Ethnologue
Languages of the World

Ethnologue
Languages of the World

Fifteenth Edition
Raymond G. Gordon, Jr., Editor

Barbara F. Grimes, Contributing Editor

Dallas

Previous Editions

First edition 1951. Second edition 1951. Third edition 1952. Fourth edition
1953. Fifth edition 1958. Sixth edition 1965. Seventh edition 1969. Eighth
edition 1974. Ninth edition 1978. Tenth edition 1984. Eleventh edition 1988.
Twelfth edition 1992. Thirteenth edition 1996. Fourteenth edition 2000.

SIL International
7500 West Camp Wisdom Road
Dallas, Texas 75236-5699 USA

Web: www.sil.org
Phone: +1 972 708 7404
Email: academic_books@sil.org

Editorial and Production Staff

Executive Editor	Gary F. Simons
Senior Editor	Mary Ruth Wise
Editor	Raymond G. Gordon, Jr.
Contributing Editor	Barbara F. Grimes
Assistant Editor	Margaret P. Frank
Editorial Assistant	Paul Walker
Copy Editor	Bonnie Brown
ISO 639/JAC Liaison	Peter G. Constable
Senior Cartographer	Irene Tucker
Cartographers	Matt Benjamin, Colin Davis
Production Manager	Robert Kaiser
Graphic Design	Kirby O'Brien
Compositors	Robert E. Chaney, Judy Benjamin
Technical Support	Ray Uehara, Stephen Tucker, Lars Huttar

Printed in the United States of America
on acid-free paper

Contents

Abbreviations

ALEM	Associação Lingüística Evangélica Missionária	**NTM**	New Tribes Mission
alt.	alternate name for	**NWFP**	Northwest Frontier Province, Pakistan
alt. dial.	alternate dialect name for	**OIEL**	Oxford International Encyclopedia of Linguistics
AMTB	Association of Brazilian Cross Cultural Missions	**OMF**	Overseas Missionary Fellowship
ANG	Anglican	**OT**	Old Testament
ANU	Australian National University	**OSV**	Object-Subject-Verb
ASL	American Sign Language	**OVS**	Object-Verb-Subject
ASSR	Autonomous Soviet Socialist Republic	**PBT**	Pioneer Bible Translators
BAP	Baptist	**pej.**	pejorative
BIA	Bureau of Indian Affairs (USA)	**PNG**	Papua New Guinea
BSI	Bible Society of India	**RC**	Roman Catholic Church
BTA	Bible Translation Association	**REF**	Reformed
BTL	Bible Translation and Literacy	**ROC**	Republic of China
CAPRO	Calvary Ministries, Nigeria	**SIL**	SIL International
CIIL	Central Institute of Indian Languages	**SIM**	SIM International
Class	Language classification	**SOV**	Subject-Object-Verb
CMA	Christian and Missionary Alliance	**SVO**	Subject-Verb-Object
CRC	Christian Reformed Church	**TEAM**	The Evangelical Alliance Mission
CV	Consonant-Vowel syllable pattern	**TILL**	The Institute for Liberian Languages
dial.	primary dialect name for	**TISLL**	The Institute for Sierra Leonean Languages
DRC	Democratic Republic of the Congo	**TV**	Television
ECP	Evangelical Church of Papua New Guinea	**UBS**	United Bible Societies
EDCL	Encyclopedic Dictionary of Chinese Linguistics	**UC**	United Church
		UFM	Unevangelized Fields Mission
EELC	Église Évangélique Lutherienne du Cameroun	**UKAW**	Artha Wacana Christian University (East Timor)
FUNAI	National Indian Foundation, Brazil	**UN**	United Nations
GILLBT	Ghana Institute of Linguistics, Literacy, and Bible Translation	**UNESCO**	United Nations Educational, Scientific, and Cultural Organization
GR	Gospel Recordings	**UNHCR**	United Nations High Commissioner for Refugees
ICDBL	International Committee for the Defense of the Breton Language	**USA**	United States of America
IEM	Indian Evangelical Mission	**USSR**	Union of Soviet Socialist Republics
IJAL	International Journal of American Linguistics	**VC**	Vowel-Consonant syllable pattern
		VDC	Village Development Committee
IMA	India Missions Association	**VOS**	Verb-Object-Subject
LBT	Lutheran Bible Translators	**VSO**	Verb-Subject-Object
Lg Dev	Language development	**WA**	World Almanac
Lg Use	Language use	**WCD**	World Christian Database
LGA	Local Government Area (Nigeria)	**WCE**	World Christian Encyclopedia (Barrett 1982)
MARC	Missions Advanced Research and Communications Center	**WT**	World Team
NT	New Testament	**YWAM**	Youth With A Mission

Note: Some institutions may be listed under more than one name because of differences among our sources.

Introduction

Since the last edition of the *Ethnologue* (2000), the publication passed the 50-year mark of compiling information concerning the languages of the world. As knowledge of the world's languages increases, so does the number of identified languages. This edition reflects an increase of 103 previously unidentified languages. Most of these are not newly discovered languages, but are ones that had been previously considered dialects of another language. Complete information on all of the world's languages is not available; thus the total number of living languages in the world cannot be known precisely. Because languages are dynamic and undergo constant change, there will never be a stable number of the living languages of the world.

The purpose of the *Ethnologue* is to provide a comprehensive listing of the known living languages of the world. Information comes from numerous sources and is confirmed by consulting both reliable published sources and a network of field correspondents. This information is compiled under several specific categories and no effort is made to gather data beyond those categories. (For a complete listing of categories, see "Layout of language entries" below.) The *Ethnologue* is intended more as a catalog than as an encyclopedia. Greater detail on a number of languages can be found in other works like the *International Encyclopedia of Linguistics* (Frawley 2003), *The World's Major Languages* (Comrie 1987), and *The Atlas of Languages* (Comrie, Matthews, and Polinsky 1997).

The information given here can be useful to linguists, translators, anthropologists, bilingual educators, government officials, aid workers, potential field investigators, missionaries, students, and others with language interests.

History of the *Ethnologue*

The *Ethnologue* was founded by Richard S. Pittman who was motivated by the desire to share information on language development needs around the world with his colleagues in SIL International as well as with other language researchers.

The first edition in 1951 was 10 mimeographed pages and included information on 46 languages or groups of languages. Maps were first included in the fourth edition (1953). The publication transitioned from mimeographed pages to a book in the fifth edition (1958). Dr. Pittman continued to expand his research through the seventh edition (1969) which listed 4,493 languages.

In 1971 Barbara F. Grimes became editor. She had assisted with the *Ethnologue* since 1953 (fourth edition) and took on the role of research editor in 1967 for the seventh edition (1969). She continued as editor through the fourteenth edition (2000). In 1971 information was expanded from primarily minority languages to encompass all known living languages of the world. Between 1967 and 1973 Ms. Grimes completed an in-depth revision of the information on Africa, the Americas, the Pacific, and a few countries of Asia. During her years as editor, the number of identified languages grew from 4,493 to 6,809, and the information recorded on each expanded so that the published work more than tripled in size.

The data given here are all taken from a computerized database on languages of the world established by then consulting editor, Joseph Grimes, in 1971 from the typesetting tapes for the seventh edition (1969). The work was done at the University of Oklahoma under a grant from the National Science Foundation. In 1974 the database was moved to a computer at Cornell University where Dr. Grimes was professor of linguistics; it was moved to a personal computer in 1979. Since 2000 it has been housed at the headquarters of SIL International in Dallas, Texas. A presentation of all languages is accessible at <http://www.ethnologue.com>. The fact that the entries are constructed by computer accounts for a certain redundancy or stiffness in the phrasing.

One feature of the database since its inception has been a system of three-letter language identifiers. The codes were first published with the following explanation in a monograph reporting the results of the grant to build the database:

> Each language is given a three-letter code on the order of international airport codes. This aids in equating languages across national boundaries, where the same language may be called by different names, and in distinguishing different languages called by the same name. (J. Grimes 1974:i)

While the codes were used behind the scenes in the database that generated the eighth and ninth editions, it was not until the tenth edition (1984) that they appeared in the publication itself.

This fifteenth edition marks an important milestone in the development of the language identifiers, namely, their emergence as a draft international standard. In 1998, the International Organization for Standardization adopted ISO 639-2—its standard for three-letter language identifiers. That was based on a convergence of ISO 639-1 (its earlier standard for two-letter language identifiers adopted in 1988) and of ANSI Z39.53 (also known as the MARC language codes, a set of three-letter identifiers developed within the library community and adopted as an American National Standard in 1987). The current standard, ISO 639-2, has proven insufficient for many purposes since it has identifiers for fewer than 400 individual languages. Thus in 2002, ISO TC37/SC2 invited SIL International to participate in the development of a new standard based on the language identifiers in the *Ethnologue* that would be a superset of ISO 639-2 and would provide identifiers for all known languages. In this edition of the *Ethnologue*, hundreds of codes have been changed in order to achieve alignment with ISO 639-2, and the proposed new standard, ISO 639-3, has passed the first round of balloting to attain the status of Draft International Standard. The three-letter language identifiers in this edition of the *Ethnologue* are thus the codes of ISO/DIS 639-3.

The problem of language identification

Due to the nature of language and the various perspectives brought to its study, it is not surprising that a number of issues prove controversial. Of preeminence in this regard is that of the definition of language itself. Since languages do not have self-identifying features, what actually constitutes a language must be operationally defined. That is, the definition of language one chooses depends on the purpose one has in identifying a language. Some base their definition on purely linguistic grounds. Others recognize that social, cultural, or political factors must also be taken into account.

Increasingly, scholars are recognizing that languages are not always easily treated as discrete isolatable units with clearly defined boundaries between them. Rather, languages are more often continua of features that extend across both geographic and social space. In addition, there is growing attention being given to the roles or functions that language varieties play within the linguistic ecology of a region or a speech community.

The *Ethnologue* approach to listing and counting languages as though they were discrete, countable units, does not preclude a more dynamic understanding of the linguistic makeup of the countries and regions in which clearly distinct varieties can be distinguished while at the same time recognizing that those languages and their "dialects" exist in a complex set of relationships to each other. Every language is characterized by variation within the speech community that uses it. Those varieties, in turn, are more or less divergent from one another. These divergent varieties are often referred to as dialects. They may be distinct enough to be considered separate languages or sufficiently similar as to be considered merely characteristic of a particular geographic region or social grouping within the speech community.

Not all scholars share the same set of criteria for what constitutes a "language" and what features define a "dialect." The *Ethnologue* applies the following basic criteria:

- Two related varieties are normally considered varieties of the same language if speakers of each variety have inherent understanding of the other variety at a functional level (that is, can understand based on knowledge of their own variety without needing to learn the other variety).

- Where spoken intelligibility between varieties is marginal, the existence of a common literature or of a common ethnolinguistic identity with a central variety that both understand can be a strong indicator that they should nevertheless be considered varieties of the same language.

- Where there is enough intelligibility between varieties to enable communication, the existence of well-established distinct ethnolinguistic identities can be a strong indicator that they should nevertheless be considered to be different languages.

Endangered languages

Language endangerment is a serious concern to which linguists and language planners have turned their attention in the last decade. For a variety of reasons, speakers of some languages are motivated to stop using their language and to use another. Parents may begin to use only that second language with their children. Eventually there may be no speakers who use the language as their first or primary language and frequently the language ceases to be used altogether and the language becomes extinct—existing, perhaps, only in recordings or written records and transcriptions. The concern about language endangerment is centered, first and foremost, around the factors which motivate speakers to abandon their language and the consequences of language death for the community of (former) speakers of that language. Since language is closely linked to culture, loss of language almost always is accompanied by social and cultural disruptions as well. Secondarily, those concerned about language endangerment recognize the implications of the loss of linguistic diversity both for the linguistic and social environment generally and for the academic community which is devoted to the study of language more specifically.

There are two dimensions to the evaluation and characterization of endangerment—the number of speakers of the language and the number and nature of the domains in which the language is used. A language may be endangered because there are fewer and fewer people who speak that language. It may also, or alternatively, be endangered because it is being used for fewer and fewer functions. The *Ethnologue* attempts to provide data on both of these dimensions whenever it is available.

Language endangerment is a matter of degree. At one end of the scale are languages that are vigorous and perhaps are even expanding in numbers of speakers or functional areas of use. At the other end are languages that are on the verge of extinction. In between are many degrees of greater or lesser endangerment. The *Ethnologue* does not attempt to identify the level of endangerment of each language listed but does specifically identify those languages at the far end of the scale by indicating "Nearly extinct" at the end of the language entry. A language is listed as nearly extinct when the speaker population is fewer than 50 or when the number of speakers is a very small fraction of the ethnic group. In this edition, 497 languages are so designated.

How to identify the level of endangerment of the other languages, however, is not necessarily clear. Linguists seek to identify trends in language use, such as a decrease in the number of speakers or a decrease in the use of the language in certain domains or functions. An increase in bilingualism, both in the number of bilinguals and in their proficiency levels, is often associated with these trends. When data are available, the following factors which may contribute to endangerment are reported in the language entries: small population size, bilingualism, urbanization, modernization, migration, industrialization, the function of each language within a society, and whether or not children are learning it. Such factors interact within a society in dynamic ways that are not necessarily predictable. As a scholarly consensus forms that can be applied worldwide, a scale of endangerment is becoming increasingly possible. In the meantime, only brief statements about the above factors are given for each language as data becomes available. (See also Hale, K., M. Krauss, L. Watahomigie, A. Yamamoto, C. Craig, L. Masayevsa Jeane, and N. England. 1992. Endangered languages. *Language* 68(1):1–42.)

Plan of the book

Following this introduction, the content of the book consists of six major sections.

Statistical Summaries. This section offers a summary view of the world language situation. Specifically, it offers numerical tabulations of living languages and number of speakers by world area, by language size, by language family, and by country.

Languages of the World. This section provides detailed information on all known living languages of the world organized by area and by country. Each country is introduced by an overview paragraph (see "Layout of country headers" below). Language entries under each country are in alphabetical order and provide a summary description of the language, structured by a set of categories (see "Layout of language entries" below). The bibliography is located at the end of this section.

Language Maps. This section provides language maps for most countries of the world. Continent maps and a world map are given to help orient the reader to the location of specific countries and continents. No political statement is intended by the placement of any boundary lines for any languages or countries on any map. See "Language maps" below for more details on the maps and how they were produced.

Language Name Index. This is an index of the 39,491 distinct names that are associated with the 7,299 languages in this edition. It is an alphabetical list of all the language names, alternate names, dialect names, and alternate dialect names that appear in the language entries. Instructions for using the index are given on its first page.

Language Code Index. This is an alphabetical index of the 7,299 three-letter language identification codes that are used throughout the volume. Instructions for using the index are given on its first page.

Country Index. This alphabetical index of country names lists the page on which the section for that country begins in the main part of the book, and the page on which its maps begin if there are any.

Layout of country headers

Languages are listed by country under each major geographic area. The entry for a country begins with a header giving summary information about the country. This header is followed by an entry for each language of the country that is not a recent immigrant. The country header has the following form:

> Official country name. Country population. National or official languages. Country literacy rates. Nonindigenous languages. Sources of information. Blind population. Deaf population. Language counts.

Official country name. This is the name used by the country in its official documents. In most cases this differs from the popular name as given in the section title and in the Country Index.

Country population. These figures are 2004 estimates from the U.S. Census Bureau.

National or official languages. National languages are those languages spoken by a large portion of the population of a nation. Official languages are those that have been designated as such by an official body.

Country literacy rates. These rates are estimates of the percentage of the population in the country that is literate in some language. Data are from various sources.

Nonindigenous languages. All languages spoken in a country are not necessarily listed as separate entries in the *Ethnologue*, especially nonindigenous or immigrant languages that are still spoken in the country of origin and apparently have no significant dialect differences between the two locations. Known nonindigenous languages are listed in the country header, with population estimate if known. They are not included in the language counts for that country. Information about nonindigenous languages is incomplete and may be incorrect. Corrections and contributions are invited for this category. See "Corrections" below for submission instructions.

Sources of information. The major sources of information for each country are given. A fuller bibliography of sources used appears in the Bibliography at the end of "Part I: Languages of the World." Sources not listed in the Bibliography are from personal communication with scholars knowledgeable in the area.

Blind population. There are reported to be from 23,000,000 to 40,000,000 or more blind people in the world. Information on the number of blind people in each country is given in the country header. Population data are from various sources. Information about the availability of Braille codes and Braille literature is given under specific languages. Readers are encouraged to submit additional information on the number of blind people in specific language groups, availability and standardization of Braille codes, and literature published or in progress.

Deaf population. There are millions of deaf and hearing-impaired people in the world. Information on the number of deaf people and an approximate count of the deaf institutions (schools, clubs, associations) is given in the country header. The deaf sign languages listed in language entries are those used exclusively within deaf communities. They do not include those, like Signed English, that spell out spoken languages used in the country. Please send additional information on deafness and deaf sign languages to the *Ethnologue* editor. See "Corrections" below for submission instructions.

Language counts. The number of languages indigenous to that country is given along with a break down of the number of living languages, the number that have become extinct since 1950 when the *Ethnologue* began tracking the living languages of the world, and the number that are used only as a second language.

Layout of language entries

Many languages are spoken in more than one country, and so are listed under several countries. (In fact this results in 9,021 entries for the 7,299 languages listed in this edition.) One of the countries is considered primary; usually the country of origin or country where most of the speakers are located. More information about a language is given in the entry for the primary country than in the others. An entry for a nonprimary country ends with the words "See more information under..." giving a cross-reference to the primary country. A complete entry for the primary country has the following form and content:

Primary language name (Alternate names) [Language identification code] Country speaker population. Monolingual population. Population remarks. Population in all countries. Ethnic population. Location. *Class*: Linguistic affiliation. *Dialects*: Dialect names. Intelligibility and dialect relations. Lexical similarity. *Lg Use*: Language function. Viability remarks. Domains. Age. Language attitudes. Bilingual proficiency levels. Bilingualism remarks. *Lg Dev*: Literacy rates. Literacy remarks. Use in elementary or secondary schools. Writing scripts. Publications and use in media. *Other*: General remarks. Linguistic typology. Geological and ecological information. Religion. Status.

Within the language entry, italicized labels are used to organize the entry into topical sections. A label appears in a given entry only if the entry contains one or more of the pieces of information associated with that topic. Five such labels are used:

- *Class* for the genetic classification of the language,
- *Dialects* for information about the dialects of the language,
- *Lg Use* for information about the viability of the language and the use of other languages by the community,
- *Lg Dev* for information about literacy rates, writing systems, written materials, use in education, and
- *Other* for any additional information.

Full information is not available for every language.

Primary language name. Each entry begins with the name used to reference that language in that country. In most cases the name is the one that the speakers prefer if such a preference is known. However, speakers within a language community may have different opinions about which name they prefer. Known preferred names are recorded using English spellings, though diacritical marks may be included. Among Khoisan languages and a few other languages in southern Africa special symbols—as submitted by sources—are used to represent the "click" sounds produced with ingressive mouth air.

Alternate names. Many languages are known by more than one name. In this edition, the 9,021 entries list 24,989 alternate names to assist the reader in identifying a language. These are given in parentheses after the main name, separated from each other by commas. Alternate names come from various sources: speakers may have more than one name for their language, or neighboring groups may use different names. Other names may have been assigned by outsiders and used in linguistic publications before the primary name was known. Another source of alternate names is variant spellings of what is essentially the same name. In many cases, languages of wider communication or regional language spellings are given. Some of the names listed may be ethnic names. An ethnic group, however, may be made up of several groups speaking several languages, or the mother-tongue speakers of a single language may be members of several different ethnic groups.

Some names in use by others are offensive to the speakers of the language; those are identified by double quotation marks.

Language identification code. Each distinct language in the world is assigned a unique three-letter code. This code is given in square brackets following the alternate names. When a given language is spoken in multiple countries, all of the entries for that language specify the same three-letter code. The code distinguishes the language from other languages with the same or similar names and identifies those cases in which the name differs across country borders. These codes ensure that each language is counted only once in world or area statistics. As explained above in "History of the Ethnologue," the codes are from the Draft International Standard version of ISO 639-3.

Country speaker population. The first population figure given refers to the estimated number of first-language speakers in the country in focus. The date and source of the population estimate are given in parentheses. Some totals given do not equal the sum of the populations given for that language in each country because of differences among sources and differences in dates when the estimates were made. The *Ethnologue* research does not extrapolate population estimates by some formula, because populations do not increase at the same rate in all language groups, and because some starting estimates themselves turn out later to have been incorrect. However, some population data submitted to the *Ethnologue* may be the result of extrapolation.

It is often difficult to get an accurate figure for the speakers of a language. All figures are only estimates—even census figures. Some sources do not include all dialects in their figures. Some sources count members of ethnic groups, whose membership does not always correspond on a one-to-one basis with speakers of languages. Some sources do not make clear whether they refer to the total number of speakers in all countries, or only to those in one of the countries. Some do not distinguish first-language speakers from second-language speakers. The *Ethnologue* provides the number of first-language speakers wherever possible.

Languages that no longer have first-language speakers are described as "Extinct" in place of a population. Effort has been made to indicate the language that is now spoken by the ethnic group. The increase in the number of extinct languages from the last edition does not indicate the number of languages that have become extinct during that period, but rather reflects better information concerning some that may have been extinct at some time previous to that publication. As discussed in the "Endangered languages" section above, it is difficult to determine just when a language becomes extinct.

Some linguists would not consider a language extinct if there are revitalization efforts and the language is being used as a second language even though there are no longer first-language speakers. The *Ethnologue* lists revitalization efforts when they are known. In some cases the "extinct" language may still be used for ritual or other cultural purposes, but only as a second language.

Monolingual population. The number of those who are monolingual can be compared with the total speaker population in estimating the viability of the language.

Population remarks. Additional information concerning populations may include population breakdowns by dialect, gender, or ethnic groups; the population of the deaf community; or other comments related to population.

Population in all countries. Since information may come from multiple sources, the sum of the country populations may not equal the figure given for all countries. In some cases, the population of one or more countries may not be available.

Ethnic population. Where it is known, the population of those who identify themselves as part of the ethnic group is given, regardless of whether they speak the language.

Location. A description of the location where the language is spoken is included in each entry where a specific area can be defined. Those languages that are scattered through a country or wide region may not have this information in the entry. A list of all countries where the language is spoken is provided in the primary entry for a language spoken in multiple countries.

Linguistic affiliation. All languages are slowly changing, and linguistically related varieties may be diverging or merging. Most languages are related to some other languages: to some more closely and to others more distantly. Linguists have used terms such as phylum, stock, family, branch, group, language, and dialect to refer to these relationships in increasing order of closeness.

The organization of linguistic relationships outlined in the Oxford University Press *International Encyclopedia of Linguistics*, 2003, Frawley, ed., is followed for most language families, because it is the most comprehensive and up-to-date guide available. For Austronesian languages, the *Comparative Austronesian Dictionary*, 1995, Darrell Tryon, ed., is generally followed. Several changes have been entered based on more recent comparative studies. In the *Ethnologue*, more inclusive group names are given first, followed by the names for less inclusive subgroups, separated by commas. The traditional numbering system used to identify different subgroups of Bantu languages in Africa has been followed. The full classification tree is available in a dynamic presentation on the *Ethnologue* website <http://www.ethnologue.com>. A listing of the highest-level language families (including number of living languages, average populations, and countries where spoken) is given in the "Statistical Summaries" section.

Dialect names. Speech varieties, which are functionally intelligible to each other's speakers because of linguistic similarity, are considered dialects of one language and listed under that language. In this edition, 10,803 dialects are listed. In addition, 6,269 alternate names for individual dialects are listed in parentheses following the primary name for the dialect. When one of these names is known to be offensive to its speakers, it is placed in double quotes. Where no dialects are listed or where the language name occurs in the dialect list, the language is known by the name of one of its dialects. Since information is not always complete, some dialect names may be ethnic group or clan names and may not reflect linguistic variation.

Intelligibility and dialect relations. Speaker intelligibility of other languages is given by a percentage indicating the level of comprehension. Values of less than 85% signal likely difficulty in comprehension of the indicated language. In some areas a number of languages show a high degree of similarity and form a linguistic group of languages and are referred to in the remarks as "clusters." They fall into the same classificatory subgroup. Alternatively, some languages may be identifiable as a distinct group for sociolinguistic reasons. In many cases both linguistic and sociolinguistic factors allow for such a grouping to be identified. Many researchers take such clusters into account when considering language development strategies.

Lexical similarity. The percentage of similarity is determined by comparing a standardized set of wordlists and counting those forms that show similarity in both form and meaning. Percentages higher than 85% usually indicate a speech variant that is likely a dialect of the language being compared.

Language function. If a language serves as a national or official language, it is indicated. A national language is one spoken by a large portion of the population of a nation. An official language is one that has been designated as such by an official body.

Viability remarks. A number of viability indicators are given. Where the language is being passed on to children as their first language, the term "vigorous" is used. Another positive indicator is the number of second-language speakers (that is, speakers of other languages who use the language as a second language). An indicator of waning viability is the degree of language shift to another language (in some cases indicated by the percentage of the ethnic community who still speak the language). General estimates of viability may be given.

Domains. When more than one language is used in a community, speakers often establish patterns of language use for specific configurations of speakers, topics, and locations. These domains of language use can be described by answering the question, "Who is speaking to whom, about what, and where?" The *Ethnologue* does not have sufficient data about each language to permit a full description of the domains of use in this technical sense, but uses the term to refer most often to a general set of locations (e.g., home, school, community) and thus only indirectly to the topics and speakers most generally associated with those locations. The knowledge of "domains of use" patterns is important to those doing language development.

Age. As language use in a community shifts from a traditional language to one of wider communication, age differences in use appear. As language shift takes place, older adults tend to be the final speakers of the traditional language. Where there is information about the ages of the speakers, the *Ethnologue* reports it.

Language attitudes. How people think about their own language is important to those promoting literacy or other development activities. Data about speakers' attitudes and the attitudes of others toward the language are reported where available.

Bilingual proficiency levels. As is common in many areas of research, there are different opinions as to how to measure bilingual proficiencies. For some language groups, estimates of proficiency in a second language are given according to Federal Interagency Language Roundtable (FILR) levels (formerly known as the Foreign Service Institute (FSI) scale). These estimates indicate the percentage of speakers for each level. These levels express increasing proficiency from 0 to 5 and are described by the FILR as: 0 No proficiency; 1 Elementary proficiency; 2 Limited working proficiency; 3 General professional proficiency; 4 Advanced professional proficiency; 5 Functionally native proficiency. Percentages have been determined by proficiency examinations of a statistical sample of speakers.

Bilingualism remarks. When speakers can use a second language, different speakers usually have varying degrees of bilingual proficiency in it, ranging from being able to use only greetings or trade in it to complete freedom to express anything in it. Language groups are sometimes reported to be bilingual if a few of the speakers can use a second language to some degree, or if there are no monolinguals; whereas other sources would not classify groups as bilingual unless a large majority of their members could use the second language very well. Because second languages are usually learned later than first languages, bilingualism is usually not uniform across a community, as mentioned above. Leaders, the educated, men, traders, those who travel, those in population centers, and people in certain age groups may be more bilingual than others. Where information is available, these factors about bilingualism are described.

Literacy rates. Where available, percentages of the speaker population who are literate are given for the first and second languages.

Literacy remarks. Information concerning motivation for literacy, government literacy programs, and comments on the writing system are given where available with additional information concerning literacy that does not appear in related categories.

Use in elementary or secondary schools. The language may be used either as a language of instruction or taught as a subject within one or more schools in the language area.

Writing scripts. Statistics on the number of languages that have written form are not available. However, the script used for written materials is given if known, e.g., Devanagari script.

Publications and use in media. Materials that have been produced in the language such as dictionaries, grammars, and broadcast media are indicated when known, but the information is very incomplete at this time. More information is welcomed though it is unlikely that the *Ethnologue* will ever be able to document existing literature in any comprehensive way. Significant publications of interest to linguists and language developers are reported whenever possible. The most widely published book in the world is the Bible with at least portions having been translated and published in 2,422 or 35% of living languages listed in the *Ethnologue*. This figure is based on the thorough archival efforts of the United Bible Societies and the American Bible Society. Information about Bible publication is given with the dates of the earliest and most recent published Bible, New Testament (NT), Old Testament (OT), or complete books (portions).

General remarks. These are general statements about the language or its context that do not fall into other specific categories.

Linguistic typology. For some languages, a little information is given on constituent order (e.g., Subject, Object, Verb = SOV), syllable patterns (e.g., Consonant, Vowel, Consonant = CVC), and other basic features that are of particular interest to linguists.

Geological and ecological information. For some languages, information on the geological and ecological environment, altitude range, and subsistence type of the speakers is given. This is not a complete typology, but a rough guide to the physical setting and general economic adaptation of the society.

Religion. The religious affiliation of the people is given where known.

Status. The phrase "Second language only" is used to indicate languages which are used as special second languages with no mother-tongue speakers such as languages of initiation, languages of herb doctors, cants, jargons, and American Plains Indian Sign Language. Such languages are listed in the body of the Ethnologue but not included among the statistical summaries of living languages. The inventory of these languages is also incomplete.

The phrase "Nearly extinct" is used to indicate those languages of fewer than 50 speakers and other languages for which the number of speakers is a very small fraction of the ethnic group.

Language maps

Maps showing the locations of language homelands are available for most countries of the world. Some maps make use of polygons to show the approximate boundaries of the language groups. No claim is made for precision in the placement of these boundaries, which in many instances overlap with those of other languages. Reference numbers are used on some maps where space does not allow the placement of language names. Finally, for some maps where the language boundaries are not known, the names or numbers alone appear. Extinct languages do not appear on the maps. Some languages are not shown due to lack of information.

Maps of countries in equatorial latitudes use a simple cylindrical projection. Generally, maps of higher latitude countries use either the Lambert conformal conic or the Robinson world projection.

Unless otherwise noted, the maps are the product of an ongoing cooperative effort between SIL International and Global Mapping International (GMI). Geographic data are from the Global Ministry Mapping System 2003. Language locations are based on the World Language Mapping System 2003. The maps were created using either Atlas GIS or ArcGIS software. The latter was kindly donated by Environmental Systems Research Institute (ESRI).

Permission to reproduce these maps in any print, electronic, or other medium must be obtained in writing from SIL International.

Acknowledgements

The compilation of a body of information such as that presented here requires a cooperative effort on the part of hundreds of contributors. Updates in this edition are largely the contribution of researchers, language field-workers, and native speakers of these languages who gave of their time and expertise to improve the accuracy and quality of the Ethnologue.

The Contributing Editor, Barbara F. Grimes, has given invaluable assistance. Colleagues in Academic Affairs of SIL International helped guide the publication through the printing process.

Other contributors include Roger Blench, Leoni Bouwer, Matthias Brenzinger, Bernard Comrie, Richard Cook, Jerry Edmondson, Bev Erasmus, Hezy Mutzafi, Nick Nicholas, Derek Nurse, Malcolm Ross, Valentin Vydrine, This edition has also benefited greatly from cooperative efforts with Dwayne Rainwater and colleagues in Pioneer Bible Translators, Jacques Rongier, Suwilai Premsrirat and staff at the Institute of Language and Culture for Rural Development, Mahidol University, Bangkok, Thailand, colleagues in Lutheran Bible Translators, and many colleagues in SIL International.

Corrections

Although this fifteenth edition contains more than 50,000 updates and corrections from the previous one, this edition makes no claims for completeness. There is still much to be learned concerning the languages of the world and the search for better knowledge goes on. A new edition is planned for publication approximately every four years.

If you believe any of the information in the *Ethnologue* to be in error, send your proposed change to the editor using one of the addresses given below. Be sure to report the source of your information. When you want to request that a language be added because you believe it to be missing altogether, use the questionnaires supplied on the *Ethnologue* web site to submit a basic profile of the language.

The *Ethnologue* staff will seek to verify the proposed change before accepting it. This process may take months as it generally involves making enquiries of individuals who are resident in the country where the language is spoken. These persons may in turn make enquiries of others in order to perform the verification. The submitter can expect to receive an acknowledgement from the *Ethnologue* editor.

Submit corrections and additions by e-mail to:

Info-SIL@sil.org

Or by post to:

Editor, *Ethnologue*
SIL International
7500 West Camp Wisdom Road
Dallas, Texas 75236
U.S.A.

Statistical Summaries

Part I, "Languages of the World," provides language-by-language information. This section steps back from the detail to offer a summary view of the world language situation. Specifically, it offers numerical tabulations of languages and number of speakers by world area, by language size, by language family, and by country.

Summary by area

The entries in Part I are organized under five world areas: Africa, the Americas, Asia, Europe, and the Pacific. Table 1 summarizes the distribution of languages and their populations by these areas. Note that the areas differ widely with respect to typical language size (Grimes 1986, 1995).

The first *Count* column in table 1 gives the number of living languages that originate in the specified area. A living language is defined as one that has at least one speaker for whom it is their first language; extinct languages and languages that are used only as a second language are excluded from these counts. In this tabulation, each language is counted only once so that the total at the bottom of the column represents the total number of living languages in the world. A language that is spoken in more than one country is counted under the area of its primary country. This has the effect of counting the languages by their area of origin.

The second *Count* column gives the total number of people who use those languages as their first language, regardless of where in the world they may live. Note, for instance, that the population given in the row for Europe is nearly twice the actual population of Europe. This is because it is a count of speakers of European languages, some of which are now used as a first language in other parts of the world due to the colonial expansion of the last few centuries. Since it is a count of first-language speakers, any given person should be counted only once. As a result the total at the bottom of the column approximates the total world population. Note, however, that the total is somewhat less than the actual world population which is currently estimated to exceed 6 billion; this is because the *Ethnologue* lacks population estimates for about 5% of the languages and because it does not automatically extrapolate population estimates but waits for reports from reliable sources.

The *Percent* columns give the share of the count for that area as a percentage of the total number listed at the bottom of the Count column. The *Mean* column gives the average number of speakers per language, while the *Median* column gives the middle value in the distribution of language populations (that is, half of the languages have more speakers than that number and half have that number or fewer).

Table 1. Distribution of languages by area of origin

Area	Living languages		Number of speakers			
	Count	Percent	Count	Percent	Mean	Median
Africa	2,092	30.3	675,887,158	11.8	323,082	25,391
Americas	1,002	14.5	47,559,381	0.8	47,464	2,000
Asia	2,269	32.8	3,489,897,147	61.0	1,538,077	10,171
Europe	239	3.5	1,504,393,183	26.3	6,294,532	220,000
Pacific	1,310	19.0	6,124,341	0.1	4,675	800
Totals	6,912	100.0	5,723,861,210	100.0	828,105	7,000

Summary by Language Size

A striking fact shown in table 1 is that there is a huge disparity between the mean size of languages and the median size. It turns out that 347 (or approximately 5%) of the world's languages have at least one million speakers and account for 94% of the world's population. By contrast, the remaining 95% of languages are spoken by only 6% of the world's people.

Table 2 summarizes the distribution of languages by size. The *Count* columns give the actual number of languages within the specified population range and the total number of first-language speakers of those languages. Where the language entry in Part I lists a range of values for the population, the midpoint of the range is used for this tabulation. The *Percent* columns give the share of the count for that population range as a percentage of the total number listed at the bottom of the Count column. Note that there are still a few hundred languages for which the Ethnologue does not have a population estimate; the calculation of percentages for speakers is therefore not able to take those languages into account. The *Cumulative* columns give the cumulative sum of the percentages going from top to bottom in the column.

Summary by language family

The genetic classifications given in the language entries of Part I name 94 different language families (that is, top-level genetic groups). Six of these, each of which has at least 5% of the world's languages, stand out as the major language families of the world. Together they account for nearly two-thirds of all languages and five-sixths of the world's population. Table 3 summarizes the distribution of languages and their populations within these six families. The columns are as for table 1, with the addition of a final column listing the countries under which the main entries for the languages of that family are found in Part I.

In addition to the other 88 language families, the genetic classification scheme also includes special categories for atificial languages, creoles, deaf sign languages, language isolates, mixed languages, pidgins, and unclassified languages. Table 4 summarizes the distribution of languages and their populations for these other language families and

Table 2. Distribution of languages by number of first-language speakers

Population range	Living languages			Number of speakers		
	Count	*Percent*	*Cumulative*	*Count*	*Percent*	*Cumulative*
100,000,000 to 999,999,999	8	0.1	0.1%	2,301,423,372	40.20753	40.20753%
10,000,000 to 99,999,999	75	1.1	1.2%	2,246,597,929	39.24969	79.45723%
1,000,000 to 9,999,999	264	3.8	5.0%	825,681,046	14.42525	93.88247%
100,000 to 999,999	892	12.9	17.9%	283,651,418	4.95560	98.83807%
10,000 to 99,999	1,779	25.7	43.7%	58,442,338	1.02103	99.85910%
1,000 to 9,999	1,967	28.5	72.1%	7,594,224	0.13268	99.99177%
100 to 999	1,071	15.5	87.6%	457,022	0.00798	99.99976%
10 to 99	344	5.0	92.6%	13,163	0.00023	99.99999%
1 to 9	204	3.0	95.5%	698	0.00001	100.00000%
Unknown	308	4.5	100.0%			
Totals	6,912	100.0		5,723,861,210	100.00000	

special categories. In most cases the population as a percentage of the world population is negligible; a figure is shown in that column only when the value is at least one-hundredth of one percent. Together tables 3 and 4 account for all known living languages of the world.

Table 3. Major language families of the world

Language family	Living languages		Number of speakers				Countries
	Count	Per-cent	Count	Per-cent	Mean	Median	
Afro-Asiatic	353	5.11	339,478,607	5.93	961,696	20,151	Afghanistan, Algeria, Bahrain, Cameroon, Chad, Cyprus, Egypt, Eritrea, Ethiopia, Georgia, Iran, Iraq, Israel, Jordan, Kenya, Libya, Mali, Malta, Mauritania, Morocco, Niger, Nigeria, Oman, Saudi Arabia, Somalia, Sudan, Syria, Tanzania, Tunisia, Turkey, United Arab Emirates, Uzbekistan, Yemen
Austronesian	1,246	18.03	311,740,132	5.45	250,193	3,384	Brunei, Cambodia, Chile, China, Cook Islands, East Timor, Fiji, French Polynesia, Guam, Indonesia, Kiribati, Madagascar, Malaysia, Marshall Islands, Mayotte, Micronesia, Myanmar, Nauru, New Caledonia, New Zealand, Niue, Northern Mariana Islands, Palau, Papua New Guinea, Philippines, Samoa, Solomon Islands, Suriname, Taiwan, Thailand, Tokelau, Tonga, Tuvalu, USA, Vanuatu, Viet Nam, Wallis and Futuna
Indo-European	430	6.22	2,562,896,428	44.78	5,960,224	150,000	Afghanistan, Albania, Armenia, Austria, Azerbaijan, Bangladesh, Belarus, Belgium, Bosnia and Herzegovina, Bulgaria, Canada, China, Croatia, Czech Republic, Denmark, Fiji, Finland, France, Georgia, Germany, Greece, Iceland, India, Iran, Iraq, Ireland, Israel, Italy, Latvia, Lithuania, Luxembourg, Macedonia, Maldives, Nepal, Netherlands, Norway, Oman, Pakistan, Peru, Poland, Portugal, Romania, Russia, Serbia and Montenegro, Slovakia, Slovenia, South Africa, Spain, Sri Lanka, Suriname, Sweden, Switzerland, Tajikistan, Turkey, Ukraine, United Kingdom, USA, Venezuela

Table 3. Major language families of the world (continued)

Language family	Living languages		Number of speakers				Countries
	Count	Per-cent	Count	Per-cent	Mean	Median	
Niger-Congo	1,495	21.63	358,091,103	6.26	239,526	26,000	Angola, Benin, Botswana, Burkina Faso, Burundi, Cameroon, Central African Republic, Chad, Comoros, Congo, Côte d'Ivoire, Democratic Republic of the Congo, Equatorial Guinea, Gabon, Gambia, Ghana, Guinea, Guinea-Bissau, Kenya, Lesotho, Liberia, Malawi, Mali, Mozambique, Namibia, Niger, Nigeria, Rwanda, Senegal, Sierra Leone, Somalia, South Africa, Sudan, Swaziland, Tanzania, Togo, Uganda, Zambia, Zimbabwe
Sino-Tibetan	399	5.77	1,275,531,921	22.28	3,196,822	18,686	Bangladesh, Bhutan, China, India, Kyrgyzstan, Laos, Myanmar, Nepal, Pakistan, Thailand, Viet Nam
Trans-New Guinea	561	8.12	3,359,894	0.06	5,989	1,245	Australia, East Timor, Indonesia, Papua New Guinea
Totals	4,484	64.87	4,851,098,085	84.75			

Table 4. Other language families of the world

Language family	Living languages		Number of speakers				Countries
	Count	Per-cent	Count	Per-cent	Mean	Median	
Alacalufan	1	0.01	20		20	20	Chile
Algic	31	0.45	194,980		6,290	3,995	Canada, USA
Altaic	64	0.93	145,069,278	2.53	2,266,707	65,000	Afghanistan, Azerbaijan, China, Georgia, Iran, Kazakhstan, Kyrgyzstan, Lithuania, Moldova, Mongolia, Russia, Turkey, Turkmenistan, Uzbekistan
Amto-Musan	2	0.03	270		135	70	Papua New Guinea
Andama-nese	4	0.06	521		130	96	India
Arauan	7	0.10	3,333		476	195	Brazil
Araucanian	2	0.03	302,000		151,000	2,000	Chile
Arawakan	49	0.71	670,565	0.01	13,685	1,300	Bolivia, Brazil, Colombia, Guyana, Honduras, Peru, Suriname, Venezuela
Artificial language	1	0.01	1,100		1,100	1,100	France
Arutani-Sape	2	0.03	24		12	5	Brazil, Venezuela
Australian	224	3.24	35,227		157	10	Australia

Table 4. Other language families of the world (continued)

Language family	Living languages		Number of speakers				Countries
	Count	Per-cent	Count	Per-cent	Mean	Median	
Austro-Asiatic	169	2.45	101,339,384	1.77	599,641	8,000	Bangladesh, Cambodia, China, India, Laos, Malaysia, Myanmar, Thailand, Viet Nam
Aymaran	3	0.04	2,228,378	0.04	742,793	736	Bolivia, Peru
Barbacoan	5	0.07	42,350		8,470	3,450	Colombia, Ecuador
Basque	3	0.04	664,308	0.01	221,436	67,500	France, Spain
Bayono-Awbono	2	0.03	200		100	100	Indonesia
Caddoan	4	0.06	68		17	20	USA
Cahuapanan	2	0.03	11,384		5,692	11,384	Peru
Carib	29	0.42	67,815		2,338	450	Brazil, Colombia, Guyana, Suriname, Venezuela
Chapacura-Wanham	4	0.06	1,978		494	40	Brazil
Chibchan	21	0.30	254,846		12,136	2,000	Colombia, Costa Rica, Ecuador, Honduras, Nicaragua, Panama
Chimakuan	1	0.01	10		10	10	USA
Choco	7	0.10	69,570		9,939	8,050	Colombia, Panama
Chon	2	0.03	6		3	2	Argentina
Chukotko-Kamchatkan	5	0.07	13,712		2,742	150	Russia
Creole	82	1.19	28,815,529	0.50	351,409	34,500	Antigua and Barbuda, Australia, Bahamas, Barbados, Belize, Brazil, Cameroon, Cape Verde Islands, Central African Republic, Chad, China, Colombia, Congo, Democratic Republic of the Congo, East Timor, Equatorial Guinea, French Guiana, Grenada, Guadeloupe, Guinea-Bissau, Guyana, Haiti, India, Indonesia, Jamaica, Kenya, Malaysia, Mauritius, Micronesia, Netherlands Antilles, New Caledonia, Nicaragua, Nigeria, Panama, Papua New Guinea, Philippines, Réunion, Saint Lucia, Saint Vincent and the Grenadines, São Tomé e Príncipe, Seychelles, Sierra Leone, Singapore, Solomon Islands, South Africa, Sri Lanka, Sudan, Suriname, Trinidad and Tobago, Turks and Caicos Islands, Uganda, U.S. Virgin Islands, USA, Vanuatu

Table 4. Other language families of the world (continued)

Language family	Living languages		Number of speakers				Countries
	Count	Per-cent	Count	Per-cent	Mean	Median	
Deaf sign language	119	1.72	Unknown				Algeria, Argentina, Armenia, Australia, Austria, Belgium, Bolivia, Brazil, Bulgaria, Canada, Chad, Chile, China, Colombia, Costa Rica, Croatia, Cuba, Czech Republic, Denmark, Dominican Republic, Ecuador, Egypt, El Salvador, Estonia, Ethiopia, Finland, France, Germany, Ghana, Greece, Guatemala, Guinea, Honduras, Hungary, Iceland, India, Indonesia, Iran, Ireland, Israel, Italy, Jamaica, Japan, Jordan, Kenya, Korea, South, Laos, Latvia, Libya, Lithuania, Madagascar, Malaysia, Mali, Malta, Mexico, Moldova, Mongolia, Morocco, Mozambique, Namibia, Nepal, Netherlands, New Zealand, Nicaragua, Nigeria, Norway, Pakistan, Peru, Philippines, Poland, Portugal, Puerto Rico, Romania, Russia, Saudi Arabia, Serbia and Montenegro, Sierra Leone, Singapore, Slovakia, Solomon Islands, South Africa, Spain, Sri Lanka, Sweden, Switzerland, Taiwan, Tanzania, Thailand, Tunisia, Turkey, Uganda, Ukraine, United Kingdom, Uruguay, USA, Venezuela, Viet Nam, Zambia, Zimbabwe
Dravidian	73	1.06	221,515,995	3.87	3,034,466	24,000	India, Nepal, Pakistan
East Bird's Head	3	0.04	34,783		11,594	12,000	Indonesia
East Papuan	33	0.48	123,095		3,730	2,200	Papua New Guinea, Solomon Islands
Eskimo-Aleut	10	0.14	89,115		8,912	4,000	Canada, Greenland, Russia, USA
Geelvink Bay	33	0.48	20,824		631	250	Indonesia
Guahiban	5	0.07	28,651		5,730	1,237	Colombia
Harakmbet	2	0.03	811		406	311	Peru
Hmong-Mien	35	0.51	6,284,271	0.11	179,551	50,000	China, Viet Nam
Hokan	19	0.27	9,500		500	75	Mexico, USA
Huavean	4	0.06	18,344		4,586	900	Mexico
Iroquoian	7	0.10	22,687		3,241	175	Canada, USA
Japanese	12	0.17	123,445,034	2.16	10,287,086	5,000	Japan
Jivaroan	4	0.06	99,292		24,823	9,333	Ecuador, Peru
Kartvelian	5	0.07	4,806,404	0.08	961,281	79,800	Georgia, Israel, Turkey
Katukinan	3	0.04	658		219	10	Brazil
Keres	2	0.03	7,971		3,986	3,391	USA

Table 4. Other language families of the world (continued)

Language family	Living languages		Number of speakers				Countries
	Count	Per-cent	Count	Per-cent	Mean	Median	
Khoisan	22	0.32	363,600		16,527	4,200	Angola, Botswana, Namibia, South Africa, Tanzania
Kiowa Tanoan	5	0.07	6,249		1,250	1,298	USA
Kwomtari-Baibai	6	0.09	3,402		567	345	Papua New Guinea
Language Isolate	36	0.52	67,284,147	1.18	1,869,004	619	Argentina, Bolivia, Brazil, Canada, Chile, Colombia, Ecuador, Honduras, India, Indonesia, Japan, Korea, South, Nigeria, Pakistan, Papua New Guinea, Peru, Russia, USA, Venezuela
Left May	6	0.09	1,990		332	330	Papua New Guinea
Lower Mamberamo	2	0.03	800		400	200	Indonesia
Lule-Vilela	1	0.01	20		20	20	Argentina
Macro-Ge	24	0.35	51,037		2,127	728	Bolivia, Brazil
Maku	6	0.09	2,551		425	300	Brazil, Colombia
Mascoian	4	0.06	16,160		4,040	2,500	Paraguay
Mataco-Guaicuru	11	0.16	92,800		8,436	2,008	Argentina, Bolivia, Brazil, Paraguay
Mayan	68	0.98	6,064,703	0.11	89,187	36,000	Belize, Guatemala, Mexico
Misumalpan	2	0.03	190,800		95,400	7,400	Nicaragua
Mixe-Zoque	17	0.25	153,330		9,019	5,200	Mexico
Mixed Language	19	0.27	678,572	0.01	35,714	2,000	Armenia, China, Denmark, Ecuador, Germany, Greece, Guatemala, Ireland, Malawi, Micronesia, Niger, Norway, Russia, Serbia and Montenegro, Spain, Sweden, Tanzania, United Kingdom, USA
Mura	1	0.01	150		150	150	Brazil
Muskogean	6	0.09	15,307		2,551	496	USA
Na-Dene	41	0.59	180,272		4,397	80	Canada, USA
Nambi-quaran	3	0.04	1,346		449	136	Brazil
Nilo-Saharan	197	2.85	34,953,324	0.61	177,428	40,000	Algeria, Benin, Burkina Faso, Central African Republic, Chad, Democratic Republic of the Congo, Eritrea, Ethiopia, Kenya, Mali, Niger, Nigeria, Sudan, Tanzania, Uganda
North Caucasian	33	0.48	4,616,040	0.08	139,880	6,693	Azerbaijan, Georgia, Russia
Oto-Manguean	172	2.49	1,903,398	0.03	11,066	4,729	Mexico
Panoan	19	0.27	42,428		2,233	387	Bolivia, Brazil, Peru

Table 4. Other language families of the world (continued)

Language family	Living languages		Number of speakers				Countries
	Count	Per-cent	Count	Per-cent	Mean	Median	
Peba-Yaguan	1	0.01	5,692		5,692	5,692	Peru
Penutian	23	0.33	5,653		246	12	Canada, USA
Pidgin	5	0.07	100		20	100	Canada, India, Liberia, Nauru, Papua New Guinea
Quechuan	45	0.65	10,100,102	0.18	224,447	25,000	Argentina, Bolivia, Chile, Colombia, Ecuador, Peru
Salishan	19	0.27	3,144		165	75	Canada, USA
Salivan	3	0.04	16,135		5,378	2,500	Colombia, Venezuela
Sepik-Ramu	100	1.45	238,123		2,381	745	Indonesia, Papua New Guinea
Siouan	12	0.17	32,614		2,718	100	Canada, USA
Sko	7	0.10	5,666		809	640	Indonesia, Papua New Guinea
Subtiaba-Tlapanec	4	0.06	70,143		17,536	3,461	Mexico
Tacanan	6	0.09	5,054		842	1,180	Bolivia
Tai-Kadai	74	1.07	78,375,999	1.37	1,059,135	25,000	China, India, Laos, Myanmar, Thailand, Viet Nam
Tarascan	2	0.03	120,000		60,000	120,000	Mexico
Torricelli	53	0.77	111,265		2,099	952	Papua New Guinea
Totonacan	11	0.16	286,670		26,061	4,000	Mexico
Tucanoan	20	0.29	22,563		1,128	550	Brazil, Colombia, Ecuador, Peru
Tupi	60	0.87	5,017,354	0.09	83,623	200	Bolivia, Brazil, French Guiana, Paraguay, Peru
Unclassified	43	0.62	501,237	0.01	11,657	622	Afghanistan, Angola, Brazil, Cameroon, Central African Republic, Chad, China, Colombia, Honduras, India, Indonesia, Mauritania, Myanmar, Nigeria, Papua New Guinea, Spain, United Kingdom, Venezuela, Viet Nam
Uralic	36	0.52	22,623,030	0.40	628,418	5,000	Estonia, Finland, Hungary, Latvia, Norway, Russia, Sweden
Uru-Chipaya	2	0.03	1,202		601	2	Bolivia
Uto-Aztecan	56	0.81	1,947,164	0.03	34,771	5,144	El Salvador, Mexico, USA
Wakashan	4	0.06	760		190	200	Canada
West Papuan	26	0.38	310,142		11,929	4,600	Indonesia
Witotoan	6	0.09	7,749		1,292	150	Colombia, Peru
Yanomam	4	0.06	32,293		8,073	5,074	Brazil, Venezuela
Yeniseian	2	0.03	772		386	2	Russia
Yukaghir	2	0.03	120		60	30	Russia

Table 4. Other language families of the world (continued)

Language family	Living languages		Number of speakers				Countries
	Count	Per-cent	Count	Per-cent	Mean	Median	
Zamucoan	2	0.03	5,571		2,786	1,800	Paraguay
Zaparoan	4	0.06	91		23	5	Ecuador, Peru
Totals	2,428	35.13	872,763,125	15.25			

Summary by country

Table 5 summarizes the distribution of languages and their populations within the countries of the world. The *Total* column gives the total number of living languages used as a first language in that country, and *Percent* translates that to a percentage of all living languages in the world. No grand totals are given for these columns since the same language can be counted as being used in multiple countries. The next two columns break the total number into *Indigenous* languages versus *Immigrant* languages. The next three columns summarize populations: *Count* gives the total number of first-language speakers in that country, *Mean* gives the average size of a language group in that country, and *Median* gives the middle size of a language (that is, half are larger and half are smaller). The last two columns are explained in the next paragraph.

Table 6 repeats the information in table 5 but presents the countries in order of their linguistic diversity, from most diverse to least diverse. The *Index* column reports Greenberg's diversity index. This is the probability that any two people of the country selected at random would have different mother tongues (Lieberson 1981). The highest possible value, 1, indicates total diversity (that is, no two people have the same mother tongue) while the lowest possible value, 0, indicates no diversity at all (that is, everyone has the same mother tongue). The computation of the diversity index is based on the population of each language as a proportion of the total population. The *Coverage* column indicates the completeness of the computation by reporting the percentage of languages in the country for which population estimates are available. Missing values are compensated for by using the total of known language populations (shown in the *Count* column) as the total population, rather than an estimate of the country's population.

Table 5. Distribution of living languages by country

Country	Living languages				Number of speakers			Diversity	
	Total	Per-cent	Indige-nous	Immi-grant	Count	Mean	Median	Index	Cover-age
Afghanistan	51	0.74	47	4	11,968,781	234,682	3,768	0.732	90%
Albania	7	0.10	7	0	3,385,000	483,571	60,000	0.257	86%
Algeria	22	0.32	18	4	24,859,164	1,129,962	40,000	0.313	64%
American Samoa	6	0.09	2	4	60,348	10,058	1,248	0.116	83%
Andorra	5	0.07	3	2	60,870	12,174	2,400	0.574	100%
Angola	41	0.59	41	0	11,018,012	268,732	39,403	0.785	93%
Anguilla	2	0.03	2	0	12,446	6,223	946	0.140	100%
Antigua and Barbuda	4	0.06	2	2	68,970	17,242	1,600	0.057	75%
Argentina	39	0.56	25	14	37,269,717	955,634	10,000	0.213	74%
Armenia	11	0.16	6	5	3,748,539	340,776	4,700	0.174	91%
Aruba	5	0.07	3	2	77,989	15,598	5,289	0.387	80%
Australia	275	3.98	231	44	16,781,815	61,025	15	0.126	90%
Austria	19	0.27	9	10	15,113,863	795,466	23,000	0.540	79%

Table 5. Distribution of living languages by country (continued)

Country	Living languages				Number of speakers			Diversity	
	Total	Per-cent	Indige-nous	Immi-grant	Count	Mean	Median	Index	Cover-age
Azerbaijan	35	0.51	14	21	7,761,112	221,746	5,208	0.373	83%
Bahamas	4	0.06	2	2	295,131	73,783	20,000	0.386	100%
Bahrain	11	0.16	3	8	557,589	50,690	25,000	0.663	82%
Bangladesh	46	0.67	39	7	123,877,068	2,692,980	17,695	0.332	78%
Barbados	2	0.03	2	0	272,000	136,000	13,000	0.091	100%
Belarus	9	0.13	1	8	8,797,031	977,448	231,000	0.397	89%
Belgium	28	0.41	9	19	12,304,650	439,452	63,600	0.734	71%
Belize	12	0.17	8	4	179,582	14,965	8,455	0.693	67%
Benin	55	0.80	54	1	6,449,442	117,263	62,000	0.901	96%
Bermuda	1	0.01	1	0	58,800	58,800	58,800	0.000	100%
Bhutan	31	0.45	24	7	657,528	21,211	8,000	0.846	74%
Bolivia	39	0.56	36	3	8,498,022	217,898	1,300	0.680	95%
Bosnia and Herzegovina	8	0.12	4	4	5,323,000	665,375	400,000	0.416	75%
Botswana	37	0.54	28	9	1,450,888	39,213	6,000	0.444	78%
Brazil	200	2.89	188	12	165,836,223	829,181	270	0.032	
British Indian Ocean Territory	1	0.01	1	0	3,500	3,500	3,500	0.000	
British Virgin Islands	2	0.03	2	0	21,730	10,865	2,000	0.167	100%
Brunei	19	0.27	17	2	341,573	17,978	6,566	0.456	79%
Bulgaria	16	0.23	11	5	9,117,720	569,858	11,000	0.224	81%
Burkina Faso	69	1.00	68	1	11,019,638	159,705	24,000	0.773	94%
Burundi	4	0.06	3	1	4,609,456	1,152,364	2,200	0.004	100%
Cambodia	24	0.35	21	3	13,204,056	550,169	5,286	0.157	92%
Cameroon	280	4.05	279	1	9,638,055	34,422	8,500	0.942	96%
Canada	145	2.10	85	60	27,388,756	188,888	2,353	0.549	81%
Cape Verde Islands	2	0.03	2	0	408,760	204,380	14,817	0.070	100%
Cayman Islands	3	0.04	1	2	42,974	14,325	20,000	0.547	100%
Central African Republic	79	1.14	69	10	3,404,818	43,099	15,000	0.960	95%
Chad	133	1.92	132	1	5,909,406	44,432	11,828	0.950	93%
Chile	12	0.17	9	3	14,041,312	1,170,109	2,000	0.034	67%
China	241	3.49	235	6	1,226,606,396	5,089,653	30,000	0.491	98%
Colombia	83	1.20	80	3	34,521,390	415,920	876	0.030	92%
Comoros	8	0.12	7	1	523,314	65,414	1,700	0.551	75%
Congo	66	0.95	62	4	2,935,116	44,471	9,599	0.820	91%
Cook Islands	6	0.09	5	1	21,619	3,603	683	0.379	100%

Table 5. Distribution of living languages by country (continued)

Country	Living languages				Number of speakers			Diversity	
	Total	Per-cent	Indige-nous	Immi-grant	Count	Mean	Median	Index	Cover-age
Costa Rica	13	0.19	9	4	3,385,392	260,415	4,500	0.050	77%
Côte d'Ivoire	92	1.33	78	14	9,220,274	100,220	26,448	0.917	87%
Croatia	8	0.12	6	2	5,025,365	628,171	22,810	0.087	75%
Cuba	4	0.06	2	2	10,003,500	2,500,875	3,500	0.001	50%
Cyprus	6	0.09	4	2	759,040	126,507	2,740	0.366	67%
Czech Republic	9	0.13	8	1	10,372,655	1,152,517	33,500	0.069	89%
Democratic Republic of the Congo	216	3.12	214	2	37,945,510	175,674	26,000	0.948	93%
Denmark	14	0.20	8	6	5,132,600	366,614	10,000	0.051	64%
Djibouti	6	0.09	5	1	660,247	110,041	52,000	0.592	83%
Dominica	3	0.04	3	0	52,800	17,600	10,000	0.313	100%
Dominican Republic	8	0.12	4	4	7,079,500	884,938	8,000	0.053	75%
East Timor	19	0.27	19	0	531,480	27,973	20,000	0.897	95%
Ecuador	25	0.36	23	2	11,139,315	445,573	4,000	0.264	96%
Egypt	21	0.30	11	10	69,089,400	3,289,971	100,000	0.509	76%
El Salvador	7	0.10	5	2	5,912,816	844,688	500	0.004	71%
Equatorial Guinea	14	0.20	14	0	355,164	25,369	5,000	0.453	93%
Eritrea	18	0.26	12	6	2,965,000	164,722	107,000	0.749	61%
Estonia	16	0.23	2	14	1,467,370	91,711	1,610	0.476	94%
Ethiopia	86	1.24	84	2	53,388,969	620,802	23,785	0.843	98%
Falkland Islands	1	0.01	1	0	1,991	1,991	1,991	0.000	100%
Fiji	20	0.29	10	10	809,457	40,473	4,929	0.607	65%
Finland	23	0.33	12	11	5,077,028	220,740	4,500	0.140	74%
France	66	0.95	29	37	59,861,314	906,990	50,000	0.272	62%
French Guiana	15	0.22	10	5	70,492	4,699	800	0.480	80%
French Polynesia	11	0.16	9	2	192,758	17,523	3,400	0.596	91%
Gabon	41	0.59	41	0	609,423	14,864	6,000	0.919	93%
Gambia	22	0.32	9	13	1,113,325	50,606	12,600	0.748	73%
Georgia	24	0.35	12	12	6,133,146	255,548	38,000	0.576	96%
Germany	69	1.00	27	42	83,674,659	1,212,676	26,000	0.189	65%
Ghana	83	1.20	79	4	20,119,660	242,406	30,000	0.805	87%
Gibraltar	3	0.04	2	1	6,200	2,067	2,900	0.498	67%
Greece	24	0.35	14	10	10,865,640	452,735	20,000	0.175	79%
Greenland	2	0.03	2	0	55,630	27,815	7,830	0.242	100%
Grenada	3	0.04	3	0	92,277	30,759	2,300	0.064	100%
Guadeloupe	4	0.06	4	0	449,500	112,375	7,300	0.084	100%

Table 5. Distribution of living languages by country (continued)

Country	Living languages				Number of speakers			Diversity	
	Total	Per-cent	Indige-nous	Immi-grant	Count	Mean	Median	Index	Cover-age
Guam	8	0.12	2	6	121,800	15,225	24,000	0.640	62%
Guatemala	54	0.78	54	0	9,141,619	169,289	33,800	0.691	96%
Guinea	38	0.55	34	4	6,647,526	174,935	13,000	0.748	79%
Guinea-Bissau	25	0.36	21	4	1,439,995	57,600	8,170	0.853	88%
Guyana	19	0.27	16	3	677,164	35,640	475	0.078	68%
Haiti	2	0.03	2	0	6,965,149	3,482,574	600	0.000	100%
Honduras	13	0.19	10	3	5,763,764	443,366	994	0.056	92%
Hungary	21	0.30	12	9	11,234,528	534,978	21,000	0.158	62%
Iceland	3	0.04	3	0	232,250	77,417	2,250	0.019	67%
India	427	6.18	415	12	943,283,395	2,209,095	28,600	0.930	94%
Indonesia	742	10.73	737	5	218,607,876	294,620	3,500	0.846	97%
Iran	79	1.14	75	4	73,367,033	928,697	80,000	0.797	68%
Iraq	25	0.36	21	4	22,595,945	903,838	40,000	0.666	88%
Ireland	5	0.07	5	0	2,966,000	593,200	100,000	0.223	80%
Israel	48	0.69	33	15	8,668,332	180,590	45,000	0.665	83%
Italy	42	0.61	33	9	88,717,451	2,112,320	50,626	0.593	86%
Jamaica	6	0.09	3	3	2,680,636	446,773	5,000	0.011	67%
Japan	16	0.23	15	1	122,801,150	7,675,072	5,000	0.028	75%
Jordan	15	0.22	9	6	5,028,193	335,213	10,000	0.484	80%
Kazakhstan	43	0.62	7	36	15,169,608	352,782	22,871	0.701	81%
Kenya	64	0.93	61	3	26,408,109	412,627	112,000	0.901	94%
Kiribati	3	0.04	2	1	59,312	19,771	500	0.033	100%
Korea, North	1	0.01	1	0	20,000,000	20,000,000	20,000,000	0.000	100%
Korea, South	4	0.06	2	2	42,063,600	10,515,900	63,600	0.003	50%
Kuwait	7	0.10	3	4	819,358	117,051	85,000	0.556	71%
Kyrgyzstan	32	0.46	3	29	5,060,314	158,135	14,000	0.670	84%
Laos	86	1.24	82	4	5,387,373	62,644	6,000	0.678	95%
Latvia	12	0.17	5	7	2,586,615	215,551	40,000	0.595	92%
Lebanon	9	0.13	6	3	4,266,500	474,056	18,000	0.161	89%
Lesotho	6	0.09	5	1	2,079,000	346,500	43,000	0.260	67%
Liberia	31	0.45	30	1	2,463,817	79,478	47,000	0.912	94%
Libya	14	0.20	9	5	5,409,186	386,370	7,000	0.362	71%
Liechtenstein	4	0.06	3	1	31,100	7,775	1,300	0.128	75%
Lithuania	11	0.16	4	7	3,675,303	334,118	45,000	0.339	73%
Luxembourg	6	0.09	3	3	447,800	74,633	13,100	0.498	100%
Macedonia	10	0.14	9	1	2,320,467	232,047	120,000	0.566	70%
Madagascar	15	0.22	13	2	10,571,000	704,733	350,000	0.656	93%

Table 5. Distribution of living languages by country (continued)

Country	Living languages				Number of speakers			Diversity	
	Total	Per-cent	Indige-nous	Immi-grant	Count	Mean	Median	Index	Cover-age
Malawi	22	0.32	14	8	10,314,480	468,840	170,000	0.519	68%
Malaysia	147	2.13	140	7	15,676,135	106,640	3,677	0.758	87%
Maldives	2	0.03	1	1	284,096	142,048	1,400	0.010	100%
Mali	54	0.78	50	4	9,031,529	167,251	50,000	0.876	89%
Malta	3	0.04	3	0	302,400	100,800	2,400	0.016	67%
Marshall Islands	2	0.03	2	0	44,500	22,250	600	0.027	100%
Martinique	3	0.04	2	1	427,784	142,595	9,000	0.043	100%
Mauritania	9	0.13	6	3	2,725,734	302,859	30,000	0.172	78%
Mauritius	13	0.19	6	7	1,157,798	89,061	31,000	0.641	85%
Mayotte	4	0.06	4	0	137,000	34,250	2,744	0.459	100%
Mexico	297	4.30	291	6	92,701,909	312,128	5,000	0.135	97%
Micronesia	19	0.27	18	1	110,053	5,792	1,631	0.792	95%
Moldova	13	0.19	5	8	4,399,547	338,427	138,000	0.589	69%
Monaco	3	0.04	3	0	27,000	9,000	5,100	0.521	100%
Mongolia	15	0.22	13	2	2,869,750	191,317	27,000	0.331	67%
Montserrat	2	0.03	2	0	7,674	3,837	100	0.026	100%
Morocco	10	0.14	9	1	26,448,925	2,644,892	80,000	0.466	80%
Mozambique	43	0.62	43	0	16,210,221	376,982	150,000	0.929	95%
Myanmar	113	1.63	108	5	46,627,310	412,631	21,000	0.521	88%
Namibia	36	0.52	28	8	1,154,615	32,073	12,000	0.808	69%
Nauru	9	0.13	3	6	10,009	1,112	714	0.596	67%
Nepal	125	1.81	123	2	22,983,905	183,871	6,533	0.742	94%
Netherlands	38	0.55	15	23	15,913,060	418,765	45,000	0.389	58%
Netherlands Antilles	6	0.09	4	2	210,000	35,000	4,000	0.266	100%
New Caledonia	41	0.59	39	2	147,491	3,597	947	0.834	100%
New Zealand	21	0.30	3	18	3,391,096	161,481	3,965	0.102	71%
Nicaragua	7	0.10	7	0	4,538,124	648,303	30,000	0.081	71%
Niger	21	0.30	21	0	9,230,862	439,565	30,000	0.646	100%
Nigeria	516	7.47	510	6	90,026,548	174,470	12,000	0.870	89%
Niue	3	0.04	2	1	2,105	702	78	0.071	67%
Norfolk Island	1	0.01	1	0	1,678	1,678	1,678	0.000	100%
Northern Mariana Islands	7	0.10	4	3	26,805	3,829	4,400	0.642	57%
Norway	21	0.30	11	10	177,168	8,437	5,000	0.657	67%
Oman	21	0.30	13	8	1,554,063	74,003	22,000	0.693	76%
Pakistan	77	1.11	72	5	137,566,712	1,786,581	50,000	0.762	87%
Palau	5	0.07	4	1	15,447	3,089	600	0.077	60%

Table 5. Distribution of living languages by country (continued)

Country	Living languages				Number of speakers			Diversity	
	Total	Per-cent	Indige-nous	Immi-grant	Count	Mean	Median	Index	Cover-age
Palestinian West Bank and Gaza	6	0.09	4	2	1,812,000	302,000	10,000	0.208	67%
Panama	18	0.26	14	4	2,580,472	143,360	3,000	0.324	72%
Papua New Guinea	820	11.86	820	0	3,665,383	4,470	1,196	0.990	100%
Paraguay	26	0.38	20	6	5,815,850	223,687	6,705	0.347	100%
Peru	94	1.36	93	1	25,447,086	270,714	5,000	0.376	96%
Philippines	180	2.60	171	9	70,556,507	391,981	16,043	0.849	96%
Pitcairn	1	0.01	1	0	46	46	46	0.000	100%
Poland	17	0.25	11	6	37,704,010	2,217,883	38,000	0.060	71%
Portugal	8	0.12	7	1	10,110,539	1,263,817	15,000	0.022	88%
Puerto Rico	13	0.19	3	10	3,525,391	271,184	1,556	0.049	54%
Qatar	6	0.09	3	3	205,250	34,208	19,950	0.608	83%
Réunion	6	0.09	3	3	573,900	95,650	8,000	0.066	67%
Romania	23	0.33	15	8	21,706,330	943,753	21,482	0.168	83%
Russia	129	1.87	101	28	139,356,854	1,080,286	10,000	0.283	91%
Rwanda	5	0.07	3	2	6,504,952	1,300,990	2,300	0.004	80%
Saint Helena	1	0.01	1	0	5,400	5,400	5,400	0.000	100%
Saint Kitts and Nevis	2	0.03	2	0	39,200	19,600	200	0.010	100%
Saint Lucia	2	0.03	2	0	159,778	79,889	1,600	0.020	100%
Saint Pierre and Miquelon	3	0.04	2	1	5,502	1,834	200	0.134	100%
Saint Vincent and the Grenadines	3	0.04	2	1	138,600	46,200	400	0.009	100%
Samoa	2	0.03	2	0	199,577	99,788	200	0.002	100%
San Marino	2	0.03	2	0	45,112	22,556	20,112	0.494	100%
São Tomé e Príncipe	5	0.07	4	1	91,450	18,290	5,000	0.389	100%
Saudi Arabia	20	0.29	5	15	16,057,746	802,887	60,000	0.609	90%
Senegal	41	0.59	36	5	9,479,825	231,215	16,700	0.772	90%
Serbia and Montenegro	14	0.20	11	3	12,953,366	925,240	80,000	0.359	71%
Seychelles	3	0.04	3	0	75,278	25,093	1,601	0.067	100%
Sierra Leone	25	0.36	24	1	4,739,450	189,578	85,000	0.817	88%
Singapore	30	0.43	21	9	2,619,376	87,313	10,000	0.748	83%
Slovakia	12	0.17	10	2	5,898,350	491,529	50,000	0.307	67%
Slovenia	10	0.14	4	6	1,908,637	190,864	4,022	0.174	80%
Solomon Islands	70	1.01	70	0	354,001	5,057	2,767	0.965	99%
Somalia	13	0.19	13	0	8,616,834	662,833	29,726	0.179	77%

Table 5. Distribution of living languages by country (continued)

Country	Living languages				Number of speakers			Diversity	
	Total	Per-cent	Indige-nous	Immi-grant	Count	Mean	Median	Index	Cover-age
South Africa	35	0.51	24	11	41,151,149	1,175,747	250,000	0.869	71%
Spain	20	0.29	13	7	38,801,740	1,940,087	25,000	0.438	70%
Sri Lanka	7	0.10	7	0	16,317,876	2,331,125	50,000	0.313	86%
Sudan	134	1.94	134	0	23,492,482	175,317	16,000	0.587	90%
Suriname	20	0.29	16	4	628,827	31,441	7,008	0.788	75%
Swaziland	4	0.06	4	0	745,000	186,250	76,000	0.228	75%
Sweden	32	0.46	15	17	8,581,331	268,167	10,000	0.167	81%
Switzerland	26	0.38	12	14	6,570,769	252,722	53,000	0.547	62%
Syria	18	0.26	15	3	12,850,000	713,889	30,000	0.503	78%
Taiwan	27	0.39	22	5	22,057,144	816,931	4,750	0.488	81%
Tajikistan	33	0.48	9	24	4,816,568	145,957	6,000	0.482	82%
Tanzania	128	1.85	127	1	25,837,668	201,857	87,000	0.965	90%
Thailand	83	1.20	74	9	53,478,502	644,319	20,000	0.753	75%
Togo	42	0.61	39	3	3,978,381	94,723	40,000	0.897	90%
Tokelau	2	0.03	2	0	1,445	722	40	0.054	100%
Tonga	3	0.04	3	0	97,024	32,341	690	0.014	67%
Trinidad and Tobago	7	0.10	6	1	74,333	10,619	4,100	0.696	100%
Tunisia	10	0.14	6	4	9,052,498	905,250	3,000	0.012	80%
Turkey	45	0.65	34	11	55,100,539	1,224,456	25,000	0.289	78%
Turkmenistan	27	0.39	3	24	4,419,733	163,694	5,289	0.386	93%
Turks and Caicos Islands	2	0.03	2	0	11,650	5,825	920	0.145	100%
Tuvalu	2	0.03	2	0	11,540	5,770	870	0.139	100%
U.S. Virgin Islands	4	0.06	2	2	65,308	16,327	4,444	0.339	100%
Uganda	46	0.67	43	3	17,009,328	369,768	200,000	0.928	89%
Ukraine	39	0.56	10	29	46,450,195	1,191,031	24,000	0.492	79%
United Arab Emirates	36	0.52	7	29	1,773,641	49,268	5,000	0.777	75%
United Kingdom	55	0.80	12	43	59,301,657	1,078,212	30,000	0.139	82%
Uruguay	11	0.16	2	9	3,150,200	286,382	28,000	0.092	55%
USA	311	4.50	162	149	262,740,392	844,824	700	0.353	73%
Uzbekistan	40	0.58	7	33	22,066,002	551,650	29,000	0.428	85%
Vanuatu	115	1.66	109	6	119,759	1,041	400	0.972	98%
Vatican State	1	0.01	1	0	1,000	1,000	1,000	0.000	100%
Venezuela	46	0.67	40	6	21,763,459	473,119	650	0.026	78%
Viet Nam	104	1.50	102	2	75,259,890	723,653	13,500	0.234	87%
Wallis and Futuna	3	0.04	3	0	13,337	4,446	3,600	0.407	100%

Table 5. Distribution of living languages by country (continued)

Country	Living languages				Number of speakers			Diversity	
	Total	Per-cent	Indige-nous	Immi-grant	Count	Mean	Median	Index	Cover-age
Yemen	14	0.20	8	6	15,720,307	1,122,879	70,643	0.579	71%
Zambia	44	0.64	41	3	10,673,160	242,572	74,800	0.855	84%
Zimbabwe	21	0.30	19	2	15,795,670	752,175	137,000	0.526	76%

Table 6. Linguistic diversity of countries (from highest to lowest)

Country	Diversity		Living languages				Number of speakers		
	Index	Cover-age	Total	Per-cent	Indig-enous	Immi-grant	Count	Mean	Median
Papua New Guinea	0.990	100%	820	11.86	820	0	3,665,383	4,470	1,196
Vanuatu	0.972	98%	115	1.66	109	6	119,759	1,041	400
Solomon Islands	0.965	99%	70	1.01	70	0	354,001	5,057	2,767
Tanzania	0.965	90%	128	1.85	127	1	25,837,668	201,857	87,000
Central African Republic	0.960	95%	79	1.14	69	10	3,404,818	43,099	15,000
Chad	0.950	93%	133	1.92	132	1	5,909,406	44,432	11,828
Democratic Republic of the Congo	0.948	93%	216	3.12	214	2	37,945,510	175,674	26,000
Cameroon	0.942	96%	280	4.05	279	1	9,638,055	34,422	8,500
India	0.930	94%	427	6.18	415	12	943,283,395	2,209,095	28,600
Mozambique	0.929	95%	43	0.62	43	0	16,210,221	376,982	150,000
Uganda	0.928	89%	46	0.67	43	3	17,009,328	369,768	200,000
Gabon	0.919	93%	41	0.59	41	0	609,423	14,864	6,000
Côte d'Ivoire	0.917	87%	92	1.33	78	14	9,220,274	100,220	26,448
Liberia	0.912	94%	31	0.45	30	1	2,463,817	79,478	47,000
Benin	0.901	96%	55	0.80	54	1	6,449,442	117,263	62,000
Kenya	0.901	94%	64	0.93	61	3	26,408,109	412,627	112,000
East Timor	0.897	95%	19	0.27	19	0	531,480	27,973	20,000
Togo	0.897	90%	42	0.61	39	3	3,978,381	94,723	40,000
Mali	0.876	89%	54	0.78	50	4	9,031,529	167,251	50,000
Nigeria	0.870	89%	516	7.47	510	6	90,026,548	174,470	12,000
South Africa	0.869	71%	35	0.51	24	11	41,151,149	1,175,747	250,000
Zambia	0.855	84%	44	0.64	41	3	10,673,160	242,572	74,800
Guinea-Bissau	0.853	88%	25	0.36	21	4	1,439,995	57,600	8,170
Philippines	0.849	96%	180	2.60	171	9	70,556,507	391,981	16,043

Table 6. Linguistic diversity of countries (from highest to lowest, continued)

Country	Diversity		Living languages				Number of speakers		
	Index	Cover-age	Total	Per-cent	Indig-enous	Immi-grant	Count	Mean	Median
Bhutan	0.846	74%	31	0.45	24	7	657,528	21,211	8,000
Indonesia	0.846	97%	742	10.73	737	5	218,607,876	294,620	3,500
Ethiopia	0.843	98%	86	1.24	84	2	53,388,969	620,802	23,785
New Caledonia	0.834	100%	41	0.59	39	2	147,491	3,597	947
Congo	0.820	91%	66	0.95	62	4	2,935,116	44,471	9,599
Sierra Leone	0.817	88%	25	0.36	24	1	4,739,450	189,578	85,000
Namibia	0.808	69%	36	0.52	28	8	1,154,615	32,073	12,000
Ghana	0.805	87%	83	1.20	79	4	20,119,660	242,406	30,000
Iran	0.797	68%	79	1.14	75	4	73,367,033	928,697	80,000
Micronesia	0.792	95%	19	0.27	18	1	110,053	5,792	1,631
Suriname	0.788	75%	20	0.29	16	4	628,827	31,441	7,008
Angola	0.785	93%	41	0.59	41	0	11,018,012	268,732	39,403
United Arab Emirates	0.777	75%	36	0.52	7	29	1,773,641	49,268	5,000
Burkina Faso	0.773	94%	69	1.00	68	1	11,019,638	159,705	24,000
Senegal	0.772	90%	41	0.59	36	5	9,479,825	231,215	16,700
Pakistan	0.762	87%	77	1.11	72	5	137,566,712	1,786,581	50,000
Malaysia	0.758	87%	147	2.13	140	7	15,676,135	106,640	3,677
Thailand	0.753	75%	83	1.20	74	9	53,478,502	644,319	20,000
Eritrea	0.749	61%	18	0.26	12	6	2,965,000	164,722	107,000
Gambia	0.748	73%	22	0.32	9	13	1,113,325	50,606	12,600
Guinea	0.748	79%	38	0.55	34	4	6,647,526	174,935	13,000
Singapore	0.748	83%	30	0.43	21	9	2,619,376	87,313	10,000
Nepal	0.742	94%	125	1.81	123	2	22,983,905	183,871	6,533
Belgium	0.734	71%	28	0.41	9	19	12,304,650	439,452	63,600
Afghanistan	0.732	90%	51	0.74	47	4	11,968,781	234,682	3,768
Kazakhstan	0.701	81%	43	0.62	7	36	15,169,608	352,782	22,871
Trinidad and Tobago	0.696	100%	7	0.10	6	1	74,333	10,619	4,100
Belize	0.693	67%	12	0.17	8	4	179,582	14,965	8,455
Oman	0.693	76%	21	0.30	13	8	1,554,063	74,003	22,000
Guatemala	0.691	96%	54	0.78	54	0	9,141,619	169,289	33,800
Bolivia	0.680	95%	39	0.56	36	3	8,498,022	217,898	1,300
Laos	0.678	95%	86	1.24	82	4	5,387,373	62,644	6,000
Kyrgyzstan	0.670	84%	32	0.46	3	29	5,060,314	158,135	14,000

Table 6. Linguistic diversity of countries (from highest to lowest, continued)

Country	Diversity		Living languages				Number of speakers		
	Index	Cover-age	Total	Per-cent	Indig-enous	Immi-grant	Count	Mean	Median
Iraq	0.666	88%	25	0.36	21	4	22,595,945	903,838	40,000
Israel	0.665	83%	48	0.69	33	15	8,668,332	180,590	45,000
Bahrain	0.663	82%	11	0.16	3	8	557,589	50,690	25,000
Norway	0.657	67%	21	0.30	11	10	177,168	8,437	5,000
Madagascar	0.656	93%	15	0.22	13	2	10,571,000	704,733	350,000
Niger	0.646	100%	21	0.30	21	0	9,230,862	439,565	30,000
Northern Mariana Islands	0.642	57%	7	0.10	4	3	26,805	3,829	4,400
Mauritius	0.641	85%	13	0.19	6	7	1,157,798	89,061	31,000
Guam	0.640	62%	8	0.12	2	6	121,800	15,225	24,000
Saudi Arabia	0.609	90%	20	0.29	5	15	16,057,746	802,887	60,000
Qatar	0.608	83%	6	0.09	3	3	205,250	34,208	19,950
Fiji	0.607	65%	20	0.29	10	10	809,457	40,473	4,929
French Polynesia	0.596	91%	11	0.16	9	2	192,758	17,523	3,400
Nauru	0.596	67%	9	0.13	3	6	10,009	1,112	714
Latvia	0.595	92%	12	0.17	5	7	2,586,615	215,551	40,000
Italy	0.593	86%	42	0.61	33	9	88,717,451	2,112,320	50,626
Djibouti	0.592	83%	6	0.09	5	1	660,247	110,041	52,000
Moldova	0.589	69%	13	0.19	5	8	4,399,547	338,427	138,000
Sudan	0.587	90%	134	1.94	134	0	23,492,482	175,317	16,000
Yemen	0.579	71%	14	0.20	8	6	15,720,307	1,122,879	70,643
Georgia	0.576	96%	24	0.35	12	12	6,133,146	255,548	38,000
Andorra	0.574	100%	5	0.07	3	2	60,870	12,174	2,400
Macedonia	0.566	70%	10	0.14	9	1	2,320,467	232,047	120,000
Kuwait	0.556	71%	7	0.10	3	4	819,358	117,051	85,000
Comoros	0.551	75%	8	0.12	7	1	523,314	65,414	1,700
Canada	0.549	81%	145	2.10	85	60	27,388,756	188,888	2,353
Cayman Islands	0.547	100%	3	0.04	1	2	42,974	14,325	20,000
Switzerland	0.547	62%	26	0.38	12	14	6,570,769	252,722	53,000
Austria	0.540	79%	19	0.27	9	10	15,113,863	795,466	23,000
Zimbabwe	0.526	76%	21	0.30	19	2	15,795,670	752,175	137,000
Monaco	0.521	100%	3	0.04	3	0	27,000	9,000	5,100
Myanmar	0.521	88%	113	1.63	108	5	46,627,310	412,631	21,000
Malawi	0.519	68%	22	0.32	14	8	10,314,480	468,840	170,000
Egypt	0.509	76%	21	0.30	11	10	69,089,400	3,289,971	100,000

Table 6. Linguistic diversity of countries (from highest to lowest, continued)

Country	Diversity		Living languages				Number of speakers		
	Index	Cover-age	Total	Per-cent	Indig-enous	Immi-grant	Count	Mean	Median
Syria	0.503	78%	18	0.26	15	3	12,850,000	713,889	30,000
Gibraltar	0.498	67%	3	0.04	2	1	6,200	2,067	2,900
Luxembourg	0.498	100%	6	0.09	3	3	447,800	74,633	13,100
San Marino	0.494	100%	2	0.03	2	0	45,112	22,556	20,112
Ukraine	0.492	79%	39	0.56	10	29	46,450,195	1,191,031	24,000
China	0.491	98%	241	3.49	235	6	1,226,606,396	5,089,653	30,000
Taiwan	0.488	81%	27	0.39	22	5	22,057,144	816,931	4,750
Jordan	0.484	80%	15	0.22	9	6	5,028,193	335,213	10,000
Tajikistan	0.482	82%	33	0.48	9	24	4,816,568	145,957	6,000
French Guiana	0.480	80%	15	0.22	10	5	70,492	4,699	800
Estonia	0.476	94%	16	0.23	2	14	1,467,370	91,711	1,610
Morocco	0.466	80%	10	0.14	9	1	26,448,925	2,644,892	80,000
Mayotte	0.459	100%	4	0.06	4	0	137,000	34,250	2,744
Brunei	0.456	79%	19	0.27	17	2	341,573	17,978	6,566
Equatorial Guinea	0.453	93%	14	0.20	14	0	355,164	25,369	5,000
Botswana	0.444	78%	37	0.54	28	9	1,450,888	39,213	6,000
Spain	0.438	70%	20	0.29	13	7	38,801,740	1,940,087	25,000
Uzbekistan	0.428	85%	40	0.58	7	33	22,066,002	551,650	29,000
Bosnia and Herzegovina	0.416	75%	8	0.12	4	4	5,323,000	665,375	400,000
Wallis and Futuna	0.407	100%	3	0.04	3	0	13,337	4,446	3,600
Belarus	0.397	89%	9	0.13	1	8	8,797,031	977,448	231,000
Netherlands	0.389	58%	38	0.55	15	23	15,913,060	418,765	45,000
São Tomé e Príncipe	0.389	100%	5	0.07	4	1	91,450	18,290	5,000
Aruba	0.387	80%	5	0.07	3	2	77,989	15,598	5,289
Bahamas	0.386	100%	4	0.06	2	2	295,131	73,783	20,000
Turkmenistan	0.386	93%	27	0.39	3	24	4,419,733	163,694	5,289
Cook Islands	0.379	100%	6	0.09	5	1	21,619	3,603	683
Peru	0.376	96%	94	1.36	93	1	25,447,086	270,714	5,000
Azerbaijan	0.373	83%	35	0.51	14	21	7,761,112	221,746	5,208
Cyprus	0.366	67%	6	0.09	4	2	759,040	126,507	2,740
Libya	0.362	71%	14	0.20	9	5	5,409,186	386,370	7,000
Serbia and Montenegro	0.359	71%	14	0.20	11	3	12,953,366	925,240	80,000
USA	0.353	73%	311	4.50	162	149	262,740,392	844,824	700

Table 6. Linguistic diversity of countries (from highest to lowest, continued)

Country	Diversity		Living languages				Number of speakers		
	Index	Cover-age	Total	Per-cent	Indig-enous	Immi-grant	Count	Mean	Median
Paraguay	0.347	100%	26	0.38	20	6	5,815,850	223,687	6,705
Lithuania	0.339	73%	11	0.16	4	7	3,675,303	334,118	45,000
U.S. Virgin Islands	0.339	100%	4	0.06	2	2	65,308	16,327	4,444
Bangladesh	0.332	78%	46	0.67	39	7	123,877,068	2,692,980	17,695
Mongolia	0.331	67%	15	0.22	13	2	2,869,750	191,317	27,000
Panama	0.324	72%	18	0.26	14	4	2,580,472	143,360	3,000
Algeria	0.313	64%	22	0.32	18	4	24,859,164	1,129,962	40,000
Dominica	0.313	100%	3	0.04	3	0	52,800	17,600	10,000
Sri Lanka	0.313	86%	7	0.10	7	0	16,317,876	2,331,125	50,000
Slovakia	0.307	67%	12	0.17	10	2	5,898,350	491,529	50,000
Turkey	0.289	78%	45	0.65	34	11	55,100,539	1,224,456	25,000
Russia	0.283	91%	129	1.87	101	28	139,356,854	1,080,286	10,000
France	0.272	62%	66	0.95	29	37	59,861,314	906,990	50,000
Netherlands Antilles	0.266	100%	6	0.09	4	2	210,000	35,000	4,000
Ecuador	0.264	96%	25	0.36	23	2	11,139,315	445,573	4,000
Lesotho	0.260	67%	6	0.09	5	1	2,079,000	346,500	43,000
Albania	0.257	86%	7	0.10	7	0	3,385,000	483,571	60,000
Greenland	0.242	100%	2	0.03	2	0	55,630	27,815	7,830
Viet Nam	0.234	87%	104	1.50	102	2	75,259,890	723,653	13,500
Swaziland	0.228	75%	4	0.06	4	0	745,000	186,250	76,000
Bulgaria	0.224	81%	16	0.23	11	5	9,117,720	569,858	11,000
Ireland	0.223	80%	5	0.07	5	0	2,966,000	593,200	100,000
Argentina	0.213	74%	39	0.56	25	14	37,269,717	955,634	10,000
Palestinian West Bank and Gaza	0.208	67%	6	0.09	4	2	1,812,000	302,000	10,000
Germany	0.189	65%	69	1.00	27	42	83,674,659	1,212,676	26,000
Somalia	0.179	77%	13	0.19	13	0	8,616,834	662,833	29,726
Greece	0.175	79%	24	0.35	14	10	10,865,640	452,735	20,000
Armenia	0.174	91%	11	0.16	6	5	3,748,539	340,776	4,700
Slovenia	0.174	80%	10	0.14	4	6	1,908,637	190,864	4,022
Mauritania	0.172	78%	9	0.13	6	3	2,725,734	302,859	30,000
Romania	0.168	83%	23	0.33	15	8	21,706,330	943,753	21,482
British Virgin Islands	0.167	100%	2	0.03	2	0	21,730	10,865	2,000

Table 6. Linguistic diversity of countries (from highest to lowest, continued)

Country	Diversity		Living languages				Number of speakers		
	Index	Cover-age	Total	Per-cent	Indig-enous	Immi-grant	Count	Mean	Median
Sweden	0.167	81%	32	0.46	15	17	8,581,331	268,167	10,000
Lebanon	0.161	89%	9	0.13	6	3	4,266,500	474,056	18,000
Hungary	0.158	62%	21	0.30	12	9	11,234,528	534,978	21,000
Cambodia	0.157	92%	24	0.35	21	3	13,204,056	550,169	5,286
Turks and Caicos Islands	0.145	100%	2	0.03	2	0	11,650	5,825	920
Anguilla	0.140	100%	2	0.03	2	0	12,446	6,223	946
Finland	0.140	74%	23	0.33	12	11	5,077,028	220,740	4,500
Tuvalu	0.139	100%	2	0.03	2	0	11,540	5,770	870
United Kingdom	0.139	82%	55	0.80	12	43	59,301,657	1,078,212	30,000
Mexico	0.135	97%	297	4.30	291	6	92,701,909	312,128	5,000
Saint Pierre and Miquelon	0.134	100%	3	0.04	2	1	5,502	1,834	200
Liechtenstein	0.128	75%	4	0.06	3	1	31,100	7,775	1,300
Australia	0.126	90%	275	3.98	231	44	16,781,815	61,025	15
American Samoa	0.116	83%	6	0.09	2	4	60,348	10,058	1,248
New Zealand	0.102	71%	21	0.30	3	18	3,391,096	161,481	3,965
Uruguay	0.092	55%	11	0.16	2	9	3,150,200	286,382	28,000
Barbados	0.091	100%	2	0.03	2	0	272,000	136,000	13,000
Croatia	0.087	75%	8	0.12	6	2	5,025,365	628,171	22,810
Guadeloupe	0.084	100%	4	0.06	4	0	449,500	112,375	7,300
Nicaragua	0.081	71%	7	0.10	7	0	4,538,124	648,303	30,000
Guyana	0.078	68%	19	0.27	16	3	677,164	35,640	475
Palau	0.077	60%	5	0.07	4	1	15,447	3,089	600
Niue	0.071	67%	3	0.04	2	1	2,105	702	78
Cape Verde Islands	0.070	100%	2	0.03	2	0	408,760	204,380	14,817
Czech Republic	0.069	89%	9	0.13	8	1	10,372,655	1,152,517	33,500
Seychelles	0.067	100%	3	0.04	3	0	75,278	25,093	1,601
Réunion	0.066	67%	6	0.09	3	3	573,900	95,650	8,000
Grenada	0.064	100%	3	0.04	3	0	92,277	30,759	2,300
Poland	0.060	71%	17	0.25	11	6	37,704,010	2,217,883	38,000
Antigua and Barbuda	0.057	75%	4	0.06	2	2	68,970	17,242	1,600
Honduras	0.056	92%	13	0.19	10	3	5,763,764	443,366	994
Tokelau	0.054	100%	2	0.03	2	0	1,445	722	40

Table 6. Linguistic diversity of countries (from highest to lowest, continued)

Country	Diversity		Living languages				Number of speakers		
	Index	*Cover-age*	*Total*	*Per-cent*	*Indig-enous*	*Immi-grant*	*Count*	*Mean*	*Median*
Dominican Republic	0.053	75%	8	0.12	4	4	7,079,500	884,938	8,000
Denmark	0.051	64%	14	0.20	8	6	5,132,600	366,614	10,000
Costa Rica	0.050	77%	13	0.19	9	4	3,385,392	260,415	4,500
Puerto Rico	0.049	54%	13	0.19	3	10	3,525,391	271,184	1,556
Martinique	0.043	100%	3	0.04	2	1	427,784	142,595	9,000
Chile	0.034	67%	12	0.17	9	3	14,041,312	1,170,109	2,000
Kiribati	0.033	100%	3	0.04	2	1	59,312	19,771	500
Brazil	0.032	92%	200	2.89	188	12	165,836,223	829,181	270
Colombia	0.030	92%	83	1.20	80	3	34,521,390	415,920	876
Japan	0.028	75%	16	0.23	15	1	122,801,150	7,675,072	5,000
Marshall Islands	0.027	100%	2	0.03	2	0	44,500	22,250	600
Montserrat	0.026	100%	2	0.03	2	0	7,674	3,837	100
Venezuela	0.026	78%	46	0.67	40	6	21,763,459	473,119	650
Portugal	0.022	88%	8	0.12	7	1	10,110,539	1,263,817	15,000
Saint Lucia	0.020	100%	2	0.03	2	0	159,778	79,889	1,600
Iceland	0.019	67%	3	0.04	3	0	232,250	77,417	2,250
Malta	0.016	67%	3	0.04	3	0	302,400	100,800	2,400
Tonga	0.014	67%	3	0.04	3	0	97,024	32,341	690
Tunisia	0.012	80%	10	0.14	6	4	9,052,498	905,250	3,000
Jamaica	0.011	67%	6	0.09	3	3	2,680,636	446,773	5,000
Maldives	0.010	100%	2	0.03	1	1	284,096	142,048	1,400
Saint Kitts and Nevis	0.010	100%	2	0.03	2	0	39,200	19,600	200
Saint Vincent and the Grenadines	0.009	100%	3	0.04	2	1	138,600	46,200	400
Burundi	0.004	100%	4	0.06	3	1	4,609,456	1,152,364	2,200
El Salvador	0.004	71%	7	0.10	5	2	5,912,816	844,688	500
Rwanda	0.004	80%	5	0.07	3	2	6,504,952	1,300,990	2,300
Korea, South	0.003	50%	4	0.06	2	2	42,063,600	10,515,900	63,600
Samoa	0.002	100%	2	0.03	2	0	199,577	99,788	200
Cuba	0.001	50%	4	0.06	2	2	10,003,500	2,500,875	3,500
Haiti	0.000	100%	2	0.03	2	0	6,965,149	3,482,574	600

Part I
Languages of the World

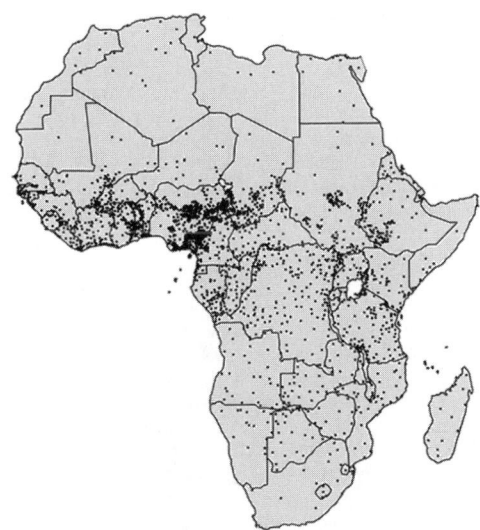

Africa

Algeria

Democratic and Popular Republic of Algeria. al-Jumhuriya al-Jazãiriya ad-Dimuqratiya ash-Shabiya. 32,129,324. 14% speak Berber languages. National or official language: Standard Arabic. Literacy rate: 50% to 52%. Also includes Catalan-Valencian-Balear, Hassaniyya Arabic (150,000), Kidal Tamasheq, Tadaksahak (1,800). Information mainly from Y. Zavadovskii 1962; M. Bateson 1967; J. Applegate 1970; Ph. Marcais 1977; W. Fischer and O. Jastrow 1980; D. Cohen 1985. Blind population: 25,000. Deaf institutions: 3. The number of languages listed for Algeria is 18. Of those, all are living languages. See map on page 677.

Algerian Sign Language [asp] *Class:* Deaf sign language. *Dialects:* It has influenced the deaf community in Oujda in northern Morocco.

Arabic, Algerian Saharan Spoken (Saharan Arabic, Tamanrasset Arabic, Tamanghasset Arabic) [aao] 100,000 in Algeria (1996). Population total all countries: 110,000. Moroccan border along the Atlas Mountains, northeast to Medea (south of Algiers), southeast to the Righ Wadi, south to 28 degrees latitude, as far as Plateau du Tademait, including some in the town of Tamanrasset. Also spoken in Niger. *Class:* Afro-Asiatic, Semitic, Central, South, Arabic. *Dialects:* Structurally distinct from other Arabic.

Arabic, Algerian Spoken (Algerian) [arq] 20,400,000 in Algeria (1996 Hunter). Population total all countries: 21,097,000. Also spoken in Belgium, France, Germany, Saint Pierre and Miquelon. *Class:* Afro-Asiatic, Semitic, Central, South, Arabic. *Dialects:* Constantine, Algiers, Oran. Eastern Algerian and Tunisian dialects are close, and Western Algerian and Moroccan dialects are close. *Lg Use:* The Ouled Nail of Biskra speak Arabic, but are ethnically separate. 3,000,000 second-language speakers. *Lg Dev:* Bible portions: 1872–1964. *Other:* Muslim (Sunni), Christian.

Arabic, Standard [arb] Middle East, North Africa. *Lg Use:* Official language. Used for written materials, formal speeches. Not a first language, but taught in schools. See main entry under Saudi Arabia.

Chenoua [cnu] 4,764 (2000 WCD). Towns are Cherchell, Hamadia, Gouraya, Damous, Oued Damous, Larhat, Marceau, Sidi Amar, Nador, Tipaza, Sidi Mousa, Ain Tagourirt. *Class:* Afro-Asiatic, Berber, Northern. *Dialects:* Lexical similarity 77% with Tachawit, 76% with Kabyle. *Lg Use:* Men and young people use Algerian Spoken Arabic as second language. *Other:* Muslim.

French [fra] 110,600 in Algeria (1993). Known more in the cities. *Lg Dev:* 20% of the population can read and write French. See main entry under France.

Kabyle (Tamazight) [kab] 2,537,000 in Algeria (1995). Estimates by some sources are up to 6,000,000 in Algeria (1998). 49,000 in Belgium. Population total all countries: 3,123,000. Grande Kabylie Mt. range, western Kabylia. Also spoken in Belgium, France. *Class:* Afro-Asiatic, Berber, Northern, Kabyle. *Dialects:* Greater Kabyle, Lesser Kabyle. *Lg Use:* Used in the home and market. Speakers have pride in Kabyle and resistance to Arabic. French is often used by men in trade and correspondence. Arabic is also used as second language, after French. *Lg Dev:* Roman script. NT: 1901–1995. *Other:* The name 'Kabyle' is reported by some sources to derive from the Arabic word for 'tribesman'. Patrilineal and patrilocal. Mountain slope. Peasant agriculturalists: olives, figs, pomegranates, peaches, apricots, pears, plums, vegetables. Muslim, secular, Christian.

Korandje [kcy] Tabelbala oasis. *Class:* Nilo-Saharan, Songhai. *Other:* The people are called 'Belbali'. They go to Libya from time to time to work.

Tachawit (Chaouia, Chawi, Shawiya, Shawia, Tacawit) [shy] 1,400,000 (1993). South and southeast of Grand Kabylie in the Aurès Mountains. *Class:* Afro-Asiatic, Berber, Northern, Zenati, Shawiya. *Lg Use:* One of the more widely used Berber languages. *Lg Dev:* Bible portions: 1950. *Other:* Muslim.

Tachelhit (Tashelhit, Tashelhait, Tashelhayt, Tasoussit, Shilha, Southern Shilha, Tachilhit) [shi] Southern Algeria near the Moroccan border around Tabelbala. *Dialect:* Susiua (Sus, Sousse). *Lg Use:* One of the more widely used Berber languages. Many men also use Arabic, but many women do not learn Arabic. *Other:* Their name for their language is 'Tachelhit'. 'Shilha' is the Arabic name for Moroccan Berber varieties in general. Muslim. See main entry under Morocco.

Tagargrent (Ouargla, Ouargli, Wargla) [oua] 5,000 (1995). South of Constantine, near Mzab. Ouargla and Ngouça are the main centers. *Class:* Afro-Asiatic, Berber, Northern, Zenati, Mzab-Wargla. *Dialects:* Ouedghir (Wadi), Temacin, Tariyit. Related to Tumzabt, Temacine Tamazight, and Taznatit. Testing showed only moderate comprehension of Tumzabt. Tariyit is a possible dialect spoken by the Haratine (former slaves of the Ouargli people). *Lg Use:* Vigorous. Positive language attitude. Speakers also use Arabic. *Lg Dev:* Dictionary. *Other:* Muslim.

Tamahaq, Tahaggart (Tamachek, Tamashekin, Tomachek, Tuareg, Touareg, Tourage) [thv] 25,000 in Algeria (1987). Population includes 20,000 Hoggar, 5,000 Ghat. Population total all countries: 62,000. Hoggar dialect in south Hoggar (Ajjer) Mountain area around Tamanghasset and south to the Niger border. The Ghat dialect is in southeast Algeria around Ganet and west. Also spoken in Libya, Niger. *Class:* Afro-Asiatic, Berber, Tamasheq, Northern. *Dialects:* Hoggar (Ahaggaren, Ajjer, Tahaggart), Ghat (Ganet, Djanet). *Lg Dev:* Traditional script called 'Shifinagh' in Niger. Bible portions: 1948–1965. *Other:* 'Tuareg' are the people, 'Targi' is the singular. Mountains. Inadan: blacksmiths; jewelry craftsmen. Muslim.

Tamazight, Central Atlas (Middle Atlas Berber, Central Shilha) [tzm] Western Algeria mountain area of Atlas and adjacent valleys to Taza, in the vicinity of Rabat, south near the Moroccan border. *Dialect:* South Oran. *Lg Use:* One of the more widely used Berber languages. *Other:* 'Berber' is the name of the people. Muslim. See main entry under Morocco.

Tamazight, Temacine (Tougourt, Touggourt, Tugurt) [tjo] 6,000 (1995). Vicinity of Temacine, Tamelhat, Ghomra, and Meggarin. *Class:* Afro-Asiatic, Berber, Northern, Zenati, Mzab-Wargla. *Dialects:* Related to Tumzabt, Tagargrent, and Taznatit. Possibly a dialect of Tagargrent, but not likely. *Lg Use:* People may have shifted to Arabic, but reports say there are still some villages where Temacine Tamazight is spoken. *Other:* Muslim.

Tamazight, Tidikelt [tia] 9,000 (1995). Tidikelt, in the vicinity of Salah, and Tit in southern Algeria. *Class:* Afro-Asiatic, Berber, Northern, Zenati, Tidikelt. *Dialects:* Tidikelt, Tit. *Lg Use:* People may have shifted to Arabic. *Other:* Muslim.

Tarifit (Tirifie, Riff, Rifi, Ruafa, Fifia, Rif, Northern Shilha, Shilha) [rif] Along the coast, eastern Alteria to Arzeu. *Dialect:* Arzeu, Igzennaian, Iznacen (Beni Iznassen). *Other:* Muslim. See main entry under Morocco.

Taznatit [grr] 40,000 (1995). Isolated, around Timimoun, near the Touat Region and around 400 miles southwest of the Mzab. *Class:* Afro-Asiatic, Berber, Northern, Zenati, Mzab-Wargla. *Dialects:* Gourara (Gurara), Touat (Tuat, Tuwat). Related to Tumzabt, Tagargrent, Temacine Tamazight, but not as close as they are to each other. Low intelligibility of other Tamazight speech forms, including Tumzabt and Tagargrent. *Lg Use:* Vigorous. *Other:* Muslim.

Tumzabt (Mzab, Mzabi, Ghardaia) [mzb] 70,000 (1995). Mzab Region 330 miles south of Algiers. 7 oases, Ghardaia being the principal one. *Class:* Afro-Asiatic, Berber, Northern, Zenati, Mzab-Wargla. *Dialects:* Only minor dialect variations. Related to Tagargrent, Temacine Tamazight, and Taznatit. *Lg Use:* Vigorous. Some speakers are probably bilingual in Arabic, French, or Spanish. Women virtually monolingual in Tumzabt. *Lg Dev:* Dictionary. *Other:* Strong cultural vitality. Tumzabt villages are interspersed among Arabic-speaking villages. Traders. Muslim.

Angola

Republic of Angola. República de Angola. 10,978,552. National or official languages: Portuguese, Koongo, Mbundu, Chokwe, Mbunda, Kwanyama (Oxikuanyama). Literacy rate: 30%. Information mainly from Redinha 1970; J. Bendor-Samuel 1989. Blind population: 12,000. The number of languages listed for Angola is 42. Of those, 41 are living languages and 1 is extinct. See map on page 678.

Bolo (Libolo, Lubolo, Haka) [blv] 2,627 (2000 WCD). Southeast of Luanda. *Class:* Niger-Congo, Atlantic-Congo, Volta-Congo, Benue-Congo, Bantoid, Southern, Narrow Bantu, Central, H, Mbundu (H.20). *Dialects:* Related to Mbundu, Nsongo, Sama.

Chokwe (Ciokwe, Cokwe, Shioko, Kioko, Quioco, Djok, Tshokwe, Tschiokloe) [cjk] 455,800 in Angola (1991). Northeastern Lunda District, and some in eastern Bie, western Moxico, and central Cuando Cubango. *Dialect:* Minungo. *Lg Use:* National language. *Other:* Traditional religion, Christian. See main entry under Democratic Republic of the Congo.

Diriku (Mbogedo, Shimbogedu, Diriko, Gciriku, Rugciriku) [diu] Southeastern border with Namibia, between Kwangali and Ndonga. See main entry under Namibia.

Holu (Kiholu, Holo, Kiholo) [hol] 23,117 in Angola (2000 WCD). Population total all countries: 28,212. Kwango River area. Also spoken in Democratic Republic of the Congo. *Class:* Niger-Congo, Atlantic-Congo, Volta-Congo, Benue-Congo, Bantoid, Southern, Narrow Bantu, Central, K, Holu (K.10). *Dialects:* Holu, Yeci. Close to Samba. Yeci may be a separate language. *Lg Dev:* Bible portions: 1943–1956. *Other:* Different from Holoholo of Democratic Republic of the Congo.

Kongo, San Salvador (Kikongo, Congo, Kisikongo, Kikoongo) [kwy] 328,361 in Angola (2000 WCD). Northern Angola and Democratic Republic of the Congo along the Congo River below Kinshasa. See main entry under Democratic Republic of the Congo.

Koongo (Kongo, Kikongo, Kikoongo, Congo, Cabinda) [kng] Northwestern corner. *Dialects:* South Kongo, South East Kongo, West Kongo (Fiote, Fioti), Ndingi, Mboka. *Lg Use:* Official language. *Other:* Christian, traditional religion. See main entry under Democratic Republic of the Congo.

Kung-Ekoka (Ekoko-!Xû, !Kung, !Ku, !Xu, !Hu, Qxû) [knw] 1,642 in Angola (2000 WCD). Primarily Namibia, Okavango, and Ovamboland Territory. *Other:* Traditional religion, Christian. See main entry under Namibia.

Kwadi (Cuepe, Cuanhoca, Curoca, Koroka, Bakoroka, Makoroko, Mucoroca) [kwz] Extinct. Southwest corner, south of Moçamedes. *Class:* Khoisan, Southern Africa, Central, Kwadi. *Dialect:* Zorotua (Vasorontu). *Lg Use:* J. C. Winter (1981) says it is extinct. There were 3 speakers in 1971 who used it regularly (E. O. J. Westphal).

Kwangali (Sikwangali, Rukwangali, Kwangari, Kwangare, Cuangar) [kwn] 10,902 in Angola (2000 WCD). South central Angola. *Dialect:* Sambyu (Shisambyu, Sambiu, Sambio). *Other:* Traditional religion, Christian. See main entry under Namibia.

Kwanyama (Ochikwanyama, Oxikuanyama, Kuanyama, Kwanjama, Kwancama, Cuanhama, Ovambo, Humba) [kua] 421,000 in Angola (1993 Johnstone). South central Angola. Also spoken in Namibia. *Class:* Niger-Congo, Atlantic-Congo, Volta-Congo, Benue-Congo, Bantoid, Southern, Narrow Bantu, Central, R, Ndonga (R.20). *Dialects:* Intelligible with Ndonga and Kwambi. *Lg Use:* National language. *Lg Dev:* Bible: 1974.

Kxoe (Kxoedam, Xun, Hukwe, !Hukwe, Xuhwe, Xu, Zama, Vazama, Cazama, "Mbarakwengo,"

"Mbarakwena," Glanda-Khwe, Black Bushman, Water Bushmen, Schekere) [xuu] 788 in Angola (2000 WCD). Huthembo (Wuthembo), northeast of Likuwa, and Lukamba (Lukanga) west of Rivungu, southeast corner of Angola. *Dialect:* Buma-Kxoe. *Other:* Traditional religion, Christian. See main entry under Namibia.

Laadi (Lari, Ladi, Kilari) [ldi] Northwestern corner. *Other:* A member of the Kongo cluster. Christian, Muslim. See main entry under Congo (Laari).

Luchazi (Chiluchazi, Lujazi, Lujash, Lutshase, Luxage, Lucazi, Lutchaz, Ponda) [lch] 155,000 in Angola (2001 Johnstone and Mandryk). Population total all countries: 209,400. Southeast, adjacent areas. Also spoken in Zambia. *Class:* Niger-Congo, Atlantic-Congo, Volta-Congo, Benue-Congo, Bantoid, Southern, Narrow Bantu, Central, K, Chokwe-Luchazi (K.20). *Lg Dev:* Bible: 1963. *Other:* Christian, traditional religion.

Luimbi (Chiluimbi, Luimbe, Lwimbe, Lwimbi) [lum] 43,869 (2000 WCD). Central, Cuanza River area. *Class:* Niger-Congo, Atlantic-Congo, Volta-Congo, Benue-Congo, Bantoid, Southern, Narrow Bantu, Central, K, Chokwe-Luchazi (K.20). *Dialects:* Related to Nkangala and Mbwela. *Lg Dev:* Bible portions: 1935.

Lunda (Chilunda) [lun] 178,000 in Angola (2001 Johnstone and Mandryk). Northeastern area. See main entry under Zambia.

Luvale (Luena, Lwena, Chiluvale, Lovale, Lubale) [lue] 464,000 in Angola (2001 Johnstone and Mandryk). Moxico, southeast provinces. *Other:* Christian, traditional religion. See main entry under Zambia.

Luyana (Luyi, Louyi, Lui, Rouyi, Luana, Luano) [lyn] 32,508 in Angola (2000 WCD). Southwestern, east of Moçamedes (Namibe). *Dialects:* Kwandi, Mbowe (Esimbowe), Mdundulu (Ndundulu, Imilangu), Mishulundu. *Other:* A cluster of dialects. Imilangu may be a dialect of Simaa. See main entry under Zambia.

Maligo [mwj] 2,233 (2000 WCD). *Class:* Khoisan, Southern Africa, Northern.

Mashi (Masi) [mho] 2,627 in Angola (2000 WCD). *Dialects:* North Kwandu, South Kwandu, Mashi. *Other:* Speakers are called 'a kwa Kwando', 'people of the Kwando River'. Nomadic. Different from Mashi (Shi) which is related to Havu of Democratic Republic of the Congo. Traditional religion. See main entry under Zambia.

Mbangala (Cimbangala, Bangala) [mxg] 22,329 (2000). North central, east of Luanda. *Class:* Niger-Congo, Atlantic-Congo, Volta-Congo, Benue-Congo, Bantoid, Southern, Narrow Bantu, Central, H, Yaka (H.30). *Dialects:* Mbangala, Yongo. Related to Yaka, Suku, Hungu, Sinji.

Mbukushu (Mbukushi, Mambukush, Mampukush, Mbukuhu, Thimbukushu, Gova, Kuso, Cusso) [mhw] 4,000 in Angola (1997 Andersson and Janson). Southeastern corner, northern bank of the Okavango River. *Other:* Traditional religion, Christian. See main entry under Namibia.

Mbunda (Chimbunda, Mbuunda) [mck] 135,000 in Angola (2001 Johnstone and Mandryk). Southeastern Angola. *Lg Use:* National language. *Other:* Different from Mbunda (Gimbunda, Kimbunu, Mbunu) which is a dialect of Yans (Iyans) in Democratic Republic of the Congo and Zambia and is in Tende-Yanzi group. See main entry under Zambia.

Mbundu (Luanda, Lunda, Loande, Loanda Mbundu, Kimbundu, Kimbundo, North Mbundu, Nbundu, N'bundo, Dongo, Ndongo, Kindongo) [kmb] 3,000,000 (1999 WA). Population includes 41,000 Ngola (1977 Voegelin and Voegelin). Northwest, Luanda Province. *Class:* Niger-Congo, Atlantic-Congo, Volta-Congo, Benue-Congo, Bantoid, Southern, Narrow Bantu, Central, H, Mbundu (H.20). *Dialects:* Njinga (Ginga, Jinga), Mbamba (Kimbamba, Bambeiro), Mbaka (Ambaquista), Ngola.

Related to Songo, Sama, Bolo. Other related languages, dialects, ethnic, or alternate names: Amboim (Mbuiyi), Kibala (Quibala), Lengue (Quilengue), Ngage, Dembo of Cacuta Caenda, Ngengu, Bondo, Quembo, Mussende, Makamba (Macamba). Mbamba may be a separate language. *Lg Use:* National language. *Lg Dev:* Bible: 1980.

Mbwela (Mbwera, Shimbwera, Mbuela, Ambuella, Ambuela) [mfu] 222,000 (2001 Johnstone and Mandryk). Central, east of Benguela. *Class:* Niger-Congo, Atlantic-Congo, Volta-Congo, Benue-Congo, Bantoid, Southern, Narrow Bantu, Central, K, Chokwe-Luchazi (K.20). *Other:* Traditional religion, Christian.

Ndombe (Dombe) [ndq] 22,329 (2000 WCD). South and southeast of Benguela. *Class:* Niger-Congo, Atlantic-Congo, Volta-Congo, Benue-Congo, Bantoid, Southern, Narrow Bantu, Central, R, South Mbundu (R.10).

Ndonga (Oshindonga, Osidonga, Ambo, Ochindonga) [ndo] 262,689 in Angola (2000 WCD). Southeast corner, Ovamboland. *Lg Dev:* Literacy rate in second language: 75%. *Other:* Highly acculturated. Christian, traditional religion. See main entry under Namibia.

Ngandyera [nne] 13,134 (2000 WCD). Southeast corner. *Class:* Niger-Congo, Atlantic-Congo, Volta-Congo, Benue-Congo, Bantoid, Southern, Narrow Bantu, Central, R, Ndonga (R.20). *Dialects:* Related to Kwanyama, Ndonga, Kwambi.

Nkangala (Cangala, Ngangala) [nkn] 22,269 (2000 WCD). Central, southeast of Mbwela. *Class:* Niger-Congo, Atlantic-Congo, Volta-Congo, Benue-Congo, Bantoid, Southern, Narrow Bantu, Central, K, Chokwe-Luchazi (K.20).

Nkhumbi (Nkumbi, Khumbi, Humbe, Ngumbi, Otjingumbi) [khu] 150,000 in Angola (1996 UBS). Southwestern, between Zemba, Luyana, Umbundu, Nyemba, and Nyaneka. Also spoken in Namibia. *Class:* Niger-Congo, Atlantic-Congo, Volta-Congo, Benue-Congo, Bantoid, Southern, Narrow Bantu, Central, R, South Mbundu (R.10). *Lg Dev:* Bible portions: 1985–1987.

Nsongo (Songo, Sungu) [nsx] 50,000 (1978 UBS). North central, Cuanza River area south of Malanje. *Class:* Niger-Congo, Atlantic-Congo, Volta-Congo, Benue-Congo, Bantoid, Southern, Narrow Bantu, Central, H, Mbundu (H.20). *Dialects:* Related to Mbundu, Sama, Bolo. *Lg Dev:* Bible portions: 1936–1978.

Nyaneka (Lunyaneka, Nhaneka, Nhaneca) [nyk] 300,000 (1996 UBS). Southwestern Angola. *Class:* Niger-Congo, Atlantic-Congo, Volta-Congo, Benue-Congo, Bantoid, Southern, Narrow Bantu, Central, R, South Mbundu (R.10). *Dialect:* Humbe, Mwila (Olumuila, Muila, Huila).

Nyemba (Ganguela, Ganguella, Ngangela, Nhemba, Gangela) [nba] 222,000 in Angola (2001 Johnstone and Mandryk). Population total all countries: 231,540. South central, Cuchi River area, southeast. Also spoken in Namibia, Zambia. *Class:* Niger-Congo, Atlantic-Congo, Volta-Congo, Benue-Congo, Bantoid, Southern, Narrow Bantu, Central, K, Chokwe-Luchazi (K.20). *Lg Dev:* Bible portions: 1955.

Nyengo (Nhengo) [nye] 9,382 (2000 WCD). Southeast corner. *Class:* Niger-Congo, Atlantic-Congo, Volta-Congo, Benue-Congo, Bantoid, Southern, Narrow Bantu, Central, K, Chokwe-Luchazi (K.20).

!O!ung (!O!kung) [oun] 5,629 (2000 WCD). Southern border with Namibia, surrounded by Luchazi. *Class:* Khoisan, Southern Africa, Northern.

Portuguese [por] 57,600 in Angola (1993). *Lg Use:* Official language. See main entry under Portugal.

Ruund (Uruund, Northern Lunda, Luunda, Chilu Wunda, Muatiamvua) [rnd] 98,508 in Angola (2000 WCD). Northeastern Angola. See main entry under Democratic Republic of the Congo.

Sama (Kissama, Quissama) [smd] 24,191 (2000 WCD). Coastal, south of Luanda. *Class:* Niger-Congo, Atlantic-Congo, Volta-Congo, Benue-Congo, Bantoid, Southern, Narrow Bantu, Central, H, Mbundu (H.20). *Dialects:* Related to Mbundu, Nsongo, Bolo.

Umbundu (Umbundo, M'bundo, Quimbundo, Ovimbundu, South Mbundu, Nano, Mbali, Mbari, Mbundu Benguella) [umb] 4,000,000 in Angola (1995 WA). Population total all countries: 4,002,880. West, Benguela District. Also spoken in Namibia. *Class:* Niger-Congo, Atlantic-Congo, Volta-Congo, Benue-Congo, Bantoid, Southern, Narrow Bantu, Central, R, South Mbundu (R.10). *Dialects:* Related to Nkhumbi, Ndombe, Nyaneka. *Lg Use:* Trade language. *Lg Dev:* Dictionary. Grammar. Bible: 1963. *Other:* Christian, traditional religion.

Yaka (Kiyaka, Iaka, Iyaka, Iaca) [yaf] 200,000 in Angola (2000 SIL). North central corner, east of the Kongo. *Dialects:* Yaka, Ngoongo. See main entry under Democratic Republic of the Congo.

Yauma [yax] 17,075 in Angola (2000 WCD). Southeast, Kwando (Cuando) River area. Also spoken in Zambia. *Class:* Unclassified. *Lg Dev:* Bible portions: 1978.

Yombe (Kiyombe, Kiombi, Iombe, Bayombe) [yom] 39,403 in Angola (2000 WCD). Cabinda. *Dialects:* Mbala (Mumbala), Vungunya (Kivungunya, Yombe Classique). *Other:* Christian, traditional religion. See main entry under Democratic Republic of the Congo.

Zemba (Dhimba, Dimba, Otjidhimba, Himba, Tjimba, Simba, Chimba, Oluthimba) [dhm] 18,000 in Angola (1996 UBS). Population total all countries: 30,000. Southwest corner. Also spoken in Namibia. *Class:* Niger-Congo, Atlantic-Congo, Volta-Congo, Benue-Congo, Bantoid, Southern, Narrow Bantu, Central, R, Herero (R.30). *Lg Dev:* Bible portions: 1970–1984.

Benin

Republic of Benin. République du Benin. Formerly Dahomey. 7,250,033. National or official language: French. Literacy rate: 28%. Also includes Mòoré. Information mainly from SIL 1972–2003; J. Bendor-Samuel 1989. Blind population: 175. Deaf institutions: 1. The number of languages listed for Benin is 54. Of those, all are living languages. See map on page 679.

Aguna (Awuna, Agunaco) [aug] 3,470 (1992 census). Zou Province, Djidja Subprefecture, around village of Agouna. *Class:* Niger-Congo, Atlantic-Congo, Volta-Congo, Kwa, Left Bank, Gbe. *Other:* Traditional religion.

Aja (Adja, Ajagbe, Hwè) [ajg] 588,100 in Benin (2002 SIL). Population total all countries: 740,400. Southwestern Benin on the Mono River. Primarily in the Couffo Province (formerly northern half of Mono Province), subprefectures of Aplahoué, Djakotomè, Dogbo, Klouékanmè, Lalo, and Tovinklin; Mono Province (formerly southern part of Mono province) subprefectures of Athiémè, Comè, and Houéyogbé. There are Aja people living in villages mixed with other language groups in the Zou Province, Djidja and Agbangnizoun subprefectures. Aja speakers can be found in Cotonou and many of the towns throughout southern Benin. Also spoken in Togo. *Class:* Niger-Congo, Atlantic-Congo, Volta-Congo, Kwa, Left Bank, Gbe, Aja. *Dialects:* Dogbo, Hwe (Ehoue), Tado (Stado, Sado, Tadou), Sikpi, Tala. The Hwe, Sikpi, Tado, and Tala varieties are linguistically closer together with Dogbo being linguistically more distinct. Differences are minor. Lexical similarity 92% with Hwe-Sikpi, 89% with Hwe-Dogbo, Hwe-Tado, and Hwe-Tala. *Lg Use:* All domains except schools and government. Most adults also use Gen. Most children understand Gen, some understand Éwé. Some adults use Éwé or French. *Lg Dev:* Literacy

rate in first language: 19%. The government selected Aja as one of the six national languages for post literacy. In Benin in 1995–96, more than 80 literacy classes and over 30 post literacy classes were organized. Roman script. Poetry. Newspapers. Radio programs. Dictionary. Grammar. *Other:* Plains. Tree Savannah. Peasants. Traditional religion, Christian.

Anii (Gisida, Basila, Bassila, Baseca, Winji-Winji, Ouinji-Ouinji) [blo] 33,600 in Benin (1992 census, village count). Population total all countries: 45,900. Both sides of the Togo-Benin border. In Benin, the southern part of the Aracora Province, Bassila Subprefecture. Also spoken in Togo. *Class:* Niger-Congo, Atlantic-Congo, Volta-Congo, Kwa, Nyo, Potou-Tano, Basila-Adele. *Dialects:* Gikolodjya, Gilempla, Giseda, Akpe, Balanka. Close to Akpe of Togo. Lexical similarity 92% between Bassila and Kouloumi, 89% between Bassila and Bodi and 74% between Bassila and Balanka. *Lg Use:* All domains except schools, government. Speakers also use Tem, Akalesem, Ede Nago, or French. *Lg Dev:* Literacy rate in first language: 10%. Literacy rate in second language: 1%. 15 literacy classes each year. Roman script. Radio programs. *Other:* Muslim.

Anufo (Chokosi, Chakosi, Chokossi, Tchokossi) [cko] 13,800 in Benin (2002 SIL). A few villages in the Atakora Province, Cobly and Boukombe subprefectures. *Lg Dev:* Literacy rate in first language: 1% to 5%. *Other:* Traditional religion, Muslim. See main entry under Ghana.

Baatonum (Baatonu, Baatombu, Baruba, Bargu, Burgu, Berba, Barba, Bogung, Bargawa, Barganchi, Bariba) [bba] 460,000 in Benin (1995 R. Jones). Population total all countries: 560,000. Central, north, Borgou Province. Also spoken in Nigeria. *Class:* Niger-Congo, Atlantic-Congo, Volta-Congo, North, Gur, Bariba. *Lg Use:* Speakers also use French. *Lg Dev:* Literacy rate in first language: 1% to 30%. Dictionary. Grammar. Bible: 1997. *Other:* The people's name for themselves is 'Baatonu', plural 'Baatombu'. Distinct from Biali (Berba). Muslim, traditional religion, Christian.

Biali (Bieri, Bjeri, Bjerb, Berba) [beh] 64,500 in Benin (1991). Population total all countries: 66,000. Atakora Province, Materi Subprefecture. There is also a sizable population in the Ouessi Subprefecture in the Borgou Province. Also spoken in Burkina Faso. *Class:* Niger-Congo, Atlantic-Congo, Volta-Congo, North, Gur, Central, Northern, Oti-Volta, Eastern. *Dialects:* Dassari, Gouande, Materi, Pingou, Tihoun, Tangeta, Porga. *Lg Use:* Many monolinguals. Others use French as second language. French and Biali in church. *Lg Dev:* Literacy rate in first language: below 1%. Literacy rate in second language: 10% French. Roman script. Radio programs. *Other:* The language is called 'Biali' or 'Bieri', the people 'Bialaba'. 'Berba' is the French name. Historical accounts claim they originated in the F'ada Ngourma area of Burkina Faso. Different from Baatonum (Berba). Traditional religion, Christian.

Boko (Bokonya, Bokko, Boo, Busa-Boko) [bqc] 70,000 in Benin (1995 R. Jones). Population total all countries: 110,000. Borgu Province. Also spoken in Nigeria. *Class:* Niger-Congo, Mande, Eastern, Eastern, Busa. *Dialects:* Closely related languages: Busa-Bisã (Nigeria), Bokobaru (Nigeria), Shanga (Nigeria). Lexical similarity 90% with Busa-Bisã, Bokobaru, Shanga, 86% with Bokobaru, 52% with Kyenga, 51% with Bissa in Burkina Faso. *Lg Use:* Positive language attitude. Bilingual level estimates for French: 0 80%, 1 10%, 2 4%, 3 3%, 4 2%, 5 1%. Speakers use French (Benin), Hausa, Yoruba, Baatonum, or Fulfulde as second language. *Lg Dev:* Literacy rate in second language: 6%. Dictionary. Grammar. Bible: 1992. *Other:* SOV; genitives before noun heads; articles, adjectives, numerals, relatives after noun heads; question word initial or final; 4 suffixes; word order distinguishes subject, object, indirect object; postpositions; person, number, aspect indicated in subject pronoun; tone indicates verb aspect; passives; CV, CCV; tonal. Interfluvial. Savannah. Peasant agriculturalists. Traditional religion, Muslim, Christian.

Dendi (Dandawa) [ddn] 30,000 in Benin (1995 Jones). Population total all countries: 32,050. Atakora and Borgou provinces, along the Niger River, from the Medru River to the Nigeria border, and down to Kandi. Many at Djogou. Most towns in northern Benin. Also spoken in Nigeria. *Class:* Nilo-Saharan, Songhai, Southern. *Dialects:* Closely related language to Zarma and Songai. They form a dialect cluster. *Lg Use:* Language of wider communication. The language is used in many of the markets as a language of wider communication. Speakers also use French. *Lg Dev:* Literacy rate in first language: 1% to 30%. Radio programs. Dictionary. Grammar. NT: 1995. *Other:* Dendi speakers are found in most of the towns of northern Benin. Muslim, Christian.

Ditammari (Ditamari, Tamari, "Somba") [tbz] 20,000 in Benin (1991 UBS). Population total all countries: 47,500. Atakora Province, Boukombe and Natitingou subprefectures. Many now live along the Djougou-Parakou road. Also spoken in Togo. *Class:* Niger-Congo, Atlantic-Congo, Volta-Congo, North, Gur, Central, Northern, Oti-Volta, Eastern. *Dialect:* Eastern Ditammari, Western Ditammari (Tamberma). *Lg Use:* Speakers also use Baatonum or French. *Lg Dev:* Literacy rate in first language: 1% to 5%. Radio programs. Grammar. NT: 1989. *Other:* "Somba" is a derogatory name applied to several related groups; mainly to the Ditammari. Muslim, traditional religion, Christian.

Ede Cabe (Caabe, Cabe) [cbj] 69,000 (2002 SIL). Borgou Province, Tchaourou Subprefecture; Zou Province, Savè and Ouèssè subprefectures. *Class:* Niger-Congo, Atlantic-Congo, Volta-Congo, Benue-Congo, Defoid, Yoruboid, Edekiri. *Dialects:* A member of the Ede language cluster. Lexical similarity 76% with Yoruba (Porto-Novo). *Lg Use:* All domains except in schools and some government offices. Yoruba and some French used along with Cabe in churches. Speakers have very high level of comprehension of Yoruba. *Lg Dev:* Literacy rate in first language: below 1%. *Other:* Traditional religion, Christian.

Ede Ica (Ica) [ica] 63,000 (2002 SIL). Zou Province, Bante subprefecture. *Class:* Niger-Congo, Atlantic-Congo, Volta-Congo, Benue-Congo, Defoid, Yoruboid, Edekiri. *Dialect:* Ica, Ilodji (Ife). A member of the Ede language cluster. Lexical similarity 83% with Yoruba of Porto-Novo. *Lg Use:* All domains. French used in schools and government. Yoruba, French, and Ica are used in churches. Yoruba and Arabic are used at mosque. Good comprehension of standard Yoruba. Standard Yoruba literacy materials are used. *Lg Dev:* Literacy rate in first language: 30%. Literacy rate in second language: 40% in French. *Other:* Traditional religion, Muslim, Christian.

Ede Idaca (Idaca, Idaaca, Idaasa, Idáîtsà) [idd] 100,000 (2002 SIL). Collines Province (northern half of former Zou Province), Dassa-Zoume and Glazoué subprefectures. *Class:* Niger-Congo, Atlantic-Congo, Volta-Congo, Benue-Congo, Defoid, Yoruboid, Edekiri. *Dialects:* One of 8 languages that make up the Ede language cluster (Yorboid) that spreads over southwestern Nigeria, southern and central Benin, and into southern and central Togo. The cluster also includes Ede Cabe, Ede Ica, Ife, Ede Ije, Ede Nago, Kura Ede Nago, Manigri-Kambole Ede Nago. The various people groups seek to maintain their individual identities yet recognize the wider 'Yoruba' community. *Lg Use:* All domains. In government offices French may be used. In school classrooms French is used. In markets some Yoruba or Fon may be used. *Lg Dev:* Literacy rate

in first language: 50%. Literacy rate in second language: 59% read Yoruba, 39% write Yoruba; 44% read and write French. The ongoing literacy program covers the whole language area due to high motivation. Radio programs. *Other:* Christian, Muslim, traditional religion.

Ede Ije (Holi, Ije) [ijj] 50,000 (2000 SIL). Plateau Province (northern part of former Oueme Province), subprefectures of Pobe and Ketou. Zou Province, Ouihni Subprefecture. In general, the rural districts between the towns of Ketou and Pobe, extending westward to the Oueme River. There is also a group of Ije villages in the Zou Province, Zogbodome Subprefecture, south of the town of Zogbodome. *Class:* Niger-Congo, Atlantic-Congo, Volta-Congo, Benue-Congo, Defoid, Yoruboid, Edekiri. *Dialects:* A member of the Ede language cluster. 99% comprehension of Yoruba, narrative text. There is a very high comprehension of Yoruba due to the linguistic and cultural closeness. Lexical similarity 85% with Yoruba of Porto-Novo, 91% with Ede Nago. *Lg Use:* All domains. In schools, French is used, some French used in government offices, Yoruba, and in some cases Fon, used in churches, Yoruba and Arabic used at mosque. *Lg Dev:* Basic literacy program using Yoruba expanded to include post-literacy. *Other:* Traditional religion, Christian, Muslim.

Ede Nago (Nago, Nagots, Nagot) [nqg] 200,000 (2002 SIL). Southeastern Benin, Plateau Province (formerly northern half of Weme Province), Ketou, Pobe, Adja-Ouere, Ifangni, and Sakete subprefectures. *Class:* Niger-Congo, Atlantic-Congo, Volta-Congo, Benue-Congo, Defoid, Yoruboid, Edekiri. *Dialects:* A member of the Ede language cluster. Lexical similarity 87 to 91% with Yoruba of Porto-Novo. *Lg Use:* French used in schools, Yoruba or French used in some government offices, and churches use primarily Yoruba with some French, Nago, or both. Yoruba has been being used for government literacy program since 1978 and since 1995 the program has been expanded to include post-literacy. 100% comprehension of Yoruba narrative text. *Lg Dev:* Roman script. *Other:* Traditional religion, Muslim, Christian.

Ede Nago, Kura (Nago) [nqk] 25,000 (2002 SIL). Donga Province (formerly southern half of Atakora Province), Bassila Subprefecture. Aledjo Koura is main center. *Class:* Niger-Congo, Atlantic-Congo, Volta-Congo, Benue-Congo, Defoid, Yoruboid, Edekiri. *Dialects:* A member of the Ede language cluster. Lexical similarity 78% with Ife of Tchetti, 76% with Manigri-Kambole Ede Nago, 68% with Yoruba of Porto-Novo, 65% with Ede Nago. *Lg Use:* All domains. Speakers also use Tem, French, or Lukpa. *Other:* Muslim.

Ede Nago, Manigri-Kambolé (Manigri, Ana) [xkb] 30,000 in Benin (2002 SIL). Population total all countries: 70,000. Donga Province (formerly southern half of Atakora Province), Bassila Subprefecture south and west of town of Bassila, Bante Subprefecture south of Bassila along route RNIE3. Also spoken in Togo. *Class:* Niger-Congo, Atlantic-Congo, Volta-Congo, Benue-Congo, Defoid, Yoruboid, Edekiri. *Dialects:* A member of the Ede language cluster. Lexical similarity 87% to 91% with Ede Nago, 77% with Yoruba of Porto-Novo, 78% with Ife of Tchetti. *Lg Use:* All domains. French used in schools, some government offices, and with outsiders. *Lg Dev:* Literacy classes using Yoruba materials were started in 1977. Post literacy activities were begun in 1995. *Other:* Muslim, Christian.

Fon (Fo, Fongbe, Fonnu, Fogbe, Dahomeen, Djedji) [fon] 1,700,000 in Benin (2000 Hoddenbagh). Population total all countries: 1,735,500. Zou Province, Atlantic Province, southern part of the Abomey-Calavi and Ouidah subprefectures, Littoral Province (Cotonou). There are many Fon interspersed with other groups throughout southern Benin and in the towns of northern Benin. Also spoken in Togo. *Class:* Niger-Congo, Atlantic-Congo, Volta-Congo, Kwa, Left Bank, Gbe, Fon. *Dialects:* Agbome, Arohun, Gbekon, Kpase. *Lg Use:* Language of wider communication. Vigorous. Limited oral use in administration, spoken use in education, religious services, commerce, and labor. Positive language attitude. Speakers also use French. *Lg Dev:* Literacy rate in first language: 10%. 10% can read Fon, 7% can write it. Newspapers. Radio programs. TV. Grammar. NT: 1993. *Other:* Coastal. Agriculturalists. Traditional religion, Christian.

Foodo [fod] 24,500 in Benin (2002 SIL). Population total all countries: 25,500. Atakora Province, Ouake Subprefecture, Semere town. Also spoken in Ghana. *Class:* Niger-Congo, Atlantic-Congo, Volta-Congo, Kwa, Nyo, Potou-Tano, Tano, Guang, North Guang. *Lg Use:* Speakers also use Tem, Kabiye, or French. *Lg Dev:* Literacy rate in first language: 1% to 5%. Radio programs. Dictionary. *Other:* Originally from Ghana; probably from the village of Salaga. Muslim.

French [fra] 16,700 in Benin (1993 Johnstone). *Lg Use:* Official language. See main entry under France.

Fulfulde, Borgu (Peulh, Peul, Fulbe-Borgu, Benin-Togo Fulfulde) [fue] 280,000 in Benin (2002 SIL). Population total all countries: 328,200. Atakora and Borgou provinces, villages, and encampments. Bakuure is spoken in the Borgou Region north of N'Dali. Korakuure is spoken in the central and south Borgou Region around Parakou. Djougoure is spoken in northern Benin in the Atacora Region, from Djougou north to the Burkina border, and may extend west into northern Togo. Tchabankeere is spoken in the Zou Region. Also spoken in Nigeria, Togo. *Class:* Niger-Congo, Atlantic-Congo, Atlantic, Northern, Senegambian, Fulani-Wolof, Fula, West Central. *Dialects:* Bakuure, Korakuure, Djougoure (Juguure), Tchabankeere (Caabankeere). *Lg Dev:* Literacy rate in first language: 1%. Among the Fulfulde speaking Gando people there are over 2,000 literates. *Other:* The Gando people speak Fulfulde, but are ethnically Boko and Baatonum. McKinstry (1998) reports Fulani living as far south as Save' and Dassa-Zoume. Animal husbandry: dairy products. Muslim, traditional religion, Christian.

Fulfulde, Gorgal (Peulh, Peul, Fulfulde, Fulfulde Western Niger) [fuh] 30,000 in Benin. Northern most part of Borgou provinces, villages and encampments. *Lg Dev:* Literacy rate in first language: 1%. *Other:* Animal husbandry: dairy products. Muslim, traditional religion. See main entry under Niger (Fulfulde, Western Niger).

Gbe, Ayizo (Ayizo, Ayzo, Ayizo-Gbe) [ayb] 328,000 (2000 SIL). Mono and Atlantique provinces. *Class:* Niger-Congo, Atlantic-Congo, Volta-Congo, Kwa, Left Bank, Gbe, Aja. *Dialects:* Kadagbe (Kada-Gbe), Ayizo-Seto, Ayizo-Tori, Ayizo-Kobe. Close to Fon. *Lg Use:* Speakers have very good comprehension of Fon. *Other:* Traditional religion, Christian.

Gbe, Ci (Ci, Cigbe, Tchi, Ayizo-Ci) [cib] 25,000 (2002 SIL). Mono Province, Lalo Subprefecture. *Class:* Niger-Congo, Atlantic-Congo, Volta-Congo, Kwa, Left Bank, Gbe. *Dialects:* A member of the Gbe language cluster. Ci is very close linguistically to Fon and is considered to be the same by Ci speakers. Lexical similarity 80% with Fon, 77% with Ayizo, 59% with Aja. *Lg Use:* All domains. French used in schools and government offices. Fon used for literacy classes and for public reading of Scriptures in churches. Comprehension of Fon is very high. *Lg Dev:* Literacy rate in first language: below 1%. *Other:* Traditional religion, Christian.

Gbe, Defi [gbh] 13,500 (2002 SIL). Southeastern corner of Benin, Oueme Province, Seme-Kpodji Subprefecture between the Oueme River to north, Cotonou-Porto-Novo railroad to west, Gulf of Guinea to south, and into Nigeria in the east. *Class:* Niger-Congo, Atlantic-Congo, Volta-Congo, Kwa, Left Bank, Gbe, Aja. *Dialects:* A member of the Gbe language cluster. Defi is close linguistically to Gun. *Lg Use:* All domains. French used in schools and government offices. Gun, French, Yoruba, and Defi used in churches. Gun, Yoruba and Defi used at mosque along with Arabic. Gun is being used for literacy. Comprehension of Gun is very high. *Lg Dev:* Literacy rate in first language: below 1%. *Other:* Traditional religion, Christian, Muslim.

Gbe, Eastern Xwla (Phla, Xwla, Offra, Ophra, Houla, Kpla, Pla, Popo) [gbx] 80,000 (2002 SIL). Southeastern Benin along coast, Oueme Province, Seme-Kpodji Subprefecture. *Class:* Niger-Congo, Atlantic-Congo, Volta-Congo, Kwa, Left Bank, Gbe. *Dialects:* A member of the Gbe language cluster. Lexical similarity 90% with Gun, 82% with Fon, 68% with Gen, 68% with Aja. *Lg Use:* All domains. French used in schools (French) and some government offices. In churches Gun is mostly used with some French and some Fon. Gun is mostly used for nonformal education. Good comprehension of Gun, comprehension of Fon is good or partial depending on location. *Other:* Traditional religion, Christian, Muslim.

Gbe, Gbesi [gbs] 65,000 (2002 SIL). In the Atlantic Province, several individual and mixed villages, Kpomasse, Alada, and Tori-Bossito subprefectures and in the Mono Province, Bopa Subprefecture along Lake Aheme. *Class:* Niger-Congo, Atlantic-Congo, Volta-Congo, Kwa, Left Bank, Gbe. *Dialect:* Gbokpa. A member of the Gbe language cluster. Lexical similarity 91% with Kotafon, 85% with Fon, 73% with Aja, 70% with Gen. *Lg Use:* All domains. French used in schools and government offices. Fon is used for literacy classes and for public reading of Scriptures in the churches. Saxwe is used for literacy in the Bopa Subprefecture. Good comprehension of Fon and slightly less for Gen. *Other:* Traditional religion, Christian.

Gbe, Kotafon (Ko, Kogbe) [kqk] 100,000 (2002 SIL). Mono Province, the main area is the subprefectures of Lokassa and Athieme. There are some villages in the Bopa Subprefecture north and south of Bopa along Lake Aheme. There are also a few Kotafon communities in the Grand Popo Subprefecture, north of Grand-Popo. *Class:* Niger-Congo, Atlantic-Congo, Volta-Congo, Kwa, Left Bank, Gbe. *Dialects:* A member of the Gbe language cluster. Lexical similarity 82% with Gbe Ayizo, 81% with Fon, 69% with Gen, 65% with Aja. *Lg Use:* All domains except where external pressures require use of other language. French in schools and some government offices. Churches use mostly Gen, some use French, Gun, Éwé, or Fon. *Other:* Traditional religion, Christian, Muslim.

Gbe, Maxi (Maxi, Maxi-Gbe, Mahi) [mxl] 66,000 in Benin (1993 Johnstone). Population total all countries: 91,300. Collines Province (formerly northern half of Zou Province), Dassa-Zoume, Savalou, Bante, Glazoue, and Ouessi subprefectures. Also spoken in Togo. *Class:* Niger-Congo, Atlantic-Congo, Volta-Congo, Kwa, Left Bank, Gbe, Fon. *Dialects:* A member of the Gbe language cluster. Lexical similarity 80% with Fon, 68% with Ayizo, 51% with Aja. *Lg Use:* Good comprehension of Fon. Speakers also use French. *Other:* Traditional religion.

Gbe, Saxwe (Saxwe, Saxwe-Gbe) [sxw] 6,272 (2000 WCD). Mono Province. *Class:* Niger-Congo, Atlantic-Congo, Volta-Congo, Kwa, Left Bank, Gbe. *Dialects:* Saxwe, Daxe, Se. *Other:* Traditional religion.

Gbe, Tofin (Tofin, Tofingbe, Tofi) [tfi] 90,000 (2002 SIL). Atlantique Province, So-Ava Subprefecture. *Class:* Niger-Congo, Atlantic-Congo, Volta-Congo, Kwa, Left Bank, Gbe, Aja. *Dialects:* A member of the Gbe language cluster. Lexical similarity 88% with Gun, 87% with Fon, 82% with Eastern Xwla, 75% with Ayizo, 66% with Gen.

Lg Use: All domains. French is used in schools and some government offices. Gun, Fon, and some French used in churches besides some Tofin. Good comprehension of Fon and of Gun. *Lg Dev:* Literacy efforts are underway using Fon, Gun, and Tofin. *Other:* Christian, traditional religion, Muslim.

Gbe, Waci (Watyu, Waci, Ouatchi, Waci-Gbe) [wci] 110,000 in Benin (1993 Johnstone). Mono Province. *Lg Use:* Speakers also use French or Éwé. *Lg Dev:* Literacy rate in first language: below 1%. *Other:* Traditional religion. See main entry under Togo.

Gbe, Weme (Weme, Weme-Gbe) [wem] 60,000 (1991 L. Vanderaa). Weme and Atlantic provinces. *Class:* Niger-Congo, Atlantic-Congo, Volta-Congo, Kwa, Left Bank, Gbe, Aja. *Lg Use:* Speakers also use French or Fon. *Other:* Traditional religion.

Gbe, Western Xwla (Phla, Xwla, Xwla-Gbe) [xwl] 50,000 in Benin (2002 SIL). Population total all countries: 71,000. Southern Benin along the western coast in the Mono Province, Grand-Popo Subprefecture, Atlantique Province, Ouidali Subprefecture, and Littoral Province (Cotonou). Also spoken in Togo. *Class:* Niger-Congo, Atlantic-Congo, Volta-Congo, Kwa, Left Bank, Gbe. *Dialects:* A member of the Gbe language cluster. Lexical similarity 86% with Gun, 84% with Fon, 73% with Gen, 68% with Aja, 90% with Xwela, 88% with Saxwe. *Lg Use:* All domains. French used in schools and some government offices. In churches Gen is mostly used with some French and some Fon. Gen is mostly used for nonformal education, some Fon is used in the eastern edge of the area around Ouidah. Good comprehension of Gen, comprehension of Fon is good or partial depending on location. *Other:* Traditional religion, Christian.

Gbe, Xwela (Phera, Xwela, Xwela-Gba, Houeda, Peda) [xwe] 65,000 (2002 SIL). Mono Province, Come Subprefecture near Lake Aheme, southernmost part of Bopa Subprefecture; Atlantic Province, Kpomasse and Ouidah subprefectures. *Class:* Niger-Congo, Atlantic-Congo, Volta-Congo, Kwa, Left Bank, Gbe. *Dialects:* A member of the Gbe language cluster. Lexical similarity 90% with Western Xwla, 85% with Fon, 71% with Gen, 82% with Saxwe, 68% with Aja. *Lg Use:* All domains. French is used in schools; Fon, Waci-Gen, or Saxwe are used for nonformal education; French, Fon, or Gen are used in government offices; Gen and some Fon and French are used in churches. Good comprehension of Fon and of Gen. Fon, Waci-Gen, and Saxwe are used for adult literacy depending on the village location. *Other:* Traditional religion, Christian.

Gen (Ge, Gen-Gbe, Mina-Gen, Mina, Guin, Gegbe, Popo) [gej] 158,000 in Benin (2001 Johnstone and Mandryk). Mono and Atlantique provinces. *Dialects:* Anexo, Agoi, Gen, Gliji. *Lg Use:* Language of wider communication. Speakers also use French. *Lg Dev:* Literacy rate in first language: 1% to 5%. Gen is one of the languages used for adult literacy by the Benin government and one of the six with government post-literacy programs. *Other:* The name of the people is 'Mina'. Traditional religion, Christian. See main entry under Togo.

Gourmanchéma (Gourmantche, Gurma, Goulmancema, Gulimancema, Migulimancema) [gux] 62,000 in Benin (2001 Johnstone and Mandryk). Northern Benin, Atacora Province, primarly Tanguieta and Kerou subprefectures. There are some individual villages in the Materi and Cobly subprefectures; Borgou Province, Banikoara and Karimama subprefectures. *Lg Dev:* Literacy rate in first language: 5% to 10%. *Other:* Traditional religion, Christian. See main entry under Burkina Faso.

Gun (Alada, Alada-Gbe, Gun-Alada, Gun-Gbe, Goun, Egun, Gu, Gugbe, Seto-Gbe, Toli-Gbe) [guw] 243,000 in Benin (2001 Johnstone and Mandryk). Population total all countries: 501,804. Southeast Benin, Weme Province, Akpro-Misserete, Avrankou, Adjara, and Porto-Novo subprefectures. Also spoken in Nigeria. *Class:* Niger-Congo, Atlantic-Congo, Volta-Congo, Kwa, Left Bank, Gbe, Aja. *Dialects:* Ajra, Alada, Seto, Toli. *Lg Use:* Speakers also use Fon or French. *Lg Dev:* Literacy rate in first language: 1% to 5%. Radio programs. Bible: 1923–1972. *Other:* Traditional religion, Christian.

Hausa [hau] Atacora and Borgou provinces mainly in larger towns and large market villages. *Lg Use:* Trade language. *Other:* Muslim, traditional religion, Christian. See main entry under Nigeria.

Ifè (Baate, Ana, Ana-Ife, Anago, Ede Ife) [ife] 80,000 in Benin (1990 SIL). Collines Province (northern part of former Zou Province), Savalou Subprefecture, Tchetti is main center. *Lg Dev:* Literacy rate in first language: below 1%. *Other:* Traditional religion, Christian. See main entry under Togo.

Kabiyé (Kabre, Kabye, Kabure, Cabrais, Cabrai) [kbp] 30,000 in Benin (1991 Vanderaa). Scattered villages in Donga Province (formerly southern half of Atakora Province), Ouake, Djougou, and Bassila subprefectures. *Other:* Traditional religion, Christian. See main entry under Togo.

Kyenga (Cenka, Tyenga) [tye] 1,000 in Benin (1995 Ross Jones SIM). Alibori Province (formerly northern half of Borgou Province), Segbana Subprefecture, around the village of Tungan Bage. See main entry under Nigeria.

Lama (Lamba, Losso) [las] 69,000 in Benin (2001 Johnstone and Mandryk). Atakora Province, several villages, Boukombe Subprefecture, northwest of Boukombe and in the Donga Province (formerly southern half of Atakora Province), Djougou and Bassila subprefectures. *Dialects:* Kande (Kante), Kadjala (Kadjalla). *Lg Use:* Speakers also use French. *Lg Dev:* Literacy rate in first language: 1% to 5%. *Other:* 'Lama' is their name for the people and language. 'Losso' refers to people on the Losso Plain who can either be Lama or Nawdm. Traditional religion, Christian. See main entry under Togo.

Lukpa (Lokpa, Logba, Legba, Lugba, Dompago) [dop] 50,000 in Benin (2001 Johnstone and Mandryk). Population total all countries: 63,581. West Djougou and border areas, Atakora Province. Primarily around Kémérida. Also spoken in Togo. *Class:* Niger-Congo, Atlantic-Congo, Volta-Congo, North, Gur, Central, Southern, Grusi, Eastern. *Lg Dev:* Literacy rate in first language: 5% to 30%. Dictionary. NT: 1977. *Other:* Different from Logba of Ghana. Traditional religion, Christian, Muslim.

Mbelime (Mbilme, "Niendi," "Niende") [mql] 24,500 (1991 Vanderaa). Atakora Province, Cobly Subprefecture and 5 villages in the Boukombe Subprefecture. *Class:* Niger-Congo, Atlantic-Congo, Volta-Congo, North, Gur, Central, Northern, Oti-Volta, Eastern. *Lg Use:* Speakers also use French or Ditammari. *Lg Dev:* Roman script. Radio programs. *Other:* People call themselves 'Bèbèdibè'. "Niende" is derogatory. Traditional religion, Christian.

Miyobe (Soruba, Bijobe, Biyobe, Sorouba, Solla, Uyobe, Meyobe, Kayobe, Kuyobe, Sola, Solamba) [soy] 7,000 in Benin (1991). Population total all countries: 8,700. Atakora Province. Also spoken in Togo. *Class:* Niger-Congo, Atlantic-Congo, Volta-Congo, North, Gur, Central, Northern, Oti-Volta, Gurma. *Dialects:* Lexical similarity 27% with Moba, 25% with Tamberma (Ditammari), 47% with Ngangam. *Lg Use:* Speakers also use French. *Lg Dev:* Literacy rate in first language: below 1%. Roman script in Togo. *Other:* Traditional religion, Christian.

Mokole (Mokollé, Mokwale, Monkole, Féri) [mkl] 65,500 (1991 L. Vanderaa). Borgou Province, Kandi and villages to the north and east. *Class:* Niger-Congo, Atlantic-Congo, Volta-Congo, Benue-Congo, Defoid, Yoruboid, Edekiri. *Lg Use:* Speakers also use French. *Lg Dev:* Literacy rate in first language: below 1%. *Other:* Traditional religion, Muslim, Christian.

Nateni [ntm] 66,000 (2001 Johnstone and Mandryk). Atakora Province. The Natemba are in Toukountouna District, Tayaba in Tanguiéta District, Kuntemba in Kobly, Matiri, and Tanguiéta districts, Okoma in Tanguiéta and Kouandé districts. Tayakou is the center of traditional beliefs and practices. *Class:* Niger-Congo, Atlantic-Congo, Volta-Congo, North, Gur, Central, Northern, Oti-Volta, Gurma. *Dialects:* Nateni (Natemba, Natimba), Tayari (Tayaba), Kunteni (Kuntemba), Okoni (Okoma). *Lg Use:* Speakers also use Baatonum or French. *Lg Dev:* Literacy rate in first language: 1% to 5%. Roman script. Radio programs. Grammar. *Other:* Traditional religion, Christian.

Ngangam (Dye, Gamgan) [gng] 20,000 in Benin (2002 SIL). *Other:* Traditional religion, Christian, Muslim. See main entry under Togo.

Notre (Bulba, Nootre, Burusa, Boulba) [bly] 1,500 (2002 SIL). Atakora Province, Tanguiéta Subprefecture, northwest, north, and northeast of town of Tanguiéta including Yarka section on the northeast side. *Class:* Niger-Congo, Atlantic-Congo, Volta-Congo, North, Gur, Central, Northern, Oti-Volta, Western, Nootre. *Lg Use:* Most all domains except schools and church. Biali or French used for some meetings. Some speakers also use Waama. *Other:* Traditional religion, Christian.

Tchumbuli (Basa, Tshummbuli, Chombulon, Tchombolo) [bqa] 2,500 (2000 SIL). Departement des Collines, subprefectures of Save and Ouessi, three villages: Okounfo, Edaningbe, and Gbede. *Class:* Niger-Congo, Atlantic-Congo, Volta-Congo, Kwa, Nyo, Potou-Tano, Tano, Central, Akan. *Dialects:* Cobecha, Tchumbuli. Lexical similarity 80% with Chumburung. *Lg Use:* Tchumbuli is used most in Gbédé and least in Edaningbe. Most domains, home. All speakers older than 60 years. Positive language attitude. Children in Okounfo and Edaningbe use Ede Cabe or Maxi, respectively. For ceremonies and the council of elders, Ede Cabe or Maxi are used. In village and regional meetings, Tchumbuli and Ede Cabe or Maxi are used alongside each other. In Edaningbe, Maxi dominates in ceremonies, used exclusively in announcements. In churches, Yoruba is used most along with French. Fon is also used by some. *Other:* Tchumbuli and Cobecha are peoples of differing origins but share a common language. In the villages of Okounfo and Edaningbe they call their language 'Cobecha', in the village of Gbede 'Tchumbuli'. Christian, Muslim.

Tem (Kotokoli, Cotocoli, Tim, Timu, Tembe) [kdh] 50,000 in Benin (2001 Johnstone and Mandryk). *Lg Use:* Language of wider communication. Speakers also use French. *Lg Dev:* Literacy rate in first language: 1% to 5%. *Other:* Muslim. See main entry under Togo.

Waama (Yoabu, Yoabou) [wwa] 50,000 (2000 SIL). 20,000 monolinguals. Atakora Province, at least 20 villages. Natitingou is the cultural center. Several thousand in Cotonou, around Parakou, and in western Nigeria. *Class:* Niger-Congo, Atlantic-Congo, Volta-Congo, North, Gur, Central, Northern, Oti-Volta, Eastern. *Dialects:* Waama, Tangamma. *Lg Use:* Vigorous. Speakers of other languages often speak Waama in the market. Used in preschools, traditional religion, some in church. Positive language attitude. Most of the younger generation know at least some French. Many of the older generation know Baatonum, Ditammari, or Nateni. *Lg Dev:* Literacy rate in first language: 1% to 10%. Newspapers. Radio programs. TV. Dictionary. Grammar. NT: 1994. *Other:* Mountain slope. Savannah. Agriculturalists. Traditional religion, Christian.

Yom (Pila, Pilapila, Kpilakpila) [pil] 74,000 (2001 Johnstone and Mandryk). Djougou area, Atakora Province. *Class:* Niger-Congo, Atlantic-Congo, Volta-Congo, North, Gur, Central, Northern, Oti-Volta, Yom-Nawdm. *Lg Use:* 10% speak Dendi and 3% speak Dompago as second language. *Lg Dev:* Literacy rate in first language: 2%. NT: 1985. *Other:* Ethnic groups: Temba (upland), Yoba (lowland). Related to Nawdm of Togo. Traditional religion, Muslim, Christian.

Yoruba (Yooba, Yariba, Ede-Yoruba) [yor] 465,000 in Benin (1993 Johnstone). Porto-Novo and throughout the country in the towns and major villages. *Dialect:* Egba. *Lg Use:* Speakers also use French. *Lg Dev:* Literacy rate in first language: 1% to 30%. *Other:* Traditional religion, Christian, Muslim. See main entry under Nigeria.

Botswana

Republic of Botswana. Formerly Bechuanaland. 1,561,973. National or official languages: English, Tswana. 220,000 sq. miles. Capital: Gaborone. Literacy rate: 68.9% over 15 years old in Tswana (1997 Central Statistics Office), 25% to 30% in English. Also includes Bemba, Hindi, Lozi (2,000), Northern Sotho (13,871), Nyanja, Southern Sotho, Urdu, Xhosa, Zulu, Chinese (1,000). Information mainly from J. Bendor-Samuel 1989; Andersson and Janson 1997; Sue Hasselbring LBT 1995–2002. Blind population: 3,347 blind, 11,211 seeing impaired (1991 census). Deaf population: 990 deaf, 6,477 hearing impaired (1991 census). The number of languages listed for Botswana is 28. Of those, all are living languages. See map on page 680.

Afrikaans [afr] 6,000 in Botswana (2004 Cook). Spoken as first language mainly in commercial farms and Ghanzi village, Ghanzi District, in the southern half of Kgalagadi District, especially near the South Africa border, and in Takatokwane village, Kweneng District. *Lg Use:* Spoken as first language by Afrikaners (Ghanzi District) and by people of mixed racial background (Kweneng and Kgalagadi districts). *Lg Dev:* Literacy rate in first language: 100% in Ghanzi, 50% in Kweneng and Kgalagadi. Literacy rate in second language: 75% in Kweneng and Kgalagadi districts in Tswana, 50% in English; few use Tswana in Ghanzi District, most use English. *Other:* Christian. See main entry under South Africa.

‖Ani (Handá, ‖Anda, Handádam, Handakwe-Dam, Handa-Khwe, Ts'éxa, Ts'exa) [hnh] 1,000 (1997 Brenzinger). Northwest District, Khwai River, Mababe. Near the Khwe. *Class:* Khoisan, Southern Africa, Central, Tshu-Khwe, Northwest. *Dialects:* Related to Khwe. *Lg Dev:* Literacy rate in second language: 15 to 29 years 70% Tswana, 50% English; 30 to 54 years 40% Tswana, 10% English. *Other:* Traditional religion, Christian.

Birwa [brl] 15,000 in Botswana (2004 Cook). Central District, Bobonong Subdistrict. East of Selebi-Phikwe in the villages: Bobonong, Kobojango, Semolale, Motalatau, and Mathathane. Also spoken in South Africa. *Class:* Niger-Congo, Atlantic-Congo, Volta-Congo, Benue-Congo, Bantoid, Southern, Narrow Bantu, Central, S, Sotho-Tswana (S.30), Sotho.

English (Sekgoa) [eng] *Lg Use:* Official language. International trade, medium of western influences, language of instruction from fifth grade, written language, official purposes, as second language. Taught from the beginning of primary school as a required subject. See main entry under United Kingdom.

‖Gana (G‖ana, G‖ana-Khwe, Gxana, Gxanna, Dxana, Kanakhoe) [gnk] 2,000 (2004 Cook). Ghanzi District, New Xadi and Ghanzi villages, Ghanzi commercial farms, Central Kalahari Game Reserve. Central District, Boteti

Subdistrict, cattleposts south and west of Rakops village. East of Naro, north of |Gwi. *Class:* Khoisan, Southern Africa, Central, Tshu-Khwe, Northwest. *Dialects:* Domkhoe, G‖aakhwe (G‖aa), G‖anakhwe (Kanakhoe), |Khessákhoe. *Lg Use:* Speakers also use |Gwi or Naro. *Lg Dev:* Literacy rate in second language: 15 to 29 years 40% Tswana, 2% English; 30 to 54 years 2% Tswana, 0% English; 55+ years 0%. *Other:* Desert. Hunter-gatherers; herders employed by cattleowners.

Gciriku (Diriku, Diriko, Rugciriku, Mbogedo, Mbogedu, Shimbogedu) [diu] 2,000 in Botswana (2004 Cook). See main entry under Namibia (Diriku).

|Gwi (G‖wikhwe, G‖wi, G|wi, Gcwi, G!wikwe, G|wikhwe, Dcui) [gwj] 2,500 (2004 Cook). Kweneng District: Dutlwe, Serinane, Takotokwane, Kautwane, Khekhenye, Letihakeng, Morwamosu, and Tsetseng villages. Ghanzi District: New Xade, East Hanahai, and Kacgae villages. *Class:* Khoisan, Southern Africa, Central, Tshu-Khwe, Southwest. *Dialect:* Khute. *Lg Use:* Speakers also use ‖Gana or Naro. *Lg Dev:* Literacy rate in second language: 15 to 29 years 40% Tswana, 2% English; 30 to 54 years 2% Tswana, 0% English; 55+ years 0%. *Other:* Desert. Hunter-gatherers.

Herero (Otjiherero, Ochiherero) [her] 20,000 in Botswana (2004 Cook). Scattered among many ethnic groups, usually having their own areas within larger towns and villages: Northwest District (Maun, Gomare, Sehitwa, Makakung, Nokaneng, Shakawe, Nxaunxau, and western cattleposts), Central District (Mahalapye, Toromoja, Rakops, Mokoboxane, Letlhakane), Ghanzi District (Charles Hill, Ghanzi, Makunda, Dryhoek, New Kanagas, Dekar), Kgalagadi District (Tsabong, Omaweneno, Werda), Kgatleng District (Morwa). *Lg Use:* All ages. Some older speakers are moving back to Namibia. *Lg Dev:* Literacy rate in first language: Nearly 60%. Literacy rate in second language: Nearly 60% in Tswana. *Other:* Spoken by the Ovaherero and Ovambanderu peoples. Erroneously called 'Damara'. Most came to Botswana as refugees from Namibia in the early 1900s. Christian, traditional religion. See main entry under Namibia.

‡Hua (‡Hua-Owani, |Hua, |Hû, ‡Hoan, ‡Hoa) [huc] 200 (2004 Cook). Southern Kalahari Desert, Kweneng District. Sasi is in southwestern Mahalapye Subdistrict of the Central District. *Class:* Khoisan, Southern Africa, Southern, Hua. *Dialects:* ‡Hua, Sasi. Related to !Xóõ. *Lg Use:* Diminishing in number of speakers. Speakers are older adults. *Other:* SOV; genitives before noun head; adjectives, numerals, demonstratives, relatives after noun head; tonal.

Ju|'hoan (Kung-Tsumkwe, Xû, Xun, Kung, !Xo, Ju'oasi, Zhu'oasi, Dzu'oasi, Tsumkwe, Dobe Kung, Xaixai) [ktz] 5,000 in Botswana (2002). Northwest District, on Namibia and Angola borders, north of ‡Kx'au‖'ein. Also spoken in Namibia. *Class:* Khoisan, Southern Africa, Northern. *Dialects:* Dzu'oasi (Ssu Ghassi, Zhu'oase), Nogau (Agau). May be intelligible with ‡Kx'au‖'ein. *Lg Dev:* Dictionary. Grammar. Bible portions: 1974. *Other:* Traditional religion, Christian.

Kalanga (Ikalanga, Chikalanga, Tjikalanga, Kalaka, Sekalaña, Sekalaka) [kck] 150,000 in Botswana (2004 Cook). The entire Northeast District and the eastern third of Central District. Lilima dialect is mainly in Botswana, Kalanga mainly in Zimbabwe. *Dialects:* Nyai (Nyayi), Ikalanga, Talahundra, Lilima (Humbe), Peri. *Lg Use:* The Talaunda dialect is extinct. Resistance to pressures to adopt Tswana language and culture is led by men. Speakers also use Tswana. *Lg Dev:* Literacy rate in first language: 90%. Literacy rate in second language: 70% in Tswana, 85% in English. *Other:* Different from Holoholo of Democratic Republic of the Congo. Speakers of the

Najwa dialect were Nambya speakers from Zimbabwe who moved to Botswana and settled along the Boteti River. Some Kalanga speakers also moved there. Najwa is now more similar to Kalanga than to Nambya. But the Najwa are borrowing many Tswana words. The Kalanga spoken in Boteti is more like Najwa than to other Kalanga dialects. Najwa are similar to the Zimbabwean Nambya. See main entry under Zimbabwe.

Kgalagadi (Khalagari, Khalakadi, Kxhalaxadi, Qhalaxarzi, Shekgalagadi) [xkv] 40,000 in Botswana (2004 Cook). South and central, along the South Africa border, northern half of Kgalagadi District, western half of Kweneng, and western half of Southern districts. Ghanzi District: Ghanzi, Kanagas, Tsotsha, Kuke, Karakobis, Ncojane, Kule, Charles Hill, New Xade, Dekar, and Grootlaagte villages. Northwest District: Sehitwa and Maun. Also spoken in Namibia. *Class:* Niger-Congo, Atlantic-Congo, Volta-Congo, Benue-Congo, Bantoid, Southern, Narrow Bantu, Central, S, Sotho-Tswana (S.30), Kgalagadi. *Dialects:* Ngologa, Shaga, Kgalagadi, Balaongwe, Pedi, Phaleng, Kenyi, Khakhae, Koma, Rhiti, Siwane. Ngologa is the largest dialect. It may be 2 separate languages. A separate language from Tswana. *Lg Use:* Speakers also use Tswana, English, or Afrikaans. *Lg Dev:* Literacy rate in second language: Ages 15 to 29, 85% Tswana, 55% English; ages 30 to 54, 50% Tswana, 15% English; ages 55+, 20% Tswana, 2% English. *Other:* SVO; genitives, articles, adjectives, numerals, relatives after noun heads; question word final; word order distinguishes subject, object, indirect object; verb affixes mark person and number; passives formed by suffix -w; causatives formed by suffix -is; comparative locatives; CV; tonal. Plains. Semiarid desert. Pastoralists. Christian.

Khwe (Khoe, Kxoe, Xun, "Water Bushmen," "Mbarakwena") [xuu] 4,000 in Botswana (2004 Cook). Northwest District: Gan, Cadikarauwe, Mohembo, Shakawe, Kaputura, |Ao-Kyao, Sikondomboro, Ngarange, Sekanduko, Xongoa, Cauwe, Moxatce, Dungu, Seronga, Beyetca, Gudigoa, Sicokora, Geixa, |Qom-ca, Tobere, ‡Umbexa, Djaxo, Kangwara villages. *Dialect:* Buga-Kxoe (Boga, Buga-Khwe, Bukakhwe, "River Bushman," ‖Anikxoe, ‖Ani-Khoe, Tannekwe, Gani-Khwe). *Lg Dev:* Literacy rate in second language: Buga: 15 to 29 years 70% Tswana, 50% English; 30 to 54 years 40% Tswana, 10% English. *Other:* Hunter-gatherers; fishermen. Traditional religion, Christian. See main entry under Namibia (Kxoe).

Kua (Cua, Tyua, Tyhua) [tyu] 817 (2004 Cook). Central District, especially Mahalapye, Serowe subdistricts and Northeast District. Primarily on cattleposts and in 'settlements'. *Class:* Khoisan, Southern Africa, Central, Tshu-Khwe, Northeast. *Other:* Nomadic. Herdsmen on cattleposts for owners; some gathering. Traditional religion, Christian.

Kuhane (Echisubia, Subia, Supia, Kwahane, Kuahane, Sesubea, Subiya, Chikuhane) [sbs] 12,000 in Botswana (1993 Johnstone). Northwest District, Chobe Subdistrict. *Other:* 'Subiya' is the Tswana name. Traditional religion, Christian. See main entry under Namibia (Subiya).

‡Kx'au‖'ein (Kung-Gobabis, ‖Au‖ei, ‖X'au‖'e, ‡Kx'au‖'ei, Auen, Kaukau, Koko) [aue] 2,000 in Botswana (2004 Cook). Ghanzi District: Grootelaagte, Kanagas, Ghanzi villages, and on the commercial farms. *Dialect:* Nogau. *Lg Use:* Most bilinguals use Naro as second language; next most common is Tswana. *Lg Dev:* Literacy rate in second language: 14 to 29 years 40% Tswana, 10% English; 30 to 54 years 2% Tswana, English 0%; 55+ years 0%. *Other:* Traditional religion, Christian. See main entry under Namibia.

Mbukushu (Mbukushi, Mambukush, Mampukush, Mbukuhu, Thimbukushu, Gova, Kusso) [mhw] 20,000 in

Botswana (2004 Cook). Northwest District, in all villages north of Gomare which are within 30 km of the Okavango River. *Lg Use:* Vigorous. All ages. *Lg Dev:* Literacy rate in second language: 15 to 29 years 90% Tswana, 50% English; 30 to 54 3% in Tswana, 10% English; 55 + 0%. *Other:* Traditional religion, Christian. See main entry under Namibia.

Nama (Naman, Namakwa, Namaqua, Dama, Damara, Damaqua, Tama, Tamma, Tamakwa, Berdama, Bergdamara, Kakuya Bushman Nasie, Rooi Nasie, "Hottentot," "Kupkaffer," "Kupkaferrn," Koekhoegowap) [naq] 1,500 in Botswana (2002). Kgalagadi District, Tsabong, Makopong, Omaweneno, Tshane villages; Ghanzi District, villages along the Ghanzi-Mamuno road. *Lg Dev:* Literacy rate in second language: 80% Tswana, 10% English. See main entry under Namibia.

Nambya (Chinambya, Nanzva, Nambzya) [nmq] 15,000 in Botswana (2004 Cook). *Other:* Christian. See main entry under Zimbabwe.

Naro (Nharo, Nharon, Nhauru, Nhaurun, ǁAikwe, ǀAikwe, ǁAiǁen, ǁAisan, ǁAiǁe) [nhr] 10,000 in Botswana (2004 Cook). Population total all countries: 14,000. Ghanzi District: Ghanzi, Bere, Dekar, East Hanahai, West Hanahai, Kuke, New Kanagas, Tshobokwane, Makunda, Grootelaagte, Karakobis, Kanagas, Charles Hill villages, and on commercial farms. Also spoken in Namibia. *Class:* Khoisan, Southern Africa, Central, Tshu-Khwe, Southwest. *Dialects:* ǀAmkwe, ǀAnekwe, G!inkwe, !Gingkwe, G!okwe, Qabekhoe (Qabekho, !Kabbakwe), Ts'aokhoe (Tsaukwe, Tsaokhwe), Tserekwe, Tsorokwe, Nǁhai-Ntse'e (Nǁhai, Ts'ao). *Lg Use:* Trade language among speakers of other Khoisan languages in Ghanzi District. *Lg Dev:* Literacy rate in second language: 15 to 29 years 70% Tswana, 15% English; 30 to 54 years 10% Tswana 2% English; 55 + year 2% Tswana, 0% English. Dictionary. Grammar. *Other:* Plains. Savannah, scrub forest. Herdsmen on cattle ranches; nannies; cooks; laborers; gatherers. Traditional religion, Christian.

Ndebele (Tabele, Tebele, Isinde'bele, Sindebele, Northern Ndebele) [nde] 8,000 in Botswana (2002). Northeast District, a few villages. See main entry under Zimbabwe.

Shua (Shua-Khwe, Mashuakwe, Tshumakwe) [shg] 6,000 (2004 Cook). Population includes 100 Danisi (1977 Voegelin and Voegelin). Central District, Tutume Subdistrict: Nata, Gweta; Boteti Subdistrict: Motopi, Popipi, Mokoboxane, Mmatshumu, Letlhakane. *Class:* Khoisan, Southern Africa, Central, Tshu-Khwe, North Central. *Dialects:* Shua-Khwe (Mashuakwe), Nǀoo-Khwe (Nǀoo, Nǁookhwe), ǀOree-Khwe (ǀOree, ǀKoree-Khoe), ǁ'Aiye (ǀAaye), ǀXaise (ǀHaise, ǀTaise, ǀHais, ǀAis), Tshidi-Khwe (Tsh'iti, Tcaiti, Sili, Shete Tsere), Danisi (Danisis, Danisa, Demisa, Madenasse, Madenassa, Madinnisane), Cara, Deti, Ganádi. *Lg Dev:* Bible portions: 1978.

Tsoa (Chware, Tshwa, Sarwa, Sesarwa, Haitshuari, Hietshware, Hiotshuwau, Hiochuwau, Tshuwau, Chuwau, Gabake-Ntshori, Gǁabake, Masarwa, Tati, Tati Bushman, Kwe-Etshori Kwee, Kwe, Kwe-Tshori) [hio] 5,000 in Botswana (2004 Cook). Population total all countries: 8,536. Central District, especially Mahalapye, Serowe subdistricts; Northeast District. Primarily on cattleposts and in 'settlements'. Also spoken in Zimbabwe. *Class:* Khoisan, Southern Africa, Central, Tshu-Khwe, Northeast. *Lg Use:* Many children speak only Tswana, some only Tsoa, some both. *Lg Dev:* Literacy rate in second language: 15 to 29 years 25% in Tswana, 20% in English; 30 to 54 years 2% in Tswana, 2% in English; 55 + years 0%. *Other:* Nomadic. Herdsmen on cattleposts for owners; some gathering. Traditional religion, Christian.

Tswana (Chuana, Coana, Cuana, Setswana, Sechuana, Beetjuans) [tsn] 1,070,000 in Botswana (1993 Johnstone). Population total all countries: 4,407,174. Spoken throughout the country as lingua franca, and as first language primarily in the Southeast and Kgatleng districts, the eastern half of Southern and Kweneng districts, in the Serowe-Palapye and Mahalapye subdistricts of Central District, and around Maun village in Northwest District. Also spoken in Namibia, South Africa, Zimbabwe. *Class:* Niger-Congo, Atlantic-Congo, Volta-Congo, Benue-Congo, Bantoid, Southern, Narrow Bantu, Central, S, Sotho-Tswana (S.30), Tswana. *Dialects:* Tlhaping (Tlapi), Rolong, Kwena, Kgatla, Ngwatu (Ngwato), Tawana, Lete, Ngwaketse, Tlokwa. Southern Sotho, Northern Sotho, and Tswana are largely inherently intelligible but have generally been considered separate languages. Standard Tswana uses Kgatla dialect. *Lg Use:* National language. Vigorous. 150,000 second-language speakers. Used among the educated. Used more for spoken purposes than written. Officially used as language of instruction in grades 1 to 4 in all government primary schools. All ages. *Lg Dev:* Literacy rate in first language: 80% to 90%. Taught in primary schools. Magazines. Newspapers. Radio programs. TV. Dictionary. Grammar. Bible: 1857–1993. *Other:* 90% to 95% of children complete standard 7 in primary school. Agriculturalists; pastoralists: cattle. Christian, traditional religion.

Tswapong (Setswapong) [two] 2,000 (1997 Andersson and Janson). Central District, Mahalapye Subdistrict: all villages east of Mahalapye. *Class:* Niger-Congo, Atlantic-Congo, Volta-Congo, Benue-Congo, Bantoid, Southern, Narrow Bantu, Central, S, Sotho-Tswana (S.30). *Dialects:* Some similarities to Pedi (N. Sotho) and some to Tswana, but it is not clearly a dialect of either. Some intelligibility to speakers of a northern dialect of Tswana (Sengwato and Setawana), and to speakers of a northwestern dialect of Pedi (Hananwa and Setokwa). Some speakers of Birwa and Tswapong have said that their varieties are closer to one another than to Tswana or Pedi. *Other:* Several groups: the Ramokgonami, Maifela, Chadibe, Sefbare, Tupsa.

!Xóõ (Ngǀamani, Tsasi) [nmn] 4,000 in Botswana (2002). Population total all countries: 4,200. Southern Gantsi District, northern Kgalagadi District, western Southern and western Kweneng districts. Also spoken in Namibia. *Class:* Khoisan, Southern Africa, Southern, Hua. *Dialects:* Auni (ǀAuni, ǀAuo), Kakia (Masarwa), Kiǀhazi, Ngǀuǁen (Nuǁen, ǀUǁen, Ngǀuǀei, ǀNuǁen, ǀUǁen), Nusan (Ngǀusan, Nu-San, Noosan), Xatia (Katia, Kattea, Khatia, Vaalpens, ǀKusi, ǀEikusi), !Kwi. *Lg Use:* People older than 10 who have been to school or have lived with speakers of other languages also use Tswana, Kgalagadi, Herero, Naro, or ǀGwi. *Lg Dev:* Dictionary. Grammar. *Other:* Nusan are in Botswana. Nuǁen dialect is extinct. SVO; prepositions; genitives, adjectives, numerals, relatives after noun heads; question word initial; 2 prefixes, 3 suffixes; word order distinguishes subjects, objects, indirect objects; verb affixes mark number, gender of subject and object, and is obligatory; passives; reduplication on periphrastics for causatives; periphrastic comparatives; CV, CVV, CVCV; tonal. Plains. Savannah. 1,100 meters. Hunter-gatherers. Nusan: traditional religion, Christian.

Yeyi (Shiyeyi, Yeei, Yei, Ciyei, Koba, Kuba) [yey] 20,000 in Botswana (2004 Cook). Population total all countries: 25,200. Ethnic population: 47,000 in Botswana. North West District, Maun, Shorobe up to Mababe, Sankoyo, Daunara, Nokaneng, Gumare, Sepopo, Ikoga, Shakawe, and Seronga. Central District, Letihakane, Xumu, Rakops, Motopi. Capitals for Wayei Maun and Gumare. Also spoken in Namibia. *Class:* Niger-Congo, Atlantic-Congo, Volta-Congo, Benue-Congo, Bantoid, Southern, Narrow Bantu, Central, R, Yeye (R.40). *Dialect:* Shirwanga. Not closely related to other languages. Lexical similarity 47% with Luyana, 30% with Herero. *Lg Use:* 43% of those who learned Yeyi from their parents say they speak Yeyi best, 57% say they speak Tswana best. Few speak Yeyi as second language. 12% of respondents say they speak only Yeyi to their children, 9% speak Yeyi and Tswana to their children. In some villages, children speak Yeyi, including Seronga, Sepopa, Ikoga, Jau. In many villages only those over 40 speak Yeyi. All speakers use Tswana as second language. 73% of respondents say they speak Tswana well. Young people who have attended secondary school also speak English. *Lg Dev:* Literacy rate in second language: Age 15 to 29: 95% Tswana, 68% English; age 30 to 54: 33% Tswana, 20% English; age 55 and over: 33% Tswana, 6% English. Motivation for literacy is high. Dictionary. *Other:* SVO; postpositions; articles, adjectives, numerals after noun heads; relatives before or after; question word initial; 4 prefixes, one suffix; word order distinguishes subjects, objects, indirect objects; noun affixes indicate case; verb affixes mark person, number, gender; CVC; nontonal. Plains. Delta. 850 to 1,000 meters. Fishermen; hunters; peasant agriculturalists. Christian.

Zezuru (Shona) [sna] 11,000 in Botswana (2004 Cook). *Dialect:* Karanga. See main entry under Zimbabwe (Shona).

British Indian Ocean Territory

British Indian Ocean Territory. 3,500 (2002). National or official language: English. Chagos Archipelago including Diego Garcia. Also includes a few from the Philippines and Mauritius along with military personnel. The number of languages listed for British Indian Ocean Territory is 1.

English [eng] 3,500 in British Indian Ocean Territory (2004). *Lg Use:* Official language. *Other:* The indigenous population no longer resides in the islands. Current residents include members of the USA military, a small detachment of British officials, and support staff, mainly of Mauritian and Philippine origin. See main entry under United Kingdom.

Burkina Faso

Formerly Upper Volta. 13,574,820. National or official language: French. Literacy rate: 19.2%: 29.5% males, 9.2% females (1998 UNESCO). Also includes Jowulu (1,000). Information mainly from J. Bendor-Samuel 1989; SIL 1973–2003; Institut de Recherche des Sciences Sociales et Humaines and the Centre Nationale de Recherche Scientifique et Technique (Tiendrebeogo 1983). Blind population: 50,000. The number of languages listed for Burkina Faso is 68. Of those, all are living languages. See map on page 681.

Bambara (Bamana, Bamanakan) [bam] 300 in Burkina Faso (1991 Vanderaa). Kénédougou Province, near N'Dorola. *Other:* Muslim. See main entry under Mali (Bamanankan).

Biali (Bieri, Bjeri, Bjerb, Berba, Burba) [beh] 1,500 in Burkina Faso (1991). Tapoa and Gourma provinces, at the Benin border, south of Arli. *Lg Use:* All ages. 30% to 40% are monolingual. *Lg Dev:* Literacy rate in second language: 9%. *Other:* Different from Baatonum (Berba). Traditional religion, Muslim, Christian. See main entry under Benin.

Birifor, Malba (Birifo, Malba-Birifor, Northern Birifor) [bfo] 108,000 in Burkina Faso (1993). Southwestern Burkina Faso, Poni Province. Also spoken in Côte d'Ivoire. *Class:* Niger-Congo, Atlantic-Congo, Volta-Congo, North, Gur, Central, Northern, Oti-Volta, Western, Northwest, Dagaari-Birifor, Birifor. *Dialects:* Wile, Birifor. *Lg Use:* All ages. Speakers also use Lobi, Mòoré, Jula, or French. *Lg Dev:* NT: 1994. *Other:* Dagaari, Wali,

and Birifor of Ghana are separate languages. Many monolinguals. Traditional religion, Christian, Muslim.

Bissa (Bisa) [bib] 350,000 in Burkina Faso (1999 SIL). Population does not include the Bissa southern Barka region. Population total all countries: 581,900. South central, Boulgou and Zoundweogo provinces, in the cities of Garango, Zabré, Gomboussougou, Tenkodogo. Also spoken in Côte d'Ivoire, Ghana, Togo. *Class:* Niger-Congo, Mande, Eastern, Eastern, Bissa. *Dialects:* Barka, Lebir, Lere. Related to Samo. *Lg Use:* All ages. Some also use Mòoré, some French. *Lg Dev:* Dictionary. Grammar. NT: 2000. *Other:* Not the same as Busa of Benin and Nigeria. The Mòoré name for the people is 'Boussanse'. Muslim, traditional religion, Christian.

Bobo Madaré, Northern (Bobo Fing, Bobo Fign, Bobo Fi, Black Bobo, Bobo, Boboda) [bbo] 35,000 in Burkina Faso (1995 SIL). Population total all countries: 53,400. Banwa Province. Tansilla is the center, with a radius of about 25 km. Also spoken in Mali. *Class:* Niger-Congo, Mande, Western, Northwestern, Soninke-Bobo, Bobo. *Dialects:* Yaba, Sankuma (Sarokama), Jèrè, Tankri, Kure, Kukoma. Northern Bobo Madaré has 20% to 30% intelligibility of Southern Bobo Madaré. All dialects of Northern understand Yaba, centered in Tansilla. Tankri is difficult for others to understand. Different from other Mande languages. Separate literature may be needed for the Mali dialect. Some linguists treat Bobo as a separate major branch of Mande. Sya is the prestige dialect in Mali and used for literature. *Lg Use:* Bobo Madaré is spoken at home. Koma, a simplified form of Kukoma, has some negative attitudes held toward it. Jula is also used by most men with good proficiency and some women for common topics, government, and trade. French is spoken by the educated. *Lg Dev:* Literacy rate in second language: 5% or below. Grammar. *Other:* Bobo Fing call themselves 'Bobo' and their language 'Boboda'. The government calls them 'Bobo Madaré'. 'Bobo' is the general Bambara word for Bobo Madaré, Buamu or Bomu. CV, CVC, CVV, CCV; tonal. Plains. Savannah, scrub forest. 400 to 500 meters. Peasant agriculturalists. Traditional religion, Muslim, Christian.

Bobo Madaré, Southern (Bobo Fing, Bobo Fi, Black Bobo, Bobo) [bwq] 311,691 (2000 WCD). Population includes 15,000 speakers of Zara. Ethnic population: 160,000 to 190,000 (1999 SIL). Mainly Houet Province, from 20 km west of Bobo Dioulasso to 40 km east, north to Kouka Region in Kossi Province. *Class:* Niger-Congo, Mande, Western, Northwestern, Soninke-Bobo, Bobo. *Dialects:* Benge, Sogokiré, Voré, Syabéré (Sya), Zara (Bobo Dioula, Bobo Jula). *Lg Use:* All ages. Syabéré in Bobo Dioulasso Region is the prestige dialect, and the one used for literature. Jula is also used by most men and some women with varying proficiency. French is spoken by the educated. *Lg Dev:* Literacy rate in second language: 10% Jula. NT: 1981. *Other:* They call themselves 'Bobo' and the language 'Boboda'. The government calls them 'Bobo Madaré'. 'Bobo' is the general Bambara word for Bobo Fing, Buamu, or Bomu. Tonal. Plains. Savannah, scrub forest. 200 to 500 meters. Peasant agriculturalists. Traditional religion, Muslim, Christian.

Bolon (Boka, Bo) [bof] 17,000 (1998 SIL). Kénédougou and Houet provinces, 12 villages around N'Dorola and Samorogouan. *Class:* Niger-Congo, Mande, Western, Central-Southwestern, Central, Manding-Jogo, Manding-Vai, Manding-Mokole, Manding. *Dialects:* Black Bolon (Northern Bolon), White Bolon (Southern Bolon). White Bolon has higher inherent intelligibility with Jula (81%) than Black Bolon (52%). *Lg Use:* All ages. High bilingualism in Jula. *Other:* Muslim, traditional religion.

Bomu (Boomu, Bore, Western Bobo Wule, Bobo Oule) [bmq] 56,000 in Burkina Faso (1991). Kossi Province.

Lg Use: All ages. Bilingual level estimates for Jula: 0 0%, 1 58%, 2 20%, 3 20%, 4 2%, 5 0%. Men can speak Jula for common topics with outsiders, women for trading. *Lg Dev:* Literacy rate in first language: Adults over 30: 2%, young people 20%. Literacy rate in second language: Young people 10% in Jula; 2% in French. *Other:* The people are called 'Bonuu' (sg.) or 'Bwa' (pl.). Plains. Savannah. Peasant agriculturalists. Traditional religion, Christian. See main entry under Mali.

Buamu (Eastern Bobo Wule, Eastern Bobo Oule, Red Bobo, Bouamou, Bwamu) [box] 185,945 (2000 WCD). Kossi, Mouhoun, Tuy, Banwa, and Les Balés provinces. Approximately 80 km east-west and 200 km north-south. *Class:* Niger-Congo, Atlantic-Congo, Volta-Congo, North, Gur, Central, Northern, Bwamu. *Dialect:* Ouarkoye. *Lg Use:* All domains, home, churches. All ages. Many men can speak Jula for common topics with outsiders, women for trading. French is also used. *Lg Dev:* Literacy rate in first language: 5%. Literacy rate in second language: 2%. Active literacy program. Radio programs. Bible portions: 1957–2002. *Other:* 'Bwa' is their name for themselves ('Bwaba' is plural) in the Dedougou dialect. 'Buamu' (Bouamou) is the language. 'Bobo' is the general Bambara name for Buamu, Bomo, or Bobo Fing, but properly applies only to the Bobo Fing. Pwe is the name of a town, not a dialect (D. Shady CMA 1973). SVO; postpositions; relatives before noun heads, numerals, adjectives after noun heads; tonal. Plains. Savannah, scrub forest. Peasant agriculturalists. Traditional religion, Christian, Muslim.

Bwamu, Cwi (Coo, Cwi, Twi) [bwy] 24,000 (1999 SIL). South of Boromo, border area between Bougouriba and Sissili provinces, area 10 km north to south, and 40 km east to west, from Founzan (Bougouriba Province) to Kabourou (Sissili Province). *Class:* Niger-Congo, Atlantic-Congo, Volta-Congo, North, Gur, Central, Northern, Bwamu. *Dialects:* Intelligibility within Cwi area is over 90%, 50% to 70% of Láá Láá Bwamu, 30% of Ouarkoye Buamu, and 65% to 70% of Dakwi Bwamu. *Lg Use:* Cwi is used in the home. All ages. Some over 7 years old have low proficiency in Jula (trade, common topics) or French (greetings, weather). *Lg Dev:* Literacy rate in second language: 3% Jula. Unable to use other Bwamu literature. Motivation for literacy is high. *Other:* Tonal. Plains. Savannah, scrub forest. 250 meters. Peasant agriculturalists. Traditional religion, Christian, Muslim.

Bwamu, Láá Láá (Kàdenbà, Yere) [bwj] 69,210 (2000 WCD). Tuy and Les Balés provinces, in and around the villages of Bagassi, Pâ, and Boni. *Class:* Niger-Congo, Atlantic-Congo, Volta-Congo, North, Gur, Central, Northern, Bwamu. *Dialects:* Close to Ouarkoye dialect of Buamu and Bwamu Twi. Speakers unable to use other Bwamu dialects for literature. *Lg Use:* Used in the home. All ages. Speakers over 7 years old can speak some Jula as second language for trade, government services, and common topics with those from other ethnic groups; French for government services. *Lg Dev:* Literacy rate in first language: 1% to 2% are fluent readers of Ouarkoye Buamu. Literacy rate in second language: 1% to 2% are fluent readers of French or Jula. Literacy program. Grammar. Bible portions: 1977–1995. *Other:* Tonal. Plains. Scrub forest. 250 meters. Peasant agriculturalists. Traditional religion, Christian, Muslim.

Cerma (Gouin, Gwe, Gwen, Kirma) [cme] 61,400 in Burkina Faso (1991). Population total all countries: 63,100. From just north of Ouagadougou, Côte d'Ivoire, along the main road to Banfora, Comoé Province. Also spoken in Côte d'Ivoire. *Class:* Niger-Congo, Atlantic-Congo, Volta-Congo, North, Gur, Central, Southern, Kirma-Tyurama. *Dialects:* Banfora-Sienena, Niangoloko-Diarabakoko, Soubakanedougou, Gouindougouba. The

Gouindougouba dialect is spoken in 1 or 2 villages. Turka is the closest language, but not inherently intelligible. *Lg Use:* Used for instruction in grades 1 to 3. All ages. Most also use Jula. Those who have been to school speak some French. *Lg Dev:* Literacy rate in first language: 12%. Literacy rate in second language: 15% Jula or French. Literacy program run by language committee. Satellite school project. Dictionary. Bible portions: 1995. *Other:* The people are called 'Gouin' or 'Ciramba'. SVO; postpositions, articles, numerals, relatives after noun heads; question word final; no more than one affix per word; word order distinguishes objects and indirect objects; verb changes with tense and aspect; causatives by sentence order; comparatives; CV, CVC, CVV, VV, V; tonal. Plains. Savannah. Peasant agriculturalists. Traditional religion, Muslim, Christian.

Dagaari Dioula (Dagari Dyoula, Dagaari Jula, Jari, Yari, Wala) [dgd] 21,000 (1999 SIL). Diébougou, To, Boromo, Soukoulaye, Silly, Pa, Dano, Leo, Gao, Dissin, Wessa, Fara, French Hamele. *Class:* Niger-Congo, Atlantic-Congo, Volta-Congo, North, Gur, Central, Northern, Oti-Volta, Western, Northwest, Dagaari-Birifor, Dagaari. *Dialects:* Not inherently intelligible with Dagaare, Jula, or Mòoré. Lexical similarity 65% to 70% with Dagaare. *Lg Use:* West of the Mouhoun River some men have routine proficiency in Jula, but women have lower proficiency. In some western locations some also speak Mòoré. *Other:* Muslim.

Dagara, Northern (Northern Dagaare, Dagari, Degati, Dagati, Dogaari, Daagari, Dagaare) [dgi] 388,000 (2001 Johnstoneand Mandryk). Southwest Burkina Faso, Poni, Bougouriba, Sissili, Mouhoun provinces. *Class:* Niger-Congo, Atlantic-Congo, Volta-Congo, North, Gur, Central, Northern, Oti-Volta, Western, Northwest, Dagaari-Birifor, Dagaari. *Dialects:* Lober (Lobr), Wule, Nura (Lawra Lobi). Dagara and Birifor are partly intelligible. *Lg Use:* All ages. Dagara is more prominent politically and socially. *Lg Dev:* Radio programs. TV. Dictionary. Grammar. *Other:* The people are called 'Dagaaba'. Different from Southern Dagaare in Ghana. Traditional religion, Christian, Muslim.

Dogon, Jamsay (Dyamsay Tegu) [djm] Northern border with Mali. *Dialects:* Domno, Gono, Bama, Guru. *Other:* Agriculturalists. See main entry under Mali.

Dogon, Tomo Kan (Tomo-Kan) [dtm] A few villages. *Other:* Agriculturalists. See main entry under Mali.

Dogosé (Dorosie, Dorhosye, Dokhosié, Doghosié, Doro Doghosié, Dokhobe, Dorobé, Doghose, Dorhossié, Dorossé) [dos] 20,000 (1991 Ouattara). Villages of Ouo, Sidéradougou, Kouere, Koro, and Sirakoro, Comoé Province, Sidéradougou Subdistrict, southwest Burkina Faso. *Class:* Niger-Congo, Atlantic-Congo, Volta-Congo, North, Gur, Central, Southern, Gan-Dogose. *Dialects:* Klamaasise, Mesise, Lutise, Gbeyãse, Sukurase, Gbogorose. Different from Bambadion dialects Dogoso and Khe. The regional dialects are inherently intelligible with each other. Lexical similarity 82% with Khisa, 68% with Kaansa, 15% with Dogoso, 14% with Khe. *Lg Use:* All ages. Speakers also use Jula. *Lg Dev:* Literacy rate in first language: 1%. Literacy rate in second language: 3%. *Other:* Clans are Ouattara or Coulibaly. Muslim, traditional religion.

Dogoso (Dorossié-Fing, Dorhosié-Finng, Black Dogose, Dorhosié-Noirs, Bambadion-Dogoso, Bambadion-Dokhosié) [dgs] 9,000 in Burkina Faso (1999 SIL). Villages are Dandougou, Torokoro, Sokoura, Bondokoro, Tolandougou, Sakédougou. Near the Dogose, Khisa, and Khe. Also spoken in Côte d'Ivoire. *Class:* Niger-Congo, Atlantic-Congo, Volta-Congo, North, Gur, Central, Southern, Dogoso-Khe. *Dialects:* Lexical similarity 56% with Khe, 15% with Dogosé, 16% with Khisa. *Lg Use:*

All ages. Speakers have some proficiency in Jula. *Other:* Traditional religion.

Dyan (Dian, Dya, Dyane, Dyanu, Dan) [dya] 14,100 (1991 Vanderaa). Bougouriba Province, Dolo, near Diébougou. *Class:* Niger-Congo, Atlantic-Congo, Volta-Congo, North, Gur, Central, Southern, Dyan. *Dialect:* Zanga. Zanga is a dialect or closely related language. Not close enough to Lobi to be intelligible. Distinct from Dan (Gio, Yacouba). *Lg Use:* Some speakers also use Jula. *Other:* Traditional religion, Muslim.

Dzùùngoo (Samogho, Samogo, Samoro, Kpango, Eastern Duun) [dnn] 13,400 (1998 Solomiac, Entz). 30% monolinguals. Kénédougou Province, Samorogouan and Samogohiri departments, west of Bobo-Dioulasso near the town of Orodara; villages of Samogo-Iri, Saraba, Diomou, Gnalé, Sokouraba, Todié, and Samogogouan. *Class:* Niger-Congo, Mande, Western, Northwestern, Samogo. *Dialects:* Kpango (Samorogouan), Dzùùngoo (Samogohiri). The two dialects are intelligible to each other's speakers. *Lg Use:* All ages. Positive language attitude. Bilingual level estimates for Jula: 0 0%, 1 10%, 2 10%, 3 30%, 4 40%, 5 10%. They speak Jula to outsiders. All men are fluent in Jula, all women are not. Some men also speak French. *Lg Dev:* Literacy rate in second language: 5% French. Dictionary. Bible portions: 2002. *Other:* 'Dzùùn' is the name for the people. 'Samogo' is the Jula name. SOV; postpositions; genitives before noun heads; articles, adjectives, numerals, relatives after noun heads; question word final; 2 suffixes; word order distinguishes subjects, objects, topic; causatives; comparatives; V, CV, CCV; tonal. Plains. Scrub forest. 500 meters. Peasant agriculturalists. Muslim.

French [fra] *Lg Use:* Official language. See main entry under France.

Fulfulde, Northeastern Burkina Faso [fuh] 750,000 in Burkina Faso (1999 SIL). Northeastern Burkina Faso corner. *Dialects:* Barani (Barain, Baraniire), Gourmantche, Bogandé, Jelgoore, Liptaakoore, Barkoundouba, Seeba-Yaga (Yaaga) Ouhiguyua, Fada Ngurma. *Other:* Animal husbandry: cattle. Muslim. See main entry under Niger (Fulfulde, Western Niger).

Gourmanchéma (Gourma, Gourmantche, Gurma, Migulimancema, Goulmacema, Gulmancema, Gulimancema) [gux] 600,000 in Burkina Faso (1999 SIL). Population total all countries: 812,500. Eastern Burkina Faso, Gourma, Tapoa, Gnagna, Komandjari, Yagha, and Kompienga provinces, just below the scrub land that blends into the Sahara. Also spoken in Benin, Niger, Togo. *Class:* Niger-Congo, Atlantic-Congo, Volta-Congo, North, Gur, Central, Northern, Oti-Volta, Gurma. *Dialects:* Northern Gourmanchema, Central Gourmanchema, Southern Gourmanchema. Central and eastern dialects are inherently intelligible, northern only with difficulty. *Lg Use:* All ages. Central is the prestige dialect and used for writing. Bilingual level estimates for Mòoré: 0 90%, 1 3%, 2 3%, 3 2%, 4 1%, 5 1%. Those who have been to school or live in town (about 10%) can use French for common topics. Some also use Zarma or Fulfulde. *Lg Dev:* Literacy rate in second language: 5% to 10%. Newspapers. Radio programs. Films. NT: 1958–1990. *Other:* The people are called 'Bigulimanceba' or 'Gourma'. SVO; postpositions; genitives, articles before noun heads; numerals after; CV; tonal, 3 tones. Plains. Savannah. Peasant agriculturalists: over 90% are able to meet all their food requirements. Traditional religion, Muslim, Christian.

Hausa (Haoussa) [hau] 500 in Burkina Faso (1991 Vanderaa). Boulgou and Gourma provinces. *Other:* Muslim. See main entry under Nigeria.

Jalkunan (Dyala, Dyalanu, Jalkuna, Blé) [bxl] 500 (1995 SIL). Ethnic population: 800 to 1,000 (1995 SIL). Village

of Blédougou, west of Banfora, near the town of Sindou, Leraba Province. *Class:* Niger-Congo, Mande, Western, Central-Southwestern, Central, Manding-Jogo, Jogo-Jeri, Jeri-Jalkuna. *Dialects:* Lexical similarity 19% with Jula, 17% with Bolon. *Lg Use:* Used in the home. All ages. All also use Jula. Jula is used for government administrative purposes. *Lg Dev:* Government literacy program in Jula. *Other:* The people are called 'Jalanu'. Tonal. Plains. Savannah, scrub forest. 300 to 400 meters. Peasant agriculturalists. Muslim.

Jula (Dyula, Dyoula, Diula, Dioula, Djula) [dyu] 1,000,000 in Burkina Faso, (1990 SIL). Population total all countries: 1,229,100. Comoé, Kénédougou, Houet, and Leraba provinces. Also spoken in Côte d'Ivoire, Mali. *Class:* Niger-Congo, Mande, Western, Central-Southwestern, Central, Manding-Jogo, Manding-Vai, Manding-Mokole, Manding, Manding-East, Northeastern Manding, Bamana. *Dialects:* Jula is a trade language of western Burkina Faso and northern Côte d'Ivoire. It is a separate language from Bambara and Malinke, and ethnically distinct. *Lg Use:* Trade language. 3,000,000 to 4,000,000 second-language speakers. All ages. *Lg Dev:* Radio programs. Films. Dictionary. Grammar. NT: 1993–1997. *Other:* Different than Jola (Diola) of Senegal. Muslim.

Kaansa (Kaanse, Kãasa, Kan, Kaan, Gan, Gã, Gane) [gna] 6,000 (1990 S. Showalter). Poni Province, Gaoua Subdistrict, Loropéni Department, bounded by Loropéni on the west, Derbi on the east, Djigoué on the south, and Yérifoula on the north. Obiré, 10 km northwest of Loropéni, is the cultural center and residence of the Kaan king. *Class:* Niger-Congo, Atlantic-Congo, Volta-Congo, North, Gur, Central, Southern, Gan-Dogose. *Dialect:* Kaansa, Kpatogo (Kpatogoso, Gbadogo, Padoro, Padogho, Padorho, Bodoro). Lexical similarity 81% between dialects, 71% with Khisa, 68% with Dogosé. *Lg Use:* All ages. Bilingual level estimates for Jula: 0 0%, 1 9%, 2 12%, 3 43%, 4 36%, 5 0%. All speakers can use Jula as second language, 30% to 50% can use Lobi, less than 20% French. *Lg Dev:* Literacy rate in second language: 3%. *Other:* The people are called 'Kamba' (pl.), 'Kaan' (sg.). Four clans: Farma, Suwa, Khama, Thaama. The Kpatogo separated politically and geographically from the Kamba. 5 primary schools in the area. Interfluvial. Gallery forest. 150 to 400 meters. Swidden or peasant agriculturalists. Muslim, traditional religion, Christian.

Kalamsé (Kalemsé, Kalenga, Sàmòmá, Sàmó) [knz] 9,568 in Burkina Faso (1985 census). Sourou Province, Tougan Subdistrict, 540 square km bordering Mali. Also spoken in Mali. *Class:* Niger-Congo, Atlantic-Congo, Volta-Congo, North, Gur, Central, Southern, Grusi, Northern. *Dialects:* Kasoma (East Kalamsé), Logremma (Logma, West Kalamsé). *Lg Use:* All ages. *Lg Dev:* Grammar. *Other:* Speakers call themselves 'Sàmó' (sg.) or 'Sàmóyá' (pl.). The administrative name is 'Kalemse' (pl.) or 'Kalenga' (sg.). Distinct from other languages called 'Samo'. Traditional religion, Muslim, Christian.

Kantosi (Kantonsi, Yare, Yarsi, Dagaari Dioula) [xkt] *Other:* Muslim. See main entry under Ghana.

Karaboro, Eastern (Kar, Ker, Kler) [xrb] 35,000 in Burkina Faso (1995 SIL). Population total all countries: 40,605. East of the main Ferké to Bobo-Dioulosso road and Banfora, southern Burkina Faso. Comoé Province. Also spoken in Côte d'Ivoire. *Class:* Niger-Congo, Atlantic-Congo, Volta-Congo, North, Gur, Senufo, Karaboro. *Dialects:* Kar averages 70% comprehension by Tenyer and Syer speakers, but the reverse is 30%. *Lg Use:* All ages. Some bilingualism in Jula. *Lg Dev:* Dictionary. Grammar. NT: 1994. *Other:* Agriculturalists: maize, millet, peanuts. Traditional religion, Muslim, Christian.

Karaboro, Western (Syer-Tenyer) [kza] 30,200 (1991 Vanderaa). West of the main Ferké to Bobo-Dioulosso road and Banfora, southern Burkina Faso. *Class:* Niger-Congo, Atlantic-Congo, Volta-Congo, North, Gur, Senufo, Karaboro. *Dialects:* Tenyer, Syer. Kar averages 70% comprehension by Tenyer and Syer speakers, but the reverse is 30%. *Lg Use:* High bilingual proficiency in Jula. *Other:* Muslim, traditional religion.

Kasem (Kassem, Kasim, Kasena, Kassena) [xsm] 120,000 in Burkina Faso (1998 SIL). Population total all countries: 250,000. Nahouri Province, Po and Tiébélé towns. Also spoken in Ghana. *Class:* Niger-Congo, Atlantic-Congo, Volta-Congo, North, Gur, Central, Southern, Grusi, Northern. *Dialects:* East Kasem, West Kasem. West and East Kasem are inherently intelligible to each other's speakers. Closest to Nuni and Lyélé. *Lg Use:* All ages. Speakers also use Mòoré or French. *Lg Dev:* Literacy rate in first language: 15% Kasem. Literacy rate in second language: 15% French, 15% Mòoré. Roman script. Grammar. NT: 1988–1997. *Other:* The people are 'Kasena', the language is 'Kasem'. East Kasem is more prestigious. Loanwords from French and Mòoré in Burkina Faso, English and Ashanti in Ghana. SVO; postpositions; genitives, articles, adjectives, numerals after noun heads; relatives after or without noun heads; no more than one affix per word; word order distinguishes subjects, objects, indirect objects, topic and comment; causatives; comparatives; CV, CVC, CVV; tonal. Plains. Savannah, scrub forest. 200 to 300 meters. Peasant agriculturalists. Traditional religion, Christian, Muslim.

Khe (Kheso, Bambadion-Kheso) [kqg] 1,300 in Burkina Faso (1983 SIL). Near the Dogose, Khisa, and Dogoso. Villages are Noumoukiedougou, Tiébata, Moromoro, Boli, Sessagbo, and Lobo. Also spoken in Côte d'Ivoire. *Class:* Niger-Congo, Atlantic-Congo, Volta-Congo, North, Gur, Central, Southern, Dogoso-Khe. *Dialects:* Lexical similarity 56% with Dogoso (Bambadion-Dogoso), 14% with Dogosé, 13% with Khisa. *Other:* Traditional religion.

Khisa (Komono, Khi, Khi Khipa, Kumwenu) [kqm] 3,000 in Burkina Faso (1991 SIL). Comoé Province, around Mangodara Prefecture, in southwest Burkina Faso near the Côte d'Ivoire border. 25 villages. *Lg Use:* Quite bilingual in Jula. The people in Dabokiri village have shifted to Jula. *Other:* 'Komono' is the Jula name. Agriculturalists: millet, maize, yams. Muslim. See main entry under Côte d'Ivoire.

Koromfé (Kurumfe, Kuruma, Fula, Fulse) [kfz] 196,000 in Burkina Faso (2001 Johnstone and Mandryk). Population total all countries: 196,100. Yatenga Province, Titao Subdistrict, Soum and Oudalan provinces, Djibo-Aribinda Subdistrict. A few in Mali at Bandiagara and Yoro, several villages. The Koromba are east, the Fulse west. Also spoken in Mali. *Class:* Niger-Congo, Atlantic-Congo, Volta-Congo, North, Gur, Central, Northern, Kurumfe. *Dialects:* Koromba, Fulse. *Lg Use:* They use Mòoré or Fulfulde as second language. *Lg Dev:* Literacy program in progress. Dictionary. Grammar. *Other:* Plains. Savannah. Agriculturalists. Muslim, Christian.

Kusaal (Kusale, Kusasi, Koussassé) [kus] 17,000 in Burkina Faso (1998 SIL). Nahouiri, Boulgou provinces, some villages south of Zabré, south central. *Dialect:* Toende (Western Kusaal). *Lg Use:* All ages. *Other:* Traditional religion, Muslim, Christian. See main entry under Ghana.

Lobi (Lobiri, Miwa) [lob] 285,500 in Burkina Faso (1991 Vanderaa). Population total all countries: 441,300. Poni Province, southwest border area around Gaoua. A few villages in northwest Ghana along the Volta River; known as Miwa. Also spoken in Côte d'Ivoire, Ghana. *Class:* Niger-Congo, Atlantic-Congo, Volta-Congo, North, Gur,

Lobi. *Dialect:* Gongon Lobi. *Lg Use:* All ages. Speakers also use Jula or French. *Lg Dev:* NT: 1965–1985. *Other:* Traditional religion, Christian, Muslim.

Lyélé (Lele) [lee] 130,000 (2001 Johnstone and Mandryk). Northern and central portion of Sanguié Province: Réo, Kyon, Tenado, Dassa, Didyr, Godyr, and Kordie subdistricts, with principal center in Réo. Thousands of migrants in neighboring countries, especially Côte d'Ivoire. *Class:* Niger-Congo, Atlantic-Congo, Volta-Congo, North, Gur, Central, Southern, Grusi, Northern. *Dialects:* Southern Lyélé (Reo), Central Lyélé, Northern Lyélé, Kandéré. Most Central and Northern Lyélé speakers have nearly 100% comprehension of the Southern Lyélé, the one being developed. Kandéré speakers have 75% comprehension of Southern Lyélé. Southern Lyélé speakers understand all dialects except Kandéré well. Close to Nuni, but inherent intelligibility between them is low. *Lg Use:* About 50% of speakers are age 15 or under. A few speakers can use Jula. Under 20% have been to school, and they can use some French. Mòoré is used to some extent for trading and other contact with the Mossi, mainly by those living near the edges of the Lyélé region. *Lg Dev:* Literacy rate in first language: Growing number in Lyélé. Literacy rate in second language: 18% mainly in French, some in Mòoré. Government coordinated literacy program, 110 classes (1998). In satellite school project. NT: 2001. *Other:* The ethnic group is called 'Lyela' or 'Lela'. 'Gurunsi' is also used, but that applies more properly to the wider grouping. SVO; postpositions; genitives before noun heads; articles, adjectives, numerals, relatives after noun heads; question word initial; 1 prefix, 2 suffix; word order distinguishes subject and object; causatives; comparatives; CV, CVV; tonal. Plains. Savannah. 300 meters. Peasant agriculturalists. Traditional religion, Christian, Muslim.

Marka (Marka Dafing, Meka) [rkm] 200,000 in Burkina Faso (1992 CMA). Population total all countries: 225,000. Kossi and Mouhoun provinces, northwest, around Nouna, Dedougou. Also spoken in Mali. *Class:* Niger-Congo, Mande, Western, Central-Southwestern, Central, Manding-Jogo, Manding-Vai, Manding-Mokole, Manding, Manding-East, Marka-Dafin. *Dialects:* Safané, Nouna, Gassan. Speakers of most dialects have more than 80% inherent intelligibility of the southeastern dialect around Safané, except for those in the northwestern dialect region, who have 70% intelligibility of it. The central dialect around Dembo village is also well understood. Reported to be close to Bambara or a variant of Jula. B. Coulibaly, a Bambara speaker and linguist, says it is harder for him to understand than the Jula on Radio Abidjan. *Lg Use:* All ages. Men who travel speak Jula to outsiders, but women and children do not speak Jula. Comprehension of Jula ranges from 45% in a southeastern village to 85% in the northwest. *Lg Dev:* Literacy rate in second language: 5% haltingly in French, some in Jula. Radio programs. Grammar. Bible portions. *Other:* 'Marka' is used for followers of the traditional religion, 'Dafing' for Muslim speakers. Different from the Marka dialect of Soninke. SOV; postpositions; genitives, articles, adjectives, numerals, relatives after noun heads; question word final; word order distinguishes subject, object, indirect object; CV. Plains. Savannah. Peasant agriculturalists. Muslim, traditional religion, Christian.

Moba (Moa, Moab, Moare, Ben) [mfq] 1,800 in Burkina Faso (1991 L. Vanderaa CRC). Boulgou Province, Ouargaye Subdistrict. *Lg Use:* All ages. See main entry under Togo.

Mòoré (Moose, More, Mole, Mossi, Moshi) [mos] 5,000,000 in Burkina Faso. Population includes 15,700 Yana (1991). Population total all countries: 5,036,700. Central Ouagadougou area and throughout the country.

Also spoken in Benin, Côte d'Ivoire, Ghana, Mali, Togo. *Class:* Niger-Congo, Atlantic-Congo, Volta-Congo, North, Gur, Central, Northern, Oti-Volta, Western, Northwest. *Dialects:* Saremdé, Taolendé, Yaadré, Ouapadoupou, Yaande, Zaore (Joore), Yana (Yanga, Jaan). Yana has over 90% intelligibility of Ouagadougou Mòoré, 75% to 80% of Joore. Joore with Ouagadougou varies from 88% in Tibga to 95% in Diabo. Yanga dialect is in Togo, completely intelligible with Central Mòoré. *Lg Use:* Dominant African language of Burkina Faso. All ages. Some who have traveled outside the area speak Jula as second language. *Lg Dev:* Radio programs. Dictionary. Grammar. Bible: 1983. *Other:* 'Moose' is the name of the people (pl.) or 'Moaaga' (sg.); 'Mòoré' of the language. Other spellings reflect obsolete spellings or pronunciations of nonspeakers. SOV; postpositions; genitives, articles, adjectives, numerals after noun heads; question word final; word order distinguishes subjects, objects; CV, CVC, CVV, CCV; tonal. Savannah. Peasant agriculturalists. Traditional religion, Muslim, Christian.

Natioro (Koo'ra, Natyoro, Natjoro) [nti] 2,400 (1991 Vanderaa). Léraba Province, Sindou Subdistrict, extreme west, almost due west of Banfora, around the town of Sindou; and in Dinaoro, Timba, and Kawara. The presence of Natioro in Mali or Côte d'Ivoire is unconfirmed. *Class:* Niger-Congo, Atlantic-Congo, Volta-Congo, North, Gur, Wara-Natioro. *Dialects:* Kaouara-Timba-Sindou-Koroni, Ginaourou. Similar to Wara but not inherently intelligible. *Lg Use:* All ages. They live among the Jula, Sénoufo. Blacksmiths are quite bilingual in Jula. *Other:* Muslim, traditional religion.

Ninkare (Gurenne, Gurne, Frafra, Nankani) [gur] 25,100 in Burkina Faso (1991). Nahouri Province, subdistrict of Zecco and Ziou. *Dialects:* Gudeni, Nankani, Booni, Frafra, Nankana. *Lg Use:* All ages. *Other:* The people call themselves either 'Ninkarsé' or 'Gursi', preferring 'Ninkarsé' in order to be clearly distinct from the Gurunsi peoples. Traditional religion, Christian, Muslim. See main entry under Ghana (Farefare).

Nuni, Northern (Nouni, Nunuma, Nounouma, Nuna, Nune, Nibulu, Nuruma) [nuv] 45,000 to 55,000 (1995 SIL). 15,000 to 25,000 in Northwestern Nuni, 25,000 to 35,000 in Northeastern Nuni. Sissili and Sanguié provinces, near Boromo. The dividing line between the dialects is the Mouhoun River. *Class:* Niger-Congo, Atlantic-Congo, Volta-Congo, North, Gur, Central, Southern, Grusi, Northern. *Dialect:* Northwestern Nuni. Northeastern Nuni. Speakers of Northern Nuni cannot understand Southern Nuni. Close to Kasem and Lyélé. *Lg Use:* All ages. Children and those older among Northwestern dialect speakers also use Jula; Lyélé by Northeastern dialect speakers who trade at local markets; French by leaders and young people who have been to school. *Lg Dev:* Literacy rate in first language: 1%. Literacy rate in second language: 5% in French. High motivation for literacy. Government coordinated literacy program in Sanguié and Sissili provinces. *Other:* The people are called 'Nuna'. SVO; postpositions; genitives before noun heads; articles, adjectives, numerals, relatives after noun heads; question word initial; 1 prefix, 1 suffix; word order distinguishes subject and object; causatives; comparatives; CV, CVV, CVCV; tonal. Plains. Savannah. 250 meters. Peasant agriculturalists. Traditional religion, Muslim, Christian.

Nuni, Southern (Nouni, Nunuma, Nounouma, Nuna, Nune, Nibulu, Nuruma) [nnw] 167,670 (2000 WCD). Sissili Province, around Léo, in eastern Mouhoun Province, southern Boulkiemdé and Sanguié provinces, western Nahouri and Kossi provinces. Over 100 villages. *Class:* Niger-Congo, Atlantic-Congo, Volta-Congo, North, Gur, Central, Southern, Grusi, Northern. *Dialects:* Micari,

Basinyari (Sundoni), Yatini, Gori, Bwana, Sankura. Close to Kasena and Lyélé. *Lg Use:* All ages. Mòoré is sometimes used as a second language mainly by men; French by leaders and young people. *Lg Dev:* Literacy rate in first language: 10%. Literacy rate in second language: 5% in French. NT: 1999. *Other:* The people are called 'Nuna'. SVO; postpositions; genitives before noun heads; articles, adjectives, numerals, relatives after noun heads; question word initial; 1 prefix, 1 suffix; word order distinguishes subject and object; causatives; comparatives; CV, CVV, CVCV; tonal. Plains. Savannah. 300 meters. Peasant agriculturalists. Traditional religion, Muslim, Christian.

Pana (Sama) [pnq] 5,000 in Burkina Faso (1998). Population total all countries: 7,800. Sourou Province, Kassoum Subdistrict, around the town of Oué in the valley of the Sourou River where it enters from Mali, on the border due north of Dedougou. Also spoken in Mali. *Class:* Niger-Congo, Atlantic-Congo, Volta-Congo, North, Gur, Central, Southern, Grusi, Northern. *Dialects:* Pana North, Pana South. *Lg Use:* All ages. Bambara or Jula are used as second languages. Young people are free to use Jula and Marka-Dafin in the home. *Other:* The people call themselves and their language 'Pana'. Muslim, traditional religion, Christian.

Phuie (Puguli, Buguli, Pougouli, Pwien, Pwe, Pwa, Pwo, Buguri, Phuien, Pwie) [pug] 14,285 (2000 WCD). Tuy, Ioba, Bougouriba, and Poni provinces. One area is between 10 and 50 km north and west of Diébougou, the other is between 25 and 40 km northeast of Dano. Other villages are scattered throughout the Dagaari territory. 450 sq km. *Class:* Niger-Congo, Atlantic-Congo, Volta-Congo, North, Gur, Central, Southern, Grusi, Western. *Dialects:* Phuie is closely related to Winye and Sisaala languages. *Lg Use:* Vigorous. All ages. Positive language attitude. Bilingualism in Northern Dagaari (women more fluent, used in markets), Jula (men more fluent, used for trade, common topics), and French (those who have been to school) varies among villages and speakers. *Lg Dev:* Literacy rate in first language: 0%. Literacy rate in second language: 1% in French. Motivation for literacy is high. *Other:* 'Puguli' is used by outsiders, 'Phu' is their name for one person, 'Phuo' for the people. Tonal. Plains. Scrub forest, savannah. 250 meters. Peasant agriculturalists. Traditional religion, Christian.

Samo, Matya (Tougan, West Central Goe, San, Sane, Northwestern Samo) [stj] 105,000 in Burkina Faso (1995 R. Jones SIM). Sourou Province, concentrations in Mouna and Solenzo areas, and Ouaga, Bobo, Dedougou, and Koudougou cities. Also spoken in Mali. *Class:* Niger-Congo, Mande, Eastern, Eastern, Samo. *Lg Use:* Tougan is a large and politically important dialect. Speakers of other dialects tend to use Jula with speakers from Tougan. Jula is used in some churches. Reciprocal bilingualism with Mòoré along the eastern border of the area. *Lg Dev:* Motivation to read French is high. A literacy center near Tougan teaches Jula. *Other:* The Rimaïbé are Samo who were former Fula slaves, now speak Fulfulde as second language, and live in Kawara, Kassan, Zoumou, Teri, in the Tougan area. Traditional religion, Christian.

Samo, Maya (San, Sa, Northeastern Samo) [sym] 38,000 (1999). North central Burkina Faso, Sourou Province. *Class:* Niger-Congo, Mande, Eastern, Eastern, Samo. *Dialects:* Bounou, Kiembara (Northeastern Goe), Bangassogo, Gomboro. Intelligibility of Matya Samo varies between 28% and 50%, depending on the village and text tested; of Southern Samo it is less than 10%. *Lg Use:* Vigorous. All domains. All ages. Less than 10% are monolingual. In the east, young people learn Mòoré well and it is the trade language; in the west Jula is the more important trade language. French is used in elementary and secondary schools. *Lg Dev:* Literacy rate in first language: below 2%. Literacy rate in second language: below 20% French, below 10% Mòoré. *Other:* Plains. Savannah. 200 to 400 meters. Peasant agriculturalists. Muslim, traditional religion, Christian.

Samo, Southern (San, Sane) [sbd] 85,000 (1998). Nayala Province, concentrations in Nouna and Solenzo areas, and Ouaga, Bobo, Dedougou, and Koudougou cities. Toma dialect is in Toma, Yaba, Gossina, Ye, Kougny, and Gassan departments. *Class:* Niger-Congo, Mande, Eastern, Eastern, Samo. *Dialect:* Toma (Nyaana, Makaa). Some serious difficulty in intelligibility among Samo varieties. Northern Samo speakers have below 10% inherent intelligibility of Southern Samo. *Lg Use:* Used in the home, religion, commerce. All ages. Toma is the larger and more politically important dialect. Toma speakers are more bilingual in French; others in Jula. Older men who have traveled a lot also use Jula; otherwise it is mainly youth who use Jula. Reciprocal bilingualism with Mòoré along the eastern border of the area. *Lg Dev:* Literacy rate in second language: Higher among Toma. Motivation to read French and Toma Samo is high. A literacy center in Toma teaches Toma. Grammar. NT: 1995. *Other:* The Rimaïbé are Samo who were former Fula slaves, now speak Fulfulde as second language, and live in Kawara, Kassan, Zoumou, Teri, in the Tougan area. Traditional religion, Muslim, Christian.

Seeku (Sambla, Sembla, Southern Samo, Samogho) [sos] 17,000. Population includes 5,000 in the northern dialect, 4 villages, 12,000 in the southern, 7 villages. Houet Province, Bobo-Dioulasso Department, west of Bobo-Dioulasso, villages of Karankasso, Bouendé, Torosso, Banzo, Tiara, Bama. *Class:* Niger-Congo, Mande, Western, Northwestern, Samogo. *Dialects:* Northern Seeku (Timiku), Southern Seeku (Gbeneku). Dialects have good inherent intelligibility. Close to Dzùùngo. 3 minor dialects. Prost says lexical correspondence to Samogho Gouan and Samogho Ire is 50%. *Lg Use:* All domains. All ages. Bilingual proficiency in Jula is uneven across the population; higher in adults. French is used mainly by the young people. *Lg Dev:* Literacy rate in second language: below 5%. Motivation for literacy is high. *Other:* The people are called 'Seemogo'. Mixed with Toussian speakers in the south and Bobo Dioula in the north. SOV; tonal. Plains. Savannah. 400 meters. Peasant agriculturalists. Muslim, Christian.

Sénoufo, Nanerigé (Nandergé, Nanergé, Nanergué, Nandereke, Naani) [sen] 50,000 (1985 census). Northern part of Kénédougou Province, from Djigouéra and north. *Class:* Niger-Congo, Atlantic-Congo, Volta-Congo, North, Gur, Senufo, Suppire-Mamara. *Dialects:* Some intelligibility of Tagba. No significant dialects or subgroups. *Lg Use:* All ages. Most men speak Jula for trade and contact with non-Senoufo, though not all speak it in the home or village. Most women speak minimal Jula and seldom use it. French is spoken only by those who have been to school, but is not used in the home or village. *Lg Dev:* Literacy rate in second language: Some in Jula or French. *Other:* 'Nanerige' is the name of the people. Plains. Savannah. Peasant agriculturalists. Traditional religion, Muslim, Christian.

Sénoufo, Senara (Sénoufo, Niangolo) [seq] 50,000 (1995 SIL). Southwest Burkina Faso, Leraba Province. *Class:* Niger-Congo, Atlantic-Congo, Volta-Congo, North, Gur, Senufo, Senari. *Dialects:* Intelligibility testing of Cebaara varies from 51% in Konadougou to 71% in Niankorodougou; of Pomoro of Mali varies from 42% in Konadougou to 74% in Niankorodougou. *Lg Use:* All ages. *Other:* Traditional religion, Muslim.

Sénoufo, Sìcìté (Sìcìté, Sìpìté, Sìcìré, Sucite, Tagba) [sep] 35,000 in Burkina Faso (1999 SIL). Kénédougou Province, Tagouara Plateau, Koloko and Ouelaní prefectures, west of Bobo-Dioulasso, to the Mali border. Also spoken in Côte d'Ivoire, Mali. *Class:* Niger-Congo, Atlantic-Congo, Volta-Congo, North, Gur, Senufo, Suppire-Mamara. *Dialects:* Difficult intelligibility of Nanerige. *Lg Use:* All ages. Bilingual level estimates for Jula: 0 5%, 1 13%, 2 55%, 3 12%, 4 9%, 5 6%. Some bilingualism in Jula, but it is used only with outsiders, as in the market. The educated use French only if an outsider does not know Jula. *Lg Dev:* Literacy rate in first language: A few. Literacy rate in second language: 20% Jula or French. Radio programs. Bible portions: 1995. *Other:* They call themselves 'Sìcijuubíí' (pl.), or 'Sìcijuungé' (sg.), and their region 'Tagba'. 'Tagba' is used by outsiders for them. Little intermarriage with others in the southern area. SOV; postpositions; genitives before nouns, articles, adjectives, numerals after noun head, question word initial; 1 prefix, 2 suffixes; word order distinguishes subjects, objects, indirect objects; CV, CVV; tonal, 3 tones. Plateau, interfluvial. Scrub forest, gallery forest. Swidden agriculturalists. Traditional religion, Muslim, Christian.

Siamou (Siémou, Siemu, Syémou, Sému, Seme) [sif] 20,000 in Burkina Faso (1999). Population total all countries: 40,000. Kénédougou Province, 80 km west of Bobo-Dioulasso, centering in Orodara, plus several small villages: Tin, Diossogou, Diéri, Kotoudéni, Diéridéni, Didéri, Lidara, and Bandougou. Also spoken in Côte d'Ivoire, Mali. *Class:* Niger-Congo, Atlantic-Congo, Volta-Congo, Kru, Seme. *Dialect:* Bandougou. Minor dialect differences between villages and within Orodara. The Bandougou dialect is considered different, but intelligibility among dialects seems adequate. No closely related languages. *Lg Use:* Vigorous. They are reserved toward people who cannot speak Siamou. Bilingual level estimates for Jula: 0 1%, 1 4%, 2 10%, 3 30%, 4 50%, 5 5%. Jula is widely used as a second language. A few also speak French. *Lg Dev:* Literacy rate in second language: A few in Jula, some in French. *Other:* Previously classified as Mande. Their tradition says they came from the south. SOV; postpositions; genitives, articles, personal pronouns before noun heads; adjectives, numerals after noun heads; question word final for yes-no questions; content question words appear in normal position: e.g., S-O-adverbial-O of prep; word order distinguishes subjects and objects; CV, CVC, CCV; tonal. Plains, interfluvial. Savannah, scrub forest. Swidden agriculturalists. Traditional religion, Muslim, Christian.

Sininkere (Silinkere, Silanke) [skq] 6,000 (1999 SIL). Sanmatenga Province, near Pensa. *Class:* Niger-Congo, Mande, Western, Central-Southwestern, Central, Manding-Jogo, Manding-Vai, Manding-Mokole, Manding. *Lg Use:* All ages. Ability in Fulfulde is good community wide. Some prefer to speak Fulfulde. A lot of intermarriage with the Fulfulde. Proficiency in Mòoré is less. *Other:* Muslim.

Sissala (Sisaali) [sld] 13,000 (1991 SIL). Sissili Province, between Léo and Hamale. 30 villages. *Class:* Niger-Congo, Atlantic-Congo, Volta-Congo, North, Gur, Central, Southern, Grusi, Western. *Dialects:* All one dialect in Burkina Faso. A separate language from the Sisaala languages in Ghana, although closest to Busilli (Western Sisaala). *Lg Use:* All ages. *Lg Dev:* NT: 1999. *Other:* Traditional religion, Muslim, Christian.

Songhay (Songay Senni, Songoy, Songai, Songhai, Songay, Songoi, Sonrai, Sonrhai, Central Songai) [hmb] 125,000 in Burkina Faso (1999). Population total all countries: 140,000. Hombori area, halfway between Gao and Mopti. Also spoken in Mali. *Class:* Nilo-Saharan, Songhai, Southern. *Dialect:* Marensé (Maransé, Koroboré). Closely related languages: Koyraboro Senni, Kaado, Zarma, Dendi, Tadaksahak. *Lg Use:* All ages.

Lg Dev: Dictionary. Grammar. *Other:* SOV; tonal. Marensé: indigo dyeing. Muslim.

Tamasheq, Kidal (Timbuktu, Tomacheck, Tamashekin, Tuareg) [taq] 31,169 in Burkina Faso (2000 WCD). Oudalan Province. *Dialects:* Timbuktu (Tombouctou, Tanaslamt), Tadghaq (Kidal). *Other:* People are called 'Tuareg' ('Targi', singular). Muslim. See main entry under Mali (Tamasheq).

Téén (Ténhé, Tegesie, Lorhon, Loghon, Loron, Nabe) [lor] 2,000 in Burkina Faso (1999). Poni Province, Kampti Subdistrict, two pockets just west of Kampti. *Lg Use:* Speakers also use Lobi, Jula, Loma, or French. *Other:* The people are called 'Ténsé' (sg.), 'Ténbó' (pl.). Savannah. Traditional religion, Christian. See main entry under Côte d'Ivoire.

Tiéfo (Tyefo, Tyeforo, Kiefo) [tiq] 1,000 (1995 SIL). Ethnic population: 12,000 to 15,000 (1995 SIL). Comoé Province, east of Toussiana, Dramandougou Tiéfo, one village. Other ethnic Tiéfo in about 20 villages, extending into Houet Province, speak Jula as first language. *Class:* Niger-Congo, Atlantic-Congo, Volta-Congo, North, Gur, Tiefo. *Dialects:* Noumoudara-Koumoudara, Dramandougou-Nyarafo. *Lg Use:* Noumoudara-Koumoudara dialect is extinct. All domains. All ages. Five of nine respondents are not upset when Tiéfo young people use Jula in the home. Jula is used with those who do not speak Tiéfo. *Lg Dev:* Literacy rate in second language: 1% in French. Nine of ten respondents state they would prefer to learn to read and write Tiéfo. *Other:* They are endogamous within the village. Tonal. Plains. Savannah, scrub forest. 300 to 400 meters. Peasant agriculturalists. Traditional religion.

Toussian, Northern (Tusia, Tusian) [tsp] 19,500 (1995 SIL). Population includes 1,000 in Wenteene dialect, 18,500 in the other dialects. Comoé Province, north, east, and south of Oradara. *Class:* Niger-Congo, Atlantic-Congo, Volta-Congo, North, Gur, Tusia. *Dialects:* Ter. Tru, Kebeenton, Wenteene. Dialects in the northern region are inherently intelligible to their speakers, but they have 45% inherent intelligibility of Southern Toussian. *Lg Use:* Used in the home. All ages. Jula is used as second language with high competence among all subgroups to outsiders, for government, and trade. French is used some for government contacts. *Lg Dev:* Literacy rate in second language: 5% in French, 3% in Jula. *Other:* SOV; postpositions; genitives, articles, adjectives, numerals, relatives after noun heads; word order distinguishes subjects, objects, indirect objects, passives; V, CV, CVC, CCV; tonal. Plains. Savannah. 400 to 700 meters. Peasant agriculturalists. Traditional religion, Muslim, Christian.

Toussian, Southern (Win, Tusia, Tusian) [wib] 19,500 in Burkina Faso (1995 SIL). Comoé and Houet provinces, about halfway between Banfora and Bobo-Dioulasso, around center of Toussiana. Also spoken in Côte d'Ivoire. *Class:* Niger-Congo, Atlantic-Congo, Volta-Congo, North, Gur, Tusia. *Dialects:* 40% inherent intelligibility of Northern Toussian. Nianha dialect is central. Each village has a separate dialect. *Lg Use:* All domains. All ages. All are fairly fluent in Jula (all ages and sexes, adults more than young people, men more than women), and some have low proficiency in French. *Lg Dev:* Literacy rate in second language: 5% in French, 3% in Jula. Bible portions: 2001. *Other:* SOV; postpositions; genitives before noun heads; articles, adjectives, numerals, relatives after noun heads; word order distinguishes subjects, objects, indirect objects, passives; causatives; comparatives; V, CV, CVC, CCV; tonal. Plains. Savannah. 400 to 500 meters. Peasant agriculturalists. Traditional religion, Muslim, Christian.

Turka (Tourka, Turuka, Curama, Tyurama) [tuz] 37,000 in Burkina Faso (1998 SIL). Comoé Province, north and west of Banfora. The principal villages are the dialects named. Also spoken in Côte d'Ivoire. *Class:* Niger-Congo, Atlantic-Congo, Volta-Congo, North, Gur, Central, Southern, Kirma-Tyurama. *Dialects:* Douna, Beregadougou-Toumousseni. Cerma is the closest language, but it is not inherently intelligible with Turka. *Lg Use:* All ages. Speakers also use Jula. *Other:* Muslim, traditional religion, Christian.

Viemo (Vigué, Vige, Vigye) [vig] 8,000 (1995 SIL). Houet Province, Karankasso Vigué Department, 40 km southeast of Bobo Dioulasso. *Class:* Niger-Congo, Atlantic-Congo, Volta-Congo, North, Gur, Viemo. *Lg Use:* Vigorous. Used in the homes and village. All ages. All use Jula widely. Few have learned French. *Lg Dev:* Literacy rate in second language: 5% in Jula, 1% in French. *Other:* Tonal. Plains. Savannah, scrub forest. 200 to 400 meters. Peasant agriculturalists. Traditional religion, Muslim.

Wara (Ouara, Ouala, Samoe) [wbf] 4,500 (1993 Johnstone). Comoé Province, west of Banfora, near the town of Sindou. The main village is Néguéni. *Class:* Niger-Congo, Atlantic-Congo, Volta-Congo, North, Gur, Wara-Natioro. *Dialects:* Negueni-Klani, Ouatourou-Niasogoni, Soulani, Faniagara. Negueni has over 95% intelligibility of Niansogoni, but the reverse is below 80%. No intelligibility of Natioro. *Lg Use:* All ages. Positive language attitude. They speak Jula to outsiders. Everyone but the youngest children speaks Jula, but proficiency is limited. *Other:* Traditional religion, Muslim, Christian.

Winyé (Kõ, Kols, Kolsi) [kst] 20,000 (1999 SIL). Bali Province, Boromo Subdistrict, around Boromo, about halfway between Bobo-Dioulosso and Ouagadougou on main route. 17 to 18 villages. *Class:* Niger-Congo, Atlantic-Congo, Volta-Congo, North, Gur, Central, Southern, Grusi, Western. *Dialects:* Close to Sisaala languages. *Lg Use:* Almost entirely monolingual. *Other:* Traditional religion, Christian, Muslim.

Zarma (Dyerma, Dyarma, Dyabarma, Zabarma, Adzerma, Djerma, Zarbarma) [dje] 600 in Burkina Faso (1987 SIL). *Other:* Muslim. See main entry under Niger.

Burundi

Republic of Burundi. Republika y'Uburundi. Formerly part of Ruanda-Urundi. 6,231,221. National or official languages: Rundi, French. Literacy rate: 14% to 30%. Also includes Rwanda (900). Information mainly from J. Bendor-Samuel 1989. Blind population: 11,000 (1982 WCE). The number of languages listed for Burundi is 3. Of those, all are living languages.

French [fra] 2,200 in Burundi (2004). *Lg Use:* Official language. See main entry under France.

Rundi (Kirundi, Urundi) [run] 4,600,000 in Burundi (1986). Population total all countries: 4,850,903. Also spoken in Rwanda, Tanzania, Uganda. *Class:* Niger-Congo, Atlantic-Congo, Volta-Congo, Benue-Congo, Bantoid, Southern, Narrow Bantu, Central, J, Rwanda-Rundi (J.60). *Dialects:* Dialects of the Hutu and Tutsi are similar. Twa is distinct but all are inherently intelligible, and also intelligible with Kinyarwanda (Rwanda). *Lg Use:* Official language. Hima is an ethnic group speaking Rundi or Rwanda. Some speakers use Swahili as a lingua franca. *Lg Dev:* Literacy rate in first language: 55%. Bible: 1967. *Other:* Ethnic groups: Hutu 80% to 85%, Tutsi 14% to 15%, Twa (Gesera, pygmy) 1% (30,000; 1972 Barrett). Christian, traditional religion, Muslim; Twa: traditional religion, Christian.

Swahili [swh] 6,356 in Burundi (2000 WCD). Widely spoken in the capital. Spoken as first language in Buyenzi, Quartier asiatique, Muslim neighborhoods, and Congolese neighborhoods (probably Congo Swahili). Spoken by Muslims in other cities like Gitega. *Lg Use:* Used in religious services. *Other:* Muslim. See main entry under Tanzania.

Cameroon

Republic of Cameroon. Formerly French Cameroun and British Cameroons. 16,063,678. National or official languages: English, French. Literacy rate: 63.4%, including 75% males, 52.1% females (1995 Encyclopedia Britannica). Also includes Efai (893). Information mainly from J. Bendor-Samuel 1989; R. Breton 1991; SIL 1973–2003. Blind population: 15,630 (1982 WCE). The number of languages listed for Cameroon is 286. Of those, 279 are living languages, 3 are second language without mother-tongue speakers, and 4 are extinct. See maps beginning on page 682.

Abar (Mijong, Missong) [mij] 2,000 (2001 SIL). North West Province, Menchum Division, Wum Subdivision, centered around village of Missong, including villages of Munken and Abar. *Class:* Niger-Congo, Atlantic-Congo, Volta-Congo, Benue-Congo, Bantoid, Southern, Beboid, Western. *Other:* 'Dzaiven Boka' may be an alternate name.

Afade (Affade, Afadeh, Mandage) [aal] 5,000 in Cameroon (2004 SIL). Far North Province, Logone-and-Chari Division, southern part of Makari Subdivision, centered around Afade. *Other:* The name 'Mandage', etc., is applied to the northern Kotoko languages. See main entry under Nigeria.

Aghem (Wum, Yum) [agq] 26,727 (2000 WCD). North West Province, Menchum Division, Wum Central Subdivision, in and around Wum. *Class:* Niger-Congo, Atlantic-Congo, Volta-Congo, Benue-Congo, Bantoid, Southern, Wide Grassfields, Narrow Grassfields, Ring, West. *Dialects:* Close to Isu and Weh. Regional differences in speech are minimal. *Lg Use:* English is used as second language. Some use Cameroon Pidgin. Some multilingualism with Weh and Isu. *Lg Dev:* Literacy rate in second language: 15% to 25%. *Other:* Aghem Cultural and Development Association active in language development. Traditional religion, Christian.

Akoose (Bakossi, Bekoose, Akosi, Koose, Kosi, Nkosi, Nkoosi) [bss] 100,000 (2001 SIL). South West Province, Kupe-Muanenguba Division, Bangem and Tombel subdivisions; Littoral Province, Moungo Division, Manjo Subdivision. *Class:* Niger-Congo, Atlantic-Congo, Volta-Congo, Benue-Congo, Bantoid, Southern, Narrow Bantu, Northwest, A, Lundu-Balong (A.10), Ngoe. *Dialects:* Northern Bakossi, Western Bakossi, Southern Bakossi, Mwambong, Ninong, Elung (Elong, Along, Nlong), Mwamenam (Mouamenam). *Lg Dev:* Literacy rate in second language: 25%. Dictionary. Bible portions: 1998.

Akum (Anyar, Okum) [aku] 1,400 in Cameroon (2002 SIL). Near the Nigerian border, North West Province, Menchum Division, Furu-Awa Subdivision, Akum village. 3 villages in Nigeria (Manga, Ekban, Konkom). Also spoken in Nigeria. *Class:* Niger-Congo, Atlantic-Congo, Volta-Congo, Benue-Congo, Jukunoid, Yukuben-Kuteb. *Lg Use:* Speakers have low proficiency in Jukun. Cameroon Pidgin is also spoken in the area. *Other:* The people are called 'Anyar'. Mountain slope.

Ambele [ael] 2,600 (2000 SIL). North West Province, Momo Division, western Widikum-Menka Subdivision, about 11 villages. *Class:* Niger-Congo, Atlantic-Congo, Volta-Congo, Benue-Congo, Bantoid, Southern, Wide Grassfields, Western Momo. *Dialects:* May be related to Busam or Atong.

Arabic, Shuwa (Arabe Choa, Shua Arabic, Choa, Chowa, Shua, Chadian Spoken Arabic) [shu] 63,600 in Cameroon (1982 SIL). Far North Province, Mayo-Sava,

Diamare, Mayo-Danay and Logone and Chari divisions. Mostly between Lake Chad and Kousseri, with some pockets of speakers south of Kousseri. *Lg Use:* Trade language. *Other:* Muslim. See main entry under Chad (Arabic, Chadian Spoken).

Atong (Etoh) [ato] 4,200 (2000 SIL). Northwest Province, Momo Division, extreme northwestern part of Widikum-Menka Subdivision, 5 villages. *Class:* Niger-Congo, Atlantic-Congo, Volta-Congo, Benue-Congo, Bantoid, Southern, Wide Grassfields, Western Momo. *Dialects:* Related to Menka and Manta.

Awing (Awi, Bambuluwe, Mbwe'wi) [azo] 19,000 (2001 SIL). North West Province, Mezam Division, Awing-Bambaluwe village. *Class:* Niger-Congo, Atlantic-Congo, Volta-Congo, Benue-Congo, Bantoid, Southern, Wide Grassfields, Narrow Grassfields, Mbam-Nkam, Ngemba. *Dialects:* Related to Bafut, Bambili-Bambui, Kpati, Mendankwe-Nkwen, Ngemba, and Pinyin. Lexical similarity 74% with Bamukumbit.

Baba (Papia, Bapa, Bapakum) [bbw] 12,750 (1982 SIL). North West Province, Mezam Division, east of Ndop on Ndop Plain. *Class:* Niger-Congo, Atlantic-Congo, Volta-Congo, Benue-Congo, Bantoid, Southern, Wide Grassfields, Narrow Grassfields, Mbam-Nkam, Nun. *Dialects:* Related to Mungaka. *Other:* Speakers refer to their language as 'Papia'.

Babanki (Kidzem, Kidzom, Finge, Kejeng, Kedjom, Kejom) [bbk] 22,500 (2000 SIL). North West Province, Mezam Division, Tuba Subdivision, villages of Kejom-Ketingo and Kejom-Keku. *Class:* Niger-Congo, Atlantic-Congo, Volta-Congo, Benue-Congo, Bantoid, Southern, Wide Grassfields, Narrow Grassfields, Ring, Center. *Lg Use:* Pidgin English is used at the markets and health clinics. Schooling is in English.

Bafanji (Bafanyi, Bafangi, Chuufi, Nchufie) [bfj] 8,500 (1982 SIL). North West Province, Ngo-Ketunjia Division, south of Ndop on Ndop Plain. *Class:* Niger-Congo, Atlantic-Congo, Volta-Congo, Benue-Congo, Bantoid, Southern, Wide Grassfields, Narrow Grassfields, Mbam-Nkam, Nun. *Dialects:* Close to Bamali, Bamenyam, Bambalang. *Other:* Speakers refer to the language as 'Chuufi'.

Bafaw-Balong (Ngoe) [bwt] 8,400 (1982 SIL). South West Province, Meme Division, north of Kumba along Kumba-Mamfe Road and southeast of Ekondo-Titi; Littoral Province, Moungo Division. *Class:* Niger-Congo, Atlantic-Congo, Volta-Congo, Benue-Congo, Bantoid, Southern, Narrow Bantu, Northwest, A, Lundu-Balong (A.10), Ngoe. *Dialects:* Bafaw (Bafo, Bafowu, Afo, Nho, Lefo'), Balong (Balon, Balung, Nlong, Valongi, Bayi, Bai). Some linguists consider this to be 2 languages. *Lg Use:* Speakers also use Duala. *Other:* Language community is heterogeneous.

Bafia (Rikpa, Ripey, Rikpa', Bekpak) [ksf] 60,000 (1991 UBS). Center Province, Mbam Division, Deuk Subdivision. *Class:* Niger-Congo, Atlantic-Congo, Volta-Congo, Benue-Congo, Bantoid, Southern, Narrow Bantu, Northwest, A, Bafia (A.50). *Dialects:* Kpa, Bape. *Lg Dev:* NT: 1996. *Other:* Speakers refer to their language as 'Rikpa' and to themselves as 'Bekpak'.

Bafut (Bufe, Fu, Fut, Befe) [bfd] 50,000 (1987 Mfonyam). North West Province, Mezam Division, Tuba Subdivision, in Bafut. *Class:* Niger-Congo, Atlantic-Congo, Volta-Congo, Benue-Congo, Bantoid, Southern, Wide Grassfields, Narrow Grassfields, Mbam-Nkam, Ngemba. *Dialect:* Bafut, Bufe (Afughe). *Lg Dev:* Literacy rate in first language: 30%. Literacy programs in about 10 schools and 30 churches. NT: 1999. *Other:* Traditional religion, Christian.

Baka (Pygmy-E, Pygmee, Bebayaka, Bebayaga, Bibaya, Pygmees de L'est, Babinga) [bkc] 25,000 in Cameroon

(1980 Phillips). Population total all countries: 28,200. Scattered in the southeast of East Province: Boumba and Ngoko, Kadey, and Upper Nyong divisions; South Province, Dja and Lobo Division. Also spoken in Gabon. *Class:* Niger-Congo, Atlantic-Congo, Volta-Congo, North, Adamawa-Ubangi, Ubangi, Sere-Ngbaka-Mba, Ngbaka-Mba, Ngbaka, Western, Baka-Gundi. *Lg Dev:* Dictionary. *Other:* Nomadic but being encouraged by the government to settle along the roadways. Different from Baka of Democratic Republic of the Congo and Sudan. Tropical forest.

Bakaka (Central Mbo) [bqz] 30,000 (1998 SIL). Littoral Province, Moungo Division, Nlonako, Manjo, western Loum, and southern Nkongsamba subdivisions. *Class:* Niger-Congo, Atlantic-Congo, Volta-Congo, Benue-Congo, Bantoid, Southern, Narrow Bantu, Northwest, A, Lundu-Balong (A.10), Ngoe. *Dialects:* Babong (Ihobe Mbog, Ihobe Mboong), Baneka (Mwaneka), Bakaka (Ehob Mkaa, Kaa, Kaka), Manehas (Mwahed, Mwahet, Mvae), Balondo (Ehobe Belon), Bafun (Mbwase Nghuy, Miamilo, Pendia). Related to Akoose, Bassossi, Mbo. *Lg Use:* Young people speak some French; older generations speak some Duala. *Lg Dev:* Literacy rate in first language: below 1%. Literacy rate in second language: 25%. Dictionary.

Bakoko (Basoo) [bkh] 50,000 (1982 SIL). Littoral Province, scattered communities: Wouri Division, south of Douala; Moungo Division, south of Dibombari; Nkam Division, around Nkondjok; and Sanaga-Maritime Division, southwest of Edea; South Province, northwest area of Ocean Division. *Class:* Niger-Congo, Atlantic-Congo, Volta-Congo, Benue-Congo, Bantoid, Southern, Narrow Bantu, Northwest, A, Basaa (A.40). *Dialects:* Adie (Elog Mpoo, Basoo Ba Die, Basoo D'edea), Bisoo (Basso, Basoo Ba Likol, Adiangok), Mbang (Dimbam-bang), Yabyang (Yabyang-Yapeke), Yakalak (Yakalag), Yapoma, Yassuku (Yasoukou, Yasug, Yasuku). *Other:* Coastal. Swamp. Agriculturalists: cocoyams, cassava, maize, plantains, rubber, oil palms, coffee, tea, cocoa, bananas; animal husbandry: goats, sheep.

Bakole (Bakolle, Kole, Bamusso) [kme] 300 (1982 SIL). South West Province, Ndian Division, south of the Meme estuary, around Bamusso. *Class:* Niger-Congo, Atlantic-Congo, Volta-Congo, Benue-Congo, Bantoid, Southern, Narrow Bantu, Northwest, A, Duala (A.20). *Dialects:* May be intelligible with or bilingual in Mokpwe.

Baldemu (Mbazla, Baldamu, Baldare) [bdn] 3 to 6 (2003 SIL). Far North Province, Diamare Division, Bogo, Balda, and Guingley are east of Maroua, Lara is south of Maroua. *Class:* Afro-Asiatic, Chadic, Biu-Mandara, A, A.5. *Other:* Shift has been to Fulfude. Nearly extinct.

Balo [bqo] 2,231 (2000 WCD). South West Province, Manyu Division, Akwaya Subdivision. *Class:* Niger-Congo, Atlantic-Congo, Volta-Congo, Benue-Congo, Bantoid, Southern, Tivoid. *Dialects:* Lexical similarity 60% with Osatu, 40% with Ipulo and Caka, 35% with Esimbi and Mesaka. *Lg Use:* Speakers also use Cameroon Pidgin. *Lg Dev:* Literacy is in English, as it is with all languages in NW and SW provinces. *Other:* Mountain slope. Traditional religion.

Bamali (Ngoobechop, Chopechop) [bbq] 5,300 (1982 SIL). North West Province, Ngo-Ketunjia Division, south of Ndop. *Class:* Niger-Congo, Atlantic-Congo, Volta-Congo, Benue-Congo, Bantoid, Southern, Wide Grassfields, Narrow Grassfields, Mbam-Nkam, Nun. *Dialects:* Related to Bafanji, Bamenyam, Bambalang, Bangolan. *Other:* Speakers refer to the language as 'Ngoobechop'.

Bambalang (Bambolang, Tshirambo, Mboyakum) [bmo] 14,500 (1982 SIL). North West Province, Ngo-Ketunjia Division, southeast of Ndop. *Class:* Niger-Congo, Atlantic-Congo, Volta-Congo, Benue-Congo, Bantoid,

Southern, Wide Grassfields, Narrow Grassfields, Mbam-Nkam, Nun. *Dialects:* Related to Bafanji, Bamenyam, Bamun, Bamali, Bangolan. *Other:* Speakers refer to the language as 'Mboyakum'.

Bambili-Bambui (Bambili) [baw] 10,000 (1983 Atlas Linguistique du Cameroun). North West Province, Mezam Division, Tuba Subdivision, along Ring Road, east of Bamenda, Bambili, and Bambui villages. *Class:* Niger-Congo, Atlantic-Congo, Volta-Congo, Benue-Congo, Bantoid, Southern, Wide Grassfields, Narrow Grassfields, Mbam-Nkam, Ngemba. *Dialects:* Bambili (Mbili, Mbele, Mbogoe), Bambui (Mbui). Inherent intelligibility is low between them and Nkwen and Mendankwe-Nkwen. *Lg Dev:* Literacy rate in second language: 15% to 25%. Grammar. *Other:* They associate more with Bafut than with Nkwen and Mendankwe-Nkwen.

Bamenyam (Mamenyan, Pamenyan, Bamenyan, Mengambo) [bce] 4,000 (1994 SIL). West Province, Bamboutos Division, northwestern Galim Subdivision, around Bamenyam; North West Province, southeastern Mezam Division. *Class:* Niger-Congo, Atlantic-Congo, Volta-Congo, Benue-Congo, Bantoid, Southern, Wide Grassfields, Narrow Grassfields, Mbam-Nkam, Nun. *Dialects:* Bati may be a dialect of Bamenyam. Close to Bamali, Bafanji, Bambalang. *Lg Use:* Some bilingualism in French and Cameroon Pidgin. *Other:* Stronger commercial links with Mbouda than with Ndop. Traditional religion, Christian.

Bamukumbit (Bamunkum, Bamoukoumbit, Bamenkoumbit, Bamenkombit, Mangkong) [bqt] 7,300 (1987 census). North West Province, Ngo-Ketunjia Division, Balikumbat Subdivision, southwest of Ndop on Ndop Plain, Bamukumbit village. *Class:* Niger-Congo, Atlantic-Congo, Volta-Congo, Benue-Congo, Bantoid, Southern, Wide Grassfields, Narrow Grassfields, Mbam-Nkam, Ngemba. *Dialects:* Lexical similarity 74% with Awing. *Lg Use:* Adults can use Bafanji and Bamali. The few educated beyond primary level can use English as a second language. Cameroon Pidgin is generally spoken and understood. *Other:* Traditional religion, Christian.

Bamun (Bamoun, Bamoum, Bamum, Shupamem) [bax] 215,000 (1982 SIL). West Province, most of Noun Division around Foumban, plus the extreme north of Mifi Division and the extreme southeast of Bamboutos Division. *Class:* Niger-Congo, Atlantic-Congo, Volta-Congo, Benue-Congo, Bantoid, Southern, Wide Grassfields, Narrow Grassfields, Mbam-Nkam, Nun. *Dialects:* Related to Bafanji, Bamali, Bambalang, Bangolan. *Lg Use:* Trade language. *Lg Dev:* Bible: 1988. *Other:* Has its own script, though not used for current orthography.

Bamunka (Ndop-Bamunka, Bamunkun, Niemeng, Mbika, Muka) [bvm] 15,200 (1982 SIL). North West Province, Mezam Division, Ndop Subdivision, around village of Bamunka. *Class:* Niger-Congo, Atlantic-Congo, Volta-Congo, Benue-Congo, Bantoid, Southern, Wide Grassfields, Narrow Grassfields, Ring, North. *Other:* Speakers refer to the language as 'Niemeng'.

Bana (Baza, Koma, Ka-Bana, Parole des Bana, Mizeran) [bcw] 13,000 (1987 SIL). Population includes 8,000 Gamboura and 5,000 Guili. On Nigerian border, Far North Province, Mayo-Tsanaga Division, Bourrah Subdivision, north and northeast of Bourrah. *Class:* Afro-Asiatic, Chadic, Biu-Mandara, A, A.3. *Dialect:* Gamboura, Gili (Guili). Close to Psikye and Hya in Cameroon and Kamwe in Nigeria. *Lg Dev:* Bible portions: 1985.

Bangandu (Bagando, Bangando, Bangantu, Southern Bangantu) [bgf] 2,700 in Cameroon (1977 Voegelin and Voegelin). East Province, Boumba and Ngoko Division, Moloundou Subdivision. Also spoken in Congo. *Class:* Niger-Congo, Atlantic-Congo, Volta-Congo, North,

Adamawa-Ubangi, Ubangi, Gbaya-Manza-Ngbaka, Southwest. *Dialects:* May be related to Ngombe in Central African Republic.

Bangolan [bgj] 13,534 (2000 WCD). North West Province, Ngo-Ketunjia Division, east of Ndop and south of Jakiri. *Class:* Niger-Congo, Atlantic-Congo, Volta-Congo, Benue-Congo, Bantoid, Southern, Wide Grassfields, Narrow Grassfields, Mbam-Nkam, Nun. *Dialects:* The most distinct linguistically and culturally of the Ndop languages. Most closely related to Bambalang. *Lg Use:* Speakers also use Cameroon Pidgin. *Other:* Traditional religion, Muslim, Christian.

Bankon (Bo, Abaw, Abo, Bon) [abb] 12,000 (2001 SIL). Littoral Province, Moungo Division, north of Douala and west of the Wouri River, and Dibombari. *Class:* Niger-Congo, Atlantic-Congo, Volta-Congo, Benue-Congo, Bantoid, Southern, Narrow Bantu, Northwest, A, Basaa (A.40). *Dialects:* Lexical similarity 86% with Barombi.

Barombi (Lombi, Lambi, Rombi, Rambi, Lombe, Balombi, Barumbi) [bbi] 3,000 (2001 SIL). South West Province, Meme Division, north of Mount Cameroon around Lake Barombi-Koto and west of Kumba around Lake Barombi-Mbo; and Ndian Division, northeast of Ekondo-Titi. *Class:* Niger-Congo, Atlantic-Congo, Volta-Congo, Benue-Congo, Bantoid, Southern, Narrow Bantu, Northwest, A, Basaa (A.40). *Dialects:* Lexical similarity 86% with Bankon.

Basaa (Bassa, Basa, Bisaa, Northern Mbene, Mvele, Mbele, Mee, Tupen, Bikyek, Bicek) [bas] 230,000 (1982 SIL). Center Province, spread all over Nyong-and-Kelle Division; Littoral Province, Nkam and Sanaga-Maritime divisions. *Class:* Niger-Congo, Atlantic-Congo, Volta-Congo, Benue-Congo, Bantoid, Southern, Narrow Bantu, Northwest, A, Basaa (A.40). *Dialects:* Bakem, Bon, Bibeng, Diboum, Log, Mpo, Mbang, Ndokama, Basso, Ndokbele, Ndokpenda, Nyamtam. *Lg Dev:* Literacy rate in second language: 25% to 50%. Dictionary. Bible: 1969.

Bassossi (Basosi, Basossi, Sosi, Nswase, Nswose, Nsose, Swose, Asobse, Ngen) [bsi] 5,000 (2004 SIL). South West Province, Kupe-Muanenguba Division, central part of Nguti Subdivision, in Nguti town and east and south of it. *Class:* Niger-Congo, Atlantic-Congo, Volta-Congo, Benue-Congo, Bantoid, Southern, Narrow Bantu, Northwest, A, Lundu-Balong (A.10), Ngoe. *Dialect:* Mienge (Lower Mbo). Related to Mbo, Akoose, Bakaka.

Bata (Gbwata, Batta, Gwate, Dii) [bta] 2,500 in Cameroon. North Province, Benoue Division, along the Nigerian border (30 km northeast of Garoua), along the Benoue River, west of Garoua and along a small section of the Faro River. *Dialect:* Ndeewe (Bata-Ndeewe). See main entry under Nigeria.

Batanga (Banoho, Bano'o, Noho, Noku, Banoo) [bnm] 6,000 in Cameroon (1982 SIL). South Province, Ocean Division, scattered along the coast around Kribi. *Dialects:* Bano'o (Banoo, Banaka, Banoko), Bapuku (Puku, Poko, Naka, Bapuu), Batanga. *Other:* Different from Batanga of South West Province (Oroko). See main entry under Equatorial Guinea.

Bati (Bati Ba Ngong, Bati de Brousse) [btc] 800 (1975 census). Littoral Province, Sanaga-Maritime Division, Ndom Subdivision, 4 villages in the Bati Canton. *Class:* Niger-Congo, Atlantic-Congo, Volta-Congo, Benue-Congo, Bantoid, Southern, Mbam, West (A.40). *Lg Use:* All ages. Most older Bati adults have little problem understanding Basaa, because their schooling used to be in that, and Basaa is used in church. Children up to 14 years old are exposed to French for primary education. Markets are in Bakoko- and Yambassa-speaking areas, so those languages are used.

Beba (Beba', Mubadji, Batadji, Babadji, Bebadji, Bazhi, Baba'zhi, Biba, Shishong, Bombe) [bfp] 3,000 (2002 SIL).

South West Province, Manyu Division, Akwaya Subdivision; North West Province, Mezam Division, Benakuma Subdivision. *Class:* Niger-Congo, Atlantic-Congo, Volta-Congo, Benue-Congo, Bantoid, Southern, Wide Grassfields, Narrow Grassfields, Mbam-Nkam, Ngemba. *Other:* Traditional religion, Christian.

Bebe (Naami, Yi Be Wu) [bzv] 2,500 (2001 SIL). North West Province, Donga-Mantung Division, west part of Ako Subdivision, west of Nkambe and north of Ring Road, Bebe-Jama and Bebe-Jatto villages. *Class:* Niger-Congo, Atlantic-Congo, Volta-Congo, Benue-Congo, Bantoid, Southern, Beboid, Eastern. *Dialects:* Member of the Eastern Beboid cluster. Lexical similarity 85% with Kemezung. *Lg Use:* All domains. Cameroon Pidgin, Kemezung, or Nsari are also used. Schooling is in English. *Other:* Speakers call the language Naami. Agriculturalists.

Bebele (Bamvele) [beb] 24,000 (1971 Welmers). Center Province, Upper Sanaga Division, Minta Subdivision; East Province, Lom-and Djerem Division, Diang Subdivision. *Class:* Niger-Congo, Atlantic-Congo, Volta-Congo, Benue-Congo, Bantoid, Southern, Narrow Bantu, Northwest, A, Yaunde-Fang (A.70). *Dialects:* Eki, Manyok. Related to Beti, Bulu, Eton, Ewondo, Fang, Mengisa. *Lg Use:* Speakers also use Beti.

Bebil (Bobilis, Gbigbil) [bxp] 6,000 (1991 SIL). East Province, Lom-and-Djerem Division, Belabo Subdivision, around Belabo. *Class:* Niger-Congo, Atlantic-Congo, Volta-Congo, Benue-Congo, Bantoid, Southern, Narrow Bantu, Northwest, A, Yaunde-Fang (A.70). *Dialects:* Different from Bebele, although related. *Lg Use:* Speakers also use Beti or Bebele.

Beezen [bnz] 450 (2001 SIL). North West Province, Menchum Division, Furu-Awa Subdivision, Kpep (Beezen) village. *Class:* Niger-Congo, Atlantic-Congo, Volta-Congo, Benue-Congo, Jukunoid, Yukuben-Kuteb. *Lg Use:* Most speakers have low proficiency in Jukun. Cameroon Pidgin is spoken in the area. Schooling is in English. *Other:* Mountain slope.

Befang (Menchum, Bifang, Beba-Befang, Biba-Bifang) [bby] 2,975 (2000 WCD). North West Province, straddling Mezam Division, Tuba Subdivision and Menchum Division, Wum Subdivision, around Befang. *Class:* Niger-Congo, Atlantic-Congo, Volta-Congo, Benue-Congo, Bantoid, Southern, Wide Grassfields, Menchum. *Dialects:* Modele (Beekuru, Iku, Aku, Usheida, Modelle, Modeli, Idele, Ambabiko), Ushaku (Mukuru, Mokuru), Befang (Ge, Beba-Befang, Bifang, Abefang), Bangui (Bangwe, Bangwi), Obang, Okomanjang (Okoromandjang).

Bekwil (Bakwele, Bakwil, Bekwel, Okpele) [bkw] East Province, Boumba-and-Ngoko Division, along the north side of the Ngoko River, at and near Moloundou. *Dialect:* Esel (Essel). *Lg Use:* Speakers also use Mpongmpong. *Other:* Traditional religion, Christian. See main entry under Congo.

Beti [btb] 2,000,000. Population includes Fang, Ewondo, Bulu, Mengisa, etc. Major part of Center and South provinces; East Province, Lom-and-Djerem and Upper Nyong divisions. *Class:* Niger-Congo, Atlantic-Congo, Volta-Congo, Benue-Congo, Bantoid, Southern, Narrow Bantu, Northwest, A, Yaunde-Fang (A.70). *Dialects:* Consists of a set of 'languages' (Bebele, Bebil, Bulu, Eton, Ewondo, Fang, Mengisa) which are partially intelligible but ethnically distinct. *Lg Use:* Trade language. *Lg Dev:* Bible: 1970. *Other:* Different from Bette-Bende of Nigeria or the Bété languages of Côte d'Ivoire.

Bikya (Furu) [byb] 1 (1986 R. Breton). North West Province, Menchum Division, Furu-Awa Subdivision, Furubana village. *Class:* Niger-Congo, Atlantic-Congo, Volta-Congo, Benue-Congo, Bantoid, Southern, Unclassified. *Dialects:* Reported to be in Furu cluster (2000

B. Connell). May be Eastern Beboid. Lexical similarity 24% with Nsaa and Noone (Beboid), 14% with Akum. *Lg Use:* Members of the ethnic group now speak Jukun. The speaker is older than 70 years (1986 R. Breton). *Other:* The people are now called 'Furu'. They were formerly called 'Bikya'. Mountain slope. Nearly extinct.

Bishuo (Biyam, Furu) [bwh] 1 (1986 R. Breton). North West Province, Menchum Division, Furu-Awa Subdivision, Ntjieka, Furu-Turuwa, and Furu-Sambari villages. *Class:* Niger-Congo, Atlantic-Congo, Volta-Congo, Benue-Congo, Bantoid, Southern, Unclassified. *Dialects:* Reported to be in Furu cluster (2000 B. Connell). May be Jukunoid. Lexical similarity 16% to 17% with Nsaa and Noone, 11% with Bikya. *Lg Use:* The speaker is older than 60 years (1986 R. Breton). *Other:* The people are called 'Furu' and now speak Jukun. They were formerly called 'Biyam'. Mountain slope. Nearly extinct.

Bitare (Njwande, Yukutare) [brt] 6,034 in Cameroon (2000 WCD). Adamawa Province, Mayo-Banyo Division, near Banyo. See main entry under Nigeria.

Bokyi (Boki, Byoki, Nki, Okii, Uki, Nfua, Osikom, Osukam, Vaaneroki) [bky] 3,700 in Cameroon. South West Province, Manyu Division, Akwaya Subdivision, along Nigerian border northwest of Mamfe. *Dialects:* Basua, Boki, Iruan. See main entry under Nigeria.

Bomwali (Bomali, Boumoali, Bumali, Lino, "Sangasanga") [bmw] 6,077 in Cameroon (2000 WCD). East of Moloundou, Malapa village. *Other:* A distinct language from Bekwil. See main entry under Congo.

Bonkeng (Bongken, Bonkenge, Bonkeng-Pendia) [bvg] 2,975 (2000 WCD). Littoral Province, Moungo Division, Loum Subdivision. *Class:* Niger-Congo, Atlantic-Congo, Volta-Congo, Benue-Congo, Bantoid, Southern, Narrow Bantu, Northwest, A, Lundu-Balong (A.10). *Lg Dev:* Literacy rate in second language: 15% to 25%.

Bubia (Bobe, Bobea, Wovea, Bota, Ewota) [bbx] 600 (1977 Voegelin and Voegelin). South West Province, Fako Division, Limbe Subdivision. *Class:* Niger-Congo, Atlantic-Congo, Volta-Congo, Benue-Congo, Bantoid, Southern, Narrow Bantu, Northwest, A, Duala (A.20). *Lg Use:* Speakers also use Duala.

Buduma (Boudouma, Yedina, Yadena, Yedima) [bdm] 200 in Cameroon. Far North Province, Logone and Chari Division, islands of Lake Chad. *Other:* Muslim, traditional religion. See main entry under Chad.

Bulu (Boulou) [bum] 174,000 (1982 SIL). South Province, entire Ntem and Dja-and-Lobo divisions; the south of Upper Sanaga Division; Center Province, the north of Nyong-and-Mfoumou Division; East Province, part of Upper Nyong Division. *Class:* Niger-Congo, Atlantic-Congo, Volta-Congo, Benue-Congo, Bantoid, Southern, Narrow Bantu, Northwest, A, Yaunde-Fang (A.70). *Dialects:* Yelinda, Yembana, Yengono, Zaman, Bene. Intelligible with Eton, Ewondo, and Fang as part of the Beti group. *Lg Use:* Language of wider communication. 800,000 second-language speakers (1991 UBS). Formerly used for education, religion, and commerce, but now in decline as language of wider communication. *Lg Dev:* Bible: 1940. *Other:* Different from Bulu (Sekiyani) of Gabon.

Bum (Bom) [bmv] 21,400 (2001 SIL). North West Province, Boyo Division, Bum Subdivision, mainly in the village of Fonfuka. *Class:* Niger-Congo, Atlantic-Congo, Volta-Congo, Benue-Congo, Bantoid, Southern, Wide Grassfields, Narrow Grassfields, Ring, Center. *Dialects:* Lexical similarity with Kom 71%.

Bung [bqd] 3 (1995 Connell). Near the Kwanja language. *Class:* Unclassified. *Dialects:* It may have been a form of Kwanja. *Lg Use:* People now use Kwanja. May be extinct. *Other:* Nearly extinct.

Busam [bxs] 1,488 (2000 WCD). North West Province, Momo Division, Batibo Subdivision, in villages of Bifang,

Ambambo, and Dinku. *Class:* Niger-Congo, Atlantic-Congo, Volta-Congo, Benue-Congo, Bantoid, Southern, Wide Grassfields, Western Momo. *Dialects:* Related to Ambele and Atong.

Busuu (Awa, Furu) [bju] 8 (1986 Breton). North West Province, Menchum Division, Furu-Awa Subdivision, Furu-Awa and Furu-Nangwa villages. *Class:* Niger-Congo, Atlantic-Congo, Volta-Congo, Benue-Congo, Bantoid, Southern, Unclassified. *Dialects:* Reported to be in Furu cluster (2000 B. Connell). May be Jukunoid. Lexical similarity 10% with Jukun languages, 7% to 8% with Beboid languages. *Lg Use:* Used by older adults at reunions. Children learn only Jukun. *Other:* People are called 'Furu', and now speak Jukun. Formerly called 'Awa'. Mountain slope. Nearly extinct.

Buwal (Ma Buwal, Bual, Gadala) [bhs] 7,000 (2001 SIL). Far North Province, Mayo-Tsanaga Division, Mokolo Subdivision, in and around Gadala, south of Mokolo. *Class:* Afro-Asiatic, Chadic, Biu-Mandara, A, A.7. *Dialects:* Lexical similarity 90% with Gavar. *Lg Use:* All domains, church. Speakers have low proficiency in Fulfulde and French. Schooling is in French.

Byep (North Makaa, Meka, Maka, Makya, Mekye, Mekae, Mekay, Mekey, Moka, Mika) [mkk] 9,500 (1988 SIL). East Province, essentially the whole northern part of Upper Nyong Division (Messamena, Abong-Mbang, Doume, Nguelemendouka subdivisions); Lom and Djerem Division, eastern Diang Subdivision (west of Bertoua). *Class:* Niger-Congo, Atlantic-Congo, Volta-Congo, Benue-Congo, Bantoid, Southern, Narrow Bantu, Northwest, A, Makaa-Njem (A.80). *Dialect:* Byep, Besep (Besha, Bindafum). Not intelligible with South Makaa. Related to South Makaa and Kol.

Caka [ckx] 5,000 (1983 Atlas Linguistique du Cameroun). South West Province, Manyu Division, Akwaya Subdivision, Asaka, Basaka and Batanga villages. *Class:* Niger-Congo, Atlantic-Congo, Volta-Congo, Benue-Congo, Bantoid, Southern, Tivoid. *Dialects:* Assaka (Adzu Balaka), Batanga (Adzu Batanga). Lexical similarity 50% with Ipulo, 40% with Balo, Osatu, Iceve-Maci, and Otank, 35% with Esimbi, 30% with Mesaka. Assaka and Batanga have 80% lexical similarity. *Lg Use:* Some Ipulo use Caka as second language. Cameroon Pidgin and English used as second languages. English is used for literacy. *Other:* Different from Batanga in the Bube-Benga group and the Batanga dialect of Oroko. Mountain slope. Traditional religion.

Cung [cug] 2,000 (2001 SIL). North West Province, Menchum Division, west of Nkambe, northeast of Wum. *Class:* Niger-Congo, Atlantic-Congo, Volta-Congo, Benue-Congo, Bantoid, Southern, Beboid, Eastern.

Cuvok (Tchouvok) [cuv] 5,000 (1983 Atlas Linguistique du Cameroun). Far North Province, Mayo-Tsanaga Division, Mokolo Subdivision, in and around Tchouvok, Matakam South Canton, near Zamay. *Class:* Afro-Asiatic, Chadic, Biu-Mandara, A, A.5. *Lg Use:* Used in the home, village, and market. Limited use of Fulfulde with outsiders and French by the few who have gone to school. Most do not know nearby languages well (Mefele, Mofu South, Mafa).

Daba (Dabba) [dbq] 17,500 in Cameroon (1997). Population total all countries: 18,500. North Province, Mayo-Louti Division, northwest of Guider in Mayo-Oulo and Guider subdivisions; Far North Province, Mayo-Tsanaga Division, Hina and Bourrah subdivisions. Also spoken in Nigeria. *Class:* Afro-Asiatic, Chadic, Biu-Mandara, A, A.7. *Dialects:* Nive, Pologozom. *Lg Dev:* NT: 1992.

Dama [dmm] 50. North Province, Benoue Division, Rey-Bouba Subdivision, a small group. *Class:* Niger-Congo, Atlantic-Congo, Volta-Congo, North, Adamawa-Ubangi,

Adamawa, Mbum-Day, Mbum, Northern, Dama-Galke. *Dialects:* May be a dialect of Mono. *Lg Use:* All speakers are older adults. Speakers are shifting to Fulfulde. *Other:* Nearly extinct.

Dek [dek] 2,975 (2000 WCD). North Province. *Class:* Niger-Congo, Atlantic-Congo, Volta-Congo, North, Adamawa-Ubangi, Adamawa, Mbum-Day, Mbum, Unclassified. *Dialects:* It may be intelligible with Kari or Mbum.

Denya (Anyang, Agnang, Anyan, Anyah, Eyan, Takamanda, Obonya, Nyang) [anv] 11,200 (1982 SIL). South West Province, Manyu Division, central and southern parts of Akwaya Subdivision and northern part of Mamfe Central Subdivision. Partially in Takamanda Forest Reserve. *Class:* Niger-Congo, Atlantic-Congo, Volta-Congo, Benue-Congo, Bantoid, Southern, Mamfe. *Dialects:* Basho, Bitieku, Takamanda, Bajwo. Dialect cluster. Kendem is linguistically between Denya and Kenyang. Lexical similarity 70% to 80% among dialects. *Lg Dev:* Literacy rate in second language: 15% to 25%.

Dii (Duru, Dourou, Durru, Nyag Dii, Yag Dii, Zaa) [dur] 47,000 (1982 SIL). North Province, Mayo-Rey Division, Tchollire Subdivision; Adamawa Province, Vina Division, Ngaoundere Subdivision, north and east of Ngaoundere. *Class:* Niger-Congo, Atlantic-Congo, Volta-Congo, North, Adamawa-Ubangi, Adamawa, Leko-Nimbari, Duru, Dii. *Dialects:* Mambe', Mamna'a, Goom, Boow, Ngbang, Sagzee (Saadje, Saakye), Vaazin, Home, Nyok. Goom may be a separate language. *Lg Dev:* Dictionary. Grammar. NT: 2001. *Other:* Speakers refer to themselves as 'Yag Dii'. Traditional religion.

Dimbong (Bumbong, Kalong, Kaalong, Lakaalong, Mbong, Lambong, Bape, Palong) [dii] 140 (1992 SIL). Ethnic population: 50,000. Center Province, Mbam Division, northwest of Bafia, 2 villages. *Class:* Niger-Congo, Atlantic-Congo, Volta-Congo, Benue-Congo, Bantoid, Southern, Narrow Bantu, Northwest, A, Bafia (A.50). *Dialects:* Related to Bafia, Hijuk, Tibea. *Lg Use:* Comprehension of Bafia is generally acquired at an early age. Comprehension of Yambeta is generalized.

Doyayo (Doohyaayo, Dowayayo, Doyaayo, Doyau, Donyayo, Donyanyo, Doayo, Dooyayo, Dooyaayo, Dowayo, Doowaayo, Tunga, Tuuno, Tungbo, Nomai, "Namshi," "Namchi," "Namci") [dow] 18,000 (1985 EELC). North Province, Benoue Division, northern Poli Subdivision and around Poli. *Class:* Niger-Congo, Atlantic-Congo, Volta-Congo, North, Adamawa-Ubangi, Adamawa, Leko-Nimbari, Duru, Voko-Dowayo, Vere-Dowayo, Dowayo. *Dialects:* Marke, Teere (Poli), Sewe. *Lg Use:* Perhaps 20% of the men have proficiency in Bilkire Fulani for trading and everyday conversation. Perhaps 5% also use French. *Lg Dev:* NT: 1991. *Other:* "Namshi" is a derogatory name sometimes used for them. People are called 'Doowaayo'. Some form of whistle speech reported. Traditional religion, Christian, Muslim.

Duala (Douala, Diwala, Dwela, Dualla, Dwala) [dua] 87,700 (1982 SIL). Littoral Province, Nkam Division, towards Yabassi and along the Wouri River; Moungo Division, around Dibombari; Wouri Division, around Cameroon estuary; South West Province, Fako Division, both sides of the Mungo River. *Class:* Niger-Congo, Atlantic-Congo, Volta-Congo, Benue-Congo, Bantoid, Southern, Narrow Bantu, Northwest, A, Duala (A.20). *Dialects:* Bodiman, Mungo (Mungu, Muungo), Oli (Ewodi, Ouri, Uli, Wuri, Wouri, Koli), Pongo. Related to Malimba. *Lg Use:* Trade language in the western area. *Lg Dev:* Literacy rate in second language: 25% to 50%. Dictionary. Grammar. Bible: 1872-1970. *Other:* Coastal. Christian.

Dugun (Panon, Pa'non, Pani, Saa, Pape) [ndu] 7,000 (1997 Lars Lode). North Province, Faro Division, Poli Subdivision, southeast of Poli. *Class:* Niger-Congo,

Atlantic-Congo, Volta-Congo, North, Adamawa-Ubangi, Adamawa, Leko-Nimbari, Duru, Dii. *Dialects:* Saan, Naan. Close to Duupa. Lexical similarity 80% with Dii. *Other:* EELC primer.

Dugwor (Dougour, Memekere, Mofu-Dugwor, Tchakidjebe) [dme] 5,000 (2001 SIL). Far North Province, Diamare Division, Meri Subdivision, west of Tchere Canton between Maroua and Meri, in six villages. *Class:* Afro-Asiatic, Chadic, Biu-Mandara, A, A.5. *Dialect:* Mikere. *Lg Use:* Used in the home, with friends, traditional ceremonies, church (partly), local market. Positive language attitude. Speakers also use Fulfulde or French.

Duli (Dui) [duz] Extinct. North Province, Benoue Division, near Pitoa. *Class:* Niger-Congo, Atlantic-Congo, Volta-Congo, North, Adamawa-Ubangi, Adamawa, Leko-Nimbari, Duru, Duli. *Dialects:* Might have been the same as Gey, as reported by Barreteau, Breton, and Dieu 1984.

Duupa (Nduupa, Doupa, Dupa, Saa) [dae] 5,000 (1991 UBS). North Province, Faro and Benoue divisions, East of Poli. *Class:* Niger-Congo, Atlantic-Congo, Volta-Congo, North, Adamawa-Ubangi, Adamawa, Leko-Nimbari, Duru, Dii. *Dialects:* Related to Dugun. *Lg Dev:* Bible portions: 1982. *Other:* Traditional religion, Christian, Muslim.

Dzodinka (Adere, Adiri, Arderi, Dzodzinka) [add] 2,600 in Cameroon (2000 WCD). North West Province, Donga-Mantung Division, extreme northern part of Nwa Subdivision, village of Adere. Also spoken in Nigeria. *Class:* Niger-Congo, Atlantic-Congo, Volta-Congo, Benue-Congo, Bantoid, Southern, Wide Grassfields, Narrow Grassfields, Mbam-Nkam, Nkambe. *Lg Dev:* Bible portions: 1923-1932. *Other:* Speakers consider themselves to be ethnically Mfumte.

Ejagham (Ejaham, Ekoi, Etung, Ejwe, Edjagam, Keaka, Kwa, Obang, Ejagam) [etu] 49,394 in Cameroon (2000 WCD). South West Province, Manyu Division, whole of Eyumodjok Subdivision and southern part of Mamfe Subdivision west of Mamfe. *Dialect:* Western Ejagham, Eastern Ejagham, Southern Ejagham (Ekin, Kwa, Qua, Aqua, Abakpa). *Other:* Western Ejagham includes Bendeghe Etung (Bindege, Dindiga, Mbuma), Northern Etung, Southern Etung, Ekwe, Akamkpa-Ejagham. Eastern Ejagham includes Keaka (Keaqa, Kejaka, Edjagam), Obang (Eeafeng). See main entry under Nigeria.

Elip (Belip, Belibi, Libie, Nuasue, Nulibie) [ekm] 6,400 (1982 SIL). Center Province, Mbam Division, Elip canton, southeast of Bokito towards the Mbam and Sanaga rivers, in Yambasa. *Class:* Niger-Congo, Atlantic-Congo, Volta-Congo, Benue-Congo, Bantoid, Southern, Mbam, Yambasa (A.60). *Dialects:* It may be possible to standardize a written form with Mmaala and Yangben, related languages. *Lg Use:* People do not think French will replace Elip. French is the language of instruction in primary and secondary education. Ewondo or Bulu are used in some churches, without interpretation. Speakers acquire comprehension of Mmala and Yangben in early adulthood.

Eman (Emane) [emn] 800 (1990 SIL). South West Province, Manyu Division, Akwaya Subdivision, towns of Amayo, Amanavil, Akalabo, and Akalam Gomo. No permanent settlements in Nigeria. *Class:* Niger-Congo, Atlantic-Congo, Volta-Congo, Benue-Congo, Bantoid, Southern, Tivoid. *Dialect:* Amayo, Amanavil (Aman, Amana, Amani, Elaka). Lexical similarity 70% with Caka, 60% with Ipulo, 40% with Iceve-Maci and Otank, 35% with Esimbi, 30% with Mesaka. Amayo and Amanavil have 80% lexical similarity. *Lg Use:* Speakers have high bilingualism in Ipulo. Cameroon Pidgin is also used. *Other:* Mountain slope. Traditional religion.

English [eng] Used mainly in South West and North West provinces. *Lg Use:* Official language. See main entry under United Kingdom.

Esimbi (Essimbi, Isimbi, Simpi, Age, Aage, Bogue, Mburugam) [ags] 20,000 (1982 SIL). North West Province, Menchum Division, western part of Wum Subdivision, centered around Benakuma. *Class:* Niger-Congo, Atlantic-Congo, Volta-Congo, Benue-Congo, Bantoid, Southern, Tivoid. *Dialects:* Lexical similarity 35% with Balo, Ipulo, and Iceve-Maci.

Eton (Iton) [eto] 52,000 (1982 SIL). Center Province, almost all of Lekie Division. *Class:* Niger-Congo, Atlantic-Congo, Volta-Congo, Benue-Congo, Bantoid, Southern, Narrow Bantu, Northwest, A, Yaunde-Fang (A.70). *Dialects:* Essele, Mvog-Namve, Mvo-Nangkok, Beyidzolo. Intelligible with Bulu, Ewondo, and Fang as part of the Beti language. Closest to Mangisa. *Lg Use:* Speakers also use French.

Evant (Evand, Avand, Avande, Ovande, Ovand, Ovando, Balegete, Belegete) [bzz] 1,000 in Cameroon (1996 SIL). South West Province, Manyu Division, Akwaya Subdivision, Atolo and Matene I villages. *Lg Use:* Speakers also use Cameroon Pidgin. *Lg Dev:* Literacy is in English. *Other:* Mountain slope. Traditional religion. See main entry under Nigeria.

Ewondo (Ewundu, Jaunde, Yaounde, Yaunde) [ewo] 577,700 (1982 SIL). Center Province, all except the eastern part of Mefou Division; the entire Mfoundi and Nyong-and-So divisions; the southern half of Nyong-and-Mfoumou Division; South Province, the northern part of Ocean Division. *Class:* Niger-Congo, Atlantic-Congo, Volta-Congo, Benue-Congo, Bantoid, Southern, Narrow Bantu, Northwest, A, Yaunde-Fang (A.70). *Dialects:* Badjia (Bakjo), Bafeuk, Bamvele (Mvele, Yezum, Yesoum), Bane, Beti, Fong, Mbida-Bani, Mvete, Mvog-Niengue, Omvang, Yabekolo (Yebekolo), Yabeka, Yabekanga, Enoah, Evouzok. It is intelligible with Bulu, Eton, and Fang as part of the Beti language. *Lg Use:* Trade language. *Lg Dev:* Literacy rate in second language: 15% to 25%. NT: 1959–1962.

Fali, North [fll] 16,000 (1982 SIL). North Province, Mayo-Louti Division, Mayo-Oulo Subdivision, around Dourbeye and Mayo-Oulo. *Class:* Niger-Congo, Atlantic-Congo, Volta-Congo, North, Adamawa-Ubangi, Adamawa, Fali. *Dialects:* Dourbeye (Fali-Dourbeye), Bossoum (Fali-Bossoum, Bonum), Bveri (Fali du Peske-Bori, Peske, Bori). *Lg Use:* Speakers are rapidly shifting to Adamawa Fulfulde. *Other:* Muslim, traditional religion.

Fali, South [fal] 20,000 (1982 SIL). Around Hossere Bapara, Tsolaram, Hossere Toro, and Ndoudja; North Province, Benoue Division, northeast of Garoua, Pitoa Subdivision, south of Dembo. *Class:* Niger-Congo, Atlantic-Congo, Volta-Congo, North, Adamawa-Ubangi, Adamawa, Fali. *Dialects:* Fali-Tinguelin (Ndoudja, Mango, Ram, Toro), Kangou (Kaang, Kangu, Fali Kangou), Bele (Ngoutchoumi, Fali-Bele, Fali du Bele-Fere). *Lg Dev:* NT: 1975. *Other:* Different from North Fali and Fali (Bana) of Nigeria and Cameroon, which is Chadic; or Vin of Nigeria.

Fang (Pamue, Pahouin) [fan] 110,552 in Cameroon (2000 WCD). South Province, half of Dja-and-Lobo Division (south of Djoum); southeastern part of Ntem Division (south of Mvangan); Ocean Division, between Lolodorf and Kribi. *Dialects:* Fang (Okak), Mvae (Mvan, Mvay), Ntoumou (Ntumu). *Lg Dev:* Literacy rate in second language: 15% to 25%. *Other:* Different from Fang which is Beboid. See main entry under Equatorial Guinea.

Fang [fak] 2,400 (2001 SIL). North West Province, Menchum Division, Wum Subdivision, northeast of Wum, village of Fang. *Class:* Niger-Congo, Atlantic-Congo, Volta-Congo, Benue-Congo, Bantoid, Southern, Beboid, Western. *Other:* Different from Fang which is Narrow Bantu.

Fe'fe' (Fe'efe'e, Feefee, Fefe, Fotouni, Bafang, Bamileke-Fe'fe', Nufi) [fmp] 123,700 (1982 SIL). West Province, Upper Nkam Division (except for the vicinity of Kekem and a small section in the southeast corner); some in Mifi Division, Bangam. *Class:* Niger-Congo, Atlantic-Congo, Volta-Congo, Benue-Congo, Bantoid, Southern, Wide Grassfields, Narrow Grassfields, Mbam-Nkam, Bamileke. *Dialects:* Fa' (Bafang), Nka' (Banka), Nee (Bana), Njee-Poantu (Bandja-Babountou), Ntii (Fondanti), Mkwet (Fondjomekwet), La'fi (Balafi), Tungi' (Fotouni), Ngam (Bangan), Ca'. First 4 dialects listed belong to Central Fe'fe', next 5 belong to North Fe'fe'. *Lg Dev:* Literacy rate in second language: 25% to 50%. Bible portions: 1960.

French [fra] Used mainly in the Littoral, West, Center, South, East, Adamawa, North, and Far North provinces. *Lg Use:* Official language. See main entry under France.

Fulfulde, Adamawa (Adamawa Fulani, Peul, Peulh, Ful, Fula, Fulbe, Boulbe, Eastern Fulani, Fulfulde, Foulfoulde, Pullo, Gapelta, Pelta Hay, Domona, Pladina, Palata, Paldida, Paldena, Dzemay, Zemay, Zaakosa, Pule, Taareyo, Sanyo, Biira) [fub] 668,700 in Cameroon (1986). Possibly 13,000,000 speakers of all Fulfulde. Population total all countries: 886,700. It is spread all over the Far North, North, and Adamawa provinces. Also spoken in Chad, Nigeria, Sudan. *Class:* Niger-Congo, Atlantic-Congo, Atlantic, Northern, Senegambian, Fulani-Wolof, Fula, Eastern. *Dialect:* Maroua, Garoua, Ngaondéré, Kambariire, Nomadic Fulfulde, Bilkire Fulani (Bilkiri). There are some serious problems in intelligibility among Cameroon dialects, and elsewhere with Cameroon dialects. *Lg Use:* Trade language in north Cameroon. Bilkire is spoken by second-language Fulfulde speakers. *Lg Dev:* Dictionary. Grammar. Bible: 1983. *Other:* 'Fulfulde' is the language, 'Fulbe' the people. Adamawa is one of the major Fula geopolitical states. SVO. Traditional religion, Muslim.

Fulfulde, Kano-Katsina-Bororro (Peul, Fulbe) [fuv] Northern Cameroon. *Dialect:* Kano-Katsina, Bororro (Bororo, Mbororo, Ako, Nomadic Fulfulde). *Other:* Muslim. See main entry under Nigeria (Fulfulde, Nigerian).

Gavar (Gawar, Gouwar, Gauar, Rtchi, Kortchi, Ma-Gavar) [gou] 7,000 (2001 SIL). Far North Province, Mayo-Tsanaga Division, Mokolo Subdivision, around Gawar, Mogode Canton, south of Mokolo. One group of Gavar Hossere lives among the Gavar-Fulfulde, and another in relative isolation in the mountains around Kortchi village. *Class:* Afro-Asiatic, Chadic, Biu-Mandara, A, A.7. *Dialects:* Lexical similarity 90% with Buwal. *Lg Use:* The Gavar Hossere speak Gavar; the Gavar Fulfulde speak Fulfulde. Used in the home and village. The Gavar Hossere use Fulfulde in the market and for outside contacts. French is learned by the few who go to school. Comprehension of surrounding languages is limited (Mofu South, Mafa, Daba). *Other:* Agriculturalists. Traditional religion, Christian.

Gbaya, Northwest (Baya) [gya] 65,000 to 80,000 in Cameroon (1980). Vast area spread out between: North Province, Mayo-Rey Division, south of Touboro; Adamawa Province, Mbere Division, Meiganga Subdivision; Djerem Division, Ngaoundal and Tibati subdivisions; Faro and Deo Division, Tignere Subdivision; East Province, Lom and Djerem Division, Garoua Boulay, Betare-Oya, and Bertoua subdivisions; Kadey Division, Kette Subdivision; Boumba and Ngoko Division, Gari-Gombo Subdivision. *Dialects:* Banginda, Mbai, Gaymona, Lai (Lay), Lombu, Mbere, Mombe, Yaáyuwee (Yaiwe, Kalla). *Other:* Primer. See main entry under Central African Republic.

Gbaya, Southwest [mdo] 13,000 to 18,000 in
Cameroon (1998 SIL). Population includes 5,000 to 8,000
Dooka, 8,000 to 10,000 Mbodomo. East Province, Lom
and Djerem Division, Bétaré-Oya Subdivision, Ngoura
District. *Dialect:* Dooka, Mbodomo (Gbaya-Mbodomo,
Bodomo). *Lg Use:* Vigorous. Minimal Fulfulde is used in
the markets. Proficiency is greater where there are more
Fulani people: Yangamo has a 30% Fulani population. A
small number also use French, mainly educated men.
Other: Traditional religion, Christian. See main entry
under Central African Republic.

Gey (Gueve, Gewe) [guv] Extinct. Ethnic population: 1,900
(1982 SIL). North Province, Benoue Division, east of
Pitoa. *Class:* Niger-Congo, Atlantic-Congo, Volta-Congo,
North, Adamawa-Ubangi, Adamawa, Gueve. *Lg Use:*
Members of the ethnic group now speak Fulfulde.

Ghomálá' (Banjun, Bandjoun, Banjoun-Baham,
Baloum, Batie, Bamileke-Bandjoun, Mandju, Mahum)
[bbj] 260,000 (1982 SIL). West Province, most of Mifi
Division (except the extreme south and pockets in the
north and west); Mifi Division, Bamendjou
Subdivision; eastern part of Menoua Division; a
pocket in southern Bamboutos Division. *Class:* Niger-
Congo, Atlantic-Congo, Volta-Congo, Benue-Congo,
Bantoid, Southern, Wide Grassfields, Narrow
Grassfields, Mbam-Nkam, Bamileke. *Dialects:*
Ghomálá' Central (Bandjoun, Jo, We, Hom, Yogam,
Baham), Ghomálá' North (Fusap, Lang), Ghomálá'
South (Te, Pa, Dengkwop), Ngemba (Bamenjou,
Fu'da, Sa, Monjo, Meka, Mugum). Based on inherent
intelligibility, Bameka, Bansoa, and Balessing are
subdialects of South Ghomálá', North Ghomálá' has 2
subdialects, Central Ghomálá' 4, and Ngemba 5.
Lg Use: Taught informally to adults since the early
1900s. Adopted by UNESCO in the 1960s and 1970s
as one of 9 languages of wider communication for
Cameroon. Taught formally in 6 Roman Catholic
schools since 1995. *Lg Dev:* Literacy rate in second
language: 25% to 50%. NT: 2002. *Other:* Traditional
religion, Christian.

Gidar (Guider, Guidar, Gidder, Kada, Baynawa) [gid]
54,000 in Cameroon (1982 SIL). Population total all
countries: 65,687. North Province, Mayo-Louti Division,
Guider and Figuil subdivisions; Far North Province, a
small section of Diamare Division. Also spoken in Chad.
Class: Afro-Asiatic, Chadic, Biu-Mandara, C. *Dialect:*
Lam. *Lg Dev:* NT: 1986.

Gimme (Kompara, Kompana, Koma Kompana, Panbe,
Gimma) [kmp] 3,000 (1982 SIL). North Province, Faro
Division, on Saptou Plain, west of Poli along the Nigerian
border in the Alantika Mountains. *Class:* Niger-Congo,
Atlantic-Congo, Volta-Congo, North, Adamawa-Ubangi,
Adamawa, Leko-Nimbari, Duru, Voko-Dowayo, Vere-
Dowayo, Vere-Gimme, Gimme. *Lg Use:* Church activities
in Fulfulde. Fulfulde is used as second language. French
proficiency is low. *Other:* Distinct from Koma (Koma
Ndera) and Gimnime (Komlama). Their name for the
language is 'Gimma'.

Gimnime (Kadam, Komlama, Gimbe, Koma Kadam,
Laame, Yotubo) [gmn] 3,000 (1982 SIL). North Province,
Faro Division, around Wangay in the Alantika Mountains,
northwest of Poli along Nigerian border. *Class:* Niger-
Congo, Atlantic-Congo, Volta-Congo, North, Adamawa-
Ubangi, Adamawa, Leko-Nimbari, Duru, Voko-Dowayo,
Vere-Dowayo, Vere-Gimme, Gimme. *Dialect:* Ritime.
Close to Gimme. *Other:* Different from Koma (Koma
Ndera) of Cameroon.

Giziga, North (Guiziga, Gisiga, Gisika, Tchere, Mi
Marva, Giziga de Maroua, Dogba, Marva) [gis] 20,000
(1982 SIL). Far North Province, Diamare Division, Meri
Subdivision, in Tchere and Mogazang massifs and

neighboring Dogba plains, north and west of Maroua.
Class: Afro-Asiatic, Chadic, Biu-Mandara, A, A.5. *Other:*
Traditional religion, Christian.

Giziga, South (Guiziga, Gisiga, Gisika) [giz] 60,000
(1991 UBS). Far North Province, Diamare and Kaele
divisions, in Diamare plains, southwest of Maroua. *Class:*
Afro-Asiatic, Chadic, Biu-Mandara, A, A.5. *Dialects:*
Muturami (Muturwa, Muturua, Giziga de Moutouroua,
Loulou), Mi Mijivin (Giziga de Midjivin), Rum. *Lg Dev:*
NT: 1996. *Other:* Traditional religion, Christian.

Glavda (Gelvaxdaxa, Galvaxdaxa, Guelebda, Galavda,
Vale) [glw] 2,800 in Cameroon (1982 SIL). Far North
Province, Mayo-Tsanaga Division, Koza Subdivision, on
the Nigerian Border, south of Ashigashia, around the
village of Gelvaxdaxa. *Other:* Different from Vale of
Chad and Central African Republic, which is Central
Sudanic. See main entry under Nigeria.

Gude (Goude, Mubi, Tchade, Shede, Mapodi, Mudaye,
Mocigin, Motchekin, Cheke, Tcheke) [gde] 28,000 in
Cameroon. Far North Province, Mayo-Tsanaga Division,
straddling the southern part of Bourrah Subdivision, north
and northwest of Dourbeye; North Province, Mayo-Louti
Division, extreme north-western part of Mayo-Oulo
Subdivision. *Other:* Traditional religion. See main entry
under Nigeria.

Gvoko (Gevoko, Ghboko, Gavoko, Kuvoko, Ngossi,
Ngoshi, Ngoshe-Ndhang) [ngs] 1,000 in Cameroon (2000
SIL). Far North Province, Mayo-Tsanaga Division,
Mokolo Subdivision, north of Tourou, Ngoshi village
(different from Nggoshe). *Lg Use:* Positive language
attitude. High level of acquired intelligibility with Hdi. See
main entry under Nigeria.

Gyele (Giele, Gieli, Gyeli, Bagyele, Bagiele, Bajeli, Bajele,
Bogyeli, Bogyel, Bondjiel, Bako, Bekoe, Bakola, Bakuele,
Likoya, Babinga) [gyi] 4,250 in Cameroon. Population
total all countries: 4,279. South Province, Ocean Division,
Kribi and Lolodorf subdivisions, in forests around Kribi
and along the road from Kribi to Lolodorf. Also spoken in
Equatorial Guinea. *Class:* Niger-Congo, Atlantic-Congo,
Volta-Congo, Benue-Congo, Bantoid, Southern, Narrow
Bantu, Northwest, A, Makaa-Njem (A.80). *Lg Dev:* Bible
portions: 1969. *Other:* Pygmies, dispersed in small groups
in the forest. Forest.

Hausa (Haoussa, Hawsa) [hau] 23,500 in Cameroon (1982
SIL). Scattered. *Other:* Muslim. See main entry under
Nigeria.

Hdi (Xedi, Hedi, Hide, Turu-Hide, Xadi) [xed] 25,000 in
Cameroon (2001 SIL). Population total all countries:
29,000. Far North Province, Mayo-Tsanaga Division,
Mokolo Subdivision, fifteen villages on Nigerian border
northwest of Mokolo. Also spoken in Nigeria. *Class:*
Afro-Asiatic, Chadic, Biu-Mandara, A, A.4, Lamang.
Dialect: Tur (Turu, Tourou, Ftour). 51% intelligibility of
Mabas, 48% of Lamang, 35% of Gvoko. Lexical
similarity 78% with Mabas, 64% with Lamang, 56% with
Gvoko. *Lg Dev:* 700 adult students each year in literacy
program. Grammar. *Other:* The name is Hide in French,
pronounced [Xdi].

Hijuk [hij] 400 (1992 SIL). Center Province, Mbam
Division, Bokito Subdivision, southwest of Bokito, part of
1 village. *Class:* Niger-Congo, Atlantic-Congo, Volta-
Congo, Benue-Congo, Bantoid, Southern, Narrow Bantu,
Northwest, A, Bafia (A.50). *Dialects:* Lexical similarity
45% with Bafia, 84% with Basaa. *Lg Use:* Speakers
understand Yangben, spoken by some in their village.
Some comprehension of Basaa and Nugunu. High degree
of generalized bilingualism in French.

Hya (Ghye, Za) [hya] 940 in Cameroon (2002 SIL). Far
North Province, Mayo-Tsanaga Division, Mokolo
Subdivision, only in Amsa. Also spoken in Nigeria.
Class: Afro-Asiatic, Chadic, Biu-Mandara, A, A.3.

Dialects: Close to Kamwe of Nigeria and Psikye of Cameroon. Lexical similarity 62% with Psikye. *Lg Use:* Used in most areas of life. Speakers also use Psikye. *Lg Dev:* Positive attitude toward literacy. *Other:* Mountain slope. Agriculturalists.

Iceve-Maci (Icheve, Becheve, Bechere, Bacheve, Ochebe, Ocebe, Ocheve, Utse, Utser, Utseu) [bec] 7,000 in Cameroon (1990). Population total all countries: 12,000. South West Province, Manyu Division, north and south of Akwaya. Also spoken in Nigeria. *Class:* Niger-Congo, Atlantic-Congo, Volta-Congo, Benue-Congo, Bantoid, Southern, Tivoid. *Dialects:* Icheve (Bacheve), Oliti (Maci, Matchi, Oliti-Akwaya, Olithi, Olit, Kwaya, Akwaya Motom, Motomo, Ihekwot). Lexical similarity 80% between Maci and Bacheve dialects, 60% with Otank, 50% with Evant and Tiv, 40% with Eman and Mesaka, 35% with Esimbi. *Lg Use:* Some use Evant, and older males can speak some Denya-Kenyang. Cameroon Pidgin is also used. *Other:* Mountain slope. Traditional religion.

Ipulo (Assumbo, Asumbo, Badzumbo) [ass] 2,500 (1990 SIL). South West Province, Manyu Division, Akwaya Subdivision, southeast of Akwaya. *Class:* Niger-Congo, Atlantic-Congo, Volta-Congo, Benue-Congo, Bantoid, Southern, Tivoid. *Dialects:* Olulu, Tinta, Etongo. Lexical similarity 90% between Olulu and Tinta. Lexical similarity 60% with Eman, 50% with Caka, 40% with Balo and Osatu, 35% with Esimbi. *Lg Use:* Some speakers also use Cameroon Pidgin, Eman, or Caka. *Other:* Communications are difficult in the area. Mountain slope. Agriculturalists. Traditional religion.

Isu [isu] 10,400 (1994 SIL). North West Province, Menchum Division, Wum Central Subdivision. Reported to be spread over a wide area up to the Nigerian border. *Class:* Niger-Congo, Atlantic-Congo, Volta-Congo, Benue-Congo, Bantoid, Southern, Wide Grassfields, Narrow Grassfields, Ring, West. *Dialects:* Little dialect variation. Considered to be a distinct language from Aghem and Weh; some comprehension of those languages. *Lg Use:* Speakers also use Cameroon Pidgin or English. *Other:* Not the same as Isu (Subu, Bimbia) which is Narrow Bantu A.20. Traditional religion, Christian.

Isu (Su, Isubu, Isuwu, Subu, Bimbia) [szv] 800 (1982 SIL). South West Province, Fako Division, Tiko Subdivision, around Bimbia estuary east of Limbe and west of Douala. *Class:* Niger-Congo, Atlantic-Congo, Volta-Congo, Benue-Congo, Bantoid, Southern, Narrow Bantu, Northwest, A, Duala (A.20). *Lg Use:* All also use Mokpwe, Duala. *Lg Dev:* Bible portions: 1843–1852. *Other:* Distinct from Isu which is Narrow Grassfields.

Iyive (Uive, Yiive) [uiv] 1,000 in Cameroon (1996 WT). Population total all countries: 2,000. South West Province, Manyu Division, northeast of Akwaya on the Nigerian border, Yive village. Also spoken in Nigeria. *Class:* Niger-Congo, Atlantic-Congo, Volta-Congo, Benue-Congo, Bantoid, Southern, Tivoid. *Dialects:* Lexical similarity 75% with Tiv.

Jimi (Djimi, Jimjimen, 'Um Falin) [jim] 3,500 (1982 SIL). Far North Province, Mayo-Tsanaga Division, on Nigerian border in and around Bourrha. *Class:* Afro-Asiatic, Chadic, Biu-Mandara, A, A.8. *Dialects:* Djimi, Zumo (Zumu, Zomo, Zame), Jimo, Wadi (Wa'i), Malabu. Close to Gude. *Lg Use:* Speakers also use Fulfude or French. *Other:* Different from Jimi of Nigeria in Bauchi State, which is West Chadic. Muslim, traditional religion.

Jina (Zina) [jia] 1,500 (2004 SIL). Far North Province, Logone-and-Chari Division, near the south of Logone-Birni Subdivision, around Zina and east of Waza. *Class:* Afro-Asiatic, Chadic, Biu-Mandara, B, B.1, Jina. *Dialects:* Jina (Zine), Sarassara, Tchide (Sede), Muxule (Muxuli, Ngodeni), Mae. People in Zina say they understand Lagwan and Musgu better than Muxule. *Lg Use:* Lagwan

is used as a second language. *Other:* Muxule may be a separate language.

Jukun Takum (Njikum, Jukun, Diyu) [jbu] 2,438 in Cameroon (2000 WCD). North West Province, Menchum Division, Furu-Awa Subdivision, Ntjieka, Furu-Turuwa, and Furu-Sambari villages. Also spoken in Nigeria. *Class:* Niger-Congo, Atlantic-Congo, Volta-Congo, Benue-Congo, Jukunoid, Central, Jukun-Mbembe-Wurbo, Jukun. *Dialect:* Takum, Donga (Akpanzhi). *Lg Use:* Trade language. *Lg Dev:* Dictionary. Grammar. NT: 1980. *Other:* The name 'Njikum' is preferred in Cameroon. People are called 'Jukun'. Mountain slope.

Kako (Yaka, Kaka, Nkoxo, Dikaka, Mkako) [kkj] 100,000 in Cameroon (2003 SIL). Population total all countries: 119,455. East Province, major part of Kadey Division, Batouri and Ndelele subdivisions. Also spoken in Central African Republic, Congo. *Class:* Niger-Congo, Atlantic-Congo, Volta-Congo, Benue-Congo, Bantoid, Southern, Narrow Bantu, Northwest, A, Kako (A.90). *Dialects:* Mbonjoku, Besembo, Bera, Ngbako. *Lg Dev:* Literacy rate in second language: 15% to 25%. Dictionary. NT: 1999. *Other:* Different from Kaka (Yamba) which is Grassfields Bantu.

Kamkam (Bungnu, Bunu, Bungun, Gbunhu, Kakaba, Mbongno) [bgu] Adamawa Province, Mayo-Banyo Division, on the Mambila Plateau. *Other:* Muslim, traditional religion. See main entry under Nigeria (Mbongno).

Kanuri, Central (Yerwa Kanuri, Kole, Kolere, Sirata, "Baribari," "Beriberi," Kanouri, Kanoury, Bornu, Bornouans, Bornouan) [knc] 56,500 in Cameroon (1982 SIL). Far North Province, Mayo-Sava Division, mainly north of Mora between Limani and Bounderi and in Kolofata Subdivision; Diamare Division, Maroua and Bogo subdivisions; Kaele and Mayo-Danay divisions, as far as Mindif and Guirvidig. *Dialects:* Mowor (Movar), Dagara, Kaga (Kagama), Sugurti, Lare, Kwayam, Njesko, Kabari (Kuvuri), Ngazar, Guvja, Mao, Temageri, Fadawa, Maiduguri. *Other:* "Beriberi" is considered a derogatory name. Muslim. See main entry under Nigeria.

Karang (Kareng, Mbum, Mbum-East, Laka, Lakka) [kzr] 17,000 in Cameroon (1991 SIL). Population total all countries: 18,000. North Province, Mayo-Rey Division, in Padjama and from Tcholliere to Touboro. Also spoken in Chad. *Class:* Niger-Congo, Atlantic-Congo, Volta-Congo, North, Adamawa-Ubangi, Adamawa, Mbum-Day, Mbum, Central, Karang. *Dialects:* Sakpu (Pandama, Tu'boro), Karang, Ngomi, Mbere. Related to Pana, Nzakambay, and Kuo. *Lg Dev:* Dictionary. Bible portions: 1999. *Other:* Different from Laka (Kabba Laka) of Central African Republic and Chad, and from Laka of Nigeria. Christian, traditional religion, Muslim.

Kare (Karré, Kari, Kali) [kbn] 4,463 in Cameroon (2000). Adamawa Province, Vina Division, around Belel; North Province, Mayo-Rey Division. *Dialects:* Tale, Kari. *Other:* Different from the Kari of Democratic Republic of the Congo, which is Benue-Congo. See main entry under Central African Republic.

Kemezung (Dumbo, Dzumbo, Kumaju) [dmo] 4,500 (2001 SIL). North West Province, Donga-Mantung Division, southwest corner of Ako Subdivision, northwest of Nkambe, town of Dumbu and village of Kwei. *Class:* Niger-Congo, Atlantic-Congo, Volta-Congo, Benue-Congo, Bantoid, Southern, Beboid, Eastern. *Dialects:* Member of the Eastern Beboid cluster. Lexical similarity 85% with Bebe. *Lg Use:* All domains. Schooling is in English. Some use Cameroon Pidgin or Bebe as a second language. *Other:* Agriculturalists; businessmen; traders.

Kendem (Bokwa-Kendem) [kvm] 1,500 (2001 SIL). South West Province, Manyu Division, partly in Tinto Subdivision and partly in Upper Bayang Subdivision, villages of Kendem, Kekpoti, and Bokwa east of Mamfe. *Class:* Niger-Congo, Atlantic-Congo, Volta-Congo, Benue-Congo, Bantoid, Southern, Mamfe. *Dialects:* Higher lexical similarity with Denya but higher intelligibility of Kenyang. *Lg Use:* Some also use Kenyang and certain dialects of Denya or Cameroon Pidgin.

Kenswei Nsei (Bamessing, Ndop-Bamessing, Melamba, Nsei, Veteng, Vetweng, Calebasses, Befi, Mesing, Kensense) [ndb] 12,500 (1982 SIL). North West Province, Mezam Division, Ndop Subdivision, west of Ndop on Ndop Plain, centered around the village of Bamessing. *Class:* Niger-Congo, Atlantic-Congo, Volta-Congo, Benue-Congo, Bantoid, Southern, Wide Grassfields, Narrow Grassfields, Ring, North. *Dialects:* Close to Vengo, Wushi, Bamunka. *Other:* Speakers refer to the language as 'Nsei'.

Kenyang (Nyang, Bayangi, Banyang, Banyangi, Banjangi, Manyang) [ken] 65,000 (1992 SIL). South West Province, Manyu Division, Mamfe Central Subdivision and Upper Banyang Subdivision, around and southwest of Mamfe; Kupe-Muanenguba Division, western corner of Nguti Subdivision. *Class:* Niger-Congo, Atlantic-Congo, Volta-Congo, Benue-Congo, Bantoid, Southern, Mamfe. *Dialects:* Upper Kenyang (Haut-Kenyang), Lower Kenyang (Bas-Kenyang), Bakoni (Upper Balong, Northern Balong, Manyemen, Kicwe, Kitwii, Twii, Manyeman). *Lg Dev:* Dictionary. Bible portions: 2001. *Other:* Upper Balong is distinct from Bafaw-Balong. SVO; prepositions; genitives, articles, adjectives, numerals, relatives after noun heads; question word final; maximum prefixes 3. Interfluvial. Deciduous forest. 1,000 meters. Swidden agriculturalists.

Kera [ker] 6,000 in Cameroon. Far North Province, Mayo-Danay Division, Southeast of Doukoula. *Lg Dev:* Literacy rate in second language: 5% to 25%. See main entry under Chad.

Kol (Bikele-Bikeng, Bikele-Bikay, Bekol) [biw] 12,000 (1988 SIL). Population includes 1,000 in Bikeng. East Province, Upper Nyong Division, vicinity of Messamena. *Class:* Niger-Congo, Atlantic-Congo, Volta-Congo, Benue-Congo, Bantoid, Southern, Narrow Bantu, Northwest, A, Makaa-Njem (A.80). *Dialects:* Bikele, Bikeng, Kol North, Kol South. *Lg Use:* Speakers also use Makaa or Koonzime.

Kolbila (Kolbilari, Kolbilla, Kolena, Kolbili, Zoono) [klc] 2,500 (1997 Lars Lode). North Province, Faro Division, Bantadje Canton, southeast of Poli, and some to the east on the main road between Ngaoundere and Garoua. Not in Nigeria. *Class:* Niger-Congo, Atlantic-Congo, Volta-Congo, North, Adamawa-Ubangi, Adamawa, Leko-Nimbari, Leko. *Dialects:* Related to Chamba Leko. *Lg Use:* Speakers also use French. *Lg Dev:* Bible portions: 1982–1985. *Other:* Mountain slope. Traditional religion, Christian, Muslim.

Kom (Nkom, Bikom, Bamekon, Itangikom, Kong) [bkm] 170,000 (2000 SIL). North West Province, southern part of Boyo Division, and 20,000 in major urban centers. *Class:* Niger-Congo, Atlantic-Congo, Volta-Congo, Benue-Congo, Bantoid, Southern, Wide Grassfields, Narrow Grassfields, Ring, Center. *Dialect:* Mbizenaku (Mbesa, Itangimbesa). *Lg Use:* Vigorous. Speakers of other languages (Aghem, Arbore, Babanki, Bum, Bussa, Dirasha, Gawwada, Koma, Komo, Laimbue, Lengola, Mmen, Noni, Ntcham, Tsamai) use it as second language. About 30% are monolingual. All domains. Oral use in local administration, oral use in religious services and written use in church, oral use in commerce, written use in letters. All ages. Positive language attitude. Many speak Cameroon Pidgin, a few speak English, very few French as second language. Some also speak Bum, Babanki,

Mmen, Oku, Lamnso'. *Lg Dev:* Literacy rate in first language: 10%. Literacy rate in second language: 15% to 25%. 5% can write Kom. 45 out of 80 schools have bilingual education. A few secondary schools have Kom language clubs, and Kom is a subject in extracurricular activities. Radio programs. Bible portions: 1998–2001. *Other:* Tonal. Mountain slope, hills, valleys. Agriculturalists. Traditional religion, Christian.

Koma (Kuma) [kmy] 3,000 in Cameroon (1984 SIL). North Province, Faro Division, northwest of Tchamba in Alantika Mountains along Nigerian border. *Dialects:* Koma Ndera, Koma Damti, Leelu, Bangru, Zanu, Liu, Yeru. *Lg Use:* Limited bilingualism in Hausa. *Other:* Different from Gimme (Kompara), Gimnime (Komlama), Komo of Ethiopia and Central Koma of Sudan. Traditional religion. See main entry under Nigeria.

Koonzime (Nzime, Djimu, Zimu, Koozime, Koozhime, Kooncimo, Dzimou) [ozm] 30,000 (2000 SIL). East Province, Upper Nyong Division, around Lomie (north and northwest, south and southeast to Dja River). *Class:* Niger-Congo, Atlantic-Congo, Volta-Congo, Benue-Congo, Bantoid, Southern, Narrow Bantu, Northwest, A, Makaa-Njem (A.80). *Dialects:* Nzime (Koonzime), Badwe'e (Badjoue, Bajwe'e, Koozime). *Lg Use:* Many Baka Pygmies speak it as a second language. All domains, public discourse, promulgate government information, oral and written use in church, oral literature. Positive language attitude. 80% speak French as second language. *Lg Dev:* 2,000 can read it, 50 can write it. Taught in primary schools. Radio programs. Dictionary. NT: 1998–2002. *Other:* 'Koonzime' refers to the Nzime dialect, 'Koozime' to the Badwe'e dialect. Hills. Tropical forest, some swamp. Agriculturalists: coffee, cocoa; trappers. Christian.

Korop (Ododop, Durop, Dyurop, Erorup) [krp] 7,438 in Cameroon (2000 WCD). South West Province, Ndian Division, along Nigerian border, northwest of Mundemba. See main entry under Nigeria.

Koshin (Kosin, Kaw) [kid] 1,000 (2001 SIL). North West Province, Menchum Division, Wum Subdivision, Village of Koshin. *Class:* Niger-Congo, Atlantic-Congo, Volta-Congo, Benue-Congo, Bantoid, Southern, Beboid, Western.

Kuk [kfn] 3,000 (2001 SIL). North-West Province, Menchum Division, Fungom Subdivision, six villages along Ring Road between Weh and Bafmeng. *Class:* Niger-Congo, Atlantic-Congo, Volta-Congo, Benue-Congo, Bantoid, Southern, Wide Grassfields, Narrow Grassfields, Ring, Center. *Other:* Traditional religion, Christian.

Kung [kfl] 1,750 (2001 SIL). North-West Province, Menchum Division, one village of Fungom Subdivision. *Class:* Niger-Congo, Atlantic-Congo, Volta-Congo, Benue-Congo, Bantoid, Southern, Wide Grassfields, Narrow Grassfields, Ring, Center. *Other:* Traditional religion, Christian.

Kuo (Ko, Koh) [xuo] 2,975 in Cameroon (2000 WCD). North Province, between Sorombeo and Chad border, and around Garoua. *Lg Dev:* Literacy rate in second language: 25% to 50%. *Other:* Different from Kuo which is Narrow Grassfields. Second-generation speakers and refugees only in Cameroon. See main entry under Chad.

Kutep (Kuteb, Kutev, Mbarike, Zumper, Ati, "Jompre") [kub] 1,400 in Cameroon (1986 R. Breton). North West Province, Menchum Division, Furu-Awa Subdivision, Baji and Lubu villages near the Nigerian border. *Dialects:* Jenuwa, Lissam, Fikyu, Kunabe, Kentin. *Lg Use:* High bilingualism in Jukun Takum. Cameroon Pidgin is also spoken in the area. *Lg Dev:* Literacy rate in second language: 15% to 25%. *Other:* People are called 'Ati'. "Jompre" is an offensive name. Mountain slope. Christian, traditional religion. See main entry under Nigeria.

Kwa' (Bakwa, Bakoa, Bamileke-Kwa) [bko] 1,000 (2000 SIL). Littoral Province, Nkam Division, eastern Nkondjok Subdivision; West Province, southwest corner of Nde Division. *Class:* Niger-Congo, Atlantic-Congo, Volta-Congo, Benue-Congo, Bantoid, Southern, Wide Grassfields, Narrow Grassfields, Mbam-Nkam, Bamileke. *Dialects:* Kwa' (Bekwa', Bakoua, Babwa, Mipa), Mbyam. *Lg Use:* Speakers also use French. *Other:* 'Bamaha' may be an alternate name. Distinct from Kwa (Ba) of Nigeria in the Adamawa branch.

Kwaja [kdz] 2,975 (2000 WCD). North West Province, Donga-Mantung Division, Nkambe Subdivision. *Class:* Niger-Congo, Atlantic-Congo, Volta-Congo, Benue-Congo, Bantoid, Southern, Wide Grassfields, Narrow Grassfields, Mbam-Nkam, Nkambe. *Dialects:* Possibly intelligible with other Mfumte languages. *Other:* Speakers consider themselves to be ethnically Mfumte.

Kwakum (Akpwakum, Abakoum, Pakum, Kpakum, Bakum, Abakum) [kwu] 10,000 (2002 SIL). East Province, Upper Nyong Division, Dimako and Doume subdivisions; Lom-and-Djerem Division, north of Bertoua and in Belabo Subdivision. *Class:* Niger-Congo, Atlantic-Congo, Volta-Congo, Benue-Congo, Bantoid, Southern, Narrow Bantu, Northwest, A, Kako (A.90). *Dialects:* Kwakum, Beten (Bethen, Petem), Til, Baki (Mbaki).

Kwanja (Konja, Kondja) [knp] 20,000 (1991 UBS). Adamawa Province, Mayo-Banyo Division, between Banyo and Bankim in the northeastern Tikar Plain, south of Mayo-Darle. *Class:* Niger-Congo, Atlantic-Congo, Volta-Congo, Benue-Congo, Bantoid, Northern, Mambiloid, Mambila-Konja, Konja. *Dialect:* Nyasunda, Nyandung, Nyanjang (Njang, Njanga). *Lg Use:* Now Cambap people mainly speak Kwanja. Speakers include a few older adults who speak the Njanga dialect (1995 Bruce Connell).

La'bi [lbi] North Province, Mayo-Rey Division, Touboro Subdivision. *Class:* Niger-Congo, Atlantic-Congo, Volta-Congo, North, Adamawa-Ubangi, Adamawa, La'bi. *Other:* The language of initiation rites practiced by the Gbaya, Mbum, and some Sara-Laka. Samarin says the vocabulary is borrowed from Sara languages. Second language only.

Lagwan (Kotoko-Logone, Logone, Lagwane, Lagouane) [kot] 10,000 in Cameroon (SIL 2003). All Kotoko languages: 167,471. Far North Province, Logone-and-Chari Division, north of Waza National Park in Logone-Birni Subdivision, from the bank of the Logone River across to the Nigerian border. Also spoken in Chad. *Class:* Afro-Asiatic, Chadic, Biu-Mandara, B, B.1, Kotoko Proper. *Dialect:* Logone-Birni, Logone-Gana (Kotoko-Gana). Related to Afade, Mser, Malgbe, Maslam, Mpade. *Lg Dev:* Grammar. *Other:* Muslim.

Laimbue [lmx] 5,000 (1994 SIL). North West Province, Menchum Division, Wum Central Subdivision, several villages; Boyo Division, Fondong Subdivision. *Class:* Niger-Congo, Atlantic-Congo, Volta-Congo, Benue-Congo, Bantoid, Southern, Wide Grassfields, Narrow Grassfields, Ring, West. *Lg Use:* Speakers in Wum Central Subdivision have some knowledge of Aghem. *Other:* Traditional religion, Christian.

Lamnso' (Nso, Nso', Nsaw, Nsho', Lamso, Lamnsok, Banso, Banso', Bansaw, Panso) [lns] 125,000 in Cameroon (1987 SIL). North West Province, Bui Division, eastern Kumbo and Jakiri subdivisions, northeast of Bamenda around Kumbo. Also spoken in Nigeria. *Class:* Niger-Congo, Atlantic-Congo, Volta-Congo, Benue-Congo, Bantoid, Southern, Wide Grassfields, Narrow Grassfields, Ring, East. *Lg Dev:* Literacy rate in second language: 15% to 25%. NT: 1990.

Lefa (Balom, Fak, Lefa') [lfa] 10,000. Center Province, Mbam and Inoubou Division, Bafia Subdivision. *Class:*

Niger-Congo, Atlantic-Congo, Volta-Congo, Benue-Congo, Bantoid, Southern, Narrow Bantu, Northwest, A, Bafia (A.50). *Dialects:* Lefa, Cama (Tempanye), Tingong, Letia.

Leti [leo] Center Province, Lekie Division, northern Sa'a Subdivision, along the bend of the Sanaga River. *Class:* Niger-Congo, Atlantic-Congo, Volta-Congo, Benue-Congo, Bantoid, Southern, Mbam, Sanaga (A.60). *Lg Use:* The Mangisa people are reported to speak two languages: Mengisa-Njowi, spoken daily, and Leti, a secret language of tradition (see Mengisa). *Other:* Second language only.

Limbum (Limbom, Nsungli, Ndzungle, Ndzungli, Njungene, Nsungali, Nsungni, Llimbumi, Wimbum, Bojiin) [lmp] 73,000 in Cameroon (1982 SIL). North West Province, Donga-Mantung Division, entire Nkambe Subdivision around Nkambe and Ndu. Also spoken in Nigeria. *Class:* Niger-Congo, Atlantic-Congo, Volta-Congo, Benue-Congo, Bantoid, Southern, Wide Grassfields, Narrow Grassfields, Mbam-Nkam, Nkambe. *Dialects:* Wiyeh, Tang, Wat. *Lg Use:* Trade language. *Lg Dev:* Literacy rate in second language: 15% to 25%. Literacy classes in 6 villages (1995). Grammar. NT: 2002.

Longto (Voko, Woko, Boko, Lonto, Longbo, Longa, Gobeyo) [wok] 2,400 (1982 SIL). North Province, Faro Division, Poli Subdivision, southwest of Poli to Faro Reserve, around Voko. *Class:* Niger-Congo, Atlantic-Congo, Volta-Congo, North, Adamawa-Ubangi, Adamawa, Leko-Nimbari, Duru, Voko-Dowayo, Voko. *Other:* Muslim.

Luo [luw] 1 (1995 Connell). A section of Atta. *Class:* Unclassified. *Other:* May be extinct. Nearly extinct.

Mada [mxu] 17,000 (1982 SIL). Far North Province, Mayo-Sava Division, Tokombere Subdivision, Mada massif at edge of Mandara Mountains and neighboring plain. *Class:* Afro-Asiatic, Chadic, Biu-Mandara, A, A.5. *Lg Dev:* Bible portions: 1989. *Other:* Distinct from Mada of Nigeria, which is Benue-Congo.

Mafa ("Matakam," Mofa, Natakan) [maf] 136,000 in Cameroon (1982 SIL). Population total all countries: 140,907. Far North Province, from Mokolo north in Mayo-Tsanaga Division. Also spoken in Nigeria. *Class:* Afro-Asiatic, Chadic, Biu-Mandara, A, A.5. *Dialects:* West Mafa, Central Mafa, East Mafa. Subdialects of West Mafa: Magoumaz, Mavoumay; Central Mafa: Ouzal, Koza, Mokola, Mokolo, Ldamtsai; East Mafa: Soulede, Roua. *Lg Dev:* Dictionary. Bible: 1978–1989. *Other:* The name "Matakam" has a derogatory connotation in Cameroon. Traditional religion, Christian.

Majera (Midah, Mida'a, Da'a) [xmj] 500 in Cameroon (2004 SIL). Far North Province, Logone-and-Chari Division, around Majera in extreme southern Logone-Birni Subdivision. Also spoken in Chad. *Class:* Afro-Asiatic, Chadic, Biu-Mandara, B, B.1, Jina. *Dialects:* Majera (Mazra), Kajire-'dulo, Hwalem (Holom). *Lg Use:* In rapid decline. The young generation is not speaking it or only speak a reduced form (H Tourneux). *Other:* Included in what the Mandage call 'Mida'a' and 'Da'a'.

Makaa (Mekaa, South Makaa, South Mekaa) [mcp] 80,000 (1987 SIL). East Province, essentially the whole northern part of Upper Nyong Division (Messamena, Abong-Mbang, Doume, Nguelemendouka subdivisions). *Class:* Niger-Congo, Atlantic-Congo, Volta-Congo, Benue-Congo, Bantoid, Southern, Narrow Bantu, Northwest, A, Makaa-Njem (A.80). *Dialects:* Bebent (Bebende, Biken, Bewil, Bemina), Mbwaanz, Sekunda. Related to Byep and Kol. *Lg Dev:* Dictionary. Bible portions: 2000.

Malgbe (Malgwe, Gulfe, Gulfei, Goulfei, Sanbalbe, Malbe, Ngwalkwe) [mxf] 6,000 in Cameroon (2004 SIL). Far North Province, Logone-and-Chari Division, along the Chari River, north of Kousseri in a town of Goulfey and

Goulfey Subdivision. Also spoken in Chad. *Class:* Afro-Asiatic, Chadic, Biu-Mandara, B, B.1, Kotoko Proper. *Dialects:* Malgbe (Goulfei), Mara, Dro, Douguia (Dugiya). Related to Afade, Mser, Lagwan, Maslam, Mpade.

Malimba (Mulimba, Mudima, Limba, Lemba) [mzd] 2,230 (2001 SIL). Littoral Province, Sanaga-Maritime Division, small pocket north of Edea, and around the mouth of the Sanaga River. *Class:* Niger-Congo, Atlantic-Congo, Volta-Congo, Benue-Congo, Bantoid, Southern, Narrow Bantu, Northwest, A, Duala (A.20). *Dialects:* Self reported high comprehension of Duala. *Lg Use:* Little interest in developing Malimba.

Mambai (Mangbai, Mangbei, Manbai, Mambay, Mamgbay, Mamgbei, Mongbay) [mcs] 8,000 in Cameroon (2002 SIL). Population total all countries: 10,000. Along Mayo-Kebi River near the Chad border in extreme northern Bibemi Subdivision, Benoue Division, North Province. Also spoken in Chad. *Class:* Niger-Congo, Atlantic-Congo, Volta-Congo, North, Adamawa-Ubangi, Adamawa, Mbum-Day, Mbum, Northern, Tupuri-Mambai.

Mambila, Cameroon (Mambilla, Mambere, Nor, Torbi, Lagubi, Tagbo, Tongbo, Bang, Ble, Juli, Bea) [mcu] 30,000 (1993 UBS). Adamawa Province, on Nigerian border in northwestern Mayo-Banyo Division, Banyo and Bankim subdivisions. *Class:* Niger-Congo, Atlantic-Congo, Volta-Congo, Benue-Congo, Bantoid, Northern, Mambiloid, Mambila-Konja, Mambila. *Dialects:* Ju Ba, Sunu Torbi (Torbi), Ju Naare (Mambila de Gembu), Langa. Closely related language: Mvanlip (Magu) in Nigeria. Close to Mambila of Nigeria, but different. Dialects form a chain; one end unintelligible to speakers of the other. Langa is inherently intelligible to speakers of some, but not most dialects. At least four dialects in Cameroon. *Lg Dev:* Dictionary. NT: 2001. *Other:* Traditional religion, Muslim.

Manta (Menta, Bantakpa, Banta, Anta, Kisam, Tinta) [myg] 5,300 (2001 SIL). South West Province, over a 30 km stretch in Manyu Division northeast of Mamfe, from the border of Mom (Akwaya Subdivision) to Manta (Mamfe Subdivision), approximately 20 villages. *Class:* Niger-Congo, Atlantic-Congo, Volta-Congo, Benue-Congo, Bantoid, Southern, Tivoid. *Dialects:* Atong is the closest known related language.

Masana (Masa, Massa, Walia, "Banana") [mcn] 103,000 in Cameroon (1982 SIL). Far North Province, southeastern Mayo-Danay Division, around Yagoua. *Dialects:* Yagwa (Yagoua), Domo, Walya, Bongor, Wina (Viri), Gizay (Guissey), Budugum. *Other:* The first three dialects listed are West Masa, Wina and Gizay are Central Masa. Traditional religion, Christian, Muslim. See main entry under Chad.

Maslam [msv] 250 in Cameroon (2004 SIL). Population total all countries: 723. Far North Province, Logone-and-Chari Division, Makari Subdivision, in Maltam and Saho northwest of Kousseri. Also spoken in Chad. *Class:* Afro-Asiatic, Chadic, Biu-Mandara, B, B.1, Kotoko Proper. *Dialects:* Maslam (Maltam), Sao (Sahu). Related to Afade, Mser, Lagwan, Malgbe, Mpade. Speakers may be able to use literature in one of those languages. *Lg Use:* In rapid decline. The young generation is not speaking it or only speak a reduced form (H. Tourneux).

Matal (Mouktele, Muktile, Muktele, Balda) [mfh] 18,000 (1982 SIL). Far North Province, Mayo-Sava Division, Mora Subdivision, southwest of Mora, to the south, eastern edge of Mandara Mountains. *Class:* Afro-Asiatic, Chadic, Biu-Mandara, A, A.5. *Lg Dev:* NT: 1989.

Mazagway (Mazagway-Hidi) [dkx] 17,000 (1997). North Province, Mayo-Louti Division, northwest of Guider; Far North Province, southwestern corner of Diamare Division, Ndoukoula Region. *Class:* Afro-Asiatic, Chadic, Biu-Mandara, A, A.7. *Dialects:*

Musgoi (Musgoy, Daba-Mousgoy), Kola (Daba-Kola, Kpala). *Lg Dev:* Bible portions: 1972. *Other:* Muslim, Christian.

Mbe' (Mbo, Mbaw) [mtk] 1,488 (2000 WCD). North West Province, Donga-Mantung Division, Nwa Subdivision, Canton of Mbo. *Class:* Niger-Congo, Atlantic-Congo, Volta-Congo, Benue-Congo, Bantoid, Southern, Wide Grassfields, Narrow Grassfields, Mbam-Nkam, Nkambe. *Other:* People are shifting to Tikar outside of the home. Distinct from Mbe of Nigeria, which is in the Ekoid group.

Mbedam [xmd] 6,000 (2001 SIL). Far North Province, Mayo-Tsanaga Division, Mokolo Subdivision, Northeast of Hina. *Class:* Afro-Asiatic, Chadic, Biu-Mandara, A, A.7. *Lg Use:* Positive language attitude. Schooling is in French. Some use Fulfulde as a second language. *Lg Dev:* Taught in primary schools. *Other:* Agriculturalists: millet, peanuts, rice, cotton.

Mbembe, Tigon (Tigum, Tigon, Tigong, Tigun, Tikun, Akonto) [nza] 36,000 in Cameroon (1982 SIL). Population total all countries: 56,000. North West Province, Donga-Mantung Division, Ako Subdivision, north of Nkambe. Also spoken in Nigeria. *Class:* Niger-Congo, Atlantic-Congo, Volta-Congo, Benue-Congo, Jukunoid, Central, Jukun-Mbembe-Wurbo, Mbembe. *Dialects:* Ashuku (Kitsipki), Nama (Dama, Namu), Nzare (Ndzale, Nsare, Izale, Izare, Njari), Kporo, Eneeme. *Lg Dev:* Literacy rate in second language: 15% to 25%. *Other:* Entirely different from Mbembe of Nigeria which is in Cross River group. Traditional religion.

Mbo (Mboo, Sambo) [mbo] 45,000 (1995 Ewane). Mbo plain: Littoral Province, Moungo Division, Nkongsamba and Melong subdivisions; West Province, Menoua Division, Santchou Subdivision and Upper Nkam Division, Kekem Subdivision. *Class:* Niger-Congo, Atlantic-Congo, Volta-Congo, Benue-Congo, Bantoid, Southern, Narrow Bantu, Northwest, A, Lundu-Balong (A.10), Ngoe. *Dialects:* Melong (Eho Mbo), Bareko (Ehow Mba, Minahe), Kekem (Nlembuu), Santchou (Nla Mboo). Related to Akoose and Bassossi. *Lg Dev:* Literacy rate in second language: 25%. *Other:* Different from Mbo of Democratic Republic of the Congo, which is Bantu D.30.

Mbonga (Mboa) [xmb] 1,488 (2000 WCD). East Province, Lom-and-Djerem Division, near Betare-Oya. *Class:* Niger-Congo, Atlantic-Congo, Volta-Congo, Benue-Congo, Bantoid, Southern, Jarawan, Cameroon.

Mbu' [muc] 1,000 (2001 SIL). North West Province, Menchum Division, Wum Subdivision, northeast of Wum, village of Mbu'. *Class:* Niger-Congo, Atlantic-Congo, Volta-Congo, Benue-Congo, Bantoid, Southern, Beboid, Western.

Mbuko (Mbuku, Mboku, Mbokou) [mqb] 13,000 (2002 SIL). Far North Province, Diamare Division, Meri Subdivision east of Meri, Mbuko massif and neighboring Mayo-Raneo plain. *Class:* Afro-Asiatic, Chadic, Biu-Mandara, A, A.5.

Mbule (Dumbule, Mbola) [mlb] 1,488 (2000 WCD). Center Province, Mbam Division, southern part of Bokito Subdivision, Mbola village. *Class:* Niger-Congo, Atlantic-Congo, Volta-Congo, Benue-Congo, Bantoid, Southern, Mbam, Yambasa (A.60). *Dialects:* Intelligibility of Yangben and Nu Baca is not fully determined. Related to Nu Baca, Elip, Mmaala.

Mbum (Mboum, Mboumtiba, Wuna, Buna) [mdd] 38,600 in Cameroon (1982 SIL). Population total all countries: 51,100. West Mbum is spread out in isolated groups: south and southwest of Ngaoundere (Adamawa Province, Vina and Djerem divisions); North Province, around Ngaoundere to border of Faro Reserve in Faro Division. Gbete is in East Province, Lom-and-Djerem Division, Belabo Subdivision. Not in Chad. Also spoken in Central

African Republic. *Class:* Niger-Congo, Atlantic-Congo, Volta-Congo, North, Adamawa-Ubangi, Adamawa, Mbum-Day, Mbum, Southern. *Dialects:* Mboum (West Mbum, Bum), Gbete (Kepere, Kpere, Pere, Ripere, Byrre, Pono, Vana). *Lg Use:* Speakers are rapidly becoming bilingual in Fulfulde. *Lg Dev:* Dictionary. Grammar. NT: 1965. *Other:* Muslim, traditional religion.

Medumba (Bagangte, Bangangte, Bamileke-Medumba) [byv] 210,000 (1991 UBS). West Province, major part of Nde Division, Tonga Subdivision and Bangangte Subdivision east of Bangangte. *Class:* Niger-Congo, Atlantic-Congo, Volta-Congo, Benue-Congo, Bantoid, Southern, Wide Grassfields, Narrow Grassfields, Mbam-Nkam, Bamileke. *Dialect:* Batongtou. *Lg Dev:* Literacy rate in second language: 15% to 25%. Bible: 1992. *Other:* Traditional religion, Christian.

Mefele (Bula, Bulahai, Boulahay) [mfj] 11,000 (2002 SIL). Far North Province, Mayo-Tsanaga Division, Mokolo Subdivision, south and east of Mokolo, 6 villages. *Class:* Afro-Asiatic, Chadic, Biu-Mandara, A, A.5. *Dialects:* Mefele, Serak (Sirak), Muhura (Mouhour), Shugule (Chougoule). *Lg Use:* Vigorous. All domains. Bilingualism in Fulfulde is increasing by those who travel, and in French by the few children in school. Bilingualism in Mafa appears to be increasing among the children, who learn it at school and market.

Mendankwe-Nkwen (Mandankwe, Mendankwe) [mfd] 23,050 (2001 SIL). North West Province, Mezam Division, Bamenda Central Subdivision, north and east of Bamenda, either side of Ring Road, and in the mountainous circle of Menda Nkwe. *Class:* Niger-Congo, Atlantic-Congo, Volta-Congo, Benue-Congo, Bantoid, Southern, Wide Grassfields, Narrow Grassfields, Mbam-Nkam, Ngemba. *Dialects:* Nkwen (Bafreng), Mendankwe (Munda, Bamenda). Mendankwe 74% intelligibility of Nkwen; Nkwen 79% intelligibility of Mendankwe. Socially very distinct groups. Related to Ngemba, Bafut, Pinyin, Awing, Bambili-Bambui. *Lg Dev:* Literacy rate in second language: 15% to 25%.

Mengaka (Ghap, Benzing, Megaka, Bamileke-Mengaka) [xmg] 20,000 (1993 SIL). West Province, Bamboutos Division, Southern Galim Subdivision, Bagam, Galim, and Bamendjing. *Class:* Niger-Congo, Atlantic-Congo, Volta-Congo, Benue-Congo, Bantoid, Southern, Wide Grassfields, Narrow Grassfields, Mbam-Nkam, Bamileke. *Dialect:* Bagam, Bamendjing (Bamendjin). Lexical similarity 91% among villages, but speakers report no dialect differences. *Lg Use:* Some bilingualism in French among younger speakers and Bamun among older ones. *Lg Dev:* Interest in language development for schools and individual literacy. Bagam script. *Other:* They call themselves 'Eghap'. Outsiders call them 'Bagam'. Distinct from Mungaka (Bali) which is Mbam-Nkam, Nun.

Mengisa (Mangisa, Mengisa-Njowe) [mct] 20,000 (1979 SIL). Center Province, Lekie Division, Sa'a Subdivision, along the bend of the Sanaga River between the river and Sa'a. *Class:* Niger-Congo, Atlantic-Congo, Volta-Congo, Benue-Congo, Bantoid, Southern, Narrow Bantu, Northwest, A, Yaunde-Fang (A.70). *Dialects:* May be intelligible with Ewondo. The Mangisa people are reported to speak 2 languages: Mengisa Njowi, spoken daily and Leti, a secret language of tradition.

Menka (Wando Bando, Mamwoh) [mea] 5,200 (2000 SIL). North West Province, Momo Division, Widikum-Menka Subdivision, west of Mbwengi, northwest of Batibo, in 10 villages. *Class:* Niger-Congo, Atlantic-Congo, Volta-Congo, Benue-Congo, Bantoid, Southern, Wide Grassfields, Narrow Grassfields, Momo. *Dialects:* Related to Atong and Manta.

Merey (Meri, Mere, Mofu de Meri) [meq] 10,000 (1982 SIL). Far North Province, Diamare Division, west of Meri on Meri Massif. *Class:* Afro-Asiatic, Chadic, Biu-Mandara, A, A.5. *Dialect:* Dugur. *Lg Dev:* Bible portions: 1986.

Mesaka (Ugare, Messaga, Messaga-Ekol, Messaka, Iyon, Banagere) [iyo] 14,000 (1982 SIL). South West Province, Manyu Division, on the Nigerian border northeast of Akwaya, in an isolated area. *Class:* Niger-Congo, Atlantic-Congo, Volta-Congo, Benue-Congo, Bantoid, Southern, Tivoid. *Dialect:* Batomo (Babasi). Batomo may be a separate language, or may be the same as Motomo (Oliti, Matchi), a dialect of Iceve-Maci. Lexical similarity 70% with Tiv. *Lg Use:* Speakers also use Tiv or Cameroon Pidgin. *Other:* 'Banagere' is the name used by the people for themselves, 'Ugare' for their language. 'Mesaka' is used by the government, 'Iyon' by the Tiv. Mountain slope. Traditional religion.

Meta' (Moghamo-Menemo, Menemo-Mogamo, Widikum-Tadkon, Chubo, Batibo, Metta, Bameta, Muta, Mitaa) [mgo] 87,000 (1982 SIL). North West Province, Momo Division, eastern and southeastern Mbengwi and eastern Batibo subdivisions; Bamenda Subdivision, around villages of Bafuchu and Nja. *Class:* Niger-Congo, Atlantic-Congo, Volta-Congo, Benue-Congo, Bantoid, Southern, Wide Grassfields, Narrow Grassfields, Momo. *Dialects:* Menemo (Metta, Meta', Uta', Bameta), Moghamo (Muywi, Iyirikum, Widekum, Tiwirkum, Batibo, Besi, Kugwe). *Lg Dev:* Literacy rate in second language: 50% to 75%.

Mfumte (Nfumte) [nfu] 24,700 (1982 SIL). North West Province, Donga-Mantung Division, Nwa Subdivision, mostly in canton of Mfumte north of Nwa and east of Nkambe, 14 villages. *Class:* Niger-Congo, Atlantic-Congo, Volta-Congo, Benue-Congo, Bantoid, Southern, Wide Grassfields, Narrow Grassfields, Mbam-Nkam, Nkambe. *Dialects:* Lus, Kom, Mballa, Bang, Koffa (Kofa), Jui, Mbat, Manang, Mbibji, Mbah. *Other:* Christian, traditional religion.

Mina (Hina, Besleri) [hna] 10,987 (2000 WCD). Far North Province, Mayo-Tsanaga Division, Hina Subdivision, south of Mokolo, 20 villages. *Class:* Afro-Asiatic, Chadic, Biu-Mandara, A, A.7. *Dialects:* Besleri, Jingjing (Dzumdzum), Gamdugun. *Lg Use:* Vigorous. All ages. Fulfulde is used at the market. French is learned in school, but few children attend school. Speakers are not generally bilingual in Daba. *Lg Dev:* Positive towards literacy. *Other:* Muslim, traditional religion.

Mmaala (Mmala, Benyi, Nuasue) [mmu] 5,300 (1982 SIL). Center Province, Mbam Division, Mmala canton, in and south of Bokito. *Class:* Niger-Congo, Atlantic-Congo, Volta-Congo, Benue-Congo, Bantoid, Southern, Mbam, Yambasa (A.60). *Dialects:* A standardized written form may be possible with Elip and Yangben, related languages. *Lg Use:* Used in religious services. Speakers do not think French will replace Mmaala. French is used for instruction in primary and secondary school. Ewondo or Bulu are used in other churches. Speakers acquire comprehension of Elip and Yangben in early adulthood.

Mmen (Bafmen, Bafumen, Bafmeng, Bafoumeng, Mme) [bfm] 35,000 (2001 SIL). Population includes 1,000 Fungom (1994 SIL). North West Province, Menchum Division, Wum Subdivision, along the Fundong Road northwest of Fundong. *Class:* Niger-Congo, Atlantic-Congo, Volta-Congo, Benue-Congo, Bantoid, Southern, Wide Grassfields, Narrow Grassfields, Ring, Center. *Dialects:* Fungom (Northern Fungom, We), Cha', Nyos. *Lg Dev:* Literacy rate in second language: 15% to 25% (Fungom). *Other:* Traditional religion, Christian.

Mofu, North (Mofu-Douvangar, Douvangar, Mofu-Nord) [mfk] 27,500 (1982 SIL). Far North Province, Diamare Division, Massifs south of Meri. *Class:* Afro-Asiatic,

Chadic, Biu-Mandara, A, A.5. *Dialects:* Douroun (Mofu de Douroum, Durum), Wazan (Wazang). *Lg Dev:* NT: 1975.

Mofu-Gudur (Mofou, Mofou de Goudour, Mofu-Sud, Mofu South) [mif] 60,000 (1998 SIL). Far North Province, Mayo-Tsanaga Division extending into Diamare Division, Mokolo Subdivision, massifs south of Tsanaga River to the Mayo-Louti River. *Class:* Afro-Asiatic, Chadic, Biu-Mandara, A, A.5. *Dialects:* Mokong, Gudur, Zidim, Dimeo, Massagal (Massakal), Njeleng. *Lg Dev:* Dictionary. Bible portions: 1985–1995.

Mokpwe (Bakweri, Bekwiri, Bakpwe, Bakwedi, Bakwele, Vakweli, Kwedi, Kweli, Kwili, Kwiri, Mokpe, Vambeng, Ujuwa) [bri] 32,200 (1982 SIL). South West Province, a large part of the Fako Division, Muyuka, Tiko, Buea, and Limbe subdivisions. *Class:* Niger-Congo, Atlantic-Congo, Volta-Congo, Benue-Congo, Bantoid, Southern, Narrow Bantu, Northwest, A, Duala (A.20). *Dialects:* Reported to include Wumboko. Literature may serve Wumboko, Bubia, and Isu. *Lg Use:* Widespread use of Cameroon Pidgin and Duala. *Lg Dev:* Literacy rate in second language: 15% to 25%.

Moloko (Molokwo, Mokyo, Molkoa, Molkwo, Molko, Melokwo) [mlw] 8,500 (1992 SIL). Far North Province, Mayo-Sava Division, Tokombere Subdivision, Makalingay Canton, on Melokwo Mountain and in the plains around its base. *Class:* Afro-Asiatic, Chadic, Biu-Mandara, A, A.5. *Dialects:* Only one dialect. Surrounded by 4 related languages (including Muyang, Giziga North, and the Mikiri dialect of Dugwor) plus one other. *Lg Use:* All domains. Little bilingualism except in outlying areas where there has been intermarriage with speakers of other languages. Fulfulde is used in the market, but interpretation is necessary when it is used in church. A few educated speakers can use French. *Other:* Christian.

Mom Jango (Vere, Verre, Were, Kobo) [ver] 6,523 in Cameroon (2000 WCD). North Province, Faro Division, Beka Subdivision, north of Tchamba on Nigerian border. See main entry under Nigeria.

Mono (Mon-Non) [mru] 300 (2001 SIL). North Province, Mayo-Rey Division, north of Rey-Bouba around Kongrong along the Mayo-Godi River. *Class:* Niger-Congo, Atlantic-Congo, Volta-Congo, North, Adamawa-Ubangi, Adamawa, Mbum-Day, Mbum, Northern, Dama-Galke. *Dialects:* Related to Dama. *Lg Use:* Speakers are older adults. Speakers are shifting to Fulfulde. *Other:* Distinct from Mono in Democratic Republic of the Congo in Banda group.

Mpade (Makari, Makary, Mendage, Mandage, Mandagué) [mpi] 16,000 in Cameroon (2004 SIL). Population total all countries: 18,366. Far North Province, Logone-and-Chari Division, centered around Makari next to Lake Chad, and Goulfey along the Chari River. Also spoken in Chad, Nigeria. *Class:* Afro-Asiatic, Chadic, Biu-Mandara, B, B.1, Kotoko Proper. *Dialects:* Shoe (Shawe, Chaoue, Schoe, Mani), Mpade (Makari), Bodo, Woulki, Digam.

Mpiemo (Mbimu, Mbimou, Mpyemo, Mpo, Bimu) [mcx] 5,000 in Cameroon (1991 SIL). East Province, Boumba-and-Ngoko Division, Gari-Gombo Subdivision along the road from Gribi to Yokadouma. *Dialects:* Jasua (Jasoa), Bidjuki (Bidjouki). *Lg Use:* Used in church together with Mpongmpong. *Other:* Traditional religion, Christian. See main entry under Central African Republic.

Mpongmpong (Mpompo, Bombo, Mpopo, Mbombo, Pongpong) [mgg] 45,000 (1991 SIL). East Province. Menzime and Bangantu are in Kadey Division, Mbang Subdivision, south of Batouri; other dialects cover most of the Boumba-and-Ngoko Division, south and west of Yokadouma. *Class:* Niger-Congo, Atlantic-Congo, Volta-Congo, Benue-Congo, Bantoid, Southern, Narrow Bantu, Northwest, A, Makaa-Njem (A.80). *Dialects:* Mbobyeng (Pobyeng), Menzime (Medzime, Mezime, Mendzime), Bageto (Baagato, Bangantu, Northern Bangantu), Kunabembe (Konabembe, Nkumabem, Kunabeeb, Konabem), Mpomam (Boman, Mboman). *Lg Use:* A few speakers understand Ewondo. *Lg Dev:* Radio programs.

Mser (Kotoko-Kuseri, Kuseri, Kouseri, Kousseri, Mandage) [kqx] 500 in Cameroon (2004 SIL). Far North Province, Logone-and-Chari Division, Kousseri Subdivision. Also spoken in Chad. *Class:* Afro-Asiatic, Chadic, Biu-Mandara, B, B.1, Kotoko Proper. *Dialects:* Mser (Kousseri), Kalo (Kalakafra), Gawi, Houlouf, Kabe. Related to Afade, Lagwan, Malgbe, Maslam, Mpade. Comprehension of Lagwan is marginal. *Lg Use:* In rapid decline. The young generation is not speaking it or only speak a reduced form (H Tourneux). *Other:* Muslim.

Mundabli (Bu) [boe] 1,000 (2001 SIL). North West Province, Menchum Division, Wum Subdivision, northeast of Wum, villages of Mundabli, Bu, and Ngwen. *Class:* Niger-Congo, Atlantic-Congo, Volta-Congo, Benue-Congo, Bantoid, Southern, Beboid, Western.

Mundang (Moundang, Moundan, Kaele, Nda, Marhay, Musemban) [mua] 44,700 in Cameroon (1982 SIL). Far North Province, Kaele Division, Kaele Subdivision, near Chad border to north and west of Kaele; North Province, Benoue Division, south of Mayo-Kebi near Chad border. The Torrock-Kaele subdialect of Zasing is spoken in Kaele and Torrock, Cameroon. *Dialects:* Kiziere, Imbana (Bana, Mbana, Imbara), Zasing (Yassing, Djasing, Yasing, Jasing, Zazing), Gelama. *Other:* Gelama may be a separate language. Traditional religion, Christian. See main entry under Chad.

Mundani [mnf] 34,000 (1987 SIL). South West Province, Manyu Division, Mamfe and northern Fontem subdivisions, south of Batibo. *Class:* Niger-Congo, Atlantic-Congo, Volta-Congo, Benue-Congo, Bantoid, Southern, Wide Grassfields, Narrow Grassfields, Momo. *Dialects:* Bamumbo (Bamumbu), Bechati, Besali, Banti, Folepi, Iguambo (Igumbo), Bangang, Nko (Nkong). *Lg Dev:* Literacy rate in first language: 5% to 10%. Literacy rate in second language: 25% to 50%. Dictionary. Bible portions: 1989–1990. *Other:* Mountain slope.

Mungaka (Bali, Li, Ngaaka, Nga'ka, Munga'ka) [mhk] 50,100 (1982 SIL). North West Province, Mezam Division, Bali Subdivision; West Province, Bamboutos Division, southeastern Galim Subdivision and Mifi Division, northern Bafoussam Subdivision. *Class:* Niger-Congo, Atlantic-Congo, Volta-Congo, Benue-Congo, Bantoid, Southern, Wide Grassfields, Narrow Grassfields, Mbam-Nkam, Nun. *Dialects:* Bali Nyonga (Bali), Ti (Bati), Nde (Bandeng). *Lg Dev:* Literacy rate in second language: 25% to 50%. Bible: 1961. *Other:* People are called 'Bali'. Different from three languages in Democratic Republic of the Congo called 'Bali', Bali of Nigeria, or Bali which is a dialect of Chamba of Nigeria and Cameroon, although many of these people have Chamba ethnic origins. Traditional religion, Christian.

Musey (Musiina, Musaya, Musoi, Moussei, Musei, Mussoi, Moussey, Mussoy, Mosi, Bananna, Bananna Ho, Ho, Museyna) [mse] 20,000 in Cameroon. Far North Province, Mayo-Danay Division, east of Guere on Chad border. *Dialect:* Pe. *Other:* Traditional religion. See main entry under Chad.

Musgu (Mousgou, Mousgoun, Musgum, Mousgoum, Musuk, Muzuk, Munjuk, Mulwi) [mug] 61,500 in Cameroon (1982 SIL). Population total all countries: 85,908. Far North Province, Mayo-Danay Division, Entire Maga Subdivision. Also spoken in Chad. *Class:* Afro-Asiatic, Chadic, Biu-Mandara, B, B.2. *Dialects:* Mpus (Pus, Pouss, Mousgoum de Pouss), Beege (Jafga), Vulum (Vlum, Mulwi), Ngilemong, Luggoy, Maniling (Mani-Iling), Muzuk (Mousgoum de Guirvidig). Vulum dialect is mainly in Chad. *Lg Dev:* NT: 1964. *Other:* They call themselves 'Mulwi'. Traditional religion, Muslim.

Muyang (Myau, Myenge, Muyenge, Mouyenge, Mouyengue) [muy] 15,000 (1982 SIL). Far North Province, Mayo-Sava Division, northeast of Tokombere, Muyang, Mougouba, Gouadagouada, and Palbarar massifs. *Class:* Afro-Asiatic, Chadic, Biu-Mandara, A, A.5.

Nagumi (Bama, Mbama) [ngv] Extinct. Formerly spoken in North Province, Benoue Division, Garoua Subdivision between Benoue and Faro rivers and Poli Mountains. *Class:* Niger-Congo, Atlantic-Congo, Volta-Congo, Benue-Congo, Bantoid, Southern, Jarawan, Cameroon. *Other:* Voegelin and Voegelin (1977:55) say this was the same as Ngong.

Naki (Mekaf, Munkaf, Nkap, Bunaki) [mff] 3,000 (1993 R. Breton). Population includes 300 in Nse chiefdom. North West Province, Menchum Division, Furu-Awa Subdivision, Nse chiefdom, Naki, Mekaf, Bukpang II, and Lebo villages. *Class:* Niger-Congo, Atlantic-Congo, Volta-Congo, Benue-Congo, Bantoid, Southern, Beboid, Eastern. *Dialects:* Member of the Eastern Beboid cluster. *Lg Use:* In Nse chiefdom they speak Nsaa and are called 'Bunsaa'. Some speakers also use Nse or Lebo, although Jukun is the trade language. In Bukpang II few speak Jukun. Cameroon Pidgin is used in the area. *Other:* The people are called 'Bunaki'.

Ncane (Nchanti, Ntshanti, Cane) [ncr] 15,500 (2002 SIL). North West Province, Donga-Mantung Division, western Nkambe Subdivision, Nkanchi, Nfume, Chunge, Bem, Kibbo and Mungong villages. *Class:* Niger-Congo, Atlantic-Congo, Volta-Congo, Benue-Congo, Bantoid, Southern, Beboid, Eastern. *Dialect:* Ncane, Mungong (Mungom). Member of the Eastern Beboid cluster. Lexical similarity 84% with Nsari, 88% with Noone. *Lg Use:* All domains. Churches use Cameroon Pidgin and English. Schooling is in English. *Other:* Hills. Agriculturalists; traders.

Ndai (Galke, Pormi) [gke] 5. North Province, Mayo-Rey Division, Tchollire. *Class:* Niger-Congo, Atlantic-Congo, Volta-Congo, North, Adamawa-Ubangi, Adamawa, Mbum-Day, Mbum, Northern, Dama-Galke. *Lg Use:* All speakers are older adults. Language shift to Fulfulde. *Other:* Nearly extinct.

Ndaktup [ncp] 2,975 (2000 WCD). North West Province, Donga-Mantung Division, northeast of Nkambe. *Class:* Niger-Congo, Atlantic-Congo, Volta-Congo, Benue-Congo, Bantoid, Southern, Wide Grassfields, Narrow Grassfields, Mbam-Nkam, Nkambe. *Dialect:* Ncha, Bitui (Bitwi). Possibly intelligible with or bilingual in other Mfumte languages. *Other:* Speakers consider themselves to be ethnically Mfumte.

Nda'nda' (Bamileke-Nda'nda') [nnz] 10,000 (1990 SIL). West Province, straddling Upper Nkam (east of Bana), Nde (north and west of Bangante), and Mifi (south of Bangou) divisions. *Class:* Niger-Congo, Atlantic-Congo, Volta-Congo, Benue-Congo, Bantoid, Southern, Wide Grassfields, Narrow Grassfields, Mbam-Nkam, Bamileke. *Dialects:* Undimeha (East Nda'nda'), Ungameha (West Nda'nda'-South Nda'nda'). Batoufam is a subdialect of East Nda'nda'. *Lg Use:* Speakers also use French. *Lg Dev:* Literacy rate in second language: 15% to 25%.

Ndemli (Ndemba, Bandem, Bayong) [nml] 5,950 (2000 WCD). Littoral Province, Nkam Division, between Yabassi, Yingui, and Nkondjok. *Class:* Niger-Congo, Atlantic-Congo, Volta-Congo, Benue-Congo, Bantoid, Southern, Ndemli. *Dialects:* Related to Tikar and Bandobo. May be the same as Bandobo.

Ndoola (Ndoro, Njoyame, Nundoro) [ndr] 2,120 in Cameroon (2000 WCD). Adamawa Province, Faro-and-Deo Division, southern Mayo-Baleo Subdivision, on the upper Mayo-Deo River, Dodeo village near the Nigerian border; North West Province, Donga-Mantung Division, north of Nkambe. See main entry under Nigeria.

Ngamambo (Mbu, Mungyen, Bafuchu, Banja, Nga, Ngembo) [nbv] 8,000 (2002 SIL). North West Province, Momo Division, eastern and southeastern Mbengwi and eastern Batibo subdivisions; Mezam Division, Santa Subdivision, around villages of Bafuchu and Nja. *Class:* Niger-Congo, Atlantic-Congo, Volta-Congo, Benue-Congo, Bantoid, Southern, Wide Grassfields, Narrow Grassfields, Momo. *Dialects:* Lexical similarity 88% with Meta' and Moghamo. *Lg Dev:* Literacy rate in second language: 50% to 75%.

Ngambay (Sara, Sara Ngambai, Gamba, Gambaye, Gamb-Lai, Ngambai, Gambai) [sba] North Province, along the route to Garoua, Mayo-Rey Division, Rey-Bouba Subdivision, near the Chad border east of Tchollire; Benoue Division, in Garoua. Primarily in Chad, some in Nigeria. See main entry under Chad.

Ngemba (Megimba, Mogimba, Ngomba, Nguemba) [nge] 18,800 (2002 SIL). North West Province, Mezam Division, Tuba and western Bamenda subdivisions. *Class:* Niger-Congo, Atlantic-Congo, Volta-Congo, Benue-Congo, Bantoid, Southern, Wide Grassfields, Narrow Grassfields, Mbam-Nkam, Ngemba. *Dialects:* Bagangu (Akum), Njong (Banjong), Mbutu (Bambutu, Alamatu, Mbotu), Songwa (Nsongwa, Bangwa, Ngwa), Mankon (Bida), Shomba (Bamechom, Almatson), Mangkunge (Ngemba, Bandeng, Bande, Bande', Nkune, Mukohn), Mbrerewi (Mundum 1, Bamundum 1), Anyang (Mundum 2, Bamundum 2), Alatening (Alatining). Related to Bafut, Mandankwe, Pinyin, Awing. Distinct from Ngiemboon (Nguemba). Lexical similarity of Mbrerewi dialect 87% with Anyang dialect, of Mbrerewi dialect 78% with Bafut, of Mbrerewi dialect 82% with Mankon dialect, of Bafut 74% with Mankon dialect. *Lg Use:* Speakers also use Cameroon Pidgin or Bafut.

Ngie (Ngi, Angie, Baninge, Baminge, Mingi, Ugie, Ungie) [ngj] 37,000 (2001 SIL). North West Province, Momo Division, western Mbengwi Subdivision, around Andek. *Class:* Niger-Congo, Atlantic-Congo, Volta-Congo, Benue-Congo, Bantoid, Southern, Wide Grassfields, Narrow Grassfields, Momo. *Dialect:* Mengum. Lexical similarity 56% between Ngie and Mengum. Mengum may therefore be a separate language. *Lg Dev:* Literacy rate in second language: 15% to 25%.

Ngiemboon (Nguemba, Ngyemboon, Bamileke-Ngyemboon, Bamileke-Ngiemboon) [nnh] 100,000 (1987 SIL). 50,000 monolinguals. West Province, Bamboutos Division, Batcham Subdivision and western Mbouda Subdivision in Balatchi; Menoua Division, north of Penka-Michel. *Class:* Niger-Congo, Atlantic-Congo, Volta-Congo, Benue-Congo, Bantoid, Southern, Wide Grassfields, Narrow Grassfields, Mbam-Nkam, Bamileke. *Dialects:* Batcham, Balatchi, Bamoungong. *Lg Use:* Vigorous. All domains. Oral use in traditional religion, oral and written in church, oral use in commerce. Positive language attitude. 50% speak French or 1% English as other languages. A few also speak Fulani. *Lg Dev:* Literacy rate in second language: 25% to 50%. Radio programs. Bible portions: 1984–1999. *Other:* Distinct from Ngemba. Foot of Mt. Bamboutos, red soil. Savannah. Agriculturalists: various crops, coffee. Traditional religion, Christian.

Ngomba (Ndaa, Nda'a, Bamileke-Ngomba) [jgo] 63,000 (1999 SIL). West Province, Bamboutos Division, southern Mbouda Subdivision, southeast of Mbouda, 5 villages; each a separate dialect. *Class:* Niger-Congo, Atlantic-Congo, Volta-Congo, Benue-Congo, Bantoid, Southern, Wide Grassfields, Narrow Grassfields, Mbam-Nkam, Bamileke. *Dialects:* Bamendjinda, Bamenkumbo, Bamesso, Babete (Bamete), Bamendjo. Dialect speakers appear to understand each other well. Bamendjinda, Bamesso, and Bamenkumbo are the most similar. *Lg Use:* All domains. Interest expressed in language development. Second languages are French and Cameroon Pidgin. Church languages are Ngomba, French, Ngiemboon, Medumba, or Bafunda. *Lg Dev:* Literacy rate in second language: 15% to 25%. *Other:* 'Nda'a' is their name for themselves. Bafounda is a separate town and language (see Ghomala), but ethnically Nda'a. Different from Ngumba in the Maka-Njem group.

Ngombale (Bamileke-Ngombale) [nla] 45,000 (1993 SIL). West Province, Bamboutos Division, northern Mbouda Subdivision, northwest of Mbouda. *Class:* Niger-Congo, Atlantic-Congo, Volta-Congo, Benue-Congo, Bantoid, Southern, Wide Grassfields, Narrow Grassfields, Mbam-Nkam, Bamileke. *Dialects:* Babadjou (Basso, Nchobela), Bamessingue (Bassing). *Lg Use:* Interest expressed in language development. All domains, including religious services. Many adults are bilingual in Ngomba and Ngiemboon, and young people in French. Cameroon Pidgin is also used. *Lg Dev:* Literacy rate in second language: 15% to 25%. *Other:* Traders. Traditional religion, Christian.

Ngong (Gong, Puuri, Nagumi) [nnx] 2 (1983 Atlas Linguistique du Cameroun). North Province, Benoue Division, south of Garoua on road to Ngaoundere, Ngong village. *Class:* Niger-Congo, Atlantic-Congo, Volta-Congo, Benue-Congo, Bantoid, Southern, Jarawan, Cameroon. *Other:* Voegelin and Voegelin (1977:55) say this is the same as Nagumi. Nearly extinct.

Ngoshie (Oshie, Ngishe) [nsh] 9,200 (2001 SIL). North West Province, Momo Division, eastern Njikwa Subdivision. *Class:* Niger-Congo, Atlantic-Congo, Volta-Congo, Benue-Congo, Bantoid, Southern, Wide Grassfields, Narrow Grassfields, Momo. *Lg Dev:* Literacy rate in second language: 15% to 25%.

Ngumba [nmg] 9,000 in Cameroon (1982 SIL). Population total all countries: 17,500. South Province, Ocean Division, Kribi and Lolodorf subdivisions, in forests around Kribi, and along the road from Kribi to Lolodorf. Also spoken in Equatorial Guinea. *Class:* Niger-Congo, Atlantic-Congo, Volta-Congo, Benue-Congo, Bantoid, Southern, Narrow Bantu, Northwest, A, Makaa-Njem (A.80). *Dialects:* Kwasio (Kwassio, Bisio), Mvumbo (Ngumba, Ngoumba, Mgoumba, Mekuk), Mabi (Mabea). *Lg Dev:* Bible portions: 1957. *Other:* Distinct from Ngomba, which is in West Province. Christian, traditional religion.

Ngwe (Nwe, Fontem, Fomopea, Bamileke-Ngwe) [nwe] 73,200 (2001 SIL). South West Province, most of Lebialem Division. *Class:* Niger-Congo, Atlantic-Congo, Volta-Congo, Benue-Congo, Bantoid, Southern, Wide Grassfields, Narrow Grassfields, Mbam-Nkam, Bamileke. *Other:* Part of a language cluster which includes Yemba and Ngiemboon.

Ngwo (Ngwaw) [ngn] 50,547 (2000 WCD). North West Province, Momo Division, Njikwa Subdivision. *Class:* Niger-Congo, Atlantic-Congo, Volta-Congo, Benue-Congo, Bantoid, Southern, Wide Grassfields, Narrow Grassfields, Momo. *Dialects:* Ngwo (Nguni, Ngwaw, Miguhni, Ngunu), Konda, Basa (Bassa), Ikweri (Ekperi), Banya, Bako, Okorobi, Zang. *Lg Dev:* Literacy rate in first language: below 1%. Literacy rate in second language: 15% to 25%.

Nimbari (Nyamnyam, Niamniam, Bari, Nimbari-Kebi, Nyam-Nyam du Mayo-Kebi) [nmr] 130 (2002 SIL). North Province, Benoue Division, Basheo Subdivision, Gorimbari village; Mayo-Louti Division, Guider Subdivision, Padjara-Djabi and Badjire villages. None in Chad or Nigeria. *Class:* Niger-Congo, Atlantic-Congo, Volta-Congo, North, Adamawa-Ubangi,

Adamawa, Leko-Nimbari, Nimbari. *Other:* Different from Suga (Nyamnyam).

Njen (Nyen, Nzin) [njj] 1,800 (2002 SIL). North West Province, Momo Division, southeast of Batibo, village of Njen. *Class:* Niger-Congo, Atlantic-Congo, Volta-Congo, Benue-Congo, Bantoid, Southern, Wide Grassfields, Narrow Grassfields, Momo. *Dialects:* Lexical similarity 47% with Moghamo. *Lg Use:* Many also speak Moghamo.

Njyem (Ndzem, Dzem, Nyem, Ndjem, Njem, Djem, Ndjeme, Ngyeme) [njy] 3,500 in Cameroon (2003 SIL). 85% monolingual. Population total all countries: 7,000. East Province, Upper Nyong Division, in Ngoila Subdivision. Also spoken in Congo. *Class:* Niger-Congo, Atlantic-Congo, Volta-Congo, Benue-Congo, Bantoid, Southern, Narrow Bantu, Northwest, A, Makaa-Njem (A.80). *Lg Use:* Many Baka Pygmies speak it as a second language. All domains, public discourse, promulgate government information, oral and written use in church, oral literature. Positive language attitude. 15% speak French as second language. *Lg Dev:* 50 can read it, 10 can write it. Bible portions: 2002. *Other:* Hills. Tropical forest, some swamp. Agriculturalists: coffee, cocoa; trappers. Christian.

Nkongho (Kinkwa, Lekongo, Upper Mbo) [nkc] 2,231 (2000 WCD). South West Province, Kupe-Muanenguba Division, Nguti Subdivision. *Class:* Niger-Congo, Atlantic-Congo, Volta-Congo, Benue-Congo, Bantoid, Southern, Narrow Bantu, Northwest, A, Lundu-Balong (A.10). *Lg Dev:* Literacy rate in second language: 15% to 25%.

Nomaande (Noomaante, Numand, Lemande, Mandi, Mande, Pimenc) [lem] 6,000 (1982 SIL). Center Province, Mbam Division, western and northern Bokito Subdivision, southwest of Bafia. *Class:* Niger-Congo, Atlantic-Congo, Volta-Congo, Benue-Congo, Bantoid, Southern, Mbam, West (A.40). *Lg Dev:* Literacy rate in second language: 25% to 50%. Bible portions: 1994–1998.

Noone (Noni, Nooni) [nhu] 25,000 (2001 SIL). North West Province, Bui Division, northwestern Kumbo Subdivision. *Class:* Niger-Congo, Atlantic-Congo, Volta-Congo, Benue-Congo, Bantoid, Southern, Beboid, Eastern. *Dialects:* Member of the Eastern Beboid cluster. Lexical similarity 88% with Ncane. *Lg Dev:* Literacy rate in second language: 25% to 50%. Dictionary.

Nsari (Akweto, Pesaa, Sali) [asj] 7,000 (2001 SIL). North West Province, Donga-Mantung Division, western part of Nkambe Subdivision, on both sides of Ring Road between Misaje and Nkambe, three villages: Mbissa, Kamine, and Akweto. *Class:* Niger-Congo, Atlantic-Congo, Volta-Congo, Benue-Congo, Bantoid, Southern, Beboid, Eastern. *Dialects:* Member of the Eastern Beboid cluster. Lexical similarity 84% with Ncane. *Lg Use:* Some bilingualism in Ncane and Cameroon Pidgin. Schooling is in English. *Other:* Agriculturalists.

Nubaca (Bango, Bongo, Baca, Nu Baca) [baf] 800 (1994 SIL). Center Province, Mbam Division, Bokito Subdivision, Yangben Canton, south of Yangben, village of Bongo, 4 quarters. *Class:* Niger-Congo, Atlantic-Congo, Volta-Congo, Benue-Congo, Bantoid, Southern, Mbam, Yambasa (A.60). *Dialects:* No significant dialect differences. Not intelligible with other Yambassa language varieties. Related to Elip, Dumbule, and Mmaala. *Lg Use:* French used by the younger generation as their main language. Ewondo is understood by most of the older generation. Basaa is only used by the older generation, not the youth. French is learned and spoken from early childhood in school, and in nearly every aspect of daily life, including the family, although interpretation into Nubaca is made in church.

Nugunu (Gunu, Gounou, Nu Gunu, Yambassa, Yambasa, Ombessa, Beke, Behie) [yas] 35,000 (1987 SIL). Center

Province, Mbam Division, Ombessa and Bokito subdivisions, in and around Ombessa to southwest. *Class:* Niger-Congo, Atlantic-Congo, Volta-Congo, Benue-Congo, Bantoid, Southern, Mbam, Yambasa (A.60). *Dialects:* Northern Gunu, Southern Gunu. *Lg Dev:* Literacy rate in second language: 50% to 75%.

Nyong (Daganyonga, Daganonga, Nyongnepa, Mumbake, Mubako, Ndagam, Samba Bali) [muo] 17,000 in Cameroon (1987 census). North West Province, Ngo-Ketunjia Division, near the Ndop Plain in Balikumbat, Baligansin, and Baligashu villages; Mezam Division, Baligham. Also spoken in Nigeria. *Class:* Niger-Congo, Atlantic-Congo, Volta-Congo, North, Adamawa-Ubangi, Adamawa, Leko-Nimbari, Leko. *Dialects:* They consider themselves to be the same ethnically as speakers of Samba Leko, but there is significant difficulty in inherent intelligibility. *Lg Use:* Speakers use Cameroon Pidgin (generally spoken and understood) or Standard English (by those educated beyond primary level) as second languages. *Other:* The people are called 'Chamba', 'Samba', 'Chamba-Bali', or 'Samba-Bali'. Traditional religion, Christian.

Nzakambay (Nzakmbay, Mbay, Nzak Mbai, Nzak Mbay) [nzy] 12,998 in Cameroon (2000 WCD). North Province, Mayo-Rey Division, Touboro Subdivision, around Touboro. *Dialect:* Gonge (Ngonge). *Lg Dev:* Literacy rate in second language: 15% to 25%. See main entry under Chad.

Nzanyi (Njanyi, Nzangi, Zani, Zany, Njeny, Jeng, Njegn, Njeng, Njai, Njei, Mzangyim, Kobochi, Kobotshi) [nja] 9,000 in Cameroon. North Province, Mayo-Louti Division, Mayo-Oulo Subdivision, west of Dourbeye near Nigerian border in Doumo Region. *Dialect:* Holma. *Other:* Muslim, traditional religion. See main entry under Nigeria.

Oblo [obl] Benoue Division, Pitoa Subdivision, around Gobtikéré, Ouro Bé, and Ouro Badjouma. *Class:* Niger-Congo, Atlantic-Congo, Volta-Congo, North, Adamawa-Ubangi, Adamawa, Unclassified. *Lg Use:* Possibly extinct. *Other:* Nearly extinct.

Oku (Kuo, Ebkuo, Ekpwo, Bvukoo, Uku, Ukfwo) [oku] 40,000 (1991 SIL). North West Province, Bui Division, western Jakiri Subdivision, around Mt. Oku and Lake Oku. *Class:* Niger-Congo, Atlantic-Congo, Volta-Congo, Benue-Congo, Bantoid, Southern, Wide Grassfields, Narrow Grassfields, Ring, Center. *Lg Dev:* Literacy rate in second language: 5% to 15%. *Other:* Distinct from Kuo which is Adamawa.

Oroko (Oroko-East, Oroko-West, Bakundu-Balue) [bdu] 105,985 (2000 WCD). South West Province, Meme Division, Kumba Subdivision, west, north, and south of Kumba; Ndian Division, eastern Ekondo-Titi Subdivision. *Class:* Niger-Congo, Atlantic-Congo, Volta-Congo, Benue-Congo, Bantoid, Southern, Narrow Bantu, Northwest, A, Lundu-Balong (A.10), Oroko. *Dialects:* Lokundu (Bakundu, Kundu, Lakundu, Bekunde, Bawo, Nkundu), Lolue (Balue, Barue, Babue, Western Kundu, Lue), Mbonge, Ekombe (Bekombo, Ekumbe), Londo (Balondo Ba Nanga, Balondo Ba Diko), Longolo (Ngolo), Bima, Lotanga (Batanga), Lokoko (Bakoko). Batanga is distinct from Batanga (Banoho) of Bantu A.30, and the Batanga dialect of Caka; Bakoko is distinct from Bakoko of Bantu A.40. *Other:* Traditional religion.

Osatu (Ossatu, Ihatum) [ost] 400 (2002 SIL). South West Province, Manyu Division, Akwaya Subdivision, southeast of Asumbo. *Class:* Niger-Congo, Atlantic-Congo, Volta-Congo, Benue-Congo, Bantoid, Southern, Tivoid. *Dialects:* Lexical similarity 60% with Balo, 40% with Ipulo and Caka, 35% with Mesaka and Esimbi. *Lg Use:* Speakers also use Cameroon Pidgin. *Lg Dev:* Literacy is in English. *Other:* Mountain slope. Traditional religion.

Pam [pmn] 30 (2003 SIL). North Province, Mayo-Rey Division, near Tchollire. *Class:* Niger-Congo,

Atlantic-Congo, Volta-Congo, North, Adamawa-Ubangi, Adamawa, Mbum-Day, Mbum, Unclassified. *Lg Use:* Speakers are older adults. Language shift to Fulfulde. *Other:* Nearly extinct.

Pana (Pani) [pnz] 2,975 in Cameroon (2000 WCD). North Province, Mayo-Rey Division, Touboro Subdivision. Some are in urban areas. *Dialect:* Man. *Other:* Man may be a separate language. See main entry under Central African Republic.

Parkwa (Podoko, Paduko, Podokwo, Podogo, Padogo, Padokwa, Pawdawkwa, Parekwa, Gwadi Parekwa, Kudala) [pbi] 30,000 (1993 SIL). Far North Province, Mayo-Sava Division, Mora Subdivision, west and southwest of Mora. *Class:* Afro-Asiatic, Chadic, Biu-Mandara, A, A.4, Mandara Proper, Podoko. *Lg Dev:* Dictionary. NT: 1992. *Other:* Traditional religion.

Peere (Pere, Peer, Kutin, Koutin, Koutine, Kutine, Kutinn, Kotopo, Kotofo, Kotpojo, Potopo, Potopore, Patapori) [pfe] 15,000 in Cameroon (1993). Northwestern Tignere Subdivision between Tignere and Nigerian border, Faro and Deo Division; northeast of Banyo, Mayo-Banyo Division, Adamawa Province. Also spoken in Nigeria. *Class:* Niger-Congo, Atlantic-Congo, Volta-Congo, North, Adamawa-Ubangi, Adamawa, Leko-Nimbari, Duru, Voko-Dowayo, Kutin. *Dialects:* Peer Muure, Zongbi (Djonbi), Dan Muure (Potopo, Kotopo, Kpotopo, Kotofo). *Lg Dev:* Dictionary. Grammar. NT: 1986. *Other:* 'Peer' is the name the people use for themselves. Primer. Traditional religion.

Péve (Ka'do, Lamé) [lme] 5,720 in Cameroon (2000 WCD). North Province, Mayo-Rey Division, northeast of Tchollire around Bouba-Ndjida Park. *Other:* Different from Lame of Nigeria. See main entry under Chad.

Pidgin, Cameroon (Wes Cos, Cameroon Creole English) [wes] Primarily in South West and North West provinces, and widespread elsewhere. *Class:* Creole, English based, Atlantic, Krio. *Dialects:* Similar to Krio of Sierra Leone and Pidgin English of various West African countries; probably an offshoot of 19th century Krio. Also similar to Sranan (Ian Hancock). There are dialect variations. *Lg Use:* Trade language. 2,000,000 mainly second-language users (1989 UBSA). Growing number of first-language speakers. Used by the police, prisons, urban school children at play since 1884. Now the most widespread lingua franca in Cameroon, used by about half the population (Todd and Hancock 1986). *Lg Dev:* NT: 2002.

Pinyin (Bapinyi, Pelimpo) [pny] 24,600 (2001 SIL). North West Province, Mezam Division, southwestern Bamenda Subdivision, southwest of Bamenda. *Class:* Niger-Congo, Atlantic-Congo, Volta-Congo, Benue-Congo, Bantoid, Southern, Wide Grassfields, Narrow Grassfields, Mbam-Nkam, Ngemba. *Dialects:* Related to Awing, Ngemba, Bafut, Mendankwe-Nkwen. *Lg Dev:* Literacy rate in second language: 15% to 25%.

Pol (Pori, Pomo, Pul, Congo Pol) [pmm] 38,676 in Cameroon (2000 WCD). Population total all countries: 44,109. East Province, Upper Nyong Division, Dimako Subdivision, east of Doume; Lom and Djerem Division, east of Belabo. Not in Central African Republic. Also spoken in Congo. *Class:* Niger-Congo, Atlantic-Congo, Volta-Congo, Benue-Congo, Bantoid, Southern, Narrow Bantu, Northwest, A, Kako (A.90). *Dialects:* Azom (Pori Asom, Asom), Bobili, Dondi, Mambaya, Pori Kinda (Kinda).

Psikye (Kapsiki, Kamsiki, Ptsake) [kvj] 40,500 in Cameroon (1982 SIL). Population total all countries: 52,500. Far North Province, Mayo-Tsanaga Division, southwestern part of Mokolo Subdivision. Some in Nigeria. Also spoken in Nigeria. *Class:* Afro-Asiatic, Chadic, Biu-Mandara, A, A.3. *Dialects:* Psikye (Kapsiki,

Kamu), Zlenge. Close to Hya and Kamwe of Nigeria. *Lg Dev:* NT: 1988. *Other:* Traditional religion.

Samba Leko (Chamba Leeko, Samba) [ndi] North Province, Faro Division, approximately between Tchamba and the Mayo-Louti River, west of Poli and in south Beka Subdivision along the Nigerian border. *Dialects:* Samba Leko (Ndii, Lekon, Lego, Leko, Laeko, Suntai), Deenu (Koola), Bangla, Samba de Wangai, Sampara. *Other:* Different from Samba Daka. See main entry under Nigeria.

Sharwa (Tchevi, Sherwin, Sarwaye) [swq] 5,100 (2000 SIL). Far North Province, Mayo-Tsanaga Division, Southern Bourrah Subdivision; a few in North Province, Mayo-Louti Division. *Class:* Afro-Asiatic, Chadic, Biu-Mandara, A, A.8. *Lg Use:* Signs of language shift to Fulfulde. *Other:* Different from Sarua (Sarwa) of Chad. Muslim.

So (Sso, Shwo, Fo) [sox] 9,000 (1992 SIL). Center Province, Nyong-and-Mfoumou Division, Akonolinga Subdivision, Melan and Emvane cantons; East Province, a few in Upper Nyong Division. *Class:* Niger-Congo, Atlantic-Congo, Volta-Congo, Benue-Congo, Bantoid, Southern, Narrow Bantu, Northwest, A, Makaa-Njem (A.80). *Dialects:* Melan So, Emvane So. The two dialects have vocabulary and pronunciation differences, but no reported problem with intelligibility between them. Melan So has been influenced by Beti (Ewondo and Bulu). *Lg Use:* So is the language of the home and village. Beti is also used in home and village. Children are increasingly learning Beti and French. Beti is used in church and the marketplace. There is a lot of intermarriage with the Beti. French is used in schools and government offices. *Other:* Different from So (Heso) of Democratic Republic of the Congo.

Suga (Nizaa, Ssuga, Galim, "Nyamnyam," "Njemnjem," "Jemjem") [sgi] 10,000 (1985). Adamawa Province, Faro-and-Deo Division, around Galim southwest of Tignere; Mayo-Banyo Division, northern Banyo Subdivision, around Sambolabbo. *Class:* Niger-Congo, Atlantic-Congo, Volta-Congo, Benue-Congo, Bantoid, Northern, Mambiloid, Suga-Vute, Suga. *Lg Dev:* Literacy rate in second language: A few adults in Fulfulde, Arabic script. Few can read Roman script. Dictionary. Grammar. *Other:* Different from Nimbari (Nyamnyam) of Cameroon. 'Sewe' may be an alternate name. 'Baghap' is their name for themselves; 'Nizaa' for their language. Agriculturalists. Muslim, traditional religion, Christian.

Tibea (Ngayaba, Nyabea, Minjanti, Zangnte, Djanti, Njanti) [ngy] 1,400 (1992 SIL). Center Province, Mbam Division, in extreme north of Ngoro Subdivision, northeast of Bafia, 3 villages. *Class:* Niger-Congo, Atlantic-Congo, Volta-Congo, Benue-Congo, Bantoid, Southern, Narrow Bantu, Northwest, A, Bafia (A.50). *Lg Use:* Speakers not bilingual in nearby languages. Younger people learning French.

Tikar (Tikar-East, Tikari, Tikali, Ndob, Tingkala, Ndome) [tik] 25,000 (1989 SIL). Center Province, Mbam Division, Ngambe-Tikar Subdivision, scattered over a wide area northwest of Yoko and northeast of Foumban; Adamawa Province, Mayo-Banyo Division, Bankim Subdivision; West Province, Noun Division, Magba Subdivision. *Class:* Niger-Congo, Atlantic-Congo, Volta-Congo, Benue-Congo, Bantoid, Southern, Tikar. *Dialects:* Twumwu (Tumu, Tikar de Bankim), Tige (Tikar de Ngambe), Nditam, Kong, Mankim, Gambai, Bandobo. Bandobo is a dialect or closely related language. The Bankim call their dialect 'Twumwu', the Ngambe call theirs 'Tige'. *Lg Dev:* Literacy rate in second language: 25% to 50%. NT: 1989.

Tiv [tiv] Few speakers in Cameroon. South West Province, Manyu Division, northeast of Akwaya on the Nigerian border, only in the village of Njobo (Njawbaw). *Lg Dev:* Literacy rate in second language: 15% to 25%. *Other:* Christian, traditional religion. See main entry under Nigeria.

To [toz] North Province, Mayo-Rey Division, Touboro Subdivision. Also spoken in Central African Republic. *Class:* Niger-Congo, Atlantic-Congo, Volta-Congo, North, Adamawa-Ubangi, Adamawa, Mbum-Day, Mbum, Unclassified. *Other:* An ancient secret male initiation language of the Gbaya. Second language only.

Tsuvan (Matsuvan, Motsuvan, Terki, Telaki, Teleki, Tchede) [tsh] 2,300 (2000 SIL). Far North Province, Mayo-Tsanaga Division, southeastern Bourrah Subdivision, northeast of Dourbeye in the village of Tchevi consisting of 5 quarters found in an area of 10 km in diameter; some in North Province, Mayo-Louti Division. *Class:* Afro-Asiatic, Chadic, Biu-Mandara, A, A.8. *Lg Use:* Diglossia with Fulfulde. Schooling is in French.

Tuki (Sanaga, Betsinga, Betzinga, Bacenga, Batchenga, Oki, Baki, Ki, Osa Nanga) [bag] 26,000 (1982 SIL). Center Province, Mbam Division, along the Sanaga River north of Saa, and north of the Sanaga River between Ombessa and Ntui. *Class:* Niger-Congo, Atlantic-Congo, Volta-Congo, Benue-Congo, Bantoid, Southern, Mbam, Sanaga (A.60). *Dialects:* Kombe (Tukombe, Wakombe, Bakombe), Tocenga (Tiki, Bacenga), Tsinga (Chinga, Tutsingo, Batsingo), Bundum, Tonjo (Bunju, Boudjou), Ngoro (Tu Ngoro, Uki, Aki), Mbere (Tumbele, Mbele, Bambele, Mvele, Bamvele).

Tunen (Banen, Banend, Penin, Penyin, Nenni Nyo'o) [baz] 35,300 (1982 SIL). Center Province, Mbam Division, Ndikinimeki and Makenene subdivisions; Littoral Province, Nkam Division, south to the eastern part of Yingui Subdivision. *Class:* Niger-Congo, Atlantic-Congo, Volta-Congo, Benue-Congo, Bantoid, Southern, Mbam, West (A.60). *Dialects:* Eling (Alinga, Tuling), Itundu, Logananga, Ndogbang, Ndokbiakat, Ndoktuna, Ni Nyo'o (Nyo'on, Nyokon, Fung), Mese (Paningesen, Ninguessen, Sese). *Lg Dev:* Dictionary. Grammar. *Other:* May be in Bantu A.60. Distinct from Pinyin in the Ngemba group. Traditional religion, Christian.

Tuotomb (Ponek, Bonek) [ttf] 1,000 (1984). Center Province, Mbam Division, Bafia Subdivision, village of Bonek near Ndikinemeki. Many live in urban areas. *Class:* Niger-Congo, Atlantic-Congo, Volta-Congo, Benue-Congo, Bantoid, Southern, Mbam, West (A.40). *Lg Use:* Speakers also use Tunen, Yambeta, or Cameroon Pidgin.

Tupuri (Toupouri, Tuburi, Toubouri, Ndore, Ndoore, Wina, Tongoyna, Honya, Dema, Mata) [tui] 125,000 in Cameroon. Population total all countries: 215,785. Far North Province, Kaele Division, southeastern Moulvouday plain east of Kaele; Mayo-Danay Division, Kar-Hay Subdivision. Also spoken in Chad. *Class:* Niger-Congo, Atlantic-Congo, Volta-Congo, North, Adamawa-Ubangi, Adamawa, Mbum-Day, Mbum, Northern, Tupuri-Mambai. *Lg Dev:* Dictionary. NT: 1988. *Other:* Traditional religion, Christian.

Twendi (Cambap) [twn] 30 (2000 B. Connell). Ethnic population: 1,000 or fewer (1991 SIL). Adamawa Province, Mayo-Banyo Division, north of Bankim, Sanga village. *Class:* Niger-Congo, Atlantic-Congo, Volta-Congo, Benue-Congo, Bantoid, Northern, Mambiloid, Mambila-Konja, Konja. *Lg Use:* The language appears to be diminishing in use. Speakers are shifting to Kwanja. Speakers are older adults. *Other:* 'Cambap' is the speakers' own name for the language. Nearly extinct.

Usaghade (Usakade, Usakedet, Isangele) [usk] 10,000 in Cameroon (1990 Bruce Connell). Mainly in Cameroon, South West Province, Ndian Division, Isangele

Subdivision, near the coast. Also spoken in Nigeria. *Class:* Niger-Congo, Atlantic-Congo, Volta-Congo, Benue-Congo, Cross River, Delta Cross, Lower Cross, Obolo, Usaghade. *Dialects:* Distinct from Efik (B. Connell 1998, Crozier and Blench 1992).

Vame (Maslava, Pelasla) [mlr] 8,500 (1992 SIL). Far North Province, Mayo-Sava Division, Mora and Tokombere subdivisions, Southern Mora massif south of Mora. *Class:* Afro-Asiatic, Chadic, Biu-Mandara, A, A.5. *Dialects:* Mayo-Plata (Pelasla, Plasla, Platla, Plata, Gwendele, Damlale), Mberem (Mbreme, Maslava), Demwa (Dmwa, Doume), Hurza (Hurzo, Ourza, Ourzo, Ouzza), Ndreme. The 5 dialects are inherently intelligible to each other's speakers. Mayo-Plata is closer to Wuzlam than the other dialects are to Wuzlam. *Lg Use:* Few know Fulfulde except a few in the Hurza area. Wandala is also used. *Other:* 'Pelasla' is their own name. Ethnic groups are Pelasla, Mbreme, Ndereme, Afem, Dumwa, Hurzo.

Vemgo-Mabas [vem] 5,000 in Cameroon (1984). Far North Province, Mayo-Tsanaga Division, village of Mabas on Nigerian border northwest of Mokolo. *Dialects:* Vemgo, Mabas. *Lg Use:* Some also use Mafa, Lamang, Hdi. *Other:* Different from Maba of Chad. 'Maya' may be an alternate name. See main entry under Nigeria.

Vengo (Babungo, Vengoo, Vengi, Pengo, Ngo, Nguu, Ngwa, Nge) [bav] 13,500 (1982 SIL). North West Province, Mezam Division, north of Ndop on the Ndop Plain. *Class:* Niger-Congo, Atlantic-Congo, Volta-Congo, Benue-Congo, Bantoid, Southern, Wide Grassfields, Narrow Grassfields, Ring, North. *Dialects:* Close to Wushi, Kenswei-Nsei, Bamunka. *Lg Dev:* Literacy rate in second language: 25% to 50%. Dictionary. Grammar. NT: 1993. *Other:* Their name for themselves is 'Vengoo'.

Vute (Voute, Woute, Baboute, Bute, Pute, Wute, Bamboute, Foute, Boute, Voutere, Bubure, Luvure, Bule, Nbule, 'Abotee, 'Abwetee) [vut] 20,000 in Cameroon (1997 Lars Lode). Population includes 300 in Banyo (1995 Bruce Connell). Population total all countries: 21,000. Center Province, northeastern Mbam Division; Upper Sanaga Division, near Nanga-Eboko and Mbandjok; Adamawa Province, Mayo-Banyo and Djerem divisions (near Tibati and Banyo); some in East Province, western Lom and Djerem Division. Also spoken in Nigeria. *Class:* Niger-Congo, Atlantic-Congo, Volta-Congo, Benue-Congo, Bantoid, Northern, Mambiloid, Suga-Vute, Vute. *Dialects:* Bute Bamnyo (Vute de Banyo), Vute Mbanjo (Vute de Mbandjok), Nudoo (Vute de Yangba), Nujum (Vute de Linte), Nduvum (Vute de Tibati), Nugane (Vute de Doume), Kumbere (Vute de Sangbe), Ngoro (Vute de Ngorro). *Lg Use:* Banyo Vute is still used daily, but seems heavily influenced by Fulfulde. *Lg Dev:* Literacy rate in second language: 15% to 25%. Bible portions: 1988. *Other:* Traditional religion, Christian.

Wandala (Mandara, Ndara, Mandara Montagnard) [mfi] 23,500 in Cameroon (1982 SIL). Population total all countries: 43,500. Far North Province, Mayo-Sava Division, in a belt starting east of Mora, around it to the north in a semicircle, and northwest to the Nigerian border. Also spoken in Nigeria. *Class:* Afro-Asiatic, Chadic, Biu-Mandara, A, A.4, Mandara Proper, Mandara. *Dialects:* Kamburwama, Masfeima, Jampalam, Ziogba, Mazagwa, Gwanje, Wandala (Mandara), Mura (Kirdi-Mora, Mora Brousse, Mora Massif, Duwe), Gamargu (Gamergou, Gamergu, Malgo, Malgwa). A dialect cluster. *Lg Use:* Vigorous. The Vame speak it as second language. All domains. Used in religious services, commerce. Positive language attitude. Some speak French or Fulani. *Lg Dev:* 200 to 300 read Wandala. Grammar. NT: 1988. *Other:* Plains. Agriculturalists. Muslim.

Wawa [www] 3,000 (1991 SIL). Adamawa Province, Mayo-Banyo Division, Bankim Subdivision, west of

Banyo, 13 villages. There may be some in Nigeria. *Class:* Niger-Congo, Atlantic-Congo, Volta-Congo, Benue-Congo, Bantoid, Northern, Mambiloid, Suga-Vute, Vute. *Dialect:* Gandua. *Lg Use:* Speakers also use Fulfulde.

Weh [weh] 6,900 (1994 SIL). North West Province, Menchum Division, Wum Central Subdivision, village of Weh. *Class:* Niger-Congo, Atlantic-Congo, Volta-Congo, Benue-Congo, Bantoid, Southern, Wide Grassfields, Narrow Grassfields, Ring, West. *Dialects:* Little dialect variation. Close to Aghem. *Lg Use:* Some speakers use Cameroon Pidgin as second language; some multilingualism with Isu. *Other:* Traditional religion, Christian.

Wumboko (Bamboko, Bomboko, Bambuku, Bumboko, Womboko, Mboko) [bqm] 4,000 (2000). South West Province, Fako Division, Buea Subdivision; Meme Division, Kumba Subdivision. *Class:* Niger-Congo, Atlantic-Congo, Volta-Congo, Benue-Congo, Bantoid, Southern, Narrow Bantu, Northwest, A, Duala (A.20). *Dialects:* Probably intelligible with Mokpwe, but different enough from Duala to possibly need separate literature.

Wushi (Babessi, Vesi, Pesii, Sii) [bse] 12,350 (1982 SIL). North West Province, Mezam Division, Ndop Subdivision, east of Ndop. *Class:* Niger-Congo, Atlantic-Congo, Volta-Congo, Benue-Congo, Bantoid, Southern, Wide Grassfields, Narrow Grassfields, Ring, North. *Dialects:* Close to Vengo, Kenswei-Nsei, Bamunka. *Other:* 'Wushi' is their name for themselves.

Wuzlam (Uldeme, Ouldeme, Uzam, Udlam, Uzlam, Mizlime) [udl] 10,500 (1982 SIL). Far North Province, Mayo-Sava Division, Tokombere Subdivision, Wuzlam Massif south of Mora. *Class:* Afro-Asiatic, Chadic, Biu-Mandara, A, A.5.

Yamba ("Kaka," Mbem, Mbubem, Kakayamba, Bebaroe, Boenga Ko Muzok, Swe'nga) [yam] 40,763 in Cameroon (2000 WCD). North West Province, Donga-Mantung Division, Central Nwa Subdivision. Seasonal immigrants in Nigeria, Mambila Plateau. Also spoken in Nigeria. *Class:* Niger-Congo, Atlantic-Congo, Volta-Congo, Benue-Congo, Bantoid, Southern, Wide Grassfields, Narrow Grassfields, Mbam-Nkam, Nkambe. *Dialects:* Ntem, Mfe, Nkot, Ntong, Kwak. *Lg Dev:* Literacy rate in second language: 15% to 25%. NT: 1992.

Yambeta (Yambetta, Njambeta) [yat] 3,700 (1982 SIL). Center Province, Mbam Division, Bafia Subdivision northwest of Bafia. *Class:* Niger-Congo, Atlantic-Congo, Volta-Congo, Benue-Congo, Bantoid, Southern, Mbam, West (A.40). *Dialect:* Nedek, Nigii (Nigi, Begi-Nibum, Kibum). Related to Bati, Mbule, Elip, Leti, Mmaala, Nubaca, Nugunu, Tuki, Yangben. *Lg Dev:* Literacy rate in second language: 15% to 25%.

Yangben (Nuasue) [yav] 2,300 (1994 SIL). Center Province, Mbam Division, Bokito Subdivision, Yangben Canton south of Bokito. *Class:* Niger-Congo, Atlantic-Congo, Volta-Congo, Benue-Congo, Bantoid, Southern, Mbam, Yambasa (A.60). *Dialects:* A standardized written form may be possible with Mmaala and Elip, related languages. *Lg Use:* Used in religious services. Speakers do not think French will replace Yangben. French is used in primary and secondary education. Ewondo or Bulu are used in other than RC churches. Speakers acquire comprehension of Mmaala and Elip in early adulthood.

Yasa (Yassa, Lyaasa, Maasa, Bongwe) [yko] 1,488 in Cameroon (2000 WCD). Population total all countries: 2,401. South Province, Ocean Division, Campo Subdivision, on the coast near Equatorial Guinea. Also spoken in Equatorial Guinea, Gabon. *Class:* Niger-Congo, Atlantic-Congo, Volta-Congo, Benue-Congo, Bantoid, Southern, Narrow Bantu, Northwest, A, Bube-Benga (A.30), Yasa. *Dialects:* A cluster of dialects. *Lg Dev:* Grammar.

Yemba (Tchang, Dschang, Bafou, Atsang-Bangwa, Bangwa, Bamileke-Yemba) [ybb] 300,000. West Province, major part of Menoua Division, centered around Dschang. *Class:* Niger-Congo, Atlantic-Congo, Volta-Congo, Benue-Congo, Bantoid, Southern, Wide Grassfields, Narrow Grassfields, Mbam-Nkam, Bamileke. *Dialect:* Yemba, Foreke Dschang (Dschang, Tchang). *Lg Dev:* Bible portions: 2000. *Other:* Part of a language cluster which includes Ngwe and Ngiemboon.

Yeni [yei] Extinct. Not far north of Mayo Darle village in Nyalang area. *Class:* Unclassified. *Lg Use:* Apparently all that remains of the language is a song, known by speakers of Sandani (Kwanja).

Yukuben (Nyikuben, Nyikobe, Ayikiben, Boritsu, Balaabe, Balaaben, Gohum, Uuhum, Uuhum-Gigi) [ybl] 950 in Cameroon (1986 R. Breton). North West Province, Menchum Division, west of Furu-Awa, near Nigerian border. *Lg Use:* Speakers in Cameroon want to have their language written and form a language committee. High bilingualism in Jukun Takum. Cameroon Pidgin is also spoken in the area. *Other:* The name 'Uuhum Gigi' is preferred in Cameroon. The people are called 'Yukuben'. Mountain slope. See main entry under Nigeria.

Zhoa [zhw] North-West Province, Menchum Division, one village of Fungom Subdivision. *Class:* Niger-Congo, Atlantic-Congo, Volta-Congo, Benue-Congo, Bantoid, Southern, Wide Grassfields, Narrow Grassfields, Ring, West. *Dialects:* Closest to Weh. *Other:* Traditional religion, Christian.

Zizilivakan (Ziziliveken, Ziliva, Àmzírív, Fali of Jilbu) [ziz] 2,800 in Cameroon (2002). Far North Province, Mayo-Tsanaga Division, Bourrah Subdivision, near Nigerian border. Also spoken in Nigeria. *Class:* Afro-Asiatic, Chadic, Biu-Mandara, A, A.8. *Other:* People are called 'Fali of Jilbu'.

Zulgo-Gemzek (Gemjek, Guemshek, Zulgo) [gnd] 26,000 (2002 SIL). Far North Province, Mayo-Sava Division, Tokombere Subdivision, eastern edge of Mandara Mountains, north of Maroua, 16 villages. *Class:* Afro-Asiatic, Chadic, Biu-Mandara, A, A.5. *Dialects:* Gemzek (Gaduwa), Mineo (Minew), Zulgo (Zoulgo, Zulgwa, Zelgwa). Slight dialect differences between villages. *Lg Use:* Fulfulde often used in church, but interpreted into Gemzek or Zulgo. If Zulgo is used in church, interpretation is not given into Gemzek. *Lg Dev:* Literacy rate in first language: below 1%. Literacy rate in second language: 10%. NT: 1988. *Other:* The Meri, Mbuko, Muyang, and Mada languages are in the surrounding area. Agriculturalists: millet. Christian, traditional religion.

Zumaya [zuy] 25 (1987 SIL). Far North Province, Diamare Division, Maroua Subdivision, Ouro-Lamorde. *Class:* Afro-Asiatic, Chadic, Masa. *Other:* Nearly extinct.

Cape Verde Islands

Republic of Cape Verde. República de Cabo Verde. 415,294. National or official languages: Portuguese, Kabuverdianu. Literacy rate: 37% to 70%. Information mainly from J. Holm 1989; S. and T. Graham 2002. The number of languages listed for Cape Verde Islands is 2. Of those, both are living languages.

Kabuverdianu (Caboverdiano) [kea] 393,943 in Cape Verde Islands (1998 S. Graham). Population includes 255,101 in Sotavento or 65% of the speakers, 138,842 in Barlavento or 35% of the speakers. Population total all countries: 926,078. Sotavento dialect is on Santiago, Maio, Fogo, and Brava islands; Barlavento dialect is on Santo Antão, São Vicente, São Nicolau, Sal, and Boa Vista islands. Also spoken in France, Germany, Italy, Luxembourg, Netherlands, Portugal, Senegal, Spain, USA. *Class:* Creole, Portuguese based. *Dialects:* Sotavento, Barlavento. There is a creole continuum and some decreolization. Lexical similarity 59% with the Gulf of Guinea creoles. *Lg Use:* National language. 29% are comfortable in Portuguese, 36% uncomfortable, 34% not functional. Since independence in 1975, the domains of spoken Portuguese have receded in favor of Creole. Portuguese used primarily on TV and radio, in Congress, classrooms, churches, and with foreigners. Portuguese is the primary language of instruction in 12 grades. *Lg Dev:* Literacy rate in second language: 29% Portuguese. Radio programs. Dictionary. Grammar. Bible portions: 1936. *Other:* Christian.

Portuguese [por] 14,817 in Cape Verde Islands (2004). *Lg Use:* Official language. See main entry under Portugal.

Central African Republic

République Centrafricaine, RCA, CAR. Formerly Central African Empire. 3,742,482. 500,000 to 600,000 did not indicate their first language in the 1988 census. National or official languages: Sango, French. Literacy rate: 27%. Also includes Bangi (7,435), Bomitaba (224), Gbaya, Hausa (20,000), Lingala (10,720), Mbandja (1,400), Ngbaka (3,000), Ngundi, Northern Ngbandi (294), Shuwa Arabic (63,000). Information mainly from Atlas Linguistique de l'Afrique Central 1984; Moñino 1988; J. Bendor-Samuel 1989; SIL 1972–2003. Blind population: 27,000 (1982 WCE). The number of languages listed for Central African Republic is 70. Of those, 69 are living languages and 1 is a second language without mother-tongue speakers. See map on page 687.

Ali [aiy] 35,000 (1996). Boali, Bimbo, Boda, and Yaloke subprefectures. *Class:* Niger-Congo, Atlantic-Congo, Volta-Congo, North, Adamawa-Ubangi, Ubangi, Gbaya-Manza-Ngbaka, East. *Lg Use:* Speakers also use Sango. Many children learn Sango as their first language.

Banda, Mid-Southern (Banda Central Sud) [bjo] 100,000 in Central African Republic (1996). Population total all countries: 102,000. Alindao, Mobaye, Mingala, Kembe, Kouango subprefectures. Also spoken in Democratic Republic of the Congo, Sudan. *Class:* Niger-Congo, Atlantic-Congo, Volta-Congo, North, Adamawa-Ubangi, Ubangi, Banda, Central, Central Core, Mid-Southern. *Dialects:* Bongo, Dukpu, Yakpa (Yacoua, Yakpwa, Yakwa, Bayaka), Wasa (Ouassa). Closest to Gubu, but speakers have better relations with Mbanza speakers. *Lg Use:* Speakers use Sango as second language in Central African Republic, Lingala in Democratic Republic of the Congo.

Banda, South Central [lnl] 150,000 in Central African Republic (1996). Population includes 55,000 Langba, 95,000 Ngbugu. Population total all countries: 153,000. Sibut, Mobaye, Alindao, Kembe, Mingala subprefectures. Also spoken in Democratic Republic of the Congo. *Class:* Niger-Congo, Atlantic-Congo, Volta-Congo, North, Adamawa-Ubangi, Ubangi, Banda, South Central. *Dialects:* Langba (Lagba), Ngbugu (Ngbougou). May be intelligible with Langbashe.

Banda, Togbo-Vara [tor] 12,000 in Central African Republic (1996). Bria (Togbo) and Bambari (Vara) subprefectures. *Dialects:* Togbo (Tohgboh, Tagbo, Tagbwali), Vara (Vora, Vera). *Lg Use:* Speakers also use Sango. *Other:* Distinct from Tagbu (Tagbo, Tagba) of Democratic Republic of the Congo in Sere group. They view themselves as very different from Mono. See main entry under Democratic Republic of the Congo.

Banda, West Central [bbp] 4,500 in Central African Republic (1996). Population includes 1,000 Wojo.

Population total all countries: 7,500. Bambari, Bakala (Dakpa), Grimari (Gbi, Wojo), Kaga Bandoro (Wojo), Bamingui (Gbaga-Nord) subprefectures. Also spoken in Sudan. *Class:* Niger-Congo, Atlantic-Congo, Volta-Congo, North, Adamawa-Ubangi, Ubangi, Banda, West Central. *Dialects:* Dakpa, Gbaga-Nord (Gbaga-2), Gbi, Vita, Wojo (Hodjo). *Lg Use:* Speakers also use Sango.

Banda-Bambari (Banda of Bambari) [liy] 183,000 (1996). Population includes 4,000 Gbende, 2,000 Joto, mainly Linda. Bambari, Ippy, Grimari, Bakala, Alindao subprefectures. *Class:* Niger-Congo, Atlantic-Congo, Volta-Congo, North, Adamawa-Ubangi, Ubangi, Banda, Central, Central Core, Banda-Bambari. *Dialects:* Linda, Joto (Jeto), Ndokpa, Ngapo (Ngapu), Gbende. *Lg Use:* Speakers also use Sango.

Banda-Banda [bpd] 102,000 in Central African Republic (1996). Bria (Bereya), Yalinga (Vidiri), Bakouma, Sibut (Ka, Gbaga-South), Dekoa, Damara, Grimari (Mbi), Bossangoa (Gbambiya), Bozoum, Bocarangoa, Paoua (Hai) subprefectures. Also spoken in Sudan. *Class:* Niger-Congo, Atlantic-Congo, Volta-Congo, North, Adamawa-Ubangi, Ubangi, Banda, Central, Central Core, Banda-Banda. *Dialects:* Banda-Banda, Bereya (Bria, Banda of Bria, Banda de Bria), Buru, Gbaga-South (Gbaga 1), Gbambiya, Hai, Ka, Mbi (Mbiyi), Ndi (Ndri), Ngalabo, Ngola, Vidiri (Mvedere, Vodere, Vidri, Vadara). May be intelligible with Banda-Bambari. *Lg Use:* Speakers also use Sango.

Banda-Mbrès (Banda of Mbrès, Banda-Mbre) [bqk] 42,500 in Central African Republic (1996). Mbrès Subprefecture (Mbre, Moruba), Kaga Bandoro, Bouca (Buka), Bakala (Sabanga, Moruba). Also spoken in Sudan. *Class:* Niger-Congo, Atlantic-Congo, Volta-Congo, North, Adamawa-Ubangi, Ubangi, Banda, Central, Central Core, Banda-Mbres. *Dialects:* Buka (Bouka), Mbre (Mbere, Mbele), Moruba (Morouba, Maraba), Sabanga (Sangbanga), Wada (Ouadda).

Banda-Ndélé (Banda of Ndélé, Nyele) [bfl] 35,500 in Central African Republic (1996). Ndili, Bamingui, Ouadda, Kaga Bandoro subprefectures. Also spoken in Sudan. *Class:* Niger-Congo, Atlantic-Congo, Volta-Congo, North, Adamawa-Ubangi, Ubangi, Banda, Central, Central Core, Banda-Ndele. *Dialects:* Banda-Ndélé, Junguru (Djingburu, Nguru), Tangbago (Tambolo, Tambaggo, Tombaggo, Tangago), Ngao (Ngau, Bandangao), Ngbala. *Lg Use:* Speakers also use Sango.

Banda-Yangere (Yangere, Yanguere) [yaj] 26,500 (1996). Nola, Bambio, Berberati, and Carnot subprefectures. *Class:* Niger-Congo, Atlantic-Congo, Volta-Congo, North, Adamawa-Ubangi, Ubangi, Banda, Central, Western. *Lg Use:* Speakers also use Sango.

Birri (Biri, Viri, Bviri) [bvq] 200 (1996). Ethnic population: 5,000 in Central African Republic. Extinct in Sudan (1993). Scattered throughout southwestern corner of Central African Republic, and formerly in Deim Zubeir, Bahr el Ghazal Province, Sudan. *Class:* Nilo-Saharan, Central Sudanic, West, Bongo-Bagirmi, Sara-Bagirmi. *Dialects:* Mboto, Munga. Only one dialect spoken in Central African Republic. *Lg Use:* Speakers also use Zande. *Other:* Different from Viri, Biri, Bviri.

Bodo [boy] 15 (1996). Haut-Mbomou Prefecture, scattered throughout the eastern tip of Central African Republic. Not more than 3 speakers in the same village. None in the original area or Sudan. *Class:* Niger-Congo, Atlantic-Congo, Volta-Congo, Benue-Congo, Bantoid, Southern, Narrow Bantu, Central, D, Bira-Huku (D.30). *Other:* Nearly extinct.

Bofi (Boffi) [bff] 23,500 (1996). Boda and Bimbo subprefectures. *Class:* Niger-Congo, Atlantic-Congo, Volta-Congo, North, Adamawa-Ubangi, Ubangi, Gbaya-Manza-Ngbaka, East. *Lg Use:* Speakers also use Sango.

Other: Those in Bimbo Subprefecture are reported to be mostly pygmies.

Bokoto (Bokodo, Bogoto, Bogodo, Bokpoto) [bdt] 130,000 (1996). Baoro, Carnot, Boda subprefectures. *Class:* Niger-Congo, Atlantic-Congo, Volta-Congo, North, Adamawa-Ubangi, Ubangi, Gbaya-Manza-Ngbaka, Central. *Dialects:* Gbaya of Boda (Gbaya de Boda), Bokpan, Bokoto. May be intelligible with Northwest Gbaya. *Lg Use:* Speakers use Sango as lingua franca.

Buraka (Bouraka, Boraka, Bolaka) [bkg] 2,500 in Central African Republic (1996). Population total all countries: 3,800. Mobaye Subprefecture, along the Ubangi River. Also spoken in Democratic Republic of the Congo. *Class:* Niger-Congo, Atlantic-Congo, Volta-Congo, North, Adamawa-Ubangi, Ubangi, Sere-Ngbaka-Mba, Ngbaka-Mba, Ngbaka, Western, Gbanzili. *Dialects:* May not be inherently intelligible with Gbanziri.

Dagba [dgk] 40,000 in Central African Republic (1996). Batangafo, Kabo, and Bossangoa subprefectures. Also spoken in Chad. *Class:* Nilo-Saharan, Central Sudanic, West, Bongo-Bagirmi, Sara-Bagirmi, Sara, Sara Proper. *Dialects:* May be intelligible with Kaba.

Dendi [deq] 10,000 (1996). Ouango Subprefecture. *Class:* Niger-Congo, Atlantic-Congo, Volta-Congo, North, Adamawa-Ubangi, Ubangi, Ngbandi. *Dialects:* High intelligibility of Yakoma. Ngbandi and Mbangi may be inherently intelligible with Dendi. *Lg Use:* High bilingualism in Sango. *Other:* Different from Dendi in Benin, Nigeria, and Niger.

French [fra] 9,000 in Central African Republic (1996). Scattered. *Lg Use:* Official language. See main entry under France.

Fulfulde, Bagirmi (Baghirmi Peul, Bagirmi Fula) [fui] 156,000 in Central African Republic (1996). Scattered. *Lg Use:* Speakers also use Sango. *Other:* Spoken by people of Wodaabe lineage who are also in northern Niger, northern Cameroon, Central African Republic. Nomadic. Different from the Bagirmi language of Chad, which is Nilo-Saharan. See main entry under Chad.

Furu (Bagero, Bagiro, Baguero, Baguiro) [fuu] 4,000 in Central African Republic (1996). Mobaye Subprefecture, 11 villages. *Lg Use:* Speakers also use Sango or Mono. See main entry under Democratic Republic of the Congo.

Ganzi [gnz] 1,400 (1996). Scattered throughout Central African Republic. *Class:* Niger-Congo, Atlantic-Congo, Volta-Congo, North, Adamawa-Ubangi, Ubangi, Sere-Ngbaka-Mba, Ngbaka-Mba, Ngbaka, Western, Baka-Gundi. *Dialects:* Ganzi, Yaka. May be intelligible with Baka. *Other:* Pygmies.

Gbanu (Gbanou, Banu) [gbv] 95,000 (1996). Carnot and Bossembélé subprefectures, north of Bogangolo. *Class:* Niger-Congo, Atlantic-Congo, Volta-Congo, North, Adamawa-Ubangi, Ubangi, Gbaya-Manza-Ngbaka, Central. *Dialects:* Gbanu, Gbagiri (Gbagili, Bagili, Baguili), Budigri (Bidikili). *Lg Use:* Have relatively high bilingualism in Sango. *Lg Dev:* Bible portions: 1932–1939.

Gbanziri (Gbanzili, Banziri, Gbandere) [gbg] 14,500 in Central African Republic (1996). Population total all countries: 17,500. Kouango Subprefecture, along the Ubangi River. Also spoken in Democratic Republic of the Congo. *Class:* Niger-Congo, Atlantic-Congo, Volta-Congo, North, Adamawa-Ubangi, Ubangi, Sere-Ngbaka-Mba, Ngbaka-Mba, Ngbaka, Western, Gbanzili. *Lg Use:* Speakers also use Sango.

Gbaya, Northwest (Gbaya Nord-Ouest, Gbaya) [gya] 200,000 in Central African Republic (1996). Population total all countries: 267,000 to 282,000. Bouar, Baboua, Bocaranga, Paoua subprefectures. Also spoken in Cameroon, Congo, Nigeria. *Class:* Niger-Congo, Atlantic-Congo, Volta-Congo, North, Adamawa-Ubangi,

Ubangi, Gbaya-Manza-Ngbaka, Northwest. *Dialects:* Gbaya Kara (Gbaya de Bouar, Boar), Bodoe, Lai (Lay), Yaáyuwee (Yaiwe, Kalla). *Lg Use:* They use Sango as lingua franca. *Lg Dev:* Dictionary. Grammar. Bible: 1995. *Other:* Christian, traditional religion, Muslim.

Gbaya, Southwest (Gbaya Sud-Ouest) [mdo] 164,000 in Central African Republic (1996). Population total all countries: 177,000. Berberati, Carnot, Gamboula, Nola subprefectures. Also spoken in Cameroon. *Class:* Niger-Congo, Atlantic-Congo, Volta-Congo, North, Adamawa-Ubangi, Ubangi, Gbaya-Manza-Ngbaka, Southwest. *Dialects:* Biyanda (Bianda), Buli (Boli), Mbondomo (Mbodomo), Bokare (Bokari), Mboundja (Mbunza), Bosoko (Bossouka, Mbusuku), Toongo, Yangele, Mbakolo (Yasua), Budamono, Mbombeleng. Mbodomo has subdialects Yangamo-Garga-Sarali, Petit-Belo-Doumba. They have high inherent intelligibility with each other. *Lg Use:* Use Sango as lingua franca. *Lg Dev:* Bible portions: 1980.

Gbaya-Bossangoa (Gbaya of Bossangoa, Gbaya de Bosangoa, Gbea, Gbeya, Gbaya of Borro, Gbaya-Borro) [gbp] 176,000 (1996). Bossangoa, Batangafo (Gbabana) subprefectures. *Class:* Niger-Congo, Atlantic-Congo, Volta-Congo, North, Adamawa-Ubangi, Ubangi, Gbaya-Manza-Ngbaka, Central. *Dialects:* Gbabana, Bossangoa. May be inherently intelligible with Gbaya-Bosoum or Suma. *Lg Use:* Speakers use Sango as lingua franca, but women have low proficiency outside towns. *Lg Dev:* Bible portions: 1934–2001.

Gbaya-Bozoum (Gbaya de Bozoum, Bozom) [gbq] 32,500 (1996). Bozoum Subprefecture. *Class:* Niger-Congo, Atlantic-Congo, Volta-Congo, North, Adamawa-Ubangi, Ubangi, Gbaya-Manza-Ngbaka, Central. *Dialects:* Diabe, Boyali, Bozom. May be inherently intelligible with Gbaya-Bossangoa. *Lg Use:* Use Sango as lingua franca.

Gbayi (Kpasiya) [gyg] 5,000 (1996). Northern Mingala Prefecture. *Class:* Niger-Congo, Atlantic-Congo, Volta-Congo, North, Adamawa-Ubangi, Ubangi, Ngbandi. *Dialects:* Related to Ngbandi. Ethnically Kpatili, but not intelligible with Kpatili.

Geme (Jeme, Ngba Geme, Gueme) [geq] 550 (1996). Ndélé Subprefecture, 2 villages north of Ndélé. *Class:* Niger-Congo, Atlantic-Congo, Volta-Congo, North, Adamawa-Ubangi, Ubangi, Zande, Zande-Nzakara. *Dialects:* Geme Tulu, Geme Kulagbolu. *Lg Use:* Speakers also use Sango.

Gubu (Gobu, Ngobo, Ngobu, Gabou, Gabu) [gox] *Lg Use:* Speakers also use Sango. *Other:* Few speakers in Central African Republic. See main entry under Democratic Republic of the Congo (Gobu).

Gula (Kara of Sudan, Kara de Soudan, Kara, Tar Gula, Gula du Mamoun, Goula, Yamegi) [kcm] 13,000 in Central African Republic (1996). Population total all countries: 13,200. Birao Subprefecture, near Sudan border at Kafia Kingi. Also spoken in Sudan. *Class:* Nilo-Saharan, Central Sudanic, West, Bongo-Bagirmi, Kara. *Dialects:* Molo, Mele, Mot-Mar (Moto-Mara), Sar (Sara), Mere, Zura (Koto). *Other:* Different from Kara of Central African Republic, Kare of Chad, or Gula of Chad. Muslim.

Gundi (Ngundi, Ngondi) [gdi] 9,000 (1988 census). Nola Subprefecture, south and east of Nola. The Sangha River is the border to the Yaka Region. *Class:* Niger-Congo, Atlantic-Congo, Volta-Congo, North, Adamawa-Ubangi, Ubangi, Sere-Ngbaka-Mba, Ngbaka-Mba, Ngbaka, Western, Baka-Gundi. *Dialects:* May be intelligible with Baka. *Other:* Most Pygmies have not been contacted by census takers. Distinct from Ngundi of Congo and Central African Republic, which is Bantu. Pygmies.

Kaba (Kabba, Sara Kaba, Sara) [ksp] 72,000 in Central African Republic (1996). Population total all countries:

83,000. Paoua and Marounda subprefectures. Also spoken in Chad. *Class:* Nilo-Saharan, Central Sudanic, West, Bongo-Bagirmi, Sara-Bagirmi, Sara, Sara Proper. *Other:* Different from Kaba Deme, Kaba Na, Kulfa (Kaba So), Sara Kaba, Laka (Kabba Laka), or Kaba of Ethiopia, a dialect of Bench.

Kako (Kaka, Yaka, Nkoxo) [kkj] 10,400 in Central African Republic (1996). Gambula town at the Cameroon border near Berberati, west Central African Republic. See main entry under Cameroon.

Kara (Fer, Dam Fer, Fertit) [kah] 4,800 (1996). Birao Subprefecture. *Class:* Unclassified. *Other:* Different from Gula (Kara of Sudan). Muslim.

Kare (Karré, Kari, Kali) [kbn] 93,000 in Central African Republic. Population includes 57,500 Kare, 35,500 Tale (1996). Population total all countries: 97,463. Bozoum and Bocaranga subprefectures. Also spoken in Cameroon. *Class:* Niger-Congo, Atlantic-Congo, Volta-Congo, North, Adamawa-Ubangi, Adamawa, Mbum-Day, Mbum, Central, Karang. *Dialects:* Tale (Tali), Kari. Intelligible with Mbum. *Lg Dev:* NT: 1947. *Other:* Different from the Kari of Democratic Republic of the Congo, which is Benue-Congo.

Kpagua (Kpagwa) [kuw] 3,830 (2000 WCD). Not in Democratic Republic of the Congo. *Class:* Niger-Congo, Atlantic-Congo, Volta-Congo, North, Adamawa-Ubangi, Ubangi, Banda, Central, Central Core, Mid-Southern. *Dialects:* Closest to Ngundu.

Kpatili (Kpatiri, Kpatere, Ngindere) [kym] 4,500 (1996). Southern Mingala Prefecture. *Class:* Niger-Congo, Atlantic-Congo, Volta-Congo, North, Adamawa-Ubangi, Ubangi, Zande, Zande-Nzakara. *Dialects:* Related to Nzakara. Not intelligible with Gbayi, who are ethnically Kpatili.

Laka (Kabba Laka) [lap] 2,050 in Central African Republic (1996). Bocaranga Subprefecture, 9 villages at the Chad border. *Other:* Different from Laka of Nigeria, which is Adamawa-Ubangi, and from Kaba of Central African Republic and Chad. See main entry under Chad.

Langbashe (Langbashi, Langbase, Langbasi, Langwasi, Langbwasse) [lna] 40,000 in Central African Republic (1996). Population total all countries: 43,000. Kouango Subprefecture. Also spoken in Democratic Republic of the Congo. *Class:* Niger-Congo, Atlantic-Congo, Volta-Congo, North, Adamawa-Ubangi, Ubangi, Banda, South Central. *Dialects:* May be intelligible with South Central Banda.

Limassa (Bomasa, Bomassa, Bamassa) [bme] Few speakers in Ngundi villages. Along the border with Democratic Republic of the Congo. *Class:* Niger-Congo, Atlantic-Congo, Volta-Congo, North, Adamawa-Ubangi, Ubangi, Sere-Ngbaka-Mba, Ngbaka-Mba, Ngbaka, Western, Baka-Gundi. *Lg Use:* Most have shifted to Idzali or Ngundi.

Lutos (Ruto) [ndy] 17,000 in Central African Republic (1996). Population total all countries: 18,978. Ndélé, Kaga Andoro, and Kabo subprefectures. Also spoken in Chad. *Class:* Nilo-Saharan, Central Sudanic, West, Bongo-Bagirmi, Sara-Bagirmi, Sara, Vale. *Dialects:* Nduka (Ndouka, Ndoukwa), Lutos (Ruto, Routo, Rito, Luto, Louto), Wada (Wad), Nduga (Ngougua), Konga. Only Lutos dialect is in Chad; Ruto and Nduka dialects are in Central African Republic. Not intelligible with Sar or Ngambai.

Manza (Mandja, Manja) [mzv] 220,000 (1996). Bouca, Kaga Bandoro, Mbrès, Dekoa, Sibut, Grimari subprefectures. Possibly in Chad or Democratic Republic of the Congo. *Class:* Niger-Congo, Atlantic-Congo, Volta-Congo, North, Adamawa-Ubangi, Ubangi, Gbaya-Manza-Ngbaka, East. *Dialects:* Close to Ngbaka-Minangende of Democratic Republic of the Congo.

Lg Use: Speakers use Sango as lingua franca. *Other:* Christian, traditional religion, Muslim.

Mbangi (Mbangui) [mgn] 2,750 (1996). Bangassou, Ouango, and Alindao subprefectures. *Class:* Niger-Congo, Atlantic-Congo, Volta-Congo, North, Adamawa-Ubangi, Ubangi, Ngbandi. *Dialects:* High intelligibility of Yakoma. May be intelligible with Ngbandi or Dendi. *Lg Use:* Reported to be highly bilingual in Sango.

Mbati (Songo, Lisongo, Isongo, Issongo, Lissongo) [mdn] 60,000 (1996). Mbaiki Subprefecture. *Class:* Niger-Congo, Atlantic-Congo, Volta-Congo, Benue-Congo, Bantoid, Southern, Narrow Bantu, Northwest, C, Ngundi (C.20). *Dialects:* Bolemba, Mbati of Mbaïki, Bwaka, Bonzio. *Lg Use:* Speakers have high bilingual proficiency in Sango.

Mbay (Mbai) [myb] 8,300 in Central African Republic (1996). Markounda and Batangafo subprefectures. *Lg Dev:* Literacy rate in second language: Fair. *Other:* Different from Mbai, a dialect of Nandi of Kenya. See main entry under Chad.

Mbum (Mboum) [mdd] 12,500 in Central African Republic (1996). Bocaranga Subprefecture, along the Cameroon border. Not in Chad. See main entry under Cameroon.

Monzombo (Monjombo, Mondjembo, Monzumbo) [moj] 1,600 in Central African Republic (1996). Mongoumba Subprefecture. See main entry under Congo.

Mpiemo (Mpo, Mbimu, Bimu, Mbimou, Mpyemo, Mbyemo) [mcx] 24,000 in Central African Republic (1996). Population total all countries: 29,000. Nola Subprefecture. Also spoken in Cameroon, Congo. *Class:* Niger-Congo, Atlantic-Congo, Volta-Congo, Benue-Congo, Bantoid, Southern, Narrow Bantu, Northwest, A, Makaa-Njem (A.80). *Dialects:* Jasoa (Jasua), Bidjuki (Bidjouki), Mpyemo. The Jasua dialect is spoken by most people and is well understood by others. *Lg Use:* Speakers have low bilingual proficiency in Sango. *Other:* Traditional religion, Christian, Muslim.

Ngam (Ngama) [nmc] 17,700 in Central African Republic (1996). Kabo Subprefecture. *Other:* Different from Ndam of Chad. See main entry under Chad.

Ngando (Dingando, Bodzanga, Bangandou, Bagandou, Ngando-Kota) [ngd] 5,000 (1996). Mbaïki Subprefecture. *Class:* Niger-Congo, Atlantic-Congo, Volta-Congo, Benue-Congo, Bantoid, Southern, Narrow Bantu, Northwest, C, Ngando (C.10). *Dialect:* Dikuta, Dikota (Kota). Close to Yaka. Kota may be a separate language. *Other:* Not related to Ngando of Democratic Republic of the Congo or Bangandu of Congo and Cameroon.

Ngbaka Ma'bo (Ngbaka Limba, Mbaka, Mbacca, Bwaka, Bouaka, Nbwaka, Gbaka, Ma'bo) [nbm] 88,000 in Central African Republic (1996). Population total all countries: 189,553. Mbaiki, Bimbo, and Mongoumba subprefectures. Also spoken in Congo, Democratic Republic of the Congo. *Class:* Niger-Congo, Atlantic-Congo, Volta-Congo, North, Adamawa-Ubangi, Ubangi, Sere-Ngbaka-Mba, Ngbaka-Mba, Ngbaka, Western, Bwaka. *Dialects:* Close to Gilima. *Lg Use:* Speakers in Central African Republic have high bilingual proficiency in Sango. *Lg Dev:* Bible portions: 1936–1937.

Ngbaka Manza [ngg] 29,000 (1996). Damara, Bogangolo, and Boali subprefectures. *Class:* Niger-Congo, Atlantic-Congo, Volta-Congo, North, Adamawa-Ubangi, Ubangi, Gbaya-Manza-Ngbaka, East. *Dialects:* May be intelligible with Manza. *Lg Use:* Speakers use Sango as lingua franca.

Ngombe (Ngombe-Kaka, Bagando-Ngombe, Bangando-Ngombe) [nmj] 1,450 (1996). Mambere Kadeï Prefecture. *Class:* Niger-Congo, Atlantic-Congo, Volta-Congo, North, Adamawa-Ubangi, Ubangi, Sere-Ngbaka-Mba, Ngbaka-Mba, Ngbaka, Western, Baka-Gundi. *Dialects:* May be intelligible with Southwest Gbaya. *Lg Use:* The younger generation in Central African Republic seems to not be using or controlling Ngombe. *Other:* Different from Ngombe in Democratic Republic of the Congo. May not be Baka-Gundi group but Gbaya group.

Nzakara (Ansakara, N'sakara, Sakara, Zakara) [nzk] 50,000 in Central African Republic (1996). Bangassou, Bakouma, and Gambo subprefectures. Also spoken in Democratic Republic of the Congo. *Class:* Niger-Congo, Atlantic-Congo, Volta-Congo, North, Adamawa-Ubangi, Ubangi, Zande, Zande-Nzakara.

Pana (Pani) [pnz] 82,000 in Central African Republic. Population includes 63,000 Pana, 10,000 Pondo, 9,000 Gonge (1996). Population total all countries: 85,975. Bocaranga Subprefecture. Also spoken in Cameroon, Chad, Nigeria. *Class:* Niger-Congo, Atlantic-Congo, Volta-Congo, North, Adamawa-Ubangi, Adamawa, Mbum-Day, Mbum, Central, Karang. *Dialects:* Pana, Pondo, Gonge. *Lg Dev:* Bible portions: 1953. *Other:* Traditional religion, Christian.

Pande (Ipande) [bkj] 9,700 (1996). Nola and Berberati subprefectures. *Class:* Niger-Congo, Atlantic-Congo, Volta-Congo, Benue-Congo, Bantoid, Southern, Narrow Bantu, Northwest, C, Ngundi (C.20). *Dialects:* Pande (Ndjeli, Njeli, Linyeli, Linzeli, Ngili), Bogongo (Bugongo, Bukongo). *Lg Use:* Speakers also use Sango.

Runga (Rounga, Runga de Ndele, Ayki, Aykindang) [rou] 21,500 in Central African Republic (1996). Bamingui-Bangoran Prefecture, capital city of Bangui. *Lg Use:* Several villages of ethnic Runga near Ndélé speak Arabic as first language: 3,280 (1988 census). Speakers also use Shua Arabic. *Other:* Agriculturalists: sorghum; hunter-gatherers; fishermen; traders. Traditional religion, Muslim. See main entry under Chad.

Sango (Sangho) [sag] 350,000 in Central African Republic (1988 census). Population includes 24,573 Sango Riverain. Population total all countries: 404,000. Scattered. Not in Cameroon. Also spoken in Chad, Congo, Democratic Republic of the Congo. *Class:* Creole, Ngbandi based. *Dialects:* A rapidly spreading creole derived from Ngbandi. Lexical similarity 51% with French, 49% from African languages. However, the African-based words are used more frequently. *Lg Use:* National language. 1,600,000 second-language speakers. More men than women speak it as second language. All domains. Spoken and written for informal use, used for instruction in community schools, in public schools when students do not understand French, church and mission publications. *Lg Dev:* Radio programs. TV. Bible: 1966. *Other:* SVO.

Sango, Riverain [snj] 34,500 (1996). Mobaye Subprefecture, along the Ubangi River. *Class:* Creole, Ngbandi based. *Dialects:* High intelligibility of Sango.

Sara Dunjo (Kaba Dunjo, Sara Dinjo) [koj] 4,000 (1996). Ndélé Subprefecture, close to the Chadian border. 9 villages. *Class:* Nilo-Saharan, Central Sudanic, West, Bongo-Bagirmi, Sara-Bagirmi, Sara, Sara Proper, Sara Kaba. *Dialects:* May be the same as Kaba Na of Chad. May be intelligible with Sara.

Sara Kaba (Ta Sara) [sbz] 13,600 (1996). Ndélé and Birao subprefectures. *Class:* Nilo-Saharan, Central Sudanic, West, Bongo-Bagirmi, Sara-Bagirmi, Sara, Sara Proper, Sara Kaba. *Dialects:* May be intelligible with Sara Dunjo of Central African Republic or Kaba Na of Chad.

Suma (Souma) [sqm] 50,000 (1996). Bossangoa, Markounda, and Paoua subprefectures. *Class:* Niger-Congo, Atlantic-Congo, Volta-Congo, North, Adamawa-Ubangi, Ubangi, Gbaya-Manza-Ngbaka. *Dialects:* May be intelligible with Gbaya-Bossangoa.

To [toz] *Other:* Ancient secret male initiation language of the Gbaya practiced in Cameroon and Central African Republic. Second language only. See main entry under Cameroon.

Ukhwejo (Benkonjo) [ukh] 2,000 (1996 SIL). Sangha Province, south of Nola. Ukhwejo dialect at Ngulo; Bikaka at Nalimo, Salo, Bayanga, and Gbaso; Piiga at Koola, Ambasila; Kamsili at Bomanzoku, Linjombo. 7 villages on both sides of the Sanga River. *Class:* Niger-Congo, Atlantic-Congo, Volta-Congo, Benue-Congo, Bantoid, Southern, Narrow Bantu, Northwest, A, Makaa-Njem (A.80). *Dialect:* Ukhwejo, Bikaka, Piiga, Kamsili (Ngamsile). Close to Koonzime, Mpiemo, Bomwali, Makaa. *Other:* Population threatened by sleeping sickness.

Vale [vae] 5,400 (1996). Batangafo, Kabo, and Kaga Bandoro subprefectures. Not in Chad. *Class:* Nilo-Saharan, Central Sudanic, West, Bongo-Bagirmi, Sara-Bagirmi, Sara, Vale. *Dialect:* Vale, Tana (Tane, Tele). Related to Lutos. Not intelligible with Sara or Ngambai. *Lg Use:* High bilingualism in Sango.

Yaka (Aka, Nyoyaka, Beká, Pygmée de Mongoumba, Pygmée de la Lobaye, Pygmées de la Sanghas, "Babinga," "Bambenga") [axk] 15,000 in Central African Republic (1996). Population total all countries: 30,000. Nola, Bambio, Mbaïki, Mongoumba subprefectures, all along the Congo border in the forest. The Sangha River is the border with the Baka Region. Also spoken in Congo. *Class:* Niger-Congo, Atlantic-Congo, Volta-Congo, Benue-Congo, Bantoid, Southern, Narrow Bantu, Northwest, C, Ngando (C.10). *Dialects:* Beka (Gbayaka, Bayaka, Moyaka), Nzari. *Lg Use:* Literacy classes are conducted in Sango. *Other:* "Babinga" is derogatory. The people are 'Bayaka' or 'Biaka'. Different from Baka, which is Ubangi. Pygmies. Forest. Hunter-gatherers. Traditional religion, Christian.

Yakoma [yky] 100,000 in Central African Republic (1996). Population total all countries: 110,000. Kembi and Ouango subprefectures. Mainly along the Ubangi River, and in administrative centers throughout Central African Republic. Also spoken in Democratic Republic of the Congo. *Class:* Niger-Congo, Atlantic-Congo, Volta-Congo, North, Adamawa-Ubangi, Ubangi, Ngbandi. *Dialects:* High intelligibility of Ngbandi and Sango. *Lg Use:* Speakers also use Sango.

Yulu (Youlou) [yul] 4,000 in Central African Republic (1996). Population total all countries: 7,000. Ouadda-Djaléi and Ouadda subprefectures. Yulu are in Central African Republic and Sudan; Binga are in Sudan and Democratic Republic of the Congo. Also spoken in Democratic Republic of the Congo, Sudan. *Class:* Nilo-Saharan, Central Sudanic, West, Bongo-Bagirmi, Kara. *Dialects:* Binga, Yulu. Aja is not a dialect of Yulu, but of Kresh (R. Brown). *Lg Use:* Many also use Kresh or Arabic in Sudan.

Zande (Azande, Zandi, Pazande, Sande, Badjande) [zne] 62,000 in Central African Republic (1996). Rafaï, Zémio, and Obo subprefectures. *Lg Use:* Speakers also use Sango. *Other:* Traditional religion, Christian. See main entry under Democratic Republic of the Congo.

Chad

Republic of Chad. République du Tchad. 9,538,544. National or official languages: Standard Arabic, French. Literacy rate: 11%. Also includes Hausa (100,000). Information mainly from P. Boyeldieu 1977, 1985; J. P. Caprile 1977; D. Barreteau 1978; H. Jungraithmayr 1981; P. Doornbos and M. L. Bender 1983; J. Bendor-Samuel 1989; SIL 1971–2003. Blind population: 110,000 to 175,000. The number of languages listed for Chad is 134. Of those, 132 are living languages and 2 are extinct. See maps beginning on page 688.

Amdang (Mimi, Mima, Mututu, Biltine, Andang, Andangti) [amj] 41,069 (2000 WCD). East, Biltine Prefecture, Biltine Subprefecture, Southeast of Biltine. *Class:* Nilo-Saharan, Fur. *Other:* Thoroughly Arabicized. Often confused with other languages called 'Mimi' (Bender). Called 'Mima' by the Arabs and 'Mututu' by the Maba. They call themselves 'Andang'. Muslim.

Arabic, Babalia Creole (Babalia, Bubalia, Babaliya) [bbz] 3,937 (1993 census). West, Chari Baguirmi Prefecture, N'Djamena Subprefecture. North of Djermaya and between Karal and Tourba. Possibly also in the Bokoro Subprefecture around Ngoura. 23 villages. *Class:* Creole, Arabic based. *Dialects:* A creole developed from Chadian Arabic (90% of the vocabulary) and Berakou (10%; Decobert). Babalia shares structural similarities with Juba Arabic. There is a post-creole continuum from Chadian Arabic to the Bagirmian basilect. *Other:* The ethnic group is called 'Babalia'. The original language of the ethnic group was Berakou. Muslim.

Arabic, Chadian Spoken (Arabe Choa, Shuwa Arabic, Shua Arabic, Shua, Chowa, Chad Arabic, Chadian Arabic, Suwa, L'arabe du Tchad) [shu] 754,590 in Chad. Population total all countries: 986,190. Salamat, Ouaddaï, Biltine, center of the Batha Region and to the west, much of Chari-Baguirmi. Beginning to be more widely used in the Mayo-Kebbi, in the north of the Tandjilé and in the Guéra. Also spoken in Cameroon, Central African Republic, Niger, Nigeria. *Class:* Afro-Asiatic, Semitic, Central, South, Arabic. *Dialects:* Batha (Biltine), Chari-Baguirmi (Salamat). A pidginized variety of this, commonly called 'Bongor Arabic', is spoken as a second language by many people in the Mayo-Kebbi and other parts of south Chad. *Lg Use:* Language of wider communication. No diglossia with Modern Standard Arabic. *Lg Dev:* Dictionary. Grammar. NT: 1967–1991. *Other:* 'Shuwa Arabic' is the name used in various other countries for the variety near Lake Chad. Muslim.

Arabic, Standard [arb] Middle East, North Africa. *Lg Use:* Official language. See main entry under Saudi Arabia.

Assangori (Sungor, Soungor, Assoungor, Azanguri, Asong, Asungore, Bognak-Asungorung, Madungore) [sjg] 23,479 in Chad (1993 census). Population total all countries: 38,479. East, Ouaddaï Prefecture, Adré Sub-prefecture, northwest of Adré and of the Masalit. Also spoken in Sudan. *Class:* Nilo-Saharan, Eastern Sudanic, Western, Tama, Tama-Sungor. *Dialects:* Sungor, Walad Dulla. Girga and Walad Dulla are ethnic groups which may or may not speak different dialects. Madungore may be a dialect of Tama. Lexical similarity 62% to 73% with Tama. *Lg Use:* The majority use Chadian Arabic as second language, although at a low proficiency level. *Other:* Muslim.

Bagirmi (Baguirmi, Baghirmi, Baguirme, Tar Barma, Barma, Mbarma, Tar Bagrimma, Bagrimma, Lis, Lisi) [bmi] 44,761 in Chad (1993 census). West, Chari Baguirmi Prefecture. Two groups: Massénya Subprefecture around Massénya; Bousso Subprefecture around Bousso. The Gol are at Massénya, the Kibar east of Massénya, the Bangri west of Massénya and along the Chari River between Guélendeng and N'Djaména, and the Dam along the Chari River from Bousso to Gezlendeng. Also spoken in Nigeria. *Class:* Nilo-Saharan, Central Sudanic, West, Bongo-Bagirmi, Sara-Bagirmi, Bagirmi. *Dialects:* Gol, Kibar, Bangri, Dam. Many dialects. *Lg Use:* Trade language. It was the language of the ancient Bagirmi kingdom. It is widely spoken as a second language. The majority use Arabic as second language. *Lg Dev:* Grammar. *Other:* Muslim.

Barein (Baraïn, Guilia, Jalkia) [bva] 4,100 (1993 census). South central, north Guéra Prefecture, Melfi Subprefecture, west (Jalkia), south, southwest (Komi), and east (Sakaya) of Melfi. *Class:* Afro-Asiatic, Chadic, East, B,

B.3. *Dialects:* Jalkia, Guilia, Sakaya (Dagne, Jelkin), Komi. Lexical similarity 92% between Jalkia and Guilia, 70% between Sakaya and both Jalkia and Guilia. *Lg Use:* Speakers also use Chadian Arabic. *Other:* Muslim.

Bedjond (Mbay Bediondo, Mbay Bejondo, Bediondo Mbai, Bédjonde, Bedjondo, Bediondo, Nangnda) [bjv] 36,000 (1969 Caprile and Fedry). Southwest, Moyen-Chari Prefecture, Koumra and Moïssala subprefectures, centered around Bediondo. West of the Day. *Class:* Nilo-Saharan, Central Sudanic, West, Bongo-Bagirmi, Sara-Bagirmi, Sara, Sara Proper. *Dialects:* Bedjond, Bébote, Yom. *Other:* A distinct language from Sar or Ngambai.

Berakou (Babalia, Bubalia) [bxv] 2 (1995 Djarangar). West, Chari Baguirmi Prefecture; N'Djamena Sub-prefecture, north of Djermaya and between Karal and Tourba; Bokoro Subprefecture, around Ngoura. 23 villages. *Class:* Nilo-Saharan, Central Sudanic, West, Bongo-Bagirmi, Sara-Bagirmi, Bagirmi. *Dialects:* Bolo Djarma, Mondogossou, Manawadji, Yiryo. *Lg Use:* The Babalia have been shifting to Chadian Arabic or Kotoko languages. All speakers older than 60 years (1995). *Other:* The people are called 'Babalia', the language 'Berakou'. Muslim. Nearly extinct.

Bernde (Morom, Tar Murba) [bdo] 2,000 (1999 SIL). Central, Guéra Prefecture, Bitkine Subprefecture, west of the village of Bolong to the border of Chari Baguirmi Prefecture. *Class:* Nilo-Saharan, Central Sudanic, West, Bongo-Bagirmi, Sara-Bagirmi, Bagirmi. *Dialects:* Bayo, Morbo, Morom. Bolong may be a separate language. Lexical similarity 59% with Bagirmi, 53% to 72% with Kenga, 51% with Jaya, 47% with Naba, 55% to 70% with Bilala, 54% to 73% with Djaya.

Besme (Huner, Hounar, 'Unar, Beseme, Besemme, Bodor) [bes] 1,228 (1993 census). Southwest, Tandjilé Prefecture, Kélo and Laï subprefectures, in Besmé, Bodor, and 3 other villages along the Logone River northwest of Laï. *Class:* Niger-Congo, Atlantic-Congo, Volta-Congo, North, Adamawa-Ubangi, Adamawa, Mbum-Day, Kim. *Dialects:* Lexical similarity 51% with Kim. *Lg Use:* Some bilingualism in Nancere and Chadian Arabic, but not universal nor at a high level. *Other:* Christian, traditional religion.

Bidiyo (Bidyo, Bidio, 'Bidio, 'Bidiyo, Bidiyo-Waana, Bidiya) [bid] 14,000 (1981 Jungraithmayr). South central, north Guéra Prefecture, Mongo Subprefecture, south of Mongo and west of Abou Telfane. *Class:* Afro-Asiatic, Chadic, East, B, B.1, 1. *Dialects:* Garawgino (Kafila), Jekkino (Kofilo), Bigawguno (Tounkoul), Nalguno (Niergui), 'Oboyguno (Zerli). The first 2 dialects listed are eastern, the others western. Dambiya is probably a Bidiyo dialect instead of a Migaama dialect. *Lg Use:* The majority use Chadian Arabic as second language. *Lg Dev:* Dictionary. Grammar. *Other:* Muslim.

Birgit (Bergit, Birgid, Berguid) [btf] 10,398 (2000 WCD). Southeast, Salamat Prefecture, Abou Déïa and Am Timan subprefectures, and Ouaddaï Prefecture, Am Dam Subprefecture. South of the Mubi, centered in Abgué. *Class:* Afro-Asiatic, Chadic, East, B, B.1, 2. *Dialects:* Abgue, Eastern Birgit, Duguri, Agrab. *Other:* All sources since Greenberg list it as a separate language from other Dangla languages. Different from Birked (Birgit) of Sudan, a Nilo-Saharan language.

Bolgo [bvo] 1,800 (1993 census). South central, Guéra Prefecture, Melfi Subprefecture, east of the Barain, southeast of Melfi. *Class:* Niger-Congo, Atlantic-Congo, Volta-Congo, North, Adamawa-Ubangi, Adamawa, Mbum-Day, Bua. *Dialects:* Bolgo Dugag (Small Bolgo), Bolgo Kubar (Big Bolgo). Lexical similarity 68% between the two dialects and between Bolgo Dugag and a form of Koke spoken in Daguéla. *Lg Use:* Vigorous. Most use

Chadian Arabic as second language. *Other:* Traditional religion, Muslim.

Bon Gula (Taataal, Poun, Bon, Bun, Gula Guera, Bon Goula) [glc] 1,200 (1997 SIL). Southeast, Guéra Prefecture, Melfi Subprefecture. North of Lake Iro, northeast of Zan. Bon and Ibir villages. *Class:* Niger-Congo, Atlantic-Congo, Volta-Congo, North, Adamawa-Ubangi, Adamawa, Mbum-Day, Bua. *Dialects:* Lexical similarity 46% with Zan Gula. *Lg Use:* Vigorous. The majority use Chadian Arabic as second language. *Other:* Bon Gula and Zan Gula are referred to together as 'Gula Guera'. Traditional religion, Muslim.

Boor (Bwara, Damraw) [bvf] 100 (1999 SIL). South, Chari-Baguirmi Prefecture, Bousso Subprefecture, and Moyen-Chari Prefecture, Sarh Rural Subprefecture, in and around Dumraw (Bwara) village on the north bank of the Chari River, just east of Miltu. *Class:* Afro-Asiatic, Chadic, East, A, A.1, 2. *Dialects:* Some have classified it as a dialect of Miltu. Lexical similarity 36% with Miltu (closest). *Lg Use:* There may be a high degree of bilingualism in Bagirmi.

Bua (Boa, Boua, Bwa, 'Ba) [bub] 7,708 (1993 census). South, Moyen-Chari Prefecture, Sarh Subprefecture, around and to the northeast of Korbol; Guéra Prefecture, Melfi Subprefecture. *Class:* Niger-Congo, Atlantic-Congo, Volta-Congo, North, Adamawa-Ubangi, Adamawa, Mbum-Day, Bua. *Dialects:* A separate language from Niellim, Fania, Tounia, and Day. 'Mana', or 'Kobe' may be an alternate name or dialect. *Lg Use:* Most speakers have low proficiency in Arabic. *Other:* Different from Bua (Bwa) of Democratic Republic of the Congo, which is Benue-Congo. Traditional religion, Muslim.

Buduma (Boudouma, Yidena, Yedima, Yedina, Yidana) [bdm] 51,600 in Chad (1993 census). Population total all countries: 54,800. West, Lac Prefecture, Bol Subprefecture, islands and northern shore of Lake Chad. No longer in Niger. Also spoken in Cameroon, Nigeria. *Class:* Afro-Asiatic, Chadic, Biu-Mandara, B, B.1, Buduma. *Dialects:* Southern Buduma, Northern Buduma. 90% inherent intelligibility between the dialects. *Lg Use:* Vigorous. Most domains, home. 60% have good to excellent oral proficiency in Kanembu as second language, about 50% in Kanuri. Some can use Arabic. *Lg Dev:* Literacy rate in first language: below 1%. Literacy rate in second language: below 5%. Grammar. *Other:* Islands, lake shore. Fishermen; agriculturalists. Muslim, traditional religion.

Buso (Busso, Dam de Bousso, Bousso) [bso] 40 (1971 Welmers). West, Chari-Baguirmi Prefecture, Bousso Subprefecture, in Maffaling and Bousso. *Class:* Afro-Asiatic, Chadic, East, A, A.1. *Dialects:* Boyeldieu says it is not in the Bua group, but Chadic. *Other:* Nearly extinct.

Chadian Sign Language [cds] 390 (1989 M. Yonadjiel). Ethnic population: Large deaf population (1989). Schools and an association for the deaf in N'Djamena, Sarh, and Moundou. *Class:* Deaf sign language. *Other:* Influences from American Sign Language. Some signs are traditional. Teachers were trained in Nigeria. Muslim, Christian.

Dagba [dgk] See main entry under Central African Republic.

Daju, Dar Daju (Dadjo, Dadju, Dajou, Daju, Dajo, Daju Mongo, Daju Oum Hadjer, Saaronge) [djc] 34,000 (1993 census). Central, Guéra Prefecture, Mongo Subprefecture, around Mongo and Eref. *Class:* Nilo-Saharan, Eastern Sudanic, Western, Daju, Western Daju. *Dialects:* Bardangal, Eref, Gadjira. Not inherently intelligible with Dar Sila Daju. Lexical similarity 64% with Dar Sila Daju. *Lg Use:* The majority use Chadian Arabic as second language. *Other:* They call themselves 'Saaronge'. Muslim.

Daju, Dar Šila (Sila, Sula, Daju, Dadjo, Dajou, Bokoruge, Bokorike) [dau] 63,082 in Chad (2000 WCD). Eastern, Ouaddaï Prefecture, Goz-Beïda Subprefecture, around Goz-Beïda and east to the Sudan border. Also spoken in Sudan. *Class:* Nilo-Saharan, Eastern Sudanic, Western, Daju, Western Daju. *Dialects:* Not inherently intelligible with Dar Daju Daju. Lexical similarity 74% with Daju of Dar Fur (Nyala and Lagowa), 60% with Shatt, 57% with Logorik. *Lg Use:* The majority use Chadian Arabic as second language. *Other:* They call themselves 'Bokoruge'. Muslim.

Dangaléat (Dangla, Danal, Dangal) [daa] 45,000 (1999 SIL). Population includes 30,000 in Dangaléat Canton. Central, Guéra Prefecture, Mongo and Bitkine subprefectures, west of Mongo. The western dialect is around Korbo; central dialect around Barlo, Koubo Adougoul; eastern dialect around Korlongo. *Class:* Afro-Asiatic, Chadic, East, B, B.1, 1. *Dialects:* West Dangaléat (Korbo, Karbo), Central Dangaleat, East Dangaleat. Intelligibility between speakers of the eastern and western dialects is low, but both understand the central dialect well. *Lg Use:* The majority use Arabic as second language. *Lg Dev:* Literacy rate in first language: 1% to 5%. Literacy rate in second language: below 5%. Dictionary. Grammar. *Other:* Traditional religion (Margaï), Muslim, Christian.

Day (Dai) [dai] 49,916 (1993 census). Southwest, Moyen-Chari Prefecture, Sarh and Moïssala subprefectures, southwest of Sarh. *Class:* Niger-Congo, Atlantic-Congo, Volta-Congo, North, Adamawa-Ubangi, Adamawa, Mbum-Day, Day. *Dialects:* Bouna, Bangoul, Ngalo, Takawa-Béngoro. The dialects are inherently intelligible to each other's speakers. *Lg Dev:* Dictionary. Grammar. NT: 1989.

Dazaga (Daza, Dasa, Dazza) [dzg] 282,281 in Chad (1993 census). Population total all countries: 312,281. North, Kanem and B.E.T. prefectures, Borkou and Ennedi subprefectures, north of Lake Chad and in the area of Largeau. Also spoken in Niger. *Class:* Nilo-Saharan, Saharan, Western, Tebu. *Dialects:* Close to Tedaga. Azzaga, the speech of the Azza, a caste division, is different from Dazaga. Its relation to Dazaga and to the speech of the Azza among the Teda is not known. *Lg Use:* The majority use Arabic as second language. *Other:* 'Daza' is the name for the people, 'Dazaga' for the language. Distinct from Daza in Nigeria, which is Chadic. Muslim.

Disa [dsi] 2,366 (2000 WCD). South, Moyen-Chari Prefecture, Kyabé Subprefecture, northwest of Lake Iro. *Class:* Nilo-Saharan, Central Sudanic, West, Bongo-Bagirmi, Sara-Bagirmi, Bagirmi. *Other:* Little is known about it. It is probably similar or related to Gula (Sara Gula) of Chad.

Fania (Fagnia, Fanya, Fanyan, Fana, Fanian, Mana, Kobe) [fni] 1,100 (1997 SIL). Southeast, Guéra Prefecture, Melfi Subprefecture, west of Lake Iro, and north of Sarh, around Mouraye, Sengué, Malakonjo, Rim, Sisi, Karo villages. *Class:* Niger-Congo, Atlantic-Congo, Volta-Congo, North, Adamawa-Ubangi, Adamawa, Mbum-Day, Bua. *Dialects:* Northern Fania, Southern Fania. A separate language from Bua. Lexical similarity 79% between dialects. *Lg Use:* Vigorous. Most use Chadian Arabic as second language. *Other:* Traditional religion, Muslim.

Fongoro (Gele, Kole) [fgr] 1,000 (1983 Doornbos and Bender). East, Ouaddaï Prefecture, Goz Beida Sub-prefecture, canton Fongoro, along the Sudan border in the Dar Fongoro Region south of Mongororo and the Sinyar, in a rather inaccessible area. *Class:* Nilo-Saharan, Central Sudanic, West, Bongo-Bagirmi, Sara-Bagirmi. *Lg Use:* Speakers are shifting to Fur. There may be a few older adult speakers left and some living in isolated places.

Extinct in Sudan. *Other:* The tse-tse fly is a problem in the area. Mountain slope. Hunter-gatherers: honey, hides; fishermen: dried fish.

French [fra] 3,000 in Chad (1993). *Lg Use:* Official language. See main entry under France.

Fulfulde, Adamawa (Adamawa Fulani, Peul, Peulh, Pullo, Pule, Ful, Fula Fulbe, Boulbe, Eastern Fulani, Foulfoulde, Nagapelta, Pelta Hay, Domona, Pladina, Palata, Paldida, Paldena, Dzemay, Zemay, Taareyo, Zaakosa, Biira, Sanyo) [fub] 128,000 in Chad, (1993 census). Population includes Kano-Katsina-Bororro Fulfulde. 152,146 all Fulfulde varieties in Chad. Southwest, Mayo-Kebbi Prefecture, around Léré. *Dialect:* Maroua, Garoua, Ngaoundéré, Kambariire, Nomadic Fulfulde, Bilkire Fulani (Bilkiri). *Other:* Fulfulde is the language, Fulbe the people. Traditional religion, Muslim. See main entry under Cameroon.

Fulfulde, Bagirmi (Baghirmi Peul, Bagirmi Fula) [fui] 24,000 in Chad. Population total all countries: 180,000. West, Chari-Baguirmi Prefecture, Masséya and Bokoro subprefectures, between Bokoro and Masséya. Also spoken in Central African Republic. *Class:* Niger-Congo, Atlantic-Congo, Atlantic, Northern, Senegambian, Fulani-Wolof, Fula, Eastern. *Dialects:* May be close to Bororo Fulfulde; reported to be a nomadic group of Mbororo. *Lg Use:* Trade language. *Other:* Spoken by people of Wodaabe lineage who are also in northern Niger, northern Cameroon, Central African Republic. Nomadic. Different from the Bagirmi language of Chad, which is Nilo-Saharan.

Fulfulde, Kano-Katsina-Bororro (Fulbe, Peul) [fuv] Mayo-Kebbi Prefecture, in the area of Pala and Léré; Chari-Baguirmi Prefecture, between Massakory and Masséya, and Lac Prefecture, north of Lake Chad near Rig-Rig. Nomadic Bororro travel along the banks of the Chari River and elsewhere. *Dialect:* Kano-Katsina, Bororro (Bororo, Mbororo, Ako, Nomadic Fulfulde). *Other:* Muslim. See main entry under Nigeria (Fulfulde, Nigerian).

Fur (For, Four, Konjara, Kondjara) [fvr] 1,800 in Chad. *Lg Dev:* Orthography developed and literacy materials in use. *Other:* Several small groups. Muslim. See main entry under Sudan.

Gabri (Gaberi, Gabere, Ngabre, Southern Gabri) [gab] 34,387 (2000 WCD). Southwest, Tandjilé Prefecture, Laï Subprefecture, northwest of Laï around Dormo and Darbé villages. *Class:* Afro-Asiatic, Chadic, East, A, A.2, 2. *Dialects:* Darbé, Dormon. *Other:* Dormo and Chiri are Gabri villages, erroneously listed as languages in some sources. Traditional religion, Christian.

Gadang [gdk] 2,500 (1997 SIL). Southwest, Chari-Baguirmi Prefecture, Bousso Subprefecture, southeast of Bousso, along the N'Djaména-Sarh road, between Mogo and Mbarlé, Somrai Region. *Class:* Afro-Asiatic, Chadic, East, A, A.1, 2. *Dialects:* Related to Sarwa, Miltu. *Lg Use:* Speakers also use Bagirmi.

Gidar (Guidar, Gidder, Kada, "Baynawa") [gid] 11,687 in Chad (1993 census). Southwest, Mayo-Kebbi Prefecture, Léré Subprefecture, northwest of Léré in Chad to Guider in Cameroon, at least 25 villages. See main entry under Cameroon.

Gor (Bodo) [gqr] 75,000 (1999 SIL). Logone Oriental Prefecture, Doba Subprefecture, centered around Bodo. *Class:* Nilo-Saharan, Central Sudanic, West, Bongo-Bagirmi, Sara-Bagirmi, Sara, Sara Proper. *Dialects:* Bodo, Yamod. Close to Bedjond and Gor, with high inherent intelligibility. *Lg Use:* There is a Gor Language Committee. The speakers have a clear understanding of their identity as separate from Mango and Bedjond. *Lg Dev:* Primer, literacy classes. *Other:* Christian, traditional religion.

Goundo [goy] 30 (1998). Tanjilé Prefecture, Laï and Kélo subprefectures, Goundo-Bengli, Goundo-Nangom, and Goundo-Yila villages. *Class:* Niger-Congo, Atlantic-Congo, Volta-Congo, North, Adamawa-Ubangi, Adamawa, Mbum-Day, Kim. *Dialects:* Lexical similarity with Besmé 60%, Kim 51%. *Lg Use:* Younger people have shifted to Kabalai and Nancere. All speakers are older adults. *Other:* Nearly extinct.

Gula (Sara Goula, Sara Gula, Goula) [glu] 10,251 (2000 WCD). Moyen-Chari Prefecture, Kyabé Subprefecture, southwest of Lake Iro. *Class:* Nilo-Saharan, Central Sudanic, West, Bongo-Bagirmi, Sara-Bagirmi, Bagirmi. *Dialects:* Probably related to Disa. *Other:* Different from Gula Iro of Chad which is Adamawa and from Gula of Central African Republic and Sudan.

Gula Iro (Goula Iro, Goula d'Iro, Kulaal) [glj] 3,500 (1991 SIL). Population includes 2,000 Pongaal, 725 Tiaala, 200 (?) Tiitaal, 350 Patool, 165 Korintal. Southeast, Moyen-Chari and Salamat prefectures, Kyabé and Am Timan subprefectures. Around Lake Iro, in and around Boum Kabir, northeast of Sarh. Pongaal dialect is in Boum Kabir, Boum Saher, Madjok, Teonen, and Karou; Tiaala in Masidjanga (Cheroba), Bouni, and Kore; Patool in Badi and Foundouk; Korintal in Cheou (Tieou); Tiitaal in western Salamat Prefecture. *Class:* Niger-Congo, Atlantic-Congo, Volta-Congo, North, Adamawa-Ubangi, Adamawa, Mbum-Day, Bua. *Dialects:* Pongaal (Ponaal), Tiaala, Tiitaal, Patool, Korintal. Not intelligible with Bon Gula or Zan Gula. *Lg Use:* Some speakers also use Arabic. There is almost no use of Sara. *Other:* 'Kulaal' is their name for themselves. Different from Gula of Chad and Sudan which is Nilo-Saharan, and from Gula of Central African Republic. Traditional religion, Christian.

Gulay (Goulai, Goulei, Gulei, Gulai, Goulaye) [gvl] 163,271 (1993 census). Population includes 23,500 Pen in 26 villages (1995 Djarangar). Southwest, Moyen-Chari (6 cantons), Logone Oriental (1 canton) and Tandjilé (1 canton) prefectures, between Koumra, Laï, and Doba. *Class:* Nilo-Saharan, Central Sudanic, West, Bongo-Bagirmi, Sara-Bagirmi, Sara, Sara Proper. *Dialect:* Gulay, Pen (Peni). *Lg Use:* Sar is the lingua franca. *Lg Dev:* Bible portions: 1956. *Other:* The Pen do not like to be called 'Gulay'.

Herdé (Ka'do Herdé, He'dé, "Kado," Zime) [hed] 40,000 (1999 SIL). Southwest, Mayo-Kebbi Prefecture, Pala and Léré subprefectures. Around Pala and Lamé. Near the Pevé, west of the Ngueté. *Class:* Afro-Asiatic, Chadic, Masa. *Lg Dev:* NT: 1980. *Other:* Linguistic and sociolinguistic differences make separate literature from Pévé and Ngueté necessary.

Horo (Hor) [hor] Extinct. Béhor north of Sarh on the Chari River. *Class:* Nilo-Saharan, Central Sudanic, West, Bongo-Bagirmi, Sara-Bagirmi, Sara, Sara Proper. *Lg Use:* Extinct. Members of the ethnic group now speak the Kle dialect of Ngam.

Jaya [jyy] 2,200 (1993 census). Central, Guéra Prefecture, Bitkine Subprefecture, 50 km north-northwest of Bitkine. *Class:* Nilo-Saharan, Central Sudanic, West, Bongo-Bagirmi, Sara-Bagirmi, Bagirmi. *Dialects:* Lexical similarity 44% with Naba.

Jonkor Bourmataguil (Djongor Bourmataguil, Dougne, Karakir) [jeu] 1,500 (1993 SIL). Salamat Prefecture, Abou Deïa Subprefecture, west of Abou Deïa. Originally centered in Bourmataguil village, now centered in Ader-Ader. *Class:* Afro-Asiatic, Chadic, East, B, B.1, 1. *Dialects:* Dougne, Musunye. Relationship with other Dangla languages needs investigation, especially Toram and Mogum. *Lg Use:* A large number of the ethnic group have given up the traditional language for Chadian Arabic, but in two villages the children still learn Jonkor Bourmataguil. *Other:* 'Karakir' means 'cave-dwellers' in

Arabic. The name 'Jegu' has been applied to this language, but Jegu is a dialect of Mogum.

Kaba (Kabba, Kaba de Paoua, Kaba de Baibokoum, Western Kaba) [ksp] 11,000 in Chad (1971 Welmers). Southwest, Logone Oriental Prefecture, Goré Subprefecture, around Goré and to the southeast. *Other:* Different from Kaba Deme, Kaba Na, Kaba So (Kulfa), or Kabba Laka (Laka). See main entry under Central African Republic.

Kaba Deme (Kaba Demi, Kaba 'Dem, Tà Sàra, Sara Kaba Dem) [kwg] 40,000 (1993 UBS). Southeast, Moyen-Chari Prefecture, Sarh and Kyabé subprefectures, between Sarh and Kyabé. Along the Chari River, Bobé, Hélibongo, Banda, Moussafoyo, Kemata villages. *Class:* Nilo-Saharan, Central Sudanic, West, Bongo-Bagirmi, Sara-Bagirmi, Sara, Sara Proper, Sara Kaba. *Dialects:* Siime, Mara, Kuruwer. *Lg Dev:* NT: 1999. *Other:* Different from Kaba, Kaba So (Kulfa), Kaba Na, or Kabba Laka (Laka). Fishermen.

Kaba Na (Kaba Nar, Kaba Naa, Na, Dana, Sara Kaba) [kwv] 35,000 (1993 UBS). Population includes 5,564 in Bale village, 4,937 in Koskabo, 4,548 in Kyabé. Southeast, Moyen-Chari Prefecture, Kyabé Subprefecture, centered in Kyabé. *Class:* Nilo-Saharan, Central Sudanic, West, Bongo-Bagirmi, Sara-Bagirmi, Sara, Sara Proper, Sara Kaba. *Dialects:* Dunje (Dendje, Dindje, Dinje, Denje, Dounje), Na, Banga (Mbanga), Tie (Tiye). Dunje may be the same as Kaba Dunjo of Central African Republic. Kaba Na may be the same as Sara Kaba of Central African Republic. *Lg Dev:* NT: 1988. *Other:* Not the same as Kaba, Kaba Deme, Kaba So (Kulfa), or Kabba Laka (Laka).

Kabalai (Kaba-Lai, Kabalay, Kabalaye, Keb-Kaye, Gablai, Lay, Lai) [kvf] 17,885 (1993 census). Southwest Chad, Tandjile Prefecture, Lai Subprefecture; Lai and to the south on the eastern bank of the Logone River. Not in Central African Republic. *Class:* Afro-Asiatic, Chadic, East, A, A.2, 2. *Dialects:* May be intelligible with Nancere. *Other:* Erroneously called 'Sara' or 'Kaba of Lai'.

Kajakse (Kadjakse, Kajeske, Kujarke, Mini, Kawa Tadimini) [ckq] 10,000 (1983 Bender). East, Ouaddaï Prefecture, Am Dam Subprefecture. South and southeast of Am Dam. Some refugees in Sudan near the border. *Class:* Afro-Asiatic, Chadic, East, B, B.1, 2. *Dialects:* Partially intelligible with Mesmedje and Mubi. *Other:* Hills. Hunter-gatherers; little livestock; traders: hides.

Kanembu (Kanambu, Kanembou) [kbl] 389,028 (1993 census). Population includes 168,441 in Lac Prefecture, 68,032 in Chari-Baguirmi Prefecture. Northwest, Kanem, Lac prefectures, and Chari-Baguirmi Prefecture, Massakory Subprefecture, northeast of Lake Chad. *Class:* Nilo-Saharan, Saharan, Western, Kanuri. *Dialects:* Karkawu, Mando, Nguri. There is a gradual differentiation between dialects of Kanembu and Kanuri. *Lg Use:* The majority use Arabic as second language. *Other:* Ethnic groups: Badé (Badde 2,646), Baribu, Chiroa, Diabu, Galabu, Kadjidi (5,638), Kankena, Kanku, Kenguina (1,944), Koubri (Koubouri 2,817), Maguirmi (1,825), Nguiguim (7,233). Muslim, traditional religion.

Kanuri, Central (Yerwa Kanuri, Kanoury, Kanouri, Bornu, Bornouans, Bornouan, Aga, Kole, Kolere, Sirata, "Baribari," "Beriberi") [knc] 93,638 in Chad (1993 census). Population includes 34,549 in Chari-Baguirmi and 23,287 in N'Djaména. Communities of speakers in Chari-Baguirmi, Batha, Guéra, and Mayo-Kebbi prefectures. *Dialects:* Dagara, Kaga (Kagama), Sugurti, Lare, Kwayam, Njesko, Kabari (Kuvuri), Ngazar, Guvja, Mao, Temageri, Fadawa. *Other:* 'Beriberi' is considered a derogatory name. Muslim. See main entry under Nigeria.

Karang (Laka, Lakka, Kareng, Eastern Mbum, Lakka Mbum, Mbum Bakal, Nzák Kàráng) [kzr] 1,000 in Chad

(1995 SIL). Southwest, Logone Oriental Prefecture, Baibokoum Subprefecture, northwest of Baïbokoum along the Cameroon border: Loumbogo, Lawtiko I, Lawtiko II, Sarkaluki villages, and possibly another, as well as two Sakpu villages. *Dialects:* Karang, Sakpu, Ngomi, Mbere. *Other:* Different from Laka (Kabba Laka) of Central African Republic and Chad, and from Laka of Nigeria. Traditional religion. See main entry under Cameroon.

Karanga (Kurunga) [kth] 10,000 (1999 SIL). Population includes 4,696 Karanga and 1,419 Bakha. East, Ouaddaï Prefecture, Abéché and Am Dam subprefectures. Around Am Dam and between Am Dam and Abéché, south of the Maba. The Bakha are southwest of Am Dam, and the Karanga and the Koniéré are northeast of Am Dam. The Kashmere are south of Abéché and north of the Karanga. *Class:* Nilo-Saharan, Maban. *Dialects:* Karanga (Kurunga), Kashmere (Kachmere), Bakha (Baxa, Bakhat, Faala, Fala), Koniéré (Konyare, Kognere, Mooyo, Moyo). Lexical similarity 73% with Maba, 94% between Karanga and Kashmere dialects. *Other:* The four dialects are distinct ethnic groups. Muslim.

Kendeje (Yaali) [klf] 1,859 (2000 WCD). East, Ouaddaï Prefecture, rural Abéché and Adré subprefectures, north and west of Hadjer Hadid. *Class:* Nilo-Saharan, Maban, Mabang. *Dialects:* Yaali, Faranga. Lexical similarity 89% between the dialects with little contact between them. *Lg Use:* Reported high bilingualism in Maba and Masalit. *Other:* Muslim.

Kenga (Kenge, Cenge) [kyq] 40,000 (1997 SIL). Central, Guéra Prefecture, Bitkine Subprefecture, around Bitkine, 52 villages, including Bolongo, Bokiyo. *Class:* Nilo-Saharan, Central Sudanic, West, Bongo-Bagirmi, Sara-Bagirmi, Bagirmi. *Dialects:* Cenge (Tar Cenge), Banama (Tar Banama), Bidjir, Banala (Tar Banala), Bolong (Tar Bolongo). Related to Naba, and Jaya, but not inherently intelligible. Lexical similarity 62% with Jaya. *Lg Use:* Positive language attitude. The majority of men use Chadian Arabic as second language for trade. Some also use French. *Lg Dev:* Literacy rate in first language: 1% to 5%. Literacy rate in second language: Men: 15% or below in French, 1% in Arabic; women: below 1%. RC song book and prayer book, good orthography. Grammar. *Other:* SVO. Agriculturalists: millet, sorghum, peanuts, okra. Muslim, Christian, traditional religion.

Kera [ker] 44,523 in Chad (1993 census). Population total all countries: 50,523. Southwest, Mayo-Kebbi Prefecture, Fianga Subprefecture, south of Fianga, near Lake Tikem. Also spoken in Cameroon. *Class:* Afro-Asiatic, Chadic, East, A, A.3. *Dialects:* Lexical similarity 42% with Kwang. *Lg Dev:* Literacy rate in first language: 5% to 10%. Literacy rate in second language: 10% to 15%. Bible portions: 1988–2001. *Other:* It has been confused with neighboring Tupuri in some publications. SVO.

Kibet (Kibeit, Kibeet, Kaben, Kabentang) [kie] 18,500 (1983 Bender). East, Salamat Prefecture, Am Timan Subprefecture, and Ouaddaï Prefecture, Goz Beïda Subprefecture. Northeast of Am Timan and southwest of Goz Beïda. *Class:* Nilo-Saharan, Maban, Mabang, Runga-Kibet. *Dialects:* Dagel (Daggal), Murru (Muro, Mourro), Kibet. Close to Runga. The dialects listed, including Murru, may be separate languages. Not a Tama variety, as reported in some sources. *Lg Use:* The majority also use Arabic. *Other:* The area is flooded for 6 months each year. The tse-tse fly is a problem. Agriculturalists: sorghum, peanuts; animal husbandry; fishermen; hunter-gatherers. Muslim.

Kim [kia] 15,354 (1993 census). Southwest, Mayo-Kebbi Prefecture, Bongor Subprefecture, Logone River area, southeast of Bongor. *Class:* Niger-Congo, Atlantic-Congo, Volta-Congo, North, Adamawa-Ubangi, Adamawa, Mbum-Day, Kim. *Dialects:* Garap (Éré), Gerep

(Djouman, Jumam), Kolop (Kilop, Kolobo), Kosop (Kwasap, Kim). Dialects listed may be closely related languages. Formerly classified as Chadic. *Lg Dev:* NT: 1955. *Other:* Incorrectly called 'Masa'.

Kimré (Gabri-Kimré) [kqp] 15,000 (1990 census). Population includes 700 Tchere-Aïba. Southwest Chad, Tandjilé Prefecture, Kélo Subprefecture, east of Laï, including Tchere-Aïba village. *Class:* Afro-Asiatic, Chadic, East, A, A.2, 1. *Dialects:* Kimruwa (Kim-Ruwa, Kimré), Buruwa (Bordo), Tchire (Tchere-Aïba). Popularly called 'Gabri', but it is not intelligible with Gabri. *Other:* The 'Kimre' name is also used for Tobanga and Southern Gabri.

Koke (Khoke) [kou] 600 (1993 census). Southeast, Guéra Prefecture, Melfi Subprefecture, southeast of Melfi; around Daguéla, Sengué, and Djourab villages. *Class:* Niger-Congo, Atlantic-Congo, Volta-Congo, North, Adamawa-Ubangi, Adamawa, Mbum-Day, Bua. *Dialects:* Lexical similarity 60% with Bolgo Dugag. *Lg Use:* The majority may be bilingual in Chadian Arabic or Fania.

Kujarge [vkj] 1,000 (1983 Bender). Dar Fongoro, 7 villages near Jebel Mirra, and scattered among the Fur and Sinyar in Sudanese villages along the lower Wadis Salih and Azum rivers. The Daju Galfigé are to the west, Sinyar to the north, Fur-Dalinga, Fongoro, Formono, and Runga to the east and south. *Class:* Unclassified. *Lg Use:* Fur is used as second language and some use Daju. *Other:* A few groups. Hunter-gatherers: honey; little agriculture or animal husbandry.

Kulfa (Kulfe, Kurmi, Kurumi, "Kaba So") [kxj] 2,200 (2004). Southeast, Moyen Chari Prefecture, Kyabé Subprefecture, southwest of Lake Iro. Centered in Alako, Male, and Moufa. *Class:* Nilo-Saharan, Central Sudanic, West, Bongo-Bagirmi, Sara-Bagirmi, Sara, Sara Proper, Sara Kaba. *Dialect:* Kurmi, So (Suka, Souka, Soko). Lexical similarity 80% with Kaba Na. *Other:* Not the same as Kaba, Kaba Deme, Kaba Na, or Laka (Kabba Laka). The name "Kaba So" is considered to be derogatory by the speakers.

Kuo (Ko, Koh) [xuo] 11,828 in Chad (2000 WCD). Population total all countries: 14,803. Southwest, Logone Oriental Prefecture, Baibokoum Subprefecture, near Baibokoum, Pao, and Bouroum cantons. The villages are on the north-south road from Pao to Laramanay, on the road northwest from Pao, and on the road northwest from Laramanay to Bouroum. Also spoken in Cameroon. *Class:* Niger-Congo, Atlantic-Congo, Volta-Congo, North, Adamawa-Ubangi, Adamawa, Mbum-Day, Mbum, Central, Koh. *Dialects:* Close to Karang and Nzakambay. *Lg Dev:* Literacy rate in first language: 1% to 5%. Literacy rate in second language: below 5%. Bible portions: 1987.

Kwang (Kuang, Kouang, Kwong) [kvi] 16,805 (1993 census). Population includes 10,000 or more Kwang, 2,000 Mobou, 250 Aloa. Southwest Chad, Tandjilé Prefecture, Laï Subprefecture. North of Laï, east of Bongor, southwest of Bousso. The Mobou are in Mobou, south of Bousso. The Aloa are in Mogo. *Class:* Afro-Asiatic, Chadic, East, A, A.3. *Dialects:* Kwang, Mobou (Mobu), Ngam (Gam, Modgel), Tchagin (Tchakin), Aloa, Kawalké, Gaya, Mindéra. The dialects listed are inherently intelligible to each other's speakers. Includes Midigil village, sometimes erroneously listed as a language named 'Modgel' (Medegel) in some sources. Lexical similarity 42% with Kera. *Lg Use:* The Aloa are Muslim and fully bilingual in Bagirmi. The Ngam use Sara as second language. *Other:* Ngam is different from Ngam of Chad and Central African Republic in the Sara group of Nilo-Saharan. Traditional religion, Christian, Muslim.

Laal (Gori) [gdm] 749 (2000 WCD). Damtar village had its own dialect, called 'Laabe' with 3 speakers left in 1977.

Southwest, Moyen-Chari Prefecture, Sarh Subprefecture, between Korbol and Dik. Centered in Gori, villages of Gori, Damtar, and Mailao near Kouno, northwest of Sarh. *Class:* Unclassified. *Dialects:* Laal, Laabe. *Other:* Some lexical relationship to the Bua group, but Boyeldieu says it should not be classified with Bua. Probably Adamawa, some sources say Chadic.

Lagwan (Kotoko-Logone, Logone, Lagwane, Lagouane) [kot] West, Chari-Baguirmi Prefecture, N'Djaména Subprefecture, south of N'Djaména along the Logone River, in the vicinity of Logone-Gana. *Dialect:* Logone-Birni, Logone-Gana (Kotoko-Gana). *Other:* A member of the Kotoko ethnic and linguistic group: Afade, Mser, Malgbe, Maslam, Mpade, and Jilbe (in Nigeria). Muslim. See main entry under Cameroon.

Laka (Kabba Laka) [lap] 55,143 in Chad (1991 census). Population total all countries: 57,193. Southwest, Logone Oriental Prefecture, Baïbokoum and Goré subprefectures. Mang is in Ngadjibian Canton, north of Bessao, and in parts of the Békan and Timbéri cantons, Goré Subprefecture. Bémour is in Bessao and Pandzangué cantons south of Moundou. Maïngao is along the Ngamadja-Dodang II axis and along the Bessao-Oudoumian axis. Goula is in Andoum Canton and in the area around Pan in Pandzangué Canton. Païis at Oudoumian. Total of 310 villages. Also spoken in Central African Republic. *Class:* Nilo-Saharan, Central Sudanic, West, Bongo-Bagirmi, Sara-Bagirmi, Sara, Sara Proper. *Dialects:* Mang, Bémour, Maïngao, Goula, Païi. Some consider it to be a dialect of Ngambai. *Lg Dev:* NT: 1960. *Other:* Different from Laka of Nigeria, which is Adamawa-Ubangi, and from Kaba of Central African Republic and Chad.

Lele [lln] 26,000 (1991 UBS). Southwest Chad, Tandjilé Prefecture, Kélo Subprefecture, south of Kélo. *Class:* Afro-Asiatic, Chadic, East, A, A.2, 1. *Lg Dev:* NT: 1991. *Other:* Different from Lele of Democratic Republic of the Congo and Lela (Kasem) of Ghana and Burkina Faso.

Lutos [ndy] 1,978 in Chad (1993 census). Southwest, Moyen-Chari Prefecture, Maro Subprefecture, south of the Ngam. *Dialect:* Ruto (Routo, Rito, Louto, Luto). See main entry under Central African Republic.

Maba (Mabang, Mabaa, Mabak, Bura Mabang, Kana Mabang, Ouaddaien, Waddayen, Wadai, Ouaddai, Borgu) [mde] 250,000 (1999 SIL). East, Ouaddaï Prefecture, Abéché and Am Dam subprefectures, and Biltine Prefecture, Biltine Subprefecture; almost all of Abéché Subprefecture and the area around Biltine. *Class:* Nilo-Saharan, Maban, Mabang, Maba. *Dialects:* Bakha, Abkar, Kajanga (Kajangan), Kelingan, Malanga, Mandaba (Ma Ndaba), Mandala (Ma Dala), Nyabadan, Kodoo, Ouled Djemma, Kujinga, Dondongo. Lexical similarity 73% with Karanga and Kachmere, 63% with Marfa, 42% with Masalit. *Lg Use:* Trade language. *Other:* Ethnic groups: Uled Djemma (Aulad Djema, Awlad Djema). Mountain slope. Agriculturalists: millet, peanuts, corn, beans, sesame, chick-peas, and various leaves. Muslim.

Mabire [muj] 3 (2001 SIL). Guéra Province, Bidiyo canton, Mongo-Rural subprefecture, village of Oulek. *Class:* Afro-Asiatic, Chadic, East, B, B.1, 1. *Dialects:* Similar to Jegu dialect of Mogum and Tounkoul dialect of Bidiyo. Lexical similarity 37% to 52% with Jegu (Mogum). *Lg Use:* Speakers also use Chadic Arabic or Kofa. *Other:* Nearly extinct.

Majera (Mazera, Midah, Mida'a, Da'a) [xmj] West, Mayo-Kebbi Prefecture, Bongor Subprefecture, north of Gelengdeng, Dogwea village. *Dialects:* Majera (Mazra), Kajire-'dulo, Hwalem (Holom). *Other:* Included in what the Mandage call 'Mida'a' and 'Da'a'. See main entry under Cameroon.

Malgbe (Gulfei, Goulfei, Goulfey, Malbe, Malgwe, Ngwalkwe, Mandage, Sanbalbe, Kotoko-Gulfei) [mxf] West, Chari-Baguirmi Prefecture, N'Djamena Sub-prefecture, north of N'Djamena along the Chari River. Douguia, Malalie, and Oulio (Walia) villages, and others. *Dialects:* Goulfey, Walia, Mara, Douguia. *Other:* Related to other Kotoko ethnic and linguistic groups: Afade, Lagwan, Maslam, Mpade, Mser, and Jilbe (of Nigeria). 'Mandage' is a name applied to the northern Kotoko languages. See main entry under Cameroon.

Mambai (Mangbai, Mangbei, Manbai, Mambay, Mamgbay, Mamgbei, Mongbay, Mangbaï de Biparé, Momboi) [mcs] 2,000 in Chad (2002 SIL). Southwest, Mayo-Kebbi Prefecture, Lere Subprefecture, Cameroon border west of Lere. *Lg Use:* Speakers are reported to understand Mundang. See main entry under Cameroon.

Mango (Mongo, Mbay Doba, Doba) [mge] 50,000 (1981 Bernard Lanne). Logone Oriental Prefecture, Doba Subprefecture, centered around Bodo. *Class:* Nilo-Saharan, Central Sudanic, West, Bongo-Bagirmi, Sara-Bagirmi, Sara, Sara Proper. *Dialects:* Close to Bedjond and Gor, with high inherent intelligibility. *Lg Use:* There is a Mango Language Committee. The speakers have a clear understanding of their identity as separate from Gor and Bedjond. *Lg Dev:* Primer, literacy classes. Bible portions: 1968. *Other:* Christian, traditional religion.

Mararit (Mararet, Merarit, Abiyi, Abiri, Ebiri) [mgb] 42,388 (1993 census). Population includes 15,376 Mararit, 27,012 Abou Charib. East, Biltine Prefecture, Am Zoer Subprefecture (Abou Charib), and Ouaddaï Prefecture, Adré Subprefecture, Mabrone Canton (Mararit). *Class:* Nilo-Saharan, Eastern Sudanic, Western, Tama, Mararit. *Dialect:* Mararit, Abou Charib (Abu Sharib, Abu Sharin). Limited intelligibility between Abou Charib and Mararit. Very difficult intelligibility of Tama. Not intelligible with Sungor. Lexical similarity 62% with Tama, 75% between Abou Charib and Mararit. *Lg Use:* The majority use Chadian Arabic as second language. *Other:* The Abou Charib live north of the Mararit and trace their ancestry to them. Mountain slope. Agriculturalists; pastoralists: cattle, camels. Muslim.

Marba ('Azumeina, Azumeina, Maraba, Kolong, Kulung) [mpg] 124,357 (1993 census). Southwest, Tandjilé Prefecture, Kélo Subprefecture, north of Kélo. *Class:* Afro-Asiatic, Chadic, Masa. *Dialect:* Monogoy. *Lg Dev:* NT: 1978. *Other:* 'Kulung' is a place in the Marba-speaking area, not a dialect or language. Different from Marfa (Marba) of Chad, which is Maban.

Marfa (Marba) [mvu] 5,000 to 10,000 (1999 SIL). East, Ouaddaï Prefecture, Abéché Subprefecture, south of Abéché. *Class:* Nilo-Saharan, Maban, Mabang, Maba. *Dialects:* Not a dialect of Masalit, as some have implied. Lexical similarity 63% with Maba, 69% with Karanga, 45% with Masalit. *Lg Use:* Chadian Arabic is used as second language, and the majority use Maba. *Other:* Different from Marba which is Chadic.

Masalit (Massalit, Massolit, Kaana Masala, Masara, Masale) [mls] 66,710 in Chad (2000 WCD). East, Ouaddaï Prefecture, Adré Subprefecture, around Adré. Northern Masalit is north and east of Geneina in Sudan, Western Masalit in Ouaddaï, Southern Masalit in Sudan. *Dialects:* Northern Masalit, Western Masalit, Southern Masalit. *Lg Use:* The majority use Chadian Arabic as second language. *Lg Dev:* Literacy rate in first language: below 1%. Literacy rate in second language: below 5%. *Other:* Muslim. See main entry under Sudan.

Masana (Masa, Massa, "Banana") [mcn] 109,093 in Chad (1993 census). Population total all countries: 212,093. Southwest, Mayo-Kebbi Prefecture, Bongo Subprefecture, along the Logone River, Bongor Region. Also spoken in Cameroon. *Class:* Afro-Asiatic, Chadic, Masa. *Dialects:*

Yagwa (Yagoua), Bongor, Wina (Viri), Walia (Walya), Domo, Gizay (Guissey, Gisey), Bugudum (Budugum), Gumay (Goumaye), Ham. All dialects understand Yagoua well, although Gizay and Yagoua have 80% intelligibility. Budugum has 97% lexical similarity to the closest other dialect. *Lg Dev:* Dictionary. NT: 1950–1955. *Other:* "Banana" has been used perjoratively by some neighboring groups. Traditional religion, Christian, Muslim.

Maslam (Mandage, Mendage, Mandagué, Maltam, Kotoko-Maltam) [msv] 473 in Chad (2000 WCD). West, Chari-Baguirmi Prefecture, N'Djamena Subprefecture. North of N'Djamena, along the Chari River. Maltam is in Miskini and Blabli villages, Sao in Farcha-Milezi and Ngara-Mandju (or 'Gourmadjo') villages. *Dialects:* Maslam (Maltam), Sao (Sahu). *Other:* In the Kotoko ethnic and linguistic group. See main entry under Cameroon.

Masmaje (Masmadje, Mesmedje) [mes] 25,727 (1993 census). Central, Batha Prefecture, Oum Hadjer Subprefecture, southwest of Oum Hadjer, north of the Mubi. *Class:* Afro-Asiatic, Chadic, East, B, B.1, 2. *Other:* Arabicized and Islamicized.

Massalat [mdg] 10 (1991 R. Blench). Ethnic population: 29,836 (1993 census). East Batha Prefecture, Oum Hadjer Subprefecture, and Ouaddaï Prefecture, Am Dam Subprefecture. *Class:* Nilo-Saharan, Maban, Mabang, Masalit. *Lg Use:* Speakers are shifting to Chadian Arabic. *Other:* The Massalat originally separated from the Masalit along the Sudan border and moved west. Muslim. Nearly extinct.

Mawa (Mahwa, Mahoua) [mcw] 6,560 (2000 WCD). Central, north Guéra Prefecture, Bitkine Subprefecture, about 30 km south of Bitkine, centered around the village of Mahoua. Southeast of the Mukulu. *Class:* Afro-Asiatic, Chadic, East, B, B.1, 1. *Dialects:* 'Gurara' and 'Roffono' ('Reupan') are villages in which the speech is very similar to that of Mahoua. Lexical similarity 8% with Ubi. *Lg Use:* The majority use Shuwa Arabic as second language, some use Kenga.

Mbara (Massa de Guelengdeng, Guelengdeng, G'kelendeng, G'kelendeg) [mpk] 1,000 (1980 Tourneux). East, Chari-Baguirmi Prefecture, Massénya Subprefecture, and Mayo-Kebbi Prefecture, Bongor Subprefecture, along the Chari River, around Guélengdeng. *Class:* Afro-Asiatic, Chadic, Biu-Mandara, B, B.2.

Mbay (Mbai, Mbaye, Sara Mbai, Moissala Mbai, Mbay Moissala) [myb] 80,000 in Chad (1990 Keegan). Population total all countries: 88,300. Southwest, Moyen-Chari Prefecture, Moïssala Subprefecture. Around Moïssala. The traditional area is on the border of Chad and Central African Republic. Also spoken in Central African Republic, Nigeria. *Class:* Nilo-Saharan, Central Sudanic, West, Bongo-Bagirmi, Sara-Bagirmi, Sara, Sara Proper. *Dialects:* Bédjou, Kan (Mbay-Kan), Ngoka (Mbang), Bédégué, Mougo, Bbate. *Lg Dev:* Dictionary. Grammar. Bible: 1980. *Other:* Traditional religion, Christian, Muslim.

Mesme (Zime, Djime, Djiwe) [zim] 20,120 (1993 census). Southwest, Tandjilé Prefecture, Kélo Subprefecture, south and west of Kélo, between Kélo and Pala. *Class:* Afro-Asiatic, Chadic, Masa. *Dialects:* Bero, Zamre. Mesmé is a separate but related language to Pévé, Nguété, and Herdé. They call themselves 'Zime', but that name is commonly used by outsiders to refer to all languages and dialects of this group. The name 'Mesmé' is used by outsiders to distinguish this group from the other groups they call 'Zime'. *Lg Dev:* NT: 1995.

Migaama (Migama, Jongor, Djonkor, Dionkor, Dyongor, Djonkor Abou Telfane) [mmy] 20,000 (2000 W. Chesley). 2,000 monolinguals. Ethnic population: 23,000 (1991 census). Central, Guéra Prefecture, Mongo Subprefecture, east of Mongo, Abou Telfane Canton centered in Baro, around Abu Telfan. Migaama dialect is in Baro, Doga in Fityari, Gamiya in Game and Julkulkili, and Dambiya in Mala. *Class:* Afro-Asiatic, Chadic, East, B, B.1, 1. *Dialect:* Migaama, Doga, Gamiya, Dambiya (Ndambiya). Dialect cluster. Dambiya is probably a Bidiyo dialect rather than a Migaama dialect. *Lg Use:* Vigorous. All domains except to Arabs in market, French to teachers in school. Oral use in administration, a little in school, some in church, commerce. Positive language attitude. 18,000 to 19,000 also use Chadian Arabic as second language, men at a high proficiency level, women at a low proficiency level. 6,000 can speak French. Modern Standard Arabic taught in school. *Lg Dev:* 100 can read Migaama, 10 can write it. Bible portions. *Other:* Mountain slope. Scrub brush, thorn trees. Agriculturalists: millet, peanuts, sesame seeds. Muslim, Christian.

Miltu (Miltou) [mlj] 272 (1993 census). Southwest, Chari-Baguirmi Prefecture, Bousso Subprefecture, around the town of Miltou. *Class:* Afro-Asiatic, Chadic, East, A, A.1, 2. *Dialects:* Lexical similarity 27% with Sarua, Somrai, Gadang, and Ndam, 36% with Boor. *Lg Use:* Speakers are shifting to Bagirmi in all domains.

Mimi (Mime) [miv] 5,000 (1983). Ethnic population: 39,945 (1993 census). Eastern, north of Biltine, near Jebels Batran and Agán, and scattered through Ouaddaï. Possibly in Sudan, in Dar Fur. *Class:* Nilo-Saharan, Fur. *Dialects:* May be the same as Amdang. This Mimi is different from the Mimi of Gaudefroy-Demombynes and the Mimi of Nachtigal (hitherto unidentified), which may be Maban (Doornbos and Bender 1983). *Lg Use:* Most also use Chadian Arabic. *Other:* Mountain slope, plains. Pastoralists; agriculturalists. Muslim.

Mire [mvh] 1,400 (1990 census). Southwest, Tandjile Prefecture, Lai Subprefecture, between the Ndam and the Kimré language areas. *Class:* Afro-Asiatic, Chadic, East, A, A.1, 1. *Dialects:* Lexical similarity 65% with Ndam, 32% with Kimré. *Lg Use:* Most use Kimré or Ndam as second language. *Other:* Traditional religion, Christian.

Mogum (Mogoum) [mou] 7,000 (1997 SIL). South central Chad, north Guéra Prefecture, Bitkine, Melfi, and Mongo subprefectures, south of the Bidiyo. *Class:* Afro-Asiatic, Chadic, East, B, B.1, 1. *Dialects:* Jegu, Koffa (Kofa), Mogum Déle, Mogum Diguimi, Mogum Urmi. Dialect cluster. Mogum Diguimi may not be a separate dialect. Lexical similarity above 96% among dialects.

Mpade (Makari, Mendage, Mandage, Mandague, Kotoko-Makari) [mpi] 2,366 in Chad (2000 WCD). West, Chari-Baguirmi Prefecture, N'Djaména Subprefecture, south of Lake Chad, in and around Mani on the Logone River, north of N'Djaména. *Dialects:* Makari, Shoe (Shawe, Chaoue, Mani), Bodo, Woulki, Digam. *Other:* In the Kotoko ethnic and linguistic group. 'Mandage', etc., is applied to the northern Kotoko languages (Afade, Malgbe, Maslam, Mpade, Mser). See main entry under Cameroon.

Mser (Kotoko-Kuseri, Kuseri, Kousseri, Klesem, Mandage, Mandague, Mendage) [kqx] West, Chari-Baguirmi Prefecture, N'Djaména Subprefecture, Cameroon border near N'Djaména. *Dialects:* Mser (Kousseri, Msir), Kalo (Kalakafra), Gawi, Houlouf, Kabe. *Lg Use:* The people of Klesem village no longer speak Mser. The majority also use Chadian Arabic or Kanuri. *Other:* The term 'Mandage', etc. is applied to all the northern Kotoko languages (Afade, Malgbe, Maslam, Mpade, Mser). Muslim. See main entry under Cameroon.

Mubi (Moubi) [mub] 35,277 (1993 census). Central, Guéra Prefecture, Mangalmé Subprefecture, east of Mongo, centered in and around Mangalmé. 135 villages. There may be some in Sudan. *Class:* Afro-Asiatic, Chadic, East, B, B.1, 2. *Dialects:* Lexical similarity 71% with Zirenkel, 35% with Dangaléat. *Lg Use:* The majority use Arabic as second language. *Other:* Different from Mubi (Gude) of Cameroon and Nigeria. Muslim.

Mukulu (Mokulu, Mokoulou, Djonkor Guera, Dyongor Guera, Diongor Guera, Jonkor-Gera, Mokilko) [moz] 12,000 (1990 SIL). Central, Guéra Prefecture, Bitkine Subprefecture, at the foot of the Guéra Massif: Moukoulou, Séguine, Doli, Morgué, Djarkatché (Mezimi), and Gougué villages. *Class:* Afro-Asiatic, Chadic, East, B, B.2. *Dialects:* Mokilko, Seginki, Doliki, Moriko, Mezimko, Gugiko. *Lg Use:* Speakers have low proficiency in Chadian Arabic. *Lg Dev:* Literacy rate in first language: 1%. Literacy rate in second language: below 5%. *Other:* Traditional religion, Christian, Muslim.

Mundang (Moundan, Moundang, Kaele, Nda) [mua] 160,880 in Chad (1993 census). Population total all countries: 205,580. Southwest, Mayo-Kebbi Prefecture, Léré, Pala, and Fianga subprefectures, centered around Léré. The Kieziere subdialect is on the border with Pévé. The Torrock-Kaélé subdialect is in Torrock. Also spoken in Cameroon. *Class:* Niger-Congo, Atlantic-Congo, Volta-Congo, North, Adamawa-Ubangi, Adamawa, Mbum-Day, Mbum, Northern, Tupuri-Mambai. *Dialect:* Kabi, Zasing (Yasing). A subdialect of Kabi is Kiziere, of Zasing is Torrock-Kaélé. *Lg Dev:* Bible: 1983.

Musey (Moussei, Musei, Mussoi, Moussey, Mussoy, Mosi, Bananna, Bananna Ho Ho, Museyna) [mse] 175,640 in Chad (1993 census). Population total all countries: 195,640. Southwest, Mayo-Kebbi Prefecture, Fianga and Gounou Gaya subprefectures, and Tandjilé Prefecture, Kélo Subprefecture, southeast of Fianga. Gounou Gaya is the commercial and administrative center. Also spoken in Cameroon. *Class:* Afro-Asiatic, Chadic, Masa. *Dialects:* Bongor-Jodo-Tagal-Berem-Gunu, Pe-Holom-Gamé, Jaraw-Domo, Lew. Some intelligibility of Masa. Marba (Azumeina) is closest linguistically. The Lew dialect is closest to Marba. All dialects are intelligible with each other. Dialect names are village names. The Pe dialect is in Cameroon. *Lg Use:* Kera and other nearby groups are bilingual in Musey. Bilingual level estimates for French: 0 0%, 1 20%, 2 30%, 3 30%, 4 19%, 5 1%. *Lg Dev:* NT: 1996. *Other:* Traditional religion.

Musgu (Mousgou, Musgum, Mousgoum, Musuk, Mousgoun, Munjuk, Moulaui, Mulwi) [mug] 24,408 in Chad (1993 census). West Chad, Mayo-Kebbi Prefecture, Bongor Subprefecture, and Chari-Baguirmi Prefecture, N'Djaména Subprefecture. Between the Chari and Logone rivers, west of Guélengdeng. *Dialects:* Mpus (Pus, Pouss, Mousgoum de Pouss, Musgum-Pouss), Beege (Jafga), Vulum (Vlum, Mulwi-Mogroum), Muzuk (Mousgoum de Guirvidig, Mousgoum de Guirvidik, Guirvidig). *Other:* Their name for themselves is 'Mulwi'. Distinct from the Muskum language in Mouskoun village. See main entry under Cameroon.

Muskum (Muzgum) [mje] Extinct. West, Mayo-Kebbi Prefecture, Bongor Subprefecture. Along the Logone River, west of Guélengdeng, village of Muskum (Mouskoun), 10 km north of Katoa. *Class:* Afro-Asiatic, Chadic, Biu-Mandara, B, B.2. *Dialects:* Lexical similarity 40% with Musgu. *Lg Use:* There was 1 speaker in 1976. Speakers now speak the Vulum dialect of Musgu.

Naba [mne] 232,448 (1993 census). Population includes 136,629 Bilala, 76,660 Kuka, and 19,159 Medogo. Central, Batha Prefecture, Ati and Oum subprefectures, and Chari-Baguirmi Prefecture, Bokoro Subprefecture. The Bilala are around Lake Fitri and toward the east to Ati. The Kuka are between Moïto and Bokoro in Bokoro Subprefecture, and between Ati and Oum Hadjer. The Medogo are southwest of Ati. *Class:* Nilo-Saharan, Central Sudanic, West, Bongo-Bagirmi, Sara-Bagirmi, Bagirmi. *Dialects:* Bilala (Bilaala, Boulala, Bulala, Mage,

Ma), Kuka (Kouka, Lisi), Medogo (Modogo, Mud). Related but not inherently intelligible with Berakou or Kenga. Lexical similarity among Bilala, Kuka, and Medogo is 99%. *Lg Use:* Some use Chadian Arabic as second language. One part of the Kuka ethnic group, who live near Oum Hadjer, have shifted from the Naba language to Chadian Arabic. *Other:* Bilala, Kuka, and Medogo are 3 ethnic groups who share a common culture and speak essentially the same language, called 'Naba' by all 3 groups. Muslim.

Nancere (Nanjeri, Nanchere, Nantcere, Nangjere, Nangcere) [nnc] 71,609 (1993 census). Southwest, Tandjilé Prefecture, Béré and Kélo subprefectures. *Class:* Afro-Asiatic, Chadic, East, A, A.2, 1. *Lg Dev:* Bible: 1986. *Other:* Traditional religion, Christian.

Ndam (Dam, Ndamm) [ndm] 6,500 (1990 census). Southwest, Tandjilé Prefecture, Laï Subprefecture, northeast of Laï, and southeast of Bousso. *Class:* Afro-Asiatic, Chadic, East, A, A.1, 1. *Dialects:* Ndam-Ndam (Southern Ndam), Ndam Dik (Northern Ndam). *Other:* Distinct from Dam of Bousso. Traditional religion, Muslim, Christian.

Ngam (Ngama, Sarngam, Ngahm, Ngamh) [nmc] 43,743 in Chad (1993 census). Population total all countries: 61,443. Southwestern Chad, Moyen-Chari Prefecture, Maro and Dembo subprefectures, centered in Maro. Ngam Tel is in Maro Canton and Moussafoyo. Ngam Tira is at Maro, Moyo, and Danamadji. Kon Ngam is in Djéké Canton. Kle is at Nara in Djéké Canton. Ngam Gir Bor is in Kabo in Central African Republic. Also spoken in Central African Republic. *Class:* Nilo-Saharan, Central Sudanic, West, Bongo-Bagirmi, Sara-Bagirmi, Sara, Sara Proper. *Dialects:* Ngam Tel, Ngam Tira, Kon Ngam, Kle, Ngam Gir Bor. *Lg Use:* Sara Madjingay is the lingua franca. *Lg Dev:* NT: 1999. *Other:* The Horo (Hor) are reported to no longer use their language and now speak the Kle dialect of Ngam. They consecrate the traditional chiefs of the Ngam.

Ngambay (Sara, Sara Ngambai, Gamba, Gambaye, Gamblai, Ngambai) [sba] 750,000 in Chad (1999 SIL). Southwest, all of Logone Occidental Prefecture; also Logone Oriental Prefecture, Bébedjia and Goré subprefectures, and Mayo-Kebbi Prefecture, Pala Subprefecture. Centered in and around Moundou. Also spoken in Cameroon, Nigeria. *Class:* Nilo-Saharan, Central Sudanic, West, Bongo-Bagirmi, Sara-Bagirmi, Sara, Sara Proper. *Dialects:* Lara, Benoye, Murum (Mouroum), Kere, Bemar (Daba de Goré). The dialects are reported to be completely intelligible with each other. The Laka language is considered by some to be a dialect of Ngambay. *Lg Use:* Trade language. Largest language of the Sara-Bagirmi group. *Lg Dev:* Bible: 1993. *Other:* Traditional religion, Christian, Muslim.

Ngete (Nguété, Nguetté, Nge'dé, Ka'do Ngueté, Zime) [nnn] 10,000 (1991 UBS). Southwest, Mayo-Kebbi Prefecture, Pala Subprefecture, east of Pala around Ngeté village; near the Pévé, east of the Herdé. *Class:* Afro-Asiatic, Chadic, Masa. *Dialects:* Linguistic and sociolinguistic differences with Pévé and Herdé make separate literature necessary. Also close to Marba. The term 'Zime' is used by outsiders to refer to this and related languages: Herdé, Pévé, Mesmé.

Niellim (Mjillem, Nyilem, Nielim, Lua) [nie] 5,157 (1993 census). Population includes 1,000 in the city of Sarh and 400 in Niou dialect. Southwest, Moyen-Chari Prefecture, Sarh Subprefecture, around Niellim town, on the southwest bank of the Chari River. Niou dialect is in Niou on the northeast bank. *Class:* Niger-Congo, Atlantic-Congo, Volta-Congo, North, Adamawa-Ubangi, Adamawa, Mbum-Day, Bua. *Dialects:* Niellim, Tchini (Cuni, Cini), Niou. *Lg Use:* Tchini dialect is extinct.

Other: The government calls them 'Niellim'. Their own name is 'Lua'. Traditional religion.

Noy (Loo) [noy] 36 (1993 census). South, Moyen-Chari Prefecture, Sarh and Koumra subprefectures, in the area between Sarh, Djoli, Bédaya, Koumra, and Koumogo villages. *Class:* Niger-Congo, Atlantic-Congo, Volta-Congo, North, Adamawa-Ubangi, Adamawa, Mbum-Day, Bua. *Lg Use:* Boyd (1989) indicates speakers are shifting to Sar. *Other:* Nearly extinct.

Nzakambay (Nzakmbay, Nzak Mbai, Nzaka Mbay, Mbum, Mboum, Njakambai, Mbum Nzakambay) [nzy] 18,503 in Chad (2000 WCD). Population total all countries: 31,501. Southwest, Logone Oriental Prefecture, Baïbokoum Subprefecture, Cameroon border, near Baïbokoum. Zoli is in the Monts de Lam area. Also spoken in Cameroon. *Class:* Niger-Congo, Atlantic-Congo, Volta-Congo, North, Adamawa-Ubangi, Adamawa, Mbum-Day, Mbum, Central, Karang. *Dialects:* Nzakambay, Zoli. Close to Karang and Kuo. *Lg Dev:* NT: 1968–1994. *Other:* Different from Mbai, which is Nilo-Saharan, and from Mbum of Cameroon. Traditional religion.

Pana (Pani) [pnz] 1,000 in Chad (1999 SIL). The Pana dialect is in Makele village, and the Gonge dialect in Giriwon and Diahoke villages. *Dialects:* Pana, Gonge. See main entry under Central African Republic.

Pévé (Ka'do Pevé, Lamé, "Kado," Zime) [lme] 30,000 in Chad (1999 SIL). Population total all countries: 35,720. Southwest near the Cameroon border, Mayo-Kebbi Prefecture, Pala and Léré subprefectures. Lamé is the largest village, home of the Chef de Canton, and administrative center. Also spoken in Cameroon. *Class:* Afro-Asiatic, Chadic, Masa. *Dialects:* Lamé, Doe (Doué), Dari. Related to Herdé and Ngueté, but phonology and grammar differences and ethnic attitudes make separate literature necessary. *Lg Dev:* NT: 1986. *Other:* Different from Lame of Nigeria. 'Zime' is used by outsiders to refer to Herdé, Ngeté, Pévé, and Mesmé.

Runga (Rounga, Roungo, Aiki, Ayki, Aykindang) [rou] 21,479 in Chad (1993 census). Population total all countries: 42,979. Southeast, Salamat Prefecture, Haraze-Mangueigne Subprefecture; Ouaddaï Prefecture, Goz-Beïda Subprefecture, along the border of Central African Republic. Also spoken in Central African Republic. *Class:* Nilo-Saharan, Maban, Mabang, Runga-Kibet. *Lg Use:* The majority of the men use Arabic as second language. *Other:* The area is flooded for 6 months each year. The tse-tse fly is a problem. Agriculturalists: sorghum; hunter-gatherers; fishermen. Traditional religion, Muslim.

Saba (Jelkung) [saa] 1,335 (2000). South central, Guéra Prefecture, Melfi Subprefecture, northeast of Melfi. *Class:* Afro-Asiatic, Chadic, East, B, B.3. *Lg Use:* Chadian Arabic is the second language of speakers, but with low proficiency. *Other:* Plains. Arid. Agriculturalists: millet. Muslim, traditional religion.

Sango (Sangho) [sag] Southern Chad. *Lg Use:* Trade language. A trade language derived from Ngbandi, with decreasing usage in Chad. Probably no first-language speakers in Chad. See main entry under Central African Republic.

Sar (Sara, Sara Madjingay) [mwm] 183,471 (1993 census). Population includes 74,670 Madjingay (1964), 16,260 No (1964), 32,000 Nar (1977). Southwest, Moyen-Chari prefecture, Sarh, Koumra, and Moïssala subprefectures in and around Sarh, Koumra, Balimba, Bessada, Bédaya, Djoli, Matékaga, and Koumogo cantons. *Class:* Nilo-Saharan, Central Sudanic, West, Bongo-Bagirmi, Sara-Bagirmi, Sara, Sara Proper. *Dialects:* Majingai (Majinngay, Madjingaye, Madjingay, Madja Ngai), Nar, No. *Lg Use:* Trade language. The principal language of Sarh. *Lg Dev:* Dictionary. NT: 1972–1986. *Other:* Traditional religion, Christian, Muslim.

Sarua (Sarwa, Saroua) [swy] 2,000 (1997 SIL). Southwest, Chari-Baguirmi Prefecture, Bousso Subprefecture, between Bousso and Miltou, along the Chari River. *Class:* Afro-Asiatic, Chadic, East, A, A.1, 2. *Dialects:* Lexical similarity 42% with Gadang, 27% with Miltu. *Lg Use:* The majority use Bagirmi as second language. *Other:* Different from Sharwa in Cameroon. Traditional religion, Christian.

Sinyar (Sinya, Shemya, Shamya, Symiarta, Shamyan, Zimirra, Taar Shamyan) [sys] 12,321 in Chad (2000 WCD). East, Ouaddaï Prefecture, Goz-Beïda Subprefecture, north of Mongororo, near the confluence of the Kaja, Azum, and Salih rivers. Also spoken in Sudan. *Class:* Nilo-Saharan, Central Sudanic, West, Bongo-Bagirmi, Sinyar. *Lg Use:* Vigorous. Most are trilingual in Sinyar, Fur, and Chadian Arabic. Many speak Daju or Masalit. *Other:* They are culturally Fur. Little education. It is geographically cut off from languages of the Bongo-Bagirmi group. Possibly no longer any speakers in Sudan (2001). Agriculturalists: grain; animal husbandry. Muslim.

Sokoro [sok] 5,000 (1994 SIL). Central, Guéra Prefecture, Melfi Subprefecture, north and northwest of Melfi, from Gogmi to Badanga. *Class:* Afro-Asiatic, Chadic, East, B, B.3. *Dialects:* Sokoro, Bedanga. Related to Mahoua. Lexical similarity 55% with Tamki. *Lg Use:* Most men speak Chadian Arabic as second language. *Other:* A group called the 'Tunjur of Melfi' in the area around Djebren may have spoken a now extinct dialect of Sokoro and are reported to mainly speak Arabic now. Muslim.

Somrai (Sounrai, Somrei, Somre, Soumray, Soumrai, Sumrai, Sibine, Shibne) [sor] 7,414 (1993 census). Southwest, Tandjilé Prefecture, Laï Subprefecture, northeast of Laï, centered at Domogou. *Class:* Afro-Asiatic, Chadic, East, A, A.1, 1. *Dialects:* Not intelligible with any other language. Lexical similarity 47% with Ndam, 39% with Sarua, 35% with Gadang, 33% with Tumak, 28% with Miltu. *Lg Use:* Speakers are not bilingual. *Other:* They call themselves 'Shibne' or 'Sibine'. Traditional religion, Christian, Muslim.

Surbakhal (Sourbakhal) [sbj] 7,885 (2000 WCD). East, Ouaddaï Prefecture, Adré Subprefecture, between Hadjer Hadid and Alacha. *Class:* Nilo-Saharan, Maban, Mabang, Masalit. *Dialects:* Lexical similarity 74% with Masalit. *Lg Use:* The majority use Maba or Masalit as second language. *Other:* Muslim.

Tama (Tamongobo, Tamok, Tamot) [tma] 62,931 (1993 census). Eastern, Biltine Prefecture, Guéréda Subprefecture, around Guéréda. Gimr dialect is east of the Tama. *Class:* Nilo-Saharan, Eastern Sudanic, Western, Tama, Tama-Sungor. *Dialects:* Tama, Orra, Haura, Girga. Lexical similarity 62% to 73% with Assangori. *Lg Use:* The majority use Chadian Arabic as second language, although at a low proficiency level. Some also use Masalit. *Other:* Muslim.

Tamki (Temki) [tax] 500 (1999 SIL). Central, Guéra Prefecture, Melfi Subprefecture, about 60 km northeast of Melfi, Tamki village. *Class:* Afro-Asiatic, Chadic, East, B, B.3. *Dialects:* Not inherently intelligible with Sokoro. Lexical similarity 62% with Saba, 55% with Sokoro, 32% with Mawa. *Lg Use:* Speakers are positive toward Tamki. They consider themselves to be ethnically Sokoro, but their attitudes are not more positive toward Sokoro than toward other neighboring languages. Most speak Chadian Arabic, Kenga, or Saba as second languages. *Other:* Traditional religion.

Tedaga (Teda, Toda, Todaga, Todga, Tuda, Tudaga, Tubu, Tebu, Tebou, Tibbu, Toubou) [tuq] 28,501 in Chad (1993 census). Population total all countries: 42,501. Far northern desert, Borkou Ennedi Tibesti Prefecture, primarily in the Tibesti Subprefecture around Bardai. Also spoken in Libya, Niger, Nigeria. *Class:* Nilo-Saharan,

Saharan, Western, Tebu. *Dialects:* Lexical similarity 67% with Daza. *Lg Use:* The majority use Dazaga as a second language, although at a low proficiency level. Some bilingualism in Chadian Arabic. *Other:* 'Teda' is the name for the people. Many separate groups. Seminomadic. Well diggers; pastoralists: camels; warriors (Tubu). Muslim.

Tobanga (Gabri-North, Gabri-Nord, Northern Gabri, Gabri) [tng] 30,000 (1999 SIL). Southwest, Tandjilé Prefecture, Laï Subprefecture, around Deressia. *Class:* Afro-Asiatic, Chadic, East, A, A.2, 2. *Dialects:* Tobanga (Deressia), Moonde. *Lg Dev:* NT: 1978. *Other:* A separate language from Gabri (Southern Gabri). Traditional religion, Christian.

Toram (Torom, Torum) [trj] 8,456 (2000). Central, Salamat Prefecture, Abou Deïa Subprefecture, southeast of Abou Deïa, south of the Birgit, in and west of Ter. *Class:* Afro-Asiatic, Chadic, East, B, B.1, 2. *Lg Use:* Speakers seem to be shifting to Chadian Arabic. *Other:* Muslim.

Tumak (Toumak, Tummok, Tumac, Dije, Sara Toumak, Tumag) [tmc] 25,249 (1993 census). Southwest, Moyen-Chari Prefecture, Koumra Subprefecture, around Goundil, southwest of Niellim. *Class:* Afro-Asiatic, Chadic, East, A, A.1, 1. *Dialect:* Tumak, Motun (Mawer, Moden, Modin, Mod, Mot, Motin). Lexical similarity 71% between Motun and Tumak. *Lg Use:* Most Motun speak Sara as second language, but with low proficiency. *Lg Dev:* Dictionary. NT: 1988. *Other:* Erroneously called 'Sara Toumak'.

Tunia (Tounia, Tunya, Tun) [tug] 2,255 (1993 census). South, Moyen-Chari Prefecture, Sarh Subprefecture, in Sarh and about three small villages north of Sarh. *Class:* Niger-Congo, Atlantic-Congo, Volta-Congo, North, Adamawa-Ubangi, Adamawa, Mbum-Day, Bua. *Dialects:* Tunya, Perim. Not intelligible with other Bua languages. *Lg Use:* Perim dialect is extinct. 25% also use Niellim, Sara (the majority, but with low proficiency), Chadian Arabic, or French. *Other:* Traditional religion, Christian.

Tupuri (Tuburi, Toubouri, Toupouri, Ndore) [tui] 90,785 in Chad (1993 census). Southwest, Mayo-Kebbi Prefecture, Fianga Subprefecture, around Fianga. *Dialects:* Bang-Ling, Bang-Were, Faale-Piyew, Podokge. See main entry under Cameroon.

Ubi (Oubi) [ubi] 1,100 (1995 SIL). Central, Guéra Prefecture, Mongo Subprefecture, southwest of Tounkoul, around Oubi village. *Class:* Afro-Asiatic, Chadic, East, B, B.1, 1. *Dialects:* Lexical similarity 48% with Mawa (closest).

Zaghawa (Soghaua, Zeggaoua, Zagaoua, Zorhaua, Zagawa, Zeghawa, Berri, Beri-Aa, Beria, Beri, Merida, Kebadi, Kuyuk, Zauge) [zag] 77,834 in Chad (1993 census). Population includes 3,000 Bideyat. East, Biltine Prefecture, Iriba Subprefecture, and Borkou Ennedi Tibesti Prefecture, Ennedi Subprefecture. *Dialects:* Tuer-Gala (Bideyat, Baele, Anna, Awe, Terawia, Beria), Kobe-Kapka, Dirong-Guruf. *Lg Use:* The majority use Chadian Arabic as second language. *Other:* Bideyat and Zaghawa are sometimes called 'Beria' (Beri). Mountain slope. 600 meters. Animal husbandry: livestock, hides, butter, salt; agriculturalists. Muslim. See main entry under Sudan.

Zan Gula (Gula Guera, Goula, Moriil, Morre) [zna] 5,000 (2003 SIL). Melfi Prefecture, Chinguil Subprefecture, northwest of Lake Iro. *Class:* Niger-Congo, Atlantic-Congo, Volta-Congo, North, Adamawa-Ubangi, Adamawa, Mbum-Day, Bua. *Dialects:* Zan, Chinguil. Lexical similarity 46% with Bon Gula. *Lg Use:* The majority use Chadian Arabic as second language. *Other:* Together with Bon Gula called 'Gula Guera'. The Gula Iro call the two groups 'Moriil'. Traditional religion, Muslim.

Zirenkel [zrn] 2,237 (1993 census). *Class:* Afro-Asiatic, Chadic, East, B, B.1, 2. *Dialects:* Lexical similarity 71% with Mubi, 34% to 36% with Dangaléat (East, Central,

and Western). *Lg Use:* The majority use Arabic as second language. Some also use Dadjo or Dangaléat.

Comoros

Federal Islamic Republic of the Comoros. Jumhuriyat al-Qumural-Itthadiyah Al-Islamiyah, Comores. 651,901. National or official languages: Standard Arabic, French. Islands of Grande Comore, Mohéli, and Anjouan. Literacy rate: 15% to 46%. Also includes Réunion Creole French (500). Information mainly from M. Chamanga and N. Guernie 1966–1967; H. and M. Ottenheimer 1976; H. Chagnoux and A. Naribou 1980. The number of languages listed for Comoros is 7. Of those, all are living languages. See map on page 690.

Arabic, Standard [arb] Throughout the island. *Lg Use:* Official language. Not a first language. See main entry under Saudi Arabia.

Comorian (Comores Swahili, Komoro, Comoro) [swb] 228,896 in Comoros (2004). Population includes Shingazidja Comorian. Population total all countries: 350,702. Anjouan Island. Also spoken in Madagascar, Mayotte, Réunion. *Class:* Niger-Congo, Atlantic-Congo, Volta-Congo, Benue-Congo, Bantoid, Southern, Narrow Bantu, Central, G, Swahili (G.40). *Dialects:* Shindzwani (Anjouan, Shindzuani), Maore (Mayotte). All dialects sufficiently distinct from mainland Swahili to warrant separate literature. *Lg Use:* Speakers also use Swahili, French, or Arabic. *Lg Dev:* Literacy rate in second language: 25%. NT: 1995. *Other:* Vanilla, perfume production. Muslim, Christian.

Comorian, Mwali (Shimwali) [wlc] 27,194 (2000 WCD). Moheli Island. *Class:* Niger-Congo, Atlantic-Congo, Volta-Congo, Benue-Congo, Bantoid, Southern, Narrow Bantu, Central, G, Swahili (G.40). *Other:* Muslim.

Comorian, Ndzwani (Shindzwani) [wni] 264,324 (2000). Anjouan Island. *Class:* Niger-Congo, Atlantic-Congo, Volta-Congo, Benue-Congo, Bantoid, Southern, Narrow Bantu, Central, G, Swahili (G.40). *Other:* Muslim.

Comorian, Ngazidja (Shingazidja, Ngazidja) [zdj] Grande Comore. *Class:* Niger-Congo, Atlantic-Congo, Volta-Congo, Benue-Congo, Bantoid, Southern, Narrow Bantu, Central, G, Swahili (G.40). *Lg Dev:* Bible portions: 1976. *Other:* Muslim.

French [fra] 1,700 in Comoros (1993). *Lg Use:* Official language. *Other:* Language of all formal education except Koranic. See main entry under France.

Malagasy [plt] 700 in Comoros (1993 Johnstone). *Lg Use:* It is spoken by a substantial number of residents of Madagascar origin. Most also use Comorian. *Other:* Traditional religion, Christian, Muslim. See main entry under Madagascar (Malagasy, Plateau).

Congo

Republic of Congo. République du Congo. Congo Brazzaville. Formerly People's Republic of the Congo. 2,998,040. National or official languages: Lingala, Kituba, French. Literacy rate: 63% to 80% (1996). Also includes Greek (400), Hausa (4,000), Portuguese (600), Sango (54,000). Information mainly from A. Jacquot 1971; J. Bendor-Samuel 1989; SIL 1982–2003. Blind population: 4,000 (1982 WCE). The number of languages listed for Congo is 62. Of those, all are living languages. See map on page 691.

Aka (Babinga, Binga, Beka, Mòáka, Yaka) [axk] 15,000 in Congo (1986 Cavalli-Storza). Northeast corner. *Dialects:*

Ethnologue

Basese (Eastern Aka), Bambenzele (Western Aka). *Other:* Mraka is singular, Beka plural. Different from the Baka language of Cameroon and Gabon, which is Ubangi. There may be more than one pygmy language in Congo. Nomadic. Pygmies. Forest. Hunter-gatherers. Traditional religion. See main entry under Central African Republic (Yaka).

Akwa [akw] 24,147 (2000 WCD). Cuvette Region, Makoua District. *Class:* Niger-Congo, Atlantic-Congo, Volta-Congo, Benue-Congo, Bantoid, Southern, Narrow Bantu, Northwest, C, Mbosi (C.30).

Bangandu (Bagando, Bangando) [bgf] Sangha Region, along the Cameroon border. *Dialects:* Baagato, North Bangato. See main entry under Cameroon.

Beembe (Kibeembe, Bembe) [beq] 3,200 (2004). Bouenza Region, district of Mouyondzi. *Class:* Niger-Congo, Atlantic-Congo, Volta-Congo, Benue-Congo, Bantoid, Southern, Narrow Bantu, Central, H, Kongo (H.10). *Dialects:* Keenge (Kikeenge), Yari (Kiyari). Dialect cluster. *Other:* Different from Bembe of Democratic Republic of the Congo.

Bekwil (Bakwele, Bakwil, Bekwel) [bkw] 9,600 in Congo (2003). Population total all countries: 12,060. Sangha Region, parallel to the border with Cameroon, from close to the Gabon border almost to Ouesso. Also spoken in Cameroon, Gabon. *Class:* Niger-Congo, Atlantic-Congo, Volta-Congo, Benue-Congo, Bantoid, Southern, Narrow Bantu, Northwest, A, Makaa-Njem (A.80). *Dialects:* Close to Konabembe. Lexical similarity 85% with Koonzime. *Other:* Different from Baakpe (Bakwiri) of Cameroon. Traditional religion, Christian.

Bobangi (Bubangi, Lobobangi, Rebu, Dzamba, Bungi, Bangi) [bni] 60,369 in Congo (2000 WCD). On Congo River, Cuvette Region, Mossaka District. See main entry under Democratic Republic of the Congo (Bangi).

Bomitaba (Mbomitaba, Mbomotaba, Bamitaba) [zmx] 9,599 in Congo (2000 WCD). Population total all countries: 9,823. Likouala Region, Epena District, along Likouala-aux-Herbes River. Also spoken in Central African Republic. *Class:* Niger-Congo, Atlantic-Congo, Volta-Congo, Benue-Congo, Bantoid, Southern, Narrow Bantu, Northwest, C, Ngundi (C.20). *Dialects:* Northern Bomitaba (Matoki), Central Bomitaba (Epena). Related to Bongili. *Other:* Traditional religion, Christian.

Bomwali (Bomali, Boumoali, Bumali, Lino, Sangasanga) [bmw] 33,203 in Congo (2002). Population total all countries: 39,280. Sangha Region, around Ouesso. Also spoken in Cameroon. *Class:* Niger-Congo, Atlantic-Congo, Volta-Congo, Benue-Congo, Bantoid, Southern, Narrow Bantu, Northwest, A, Makaa-Njem (A.80).

Bongili (Bongiri, Bungili, Bungiri, Bokiba) [bui] 4,000. Sangha Region, on and near Sangha River, southeast of Ouesso, as far as Pikounda area and southwest of Ouesso, Liouesso area. *Class:* Niger-Congo, Atlantic-Congo, Volta-Congo, Benue-Congo, Bantoid, Southern, Narrow Bantu, Northwest, C, Ngundi (C.20). *Lg Dev:* NT: 1947. *Other:* Different from Bukongo of Central African Republic.

Bonjo [bok] 3,000. Likouala Region, on and near Oubangui, Motaba, and Ibenga rivers, Dongou and Impfondo districts. *Class:* Niger-Congo, Atlantic-Congo, Volta-Congo, North, Adamawa-Ubangi, Ubangi, Gbaya-Manza-Ngbaka, East. *Lg Use:* Speakers are shifting to Lingala (2000 B. Connell).

Bwisi (Ibwisi, Mbwisi) [bwz] 3,018 in Congo (2000 WCD). Population total all countries: 4,248. Niari Region, Kibangou District, Banda area, on Gabon border. Also spoken in Gabon. *Class:* Niger-Congo, Atlantic-Congo, Volta-Congo, Benue-Congo, Bantoid, Southern, Narrow Bantu, Northwest, B, Sira (B.40). *Other:* Different from Talinga-Bwisi of Democratic Republic of the Congo and Uganda.

Dibole (Babole, Southern Bomitaba) [bvx] 4,000 (1989 SIL). Ethnic population: 4,000 to 5,000. Southern half of the Epena District, northeastern Congo, 16 villages. *Class:* Niger-Congo, Atlantic-Congo, Volta-Congo, Benue-Congo, Bantoid, Southern, Narrow Bantu, Northwest, C, Ngundi (C.20). *Dialects:* Northern Dibole (Dzeke), Central Dibole (Kinami), Southern Dibole (Bouanila). *Lg Use:* All domains. Positive language attitude. *Other:* Fishermen; hunters; agriculturalists: manioc. Traditional religion, Christian.

Doondo (Kidoondo, Dondo) [dde] 3,018 (2000 WCD). Bouenza Region; Nkayi, Madingou, Mfouati, and Boko-Songho districts. *Class:* Niger-Congo, Atlantic-Congo, Volta-Congo, Benue-Congo, Bantoid, Southern, Narrow Bantu, Central, H, Kongo (H.10). *Dialects:* A member of the Kongo cluster.

Fang (Pamue, Pahouin) [fan] 6,037 in Congo (2000 WCD). Few speakers in Congo. Small area in extreme northwest. *Dialects:* Make, Ntum, Ogowe. See main entry under Equatorial Guinea.

French [fra] 28,000 in Congo (1993). *Lg Use:* Official language. *Other:* Sole language of formal education. See main entry under France.

Gbaya (Baya, Northwest Gbaya) [gya] 2,000 in Congo (1993 Johnstone). Sangha Region, a few scattered areas on Cameroon border. See main entry under Central African Republic (Gbaya, Northwest).

Kaamba (Kikaamba) [xku] 3,018 (2000 WCD). Bouenza Region; Nkayi, Madingou, Mfouati, and Boko-Songho districts. *Class:* Niger-Congo, Atlantic-Congo, Volta-Congo, Benue-Congo, Bantoid, Southern, Narrow Bantu, Central, H, Kongo (H.10). *Dialects:* A member of the Kongo cluster.

Kako (Kaka, Yaka, Nkoxo) [kkj] 9,055 in Congo (2002). Scattered areas in extreme north of Likouala Region, on Ibenga and Motaba rivers. See main entry under Cameroon.

Kituba (Munukutuba, Kikoongo) [mkw] 1,156,800 (1987 SIL). Spoken mainly between Brazzaville and Pointe-Noire. *Class:* Creole, Kongo based. *Dialects:* Close to Kituba of Democratic Republic of the Congo. *Lg Use:* National language. The main language of the south and one of the two national languages of Congo. *Lg Dev:* Literacy rate in first language: 5% to 10%. Literacy rate in second language: 15% to 25%. Bible portions: 1989.

Koongo (Kikongo, Congo, Kikoongo) [kng] Pool Region, around Boko, west and northwest of Brazzaville. *Other:* A member of the Kongo cluster. Christian, Muslim. See main entry under Democratic Republic of the Congo.

Kota (Ikota, Ikuta) [koq] 9,055 in Congo (2000 WCD). Cuvette Region, west of Mbomo; Sangha Region, Liouesso area. Primarily in Gabon. See main entry under Gabon.

Koyo (Ekoyo, Kouyou) [koh] 1,000. Cuvette Region, Owando District, around Owando. *Class:* Niger-Congo, Atlantic-Congo, Volta-Congo, Benue-Congo, Bantoid, Southern, Narrow Bantu, Northwest, C, Mbosi (C.30). *Other:* SVO.

Kunyi (Kikunyi, Kugni) [njx] 52,000 (1984 census). Bouenza and Niari regions, south and southeast from Makabana to the Democratic Republic of the Congo border. *Class:* Niger-Congo, Atlantic-Congo, Volta-Congo, Benue-Congo, Bantoid, Southern, Narrow Bantu, Central, H, Kongo (H.10). *Dialect:* Nyaanga (Kinyaanga). A member of the Kongo cluster.

Laari (Lari, Laadi, Ladi, Kilari) [ldi] 90,553 in Congo (2000 WCD). South of Pool Region, west and northwest of Brazzaville. Also spoken in Angola. *Class:* Niger-Congo, Atlantic-Congo, Volta-Congo, Benue-Congo, Bantoid, Southern, Narrow Bantu, Central, H, Kongo (H.10). *Dialect:* Ghaangala (Kighaangala, Hangala). *Other:* A member of the Kongo cluster. Christian, Muslim.

Likuba (Kuba) [kxx] 30,184 (2000 WCD). Cuvette Region, on the Congo River, just above the mouth of the Sangha River. *Class:* Niger-Congo, Atlantic-Congo, Volta-Congo, Benue-Congo, Bantoid, Southern, Narrow Bantu, Northwest, C, Mbosi (C.30). *Dialects:* Mutual intelligibility with Likwala.

Likwala (Likouala, Kwala, Ekwala) [kwc] 45,276 (2000 WCD). Cuvette Region, on lower reaches of the Likouala-Mossaka, Sangha, and Likouala-aux-Herbes rivers. *Class:* Niger-Congo, Atlantic-Congo, Volta-Congo, Benue-Congo, Bantoid, Southern, Narrow Bantu, Northwest, C, Mbosi (C.30). *Dialects:* Mutual intelligibility with Likuba.

Lingala (Ngala) [lin] 90,553 in Congo (2000 WCD). Spoken mainly in Brazzaville and the north of Congo. *Lg Use:* National language. *Lg Dev:* Literacy rate in first language: 10% to 30%. Literacy rate in second language: 25% to 75%. See main entry under Democratic Republic of the Congo.

Lumbu (Ilumbu) [lup] 3,018 in Congo (2000 WCD). Niari Region, Kibangou District, between Kibangou and Gabon border. See main entry under Gabon.

Mbandja (Mbanza, Mbanja, Banja) [zmz] 9,055 in Congo (2000). Extreme north of Likouala Region, close to Oubangui River. See main entry under Democratic Republic of the Congo.

Mbangwe (Mbahouin, M'bahouin) [zmn] 1,509 in Congo (2000 WCD). Lekoumou Region, small groups in Bambama District. See main entry under Gabon.

Mbere (Mbédé, Mbété, Limbede) [mdt] 60,369 in Congo (2000 WCD). Population total all countries: 105,882. Cuvette-West Region, Kelle and northern Ewo districts. Also spoken in Gabon. *Class:* Niger-Congo, Atlantic-Congo, Volta-Congo, Benue-Congo, Bantoid, Southern, Narrow Bantu, Northwest, B, Mbere (B.60). *Dialect:* Ngwii. Related to Kaningi, Ndumu, Yangho. Lexical similarity 77% with Mbamba, 76% with Ngungwel, 74% with Teghe, 70% with Tsaayi. *Other:* The people are called 'Ambede'. Traditional religion, Christian.

Mboko (Mboxo, Mbuku) [mdu] 27,166 (2000 WCD). Cuvette Region, western part of Makoua District. *Class:* Niger-Congo, Atlantic-Congo, Volta-Congo, Benue-Congo, Bantoid, Southern, Narrow Bantu, Northwest, C, Mbosi (C.30). *Dialect:* Ngare. A dialect cluster.

Mbosi (Mboshi, Mbochi, Mboshe, Embosi) [mdw] 108,361 (2000 WCD). Cuvette Region, Owando and Mossaka districts, but not as far north as Owando. Plateaux Region, Abala District. *Class:* Niger-Congo, Atlantic-Congo, Volta-Congo, Benue-Congo, Bantoid, Southern, Narrow Bantu, Northwest, C, Mbosi (C.30). *Lg Use:* All domains. Younger speakers do not control some of the richness of the language. They desire proficiency in French and go to cities for higher education. Speakers are proud of Mbosi. It is viewed as a spoken language only. French is viewed as the language for reading and writing. Few monolinguals. Most have some ability in Lingala, French, and Teke-Tege. *Other:* Plateau, hills. Savannah, forest. Agriculturalists. Traditional religion, Christian.

Moi (Lemoi) [mow] 3,018 (2000 WCD). West bank of Oubangui River, at mouth of Alima River, south of Mossaka. *Class:* Niger-Congo, Atlantic-Congo, Volta-Congo, Benue-Congo, Bantoid, Southern, Narrow Bantu, Northwest, C, Bangi-Ntomba (C.40).

Monzombo (Monjombo, Mondjembo, Munzombo) [moj] 6,000 in Congo (1993 Johnstone). Population total all countries: 12,600. Extreme northeast, on Oubangui River. Also spoken in Central African Republic, Democratic Republic of the Congo. *Class:* Niger-Congo, Atlantic-Congo, Volta-Congo, North, Adamawa-Ubangi, Ubangi, Sere-Ngbaka-Mba, Ngbaka-Mba, Ngbaka, Western, Monzombo.

Mpyemo (Mpo, Mbimu, Bimu, Mbimou, Mbyemo) [mcx] Sangha Region, along Cameroon border. *Dialects:* Jasoa (Jasua), Bidjuki (Bidjouki), Mpyemo. *Other:* Traditional religion, Christian, Muslim. See main entry under Central African Republic (Mpiemo).

Ndasa (Andasa) [nda] 4,528 in Congo (2000 WCD). Population total all countries: 6,988. Lekoumou Region, west of Zanaga. Also spoken in Gabon. *Class:* Niger-Congo, Atlantic-Congo, Volta-Congo, Benue-Congo, Bantoid, Southern, Narrow Bantu, Northwest, B, Kele (B.20).

Ngbaka [nga] 3,652 in Congo (2000 WCD). Likouala Region, small group on west bank of Oubangui River, midway between Impfondo and confluence with the Congo River. *Other:* Different from Ngbaka Ma'bo. See main entry under Democratic Republic of the Congo.

Ngbaka Ma'bo (Ngbaka Limba, Mbaka, Mbacca, Bwaka, Bouaka, Nbwaka, Gbala, Ma'bo) [nbm] 90,553 in Congo (2000 WCD). *Lg Use:* Speakers also use Lingala. See main entry under Central African Republic.

Ngom (Ungom, Angom, Bangom, Bangomo, Ongom) [nra] 4,528 in Congo (2000). Cuvette-West Region, northwest of Mbomo. See main entry under Gabon.

Ngundi (Ingundi, Ngondi) [ndn] 3,000 in Congo (2004). Sangha Region, east of Ouesso. Also spoken in Central African Republic. *Class:* Niger-Congo, Atlantic-Congo, Volta-Congo, Benue-Congo, Bantoid, Southern, Narrow Bantu, Northwest, C, Ngundi (C.20). *Other:* Different from Gundi of Central African Republic, which is Adamawa-Ubangi.

Ngungwel (Ngungulu, Ngangoulou, Engungwel, Northeastern Teke) [ngz] 45,000 (1988 SIL). Plateaux Province, Gamboma District. *Class:* Niger-Congo, Atlantic-Congo, Volta-Congo, Benue-Congo, Bantoid, Southern, Narrow Bantu, Northwest, B, Teke (B.70). *Dialect:* Mpu (Mpumpum). Lexical similarity 89% with Boo, 81% with Kukua, 77% with Teghe, 76% with Tsaayi and Mbere, 75% with Tyee, 68% with Laali, 61% with Yaa. *Lg Use:* The speakers would not accept Teke-Eboo or Teke-Kukuya literature. They consider themselves a distinct people from other Teke groups. *Other:* The people are called 'Angungwel'.

Njebi (Nzebi, Injebi, Ndjabi, Njevi, Binzabi, Njabi, Yinzebi, Yinjebi) [nzb] 15,092 in Congo (2000). Niari Province, Mayoko District. See main entry under Gabon.

Njyem (Ndzem, Dzem, Nyem, Ndjem, Njem, Djem, Ndjeme, Ngyeme) [njy] 3,500 in Congo. 85% monolingual. Sangha Region, Souanke District, along paths leading north to Cameroon. *Lg Use:* Many Baka Pygmies speak it as a second language. All domains, public discourse, promulgate government information, oral and written use in church, oral literature. Positive language attitude. 15% speak French as second language. *Lg Dev:* 15 people can read. *Other:* Hills. Tropical forest, some swamp. Agriculturalists: cocoa; trappers. Christian. See main entry under Cameroon.

Ombamba (Lembaamba, Mbama, Mbamba, Mbaama) [mbm] 15,092 in Congo (2000). Lekoumou Region, Bambama District. Also spoken in Gabon. *Class:* Niger-Congo, Atlantic-Congo, Volta-Congo, Benue-Congo, Bantoid, Southern, Narrow Bantu, Northwest, B, Mbere (B.60). *Dialects:* Lexical similarity 81% with Teghe, 77% with Mbere, 66% with Tsaayi.

Pomo (Pol, Pori, Pul, Congo Pol) [pmm] 5,433 in Congo (2000 WCD). Sangha Region, north of Ouesso, on borders with Cameroon and Central African Republic. Not in Central African Republic. See main entry under Cameroon (Pol).

Punu (Ipunu, Yipunu, Puno, Pouno, Ipounou) [puu] 9,055 in Congo (2000 WCD). Total of all Sira-Punu languages in Congo 80,000. Spoken in Nyari Region toward the Gabon border. See main entry under Gabon.

Suundi (Kisuundi, Suundi de Kimongo) [sdj] 120,737 (2000 WCD). Around Kimongo in Bouenza and Niari regions, south and southeast from Makabana to the Democratic Republic of the Congo border. *Class:* Niger-Congo, Atlantic-Congo, Volta-Congo, Benue-Congo, Bantoid, Southern, Narrow Bantu, Central, H, Kongo (H.10). *Dialects:* A member of the Kongo cluster.

Teke-Eboo (Boma, Boo, Boõ, Iboo, Eboom, Bamboma, Eboo Teke, Central Teke, Teke-Boma) [ebo] 20,379 in Congo (2000 WCD). 454,000 all Teke languages in Congo (2001 Johnstone and Mandryk). Pool Region eastward to Congo River. Also spoken in Democratic Republic of the Congo. *Class:* Niger-Congo, Atlantic-Congo, Volta-Congo, Benue-Congo, Bantoid, Southern, Narrow Bantu, Northwest, B, Teke (B.70). *Dialects:* Eboo is the language of the ancient Teke kings. Lexical similarity 63% with Iyaa, 69% with Laali, 75% with Tsaayi, 85% with Tyee, 86% with Kukua, 89% with Ngungwel, 79% with Tege. *Lg Dev:* Literacy rate in first language: 0%. *Other:* Ethnic group name is 'Aboo'. Plateau. Savannah, scrub trees, small areas of tropical forest. High altitude. Traditional religion.

Teke-Fuumu (Kiteke, Teke du Pool, South Central Teke) [ifm] 8,150 (2000 WCD). Pool Region. Fuumu is immediately north of Brazzaville; Wuumu extends north and northwest to the Lefini River. *Class:* Niger-Congo, Atlantic-Congo, Volta-Congo, Benue-Congo, Bantoid, Southern, Narrow Bantu, Northwest, B, Teke (B.70). *Dialects:* Fuumu (Ifuumu, Mfumu), Wuumu (Iwuumu, Wumbu).

Teke-Ibali (Kiteke, Ibali, Eastern Teke) [tek] 36,221 in Congo (2000 WCD). On Congo River, Pool Region, close to Brazzaville. *Dialect:* Ngee. See main entry under Democratic Republic of the Congo (Teke, Ibali).

Teke-Kukuya (Kukwa, Kikuwa, Chikuya, Koukouya, Southern Teke) [kkw] 38,787 (2000 WCD). Plateaux Province, Lekana District, east of Leketi River. *Class:* Niger-Congo, Atlantic-Congo, Volta-Congo, Benue-Congo, Bantoid, Southern, Narrow Bantu, B, Teke (B.70). *Dialects:* Lexical similarity 86% with Boo, 85% with Tyee, 81% with Ngungwel, 80% with Tsaayi, 79% with Teghe, 75% with Laali, 70% with Yaa. *Lg Use:* They do not accept Ngungwel (Northeastern Teke) literature. Strong ethnic pride.

Teke-Laali (Ilaali) [lli] Lekoumou Region, south of Komono. *Class:* Niger-Congo, Atlantic-Congo, Volta-Congo, Benue-Congo, Bantoid, Southern, Narrow Bantu, Northwest, B, Teke (B.70). *Dialects:* Lexical similarity 81% with Tsaayi, 78% with Tyee.

Teke-Nzikou (Njyunjyu, Njiunjiu) [nzu] 490,000 all Teke languages in Congo (1993 Johnstone). Plateaux Region, around Djambala. *Class:* Niger-Congo, Atlantic-Congo, Volta-Congo, Benue-Congo, Bantoid, Southern, Narrow Bantu, Northwest, B, Teke (B.70). *Other:* Plateau. Savannah, scrub trees, small areas of tropical forest. High altitude. Traditional religion.

Teke-Tege (Teghe, Iteghe, Teke Alima, Teke Kali, Northern Teke) [teg] 49,291 in Congo (2000 WCD). Population includes 9,000 Nzkini, 15,000 Teghe. Population total all countries: 65,036. Cuvette Region, Ewo and Okoyo districts. Some in Plateaux Region, Abala District, west of Mpama River. Also spoken in Gabon. *Class:* Niger-Congo, Atlantic-Congo, Volta-Congo, Benue-Congo, Bantoid, Southern, Narrow Bantu, Northwest, B, Teke (B.70). *Dialects:* Kateghe (Nzikini), Keteghe. Lexical similarity 81% with Mbamba, 79% with Kukua, 77% with Ngungwel, 76% with Boo, 75% with Tyee, 74% with Mbere, 73% with Laali and Tsaayi, 67% with Teghe.

Teke-Tsaayi (Getsaayi, Tsaya, Tsaye, Tsayi) [tyi] 95,926 (2000 WCD). Lekoumou Region, to the north, east of Mossendjo. *Class:* Niger-Congo, Atlantic-Congo, Volta-Congo, Benue-Congo, Bantoid, Southern, Narrow Bantu, Northwest, B, Teke (B.70). *Dialects:* Lexical similarity 76% with Tyee, 80% with Kukua.

Teke-Tyee (West Teke) [tyx] 14,400. 490,000 all Teke languages in Congo (1993 Johnstone). Lekoumou Region, Bouenza. *Class:* Niger-Congo, Atlantic-Congo, Volta-Congo, Benue-Congo, Bantoid, Southern, Narrow Bantu, Northwest, B, Teke (B.70). *Dialects:* Lexical similarity 85% with Kukuya and Eboo. *Other:* Plateau. Savannah, scrub trees, small areas of tropical forest. High altitude. Traditional religion.

Tsaangi (Itsangi, Tcengui, Tchangui, Icaangi) [tsa] 13,583 in Congo (2000 WCD). Population total all countries: 22,194. Niari Region, north and northwest of Mossendjo. Also spoken in Gabon. *Class:* Niger-Congo, Atlantic-Congo, Volta-Congo, Benue-Congo, Bantoid, Southern, Narrow Bantu, Northwest, B, Njebi (B.50).

Vili (Tsivili, Civili, Fiote, Fiot) [vif] 7,305 in Congo (2000 WCD). Population total all countries: 10,995. Kouilou Province, along the coast between the Angola and Gabon borders. Yoombe Island. Also spoken in Gabon. *Class:* Niger-Congo, Atlantic-Congo, Volta-Congo, Benue-Congo, Bantoid, Southern, Narrow Bantu, Central, H, Kongo (H.10). *Dialect:* Yoombe (Yombe, Ciyoombe). A dialect cluster. *Other:* The people are called 'Bavili'. Coastal.

Wumbvu (Wumvu) [wum] Niari Region, northward to the Gabonese border. See main entry under Gabon.

Yaka (West Teke, Yaa, Iyaka) [iyx] 10,000 (1988). Lekoumou Region, in and around Sibiti. *Class:* Niger-Congo, Atlantic-Congo, Volta-Congo, Benue-Congo, Bantoid, Southern, Narrow Bantu, Northwest, B, Teke (B.70). *Dialects:* Lexical similarity 91% with Laali, 74% with Tsaayi, 69% with Tyee.

Yombe (Kiyombe, Kiombi, Bayombe) [yom] 347,723 in Congo (2000 WCD). *Dialects:* Mbala (Mumbala), Vungunya (Kivungunya, Yombe Classique). *Other:* Distinct enough from Vili to need separate literature. Christian, traditional religion. See main entry under Democratic Republic of the Congo.

Côte d'Ivoire

Ivory Coast. République de la Côte d'Ivoire. 17,327,724. National or official language: French. Literacy rate: 42.4% to 45%. Also includes Bissa (63,000), Dogoso, Eastern Karaboro (5,605), Glaro-Twabo, Khe, Maasina Fulfulde (1,200), Malba Birifor, Mòoré, Nafaanra, Siamou, Sìcìté Sénoufo, Southern Toussian, Turka, Vietnamese, people from Burkina Faso (1,600,000), from Mali (754,000), from Guinea (238,000), from Liberia (200,000) or more, others (345,000). Information mainly from M. Delafosse 1904; J. Bendor-Samuel 1989; SIL 1973–2003. Blind population: 50,000 (1982 WCE). Deaf institutions: 1. The number of languages listed for Côte d'Ivoire is 80. Of those, 78 are living languages and 2 are extinct. See map on page 692.

Abé (Abbé, Abbey, Abi) [aba] 170,000 (1995 SIL). Southern Department, Subprefecture of Agboville (except Krobou Canton) and Abbe Canton of Tiassale Subprefecture. 70 villages. *Class:* Niger-Congo, Atlantic-Congo, Volta-Congo, Kwa, Nyo, Agneby. *Dialect:* Tioffo, Morie, Abbey-Ve, Kos (Khos). *Lg Dev:* Literacy rate in first language: 5% to 10%. Literacy rate in second language: 50% to 75%. Bible portions: 1967–1980. *Other:* SVO; postpositions; tonal. Coastal. Tropical forest. Sea level to 30 meters. Agriculturalists: manioc, yams, plantains, tomatoes, hot peppers; cash crops: cocoa, coffee, palm oil; some professionals. Christian, traditional religion, Muslim.

Abidji (Abiji) [abi] 50,500 (1993 SIL). Department of Abidjan, Subprefecture of Sikensi (12 villages), and a few villages in Subprefecture of Dabou. *Class:* Niger-Congo, Atlantic-Congo, Volta-Congo, Kwa, Nyo, Agneby. *Dialects:* Enyembe, Ogbru. *Lg Use:* Speakers also use French, Jula, Baoule, or Adioukrou. *Lg Dev:* Literacy rate in first language: 1% to 5%. Literacy rate in second language: 25% to 50%. NT: 2001. *Other:* Nasalization on syllable; tonal. Christian, other.

Abron (Brong, Bron, Doma, Gyaman) [abr] 131,700 in Côte d'Ivoire (1993 SIL). Eastern Department, subprefectures of Tanda and Bondoukou. *Lg Use:* Some use Kulango or Jula. Most have good comprehension of Asante Twi in Ghana. *Other:* Called 'Abron' in Côte d'Ivoire and 'Brong' in Ghana. Christian, Muslim, traditional religion, other. See main entry under Ghana.

Abure (Abouré, Abule, Akaplass, Abonwa) [abu] 55,120 (1993 SIL). Southern Department, Subprefecture of Bonoua, some in Subprefecture of Grand Bassam, many in Abidjan. *Class:* Niger-Congo, Atlantic-Congo, Volta-Congo, Kwa, Nyo, Potou-Tano, Tano, Western. *Dialects:* Closest to Anyin. Also close to Baule and Nzema. *Lg Use:* Many speakers use Anyin. *Lg Dev:* Literacy rate in first language: 5% to 10%. Literacy rate in second language: 25% to 50%. *Other:* Ethnic subgroups: Eyive (majority), Ehie, Ossouon. Christian, traditional religion, Muslim, other.

Adioukrou (Adyukru, Adjukru, Adyoukrou, Ajukru) [adj] 100,000 (1999 SIL). Southern Department, Subprefecture of Dabou, in 49 villages. *Class:* Niger-Congo, Atlantic-Congo, Volta-Congo, Kwa, Nyo, Agneby. *Lg Dev:* Literacy rate in first language: 30% to 60%. Literacy rate in second language: 25% to 50%. NT: 1998. *Other:* Christian, Muslim, traditional religion.

Aizi, Aproumu (Ahizi, Aprwe, Aprou, Oprou, Aproumu) [ahp] 6,500 (1999 SIL). Southern Department, on both banks of the Ebrié Lagoon in Jacqueville Subprefecture, villages of Attoutou A (new quarter), Attoutou B, Tefredji, Koko, Bapo (Allaba B, Taboth), and in the village of Allaba in Dabou Subprefecture. *Class:* Niger-Congo, Atlantic-Congo, Volta-Congo, Kru, Aizi. *Lg Use:* Young people learn French in school. *Lg Dev:* Literacy rate in second language: 25% to 50%. *Other:* Their name for the Aizi people: 'Aproin'. They call Lélémrin (Tiagbamrin) 'Chicalé' and Mobumrin 'Amaboué'. 'Akabu', 'Opro', 'Saptomrin' and 'Tchavamrin' are names used in different Mobu and Lélé villages to refer to Apro. The Adioukrou say 'Ed-eyng' and Alladian 'Ezibo' to refer to all the Aizi groups. Fishermen, fish merchants. Christian, Muslim, other.

Aizi, Mobumrin (Ahizi) [ahm] 2,000 (1999 SIL). Southern Department, Jacqueville Subprefecture, 2 villages (Abraco and Abraniamiambo) on the north bank of the Ebrié Lagoon. *Class:* Niger-Congo, Atlantic-Congo, Volta-Congo, Kru, Aizi. *Lg Use:* Older speakers use Adioukrou. Young people learn French in school. *Lg Dev:* Literacy rate in second language: 25% to 50%. *Other:* Speakers are 'Mouin'. Their name for the Aizi people: 'Frukpu'. The Adioukrou say 'Ed-eyng' and the Alladian 'Ezibo' to refer to all the Aizi groups. Fish merchants. Christian, Muslim, other.

Aizi, Tiagbamrin (Ahizi, Tiagba, Lélémrin) [ahi] 9,000 (1999 SIL). Southern Department, Jacqueville Subprefecture, both banks of the Ebrié Lagoon, in the villages of Tiagba, Nigui-Assoko, Nigui-Saff, Tiémié, and Attoutou B (old quarter). *Class:* Niger-Congo, Atlantic-Congo, Volta-Congo, Kru, Aizi. *Dialects:* Not intelligible with Mobumrin Aizi, even though both are Kru languages. *Lg Use:* Older speakers use Adioukrou. Young people

learn French in school. *Lg Dev:* Literacy rate in second language: 25% to 50%. *Other:* Their name for the Aizi people is 'Prokpo' ('Krokpo' in Tiagba town). 'Tiagbamrin' means 'language of Tiagba'. People in other villages say they speak 'Lélémrin'. The Adioukrou say 'Ed-eyng' and the Alladian 'Ezibo' to refer to all the Aizi groups. Fishermen, fish merchants. Christian, Muslim, other.

Alladian (Alladyan, Allagia, Allagian) [ald] 23,000 (1993 SIL). Southern Department, along the plain between the coast and the Ebrie Lagoon in 21 villages in the Subprefecture of Jacqueville. *Class:* Niger-Congo, Atlantic-Congo, Volta-Congo, Kwa, Nyo, Avikam-Alladian. *Lg Dev:* Literacy rate in second language: 25% to 50%. Bible portions: 1937–1968. *Other:* Christian, Muslim, traditional religion, other.

Anyin (Anyi, Agni) [any] 610,000 in Côte d'Ivoire (1993 SIL). Population total all countries: 860,000. Southern Region, Abidjan and Aboisso departments; East-Central Region, Abengourou and Agnibilekrou departments; North-East Region, Bondoukou and Tanda departments; North-Central Region, M'bahiakro Department; and Central Region, Bongouanou and Daoukro departments. Between Kulango and Abron to the north; Nzema, Abure, and the Lagoon languages to the south; Baulé to the west; Twi in Ghana to the east. Also spoken in Ghana. *Class:* Niger-Congo, Atlantic-Congo, Volta-Congo, Kwa, Nyo, Potou-Tano, Tano, Central, Bia, Northern. *Dialects:* Sanvi, Indenie, Bini, Bona, Moronou, Djuablin, Ano, Abe, Barabo, Alangua. Closest to Baoulé. Also close to Nzema and Sehwi. *Lg Use:* 10,000 to 100,000 second-language users. Speakers also use French, Jula, or Twi. *Lg Dev:* Literacy rate in first language: 1% to 5%. Literacy rate in second language: 25% to 50%. Radio programs. NT: 1997. *Other:* Christian, traditional religion, Muslim, other.

Anyin Morofo (Morofo) [mtb] 300,000 (2002 SIL). Southern, Eastern, and Central departments, Moronou. *Class:* Niger-Congo, Atlantic-Congo, Volta-Congo, Kwa, Nyo, Potou-Tano, Tano, Central, Bia, Northern. *Other:* 'Morofue' refers to a Morofo speaker.

Attié (Atie, Akye, Akie, Atche, Atshe) [ati] 381,000 (1993 SIL). Abidjan Department, subprefectures of Anyama and Alepe; Adzope Department, subprefectures of Adzope, Affery, Agou, Akoupe, Yakasse-Attobrou. *Class:* Niger-Congo, Atlantic-Congo, Volta-Congo, Kwa, Nyo, Attie. *Dialects:* Naindin, Ketin, Bodin. The Bodin dialect is the most prestigious and numerous. *Lg Use:* Speakers also use French, Jula, Anyin, Ebrie, Abbey, or Baoule. *Lg Dev:* Literacy rate in first language: 1% to 5%. Literacy rate in second language: 50% to 75%. Radio programs. NT: 1995. *Other:* Some form of whistle speech reported. Christian, traditional religion, other.

Avikam (Avekom, Brignan, Brinya, Gbanda, Kwakwa, Lahu) [avi] 21,000 (1993 SIL). Southern Department, along the coastal plain of Grand Lahou, Avikam Canton. *Class:* Niger-Congo, Atlantic-Congo, Volta-Congo, Kwa, Nyo, Avikam-Alladian. *Lg Dev:* Literacy rate in second language: 25% to 50%. Bible portions: 1957. *Other:* Christian, traditional religion, Muslim, other.

Bakwé [bjw] 10,300 (1993 SIL). Southern and West Central departments, prefectures of Sassandra, Soubre, San Pedro. *Class:* Niger-Congo, Atlantic-Congo, Volta-Congo, Kru, Eastern, Bakwe. *Dialects:* Defa, Deple, Dafa, Nigagba, Nyinagbi. Closest to Godié. *Lg Dev:* Literacy rate in first language: below 1%. Literacy rate in second language: 5% to 15%. *Other:* Christian, traditional religion, Muslim, other.

Bambara (Bamana, Bamanakan) [bam] 5,500 in Côte d'Ivoire (1993 SIL). *Lg Use:* Trade language. *Other:* Traders. Muslim, Christian, traditional religion, other. See main entry under Mali (Bamanankan).

Baoulé (Baule, Bawule) [bci] 2,130,000 (1993 SIL).
Central Department, widespread throughout southern Côte
d'Ivoire. *Class:* Niger-Congo, Atlantic-Congo, Volta-
Congo, Kwa, Nyo, Potou-Tano, Tano, Central, Bia,
Northern. *Dialects:* Close to Anyin. Many subgroups, but
all claim to understand the standard variety. *Lg Dev:*
Literacy rate in first language: 10% to 30%. Literacy rate
in second language: 25% to 50%. Radio programs. Bible:
1998. *Other:* Largest ethnic group in Côte d'Ivoire.
Traditional religion, Christian, Muslim, other.

Beng (Ngain, Ngan, Nguin, Ngin, Ngen, Gan, Ben) [nhb]
17,000 (1993 SIL). Central Department. 20 villages in the
northeast corner of M'bahiakro Subprefecture and 2
villages in Prikro Subprefecture. *Class:* Niger-Congo,
Mande, Eastern, Southeastern, Nwa-Ben, Ben-Gban.
Lg Use: Speakers have some proficiency in Baoulé, Jula,
or French. *Lg Dev:* Literacy rate in first language: below
1%. Literacy rate in second language: below 5%. *Other:*
Traditional religion, Muslim, Christian.

Bété, Daloa (Daloua Bété, Northern Bété) [bev] 130,000
(1993 SIL). West Central Department, Daloa
Subprefecture. *Class:* Niger-Congo, Atlantic-Congo,
Volta-Congo, Kru, Eastern, Bete, Western. *Lg Dev:*
Literacy rate in first language: 1% to 5%. Literacy rate in
second language: 25% to 50%. NT: 1996. *Other:*
Christian, traditional religion, Christian, Muslim, other.

Bété, Gagnoa (Gagnoua-Bété, Shyen, Eastern Bété)
[btg] 150,000 (1989 SIL). Gagnoa Subprefecture. *Class:*
Niger-Congo, Atlantic-Congo, Volta-Congo, Kru, Eastern,
Bete, Eastern. *Dialect:* Nekedi, Zadie, Niabre, Kpakolo,
Zebie, Guebie, Gbadi (Gbadie, Badie). *Lg Dev:* Literacy
rate in first language: below 1%. Literacy rate in second
language: 25% to 50%. *Other:* Christian, traditional
religion, Muslim, other.

Béte, Guiberoua (Central Bété, Western Bété) [bet]
130,000 (1993 SIL). West Central Department, Daloua,
Issia, Guiberoua, Soubre, Buyo, Gregbeu, and Ouaragahio
subprefectures. *Class:* Niger-Congo, Atlantic-Congo,
Volta-Congo, Kru, Eastern, Bete, Western. *Dialects:*
Soubré, Guiberoua. Closest to Godié. There are 18
dialects. *Lg Dev:* Literacy rate in first language: below
1%. Literacy rate in second language: 15% to 25%. NT:
1982. *Other:* Different from Bete of Nigeria and
Cameroon. Christian, traditional religion, Muslim, other.

Beti (Eotile) [eot] 200 (1999 R. Blench). Ethnic population:
3,181 (1988 census). Southern Department, villages of
Vitre I and Vitre II, Subprefecture of Grand Bassam.
Class: Niger-Congo, Atlantic-Congo, Volta-Congo, Kwa,
Nyo, Potou-Tano, Tano, Western. *Lg Use:* The last
speaker of the 'pure' form of Beti died about 1993.
Present speakers use a variety that is heavily influenced by
surrounding languages. Only a few elderly men remember
a few words from the 'pure' Beti dialect. Speakers shifting
to Anyin (Blench 2000). Some also speak Nzema, Abure,
Ebrie, Mbato, or Attié. *Other:* Christian, traditional
religion, other.

Birifor, Southern (Birifo) [biv] 4,308 in Côte d'Ivoire
(1993 SIL). Northeast corner. *Other:* Traditional religion,
Christian, Muslim, other. See main entry under Ghana.

Cerma (Gouin, Guin, Gwe, Gwen, Kirma) [cme] 1,700 in
Côte d'Ivoire (1991). Five villages around
Ouangolodougo, north of Ferkessedougou. *Other:*
Traditional religion. See main entry under Burkina Faso.

Daho-Doo [das] 4,000 (1996 SIL). Western Department,
just north of Tai and south of the Guéré. Doo are in 5
villages just south of Guiglo. Before 1933 they lived on
the right bank of the Nzo, near its junction with the
Sassandra. *Class:* Niger-Congo, Atlantic-Congo, Volta-
Congo, Kru, Western, Wee, Guere-Krahn. *Dialects:*
Although the Daho and Doo are considered to be Wè,
their speech is not understood by other Wè. The closest

lexical similarity they have to any Wè variety is 80%, and
the lowest is 30%. Lexical similarity 92% between Daho
and Doo. *Lg Use:* The Daho and Doo consider themselves
to be Guéré. All speak Wè Southern as second language,
but the Wè Southern do not understand Daho or Doo.

Dan (Yacouba, Yakuba, Da, Gio, Gio-Dan) [daf] 800,000
in Cote d'Ivoire (1993 SIL). Population includes 400,000
in Eastern Dan, 400,000 in western Dan. Population total
all countries: 951,600. Prefectures of Man (except Kouibly
and Facoubly), Danané, Biankouma (except Toura), plus
19 villages in the Prefecture of Touba. Also spoken in
Guinea, Liberia. *Class:* Niger-Congo, Mande, Eastern,
Southeastern, Guro-Tura, Tura-Dan-Mano, Tura-Dan.
Dialects: Gweetaawu (Eastern Dan), Blowo (Western
Dan). At least 38 subdialects. In Liberia speakers in
Garplay understood Côte d'Ivoire Yacouba dialect tapes as
follows: Danane, Koulinle, Kale: very well; Blosse: quite
well; Bloundo: reasonably well; dialects east of Blouno:
considerable difficulty (M. Bolli SIL 1971). *Lg Use:*
Speakers also use Jula or French. *Lg Dev:* Literacy rate in
first language: 1% or more. Literacy rate in second
language: 25% to 50%. NT: 1981–1993. *Other:* Called
'Gio' in Liberia. Some form of whistle speech reported.
Agriculturalists: rice, manioc, coffee, cocoa. Traditional
religion, Christian, Muslim, other.

Deg (Degha, Aculo, Janela, Mo, Buro, Mmfo) [mzw] 1,100
in Côte d'Ivoire (1991). See main entry under Ghana.

Dida, Lakota (Dieko, Gabo, Satro, Guébie, Brabori, Ziki)
[dic] 93,800 (1993 SIL). All Dida: 195,400 (1993 SIL).
Region around the town of Lakota. *Class:* Niger-Congo,
Atlantic-Congo, Volta-Congo, Kru, Eastern, Dida.
Dialect: Vata. *Lg Dev:* Literacy rate in first language:
below 1%. Literacy rate in second language: 25% to 50%.
Other: A separate language from Yocoboué Dida.
Traditional religion.

Dida, Yocoboué [gud] 101,600 (1993 SIL). Population
includes 7,100 Guitry, 94,500 Divo. Southern Department,
Guitry Subprefecture, area around town of Guitry. *Class:*
Niger-Congo, Atlantic-Congo, Volta-Congo, Kru, Eastern,
Dida. *Dialects:* Lozoua (Guitry, Yocoboue, Yokouboué,
Gakpa, Goudou, Kagoué), Divo. Lakota Dida is
marginally intelligible with Yocoboué. *Lg Use:* Guitry is
prestigious. Speakers also use French. *Lg Dev:* Literacy
rate in first language: 1% to 5%. Literacy rate in second
language: 25% to 50%. Radio programs. TV. Bible
portions: 1930–1972. *Other:* More survey is needed in
Dida area. Christian, Muslim, traditional religion, other.

Ebrié (Tyama, Kyama, Tsama, Cama, Caman, Tchaman)
[ebr] 75,859 (1988 census). Abidjan Department, urban
Abidjan, the Subprefecture of Dabou, and the
Subprefecture of Bingerville. 57 villages, including 27 in
Abidjan. *Class:* Niger-Congo, Atlantic-Congo, Volta-
Congo, Kwa, Nyo, Potou-Tano, Potou. *Dialects:* Low
lexical similarity and structurally different from
surrounding languages. *Lg Use:* More use of French than
other groups because of their proximity to the capital.
Lg Dev: Literacy rate in second language: 50% to 75%.
Radio programs. NT: 1998. *Other:* Christian, other.

Ega (Diés, Egwa) [ega] 2,500 (2001 Connell). Southern
Department, Diés Canton, Borondoukou village near Gly.
Class: Niger-Congo, Atlantic-Congo, Volta-Congo, Kwa,
Nyo, Potou-Tano, Ega. *Lg Use:* More vigorous than was
previously thought (R. Blench 2001). The ethnic group is
growing, but some are shifting to the Dida language
because of intermarriage and other influences. Some count
themselves as ethnic Dida in the census. *Other:*
Traditional religion, Christian, Muslim, other.

Esuma (Essouma) [esm] Extinct. Ethnic population: 164
(1988 census). Southern Department, Essouma Canton of
Adiake Subprefecture. Two villages of Assinie and Mafia.
Class: Niger-Congo, Atlantic-Congo, Volta-Congo, Kwa,

Nyo, Unclassified. *Lg Use:* Became extinct about 200 years ago. Members of the ethnic group now speak Anyin and Nzema. *Other:* Christian, Muslim, other.

French [fra] 17,470 in Côte d'Ivoire (1988 census). *Lg Use:* Official language. See main entry under France.

Gagu (Gagou, Gban) [ggu] 36,595 (1993). West Central Department, Oume Subprefecture. *Class:* Niger-Congo, Mande, Eastern, Southeastern, Nwa-Ben, Ben-Gban. *Dialects:* Bokwa, N'da, Bokabo, Tuka. N'da dialect is central. *Lg Use:* Speakers also use French, Bété, Gouro, Dida, or Jula. *Lg Dev:* Bible portions: 1970. *Other:* Christian, traditional religion, Muslim, other.

Glio-Oubi (Oubi, Ubi, Glio) [oub] 2,500 in Côte d'Ivoire (1991). Western Department. Tai Canton, Tai Subprefecture. 6 towns on each side of the border. *Lg Use:* High bilingualism with several surrounding languages in Côte d'Ivoire. *Other:* They are called 'Glio' in Liberia. Traditional religion. See main entry under Liberia.

Godié (Godye) [god] 26,448 (1993 SIL). Southern Department, Sassandra and Fresco subprefectures. Koyo dialect is in Kotrohou Canton. *Class:* Niger-Congo, Atlantic-Congo, Volta-Congo, Kru, Eastern, Bete, Western. *Dialects:* Tiglu, Glibe, Kagbo, Dagli, Nugbo, Dlogo, Jluko, Nyago, Koyo. The Koyo dialect may be closer to Dida than to Godié. Kagbo is the most widely understood dialect. *Lg Dev:* Radio programs. TV. Bible portions: 1977. *Other:* Christian, traditional religion, Muslim, other.

Grebo, Southern [grj] *Dialect:* Seaside Grebo. *Other:* Mainly refugees in Côte d'Ivoire. Traditional religion. See main entry under Liberia.

Guro (Gouro, Kweni, Lo, Kwéndré) [goa] 332,100 (1993 SIL). West Central and Central departments, subprefectures of Zuénoula, Vavoua, Gouitafla, Bouafle, Sinfra, Oumé. *Class:* Niger-Congo, Mande, Eastern, Southeastern, Guro-Tura, Guro-Yaoure. *Lg Dev:* Literacy rate in second language: 25%. Radio programs. Bible: 1979. *Other:* Muslim, Christian, other.

Jeri Kuo (Jeli Kuo, Celle) [jek] 1,500 (1990 Kastenholz). Ethnic population: 20,000 (1990 Kastenholz). Mainly to the southwest and some to the north of Korhogo. *Class:* Niger-Congo, Mande, Western, Central-Southwestern, Central, Manding-Jogo, Jogo-Jeri. *Dialects:* Related to Jogo (Ligbi) of Ghana and Tongon, an extinct blacksmith language of the Djimini Senoufo. *Other:* Leatherworkers.

Jula (Dyula, Dyoula, Diula, Dioula, Djula) [dyu] 179,100 in Côte d'Ivoire (1991). Northern Region, Ferkessédougou Department, Kong Subprefecture, and major cities throughout Côte d'Ivoire. *Dialect:* Kong Jula, Tagboussikan, Dioula Véhiculaire (Trade Jula). *Lg Use:* Trade language. *Lg Dev:* Literacy rate in first language: below 1%. Literacy rate in second language: 15% to 25%. *Other:* Designated by the government as one of five languages to be developed for literature. Muslim. See main entry under Burkina Faso.

Khisa (Komono, Khi Khipa, Kumwenu) [kqm] 5,000 in Côte d'Ivoire (1991 Vanderaa). Population total all countries: 8,000. Also spoken in Burkina Faso. *Class:* Niger-Congo, Atlantic-Congo, Volta-Congo, North, Gur, Central, Southern, Gan-Dogose. *Dialects:* Speakers say they can understand Kaansa after a time. Also reported to be Senoufo. Lexical similarity 82% with Dogosé, 72% with Kpatogo, 71% with Kaansa, 16% with Dogoso, 13% with Khe. *Other:* Muslim.

Kodia (Kwadia, Kwadya) [kwp] 837 (1993 SIL). South central. *Class:* Niger-Congo, Atlantic-Congo, Volta-Congo, Kru, Eastern, Kwadia. *Lg Dev:* Literacy rate in first language: below 1%. Literacy rate in second language: 15% to 25%. *Other:* Déima (African syncretism), Christian, traditional religion, Muslim.

Koro (Koro Jula) [kfo] 40,000 (1999 SIL). Mankono Department, Tiéningboué Subprefecture. *Class:* Niger-

Congo, Mande, Western, Central-Southwestern, Central, Manding-Jogo, Manding-Vai, Manding-Mokole, Manding, Manding-East, Southeastern Manding, Maninka-Mori. *Dialects:* High comprehension of Koyaga. *Other:* They have their own ethnic identity, although they live near the Koyaga. Muslim.

Kouya (Kowya, Sokya, Kuya) [kyf] 10,117 (1993 SIL). West Central Department, Kouya Canton of Vavoua Subprefecture, 12 villages. *Class:* Niger-Congo, Atlantic-Congo, Volta-Congo, Kru, Eastern, Bete, Eastern. *Dialects:* Closest to Gbadi Bété and Dida. *Lg Use:* 50% of speakers have some proficiency in Guro. *Lg Dev:* Literacy rate in first language: below 1%. Literacy rate in second language: 15% to 25%. NT: 2002. *Other:* Tropical forest, savannah. Agriculturalists. Traditional religion, Christian, Muslim, other.

Koyaga (Koyaga Jula, Koyaka, Koyara, Koyaa, Koya, Koyagakan) [kga] 60,000 (1999 SIL). Mankono Department, western four subprefectures. *Class:* Niger-Congo, Mande, Western, Central-Southwestern, Central, Manding-Jogo, Manding-Vai, Manding-Mokole, Manding, Manding-East, Southeastern Manding, Maninka-Mori. *Dialects:* Koyaga, Siaka, Sagaka, Nigbi. High comprehension of Koro. *Other:* They have their own ethnic identity, although they live near the Koro. Muslim, Christian, traditional religion, other.

Krahn, Western (Krahn, Northern Krahn) [krw] 12,200 in Côte d'Ivoire (1993 SIL). Western Côte d'Ivoire, around Toulépleu. *Dialects:* Pewa (Peewa), Biai. *Lg Dev:* Literacy rate in first language: below 1%. Literacy rate in second language: 25% to 50%. *Other:* There are influences from local French, but in Liberia from Liberian English. There are orthographic differences from that of Liberia. Traditional religion, Christian, Muslim. See main entry under Liberia.

Krobu (Krobou) [kxb] 9,920 (1993 SIL). Southern Department, Subprefecture of Agboville. Four villages. *Class:* Niger-Congo, Atlantic-Congo, Volta-Congo, Kwa, Nyo, Potou-Tano, Tano, Krobu. *Lg Use:* Speakers also use Baule, Abe. *Other:* Christian, Muslim, traditional religion, other.

Krumen, Plapo (Plapo) [ktj] 100 (2004). Southwest corner of Côte d'Ivoire, between Bapo and Honpo dialects of Tepo Krumen. *Class:* Niger-Congo, Atlantic-Congo, Volta-Congo, Kru, Western, Grebo, Ivorian. *Lg Dev:* NT: 2002. *Other:* Coastal.

Krumen, Pye (Kroumen, Southeastern Krumen, Northeastern Krumen) [pye] 20,000 (1993 SIL). All Krumen: 48,300 (1993 SIL). Southwestern Côte d'Ivoire between San Pedro and Tai, subprefectures of Tai, Bereby, and part of San Pedro. *Class:* Niger-Congo, Atlantic-Congo, Volta-Congo, Kru, Western, Grebo, Ivorian. *Dialects:* Trepo, Wluwe-Hawlo (Haoulo), Gbowe-Hran, Wlepo, Dugbo, Yrewe (Giriwe), Yapo, Pie (Pye, Pie-Pli-Mahon-Kuse-Gblapo-Henekwe). *Lg Dev:* Literacy rate in first language: below 1%. Literacy rate in second language: 25% to 50%. *Other:* Christian, traditional religion, Muslim, other.

Krumen, Tepo (Southern Krumen, Southwestern Kroumen, Krumen, Kroumen, Kru) [ted] 28,300 in Côte d'Ivoire (1993 SIL). All Krumen: 48,300 (1993 SIL). Population total all countries: 31,213. Southwest corner of Côte d'Ivoire, subprefectures of Tabou and Grabo. Glawlo dialect is in Liberia. Also spoken in Liberia. *Class:* Niger-Congo, Atlantic-Congo, Volta-Congo, Kru, Western, Grebo, Ivorian. *Dialects:* Tepo, Bapo, Wlopo (Ropo), Dapo, Honpo, Yrepo (Kapo), Glawlo. *Lg Use:* Speakers also use French or Jula. *Lg Dev:* Literacy rate in first language: 1% to 5%. Literacy rate in second language: 25% to 50%. Grammar. NT: 1995. *Other:* Christian, traditional religion, Muslim, other.

Kulango, Bondoukou [kzc] 77,000 in Côte d'Ivoire (1993 SIL). Population total all countries: 104,000. Eastern Department, Subprefecture of Bondoukou. Also spoken in Ghana. *Class:* Niger-Congo, Atlantic-Congo, Volta-Congo, North, Gur, Kulango. *Lg Dev:* Literacy rate in first language: below 1%. Literacy rate in second language: 15% to 25%. Roman script. NT: 1975. *Other:* Muslim, Christian, traditional religion, other.

Kulango, Bouna (Koulango, Kulange, Nkuraeng, Nkurange) [nku] 142,000 in Côte d'Ivoire (1993). Population total all countries: 157,500. Eastern Department, Subprefecture of Nassian. Also spoken in Ghana. *Class:* Niger-Congo, Atlantic-Congo, Volta-Congo, North, Gur, Kulango. *Dialect:* Nabanj. Speakers of the Bouna dialect understand Bondoukou, but the reverse is not true. *Lg Dev:* Literacy rate in first language: below 1%. Literacy rate in second language: 15% to 25%. *Other:* Traditional religion, Christian, Muslim.

Ligbi (Ligwi, Nigbi, Nigwi, Tuba, Banda, Jogo) [lig] 4,000 in Côte d'Ivoire (1991 Vanderaa). Eastern Department, one large village called Bineto, one community at Bouna, the town of Slil near Boundoukou, some at Ourodougou on the edge of Malinke territory. *Lg Use:* In other countries, blacksmiths speaking Manding languages are also called 'Noumou', but in Côte d'Ivoire and Ghana, the Noumou speak Ligbi. *Lg Dev:* Literacy rate in first language: below 1%. Literacy rate in second language: 15% to 25%. *Other:* 'Numu' (Noumou, Numun) is the name of a caste of blacksmiths; not a separate language. 'Banda' is the name for the people, which is also the name for speakers of the Nafaanra language. Traditional religion, Muslim. See main entry under Ghana.

Lobi (Lobiri, Miwa) [lob] 155,800 in Côte d'Ivoire (1993 SIL). Eastern Department, northern strip. *Lg Dev:* Literacy rate in first language: below 1%. Literacy rate in second language: 5% to 15%. *Other:* Traditional religion, Christian, Muslim, other. See main entry under Burkina Faso.

Loma (Lomakka, Lomasse, Lomapo, Malinke) [loi] 8,007 (2000 WCD). Near Tèèn and Kulango areas. *Class:* Niger-Congo, Atlantic-Congo, Volta-Congo, North, Gur, Teen. *Dialects:* Close to Tèèn and Kulango, but not inherently intelligible. Closer to Kulango than Tèèn is to Kulango. *Lg Use:* Speakers also use Tèèn. *Other:* The people are called 'Lomapo'. Different from Loma of Liberia.

Mahou (Maou, Mau, Mahu, Mauka, Mauke) [mxx] 169,100 (1993 SIL). Northwest Region, Touba Department. *Class:* Niger-Congo, Mande, Western, Central-Southwestern, Central, Manding-Jogo, Manding-Vai, Manding-Mokole, Manding, Manding-East, Southeastern Manding, Maninka-Mori. *Dialect:* Mahouka, Koroka, Tenenga, Finanga, Baralaka (Barala). Speakers of some listed dialects may not be able to use Mahou literature. Barala may be a dialect of Wojenaka. *Lg Dev:* Literacy rate in first language: below 1%. Literacy rate in second language: 5% to 15%. *Other:* Muslim, traditional religion, other.

Maninka, Forest [myq] 15,000. Northwest Region, Odienné Department, near Mali and Guinea borders. *Class:* Niger-Congo, Mande, Western, Central-Southwestern, Central, Manding-Jogo, Manding-Vai, Manding-Mokole, Manding, Manding-East, Southeastern Manding, Maninka-Mori. *Dialect:* Wasulu (Wassulunka, Wassoulounka, Wassulunke). This may be the same language as Eastern Maninkakan, Wojenaka, or different from both. *Other:* Ethnic Fulani who now speak a Manding language. Muslim.

Mbato (Gwa, Goaa, M'bato, Mbatto, Mgbato, Ogwia, Potu, N-Batto) [gwa] 25,000 (1993 SIL). Southern Department, Subprefecture of Petit Alépé. *Class:* Niger-Congo, Atlantic-Congo, Volta-Congo, Kwa, Nyo, Potou-Tano, Potou. *Dialects:* Related to Ebrii. *Lg Use:* Some bilingualism with Attié or Anyin. *Lg Dev:* Literacy rate in first language: below 1%. Literacy rate in second language: 25% to 50%. *Other:* Christian, traditional religion, Muslim, other.

Mbre (Bre, Bere, Pre, Pre Pisia) [mka] 200 (2000 SIL). Ethnic population: 700. About 20 km from Marabadiassa, northwest of Bouake and Diabo, in villages of Bondosso and Niantibo, having shrunk from 15 villages a few years ago. *Class:* Niger-Congo, Unclassified. *Dialects:* Considerably different from surrounding Mande and nearby Kwa languages. *Lg Use:* Speakers are shifting to Koro.

Mwan (Muan, Mona, Mouan, Muana, Mwa) [moa] 17,000 (1993 SIL). Kongasso Subprefecture and the southern part of Mankono Subprefecture. *Class:* Niger-Congo, Mande, Eastern, Southeastern, Nwa-Ben, Wan-Mwan. *Lg Use:* Speakers also use Jula or Guro. *Lg Dev:* Literacy rate in first language: below 1%. Literacy rate in second language: 15% to 25%. Bible portions: 1982–1995. *Other:* Traditional religion, Muslim, Christian, other.

Neyo (Gwibwen, Towi) [ney] 9,200 (1993 SIL). Southern Department, Sassandra Subprefecture, Neyo, and Kébé cantons, from Niégba in the west to Dagbégo in the east and Niabayo in the north. *Class:* Niger-Congo, Atlantic-Congo, Volta-Congo, Kru, Eastern, Dida. *Dialects:* Closest to Kagbo dialect of Godié, but they consider themselves to be a separate ethnic group. May be closer to Dida than to Bété. *Lg Dev:* Literacy rate in first language: below 1%. Literacy rate in second language: 25% to 50%. *Other:* 'Neyo' is their name for themselves. Christian, traditional religion, Muslim, other.

Nyabwa (Nyaboa, Niaboua, Nyabwa-Nyédébwa) [nwb] 42,700 (1993 SIL). Population includes 32,500 Nyabwa, 7,700 Nyedebwa, 2,500 Kouzié. West Central Department, northwest corner, subprefectures of Vavoua (Nyedebwa), Issia, Buyo, Zoukougbeu (Nyabwa), Daloua. *Class:* Niger-Congo, Atlantic-Congo, Volta-Congo, Kru, Western, Wee, Nyabwa. *Dialect:* Nyabwa, Nyedebwa (Niédéboua). Lexical similarity 90% between Nyabwa and Nyedebwa, 74% to 80% between them and Guéré and Wobe dialects. *Lg Use:* Speakers also use French, Dioula, Guéré, Wobe, or Biti. *Lg Dev:* Literacy rate in first language: 5% to 10%. Literacy rate in second language: 15% to 25%. NT: 1991. *Other:* They do not want to be called 'Bété'. Kouzii is an ethnic subgroup of Nyabwa, not a dialect. Some form of whistle speech reported. Christian, traditional religion, Muslim, other.

Nzema (Nzima, Appolo) [nzi] 66,700 in Côte d'Ivoire (1993 SIL). Aboisso Department, Tiapoum Subprefecture, southeastern coast. Many in Abidjan. *Lg Dev:* Literacy rate in first language: 1% to 5%. Literacy rate in second language: 25% to 50%. *Other:* Christian, traditional religion, Muslim, other. See main entry under Ghana.

Senoufo, Cebaara (Senadi, Senari, Syenere, Tiebaara, Tyebala) [sef] 862,000 (1993 SIL). Northern, around Korhogo. *Class:* Niger-Congo, Atlantic-Congo, Volta-Congo, North, Gur, Senufo, Senari. *Dialects:* Kafire, Kasara, Kufuru, Tagbari (Mbengui-Niellé), Patara, Pogara, Tyebara, Tagara, Tenere, Takpasyeeri (Messeni), Southwest Senari, Kandere (Tengrela), Papara, Fodara, Kulere, Nafara. Korhogo dialect is central. The Kulele speak the Kulere dialect scattered throughout the Senoufo area. *Lg Use:* The Tyelibele (Tyeliri) are leather workers scattered throughout the Senoufo area, speaking, as first language, the various Senoufo languages where they live. Speakers also use Jula. *Lg Dev:* Literacy rate in first language: 1% to 5%. Literacy rate in second language: 5% to 15%. NT: 1982–1995. *Other:* Tyeliri: leather workers; Kulere: wood-carvers. Traditional religion, Muslim, Christian.

Senoufo, Djimini (Dyimini, Djimini, Jinmini) [dyi] 95,500 (1993 SIL). Dabakala Department, northwest corner. *Class:* Niger-Congo, Atlantic-Congo, Volta-Congo, North, Gur, Senufo, Tagwana-Djimini. *Dialects:* Diamala (Djamala, Dyamala), Djafolo, Dofana, Foolo, Singala. Singala is the prestige dialect of Dabakala. Lexical similarity 76% to 81% with Tagwana. *Lg Use:* Speakers also use Djoula. *Lg Dev:* Literacy rate in first language: below 1%. Literacy rate in second language: 5% to 15%. NT: 1993. *Other:* Muslim, Christian, traditional religion, other.

Senoufo, Nyarafolo (Nyarafolo-Niafolo) [sev] 48,000 (2003 SIL). Northeast around Ferkessédougou. *Class:* Niger-Congo, Atlantic-Congo, Volta-Congo, North, Gur, Senufo, Senari. *Lg Dev:* Literacy rate in first language: below 1%. Literacy rate in second language: 5% to 15%. *Other:* Traditional religion, Muslim.

Senoufo, Palaka (Palara, Palaka, Kpalagha, Pallakha, Pilara) [plr] 8,000 (1995 SIL). Central Department, area around Sikolo, north of Djimini. *Class:* Niger-Congo, Atlantic-Congo, Volta-Congo, North, Gur, Senufo, Kpalaga. *Dialects:* Lexical similarity 65% to 70% with other Senufo languages and dialects. *Lg Dev:* Literacy rate in first language: below 1%. Literacy rate in second language: 5% to 15%. *Other:* Traditional religion, Muslim.

Senoufo, Shempire (Syempire, Shenpire) [seb] 100,000 (1996). North of Tingréla. *Class:* Niger-Congo, Atlantic-Congo, Volta-Congo, North, Gur, Senufo, Suppire-Mamara. *Dialects:* 3 or 4 dialects. Relationship to Supyire Senoufo in Mali is undetermined. *Lg Dev:* Literacy rate in first language: 0%. Literacy rate in second language: below 5%.

Senoufo, Tagwana (Tagbana, Tagwana, Tagouna) [tgw] 138,100 (1993 SIL). Central Department, north central area, west of Djimini. *Class:* Niger-Congo, Atlantic-Congo, Volta-Congo, North, Gur, Senufo, Tagwana-Djimini. *Dialects:* Gbo (Zoro), Tafire, Niediekaha, Niangbo, Niakaramadougou, Fondebougou, Djidanan, Fourgoula, Katiara, Katiola. Lexical similarity 76% to 81% with Djimini dialects. *Lg Dev:* Literacy rate in first language: below 1%. Literacy rate in second language: 15% to 25%. NT: 1987. *Other:* Christian, Muslim, traditional religion, other.

Soninke (Marka, Sarakole, Sarawule, Toubakai, Wakore, Gadyaga, Serahuli, Aswanik, Silabe) [snk] 100,000 in Côte d'Ivoire (1991 Vanderaa). *Dialect:* Azer (Adjer, Aser). *Other:* Muslim. See main entry under Mali.

Téén (Ténhé, Tegesie, Lorhon, Loron, Loghon, Nabe) [lor] 6,100 in Côte d'Ivoire (1991). Population total all countries: 8,100. Bouna Department, mainly Téhini Subprefecture. Also spoken in Burkina Faso. *Class:* Niger-Congo, Atlantic-Congo, Volta-Congo, North, Gur, Teen. *Dialects:* Different from Kulango. Closest to Loma, Kulango, Nabanj. *Lg Use:* Speakers also use Lobi, Jula, Loma, or French. *Lg Dev:* Literacy rate in first language: below 1%. Literacy rate in second language: below 5%. Bible portions: 1985–1995. *Other:* The name of the people is 'Ténbó' (pl.), 'Ténsé' (sg.); the language 'Téén'. Savannah. Traditional religion, Christian.

Tonjon [tjn] Extinct. Dabakala Department, among the Djimini Senoufo. *Class:* Niger-Congo, Mande, Western, Central-Southwestern, Central, Manding-Jogo, Jogo-Jeri, Jogo. *Dialects:* Related to Jogo (Ligbi) of Ghana and Jeri Kuo of Côte d'Ivoire. *Other:* Formerly spoken by blacksmiths.

Toura (Tura, Ween) [neb] 38,500 (1993 SIL). Department of Biankouma, eastern part, mountainous region east of the main road from Man to Touba, north of the main road from Man to Seguela, a little north of the Bafing River, otherwise the Bafing and Sassandra rivers from the

northern and eastern borders. *Class:* Niger-Congo, Mande, Eastern, Southeastern, Guro-Tura, Tura-Dan-Mano, Tura-Dan. *Dialects:* Naò, Boo, Yiligele, Gwéò, Wáádú, Guse. Probably closest to Dan. Also close to Gouro, Gban, Mann (in Liberia). *Lg Use:* Speakers also use Dan, Wobe, Jula, or French. *Lg Dev:* Literacy rate in first language: below 1%. Literacy rate in second language: 5% to 15%. NT: 1986. *Other:* Traditional religion.

Wan (Nwa) [wan] 22,000 (1993 UBS). Subprefectures of Kounahiri and the western part of Beoumi. *Class:* Niger-Congo, Mande, Eastern, Southeastern, Nwa-Ben, Wan-Mwan. *Dialects:* Miamu, Kemu. *Lg Use:* Speakers also use French, Jula, or Muan. *Other:* Traditional religion, Christian, Muslim, other.

Wané (Ngwané, Hwane) [hwa] 2,100 (1993 SIL). Southwestern coast. *Class:* Niger-Congo, Atlantic-Congo, Volta-Congo, Kru, Eastern, Bakwe. *Lg Use:* They do not like to be identified as Bakwe and are vocal about their identity as being separate. Some young people understand Bakwe, and they seem to understand French. *Lg Dev:* Literacy rate in first language: below 1%. Literacy rate in second language: 15% to 25%. *Other:* They intermarry frequently with the Bakwe. Traditional religion, Christian, Muslim, other.

Wè Northern (Wobé, Ouobe, Wèè) [wob] 156,300 (1993 SIL). Western Department, subprefectures of Kouibly and Fakobly. *Class:* Niger-Congo, Atlantic-Congo, Volta-Congo, Kru, Western, Wee, Wobe. *Dialect:* Tao, Péomé, Sémien (Gbéan). Kouibly dialect is intelligible for about half of the Wè Southern speakers. Lexical similarity 90% to 94% among dialects, Kouibly dialect (Tao and Gbean) has 84% to 89% lexical similarity with Wè Southern dialects. *Lg Use:* Speakers also use French. *Lg Dev:* Literacy rate in first language: 1% to 5%. Literacy rate in second language: 15% to 25%. Grammar. NT: 1984. *Other:* Some form of whistle speech reported. Christian, traditional religion, Muslim, other.

Wè Southern (Guéré, Central Guéré, Gere, Wèè) [gxx] 292,500 (1999 SIL). Population includes 20,000 Niao (1995 SIL). Western Department, subprefectures of Guiglo, Duékoué, Bangolo, Tai. *Class:* Niger-Congo, Atlantic-Congo, Volta-Congo, Kru, Western, Wee, Guere-Krahn. *Dialects:* Zibiao, Zagne, Zagna, Beu (Zarabaon), Zaa (Zaha), Neao (Niabo, Neabo), Gboo (Gbobo), Fleo, Nyeo. Southern Wè has 7 more consonants than Northern Wè. *Lg Use:* Speakers consider Wè to be one language with many dialects. They are one ethnic group, together with Krahn in Liberia. Most bilingual comprehension in French and Jula is limited to greetings and trade. *Lg Dev:* Literacy rate in first language: below 1%. Literacy rate in second language: 25% to 40%. Radio programs. TV. NT: 1982. *Other:* 'Wèè' is their name for people and language. Christian, traditional religion, Muslim, other.

Wè Western (Guéré, Gere, Wèè, Neyo) [wec] 25,188 (1998 SIL). Population includes 20,000 Kaoro (1995 SIL). Western Department, Subprefecture of Toulépleu. *Class:* Niger-Congo, Atlantic-Congo, Volta-Congo, Kru, Western, Wee, Guere-Krahn. *Dialects:* Nidrou (Nidru), Kaoro (Kaawlu, Kaowlu). *Lg Use:* Most bilingual comprehension in French and Jula is limited to greetings and trade. *Lg Dev:* Literacy rate in first language: below 1%. Literacy rate in second language: 15% to 25%. NT: 1991. *Other:* 'Wèè' is their name for people and language. Neyo is distinct from another Kru language by that name. Christian, traditional religion.

Wojenaka (Odiennekakan, Malinké, Odienné Jula) [jod] 120,000 (1999 SIL). Population includes 15,000 Wasulu. Northwest Region, Odienné Department. *Class:* Niger-Congo, Mande, Western, Central-Southwestern, Central, Manding-Jogo, Manding-Vai, Manding-Mokole, Manding,

Manding-East, Southeastern Manding, Maninka-Mori. *Dialect:* Odienneka, Sienkoka, Nafana, Bodougouka, Toudougouka, Vandougouka, Wasulu (Wassulunka, Wassoulounka, Wassulunke, Forest Maninka). Some of the dialects listed may be separate languages. Forest Maninka may be Folongakan, a dialect of Wojenaka. Barala may be a dialect of Wojenaka. *Other:* Wasulu are ethnic Fulani who have adopted a Manding language. In Côte d'Ivoire this may be Eastern Maninkakan, Forest Maninka, or separate from both. Muslim.

Worodougou (Worodougou Jula, Ouorodougou, Worodugu, Worodougoukakan, Bakokan) [jud] 80,000 (1999 SIL). Northwest Region, Séguéla Department. *Class:* Niger-Congo, Mande, Western, Central-Southwestern, Central, Manding-Jogo, Manding-Vai, Manding-Mokole, Manding, Manding-East, Southeastern Manding, Maninka-Mori. *Dialects:* Worodougouka, Karanjan, Kanika. Karanjan may be a separate language. *Other:* Called 'Bakokan' by people in Mankono Department. Muslim.

Yaouré (Yaure, Yohowré, Youré) [yre] 24,600 (1991 Vanderaa). Population includes 13,000 in villages, 7,000 in cities (1982 SIL). Bouaflé Department, Yaoure Canton of Bouafli Subprefecture, bounded on the south by Red Bandama, the east by the White Bandama River, the north by Lake Kossou, the west by Bouaflé. *Class:* Niger-Congo, Mande, Eastern, Southeastern, Guro-Tura, Guro-Yaoure. *Dialects:* Klan, Yaan, Taan, Yoo, Bhoo. Closest to Guro. *Lg Use:* Speakers also use Gouro, Baoule, or Jula. *Lg Dev:* Literacy rate in first language: 1% to 5%. Literacy rate in second language: 25% to 50%. NT: 1999. *Other:* Traditional religion.

Democratic Republic of the Congo

Democratic Republic of the Congo, République Démocratique du Congo. Formerly Belgian Congo, Congo-Leopoldville, Congo-Kinshasa, Republic of Zaïre. 58,317,930. National or official languages: Koongo, Lingala, Luba-Kasai, Congo Swahili, French. Literacy rate: 55% to 61%. Also includes Boguru, Fanagalo, Greek, people from India. Information mainly from Y. Bastin 1978; K. S. Olson 1996; John Bendor-Samuel 1989; SIL 1977–2003. Blind population: 73,000 (1982 WCE). Deaf institutions: 12 (CMD). The number of languages listed for Democratic Republic of the Congo is 215. Of those, 214 are living languages and 1 is extinct. See maps beginning on page 694.

Alur (Lur, Aloro, Alua, Alulu, Luri, Dho Alur, Jo Alur) [alz] 750,000 in Democratic Republic of the Congo (2001 Johnstone and Mandryk). Population total all countries: 1,209,000. Orientale Province: Mahagi Territory and northwest to Djalasiga area. Also spoken in Uganda. *Class:* Nilo-Saharan, Eastern Sudanic, Nilotic, Western, Luo, Southern, Luo-Acholi, Alur-Acholi, Alur. *Dialects:* Lexical similarity 96% between Jonam and Ngora. *Lg Dev:* Newspapers. Radio programs. Bible: 1936–1955. *Other:* Christian.

Amba (Kwamba, Kuamba, Rwamba, Hambo, Ruwenzori Kibira, Humu, Kiumu) [rwm] 4,500 in Democratic Republic of the Congo (1991 SIL). Nord-Kivu Province, Uganda border area south of Lake Albert, northern foothills of Ruwenzori. *Dialects:* Kigumu (Kuamba, Hamba, Lubulebule), Kihyanzi, Kusuwa. *Lg Use:* Many also use Talinga-Bwisi. See main entry under Uganda.

Asoa (Asua, Asuati, Asuae, Aka) [asv] 25,474 (2000 WCD). Orientale Province, Rungu Territory, Ituri Forest, among Mangbetu groups Maele, Meje, Aberu, and Popoi. *Class:* Nilo-Saharan, Central Sudanic, East, Mangbetu. *Lg Use:* Some Asoa learn Mangbetu-Meje. Mangbetu men sometimes take Asoa wives, but Mangbetu women do not ordinarily marry Asoa men. *Other:* A pygmy group. 'Aka' may be derogatory. Hunter-gatherers.

Aushi (Avaushi, Vouaousi, Ushi, Usi, Uzhili) [auh] Haut Katanga Province to the east of Lubumbashi. *Lg Use:* Language of wider communication. See main entry under Zambia.

Avokaya (Abukeia, Avukaya) [avu] 25,000 in Democratic Republic of the Congo (1989 SIL). Population includes 2,000 Ojila, 10,000 Northern Ogambi. Orientale Province, Faradje Territory, close to Sudan border. *Dialects:* Ojila, Ajigu (Ajugu), Northern Ogambi, Avokaya Pur. See main entry under Sudan.

Babango (Mobango) [bbm] 2,547 (2000 WCD). Orientale Province, Basoko Territory. *Class:* Niger-Congo, Atlantic-Congo, Volta-Congo, Benue-Congo, Bantoid, Southern, Narrow Bantu, Northwest, C, Bangi-Ntomba (C.40), Lusengo. *Dialects:* Close to Budza which is immediately downriver; possibly a dialect.

Baka (Tara Baaka) [bdh] 1,300 in Democratic Republic of the Congo (1993 UBS). Orientale Province, between Garamba National Park and Sudan border. A few among the Logo. *Other:* Different from Baka of Cameroon. Refugees in Democratic Republic of the Congo. See main entry under Sudan.

Bali (Kibali, Kibaali, Baali, Kibala, Libaali, Dhibali) [bcp] 42,000 (1987 UBS). 5% to 10% monolingual. Orientale Province, Tshopo District, Bafwasende Territory, between the Tshopo River to the south and the Ituri River to the north, and on the north bank of the Ituri River. *Class:* Niger-Congo, Atlantic-Congo, Volta-Congo, Benue-Congo, Bantoid, Southern, Narrow Bantu, Central, D, Lega-Kalanga (D.20). *Dialects:* Bemili, Bakundumu, Bafwandaka, Bekeni. Bemili is central linguistically and geographically. Lexical similarity 52% with Lika; 40% to 45% with Bwa and Pagibete; 46% with Komo; 40% with Bhele, Bila, and Bera; 30% with Budu and Ndaka; 25% with Lega languages and Lingala. *Lg Use:* Bilingual level estimates for Lingala: 0 10%, 1 15%, 2 30%, 3 30%, 4 10%, 5 5%. Congo Swahili is spoken by (1) all leaders, nearly all young people and men (speak well in certain domains), (2) most women and older men (less fluent), (3) many older women and young children (low proficiency). Lingala is used mainly by those who travel or have been in military service. French is spoken by those with secondary school education, less than 5%. *Lg Dev:* Literacy rate in first language: 1% to 2%. Literacy rate in second language: 30% to 40% in Congo Swahili. *Other:* 'Kibali' is the official name. 'Dhibali' is their own name. Speakers are called 'Babali'. SVO; prepositions; genitives before nouns; articles, adjectives, numerals, relatives after nouns; question word sentence final; 1–3 prefixes; 1–5 suffixes; word order distinguishes role; affixes mark person, number of subject and object in one noun group; active, passive, reflexive; 2 causatives; aspect; comparatives; 3 tones; stress; 9 vowels. Riverine. Tropical forest. 500 meters. Swidden agriculturalists.

Baloi (Loi, Boloi, Baato Baloi, Rebu) [biz] 20,000 (2002). Equateur Province, south, west, and east of Bomongo. *Class:* Niger-Congo, Atlantic-Congo, Volta-Congo, Benue-Congo, Bantoid, Southern, Narrow Bantu, Northwest, C, Bangi-Ntomba (C.40), Ngiri. *Dialects:* Loi, Dzamba (Jamba), Makutu, Mampoko. Close to Balobo (Likila), Ndobo.

Bamwe [bmg] 20,000 (1983 census). Equateur Province, Sud Ubangi, Kungu Territory, in Mwanda Collectivité, upper reaches of Ngiri River between the villages of Limpoko and Sombe, including villages of Moniongo, Libobi, Likata, Mondongo, Lifunga, Bomole, Lokutu, Botunia; 10 villages. *Class:* Niger-Congo, Atlantic-Congo, Volta-Congo, Benue-Congo, Bantoid, Southern,

Narrow Bantu, Northwest, C, Bangi-Ntomba (C.40). *Dialects:* All village dialects are highly intelligible to each other. Dzando and Ndolo are the most closely related languages. *Lg Use:* Nearly everyone speaks Lingala except oldest women. Many other women speak only market Lingala. *Lg Dev:* Literacy rate in second language: 30% to 50% in Lingala. *Other:* Riverine.

Banda, Mid-Southern [bjo] 2,000 in Democratic Republic of the Congo (1986 SIL). Equateur Province, Bosobolo Territory in a few villages north of Dubulu, and Mobaye Territory. *Dialect:* Yakpa (Yacoua, Yakpwa, Yakwa, Bayaka). *Lg Use:* Many villages in Democratic Republic of the Congo where Yakpa was formerly spoken now speak Mono or Mbandja. All speakers also use Mono, Mbanza, or Lingala. See main entry under Central African Republic.

Banda, South Central [lnl] 3,000 in Democratic Republic of the Congo. Equateur Province. *Dialect:* Ngbugu (Ngubu, Ngbougou). *Lg Use:* Some men are fluent in Lingala and Sango. Some use Mono, but they may not accept Mono literature. *Lg Dev:* Literacy rate in second language: Low. *Other:* Fishermen. See main entry under Central African Republic.

Banda, Togbo-Vara [tor] 12,000 in Democratic Republic of the Congo (1984 census). Population total all countries: 24,000. Equateur Province, Nord Ubangi, Bosobolo Territory mainly, around towns of Badja and Baya, between villages of Vongba II and Bandema, on the road as far as Gwara II, and scattered villages in the area. Also spoken in Central African Republic, Sudan. *Class:* Niger-Congo, Atlantic-Congo, Volta-Congo, North, Adamawa-Ubangi, Ubangi, Banda, Central, Central Core, Togbo-Vara. *Dialect:* Togbo (Tohgboh, Tagbo). *Lg Use:* High bilingualism in Mono, but they view themselves as very different from Mono. Many men, especially younger ones, speak Lingala and Sango. *Lg Dev:* Literacy rate in second language: Low in Lingala and not increasing. *Other:* Different from Tagbu of Democratic Republic of the Congo in Sere group.

Bangala (Ngala) [bxg] Few first-language speakers. Orientale Province. *Class:* Niger-Congo, Atlantic-Congo, Volta-Congo, Benue-Congo, Bantoid, Southern, Narrow Bantu, Northwest, C, Bangi-Ntomba (C.40), Lusengo. *Dialects:* Related to Lusengo and Lingala. There is a trend toward becoming more like Lingala. *Lg Use:* Trade language. 3,500,000 second-language speakers (1991 UBS). *Lg Dev:* Bible: 1953–1995.

Bangba (Abangba) [bbe] 11,000 (1993 SIL). Orientale Province, Kopa Collectivité of the Niangara Territory, and the area around Tora in the Watsa Territory. *Class:* Niger-Congo, Atlantic-Congo, Volta-Congo, North, Adamawa-Ubangi, Ubangi, Sere-Ngbaka-Mba, Ngbaka-Mba, Ngbaka, Eastern, Mayogo-Bangba. *Dialects:* Kopa, Tora. Lexical similarity 70% with Mayogo, 72% with Mündü, 90% among dialects.

Bangi (Bobangi, Bubangi, Lobobangi, Rebu, Dzamba) [bni] 50,948 in Democratic Republic of the Congo (2000 WCD). Population total all countries: 118,752. Equateur Province, east of Congo River from Bolobo to Mbandaka. Also spoken in Central African Republic, Congo. *Class:* Niger-Congo, Atlantic-Congo, Volta-Congo, Benue-Congo, Bantoid, Southern, Narrow Bantu, Northwest, C, Bangi-Ntomba (C.40). *Lg Dev:* NT: 1909–1922.

Bangubangu (Kibangubangu, Bangobango, Kibangobango) [bnx] 171,000 (1995 SIL). Population includes 85,000 Bangubangu, 30,000 Mikebwe, 20,000 Kasenga, 32,000 Nonda, 4,000 Hombo. Maniema Province, Kasongo District, Kabambare Territory. *Class:* Niger-Congo, Atlantic-Congo, Volta-Congo, Benue-Congo, Bantoid, Southern, Narrow Bantu, Central, L,

Songye (L.20). *Dialects:* Bangubangu, Mikebwe, Kasenga, Nonda, Hombo, Sanzi. Dialects listed are probably separate languages. Most closely related to Hemba (lexical similarity 67%) and Songe (58%). Lexical similarity 81% with Mikebwe, 80% with Kasenga, 80% with Nonda, 71% with Hombo. *Other:* Muslim, Christian, traditional religion.

Barambu (Barambo, Amiangba, Amiangbwa, Balambu, Abarambo, Duga) [brm] 25,570 (1990 census). A few hundred living among the Bangba (1996). Orientale Province, Poko Territory, between the Bomokandi and Uélé rivers. *Class:* Niger-Congo, Atlantic-Congo, Volta-Congo, North, Adamawa-Ubangi, Ubangi, Zande, Barambo-Pambia. *Dialects:* Unconfirmed reports of a 'Pamiaangba' dialect near Dungu in Niangara Territory. *Lg Use:* Extinct in Sudan in 1975.

Beeke (Beke, Ibeeke) [bkf] 1,000 (1994 SIL). Orientale Province, Ituri District, Mambasa Territory, one village in each of the Bandaka and Bombo collectivités. *Class:* Niger-Congo, Atlantic-Congo, Volta-Congo, Benue-Congo, Bantoid, Southern, Narrow Bantu, Central, D, Lega-Kalanga (D.20). *Dialects:* Lexical similarity 65% with Bali, 46% with Lika and Bila, 40% with Bera, 38% with Ndaka. *Lg Use:* Nearly all speakers also use Ndaka. Ndaka is preferred by most speakers. *Other:* Probably ethnic Bali who moved away from Bali territory, first to 2 villages south of the Ituri River, and in the 1960s to Ndaka and Mbo territory along the main road from Mambasa to Kisangani.

Bemba (Ichibemba, Wemba, Chiwemba) [bem] 300,000 in Democratic Republic of the Congo (2000). Near southeastern border of Katanga Province. Possibly in Zimbabwe. *Dialects:* Lembue, Lomotua (Lomotwa), Ngoma, Nwesi, Shila. *Lg Use:* Language of wider communication. *Other:* Distinct from Beembe (Bembe) of Congo-Brazzaville. Shila: traditional religion, Christian. See main entry under Zambia.

Bemba (Kinyabemba) [bmy] 295,780 (2000 WCD). Southern Kivu Province. *Class:* Niger-Congo, Atlantic-Congo, Volta-Congo, Benue-Congo, Bantoid, Southern, Narrow Bantu, Unclassified. *Other:* Distinct from Bemba (Ichibemba) in southeastern Katanga Province, Zambia, and Tanzania; or Bembe (IBembe) in Kivu Province, Fizi Territory.

Bembe (Ibembe, Beembe, Ebembe) [bmb] 252,000 in Democratic Republic of the Congo (1991 UBS). Sud-Kivu Province, Fizi Territory, west of Lake Tanganyika. Also spoken in Tanzania. *Class:* Niger-Congo, Atlantic-Congo, Volta-Congo, Benue-Congo, Bantoid, Southern, Narrow Bantu, Central, D, Bembe (D.50). *Dialects:* Lexical similarity 76% to 84% with Lega-Mwenga dialects, 68% with Buyu, 60% with Lega-Shabunda, 55% with Zimba, 50% with Enya, 45% with Nyanga, 40% with Tembo, 30% with Lengola. *Lg Dev:* Bible: 1991. *Other:* Bryan classifies it with the Lega group. Distinct from Beembe (Bembe) of Congo-Brazzaville. Traditional religion, Christian, Muslim.

Bendi (Mabendi, Mabeni) [bct] 32,000 (1991 SIL). Orientale Province, Djugu Territory, midway between Bunia and Djalasiga. *Class:* Nilo-Saharan, Central Sudanic, East, Lendu. *Other:* Also reported to be Mangbutu-Efe. Different from Ngiti (Bindi) or Bendi, which is a dialect of Banda.

Bera (Kibira, Plains Bira) [brf] 120,000 (1992 SIL). Orientale Province, Ituri District, Irumu Territory. *Class:* Niger-Congo, Atlantic-Congo, Volta-Congo, Benue-Congo, Bantoid, Southern, Narrow Bantu, Central, D, Bira-Huku (D.30). *Dialects:* One dialect, but some variation around Solenyama. Lexical similarity 70% with Amba; 56% to 59% with Bila, Kaiku, Bhele, and Komo; 47% with Bwa, Lika, and Bali; 22% with Nyali and Budu.

Lg Use: Older adults do not understand Congo Swahili, but others do. *Lg Dev:* Bible portions: 1930.

Bhele (Ebhele, Kipere, Ipere, Pere, Peri, Piri, Pili, Bili, Kipili) [bhy] 15,000 (1989). Nord-Kivu Province, Lubero Territory, west of Butembo. Southern Bhele is in Munjoa. *Class:* Niger-Congo, Atlantic-Congo, Volta-Congo, Benue-Congo, Bantoid, Southern, Narrow Bantu, Central, D, Bira-Huku (D.30). *Dialect:* Bugombe (Ebugombe). Lexical similarity 80% with Kaiku and Komo, 70% with Bila, less than 60% with Bera and Amba, 40% with Bali and Lika. *Lg Use:* Swahili is their main second language, then Nande. *Lg Dev:* Bible portions: 1939–1986. *Other:* Different from Peri, which is a dialect of Kalanga of Zimbabwe. Names of ethnic groups: Babeka, Baleje, Batike, Babhogombe (Bapakombe, Bugombe, Ebugombe), Babhaidhomba, Babhogala (Bapokara).

Bila (Kibila, Forest Bira, Ebila, Western Bila) [bip] 40,000 (1993 SIL). Orientale Province, Ituri District, Irumu Territory. *Class:* Niger-Congo, Atlantic-Congo, Volta-Congo, Benue-Congo, Bantoid, Southern, Narrow Bantu, Central, D, Bira-Huku (D.30). *Dialects:* Bombi-Ngbanja, Nyaku. Lexical similarity 94% between dialects. Closely related to other 'Bira' languages: lexical similarity 80% with Kaiku, 72% with Bhele, 70% with Komo, nearly 60% with Bera and Amba, 46% with Beeke, 45% with Bwa, 40% with Lika and Bali, 26% with Mbo, 22% with Budu and Ndaka. *Lg Use:* About 25% of men, 10% to 15% of women have routine proficiency in Congo Swahili, older adults have none. *Other:* Traditional religion, Christian, Muslim.

Binji (Bindji) [bpj] 165,000 (2000). Kasaï Occidental Province, Kazumba Territory. *Class:* Niger-Congo, Atlantic-Congo, Volta-Congo, Benue-Congo, Bantoid, Southern, Narrow Bantu, Central, L, Songye (L.20). *Lg Dev:* NT: 1962.

Boko (Iboko) [bkp] 21,000. Equateur Province, on Congo River, upstream from Mbandaka. *Class:* Niger-Congo, Atlantic-Congo, Volta-Congo, Benue-Congo, Bantoid, Southern, Narrow Bantu, Northwest, C, Bangi-Ntomba (C.40). *Other:* Different from Boko (Woko) of Cameroon and Boko (Busa) of Benin and Nigeria.

Bolia (Bulia, Bokoki) [bli] 100,000 (2000). Bandundu Province, north of Lake Mai-Ndombe. *Class:* Niger-Congo, Atlantic-Congo, Volta-Congo, Benue-Congo, Bantoid, Southern, Narrow Bantu, Northwest, C, Bangi-Ntomba (C.40). *Dialects:* Close to, or possibly a dialect of, Ntomba. *Lg Dev:* Bible portions: 1936.

Boloki (Baloki, Buluki, Boleki, River Ruki) [bkt] 4,200. Equateur Province, both sides of the Congo River, upstream from Mbandaka. *Class:* Niger-Congo, Atlantic-Congo, Volta-Congo, Benue-Congo, Bantoid, Southern, Narrow Bantu, Northwest, C, Bangi-Ntomba (C.40), Lusengo. *Lg Use:* Speakers are shifting to Lingala. *Lg Dev:* Bible portions: 1895–1904.

Bolondo [bzm] 3,000 (1983 census). Equateur Province, Sud Ubangi, Budjala Territory on the Saw River south of Budjala, around the village of Bamba. *Class:* Niger-Congo, Atlantic-Congo, Volta-Congo, Benue-Congo, Bantoid, Southern, Narrow Bantu, Northwest, C, Bangi-Ntomba (C.40). *Dialects:* Most closely related to Motembo. *Lg Use:* Lingala is used widely in the main market towns among 'Water People', but hardly at all in the other villages, where comprehension is lower. Many villagers also speak Ngbandi. *Other:* Riverine.

Boma (Buma, Kiboma, Boma Kasai) [boh] 20,500 (2000). Bandundu Province. *Class:* Niger-Congo, Atlantic-Congo, Volta-Congo, Benue-Congo, Bantoid, Southern, Narrow Bantu, Northwest, B, Yanzi (B.80).

Bomboli (Bombongo) [bml] 2,500 (1986 SIL). Equateur Province, Sud Ubangi, Kungu Territory, Dongo Collectivité, north of Bomongo on one of the canals flowing into the Ngiri River, between the villages of Bokondo and Bodjinga. *Class:* Niger-Congo, Atlantic-Congo, Volta-Congo, Benue-Congo, Bantoid, Southern, Narrow Bantu, Northwest, C, Bangi-Ntomba (C.40). *Dialects:* Closest to Bozaba and Lobala. 3 dialects. *Lg Use:* They consider themselves ethnically distinct from the Lobala. They may accept Lobala literature. Use of Lobala is receptive only. Speakers use Lingala as second language. *Other:* Riverine.

Bomboma (Boba) [bws] 23,000 (1983 census). Population includes 1,279 in Lingonda. Equateur Province, Sud Ubangi, Kungu Territory, Bomboma Collectivité on the southern Roa Dongo between the villages of Bomboma and Bokonzi, and including the villages of Lingonda, Ebuku, Makengo, Ndzubele, Motuba: 7 villages. *Class:* Niger-Congo, Atlantic-Congo, Volta-Congo, Benue-Congo, Bantoid, Southern, Narrow Bantu, Northwest, C, Bangi-Ntomba (C.40). *Dialects:* Likaw, Lingonda, Ebuku, Bokonzi. The Likaw in Budjala Territory, southwest of Budjala, are reported to be ethnically one with Bomboma and to have good inter-comprehension. Lexical similarity 93% with Ebuku and Lingonda. *Lg Use:* Lingala is widely spoken by nearly everyone. *Other:* Riverine (Lingonda).

Borna (Eborna) [bxx] *Class:* Niger-Congo, Atlantic-Congo, Volta-Congo, Benue-Congo, Bantoid, Southern, Unclassified. *Other:* May not exist (J. Ellington 1982) or may be same as Boma.

Bozaba (Buzaba, Budzaba) [bzo] 5,500 (1983 census). Equateur Province, Sud Ubangi, Kungu Territory, Mwanda Collectivité, on the islands and canals northwest of the confluence of the Ngiri and Mwanda rivers. *Class:* Niger-Congo, Atlantic-Congo, Volta-Congo, Benue-Congo, Bantoid, Southern, Narrow Bantu, Northwest, C, Bangi-Ntomba (C.40). *Dialects:* Most closely related to Bomboli, then Bomboma and Lobala. *Lg Use:* Bilingual in Lingala but largely only for market use. *Other:* Riverine.

Budu (Ebudu, Kibudu, Bodo) [buu] 180,000 (1991 SIL). Orientale Province, Wamba Territory, 8 collectivités. *Class:* Niger-Congo, Atlantic-Congo, Volta-Congo, Benue-Congo, Bantoid, Southern, Narrow Bantu, Central, D, Bira-Huku (D.30). *Dialects:* Ineta (Timoniko), Wadimbisa (Isombi), Makoda, West Bafwangada (Bafanio), East Bafwangada, Bafwakoyi, Malamba, Mahaa. The first four dialects listed are on the Ibambi side of the Nepoko River; the last four on the Wamba side. The Ibambi group and the Wamba group consider themselves to be one people and language. Lexical similarity 92% within dialects, 85% lexical similarity with Ndaka, 78% with Mbo, 74% with Nyali and Vanuma, 30% with Bali, Lika, and Komo, 20% to 25% with Bhele, Kaiku, Bila, and Bera, 14% with Swahili. *Lg Use:* Most speakers also use Swahili. *Other:* Traditional religion, Christian.

Budza (Ebuja, Buja, Budja, Mbudja, Embudja, Limbudza) [bja] 226,000 (1985 census). Equateur Province, Mongala, Bumba, and parts of Bongandanga territories. *Class:* Niger-Congo, Atlantic-Congo, Volta-Congo, Benue-Congo, Bantoid, Southern, Narrow Bantu, Northwest, C, Bangi-Ntomba (C.40), Lusengo. *Dialects:* Mbila, Monzamboli, Bosambi, Yaliambi. Close to Babango. Lexical similarity 89% with Babango, 59% with Ngombe, 48% with Lingala, 35% to 40% with Pagibete and Bwa. *Lg Use:* Lingala is the lingua franca, spoken by all ages and sexes. Some young people speak only Lingala. *Lg Dev:* Literacy rate in second language: High in Lingala.

Buraka (Bouraka, Boraka) [bkg] 1,300 in Democratic Republic of the Congo. Equateur Province, scattered groups along the Ubangi River, north and northeast of Bosobolo. See main entry under Central African Republic.

Bushoong (Bushong, Busoong, Bushongo, Shongo, Mbale, Bamongo, Mongo, Kuba, Ganga) [buf] 155,137

(2000 WCD). Kasaï Occidental Province, Mweka and northern Ilebo territories. *Class:* Niger-Congo, Atlantic-Congo, Volta-Congo, Benue-Congo, Bantoid, Southern, Narrow Bantu, Northwest, C, Bushong (C.90). *Dialects:* Djembe, Ngende, Ngombe (Ngombia), Ngongo, Pianga (Panga, Tsobwa, Shobwa, Shoba). *Lg Dev:* Bible: 1927. *Other:* Traditional religion, Christian.

Buya (Ibuya) [byy] 13,000 (2002). *Class:* Niger-Congo, Atlantic-Congo, Volta-Congo, Benue-Congo, Bantoid, Southern, Unclassified.

Buyu (Buyi, Kibuyu, Bujwe) [byi] 10,000 (2002). On Lake Tanganyika, on the border between Sud-Kivu and Katanga provinces. *Class:* Niger-Congo, Atlantic-Congo, Volta-Congo, Benue-Congo, Bantoid, Southern, Narrow Bantu, Central, D, Bembe (D.50). *Dialects:* Lexical similarity 68% with Bembe, 60% with Lega-Mwenga, 55% with Lega-Shabunda, 50% with Zimba and Enya, 40% with Bangubangu.

Bwa (Boa, Bua, Boua, Libua, Libwali, Libenge, Kibua, Kibwa) [bww] 200,000 (1994 SIL). Orientale Province, Buta, Bambesa, Banalia, Aketi, and Bondo territories. Buta is considered the center. Most people in Buta and Bambesa territories speak similar dialects. Kiba is in Banalia Territory, Benge and Bati in Aketi and Bondo territories. *Class:* Niger-Congo, Atlantic-Congo, Volta-Congo, Benue-Congo, Bantoid, Southern, Narrow Bantu, Northwest, C, Ngombe (C.50). *Dialect:* Leboa-Le, Yewu, Kiba, Benge, Bati (Baati). Leboa-le, Yewu, and Kiba have 90% lexical similarity to Benge and Bati, 80% to 85% with Pagibete, 60% to 80% with Kango, 60% to 65% with Ngelima, 55% to 60% with Lika, 48% with Komo, 43% with Bali, 37% with Ngombe, 35% with Budza, 30% with Lingala. *Lg Dev:* Bible portions: 1938. *Other:* Clan names: Bangingita, Bagunzulu, Bokipa. Different from Bua of Chad. The Ngombe group is sometimes called Bantu C.40. Some noun classes have suffixes in addition to the usual prefixes.

Bwela (Buela, Lingi) [bwl] 8,400 (2002). *Class:* Niger-Congo, Atlantic-Congo, Volta-Congo, Benue-Congo, Bantoid, Southern, Narrow Bantu, Northwest, C, Ngombe (C.50).

Bwile [bwc] 12,400 in Democratic Republic of the Congo (2002). Haut Katanga Province, north of Aushi in Pweto area at the north end of Lake Mweru. See main entry under Zambia.

Chokwe (Cokwe, Ciokwe, Tshokwe, Tschiokwe, Shioko, Djok, Imo) [cjk] 504,000 in Democratic Republic of the Congo (1990 UBS). Population total all countries: 1,009,580. Close to Angola border in southeastern Bandundu, Kasaï Occidental, and Katanga provinces. Also spoken in Angola, Namibia, Zambia. *Class:* Niger-Congo, Atlantic-Congo, Volta-Congo, Benue-Congo, Bantoid, Southern, Narrow Bantu, Central, K, Chokwe-Luchazi (K.20). *Lg Dev:* Bible: 1970–1990.

Dengese (Ndengese, Lengese, Ileo) [dez] 8,600 (2000). Kasaï Occidental Province, Dekese Territory. *Class:* Niger-Congo, Atlantic-Congo, Volta-Congo, Benue-Congo, Bantoid, Southern, Narrow Bantu, Northwest, C, Bushong (C.90).

Ding (Di, Din, Dzing) [diz] 155,000 (2002). Bandundu Province, Idiofa Territory, on the Kasaï River. *Class:* Niger-Congo, Atlantic-Congo, Volta-Congo, Benue-Congo, Bantoid, Southern, Narrow Bantu, Northwest, B, Yanzi (B.80). *Dialects:* Close to Yansi.

Dongo (Donga, Dongo Ko) [doo] 12,900 (2000). Orientale Province, east of Watsa. *Class:* Niger-Congo, Atlantic-Congo, Volta-Congo, North, Adamawa-Ubangi, Ubangi, Sere-Ngbaka-Mba, Ngbaka-Mba, Mba. *Other:* Different from Dongo which is a dialect of Kresh of Sudan, Dong (Donga) of Nigeria which is in the Chamba group of Adamawa, and Ndo which is Nilo-Saharan.

Dzando [dzn] 6,000 (1983 census). Equateur Province, Sud Ubangi, Kungu Territory, Mwanda Collectivité, between the Ngiri and Mwanda rivers in the swamp lands in the villages of Lokay, Molunga, Maboko, and Moliba. *Class:* Niger-Congo, Atlantic-Congo, Volta-Congo, Benue-Congo, Bantoid, Southern, Narrow Bantu, Northwest, C, Bangi-Ntomba (C.40). *Dialects:* Lokay, Molunga, Maboko, Moliba. Comprehension of Lifunga dialect of Bamwe is very high. Lexical similarity 6% with Lifunga dialect of Bamwe. *Lg Use:* Nearly everyone speaks Lingala except the oldest women. Other women speak only market Lingala. *Other:* Riverine.

Efe [efe] 20,000 (1991 SIL). Orientale Province, Mambasa, Watsa, Irumu, and Djugu territories. *Class:* Nilo-Saharan, Central Sudanic, East, Mangbutu-Efe. *Dialects:* Related to Lese. *Other:* They live among the Balese and trade with them. A pygmy group. Forest, savannah. Hunter-gatherers: honey, meat. Traditional religion.

Enya (Tsheenya, Ena, Genya) [gey] 15,000 (2000). On Lualaba River from Kisangani upriver to Kongolo, Orientale Province, Ubundu Territory. *Class:* Niger-Congo, Atlantic-Congo, Volta-Congo, Benue-Congo, Bantoid, Southern, Narrow Bantu, Central, D, Enya (D.10). *Dialects:* Lexical similarity 67% with Mituku, 54% with Lega-Shabunda, 50% with Lega-Mwenga, Bembe, Buyu, and Zimba, 47% with Nyanga, 40% with Lengola, 30% with Komo and Lingala. *Other:* Fishermen.

Foma (Lifoma, Fuma) [fom] 13,000 (2002). Orientale Province, on the north side of the Congo River upstream from Basoko. *Class:* Niger-Congo, Atlantic-Congo, Volta-Congo, Benue-Congo, Bantoid, Southern, Narrow Bantu, Northwest, C, Kele (C.60). *Other:* Also called 'Pseudo-Bambole'.

French [fra] *Lg Use:* Official language. *Lg Dev:* Taught in secondary schools. See main entry under France.

Fuliiru (Fuliru, Kifuliiru, Fulero, Kifulero) [flr] 300,000 (1999 SIL). Sud-Kivu Province, Uvira Territory, north and northwest of Uvira. *Class:* Niger-Congo, Atlantic-Congo, Volta-Congo, Benue-Congo, Bantoid, Southern, Narrow Bantu, Central, J, Shi-Havu (J.50). *Dialects:* Lexical similarity 70% with Mashi, 90% with Nyindu and Joba. *Lg Use:* Speakers also use Swahili. *Lg Dev:* NT: 1999.

Furu (Bagero, Bagiro, Baguero, Baguiro) [fuu] 12,000 in Democratic Republic of the Congo (1984 census). Population total all countries: 16,000. Equateur Province, Nord Ubangi, east of Bosobolo in Bosobolo and Mobaye territories. Also spoken in Central African Republic. *Class:* Nilo-Saharan, Central Sudanic, West, Bongo-Bagirmi, Kara. *Lg Use:* Most also use Lingala, Sango, Mono, or Gbanziri. Lingala comprehension is limited.

Gbanziri (Gbanzili, Banziri, Gbandere) [gbg] 3,000 in Democratic Republic of the Congo (1986 SIL). Equateur Province, Nord Ubangi, Bosobolo Territory, a few villages along Ubangi River. *Lg Use:* Speakers also use Lingala or Mono. See main entry under Central African Republic.

Gbati-ri (Gbote) [gti] 21,000 (2002). Orientale Province, between Isiro and Watsa, north of Mungbere. *Class:* Niger-Congo, Atlantic-Congo, Volta-Congo, Benue-Congo, Bantoid, Southern, Narrow Bantu, Central, Unclassified. *Other:* Part of a cluster with Nyanga-li and Mayeka.

Gilima [gix] 12,000 (1984 census). Equateur Province, Sud Ubangi, in the north of the Libenge Territory in 3 groups: Bogon in the north, Mbanza-Balakpa in the southeast, and Bandi in the southwest. It may also be in Central African Republic. *Class:* Niger-Congo, Atlantic-Congo, Volta-Congo, North, Adamawa-Ubangi, Ubangi, Sere-Ngbaka-Mba, Ngbaka-Mba, Ngbaka, Western, Bwaka. *Dialects:* Close to Ngbaka Ma'bo. *Lg Use:* Very low bilingualism in Lingala. Gilima has recently taken over from Mbandja, Ngbaka, and Ngbaka Ma'bo in the

Libenge Zone north of Zongo. Older adults speak Mbandja or Ngbaka. *Lg Dev:* Literacy rate in second language: Low.

Gobu (Gubu, Ngobo, Ngobu, Gabou, Gabu) [gox] 12,000 in Democratic Republic of the Congo (1984 census). Equateur Province, Nord Ubangi, Bosobolo Territory, in two areas, north of Bili between Duguru and Borunu on the Sidi road, and in a wide area around Pandu between the villages of Denbili and Bele II. Also spoken in Central African Republic. *Class:* Niger-Congo, Atlantic-Congo, Volta-Congo, North, Adamawa-Ubangi, Ubangi, Banda, Central, Central Core, Mid-Southern. *Dialects:* Closest to Togbo and Mono. *Lg Use:* Ethnic attitudes may hinder use of Mono literature. High bilingualism in Mono. Most younger men also use Lingala or Sango. *Lg Dev:* Literacy rate in second language: Low in Lingala.

Hamba [hba] 13,000 (2002). Kasaï Oriental Province, Lodja Territory. *Class:* Niger-Congo, Atlantic-Congo, Volta-Congo, Benue-Congo, Bantoid, Southern, Narrow Bantu, Central, D, Lega-Kalanga (D.20). *Other:* Different from Hamba which is a dialect of Haya of Tanzania.

Havu (Kihavu, Haavu) [hav] 506,000 (2002). Sud-Kivu Province, Kalehe Territory. *Class:* Niger-Congo, Atlantic-Congo, Volta-Congo, Benue-Congo, Bantoid, Southern, Narrow Bantu, Central, J, Shi-Havu (J.50). *Dialects:* Lexical similarity 70% with Shi. *Lg Use:* Havu learn Shi, but not vice versa.

Hema (Hema-Sud, Southern Hema, Kihema, Congo Nyoro, Nyoro, Runyoro) [nix] 124,650 in Democratic Republic of the Congo (2000 WCD). Orientale Province, Ituri District, Irumu and Djugu territories. Also spoken in Uganda. *Class:* Niger-Congo, Atlantic-Congo, Volta-Congo, Benue-Congo, Bantoid, Southern, Narrow Bantu, Central, J, Nyoro-Ganda (J.10). *Dialect:* Toro (Orutoro, Tooro). Toro dialect in Democratic Republic of the Congo is quite different from Nyoro of Uganda. Lexical similarity 78% between Toro and Nyoro. *Other:* Hema is spoken by the Southern Hema people, of the same ethnic stock as the Northern Hema (who speak Lendu), and of the same ethnic stock as speakers of the Hima dialect of Nyankore in Uganda.

Hemba (Kihemba, Emba, Kiemba, Luba-Hemba, Eastern Luba) [hem] 180,958 (2000 WCD). Katanga Province, eastern Kongolo Territory. *Class:* Niger-Congo, Atlantic-Congo, Volta-Congo, Benue-Congo, Bantoid, Southern, Narrow Bantu, Central, L, Luba (L.30). *Dialects:* Lexical similarity 67% with Bangubangu, 64% with Songe, higher than 67% with Mikebwe and Hombo.

Holoholo (Kiholoholo, Horohoro, Guha, Kalanga, Kikalanga) [hoo] 15,500 (2002). Katanga Province, area northwest of Kalemie. Not in Tanzania. *Class:* Niger-Congo, Atlantic-Congo, Volta-Congo, Benue-Congo, Bantoid, Southern, Narrow Bantu, Central, D, Lega-Kalanga (D.20). *Lg Dev:* Bible portions: 1948. *Other:* Different from Holu (Kiholo, Holo).

Holu (Kiholu, Holo, Kiholo) [hol] 5,095 in Democratic Republic of the Congo. Extreme southwest corner of Bandundu Province. See main entry under Angola.

Hunde (Kihunde, Kobi, Rukobi) [hke] 200,000 (1980 UBS). Nord-Kivu Province, Masisi and Rutshuru territories. Apparently none in Uganda. *Class:* Niger-Congo, Atlantic-Congo, Volta-Congo, Benue-Congo, Bantoid, Southern, Narrow Bantu, Central, J, Shi-Havu (J.50). *Dialects:* Lexical similarity 75% with Tembo, 65% with Nande, 57% with Nyanga and Shi, 50% with Lega-Shabunda. *Lg Dev:* NT: 1987. *Other:* Traditional religion, Christian.

Hungana (Hunganna, Huana, Kihungana, Hungaan) [hum] 400. Bandundu Province, Bulungu Territory. *Class:* Niger-Congo, Atlantic-Congo, Volta-Congo, Benue-Congo, Bantoid, Southern, Narrow Bantu, Central, H,

Hungana (H.40). *Lg Dev:* Bible portions: 1920–1935. *Other:* SVO.

Joba (Kijoba, Vira, Kivira, Loba) [job] 10,000 (1989 SIL). Sud-Kivu Province, Uvira Territory, north and northwest of Uvira. *Class:* Niger-Congo, Atlantic-Congo, Volta-Congo, Benue-Congo, Bantoid, Southern, Narrow Bantu, Central, J, Shi-Havu (J.50). *Lg Use:* Speakers are highly bilingual in Fuliiru.

Kabwari [kcw] 8,400 (2002). Sud-Kivu Province, Fizi Territory. *Class:* Niger-Congo, Atlantic-Congo, Volta-Congo, Benue-Congo, Bantoid, Southern, Narrow Bantu, Central, J, Shi-Havu (J.50).

Kaiku (Ikaiku, Kaiko) [kkq] 13,000 (2002). Orientale Province, Ituri District, Mambasa Territory, Babombi Collectivité. *Class:* Niger-Congo, Atlantic-Congo, Volta-Congo, Benue-Congo, Bantoid, Southern, Narrow Bantu, Central, D, Bira-Huku (D.30). *Dialects:* Closest to Bila and Bhele. Lexical similarity 80% with Bhele and Bila, 70% with Komo, 56% with Bera, 20% to 25% with Mbo, Ndaka, and Budu. *Other:* The people are considered to be Bila.

Kakwa (Bari Kakwa) [keo] 20,000 in Democratic Republic of the Congo. Orientale Province, Aru Territory, north of Aru, and Faradje Territory. *Other:* Christian. See main entry under Uganda.

Kaliko (Keliko, Kaliko-Ma'di, Ma'di, Maditi) [kbo] 7,500 in Democratic Republic of the Congo (1989 SIL). Orientale Province, northern Aru Territory, along the Sudan border. *Dialects:* Didi, Dogo. *Other:* Dogo dialect is more like Sudanese Kaliko. See main entry under Sudan (Keliko).

Kango (Likango) [kty] 5,900 (2002). Orientale Province, Bas-Uélé District, along the banks of the Uélé River and its tributaries. *Class:* Niger-Congo, Atlantic-Congo, Volta-Congo, Benue-Congo, Bantoid, Southern, Narrow Bantu, Northwest, C, Ngombe (C.50). *Dialects:* Bomokandi, Uélé. One dialect has 70% to 75% lexical similarity with Pagibete, 66% with Ngelima, 75% to 80% with Bwa, 60% with Lika. Bomokandi has 60% to 65% with Bwa and Pagibete, 68% with Lika, 58% with Ngelima. Both dialects have 50% with Bali and Komo. *Other:* Said to be a pidginized language. It may be a cover term for a variety of dialects spoken by fishermen, called 'Bakango'. Different from Kango, a pygmy language spoken among the Bali. The Ngombe group is sometimes called Bantu C.40 rather than C.50. Fishermen.

Kango (Dikango, Kango Pygmy, Likango, Kikango, "Kibatchua," "Dibatchua") [kzy] 2,000 (1998 T. Harvey). Orientale Province, Tshopo District, Bafwasende Territory, among the Bali, primarily in the Bakundumu and Bemili collectivités. The smaller dialect has 7 villages just to the south of where the Nepoki River meets the Ituri to become the Aruwimi River. *Class:* Niger-Congo, Atlantic-Congo, Volta-Congo, Benue-Congo, Bantoid, Southern, Narrow Bantu, Central, D, Bira-Huku (D.30). *Dialects:* 2 dialects, inherently intelligible with each other. Related to Komo and Bali. Lexical similarity 78% with Komo, 72% with Bila, 60% with Bali, 50% with Lika. *Lg Use:* Speakers also use Bali. Bangala is preferred by those whose permanent villages are to the north, and Congo Swahili by those whose permanent villages are to the south. *Lg Dev:* Literacy rate in second language: 1%. *Other:* The people call themselves 'Bakango' and their language 'Dikango'. The language is evidently a combination of Komo and Bali, with some borrowings from the Bila-based Mbuti pygmy language. Different from the riverine Kango to the north, who are fishermen. Those who attend school have completed Standard 1 or 2 classes. 5 vowels. Riverine. Tropical forest. 500 meters. Hunter-gatherers. Traditional religion, Christian.

Kanu (Likanu, Kaanu, Kano) [khx] 3,500 (1971 Welmers). Nord-Kivu Province, Walikale Territory, Kabunga area.

Class: Niger-Congo, Atlantic-Congo, Volta-Congo, Benue-Congo, Bantoid, Southern, Narrow Bantu, Central, D, Lega-Kalanga (D.20). *Dialects:* Probably a dialect of Lega-Shabunda.

Kanyok (Kanyoka, Kanioka) [kny] 200,000 (1991 UBS). Kasaï Oriental Province, Mwene-Ditu Territory, between the Bushimaie and Luembe rivers. *Class:* Niger-Congo, Atlantic-Congo, Volta-Congo, Benue-Congo, Bantoid, Southern, Narrow Bantu, Central, L, Luba (L.30). *Lg Dev:* Bible portions: 1979–1991.

Kaonde (Chikaonde, Kawonde, Chikahonde) [kqn] 36,000 in Democratic Republic of the Congo (1995). Katanga Province, eastern part of Kolwezi Territory. See main entry under Zambia.

Kari (Kare, Li-Kari-Li) [kbj] 1,000. Scattered groups in northwestern Orientale Province, north of Uele River. Only scattered speakers in Central African Republic (1996). *Class:* Niger-Congo, Atlantic-Congo, Volta-Congo, Benue-Congo, Bantoid, Southern, Narrow Bantu, Central, Unclassified.

Kela (Okela, Ikela, Lemba) [kel] 180,000 (1972 Barrett). Kasaï Oriental Province, Lomela Territory. *Class:* Niger-Congo, Atlantic-Congo, Volta-Congo, Benue-Congo, Bantoid, Southern, Narrow Bantu, Northwest, C, Tetela (C.80). *Lg Dev:* Bible portions: 1940. *Other:* Traditional religion, Christian.

Kele (Lokele, Ekele, Kili, Likelo, Yakusu) [khy] 160,000 (1980 UBS). Population includes 7,000 Yalikoka (1977 Voegelin and Voegelin). Orientale Province, Isangi Territory, on Lomami and Congo rivers. *Class:* Niger-Congo, Atlantic-Congo, Volta-Congo, Benue-Congo, Bantoid, Southern, Narrow Bantu, Northwest, C, Kele (C.60). *Lg Use:* Trade language. *Lg Dev:* NT: 1918–1958. *Other:* Distinct from Kele (Dikele) of Gabon. Ethnic groups: Lileko, Mbooso, Yalikoka, Yaokandja, Yawemba. Christian, traditional religion.

Kete (Lukete, Kikete) [kcv] 8,400 (2002). Kasaï Occidental Province, northeast of Mweka. *Class:* Niger-Congo, Atlantic-Congo, Volta-Congo, Benue-Congo, Bantoid, Southern, Narrow Bantu, Central, L, Songye (L.20).

Kituba (Kikongo-Kutuba, Kikongo Simplifié, Kikongo Ya Leta, Kileta, Kikongo Commercial, Kibulamatadi) [ktu] 4,200,000 (1990 UBS). Bas-Congo and southern Bandundu provinces. *Class:* Creole, Kongo based. *Dialects:* Ikeleve, Western Kituba, Eastern Kituba. A creole based on the Kongo dialect spoken in Manianga area (Bas-Congo), but unintelligible to speakers of it or other Kongo dialects. Influenced by Lingala, French, restructured Swahili, Portuguese, and other local dialects. Kituba of Congo is closely related. *Lg Use:* Means of communication among various language groups. 800,000 second-language speakers. *Lg Dev:* Bible: 1990.

Komo (Kikomo, Kikumu, Kikuumu, Kikumo, Kuumu, Kumu, Kumo) [kmw] 400,000 (1998 SIL). Maniema Province, and into Orientale and Nord-Kivu provinces, as far as Walikale, Opienge, and Punia. Lubutu is the center. *Class:* Niger-Congo, Atlantic-Congo, Volta-Congo, Benue-Congo, Bantoid, Southern, Narrow Bantu, Central, D, Bira-Huku (D.30). *Dialects:* No dialects, but speech varieties have the following differences: up to 10% lexical differences, in comparison with the reference lexicon as found in Lubutu. Most noticeable phonological variation: presence of [l]. Most noticeable relational word variation: shape of the alienable possession marker. Lexical similarity 80% with Bhele, 70% with Bila, 58% with Bera, 48% with Bwa, 46% with Bali, Lika, and Pagibete, 30% with Lingala, Lega-Shabunda, and Budu. *Lg Use:* Used by Lengola speakers as their second language. All ages except in population centers where the first language is Congo Swahili, and then it is 7 and older for boys. Bilingual level estimates for Congo Swahili: 0 5%, 1 5%, 2 5%, 3 10%, 4

60%, 5 15%. Those around Kisangani are more likely to know Lingala than Congo Swahili (more than 10% of the men). *Lg Dev:* Literacy rate in first language: 1%. Literacy rate in second language: 50% older men (born before 1970), 30% younger men, less than 10% women. Poetry. Bible portions: 1991. *Other:* SVO; prepositions; noun head followed by genitive and relative clause; question word initial; 7 prefixes; 4 suffixes; word order distinguishes subject, object, indirect object; human-animate-inanimate contrast in plural and adjective agreement (no Bantu concord); verb affixes obligatorily mark person and number of subject and object; some ergativity in gerund phrase; middle, stative, unaccusative marked by suffix; causatives marked by suffix; comparisons; CV, V, Nasal CV, CV Nasal, Nasal; tonal. Interfluvial, mountain valley. Tropical forest. 450 to 600 meters. Swidden agriculturalists. Christian, traditional religion, Muslim, other.

Kongo, San Salvador (Kikongo, Congo, Kisikongo, Kikoongo) [kwy] 536,994 in Democratic Republic of the Congo (2000 WCD). Population total all countries: 865,355. Along the Congo River below Kinshasa in Democratic Republic of the Congo and northern Angola. Also spoken in Angola. *Class:* Niger-Congo, Atlantic-Congo, Volta-Congo, Benue-Congo, Bantoid, Southern, Narrow Bantu, Central, H, Kongo (H.10). *Dialects:* Fioti and San Salvador are different enough to need separate literature. *Lg Dev:* Bible: 1916–1926.

Konjo (Konzo) [koo] Western slope of the Ruwenzori Mountains. *Dialect:* Sanza (Ekisanza). *Other:* Mountain slope, plains. Up to 2,200 meters. Agriculturalists: yams, beans, sweet potatoes, peanuts, soy beans, potatoes, rice, wheat, cassava, coffee, bananas, cotton; animal husbandry: goats, sheep, poultry. Traditional religion, Christian. See main entry under Uganda.

Koongo (Kongo, Kikongo, Congo, Kikoongo) [kng] 1,000,000 in Democratic Republic of the Congo (1986 UBS). Bas-Congo Province. Cataract dialect in Bas-Congo Province and around Mbanza Manteke, Fioti north of Boma, and scattered communities along the Congo River from Brazzaville to its mouth. Also spoken in Angola, Congo. *Class:* Niger-Congo, Atlantic-Congo, Volta-Congo, Benue-Congo, Bantoid, Southern, Narrow Bantu, Central, H, Kongo (H.10). *Dialects:* South Congo, Central Kongo, West Kongo (Fiote, Fioti), Bwende (Buende), East Kongo, Southeast Kongo, Nzamba (Dzamba). Other languages of the Kongo group are sometimes regarded as dialects of Kongo (see separate entries for Beembe, Doondo, Kunyi, Vili, Monokutuba, and Kituba). In Angola Ndingi and Mboka may be separate languages. *Lg Use:* National language. *Lg Dev:* Bible: 1905–1933. *Other:* Fioti is also spoken by the Buende and Vili peoples. SVO (for Dzamba). Christian.

Kpala (Kwala, Kpwaala, Gbakpwa) [kpl] 3,000 (1986 SIL). Equateur Province, small groups in Libenge and Bosobolo territories. *Class:* Niger-Congo, Atlantic-Congo, Volta-Congo, North, Adamawa-Ubangi, Ubangi, Sere-Ngbaka-Mba, Ngbaka-Mba, Ngbaka, Western, Monzombo. *Dialects:* Close to Monzombo. *Lg Use:* Vigorous. Speakers also use Lingala. *Other:* Different from Kpala which is a dialect of Kresh of Sudan.

Kusu (Kikusu, Kutsu, Lokutsu, Kongola, Fuluka) [ksv] 26,000 (1971 Welmers). Southwestern corner of Maniema Province, Kibombo Territory. *Class:* Niger-Congo, Atlantic-Congo, Volta-Congo, Benue-Congo, Bantoid, Southern, Narrow Bantu, Northwest, C, Tetela (C.80).

Kwami (Kikwami, Kikwame, Kwame) [ktf] 400. Maniema and Nord-Kivu provinces, between Kasese and Walikale. *Class:* Niger-Congo, Atlantic-Congo, Volta-Congo, Benue-Congo, Bantoid, Southern, Narrow Bantu, Central, D, Lega-Kalanga (D.20). *Dialects:* Lexical similarity 70%

with Nyanga, 68% with Lega-Shabunda, 66% with Kanu and Enya, 61% with Mituku, 57% with Zimba, 55% with Bembe, 52% with Lega-Mwenga, 49% with Hunde and Shi, 48% with Buyu, 47% with Tembo, 46% with Nande, 41% with Lengola, 34% with Komo. *Other:* More influence from Lega than from Komo.

Kwese (Pindi, Kikwese, Ukwese) [kws] 60,000. Eastern Bandundu Province, west of Kikwit. *Class:* Niger-Congo, Atlantic-Congo, Volta-Congo, Benue-Congo, Bantoid, Southern, Narrow Bantu, Central, K, Holu (K.10). *Lg Dev:* Bible portions: 1929.

Lala-Bisa [leb] Extreme southeast corner of Katanga Province. *Dialects:* Ambo (Bambo, Kambonsenga), Luano, Swaka, Wulima, Lala (Ichilala), Bisa (Ichibisa, Wiza). See main entry under Zambia.

Lalia [lal] 55,000 (1993). Southeast corner of Equateur Province, Ikela Territory, collectivités of Tumbenga, Lokina, Lofume, Tshwapa, and Loile. Yalosaka is the center. *Class:* Niger-Congo, Atlantic-Congo, Volta-Congo, Benue-Congo, Bantoid, Southern, Narrow Bantu, Northwest, C, Mongo (C.70). *Lg Use:* Young people continue to use Lalia. Mongo and Lingala are used in church. *Other:* Distinct from Mongo.

Lamba (Ichilamba, Chilamba) [lam] Southeast corner of Katanga Province. See main entry under Zambia.

Langbashe (Langbashi, Langbase, Langbasi, Langwasi, Langbwasse) [lna] 3,000 in Democratic Republic of the Congo (1984 census). Equateur Province, Nord Ubangi, Bosobolo Territory, along the Ubangi River, villages of Sidi, Bada, Zimango, Banga, Boduna, and a few other villages elsewhere in the territory. See main entry under Central African Republic.

Lega-Mwenga (Shile, Kilega, Rega, Kirega, Leka-Shile, Leka-Sile, Ishile, Ileka Ishile) [lgm] 44,896 (2000 WCD). Sud-Kivu Province, Mwenga Territory. *Class:* Niger-Congo, Atlantic-Congo, Volta-Congo, Benue-Congo, Bantoid, Southern, Narrow Bantu, Central, D, Lega-Kalanga (D.20). *Dialects:* Iyoko, Ibanda, Isopo, Lusenge, Bilembo-Mango, Mizulo. 20 dialects. Speakers say Lega-Shabunda and Bembe are difficult to understand. Lexical similarity 96% to 88% among dialects, 84% to 76% with Bembe, 81% to 67% with Lega-Shabunda, 60% with Buyu, 50% with Zimba, Enya, and Mituku, 45% with Nyanga. *Lg Use:* Congo Swahili is the language of instruction in school.

Lega-Shabunda (Kilega, Rega, Kirega, Ileka-Igonzabale, Leka-Igonzabale, Igonzabale) [lea] 400,000 (1982 UBS). Sud-Kivu and Maniema provinces, Shabunda and Pangi territories. The first 5 dialects are in Shabunda Territory, Kinyamunsange is in Pangi Territory. *Class:* Niger-Congo, Atlantic-Congo, Volta-Congo, Benue-Congo, Bantoid, Southern, Narrow Bantu, Central, D, Lega-Kalanga (D.20). *Dialect:* Kigala, Kigyoma, Liliga, Kisede, Kinyabanga, Kinyamunsange (Pangi). Lexical similarity 67% to 81% with Lega-Mwenga, 65% with Kwami, 60% with Bembe, 55% with Budu, Mituku, and Enya, 50% with Zimba, Nyanga, and Hunde, 45% with Nande, 30% with Komo. Kanu is probably a dialect with 92% similarity. *Lg Dev:* NT: 1957. *Other:* Traditional religion, Christian.

Lele (Usilele, Bashilele) [lel] 26,000 (1971 Welmers). Western edge of Kasaï Occidental Province, Ilebo and Tshikapa territories, and extreme east of Bandundu Province, Idiofa and Gungu territories. *Class:* Niger-Congo, Atlantic-Congo, Volta-Congo, Benue-Congo, Bantoid, Southern, Narrow Bantu, Northwest, C, Bushong (C.90). *Dialects:* Intelligible with Wongo. *Other:* Different from Lele of Chad.

Lendu (Bbadha, Bbaledha, Kilendu, Baletha, Batha, Balendru, Bale, Hema-Nord, Kihema-Nord) [led] 750,000 in Democratic Republic of the Congo (1996 SIL).

Population total all countries: 760,000. Orientale Province, Ituri District, Djugu Territory, west and northwest of Lake Albert. Also spoken in Uganda. *Class:* Nilo-Saharan, Central Sudanic, East, Lendu. *Dialects:* Djadha (Jidha), Tadha, Pidha, Ddralo (Ddradha), Njawlo (Njawdha). Tadha is the standard dialect. Djadha is the largest dialect and the one used for literature. Jidha is the speech variety of the Bagegere (Northern Hema) who have adopted Lendu. *Lg Use:* Spoken as first language by people from 4 ethnic backgrounds: Lendu, Hema-North, Alur, and Okebu. Speakers also use Swahili. *Lg Dev:* NT: 1936–1989. *Other:* Christian.

Lengola (Kilengola, Lengora) [lej] 100,000 (1998). Orientale Province, Ubundu Territory, Maniema Province, Lubutu and Punia territories, both sides of the Lualaba River, but more on the west side within a triangle between Opienge, Lowa, and a point called 'Km 100' on the Kisangani-Lubutu road. *Class:* Niger-Congo, Atlantic-Congo, Volta-Congo, Benue-Congo, Bantoid, Southern, Narrow Bantu, Central, D, Enya (D.10). *Dialects:* 2 dialects which differ in pronunciation. Lexical similarity 40% with Enya and Mituku, 35% to 40% with Budu and Komo, 30% to 35% with Lega-Shabunda, Lega-Mwenga, and Zimba, 25% to 30% with Bembe, Buyu, and Bali. *Lg Use:* Some speakers also use Congo Swahili or Komo. *Other:* Riverine. Agriculturalists; fishermen; hunters. Christian, Muslim.

Lese (Lesa, Lesse, Lissi, Walisi, Walese, Balese, Mbuti) [les] 50,000 (1991 SIL). Orientale Province, Watsa, Djugu, Irumu, and Mambasa territories. *Class:* Nilo-Saharan, Central Sudanic, East, Mangbutu-Efe. *Dialects:* Lese Karo, Arumbi (Upstream Lese), Ndese (Lese Dese), Vukutu (Vonkutu, Obi), Fare. Close to Mamvu, Bendi, Mangbutu, Efe. *Lg Use:* Congo Swahili (Kingwana) and Bangala are the lingua francas, but their use is somewhat limited, especially among the women. *Other:* Agriculturalists. Traditional religion, Christian.

Libinza (Libinja) [liz] 10,000 (1986 SIL). Equateur Province, Sud Ubangi and Equateur districts, in Kungu and northern Bomongo districts, on the Ngiri and Mwanda rivers, from the villages of Monia and Boniange southward, on islands as far as Bomongo. *Class:* Niger-Congo, Atlantic-Congo, Volta-Congo, Benue-Congo, Bantoid, Southern, Narrow Bantu, Northwest, C, Bangi-Ntomba (C.40), Ngiri. *Dialects:* Monia, Boniange, Kutu. There are other dialects besides those listed. Dialects or closely related languages: Balobo (Likila), Ndobo. *Other:* Distinct from the Libinja dialect of Ngombe.

Ligenza (Gendja, Digenja, Gendza-Bali) [lgz] 43,000 (1986 SIL). Equateur Province, Bumba Territory, 3 or 4 small areas. *Class:* Niger-Congo, Atlantic-Congo, Volta-Congo, Benue-Congo, Bantoid, Southern, Narrow Bantu, Northwest, C, Ngombe (C.50). *Dialects:* Bokoy, Elowa, Benza, Bolupi. *Lg Use:* High bilingualism in Lingala for all speakers. *Lg Dev:* Literacy rate in second language: High in Lingala.

Lika (Kilika, Toriko, Kpongo, Mabiti) [lik] 60,000 (1989 SIL). Population includes 57,000 in Wamba District, 3,000 in Rungu District. Orientale Province, Upper-Uele District, Wamba Territory, Balika-Toriko Collectivité. Some in Rungu Territory, Mongomasi Collectivité. *Class:* Niger-Congo, Atlantic-Congo, Volta-Congo, Benue-Congo, Bantoid, Southern, Narrow Bantu, Central, D, Lega-Kalanga (D.20). *Dialects:* Likó (Ikó), Lilikó, Liliká (Liká). Lexical similarity 65% to 70% with Bomokandi Kango, 55% to 60% with Pagibete, Bwa, and Uélé Kango, 52% with Bali, 51% with Ngelima, 46% with Komo, 40% with Bhele, Bila, and Bera, 30% with Budu, 25% with Lega languages and Lingala. *Lg Use:* Swahili is used as second language in southern Wamba Zone, Bangala in Rungu Zone, some Meje and Budu also. *Other:* Ethnic groups: Mabiti and Maliko. 2 secondary schools, 15 primary schools, but Lika is not used in the schools. Forest. Agriculturalists: coffee, manioc, peanuts, bananas, palm oil, rice, papaya, pineapple, sugarcane, sweet potatoes, yams, eggplant; animal husbandry: poultry; fishermen. Christian, Muslim.

Likila (Bangela, Balobo) [lie] 8,400 (2002). Equateur Province, around Makanza town on the northern bank of the Congo River. *Class:* Niger-Congo, Atlantic-Congo, Volta-Congo, Benue-Congo, Bantoid, Southern, Narrow Bantu, Northwest, C, Bangi-Ntomba (C.40), Ngiri. *Dialects:* Dialect or closely related language to Libinza or Baloi.

Lingala (Ngala) [lin] 2,037,929 in Democratic Republic of the Congo (2000 WCD). Second-language speakers together with Bangala in Democratic Republic of the Congo: 7,000,000 (1999 WA). Population total all countries: 2,139,202. Widely used in Bandundu, Equateur, and Orientale provinces, except the southeast of Orientale. Also spoken in Central African Republic, Congo. *Class:* Niger-Congo, Atlantic-Congo, Volta-Congo, Benue-Congo, Bantoid, Southern, Narrow Bantu, Northwest, C, Bangi-Ntomba (C.40), Lusengo. *Dialects:* Close to Lusengo and Bangala. Lexical similarity 33% with Bobangi. *Lg Use:* National language. Variation in communities. *Lg Dev:* Dictionary. Bible: 1970–2000. *Other:* SVO.

Lobala [loq] 60,000 (2000 D. Morgan). Very few monolinguals. Equateur Province, Sud Ubangi and Equateur districts, Kungu and Bomongo territories, on the road northeast of Dongo as far as the village of Mokusi, and on the road south from Dongo following the Ubangi River, and forest south and west of this road. *Class:* Niger-Congo, Atlantic-Congo, Volta-Congo, Benue-Congo, Bantoid, Southern, Narrow Bantu, Northwest, C, Bangi-Ntomba (C.40). *Dialects:* Poko, South Lobala, Tanda, Likoka. Closest to Bomboma and Libinza in Democratic Republic of the Congo. Lexical similarity 65% with Lingala. *Lg Use:* Parents in the forest are passing on Lobala to children, and some along the Ubangi River. Bomboli speakers use Lobala as second language. Used in literacy classes, religious services, oral use in commerce. Positive language attitude. Speakers are increasing their use of Lingala, especially along the Ubangi River. *Other:* Forest. Fishermen; cocoa.

Logo (Logoti) [log] 210,000 (1989 SIL). Population includes 100,000 Ogambi. Orientale Province, Faradje Territory, and town of Watsa. *Class:* Nilo-Saharan, Central Sudanic, East, Moru-Madi, Central. *Dialects:* Ogambi (Ogamaru, Northern Logo), Doka, Lolya, Obilebha (Obelebha, Obileba), Bhagira (Bagela), Bari (Bari-Logo, Bariti). A dialect cluster, with Lolya as central. Close to Avokaya and Omi. Avokaya in Democratic Republic of the Congo spoken in the northern Ogambi Area, may be closer to Logo than to Avokaya in Sudan. *Lg Dev:* Bible portions: 1924–2000. *Other:* Christian, traditional religion.

Lombi (Lumbi, Rombi, Rumli, Odyalombito) [lmi] 12,000 (1993 SIL). Orientale Province, Tshopo District, Bafwasende Territory, Barumi and Bekeni collectivités. Opienge, Banguruye, and Bangolu are centers. *Class:* Nilo-Saharan, Central Sudanic, East, Mangbetu. *Dialects:* Close to Mangbetu, but not as close as Mangbetu dialects are to each other. *Other:* Different than the Lombi dialect of Basa in Cameroon.

Lombo (Olombo, Ulumbu, Turumbu) [loo] 10,000 (1971 Welmers). Orientale Province, both sides of Congo River in Isangi area. *Class:* Niger-Congo, Atlantic-Congo, Volta-Congo, Benue-Congo, Bantoid, Southern, Narrow Bantu, Northwest, C, Kele (C.60). *Other:* Reported to readily understand Kele.

Lonzo [lnz] 300. Bandundu Province, Kenge Territory. *Class:* Niger-Congo, Atlantic-Congo, Volta-Congo, Benue-Congo, Bantoid, Southern, Narrow Bantu, Central, H, Yaka (H.30).

Luba-Kasai (Luba-Lulua, Tshiluba, Western Luba, Luva) [lua] 6,300,000 (1991 UBS). Used throughout Kasaï Occidental and Kasaï Oriental provinces. *Class:* Niger-Congo, Atlantic-Congo, Volta-Congo, Benue-Congo, Bantoid, Southern, Narrow Bantu, Central, L, Luba (L.30). *Dialects:* Significant dialect differences between East Kasai Region (Baluba people) and West Kasai Region (Bena Lulua people). Hemba is a closely related language. *Lg Use:* National language. 700,000 second-language speakers. *Lg Dev:* Literacy rate in second language: Over 60% among Christians. Bible: 1927–1996. *Other:* Christian.

Luba-Katanga (Luba-Shaba, Kiluba) [lub] 1,505,000 (1991 UBS). Katanga Province, Haut-Lomami District. *Class:* Niger-Congo, Atlantic-Congo, Volta-Congo, Benue-Congo, Bantoid, Southern, Narrow Bantu, Central, L, Luba (L.30). *Lg Dev:* Bible: 1951.

Lugbara (High Lugbara) [lgg] 840,000 in Democratic Republic of the Congo (2001 Johnstone and Mandryk). Orientale Province, Aru Territory, 6 collectivités. *Dialects:* Zaki, Abedju-Azaki, Lu, Aluru, Nio, Otsho. *Other:* Aluru is reported to be influenced by Ndo; Nio and Otsho are similar to Uganda Lugbara. Christian. See main entry under Uganda.

Luna (Inkongo, Kuba, Northern Luba) [luj] 50,000. Kasaï Oriental Province, Lusambo Territory. *Class:* Niger-Congo, Atlantic-Congo, Volta-Congo, Benue-Congo, Bantoid, Southern, Narrow Bantu, Central, L, Songye (L.20). *Lg Dev:* Bible: 1927–1932.

Lunda (Chilunda) [lun] Southern and southwestern Katanga Province, Lualaba District; extreme south of Bandundu Province, Kahemba Territory. *Dialects:* Lunda Ndembu, Lunda Kalunda, Lunda Kambove. See main entry under Zambia.

Lusengo (Losengo) [lse] 42,000 (2002). Primarily on the Congo River in Equateur Province, Mankanza, Lisala, and Bumba territories. *Class:* Niger-Congo, Atlantic-Congo, Volta-Congo, Benue-Congo, Bantoid, Southern, Narrow Bantu, Northwest, C, Bangi-Ntomba (C.40), Lusengo. *Dialects:* Kangana, Iliku (Eleko, Leko, Eleku, Loleko, Leku), Limpesa, Lipoto (Upoto, Kele, Ingundji), Bumwangi, Busu Djanga, Empesa Poko, Esumbu, Kunda, Kumba, Lusengo Poto, Mongala Poto, Ngundi, Mongo. *Lg Dev:* Bible portions: 1898–1920.

Lwalu [lwa] 21,000 (1971 Welmers). Kasaï Occidental Province, Luiza Territory. *Class:* Niger-Congo, Atlantic-Congo, Volta-Congo, Benue-Congo, Bantoid, Southern, Narrow Bantu, Central, L, Luba (L.30).

Ma (Amadi, Madi, Madyo) [msj] 4,700 (1977 Voegelin and Voegelin). Orientale Province, north of Niangara, close to Kapili River. *Class:* Niger-Congo, Atlantic-Congo, Volta-Congo, North, Adamawa-Ubangi, Ubangi, Sere-Ngbaka-Mba, Ngbaka-Mba, Mba. *Dialects:* Closest to Dongo.

Mabaale (Lomabaale, Mabale, Mbali) [mmz] 42,000 (2002). Equateur Province, Ngiri River area. *Class:* Niger-Congo, Atlantic-Congo, Volta-Congo, Benue-Congo, Bantoid, Southern, Narrow Bantu, Northwest, C, Bangi-Ntomba (C.40). *Dialect:* Bembe, Lipanja, Banza, Mbinga, Lobo (Balobo).

Mamvu (Tengo) [mdi] 60,000 (1991 SIL). Orientale Province, west and southwest of Watsa in Watsa Territory. Possibly some in Uganda. *Class:* Nilo-Saharan, Central Sudanic, East, Mangbutu-Efe. *Dialect:* Amengi, Mamvu (Momvu, Momfu). *Lg Dev:* Bible portions: 1931. *Other:* They call their language 'Tengo'. A separate language from Efe.

Mangbetu (Nemangbetu, Mangbettu, Mambetto, Amangbetu, Kingbetu) [mdj] 620,000. Orientale Province, Rungu, Niangara, Poko, Watsa, Wamba, and northeast corner of Banalia territories. The Popoi group is in Banalia Territory, and the Aberu group is in Wamba Territory. None in Uganda. *Class:* Nilo-Saharan, Central Sudanic, East, Mangbetu. *Dialects:* Meje (Medje), Mangbetu, Makere, Malele, Popoi. The Medje dialect is reported to have the most speakers, and is the most widely understood. Lombi and Asua are related separate languages. *Lg Use:* Perhaps 50% know Bangala, another 10% have low proficiency. Popoi and Aberu are in Swahili-speaking areas. *Other:* Names of ethnic groups: Mangbetu, Mabisanga (clan name), Medje, Makere, Aberu, Popoi, Malele.

Mangbutu (Mombuttu, Wambutu, Mangu-Ngutu) [mdk] 15,000 (1991 SIL). Population includes 1,200 Andinai. Orientale Province, south of the Kibali River and east of the Moto River in Watsa Territory. *Class:* Nilo-Saharan, Central Sudanic, East, Mangbutu-Efe. *Dialect:* Andinai, Makutana, Angwe (Andali). The Andinai are separated from the other Mangbutu by the Lese. The Andali are a clan speaking the Angwe dialect. *Other:* Savannah. Christian.

Mayeka [myc] 21,000 (2004). Ethnic population: 25,474 (2000 WCD). Vicinity of Congo, Central African Republic, Democratic Republic of the Congo borders. Not in Central African Republic. *Class:* Niger-Congo, Atlantic-Congo, Volta-Congo, Benue-Congo, Bantoid, Southern, Narrow Bantu, Central, Unclassified. *Dialects:* A member of the same dialect cluster as Nyanga-li, Gbati-ri.

Mayogo (Maigo, Maiko, Mayko, Kiyogo, Majugu, Mayugo) [mdm] 100,000 (1991 SIL). Orientale Province, Isiro area. Most are in the Rungu and Wamba territories. *Class:* Niger-Congo, Atlantic-Congo, Volta-Congo, North, Adamawa-Ubangi, Ubangi, Sere-Ngbaka-Mba, Ngbaka-Mba, Ngbaka, Eastern, Mayogo-Bangba. *Dialect:* Madimadoko, Madipia (Mabozo, Magbai, Mabodese, Madjedje). Lexical similarity 70% to 75% with Bangba, 62% with Mündü. *Lg Use:* Bangala is the main lingua franca, then Lingala. Bangala used by the older generation. Increasingly the young are using Lingala. *Other:* Ethnic groups: Bakango, Dai (Day, Angai), Maambi, Mangbele. Christian, traditional religion.

Mba (Kimanga, Manga, Kimbanga) [mfc] 36,087 (2000 WCD). Orientale Province, Banalia Territory, Banjwade area. *Class:* Niger-Congo, Atlantic-Congo, Volta-Congo, North, Adamawa-Ubangi, Ubangi, Sere-Ngbaka-Mba, Ngbaka-Mba, Mba. *Lg Use:* Vigorous. Children have difficulty with Congo Swahili. *Other:* Perhaps 45% of children are in school. SVO, SOV.

Mbala (Gimbala, Rumbala) [mdp] 200,000 (1972 Nida). Bandundu Province, Bagata and Bulungu territories, between Kwango and Kwilu rivers. *Class:* Niger-Congo, Atlantic-Congo, Volta-Congo, Benue-Congo, Bantoid, Southern, Narrow Bantu, Central, K, Mbala (K.60). *Lg Use:* Speakers also use Kituba. *Lg Dev:* Bible portions: 1931–1968.

Mbandja (Mbanza, Mbanja, Mbandza) [zmz] 351,543 in Democratic Republic of the Congo (2000 WCD). Population total all countries: 361,998. Equateur Province, various areas in Sud Ubangi, Nord Ubangi, and western Mongala districts, to west, southwest, and east of the Ngbaka language. Also spoken in Central African Republic, Congo. *Class:* Niger-Congo, Atlantic-Congo, Volta-Congo, North, Adamawa-Ubangi, Ubangi, Banda, Southern. *Dialects:* Kala, Gbado. *Lg Use:* Lingala is the lingua franca; in some areas up to 60% speak it and 40% understand it in varying degrees. *Lg Dev:* NT: 1998.

Mbesa (Mombesa, Mobesa) [zms] 8,400 (2002). Orientale Province, northern Yahuma Territory, south of Congo River. *Class:* Niger-Congo, Atlantic-Congo, Volta-Congo, Benue-Congo, Bantoid, Southern, Narrow Bantu, Northwest, C, Kele (C.60).

Mbo (Kimbo, Imbo) [zmw] 11,000 (1994 SIL). Orientale Province, Ituri District, Mambasa Territory, Bombo Collectivité. *Class:* Niger-Congo, Atlantic-Congo, Volta-Congo, Benue-Congo, Bantoid, Southern, Narrow Bantu, Central, D, Bira-Huku (D.30). *Dialects:* Speakers of Ndaka, Budu, Vanuma, Nyali, and Mbo agree that their languages are closer to each other than to other border Bantu languages. One dialect. Lexical similarity 87% with Ndaka, 78% with Budu, 77% with Vanuma, 76% with Nyali, 30% with Komo, 25% with Bhele, Kaiku, Bila, Bera. *Other:* Different from Mbo of Cameroon, which is Bantu A.10. Traditional religion, Muslim.

Mbole (Lombole) [mdq] 100,000 (1971 Welmers). Orientale Province, southwest of Kisangani. *Class:* Niger-Congo, Atlantic-Congo, Volta-Congo, Benue-Congo, Bantoid, Southern, Narrow Bantu, Central, D, Enya (D.10). *Dialects:* Keembo, Nkimbe (Nkembe), Yangonda, Yaisu, Inja, Botunga, Yaamba, Yaikole. Close to Mituku. *Other:* Apparently different from the Mbole dialect of Ombo.

Mfinu (Emfinu, Funika, Mfununga) [zmf] 8,400 (2002). Bandundu Province. *Class:* Niger-Congo, Atlantic-Congo, Volta-Congo, Benue-Congo, Bantoid, Southern, Narrow Bantu, Northwest, B, Yanzi (B.80). *Dialects:* Ntsiam, Ntswar.

Mituku (Kinya-Mituku, Metoko) [zmq] 50,948 (2000 WCD). Orientale Province, Ubundu Territory, west of Lualaba River. *Class:* Niger-Congo, Atlantic-Congo, Volta-Congo, Benue-Congo, Bantoid, Southern, Narrow Bantu, Central, D, Enya (D.10). *Dialects:* Close to Mbole. Lexical similarity 67% with Enya, 55% with Lega-Shabunda, 50% with Nyanga, Lega-Mwenga, Bembe, Buyu, and Zimba, 40% with Lengola.

Moingi [mwz] 4,200 (2002). Orientale Province, Yahuma Territory, south of Congo River, opposite the town of Basoko. *Class:* Niger-Congo, Atlantic-Congo, Volta-Congo, Benue-Congo, Bantoid, Southern, Unclassified.

Mongo-Nkundu (Mongo, Lomongo) [lol] 400,000 (1995). Southern half of Equateur Province and northeastern part of Bandundu Province. *Class:* Niger-Congo, Atlantic-Congo, Volta-Congo, Benue-Congo, Bantoid, Southern, Narrow Bantu, Northwest, C, Mongo (C.70). *Dialects:* Mpama, Wangata, Panga (Ipanga, Titu, Buli, South Nkundo), Bukala (Kala), Yalima (Yajima), Kutu (Bakutu), Ekonda Mongo (Lomongo), Longo (Bolongo), Nkundo (Nkundu, Lonkundu, Lonkundo, Lolo), Ntomba-Inongo, Ntomba-Bikoro, Konda (Ekonda, Lokonda, Lokwala), Longombe. Dialect or language cluster: Lalia, Mongo-Nkundu, Ngando, Ombo. The Longombe dialect is spoken along the road between Boende and Wema, is closest to the Bakutu dialect, and is distinct from the Lingombe language. Ntomba-Inongo, Ntomba-Bikoro, and Konda may be separate languages. Konda is in Equateur Province, Equateur District, Mai-Ndombe District, Kiri Territory. In Mbandaka, speakers called their dialect 'Lonkundo'. *Lg Use:* Lingala is increasing in use. *Lg Dev:* Bible: 1930.

Mono (Amono) [mnh] 65,000 (1984 census). Equateur Province, Nord Ubangi, Bosobolo Territory, and some in Libenge Territory. Bili is the center. *Class:* Niger-Congo, Atlantic-Congo, Volta-Congo, North, Adamawa-Ubangi, Ubangi, Banda, Central, Central Core, Mid-Southern. *Dialects:* Bili, Bubanda, Galaba, Kaga, Mpaka. Closest linguistically to Togbo and Gobu, but quite different ethnically from Togbo. *Lg Use:* Lingala is widely understood by men and most young people, but poorly understood by women. Most understand Sango. *Lg Dev:* Literacy rate in second language: Low in Lingala, women below 10%.

Monzombo (Monjombo, Mono-Jembo, Monzumbo) [moj] 5,000 in Democratic Republic of the Congo (1986 SIL). Equateur Province, on east bank of Ubangi River south of Libenge. *Lg Use:* Speakers also use Lingala. *Other:* Fishermen. See main entry under Congo.

Mpuono [zmp] 165,000 (1972 Nida). Bandundu Province, Idiofa Territory. *Class:* Niger-Congo, Atlantic-Congo, Volta-Congo, Benue-Congo, Bantoid, Southern, Narrow Bantu, Northwest, B, Yanzi (B.80). *Dialect:* Mpuono, Mpuun (Mbuun, Kimbuun, Mbunda, Gimbunda). Close to Yansi. *Lg Dev:* Bible portions: 1935–1951. *Other:* Different from Mbunda of Democratic Republic of the Congo and Angola in Chokwe-Luchazi group.

Mündü (Mundo, Mountou, Mondo) [muh] 2,800 in Democratic Republic of the Congo. Orientale Province, north and northeast of Faradje. *Lg Use:* Bangala is the lingua franca, but most have difficulty understanding it. See main entry under Sudan.

Mvuba (Mbuba, Bambuba, Bamvuba, Mvuba-A, Obiye) [mxh] 5,095 in Democratic Republic of the Congo (2000 WCD). Nord-Kivu Province, Beni Territory, around Oicha. Also spoken in Uganda. *Class:* Nilo-Saharan, Central Sudanic, East, Mangbutu-Efe. *Dialects:* Close to Lese.

Nande (Kinandi, Kinande, Nandi, Northern Nande, Ndande, Orundande) [nnb] 903,000 (1991 UBS). Nord-Kivu Province, mainly in Beni and Lubero territories. *Class:* Niger-Congo, Atlantic-Congo, Volta-Congo, Benue-Congo, Bantoid, Southern, Narrow Bantu, Central, J, Konzo (J.40). *Dialects:* Nande, Kumbule (Ekikumbule), Mate (Ekimate), Tangi (Ekitangi), Sanza (Ekisanza), Shu (Ekishu), Ekisongoora (Songola, Nyangala), Swaga (Ekiswaga, Ekikira), Yira (Ekiyira). Lexical similarity 75% with Konjo, 65% with Hunde, 55% with Tembo and Shi, 45% with Nyoro, Nyanga, and Lega-Shabunda, 40% with Talinga-Bwisi, 30% with Bhele, 25% with Amba. *Lg Dev:* Bible: 1980–1996. *Other:* Different from Nandi dialect of Kalenjin of Kenya. Christian.

Ndaka (Ndaaka, Indaaka) [ndk] 25,000 (1994 SIL). Orientale Province, Ituri District, Mambasa Territory, Bandaka Collectivité, along the road between Bunia and NiaNia. Roads also go to Kisangani and Isiro. *Class:* Niger-Congo, Atlantic-Congo, Volta-Congo, Benue-Congo, Bantoid, Southern, Narrow Bantu, Central, D, Bira-Huku (D.30). *Dialects:* Only 1 dialect. Speakers of Mbo, Budu, Vanuma, Nyali, and Ndaka agree that their languages are closer to each other than to other border Bantu languages. Lexical similarity 87% with Mbo, 85% with Budu, 76% with Vanuma, 73% with Nyali, 30% with Komo, 22% with Bhele, Kaiku, Bila, and Bera. *Lg Dev:* Literacy rate in second language: 25% to 40%. *Other:* Traditional religion.

Ndo (Ke'bu, Oke'bu, Kebutu, Ndu) [ndp] 100,000 in Democratic Republic of the Congo. Orientale Province, Mahagi and Aru territories, south of the Lowa River, west and northwest of Djalasiga, a pocket of Okebu on the border with Uganda. *Dialects:* Avari (Avare, Avere, Aviritu), Oke'bu, Membi (Membitu, Meembi, Mombi, Ndo). *Lg Use:* Vigorous. Speakers also use Bangala or Swahili. *Other:* In some areas Bangala is the lingua franca, in others Swahili. Blacksmiths. Christian. See main entry under Uganda.

Ndobo (Ndoobo) [ndw] 10,190 (2000 WCD). Equateur Province, between Bomongo and the Congo River. *Class:* Niger-Congo, Atlantic-Congo, Volta-Congo, Benue-Congo, Bantoid, Southern, Narrow Bantu, Northwest, C, Bangi-Ntomba (C.40), Ngiri. *Dialects:* It may be a dialect of Baloi or Libinza.

Ndolo (Ndoolo, Mosange, Tando) [ndl] 8,000 (1983 census). Equateur Province, Sud Ubangi, Budjala Territory, Ndolo-Liboko Collectivité, on the Moeko River, south of Budjala between Ndama and Bokala villages, and

in Tando and Lisombo villages. *Class:* Niger-Congo, Atlantic-Congo, Volta-Congo, Benue-Congo, Bantoid, Southern, Narrow Bantu, Northwest, C, Bangi-Ntomba (C.40), Lusengo. *Lg Use:* Might not accept Bamwe literature. Speakers also use Lingala. *Other:* Riverine.

Ndunga (Mondunga, Mondugu, Bondonga, Modunga) [ndt] 2,500 (1977 Voegelin and Voegelin). Equateur Province, 8 villages in Lisala Territory. *Class:* Niger-Congo, Atlantic-Congo, Volta-Congo, North, Adamawa-Ubangi, Ubangi, Sere-Ngbaka-Mba, Ngbaka-Mba, Mba. *Dialects:* Close to Mba (Kimanga).

Ngando (Ngandu, Longandu) [nxd] 220,000 (1995). Equateur Province, Maringa River area, north of Ikela. *Class:* Niger-Congo, Atlantic-Congo, Volta-Congo, Benue-Congo, Bantoid, Southern, Narrow Bantu, Northwest, C, Mongo (C.70). *Dialects:* Related to Lalia. *Lg Dev:* NT: 1941. *Other:* Not related to Ngando of Central African Republic.

Ngbaka (Ngbaka Minangende, Ngbaka Gbaya) [nga] 1,012,184 in Democratic Republic of the Congo (2000 WCD). 600,000 monolinguals. Population total all countries: 1,018,836. Equateur Province, Gemena Territory and surrounding area, 850 villages. Also spoken in Central African Republic, Congo. *Class:* Niger-Congo, Atlantic-Congo, Volta-Congo, North, Adamawa-Ubangi, Ubangi, Gbaya-Manza-Ngbaka, East. *Dialects:* Dialect differences are minor. Related to Gbaya of Central African Republic and Cameroon. *Lg Use:* Vigorous. Speakers of Gilima, Ngbundu, Mbandja, and Mono use it as second language. All domains. Oral and written use in administration, religion, oral use in commerce, oral literature. Used in some schools for first three years. All ages. Positive language attitude. One-third speak Lingala, 5% speak French. *Lg Dev:* Possibly 150,000 read it, 100,000 can write it. Taught in primary schools. Bible: 1995. *Other:* Ngbaka is a different language from Ngbaka Ma'bo. Savannah, tropical forest. Agriculturalists. Christian, traditional religion, syncretism.

Ngbaka Ma'bo (Ngbaka Limba, Mbaka, Mbacca, Bwaka, Bouaka, Nbwaka, Gbaka, Gwaka, Mbwaka, Ma'bo) [nbm] 11,000 in Democratic Republic of the Congo (1984 census). Equateur Province, Libenge District, and Zongo Territory, on the road north and south of Zongo, and in a belt just north of Libenge. *Lg Use:* Most also use Lingala. See main entry under Central African Republic.

Ngbandi, Northern (Ngwandi, Mongwandi, Baza) [ngb] 250,000 in Democratic Republic of the Congo (2000 SIL). 75,000 monolinguals. Population total all countries: 250,294. Equateur Province, Mobaye and Yakoma territories, extending into Orientale Province, Bondo Territory. Also spoken in Central African Republic. *Class:* Niger-Congo, Atlantic-Congo, Volta-Congo, North, Adamawa-Ubangi, Ubangi, Ngbandi. *Dialects:* 2 dialects, about equal in size. Sango is derived from Ngbandi. *Lg Use:* Vigorous. Some speakers of other languages use it for trade in border areas. All domains. Oral use in some churches. Oral literature. Positive language attitude. 70% have routine proficiency in Lingala; 10% can speak French. *Lg Dev:* Literacy rate in first language: 8%. 20,000 read it; 5,000 can write it. NT: 1988. *Other:* Ethnic groups: Abasango, Bwato, Mbaati, Nzomboy (Monjomboli). Savannah, tropical forest. Agriculturalists. Christian.

Ngbandi, Southern (Mongbandi, Mbati, Ngbandi-Sud, Ngbandi-Ngiri, Ngwandi, Mongwandi) [nbw] 105,000. Equateur Province, Businga, Budjala, Kungu, and Libenge territories. *Class:* Niger-Congo, Atlantic-Congo, Volta-Congo, North, Adamawa-Ubangi, Ubangi, Ngbandi. *Dialects:* Different enough from Northern Ngbandi that separate literature is needed. *Lg Use:* Positive language attitude. The majority speak Lingala as second language. *Lg Dev:* Bible portions: 1984. *Other:* Villages are interspersed with Mbandja villages. Riverine, plains. Forest. Agriculturalists. Christian.

Ngbee (Lingbee, Lingbe, Mangbele, Majuu) [jgb] Extinct. Orientale Province, scattered in Rungu, Niangara, Wamba, and Watsa territories. *Class:* Niger-Congo, Atlantic-Congo, Volta-Congo, Benue-Congo, Bantoid, Southern, Narrow Bantu, Central, Unclassified. *Lg Use:* Members of the ethnic group now speak Mangbetu or Mayogo.

Ngbinda (Bungbinda, Bangbinda) [nbd] 4,200 (2002). *Class:* Niger-Congo, Atlantic-Congo, Volta-Congo, Benue-Congo, Bantoid, Southern, Narrow Bantu, Central, Unclassified. *Other:* Became extinct linguistically in Sudan by 1975.

Ngbundu [nuu] 16,000 (1984 census). Equateur Province, Sud Ubangi, Libenge Territory. Northern group is north of Libenge from the Boyabo crossroads east to Budu and north to Oro. Southern group is south of Libenge, mixed with Mbandja and other language groups. Not in Central African Republic. *Class:* Niger-Congo, Atlantic-Congo, Volta-Congo, North, Adamawa-Ubangi, Ubangi, Banda, Southwestern. *Lg Use:* Bilingual in Lingala. Use of Mono, Mbandja, or Ngbaka is receptive only.

Ngelima (Bangelima, Bangalema, Angba, Leangba) [agh] 13,588 (2000 WCD). Orientale Province, Banalia and Basoko territories. *Class:* Niger-Congo, Atlantic-Congo, Volta-Congo, Benue-Congo, Bantoid, Southern, Narrow Bantu, Northwest, C, Ngombe (C.50). *Dialects:* Beo, Buru (Boro, Leboro), Tungu, Hanga. May be more than one language. Close to Bwa. The Ngombe group is sometimes called Bantu C.40. Lexical similarity 60% to 65% with Bwa, Kango, and Pagibete, 50% with Lika and Komo, 40% with Ngombe, Benza, and Budza.

Ngiti (Kingiti, Ngeti, Kingeti, Ndruna, Druna, Bindi, Lendu-Sud) [niy] 100,000 (1991). Orientale Province, Irumu Territory, south of Bunia. *Class:* Nilo-Saharan, Central Sudanic, East, Lendu. *Other:* 'Ndruna' is the name speakers use for their language. Different from Bendi.

Ngombe (Lingombe) [ngc] 150,000 (1971 Welmers). Equateur Province, extensive area along both sides of Congo River, primarily in Mongala District and in adjacent parts of Southern Ubangi and Equateur districts. Binja is in Orientale Province, Aketi Territory. *Class:* Niger-Congo, Atlantic-Congo, Volta-Congo, Benue-Congo, Bantoid, Southern, Narrow Bantu, Northwest, C, Ngombe (C.50). *Dialects:* Binja (Binza, Libindja, Libinja), Wiindza-Baali, Doko. Close to Bwela (Lingi), Doko, Libale. Lexical similarity 78% between standard Ngombe and Binja, 59% with Ngombe, 40% with Lingala, Pagibete, and Ngelima, 37% with Bwa. *Lg Dev:* NT: 1915–1956. *Other:* Different from Ngombe in Central African Republic.

Ngongo [noq] 4,076 (2000 WCD). Bandundu Province. *Class:* Niger-Congo, Atlantic-Congo, Volta-Congo, Benue-Congo, Bantoid, Southern, Narrow Bantu, Central, H, Yaka (H.30). *Lg Use:* Speakers are quite bilingual in Kituba.

Ngul (Ngoli, Ingul, Nguli, Ngulu) [nlo] 8,400 (2002). Western Bandundu Province along the Kasaï River north of Idiofa. *Class:* Niger-Congo, Atlantic-Congo, Volta-Congo, Benue-Congo, Bantoid, Southern, Narrow Bantu, Northwest, B, Mbere (B.60).

Ngundu [nue] 5,095 (2000 WCD). *Class:* Niger-Congo, Atlantic-Congo, Volta-Congo, North, Adamawa-Ubangi, Ubangi, Banda, Central, Central Core, Mid-Southern. *Dialects:* Closest to Kpagua.

Nkutu (Nkuchu, Nkutshu, Bankutu) [nkw] 40,000 (1972 Nida). Northern Kasaï Oriental Province. *Class:* Niger-Congo, Atlantic-Congo, Volta-Congo, Benue-Congo,

Bantoid, Southern, Narrow Bantu, Northwest, C, Tetela (C.80). *Dialects:* Elembe, Hamba, Lokalo (Kalo), Kongola-Meno, Ngongo, Saka (Losaka). *Lg Dev:* Bible portions: 1937–1940. *Other:* Descendants of the ancient Mongo empire. Traditional religion.

Ntomba (Lontomba, Ntumba, Luntumba, Ntomba-Bolia) [nto] 100,000 (1980 UBS). Bandundu Province, northeast of Lake Tumba. *Class:* Niger-Congo, Atlantic-Congo, Volta-Congo, Benue-Congo, Bantoid, Southern, Narrow Bantu, Northwest, C, Bangi-Ntomba (C.40). *Dialects:* Imona, Mpongo, Nkole, Ntomba, Sakanyi, Soko, Saw. Close to Saw, Bolia (Bokoki). *Lg Dev:* Bible portions: 1916–1947.

Nyali (Linyali, Nyari, Huku, Nyali-Kilo, North Nyali) [nlj] 43,000 (1993 SIL). Orientale Province, Ituri District, Djugu Territory, Kilo Collectivité. *Class:* Niger-Congo, Atlantic-Congo, Volta-Congo, Benue-Congo, Bantoid, Southern, Narrow Bantu, Central, D, Bira-Huku (D.30). *Dialects:* Only one dialect, since 'Nyali-South' is actually Vanuma. Speakers of Vanuma, Mbo, Ndaka, Budu, and Nyali are closer to each other than to other border Bantu languages. Lexical similarity 85% with Vanuma, 76% with Mbo, 73% with Ndaka and Budu. *Lg Use:* A local language committee has been promoting Nyali since 1982. *Other:* The name 'Huku' is reported to be a Hema term used for anyone who is not a Hema.

Nyanga (Kinyanga, Inyanga) [nyj] 150,000 (1994 census). Nord-Kivu Province, Walikale Territory, Wanyanga Collectivité. *Class:* Niger-Congo, Atlantic-Congo, Volta-Congo, Benue-Congo, Bantoid, Southern, Narrow Bantu, Central, D, Nyanga (D.40). *Dialects:* Inyanga, Ifuna, Ikumbure, Itiri. The dialects do not differ much. Itiri appears to be the most divergent. The dialect around Bana-Bangi is reported to be the best understood. Lexical similarity 70% with Kwami, 57% with Hunde, 54% with Kanu, 50% with Lega-Shabunda and Tembo, 45% with Nande, Lega-Mwenga, and Bembe, 42% with Shi, 40% with Buyu and Zimba, 30% with Komo. *Lg Use:* Many also use Congo Swahili. *Lg Dev:* Literacy rate in second language: 20% to 30%. *Other:* Different from Nyanga-li. Agriculturalists: rice, beans, greens, manioc, tomato, onion, banana, avocado, papaya, pineapple, mango. Traditional religion, Christian, Muslim.

Nyanga-li (Linyanga-le) [nyc] 48,000 (2002). Orientale Province, Watsa Territory, southwest of Watsa. *Class:* Niger-Congo, Atlantic-Congo, Volta-Congo, Benue-Congo, Bantoid, Southern, Narrow Bantu, Central, Unclassified. *Dialects:* A member of the same dialect cluster as Gbati-ri, Mayeka. *Other:* Different from Nyanga.

Nyindu [nyg] 8,400 (2002). Sud-Kivu Province, west of Lake Kivu. *Class:* Niger-Congo, Atlantic-Congo, Volta-Congo, Benue-Congo, Bantoid, Southern, Narrow Bantu, Central, J, Shi-Havu (J.50). *Dialects:* Many Nyindu speakers consider themselves to be Lega-Mwenga, but Lega and Shi speakers consider them to be Shi. Their speech is reported to be a mixture of Lega-Mwenga and Shi.

Nzakara (N'sakara, Sakara, Zakara, Ansakara) [nzk] Orientale Province, northwestern part of Bondo Territory, on the border with Central African Republic. See main entry under Central African Republic.

Ombo (Loombo, Hombo, Songola) [oml] 8,400 (2002). Maniema Province, northwest of Kindu. *Class:* Niger-Congo, Atlantic-Congo, Volta-Congo, Benue-Congo, Bantoid, Southern, Narrow Bantu, Northwest, C, Mongo (C.70). *Dialect:* Mbuli (Mbole). Jongo and Langa may be dialects. *Other:* Mbole is apparently distinct from Mbole in the Enya group.

Omi (Kaliko-Omi) [omi] 39,500 (1989 SIL). Orientale Province, Aru Territory, between the Nzoro and Lowa rivers along the Aru to Aba road. *Class:* Nilo-Saharan, Central Sudanic, East, Moru-Madi, Central. *Dialects:* Close to Kaliko, but not close enough to Kaliko or Ma'di to use literature in those languages. Previously considered to be a Kaliko dialect.

Pagibete (Apakabeti, Apakibeti, Apagibete, Apagibeti, Pagabete) [pae] 28,000 (2000 SIL). Population includes 6,000 Momveda, 4,500 Mongbapele. Equateur Province, Businga, Yakoma, and Bumba territories. Mongbapele is along the road south of Businga. Momveda is in the area around Ngakpo on the north side of the Dua River, across from Gumba, and in Butu, Yakoma Territory. Ndundusana is to the south of Butu and at Ndundu-Sana in the northern Bumba Territory. Before the civil war they also lived in Businga, Lisala, and Gbadolite towns. *Class:* Niger-Congo, Atlantic-Congo, Volta-Congo, Benue-Congo, Bantoid, Southern, Narrow Bantu, Northwest, C, Ngombe (C.50). *Dialect:* Momveda, Mongbapele, Ndundusana (Gezon, Egezon, Egezo, Egejo). Momveda and Mongbapele are similar, and have 90% lexical similarity with Ndundusana. Momveda and Mongbapele have 80% lexical similarity with Bwa, Ndundusana has 85%. Dialects have 60% to 75% with Kango, 60% to 65% with Ngelima, 55% to 60% with Lika, 46% with Komo, 40% to 45% with Bali, 35% to 40% with Ngombe and Budza, 30% with Lingala. *Lg Use:* Vigorous in most families. 20% of Pagibete men marry speakers of other languages, and those women experience pressure to learn it. Children of women who marry men from other languages speak it when visiting Pagibete villages. All domains. Local administration, religious services. Some Ebale speakers use Pagibete for trading. Positive language attitude. Fewer than 1% of adults are monolingual—mainly older women. Most are partially bilingual in Lingala. Possibly 30% have intermarried with Ngombe or Ngbandi speakers and understand or speak those languages. About 5% have some secondary education and have varying proficiency in French. *Lg Dev:* 400 can read it, 50 can write it. *Other:* Hills. Tropical forest. Agriculturalists (women), hunters (men). Christian, traditional religion.

Pambia (Apambia) [pmb] 21,000 (1982 SIL). Northern Orientale Province. *Class:* Niger-Congo, Atlantic-Congo, Volta-Congo, North, Adamawa-Ubangi, Ubangi, Zande, Barambo-Pambia. *Other:* None in Sudan or Central African Republic.

Pelende [ppp] 8,400 (2002). Bandundu Province, Kenge Territory. *Class:* Niger-Congo, Atlantic-Congo, Volta-Congo, Benue-Congo, Bantoid, Southern, Narrow Bantu, Central, H, Yaka (H.30). *Other:* Similar to Lonzo, Ngongo.

Phende (Kipende, Giphende, Pende, Gipende, Pindi, Pinji) [pem] 420,000 (1991 UBS). Bandundu Province, Idiofa and Gungu territories, south of the Kasaï River. *Class:* Niger-Congo, Atlantic-Congo, Volta-Congo, Benue-Congo, Bantoid, Southern, Narrow Bantu, Central, K, Holu (K.10). *Lg Use:* Kituba is the lingua franca. *Lg Dev:* NT: 1935-1977. *Other:* Traditional religion.

Poke (Topoke, Tofoke, Tovoke, Puki) [pof] 46,000 (1971 Welmers). Orientale Province, Isangi Territory, south of Congo River downstream from Kisangani. *Class:* Niger-Congo, Atlantic-Congo, Volta-Congo, Benue-Congo, Bantoid, Southern, Narrow Bantu, Northwest, C, Kele (C.60). *Dialects:* Baluombila, Likolo, Liutwa, Lombooki. May be able to use Lokele literature. *Lg Dev:* Bible portions: 1923. *Other:* Also called 'Pseudo-Lokele'. Christian, traditional religion.

Ruund (Uruund, Northern Lunda, Luunda, Chiluwunda, Muatiamvua, Luwunda, Lunda-Kamboro, Lunda Kambove) [rnd] 152,845 in Democratic Republic of the Congo (2000 WCD). Population total all countries: 251,353. Katanga Province, Lualaba District. Also spoken

in Angola. *Class:* Niger-Congo, Atlantic-Congo, Volta-Congo, Benue-Congo, Bantoid, Southern, Narrow Bantu, Central, K, Salampasu-Ndembo (K.30). *Lg Dev:* NT: 1933-1996.

Rwanda (Kinyarwanda, Ruanda) [kin] 250,000 in Democratic Republic of the Congo (UBS). Nord-Kivu Province, Rwanda border area between Lakes Edward and Kivu and extending westward. *Dialects:* Bwisha (Kinyabwisha), Mulenge (Kinyamulenge), Twa. *Other:* Dialects in Democratic Republic of the Congo may need separate literature. Twa: traditional religion, Christian. See main entry under Rwanda.

Sakata (Kisakata, Saka, Lesa, Odual) [skt] 75,000 (1982 UBS). Bandundu Province, Kutu, Mushie, and Inongo territories, Lukenie River, and Semendua area. *Class:* Niger-Congo, Atlantic-Congo, Volta-Congo, Benue-Congo, Bantoid, Southern, Narrow Bantu, Northwest, C, Bangi-Ntomba (C.40). *Dialects:* Sakata, Djia (Kidjia, Dia, Dja), Bai (Kibai). A cluster of dialects. Descendants of the ancient Mongo empire. *Lg Use:* All ages. Lingala is the lingua franca. *Lg Dev:* Bible portions: 1932-1951.

Salampasu (Chisalampasu) [slx] 60,000 (1977 Voegelin and Voegelin). Southeastern part of Kasaï Occidental Province, east of Luiza. *Class:* Niger-Congo, Atlantic-Congo, Volta-Congo, Benue-Congo, Bantoid, Southern, Narrow Bantu, Central, K, Salampasu-Ndembo (K.30). *Dialect:* Luntu. *Lg Dev:* Bible portions: 1938.

Samba (Tsamba, Usamba, Tsaam, Shankadi) [smx] 4,200 (2002). Bandundu Province, northern part of Kasongo-Lunda Territory. *Class:* Niger-Congo, Atlantic-Congo, Volta-Congo, Benue-Congo, Bantoid, Southern, Narrow Bantu, Central, K, Holu (K.10). *Dialects:* Close to Holu.

Sanga (Kisanga, Southern Luba, Luba-Sanga, Luba-Garenganze) [sng] 431,000 (1991 UBS). Katanga Province, north of Likasi, widely dispersed in Lubudi, Mitwaba, and Pweto territories. *Class:* Niger-Congo, Atlantic-Congo, Volta-Congo, Benue-Congo, Bantoid, Southern, Narrow Bantu, Central, L, Luba (L.30). *Lg Dev:* Bible: 1928-1994.

Sango (Sangho) [sag] Few speakers in Democratic Republic of the Congo. Extreme northern border of Equateur Province (Oubangui River). *Lg Use:* Trade language. *Other:* A rapidly spreading language derived from Ngbandi with loans from Bantu languages and French. See main entry under Central African Republic.

Seba (Sewa, Shishi, Kunda) [kdg] 167,000 (2002). Katanga Province, Kasenga Territory. *Class:* Niger-Congo, Atlantic-Congo, Volta-Congo, Benue-Congo, Bantoid, Southern, Narrow Bantu, Central, M, Bisa-Lamba (M.50), Bisa. *Other:* Distinct from Kunda dialect of Lusengo, the Kunda of Zimbabwe and Mozambique in the Senga-Sena group, the Kunda dialect of Nyanja, and the Konda dialect or language in Mongo group.

Sengele (Kesengele, Sengere) [szg] 17,000 (2002). Bandundu Province, west of Lake Mai-Ndombe. *Class:* Niger-Congo, Atlantic-Congo, Volta-Congo, Benue-Congo, Bantoid, Southern, Narrow Bantu, Northwest, C, Bangi-Ntomba (C.40). *Lg Dev:* Bible portions: 1915-1917.

Sere (Shere, Sheri, Chere, Serre, Shaire, Siri, Sili, Basiri, Basili) [swf] 2,500 in Democratic Republic of the Congo. Population total all countries: 2,528. Groups live among the Zande in Orientale Province, northeast of Ango. No speakers in Sudan. Also spoken in Central African Republic. *Class:* Niger-Congo, Atlantic-Congo, Volta-Congo, North, Adamawa-Ubangi, Ubangi, Sere-Ngbaka-Mba, Sere, Sere-Bviri, Ndogo-Sere. *Dialects:* Closest to Ndogo and Tagbu. Slight dialect differences in Democratic Republic of the Congo and Central African Republic.

Shi (Mashi) [shr] 654,000 (1991 UBS). Sud-Kivu Province, north, west, and south of Bukavu. *Class:* Niger-Congo, Atlantic-Congo, Volta-Congo, Benue-Congo, Bantoid,

Southern, Narrow Bantu, Central, J, Shi-Havu (J.50). *Dialects:* Lindja, Hwindja (Lwindja), Ziba, Longe-Longe. Lexical similarity 70% to Havu and Tembo, 57% with Hunde, 55% with Nande, 44% with Lega-Shabunda, 42% with Nyanga. *Lg Dev:* Bible: 1997. *Other:* Different from Mashi of Zambia.

So (Heso, Eso, Soko, Soa, Gesogo) [soc] 6,000 (1971 Welmers). Orientale Province, north of Basoko. May also be in Uganda. *Class:* Niger-Congo, Atlantic-Congo, Volta-Congo, Benue-Congo, Bantoid, Southern, Narrow Bantu, Northwest, C, Kele (C.60). *Lg Dev:* NT: 1920. *Other:* Distinct from So of Cameroon.

Sonde (Kisonde, Soonde, Kisoonde) [shc] 96,000 (2002). Southeastern Bandundu Province, Feshi Territory. *Class:* Niger-Congo, Atlantic-Congo, Volta-Congo, Benue-Congo, Bantoid, Southern, Narrow Bantu, Central, H, Yaka (H.30). *Other:* 'Kilua' may be a name of the language.

Songa (Kisonga) [sgo] Southern Kivu Province. *Class:* Niger-Congo, Atlantic-Congo, Volta-Congo, Benue-Congo, Bantoid, Southern, Narrow Bantu, Unclassified.

Songe (Songye, Kisongye, Lusonge, Kalebwe, Northeast Luba, Yembe, Kisonge, Luba-Songi, Kisongi) [sop] 1,000,000 (1991 WA). Population includes 150,000 in Western Kalebwe (1982 UBS). Kasaï Oriental Province, between Sankuru and Lualaba rivers, mainly in Kabinda Zone and eastward into Kongolo and Kabolo territories of Katanga Province. *Class:* Niger-Congo, Atlantic-Congo, Volta-Congo, Benue-Congo, Bantoid, Southern, Narrow Bantu, Central, L, Songye (L.20). *Dialects:* Western Kalebwe (Esambi Kipya, Songe), Eastern Kalebwe (Kilombeno Kibya, Ikalebwe), Mbagani. Related to Mbagani. *Lg Dev:* NT: 1952–1978. *Other:* Ethnic subgroups are Bena Tshofwe, Bekalebwe, Beneki, Belande, Babembe, Balaa, Bambo, Befundu.

Songo (Kisongo, Itsong) [soo] 13,000 (2002). Bandundu Province, Bulungu Territory. Possibly also in Angola. *Class:* Niger-Congo, Atlantic-Congo, Volta-Congo, Benue-Congo, Bantoid, Southern, Narrow Bantu, Central, Unclassified. *Other:* Possibly same as Nsongo (Songo) of Angola.

Songomeno [soe] 50,000 (1972 Barrett). Kasaï Occidental Province, Dekese Territory. *Class:* Niger-Congo, Atlantic-Congo, Volta-Congo, Benue-Congo, Bantoid, Southern, Narrow Bantu, Northwest, C, Bushong (C.90). *Other:* Traditional religion, Christian.

Songoora (Songola, Kesongola, Binja) [sod] 1,300 (1971 Welmers). Maniema Province, Punia, Kindu, and Shabunda territories. Gengele is in Kindu Territory. *Class:* Niger-Congo, Atlantic-Congo, Volta-Congo, Benue-Congo, Bantoid, Southern, Narrow Bantu, Central, D, Lega-Kalanga (D.20). *Dialects:* Gengele (Kegengele), North Binja, South Binja. North and South Binja may be separate languages. Gengele is reported to be a creole based on Lega-Shabunda, Kusu, and other languages (W. B. Mwangati 1991). *Other:* Different from the Songoora (Edi Songoora) dialect of Nande.

Suku (Kisuku) [sub] 50,000 (1980 UBS). Southern Bandundu Province, west of Feshi, in areas of Moanza and Mwela. *Class:* Niger-Congo, Atlantic-Congo, Volta-Congo, Benue-Congo, Bantoid, Southern, Narrow Bantu, Central, H, Yaka (H.30). *Dialects:* One report says that it is not in the Yaka (H.30) subgroup, but in the Kongo subgroup (H.10). Another says it is in Holu (K.10). *Lg Use:* Vigorous. Kituba is the lingua franca but its use seems limited. *Lg Dev:* Bible portions: 1973.

Swahili, Congo (Zaïre Swahili) [swc] 1,000. Throughout the Katanga, Nord-Kivu, Sud-Kivu, and Maniema provinces and the southeastern part of the Orientale Province. There are other varieties of Swahili in East Africa. *Class:* Niger-Congo, Atlantic-Congo, Volta-Congo, Benue-Congo, Bantoid, Southern, Narrow Bantu, Central, G, Swahili (G.40). *Dialects:* Ituri Kingwana, Lualaba Kingwana, Katanga Swahili, Kivu Swahili. Kingwana is a pidgin Swahili which functions socio-linguistically as a dialect. There are several regional dialects, with that of the formerly Arabized areas being closest to Swahili of Kenya and Tanzania. Lexical similarity 30% with Lingala and with the Lega group, 15% to 20% with Bira-Huku group, Bali, and Lika. *Lg Use:* National language. Second language for 9,100,000 (1991 UBS). *Lg Dev:* Taught in primary schools. Bible: 1960–1997.

Taabwa (Rungu, Ichitaabwa, Tabwa) [tap] 250,000 in Democratic Republic of the Congo (1972 Barrett). Population total all countries: 310,000. Katanga Province, on Lake Tanganyika, south of Moba. Also spoken in Zambia. *Class:* Niger-Congo, Atlantic-Congo, Volta-Congo, Benue-Congo, Bantoid, Southern, Narrow Bantu, Central, M, Bemba (M.40). *Dialect:* Shila. *Other:* Traditional religion, Christian, Muslim.

Tagbu (Tagbo, Tagba) [tbm] 17,000 (2002). Widely scattered. None in Sudan or Central African Republic. *Class:* Niger-Congo, Atlantic-Congo, Volta-Congo, North, Adamawa-Ubangi, Ubangi, Sere-Ngbaka-Mba, Sere, Sere-Bviri, Ndogo-Sere. *Dialects:* Closest to Sere and Ndogo. *Other:* Different from Togbo (Tagbo) of Democratic Republic of the Congo in Banda group.

Talinga-Bwisi (Kitalinga, Lubwisi, Olubwisi, Bwissi, Mawissi, Lubwissi) [tlj] 30,890 in Democratic Republic of the Congo (2000 WCD). Nord-Kivu Province, Beni Territory, Butalinga County, within the boundaries of the Virunga National Park, up to the Uganda border. *Lg Use:* Congo Swahili is the lingua franca in the area. *Other:* Different from Bwisi of Congo-Brazzaville and Gabon. The name 'Talinga' is used in Democratic Republic of the Congo and 'Bwisi' in Uganda. See main entry under Uganda.

Teke, Eboo [ebo] 454,000 all Teke languages in Congo (2001 Johnstone and Mandryk). Bandundo Province, Mushie Territory. *Other:* Ethnic group name is 'Aboo'. Plateau. Savannah, scrub trees, small areas of tropical forest. High altitude. Traditional religion. See main entry under Congo (Teke-Eboo).

Teke, Ibali (Kiteke, Ibali, Eastern Teke) [tek] 71,000 in Democratic Republic of the Congo. Population total all countries: 107,221. Kwamouth, Masia, Kinshasa, near Banbana on road to Kenga. Upstream from Kinshasa to Kwa (Kasaï) River and inland to Fatunda area. Also spoken in Congo. *Class:* Niger-Congo, Atlantic-Congo, Volta-Congo, Benue-Congo, Bantoid, Southern, Narrow Bantu, Northwest, B, Teke (B.70). *Dialects:* Mosieno, Ngee (Esingee), Bali (Ambali, Teo, Tio, Tyo). Ngee may be a separate language. *Lg Use:* Lingala or Kituba are used as trade languages. *Lg Dev:* Literacy rate in second language: 65% to 85%. Bible portions: 1889–1905.

Tembo (Kitembo, Chitembo, Nyabungu) [tbt] 150,000 (1994 SIL). Sud-Kivu and Nord-Kivu provinces, almost all in Kalehe Territory. *Class:* Niger-Congo, Atlantic-Congo, Volta-Congo, Benue-Congo, Bantoid, Southern, Narrow Bantu, Central, J, Shi-Havu (J.50). *Dialects:* Tembo (Kitembo), Rhinyihinyi. No major dialect differences. Related to Havu, Hunde, Shi, Fuliiru. Lexical similarity 75% with Hunde, 70% with Shi, 55% with Nande, 50% with Nyanga, 45% with Lega Shabunda. *Lg Dev:* Bible portions: 1977. *Other:* Different from Tembo in the Ngombe group, Tembo (Tambo) in the Nyika-Safwa group, and Tembo in the Yaka group.

Tembo (Motembo, Litembo) [tmv] 5,000 (1986 SIL). Equateur Province, Sud Ubangi and Equateur districts, Budjala and Bomongo districts, villages of Libanza, Bokele, and Bosanga on the Banga-Melo River, at 1 or 2 villages on the Mongala River southwest of Akula, and

Sumba Island. *Class:* Niger-Congo, Atlantic-Congo, Volta-Congo, Benue-Congo, Bantoid, Southern, Narrow Bantu, Northwest, C, Ngombe (C.50). *Dialects:* There may be wide dialect variations. *Lg Use:* Speakers also use Lingala. *Other:* Riverine.

Tetela (Otetela, Sungu) [tll] 750,000 (1991 UBS). Northern Kasaï Oriental Province. *Class:* Niger-Congo, Atlantic-Congo, Volta-Congo, Benue-Congo, Bantoid, Southern, Narrow Bantu, Northwest, C, Tetela (C.80). *Lg Dev:* Bible: 1966. *Other:* Christian, traditional religion, Muslim.

Tiene (Kitiene, Kitiini, Tende) [tii] 24,500 (1977 SIL). Bandundu Province, Bolobo area on Congo River and inland savannah and forest. *Class:* Niger-Congo, Atlantic-Congo, Volta-Congo, Benue-Congo, Bantoid, Southern, Narrow Bantu, Northwest, B, Yanzi (B.80). *Lg Use:* Lingala is the lingua franca, but its use is limited.

Vanuma (Bvanuma, Livanuma, Bambutuku) [vau] 6,700 (1993 SIL). Orientale Province, Ituri District, Irumu Territory, Tchabi Collectivité. *Class:* Niger-Congo, Atlantic-Congo, Volta-Congo, Benue-Congo, Bantoid, Southern, Narrow Bantu, Central, D, Bira-Huku (D.30). *Dialects:* Lexical similarity 85% with Nyali, 75% with Budu, Ndaka, and Mbo, 76% with Bila. *Lg Dev:* Literacy rate in second language: 30%.

Wongo (Gongo, Ndjembe, Tukkongo, Tukongo, Bakong) [won] 12,691 (2000 WCD). Kasaï Occidental Province, Ilebo and Tshikapa territories. Bandundu Province, Guagu and Idiofa territories, in area of Lubue River. *Class:* Niger-Congo, Atlantic-Congo, Volta-Congo, Benue-Congo, Bantoid, Southern, Narrow Bantu, Northwest, C, Bushong (C.90). *Dialects:* Intelligible with Lele. *Lg Dev:* Bible portions: 1938–1940.

Yaka (Kiyaka, Iaka, Iyaka) [yaf] 700,000 in Democratic Republic of the Congo (2000 SIL). Population total all countries: 900,000. Bandundu Province (400,000), Popokabaka and Kasongo Lunda territories. Also spoken in Angola. *Class:* Niger-Congo, Atlantic-Congo, Volta-Congo, Benue-Congo, Bantoid, Southern, Narrow Bantu, Central, H, Yaka (H.30). *Dialect:* Ngoongo. *Lg Use:* Kituba is the lingua franca. *Lg Dev:* Bible portions: 1938–1957.

Yakoma [yky] 10,000 in Democratic Republic of the Congo. See main entry under Central African Republic.

Yamongeri (Yamongiri) [ymg] 13,000 (2002). Equateur Province, south of the Congo River. *Class:* Niger-Congo, Atlantic-Congo, Volta-Congo, Benue-Congo, Bantoid, Southern, Narrow Bantu, Northwest, C, Bangi-Ntomba (C.40). *Dialects:* Related to Budza.

Yango (Gbendere) [yng] 3,000 (1986 SIL). Equateur Province, Kungu and Libenge districts, around Esobe River and in village of Gbendere. *Class:* Niger-Congo, Atlantic-Congo, Volta-Congo, North, Adamawa-Ubangi, Ubangi, Sere-Ngbaka-Mba, Ngbaka-Mba, Ngbaka, Western, Monzombo. *Dialects:* Close to Monzombo. *Lg Use:* Lingala is widely spoken; also Ngbandi and Mbandja.

Yansi (Yanzi, Eyanzi, Kiyanzi, Eyansi, Yans) [yns] 100,000 (1997 Salikoko Mufwene). Bandundu Province, Bulungu Territory, Loange River area. *Class:* Niger-Congo, Atlantic-Congo, Volta-Congo, Benue-Congo, Bantoid, Southern, Narrow Bantu, Northwest, B, Yanzi (B.80). *Dialect:* Yeei (Yey). Related to Ding, Mbuun. *Lg Use:* 75% of the speakers have routine proficiency in Kituba.

Yela (Boyela, Kutu) [yel] 33,000 (1977 Voegelin and Voegelin). Equateur Province, mainly in Bokungu Territory. *Class:* Niger-Congo, Atlantic-Congo, Volta-Congo, Benue-Congo, Bantoid, Southern, Narrow Bantu, Northwest, C, Tetela (C.80).

Yombe (Kiyombe, Kiombi, Bayombe) [yom] 669,000 in Democratic Republic of the Congo (2002). Population total all countries: 1,056,126. Western Bas-Congo Province, Mayombe Forest. Also spoken in Angola, Congo. *Class:*

Niger-Congo, Atlantic-Congo, Volta-Congo, Benue-Congo, Bantoid, Southern, Narrow Bantu, Central, H, Kongo (H.10). *Dialects:* Mbala (Mumbala), Vungunya (Kivungunya, Yombe Classique). *Other:* Distinct enough from Kongo-Fioti to need separate literature. Forest. Christian, traditional religion.

Yulu (Youlou) [yul] Binga are in Democratic Republic of the Congo and Sudan; Yulu are in Sudan and Central African Republic. *Dialects:* Binga, Yulu. *Lg Use:* Many in Sudan also use Kresh or Arabic. See main entry under Central African Republic.

Zande (Pazande, Zandi, Azande, Sande, Asande, Badjande, Bazenda) [zne] 730,000 in Democratic Republic of the Congo. Population total all countries: 1,142,000. Far north of Orientale Province, Bas-Uele District. Also spoken in Central African Republic, Sudan. *Class:* Niger-Congo, Atlantic-Congo, Volta-Congo, North, Adamawa-Ubangi, Ubangi, Zande, Zande-Nzakara. *Lg Dev:* Bible: 1978. *Other:* SVO, VSO. Traditional religion, Christian.

Zimba [zmb] 120,000 (1994 census). Maniema Province, Kasongo Territory, Mulu and Maringa collectivités. *Class:* Niger-Congo, Atlantic-Congo, Volta-Congo, Benue-Congo, Bantoid, Southern, Narrow Bantu, Central, D, Lega-Kalanga (D.20). *Dialects:* Binja (Soe, Sole), Semulu (Semolo, Nyembombo, Kisembombo), Semalinga, Kwange, Mamba (Kyenyemamba). Kwange and Mamba may be separate languages. Lexical similarity 55% with Bembe, 50% with Lega-Mwenga, Lega-Shabunda, Buyu, Mituku, Enya, 40% with Nyanga, 34% with Bangubangu, 32% with Komo. *Lg Use:* The majority speak Binja dialect. Semulu is spoken in the northeast, Semalinga in the west. Many also use Congo Swahili. *Other:* Agriculturalists: rice, beans, greens, tomato, onion, cabbage, peanuts, papaya, pineapple, mango. Christian, Muslim, Kimbanguist, traditional religion.

Djibouti

Republic of Djibouti. Jumhouriyya Djibouti. République de Djibouti. Formerly part of Somaliland and French Territory of the Afars and the Issas. 466,900. National or official languages: French, Standard Arabic. Literacy rate: 20% to 34% (1996). Also includes Greek (1,600). The number of languages listed for Djibouti is 5. Of those, all are living languages. See map on page 698.

Afar (Afaraf, "Danakil") [aar] 300,000 in Djibouti (1996). Red Sea Coast. *Lg Dev:* Literacy rate in second language: below 1%. *Other:* The people are called "Danakil" by others, but this is considered offensive. Nomadic. Coastal, mountain slope. Desert. Pastoralists. Muslim. See main entry under Ethiopia.

Arabic, Standard [arb] *Lg Use:* Official language. See main entry under Saudi Arabia.

Arabic, Ta'izzi-Adeni Spoken (Djibouti Arabic) [acq] 52,000 in Djibouti (1995). *Other:* Muslim. See main entry under Yemen.

French [fra] 15,440 in Djibouti (1988). *Lg Use:* Official language. See main entry under France.

Somali [som] 291,207 in Djibouti (2000 WCD). *Other:* Nomadic. 3 clans: Issa, Gadaboursi, Issaq. Pastoralists. Muslim. See main entry under Somalia.

Egypt

Arab Republic of Egypt. Jumhuriyat Misr al-Arabiyah. 76,117,421. National or official languages: Standard Arabic, Egyptian Spoken Arabic. Literacy rate: 55% (1993 govt. figure). Also includes Adyghe, Amharic (5,000), Armenian (100,000), Bedawi (77,000), Italian (72,400), Moroccan Spoken Arabic, South Levantine Spoken Arabic (50,000),

Sudanese Spoken Arabic (3,800,000), Tosk Albanian (18,000), West Central Oromo. Information mainly from Applegate 1970; J. Milton Cowan 1973. Blind population: 1,000,000. Deaf institutions: 4. The number of languages listed for Egypt is 12. Of those, 11 are living languages and 1 is extinct. See map on page 693.

Arabic, Eastern Egyptian Bedawi Spoken
(Bedawi, Levantine Bedawi Arabic) [avl] 780,000 in Egypt (1996). Population total all countries: 1,610,000. Bedouin regions in Sinai and along parts of the Red Sea coast, most of the way to the southern border, along the whole east bank until it reaches the Bedawi language. Also spoken in Israel, Jordan, Palestinian West Bank and Gaza, Syria. *Class:* Afro-Asiatic, Semitic, Central, South, Arabic. *Dialects:* Northeast Egyptian Bedawi Arabic, South Levantine Bedawi Arabic, North Levantine Bedawi Arabic. Similar to some Hijazi dialects in northwestern Saudi Arabia. *Lg Dev:* TV. *Other:* Muslim (Sunni).

Arabic, Egyptian Spoken (Lower Egypt Arabic, Normal Egyptian Arabic, Massry) [arz] 44,406,000 in Egypt (1998). Population total all countries: 46,321,000. Also spoken in Iraq, Israel, Jordan, Kuwait, Libya, Saudi Arabia, United Arab Emirates, Yemen. *Class:* Afro-Asiatic, Semitic, Central, South, Arabic. *Dialects:* North Delta Arabic, South Central Delta Arabic, Cairene Arabic. The media have established a normal Egyptian Spoken Arabic based on Cairo speech. Cairene is the most widely understood dialect used for nonprint media, both in Egypt and throughout the sedentary Arab world. It is an amalgam of Delta Arabic and Middle Egypt Arabic, with borrowings from literary Arabic. *Lg Use:* National language. All domains. English or French used in academic settings. *Lg Dev:* Radio programs. TV. NT: 1932. *Other:* Muslim.

Arabic, Sa'idi Spoken (Sa'idi, Upper Egypt Arabic) [aec] 18,900,000 (1996). Southern Egypt from the edge of Cairo to the Sudan border. The Middle Egypt dialect is in Bani Sweef, Fayyuum, and Gizeh. Upper Egypt dialect is from Asyuut to Edfu and south. Some might be in Libya or the Gulf. *Class:* Afro-Asiatic, Semitic, Central, South, Arabic. *Dialects:* Middle Egypt Arabic, Upper Egypt Arabic. *Lg Use:* Speakers prefer Cairene over Sudanese. Speakers of Cairene do not understand Sa'idi, but speakers of Sa'idi understand Cairene and some use it as second language. *Other:* Similar to Sudanese Arabic, especially in the south, but heavily influenced by Cairene Arabic.

Arabic, Standard [arb] Middle East, North Africa. *Lg Use:* Official language. Not a first language. Used for nearly all written materials and formal speeches. Taught in schools. See main entry under Saudi Arabia.

Arabic, Western Egyptian Bedawi Spoken
(Bedawi, Libyan Spoken Arabic, Sulaimitian Arabic, Maghrebi Arabic) [ayl] 300,000 in Egypt (1996). Bedouin regions from the edge of Alexandria west to the Libyan border. Some in western oases. *Dialects:* Western Egyptian Bedawi Arabic, Tripolitanian Arabic, Southern Libyan Arabic, Eastern Libyan Arabic. *Other:* Muslim (Sunni). See main entry under Libya (Arabic, Libyan Spoken).

Coptic (Neo-Egyptian) [cop] Extinct. *Class:* Afro-Asiatic, Egyptian. *Dialects:* Bohairic, Sahidic. *Lg Use:* Liturgical language of the Coptic Church, Bohairic dialect. No first-language speakers; it probably became extinct in the 16th century. *Lg Dev:* NT: 1716–1924.

Domari [rmt] 234,000 in Egypt (2004). Muslim Gypsies in Egypt: 1,080,000. The Ghagar live mainly in Dakahlia Governorate, north of Cairo. *Dialects:* Nawar (Ghagar), Helebi. *Lg Use:* Reports that many now speak Arabic. *Other:* Muslim. See main entry under Iran.

Egypt Sign Language [esl] *Class:* Deaf sign language.

Greek [ell] 42,000 in Egypt (2004). Alexandria. See main entry under Greece.

Kenuzi-Dongola (Dongola-Kenuz, Nile Nubian, Dongolawi, Metoki) [kzh] 100,000 in Egypt (1996). Ethnic population: 100,000 in Egypt. 40% in the Upper Nile valley, mainly at Kom Ombo, the rest in various cities. *Dialect:* Dongola, Kenuz (Kenuzi, Kunuzi, Kenzi). *Lg Use:* There may be fewer speakers (1996). The language is the central feature of Nubian identity. The ethnic group is larger in Egypt than Sudan, but many are now monolingual in Egyptian or Sa'idi Arabic. The shift to Arabic is expected to continue in the cities. *Other:* Muslim. See main entry under Sudan.

Nobiin (Fiadidja-Mahas, Mahas-Fiadidja, Fadicca, Fadicha, Fedija, Fadija, Fiadidja, Fiyadikkya, Fedicca, Nile Nubian, Mahas, Sukot) [fia] 200,000 in Egypt (1996). Northern Province, northwards from Burgeg to the Egyptian border at Wadi Halfa. Also at New Halfa in Kassala Province. 40% in the Upper Nile Valley, mainly near Kom Ombo; the rest in various cities. *Lg Use:* The language is the center of Nubian identity. The ethnic group is larger in Egypt than Sudan, but most are now monolingual in Egyptian or Sa'idi Arabic. The shift to Arabic is expected to continue in the cities. *Other:* Spoken by the Fedicca in Egypt and the Mahas in Sudan. Muslim. See main entry under Sudan.

Siwi (Siwa, Sioua, Oasis Berber, Zenati) [siz] 5,000 (1995). Northwestern desert, Siwa Oasis, several isolated villages in the western oasis. *Class:* Afro-Asiatic, Berber, Eastern, Siwa. *Dialects:* Not closely related to other Berber languages. *Lg Use:* Speakers also use Arabic. *Other:* Muslim.

Equatorial Guinea

Republic of Equatorial Guinea. República de Guinea Ecuatorial. Formerly Spanish Guinea. 523,051. National or official languages: Spanish, French. Literacy rate: 55% to 72%. Also includes people from Nigeria, Europe, India. Information mainly from A. Jacquot 1978; J. Holm 1989; J. Bendor-Samuel 1989; A. Iyanga Pendi 1991; SIL 1987–2003. Blind population: 800 (1982 WCE). The number of languages listed for Equatorial Guinea is 14. Of those, all are living languages. See map on page 700.

Batanga (Banoho, Bano'o, Noho, Nohu, Noku, Banoo) [bnm] 9,000 in Equatorial Guinea (2001 Johnstone and Mandryk). Population total all countries: 15,000. Also spoken in Cameroon. *Class:* Niger-Congo, Atlantic-Congo, Volta-Congo, Benue-Congo, Bantoid, Southern, Narrow Bantu, Northwest, A, Bube-Benga (A.30). *Dialect:* Bapuku (Puku, Naka, Bapuu). The Puku are one of the Ndowe coastal peoples. *Lg Dev:* Bible portions: 1953. *Other:* Different from Batanga of South West Province in Cameroon (Balundu-Bima), and the Batanga dialect of Caka. Coastal. Tropical forest. Sea level to 50 meters. Fishermen.

Benga [bng] 3,000 in Equatorial Guinea (1995). Population includes 400 on Corisco Island. Rio Muni. Corisco Island. 80% have moved to Libreville, Gabon to Bata in EG. Also spoken in Gabon. *Class:* Niger-Congo, Atlantic-Congo, Volta-Congo, Benue-Congo, Bantoid, Southern, Narrow Bantu, Northwest, A, Bube-Benga (A.30). *Dialects:* Related to Batanga. *Lg Dev:* NT: 1871–1893. *Other:* One of the Ndowe 'coastal' peoples. Coastal, volcanic island. Tropical forest. 1 to 30 meters. Fishermen; coconut palms. Christian.

Bube (Boombe, Bobe, Bubi, Ediya, Adija, Adeeyah, Boobe, Fernandian) [bvb] 40,000 (1995 UBS). Fernando Po, Biombo Island. *Class:* Niger-Congo, Atlantic-Congo, Volta-Congo, Benue-Congo, Bantoid, Southern, Narrow

Bantu, Northwest, A, Bube-Benga (A.30). *Dialects:* North Bobe, Southwest Bobe, Southeast Bobe. *Lg Dev:* Bible portions: 1849. *Other:* Volcanic island. Tropical forest. Sea level to 1,500 meters. Swidden agriculturalists; fishermen.

Fa D'ambu (Annobonés, Annobonese, Annobonense) [fab] 2,500 in Equatorial Guinea (1999 SIL). Population total all countries: 3,100. Annobón Island, isolated from the mainland by 360 km of ocean (2,000), and in a community from Annobón living in Malabo on Bioko Island (500), a few on continental Equatorial Guinea. Also spoken in Spain. *Class:* Creole, Portuguese based. *Dialects:* Different from Fernando Po Krio and Crioulo of Guinea-Bissau and Kabuverdianu. Little variation between Annobonese in Annobón and Malabo. Lexical similarity 62.5% with São Tomense. 10% of the lexicon comes from Spanish. *Lg Use:* Vigorous use in Annobón and Malabo. All domains except government and education. Language closely related to cultural identity and solidarity. Many on Bioko learn Spanish, but less so on Annobón. Women on Annobón seem uncomfortable in Spanish. Spanish is used in government and education. Many on Bioko learn the local trade language, Fernando Po Creole English. Noncreolized Portuguese used as liturgical language by local Catholics. *Other:* The Portuguese took slaves from São Tomé and Angola to establish a population on Annobón. It was later traded to Spain. Also influenced by the Creole English of Bioko. They are famed swimmers, fishermen, and whalers. Possible vowel length; vowel harmony; tone sandhi. Volcanic island. Tropical forest. Sea level to 500 meters. Fishermen; agricultural laborers; coconut palms; whalers. Christian.

Fang (Pamue, Pahoun) [fan] 258,722 in Equatorial Guinea (2000 WCD). Population total all countries: 450,586. Interior. Also spoken in Cameroon, Congo, Gabon, São Tomé e Príncipe. *Class:* Niger-Congo, Atlantic-Congo, Volta-Congo, Benue-Congo, Bantoid, Southern, Narrow Bantu, Northwest, A, Yaunde-Fang (A.70). *Dialect:* Make, Ntum (Ntumu). Intelligible with Bulu and Ewondo as part of the Beti language cluster. *Lg Dev:* Bible: 1951. *Other:* Ethnic groups are Okak, Ntumu. They are known as 'warriors of the jungle'. Their knowledge of jungle plants, animals, survival is legendary. Interfluvial. Tropical forest. Sea level to 700 meters. Hunter-gatherers. Christian, traditional religion.

Fernando Po Creole English (Pidginglis, Fernandino, Fernando Po Krio, Criollo) [fpe] 5,000 (1998 SIL). North central Bioko Island (Fernando Po), 6 communities in or near Malabo: Musola, Las Palmas, Sampaca, Basupu, Fiston, Balveri de Cristo Rey. *Class:* Creole, English based, Atlantic, Krio. *Dialects:* Pidginglis may be a separate language from Krio. *Lg Use:* Trade language. 70,000 or 17.5% speak it as trade language. About 1,000 are monolingual. Language of instruction in school is Spanish. English and some Bubi are also used. *Lg Dev:* Literacy rate in second language: 75% in Spanish. *Other:* Speakers came from Sierra Leone in 1827. Volcanic island. Tropical forest. Sea level to 300 meters. Agriculturalists. Christian.

French [fra] Known more in the cities. *Lg Use:* Official language. 75,000 to 100,000 second-language speakers in Equatorial Guinea. Used in commerce and government. *Other:* Declared an official language in 1997. Increasingly becoming a language of wider communication. See main entry under France.

Gyele (Giele, Gieli, Gyeli, Bagyele, Bagiele, Bajeli, Bajele, Bogyeli, Bogyel, Bondjiel, Bako, Bekoe, Bakola, Bakuele, Likoya, Babinga) [gyi] 29 in Equatorial Guinea (1998 govt.). Near the coast, northwest corner of Equatorial Guinea. *Other:* Pygmies, dispersed in small groups in the forest. Forest. See main entry under Cameroon.

Molengue (Molendji, Balengue) [bxc] 1,000 (2002 SIL). Southern, just inland from coast, about half of the way up, between the southern tip of the country and the Rio Benito. *Class:* Niger-Congo, Atlantic-Congo, Volta-Congo, Benue-Congo, Bantoid, Southern, Narrow Bantu, Northwest, B, Unclassified. *Other:* One of 3 groups known as 'semi-playeros', who function well on the coast and in the jungle. Coastal, riverine. Tropical forest. Sea level to 100 meters. Swidden agriculturalists.

Ngumba (Mvumbo, Ngoumba, Mgoumba, Mabi, Mabea, Bujeba) [nmg] 8,500 in Equatorial Guinea (1982 SIL). Rio Muni. *Dialect:* Kwasio (Bisio, Bissio, Bisiwo). *Other:* One of 3 groups known as 'semi-playeros', because they function well on the coast and in the jungle. Coastal, riverine. Tropical forest. Sea level to 100 meters. Swidden agriculturalists. See main entry under Cameroon.

Ngumbi (Combe, Kombe) [nui] 4,000 (1995). Rio Muni coast, including Ecuco village. *Class:* Niger-Congo, Atlantic-Congo, Volta-Congo, Benue-Congo, Bantoid, Southern, Narrow Bantu, Northwest, A, Bube-Benga (A.30), Yasa. *Dialects:* Asonga, Bomudi, Moganda. In Yasa (Bongwe) cluster. May be a dialect of Yasa. One of the Ndowe coastal peoples. *Lg Dev:* NT: 1940. *Other:* Coastal. Tropical forest. Sea level to 50 meters. Fishermen; swidden agriculturalists. Christian.

Seki (Sekyani, Sekiani, Sekiyani, Sekiana, Shekiyana, Sheke, Seke, Beseki, Bulu) [syi] 11,000 in Equatorial Guinea (2001 Johnstone and Mandryk). Population total all countries: 14,690. Coastal. Also spoken in Gabon. *Class:* Niger-Congo, Atlantic-Congo, Volta-Congo, Benue-Congo, Bantoid, Southern, Narrow Bantu, Northwest, B, Kele (B.20). *Dialects:* Different from Bulu of Cameroon. One of 3 groups known as 'semi-playeros' because they function well on the coast and in the jungle. *Other:* Coastal, riverine. Tropical forest. Sea level to 100 meters. Swidden agriculturalists.

Spanish [spa] 11,500 in Equatorial Guinea (1993 Johnstone). Mainly on Biombo Island. *Lg Use:* Official language. See main entry under Spain.

Yasa (Yassa, Lyassa, Maasa, Bongwe) [yko] 913 in Equatorial Guinea (2000 WCD). Rio Muni. Yasa dialect is in Cameroon and 1 village (Rio Ntem). *Dialects:* Iyasa, Bweko, Vendo, Bodele, Marry, One, Asonga, Bomui, Mogana, Mooma, Mapanga. *Other:* One of the Ndowe coastal peoples. Coastal. Tropical forest. 1 to 50 meters. Fishermen. See main entry under Cameroon.

Eritrea

State of Eritrea. 4,447,307. National or official languages: English, Standard Arabic, Tigrinya. Capital: Asmara. Independence from Ethiopia 1993. Literacy rate: 37%. Also includes Central Kanuri, Hadrami Spoken Arabic (100,000), Hausa, Qimant, Sudanese Spoken Arabic (100,000), Ta'izzi-Adeni Spoken Arabic (18,000). The number of languages listed for Eritrea is 13. Of those, 12 are living languages and 1 is extinct. See map on page 698.

Afar (Afaraf, "Danakil," "Denkel") [aar] 160,000 in Eritrea (2001 Johnstone and Mandryk). Southern Eritrea. May also be in Somalia. *Dialects:* Central Afar, Northern Afar, Aussa, Ba'adu. *Lg Use:* Speakers also use Arabic. *Lg Dev:* Literacy rate in second language: 8%. *Other:* The people are called "Danakil" by others, but that is considered to be offensive by the Afar. Nomadic. Muslim, Christian. See main entry under Ethiopia.

Arabic, Hijazi Spoken (Hijazi) [acw] Red Sea coast. *Other:* Rashaydah nomadic camel-herders migrated from Arabia to the Red Sea hills of Sudan and Eritrea in the middle of the 19th century. See main entry under Saudi Arabia.

Arabic, Standard [arb] Middle East, North Africa. *Lg Use:* Official language. Used in some schools. See main entry under Saudi Arabia.

Bedawi (Bedàwie, Beja, Bedawiye, Bedawye, Bedauye, Bedwi, Bedya, Bedja, Lobat) [bej] 150,000 in Eritrea (2001 Johnstone and Mandryk). Population includes 20,000 Hadendoa (1970 Bendor). *Dialects:* Hadareb (Hadaareb), Bisharin (Bisarin, Bisariab), Hadendoa (Hadendowa), Beni-Amir, Ababda, Amara. *Other:* The Beja people call their language 'Bedàwie'. Muslim. See main entry under Sudan.

Bilen (Bogo, Bogos, Bilayn, Bilin, Balen, Beleni, Belen, Bilein, Bileno, North Agaw) [byn] 70,000 (1995). Central Eritrea, in and around the town of Keren. *Class:* Afro-Asiatic, Cushitic, Central, Northern. *Lg Use:* 60% of the Christians are partly bilingual in Tigrinya, 70% of the Muslims also use Tigré. The younger generation mixes their speech with Arabic. Some also use Nara or Kunama. *Lg Dev:* Bible portions: 1882–1984. *Other:* SOV. Muslim, Christian.

English [eng] *Lg Use:* National language. *Other:* Language of higher education and many technical fields. See main entry under United Kingdom.

Geez (Ancient Ethiopic, Ethiopic, Ge'ez, Giiz) [gez] Extinct. *Lg Use:* Liturgical language only. *Other:* Christian. See main entry under Ethiopia.

Italian [ita] A few monolinguals. *Lg Use:* Spoken as a second language. See main entry under Italy.

Kunama (Baza, Baaza, Bazen, Baazen, Baazayn, Baden, Baaden, Bada, Baada, Cunama, Diila) [kun] 107,000 in Eritrea (2001 Johnstone and Mandryk). Population includes 1,000 in Ilit, 600 in Odasa. Population total all countries: 108,883. Western Eritrea, on the Gash and Setit rivers, Sudan border and into Tigray Province. Barka is south of Barentu; Marda is north, northeast, and east of Barentu and in Barentu; Aimara is west of Barentu; Laki-Tukura is south of Aimara, west of Barka; Tika is south of Laki-Tukura, west of Barka. None in Sudan. Also spoken in Ethiopia. *Class:* Nilo-Saharan, Kunama. *Dialects:* Barka (Berka), Marda, Aimara (Aaimasa, Aymasa, Odasa), Tika (Tiika, Lakatakura-Tika), Ilit (Iliit, Iiliit, Iilit), Bitama (Bitaama), Sokodasa (Sogodas, Sogadas), Takazze-Setiit (Setiit, Setit), Tigray. Bitama and Ilit are nearly unintelligible to speakers of other Kunama. Barka is the largest dialect and intelligible to speakers of all others. *Lg Dev:* Literacy rate in second language: Low. NT: 1927. *Other:* Laka-Takura and Tika have been influenced by Arab culture and by the Beni-Amer. SOV; postpositions; case suffixes. Mountains, savannah, thorn trees. Agriculturalists: sorghum, millet, sesame; animal husbandry: cattle, sheep, goats, donkeys, poultry. Traditional religion, Muslim (Ilit, Bitama).

Nara (Nera, "Barea," "Barya," "Baria," Higir, Koyta, Mogareb, Santora) [nrb] 80,000 (2001 Johnstone and Mandryk). In and north of Barentu, western Eritrea, adjoining Kunama territory which is to the south. *Class:* Nilo-Saharan, Eastern Sudanic, Eastern, Nara. *Dialects:* Considerable dialect variation within the four main groups: Higir, Mogareb, Koyta, Santora. Little intelligibility of Kunama. *Lg Use:* They use Tigré for intercommunication, or Arabic. The Koyta use Kunama. *Other:* "Barya" is a derogatory name. SOV; case suffixes; passive verbs; reciprocal verbs. Muslim, traditional religion.

Saho (Sao, Shaho, Shoho, Shiho) [ssy] 180,000 in Eritrea (2001 Johnstone and Mandryk). Population total all countries: 202,759. Southern Eritrea. Also spoken in Ethiopia. *Class:* Afro-Asiatic, Cushitic, East, Saho-Afar. *Dialects:* Very close to Afar. The Irob dialect is only in Ethiopia. *Lg Dev:* Literacy rate in first language: below 1%. Literacy rate in second language: below 5%. Dictionary. Bible portions: 1964. *Other:* Ethnic group

names are Asa'orta, Hadu (Hazu), Miniferi. Nomadic. They do not accept outsiders. They have suffered from recent famines. SOV. Muslim, Christian.

Tigré (Khasa, Xasa) [tig] 800,000 in Eritrea (1997 census). Also spoken in Sudan. *Class:* Afro-Asiatic, Semitic, South, Ethiopian, North. *Dialect:* Mansa' (Mensa). *Lg Use:* Used as second language by the Tukrir. *Lg Dev:* Bible: 1988. *Other:* Spoken by some Beni-Amer called 'Lobot'. Other ethnic groups are Ad Aha, Geden Sikta, Iddifer, Teroa Beit Mushe. Believed by some to be the direct linguistic descendant of Ge'ez. Incorrectly called 'Ge'ez'. SOV. Muslim.

Tigrigna (Tigrinya, Tigray) [tir] 1,200,000 in Eritrea (2001 Johnstone and Mandryk). South and central Eritrea. *Lg Use:* Official language. *Lg Dev:* Literacy rate in first language: 1% to 10%. Literacy rate in second language: 5% to 25%. *Other:* Christian, Muslim. See main entry under Ethiopia.

Ethiopia

Republic of Ethiopia. Federal Democratic Republic of Ethiopia. Ye Etiyop'iya Hizbawi Dimokrasiyawi Ripublik. 67,851,281. National or official languages: Amharic, English, Tigrigna. Literacy rate: 23.4% (1998 CSA). Also includes Kunama (1,883), Sudanese Spoken Arabic. Information mainly from M. L. Bender 1971, 1975, 1976, 1983, 1989; Ralph Siebert 1998–1999. Blind population: 117,739; totally blind, 201,455; partially blind (1998 census). Deaf population: 131,359 hearing problems, 58,415 hearing and speaking problems (1998 census). Deaf institutions: 7. The number of languages listed for Ethiopia is 89. Of those, 84 are living languages and 5 are extinct. See maps beginning on page 698.

Aari (Ari, Ara, Aro, Aarai, "Shankilla," "Shankillinya," "Shankilligna") [aiz] 158,857 (1998 census). 129,350 monolinguals. Ethnic population: 155,002 (1989 census). North central Omo Region, southern tip of Ethiopian plateau, near the Hamer-Banna. *Class:* Afro-Asiatic, Omotic, South. *Dialects:* Gozza, Bako (Baco), Biyo (Bio), Galila, Laydo, Seyki, Shangama, Sido, Wubahamer (Ubamer), Zeddo. Galila is a significantly divergent dialect. *Lg Use:* 13,319 second-language users. Used in the home, market. Some bilingualism in Amharic and Gofa (Wolaytta). *Lg Dev:* Literacy rate in first language: below 1%. Literacy rate in second language: 8.3%. NT: 1998. *Other:* "Shankilla" is a derogatory name. Patrilineal. SOV. Plateau. Agriculturalists; traders; cottage industries. Traditional religion, Christian.

Afar (Afaraf, "Danakil," "Denkel," 'Afar Af, Adal) [aar] 979,367 in Ethiopia. 905,872 monolinguals (1998 census). Population total all countries: 1,439,367. Eastern lowlands, Afar Region. May also be in Somalia. Also spoken in Djibouti, Eritrea. *Class:* Afro-Asiatic, Cushitic, East, Saho-Afar. *Dialect:* Northern Afar, Central Afar, Aussa, Baadu (Ba'adu). Related to Saho. *Lg Use:* 22,848 second-language users. Speakers also use Arabic. *Lg Dev:* Literacy rate in first language: below 1%. Literacy rate in second language: 3%. Radio programs. Dictionary. Grammar. NT: 1994. *Other:* The people are called "Danakil" in Arabic and by others, but that is considered to be offensive by the Afar; called 'Adal' in Amharic. Nomadic. People have suffered from recent famines. SOV. Coastal, salt flats, volcanic rock. Desert, plain. Pastoralists; agriculturalists. Muslim, Christian.

Alaba (Allaaba, Halaba) [alw] 126,257 (1998 census). 95,388 monolinguals (1998 census). Ethnic population: 125,900 (1998 census). Rift Valley southwest of Lake Shala. Separated by a river from the Kambatta. *Class:* Afro-Asiatic, Cushitic, East, Highland. *Dialects:* Lexical similarity 81% with Kambaata, 64% with Sidamo, 56% with Libido, 54% with Hadiyya. *Lg Use:* 25,271 second-language users. There is interest in using Alaba for primary education. *Lg Dev:* Literacy rate in first language: below 1%. Literacy rate in second language: 8.6%. *Other:* SOV. Muslim, Christian.

Amharic (Abyssinian, Ethiopian, Amarinya, Amarigna) [amh] 17,372,913 in Ethiopia (1998 census). 14,743,556 monolinguals. Population total all countries: 17,417,913. Ethnic population: 16,007,933 (1998 census). North central Ethiopia, Amhara Region, and in Addis Ababa. Also spoken in Egypt, Israel, Sweden. *Class:* Afro-Asiatic, Semitic, South, Ethiopian, South, Transversal, Amharic-Argobba. *Lg Use:* National language. 4,000,000 second-language speakers. Used in government, public media, national commerce, education to seventh grade in many areas, wide variety of literature (fiction, poetry, plays, magazines). Speakers also use English, Arabic, Oromo, or Tigrinya. *Lg Dev:* Literacy rate in first language: 28.1%. Literacy rate in second language: 28.1%. Radio programs. TV. Dictionary. Grammar. Bible: 1840–1988. *Other:* People have suffered from recent famines. SOV; prepositions, postpositions, genitives, articles, and relatives precede noun heads; question word initial; case affixes; verb suffixes show person, number, gender of subject and (optionally) object; passives including deponents, causatives, CV, CVC, V, CVCC. Christian, Jewish.

Anfillo (Southern Mao) [myo] 500 (1990 SIL). Ethnic population: 1,000 (1990 SIL). Anfillo Forest, west of Dembi Dolo. *Class:* Afro-Asiatic, Omotic, North, Gonga-Gimojan, Gonga, Central. *Dialects:* Lexical similarity 53% with Shekkacho. *Lg Use:* Speakers are older adults. Members of the ethnic group mainly speak Western Oromo. *Lg Dev:* Literacy rate in second language: 5%. *Other:* SOV.

Anuak (Anywak, Anyuak, Anywa, Yambo, Jambo, Yembo, Bar, Burjin, Miroy, Moojanga, Nuro) [anu] 45,646 in Ethiopia (1998 census). 34,311 monolinguals. Ethnic population: 45,665 (1998 census). Gambela Region in the southwest. Along the Baro, Alworo, and Gilo rivers and on the right bank of the Akobo River. Gambela town is the main center. *Dialects:* Adoyo, Coro, Lul, Opëno. *Lg Use:* 2,114 second-language users. *Lg Dev:* Literacy rate in second language: 37%. *Other:* Agriculturalists: maize, sorghum; animal husbandry; fishermen; hunters. Traditional religion. See main entry under Sudan.

Arbore (Arbora, Erbore, Irbore) [arv] 4,441 (1998 census). 3,907 monolinguals (1998 census). Ethnic population: 6,559 (1998 census). Extreme southwest, Omo Region, near Lake Stefanie. *Class:* Afro-Asiatic, Cushitic, East, Western Omo-Tana. *Lg Use:* 3,108 second-language speakers. Komso is the lingua franca. *Lg Dev:* Literacy rate in second language: 13.9%. *Other:* SOV.

Argobba [agj] 10,860 (1998 census). 44,737 monolinguals. Population includes 47,285 in Amharic, 3,771 in Oromo, 541 in Tigrigna (1998 census). Ethnic population: 62,831 (1998 census). Fragmented areas along the Rift Valley in settlements like Yimlawo, Gusa, Shonke, Berket, Keramba, Mellajillo, Metehara, Shewa Robit, and surrounding rural villages. *Class:* Afro-Asiatic, Semitic, South, Ethiopian, South, Transversal, Amharic-Argobba. *Dialects:* Ankober, Shonke. It is reported that the 'purest' Argobba is spoken in Shonke and T'olaha. Lexical similarity 75% to 85% with Amharic. *Lg Use:* 3,236 second-language speakers. The ethnic group near Ankober mainly speaks Amharic; the group near Harar mainly speaks Oromo. The ethnic group is working to foster ethnic recognition. Speakers also use Amharic or Oromo. *Lg Dev:* Literacy rate in second language: 16.4%. *Other:* Traders; agriculturalists. Muslim.

Awngi (Awiya, Awi, Agaw, Agau, Agew, Agow, Awawar, Damot, Kwollanyoch) [awn] 356,980 (1998 census).

279,326 monolinguals. Ethnic population: 397,491 (1998 census). Amhara Region. Widely scattered parts of Agew Midir and Metekel, southwest of Lake Tana. *Class:* Afro-Asiatic, Cushitic, Central, Southern. *Lg Use:* 64,425 second-language speakers. 80% to 90% of speakers use Amharic as second language. *Other:* SOV. Agriculturalists.

Baiso (Bayso, Alkali) [bsw] 1,010 (1995 SIL). Ethnic population: 3,260 (1994 M. Brenzinger). Alge village near Merab Abaya, halfway between Soddo and Arba Minch (390); Gidicho Island, Baiso and Shigima villages (200); and Welege Island on Lake Abaya (420), and the western shore of the lake. *Class:* Afro-Asiatic, Cushitic, East, Western Omo-Tana. *Lg Use:* The people have resisted extinction for at least 1,000 years (Brenzinger, Heine, and Sommer 1991). Most domains. Most children learn Baiso. Older adults and those living on Gidicho Island also use Afan Oromo. The youth have better proficiency in Gamo and Wolaytta, and little knowledge of Afan Oromo. *Lg Dev:* Speakers are positive toward the idea of Baiso literature. *Other:* Speakers are now the minority in all their locations. SOV. Fishermen; agriculturalists; weavers; hippo hunters.

Bambassi (Bambeshi, Siggoyo, Amam, Fadiro, Northern Mao, Didessa) [myf] 5,000 (1982 SIL). Beni Shangul Region, in and around Bambesi. *Class:* Afro-Asiatic, Omotic, North, Mao, East. *Dialects:* Kere, Bambassi. Lexical similarity 31% with other Omotic languages, 17% with Hozo-Sezo (Bender 1983). *Lg Use:* Attitudes toward Oromo vary. Some speakers also use Oromo or Arabic, and almost none use Amharic. *Lg Dev:* Literacy rate in second language: 5.3%. *Other:* SOV. Muslim.

Basketo (Basketto, Baskatta, Mesketo) [bst] 57,805 (1998 census). 42,726 monolinguals. Ethnic population: 51,097 (1998 census). North Omo Region, on a plateau west of Bulki. *Class:* Afro-Asiatic, Omotic, North, Gonga-Gimojan, Gimojan, Ometo-Gimira, Ometo, West. *Dialects:* Lexical similarity 61% with Oyda. *Lg Use:* 8,961 second-language speakers. Speakers have low proficiency in Wolaytta. *Lg Dev:* Literacy rate in first language: below 1%. Literacy rate in second language: 10.2%. *Other:* SOV. Plateau. Christian.

Bench (Gimira, Ghimarra, Gimarra, Dizu) [bcq] 173,586 (1998 census). 149,293 monolinguals. Population includes 10,002 She, 1,070 Mer. Ethnic population: 173,123 (1998 census). Kafa Region, in and around Mizan Teferi and Shewa Bench towns. *Class:* Afro-Asiatic, Omotic, North, Gonga-Gimojan, Gimojan, Ometo-Gimira, Gimira. *Dialects:* Bench (Bencho, Benesho), Mer (Mieru), She (Sce, Kaba). *Lg Use:* 22,640 second-language speakers. Speakers also use Amharic. *Lg Dev:* Literacy rate in first language: below 1%. Literacy rate in second language: 12% Amharic. NT: 1990. *Other:* SOV; tonal, 5 level tones, 1 glide. Forest, savannah. 1,700 to 2,000 meters. Agriculturalists: wheat, barley, maize, sorghum. Traditional religion, Christian.

Berta (Beni Shangul, Bertha, Barta, Burta, Wetawit, Jebelawi) [wti] 124,799 in Ethiopia (1998 census). 99,689 monolinguals including 4,146 Fadashi. Population includes 8,715 Fadashi. Population total all countries: 146,799. Ethnic population: 125,853 including 7,323 Fadashi (1998 census). Beni Shangul Region, the corner formed by the Blue Nile River and Sudan border north of Asosa, and Dalati, a village east of the Dabus River. Also spoken in Sudan. *Class:* Nilo-Saharan, Berta. *Dialects:* Shuru, Bake, Undu, Mayu, Fadashi, Dabuso, Gobato. Probably two or more languages. Fadashi may be separate. *Lg Use:* 16,533 second-language speakers including 795 of Fadashi. *Lg Dev:* Literacy rate in second language: Berta: 9.7%, Gobato: 55.4%. *Other:* 'Beni Shangul' is the Arabic name. SVO; case suffixes, passive, causative; prepositions; tonal. Agriculturalists. Muslim.

Birale ('Ongota, Birelle, Ifa'ongota, "Shanqilla") [bxe] 19 (2000 M. Brenzinger). Ethnic population: 89 (2000 M. Brenzinger). One village on the west bank of the Weyt'o River, southeast Omo Region. *Class:* Afro-Asiatic, Unclassified. *Lg Use:* All speakers are older adults. Not supportive of language maintenance. Members of the ethnic group who do not speak Birale conduct their affairs in Tsamai. *Other:* SOV; postpositions, genitives follow noun heads, suffixes indicate noun case, verb affixes mark subject person, number, and gender, passive, causative. Agriculturalists; hunters. Nearly extinct.

Boro (Bworo, Shinasha, Scinacia) [bwo] 19,878 (1998 census). Population includes 144 Gamila; 2,276 second-language speakers including 45 Gamila; 18,567 monolinguals including 77 Gamila. Ethnic population: 32,894 including 186 Gamila (1998 census). Southwest Amhara Region, near the Blue Nile River. *Class:* Afro-Asiatic, Omotic, North, Gonga-Gimojan, Gonga, North. *Dialects:* Amuru, Wembera, Gamila, Guba. Related to Kafa. Scattered dialect groups. Lexical similarity 46% with Shekkacho. *Lg Use:* Speakers also use Amharic or Oromo. *Lg Dev:* Literacy rate in second language: 25.1%. *Other:* SOV.

Burji (Bambala, Bembala, Daashi) [bji] 35,731 in Ethiopia (1998 census). 29,259 monolinguals. Population total all countries: 42,731. Ethnic population: 46,565 (1998 census). South of Lake Ciamo. Also spoken in Kenya. *Class:* Afro-Asiatic, Cushitic, East, Highland. *Dialects:* Lexical similarity 41% with Sidamo (closest). *Lg Use:* 3,045 second-language speakers. Many speakers in Ethiopia are older adults. *Lg Dev:* Literacy rate in first language: below 1%. Literacy rate in second language: 29.1%. Dictionary. NT: 1993. *Other:* SOV; passives; middle voice; causatives; subject suffixes distinguish person, number, gender. Christian, Muslim.

Bussa (Dobase, D'oopace, D'opaasunte, Lohu, Mashile, Mashelle, Masholle, Mosiye, Musiye, Gobeze, Gowase, Goraze, Orase) [dox] 6,624 (1998 census). 4,955 monolinguals. Ethnic population: 9,207 (1998 census). Omo Region, west of Lake Chamo. *Class:* Afro-Asiatic, Cushitic, East, Dullay. *Dialects:* There is a dialect chain with Komso-Dirasha-Dobase. Lexical similarity 78% with Gawwada, 51% with Komso, 86% with Gollango, 80% with Harso, 61% with Tsamai. *Lg Use:* 920 second-language speakers. Bilingualism reinforces intelligibility of Komso and Dirasha. *Lg Dev:* Literacy rate in second language: 13.8%. *Other:* SOV. Mountain slope. Deciduous forest. Peasant agriculturalists.

Chara (Ciara) [cra] 6,932. 5,556 monolinguals. Ethnic population: 6,984 (1998 census). Central Kafa Region, just north of the Omo River. *Class:* Afro-Asiatic, Omotic, North, Gonga-Gimojan, Gimojan, Ometo-Gimira, Chara. *Dialects:* Lexical similarity 54% with Wolaytta. *Lg Use:* 668 second-language speakers. All domains. Some also use Wolaytta to the east or Kafa to the west. *Lg Dev:* Literacy rate in second language: 0.8%. *Other:* SOV; noun case suffixes; postpositions. Agriculturalists: small grain. Traditional religion.

Daasanach (Dasenech, Daasanech, Dathanaik, Dathanaic, Dathanik, Gheleba, Geleba, Geleb, Gelebinya, Gallab, Galuba, Gelab, Gelubba, Dama, Marille, Merile, Merille, Morille, Reshiat, Russia, "Shangilla") [dsh] 32,064 in Ethiopia (1998 census). 31,368 monolinguals. Population total all countries: 34,564. Ethnic population: 32,099 (1998 census). Lower Omo River, along Lake Turkana, extending into Kenya. Also spoken in Kenya. *Class:* Afro-Asiatic, Cushitic, East, Western Omo-Tana. *Lg Use:* 231 second-language speakers. *Lg Dev:* Literacy rate in second language: 1.7%. Bible portions: 1997–2000. *Other:* An ethnic group name is 'Reshiat' (Russia). SOV.

Plains. Semiarid, desert. Pastoralists; agriculturalists: sorghum. Traditional religion, Christian.

Dime (Dima) [dim] 6,501 (1998 census). 4,785 monolinguals. Ethnic population: 6,197 (1998 census). Kafa Region, north of the Omo River, just before it turns south. *Class:* Afro-Asiatic, Omotic, South. *Dialects:* Lexical similarity 47% with Banna. *Lg Use:* 529 second-language speakers. Not bilingual in neighboring languages, except possibly Aari. *Lg Dev:* Literacy rate in first language: below 1%. Literacy rate in second language: 9.9%. *Other:* Population has diminished because of disease and war. SOV.

Dirasha (Dhirasha, Diraasha, Dirayta, Gardulla, Ghidole, Gidole) [gdl] 50,328 (1998 census). 41,685 monolinguals. Ethnic population: 54,354 (1998 census). Omo Region, in the hills west of Lake Chamo, around Gidole town. *Class:* Afro-Asiatic, Cushitic, East, Konso-Gidole. *Dialects:* Part of a dialect cluster with Komso and Bussa. Lexical similarity 55% with Komso. *Lg Use:* 1,974 second-language speakers. Many also use Oromo or Komso. *Other:* SOV; verb suffix morphology shows causative, reflexive, subject person, number, gender.

Dizi (Maji, Dizi-Maji, Sizi, Twoyu) [mdx] 21,075 (1998 census). 17,583 monolinguals. Ethnic population: 21,894 (1998 census). Kafa Region, near Maji town. *Class:* Afro-Asiatic, Omotic, North, Dizoid. *Dialects:* Related to Sheko, Nayi. *Lg Use:* 2,054 second-language speakers. *Lg Dev:* Literacy rate in first language: below 1%. Literacy rate in second language: 16.8%. *Other:* SOV; tonal. Traditional religion, Christian.

Dorze [doz] 20,782 (1998 census). 9,905 monolinguals. Ethnic population: 28,990 (1998 census). Mostly in North Omo Region in and around Chencha, but a significant community is in Addis Ababa. *Class:* Afro-Asiatic, Omotic, North, Gonga-Gimojan, Gimojan, Ometo-Gimira, Ometo, Central. *Dialects:* Lexical similarity 82% to 87% with Gamo, 77% to 81% with Gofa, 80% with Wolaytta, 73% to 75% with Kullo, 54% with Koorete, 48% with Male. *Lg Use:* 3,597 second-language speakers. *Lg Dev:* Literacy rate in second language: 56.8%. *Other:* SOV. Weavers.

English [eng] 1,986 in Ethiopia (1998 census). *Lg Use:* Official language. 169,726 second-language users. Language of higher education, many technical fields, and international communication. See main entry under United Kingdom.

Ethiopian Sign Language [eth] *Class:* Deaf sign language. *Lg Use:* There are several sign languages used in different schools for the deaf. Little research. Used since 1971. There have been elementary schools for deaf children since 1956. *Other:* There is a manual alphabet for spelling.

Gafat [gft] Extinct. South Blue Nile area. *Class:* Afro-Asiatic, Semitic, South, Ethiopian, South, Outer, n-Group. *Lg Use:* Members of the ethnic group now speak Amharic. *Lg Dev:* Bible portions: 1945.

Gamo-Gofa-Dawro [gmo] 1,236,637 (1998 census). 1,046,084 monolinguals including 597,130 Gamo, 259,633 Dawro, 189,321 Gofa. Population includes 690,069 Gamo, 313,228 Dawro, 233,340 Gofa. Ethnic population: 1,292,860 (1998 census) including 719,847 Gamo, 331,483 Dawro, 241,530 Gofa (1998 census). Omo Region, in and around Arba Minch, and in the mountains west to Lake Abaya. Dache is a place name, not a language. *Class:* Afro-Asiatic, Omotic, North, Gonga-Gimojan, Gimojan, Ometo-Gimira, Ometo, Central. *Dialects:* Gamo (Gemu), Gofa (Goffa), Dawro (Dauro, Kullo, Cullo, Ometay). Subdialects of Dawro are Konta (Conta) and Kucha (Kusha, Koysha). Gamo has 79% to 91% lexical similarity with Gofa, 79% to 89% with Wolaytta, 82% to 87% with Dorze, 73% to 80% with

Dawro, 49% with Koorete, 44% with Male. Dawro has 76% with Gofa, 80% with Wolaytta, 73% to 75% with Dorze, 48% with Koorete, 43% with Male. *Lg Use:* 77,883 second-language users including 24,438 Gamo, 19,996 Dawro, 33,449 Gofa. *Lg Dev:* Literacy rate in first language: below 1%. Literacy rate in second language: Gamo: 18.2%, Gofa: 18.5%, Dawro: 23.8%. *Other:* The government is developing joint educational materials for these 3 groups. SOV; derived nouns formed by suffixation of verbs; passives; case suffixes; postpositions; tonal, tonal.

Ganza (Ganzo, Koma) [gza] 5,400 (2004). Ethnic population: 6,291 (2000 WCD). Western Oromo, near the Blue Nile. *Class:* Afro-Asiatic, Omotic, North, Mao, West. *Dialects:* Related to Hozo-Sezo (Ruhlen 1987.322). Lexical similarity 14% with Omotic languages, 6% with Mao. *Lg Use:* Oromo-Wellega is the lingua franca of the area, but possibly not for Ganza. *Other:* Different from Gumuz. SOV.

Gawwada (Gauwada, Gawata, Kawwad'a, Kawwada) [gwd] 32,698 (1998 census). 27,477 monolinguals. Ethnic population: 33,971 (1998 census). Omo Region, west of Lake Chamo. *Class:* Afro-Asiatic, Cushitic, East, Dullay. *Dialects:* Dihina (Tihina, Tihinte), Gergere (K'ark'arte), Gobeze, Gollango (Kollanko), Gorose (Gorrose, Korrose), Harso (Worase). Lexical similarity 78% with Bussa, 73% with Tsamai, 77% with Harso, 92% with Gollango, 41% with Komso. Harso has 80% with Dobase, 56% with Tsamai. *Lg Use:* 1,367 second-language speakers. Amharic and Oromo are used as second language. Leaders use Komso. *Lg Dev:* Literacy rate in first language: below 1%. Literacy rate in second language: 22.3%. *Other:* SOV. Mountain slope. Deciduous forest. Peasant agriculturalists.

Gedeo (Geddeo, Deresa, Derasa, Darasa, Derasanya, Darassa) [drs] 637,082 (1998 census). 438,958 monolinguals. Ethnic population: 639,905 (1998 census). Central highland area, southwest of Dilla and east of Lake Abaya. *Class:* Afro-Asiatic, Cushitic, East, Highland. *Dialects:* Lexical similarity 60% with Sidamo (closest), 57% with Alaba, 54% with Kambaata, 51% with Hadiyya. *Lg Use:* 47,950 second-language speakers. *Lg Dev:* Literacy rate in first language: below 1%. Literacy rate in second language: 5.2%. NT: 1986. *Other:* SOV; causative; middle; passive verbs. Traditional religion, Christian, Muslim.

Geez (Ancient Ethiopic, Ethiopic, Ge'ez, Giiz) [gez] Extinct. Also spoken in Eritrea. *Class:* Afro-Asiatic, Semitic, South, Ethiopian, North. *Lg Use:* Official liturgical language of the Ethiopian Orthodox Church. Ancient language of the Aksumites. *Lg Dev:* Grammar. Bible: 1918. *Other:* VSO. Christian.

Gumuz (Bega-Tse, Sigumza, Gumuzinya, Gumis, Gombo, Mendeya, "Shankillinya," "Shankilligna," "Shanqilla," Debatsa, Debuga, Dehenda, Bega) [guk] 120,424 in Ethiopia (1998 census). 88,192 monolinguals. Population total all countries: 160,424. Ethnic population: 121,487 (1998 census). Near Metemma on Sudan border south through Gondar and Gojjam, along Blue Nile and south into Wellaga and Didessa Valley up to Leqemt-Gimbi Road, and villages southwest of Addis Ababa, around Welqite (possibly 1,000). Also spoken in Sudan. *Class:* Nilo-Saharan, Komuz, Gumuz. *Dialects:* Guba, Wenbera, Sirba, Agalo, Yaso, Mandura, Dibate, Metemma. There are noticeable dialect differences, and not all dialects are inherently intelligible. Mandura, Dibate, and Metemma form a distinct dialect cluster. *Lg Use:* 4,379 second-language speakers. Limited comprehension of Oromo. *Lg Dev:* Literacy rate in first language: below 1%. Literacy rate in second language: 6.2%. *Other:* "Shankillinya" is a derogatory name. There are connections between villages for intermarriage and trade. SVO; verb affixes show person, number of subject, first plural inclusive and

exclusive; tonal, 3 tones. Traditional religion, Muslim, Christian.

Hadiyya (Adiya, Adiye, Hadiya, Hadya, Adea, Hadia) [hdy] 923,958 (1998 census). 595,107 monolinguals. Ethnic population: 927,933 (1998 census). Gurage, Kambaata, Hadiyya Region, between the Omo and Billate rivers, in and around Hosaina town. *Class:* Afro-Asiatic, Cushitic, East, Highland. *Dialects:* Leemo, Soro. Lexical similarity 82% with Libido, 56% with Kambaata, 54% with Alaba, 53% with Sidamo. *Lg Use:* 150,889 second-language speakers. Speakers also use Amharic. *Lg Dev:* Literacy rate in first language: below 1%. Literacy rate in second language: 34.4%. NT: 1992. *Other:* SOV; passive, reflexive, causative, middle verbs. Christian, Muslim.

Hamer-Banna (Hamar-Koke, Hammercoche, Amarcocche, Cocche, Beshada, Hamer, Hammer, Hamar, Amer, Amar, Ammar, Banna, Bana, Kara Kerre) [amf] 42,838 (1998 census). 38,354 monolinguals (1998 census). Ethnic population: 42,466 (1998 census). South Omo Region, near the Omo River, and north of Lake Turkana, in the southwest corner, near the Kenya, Uganda, Sudan borders. *Class:* Afro-Asiatic, Omotic, South. *Dialects:* Hamer and Banna are separate ethnic groups who speak virtually the same language. *Lg Use:* 7,120 second-language speakers. *Lg Dev:* Literacy rate in first language: below 1%. Literacy rate in second language: 1.4%. *Other:* SOV. Pastoralists. Traditional religion, Christian.

Harari (Hararri, Adare, Adere, Aderinya, Adarinnya, Gey Sinan) [har] 21,283 (1998 census). 2,351 monolinguals. 20,000 in Addis Ababa, outside Harar city (Hetzron 1997:486). Ethnic population: 21,757 (1998 census). Homeland Eastern, traditionally within the walled city of Harar. Large communities in Addis Ababa, Nazareth, and Dire Dawa. *Class:* Afro-Asiatic, Semitic, South, Ethiopian, South, Transversal, Harari-East Gurage. *Lg Use:* 7,766 second-language speakers. Positive language attitude. *Lg Dev:* Literacy rate in first language: below 1%. Literacy rate in second language: 81.3%. Dictionary. *Other:* SOV. Muslim.

Hozo (Begi-Mao) [hoz] 3,000 (1995 SIL). Western Oromo Region, Begi area, 50 or more villages. *Class:* Afro-Asiatic, Omotic, North, Mao, West. *Dialects:* Related to Bambassi (Bender 1975). *Lg Use:* Western Oromo is the lingua franca of the area, but there are some negative attitudes toward it. Bilingual proficiency in Amharic and Arabic is low. *Lg Dev:* Literacy rate in second language: 5.1%.

Inor (Ennemor) [ior] 280,000. Population includes 50,000 Endegeny. West Gurage Region, Innemor and Endegeny woredas. *Class:* Afro-Asiatic, Semitic, South, Ethiopian, South, Outer, tt-Group. *Dialect:* Enegegny (Enner). Part of a Gurage cluster of languages.

Kachama-Ganjule (Gats'ame, Get'eme, Gatame) [kcx] 4,072 (1998 census). 1,002 monolinguals including 816 Kachama, 186 Ganjule. Population includes 2,682 Kachama,1,390 Ganjule; 419 second-language speakers including 223 Kachama, 196 Ganjule. Ethnic population: 3,886 (1998 census) including 2,740 Kachama, 1,146 Ganjule. Kachama is on Gidicho Island in Lake Abaya. Ganjule originally on a small island in Lake Chamo. Ganjule have recently relocated to Shela-Mela on the west shore of Lake Chamo. *Class:* Afro-Asiatic, Omotic, North, Gonga-Gimojan, Gimojan, Ometo-Gimira, Ometo, East. *Dialects:* Ganjule (Ganjawle), Ganta, Kachama. Lexical similarity 46% with Wolaytta. *Lg Use:* Some also use Wolaytta. *Lg Dev:* Literacy rate in second language: Kachama: 35.2%. *Other:* SOV.

Kacipo-Balesi [koe] 4,120 in Ethiopia (2000 WCD). Southern Ethiopia-Sudan border, Boma Plateau in Sudan (Kacipo). *Dialects:* Balesi (Baale, Bale), Zilmamu

(Silmamo, Zelmamu, Zulmamu, Tsilmano), Kacipo
(Kachepo, Suri, Western Suri). *Lg Use:* Some use Surma
as second language. *Lg Dev:* Literacy rate in first
language: below 1%. Literacy rate in second language:
0.6%. See main entry under Sudan.

Kafa (Kaficho, Kefa, Keffa, Kaffa, Caffino, Manjo) [kbr]
569,626. 445,018 monolinguals (1998 census). Ethnic
population: 599,188 (1998 census). Kafa Region, in and
around the town of Bonga. There may be some in Sudan.
Class: Afro-Asiatic, Omotic, North, Gonga-Gimojan,
Gonga, South. *Dialect:* Kafa, Bosha (Garo). Related to
Shekkacho. Bosha may be a separate language. Manjo is
an argot based on Kafa (Bender 1983). *Lg Use:* 46,720
second-language speakers. *Lg Dev:* Literacy rate in
second language: 22%. NT: 2001. *Other:* SOV.
Agriculturalists. Traditional religion, Christian, Muslim.

Kambaata (Kambatta, Kambata, Kembata, Kemata,
Kambara, Donga) [ktb] 606,241 (1998 census). 345,797
monolinguals including 278,567 Kambaata, 51,541
Timbaro, 15,689 Qebena (1998 census). Population
includes 487,655 Kambaata, 82,803 Timbaro, 35,783
Qebena. Ethnic population: 621,407 (1998 census).
Southwest Gurage, Kambaata, Hadiyya Region. Durame
is the main town. *Class:* Afro-Asiatic, Cushitic, East,
Highland. *Dialects:* Tambaro, Timbaro (Timbara,
Timbaaro), Qebena (Qabena, Kebena, K'abena). Qebena
may be a separate language. Lexical similarity 95% with
Timbaro dialect, 81% with Allaaba, 62% with Sidamo,
57% with Libido, 56% with Hadiyya. *Lg Use:* 83,750
second-language speakers including 68,607 Kambaata,
10,715 Timbaro, 4,428 Qebena. *Lg Dev:* Literacy rate in
first language: below 1%. Literacy rate in second
language: 43.7%. NT: 1992. *Other:* SOV; passive, middle,
causative verbs; subject suffixes distinguish person,
number, gender. Christian, Muslim.

Karo (Kerre, Cherre, Kere) [kxh] 200 (1998 M. Yigezu).
South Omo Region, upstream from the Daasanach,
riverside settlements near the Hamer-Banna. *Class:* Afro-
Asiatic, Omotic, South. *Dialects:* Dialect or closely
related language to Hamer-Banna. Lexical similarity 81%
with Hamer-Banna. *Lg Use:* Many use Nyangatom as
second language. *Lg Dev:* Literacy rate in second
language: 1.5%. *Other:* Different from Kara of Sudan
which is Central Sudanic. They have a service relationship
with the Banna. SOV. Agriculturalists.

Kistane (Soddo, Soddo Gurage, North Gurage) [gru]
254,682 (1998 census). Ethnic population: 363,867 (1998
census) including 4,000 Gogot. Gurage, Kambaata,
Hadiyya Region, just southwest of Addis Ababa. *Class:*
Afro-Asiatic, Semitic, South, Ethiopian, South, Outer, n-
Group. *Dialects:* Soddo (Aymallal, Aymellel, Kestane,
Kistane), Dobi (Dobbi, Gogot, Goggot). Not intelligible
with Silte or West Gurage. Dobi speakers' comprehension
of Soddo is 76%, and Soddo speakers' comprehension of
Dobi is 90%. *Lg Use:* 60,538 second-language speakers.
People along the roads have contact with Amharic; some
men are partially bilingual. People in the interior are not
generally bilingual (B. Denboba 1989). *Lg Dev:* Literacy
rate in second language: 21.5%. *Other:* SOV. Christian.

Komo (Madiin, Koma, South Koma, Central Koma) [xom]
1,500 in Ethiopia (1975 Bender). South and west of
Kwama. *Dialects:* Koma of Begi, Koma of Daga. *Lg Dev:*
Literacy rate in second language: 12.8%. *Other:* Different
from Koma of Cameroon. See main entry under Sudan.

Komso (Konso, Conso, Gato, Af-Kareti, Karate, Kareti)
[kxc] 149,508 (1998 census). 138,696 monolinguals.
Ethnic population: 153,419 (1998 census). South of Lake
Ciamo in the bend of the Sagan River. A few migrants in
Kenya. *Class:* Afro-Asiatic, Cushitic, East, Konso-Gidole.
Dialects: Lexical similarity 51% with Bussa, 41% with
Gawwada, 31% with Tsamai. *Lg Use:* 5,658 second-

language speakers. *Lg Dev:* Literacy rate in first language:
below 1%. Literacy rate in second language: 7.2%. NT:
2002. *Other:* SOV. Mountain slope. Deciduous forest.
Peasant agriculturalists. Traditional religion.

Koorete (Amarro, Amaarro, Badittu, Nuna, Koyra, Koore,
Kwera) [kqy] 103,879. 84,388 monolinguals (1998
census). About 60 Harro families in Harro village on
Gidicho (Gidicció) Island. Ethnic population: 107,595
(1998 census). In the Amaro mountains east of Lake
Abaya, Sidama Region. *Class:* Afro-Asiatic, Omotic,
North, Gonga-Gimojan, Gimojan, Ometo-Gimira, Ometo,
East. *Dialects:* Lexical similarity 54% with Dorze, 53%
with Wolaytta, 52% with Gofa, 49% with Gamo, 48%
with Kullo, 45% with Male. *Lg Use:* 2,371 second-
language speakers. *Lg Dev:* Literacy rate in first language:
below 1%. Literacy rate in second language: 24.1%. Bible
portions: 1999–2001. *Other:* 'Koorete' is their name for
themselves. 'Amaro' is the name of the mountain area
where they live. SOV.

Kunfal (Kunfäl, Kunfel, Kumfel) [xuf] 2,000 (2000 M.
Brenzinger). West of Lake Tana. *Class:* Afro-Asiatic,
Cushitic, Central, Southern. *Dialects:* Related to Awngi.
Lg Use: Most also use Amharic. *Other:* SOV.

Kwama (Takwama, Gwama, Goma, Gogwama, Koma of
Asosa, North Koma, Nokanoka, Afan Mao, Amam, T'wa
Kwama) [kmq] 15,000 (1982 SIL). Along Sudan border in
southern Beni Shangul Region, from south of Asosa to
Gidami, and in Gambela and Bonga. 19 villages, including
one (Yabus) in Sudan. *Class:* Nilo-Saharan, Komuz,
Koman. *Lg Use:* Vigorous. Oromo is their second
language. Arabic has some influence, and speakers have
low to moderate proficiency in it. Amharic has little
influence. *Lg Dev:* Literacy rate in second language:
68.4%. *Other:* Muslim.

Kwegu (Koegu, Kwegi, Bacha, Menja, Nidi) [xwg] 103
(1998 census). 73 monolinguals. Ethnic population: 173
(1998 census). Kuchur village on the western bank of the
Omo River in southwestern Ethiopia. *Class:* Nilo-
Saharan, Eastern Sudanic, Eastern, Surmic, South,
Southeast, Kwegu. *Dialects:* Yidinich (Yidinit, Yidi),
Muguji. The dialects listed may not be inherently
intelligible with Kwegu; it may be a name for several
hunter groups. Lexical similarity 36% with Mursi.
Lg Use: Diminishing among adults. 51 second-language
speakers. The Kwegu use the Bodi dialect of Me'en or
Mursi as second language, depending on the area. *Other:*
They are under the Bodi and Mursi, and looked down on
by them. Mursi and Bodi men may marry Kwegu women.
SVO; postpositions. Hunter-gatherers: hippopotamus, wild
fruit, honey; flood and rain cultivation: maize, durra.

Libido (Maraqo, Marako) [liq] 36,612 (1998 census).
14,623 monolinguals. Ethnic population: 38,096 (1998
census). Hadiyya, Kambaata, Gurage Region, northeast of
Hosaina. *Class:* Afro-Asiatic, Cushitic, East, Highland.
Dialects: Syntactic, morphological, and lexical differences
from Hadiyya. Lexical similarity 82% with Hadiyya, 57%
with Kambaata, 56% with Allaaba, 53% with Sidamo.
Lg Use: 9,208 second-language speakers. *Lg Dev:*
Literacy rate in first language: below 1%. Literacy rate in
second language: 15.7%. *Other:* SOV; passive, reflexive,
causative, middle voice verbs. Muslim.

Majang (Mesengo, Masongo, Masango, Majanjiro, Tama,
Ojanjur, Ajo, Ato Majang, Ato Majanger-Onk) [mpe]
15,341 (1998 census). 10,752 monolinguals. Ethnic
population: 15,341 (1998 census). Southwest. Mainly
within a long, narrow belt between Bure (east of Gambela)
and Guraferda to the south. Covers part of Gambela,
Oromo, and Kafa administrative regions. They have been
scattered, but are now settling in villages. *Class:* Nilo-
Saharan, Eastern Sudanic, Eastern, Surmic, North,
Majang. *Dialects:* Minor dialect variation. *Lg Use:* 438

second-language speakers. *Lg Dev:* Literacy rate in first language: below 1%. Literacy rate in second language: 21.1%. *Other:* The people are called 'Majang' or 'Majangir'. VSO, postpositions; genitives, articles, adjectives, numerals, relatives after noun heads; question words final; suffixes indicate case, passives; causative prefix; reciprocal verb forms; verb affixes mark person, number, subject, object; many syllable patterns; tonal. Mountain slope. Rainforest. Swidden agriculturalists; beekeepers; hunters. Traditional religion, Christian.

Male [mdy] 53,779 (1998 census). 40,660 monolinguals. Ethnic population: 46,458 (1998 census). Omo Region, southeast of Jinka. *Class:* Afro-Asiatic, Omotic, North, Gonga-Gimojan, Gimojan, Ometo-Gimira, Ometo. *Dialects:* Lexical similarity 48% with Dorze, 46% with Gofa, 45% with Kooree, 44% with Gamo, 43% with Wolaytta and Kullo. *Lg Use:* 6,730 second-language speakers. Male is the language of the home. *Lg Dev:* Literacy rate in second language: 4.5%. Interest in Male literature. *Other:* Different from Malo (see Zayse). SOV.

Me'en (Mekan, Mie'en, Mieken, Meqan, Men) [mym] 56,585 (1998 census). 51,446 monolinguals including 4,553 Bodi. Population includes 4,570 Bodi. Ethnic population: 57,501 (1998 census) including 4,686 Bodi. Central Kafa Region, the Tishena in and around Bachuma, the Bodi in lowlands to the south, near the Omo River. Not in Sudan. *Class:* Nilo-Saharan, Eastern Sudanic, Eastern, Surmic, South, Southeast, Pastoral, Me'en. *Dialects:* Bodi (Podi), Tishena (Teshina, Teshenna). Tishena is inherently intelligible with Bodi. Close to Mursi. Lexical similarity 65% with Surma, 30% with Murle. *Lg Use:* 6,300 second-language speakers including 342 Bodi. *Lg Dev:* Literacy rate in first language: below 1%. Literacy rate in second language: 3.3%. The number of literates is increasing. *Other:* Geographical names: Bachuma, Bachuman, Golda, Goldea, Goldiya, Guldiya. SVO; postpositions; genitives, adjective, articles, and relatives follow noun heads; question word final; prefixes and suffixes; verbs inflected; tonal. Highland, lowland. Tishena, Me'en: agriculturalists; Bodi (nomadic): pastoralists: cattle. Traditional religion, Christian.

Melo (Malo) [mfx] 20,151 (1998 census). 13,264 monolinguals. Ethnic population: 20,189 (1998 census). North Omo Region, in and around Malo-Koza, northeast of the Basketo. *Class:* Afro-Asiatic, Omotic, North, Gonga-Gimojan, Gimojan, Ometo-Gimira, Ometo, Central. *Dialects:* Related to Gamo-Gofa-Dawro, but may not be inherently intelligible. The Language Academy said it should be considered a separate speech variety. Lexical similarity 70% with the majority of Ometo language varieties. *Lg Use:* 4,657 second-language speakers. *Lg Dev:* Literacy rate in second language: 9.5%.

Mesmes [mys] Extinct. Gurage, Hadiyya, Kambatta Region. *Class:* Afro-Asiatic, Semitic, South, Ethiopian, South, Outer, tt-Group. *Dialects:* Related to West Gurage. *Other:* SOV.

Mesqan (Masqan, Meskan) [mvz] 25,000 (2002). West Gurage Region, Mareqo woreda, principle villages: Mikayelo, Mesqan, and Hudat. *Class:* Afro-Asiatic, Semitic, South, Ethiopian, South, Outer, tt-Group.

Murle (Murele, Merule, Mourle, Murule, Beir, Ajibba) [mur] 200 in Ethiopia (1975 Tournay). South of the Akobo River. Olam is in southwest Ethiopia and on the Sudan border. It is between Murle and Majang culturally and linguistically (Bender 1983). *Dialect:* Olam (Ngalam, Bangalam). *Lg Use:* They speak Nyangatom as second language. *Other:* There is a lot of intermarriage with the Nyangatom. Pastoralists; agriculturalists. Traditional religion. See main entry under Sudan.

Mursi (Murzi, Murzu, Merdu, Meritu, Dama) [muz] 3,278 (1998 census). 3,155 monolinguals. Ethnic population:

3,258 (1998 census). Central Omo Region, lowlands southwest of Jinka. *Class:* Nilo-Saharan, Eastern Sudanic, Eastern, Surmic, South, Southeast, Pastoral, Suri. *Dialects:* Close to Suri of Sudan. *Lg Use:* 34 second-language speakers. *Lg Dev:* Literacy rate in first language: below 1%. Literacy rate in second language: 1.2%. *Other:* SVO; postpositions; tonal; case suffixes; verb affixes show subject person and number; question words final. Pastoralists. Traditional religion.

Nayi (Na'o, Nao) [noz] 3,656 (1998 census). 1,137 monolinguals. Ethnic population: 4,005 (1998 census). Decha Awraja, Kafa Region, and scattered in other parts of Kafa. The nearest town is Bonga. A few in Dulkuma village of the Shoa Bench Wereda, and Aybera, Kosa, and Jomdos villages of Sheko Wereda. *Class:* Afro-Asiatic, Omotic, North, Dizoid. *Dialects:* Related to Dizi, Sheko. Lexical similarity 58% with Dizi. *Lg Use:* 1,876 second-language speakers. Speakers are adults. Young people speak only Kafa. Kafa is the trade language. *Lg Dev:* Literacy rate in second language: 6.5%. *Other:* SOV. Agriculturalists.

Nuer (Naath) [nus] 64,907 in Ethiopia (1998 census). 61,640 monolinguals. Ethnic population: 64,534 (1998 census). Along the Baro River, in Gambela Region. *Dialect:* Eastern Nuer (Ji, Kany, Jikany, Door, Abigar). *Lg Use:* 1,122 second-language speakers. Speakers also use Arabic. *Lg Dev:* Literacy rate in second language: 7.9%. *Other:* 'Naath' is their name for themselves. Severe disruption in residence patterns caused by fighting in Ethiopia and Sudan. Many are refugees or homeless (1991). Traditional religion. See main entry under Sudan.

Nyangatom (Inyangatom, Donyiro, Dongiro, Idongiro) [nnj] 14,177 (1998 census). 13,797 monolinguals. Ethnic population: 14,201 (1998 census). Extreme southwest corner of Ethiopia, Omo Region. Two settlement centers: Omo River and Kibish River. Transhumance into the region of Moru Angipi in Sudan. *Class:* Nilo-Saharan, Eastern Sudanic, Nilotic, Eastern, Lotuxo-Teso, Teso-Turkana, Turkana. *Dialects:* Inherently intelligible with Toposa and Turkana. *Lg Use:* 123 second-language speakers. Ethnic identity attitudes are strong. Mutual nonagression pact with the Toposa. Occasionally unfriendly with the Turkana and Sudan Jiye. *Lg Dev:* Literacy rate in second language: 1.9%. *Other:* Seminomadic. VSO; highly inflectional, grammatical tone (tense, case); vowel harmony; voiceless vowels. Pastoralists: cattle herders; agriculturalists: sorghum, beans. Traditional religion.

Opuuo (Opo-Shita, Opo, Opuo, Cita, Ciita, Shita, Shiita, Ansita, Kina, Kwina, "Langa") [lgn] 301 in Ethiopia. 235 monolinguals. Ethnic population: 307 (1998 census). 5 villages along the Sudan border north of the Anuak and Nuer. Also spoken in Sudan. *Class:* Nilo-Saharan, Komuz, Koman. *Dialects:* Lexical similarity 24% with Koma. *Lg Use:* West-Central Oromo is the lingua franca of the area. *Lg Dev:* Literacy rate in second language: 35.9%. *Other:* "Langa" is a derogatory name used by the Anuak for them.

Oromo, Borana-Arsi-Guji (Afan Oromo, Southern Oromo, "Galla," "Gallinya," "Galligna") [gax] 3,634,000 in Ethiopia. Population total all countries: 3,827,616. South Oromo Region. Also spoken in Kenya, Somalia. *Class:* Afro-Asiatic, Cushitic, East, Oromo. *Dialects:* Borana (Boran, Borena), Arsi (Arussi, Arusi), Guji (Gujji, Jemjem), Kereyu, Salale (Selale), Gabra (Gabbra, Gebra). Harar is closely related, but distinct enough to need separate literature. In Kenya, Gabra and Sakuye may have significant dialect and language attitude differences from the Boran dialect. *Lg Use:* Oromo is viewed as one people speaking one language. *Lg Dev:* Literacy rate in first language: below 1%. Literacy rate in second language: 16%. Bible: 1995. *Other:* Called 'Borana' in Kenya. The name "Galla" is derogatory. SOV. Muslim, traditional religion.

Oromo, Eastern ("Qotu" Oromo, Harar, Harer, "Qottu," "Quottu," "Qwottu," "Kwottu," Ittu) [hae] 4,526,000 (1998 census). Eastern and western Hararghe zone in northern Bale zone. *Class:* Afro-Asiatic, Cushitic, East, Oromo. *Dialects:* Close to Borana Oromo, but divergent. *Lg Use:* The Oromo view themselves as one people speaking one language. Speakers also use Amharic. *Lg Dev:* Literacy rate in second language: 15%. *Other:* SOV. Muslim.

Oromo, West Central (Afan Oromo, Oromiffa, Oromoo, "Galla") [gaz] 8,920,000 in Ethiopia (1998 census). Ethnic population: All ethnic Oromo are 30,000,000 in Ethiopia. Oromo Region, West and Central Ethiopia, and along the Rift Valley escarpment east of Dessie and Woldiya. Also spoken in Egypt. *Class:* Afro-Asiatic, Cushitic, East, Oromo. *Dialects:* Western Oromo, Central Oromo. Subdialects are Mecha (Maccha, Wellaga, Wallaga, Wollega), Raya, Wello (Wollo), Tulema (Tulama, Shoa, Shewa). Harar and Boran are different enough to need separate literature. *Lg Use:* Trade language. Used by regional and national government, public media, national commerce, education to eighth grade, variety of literature. The Oromo are viewed as one people speaking one language. *Lg Dev:* Literacy rate in first language: 1% to 5%. Literacy rate in second language: 22.4%. Roman script. Newspapers. Radio programs. TV. Dictionary. Grammar. Bible: 1899–1998. *Other:* SOV. Agriculturalists: variety of crops, spices, coffee; animal husbandry; miners; tourism; textiles; meat packing; refineries. Traditional religion (Waaqqefata), Christian, Muslim.

Oyda [oyd] 16,597 (1998 census). 6,244 monolinguals. Ethnic population: 14,075 (1998 census). Northwest Omo Region, southwest of Sawla. *Class:* Afro-Asiatic, Omotic, North, Gonga-Gimojan, Gimojan, Ometo-Gimira, Ometo, Central. *Dialects:* Lexical similarity 69% with Wolaytta, 61% with Basketo. *Lg Use:* 4,040 second-language speakers. Some also use Wolaytta. *Lg Dev:* Literacy rate in second language: 18.7%. *Other:* SOV.

Qimant (Kimanteney, Western Agaw) [ahg] 1,650 in Ethiopia (1998 census). Ethnic population: 172,327 (1998 census). Northwest Amhara Region, north of Lake Tana. Communities of Qwara or Kayla are near Addis Ababa and in Eritrea. None in Sudan. Also spoken in Eritrea. *Class:* Afro-Asiatic, Cushitic, Central, Western. *Dialects:* Qimant (Kemant, Kimant, Kemanat, Kamant, Chemant, Qemant), Dembiya (Dembya, Dambya), Hwarasa (Qwara, Qwarina, "Kara"), Kayla, Semyen, Achpar, Kwolasa (Kwolacha). Distinct from Awngi, Bilen, and Xamtanga. *Lg Use:* 3,181 second-language speakers. Qwara dialect is extinct. 170,747 ethnic Western Agaw are monolingual in Amharic in Ethiopia. It is reported that all Qimant also use Amharic. Ge'ez is used as liturgical language, but many use a few Hebrew words in prayer. *Lg Dev:* Literacy rate in second language: 14.7%. Bible portions: 1885. *Other:* Kayla or Qwara people are called 'Falashi', the so-called 'Black Jews'. 2,321 Falashas in Ethiopia. Most of the remaining Falasha went to Israel in 1999. No evidence of a distinct Jewish language. 'Kara' is an incorrect spelling. SOV. Christian (Qimant), Jewish (Kayla).

Rer Bare (Rerebere, Adona) [rer] Extinct. Wabi Shebelle River around Gode, eastern Ogaden, near Somali border, and along the Ganale and Dawa rivers. *Class:* Unclassified. *Lg Use:* Members of the ethnic group now speak Somali. *Other:* They are called 'Rer Bare' in Somali, which means 'tribe Bare'.

Saho (Sao, Shaho, Shoho, Shiho) [ssy] 22,759 in Ethiopia (1998 census). Tigray. *Dialect:* Irob. *Lg Use:* 3,378

second-language speakers. They do not accept outsiders. *Lg Dev:* Literacy rate in second language: High. *Other:* Ethnic group names are Asa'orta, Hadu (Hazu), Miniferi. They have suffered from recent famines. The Irob are not nomadic. Christian. See main entry under Eritrea.

Sebat Bet Gurage (Central West Gurage, West Gurage, Guragie, Gouraghie, Gurague) [sgw] 440,000. Population includes Chaha 130,000, Gura 20,000, Muher 90,000, Gyeto 80,000, Ezha 120,000. West Gurage Region, Chaha is spoken in and around Emdibir, Gura is spoken in and around Gura Megenase and Wirir, Muher is spoken in and around Ch'eza and in the mountains north of Chaha and Ezha, Gyeto is spoken south of Ark'it' in K'abul and K'want'e, Ezha is spoken in Agenna. *Class:* Afro-Asiatic, Semitic, South, Ethiopian, South, Outer, tt-Group. *Dialects:* Chaha (Cheha), Ezha (Eza, Izha), Gumer (Gwemarra), Gura, Gyeto, Muher. A member of the Gurage cluster of languages. *Lg Dev:* Literacy rate in first language: below 1%. Literacy rate in second language: 25.3%. NT: 1983. *Other:* SOV.

Seze (Sezo) [sze] 3,000 (1995 SIL). Western Oromo Region, near Begi, north of the Hozo. *Class:* Afro-Asiatic, Omotic, North, Mao, West. *Dialects:* Related to Bambassi (Bender 1975). *Lg Use:* Oromo-Wellega is the lingua franca of the area, but there are some negative attitudes toward it. Bilingual proficiency in Amharic and Arabic is low. *Lg Dev:* Literacy rate in second language: 5%.

Shabo (Shako, "Mekeyer," "Mikeyir," "Mikair") [sbf] 400 to 500 (2000 M. Brenzinger). Ethnic population: 600 or more (2000). Kafa Region, between Godere and Mashi, among the Majang and Shekkacho. *Class:* Nilo-Saharan, Unclassified. *Dialects:* Apparently a hybrid. Distinct from Sheko. Lexical similarity 30% with Majang, 12% with other West Cushitic (Omotic) languages. *Lg Use:* Most domains. About half the children learn Shabo. Speakers also use Majang or Shekkacho. *Other:* They do not like the name "Mekeyer" used by outsiders. They live in family units, not villages. SOV; postpositions; gender in all 3 persons. Hunter-gatherers; beekeepers. Traditional religion, Christian.

Shekkacho (Mocha, Shakacho, Shekka) [moy] 54,894 (1998 census). 36,449 monolinguals. Ethnic population: 53,897 (1998 census). North Kafa Region, in and around Maasha. *Class:* Afro-Asiatic, Omotic, North, Gonga-Gimojan, Gonga, South. *Dialects:* Close to Kafa. *Lg Use:* 3,476 second-language speakers. *Lg Dev:* Literacy rate in first language: below 1%. Literacy rate in second language: 38.9%. *Other:* 'Shekkacho' is their self name. SOV; tonal. Traditional religion, Christian.

Sheko (Shekko, Shekka, Tschako, Shako, Shak) [she] 23,785. 13,611 monolinguals (1998 census). Ethnic population: 23,785 (1998 census). Kafa Region, Shako District. Gaizek'a is a monolingual community. Bajek'a, Selale, and Shimi are multilingual. *Class:* Afro-Asiatic, Omotic, North, Dizoid. *Dialect:* Dorsha, Bulla (Daan, Dan, Daanyir). *Lg Use:* 4,920 second-language speakers. Used in the home, religion, and community. Some bilingualism in Amharic and Bench. *Lg Dev:* Literacy rate in first language: below 1%. Literacy rate in second language: 16.3%. *Other:* SOV; postpositions; genitives, articles, adjectives, numerals, relatives after noun heads; question word initial; 1 prefix, 5 suffixes; word order distinguishes subjects, objects, indirect objects; affixes indicate case of noun phrases; verb affixes mark person, number, gender of subject; passives, causatives, comparatives; CV, CVC, CVV, CV:C, CVCC; tonal, 3 tones. Agriculturalists. Traditional religion, Christian.

Sidamo (Sidámo 'Afó, Sidaminya) [sid] 1,876,329 (1998 census). 1,632,902 monolinguals. Ethnic population: 1,842,314 (1998 census). South central Ethiopia, northeast of Lake Abaya and southeast of Lake Awasa (Sidamo Awraja). Awasa is the capital of the Sidama Region. _Class:_ Afro-Asiatic, Cushitic, East, Highland. _Dialects:_ Lexical similarity 64% with Allaaba, 62% with Kambaata, 53% with Hadiyya. _Lg Use:_ 101,340 second-language speakers. _Lg Dev:_ Literacy rate in first language: 1% to 5%. Literacy rate in second language: 20.3%. Dictionary. Grammar. NT: 1990. _Other:_ SOV.

Silt'e (East Gurage, Selti, Silti) [xst] 827,764 (1998 census). Ethnic population: 900,348 (1998 census). About 150 km south of Addis Ababa. _Class:_ Afro-Asiatic, Semitic, South, Ethiopian, South, Transversal, Harari-East Gurage. _Dialects:_ Enneqor (Inneqor), Ulbarag (Urbareg), Wolane (Walane). Not intelligible with West or North Gurage. 40% or less intelligible with Chaha (Central West Gurage). _Lg Use:_ 89,042 second-language speakers. _Lg Dev:_ Literacy rate in first language: below 1%. Literacy rate in second language: 16.6%. Dictionary. Bible portions: 1981. _Other:_ SOV; prepositions and postpositions; genitives, adjectives, numerals, relatives before noun heads; articles after noun heads; passives; causatives; CV, CVC; nontonal.

Somali (Standard Somali, Common Somali) [som] 3,334,113 in Ethiopia (2000 WCD). 2,878,371 monolinguals. Southeast Ethiopia, Somali Region. _Lg Use:_ 95,572 second-language speakers. 10% use Amharic or Arabic as second language. _Lg Dev:_ Literacy rate in second language: 7.3%. _Other:_ Daarood, Ogaadeen, Dir, Gadabuursi, Hawiye, and Isxaaq are major clan families in Ethiopia. Agriculturalists. Muslim, Christian. See main entry under Somalia.

Suri (Surma, Shuri, Churi, Dhuri, Shuro, Eastern Suri) [suq] 19,622 in Ethiopia (1998 census). 19,269 monolinguals. Population total all countries: 20,622. Ethnic population: 19,632 (1998 census). Southwestern Kafa Region toward the Sudan border. Some are west of Mizan Teferi. Also spoken in Sudan. _Class:_ Nilo-Saharan, Eastern Sudanic, Eastern, Surmic, South, Southeast, Pastoral, Suri. _Dialects:_ Tirma (Tirima, Terema, Terna, Dirma, Cirma, Tirmaga, Tirmagi, Tid), Chai (Cai, Caci). Lexical similarity 81% with Mursi. _Lg Use:_ 212 second-language speakers. _Lg Dev:_ Literacy rate in first language: below 1%. Literacy rate in second language: 0.6%. Dictionary. _Other:_ Names of ethnic groups: Dama, Dhuak. SVO. Mountain valley. Savannah, scrub forest. 800 to 1,800 meters. Transhumant pastoralists; swidden agriculturalists. Traditional religion.

Tigrigna (Tigrinya, Tigray) [tir] 3,224,875 in Ethiopia (1998 census). 2,819,755 monolinguals. Population total all countries: 4,449,875. Ethnic population: 3,284,568 (1998 census). Tigray Province. Also spoken in Eritrea, Germany, Israel. _Class:_ Afro-Asiatic, Semitic, South, Ethiopian, North. _Lg Use:_ National language. 146,933 second-language speakers. _Lg Dev:_ Literacy rate in first language: 1% to 10%. Literacy rate in second language: 26.5%. Ethiopic script. Radio programs. Grammar. Bible: 1956. _Other:_ Speakers are called 'Tigrai'. Christian.

Tsamai (Ts'amay, S'amai, Tamaha, Tsamako, Tsamakko, Bago S'aamakk-Ulo, Kuile, Kule, Cule) [tsb] 8,621 (1998 census). 5,298 monolinguals. Ethnic population: 9,702 (1998 census). Omo Region, lowlands west of Lake Chamo. _Class:_ Afro-Asiatic, Cushitic, East, Dullay. _Dialects:_ The Tsamai say Gawwada is difficult to understand. Possibly related to Birale. The most aberrant Dullay variety. Lexical similarity 56% to 73% with Gawwada dialects, 61% with Bussa, 31% with Komso. _Lg Use:_ 1,200 second-language speakers. They use Komso for trade. _Lg Dev:_ Literacy rate in first language: below 1%. Literacy rate in second language: 2.8%. _Other:_ SOV. Mountain slope. Deciduous forest. Peasant agriculturalists.

Turkana [tuv] 25,163 in Ethiopia (2000 WCD). Southwestern region west of the Omo River. _Other:_ Seminomadic. Plains. Semiarid desert. 350 to 2,000 meters. Pastoralists: cattle, sheep, goats, camels, donkeys; fishermen. Traditional religion, Christian. See main entry under Kenya.

Uduk (Twampa, Kwanim Pa, Burun, Kebeirka, Othan, Korara, Kumus) [udu] 20,000 in Ethiopia (1995 W. James). Large refugee camp at Bonga, near Gambela town, Gambela Region. Some still in Sudan (1995). Also spoken in Sudan. _Class:_ Nilo-Saharan, Komuz, Koman. _Lg Dev:_ NT: 1963. _Other:_ Most have come from Sudan. SVO. Traditional religion, Christian.

Weyto (Wayto, Weyt'o) [woy] Extinct. Ethnic population: 1,631 of whom 1,519 (93%) speak Amharic as first language, others speak other first languages. Lake Tana Region. _Class:_ Unclassified. _Dialects:_ The former language was possibly Eastern Sudanic or an Awngi variety (Bender 1983), or Cushitic (Bender, Bowen, Cooper, and Ferguson 1976:14). _Lg Dev:_ Literacy rate in second language: 16.2%. _Other:_ Hunters: hippopotamus.

Wolaytta (Wellamo, Welamo, Wollamo, Wallamo, Walamo, Ualamo, Uollamo, Wolaitta, Wolaita, Wolayta, Wolataita, Borodda, Uba, Ometo) [wal] 1,231,673 (1998 census). 999,694 monolinguals. Ethnic population: 1,269,216 (1998 census). Wolaytta Region, Lake Abaya area. _Class:_ Afro-Asiatic, Omotic, North, Gonga-Gimojan, Gimojan, Ometo-Gimira, Ometo, Central. _Dialect:_ Zala. Dorze, Melo, Oyda may be dialects of Wolaytta or of Gamo-Gofa-Dawro. Lexical similarity 79% to 93% with Gamo, 84% with Gofa, 80% with Kullo and Dorze, 48% with Koorete, 43% with Male. _Lg Use:_ 89,801 second-language speakers. _Lg Dev:_ Literacy rate in first language: 1% to 5%. Literacy rate in second language: 29.6%. NT: 1981. _Other:_ Geographic names: Balta, Borodda, Ganta, Otschollo, Uba. SOV. Traditional religion, Christian.

Xamtanga (Khamtanga, Simt'anga, Agawinya, Xamta, Xamir) [xan] 143,369 (1998 census). 93,889 monolinguals. Ethnic population: 158,231 (1998 census). North Amhara Region, Avergele District and Lasta and Waag zones, 100 km north of Weldiya. _Class:_ Afro-Asiatic, Cushitic, Central, Eastern. _Dialects:_ Low inherent intelligibility of Qemant. Lexical similarity 45% with Qemant. _Lg Use:_ A few Xamir do not speak Xamtanga, but most do, and have a strong desire to have literature. There is an association of Xamtanga speakers in Weldiya. 11,026 second-language speakers. The monolinguals are older people or women. Others also use Amharic. _Lg Dev:_ Literacy rate in second language: 6.5%. _Other:_ Surrounded by Amharic and Tigrigna speakers. A different language from Awngi, also sometimes called 'Agaw'. The people are called 'Xamir'. SOV. 2,000 to 3,000 meters. Agriculturalists: wheat, sorghum. Christian.

Yemsa (Yem, Yemma, "Janjero," "Janjerinya," "Janjor," "Yangaro," "Zinjero") [jnj] 81,613 (1998 census). Ethnic population: 165,184 (1998 census). Oromo Region, recognized as separate district, northeast of Jimma, southwestern Ethiopia, Fofa, and mixed with the Oromo in their villages; Sokoru, Saja, Deedoo, Sak'a, Jimma. _Class:_ Afro-Asiatic, Omotic, North, Gonga-Gimojan, Gimojan, Janjero. _Dialects:_ Fuga of Jimma, Toba. Fuga of Jimma may be a separate language. Lexical similarity 24% with Mocha language. _Lg Use:_ 4,356 second-language speakers. Some negative attitudes toward Oromo. Speakers want literature in their language. Young people also use Amharic, older adults use Oromo. _Lg Dev:_ Literacy rate in second language: 24.2%. _Other:_ 'Yemma' is the name for the ethnic group, 'Yemsa' for the language. "Janjero" is derogatory. SOV; tonal. Traditional religion, Christian.

Zay (Zway, Lak'i, Laqi, Gelilla) [zwa] 4,880 (1994 SIL). Ethnic population: 4,880. Shores of Lake Zway and eastern islands in Lake Zway. *Class:* Afro-Asiatic, Semitic, South, Ethiopian, South, Transversal, Harari-East Gurage. *Dialects:* No dialect variations. Lexical similarity 61% with Harari, 70% with Silte (M. L. Bender 1971). *Lg Use:* Speakers also used Oromo or Amharic. *Other:* 'Zway' refers to the lake and town, 'Zay' to the people and language. 'Lak'i' ('Laqi') is the Oromo name for the people. Agriculturalists; fishermen.

Zayse-Zergulla (Zaysse) [zay] 17,800 (1998 census). 7,530 monolinguals including 7,371 Zayse, 159 Zergulla. Population includes 10,172 Zayse, 7,625 Zergulla. Ethnic population: 11,232 (1998 census) including 10,842 Zayse, 390 Zergulla. Omo Region, west of Lake Chamo. *Class:* Afro-Asiatic, Omotic, North, Gonga-Gimojan, Gimojan, Ometo-Gimira, Ometo, East. *Dialects:* Zergulla (Zergullinya), Zayse. Close to the Gidicho dialect of Kooreete. *Lg Use:* Vigorous. Approximately 7,000 ethnic Gamo speak Zergulla as first language, which is reflected in the population figure. *Lg Dev:* Literacy rate in second language: 32.5%. *Other:* The culture is vigorous. SOV.

Gabon

Gabonese Republic. République Gabonaise. 1,355,246. National or official language: French. Literacy rate: 70% to 77%. Also includes people from Lebanon (1,000), from Cameroon, Equatorial Guinea, and West Africa 12% of the population. Information mainly from A. Jacquot 1978; J. Bendor-Samuel 1989. Blind population: 1,300 (1982 WCE). The number of languages listed for Gabon is 41. Of those, all are living languages. See map on page 700.

Baka (Babinga) [bkc] 3,200 in Gabon (1990 CMA). Cameroon border area. *Other:* 'Babinga' is used for the Baka, Aka, and Gieli; separate Pygmy languages; it means 'Pygmy'. The name 'Aka' may not be used in Gabon. Dispersed in small groups. Nomadic. Tropical forest. Hunter-gatherers; fishermen. Traditional religion. See main entry under Cameroon.

Barama (Gibarama, Ghibarama, Bavarama, Yibarambu) [bbg] 6,000 (1990 CMA). Ogooue Maritime Province, east of Omboue. Nyanga Province, west of Moabi. *Class:* Niger-Congo, Atlantic-Congo, Volta-Congo, Benue-Congo, Bantoid, Southern, Narrow Bantu, Northwest, B, Sira (B.40). *Other:* The people are called 'Yibarambu'. Traditional religion.

Bekwil (Bekwel, Bekwie, Bakwele, Bakwil) [bkw] 2,460 in Gabon (2000 WCD). Extreme northeast corner, Ogooue Ivindo Province, northeast of Mekambo. *Other:* Different from Bakwiri (Mokpwe) of Cameroon. Forest. Traditional religion, Christian. See main entry under Congo.

Benga [bng] North of Libreville. *Lg Use:* All speakers are older adults. *Other:* Spoken by small groups. See main entry under Equatorial Guinea.

Bubi (Bhubhi, Ibubi, Ibhubhi, Pove, Eviia) [buw] 5,000 (1990 CMA). Ogooue-Lolo Province, west of Koulamoutou, between M'Bigou and N'djoli. *Class:* Niger-Congo, Atlantic-Congo, Volta-Congo, Benue-Congo, Bantoid, Southern, Narrow Bantu, Northwest, B, Tsogo (B.30). *Lg Use:* Speakers are reported to understand Getsogo. *Other:* They are called 'Bapove'. Distinct from the Bubi dialect of Kele, and from Bube of Equatorial Guinea. Traditional religion.

Bwisi (Ibwisi, Mbwisi) [bwz] 1,230 in Gabon (2000 WCD). Far south, Nyanga Province, Ndende area on the border with Congo. *Other:* Different from Talinga-Bwisi of Democratic Republic of the Congo and Uganda. See main entry under Congo.

Duma (Liduma, Aduma, Douma, Adouma, Badouma) [dma] 9,841 (2000 WCD). Upper Ogooue Province, Franceville area near Lastourville. *Class:* Niger-Congo, Atlantic-Congo, Volta-Congo, Benue-Congo, Bantoid, Southern, Narrow Bantu, Northwest, B, Njebi (B.50). *Other:* They can understand Njebi.

Fang (Pamue, Pahouin) [fan] 61,504 in Gabon (2000 WCD). Northwest, Estuary and Woleu-Ntem provinces. *Dialects:* Make, Ntum, Ogowe. See main entry under Equatorial Guinea.

French [fra] 37,500 in Gabon (1993 Johnstone). *Lg Use:* Official language. *Other:* The only language of formal education. See main entry under France.

Kande (Kanda, Okande) [kbs] 1,000 (1990 CMA). Ogooue-Ivindo Province, west of Booue. *Class:* Niger-Congo, Atlantic-Congo, Volta-Congo, Benue-Congo, Bantoid, Southern, Narrow Bantu, Northwest, B, Tsogo (B.30). *Other:* The people are called 'Okande'. They are threatened and undocumented linguistically (2000 B. Connell). Traditional religion.

Kaningi (Lekaningi, Bakanike) [kzo] 6,000 (1990 CMA). Upper Ogooue Province, south of Franceville. *Class:* Niger-Congo, Atlantic-Congo, Volta-Congo, Benue-Congo, Bantoid, Southern, Narrow Bantu, Northwest, B, Mbere (B.60). *Other:* Traditional religion.

Kélé (Akele, Dikele, Western Kele) [keb] 9,226 (2000 WCD). Scattered groups in or near Middle Ogooue Province, around Mimongo. *Class:* Niger-Congo, Atlantic-Congo, Volta-Congo, Benue-Congo, Bantoid, Southern, Narrow Bantu, Northwest, B, Kele (B.20). *Dialects:* Bubi, Western Kele. Close to Ngom. Also related to Kota, Mahongwe, Mbangwe, Ndasa, Sake, Seki, Sighu, Wumbvu. *Lg Dev:* Bible portions: 1855–1879. *Other:* Not the same as Lokele of Democratic Republic of the Congo. They interact with the Tsogo and the Sangu around Mimongo. Traditional religion.

Kota (Ikota, Ikuta, Kotu) [koq] 34,442 in Gabon (2000 WCD). Population total all countries: 43,497. A large area in Ogooue-Iwindo Province. Also spoken in Congo. *Class:* Niger-Congo, Atlantic-Congo, Volta-Congo, Benue-Congo, Bantoid, Southern, Narrow Bantu, Northwest, B, Kele (B.20). *Dialects:* Many dialects. *Lg Dev:* Bible portions: 1938–1948. *Other:* Traditional religion.

Lumbu (Ilumbu, Baloumbou) [lup] 19,681 in Gabon (2000 WCD). Population total all countries: 22,699. Nyanga Province, between the Nyanga and Bangua rivers, on the southwest coast, and the Congo border. Also spoken in Congo. *Class:* Niger-Congo, Atlantic-Congo, Volta-Congo, Benue-Congo, Bantoid, Southern, Narrow Bantu, Northwest, B, Sira (B.40). *Lg Dev:* Bible portions: 1933–1966. *Other:* Some intermarriage with Vili women. Coastal. Fishermen; hunters. Traditional religion.

Mahongwe [mhb] 1,000 (2000 B. Connell). Northeast corner, Mekambo area. *Class:* Niger-Congo, Atlantic-Congo, Volta-Congo, Benue-Congo, Bantoid, Southern, Narrow Bantu, Northwest, B, Kele (B.20). *Lg Use:* Reported to be threatened and undocumented linguistically (2000 Connell).

Mbama (Lembaamba, Gimbaama, Bambaama, Mbamba, Mbaama, Obamba, Bakota) [mbm] Upper Ogooue Province, south of Okondja. *Other:* Intermarriage with the Sake. Traditional religion. See main entry under Congo (Ombamba).

Mbangwe (Mbahouin, M'bahouin) [zmn] 3,690 in Gabon (2000 WCD). Population total all countries: 5,199. Upper Ogooue Province, south and west of Franceville. Also spoken in Congo. *Class:* Niger-Congo, Atlantic-Congo, Volta-Congo, Benue-Congo, Bantoid, Southern, Narrow Bantu, Northwest, B, Kele (B.20). *Other:* Traditional religion.

Mbere (Mbédé, Limbede, Mbété, Ambede) [mdt] 45,513 in Gabon (2000 WCD). All Mbere languages in Gabon: 110,000 (1993 Johnstone). Upper Ogooue Province, Okondja area. *Dialect:* Ngwii. *Other:* The people are called 'Ambede'. Traditional religion. See main entry under Congo.

Myene (Omyene, Pangwe) [mye] 46,743 (2000 WCD). Population includes 1,000 to 2,000 Dyumba, 1,000 to 5,000 Enenga, 2,000 to 11,000 Galwa, 1,000 to 4,000 Mpongwe, 10,000 Orungu, 20,000 Nkomi. Mainly in Ogooue-Maritime and Middle Ogooue provinces, from Lambarene area to coast. Mpongwe dialect is spoken on both sides of the Gabon Estuary, south of Libreville, Port Gentil area. Ajumba is north of Lambarene, Enenga northeast of Lambarene, Galwa in the Lambarene area and westward, Nkomi is on the coast, southeast of Port Gentil. *Class:* Niger-Congo, Atlantic-Congo, Volta-Congo, Benue-Congo, Bantoid, Southern, Narrow Bantu, Northwest, B, Myene (B.10). *Dialects:* Ajumba (Dyumba, Adyumba, Adjumba), Enenga, Galwa (Galoa, Galua, Galloa, Omyene), Mpongwe (Mpungwe, Npongwe, Pongoué, Mpongoué, Npongué), Nkomi (N'komi), Orungu (Rongo, Rungu). A dialect cluster. *Lg Use:* Reported to have been partly submerged by the Fang. *Lg Dev:* Bible: 1927. *Other:* Nkomi: fishermen; oil field workers.

Ndasa (Andasa, Ndash, Ndassa) [nda] 2,460 in Gabon (2000 WCD). Upper Ogooue Province, south of Franceville. *Other:* The people are called 'Bandasa'. Traditional religion. See main entry under Congo.

Ndumu (Minduumo, Mindoumou, Lendumu, Ndumbu, Nduumo, Ndumbo, Ondoumbo, Ondumbo, Mindumbu, Doumbou, Dumbu, Bandoumou) [nmd] 4,305 (2000 WCD). Upper Ogooue Province, from Lastoursville to the north of Franceville. *Class:* Niger-Congo, Atlantic-Congo, Volta-Congo, Benue-Congo, Bantoid, Southern, Narrow Bantu, Northwest, B, Mbere (B.60). *Dialects:* Epigi, Kanandjoho, Kuya, Nyani. *Other:* The people are called 'Bandoumu'. Riverine. Traditional religion.

Ngom (Ungom, Angom, Bangom, Bangomo, Ongom, Ngomo) [nra] 8,242 in Gabon (2000 WCD). Population total all countries: 12,770. Extreme northeast, around Mekambo and in Ogooue-Lolo Province, Koulamoutou area. Also spoken in Congo. *Class:* Niger-Congo, Atlantic-Congo, Volta-Congo, Benue-Congo, Bantoid, Southern, Narrow Bantu, Northwest, B, Kele (B.20). *Dialects:* Close to Kele. *Lg Dev:* Bible portions: 1910.

Njebi (Nzebi, Injebi, Yinzebi, Yinjebi, Njabi, Bandzabi, Ndjabi, Ndjevi) [nzb] 25,000 in Gabon. Population total all countries: 40,092. Ogooue-Lolo and Ngounie provinces, west of Franceville, and extending to Lebamba area. Also spoken in Congo. *Class:* Niger-Congo, Atlantic-Congo, Volta-Congo, Benue-Congo, Bantoid, Southern, Narrow Bantu, Northwest, B, Njebi (B.50). *Lg Dev:* NT: 1968–1979.

Pinji (Gapinji, Apinji, Apindji, Apindje) [pic] 5,000 (1990 CMA). Ngounie Province, east of Mouila, between Eleke and Fougamou. *Class:* Niger-Congo, Atlantic-Congo, Volta-Congo, Benue-Congo, Bantoid, Southern, Narrow Bantu, Northwest, B, Tsogo (B.30). *Lg Use:* Speakers also use Getsogo. *Other:* Different from Pende of Democratic Republic of the Congo. Forest. Traditional religion.

Punu (Ipunu, Yipunu, Pouno, Puno, Yipounou) [puu] 123,009 in Gabon (2000 WCD). Population total all countries: 132,064. Nyanga and Ngounie provinces, Tchibanga and Ndende areas. Also spoken in Congo. *Class:* Niger-Congo, Atlantic-Congo, Volta-Congo, Benue-Congo, Bantoid, Southern, Narrow Bantu, Northwest, B, Sira (B.40). *Lg Dev:* NT: 1977.

Sake (Asake, Shake) [sak] 1,000 (2000 B. Connell). Central, Ogooue-Iwindo Province, Booue area. *Class:* Niger-Congo, Atlantic-Congo, Volta-Congo, Benue-

Congo, Bantoid, Southern, Narrow Bantu, Northwest, B, Kele (B.20). *Other:* Threatened and undocumented linguistically (2000 B. Connell).

Sangu (Isangu, Yisangu, Chango, Shango, Yisangou) [snq] 20,911 (2000 WCD). Ngounie Province, Mimongo and Iboundji area. *Class:* Niger-Congo, Atlantic-Congo, Volta-Congo, Benue-Congo, Bantoid, Southern, Narrow Bantu, Northwest, B, Sira (B.40). *Lg Dev:* Bible portions: 1943–1959. *Other:* The people are called 'Masangu' or 'Massangou'. Not related to Sangu of Tanzania or Sango of Central African Republic, Chad, and Democratic Republic of the Congo. Traditional religion.

Seki (Sekyani, Sekiani, Sekiyani, Sekiana, Shekiyana, Sheke, Seke, Seseki) [syi] 3,690 in Gabon (2000 WCD). Northwest coast around Cocobeach. *Other:* Different from Bulu of Cameroon. See main entry under Equatorial Guinea.

Sighu (Lesighu, Mississiou) [sxe] 1,000 (1990 CMA). Ogooue-Lolo Province, Koulamoutou-Lastourville area. *Class:* Niger-Congo, Atlantic-Congo, Volta-Congo, Benue-Congo, Bantoid, Southern, Narrow Bantu, Northwest, B, Kele (B.20). *Other:* Threatened and undocumented linguistically (2000 B. Connell).

Simba (Nsindak) [sbw] 3,000 (1990 CMA). Ogooue-Lolo Province, between Sindare and Mimongo. *Class:* Niger-Congo, Atlantic-Congo, Volta-Congo, Benue-Congo, Bantoid, Southern, Narrow Bantu, Northwest, B, Tsogo (B.30). *Other:* Traditional religion.

Sira (Gisira, Eshira, Isira, Ichira, Ishira, Yichira, Shira, Shire) [swj] 39,449 (2000 WCD). 250,000 in all Sira languages in Gabon (1993 Johnstone). Ngounie Province, west of Mouila, southwest of Fougamou and Mandji. *Class:* Niger-Congo, Atlantic-Congo, Volta-Congo, Benue-Congo, Bantoid, Southern, Narrow Bantu, Northwest, B, Sira (B.40). *Lg Use:* Speakers also use Punu. *Lg Dev:* Grammar. Bible portions: 1954. *Other:* The people are called 'Eshira'. Traditional religion.

Tchitchege [tck] 2,000 (2003). Mboua village, on the road south from Franceville to Boumango. *Class:* Niger-Congo, Atlantic-Congo, Volta-Congo, Benue-Congo, Bantoid, Southern, Narrow Bantu, Northwest, B, Teke (B.70).

Teke, Northern (Teghe, Katege, Iteghe, Tege, Teke, Ketego) [teg] 15,745 in Gabon (2000 WCD). Upper Ogooue Province, east of Franceville. *Dialects:* Njiningi (Kanjiningi, Ndjinini, Njikini, Nzikini, Djikini), Tegekali (Katege, Tege, Tégué). *Other:* Traditional religion, Christian. See main entry under Congo (Teke-Tege).

Tsaangi (Itsaangi, Tsangi, Itsangi, Icaangui, Tcengui, Tchangui, Batsangui) [tsa] 8,611 in Gabon (2000 WCD). Upper Ogooue Province, west and southwest of Franceville. *Other:* The people are called 'Batsangui'. Traditional religion. See main entry under Congo.

Tsogo (Getsogo, Ghetsogo, Mitsogo) [tsv] 12,000 (1982 UBS). Ngounie Province, north and east of Mouila. *Class:* Niger-Congo, Atlantic-Congo, Volta-Congo, Benue-Congo, Bantoid, Southern, Narrow Bantu, Northwest, B, Tsogo (B.30). *Lg Dev:* Grammar. NT: 1983. *Other:* The people are called 'Mitsogo'.

Vili (Tsivili, Civili, Fiote, Fiot) [vif] 3,690 in Gabon (2000 WCD). Extreme south, on the coast near Mayumba. *Dialect:* Yoombe (Ciyoombe). *Lg Dev:* Some people are literate in Ipunu or Lumbu. *Other:* The people are called 'Bavili'. Traditional religion, Christian. See main entry under Congo.

Vumbu (Yivoumbou) [vum] 2,460 (2000 WCD). Yetsou area, west of Mouila. *Class:* Niger-Congo, Atlantic-Congo, Volta-Congo, Benue-Congo, Bantoid, Southern, Narrow Bantu, Northwest, B, Sira (B.40). *Dialects:* Related to Yipunu. *Other:* Distinct from Wumbvu in the Kele subgroup (B.20).

Wandji (Bawandji) [wdd] 10,493 (2000 WCD). Ogooue-Lolo and Haut Ogooue. *Class:* Niger-Congo, Atlantic-Congo, Volta-Congo, Benue-Congo, Bantoid, Southern, Narrow Bantu, Northwest, B, Njebi (B.50). *Dialects:* May be a dialect of Njebi. Reported that speakers can understand Njebi. *Other:* The people are called 'Bawandji'. Traditional religion.

Wumbvu (Wumvu) [wum] 18,328 in Gabon (2000 WCD). Ngounie Province, east of Lebamba. Also spoken in Congo. *Class:* Niger-Congo, Atlantic-Congo, Volta-Congo, Benue-Congo, Bantoid, Southern, Narrow Bantu, Northwest, B, Kele (B.20). *Other:* Traditional religion.

Yangho (Yongho, Miyangho, Bayongho) [ynh] 5,000 (1990). Haut Ogooue around Mamidi and Bakoumba. *Class:* Niger-Congo, Atlantic-Congo, Volta-Congo, Benue-Congo, Bantoid, Southern, Narrow Bantu, Northwest, B, Mbere (B.60). *Other:* Traditional religion.

Yasa (Yassa, Lyassa, Maasa, Bongwe) [yko] *Dialects:* Iyasa, Bweko, Vendo, Bodele, Marry, One, Asonga, Bomui, Mogana, Mooma, Mapanga. *Other:* Some or all speakers are reported to be pygmies. See main entry under Cameroon.

Gambia

The Gambia. Republic of The Gambia. 1,546,848. National or official language: English. Literacy rate: 35%. Also includes Bainouk-Gunyaamolo, Balanta-Kentohe (26,000), Bambara (5,740), Bayot (500), Jola-Kasa, Karon (1,350), Krio (9,000), Mankanya (1,650), Mansoanka (1,000), Pular, Upper Guinea Crioulo, Wolof, Xasonga. Information mainly from J. Bendor-Samuel 1989; Central Statistics Department, Banjul 1996. Blind population: 2,700 (1982 WCE). The number of languages listed for Gambia is 9. Of those, all are living languages. See map on page 727.

English [eng] 1,000 in Gambia (2004). *Lg Use:* Official language. See main entry under United Kingdom.

Jola-Fonyi (Kujamataak, Kújoolaak Kati Fooñi, Jola-Fogny, Diola-Fogny, Yola, Jola) [dyo] 59,650 in Gambia (2002 SIL). Southwestern districts. *Lg Use:* Fonyi is the largest and most widely understood Jola variety. *Other:* Muslim, traditional religion, Christian. See main entry under Senegal.

Mandinka (Mandinque, Mandingo, Manding, Mandé, Socé) [mnk] 453,500 in Gambia (2002). Most of the western half of Gambia. *Lg Use:* The main language of middle Gambia. *Lg Dev:* Literacy rate in second language: 50% in Mandinka in Arabic script. *Other:* Muslim. See main entry under Senegal.

Mandjak (Mandjaque, Manjaca, Manjaco, Manjiak, Manjacu, Manjack, Mandyak, Ndyak, Kanyop) [mfv] 19,250 in Gambia (2002). Western, south of the Gambia River. *Dialects:* Bok (Babok), Sarar, Teixeira Pinto, Tsaamo, Likes-Utsia (Baraa, Kalkus), Cur (Churo), Lund, Yu (Pecixe). *Other:* Traditional religion, Christian. See main entry under Guinea-Bissau.

Maninkakan, Western (Northwestern Maninka, Malinke, Malinka) [mlq] 12,600 in Gambia (2004). Eastern Gambia. *Dialect:* Jahanka. *Other:* Jahanka in Gambia may be a dialect of Western Maninkakan, or a separate language. Muslim. See main entry under Senegal.

Pulaar (Fulfulde-Pulaar, Pulaar Fulfulde, Peul, Peulh, Fulbe Jeeri, Fulani) [fuc] 262,550 in Gambia (2002). *Dialects:* Fulacunda (Fulakunda, Fulkunda), Toucouleur (Tukolor, Tukulor, Halpulaar, Haalpulaar). *Lg Use:* Fulbe Jeeri, Toucouleur, and Fulacunda are ethnic groups that speak Pulaar. Speakers also use Mandinka. *Lg Dev:* An official literacy committee is concerned with Pulaar. *Other:* Muslim, Christian. See main entry under Senegal.

Serer-Sine (Serer, Serrer, Seereer, Serer-Sin, Sine-Saloum) [srr] 28,360 in Gambia (2002). Northwestern Gambia. *Dialect:* Segum, Fadyut-Palmerin, Sine, Dyegueme (Gyegem). *Other:* Traditional religion, Muslim, Christian. See main entry under Senegal.

Soninke (Marka, Maraka, Sarahole, Sarawule, Sarahuli, Silabe, Toubakai, Wakore, Gadyaga, Aswanik) [snk] 66,175 in Gambia (2002). Southeastern corner. *Dialect:* Azer (Adjer, Aser). *Other:* Muslim, Christian. See main entry under Mali.

Wolof, Gambian [wof] 165,000 (2002). Western Division, south bank of the Gambia River and central. Wolof on the north bank speak Wolof of Senegal. *Class:* Niger-Congo, Atlantic-Congo, Atlantic, Northern, Senegambian, Fula-Wolof, Wolof. *Dialects:* Wolof of Senegal is intelligible with that of Gambia but with significant enough differences to require adaptation of materials. Needs further investigation. *Lg Dev:* Bible portions: 1882–1967. *Other:* Riverine. Tropical forest. 46 meters. Fishermen; peasant agriculturalists. Muslim.

Ghana

Republic of Ghana. Formerly Gold Coast and British Togoland. 20,757,032. National or official language: English. Literacy rate: 36% (1992 UNESCO). Also includes Foodo (1,000), Klao, Lobi, Mòoré. Information mainly from E. Hall 1983; J. Bendor-Samuel 1989; GILLBT 1970–1999. Blind population: 60,418. Deaf institutions: 20. The number of languages listed for Ghana is 79. Of those, all are living languages. See map on page 701.

Abron (Brong, Bron, Doma, Gyaman) [abr] 1,050,000 in Ghana (2003). Population total all countries: 1,181,700. Southwestern Ghana, northwest of Asante Twi. Also spoken in Côte d'Ivoire. *Class:* Niger-Congo, Atlantic-Congo, Volta-Congo, Kwa, Nyo, Potou-Tano, Tano, Central, Akan. *Lg Dev:* Literacy rate in first language: below 1%. Literacy rate in second language: 25% to 50%. *Other:* Muslim.

Adamorobe Sign Language [ads] 3,400 including hearing people (2003). Adamorobe, a village in the Eastern Region. The district capital is Aburi. *Class:* Deaf sign language. *Lg Use:* 15% deafness in the population; one of the highest percentages in the world, caused by genetic recessive autosome. The village has been settled for 200 years. It is an indigenous deaf sign language, also used by many hearing people. Most users have no contact with Ghanaian Sign Language. All ages, evenly distributed. *Other:* Agriculturalists; firewood traders.

Adangbe (Dangbe, Adantonwi, Agotime, Adan) [adq] Population total all countries: 2,000. Border area with Togo directly east of Ho. Agotime are mainly in Ghana. Volta Region. Ghana towns are Kpoeta, Apegame, and others. Also spoken in Togo. *Class:* Niger-Congo, Atlantic-Congo, Volta-Congo, Kwa, Left Bank, Kposo-Ahlo-Bowili. *Dialects:* Close to Igo. *Other:* Different from Adangme. The Adan and Agotime are separate ethnic groups who speak Adangbe.

Adele (Gidire, Bidire) [ade] 11,000 in Ghana (2003). East central border with Togo. Upper Adele is in Togo, Lower Adele in Ghana. *Dialects:* Upper Adele, Lower Adele. *Lg Use:* Speakers also use Twi. *Lg Dev:* Literacy rate in first language: below 1%. Literacy rate in second language: 5% to 15%. *Other:* Speakers' name for the language is 'Gidire', for themselves, 'Bidire'. 'Adele' is the name used by others. Different from Adere of Cameroon. Valleys. Forest, savannah. Subsistence agriculturalists: crop diversity. Traditional religion, Christian. See main entry under Togo.

Ahanta [aha] 142,000 (2003). Southwest coast. *Class:* Niger-Congo, Atlantic-Congo, Volta-Congo, Kwa, Nyo, Potou-Tano, Tano, Central, Bia, Southern. *Lg Use:* Vigorous. Partial bilingualism in Fante and Nzema. *Lg Dev:* Literacy rate in first language: below 1%. Literacy rate in second language: 5% to 15%. Radio programs. Bible portions: 2002. *Other:* Agriculturalists. Traditional religion, Christian.

Akan [aka] 8,300,000 (2004 SIL). Population includes 2,800,000 Asante Twi, 1,900,000 Fante, 555,000 Akuapem Twi (2004). The Asante are south central, Ashanti Province. The Akuapem are southeast, in areas north of Accra. The Fante are south central, between Winneba, Takoradi, and Obuasi. *Class:* Niger-Congo, Atlantic-Congo, Volta-Congo, Kwa, Nyo, Potou-Tano, Tano, Central, Akan. *Dialects:* Fante (Fanti, Mfantse), Akuapem (Akwapem Twi, Twi, Akuapim, Akwapi), Asante (Ashante Twi, Asanti, Achanti), Agona, Dankyira, Asen, Akyem Bosome, Kwawu (Kwahu), Ahafo. *Lg Use:* 1,000,000 second-language speakers. *Lg Dev:* Literacy rate in first language: 30% to 60%. Literacy rate in second language: 5% to 10%. Taught in primary and secondary schools. Roman script. Dictionary. Grammar. Bible: 1871–1964. *Other:* The speech of the Asante and Akuapem is called 'Twi'. svo.

Akposo (Kposo, Ikposo, Akposso) [kpo] 7,500 in Ghana (2003). Southern. *Dialects:* Amou Oblou, Ikponu, Iwi (Uwi), Litime (Badou), Logbo, Uma. *Lg Use:* Positive language attitude. Speakers have some proficiency in Éwé. *Lg Dev:* Literacy rate in first language: below 1%. Literacy rate in second language: 5% to 15%. Community-sponsored vernacular literacy materials are available. *Other:* Traditional religion. See main entry under Togo (Ikposo).

Animere (Anyimere, Kunda) [anf] 700 (2003). East central, Kecheibi and Kunda villages, remote location. None in Togo. *Class:* Niger-Congo, Atlantic-Congo, Volta-Congo, Kwa, Left Bank, Kebu-Animere. *Lg Use:* Reported as not being passed on to children any longer. Twi may be the second language. *Lg Dev:* Literacy rate in second language: 5% to 15%. *Other:* Traditional religion.

Anufo (Chokosi, Chakosi, Kyokosi, Tchokossi, Tiokossi) [cko] 66,000 in Ghana (2003). Population total all countries: 137,600. Northeast around Wawjayga. Also spoken in Benin, Togo. *Class:* Niger-Congo, Atlantic-Congo, Volta-Congo, Kwa, Nyo, Potou-Tano, Tano, Central, Bia, Northern. *Lg Dev:* Literacy rate in first language: below 1%. Literacy rate in second language: below 5%. Radio programs. Dictionary. Grammar. Bible portions: 1993. *Other:* Large migration across the border. 'Anufo' is the name the people use for themselves; 'Chokosi' is used by others. Traditional religion, Muslim, Christian.

Anyin (Anyi, Agni) [any] 250,000 in Ghana (2003). Between Abron to the north, Nzema to the south, Côte d'Ivoire to the west, Twi to the east. The Aowin dialect is in Ghana. *Dialect:* Aowin (Brissa, Brosa). *Lg Use:* Speakers also use Twi. *Lg Dev:* Literacy rate in second language: below 5%. *Other:* Traditional religion. See main entry under Côte d'Ivoire.

Avatime (Afatime, Sideme, Sia) [avn] 24,000 (2003). Southeast, center at Amedzofe (Amajofe). *Class:* Niger-Congo, Atlantic-Congo, Volta-Congo, Kwa, Left Bank, Avatime-Nyangbo. *Dialects:* Close to Nyangbo, Tafi. *Lg Use:* Understood somewhat as a second language by speakers of nearby languages. Diminishing contact with Éwé. *Lg Dev:* Literacy rate in first language: below 1%. Literacy rate in second language: 5% to 15%. Grammar. *Other:* Traditional religion.

Awutu [afu] 180,000 (2003). Coast, west of Accra. *Class:* Niger-Congo, Atlantic-Congo, Volta-Congo, Kwa, Nyo, Potou-Tano, Tano, Guang, South Guang. *Dialects:* Awutu, Efutu, Senya. *Lg Use:* Speakers also use Fante. *Lg Dev:*

Literacy rate in first language: below 1%. Literacy rate in second language: 5% to 15%. *Other:* A high proportion of the people have school education. Christian, Muslim, traditional religion, secular.

Bimoba (Moar, Moor) [bim] 120,000 (2004 SIL). Ethnic population: 200,000. Northeast, Gambaga District, south of Kusaasi, north of Konkomba. *Class:* Niger-Congo, Atlantic-Congo, Volta-Congo, North, Gur, Central, Northern, Oti-Volta, Gurma, Moba. *Dialects:* Related to Moba of Togo, but not inherently intelligible with it. *Lg Dev:* Literacy rate in first language: 10% to 30%. Literacy rate in second language: 15% to 25%. Grammar. Bible: 2003. *Other:* Traditional religion, Muslim, Christian.

Birifor, Southern (Birifo, Ghana Birifor) [biv] 125,000 in Ghana (2003). Population total all countries: 129,308. Northwest corner. Also spoken in Côte d'Ivoire. *Class:* Niger-Congo, Atlantic-Congo, Volta-Congo, North, Gur, Central, Northern, Oti-Volta, Western, Northwest, Dagaari-Birifor, Birifor. *Dialects:* A separate language from Wali, Dagaari, Malba-Birifor of Burkina Faso. *Lg Use:* Vigorous. All domains. All ages. *Lg Dev:* Literacy rate in first language: 1%. Literacy rate in second language: 5% or more. Radio programs. Dictionary. Bible portions: 1993–2001. *Other:* Traditional religion.

Bissa (Bisa) [bib] 165,900 in Ghana (2003). Northeast. *Dialects:* Lebir (Western Bisa), Baraka (Eastern Bisa). *Lg Use:* Some bilingualism in Mòoré. *Lg Dev:* Literacy rate in second language: 7%. *Other:* Not the same as Busa of Benin and Nigeria. The name of the people is 'Busansi'. Traditional religion, Muslim, Christian. See main entry under Burkina Faso.

Buli (Builsa, Bulisa, Kanjaga, Guresha) [bwu] 150,000 (2003 GILLBT). Sandema District. None in Burkina Faso. *Class:* Niger-Congo, Atlantic-Congo, Volta-Congo, North, Gur, Central, Northern, Oti-Volta, Buli-Koma. *Dialects:* Konni is the closest language. Lexical similarity 77% with Mampruli. *Lg Use:* Vigorous. All domains. All ages. *Lg Dev:* Literacy rate in first language: Around 10%. Literacy rate in second language: 5% to 15%. Dictionary. Grammar. NT: 1995. *Other:* The people call themselves 'Bulisa' or 'Builsa'. 'Kanjaga' and 'Guresha' are names given by others. Traditional religion, Christian, Muslim.

Chakali [cli] 6,000 (2003 GILLBT). East of Wa. Ducie is largest village. *Class:* Niger-Congo, Atlantic-Congo, Volta-Congo, North, Gur, Central, Southern, Grusi, Western. *Dialects:* Lexical similarity is 62% with Tampulma, 68% with Vagla. *Lg Use:* Used in the home. In Tuasa, only older people; in other villages children are also speakers. The Chakali seem to accept the Wali language, but do not approve of it being used in their homes. Speakers also use Wali. *Other:* Muslim, traditional religion, Christian.

Chala (Tshala, Cala) [cll] 3,000 (2003 GILLBT). Villages of Nkwanta, Odomi, Ago in the Volta Region. Jadigbe village near Seipe, south of Ekumdipe in the Northern Region is 35% Chala. None in Togo. *Class:* Niger-Congo, Atlantic-Congo, Volta-Congo, North, Gur, Central, Southern, Grusi, Eastern. *Lg Use:* Some also use Gikyode; proficiency is higher than in Twi. Twi is spoken to outsiders. *Other:* Different from Chala (Ron) of Nigeria. They are under the Gikyode paramount chief. Traditional religion.

Cherepon (Okere, Kyerepong, Chiripong, Chiripon) [cpn] 111,000 (2003). A pocket between the Ga and Twi areas, north of Larteh. *Class:* Niger-Congo, Atlantic-Congo, Volta-Congo, Kwa, Nyo, Potou-Tano, Tano, Guang, South Guang. *Lg Use:* Speakers also use Twi (Akan). *Lg Dev:* Literacy rate in first language: 1% to 5%. Literacy rate in second language: 5% to 15%. *Other:* Traditional religion.

Chumburung (Nchumburung, Nchimburu, Nchummuru, Kyongborong) [ncu] 69,000 (2004 SIL). Population includes 2,700 Yeji. A triangular area with Volta Lake on the south, Daka River on the northwest, Yeji south of the lake. *Class:* Niger-Congo, Atlantic-Congo, Volta-Congo, Kwa, Nyo, Potou-Tano, Tano, Guang, North Guang. *Dialects:* Northern Chumburung (Banda), Southern Chumburung (Lonto, Gurubi, Chinderi, Bejamse, Borae), Yeji (Yedji). Reported to be intelligible with Krache; however, Krache speakers are not inclined to use Chumburung materials. Lexical similarity 77% with Yeji, 79% with Kplang, 78% with Krache, 69% with Dwang, 67% with Nawuri and Gichode, 60% with Gonja. *Lg Use:* Vigorous. All domains. All ages. Most also use Twi. *Lg Dev:* Literacy rate in first language: below 1%. Literacy rate in second language: below 5%. Yeji can read Chumburung material with literacy help. Dictionary. Grammar. NT: 1988. *Other:* 'Chumburung' is the language, 'Nchumburung' the people. Traditional religion, Christian, Muslim.

Dagaare, Southern (Southern Dagari, Dagari, Dagara, Degati, Dagati, Dogaari, Dagaare) [dga] 700,000 (2003). 1,000,000 including Northern Dagara in Burkina Faso (2003). Northwest corner of Ghana, western part of Upper West Region. *Class:* Niger-Congo, Atlantic-Congo, Volta-Congo, North, Gur, Central, Northern, Oti-Volta, Western, Northwest, Dagaari-Birifor, Dagaari. *Dialects:* Dagaare and Birifor are partially intelligible. It is distinct from Northern Dagara in Burkina Faso. *Lg Use:* National language. Vigorous. All domains. All ages. *Lg Dev:* Literacy rate in first language: 5% to 10%. Literacy rate in second language: 5% to 15%. Taught in primary and secondary schools. Radio programs. Dictionary. Grammar. Bible portions: 1970. *Other:* The people are called 'Dagaaba'. Dagaare is more prominent politically and socially than Birifor. Traditional religion, Christian, Muslim.

Dagbani (Dagbane, Dagomba, Dagbamba) [dag] 800,000 (2004 SIL). Northeast around Tamale and as far as Yendi. *Class:* Niger-Congo, Atlantic-Congo, Volta-Congo, North, Gur, Central, Northern, Oti-Volta, Western, Southeast. *Dialect:* Nanuni (Nanumba). Lexical similarity 95% with Mampruli, 90% with Talni, 89% with Kusaal. *Lg Use:* National language. Trade language. Vigorous. All domains. All ages. *Lg Dev:* Literacy rate in first language: 3%. Literacy rate in second language: 2%. Taught in primary and secondary schools. Radio programs. Dictionary. Grammar. NT: 1974. *Other:* The people are called 'Dagbamba' or 'Dagomba', the language 'Dagbanli' ('Dagbani' by outsiders). SVO. Agriculturalists. Muslim, traditional religion, Christian.

Dangme (Adangme) [ada] 800,000 (2004 SIL). Southeast, coast east of Accra and inland. *Class:* Niger-Congo, Atlantic-Congo, Volta-Congo, Kwa, Nyo, Ga-Dangme. *Dialects:* Ada, Ningo, Osu, Shai, Gbugbla, Krobo. *Lg Dev:* Literacy rate in first language: 30% to 60%. Literacy rate in second language: 75% to 100%. Bible: 1999. *Other:* Traditional religion.

Deg (Degha, Mo, Mmfo, Aculo, Janela, Buru) [mzw] 26,400 in Ghana (2003). Population total all countries: 27,500. West central, west of Volta Lake. Also spoken in Côte d'Ivoire. *Class:* Niger-Congo, Atlantic-Congo, Volta-Congo, North, Gur, Central, Southern, Grusi, Western. *Dialects:* Longoro, Mangum, Boe. Lexical similarity 78% with Vagla. *Lg Use:* Vigorous. All domains. All ages. Twi (Akan) is widely spoken as second language. English is also used. *Lg Dev:* Literacy rate in first language: 5% to 10%. Literacy rate in second language: 5% to 15%. NT: 1996. *Other:* 'Deg' is their name for themselves; 'Mo' is used by outsiders. Traditional religion, Christian.

Delo (Ntrubo, Ntribu, Ntribou) [ntr] 10,900 in Ghana (2003). Population total all countries: 16,300. East central border with Togo. The paramount chief is at Brewaniase, 20 miles south of Nkwanta. Also spoken in Togo. *Class:* Niger-Congo, Atlantic-Congo, Volta-Congo, North, Gur, Central, Southern, Grusi, Eastern. *Dialects:* It has been reclassified from Kwa to Gur family. *Lg Use:* Vigorous. All domains. All ages. Speakers also use Twi or English. *Lg Dev:* Literacy rate in first language: below 1%. Literacy rate in second language: 5% to 15%. Bible portions. *Other:* 'Ntrubo' is the name of the people. Traditional religion, Christian.

Dompo (Dumpo, Ndmpo) [doy] 60 to 70 (1999 Blench). Ethnic population: 965 (2000 WCD). Brong-Ahafo Region, a quarter of Banda called Dompofie. *Class:* Niger-Congo, Atlantic-Congo, Volta-Congo, Kwa, Nyo, Potou-Tano, Tano, Guang, North Guang. *Lg Use:* Speakers also use Nafaanra. *Other:* 'Dompo' is the name of people and language.

Dwang (Dwan, Nchumunu) [nnu] 8,200 (2003 GILLBT). Population includes 1,600 Bekye, 3,300 Kenyen, 3,300 Wiase. South of Volta Lake and the Chumburung, east of Atebubu. *Class:* Niger-Congo, Atlantic-Congo, Volta-Congo, Kwa, Nyo, Potou-Tano, Tano, Guang, North Guang. *Dialects:* Bekye, Kenyen, Wiase. A dialect cluster. Closest to Kplang. 75% comprehension of Chumburung. Krache is understood well because of contact. *Lg Use:* Vigorous. Most domains. All ages. Most also use Twi (Akan). Twi used in several public functions. *Other:* The people were historically known as 'Bassa'.

English [eng] *Lg Use:* Official language. Second-language speakers in Ghana: 1,000,000 (1977 Voegelin and Voegelin). See main entry under United Kingdom.

Éwé (Eibe, Ebwe, Eve, Efe, Eue, Vhe, Gbe, Krepi, Krepe, Popo) [ewe] 2,250,500 in Ghana (2003). Population total all countries: 3,112,400. Southeast corner. Also spoken in Togo. *Class:* Niger-Congo, Atlantic-Congo, Volta-Congo, Kwa, Left Bank, Gbe. *Dialects:* Anglo (Anlo), Awuna, Hudu, Kotafoa. Westernmost language of the Gbe language cluster. *Lg Use:* Language of wider communication. Vigorous. 500,000 second-language speakers. All domains. *Lg Dev:* Literacy rate in first language: 30% to 60%. Literacy rate in second language: 75% to 100%. Taught in primary and secondary schools. Roman script. Newspapers. Radio programs. TV. Dictionary. Grammar. Bible: 1913–1931. *Other:* Some form of whistle speech reported. Christian, traditional religion.

Farefare (Frafra, Gurenne, Gurune, Nankani) [gur] 820,000 in Ghana (2003). Population includes up to 656,000 in the Upper East Region, and at least 164,000 in various towns and cities in other regions (2003). Population total all countries: 845,100. Northeast Ghana, Upper East Region around Bolgatanga, Frafra District, and as far west as Navrongo. Also spoken in Burkina Faso. *Class:* Niger-Congo, Atlantic-Congo, Volta-Congo, North, Gur, Central, Northern, Oti-Volta, Western, Northwest. *Dialects:* Gurune (Gudenne, Gurenne, Gudeni, Zuadeni), Nankani (Naani, Nankanse), Booni, Talni (Talensi, Talene), Nabt (Nabit, Nabde, Nabte, Nabdam, Nabdug, Nabrug, Nabnam, Namnam). 5 major dialects and many minor ones, all able to use the published materials. The dialects are divided according to geography and ethnic sub-boundaries. Some dialects are named after towns or localities. Speakers consider Dagaare in particular to be a sister language. *Lg Use:* National language. Vigorous. All domains. All ages. *Lg Dev:* Literacy rate in first language: 1% to 5%. Literacy rate in second language: 5% to 15%. Taught in primary and secondary schools. Roman script. Radio programs. Videos. Dictionary. Grammar. NT: 1986. *Other:* They call themselves their clan or dialect name, and their language 'Farefare'. Speakers of Talni are called 'Talensi'. Traditional religion, Christian, Muslim.

Fulfulde, Maasina (Peul, Fulbe, Maacina) [ffm] 7,300 in Ghana (1991). Northern, in small groups. *Lg Use:* Speakers also use Hausa. *Other:* Nomadic. They are considered to be foreigners by Ghanaians. Pastoralists. Muslim. See main entry under Mali.

Ga (Amina, Gain, Accra, Acra) [gaa] 600,000 (2004 SIL). Southeast, coast around Accra. *Class:* Niger-Congo, Atlantic-Congo, Volta-Congo, Kwa, Nyo, Ga-Dangme. *Lg Use:* National language. Ga is the major language of Accrá, the capital. *Lg Dev:* Literacy rate in first language: 30% to 60%. Literacy rate in second language: 75% to 100%. Taught in primary and secondary schools. Dictionary. Bible: 1866–1997. *Other:* Traditional religion.

Ghanaian Sign Language [gse] *Class:* Deaf sign language. *Dialects:* Related to American and Nigerian sign languages. Brought in 1957 by missionary Andrew Foster. Differs from American Sign Language in lexicon. There are new and local signs, and some modified from ASL. *Lg Use:* 9 deaf schools. Other deaf people use home signs. Elementary schools for deaf children since 1957. Sign language interpreters are required for deaf people in court. Little research. Some sign language classes for hearing people. *Other:* There is a manual alphabet for signing.

Gikyode (Kyode, Chode) [acd] 10,400 (2003). East central, on the border with Togo. Remote. 9 villages. *Class:* Niger-Congo, Atlantic-Congo, Volta-Congo, Kwa, Nyo, Potou-Tano, Tano, Guang, North Guang. *Dialects:* Lexical similarity 75% with Ginyanga of Togo. *Lg Use:* Vigorous. All domains. All ages. Twi (Akan) is used for trade. *Lg Dev:* Literacy rate in first language: 1% to 2% first-language literates, 5% second-language literates. Literacy rate in second language: 5% to 20%. NT: 2001. *Other:* The name of the people is 'Akyode' (Achode), the language is 'Gikyode' (correct spelling), 'Gichode' is the correct English pronunciation. Foothills, mountain slope. Forest, savannah. Agriculturalists: cassava, yams, plantain, peanuts, rice, cocoa, coffee. Traditional religion, Christian.

Gonja (Ngbanyito) [gjn] 230,000 (2004 SIL). In the southern part of the Northern Region, west central Ghana, around the upper branches of the Volta Lake, and from the Black Volta River to the area on both sides of the White Volta. *Class:* Niger-Congo, Atlantic-Congo, Volta-Congo, Kwa, Nyo, Potou-Tano, Tano, Guang, North Guang. *Dialect:* Gonja, Choruba (Choroba). It is not intelligible with Chumburung. *Lg Use:* National language. Language of wider communication. Vigorous. All domains. All ages. *Lg Dev:* Literacy rate in first language: 1% to 5%. Literacy rate in second language: below 5%. Taught in primary and secondary schools. Dictionary. Grammar. NT: 1984. *Other:* Traditional religion, Muslim, Christian.

Gua (Anum-Boso, Gwa) [gwx] 60,200 (2003). A pocket in Éwé area. *Class:* Niger-Congo, Atlantic-Congo, Volta-Congo, Kwa, Nyo, Potou-Tano, Tano, Guang, South Guang. *Dialects:* Anu (Anum), Boso. *Lg Use:* Speakers of all dialects use Twi (Akan) as second language. *Lg Dev:* Literacy rate in first language: 1% to 5%. Literacy rate in second language: 5% to 15%. Grammar. *Other:* Traditional religion.

Hanga (Anga) [hag] 6,800 (2003 GILLBT). Population includes 4,100 in the traditional area, 2,700 elsewhere. North central, southeast of the Mole game reserve, Damongo District. The biggest village is Murugu. *Class:* Niger-Congo, Atlantic-Congo, Volta-Congo, North, Gur, Central, Northern, Oti-Volta, Western, Southeast. *Dialects:* Northern Hanga, Southern Hanga. Kamara is a separate language. Subdialects of Southern Hanga are Langantere, Murugu, Damongo; subdialects of Northern Hanga are Yazori and Bowena. Lexical similarity 84% with Dagaare and Farefare. *Lg Use:* Vigorous. All

domains. Speakers also use Gonja. *Lg Dev:* Literacy rate in first language: 10% to 30%. Literacy rate in second language: 5% to 15%. NT: 1983. *Other:* Politically a subgroup of the Gonja. Savannah. Agriculturalists: maize, sorghum, millet, yams, cassava.

Hausa [hau] *Lg Use:* Trade language in Northern Ghana. *Other:* Muslim. See main entry under Nigeria.

Jwira-Pepesa (Pepesa-Jwira) [jwi] 18,000 (2003 GILLBT). Southwest corner. The Jwira live north of Axim from Bamiankaw to Humjibere along the Ankobra River (18 villages). The Pepesa live on Wasa land between Agona Junction and Tarkwa. Dompim is the main town. A mountain range separates the two groups. *Class:* Niger-Congo, Atlantic-Congo, Volta-Congo, Kwa, Nyo, Potou-Tano, Tano, Central, Bia, Southern. *Dialects:* Jwira, Pepesa. 60% intelligibility of Nzema. *Lg Use:* In the north, some Jwira speak Wasa as a second language; in the south, some speak Nzema as a second language. The Pepesa use Wasa as second language. *Lg Dev:* Literacy rate in second language: 50% to 75%. *Other:* Traditional religion, Christian.

Kabiyé (Kabire, Cabrai, Kabure, Kabye, Cabrais) [kbp] North. *Other:* Traditional religion. See main entry under Togo.

Kamara [jmr] 3,000 (2003 GILLBT). Ethnic population: 5,000 in Ghana (2003 GILLBT). Larabanga village, about 10 miles along the road west of Damongo, in the middle of the Northern Region, on the edge of the Hanga area. Safaliba sources report another small village about 15 to 20 miles south of Bole. Some ethnic Kamara in Mandari speak Safaliba, not Kamara. J. Becuwe reports a population of 3,000 in Bouna, Côte d'Ivoire (1981). *Class:* Niger-Congo, Atlantic-Congo, Volta-Congo, North, Gur, Central, Northern, Oti-Volta, Western, Southeast. *Dialects:* Significantly different from Hanga, and distinct culturally. Closer to Dagbani than to Hanga (G. Hunt 1997). *Lg Use:* Vigorous. The Kamara in Larabanga speak Kamara. It is not known if those in Côte d'Ivoire speak Kamara. All domains. All ages. Those in Mandari are bilingual or speak only Safaliba. *Other:* Muslim.

Kantosi (Kantonsi, Yare, Yarsi, Dagaare-Dioula) [xkt] 2,300 in Ghana (2003 GILLBT). Population includes 280 to 400 in Sandema District, probably about 280 in Kpaliwongo. North central Ghana, Sandema District, among the Bulsa (Buli language). Other settlements near Wa, in Navrongo, Bolgatonga, Nalerigu, and Kpaliwogo. They say Kpaliwongo, a village southeast of Funsi (Upper West Region), is their place of origin. After being destroyed during the days of slave-raiding, it was rebuilt and Kantosis have moved back. Also spoken in Burkina Faso. *Class:* Niger-Congo, Atlantic-Congo, Volta-Congo, North, Gur, Central, Northern, Oti-Volta, Western, Southeast. *Dialects:* Close to Kamara, Farefare, Dagbani. *Lg Use:* Vigorous. Endangered because people in some of the settlements now speak the language of those they have settled among: those in Funsi now speak Pasaale, those near Wa now speak Wali. Used in the home. All ages. Those in Sandema use Buli as second language. *Lg Dev:* Taught in primary schools. *Other:* One source says they are from Niger or Mali. Kantosi is referred to as 'Yare' or 'Yarsi' by the Bulsa. Distinct from Dagaare-Dioula in Burkina Faso. Muslim.

Kasem (Kasena, Kassena, Kassene) [xsm] 130,000 in Ghana (2004 SIL). North central (Navrongo District). *Dialects:* Nunuma, Lela, Kasem, Fere. *Lg Use:* National language. Vigorous. All domains. All ages. *Lg Dev:* Literacy rate in first language: 1% to 5%. Literacy rate in second language: 15% to 25%. Taught in primary and secondary schools. *Other:* The people are 'Kasena', the language 'Kasem'. Traditional religion, Christian, secular, Muslim. See main entry under Burkina Faso.

Konkomba (Likpakpaln, Kpankpam, Kom Komba) [xon] 500,000 in Ghana (2003). Population total all countries: 550,100. Northeast border area around Guerin, Yendi District. Many groups are scattered throughout north central Ghana. Also spoken in Togo. *Class:* Niger-Congo, Atlantic-Congo, Volta-Congo, North, Gur, Central, Northern, Oti-Volta, Gurma. *Dialects:* Lichabool-Nalong, Limonkpel, Linafiel, Likoonli, Ligbeln. *Lg Use:* Vigorous. All domains. All ages. Speakers also use Twi, Bassari, Hausa, or English. *Lg Dev:* Literacy rate in first language: 1% to 10%. Literacy rate in second language: 5% to 15%. Dictionary. Bible: 1998. *Other:* 'Likpakpaln' is the self name for the language, 'Bikpakpaln' for the people. Patrilineal, patrilocal. Agriculturalists: yams. Traditional religion, Muslim, Christian.

Konni (Koni, Koma, Komung) [kma] 3,800 (2003 GILLBT). Remote and isolated. Southeast of the Sisaala and west of the Mamprusi. No roads. 5 villages; Yikpabongo is the main one, Nangurima is another. *Class:* Niger-Congo, Atlantic-Congo, Volta-Congo, North, Gur, Central, Northern, Oti-Volta, Buli-Koma. *Dialects:* Related to Mampruli, Hanga, Buli. Lexical similarity 60% with Buli. *Lg Use:* Vigorous, with a strong sense of ethnic identity. Women from other language groups who marry Koma men learn the Konni language. All domains. All ages. They also speak several nearby languages including Mampruli and Sisaala. *Lg Dev:* Literacy rate in first language: 0%. Literacy rate in second language: 0%. *Other:* Politically under the Mampruli chief. The people are called 'Koma'. A high percentage of blindness from onchocerciasis. Agriculturalists: yams, cassava, millet, guinea corn, maize, peanuts. Traditional religion, Christian, Muslim.

Kplang (Prang) [kph] 1,600 (2003 GILLBT). South of Volta Lake, south of Yeji (Chumburung). *Class:* Niger-Congo, Atlantic-Congo, Volta-Congo, Kwa, Nyo, Potou-Tano, Tano, Guang, North Guang. *Dialects:* 73% intelligibility of Chumburung. 96% comprehension of Yeji due to proximity. Lexical similarity 92% with Yeji Chumburung, 79% with Chumburung. *Lg Use:* Vigorous. Most domains. All ages. Most people are somewhat bilingual in Twi (Akan). Public functions in Asante Twi (Akan). *Other:* Traditional religion.

Krache (Krachi, Krakye, Kaakyi) [kye] 58,000 (2004 SIL). Central, near Nchimburu, area of Kete Krachi. *Class:* Niger-Congo, Atlantic-Congo, Volta-Congo, Kwa, Nyo, Potou-Tano, Tano, Guang, North Guang. *Lg Use:* Vigorous. All domains. All ages. Some speakers also use Twi (Akan). *Lg Dev:* High level of school attendance. *Other:* Traditional religion.

Kulango, Bondoukou (Nkuraeng, Nkurange, Koulango, Kulange, Kolango, Bonduku Kulango) [kzc] 27,000 in Ghana (2003 GILLBT). West central, west of Wenchi. *Other:* Traditional religion. See main entry under Côte d'Ivoire.

Kulango, Bouna (Nkuraeng, Buna Kulango, Bouna Koulango) [nku] 15,500 in Ghana (1991). West central border area. *Dialects:* Sekwa, Nabanj. *Other:* Traditional religion. See main entry under Côte d'Ivoire.

Kusaal (Kusale, Kusasi) [kus] 420,000 in Ghana (2004 SIL). Population includes 350,000 Angole, 70,000 Toende. Population total all countries: 437,000. Northeast corner, Bawku District. Also spoken in Burkina Faso. *Class:* Niger-Congo, Atlantic-Congo, Volta-Congo, North, Gur, Central, Northern, Oti-Volta, Western, Southeast, Kusaal. *Dialects:* Angole (Eastern Kusaal), Toende (Western Kusaal). Further investigation of Toende in Burkina Faso is needed, including inherent intelligibility and language attitudes. Possible marginal intelligibility of Eastern (Angole) Kusaal. Many claim to be able to understand the related languages: Mòoré, Dagbani, Mampruli, Farefare

(Gurenne). Kusaal is a member of the Mòoré-Dagbani cluster. *Lg Use:* Vigorous. All domains. All ages. Speakers also use Hausa. *Lg Dev:* Literacy rate in first language: 1% to 5%. Literacy rate in second language: 15% to 25%. Roman script. Dictionary. Grammar. NT: 1976–1995. *Other:* The people are called 'Kusasi'. Traditional religion, Muslim, Christian.

Lama (Lamba, Losso) [las] Several hundred or perhaps thousands in Ghana (1996). About 100 km south of Bassar, over to Yendi, and even as far as Tamale, and southeast of Tamale. *Dialect:* Kadjala (Kadjalla). *Other:* Sometimes called Kabiye or Losso in Ghana. See main entry under Togo.

Larteh (Late, Lete, Gua) [lar] 74,000 (2003 GILLBT). A pocket in the Ga and Twi areas, south of Cherepon. *Class:* Niger-Congo, Atlantic-Congo, Volta-Congo, Kwa, Nyo, Potou-Tano, Tano, Guang, South Guang. *Lg Use:* Speakers also use Twi (Akan). *Lg Dev:* Literacy rate in first language: 1% to 5%. Literacy rate in second language: 5% to 15%. *Other:* Traditional religion.

Lelemi (Lefana, Lafana, Buem) [lef] 48,900 (2003). Southeast, town of Jasikan. *Class:* Niger-Congo, Atlantic-Congo, Volta-Congo, Kwa, Nyo, Potou-Tano, Lelemi, Lelemi-Akpafu. *Lg Use:* Vigorous. All domains. All ages. Some bilingualism in Twi (Akan). *Lg Dev:* Literacy rate in first language: below 1%. Literacy rate in second language: 5% to 15%. Grammar. NT: 1995. *Other:* The people are called 'Buem'. SVO. Christian, traditional religion.

Ligbi (Ligwi, Nigbi, Nigwi, Tuba, Banda, Dzowo, Namasa, Tsie, Weila, Wiila, Weela, Jogo) [lig] 15,000 in Ghana (2003 GILLBT). Population total all countries: 19,000. Numasa, northwest Brong-Ahafo, East of Sampa and northwest of Wenchi. Also spoken in Côte d'Ivoire. *Class:* Niger-Congo, Mande, Western, Central-Southwestern, Central, Manding-Jogo, Jogo-Jeri, Jogo. *Dialects:* Bungase, Gyogo, Hwela (Weila, Wiila, Weela, Vwela), Dwera (Manji-Kasa), Atumfuor (Atumfuor-Kasa), Ntoleh. *Lg Use:* Blacksmiths in other countries speaking Manding languages are also called 'Noumou', but in Ghana and Côte d'Ivoire the Noumou speak Ligbi. Speakers also use Asante Twi. *Lg Dev:* Grammar. *Other:* 'Banda' is the name of the people, which also refers to speakers of the Nafaanra language. 'Numu' is a caste of blacksmiths who speak the same dialect as others. Muslim, traditional religion.

Logba [lgq] 7,500 (2003). Southeast. *Class:* Niger-Congo, Atlantic-Congo, Volta-Congo, Kwa, Nyo, Potou-Tano, Logba. *Lg Use:* A population sample averaged 87% comprehension of Éwé mixed discourse types. *Other:* Different from Dompago (Logba) of Benin and Togo.

Mampruli (Mamprule, Manpelle, Ngmamperli) [maw] 220,000 in Ghana (2004 SIL). East and west of Gambaga, northeast Northern Region. Also spoken in Togo. *Class:* Niger-Congo, Atlantic-Congo, Volta-Congo, North, Gur, Central, Northern, Oti-Volta, Western, Southeast. *Dialects:* Eastern Mampruli, Western Mampruli. 50% intelligibility of Dagbani. Lexical similarity 95% with Dagbani, 90% with Farefare. *Lg Use:* Vigorous. All domains. All ages. Speakers also use Farefare, Bimoba, or Bissa. *Lg Dev:* Literacy rate in first language: below 1%. Literacy rate in second language: 5% to 10%. 48 literacy teachers. Dictionary. NT: 2001. *Other:* The people are called 'Mamprusi'. About 20 primary schools, 10 junior secondary schools, 3 secondary schools. Traditional religion, Muslim.

Nafaanra (Nafana, Nafaara, Pantera-Fantera, Banda, Dzama, Gambo) [nfr] 61,000 in Ghana (2003 GILLBT). Western border, east of Bondoukou in Côte d'Ivoire. Also spoken in Côte d'Ivoire. *Class:* Niger-Congo, Atlantic-Congo, Volta-Congo, North, Gur, Senufo, Nafaanra.

Dialects: Pantera, Fantera. *Lg Use:* Vigorous. All domains. All ages. Bilingual level estimates for Twi (Akan): 0 15%, 1 15%, 2 50%, 3 20%, 4 0%, 5 0%. *Lg Dev:* Literacy rate in first language: 1% to 5%. Literacy rate in second language: 15% to 25%. Grammar. NT: 1984. *Other:* 'Banda', 'Banafo', or 'Nafana' are names for the people. Different from Nafara Senoufo of Côte d'Ivoire. SOV; postpositions; genitives before noun heads; articles, adjectives, numerals, relatives after noun heads; question word initial; word order distinguishes subject, object, indirect object; ergativity; causatives; comparatives; CV, CVV; tonal. Plains, mountain slope. Savannah, tropical forest. 200 to 300 meters. Intensive agriculturalists: tobacco, yams, cotton, peanuts; animal husbandry: cattle guarded by Fulani. Traditional religion, Muslim, Christian.

Nawdm (Naudm, Nawdam, Naoudem) [nmz] In Accra, Ho, Kpandu, and Volta Region. See main entry under Togo.

Nawuri [naw] 14,000 (2003 GILLBT). East central, mostly on the western bank of the Oti River branch of Lake Volta. *Class:* Niger-Congo, Atlantic-Congo, Volta-Congo, Kwa, Nyo, Potou-Tano, Tano, Guang, North Guang. *Dialects:* Closest inherent intelligibility of Gikyode. Not intelligible with Chumburung. Highest lexical similarity with the Buipe dialect of Gonja (72%). *Lg Use:* Vigorous. All domains. All ages. *Lg Dev:* Literacy rate in first language: below 1%. Literacy rate in second language: 5% to 15%. Grammar. Bible portions: 1999. *Other:* SVO; post-positions; genitives before noun heads; articles, adjectives, numerals, relatives after noun heads; question word initial; word order distinguishes subjects, objects, indirect objects, given and new information, topic and comment; subject pronouns are clitics, objects (postverbal) can be treated as independent words; subject and object pronouns indicate person and number; limited noun class agreement of head nouns with modifiers; verb agreement with prefix concord marker which is usually a copy of the head noun (agreement both within noun phrase and subject-verb), but less extensive than in many Bantu languages; semiproductive causative suffix on verbs; comparison typically indicated by a serial verb or serial clause construction; CV, CVC, limited V(C); tonal. Traditional religion, Christian.

Nchumbulu [nlu] 1,800 (2003 SIL). Three villages west of Volta Lake near Kplang. *Class:* Niger-Congo, Atlantic-Congo, Volta-Congo, Kwa, Nyo, Potou-Tano, Tano, Guang, North Guang. *Dialects:* May use Chumburung or Dwan literature. *Lg Use:* Speakers also use Twi. *Other:* Some form of whistle speech reported.

Nkonya [nko] 28,000 (2004 SIL). Southeast Ghana, northwest of the Éwé. Some among the Gua. *Class:* Niger-Congo, Atlantic-Congo, Volta-Congo, Kwa, Nyo, Potou-Tano, Tano, Guang, North Guang. *Lg Use:* Speakers also use Éwé or Twi. *Lg Dev:* Literacy rate in first language: below 1%. Literacy rate in second language: 5% to 15%. Bible portions. *Other:* Traditional religion.

Ntcham (Tobote, Ncham, Bassar, Bassari, Basari, Basar, Basare) [bud] 57,000 in Ghana (2004 SIL). *Dialect:* Bitaapul. *Lg Dev:* Literacy rate in first language: below 1%. Literacy rate in second language: 15% to 25%. *Other:* Traditional religion. See main entry under Togo.

Nyangbo (Tutrugbu) [nyb] 6,400 (2003). Southeast Ghana. *Class:* Niger-Congo, Atlantic-Congo, Volta-Congo, Kwa, Left Bank, Avatime-Nyangbo. *Dialects:* People who have had no contact with Tafi had 67% intelligibility of it on tests; people 30 to 50 years old had nearly perfect comprehension. There are reported to be only phonological differences. *Lg Use:* A population sample averaged 72% comprehension of Éwé mixed discourse types. *Other:* Traditional religion.

Nzema (Nzima, Appolo) [nzi] 262,000 in Ghana (2004 SIL). Population total all countries: 328,700. Southwest

corner. Also spoken in Côte d'Ivoire. *Class:* Niger-Congo, Atlantic-Congo, Volta-Congo, Kwa, Nyo, Potou-Tano, Tano, Central, Bia, Southern. *Dialect:* Evalue. *Lg Use:* Speakers also use Fante. *Lg Dev:* Literacy rate in first language: 1% to 5%. Literacy rate in second language: 50% to 75%. Bible: 1999. *Other:* Traditional religion.

Paasaal (Pasaale, Funsile, Southern Sisaala, Pasaale Sisaala) [sig] 36,000 (2003 GILLBT). Upper West Region, 80 km south of Tumu, 105 km east of Wa, about 18 villages. *Class:* Niger-Congo, Atlantic-Congo, Volta-Congo, North, Gur, Central, Southern, Grusi, Western. *Dialects:* Gilbagala, Pasaali. Gilbagala is closer to Paasaal than to Tumulung Sisaala. The dialect in Funsi Kundogo is predominant among the Paasaal villages. *Lg Use:* Vigorous. All domains. All ages. Speakers also use Wali, Sisaala, Hausa, or English. *Lg Dev:* Literacy rate in first language: 1% to 2%. Literacy rate in second language: 5% to 15%. About 50% of children begin school; 10% to 20% complete junior secondary school. Grammar. NT: 2001. *Other:* SVO; prepositions; articles, adjectives, numerals after noun heads; question word initial; word order distinguishes object; ergativity; CV, CVC, CVV; tonal. Plains. Savannah. Agriculturalists: guinea corn. Traditional religion, Muslim, Christian.

Safaliba (Safali, Safalaba, Safalba) [saf] 4,000 (2003). Immediately west and south of Bole, western Northern Region. Villages of Mandari, Tanyire, Manfuli, and Gbenfu, and settlements in the nearby towns of Bote, Sawla, Kalba. Speakers also reported in Vonkoro and Bouna, Côte d'Ivoire. *Class:* Niger-Congo, Atlantic-Congo, Volta-Congo, North, Gur, Central, Northern, Oti-Volta, Western, Northwest. *Dialects:* Lexical similarity 79% with Dagaari. *Lg Use:* Vigorous. All domains. All ages. Speakers also use Gonja. *Lg Dev:* Literacy rate in first language: below 1%. Literacy rate in second language: 8% English, Gonja. Bible portions: 2003. *Other:* Plains, hills. Savannah. Agriculturalists: yams, maize. Traditional religion, Muslim, Christian.

Sehwi (Sefwi, Asahyue) [sfw] 250,000 (2003). Southwest Ghana. *Class:* Niger-Congo, Atlantic-Congo, Volta-Congo, Kwa, Nyo, Potou-Tano, Tano, Central, Bia, Northern. *Dialects:* Close to Anyin of Côte d'Ivoire. *Lg Use:* Speakers also use Twi. *Lg Dev:* Bible portions: 1998. *Other:* Traditional religion, Christian.

Sekpele (Likpe, Mu, Bosele) [lip] 23,400 (2003). Southeast, north of Hohoe. *Class:* Niger-Congo, Atlantic-Congo, Volta-Congo, Kwa, Nyo, Potou-Tano, Lelemi, Likpe-Santrokofi. *Dialects:* Sekwa, Sekpele. *Lg Use:* Vigorous. All domains. All ages. A population sample averaged 75% comprehension of Éwé mixed discourse types. Twi is also used. *Lg Dev:* Literacy rate in first language: below 1%. Literacy rate in second language: 5% to 15%. *Other:* Traditional religion.

Selee (Santrokofi, Sentrokofi, Bale, Sele) [snw] 11,300 (2003 GILLBT). Southeast, villages of Benua, Bume, Gbodome. *Class:* Niger-Congo, Atlantic-Congo, Volta-Congo, Kwa, Nyo, Potou-Tano, Lelemi, Likpe-Santrokofi. *Lg Use:* Vigorous. All domains. All ages. Diminishing contact with Éwé. *Lg Dev:* Literacy rate in first language: below 1%. Literacy rate in second language: 5% to 15%. *Other:* The people call themselves 'Bale'. Outsiders call them 'Santrokofi'. Traditional religion, Christian.

Sisaala, Tumulung (Sisai, Issala, Hissala, Sisala Tumu, Isaalung) [sil] 105,000 (2003 GILLBT). North central, Tumu District. *Class:* Niger-Congo, Atlantic-Congo, Volta-Congo, North, Gur, Central, Southern, Grusi, Western. *Dialects:* Isala, Gil Bagale (Galebagla), Nsihaa, Potule. *Lg Use:* Vigorous. All domains. All ages. Speakers also use Twi or Hausa. *Lg Dev:* Literacy rate in first language: 1% to 5%. Literacy rate in second language: 5% to 15%. Dictionary. NT: 1984. *Other:* Traditional religion, Muslim, Christian.

Sisaala, Western (Busillu Sisala, Sisai, Issala, Hissala) [ssl] 30,000 (2003 GILLBT). North central, Lambusie and surrounding towns. *Class:* Niger-Congo, Atlantic-Congo, Volta-Congo, North, Gur, Central, Southern, Grusi, Western. *Dialects:* Close to Sissala of Burkina Faso. *Other:* Traditional religion, Muslim.

Siwu (Akpafu-Lolobi, Lolobi-Akpafu, Siwusi) [akp] 27,000 (2003). Southeast, north of Hohoé. *Class:* Niger-Congo, Atlantic-Congo, Volta-Congo, Kwa, Nyo, Potou-Tano, Lelemi, Lelemi-Akpafu. *Dialects:* Akpafu, Lolobi. Lolobi and Akpafu are inherently intelligible, but have been politically separate since the 1800s. A population sample averaged 66% comprehension of Éwé mixed discourse types. *Lg Use:* Vigorous. All domains. All ages. *Lg Dev:* Literacy rate in second language: 25% to 50%. *Other:* 'Lolobi' and 'Akpafu' are names for town and people. Their own name for the language is 'Siwu'. Community sponsored vernacular literacy materials are available. Traditional religion, Christian.

Tafi (Tegbo) [tcd] 4,400 (2003). East central, near the Togo border. None in Togo. *Class:* Niger-Congo, Atlantic-Congo, Volta-Congo, Kwa, Left Bank, Avatime-Nyangbo. *Lg Use:* Speakers also use Éwé. *Other:* A population sample averaged 73% comprehension of Éwé mixed discourse types. 83% understand Nyangbo narrative well. Muslim, traditional religion.

Tampulma (Tamprusi, Tampole, Tampolem, Tampolense, Tamplima, Tampele) [tpm] 16,000 (2003). North central, south of Sisaala, Damongo District, 25 villages. *Class:* Niger-Congo, Atlantic-Congo, Volta-Congo, North, Gur, Central, Southern, Grusi, Western. *Dialects:* 2 inherently intelligible dialects. Lexical similarity 62% with Chakali. *Lg Use:* Vigorous. All domains. All ages. *Lg Dev:* Literacy rate in first language: 1% to 5%. Literacy rate in second language: 15% to 25%. Roman script. Bible: 2000. *Other:* 'Tamprusi' is the name of the people. Agriculturalists: guinea corn, millet, yams; fishermen. Christian, traditional religion.

Tem (Kotokoli, Cotocoli, Tim, Timu, Temba) [kdh] 53,000 in Ghana. Most in Accra. *Other:* Muslim. See main entry under Togo.

Tuwuli (Bowiri, Bowili, Liwuli, Siwuri, Bawuli, Tuwili) [bov] 11,400 (2003 GILLBT). Volta Region, from Volta Lake eastward to Amanfro on the Hohoe-Jasikan road. Not found in Togo. *Class:* Niger-Congo, Atlantic-Congo, Volta-Congo, Kwa, Left Bank, Kposo-Ahlo-Bowili. *Lg Use:* Vigorous. All domains. All ages. Diminishing contact with Éwé. *Lg Dev:* Literacy rate in second language: 25% to 50%. *Other:* Traditional religion.

Vagla (Vagala, Sitigo, Kira, Konosarola, Paxala) [vag] 13,500 (2003 GILLBT). West central near Sawla, Northern Province, Damongo District. *Class:* Niger-Congo, Atlantic-Congo, Volta-Congo, North, Gur, Central, Southern, Grusi, Western. *Dialects:* Bole, Buge. Lexical similarity 68% with Chakali. *Lg Use:* Vigorous. All domains. All ages. 75% use Waali as second language. *Lg Dev:* Literacy rate in first language: 1% to 5%. Literacy rate in second language: 15% to 25%. Roman script. Dictionary. Grammar. NT: 1977. *Other:* Traditional religion.

Wali (Waali, Wala, Ala, Ouala) [wlx] 138,000 (2003). Northwest corner. *Class:* Niger-Congo, Atlantic-Congo, Volta-Congo, North, Gur, Central, Northern, Oti-Volta, Western, Northwest. *Dialects:* Fufula, Yeri Waali, Cherii, 'Bulengee, 'Dolimi. Distinct from Birifor and Dagaari. *Lg Use:* Language of wider communication. Vigorous. The Chakali are bilingual in Wali. All domains. All ages. *Lg Dev:* Literacy rate in first language: below 1%. Literacy rate in second language: 15% to 25%. NT: 1984.

Other: The ' before dialect names indicates a change in vowel quality. Traditional religion, Muslim, Christian.

Wasa (Wasaw, Wassa) [wss] 309,000 (2003). Southwestern Ghana. *Class:* Niger-Congo, Atlantic-Congo, Volta-Congo, Kwa, Nyo, Potou-Tano, Tano, Central, Akan. *Dialects:* Amenfi, Fianse. Some intelligibility of Abron. *Lg Use:* Twi (Akan) is used as second language. Low Asante and Fante comprehension in rural areas. *Lg Dev:* Literacy rate in first language: below 1%. Literacy rate in second language: 5% to 15%. *Other:* Traditional religion.Ghana

Guinea

Republic of Guinea. République de Guinée. 9,246,462. National or official languages: French, regional languages: Northern Kissi, Guinea Kpelle, Eastern Maninkakan, Pular, Susu, Toma. Literacy rate: 28% to 35%. Also includes Bambara, Bandi (7,000), Krio, Soninke, people from Lebanon and Europe. Information mainly from Voegelin and Voegelin 1977; J. Bendor-Samuel 1989. Blind population: 45,000 (1982 WCE). Deaf institutions: 3. The number of languages listed for Guinea is 36. Of those, 34 are living languages and 2 are extinct. See map on page 702.

Badyara (Badara, Badian, Badjara, Badyaranke, Pajade, Pajadinka, Gola, Bigola) [pbp] 6,300 in Guinea (1998 NTM). Population total all countries: 12,205. Koundara Region. Also spoken in Guinea-Bissau, Senegal. *Class:* Niger-Congo, Atlantic-Congo, Atlantic, Northern, Eastern Senegal-Guinea, Tenda. *Dialects:* Biafada is the closest language, with 52% lexical similarity. *Other:* They maintain cultural autonomy. Beekeepers; agriculturalists; cotton cloth weavers. Muslim.

Baga Binari (Barka, Binari, Kalum, Mborin) [bcg] 3,000. Coast east of the Nunez River in Boké Region. *Class:* Niger-Congo, Atlantic-Congo, Atlantic, Southern, Mel, Temne, Baga. *Dialects:* Close to Landoma and Temne. *Lg Use:* Speakers also use Susu. *Other:* Muslim, traditional religion.

Baga Kaloum [bqf] Extinct. *Class:* Niger-Congo, Atlantic-Congo, Atlantic, Southern, Mel, Temne, Baga. *Lg Use:* Members of the ethnic group now speak Susu. *Other:* Muslim, traditional religion.

Baga Koga (Barka, Koga, Koba) [bgo] Ethnic population: 5,000. Coast between the Pongo and Konkouré rivers, extending to the Île de Kito. *Class:* Niger-Congo, Atlantic-Congo, Atlantic, Southern, Mel, Temne, Baga. *Dialects:* Close to Landoma, Temne. *Lg Use:* Speakers also use Susu. *Other:* Muslim, traditional religion. Nearly extinct.

Baga Manduri (Barka, Mandari, Maduri, Manduri) [bmd] 4,000. Islands in Nunez River delta, around Dobale, Kanfarande Subprefecture. *Class:* Niger-Congo, Atlantic-Congo, Atlantic, Southern, Mel, Temne, Baga. *Dialects:* Close to Landoma, Temne. *Lg Use:* Speakers also use Susu. *Other:* Muslim, traditional religion.

Baga Mboteni [bgm] Ethnic population: 4,893. South of the Nunez River. *Class:* Niger-Congo, Atlantic-Congo, Atlantic, Northern, Mbulungish-Nalu. *Dialects:* Related to Nalu, Mbulungish. *Lg Use:* Speakers also use Susu. *Other:* Muslim, traditional religion. Nearly extinct.

Baga Sitemu (Barka, Sitemuú, Tchitem, Stem Baga, Rio Pongo Baga) [bsp] 4,000. Southern bank of the Nunez River in the Boké and Boffa regions. Baga Marara is spoken on Marara islands south of the Rio Pongo Inlet. *Class:* Niger-Congo, Atlantic-Congo, Atlantic, Southern, Mel, Temne, Baga. *Dialect:* Marara. Close to Landoma, Temne. *Lg Use:* Speakers also use Susu. *Other:* Muslim, traditional religion.

Baga Sobané (Barka, Sobané, Baga Kakissa) [bsv] Extinct. Between the Kapatchez and Pongo rivers. *Class:*

Niger-Congo, Atlantic-Congo, Atlantic, Southern, Mel, Temne, Baga. *Dialects:* Was close to Landoma, Temne. *Lg Use:* Members of the ethnic group now speak Susu. *Other:* Muslim, traditional religion.

Bassari (Basari, Onian, Ayan, Biyan, Wo, Tenda Basari) [bsc] 8,600 in Guinea (1991 Vanderaa). *Other:* Matrilineal. Traditional religion. See main entry under Senegal.

Bullom So (Northern Bullom, Bolom, Bulem, Bullun, Bullin, Mmani, Mandingi, Mandenyi) [buy] Few speakers in Guinea (2001). Along the coast from the Guinea border to the Sierra Leone border. *Lg Use:* All speakers are older adults. See main entry under Sierra Leone.

Dan (Yacouba, Yakuba, Gio, Gyo, Gio-Dan, Da) [daf] 800 in Guinea (2001 Pruett). Lola Prefecture, one village named Kogota east of Nzoo on the Côte d'Ivoire border. *Other:* Traditional religion, Christian. See main entry under Côte d'Ivoire.

French [fra] *Lg Use:* Official language. See main entry under France.

Guinean Sign Language [gus] Conakry. *Class:* Deaf sign language. *Lg Use:* Used in the deaf school in Conakry. *Other:* Appears to be heavily influenced by, or based on, ASL, with some influence from French Sign Language.

Jahanka (Jahanque, Jahonque, Diakkanke, Diakhanke, Dyakanke) [jad] 12,600 in Guinea (1991). Population total all countries: 13,100. Around Touba and Toubadinque near Gaoual, border area of Mali and Guinea. Also spoken in Mali. *Class:* Niger-Congo, Mande, Western, Central-Southwestern, Central, Manding-Jogo, Manding-Vai, Manding-Mokole, Manding. *Dialects:* Jahanka in Gambia may be the same as this, or a dialect of Western Maninkakan. Jahanka in Senegal and Guinea-Bissau is a dialect of Western Maninkakan. Lexical similarity 75% with Mandinka. *Lg Dev:* Arabic script. *Other:* They are reported to have come from Mali in the 18th century. They trace their origins to Soninke, but now speak a separate language. Rice merchants; Muslim scholars. Muslim.

Kakabe (Jon Kule, Fulajon Kan, Ourekabakan) [kke] East of Timbo, Sokotoro, Wure Kaba, and 33 other villages. *Class:* Niger-Congo, Mande, Western, Central-Southwestern, Central, Manding-Jogo, Manding-Vai, Manding-Mokole, Mokole. *Dialects:* Close to Mixifore linguistically, but 250 km apart. Lexically similarity 50% with Eastern Maninkakan, 58% with Mixifore (Rainwater 2002). *Lg Use:* Most speakers are trilingual in Kakabe, Pular, and Eastern Maninkakan. *Lg Dev:* Some are literate in Pular (Arabic script) or French. *Other:* Agriculturalists. Muslim.

Kissi, Northern (Gizi, Kisi, Kissien, Kisie) [kqs] 286,500 in Guinea (1991 Vanderaa). Population total all countries: 326,500. South central, Kissidougou Region. Also spoken in Sierra Leone. *Class:* Niger-Congo, Atlantic-Congo, Atlantic, Southern, Mel, Bullom-Kissi, Kissi. *Dialects:* Liaro, Kama, Teng, Tung. Close to Sherbro. Southern Kissi of Liberia and Sierra Leone is different. *Lg Use:* Official regional language. *Lg Dev:* Literacy rate in second language: 10% in French. Literacy materials taught in school. Grammar. NT: 1966–1986. *Other:* Many loanwords from Malinke. Traditional religion, Muslim, Christian.

Kono [knu] 90,000 (2001). Southeast at Liberia border. *Class:* Niger-Congo, Mande, Western, Central-Southwestern, Southwestern, Kpelle. *Dialects:* Lexical similarity 52% to 67% between Kpelle and Kono. *Other:* Different from Kono of Sierra Leone.

Kpelle, Guinea (Kpele, Guerze, Gerze, Gerse, Gbese, Pessa, Pessy, Kpwessi, Akpese, Kpelese, Kpelesetina, Kpese, Kperese, Northern Kpele) [gkp] 308,000 (1991 Vanderaa). Southeast at Liberia border. *Class:* Niger-Congo, Mande, Western, Central-Southwestern, Southwestern, Kpelle. *Dialects:* Different enough from Kpelle of Liberia to need separate materials. Lexical

similarity 52% to 67% with Kono. *Lg Use:* Official regional language. *Lg Dev:* Literacy materials taught in school. Bible portions: 1945–1969. *Other:* 'Guerzé' is the French name. Traditional religion, Christian, Muslim.

Kuranko (Koranko) [knk] 55,200 in Guinea (1991). Between Faranah and Kissidougou and toward Kerouané. *Other:* Ethnically separate from Eastern Maninkakan. Traditional religion, Muslim. See main entry under Sierra Leone.

Landoma (Landouman, Landuma, Tyapi, Tyopi, Tiapi, Cocoli) [ldm] 14,400 (1991 Vanderaa). Between the upper Rio Nunez and the upper Rio Pongas. Not in Guinea-Bissau. *Class:* Niger-Congo, Atlantic-Congo, Atlantic, Southern, Mel, Temne, Baga. *Dialect:* Tiapi (Tapessi). Close to Baga and Temne. *Other:* Traditional religion, Muslim.

Lele [llc] 23,000 (1998 Willits). Population includes 12,000 in Kissidougou Prefecture and 11,000 in Guekedou. Kissidougou vicinity, with Mato River on the west. Main centers are Yombiro, Tangalto, and Kassadou, west and southwest of Kissidou. Not in Sierra Leone. *Class:* Niger-Congo, Mande, Western, Central-Southwestern, Central, Manding-Jogo, Manding-Vai, Manding-Mokole, Mokole. *Dialects:* Yombiro Lele (North Lele), Tangalto Lele (East Lele), Kassadou Lele (South Lele), Kounte Lele (Central Lele). Kassadou people cannot understand Tangalto dialect. Lexical similarity 55% with Eastern Maninkakan and Mixifore, 73% with Kuranko of Sierra Leone. *Lg Use:* Positive language attitude. *Other:* Muslim.

Limba, East (Yimba, Yumba) [lma] 4,000 in Guinea (1993 Johnstone). Population includes 2,000 speakers of the Ke subdialect of Northern Limba (1991 J. Kaiser). Also spoken in Sierra Leone. *Class:* Niger-Congo, Atlantic-Congo, Atlantic, Southern, Limba. *Dialect:* Northern Limba (Warawara, Ke-Woya-Yaka). *Other:* Quite different from West-Central Limba of Sierra Leone. Traditional religion, Muslim.

Maninka, Konyanka (Konya, Konyakakan) [mku] 128,400 in Guinea (1986). Beyla Region. Also spoken in Liberia. *Class:* Niger-Congo, Mande, Western, Central-Southwestern, Central, Manding-Jogo, Manding-Vai, Manding-Mokole, Manding, Manding-East, Southeastern Manding. *Dialects:* Lexical similarity 72% with Eastern Maninkakan. *Other:* Muslim.

Maninka, Sankaran (Faranah, Sankarankan) [msc] *Class:* Niger-Congo, Mande, Western, Central-Southwestern, Central, Manding-Jogo, Manding-Vai, Manding-Mokole, Manding, Manding-East, Southeastern Manding. *Dialects:* Lexical similarity 79% with Eastern Maninkakan. *Other:* Muslim.

Maninkakan, Eastern (Maninka, Mande, Southern Maninka, Kankan Maninka, Eastern Malinke) [emk] 1,890,000 in Guinea (1986). Population includes 73,500 Wasulu. Population total all countries: 2,013,800. Central, Kankan Region, all over upper Guinea, and the forest region near Liberia. Also spoken in Liberia, Sierra Leone. *Class:* Niger-Congo, Mande, Western, Central-Southwestern, Central, Manding-Jogo, Manding-Vai, Manding-Mokole, Manding, Manding-East, Southeastern Manding. *Dialects:* Bö, Amana (Kourousa), Koulounkalan, Maninka-Mori (Mori), Wasulu (Wassulu, Wassulunka, Wassulunke). Maninka of Liberia is the same as Maninka of Guinea (Eastern Maninkakan), Bambara of Mali and parts of Senegal is not vastly different. Eastern Maninkakan of Côte d'Ivoire is close to Bambara; Western Maninkakan of south central and southeast Senegal is considerably different. Wasulu is a dialect of Eastern Maninkakan in Guinea, but of Bambara in Mali. Eastern Maninkakan has 92% lexical similarity with Wasulu, 79% with Sankaran, 72% with Konyanka.

Lg Use: Official regional language. *Lg Dev:* Literacy materials taught in school. Nko script. Dictionary. NT: 1932–1966. *Other:* Nko script is popular, created in 1948 by Sulemana Kante, with about 50 publications, and schools teaching it. Muslim.

Mann (Maa, Mah, Mano, Mawe) [mev] 71,022 in Guinea (1997 Mamy). East of Kpelle in Nzérékore Prefecture (40,536), Lola Prefecture (16,486), Yomou Prefecture (14,000). *Other:* Traditional religion. See main entry under Liberia.

Manya (Manya Kan, Mandingo, Maniya) [mzj] 25,000 in Guinea (1997 Pruett). Macenta Prefecture. *Lg Use:* Speakers do not consider themselves to be Eastern Maninkakan. *Other:* Muslim, Christian. See main entry under Liberia.

Mbulungish (Baga Foré, Baga Monson, Monshon, Monchon, Bulunits, Longich, Black Baga) [mbv] 5,000 (1998 Willits). On the coast north of the Nunez River, 22 villages. *Class:* Niger-Congo, Atlantic-Congo, Atlantic, Northern, Mbulungish-Nalu. *Dialects:* Related to Nalu, Baga Mboteni. *Lg Use:* Children were reported to be speaking the language actively in 1995–1996. *Other:* Muslim, traditional religion.

Mixifore (Mogofin, Mikifore) [mfg] 3,600 (1991). Central. *Class:* Niger-Congo, Mande, Western, Central-Southwestern, Central, Manding-Jogo, Manding-Vai, Manding-Mokole, Mokole. *Dialects:* It seems to be close to the Vai-Kono-Kuranko subgroup (Vydrine). Lexical similarity 51% with Eastern Maninkakan, 55% with Lele, 54% to 58% with varieties of Kuranko. *Other:* 'Mixifore' means 'black person' in Susu. 'Mogofin' means the same thing, and is their name for themselves. Muslim.

Nalu (Nalou) [naj] 13,000 in Guinea (1993 Johnstone). Population total all countries: 21,150. Near Boke, Katchek Island. Also spoken in Guinea-Bissau. *Class:* Niger-Congo, Atlantic-Congo, Atlantic, Northern, Mbulungish-Nalu. *Dialects:* Related to Mbulungish and Baga Mboteni. *Lg Use:* Speakers also use Susu. *Other:* Muslim, traditional religion.

Pulaar (Fulfulde Pulaar, Peul, Peulh, Haalpulaar) [fuc] 24,000 in Guinea (1991). One community near Dinguiray (Pulaar), and a few communities in the north near Sareboido. *Dialects:* Toucouleur (Tukulor, Tukolor, Pulaar, Futa Toro), Fulacunda (Fulakunda, Fulkunda, Fula Preto). *Other:* Many Arabic loans. The official orthography is different from that used elsewhere. Muslim. See main entry under Senegal.

Pular (Fuuta Jalon, Futa Jallon, Fouta Dyalon, Fulbe, Fullo Fuuta, Futa Fula, Foula Fouta, Fulfulde Jalon, Jalon) [fuf] 2,550,000 in Guinea (1991 Vanderaa). Population total all countries: 2,915,784. Northwest, Fouta Djallon area. Also spoken in Gambia, Guinea-Bissau, Mali, Senegal, Sierra Leone. *Class:* Niger-Congo, Atlantic-Congo, Atlantic, Northern, Senegambian, Fulani-Wolof, Fula, West Central. *Dialects:* Kebu Fula, Fula Peta. Different enough from Pulaar in Senegal to need separate literature. In Sierra Leone, recent immigrants from Guinea speak the original Futa Jalon or the Kebu dialect (Dalby 1962). It is intelligible with Fula Peta of Guinea and with dialects of Guinea, Guinea-Bissau, and Senegal. A slightly modified form of Futa Jalon is known as Krio Fula with many loans from Sierra Leone languages. *Lg Use:* Official regional language. Many monolinguals. Eastern Maninkakan and Susu used as second language by others. *Lg Dev:* Grammar. Bible portions: 1929–1986. *Other:* Heavy borrowing from Arabic. Guinea has had an extensive literature in Pular, but little still exists. Muslim, Christian.

Susu (Soso, Susoo, Soussou, Sose) [sus] 905,500 in Guinea (2001 Johnstone and Mandryk). Population total all countries: 1,029,380. Western Guinea, and mainly in the southwest. Also spoken in Guinea-Bissau, Sierra

Leone. *Class:* Niger-Congo, Mande, Western, Central-Southwestern, Central, Susu-Yalunka. *Dialects:* Distinct from Yalunka. *Lg Use:* Official regional language. Some also use French. *Lg Dev:* Literacy materials taught in school. Roman and Arabic scripts. NT: 1884–1988. *Other:* Muslim, traditional religion, Christian.

Toma (Toa, Toale, Toali, Tooma) [tod] 143,800 (1991 Vanderaa). Southern, between Macenta and Kissidougou. *Class:* Niger-Congo, Mande, Western, Central-Southwestern, Southwestern, Mende-Loma, Loma. *Dialects:* Distinct enough from Loma of Liberia to need separate literature. *Lg Use:* Official regional language. *Lg Dev:* Literacy materials taught in school. NT: 1981. *Other:* Traditional religion, Muslim, Christian.

Wamey (Wamay, Wamei, Konyagi, Coniagui, Cogniagui, Koniagi, Conhague, Tenda) [cou] 5,270 in Guinea (2001 Pruett). Koundara Region and around Youkounkoun, extending to the Senegal border. *Other:* 'Wamey' is their own name. Konyagi is a Peul word meaning 'bees'. Nomadic. Over 3,000 migrate from Guinea to Senegal annually. Many stay longer. Traditional religion, Christian, Muslim. See main entry under Senegal.

Yalunka (Djallonke, Dyalonke, Dialonke, Jalonke, Yalunke) [yal] 55,514 in Guinea (2002 SIL). Population total all countries: 105,764. West of Faranah, south toward the Sierra Leone border and north to Passaya. Also on the Senegal-Mali border in the Balaki souspréfecture. Also spoken in Mali, Senegal, Sierra Leone. *Class:* Niger-Congo, Mande, Western, Central-Southwestern, Central, Susu-Yalunka. *Dialects:* Sulima, Firia. Close to Susu, but only marginally intelligible. Lexical similarity 83% to 92% among dialects. *Lg Dev:* NT: 1976. *Other:* Muslim.

Guinea-Bissau

Republic of Guinea-Bissau. República da Guiné-Bissau. Formerly Portuguese Guinea. 1,388,363. National or official language: Portuguese. Literacy rate: 6%. Also includes Pular (1,199), Susu (3,880), Western Maninkakan, Wolof, people from Cape Verde, Guinea, Europe. Information mainly from J. Bendor-Samuel 1989; J. Holm 1989. Blind population: 5,000 (1982 WCE). The number of languages listed for Guinea-Bissau is 21. Of those, all are living languages. See map on page 702.

Badyara (Badian, Badjara, Badyaranke, Pajade, Pajadinca, Pajadinka, Gola, Bigola) [pbp] 4,220 in Guinea-Bissau (2002). Northeast corner. *Lg Use:* The speakers may be bilingual in Mandinka. *Other:* Muslim. See main entry under Guinea.

Bainouk-Gunyuño (Banyum, Banyun, Bagnoun, Banhum, Bainuk, Banyuk, Banyung, Elomay, Elunay) [bab] 8,170 (2002). South of the Casamance River. *Class:* Niger-Congo, Atlantic-Congo, Atlantic, Northern, Eastern Senegal-Guinea, Banyun. *Dialects:* A distinct language from Bainouk-Gunyamoolo of Senegal and Gambia. Related to Kobiana and Kasanga of Senegal and Guinea-Bissau. More closely related to the Tenda languages of eastern Senegal than to Diola and Balanta. *Other:* Muslim, traditional religion.

Balanta-Kentohe (Balanta, Balant, Balante, Balanda, Ballante, Belante, Bulanda, Brassa, Alante, Frase) [ble] 367,000 in Guinea-Bissau (2002). Population total all countries: 393,000. North central and central coast. Also spoken in Gambia. *Class:* Niger-Congo, Atlantic-Congo, Atlantic, Northern, Bak, Balant-Ganja. *Dialects:* Fora, Kantohe (Kentohe, Queuthoe), Naga, Mane. Naga, Mane, and Kantohe may be separate languages. A separate language from Balanta-Ganja in Senegal. Not intelligible with Mansoanka. *Lg Dev:* Bible portions: 1980. *Other:* Traditional religion, Christian, Muslim.

Bassari (Onian, Onëyan, Ayan, Biyan, Wo, Basari) [bsc] 475 in Guinea-Bissau (2002). Northeastern. *Other:* Traditional religion, Christian. See main entry under Senegal.

Bayot (Bayote, Baiot, Bayotte) [bda] 2,025 in Guinea-Bissau (2002). Northwestern, along the border with Senegal. *Other:* Traditional religion. See main entry under Senegal.

Biafada (Beafada, Biafar, Bidyola, Bedfola, Dfola, Fada) [bif] 41,420 (2002). Central south, north of the Nalu. *Class:* Niger-Congo, Atlantic-Congo, Atlantic, Northern, Eastern Senegal-Guinea, Tenda. *Dialects:* Lexical similarity 52% with Badyara. *Other:* Muslim.

Bidyogo (Bijago, Bijogo, Bijougot, Budjago, Bugago, Bijuga) [bjg] 27,575 (2002). Roxa and Bijago islands. Anhaki is on Canhabaque (Roxa) Island, Kagbaaga on Bubaque Island, Kamona on Caravela and Caraxe islands, Kajoko on Orango and Uno islands. *Class:* Niger-Congo, Atlantic-Congo, Atlantic, Bijago. *Dialects:* Anhaqui (Anhaki), Kagbaaga, Kamona, Kajoko (Orango). Some intelligibility problems are reported between dialects. Only Kamona is said to be unintelligible to others. There are important grammatical differences between Kagbaaga and Anhaki, Kagbaaga and Kajoko. No information about dialects on Galinhas and Formosa islands. *Lg Use:* Crioulo is also spoken. *Lg Dev:* Little literacy work has been done. NT: 1975. *Other:* Anhaki spoken on Canhabaque, Kagbaaga spoken on Bubaque, Kamona spoken on Caravela and Caraxe, and Kajoko spoken on Orango and Uno. Other dialects may be spoken on Galinhas and Formosa islands. Traditional religion, Christian.

Crioulo, Upper Guinea (Kiryol, Portuguese Creole, Kriulo, Guinea-Bissau Creole) [pov] 189,850 in Guinea-Bissau (2002). Population total all countries: 392,350. Also spoken in Gambia, Senegal, USA. Also Bijagos Islands. *Class:* Creole, Portuguese based. *Dialects:* Bissau-Bolama Creole, Bafatá Creole, Cacheu-Ziguinchor Creole. *Lg Use:* Trade language. 600,000 or more second-language users (Chataigner ms.). Portuguese not well known. *Lg Dev:* Grammar. Bible: 1999.

Ejamat (Ediamat, Fulup, Feloup, Felup, Felupe, Floup, Flup) [eja] 22,000 in Guinea-Bissau (2002). Population total all countries: 24,025. Northwest corner, San Domingo District. Also spoken in Senegal. *Class:* Niger-Congo, Atlantic-Congo, Atlantic, Northern, Bak, Jola, Jola Proper, Jola Central, Her-Ejamat. *Dialects:* Lexical similarity 63% between Her-Ejamat and Jola-Fonyi or Jola-Kasa; 50% with Gusilay or Elun. *Other:* Muslim, traditional religion.

Jola-Fonyi (Kujamataak, Kújoolaak Kati Fooñi, Jola-Fogny, Diola-Fogny, Jola) [dyo] 5,996 in Guinea-Bissau (2000 WCD). *Lg Use:* Fonyi is the largest and most widely understood Jola variety. See main entry under Senegal.

Kasanga (Cassanga, Kassanga, I-Hadja, Haal) [ccj] 650 (2002). A remnant is living near Felupe, northwest, in a sparsely populated border area. None in Senegal. *Class:* Niger-Congo, Atlantic-Congo, Atlantic, Northern, Eastern Senegal-Guinea, Nun. *Dialects:* Close to Banyun. *Lg Use:* Speakers also use Mandinka. *Other:* Traditional religion.

Kobiana (Cobiana, Uboi, Buy) [kcj] 650 in Guinea-Bissau (2002). Ethnic population: 650. Near Banyun. Also spoken in Senegal. *Class:* Niger-Congo, Atlantic-Congo, Atlantic, Northern, Eastern Senegal-Guinea, Nun. *Dialects:* Close to Bainouk and Kasanga. *Lg Use:* Speakers also use Mandyak, but not vice versa. *Other:* Traditional religion.

Mandinka (Mandinga, Mandingue, Mandingo, Mandinque, Manding) [mnk] 154,200 in Guinea-Bissau (2002). North central, central, and northeastern. *Other:* Muslim. See main entry under Senegal.

Mandjak (Mandjaque, Manjaca, Manjaco, Manjiak, Mandyak, Manjaku, Manjack, Ndyak, Mendyako, Kanyop)

[mfv] 170,230 in Guinea-Bissau (2002). Population total all countries: 285,150. West and northwest of Bissau. Also spoken in France, Gambia, Senegal. *Class:* Niger-Congo, Atlantic-Congo, Atlantic, Northern, Bak, Manjaku-Papel. *Dialects:* Bok (Babok, Sarar, Teixeira Pinto, Tsaam), Likes-Utsia (Baraa, Kalkus), Cur (Churo), Lund, Yu (Pecixe, Siis, Pulhilh). Some dialects listed may be separate languages. Close to Mankanya and Papel. *Lg Use:* Important politically. Thousands have emigrated to France. *Lg Dev:* Bible portions: 1968. *Other:* Nominal prefixes, 2 plural forms; complex auxiliary verbs and aspect particles; verb suffixes; relative clauses functioning as adjectives, with nominal markers at beginning and end; pitch distinction on verbal and nominal forms; emphatic markers. Traditional religion, Christian, Muslim.

Mankanya (Mankanha, Mancanha, Mancagne, Mancang, Bola) [knf] 40,855 in Guinea-Bissau (2002). Population total all countries: 68,955. Northwest of Bissau. Also spoken in Gambia, Senegal. *Class:* Niger-Congo, Atlantic-Congo, Atlantic, Northern, Bak, Manjaku-Papel. *Dialects:* Burama (Bulama, Buram, Brame), Shadal (Sadar). Related to Mandjak. *Lg Dev:* Grammar. *Other:* Speakers are fairly well educated. Traditional religion.

Mansoanka (Mansoanca, Maswanka, Sua, Kunant, Kunante) [msw] 14,300 in Guinea-Bissau (2002). Population total all countries: 15,300. North central. Also spoken in Gambia. *Class:* Niger-Congo, Atlantic-Congo, Atlantic, Southern, Sua. *Dialects:* Not inherently intelligible with Balanta or Mandinka, although called 'Mandinkanized Balanta'. *Other:* Muslim.

Nalu (Nalou) [naj] 8,150 in Guinea-Bissau (2002). Southwest near the coast. *Lg Use:* Reported to be closed to outsiders. Many also use Susu. *Other:* Intermarriage in the border area with another group. Muslim, traditional religion. See main entry under Guinea.

Papel (Pepel, Papei, Moium, Oium) [pbo] 125,550 (2002). Bissau Island. *Class:* Niger-Congo, Atlantic-Congo, Atlantic, Northern, Bak, Manjaku-Papel. *Dialects:* Close to Mankanya and Mandyak. 3 dialects. *Lg Dev:* NT: 1996. *Other:* Traditional religion, Christian.

Portuguese [por] *Lg Use:* Official language. See main entry under Portugal.

Pulaar (Fulfulde-Pulaar, Pulaar Fulfulde, Peul, Peulh) [fuc] 245,130 in Guinea-Bissau (2002). North central and northeastern Guinea-Bissau. *Dialect:* Fulacunda (Fulakunda, Fulkunda, Fula Preto, Fula Forro). *Other:* Fula Forro are 'free' Fulas; Fulacunda are 'slave' Fulas. Muslim. See main entry under Senegal.

Soninke (Sarakole, Marka) [snk] 6,470 in Guinea-Bissau (2002). *Dialect:* Azer (Adjer, Aser, Ajer, Masiin, Taghdansh). *Lg Use:* They live among the Fula and Mandinka and speak those languages as second languages. *Other:* Ethnic groups: Aser, Aswanik, Gadyaga, Marka, Markanka, Nono, Saracole, Serahuli, Sarawule, Tonbakai, Wakove. Muslim. See main entry under Mali.

Kenya

Republic of Kenya. Jamhuriya Ya Kenya. 32,021,856. National or official languages: Swahili, English. Literacy rate: 45% (1987 official government figure). Also includes Hadrami Spoken Arabic (10,000), Hindi, Ta'izzi-Adeni Spoken Arabic (10,000). Information mainly from W. Whiteley 1969, 1974; Heine and Möhlig 1980; J. Bendor-Samuel 1989; BTL 1983–1999. Blind population: 70,000. Deaf institutions: 25. The number of languages listed for Kenya is 61. Of those, all are living languages. See map on page 703.

Arabic, Omani Spoken [acx] 15,000 in Kenya (1995). Along the coast. *Lg Dev:* Literacy is in Arabic. *Other:*

Swahili is the first language of most or all. It is reported that they came to Kenya as early as 900 A.D., originally from Yemen and Oman. Muslim. See main entry under Oman.

Boni (Aweera, Aweer, Waata, Wata, Sanye, Wasanye, Waboni, Bon, Ogoda, Wata-Bala) [bob] 3,500 in Kenya (1994). In forest hinterland behind Lamu, Lamu, and Tana River districts, Coast Province; Garissa District, North-Eastern Province. At least 11 villages. Also spoken in Somalia. *Class:* Afro-Asiatic, Cushitic, East, Rendille-Boni. *Dialects:* Close to Garre of Somalia, but not close in culture or appearance. *Lg Use:* Many are monolingual. Some also use Somali, Orma, or Swahili. *Lg Dev:* Literacy rate in first language: 10% to 30%. Literacy rate in second language: 50% to 75%. *Other:* Different from Sanye (Waat) of the Oromo Group or Dahalo (Sanye) of Southern Cushitic. Vernacular literature is desired. They are being settled in scattered villages and encouraged to switch to farming. Forest. Hunter-gatherers; agriculturalists: maize, beans. Traditional religion, Muslim.

Borana (Boran, Booran, Boraan, Southern Oromo, Oromo, "Galla") [gax] 152,000 in Kenya (1994 I. Larsen BTL). Population includes 96,000 Borana (1994), 43,000 Gabra (1994), 13,000 Sakuye (1994). Marsabit and Isiolo districts, Eastern Province. *Dialects:* Boran, Gabra (Gabbra, Gebra), Sakuye (Saguye). *Lg Use:* Also spoken by the younger Burji population around Marsabit and Moyale. *Other:* The name 'Borana' is used almost exclusively in Kenya, but 'Oromo' is used in Ethiopia. Seminomadic. Desert. Pastoralists: camel, cattle. Muslim, Christian, traditional religion. See main entry under Ethiopia (Oromo, Borana-Arsi-Guji).

Bukusu (Lubukusu) [bxk] 565,000 (1987 BTL). Population includes 47,000 Tachon (1980 Heine and Möhlig). Western Province, Bungoma District, Mt. Elgon. *Class:* Niger-Congo, Atlantic-Congo, Volta-Congo, Benue-Congo, Bantoid, Southern, Narrow Bantu, Central, J, Masaba-Luyia (J.30), Luyia. *Dialect:* Bukusu, Tachoni (Tachon). *Lg Dev:* Literacy rate in first language: 1% to 5%. Literacy rate in second language: 25% to 50%. NT: 1993. *Other:* Mountain slope. Christian.

Burji (Bambala) [bji] 7,000 in Kenya (1994 I. Larsen). Mainly around Marsabit township, Moyale. *Lg Use:* All speakers older than 20 years. Speakers below 40 years are apparently functionally bilingual in Boran. *Lg Dev:* Literacy rate in first language: below 1%. Literacy rate in second language: 15% to 25%. *Other:* Brought from Ethiopia in the 1930s to build roads from Moyale to other north Kenya towns. Mountain slope. Businessmen, agriculturalists. Christian, traditional religion. See main entry under Ethiopia.

Chonyi (Chichonyi) [coh] 121,000 (1994 I. Larsen BTL). Kilifi District, Coast Province. *Class:* Niger-Congo, Atlantic-Congo, Volta-Congo, Benue-Congo, Bantoid, Southern, Narrow Bantu, Central, E, Nyika (E.40), Mijikenda. *Dialects:* Chonyi speakers may understand Giryama. *Other:* Christian, Muslim.

Chuka (Suka, Chuku) [cuh] 70,000 (1980 SIL). Southern Meru District, Eastern Province. *Class:* Niger-Congo, Atlantic-Congo, Volta-Congo, Benue-Congo, Bantoid, Southern, Narrow Bantu, Central, E, Kikuyu-Kamba (E.20), Meru. *Dialects:* Comprehension of northern Meru dialects is borderline. Close to Tharaka. Lexical similarity 73% with Embu, 70% with Gikuyu, 67% with Meru, 63% with Kamba. *Lg Use:* Speakers in different regions also use Meru, Gikuyu, Kamba, or Swahili. *Other:* Christian.

Cutchi-Swahili (Asian Swahili) [ccl] 46,003 in Kenya (2000 WCD). Also spoken in Tanzania. *Class:* Creole, Swahili based. *Dialects:* May be adequately intelligible to speakers of standard Swahili. Cutchi-Swahili and Asian Swahili may not be the same. *Lg Use:* Asian Swahili is

used by other Asians in communicating with non-English speaking Africans and other Asians who share no other common language. Speakers also use English. *Lg Dev:* Literacy rate in first language: below 1%. Literacy rate in second language: 15% to 25%. *Other:* The first language of some Gujarati Muslims who have come from Zanzibar. It has regular but distinct phonology, lexical, and grammatical differences from Swahili, described by Whitely (1974:73–79). Muslim (Ismaili and Ithnasheri).

Daasanach (Geleb, Dama, Marille, Reshiat, "Shangilla," Daasanech, Dasenech, Dathanaik, Geleba, Gheleba) [dsh] 2,500 in Kenya (1980 SIL). Northeastern shore of Lake Turkana, around Illeret, Marsabit District, Eastern Province. *Lg Dev:* Literacy rate in first language: below 1%. Literacy rate in second language: below 5%. *Other:* "Shangilla" is a derogatory name. 8 ethnic groups: Inkabelo (7,000), Inkoria (2,000), Naritch (Naarich 1,800), Elele (1,500), Randal (1,000), Oro (800), Koro (500), Riele (400). Plains. Semiarid desert. Animal husbandry: cattle; agriculturalists: millet, tobacco; fishermen. Traditional religion, Christian. See main entry under Ethiopia.

Dahalo (Sanye, Guo Garimani) [dal] 400 (1992 Brenzinger). Ethnic population: 400. Near the mouth of the Tana River, Lamu and Tana River districts, Coast Province. *Class:* Afro-Asiatic, Cushitic, South. *Dialects:* The language has clicks, although unrelated to Khoisan languages. *Lg Use:* Highly assimilated and bilingual in Swahili. *Other:* Different from Sanye (Waata). The name "Dahalo" is derogatory. Traditional religion.

Digo (Kidigo, Chidigo) [dig] 217,000 in Kenya (1994 I. Larsen BTL). Population total all countries: 305,000. Kwale District, Coast Province, south of Mombasa. Also spoken in Tanzania. *Class:* Niger-Congo, Atlantic-Congo, Volta-Congo, Benue-Congo, Bantoid, Southern, Narrow Bantu, Central, E, Nyika (E.40), Mijikenda. *Dialects:* Partially intelligible with Giryama but the most remote from Giryama of the Mijikenda Subgroup. Lexical similarity 74% with Duruma, 72% with Chonyi and Swahili, 71% with Swahili dialects Mrima and Mvita, 67% with Amu, 62% with Bajun, 58% with Lower Pokomo. *Lg Use:* Vigorous. Speakers also use Swahili. *Lg Dev:* Literacy rate in first language: below 1%. Literacy rate in second language: 45% in Swahili. Bible portions: 1982–2000. *Other:* A moderate degree of Swahili influence. Coastal. Agriculturalists; fishermen; traders; industry workers. Muslim, traditional religion, Christian.

Duruma [dug] 247,000 (1994 SIL). West Kwale District, Coast Province, south of Mombasa to the Tanzanian border. *Class:* Niger-Congo, Atlantic-Congo, Volta-Congo, Benue-Congo, Bantoid, Southern, Narrow Bantu, Central, E, Nyika (E.40), Mijikenda. *Dialects:* Of the nine Mijikenda dialects, Duruma is the second most remote from Giryama linguistically. Lexical similarity 4% with Digo, 66% with Swahili. *Lg Use:* Vigorous. Language attitudes toward Giryama indicate the need for separate Duruma literature. Comprehension of Swahili and Digo is low. *Lg Dev:* Literacy rate in first language: below 1%. Literacy rate in second language: 13%. NT: 1999. *Other:* Traditional religion, Christian, Muslim.

El Molo (Elmolo, Fura-Pawa, Ldes, Dehes, "Ndorobo") [elo] 8 (1994 Larsen). Ethnic population: 400 (2000 M. Brenzinger). Southeastern shore of Lake Turkana, Elmolo Bay, Marsabit District, Eastern Province. *Class:* Afro-Asiatic, Cushitic, East, Western Omo-Tana. *Dialects:* The original language is close to Daasanach. *Lg Use:* May be extinct. All speakers older than 50 years (1994). Most of the ethnic group now speak Samburu. They are affiliated with the Samburu. *Other:* Plains. Semiarid desert. Fishermen. Traditional religion, Christian. Nearly extinct.

Embu (Kiembu) [ebu] 429,000 (1994 I. Larsen BTL). Population includes 150,000 in Embu, 61,725 in Mbeere

(1980 Heine and Möhlig). Embu District, Eastern Province. *Class:* Niger-Congo, Atlantic-Congo, Volta-Congo, Benue-Congo, Bantoid, Southern, Narrow Bantu, Central, E, Kikuyu-Kamba (E.20). *Dialects:* Mbeere (Mbere, Kimbeere), Embu. Mbeere is reported to have adequate intelligibility of Embu. The population estimate may include Chuka and Mwimbi-Muthambi. Lexical similarity 85% with Mbeere, 73% with Gikuyu and Chuka, 66% with Kamba, 63% to 65% with Meru. *Lg Use:* Some speakers have proficiency in Gikuyu because of previous teaching in the schools, but it is limited in rural areas. Up to 70% have low proficiency in Swahili. Comprehension of Meru is limited. *Lg Dev:* Literacy rate in first language: below 1%. Literacy rate in second language: 25% to 50%. *Other:* 'Embo' is an incorrect spelling. There are government literacy materials in Embu. Embu: Christian, traditional religion; Mbeere: traditional religion, Christian.

Endo (Endo-Marakwet, Marakuet, Markweta) [enb] 80,000 (1997 SIL). Rift Valley Province, Elgeyo Marakwet District. *Class:* Nilo-Saharan, Eastern Sudanic, Nilotic, Southern, Kalenjin, Nandi-Markweta, Markweta. *Dialects:* Endo, Sambirir. Low intelligibility with major Kalenjin dialects and Talai. *Lg Dev:* Literacy rate in first language: below 1%. Literacy rate in second language: 5% to 15%. Bible portions: 1998–2000. *Other:* Marakwet is a cover term for Endo-Sambirir and Talai. Animal husbandry: cattle, goats, sheep; hunters; agriculturalists. Traditional religion, Christian.

English [eng] *Lg Use:* Official language. Mainly second-language speakers in Kenya. See main entry under United Kingdom.

Garreh-Ajuran [ggh] 128,000 (1994 I. Larsen BTL). Population includes 96,000 Garreh, 32,000 Ajuran. Mandera and Wajir districts, North Eastern Province. *Class:* Afro-Asiatic, Cushitic, East, Oromo. *Dialects:* Garreh (Gurreh, Garre, Gari), Ajuran (Ajuuraan, Ujuuraan). Part of a dialect cluster. Lexical similarity 85% with Boran. *Lg Use:* The Ajuran in Kenya speak Somali as second language. Swahili is also used, and some can also speak the Garre of Somalia, which their ancestors spoke. In Somalia (not Kenya), the Ajuran ethnic group speak a variety of Common Somali as first language, and the Garre ethnic group apparently speak a language related to Somali. *Lg Dev:* Literacy rate in second language: 2%. *Other:* Seminomadic. Pastoralists. Muslim, Christian.

Gikuyu (Kikuyu, Gekoyo, Gigikuyu) [kik] 5,347,000 (1994 I. Larsen BTL). West central Kenya, in Kiambu, Murang'a, Nyeri, and Kirinyaga districts, Central Province. *Class:* Niger-Congo, Atlantic-Congo, Volta-Congo, Benue-Congo, Bantoid, Southern, Narrow Bantu, Central, E, Kikuyu-Kamba (E.20). *Dialects:* Southern Gikuyu (Kiambu, Southern Murang'a), Ndia (Southern Kirinyaga), Gichugu (Northern Kirinyaga), Mathira (Karatina), Northern Gikuyu (Northern Murang'a, Nyeri). Lexical similarity 73% with Embu, 70% with Chuka, 67% with Kamba, 63% with Meru. *Lg Use:* Speakers also use Swahili or English. *Lg Dev:* Literacy rate in first language: 30% to 60%. Literacy rate in second language: 75% to 100%. 95% of the children are in school. Grammar. Bible: 1951–1965. *Other:* Mountain slope, hills, plains. Agriculturalists: sorghum, millet, beans, sweet potatoes, maize, potatoes, cassava, bananas, sugarcane, yams, fruit, tobacco, coffee, castor oil, tea, pyrethrum, peas; animal husbandry: goats, sheep, cattle. Christian, traditional religion.

Giryama (Giriama, Agiryama, Kigiriama, Nika, Nyika, Kinyika) [nyf] 623,000 (1994 I. Larsen BTL). Population includes 496,000 Giryama, 17,000 Kauma, 19,000 Jibana, 13,000 Kambe, 72,000 Rabai, 6,000 Ribe. North of Mombasa, Kilifi and Kwale districts, Coast Province.

Class: Niger-Congo, Atlantic-Congo, Volta-Congo, Benue-Congo, Bantoid, Southern, Narrow Bantu, Central, E, Nyika (E.40), Mijikenda. *Dialects:* Kauma, Ribe (Rihe), Jibana (Dzihana), Kambe, Giryama, Chwaka, Rabai. Digo and Duruma are the most distinct from Giryama. Dialect speakers may understand Chonyi. Lexical similarity 72% with Digo, 63% with Mrima, 62% with Mvita, 61% with Amu, 59% with Lower Pokomo and Bajun. *Lg Use:* Most speak Swahili fairly well. Many school children are learning English. *Lg Dev:* Literacy rate in first language: below 1%. Literacy rate in second language: 15% to 25%. Bible: 1901. *Other:* Different from Nyiha (Nyika) of Tanzania and Zambia. Strong traditional social system. Nine ethnic groups, all called 'Mijikenda'. Coastal. Agriculturalists, cash crops. Traditional religion, Christian, Muslim.

Gujarati [guj] 50,000 in Kenya (1995 SIL). Mainly in Nairobi. *Other:* Most have lived in Kenya for several generations. Hindu, Jain, Muslim. See main entry under India.

Gusii (Kisii, Kosova, Guzii, Ekegusii) [guz] 1,582,000 (1994 I. Larsen BTL). Southwestern, south of Kavirondo Gulf, Kisii District, Nyanza Province. *Class:* Niger-Congo, Atlantic-Congo, Volta-Congo, Benue-Congo, Bantoid, Southern, Narrow Bantu, Central, E, Kuria (E.10). *Lg Use:* 500,000 second-language speakers. *Lg Dev:* Literacy rate in second language: 15% to 25%. Bible: 1988. *Other:* Different from Kisi of Tanzania. Christian, traditional religion.

Idakho-Isukha-Tiriki [ida] 306,000 (1987 BTL). Population includes Idakho 65,000, Isukha 90,000, Tiriki 100,000 (1980 Heine and Möhlig). Kakamega District, Western Province. *Class:* Niger-Congo, Atlantic-Congo, Volta-Congo, Benue-Congo, Bantoid, Southern, Narrow Bantu, Central, J, Masaba-Luyia (J.30), Luyia. *Dialects:* Idakho (Idaxo, Itakho, Kakamega, Kakumega), Isukha (Isuxa, Lwisukha), Tiriki. Speakers have high comprehension of Logooli, but there is resistance to each other's pronunciation. *Lg Use:* Lexical similarity 70% with Logooli, 52% with Masaba (Uganda) and Saamia. *Lg Dev:* Literacy rate in first language: below 1%. Literacy rate in second language: 15% to 25%. Bible portions: 2000. *Other:* Christian.

Kachchi (Cutchi, Kacchi, Katchi, Cutch) [kfr] 10,000 in Kenya (1995 SIL). Nairobi, Mombasa, and main trade routes. *Lg Use:* Used in the home. Speakers also use Gujarati, English, or Swahili. *Other:* Masons; merchants (70% of Kenyan Asians). Hindu (Swami Narayan), Muslim (Memon and Shi'a Ismaili), Christian. See main entry under India.

Kalenjin [kln] 2,458,123 (1989 census). Population includes 471,459 Kipsigis, 261,969 Nandi, 110,908 Keiyo, 130,249 Tugen (1980 Heine and Möhlig). Mainly Nandi, Kericho, and Uasin Gishu districts, Rift Valley Province. *Class:* Nilo-Saharan, Eastern Sudanic, Nilotic, Southern, Kalenjin, Nandi-Markweta, Nandi. *Dialects:* Nandi (Naandi, Cemual), Terik (Nyang'ori), Kipsigis (Kipsiikis, Kipsikis, Kipsikiis), Keiyo (Keyo, Elgeyo), South Tugen (Tuken), Cherangany. Lexical similarity 60% with Omotik, 50% with Datooga. *Lg Dev:* Literacy rate in first language: below 1%. Literacy rate in second language: 15% to 25%. Bible: 1939–1969. *Other:* VSO. Agriculturalists: millet, maize, potatoes, beans, pumpkins, tobacco, bananas, tea, sweet potatoes, sugarcane, peas, fruit, coffee, pyrethrum; animal husbandry: cattle, goats, sheep, poultry. Keiyo: Christian, traditional religion; Kipsigis: Christian, traditional religion; Nandi: Christian, traditional religion.

Kamba (Kikamba, Kekamba) [kam] 2,448,300 (1989 census). South central, Machakos and Kitui districts, Eastern Province. Some in Kwale District, Coast Province.

Class: Niger-Congo, Atlantic-Congo, Volta-Congo, Benue-Congo, Bantoid, Southern, Narrow Bantu, Central, E, Kikuyu-Kamba (E.20). *Dialects:* Masaku, South Kitui, North Kitui, Mumoni. Lexical similarity 67% with Gikuyu, 66% with Embu, 63% with Chuka, 57% to 59% with Meru. *Lg Use:* 600,000 second-language speakers. *Lg Dev:* Literacy rate in first language: below 1%. Literacy rate in second language: 25% to 50%. Bible: 1956. *Other:* Mountain slope. 450 to 1,600 meters. Agriculturalists: sorghum, millet, maize, beans, peas, sweet potatoes, yams, cassava, sugarcane, bananas, tobacco; animal husbandry: cattle, sheep, goats; traders; woodcarvers. Christian, traditional religion, Muslim.

Kenyan Sign Language (KSL) [xki] Students in primary schools in 1990: 2,600. There are around 200,000 deaf people in Kenya. It is not known how many know KSL. 32 primary schools for the deaf in Hola, Kapsabet, Karatina, Karen, Kerugoya, Kilifi, Kisumu, Kitui, Kwale, Meru, Mombasa, Mumias, Murang'a, Nairobi, Nakuru, North Kinangop, Ruiru, Sakwa. Schools under the Kenya Institute of Education (KIE) use a Kenyan version of (American) Exact Signed English, including one at Machakos. KSL is used at Nyangoma School at Bondo, a primary and boys' technical school (Sakwa), and in one girl's school. A school in Mombasa uses British Sign Language. Some Belgian brothers use Belgian Sign language in a school near Oyugis. 4 churches in Nairobi: 2 use KIE Signed English, 1 a mixture of that and KSL, the other uses a mixture of Korean, American, and Kenyan Sign Languages. *Class:* Deaf sign language. *Dialects:* Mainly unrelated to other sign languages. It has become standardized with slight variations since 1961, when elementary schools for deaf children were begun. The deaf from Kisumu (western Kenya) to the deaf in Mombasa (eastern Kenya) can understand each other completely even with some dialect differences. The deaf in Uganda and Tanzania do not really understand KSL, though they have much in common. *Lg Use:* Used in court cases involving deaf people. The Kenya National Association of the Deaf which has 12 branches. The government is using KIE (Kenya Signed English). The University of Nairobi backs KSL. Little research. *Lg Dev:* Dictionary. *Other:* Communication with those who do not know KSL is superficial only. KSL fits Kenyan culture and ties students back to their families and friends who know it. There is a manual alphabet for spelling.

Konkani, Goanese (Gomataki, Goan, Goanese) [gom] 3,900 in Kenya (1987). Nairobi. *Lg Use:* Used by many Asians whose ancestors came from Goa or north India. Not used in schools. Goanese Konkani is the language of the home and community. Speakers also use English. See main entry under India.

Kuria (Kikuria, Igikuria, Ekiguria, Kurya, Tende) [kuj] 135,000 in Kenya (1994 I. Larsen BTL). The first four dialects listed are in Kenya, Kuria District, Nyanza Province. The last three dialects are in Tanzania. *Dialects:* Nyabasi, Bugumbe, Bukira, Bwirege, Kiroba, Simbiti, Sweta. *Other:* 'Koria' is not considered proper spelling. Christian, traditional religion. See main entry under Tanzania.

Logooli (Ragoli, Uluragooli, Llugule, Lugooli, Maragooli, Luragoli, Llogole, Maragoli) [rag] 197,000 (1987 BTL). Kakamega District, Western Province. *Class:* Niger-Congo, Atlantic-Congo, Volta-Congo, Benue-Congo, Bantoid, Southern, Narrow Bantu, Central, J, Masaba-Luyia (J.30), Luyia. *Dialects:* Lexical similarity 70% to 80% with Idakho-Isukha-Tiriki. *Lg Dev:* Literacy rate in first language: 10% to 30%. Literacy rate in second language: 50% to 75%. Bible: 1951. *Other:* The people are called 'Avalogoli'. 'Mulogoli' is a person from Maragoli.

Luo (Dholuo, Nilotic Kavirondo, Kavirondo Luo) [luo] 3,185,000 in Kenya (1994 I. Larsen BTL). Population total all countries: 3,465,000. Nyanza Province. Also spoken in Tanzania. *Class:* Nilo-Saharan, Eastern Sudanic, Nilotic, Western, Luo, Southern, Luo-Acholi, Luo. *Lg Dev:* Literacy rate in first language: 10% to 30%. Literacy rate in second language: 50% to 75%. Bible: 1953–1977. *Other:* Different from Lwo of Uganda or Lwo (Luo, Jur Lwo) of Sudan. Fishermen. Christian, traditional religion, Muslim.

Luyia (Luluyia, Luhya) [luy] 3,418,083 in Kenya (1989 census). Population includes 135,000 Wanga, 65,000 Marama, 45,000 Tsotso 60,000 Kisa, 105,000 Kabras, 50,000 Saamia, 35,000 West Nyala, 60,000 Khayo, 60,000 Marachi (1980 SIL). Population total all countries: 3,643,461. Lake Victoria area, Western Province. Saamia and Songa dialects are in Uganda. Also spoken in Uganda. *Class:* Niger-Congo, Atlantic-Congo, Volta-Congo, Benue-Congo, Bantoid, Southern, Narrow Bantu, Central, J, Masaba-Luyia (J.30), Luyia. *Dialects:* Kisa (Shisa, Lushisa), Marama, Wanga (Hanga, Luhanga, Oluhanga, Kawanga, Oluwanga), Tsotso, Saamia (Samia, Olusamia, Lusamia, Lusaamia, Samya), West Nyala (Nyala-B), Khayo, Songa, Marachi, Kabras. Saamia has 88% lexical similarity with Wanga, 80% with Nyore, 62% with Masaba, 59% to 61% with Ganda, 52% with Isuxa, 51% with Gwere. Dialects in Uganda have 92% lexical similarity. *Lg Dev:* Literacy rate in first language: 10% to 30%. Literacy rate in second language: 50% to 75%. Bible: 1975. *Other:* The people are called 'Abaluyia', singular 'Muluyia'. Christian, traditional religion, Muslim.

Maasai (Masai) [mas] 453,000 in Kenya (1994 I. Larsen BTL). Population total all countries: 883,000. Kajiado and Narok districts, Rift Valley Province. Also spoken in Tanzania. *Class:* Nilo-Saharan, Eastern Sudanic, Nilotic, Eastern, Lotuxo-Teso, Lotuxo-Maa, Ongamo-Maa. *Dialects:* Kaputiei, Keekonyokie, Matapo, Laitokitok, Iloodokilani, Damat, Purko, Loitai, Siria, Moitanik (Wuasinkishu), Kore, Arusa (Arusha), Parakuyo (Baraguyu, Kwavi), Kisonko. Arusha is distinct from the Bantu Chaga-related variety. One source reports that Arusha who are pastoralists dress like the Maasai and speak a Maasai-related variety, whereas those who are agriculturalists intermarry with the Chaga. Other sources say the Arusha originally spoke a Bantu language. The dialects listed in Tanzania have 82% to 86% lexical similarity with Kenya dialects. In Kenya, Purko has 91% to 96% lexical similarity with other Kenya dialects, 82% with Baraguyu, 86% with Arusha, 77% to 89% with Samburu, 82% to 89% with Chamus, 60% to 90% with Ngasa (Ongamo). *Lg Use:* The Kore now speak Somali as first language. *Lg Dev:* Literacy rate in first language: below 1%. Literacy rate in second language: 18%. Bible: 1991. *Other:* Seminomadic. Purko is the largest dialect in Kenya and centrally located. VSO. Pastoralists: cattle, goats; agriculturalists. Traditional religion, Christian.

Malakote (Ilwana) [mlk] 8,000 (1994 I. Larsen BTL). Tana River north of Pokomo, between Bura and Garissa, Tana River District, Coast Province. *Class:* Niger-Congo, Atlantic-Congo, Volta-Congo, Benue-Congo, Bantoid, Southern, Narrow Bantu, Central, E, Nyika (E.40), Malakote. *Dialects:* Not intelligible with Upper Pokomo or Lower Pokomo. Lexical similarity 57% with Lower Pokomo, 55% with Upper Pokomo. *Lg Dev:* Literacy rate in first language: below 1%. Literacy rate in second language: below 5%. *Other:* Cushitic influence. Agriculturalists; fishermen. Muslim.

Meru (Kimeru) [mer] 1,305,000 (1994 I. Larsen BTL). Population includes 540,000 Meru, 26,400 Igoji (1980 Berne and Mölig). Meru District, Eastern Province, northeast of Mt. Kenya. *Class:* Niger-Congo, Atlantic-Congo, Volta-Congo, Benue-Congo, Bantoid, Southern,

Narrow Bantu, Central, E, Kikuyu-Kamba (E.20), Meru. *Dialects:* Meru, Igembe, Tigania, Imenti, Miutini, Igoji. Lexical similarity 85% between Imenti and Tigania. 67% similarity with Chuka, 63% with Embu and Gikuyu, 57% with Kamba. *Lg Dev:* Literacy rate in first language: 5% to 10%. Literacy rate in second language: 25% to 50%. Bible: 1964. *Other:* 'Mero' is not a correct spelling. Different from Meru of Tanzania. Traditional religion, Christian, Muslim.

Mwimbi-Muthambi [mws] 70,000 (1980 SIL). Central Meru District, Eastern Province. *Class:* Niger-Congo, Atlantic-Congo, Volta-Congo, Benue-Congo, Bantoid, Southern, Narrow Bantu, Central, E, Kikuyu-Kamba (E.20), Meru. *Dialects:* Mwimbi (Kimwimbi), Muthambi. People may be able to use Meru literature. *Other:* Christian.

Nubi (Ki-Nubi, Kinubi) [kcn] 10,000 in Kenya. Population includes 3,000 to 6,000 in Kibera. Kibera, outside Nairobi. *Lg Use:* Speakers use Swahili for out-group communication and Nubi for in-group communication, with a stable bilingualism. 30% can also use English. Non-Nubi wives of Nubi men are expected to learn Nubi. *Lg Dev:* Literacy rate in first language: below 1%. Literacy rate in second language: below 5%. *Other:* Muslim. See main entry under Uganda.

Nyala, East [nle] 35,000 (1980 SIL). Lake Victoria area, Western Province. *Class:* Niger-Congo, Atlantic-Congo, Volta-Congo, Benue-Congo, Bantoid, Southern, Narrow Bantu, Central, J, Masaba-Luyia (J.30), Luyia.

Nyore (Olunyore, Lunyore, Nyole, Nyoole, Lunyole, Olunyole) [nyd] 120,000 (1980 Heine and Möhlig). Above Kavirondo Gulf, Kakamega District, Western Province. *Class:* Niger-Congo, Atlantic-Congo, Volta-Congo, Benue-Congo, Bantoid, Southern, Narrow Bantu, Central, J, Masaba-Luyia (J.30), Luyia. *Dialects:* Lexical similarity 61% with Nyole of Uganda. *Lg Dev:* NT: 1936–1996. *Other:* SVO. Christian.

Okiek (Akiek, Akie, Ogiek, "Ndorobo," Kinare) [oki] Few speakers in Kenya (1980 Heine and Möhlig). Population total all countries 500. Ethnic population: 36,869 (2000). On East Mau Escarpment, Nakuru District, Rift Valley Province. The Sogoo live in the southern Mau Forest between the Amala and Ewas Ng'iro rivers near the Nosogami stream. Also spoken in Tanzania. *Class:* Nilo-Saharan, Eastern Sudanic, Nilotic, Southern, Kalenjin, Okiek. *Dialect:* Okiek, Suiei, Sogoo (Sokoo). *Lg Use:* Some "Ndorobo" languages are nearly extinct. The Akiek in northern Tanzania now speak Maasai. The Akiek of Kinare in Kenya now speak Kikuyu. Those in Tanzania and Kenya are not in contact with each other. Sogoo may be extinct. "The language is remembered by a few old men married to Kikuyu women and living in Kikuyu communities" (Dimmendaal 1989). Some also use Kalenjin. Most or all Okiek have high proficiency in an adopted language. *Other:* "Ndorobo" is a derogatory cover term for several small hunter or forest groups, not linguistically related (El Molo, Yaaku, Okiek, Omotik, Aasax). Forest, mountain slope. Hunter-gatherers (formerly); beekeepers. Christian.

Omotik (Omotic, Laamoot, "Ndorobo") [omt] 50 (1980). Ethnic population: 200 or more (2000). Around Lemek, Narok District, Rift Valley Province. *Class:* Nilo-Saharan, Eastern Sudanic, Nilotic, Southern, Tatoga. *Dialect:* Suiei. Lexical similarity 60% with Kalenjin, 50% with Datooga. *Lg Use:* Speakers are older adults. The majority of ethnic group now speak Maasai. Most or all "Ndorobo" language speakers are highly bilingual in an adopted language. *Other:* "Ndorobo" is a derogatory cover term for several small hunter or forest groups, not linguistically related (El Molo, Yaaku, Okiek, Omotik). Some are nearly extinct. Traditional religion. Nearly extinct.

Orma (Uardai, Wadai, Warday, Wardei) [orc] 55,000 (1994 I. Larsen BTL). Population includes 5,000 Munyo. Garissa and Tana River districts, Northeastern and Coast provinces. The Oromo spoken in the Lower Jubba Region of Somalia may actually be Orma. The Orma controlled that area until the mid or late 19th century. They move from the lower Tana River inland toward Kitui District during rainy season. *Class:* Afro-Asiatic, Cushitic, East, Oromo. *Dialects:* Munyo (Korokoro, Munyo Yaya), Waata (Sanye), Orma. Distinct from Boran. Munyoyaya is an ethnic group speaking a dialect of Orma. *Lg Dev:* Bible portions: 2000. *Other:* Savannah, semiarid. Orma: pastoralists: cattle, sheep, goats; Munyo: fishermen. Muslim.

Panjabi, Eastern (Punjabi, Gurmukhi, Gurumukhi) [pan] 10,000 in Kenya (1995 SIL). Nairobi. *Dialect:* Panjabi Proper. *Other:* Most came to Kenya with the building of the railroad at the turn of the 20th century. Sikh, Hindu, Muslim. See main entry under India.

Pokomo, Lower (Kipokomo, Pfokomo, Malachini) [poj] 29,000 (1994 I. Larsen BTL). Lower Tana River, Tana River District, Coast Province. *Class:* Niger-Congo, Atlantic-Congo, Volta-Congo, Benue-Congo, Bantoid, Southern, Narrow Bantu, Central, E, Nyika (E.40), Pokomo. *Dialects:* Mwina, Buu I, Buu II, Buu III, Kulesa, Ngatana, Dzunza, Kalindi. Lexical similarity 76% with Upper Pokomo, 63% with Mvita, 61% with Amu, 60% with Mrima, 59% with Giryama, 58% with Digo, 57% with Bajun. *Lg Use:* 75% of the speakers have some degree of bilingual proficiency in Swahili. *Lg Dev:* Literacy rate in first language: below 1%. Literacy rate in second language: 25% to 50%. NT: 1902. *Other:* Agriculturalists; fishermen. Traditional religion, Christian.

Pokomo, Upper [pkb] 34,000 (1994 I. Larsen BTL). Population includes 5,000 Malalulu, 6,000 Zubaki, 2,100 Ndura, 2,600 Kinakomba, 1,500 Gwano, 6,150 Ndera. Upper Tana River, Tana River District, Coast Province. *Class:* Niger-Congo, Atlantic-Congo, Volta-Congo, Benue-Congo, Bantoid, Southern, Narrow Bantu, Central, E, Nyika (E.40), Pokomo. *Dialects:* Malalulu, Zubaki, Ndura, Kinakomba, Gwano, Ndera. *Lg Dev:* Literacy rate in first language: below 1%. Literacy rate in second language: 15% to 25%. *Other:* Riverine. Agriculturalists; fishermen. Muslim.

Pökoot (Pökot, Suk, Pakot) [pko] 264,000 in Kenya (1994 I. Larsen BTL). Baringo and West Pokot districts, Rift Valley Province. Also spoken in Uganda. *Class:* Nilo-Saharan, Eastern Sudanic, Nilotic, Southern, Kalenjin, Pokot. *Dialects:* East Pokot, West Pokot. *Lg Dev:* Literacy rate in first language: below 1%. Literacy rate in second language: 15% to 25%. NT: 1967–1987. *Other:* Seminomadic. Mountain slope, plains. Pastoralists: cattle, sheep, goats; agriculturalists. Traditional religion, Christian.

Rendille (Rendile, Randile) [rel] 32,000 (1994 I. Larsen BTL). Marsabit District, between Lake Turkana and Marsabit Mt., Eastern Province. *Class:* Afro-Asiatic, Cushitic, East, Rendille-Boni. *Lg Dev:* Literacy rate in first language: below 1%. Literacy rate in second language: 5% to 15%. Bible portions: 1993–2000. *Other:* Nomadic. The Ariaal Rendille people live in inter-dependent relationship with the Samburu and speak Samburu. SOV. Semiarid desert. Pastoralists: camels, sheep, goats, cattle. Traditional religion, Muslim, Christian.

Sabaot (Mt. Elgon Maasai) [spy] 143,000 (1994 I. Larsen BTL). Mt. Elgon District, Western Province. Also Trans-Nzoia District in Rift Valley Province. *Class:* Nilo-Saharan, Eastern Sudanic, Nilotic, Southern, Kalenjin, Elgon. *Dialects:* Bong'omeek (Bong'om, Pong'om), Koony (Kony), Book (Bok, Pok). Related to Sebei of

Uganda. *Lg Use:* Bung'omek is being absorbed by Bukusu. *Lg Dev:* Literacy rate in first language: below 1%. Literacy rate in second language: 27%. NT: 1998. *Other:* Pastoralists: cattle; agriculturalists. Christian, traditional religion.

Sagalla (Kisagala, Kisagalla, Sagala, Teri, Saghala) [tga] 10,000 (1980 Heine and Möhlig). Taita Hills, slopes of Sagala Hill, Taita District, Coast Province. *Class:* Niger-Congo, Atlantic-Congo, Volta-Congo, Benue-Congo, Bantoid, Southern, Narrow Bantu, Central, E, Nyika (E.40), Taita. *Dialects:* Dambi, Mugange, Teri, Kishamba, Gimba, Kasigau. Lexical similarity 62% with Taita. *Lg Dev:* Literacy rate in first language: below 1%. Literacy rate in second language: 15% to 25%. NT: 1994. *Other:* Distinct from Sagala of Tanzania. Traditional religion, Christian, Muslim.

Samburu (Sambur, Sampur, Burkeneji, Lokop, E Lokop, Nkutuk) [saq] 147,000 (1994 I. Larsen BTL). Population includes 128,000 Samburu, 19,000 Chamus. Samburu District, and south and east shores of Lake Baringo, Baringo District, Rift Valley Province (Chamus). *Class:* Nilo-Saharan, Eastern Sudanic, Nilotic, Eastern, Lotuxo-Teso, Lotuxo-Maa, Ongamo-Maa. *Dialect:* Chamus (Ilcamus, Njemps). Lexical similarity 94% to 88% with Chamus, 89% to 77% with Maasai, 59% with Ngasa (Ongamo), 82% between Chamus and Maasai. *Lg Use:* The El Molo mainly speak Samburu now, a slightly different dialect. *Lg Dev:* Literacy rate in first language: below 1%. Literacy rate in second language: Samburu: 15% to 25%, Chamus: 41%. *Other:* Nomadic. Pastoralists: cattle, goats, sheep. Samburu: traditional religion, Christian; Chamus: traditional religion, Christian.

Sanye (Sanya, Wasanye, Ariangulu, Langulo, Waata, Waat) [ssn] 5,000 (1980 SIL). Lower parts of Tana River, Lamu District, Coast Province. *Class:* Afro-Asiatic, Cushitic, East, Oromo. *Lg Dev:* Literacy rate in first language: below 1%. Literacy rate in second language: 15% to 25%. *Other:* They have maintained their language in spite of change in economy and pressure from other languages. Distinct language from Dahalo (Sanye) or Boni. Forest dwellers. Formerly hunter-gatherers; now agriculturalists. Muslim, Christian.

Somali (Standard Somali) [som] 420,354 in Kenya (2000 WCD). Population includes 45,098 Somali, 27,244 Hawiyah, 100,400 Degodia,139,597 Ogaden (1989 census). Northeastern Province around Wajir. *Dialects:* Degodia, Ogaden. *Lg Dev:* Literacy rate in first language: below 1%. Literacy rate in second language: Somali: 15% to 25%, Ogaadeen: 1%. *Other:* Daarood, Dir, Hawiye, Ogaadeen are clan families in Kenya. The people are nomadic. Dialect differences cut across clan differences. Pastoralists: camel, sheep, goats. Muslim. See main entry under Somalia.

Suba [suh] 129,000 in Kenya (1994 I. Larsen BTL). Population includes 37,000 Mfangano, 32,000 Gwasi, 22,000 Kaksingri, 15,000 Muhuru, 10,000 Suna, 8,000 Wiregi, 5,000 Ungoe (1997). Population total all countries: 159,000. Eastern shores of Lake Victoria, Mfangano and Rusinga islands. Also spoken in Tanzania. *Class:* Niger-Congo, Atlantic-Congo, Volta-Congo, Benue-Congo, Bantoid, Southern, Narrow Bantu, Central, E, Kuria (E.10). *Dialects:* Mfangano, Gwasi, Kaksingri, Muhuru, Suna, Wiregi, Ungoe. Suba is a major part of the Kuria subgroup. *Lg Use:* Vigorous use of Suba in Kaksingiri and Mfangano Island. The majority use Luo as second language. *Lg Dev:* Literacy rate in first language: below 1%. Literacy rate in second language: 25% to 50%. Bible portions: 1993–1999.

Swahili (Kiswaheli, Kiswahili, Suahili, Kisuahili, Arab-Swahili) [swh] 131,000 in Kenya. Population includes 66,000 Bajuni (1994 I. Larsen BTL), 6,000 Siyu, 3,000

Pate, 15,000 Amu, 25,000 to 30,000 Mvita, 13,900 Shirazi (1989 census), 2,000 Vumba (1980 Heine and Möhlig). Coast Province. *Dialects:* Amu, Mvita (Kimvita, Mombasa), Bajuni (Bajun, T'ik'uu, Tikulu, Tukulu, Gunya, Mbalazi, Chimbalazi), Pate, Pemba (Phemba, Hadimu, Tambatu), Mrima, Fundi, Siu (Siyu), Shamba (Kishamba), Matondoni. *Lg Use:* Official language. Classical and modern literature. *Lg Dev:* Literacy rate in second language: 51%. Swahili is compulsory in primary education. *Other:* In the Mombasa area they call themselves 'Arab' or 'Shirazi', in Lamu area they call themselves 'Bajun'. The dialects listed are in Kenya. Bajuni is the most divergent. Bajuni and Pemba may be separate languages. Coastal, valley. Traders; small businessmen; Bajun: fishermen; agriculturalists. Muslim. See main entry under Tanzania.

Taita (Dabida, Davida, Kidabida, Teita, Kitaita, Dawida) [dav] 203,389 (1989 census). Taita hills, Taita District, Coast Province. *Class:* Niger-Congo, Atlantic-Congo, Volta-Congo, Benue-Congo, Bantoid, Southern, Narrow Bantu, Central, E, Nyika (E.40), Taita. *Dialects:* Mbololo, Werugha, Mbale, Chawia, Bura, Mwanda. Lexical similarity 62% with Sagalla, 46% with Gweno, 41% to 44% with Chaga. *Lg Use:* Speakers are highly bilingual in Swahili. *Lg Dev:* Literacy rate in first language: 1% to 5%. Literacy rate in second language: 25% to 50%. NT: 1922–1990. *Other:* Christian, traditional religion, Muslim.

Talai (Marakwet) [tle] 38,091 (2000 WCD). Rift Valley Province. *Class:* Nilo-Saharan, Eastern Sudanic, Nilotic, Southern, Kalenjin, Nandi-Markweta, Markweta. *Dialects:* Low intelligibility of basic Kalenjin dialects and Endo. *Lg Dev:* Literacy rate in first language: below 1%. Literacy rate in second language: 15% to 25%. *Other:* 'Marakwet' is a cover term for Talai and Endo. Traditional religion, Christian.

Taveta (Kitaveta, Kitubeta, Tubeta) [tvs] 14,358 (1989 census). Around Taveta in adjacent areas. Taita District, Coast Province. *Class:* Niger-Congo, Atlantic-Congo, Volta-Congo, Benue-Congo, Bantoid, Southern, Narrow Bantu, Central, G, Shambala (G.20). *Dialects:* Closely related to Asu. *Lg Use:* Those younger than 30 years old in Kenya are highly bilingual in Swahili. *Lg Dev:* Literacy rate in first language: 1% to 5%. Literacy rate in second language: 25% to 50%. NT: 1906. *Other:* Christian.

Teso (Ateso) [teo] 279,000 in Kenya (2001 Johnstone and Mandryk). Busia District, Western Province. *Other:* Christian, traditional religion. See main entry under Uganda.

Tharaka (Kitharaka, Saraka, Sharoka) [thk] 112,000 (1994 I. Larsen BTL). Eastern Meru District, Embu District, and some in Kitui District, Eastern Province. *Class:* Niger-Congo, Atlantic-Congo, Volta-Congo, Benue-Congo, Bantoid, Southern, Narrow Bantu, Central, E, Kikuyu-Kamba (E.20), Meru. *Dialects:* Gatue (North Tharaka), Thagichu (Kitui), Ntugi (Central Tharaka), Tharaka (South Tharaka). Thagichu dialect has extensive Kamba borrowings. Gatue dialect is influential. Difficult intelligibility of northern Meru dialects. Some Meru words have offensive meanings in Tharaka. Close to Chuka. *Lg Use:* Older people's dialect is more prestigious because of lack of borrowings, but few people use it. English is used in schools and offices; Swahili in churches, schools, jobs, and sometimes in the home. Gikuyu and Meru also used. *Lg Dev:* Literacy rate in first language: below 1%. Literacy rate in second language: 30% Swahili or English. NT: 2000. *Other:* Agriculturalists: millet, sorghum. Traditional religion, Christian.

Tugen, North (North Tuken, Tuken) [tuy] 144,000 (1987 BTL). West central, west of the Kalenjin. *Class:* Nilo-Saharan, Eastern Sudanic, Nilotic, Southern, Kalenjin, Nandi-Markweta, Nandi. *Dialects:* People may not be able to use Kalenjin literature. *Other:* Traditional religion, Christian.

Turkana (Bume, Buma, Turkwana) [tuv] 340,000 in Kenya (1994 I. Larsen BTL). Population total all countries: 365,163. Turkana, Samburu, Trans-Nzoia, Laikipia, Isiolo districts, Rift Valley Province, west and south of Lake Turkana, and Turkwel and Kerio rivers. Also spoken in Ethiopia. *Class:* Nilo-Saharan, Eastern Sudanic, Nilotic, Eastern, Lotuxo-Teso, Teso-Turkana, Turkana. *Dialects:* Northern Turkana, Southern Turkana. Inherently intelligible with Toposa, but hostile toward the speakers. Also partially intelligible with Karamojong, Jie, and Nyangatom, but all five are ethnically distinct. There are a few phonological, lexical, and discourse marker differences between them. Northern Turkana and Eastern Toposa are closer; Southern Turkana and Western Toposa are farther apart linguistically. The four varieties form a cluster divided in the middle by the Kenya-Sudan border. Lexical similarity 85% similarity with Karamojong, 76% with Teso. *Lg Use:* Vigorous. Unfriendly toward the Karamojong and Pokot; friendly with Jie. Most are monolingual. Only a few adults have mastered upcountry Swahili as lingua franca. More are learning Swahili because of a new road. A few can speak Pokot or Daasenech. *Lg Dev:* Literacy rate in first language: 5% to 10%. Literacy rate in second language: 25% to 50%. NT: 1986. *Other:* A few Somali and Gikuyu have shops in the area. Seminomadic. VSO; highly inflectional; grammatical tone; vowel harmony; voiceless vowels. Plains. Semiarid desert. 350 to 2,000 meters. Pastoralists: cattle, sheep, goats, camels, donkeys; fishermen. Traditional religion, Christian.

Yaaku (Mukogodo, Mogogodo, Mukoquodo, Siegu, Yaakua, "Ndorobo") [muu] 50 (1983). Ethnic population: 250 (1983). Laikipia District, Mukogodo Division, Mukogodo Forest west of Doldol, foothills north of Mt. Kenya. *Class:* Afro-Asiatic, Cushitic, East, Yaaku. *Lg Use:* Few domains. Speakers are older adults. Negative language attitude. Most or all "Ndorobo" groups are highly bilingual in an adopted language. *Other:* "Ndorobo" is a derogatory cover term for several small hunter or forest groups, which are not linguistically related (El Molo, Yaaku, Okiek, Omotik). Forest. Hunter-gatherers; pastoralists. Christian. Nearly extinct.

Lesotho

Kingdom of Lesotho. Formerly Basutoland. 1,865,040. National or official languages: South Sotho, English. Literacy rate: 59% to 74%. Also includes Afrikaans, people from France, India, Pakistan. Information mainly from J. Bendor-Samuel 1989. Blind population: 3,000 (1982 WCE). Deaf institutions: 1. The number of languages listed for Lesotho is 5. Of those, all are living languages. See map on page 704.

English [eng] *Lg Use:* Official language. See main entry under United Kingdom.

Phuthi [ssw] 43,000 in Lesotho (2002). See main entry under Swaziland (Swati).

Sotho, Southern (Suto, Suthu, Souto, Sesotho, Sisutho) [sot] 1,770,000 in Lesotho (2001 Johnstone and Mandryk). Population total all countries: 4,874,197. Also spoken in Botswana, South Africa. *Class:* Niger-Congo, Atlantic-Congo, Volta-Congo, Benue-Congo, Bantoid, Southern, Narrow Bantu, Central, S, Sotho-Tswana (S.30), Sotho, Southern. *Dialects:* Sotho, Pedi, and Tswana are largely inherently intelligible but have generally been considered separate languages. *Lg Use:* National language. *Lg Dev:* Magazines. Newspapers. Radio programs. TV. Bible: 1878–1989. *Other:* Christian, traditional religion.

Xhosa [xho] 18,000 in Lesotho (1993 Johnstone). Sebapala Valley, villages near Tosing; Tele Valley, Sinxondo. See main entry under South Africa.

Zulu [zul] 248,000 in Lesotho (1993). Butha-Buthe District, Caledonspoort Border Post. See main entry under South Africa.

Liberia

Republic of Liberia. 3,390,635. National or official language: English. Literacy rate: 25% (1989 WA). Also includes Eastern Maninkakan (33,800), people from Lebanon, elsewhere in West Africa. Information mainly from J. Bendor-Samuel 1989; TILL 1973–1998. Blind population: 15,000 (1982 WCE). Deaf institutions: 1. The number of languages listed for Liberia is 30. Of those, all are living languages. See map on page 705.

Bandi (Bande, Gbandi, Gbande, Gbunde) [bza] 100,000 in Liberia (2001 Johnstone and Mandryk). 50,000 have fled to Guinea (1993 Johnstone). Population total all countries: 107,000. Lofa County, northwest Liberia. Also spoken in Guinea. *Class:* Niger-Congo, Mande, Western, Central-Southwestern, Southwestern, Mende-Loma, Mende-Bandi, Bandi. *Dialects:* Tahamba, Wawana, Wulukoha, Hasala, Lukasa, Hembeh. Tahamba dialect used for literature. Lexical similarity 96% among the 6 dialects, 83% with the closest Mende dialect. *Lg Dev:* Grammar. NT: 2000. *Other:* Erroneously but often called 'Gbandi' or 'Gbande'. Traditional religion, Muslim, Christian.

Bassa [bsq] 347,600 in Liberia (1991 Vanderaa). Population total all countries: 352,600. Grand Bassa, Rivercess, and Montserrado counties, central Liberia. Gbii overlaps into Nimba County. Also spoken in Sierra Leone. *Class:* Niger-Congo, Atlantic-Congo, Volta-Congo, Kru, Western, Bassa. *Dialects:* Gbor, Gba Sor, Mabahn, Hwen Gba Kon, Central Bassa, Rivercess Bassa. *Lg Use:* Speakers also use Liberian English. *Lg Dev:* NT: 1970. *Other:* Different from Bassa of Nigeria or Bassa (Basaa) of Cameroon. Indigenous Vah script, developed around 1900 by Dr. Lewis, alphabetical, with tone marked, is still used by older men. SVO. Hills. Tropical forest, swamp. Agriculturalists: upland rice. Christian, traditional religion.

Dan (Yacouba, Yakuba, Gio, Gyo, Da, Gio-Dan) [daf] 150,800 to 200,000 in Liberia (1993 SIL). Nimba County, north central Liberia. *Dialects:* Upper Gio, Lower Gio, River Cess Gio. *Other:* Traditional religion. See main entry under Côte d'Ivoire.

Dewoin (De, Dey, Dei, Dewoi) [dee] 8,100 (1991 Vanderaa). Montserrado County near the coast and Monrovia, primarily between the Lofa and St. Paul rivers. *Class:* Niger-Congo, Atlantic-Congo, Volta-Congo, Kru, Western, Bassa. *Dialects:* No significant dialect differences. Lexical similarity 72% with Bassa. *Lg Use:* Many also use English. *Lg Dev:* Literacy rate in second language: 5%. *Other:* Many loans from other languages. Muslim, traditional religion, Christian.

English [eng] 69,000 in Liberia (1993). *Dialect:* Liberian Standard English. *Lg Use:* Official language. See main entry under United Kingdom.

Gbii (Gbi-Dowlu, Gbee) [ggb] 5,600 (1991 Vanderaa). Nimba County, central Liberia, west of Cestos River. *Class:* Niger-Congo, Atlantic-Congo, Volta-Congo, Kru, Western, Bassa. *Dialects:* Kplor, Dorbor. Lexical similarity 78% with Bassa. *Lg Use:* Many understand Bassa, but the reverse is not true. Many understand English. Liberian English is also used. *Other:* Traditional religion.

Glaro-Twabo [glr] 4,273 in Liberia (2000 WCD). Grand Gedeh County, northeastern Liberia. Refugees in Côte d'Ivoire. Also spoken in Côte d'Ivoire. *Class:* Niger-Congo, Atlantic-Congo, Volta-Congo, Kru, Western, Wee, Guere-Krahn. *Dialects:* Glaro, Twabo. Minimal intelligibility between Twabo and some Eastern Krahn dialects, but not between Glaro and Eastern Krahn. Lexical similarity 82% with some Eastern Krahn dialects. Glaro and Twabo have 87% lexical similarity. *Other:* Tropical forest. Traditional religion.

Glio-Oubi (Glio, Oubi, Ubi) [oub] 3,500 in Liberia (1991). Population total all countries: 6,000. Northeast. Six towns on each side of the border. Also spoken in Côte d'Ivoire. *Class:* Niger-Congo, Atlantic-Congo, Volta-Congo, Kru, Western, Grebo, Glio-Oubi. *Dialects:* Closest lexical similarity is 75% with Twabo of Liberia and 73% with Trepo of Côte d'Ivoire. *Other:* Called 'Glio' in Liberia and 'Oubi' in Côte d'Ivoire. Traditional religion.

Gola [gol] 99,300 in Liberia (1991 Vanderaa). Population total all countries: 107,300. Western Liberia, between the Mano and St. Paul rivers. Also spoken in Sierra Leone. *Class:* Niger-Congo, Atlantic-Congo, Atlantic, Southern, Mel, Gola. *Dialects:* Deng (Todii), Kongba, Senje. *Lg Dev:* Bible portions. *Other:* Different from Gola of Nigeria or Gola (Badyara) of Guinea and Guinea-Bissau. SVO; CV; tonal. Muslim, Christian, traditional religion.

Grebo, Barclayville (Wedebo Grebo) [gry] 23,700 (1991 Vanderaa). 387,000 all Grebo languages in Liberia (2001 Johnstone and Mandryk). Grand Gedeh County. Southeast coast and inland, between Klao and Jabo Grebo. *Class:* Niger-Congo, Atlantic-Congo, Volta-Congo, Kru, Western, Grebo, Liberian. *Dialects:* Wedebo, Kplebo. A dialect cluster. Dialects are quite distinct. Many phonological differences with Jabo, which would make literacy difficult if they were combined. *Lg Use:* They identify with Klao, but understand Grebo better. There are strong ethnocentric attitudes between subgroups. *Other:* Traditional religion.

Grebo, Central [grv] 29,131 (2000 WCD). Eastern border, including Barrobo. *Class:* Niger-Congo, Atlantic-Congo, Volta-Congo, Kru, Western, Grebo, Liberian. *Dialects:* Globo, Nyenebo, Dorobo, Borobo, Trembo. Distinct from Gboloo. Dialects may be quite distinct. *Other:* Traditional religion.

Grebo, Gboloo (Gboloo, Gblou Grebo) [gec] 56,300 (1991 Vanderaa). Eastern Province, Maryland County, eastern border, north of Jabo Grebo. *Class:* Niger-Congo, Atlantic-Congo, Volta-Congo, Kru, Western, Grebo, Liberian. *Dialects:* Gederobo, Nyanoun, Tuobo, Biabo, Dediebo. *Other:* Tropical forest. Traditional religion.

Grebo, Northern [gbo] 84,500 (1999 LBT). Southeast, Grand Gedeh, Maryland, and Kru Coast counties near the Côte d'Ivoire border, south of Krahn, north of Klao, west of Glaro. *Class:* Niger-Congo, Atlantic-Congo, Volta-Congo, Kru, Western, Grebo, Liberian. *Dialects:* Chedepo, E Je (Eh Je), Palipo, Gbepo (Gbeapo), Jedepo, Tienpo, Klepo, Fopo-Bua, Northeastern Grebo. Dialect cluster. Dialects are quite distinct. Subdialects of Northeastern dialect are Nitiabo, Sabo, Tuobo, Ketiepo, Webo. *Lg Use:* Ethnocentric attitudes are strong between different subgroups. *Lg Dev:* NT: 1989. *Other:* Traditional religion.

Grebo, Southern [grj] 28,700 in Liberia (1999 LBT). Eastern Province, Grand Gedeh and Maryland counties, southeastern coast and inland. Also spoken in Côte d'Ivoire. *Class:* Niger-Congo, Atlantic-Congo, Volta-Congo, Kru, Western, Grebo, Liberian. *Dialects:* Glebo (Seaside Grebo), Jabo, Nyabo, Wrelpo. A dialect cluster. Dialects are quite distinct. *Lg Use:* Ethnocentric attitudes are strong between subgroups. *Other:* Traditional religion.

Kisi, Southern (Kissi, Gizi, Gisi, Kissien) [kss] 115,000 in Liberia (1995). Population total all countries: 200,000. Lofa County, extreme northwest corner of Liberia. Also spoken in Sierra Leone. *Class:* Niger-Congo, Atlantic-Congo, Atlantic, Southern, Mel, Bullom-Kissi, Kissi. *Dialects:* Luangkori, Tengia, Warn. Different from Northern Kissi of Guinea. *Lg Dev:* Literacy rate in second

language: 20%. NT: 1991. *Other:* Traditional religion, Christian, Muslim.

Klao (Kru, Kroo, Klaoh, Klau) [klu] 184,000 in Liberia (1991 Vanderaa). Population total all countries: 192,000. Coastal and inland, Eastern Province. Also spoken in Ghana, Nigeria, Sierra Leone, USA. *Class:* Niger-Congo, Atlantic-Congo, Volta-Congo, Kru, Western, Klao. *Dialects:* Western Klaoh, West Central Klaoh, Central Klaoh, Eastern Klaoh. *Lg Dev:* NT: 1999. *Other:* SVO main clause; SOV embedded clause. Traditional religion.

Kpelle, Liberia (Kpele, Gbese, Pessa, Pessy, Kpwessi) [xpe] 487,400 (1991 Vanderaa). Central. *Class:* Niger-Congo, Mande, Western, Central-Southwestern, Southwestern, Kpelle. *Dialects:* Dialect differences are slight. Different enough from Kpelle of Guinea to need separate literature. *Lg Dev:* NT: 1967. *Other:* Largest group in Liberia. Traditional religion, Christian.

Krahn, Eastern (Eastern Kran, Kran) [kqo] 47,000 (1991 L. Vanderaa CRC). Population includes 20,000 Tchien (1992 UBS). Northeast near Côte d'Ivoire border. *Class:* Niger-Congo, Atlantic-Congo, Volta-Congo, Kru, Western, Wee, Konobo. *Dialect:* Gorbo, Kanneh, Konobo, Tchien (Chiehn). Minimal intelligibility between some dialects and Twabo. Distinct from Western Krahn, Sapo, and Central Guéré. Lexical similarity 93% between Gorbo and Kanneh, 87% between Gorbo and Konobo. *Lg Dev:* Bible portions: 1953–1994. *Other:* Traditional religion, Christian, Muslim.

Krahn, Western (Krahn, Northern Krahn, Western Kran, Kran) [krw] 47,800 in Liberia (1991). Population total all countries: 60,000. Near the border of Côte d'Ivoire, Grand Gedeh County. Also spoken in Côte d'Ivoire. *Class:* Niger-Congo, Atlantic-Congo, Volta-Congo, Kru, Western, Wee, Guere-Krahn. *Dialects:* Gbo, Gbaeson (Gbaison, Gbarzon), Plo, Biai, Gbarbo, Gborbo (Gbobo), Kpeaply. Dialects in Côte d'Ivoire have French influences. *Lg Dev:* Côte d'Ivoire orthography differs from Liberia. NT: 1992–1995. *Other:* Traditional religion, Christian, Muslim.

Krumen, Tepo (Southern Krumen, Krumen, Kroumen, Kru) [ted] 2,913 in Liberia (2000 WCD). Glawlo dialect is in southeastern Liberia. Other dialects are in southwestern Côte d'Ivoire. *Dialects:* Tepo, Bapo, Plapo, Wlopo (Ropo), Dapo, Honpo, Yrepo (Kapo), Glawlo. *Other:* Traditional religion. See main entry under Côte d'Ivoire.

Kuwaa (Kwaa, Kowaao, Belleh, Belle) [blh] 12,800 (1991 Vanderaa). Lofa County, south of Bandi and Loma, north of Kpelle. *Class:* Niger-Congo, Atlantic-Congo, Volta-Congo, Kru, Kuwaa. *Dialects:* Only minor pronunciation differences exist between the two Kuwaa clans; Lubaisu and Gbade. *Lg Use:* Many of the Kuwaa also speak the nearby languages Bandi, Loma, and Kpelle. *Lg Dev:* Literacy rate in second language: 5%. NT: 1989. *Other:* Traditional religion, Christian, Muslim.

Liberian English (Liberian Pidgin English) [lir] *Class:* Pidgin, English based, Atlantic. *Dialect:* Kru Pidgin English. Regional dialects. *Lg Use:* Trade language. 1,500,000 second-language speakers (1984 census). Used as a second language for communication between different language groups. *Lg Dev:* Radio programs. *Other:* As different from Standard English as is Sierra Leone Krio. Repidginized from American Black English of the 1800s (J. Holm).

Loma (Looma, Loghoma, Lorma, "Buzi," "Busy," "Bouze") [lom] 141,800 (1991 Vanderaa). Northwest Liberia Loffa County, border area. *Class:* Niger-Congo, Mande, Western, Central-Southwestern, Southwestern, Mende-Loma, Loma. *Dialects:* Gizima, Wubomei, Ziema, Bunde, Buluyiema. Distinct enough from Toma of Guinea to need separate literature. *Lg Dev:* Literature and literacy program in progress. NT: 1971. *Other:* "Buzi" is an offensive name. Different from Loma of Côte d'Ivoire. Traditional religion, Christian.

Maninka, Konyanka (Konya, Konyakakan) [mku] North area bordering Guinea. *Other:* Differs from Guinea variety in the use of English loans. Muslim. See main entry under Guinea.

Mann (Maa, Mah, Mano, Mawe) [mev] 185,000 in Liberia (1995). Population total all countries: 256,022. Nimba County, north central Liberia. Also spoken in Guinea. *Class:* Niger-Congo, Mande, Eastern, Southeastern, Guro-Tura, Tura-Dan-Mano, Mano. *Lg Dev:* NT: 1978. *Other:* Traditional religion, Christian.

Manya (Manya Kan, Mandingo) [mzj] 45,400 in Liberia (1991 Vanderaa). Population total all countries: 70,400. Also spoken in Guinea. *Class:* Niger-Congo, Mande, Western, Central-Southwestern, Central, Manding-Jogo, Manding-Vai, Manding-Mokole, Manding, Manding-East, Southeastern Manding. *Dialects:* Lexical similarity 70% with Konyanka, 66% with Eastern Maninkakan. *Other:* Muslim, Christian.

Mende (Boumpe, Hulo, Kossa, Kosso) [men] 19,700 in Liberia (1991 Vanderaa). *Other:* Muslim. See main entry under Sierra Leone.

Sapo (Southern Krahn, Sarpo) [krn] 31,600 (1991 Vanderaa). Eastern, Sinoe County, and Grand-Gedeh County (Putu). Adjacent to Eastern Krahn, Tchien dialect. *Class:* Niger-Congo, Atlantic-Congo, Volta-Congo, Kru, Western, Wee, Guere-Krahn. *Dialects:* Nomopo (Nimpo), Waya (Wedjah), Juarzon, Sinkon (Senkon), Putu, Kabade (Karbardae). All Western Wè and Sapo dialects are related by 84% to 97% lexical similarity, including some Wè dialects in Côte d'Ivoire. *Lg Dev:* Bible portions: 1956. *Other:* Traditional religion, Christian.

Tajuasohn (Tajuosohn, Tajuoso, Tajuason) [tja] 9,600 (1991 Vanderaa). Sino County, north of Greenville. *Class:* Niger-Congo, Atlantic-Congo, Volta-Congo, Kru, Western, Klao. *Dialects:* Five clans speaking inherently intelligible dialects. Many can understand Klao, but the reverse is not true. *Other:* Traditional religion.

Vai (Vei, Vy, Gallinas, Gallines) [vai] 89,500 in Liberia (1991 L. Vanderaa CRC). Population total all countries: 105,000. Western. Also spoken in Sierra Leone. *Class:* Niger-Congo, Mande, Western, Central-Southwestern, Central, Manding-Jogo, Manding-Vai, Vai-Kono. *Dialects:* Different from Kono. *Lg Use:* 20% use English, 10% Mende, 5% Gola as second language. *Lg Dev:* Literacy rate in second language: 10%. Grammar. NT: 2002. *Other:* Indigenous script, a syllabary invented by Duala Bukare in the 1820s or 1830s. SOV. Muslim, traditional religion, Christian.

Libya

Socialist People's Libyan Arab Jamahiriya. al-Jamahiriyah al-Arabiya al-Libya al-Shabiya al-Ishtirakiya. 5,631,585. 500,000 resident foreign workers (1986 USA Today). National or official language: Standard Arabic. Literacy rate: 22% to 60%. Also includes Egyptian Spoken Arabic (1,000,000), Italian, Tedaga (2,000), Western Cham, Zaghawa (7,000), many laborers from Sudan, North Africa, Chad, Korea, Pakistan, Bangladesh, Europe. Information mainly from J. Applegate 1970; D. Cohen 1985. Deaf institutions: 2. The number of languages listed for Libya is 9. Of those, all are living languages. See map on page 693.

Arabic, Libyan Spoken (Libyan Vernacular Arabic, Sulaimitian Arabic) [ayl] 4,200,000 in Libya (1995). Population total all countries: 4,505,000. Especially in the northern half of Libya. Also spoken in Egypt, Niger. *Class:* Afro-Asiatic, Semitic, Central, South, Arabic.

Dialects: Tripolitanian Arabic, Southern Libyan Arabic, Eastern Libyan Arabic. In the west, it is similar to the Bedouin Arabic of southern Tunisia. *Lg Use:* French is used as second language; 20% use Italian. *Lg Dev:* Literacy rate in second language: 50%. *Other:* Agriculturalists: wheat, barley, olives, citrus, dates; animal husbandry. Muslim (Sunni).

Arabic, Standard [arb] *Lg Use:* National language. Used for nearly all written materials, formal speeches. Not a first language, but taught in schools. See main entry under Saudi Arabia.

Awjilah (Aujila, Augila, Aoudjila) [auj] 3,000 (2000). Women are monolingual. Cyrenaica, eastern Libya. *Class:* Afro-Asiatic, Berber, Eastern, Awjila-Sokna. *Lg Use:* Mainly older speakers. Most men also use Libyan Spoken Arabic. *Other:* Outsiders moving into their territory. They cultivate small gardens using subsoil water from 6 to 12 meters below the surface. Muslim (Sunni).

Domari [rmt] 31,738 in Libya (2000 WCD). *Dialect:* Helebi. *Other:* Muslim. See main entry under Iran.

Ghadamès [gha] 2,000 in Libya. Population total all countries: 4,000. Ghadamès, a small oasis near the Algeria-Tunisia border. Also spoken in Tunisia. *Class:* Afro-Asiatic, Berber, Northern, Zenati, East. *Dialects:* Ayt Waziten, Elt Ulid. *Other:* Muslim.

Libyan Sign Language [lbs] *Class:* Deaf sign language.

Nafusi (Djerbi, Nefusi, Jabal Nafusi, Jebel Nefusi, Jbel Nafusi) [jbn] 141,000 in Libya (1998). Population total all countries: 167,000. Tripolitania, western Libya, isolated area around the towns of Nalut and Yafran, Jabal Nafusah Region, coastal area around Zuara, west of Tripoli. Also spoken in Tunisia. *Class:* Afro-Asiatic, Berber, Northern, Zenati, East. *Dialects:* Zuara (Zouara, Zuwarah, Zwara, Zuraa), Tamezret (Duwinna), Jerbi (Jerba). Zuara dialect well known in Jebel Nafusa area and in Jerba Tunisia. Some visit Zuara, but not vice versa. Dialect of Matmata and Tatawine area less well understood by speakers in Jerba or Zuara. Speakers in Zuara and Jebel areas understand Jerba stories well. *Lg Use:* All domains. All ages. Speakers take pride in using Nafusi. Preschool children are monolingual in Nafusi. *Other:* Most live apart from Arabized inhabitants of the region. Semiarid. Dam builders; agriculturalists. Muslim (Ibadi).

Sawknah (Sokna) [swn] 5,448 (2000 WCD). Tripolitania. *Class:* Afro-Asiatic, Berber, Eastern, Awjila-Sokna. *Other:* Muslim.

Tamahaq, Tahaggart (Tamashekin, Tourage, Tomachek, Tamachek, Tuareg, Toureg) [thv] 17,000 in Libya (1993 Johnstone). The Hoggar dialect is in the south Hoggar (Ajjer) Mountain area around Tamanrasset and south into Niger. The Ghat dialect is in southeast Algeria around Ganet and west Libyan oases around Ghat. *Dialects:* Hoggar (Ahaggaren, Ajjer, Tahaggart), Ghat (Ganet, Djanet). *Other:* 'Tuareg' are the people ('Targi' is the singular); 'Tamahaq' is the language. Volcanic mountain slope. Inadan: blacksmiths; jewelry craftsmen. Muslim. See main entry under Algeria.

Madagascar

Democratic Republic of Madagascar. Repolika Demokratika Malagasy. 17,501,871. National or official languages: Standard Malagasy, French. Literacy rate: 46%. Also includes Morisyen (4,000), Réunion Creole French (45,000), Arabic (20,000), Chinese (16,000). Information mainly from P. Verin, Kottak, and Gorlin 1969; A. Ramer 1995. Blind population: 40,000 (1982 WCE). Deaf institutions: 2. The number of languages listed for Madagascar is 13. Of those, all are living languages. See map on page 690.

Comorian (Comores Swahili, Komoro, Comoro) [swb]
20,000 in Madagascar (2001 Johnstone and Mandryk).
Dialects: Shinzwani (Anjouan), Shimaore (Mayotte).
Other: Vanilla, perfume production. Muslim. See main
entry under Comoros.
French [fra] 18,000 in Madagascar (1993 Johnstone).
Lg Use: Official language. See main entry under France.
Madagascar Sign Language [mzc] *Class:* Deaf sign
language. *Dialects:* Similar to Norwegian Sign Language.
Other: Deaf people learn to sign at school, not first
language.
Malagasy, Antankarana (Tankarana) [xmv] 88,000
(1996). Northern tip, Antananarivo. *Class:* Austronesian,
Malayo-Polynesian, Barito, East, Malagasy. *Dialects:*
Lexical similarity 71% with Merina. *Other:* VOS.
Agriculturalists.
Malagasy, Bara [bhr] 500,000 (2002). South central
Madagascar, Ibara, south of Betsileo, west of Tesaka, east
of Masikoro, north of Anosy, Androy, and Mahafaly.
Class: Austronesian, Malayo-Polynesian, Barito, East,
Malagasy. *Dialects:* Lexical similarity 69% with Merina.
Malagasy, Masikoro [msh] 90,000 (2001). Southwest
Madagascar, Toliara Province, Toliara and Morombe
districts. *Class:* Austronesian, Malayo-Polynesian, Barito,
East, Malagasy. *Dialects:* Lexical similarity 72% with
Merina.
Malagasy, Northern Betsimisaraka [bmm] 900,000
(2001). East coast of Madagascar, Toamasina Province,
Mananara Avaratra, Soanierana-Ivongo, Fenoarivo
Antsinana, Vavatenina, Toamasina districts. *Class:*
Austronesian, Malayo-Polynesian, Barito, East, Malagasy.
Malagasy, Plateau [plt] 5,940,000 in Madagascar
(2002). Population total all countries: 5,948,700. The
central part of the Island. Also spoken in Comoros,
Réunion. *Class:* Austronesian, Malayo-Polynesian, Barito,
East, Malagasy. *Dialects:* Merina, Betsileo, Sihanaka,
Bezanozano, Tanala. The closest language outside of
Madagascar is Ma'anyan in south Borneo (Kalimantan,
Indonesia). *Lg Use:* Official language. *Lg Dev:*
Dictionary. Grammar. Bible: 1835–1938. *Other:* Loans
from Bantu languages, Swahili, Arabic, English, French.
VOS. Agriculturalists: coffee, cloves, vanilla, rice;
perfume. Traditional religion, Christian, Muslim.
Malagasy, Sakalava [skg] 350,000 (2001). Northwest
Madagascar, Mahajanga Province, Maintirano, Morafenobe,
Besalampy, Soalala, Mitsinjo, Ambato Boina, Marovoay,
Mahajanga, Analalava districts; Antsiranana Province,
Ambanja District. *Class:* Austronesian, Malayo-Polynesian,
Barito, East, Malagasy. *Dialects:* Northern Sakalava, Vezo.
Malagasy, Southern Betsimisaraka (Antesaka)
[bjq] 600,000 (2001). East coast of Madagascar,
Toamasina Province, Mahanoro District; Fianarantsoa
Province, Nosy Varika, Mananjary, Manakara Atsimo
districts. *Class:* Austronesian, Malayo-Polynesian, Barito,
East, Malagasy.
Malagasy, Tandroy-Mahafaly (Tandroy) [tdx]
650,000 (2001). Southern Madagascar, Toliara Province,
Beloha, Tsihombe, Ambovombe, Bekily districts. *Class:*
Austronesian, Malayo-Polynesian, Barito, East, Malagasy.
Dialects: Lexical similarity 62% with Merina.
Malagasy, Tanosy [txy] 350,000 (2002 SIL). Southeast
Madagascar, along the coast. Others south of the Onilahy
River, south of Ibara and north of Androy, northeast of
Mahafaly and the area in between. *Class:* Austronesian,
Malayo-Polynesian, Barito, East, Malagasy. *Dialects:*
Lexical similarity 75% with Merina.
Malagasy, Tsimihety (Tsimihety) [xmw] 1,016,000
(1996). North central. *Class:* Austronesian, Malayo-
Polynesian, Barito, East, Malagasy. *Dialects:* Lexical
similarity 68% with Merina. *Lg Dev:* Bible portions:
1924. *Other:* VOS. Agriculturalists.

Malawi

Republic of Malawi. Formerly Nyasaland. 11,906,855.
National or official languages: Nyanja (Chewa), Tumbuka,
English. Literacy rate: 25% to 41%. Also includes Bemba,
Bengali, Fipa, Greek (2,000), Gujarati (5,000), Portuguese
(9,000), Shona, Urdu. Information mainly from R. B.
Boeder; Patai 1972; J. Bendor-Samuel 1989. Blind
population: 18,000 (1982 WCE). The number of languages
listed for Malawi is 14. Of those, all are living languages.
See map on page 708.

Afrikaans [afr] *Other:* Spoken by people of Dutch descent
from South Africa. See main entry under South Africa.
English [eng] 16,000 in Malawi (1993). *Lg Use:* Official
language. See main entry under United Kingdom.
Kachchi (Katchi, Kacchi, Kachi, Cuchi, Cutch) [kfr]
Lg Use: Spoken by the majority of Asians in Malawi.
Other: Muslim. See main entry under India.
Kokola (Kokhola) [kzn] 200,000 in Malawi (2000).
Southeastern border, south of Mlanje and Cholo, north of
Chiromo. Also spoken in Mozambique. *Class:* Niger-
Congo, Atlantic-Congo, Volta-Congo, Benue-Congo,
Bantoid, Southern, Narrow Bantu, Central, P, Makua
(P.30). *Dialects:* One source says they are a subgroup of
Lolo, which is a subgroup of Lomwe. May be intelligible
with Lomwe. Close to Marendje and Takwane. *Lg Use:*
Most speakers use Chewa (Nyanja) as second language.
Lambya (Ichilambya, Lambia, Lambwe, Rambia) [lai]
45,000 in Malawi (2001 Johnstone and Mandryk).
Population total all countries: 85,000. Northwestern tip,
bordering Tanzania and Zambia. Also spoken in Tanzania.
Class: Niger-Congo, Atlantic-Congo, Volta-Congo,
Benue-Congo, Bantoid, Southern, Narrow Bantu, Central,
M, Nyika-Safwa (N.20). *Dialects:* Sukwa (1,000 to 3,000
in 1992) in the Sukwa Hills, northern Malawi, came from
Tanzania, and may be intelligible with Lambya.
Lomwe, Malawi (Nguru, Anguru) [lon] 250,000 (2001
Johnstone and Mandryk). Southeastern, south of Lake
Kilwa, south of the Yao, northeast of the Sena. *Class:*
Mixed Language, Makhua-Nyanja. *Dialects:* Not
intelligible with Lomwe of Mozambique. Different from
Ngulu (Kingulu) of Tanzania. *Lg Use:* Speakers also use
Nyanja (Chewa). *Other:* Traditional religion.
Ndali [ndh] 70,000 in Malawi (2003 SIL). *Dialect:* Sukwa.
See main entry under Tanzania.
Nyakyusa-Ngonde (Kinyakyusa, Ikinyikyusa,
Nyekyosa, Ngonde, Ikingonde, Konde, Nkonde, Nkhonde,
Mombe, Sochile, Sokile, Kukwe, Nyakusa) [nyy] 300,000
in Malawi (1993 Johnstone). Northern tip, south of the
Lambya, west of Lake Malawi. *Dialects:* Nyakyusa,
Nkonde. See main entry under Tanzania.
Nyanja (Chinyanja, Chewa) [nya] 7,000,000 in Malawi
(2001 Johnstone and Mandryk). Population total all
countries: 9,349,471. West central and southwestern. Also
spoken in Botswana, Mozambique, Zambia, Zimbabwe.
Class: Niger-Congo, Atlantic-Congo, Volta-Congo,
Benue-Congo, Bantoid, Southern, Narrow Bantu, Central,
N, Nyanja (N.30). *Dialects:* Chewa (Chichewa, Cheva,
Sheva), Ngoni, Manganja (Waganga, Cimanganja), Nyasa,
Peta (Cipeta, Maravi, Marave, Malawi). Most Ngoni in
Malawi speak Chewa or Tumbuka. *Lg Use:* Official
language. 400,000 second-language speakers (1999 WA).
Lg Dev: Newspapers. Radio programs. Dictionary.
Grammar. Bible: 1905. *Other:* SVO. Traditional religion,
Christian.
Sena, Malawi (Cisena, Chisena) [swk] 270,000 (2001
Johnstone and Mandryk). Southern tip bordering
Mozambique. *Class:* Niger-Congo, Atlantic-Congo,
Volta-Congo, Benue-Congo, Bantoid, Southern, Narrow

Bantu, Central, N, Senga-Sena (N.40), Sena. *Dialects:* Closely related to Kunda. *Lg Dev:* NT: 2000.

Tonga (Chitonga, Siska, Sisya, Western Nyasa, Kitonga) [tog] 170,000 (2001 Johnstone and Mandryk). North of Bandawe, west shore of Lake Malawi, Northern Province. *Class:* Niger-Congo, Atlantic-Congo, Volta-Congo, Benue-Congo, Bantoid, Southern, Narrow Bantu, Central, N, Manda (N.10). *Lg Dev:* Bible: 1987. *Other:* Different from Tonga of Zimbabwe and Zambia and Gitonga of Mozambique.

Tumbuka (Tumboka, Chitumbuka, Tamboka, Tambuka, Timbuka, Tombucas) [tum] 940,000 in Malawi (2001 Johnstone and Mandryk). Population total all countries: 1,332,000. Northern Province, west shore of Lake Malawi, south of the Ngonde, north of the Tonga and Ngoni. Also spoken in Zambia. *Class:* Niger-Congo, Atlantic-Congo, Volta-Congo, Benue-Congo, Bantoid, Southern, Narrow Bantu, Central, N, Tumbuka (N.20). *Dialects:* Chitumbuka, Chikamanga (Kamanga, Henga), Nenya, Poka (Chipoka, Phoka), Yombe, Senga, Nthali, Fungwe, Wenya, Hewe (Hewa). Most Ngoni in Malawi speak Tumbuka or Chewa. *Lg Use:* National language. *Lg Dev:* Bible: 1957–1980. *Other:* Kandawire and Fulirwa are clans, not dialects. Christian, traditional religion.

Yao (Chiyao, Achawa, Adsawa, Adsoa, Ajawa, Ayawa, Ayo, Ayao, Djao, Haiao, Hiao, Hyao, Jao, Veiao, Wajao) [yao] 1,000,000 in Malawi (2001 Johnstone and Mandryk). Population total all countries: 1,942,000. Around the southeastern tip of Lake Malawi, bordering Mozambique. Also spoken in Mozambique, Tanzania, Zambia. *Class:* Niger-Congo, Atlantic-Congo, Volta-Congo, Benue-Congo, Bantoid, Southern, Narrow Bantu, Central, P, Yao (P.20). *Dialect:* Mangoche. *Lg Dev:* Literacy rate in first language: 5%. Literacy rate in second language: 60% Chewa, 30% Arabic. Dictionary. Grammar. Bible: 1920. *Other:* Yao in Tanzania use a different orthography from Malawi. Muslim, Christian, traditional religion.

Zulu (Ngoni, Kingoni, Isizulu, Zunda) [zul] 37,480 in Malawi (1966 census). *Other:* Ngoni is a dialect of Zulu or Swazi spoken in Malawi. 'Ngoni' also used as an alternate name for Chichewa and possibly for Matengo. See main entry under South Africa.

Mali

Republic of Mali. République du Mali. Formerly French Sudan. 11,956,788. National or official languages: French, Bamanankan, Bomu, Tieyaxo Bozo, Toro So Dogon, Maasina Fulfulde, Hasanya Arabic, Mamara Senoufo, Kita Maninkakan, Soninke, Koyraboro Senni Songhay, Syenara Senoufo, Tamasheq, Xaasongaxango. Literacy rate: Men 26.6%, women 11.4% (1987). Also includes Matya Samo, North Levantine Spoken Arabic (550), Siamou (20,000), Wolof. Information mainly from G. Manessy 1961, 1975, 1981; J. Capron 1973; R. Nicolai 1979, 1981, 1983; J. Bendor-Samuel 1989. Blind population: 110,000 (1982 WCE). The number of languages listed for Mali is 50. Of those, all are living languages. See maps beginning on page 706.

Arabic, Hasanya (Maure, Mauri, Moor, Suraka, Suraxxé, Hassaniyya, Hassani) [mey] 106,100 in Mali (1991). Nioro and Nara. *Lg Use:* National language. *Other:* Speakers are called 'Maures' ('Moors'). The language is called 'Suraka' by the Bambara and 'Suraxxé' by the Soninke. Hunter-gatherers. Muslim. See main entry under Mauritania (Hassaniyya).

Bamako Sign Language [bog] Bamako school for deaf children, separated into 3 grade classes. It is not known if it is widely used elsewhere or not. *Class:* Deaf sign language. *Dialects:* Not related to other sign languages.

Lg Use: Some hearing people use it to communicate with deaf people. 6 to 50 years old. They have some knowledge of French and possibly Bambara. *Lg Dev:* Dictionary. *Other:* Another community of deaf people in Bamako use a West African variety of American Sign Language.

Bamanankan (Bambara, Bamanakan) [bam] 2,700,000 in Mali (1995). Population includes 75,000 Ganadugu (1991 Vanderaa), 41,200 Wasulu. Population total all countries: 2,786,385. Also spoken in Burkina Faso, Côte d'Ivoire, Gambia, Guinea, Mauritania, Senegal. *Class:* Niger-Congo, Mande, Western, Central-Southwestern, Central, Manding-Jogo, Manding-Vai, Manding-Mokole, Manding, Manding-East, Northeastern Manding, Bamana. *Dialects:* Standard Bambara, Somono, Segou, San, Beledugu, Ganadugu, Wasulu (Wasuu, Wassulunka, Wassulunke), Sikasso. There are many local dialects. The main division is Standard Bambara, influenced heavily by Western Maninkakan, and rural dialects. Bamanankan dialects are spoken in varying degrees by 80% of the population. Wasulu is a dialect of Bamanankan in Mali and of Western Maninkakan in Guinea. *Lg Use:* National language. Language of wider communication. Used for adult education. *Lg Dev:* Radio programs. Dictionary. Grammar. Bible: 1961–1987. *Other:* Wasulu are former Fulbe. Muslim, traditional religion, Christian.

Bankagooma (Banka, Bankagoma, Bankagoroma, Bankaje) [bxw] 5,085 (1995 SIL). Ethnic population: 5,085. North of Sikasso in Danderesso Administrative District, towns of Nougoussouala (Nonko), Fourouma, Mamarasso (Mora), Famsara, and Zantiguila. *Class:* Niger-Congo, Mande, Western, Northwestern, Samogo. *Lg Use:* Bankagooma is no longer spoken in Bambadougou (Faijanta), Nyaradougou (Jaata), Samogossoni, and possibly other towns, where the people now speak Bambara. A few villages are still stable. Spoken by children and adults as first language in some towns. Speakers also use Bambara.

Bobo Madaré, Northern (Bobo Fing, Bobo Fign, Bobo Fi, Bobo, Black Bobo, Finng, Bobo Da) [bbo] 18,400 in Mali (2000 WCD). An approximate rectangle in Mali around Bura and Mafune. *Dialects:* Benge, Sogokiri, Sya (Sia), Vore. *Lg Use:* Speakers also use Jula or French. *Other:* The term 'Bobo' has been carelessly applied to the Bwa people or their languages Buamu and Boomu. The Bambara names 'Black Bobo' (Bobo Fing) and 'Red Bobo' (Bobo Oule for Buamu and Bomu) only add confusion. Traditional religion, Muslim. See main entry under Burkina Faso.

Bomu (Boomu, Bore, Western Bobo Oule, Western Red Bobo, Western Bwamu, Bobo Wule) [bmq] 102,000 in Mali (1976 census). Population total all countries: 158,000. A triangle between San and Sofara on the Bani River in Mali, and Soumbara, west of Nouna, in Burkina Faso. The Mao subdialect is separate from the others and straddles the Mali-Burkina Faso border about 40 km east-west by 20 km north-south, and is on the main San to Bobo-Dioulasso road. Also spoken in Burkina Faso. *Class:* Niger-Congo, Atlantic-Congo, Volta-Congo, North, Gur, Central, Northern, Bwamu. *Dialects:* Dwemu, Dahanmu. Dwemu subdialects are Terekongo (Terekoungo), Wahu (between Téné and the Bani River), Togo. Dahanmu subdialects are Koniko, Mandiakuy, Bomborokuy, and Mao (Mahou). *Lg Use:* National language. *Lg Dev:* Grammar. NT: 1954–1994. *Other:* 'Bomu' is the official spelling. The people call themselves 'Bo' (sg.), 'Bwa' (pl.), and the language 'Bomu' or 'Boré'. The so-called 'Bobo Gbe (White Bobo, Kyan, Tian, Tyan)' were a mistakenly identified group of Bwa. SOV; postpositions; genitives, relatives before noun heads; articles, adjectives, numerals after noun heads; word order distinguishes subjects, objects, indirect objects; V, CV, CVV; tonal. Traditional religion.

Bozo, Hainyaxo (Hainyaxo, Hanyaxo, Xanyaxo, Xan, Hain, Kelenga, Kélinga, Kéllingua, Boso) [bzx] 117,696 (1987 census). From Miérou (near Ke-Maacina) to Tamani on the Niger River. They can be found working the major rivers in much of West Africa. *Class:* Niger-Congo, Mande, Western, Northwestern, Soninke-Bobo, Soninke-Boso, Boso, Eastern. *Dialects:* Lexical similarity 48% with Tieyaxo Boso (closest). *Lg Use:* All Bozo speakers are 6 years and older (1987). Speakers also use Bambara. *Other:* They call themselves 'Hain' (Xan; sg.) and their language 'Hainyaxo'. They accept the Bambara term 'Boso' to refer to all ethnic Boso. Fishermen. Muslim.

Bozo, Jenaama (Sorogaama, Corogaama, Sarkanci, Sarkawa, Djenaama, Nononke, Boso) [bze] 100,000 in Mali (1991 Vanderaa). Administrative circles of Djenné, Mopti, Youwarou, Tenenkou and Bandiagara. Between the Bani and Niger rivers (Pondori dialect), between the Diaka and Niger rivers (Kotya dialect), along the Niger River from Mopti to Lake Débo (Korondougou dialect), north of Kotya and around Lake Debo (Debo dialect). Some in Côte d'Ivoire around the Kosson and Ayamé dams. Also spoken in Nigeria. *Class:* Niger-Congo, Mande, Western, Northwestern, Soninke-Bobo, Soninke-Boso, Boso, Jenaama. *Dialects:* Pondori, Kotya (Kotyaxo), Korondougou, Débo. Lexical similarity 53% with Tieyaxo Bozo (closest). *Lg Use:* Nononke and Somono who live in the same area speak Jenaama as first language. Speakers of the northern dialects have some proficiency in Songai or Fulfulde; of the southern dialects in Bambara. *Other:* The Bozos call themselves 'Sorogo' (sg.), 'Sorogoye' (pl.), and their language 'Sorogama' which means 'language of the Bozos'. They accept the Bambara term 'Boso' to refer to the entire ethnic group. Nononkes are often also called Marka or 'dry Marka', referring to the fact that they were originally Soninke or Malinke but no longer speak their language. Somono call themselves 'Komuo' (sg.), 'Kombye' (pl.). Fishermen (traditionally), agriculturalists: rice. Muslim.

Bozo, Tièma Cièwè (Tièma Cièwè, Tié, Boso) [boo] 2,500 (1991). Population includes 831 in Enguem, 1,315 in Aouré. Administrative circle of Youwarou, Arrondissement Guidio Saré; Enghem (Enguem), Aouré (Aoré), and Kamago Sébi villages, where the Niger River leaves Lake Debo. *Class:* Niger-Congo, Mande, Western, Northwestern, Soninke-Bobo, Soninke-Boso, Boso, Eastern. *Dialects:* Lexical similarity 60% with Tieyaxo Boso. *Lg Use:* Speakers also use Fulfulde or Songai. *Other:* They call themselves 'Tié' (sg.) and the language 'Tièma Cèwè'. The Bambara term 'Boso' is accepted to refer to the entire ethnic group. Fishermen. Muslim.

Bozo, Tiéyaxo (Tieyaxo, Tigemaxo, Tiemaxo, Tyeyaxo, Tiéyakho, Tiguémakho, Tie, Tégué, Boso) [boz] 117,696 (1987 census). From Koa to Miérou on the Niger River, and Diafarabié to Sendédaga on the Diaka River (a tributary). They work the major rivers in much of West Africa. *Class:* Niger-Congo, Mande, Western, Northwestern, Soninke-Bobo, Soninke-Boso, Boso, Eastern. *Dialects:* Lexical similarity 53% with Sorogama Boso (closest), 30% with Soninke. *Lg Use:* National language. Some ethnic Marka and Somono live among them and speak Tiéyaxo as their first language. 6 years and older (1987). Some also use Bambara or Fulfulde, depending on the region. *Other:* They call themselves 'Tié' (sg.), 'Tieye' (pl.), and the language 'Tiéyaxo'. The term 'Boso' (Bambara term meaning 'house of bamboo') is accepted to refer to their ethnic group. Swamp. Fishermen. Muslim.

Dogon, Bangeri Me (Bangeri Me, Numadaw) [dba] 1,200 (1998 Durieux). Spoken in 7 villages in the extreme northwest of the plateau. Numadaw might relate to ethnonym 'Nononke'. *Class:* Niger-Congo, Atlantic-Congo, Volta-Congo, Dogon. *Other:* Agriculturalists.

Dogon, Bondum Dom (Bondum-Dom) [dbu] 24,700 (1998 Durieux). Along the northern border of the plateau, separated from the Tommo So area to its south by a mainly uninhabited plain east of Dia, and a deep ravine running westward from Dia to the cliff that ends the plateau. Borko village (14,57 N; 3,21 W) is about center of the language area. *Class:* Niger-Congo, Atlantic-Congo, Volta-Congo, Dogon. *Dialects:* Kindjim, Nadjamba. *Other:* Agriculturalists.

Dogon, Dogul Dom (Dogul-Dom) [dbg] 15,700 (1998 Durieux). 14 villages about 20 km northeast of Bandiagara with Nandoli as center. *Class:* Niger-Congo, Atlantic-Congo, Volta-Congo, Dogon. *Other:* Called 'Omogo' by Tommo So speakers, and 'Dogulu So' by Toro So speakers. Agriculturalists.

Dogon, Donno So (Kamba So) [dds] 45,300 (1998 Durieux). Kamba So is spoken around Kamba, and Donno So around Bandiagara. *Class:* Niger-Congo, Atlantic-Congo, Volta-Congo, Dogon. *Dialects:* Kamma So, Donno So. Similar to Tommo So. *Lg Dev:* Literacy and numeracy primers available but not in use because government language policy only allows Toro So materials. Dictionary. Grammar. NT: 1988. *Other:* Agriculturalists.

Dogon, Jamsay (Dyamsay Tegu) [djm] 130,000 in Mali (1998 Durieux). Large but sparsely populated area east of the Dogon cliffs extending into Burkina Faso. Also spoken in Burkina Faso. *Class:* Niger-Congo, Atlantic-Congo, Volta-Congo, Dogon. *Dialects:* Domno, Gono, Bama, Guru. Degree of comprehension between dialects uncertain. *Other:* Agriculturalists.

Dogon, Kolum So (Edyenge Dom, Idyoli Donge, Piniari) [dkl] 24,000 (1998 Durieux). Area between Sevare and Bandiagara, in Pinia administrative area. *Class:* Niger-Congo, Atlantic-Congo, Volta-Congo, Dogon. *Dialects:* Mombo (Helabo, Miambo), Ambange (Ampari). *Other:* Called 'Kulum So', meaning 'sunset dialects', by central Dogons. Called 'Piniari' by Fulani. Agriculturalists.

Dogon, Tene Kan (Tene Tingi, Tene Kan) [dtk] 127,000 (1998 Durieux). From Bankass nearly to Koro. *Class:* Niger-Congo, Atlantic-Congo, Volta-Congo, Dogon. *Dialects:* Tengu Tingi, Togo Kan, Sagara, Guimini Kan. *Other:* Agriculturalists.

Dogon, Tomo Kan (Tomo-Kan) [dtm] 132,800 in Mali (1998 Durieux). Large area southwest of Bankass. Also spoken in Burkina Faso. *Class:* Niger-Congo, Atlantic-Congo, Volta-Congo, Dogon. *Dialects:* Distinct from Tommo So (Tombo). *Lg Dev:* Dictionary. Grammar. *Other:* A few villages in Burkina Faso. Agriculturalists.

Dogon, Toro So (Dogoso, Bomu Tegu, Toro So) [dts] 50,000 (1998 Durieux). Spoken along the cliff from Yendoumman to Idyeli. *Class:* Niger-Congo, Atlantic-Congo, Volta-Congo, Dogon. *Dialects:* Different from Dogoso and Dogosé in Burkina Faso. *Lg Use:* National language. *Lg Dev:* Dictionary. NT: 1957–1994. *Other:* Cliff dwellers. The language is called 'Bomu Tegu' by their neighbors in the plains. Agriculturalists.

Dogon, Toro Tegu (Tandam) [dtt] 2,900 (1998 Durieux). About 80 km east of Douentza along a paved road. Approximately 15 villages. *Class:* Niger-Congo, Atlantic-Congo, Volta-Congo, Dogon. *Other:* Agriculturalists.

Duungooma (Samogho, Samogo, Samoro, Du, Mali Duun, Duungo, Western Duun) [dux] 70,000 (1991 Vanderaa). 3rd Region (Sikasso), prefectures of Kadiolo and Sikasso. Kai is the largest town. *Class:* Niger-Congo, Mande, Western, Northwestern, Samogo. *Lg Use:* Nearly everyone can speak Bambara. Students also speak French. *Other:* 'Samogho' is the ethnic name used in Bambara, and is a cover term to include Duungooma, Bankagooma, and Jowulu speakers. Muslim, traditional religion.

French [fra] 9,000 in Mali (1993 Johnstone). *Lg Use:* Official language. *Other:* Official language for instruction in schools. See main entry under France.

Fulfulde, Maasina (Peul, Macina) [ffm] 911,200 in Mali (1991). Population total all countries: 919,700. Central Mali. The western dialect is spoken around Segou and Macina. The eastern dialect is spoken from north of Mopti to Boni in the east. Also spoken in Côte d'Ivoire, Ghana. *Class:* Niger-Congo, Atlantic-Congo, Atlantic, Northern, Senegambian, Fulani-Wolof, Fula, West Central. *Dialects:* Western Macina, Eastern Macina. There are some dialect differences, but popular opinion is that all dialects in Mali are inherently intelligible. Substantial Bambara influence. There is skewing between the ethnic and linguistic relationships. *Lg Use:* National language. All domains, local administration, trade language, some oral use in first 2 grades, oral and written use in religious services, and oral use in commerce. Positive language attitude. Speakers also use Bambara. *Lg Dev:* Newspapers. Radio programs. Dictionary. Grammar. Bible portions: 1934. *Other:* Maasina in Mali is a major Fula geopolitical state. The people are called 'Fulbe' in Fulfulde and 'Fulani' in English and the language 'Peul' or 'Toucouleur' in French. Delta. Nomadic pastoralists: cattle. Muslim, syncretism, Christian.

Jahanka (Jahanque, Jahonque, Diakkanke, Diakhanke, Dyakanke) [jad] 500 in Mali (2001). Kotema and Niebore villages, near the Guinea border. Possibly more villages farther east. *Other:* They are reported to have originated in Mali. They trace their origins to Soninke, but now speak a separate language. Muslim. See main entry under Guinea.

Jalunga (Yalunka, Djallonke, Dyalonke, Dialonke, Jalonke, Yalunke) [yal] 9,000 in Mali (2002 SIL). Extreme southwest corner along the Guinea border, Faleya Region, to where the Baafing River comes to the Mali-Guinea border. *Other:* Muslim. See main entry under Guinea (Yalunka).

Jowulu (Jo, Samogho) [jow] 10,000 in Mali (2002). Population total all countries: 11,000. 3rd Region, Prefecture of Kadiolo, Subprefecture of Loulouni. Also spoken in Burkina Faso. *Class:* Niger-Congo, Mande, Western, Northwestern, Samogo. *Lg Use:* The men speak Bambara fairly well. The few who have been to school speak and read French. A few use Supyire or Duungooma as a second language. *Other:* They call themselves 'Jotoni' (pl.) and their language 'Jowulu'. 'Samogho' is a cover term including the Dzuungoo, Duungooma, Bankagooma, Samo, Jowulu, and possibly other languages. Traditional religion.

Jula (Dyoula, Diula, Dioula, Djula, Dyula) [dyu] 50,000 in Mali (1991). *Lg Use:* Trade language. *Other:* Muslim. See main entry under Burkina Faso.

Kagoro (Kakolo) [xkg] 15,000 (1998 Valentin Vydrine). Ethnic population: 21,500 (1991 Vanderaa). Kaarta-Bine and Gumbu regions, about 70 ethnic Kagoro villages (Vydrine 1998). *Class:* Niger-Congo, Mande, Western, Central-Southwestern, Central, Manding-Jogo, Manding-Vai, Manding-Mokole, Manding, Manding-West. *Dialects:* Close to Khasonke. Bamanankan speakers have poor comprehension of Kagoro. Lexical similarity 86% with Kita Maninkakan. *Lg Use:* Being replaced by Bambara. Kagoro now spoken only in a few corners of Kaarta. Most can use Bamanankan, Soninke, or Hasanya as second language (1998 Vydrine). *Other:* Some lexical influence from Soninke. Recent heavy Bambara influence. Muslim, traditional religion.

Koromfé [kfz] 100 in Mali. Near Burkina Faso border southeast of Dinangourou (east of Sangha) including Yoro,

Kindi, Bougal, Nassouwele, Youmnetao, Ouri, Boutou, Lou, Tidore, Boulagadji, Kalalgaobe. *Dialects:* Eastern Koromfe, Western Koromfe. *Other:* The people call themselves 'Koromba'. The people are called 'Tellem' by Dogon, 'Foulsé' by Mossi and French, 'Foula' by Mossi, and 'Kurum-Korey' by Peul. See main entry under Burkina Faso.

Maninkakan, Kita (Malinke, Kita Maninka, Central Malinke) [mwk] 600,000 (1991 Vanderaa). Population includes 50,000 Fulanke (based on 1991 Vanderaa). From Kita west to the Tambaoura cliff range. *Class:* Niger-Congo, Mande, Western, Central-Southwestern, Central, Manding-Jogo, Manding-Vai, Manding-Mokole, Manding, Manding-West. *Dialect:* Fulanke. Kita speakers have 64% intelligibility of Bambara. *Lg Use:* National language. *Lg Dev:* Grammar. *Other:* The Fulanke is an ethnic group that lives in the Kita area. They have a Fulbe (Fulani) background, but have adopted the Maninkakan language of the surrounding Western Maninkakan. Muslim.

Maninkakan, Western (Northwestern Maninka, Malinke, Malinka, Western Malinke) [mlq] 100,000 in Mali (based on Vanderaa 1991). West of Tambaoura cliff range at border of Mali and Guinea. *Dialects:* Kenieba Maninka, Nyoxolonkan. *Other:* Muslim, traditional religion, Christian. See main entry under Senegal.

Marka (Marka-Dafin, Dafing, Meka) [rkm] 25,000 in Mali (1991). Around the villages of Koula, Diarani, Yelené, Kuna; Dialassagou, Ouenkoro, Bai. *Lg Use:* Most Pana people also speak Marka-Dafin very well. *Other:* 'Marka' is used for followers of the traditional religion, 'Dafing' for Muslim speakers. Different from the Marka name for Soninke, and the Marka-Jalan who speak the San dialect of Bamanankan. Traditional religion, Muslim, Christian. See main entry under Burkina Faso.

Mòoré (More, Mole, Mossi, Moshi) [mos] 17,000 in Mali (1980). Some villages in the Dogon area, near the Burkina Faso border, and elsewhere. *Other:* Speakers came into Mali from Burkina Faso during the colonial period. Traditional religion, Muslim. See main entry under Burkina Faso.

Pana (Sama) [pnq] 2,800 in Mali (1982 SIL). South of Bandiagara, straddling the Mali-Burkina Faso border east of the Sourou River, due north of Kassoum in Burkina Faso. *Dialects:* Pana North, Pana South. *Lg Use:* Speakers are favorable toward using Marka-Dafin, Jula, or Bamanankan. They are reported to be bilingual in Jula. *Other:* The people call themselves and their language 'Pana'. See main entry under Burkina Faso.

Pulaar (Pulaar Fulfulde, Peul, Peuhl) [fuc] 175,000 in Mali (1995). Population includes 40,000 Fulbe Jeeri. Settled primarily in northwestern Mali around Nioro and Kayes. Pockets found in Segou and Bandiagara, which are remnants of Umar Tal's conquest in the middle 1800s. *Dialect:* Toucouleur (Tukolor, Tukulor, Pulaar, Halpulaar, Haalpulaar, Fulbe Jeeri). *Lg Use:* Fulbe Jeeri is an ethnic group which speaks this language as first language. *Other:* Muslim. See main entry under Senegal.

Pular (Fuuta Jalon, Futa Jallon, Fouta Dyalon, Fulfulde Jalon, Fullo Fuuta, Futa Fula, Foula Fouta) [fuf] 50,000 in Mali (1991). Western Mali from Guinea up to about Keniéba, especially in the administrative districts of Faléa and Faraba. *Other:* Muslim. See main entry under Guinea.

Sàmòmá (Kalamsé, Kalemsé, Kalenga, Sàmó) [knz] Lògrèmmá dialect spoken in at least six villages in Mali: Dian, Sougou, Zon, Ponghon, Gako, and Soyma. *Dialect:* Logremma (Logma, West Kalamsé). *Lg Use:* Several Mali villages have shifted to Dogon. *Other:* Speakers call themselves 'Sàmó' (sg.) or 'Sàmóyá' (pl.); distinct from other languages called 'Samo'. Traditional religion, Muslim, Christian. See main entry under Burkina Faso (Kalamsé).

Senoufo, Mamara (Miniyanka, Minya, Mianka, Minianka, Mamara, Tupiire) [myk] 737,802 (2000 WCD). *Class:* Niger-Congo, Atlantic-Congo, Volta-Congo, North, Gur, Senufo, Suppire-Mamara. *Dialects:* Sõghoo, Bàjii, Nafãã, Mìjuu, Kle Noehmõ, Nejuu, Koloo, Kujaa, Suõõ. Close to Supyire Senoufo, but intercomprehension is difficult. *Lg Use:* National language. Speakers also use Bambara. *Lg Dev:* Grammar. Bible portions: 1967–1975. *Other:* Their name for themselves is 'Bamana', but this is different from the Bambara dialect called 'Bamana'. Traditional religion, Muslim, Christian.

Sénoufo, Sìcìté (Sìcìté, Sìpììté, Sìcìré, Sucite, Tagba) [sep] Villages of Bakoronidougou, Gouaniéresso, Finkolo-Zanso, and Missidougou, east of Sikasso near the Burkina Faso border. *Other:* They call themselves 'Sìcijuubíí' (pl.), or 'Sìcijuungé' (sg.), and their region 'Tagba'. 'Tagba' is used by outsiders for them. Little intermarriage with others in the southern area. Plateau, interfluvial. Scrub forest, gallery forest. Swidden agriculturalists. Traditional religion, Muslim. See main entry under Burkina Faso.

Senoufo, Supyire (Supyire, Sup'ide, Suppire) [spp] 364,000 (1991). At Sikasso. *Class:* Niger-Congo, Atlantic-Congo, Volta-Congo, North, Gur, Senufo, Suppire-Mamara. *Lg Dev:* Grammar. Bible portions: 1979–1998. *Other:* Traditional religion, Muslim.

Senoufo, Syenara (Syenara, Shenara, Senare, Senari) [shz] 136,500 (1991 Vanderaa). South of the Duun language area around Kadiolo. *Class:* Niger-Congo, Atlantic-Congo, Volta-Congo, North, Gur, Senufo, Senari. *Lg Use:* National language. *Other:* Traditional religion, Muslim.

Songhay, Humburi Senni (Songay Senni, Songoy, Songhoy, Songai, Songhai, Songay, Songoi, Songhay, Sonrai, Sonrhai, Central Songai, Hombori Songhay) [hmb] 15,000 in Mali (1999 Heath). Hombori area, halfway between Gao and Mopti. *Dialect:* Djenne Chiini. *Other:* Muslim, traditional religion. See main entry under Burkina Faso (Songhay).

Songhay, Koyra Chiini (Songay, Songoy, Songhoy, Songai, Songhai, Songoi, Songhay, Sonrai, Sonrhai, West Songhoy, Timbuktu Songhoy) [khq] 200,000 (1999 SIL). On the Niger River from Djenné to just east of Timbuktu. *Class:* Nilo-Saharan, Songhai, Southern. *Dialects:* Koyra Chiini, Djenné Chiini. The main dialect division is between Timbuktu and the upriver towns from Diré to Niafunké. A very distinct dialect is in Djenné city. Closely related languages: Koyraboro Senni Songhay, Humburi Senni Songhay, Zarma, Dendi. Lexical similarity 77% between Gao and Timbuktu dialects, 50% lexical similarity with Tadaksahak. *Lg Use:* All ages. Timbuktu has more prestige than other West Songhoy dialects. In Timbuktu they are mainly monolingual, some French, Tamasheq, Arabic; In Djenné most are bilingual or multilingual in French, Bambara, or other languages. *Lg Dev:* Dictionary. Grammar. NT: 1936. *Other:* Kaado (Zarma dialect) is SOV; West Songhay SVO. Djenné Chiini phonology, lexicon, basic inflection almost identical to Koyra Chiini, but syntax (especially relativization and focalization) very different; Djenné has 7 vowels to 5 for Koyra Chinni (J. Heath); Kaado has 3 tones, West Songhay no tones. Muslim, traditional religion.

Songhay, Koyraboro Senni (Koyra Senni, Koroboro Senni, Songay Senni, Songoy, Songai, Songhai, Songay, Songoi, Songhay, Sonrai, Sonrhai, East Songhay, Gao Songhay, Koyra Senni Songhay) [ses] 400,000 (1999 Dan Stauffer). Southeast, along the Niger River from Gourma Rharous, just east of Timbuktu, through Bourem, Goa, and Ansongo on to the Mali-Niger border. Borders Kaado (Zarma) in Niger, but boundary zone not well studied. *Class:* Nilo-Saharan, Songhai, Southern. *Dialects:*

Intelligibility is good of all dialects on the Niger River. Fulan Kirya variety has more limited intelligibility because of heavy lexical borrowing from Fulfulde and Humburi Senni Songhay. Closely related languages: Koyra Chiini Songhay, Humburi Senni Songhay, Zarma, Dendi. Lexical similarity 77% between Gao and Timbuktu dialects, lexical similarity 50% with Tadaksahak. *Lg Use:* National language. Trade language. Language of instruction at primary level in some experimental schools. All ages. Gao variety is dominant in all respects. Many are monolingual. Some know Bambara, French, or Tamasheq, but there is no extensive bilingualism (J. Heath 1999). *Lg Dev:* Actively promoted by the government through adult literacy classes and as the language of instruction at the primary level in some experimental schools. Some French literacy. Dictionary. Grammar. *Other:* SOV; nontonal. Muslim, traditional religion.

Soninke (Marka, Maraka, Sarakole, Sarakule, Sarawule, Serahuli, Silabe, Toubakai, Wakore, Gadyaga, Aswanik, Diawara) [snk] 700,000 in Mali (1991). Population includes 125,000 Diawara (1991 Vanderaa), 374,042 first-language Marka speakers (1987 census). Population total all countries: 1,096,795. Nioro, Nara, Banamba, Yélémané, Kayes are principal towns in Mali. Also possibly Niger. Also spoken in Côte d'Ivoire, Gambia, Guinea, Guinea-Bissau, Mauritania, Senegal. *Class:* Niger-Congo, Mande, Western, Northwestern, Soninke-Bobo, Soninke-Boso, Soninke. *Dialects:* Azer (Adjer, Aser), Kinbakka, Xenqenna. Dialects in Mali, Senegal, Mauritania, and possibly Gambia are close enough to use the same literature. *Lg Use:* National language. The Diawara (125,000 in 1993; Johnstone) live among the Soninke and speak Sarakole, but consider themselves to be separate from the Soninke. Speakers also use Bambara or Fula. *Lg Dev:* Radio programs. TV. Dictionary. Grammar. Bible portions: 2001. *Other:* Their own name for the language is 'Soninkanxaane'. The 'Marka' name used for Soninke is different from the Marka language. Muslim.

Tadaksahak (Dausahaq, Daoussak, Daoussahaq, Dawsahaq, Daosahaq) [dsq] 30,000 in Mali (1995). Population total all countries: 31,800. 7th region, about 300 km east-west by 200 km north-south with Ménaka as geographic center. They travel into Niger and Algeria. Also spoken in Algeria. *Class:* Nilo-Saharan, Songhai, Northern. *Dialects:* Close to Tagdal (Niger), Tasawaq (Niger), Korandje (Algeria). Northern Songhay Languages share features from Songhay and Tamasheq. *Lg Use:* Vigorous. All ages. Reported to also use Tamasheq, although women and children in isolated encampments understand very little. *Other:* They call themselves 'Idaksahak' (pl.). The culture is shared with Tamasheq. SVO; stress system. Traditionally nomadic herdsmen for the Iwellemmeden Tuareg nobility.

Tamajaq (Tamajeq, Tamasheq, Tomacheck, Tamashekin, "Tuareg," "Tourage," Tahoua, Tajag) [ttq] 190,000 in Mali (1991). East Mali, Menaka, and Gao regions. *Dialects:* Tawallammet Tan Dannag (Ioullemmeden), Tawallammat Tan Ataram. *Other:* The people call themselves 'Kal Tamajaq'. Muslim. See main entry under Niger (Tamajaq, Tawallammat).

Tamasheq (Kidal Tamasheq, Tomacheck, Tamashekin, "Tuareg," Timbuktu, Kidal) [taq] 250,000 in Mali (1991). Population total all countries: 281,169. Central, Timbuktu area, and northeast Mali. Also spoken in Algeria, Burkina Faso. *Class:* Afro-Asiatic, Berber, Tamasheq, Southern. *Dialects:* Timbuktu (Tombouctou, Tanaslamt), Tadhaq (Kidal). It may be two separate languages. *Lg Use:* National language. Language of instruction at primary level in some experimental schools. *Lg Dev:* The government is actively promoting the language through adult literacy classes. Taught in primary schools. NT:

Ethnologue

2003. *Other:* The people are called 'Kel Tamasheq'. The Bellah were formerly under the Tuareg economically. Pastoralists: cattle, goats, camels, donkeys. Muslim.

Xaasongaxango (Xasonga, Kassonke, Khassonka, Khassonké, Khasonke, Kasonke, Kasson, Kasso, Xaasonga, Xasonke) [kao] 120,000 in Mali (1991). Population total all countries: 128,170. Principal towns are Bafoulabé, Kayes. Also spoken in Gambia, Senegal. *Class:* Niger-Congo, Mande, Western, Central-Southwestern, Central, Manding-Jogo, Manding-Vai, Manding-Mokole, Manding, Manding-West. *Dialects:* Highly intelligible with Western Maninkakan and a little less with Bambara, but for sociolinguistic reasons they are not considered dialects. 90% inherent intelligibility of Malinke in eastern Senegal. Lexical similarity 70% with Mandinka of Gambia and Senegal. *Lg Use:* National language. Most Xasonga and Bambara manage to understand each other. *Lg Dev:* Grammar. Bible portions: 1997. *Other:* The people call themselves 'Xasongo' or 'Xasonga' (sg.), Xasongolu (pl.). The French spelling is Khassonké. Muslim, traditional religion.

Zarmaci (Zarma, Dyerma, Dyarma, Dyabarma, Adzerma, Djerma, Zabarma, Zarbarma) [dje] Tabankort and Akabar villages south of Menaka at Niger border. *Other:* Muslim, traditional religion. See main entry under Niger (Zarma).

Mauritania

Islamic Republic of Mauritania. République Islamique de Mauritanie. 2,998,563. National or official language: Hassaniyya. There are many tribes, castes, or clans of whom little is known. Literacy rate: 17% to 28%. Also includes Bambara, French, Korean (60,000), Tamasheq. Information mainly from A. Gerteiny 1967; Applegate 1970. The number of languages listed for Mauritania is 6. Of those, all are living languages. See map on page 709.

Hassaniyya (Klem El Bithan, Hasanya, Hassani, Hassaniya) [mey] 2,475,000 in Mauritania (2002). Population total all countries: 2,787,625. Throughout the country. Also spoken in Algeria, Mali, Morocco, Niger, Senegal. *Class:* Afro-Asiatic, Semitic, Central, South, Arabic. *Dialects:* Not intelligible with other Arabic varieties. The 'Nemadi' (Ikoku) are an ethnic group of 200 (1967) that speak Hassaniyya, but they have special morphemes for dogs, hunting, and houses. They are nomadic between Mali and Mauritania. *Lg Use:* Official language. *Lg Dev:* Radio programs. Dictionary. *Other:* Speakers are called 'Maures' ('Moors'). White Maure are called 'Bithan', which may also be used for the Maure in general. Black Maure are called 'Haratine'. They are nomadic between Mauritania and Mali. Pastoralists; traders. Muslim.

Imeraguen (Imraguen) [ime] 534 (2000). Near Nouakchott, the region stretching from Cape Timiris to Nouadhibou. *Class:* Unclassified. *Dialects:* The language is reported to be a variety of Hassaniyya structured on an Azer (Soninke) base. *Other:* Vassals to important Hassan tribes, especially the Oulad Bou Sba. Reported to be remnants of the Bafours. They use nets for fishing. Coastal. Fishermen.

Pulaar (Peul) [fuc] 150,000 in Mauritania. *Dialect:* Toucouleur (Tukulor, Pulaar, Haalpulaar). *Other:* Fuuta Tooro (Fouta Toro) was a major Toucouleur geopolitical state, which has its seat in northern Senegal and is also in Mauritania. Muslim. See main entry under Senegal.

Soninke (Marka, Sarakole, Sarawule, Toubakai, Wakore, Gadyaga, Serahuli, Aswanik, Silabe) [snk] 30,000 in Mauritania. Chamama Region. *Dialect:* Azer (Adjer, Aser). *Other:* Muslim. See main entry under Mali.

Wolof (Ouolof, Yallof, Walaf, Volof) [wol] 10,000 in Mauritania (1993 Johnstone). *Dialects:* Baol, Cayor, Dyolof (Djolof, Jolof), Lebou, Ndyanger. *Lg Use:* Language of wider communication. *Other:* Muslim. See main entry under Senegal.

Zenaga [zen] 200 to 300 (1998). Between Mederdra and the Atlantic coast, southern Mauritania. *Class:* Afro-Asiatic, Berber, Zenaga. *Dialects:* The language is related to other Berber languages in basic structure though specific features are quite different. *Lg Use:* Few adult speakers. Speakers also use Hassaniyya. *Other:* People are bedouins, reported to travel mainly in caravans. Racially, they are both white and black; the latter are descendants of slaves captured centuries ago. Pastoralists. Muslim.

Mauritius

Mauritius. 1,220,481. Ethnically 685,170 or 69% of the population from India. National or official languages: English, French. Includes Rodrigues; 4 islands. Literacy rate: 90% to 94%. Also includes Eastern Panjabi (26,000), Gujarati (3,336), Hakka Chinese (35,000), Mandarin Chinese, Marathi (11,787), Telugu (10,675), Yue Chinese. Information mainly from P. Baker 1972; P. Baker and R. Ramnak 1985; R. Barz and J. Siegel 1988; T. Eriksen 1990. Blind population: 250. Deaf institutions: 2. The number of languages listed for Mauritius is 6. Of those, all are living languages.

Bhojpuri [bho] 336,000 in Mauritius (2001 Johnstone and Mandryk). Urban and rural areas. *Dialects:* Mauritian Bhojpuri, Bojpury. *Lg Use:* Often used in government and politics. *Other:* Although often called 'Hindi', the language is Bhojpuri. Hindu. See main entry under India.

English [eng] 3,000 in Mauritius (1993 Johnstone). *Lg Use:* Official language. Not widely known. Used in secondary school, courts, for road signs. See main entry under United Kingdom.

French [fra] 37,000 in Mauritius. *Lg Use:* Official language. Used in stores. Widely used by young people as second language. Older adults tend to use creole. See main entry under France.

Morisyen (Mauritius Creole French, Kreole, Kreol, Mauritian, Maurysen) [mfe] 600,000 in Mauritius (1989). Population total all countries: 604,000. Also spoken in Madagascar. *Class:* Creole, French based. *Dialect:* Rodrigues Creole. Closer to French creoles of the Caribbean than to Réunion Creole (Philip Baker). Nearly identical to Rodrigues. *Lg Use:* Trade language. Lower prestige than French or English. Speakers also use French. *Lg Dev:* Dictionary. Grammar. Bible portions: 1885–1900.

Tamil [tam] 31,000 in Mauritius (2001 Johnstone and Mandryk). *Lg Use:* Used in government and politics. *Other:* Hindu. See main entry under India.

Urdu [urd] 64,000 in Mauritius (1993 Johnstone). *Lg Use:* Used in government and politics. *Other:* Muslim. See main entry under Pakistan.

Mayotte

Mayotte. 186,026. National or official language: French. A French department. Literacy rate: 32% to 58.4%. The number of languages listed for Mayotte is 4. Of those, all are living languages. See map on page 690.

Bushi (Shibushi, Kibushi, Kibuki, Shibushi Shimaore, Sakalava, Antalaotra) [buc] 39,000 (2001). *Class:* Austronesian, Malayo-Polynesian, Barito, East, Malagasy. *Dialects:* Kibushi-Kimaore, Kiantalaotse. *Other:* VOS.

French [fra] 2,450 in Mayotte (1993 Johnstone). *Lg Use:* Official language. See main entry under France.

Maore (Comores Swahili, Komoro, Comoro, Comorian, Shimaore) [swb] 92,806 in Mayotte (1993 Johnstone). *Dialect:* Shinzwani (Anjouan). *Other:* Vanilla, perfume production. Muslim. See main entry under Comoros (Comorian).

Swahili [swh] 2,744 in Mayotte (1993 Johnstone). *Other:* Muslim. See main entry under Tanzania.

Morocco

Kingdom of Morocco. al-Mamlaka al-Maghrebia. 32,209,101. National or official language: Standard Arabic. Literacy rate: 30% to 50%. Also includes French (80,000). Information mainly from C. Coon 1931; Y. Zavadovskii 1962; D. Cohen 1963, 1985; J. Applegate 1970; J. Chetrit 1985. Blind population: 35,000 (1982 WCE). Deaf institutions: 1. The number of languages listed for Morocco is 11. Of those, 9 are living languages and 2 are extinct. See map on page 677.

Arabic, Hassaniyya (Sahrawi, Maure, Mauri, Moor, Sulaka, Hasanya, Hassani) [mey] 40,000 in Morocco (1995). Southern Morocco, from Laayoune on down. See main entry under Mauritania (Hassaniyya).

Arabic, Judeo-Moroccan [aju] 8,925 in Morocco (2000 WCD). Casablanca. *Lg Use:* Younger generation speakers have French as first language. Their Arabic is closer to Moroccan Arabic than to Moroccan Judeo-Arabic. Most speakers in Morocco are older adults. Many older adults speak Spanish or French as first language. Some bilingualism in Spanish, French, and Hebrew. *Other:* A large number of borrowings from Spanish, Ladino, and French. In Casablanca, the Jewish community is well educated and well off. Several Jewish schools taught almost exclusively in Hebrew. Jewish. See main entry under Israel.

Arabic, Moroccan Spoken (Moroccan Arabic, Moroccan Colloquial Arabic, Moroccan Darija, Maghrebi Arabic, Maghribi Colloquial Arabic) [ary] 18,800,000 in Morocco (1995). Population total all countries: 19,480,600. Northern Morocco and southern Morocco south of the Atlas Mountains, and including the port cities of the Sahara. Also spoken in Belgium, Egypt, France, Germany, Gibraltar, Netherlands, United Kingdom. *Class:* Afro-Asiatic, Semitic, Central, South, Arabic. *Dialects:* Rabat-Casablanca Arabic, Fez. Meknes, Tangier, Oujda, Jebli (Jebelia, Jbala), Southern Morocco Arabic, Marrakech. *Lg Use:* 5,000,000 second-language speakers. Speakers are keenly aware of differences with other Arabic varieties. *Lg Dev:* NT: 1932. *Other:* Speakers across North Africa call their spoken Arabic varieties 'darija' or 'darijah', so it is not specific for this variety. SVO; prepositions; genitives, adjectives, relatives after noun heads; articles and numerals before noun heads; question word initial; prefixes 3. suffixes 4; word order distinguishes subjects, objects, indirect objects, topic and comment; affixes do not indicate case of noun phrase; verb affixes mark person, number, gender of subject, object-obligatory; CCVCC; nontonal. Muslim (Sunni).

Arabic, Standard [arb] *Lg Use:* Official language. Used for education, official purposes, communication among Arabic speaking countries. See main entry under Saudi Arabia.

Ghomara [gho] Extinct. North and west of Tamazight, a small region near Chechaouen, western Rif mountains, Oued Laou Valley. *Class:* Afro-Asiatic, Berber, Northern, Zenati, Ghomara. *Dialects:* Coon says Ghomara is intelligible with Tarifit. *Lg Use:* Members of the ethnic group now speak Moroccan Spoken Arabic. *Other:* Muslim.

Moroccan Sign Language [xms] Used in Tetouan and other cities. *Class:* Deaf sign language. *Dialects:* Algerian Sign Language has influenced the strong deaf community of 60 to 70 men in the city of Oujda in the north. Lexical similarity less than 50% with American Sign Language. *Lg Use:* Many deaf women do not leave their homes, or do not sign in the streets, so it is difficult to determine numbers. Association Nanane, a school in the north, had about 30 students, ages 4 to 21. MSL used in 3 programs for the deaf. Communities in Rabat, Tangier, and Casa Blanca do not use MSL. Used by USA Peace Corps. Most deaf people cannot read or write or understand Arabic. *Lg Dev:* Dictionary. *Other:* Developed from local signs and introduced signs.

Senhaja de Srair (Sanhaja of Srair, Sinhaja Srir) [sjs] Extinct. Northern, west of Tarifit. *Class:* Afro-Asiatic, Berber, Northern, Zenati, Riff. *Dialects:* Coon (1939) says it was a separate language from Tarifit. *Lg Use:* Members of the ethnic group now speak Moroccan Spoken Arabic. *Other:* Muslim.

Spanish [spa] 20,000 in Morocco (1993 Johnstone). Melilla and scattered across the north coast. See main entry under Spain.

Tachelhit (Tashilheet, Tashelheyt, Tachilhit, Tashelhit, Tasoussit, Shilha, Susiua, Southern Shilha) [shi] 3,000,000 in Morocco (1998). Southwestern Morocco, from coast south to Ifni and north to near Agadir, northeast to outskirts of Marrakech, and east to Draa, including the valley of the Sous, and south near the border. Also spoken in Algeria, France. *Class:* Afro-Asiatic, Berber, Northern, Atlas. *Lg Use:* Many men also use Arabic. Many women do not learn Arabic. *Lg Dev:* Bible portions: 1906–1925. *Other:* 'Tachelhit' is their name for their language. 'Shilha' is the Arabic name for Moroccan Berber language varieties in general. Soussi: shopkeepers. Muslim.

Tamazight, Central Atlas (Central Shilha, Middle Atlas Berber, Shilha) [tzm] 3,000,000 in Morocco (1998). Population total all countries: 3,150,000. Middle Atlas, High Atlas, eastern High Atlas Mountains. 1,200,000 in rural areas between Taza, Khemisset, Azilal, Errachidia; 100,000 outside the language area. Also spoken in Algeria, France. *Class:* Afro-Asiatic, Berber, Northern, Atlas. *Dialects:* Central Atlas, South Oran. Much variety in dialects. May be more than one language. *Lg Use:* One of the major Berber languages. 40% monolingual. Others use Arabic as second language. *Lg Dev:* Literacy rate in second language: Men 25%, women 5%. Bible portions: 1919–1981. *Other:* 65% live in rural areas, 10% live outside the traditional area. VSO (for Berber).

Tarifit (Rifi, Rifia, Northern Shilha, Shilha) [rif] 1,500,000 in Morocco (1991). Population total all countries: 1,700,000. Northern Morocco. The dialects listed are near Al Hoceima. Also spoken in Algeria, Belgium, France, Germany, Netherlands, Spain. *Class:* Afro-Asiatic, Berber, Northern, Zenati, Riff. *Dialect:* Urrighel, Beni Iznassen (Beni Snassen). There may be other dialects. Beni Snassen may be a separate language. *Lg Dev:* Bible portions: 1887–2001. *Other:* 'Rifia' is the Arabic name for their language; 'Rifi' (sg.) or 'Ruafa' (pl.) are names for the people; 'Rif' or 'Riff' are geographical names. Coastal. Deciduous forest. Fishermen. Muslim.

Mozambique

Republic of Mozambique. República de Moçambique. 18,811,731. National or official language: Portuguese. Literacy rate: 20%. Also includes Chinese (7,000) or fewer, people from India (15,000). Information mainly from J.

Rennie 1973; R. B. Boeder n.d.; P. Afido et al. 1989. Blind population: 28,000 (1982 WCE). The number of languages listed for Mozambique is 43. Of those, all are living languages. See map on page 710.

Barwe (Balke, Cibalke) [bwg] 15,000 (1999). Tete Province. *Class:* Niger-Congo, Atlantic-Congo, Volta-Congo, Benue-Congo, Bantoid, Southern, Narrow Bantu, Central, N, Senga-Sena (N.40), Sena. *Dialects:* Speakers probably have good comprehension of Nyungwe or Sena.

Chopi (Shichopi, Copi, Cicopi, Shicopi, Tschopi, Txopi, Txitxopi) [cce] 800,000 (2001 Johnstone and Mandryk). Southern coast, north of Limpopo River. Center is Quissico, southern part of Zavala District, approximately 100 km coastal strip between Inharrime and Chidunguela. *Class:* Niger-Congo, Atlantic-Congo, Volta-Congo, Benue-Congo, Bantoid, Southern, Narrow Bantu, Central, S, Chopi (S.60). *Dialects:* Copi, Ndonge, Lengue (Lenge, Kilenge), Tonga, Lambwe, Khambani. Many dialects; all inherently intelligible with each other. Lexical similarity 44% with Gitonga. *Lg Use:* About half of the speakers understand Tswa. *Lg Dev:* Literacy rate in second language: 10%. Dictionary. Grammar. NT: 2000. *Other:* Distinct from Chopi (Dhopaluo), a dialect of Acholi of Uganda.

Chuwabu (Chuwabo, Chwabo, Cuwabu, Cuabo, Chuabo, Chichwabo, Cicuabo, Txuwabo, Echuwabo, Echuabo) [chw] 786,715 (1997 census). Central coast between Quelimane and the Mlanje Mountains. *Class:* Niger-Congo, Atlantic-Congo, Volta-Congo, Benue-Congo, Bantoid, Southern, Narrow Bantu, Central, P, Makua (P.30). *Dialects:* Central Chuwabo, Nyaringa, Marale, Karungu, Maindo. Lexical similarity 78% between Chuwabo of Makusi District and Marrare. *Lg Dev:* Grammar. NT: 1978–2003. *Other:* Traditional religion, Christian, Muslim.

Dema [dmx] 5,000 (2000 Bister). Population displaced during Cabora Bassa Dam construction. Far western Mozambique, just north of Zimbabwe. *Class:* Niger-Congo, Atlantic-Congo, Volta-Congo, Benue-Congo, Bantoid, Southern, Narrow Bantu, Central, S, Shona (S.10). *Lg Use:* Strong pressure toward assimilation to Nyungwe.

Kokola [kzn] Western Zambesia Province. See main entry under Malawi.

Koti (Coti, Ekoti, Angoche, Angoxe) [eko] 64,200 (1997 Mucanheia). Nampula Province, Angoche District, coastal around Angoche Island; also a community in Nampula City. *Class:* Niger-Congo, Atlantic-Congo, Volta-Congo, Benue-Congo, Bantoid, Southern, Narrow Bantu, Central, P, Makua (P.30). *Dialect:* Ekoti, Enatthembo (Sangaje, Esangaje, Esakaji, Esangaji, "Edheidhei," "Etteittei"). A separate language within the Makhuwa group. *Lg Use:* Used in the home, market, and trading. All ages. Those living on the mainland can use Makhuwa (trading, contacts with neighbors), Portuguese (school, church, government), but little Swahili or Arabic. *Lg Dev:* Literacy rate in second language: 20% Portuguese. Grammar. *Other:* Lexicon heavily influenced by Swahili. Muslim, Christian.

Kunda (Chikunda, Cikunda, Chicunda) [kdn] 4,929 in Mozambique (2000 WCD). Around confluence of the Luangwe and Zambezi rivers. *Other:* Different from Kunda which is a dialect of Nyanja, and different from Kunda dialect of Lusengo in the Democratic Republic of the Congo. Traditional religion, Christian. See main entry under Zimbabwe.

Lolo (Ilolo) [llb] 150,000 (2002 SIL). Western Zambesia Province. *Class:* Niger-Congo, Atlantic-Congo, Volta-Congo, Benue-Congo, Bantoid, Southern, Narrow Bantu, Central, P, Makua (P.30). *Dialects:* May be a dialect of Lomwe or Makhuwa. Close to Takwane.

Lomwe (Ngulu, Ingulu, Nguru, Mihavane, Mihavani, Mihawani, Western Makua, Lomue, Ilomwe, Elomwe, Alomwe, Walomwe, Chilowe, Cilowe, Acilowe) [ngl] 1,300,000 (1991). Northeast and central, most of Zambezia Province, southern Nampula Province. The prestige center is Alto Molocue, Zambezia. *Class:* Niger-Congo, Atlantic-Congo, Volta-Congo, Benue-Congo, Bantoid, Southern, Narrow Bantu, Central, P, Makua (P.30). *Dialects:* Closest to Makhuwa, Chwabo. *Lg Dev:* NT: 1930–1983. *Other:* Different from Ngulu (Kingulu) of Tanzania. Traditional religion, Christian, Muslim.

Maindo (Chwambo) [cwb] 20,000 (2003). Micaune, just northeast of Chinde, at the mouth of the Zambezi River. *Class:* Niger-Congo, Atlantic-Congo, Volta-Congo, Benue-Congo, Bantoid, Southern, Narrow Bantu, Central, P, Makua (P.30). *Dialects:* Mitange, Badoni. Lexical similarity 84% with Chuabo. *Other:* Traditional religion, Christian, Muslim.

Makhuwa (Central Makhuwa, Makhuwa-Makhuwana, Macua, Emakua, Makua, Makoane, Maquoua, Makhuwwa of Nampula, Emakhuwa) [vmw] 2,500,000 (1996). Nampula, south of Meeto area. *Class:* Niger-Congo, Atlantic-Congo, Volta-Congo, Benue-Congo, Bantoid, Southern, Narrow Bantu, Central, P, Makua (P.30). *Dialects:* Emwaja, Enaharra (Maharra, Nahara, Emathipane), Enyara, Central Makua (Makhuwana, Makuana, Emakhuwana), Empamela (Nampamela), Enlai (Mulai). *Lg Dev:* Bible: 1982–2000. *Other:* Traditional religion, Muslim, Christian.

Makhuwa-Marrevone (Maca, Maka, Coastal Makhuwa, South Maca, Emaka, Marevone, Marrevone) [xmc] 420,101 (2000 WCD). Coast of central Delgado Province from Moma to Angoche. *Class:* Niger-Congo, Atlantic-Congo, Volta-Congo, Benue-Congo, Bantoid, Southern, Narrow Bantu, Central, P, Makua (P.30). *Dialects:* Makhuwana (Emakhuwana), Naharra (Enaharra), Enlai, Nampamela (Empamela). *Other:* Traditional religion, Muslim, Christian.

Makhuwa-Meetto (Meetto, Mêto, Meto, Metto, Emeto, Imeetto, Medo) [mgh] 800,000 in Mozambique (1997 census). Population total all countries: 1,160,000. Cabo Delgado and Niassa provinces. Also spoken in Tanzania. *Class:* Niger-Congo, Atlantic-Congo, Volta-Congo, Benue-Congo, Bantoid, Southern, Narrow Bantu, Central, P, Makua (P.30). *Dialects:* Imeetto has 81% to 88% lexical similarity with Saka, 78% to 82% with Nahara, 78% to 80% with Makua, 66% to 68% with Lomwe. *Lg Dev:* Dictionary. Grammar. Bible portions: 1927. *Other:* Traditional religion, Muslim, Christian.

Makhuwa-Moniga (Emoniga, Moniga, Emakhuwa-Emoniga) [mhm] 200,000 (2003 Kröger). Delgado Province. *Class:* Niger-Congo, Atlantic-Congo, Volta-Congo, Benue-Congo, Bantoid, Southern, Narrow Bantu, Central, P, Makua (P.30). *Dialects:* Lexical similarity 56% with Lomwe. *Other:* Traditional religion, Muslim, Christian.

Makhuwa-Saka (Saaka, Esaaka, Saka, Saanga, Isaanga, Ishanga, Sanga) [xsq] 200,000 (2003 Kröger). Delgado Province. *Class:* Niger-Congo, Atlantic-Congo, Volta-Congo, Benue-Congo, Bantoid, Southern, Narrow Bantu, Central, P, Makua (P.30). *Dialects:* Saka (Esaaka), Rati (Erati). Lexical similarity 81% to 88% with Makhuwa-Meetto, 78% to 80% with Makhuwa. *Lg Use:* Positive language attitude. *Lg Dev:* Grammar. *Other:* Traditional religion, Muslim, Christian.

Makhuwa-Shirima (West Makua, Xirima, Eshirima, Chirima, Shirima, Makhuwa-Niassa, Makhuwa-Xirima, Makhuwa-Exirima) [vmk] 500,000 (1996). South of Niassa Province. *Class:* Niger-Congo, Atlantic-Congo, Volta-Congo, Benue-Congo, Bantoid, Southern, Narrow Bantu, Central, P, Makua (P.30). *Dialects:* Probably not intelligible with the Metto, Makhuwa, or Lomwe. *Lg Dev:* NT: 2000.

Makonde (Chimakonde, Chinimakonde, Cimakonde, Konde, Makonda, Maconde, Shimakonde, Matambwe) [kde] 233,358 in Mozambique (1997 census). Population includes 12,000 Ndonde (1980). Northeast Mozambique. Maviha is in Mueda, Mozambique. *Dialects:* Vadonde (Donde, Ndonde), Vamwalu (Mwalu), Vamwambe (Mwambe), Vamakonde (Makonde), Maviha (Chimaviha, Kimawiha, Mavia, Mabiha, Mawia). *Lg Use:* Speakers are reserved toward outsiders. *Other:* Woodcarvers; agriculturalists. Muslim, traditional religion, Christian. See main entry under Tanzania.

Makwe (Kimakwe, Palma, Macue) [ymk] 22,000 in Mozambique (2003). Population total all countries: 32,000. Cabo Delgado Province, on the coast from the Tanzania border south to Quionga, Palma, until just south of Olumbe; and in the interior along the Rovuma River until Pundanhar. Also spoken in Tanzania. *Class:* Niger-Congo, Atlantic-Congo, Volta-Congo, Benue-Congo, Bantoid, Southern, Narrow Bantu, Central, G, Swahili (G.40). *Dialects:* Coastal Makwe (Palma), Interior Makwe. Not inherently intelligible with Swahili. Lexical similarity 60% with Swahili, 57% with Mwani, 48% with Yao. *Lg Use:* All men appear to speak Swahili, not all women understand it well. Most Palma men can speak Mwani. Most Rovuma people can speak Makonde. Those who have been to school can read Portuguese or Swahili. *Lg Dev:* Literacy rate in second language: 20%. Motivation for literacy is high. Grammar. *Other:* Muslim.

Manyawa [mny] 150,000 (1999). 85% are monolingual in Lugela District. Western Zambezia Province, including Lugela District. *Class:* Niger-Congo, Atlantic-Congo, Volta-Congo, Benue-Congo, Bantoid, Southern, Narrow Bantu, Central, P, Makua (P.30). *Dialects:* Close to Takwane. Lexical similarity 69% with Takwane. *Lg Use:* Speakers have low proficiency in Lomwe.

Manyika (Chimanyika, Manika) [mxc] 145,331 in Mozambique (2000 WCD). 759,923 Shona in Mozambique (1980 census) probably included Manyika, Ndau, Tewe, and Tawala. Northern half of Manica Province, north of Ndau, west of Tewe. *Dialects:* Bocha (Boka), Bunji, Bvumba, Domba, Guta, Here, Hungwe, Jindwi, Karombe, Nyamuka, Nyatwe, Unyama. *Other:* Traditional religion, Christian, Muslim. See main entry under Zimbabwe.

Marenje (Emarendje, Marendje) [vmr] 75,000 (1997 census). Western Zambezia. *Class:* Niger-Congo, Atlantic-Congo, Volta-Congo, Benue-Congo, Bantoid, Southern, Narrow Bantu, Central, P, Makua (P.30). *Dialects:* Related to Lolo and Kokola.

Mozambican Sign Language [mzy] In at least the 3 largest cities: Maputo, Beira, and Nampula. *Class:* Deaf sign language. *Dialects:* Some dialectal variation. Standardization efforts are in progress (1999). Not related to or based on Portuguese nor Portuguese Sign Language. *Other:* Being taught and developed.

Mwani (Kimwani, Mwane, Muane, Quimuane, Ibo) [wmw] 80,000 (2000). Cabo Delgado Province, on the coast north of Pemba from Arimba to Palma, including Ibo and Mocimboa da Praia, and the offshore Querimba Archipelago. *Class:* Niger-Congo, Atlantic-Congo, Volta-Congo, Benue-Congo, Bantoid, Southern, Narrow Bantu, Central, G, Swahili (G.40). *Dialects:* Wibo (Kiwibo), Kisanga (Kikisanga, Quissanga), Nkojo (Kinkojo), Nsimbwa (Kinsimbwa). Not intelligible with Swahili. Kiwibo is the prestige dialect. Kinsimbwa, the northernmost Mocimboa da Praia dialect is inherently intelligible with others, even though it is the most distinct. Lexical similarity 60% with Swahili, 48% with Yao. *Lg Use:* 20,000 second-language speakers. Used in the home, for

social purposes, religion, commerce. 30% to 40% also use Portuguese, 30% Swahili (mainly in the north), and 30% to 40% Makhuwa. Men are more bilingual than women. Traders and schoolchildren can use Portuguese. Portuguese is used for school, government, and trading. Swahili is used for trading in the north. *Lg Dev:* Literacy rate in second language: 30% to 40% Arabic script, 30% to 40% in Portuguese. Dictionary. *Other:* People are called 'Namwaní' or 'Mwaní' by Portuguese speakers. Traders. Muslim.

Nathembo (Sakaji, Esakaji, Sankaji, Sanagage, Sangaji, Theithei) [nte] 18,000 (1993 Johnstone). Southeastern Nampula Province, just north of Angohe, on the Sangange Peninsula, at Zubairi, Charamatane, Amisse, Mutembua, Namaeca, Namaponda, and up to Mogincual and Khibulani. *Class:* Niger-Congo, Atlantic-Congo, Volta-Congo, Benue-Congo, Bantoid, Southern, Narrow Bantu, Central, P, Makua (P.30). *Other:* Similar to Makhuwa and Swahili. 'Sakaji' is a place name. Coastal.

Ndau (Chindau, Njao, Ndzawu, Southeast Shona, Sofala) [ndc] 1,900,000 in Mozambique (2000 Chebanne). Population total all countries: 2,700,000. South central region, south of Beira in Sofala and Manica Province. Also spoken in Zimbabwe. *Class:* Niger-Congo, Atlantic-Congo, Volta-Congo, Benue-Congo, Bantoid, Southern, Narrow Bantu, Central, S, Shona (S.10). *Dialects:* Ndau (Cindau), Shanga (Cimashanga, Mashanga, Chichanga, Chixanga, Xanga, Changa, Senji, Chisenji), Danda (Cidanda, Ndanda, Cindanda, Vadanda, Watande), Dondo (Cidondo, Wadondo, Chibabava), Gova (Cigova). Closer to Manyika, and much more divergent from Union Shona. Danda and Ndanda may be the same. Gova in Mozambique is closer to Ndau, but in Zambia and Zimbabwe it is closer to Korekore dialect of Shona. Lexical similarity 92% between Danda and Dondo dialects, 85% between Dondo and Shanga; 74% to 81% between Ndau dialects and Manyika. *Lg Dev:* Bible: 1957. *Other:* Other geographical or ethnic names: Dzika, Hijo, Buzi (Buji), Tomboji, Mukwilo. Traditional religion, Christian.

Ngoni (Chingoni, Kingoni, Angoni, Kisutu, Sutu) [ngo] 35,000 in Mozambique (1989). Central Cabo Delgado Province, around Macuaida in Niassa Province, in northeast Tete Province. *Other:* Speakers formerly spoke Zulu. The Ngoni people in Malawi do not speak Ngoni, but all speak Nyanja as their first language. Muslim. See main entry under Tanzania.

Nsenga (Chinsenga, Senga) [nse] 141,000 in Mozambique (1993 Johnstone). *Other:* Different from Senga dialect of Tumbuka of Zambia, Malawi, and Tanzania. Traditional religion, Christian. See main entry under Zambia.

Nyanja (Chinyanja) [nya] 497,671 in Mozambique (1997 census). Niassa, Zambezia, and Tete provinces. Chewa is in Macanga District, Tete; Ngoni is in Sanga and Lago in Niassa, Angonia in Tete; Nsenga is in Zumbo in Tete; Nyanja is along Lake Niassa in Niassa and Tete. *Dialects:* Chewa (Cewa, Chichewa, Cicewa), Ngoni (Cingoni), Nyanja (Cinyanja). *Other:* The Ngoni people in Angonia District of Tete Province in western Mozambique have adopted Nyanja as their first language. Traditional religion, Christian. See main entry under Malawi.

Nyungwe (Chinyungwi, Cinyungwe, Nyongwe, Teta, Tete, Yungwe) [nyu] 262,455 (1980 census). Central, banks of Zambezi River above the Sena. *Class:* Niger-Congo, Atlantic-Congo, Volta-Congo, Benue-Congo, Bantoid, Southern, Narrow Bantu, Central, N, Senga-Sena (N.40), Sena. *Dialects:* Close to Sena. *Lg Use:* Language of wider communication. *Lg Dev:* Dictionary. Grammar. Bible portions: 1897.

Phimbi (Pimbi) [phm] 6,000. Central, banks of Zambezi River above the Sena. *Class:* Niger-Congo, Atlantic-Congo, Volta-Congo, Benue-Congo, Bantoid, Southern,

Narrow Bantu, Central, N, Senga-Sena (N.40), Sena. *Dialects:* Close to Sena. *Lg Use:* Some speakers also use Chewa or Nyungwe.

Portuguese [por] 30,000 in Mozambique (1998 SIL). *Lg Use:* Official language. 27% speak it as second language. See main entry under Portugal.

Ronga (Shironga, Xironga, Gironga) [rng] 640,947 in Mozambique (2000 WCD). Population total all countries: 727,565. South of Maputo Province, coastal areas. Also spoken in South Africa. *Class:* Niger-Congo, Atlantic-Congo, Volta-Congo, Benue-Congo, Bantoid, Southern, Narrow Bantu, Central, S, Tswa-Ronga (S.50). *Dialects:* Konde, Putru, Kalanga. Partially intelligible with Tsonga and Tswa. *Lg Dev:* Grammar. Bible: 1923.

Sena (Cisena, Chisena) [seh] 876,570 (1997 census). 86,000 Podzo in Mozambique (1993 Johnstone). Northwest, Sofala, Manica, Tete, and Zambezia provinces, lower Zambezi River Region. *Class:* Niger-Congo, Atlantic-Congo, Volta-Congo, Benue-Congo, Bantoid, Southern, Narrow Bantu, Central, N, Senga-Sena (N.40), Sena. *Dialects:* Caia (Care, Sare, North Sena), Bangwe (South Sena), Rue (Chirue), Gombe, Sangwe, Podzo (Phodzo, Chipodzo, Cipodzo, Puthsu, Shiputhsu), Gorongosa. Different literature needed for Malawi. Close to Nyungwe, Nyanja, Kunda. Lexical similarity 92% between Podzo and Sena-Sare. *Lg Use:* Sena Central is the prestige dialect. Limited comprehension of Ndau in Beira Region. Ndau is the church language in Beira; Shona and Nyanja are used in Tâte. They use Ndau to Ndau speakers, Portuguese to other non-Sena. *Lg Dev:* Dictionary. Grammar. NT: 1983. *Other:* Traditional religion, Christian, Muslim.

Swahili [swh] 9,232 in Mozambique (2000 WCD). Northern. *Lg Use:* Second-language speakers in Mozambique. See main entry under Tanzania.

Swati (Swazi, Siswazi, Siswati, Tekela, Tekeza) [ssw] 731 in Mozambique (1980 census). See main entry under Swaziland.

Takwane (Thakwani) [tke] 150,000 (1997 census). Western Zambezia Province. *Class:* Niger-Congo, Atlantic-Congo, Volta-Congo, Benue-Congo, Bantoid, Southern, Narrow Bantu, Central, P, Makua (P.30). *Dialects:* Related to Manyawa.

Tawara (Tawala) [twl] 50,000 (1997). South of Tete Province, just north of Zimbabwe. *Class:* Niger-Congo, Atlantic-Congo, Volta-Congo, Benue-Congo, Bantoid, Southern, Narrow Bantu, Central, S, Shona (S.10). *Dialects:* Tawara-Chioco, Tawara-Daque. The northernmost variety related to Korekore. It appears to have been influenced by Nyungwe.

Tewe (Ciute, Chiute, Teve, Vateve, Wateve) [twx] 250,000 (2000 Nelimo). Manica Province, Chimoio City and District. *Class:* Niger-Congo, Atlantic-Congo, Volta-Congo, Benue-Congo, Bantoid, Southern, Narrow Bantu, Central, S, Shona (S.10). *Dialects:* Considered by many to be a Manyika dialect.

Tonga (Inhambane, Shengwe, Bitonga, Tonga-Inhambane) [toh] 223,971 (1980 census). South, Inhambane area up to Morrumbane. *Class:* Niger-Congo, Atlantic-Congo, Volta-Congo, Benue-Congo, Bantoid, Southern, Narrow Bantu, Central, S, Chopi (S.60). *Dialects:* Gitonga Gy Khogani, Nyambe (Cinyambe), Sewi (Gisewi). Lexical similarity 44% with Chopi. *Lg Dev:* NT: 1890–1996. *Other:* Different from Chitonga of Malawi, Chitonga of Zambia and Zimbabwe, or Tonga dialect of Ndau.

Tsonga (Shitsonga, Xitsonga, Thonga, Tonga, Gwamba) [tso] 1,500,000 in Mozambique (1989 UBS). South of Maputo, most of Maputo and Gaza provinces. *Dialects:* Bila (Vila), Changana (Xichangana, Changa, Shangaan, Hlanganu, Hanganu, Langanu, Shilanganu, Shangana), Jonga (Djonga, Dzonga), Ngwalungu (Shingwalungu).

Other: Christian, traditional religion, Muslim. See main entry under South Africa.

Tswa (Shitshwa, Kitshwa, Sheetshwa, Xitshwa, Tshwa) [tsc] 695,212 in Mozambique (1980 census). Southern Region, most of Inhambane Province. Also spoken in South Africa, Zimbabwe. *Class:* Niger-Congo, Atlantic-Congo, Volta-Congo, Benue-Congo, Bantoid, Southern, Narrow Bantu, Central, S, Tswa-Ronga (S.50). *Dialects:* Hlengwe (Lengwe, Shilengwe, Lhengwe, Makwakwe-Khambana, Khambana-Makwakwe, Khambani), Tshwa (Dzibi-Dzonga, Dzonga-Dzibi, Dzivi, Xidzivi), Mandla, Ndxhonge, Nhayi. Partially intelligible of Ronga and Tsonga. *Lg Dev:* Dictionary. Grammar. Bible: 1910–1955.

Yao (Chiyao, Ciyao, Achawa, Adsawa, Adsoa, Ajawa, Ayawa, Ayo, Djao, Haiao, Hiao, Hyao, Jao, Veiao, Wajao) [yao] 450,000 in Mozambique (2001 Johnstone and Mandryk). Niassa Province, south and west of Lake Malawi. Also possibly Zimbabwe. *Dialects:* Makale (Cimakale), Massaninga (Cimassaninga), Machinga, Mangochi, Tunduru Yao, Chikonono (Cikonono). *Other:* Muslim, Christian, traditional religion. See main entry under Malawi.

Zulu (Isizulu, Zunda) [zul] 1,798 in Mozambique (1980 census). See main entry under South Africa.

Namibia

Republic of Namibia. Formerly South West Africa. 1,954,033. National or official languages: English, regional languages: Diriku, Herero, Kwangali, Kwanyama, Lozi, Mbukushu, Nama, Ndonga, Tswana. Literacy rate: 16% (1989 WA). Also includes Chokwe (5,580), Fanagalo, Kgalagadi, Luyana, Nkhumbi, Nyemba (9,540), Portuguese, Standard German (12,827), Umbundu (2,880). Information mainly from G. Stanley 1968; M. Brenzinger 1997; W. Haacke and E. Elderkin 1997; T. Güldemann 1998; J. Maho 1998. Blind population: 1,400 (1982 WCE). The number of languages listed for Namibia is 28. Of those, all are living languages. See map on page 711.

Afrikaans [afr] 133,324 in Namibia (1991 census). Not known in the north, in the Owambo tribes, and the Kavango and Caprivi regions. *Lg Use:* Used by 25% of the population in Windhoek in their homes (1995 census). *Other:* It formerly had official status. See main entry under South Africa.

Diriku (Diriko, Gciriku, Rugciriku, Mbogedo, Mbogedu, Shimbogedu) [diu] 29,400 in Namibia (1982 Prinloo et al.). Population total all countries: 31,400. Okavango. Also spoken in Angola, Botswana. *Class:* Niger-Congo, Atlantic-Congo, Volta-Congo, Benue-Congo, Bantoid, Southern, Narrow Bantu, Central, K, Diriku (K.70). *Dialects:* May be close to Sambya, Kwangali. *Lg Use:* National language. Used in schools, administration. *Lg Dev:* Radio programs. Dictionary. NT: 1988.

English [eng] 10,941 in Namibia (1991 census). *Lg Use:* Official language. Not understood or spoken by everyone. See main entry under United Kingdom.

Fwe [fwe] 7,400 (1998). Western East Caprivi. *Class:* Niger-Congo, Atlantic-Congo, Volta-Congo, Benue-Congo, Bantoid, Southern, Narrow Bantu, Central, K, Subia (K.50). *Dialects:* Close to Subiya. *Other:* Not the same as the We dialect of Tonga.

Hai‖om ("San," "Saan") [hgm] 16,000 in Namibia (1995 A. Miller-Ockhuizen). Mangetti Dune, Omataku, Grootfontein, Baghani, Tsintsabis. 'Maroelaboom' is the area of Namibia next to the Agricultural gate entering the former Bushmanland. Some moved to Kimberley, South Africa. Possibly in Angola, where they are reported to have come from. Also spoken in South Africa. *Class:*

Khoisan, Southern Africa, Central, Hain‖um. *Dialects:* Kedi (Kedde, Keddi), Chwagga, Hain‖um (Hei‖om, Heikom, Heikum, Heikom Bushman). Somewhat intelligible with Kung-Tsumkwe (Juǀ'hoan), but a different language. Also reported to speak a language or dialect similar to Nama and Damara. *Lg Use:* Speakers use Afrikaans, English, Damara, or Kwangali as second languages. Afrikaans is more widely known than English, but English is now learned in school instead of Afrikaans. Used for interlanguage contact. Many men speak Afrikaans well. Many who live near the Damara or Kwangali speak those languages well or at least understand them. *Lg Dev:* Literacy rate in second language: Low in Afrikaans. *Other:* "San" is a derogatory Nama name for all bushmen. Hunter-gatherers. Traditional religion, Christian.

Herero (Otjiherero, Ochiherero) [her] 113,000 in Namibia (1991 census). Population total all countries: 133,000. Damaraland and northwest Ovamboland territory, Kaokoveld. Also spoken in Botswana. *Class:* Niger-Congo, Atlantic-Congo, Volta-Congo, Benue-Congo, Bantoid, Southern, Narrow Bantu, Central, R, Herero (R.30). *Dialects:* Mbandieru, Kuvale. *Lg Use:* National language. *Lg Dev:* Dictionary. Grammar. Bible: 1987. *Other:* Erroneously called 'Damara'. The people are 'Ovaherero'. Traditional religion, Christian.

Juǀ'hoan (Kung-Tsumkwe, Xû, Xun, Kung, !Xo, Ju'oasi, Zhu'oasi, Dzu'oasi, Tshumkwe, Dobe Kung, Xaixai) [ktz] 25,000 to 30,000 in Namibia together with the Vasekela, the !Xung, and the ǂKx'auǁein (1998 J. F. Maho, p.113). Northeast. *Dialects:* Dzu'oasi (Ssu Ghassi, Zhu'oase), Nogau (Agau). *Lg Dev:* Nyaenyae Development Trust is teaching reading in Namibia. *Other:* Speakers use the name 'Juǀ'hoan' for themselves. Traditional religion, Christian. See main entry under Botswana.

Kung-Ekoka (Ekoka-!Xû, Kung, !Kung, !Ku, !Xu, !Hu, Qxü, !Xun, !Khung, !Xung) [knw] 1,757 in Namibia (2000). Population total all countries: 6,899. Okavango and Ovamboland Territory. Also spoken in Angola, South Africa. *Class:* Khoisan, Southern Africa, Northern. *Dialect:* Akhoe. *Lg Dev:* Bible portions: 1975–1980. *Other:* Possibly the same as Vasekela. Traditional religion, Christian.

Kwambi [kwm] 30,000 (1972 Nida). Ovamboland north. Possibly also in Angola. *Class:* Niger-Congo, Atlantic-Congo, Volta-Congo, Benue-Congo, Bantoid, Southern, Narrow Bantu, Central, R, Ndonga (R.20). *Lg Dev:* NT: 1951.

Kwangali (Sikwangali, Rukwangali, Kwangari, Kwangare) [kwn] 73,074 in Namibia (2000 WCD). Population includes 2,000 Sambyu. Population total all countries: 83,976. Okavango. Also spoken in Angola. *Class:* Niger-Congo, Atlantic-Congo, Volta-Congo, Benue-Congo, Bantoid, Southern, Narrow Bantu, Central, K, Kwangwa (K.40). *Dialect:* Sambyu (Shisambyu, Sambiu, Sambio). Sambyu may be intelligible with Diriku. *Lg Use:* National language. Used in education, administration. *Lg Dev:* Radio programs. Dictionary. Grammar. Bible: 1987.

Kwanyama (Ochikwanyama, Kuanyama, Ovambo, Humba, Kwanjama, Kwancama, Otjiwambo, Owambo) [kua] 713,919 in Namibia together with Ndonga and Kwambi; 1991 census. Northern Okavangoland. *Lg Use:* National language. *Lg Dev:* Literacy rate in second language: 50%. *Other:* Called 'Otjiwambo' and 'Owambo' together with Ndonga. See main entry under Angola.

ǂKx'auǁ'ein (Kung-Gobabis, ‖Auǁei, ‖X'auǁ'e, ǂKx'auǁ'ei, Auen, Kaukau, Koko) [aue] 2,000 in Namibia. Population total all countries: 4,000. Ovamboland Territory, Ekoka. Also spoken in Botswana. *Class:* Khoisan, Southern

Africa, Northern. *Dialect:* Nogau. *Lg Dev:* NT. *Other:* Traditional religion, Christian.

Kxoe (Kxoedam, Khwedam, Khoe, Xun, "Water Bushmen," "Mbarakwena," "Barakwena" "Barakwengo") [xuu] 4,000 in Namibia. Population includes 3,600 in West Caprivi and 400 in East Caprivi. Population total all countries: 9,988. West Caprivi in Namibia is recognized as the 'core land' of the Kxoe people by the Kxoe and the Namibian government. They also live in East Caprivi. Also spoken in Angola, Botswana, South Africa, Zambia. *Class:* Khoisan, Southern Africa, Central, Tshu-Khwe, Northwest. *Dialects:* ‖Xo-Kxoe, ‖Xom-Kxoe, Buma-Kxoe, Buga-Kxoe. Minor dialect differences within Kxoe. Related to ‖Ani, ǀAnda, Naro, Khoekhoegowap but is quite distinct from each of these and not mutually intelligible. *Lg Use:* Vigorous. Many non-Kxoe learn Kxoe for interaction with Kxoe. Positive language attitude. Many young people in West Caprivi claim not to understand Mbukushu at all. English, Afrikaans, and Kxoe used for oral teaching in schools; textbooks are in English. *Lg Dev:* Dictionary. Grammar. *Other:* Hunter-gatherers; fishermen: they still get 25% to 50% of their food this way; agriculturalists.

Lozi (Silozi, Rozi, Tozvi, Rotse, Rutse, Kololo) [loz] 25,200 in Namibia (1982 Prinsloo et al.). East Caprivi Strip. *Lg Use:* National language. Spoken as lingua franca by all East Caprivians. Used in education, administration. See main entry under Zambia.

Mashi (Masi) [mho] Few speakers in Namibia. East Caprivi. *Dialects:* North Kwandu, South Kwandu, Mashi. *Other:* Nomadic. Distinct from Mashi (Shi) which is related to Havu of Democratic Republic of the Congo. Traditional religion. See main entry under Zambia.

Mbalanhu (Mbalantu, Mbaanhu, Mbaluntu) [lnb] Northern. *Class:* Niger-Congo, Atlantic-Congo, Volta-Congo, Benue-Congo, Bantoid, Southern, Narrow Bantu, Central, R, Ndonga (R.20).

Mbukushu (Mbukushi, Mambukush, Mampukush, Mbukuhu, Thimbukushu, Gova, Kusso) [mhw] 20,000 in Namibia (1997 Andersson and Janson). Population total all countries: 44,000. Northwest Ovambo and northeast Okavango area, Andara. Also spoken in Angola, Botswana, Zambia. *Class:* Niger-Congo, Atlantic-Congo, Volta-Congo, Benue-Congo, Bantoid, Southern, Narrow Bantu, Central, K, Kwangwa (K.40). *Dialects:* Close to Kwangali. *Lg Use:* National language. *Lg Dev:* Radio programs. Dictionary. Grammar. NT: 1986. *Other:* Traditional religion, Christian.

Nama (Naman, Namakwa, Namaqua, Maqua, Tama, Tamma, Tamakwa, Berdama, Bergdamara, Kakuya Bushman Nasie, Rooi Nasie, "Hottentot," "Klipkaffer," "Klipkaffern," "Khoekhoegowap," "Khoekhoegowab") [naq] 176,201 in Namibia (1992 Barnard). Population includes 70,000 Nama, 105,000 Damara (1998 J.F. Maho). Population total all countries: 233,701. South central to the Orange River, Great Namaland. Also spoken in Botswana, South Africa. *Class:* Khoisan, Southern Africa, Central, Nama. *Dialects:* Damara, Sesfontein Damara, Namidama, Central Damara, Nama. Sesfontein Damara is reported to be unintelligible to speakers of other dialects. *Lg Use:* National language. Offered as a school subject. Can be studied up to doctoral level at U. of Namibia, also used in administration. *Lg Dev:* Radio programs. Dictionary. Grammar. Bible: 1966. *Other:* SOV. Pastoralist.

Namibian Sign Language [nbs] *Class:* Deaf sign language. *Lg Dev:* Dictionary.

Naro (Nharo) [nhr] 4,000 in Namibia (1998 Maho). Eastern Namibia. *Other:* Agriculturalists. See main entry under Botswana.

Ndonga (Ochindonga, Oshindonga, Osindonga, Otjiwambo, Owambo, Ambo) [ndo] 429,541 in Namibia

(2000 WCD). 713,919 in Namibia, including Kwanyama and Kwambi; 1991 census. Population total all countries: 692,230. Ovamboland. Also spoken in Angola. *Class:* Niger-Congo, Atlantic-Congo, Volta-Congo, Benue-Congo, Bantoid, Southern, Narrow Bantu, Central, R, Ndonga (R.20). *Dialects:* Ngandyera, Eunda Kolonkadhi, Kwaludhi. Ngandyera may be a separate language. Partially intelligible with Kwanyama. *Lg Use:* National language. *Lg Dev:* Literacy rate in second language: 75%. Dictionary. Grammar. Bible: 1954–1986. *Other:* Called 'Otjiwambo' and 'Owambo', together with the Kwanyama and Kwambi. Highly acculturated. Christian, traditional religion.

Subiya (Echisubia, Subia, Supia, Chikwahane, Chikuahane, Ciikuhane, Mbalangwe) [sbs] 24,500 in Namibia (1991). Population total all countries: 41,985. East Caprivi. Also spoken in Botswana, Zambia. *Class:* Niger-Congo, Atlantic-Congo, Volta-Congo, Benue-Congo, Bantoid, Southern, Narrow Bantu, Central, K, Subia (K.50). *Dialects:* Lexical similarity 61% with Luyana, 60% with Tonga. *Lg Dev:* Grammar. *Other:* 'Subiya' is the Tswana name. Tonga is a separate language. 'Mbalangwe' is applied to Subiya speakers living in the Mafwe area (Anton Bredell, J. F. Maho 1998:51). Traditional religion, Christian.

Totela (Echitotela) [ttl] East Caprivi. *Other:* Apparently no linguistic descriptions have been written. See main entry under Zambia.

Tswana [tsn] 6,050 in Namibia (1991 census). East central Namibia and Eastern Caprivi. *Dialects:* Tlharo, Tlhaping, Tawana. *Lg Use:* National language. Used in education, administration. *Other:* Animal husbandry: cattle; agriculturalists. See main entry under Botswana.

Vasekela Bushman (!'O-!Khung) [vaj] Western Caprivi area. *Class:* Khoisan, Southern Africa, Northern. *Dialects:* May be the same as 'Akhoe or Kung-Ekoka. *Other:* Large numbers migrated to Namibia and South Africa because of the war in Angola.

!Xóõ [nmn] 200 in Namibia (1985 Traill). Along the east central Botswana border in the vicinity of Aranos and Leonardville. *Dialects:* Auni (|Auni, |Auo), Kakia (Masarwa), Ki|hazi, Ng|u|en (Nu||en, |U||en, Ng|u|ei, |Nu||en, ||U||en), Nusan (Ng|usan, Nu-San, Noosan), Xatia (Katia, Khatia, Kattea, Vaalpens, |Kusi, |Eikusi), !Kwi. *Lg Use:* The N|gamani, |Nu||en, |'Auni, and Ki|hazi are extinct. See main entry under Botswana.

Yeyi (Shiyeyi, Yei, Yeei, Ciyei, Koba, Kuba) [yey] 5,200 in Namibia (1998 Maho). East Caprivi strip. *Dialect:* Shirwanga. *Lg Use:* All ages. Second languages are Subiya, Mbukushu, Mashi, and Lozi. They speak many languages of the Caprivi with those speakers. *Lg Dev:* Literacy rate in second language: 45% in Lozi. *Other:* Christian. See main entry under Botswana.

Zemba (Dhimba, Otjidhimba, Himba, Simba, Oluthimba, Luzimba) [dhm] 12,000 in Namibia (1996 UBS). Kunene Region, northwest Namibia, especially around Etoto and Ruacana, near the Herero. *Other:* Speakers are called 'Luzimba', 'Ovazemba', or 'Ovazimba'. See main entry under Angola.

Niger

Republic of Niger. République du Niger. 11,360,538. National or official languages: French, Arabic, Fulfulde, Gourmanchéma, Hausa, Manga Kanuri, Tamajaq, Zarma. Literacy rate: 17%. Information mainly from J. Lukas 1937; J. Applegate 1970; D. Sapir 1971; R. Nicolaï 1979, 1981, 1983; J. Bendor-Samuel 1989; K. Isaac 1998. Blind population: 30,000 (1998). Deaf population: 20,000 (1998). The number of languages listed for Niger is 21. Of those, all are living languages. See maps beginning on page 712.

Arabic, Algerian Saharan Spoken [aao] 10,000 in Niger (1998). Around Agadez and northwest Niger. *Lg Use:* Speakers also use Tamajaq. *Other:* Originally from Algeria. Muslim. See main entry under Algeria.

Arabic, Hassaniyya (Maure, Mauri, Moor, Sulaka, Hasanya, Hassani) [mey] 10,000 in Niger (1998). *Other:* Muslim. See main entry under Mauritania (Hassaniyya).

Arabic, Libyan Spoken (Libyan Vernacular Arabic, Sulaimitian Arabic) [ayl] 5,000 in Niger (1998). Eastern Niger north of N'guigmi near Ngourti. *Other:* Muslim. See main entry under Libya.

Arabic, Shuwa (Arabe Choa, Shuwa Arabic, Shua, Chadic Arabic) [shu] 5,000 in Niger (1998). Eastern Niger. *Other:* Muslim. See main entry under Chad (Arabic, Chadian Spoken).

Dazaga (Dasa, Dazza, Daza, Tubu, Tebu, Tibbu, Toubou) [dzg] 30,000 in Niger (1998 SIL). Eastern Niger in the south near the Chad border. *Dialect:* Dazaga, Azzaga (Azza, Aza). *Lg Use:* Official language. The government plans to develop Dazaga for formal and informal education. Low bilingualism in Arabic. *Other:* 'Daza' is the name for the people, 'Dazaga' for the language. In Niger the outsider term 'Tubu' groups Dazaga and Tedaga. Different from Daza in Nigeria, which is Chadic. Muslim. See main entry under Chad.

French [fra] 6,000 in Niger (1993 Johnstone). *Lg Use:* Official language. See main entry under France.

Fulfulde, Central-Eastern Niger (Peul, Peulh, Fulani, Fula, Fulbe) [fuq] 450,000 (1998). Central and eastern Niger, from around Dogondoutchi on eastward to the Chad border. *Class:* Niger-Congo, Atlantic-Congo, Atlantic, Northern, Senegambian, Fulani-Wolof, Fula, East Central. *Dialect:* Wodaabe. Wodaabe culture is distinct from other Fulfulde varieties. *Lg Use:* Official language. The Fulbe (15,000,000) from Senegal to Sudan consider themselves to be one ethnic group and to speak one language, while acknowledging differences in speech. Many use Hausa as second language. *Lg Dev:* Taught in primary schools. Radio programs. TV. *Other:* The people are 'Pullo' (sing.) or 'Fulbe' (pl.), the language 'Fulfulde'. The English name is 'Fulani' and the French 'Peul'. Many loanwords from Hausa. SVO; prepositions and postpositions; genitives, articles, adjectives, numerals, relatives after noun heads; question word final; 1 prefix, 9 suffixes; word order distinguishes subjects, objects, indirect objects, given and new information, topic and comment; verb affixes mark number, subject (obligatory); class marking with participle obligatory; middle and passive voice; causatives; CV, CVC, CVV, CVVC; nontonal. Muslim, traditional religion.

Fulfulde, Western Niger (Peul, Peulh, Fulani, Fula, Fulbe) [fuh] 400,000 in Niger (1998). Population total all countries: 1,180,000. Western Niger, from Burkina Faso border east to around Dogondoutchi. Also spoken in Benin, Burkina Faso. *Class:* Niger-Congo, Atlantic-Congo, Atlantic, Northern, Senegambian, Fulani-Wolof, Fula, East Central. *Dialects:* Dallol, Bitinkoore. *Lg Use:* Official language. The Fulbe from Senegal to Sudan consider themselves to be one ethnic group and to speak one language, while acknowledging differences in speech. Many use Zarma as second language. *Lg Dev:* Taught in primary schools. Radio programs. TV. *Other:* The Fulbe call their language 'Fulfulde' and the people 'Fulbe' (pl.), 'Pullo' (sing.). SVO; prepositions and postpositions; genitives, articles, adjectives, numerals, relatives after noun heads; question word final; 1 prefix, 9 suffixes; word order distinguishes subjects, objects, indirect objects, given and new information, topic and comment; verb affixes mark number, subject (obligatory); class marking with participle obligatory; middle and passive voice; causatives; CV, CVC, CVV, CVVC; nontonal. Muslim.

Gourmanchéma (Gourma, Gurma, Gourmantche, Goulimancema) [gux] 30,000 in Niger (1998). Southwest, near Burkina Faso border. *Lg Use:* Official language. *Other:* Traditional religion, Muslim, Christian. See main entry under Burkina Faso.

Hausa (Haussa, Haoussa, Hausawa) [hau] 5,000,000 in Niger (1998). First-language speakers in central Niger along the Nigeria border. Spoken in cities throughout Niger. *Dialects:* Dawra, Katsina, Damagaram, Gobirawa, Aderawa, Arewa, Kurfey, Gaya. *Lg Use:* Official language. Spoken by 55% of the population as first language, by 25% as second language. The main trade language of Niger. *Lg Dev:* Taught in primary schools. *Other:* Muslim. See main entry under Nigeria.

Kanuri, Bilma (Bla Bla, Kanouri, Kanoury) [bms] 20,000 (2003). Northeast Niger, Kawar Region. *Class:* Nilo-Saharan, Saharan, Western, Kanuri. *Dialects:* Bilma, Fachi. A member of the Kanuri cluster. *Other:* Muslim.

Kanuri, Central (Yerwa Kanuri, Kanoury, Kanouri, Bornu, Bornouans, Kole, Sirata, "Beriberi") [knc] 80,000 in Niger (1998). Eastern Niger along the Nigeria border. *Dialect:* Movar (Mowor, Mober, Mobber, Mavar). *Other:* "Beriberi" is considered a derogatory name. Movar may be a separate language. Muslim. See main entry under Nigeria.

Kanuri, Manga (Manga, Kanouri, Kanoury) [kby] 280,000 in Niger (1998). Population total all countries: 480,000. Eastern Niger along the Nigeria border. Also spoken in Nigeria. *Class:* Nilo-Saharan, Saharan, Western, Kanuri. *Dialects:* Manga, Dagara. Part of a dialect cluster that includes other Kanuri varieties and Kanembu in Chad. *Lg Use:* Official language. *Lg Dev:* Literacy rate in second language: 20%. 2 bilingual primary schools. Radio programs. TV. Bible portions. *Other:* Dagara may be a separate language. Muslim.

Kanuri, Tumari (Kanembu, Kanambu) [krt] 40,000 (1998). 50% monolingual. Tumari in N'guigmi and the other dialects in neighboring villages. *Class:* Nilo-Saharan, Saharan, Western, Kanuri. *Dialects:* Tumari, Sugurti (Suwurti), Kubari (Kuwuri). Not the same as Kanembu in Chad, although referred to as 'Kanembu' in Niger. There is a gradual differentiation between Kanembu in Chad and Kanuri dialects. Closest to Manga Kanuri. *Lg Use:* About half the population use Hausa as second language. A few use Dazaga. *Other:* Muslim, traditional religion.

Tagdal [tda] 26,862 (2000 WCD). Between Tahoua in central Niger, Agadez in north central Niger, and Ingall in northeast Niger. *Class:* Mixed Language, Songhay-Berber. *Dialects:* Azawagh (Southern Tagdal), Air (Northern Tagdal). Tagdal lexicon is about 75% to 80% Berber. Everyday vocabulary is about 50% Berber and 50% Songhay. *Lg Use:* Most women and many men are monolingual in Tagdal. If they speak a second language it is Tamajaq or Hausa. *Lg Dev:* Literacy rate in second language: Low in French, lower in Arabic. *Other:* Nomadic. The speakers are called Igalan (pl.), Agdal (sg.). Pastoralists; agriculturalists. Muslim.

Tamahaq, Tahaggart (Tamasheq, Tamachek, Tamashekin, Tomachek, Tuareg, Touareg, Tourage) [thv] 20,000 in Niger (1998). The Hoggar dialect is in the south Hoggar (Ajjer) Mountain area around Tamanrasset and south into Niger. The Ghat dialect is in southeast Algeria around Ganet and west Libyan oases around Ghat. *Dialects:* Hoggar (Ahaggaren, Ajjer, Tahaggart), Ghat (Ganet, Djanet). *Other:* 'Tamahaq' is the speakers' name for their language. 'Tuareg' is an Arabic name for the people. Nomadic. Volcanic mountain slope. Nomadic. Inadan caste: blacksmiths; jewelry craftsmen. Muslim. See main entry under Algeria.

Tamajaq, Tawallammat (Tamasheq, Tamachek, Tomacheck, Tamashekin, Tuareg, Touareg, Tourage, Amazigh, Tahoua, Tewellemet, Tahoua Tamajeq) [ttq]

450,000 in Niger (1998). Population total all countries: 640,000. The eastern dialect is in central Niger, around Tahoua from Ingal to the Mali border. The western dialect is in western Niger, north and northwest of Niamey and in eastern Mali, Menaka Region. Also spoken in Mali, Nigeria. *Class:* Afro-Asiatic, Berber, Tamasheq, Southern. *Dialects:* Tawallammat Tan Dannag (Ioullemmeden), Tawallammat Tan Ataram. *Lg Use:* Official language. *Lg Dev:* Traditional script called 'Shifinagh'. Radio programs. Bible portions: 1979–1985. *Other:* 'Tuareg' is an Arabic name for the people. They call their language 'Tamajaq' and themselves 'Kel Tamajaq'. Nomadic. Pastoralists; agriculturalists. Muslim.

Tamajeq, Tayart (Tamachek, Tomacheck, Amazigh, Tuareg, Touareg) [thz] 250,000 (1998). Central, Agadez area. *Class:* Afro-Asiatic, Berber, Tamasheq, Southern. *Dialects:* Air (Agadez, Tayart, Tayert, Tamestayert), Tanassfarwat (Tamagarast). *Lg Dev:* Taught in primary schools. Traditional script called 'Shifinagh'. Radio programs. NT: 1990. *Other:* The speakers' name for their language is 'Tamajeq'. Nomadic. Muslim.

Tasawaq (Ingelshi) [twq] 8,000 (1998 SIL). Central Niger, Ingal and Teguidda-n-Tessoumt, near Agadez. *Class:* Nilo-Saharan, Songhai, Northern. *Dialects:* Close to Tagdal (Niger), Tadaksahak (Mali), Korandje (Algeria). *Lg Use:* Some also speak Hausa or Tamajaq. *Other:* Shares features of Songai and Tamajaq. The people call themselves 'Ingalkoyyu', 'The lords of Ingal'. Businessmen: salt and date trade; agriculturalists. Muslim.

Tedaga (Teda, Tubu, Tebu, Tibbu, Toubou) [tuq] 10,000 in Niger (1998 SIL). Seguedine, Bilma, Termit-Kaoboul. *Lg Use:* Speakers also use Dazaga. The majority use Arabic. *Other:* 'Teda' is the name for the people. In Niger the outsider term 'Tubu' groups Dazaga and Tedaga. Seminomadic. Close to Dazaga. Azzaga, the speech of the Azza, a caste division, is different from Tedaga, but its relation to Tedaga and to the speech of the Azza among the Daza is not known. Welldiggers; pastoralists: camels. Muslim. See main entry under Chad.

Zarma (Dyerma, Dyarma, Dyabarma, Adzerma, Djerma, Zabarma, Zarbarma, Zarmaci) [dje] 2,100,000 in Niger (1998). Population total all countries: 2,188,400. Southwestern Niger. Also spoken in Burkina Faso, Mali, Nigeria. *Class:* Nilo-Saharan, Songhai, Southern. *Dialect:* Kaado. In Niger, dialects from Dendi and Songai blend into Zarma. Intelligibility is high, although they use ethnic names 'Dendi' or 'Songai' for themselves. Speakers cannot understand Gao Songai in Mali. *Lg Use:* Official language. *Lg Dev:* Taught in primary schools. Radio programs. TV. Dictionary. Bible: 1990. *Other:* Ethnic groups include Kurtey (32,000), Wogo (28,000), Songai (400,000), Dendi (40,000). Muslim, traditional religion, Christian.

Nigeria

Federal Republic of Nigeria. 137,253,133. National or official languages: Edo, Efik, Adamawa Fulfulde, Hausa, Idoma, Igbo, Central Kanuri, Yoruba, English. Literacy rate: 42% to 51%. Also includes Bagirmi, Klao, Mbay, Mpade, Ngambay, Pana, people from Lebanon, Europe. Information mainly from K. Hansford, J. Bendor-Samuel, and R. Stanford 1976; J. Bendor-Samuel 1989; D. Crozier and R. Blench 1992; R. Blench 1998, 2004; B. Connell 1998, 2002; U. Siebert 1998, 2002. Blind population: 800,000 (1982 WCE). Deaf institutions: 22. The number of languages listed for Nigeria is 521. Of those, 510 are living languages, 2 are second language without mother-tongue speakers, and 9 are extinct. See maps beginning on page 714.

Abanyom (Abanyum, Befun, Bofon, Mbofon) [abm] 12,500 (1986). Cross River State, Ikom LGA, Abangkang the main village. *Class:* Niger-Congo, Atlantic-Congo, Volta-Congo, Benue-Congo, Bantoid, Southern, Ekoid.

Abon (Abong, Abõ, Ba'ban) [abo] 1,000 (1973 SIL). Taraba State, Sardauna LGA, Abong town, east of Baissa. *Class:* Niger-Congo, Atlantic-Congo, Volta-Congo, Benue-Congo, Bantoid, Southern, Tivoid.

Abua (Abuan) [abn] 25,000 (1989 Faraclas). Rivers State, Degema and Ahoada LGAs. *Class:* Niger-Congo, Atlantic-Congo, Volta-Congo, Benue-Congo, Cross River, Delta Cross, Central Delta, Abua-Odual. *Dialects:* Central Abuan, Emughan, Otapha, Okpeden. The central dialect is understood by all others. Odual is the most closely related language. Lexical similarity 70% with Odual. *Lg Dev:* Dictionary. NT: 1978.

Abureni (Mini) [mgj] Bayelsa State, four towns: Brass LGA, Agrisaba (Obo-Emeke); Ogbia LGA, Idema; Nembe LGA, Okoroba; Ogbia LGA, Opume, which is politically part of Oloibiri. *Class:* Niger-Congo, Atlantic-Congo, Volta-Congo, Benue-Congo, Cross River, Delta Cross, Central Delta. *Other:* 'Mini' is the Nembe name.

Acipa, Eastern (Acipanci, Achipa, Sagamuk) [acp] 5,000 (1993). Niger State, Kontagora LGA; Kaduna State, Birnin Gwari LGA. Towns include Randeggi and Bobi. *Class:* Niger-Congo, Atlantic-Congo, Volta-Congo, Benue-Congo, Kainji, Western, Kamuku. *Dialect:* Boroma (Taboroma). Lexical similarity 83% between Randeggi and Bobi; 52% with Shama; 47% to 50% with Kamuku; 42% to 44% with Hungworo; 15% to 20% with Western Acipa. *Lg Use:* The influence of the Hausa language is slight. *Other:* The people are called 'Acipawa'. Traditional religion.

Acipa, Western (Acipanci, Achipa, Sagamuk) [awc] 20,000 (1995 CAPRO). Niger State, Kontagora LGA; Kebbi State, Sakaba LGA. Towns include Kumbashi, Kakihum, and Karisen. *Class:* Niger-Congo, Atlantic-Congo, Volta-Congo, Benue-Congo, Kainji, Western, Kamuku. *Dialect:* Cep (Tochipo, Tacep, Western Acipanci). Morphological evidence suggests its affiliation with the Kamuku language cluster. Lexical similarity 89% to 95% among the dialects; 15% to 20% with Eastern Acipa; 18% with Hungworo; 16% to 17% with Shama; 15% to 17% with Kamuku. *Lg Use:* The influence of the Hausa language is slight. *Other:* The people are called 'Acipawa'. Traditional religion.

Aduge [adu] 1,904 (1992 Crozier and Blench). Anambra State, Oyi LGA. *Class:* Niger-Congo, Atlantic-Congo, Volta-Congo, Benue-Congo, Edoid, Northwestern. *Lg Dev:* Grammar.

Afade (Affade, Afadeh, Afada, Kotoko, Mogari) [aal] 25,000 in Nigeria (1998 R. M. Blench). Population total all countries: 30,000. Borno State, Ngala LGA, 12 rather dense villages. Also spoken in Cameroon. *Class:* Afro-Asiatic, Chadic, Biu-Mandara, B, B.1, Kotoko Proper. *Other:* All Kotoko language speakers in Nigeria may speak Hausa.

Agatu (North Idoma, Ochekwu) [agc] 70,000 (1987 UBS). Benue State, Otuko Division, districts of Agatu, Ochekwu, and Adoka; Nasarawa State, Awe and Nasarawa LGAs. *Class:* Niger-Congo, Atlantic-Congo, Volta-Congo, Benue-Congo, Idomoid, Akweya, Etulo-Idoma, Idoma. *Dialects:* Member of the Idoma dialect cluster. *Lg Dev:* NT: 1984.

Agoi (Wagoi, Ro Bambami, Wa Bambani, Ibami) [ibm] 12,000 (1989 Faraclas). Cross River State, Obubra LGA, Agoi-Ekpo, Ekom-Agoi, Agoi-Ibami, and Itu-Agoi towns. *Class:* Niger-Congo, Atlantic-Congo, Volta-Congo, Benue-Congo, Cross River, Delta Cross, Upper Cross, Agoi-Doko-Iyoniyong. *Dialect:* Iko.

Agwagwune ("Akunakuna," Agwaguna, Gwune, Akurakura, Okurikan) [yay] 20,000 (1973 SIL). Cross River State, Akamkpa LGA. *Class:* Niger-Congo, Atlantic-Congo, Volta-Congo, Benue-Congo, Cross River, Delta Cross, Upper Cross, Central, North-South,

Ubaghara-Kohumono, Kohumono. *Dialects:* Abayongo (Bayono, Bayino), Abini (Obini, Abiri), Adim (Odim, Dim), Orum, Erei (Enna, Ezei), Agwagwune, Etono (Etuno). A dialect cluster. *Lg Dev:* Bible portions: 1894.

Àhàn (Ahaan) [ahn] 300 (2000 Blench). Ondo State, Ekiti LGA, Ajowa, Igashi, and Omou towns. *Class:* Niger-Congo, Atlantic-Congo, Volta-Congo, Benue-Congo, Ayere-Ahan.

Ajawa (Aja, Ajanci) [ajw] Extinct. Bauchi State. *Class:* Afro-Asiatic, Chadic, West, B, B.2. *Dialects:* Related to Miya. *Lg Use:* Became extinct between 1920 and 1940. Members of the ethnic group now speak Hausa.

Ake (Aike, Akye) [aik] 2,000 (1999 R. Blench). Nasarawa State, Lafia LGA, 3 villages. *Class:* Niger-Congo, Atlantic-Congo, Volta-Congo, Benue-Congo, Plateau, Western, Southwestern, B. *Dialects:* The closest language is Eggon. *Lg Use:* There is concern in the largest village that people are losing the language to Hausa.

Akpa (Akweya) [akf] 26,894 (2000 WCD). Benue State, Otukpo LGA. *Class:* Niger-Congo, Atlantic-Congo, Volta-Congo, Benue-Congo, Idomoid, Yatye-Akpa. *Dialects:* Dialect cluster. Lexical similarity 84% with Ekpari.

Akpes (Ibaram-Efifa) [ibe] 10,000 (1992 Crozier and Blench). Ondo State, Akoko North LGA. *Class:* Niger-Congo, Atlantic-Congo, Volta-Congo, Benue-Congo, Akpes. *Dialects:* Akunnu (Akpes), Ase, Daja, Efifa, Esuku (Echuku), Gedegede, Ikorom, Ibaram, Iyani. A dialect cluster. *Lg Use:* Yoruba is the lingua franca.

Akuku [ayk] Edo State, Akoko-Edo LGA. *Class:* Niger-Congo, Atlantic-Congo, Volta-Congo, Benue-Congo, Edoid, Northwestern, Southern. *Dialects:* Related to Oloma.

Akum (Anyar) [aku] Taraba State, near the Cameroon border, 3 villages in Nigeria (Manga, Ekban, Konkom). *Lg Use:* Most speakers have low proficiency in Jukun. Cameroon Pidgin is also spoken in the area. *Other:* The people are called 'Anyar'. Mountain slope. See main entry under Cameroon.

Alago (Aragu, Arago, Argo, Idoma Nokwu) [ala] 35,052 (2000). Nasarawa State, Awe and Lafia LGAs. *Class:* Niger-Congo, Atlantic-Congo, Volta-Congo, Benue-Congo, Idomoid, Akweya, Etulo-Idoma, Idoma. *Dialects:* Doma, Agwatashi, Keana, Assaikio. *Lg Use:* Speakers also use Hausa. *Lg Dev:* Literacy rate in second language: 5%. Bible portions: 1929. *Other:* Traditional religion, Muslim, Christian.

Alege (Alegi, Uge, Ugbe) [alf] 1,200 (1973 SIL). Cross River State, Obudu LGA. *Class:* Niger-Congo, Atlantic-Congo, Volta-Congo, Benue-Congo, Cross River, Bendi. *Dialects:* Related to Gayi (Bisu of Obanliku cluster) of Nigeria and Cameroon.

Alumu-Tesu (Arum-Cesu, Arum-Chessu, Arum-Tesu, Alumu) [aab] 4,702 (2000 WCD). Nasarawa State, Akwanga LGA, near Wamba. Alumu is 7 villages and Tesu is 1. *Class:* Niger-Congo, Atlantic-Congo, Volta-Congo, Benue-Congo, Plateau, Alumic. *Dialects:* Alumu (Arum), Tesu. Related to Toro. The two dialects have only intonation differences. *Lg Use:* Spoken fluently by young people.

Ambo [amb] 1,000. Taraba State, Sardauna LGA, 1 village east of Baissa. *Class:* Niger-Congo, Atlantic-Congo, Volta-Congo, Benue-Congo, Bantoid, Southern, Tivoid.

Amo (Amon, Among, Timap, Ba) [amo] 12,263 (2000 WCD). Plateau State, Bassa LGA; Kaduna State, Saminaka LGA. *Class:* Niger-Congo, Atlantic-Congo, Volta-Congo, Benue-Congo, Kainji, Eastern, Amo. *Dialects:* Not close to other languages. *Lg Dev:* Grammar. *Other:* 'Timap' is the language, 'Kumap' a speaker, 'Amap' the people.

Anaang (Anang, Annang) [anw] 1,000,000 (1990). Akwa Ibom State, Ikot Ekpene, Essien Udim, Abak, Ukanafun, and Oruk-Anam LGAs. *Class:* Niger-Congo, Atlantic-Congo, Volta-Congo, Benue-Congo, Cross River, Delta Cross, Lower Cross, Obolo, Efik. *Dialects:* Ikot Ekpene, Abak, Ukanafun. *Lg Dev:* Taught in primary schools. TV. *Other:* Referred to locally as 'Ekpene', 'Abak', and 'Ukanafun'.

Áncá (Bunta) [acb] Taraba State, Sardauna LGA, Antere, Nca village. *Class:* Niger-Congo, Atlantic-Congo, Volta-Congo, Benue-Congo, Bantoid, Unclassified. *Other:* May be the same as Manta.

Arabic, Shuwa (Arabe Choa, Shuwa, Shua Arabic, Chadian Arabic) [shu] 100,000 in Nigeria (1973 SIL). Borno State, Dikwa, Konduga, Ngala, and Bama LGAs, and ranging widely across Borno and Yobe states on transhumance. *Lg Use:* Trade language. No diglossia with Modern Standard Arabic. *Other:* The term 'Shua' is considered perjorative by some people. Muslim. See main entry under Chad (Arabic, Chadian Spoken).

Arigidi (North Akoko) [aqg] 48,000 (1986 in Crozier and Blench 1992). Population includes 45,000 Igasi, 3,000 Uro. Ondo State, Akoko North LGA; Kogi State, Kogi LGA. *Class:* Niger-Congo, Atlantic-Congo, Volta-Congo, Benue-Congo, Defoid, Akokoid. *Dialects:* Oyin, Uro, Arigidí, Erúsú (Erushu), Ojo, Udo (Ido, Òwòn Ùdò, Oke-Agbe), Afa (Affa, Òwòn Àfá), Òge (Òwòn Ògè), Aje, Ese (Òwòn Èsé), Igasi (Ìgàshí, Òwòn Ìgásí). A dialect cluster.

Ashe (Koron Ache, Ache, Ala, Koron Ala, Koro Makama) [ahs] 35,000 (1972 Barrett). Population includes Begbere-Ejar. Kaduna State, Kachia LGA. *Class:* Niger-Congo, Atlantic-Congo, Volta-Congo, Benue-Congo, Plateau, Western, Northwestern, Koro. *Dialects:* Related to Begbere-Ejar.

Asu (Abewa, Ebe) [aum] 5,000 (1998 Blench). Niger State, Mariga LGA, several villages south of Kontagora. *Class:* Niger-Congo, Atlantic-Congo, Volta-Congo, Benue-Congo, Nupoid, Nupe-Gbagyi, Nupe. *Lg Use:* Vigorous. Speakers also use Nupe. *Other:* Vocabulary has been heavily influenced by Nupe in recent years (Blench 1991).

Atsam (Cawai, Cawe, Cawi, Chawai, Chawe, Chawi) [cch] 30,000 (1972 Barrett). Kaduna State, Kachia LGA. *Class:* Niger-Congo, Atlantic-Congo, Volta-Congo, Benue-Congo, Kainji, Eastern, Piti-Atsam. *Dialects:* Closest to Piti. *Lg Dev:* Bible portions: 1923–1932. *Other:* Traditional religion.

Auyokawa (Auyakawa, Awiaka) [auo] Extinct. Jigawa State, Keffin Hausa and Auyo LGAs. *Class:* Afro-Asiatic, Chadic, West, B, B.1.

Awak (Awok, Yebu) [awo] 6,000 (1995 CAPRO). Gombe State, Kaltungo LGA. *Class:* Niger-Congo, Atlantic-Congo, Volta-Congo, North, Adamawa-Ubangi, Adamawa, Waja-Jen, Waja, Awak. *Other:* Agriculturalists: millet, maize, peanuts, guinea corn. Christian, traditional religion.

Ayere [aye] 3,000 (1992 Blench). Kwara State, Oyi LGA, Kabba District. *Class:* Niger-Congo, Atlantic-Congo, Volta-Congo, Benue-Congo, Defoid, Ayere-Ahan.

Ayu (Aya) [ayu] 800 (2003 SIL). Kaduna State, Jema'a LGA, Kongon, Gwade, Tayu, Arau, Diger, Ikwa, Agamati, Anka Ambel, and Amantu villages. *Class:* Niger-Congo, Atlantic-Congo, Volta-Congo, Benue-Congo, Plateau, Ayu. *Lg Use:* Children do not use Ayu. Most speakers also fluent in Hausa. *Other:* Muslim.

Baan (Baan-Ogoi, Goi, Ogoi) [bvj] 5,000 (1990). Rivers State, Gokana, Tai, and Eleme LGAs, Ban-Ogoi plus villages. *Class:* Niger-Congo, Atlantic-Congo, Volta-Congo, Benue-Congo, Cross River, Delta Cross, Ogoni, West. *Dialects:* Ka-Ban, Kesari. *Lg Dev:* Dictionary.

Baangi (Cibaangi) [bqx] 15,000 (1996). Northern Niger State. *Class:* Niger-Congo, Atlantic-Congo, Volta-Congo, Benue-Congo, Kainji, Western, Kambari.

Baatonum (Baatonun, Bariba, Batonnum, Batonu, Baatonun-Kwara, Bargu, Burgu, Borgu, Borgawa, Berba, Barba, Bogung, Zana) [bba] 100,000 in Nigeria (1995 Jones). Kwara State, Borgu LGA; Niger State. *Other:* Traditional religion, Muslim, Christian. See main entry under Benin.

Bacama (Bachama, Bashamma, Abacama, Besema, Bwareba, Gboare) [bcy] 150,000 (1992 CAPRO). Adamawa State, Numan and Guyuk LGAs, Kaduna State, northeast of Kaduna town. *Class:* Afro-Asiatic, Chadic, Biu-Mandara, A, A.8. *Dialects:* Mulyen (Mulwyin, Mwulyin), Opalo, Wa-Duku. In Bata dialect cluster. *Lg Use:* Trade language. *Lg Dev:* Grammar. Bible portions: 1915. *Other:* Bacama fishermen migrate long distances down the Benue with camps as far as the confluence. Agriculturalists; fishermen.

Bada (Badawa, Badanchi, Bat, Mbada, Mbat, Mbadawa, Kanna, Jar, Jarawan Kogi, Garaka, River Jarawa, Plains Jarawa) [bau] 10,000 (1991 SIL). Plateau State, Kanam LGA; Bauchi State, Tafawa Balewa LGA. *Class:* Niger-Congo, Atlantic-Congo, Volta-Congo, Benue-Congo, Bantoid, Southern, Jarawan, Nigerian. *Dialect:* Gar. A member of the Jarawa dialect cluster. *Other:* Traditional religion, Christian, Muslim.

Bade (Bedde, Bede, Gidgid) [bde] 250,000 (1993). Yobe State, Bade LGA; Jigawa State, Hadejia LGA. *Class:* Afro-Asiatic, Chadic, West, B, B.1, Bade Proper. *Dialects:* Gashua Bade (Mazgarwa), Southern Bade (Bade-Kado), Western Bade (Magwaram. Maagwaram), Shirawa. Close to Duwai and Ngizim. *Lg Use:* Speakers are shifting to Hausa. Shirawa dialect is extinct. Speakers have a routine proficiency in Hausa, Kanuri, or Fulani. *Other:* Muslim, traditional religion, Christian.

Bakpinka (Begbungba, Uwet, Iyongiyong, Iyoniyong) [bbs] Ethnic population: 3,416 (2000 WCD). Cross River State, Akamkpa LGA. *Class:* Niger-Congo, Atlantic-Congo, Volta-Congo, Benue-Congo, Cross River, Delta Cross, Upper Cross, Agoi-Doko-Iyoniyong. *Lg Use:* Reported to be dying out.

Bali (Bibaali, Maya, Abaali, Ibaali) [bcn] 2,000 (1991 Blench). Adamawa State, Numan LGA, at Bali, 30 km from Numan on the road to Jalingo. *Class:* Niger-Congo, Atlantic-Congo, Volta-Congo, North, Adamawa-Ubangi, Adamawa, Leko-Nimbari, Mumuye-Yandang, Yandang. *Dialects:* Close to Kpasam. *Lg Use:* They speak Hausa as second language, and some Bacama or Fulfulde. *Other:* 'Maya' or 'Abaali' is their name for the language, 'Ibaali' for the people. Agriculturalists: guinea corn, peanuts, rice. Christian, traditional religion, Muslim.

Bangwinji (Bangunji, Bangjinge) [bsj] 6,000 (1992 Crozier and Blench). Bauchi State, Balanga, Billiri, and Kaltungo LGAs. *Class:* Niger-Congo, Atlantic-Congo, Volta-Congo, North, Adamawa-Ubangi, Adamawa, Waja-Jen, Waja, Tula. *Dialects:* Kaalo, Naaban. Noun class system is closer to Waja and Tula. *Other:* Agriculturalists: guinea corn, beans, millet, beniseed, cotton, peanuts. Traditional religion.

Barikanchi [bxo] *Class:* Pidgin, Hausa based. *Lg Use:* Used in military barracks. *Other:* Second language only.

Basa (Basa-Benue, Rubasa, Rubassa, "Bassa-Kwomu," "Bassa-Komo," Abatsa, Abacha) [bzw] 100,000 (1973 SIL). Kogi State, Bassa and Ankpa LGAs; Plateau State, Nasarawa LGA; Federal Capital Territory, Yaba and Kwali LGAs; Benue State, Makurdi LGA. *Class:* Niger-Congo, Atlantic-Congo, Volta-Congo, Benue-Congo, Kainji, Western, Basa. *Dialects:* North-south dialect division along the Benue River. *Lg Use:* Speakers also use Igala or Nupe. *Lg Dev:* Literacy rate in second language: 5%. NT: 1972. *Other:* Speakers do not like the name "Bassa-Kwomu" or "Basa-Komo." Traditional religion, Christian, Muslim.

Basa-Gumna (Basa-Kaduna, Bassa-Kaduna, Gwadara Basa, Basa Kuta) [bsl] Extinct. Niger State, Chanchaga LGA; Plateau State, Nasarawa LGA. *Class:* Niger-Congo, Atlantic-Congo, Volta-Congo, Benue-Congo, Kainji, Western, Basa. *Lg Use:* Extinct in 1987. The ethnic group speaks Hausa.

Basa-Gurmana (Koromba) [buj] 2,000 (1987 Blench). Niger State, border of Rafi and Chanchaga LGAs, Kafin Gurmana. *Class:* Niger-Congo, Atlantic-Congo, Volta-Congo, Benue-Congo, Kainji, Western, Basa.

Bassa-Kontagora [bsr] 10 (1987). Ethnic population: 30,000. Niger State, Mariga LGA, northeast of Kontagora. *Class:* Niger-Congo, Atlantic-Congo, Volta-Congo, Benue-Congo, Kainji, Western, Basa. *Other:* Probably extinct. Nearly extinct.

Bata (Gbwata, Batta, Demsa Bata, Gboati, Gbwate, Bete, Birsa, Dunu) [bta] 150,000 in Nigeria (1992). Population total all countries: 152,500. Adamawa State, Numan, Song, Fufore, and Mubi LGAs. Also spoken in Cameroon. *Class:* Afro-Asiatic, Chadic, Biu-Mandara, A, A.8. *Dialects:* Zumu (Zomo, Jimo), Wadi (Wa'i), Malabu, Kobotachi, Ribaw (Ribow), Demsa, Garoua (Garua), Jirai. Closely related languages: Bacama, Gude, Nzanyi, Vin, Fali, Zizilivakan. They have joined with the Bacama in the Bwatiye Association. *Lg Dev:* Dictionary. *Other:* Agriculturalists; fishermen; animal husbandry: pigs, goats. Traditional religion, Muslim, Christian.

Batu [btu] 25,000. Taraba State, Sardauna LGA, several villages east of Baissa, below the Mambila escarpment. *Class:* Niger-Congo, Atlantic-Congo, Volta-Congo, Benue-Congo, Bantoid, Southern, Tivoid. *Dialects:* Amanda-Afi, Angwe, Kamino. A language cluster.

Bauchi (Bauci, Baushi, Kushi) [bsf] 20,000 (1988 Blench). Niger State, Rafi and Shiroro LGAs. *Class:* Niger-Congo, Atlantic-Congo, Volta-Congo, Benue-Congo, Kainji, Western, Baushi-Gurmana. *Dialects:* Wayam-Rubu, Madaka (Adeka), Supana.

Beele (Bele, Àbéélé, Bellawa) [bxq] 120 (1922 Temple). Bauchi State, near the Bole, a few villages. *Class:* Afro-Asiatic, Chadic, West, A, A.2, Bole, Bole Proper. *Dialects:* A separate language from Bole. *Other:* Muslim.

Begbere-Ejar (Koro Agwe, Agere, Koro Makama, Koro Myamya, Miamia, Miamiya) [bqv] 35,000 (1972 Barrett). Population includes Ashe. Kaduna State, Kachia LGA, Plateau State, Keffi LGA. *Class:* Niger-Congo, Atlantic-Congo, Volta-Congo, Benue-Congo, Plateau, Western, Northwestern, Koro. *Dialects:* Koron Panda, Koron Ache, Ejar. *Other:* The alternate names listed refer to the people. 'Koro' is used as a cover term for several groups. Traditional religion, Muslim, Christian.

Bekwarra (Ebekwara, Bekworra, Yakoro) [bkv] 100,000 (1989 SIL). Cross River State, Ogoja LGA. *Class:* Niger-Congo, Atlantic-Congo, Volta-Congo, Benue-Congo, Cross River, Bendi. *Lg Dev:* Radio programs. TV. Grammar. NT: 1983.

Bena (Ebina, Binna, Gbinna, Ebuna, Buna, Yongor, Yungur, Yangeru, Purra, "Lala") [yun] 95,000 (1992). Adamawa State, Guyuk, Gombi, and Song LGAs, new settlements along the road from Song to Yola. *Class:* Niger-Congo, Atlantic-Congo, Volta-Congo, North, Adamawa-Ubangi, Adamawa, Waja-Jen, Yungur, Yungur-Roba. *Lg Use:* Speakers also use Fulfulde, Dera, or Hausa. *Other:* The name "Lala" is offensive. 'Purra' is a cover term for the northern clans. 17 clans. Traditional religion, Christian, Muslim.

Berom (Birom, Berum, Gbang, Kibo, Kibbo, Kibbun, Kibyen, "Shosho," Aboro, Boro-Aboro, Afango, Chenberom, Cen Berom) [bom] 300,000 (1993 SIL). Population includes Cen 2,000. Plateau State, Berakin Ladi and Jos LGAs; Kaduna State, Jema'a LGA; Bauchi State. *Class:* Niger-Congo, Atlantic-Congo, Volta-Congo, Benue-Congo, Plateau, Beromic. *Dialects:* Gyell-Kuru-Vwang (Ngell-Kuru-Vwang), Fan-Foron-Heikpang, Bachit-Gashish, Du-Ropp-Rim, Hoss, Cen. *Lg Dev:* Literacy rate in first language: 10% to 30%. Literacy rate in second language: 25% to 50%. Dictionary. Grammar. NT: 1984. *Other:* "Shosho" is an offensive name. Cen may be a separate language.

Bete [byf] 50 (1992). Ethnic population: 3,000. Taraba State, Takum LGA, Bete town, at the foot of Bete mountain, south of Wukari. *Class:* Niger-Congo, Atlantic-Congo, Volta-Congo, Benue-Congo, Jukunoid. *Dialects:* Reported to have been close to Lufu. *Lg Use:* Members of the ethnic group now speak Jukun. *Other:* 6 subgroups: Aphan (Afan), Ruke, Osu, Agu, Botsu, Humiyan. Formerly had land disputes with the Tiv. Christian, traditional religion. Nearly extinct.

Bete-Bendi (Bette-Bendi, Dama) [btt] 36,800 (1963). Cross River State, Obudu LGA. *Class:* Niger-Congo, Atlantic-Congo, Volta-Congo, Benue-Congo, Cross River, Bendi. *Dialects:* Bete (Bette, Mbete), Bendi. *Lg Dev:* NT: 1982. *Other:* Not the same as Bete of Nigeria in Gongola State, Bete of Cameroon, or Bété of Côte d'Ivoire.

Bile (Bille, Billanchi, Kunbille, Bili) [bil] 30,000 (1992). East of Numan, along Benue River, Adamawa State, Numan LGAs, southwest of Numan. *Class:* Niger-Congo, Atlantic-Congo, Volta-Congo, Benue-Congo, Bantoid, Southern, Jarawan, Nigerian. *Dialects:* Related to Mbula-Bwazza. *Lg Use:* Speakers also use Hausa or Fulfulde. *Other:* Traditional religion, Christian, Muslim.

Bina (Bogana, Binawa) [byj] 7,000 (2000). Kaduna State, Saminaka LGA. *Class:* Niger-Congo, Atlantic-Congo, Volta-Congo, Benue-Congo, Kainji, Eastern, Northern Jos, Kauru.

Biseni (Buseni, Amegi, Northeast Central Ijo) [ije] 4,800 (1977 Voegelin and Voegelin). Bayelsa State, Biseni-Okordia LGA. *Class:* Niger-Congo, Atlantic-Congo, Ijoid, Ijo, Inland Ijo. *Dialects:* Not fully intelligible with other languages in the Ijo language cluster. *Lg Use:* Use Kolokuma for wider communication.

Bitare (Njwande, Yukutare) [brt] 113,862 in Nigeria (2000 WCD). Population total all countries: 119,896. Taraba State, Sardauna LGA, near Baissa. Also spoken in Cameroon. *Class:* Niger-Congo, Atlantic-Congo, Volta-Congo, Benue-Congo, Bantoid, Southern, Tivoid. *Dialects:* Close to Abong.

Bo-Rukul (Mabo-Barkul, Mabo-Barukul, "Kaleri") [mae] 2,000 (1999 R. Blench). Population includes 1,000 in each dialect. Plateau State, Bokkos LGA, Barkul, Mabo, Richa, Mwa villages. *Class:* Niger-Congo, Atlantic-Congo, Volta-Congo, Benue-Congo, Plateau, Southeastern. *Dialects:* Bo, Rukul. A language cluster. *Lg Use:* Vigorous. They speak Hausa and Kulere outside the village. Hausa is the lingua franca. English is restricted to young people, especially men, used in education and government. *Lg Dev:* Literacy rate in second language: 50% of young people read Hausa haltingly. *Other:* 'ma-' sg. and 'ba-' pl. are prefixes referring to speakers. Culturally they are considered to be Kulere, but the language is different. "Kaleri" is a derogatory name. Christian.

Boga (Boka) [bvw] 10,000 (1990 Blench). Adamawa State, Gombi LGA. *Class:* Afro-Asiatic, Chadic, Biu-Mandara, A, A.1, Eastern.

Boghom (Bogghom, Bohom, Burom, Burum, Burrum, Burma, Borrom, Boghorom, Bokiyim) [bux] 50,000 (1973 SIL). Plateau State, Kanam, Wase, and Shendam LGAs. *Class:* Afro-Asiatic, Chadic, West, B, B.3, Boghom. *Dialects:* Related to Mangas. *Lg Dev:* Bible portions: 1955.

Boko (Bokko, Bokonya, Boo) [bqc] 40,000 in Nigeria (1995 R. Jones). Niger State, Borgu LGA; Kebbi State,

Bagudo LGA, from Senji in the north to Kenugbe and Kaoje, 150 km to the south and Demmo, 50 km to the east, 35 villages. *Lg Use:* Positive language attitude. Speakers also use Baatonum, Hausa, or English. *Lg Dev:* Adult literacy program. *Other:* They call their language 'Boo'; the Hausa call all Busa languages 'Busanchi' and the people 'Busawa'. Muslim, traditional religion, Christian. See main entry under Benin.

Bokobaru (Busa-Bokobaru, Zongben, Zõgbe) [bus] 30,000 (1997 Jones). Population includes 6,000 in Kaiama, 24,000 in other villages. Kwara State, primarily Kaiama LGA, some in Baruten LGA. 35 villages. *Class:* Niger-Congo, Mande, Eastern, Eastern, Busa. *Dialects:* Kaiama, Village Bokobaru. Speakers of Kaiama and dialect in other villages have good inherent intelligibility of each other's dialects. The Bokobaru variety is distinct enough to require separate literature from Boko of Benin. The Busa variety of Nigeria may also require separate literature. Lexical similarity 86% with Boko, 91% with Busa, 53% with Kyenga, 50% with Bissa of Burkina Faso and Ghana. *Lg Use:* Positive language attitude. Bilingual level estimates for English: 0 80%, 1 10%, 2 4%, 3 3%, 4 2%, 5 1%. Some speakers use Hausa, Yoruba, English, Baatonum, Fulfulde as second languages to speakers from those groups. Some use Hausa among themselves. *Lg Dev:* Literacy rate in second language: 10%. High motivation for literacy. Adult literacy program. Dictionary. Grammar. Bible portions: 1972–1998. *Other:* The people are Bussawa. They call the language 'Bussagwe'. The Hausa call the language 'Busanchi'. SOV; genitives before noun heads; articles, adjective, numerals, relatives after noun heads; question word initial or final; 4 suffixes; word order distinguishes subject, object, indirect object; postpositions; person, number, aspect included in subject pronouns; tone changes some verb aspect; passives; CV, CVV, CCV; tonal. Interfluvial. Savannah. Peasant agriculturalists. Muslim, traditional religion, Christian.

Bokyi (Boki, Nki, Okii, Uki, Nfua, Osikom, Osukam, Vaaneroki) [bky] 140,000 in Nigeria (1989 SIL). Population total all countries: 143,700. Cross River State, Ikom, Obudu, and Ogoja LGAs. Also spoken in Cameroon. *Class:* Niger-Congo, Atlantic-Congo, Volta-Congo, Benue-Congo, Cross River, Bendi. *Dialects:* Basua (Bashua), Irruan (Erwan, Eerwee), Boje (Bojie), Kwakwagom, Nsadop, Osokom, Wula (Baswo, Okundi, Kecwan), Oku, Boorim, Oyokom, Abo (Abu), Eastern Bokyi (East Boki). *Lg Use:* Important district language. *Lg Dev:* Bible: 1987. *Other:* Ethnic groups: Ndir, Ukwese, Utang, Yon.

Bole (Bolanchi, Ampika, Borpika, Bolewa, Bolawa) [bol] 100,000 (1990). Bauchi State, Dukku, Alkaleri, and Darazo LGAs; Gombe State, Dukku LGA; Yobe State, Fika LGA; Plateau State, Wase LGA. *Class:* Afro-Asiatic, Chadic, West, A, A.2, Bole, Bole Proper. *Dialect:* Bara, Fika (Fikankayen, Anpika). *Lg Dev:* Grammar. *Other:* Speakers are called 'Bolewa' or 'Bolawa'. Bele is a separate language. The Ngara (2,000 in 1993) claim to be part of Bole, but the Bolewa disagree. Muslim.

Bu (Jida-Abu, Jidda-Abu, Jida, Ibut, Nakare) [jid] 6,000 (1999 R. Blench). Population includes 4,000 Bu and 2,000 Ninkada. Nasarawa State, Akwanga LGA, 4 villages. *Class:* Niger-Congo, Atlantic-Congo, Volta-Congo, Benue-Congo, Plateau, Ninzic. *Dialects:* Bu (Abu), Ninkada (Jida). The 2 dialects are ethnically and geographically distinct, but linguistically similar.

Bukwen [buz] 1,000. Taraba State, near Takum, 1 village. *Class:* Niger-Congo, Atlantic-Congo, Volta-Congo, Benue-Congo, Bantoid, Southern, Beboid.

Bumaji [byp] 11,386 (2000 WCD). Cross River State, Obudu LGA, Bumaji town. *Class:* Niger-Congo, Atlantic-Congo, Volta-Congo, Benue-Congo, Cross River, Bendi.

Bura-Pabir (Bura, Burra, Bourrah, Pabir, Babir, Babur, Barburr, Mya Bura, Kwojeffa, Huve, Huviya) [bwr] 250,000 (1987 UBS). Population includes 200,000 Pabir (1993). 32,000 in Adamawa State (1992). Borno State, Biu and Askira-Uba LGAs; Adamawa State, Gombi LGA. *Class:* Afro-Asiatic, Chadic, Biu-Mandara, A, A.2, 1. *Dialects:* Pela (Bura Pela, Hill Bura), Hyil Hawul (Bura Hyilhawul, Plain Bura). Kofa may be a related language. *Lg Dev:* Literacy rate in second language: 3%. Dictionary. Grammar. NT: 1937–1987. *Other:* Ngohi is a small subgroup. Agriculturalists; weavers; hunters; fishermen; wood carvers. Traditional religion, Muslim, Christian.

Burak (Buurak) [bys] 4,000 (1992 Crozier and Blench). Bauchi State, Billiri and Kaltungo LGAs, Burak town. *Class:* Niger-Congo, Atlantic-Congo, Volta-Congo, North, Adamawa-Ubangi, Adamawa, Waja-Jen, Jen. *Other:* Mountain slope. Traditional religion, Christian.

Bure (Bubure) [bvh] 500. Bauchi State, Darazo LGA, one village southeast of Darazo town. *Class:* Afro-Asiatic, Chadic, West, A, A.2, Bole.

Buru [bqw] 1,000. Taraba State, Sardauna LGA, east of Baissa, a village near Batu. *Class:* Niger-Congo, Atlantic-Congo, Volta-Congo, Benue-Congo, Bantoid, Unclassified.

Busa (Bisã, Bisayã, Busa-Bisã, Busano, Bussanchi) [bqp] 20,000 (1998 Ross Jones SIM). Niger State, Borgu LGA, Kebbi State, Bagudo LGA, 35 villages. *Class:* Niger-Congo, Mande, Eastern, Eastern, Busa. *Dialects:* New Busa, Wawa, Illo. The two dialects are inherently intelligible to each other's speakers. Busa has more prestige, but Wawa viewed as purer, and used for literature. New Busa has Hausa-influenced phonology. Illo Busa has Boko influence. Other Busa languages (Boko, Bokobaru) require separate literature. Lexical similarity 91% with Bokobaru, 85% with Boko, 54% with Kyenga, 50% with Bissa in Burkina Faso. *Lg Use:* 20,000 second-language users. Positive language attitude. Bilingual level estimates for Hausa: 0 30%, 1 40%, 2 13%, 3 10%, 4 5%, 5 2%. Speakers also use Hausa, Kambari, and English. Hausa is used in school. *Lg Dev:* Literacy rate in second language: 5%. Busa and Hausa adult literacy programs. Busa literature is available. Dictionary. Grammar. Bible portions: 1993–1998. *Other:* Speakers call themselves 'Bisã'. Different from Bissa of Burkina Faso and Ghana. SOV; postpositions; genitives before noun heads; articles, adjectives, numerals, relatives after noun heads; question word initial or final; 4 suffixes; word order distinguishes subject, object, direct object; person, number, aspect included in subject pronouns; tone indicates some verb aspect; passive; CV, CVV, CCV; grammatical tone affects NPs, verbs, and pronouns; tonal, 3 level tones. Riverine. Savannah. Peasant agriculturalists. Muslim, Christian.

Cakfem-Mushere (Chakfem, Chokfem) [cky] 5,000 (1990 SIL). Plateau State, Mangu LGA. *Class:* Afro-Asiatic, Chadic, West, A, A.3, Angas Proper, 1. *Dialects:* Kadim-Kaban, Jajura.

Cara (Chara, Fachara, Nfachara, Fakara, Pakara, Tera, Teriya, Terri, Tariya) [cfd] 3,000 (1999 R. Blench). Plateau State, Bassa LGA, Teriya village. *Class:* Niger-Congo, Atlantic-Congo, Volta-Congo, Benue-Congo, Plateau, Central, North-Central. *Lg Use:* The adults think that younger people are shifting to Hausa. They tend to know Hausa, and some youth also speak English. They generally do not speak the languages of their neighbors. *Other:* Complex morphology.

Centúúm (Cen Tuum) [cet] 200 (1992 Crozier and Blench). Bauchi State, Balanga LGA, Cham town, among the Dijim. *Class:* Language Isolate. *Lg Use:* All speakers are older adults. *Other:* The Dijim call the people 'Jalabe' or 'Jaabe'.

Che (Rukuba, Kuche, Bache, Inchazi, Sale) [ruk] 100,000 (2003 Blench). Plateau State, Bassa LGA.

Class: Niger-Congo, Atlantic-Congo, Volta-Congo, Benue-Congo, Plateau, Western, Southwestern, A. *Lg Dev:* Grammar. Bible portions: 1924–1931. *Other:* The language is 'Kuche', a speaker 'Ache', the people 'Bache'.

Cibak (Chibuk, Chibok, Chibbak, Chibbuk, Kyibaku, Kibbaku, Kikuk) [ckl] 100,000 (1993 CAPRO). Borno State, Damboa LGA. *Class:* Afro-Asiatic, Chadic, Biu-Mandara, A, A.2, 1.

Cinda-Regi-Tiyal (Kamuku) [cdr] 30,000 (1995 S. and S. Dettweiler). Niger State, Chanchaga, Rafi, and Mariga LGAs; Kaduna State, Birnin Gwari LGA. *Class:* Niger-Congo, Atlantic-Congo, Volta-Congo, Benue-Congo, Kainji, Western, Kamuku. *Dialects:* Cinda (Ucinda, Jinda, Majinda, Tegina, Makangara), Regi, Tiyal (Tiyar, Kuki). Lexical similarity 90% to 95% among the three dialects. *Lg Use:* Speakers also use Hausa. *Lg Dev:* Literacy rate in second language: 10%. *Other:* Clans are Uregi, Urogo, Tiyar (Kuki), Ucinda (Jinda), and Ushana. Laka, or Kamuku Laka, are Hausa-speaking ethnic Kamuku. Traditional religion, Muslim, Christian.

Cineni [cie] 3,000 (1998). Borno State, Gwoza LGA, Cineni village. *Class:* Afro-Asiatic, Chadic, Biu-Mandara, A, A.4, Mandara Proper, Glavda.

Cishingini (Ashaganna, Ashingini, Aschingini, Chisingini, "Maunchi," "Mawanchi," Kambari, Kamberri, Kamberchi, Yauri, Agwara Kambari) [asg] 100,000 (2004 SIL). Niger State, Borgu and Agwara LGAs, just west of the Niger River and north of the Kainji Lake National Park; and Kebbi State, east of the Niger River from the Yelwa area south to Ngaski and Nasko. *Class:* Niger-Congo, Atlantic-Congo, Volta-Congo, Benue-Congo, Kainji, Western, Kambari. *Dialect:* Rofia. A member of the Kambari cluster, which includes Tsishingini and Tsikimba. *Lg Use:* Speakers can use Hausa and some can use English or other Kambari languages. *Lg Dev:* Literacy rate in first language: 5%. Bible portions: 1994. *Other:* Speakers are called 'Ashingini'. Traditional religion, Christian, Muslim.

Ciwogai (Tsagu, Sago) [tgd] 2,000 (1995 CAPRO). Bauchi State, Ganjuwa LGA, Tsagu village and farms in the vicinity. Near the Diri. *Class:* Afro-Asiatic, Chadic, West, B, B.2. *Dialects:* Related to Diri. *Other:* Traditional religion.

C'lela (Lela, Lalawa, Kolela, Cala-Cala, Chilela, Chilala, Dakarkari, Dakakari, Dakkarkari) [dri] 90,000 (1993 SIL). Eastern Kebbi State, Zuru, Sakaba, and Donko-Wasagu LGAs; Niger State, Rijau LGA; and migrants farther south. *Class:* Niger-Congo, Atlantic-Congo, Volta-Congo, Benue-Congo, Kainji, Western, Duka. *Dialects:* Lila (Zuru, Senchi, Southern Lela), Dabai (Central Lela), Ribah, Adoma (Aroma, Roma-Na, Roma, Yelmo, Northern Lela). Lexical similarity 93% to 98% among dialects at Rade, Ribah, Dabai, and Senchi. Lexical similarity 55% with Duka, 54% with the Fakai cluster, 47% with Gwamhi-Wuri, 20% with Acipa. *Lg Use:* Speakers also use Hausa. *Lg Dev:* Radio programs. Bible portions: 1931. *Other:* 'Dakarkari' is the Hausa name for the people. 'Lela' is their own name for people and language. Hills, plains. Savannah. 250 to 500 meters. Agriculturalists: guinea corn, millet, maize, acha, peanuts, beans, sugarcane, cotton; brewing alcohol; blacksmiths; mat makers; smelting; potters. Traditional religion, Muslim, Christian.

Como Karim (Chomo, Shomong, Shomoh, Nuadhu, Shomo Karim, Kirim, Kiyu, Kinzimba, Asom) [cfg] 11,386 (2000 WCD). Taraba State, Jalingo, Karim Lamido LGAs, near Lau. *Class:* Niger-Congo, Atlantic-Congo, Volta-Congo, Benue-Congo, Jukunoid, Central, Jukun-Mbembe-Wurbo, Wurbo. *Other:* Called 'Bakula' together with Shoo-Minda-Nyem, Jiru, and Jessi. Hunters; fishermen. Traditional religion, Muslim, Christian.

Cori (Chori) [cry] 1,000 (2004). Kaduna State, Jema'a LGA, one village and associated hamlets. *Class:* Niger-Congo, Atlantic-Congo, Volta-Congo, Benue-Congo, Plateau, Western, Northwestern, Hyamic. *Lg Dev:* Grammar.

Daba (Dabba) [dbq] 1,000 in Nigeria (1992 Crozier and Blench). Adamawa State, Mubi LGA, between Mubi and Bahuli, 1 village. See main entry under Cameroon.

Dadiya (Dadia, Daadiya, Loodiya) [dbd] 30,000 (1998). Bauchi State, Balanga LGA; Taraba State, Karim Lamido LGA; Adamawa State, Numan LGA, between Dadiya and Bambam. *Class:* Niger-Congo, Atlantic-Congo, Volta-Congo, North, Adamawa-Ubangi, Adamawa, Waja-Jen, Waja, Dadiya. *Dialects:* Tunga (Boleri), Loofiyo, Kookwila, Loofaa. The dialect names are also names of settlements. *Other:* Mountain slope, plains. Agriculturalists: grain, peanuts, beans, rice, cotton. Traditional religion.

Dass (Barawa) [dot] 8,830. Population includes 1,130 Lukshi, 4,700 Durr-Baraza, 700 Wandi and Zumbul, 2,300 Dot (1971 census). Bauchi State, Akleri, Toro, and Dass LGAs; Plateau State, Shendam LGA. *Class:* Afro-Asiatic, Chadic, West, B, B.3. *Dialects:* Lukshi (Dekshi), Durr-Baraza (Bandas), Zumbul (Boodla), Wandi (Wangday), Dot (Dwat, Zodi, Dott). A dialect cluster.

Daza (Dazawa) [dzd] Bauchi State, Darazo LGA, a few villages. *Class:* Afro-Asiatic, Chadic, West, A. *Other:* Different from Dazaga in Chad and Niger, which is Saharan.

Defaka (Afakani) [afn] 200 (2001 Blench). Rivers State, Opobo-Nkoro LGA, in the Niger Delta, town of Nkoro. *Class:* Niger-Congo, Atlantic-Congo, Ijoid, Defaka. *Dialects:* Related to the Ijo group. *Lg Use:* Speakers are shifting to Nkoroo.

Degema ("Udekama") [deg] 10,000 (1999 SIL). Rivers State, Degema LGA, Usokun-Degema (Usokun) and Degema Town (Atala) communities. *Class:* Niger-Congo, Atlantic-Congo, Volta-Congo, Benue-Congo, Edoid, Delta. *Dialect:* Atala, Usokun (Kala Degema). *Lg Use:* There is no standard variety of Degema. *Lg Dev:* Grammar. *Other:* 'Degema' refers to the people, the area, and the language. The Kalabari call the people and language 'Udekama'; this name is disliked by the Degema. The Obonoma (Ekomburu) in Akuku-Toru LGA shifted from Degema to Kalabari in the past.

Dendi (Dandawa) [ddn] 2,050 in Nigeria (2000 WCD). Kebbi State, Argungu and Bagudo LGAs, on upper Niger River. See main entry under Benin.

Deno (Denawa, Denwa, Be) [dbb] 6,000 (1995 CAPRO). Bauchi State, Darazo LGA, 45 km northeast of Bauchi town. *Class:* Afro-Asiatic, Chadic, West, A, A.2, Bole, Bole Proper. *Lg Use:* Speakers are shifting to Hausa and Fulfulde. *Other:* Agriculturalists: guinea corn, maize, millet, cassava, beans, rice. Traditional religion, Muslim.

Dera (Kanakuru) [kna] 20,000 (1973 SIL). Gongola State, Guyuk LGA; Borno State, Biu LGA. *Class:* Afro-Asiatic, Chadic, West, A, A.2, Tangale, Dera. *Dialects:* Shani, Shellen, Gasi. *Lg Use:* Some speakers use Hausa, Bura, Lala, Fulfulde, Longuda, or English as second language. *Lg Dev:* Many are educated. Most villages have primary schools. Grammar. Bible portions: 1937. *Other:* Agriculturalists: guinea corn, peanuts, cotton; hunters; fishermen. Traditional religion, Muslim, Christian.

Dghwede (Hude, Johode, Traude, Dehoxde, Tghuade, Toghwede, Wa'a, Azaghvana, Zaghvana) [dgh] 30,000 (1980 UBS). Borno State, Gwoza LGA. *Class:* Afro-Asiatic, Chadic, Biu-Mandara, A, A.4, Mandara Proper, Glavda. *Lg Dev:* NT: 1980.

Dibo (Shitako, Zitako, Zhitako. Ganagana, Ganagawa) [dio] 100,000 (1992 Crozier and Blench). Niger State, Lapai LGA; Federal Capital Territory; Plateau State, Nasarawa LGA. *Class:* Niger-Congo, Atlantic-Congo,

Volta-Congo, Benue-Congo, Nupoid, Nupe-Gbagyi. *Lg Use:* An unknown number living among the Gbari no longer speak their own language (Blench 1990). *Other:* 'Ganagana' and 'Ganagawa' are names for the people. Muslim, traditional religion, Christian.

Dijim-Bwilim [cfa] 25,000 (1998). Bauchi State, Balanga LGA; Gongola State, Numan LGA. *Class:* Niger-Congo, Atlantic-Congo, Volta-Congo, North, Adamawa-Ubangi, Adamawa, Waja-Jen, Waja, Cham-Mona. *Dialects:* Dijim (Cham, Cam), Bwilim (Mwano, Mwona, Mwomo, Mona, Mwana, Fitilai). Related to Lotsu-Piri. *Other:* Some form of whistle speech reported. Traditional religion, Christian.

Diri (Dirya, Diriya, Diryawa) [dwa] 7,196 (2000 WCD). Bauchi State, Ningi and Darazo LGAs. *Class:* Afro-Asiatic, Chadic, West, B, B.2. *Other:* A separate language from Tsagu.

Dirim (Dirin, Dirrim, Daka, Dakka) [dir] 9,000 (1992). Taraba State, Bali LGA. *Class:* Niger-Congo, Atlantic-Congo, Volta-Congo, Benue-Congo, Dakoid. *Dialects:* Close to Samba Daka and may be a dialect. *Other:* Many blind people, caused by filaria. Traditional religion, Muslim, Christian.

Doka [dbi] 11,386 (2000 WCD). Kaduna State, Kachia LGA, 1 village. *Class:* Niger-Congo, Atlantic-Congo, Volta-Congo, Benue-Congo, Plateau, Northern. *Other:* Distinct from Duka (dialect of Hun-Saare).

Doko-Uyanga (Uyanga, Dosanga, Basanga, Iko) [uya] 200. Cross River State, Akamkpa LGA, several villages. *Class:* Niger-Congo, Atlantic-Congo, Volta-Congo, Benue-Congo, Cross River, Delta Cross, Upper Cross, Agoi-Doko-Iyoniyong.

Dong (Donga) [doh] 5,000 (1998 Blench). Taraba State, Zing LGA; Adamawa State, Mayo Belwa LGA. *Class:* Niger-Congo, Atlantic-Congo, Volta-Congo, Benue-Congo, Bantoid, Northern, Dakoid. *Other:* Distinct from Dongo (Donga) of Democratic Republic of the Congo, which is in the Amadi group of Ubangi (Adamawa-Ubangi).

Duguri (Dugurawa, Dugarwa, Duguranchi, Dukuri) [dbm] 20,000 (1995 CAPRO). Bauchi State, Alkaleri and Tafawa Balewa LGAs; Plateau State, Kanam LGA. *Class:* Niger-Congo, Atlantic-Congo, Volta-Congo, Benue-Congo, Bantoid, Southern, Jarawan, Nigerian. *Dialects:* Gar Duguri, Badara Duguri, Northeast Duguri, Southwest Duguri. A member of the Jarawa dialect cluster. *Lg Dev:* Literacy rate in second language: 20%. *Other:* 21 elementary schools, a senior and a junior secondary school. Agriculturalists: guinea corn, peanuts, millet, beans, rice; animal husbandry. Traditional religion, Muslim, Christian.

Duguza (Dugusa) [dza] 2,000 (1973 SIL). Bauchi State, Toro LGA; Plateau State, Jos South LGA. *Class:* Niger-Congo, Atlantic-Congo, Volta-Congo, Benue-Congo, Kainji, Eastern, Northern Jos, Jera.

Duhwa (Karfa, Kerifa, Nzuhwi) [kbz] 800 (1973 SIL). Nasarawa State, Akwanga LGA, Kerifa village. *Class:* Afro-Asiatic, Chadic, West, A, A.4, Ron Proper. *Other:* 'Duhwa' is their own name.

Dulbu [dbo] 100 (1993). Bauchi State, Bauchi LGA, Dulbu village southeast of Bauchi town. *Class:* Niger-Congo, Atlantic-Congo, Volta-Congo, Benue-Congo, Bantoid, Southern, Jarawan, Nigerian. *Lg Use:* Speakers are shifting to Hausa.

Dungu (Dungi, Dingi, Dwingi, Dunjawa) [dbv] 1,104 (2000 WCD). Kaduna State, Saminaka LGA, Dungi town. *Class:* Niger-Congo, Atlantic-Congo, Volta-Congo, Benue-Congo, Kainji, Eastern, Northern Jos, Kauru.

Duwai (Evji, Eastern Bade) [dbp] 11,386 (2000 WCD). Yobe State, Bade LGA; Kano State, Hadejia LGA. *Class:* Afro-Asiatic, Chadic, West, B, B.1, Duwai. *Other:* In Bade language cluster.

Dza (Janjo, Jenjo, Jen) [jen] 20,131 (2000 WCD). Taraba State, Karim Lamido LGA, and Adamawa State, Numan LGA, Jen town, east of Karim-Lamido town, south of Bambuka town, by the Benue River bank. *Class:* Niger-Congo, Atlantic-Congo, Volta-Congo, North, Adamawa-Ubangi, Adamawa, Waja-Jen, Jen. *Dialects:* Kaigama, Laredo (Ardido), Jaule (Joole). *Other:* Agriculturalists; hunters. Traditional religion, Christian, Muslim.

Dzodinka (Adere, Adiri) [add] Taraba State, Sardauna LGA, 1 village on the Cameroon border. *Other:* Different from Adele of Ghana and Togo. See main entry under Cameroon.

Ebira (Igbirra, Igbarra, Ibara, Kotokori, Katawa, Kwotto, Igbira, Egbira, Egbura) [igb] 1,000,000 (1989 J. Adive). About 90% are monolingual. Kwara State, Okene, Okehi, and Kogi LGAs; Nasarawa State, Nasarawa LGA; Edo State, Akoko-Edo LGA. *Class:* Niger-Congo, Atlantic-Congo, Volta-Congo, Benue-Congo, Nupoid, Ebira-Gade. *Dialects:* Okene (Hima, Ihima), Igara (Etuno), Koto (Igu, Egu, Ika, Bira, Biri, Panda). A dialect cluster. *Lg Use:* Vigorous. Speakers of other languages use Ebira to communicate with Ebira people. Taught as a subject at the College of Education. All domains. Used in administration, commerce, oral and written use in religious services. Positive language attitude. 10% bilingual in Yoruba, Hausa, English, or Igara. *Lg Dev:* Literacy rate in first language: 5% to 10%. Literacy rate in second language: 25%. High literacy motivation. Taught in primary schools. Radio programs. TV. Grammar. NT: 1981. *Other:* Hills, valleys. Agriculturalists; weavers. Muslim, traditional religion, Christian.

Ebughu (Oron) [ebg] 5,000 (1988). Akwa Ibom State, Mbo and Oron LGAs. *Class:* Niger-Congo, Atlantic-Congo, Volta-Congo, Benue-Congo, Cross River, Delta Cross, Lower Cross, Obolo, Ebughu. *Dialects:* Listed separately in Crozier and Blench 1992.

Edo (Bini, Benin, Addo, Oviedo, Ovioba) [bin] 1,000,000 (1999 WA). Bendel State, Ovia, Oredo, and Orhionmwon LGAs. *Class:* Niger-Congo, Atlantic-Congo, Volta-Congo, Benue-Congo, Edoid, North-Central, Edo-Esan-Ora. *Lg Use:* Official language. Used in adult education, history text. *Lg Dev:* Taught in primary and secondary schools. Roman script. Radio programs. TV. Dictionary. Bible: 1996.

Efai (Effiat) [efa] 6,319 in Nigeria (2000 WCD). Population total all countries: 7,212. Akwa Ibom State, Mbo LGA. Also spoken in Cameroon. *Class:* Niger-Congo, Atlantic-Congo, Volta-Congo, Benue-Congo, Cross River, Delta Cross, Lower Cross, Obolo, Efai. *Dialects:* Listed separately in Crozier and Blench 1992.

Efik (Calabar) [efi] 400,000 (1998). Cross River State, Calabar Municipality, Odukpani and Akamkpa LGAs; Akwa Ibom State, town of Itu. *Class:* Niger-Congo, Atlantic-Congo, Volta-Congo, Benue-Congo, Cross River, Delta Cross, Lower Cross, Obolo, Efik. *Lg Use:* Official language. 2,000,000 second-language speakers. The major dialect and language of the Ibibio-Efik group. Used in adult education, university courses. Decreasing in use as a second language. *Lg Dev:* Taught in primary and secondary schools. Roman script. Radio programs. TV. Dictionary. Grammar. Bible: 1868–1995. *Other:* SVO. Christian.

Efutop (Ofutop, Agbaragba) [ofu] 10,000 (1973 SIL). Cross River State, Ikom LGA. *Class:* Niger-Congo, Atlantic-Congo, Volta-Congo, Benue-Congo, Bantoid, Southern, Ekoid.

Eggon (Egon, Mo Egon, Mada Eggon, Hill Mada, Mada Dutse) [ego] 140,368 (1990). Nasarawa State, Nasarawa Eggon, Akwanga, Lafia, Awe, and Obi LGAs. *Class:* Niger-Congo, Atlantic-Congo, Volta-Congo, Benue-Congo, Plateau, Western, Southwestern, B. *Dialects:* 25 dialects are locally recognized, but their status is unclear. *Lg Use:* Speakers also use Hausa. *Lg Dev:* Dictionary. NT: 1974. *Other:* Traditional religion, Christian, Muslim.

Ehueun (Ekpimi, Ekpenmen, Epimi) [ehu] 14,244 (2000 WCD). Ondo State, Akoko South LGA. *Class:* Niger-Congo, Atlantic-Congo, Volta-Congo, Benue-Congo, Edoid, Northwestern, Osse. *Dialects:* Related to Ukue.

Ejagham (Ekoi) [etu] 67,281 in Nigeria (2000 WCD). Population total all countries: 116,675. Cross River State, Akampka, Idom, Odukpani, Calabar LGAs. Also spoken in Cameroon. *Class:* Niger-Congo, Atlantic-Congo, Volta-Congo, Benue-Congo, Bantoid, Southern, Ekoid. *Dialects:* Southern Ejagham (Ekin, Qua, Kwa, Aqua, Abakpa), Western Ejagham, Eastern Ejagham. *Lg Dev:* Radio programs. TV. Grammar. NT: 1997. *Other:* Western Ejagham includes Bendeghe Etung (Bindege, Dindiga, Mbuma), Northern Etung, Southern Etung, Ekwe, Akamkpa-Ejagham. Eastern Ejagham includes Keaka (Keaqa, Kejaka, Edjagam), Obang (Eeafeng).

Ekajuk (Akajo, Akajuk) [eka] 30,000 (1986 Asinya). Cross River State, Ogoja LGA, Bansara, Nwang, Ntara 1, 2, and 3, and Ebanibim towns. *Class:* Niger-Congo, Atlantic-Congo, Volta-Congo, Benue-Congo, Bantoid, Southern, Ekoid. *Lg Dev:* NT: 1971.

Eki [eki] 5,000 (1988, in Crozier and Blench 1992:36). Cross River State, northeast of Efik, south of Idere. *Class:* Niger-Congo, Atlantic-Congo, Volta-Congo, Benue-Congo, Cross River, Delta Cross, Lower Cross, Obolo. *Dialects:* Listed separately in Crozier and Blench 1992. Probably Central Lower Cross, related to Anaang. Close to Idere (B. Connell 1998).

Ekit (Eket) [eke] 200,000 (1989). Akwa Ibom State, Uquo Ibeno and Eket LGAs. *Class:* Niger-Congo, Atlantic-Congo, Volta-Congo, Benue-Congo, Cross River, Delta Cross, Lower Cross, Obolo, Ekit. *Dialects:* Listed separately in Crozier and Blench 1992. Some dialect variation.

Ekpeye (Ekpabya, Ekkpahia, Ekpaffia) [ekp] 30,000 (1973 SIL). Rivers State, Ahoada East and Ahoada West LGAs. *Class:* Niger-Congo, Atlantic-Congo, Volta-Congo, Benue-Congo, Igboid, Ekpeye. *Dialects:* Ako, Upata, Ubye, Igbuduya. Related to Igbo. *Lg Dev:* Grammar.

Eleme [elm] 58,000 (1990 UBS). Rivers State, Eleme LGA. *Class:* Niger-Congo, Atlantic-Congo, Volta-Congo, Benue-Congo, Cross River, Delta Cross, Ogoni, West. *Lg Dev:* Grammar. Bible portions: 1988.

Eloyi (Afo, Afu, Aho, Afao, Epe, Keffi) [afo] 25,000 (2000 SIL). Plateau State, Awe and Nasarawa LGAs; Benue State, Otukpo LGA. *Class:* Niger-Congo, Atlantic-Congo, Volta-Congo, Benue-Congo, Idomoid, Akweya, Eloyi. *Dialects:* Mbeci, Mbeji, Mbamu. *Lg Use:* Speakers also use Hausa. *Lg Dev:* Literacy rate in second language: 5%. *Other:* Traditional religion, Muslim, Christian.

Emai-Iuleha-Ora (Kunibum, Ivbiosakon) [ema] 100,000 (1987 Schaefer). Edo State, Owan LGA. *Class:* Niger-Congo, Atlantic-Congo, Volta-Congo, Benue-Congo, Edoid, North-Central, Edo-Esan-Ora. *Dialects:* Ivhimion, Emai, Iuleha, Ora. Dialect cluster. *Lg Use:* Ora is used in initial primary education. Dictionary. Bible portions: 1908–1910. *Other:* Traditional religion.

Engenni (Ngene, Egene) [enn] 20,000 (1980 UBS). Rivers State, Ahoada West LGA; Bayelsa State, Yenagoa LGA. *Class:* Niger-Congo, Atlantic-Congo, Volta-Congo, Benue-Congo, Edoid, Delta. *Dialects:* Ediro, Inedua, Ogua, Zarama. *Lg Dev:* Grammar. NT: 1977.

English [eng] *Lg Use:* Official language. Second-language speakers in Nigeria: 1,000,000 (1977 Voegelin and Voegelin). Used in government and education. See main entry under United Kingdom.

Enwan (Oron) [enw] 15,000 (1998 B. Connell). Akwa Ibom State, Mbo LGA. *Class:* Niger-Congo, Atlantic-Congo, Volta-Congo, Benue-Congo, Cross River, Delta Cross, Lower Cross, Obolo, Enwang-Uda. *Dialects:*

Listed separately in Crozier and Blench 1992. *Other:* Incorrectly referred to as 'Oron'.

Enwan [env] Edo State, Akoko-Edo LGA. *Class:* Niger-Congo, Atlantic-Congo, Volta-Congo, Benue-Congo, Edoid, North-Central, Ghotuo-Uneme-Yekhee.

Epie (Epie-Atissa) [epi] 12,000 (1973 SIL). Bayelsa State, Yenagoa LGA. *Class:* Niger-Congo, Atlantic-Congo, Volta-Congo, Benue-Congo, Edoid, Delta. *Dialect:* Atisa (Atissa). *Lg Use:* Most speakers of Atisa also use Izon. *Lg Dev:* Dictionary.

Eruwa (Erohwa, Erakwa, Arokwa) [erh] 64,000 (2004). Delta State, Isoko LGA. *Class:* Niger-Congo, Atlantic-Congo, Volta-Congo, Benue-Congo, Edoid, Southwestern. *Dialects:* Related to Urhobo. Not intelligible with any Isoko dialect. *Lg Use:* Most speakers also use Central Isoko, which is replacing Eruwa.

Esan (Ishan, Isa, Esa, Anwain) [ish] 200,000 (1973 SIL). Population includes 7,000 Ekpon in 7 villages (1998). Edo State, Agbazko, Okpebho, Owan, and Etsako LGAs. *Class:* Niger-Congo, Atlantic-Congo, Volta-Congo, Benue-Congo, Edoid, North-Central, Edo-Esan-Ora. *Dialects:* Ekpon, Igueben. *Lg Use:* Used in initial primary education. 90% speak or understand Nigerian Pidgin English. English and possibly Ika are also used as second languages. *Lg Dev:* Taught in primary schools. Radio programs. TV. Bible portions: 1974. *Other:* Plains. Tropical forest. Peasant agriculturalists: yams, bananas, oranges, plantains, cassava; hunters. Christian, traditional religion, Muslim.

Etebi [etb] 15,000 (1989). Akwa Ibom State, Uquo Ibeno LGA. *Class:* Niger-Congo, Atlantic-Congo, Volta-Congo, Benue-Congo, Cross River, Delta Cross, Lower Cross, Obolo, Ekit. *Dialects:* Listed separately in Crozier and Blench 1992. *Other:* 'Oron' and 'Ekit' are incorrect names.

Eten (Ganawuri, Etien, Jal, Ten, Niten, Aten, Iten) [etx] 40,000 (2003 Blench). Plateau State, Barakin Ladi LGA; Kaduna State, Jema'a LGA. *Class:* Niger-Congo, Atlantic-Congo, Volta-Congo, Benue-Congo, Plateau, Beromic. *Lg Dev:* Dictionary. Bible portions: 1940.

Etkywan (Icen, Ichen, Itchen, Etekwe, Kyato, Kyanton, Kentu, Nyidu) [ich] 50,167 (2000 WCD). Taraba State, Takum, Sardauna, Bali, and part of Wukari LGAs. *Class:* Niger-Congo, Atlantic-Congo, Volta-Congo, Benue-Congo, Jukunoid, Central, Kpan-Icen. *Lg Use:* Some speak Hausa as second language. *Other:* Christian, traditional religion, Muslim.

Etulo (Eturo, Utur, Turumawa) [utr] 10,000 (1988 Shain). Benue State, Gboko LGA; Taraba State, Wukari LGA. *Class:* Niger-Congo, Atlantic-Congo, Volta-Congo, Benue-Congo, Idomoid, Akweya, Etulo-Idoma, Etulo. *Other:* Traditional religion, Christian.

Evant (Evand, Avand, Avande, Ovand, Ovande, Ovando, Balegete, Belegete) [bzz] 10,000 in Nigeria (1996 SIL). Population total all countries: 11,000. Cross River State, Obudu LGA. Also spoken in Cameroon. *Class:* Niger-Congo, Atlantic-Congo, Volta-Congo, Benue-Congo, Bantoid, Southern, Tivoid. *Dialects:* Lexical similarity 50% with Iceve-Maci, Tiv, and Otank. *Other:* Mountain slope. Traditional religion.

Fali (Fali of Mubi, Fali of Muchella, Vimtim, Yimtim) [fli] 20,000 (1990 in Crozier and Blench 1992:39). Population includes 5,000 or fewer in Vin dialect. Adamawa State, Mubi and Michika LGAs, 4 principal villages. *Class:* Afro-Asiatic, Chadic, Biu-Mandara, A, A.8. *Dialects:* Vin (Uroovin, Uvin, Vimtim), Huli (Bahuli, Urahuli), Madzarin (Ura Madzarin, Muchella), Bween (Urambween, Bagira). Dialects are named after villages. *Lg Use:* Speakers also use Fulfulde or Hausa. *Lg Dev:* Little formal education. *Other:* Hills, plains. Agriculturalists: guinea corn, maize, peanuts, bambara nuts, tiger nuts, rice; animal husbandry: cows, sheep, goats, chickens. Traditional religion.

Fali of Baissa [fah] Few speakers left (1992 Crozier and Blench). Southern Taraba State, Falinga Plateau Region. *Class:* Niger-Congo, Atlantic-Congo, Volta-Congo, Benue-Congo, Unclassified. *Other:* Nearly extinct.

Fam [fam] 1,000 (1984). Taraba State, Bali LGA, 17 km east of Kungana. *Class:* Niger-Congo, Atlantic-Congo, Volta-Congo, Benue-Congo, Bantoid, Northern, Fam. *Dialects:* Not closely related to other languages.

Firan (Faran, Foron, Yes Firan, Kwakwi) [fir] 2,500 (2003 Blench). Plateau State, Barkin Ladi LGA, Kwakwi Station south of Jos. *Class:* Niger-Congo, Atlantic-Congo, Volta-Congo, Benue-Congo, Plateau, Central, Izeric. *Dialects:* Related to Izere.

Fulfulde, Adamawa (Eastern Fulfulde, Fulatanchi, Fulani, Fula, Fillanci) [fub] 7,611,000 includes all Fulfulde in Nigeria (1991 SIL). East central Nigeria, Taraba and Adamawa States, center in Yola. *Lg Use:* Official language. *Other:* The language is 'Fulatanchi', 'Fillanci', or 'Fula'; a speaker is 'Pullo'; the people are 'Fulbe' or 'Fulani'. Muslim, traditional religion. See main entry under Cameroon.

Fulfulde, Benin-Togo [fue] South and west of the Niger River, from the corner where Nigeria, Niger, and Benin meet, down to about 50 km south of where a big tributary joins the Niger River from the east, and following the Niger River south to the delta. The southern boundary is a rough east-west line from a point below the intersection of the rivers to about 75 km south of the angle in the Benin-Nigeria border, where the border bends from almost straight north-south to about 30 km nearly due east. See main entry under Benin (Fulfulde, Borgu).

Fulfulde, Nigerian (Kano-Katsina-Bororo Fulfulde) [fuv] 1,707,926 in Nigeria (2000 WCD). Population includes 340,000 in Sokoto. Kano-Katsina dialect is spoken in the area of Kano, Katsina, Zaria, Jos Plateau and southeast to Bauchi; Gombe is the center. The Bororro dialect is in Bornu State; Maiduguri is the center. Sokoto is in Sokoto State. Also spoken in Cameroon, Chad. *Class:* Niger-Congo, Atlantic-Congo, Atlantic, Northern, Senegambian, Fulani-Wolof, Fula, East Central. *Dialects:* Kano-Katsina, Bororo (Mbororo, Ako, Nomadic Fulfulde), Sokoto. *Other:* Sokoto is a major Fulbe geopolitical unit. Muslim.

Fum [fum] Taraba State, Sardauna LGA, Antere, on the Cameroon border. *Class:* Niger-Congo, Atlantic-Congo, Volta-Congo, Benue-Congo, Bantoid, Southern, Wide Grassfields, Narrow Grassfields. *Other:* May be the same as Mfumte in Cameroon.

Fungwa (Tufungwa, Afungwa, Ura, Ula) [ula] 1,000 (1992 Blench). Niger State, Rafi LGA. *Class:* Niger-Congo, Atlantic-Congo, Volta-Congo, Benue-Congo, Kainji, Western, Kamuku.

Fyam (Fyem, Pyem, Paiem, Gyem, Fem, Pem, Genawa, Gyema) [pym] 3,000. Plateau State, Jos, Barkin Ladi, and Mangu LGAs. *Class:* Niger-Congo, Atlantic-Congo, Volta-Congo, Benue-Congo, Plateau, Southeastern. *Dialects:* Closest to Horom. Chadic influence. *Lg Use:* In some villages, young people use Fyam only in special contexts. Shift to Hausa in progress. Fyam is used at home and in the village in some cases. Hausa is used generally, English in education and government. English is restricted to young people, especially men. *Lg Dev:* 50% of the young read haltingly in Hausa. Radio programs. Grammar. *Other:* Muslim, Christian.

Fyer (Fier) [fie] 26,131 (2000 WCD). Plateau State, Mangu LGA, Fyer District. *Class:* Afro-Asiatic, Chadic, West, A, A.4, Fyer. *Lg Use:* Vigorous. *Lg Dev:* Grammar.

Gaa (Tiba) [ttb] 10,000 (1997 Boyd). Adamawa State, Ganye LGA; Tiba Plateau, between Garba Sbege and Jada, north of the Shebshi Mountains. *Class:* Niger-Congo, Atlantic-Congo, Volta-Congo, Benue-Congo, Bantoid, Northern, Dakoid.

Ga'anda (Ga'andu, Ganda, Mokar, Makwar) [gqa] 43,000 (1992). Adamawa State, Gombi LGA. Some also in Song, Guyuk, and Mubi LGAs, and Borno State, Biu LGA. *Class:* Afro-Asiatic, Chadic, Biu-Mandara, A, A.1, Eastern. *Dialects:* Ga'anda, Gabin. *Lg Use:* Speakers also use Hausa or Fulfulde. *Lg Dev:* Grammar. *Other:* 14 villages have primary schools, and Ga'anda has a secondary school. Speakers are becoming more interested in education. Traditional religion, Christian, Muslim.

Gade (Gede) [ged] 72,100 (2000). Federal Capital Territory and Nasarawa State, Nasarawa LGA. *Class:* Niger-Congo, Atlantic-Congo, Volta-Congo, Benue-Congo, Nupoid, Ebira-Gade. *Lg Dev:* Dictionary. Grammar. *Other:* Considered to be conservative by neighbors. Traditional religion, Muslim.

Galambu (Galambi, Galambe, Galembi) [glo] Ethnic population: 21,622 (2000 WCD). Bauchi State, Bauchi LGA. *Class:* Afro-Asiatic, Chadic, West, A, A.2, Bole, Bole Proper. *Lg Use:* Most members of the ethnic group do not speak Galambu. *Other:* Agriculturalists: guinea corn, maize, beans. Muslim.

Gamo-Ningi [bte] Extinct. Ethnic population: 15,000 (1992 Crozier and Blench). Bauchi State, Ningi LGA. *Class:* Niger-Congo, Atlantic-Congo, Volta-Congo, Benue-Congo, Kainji, Eastern, Northern Jos, Jera. *Dialects:* Gamo (Buta, Mbuta, Mbotu, Ba-Buche, Ba-Mbutu), Ningi. Formerly a dialect cluster. *Lg Use:* Members of the ethnic group now speak Hausa.

Gbagyi (Ibagyi, Gbagye, Gwari, East Gwari, Gwari Matai) [gbr] 700,000 (1991 SIL). Niger State, Rafi, Chanchaga, Shiroro, Suleija LGAs; Kaduna State, Kachia LGA; Nasarawa State, Keffi, Nasarawa LGAs; Federal Capital Territory. *Class:* Niger-Congo, Atlantic-Congo, Volta-Congo, Benue-Congo, Nupoid, Nupe-Gbagyi, Gbagyi-Gbari. *Dialect:* Tawari, Kuta, Diko, Karu, Kaduna, Louome, Vwezhi, Ngenge (Genge, Gyange, Gyengyen). *Lg Dev:* NT: 1956. *Other:* Agriculturalists; pastoralists. Traditional religion, Christian, Muslim.

Gbari (Gbari Yamma, Gwari Yamma, West Gwari, Nkwa) [gby] 350,000 (2002 SIL). From Zungeru in Niger State to the Kaduna River in the north, southeast through Minna and Paiko to a little past Kwali in the Federal Capital Territory. Niger State, Chanchaga, Suleija, Agaie, Rafi, and Lapai LGAs; Nasarawa State, Nasarawa LGA. *Class:* Niger-Congo, Atlantic-Congo, Volta-Congo, Benue-Congo, Nupoid, Nupe-Gbagyi, Gbagyi-Gbari. *Dialects:* Kwali, Izem, Gayegi, Gbagyi Nkwa, Paiko, Botai, Jezhu, Kong, Kwange (Kangye, Agbawi, Wake, Wi), Wahe. Lexical similarity 89% to 98% among dialects, 66% to 78% with Gbagyi dialects. *Lg Use:* Speakers do not want to be considered Gbagyi. *Lg Dev:* Literacy rate in first language: below 1%. Literacy rate in second language: 5% to 15%. Dictionary. Grammar. Bible portions: 1925–1926. *Other:* Mountain slope. Agriculturalists. Traditional religion, Muslim.

Gbaya, Northwest (Baya) [gya] Very few speakers in Nigeria. Taraba State, Bali LGA. *Dialect:* Gbeya (Gbea). See main entry under Central African Republic.

Gbiri-Niragu (Gure-Kahugu) [grh] 25,000 (2000). Kaduna State, Saminaka LGA. *Class:* Niger-Congo, Atlantic-Congo, Volta-Congo, Benue-Congo, Kainji, Eastern, Northern Jos, Kauru. *Dialects:* Gbiri (Igbiri, Agari, Agbiri, Gura, Gure), Niragu (Kahugu, Kapugu, Kafugu, Kagu, Anirago). *Lg Use:* Speakers are shifting to Hausa.

Geji (Gezawa, Gejawa, Kayauri) [gji] 6,000 (1995 CAPRO). Bauchi State, Toro LGA. *Class:* Afro-Asiatic, Chadic, West, B, B.3, Zaar Proper. *Dialects:* Bolu (Magang, Pelu), Geji (Gyaazi, Gezawa, Gaejawa), Zaranda (Buu). Geji dialect cluster, in Barawa language cluster.

Other: Agriculturalists: guinea corn, maize, millet, rice, peanuts, cassava. Traditional religion.

Gengle (Wegele, Momu, Yagele) [geg] 4,000. Adamawa State, Mayo Belwa and Fufore LGAs. *Class:* Niger-Congo, Atlantic-Congo, Volta-Congo, North, Adamawa-Ubangi, Adamawa, Leko-Nimbari, Mumuye-Yandang, Mumuye. *Lg Use:* Speakers also use Hausa. *Other:* Not the same as Gongla. Traditional religion, Christian, Muslim.

Gera (Gerawa) [gew] 200,000 (1995 CAPRO). Bauchi State, Bauchi and Ganjuwa LGAs, Bauchi town. *Class:* Afro-Asiatic, Chadic, West, A, A.2, Bole, Bole Proper. *Lg Use:* Speakers are shifting to Hausa. *Other:* Traditional religion, Muslim.

Geruma (Gerema, Germa) [gea] 9,029 (2000 WCD). Bauchi State, Toro, Ganjuwa, Bauchi, and Southjern Ningi LGAs. *Class:* Afro-Asiatic, Chadic, West, A, A.2, Bole, Bole Proper. *Dialects:* Sum, Duurum. Gamsawa (Gamshi) mentioned by Temple (1922) could be another dialect. *Lg Use:* Speakers are shifting to Hausa. *Other:* Agriculturalists: guinea corn, millet, maize, peanuts, beans, rice. Muslim, traditional religion.

Ghotuo (Otwa, Otuo) [aaa] 9,000 (1994). Edo State, Owan, and Akoko-Edo LGAs. *Class:* Niger-Congo, Atlantic-Congo, Volta-Congo, Benue-Congo, Edoid, North-Central, Ghotuo-Uneme-Yekhee.

Gibanawa (Gembanawa, Gimbanawa, Jega) [gib] Sokoto State, Jega LGA, near the Dukawa. *Class:* Pidgin, Hausa based. *Dialects:* Hausa-speaking Fulani. *Lg Use:* The largest group in Jega LGA. They use Gibanawa as a contact language. *Other:* Second language only.

Giiwo (Bu Giiwo, Kirfi, Kirifi, Kirifawa) [kks] 14,000 (1998 SIL). Bauchi State, Alkaleri, Bauchi, and Darazo LGAs. *Class:* Afro-Asiatic, Chadic, West, A, A.2, Bole, Bole Proper. *Lg Use:* Speakers also use Hausa. *Other:* Agriculturalists: guinea corn, beans, peanuts, maize. Muslim.

Glavda (Galavda, Gelebda, Glanda, Guelebda, Galvaxdaxa) [glw] 28,465 in Nigeria (2000 WCD). Population total all countries: 31,265. Borno State, Gwoza LGA, mainly in Nggoshe village (different from Ngoshi), and in Agapalawa, Amuda, Vale, Ashigashiya, Kerawa, Pelekwa villages. Also spoken in Cameroon. *Class:* Afro-Asiatic, Chadic, Biu-Mandara, A, A.4, Mandara Proper, Glavda. *Dialects:* Bokwa, Ngoshie (Ngweshe), Glavda. Close to Guduf. Wolff (1971) separates Glavda from Guduf and Gvoko. *Lg Dev:* Literacy rate in second language: 5%. Dictionary. Bible portions: 1967. *Other:* Traditional religion, Christian, Muslim.

Goemai (Ankwai, Ankwei, Ankwe, Kemai) [ank] 200,000 (1995). Plateau State, Shendam; Nasarawa State, Lafia and Awe LGAs. *Class:* Afro-Asiatic, Chadic, West, A, A.3, Angas Proper, 2. *Lg Use:* Hausa is used as lingua franca. *Lg Dev:* Radio programs. Dictionary. Grammar. *Other:* Traditional religion, Muslim.

Gokana [gkn] 100,000 (1989). Rivers State, Gokana LGA. *Class:* Niger-Congo, Atlantic-Congo, Volta-Congo, Benue-Congo, Cross River, Delta Cross, Ogoni, East. *Dialects:* Bodo, Bomu, Dere, Kibangha. *Lg Dev:* NT: 1996.

Gude (Goude, Cheke, Tchade, Shede, Mapodi, Mapuda, Mudaye, Mocigin, Motchekin) [gde] 68,000 in Nigeria (1987). Population total all countries: 96,000. Adamawa State, Mubi LGA; Borno State, Askira-Uba LGA. Also spoken in Cameroon. *Class:* Afro-Asiatic, Chadic, Biu-Mandara, A, A.8. *Dialects:* Different dialects are spoken in Cameroon and Nigeria but they are inherently intelligible. *Lg Use:* Speakers also use Hausa, Nzanyi, Fulfulde, or English. *Lg Dev:* Literacy program in progress. Grammar. NT: 1999. *Other:* Muslim, traditional religion, Christian.

Gudu (Gudo, Gutu) [gdu] 5,000 (1993). Adamawa State, Song LGA. *Class:* Afro-Asiatic, Chadic, Biu-Mandara, A, A.8. *Dialect:* Kumbi. *Other:* Formerly the culture and religion were similar to the Ngwaba. Muslim.

Guduf-Gava (Gudupe, Afkabiye) [gdf] 55,918 (2000 WCD). Borno State, Gwoza LGA, mainly in Gava, Cikide, and Guduf. *Class:* Afro-Asiatic, Chadic, Biu-Mandara, A, A.4, Mandara Proper, Glavda. *Dialects:* Cikide (Chikide), Guduf, Gava (Yaghwatadaxa, Yawotataxa). Close to Glavda. Hedi speakers have 35% intelligibility of Guduf. Wolff (1971) separates Guduf from Gvoko and Glavda. Lexical similarity 56% with Hedi, 50% with Lamang and Mabas. *Lg Dev:* Bible portions: 1966. *Other:* Mountain slope.

Gun (Gugbe, Gun-Alada, Gun-Gbe, Seto-Gbe) [guw] 258,804 in Nigeria (2000 WCD). Lagos State, Badagry LGA. *Dialects:* Alada (Alada-Gbe), Asento, Gbekon, Gun (Gu, Egun, Goun), Phela, Savi, Weme, Seto. See main entry under Benin.

Gupa-Abawa [gpa] 15,000 (1989). Population includes 10,000 or more Gupa, 5,000 Abawa. Niger State, Lapai LGA, around Gupa and Edzu villages. *Class:* Niger-Congo, Atlantic-Congo, Volta-Congo, Benue-Congo, Nupoid, Nupe-Gbagyi, Nupe. *Dialects:* Gupa, Abawa.

Gurmana [gvm] 3,000 (1989). Niger State, Shiroro LGA, Gurmana town and nearby hamlets. *Class:* Niger-Congo, Atlantic-Congo, Volta-Congo, Benue-Congo, Kainji, Western, Baushi-Gurmana.

Guruntum-Mbaaru (Guruntum, Gurdung) [grd] 15,000 (1993). Bauchi State, Bauchi and Alkaleri LGAs. *Class:* Afro-Asiatic, Chadic, West, B, B.3, Guruntum. *Dialects:* Dooka, Gar, Gayar, Karakara, Kuuku, Mbaaru. *Lg Use:* Speakers are shifting to Hausa. *Other:* Agriculturalists: beans, maize, millet. Muslim.

Gvoko (Gevoko, Ghboko, Gavoko, Kuvoko, Ngossi, Ngoshi, Ngoshe-Ndhang, Ngweshe-Ndaghan, Ngoshe Sama, Nggweshe) [ngs] 20,000 in Nigeria (1990). Population total all countries: 21,000. Borno State, Gwoza LGA; Adamawa State, Michika LGA. Also spoken in Cameroon. *Class:* Afro-Asiatic, Chadic, Biu-Mandara, A, A.4, Mandara Proper, Glavda. *Dialects:* A separate but related language to Glavda and Guduf.

Gwa [gwb] 979 (2000 WCD). Bauchi State, Toro LGA. *Class:* Niger-Congo, Atlantic-Congo, Volta-Congo, Benue-Congo, Bantoid, Southern, Jarawan, Nigerian. *Dialects:* Related to Lame. *Lg Use:* Speakers also use Hausa.

Gwamhi-Wuri (Lyase, Lyase-Ne) [bga] 16,000 (2000). Kebbi State, Wasugu LGA, Danko-Maga area, and Niger State, Magama LGA, Dusai and Kwimu. The Gwamfawa are around Danko and the Wurawa around Maga. Migrants are in Niger State. *Class:* Niger-Congo, Atlantic-Congo, Volta-Congo, Benue-Congo, Kainji, Western, Duka. *Dialects:* Gwamhi (Gwamfanci, Gwamfi Gwamfawa, Abaangi, Banga, Banganci, Bangawa), Wuri (Wuranci, Wurawa). The two dialects have slight lexical and tonal differences. Lexical similarity 57% with Puku-Geeri-Keri-Wipsi, 47% with Duka, 43% with Lela. *Lg Use:* Many Gwamfawa are assimilating to Lela culture and language, while the Wurawa are assimilating to Hausa. Speakers also use Lela or Hausa. *Other:* 'Bangawa' is the Hausa name for the people, 'Banganci' for the language; 'Lyase' means 'mother tongue'.

Gwandara (Kwandara) [gwn] 27,349 (2000). Niger State, Suleija LGA; Federal Capital Territory; Kaduna State, Kachia LGA; Nasarawa State, Keffi, Lafia, Nasarawa, and Akwanga LGAs. *Class:* Afro-Asiatic, Chadic, West, A, A.1. *Dialects:* Gwandara Karashi, Gwandara Koro, Gwandara Southern (Kyan Kyar), Gwandara Eastern (Toni), Gwandara Gitata, Nimbia. *Lg Use:* Speakers also use Hausa. *Lg Dev:* Dictionary. *Other:* Traditional religion, Muslim.

Gyem (Gyemawa, Gema, Gemawa, Gyam) [gye] 1,000 (1995 CAPRO). Bauchi State, Toro LGA. *Class:* Niger-Congo, Atlantic-Congo, Volta-Congo, Benue-Congo, Kainji, Eastern, Northern Jos, Jera. *Lg Use:* Speakers are shifting to Hausa. *Other:* Different from Fyam (Gyem). Agriculturalists. Traditional religion.

Hasha (Yashi) [ybj] 3,000 (1999 Blench). Nasarawa State, Akwanga LGA, 3 villages: Hashasu, Kusu, and Bwora. *Class:* Niger-Congo, Atlantic-Congo, Volta-Congo, Benue-Congo, Plateau, Western, Southwestern, B. *Lg Use:* Hausa widely known. English spoken by some secondary school students.

Hausa (Hausawa, Haoussa, Abakwariga, Mgbakpa, Habe, Kado) [hau] 18,525,000 in Nigeria (1991 SIL). Population total all countries: 24,162,000. Spoken as a first language in large areas of Sokoto, Kaduna, Katsina, Kano, Bauchi, Jigawa, Zamfara, Kebbi, and Gombe states. Spoken as a second language in the northern half of Nigeria. Also spoken in Benin, Burkina Faso, Cameroon, Central African Republic, Chad, Congo, Eritrea, Germany, Ghana, Niger, Sudan, Togo. *Class:* Afro-Asiatic, Chadic, West, A, A.1. *Dialects:* Kano, Katagum, Hadejiya, Sokoto, Gobirawa, Adarawa, Kebbawa, Zamfarawa, Katsina, Arewa. Barikanchi is a Hausa pidgin used in military barracks. There is a pidgin or market Hausa. Subdialects of Eastern Hausa: Kano, Katagum, Hadejiya; of Western Hausa: Sokoto, Katsina, Gobirawa, Adarawa, Kebbawa, Zamfarawa; of North Hausa: Arewa, Arawa. Abakwariga is a subgroup. *Lg Use:* Official language in northern region. Trade language. 15,0000,000 second-language speakers. *Lg Dev:* Roman and Ajami scripts; Roman and Arabic scripts in Cameroon. Radio programs. TV. Dictionary. Grammar. Bible: 1932–1996. *Other:* Official regional language in the north. SVO. Muslim, traditional religion (Maguzawa), Christian.

Hausa Sign Language [hsl] *Class:* Deaf sign language.

Hide (Hdi, Hedi, Turu-Hide, Tur, Turu, Tourou, Ftour, Xedi) [xed] 4,000 in Nigeria (2001 SIL). Borno State, Gwoza LGA; Adamawa State, Michika LGA; along the Cameroon border, across from Tourou; part of one village. *Other:* In Nigeria the name 'Hide' is preferred, in Cameroon 'Hdi'. Little education. 1 primary school. Mountain slope. Agriculturalists: guinea corn, beans, millet. Traditional religion, Christian, Muslim. See main entry under Cameroon (Hdi).

Holma (Da Holmaci, Bali Holma) [hod] Extinct. Adamawa State, north of Sorau on the Cameroon border. *Class:* Afro-Asiatic, Chadic, Biu-Mandara, A, A.8. *Dialects:* Related to Nzanyi. *Lg Use:* Members of the ethnic group now speak Fulfulde.

Hõne [juh] 7,000 (1999 Anne Storch). Population includes 6,250 in Gwana area, 750 in Pindiga area. Ethnic population: Much more than 7,000 (1999 Anne Storch). Gombe State, Akko LGA. One dialect is in Pindiga and adjacent villages (Tumu, Kashere, Futuk, Kaltanga), the other in Gwana and adjacent villages (Kasan Dare, Gobirawa, Katagum, Kwaya, Dizi, Digare, Jukon, Konan Kuka, Andamin). *Class:* Niger-Congo, Atlantic-Congo, Volta-Congo, Benue-Congo, Jukunoid, Central, Jukun-Mbembe-Wurbo, Jukun. *Dialects:* Pindiga, Gwana. Gwana and Pindiga dialects are intelligible to each other's speakers with difficulty. Close to Wãpha, Jiba, Wapan, Jukun Takum, Jibu, but not intelligible with them. *Lg Use:* A few hundred Jiba (Kona, Jukun of Kona) speak it occasionally as second language. Used in the home. Few children. Almost entirely above 30 in Pindiga area, but also below 30 in Gwana area. Gwana is historically more important, but Pindiga currently holds more political

power. They appear to have shame toward Hõne. Negative attitudes toward Tangale and Fulbe for historical reasons. They speak Hausa, English, or Fulfulde for official purposes, at school, at Emir's palace; Tangale, Bole, Pero, or Jiba for trade. *Lg Dev:* Literacy rate in second language: 15% in Hausa or English. Motivation to read is high. *Other:* Muslim, traditional religion (Maam).

Horom ("Kaleri") [hoe] 1,500 (1998 Blench). Plateau State, Bokkos LGA. *Class:* Niger-Congo, Atlantic-Congo, Volta-Congo, Benue-Congo, Plateau, Southeastern. *Other:* Horom is the name of a village in the Kulere-speaking area, therefore they have been erroneously referred to as "Kaleri," which is a derogatory name.

Huba (Kilba, Chobba) [hbb] 175,000 (1992). Adamawa State, Hong, Maiha, Gombi, and Mubi LGAs. *Class:* Afro-Asiatic, Chadic, Biu-Mandara, A, A.2, 2. *Dialect:* Luwa. *Lg Use:* Speakers also use Hausa or Fulfulde. *Lg Dev:* Nearly all villages have primary schools; some have secondary schools. Literacy program in progress. Bible portions: 1976. *Other:* Mountain slope. Agriculturalists; animal husbandry: cattle; weavers, cloth dyers.

Hun-Saare (Duka, Dukawa, Dukwa, Dukanci, Dukanchi) [dud] 73,000 (1985 Patience Ahmed). Population includes 10,000 outside the traditional area. Kebbi State, Wasagu and Yauri LGAs; Niger State, Rijau LGA, and migrants farther south. Dialect centers are Rijau-Senjir, Dukku-Iri, Zente-Dogo, and Darengi. *Class:* Niger-Congo, Atlantic-Congo, Volta-Congo, Benue-Congo, Kainji, Western, Duka. *Dialects:* Eastern Duka (Hun, Et-Hun, Hune), Western Duka (Es-Saare). Lexical similarity 85% between Rijau and Dukku dialects; 63% Duka with Puku-Geeri-Keri-Wipsi, 50% with Lela, 47% with Gwamhi-Wuri. *Lg Dev:* Literacy rate in first language: below 1%. Literacy rate in second language: 2%. Bible portions: 1974–1979. *Other:* Dukawa from the west refer to the speech of the east as 'Es-Saare', just as they refer to their own. Plains, hills. Savannah. 200 to 500 meters. Peasant agriculturalists; hunters. Traditional religion, Muslim, Christian.

Hungworo (Ngwoi, Nkwoi, Ngwe, Ingwo, Ingwe, Ungwe) [nat] 20,000 (2003 SIL). Niger State, Rafi LGA, around Kagara and Maikujeri towns. *Class:* Niger-Congo, Atlantic-Congo, Volta-Congo, Benue-Congo, Kainji, Western, Kamuku. *Dialects:* Lexical similarity 50% to 52% with Kamuku dialects.

Hwana (Hwona, Hona, Tuftera, Fiterya) [hwo] 32,000 (1992). Adamawa State, Gombi LGA, and some in Song and Hong LGAs. *Class:* Afro-Asiatic, Chadic, Biu-Mandara, A, A.1, Eastern. *Lg Use:* Speakers also use Fulfulde, Hausa, Kilba, or Gaanda. *Other:* 'Tuftera' is their name for their language, 'Fiterya' for themselves. Four divisions: Hwana Guyaku, Hwana Tawa, Ngithambara, and Hwana Barni. Agriculturalists; animal husbandry: cattle, goats; hunters. Traditional religion, Christian, Muslim.

Hya (Ghye, Za) [hya] Tukwri, Shike, Ligwe and Gameta villages. See main entry under Cameroon.

Hyam (Ham, Hyamhum, Jabba, Jeba) [jab] 100,000 (1994 UBS). Kaduna State, Kachia and Jema'a LGAs. *Class:* Niger-Congo, Atlantic-Congo, Volta-Congo, Benue-Congo, Plateau, Hyamic. *Dialects:* A dialect cluster. *Lg Dev:* Bible portions: 1921–1923. *Other:* Traditional religion.

Ibani (Bonny, Ubani) [iby] 60,000 (1989 UBS). Rivers State, Bonny. *Class:* Niger-Congo, Atlantic-Congo, Ijoid, Ijo, Eastern, Northeastern, Ibani-Okrika-Kalabari. *Dialects:* A member of Koin cluster within the Ijo cluster. *Lg Dev:* Bible portions: 1892–1986.

Ibibio [ibb] 1,500,000 to 2,000,000 (1998 B. Connell). Akwa Ibom State, Itu, Uyo, Etinan, Ikot Abasi, Ikono,

Ekpe-Atai, Uruan, Onna, Nsit-Ubium, and Mkpat Enin LGAs. *Class:* Niger-Congo, Atlantic-Congo, Volta-Congo, Benue-Congo, Cross River, Delta Cross, Lower Cross, Obolo, Efik. *Dialects:* Enyong, Central Ibibio, Itak, Nsit. Several dialects. *Lg Use:* Trade language. Ibibio is the main trade language of Akwa Ibom State. Used in university courses. Efik is decreasing in use as literary language. *Lg Dev:* Taught in primary and secondary schools. Roman script. Radio programs. TV. Dictionary. Grammar. *Other:* SVO. Christian.

Ibilo [ibi] 5,000. Edo State, single town of Ibilo. *Class:* Niger-Congo, Atlantic-Congo, Volta-Congo, Benue-Congo, Edoid, North-Central, Edo-Esan-Ora.

Ibino (Ibeno, Ibuno) [ibn] 10,000 (1989 Faraclas). Akwa Ibom State, Uquo-Ibeno LGA. *Class:* Niger-Congo, Atlantic-Congo, Volta-Congo, Benue-Congo, Cross River, Delta Cross, Lower Cross, Obolo, Ibino.

Ibuoro [ibr] 5,000 (1988). Akwa Ibom State, Itu and Ikono LGAs. *Class:* Niger-Congo, Atlantic-Congo, Volta-Congo, Benue-Congo, Cross River, Delta Cross, Lower Cross, Obolo, Ibuoro. *Dialects:* Listed separately in Crozier and Blench 1992.

Iceve-Maci (Icheve, Ochebe, Ocheve, Oceve, Utse, Utser, Utseu) [bec] 5,000 in Nigeria (1990). Cross River State, Obudu LGA. *Dialects:* Maci (Matchi, Oliti, Olithi, Olit, Kwaya, Oliti-Akwaya, Motom, Motomo), Bacheve (Becheve, Bechere, Beheve, Baceve). See main entry under Cameroon.

Idere [ide] 5,000 (1988). Akwa Ibom State, Itu LGA. *Class:* Niger-Congo, Atlantic-Congo, Volta-Congo, Benue-Congo, Cross River, Delta Cross, Lower Cross, Obolo. *Dialects:* Listed separately in Crozier and Blench 1992. Probably Central Lower Cross, related to Anaang. Close to Eki (B. Connell 1998).

Idesa [ids] 5,693 (2000 WCD). Edo State, Akoko-Edo LGA. *Class:* Niger-Congo, Atlantic-Congo, Volta-Congo, Benue-Congo, Edoid, Northwestern, Southern. *Dialects:* Related to Oloma.

Idoma [idu] 600,000 (1991 UBS). Benue State, Otukpo and Okpokwu LGAs. *Class:* Niger-Congo, Atlantic-Congo, Volta-Congo, Benue-Congo, Idomoid, Akweya, Etulo-Idoma, Idoma. *Dialects:* Idoma Central (Oturkpo, Akpoto), Idoma West, Idoma South (Igumale, Igwaale, Ijigbam), Okpogu. Dialect cluster. *Lg Use:* Official language. Used in adult education. *Lg Dev:* Taught in primary schools. Radio programs. TV. Grammar. NT: 1970. *Other:* Agriculturalists: yams, guinea corn, cassava, maize, beniseed, rice, millet; hunters; fishermen.

Idon (Idong) [idc] 5,000. Kaduna State, Kachia LGA. *Class:* Niger-Congo, Atlantic-Congo, Volta-Congo, Benue-Congo, Plateau, Northern.

Idun (Lungu, Ungu, Adong) [ldb] 10,000 (1972 Barrett). Kaduna State, Jema'a LGA. *Class:* Niger-Congo, Atlantic-Congo, Volta-Congo, Benue-Congo, Plateau, Western, Northwestern, Koro. *Other:* Different from Idon. Traditional religion.

Igala (Igara) [igl] 800,000 (1989 UBS). Kogi State, Ankpa, Idah, Dekina, and Bassa LGAs; Edo State, Oshimili LGA; Anambra State, Anambra LGA. *Class:* Niger-Congo, Atlantic-Congo, Volta-Congo, Benue-Congo, Defoid, Yoruboid, Igala. *Dialects:* Ebu, Idah, Ankpa, Ogugu, Ibaji, Ife, Anyugba. *Lg Use:* Agatu, Idoma, and Bassa people use Igala for attending Ika Bible School. All domains. Used in initial primary education. *Lg Dev:* Taught in primary schools. Bible: 1968. *Other:* Traditional religion, Christian, Muslim.

Igbo (Ibo) [ibo] 18,000,000 (1999 WA). Abia State, Anambra State, Aguata, Anambra, Awka, Idemili, Ihiala, Njikoka, Nnewi, and Onitsha LGAs; Enugu State, Awgu, Enugu, Ezeagu, Igo-Etiti, Igbo-Eze, Isi-Uzo, Nkanu, Nsukka, Udi, and Uzo-Uwani LGAs; Imo State; Rivers

State, Ikwerre, Bonny, and Ahoada LGAs; Delta State, Oshimili, Aniocha, and Ndokwa LGAs; Akwa Ibom State, Ika LGA. The states where Igbo is spoken as the only or majority language are Abia, Anambra, Ebonyi, Enugu, and Imo. It is also spoken in the northeast of Delta State and the southeast of Rivers State, Oyigbo LGA and the Opobo part of Opobo-Nkoro LGA, and alongside Ibani in Bonny LGA. *Class:* Niger-Congo, Atlantic-Congo, Volta-Congo, Benue-Congo, Igboid, Igbo. *Dialects:* Owerri (Isuama), Onitsha, Umuahia, Orlu, Ngwa, Afikpo, Nsa, Oguta, Aniocha, Eche, Egbema, Oka (Awka), Bonny-Opobo, Mbaise, Nsuka, Ohuhu, Unwana. 30 dialects vary in inherent intelligibility. The standard literary form is developing based on the dialects of Owerri and Umuahia, omitting the nasality and aspiration found in those dialects. *Lg Use:* Official language in the southwest. The main trade language of Abia, Anambra, Ebonyi, Enugu, and Imo states. Used for government notices. *Lg Dev:* Roman script. Radio programs. TV. Dictionary. Grammar. Bible: 1906–1988. *Other:* Christian, traditional religion.

Igede (Igedde, Egede) [ige] 250,000 (1991 UBS). Benue State, Oju, Otukpo, and Okpokwu LGAs; Cross River State, Ogoja LGA. *Class:* Niger-Congo, Atlantic-Congo, Volta-Congo, Benue-Congo, Idomoid, Akweya, Etulo-Idoma, Idoma. *Dialects:* Ito, Oju (Central Igede), Worku, Gabu. *Lg Dev:* Grammar. NT: 1981.

Iguta (Naraguta, Anaguta) [nar] 6,123 (1990). Plateau State, Bassa LGA. *Class:* Niger-Congo, Atlantic-Congo, Volta-Congo, Benue-Congo, Kainji, Eastern, Northern Jos, Jera. *Other:* 'Iguta' is the language, 'Unaguta' a speaker, 'Anaguta' or 'Naragutawa' the people.

Igwe [igw] 47,845 (2000 WCD). Edo State, Akoko-Edo LGA. *Class:* Niger-Congo, Atlantic-Congo, Volta-Congo, Benue-Congo, Edoid, North-Central, Ghotuo-Uneme-Yekhee.

Ihievbe [ihi] North and east of Afuze, Owan LGA, villages of Ihievbe Ogbe, Ebetse, and Iyakhora. *Class:* Niger-Congo, Atlantic-Congo, Volta-Congo, Benue-Congo, Edoid, North-Central.

Ija-Zuba (Koro Afiki, Koro Ija, Koro Zuba) [vki] Federal Capital Territory, south of Abuja, north of the Minna Suleja road. *Class:* Niger-Congo, Atlantic-Congo, Volta-Congo, Benue-Congo, Unclassified. *Dialects:* A dialect cluster. Listed separately in Crozier and Blench 1992. Different from Koro of Lafia, Begbere-Ejar, or Tanjijili. 'Koro' is used as a cover term for several languages.

Ijo, Southeast (Ijaw, Brass Ijo) [ijs] 71,500 (1977 Voegelin and Voegelin). Population includes 66,600 Nembe, 4,900 Akassa. Bayelsa State, Brass LGA. *Class:* Niger-Congo, Atlantic-Congo, Ijoid, Ijo, East. *Dialects:* Nembe (Nimbe), Akassa (Akaha). *Lg Dev:* Literacy rate in second language: 60%. Dictionary. Bible: 1956. *Other:* A separate language within the Ijo cluster. Christian, traditional religion.

Ika [ikk] 22,772 (2000 WCD). Delta State, Ika LGA. *Class:* Niger-Congo, Atlantic-Congo, Volta-Congo, Benue-Congo, Igboid, Igbo. *Dialects:* A separate language in the Igbo language cluster. The dialect around Agbor, the administrative and commercial center, appears to be developing into a standard form. Further east and south from there, the varieties become more similar to Igbo (Report of the Committee on Languages of Midwestern State: 12). *Lg Dev:* Grammar.

Iko [iki] 5,000 (1988). Akwa Ibom State, Ikot Abasi LGA, 3 villages. *Class:* Niger-Congo, Atlantic-Congo, Volta-Congo, Benue-Congo, Cross River, Delta Cross, Lower Cross, Obolo, Iko. *Dialects:* Culturally they consider themselves Obolo, but they cannot use Obolo literature. The language is closer to other Lower Cross languages than to Obolo. Listed separately by Crozier and Blench 1992.

Ikpeshi (Ikpeshe, Ekpeshe) [ikp] 5,317 (2000 WCD). Bendel State, Etsako LGA. *Class:* Niger-Congo, Atlantic-Congo, Volta-Congo, Benue-Congo, Edoid, North-Central, Ghotuo-Uneme-Yekhee.

Iku-Gora-Ankwa (Iku) [ikv] Kaduna State, Kachia LGA. *Class:* Niger-Congo, Atlantic-Congo, Volta-Congo, Benue-Congo, Plateau, Northern.

Ikulu (Ikolu, Ankulu) [ikl] 50,000 (1998). Kaduna State, Kachia LGA. *Class:* Niger-Congo, Atlantic-Congo, Volta-Congo, Benue-Congo, Plateau, Northern.

Ikwere (Ikwerre, Ikwerri) [ikw] 200,000 (1973 SIL). Rivers State, Ikwerre, Port Harcourt, and Obio-Akpor LGAs. *Class:* Niger-Congo, Atlantic-Congo, Volta-Congo, Benue-Congo, Igboid, Igbo. *Dialects:* Apani, Akpo-Mgbu-Tolu, Ogbakiri, Emowhua, Ndele, Elele, Omerelu, Egbedna, Aluu, Igwuruta, Ibaa, Isiokpo, Omagwna, Ubima, Ipo, Omudioga, Obio, Rumuji. A separate language in the Igbo language cluster. *Lg Dev:* Considerable local interest in language and literacy. Grammar.

Ilue (Idua) [ilv] 5,000 (1988). Akwa Ibom State, Oron LGA. *Class:* Niger-Congo, Atlantic-Congo, Volta-Congo, Benue-Congo, Cross River, Delta Cross, Lower Cross, Obolo, Ilue. *Dialects:* Listed separately in Crozier and Blench 1992. *Lg Use:* Diminishing in size. Speakers are shifting to Efik or Oron (Blench 2000). Generally not used by younger people.

Irigwe (Iregwe, Aregwe, Rigwe, Nnerigwe, Kwoll, Kwal, Miango, Nyango, Idafan, Kwan, Nkarigwe) [iri] 40,000 (1985 UBS). Plateau State, Bassa and Barakin Ladi LGAs; Kaduna State, Saminaka LGA. *Class:* Niger-Congo, Atlantic-Congo, Volta-Congo, Benue-Congo, Plateau, Central, South-Central. *Lg Dev:* Bible portions: 1923–1935. *Other:* The language is 'Nkarigwe' or 'Rigwe', the people are 'Nnerigwe' or 'Miyango'.

Isekiri (Itsekiri, Ishekiri, Shekiri, Jekri, Chekiri, Iwere, Irhobo, Warri, Iselema-Otu, Selemo) [its] 510,000 (1991 UBS). Delta State, Warri, Bomadi, and Ethiope LGAs. *Class:* Niger-Congo, Atlantic-Congo, Volta-Congo, Benue-Congo, Defoid, Yoruboid, Edekiri. *Dialects:* Close to Yoruba. *Lg Use:* Used in initial primary education. *Lg Dev:* Taught in primary schools. Grammar. NT: 1985.

Isoko ("Igabo," "Sobo," "Biotu") [iso] 423,000 (2001 Johnstone and Mandryk). Delta State, Isoko and Ndokwa LGAs. *Class:* Niger-Congo, Atlantic-Congo, Volta-Congo, Benue-Congo, Edoid, Southwestern. *Dialects:* Ozoro, Ofagbe, Emede, Owe (Owhe), Elu, Aviara, Iyede, Imiv, Enhwe, Ume, Iwire (Igbide), Olomoro, Iyede-Ami, Unogboko, Itebiege, Uti, Iyowo, Ibiede, Oyede, Uzere, Irri (Iri) Ole (Oleh). *Lg Use:* Used in initial primary education. *Lg Dev:* Taught in primary schools. Grammar. Bible: 1977. *Other:* "Sobo" and "Igabo" are offensive names. "Biotu" not recommended; it is the Izon name for the Isoko, meaning 'interior people' and is not meant offensively by the Izon; however, the Isoko do not like it.

Ito [itw] 5,000 (1988). Akwa Ibom State, Akamkpa LGA. *Class:* Niger-Congo, Atlantic-Congo, Volta-Congo, Benue-Congo, Cross River, Delta Cross, Lower Cross, Obolo, Ibuoro. *Dialects:* Listed separately in Crozier and Blench 1992.

Itu Mbon Uzo (Itu Mbon Uso, Itu Mbuzo) [itm] 5,000 (1988). Akwa Ibom State, Ikono and Itu LGAs. *Class:* Niger-Congo, Atlantic-Congo, Volta-Congo, Benue-Congo, Cross River, Delta Cross, Lower Cross, Obolo, Ibuoro. *Dialects:* Listed separately in Crozier and Blench 1992.

Ivbie North-Okpela-Arhe [atg] 20,000 (1973 SIL). Edo State, Etsako and Akoko-Edo LGAs, villages of Ate, Okpekpe and Okpella. *Class:* Niger-Congo, Atlantic-Congo, Volta-Congo, Benue-Congo, Edoid, North-Central, Ghotuo-Uneme-Yekhee. *Dialects:* Ivbie North (Ibie North), Okpela (Okpella, Ukpella, Upella), Arhe (Atte, Ate). Dialect cluster.

Iyayu (Idoani) [iya] 24,651 (2000 WCD). Ondo State, one-quarter of Idoani town. *Class:* Niger-Congo, Atlantic-Congo, Volta-Congo, Benue-Congo, Edoid, Northwestern, Osse. *Other:* Listed separately from Uhami in Crozier and Blench 1992. The people are sometimes called 'Idoani'.

Iyive (Uive, Yiive, Ndir, Asumbo) [uiv] 1,000 in Nigeria (1992 Crozier and Blench). Benue State, Kwande LGA, near Turan. *Other:* The people's name for themselves is 'Ndir'. See main entry under Cameroon.

Izere (Izarek, Fizere, Fezere, Feserek, Afizarek, Afizare, Afusare, Jari, Jarawa, Jarawan Dutse, Hill Jarawa, Jos-Zarazon) [fiz] 50,000 (1993 SIL). Southern dialects: Plateau State, Barikin Ladi LGA; Northern dialects: Plateau State, Jos LGA; Bauchi State, Toro LGA; and Kaduna State, Jema'a LGA. *Class:* Niger-Congo, Atlantic-Congo, Volta-Congo, Benue-Congo, Plateau, Central, South-Central. *Dialects:* Northwest Izere, Northeast Izere, South Izere, Ganang-Faishang. The Fobor dialect is prestigious. Northwest Izere subdialects: Fobor (Fobur) and Shere; Northeast Izere: Fedare (Zandi, Zendi), Jarawan Kogi (Maigemu), and Fursom (Fursum); South Izere: Forom (Ichen); Ganang and Faishang. Firan is a separate language. *Lg Dev:* Literacy rate in first language: below 1%. Literacy rate in second language: 25% to 50%. Radio programs. Bible portions: 1940. *Other:* The language is called 'Izarek', 'Izere', or 'Izer'; a speaker 'Bajari', the people 'Jarawa', 'Afizarek', 'Afizere', 'Afudelek', 'Fizere', 'Feserek', 'Fezere', 'Hill Jarawa', 'Jarawan Dutse'. 'Jos-Zarazon' is the name of indigenous speakers in Jos.

Izi-Ezaa-Ikwo-Mgbo [izi] 593,000 (1973 SIL). Population includes 200,000 Izi, 180,000 Ezaa, 150,000 Ikwo, 63,000 Mgbo. Ebonyi State, Abakaliki, Ezza, Ohaozara, and Ishielu LGAs; Benue State, Okpokwu LGA. *Class:* Niger-Congo, Atlantic-Congo, Volta-Congo, Benue-Congo, Igboid, Igbo. *Dialects:* Izi (Izzi), Ezaa (Eza), Ikwo, Mgbo (Ngbo). Dialect cluster within the Igbo language cluster. *Lg Dev:* Grammar. Bible: 2002.

Izon (Izo, Uzo, Ijo, Ijaw, Central-Western Ijo) [ijc] 1,000,000 (1989 Williamson). Population includes 100,000 Kolokuma (1991 UBS). 1,770,000 all Ijo languages. Bayelsa State, Yenagoa, Southern Ijaw, Kolokuma-Opokuma, Ekeremor,and Sagbama LGAs; Delta State, Burutu, Warri, and Ughelli LGAs; Ondo State, Ilaje Ese-Odo LGAs; Ekiti State, Ikole LGA. *Class:* Niger-Congo, Atlantic-Congo, Ijoid, Ijo, West Ijo. *Dialects:* Arogbo, Furupagha, Egbema, West Olodiama, Oporoza (Gbaranmatu), Ogulagha, Iduwini, Ikibiri, Ogboin, West Tarakiri, Kabo(Kabowei), Kumbo(Kumbowei), Mein, Operemo, Tuomo, Ogbe Ijo, Gbarain, Kolokuma-Opokuma, Ekpetiama, Apoi, Koluama, Basan (Bassan), East Olodiama, East Tarakiri, Oyiakiri, Oporomo (Oporoma), Bumo (Boma). The Ijo (Ijaw) cluster is made up of seven separate languages. Izon has about 30 inherently intelligible dialects. *Lg Use:* The Kolokuma dialect is used in adult and primary education. *Lg Dev:* Radio programs. TV. Dictionary. Grammar. Bible portions: 1912–1924.

Izora (Chokobo, Cokobo, Cikobu, Chikobo, Cokobanci, Azora) [cbo] 4,816 (2000 WCD). Plateau State, Bassa LGA. *Class:* Niger-Congo, Atlantic-Congo, Volta-Congo, Benue-Congo, Kainji, Eastern, Northern Jos, Jera. *Other:* The language is 'Izora' or 'Cokobanci'; a speaker is 'Bacokobi'; the speakers are 'Cokobawa' or 'Ndazora'.

Janji (Anafejanzi, Jenji, Tijanji, Ajanji) [jni] 1,150 (2000 WCD). Plateau State, Bassa LGA. *Class:* Niger-Congo, Atlantic-Congo, Volta-Congo, Benue-Congo, Kainji, Eastern, Northern Jos, Jera. *Other:* 'Tijanji' is the language, 'Ujanji' a speaker, 'Ajanji' the people.

Jara (Jera) [jaf] 46,251 (2000 WCD). Borno State, Biu and Kwaya-Kusar LGAs; Gombei State, Akko and

Yamaltu-Deba LGAs. *Class:* Afro-Asiatic, Chadic, Biu-Mandara, A, A.1, Western. *Lg Use:* Jara is being replaced by Fulfulde and Hausa. *Other:* Different from Jera, which is Benue-Congo.

Jarawa (Jaranchi, Jar, Jara, Jarawan Kogi) [jar] 150,000 (1978 MARC). Population includes 20,000 Bankal, 19,000 Gingwak. Bauchi, Adamawa, and Plateau States. *Class:* Niger-Congo, Atlantic-Congo, Volta-Congo, Benue-Congo, Bantoid, Southern, Jarawan, Nigerian. *Dialects:* Bankal (Bankala, Baranci, Zhar), Ligri, Kanam, Bobar, Gingwak (Gwak, Jarawan Bununu, Jaracin Kasa). Dialect cluster. *Lg Use:* Most men speak Hausa but most women understand little Hausa. *Lg Dev:* Bible portions: 1940. *Other:* Agriculturalists: guinea corn, maize, millet. Traditional religion, Muslim, Christian.

Jere (Jeere, Jera) [jer] 64,850 (1998 CAPRO). Population includes 15,000 Buji (1998), 15,000 Gusu (1998), 30,000 Jere (1998), 4,000 Ribina (1996 CAPRO), 850 Gurrum (1936). Plateau State, Bassa LGA; Bauchi State, Toro LGA; Kaduna State, Saminaka LGA. *Class:* Niger-Congo, Atlantic-Congo, Volta-Congo, Benue-Congo, Kainji, Eastern, Northern Jos, Jera. *Dialects:* Buji (Eboze, Anabeze), Gusu (Gusawa, Gussum, Gesawa, Guzawa, Isanga, Asanga, Anibau, Anosangobari), Jere (Jeriyawa, Ezelle, Azelle, Jengre), Ribina (Rebina, Bunu, Ibunu, Narabunu, Anorubuna, Gurrum, Anegorom). A dialect cluster. For Ezelle dialect, a speaker is 'Ozelle' or 'Bajere'; the speakers are 'Azelle' or 'Jarawa'. For Eboze dialect, a speaker is 'Unabeze', speakers are 'Anabeze'. *Other:* Different from Jara, which is Chadic. Agriculturalists: guinea corn, maize, potatoes, cocoyam, tomatoes. Traditional religion, Christian.

Jiba (Kona, Jukun Kona, Jibi, Jibe) [juo] 2,000 (1977 Voegelin and Voegelin). Taraba State, Wukari and Karim Lamido LGAs; Plateau State, Langtang and Wase LGAs; Bauchi State, Alkaleri and Akko LGAs; villages north and west of Kalingo. *Class:* Niger-Congo, Atlantic-Congo, Volta-Congo, Benue-Congo, Jukunoid, Central, Jukun-Mbembe-Wurbo, Kororofa. *Dialects:* A member of the Kororofa language cluster. *Lg Dev:* Bible portions: 1927–1950. *Other:* The ethnic group is called 'Bajibaro'. Traditional religion.

Jibu (Jibawa, Jibanci) [jib] 30,000 (1997 SIL). Taraba State, Gashaka and Bali LGA. *Class:* Niger-Congo, Atlantic-Congo, Volta-Congo, Benue-Congo, Jukunoid, Central, Jukun-Mbembe-Wurbo, Jukun. *Dialects:* Gayam, Garbabi, Galamjina. *Lg Use:* Some living near the main roads also speak Fulfulde and Hausa. *Lg Dev:* Literacy rate in first language: 1% to 3%. Literacy rate in second language: 5% to 7%. Few have finished secondary school. NT: 1996. *Other:* Mountain slope, plains. Agriculturalists. Traditional religion, Christian, Muslim.

Jilbe (Zoulbou) [jie] 100 (1999 H. Tourneux). Borno State, Jilbe town, on the border of Cameroon across from the town of Dabanga. 1 village only. *Class:* Afro-Asiatic, Chadic, Biu-Mandara, B, B.1. *Dialects:* Speakers of Kotoko languages in Cameroon and Chad consistently report low intelligibility of Jilbe. Not the same as Zizilivakan. *Other:* Muslim.

Jimi (Bi-Gimu) [jmi] 1,000 (1995 CAPRO). Bauchi State, Ganjuwa LGA, Jimi village. *Class:* Afro-Asiatic, Chadic, West, B, B.3, Eastern. *Dialect:* Zumo. *Lg Use:* Speakers are older adults. *Other:* Different from Jimi in Cameroon in the Biu-Mandara group. Muslim.

Jiru (Wiyap, Kir, Atak, Zhiru) [jrr] 3,416 (2000 WCD). Taraba State, Karim Lamido LGA. *Class:* Niger-Congo, Atlantic-Congo, Volta-Congo, Benue-Congo, Jukunoid, Central, Jukun-Mbembe-Wurbo, Wurbo. *Other:* Traditional religion, Muslim, Christian.

Jju (Kaje, Kajji, Kache) [kaj] 300,000 (1988 SIL). Kaduna State, Kachia and Jema'a LGAs. *Class:* Niger-Congo,

Atlantic-Congo, Volta-Congo, Benue-Congo, Plateau, Central, South-Central. *Lg Dev:* Literacy rate in first language: 10% to 30%. Literacy rate in second language: 50% to 75%. Literacy program in progress. Grammar. NT: 1982.

Jorto [jrt] 17,284 (2000). Plateau State, Shendam LGA, at Dokan Kasuwa. *Class:* Afro-Asiatic, Chadic, West, A, A.3, Angas Proper, 1.

Ju [juu] 900 (1993). Bauchi State, Bauchi LGA, Ju village. *Class:* Afro-Asiatic, Chadic, West, B, B.3, Guruntum. *Other:* Agriculturalists: sweet potato, millet, maize; animal husbandry; hunters. Traditional religion, Christian.

Jukun Takum (Diyi, Njikum, Jukun) [jbu] Taraba State, Takum, Sardauna, and Bali LGAs. *Dialect:* Takum, Donga (Akpanzhi). *Lg Use:* Trade language. Second-language speakers in Nigeria: 40,000 (1979 UBS). No first-language speakers in Nigeria. *Lg Dev:* Literacy program in progress. *Other:* The name 'Njikum' is preferred in Cameroon. Formerly founders of the Kwararafa Kingdom, which existed from the 16th to the 19th centuries. Christian, traditional religion, Muslim. See main entry under Cameroon.

Kaan (Libo, Libbo, Kan) [ldl] 10,000 (1992). Adamawa State, Shellen, Song, and Numan LGAs. *Class:* Niger-Congo, Atlantic-Congo, Volta-Congo, North, Adamawa-Ubangi, Adamawa, Waja-Jen, Yungur, Libo. *Lg Use:* Most adults speak Hausa, Fulfulde, Mbula-Bwaza, Tambo, or Dera as second language. *Lg Dev:* No primary schools in the area. Many desire education. *Other:* Agriculturalists. Traditional religion, Christian, Muslim.

Kadara (Adara) [kad] 40,000 (1972 Barrett). Kaduna State, Kachia LGA; Niger State, Chanchaga LGA. *Class:* Niger-Congo, Atlantic-Congo, Volta-Congo, Benue-Congo, Plateau, Northern. *Dialects:* Kajuru (Ajure), Minna, Kachia, Iri. *Lg Dev:* Literacy rate in second language: 20%. *Other:* Traditional religion, Christian, Muslim.

Kag-Fer-Jiir-Koor-Ror-Us-Zuksun (Fakanci, Fakkanci, Puku-Geeri-Keri-Wipsi) [gel] 36,000 (1992 SIL). Kebbi State, Zuru LGA, Fakai District, with migrants farther south. Kur is also in Kebbi State, Sakaba LGA. *Class:* Niger-Congo, Atlantic-Congo, Volta-Congo, Benue-Congo, Kainji, Western, Duka. *Dialects:* Kag (Puku, Fakanchi, Et-Kag), Jiir (Gelanchi, Et-Jiir), Kur (Kere, Kar, Keri-Ni, Kelli-Ni, Kelanchi, Kelinci), Zuksun (Zussun, Et-Zuksun), Ror (Et-Maror, Tudanchi, Er-Gwar), Fer (Fere. Et-Fer, Wipsi-Ni, Kukum), Us (Et-Us), Koor (Kulu). Kag, Ker, Jiir, and Fer speakers have 79% to 92% inherent intelligibility of Ror. Ror and Kag are the largest dialects, Koor and Us the smallest. Lexical similarity 81% to 97% among dialects, 63% with Duka, 50% with Lela, 57% with Gwamhi-Wuri. *Lg Use:* Hausa bilingual proficiency differs regionally. *Other:* Speakers are interested in literature in their language. Traditional religion, Muslim, Christian.

Kagoma (Gwong, Gyong, Kwong, Agoma) [kdm] 25,391 (2000 WCD). Kaduna State, Jema'a LGA. *Class:* Niger-Congo, Atlantic-Congo, Volta-Congo, Benue-Congo, Plateau, Western, Northwestern, Hyamic. *Lg Dev:* Grammar.

Kaivi (Kaibi) [kce] 2,323 (2000 WCD). Kaduna State, Saminaka LGA. *Class:* Niger-Congo, Atlantic-Congo, Volta-Congo, Benue-Congo, Kainji, Eastern, Northern Jos, Kauru.

Kakanda (Akanda, Hyabe, Adyaktye) [kka] 20,000 (1989 Blench). Niger State, Agaie and Lapai LGAs; Kwara State, Kogi LGA, and communities along the Niger River centered on Budã. *Class:* Niger-Congo, Atlantic-Congo, Volta-Congo, Benue-Congo, Nupoid, Nupe-Gbagyi, Nupe. *Dialects:* Budon Kakanda, Gbanmi-Sokun Kakanda.

Kakihum [kxe] 15,000 (1996). Northern Niger State. *Class:* Niger-Congo, Atlantic-Congo, Volta-Congo, Benue-Congo, Kainji, Western, Kambari.

Kalabari [ijn] 257,764 (1989 Jenewari). Rivers State, Degema, Asaritoru, and Port Harcourt LGAs. *Class:* Niger-Congo, Atlantic-Congo, Ijoid, Ijo, East, Ibani-Okrika-Kalabari. *Dialects:* Mutually intelligible with Bile (Bille), Okrika, and Ibani within East Ijo. *Lg Dev:* Grammar. Bible portions: 1980–1991.

Kam (Yimwom, Nyiwom, Nyingwom) [kdx] 5,000 (1993). Taraba State, Bali LGA, 2 villages between Mayo Kam and Garba Chede. *Class:* Niger-Congo, Atlantic-Congo, Volta-Congo, North, Adamawa-Ubangi, Adamawa, Kam. *Lg Use:* Speakers also use Hausa or Fulfulde. *Other:* Traditional religion, Christian, Muslim.

Kamantan (Kamanton, Angan) [kci] 10,000 (1972 Barrett). Kaduna State, Kachia LGA. *Class:* Niger-Congo, Atlantic-Congo, Volta-Congo, Benue-Congo, Plateau, Ninzic. *Other:* Traditional religion.

Kami [kmi] 5,000 (1992 Crozier and Blench). Niger State, Lapai LGA, Ebo town, and 11 villages. *Class:* Niger-Congo, Atlantic-Congo, Volta-Congo, Benue-Congo, Nupoid, Nupe-Gbagyi, Nupe.

Kamo (Kamu, Nubama, Nyima, Ma) [kcq] 20,000 (1995 CAPRO). Gombe State, Billiri, Kaltungo and Akko LGAs. *Class:* Niger-Congo, Atlantic-Congo, Volta-Congo, North, Adamawa-Ubangi, Adamawa, Waja-Jen, Waja, Awak. *Dialects:* Typologically closer to Awak (no singular-plural noun suffixes). *Other:* 5 primary schools, 1 junior secondary school. Agriculturalists: guinea corn, rice, millet, peanuts. Traditional religion, Christian.

Kamwe (Higi, Hiji, Higgi, Vacamwe) [hig] 300,000 (1992). Adamawa State, Michika LGA, in the Mandara Mountains. *Class:* Afro-Asiatic, Chadic, Biu-Mandara, A, A.3. *Dialects:* Nkafa, Dakwa (Bazza), Sina, Futu, Tili Pte, Fali of Kiriya, Fali of Mijilu, Modi, Humsi. Close to Psikye and Hya of Cameroon. *Lg Dev:* Primary schools. People in lowland towns have more education. NT: 1975–1999. *Other:* Mountain slope. Agriculturalists: guinea corn, peanuts, beans, sweet potato, millet; animal husbandry; hunters. Traditional religion, Christian, Muslim.

Kaningdon-Nindem [kdp] 2,291 (1934). Kaduna State, Jema'a LGA. *Class:* Niger-Congo, Atlantic-Congo, Volta-Congo, Benue-Congo, Plateau, Western, Southwestern, A. *Dialects:* Kaningdom (Kaninkon, Kaningkwom, Kaningkon), Nindem (Inidem, Nidem). Dialect cluster.

Kanufi (Karshi) [kni] 10,361 (2000 WCD). Kaduna State, Jema'a LGA. *Class:* Niger-Congo, Atlantic-Congo, Volta-Congo, Benue-Congo, Plateau, Ninzic.

Kanuri, Central (Yerwa Kanuri, Kanouri, Beriberi, Bornu, Kanoury) [knc] 3,000,000 in Nigeria (1985 Gunnemark and Kenrick). Population total all countries: 3,425,138. Borno State, Kukawa, Kaga, Konduga, Maiduguri, Monguno, Ngala, Bama, Gwoza LGAs; Yobe State, Nguru, Geidam, Damaturu, Fika, Fune, and Gujba LGAs; Jigawa State, Hadejia LGA. Also spoken in Cameroon, Chad, Eritrea, Niger, Sudan. *Class:* Nilo-Saharan, Saharan, Western, Kanuri. *Dialects:* Kaga (Kagama), Lare (Lere), Kwayam, Njesko, Kabari (Kuvuri), Ngazar, Guvja, Mao, Temageri, Fadawa, Yerwa. Lukas says Kwayam is not understood by other Kanuri. All can understand the Maiduguri dialect. Closest to Manga Kanuri and Kanembu. Yerwa is the central dialect. Part of a dialect cluster that includes other Kanuri dialects and Kanembu in Chad. *Lg Use:* Official language. 500,000 second-language speakers. *Lg Dev:* Ajami script. Radio programs. TV. Dictionary. Grammar. NT: 1997. *Other:* SOV. Muslim.

Kanuri, Manga (Manga, Kanouri, Kanoury) [kby] 200,000 in Nigeria (1993). Mainly Yobe State, some in Jigawa and Bauchi states. *Dialects:* Dagara, Manga. *Lg Use:* Trade language. *Other:* Muslim. See main entry under Niger.

Kapya [klo] 200 (2004). Taraba State, Takum LGA, at Kapya. *Class:* Niger-Congo, Atlantic-Congo, Volta-Congo, Benue-Congo, Jukunoid, Yukuben-Kuteb. *Dialects:* Related to Kutep.

Karekare (Karaikarai, Karai Karai, Kerekere, Kerrikerri) [kai] 150,000 to 200,000 (1993 CAPRO). Bauchi State, Gamawa and Misau LGAs; Yobe State, Fika and Nangere LGAs. *Class:* Afro-Asiatic, Chadic, West, A, A.2, Bole, Karekare. *Dialects:* Jalalam (West Karekare), Birkai, Kwarta Mataci. *Lg Dev:* Grammar. *Other:* Muslim, traditional religion, Christian.

Kariya (Kariyu, Kauyawa, Lipkawa, Vinahe, Wihe) [kil] 2,000 (1995 CAPRO). Bauchi State, Ganjuwa LGA, Kariya village near Miya town. *Class:* Afro-Asiatic, Chadic, West, B, B.2. *Other:* Agriculturalists: maize, guinea corn, peanuts, millet. Muslim, traditional religion.

Khana (Kana, Ogoni) [ogo] 200,000 (1989). Rivers State, Khana LGA; Akwa Ibom State, Oruk Anam LGA (only the village Wiisoe). *Class:* Niger-Congo, Atlantic-Congo, Volta-Congo, Benue-Congo, Cross River, Delta Cross, Ogoni, East. *Dialects:* Yeghe, Norkhana, Ken-Khana, Boúe, Nyo-Kana, Babbe. Close to Gokana, Tee. *Lg Use:* Khana is the largest language of the Ogonoid group and therefore speakers of Gokana, Baan, and Tee tend to learn it. *Lg Dev:* Grammar. Bible: 1968.

Kholok (Kode, Koode, Kwoode, Pia, Pitiko, Widala, Wurkum) [ktc] 2,500 (1977 Voegelin and Voegelin). Taraba State, Karim Lamido LGA, near Didango. *Class:* Afro-Asiatic, Chadic, West, A, A.2, Bole, Bole Proper.

Kinuku (Kinuka, Kinugu) [kkd] 500 (1973 SIL). Kaduna State, Saminaka LGA. *Class:* Niger-Congo, Atlantic-Congo, Volta-Congo, Benue-Congo, Kainji, Eastern, Northern Jos, Kauru.

Kiong (Akayon, Akoiyang, Okonyong, Okoyong, Iyoniyong) [kkm] 100 (2004). Ethnic population: 569 (2000 WCD). Cross River State, Odukpani and Akampka LGAs. *Class:* Niger-Congo, Atlantic-Congo, Volta-Congo, Benue-Congo, Cross River, Delta Cross, Upper Cross, Kiong-Korop. *Lg Use:* Speakers are older adults; the younger generation speaks Efik. For several generations before now, the people were bilingual in Kiong and Efik. *Other:* Nearly extinct.

Kir-Balar (Kir, Kirr) [kkr] 3,050 (1993). Bauchi State, Bauchi LGA, Kir Bengbet and Kir Bajang'le villages. *Class:* Afro-Asiatic, Chadic, West, B, B.3, Boghom. *Dialect:* Kir, Balar (Larbawa). *Other:* Muslim.

Kirike (Okrika) [okr] 248,000 (1995 UBS). Rivers State, Okrika, Port Harcourt, and Ogu-Bolo LGAs. *Class:* Niger-Congo, Atlantic-Congo, Ijoid, Ijo, East, Ibani-Okrika-Kalabari. *Lg Dev:* Bible portions: 1979–1991.

Koenoem (Kanam) [kcs] 3,000 (1973 SIL). Plateau State, Shendam LGA. *Class:* Afro-Asiatic, Chadic, West, A, A.3, Angas Proper, 2.

Kofa (Kota) [kso] Adamawa State, Song LGA, north of Betul road, north of Yola. *Class:* Afro-Asiatic, Chadic, Biu-Mandara, A, A.2, 1. *Dialects:* Reported to be a separate language from Bura-Pabir.

Kofyar [kwl] 109,943 (2000). Plateau State, Qua'an Pan and Mangu LGAs; Nasarawa State, Lafia LGA. *Class:* Afro-Asiatic, Chadic, West, A, A.3, Angas Proper, 1. *Dialects:* Kofyar (Kwong), Kwagallak (Kwa'alang, Kwalla), Dimmuk (Dimuk, Doemak), Mirriam (Mernyang), Bwol (Bwal, Mbol), Gworam (Giverom, Goram), Jipal (Jepel, Jepal, Jibyal). Dialect cluster. *Other:* Traditional religion.

Kohumono (Bahumono, Ohumono, Ediba, Humono, Ekumuru) [bcs] 30,000 (1989). Cross River State, Obubra LGA. *Class:* Niger-Congo, Atlantic-Congo, Volta-Congo,

Benue-Congo, Cross River, Delta Cross, Upper Cross, Central, North-South, Ubaghara-Kohumono, Kohumono.
Koma (Kuma) [kmy] 32,000 in Nigeria (1989). Population total all countries: 35,000. Adamawa State, Ganye and Fufore LGAs, Koma Vomni, Alantika Mountains. Also spoken in Cameroon. *Class:* Niger-Congo, Atlantic-Congo, Volta-Congo, North, Adamawa-Ubangi, Adamawa, Leko-Nimbari, Duru, Voko-Dowayo, Vere-Dowayo, Vere-Gimme, Vere. *Dialects:* Gomme (Damti, Koma Kampana, Panbe), Gomnome (Mbeya, Gimbe, Koma Kadam, Laame, Youtubo), Ndera (Vomni, Doome, Doobe). A language cluster. 3 subdialects: Koma Vomni, Koma Beiya, and Koma Damti. Ndera and Gomnome speakers barely understand each other, but both understand Gomme. Related to Mom Jango. *Lg Use:* Some speakers understand Hausa, especially those on the plains, but the majority speak only Koma. *Lg Dev:* Literacy rate in second language: Low. *Other:* Different from Koma of Ethiopia and Sudan. 7 primary schools. Mountain slope, plains. Traditional religion, Christian, Muslim.
Kono (Konu, Kwono) [klk] 5,522 (2000 WCD). Kaduna State, Saminaka LGA, Kona village. *Class:* Niger-Congo, Atlantic-Congo, Volta-Congo, Benue-Congo, Kainji, Eastern, Northern Jos, Kauru.
Korop (Ododop, Durop, Kurop) [krp] 10,248 in Nigeria (2000 WCD). Population total all countries: 17,686. Cross River State, Odukpani and Akampka LGAs. Also spoken in Cameroon. *Class:* Niger-Congo, Atlantic-Congo, Volta-Congo, Benue-Congo, Cross River, Delta Cross, Upper Cross, Kiong-Korop.
Kpan (Yorda, Ibukwo, Kpwate, Hwaye, Hwaso, Nyatso, Kpanten, Ikpan, Abakan, Nyonyo) [kpk] 11,386 (2000 WCD). Taraba State, Wukari, Takum, and Sardauna LGAs, Kato Bagha, Wukari, Suntai, Gayan, Gindin Dutse, Likam. *Class:* Niger-Congo, Atlantic-Congo, Volta-Congo, Benue-Congo, Jukunoid, Central, Kpan-Icen. *Dialects:* Bissaula, Kumbo (Kpanzon), Takum, Donga (Akpanzhi), Apa, Kente (Kentu, Kyentu, Etkye), Eregba. Related to Icen. *Lg Use:* The Bissaula dialect is extinct.
Kpasam (Passam, Kpasham, Nyisam, 'Balo') [pbn] 3,000. Adamawa State, Numan LGA, Kpasham town, on the Numan-Jalingo road. *Class:* Niger-Congo, Atlantic-Congo, Volta-Congo, North, Adamawa-Ubangi, Adamawa, Leko-Nimbari, Mumuye-Yandang, Yandang. *Lg Use:* Speakers also use Hausa, Fulfulde, or Bacama. *Other:* There are primary schools in the village and speakers want to send their children to school. One junior secondary school. Agriculturalists. Christian, traditional religion, Muslim.
Kpati [koc] Extinct. Taraba State, Wukari, Takum LGAs. *Class:* Niger-Congo, Atlantic-Congo, Volta-Congo, Benue-Congo, Bantoid, Southern, Wide Grassfields, Narrow Grassfields, Mbam-Nkam, Ngemba.
Kubi (Kuba, Kubawa) [kof] Extinct. Ethnic population: 1,500 (1995 CAPRO). Bauchi State, Gunjawa LGA, Kubi town. *Class:* Afro-Asiatic, Chadic, West, A, A.2, Bole, Bole Proper. *Lg Use:* Members of the ethnic group now speak Hausa. *Other:* Muslim.
Kudu-Camo (Kuda-Chamo, Kudawa) [kov] 42 (1990 Michael Bross). Bauchi State, Ningi LGA. *Class:* Niger-Congo, Atlantic-Congo, Volta-Congo, Benue-Congo, Kainji, Eastern, Northern Jos, Jera. *Dialects:* Kudu (Kuda), Camo (Chamo). Related to Butu-Ningi. A dialect cluster. *Lg Use:* Speakers are shifting to Hausa (2000 Blench). *Other:* Nearly extinct.
Kugama (Kugamma, Wegam, Yamale, Yamalo) [kow] 5,000 (1995). Adamawa State, Fufore LGA. *Class:* Niger-Congo, Atlantic-Congo, Volta-Congo, North, Adamawa-Ubangi, Adamawa, Leko-Nimbari, Mumuye-Yandang, Yandang. *Lg Use:* Speakers also use Hausa, Gengle, Yandang, Kumba, Jiba, or Poli. *Other:* Traditional religion, Christian, Muslim.

Kugbo [kes] 2,000 (1973 SIL). Rivers State, Brass LGA. *Class:* Niger-Congo, Atlantic-Congo, Volta-Congo, Benue-Congo, Cross River, Delta Cross, Central Delta, Kugbo.
Kukele (Ukele, Bakele) [kez] 95,000 (1989). Cross River State, Ogoja LGA; Ebonyi State, Abakaliki LGA; Benue State, Okpokwu and Oju LGAs. *Class:* Niger-Congo, Atlantic-Congo, Volta-Congo, Benue-Congo, Cross River, Delta Cross, Upper Cross, Central, North-South, Koring-Kukele, Kukele. *Dialects:* Mtezi, Ugbala, Iteeji. Four dialects in the north, three in the south, besides those named. *Lg Dev:* Literacy program in progress. NT: 1979.
Kulere (Tof, Korom Boye, Akandi, Akande, Kande) [kul] 15,570 (1990). Plateau State, Bokkos LGA. *Class:* Afro-Asiatic, Chadic, West, A, A.4, Ron Proper. *Dialects:* Tof, Richa, Kamwai-Marhai. *Lg Dev:* Grammar. *Other:* Different from Kulere of Côte d'Ivoire, a trade dialect of Senoufo.
Kulung (Bambur, Kuluno, Bakulung, Bakulu, Bakuli, Kulu, Kukulung, Wo, Wurkum) [bbu] 15,000 (1973 SIL). Taraba State, Karim Lamido LGA, at Balasa, Bambur, and Kirim; Wukari LGA at Gada Mayo. *Class:* Niger-Congo, Atlantic-Congo, Volta-Congo, Benue-Congo, Bantoid, Southern, Jarawan, Nigerian. *Lg Dev:* Bible portions: 1950. *Other:* 4 clans: Bambur, Balassa, Banyam, Bamingun. Different from Kulung of Chad which is Chadic. Similar in culture to Piya, Kodei, Kwanchi, Pelang, and Pero. Agriculturalists. Traditional religion, Christian, Muslim.
Kumba (Sate, Yofo, Isaro) [ksm] 3,416 (2000 WCD). Adamawa State, Mayo Belwa and Fufore LGAs. *Class:* Niger-Congo, Atlantic-Congo, Volta-Congo, North, Adamawa-Ubangi, Adamawa, Leko-Nimbari, Mumuye-Yandang, Mumuye. *Lg Use:* Speakers also use Fulfulde or Hausa. *Lg Dev:* No schools. *Other:* Agriculturalists; animal husbandry: cows. Traditional religion, Christian, Muslim.
Kupa [kug] 20,000 (1998 Blench). Kwara State, Kogi LGA, around Abugi. 52 villages. *Class:* Niger-Congo, Atlantic-Congo, Volta-Congo, Benue-Congo, Nupoid, Nupe-Gbagyi, Nupe.
Kurama (Tikurami, Akurumi, Bagwama, Akurmi, Azumu, Bukurumi) [krh] 40,284 (2000 WCD). Kaduna State, Saminaka and Ikara LGAs; Kano State, Tudun Waya LGA. *Class:* Niger-Congo, Atlantic-Congo, Volta-Congo, Benue-Congo, Kainji, Eastern, Northern Jos, Kauru. *Other:* 'Tukurami' is the language, 'Bukurumi' a speaker, 'Akurumi' the people.
Kushi (Chong'e, Kushe, Goji) [kuh] 11,000 (1995 CAPRO). Bauchi State, Billiri, and Kaltungo LGAs, Kushi village. *Class:* Afro-Asiatic, Chadic, West, A, A.2, Tangale, Tangale Proper. *Other:* Agriculturalists: guinea corn, maize, beans, peanuts, cotton, rice.
Kutep (Kuteb, Kutev, Mbarike, Zumper, "Jompre," Ati) [kub] 44,588 in Nigeria (2000 WCD). Population total all countries: 45,988. Taraba State, Takum LGA. Also spoken in Cameroon. *Class:* Niger-Congo, Atlantic-Congo, Volta-Congo, Benue-Congo, Jukunoid, Yukuben-Kuteb. *Dialects:* Jenuwa, Lissam, Fikyu, Kunabe, Kentin. Fikyu has subdialects. *Lg Use:* Speakers also use Hausa or Jukun. *Lg Dev:* Literacy program in progress. Grammar. NT: 1986–1995. *Other:* "Jompre" is an offensive name. Christian, traditional religion.
Kutto (Kupto, Kúttò) [kpa] 3,000 (1995). Bauchi State, Bajoga LGA; Borno State, Gujba LGA, 2 villages. *Class:* Afro-Asiatic, Chadic, West, A, A.2, Tangale, Tangale Proper.
Kuturmi (Ada) [khj] 10,521 (2000 WCD). Kaduna State, Kachia LGA. *Class:* Niger-Congo, Atlantic-Congo, Volta-Congo, Benue-Congo, Plateau, Northern.
Kwa (Kwah, Baa) [kwb] 7,000 (1992). Adamawa State, Numan LGA, Gyakan and Kwa towns, near Munga.

Class: Niger-Congo, Atlantic-Congo, Volta-Congo, North, Adamawa-Ubangi, Adamawa, Kwa. *Dialects:* Gyakan, Kwa. *Lg Use:* Speakers also use Bacama. *Other:* Different from Kwa' of Cameroon in the Bamileke group. Tradesmen. Traditional religion, Christian.

Kwaami (Kwami, Kwam, Kwamanchi, Kwom, Komawa) [ksq] 10,000 (1990). Bauchi State, Gombe LGA. *Class:* Afro-Asiatic, Chadic, West, A, A.2, Tangale, Tangale Proper. *Lg Dev:* Grammar.

Kwak (Bùkwák) [kwq] Taraba State, Sardauna LGA, Antere. *Class:* Niger-Congo, Atlantic-Congo, Volta-Congo, Benue-Congo, Bantoid, Unclassified. *Other:* May be the same as Yamba.

Kyak (Bambuka, Nyakyak) [bka] 5,000 (1995 Adelberger). Taraba State, Karim Lamido LGA. *Class:* Niger-Congo, Atlantic-Congo, Volta-Congo, North, Adamawa-Ubangi, Adamawa, Waja-Jen, Jen. *Other:* Agriculturalists. Traditional religion, Christian.

Kyenga (Tyanga, Tienga, Tyenga, Kenga) [tye] 4,000 in Nigeria (1995 Ross Jones SIM). Population total all countries: 5,000. Kebbi State, Geshuru, Kaele, Saufu, and Tuni villages, all west of Illo, and in the Boko villages of Maze, Samia, Baikinrua, and Pisa. Also spoken in Benin. *Class:* Niger-Congo, Mande, Eastern, Eastern, Busa. *Dialects:* Lexical similarity 70% with Shanga, 38% to 40% with the Busa group. *Lg Use:* Little Kyenga use, shifting to Hausa or Dendi. Speakers also use Hausa. *Other:* Traditional religion, Muslim.

Labir (Jaku, Jakun, Jakanci) [jku] Ethnic population: 11,386 (2000 WCD). Bauchi State, Bauchi and Alkaleri LGAs. *Class:* Niger-Congo, Atlantic-Congo, Volta-Congo, Benue-Congo, Bantoid, Southern, Jarawan, Nigerian. *Other:* Agriculturalists. Muslim, Christian. Nearly extinct.

Laka (Lakka, Lau, Lao Habe, Godogodo) [lak] 5,000 (1995). Taraba State, Karim Lamido LGA; Adamawa State, Yola LGA. *Class:* Niger-Congo, Atlantic-Congo, Volta-Congo, North, Adamawa-Ubangi, Adamawa, Mbum-Day, Mbum, Unclassified. *Dialects:* Related to Karang. *Other:* Different from Laka (Kabba Laka) of Central African Republic and Chad, or from Karang (Laka) of Cameroon and Chad. Muslim, Christian.

Lala-Roba (Gworam) [lla] 46,000 (1993). Adamawa State, Gombi LGA, and Borno State. *Class:* Niger-Congo, Atlantic-Congo, Volta-Congo, North, Adamawa-Ubangi, Adamawa, Waja-Jen, Yungur, Yungur-Roba. *Dialects:* Lala (Lalla), Roba (Robba), Ebode. *Lg Use:* Speakers also use Fulfulde, Gaanda, or Hausa. *Other:* Hunters (January to April); agriculturalists (May to December): peanuts, guinea corn, bambara nuts, tiger nuts; animal husbandry: goats, poultry, sheep, dogs. Traditional religion, Christian.

Lamang (Laamang, Gbuhwe, Waha) [hia] 40,000 (1993). Borno State, Gwoza LGA; Adamawa State, Michika LGA. *Class:* Afro-Asiatic, Chadic, Biu-Mandara, A, A.4, Lamang. *Dialects:* North Laamang, Central Laamang, South Laamang. Speakers have 37% intelligibility of Mabas, 31% of Hedi. Subdialects of North Lamang: Zaladeva (Alataghwa), Dzuba, Leghva (Luhuva), Gwoza-Wakane; of Central Lamang: Hedkala (Hidkala, Xidkala, Hitkala, Hitkalanchi), Waga (Waha, Woga, Wagga), Dlige; of South Lamang: Ghudavan. Lexical similarity 64% with Hedi and Mabas, 50% with Gevoko. *Lg Dev:* Literacy rate in first language: below 1%. Literacy rate in second language: 25% to 50%. Grammar. Bible portions: 1992.

Lame [bma] 10,000 (1995 CAPRO). Bauchi State, Toro LGA, Lame District. *Class:* Niger-Congo, Atlantic-Congo, Volta-Congo, Benue-Congo, Bantoid, Southern, Jarawan, Nigerian. *Dialects:* Ruhu (Rufu, Rufawa), Mbaru (Bambaro, Bombaro, Bomberawa, Bunberawa, Bambara, Bamburo), Gura (Tugura, Agari, Agbiri).

Dialect cluster. *Lg Use:* There were reported to be no speakers of Ruhu left in 1987 (Blench). *Other:* Different from Pévé (Lamé) of Cameroon and Chad.

Lamja-Dengsa-Tola [ldh] 3,416 (2000 WCD). Adamawa State, Mayo Belwa LGA, around Ganglamja (Lamja Mt.), near the road between Mayo Belwa and Tola. 13 villages of Lamja and Dengsa. The central town of the Lamja is Ganglamja. The Dengsa live south of the Lamja. *Class:* Niger-Congo, Atlantic-Congo, Volta-Congo, Benue-Congo, Bantoid, Northern, Dakoid. *Dialects:* Lamja, Dengsa, Tola. A dialect cluster. The three dialects are inherently intelligible to each other's speakers. They may not be sufficiently distinct from Samba Daka to be a separate language. *Lg Dev:* Literacy rate in second language: low. *Other:* 8 primary schools. Agriculturalists: guinea corn, peanuts, maize, rice, cassava; hunters (dry season). Muslim, traditional religion, Christian.

Lamnso' (Nsho', Lamso, Lamnsok, Banso, Banso', Bansaw, Panso, Nso, Nso', Nsaw) [lns] Taraba State, Sardauna LGA, scattered in settlements sometimes mixed with speakers of other languages. *Lg Use:* Speakers also use Fulfulde. *Other:* Most Lamnso' have fled to Cameroon. Agriculturalists. Traditional religion, Christian. See main entry under Cameroon.

Laru (Larawa, Laranchi, Laro) [lan] 5,000 (1995 Jones). Niger State, Borgu LGA, on the banks of the Niger River, Karabonde, Monnai, Leshigbe, Luma, Sansanni, Shagunu villages. *Class:* Niger-Congo, Atlantic-Congo, Volta-Congo, Benue-Congo, Kainji, Western, Kainji Lake. *Other:* They are reported to be assimilating to Bisã language and culture. Muslim.

Leelau (Lelau, Lelo, Munga Lelau, Munga) [ldk] 5,000 (1995 Adelberger). Taraba State, Karim Lamido LGA, between Bambuka and Karim-Lamido town, near Lake Mungah. *Class:* Niger-Congo, Atlantic-Congo, Volta-Congo, North, Adamawa-Ubangi, Adamawa, Waja-Jen, Jen. *Dialects:* A member of the Munga dialect cluster. *Other:* In the Bikwin ethnic cluster. Clan names: Tanyam, Munzigah, Brem, Gopi. Agriculturalists; animal husbandry; fishermen. Traditional religion, Christian.

Legbo (Agbo, Gbo, Igbo, Imaban, Itigidi) [agb] 60,000 (1989). Cross River State, Obubra LGA; Ebonyi State, Afikpo LGA. *Class:* Niger-Congo, Atlantic-Congo, Volta-Congo, Benue-Congo, Cross River, Delta Cross, Upper Cross, Central, East-West, Mbembe-Legbo, Legbo.

Lemoro (Limoro, Limorro, Emoro, Anemoro, Anowuru) [ldj] 10,000 (1998 CAPRO). Plateau State, Bassa LGA; Bauchi State, Toro LGA. *Class:* Niger-Congo, Atlantic-Congo, Volta-Congo, Benue-Congo, Kainji, Eastern, Northern Jos, Jera. *Other:* The language is 'Emoro', a speaker is 'Limoro', the speakers are 'Anemoro'. Traditional religion, Christian, Muslim.

Lenyima (Anyima, Inyima) [ldg] Cross River State, Obubra LGA. *Class:* Niger-Congo, Atlantic-Congo, Volta-Congo, Benue-Congo, Cross River, Delta Cross, Upper Cross, Central, East-West, Mbembe-Legbo, Legbo. *Other:* The people are 'Anyima'.

Lere [gnh] Ethnic population: 16,328. Bauchi State, Toro LGA. *Class:* Niger-Congo, Atlantic-Congo, Volta-Congo, Benue-Congo, Kainji, Eastern, Northern Jos, Jera. *Dialects:* Si (Rishuwa, Kauru, Kuzamani), Gana, Takaya (Taura). Language cluster. *Other:* There may be few speakers left. Nearly extinct.

Leyigha (Asiga, Assiga, Ayigha, Ayiga, Yigha) [ayi] 10,000 (1989). Cross River State, Obubra LGA. *Class:* Niger-Congo, Atlantic-Congo, Volta-Congo, Benue-Congo, Cross River, Delta Cross, Upper Cross, Central, East-West, Mbembe-Legbo, Legbo. *Other:* The people are called 'Ayigha'.

Lijili (Ligili, Mijili, Migili, Megili, Koro Lafia, Koro of Lafia) [mgi] 50,000 (1985 UBS). Nasarawa State, Awe and Lafia LGAs. *Class:* Niger-Congo, Atlantic-Congo, Volta-Congo, Benue-Congo, Plateau, Southern. *Lg Dev:* Grammar. NT: 1986. *Other:* 'Migili' is the name of the people.

Limbum (Wimbum, Kambu) [lmp] Few speakers in Nigeria (1992 Crozier and Blench). Taraba State, Sardauna LGA, Mambila uplands. See main entry under Cameroon.

Lokaa (Yakurr, Yakö, Loko, Loke, Luko) [yaz] 120,000 (1989). Cross River State, Obubra LGA. *Class:* Niger-Congo, Atlantic-Congo, Volta-Congo, Benue-Congo, Cross River, Delta Cross, Upper Cross, Central, East-West, Loko. *Dialects:* Ugep, Nkpam. *Lg Dev:* Grammar. Bible portions: 1967–1984. *Other:* Agriculturalists: yams.

Longuda (Nunguda, Nunguraba, Nungura, Languda, Longura) [lnu] 32,000 (1973 SIL). Adamawa State, Guyuk LGA; Bauchi State, Balanga LGA. *Class:* Niger-Congo, Atlantic-Congo, Volta-Congo, North, Adamawa-Ubangi, Adamawa, Waja-Jen, Longuda. *Dialects:* Nya Ceriya (Banjiram, Cirimba), Nya Gwanda (Nyuwar, Gwandaba), Nya Guyuwa (Guyuk, Plain, Turuba), Nya Dele (Jessu), Nya Tariya (Taraba). *Lg Use:* Speakers also use Hausa, Fulfulde, Dera, Waja, or English. *Lg Dev:* Literacy rate in second language: 20% Hausa. NT: 1978. *Other:* Traditional religion, Christian.

Loo (Lo, Loh, Shunhu, Shungo) [ldo] 8,000 (1992 Crozier and Blench). Gombe State, Kaltungo LGA; Taraba State, Karim Lamido LGA, northeast of Karim Lamido town, off the Bambuka to Karim-Lamido road. *Class:* Niger-Congo, Atlantic-Congo, Volta-Congo, North, Adamawa-Ubangi, Adamawa, Waja-Jen, Jen. *Other:* Clan names: Fore (Kyilayo), Bene, Tamu, Bana, Talau, Tadam, Wawa. Agriculturalists; animal husbandry; fishermen. Traditional religion, Christian.

Lopa (Lopawa, Lupa, Kirikjir, Djiri) [lop] 5,000 (1996 Blench). Niger State, Borgu LGA, Amboshidi and Tungan Bori, islands in the Niger River; Kebbi State, Yauri LGA. *Class:* Niger-Congo, Atlantic-Congo, Volta-Congo, Benue-Congo, Kainji, Western, Kainji Lake. *Other:* Those in Borgu LGA are reported to be assimilating to Bisã language and culture.

Lubila (Lubilo, Kabila, Kabire, Ojor, Ofor) [kcc] 11,386 (2000 WCD). Cross River State, Akamkpa LGA, at Ojo Nkomba and Ojo Akangba. *Class:* Niger-Congo, Atlantic-Congo, Volta-Congo, Benue-Congo, Cross River, Delta Cross, Upper Cross, Central, East-West, Loko.

Lufu [ldq] Ethnic population: 2,000 to 3,000 (1992). Taraba State, Takum LGA, Lufu, and Lufu Jauro. *Class:* Unclassified. *Lg Use:* Speakers are shifting to Jukun. Culture and religion similar to the Jukun Kapya. Language reported to have been close to Bete and Bibi. Former speakers at Arufu near Wukari have lost the language. Speakers are older adults. *Other:* Christian, traditional religion. Nearly extinct.

Luri [ldd] 30 (1973 SIL). Bauchi State, Bauchi LGA, Kayarda and Luri villages. *Class:* Afro-Asiatic, Chadic, West. *Other:* Muslim. Nearly extinct.

Maaka (Maha, Maka, Maga, Magha) [mew] 10,000 (1993). Borno State, Gujba LGA, Bara town and associated hamlets. *Class:* Afro-Asiatic, Chadic, West, A, A.2, Bole, Bole Proper. *Other:* Muslim, traditional religion.

Mada (Madda, Yidda) [mda] 100,000 (1993 SIL). Plateau State, Akwanga and Keffi LGAs; Kaduna State, Jema'a LGA. *Class:* Niger-Congo, Atlantic-Congo, Volta-Congo, Benue-Congo, Plateau, Ninzic. *Lg Dev:* Literacy rate in first language: below 1%. Literacy rate in second language: 25% to 50%. Grammar. NT: 1999. *Other:* Different from Mada of Cameroon. Traditional religion, Christian, Muslim.

Mafa ("Matakam," Natakan, Bulahai, Bula) [maf] 4,907 in Nigeria (2000 WCD). Borno State, Gwoza LGA. *Dialect:*

Mafa. *Other:* "Matakam" is derogatory. See main entry under Cameroon.

Mághdì (Tala, Widala) [gmd] 2,000 (1992). Taraba State, Karim Lamido LGA, a section of the Widala. *Class:* Niger-Congo, Atlantic-Congo, Volta-Congo, North, Adamawa-Ubangi, Adamawa, Waja-Jen, Jen. *Other:* 'Widala' applies to the people. Kholok is also called 'Widala'.

Mak (Panyam, Panya, Leemak, Lemak, Zo) [pbl] 5,693 (2000 WCD). Taraba State, Karim Lamido LGA, northeast of Karim Lamido town, off the Banbuka to Karim-Lamido road. *Class:* Niger-Congo, Atlantic-Congo, Volta-Congo, North, Adamawa-Ubangi, Adamawa, Waja-Jen, Jen. *Dialects:* Panya, Zo. *Other:* In the Bikwin ethnic cluster. Clan names: Guma, Zidah, Togon, Mungok, Tawok, Tagwam. Traditional religion, Christian.

Mala (Rumaya, Rumaiya, Amala, Tumala) [ruy] 6,627 (2000 WCD). Kaduna State, Saminaka LGA. *Class:* Niger-Congo, Atlantic-Congo, Volta-Congo, Benue-Congo, Kainji, Eastern, Northern Jos, Kauru.

Mama (Kantana, Kwarra) [mma] 20,000 (1973 SIL). Nasarawa State, Akwanga LGA. *Class:* Niger-Congo, Atlantic-Congo, Volta-Congo, Benue-Congo, Bantoid, Southern, Jarawan, Nigerian.

Mambila, Nigeria (Mambilla, Mabila, Mambere, Nor, Nor Tagbo, Lagubi, Tongbo, Bang) [mzk] 99,000 (1993). Taraba State, Sardauna LGA, Mambila Plateau. *Class:* Niger-Congo, Atlantic-Congo, Volta-Congo, Benue-Congo, Bantoid, Northern, Mambiloid, Mambila-Konja, Mambila. *Dialect:* Barup. Nearly every village has a separate dialect, forming a chain. Dialect centers are Bang, Dorofi, Gembu, Hainari, Kabri, Mayo Ndaga, Mbamnga, Tamien, Tepo, Warwar. Close to Mambila of Cameroon. *Lg Use:* Speakers also use Fulfulde or English. *Lg Dev:* NT: 1977. *Other:* Traditional religion, Christian, Muslim.

Mangas [zns] 100 (1995 CAPRO). Bauchi State, Bauchi LGA. Mangas town. *Class:* Afro-Asiatic, Chadic, West, B, B.3, Boghom. *Lg Use:* Speakers also use Hausa. *Other:* Muslim, traditional religion, Christian.

Marghi Central (Marghi, Margi) [mrt] 135,000 in Marghi Central, Marghi South, and Putai languages (1999). Borno State, Askira-Uba and Damboa LGAs; Adamawa State, Mubi and Michika LGAs. *Class:* Afro-Asiatic, Chadic, Biu-Mandara, A, A.2, 2. *Dialects:* Lassa (Babal), Gulak (Dzerngu), Madube (Gwara), Mulgwe (Malgwa), Wurga. *Lg Dev:* Grammar. NT: 1987. *Other:* Marghi South, Marghi Central, and Putai form a language cluster. SVO.

Marghi South [mfm] Borno State, Askira-Uba LGA; Adamawa State, Mubi and Michika LGAs. *Class:* Afro-Asiatic, Chadic, Biu-Mandara, A, A.2, 2. *Dialects:* Wamdiu, Hildi. Marghi South, Marghi Central, and Putai form a language cluster. Hoffman (1963) relates Marghi South to Huba rather than to Margi.

Mashi [jms] 1,000. Taraba State, near Takum. *Class:* Niger-Congo, Atlantic-Congo, Volta-Congo, Benue-Congo, Bantoid, Southern, Beboid.

Mawa [wma] Extinct. Bauchi State, Toro LGA, possibly Mara village. *Class:* Unclassified. *Other:* Apparently different from the Mawa language of Chad, which is Chadic.

Mbe (Western Mbube, Ketuen) [mfo] 14,300 (1973 SIL). Cross River State, Ogoja LGA. *Class:* Niger-Congo, Atlantic-Congo, Volta-Congo, Benue-Congo, Bantoid, Southern, Mbe. *Dialects:* Idum, Ikumtale, Odaje. *Lg Dev:* Bible portions: 1992. *Other:* Distinct from Mbe' of Cameroon, a Grassfields language.

Mbembe, Cross River (Okam, Oderiga, Wakande, Ifunubwa, Ekokoma, Ofunobwam) [mfn] 100,000 (1982

UBS). Cross River State, Obubra and Ikom LGAs; Anambra State, Abakaliki LGA. *Class:* Niger-Congo, Atlantic-Congo, Volta-Congo, Benue-Congo, Cross River, Delta Cross, Upper Cross, Central, East-West, Mbembe-Legbo, Mbembe. *Dialects:* Okom (Eghom, Ohana-Onyen), Apiapum, Adun, Osopong (Osophong, Ezopong), Ofombonga (Ewumbonga), Ofonokpan, Ekama (Ekamu), Oferikpe. *Lg Dev:* Grammar. NT: 1985. *Other:* Different than Tigon Mbembe.

Mbembe, Tigon (Akonto, Akwanto, Tigon, Tigong, Tigim, Tukun, Noale) [nza] 20,000 in Nigeria (1987). Taraba State, Sardauna LGA, Kurmi District. *Dialects:* Ashuku (Kitsipki), Nama (Dama, Namu, Nzare, Kporo, Eneeme). *Lg Use:* Speakers also use Hausa. *Lg Dev:* Every village has a primary school. *Other:* Entirely different from Mbembe in the Cross River group. Dialects form a cluster. Hills. Forest. Agriculturalists: palm nuts, palm oil. Traditional religion, Christian. See main entry under Cameroon.

Mboi (Mboire, Mboyi, Gena) [moi] 19,000 (1992). Adamawa State, Song, Fufore, and Gombi LGAs. *Class:* Niger-Congo, Atlantic-Congo, Volta-Congo, North, Adamawa-Ubangi, Adamawa, Waja-Jen, Yungur, Mboi. *Dialects:* Banga, Mboi, Handa. Dialect cluster. *Lg Use:* Speakers also use Hausa, Fulfulde, Yungur, Gudu, or Gaanda. *Lg Dev:* Primary schools are in all the major villages. They desire education. *Other:* Traditional religion, Christian, Muslim.

Mbongno (Bungnu, Bunu, Bungun, Gbunhu, Kakaba, Kamkam) [bgu] 3,000 in Nigeria (1999 Blench and Connell). Taraba State, Sardauna LGA, Kakara town. Also spoken in Cameroon. *Class:* Niger-Congo, Atlantic-Congo, Volta-Congo, Benue-Congo, Bantoid, Northern, Mambiloid, Mambila-Konja, Magu-Kamkam-Kila. *Dialects:* Several minor dialects. *Lg Use:* Speakers also use Fulfulde, Hausa, or Mambila. *Other:* Agriculturalists. Muslim, traditional religion.

Mbula-Bwazza [mbu] 40,558 (2000 WCD). Population includes 10,000 Bwazza, 20,000 Tambo, 5,000 to 10,000 Mbula. Adamawa State, Numan, Guyuk, Song, Demsa LGAs. *Class:* Niger-Congo, Atlantic-Congo, Volta-Congo, Benue-Congo, Bantoid, Southern, Jarawan, Nigerian. *Dialects:* Bwazza (Bwaza, Bwa'za, Bare, Bere, Tambo), Mbula. *Lg Use:* Many also speak Kanakuru, Longuda, Bacama, or Bata. In some areas they live with the Libo and also speak Libo. Some older ones also speak Hausa or Fulfulde. Some speak English. *Other:* Primary schools in the major villages, and a few secondary schools. Agriculturalists: maize, millet, guinea corn, peanuts, cassava, sweet potatoes, cocoyam, bananas, sugarcane; fishermen; animal husbandry: horses, goats, sheep, pigs. Traditional religion, Christian.

Mburku (Barke, Barko, Burkanawa, Lipkawa, Mburkanci, Wudufu, Kariya Wuufu) [bbt] 12,000 (2000). Bauchi State, Darazo LGA. *Class:* Afro-Asiatic, Chadic, West, B, B.2.

Mingang Doso (Munga Doso, Ngwai Mungàn, Doso) [mko] 3,000 (1995 SIL). Taraba State, Karim Lamido LGA, 15 km east of Karim Lamido town. 1 village and associated hamlets. *Class:* Niger-Congo, Atlantic-Congo, Volta-Congo, North, Adamawa-Ubangi, Adamawa, Waja-Jen, Jen. *Other:* Traditional religion.

Miship (Chip, Cip, Ship) [mjs] 6,000 (1976 SIL). Plateau State, Pankshin, Mangu, Shendam LGAs. *Class:* Afro-Asiatic, Chadic, West, A, A.3, Angas Proper, 1. *Dialect:* Doka.

Miya (Miyawa, Muya) [mkf] 30,000 (1995 CAPRO). Bauchi State, Ganjuwa LGA, Miya town. *Class:* Afro-Asiatic, Chadic, West, B, B.2. *Dialects:* Gala, Faishang, Fursum, Demshin, Federe. *Lg Use:* Speakers also use Hausa. *Lg Dev:* Grammar. *Other:* Agriculturalists: guinea

corn, maize, rice, millet, peanuts. Traditional religion, Muslim, Christian.

Mom Jango (Vere, Verre, Were, Kobo) [ver] 104,275 in Nigeria (2000 WCD). Population total all countries: 110,798. Adamawa State, Yola and Fufore LGAs, Verre hills. Also spoken in Cameroon. *Class:* Niger-Congo, Atlantic-Congo, Volta-Congo, North, Adamawa-Ubangi, Adamawa, Leko-Nimbari, Duru, Voko-Dowayo, Vere-Dowayo, Vere-Gimme, Vere. *Dialect:* Mom Jango, Momi (Ziri). Mom Jango and Momi are probably separate languages. *Lg Use:* 90% use Fulfulde as second language. *Other:* Traditional religion, Christian, Muslim.

Montol (Montal, Baltap, Teel) [mtl] 21,858 (1990). Plateau State, Shendam LGA. *Class:* Afro-Asiatic, Chadic, West, A, A.3, Angas Proper, 2. *Dialects:* Montol, Baltap-Lalin. Related to Tal.

Moo (Gwomu, Gwomo, Gwom, Gomu, Ngwaa Móò, Yáá Mòò) [gwg] 5,000 (1998). Taraba State, Karim Lamido LGA, northeast of Karim Lamido town, off the Bambuka to Karim-Lamido road, close to Gomu Mountain. *Class:* Niger-Congo, Atlantic-Congo, Volta-Congo, North, Adamawa-Ubangi, Adamawa, Waja-Jen, Jen. *Other:* In the Bikwin ethnic cluster. Agriculturalists; animal husbandry, fishermen. Traditional religion, Christian.

Mumuye (Yoro) [mzm] 400,000 (1993 SIL). Taraba State, Jalingo, Zing, Karim Lamido, Yorro, Bali LGAs; Adamawa State, Ganye, Fufore, Yola, Numan, and Mayo Belwa LGAs. *Class:* Niger-Congo, Atlantic-Congo, Volta-Congo, North, Adamawa-Ubangi, Adamawa, Leko-Nimbari, Mumuye-Yandang, Mumuye. *Dialects:* Zinna, Dong, Yoro, Lankaviri, Gola (Bajama), Gongla, Kasaa, Saawa, Jalingo, Nyaaja, Jeng, Gnoore, Yaa, Sagbee, Shaari, Kugong, Mang, Kwaji, Meeka, Yakoko. Lankaviri dialect is sufficiently different from Zing to need separate literature. *Lg Dev:* Literacy rate in first language: below 1%. Literacy rate in second language: 25% to 50%. Grammar. NT: 1995. *Other:* Agriculturalists. Traditional religion, Muslim, Christian.

Mundat [mmf] 1,000 (1998 SIL). Plateau State, Bokkos LGA, Mundat village near Sha. *Class:* Afro-Asiatic, Chadic, West, A, A.4, Ron Proper. *Dialects:* Close to Sha and Karfa.

Mvanip (Mvanöp, Mvanon, Mvanlip, Mvano, Magu) [mcj] 100 (1999 Connell and Blench). Taraba State, Sardauna LGA, 25% of Zongo Ajiya and related hamlets in the northwest of the Mambila Plateau. *Class:* Niger-Congo, Atlantic-Congo, Volta-Congo, Benue-Congo, Bantoid, Northern, Mambiloid, Mambila-Konja, Magu-Kamkam-Kila. *Lg Use:* Vigorous. All ages.

Mwaghavul (Sura) [sur] 295,000 (1993 SIL). Plateau State, Barakin-Ladi and Mangu LGAs. *Class:* Afro-Asiatic, Chadic, West, A, A.3, Angas Proper, 1. *Dialects:* Mupun (Mapan, Mapun), Panyam. *Lg Use:* Trade language. Several smaller language groups nearby use Mwaghavul as second language. *Lg Dev:* Literacy rate in first language: 10% to 30%. Literacy rate in second language: 50% to 75%. Dictionary. Grammar. NT: 1991–1995.

Nde-Gbite (Biti, Bötö) [ned] Taraba State, Sardauna LGA, Antere. *Class:* Niger-Congo, Atlantic-Congo, Volta-Congo, Benue-Congo, Bantoid, Southern, Wide Grassfields, Narrow Grassfields, Unclassified.

Nde-Nsele-Nta [ndd] 19,500 (1987). Population includes 12,000 Nde, 3,000 Nsele, 4,500 Nsa. Cross River State, Ikom LGA. *Class:* Niger-Congo, Atlantic-Congo, Volta-Congo, Benue-Congo, Bantoid, Southern, Ekoid. *Dialects:* Nde (Ekamtulufu, Mbenkpe, Udom, Mbofon, Befon), Nsele, Nta (Atam, Afunatam).

Ndoe [nbb] 7,344 (2000 WCD). Cross River State, Ikom LGA. *Class:* Niger-Congo, Atlantic-Congo, Volta-Congo, Benue-Congo, Bantoid, Southern, Ekoid. *Dialects:* Ekparabong (Akparabong), Balep (Anep, Anyep).

Ndoola (Ndoro, Nundoro, Njoyame, Ndola) [ndr] 60,449 in Nigeria (2000 WCD). Population total all countries: 62,569. Taraba State, Bali, Gashaka, Sardauna LGAs. Also spoken in Cameroon. *Class:* Niger-Congo, Atlantic-Congo, Volta-Congo, Benue-Congo, Bantoid, Northern, Mambiloid, Ndoro. *Dialects:* There are at least two distinct dialects, those on and at the foot of the Mambila Plateau and those around Baissa, which seem to be similar to Serti. *Lg Use:* Speakers also use Fulfulde or Hausa. *Other:* Traditional religion, Christian, Muslim.

Ndun (Nandu, Indun) [nfd] 3,000 (2003 Blench). Kaduna State, southwest of Fadan Karshe, villages of Ankpong, Anfufalim, Ngbok, Ankara, Banyeng, Ungwar Rimi. *Class:* Niger-Congo, Atlantic-Congo, Volta-Congo, Benue-Congo, Plateau, Central, West-Central. *Lg Use:* Speakers also use Hausa.

Ndunda [nuh] 300 to 400 (1999 Blench and Connell). Taraba State, Sardauna LGA, near Mvanip, 5 km from Yerimaru, past Kakara on the tea estate road, northwest of Gembu. *Class:* Niger-Congo, Atlantic-Congo, Volta-Congo, Benue-Congo, Bantoid, Northern, Mambiloid, Mambila-Konja, Magu-Kamkam-Kila. *Lg Use:* All ages.

Ngamo (Ngamawa, Gamo, Gamawa) [nbh] 60,000 (1993). Yobe State, Fika LGA; Gambe State, Nafada-Bajoga LGA. *Class:* Afro-Asiatic, Chadic, West, A, A.2, Bole, Bole Proper. *Other:* Traditional religion, Muslim, Christian.

Ngas (Angas, Kerang, Karang) [anc] 400,000 (1998 SIL). Plateau State, Pankshin, Kanam, and Langtang LGAs. *Class:* Afro-Asiatic, Chadic, West, A, A.3, Angas Proper, 1. *Dialects:* Hill Angas, Plain Angas. *Lg Dev:* Dictionary. Grammar. NT: 1979. *Other:* 'Kerang' or 'Karang' is a place name. Speakers prefer 'Ngas' as language name.

Nggwahyi (Ngwaxi, Ngwohi) [ngx] 2,000 (1995). Borno State, Askira-Uba LGA. *Class:* Afro-Asiatic, Chadic, Biu-Mandara, A, A.2.

Ngizim (Ngizmawa, Ngezzim) [ngi] 80,000 (1993). Yobe State, Damaturu LGA. *Class:* Afro-Asiatic, Chadic, West, B, B.1, Bade Proper. *Lg Dev:* Dictionary. Grammar. *Other:* Muslim, traditional religion, Christian.

Ngwaba (Gombi, Goba) [ngw] 10,000 (1993 CAPRO). Adamawa State, Gombi LGA at Fachi and Guduniya, and Hong LGA. 2 villages. *Class:* Afro-Asiatic, Chadic, Biu-Mandara, A, A.8. *Lg Use:* Speakers also use Fulfulde, Hausa, Gudu, or Nzanyi. *Other:* Agriculturalists; hunters; butchers. Traditional religion, Christian, Muslim.

Nigerian Sign Language [nsi] *Class:* Deaf sign language. *Other:* Influences from American and Ghanaian sign languages. Originated in 1960.

Ningye [nns] 3,985 (2000 WCD). Kaduna State, Jema'a LGA, Ningeshen Kurmi village and 3 small settlements: Akwankwan, Kobin, and Ningeshen Dutse. *Class:* Niger-Congo, Atlantic-Congo, Volta-Congo, Benue-Congo, Plateau, Western, Southwestern, A. *Lg Use:* Language is spoken fluently by young people and others. Numana and Gbantu are the main second languages. Hausa widely known. Some young people also speak English.

Ninzo (Ninzam, Nunzo, Gbhu D Amar Randfa, Amar Tita, Ancha, Incha, Kwasu, Akiza, Sambe, Fadan Wate, Hate) [nin] 35,000 (1973 SIL). Kaduna State, Jema'a LGA; Nasarawa State, Akwanga LGA. *Class:* Niger-Congo, Atlantic-Congo, Volta-Congo, Benue-Congo, Plateau, Ninzic. *Lg Use:* Speakers have a considerable degree of bilingualism in Hausa. *Lg Dev:* Grammar.

Njerep (Njerup) [njr] 6 (2000 B. Connell). Southeast, near the Mambila. Not used in Cameroon any longer. *Class:* Niger-Congo, Atlantic-Congo, Volta-Congo, Benue-Congo, Bantoid, Northern, Mambiloid, Mambila-Konja, Njerup. *Lg Use:* Speakers are older adults. People now speak Mambila. *Other:* Nearly extinct.

Nkari [nkz] 5,000 (1998 B. Connell). Akwa Ibom State, Ikono LGA. *Class:* Niger-Congo, Atlantic-Congo, Volta-Congo, Benue-Congo, Cross River, Delta Cross, Lower Cross, Obolo, Ibuoro. *Dialects:* Formerly thought to be a dialect of Ibibio. *Lg Use:* Ibibio is the main trade language of Akwa Ibom State.

Nkem-Nkum [isi] 34,500 (1987 Asinya). Population includes 18,000 Nkem, 16,500 Nkum. Cross River State, Ogoja LGA. *Class:* Niger-Congo, Atlantic-Congo, Volta-Congo, Benue-Congo, Bantoid, Southern, Ekoid. *Dialects:* Nkem (Nkim, Ogoja, Ishibori, Isibiri, Ogboja), Nkum. Dialect cluster.

Nkoroo (Nkoro) [nkx] 4,550 (1989 UBS). Rivers State, Opobo-Nkoro LGA. *Class:* Niger-Congo, Atlantic-Congo, Ijoid, Ijo, East Nkoroo. *Other:* A separate language within the Ijo cluster.

Nkukoli (Lokoli, Lokukoli, Nkokolle, Ekuri) [nbo] 1,000 (1973 SIL). Cross River State, at the juncture of Ikom, Obubra and Akamkpa LGAs, Iko Ekperem Development Area. *Class:* Niger-Congo, Atlantic-Congo, Volta-Congo, Benue-Congo, Cross River, Delta Cross, Upper Cross, Central, East-West, Loko.

Nnam (Ndem) [nbp] 3,000 (1987 Asinya). Cross River State, Ikom and Ogoja LGAs. *Class:* Niger-Congo, Atlantic-Congo, Volta-Congo, Benue-Congo, Bantoid, Southern, Ekoid.

Nshi [nsc] Taraba State, Sardauna LGA, Antere, Nkiri. *Class:* Niger-Congo, Atlantic-Congo, Volta-Congo, Benue-Congo, Bantoid, Unclassified. *Other:* May be the same as Wushi.

Numana-Nunku-Gbantu-Numbu (Sanga) [nbr] 30,000 (2003 Blench). Kaduna State, Jema'a LGA; Plateau State, Akwanga LGA. *Class:* Niger-Congo, Atlantic-Congo, Volta-Congo, Benue-Congo, Plateau, Western, Southwestern, A. *Dialects:* Nunku, Numana (Nimana), Gbantu (Gwantu, Gwanto), Numbu. Dialect cluster.

Nungu (Rindre, Rendre, Rindiri, Lindiri) [rin] 50,000 (1999). Plateau State, Akwanga LGA. *Class:* Niger-Congo, Atlantic-Congo, Volta-Congo, Benue-Congo, Plateau, Ninzic. *Dialects:* Rindre, Gudi.

Nupe-Nupe-Tako (Nupe, Nufawa, Nupeci, Nupenchi, Nupecidji, Nupencizi) [nup] 800,000 (1990). Niger State, Mariga, Gbako, Agaie, and Lapai LGAs; Kwara State, Edu LGA; KoGi State, Kogi LGA; Federal Capital Territory. *Class:* Niger-Congo, Atlantic-Congo, Volta-Congo, Benue-Congo, Nupoid, Nupe-Gbagyi, Nupe. *Dialects:* Nupe Central (Nife, Anupe, Nupecizi, Nupencizi, Ampeyi, Anupecwayi, Anuperi, Tapa, Tappah, Takpa), Nupe Tako (Bassa Nge). Nupe Central has become the literary norm. *Lg Use:* Trade language. A regionally important language. 200,000 second-language speakers (1999 WA). *Lg Dev:* Literacy rate in second language: 60%. Dictionary. Grammar. Bible: 1953–1989. *Other:* Fishermen. Muslim, traditional religion, Christian.

Nyam (Nyambolo) [nmi] Taraba State, Karim Lamido LGA, at Andami village. 1 village. *Class:* Afro-Asiatic, Chadic, West, A, A.2, Bole, Bole Proper.

Nyeng (Ningon, Hanyeng) [nfg] 2,000 (2003 Blench). Kaduna State, Adu village. *Class:* Niger-Congo, Atlantic-Congo, Volta-Congo, Benue-Congo, Plateau, Central, West-Central. *Lg Use:* Speakers also use Hausa.

Nyong (Mumbake, Mubako, Nyongnepa, Nyoking, Daganyonga, Teteka, Chukkol, Yapeli, Peti) [muo] Adamawa State, Mayo Belwa LGA, 6 villages. *Lg Use:* Speakers also use Hausa, Fulfulde, Samba, Yendang, Kumba, or Mumuye. *Lg Dev:* Growing interest in education. *Other:* Agriculturalists; traders; hunters. Traditional religion, Christian, Muslim. See main entry under Cameroon.

Nzanyi (Njanyi, Nzangi, Njai, Njeny, Zani, Zany, Jeng, Jenge, Njei, Njeing, Kobotshi) [nja] 77,000 in Nigeria (1993). Population total all countries: 86,000. Adamawa

State, Maiha LGA. Also spoken in Cameroon. *Class:* Afro-Asiatic, Chadic, Biu-Mandara, A, A.8. *Dialects:* Paka, Rogede, Nggwoli, Hoode, Maiha, Magara, Dede, Mutidi, Lovi. *Lg Dev:* Schools in nearly every village, but enrollment is usually low. *Other:* Agriculturalists. Muslim, traditional religion, Christian.

Obanliku (Abanliku) [bzy] 65,000 (1989 Faraclas). Cross River State, Obudu LGA. *Class:* Niger-Congo, Atlantic-Congo, Volta-Congo, Benue-Congo, Cross River, Bendi. *Dialects:* Bebi, Busi, Basang, Bisu (Gayi), Bishiri. Dialect cluster. Related to Alege.

Obolo (Andoni, Andone, Andonni) [ann] 200,000 (1996 National Population Commission). Rivers State, Andoni LGA; Akwa Ibom State, Ikot Abasi LGA, islands off southern coast. Bounded on the east and northeast by the Ibibio, on the northwest by the Ogoni, on the west by the Ibani, on the south by the Atlantic Ocean. *Class:* Niger-Congo, Atlantic-Congo, Volta-Congo, Benue-Congo, Cross River, Delta Cross, Lower Cross, Obolo. *Dialects:* Ngo, Ataba, Unyeada, Okoroete, Ibot Obolo. Ngo (in the Central area) is the prestige dialect. *Lg Use:* In the east there is a movement toward establishing a stronger Obolo ethnic identity and getting rid of borrowed words from Ibibio. Ibibio and Igbo are the trade languages. English is learned in school. *Lg Dev:* Literacy rate in first language: 5% to 10%. Literacy rate in second language: 25% to 50%. There are church adult literacy classes throughout the area. Taught in primary and secondary schools. Magazines. Grammar. NT: 1991. *Other:* 'Obolo' is their own name, 'Andoni' is the government's name. Riverine. Fishermen; agriculturalists.

Obulom (Abuloma) [obu] 3,416 (2000 WCD). Rivers State, Port Harcourt LGA, Abuloma town. *Class:* Niger-Congo, Atlantic-Congo, Volta-Congo, Benue-Congo, Cross River, Delta Cross, Central Delta.

Odual (Saka) [odu] 18,000 (1989). Rivers State, Abua-Odual LGA. *Class:* Niger-Congo, Atlantic-Congo, Volta-Congo, Benue-Congo, Cross River, Delta Cross, Central Delta, Abua-Odual. *Dialects:* Arughunya, Adibom. Lexical similarity 70% with Abua (closest). *Lg Dev:* NT: 1981–2002.

Odut [oda] 20 (1980s, from Blench 2000). Cross River State, Odukpani LGA. *Class:* Niger-Congo, Atlantic-Congo, Volta-Congo, Benue-Congo, Cross River, Delta Cross, Upper Cross, Kiong-Korop. *Other:* It may be extinct. Nearly extinct.

Ogbah (Ogba) [ogc] 170,000 (1993 A. Ahiamadu). Rivers State, Ogba-Egbema-Ndoni LGA, northern Niger Delta. *Class:* Niger-Congo, Atlantic-Congo, Volta-Congo, Benue-Congo, Igboid, Igbo. *Dialects:* Egnih, Igburu-Usomini. A member of the Igbo language cluster. Lexical similarity 81% to 94% among dialects; Ogbah has 45% lexical similarity with Ndoni, 41% with Egbema, 32% with Ikwere, 23% with Ekpeye. *Lg Use:* Speakers also use Igbo, Nigerian Pidgin, or English. *Lg Dev:* Literacy rate in first language: Low. Grammar. Bible portions: 1999. *Other:* About 64 primary schools, 8 post-primary schools, technical college in the area. Riverine. Swamp. Agriculturalists; fishermen; traders. Christian, traditional religion.

Ogbia (Ogbinya) [ogb] 200,000 (1989). Bayelsa State, Brass LGA. *Class:* Niger-Congo, Atlantic-Congo, Volta-Congo, Benue-Congo, Cross River, Delta Cross, Central Delta. *Dialects:* Agholo (Kolo), Oloibiri, Anyama. Dialect cluster but all inherently intelligible.

Ogbogolo (Obogolo) [ogg] 10,000 (1995). Rivers State, Ahoada LGA, 1 town. *Class:* Niger-Congo, Atlantic-Congo, Volta-Congo, Benue-Congo, Cross River, Delta Cross, Central Delta.

Ogbronuagum (Bukuma) [ogu] 12,000 (2000 E. Kari). Ethnic population: 12,000 (2000 E. Kari). Rivers State, Degema LGA, Bukuma village near Buguma. *Class:*

Niger-Congo, Atlantic-Congo, Volta-Congo, Benue-Congo, Cross River, Delta Cross, Central Delta. *Lg Dev:* Grammar.

Oko-Eni-Osayen (Oko, Ogori-Magongo) [oks] 10,000 (1989 Williamson). Population includes 4,000 in Ogori, 3,000 in Magongo, 3,000 in Eni. Kogi State, Okene LGA, Ogori and Magongo towns, ten miles south southwest of Okene. *Class:* Niger-Congo, Atlantic-Congo, Volta-Congo, Benue-Congo, Oko. *Dialects:* Oko (Ogori, Uku), Osayen (Magongo, Osanyin), Eni. A dialect cluster. It seems to be equally distantly related to Yoruba, Ebira, Edo, Igbo, and Idoma.

Okobo [okb] 50,000 (1991 Connell). Akwa Ibom State, Okobo LGA. *Class:* Niger-Congo, Atlantic-Congo, Volta-Congo, Benue-Congo, Cross River, Delta Cross, Lower Cross, Obolo, Okobo. *Dialects:* Possibly two dialects.

Okodia (Okordia, Akita) [okd] 3,600 (1977 Voegelin and Voegelin). Bayelsa State, Yenagoa LGA. *Class:* Niger-Congo, Atlantic-Congo, Ijoid, Ijo, West, Inland Ijo. *Dialects:* Not fully intelligible with Biseni or other Ijo languages. Speakers tend to learn Kolokuma for wider communication.

Okpamheri (Opameri) [opa] 30,000 (1973 SIL). Edo State, Akoko-Edo LGA. *Class:* Niger-Congo, Atlantic-Congo, Volta-Congo, Benue-Congo, Edoid, Northwestern, Southern. *Dialects:* Okulosho (Okurosho), Western Okpamheri, Emhalhe (Emarle, Somorika, Semolika). Subdialects of Okulosho: Ojirami (Eekunu), Dagbala (Dangbala), Oja (Oza), Makeke (Uuma), Oma. Subdialects of Western Okpamheri: Ekpe, Bekuma, Lankpese (Lampese, Lankpeshi), Imoga (Imorga, Uma), Eko (Ekon, Ekor), Ikaran-Oke (Ikeram-Oke), Ebunn-Oke, Ikaran-Ele (Ikeran-Ile), Ebunn-Ugbo, Ikpesa, Igbo-Ola-Sale (Ugboshi-Sale), Aiyegunle (Oshi), Igbo-Ola-Oke (Ugboshi-Oke), Onumo (Onumu), Ogugu, Ogbe-Sale, Ogbe-Oke. *Lg Dev:* Grammar. *Other:* Traditional religion, Christian.

Okpe [oke] 25,425 (2000 WCD). Edo State, Okpe LGA. *Class:* Niger-Congo, Atlantic-Congo, Volta-Congo, Benue-Congo, Edoid, Southwestern. *Other:* Distinct from Okpe-Idesa-Oloma-Akuku, which is Northwestern Edoid.

Okpe [okx] 8,700 (2004). Edo State, Akoko-Edo LGA. *Class:* Niger-Congo, Atlantic-Congo, Volta-Congo, Benue-Congo, Edoid, Northwestern, Southern. *Dialects:* Related to Oloma. *Other:* Distinct from Okpe, which is Southwestern Edoid.

Oloma [olm] Edo State, Akoko-Edo LGA. *Class:* Niger-Congo, Atlantic-Congo, Volta-Congo, Benue-Congo, Edoid, Northwestern, Southern. *Dialects:* Related to Okpe-Idesa-Akuku.

Olulumo-Ikom (Lulumo) [iko] 30,000 (1989 Faraclas). Population includes 5,000 Olulumo, 25,000 Ikom. Cross River State, Ikom LGA. May also be in Cameroon. *Class:* Niger-Congo, Atlantic-Congo, Volta-Congo, Benue-Congo, Cross River, Delta Cross, Upper Cross, Central, East-West, Ikom. *Dialects:* Okuni, Olulumo, Ikom.

Oring (Orri, Orrin, Orringorrin, Koring) [org] 75,000 (1989). Population includes 12,300 Ufia, 3,000 Effium, 6,350 Okpoto (1955 R. G. Armstrong). Benue State, Okpokwu LGA; Ebonyi State, Ishielu LGA. *Class:* Niger-Congo, Atlantic-Congo, Volta-Congo, Benue-Congo, Cross River, Delta Cross, Upper Cross, Central, North-South, Koring-Kukele, Koring. *Dialects:* Okpoto, Ufia (Utonkon), Ufiom (Effium).

Oro (Oron) [orx] 75,000 (1989). Akwa-Ibom State, Oron LGA. *Class:* Niger-Congo, Atlantic-Congo, Volta-Congo, Benue-Congo, Cross River, Delta Cross, Lower Cross, Obolo, Oro. *Dialects:* Some dialect variation. *Lg Dev:* Grammar.

Oruma [orr] 5,000 (1995). Bayelsa State, Ogbia LGA, towns of Oruma and Ibelebiri. *Class:* Niger-Congo,

Atlantic-Congo, Ijoid, Ijo, West, Inland Ijo. *Other:* A separate language within the Ijo cluster.

Ososo [oso] 19,038 (2000 WCD). Edo State, Akoko-Edo LGA. *Class:* Niger-Congo, Atlantic-Congo, Volta-Congo, Benue-Congo, Edoid, North-Central, Ghotuo-Uneme-Yekhee.

Otank (Otanga, Utanga, Utange, Otang, Utank) [uta] 3,000 (1973 SIL). Cross River State, Obudu LGA; Benue State, Kwande LGA. *Class:* Niger-Congo, Atlantic-Congo, Volta-Congo, Benue-Congo, Bantoid, Southern, Tivoid. *Dialects:* Lexical similarity 70% with Tiv, 60% with Iceve-Maci, 50% with Evant, 40% with Mesaka and Eman. *Other:* Mountain slope. Traditional religion.

Pa'a (Afawa, Afanci, Pala, Pa'awa, Fa'awa, Foni, Afa, Fucaka) [pqa] 8,000 (1995 CAPRO). Bauchi State, Ningi and Bauchi LGAs. *Class:* Afro-Asiatic, Chadic, West, B, B.2. *Lg Use:* Speakers are shifting to Hausa. *Lg Dev:* Literacy rate in second language: 1%. Grammar. *Other:* Agriculturalists: guinea corn, millet, maize, peanuts, beans; fishermen. Traditional religion, Muslim, Christian.

Pangseng [pgs] Taraba State, Karim Lamido LGA. *Class:* Niger-Congo, Atlantic-Congo, Volta-Congo, North, Adamawa-Ubangi, Adamawa, Leko-Nimbari, Mumuye-Yandang, Mumuye. *Dialects:* Pangseng, Komo, Jega.

Pe (Dalong, Pai) [pai] 4,000 (2003 Blench). Plateau State, Pankshin LGA, 17 km south of the main road from Jos-Amper, turning a few kilometers before Amper. 7 villages. *Class:* Niger-Congo, Atlantic-Congo, Volta-Congo, Benue-Congo, Plateau, Tarokoid. *Lg Use:* Vigorous. All ages.

Peere (Pere, Peer, Pare, Potopo, Potopore, Patapori, Kutin, Koutin, Kutine, Kutinn, Kotopo, Kotofo, Kotpojo) [pfe] Few speakers in Nigeria. Adamawa State, Ganye LGA. *Lg Use:* Speakers also use Fulfulde. *Other:* It is reported that all Peere speakers have moved to Cameroon since Gashaka-Gumti National Park was created. Hunters. Muslim, traditional religion, Christian. See main entry under Cameroon.

Pero (Pipero, Filiya) [pip] 25,000 (1995 CAPRO). Bauchi State, Kaltungo LGA, Gwandum, Gundalf, Kushi, Yapito, Burak and Bangunji. *Class:* Afro-Asiatic, Chadic, West, A, A.2, Tangale, Tangale Proper. *Lg Use:* They use Hausa as lingua franca. *Lg Dev:* Dictionary. Grammar. Bible portions: 1936–1938. *Other:* Agriculturalists: guinea corn, peanuts, beniseed, millet, maize, cotton, beans, fruit. Christian.

Pidgin, Nigerian (Nigerian Creole English, Nigerian Pidgin English) [pcm] Southern states and in Sabon Garis of the northern states, coastal and urban areas. *Class:* Creole, English based, Atlantic, Krio. *Dialects:* Lagos Pidgin, Delta Pidgin, Cross River Pidgin, Benin Pidgin. No unified standard. The dialects listed may be very different from each other. Partially intelligible with Krio of Sierra Leone and Cameroon Pidgin. *Lg Use:* Trade language. Increasing in importance and use. It is a creole with native speakers, as well as used as a pidgin between Africans and Europeans, and Africans from different languages. Used in novels, plays, advertising. *Lg Dev:* Poetry. Radio programs. TV. Dictionary. Grammar. Bible portions: 1957.

Piti (Pitti, Abisi, Bisi) [pcn] 5,534 (2000 WCD). Kaduna State, Saminaka LGA. *Class:* Niger-Congo, Atlantic-Congo, Volta-Congo, Benue-Congo, Kainji, Eastern, Piti-Atsam. *Dialect:* Riban (Ribam).

Piya-Kwonci (Piya, Pia, Pitiko, Wurkum, Ambandi) [piy] 5,000 (1992). Taraba State, Karim Lamido LGA; and some in Bauchi State. 21 villages or more. *Class:* Afro-Asiatic, Chadic, West, A, A.2, Tangale, Tangale Proper. *Dialects:* Piya, Kwonci. *Lg Use:* Speakers use Hausa, Kulung, Pelang, Tangale or some English as second language. *Lg Dev:* Bible portions: 1950. *Other:* Similar in culture to the Kulung, Kodei, Kwanchi, Pelang, and Pero.

'Ambandi' is their name for themselves. Agriculturalists. Christian, Muslim.

Polci (Palci, Palchi, Polchi) [plj] 22,000 (1995 CAPRO). Population includes 2,000 Zul (1995), 4,000 Buli (1993), 400 Langas (1993), 15,000 Polci, 250 Baram (1993), 800 Dir (1993). Bauchi State, Dass, Toro, and Bauchi LGAs. *Class:* Afro-Asiatic, Chadic, West, B, B.3, Zaar Proper. *Dialects:* Zul (Mbarmi, Barma), Baram (Mbaram, Barang), Dir (Diir, Dra, Baram Dutse), Buli, Langas (Nyamzax, Lundur), Polci (Posa, Polshi, Palci). Polci dialect cluster in Barawa language cluster. *Lg Use:* Speakers are shifting to Hausa (2000 Blench). *Lg Dev:* Grammar. *Other:* Agriculturalists: guinea corn, peanuts, acha, maize; animal husbandry: poultry, goats; hunters.

Pongu (Pongo, Pangu, Arringeu, Tarya) [png] 30,000 (2003 SIL). Niger State, Rafi LGA, Gumna and Tegina districts, widespread small villages between Kusheriki in the north, Zungeru in the south, and along the new road to the southwest, with center in Sabon Gari Pangu. Bordered by the Kamuku, Ngwoi, Ura, Basa-Kaduna, Baushi, Basa-Gurmana, Gurmana, and Gbari. Small numbers are in Kaduna, Minna, Kontagora, and Bida towns. *Class:* Niger-Congo, Atlantic-Congo, Volta-Congo, Benue-Congo, Kainji, Western, Kamuku. *Dialects:* Akwa, Asebi, Awege, Azhiga, Cagere, Camajere, Cansu, Caundu, Ubwebwe. Dialect variation is slight, with 94% to 99% similarity. *Lg Use:* All domains. Used in church when only Pongu are present. Hausa is used as second language with outsiders. English is used in education and for national government purposes. *Lg Dev:* Some children and adults are literate in Hausa or English. *Other:* They call their language 'Tarya', themselves 'Arya'. Sister exchange pattern in marriage. Savannah. 200 to 500 meters. Peasant agriculturalists. Muslim, traditional religion (Mai-Giro), Christian.

Psikye (Kapsiki, Kamsiki, Ptsake) [kvj] 12,000 in Nigeria (1992). Adamawa State, north and east of Michika, south of Madagali, in the Mandara Mountains. *Dialects:* Psikye (Kapsiki, Kamu), Zlenge, Wula (Oula, Ula-Xangku, Lying). *Lg Dev:* Literacy rate in second language: Low. *Other:* Mountain slope. Agriculturalists: guinea corn, peanuts, rice, beans; animal husbandry. Traditional religion, Christian, Muslim. See main entry under Cameroon.

Putai (Marghi West) [mfl] 50. Borno State, Damboa LGA. *Class:* Afro-Asiatic, Chadic, Biu-Mandara, A, A.2, 1. *Lg Use:* Speakers also use Kanuri. *Other:* The language is dying out in favor of Kanuri, but the ethnic population is large. Nearly extinct.

Putukwam (Utugwang, Mbe Afal, Mbube Eastern) [afe] 12,000 (1973 SIL). Population includes 3,500 Afrike. Cross River State, Obudu and Ogoja LGAs. *Class:* Niger-Congo, Atlantic-Congo, Volta-Congo, Benue-Congo, Cross River, Bendi. *Dialects:* Utugwang (Otukwang), Okorogung, Okorotung, Afrike (Aferike), Obe (Mbe East), Oboso. Member of the Obe cluster. *Lg Use:* Speakers are reported to understand Bekwarra well. *Other:* Traditional religion, Christian.

Pyapun [pcw] 17,284 (2000 WCD). Plateau State, Shendam LGA. *Class:* Afro-Asiatic, Chadic, West, A, A.3, Angas Proper, 2. *Dialects:* Related to Tal and Montol.

Rang [rax] Taraba State, Zing LGA. *Class:* Niger-Congo, Atlantic-Congo, Volta-Congo, North, Adamawa-Ubangi, Adamawa, Leko-Nimbari, Mumuye-Yandang, Mumuye. *Dialects:* Close to Mumuye.

Reshe (Tsureshe, Tsureja, Bareshe, Gunga, Gungawa, Gunganchi, Yaurawa) [res] 44,000 (1993 SIL). Kebbi State, Yauri LGA; Niger State, Borgu LGA; southern Kebbi State, western Niger State, banks of the Niger

River, north of Busa. *Class:* Niger-Congo, Atlantic-Congo, Volta-Congo, Benue-Congo, Kainji, Western, Reshe. *Dialects:* Blench says it is the most divergent of the Western Kainji languages. Lexical similarity 43% with Lopa, 33% with Laru, 20% with Duka, 11% with Kamabari (Salka). *Lg Use:* Speakers are shifting to Hausa (Blench 2000). There is a strong association between wrestling, the traditional religion, and ethnic identity. *Lg Dev:* Bible portions: 1970. *Other:* The people are 'Bareshe', the language 'Reshe' or 'Tsureshe'. Ethnic subgroups: Gungawa, Yaurawa (Yauri). 180 to 300 meters. Agriculturalists: guinea corn, beans, rice, onions; fishermen; canoe makers; mat makers. Muslim, traditional religion, Christian.

Rogo (Urogo, Burogo, Ucanja Kamuku) [rod] Niger State, Rafi and Mariga LGAs, around Ucanja town, 30 km northwest of Kagara; Kaduna State, Birnin Gwari LGA. *Class:* Niger-Congo, Atlantic-Congo, Volta-Congo, Benue-Congo, Kainji, Western, Kamuku.

Ron ("Challa," "Chala") [cla] 115,000 (1995). Population includes 20,000 Shagawu. Plateau State, Bokkos, Barakin-Ladi and Mangu LGAs. *Class:* Afro-Asiatic, Chadic, West, A, A.4, Ron Proper. *Dialects:* Bokkos (Alis I Run), Daffo-Butura (Lis Ma Run), Monguna (Shagawu, Shagau, Nafunfia, Maleni). *Lg Dev:* Radio programs. Grammar.

Ruma (Ruruma, Rurama, Turama, Bagwama) [ruz] 5,090 (2000 WCD). Kaduna State, Saminaka LGA. *Class:* Niger-Congo, Atlantic-Congo, Volta-Congo, Benue-Congo, Kainji, Eastern, Northern Jos, Kauru.

Samba Daka (Chamba Daka, Tsamba, Tchamba, Sama, Samba, Jama, Daka, Dakka, Dekka, Nakanyare, Deng, Tikk) [ccg] 107,000 (2000). Taraba State, Gashaka, Jalingo, Bali, Zing LGAs, and Adamawa State, Ganye and Mayo Belwa LGAs. *Class:* Niger-Congo, Atlantic-Congo, Volta-Congo, Benue-Congo, Bantoid, Northern, Dakoid. *Dialects:* Samba Daka, Samba Jangani, Samba Nnakenyare, Samba of Mapeo, Taram, Dirim. A dialect cluster. Together with Lamja-Dengsa-Tola it may form a language cluster. Close to Dirim. *Lg Use:* Speakers also use Fulfulde or Hausa. *Lg Dev:* Literacy rate in second language: 3%. Bible portions: 1933. *Other:* Different from Samba Leko or Chamba (Akaselem) of Togo. Traditional religion, Muslim, Christian.

Samba Leko (Chamba Leko, Samba Leeko, Samba, Ndi, Lekon, Lego, Leko, Suntai) [ndi] 62,020 in Nigeria (2000 WCD). Adamawa State, Ganye, Fufore, Wukari, and Takum LGAs. Also spoken in Cameroon. *Class:* Niger-Congo, Atlantic-Congo, Volta-Congo, North, Adamawa-Ubangi, Adamawa, Leko-Nimbari, Leko. *Dialects:* Close to Kolbila. *Lg Use:* Those in Donga now speak Jukun. *Lg Dev:* Grammar. NT: 2001. *Other:* Traditional religion, Christian, Muslim.

Sanga (Isanga, Asanga) [xsn] 20,142 (2000 WCD). Population includes 1,600 Bujiyel (1995 CAPRO). Bauchi State, Toro LGA. *Class:* Niger-Congo, Atlantic-Congo, Volta-Congo, Benue-Congo, Kainji, Eastern, Northern Jos, Jera. *Dialect:* Bujiyel. *Other:* The language is 'Isanga', a speaker 'Osanga', the speakers 'Asanga'. Distinct from Numana-Nunku-Gbantu (Sanga) of Kaduna and Plateau states. Traditional religion, Christian.

Sasaru [sxs] 12,456 (2000 WCD). Edo State, Akoko-Edo LGA. *Class:* Niger-Congo, Atlantic-Congo, Volta-Congo, Benue-Congo, Edoid, North-Central, Ghotuo-Uneme-Yekhee.

Saya (Sayawa, Seya, Seyawa, Sayanci, Seiyara, Sayara) [say] 50,000 (1973 SIL). Population includes 7,000 Sigdi (1995 CAPRO). Bauchi State, Tafawa Balewa LGA. *Class:* Afro-Asiatic, Chadic, West, B, B.3, Zaar Proper. *Dialects:* Sigidi (Sugudi, Sigdi, Segiddi), Zaar (Vikzar, Vigzar, Kal, Gambar Leere, Lusa). Saya dialect cluster in Barawa language cluster. *Other:* Mountain slope.

Agriculturalists: guinea corn, peanuts, sweet potato, acha, rice, yams, cocoyam, maize, cotton, onions, tomato, pepper; weavers; basket makers; gourd carvers; sculptors; leatherwork; hunters. Traditional religion, Christian.

Sha [scw] 3,000 (1998 SIL). Plateau State, Bokkos LGA, Sha District. *Class:* Afro-Asiatic, Chadic, West, A, A.4, Ron Proper. *Lg Dev:* Grammar.

Shakara (Isakara, Tari) [nfk] 3,000 (2003 Blench). Kaduna State, 13 villages. *Class:* Niger-Congo, Atlantic-Congo, Volta-Congo, Benue-Congo, Plateau, Central, West-Central. *Lg Use:* Speakers also use Hausa.

Shall-Zwall [sha] 8,900 (2004). Bauchi State, Dass LGA. *Class:* Niger-Congo, Atlantic-Congo, Volta-Congo, Benue-Congo, Plateau, Beromic. *Dialects:* Shall (Shal), Zwall. Dialect cluster.

Shama-Sambuga (Tushama, Bushama) [sqa] 5,000 (1995 S. and S. Dettweiler). Niger State, Rafi and Mariga LGAs; Kaduna State, Birnin Gwari LGA. *Class:* Niger-Congo, Atlantic-Congo, Volta-Congo, Benue-Congo, Kainji, Western, Kamuku. *Dialects:* Shama, Sambuga. Lexical similarity 64% to 66% with the three Kamuku dialects, 69% with Hungworo, 52% with Eastern Acipa, 16% to 17% with Western Acipa. *Lg Use:* Speakers also use Hausa.

Shamang (Samban, Samang) [xsh] Kaduna State, Kachia and Jema'a LGAs. *Class:* Niger-Congo, Atlantic-Congo, Volta-Congo, Benue-Congo, Plateau, Western, Northwestern, Hyamic. *Dialects:* Related to Hyam.

Shanga (Shangawa, Shonga, Shongawa) [sho] 5,000 (1995). Kebbi State between Kaoje and Yauri, on both sides of the Niger River, but especially on the north bank; Gante, Lafugu, Zaria, Besse, Shanga, Dugu Raha, Dugu Tsofo, Bakin Turu villages. *Class:* Niger-Congo, Mande, Eastern, Eastern, Busa. *Dialects:* Not inherently intelligible with the Busa group. Lexical similarity 70% with Tyenga, 38% to 40% lexical similarity with the Busa group. *Lg Use:* Speakers are shifting to Hausa. *Other:* Traditional religion, Muslim.

Shau (Sho, Lìsháù) [sqh] Bauchi State, Toro LGA, Shau and Mana villages. *Class:* Niger-Congo, Atlantic-Congo, Volta-Congo, Benue-Congo, Kainji, Eastern, Northern Jos, Jera. *Other:* Nearly extinct.

Sheni (Shani, Shaini) [scv] 200 (1925). Kaduna State, Saminaka LGA. *Class:* Niger-Congo, Atlantic-Congo, Volta-Congo, Benue-Congo, Kainji, Eastern, Northern Jos, Jera.

Shiki (Gubi, Guba, Gubawa, Mashiki) [gua] Bauchi State, Bauchi LGA. Gubi and Guru towns north of Bauchi town. *Class:* Niger-Congo, Atlantic-Congo, Volta-Congo, Benue-Congo, Bantoid, Southern, Jarawan, Nigerian. *Dialects:* Gubi, Guru. *Lg Use:* All speakers are older adults (CAPRO 1995:153). Speakers also use Gera or Hausa. *Lg Dev:* Literacy rate in second language: 30% or less. *Other:* Agriculturalists: guinea corn, peanuts, rice, maize, yams; animal husbandry: cattle, sheep. Muslim.

Shoo-Minda-Nye [bcv] 10,000 (1973 SIL). Taraba State, Karim Lamido LGA, villages on the banks of the Benue River. *Class:* Niger-Congo, Atlantic-Congo, Volta-Congo, Benue-Congo, Jukunoid, Central, Jukun-Mbembe-Wurbo, Unclassified. *Dialects:* Shoo (Banda, Bandawa), Minda (Jinleri), Nye (Kunini). *Lg Use:* All 3 dialects are of equal status. Some speakers also use Fulfulde, Hausa, and Jenjo. *Other:* Called 'Bakula' together with Como Karim, Munga, Jiru, and Jessi. Ethnic groups: Banda, Kunini, Lau Habe. Fishermen. Christian, traditional religion, Muslim.

Shuwa-Zamani (Kuzamani, Rishuwa, Kauru) [ksa] 1,000 (1973 SIL). Bauchi State, Toro LGA. *Class:* Niger-Congo, Atlantic-Congo, Volta-Congo, Benue-Congo, Kainji, Eastern, Northern Jos, Kauru.

Siri (Sirawa) [sir] Ethnic population: 3,234 (2000 WCD). Bauchi State, Ningi LGA. *Class:* Afro-Asiatic, Chadic, West, B, B.2. *Lg Use:* Spoken by only a few older adults. *Other:* Agriculturalists: guinea corn, millet, maize, orchards. Muslim, Christian.

Somyev (Somyewe, Kila) [kgt] 15 to 20 (2000 B. Connell). Taraba State, Sardauna LGA, Kila Yang, Njike, Kuma, Jabu, Kikau, and Mayo Daga towns. Apparently extinct in Cameroon. *Class:* Niger-Congo, Atlantic-Congo, Volta-Congo, Benue-Congo, Bantoid, Northern, Mambiloid, Mambila-Konja, Magu-Kamkam-Kila. *Lg Use:* Speakers are older adults. *Other:* They live among the Mambila. Blacksmiths. Muslim. Nearly extinct.

Sorko (Sorogama, Corogama, Sarkanci, Sarkawa, Jenama, Nononke, "Boso" Bozo, Jenaama Bozo) [bze] Niger, Kwara, and Kebbi states, Lake Kainji. *Lg Use:* Those in Nigeria speak Hausa as first language. *Other:* New Sorko speaking groups have been migrating down the river into Nigeria. Fishermen. Muslim. See main entry under Mali (Bozo, Jenaama).

Sukur (Sugur, Adikimmu Sukur, Gemasakun, Sakul) [syk] 14,779 (1992). Northern tip of Adamawa State, Michika LGA, Mandara Mountains. *Class:* Afro-Asiatic, Chadic, Biu-Mandara, A, A.6. *Lg Use:* Speakers use Fulfulde, Hausa, Wula (Psikye), Kamwe, or some English as second languages. Hausa used in most churches. *Other:* Mountain slope. Agriculturalists; animal husbandry. Traditional religion, Christian, Muslim.

Sur (Tapshin, Tapshinawa, Suru, Myet, Nsur, Dishili) [tdl] 5,000 (1998 Blench). Bauchi State, Tafawa Balewa LGA; Plateau State, Pankshin LGA. *Class:* Niger-Congo, Atlantic-Congo, Volta-Congo, Benue-Congo, Plateau, Tarokoid. *Lg Use:* Speakers also use Ngas. *Other:* Traditional religion.

Surubu (Srubu, Fiti, Skrubu, Zurubu) [sde] 7,173 (2000 WCD). Kaduna State, Saminaka LGA. *Class:* Niger-Congo, Atlantic-Congo, Volta-Congo, Benue-Congo, Kainji, Eastern, Northern Jos, Kauru.

Tal (Amtul, Kwabzak) [tal] 10,000 (1973 SIL). Plateau State, Pankshin LGA. *Class:* Afro-Asiatic, Chadic, West, A, A.3, Angas Proper, 2. *Dialects:* Related to Montol, Goemai, Pyapun, Koenoem.

Tala [tak] 1,000 (1993). Bauchi State, Bauchi LGA, Kuka and Talan Kasa villages. *Class:* Afro-Asiatic, Chadic, West, B, B.3, Guruntum. *Other:* Agriculturalists: guinea corn, maize; animal husbandry: livestock. Traditional religion, Christian.

Tamajaq, Tawallammat (Tamasheq, Tomacheck, Tahoua Tamajeq, Tuareg, Buzu, Azbinawa) [ttq] Few speakers in Nigeria. A few villages in the far northwest in Sokoto State. *Dialect:* Ioullemmeden. *Other:* Only seasonal migrants and laborers. No resident villages. It may be the eastern rather than the western dialect in Nigeria. Muslim. See main entry under Niger.

Tambas (Tambes, Tembis) [tdk] 3,000 (2001 Blench). Plateau State, Pankshin LGA. *Class:* Afro-Asiatic, Chadic, West, A, A.4, Fyer.

Tangale (Tangle) [tan] 130,000 (1995 CAPRO). Gombe State, Billiri, Kaltungo, Akko, and Balanga LGAs. *Class:* Afro-Asiatic, Chadic, West, A, A.2, Tangale, Tangale Proper. *Dialects:* Kaltungo, Biliri, Shongom, Ture. *Lg Dev:* Dictionary. Grammar. NT: 1932–1963. *Other:* Agriculturalists: guinea corn, peanuts, maize, beans, millet, cotton, rice; small businesses. Christian, traditional religion.

Tanjijili (Jijili, Ujijili, Koro Funtu of Kafin Koro, Koro Funtu of Minna, Koro of Shakoyi) [uji] 8,540 (2000 WCD). Niger State, Chanchaga and Suleija LGAs, on the road from Minna to Abuja at Kafin Koro, about 10 villages. *Class:* Niger-Congo, Atlantic-Congo, Volta-Congo, Benue-Congo, Plateau, Southern. *Other:* All the alternate names listed, except 'Tanjijili', are names of the people.

Tarok (Yergam, Yergum, Appa) [yer] 300,000 (1998 Blench). Plateau State, Kanam, Wase, and Langtang LGAs; Gongola State, Wukari LGA. *Class:* Niger-Congo, Atlantic-Congo, Volta-Congo, Benue-Congo, Plateau, Tarokoid. *Dialects:* Izini (Hill Tarok), Itarok (Plain Tarok), Selyer, Itarok Oga Asa, Igyang. *Lg Dev:* Literacy rate in first language: 5% to 10%. Literacy rate in second language: 50% to 75%. Literacy program in progress. Dictionary. NT: 1988.

Tedaga [tuq] 2,000 in Nigeria (1990 Blench). Borno State, northeastern LGAs, a few villages. *Dialect:* Kecherda. *Other:* 'Teda' is the name for the people. Muslim. See main entry under Chad.

Tee (Tai) [tkq] Rivers State, Tai LGA. *Class:* Niger-Congo, Atlantic-Congo, Volta-Congo, Benue-Congo, Cross River, Delta Cross, Ogoni, East. *Dialects:* Previously regarded as a dialect of Khana. Has a number of sounds not found in Khana. *Lg Dev:* Dictionary.

Teme (Tema) [tdo] 4,000 (1995). Adamawa State, Mayo Belwa LGA, along the banks of the Mayo Belwa River. *Class:* Niger-Congo, Atlantic-Congo, Volta-Congo, North, Adamawa-Ubangi, Adamawa, Leko-Nimbari, Mumuye-Yandang, Mumuye. *Lg Use:* Speakers use Hausa or Fulfulde as second language. Some can speak Sate (Kumba), Yendang, or Gengle. *Lg Dev:* Literacy rate in second language: Low. *Other:* Agriculturalists. Traditional religion, Muslim.

Tera [ttr] 100,620 (2000 WCD). Bauchi State, Yamaltu-Deba LGA; Borno State, Kwayakusar LGA. *Class:* Afro-Asiatic, Chadic, Biu-Mandara, A, A.1, Western. *Dialects:* Nyimatli (Nyemathi, Yamaltu, Nimalto, Nyimatali), Pidlimdi (Hina, Hinna, Ghuna, Ghena), Bura Kokura. Dialect cluster. *Lg Use:* Speakers also use Hausa. *Lg Dev:* Grammar. Bible portions: 1930. *Other:* Agriculturalists: guinea corn, millet, maize, rice, wheat, orchards; fishermen; weavers.

Teshenawa [twc] Extinct. Jigawa State, Keffin Hausa LGA, Teshena town. *Class:* Afro-Asiatic, Chadic, West, B, B.1, Bade Proper.

Tha (Joole Manga, Kapawa) [thy] 1,000 (1998 Kleinewillinghöfer). Taraba State, near Lau. *Class:* Niger-Congo, Atlantic-Congo, Volta-Congo, North, Adamawa-Ubangi, Adamawa, Waja-Jen, Jen.

Tita (Hoai Petel) [tdq] 3,416 (2000 WCD). Taraba State, Jalingo LGA, at Hoai Petel. *Class:* Niger-Congo, Atlantic-Congo, Volta-Congo, Benue-Congo, Jukunoid, Central, Jukun-Mbembe-Wurbo, Wurbo. *Other:* May be extinct.

Tiv ("Munshi") [tiv] 2,212,000 in Nigeria (1991 UBS). Benue State, Makurdi, Gwer, Gboko Kwande, Vandeikya, and Katsina Ala LGAs; Plateau State, Lafia LGA; Taraba State, Bali, Takum, and Wukari LGAs. A few in Cameroon. Also spoken in Cameroon. *Class:* Niger-Congo, Atlantic-Congo, Volta-Congo, Benue-Congo, Bantoid, Southern, Tivoid. *Lg Use:* Used as a language of wider communication. *Lg Dev:* Taught in primary schools. Dictionary. Grammar. Bible: 1964. *Other:* "Munshi" is a perjorative name. Christian, traditional religion.

Toro (Turkwam) [tdv] 3,928 (2000 WCD). Nasarawa State, Akwanga LGA, northeast of Wamba, Turkwam village. *Class:* Niger-Congo, Atlantic-Congo, Volta-Congo, Benue-Congo, Plateau. *Lg Use:* Vigorous. They identify culturally with the Kantana.

Tsikimba (Agaushi, Auna, Kimba, Akimba, Kambari, Kamberri, Kamberchi) [kdl] 100,000 (2004 SIL). Niger State, Magama and Mariga LGAs, Auna and Wara areas, just west of Kainji Lake on the Niger River. *Class:* Niger-Congo, Atlantic-Congo, Volta-Congo, Benue-Congo, Kainji, Western, Kambari. *Dialects:* Agaunshe, Ashen.

A member of the Kambari cluster, which includes Tsishingini and Cishingini. *Lg Use:* All ages. Speakers also use Hausa, English, or other Kambari languages. *Lg Dev:* Literacy rate in first language: 5%. Literacy rate in second language: 20% Hausa. Bible portions: 2001. *Other:* Speakers are called 'Akimba'. Muslim, traditional religion, Christian.

Tsishingini (Kambari, Kamberri, Kamberchi, Salka, Ashingini) [tsw] 100,000 (2004 SIL). Niger State, Magama and Mariga LGAs, Salka area. *Class:* Niger-Congo, Atlantic-Congo, Volta-Congo, Benue-Congo, Kainji, Western, Kambari. *Dialect:* Ibeto. A member of the Kambari language cluster, which includes Cishingini and Tsikimba. *Lg Use:* All ages. Speakers also use Hausa, English, or other Kambari languages. *Lg Dev:* Literacy rate in first language: below 5%. Literacy rate in second language: 15% to 20% Hausa. Grammar. Bible portions: 1933–2001. *Other:* Speakers are called 'Ashingini'. Area opened by large dam. Primarily rural. Christian, Muslim, traditional religion.

Tso (Lotsu-Piri, Cibbo, Tsóbó, Cuyi Tsó, Pire, Piri, Kitta) [ldp] 16,000 (1992 CAPRO). Adamawa State, Numan LGA; Bauchi State, Kaltungo LGA. *Class:* Niger-Congo, Atlantic-Congo, Volta-Congo, North, Adamawa-Ubangi, Adamawa, Waja-Jen, Waja, Cham-Mona. *Dialects:* Berbou, Gusubou, Swabou.

Tsuvadi (Avadi, Abadi, Evadi, Kamberi, Ibeto) [tvd] 150,000 (1998). Niger State, Bangi, Kontagora, and Rijau LGAs. *Class:* Niger-Congo, Atlantic-Congo, Volta-Congo, Benue-Congo, Kainji, Western, Kambari. *Lg Dev:* Literacy rate in second language: 2%. Bible portions: 1997–2001. *Other:* The people are called 'Avadi'.

Tula (Kotule, Kutule) [tul] 30,000 (1998 Kleinewillinghöfer). Gombe State, Kaltungo LGA, 30 km east of Billiri. *Class:* Niger-Congo, Atlantic-Congo, Volta-Congo, North, Adamawa-Ubangi, Adamawa, Waja-Jen, Waja, Tula. *Dialects:* Kutule, Baule, Yili. *Lg Dev:* Grammar. Bible portions: 1929. *Other:* Several primary and secondary schools. Agriculturalists: guinea corn, maize, peanuts, millet, beans, fruits.

Tumi (Tutumi, Kitimi) [kku] 2,266 (2000 WCD). Kaduna State, Saminaka LGA. *Class:* Niger-Congo, Atlantic-Congo, Volta-Congo, Benue-Congo, Kainji, Eastern, Northern Jos, Kauru.

Tyap (Katab, Kataf) [kcg] 130,000 (1993 SIL). Kaduna State, Kachia, Saminaka, and Jema'a LGAs. *Class:* Niger-Congo, Atlantic-Congo, Volta-Congo, Benue-Congo, Plateau, Central, South-Central. *Dialects:* Kafanchan (Fantuan, Kpashan), Kachichere (Aticherak, Daroro), Katab (Atyap, Tyap), Kagoro (Agwolok, Agolok, Agwot, Aguro), Atakat (Atakar, Attaka, Attakar, Takat), Sholio (Asholio, Asolio, Osholio, Aholio, Marwa, Morwa, Moroa, Maruwa, Maroa). *Lg Dev:* Literacy rate in first language: below 1%. Literacy rate in second language: 25% to 50%. Bible portions: 1940. *Other:* An important district language.

Ubaghara [byc] 30,000 (1985 UBS). Population includes 24,000 Biakpan. Cross River State, Akampka LGA. *Class:* Niger-Congo, Atlantic-Congo, Volta-Congo, Benue-Congo, Cross River, Delta Cross, Upper Cross, Central, North-South, Ubaghara-Kohumono, Ubaghara. *Dialect:* Biakpan, Ikun, Etono, Ugbem, Utuma (Utama, Utamu). Dialect cluster. *Lg Dev:* Bible portions: 1984.

Ubang [uba] 3,416 (2000 WCD). Cross River State, Obudu LGA. *Class:* Niger-Congo, Atlantic-Congo, Volta-Congo, Benue-Congo, Cross River, Bendi.

Uda [uda] 10,000 (1988). Akwa Ibom State, Mbo LGA. *Class:* Niger-Congo, Atlantic-Congo, Volta-Congo, Benue-Congo, Cross River, Delta Cross, Lower Cross, Obolo, Enwang-Uda. *Dialects:* Listed separately by Crozier and Blench 1992.

Uhami (Ishua) [uha] 13,584 (2000 WCD). Ondo State, Akoko South and Owo LGAs. *Class:* Niger-Congo, Atlantic-Congo, Volta-Congo, Benue-Congo, Edoid, Northwestern, Osse. *Other:* Listed separately from Iyayu by Crozier and Blench 1992.

Ukaan (Ikan, Anyaran, Auga, Kakumo) [kcf] 18,000 (1973 SIL). Ondo State, Akoko North LGA, towns of Kakumo-Akoko, Auga, Ishe; Edo State, Akoko Edo LGA, town of Anyaran, Kakumo-Aworo. *Class:* Niger-Congo, Atlantic-Congo, Volta-Congo, Benue-Congo, Ukaan. *Dialects:* Ishe, Kakumo, Auga. *Lg Use:* Yoruba is lingua franca.

Ukpe-Bayobiri [ukp] 12,000 (1973 SIL). Cross River State, Obudu and Ikom LGAs. *Class:* Niger-Congo, Atlantic-Congo, Volta-Congo, Benue-Congo, Cross River, Bendi. *Dialects:* Ukpe, Bayobiri. Dialect cluster.

Ukpet-Ehom (Akpet-Ehom) [akd] 11,386 (2000 WCD). Cross River State, Akamkpa LGA. *Class:* Niger-Congo, Atlantic-Congo, Volta-Congo, Benue-Congo, Cross River, Delta Cross, Upper Cross, Akpet. *Dialects:* Ukpet (Akpet), Ehom (Ubeteng, Ebeteng). A dialect cluster.

Ukue (Ukpe, Ekpenmi, Ekpenmen, Epinmi) [uku] 14,085 (2000 WCD). Ondo State, Akoko South LGA. *Class:* Niger-Congo, Atlantic-Congo, Volta-Congo, Benue-Congo, Edoid, Northwestern, Osse. *Dialects:* Related to Ehuen.

Ukwa [ukq] 100 (2004). Cross River State, Akampka LGA. *Class:* Niger-Congo, Atlantic-Congo, Volta-Congo, Benue-Congo, Cross River, Delta Cross, Lower Cross, Obolo, Efik. *Dialects:* Listed separately by Crozier and Blench 1992.

Ukwuani-Aboh-Ndoni [ukw] 150,000 (1973 SIL). Delta State, Ndokwa LGA; Rivers State, Ogba-Egbema-Ndoni LGA. *Class:* Niger-Congo, Atlantic-Congo, Volta-Congo, Benue-Congo, Igboid, Igbo. *Dialects:* Ukwuani (Ukwani, Ukwali, Kwale), Abo (Aboh, Eboh), Ndoni. A dialect cluster within the Igbo language cluster. *Lg Dev:* Grammar.

Ulukwumi [ulb] 10,000 (1992 Crozier and Blench). Delta State, Aniocha and Oshimili LGAs. *Class:* Niger-Congo, Atlantic-Congo, Volta-Congo, Benue-Congo, Defoid, Yoruboid, Edekiri.

Umon (Amon) [umm] 20,000 (1995). Cross River State, Akampka LGA, 25 villages. *Class:* Niger-Congo, Atlantic-Congo, Volta-Congo, Benue-Congo, Cross River, Delta Cross, Upper Cross, Central, North-South, Ubaghara-Kohumono, Kohumono. *Lg Dev:* Bible portions: 1895.

Uneme (Uleme, Ileme, Ineme) [une] 19,846 (2000 WCD). Edo State, Etsako, Agbazko, and Akoko-Edo LGAs. *Class:* Niger-Congo, Atlantic-Congo, Volta-Congo, Benue-Congo, Edoid, North-Central, Ghotuo-Uneme-Yekhee.

Uokha [uok] North and west of Afuze, Owan LGA. *Class:* Niger-Congo, Atlantic-Congo, Volta-Congo, Benue-Congo, Edoid, North-Central.

Urhobo ("Sobo") [urh] 546,000 (1993 Johnstone). Delta State, Ethiope and Ughelli LGAs. *Class:* Niger-Congo, Atlantic-Congo, Volta-Congo, Benue-Congo, Edoid, Southwestern. *Dialects:* Agbarho, Ujevwe, Agbon, Udu. *Lg Dev:* Taught in primary schools. Bible: 1977. *Other:* "Sobo" is offensive.

Usaghade (Usakade, Usakedet, Isangele) [usk] Cross River State, Odukpani LGA, half of a village. In and around Calabar. See main entry under Cameroon.

Uvbie ("Evhro," Uvhria, Uvwie, Evrie, Effurun) [evh] 19,801 (2000 WCD). Delta State, Ethiope LGA. *Class:* Niger-Congo, Atlantic-Congo, Volta-Congo, Benue-Congo, Edoid, Southwestern. *Dialects:* Related to Urhobo. *Other:* The name "Evhro" is offensive.

Uzekwe (Ezekwe) [eze] 5,000 (1973 SIL). Cross River State, Ogoja LGA. *Class:* Niger-Congo, Atlantic-Congo,

Volta-Congo, Benue-Congo, Cross River, Delta Cross, Upper Cross, Central, North-South, Koring-Kukele, Kukele.

Vaghat-Ya-Bijim-Legeri (Kwanka) [bij] 20,000 (2003). Plateau State, Mangu LGA; Bauchi State, Tafawa Balewa LGA, 10 villages 20 km south of Tafawa Balewa. *Class:* Niger-Congo, Atlantic-Congo, Volta-Congo, Benue-Congo, Plateau, Western, Southwestern, A. *Dialects:* Vaghat (Tivaghat, Kadun, Kwanka), Ya (Tiya, Boi), Bijim, Legeri. Dialect cluster. *Other:* Traditional religion, Christian.

Vemgo-Mabas [vem] 10,000 in Nigeria (1993). Population total all countries: 15,000. Adamawa State, Michika LGA, Madagali District. Also spoken in Cameroon. *Class:* Afro-Asiatic, Chadic, Biu-Mandara, A, A.4, Lamang. *Dialect:* Vemgo, Mabas, Visik (Vizik). 56% intelligibility of Lamang, 36% intelligibility of Hedi. Possibly intelligible with Mafa. Lexical similarity 78% with Hide, 64% with Lamang, 50% with Gvoko. *Lg Use:* Speakers use Fulfulde, Mafa, or Wula (Psikye) as second language. Some speak Hide. *Other:* 'Maya' may be an alternate name. Different from Maba of Chad. Pastoralists; agriculturalists. Traditional religion, Christian.

Viti (Vötö) [vit] Taraba State, Sardauna LGA, Antere. *Class:* Niger-Congo, Atlantic-Congo, Volta-Congo, Benue-Congo, Bantoid, Southern, Wide Grassfields, Narrow Grassfields, Unclassified.

Vono (Kiballo, Kiwollo) [kch] 500 (1973 SIL). Kaduna State, Saminaka LGA. *Class:* Niger-Congo, Atlantic-Congo, Volta-Congo, Benue-Congo, Kainji, Eastern, Northern Jos, Kauru.

Voro (Ebina, Ebuna, Buna, Bena, Woro, Yungur) [vor] Adamawa State, Guyuk and Song LGAs, south of the Dumne road, Waltande and associated hamlets. *Class:* Niger-Congo, Atlantic-Congo, Volta-Congo, North, Adamawa-Ubangi, Adamawa, Waja-Jen, Yungur, Yungur-Roba.

Vute (Mbute, Mbutere, Bute, Wute, Fute, Buti, Babute, Mfuti, Wetere, Vutere) [vut] 1,000 in Nigeria (1973 SIL). Taraba State, Sardauna LGA, Northeast Mambila Plateau. See main entry under Cameroon.

Waja (Wiyaa, Wuya, Nyan Wiyau) [wja] 60,000 (1989 Kleinewillinghöfer). Gombe State, Balanga, Akko, Yamaltu Deba LGAs; Adamawa State, northern Michika LGA; Borno State, Gwoza LGA; Taraba State, Bali LGA. *Class:* Niger-Congo, Atlantic-Congo, Volta-Congo, North, Adamawa-Ubangi, Adamawa, Waja-Jen, Waja, Tula. *Dialects:* Deruwo (Wajan Dutse), Waja (Wajan Kasa). Only small dialect differences. *Lg Use:* Speakers also use Fulfulde. *Lg Dev:* Grammar. Bible portions: 1926–1935. *Other:* Agriculturalists: wheat, guinea corn, maize, rice; hunters; animal husbandry: cattle, goats, sheep. Traditional religion, Christian, Muslim.

Waka [wav] 5,000 (1992). Taraba State, Karim Lamido LGA. *Class:* Niger-Congo, Atlantic-Congo, Volta-Congo, North, Adamawa-Ubangi, Adamawa, Leko-Nimbari, Mumuye-Yandang, Mumuye.

Wandala (Mandara, Ndara) [mfi] 20,000 in Nigeria (1993). Population includes 10,000 Gamargu, 9,300 Kirawa. Borno State, Damboa, Bama, Gwoza, and Konduga LGAs. *Dialects:* Kamburwama, Masfeima, Jampalam, Ziogba, Mazagwa, Gwanje, Gamargu (Gamergu, Malgo, Malgwa), Kirawa. *Lg Use:* Vigorous. Some speak Hausa or English. *Other:* Muslim, traditional religion. See main entry under Cameroon.

Wannu (Awannu, Abinsi, Jukun Abinsi, River Jukun) [jub] 4,000. A few thousand (1998 Storch). Gongola State, Makurdi Division, Iharev District at Abinsi town. *Class:* Niger-Congo, Atlantic-Congo, Volta-Congo, Benue-Congo, Jukunoid, Central, Jukun-Mbembe-Wurbo, Kororofa. *Dialects:* A member of the Kororofa language cluster. *Other:* Traditional religion.

Wapan (Jukun Wukari, Wukari, Wakari, Wapã, Jukun Wapan, Juku, Jukum, Jukon, Juku Junkun, Jinkum) [juk] 100,000 (1994 UBS). Taraba State, Wukari LGA; Plateau State, Shendam and Langtang LGAs; Nasarawa State, Lafia and Awe LGAs. *Class:* Niger-Congo, Atlantic-Congo, Volta-Congo, Benue-Congo, Jukunoid, Central, Jukun-Mbembe-Wurbo, Kororofa. *Dialect:* Wukan. A member of the Kororofa language cluster. *Lg Dev:* NT: 1994. *Other:* Traditional religion.

Wãpha (Wase, Wase Tofa) [juw] 1,605 (2000 WCD). Plateau State, Shendam, Wase LGA, Wase Tofa village, and Kumbur village, Langtang LGA. *Class:* Niger-Congo, Atlantic-Congo, Volta-Congo, Benue-Congo, Jukunoid, Central, Jukun-Mbembe-Wurbo, Jukun. *Other:* In Jukun language cluster. Traditional religion.

Warji (Warja, Warjawa, Sar, Sarawa) [wji] 77,665 (2000 WCD). Bauchi State, Ningi LGA; Jigawa State, Birnin Kudu LGA. *Class:* Afro-Asiatic, Chadic, West, B, B.2. *Dialects:* Gala may be a dialect. *Lg Use:* Speakers are shifting to Hausa. *Lg Dev:* Literacy rate in second language: 10%. *Other:* Agriculturalists: guinea corn, maize, peanuts, beans, rice, millet, wheat, onions, pepper, tomato. Traditional religion, Muslim, Christian.

Wom (Pere, Perema, Pereba) [wom] 5,000 (1989 Blench). Adamawa State, Fufore LGA. *Class:* Niger-Congo, Atlantic-Congo, Volta-Congo, North, Adamawa-Ubangi, Adamawa, Leko-Nimbari, Leko. *Dialects:* Close to Samba Leko. *Other:* It is reported that they intermarry with Mom Jango speakers. 'Wom' is a town name. Traditional religion, Christian, Muslim.

Yace (Yache, Yatye, Iyace, Ekpari) [ekr] 50,000 (2002). Cross River State, Yala Local Government Area, Osina, Imbuor, Aliforkpa (Ewor), Wonyer, Maa (formerly Ijiegu). *Class:* Niger-Congo, Atlantic-Congo, Volta-Congo, Benue-Congo, Idomoid, Yatye-Akpa. *Dialects:* Alifokpa, Ijiegu. Lexical similarity 84% with Akpa. *Lg Use:* Speakers also use Yala, Bekwarra, Tiv, or Igede. *Lg Dev:* Bible portions: 1980.

Yala (Iyala) [yba] 50,000 (1973 SIL). Cross River State, Ogoja, Obubra, and Ikom LGAs. *Class:* Niger-Congo, Atlantic-Congo, Volta-Congo, Benue-Congo, Idomoid, Akweya, Etulo-Idoma, Idoma. *Dialects:* Nkum (Yala Ikom), Nkum Akpambe (Yala Obubra), Yala Ogoja. *Lg Dev:* Grammar. NT: 1979.

Yamba (Mbem, "Kaka") [yam] Few speakers in Nigeria (1990 Blench). Taraba State, Sardauna and Gashaka LGAs, Antere, and other border villages. See main entry under Cameroon.

Yangkam (Yankam, Basharawa, Bashiri, Bashar) [bsx] 100 (1996 Blench). Plateau State, Kanam, Langtang, and Wase LGAs, west of Bashar, 25 km north of Jarme on the Amper-Bashar road. 4 villages: Tukur, Bayar, Pyaksam, and Kiram; and 2 older adult men in Yuli, 15 km northwest of Bashar. *Class:* Niger-Congo, Atlantic-Congo, Volta-Congo, Benue-Congo, Plateau, Tarokoid. *Dialects:* Close to Pe. *Lg Use:* Most have shifted to Hausa, while still retaining their Bashar identity. All speakers older than 50 years (1996). *Other:* Heavily influenced by 19th century slave raids. Muslim.

Yedina (Boudouma, Buduma, Yedana, Yedima, Yidana) [bdm] 3,000 in Nigeria. Borno State, on islands in Lake Chad. *Dialect:* Buduma, Kuri (Kouri, Kakaa). *Other:* Seminomadic. Pastoralists; fishermen. Muslim, traditional religion. See main entry under Chad (Buduma).

Yekhee (Etsako, Etsakor, Afenmai, Iyekhee, "Kukuruku") [ets] 274,000 (1995 UBS). Edo State, Etsako, Agbako, and Okpebho LGAs. *Class:* Niger-Congo, Atlantic-Congo, Volta-Congo, Benue-Congo, Edoid, North-Central, Ghotuo-Uneme-Yekhee. *Dialects:* Auchi, Uzairue, South Ibie (South Ivbie), Uwepa-Uwano (Weppa Wano), Avianwu (Fugar), Aviele, Ivhiadaobi, Ekperi. *Lg Dev:*

Bible portions: 1980. *Other:* Not all speakers of the language recognize 'Yekhee' as the name of the language; some prefer 'Etsako'. However, 'Etsako' is not the only language listed as being spoken in Etsako LGA. The name "Kukuruku" is derogatory.

Yendang (Yendam, Yandang, Nyandang, Yundum) [yen] 62,640 (1987). Adamawa State, Mayo Belwa and Numan LGAs; Taraba State, Yoro, Jalingo, Zing, and Karim Lamido LGAs. *Class:* Niger-Congo, Atlantic-Congo, Volta-Congo, North, Adamawa-Ubangi, Adamawa, Leko-Nimbari, Mumuye-Yandang, Yandang. *Dialects:* Kuseki, Yofo, Poli (Akule, Yakule), Yoti. *Lg Use:* Speakers also use Hausa, Fulfulde, Mumuye, or English. *Other:* Agriculturalists; animal husbandry.

Yeskwa (Yasgua) [yes] 13,000 (1973 SIL). Kaduna State, Jema'a LGA; Nasarawa State, Keffi LGA. *Class:* Niger-Congo, Atlantic-Congo, Volta-Congo, Benue-Congo, Plateau, Western, Northwestern, Koro. *Dialects:* Panda, Nyenkpa, Tattara, Bede, Buzi. *Other:* Tattara is said to be the 'standard' form of Yeskwa.

Yiwom (Gerka, Gerkawa, Gerkanchi, Gurka) [gek] 14,050 (2000). Plateau State, Shendam and Langtang South LGAs. *Class:* Afro-Asiatic, Chadic, West, A, A.3, Yiwom. *Lg Dev:* Radio programs.

Yoruba (Yooba, Yariba) [yor] 18,850,000 in Nigeria (1993 Johnstone). Population total all countries: 19,327,000. Most of Oyo, Ogun, Ondo Osun, Kwara, and Lagos states; and western LGAs of Kogi State. Also spoken in Benin, Togo, United Kingdom, USA. *Class:* Niger-Congo, Atlantic-Congo, Volta-Congo, Benue-Congo, Defoid, Yoruboid, Edekiri. *Dialects:* Oyo, Ijesha, Ila, Ijebu, Ondo, Wo, Owe, Jumu, Iworro, Igbonna, Yagba, Gbedde, Egba, Akono, Aworo, Bunu (Bini), Ekiti, Ilaje, Ikale, Awori. *Lg Use:* Official language in southwest. Used for government notices. 2,000,000 second-language speakers. *Lg Dev:* Literacy rate in second language: 35%. Taught in primary and secondary schools. Roman script. Newspapers. Radio programs. TV. Dictionary. Grammar. Bible: 1884–1966. *Other:* SVO. Christian, Muslim, traditional religion.

Yukuben (Nyikuben, Nyikobe, Ayikiben, Boritsu, Balaabe, Balaaben, Oohum, Uuhum, Uuhum-Gigi, Uhumkhegi) [ybl] 15,000 in Nigeria (1992). Population total all countries: 15,950. Taraba State, Takum LGA, between the Katsina Ala and Gamana rivers. About 20 villages in Nigeria. Also spoken in Cameroon. *Class:* Niger-Congo, Atlantic-Congo, Volta-Congo, Benue-Congo, Jukunoid, Yukuben-Kuteb. *Lg Use:* Trade language. Speakers use Jukun, Kuteb (in areas close to Kuteb), or Hausa as second languages. Many women, especially in the mountains, do not understand Hausa. *Other:* Traditional religion, Christian.

Zangwal (Zwangal, Twar) [zah] 100 (1993). Bauchi State, Bauchi LGA. *Class:* Afro-Asiatic, Chadic, West, B, B.3, Guruntum. *Other:* Agriculturalists: millet, peanuts, guinea corn. Muslim.

Zari (Zariwa) [zaz] 20,746 (2000 WCD). Population includes 20,000 Zakshi (1995 CAPRO), 1,000 Boto. Bauchi State, Toro, Dass, and Tafawa Balewa LGAs, and Plateau State. *Class:* Afro-Asiatic, Chadic, West, B, B.3, Zaar Proper. *Dialects:* Zakshi (Zaksa), Boto (Boot, Bibot), Zari (Kopti, Kwapm). In the Zari dialect cluster in the Barawa language cluster. *Other:* Traditional religion, Muslim, Christian.

Zarma (Dyerma, Dyarma, Dyabarma, Zabarma, Adzerma, Djerma, Zarbarma, Zerma) [dje] 87,800 in Nigeria (2000). Kebbi State, Argungu, Birnin Kebbi, and Bunza LGAs; north of Mokwa in villages along the road to Kontagora in Niger State; several villages north of Nguru in Yobe State. *Dialect:* Kaado. *Other:* Muslim. See main entry under Niger.

Zeem [zua] 1,708 (2000 WCD). Bauchi State, Toro LGA. *Class:* Afro-Asiatic, Chadic, West, B, B.3, Zaar Proper. *Dialects:* Zeem (Tulai), Danshe (Chaari), Lushi (Lukshi, Dokshi). The Zeem dialect cluster in the Barawa language cluster.

Zhire (Kenyi) [zhi] Kaduna State, Kachia and Jema'a LGAs. *Class:* Niger-Congo, Atlantic-Congo, Volta-Congo, Benue-Congo, Plateau, Western, Northwestern, Hyamic. *Dialects:* Related to Hyam.

Ziriya (Jiriya) [zir] Bauchi State, Toro LGA, Kere and Ziriya. *Class:* Niger-Congo, Atlantic-Congo, Volta-Congo, Benue-Congo, Kainji, Eastern, Northern Jos, Jera. *Other:* Nearly extinct.

Zizilivakan (Ziziliveken, Ziliva, Àmzírív, Fali of Jilbu) [ziz] Adamawa State, Mubi LGA, Jilbu town, near Cameroon border. *Other:* People are called 'Fali of Jilbu'. Muslim. See main entry under Cameroon.

Zumbun (Jimbin, Jimbinawa) [jmb] 2,000 (1995 CAPRO). Bauchi State, Darazo LGA, Jimbim settlement. *Class:* Afro-Asiatic, Chadic, West, B, B.2. *Other:* Traditional religion.

Réunion

French Department of Réunion. 766,153. National or official language: French. Literacy rate: 61.2% (1975 WA). Also includes Comorian (9,000), Gujarati, Malagasy (8,000), Chinese (21,000). Information mainly from J. Holm 1989. The number of languages listed for Réunion is 3. Of those, all are living languages.

French [fra] 2,400 in Réunion (1993 Johnstone). *Lg Use:* Official language. 160,500 second-language speakers. See main entry under France.

Réunion Creole French [rcf] 554,500 in Réunion (1987). Population total all countries: 600,000. Also spoken in Comoros, Madagascar. *Class:* Creole, French based. *Dialects:* Two dialects: urban and popular; the former is closer to French, the latter more similar to Bantu and West African languages. *Lg Use:* 25% of the speakers are white, poor, living in the mountainous interior, and speak archaic highland varieties. 25% are Indian, live in the coastal lowlands, and speak the basilect or deep creole. 45% are African and mixed, live in the coastal lowlands, and speak the basilect. The creole is gaining status on Réunion. Education is in French. *Lg Dev:* Dictionary. *Other:* Sugar, perfume production.

Tamil [tam] Including second-language speakers: 120,000 in Réunion (1991 Froise). *Other:* 90% describe themselves as of Indian origin. Hindu. See main entry under India.

Rwanda

Republic of Rwanda. Republika y'u Rwanda. Formerly part of Ruanda-Urundi. 7,954,013. National or official languages: Rwanda, English, French. Literacy rate: 50%. Also includes Rundi, Swahili (10,652). Information mainly from J. Bendor-Samuel 1989. Blind population: 12,000 (1982 WCE). The number of languages listed for Rwanda is 3. Of those, all are living languages.

English [eng] 300 in Rwanda (2004). *Lg Use:* Official language. Mainly second-language speakers in Rwanda. There may be more users of English than of French. See main entry under United Kingdom.

French [fra] 2,300 in Rwanda (2004). *Lg Use:* Official language. See main entry under France.

Rwanda (Ruanda, Kinyarwanda, Ikinyarwanda, Orunyarwanda, Urunyaruanda) [kin] 6,491,700 in Rwanda (1998). Population total all countries: 7,275,292. Also spoken in Burundi, Democratic Republic of the Congo,

Uganda. *Class:* Niger-Congo, Atlantic-Congo, Volta-Congo, Benue-Congo, Bantoid, Southern, Narrow Bantu, Central, J, Rwanda-Rundi (J.60). *Dialects:* Igikiga (Kiga, Tshiga), Bufumbwa, Hutu (Lera, Ululera, Hera, Ndara, Shobyo, Tshogo, Ndogo), Rutwa (Twa). Intelligible with Rundi. *Lg Use:* Official language. Hima is an ethnic group speaking Rwanda or Rundi, not a language. *Lg Dev:* Bible: 1954–1993. *Other:* Ethnic groups: Hutu 89%, Tutsi 10%, Twa (pygmies, 30,000; 1972 Barrett) 1%. Possibly 75% of the Batwa killed in the 1994 war. SVO. Christian, traditional religion, Muslim; Twa: traditional religion, Christian.

Saint Helena

Saint Helena. 7,415. Population includes 5,400 Saint Helena (1985 WA), 262 Tristen de Cunha (1983 WA), 1,500 Ascension (1985 WA). National or official language: English. British dependency. The number of languages listed for Saint Helena is 1.

English [eng] 5,400 in Saint Helena (2004). *Lg Use:* National language. See main entry under United Kingdom.

São Tomé e Príncipe

Democratic Republic of São Tomé and Príncipe. República Democrática de São Tomé e Príncipe. 181,565. National or official languages: Portuguese, Sãotomense, Principense. Literacy rate: 50% to 74%. Also includes Fang (13,771), people from Angola, Cape Verde, Mozambique. Information mainly from J. Holm 1989; P. Maurer 1995; G. Lorenzino 1999; S. and T. Graham 1998. The number of languages listed for São Tomé e Príncipe is 4. Of those, all are living languages. See map on page 700.

Angolar (Ngola) [aoa] 5,000 (1998 S. and T. Graham). Angolar is spoken on the southern tip of São Tomé Island. Most are around the town of São João dos Angolares, and some in the southern region of Caué. *Class:* Creole, Portuguese based. *Dialects:* The substratum was largely Kwa and Western Bantu languages; quite distinct from the creoles of Guinea-Bissau, Senegal, Gambia, and Cape Verde. The 33% of the Angolar lexicon not shared with São Tomense is largely of Bantu origin, apparently Kimbundu of Angola, with some from Kongo, Bini, and Ndingi. Lexical similarity 70% with São Tomense, 67% with Principense, 53% with Annobonese. *Lg Use:* Used in the home and community. Some Angolares speak São Tomense also, and are tending to be absorbed into the Forros. Many speak Portuguese, but many of those are not comfortable in speaking it. *Lg Dev:* Literacy rate in second language: 50% Portuguese. Grammar. *Other:* The Angolares are a distinct ethnolinguistic group from the Forros ('freedmen'). Tonal. Christian.

Portuguese [por] 2,580 in São Tomé (1993). *Lg Use:* Official language. Used by many people as their primary language until their late 20s, when they become more active in São Tomense society, and relearn São Tomense, the language of social networks above age 30. Used as a second language by some people. See main entry under Portugal.

Principense (Lun'gwiye, "Moncó") [pre] 200 (1999 S. Graham). Ethnic population: 1,558. On Príncipe Island. *Class:* Creole, Portuguese based. *Dialects:* The substratum was largely Kwa and Western Bantu languages; quite distinct from the creoles of Guinea-Bissau, Senegal, Gambia, and Cape Verde. Principense shares 77% lexical similarity with São Tomense, 67% with Angolar, 62% with Annobonese. *Lg Use:* National language. Speakers are older adults. Most speak Portuguese, and some learn Sãotomense.

Sãotomense (São Tomense) [cri] 69,899 (1999 S. Graham). São Tomense is spoken on São Tomé Island, all but the southern tip. *Class:* Creole, Portuguese based. *Dialects:* The substratum was largely Kwa and Western Bantu languages; quite distinct from the creoles of Guinea-Bissau, Senegal, Gambia, and Cape Verde. Lexical similarity 77% with Principense, 62% with Fa D'Ambu (Annobonese), 70% with Angolar. *Lg Use:* National language on São Tomé Island. The language of social identity in most São Tomé social networks for age 30 and above. The Angolares are a distinct ethnolinguistic group from the Forros ('freedmen'), Sãotomense speakers also on São Tomé Island. Most Angolares speak Sãotomense also, and are tending to be absorbed into the Forros. Most speak Portuguese. Some older adult women may not understand Portuguese adequately. *Lg Dev:* Literacy rate in second language: 50% Portuguese.

Senegal

Republic of Senegal. République du Sénégal. 10,852,147. National or official languages: Balanta-Ganja, Hassaniyya, Jola-Fonyi, Mandinka, Mandjak, Mankanya, Noon, Pulaar, Serer-Sine, Soninke, Wolof, French. Literacy rate: 21.7% (1988 census), 28.6% men, 15.6% women. Also includes Bambara (74,845), Hassaniyya (6,525), Kabuverdianu (28,135), Krio, Vietnamese. Information mainly from D. Sapir 1971; Atlas National du Senegal 1977; J. Lopis 1980; A. Barry 1987; J. Bendor-Samuel 1989; G. Williams 1993, 2003; B. Hopkins 1995. Blind population: 22,000 (1982 WCE). Deaf institutions: 6. The number of languages listed for Senegal is 36. Of those, all are living languages. See map on page 727.

Badyara (Badian, Badjara, Badjaranke, Pajade, Pajadinca, Pajadinka, Gola, Bigola) [pbp] 1,685 in Senegal (2002). South central, one village that is all Bajara. *Lg Use:* The speakers may use Mandinka as second language. *Other:* Muslim. See main entry under Guinea.

Bainouk-Gunyaamolo (Banyum, Banyun, Bagnoun, Banhum, Bainuk, Banyuk, Banyung, Elomay, Elunay, Ñuñ) [bcz] 5,635 in Senegal (2002). North of the Casamance River in the triangle formed by the towns of Bignona, Tobor, and Niamone, north of Ziguinchor, across the Casamance River. Also spoken in Gambia. *Class:* Niger-Congo, Atlantic-Congo, Atlantic, Northern, Eastern Senegal-Guinea, Banyun. *Dialects:* Gujaaxet, Gunyamoolo. Two dialects are intelligible to each other's speakers: the one around Niamone (Gunyaamolo) and the other around Tobor. Close to Kobiana and Kasanga of Guinea-Bissau. More closely related to the Tenda languages of eastern Senegal than to the neighboring Diola and Balanta. Gunyuño in Guinea-Bissau is distinct. *Lg Dev:* Literacy rate in first language: below 1%. Bible portions: 2003. *Other:* Muslim, traditional religion, Christian.

Bainouk-Samik [bcb] 1,685 (2002). Mainly in Samik and surrounding villages, on the south side of the Casamance River, about 20 km east of Ziguinchor; also in some scattered villages north and east of Samik. *Class:* Niger-Congo, Atlantic-Congo, Atlantic, Northern, Eastern Senegal-Guinea, Banyun.

Balanta-Ganja (Fjaa, Balant, Balante, Balanda, Ballante, Belante, Bulanda, Brassa, Alante, Fraase) [bjt] 106,350 (2002). Southwest corner of Senegal, south of the Casamance River, between Goudomp and Tanaff, and south from there. *Class:* Niger-Congo, Atlantic-Congo, Atlantic, Northern, Bak, Balant-Ganja. *Dialects:* Fganja (Ganja), Fjaalib (Blip). A separate language from Balanta-Kentohe in Guinea-Bissau. *Lg Use:* Official language. Speakers also use Mandinka. *Lg Dev:* Literacy rate in first language: below 1%. *Other:* Traditional religion, Christian.

Bandial (Banjaal) [bqj] 10,125 (2002). Villages of Affiniam, Badiate-Grand, Bandial, Brin, Enampor, Essil, Etama, Kamobeul, and Seleky. The area is bounded by the Casamance River on the north, the Komobeul Bôlon on the west, the Ziguinchor-Oussouye road on the south, and the Brin-Nyassia road on the east. The only village north of the Casamance River is Affiniam. *Class:* Niger-Congo, Atlantic-Congo, Atlantic, Northern, Bak, Jola, Jola Proper, Jola Central, Gusilay. *Dialect:* Affiniam, Bandial, Elun (Hulon, Kuluunaay). Affiniam is more intelligible with Bandial than with Gusilay. Affiniam has 74% lexical similarity with Bandial dialect and 66% with Gusilay. *Lg Use:* Speakers also use Jola-Fonyi, Jola-Kasa, Mandinka, Pulaar, or Wolof. *Lg Dev:* Literacy rate in first language: below 1%.

Bassari (Basari, Tenda Basari, Biyan, Onëyan, Onian, Ayan, Wo) [bsc] 8,835 in Senegal (2002). Population total all countries: 17,910. Southeastern, Upper Casamance, around Edun, border areas, Kedougou, Tambacounda. Also spoken in Guinea, Guinea-Bissau. *Class:* Niger-Congo, Atlantic-Congo, Atlantic, Northern, Eastern Senegal-Guinea, Tenda. *Dialects:* Closely related to Budik. *Lg Dev:* Literacy rate in first language: below 1%. NT: 1988. *Other:* 'Tenda' is used as a cover term for Bassari, Badyara, Konyagi, Budik. High mortality rate. Women intermarry with men from Fulbe and other groups; children become part of the other group. Trading is carried on with the Fulbe. Traditionally hunter-gatherers; now agriculturalists: millet, peanuts, fonyo, beans; in cities: bamboo fence makers; domestic help. Traditional religion, Christian.

Bayot (Baiote, Baiot, Bayotte) [bda] 14,625 in Senegal (2002). Population total all countries: 17,150. A cluster of villages about 12 km southwest of Ziguinchor, grouped around the village of Nyassia. Also spoken in Gambia, Guinea-Bissau. *Class:* Niger-Congo, Atlantic-Congo, Atlantic, Northern, Bak, Jola, Bayot. *Dialect:* Essin. Essin and Bayot form a cluster that needs further investigation. Lexical similarity 15% to 18% with other Jola varieties (closest). *Lg Use:* Speakers use Jola-Kasa as second language, some Wolof, and perhaps Mankanya or Mandjak. *Lg Dev:* Literacy rate in first language: below 1%. *Other:* Traditional religion, Christian.

Budik (Bedik, Tandanke, Tendanke, Tenda, Bande, Basari du Bandemba) [tnr] 3,375 (2002 NTM). Southeastern. *Class:* Niger-Congo, Atlantic-Congo, Atlantic, Northern, Eastern Senegal-Guinea, Tenda. *Dialects:* Close to Bassari. *Lg Dev:* Literacy rate in first language: below 1%. Dictionary. Bible portions: 1997. *Other:* Reported to be a creole with elements from Bassari, Peul, and other languages. Traditional religion, Christian.

Crioulo, Upper Guinea (Portuguese Creole, Kriulo) [pov] 46,500 in Senegal (1998). Ziguinchor, Bignona, and Kolda. It overlaps from Guinea-Bissau and the Bijagos Islands. *Dialect:* Cacheu-Ziguinchor Creole. *Lg Dev:* Literacy rate in first language: below 1%. *Other:* The Senegal dialect is different from Guinea-Bissau, with some Pidgin French vocabulary. Intelligible with Guinea-Bissau Creole. Christian. See main entry under Guinea-Bissau.

Ejamat (Ediamat, Fulup, Feloup, Felup, Felupe, Floup, Flup) [eja] 2,025 in Senegal (2002 SIL). Extreme southern Senegal, a handful of villages 5 to 7 km due south of Oussouye, including Kahem, Efok, Youtou. *Lg Use:* They may use Jola-Kasa and Wolof as second languages. *Lg Dev:* Literacy rate in first language: below 1%. *Other:* Distinct from other Jola varieties. See main entry under Guinea-Bissau.

French [fra] *Lg Use:* Official language. See main entry under France.

Gusilay (Kusiilaay, Gusilaay, Gusiilay, Kusilay) [gsl] 13,950 (2002). Village of Tionk Essil, between Tendouck and Mlomp-North. *Class:* Niger-Congo, Atlantic-Congo, Atlantic, Northern, Bak, Jola, Jola Proper, Jola Central, Gusilay. *Lg Use:* Speakers also use Jola-Fonyi, Wolof, Mandinka, or Pulaar. *Lg Dev:* Literacy rate in first language: below 1%.

Jalunga (Yalunka, Yalunke, Jalonké, Dyalonke, Djallonke, Dialonké) [yal] 11,250 in Senegal (2002 S. Hejnar NTM). Southeastern, intersection of Mali, Guinea, and Senegal borders. *Other:* Called 'Yalunka' in other countries. Muslim. See main entry under Guinea (Yalunka).

Jola-Fonyi (Kújoolaak Kati Fooñi, Kujamataak, Jola-Fogny, Diola-Fogny, Dyola, Jóola, Jola, Yola) [dyo] 292,630 in Senegal (2002). Population includes 209,340 Fonyi, 83,285 Buluf. Population total all countries: 358,276. Area surrounding the city of Bignona, bounded on the south by the Casamance River, on the north by a strip just north of the Senegal-Gambia border, on the west by the Diouloulou-Marigot tributary, and on the east by the Soungrougrou River. Also in an area 15 to 20 km east and southeast of Ziguinchor, the regional capital. Also spoken in Gambia, Guinea-Bissau. *Class:* Niger-Congo, Atlantic-Congo, Atlantic, Northern, Bak, Jola, Jola Proper, Jola Central, Jola-Fonyi. *Dialects:* Buluf, Fonyi, Kombo, Kalounaye, Narang. Gusilay, Kwatay, Karon, Mlomp, Kerak, Ejamat, and Bayot are more distantly related languages, but they are close geographically. Jola-Fonyi is the largest Jola variety and the most widely understood. Lexical similarity 68% with Jola-Kasa. *Lg Use:* Official language. Vigorous. Speakers of Gusilay, Karon, Kwatay, Mlomp, and some Pulaar living in the area speak Jola-Fonyi as second language. All domains, oral and written use in administration, informal use in education. Oral use in commerce, traditional religion, some use in other religious services, oral literature. Positive language attitude. Possibly less than 10% are monolingual. Over 90% also speak Wolof, French, or Mandinka. *Lg Dev:* Literacy rate in first language: below 1%. Buluf seems to have many lexical items different from Fonyi, but Buluf speakers are willing to learn to read Fonyi. Radio programs. TV. Dictionary. Grammar. Bible portions: 2000. *Other:* Distinct from Jula (Dioula, Dyoula, Dyula) of Mali, Burkina Faso, and Côte d'Ivoire, which is Mande. Lightly forested, savannah. Intensive agriculturalists: wet rice, millet, peanuts. Muslim, Christian, traditional religion.

Jola-Kasa (Diola-Kasa, Casa, Jóola-Kasa) [csk] 40,850 in Senegal (2002). Villages around the city of Oussouye and north to the Casamance River, bounded by the Kamobeul Bôlon tributary on the east and the Kachiouane Bôlon on the west. It also includes the villages of Hitou and Niamoun north of the Casamance River. Also spoken in Gambia. *Class:* Niger-Congo, Atlantic-Congo, Atlantic, Northern, Bak, Jola, Jola Proper, Jola Central, Jola-Kasa. *Dialects:* Ayun, Esulalu (Esuulaalur, Oussouye, Mlomp South), Fluvial, Huluf, Selek, Bliss (Niomoun). Close to Jola-Fonyi. *Lg Dev:* Literacy rate in first language: below 1% to 5%. Grammar. Bible portions: 1961–1995.

Karon [krx] 9,070 in Senegal (2002). Population total all countries: 10,420. Southwest Senegal along the coast, south of Diouloulou, and surrounding the town of Kafountine. Bounded on the west by the Atlantic Ocean, on the south by the Kalisseye Inlet, on the east by the Diouloulou Marigot Estuary, and on the north by the Senegal-Gambia border. Also spoken in Gambia. *Class:* Niger-Congo, Atlantic-Congo, Atlantic, Northern, Bak, Jola, Jola Proper, Karon-Mlomp. *Dialects:* Lexical similarity 42% with the closest Jola language. *Lg Use:* Speakers also use Jola-Fonyi or Wolof. *Lg Dev:* Literacy rate in first language: below 1%.

Kerak (Her, Keerak, Keeraku) [hhr] 11,930 (2002). Kabrousse village, extreme southwestern corner of Senegal just before crossing into Guinea-Bissau, and possibly other nearby villages in both countries. *Class:* Niger-Congo, Atlantic-Congo, Atlantic, Northern, Bak, Jola, Jola Proper, Jola Central, Her-Ejamat. *Dialects:* A distinct language from other Jola varieties. Lexical similarity between Kerak and Ejamat was estimated to be 70% by early survey work. More recent estimates put it closer to 90%. *Lg Use:* Speakers may use French and Wolof as second languages. *Lg Dev:* Literacy rate in first language: below 1%.

Kobiana (Cobiana, Uboi, Buy) [kcj] *Lg Use:* Speakers also use Mandyak. *Other:* Traditional religion. See main entry under Guinea-Bissau.

Kuwaataay (Kwatay) [cwt] 5,625 (2002). In Diembering, Bouyouye, Nyikine, Boukot-Diola, and some other villages along the coast just south of the mouth of the Casamance River, and Dakar. *Class:* Niger-Congo, Atlantic-Congo, Atlantic, Northern, Bak, Jola, Jola Proper, Kwatay. *Dialects:* Distinct from other Jola varieties. Lexical similarity 40% with closest Jola language. *Lg Use:* Most speakers can speak or understand Jola-Kasa, Jola-Fonyi, and some Wolof. *Lg Dev:* Literacy rate in first language: below 1%. Dictionary. Grammar. NT: 2000.

Lehar (Lala) [cae] 10,925 (2002). North of Thies in west central Senegal, around the towns of Panbal, Mbaraglov, Dougnan. *Class:* Niger-Congo, Atlantic-Congo, Atlantic, Northern, Cangin. *Dialects:* 52% intelligibility of Non. Lexical similarity 84% with Non, 74% with Safen, 68% with Ndut and Palor, 22% with Serer-Sine. *Lg Use:* Bilingual level estimates for Wolof: 0 0–1%, 1 5%, 2 15%, 3 60%, 4 15%, 5 5%. Some speakers also use Non, Ndut, or French. *Lg Dev:* Literacy rate in first language: below 1%. *Other:* Their name for themselves is 'Lala'. SVO; nontonal. Plains. Savannah. Peasant agriculturalists: peanuts, manioc, tomatoes. Muslim, traditional religion, Christian.

Mandinka (Manding, Mandingo, Mandingue, Mandinque, Mande, Socé) [mnk] 606,645 in Senegal (2002). Population total all countries: 1,214,345. Southeastern and south central. Also spoken in Gambia, Guinea-Bissau. *Class:* Niger-Congo, Mande, Western, Central-Southwestern, Central, Manding-Jogo, Manding-Vai, Manding-Mokole, Manding, Manding-West. *Dialects:* Mandinka, Eastern Maninkakan, and Malinke are separate languages. Lexical similarity 79% with Kalanke, 75% with Jahanka, 70% with Kassonke, 59% with Malinke, 53% with Mori, 48% with Bambara. *Lg Use:* Official language. *Lg Dev:* Literacy rate in first language: below 1%. NT: 1989. *Other:* Muslim.

Mandjak (Mandjaque, Manjaca, Manjaco, Manjak, Manjaku, Manjack, Mandyak, Majak, Ndjak, Kanyop) [mfv] 95,670 in Senegal (2002). Southwest Senegal. *Dialects:* Bok (Kabok, Sara, Teixeira Pinto, Tsaam), Likes-Utsia (Baraa, Kalkus), Cur (Churo), Lund, Yu (Pecixe). *Lg Use:* Official language. *Lg Dev:* Literacy rate in first language: below 1%. *Other:* Traditional religion, Christian. See main entry under Guinea-Bissau.

Maninkakan, Western (Maninka-Western, Maninga, Malinka, Malinke, Western Malinke) [mlq] 382,670 in Senegal (2002). Population total all countries: 495,270. Eastern Senegal. Also spoken in Gambia, Guinea-Bissau, Mali. *Class:* Niger-Congo, Mande, Western, Central-Southwestern, Central, Manding-Jogo, Manding-Vai, Manding-Mokole, Manding, Manding-West. *Dialect:* Jahanka (Jahanque, Jahonque, Diakkanke, Diakhanke, Kyakanke). The Jahanka are reported to have come from Mali in the 18th century. They trace their origins to Soninke, but now speak a dialect of Malinke in Senegal (Western Maninkakan). Vocabulary and grammar differences with Mandinka. Lexical similarity 59% with Mandinka. *Lg Dev:* Literacy rate in first language: below

1%. Arabic script. Grammar. Bible portions: 1997–2003. *Other:* Muslim, traditional religion.

Mankanya (Mancagne, Mancang, Mancanha, Mankanha, Bola) [knf] 26,450 in Senegal (2002). Scattered. *Dialects:* Burama (Bulama, Buram, Brame), Shadal (Sadar). *Lg Use:* Official language. Speakers have a language association (PKUMEL), are developing an orthography and standardizing the language. Extensive bilingualism in Mandjak. *Lg Dev:* Literacy rate in first language: below 1%. *Other:* Traditional religion, Christian. See main entry under Guinea-Bissau.

Mlomp (Mlomp North, Gulompaay) [mlo] 4,895 (2002). Mainly in Mlomp village north of the Casamance River, 25 km due east of Bignona, on the road between Tendouck and Tiobon, Bignona Department, several surrounding villages, and scattered around the country. *Class:* Niger-Congo, Atlantic-Congo, Atlantic, Northern, Bak, Jola, Jola Proper, Karon-Mlomp. *Dialects:* Lexical similarity 64% with Karon (closest), 42% with the closest other Jola language. *Lg Use:* Many speak and understand Jola-Fonyi as second language, some know Wolof, and a few may know Mandinka or Pulaar. *Lg Dev:* Literacy rate in first language: below 1%.

Ndut (Ndoute) [ndv] 35,000 (2002). West central, northwest of Thiès. *Class:* Niger-Congo, Atlantic-Congo, Atlantic, Northern, Cangin. *Dialects:* 32% intelligibility of Palor. Lexical similarity 84% with Palor, 68% with Safen, Non, and Lehar, 22% with Serer-Sine. *Lg Use:* Bilingual level estimates for Wolof: 0 0–1%, 1 5%, 2 15%, 3 60%, 4 15%, 5 5%. Some also use Wolof, Lehar, Safen, or French. *Lg Dev:* Literacy rate in first language: below 1%. *Other:* 'Ndut' is their name for themselves. SVO; nontonal. Plains. Savannah. Peasant agriculturalists: peanuts, manioc, tomatoes, corn. Muslim, Christian, traditional religion.

Noon (None, Non, Serer-Noon) [snf] 29,825 (2002). Surrounding Thiès and in Thiès. Padee is in Fandene, Cangin in Thiès, Saawii north of Thiès. *Class:* Niger-Congo, Atlantic-Congo, Atlantic, Northern, Cangin. *Dialects:* Padee, Cangin, Saawii. Noon is very different from Serer-Sine. 68% intelligibility of Lehar. Lexical similarity 84% with Lehar, 74% with Safen, 68% with Ndut and Palor, 22% with Serer-Sine. *Lg Use:* Official language. Bilingual level estimates for Wolof: 0 0–1%, 1 5%, 2 15%, 3 60%, 4 15%, 5 5%. Wolof is used to communicate with Lehar speakers, and others. Some are also bilingual in French. *Lg Dev:* Literacy rate in first language: below 1%. Grammar. *Other:* 'Noon' is their name for themselves. 'Dyoba' is an alternate name for a family name, not for Noon. 'Serer-Noon' is only used to distinguish them from other languages in a context of the larger cultural group of Serer languages. SVO; nontonal. Plains. Savannah. Peasant agriculturalists. Christian, Muslim.

Palor (Falor, Palar, Sili, Sili-Sili, Waro) [fap] 9,680 (2002). West central, west southwest of Thies. *Class:* Niger-Congo, Atlantic-Congo, Atlantic, Northern, Cangin. *Dialects:* 55% intelligibility of Ndut, 27% of Safen. Lexical similarity 84% with Ndut, 74% with Safen, 68% with Non and Lehar, 22% with Serer-Sine. *Lg Use:* Used in the home. Bilingual level estimates for Wolof: 0 0–1%, 1 5%, 2 15%, 3 60%, 4 15%, 5 5%. Some speakers also use Safen or French. *Lg Dev:* Literacy rate in first language: below 1%. *Other:* 'Waro' is their name for themselves. There are no schools in the area. SVO; nontonal. Plains. Savannah. Peasant agriculturalists: peanuts, manioc, mangoes, tomatoes. Muslim, traditional religion.

Pulaar (Pulaar Fulfulde, Peul, Peulh) [fuc] 2,387,340 in Senegal (2002). Population total all countries: 3,244,020. Fulbe Jeeri and Toucouleur are primarily in the Senegal River Valley and Mauritania. Fulacunda is in the Upper

Casamance Region, from 40 miles west of Kolda to the headwaters of the Gambia River in the east, from the southern border of Senegal in the south to the Gambian border in the north. Also spoken in Gambia, Guinea, Guinea-Bissau, Mali, Mauritania. *Class:* Niger-Congo, Atlantic-Congo, Atlantic, Northern, Senegambian, Fulani-Wolof, Fula, Western. *Dialects:* Toucouleur (Tukolor, Tukulor, Tokilor, Pulaar, Haalpulaar, Fulbe Jeeri), Fulacunda (Fulakunda, Fulkunda). Fulbe Jeeri and Toucouleur (Haalpulaar'en) are separate ethnic groups speaking this form of Pulaar. Jeeri is a geographical region in which a large number of diverse lineages still follow a seminomadic life. There are 3 families subdivided into at least 20 lineages, each of which has some dialect differences; all are inherently intelligible. Bunndu is a Fula geopolitical state composed of a mix of Toucouleur and Fulbe Jeeri. Fuuta Tooro (Fouta Toro) was a major Toucouleur geopolitical state, which has its seat in northern Senegal, and is also in Mauritania. Fulacunda is an ethnic group speaking a closely related dialect of Pulaar. Their region is called Fuladu in the Upper Casamance area of Senegal. Different enough from Pular to need separate literature. There are five Fulfulde varieties in Guinea-Bissau. Related to Maasina Fulfulde. *Lg Use:* Official language. *Lg Dev:* Literacy rate in first language: 10% to 30%. Literacy rate in second language: 15% to 25%. Grammar. NT: 1997. *Other:* Desert. Fulbe Jeeri: seminomadic pastoralists. Muslim.

Pular (Fuuta Jalon, Futa Jallon, Fouta Dyalon, Fullo Fuuta, Futa Fula) [fuf] 136,185 in Senegal (2002). *Lg Use:* Looked upon as outsiders in Senegal. *Lg Dev:* Literacy rate in first language: below 1%. *Other:* Large numbers from Guinea have settled or work seasonally in Casamance, eastern Senegal, and Dakar. Muslim. See main entry under Guinea.

Saafi-Saafi (Sereer Saafen, Serer-Safen, Serere-Saafen, Safi, Saafi, Safi-Safi, Safen) [sav] 117,050 (2002). Southwest of and near Thiès, and to the ocean; the triangle between Diamniadio, Popenguine, and Thiès. 60 villages: 43 are over 80% Saafi, 8 are under 50%. *Class:* Niger-Congo, Atlantic-Congo, Atlantic, Northern, Cangin. *Dialects:* Boukhou, Sebikotane, Sindia, Hasab, Diobass. Dialects are named after villages and a zone (Diobass). Lexical similarity 74% with Non, Lehar, and Palor; 68% with Ndut; 22% with Serer-Sine. *Lg Use:* Trade language in the southern Cangin region. Vigorous. All domains, use with Saafi people, oral tradition. Positive language attitude. Bilingual level estimates for Wolof: 0 1%, 1 5%, 2 15%, 3 60%, 4 15%, 5 5%. Children and very few adults are monolingual. Some speakers are also bilingual in Ndut, French, Serer-Sine, English, Spanish, Pulaar, Palor. Wolof tends to be used in Muslim ceremonies. *Lg Dev:* Literacy rate in first language: below 1%. Literacy rate in second language: 25% in French. Desire for Saafi-Saafi literature. Roman script. Radio programs. *Other:* 'Saafen' is the name of the area, 'Saafi' is the people name. SVO; nontonal. Plains, hills, valleys. Savannah. Peasant agriculturalists: peanuts, manioc, beans, tomatoes, mango, other fruit; jobs in the capital. Muslim, syncretism, traditional religion, Christian.

Serer-Sine (Sérère-Sine, Serer, Serrer, Sereer, Seereer, Serer-Sin, Sine-Saloum, Seex, Sine-Sine) [srr] 1,154,760 in Senegal (2002). Population total all countries: 1,183,120. West central Senegal and the Sine and Saloum river valleys. Also spoken in Gambia. *Class:* Niger-Congo, Atlantic-Congo, Atlantic, Northern, Senegambian, Serer. *Dialects:* Segum, Fadyut-Palmerin, Sine, Dyegueme (Gyegem), Niominka. Niominka and Serere-Sine are inherently intelligible to each other's speakers. *Lg Use:* Official language. *Lg Dev:* Literacy rate in first language: below 1%. NT: 1987. *Other:* 'Sereer' is their

name for themselves. Traditional religion, Muslim, Christian.

Soninke (Marka, Maraka, Sarahole, Sarawule, Serahuli, Silabe, Toubakai, Walpre) [snk] 194,150 in Senegal (2002). Principally north and south of Bakel along the Senegal River. Bakel, Ouaoundé, Moudéri, and Yaféra are the principal towns. *Dialects:* Azer (Adjer, Aser), Gadyaga. *Lg Use:* Official language. *Lg Dev:* Literacy rate in first language: below 1%. *Other:* Muslim. See main entry under Mali.

Wamey (Wamay, Wamei, Konyagi, Coniagui, Conhague, Koniagui) [cou] 16,700 in Senegal (2002). Population total all countries: 21,970. Southeast. Migration from Guinea no longer taking place. Also spoken in Guinea. *Class:* Niger-Congo, Atlantic-Congo, Atlantic, Northern, Eastern Senegal-Guinea, Tenda. *Lg Dev:* Literacy rate in first language: below 1%. *Other:* 'Wamay' is their own name for their language, 'Wamey', the name in Peul, is what others call them. Agriculturalists; making wine, beer; weaving bamboo mats. Traditional religion, Christian.

Wolof (Ouolof, Yallof, Walaf, Volof, Waro-Waro) [wol] 3,568,060 in Senegal (2002). Population total all countries: 3,612,560. Western and central, left bank of Senegal River to Cape Vert. Also spoken in France, Gambia, Guinea-Bissau, Mali, Mauritania. *Class:* Niger-Congo, Atlantic-Congo, Atlantic, Northern, Senegambian, Fula-Wolof, Wolof. *Dialects:* Baol, Cayor, Dyolof (Djolof, Jolof), Lebou (Lebu), Jander. Different from Wolof of Gambia. *Lg Use:* Official language. The main African language of Senegal. Predominantly urban. Speakers also use French or Arabic. *Lg Dev:* Literacy rate in first language: 10%. Literacy rate in second language: 30%. Radio programs. Dictionary. Grammar. NT: 1988. *Other:* 'Wolof' is their name for themselves. Muslim.

Xasonga (Kassonke, Khasonke, Kasonke, Kasson, Kasso, Xaasonga, Xasonke, Xaasongaxango) [kao] 8,170 in Senegal (2002). *Lg Dev:* Literacy rate in first language: below 1%. *Other:* Muslim. See main entry under Mali (Xaasongaxango).e

Seychlles

Republic of Seychelles. 80,832. National or official languages: English, French, Seselwa Creole French. Includes Aldabra, Farquhar, Des Roches; 92 islands. Literacy rate: 62% to 80%. Information mainly from J. Holm 1989; D. Bickerton 1988. Blind population: 150 (1982 WCE). The number of languages listed for Seychelles is 3. Of those, all are living languages.

English [eng] 1,601 in Seychelles (1971 census). *Lg Use:* Official language. *Other:* Principal language of the schools. See main entry under United Kingdom.

French [fra] 977 in Seychelles (1971 census). *Lg Use:* Official language. *Other:* Spoken by the French settler families, 'grands blancs'. See main entry under France.

Seselwa Creole French (Seychellois Creole, Seychelles Creole French, Kreol, Creole, Ilois) [crs] 72,700 (1998). Ethnic population: 72,700. *Class:* Creole, French based. *Dialects:* Seychelles dialect is reported to be the same as Chagos. Structural differences with Mauritius are relatively minor. Not adequately intelligible with Réunion Creole. *Lg Use:* Official language since 1977. All domains, home, community, education, politics, health and social affairs, administration, academic discourse, literature, theater, music, art. The first 4 years of education are in Seselwa. Used for some subjects for 5 more years. Positive language attitude. *Lg Dev:* Taught in primary schools. Roman script. Radio programs. Dictionary. Grammar. NT: 2000. *Other:* Fishermen. Christian.

Sierra Leone

Republic of Sierra Leone. 5,883,889. National or official language: English. Literacy rate: 15%. Also includes Greek (700), people from Lebanon, India, Pakistan, Liberia. Information mainly from D. Dalby 1962; TISSL 1995. Blind population: 28,000 (1982 WCE). Deaf institutions: 5. The number of languages listed for Sierra Leone is 24. Of those, all are living languages. See map on page 728.

Bassa [bsq] 5,000 in Sierra Leone (1991 D. Slager). Freetown. *Other:* Traditional religion. See main entry under Liberia.

Bom (Bome, Bum, Bomo) [bmf] 250 (1991 Slager). Ethnic population: 5,000. Along the Bome River. *Class:* Niger-Congo, Atlantic-Congo, Atlantic, Southern, Mel, Bullom-Kissi, Bullom, Northern. *Lg Use:* Speakers are shifting to Mende. *Other:* Traditional religion.

Bullom So (Northern Bullom, Bolom, Bulem, Bullun, Bullin, Mmani, Mandingi, Mandenyi) [buy] 500 in Sierra Leone (1988 Vanderaa). Ethnic population: 6,800. Along the coast from the Guinea border to the Sierra Leone River. Also spoken in Guinea. *Class:* Niger-Congo, Atlantic-Congo, Atlantic, Southern, Mel, Bullom-Kissi, Bullom, Northern. *Dialects:* Mmani, Kafu. Bom is closely related. Little intelligibility of Sherbro, none of Krim. Bom has 66% to 69% lexical similarity with Sherbro dialects, 34% with Krim. *Lg Use:* Speakers shifting to Temne. *Lg Dev:* Bible portions: 1816. *Other:* The people are intermarried with the Temne and the Susu. Traditional religion.

English [eng] *Lg Use:* Official language. Used in administration, law, education, commerce. See main entry under United Kingdom.

Gola (Gula) [gol] 8,000 in Sierra Leone (1989 TISLL). Along the border and a few miles into Sierra Leone. *Dialects:* De (Deng), Managobla (Gobla), Kongbaa, Kpo, Senje (Sene), Tee (Tege), Toldil (Toodii). *Lg Use:* Speakers in Sierra Leone are shifting to Mende. *Other:* Different from Gola of Nigeria (dialect of Mumuye) or Gola (Badyara) of Guinea-Bissau and Guinea. Muslim, Christian. See main entry under Liberia.

Kisi, Southern (Kisi, Gissi, Kissien) [kss] 85,000 in Sierra Leone (1995). *Lg Dev:* Literacy rate in second language: 3%. *Other:* Different from Northern Kissi. Traditional religion, Muslim, Christian. See main entry under Liberia.

Kissi, Northern (Gizi, Kisi, Kissien, Kisie) [kqs] 40,000 in Sierra Leone (1991 LBT). *Dialects:* Liaro, Kama, Teng, Tung. *Lg Use:* Speakers also use Krio or Mende. *Other:* Traditional religion. See main entry under Guinea.

Klao (Kru, Kroo, Klaoh, Klau) [klu] 8,000 in Sierra Leone (1989 TISLL). Freetown. Originally from Liberia. *Other:* Traditional religion. See main entry under Liberia.

Kono (Konnoh) [kno] 190,000 (1989 TISLL). Northeast. *Class:* Niger-Congo, Mande, Western, Central-Southwestern, Central, Manding-Jogo, Manding-Vai, Vai-Kono. *Dialects:* Northern Kono (Sando), Central Kono (Fiama, Gbane, Gbane Kando, Gbense, Gorama Kono, Kamara, Lei, Mafindo, Nimi Koro, Nimi Yama, Penguia, Soa, Tankoro, Toli). Not intelligible with Vai. The dialects have minor differences, and can use the same literature. *Lg Use:* 25,000 second-language speakers (1981 Cranmer UBS). *Lg Dev:* Bible portions: 1919–1993. *Other:* Different from the Kono dialect of Kpelle in Guinea. Hills. Agriculturalists: rice, greens, cassava, yams, coffee, cacao; diamond miners. Traditional religion, Muslim, Christian.

Krim (Kim, Kittim, Kirim, Kimi) [krm] 500 (1990 CR). Ethnic population: 10,000 (1990 CR). On the coast between Sherbro and Vai, along the Krim River. *Class:* Niger-Congo, Atlantic-Congo, Atlantic, Southern, Mel, Bullom-Kissi, Bullom, Southern. *Dialects:* Lexical similarity 44% to 45% with Sherbro, 34% with Northern Bullom. *Lg Use:* There are 7 or 8 towns where children and others speak Krim. Speakers also use Sherbro, and are being absorbed into the Mende group. *Other:* Traditional religion, Muslim.

Krio (Creole, Patois) [kri] 472,600 in Sierra Leone (1993). Population total all countries: 481,600. Communities in Freetown, on the Peninsula, on the Banana Islands, York Island, in Bonthe, by de-tribalized Sierra Leoneans and as the lingua franca throughout the country. Also spoken in Gambia, Guinea, Senegal. *Class:* Creole, English based, Atlantic, Krio. *Dialect:* Aku. Krio and Jamaican Creole, and Krio and Sea Islands Creole may have some inter-intelligibility. *Lg Use:* Language of wider communication. Vigorous. Spoken more in provincial towns than in villages, and for interethnic communication. Possibly half the speakers use Krio in their workplace. It is the formal language for those who do not speak English. Second-language users prefer their indigenous languages for informal situations. Possibly 4,000,000 are second-language users (1987 F. Jones). All domains, education. Dominant language of the younger generation. *Lg Dev:* Literacy rate in second language: Fewer than 15% in English. Taught as an elective from primary to college level. NT: 1986–1992. *Other:* First-language Krio speakers are mainly descendants of repatriated slaves from Jamaica. There is linguistic influence from Yoruba (I. Hancock 1987). Traditional religion, Christian.

Kuranko (Koranko) [knk] 250,000 in Sierra Leone (1995). Population total all countries: 305,200. Northern Province around Kabala. Also spoken in Guinea. *Class:* Niger-Congo, Mande, Western, Central-Southwestern, Central, Manding-Jogo, Manding-Vai, Manding-Mokole, Mokole. *Dialects:* Barrawa, Nieni, Mankaliya, Sambaya, Ney, Sengbe, Mongo. The dialect near the Guinea border is similar to Eastern Maninkakan, so some have called Kuranko a dialect of Eastern Maninkakan. Farther south, the dialects are more different from Eastern Maninkakan. *Lg Dev:* Literacy rate in second language: 5%. NT: 1972. *Other:* Traditional religion, Muslim, Christian.

Limba, East (Yimba, Yumba) [lma] North central. *Dialects:* Northern Limba (Warawara, Ke-Woya-Yaka), Southern Limba (Biriwa-Saroko-Kalantuba-Sunko). *Other:* Traditional religion, Muslim. See main entry under Guinea.

Limba, West-Central (Yimba, Yumba) [lia] 335,000 (1989 J. Kaiser). Population includes East Limba. North central area north of Makeni. *Class:* Niger-Congo, Atlantic-Congo, Atlantic, Southern, Limba. *Dialects:* Western Limba (Tonko, Sela), Central (Tamiso, Gbongogbo). *Lg Dev:* NT: 1966–1983. *Other:* It is quite different from East Limba of Sierra Leone and Guinea. Traditional religion, Muslim, Christian.

Loko (Landogo) [lok] 115,000 (1989 J. Kaiser TISLL). Two separate areas; parts of the Koya, Ribbi, and Bumpe chiefdoms; Sanda Loko chiefdom. *Class:* Niger-Congo, Mande, Western, Central-Southwestern, Southwestern, Mende-Loma, Mende-Bandi, Mende-Loko. *Dialects:* Magbiambo, Gbendembu, Ngoahu, Nagbanmba, Sanda, Laia, Libisegahun, Koya, Ribbi, Buya. Close to Mende. *Lg Dev:* NT: 1983. *Other:* Traditional religion, Muslim, Christian.

Maninkakan, Eastern (Mandingo, Madingo, Mande, Maninka-Mori, Southern Maninka, Kankan Maninka, Eastern Malinke) [emk] 90,000 in Sierra Leone (1989 J. Kaiser). Kabala area and small groups throughout the country. *Lg Use:* Trade language. *Other:* Traders. Muslim. See main entry under Guinea.

Mende (Boumpe, Hulo, Kossa, Kosso) [men] 1,460,000 in Sierra Leone (1987 UBS). Population total all countries: 1,479,700. South central. Expanding along the coast and to the south and east. Also spoken in Liberia. *Class:* Niger-Congo, Mande, Western, Central-Southwestern, Southwestern, Mende-Loma, Mende-Bandi, Mende-Loko. *Dialects:* Kpa, Ko, Waanjama, Sewawa. Bandi, mainly in Liberia, is considered to be a separate language. Dialects have 92% to 98% lexical similarity with each other. *Lg Use:* Trade language. There are a number of monolinguals. Others use Krio as second language. *Lg Dev:* Taught as an elective from primary to college levels. Kikakui script. Dictionary. Grammar. Bible: 1959. *Other:* Traditional religion, Muslim, Christian.

Pular (Fuuta Jalon, Futa Jallon, Fouta Dyalon, Fulbe, Fullo Fuuta, Futa Fula) [fuf] 178,400 in Sierra Leone (1991). Throughout the country but especially in the north. *Dialects:* Krio Fula, Kebu Fula. *Other:* People live in settled and migrant communities. Muslim. See main entry under Guinea.

Sherbro (Southern Bullom, Shiba, Amampa, Mampa, Mampwa) [bun] 135,000 (1989 Kaiser). Southern Province adjoining the Western Area; York District on western peninsula, Ribbi Shenge, Dima, Sicie, Timdel, Benducha, Nongoba. *Class:* Niger-Congo, Atlantic-Congo, Atlantic, Southern, Mel, Bullom-Kissi, Bullom, Southern. *Dialects:* Shenge Sherbro, Sitia Sherbro, Ndema Sherbro, Peninsula Sherbro. Not intelligible with Krim or Bullom So. Shenge is the prestige dialect. Lexical similarity 66% to 69% with Bullom So, 44% to 45% with Krim, 83% to 89% among dialects. *Other:* Traditional religion, Muslim, Christian.

Sierra Leone Sign Language [sgx] Freetown. *Class:* Deaf sign language.

Susu (Susoo, Soussou, Soso, Sose) [sus] 120,000 in Sierra Leone (1989 J. Kaiser). Northern Province, interspersed throughout western sections. *Lg Use:* Some also use Krio or English. *Other:* Muslim. See main entry under Guinea.

Themne (Temne, Timne, Timene, Timmannee, Temen) [tem] 1,200,000 (1989 J. Kaiser). Northern Province, west of Sewa River to Little Scarcie. *Class:* Niger-Congo, Atlantic-Congo, Atlantic, Southern, Mel, Temne, Temne-Banta. *Dialects:* Banta, Konike, Yoni, Bombali, Western Temne (Pil), Sanda, Ribia, Kholifa, Koya, Masingbi, Malal. The people claim to understand all dialects. Lexical similarity 74% between Masingbi and Malal, 70% between Konike and western varieties. *Lg Use:* Trade language. The primary language of central Sierra Leone. 240,000 second-language speakers (1981 D. Cranmer). 25% use Krio, 5% use English as second language. A number of monolinguals. *Lg Dev:* Literacy rate in second language: 6%. Taught as an elective from primary to college level. NT: 1868–1955. *Other:* Agriculturalists: rice. Traditional religion, Muslim, Christian.

Vai (Vei, Vy, Gallinas, Gallines) [vai] 15,500 in Sierra Leone (1991). *Lg Use:* Most are Mende speakers in Sierra Leone. *Other:* Muslim. See main entry under Liberia.

Yalunka (Yalunke, Djallonke, Kjalonke, Dialonke, Jalonke) [yal] 30,000 in Sierra Leone (2002 SIL). Northern Province, Balaki Subprefecture around Yifin, Falaba area; Balaki, Kunsi, Bouria, Solia, Foulaya, Jouloubaya villages. *Dialects:* Musaia, Firia, Sulima. *Lg Use:* They want literature in Yalunka. Speakers also use Eastern Maninkakan, Krio. *Lg Dev:* Literacy rate in second language: 2%. *Other:* Muslim, traditional religion, Christian. See main entry under Guinea.

Somalia

Somali Democratic Republic, Jamhuriyadda Dimugradiga Somaliya. Formerly British and Italian Somaliland. 8,304,601. National or official languages: Somali, Standard Arabic, English. Most of the Arabic and all of the people from India and Italy have left. Literacy rate: 24% to 40%

(1977 C. M. Brann). Information mainly from B. W. Andrzejewski 1975, 1978; D. Biber 1984; M. Lamberti 1986; A. O. Mansur 1986; K. Menkhaus 1989. Blind population: 10,000 (1982 WCE). The number of languages listed for Somalia is 13. Of those, all are living languages. See map on page 729.

Arabic, Standard [arb] *Lg Use:* National language. Most Somalis have very limited or no proficiency in Arabic. See main entry under Saudi Arabia.

Boni [bob] Few if any speakers in Somalia (1991). *Other:* Hunters. Muslim. See main entry under Kenya.

Boon (Af-Boon) [bnl] 59 (2000 WCD). Jilib District, Middle Jubba Region, scattered in the bush and live in settlements of 2 or 3 houses with their closest relatives. *Class:* Afro-Asiatic, Cushitic, East. *Dialects:* There are similarities to Somali. *Lg Use:* In recent decades they have shifted to the Maay dialect of Jilib. All speakers older than 60 years (1986 M. Lamberti). *Other:* Not the same as Boni. 'Boon' means low caste, including Yibir, Midgaan (Midgo, language Af-Midgood), Madiban, Tumal, Yahar, Yihir, and other clans. Hunter-gatherers; leather workers. Nearly extinct.

Dabarre (Af-Dabarre) [dbr] 26,753 (2000 WCD). Spoken by the Dabarre clan around Dhiinsoor District, May Region, and the Iroole Clan in nearby Baraawe District, Lower Shabeelle Region, and in Qansax Dheere. *Class:* Afro-Asiatic, Cushitic, East, Somali. *Dialect:* Dabarre, Iroole (Af-Iroole). A very distinctive language in the Digil clan family. *Other:* Muslim.

English [eng] *Lg Use:* Official language. Used more in the north. See main entry under United Kingdom.

Garre (Af-Garre) [gex] 50,000 (1992). Ethnic population: Possibly several hundred thousand in the ethnic group (1992). Dominate areas of southern Somalia, especially in the Wanle Weyn-Buur Hakaba area; Baydhaba, Dhiinsoor, Buurhakaba, and Qoryooley districts; Middle and Lower Shabeelle and Bay regions. *Class:* Afro-Asiatic, Cushitic, East, Somali. *Dialects:* Reported to be linguistically close to Boni. *Other:* Part of the Hawiye clan family. They consider themselves to be one people with the Garreh in Kenya, although they now speak different languages. Some ethnic Garre in Somalia speak Maay as first language. Muslim.

Jiiddu (Jiddu, Af-Jiiddu) [jii] 29,726 (2000 WCD). Lower Shabeelle Bay and Middle Jubba regions, Qoryooley, Dhiinsoor, Jilib, and Buurhakaba districts. *Class:* Afro-Asiatic, Cushitic, East, Somali. *Dialects:* A distinct language from Somali and Tunni, usually grouped under the Digil dialects or languages. Different sentence structure and phonology from Somali. Closer to Somali than to Baiso. Some similarities to Konsoid languages and to Gedeo, Alaba, Hadiyya, and Kambaata. *Lg Use:* Spoken by the Jiiddu clan. Ethnic Jiiddu in Bale Province, Ethiopia speak Oromo as first language. *Other:* Muslim.

Maay (Af-Maay Tiri, Af-Maay, Af-May, Af-Maymay, Rahanween, Rahanweyn) [ymm] 594,520 (2000 WCD). 700,000 to 1,500,000 including the Digil dialects or languages. Southern Somalia, Gedo Region, Middle and Lower Shabeelle, Middle and Lower Jubba, Baay, and Bakool regions. *Class:* Afro-Asiatic, Cushitic, East, Somali. *Dialect:* Af-Helledi. It may be more than one language; the dialects form a continuum. Standard Somali is difficult or unintelligible to Maay speakers, except for those who have learned it through mass communications, urbanization, and internal movement. Different sentence structure and phonology from Somali. The Rahanwiin (Rahanweyn) clan confederacy speak various Maay dialects or languages. Af-Helledi is a Maay secret language used by hunters. *Lg Use:* Used by the Tunni, Jiiddu, Garre, and Dabarre as second language. *Other:* Little travel. Muslim.

Mushungulu (Kimushungulu, Mushunguli) [xma] 20,000 to 50,000 (1992). Southern Somalia, Jamaame District of Lower Jubba Region, centered in Jamaame District, and some in urban areas in nearby Kismaayo and in Muqdisho. *Class:* Niger-Congo, Atlantic-Congo, Volta-Congo, Benue-Congo, Bantoid, Southern, Narrow Bantu, Central, G, Zigula-Zaramo (G.30). *Dialects:* May be the same as, or intelligible with, Zigula or Shambaa. *Lg Use:* Men also use Maay or Somali. *Other:* Descended from fugitive slaves who escaped from their Somali masters in the Middle Shabeelle region around 1840. In northeast Tanzania, they were called 'Wazegua' (see Zigula). Agriculturalists. Muslim, traditional religion.

Oromo, Borana-Arsi-Guji (Southern Oromo) [gax] 41,616 in Somalia (2000 WCD). Gedo Region. *Dialect:* Borana (Booran, Boran). *Other:* The Oromo variety in Gedo is probably Borana; that in the Lower Jubba Region is probably Orma. Muslim. See main entry under Ethiopia.

Somali (Af-Soomaali, Af-Maxaad Tiri, Common Somali, Standard Somali) [som] 7,784,434 in Somalia (2000 WCD). Population total all countries: 12,653,480. Throughout the country. Also spoken in Djibouti, Ethiopia, Finland, Italy, Kenya, Oman, Saudi Arabia, Sweden, United Arab Emirates, United Kingdom, Yemen. *Class:* Afro-Asiatic, Cushitic, East, Somali. *Dialect:* Northern Somali, Benaadir, Af-Ashraaf (Ashraaf). Northern Somali is the basis for Standard Somali. It is readily intelligible to speakers of Benaadir Somali, but difficult or unintelligible to most Maay and Digil speakers. Those in Merka and Muqdisho speak Af-Ashraaf, a distinct variety which may have limited inherent intelligibility to speakers of Standard Somali. *Lg Use:* Official language. The language of most of the people of the country. Speakers also use Arabic or Italian. *Lg Dev:* Literacy rate in second language: 25% in cities, 10% rural. Taught in primary schools. Roman script. Radio programs. Dictionary. Grammar. Bible: 1979. *Other:* SOV. Pastoralists; agriculturalists: sugar, bananas, sorghum, corn, gum, incense; miners: iron, tin, gypsum, bauxite, uranium. Muslim, Christian.

Swahili [swh] 40,000 in Somalia (1992). The Mwini live in Baraawe (Brava), Lower Shabeelle, and were scattered in cities and towns of southern Somalia. Most have fled to Kenya because of the civil war. The Bajun live in Kismaayo District and the neighboring coast. *Dialects:* Mwini (Mwiini, Chimwiini, Af-Chimwiini, Barwaani, Bravanese), Bajuni (Kibajuni, Bajun, Af-Bajuun, Mbalazi, Chimbalazi). *Other:* Reported to have come centuries ago from Zanzibar. Mwini: artisans (leather goods); Bajun: fishermen. See main entry under Tanzania.

Tunni (Af-Tunni) [tqq] 29,726 (2000 WCD). Lower Shabeelle and Middle Jubba regions, Dhiinsoor, Baraawe, and Jilib districts. *Class:* Afro-Asiatic, Cushitic, East, Somali. *Dialects:* Distinct from Somali or Jiiddu, usually grouped under the Digil dialects or languages. Different sentence structure and phonology from Somali. *Other:* Maay language influences. Nomadic. Pastoralists: cattle, sheep, goats. Muslim.

South Africa

Republic of South Africa. Republiek van Suid-Afrika. 42,718,530. Population includes 24,100,000 Africans (73.8%), 5,000,000 Whites (14.8%), 2,800,000 'Coloureds' (8.7%), 890,292 Asians (2.7%) (1987 USA Today). National or official languages: Afrikaans, Ndebele, Northern Sotho, Southern Sotho, Swati, Tsonga, Tswana, Venda, Xhosa, Zulu, English. Literacy rate: 50% Africans, 62% 'Coloureds', 69% Asians, 99% Whites (1990 WA). Also includes Angloromani, Eastern Yiddish, Greek (70,000), Gujarati, Hai‖om, Hakka Chinese (6,063), Kung-Ekoka (3,500), Portuguese (617,000), Standard German (45,000),

Tamil (250,000), Yue Chinese (15,000), workers from nearby countries (2,700,000). Information mainly from F. Anderson 1987; J. Holm 1989; L-G Andersson and T. Janson 1997; M. Brenzinger 1997. Blind population: 62,000 (1982 WCE). Deaf population: 12,100 (1986 Gallaudet University). Deaf institutions: 43. The number of languages listed for South Africa is 31. Of those, 24 are living languages, 3 are second language without mother-tongue speakers, and 4 are extinct. See map on page 704.

Afrikaans [afr] 5,811,547 in South Africa (1996 census). Population total all countries: 5,965,879. Pretoria and Bloemfontein are principal centers of population. Cape Malays live mainly in Cape Town, with some in Johannesburg, Pretoria, Durban, and Port Elizabeth. Also spoken in Australia, Botswana, Canada, Lesotho, Malawi, Namibia, New Zealand, Zambia, Zimbabwe. *Class:* Indo-European, Germanic, West, Low Saxon-Low Franconian, Low Franconian. *Dialects:* Cape Afrikaans (West Cape Afrikaans), Orange River Afrikaans, East Cape Afrikaans. A variant of the Dutch spoken by the 17th century colonists, with some lexical and syntactic borrowings from Malay, Bantu languages, Khoisan languages, Portuguese, and other European languages. Their ancestors were brought from Java 300 years ago. *Lg Use:* Official language. 150,000 Cape Malays speak Afrikaans; 10,300,000 second-language speakers. Some also speak English. *Lg Dev:* Taught in primary and secondary schools. Newspapers. Radio programs. TV. Grammar. Bible: 1933–1983. *Other:* Cape Malays: builders, carpenters. Muslim, Christian.

Birwa [brl] See main entry under Botswana.

Camtho (Isicamtho, Iscamtho) [cmt] Soweto, Johannesburg, urban settings. *Class:* Mixed Language, Zulu-Bantu. *Dialects:* A development in the 1980s from the original Tsotsitaal, and sometimes called 'Tsotsitaal'. Also described as a basically Zulu or Sotho language with heavy codeswitching and many English and Afrikaans content morphemes. *Lg Use:* Mainly used by young people. *Other:* Second language only.

English [eng] 3,457,467 in South Africa (1996 census). *Lg Use:* Official language. The main means of communication in urban areas. Many second-generation people from India, Portugal, Germany, and Greece speak English as first language. See main entry under United Kingdom.

Fanagalo ("Fanakalo," "Fanekolo," "Kitchen Kaffir," "Mine Kaffir," Piki, Isipiki, "Isikula," Lololo, Isilololo, Pidgin Bantu, Basic Zulu, Silunguboi) [fng] Several hundred thousand speakers in South Africa (1975 Reinecke). Also spoken in Democratic Republic of the Congo, Namibia, Zambia, Zimbabwe. *Class:* Pidgin, Zulu based. *Dialects:* The dialect in Zambia is called 'Cikabanga', that in Zimbabwe is called 'Chilapalapa'. Influenced by Shona in Zimbabwe. About 70% of the vocabulary in Zimbabwe comes from Zulu, 24% from English, 6% from Afrikaans. Influenced by Bemba in Zambia. 70% of the vocabulary comes from Zulu, 24% from English, 6% from Afrikaans. *Lg Use:* Trade language. Used widely in towns and gold, diamond, coal, and copper mining areas. *Lg Dev:* Dictionary. *Other:* Originated in the 19th century. 'Fanagalo' and most or all other names are pejorative. Second language only.

Gail [gic] Mainly in Johannesburg, Pretoria, Cape Town, Durban, Bloemfontein, and Port Elizabeth. *Class:* Unclassified. *Dialects:* In Johannesburg it is more English based, in Pretoria more Afrikaans based. Reported to be related to Polari in the United Kingdom. *Lg Use:* 20,000 second- or third-language speakers. The first language of users is English or Afrikaans. *Other:* An in-group language among some people. Second language only.

Hindi [hin] 890,292 including all Indian languages (1986 USA Today). 2,000,000 speakers of Western Hindi languages in all Africa (1977 Voegelin and Voegelin). Mainly in Natal. *Other:* Has features of Bhojpuri in South Africa. Hindu. See main entry under India.

Korana (Koranna, !Ora, !Kora, Koraqua, Gorachouqua) [kqz] Extinct. Ethnic population: 10,000 in South Africa (1972 Barrett). Western. Possibly also Botswana. *Class:* Khoisan, Southern Africa, Central, Nama. *Lg Dev:* Bible: 1933. *Other:* Nomads. Christian, traditional religion.

Kxoe (Khoe, Xun, Water Bushmen, Mbarakwena, Mbarakwengo) [xuu] 1,100 in South Africa (2000). Smithsdrift. *Dialects:* ‖Ani, Kxoedam. *Other:* Refugees from Caprivi since 1991 living in tents. See main entry under Namibia.

Nama (Naman, Namakwa, Namaqua, Dama, Damara, Damaqua, Tama, Tamma, Tamakwa, Khoekhoe, Berdama, Bergdamara, Khoeknoegowap, Khoi, "Hottentot," Rooi Nasie, Kakuya Bushman Nasie, "Klipkaffer," "Klipkaffern") [naq] 56,000 in South Africa (1989 UBS). *Dialect:* Gimsbok Nama. *Other:* Language of secondary education. See main entry under Namibia.

Ndebele (Nrebele, Ndzundza, Transvaal Ndebele, Southern Ndebele) [nbl] 586,961 (1996 census). Transvaal, south and central. *Class:* Niger-Congo, Atlantic-Congo, Volta-Congo, Benue-Congo, Bantoid, Southern, Narrow Bantu, Central, S, Sotho-Tswana (S.30), Sotho, Northern. *Lg Use:* Official language. 1,400,000 second-language speakers. *Lg Dev:* Grammar. NT: 1986. *Other:* Different from Ndebele of Zimbabwe.

N‖u (ǂKhomani, Ng'uki, Nghuki, N‖u‖en, Nusan) [ngh] 10 (2003 Crawhall). Ethnic population: 500 (1998 Nigel Crawhall, South African San Institute). 2 at Andriesvale (near Witdraai), 1 at Witdraai, 1 at Philandersbron (near Rietfontein), 2 in Olifantshoek, 3 in Upington townships, 1 in Raaswater (outside Upington). *Class:* Khoisan, Southern Africa, Southern, !Kwi. *Dialect:* N‖u, |'Auni, ‖Kxau, ‖Ng!ke (Ng‖-|e, ‖Ng, |ing‖ke). Close to |Xam. *Lg Use:* Speakers are older adults. Speakers are concerned that N‖u is dying out. Younger people have a strong loyalty to Nama, not shared by N‖u speakers. Speakers use Afrikaans and Nama (Khoekhoegowab) fluently. *Lg Dev:* Literacy is in Afrikaans. *Other:* 'ǂKhomani' is the name for the ethnic group. 'Ng'uki' is an incorrect name. The |'Auni dialect is extinct. Christian, traditional religion. Nearly extinct.

Oorlams [oor] Transvaal. *Class:* Creole, Afrikaans based. *Lg Use:* There are first-language speakers. It also includes some Bantu words. There are a large number of small colonies of Africans.

Ronga (Shironga) [rng] 86,618 in South Africa (2000 WCD). *Dialect:* Konde. See main entry under Mozambique.

Seroa [kqu] Extinct. Also was in Lesotho. *Class:* Khoisan, Southern Africa, Southern, !Kwi. *Dialects:* !Gã!nge (!Gã!ne), ‖Ku‖e. Had three dialects.

Sotho, Northern (Pedi, Sepedi, Transvaal Sotho) [nso] 3,695,846 in South Africa (1996 census). Population total all countries: 3,709,717. Transvaal, south and central. Also spoken in Botswana. *Class:* Niger-Congo, Atlantic-Congo, Volta-Congo, Benue-Congo, Bantoid, Southern, Narrow Bantu, Central, S, Sotho-Tswana (S.30), Sotho, Northern. *Dialects:* Masemola (Masemula, Tau), Kgaga (Kxaxa, Khaga), Koni (Kone), Tswene (Tsweni), Gananwa (Xananwa, Hananwa), Pulana, Phalaborwa (Phalaburwa, Thephalaborwa), Khutswe (Khutswi, Kutswe), Lobedu (Lubedu, Lovedu, Khelobedu), Tlokwa (Tlokoa, Tokwa, Dogwa), Pai, Dzwabo (Thabine-Roka-Nareng), Kopa, Matlala-Moletshi. Dialects Pai, Kutswe, and Pulana are more divergent and sometimes called 'Eastern Sotho'. *Lg Use:* Official language. *Lg Dev:*

Taught in primary and secondary schools. Radio programs. TV. Bible: 1904–2000. *Other:* Agriculturalists; miners; tourism. Christian, traditional religion.

Sotho, Southern (Suto, Suthu, Sesotho, Souto, Sisutho) [sot] 3,104,197 in South Africa (1996 census). *Dialects:* Taung, Phuthi. *Lg Use:* Official language. *Lg Dev:* Literacy rate in second language: 15% to 20%. Language of secondary education. *Other:* Christian, traditional religion. See main entry under Lesotho.

South African Sign Language [sfs] 12,100 deaf persons including 6,000 Black, 2,000 English white, 2,000 Afrikaans white, 1,200 Coloured, 900 Indian; 1986 Gallaudet Univ. *Class:* Deaf sign language. *Dialects:* The North British sign system was used for the deaf in white English-speaking families. In 1881 a school for Afrikaans-speaking families was begun using British Sign Language. Several dialects are used unofficially in different schools. There are 9 sign language systems, 60% related to British or Australian sign languages, few to American Sign Language. *Lg Use:* Sign language is understood to some degree by most deaf people. Some interpreters are provided in courts. *Other:* The first deaf school was established about 1846. Now there are 29 schools for 4,000 children. There is a Signed Afrikaans.

Swahili (Kiswaheli, Suahili, Kisuahili, Arab-Swahili) [swh] 1,000 in South Africa (1987 Schreck and Barrett). Chatsworth, an urban area close to Durban on the Natal coast. *Other:* Zanzibaris brought from Zanzibar and northern Mozambique from 1873 to 1878. Coastal. Market gardeners. Muslim. See main entry under Tanzania.

Swati (Swazi, Siswazi, Siswati, Tekela, Tekeza, Thithiza, Yeyeza) [ssw] 1,013,193 in South Africa (1996 census). *Dialects:* Baca, Hlubi, Phuthi. *Lg Use:* Official language. *Other:* Christian, traditional religion. See main entry under Swaziland.

Tsonga (Shitsonga, Thonga, Tonga, Shangana, Shangaan) [tso] 1,756,105 in South Africa (1996 census). Population total all countries: 3,275,105. Transvaal. Also spoken in Mozambique, Swaziland, Zimbabwe. *Class:* Niger-Congo, Atlantic-Congo, Volta-Congo, Benue-Congo, Bantoid, Southern, Narrow Bantu, Central, S, Tswa-Ronga (S.50). *Dialects:* Luleke (Xiluleke), Gwamba (Gwapa), Changana, Hlave, Kande, N'walungu (Shingwalungu), Xonga, Jonga (Dzonga), Nkuma, Songa, Nhlanganu (Shihlanganu). 'Tsonga' is used to describe Changana, Tswa, and Ronga, although it is often used interchangeably with Changana, the most prestigious of the three. All are recognized as languages, although they are inherently intelligible. *Lg Use:* Official language. *Lg Dev:* A language of secondary education. Radio programs. Dictionary. Grammar. Bible: 1907–1989. *Other:* Christian, traditional religion.

Tsotsitaal (Fly Taal, Flaai Taal) [fly] It had tens of thousands of primary users; hundreds of thousands of second-language users (1984 Gilbert and Makhudu). In Gauteng province, around Johannesburg, Pretoria, Bloemfontein, and other cities. *Class:* Creole, Afrikaans based. *Dialects:* Not intelligible to Afrikaans speakers. Uses many Afrikaans, English, and Bantu words, and others of unknown origin. *Lg Use:* Originated in the gold mines in Transvaal from 1886. Creolized by 1930. Used until the 1970s or 1980s. *Other:* 'Tsotsitaal' means 'speech of young gang member, criminal, or thug'. Nearly extinct.

Tswa (Shitshwa, Kitshwa, Xitshwa, Sheetshwa, Tshwa) [tsc] *Dialects:* Hlengwe (Makawe-Khambana), Tshwa (Dzibi-Dzonga). See main entry under Mozambique.

Tswana (Tsiwaha, Beetjuans, Chuana, Coana, Cuana, Sechuana) [tsn] 3,301,774 in South Africa (1996 census). *Dialects:* Tawana, Hurutshe, Ngwaketse, Thlaro, Kwena, Ngwato, Tlokwa, Melete, Kgatla, Thlaping (Tlapi),

Rolong. *Lg Use:* Official language. *Lg Dev:* Taught in primary and secondary schools. *Other:* Christian, traditional religion. See main entry under Botswana.

Urdu [urd] 170,000 South Asian Muslims in South Africa (1987). Along the Natal coast and urban areas around Durban, Transvaal surrounding Johannesburg, and scattered smaller towns. *Lg Use:* Most speak English. *Other:* Merchants; traders; industrial, professional (medicine, computers), clerical workers; craftsmen. Muslim. See main entry under Pakistan.

Venda (Chivenda) [ven] 876,409 in South Africa (1996 census). Population total all countries: 960,409. Transvaal, north. Also spoken in Zimbabwe. *Class:* Niger-Congo, Atlantic-Congo, Volta-Congo, Benue-Congo, Bantoid, Southern, Narrow Bantu, Central, S, Venda (S.20). *Dialects:* Phani, Tavha-Tsindi, Ilafuri, Manda, Guvhu, Mbedzi, Lembetu. *Lg Use:* Official language. The Lembaa are a Venda-speaking Jewish people claiming Falasha descent. *Lg Dev:* Literacy rate in second language: Fairly low. Radio programs. Bible: 1936. *Other:* Traditional religion, Christian, Jewish (Lembaa).

|Xam (|Kham-Ka-!k'e, |Kamka!e, |Xam-Ka-!k'e) [xam] Extinct. *Class:* Khoisan, Southern Africa, Southern, !Kwi.

||Xegwi (||Xegwe, ||Xekwi, Batwa, Bush-C, Abathwa, Boroa, Tloue, Tloutle, Kloukle, Lxloukxle, Amankgqwigqwi, Nkqeshe, Amabusmana, Gi||kxigwi, Ki||kxigwi) [xeg] Extinct. Near the Swaziland border. *Class:* Khoisan, Southern Africa, Southern, !Kwi. *Other:* The last speaker died in 1988.

Xhosa (Isixhosa, Xosa, Koosa, "Kaffer," "Kaffir," "Caffre," "Cafre," "Cauzuh") [xho] 7,196,118 in South Africa (1996 census). Population total all countries: 7,214,118. Southwest Cape Province and Transkei. Also spoken in Botswana, Lesotho. *Class:* Niger-Congo, Atlantic-Congo, Volta-Congo, Benue-Congo, Bantoid, Southern, Narrow Bantu, Central, S, Nguni (S.40). *Dialects:* Gealeka, Ndlambe, Gaika (Ncqika), Thembu, Bomvana, Mpondomse (Mpondomisi), Mpondo, Xesibe, Rhathabe, Bhaca, Cele, Hlubi, Mfengu. 15% of the vocabulary is estimated to be of Khoekhoe (Khoisan) origin. *Lg Use:* Official language. Many understand Zulu, Swati, Southern Sotho. *Lg Dev:* Literacy rate in first language: 50%. Literacy rate in second language: 20% to 25%. Taught in primary and secondary schools. Magazines. Newspapers. Radio programs. TV. Bible: 1859. *Other:* "Cauzuh" is an obsolete name. Somewhat acculturated. Clicks. Agriculturalists; miners; industrial workers. Christian, traditional religion.

Xiri (Khiri, Grikwa, Griqua, Xrikwa, Xirikwa, Gry, Cape Hottentot, Gri) [xii] 87 (2000 WCD). *Class:* Khoisan, Southern Africa, Central, Nama. *Lg Use:* A few isolated speakers (2000). *Other:* Nearly extinct.

Zulu (Isizulu, Zunda) [zul] 9,200,144 in South Africa (1996 census). Population total all countries: 9,563,422. Zululand and northern Natal. Also spoken in Botswana, Lesotho, Malawi, Mozambique, Swaziland. *Class:* Niger-Congo, Atlantic-Congo, Volta-Congo, Benue-Congo, Bantoid, Southern, Narrow Bantu, Central, S, Nguni (S.40). *Dialects:* Lala, Qwabe. Close to Swazi and Xhosa. *Lg Use:* Official language. 15,700,000 second-language speakers. *Lg Dev:* Literacy rate in second language: 70%. Taught in primary and secondary schools. Newspapers. Radio programs. Dictionary. Grammar. Bible: 1883–1959. *Other:* Christian, traditional religion.

Sudan

Republic of the Sudan. Jamhuryat as-Sudan. 39,148,162. National or official language: Standard Arabic. Literacy rate: 20% to 27%. Information mainly from M. L. Bender 1976, 1983, 1989; T. Schadeberg 1981; P. Doornbos and M. L.

Bender 1983; R. Stevenson 1984; J. Bendor-Samuel 1989. Blind population: 110,000 (1982 WCE). Deaf institutions: 1. The number of languages listed for Sudan is 142. Of those, 134 are living languages and 8 are extinct. See maps beginning on page 730.

Acheron (Garme) [acz] Northern Sudan, Kordofan Province, southern Nuba Hills. *Class:* Niger-Congo, Kordofanian, Talodi, Talodi Proper, Tocho. *Dialects:* Eastern Acheron, Western Acheron. Not a dialect of Moro. *Lg Use:* Speakers also use Sudanese Arabic. *Other:* Orthography and literacy materials.

Acholi (Acoli, Atscholi, Shuli, Gang, Lwo, Akoli, Acooli, Log Acoli, Dok Acoli) [ach] 45,000 in Sudan (2000). Southern Sudan, Opari District, Acholi Hills. See main entry under Uganda.

Afitti (Ditti, Unietti, Affitti, Dinik) [aft] 4,512 (1984 R. C. Stevenson). Northern Sudan, Nuba Hills, eastern Jebel ed Dair. Main center is Sidra. *Class:* Nilo-Saharan, Eastern Sudanic, Western, Nyimang. *Dialects:* Not inherently intelligible with Ama. Lexical similarity 59% with Ama. *Other:* Muslim.

Aja (Ajja, Adja) [aja] 200 (1993 SIL). Southern Sudan, Western Bahr el Ghazal Province. Also in the western Central African Republic, along the Sudan border, near the Shinko and Sapo rivers. *Class:* Nilo-Saharan, Central Sudanic, West, Kresh. *Dialects:* They consider themselves to be a Kresh tribe, but their language is not intelligible to the Kresh. Santandrea reports it to be halfway between Banda and Kresh; nearer to Banda in vocabulary and Kresh in structure. *Lg Use:* Speakers are mostly bilingual in Gbaya (Kresh). *Other:* Plains. Wooded savannah. Swidden agriculturalists.

Aka (Sillok, Jebels Sillok, Jebel Silak, Fa-C-Aka) [soh] 300 (1989 Bender). Northern Sudan, Sillok (Silak) Hills, west of the main Berta-speaking people. *Class:* Nilo-Saharan, Eastern Sudanic, Eastern, Eastern Jebel, Aka-Kelo-Molo. *Lg Use:* Speakers also use Arabic or Berta. *Other:* Heavily Arabicized and influenced by Berta. A remnant group (1983 Bender). They call themselves 'Fa-c-aka', 'people of Aka'.

Ama (Nyimang, Inyimang, Nyima, Nyiman) [nyi] 70,000 (1982 SIL). Northern Sudan, Kordofan Province, northwest of Dilling on range of hills of which Jebel Nyimang is a part, and on the Mandal range. *Class:* Nilo-Saharan, Eastern Sudanic, Western, Nyimang. *Dialects:* Lexical similarity 59% with Afitti. *Lg Use:* Education is in Arabic. *Lg Dev:* Bible portions: 1950. *Other:* Muslim, Christian.

Anuak (Anywak, Anywa, Yambo, Jambo, Nuro, Anyuak, Dho Anywaa) [anu] 52,000 in Sudan (1991 UBS). Population total all countries: 97,646. Upper Nile Province, Pibor and Lower Akobo rivers. From Akobo Post to latitude 6.45N. Also spoken in Ethiopia. *Class:* Nilo-Saharan, Eastern Sudanic, Nilotic, Western, Luo, Northern, Anuak. *Dialects:* Closer to Acholi and Luo of Uganda than to Shilluk. *Lg Dev:* NT: 1962–1965. *Other:* SVO; prepositions; tonal. Riverine. Traditional religion, Christian, Muslim.

Arabic, Standard [arb] Middle East, North Africa. *Lg Use:* Official language. Used for nearly all written materials and formal speeches. Not a first language, but taught in schools. Very little known and even less used in the south. Serious educational and sociolinguistic problems in the north also. *Other:* Not intelligible with Sudanese Spoken Arabic or Sudanese Creole Arabic. See main entry under Saudi Arabia.

Arabic, Sudanese Creole (Juba Arabic, Southern Sudan Arabic, Pidgin Arabic) [pga] 20,000 (1987). Southern Sudan, in the towns and many villages all over Equatoria Region, and up into Bahr al Ghazal and Upper

Nile regions. Refugees have gone to other countries. *Class:* Creole, Arabic based. *Dialects:* Difficult intelligibility of Nubi, Sudanese Arabic, or Modern Standard Arabic. *Lg Use:* Trade language. 44,000 second-language speakers. Used as the major language of communication among speakers of different languages in Equatoria, south of Wau and Malakal. Used in many religious services as first or second language in Juba and a few other towns. Most people in towns speak at least two languages, and it is common for them to speak Creole Arabic, English, and 1, 2, or 3 vernaculars. *Lg Dev:* Bible portions: 1983–1985. *Other:* SVO; tonal. Muslim, Christian.

Arabic, Sudanese Spoken (Khartoum Arabic) [apd] 15,000,000 in Sudan (1991). Population total all countries: 18,986,000. Northern Sudan primarily. Also spoken in Egypt, Eritrea, Ethiopia, Saudi Arabia. *Class:* Afro-Asiatic, Semitic, Central, South, Arabic. *Dialects:* Khartoum, Western Sudanese, North Kordofan Arabic, Ja'ali, Shukri. *Lg Use:* Trade language. *Lg Dev:* NT: 1978. *Other:* Western Sudan Spoken Arabic, Juba Arabic, and Khartoum Arabic have little compatibility (Alan S. Kaye 1988). Muslim, Christian.

Avokaya (Abukeia, Avukaya) [avu] 40,000 in Sudan (2002). Population total all countries: 65,000. Southern Sudan, Western Equatorial Province. The Ajugu dialect is on the Sudan-Congo border south of Maridi, the Ojila dialect is mainly between the Naam (Era) and Olo rivers and farther east. Also spoken in Democratic Republic of the Congo. *Class:* Nilo-Saharan, Central Sudanic, East, Moru-Madi, Central. *Dialects:* Ojila (Odzila, Odziliwa), Ajugu (Adjiga, Ojiga, Agamoru). Close to Logo. Avokaya Pur near Faradje is closer to Logo than to the Ojila dialect of Sudan. *Lg Use:* There is intermarriage and bilingualism with the Baka and Mundu, especially near Maridi. *Lg Dev:* NT: 2002.

Bai (Bari) [bdj] 2,500 (1971 Welmers). Southern Sudan, Western District, on Wau-Deim Zubeir road, west of Sere. A few north of Tembura. 2 villages. *Class:* Niger-Congo, Atlantic-Congo, Volta-Congo, North, Adamawa-Ubangi, Ubangi, Sere-Ngbaka-Mba, Sere, Sere-Bviri, Bai-Viri. *Lg Use:* Speakers are bilingual in Ndogo.

Baka (Tara Baka) [bdh] 25,000 in Sudan (1993 UBS). Population total all countries: 26,300. Southern Sudan, Western Equatoria Province, south and west of Maridi, northwest of Yei. Also spoken in Democratic Republic of the Congo. *Class:* Nilo-Saharan, Central Sudanic, West, Bongo-Bagirmi, Bongo-Baka, Baka. *Lg Use:* Sudanese Creole Arabic is the main second language. Zande is taught in school and used in church. Some speakers intermarry with the Avokaya and Mundu and also use those languages. Moru also used. *Lg Dev:* Literacy rate in first language: below 1%. Literacy rate in second language: 5% to 25%. Bible portions: 1990–1993. *Other:* Different from, and unrelated to, Baka of Cameroon. Christian, traditional religion, Muslim.

Banda, Mid-Southern [bjo] Southern Sudan, town of Sopo, near Central African Republic border, and refugees in Khartoum. *Dialects:* Dukpu, Wasa. See main entry under Central African Republic.

Banda, Togbo-Vara [tor] Southern Sudan. *Dialect:* Togbo (Tohgboh, Tagbo). *Lg Use:* They view themselves as very different from Mono. *Other:* Different from Tagbu (Tagbo, Tagba) of Democratic Republic of the Congo in Sere group. Not intelligible with other Banda languages or dialects in Sudan. See main entry under Democratic Republic of the Congo.

Banda, West Central (Golo) [bbp] 3,000 in Sudan (1982 SIL). Between Wau and Mboro. *Lg Use:* Speakers are reported to be bilingual in Ndogo in Sudan. Most no longer speak Golo. See main entry under Central African Republic.

Banda-Banda [bpd] Southern Sudan, town of Sopo near Central African Republic border. Refugees in Khartoum. *Dialects:* Govoro (Govhoroh), Vidiri (Mvedere, Vodere, Vidri, Vadara), Wundu. See main entry under Central African Republic.

Banda-Mbrès (Banda of Mbrés, Banda-Mbre) [bqk] Southern Sudan, town of Sopo, near the Central African Republic border, and refugees in Khartoum. *Dialects:* Buka (Bouka), Mbre (Mbere, Mbele), Moruba (Morouba, Maraba), Sabanga (Sangbanga), Wada (Ouadda). See main entry under Central African Republic.

Banda-Ndélé (Banda of Ndélé, Nyele) [bfl] Southern Sudan, town of Sopo near the Central African Republic border, and refugees in Khartoum. *Dialects:* Junguru (Djingburu, Nguru), Tangbago (Tambolo, Tambaggo, Tombaggo, Tangago), Banda-Kpaya. *Other:* Muslim, Christian, traditional religion. See main entry under Central African Republic.

Bari (Beri) [bfa] 420,000 in Sudan (2000). Population includes 26,400 in Kuku, 18,000 in Nyangbara, 3,400 in Nyepu, 25,000 in Pojulu. Population total all countries: 480,000. Southern Sudan, both banks of the Nile, south of Terakeka on the west bank, south of Mongalla on the east bank, as far as the Kajo Kaji Escarpment, from 5.30N on left bank, 5.15N on right bank to just south of latitude 4.15N. Also spoken in Uganda. *Class:* Nilo-Saharan, Eastern Sudanic, Nilotic, Eastern, Bari. *Dialects:* Kuku, Nyangbara (Nyangwara, Nyambara), Nyepu (Nyefu, Nyepo, Nypho, Ngyepu), Pöjulu (Pajulu, Fadjulu, Fajelu, Madi), Ligo (Liggo). Lexical similarity 86% with Ngyepu, 85% with Pöjulu, 81% with Kuku, 80% with Nyanggwara, 71% with Mondari, 73% with Kakwa. *Lg Dev:* Grammar. Bible: 1979. *Other:* Ethnic groups: Dupi (serfs), Kulu'ba, Liggi, Lui (free men), Tomonok (fishing, smithing). The Marshia (Marsanit) are professional smiths within the Bari group, who live in and around Rimo (Remo), and keep to themselves. Ethnic Bari in Democratic Republic of the Congo now speak a dialect of Logo, and not Bari. Plains, shallow ravines, mountain slope. Bushy, savannah, swamps, forests. 500 to 900 meters. Blacksmiths: iron ore; pastoralists: cattle, goats, sheep; agriculturalists: millet, eleusine, simsim, peanuts, cassava, sweet potatoes. Traditional religion.

Baygo (Baigo, Bego, Beko, Beigo, Béogé, Beygo) [byg] Extinct. Ethnic population: 850 (1978 GR). Northern Sudan, Southern Dar Fur, southeast of Nyala, in the hills east of Kube (Kubbi). Jebel Beygo. *Class:* Nilo-Saharan, Eastern Sudanic, Western, Daju, Western Daju. *Dialects:* Was close to Daju of Dar Fur. *Other:* They did not use the name 'Daju'. Muslim.

Bedawi (Beja, Bedawiye, Bedauye, To-Bedawie, Bedja) [bej] 951,000 in Sudan (1982 SIL). Population includes 30,000 Hadendoa, 15,000 Bisharin (1992). Population total all countries: 1,178,000. Northeastern Sudan along the Red Sea coast. Also spoken in Egypt, Eritrea. *Class:* Afro-Asiatic, Cushitic, North. *Dialects:* Hadendoa (Hadendowa, Hadendiwa), Hadareb (Hadaareb), Bisharin (Bisariab), Beni-Amir. Little vocabulary in common with other Cushitic languages, but a great deal of the verbal morphology is similar. *Lg Use:* Speakers also use Arabic or Tigré. *Lg Dev:* Dictionary. Grammar. *Other:* 'Bedàwie' is their name for the language. Halenga and Arteiga are ethnic groups. SOV; prefixes, postpositions, causatives, reciprocals, reflexives, subject; suffixes distinguish person, number, gender. Coastal. Desert. Pastoralists. Muslim (Sunni).

Belanda Bor (De Bor) [bxb] 8,000 (1983 SIL). Southern Sudan, between Wau and Tambura; villages of Raffili, Tirga, Bazia, Ayo, Gitten, Taban in Bahr-el-Ghazal; villages of Komai, Nagero, Bangazegino, and Tambura in W. Equatoria. *Class:* Nilo-Saharan, Eastern Sudanic,

Nilotic, Western, Luo, Northern, Bor. *Lg Use:* Most speakers also use Belanda Viri. There is much intermarriage between the two groups. *Other:* Traditional religion, Christian, Muslim.

Belanda Viri (Viri, Bviri, Biri, Gumba, Gamba, Mbegumba, Mvegumba, Belanda) [bvi] 16,000 (1971 Welmers). Southern Sudan, scattered villages (Bringi, Bagari, Dadu, Ngoku, Ngisa, Farajallah, Ngotakala, Ngongba, Natabo, Momoyi, and some others), around Raffili, on the Wau road, on the Kuru River, 40 miles from Deim Zubeir, around Tembura among the Zande, on the Iba River near Yambio. *Class:* Niger-Congo, Atlantic-Congo, Volta-Congo, North, Adamawa-Ubangi, Ubangi, Sere-Ngbaka-Mba, Sere, Sere-Bviri, Bai-Viri. *Lg Use:* Speakers also use Belanda Bor. *Other:* They call themselves 'Viri'.

Beli (Behli, Beili, Jur Beli, 'Beli) [blm] 6,600 (1982 SIL). Population includes 5,000 Beli, 1,600 Sopi. Southern Sudan. One group is southwest of Rumbek, at Wulu, westward along the road to Bahr Gel and south toward the southern border of Lakes Province. In some areas they are heavily intermingled with Dinka. Another group lives east of Mvolo and has no links with the first group. They are centered around Bahri Girinti (Lake Nyiropo) just west of Yei River. *Class:* Nilo-Saharan, Central Sudanic, West, Bongo-Bagirmi, Bongo-Baka, Morokodo-Beli. *Dialect:* Wulu, Bahri Girinti, Sopi (Supi). Lexical similarity 46% with Jur Modo, 45% with Bongo, 41% with Mo'da and Morokodo, 39% with Baka. *Lg Dev:* Using Jur Modo literacy materials (1998). *Other:* Christian, traditional religion.

Berta (Barta, Burta, "Beni Shangul," Wetawit) [wti] 22,000 in Sudan. Blue Nile Province, on the Ethiopia border. *Dialects:* Shuru, Bake, Undu, Mayu, Fadashi. *Other:* "Beni Shangul" is the Arabic name, and is reported to be derogatory. Agriculturalists. Traditional religion, Muslim. See main entry under Ethiopia.

Berti [byt] Extinct. Northern Sudan. Tagabo Hills, Dar Fur, and in Kordofan. *Class:* Nilo-Saharan, Saharan, Eastern. *Other:* Muslim.

Birked (Birguid, Birgid, Birkit, Birqed, Murgi, Kajjara) [brk] Extinct. Northern Sudan, north Dar Fur, north and east of Daju and Baygo, east of Jebel Marra between Jebel Harayt and the Rizaykat (Arab) country. Also north of Nyala. A few in north Kordofan south of El Obeid. *Class:* Nilo-Saharan, Eastern Sudanic, Eastern, Nubian, Central, Birked. *Dialects:* Lexical similarity 60% with Kadaru; 51% with Meidob (closest). *Other:* Muslim.

Boguru (Koguru, Kogoro, Buguru) [bqu] 494 in Sudan. Mariko, Baambu, Ibba, Bagasu. Also spoken in Democratic Republic of the Congo. *Class:* Niger-Congo, Atlantic-Congo, Volta-Congo, Benue-Congo, Bantoid, Southern, Narrow Bantu, Central, Unclassified. *Dialect:* Boguru, Bukur (Bukum, Bukuru). *Lg Use:* Speakers in exile in Democratic Republic of the Congo are organized and wanting help with language revival.

Bongo (Bungu, Dor) [bot] 10,084 (2000 WCD). A large sparsely populated area reaching from Tonj and Wau on the north, the Beli on the east, the Zande on the south, and the Bor on the west. *Class:* Nilo-Saharan, Central Sudanic, West, Bongo-Bagirmi, Bongo-Baka, Bongo. *Dialects:* Busere Bongo, Tonj Bongo, Bungo. Slight dialect differences between those on the River Busere, who have had Zande influence, and those around Tonj. Bungo dialect has minor differences. Close to the Jur Beli cluster. *Lg Use:* Bilingualism in Jur Beli is low. Generally, adults understand Zande, and adult males understand Dinka Rek. The youth do not understand Zande or Dinka because education is mostly in Arabic with some English. Many students drop out of school because they cannot understand the language being used. *Lg Dev:* Orthography

developed and literacy materials in use. *Other:* Different from Bongo which is a dialect or closely related language to Banda of Central African Republic and Democratic Republic of the Congo. SVO. Hunters. Traditional religion, Muslim, Christian.

Burun (Barun, Lange, Cai, Borun) [bdi] 18,000 (1977 Voegelin and Voegelin). Northern Sudan, Blue Nile Province. *Class:* Nilo-Saharan, Eastern Sudanic, Nilotic, Western, Luo, Northern, Maban-Burun, Burun. *Dialects:* Ragreig, Abuldugu (Bogon, Mugo-Mborkoina), Maiak, Mufwa (Mopo), Mughaja (Mugaja, Mumughadja). Some southern dialects are intelligible with Mabaan. *Other:* There are three cultural sections: Northern, comprising Cerkom (Serkum), Morkuny (Baldugu), Mayica (Magaja); Eastern, Comprising Gengar (Kurmuk), Jorak (Jorok), Redwak (Regareg); South-West, comprising Mayak, Mofo (Mufu).

Dagik (Masakin, Masakin Dagig, Dagig, Reikha, Dengebu, Masakin Gusar, Buram) [dec] Population 38,000 including Ngile speakers (1982 SIL). Northern Sudan, Kordofan Province, Nuba Mountains, on some outlying hills in Mesakin Hills, Reika village. *Class:* Niger-Congo, Kordofanian, Talodi, Talodi Proper, Ngile-Dengebu. *Dialects:* Lexical similarity 80% with Ngile (closest). *Lg Use:* Speakers also use Sudanese Arabic.

Dair (Daier, Thaminyi) [drb] 1,000 (1978 GR). Northern Sudan, west and south parts of Jebel Dair, Kordofan. *Class:* Nilo-Saharan, Eastern Sudanic, Eastern, Nubian, Central, Hill, Unclassified. *Other:* SOV.

Daju, Dar Fur (Nyala-Lagowa, Fininga, Dagu, Daju Ferne, Beke) [daj] 143,053 (2000 WCD). Northern Sudan, Dar Fur Province, in the Daju Hills 25 miles northeast of Nyala. Also in Geneina District in Dar Masalit. The West Kordofan dialect is in the Daju Hills near Lagowa, with main settlements at Dar el Kabira (Kidong), Silecce and Warina; also Jebel Miheila, Nyukri, and Tamanyik. *Class:* Nilo-Saharan, Eastern Sudanic, Western, Daju, Western Daju. *Dialects:* Nyala, Lagowa. Lexical similarity 83% between Nyala and Lagowa, 74% with Sila, 62% with Shatt, 56% with Logorik. *Other:* Muslim.

Daju, Dar Sila (Sila, Sula, Mongo-Sila, Bokor, Bokoruge, Bokorike) [dau] Northern Sudan. Nearly all those Daju of Dar Sila who are in Sudan have migrated into Dar Fur and settled there in recent times. *Dialects:* Mongo, Sila. *Other:* Little education. Traditional religion, Muslim. See main entry under Chad.

Didinga ('Di'dinga, Xaroxa, Toi, Lango) [did] 100,000 (2000). 1997 parish survey indicated population of 117,000, but it is not clear if this is entirely Didinga. Southern Sudan, Didinga Hills (about 60km. northeast of the junction of the Sudan, Kenya and Uganda borders) and north of Nagishot. *Class:* Nilo-Saharan, Eastern Sudanic, Eastern, Surmic, South, Southwest, Didinga-Murle, Didinga-Longarim. *Dialects:* Ethnic groups: Chukudum, Lowudo. Slight differences in speech between Chukudum and Lowudo, apparently mainly phonetic. Lexical similarity 83% with Narim, 71% with Murle. *Lg Dev:* Bible portions: 1994. *Other:* Different from Lango which is related to Lotuko. Traditional religion.

Dilling (Delen, Warki, Warkimbe) [dil] 5,295 (1984 R. C. Stevenson). Northern Sudan, Southern Kordofan, town of Dilling and surrounding hills, including Kudr. *Class:* Nilo-Saharan, Eastern Sudanic, Eastern, Nubian, Central, Hill, Unclassified. *Dialects:* Dilling, Debri. Lexical similarity 94% with Debri, 93% with Kadaru. *Other:* SOV.

Dinka, Northeastern (Padang, White Nile Dinka) [dip] 320,000 (1986 UBS). Population includes 7,200 Abialang, 9,000 Dongjol, 2,500 Luac, 16,000 Ngok-Sobat, 20,000 Jok, 13,500 Ageer, 2,000 Rut, 400 Thoi. Southern Sudan, northeast of the Sudd, along both sides of the White Nile, and along the Sobat River. *Class:* Nilo-Saharan, Eastern Sudanic, Nilotic, Western, Dinka-Nuer, Dinka. *Dialects:* Abiliang (Dinka Ibrahim, Akoon, Bawom, Bowom), Dongjol, Luac (Luaic), Ngok-Sobat (Ngork, Jok), Ageer (Ager, Ageir, Abuya, Beer, Niel, Nyel, Paloc, Paloic), Rut, Thoi. Lexical similarity 92% with Northwestern Dinka, 88% with Southwestern Dinka, 88% with Southeastern Dinka, 86% with South Central Dinka. *Lg Use:* Speakers also use Sudanese Arabic. *Lg Dev:* NT: 1952. *Other:* 'Jaang' is a cover term for all Dinka languages. Traditional religion, Christian, Muslim.

Dinka, Northwestern (Ruweng) [diw] 80,000 (1986). Southern Sudan, north of the Bahr el Ghazal River, and southern Kordofan around Abyei. *Class:* Nilo-Saharan, Eastern Sudanic, Nilotic, Western, Dinka-Nuer, Dinka. *Dialects:* Alor, Ngok-Kordofan, Pan Aru, Pawany. A separate language from other Dinka (J. Duerksen SIL). Lexical similarity 88% with Southwestern Dinka and Southeastern Dinka, 84% with South Central Dinka.

Dinka, South Central (Agar, Central Dinka) [dib] 250,000. Population includes 2,000 Aker, 2,000 Thany, 22,000 Ciec, 25,000 Gok (Tucker and Bryan). (Total Dinka 2,000,000 or more). Southern Sudan, west of the Nile, south of the Sudd. Aker is southeast of the Agar; Aliap is south of the Bor in a few fishing villages mainly on the east bank of the Nile. Ciec is in Lakes District on the west bank of the Nile. Gok is between the Agar and the Rek in Jur River and Lakes districts. *Class:* Nilo-Saharan, Eastern Sudanic, Nilotic, Western, Dinka-Nuer, Dinka. *Dialects:* Aliap (Aliab, Thany, Aker), Ciec (Ciem, Cic, Chiech, Kwac, Ajak, Ador), Gok (Gauk, Cok), Agar. Gok is also influenced by Southwestern Dinka and has a number of Arabic loans. Agar is becoming accepted as the educational standard for South Central Dinka. Lexical similarity 90% with Southeastern Dinka. *Lg Use:* Speakers also use Sudanese Arabic. *Lg Dev:* Bible portions: 1866–1916. *Other:* Pastoralists; agriculturalists: grain, corn, peanuts, beans. Traditional religion, Christian, Muslim.

Dinka, Southeastern (Bor, Eastern Dinka) [dks] 250,000. Population includes 21,000 Atoc, 9,000 Ghol, 4,000 Nyarueng, 35,000 Twi, 21,000 Bor Gok (Tucker and Bryan). 500,000 including South Central (Agar) and Southeastern (Bor) (1982 UBS). Southern Sudan, east of the Nile, around Bor, and northwards. *Class:* Nilo-Saharan, Eastern Sudanic, Nilotic, Western, Dinka-Nuer, Dinka. *Dialects:* Bor (Bor Gok), Athoc (Athoic, Atoc, Borathoi, Bor Athoic), Ghol, Nyarweng (Nyarueng, Narreweng), Tuic (Twi). *Lg Use:* Sudanese Arabic is the second language. Speakers of some dialects also speak Nuer Gewaar and Nuer Lou. *Lg Dev:* NT: 1940. *Other:* Traditional religion, Christian, Muslim.

Dinka, Southwestern (Rek, Western Dinka) [dik] 450,000 (1982 UBS). Population includes 55,000 Abiem, 15,000 Luac, 40,000 Malual, 17,000 Paliet, 35,000 Palioupiny, 50,000 Tuic. Southern Sudan, north and northwest of Wau. *Class:* Nilo-Saharan, Eastern Sudanic, Nilotic, Western, Dinka-Nuer, Dinka. *Dialects:* Rek (Raik), Abiem (Ajong Dit, Ajong Thi, Akany Kok, Akern Jok, Apuoth, Apwoth, Anei), Aguok (Agwok), Apuk, Awan, Lau, Luac, Malual (Malwal, Atoktou, Duliit, Korok, Makem, Peth), Paliet (Baliet, Ajak, Buoncwai, Bon Shwai, Bwoncwai, Kongder, Kondair, Thany Bur, Tainbour), Palioping (Palioping, Akjuet, Akwang, Ayat, Cimel, Gomjuer), Tuic (Twic, Twich, Twij, Adhiang, Amiol, Nyang, Thon). Luac dialect is different from Luac dialect in Northeastern Dinka. Lexical similarity 89% with South Central Dinka, 90% with Southeastern Dinka. *Lg Use:* Speakers also use Sudanese Arabic. *Other:* Animal husbandry: cattle. Traditional religion, Christian, Muslim.

Domari [rmt] Northern Sudan. *Other:* Main clans in Sudan: Halabi, Ghajar. Muslim. See main entry under Iran.

Dongotono [ddd] 6,219 (2000 WCD). Southern Sudan, eastern Equatoria Province, Dongotono Hills southeast of Torit. *Class:* Nilo-Saharan, Eastern Sudanic, Nilotic, Eastern, Lotuxo-Teso, Lotuxo-Maa, Lotuxo. *Dialects:* Lexical similarity 60% with Otuho.

El Hugeirat (El Hagarat) [elh] 200 (2000 Brenzinger). Northern Sudan, West Kordofan on El Hugeirat Hills. *Class:* Nilo-Saharan, Eastern Sudanic, Eastern, Nubian, Central, Hill, Unclassified. *Other:* SOV.

Feroge (Ferroge, Feroghe, Kaligi, Kaliki, Kalige, Kalike) [fer] 8,000 (1982 SIL). Southern Sudan, Western Bahr el Ghazal at Khor Shamam, 8 miles northeast of Raga. *Class:* Niger-Congo, Atlantic-Congo, Volta-Congo, North, Adamawa-Ubangi, Ubangi, Sere-Ngbaka-Mba, Sere, Feroge-Mangaya. *Dialects:* Indri, Mangaya, and Togoyo are closely related languages. *Lg Use:* Many also use Sudanese Arabic. *Other:* Their own name is 'Kaligi'. 'Feroge' is the Arabic name for the people. Muslim.

Fulfulde, Adamawa (Fellata) [fub] 90,000 in Sudan (1982 SIL). Northern Sudan, Blue Nile and Kordofan regions. *Dialect:* Gombe. *Lg Use:* Few monolinguals; most are children. Many speak Sudanese Arabic; some also speak Hausa and Songai as second languages. Mahdist group is bilingual in Fulfulde and Sudanese Spoken Arabic. *Other:* Previous migrations from Sokoto, Nigeria; Maasina, Mali; Liptaako and Jelgooji, Burkina Faso; Adamawa and Gombe, Nigeria; and the Wodaabe lineage have settled in Sudan. Some also from Cameroon. Predominant Fulfulde in Sudan is Adamawa. Influenced by Arabic. Muwalid group is monolingual in Sudanese Spoken Arabic. Muslim. See main entry under Cameroon.

Fur (For, Fora, Fordunga, Furawi, Furakang, Forta, Forok, Konjara, Kungara, Yerge, Onage, Korra, Kadirgi, Kurka, Dala, Lali) [fvr] 500,000 in Sudan (1983 Bender). Population total all countries: 501,800. Northern Sudan, Dar Fur. Also spoken in Chad. *Class:* Nilo-Saharan, Fur. *Dialects:* Largely uniform with some dialect differences. *Lg Use:* Those in urban situations are shifting to Arabic. *Lg Dev:* Grammar. *Other:* SOV. Mountain slope, foothills, lowland. Agriculturalists: millet, sorghum, peanuts, vegetables, spices, fruit; animal husbandry: cattle. Muslim.

Gaam (Ingassana, Ingessana, Tabi, Metabi, Muntabi, Mamedja, Mamidza, Kamanidi) [tbi] 67,166 (2000 WCD). Northern Sudan. The main center is in and around Jebel Tabi, on Tabi Massif and outlying hills. A small community in Khartoum. Not in Ethiopia. *Class:* Nilo-Saharan, Eastern Sudanic, Eastern, Eastern Jebel, Gaam. *Dialects:* Soda (Tao), Kukur (Gor), Kulang (Kulelek, Bau), Buwahg (Buek). *Lg Dev:* Orthography developed and literacy materials in use. *Other:* Clan groups: Agadi, Bagis, Beek, Bulmut, Kilgu, Kukuli, Mugum, Sidak. Traditional religion, Muslim, Christian.

Gbaya (Kresh, Kreish, Kreich, Kredj, Kparla, Kpala, Kpara) [krs] 16,000 in Sudan (1987 SIL). Southern Sudan, Western Bahr el Ghazal Province. At Kuru, Deim Zubeir, Raga, Angbanga, Kata, Menangba, Boro, Kafia Kingi. The Dongo are reported by Fr. Santandrea to be in Hobbinya District of Southern Dar Fur Province. Also communities in Wau and Khartoum. Largest numbers in Raga and Boro. A few refugees have settled in Central African Republic and elsewhere. Also spoken in Central African Republic. *Class:* Nilo-Saharan, Central Sudanic, West, Kresh. *Dialects:* Naka (Kresh-Boro), Gbaya-Ndogo (Kresh-Ndogo), Gbaya-Ngbongbo (Kresh-Hofra), Gbaya-Gboko, Orlo (Woro), Gbaya-Dara, Dongo. 8 tribes and dialects. Gbaya-Ndogo is prestigious and understood by all. Naka is largest and also well understood. *Lg Use:* About 4,000 others speak Gbaya as second language. Men and those who have been to school speak Sudanese Arabic as second language for most common topics. They do not accept Standard Arabic, except for a few who have been to school. *Other:* SVO; prepositions; genitives, articles, relatives after noun heads; adjectives before, numerals usually before noun heads; CV, V, CCV (CVC rare); tonal, 5 tones. Plains. Wooded savanna. 400 meters (Wau), 600 meters (Raga), 700 meters (Boro). Swidden agriculturalists; craftsmen in towns. Muslim, Christian.

Ghulfan (Gulfan, Wunci, Wuncimbe) [ghl] 16,000 (1984 R. C. Stevenson). Northern Sudan, Kordofan, in two hill ranges 25 to 30 miles south of Dilling: Ghulfan Kurgul and Ghulfan Morung. *Class:* Nilo-Saharan, Eastern Sudanic, Eastern, Nubian, Central, Hill, Kadaru-Ghulfan. *Other:* SOV.

Gula (Kara, Kara of Sudan, Yamegi) [kcm] 200 to 2,000 in Sudan (1987 SIL). Southern Sudan at Kafia Kingi in extreme western Bahr el Ghazal Province and at Kata. *Dialects:* Gula (Goula), Nguru (Bubu, Koyo). *Lg Use:* Many in Sudan are reported to be bilingual in Kresh or Arabic. *Other:* Different from Kara of Central African Republic, Kare of Chad, or Gula of Chad. See main entry under Central African Republic.

Gule (Anej, Hamej, Fecakomodiyo) [gly] Extinct. Ethnic population: 1,000 (1983 Bender). Northern Sudan, Jebel Gule, San and Roro hills north of the Gaam, west of Er Roseires. *Class:* Nilo-Saharan, Komuz, Koman. *Lg Use:* Members of the ethnic group now speak Arabic. *Other:* Muslim, traditional religion.

Gumuz (Mendeya, Debatsa, Deguba, Dehenda, Gumis, Gombo, Shankillinya, Shanqilla) [guk] 40,000 in Sudan. Northern Sudan, east of Er Roseires, around Famaka and Fazoglo on the Blue Nile and northwards along the Ethiopia border. *Dialects:* Disoha (Desua), Dakunza (Degoja, Dukunza, Gunza, Ganza, Dukuna, Dugunza), Sai, Sese (Saysay), Dekoka, Dewiya, Kukwaya, Gombo, Jemhwa, Modea. See main entry under Ethiopia.

Hausa [hau] 489,000 in Sudan (2001 Johnstone and Mandryk). Northern Sudan. *Lg Use:* Trade language. In Sudan many speakers are probably ethnic Fulani who no longer speak Fulfulde. *Other:* Muslim. See main entry under Nigeria.

Heiban (Ebang, Abul) [hbn] 4,412 (1984). Northern Sudan, around Heiban, Abul (Obul), and nearby hills. In Heiban town on the Abri-Talodi road. *Class:* Niger-Congo, Kordofanian, Heiban, West-Central, Central, Ebang-Logol, Ebang-Laru. *Dialects:* Lexical similarity 90% with Laro (closest). *Lg Use:* Speakers also use Sudanese Arabic. *Lg Dev:* NT: 1966.

Homa [hom] Extinct. Southern Sudan, around towns of Mopoi and Tambura. *Class:* Niger-Congo, Atlantic-Congo, Volta-Congo, Benue-Congo, Bantoid, Southern, Narrow Bantu, Central, D, Bira-Huku (D.30). *Lg Use:* Extinct in 1975.

Indri (Yanderika, Yandirika) [idr] 700. Southern Sudan, southwest, in a small area around Raga. *Class:* Niger-Congo, Atlantic-Congo, Volta-Congo, North, Adamawa-Ubangi, Ubangi, Sere-Ngbaka-Mba, Sere, Indri-Togoyo. *Dialects:* Closest to Feroge. *Lg Use:* Speakers are reported to be bilingual in Arabic or Feroge.

Jumjum (Berin, Olga, Wadega) [jum] 50,374 (2000 WCD). Northern Upper Nile Province, along Khor Jumjum on Jebels Tunga, Terta, and Wadega. *Class:* Nilo-Saharan, Eastern Sudanic, Nilotic, Western, Luo, Northern, Maban-Burun, Maban.

Jur Modo (Modo, Jur) [bex] 100,000 (2004 SIL). Southern Sudan, vicinity of Mvolo and on the Naam (Olo) River. *Class:* Nilo-Saharan, Central Sudanic, West, Bongo-Bagirmi, Bongo-Baka, Morokodo-Beli. *Dialects:* Lori, Modo (Jur Modo, Modo Lali), Wira, Wetu. *Lg Use:* Vigorous. The Wetu dialect is not extinct. All domains, oral and written use in administration, commerce, written use in folk stories, keeping of family records. Positive language attitude. Many speakers also use Arabic, Dinka,

Moru, Baka, or Zande. *Lg Dev:* Taught in primary schools. NT: 1998. *Other:* Plains, riverine. Agriculturalists including fruit.

Kacipo-Balesi [koe] 10,000 in Sudan (2003). Almost completely monolingual. Population total all countries: 14,120. Southern Sudan, on the Boma Plateau among the Murle, near the Ethiopian border. Also spoken in Ethiopia. *Class:* Nilo-Saharan, Eastern Sudanic, Eastern, Surmic, South, Southwest, Kacipo-Balesi. *Dialects:* Kichepo, Suri, Western Suri. Related to Murle and Didinga. Pronoun differences between Balesi and Zilmamu. Lexical similarity 40% to 54% with Murle, 35% with Mursi. *Other:* They have little contact with the outside world. They call themselves 'Kacipo'. VSO. Traditional religion.

Kadaru (Kadaro, Kadero, Kaderu, Kodoro, Kodhin, Kodhinniai) [kdu] 12,360 (2000 WCD). Northern Sudan, Kordofan Province, Nuba mountains, Kadaru Hills between Dilling and Delami. *Class:* Nilo-Saharan, Eastern Sudanic, Eastern, Nubian, Central, Hill, Kadaru-Ghulfan. *Dialects:* Kadaru (Kodur), Kururu (Tagle), Kafir (Ka'e), Kurtala (Ngokra), Dabatna (Kaaral), Kuldaji (Kendal). Lexical similarity 93% with Dilling, 92% to 87% with Debri, 60% with Birked. *Other:* The dialects are spoken by clan groups living on separate hills. SOV.

Kakwa (Bari Kakwa, Kakua, Kwakwak, Kakwak) [keo] 40,000 in Sudan (1978 SIL). Southern Sudan, Yei District, extending into Democratic Republic of the Congo in the west at Aba and in the south around Mahagi. *Other:* Agriculturalists: maize, eleusine, peanuts, simsim, sweet potatoes, cassava, honey; pastoralists: goats, few sheep, cattle. Christian, traditional religion. See main entry under Uganda.

Kanga [kcp] 8,000 (1989). Northern Sudan, Miri Hills, west and southwest of Kadugli. The most southwesterly hills of the Nuba Mountains. The Kufa cluster of villages lies southeast of Miri, northeast of Lima, and north of Kanga. Four main villages in Kufa: Toole, Lenyaguyox, Bilenya, and 'Dologi. Toole was the main centre. *Class:* Nilo-Saharan, Unclassified. *Dialects:* Abu Sinun, Chiroro-Kursi, Kanga, Kufa-Lima, Krongo Abdalla. Lexical similarity 85% with Tumma (closest). *Lg Use:* Speakers also use Sudanese Arabic.

Kanuri, Central (Yerwa Kanuri, Kanouri, Bornu, Bornouans, Kanoury, Kole, Sirata, "Beriberi") [knc] 195,000 in Sudan (1993 Johnstone). Northern. *Dialects:* Dagara, Kaga (Kagama), Sugurti, Lare, Kwayam, Njesko, Kabari (Kuvuri), Ngazar, Guvja, Mao, Temageri, Fadawa, Maiduguri. *Other:* "Beriberi" is considered a derogatory name. Muslim. See main entry under Nigeria.

Karko (Garko, Kithonirishe) [kko] 12,986 (1984 R. C. Stevenson). Northern Sudan, Kordofan, in Karko Hills 20 miles west of Dilling, including Dulman. May also be spoken on Abu Jinik to the west (1,000) and El Tabaq southwest of Katla (800). *Class:* Nilo-Saharan, Eastern Sudanic, Eastern, Nubian, Central, Hill, Unclassified. *Lg Use:* Speakers also use Sudanese Arabic. *Other:* SOV.

Katcha-Kadugli-Miri [xtc] 81,500 (2004 SIL). Population includes 48,864 Kadugli and Katcha, 4,000 Miri (1987 Baumann) and 6,500 Tumma (1956 census). Northern Sudan, Kordofan Province, in the southern hills of the Nuba Hills area. Katcha is in villages of Katcha, Tuna, Kafina, Dabakaya (Donga), Belanya, and Farouq, a short distance south of Kadugli and southeast of the Miri Hills. Kadugli is also in villages surrounding Kadugli, namely, Murta, Kulba, 'Daalimo, Thappare, and Takko. Miri villages of Miri Bara, Miri Guwa, Umduiu, Nyimodu, Luba, Kadoda, Kya, Tulluk, Hayar al-Nimr, Kuduru, Kasari, and Sogolle lie west of Kadugli. *Class:* Nilo-Saharan, Unclassified. *Dialects:* Katcha (Tolubi, Dholubi), Kadugli (Dakalla, Talla, Dhalla, Toma Ma Dalla, Kudugli, Morta), Miri, Damba, Tumma. R. C. Stevenson treats them as dialects of one language. Ruhlen (1987) and Schadeberg (1989) treat them as separate. Samir Bulus says that Tumma is dialect of Katcha. Lexical similarity 85% among Katcha, Kadugli, and Miri, 88% between Kadugli and Damba. *Lg Use:* Speakers also use Sudanese Arabic. *Other:* Some Daju live among the Kadugli.

Katla (Akalak, Kalak) [kcr] 14,208 (1984 R. C. Stevenson). Northern Sudan, Nuba Hills, Katla Hills 35 miles southwest of Dilling. *Class:* Niger-Congo, Kordofanian, Katla. *Dialect:* Bombori, Kateik, Kiddu, Kirkpong, Karoka, Koldrong, Julud (Gulud). Related to Tima. The dialects listed are place names where variations are spoken.

Keiga (Yega, Keiga-Timero, Keiga-Al-Kheil, Demik, Aigang) [kec] 6,072 (1984 R. C. Stevenson). Northern Sudan, Nuba Hills area, Jebel Demik, north of Miri, western part of Kadugli Province. Three areas: Ambong (villages: Ambong, Ambongadi, Kandang, Kuluwaring, Tingiragadi, Lakkadi, Taffor, Arungekkaadi, Bila Ndulang, Roofik, Saadhing); Lubung (villages: Kuwaik, Tungunungunu, Miya Ntaarang, Miya Ntaluwa, Miya Ndumuru, Semalili); Tumuro (villages: Koolo, Kayide, Jughuba, Tumuro). *Class:* Nilo-Saharan, Unclassified. *Dialects:* Demik (Rofik), Keiga (Aigang). Lexical similarity 60% with closest Kadugli languages. *Lg Use:* Most domains. About half the children learn the language. Speakers also use Sudanese Arabic.

Keliko (Kaliko) [kbo] 10,000 in Sudan (1998 SIL). Population total all countries: 22,500. Southern Sudan, southern part of Yei District. Also spoken in Democratic Republic of the Congo, Uganda. *Class:* Nilo-Saharan, Central Sudanic, East, Moru-Madi, Central. *Dialects:* Eastern Keliko, Western Keliko. *Lg Dev:* Bible portions: 2002. *Other:* The name 'Keliko' is preferred in Sudan, 'Kaliko' in the other countries. Traditional religion, Christian.

Kelo (Tornasi, Kelo-Beni Sheko, Ndu-Faa-Keelo) [xel] 200. Northern Sudan, Tornasi Hills; Jebels Tornasi (Keeli village) and Beni Sheko. West of Berta speaking people. *Class:* Nilo-Saharan, Eastern Sudanic, Eastern, Eastern Jebel, Aka-Kelo-Molo. *Dialects:* Beni Sheko, Kelo. *Lg Use:* M. L. Bender reports that they are not extinct (1997). *Other:* Muslim.

Kenuzi-Dongola (Dongola-Kenuz, Nile Nubian, Dongolawi) [kzh] 180,000 in Sudan (1996). Population total all countries: 280,000. Northern Sudan, mainly at Dongola and surrounding villages in Northern Province. The northern boundary with Nobiin is at Burgeg. Also spoken in Egypt. *Class:* Nilo-Saharan, Eastern Sudanic, Eastern, Nubian, Central, Dongolawi. *Dialect:* Dongola, Kenuzi (Kenuz, Kunuzi). Not intelligible with Nobiin. Lexical similarity 67% with Nobiin, 56% with Debri. *Lg Use:* Speakers also use Sudanese Arabic. *Lg Dev:* Arabic and Roman scripts in Egypt. Bible portions: 1912.

Ko (Kau, Fungor, Fungur) [fuj] 2,683 (1984 R. C. Stevenson). Northern Sudan, on small isolated hills in the extreme eastern part of the Nuba hills, between Talodi and the White Nile. *Class:* Niger-Congo, Kordofanian, Heiban, Eastern. *Dialects:* Kau (Ko), Nyaro. Nyaro and Kau may be the same dialect. Lexical similarity 67% with Warnang (closest). *Other:* Traditional religion.

Koalib (Kawalib, Kowalib, Ngirere, Nirere, Rere, Lgalige, Abri) [kib] 44,258 (1984 R. C. Stevenson). Northern Sudan, southern Kordofan Province, Nuba Mountains, around Delami, including Umm Berumbita and Turum (Nguqwurang), south and southwest of Abri around Koalib range (Ngunduna), at and around Nyukwur, also at Umm Heitan and Hadra (Nginyukwur), in villages scattered over the plain around Abri (Ngirere). *Class:* Niger-Congo, Kordofanian, Heiban, West-Central, Central, Rere. *Dialects:* Nguqwurang, Ngunduna, Nginyukwur,

Ngirere, Ngemere. Lexical similarity 75% with closest Heiban languages. *Lg Use:* Speakers also use Sudanese Arabic. *Lg Dev:* NT: 1967–1994. *Other:* Traditional religion, Muslim, Christian.

Komo (Koma of Daga, Como, Central Koma, Gokwom, Hayahaya, Madiin) [xom] 10,000 in Sudan (1979 James). Population total all countries: 11,500. Northern Sudan, around Ahmar, Tombak, and Yabus rivers, in southern Funj Region of Blue Nile Province. Also spoken in Ethiopia. *Class:* Nilo-Saharan, Komuz, Koman. *Dialects:* Beilla, Chali. Those listed as dialects may be separate languages. Lexical similarity 52% with Uduk. *Lg Dev:* Dictionary. Bible portions: 1960–1963. *Other:* Different from Koma of Cameroon.

Krongo (Korongo, Kurungu, Kadumodi, Tabanya, Dimodongo) [kgo] 21,688 (1984 R. C. Stevenson). Northern Sudan, Krongo Hills, south of Masakin range and west of Talodi, Kordofan Province. Mainly in Tabanya, Toroji and Angolo, and also in Damaguto, Dimadragu, Dimodongo, and Dar. *Class:* Nilo-Saharan, Unclassified. *Dialect:* Fama-Teis-Kua. Lexical similarity 85% with Tumtum. *Lg Use:* Speakers also use Sudanese Arabic. *Lg Dev:* Grammar. NT: 1963. *Other:* Traditional religion, Muslim, Christian.

Lafofa [laf] 600 (2000 Brenzinger). Northern Sudan, Nuba Hills, central Eliri range, and on two hills to the south and east. *Class:* Niger-Congo, Kordofanian, Talodi, Tegem. *Dialects:* Jebel El Amira (El Amira), Jebel Tekeim (Jebel, Tekeim, Tegem), Lafofa. Lexical similarity 25% with closest languages.

Lango (Langgo) [lno] 20,000 (1987 SIL). Southern Sudan, eastern Equatoria Province, Torit District. *Class:* Nilo-Saharan, Eastern Sudanic, Nilotic, Eastern, Lotuxo-Teso, Lotuxo-Maa, Lotuxo. *Dialects:* A separate language from Otuho. *Lg Use:* Speakers also use Otuho. *Other:* Different language from Lango of Uganda, or Lango, an alternate name for Didinga of Sudan. Pastoralists: cattle; agriculturalists: millet, beans, sweet potatoes, tobacco, bananas. Traditional religion.

Laro (Laru, Aaleira, Yillaro, Ngwullaro) [lro] 40,000 (1998 local). Northern Sudan, Nuba Hills on the hills of Laro (Alleira) and a few small hills nearby. *Class:* Niger-Congo, Kordofanian, Heiban, West-Central, Central, Ebang-Logol, Ebang-Laru. *Dialects:* Tunduli, Laro. Lexical similarity 90% with Heiban (closest). *Lg Use:* Speakers also use Sudanese Arabic. *Other:* Christian, Muslim, traditional religion.

Logol (Lukha) [lof] 7,811 (2000 WCD). Northern Sudan, on small isolated hills in the extreme eastern part of the Nuba Hills, between Talodi and the White Nile. *Class:* Niger-Congo, Kordofanian, Heiban, West-Central, Central, Ebang-Logol, Logol. *Dialects:* Lexical similarity 85% with Otoro (closest). *Other:* Traditional religion.

Logorik (Liguri) [liu] 2,000 (1971 Welmers). Northern Sudan, central Nuba Mountains, Jebel Liguri and other hills northeast of Kadugli. *Class:* Nilo-Saharan, Eastern Sudanic, Western, Daju, Eastern Daju. *Dialects:* Saburi, Tallau (Talau, Talo), Liguri. Lexical similarity 64% with Shatt, 56% with Daju of Dar Fur (Nyala and Lagowa), 57% with Sila. *Lg Use:* Speakers also use Sudanese Arabic. *Other:* Christian, Muslim, traditional religion.

Lokoya (Lokoiya, Lokoja, Loquia, Lowoi, Owoi, Loirya, Oirya, Ellyria, Oxoriok, Koyo) [lky] 40,138 (2000 WCD). Southern Sudan, eastern Equatoria, Torit District. *Class:* Nilo-Saharan, Eastern Sudanic, Nilotic, Eastern, Lotuxo-Teso, Lotuxo-Maa, Lotuxo. *Dialects:* Lexical similarity 64% with Otuho, 57% with Lopit, 56% with Dongotono. *Lg Use:* Speakers are reported to be bilingual in Otuho. *Other:* Ethnic groups: Irya and Owe. Animal husbandry: sheep, goats, cattle, poultry; agriculturalists: millet, simsim, beans, tobacco. Traditional religion.

Lopit (Loppit, Lopid, Lofit, Lafite, Lafit, Lafiit) [lpx] 50,000 (1995 Scott Randal). Southern Sudan, eastern Equatoria Province, Lopit Hills, northeast of Torit. *Class:* Nilo-Saharan, Eastern Sudanic, Nilotic, Eastern, Lotuxo-Teso, Lotuxo-Maa, Lotuxo. *Dialects:* Lexical similarity 63% with Otuho. *Other:* Blacksmiths; swidden agriculturalists; animal husbandry: cattle.

Lumun (Lomon, Kuku-Lumun) [lmd] 45,000 (1980 local count). Northern Sudan, Talodi, Moro Hills; villages Toromathan, To'ri, and Canya'ru. *Class:* Niger-Congo, Kordofanian, Talodi, Talodi Proper, Tocho. *Dialects:* Lexical similarity 70% with closest Talodi languages. *Lg Use:* Speakers also use Sudanese Arabic. *Lg Dev:* Bible portions: 2001–2002.

Luwo (Lwo, Jur Luo, Jur Lwo, Jo Lwo, Dhe Lwo, Dhe Luwo, Giur) [lwo] 80,000 (1983 census). Southern Sudan, Bahr el Ghazal, north of Wau toward Aweil, southeast of Wau as far as Tonj. *Class:* Nilo-Saharan, Eastern Sudanic, Nilotic, Western, Luo, Northern, Jur. *Dialects:* Different from Lwo of Uganda, or Luo of Kenya and Tanzania, but related. *Lg Use:* Vigorous. Thuri speakers sometimes use Luwo as second language. All domains, local administration, some use in schools, churches. Positive language attitude. Speakers also use Dinka, English, or Arabic. *Lg Dev:* NT: 2003. *Other:* Forest. Agriculturalists. Traditional religion, Christian.

Mabaan (Maaban, Meban, Southern Burun, Gura, Tungan, Barga, Tonko, Ulu) [mfz] 50,418 (2000 WCD). On the border of Blue Nile and Upper Nile provinces, between Yabus and Tombak rivers in the north and Khor Daga in the south. Not in Ethiopia. *Class:* Nilo-Saharan, Eastern Sudanic, Nilotic, Western, Luo, Northern, Maban-Burun, Maban. *Dialects:* Partially intelligible with some southern dialects of Burun. *Lg Dev:* NT: 1988–2002. *Other:* Traditional religion, Christian.

Ma'di (Ma'adi, Ma'diti) [mhi] 18,000 in Sudan (1982 SIL). Southern Sudan, Equatoria Province, Madi Subdistrict, Opari District, West Nile District. *Dialects:* Pandikeri, Lokai, Burulo. See main entry under Uganda.

Mandari (Mondari, Mundari, Shir, Chir, Kir) [mqu] 115,997 (2000 WCD). Southern Sudan, near Bari; 1 division around Tali, the other on both sides of the Nile between Tombe and Mongalla. *Class:* Nilo-Saharan, Eastern Sudanic, Nilotic, Eastern, Bari. *Dialects:* A different language and culture from Bari. Lexical similarity 75% with Nyanggwara, 71% with Bari and Ngyepu, 70% with Pöjulu, 66% with Kuku, 61% with Kakwa. *Other:* Nomadic. Ethnic groups: Mondari Boronga, Sere, Böri. Plain. Arid, acacia and scrub forest. Pastoralists: cattle, goats; agriculturalists: peanuts, beans, millet, simsim, maize, sugarcane, cassava, tobacco, Indian hemp, honey; gatherers: wild vegetables; fishermen; hunters. Traditional religion.

Mangayat (Mangaya, Mongaiyat, Bug, Buga) [myj] 400 (1987 SIL). Southern Sudan, in Western Bahr el Ghazal, some in Raga, most in Mangayat, 18 miles southeast of Raga. *Class:* Niger-Congo, Atlantic-Congo, Volta-Congo, North, Adamawa-Ubangi, Ubangi, Sere-Ngbaka-Mba, Sere, Feroge-Mangaya. *Lg Use:* Many also use Gbaya (Kresh) or Arabic. *Other:* They call themselves 'Bug'.

Masalit (Massalit, Kaana Masala, Jwisince) [mls] 173,810 in Sudan (2000 WCD). Population total all countries: 240,520. Northern Sudan, Dar Fur Province, Dar Masalit and Nyala District, scattered colonies in Dar Fongoro and to the south and east, and Gedaref Region; Geneina, Mistere, and Habila Kajangise. Also spoken in Chad. *Class:* Nilo-Saharan, Maban, Mabang, Masalit. *Dialects:* The dialect in Dar Masalit in Dar Fur differs from that spoken in Nyala District. Lexical similarity 36% with Karanga, 42% with Maba, 45% with Marfa. *Lg Use:* The majority use Arabic as second language; however, people

in the central area and women know only limited Arabic. *Other:* Muslim.

Midob (Meidob, Midobi, Tidda, Tid, Tid-N-Aal) [mei] 50,000 (1993 R. Werner). Northern Sudan, Dar Fur Province, Jebel Midob, and settled communities in Omdurman and Gezira Aba. The center is Malha. *Class:* Nilo-Saharan, Eastern Sudanic, Eastern, Nubian, Western. *Dialects:* Shelkota (Shalkota), Kaageddi, Urrti (Uurti). Lexical similarity 51% with Birgid (closest). *Other:* Pastoralists. Muslim.

Mittu [mwu] Extinct. Southern Sudan. *Class:* Nilo-Saharan, Central Sudanic, West, Bongo-Bagirmi, Bongo-Baka, Morokodo-Beli.

Mo'da (Gberi, Gweri, Gbara, Muda) [gbn] 600 (1977 Voegelin and Voegelin). Southern Sudan, northwest of Mvolo on both sides of the border of Lakes and Western Equatoria provinces. *Class:* Nilo-Saharan, Central Sudanic, West, Bongo-Bagirmi, Bongo-Baka, Morokodo-Beli, Morokodo-Mo'da. *Dialects:* Lexical similarity 64% with Morokodo, 58% with Jur Modo, 41% with Beli, 49% with Bongo, 38% with Baka.

Molo (Malkan, Tura-Ka-Molo) [zmo] 100 (1988 M.L. Bender). At Jebel Malkan, near the Berta language, south of the Blue Nile, near the Ethiopian border. *Class:* Nilo-Saharan, Eastern Sudanic, Eastern, Eastern Jebel, Aka-Kelo-Molo. *Lg Use:* Reported to be bilingual in Arabic and Berta. *Other:* They call themselves 'Tura-Ka-Molo', meaning 'speech of Molo'. Muslim.

Moro (Dhimorong) [mor] 30,000 (1982 SIL). Northern Sudan, eastern Nuba Mountains, Kordofan Province. *Class:* Niger-Congo, Kordofanian, Heiban, West-Central, Western. *Dialects:* Umm Dorein (Longorban), Umm Gabralla (Toberelda), Nderre, Laiyen, Nubwa, Ulba, Werria. Lexical similarity 75% with Tira (closest). *Lg Dev:* NT: 1965–1994.

Morokodo (Ma'di) [mgc] 3,400 (1977 Voegelin and Voegelin). Population includes 280 Biti. Southern Sudan, in the area between Amadi and Maridi. *Class:* Nilo-Saharan, Central Sudanic, West, Bongo-Bagirmi, Bongo-Baka, Morokodo-Beli, Morokodo-Mo'da. *Dialects:* Biti, Ma'du, Morokodo. A dialect cluster. Lexical similarity 63% with Jur Modo, 41% with Beli, 45% with Bongo, 43% with Baka. *Lg Use:* The Ma'du dialect may be extinct (1984). Many use Moru as second language. *Lg Dev:* Orthography developed and literacy materials in use.

Moru (Kala Moru) [mgd] 70,000 (1982 SIL). Population includes 1,200 Agi, 2,500 Andri, 5,000 Kadiro, 9,000 Miza, 400 Wa'di. Southern Sudan, Mundri District, Equatoria Province. *Class:* Nilo-Saharan, Central Sudanic, East, Moru-Madi, Northern. *Dialects:* Agi, Andri, 'Bali'ba, Kadiro, Lakama'di, Miza, Moruwa'di. Andri and 'Bali'ba dialects are similar, Kadiro and Lakama'di are nearly identical. *Lg Dev:* Literacy rate in second language: 85%. Bible: 2000. *Other:* SVO, SOV.

Mündü (Mundo, Mountou, Mondu, Mondo) [muh] 23,000 in Sudan. Population total all countries: 25,800. Southern Sudan, western Equatoria Province northwest of Yei and in Moru District south of Maridi. Also spoken in Democratic Republic of the Congo. *Class:* Niger-Congo, Atlantic-Congo, Volta-Congo, North, Adamawa-Ubangi, Ubangi, Sere-Ngbaka-Mba, Ngbaka-Mba, Ngbaka, Eastern, Mundu. *Dialect:* Shatt. Closest to Mayogo and Bangba of Democratic Republic of the Congo. *Lg Use:* There is intermarriage with the Avokaya and Baka, and bilingualism in those languages. Some bilingualism also in Bangala and Arabic. *Lg Dev:* Literacy rate in first language: 10% to 15%. Literacy rate in second language: 25% to 50%. Bible portions: 1984–1995.

Murle (Murelei, Merule, Mourle, Murule, Beir, Ajibba, Agiba, Adkibba) [mur] 60,000 in Sudan (1982 SIL). Population total all countries: 60,200. Southern Sudan,

Upper Nile Province, Pibor District, south of the Akobo River, Boma Plateau, and to east and north. Also spoken in Ethiopia. *Class:* Nilo-Saharan, Eastern Sudanic, Eastern, Surmic, South, Southwest, Didinga-Murle, Murle. *Dialects:* Related to Didinga. Subgroups: Lotilla, Boma, Olam (Ngalam). Maacir may be a dialect or ethnic group. Lexical similarity 74% with Narim, 71% with Didinga. *Lg Dev:* Dictionary. Grammar. NT: 1996. *Other:* Ethnic groups: Lotilla, Boma, Olam (Ngalan). VSO, postpositions; genitives and relatives follow noun heads; suffixes indicate case; question words final; verbal affixes (prefixes and suffixes) distinguish subject person and number. Riverine. Savannah. Seminomadic pastoralists. Traditional religion, Christian.

Narim (Larim, Larimo, Lariim, Nariim, Longarim, Lariminit) [loh] 3,623 (1983 Fukui). Southern Sudan, western Boya Hills, around Mt. Kosodek and Mt. Lobuli. *Class:* Nilo-Saharan, Eastern Sudanic, Eastern, Surmic, South, Southwest, Didinga-Murle, Didinga-Longarim. *Dialects:* Lexical similarity 74% with Murle, 83% with Didinga. *Lg Dev:* Literacy rate in second language: 10%. *Other:* 'Boya' is the name for the people. 'Longarim' is the Didinga name. Pastoralists; agriculturalists. Christian.

Nding (Eliri) [eli] 400 (1971 Welmers). Northern Sudan, southern Eliri range. *Class:* Niger-Congo, Kordofanian, Talodi, Talodi Proper, Nding. *Dialects:* Lexical similarity 70% with closest Talodi languages.

Ndogo [ndz] 23,343 (2000 WCD). Few monolinguals. Southern Sudan, Western District along Wau-Deim Zubeir Road between Mboro and Kpango rivers. A few are north of Tembura among the Zande. Not in Central African Republic. *Class:* Niger-Congo, Atlantic-Congo, Volta-Congo, North, Adamawa-Ubangi, Ubangi, Sere-Ngbaka-Mba, Sere, Sere-Bviri, Ndogo-Sere. *Lg Use:* Language of wider communication. Vigorous in most areas. Spoken as a second language by the Golo, Gbaya at Deim Zubeir, Bai, West Central Banda, Balanda, Golo, Sere, some Gbaya, Woro, some Luwo. All domains. Oral use in courts, commerce, personal letters. Used in first year in some schools. Positive language attitude. Nearly all speak some Bayi, Golo, Sere, Balanda, Arabic, English, Dinka, Luwo, Gbaya, or Banda as second language. *Lg Dev:* 10,000 can read Ndogo, 2000 can write it. Taught in primary schools. NT: 2001. *Other:* Perhaps 30% displaced to Wau (regional capital) or to cities in northern Sudan. Gbaya-Ndogo is a different language. Riverine, plains. Forested savannah. Agriculturalists. Christian, traditional religion.

Ngile (Masakin, Mesakin, Daloka, Taloka, Darra) [jle] 38,000 (1982 SIL). Population includes Dajik. Northern Sudan, Kordofan Province, Nuba Mountains, in Mesakin Hills on some outlying hills. *Class:* Niger-Congo, Kordofanian, Talodi, Talodi Proper, Ngile-Dengebu. *Dialects:* Aheima (El Akheimar), Daloka (Taloka), Masakin Gusar (Mesakin Qusar, Masakin Buram), Masakin Tuwal (Tiwal, Towal).

Njalgulgule (Nyolge, Nyoolne, Ngulgule, Begi, Bege, Beko, Njangulgule) [njl] 900 (1977 Voegelin and Voegelin). Southern Sudan, on the Sopo River just above the Sopo-Boro confluence, and west of the Dinka. 1 village. *Class:* Nilo-Saharan, Eastern Sudanic, Western, Daju, Western Daju. *Lg Use:* Speakers also use Arabic. *Other:* Muslim.

Nobiin (Mahas-Fiadidja, Mahas-Fiyadikkya, Fiadidja-Mahas) [fia] 295,000 in Sudan (1996). Population total all countries: 495,000. Northern Province, northwards from Burgeg to the Egyptian border at Wadi Halfa. Also at New Halfa in Kassala Province. Also spoken in Egypt. *Class:* Nilo-Saharan, Eastern Sudanic, Eastern, Nubian, Northern. *Dialects:* Mahas (Mahasi, Mahass), Fiyadikka (Fedicca, Fadicha, Fadicca, Fadija, Fiadidja). Not intelligible with Kenuzi-Dongola.

Lexical similarity 67% with Kenuzi-Dongola. *Lg Use:* Spoken by the Mahas in Sudan and the Fedicca in Egypt. Speakers also use Sudanese Arabic. *Lg Dev:* Arabic and Roman scripts in Egypt. Bible portions: 1860–1899. *Other:* Called 'Fiadidja-Mahas' in Egypt. Muslim.

Nuer (Naath, Naadh) [nus] 740,000 in Sudan (1982 SIL). Population includes 2,935 Western Jikany, 12,500 Lou, 1,100 Nyuong, 2,500 Thiang, 5,900 Bul, 2,400 Jagai, 6,700 Laak, 4,900 Leik, 1,600 Door, 17,600 Eastern Jikany (1977 Voegelin and Voegelin). Population total all countries: 804,907. Southern Sudan, east Upper Nile Province, in the region of Nasir on the upper Sobat River, in and around a triangle formed between Bahr el Zeraf and Bahr el Jebel, and extending up the Sobat River across the Ethiopian border. Also spoken in Ethiopia. *Class:* Nilo-Saharan, Eastern Sudanic, Nilotic, Western, Dinka-Nuer, Nuer. *Dialects:* Dor (Door), Eastern Jikany (Jikain, Jekaing), Abigar, Western Jikany, Cien, Thognaath (Thok Nath), Lou (Lau), Nyuong, Thiang (Bul, Gawaar, Jagai, Laak, Leik). Dialects correspond mainly to geographic divisions. *Lg Use:* Speakers also use Arabic. *Lg Dev:* Bible: 1999. *Other:* They call themselves 'Naath'. Severe disruption in residence patterns caused by fighting in Sudan and Ethiopia. Many are refugees or homeless (1991). Plains. Pastoralists: cattle; fishermen. Traditional religion, Christian.

Nyamusa-Molo [nwm] 1,200 Nyamusa (1977 Voegelin and Voegelin). Southern Sudan, western Equatoria Province, southeast of Beli, northeast of Morokodo. *Class:* Nilo-Saharan, Central Sudanic, West, Bongo-Bagirmi, Bongo-Baka, Morokodo-Beli, Morokodo-Mo'da. *Dialects:* Nyamusa, Molo. Lexical similarity 84% between Nyamusa and Molo, 70% to 75% with Jur Modo dialect cluster.

Olu'bo (Luluba, Olubogo, Oluboti, Lulubo, Ondoe, Lolubo) [lul] 15,000 (1985 SIL). Southern Sudan, eastern Equatoria Province, about 30 miles east of the Nile River. Main town Lokiliri, between Juba-Torit and Juba-Nimule roads. *Class:* Nilo-Saharan, Central Sudanic, East, Moru-Madi, Southern. *Lg Use:* There is strong interest in using Olu'bo for education. Many also use Bari. *Other:* Pastoralists; traders. Traditional religion.

Opuuo (Opo-Shita, Opo, Opuo, "Langa," Shita, Shitta, Cita, Ciita, Ansita, Kina, Kwina) [lgn] Upper Nile Province, around Kigille and Maiwut on Ethiopia border. *Dialects:* Buldit, Kusgilo. See main entry under Ethiopia.

Otoro (Utoro, Dhitoro, Litoro, Kawama, Kawarma) [otr] 10,000 (2001). Northern Sudan, Kordofan Province, Nuba Mountains Region, Otoro Hills south of Heiban and west of the Heiban-Talodi road. *Class:* Niger-Congo, Kordofanian, Heiban, West-Central, Central, Ebang-Logol, Utoro. *Dialects:* Dugujur, Dukwara, Dorobe, Dogoridi. *Lg Use:* Speakers also use Sudanese Arabic. *Lg Dev:* NT: 1966.

Otuho (Lotuko, Lotuho, Lotuxo, Lotuka, Lattuka, Latuko, Latuka, Latooka, Otuxo, Olotorit) [lot] 135,000 (1977 Voegelin and Voegelin). Population includes Dongotono (1998), 2,500 Koriot, 1,000 Lomya. Southern Sudan, Torit District, eastern Equatoria Province, east and southeast of the Luluba and the Lokoya. *Class:* Nilo-Saharan, Eastern Sudanic, Nilotic, Eastern, Lotuxo-Teso, Lotuxo-Maa, Lotuxo. *Dialects:* Koriok, Logiri (Logir), Lomya (Lomia), Lorwama, Lowudo (Loudo, Lauda), Logotok. Lexical similarity 64% with Lokoya, 63% with Lopit, 60% with Dongotono. *Lg Dev:* Literacy rate in second language: 10%. NT: 1969. *Other:* Agriculturalists: millet, eleusine, maize, simsim, peanuts, sweet potatoes, tobacco; pastoralists: cattle, sheep; hunters; fishermen. Traditional religion, Christian, Muslim.

Päri (Lokoro) [lkr] 28,000 (1987 SIL). Southern Sudan, E. Equatoria Province, on Jebel Lafon. They are northwest of the Lopit, and northeast of the Lokoya, in villages of Bura, Pucwaa, Pugari, Kor, Angulumeere, and Wiatuo. *Class:*

Nilo-Saharan, Eastern Sudanic, Nilotic, Western, Luo, Northern, Unclassified.

Reel (Atuot, Atwot, Thok Cieng Reel) [atu] 50,000 (1998 Atuot community). Southern Sudan, Lakes Province. Bordering Ciec Dinka in the north near Panekar, Agar Dinka on the west near Lake Nyibor, Jur Modo on the south, and Ador Dinka in the east near Yirol. *Class:* Nilo-Saharan, Eastern Sudanic, Nilotic, Western, Dinka-Nuer, Nuer. *Dialects:* No dialect differences. Lexical similarity 77% with Nuer; 49% with Dinka. *Lg Use:* The Apak are fully bilingual in the Ciec dialect of South Central Dinka. The other subtribes are less bilingual. The Kuek and Rorkec have many monolinguals and are regarded as having the purest form of the language. *Other:* They live among the Dinka, 100 km from the Nuer, but have common grazing grounds with the Nuer. They are culturally Dinka. Subtribes: Apak, Luac, Jilek, Rorkec, Akot, Kuek. 'Atuot' is the Dinka name for them. The Apak call themselves 'Atuot'. Pastoralists.

Shatt (Caning) [shj] 15,000 (1984 R. C. Stevenson). Northern Sudan, Shatt Hills southwest of Kadugli (Shatt Daman, Shatt Safia, Shatt Tebeldia), and parts of Abu Hashim and Abu Sinam. *Class:* Nilo-Saharan, Eastern Sudanic, Western, Daju, Eastern Daju. *Dialects:* Lexical similarity 64% with Liguri, 62% with Daju of Dar Fur (Nyala and Lagowa), 60% with Sila. *Other:* 'Caning' is their own name for themselves. 'Shatt' is applied by Arabic speakers to inhabitants of the Kordofan Hills. It means 'dispersed', 'scattered', and is applied to various groups. Distinct from Shatt (Thuri) in the Lwo group, or the Shatt dialect of Mundu. SVO.

Shilluk (Colo, Dhocolo, Chulla, Shulla) [shk] 175,000 (1982 SIL). Southern Sudan, Upper Nile Province, between Nile and Kordofan Province boundary, from Latitude 11 in the north to about 50 miles west of Tonga; also on the east bank of the Nile around the junction of the Nile and Sobat rivers, and for about 20 miles up the Sobat River. *Class:* Nilo-Saharan, Eastern Sudanic, Nilotic, Western, Luo, Northern, Shilluk. *Dialects:* Lexical similarity 60% with Anuak, Pari, Luwo. *Lg Dev:* Literacy rate in second language: 20%. Roman script. Grammar. NT: 1977. *Other:* Traditional religion, Christian.

Shwai (Shirumba, Shuway, Ludumor, Cwaya) [shw] 3,500 (1989). Northern Sudan, Kordofan Province, Nuba Mountains, in villages in the Shwai Hills, northwest of Otoro near Heiban-Kadugli road. *Class:* Niger-Congo, Kordofanian, Heiban, West-Central, Shirumba. *Dialects:* Shabun, Cerumba (Shirumba), Ndano. *Lg Use:* Speakers also use Sudanese Arabic. *Other:* They call themselves 'Cwaya'.

Sinyar (Sinya, Shemya) [sys] The main center is at Foro Boranga. *Other:* Probably no longer any speakers in Sudan (2001). They are geographically cut off from speakers of other Bongo-Bagirmi languages. Muslim. See main entry under Chad.

Sungor (Soungor, Assagori, Azangori, Asongori, Asungore, Erenga, Madungore, Shaale) [sjg] 15,000 in Sudan. Northern Sudan, Dar Fur, Melmele in Dar Masalit. Bounded on the west by the Tama, south by the Masalit, east by Arabic-speaking nomadic groups, north by the Gimr and Jebel Mun. *Dialects:* Girga, Walad Dulla, Erenga, Murasi, Sebunkik. *Other:* Culturally Maba. Agriculturalists; animal husbandry: cattle. Muslim. See main entry under Chad (Assangori).

Suri (Surma) [suq] 1,000 Tirma in Sudan (1983 SIL). Southern Sudan, Boma Plateau near the Ethiopian border. *Dialects:* Tirma (Tirima, Terema, Terna, Dirma, Cirma, Tirmaga, Tirmagi, Tid), Chai (Caci, Cai). See main entry under Ethiopia.

Tagoi (Tagoy) [tag] 13,000 (1982 SIL). Population includes 2,000 Tagoi, 552 Moreb, 1,100 Tumale (1977

Voegelin and Voegelin). Northern Sudan, Kordofan Province, Nuba Mountains, at Moreb, Tagoi, Turjok, Tumale Hill, possibly Tuling village. Tukum and Turum are places where Tagoi dialects are spoken (1956 Tucker and Bryan). *Class:* Niger-Congo, Kordofanian, Rashad. *Dialects:* Moreb, Tumale, Tagoi.

Talodi (Gajomang, Ajomang, Jomang) [tlo] 1,500 (1989). Northern Sudan, Nuba Hills, in Talodi town and hill, including the villages of Tasomi and Tata. *Class:* Niger-Congo, Kordofanian, Talodi, Talodi Proper, Jomang. *Dialects:* The dialects are nearly identical. Lexical similarity 70% with closest Talodi languages.

Tegali (Tagale, Tegele, Togole, Tekele) [ras] 35,738 (1984 R. C. Stevenson). Northern Sudan, Kordofan Province, Nuba Mountains, Tegali Range, Rashad hills and town of Rashad. *Class:* Niger-Congo, Kordofanian, Rashad. *Dialects:* Rashad (Kom, Ngakɔm, Kome), Tegali. *Other:* Tegali and Rashad are nearly identical. SOV. Muslim.

Temein (Temainian, Rone, Ronge) [teq] 10,000 (1984 R. C. Stevenson). Northern Sudan, Nuba Hills in the Temein hills southwest of Dilling, between Jebels Ghulfan Morung and Julud (Gulud). *Class:* Nilo-Saharan, Eastern Sudanic, Western, Temein. *Dialects:* Lexical similarity 67% with Tese.

Tennet (Tenet) [tex] 4,000 (1994 SIL). Southern Sudan, Equatoria Province, Lopit Hills, northeast of Torit, 5 villages. *Class:* Nilo-Saharan, Eastern Sudanic, Eastern, Surmic, South, Southwest, Didinga-Murle, Tennet. *Dialects:* Some intelligibility of Murle, Narim, and Didinga (in descending order). *Lg Use:* All ages. A strong sense of Tenet ethnic identity. Most Tennet are fluent in Lopit, from which they borrow most of their songs. Many over 20 years old know Toposa, which is used for ox names and a few songs. Many can also understand some Otuho, which is closely related to Lopit. Those with schooling know a little Arabic. *Lg Dev:* Literacy rate in first language: 1%. Literacy rate in second language: 1% Arabic. Motivation for literacy is high. Grammar. Bible portions: 1994–2001. *Other:* They have a number of Lopit loanwords. VSO; genitives, adjectives, numerals, relatives after noun heads; question word final; 4 suffixes; word order distinguishes given and new information; noun affixes indicate case; verb affixes mark person, number; agreement obligatory; passives; antipassives; causatives; comparatives; (C)(G)V(:)(C) or (C)V(G)(C); tonal. Mountain slope. Savannah, surrounding plain, tropical forest on the hill. 600 to 1,200 meters. Swidden agriculturalists; animal husbandry: cattle; blacksmiths. Traditional religion, Christian.

Tese (Teis-Umm-Danab, Keiga Jirru, Keiga Girru) [keg] 1,400 (1971 Welmers). Northern Sudan, Nuba Hills, Keiga Jirru west of Debri, and in 6 villages, northeast of Kadugli. *Class:* Nilo-Saharan, Eastern Sudanic, Western, Temein. *Dialects:* Lexical similarity 67% with Temein. *Lg Use:* Speakers also use Sudanese Arabic.

Thuri (Dhe Thuri, Jo Thuri, Wada Thuri, Shatt) [thu] 16,720 (2000 WCD). Southern Sudan between Wau and Aweil, between Jur and Lol rivers, on Raga-Nyamlell road, and on Wau-Deim Zubeir road. *Class:* Nilo-Saharan, Eastern Sudanic, Nilotic, Western, Luo, Northern, Thuri. *Dialects:* Bodho (Dhe Boodho, Dembo, Demen, Dombo), Colo (Dhe Colo, Jur Shol, Jo Colo), Manangeer (Jur Manangeer). *Other:* Different from Shatt in the Daju group.

Tigré (Khasa, Xasa) [tig] Northern Sudan. *Dialect:* Mansa' (Mensa). *Other:* Believed by some to be a direct linguistic descendant of Ge'ez. Muslim. See main entry under Eritrea.

Tima (Lomorik, Lomuriki, Tamanik, Yibwa) [tms] 3,305 (2000 WCD). Northern Sudan, Nuba Hills in villages on and near Jebel Tima, 10 miles southwest of Katla, West

Kordofan District. *Class:* Niger-Congo, Kordofanian, Katla.

Tingal (Kajakja, Kajaja) [tie] 8,000 (1982 SIL). Northern Sudan, Tegali Hills. *Class:* Niger-Congo, Kordofanian, Rashad.

Tira (Tiro, Thiro, Lithiro) [tic] 40,000 (1982 SIL). Northern Sudan, Nuba Hills in villages extending from near Otoro to the neighborhood of Talodi. *Class:* Niger-Congo, Kordofanian, Heiban, West-Central, Western. *Dialects:* Kinderma (Kanderma), Tira El Akhdar (Tira Dagig), Tira Lumum (Luman), Tira Mandi. There are slight variations among the dialects. Lexical similarity 75% with Moro (closest). *Lg Use:* Speakers also use Sudanese Arabic. *Lg Dev:* Bible portions: 1999–2001. *Other:* Traditional religion, Muslim, Christian.

Tocho (Toicho, Tacho) [taz] 3,800 (1977 Voegelin and Voegelin). Northern Sudan, Talodi, Moro Hills. *Class:* Niger-Congo, Kordofanian, Talodi, Talodi Proper, Tocho. *Dialects:* Lexical similarity 70% with closest Talodi languages. *Lg Use:* Speakers also use Sudanese Arabic.

Togoyo (Togoy) [tgy] Extinct. Southern Sudan, west, in a small area around Raga. *Class:* Niger-Congo, Atlantic-Congo, Volta-Congo, North, Adamawa-Ubangi, Ubangi, Sere-Ngbaka-Mba, Sere, Indri-Togoyo.

Toposa (Taposa, Topotha, Akara, Kare, Kumi) [toq] 100,000 (2000 M. Schroeder). Most are monolingual. Southern Sudan, along both sides of Singaita and Lokalyen rivers. Ritual center at Loyooro River. They migrate as far as Moruangipi, and occasionally farther east into the disputed Ilemi Triangle at the Ethiopian border for seasonal grazing. They have no permanent settlements there. *Class:* Nilo-Saharan, Eastern Sudanic, Nilotic, Eastern, Lotuxo-Teso, Teso-Turkana, Turkana. *Dialects:* Eastern Toposa, Western Toposa, Jiye. Eastern Toposa and Jiye are linguistically closer to Turkana; Western Toposa to Karamojong. Inherently intelligible with Nyangatom, Karamojong, and Turkana, but each has strong ethnic attitudes. Separate literature is needed also because of loans from different second languages, and different discourse structures. Limited intelligibility of Teso. *Lg Use:* Vigorous. Neighboring groups use it in trade (Didinga, Murle, Boya-Longarim, Tennet). All domains. Positive language attitude. The Toposa are peaceful with the Karamojong, have a mutual non-aggression pact with the Nyangatom, are intermittently unfriendly to the Jiye of Sudan, permanently in tension with the Turkana, and to the Murle-Didinga group (Murle, Didinga, Boya-Longarim). A small number speak Southern Sudanese Arabic (Juba Arabic) for trading. A few know some English from school. *Lg Dev:* Literacy rate in first language: Fewer than 5%. Perhaps 2,000 can read. Taught in primary schools. Dictionary. Grammar. Bible portions: 2002. *Other:* Seminomadic. VSA (morphologically ergative); highly inflectional; grammatical tone (tense, case); vowel harmony; voiceless vowels; questions: yes and no sentence final, content questions sentence initial and final. Plains, hills. Animal husbandry: cattle; agriculturalists. Traditional religion, Christian.

Torona [tqr] Extinct. Northern Sudan, Talodi, Moro Hills. *Class:* Niger-Congo, Kordofanian, Talodi, Talodi Proper, Tocho. *Lg Use:* Members of the ethnic group now speak Tira.

Tulishi (Tulesh, Thulishi, Kuntulishi) [tey] 8,628 (1977 Voegelin and Voegelin). Population includes 3,000 Kamda, 2,500 Tulishi. Northern Sudan, hills on the western edge of the Nuba Hills on Jebel Tulishi south of Katla, on Jebel Kamdang north of Lagowa, south of Tulishi. Lagawa is the largest village, Kam'da is the administrative center, and other villages are Laati, Lawwa, Ntukungnge, Aabiisa, Nattilongke, Aliyooro Manadaha,

Thudhi, Kirakaati. *Class:* Nilo-Saharan, Unclassified. *Dialects:* Tulishi, Kamda (Kamdang), Dar El Kabira (Turuj, Truj, Logoke, Minjimmina). Dar el Kabira and Kamdang dialects are similar. *Lg Use:* Speakers also use Sudanese Arabic.

Tumtum [tbr] 7,300. Population includes 6,000 in Karondi, 1,300 in Tumtum. Northern Sudan, Nuba Hills; Kurondi south of Eliri, Talassa in the northern part of Eliri. *Class:* Nilo-Saharan, Unclassified. *Dialects:* Karondi (Kurondi, Korindi), Talassa (Talasa), Tumtum. Lexical similarity 85% with Krongo (closest).

Uduk (Twampa, Kwanim Pa, Burun, Kebeirka, Othan, Korara, Kumus) [udu] Northern Sudan, Upper Nile Province from Belila in the north, southwards along Blue Nile Province boundary to Yabus River. Most now in a refugee camp in Ethiopia. *Other:* Christian, traditional religion. See main entry under Ethiopia.

Wali (Walari, Walarishe) [wll] 487 (1977 Voegelin and Voegelin). Northern Sudan, in the Wali Hills, south of Karko Hills. *Class:* Nilo-Saharan, Eastern Sudanic, Eastern, Nubian, Central, Hill, Unclassified. *Other:* SOV.

Warnang (Werni) [wrn] 1,100 (1956 census). Northern Sudan, on small isolated hills in the extreme eastern part of the Nuba Hills between Talodi and the White Nile. *Class:* Niger-Congo, Kordofanian, Heiban, Eastern. *Dialects:* Lexical similarity 67% with Ko (closest). *Other:* Traditional religion.

Yulu (Youlou) [yul] 3,000 in Sudan (1987 SIL). Population includes 2,000 Yulu and 1,000 Binga. Southern Sudan. The Yulu are at Khor Buga, 2 miles west of Raga in Western Bahr el Ghazal Province, and in Habbaniya District of Dar Fur. The Binga are at Menangba, west of Raga and in Democratic Republic of the Congo. *Dialects:* Binga, Yulu. *Lg Use:* Many speakers also use Kresh or Arabic. See main entry under Central African Republic.

Zaghawa (Soghaua, Zeggaoua, Zagaoua, Zorhaua, Zagawa, Zeghawa, Zauge, Berri, Beri, Beri-Aa, Merida, Kebadi, Kuyuk) [zag] 102,000 in Sudan (1982 SIL). Population total all countries: 186,834. Northern Sudan, northwest Dar Fur (northern Magdumate and Dar Kabja), and scattered farther south. Also in Kordofan. Surrounded on three sides by the Sahara. Also spoken in Chad, Libya. *Class:* Nilo-Saharan, Saharan, Eastern. *Dialects:* Wagi (Twer), Kube, Tuba (Bideyat). Wagi is the main dialect in Sudan. Ethnic subgroups are Kobe, Dor, Anka, with slight dialect differences. Seminomadic. *Lg Use:* Groups in Sudan are Arabic speaking. *Other:* Better educated than other groups. Beri is their own name for the people. Mountain slope. 600 meters. Animal husbandry; gatherers; agriculturalists; traders: livestock, hides, butter, salt. Muslim, traditional religion.

Zande (Azande, Zandi, Pazande, Sande, Badjande) [zne] 350,000 in Sudan (1982 SIL). Southern Sudan, Democratic Republic of the Congo (primarily, and Central African Republic in an elongated semicircle with Uele River as its base). Some projections south. *Dialect:* Dio, Makaraka (Odio). *Other:* The speech of the Zande in Sudan is fairly uniform except for the Mbomu, Sueh-Meridi, Bile, Bandiya, Bamboy, Bomokandi, Anunga. Agriculturalists. Traditional religion, Christian. See main entry under Democratic Republic of the Congo.

Swaziland

Kingdom of Swaziland. 1,169,241. National or official languages: Swati, English. Literacy rate: 65% to 67%. Information mainly from J. Bendor-Samuel 1989. Blind population: 1,000 (1982 WCE). Deaf institutions: 1. The number of languages listed for Swaziland is 4. Of those, all are living languages. See map on page 704.

English [eng] *Lg Use:* Official language. *Other:* Taught in all government and private schools. See main entry under United Kingdom.

Swati (Swazi, Isiswazi, Siswati, Tekela, Tekeza) [ssw] 650,000 in Swaziland (1993 Johnstone). Population total all countries: 1,706,924. Also spoken in Lesotho, Mozambique, South Africa. *Class:* Niger-Congo, Atlantic-Congo, Volta-Congo, Benue-Congo, Bantoid, Southern, Narrow Bantu, Central, S, Nguni (S.40). *Dialects:* Baca, Hlubi, Phuthi. *Lg Use:* Official language. *Lg Dev:* Literacy rate in first language: High. Taught in all national schools. Newspapers. Radio programs. TV. Bible: 1996. *Other:* 'Siswati' is the Swati name, 'Swazi' is the Zulu name. The people are highly educated. Christian, traditional religion.

Tsonga (Shitsonga, Xitsonga, Changana, Xichangana) [tso] 19,000 in Swaziland (1993 Johnstone). See main entry under South Africa.

Zulu (Isizulu, Zunda) [zul] 76,000 in Swaziland (1993 Johnstone). See main entry under South Africa.

Tanzania

United Republic of Tanzania. Jamhuri ya Muungano wa Tanzania. Formerly German East Africa, Tanganyika. 36,588,225. National or official languages: Swahili, English. Literacy rate: 80% to 85%. Also includes Rundi (150,000), Konkani, Panjabi, Urdu, Chinese, people from Europe (70,000), Rwanda (25,000), Mozambique. Information mainly from F. Huntingford 1953; B. Taylor 1962; R. Willis 1966; W. Whiteley 1969; E. Polomé and C. Hill 1980; F. Rottland 1981; D. Nurse 1982; G. Dimmendaal 1989. Blind population: 40,000 (1982 WCE). Deaf institutions: 7. The number of languages listed for Tanzania is 128. Of those, 127 are living languages and 1 is extinct. See maps beginning on page 732.

Aasáx (Asax, Asá, Aasá, Assa, Asak, "Ndorobo," "Dorobo," Lamanik, Il Konono) [aas] 350 (1999 Jeff Carr). Northern Tanzania in the central Maasai Steppe. Landenai, Ndovu Okutu, Lolbeni villages, and Lemelebo, Landrobo, Naitomani, and Kilili districts are reported to have speakers. *Class:* Afro-Asiatic, Cushitic, South. *Lg Use:* Reported in 1999 to still be spoken in the central Massai Steppe. It became linguistically extinct in the eastern Maasai Steppe in 1976. They are dependent on the Maasai and became absorbed into it and nearby Bantu groups. Speakers use Maasai with the Maasai, on whom they are economically dependent. *Other:* 'Assa' is the name for the people. 'Lamanik' and 'Il Konono' apparently refer to ancestry and not the language. In the last 4 districts mentioned the Assa are nomadic and hold joint religious ceremonies with the Temi (Sonjo) to the north. Hunter-gatherers; settled and nomadic.

Alagwa (Alagwaisi, Alagwase, Alawa, Chasi, Asi, Wasi, Kialagwa) [wbj] 30,000 (2001 Kiessling). Dodoma Region, Kondoa District. *Class:* Afro-Asiatic, Cushitic, South. *Dialects:* Related to Iraqw, but not inherently intelligible. Also close to Burunge and Gorowa. *Lg Use:* Vigorous in most areas. In mixed villages children tend to speak Langi among themselves. Some speakers also use Langi. *Other:* Their name for themselves is 'Alagwa'. Agriculturalists. Muslim.

Arabic, Omani Spoken [acx] Ethnic population: 195,000 in Tanzania (1993 Johnstone). Zanzibar. *Lg Use:* Second and third generation in Tanzania, originally from Yemen and Oman. Some or all may speak Swahili as first language. *Lg Dev:* Literacy is in Arabic. *Other:* Muslim. See main entry under Oman.

Arabic, Standard [arb] Middle East, north Africa. See main entry under Saudi Arabia.

Aramanik (Laramanik, "Ndorobo," "Dorobo") [aam] 3,000 (2002). Masaai Steppe, Arusha Region. *Class:* Nilo-Saharan, Eastern Sudanic, Nilotic, Southern, Kalenjin, Nandi-Markweta, Nandi. *Lg Use:* Speakers have limited comprehension of other languages. *Other:* Kisankasa, Mediak, Mosiro, and Aasax are also called "Ndorobo."

Asu (Chiasu, Chasu, Athu, Casu, Pare) [asa] 500,000 (2000). 5% monolingual. Northeastern, Kilimanjaro Region, Pare Mountains, Mwanga and Same districts. *Class:* Niger-Congo, Atlantic-Congo, Volta-Congo, Benue-Congo, Bantoid, Southern, Narrow Bantu, Central, G, Shambala (G.20). *Dialects:* Related to Taveta. *Lg Use:* Vigorous. Used in the home, religion. 63% bilingual in Swahili, 32% trilingual in Swahili and English. *Lg Dev:* Literacy rate in second language: 80%. NT: 1922–1967. *Other:* 'Wapare' is an ethnic group name. Mountain slope. Christian, Muslim.

Bembe (Ibembe, Beembe, Ebembe, Kibembe) [bmb] Kigoma Region, Kigoma Vijinini District. On the shore of Lake Tanganyika, from Kigoma town north to the Gombe National Park. *Lg Use:* Religious services in Swahili. *Other:* Some are Tanzanian citizens, others are recent immigrants and citizens of Democratic Republic of the Congo. Different from Beembe (Bembe) of Congo. Fishermen. Traditional religion, Christian. See main entry under Democratic Republic of the Congo.

Bena (Ekibena, Kibena) [bez] 670,000 (2001 Johnstone and Mandryk). Southwest central, Iringa Region, Njombe District. *Class:* Niger-Congo, Atlantic-Congo, Volta-Congo, Benue-Congo, Bantoid, Southern, Narrow Bantu, Central, G, Bena-Kinga (G.60). *Dialects:* Lexical similarity 71% with Pangwa, 65% with Hehe, 55% with Sangu, 53% with Kinga, 51% with Wanji, 47% with Kisi. *Lg Dev:* NT: 1914–1920.

Bende (Kibende, Si'bende) [bdp] 27,000 (1999). Rukwa Region, Mpanda District, Kabungu, Karema, and Mwese divisions. *Class:* Niger-Congo, Atlantic-Congo, Volta-Congo, Benue-Congo, Bantoid, Southern, Narrow Bantu, Central, F, Tongwe (F.10). *Dialects:* Tongwe and Bende may be dialects of one language. Lexical similarity 74% with Sumbwa, 72% with Nyamwezi, 70% with Sukuma Hu, 67% with Ha, 71% with Rundi, 60% with Hangaza, 58% with Nyankore and 65% with Holoholo and 90% with Tongwe. *Lg Use:* All ages. 55% to 71% of speakers have lower than routine proficiency in Swahili. *Other:* Valley. Deciduous forest. Agriculturalists; hunters. Muslim, Christian, syncretism with traditional religion.

Bondei (Kibondei, Bonde) [bou] 80,000 (1987). Northeastern Tanzania, Tanga Region, Usambara Mountains, inland from Tanga. *Class:* Niger-Congo, Atlantic-Congo, Volta-Congo, Benue-Congo, Bantoid, Southern, Narrow Bantu, Central, G, Shambala (G.20). *Dialects:* It has been influenced linguistically by Doe and Kwere, and it has influenced them. Lexical similarity 75% with Shambala and Zigula, 73% with Ngulu. *Lg Use:* Speakers are shifting to Swahili. *Lg Dev:* Bible portions: 1887–1895. *Other:* Muslim, Christian.

Bungu (Wungu, Echiungu, Kibungu) [wun] 36,000 (1987). Chunya District of Mbeya Region. *Class:* Niger-Congo, Atlantic-Congo, Volta-Congo, Benue-Congo, Bantoid, Southern, Narrow Bantu, Central, F, Sukuma-Nyamwezi (F.20). *Lg Use:* All ages. Many have below routine ability in Swahili. *Other:* Plateau. Semiarid. Agriculturalists; animal husbandry: livestock; fishermen. Traditional religion, Christian.

Burunge (Bulunge, Mbulugwe, Burungi) [bds] 13,000 (2002). Kondoa District of Dodoma Region, southeast of the Langi, Goima, Chambalo, and Mirambu villages. *Class:* Afro-Asiatic, Cushitic, South. *Dialects:* Close to Alagwa, Gorowa, Iraqw. *Lg Use:* Used in the home, field, sometimes in churches. All ages. Low prestige language. Burunge don't like to use it in front of others. They also speak Swahili and Langi as second languages. *Other:* SOV; prepositions, genitives, articles, adjectives, numerals, relatives after noun heads; 5 suffixes; word order distinguishes subjects, objects, indirect objects, given and new information (SOV already introduced object, SVO newly introduced object), topic and comment; preverbal clitics indicate case of noun phrase; verbal suffixes mark person, number, gender of subject; preverbal clitics mark person of subject; preverbal clitics mark person, number, and gender of nonsubject noun phrase; this agreement is obligatory; mediopassive is marked by verbal derivational suffix; subject indefinite is marked by preverbal clitic; causatives; CV, CVV, CVC (restriction on second C)CV; tonal. Plains. Arid, deciduous bush (scrub forest). 1,200 meters. Agriculturalists. Traditional religion, Muslim, Christian.

Cutchi-Swahili (Asian Swahili) [ccl] Dar es Salaam, Dodoma, Mwanza, Arusha. *Lg Use:* The first language of some Gujarati Muslims who have come from Zanzibar. Asian Swahili is used by other Asians in communicating with non-English speaking Africans and other Asians who share no common language. Speakers also use English. *Other:* It has a regular but distinct phonology and lexical and grammatical differences, described by Whitely (1974.73–79). Cutchi-Swahili and Asian Swahili may not be identical. Muslim (Ismaili and Ithnasheri). See main entry under Kenya.

Datooga (Datoga, Datog, Tatoga, Tatog, Taturu, "Mangati") [tcc] 87,798 (2000 WCD). Singida and Mbulu regions. The Barabaig are mainly in the northern volcanic highlands near Mt. Hanang. *Class:* Nilo-Saharan, Eastern Sudanic, Nilotic, Southern, Tatoga. *Dialects:* Bajuta, Gisamjanga (Kisamajeng, Gisamjang), Barabayiiga (Barabaig, Barabayga, Barabaik, Barbaig), Tsimajeega (Isimijeega), Rootigaanga (Rotigenga, Rotigeenga), Buraadiiga (Buradiga, Bureadiga), Bianjiida (Biyanjiida, Utatu). Sabaot is probably the closest language linguistically. Barabaik and Kisamajeng are very close and are completely inherently intelligible. There are several other dialects or ethnic groups: Darorajega, Gidang'odiga, Bisiyeda, Daragwajega, Salawajega, Ghumbiega, Mangatiga. Lexical similarity 50% with Kalenjin and Omotik of Kenya. *Lg Use:* Vigorous. Bilingual level estimates for Swahili: 0 90%, 1 6%, 2 2%, 3 1%, 4 1%, 5 0%. Those who have been to school have routine proficiency in Swahili. A few use Iraqw, Iramba, or Nyaturu as second language for commerce. *Lg Dev:* Literacy rate in second language: 1%. *Other:* 'Mangati' or 'Ole-Mangati' is the Maasai name meaning 'enemies'. 'Taturu' is the Sukuma name. There is intermarriage with the Iraqw. Datoga orthography is different from Swahili. VSO; prepositions; genitives, articles, adjectives, numerals after noun heads; question word final; 4 prefixes, 5 suffixes on verb; case marked by tone; verb affixes mark person, number; (C)(C)V(:), VC; tonal. Plains, mountain slope. Savannah. 1,100 to 2,000 meters. Pastoralists: cattle, goats, sheep, donkeys; agriculturalists: maize, beans, millet; hunters. Traditional religion, Christian.

Dhaiso (Kidhaiso, Daiso, Daisu, Kiseguju) [dhs] 5,000 (1999). Bwiti and Magati villages at the base of the eastern Usambara Mountains on the northern side, Muheza District, Tanga Region. *Class:* Niger-Congo, Atlantic-Congo, Volta-Congo, Benue-Congo, Bantoid, Southern, Narrow Bantu, Central, E, Kikuyu-Kamba (E.20). *Dialects:* Related to Kamba of Kenya. Lexical similarity 32% with Digo. *Lg Use:* Not being transmitted by adults to children. Most older children and nearly all adults are able to speak Dhaiso, but they report speaking Swahili at least as often as Dhaiso, even at home. Most primary school-age children do not speak Dhaiso. Self reported proficiency in Swahili is high. 47% of adults claimed Swahili as first language on a questionnaire. *Other:* People were historically one with the Segeju. When speaking Swahili, the Dhaiso people call their language Kisegeju. Muslim.

Digo (Kidigo, Chidigo) [dig] 88,000 in Tanzania (1987). Northeastern coast area around Tanga. *Other:* The Segeju (Kisegeju, Sageju, Sengeju) is an ethnic group which probably once spoke Dhaiso, but speak Digo or Swahili today as first language. Muslim. See main entry under Kenya.

Doe (Dohe, Kidoe) [doe] 24,000 (1987). Pwani Region, Bagamoyo District, north of the Kwere. *Class:* Niger-Congo, Atlantic-Congo, Volta-Congo, Benue-Congo, Bantoid, Southern, Narrow Bantu, Central, G, Zigula-Zaramo (G.30). *Dialects:* Doe has influenced Zigula and Bondei linguistically, and it has been influenced by them. Lexical similarity 74% with Kwere, 64% with Kami, 61% with Kutu and Zaramo, 70% with Zigula, 54% with Luguru. *Lg Use:* Speakers also use Swahili.

English [eng] *Lg Use:* Official language. Second-language speakers in Tanzania: 1,500,000 (1977 Voegelin and Voegelin). Used by some Asian residents as first language. *Lg Dev:* Taught in primary schools. Used as medium of instruction in secondary schools and universities. See main entry under United Kingdom.

Fipa (Icifipa, Ichifipa, Cifipa, Fiba, Kifipa) [fip] 200,000 in Tanzania (1992 UBS). Sumbawanga and Nkansi Districts, Rukwa Region, a large area between lakes Tanganyika and Rukwa. Also spoken in Malawi. *Class:* Niger-Congo, Atlantic-Congo, Volta-Congo, Benue-Congo, Bantoid, Southern, Narrow Bantu, Central, F, Tongwe (F.10). *Dialects:* Kandaasi, Siiwa, Kwaafi, Ntili, Peemba, Kwa, Nkwaamba, Sukuuma. *Lg Use:* Speakers also use Swahili. *Lg Dev:* NT: 1988. *Other:* Plateau, hills, coastal, valleys. Savannah, scrub. 800 to 2,000 meters. Agriculturalists: millet, maize, lima beans, sweet potatoes, cassava, peanuts, spinach, tomatoes, onions, potatoes, chiles, sorghum, bananas, papayas, oranges, limes, mangoes, tobacco, coconuts, wheat, coffee; animal husbandry: cattle, sheep, goats, fowl, pidgeons; fishermen. Christian, traditional religion, Muslim.

Gogo (Chigogo, Kigogo) [gog] 1,300,000 (1992 UBS). Dodoma Region; Singida Region, Manyoni District. *Class:* Niger-Congo, Atlantic-Congo, Volta-Congo, Benue-Congo, Bantoid, Southern, Narrow Bantu, Central, G, Gogo (G.10). *Dialects:* Nyambwa (West Gogo), Nyaugogo (Central Gogo), Tumba (East Gogo). Lexical similarity 50% with Hehe and Sangu, 48% with Kimbu, 45% with Nilamba. *Lg Use:* Vigorous. Used in meetings by the Anglican church. *Lg Dev:* Bible: 1962. *Other:* Seminomadic. Valleys. Agriculturalists. Traditional religion, Christian, Muslim.

Gorowa (Goroa, Fiome, Gorwaa) [gow] 50,000 (1999 R. Kiessling). Arusha Region, Mbulu District; Dodoma Region, Kondoa District, near Babati, around Mt. Ufiome. *Class:* Afro-Asiatic, Cushitic, South. *Dialects:* Close to Burunge, Alagwa, Iraqw. May be a dialect of Iraqw. *Lg Use:* Speakers also use Iraqw or Swahili. *Other:* Hills. Forests. 1,300 meters. Christian, traditional religion.

Gujarati [guj] 250,000 in Tanzania (1993 Johnstone). Small communities. *Lg Use:* Vigorous. *Other:* They have their own religious institutions and evening schools. See main entry under India.

Gweno (Kigweno) [gwe] Few speakers (2000 M. Brenzinger). Ethnic population: 2,000 or more. Kilimanjaro Region, northernmost part of the North Pare Hills. *Class:* Niger-Congo, Atlantic-Congo, Volta-Congo, Benue-Congo, Bantoid, Southern, Narrow Bantu, Central, E, Chaga (E.30). *Dialects:* Lexical similarity 54% to 56%

with Chaga dialects (closest), 46% with Taita. *Lg Use:* Speakers are shifting to Asu. Most speakers are older adults. Speakers also use Swahili. *Other:* Nearly extinct.

Ha (Giha, Kiha, Ikiha) [haq] 990,000 (2001 Johnstone and Mandryk). Kigoma Region. *Class:* Niger-Congo, Atlantic-Congo, Volta-Congo, Benue-Congo, Bantoid, Southern, Narrow Bantu, Central, J, Rwanda-Rundi (J.60). *Dialects:* Dialects in border area near Burundi are reported to be intelligible with Rundi (Polomé 1980). Lexical similarity 78% with Rundi, 77% with Hangaza and Shubi, 72% with Rwanda. *Lg Use:* Vigorous. Also spoken by the Jiji people in the Ujiji area. *Lg Dev:* Bible portions: 1960–1962. *Other:* Traditional religion, Muslim, Christian.

Hadza (Hatsa, Hadzapi, Hadzabi, Kindiga, "Tindiga," Wakindiga, Kangeju) [hts] 800 (2000 Brenzinger). Ethnic population: 800. Some distance northwest of the Sandawe, southeast of Lake Victoria, Singida, Arusha, and Shinyanga regions, near Lake Eyasi. *Class:* Khoisan, Hatsa. *Dialects:* Bali may be a dialect. *Lg Use:* Vigorous. *Other:* Nomadic. Population dwindling. Pressures from outside are resulting in less land, food, and more disease. Swamps, wilderness. Hunter-gatherers. Traditional religion, Christian.

Hangaza (Kihangaza) [han] 150,000 (1987). Northwestern, southwest of Bukoba. Kagera Region, Ngara and Biharamulo districts. *Class:* Niger-Congo, Atlantic-Congo, Volta-Congo, Benue-Congo, Bantoid, Southern, Narrow Bantu, Central, J, Rwanda-Rundi (J.60). *Dialects:* Lexical similarity 85% with Shubi, 83% with Rundi, 77% with Ha, 72% with Rwanda. *Lg Use:* Positive language attitude. *Lg Dev:* Bible portions: 1938.

Haya (Ekihaya, Ruhaya, Ziba, Kihaya) [hay] 1,200,000 (1991 UBS). Kagera Region, mainly Bukoba District. *Class:* Niger-Congo, Atlantic-Congo, Volta-Congo, Benue-Congo, Bantoid, Southern, Narrow Bantu, Central, J, Haya-Jita (J.20). *Dialects:* Bumbira, Edangabo, Ganda-Kiaka, Hamba, Hangiro, Mwani, Nyakisisa, Ekiziba, Yoza. *Lg Use:* Vigorous. *Lg Dev:* Bible: 2002. *Other:* Agriculturalists: plantain, coffee, beans, maize; miners: tin, wolfram; animal husbandry: cattle, goats. Christian, traditional religion, Muslim.

Hehe (Kihehe) [heh] 750,000 (1994 UBS). Iringa Region, south of Gogo. *Class:* Niger-Congo, Atlantic-Congo, Volta-Congo, Benue-Congo, Bantoid, Southern, Narrow Bantu, Central, G, Bena-Kinga (G.60). *Dialects:* Lexical similarity 65% with Bena (closest), 59% with Pangwa, 56% with Sangu, 50% with Kinga, 48% with Wanji. *Lg Use:* Vigorous. *Lg Dev:* Bible portions: 2000.

Ikizu [ikz] 28,000 (1987). Mara Region, east of Zanaki and Kerebe. *Class:* Niger-Congo, Atlantic-Congo, Volta-Congo, Benue-Congo, Bantoid, Southern, Narrow Bantu, Central, E, Kuria (E.10). *Lg Use:* Most speakers have low proficiency in Swahili.

Ikoma (Nata, Ikinata) [ntk] 15,000 (1987). Mara Region, east of Ikizu, Zanaki, and Kerebe. *Class:* Niger-Congo, Atlantic-Congo, Volta-Congo, Benue-Congo, Bantoid, Southern, Narrow Bantu, Central, E, Kuria (E.10). *Dialect:* Issenyi (Isenyi, Ikisenyi). Lexical similarity 81% with Zanaki, 73% with Ngurimi, 68% with Kuria, 44% with Gusii. *Lg Use:* Speakers have low proficiency in Swahili.

Iraqw (Mbulu, Mbulunge, Erokh, Iraku, Kiiraqw) [irk] 462,000 (2001 Johnstone and Mandryk). Arusha Region, Mbulu District, highlands southwest of Arusha in north. *Class:* Afro-Asiatic, Cushitic, South. *Dialect:* Asa. Asa may be a separate language. *Lg Use:* Vigorous. *Lg Dev:* NT: 1977. *Other:* 1,800 meters. Agriculturalists: maize, beans, red and white sorghum, sweet potatoes, millet; animal husbandry: cattle, sheep. Traditional religion, Christian, Muslim.

Isanzu (Kinyihanzu, Kinyisanzu) [isn] 32,400 (1987). Iramba District of Singida Region. *Class:* Niger-Congo,

Atlantic-Congo, Volta-Congo, Benue-Congo, Bantoid, Southern, Narrow Bantu, Central, Unclassified. *Dialects:* Closely related to Nyaturu. *Lg Use:* Used in the home. *Other:* 1,200 to 1,600 meters. Agriculturalists: millet, maize, sorghum; animal husbandry. Christian, traditional religion, Muslim.

Jita (Echijita, Ecijita) [jit] 217,000 (1987). Mara Region, southeastern shore of Lake Victoria, between the Zanaki and Kerebe. *Class:* Niger-Congo, Atlantic-Congo, Volta-Congo, Benue-Congo, Bantoid, Southern, Narrow Bantu, Central, J, Haya-Jita (J.20). *Dialects:* Lexical similarity 83% with Kwaya, 81% with Kara, 62% with Kerewe. *Lg Use:* Vigorous. *Lg Dev:* NT: 1943–1960.

Kabwa [cwa] North central, Mara Region. *Class:* Niger-Congo, Atlantic-Congo, Volta-Congo, Benue-Congo, Bantoid, Southern, Narrow Bantu, Central, E, Kuria (E.10). *Dialects:* Close to Kiroba (Kuria).

Kachchi (Cutchi, Kacchi, Kachi, Katchi) [kfr] Cities. *Lg Use:* Speakers use Kachchi 52% of the time, Gujarati 14%, English 26%. *Other:* Hindu, Muslim. See main entry under India.

Kagulu (Chikagulu, Kaguru, Northern Sagara, Kiningo, Solwa, Kigalulu, Kigaguru) [kki] 217,000 (1987). Morogoro Region, Kodoma Region, Kilosa District. *Class:* Niger-Congo, Atlantic-Congo, Volta-Congo, Benue-Congo, Bantoid, Southern, Narrow Bantu, Central, G, Gogo (G.10). *Dialects:* Megi, Tumba, Mangehele. Lexical similarity 63% with Sagala, 56% with Gogo. *Lg Use:* Speakers also use Swahili. *Lg Dev:* Bible portions: 1885–1894. *Other:* Lowland, plateau, hills, mountain slope. Savannah, scrub, deciduous forest. 600 to 2,100 meters. Agriculturalists: maize, beans, peanuts, banana, cassava, mango, papaya, limes, cotton, sugarcane, potatoes, plantains, tobacco, coffee, citrus, pumpkins, castor, sunflowers; animal husbandry: poultry, sheep, goats, cattle. Christian, traditional religion, Muslim.

Kahe [hka] 2,700 (1987). Southeast of Moshi. *Class:* Niger-Congo, Atlantic-Congo, Volta-Congo, Benue-Congo, Bantoid, Southern, Narrow Bantu, Central, E, Chaga (E.30). *Other:* SVO.

Kami (Kikami) [kcu] 16,411 (2000 WCD). Morogoro Region, Morogoro and Kilosa districts. About 30 km north and northeast of Morogoro, on and south of the main road to Dar es Salaam, and on for about 20 km. The farthest village is about 60 km south of this road. *Class:* Niger-Congo, Atlantic-Congo, Volta-Congo, Benue-Congo, Bantoid, Southern, Narrow Bantu, Central, G, Zigula-Zaramo (G.30). *Dialects:* Lexical similarity 69% with Kutu and Kwere, 65% with Zaramo, 64% with Doe, 54% with Luguru. *Lg Use:* Use is declining. Used for traditional religious ceremonies and conflict mediation through the traditional chief. Low Swahili proficiency. *Other:* Savannah, scrub forest. 300 to 1,000 meters. Agriculturalists: citrus, mangoes, pineapples, other fruits, sorghum, millet, rice, maize, beans, cassava, bananas, sweet potatoes, other vegetables; animal husbandry: poultry, goats. Muslim, traditional religion, syncretism.

Kara (Regi) [reg] 86,000 (1987). Southeastern shore of Lake Victoria, between the Zanaki and Kerewe, on Ukerewe island. A few in Mwanza. *Class:* Niger-Congo, Atlantic-Congo, Volta-Congo, Benue-Congo, Bantoid, Southern, Narrow Bantu, Central, J, Haya-Jita (J.20). *Dialects:* Lexical similarity 81% with Jita, 80% with Kwaya. *Lg Use:* Vigorous. Younger speakers and a few adults also use Swahili. *Other:* 'Regi' is a group name. They do not travel much. Fishermen.

Kerewe (Ekikerebe, Kerebe) [ked] 100,000 (1987). Northwestern Ukerewe Island, southern Lake Victoria, Kibara. North of Sukuma, across Speke Gulf. *Class:* Niger-Congo, Atlantic-Congo, Volta-Congo, Benue-Congo, Bantoid, Southern, Narrow Bantu, Central, J,

Haya-Jita (J.20). *Dialects:* Lexical similarity 76% with Zinza, 75% with Haya, 69% with Nyambo, 68% with Nyankore, 63% with Chiga and Toro, 62% with Nyoro. *Lg Use:* Shift among younger people toward Jita. *Lg Dev:* NT: 1936–1946.

Kimbu (Kikimbu, Ikibungu, Yanzi) [kiv] 78,000 (1987). Mbeya Region, Kipembawe ward of Chunya District; Singida Region, Manyoni District; Tabora Region, Sikonge District. *Class:* Niger-Congo, Atlantic-Congo, Volta-Congo, Benue-Congo, Bantoid, Southern, Narrow Bantu, Central, F, Sukuma-Nyamwezi (F.20). *Dialects:* Lexical similarity 61% with Nilamba, 57% with Sukuma, 53% with Nyaturu, 48% with Sumbwa, 47% with Langi. *Lg Use:* Vigorous. Low prestige. In some areas, speakers identify themselves to outsiders as being from other ethnic groups. Some speakers also use Swahili or Nyamwezi. Most speakers have less than routine proficiency in Swahili. *Other:* Seminomadic. Forest. Agriculturalists: sorghum, millet, maize, rice, sweet potatoes, cassava, peanuts, beans, chick-peas, gourds, sunflowers; beekeepers. Traditional religion, Christian, Muslim.

Kinga (Kikinga, Ekikinga) [zga] 140,000 (2003). 57,000 in Makete District. Iringa Region, Makete District, in the Kipengere Mountain Range. *Class:* Niger-Congo, Atlantic-Congo, Volta-Congo, Benue-Congo, Bantoid, Southern, Narrow Bantu, Central, G, Bena-Kinga (G.60). *Dialects:* Kinga, Mahanji. *Lg Use:* Vigorous. Used in the home. All ages. Positive language attitude. Magoma speakers see themselves as a separate ethnic group. Most also use Swahili, many with low proficiency. *Lg Dev:* NT: 1961. *Other:* Mountain mesa and mountain slope. Savannah and gallery forest. 1,500 to 2,800 meters. Agriculturalists: potatoes, wheat, peas, maize, and other crops. Christian, traditional religion.

Kisankasa ("Ndorobo," "Dorobo") [kqh] 4,670 (1987). *Class:* Nilo-Saharan, Eastern Sudanic, Nilotic, Southern, Kalenjin, Nandi-Markweta, Nandi. *Dialects:* A distinct language from others called "Dorobo": Aramanik, Mediak, Mosiro. See also Aasax. *Lg Use:* Speakers have limited comprehension of other languages.

Kisi (Kikisi) [kiz] 10,200 (2001). Ethnic population: 18,000. Northwestern shore of Lake Nyasa (L. Malawi). Iringa Region, Ludewa District, Mwambao Division, Lupingu and Makonde Wards. Four primary villages: Lifuma, Lupingu, Makonde, and Nindi. *Class:* Niger-Congo, Atlantic-Congo, Volta-Congo, Benue-Congo, Bantoid, Southern, Narrow Bantu, Central, G, Bena-Kinga (G.60). *Dialects:* Lexical similarity 62% with Pangwa, 55% with Kinga, 53% with Sangu, 52% with Wanji, and 47% with Bena. *Lg Use:* Vigorous in main area. All ages. 34% to 51% below routine proficiency in Swahili. *Other:* Different from Kisii (Gusii) of Kenya. May be the same as Kichi. Coastal, riverine. Semitropical. Fishermen; agriculturalists. Christian, traditional religion.

Konongo (Kikonongo) [kcz] 51,000 (1987). Rukwa Region, in the northwest corner of Mpanda District, south of the Nyamwezi, across the Ugalla River. 25% live in the traditional area. *Class:* Niger-Congo, Atlantic-Congo, Volta-Congo, Benue-Congo, Bantoid, Southern, Narrow Bantu, Central, F, Sukuma-Nyamwezi (F.20). *Dialects:* May be a dialect of Nyamwezi. *Other:* Agriculturalists: sorghum, millet, maize, rice, sweet potatoes, cassava, peanuts, beans, chick-peas, gourds, sunflowers.

Kuria (Ikikuria, Igikuria, Tende, Kurya, Kurye) [kuj] 213,000 in Tanzania (1987). Population total all countries: 348,000. Mara Region, near the Kenya border, east of Lake Victoria. Also spoken in Kenya. *Class:* Niger-Congo, Atlantic-Congo, Volta-Congo, Benue-Congo, Bantoid, Southern, Narrow Bantu, Central, E, Kuria

(E.10). *Dialects:* Kiroba, Simbiti, Sweta. Kiroba and Simbiti may be distinct languages. *Lg Use:* Vigorous. *Lg Dev:* NT: 1996. *Other:* Koria is not a good spelling.

Kutu (Kikutu, Khutu) [kdc] 45,000 (1987). Morogoro Region, Morogoro and Kilosa districts. *Class:* Niger-Congo, Atlantic-Congo, Volta-Congo, Benue-Congo, Bantoid, Southern, Narrow Bantu, Central, G, Zigula-Zaramo (G.30). *Dialects:* Lexical similarity 69% with Kami, 68% with Zaramo, 64% with Kwere, 61% with Doe. *Lg Use:* Speakers also use Swahili. *Other:* Matrilineal. Plains. Below 160 meters. Agriculturalists: tobacco, cotton, kapok, sorghum, maize; animal husbandry: sheep, goats, poultry; hunters; fishermen. Muslim, traditional religion, Christian.

Kw'adza (Qwadza) [wka] Extinct. Mbulu District. *Class:* Afro-Asiatic, Cushitic, South. *Dialects:* Related to Iraqw. *Lg Use:* C. Ehret was reported to be working with the last speaker (M. L. Bender 1976:280). Confirmed by R. Kiessling (1999).

Kwaya [kya] 102,000 (1987). Mara Region, southeastern shore of Lake Victoria, between the Zanaki and Kerebe. *Class:* Niger-Congo, Atlantic-Congo, Volta-Congo, Benue-Congo, Bantoid, Southern, Narrow Bantu, Central, J, Haya-Jita (J.20). *Dialect:* Ruri. Lexical similarity 83% with Jita, 80% with Kara.

Kwere (Kakwere, Kwele, Ng'were, Nghwele, Tsinghwele, Kinghwele, Ngwele, Kikwere) [cwe] 98,000 (1987). Pwani Region, Bagamoyo District. Many live among the Zaramo and Luguru. *Class:* Niger-Congo, Atlantic-Congo, Volta-Congo, Benue-Congo, Bantoid, Southern, Narrow Bantu, Central, G, Zigula-Zaramo (G.30). *Dialects:* Lexical similarity 74% with Doe, 69% with Kami, 64% with Kutu, 61% with Zaramo, 62% with Zigula, 54% with Luguru. *Lg Use:* Vigorous. *Other:* The Kwere call their language 'Nghwele'. Kwere has influenced Zigula linguistically, and has been influenced by Zigula and Bondei. Matrilineal. Coastal. Agriculturalists: dry rice, maize, sorghum, peas, sesame, cotton, coconuts, fruit; fishermen; animal husbandry: small livestock; wood carvers. Traditional religion, Muslim, Christian.

Lambya (Ichilambya, Icilambya, Lambia, Lambwa, Rambia, Iramba, Ici-Rambia) [lai] 40,000 in Tanzania (1987). Southern part of Ulambya Division in Ileje District, Mbeya Region, border with Malawi. See main entry under Malawi.

Langi (Kilangi, Irangi, Rangi, Kirangi) [lag] 350,000 (1999 Hartung and Stegen). 35,000 monolinguals. Population includes many ethnic Burunge (in Chemba, Goima, and elsewhere) and some ethnic Alagwa (in Kolo, Mnenya, and elsewhere) who are Langi first-language speakers. Dodoma Region, Kondoa District, west of the Maasai, northeast of the Sandawe. Communities also in Dodoma, Mwanza, Dar es Salaam, Arusha, Tanga, Morogoro, Babati, and Singida. *Class:* Niger-Congo, Atlantic-Congo, Volta-Congo, Benue-Congo, Bantoid, Southern, Narrow Bantu, Central, F, Nyilamba-Langi (F.30). *Dialects:* Kondoa, Haubi, Kolo, Mondo. Close to Mbugwe. Limited comprehension of any other language. Lexical similarity 74% with Mbugwe, 49% with Nyaturu and Sukuma, 48% with Nyamwezi, 47% with Kimbu and Nilamba, 40% with Sumbwa. *Lg Use:* Vigorous. Used in the home, market. All ages. Proud of language and culture, yet preferring Swahili or English for personal benefit. Widespread bilingualism with Swahili. *Other:* Influenced by Cushitic languages. Speakers call their language 'Langi'; the Swahili pronunciation is 'Rangi'. SVO. Agriculturalists. Muslim, Christian.

Luguru (Lugulu, Ikiruguru, Guru, Ruguru, Kiluguru, Kiruguru) [ruf] 692,000 (2001 Johnstone and Mandryk). Morogoro Region, Morogoro and Kilosa districts; Pwani

Region, Bagamoyo District, Luguru Mountains, and Dar-es-Salaam. _Class:_ Niger-Congo, Atlantic-Congo, Volta-Congo, Benue-Congo, Bantoid, Southern, Narrow Bantu, Central, G, Zigula-Zaramo (G.30). _Dialects:_ People have little comprehension of other languages. Lexical similarity 54% with Kami. _Lg Use:_ Vigorous. _Other:_ Matrilineal. Coastal plains, hills, mountain slope. 300 to 1,000 meters. Agriculturalists: hill rice, maize, sorghum, beans, peas, cassava, bananas, sweet potatoes, vegetables, coffee, fruit; animal husbandry: sheep, goats, poultry; fishermen; some wage earners. Traditional religion, Muslim, Christian.

Luo (Dholuo, Kavirondo) [luo] 280,000 in Tanzania (2001 Johnstone and Mandryk). Mara Region, near Kenya border, east of Lake Victoria. _Lg Use:_ Vigorous. _Other:_ Different from Lwo (Lango) of Uganda or Lwo (Luo, Jur Luwo) of Sudan. See main entry under Kenya.

Maasai (Masai, Maa, Lumbwa, Kimaasai) [mas] 430,000 in Tanzania (1993). Population includes 170,000 Arusa, 30,000 Baraguyu (1987). North central, on Kenya border, east of Serengeti National Park. The Baraguyu are spread from the Indian Ocean nearly to Malawi. _Dialects:_ Arusha (Il-Arusha, L-Arusha), Parakuyo (Baraguyu, Kwavi), Kisonko. _Lg Use:_ Vigorous. The Baraguyu speak Maasai, but they consider themselves to be a separate ethnic group from the Maasai. Speakers also use Swahili. _Other:_ Nomadic. Patrilineal. Some men marry women from other language groups. Pastoralists: cattle, sheep, goats; agriculturalists. Traditional religion, Christian; Arusha: traditional religion, Christian. See main entry under Kenya.

Machame (Kimashami, Machambe) [jmc] 300,000 (1992 UBS). Chaga area. _Class:_ Niger-Congo, Atlantic-Congo, Volta-Congo, Benue-Congo, Bantoid, Southern, Narrow Bantu, Central, E, Chaga (E.30). _Dialects:_ Masama, Siha (Shira), Ng'uni, Bosho, Hai. A member of the Chaga dialect continuum which includes Rombo, Mochi, Vunjo. _Lg Dev:_ NT: 2000.

Machinga [mvw] 36,000 (1987). Lindi Region, Kilwa and Lindi districts, along the coast, above the 10th parallel south, close to the Mwera and the Ngindo. _Class:_ Niger-Congo, Atlantic-Congo, Volta-Congo, Benue-Congo, Bantoid, Southern, Narrow Bantu, Central, P, Yao (P.20). _Other:_ Muslim.

Magoma (Kimagoma) [gmx] 9,000 (SIL 2003). Iringa Region, Makete District, near the Kitulo Plateau. _Class:_ Niger-Congo, Atlantic-Congo, Volta-Congo, Benue-Congo, Bantoid, Southern, Narrow Bantu, Central, G, Bena-Kinga (G.60). _Dialects:_ Two very closely related varieties: one in the lower villages and one in the villages with a higher elevation. _Lg Use:_ Vigorous. Used in most domains. All ages. Positive language attitude. Speakers also use Swahili, some with low proficiency. Swahili used in the elementary schools, English in the secondary schools. _Other:_ Magoma is often considered part of Kinga and their language as a dialect of Kinga. However, Magoma speakers see themselves as a separate ethnic group. They say that they cannot always understand Kinga very well. Low similarity figures on wordlist comparison supports this claim. Children do not understand Kinga. Mountain mesa and mountain slope. Savannah and gallery forest. 2,100 to 2,500 meters. Subsistence agriculturalists: potatoes, wheat, peas, maize, and other crops; lumbermen. Christian, traditional religion.

Makhuwa-Meetto (Makua, Makhua, Imakua, Makoa, Mato, Maquoua, Kimakua, Makuwa) [mgh] 360,000 in Tanzania (1993). Mtwara Region, Masasi District, extreme southern Tanzania. _Dialect:_ Medo (Meto, Emeto). _Other:_ Muslim, traditional religion, Christian. See main entry under Mozambique.

Makonde (Chimakonde, Chinimakonde, Konde, Matambwe) [kde] 1,140,000 in Tanzania (2001 Johnstone

and Mandryk). Population total all countries: 1,373,358. Mtwara Region, primarily Mtwara Urban, Mtwara Rural, Tandahomba, and Newala districts. Also spoken in Mozambique. _Class:_ Niger-Congo, Atlantic-Congo, Volta-Congo, Benue-Congo, Bantoid, Southern, Narrow Bantu, Central, P, Yao (P.20). _Dialects:_ "Maviha," Maraba. Matambwe may be closer to Yao than Makonde, and may even be a separate language or a dialect of Mwera. _Lg Use:_ Vigorous. Most have low proficiency in Swahili. _Lg Dev:_ Grammar. Bible portions. _Other:_ "Mahiva" is a derogatory term for Makonde immigrants from Mozambique who have largely been assimilated into the Tanzanian Makonde culture. Muslim, Christian, traditional religion.

Malila (Malilia, Ishimalilia, Shimalilia, Kimalila) [mgq] 65,000 (2003 SIL). Mbeya Region, about 40 km southwest of the town of Mbeya. South of Safwa, north of Ndali, west of Nyakyusa, east of Nyiha. _Class:_ Niger-Congo, Atlantic-Congo, Volta-Congo, Benue-Congo, Bantoid, Southern, Narrow Bantu, Central, M, Nyika-Safwa (M.20). _Lg Use:_ Vigorous. Speakers of other languages moving into the area learn Malila. Used in most domains including church and politics. All ages. Positive language attitude. Bilingualism in Swahili is low compared to other areas. Safwa and Nyiha are understandable along the borders, but the central speech forms of Nyiha and Safwa do not appear to be comprehensible to a majority of the Malila population. _Other:_ Mountain Slopes. Savannah and tropical forest. 1,600 to 2,200 meters. Agriculturalists: maize, potatoes, sweet potatoes, peas, beans, millet, and some wheat. Cash crops include coffee and pyrethrum. Christian, traditional religion.

Mambwe-Lungu [mgr] 97,000 in Tanzania (1987). Population includes 63,000 Mambwe and 34,000 Rungu. Rukwa Region, Sumbawanga District, the southeastern shore and to the south of Lake Tanganyika. _Dialects:_ Mambwe (Icimambwe, Ichimambwe, Kimambwe), Rungu (Icilungu, Lungu, Cilungu, Kilungu, Kirungu). _Other:_ Forest, savannah. Agriculturalists: millet, sorghum, maize, peanuts, beans; animal husbandry: cattle, sheep, goats, poultry; fishermen. Traditional religion, Christian. See main entry under Zambia.

Manda (Kimanda, Kinyasa, Nyasa) [mgs] 22,000 in Ludewa District (2002). Iringa Region, Ludewa District; also Ruvuma Region, Mbinga District; eastern shore of Lake Nyasa. _Class:_ Niger-Congo, Atlantic-Congo, Volta-Congo, Benue-Congo, Bantoid, Southern, Narrow Bantu, Central, G, Bena-Kinga (G.60). _Dialect:_ Matumba. Matumba is recognized as a distinct dialect but is completely intelligible with Manda. _Lg Use:_ Vigorous. Manda is used in low domains and to discuss high domains. For high domains, Swahili is used or mixed with Manda. All ages. Positive language attitude. _Lg Dev:_ NT: 1937. _Other:_ The Matumba see themselves as a separate group related to the Manda, while the Manda view them as a subgroup of the Manda. Coastal and mountain slope. Savannah. 511 to 1,330 meters. Fishermen; agriculturalists: cassava, corn, bananas, cashews. Christian.

Maraba (Kimakwe, Makwe, Palma) [ymk] 10,000 in Tanzania (2003). Southeast Tanzania. _Lg Use:_ Speakers also use Swahili. _Lg Dev:_ Motivation for literacy is high. _Other:_ Muslim. See main entry under Mozambique (Makwe).

Matengo (Chimatengo, Kimatengo) [mgv] 150,000 (1987). Ruvuma Region, southwest, east of Lake Malawi. Also possibly in Malawi. _Class:_ Niger-Congo, Atlantic-Congo, Volta-Congo, Benue-Congo, Bantoid, Southern, Narrow Bantu, Central, N, Manda (N.10). _Lg Use:_ Speakers have little comprehension of other languages. _Lg Dev:_ Grammar.

Matumbi (Kimatumbi) [mgw] 72,000 (1978 MARC). Lindi Region, on the banks of the Ruvuma, next to the Makonde and Makhuwa (Polomé and Hill 1980). *Class:* Niger-Congo, Atlantic-Congo, Volta-Congo, Benue-Congo, Bantoid, Southern, Narrow Bantu, Central, P, Matumbi (P.10). *Dialect:* Kuchi. *Lg Use:* Speakers have little comprehension of Swahili or other languages. *Other:* Muslim, traditional religion, Christian.

Mbugu (Ma'a, Mbougou, Wama'a, Wa Maathi, Kibwyo) [mhd] 7,000 (1997). Ethnic population: 32,000. Tanga Region, Lushoto District, in Usambara Mountains. *Class:* Mixed Language, Bantu-Cushitic. *Dialects:* Cha ndani, Cha kawaida. *Lg Use:* Speakers also use Asu, Shambala, or Swahili. *Other:* People call themselves 'Wa-Ma'a'. A hybrid language; Bantu inflectional (prefix and concord) system with Cushitic vocabulary. Derivational morphemes are Bantu and Cushitic (or non-Bantu). The Bantu influence is from Pare and Shambala.

Mbugwe (Kimbugwe, Mbuwe) [mgz] 24,000 (1999). Babati District, Arusha Region. *Class:* Niger-Congo, Atlantic-Congo, Volta-Congo, Benue-Congo, Bantoid, Southern, Narrow Bantu, Central, F, Nyilamba-Langi (F.30). *Dialects:* Lexical similarity 52% with Langi. *Lg Use:* All ages.

Mbunga [mgy] 29,000 (1987). South central, southeast of the Hehe, north of the Pogolo. *Class:* Niger-Congo, Atlantic-Congo, Volta-Congo, Benue-Congo, Bantoid, Southern, Narrow Bantu, Central, P, Matumbi (P.10). *Dialects:* Lexical similarity 69% with Ndamba, 57% with Pogolu. *Other:* There may be two varieties called 'Mbunga', one Bantu P.10, and one Bantu G.50.

Mediak (Ndorobo, Dorobo) [mwx] 5,268 (2000 WCD). *Class:* Nilo-Saharan, Eastern Sudanic, Nilotic, Southern, Kalenjin, Nandi-Markweta, Nandi. *Lg Use:* Limited comprehension of other languages. *Other:* A distinct language from others called "Dorobo": Aramanik, Kisankasa, Mosiro, Aasax. Hunter-gatherers.

Mochi (Moshi, Kimoshi, Mosi, Old Moshi, Kimochi) [old] 596,656 (2000 WCD). Around Moshi, south corner Chaga area. *Class:* Niger-Congo, Atlantic-Congo, Volta-Congo, Benue-Congo, Bantoid, Southern, Narrow Bantu, Central, E, Chaga (E.30). *Dialect:* Uru. A member of the Chaga dialect continuum which includes Rombo, Machame, Vunjo. *Lg Dev:* NT: 1939.

Mosiro (Ndorobo, Dorobo) [mwy] 5,268 (2000 WCD). *Class:* Nilo-Saharan, Eastern Sudanic, Nilotic, Southern, Kalenjin, Nandi-Markweta, Nandi. *Dialects:* A distinct language from others called "Dorobo": Aramanik, Mediak, Kisankasa. *Lg Use:* Speakers have limited comprehension of other languages. *Other:* Hunter-gatherers.

Mpoto (Chimpoto, Kinyasa, Nyasa) [mpa] 80,000 (1977 Voegelin and Voegelin). Ruyuma Region, Mbinga District, southwestern, along northeast shore of Lake Nyasa. *Class:* Niger-Congo, Atlantic-Congo, Volta-Congo, Benue-Congo, Bantoid, Southern, Narrow Bantu, Central, N, Manda (N.12). *Lg Use:* Many Mpoto speakers are proficient in Matengo. *Lg Dev:* Bible portions: 1913–1924. *Other:* Both Mpoto and Manda have alternate names of 'Kinyasa'. Christian, traditional religion.

Mwera (Nyasa, Kinyasa, Nyanza) [mjh] 6,000 (2004). Ruyuma Region, Mbinga District, Mbamba Bay, Shore of Lake Nyasa, southwest Tanzania. *Class:* Niger-Congo, Atlantic-Congo, Volta-Congo, Benue-Congo, Bantoid, Southern, Narrow Bantu, Central, P, Yao (P.20). *Dialects:* Similar to Mwera in the Lindi Region, but not the same. Also reported to be similar to Nyanja (N.30) languages.

Mwera (Chimwera, Cimwera, Mwela) [mwe] 469,000 (2001 Johnstone and Mandryk). Southeast, north of Makonde, mostly in Lindi Region, primarily Nachingwea, Ruangwa, and Lindi Urban and Rural districts. *Class:*

Niger-Congo, Atlantic-Congo, Volta-Congo, Benue-Congo, Bantoid, Southern, Narrow Bantu, Central, P, Yao (P.20). *Lg Use:* Speakers also use Swahili. *Lg Dev:* Grammar. *Other:* Muslim, Christian.

Ndali (Chindali, Kindali, Ici-Ndali) [ndh] 150,000 in Tanzania (1987). Population total all countries: 220,000. Mbeya Region, Ileje District, cross into Malawi, between Lambya and Nyakyusa. Also spoken in Malawi. *Class:* Niger-Congo, Atlantic-Congo, Volta-Congo, Benue-Congo, Bantoid, Southern, Narrow Bantu, Central, M, Nyika-Safwa (M.20). *Dialect:* Sukwa. *Lg Use:* Vigorous. Used in most domains. All ages. Very positive language attitude. Lower than routine proficiency in Swahili. *Other:* Different from Ndali which is a dialect of Zanaki. Mountainous. Semi-tropical. Up to 2,458 meters. Agriculturalists: maize, beans, cassava, bananas; animal husbandry: cattle, goats, sheep. Christian, traditional religion.

Ndamba [ndj] 55,000 (1987). South central, Iringa Region, northeast of Bena, southeast of Hehe, west of Pogolo, southwest of Mbunga. *Class:* Niger-Congo, Atlantic-Congo, Volta-Congo, Benue-Congo, Bantoid, Southern, Narrow Bantu, Central, G, Pogoro (G.50). *Dialects:* Lexical similarity 69% with Mbunga, 56% with Pogolo. *Lg Use:* Speakers also use Swahili.

Ndendeule (Ndendeuli, Kindendeule, Kindendeuli) [dne] 100,000 (2000 Deo Ngonyani). Inland, east of the main Ngoni territory south of the 10th parallel, Ruvuma Region. Neighbor languages are Yao to the south and east, Ngoni to the west, Bena to the north, Nindi to the south, Ngindo to the northeast beyond the Selous Game Reserve. *Class:* Niger-Congo, Atlantic-Congo, Volta-Congo, Benue-Congo, Bantoid, Southern, Narrow Bantu, Central, P, Matumbi (P.10). *Dialects:* Closest to Ngindo, although geographically distant. *Lg Use:* Speakers have little comprehension of other languages. *Lg Dev:* Grammar.

Ndengereko (Kingengereko, Ndengeleko) [ndg] 110,000 (2000). Central coast, south of the Zaramo, north of the Rufiji. Eastern parts of Songea District, Ruvuma Region. *Class:* Niger-Congo, Atlantic-Congo, Volta-Congo, Benue-Congo, Bantoid, Southern, Narrow Bantu, Central, P, Matumbi (P.10). *Lg Use:* Speakers have low proficiency in Swahili.

Ndonde Hamba (Kimawanda, Mawanda, Ndomde, Ndonde, Kindonde Hamba, Chindonde Hamba, Chindonde) [njd] 10,000 to 20,000 (2002 PBT). Lindi Region, Nachingwea District, primarily Kilimarondo Division. *Class:* Niger-Congo, Atlantic-Congo, Volta-Congo, Benue-Congo, Bantoid, Southern, Narrow Bantu, Central, P, Yao (P.20). *Lg Use:* Speakers are shifting to Swahili. Speakers have high proficiency in Makhuwa-Metto. *Other:* Close to Mwera. It has extensive borrowing from Ngindo. 450 to 600 meters. Muslim, traditional religion, Christian.

Ngasa (Shaka, Ongamo) [nsg] 200 to 300 (1983). Ethnic population: 4,285 (2000 WCD). Eastern slopes of Mt. Kilimanjaro. *Class:* Nilo-Saharan, Eastern Sudanic, Nilotic, Eastern, Lotuxo-Teso, Lotuxo-Maa, Ongamo-Maa. *Dialects:* Lexical similarity 60% with Maasai, 59% with Samburu, 58% with Chamus. *Lg Use:* Use began to diminish in the 1950s. Members of the ethnic group speak Chaga. Speakers are older adults.

Ngindo (Kingindo, Njindo, Magingo) [nnq] 220,000 (1987). East central, south of the Rufiji, west of the Mwera. *Class:* Niger-Congo, Atlantic-Congo, Volta-Congo, Benue-Congo, Bantoid, Southern, Narrow Bantu, Central, P, Matumbi (P.10). *Lg Use:* Speakers also use Swahili.

Ngoni (Chingoni, Kingoni, Angoni, Kisutu, Sutu) [ngo] 170,000 in Tanzania (1987). Population total all countries: 205,000. South central, Ruvuma Region, south of Songea. Also spoken in Mozambique. *Class:* Niger-Congo, Atlantic-Congo, Volta-Congo, Benue-Congo, Bantoid, Southern, Narrow Bantu, Central, N, Manda (N.10).

Dialects: Different from 'Ngoni' which is an alternate name for Zulu, Ngoni dialect of Nsenga, Ngoni dialect of Tumbuka. Not related to Ngoni of Malawi. Low lexical similarity percentage with Zulu. *Lg Dev:* Bible portions: 1891–1898. *Other:* The people formerly spoke Zulu. The Ngoni people in Malawi do not speak Ngoni, but all speak Nyanja as first language.

Ngulu (Kingulu, Nguru, Nguu, Wayomba, Geja) [ngp] 132,000 (1987). Morogoro Region, Morogoro District; Tanga Region, Handeni District; Dodoma Region, Mpwapwa and Kongwa districts. *Class:* Niger-Congo, Atlantic-Congo, Volta-Congo, Benue-Congo, Bantoid, Southern, Narrow Bantu, Central, G, Zigula-Zaramo (G.30). *Dialects:* Lexical similarity 83% with Zigula, 73% with Bondei, 68% with Shambala. *Lg Use:* Speakers have a limited comprehension of Swahili. *Other:* Different from Ngulu of Mozambique and Malawi. Matrilineal. Mountain slope, foothills, plains. 300 meters and higher. Traders; agriculturalists: maize, millet, sorghum, beans, peas, bananas, sugarcane, cassava, castor, peanuts, sweet potatoes, pumpkins, fruit, mountain rice, tobacco, cotton, coffee; animal husbandry: poultry, sheep, goats, cattle. Traditional religion, Christian, Muslim.

Ngurimi (Ikingurimi, Ngoreme, Ngruimi, Nguruimi, Dengurume) [ngq] 32,000 (1987). North central border with Kenya, between the Maasai and the Kuria, Shinyanga and Mara regions. *Class:* Niger-Congo, Atlantic-Congo, Volta-Congo, Benue-Congo, Bantoid, Southern, Narrow Bantu, Central, E, Kuria (E.10). *Dialects:* Limited comprehension of other languages. Lexical similarity 84% with Kuria, 80% with Zanaki, 73% with Ikoma, 49% with Gusii.

Nilamba (Nyilamba, Ikinilamba, Iramba, Nilyamba, Ikiniramba, Ilamba, Niramba, Kiniramba, Kinilamba) [nim] 440,000 (1987). Population includes 50,000 Iambi. Western Shinyanga Region, north of the Nyaturu. *Class:* Niger-Congo, Atlantic-Congo, Volta-Congo, Benue-Congo, Bantoid, Southern, Narrow Bantu, Central, F, Nyilamba-Langi (F.30). *Dialect:* Iambi. Lexical similarity 56% with Nyamwezi, 55% with Sukuma, 45% with Sumbwa. *Lg Dev:* NT: 1967.

Nindi [nxi] 100. East Songea District, Ruvuma Region, southern Tanzania close to the Mozambique border, south of the Ndendeule. *Class:* Niger-Congo, Atlantic-Congo, Volta-Congo, Benue-Congo, Bantoid, Southern, Narrow Bantu, Central, P, Matumbi (P.10). *Dialects:* Similar to Ndendeule. *Other:* Virtually unknown outside the district.

Nyakyusa-Ngonde (Ikinyakyusa, Mombe, Ngonde, Ikingonde, Konde, Nkonde, Nyakyusa, Nyikyusa, Sochile, Sokile, Sokili, Kukwe, Nyekyosa, Kinyakyusa) [nyy] 750,000 in Tanzania (1992 UBS). Population total all countries: 1,050,000. Southern areas of Mbeya Region. North end of Lake Malawi. Some also in Iringa Region, Makete District. Also spoken in Malawi. *Class:* Niger-Congo, Atlantic-Congo, Volta-Congo, Benue-Congo, Bantoid, Southern, Narrow Bantu, Central, M, Nyakyusa (M.30). *Dialects:* Nyakyusa, Kukwe, Mwamba (Lungulu), Ngonde, Selya (Salya, Seria). *Lg Use:* Vigorous. *Lg Dev:* Dictionary. Bible: 1993–1996. *Other:* Traditional religion, Christian, Muslim.

Nyambo (Ekinyambo, Karagwe, Rukaragwe, Ururagwe, Ragwe, Runyambo, Kinyambo) [now] 400,000 (2003). Kagera Region, Karagwe District, northwest corner, Uganda border, west of Lake Victoria. *Class:* Niger-Congo, Atlantic-Congo, Volta-Congo, Benue-Congo, Bantoid, Southern, Narrow Bantu, Central, J, Haya-Jita (J.20). *Dialect:* Yakahanga. Lexical similarity 84% with Haya, 81% with Zinza, 75% with Kerewe, 78% with Nyankore, 72% with Chiga, 69% with Kerewe, 68% with Toro, 67% with Nyoro. *Lg Use:* Some also use Haya.

Nyamwanga (Chinamwanga, Mwanga, Namwanga, Kinamwanga) [mwn] 87,000 in Tanzania (1987). Rukwa Region, southeast corner of Sumbawanga District; Mbeya Region, southwest corner of Mbozi District, bordering to Zambia south of the Fipa. Southwest of Lake Rukwa. Saisi Valley in the northwest to forested plateau in the southeast. *Dialects:* Tambo, Iwa. *Other:* Agriculturalists: millet, peanuts, beans, maize; animal husbandry: cattle, sheep, goats, poultry, pidgeons. Traditional religion. See main entry under Zambia.

Nyamwezi (Kinyamwezi, Kinyamwesi, Nyamwesi, Namwezi) [nym] 1,200,000 (2001 Johnstone and Mandryk). 73% are in the traditional area. Northwest central, between Lake Victoria and Lake Rukwa. Tabora Region; Rukwa, Singida, and Shinyanga regions. *Class:* Niger-Congo, Atlantic-Congo, Volta-Congo, Benue-Congo, Bantoid, Southern, Narrow Bantu, Central, F, Sukuma-Nyamwezi (F.20). *Dialects:* Nyanyembe, Takama (Garaganza), Mweri (Sumbwa, Konongo, Kiya). Lexical similarity 84% with Sukuma, 61% with Sumbwa, 56% with Nilamba. *Lg Use:* Vigorous. *Lg Dev:* Grammar. NT: 1909–1951. *Other:* Agriculturalists: sorghum, millet, maize, rice, sweet potatoes, cassava, peanuts, beans, chick-peas, gourds, sunflowers. Traditional religion, Muslim, Christian.

Nyaturu (Turu, Kinyaturu, Rimi, Limi, Kirimi, Remi, Kiremi, Keremi) [rim] 556,000 (1993 Johnstone). Singida Region, Iramba and Singida districts, north central, south of Singida, west of the Wembere River. *Class:* Niger-Congo, Atlantic-Congo, Volta-Congo, Benue-Congo, Bantoid, Southern, Narrow Bantu, Central, F, Nyilamba-Langi (F.30). *Dialects:* Girwana (Rimi), Chahi, Ginyamunyinganyi. Lexical similarity 63% with Nilamba, 59% with Sukuma, 58% with Nyamwezi, 53% with Kimbu, 49% with Nyaturu, 44% with Sumbwa. *Lg Dev:* Bible portions: 1956–1964. *Other:* Government name is 'Kinyaturu'. Traditional religion, Christian, Muslim.

Nyiha (Ishinyiha, Shinyiha, Nyika, Nyixa, Kinyiha) [nih] 306,000 in Tanzania (1987). Population total all countries: 626,000. Mbeya Region, Mbozi District, south and west of Lake Rukwa. Also spoken in Zambia. *Class:* Niger-Congo, Atlantic-Congo, Volta-Congo, Benue-Congo, Bantoid, Southern, Narrow Bantu, Central, M, Nyika-Safwa (M.20). *Dialects:* Close to Lambya, Malila. *Lg Dev:* NT: 1913–1966. *Other:* Different from Nyika (Giryama) of Kenya. Traditionally weavers, iron workers, hunters; swidden agriculturalists: millet; animal husbandry: cattle, goats, poultry.

Okiek (Akie, Akiek) [oki] Northern Tanzania, southern part of Arusha Region; the Akie live in small groups south of Arusha among Maasai speakers. *Lg Use:* Most young Akiek do not speak Akiek. All Akiek speak Maasai as first or second language. Some young people also know Swahili. *Other:* "Ndorobo" is a derogatory name. Speakers in Tanzania and Kenya are not in touch with each other. Former hunter-gatherers. See main entry under Kenya.

Pangwa (Ekipangwa, Kipangwa) [pbr] 95,000 (2002). Iringa Region, Ludewa District; in the Livingstone mountains on the eastern shore of Lake Nyasa. *Class:* Niger-Congo, Atlantic-Congo, Volta-Congo, Benue-Congo, Bantoid, Southern, Narrow Bantu, Central, G, Bena-Kinga (G.60). *Dialect:* Kimwela. Kimwela is spoken with a distinctly different accent and the people consider themselves a separate ethnic group, but the language is completely intelligible with the main variety of Pangwa. Lexical similarity 71% with Bena, 62% with Kisi, 61% with Kinga, 59% with Hehe, 58% with Sangu, 55% with Wanji. *Lg Use:* Vigorous. Pangwa is used in low domains and often to discuss high domains. Swahili is also used in high domains. All ages. Positive language attitude. Speakers have limited comprehension of Swahili. *Lg Dev:* Grammar. *Other:* Pangwa speakers report high intelligibility with Bena. However, preliminary intelligibility testing showed that actually comprehension is not adequate to use Bena material. Mountain slope and valley. Savannah, Scrub forest, and Gallery forest. 1,330 to 2,200 meters. Agriculturalists: corn, beans, peas, coffee, tea, wheat, pyrethrum; animal husbandry. Christian, traditional religion.

Pimbwe (Ichipimbwe, Cipimbwe, Kipimbwe) [piw] 29,000 (1987). Rukwa Region, Mpanda and Mkasi districts. Rift Valley to the northwest of Lake Rukwa. *Class:* Niger-Congo, Atlantic-Congo, Volta-Congo, Benue-Congo, Bantoid, Southern, Narrow Bantu, Central, F, Tongwe (F.10). *Lg Use:* Speakers have limited comprehension of Swahili. *Other:* Agriculturalists: millet, maize, sorghum, cassava, beans, peanuts; animal husbandry: goats, poultry. Christian, traditional religion.

Pogolo (Chipogolo, Pogoro, Pogora, Chipogoro, Pogolu, Shpogolu) [poy] 185,000 (1987). Iringa and Morogoro regions, south central, south of the Mbunga, east of the Ndamba. *Class:* Niger-Congo, Atlantic-Congo, Volta-Congo, Benue-Congo, Bantoid, Southern, Narrow Bantu, Central, G, Pogoro (G.50). *Dialects:* Lexical similarity 57% with Mbunga, 56% with Ndamba.

Rombo (Kirombo) [rof] Chaga area, eastern area. *Class:* Niger-Congo, Atlantic-Congo, Volta-Congo, Benue-Congo, Bantoid, Southern, Narrow Bantu, Central, E, Chaga (E.30). *Dialects:* Keni, Mashati, Mkuu, Usseri. A member of the Chaga dialect continuum which includes Mochi, Machame, Vunjo.

Rufiji (Ruihi, Kiruihi, Fiji) [rui] 200,000 (1987). Pwani Region, Rufiji District, central coast, south of the Ndengereko, north of the Matumbi. *Class:* Niger-Congo, Atlantic-Congo, Volta-Congo, Benue-Congo, Bantoid, Southern, Narrow Bantu, Central, P, Matumbi (P.10). *Other:* Muslim.

Rungwa (Lungwa, Ichirungwa, Icilungwa, Runga) [rnw] 18,000 (1987). Rukwa Region, Mpanda District, the plains at the northern end of Lake Rukwa. *Class:* Niger-Congo, Atlantic-Congo, Volta-Congo, Benue-Congo, Bantoid, Southern, Narrow Bantu, Central, F, Tongwe (F.10). *Lg Use:* Some also use Swahili. *Other:* Agriculturalists: millet, maize, cassava, sesame seed, peanuts; animal husbandry: goats, sheep, poultry. Traditional religion.

Rwa (Rwo, Kirwo) [rwk] 90,000 (1987). Population includes 50,000 Kihai. Arusha Region, around Mt. Meru. *Class:* Niger-Congo, Atlantic-Congo, Volta-Congo, Benue-Congo, Bantoid, Southern, Narrow Bantu, Central, E, Chaga (E.30). *Dialect:* Kihai (Meru). *Lg Dev:* NT: 1964. *Other:* Distinct from Meru of Kenya.

Safwa (Ishisafwa, Cisafwa, Kisafwa) [sbk] 158,000 (1987). Mbeya and Poroto mountain ranges in the Mbeya, Chunya, and Mbozi districts of Mbeya Region. *Class:* Niger-Congo, Atlantic-Congo, Volta-Congo, Benue-Congo, Bantoid, Southern, Narrow Bantu, Central, M, Nyika-Safwa (M.20). *Dialects:* Guruka, Mbwila, Poroto, Songwe. *Lg Use:* Vigorous. Used in the home. All ages. A Swahili sentence repetition test was given to a stratified random population sample in 3 rural villages. 82% tested below routine proficiency. *Lg Dev:* Grammar. *Other:* Agriculturalists: maize, rice, sunflowers, cassava, wheat, peas. Cash crops include cotton, potatoes, and coffee; animal husbandry: goats, sheep, cows. Traditional religion, Christian.

Sagala (Kisagala, Southern Kisagala, Kisagara, Sagara) [sbm] 79,000 (1987). Morogoro Region, Kilosa and Ulanga districts; Dodoma Region, Mpwapwa District; Iringa Region. *Class:* Niger-Congo, Atlantic-Congo, Volta-Congo, Benue-Congo, Bantoid, Southern, Narrow Bantu, Central, G, Zigula-Zaramo (G.30). *Dialects:* Itumba, Kondoa (Solwe), Kweny, Nkwifiya (Kwifa, Kwiva). Lexical similarity 63% with Kagulu, 60% with Gogo. *Lg Use:* Speakers have some proficiency in Swahili. *Other:* Different from Sagalla which is in Taita

group of Kenya. Matrilineal. Mountain slope. Traditional religion, Muslim, Christian.

Sandawe (Sandaui, Sandawi, Sandwe, Sandaweeki, Kisandawe) [sad] 40,000 (2000). Dodoma Region, Kondoa District, between the Bubu and Mponde rivers. *Class:* Khoisan, Sandawe. *Dialects:* Bisa, Telha. 2 dialects. *Lg Use:* Vigorous. All domains. Positive language attitude. People think Sandawe is too difficult to read or write. Older people and those in remote areas are monolingual. Most use Swahili as second language. Most have limited comprehension of other languages. *Other:* They have intermarried with the Gogo, Turu, and Maasai. SOV. Hills. Shrubs and bushes. Hunter-gatherers; fishermen; agriculturalists; pastoralists: cattle. Traditional religion, Christian, Muslim.

Sangu (Sango, Eshisango, Rori, Kisangu) [sbp] 75,000 (1987). Usangu Plains, Mbarale District, Mbeya Region. *Class:* Niger-Congo, Atlantic-Congo, Volta-Congo, Benue-Congo, Bantoid, Southern, Narrow Bantu, Central, G, Bena-Kinga (G.60). *Lg Use:* Vigorous. All ages. Positive language attitude. Most speakers have less than routine proficiency in Swahili. *Other:* Different from Sango of Democratic Republic of the Congo, Central African Republic, and Chad, or from Sanga of Democratic Republic of the Congo and from Sangu of Gabon. Plains. Agriculturalists; animal husbandry. Muslim, traditional religion, Christian.

Segeju (Kisegeju, Sageju, Sengeju) [seg] 7,000 (2003 SIL). Ethnic population: Fewer than 15,000. Narrow strip of the northeast coast between Tanga and the Kenya border, Muheza District, Tanga region. *Class:* Niger-Congo, Atlantic-Congo, Volta-Congo, Benue-Congo, Bantoid, Southern, Narrow Bantu, Central, E, Nyika (E.40), Mijikenda. *Dialects:* Closely related to Digo. *Lg Use:* Many ethnic Segeju do not speak the Segeju language; they speak Swahili or Digo as first language. Self-reported high Swahili ability in all age groups. *Other:* People were historically one with the Dhaiso. The Dhaiso language is also called Kisegeju in Swahili. Muslim.

Shambala (Kishambala, Kishambaa, Kisambaa, Sambaa, Shambaa, Sambala, Sambara, Schambala) [ksb] 664,000 (2001 Johnstone and Mandryk). Tanga Region, Lushoto District, Usambara Mountains. *Class:* Niger-Congo, Atlantic-Congo, Volta-Congo, Benue-Congo, Bantoid, Southern, Narrow Bantu, Central, G, Shambala (G.20). *Dialects:* Lexical similarity 75% with Bondei, 68% with Ngulu and Zigula. *Lg Dev:* NT: 1908. *Other:* Muslim, Christian, traditional religion.

Shubi (Subi, Urushubi, Sinja) [suj] 153,000 (1987). Kagera Region, northwest of Sumbwa, near Lake Victoria. *Class:* Niger-Congo, Atlantic-Congo, Volta-Congo, Benue-Congo, Bantoid, Southern, Narrow Bantu, Central, J, Rwanda-Rundi (J.60). *Dialects:* Lexical similarity 85% with Hangaza, 77% with Rundi and Ha, 71% with Rwanda, 49% with Sumbwa. *Other:* Traditional religion, Christian.

Sizaki (Shashi, Sasi, Kisizaki) [szk] 82,000 (1987). Mara Region, Musoma District, near Zanaki, northeast of Kerebe, near the southeast shore of Lake Victoria. *Class:* Niger-Congo, Atlantic-Congo, Volta-Congo, Benue-Congo, Bantoid, Southern, Narrow Bantu, Central, E, Kuria (E.10). *Dialects:* Related to Zanaki. *Lg Use:* Speakers also use Swahili.

Suba [suh] 30,000 in Tanzania (1987). Mara Region, Tarime District, north central, south of Luo. *Lg Use:* Speakers have some proficiency in Swahili. See main entry under Kenya.

Subi [xsj] Kagera Region, Biharamulo District. *Class:* Niger-Congo, Atlantic-Congo, Volta-Congo, Benue-Congo, Bantoid, Southern, Narrow Bantu, Central, J, Haya-Jita (J.20). *Other:* Widely spread in multiethnic communities, but retain the language.

Sukuma (Kisukuma) [suk] 3,200,000 (2001 Johnstone and Mandryk). Northwest, between Lake Victoria and Lake Rukwa, Shinyanga to Serengeti Plain (Kiya); also Mwanza (Gwe). A small percentage in cities; 88% in the traditional area. *Class:* Niger-Congo, Atlantic-Congo, Volta-Congo, Benue-Congo, Bantoid, Southern, Narrow Bantu, Central, F, Sukuma-Nyamwezi (F.20). *Dialect:* Kiya, Gwe (Kigwe). Dialects contiguous with Nyamwezi are intelligible with it. Lexical similarity 84% with Nyamwezi, 59% with Sumbwa and Nyaturu, 57% with Kimbu, 55% with Nilamba, 49% with Langi. *Lg Use:* Vigorous. A few young people in cities do not speak Sukuma. In the country the young people borrow more Swahili in their Sukuma. Speakers also use Swahili. *Lg Dev:* Bible: 1960. *Other:* Pastoralists: cattle; agriculturalists: sorghum, millet, maize, rice, sweet potatoes, cassava, peanuts, beans, chick-peas, gourds, sunflowers, cotton, tobacco; fishermen. Traditional religion, Christian, Muslim.

Sumbwa (Kisumbwa) [suw] 191,000 (1987). Bukombe District of Shinyanga Region. *Class:* Niger-Congo, Atlantic-Congo, Volta-Congo, Benue-Congo, Bantoid, Southern, Narrow Bantu, Central, F, Sukuma-Nyamwezi (F.20). *Dialects:* Lexical similarity 61% with Nyamwezi, 59% with Sukuma, 45% with Nilamba. *Lg Use:* Many speakers have below routine ability in Swahili. *Other:* Agriculturalists: sorghum, millet, maize, rice, sweet potatoes, cassava, peanuts, beans, chick-peas, gourds, sunflowers, bananas. Christian, traditional religion, Muslim.

Swahili (Kiswahili, Kisuaheli) [swh] 540,837 in Tanzania (2000 WCD). 313,200 monolinguals. Population total all countries: 772,642. Zanzibar, coastal areas. Also spoken in Burundi, Kenya, Mayotte, Mozambique, Oman, Rwanda, Somalia, South Africa, Uganda, United Arab Emirates, USA. *Class:* Niger-Congo, Atlantic-Congo, Volta-Congo, Benue-Congo, Bantoid, Southern, Narrow Bantu, Central, G, Swahili (G.40). *Dialects:* Mrima, Unguja (Kiunguja, Zanzibar), Pemba, Mgao. Bajun has 85% lexical similarity with Amu, 78% with Mvita, 72% with Mrima; Mvita has 86% with Amu, 79% with Mrima; Mrima has 79% with Amu. *Lg Use:* Official language. 30,000,000 rural people are second-language users; they use the local language for most activities, but Swahili with outsiders. It is also common for people of numerous ethnic groups besides Swahili who grow up in certain towns to speak Swahili as first language. *Lg Dev:* Radio programs. TV. Dictionary. Bible: 1891–1996. *Other:* SVO. Muslim, Christian.

Tanzanian Sign Language (Lugha Ya Alama, "Lugha Ya Bubu") [tza] *Class:* Deaf sign language. *Lg Dev:* Dictionary. *Other:* There are schools for the deaf, in the past each using a different sign language. More recently Tanzanian sign language has been standardized by CHAVITA (Tanzania Association for the Deaf) and there are efforts to use it in most of the schools for the deaf. There have been elementary schools for deaf children since 1963. Approximately 5% of deaf children attend school. There is a committee on national sign language. Little research.

Temi (Sonjo, Sonyo, Wasonjo, Watemi, Kisonjo) [soz] 30,000 (2002 SIL). Arusha Region, Ngorongoro District, north central near the Kenya border, Maasai area, 2 hours by car from the Wasso-Loliondo area, on unimproved roads. 7 villages: Sale (Eroghata), Mdito, Samunge (Soyeta), Digodigo (Ebwe), Kisangiro (Raghari), Mugholo (Gheeri), Oldonyo Sambu (Kura). *Class:* Niger-Congo, Atlantic-Congo, Volta-Congo, Benue-Congo, Bantoid, Southern, Narrow Bantu, Central, E, Kuria (E.10). *Dialects:* The language is reported to show some similarities to Gikuyu of Kenya. *Lg Use:* About 60% of speakers also use Swahili. Swahili used in education. *Other:* The name 'Wasonjo' is a misnomer, referring to beans of the Batemi plant. They call their language

'GiTemi', and themselves the 'Batemi'. They hold joint religious ceremonies with Aasax speakers. Hilly. Scrub forest, semitropical. 1,200 to 1,600 meters. Pastoralists; agriculturalists, irrigation. Traditional religion, Christian.

Tongwe (Kitongwe, Sitongwe) [tny] 13,000 to 15,000 (2001). Ethnic population: 31,551 (2000 WCD). Within the boundaries of Kigoma District, Kigoma Region. The Tongwe live on the eastern shore of Lake Tanganyika between the villages of Ilagala (N) to Kashagulu (S), boundary between Kigoma and Rukwa regions constitutes eastern boundary of the Tongwe area. The shore of Lake Tanganyika constitutes the western border. There are also small pockets of Tongwe (up to 20% to 30% of the population) around villages of Uvinza and Nguruka. *Class:* Niger-Congo, Atlantic-Congo, Volta-Congo, Benue-Congo, Bantoid, Southern, Narrow Bantu, Central, F, Tongwe (F.10). *Dialects:* Lexical similarity 83 to 91% with Bende (with different varieties). *Lg Use:* In the mountains, vigorous all ages, in Kalya and Kashagulu some Swahili, in other areas speakers are over 40. Used mostly at home and also with the Bende. Outside the mountains, speakers are older than 40 years. Attitude testing among speakers indicates a higher prestige of Tongwe variety. Some use of Swahili in high domains. *Lg Dev:* Dictionary. *Other:* Lake shore, mountain slope; riverine. Deciduous forest. 700 to 2,000 meters. Fishermen; agriculturalists: maize, cassava, rice (close to lake shore), millet, peanuts, sweet potatoes. Traditional religion, Muslim.

Vidunda (Chividunda, Kividunda, Ndunda) [vid] 32,000 (1987). East central, east of the Hehe, west of the Kutu Morogoro Region, south of Mikumi town in the mountains west of Kidodi. *Class:* Niger-Congo, Atlantic-Congo, Volta-Congo, Benue-Congo, Bantoid, Southern, Narrow Bantu, Central, G, Zigula-Zaramo (G.30). *Lg Use:* Vigorous. Some speakers also use Swahili. *Other:* Matrilineal. Valleys, foothills, mountain slope. 300 to 2,000 meters. Animal husbandry: goats, sheep, poultry, few cattle; hunters; fishermen; agriculturalists: dry rice, maize, millet, beans, bananas, peas, sugarcane, cassava, sweet potatoes, pumpkins, tobacco, cotton, vegetables, fruit. Traditional religion, Christian, Muslim.

Vinza [vin] 10,000 (1987). Kigoma Region, Kigoma District, around and west of the town of Uvinza. West of the Nyamwezi, north of the Tongwe. *Class:* Niger-Congo, Atlantic-Congo, Volta-Congo, Benue-Congo, Bantoid, Southern, Narrow Bantu, Central, J, Rwanda-Rundi (J.60). *Lg Use:* Speakers have some proficiency in Swahili.

Vunjo (Kivunjo, Wunjo, Kiwunjo) [vun] 300,000 (1992 UBS). Kilimanjaro Region, Chaga area, southeast variety. *Class:* Niger-Congo, Atlantic-Congo, Volta-Congo, Benue-Congo, Bantoid, Southern, Narrow Bantu, Central, E, Chaga (E.30). *Dialects:* Marangu, Lema (Kilema), Mamba, Mwika. A member of the Chaga dialect continuum which includes Rombo, Mochi, Machame. *Lg Dev:* Bible portions: 1995.

Wanda (Iciwanda, Ichiwanda, Wandia, Vanda, Kiwanda) [wbh] 24,000 (1987). Mbeya Region, Mbozi District; Rukwa Region, Sumbawanga District. *Class:* Niger-Congo, Atlantic-Congo, Volta-Congo, Benue-Congo, Bantoid, Southern, Narrow Bantu, Central, M, Nyika-Safwa (M.20). *Dialect:* Sichela. Lexical similarity 68% with Nyamwanga. *Lg Use:* A significant percentage of speakers appear to have less than routine proficiency in Swahili. *Other:* Sichela is a small group associated with the Wanda. Its dialect status is undetermined. Agriculturalists: millet, maize, rice, peanuts, potatoes; animal husbandry; fishermen. Christian, traditional religion.

Wanji (Kivwanji, Kiwanji) [wbi] 28,000 (SIL 2003). Iringa Region, Makete District, in the Kipengere Mountain Range. West of the Bena, south of the Sangu, north of the

Kinga. *Class:* Niger-Congo, Atlantic-Congo, Volta-Congo, Benue-Congo, Bantoid, Southern, Narrow Bantu, Central, G, Bena-Kinga (G.60). *Lg Use:* Adolescents prefer Swahili. Those who stay in the area often go back to Wanji when they get older. All ages. Positive language attitude. *Lg Dev:* Bible portions: 1979–1985. *Other:* Mountain mesa. Savannah, gallery forest. 1,800 to 2,800 meters. Agriculturalists: potatoes, wheat, peas, maize, and other crops. Christian, traditional religion.

Ware [wre] *Class:* Niger-Congo, Atlantic-Congo, Volta-Congo, Benue-Congo, Bantoid, Southern, Narrow Bantu, Central, E, Kuria (E.10).

Yao (Chiyao, Achawa, Adsawa, Ajawa, Ayawa, Ayo, Djao, Hajao, Hiao, Hyao, Jao, Veiao, Wajao) [yao] 492,000 in Tanzania (2001 Johnstone and Mandryk). South central, east of Lake Malawi, Mozambique border area. Mtwara Region, Masasi District and Ruvuma Region, Tunduru District. Also possibly in Zimbabwe. *Other:* Yao in Tanzania use a Swahili-based orthography different from Malawi and Mozambique. Muslim, Christian, traditional religion. See main entry under Malawi.

Zanaki (Ikizanaki, Kizanaki) [zak] 62,000 (1987). Mwanza Region, Magu District; Mara Region, Bunda District, slightly inland, southeast shore, Lake Victoria above Speke Gulf. *Class:* Niger-Congo, Atlantic-Congo, Volta-Congo, Benue-Congo, Bantoid, Southern, Narrow Bantu, Central, E, Kuria (E.10). *Dialects:* Ndali, Siora, Girango. Lexical similarity 81% with Ikoma, 80% with Ngurimi, 78% with Kuria, 50% with Gusii. *Lg Dev:* Bible portions: 1948.

Zaramo (Zalamo, Kizaramo, Dzalamo, Zaramu, Saramo, Myagatwa) [zaj] Few speakers (1991 Brenzinger, Heine, and Sommer). Ethnic population: 656,730 (2000). East central coast, Pwani Region, Kisarawe and Bagamoyo districts, between Bagamoyo and Dar es Salaam. *Class:* Niger-Congo, Atlantic-Congo, Volta-Congo, Benue-Congo, Bantoid, Southern, Narrow Bantu, Central, G, Zigula-Zaramo (G.30). *Dialects:* Lexical similarity 68% with Kutu, 65% with Kami, 61% with Kwere and Doe. *Lg Use:* Speakers are older adults. Speakers are shifting rapidly to Swahili. *Lg Dev:* NT: 1975. *Other:* Matrilineal. Coastal, foothills. Scrub forest. 200 to 1,000 meters. Agriculturalists: rice, millet, sorghum, maize, cassava, peas, beans, yams, fruit, peanuts, cashews, sesame seed, tobacco, cotton, coconuts; animal husbandry: goats, sheep, poultry; fishermen. Muslim, traditional religion, Christian.

Zigula (Zigua, Zigwa, Kizigula, Zeguha, Zigoua, Zegura, Seguha, Wazegua, Wayombo) [ziw] 355,000 (1993 Johnstone). Pwani Region, Bagamoyo District; Tanga Region, northeastern, Maasai Steppe. *Class:* Niger-Congo, Atlantic-Congo, Volta-Congo, Benue-Congo, Bantoid, Southern, Narrow Bantu, Central, G, Zigula-Zaramo (G.30). *Dialects:* Lexical similarity 83% with Ngulu, 75% with Bondei, 68% with Shambala, 70% with Doe, 62% with Kwere. *Lg Use:* Some also use a nonstandard, 'street' Swahili. *Lg Dev:* Bible portions: 1906. *Other:* It has been influenced linguistically by Doe and Kwere, and has influenced them. May be the same as Mushungulu in Somalia. Coastal, hills. 200 to 300 meters. Agriculturalists: sorghum, maize, beans, yams, manioc, pumpkins, cucumbers, sesame, peanuts, tobacco, hemp, castor, coconuts; animal husbandry: cattle, goats, sheep, donkeys, poultry; hunters; fishermen; wage laborers; traders. Muslim, Christian.

Zinza (Echijinja, Echidzindza, Ecizinza, Dzinda, Jinja, Zinja, Dzindza, Kizinza) [zin] 138,000 (1987). Southwest shore of Lake Victoria and neighboring islands. *Class:* Niger-Congo, Atlantic-Congo, Volta-Congo, Benue-Congo, Bantoid, Southern, Narrow Bantu, Central, J, Haya-Jita (J.20). *Dialects:* Longo, Kula. Lexical similarity 81% with Nyambo and Nyankore, 78% with Haya, 76% with Kerewe, 75% with Chiga, 67% with Nyoro and Toro.

Lg Use: Used in the home. Most speakers have high proficiency in Swahili. *Lg Dev:* Literacy rate in first language: 5%. Bible portions: 1930–1958. *Other:* Lakeside, savannah. Agriculturalists: millet, beans, plantains; fishermen; animal husbandry: cattle, sheep, goats. Traditional religion, mixed Christian and traditional religion, Christian, Muslim.

Togo

Republic of Togo. République Togolaise. 5,556,812. National or official languages: Éwé, Kabiye, French. Literacy rate: 39% all, 40% males. Also includes Hausa, Mampruli, Yoruba, people from Lebanon (3,500). Information mainly from B. Heine 1968; J. Stewart 1971; G. Manessy 1975, 1981; J. Bendor-Samuel 1989. Blind population: 12,052 (1981 census). Deaf institutions: 1. The number of languages listed for Togo is 39. Of those, all are living languages. See map on page 734.

Adangbe (Dangbe, Adantonwi, Agotime, Adan) [adq] 2,000 in Togo (2002 SIL). Border area of Togo and Ghana directly east of Ho, Ghana. Agotime are mainly in Ghana. Volta Region. *Other:* Different from Adangme. The Adan and Agotime are separate ethnic groups who speak Adangbe. See main entry under Ghana.

Adele (Bidire, Bedere, Gidire, Gadre) [ade] 16,300 in Togo (2003 SIL). Population total all countries: 27,300. West central. There is difficult access to the area. The main centers are Koué Mpotì, Yégué. Upper Adele is in Togo, Lower Adele in Ghana. Also spoken in Ghana. *Class:* Niger-Congo, Atlantic-Congo, Volta-Congo, Kwa, Nyo, Potou-Tano, Basila-Adele. *Dialects:* Upper Adele, Lower Adele. 85% to 90% inherent intelligibility between dialects, minor differences in tone and lexicon. Ghana and Togo dialects differ. *Lg Dev:* Literacy rate in first language: below 1%. Grammar. NT: 1996. *Other:* Ethnic group is Lolo. Different from Adere of Cameroon. Traditional religion, Christian.

Aja (Ajagbe, Adja) [ajg] 152,300 in Togo (2002 SIL). Southwestern Benin and Southeastern Togo on both sides of the Mono River. In Togo in the southeast corner of the Plateau Province north and south of the 'Forêt de Togodo', in the prefecture of Moyen-Mono, as well as in the prefecture 'des Lacs' and the prefecture of Yoto. There are also Aja speakers in Lome and several other towns in southern Togo. *Dialects:* Dogo, Hwe (Ehoue), Tado (Stado, Sado, Tadou), Sikpi, Tala. *Lg Use:* All domains except schools and government. Most adults use Gen. Most children understand Gen. Some speakers also use Éwé or French. *Lg Dev:* Literacy rate in first language: 19%. *Other:* Plains. Tree Savannah. Peasants. Traditional religion, Christian. See main entry under Benin.

Akaselem (Tchamba, Akasele, Kasele, Kamba, Chamba, Cemba) [aks] 47,500 (2002 SIL). Central Region east of Sokodé, Tchamba Prefecture. *Class:* Niger-Congo, Atlantic-Congo, Volta-Congo, North, Gur, Central, Northern, Oti-Volta, Gurma, Ntcham. *Lg Use:* Positive language attitude. The men are more bilingual in Tem than the women. Some also use French. *Lg Dev:* Literacy rate in first language: below 1%. *Other:* Muslim, traditional religion.

Akebu (Akebou, Kebu, Kabu, Kegberike, Ekpeebhe) [keu] 56,400 (2002 SIL). South, Canton Akebou of Prefecture de Wawa and into Ghana. Main centers Kougnohou, Veh-Nkougna, Kamina. *Class:* Niger-Congo, Atlantic-Congo, Volta-Congo, Kwa, Left Bank, Kebu-Animere. *Lg Use:* All domains except schools and with outsiders. Positive language attitude. Some speakers bilingual in Éwé or Gen. Some also know French. In the churches Éwé is used extensively. *Lg Dev:* Literacy rate in first language: below

1%. *Other:* Mountain slope. Traditional religion, Christian.

Anii (Akpe, Gisida, Basila, Bassila, Baseca, Winji-Winji, Ounji-Ounji) [blo] 12,300 in Togo (2002 SIL). Both sides of the Togo-Benin border. In Benin, the southern part of the Aracora Province, Bassila Subprefecture. In Togo, the Central Region, Tchamba Prefecture. *Dialect:* Akpe, Balanka, Gikolodjya, Gilempla, Giseda, Gisème, Ananjubi (Anandjoobi). *Lg Use:* All domains except schools, government. General level of comprehension of Bassila Anii is high. Speakers also use Tem, Akalesem, Ifè, or French. *Lg Dev:* Literacy rate in first language: 10%. Literacy rate in second language: 1%. 15 classes each year. *Other:* Muslim. See main entry under Benin.

Anufo (Chokosi, Chakosi, Tchokossi, Tiokossi, Chokossi) [cko] 57,800 in Togo (2002 SIL). Savannah Region in northern Togo, around town of Mango and into Ghana. *Lg Use:* Trade language. About 18,000 Ngangam second-language speakers. Speakers also use Hausa or French. *Lg Dev:* Literacy rate in first language: 1% to 5%. Some can read some French or Arabic. *Other:* Traditional religion, Muslim, Christian. See main entry under Ghana.

Bago-Kusuntu (Bago, Koussountou) [bqg] 7,500 (2000 Togo govt). Ethnic population: 8,000. Central Region, Tchamba Prefecture. The main centers are Koussountou (25 km south east of Tchamba) and Bagou (35 km south of Koussountou). *Class:* Niger-Congo, Atlantic-Congo, Volta-Congo, North, Gur, Central, Southern, Grusi, Eastern. *Dialects:* Bago, Kusuntu. *Lg Use:* All domains. French used in schools, Tem used in regional meetings, and Tem or French used with outsiders. *Lg Dev:* Literacy rate in first language: below 1%. Literacy rate in second language: 5% in Tem, 5% in French. *Other:* Muslim, traditional religion, Christian.

Bissa (Bisa) [bib] 3,000 in Togo (1991 SIL). Border with Burkina Faso in the northwest corner of Togo, Savana Region, Tone Prefecture. *Lg Use:* Many speak Mòoré with Mossi who do not speak Bissa; on common topics. They also use French. *Lg Dev:* Literacy rate in first language: below 1%. *Other:* Speakers are called 'Busansi'. Traditional religion. See main entry under Burkina Faso.

Delo (Ntrubo, Ntribu, Ntribou) [ntr] 5,400 in Togo (1998). Central Region, Blitta Prefecture, border with Ghana. *Lg Use:* Speakers also use French. *Lg Dev:* Literacy rate in first language: below 1%. *Other:* People are called 'Ntrubo'. Traditional religion. See main entry under Ghana.

Ditammari (Tamari, Soma, Some, "Somba," Tamberma) [tbz] 27,500 in Togo (2002 SIL). Kara Region, Kande Prefecture, east of Kanté along Benin border. The main centers in Togo are Nadoba, Wantema, Warengo, Koutougou. *Dialect:* Eastern Ditammari, Western Ditammari (Tamberma). *Lg Use:* A little bilingualism in French. *Lg Dev:* Literacy rate in first language: below 1%. *Other:* "Somba" is a derogatory name. 'Tamberma', 'Bataba', 'Batammaraba' are names for the people in Togo. Traditional religion, Muslim, Christian. See main entry under Benin.

Ede Nago, Manigri-Kambolé (Southwest Ede, Kambolé) [xkb] 40,000 in Togo (2002 SIL). Central Region, Tchamba Prefecture in the town of Kambolé and a few surrounding villages. *Lg Use:* All domains except French in schools, some government offices and with outsiders. Speakers also use French or Yoruba. *Lg Dev:* Literacy rate in first language: below 1%. *Other:* Traditional religion, Muslim, Christian. See main entry under Benin.

Éwé (Eibe, Ehwe, Eve, Vhe, Krepe, Krepi, Popo) [ewe] 861,900 in Togo (1991 Vanderaa). Maritime Region and Plateau Region south of Atakpamé. Main centers in Kpalimé, Notsé, Tsévié. *Dialects:* Adan, Agu, Anglo (Anlo, Awlan), Aveno, Be, Gbin, Ho, Kpelen, Togo, Vlin, Vo. *Lg Use:* National language. Predominant language in southern Togo. Speakers also use French. *Lg Dev:* Literacy rate in first language: 10% to 60%. Taught in primary schools. *Other:* Christian, traditional religion. See main entry under Ghana.

Fon (Fo, Fon-Gbe, Fonnu, Fogbe, Dahomeen, Djedji) [fon] 35,500 in Togo (1991). They are widely scattered and form small minorities in the Plateau Region south and north of the town of Atakpame. *Lg Use:* Speakers also use Éwé or French. *Lg Dev:* Literacy rate in first language: 5% to 60%. *Other:* Traditional religion, Christian. See main entry under Benin.

French [fra] 3,000 in Togo (1993). *Lg Use:* Official language. See main entry under France.

French Sign Language (Langue des Signes Française, LSF) [fsl] *Other:* Taught in 1 school for the deaf in Togo. See main entry under France.

Fulfulde, Borgu (Benin-Togo Fulfulde, Peulh, Peul, Fulani) [fue] 48,200 in Togo (1993 Johnstone). North. The Djougoure dialect may extend west into Togo. *Dialect:* Atakora Fulfulde. *Other:* Muslim. See main entry under Benin.

Gbe, Maxi (Mahi, Maxi-Gbe) [mxl] 25,300 in Togo (1991). Several linguistically isolated communities in the southern part of Central Region and northwestern part of Plateau Region north and south of Atapkame. *Lg Use:* Good comprehension of Fon. *Lg Dev:* Literacy rate in first language: below 1%. *Other:* Traditional religion. See main entry under Benin.

Gbe, Waci (Ouatchi, Waci, Waci-Gbe, Wachi, Watyi) [wci] 365,500 in Togo (1991). Population total all countries: 475,500. The main centers are in Vogan, Tabligbo, Attitigon. Also spoken in Benin. *Class:* Niger-Congo, Atlantic-Congo, Volta-Congo, Kwa, Left Bank, Gbe. *Dialects:* One of 10 languages that make up the Gbe language cluster that extends from southeastern Ghana across southern Togo and southern Benin into southwestern Nigeria. The cluster also includes Ci Gbe, Defi Gbe, Gbesi Gbe, Eastern Xwla Gbe, Maxi Gbe, Kotafon Gbe, Western Xwla Gbe, Tofin Gbe, Xwela Gbe. *Lg Use:* Speakers also use Éwé or French. *Lg Dev:* Literacy rate in first language: below 1%. *Other:* Traditional religion, Christian.

Gbe, Western Xwla [xwl] 21,000 in Togo (2002 SIL). Southeastern Togo along the Mono River. *Lg Use:* Good comprehension of Gen, comprehension of Fon is good or partial depending on location. Some bilingualism in French. *Lg Dev:* Literacy rate in first language: below 1%. *Other:* Traditional religion, Christian. See main entry under Benin.

Gen (Ge, Gen-Gbe, Mina-Gen, Mina, Popo, Guin, Gebe) [gej] 200,900 in Togo (1991). Population total all countries: 358,900. Southeastern part of Togo, Maritime Region. Also spoken in Benin. *Class:* Niger-Congo, Atlantic-Congo, Volta-Congo, Kwa, Left Bank, Gbe, Mina. *Dialects:* Anexo, Gliji, Agoi, Gen. *Lg Use:* Language of wider communication. *Lg Dev:* Literacy rate in first language: 1% to 5%. Radio programs. NT: 1962. *Other:* The people are called 'Mina' by neighboring groups.

Ginyanga (Agnagan, Anyanga, Genyanga) [ayg] 12,000 (2000 census). Ethnic population: 12,500. Central Region, Blitta Prefecture, west and south of Blitta. *Class:* Niger-Congo, Atlantic-Congo, Volta-Congo, Kwa, Nyo, Potou-Tano, Tano, Guang, North Guang. *Dialects:* Lexical similarity 75% with Gichode. *Lg Use:* Some speakers also use Éwé or French. French used in schools, Éwé used in major markets and with strangers, Éwé and French used in churches. Average comprehension of Gichode is 86%

(2000 SIL). *Lg Dev:* Literacy rate in first language: below 1%. *Other:* The people call themselves 'Anyanga' or 'Agnagan'. They use Gichode language materials. Traditional religion, Muslim, Christian.

Gourmanchéma (Gourmantche, Gourma, Gurma, Migulimancema, Gulimancema) [gux] 120,500 in Togo (1991 Vanderaa). Northeastern Togo. Savana Region, Mandouri Subprefecture. Main centers: Korbongou, Mandouri. *Lg Dev:* Literacy rate in first language: 1% to 30%. *Other:* Traditional religion. See main entry under Burkina Faso.

Ifè (Ana-Ifé, Ana, Baate) [ife] 102,000 in Togo (2002 SIL). Population total all countries: 182,000. Northeastern part of Plateau Region, Ogou and Est-Mono prefectures, and in Benin. The main centers are Atakpamé, Kamina, and Dadja. Also in the village of Ese-Ana in southern Togo. Also spoken in Benin. *Class:* Niger-Congo, Atlantic-Congo, Volta-Congo, Benue-Congo, Defoid, Yoruboid, Edekiri. *Dialects:* Tschetti, Djama, Dadja. A member of the Ede language cluster. Lexical similarity 78% with Yoruba of Porto-Novo, 87% to 91% with Ede Nago. *Lg Use:* Some bilingualism in Éwé in the south and Yoruba in the north. Some also know French. *Lg Dev:* Literacy rate in first language: 1% to 5%. Literacy rate in second language: 15%. Roman script. Radio programs. Films. Videos. Dictionary. Bible portions: 1995. *Other:* Traditional religion, Christian, Muslim.

Igo (Ahlon, Achlo, Anlo, Ago, Ahlõ, Ahonlan, Ahlon-Bogo) [ahl] 6,000 (1995 H. Massanvi Gblem). No monolinguals. Ethnic population: 6,000. Plateau Region, Apeyeme prefecture a Canton Bogo-Ahlon around village of Sassanou. *Class:* Niger-Congo, Atlantic-Congo, Volta-Congo, Kwa, Left Bank, Kposo-Ahlo-Bowili. *Lg Use:* Vigorous. All domains, traditional religion, church. Speakers use French, and may use Éwé as second language. French used in education. Some also speak Ikposo, Lelemi, Likpe, Twi, or Tem. *Lg Dev:* Literacy rate in first language: 33%. 2,000 read Igo, 1,000 can write it. *Other:* 'Ahlon' was the official name. The people call themselves 'Bogo'. Mountain slope, valleys. Agriculturalists: coffee, cocoa, maize, casava, plantain, rice. Christian, traditional religion.

Ikposo (Kposo, Akposo, Akposso) [kpo] 155,000 in Togo (2002 SIL). Population total all countries: 162,500. Plateau Region, Amou, Wawa and Ogou prefectures. West of Atakpamé. The main centers are Amlamé, Amou-Oblo, Atakpamé. Also spoken in Ghana. *Class:* Niger-Congo, Atlantic-Congo, Volta-Congo, Kwa, Left Bank, Kposo-Ahlo-Bowili. *Dialects:* Amou Oblou, Ikponu, Iwi (Uwi), Litime (Badou), Logbo, Uma. *Lg Use:* Positive language attitude. High use of Éwé. Many also use French. *Lg Dev:* Literacy rate in first language: 1% to 5%. *Other:* Traditional religion, Christian.

Kabiyé (Kabre, Cabrai, Kabure, Kabye, Cabrais) [kbp] 700,000 in Togo (1998 SIL). Population total all countries: 730,000. Kara Region. Main centers in prefectures of Kozah and Binah. Two-thirds of people now live in Central and Plateau Regions. Primarly in prefectures of Sotouboua, Blitta, Kloto, Ogou, Amlame, Wawa, and Haho. Also spoken in Benin, Ghana. *Class:* Niger-Congo, Atlantic-Congo, Volta-Congo, North, Gur, Central, Southern, Grusi, Eastern. *Dialects:* Kewe, Kijang, Lama-Tissi, Boufale. Lexical similarity 60% between Kabiye, Lama, Tem and Lukpa. *Lg Use:* National language. Speakers also use French, Tem, or Éwé. *Lg Dev:* Literacy rate in first language: 1% to 30%. Magazines. Newspapers. Radio programs. TV. Dictionary. Grammar. Bible: 1999. *Other:* Traditional religion, Christian, Muslim.

Konkomba [xon] 50,100 in Togo (1991 Vanderaa). Kara Region, north of Kabou along border with Ghana. Main

centers in Guérin-Kouka, Nawaré, Kidjaloum. *Lg Use:* Speakers also use French. *Lg Dev:* Literacy rate in first language: 1% to 5%. *Other:* Traditional religion, Christian. See main entry under Ghana.

Kpessi (Kpesi, Kpétsi) [kef] 4,000 (2002 SIL). Ethnic population: 4,000. Central Togo, in the East Mono Prefecture, Kpessi and Nyamassila cantons and in Blitta Prefecture, Langabou Canton. *Class:* Niger-Congo, Atlantic-Congo, Volta-Congo, Kwa, Left Bank, Gbe. *Lg Use:* Most domains, home, formal village functions, prayer and announcements in church. All ages. Very positive language attitude and attempts by leaders to keep language in use and insure that children are learning it. Good comprehension of Éwé and Gen. Éwé language used in literacy. Some also speak French, Ifè, Tem, or Kabiye. *Lg Dev:* Literacy rate in first language: below 1%. *Other:* Traditional religion.

Lama (Lamba, Losso) [las] 117,400 in Togo (1991 Vanderaa). Population total all countries: 186,400. Kara Region, Prefectures of Kande and Doufelgou. Over 50% of the population have settled in the Central and Plateau Regions, prefectures of Sotouboua, Ogou, and Haho. There is an important minority in Lomé and a large population in Ghana. Also spoken in Benin, Ghana. *Class:* Niger-Congo, Atlantic-Congo, Volta-Congo, North, Gur, Central, Southern, Grusi, Eastern. *Dialects:* Kande (Kante), Kadjala (Kadjalla), Defale. It is related to Tem and Kabiye. Leon and Yaka, and 2 to 4 other villages south of Kande, between Lama and Kabiye, and west of Niamtougou may need separate literature. *Lg Use:* Speakers also use French, Éwé, or Kabiye. *Lg Dev:* Literacy rate in first language: 1% to 5%. Literacy rate in second language: 20%. Roman script. NT: 1993. *Other:* 'Lama' is their name for the language and people. 'Lamba' is the French name. 'Losso' refers to people on the Losso Plain, including the Nawdeba (Nawdm). Traditional religion, Muslim, Christian.

Lukpa (Lokpa, Logba, Legba, Lugba, Dompago) [dop] 13,581 in Togo (2000 WCD). Kara Region, Binah Prefecture along Benin border. Also a few villages in Central Region. *Lg Use:* Speakers also use French. *Lg Dev:* Literacy rate in first language: 1% to 5%. *Other:* Different from Logba of Ghana. Traditional religion, Christian, Muslim. See main entry under Benin.

Miyobe (Soruba, Sorouba, Bijobe, Biyobe, Uyobe, Kyobe, Kuyobe, Kuyobe, Solamba, Sola, Solla) [soy] 1,700 in Togo (1991). Kara Region, Binah Prefecture, northeast of Kpagouda in Togo, bordering Benin. Main centers in Kouyoria, Sola. There are isolated groups in Kounacire (Massédéna) and Sola (Koutougou). *Lg Use:* Most speak Kabiye with the ability to discuss common topics. Some also speak French, Lama, or Miyobe. *Lg Dev:* Literacy rate in first language: below 1%. *Other:* 'Sola' is a village name, 'Bijobe' the ethnic name. See main entry under Benin.

Moba (Moab, Moare, Moa, Ben) [mfq] 189,400 in Togo (1991 L. Vanderaa CRC). Population total all countries: 191,200. Northwest part of Savana Region. The main towns are Dapaong and Bombouaka. Also spoken in Burkina Faso. *Class:* Niger-Congo, Atlantic-Congo, Volta-Congo, North, Gur, Central, Northern, Oti-Volta, Gurma, Moba. *Dialect:* Natchaba. Related to Bimoba in Ghana, but with only limited intelligibility. Diverse dialect situation, varying almost from family to family. Possible dialect cluster. *Lg Use:* Women almost exclusively monolingual. Men and women with more education can speak limited French. French is used to talk to those from another language group. *Lg Dev:* Literacy rate in first language: 1% to 30%. More interest in learning to read French than Moba. Roman script. Bible portions: 1941–1984. *Other:* Traditional religion, Christian.

Mòoré (Moose, Mossi, More, Mole, Moshi) [mos] 19,700 in Togo (1991). Population includes 7,155 in Moore, 7,908 in Yanga dialect (1981 census). Savana Region, several villages north of Dapaon Senkanssé, Timbou, Tabi. *Dialect:* Yanga (Yana, Yan, Yam, Yaan, Jaan, Timbou). *Lg Use:* Many monolinguals. Some use French as second language. *Lg Dev:* Literacy rate in second language: Many in the younger generation can read French. See main entry under Burkina Faso.

Nawdm (Naudm, Nawdam, Naoudem, Losso, Losu) [nmz] 145,600 in Togo (1991 Vanderaa). Kara Region, around Niamtougou, Prefecture of Doufelgou. Many have settled in the Central and Plateau Regions, prefectures of Sotouboua, Ogou, and Haho. There is an important minority in Lomé. Also spoken in Ghana. *Class:* Niger-Congo, Atlantic-Congo, Volta-Congo, North, Gur, Central, Northern, Oti-Volta, Yom-Nawdm. *Dialects:* Close to Yom. *Lg Use:* Speakers also use French. *Lg Dev:* Literacy rate in first language: below 1%. Grammar. Bible portions: 1992. *Other:* 'Losso' is the name they use for themselves when talking to outsiders. Traditional religion, Christian.

Ngangam (Dye, Gangam, Gangum, Ngangan, Nbangam, Migangam, Mijiem) [gng] 46,000 in Togo (2002 SIL). Population total all countries: 66,000. Savana Region, Oti Prefecture, around Gando-Namoni, Mogou, Koumongou, and Kountouri. Also spoken in Benin. *Class:* Niger-Congo, Atlantic-Congo, Volta-Congo, North, Gur, Central, Northern, Oti-Volta, Gurma. *Dialects:* Motiem (Mogou), Koumongou. Close to Konkomba, Ntcham, Moba, Gurma. *Lg Use:* Some speak Anufo well enough to discuss abstract concepts. A small percentage of speakers, mainly men, have been educated in French. *Lg Dev:* Literacy rate in first language: below 1%. Roman script. Radio programs. Grammar. *Other:* There are Anufo villages in the area. Gando is considered to be the center of economic and religious life. Traditional religion, Christian, Muslim.

Ntcham (Bassar, Basare, Bassari, Basari, Basar, Ncham, Natchamba, Tobote) [bud] 100,000 in Togo (1993 SIL). Population total all countries: 157,000. West central, Bassar, Kabou, Kalanga, and adjacent areas. Also spoken in Ghana. *Class:* Niger-Congo, Atlantic-Congo, Volta-Congo, North, Gur, Central, Northern, Oti-Volta, Gurma, Ntcham. *Dialects:* Ncanm, Ntaapum, Ceemba, Linangmanli. *Lg Use:* Speakers also use French or Konkomba. *Lg Dev:* Literacy rate in first language: 1% to 5%. Grammar. NT: 1986–1990. *Other:* Traditional religion, Christian, Muslim.

Tem (Kotokoli, Cotocoli, Tim, Timu, Temba) [kdh] 204,100 in Togo (1991). Population total all countries: 307,100. Kara Region, Bafilo Subprefecture; Central Region, Tchoudjo and Sotouboua prefectures. Bafilo, Sokode, and Sotouboua are main centers. There are many Tem in the Plateau Region near Badou. Also spoken in Benin, Ghana. *Class:* Niger-Congo, Atlantic-Congo, Volta-Congo, North, Gur, Central, Southern, Grusi, Eastern. *Lg Use:* Language of wider communication. All domains. Some speakers also use French. Arabic used at mosque. *Lg Dev:* Literacy rate in first language: 1% to 5%. Roman script. Radio programs. Dictionary. *Other:* Muslim, traditional religion, Christian.

Wudu [wud] 2,000. The main centers are Gbékon and Glitho. *Class:* Niger-Congo, Atlantic-Congo, Volta-Congo, Kwa, Left Bank, Gbe. *Other:* Traditional religion.

Tunisia

Republic of Tunisia. alJumhuriyah at-Tunisiyah. 9,974,722. National or official language: Standard Arabic. Literacy rate: 42% to 62%. Also includes Ghadamès (2,000), Greek (298), Italian (9,700), Maltese (3,000). Information mainly from J.

Applegate 1970; D. Cohen 1985; J. Holm 1989. Blind population: 18,000. Deaf institutions: 1. The number of languages listed for Tunisia is 8. Of those, 6 are living languages and 2 are extinct. See map on page 677.

Arabic, Judeo-Tunisian [ajt] 500 in Tunisia (1994 H. Mutzafi). *Dialect:* Tunis. *Lg Use:* Most of the Jews in Tunisia now speak French. *Other:* Jewish. See main entry under Israel.

Arabic, Standard [arb] *Lg Use:* Official language. Used for written materials and formal speeches. Not a first language, but taught in schools. See main entry under Saudi Arabia.

Arabic, Tunisian Spoken (Tunisian, Tunisian Arabic, Tunisian Darija) [aeb] 9,000,000 in Tunisia (1995). Population total all countries: 9,247,800. Also spoken in Belgium, France, Germany. *Class:* Afro-Asiatic, Semitic, Central, South, Arabic. *Dialects:* Tunis, Sahil, Sfax, North-Western Tunisian, South-Western Tunisian, South-Eastern Tunisian. Close to Eastern Algerian Arabic, but clearly distinct. The Tunis dialect is used in media and in language textbooks for foreigners. Southern dialects are structurally similar to dialects in Libya. *Lg Dev:* Bible portions: 1903–1928. *Other:* Muslim.

French [fra] 11,000 in Tunisia (1993). See main entry under France.

Lingua Franca (Petit Mauresque, Ferenghi, Sabir, 'Ajnabi, Aljamia) [pml] Extinct. Tunisia; Dodecanese Islands west bank, Greece; Cyprus; other major Mediterranean ports. *Class:* Pidgin, Romance based. *Dialects:* Lexicon from Italian and Provençal. An earlier version may have been a pidginized Latin. On the Barbary Coast of North Africa in 1578, its lexicon came from Spanish and Portuguese. In Algeria in the 1830s, it drew increasingly from French, and later became the nonstandard French of that area. It may also have influenced other pidgins. There is a report of a present-day variety on the Aegean Islands, used as a pidgin in the southeastern Mediterranean region, to have mainly Arabic syntax, and vocabulary which is 65% to 70% Italian, 10% Spanish, and other Catalan, French, Ladino, and Turkish words. *Lg Dev:* Dictionary. *Other:* Documented in Djerba, Tunisia in 1353. Coastal. Sea level. Craftsmen, urban workers. Christian, Muslim (Sunni).

Sened [sds] Extinct. Sened and Tmagourt villages, northwest of Gabès. Southern Tunisia. *Class:* Afro-Asiatic, Berber, Northern, Zenati, East. *Dialects:* Tmagourt (Tmagurt), Sened. *Lg Use:* A few older adults still remember a few words (1999). *Other:* Muslim.

Shilha (Nafusi, Jabal Nafusi, Tunisian Berber, Djerbi) [jbn] 26,000 in Tunisia (1998). Southeastern Tunisia on Mediterranean islands (Jerba), isolated villages south of Jerba, southern Tunisia, and Pacha, old Medina, and Bab Souika streets in Tunis (Tamezret), Tamezret village near Zeraoua and Taoujjout, south of Gabès (Tamezret). *Dialects:* Jbali-Tamezret (Duwinna), Jerba (Djerbi, Guelili). *Lg Use:* Spoken only in the home. *Other:* 'Shilha' is also used as a cover term for Berber languages in Morocco and Tunisia. Many people from Chenini sell newspapers in Tunis. Muslim. See main entry under Libya (Nafusi).

Tunisian Sign Language [tse] *Class:* Deaf sign language. *Lg Use:* Used in a school for the deaf. Used by USA Peace Corps. *Other:* There are loans from French Sign Language and Italian Sign Language, but it is distinct.

Uganda

Republic of Uganda. 26,404,543. Population includes 16,072,548 of Ugandan citizenship (1993 SIL). National or official language: English. Literacy rate: 52% to 57%. Also includes Hema, Kaliko (5,000), Mvuba, people from

Democratic Republic of the Congo, Rwanda, Kenya, Sudan. Information mainly from C. Stigand 1925; E. Ramponi 1937; J. Middleton 1955, 1960, 1965; A. Southall 1956; B. Taylor 1962; P. Ladefoged, R. Glick, C. Criper 1972; C. Turnbull 1972; R. Vossen 1981, 1983; M.L. Bender 1989; G. Dimmendaal 1989. Blind population: 175,000. Deaf institutions: 4. The number of languages listed for Uganda is 45. Of those, 43 are living languages and 2 are extinct. See map on page 735.

Acholi (Acoli, Atscholi, Shuli, Gang, Lwo, Lwoo, Akoli, Acooli, Log Acoli, Dok Acoli) [ach] 746,796 in Uganda (1991 census). Population includes 12,089 speakers of Chopi, (1972 Ladefoged et al.). Population total all countries: 791,796. North central Acholi District. Also spoken in Sudan. *Class:* Nilo-Saharan, Eastern Sudanic, Nilotic, Western, Luo, Southern, Luo-Acholi, Alur-Acholi, Lango-Acholi. *Dialect:* Labwor, Nyakwai, Dhopaluo (Chopi, Chope). *Lg Dev:* Bible: 1986. *Other:* Ruhlen (1987) classifies Labwor as a separate language. Christian, traditional religion.

Adhola (Dhopadhola, Jopadhola, Ludama) [adh] 247,577 (1986). Eastern, Mbale District. Not in Kenya. *Class:* Nilo-Saharan, Eastern Sudanic, Nilotic, Western, Luo, Southern, Adhola. *Dialects:* The most distinct of the Western Nilotic languages in Uganda. *Lg Dev:* Newspapers. Radio programs. Bible portions: 1977–1979. *Other:* The people are called 'Jopadhola' or 'Budama'.

Alur (Lur, Luri, Aloro, Alua, Alulu, Dho Alur, Jo Alur) [alz] 459,000 in Uganda (2001 Johnstone and Mandryk). North of Lake Albert. *Dialects:* Jokot, Jonam, Mambisa, Wanyoro. *Lg Dev:* Literacy campaign ongoing. *Other:* Christian. See main entry under Democratic Republic of the Congo.

Amba (Kwamba, Kuamba, Ku-Amba, Rwamba, Lwamba, Hamba, Lubulebule, Ruwenzori Kibira, Humu, Kihumu) [rwm] 16,000 in Uganda (1991 census). Population total all countries: 20,500. Ethnic population: 62,926 (1991 census). Democratic Republic of the Congo border south of Lake Albert, Beni District, Watalinga and Bawisa subcounties, Ruwenzori Mountains, Bundibugyo District. Also spoken in Democratic Republic of the Congo. *Class:* Niger-Congo, Atlantic-Congo, Volta-Congo, Benue-Congo, Bantoid, Southern, Narrow Bantu, Central, D, Bira-Huku (D.30). *Dialects:* Kyanzi (Kihyanzi), Suwa (Kusuwa). Close to Bera, Bila, Komo, Bhele. Lexical similarity 70% with Bera, 57% to 59% with Bila, Kaiku, Komo, and Bhele, 25% with Nande, 34% with Talinga-Bwisi may indicate convergence. *Lg Use:* They use Talinga-Bwisi as a second language. Proficiency in Runyoro-Rutooro is limited. *Lg Dev:* Literacy campaign in progress. *Other:* Their name for themselves is 'Kwamba'. Called 'Kihumu' in Democratic Republic of the Congo. The people are called 'Baamba'. Savannah, forest. 750 to 1,000 meters. Agriculturalists: plantains, millet, maize, sweet potatoes, peanuts, rice, coffee, cotton, cassava; animal husbandry: goats, sheep. Traditional religion, Christian.

Aringa (Low Lugbara) [luc] 588,830 (1991 census). Northwest corner, north of Lake Albert, Aringa county, north of Lugbara, west of Ma'di. Not in Sudan. *Class:* Nilo-Saharan, Central Sudanic, East, Moru-Madi, Central. *Lg Use:* The speakers of Lugbara and Ma'di both consider Aringa to be a separate but related language.

Bari (Beri) [bfa] 60,000 in Uganda. Northwest corner. *Dialects:* Kuku, Nyepu (Ngyepu, Nyefu, Nyepo, Nypho), Pöjulu (Pajulu, Fadjulu, Fajulu, Fajelu), Nyangbara (Nyangwara, Nyambara), Mondari (Mandari, Mundari). *Lg Use:* Trade language. See main entry under Sudan.

Chiga (Oluchiga, Orukiga, Ciga, Kiga, Rukiga) [cgg] 1,391,442 (1991 census). Extreme southwest, Ankole District, Western Province. *Class:* Niger-Congo, Atlantic-Congo, Volta-Congo, Benue-Congo, Bantoid, Southern, Narrow Bantu, Central, J, Nyoro-Ganda (J.10). *Dialects:* 72% intelligible of Nyankore. Lexical similarity 84% to 94% with Nyankore, 77% with Nyoro, 75% with Zinza, 72% with Nyambo, 70% with Haya, 68% with Tooro, 63% with Kerewe. *Other:* Hills, mountain slope. Swamp. 1,200 to 1,800 meters. Agriculturalists: millet, sorghum, sweet potatoes, beans, peas, maize, wheat, peanuts, sunflower seeds, potatoes, cassava, vegetables, plantains, tobacco, flax, coffee, peas; animal husbandry: cattle. Christian, traditional religion.

English [eng] *Lg Use:* Official language. Second-language speakers: 1,000,000 in Uganda (1977 Voegelin and Voegelin). Used in primary schools, law courts. See main entry under United Kingdom.

Ganda (Luganda) [lug] 3,015,980 (1991 census). Southeast, from the northwest shore of Lake Victoria to Lake Kyoga and the Tanzania border; primarily Buganda Province. *Class:* Niger-Congo, Atlantic-Congo, Volta-Congo, Benue-Congo, Bantoid, Southern, Narrow Bantu, Central, J, Nyoro-Ganda (J.10). *Dialects:* Kooki (Olukooki), Sese (Olusese), Luvuma, Ludiopa. Luvuma, Ludiope may be dialects. Lexical similarity 71% to 86% with Soga, 68% with Gwere. *Lg Use:* Language of wider communication. The most widely spoken second language in Uganda next to English. 1,000,000 second-language speakers (1999 WA). Used in primary schools. The Kooki dialect may be extinct. *Lg Dev:* Newspapers. Radio programs. Dictionary. Bible: 1896–1968. *Other:* The people are called 'Baganda'. SVO. Plateau, hills, valleys. Swamp. 1,200 meters. Agriculturalists: bananas, tobacco, beans, millet, maize, sweet potatoes, peanuts, cassava, cotton; animal husbandry: cattle, goats, poultry; hunters.

Gujarati [guj] 147,000 in Uganda (1986). *Other:* The people migrated to Uganda during the early part of the 20th century. Hindu. See main entry under India.

Gungu (Rugungu, Lugungu) [rub] 65,000 (2000). Hoima and Masindi districts, primarily along the northeast shore of Lake Albert in the Rift Valley, Buliisa, Bilso, and Kigorobya subcounties. Also in the hills above the valley. *Class:* Niger-Congo, Atlantic-Congo, Volta-Congo, Benue-Congo, Bantoid, Southern, Narrow Bantu, Central, J, Nyoro-Ganda (J.10). *Dialects:* 58% or lower inherent intelligibility of Nyoro-Tooro. Tooro is the closest language. Lexical similarity 65% with Tooro. *Lg Use:* Vigorous. Lugungu Language Committee. Speakers of other languages use Gungu at work. All domains, oral use in administration, most churches, commerce. Positive language attitude. All speakers have minimal proficiency in Nyoro, Alur, English, or Swahili. *Lg Dev:* Taught in primary schools. Radio programs. Bible portions: 1998. *Other:* The ethnic group is called 'Bagungu'. SVO; genitives, adjectives, relatives after noun heads; question word final; word order distinguishes subject and object; subject agreement obligatory, object agreement optional; verb suffixes mark subject, object, tense, aspect, and negation; verb suffixes mark perfective, applicative, reversive, stative, reciprocal, passive, and causative; contrastive vowel length, upper 7-vowel system with vowel harmony; V, CV, CVV, (C)C(C)V where first C is a nasal and last C a semivowel; tonal. Shore, hills, coastal. Savannah, tropical forest. Fishermen; peasant agriculturalists; pastoralists. Christian, Muslim.

Gwere (Lugwere, Olugwere) [gwr] 275,608 (1991 census). Pallisa District, dominating 2 of the district's 4 counties. *Class:* Niger-Congo, Atlantic-Congo, Volta-Congo, Benue-Congo, Bantoid, Southern, Narrow Bantu, Central, J, Nyoro-Ganda (J.10). *Dialects:* Closest to Lusiki in vocabulary. Lexical similarity 68% with Ganda, 64% with Soga. *Lg Use:* Vigorous. Used in the home, village, market. Medium of instruction in the first 2 years of primary school. Luganda is used in church. *Lg Dev:* Taught in primary schools. Newspapers. Radio programs.

Hindi [hin] 2,200 in Uganda (1994). *Other:* The people migrated to Uganda in the early 20th century. Hindu. See main entry under India.

Ik (Icietot, Teuso, Teuth, Ngulak) [ikx] 2,000 (1972 C. Turnbull). Northeast part of Karamoja. *Class:* Nilo-Saharan, Eastern Sudanic, Kuliak, Ik. *Dialects:* It is very different from other Eastern Sudanic languages. *Lg Use:* Speakers are reported to use Karamojong as second language. *Other:* They call their language 'Icietot'. Mountain slope. Hunters; some cultivation. Traditional religion.

Kakwa (Bari Kakwa, Kakua, Kwakwak) [keo] 86,472 in Uganda (1991 census). Population total all countries: 146,472. Northwest corner, West Nile District. Also spoken in Democratic Republic of the Congo, Sudan. *Class:* Nilo-Saharan, Eastern Sudanic, Nilotic, Eastern, Bari. *Dialects:* Dialects of Sudan, Democratic Republic of the Congo, and Uganda differ little (Nida). Very different from other Eastern Nilotic languages of Uganda. *Lg Use:* People are friendly with the Toposa; unfriendly to the Turkana. *Lg Dev:* Literacy campaign in progress. Radio programs. Bible: 1983. *Other:* Christian, traditional religion.

Karamojong (Karimojong, Karimonjong) [kdj] 370,000 (1994 UBS). Population includes 50,000 Jie (1986 MARC). East and northeast, Karamojo District around Moroto. *Class:* Nilo-Saharan, Eastern Sudanic, Nilotic, Eastern, Lotuxo-Teso, Teso-Turkana, Turkana. *Dialects:* Karamojong, Jie (Jiye), Dodos (Dodoth). The dialects have 83% to 95% lexical similarity. Lexical similarity 85% with Turkana, 75% with Teso. *Lg Use:* People are friendly with the Toposa; unfriendly to the Turkana. *Lg Dev:* Radio programs. Dictionary. NT: 1974. *Other:* Several subdivisions represent more than one ethnic group. Seminomadic. VSO; highly inflectional; grammatical tone; vowel harmony; voiceless vowels. Pastoralists: cattle, sheep, goats, donkeys; agriculturalists: sorghum. Traditional religion, Christian; Jie: traditional religion.

Kenyi (Lukenyi) [lke] 390,115. Between Lake Victoria and Lake Kyoga, Busoga Province. *Class:* Niger-Congo, Atlantic-Congo, Volta-Congo, Benue-Congo, Bantoid, Southern, Narrow Bantu, Central, J, Nyoro-Ganda (J.10). *Dialects:* Welmers lists Olusoga and Lukenyi separately. Lexical similarity 81% with Soga, 71% to 86% with Ganda, 64% with Gwere, 58% with Saamia. *Other:* Politically distinct from Ganda. The people are called 'Bakenyi'. They say they are a displaced people of Ganda origin. Hills, valleys. Swamp. Agriculturalists: bananas, beans, millet, coffee, cotton.

Konjo (Rukonjo, Olukonjo, Konzo, Olukonzo, Lhukonzo) [koo] 361,709 in Uganda (1992 census). Southwest, Ruwenzori Mountains. Also spoken in Democratic Republic of the Congo. *Class:* Niger-Congo, Atlantic-Congo, Volta-Congo, Benue-Congo, Bantoid, Southern, Narrow Bantu, Central, J, Konzo (J.40). *Dialects:* Sanza (Ekisanza), Rukonjo. Many dialects. Lexical similarity 77% with Nande. *Lg Dev:* Radio programs. Bible portions: 1914. *Other:* Mountain slope, hills, plains. Up to 2,200 meters. Agriculturalists: yams, beans, sweet potatoes, peanuts, soy beans, potatoes, rice, wheat, cassava, coffee, bananas, cotton; animal husbandry: goats, sheep, poultry. Traditional religion, Christian.

Kumam (Kuman, Ikokolemu, Kumum, Ikumama, Akum, Akokolemu) [kdi] 112,629 (1991 census). South of Lake Kwania, western Teso District. *Class:* Nilo-Saharan, Eastern Sudanic, Nilotic, Western, Luo, Southern, Kumam. *Dialects:* Lexical similarity 82% with Dhopaluo, 81% with Lango, 77% with Acholi. *Lg Dev:* Literacy campaign in progress. Radio programs. *Other:* Ladefoged and Bender classify Kumam as Southern Luo; some linguists classify it in the Dinka group. Kumam oral tradition gives a Teso descent.

Kupsabiny (Sebei, Sapei) [kpz] 120,000 (1994 UBS). Eastern border area slightly north of Mbale, Sebei Province. *Class:* Nilo-Saharan, Eastern Sudanic, Nilotic, Southern, Kalenjin, Elgon. *Dialects:* Sabiny (Sapiny, Kupsabiny, Kupsapiny), Mbai, Sor. *Lg Dev:* Literacy campaigns. Radio programs. NT: 1996. *Other:* People called 'Sebei'.

Lango (Lwo, Lwoo, Leb-Lano, Langi) [laj] 977,680 (1991 census). 5.6% of population (1972 Ladefoged et al.). Central, north of Lake Kyoga, Lango Province. *Class:* Nilo-Saharan, Eastern Sudanic, Nilotic, Western, Luo, Southern, Luo-Acholi, Alur-Acholi, Lango-Acholi. *Lg Dev:* Literacy campaign in progress. Taught in primary schools. Roman script. Newspapers. Radio programs. Grammar. Bible: 1979. *Other:* Distinct from Acholi (Lwo), Lango of Sudan (related to Lotuko), or Lango (Didinga) of Sudan.

Lendu [led] 10,000 in Uganda (2002 SIL). *Lg Use:* Speakers also use Swahili. See main entry under Democratic Republic of the Congo.

Lugbara (High Lugbara) [lgg] 200,000 in Uganda (1983 SIL). Population includes 140,000 in Arua, 60,000 in Maracha and Terego. Population total all countries: 1,040,000. Northwest, west Nile District. Also spoken in Democratic Republic of the Congo. *Class:* Nilo-Saharan, Central Sudanic, East, Moru-Madi, Central. *Dialects:* Arua (Standard Lugbara), Maracha, Terego (Omugo). *Lg Dev:* Literacy campaign in progress. Taught in primary schools. Newspapers. Radio programs. Bible: 1966. *Other:* Plateau, mountain ridge. Few trees. 1,200 to 1,500 meters. Agriculturalists: eleusine, sorghum, simsim, peas, beans, peanuts, pumpkins, sugarcane, bananas, maize, cassava, tobacco; animal husbandry: cattle, goats, sheep, poultry. Traditional religion, Christian, Muslim, Baha'i.

Luyia (Luluyia, Luhya) [luy] 225,378 in Uganda (1991 census). Population includes 10,000 Songa, 40,074 of Lugwe. Lake Victoria area near Kenya border. *Dialects:* Saamia, Songa, Lugwe. *Lg Use:* Ganda is used in church. *Other:* The people are called 'Abaluyia', singular 'Muluyia'. Christian, traditional religion. See main entry under Kenya.

Ma'di (Ma'adi, Ma'diti) [mhi] 130,558 in Uganda (1991 census). Population total all countries: 148,558. Northwestern Sudan border area near Nimule, West Nile District, Madi Province, Madi Subdistrict, and Madi County. Moyo is in the west, Adjumani in the east. Also spoken in Sudan. *Class:* Nilo-Saharan, Central Sudanic, East, Moru-Madi, Southern. *Dialect:* Moyo, Adjumani (Oyuwi). *Lg Dev:* Literacy campaign in progress. Newspapers. Radio programs. NT: 1977.

Ma'di, Southern (Southern Ma'di) [snm] 48,000 (1983 SIL). Okollo County, on the west bank of the Nile River. Okollo town is the administrative center. *Class:* Nilo-Saharan, Central Sudanic, East, Moru-Madi, Southern. *Dialects:* Okollo, Ogoko, Rigbo. Closer to Lugbara than to Madi (Moyo), which they do not understand. Ogoko and Rigbo are closer to Lugbara than Okollo is; intelligibility testing needed. Okollo dialect is considered more 'pure' than the others.

Masaba (Lumasaba, Masaaba, Gisu, Lugisu) [myx] 751,253 (1991 census). Eastern, south of the Kupsabiny, Bugisu Province. *Class:* Niger-Congo, Atlantic-Congo, Volta-Congo, Benue-Congo, Bantoid, Southern, Narrow Bantu, Central, J, Masaba-Luyia (J.30). *Dialects:* Ulubukusu, Ulubuya, Uludadiri, Lugisu (Gishu), Ulukisu, Syan. Syan is a related dialect or language. Lexical similarity 62% with Saamia, 52% with Isuxa, 50% with

Ragooli. *Lg Dev:* Literacy campaign in progress. Radio programs. NT: 1977–1992.

Ndo (Kebu, Oke'bu, Ndu) [ndp] 200,000 in Uganda (1994 UBS). Population total all countries: 300,000. Northwestern. Mahigi is the center. Also spoken in Democratic Republic of the Congo. *Class:* Nilo-Saharan, Central Sudanic, East, Mangbutu-Efe. *Dialects:* Avari (Aviritu, Avere), Oke'bu (Ndo Oke'bu, Kebutu, Kebu), Membi. *Lg Dev:* NT: 1994. *Other:* Blacksmiths.

Nubi (Kinubi, Ki-Nubi) [kcn] 14,739 in Uganda (1991 census). Population total all countries: 24,739. Bombo, 30 miles north of Kampala, Arua, and elsewhere in Uganda. Also spoken in Kenya. *Class:* Creole, Arabic based. *Dialects:* Descendants of Emin Pasha's troops. Formerly a soldier language, which split off from Sudanese Pidgin Arabic about 1900. There are conflicting reports of intelligibility of Sudanese Creole Arabic. 90% of the lexicon comes from Arabic. 90% of the lexicon is from Arabic. *Lg Dev:* Grammar. *Other:* Traders. Muslim.

Nyang'i (Nuangeya, Nyuangia, Nyangiya, Nyangia, Ngangea, Gyangiya, Nyangeya, Ngiangeya, Nipori, Niporen, Poren, Ngapore, Upale) [nyp] Extinct. Ethnic population: 100 or fewer. Eastern. *Class:* Nilo-Saharan, Eastern Sudanic, Kuliak, Ngangea-So. *Dialects:* A separate language from Ik. *Lg Use:* Members of the ethnic group now speak Dodos (Karamojong). *Other:* Hunters; some cultivation. Traditional religion.

Nyankore (Nkole, Nyankole, Runyankole, Ulunyankole, Ulunyankore) [nyn] 1,643,193 (1991 census). Population includes 141,668 Hororo, 1,643,193 Hima. Western Province, Ankole District, east of Lake Edward. *Class:* Niger-Congo, Atlantic-Congo, Volta-Congo, Benue-Congo, Bantoid, Southern, Narrow Bantu, Central, J, Nyoro-Ganda (J.10). *Dialects:* Hororo, Orutagwenda, Hima. Hima may be a separate language. Nyankore, Nyoro, and their dialects are considered by some to be one language (lexical similarity 78% to 96%). Lexical similarity 84% to 94% with Chiga, 75% to 86% with Tooro (Nyoro), 81% with Zinza, 78% with Nyambo, 74% with Haya, 68% with Kerewe. *Lg Dev:* Taught in primary schools. Newspapers. Radio programs. Bible: 1964–1989. *Other:* The standardization of the western languages (Nyankore-Chiga and Nyoro-Tooro) is called 'Runyakitara', and is taught at the University. Ethnic groups: Bahima, Bairu. Plains, hills, plateau. Savannah, acacia scrub, tropical forest, papyrus, swamp. 900 to 1,200 meters. Agriculturalists: millet, sweet potatoes, plantains, beans, peanuts, cassava, coffee, maize, sorghum; animal husbandry: goats, sheep, cattle; fishermen. Christian, traditional religion, Muslim.

Nyole (Nyule, Nyuli, Lunyole) [nuj] 228,918 (1991 census). Southeast Uganda in Tororo District. *Class:* Niger-Congo, Atlantic-Congo, Volta-Congo, Benue-Congo, Bantoid, Southern, Narrow Bantu, Central, J, Masaba-Luyia (J.30). *Dialects:* Menya (Lumenya), Hadyo (Luhadyo), Sabi (Lusabi), Wesa (Luwesa). Lexical similarity 70% to 80% with the Saamia dialect of Luyia, 82% with the Lugwe dialect of Luyia, 67% with Ganda, 61% with Nyore of Kenya. *Lg Use:* Vigorous. There is a Lunyole Language Association. Speakers have low proficiency in Ganda, which is used in church. *Lg Dev:* Taught in primary schools. Radio programs. Dictionary. *Other:* SVO. Plains. Tropical forest. Peasant agriculturalists.

Nyoro (Runyoro) [nyo] 495,443 (1991 census). South and southeast of Lake Albert, Bunyoro and Toro provinces. *Class:* Niger-Congo, Atlantic-Congo, Volta-Congo, Benue-Congo, Bantoid, Southern, Narrow Bantu, Central, J, Nyoro-Ganda (J.10). *Dialect:* Rutagwenda, Orunyoro (Nyoro). 73% inherent intelligibility of Gungu. Hema-Sud (Nyoro-Tooro) in Democratic Republic of the Congo is

quite different. Lexical similarity 78% to 93% with Toro, 77% with Nyankore and Ciga, 67% with Nyambo and Zinza, 66% with Haya, 62% with Kerewe. *Lg Dev:* Literacy campaign in progress. Taught in primary schools. Roman script. Newspapers. Radio programs. Bible: 1912. *Other:* Coastal, plateau, mountain slope. Savannah, swamp. Animal husbandry: cattle; fishermen; agriculturalists: millet, sorghum, plantains, sweet potatoes, beans, pumpkins, cowpeas, cassava, peanuts, cotton, tobacco; hunters. Christian, traditional religion, Muslim.

Pökoot (Pokot, Pakot, Suk) [pko] East central, near Kupsabiny. *Other:* Seminomadic. Traditional religion, Christian. See main entry under Kenya.

Ruli (Ruruli, Luduuli) [ruc] 68,010 (1991 census). East of Nyoro. *Class:* Niger-Congo, Atlantic-Congo, Volta-Congo, Benue-Congo, Bantoid, Southern, Narrow Bantu, Central, J, Nyoro-Ganda (J.10). *Dialects:* Eastern Ruli, Western Ruli. Nakasongola (east) is influenced by Ganda, and in Kuyanoongo (west) by Nyoro. Lexical similarity 79% between Eastern and Western Ruli, 71% with Nyoro (closest), 70% between Eastern Ruli and Ganda. *Lg Use:* Used in the home and village.

Rundi [run] 100,903 in Uganda (1991 census). Most in Buganda. See main entry under Burundi.

Rwanda (Runyarwanda, Ruanda) [kin] 532,692 in Uganda (1991 census). Population includes 203,030 speakers of Rufumbira, 329,662 Rwanda, 1,394 Twa. Southwestern border with Rwanda. The largest group in Kisoro District. *Dialects:* Rufumbira, Twa. *Lg Use:* Vigorous. *Lg Dev:* Literacy campaign in progress. *Other:* Rufumbira may be distinct. See main entry under Rwanda.

Singa (Lusinga) [sgm] Extinct. Rusinga Island. *Class:* Niger-Congo, Atlantic-Congo, Volta-Congo, Benue-Congo, Bantoid, Southern, Narrow Bantu, Central, J, Nyoro-Ganda (J.10).

Soga (Lusoga, Olusoga) [xog] 1,370,845 (1991 census). Between Lake Victoria and Lake Kyoga, Busoga Province. Lutenga is around Jjinja, Lulamogi farther north. *Class:* Niger-Congo, Atlantic-Congo, Volta-Congo, Benue-Congo, Bantoid, Southern, Narrow Bantu, Central, J, Nyoro-Ganda (J.10). *Dialects:* Tenga (Lutenga), Lamogi (Lulamogi), Gabula (Lugabula). Welmers lists Soga and Kenyi separately. Lexical similarity 81% with Kenyi, 71% to 86% with Ganda, 64% with Gwere, 58% with Saamia. Tenga has 82% with Ganda. Lamogi dialect has 79% to 82% lexical similarity with Tenga, 89% with Siki, 88% with Soga, 82% with Gwere. *Lg Use:* Politically distinct from Ganda. *Lg Dev:* Literacy campaign in progress. Radio programs. NT: 2000. *Other:* Hills, valleys. Swamp. Agriculturalists: bananas, beans, millet, coffee, cotton.

Soo (So, Tepeth, Tepes) [teu] 5,000 (1972 Ladefoged et al.). Karamoja District of eastern Uganda on Mt. Moroto on Kenya border. *Class:* Nilo-Saharan, Eastern Sudanic, Kuliak, Ngangea-So. *Lg Use:* In some areas used mainly by those over 40 years old. Younger people speak Karamojong as primary language. *Lg Dev:* Dictionary.

Swahili (Kiswahili, Kisuaheli) [swh] 2,330 in Uganda (2000 WCD). *Dialect:* Shamba (Kishamba). *Lg Use:* The government plans to make this a mandatory subject in schools. Used by the security forces and in some regions. *Other:* Muslim. See main entry under Tanzania.

Talinga-Bwisi (Kitalinga, Lubwisi, Olubwisi, Bwissi, Mawissi, Lubwissi) [tlj] 53,467 in Uganda (1991 census). Population total all countries: 84,357. Democratic Republic of the Congo border, Bwamba County, Bundibugyo District, southwest of Fort Portal, between Albert and Edward Lakes, immediately next to the Democratic Republic of the Congo border, near Kilembe. Also spoken in Democratic Republic of the Congo. *Class:* Niger-Congo, Atlantic-Congo, Volta-Congo, Benue-Congo, Bantoid, Southern, Narrow Bantu, Central, J,

Haya-Jita (J.20). *Dialects:* 68% inherent intelligibility of Tooro. Lexical similarity 73% with Tooro, 72% with Nyoro, 40% with Nande. *Lg Use:* Used in the home, in some churches, primary school, and market if both speakers are Babwisi. Tooro is used in some churches. Speakers use Tooro as second language. The Batooro used to rule over the Babwisi, but Tooro use seems to be decreasing. English is used by men and boys who have been to higher levels of school. *Lg Dev:* Radio programs. *Other:* Called 'Bwisi' in Uganda, 'Talinga' in Democratic Republic of the Congo. Different from Bwisi of Congo and Gabon. SVO; CV, V; tonal. Mountain slope. Tropical forest. Peasant agriculturalists. Christian, Muslim.

Teso (Ateso, Ikumama, Bakedi, Bakidi, Etossio, Elgumi, Wamia) [teo] 999,537 in Uganda (1991 census). Population total all countries: 1,278,537. Sorot and Kumi regions, southeast, Teso Province. Lokathan live around Madial at the north end of the Nangeya Mountains. Also spoken in Kenya. *Class:* Nilo-Saharan, Eastern Sudanic, Nilotic, Eastern, Lotuxo-Teso, Teso-Turkana, Teso. *Dialects:* Lokathan (Biri, Ketebo), Orom (Rom). Limited intelligibility of other varieties in the Teso-Turkana group. The dialect in Ngoro is considered standard. Lexical similarity 76% with Turkana, 75% with Karamojong. *Lg Dev:* Literacy campaign in progress. Taught in primary schools. Newspapers. Radio programs. Bible: 1961. *Other:* The people are 'Iteso'. VSO; highly inflectional; grammatical tone; vowel harmony. Pastoralists; agriculturalists. Christian, traditional religion.

Tooro (Rutooro, Orutoro, Rutoro, Toro) [ttj] 488,024 (1991 census). South and southeast of Lake Albert, Toro Province. *Class:* Niger-Congo, Atlantic-Congo, Volta-Congo, Benue-Congo, Bantoid, Southern, Narrow Bantu, Central, J, Nyoro-Ganda (J.10). *Dialect:* Tuku. Hema-Sud (Nyoro-Toro) in Democratic Republic of the Congo is quite different. Lexical similarity 78% to 93% with Nyoro. *Other:* Coastal, plateau, mountain slope. Savannah, swamp. Animal husbandry: cattle; fishermen; agriculturalists: millet, sorghum, plantains, sweet potatoes, beans, pumpkins, cowpeas, cassava, peanuts, cotton, tobacco; hunters. Christian, traditional religion, Muslim.

Ugandan Sign Language (USL) [ugn] All over Uganda, but mainly in the towns. *Class:* Deaf sign language. *Lg Use:* There have been elementary schools for deaf children since 1962. Several sign languages became one in 1988. The schools allow sign language in the classroom since 1988. The sign language used in the classroom and that used by adults outside is the same. Some sign language interpreters are provided for deaf people in court. Little research. There are a few sign language classes for hearing people. It was recognized as a minority language in 1995. Interpretation provided in parliament from a deaf member. Promotion by the Uganda National Association of the Deaf. Positive language attitude. Influences from Kenyan Sign Language and ASL. Knowledge of English is not widespread or deep. *Lg Dev:* Dictionary. *Other:* There is a manual alphabet for spelling.

Zambia

Republic of Zambia. Formerly Northern Rhodesia and Mozambique. 10,462,436. National or official languages: English, regional languages: Mbukushu, Nyanja. Literacy rate: 25% to 76%. Also includes Nyemba, Urdu, people from Europe (30,000), Asia (8,000), Angola and Mozambique. Information mainly from S. Ohannessian and M. Kashoki 1978; A. Vitale 1980; J. Holm 1989; M. Brenzinger 1997. Blind population: 38,000 (1982 WCE). Deaf institutions: 5. The number of languages listed for Zambia is 43. Of those, 41 are living languages and 2 are second language without mother-tongue speakers. See map on page 736.

Afrikaans [afr] *Lg Use:* Language of wider communication. See main entry under South Africa.

Aushi (Avaushi, Vouaousi, Ushi, Usi, Uzhil) [auh] 95,200 in Zambia (2000). Northern, Luapula Province. Also spoken in Democratic Republic of the Congo. *Class:* Niger-Congo, Atlantic-Congo, Volta-Congo, Benue-Congo, Bantoid, Southern, Narrow Bantu, Central, M, Bemba (M.40). *Lg Use:* Language of wider communication. *Other:* SVO.

Bemba (Chibemba, Ichibemba, Wemba, Chiwemba) [bem] 3,300,000 in Zambia (2001 Johnstone and Mandryk). Population includes 741,114 Bemba, 32,022 Luunda, 5,190 Shila, 26,429 Tabwa, 16,833 Cishinga, 28,172 Kabende, 6,706 Mukulu, 42,298 Ng'umbo, 14,040 Twa-Unga (1969 census). Population total all countries: 3,600,000. Northern, Copperbelt, and Luapula provinces. Possibly in Zimbabwe. Also spoken in Botswana, Democratic Republic of the Congo, Malawi. *Class:* Niger-Congo, Atlantic-Congo, Volta-Congo, Benue-Congo, Bantoid, Southern, Narrow Bantu, Central, M, Bemba (M.40). *Dialects:* Lembue, Lomotua (Lomotwa), Ngoma, Nwesi, Town Bemba, Luunda (Luapula), Chishinga, Kabende, Mukulu, Ng'umbo, Twa of Bangweulu, Unga. Town Bemba has a Bemba base with heavy codeswitching with English and neighboring Bantu languages. *Lg Use:* Language of wider communication. Town Bemba is a widely used lingua franca in urban, not rural areas, and it has higher social status than other languages except English. Bemba is recognized for educational and administrative purposes. *Lg Dev:* Newspapers. Radio programs. Dictionary. Bible: 1956–1983. *Other:* SVO. Traditional religion, Christian.

Bwile [bwc] 12,362 in Zambia (1969 census). Population total all countries: 24,762. Also spoken in Democratic Republic of the Congo. *Class:* Niger-Congo, Atlantic-Congo, Volta-Congo, Benue-Congo, Bantoid, Southern, Narrow Bantu, Central, L, Bwile (L.10). *Dialects:* Not closely related to other languages.

Chokwe (Ciokwe, Cokwe, Shioko, Tshokwe, Tschiokwe, Djok) [cjk] 44,200 in Zambia, (1986). Northwestern Province, east of the Mbunda. *Dialect:* Minungo. See main entry under Democratic Republic of the Congo.

English [eng] 41,434 in Zambia (1969 census). *Lg Use:* Official language. Spoken as first language by Europeans mainly. A small minority of Zambian Africans speak it as a first language. Used as a second language. The only language of Parliament. See main entry under United Kingdom.

Fanagalo ("Fanakalo," "Fanekolo," Piki, Isipiki, Lololo, Isilololo, Pidgin Bantu, Basic Zulu, "Kitchen Kaffir," "Mine Kaffir," "Isikula") [fng] Several hundred speakers in Zambia (1975 Reinecke). Towns and mining areas. *Dialect:* Cikabanga. *Lg Use:* Trade language. Rejected by most Africans because it was imported from Zimbabwe and South Africa by Europeans who did not want Africans to learn English (Adler 1977). *Other:* Second language only. See main entry under South Africa.

Gujarati [guj] 12,000 in Zambia (1985 IEM). *Other:* Hindu. See main entry under India.

Ila (Chiila, Shukulumbwe, Sukulumbwe) [ilb] 61,200 (1986). Central and Southern provinces, west of the Sala. With Tonga it predominates in the south. West bend of Kafue River. *Class:* Niger-Congo, Atlantic-Congo, Volta-Congo, Benue-Congo, Bantoid, Southern, Narrow Bantu, Central, M, Lenje-Tonga (M.60), Tonga. *Dialects:* Lundwe, Lumbu, Ila. *Lg Dev:* Dictionary. Grammar. NT: 1915–1945.

Kaonde (Chikaonde, Chikahonde, Kawonde, Luba Kaonde) [kqn] 248,000 in Zambia (2001 Johnstone and Mandryk). Population total all countries: 284,000. Northwest of Mumbwe, Northwestern and Central provinces. Also spoken in Democratic Republic of the Congo. *Class:* Niger-Congo, Atlantic-Congo, Volta-Congo, Benue-Congo, Bantoid, Southern, Narrow Bantu, Central, L, Kaonde (L.40). *Dialects:* Not closely related to other languages. *Lg Use:* Officially taught in primary schools. *Lg Dev:* Literacy campaigns, agricultural extension services. Taught in primary schools. Newspapers. Radio programs. Bible: 1975.

Khwe (Xun, Hukwe, !Hukwe, Xuhwe, Xu, Zama, Vazama, Cazama, Mbara Kwengo, Mbarakwena, Glanda-Khwe, Black Bushman, Water Bushmen, Schekere, Kxoe) [xuu] 100 in Zambia (1998 Brenzinger). Western Zambia, east of the Zambesi River near Luzu village, 6 villages. East of Luzu in Sakulinda village; and 250 km to the northwest, in remote areas of southeastern Senaga District, and the 3 settlements Kashesha ki liwanika, Namafumbwana, and Sanze. *Dialect:* ‖Xo-Kxoe. *Lg Use:* Many in Zambia have given up Khwe to speak the language of their partners and parents. Few speak Lozi, the lingua franca of the area. See main entry under Namibia (Kxoe).

Kunda (Chikunda) [kdn] 43,770 in Zambia (2000 WCD). Southeastern Central Province. *Other:* Distinct from the Kunda dialect of Nyanja or Kunda of Democratic Republic of the Congo. See main entry under Zimbabwe.

Lala-Bisa (Biza-Lala) [leb] 371,000 in Zambia (2001 Johnstone and Mandryk). Population includes Lala 200,000 (1991 UBS). Eastern, along Luangwa River (Bisa), and southwest (Lala), Northern, Central, and Eastern provinces. Also spoken in Democratic Republic of the Congo. *Class:* Niger-Congo, Atlantic-Congo, Volta-Congo, Benue-Congo, Bantoid, Southern, Narrow Bantu, Central, M, Bisa-Lamba (M.50), Bisa. *Dialects:* Ambo, Luano, Swaka, Bisa (Ichibisa, Biisa, Wisa, Wiza), Lala (Ichilala). *Lg Dev:* NT: 1947–1977.

Lamba (Ichilamba, Chilamba) [lam] 214,000 in Zambia (2001 Johnstone and Mandryk). Population includes 89,969 Lamba, 11,782 Lima (1969 census). Copperbelt, Central, and southeastern Northwestern provinces. Also spoken in Democratic Republic of the Congo. *Class:* Niger-Congo, Atlantic-Congo, Volta-Congo, Benue-Congo, Bantoid, Southern, Narrow Bantu, Central, M, Bisa-Lamba (M.50), Lamba. *Dialects:* Lamba, Lima. *Lg Dev:* Dictionary. Bible: 1959. *Other:* Different from Ilamba of Tanzania.

Lenje (Chilenje, Lenji, Lengi, Mukuni, Chinamukuni, Ciina) [leh] 171,000 (2001 Johnstone and Mandryk). Lukanga Swamp area, Central Province. *Class:* Niger-Congo, Atlantic-Congo, Volta-Congo, Benue-Congo, Bantoid, Southern, Narrow Bantu, Central, M, Lenje-Tonga (M.60), Lenje. *Dialects:* Twa (Lukanga), Lenje. *Lg Dev:* Bible portions: 1927–1994.

Lozi (Silozi, Rozi, Tozvi, Rotse, Rutse, Kololo) [loz] 473,000 in Zambia (1993 Johnstone). Population total all countries: 570,200. Barotseland, Western Province, and Southern Province near Livingstone. Also spoken in Botswana, Namibia, Zimbabwe. *Class:* Niger-Congo, Atlantic-Congo, Volta-Congo, Benue-Congo, Bantoid, Southern, Narrow Bantu, Central, S, Sotho-Tswana (S.30). *Lg Dev:* Newspapers. Radio programs. Dictionary. Grammar. Bible: 1951–1987. *Other:* Recognized for educational and administrative purposes.

Luchazi (Chiluchazi, Lucazi, Cujazi, Lujasi, Lujash, Lutshase, Luxage, Ponda) [lch] 54,400 in Zambia (1986). West central Northwestern Province. See main entry under Angola.

Lunda (Chilunda) [lun] 222,000 in Zambia (2001 Johnstone and Mandryk). Population total all countries: 400,000. Northwestern Province, Copperbelt. Also spoken in Angola, Democratic Republic of the Congo. *Class:* Niger-Congo, Atlantic-Congo, Volta-Congo, Benue-Congo, Bantoid, Southern, Narrow Bantu, Central, K,

Salampasu-Ndembo (K.30). *Dialects:* Kosa (Koosa), Ndembu, Humbu, Kawiku. Close to Ruund. *Lg Dev:* Literacy campaigns, agricultural extension services. Taught in primary schools. Newspapers. Radio programs. Bible: 1962. *Other:* Distinct from Luunda, a dialect of Bemba.

Luvale (Luena, Lwena, Chiluvale, Lovale, Lubale) [lue] 205,000 in Zambia (2001 Johnstone and Mandryk). Population total all countries: 669,000. Northwestern and Western provinces. Also spoken in Angola. *Class:* Niger-Congo, Atlantic-Congo, Volta-Congo, Benue-Congo, Bantoid, Southern, Narrow Bantu, Central, K, Chokwe-Luchazi (K.20). *Lg Use:* Language of wider communication. Recognized for educational and administrative purposes. A dominant regional language. *Lg Dev:* Newspapers. Radio programs. Bible: 1955–1961. *Other:* Traditional religion, Christian.

Luyana (Esiluyana, Louyi, Lui, Luyi, Rouyi) [lyn] 74,800 in Zambia (1986). Population includes 12,114 Kwandi, 29,333 Kwanga, 2,692 Mbowe (1969 census). Population total all countries: 107,308. Eastern Lozi-Luyana area, Western Province. Also spoken in Angola, Namibia. *Class:* Niger-Congo, Atlantic-Congo, Volta-Congo, Benue-Congo, Bantoid, Southern, Narrow Bantu, Central, K, Kwangwa (K.40). *Dialects:* Kwandi, Kwanga, Mbowe (Esimbowe), Mbumi. Mbowe may be a separate language. *Lg Dev:* Dictionary.

Mambwe-Lungu [mgr] 262,800 in Zambia (1993 Johnstone). Population total all countries: 359,800. Northeastern Northern Province south of Lake Tanganyika. Also spoken in Tanzania. *Class:* Niger-Congo, Atlantic-Congo, Volta-Congo, Benue-Congo, Bantoid, Southern, Narrow Bantu, Central, F, Tongwe (F.10). *Dialects:* Mambwe (Ichimambwe, Kimambwe), Rungu (Lungu, Ichirungu, Adong). There are minor dialect differences between Mambwe and Lungu. *Lg Dev:* NT: 1901–1991.

Mashi (Masi) [mho] 20,795 in Zambia (1969 census). Population total all countries: 23,422. Southwestern Western Province. Also spoken in Angola, Namibia. *Class:* Niger-Congo, Atlantic-Congo, Volta-Congo, Benue-Congo, Bantoid, Southern, Narrow Bantu, Central, K, Kwangwa (K.40). *Dialects:* North Kwandu, South Kwandu, Mashi. Dialect cluster. *Other:* Nomadic. Different from Mashi (Shi) which is related to Havu of Democratic Republic of the Congo. Traditional religion.

Mbowe (Esimbowe) [mxo] 2,692 (1969 census). North central Western Province. *Class:* Niger-Congo, Atlantic-Congo, Volta-Congo, Benue-Congo, Bantoid, Southern, Narrow Bantu, Central, K, Kwangwa (K.40).

Mbukushu (Mbukushi, Mambukush, Mampukush, Mbukuhu, Thimukushu, Gova, Kusso) [mhw] Few speakers in Zambia. Southwestern corner of Western Province, along the Kwando River. *Lg Use:* Official regional language. Schools, administration, radio broadcasting. *Other:* Traditional religion, Christian. See main entry under Namibia.

Mbunda (Chimbunda, Mbuunda, Gimbunda, Kimbunda) [mck] 126,000 in Zambia (1993 Johnstone). Population total all countries: 261,000. Northern Barotseland, western Northwestern Province. Also spoken in Angola. *Class:* Niger-Congo, Atlantic-Congo, Volta-Congo, Benue-Congo, Bantoid, Southern, Narrow Bantu, Central, K, Chokwe-Luchazi (K.20). *Lg Dev:* Dictionary. NT: 1983. *Other:* Different from Mbunda (Mbuun, Mbunu) which is a dialect of Mpuono in Democratic Republic of the Congo in the Yanzi group.

Nkoya (Shinkoya) [nka] 70,000 (1995 UBS). Mankoya area, Western and Southern provinces. *Class:* Niger-Congo, Atlantic-Congo, Volta-Congo, Benue-Congo, Bantoid, Southern, Narrow Bantu, Central, L, Nkoya

(L.50). *Dialects:* Nkoya, Mbowela (Mbwela, Mbwera, Shimbwera), Lushangi, Shasha, Lukolwe, Mashasha. *Lg Dev:* NT: 1936–1991.

Nsenga (Chinsenga, Senga) [nse] 427,000 in Zambia (1993 Johnstone). Population total all countries: 584,100. Petauke District, Eastern and Central provinces. Also spoken in Mozambique, Zimbabwe. *Class:* Niger-Congo, Atlantic-Congo, Volta-Congo, Benue-Congo, Bantoid, Southern, Narrow Bantu, Central, N, Senga-Sena (N.40), Senga. *Dialect:* Nsenga, Ngoni (Mpezeni). *Lg Dev:* NT: 1923. *Other:* Distinct from Senga dialect of Tumbuka of Zambia, Malawi, and Tanzania. Christian, traditional religion.

Nyamwanga (Ichinamwanga, Mwanga, Namwanga, Inamwanga) [mwn] 169,000 in Zambia (1993 Johnstone). Population includes 14,698 Iwa and 7,171 Tambo (1969 census). Population total all countries: 256,000. Eastern Northern Province to Lake Rukwa. Also spoken in Tanzania. *Class:* Niger-Congo, Atlantic-Congo, Volta-Congo, Benue-Congo, Bantoid, Southern, Narrow Bantu, Central, M, Nyika-Safwa (M.20). *Dialect:* Iwa, Tambo (Tembo). *Lg Dev:* Bible: 1982.

Nyanja (Chinyanja) [nya] 1,600,000 in Zambia (2001 Johnstone and Mandryk). Population includes 196,640 Chewa, 256,588 Ngoni, 8,032 Kunda (1969 census). Eastern and Central provinces. *Dialects:* Chewa (Cewa), Peta (Cipeta, Chipeta, Malawi, Maravi, Marave), Chingoni (Ngoni), Manganja (Waganga), Nyasa, Kunda. *Lg Use:* The official language of the police and Zambia regiment. Nyanja is the language of education, administration. *Other:* The Kunda dialect is distinct from Kunda of Mozambique in the Senga-Sena group. See main entry under Malawi.

Nyiha (Ishinyiha, Nyika, Nyixa) [nih] 320,000 in Zambia (1993 Johnstone). Northeastern Northern Province near the Malawi border, Isoka and Chama districts. *Dialect:* Wandya. *Other:* May constitute one language with Ichilambya of Tanzania and Malawi. Different from Nyika (Nika, Giryama) of Kenya. See main entry under Tanzania.

Sala [shq] 20,400 (1986). South central Central Province. *Class:* Niger-Congo, Atlantic-Congo, Volta-Congo, Benue-Congo, Bantoid, Southern, Narrow Bantu, Central, M, Lenje-Tonga (M.60), Tonga. *Dialects:* Reported to be intelligible with Tonga and possibly Ila.

Settla (Kisettla, Kisetla) [sta] May also be in Kenya. *Class:* Pidgin, Swahili based. *Lg Use:* A 'despised' pidgin (M. Adler 1977:50). *Other:* Limited vocabulary and grammar. Second language only.

Shona (Chishona) [sna] 30,222 in Zambia (2000 WCD). Several thousand Shona in Mumbwe. Mumbwa, Central Province. Gova dialect is near the Zimbabwe border. *Dialect:* Korekore (Korikori, Makorekore, Wakorikori, Northern Shona, Goba, Gova, Gowa). *Other:* Korekore is the main dialect in Zambia, with subdialect Goba. See main entry under Zimbabwe.

Simaa [sie] 74,800 (1986). Population includes 8,000 in Makoma (1977 Voegelin and Voegelin). Western Lozi-Luyana area, Western Province. *Class:* Niger-Congo, Atlantic-Congo, Volta-Congo, Benue-Congo, Bantoid, Southern, Narrow Bantu, Central, K, Kwangwa (K.40). *Dialects:* Simaa, Mulonga, Imilangu, Mwenyi, Nyengo, Makoma, Liyuwa. Imigangu may be a dialect of Luyana.

Soli (Chisoli) [sby] 54,400 (1986). Central Province, east of Lusaka. *Class:* Niger-Congo, Atlantic-Congo, Volta-Congo, Benue-Congo, Bantoid, Southern, Narrow Bantu, Central, M, Lenje-Tonga (M.60), Tonga. *Dialects:* A more distinct language or dialect of the Tonga group. *Lg Dev:* Bible portions.

Subiya (Subia, Supia, Echisubia, Chikwahane, Chikuahane) [sbs] 5,485 in Zambia (1969 census). Southeastern corner of Western Province. *Other:*

Traditional religion, Christian. See main entry under Namibia.

Taabwa (Rungu, Ichitaabwa, Tabwa) [tap] 60,000 in Zambia. Northwestern Northern Province. *Dialect:* Shila. *Other:* Agriculturalists. Traditional religion. See main entry under Democratic Republic of the Congo.

Tonga (Chitonga, Zambezi, Plateau Tonga) [toi] 1,380,000 in Zambia (2001 Johnstone and Mandryk). Population includes 427,031 Tonga, 11,994 Toka, 7,874 Leya. Population total all countries: 1,517,000. With Ila it predominates in the south, Southern and Western provinces. Also spoken in Zimbabwe. *Class:* Niger-Congo, Atlantic-Congo, Volta-Congo, Benue-Congo, Bantoid, Southern, Narrow Bantu, Central, M, Lenje-Tonga (M.60), Tonga. *Dialects:* Chitonga, Leya, Toka (Southern Tonga), We (Valley Tonga), Shanjo (Sanjo), Twa of Kafwe, Mala. Related to Lundwe, Mala. *Lg Use:* Recognized for educational and administrative purposes. *Lg Dev:* Newspapers. Radio programs. Bible: 1963. *Other:* Different from Tonga of Malawi, Gitonga of Mozambique, or Tsonga (Tonga) of Mozambique.

Totela (Echitotela) [ttl] 14,000 in Zambia (1971 Welmers). Southeastern Western Province, north of Subia. Also spoken in Namibia. *Class:* Niger-Congo, Atlantic-Congo, Volta-Congo, Benue-Congo, Bantoid, Southern, Narrow Bantu, Central, K, Subia (K.50).

Tumbuka (Tumboka, Chitumbuka, Tew, Tambuka, Timbuka, Tombucas) [tum] 392,000 in Zambia (2001 Johnstone and Mandryk). Population includes 33,666 Senga, 1,720 Yombe. Northeastern Eastern Province. *Dialects:* Chitumbuka, Chikamanga (Kamanga, Henga), Kandawire, Chipoka, Yombe, Senga, Fungwe, Wenya, Nenya, Ngoni (Magodi), Fililwa (Filirwa), Hewe (Hewa), Nthali. *Other:* Senga dialect is distinct from Nsenga of Petauke District. See main entry under Malawi.

Yao (Chiyao, Ciyao, Achawa, Adsawa, Adsoa, Ajawa, Ayawa, Chichawa, Ayo, Djao, Haiao, Hiao, Hyao, Jao, Veiao, Wajao) [yao] 200 families or more in the 1970s (Dr. Felix Banda). Eastern Province, Chipata District, Kapata Township, and Katete District. *Dialects:* Makale (Cimakale), Massaninga (Cimassaninga). *Lg Use:* Speakers also use Nyanja or Chewa. *Other:* Workers for Asian merchants. Muslim. See main entry under Malawi.

Yauma [yax] Southwest corner, Kwando River area. See main entry under Angola.

Zambian Sign Language [zsl] *Class:* Deaf sign language.

Zimbabwe

Republic of Zimbabwe. Formerly Rhodesia and Southern Rhodesia. 12,671,860. National or official language: English. Literacy rate: 49% to 76%. Also includes Afrikaans, Gujarati (19,000), people from Europe (90,000), possibly Bemba. Information mainly from J. Bendor-Samuel 1989. Blind population: 15,000 (1982 WCE). Deaf institutions: 6. The number of languages listed for Zimbabwe is 20. Of those, 19 are living languages and 1 is a second language without mother-tongue speakers. See map on page 737.

Dombe [dov] Hwange District, around Lukosi. *Class:* Niger-Congo, Atlantic-Congo, Volta-Congo, Benue-Congo, Bantoid, Southern, Narrow Bantu, Central, M, Lenje-Tonga (M.60), Tonga. *Dialects:* Related to Tonga, with Nambya influences. *Lg Use:* Speakers of Nambya appear to understand it, and vice versa.

English [eng] 375,490 in Zimbabwe (1969 census). *Lg Use:* Official language. Spoken by most Europeans and an increasing number of Africans. Used in all or most education. See main entry under United Kingdom.

Fanagalo ("Fanakalo," "Fanekolo," Piki, Isipiki, Lololo, Isilololo, Pidgin Bantu, "Kitchen Kaffir," "Mine Kaffir," "Isikula") [fng] Several hundred thousand speakers in Zimbabwe (1975 Reinecke). *Dialect:* Chilapalapa. *Lg Use:* Trade language. Used widely in towns and mining areas. *Other:* Second language only. See main entry under South Africa.

Hietshware (Hiechware, Chware, Sarwa, Sesarwa, Tshuwau, Haitshuwau) [hio] 3,536 in Zimbabwe (2000 WCD). *Other:* Nomadic. Traditional religion, Christian. See main entry under Botswana (Tsoa).

Kalanga (Ikalanga, Chikalanga, Tjikalanga, Kanana, Sekalaña, Kalana, Western Shona, Bakaa, Makalaka, Wakalanga) [kck] 700,000 in Zimbabwe (2000 Chebanne). Population total all countries: 850,000. Southwest of Bulawayo and along the Botswana border. Most Kalanga are in Zimbabwe, and most Lilima are in Botswana. Also spoken in Botswana. *Class:* Niger-Congo, Atlantic-Congo, Volta-Congo, Benue-Congo, Bantoid, Southern, Narrow Bantu, Central, S, Shona (S.10). *Dialects:* Lilima (Humbe, Limima), Nyai (Abanyai, Banyai, Wanyai), Peri, Talahundra. The Talahundra dialect is extinct. The Peri are an ethnic group of Birwa and Tswapong assimilated into Kalanga and speak Lilima. The Humbe dialect is ethnically different from the Lilima but now speak the same language. Close to Karanga, Zezuru, and Shangwe (dialects of Shona). *Lg Use:* Rapidly being absorbed by Ndebele, though most rural members speak Kalanga. In the fall of 1985 the government introduced Kalanga primers into schools in the Kalanga area. Most speak Shona and Ndebele as second language, because they are required in school and are languages of wider communication. *Lg Dev:* Dictionary. Grammar. NT: 1999.

Kunda (Chikunda, Cikunda) [kdn] 145,214 in Zimbabwe (2000 WCD). Population total all countries: 193,913. Along the Mwazam'tanda River. Also spoken in Mozambique, Zambia. *Class:* Niger-Congo, Atlantic-Congo, Volta-Congo, Benue-Congo, Bantoid, Southern, Narrow Bantu, Central, N, Senga-Sena (N.40), Sena. *Dialects:* Closer to Nyungwe than to Sena. *Lg Dev:* Bible portions: 1988. *Other:* Different from Kunda which is a dialect of Nyanja.

Lozi (Silozi, Rozi, Rotvi, Tozvi, Rotse, Rutse, Kololo) [loz] 70,000 in Zimbabwe (1982). See main entry under Zambia.

Manyika (Chimanyika, Manika, Bamanyeka, Wamanyika, Wanyika) [mxc] 861,180 in Zimbabwe (2000 WCD). Population total all countries: 1,006,511. Manicaland Province and adjacent areas, northeast of Umtali. Also spoken in Mozambique. *Class:* Niger-Congo, Atlantic-Congo, Volta-Congo, Benue-Congo, Bantoid, Southern, Narrow Bantu, Central, S, Shona (S.10). *Dialects:* Bocha (Boka), Bunji, Bvumba, Domba, Guta, Here, Hungwe, Jindwi, Karombe, Nyamuka, Nyatwe, Unyama. A little more divergent from Shona than Karanga, Zezuru, and Korekore. At least partially intelligible with Shona. Manyika has 74% to 81% lexical similarity with Ndau. *Lg Dev:* NT: 1908.

Nambya (Chinambya, Nanzva, Nambzya) [nmq] 90,000 in Zimbabwe (2000 A. Chebanne). Population total all countries: 105,000. Primarily Hwange District of Matabeleland North, with some speakers having migrated south and west into Lupane and Binga districts. Some in Bulawayo. Also spoken in Botswana. *Class:* Niger-Congo, Atlantic-Congo, Volta-Congo, Benue-Congo, Bantoid, Southern, Narrow Bantu, Central, S, Shona (S.10). *Dialects:* Slight pronunciation difference in Jambezi area: [Cwi] versus [Cu]. Closest to Kalanga, but unintelligible to each other's speakers without several weeks of living together. *Lg Use:* Since Nambya is rarely written and not taught in school, educated young people will often choose Ndebele as their mode of communication, unless speaking to other Nambya. Ndebele is taught in school. Educated young people speak it with varying fluency. Older, uneducated people rarely speak or understand it. Both young and old mostly speak and understand Dombe. Those who have had contact with Tonga are also comfortable in it. Intermarriage with Tonga people is common. Few first-language speakers of Shona in Hwange District, it is dominant in print and electronic media, and similar to Nambya, so most Nambya understand it. Nyanja is commonly spoken and understood. Educated people have varying degrees of English ability, but few would choose to use English outside of school or work. *Lg Dev:* Literacy in Ndebele and English. NT: 1993. *Other:* 'Nanzva' is the Ndebele name for Nambya. 'Banyai' is a name for the people. Christian.

Ndau (Chindau, Ndzawu, Njao, Southeast Shona, Sofala) [ndc] 800,000 in Zimbabwe (2000 Chebanne). South of Umtali, Melsetter, and adjacent areas. *Dialects:* Changa (Chichanga, Chixanga, Shanga), Garwe, Tonga (Abatonga, Atonga, Batoka, Batonga, Watonga). *Lg Dev:* In the fall of 1985 the government introduced Ndau primers into schools in the Ndau area. *Other:* Traditional religion, Christian. See main entry under Mozambique.

Ndebele (Tabele, Tebele, Isinde'bele, Sindebele, Northern Ndebele) [nde] 1,550,000 in Zimbabwe (2001 Johnstone and Mandryk). Population total all countries: 1,558,000. Matabeleland, around Bulawayo. Also spoken in Botswana. *Class:* Niger-Congo, Atlantic-Congo, Volta-Congo, Benue-Congo, Bantoid, Southern, Narrow Bantu, Central, S, Nguni (S.40). *Dialects:* Close to Zulu. *Lg Dev:* Literacy rate in second language: 55%. Dictionary. Bible: 1978. *Other:* Different from Ndebele of Transvaal, South Africa.

Nsenga (Chinsenga, Senga) [nse] 16,100 in Zimbabwe (1969 census). *Other:* Different from Senga dialect of Tumbuka of Zambia, Malawi, and Tanzania. See main entry under Zambia.

Nyanja (Chinyanja) [nya] 251,800 in Zimbabwe (1969 census). See main entry under Malawi.

Shona ("Swina," Chishona) [sna] 10,663,000 in Zimbabwe. Population includes 4,500,000 Karanga (2000 Chebanne), 1,700,000 Korekore (2000 Chebanne), 3,200,000 Zezuru (2000 Chebanne), 1,300,000 Shona. Population total all countries: 10,704,222. Mashonaland, central, and dispersed over many areas of the country. Also spoken in Botswana, Malawi, Zambia. *Class:* Niger-Congo, Atlantic-Congo, Volta-Congo, Benue-Congo, Bantoid, Southern, Narrow Bantu, Central, S, Shona (S.10). *Dialects:* Karanga (Chikaranga), Zezuru (Chizezuru, Bazezuru, Bazuzura, Mazizuru, Vazezuru, Wazezuru), Korekore (Northern Shona, Goba, Gova, Shangwe). Subdialects: Karanga: Duma, Jena, Mhari (Mari), Ngova, Nyubi, Govera; Korekore: Budya, Gova, Tande, Tavara, Nyongwe, Pfunde, Shan Gwe; Zezuru: Shawasha, Gova, Mbire, Tsunga, Kachikwakwa, Harava, Nohwe, Njanja, Nobvu, Kwazwimba (Zimba); Shona: Toko, Hwesa. Rozvi (Rozwi, Ruzwi, Chirozwi) speak Karanga dialect and do not have their own language. Ndau and Manyika are partially intelligible with Shona. *Lg Use:* Shona is the dominant African language of Zimbabwe and is understood by a considerable number. 1,800,000 speak Shona as second or third language in all countries (2000 A. Chebanne). It is primarily a written language apparently based chiefly on Karanga and Zezuru with lexical items also from Manyika and Korekore. Urban populations tend to speak school or standard Shona. English is used with Europeans, and to Africans who don't understand nearby languages. *Lg Dev:* Literacy rate in second language: 86% in English and Shona. Taught in primary schools. Roman script. Dictionary. Grammar. Bible: 1949–1980. *Other:* "Swina" is a derogatory name. SVO. Traditional religion with Christian syncretism, Christian, secular.

Tonga (Chitonga, Zambezi) [toi] 137,000 in Zimbabwe (2001 Johnstone and Mandryk). *Dialects:* Chitonga, Leya, Toka, We. *Other:* Different from Chitonga of Malawi or Tonga of Mozambique. See main entry under Zambia.

Tsonga (Shitsonga, Xitsonga, Thonga, Tonga, Gwamba) [tso] Southeastern near Mozambique border. *Dialects:* Bila (Vila), Changana (Changa, Xichangana, Shangaan, Hlanganu, Hanganu, Langanu, Shilanganu, Shangana), Jonga (Djonga, Dzonga), Ngwalungu (Shingwalungu). See main entry under South Africa.

Tswa (Shitshwa, Kitshwa, Xitshwa, Sheetshwa, Tshwa) [tsc] South. *Dialects:* Hlengwe (Makakwe-Khambana), Tshwa (Dzibi-Dzonga). See main entry under Mozambique.

Tswana (Chuana, Sechuana, Coana, Cuana, Tshwana, Beetjuans, Chwana) [tsn] 29,350 in Zimbabwe (1969 census). *Dialects:* Ngwatu (Mangwato), Tlhaping. *Other:* Spoken by the Bakaka. See main entry under Botswana.

Venda (Chivenda, Cevenda, Tshivenda) [ven] 84,000 in Zimbabwe (1989). South-southeast along South Africa border. *Dialects:* Phani, Tavhatsindi. *Other:* Traditional religion, Christian. See main entry under South Africa.

Zimbabwe Sign Language (Zimsign) [zib] *Class:* Deaf sign language. *Dialects:* Zimbabwe School Sign, Masvingo School Sign, Zimbabwe Community Sign. The sign language used in Masvingo is different from that used in other schools. The sign language used in schools and that used by adults outside is different. It is not clear if they are inherently intelligible to each other. There is some desire for standardization among educators. There are rumors of relationships to sign languages from Germany, Ireland, Australia, England, South Africa. *Lg Use:* Deaf people go to different schools, each using a different sign language. There have been elementary schools for deaf children since the 1940s. The Ministry of Education has pushed to open more spaces for deaf students in special classes in local schools. There is little research on the sign language. The deaf community is quite strong in terms of individual identity. They live their lives around deaf social networks and activities. *Lg Dev:* Literacy in English is better among some deaf people than others, but generally limited. It is quite limited in Shona, mainly known by those from Masvingo. TV. *Other:* There is a manual alphabet used for spelling English, possibly related to that in South Africa.

Americas

Anguilla

Anguilla. 13,008. National or official language: English. Self-governing part of British West Indies. Literacy rate: 82% to 95%. Information mainly from J. Holm 1989; SIL 1977–2003. The number of languages listed for Anguilla is 2. Of those, both are living languages. See map on page 740.

Anguillan Creole English (Leeward Caribbean Creole English) [aig] 11,500 in Anguilla (2001 census). *Other:* Agriculturalists; fishermen. Christian. See main entry under Antigua and Barbuda (Antigua and Barbuda Creole English).

English [eng] 946 in Anguilla (2004). *Lg Use:* Official language. See main entry under United Kingdom.

Antigua and Barbuda

Antigua and Barbuda. 68,320. Population includes 64,000 on Antigua, 1,200 on Barbuda (1997 govt. figures). National or official language: English. Self-governing part of British West Indies. Literacy rate: 90%. Also includes North Levantine Spoken Arabic (400), Portuguese (1,600), people from India and Pakistan. Deaf institutions: 1. The number of languages listed for Antigua and Barbuda is 2. Of those, both are living languages. See map on page 740.

Antigua and Barbuda Creole English (Leeward Caribbean Creole English) [aig] 66,970 in Antigua and Barbuda (2001). Population total all countries: 125,244. Spoken throughout Antigua and Barbuda. Also spoken in Anguilla, Dominica, Montserrat, Saint Kitts and Nevis, United Kingdom. *Class:* Creole, English based, Atlantic, Eastern, Southern. *Dialects:* Antiguan Creole English, Barbuda Creole English. Slightly intelligible with Jamaican and perhaps Bahamas creoles. May be close to English Creoles of the Virgin Islands and Netherlands Antilles. There is a creole continuum with Standard English. *Lg Use:* Most villagers deny the existence of a creole, although they speak it. *Other:* Agriculturalists: sugarcane.

English [eng] *Lg Use:* Official language. See main entry under United Kingdom.

Argentina

Argentine Republic, República Argentina. 39,144,753. Population includes 100,000 to 150,000 American Indians (1997). National or official language: Spanish. Literacy rate: 92% to 95%. Also includes Catalan-Valencian-Balear, Eastern Yiddish, Italian (1,500,000), Japanese (32,000), Lithuanian, North Levantine Spoken Arabic (1,000,000), Paraguayan Guaraní (200,000), Plautdietsch (140), Slovenian (10,000), South Levantine Spoken Arabic, Standard German (400,000), Turoyo, Ukrainian, Vlax Romani. Information mainly from A. Acebes 1966; A. Tovar 1961, 1966; SIL 1969–2003; A. Buckwalter 1981–83; Nick Drayson ANG 1982–84. Blind population: 14,300 (1982 WCE) or 30,000 (1979). Deaf population: 2,056,145. Deaf institutions: 17. The number of languages listed for Argentina is 27. Of those, 25 are living languages and 2 are extinct. See map on page 741.

Abipon [axb] Extinct. *Class:* Mataco-Guaicuru, Guaicuruan. *Other:* Related to Kadiweu.

Argentine Sign Language [aed] *Class:* Deaf sign language. *Lg Use:* Deaf people go to different schools, each using a different sign language outside class. Sign language is not allowed in the classroom. There are sign language stories and drama on film. There is a committee for a national sign language, and organizations for sign language teachers and interpreters. *Lg Dev:* TV. Videos. *Other:* Deaf schools were begun in 1885. There is a manual alphabet for Spanish spelling.

Aymara, Central [ayr] *Other:* Quite a few have come from Bolivia looking for work. Sugar mill workers. See main entry under Bolivia.

Chané [caj] Extinct. Salta Province. *Class:* Arawakan, Unclassified. *Dialects:* Some have equated this name with 'Guana' (Kaskiha) of Paraguay of Mascoian affiliation, or Terena of Brazil of Arawakan affiliation, but they are distinct. *Lg Use:* The language has not been spoken for 300 years. Descendants are called

'Izoceño' and now speak a variety of Chiriguano (Eastern Bolivian Guaraní).

Chiripá (Tsiripá, Txiripá, Nhandeva, Ñandeva, Apytare) [nhd] *Dialect:* Apapocuva. *Other:* Called 'Chiripá' in Paraguay, 'Nhandeva' in Brazil. 'Ñandeva' is used in the Paraguayan Chaco for the Tapiete. See main entry under Paraguay.

Chorote, Iyojwa'ja (Choroti, Yofuaha, Eklenjuy) [crt] 800 (1982 Drayson). Northeast Salta Province. *Class:* Mataco-Guaicuru, Mataco. *Dialects:* A distinct language from Iyo'wujwa Chorote (Drayson). *Lg Dev:* NT: 1997. *Other:* Called 'Chorote' in Argentina, 'Choroti' in Paraguay, 'Eklenjuy' by the Nivaclé. River dwellers. Traditional religion.

Chorote, Iyo'wujwa (Choroti, Manjuy, Manjui) [crq] 1,500 in Argentina. 50% monolinguals. Population total all countries: 2,008. In Argentina they are mixed with the Iyojwa'ja Chorote. No more than a couple of families in Bolivia. Also spoken in Bolivia, Paraguay. *Class:* Mataco-Guaicuru, Mataco. *Lg Use:* In Argentina all children have primary education in Spanish. *Lg Dev:* Bible portions: 1992. *Other:* Traditional religion.

Guaraní, Mbyá (Mbua, Eastern Argentina Guaraní, Mbyá) [gun] 3,000 in Argentina (2002 Dooley). Northeast Argentina. *Other:* Traditional religion. See main entry under Brazil.

Guaraní, Western Argentine (Eastern Bolivian Guaraní, "Chawuncu," "Chiriguano") [gui] 15,000 in Argentina. Jujuy, Salta. *Dialect:* Chané, Izoceño (Izocenyo, Isocenio). *Lg Use:* Chané is a group that formerly spoke an Arawakan language, but now speak a variety of Western Argentine Guaraní. *Other:* 'Guarayo' is used in Argentina as a collective name; distinct from Guarayo of Bolivia. "Chawuncu," "Chabanco," "Chaguanco," "Chiriguano" are derogatory. Izoceño is a group that speaks a variety of this language. Traditional religion. See main entry under Bolivia (Guaraní, Eastern Bolivian).

Kaiwá (Caingua, Caiwá, Kayova) [kgk] 512 in Argentina. Northeast Argentina. See main entry under Brazil.

Mapudungun (Araucano, Maputongo, Mapuche, Mapudungu) [arn] 100,000 in Argentina (2000). Provinces of Neuquen, Rio Negro, Chubut, Buenos Aires, La Pampa. *Dialect:* Pehuenche. *Other:* Recent migration from Chile. See main entry under Chile.

Mocoví (Mocobí, Mbocobí) [moc] 4,525 (2000 WCD). South Chaco, northeast Santa Fe. *Class:* Mataco-Guaicuru, Guaicuruan. *Lg Dev:* NT: 1988. *Other:* Traditional religion.

Nivaclé (Ashlushlay, "Chulupi," "Churupi," "Chulupie," "Chulupe") [cag] 200 in Argentina. Salta Province, northeast. *Dialects:* Forest Nivaclé, River Nivaclé. *Other:* Traditional religion. See main entry under Paraguay.

Ona (Aona, Selknam, Shelknam) [ona] 1 to 3 (1991 Adelaar). Patagonia, Tierra del Fuego. Also formerly in Chile. *Class:* Chon. *Lg Use:* Speakers have shifted to Spanish. Probably extinct (2000 W. Adelaar). *Other:* They lost their land because of outside settlers, mines, and cattle. Island. Steppe in the north, forest in the south. Up to 800 meters. Hunter-gatherers. Nearly extinct.

Pilagá (Pilaca) [plg] 2,000 (1991 UBS). Along the valleys of the Bermejo and Pilcomayo rivers in central and western Formosa Province, also Chaco and Salta provinces. *Class:* Mataco-Guaicuru, Guaicuruan. *Dialects:* Toba-Pilagá (Toba del Oeste, Sombrero Negro), Chaco Pilagá (Toba Sur). Intelligibility between the dialects needs investigation. *Lg Dev:* NT: 1993. *Other:* Traditional religion.

Puelche (Gennaken, Pampa, Northern Tehuelche) [pue] 5 or 6. Pampas. *Class:* Language Isolate. *Other:* Distinct from Pehuenche dialect of Mapudungun. Extinct in Chile. Nearly extinct.

Quechua, South Bolivian (Central Bolivian Quechua) [quh] 855,000 in Argentina. Population includes 200,000 temporary laborers, about 100,000 looking for work, 500,000 living in Buenos Aires (1971 F. Hicks). Possibly 70,000 in Salta Province. Buenos Aires, some working on docks. Some in Salta Province. *Dialect:* Northwest Jujuy (Colla). *Other:* Different from Santiago del Estero (R. Nardi). See main entry under Bolivia.

Quichua, Santiago del Estero (Santiagueño Quichua) [qus] 60,000 (2000 SIL). Ethnic population: 60,000. Santiago del Estero Province, north central Argentina, Departments of Figueroa, Moreno, Robles, Sarmiento, Brigadier J. F. Ibarra, San Martín, Silipica, Loreto, Atamisqui, Avellaneda, Salavina, Quebrachos, Mitre, Aguirre, some in southeast Salta Province, western Taboada Department along the Salado River, and Buenos Aires. *Class:* Quechuan, Quechua II, C. *Dialects:* Different from Bolivian (lexical similarity 81%) or other Quechua (P. Landerman SIL 1968). *Lg Use:* Increased use by media, musical groups. There is a Chair of Quichua in the National University. Vigorous. Positive language attitude. Young men have some proficiency in Spanish because of serving in the armed forces; rural men also use Spanish; children are in Spanish language schools. *Lg Dev:* There is a decree authorizing promotion and teaching in schools. Roman script. Radio programs. Dictionary. Grammar. *Other:* Plains. Desert. Agriculturalists; migrations to sugarcane harvest; cotton harvesters; carbon-making industry. Christian, traditional religion, syncretism.

Spanish [spa] 33,000,000 in Argentina (1995). *Lg Use:* Official language. See main entry under Spain.

Tapieté (Guarayo, Guasurangue, Tirumbae, Yanaigua, Ñanagua) [tpj] 100 in Argentina. Northeast, Tartagal, 1 village. See main entry under Paraguay.

Tehuelche (Aoniken, Gunua-Kena, Gununa-Kena, Inaquen) [teh] 4 (2000 W. Adelaar). Ethnic population: 200 (2000 W. Adelaar). Patagonia. *Class:* Chon. *Other:* The people have come from Chile. Nomadic hunters, traditionally. Nearly extinct.

Toba (Chaco Sur, Qom, Toba Qom, Toba Sur) [tob] 19,810 in Argentina (2000 WCD). Population total all countries: 20,656. Eastern Formosa Province and Chaco Province. Also spoken in Bolivia, Paraguay. *Class:* Mataco-Guaicuru, Guaicuruan. *Dialects:* Southeast Toba, Northern Toba. *Lg Dev:* Dictionary. NT: 1980. *Other:* Different from Toba of Paraguay (Toba-Maskoy) or Toba-Pilagá of Argentina. Traditional religion, Christian.

Vilela [vil] 20 (1981 Buckwalter). Resistencia, east central Chaco Province near Paraguay border. *Class:* Lule-Vilela. *Lg Use:* Any remaining Vilela are apparently being absorbed by the Toba or losing their Indian identity in the barrios of towns and cities (1981 Buckwalter). *Other:* Nearly extinct.

Welsh [cym] 25,000 in Argentina (1998 A. Leaver). Patagonia, Chubut Territory. *Dialect:* Patagonian Welsh. *Lg Use:* First- and second-language speakers (1998). Spoken here since around 1891. Speakers also use Spanish. See main entry under United Kingdom.

Wichí Lhamtés Güisnay ("Mataco" Güisnay, Güisnay, "Mataco" Pilcomayo, "Mataco") [mzh] 15,000 (1999). Northern, Pilcomayo River area. *Class:* Mataco-Guaicuru, Mataco. *Lg Dev:* Grammar. *Other:* "Mataco" is derogatory. The self name of the people is 'Wichí'; the language 'Wichí Lhamtés'. Traditional religion.

Wichí Lhamtés Nocten ("Mataco" Nocten, Nocten, Noctenes, Oktenai) [mtp] 100 in Argentina. Northern border down to Tartagal. *Other:* Traditional religion. See main entry under Bolivia.

Wichí Lhamtés Vejoz ("Mataco" Vejoz, Vejos) [wlv] 25,000 in Argentina (1991 UBS). Northern area: Chaco, Formosa, Salta, Jujuy. Generally west of Toba, along upper Bermejo River Valley and Pilcomayo River. Also spoken in Bolivia. *Class:* Mataco-Guaicuru, Mataco. *Dialect:* Bermejo Vejoz. Not intelligible with other Chaco languages. *Lg Use:* Bilingual level estimates for Spanish: 0 0%, 1 80%, 2–3 19%, 4–5 1%. *Lg Dev:* Bible: 2002. *Other:* Language family also called 'Mataco-Mataguayo'. Traditional religion.

Aruba

Aruba. 71,218. National or official language: Dutch. Government has been autonomous since 1986 from Netherlands Antilles. By agreement of all parties, it remains part of the Kingdom of the Netherlands. Also includes Spanish (9,700), Sranan. The number of languages listed for Aruba is 3. Of those, all are living languages. See map on page 740.

Dutch [nld] 5,289. *Lg Use:* Official language. Use is declining. See main entry under Netherlands.
English [eng] 3,000. *Dialect:* Aruba English. See main entry under United Kingdom.
Papiamentu (Papiamento, Papiam, Curaçoleño, Curassese, Papiamentoe) [pap] 60,000 in Aruba (1999). *Lg Use:* Using both Papiamentu and Dutch is not considered an indication of lack of education. However, inability to use Dutch hinders social and political mobility, and leads to discontent. See main entry under Netherlands Antilles.

Bahamas

The Commonwealth of the Bahamas. 299,697. National or official language: English. 30 inhabited islands. Literacy rate: 95% (1990). Also includes Greek (800), Haitian Creole French (20,000). Deaf population: 16,451. Deaf institutions: 2. The number of languages listed for Bahamas is 3. Of those, 2 are living languages and 1 is extinct. See map on page 739.

Bahamas Creole English (Bahamian Creole English, Bahamian Dialect) [bah] 225,000 in Bahamas (1987). Also spoken in USA. *Class:* Creole, English based, Atlantic, Eastern, Northern. *Dialects:* Intelligibility with Sea Islands Creole good. Very close to Sea Islands Creole and Afro-Seminole of USA (Ian Hancock). The major differences with Sea Islands are in phonology, a few words, regional expressions, and a few grammatical differences (verbal markers). There is a spectrum of varieties from Standard USA English usage to the creole (Todd and Hancock 1986). *Lg Dev:* Another orthography may be needed, since there were negative responses to the Sea Islands orthography presently in use. Dictionary. *Other:* Christian.
English [eng] 49,331 in Bahamas (2004). *Lg Use:* Official language. See main entry under United Kingdom.
Taino [tnq] Extinct. Members of the ethnic group are also now in the USA, in Florida and New Jersey, in Puerto Rico, Santo Domingo, and Cuba. *Class:* Arawakan, Maipuran, Northern Maipuran, Caribbean. *Lg Use:* Members of the ethnic group now speak Spanish, or a Spanish-Taino mixed language, not understood by Spanish speakers. They estimate the present language to be 55% Taino and 45% Spanish. They also use Spanish or English.

Barbados

Barbados. 278,289. National or official language: English. Literacy rate: 98% to 99%. Deaf institutions: 2. The number of languages listed for Barbados is 2. Of those, both are living languages. See map on page 740.

Bajan (Barbadian Creole English) [bjs] 259,000 (1995). *Class:* Creole, English based, Atlantic, Eastern, Southern. *Dialects:* There is a basilectal variety spoken in a fishing village (Roy 1986). The speech of the poor and less educated is similar to the mesolect in nearby countries. Increasingly influenced by USA rather than United Kingdom English (Todd and Hancock 1986). Fewer than 20 lexical items are traceable to African origin (Niles 1980:148). Shares lexical features with Caribbean creoles. *Other:* Christian.
English [eng] 13,000 in Barbados (1995). *Lg Use:* National language. See main entry under United Kingdom.

Belize

Belize. 272,945. American Indians 11% (1991 census). National or official language: English. Literacy rate: 70%. Average years of schooling 7.53. Also includes Hindi (8,455), Japanese, Korean, North Levantine Spoken Arabic (187), Chinese. Information mainly from SIL 1973–2003. Blind population: 728 registered. Deaf population: 12,671. Deaf institutions: 1. The number of languages listed for Belize is 8. Of those, all are living languages. See map on page 742.

Belize Kriol English (Northern Central America Creole English, Kriol, Creola) [bzj] 55,051 in Belize (1991 census). Population total all countries: 95,051. Ethnic population: 158,000 including second-language speakers (1990). Most live in Belize City, but nearly everyone else in Belize is either a first- or second-language speaker of Creole. Many of the rural villages are Creole-speaking. Creole people tend to live along the coast or other waterways. It is the lingua franca in much of the country. Also spoken in USA. *Class:* Creole, English based, Atlantic, Western. *Dialects:* Reported to be very close to Mískito Coast, Rama Cay, and Islander (San Andrés) creoles. Historically an extension of Mískito Coast Creole. Dahufra was a creole used in the 16th to 18th centuries. *Lg Use:* Spoken by creoles and people of East Indian descent, used everywhere in most areas of life. Used in advertisements. Positive language attitude. *Lg Dev:* Newspapers. Radio programs. TV. Dictionary. Grammar. Bible portions: 1999. *Other:* Jamaican Creole is different in orthography and grammar. Timber; agriculturalists; fishermen; industrial workers; construction industry; commerce; government; teachers.
English [eng] *Lg Use:* Official language. 55,998 second-language speakers in Belize (1991 census). Used in education, government, commerce. See main entry under United Kingdom.
Garifuna (Caribe, Central American Carib, Black Carib, "Moreno") [cab] 12,274 in Belize (1991 census). Dangriga, Stann Creek, and Toledo along the coast, 6 villages. *Lg Use:* Speakers also use Belize Creole. See main entry under Honduras.
Kekchí (Ketchí, Quecchí, Cacché) [kek] 9,000 in Belize (1995 SIL). Southern Belize. See main entry under Guatemala (Q'eqchi').
Maya, Mopán (Maya Mopán, Mopane) [mop] 8,375 in Belize (2000 WCD). Population total all countries: 10,975. Toledo, Stann Creek, and Cayo districts. Also spoken in Guatemala. *Class:* Mayan, Yucatecan, Mopan-Itza. *Lg Dev:* NT: 1979. *Other:* VOS.
Maya, Yucatán (Yucateco) [yua] Ethnic population: 5,000 in Belize (1991). San Antonio and Succoths in Cayo District. It may still be spoken in the Orange Walk and Corozal districts near the Mexico border. *Lg Use:* Speakers in Belize are shifting to Spanish. Many are concerned about language loss and are trying to start classes for the youth. Speakers are older adults. People in

Succoths village say the older people speak Maya. See main entry under Mexico.

Plautdietsch (German, Mennonite German) [pdt] 5,763 in Belize (1991 census). *Lg Use:* 110,735 or more in Latin America are fairly monolingual. 15% speak German, many speak English, and some speak Creole or Spanish as second language. *Other:* Christian. See main entry under Canada.

Spanish (Español, Castellano) [spa] 80,477 in Belize (1991 census). Northern and western districts, and scattered throughout the country. See main entry under Spain.

Bermuda

Bermuda. 64,935. Population of African descent 66%. National or official language: English. British dependency. Literacy rate: 97% to 99%. The number of languages listed for Bermuda is 1.

English [eng] 58,800 in Bermuda (1989). *Dialect:* Bermudan English. *Lg Use:* Official language. *Other:* Colloquial English may not be a creole but a regional variety of uncreolized English. See main entry under United Kingdom.

Bolivia

Republic of Bolivia, República de Bolivia. 8,724,156. National or official languages: Spanish, North Bolivian Quechua, South Bolivian Quechua, Central Aymara. Literacy rate: 63% to 81%. Also includes Corsican (60,000), Standard German (160,000), Wichí Lhamtés Vejoz. Information mainly from SIL 1956–2003. Blind population: 1,070. Deaf population: 46,800. Deaf institutions: 9 or more. The number of languages listed for Bolivia is 44. Of those, 36 are living languages, 1 is a second language without mother-tongue speakers, and 7 are extinct. See map on page 743.

Araona (Cavina) [aro] 81 (2000 Adelaar). Ethnic population: 90 (2000 W. Adelaar). Northwest, headwaters of Manupari River. *Class:* Tacanan, Araona-Tacana, Araona. *Lg Use:* Vigorous. All ages. Knowledge of Spanish is increasing. *Lg Dev:* Dictionary. Bible portions: 1974–1981. *Other:* Araona and Cavina are names of two moieties of the group. SOV.

Aymara, Central [ayr] 1,785,000 in Bolivia (1987). Population total all countries: 2,227,642. Whole Altiplano west of eastern Andes. Some migration to the yungas and the lowlands. Also spoken in Argentina, Chile, Peru. *Class:* Aymaran. *Dialects:* Chilean Aymara is very close to La Paz, Bolivia dialect. *Lg Use:* Official language. All ages. *Lg Dev:* Churches are active in literacy. Openings in government schools for the use of Aymara literature. Radio programs. Dictionary. Grammar. Bible: 1987–1993. *Other:* Traditional religion, Christian.

Ayoreo (Ayoré, Morotoco, Moro, Pyeta, Yovai) [ayo] 771 in Bolivia (2000 Adelaar). Ethnic population: 856 in Bolivia (2000 W. Adelaar). Gran Chaco region, department of Santa Cruz. *Dialect:* Tsiricua. *Lg Use:* All ages. *Other:* Called 'Morotoco' in Paraguay and Ayoreo in Bolivia. See main entry under Paraguay.

Baure [brg] 13 (2000 Adelaar). Ethnic population: 631 (2000). Beni Department, northwest of Magdalena. *Class:* Arawakan, Maipuran, Southern Maipuran, Bolivia-Parana. *Lg Use:* Speakers are shifting to Spanish. Children and most adults were not using Baure 20 years ago. *Lg Dev:* Bible portions: 1960–1966. *Other:* Nearly extinct.

Bolivian Sign Language [bvl] 350 to 400 (1988 E. Powlison). Cochabamba, La Paz, Riberalta, Santa Cruz. *Class:* Deaf sign language. *Dialects:* Based on American Sign Language with necessary changes for Spanish spelling. Some groups in La Paz and Santa Cruz use the same signs with some dialect signs from their own areas. *Other:* Originated by missionaries. Other deaf schools use only the oralist approach.

Callawalla (Callahuaya) [caw] 10 or 20 speakers (1995 SIL). Highlands and high valleys, eastern Andes north of La Paz, Charazani area north of Lake Titicaca. *Class:* Mixed Language, Quechua-Puquina. *Dialects:* The language seems to have Quechua affixes and syntactic patterns, but distinctive roots from a dialect of the extinct Puquina language (Girault 1990). *Lg Use:* A special language used by the herb doctors of the Inca emperors; they continue as herb doctors. May be extinct. Women and children do not speak Callawalla, but speak Spanish, North Bolivia Quechua, or Aymara. Spoken only by the men. *Other:* Second language only.

Canichana (Kanichana) [caz] Extinct. Ethnic population: 583 (2000 W. Adelaar). Lowlands. *Class:* Language Isolate. *Dialects:* Said to be of the Tucanoan family.

Cavineña [cav] 1,180 (2000 W. Adelaar). Ethnic population: 1,736 (2000 W. Adelaar). Northern Bolivia, southeast of Riberalta, along the Beni River, east of the Beni, and 500 in the Pando on the west side of the Beni. *Class:* Tacanan, Araona-Tacana, Cavinena-Tacana, Cavinena. *Lg Use:* Bilingual level estimates for Spanish: 0 40%, 1 25%, 2 15%, 3 10%, 4 5%, 5 5%. Becoming increasingly bilingual in Spanish. 500 children in school (1995). High school in Galilea has 135 students and 15 teachers. *Lg Dev:* Dictionary. NT: 1985. *Other:* SOV. Rubber; castaña nut gatherers; agriculturalists.

Cayubaba (Cayuwaba, Cayuvava) [cyb] Extinct. Ethnic population: 794 (2000 W. H. Adelaar). Beni Department, west of Mamore River, north of Santa Ana. *Class:* Language Isolate. *Dialects:* Ruhlen and others classify it as Equatorial. *Lg Use:* Members of the ethnic group now speak Spanish.

Chácobo [cao] 550 (2000 SIL). Ethnic population: 860 (2000 SIL). Northwest Beni, south of Riberalta. *Class:* Panoan, Southern. *Lg Use:* Bolivian non-Chacobo children at Alto Ivon are learning Chácobo. All ages. Spanish bilingual schools have about 180 students, 4 teachers, 5 grades. 3 of the teachers are Chácobo. 50% are monolingual. *Lg Dev:* NT: 1979. *Other:* Agriculturalists.

Chipaya (Puquina) [cap] 1,200 (1995). Ethnic population: 1,800. Department of Oruro, Province of Atahuallpa. *Class:* Uru-Chipaya. *Dialects:* May be Arawakan or distantly related to Mayan. *Lg Use:* Vigorous. Used in religious services. Positive language attitude. Previously bilingualism was mainly in Aymara, now in Spanish. 400 children in school. 5% are monolingual. 500 speakers are multilingual in Spanish and Aymara (SIL 2000). *Lg Dev:* Literacy rate in first language: 50%. Roman script. NT: 1978. *Other:* Now have a complete high school. SOV. Plains. 3,600 meters. Agriculturalists: grain; animal husbandry: sheep, llamas. Christian, traditional religion.

Chiquitano (Chiquito, Tarapecosi) [cax] 5,855 (2000 Adelaar). Ethnic population: 47,086 (2000 W. Adelaar). Eastern region east of Santa Cruz. *Class:* Macro-Ge, Chiquito. *Dialects:* Concepción, San Ignacio de Velazco, San Javier (Javierano, Xavierano), Santiago, San Miguel. *Lg Use:* Some children learn Chiquitano either from parents or from the community. *Lg Dev:* NT: 1980. *Other:* There are grammatical differences between the dialects of men and women, but different literature not needed. VO. Agriculturalists. Traditional religion, Christian.

Chorote, Iyo'wujwa (Choroti, Manjuy, Manjui) [crq] 8 in Bolivia (1982). Southeast, Tarija Department. *Lg Use:* Possibly extinct in Bolivia. See main entry under Argentina.

Ese Ejja (Ese Eja, Ese Exa, Tiatinagua, "Chama," Huarayo) [ese] 1,300 in Bolivia (2000 SIL). Population total all countries: 1,772. Ethnic population: 1,300 in Bolivia (2000 SIL). Northwestern region, and into the foothills on the Beni and Madre de Dios rivers in Bolivia, Tambopata and Heath rivers around Puerto Maldonado in Peru. Also spoken in Peru. *Class:* Tacanan, Tiatinagua. *Dialects:* Each clan has slight dialect differences; all seem inherently intelligible. Appears to differ the most from other Tacanan languages. The Tambopata dialect in Peru is somewhat different from the Bolivian dialect. *Lg Use:* All ages. Bilingual level estimates for Spanish: 0 40%, 1 20%, 2 30%, 3 10%, 4 0%, 5 0%. *Lg Dev:* Dictionary. NT: 1984. *Other:* The name "Chama" is objectionable. SOV. Hunter-gatherers; fishermen.

Guaraní, Eastern Bolivian ("Chiriguano") [gui] 33,670 in Bolivia (2000 W. Adelaar). Population total all countries: 48,974. Ethnic population: 36,917 in Bolivia (2000 W. Adelaar). South central Parapeti River area, Tarija. Also spoken in Argentina, Paraguay. *Class:* Tupi, Tupi-Guarani, Subgroup I. *Dialects:* Izoceño (Izocenio), Ava. *Lg Use:* All ages. *Lg Dev:* Radio programs. Grammar. Bible: 2001. *Other:* Called 'Guarayo' in Paraguay and 'Guaraní Occidental', "Chiriguano," or "Chawuncu" in Argentina. "Chawuncu" and "Chiriguano" are derogatory names. Interfluvial. Tropical forest. Swidden agriculturalists. Traditional religion, Christian.

Guaraní, Western Bolivian (Simba, Simba Guaraní) [gnw] 7,000 (2002 Russell). Chuquisaca Department, south to Pilcomayo River, east to Cuevo, north to Monte Agudo. *Class:* Tupi, Tupi-Guarani, Subgroup I. *Lg Dev:* NT: 1984. *Other:* Traditional religion, Christian.

Guarayu ("Guarayo") [gyr] 5,933 (2000 W. Adelaar). Ethnic population: 7,235 (2000 W. Adelaar). Northeastern Guarayos River area. *Class:* Tupi, Tupi-Guarani, Subgroup II. *Lg Use:* All ages. *Lg Dev:* NT: 1985. *Other:* Different from Guarayo of Paraguay (which is the same as Chiriguano) or Huarayo (Ese Ejja) of Peru and Bolivia. The name "Guarayo," used for several groups, means 'savage'. 950 children in school in Urubicha. 31 of 34 teachers are Guarayu (1995). SOV. Tropical forest. Traditional religion, Christian.

Ignaciano (Moxo, Moxos, Mojos, Mojo) [ign] 4,500 (2000 SIL). Ethnic population: 20,805 with Trinitario (2000 W. Adelaar). South central Beni. *Class:* Arawakan, Maipuran, Southern Maipuran, Bolivia-Parana. *Dialects:* Limited intelligibility of Trinitario, similar to Spanish and Portuguese, with vowel reduction. *Lg Use:* Ignaciano used in town meetings unless outsiders present. Many use Ignaciano in daily life. Ignaciano a required subject in the lower school grades, one session per week. Perhaps half of the children learn Ignaciano. Bilingual level estimates for Spanish: 0 25%, 1 20%, 2 34%, 3 19%, 4 2%, 5 0%. Spanish is the language of instruction in schools. By the 1980s, fewer than 100 monolinguals, all older than 30. Most women can converse in Spanish. Much Spanish influence. *Lg Dev:* RC school. Other schools since the 1930s. Dictionary. NT: 1980. *Other:* Nearly the same culture as Trinitario. Tropical forest, savannah. Agriculturalists; pastoralists; traditionally hunter-gatherers.

Itene (Iteneo, Itenez, More) [ite] Extinct. Ethnic population: 108 (2000 W. Adelaar). North central Beni Department at junction of Mamoré and Itenez rivers. *Class:* Chapacura-Wanham, Guapore. *Dialect:* Itoreauhip. Related languages: Chapacura, Quitemoca, Cujuna, Cumana, Mataua, Uanham, Urunumacan; probably all extinct. *Lg Use:* Children were not speaking Itene and only some of the older people were actively using it 30 years ago. Members of the ethnic group now speak Spanish.

Itonama (Machoto, Saramo) [ito] 10 (2000 Crevels). Ethnic population: 5,090 (2000 W. Adelaar). Beni Department and Itonamas River. *Class:* Language Isolate. *Dialects:* Ruhlen classifies it as Paezan. *Lg Use:* Speakers

are shifting to Spanish. Speakers are older adults. *Lg Dev:* Dictionary. Bible portions: 1967. *Other:* Nearly extinct.

Jorá (Hora) [jor] Extinct. *Class:* Tupi, Tupi-Guarani, Guarayu-Siriono-Jora II. *Lg Use:* Adelaar reports 5 to 10 speakers (1991).

Leco (Leko, Rik'a) [lec] 20 (2001 Simon van de Kerke). Ethnic population: 80 (2000 W. Adelaar). East of Lake Titicaca, some in Apolo area, scattered families on the Mapiri-Kaka River in Karura, Candelaria, Tutilimundi and Uyapi and on the Coroico River in Trapichiponte in KeleKelera. *Class:* Language Isolate. *Dialects:* Reported to be Quechuan. *Other:* Preserve some folklore, dances, and music. Reported to be recently extinct linguistically. Nearly extinct.

Movima [mzp] 1,452 (2000 W. Adelaar). Ethnic population: 6,528 (2000 W. Adelaar). Central Beni Department, in and around Santa Ana on the Yacuma River. *Class:* Language Isolate. *Dialects:* Reported to be Tucanoan. *Lg Use:* Some children speakers. Speakers also use Spanish. *Lg Dev:* Dictionary. Bible portions: 1967.

Pacahuara (Pacawara) [pcp] 17 (2000 W. Adelaar). Ethnic population: 18 (2000 W. Adelaar). Northwest Beni. *Class:* Panoan, Southern. *Other:* All are integrated into the Chácobo. Tropical forest. Rubber gatherers. Nearly extinct.

Pauserna (Paucerne, Guarayu-Ta, Pauserna-Guarasugwé) [psm] Extinct. Ethnic population: 46 (2000 W. Adelaar). Southeast Beni on Guapore River. *Class:* Tupi, Tupi-Guarani, Pauserna.

Plautdietsch (German, Mennonite German) [pdt] 28,567 in Bolivia (1996 editor, Menno-Bote). *Lg Use:* 6% speak Spanish or Standard German as second language. *Other:* Christian. See main entry under Canada.

Quechua, North Bolivian (North la Paz Quechua) [qul] 116,483 in Bolivia (1978 census). 18,452 monolinguals. Apolo Region La Paz Department. Also spoken in Peru. *Class:* Quechuan, Quechua II, C. *Dialects:* Apolo, Charazani, Chuma. *Lg Use:* Official language. Vigorous. All domains. Used in religious services, commerce, and labor. Positive language attitude. Children are increasing their use of Spanish. *Lg Dev:* Some bilingual education. Roman script. Newspapers. Radio programs. TV. NT: 1985. *Other:* SOV. Mountain slope. Agriculturalists; gold miners. Christian.

Quechua, South Bolivian (Central Bolivian Quechua, Quechua Boliviano) [quh] 2,782,500 in Bolivia (1987). Population total all countries: 3,637,500. Highland regions and lowland except around Apolo, Northwest Jujuy Quechua in Argentina. Also spoken in Argentina. *Class:* Quechuan, Quechua II, C. *Dialects:* Sucre, Cochabamba, Oruro, Potosí, Chuquisaca, Northwest Jujuy. May be intelligible with Chilean Quechua. *Lg Use:* Official language. *Lg Dev:* Dictionary. Bible: 1986–1993. *Other:* SOV. Traditional religion, Christian.

Reyesano (San Borjano) [rey] Possibly a few speakers (2000 W. Adelaar). Ethnic population: 4,118 (2000 W. Adelaar). Beni Department, west central around San Borja, near Reyes. *Class:* Tacanan, Araona-Tacana, Cavinena-Tacana, Tacana Proper. *Lg Use:* There were a few speakers in 1961, including some children. Speakers are older adults. *Other:* Nearly extinct.

Saraveca [sar] Extinct. Eastern jungle. *Class:* Arawakan, Maipuran, Central Maipuran.

Shinabo [snh] Extinct. *Class:* Panoan, Southern. *Other:* Existence improbable; contact has been attempted several times. Thought to have possibly been a Chácobo group.

Sirionó (Mbia Chee, Mbya) [srq] 399 (2000 W. Adelaar). 50 monolinguals. Ethnic population: 419 (2000 W. Adelaar) to over 600 (2000 P. Priest SIL). Eastern Beni and northwestern Santa Cruz Departments, village of Ibiato (Eviato) and along the Río Blanco in farms and ranches. *Class:* Tupi, Tupi-Guarani, Subgroup II.

Dialects: Close to Yuqui. *Lg Use:* Parents pass Sirionó on to children, but want them to learn Spanish. Used in religious services. All ages. Positive language attitude. 5% to 10% are monolingual, others use Spanish as second language. *Lg Dev:* Literacy rate in first language: 40%. 250 can read, 50 can write Sirionó. Taught in primary schools. Roman script. Dictionary. NT: 1977. *Other:* Some form of whistle speech reported. Tropical forest, pampa. Lowlands. Agriculturalists. Christian.

Spanish [spa] 3,483,700 in Bolivia (1995). *Lg Use:* Official language. See main entry under Spain.

Tacana (Takana) [tna] 1,821 (2000 W. Adelaar). Ethnic population: 5,058 (2000 W. Adelaar). Beni and Madre de Dios rivers, jungle, some in foothills. *Class:* Tacanan, Araona-Tacana, Cavinena-Tacana, Tacana Proper. *Lg Use:* Speakers also use Spanish. *Lg Dev:* Dictionary. Grammar. NT: 1981.

Tapieté (Guasurango, Tirumbae, Yanaigua, Ñanagua) [tpj] 70 in Bolivia (2000 W. Adelaar). Ethnic population: 74 in Bolivia (2000 W. Adelaar). Southeast, towns of Samayhuate and Cutaiqui. *Other:* Same as Guasurango in Paraguay. See main entry under Paraguay.

Toba (Qom) [tob] 146 in Bolivia. *Other:* Different from Toba-Pilagá of Argentina or Toba of Paraguay (Toba-Maskoy). See main entry under Argentina.

Toromono (Toromona) [tno] 200 (1983 Varese). Ethnic population: 200 (2000 W. Adelaar). Northwest, close to the Araona, between the upper Madidi and the River Heath. *Class:* Tacanan, Araona-Tacana, Cavinena-Tacana, Tacana Proper. *Other:* They have not been located. May not still exist.

Trinitario (Moxos, Mojos) [trn] 5,500 (2000 SIL). Ethnic population: 20,805 with Ignaciano (2000 W. Adelaar). South central Beni. *Class:* Arawakan, Maipuran, Southern Maipuran, Bolivia-Parana. *Dialects:* Loreto (Loretano), Javierano. *Lg Dev:* NT: 1979. *Other:* Both Trinitario and Ignaciano are included under a term called 'Mojeños', and occasionally 'Moxeños'.

Tsimané (Chimané, Mosetén) [cas] 5,316 (2000 Adelaar). Ethnic population: 5,907. Southwestern Beni Department and along Maniqui River, and towns of San Miguel de Huachi and Santa Ana de Alto Beni. *Class:* Language Isolate. *Dialects:* Gill (2002) reports that Mosetén move into Tsimané communities and function with seemingly no communication difficulties. *Lg Use:* All ages. Mosetén young people are becoming bilingual in Spanish at a rate much faster than the Tsimané. *Lg Dev:* Mosetén has a different orthography but it is not used. Dictionary. NT: 1997. *Other:* Adelaar (1991) considers Mosetén and Tsimané to be 2 separate languages. Fishermen; swidden agriculturalists: bananas, manioc; hunters. Traditional religion.

Uru (Morato, Muratu, Iru-Itu) [ure] 2 (2000 W. Adelaar). Ethnic population: 142 (2000 W. Adelaar). Department of Oruro, Province of Atahuallpa, near Lake Titicaca, near where the Desaguadero River comes out of Titicaca, near Iruitu. *Class:* Uru-Chipaya. *Lg Use:* A few older people 20 years ago. The others were assimilated to Spanish or Central Aymara. *Other:* Those at the south end of Lake Poopo spoke only Aymara and Spanish 15 years ago. May be extinct. Nearly extinct.

Wichí Lhamtés Nocten ("Mataco" Nocten, Oktenai, Nocten, Noctenes, Bolivian "Mataco," Weenhayek) [mtp] 1,811 in Bolivia (1994). Population total all countries: 1,911. Ethnic population: 2,081 (1994). North central Tarija Department, southwest of Pilcomayo River, Cordillera de Pirapo. Also spoken in Argentina. *Class:* Mataco-Guaicuru, Mataco.

Yaminahua (Yaminawa, Jaminawa, Yamanawa) [yaa] 137 in Bolivia (2000 W. Adelaar). Ethnic population: 161 in Bolivia (2000 W. Adelaar). Northwest corner Pando

Department. *Lg Use:* All ages. *Other:* Same dialect or close to that of Peru and Brazil. They came from Brazil. See main entry under Peru.

Yuqui (Yuki, Bia) [yuq] 125 (2000 Adelaar). Ethnic population: 138 (2000 Adelaar). Foothills north of Cochabamba, one location on the Chimoré River. *Class:* Tupi, Tupi-Guarani, Guarayu-Siriono-Jora II. *Dialects:* Close to Sirionó. *Lg Use:* Speakers also use Spanish. *Lg Dev:* Bible portions. *Other:* Nomadic. Bia is a Guaraní name. Foothills.

Yuracare (Yura) [yuz] 2,675 (2000 W. Adelaar). Ethnic population: 3,333 (2000 W. Adelaar). Beni and Cochabamba departments, scattered primarily along the Chapare River. *Class:* Language Isolate. *Dialects:* Mansinyo, Soloto. *Lg Use:* All ages. *Lg Dev:* NT: 1999.

Brazil

Federative Republic of Brazil. República Federativa do Brasil. 184,101,109. Population includes 311,656 American Indians (1995 govt. figure). 155,000 speakers of American Indian languages (1985 Rodrigues). National or official language: Portuguese. There are reports of up to 34 groups without peaceful contact. Literacy rate: 76% (1989 WA). Also includes Assyrian Neo-Aramaic, Catalan-Valencian-Balear, Irish Gaelic, Italian (500,000), Japanese (380,000), Korean (37,000), Latvian, Lithuanian, Standard German (1,500,000), Turoyo, Ukrainian, Vlax Romani. Information mainly from D. Ribeiro 1957; A. Rodrigues 1958; J. Hopper 1967; A. Jensen 1985; D. Derbyshire and G. Pullum 1986; SIL 1957–2003. Blind population: 124,805. Deaf population: 9,624,345. Deaf institutions: 60. The number of languages listed for Brazil is 235. Of those, 188 are living languages and 47 are extinct. See map on page 744.

Acroá (Coroá) [acs] Extinct. Bahia area. *Class:* Macro-Ge, Ge-Kaingang, Ge, Central.

Agavotaguerra (Agavotokueng, Agavotoqueng) [avo] 100 (1986 SIL). Mato Grosso, Xingú Park, between the Curisevo and Culuene rivers, near the Kuikúro. *Class:* Unclassified. *Dialects:* Related to Waurá and Yawalapiti. *Other:* May be extinct.

Amahuaca (Amawáka, Amawaca, Amenguaca, Sayacu) [amc] 220 in Brazil (1995). Amazonas. *Dialects:* Inuvaken, Viwivakeu. See main entry under Peru.

Amanayé (Amanajé, Manaze, Amanage, Manaxo, Manajo, Manazo, Amanyé) [ama] Ethnic population: 60 (2000 C. Jensen). Pará, On the Capim River in São Domingos do Capim Minicipality. *Class:* Tupi, Tupi-Guarani, Subgroup VIII. *Lg Use:* Probably extinct. *Other:* Integrated culturally and linguistically to Portuguese. Nearly extinct.

Amapá Creole (Lanc-Patúa) [amd] 25,000 (1995 SIL). Throughout State of Amapá, concentrated around the capital, Macapá. *Class:* Creole, French based. *Other:* Has English and French influences. Some Indian groups in Amapá speak other creoles, like the Karipúna.

Amikoana (Amikuân) [akn] A few speakers. Northern Amapá. *Class:* Unclassified.

Amundava (Amundawa, Amondawa) [adw] 50 (2000 SIL). Rondônia, Acre, near the Jiparaná River. *Class:* Tupi, Tupi-Guarani, Subgroup VI. *Dialects:* Close to Tenharim.

Anambé [aan] 7 (1991 SIL). Ethnic population: 77 (1993 SIL). Pará, Cairari River, tributary of the Moju River. *Class:* Tupi, Tupi-Guarani, Subgroup VIII. *Dialects:* Close to Asuriní. *Other:* The ethnic group now speaks Portuguese. Nearly extinct.

Apalaí (Aparai, Apalay) [apy] 450 (1993 SIL). 100 monolinguals. Pará, mainly on the Paru Leste River with fringe groups on the Jari and Citare rivers. 20 villages.

Class: Carib, Northern, East-West Guiana, Wayana-Trio.
Lg Use: 75% bilingual in Wayana. *Lg Dev:* Literacy rate
in first language: 10% to 30%. Literacy rate in second
language: 37%. Dictionary. Grammar. NT: 1986. *Other:*
OVS, SOV.

Apiacá (Apiake, Apiaká) [api] 2 (1986 Rodrigues). Ethnic
population: 90 (2000 C. Jensen). Northern Mato Grosso,
upper Rio Tapajos, near confluence of São Manoel, near
the border between Pará and Mato Grosso. *Class:* Tupi,
Tupi-Guarani, Subgroup VI. *Other:* Assimilated into
Brazilian culture and Portuguese language. Nearly extinct.

Apinayé (Apinajé, Apinagé) [apn] 800 (1994 SIL).
Tocantins, near Tocantinópolis, 6 villages. *Class:* Macro-
Ge, Ge-Kaingang, Ge, Northwest, Apinaye. *Lg Use:* Some
speakers also use Portuguese. *Lg Dev:* Literacy rate in
first language: 5% to 10%. Literacy rate in second
language: 15% to 25%. Grammar. NT: 1999. *Other:* SOV.
Between tropical forest and savannah. Hunter-gatherers;
agriculturalists: manioc, sweet potatoes, gourds, cotton.

Apurinã (Ipurinãn, Kangite, Popengare) [apu] 2,000 (1994
SIL). Amazonas, Acre; scattered over a thousand miles of
the Purus River from Rio Branco to Manaus. *Class:*
Arawakan, Maipuran, Southern Maipuran, Purus. *Lg Dev:*
Bible portions: 1993. *Other:* OSV. Traditional religion,
Christian.

Arapaso (Arapaço, Araspaso, Koneá) [arj] 268 (1992
ALEM). São Gabriel, Iauarete, Amazonas. *Class:*
Tucanoan, Eastern Tucanoan, Northern. *Dialects:*
Reported to be a dialect of Tucano. *Lg Use:* Speakers are
shifting to Tucano. *Other:* May be extinct.

Arára, Mato Grosso (Arara do Beiradão, Arara do Rio
Branco) [axg] Extinct. Ethnic population: 100 (1998).
Mato Grosso. *Class:* Unclassified. *Lg Use:* Members of
the ethnic group now speak Portuguese.

Arára, Pará (Ajujure) [aap] 110 (1994 SIL). Pará in 2
villages. *Class:* Carib, Northern, Northern Brazil. *Dialects:*
The closest extant languages are Ikpeng and Bakairí.
Lg Use: A few can speak a little Portuguese. *Other:* Some
groups remain uncontacted. Hunter-gatherers; fishermen.

Araweté (Bïde) [awt] 184 (1994 ALEM). Amazonas, at
least one sizeable village, near Xingú River, near Altamira.
Class: Tupi, Tupi-Guarani, Subgroup V. *Dialects:* Close
to Asuriní, Parakanã, Tapirapé. *Lg Use:* Nearly all
speakers are monolingual (1986).

Arikapú (Maxubí, Aricapú) [ark] 6 (1998 SIL). Rondônia,
headwaters of the Rio Branco, tributary of the right bank
of the Guaporé. *Class:* Macro-Ge, Yabuti. *Dialects:*
Similar to Jabuti. *Lg Use:* Speakers are shifting to
Portuguese. *Other:* Integrated into Brazilian culture and
language. Nearly extinct.

Arikem (Ariken) [ait] Extinct. Rôndonia State, Candeias
and Jamari rivers, tributaries of the upper Madeira. *Class:*
Tupi, Arikem.

Arua (Arawá) [aru] Extinct. *Class:* Arauan. *Lg Use:*
Became extinct in 1877. *Other:* Known from an 1869
word list. Different from Tupi Aruá and Ge Arua.

Aruá [arx] 12 (1990). Ethnic population: 40 (2000 C.
Jensen). Rio Branco post, Branco and Guaporé rivers,
Rondônia. *Class:* Tupi, Monde. *Dialect:* Aruáshi
(Aruachi). *Lg Use:* A few still remember the language.
Most speak Portuguese. *Other:* Said to be many in Mato
Grosso. Voegelin and Voegelin (1977) treat as distinct
from Arawak Arua (Aruan, Araua) and Ge Arua. Nearly
extinct.

Arutani (Auaqué, Auake, Awake, Aoaqui, Oewaku, Uruak,
Urutani, Orotani) [atx] 17 in Brazil (1986 SIL). Population
total all countries: 19. Roraima. Also spoken in Venezuela.
Class: Arutani-Sape. *Lg Use:* Most are intermarried with
the Ninam, some with the Pemon (Arecuna) and a few with
the Sapi and do not speak Arutani fluently. The remaining
speakers also use Ninam. *Other:* Nearly extinct.

Ashéninka, Ucayali-Yurúa (Ucayali Ashéninca) [cpb]
212 to 235 in Brazil (1983 SIL). Acre. *Other:* Intermittent
contact in Brazil. See main entry under Peru.

Asuriní (Assuriní, Assuriní do Tocantins, Asuriní do
Trocará, Akwaya) [asu] 191 (1995 AMTB). Trocará near
Tucurui, on the Tocantins River, Pará. *Class:* Tupi, Tupi-
Guarani, Subgroup IV. *Dialects:* In Akwáwa cluster.
Close to Parakanã. Similar to Suruí do Pará. *Lg Use:*
Speakers are shifting to Portuguese. *Lg Dev:* Literacy rate
in first language: below 1%. Literacy rate in second
language: below 5%. Dictionary. Grammar. Bible
portions: 1973. *Other:* Different from Asuriní do Xingú.
OVS. Agriculturalists: manioc; fishermen.

Asuriní, Xingú (Awaté, Awaeté, Asuriní de Koatinema,
Asuriní do Xingu) [asn] 63 (1994 ALEM). At least one
sizeable village, on Rio Piçava off Xingú River near
Altamira, Pará. *Class:* Tupi, Tupi-Guarani, Subgroup V.
Dialects: Different from Asuriní of the Tocantins
(Akwaya), and Arawete. *Lg Use:* Most speakers have low
proficiency in Portuguese.

Atorada (Atorad, Ator'ti, Dauri, Atorai) [aox] Few
speakers in Brazil (2000). Roraima. *Lg Use:* Speakers are
older than 50 years. Speakers also use Portuguese. *Other:*
Different from Atruahí. See main entry under Guyana.

Atruahí (Atroaí, Atroarí, Atrowari, Atroahy, Ki'nya) [atr]
350 (1995 SIL). On the Alalau and Camanau rivers on the
border between the state of Amazonas and the territory of
Roraima, and on the Jatapu and Jauaperi rivers. 24 villages.
Class: Carib, Northern, East-West Guiana, Waimiri.
Dialects: Atruahi, Waimirí (Uaimirí, Wahmirí), Jawaperi
(Yauaperi). Related to Sapara, Pauxiana, Piriutite, and
Tiquiriá. *Other:* Contacted by Waiwai people in 1968.
Different from Atorada. Traditional religion.

Aurá (Auré) [aux] 2 (2004 SIL). Live with the Guajá in
Maranhão. Originally lived in Pará. *Class:* Tupi, Tupi-
Guarani. *Other:* Nearly extinct.

Avá-Canoeiro (Canoeiros, Canoe, Canoa, Avá, Abá,
Awana) [avv] 56 (1995 SIL). Goiás, Island of Bananal,
and the upper Tocantins River valley. *Class:* Tupi, Tupi-
Guarani, Subgroup IV. *Lg Use:* All monolingual
speakers. *Other:* FUNAI contacted another group of 15
in 1983 close to the Tocantins River. Seminomadic.
Traditional religion.

Awetí (Awetö, Aueto, Aueti, Auiti, Arauite, Arauine)
[awe] 90 (2000 SIL). Xingú Park, Mato Grosso, Rio
Culiseu (upper Xingú River). *Class:* Tupi, Aweti.
Lg Use: May be bilingual in Kamayurá. *Other:* Tropical
forest. Fishermen; hunter-gatherers; swidden
agriculturalists: manioc, maize.

Bakairí (Bacairí, Kurâ) [bkq] 570 (1994 SIL). Mato
Grosso in 9 or 10 villages. *Class:* Carib, Southern, Xingu
Basin. *Lg Use:* Speakers have some proficiency in
Portuguese. *Lg Dev:* Literacy rate in first language: below
1%. Literacy rate in second language: 15% to 25%.
Grammar. Bible portions: 1969–1976. *Other:* SOV, OVS.

Banawá (Kitiya, Banavá, Banauá, Jafí) [bnh] 100 (2002
SIL). Amazonas, upriver quite a distance from the
Jamamadí. Half live on the Banawá River, others on small
creeks and in scattered locations; 1 village and 2 extended
family settlements. *Class:* Arauan. *Dialects:* Not as close
to Jamamadí linguistically as previously thought. *Lg Use:*
Positive language attitude. Some speakers also use
Jamamadí or Portuguese. *Lg Dev:* Literacy rate in first
language: below 1%. Literacy rate in second language:
below 5%. *Other:* They call themselves 'Kitiya'. Tropical
forest.

Baniwa (Baniua do Içana, Maniba, Baniva, Baniba, Issana,
Dakenei) [bwi] 5,460 in Brazil (1983 SIL). Population
includes 4,057 Baniwa, 1,000 Hohodené, 403 Seuci.
Population total all countries: 5,893. Middle Içana River,
Amazonas. They go to Colombia or Venezuela mainly to

work or trade. Also spoken in Venezuela. *Class:*
Arawakan, Maipuran, Northern Maipuran, Inland.
Dialects: Hohodené (Hohodena, Kadaupuritana), Siusy-
Tapuya (Seuci, Siuci, Siusi). Related to Carutana and
Curripaco. Several groups on the middle Içana and Ayarí
rivers who speak Baniwa: Hohodené, Kadaupuritana,
Sucuriyu-Tapuya, Siusy-Tapuya, Irá-Tapuya, Kawá-
Tapuya, Waliperedakenai (Ribeiro 1967). *Lg Dev:* NT:
1965–1985. *Other:* 'Kohoroxitari' may be another name
for Baniwa.

Bororô (Boe) [bor] 850 (1994 SIL). Central Mato Grosso,
8 villages. *Class:* Macro-Ge, Bororo, Bororo Proper.
Lg Dev: Literacy rate in first language: 10% to 30%.
Literacy rate in second language: 15% to 25%. NT: 1993.
Other: SOV.

Brazilian Sign Language (Lsb, São Paulo Sign
Language) [bzs] São Paulo, Rio de Janeiro, Minas Gerais,
Santa Catarina, and elsewhere. *Class:* Deaf sign language.
Dialects: The dialects appear to be inherently intelligible,
although northern dialects above the Amazon show greater
differences. Some relationship to North American and
European sign languages. *Lg Dev:* TV. Dictionary.
Other: The fingerspelling used for proper names is similar
to a European system. The first deaf school was begun in
1857 in Rio de Janeiro, then one in Porto Alegre. The deaf
in São Paulo generally receive an oralist education.

Cafundo Creole [ccd] 40 (1978 M. Gnerre, U. Estadual
de Campinas). Cafundo, 150 miles from São Paulo.
Class: Creole, Portuguese based. *Lg Use:* Speakers are
fluent in Portuguese. *Other:* Bantu lexicon in Portuguese
morphological and syntactic framework. The creole is
considered a secret language. A similar creole has been
recently discovered in Minas Gerais. Nearly extinct.

Caló (Calo, Gitano, Iberian Romani) [rmr] 10,000 in Latin
America. *Dialect:* Brazilian Calão. *Lg Use:* Speakers also
use Portuguese. *Other:* A cryptolectal variety of
Portuguese. Christian. See main entry under Spain.

Canela (Kanela) [ram] 1,420 (1995 SIL). Population
includes 950 Ramkokamekra, 470 Apanjekra (1995 SIL).
Maranhão, southeastern Pará. *Class:* Macro-Ge, Ge-
Kaingang, Ge, Northwest, Timbira. *Dialects:* Apanjekra
(Apanhecra, Apaniekra), Ramkokamekra. *Lg Dev:*
Grammar. NT: 1990. *Other:* SOV. Hunters;
agriculturalists: maize, yams. Traditional religion.

Carib (Caribe, Cariña, Kalihna, Kalinya, Galibí,
Maraworno, Marworno) [car] 100 in Brazil (1995 SIL).
State of Amapá. *Dialect:* Tyrewuju (Eastern Carib).
Other: Called 'Galibi' in Brazil. Portuguese-Carib creole
people (Galibí do Uaça) also speak Crioulo (French
Creole). See main entry under Venezuela.

Carútana (Karutana, Arara do Amazonas) [cru] 300
(2000). Northwest Amazonas, near Curripaco. *Class:*
Arawakan, Maipuran, Northern Maipuran, Inland.
Dialects: Adaru, Arara, Dzaui (Dzawi), Jauarete
(Yawarete Tapuya), Jurupari (Yurupari Tapuya), Mapache,
Uadzoli (Wadzoli), Urubu. Close to Curripaco and
Baniwa. Arara may be distinct.

Cashinahua (Cashinahuá, Kaxinawá, Kaxinauá,
Kaxynawa, Caxinawá) [cbs] 400 in Brazil (2003). Acre.
Lg Use: Speakers have some proficiency in Portuguese.
See main entry under Peru.

Chiripá (Nhandeva, Ñandeva, Tsiripá, Txiripá, Apytare,
Guaraní) [nhd] 4,900 in Brazil (1995 AMTB). Mato
Grosso do Sul State, Paraná, Santa Catarina, Rio Grande
do Sul, São Paulo. *Dialect:* Apapocuva. *Lg Use:* In
Brazil, the group is shifting to Portuguese. Speakers are
older adults. *Other:* In Brazil it has been influenced by
Paraguayan Guaraní, Mbyá, and Kaiwá. Most speakers are
from the Apapocuva group, which has been described by
ethnographers. Called 'Nhandeva' in Brazil. The name
'Ñandeva' is used in the Paraguayan Chaco for Tapiete,

a different but related language. See main entry under
Paraguay.

Cinta Larga [cin] 1,000 (1995 SIL). Western Mato
Grosso. *Class:* Tupi, Monde. *Other:* Some are still
uncontacted. Rodrigues lists Zoró, Cinta Larga, and
Gavião as separate languages (1986).

Cocama-Cocamilla (Cocama, Kokama) [cod] 50 in
Brazil (2000 SIL). Ethnic population: 411 in Brazil (2000
D. Moore). Amazonas. *Dialect:* Cocama, Cocamilla
(Kokamilla). *Lg Use:* The speakers in Brazil are trilingual
in Spanish, Portuguese, and Cocama. See main entry
under Peru.

Cubeo (Pamié, Cuveo, Cubeu, Kobeua, Kobewa, Kubwa,
Kobéwa, Hehenawa, Pamiwa) [cub] 150 in Brazil (1986
SIL). Northwest Amazonas, near São Gabriel. See main
entry under Colombia.

Culina (Kulína, Kulyna, Corina, Madija, Madihá) [cul] 903
in Brazil (2000 WCD). Population total all countries:
1,303. Amazonas, Acre. Also spoken in Peru. *Class:*
Arauan. *Dialects:* Minor changes from Peruvian dialect.
Lg Dev: Bible portions: 1965–1985. *Other:* SOV.

Curripaco (Curipaco, Kuripako, Koripako, Korispaso)
[kpc] 810 in Brazil (1995 AMTB). Northwest Amazonas.
Dialects: Korripako (Karupaka), Unhun (Cadauapuritana,
Enhen). See main entry under Colombia.

Dâw ("Kamã," Kamã Makú) [kwa] 83 (1994 ALEM).
Amazonas, across the river from São Gabriel de
Cochoeira, a county seat just below the confluence of
the Vaupés and Negro rivers. *Class:* Maku. *Other:* They
call themselves 'Dâw'.

Dení (Dani) [dny] 750 (2002 SIL). Amazonas. *Class:*
Arauan. *Dialect:* Inauini. *Lg Dev:* Dictionary. *Other:*
Sometimes called 'Jamamadí', but that is a separate
language.

Desano (Desâna, Dessano, Wina, Uina, Wirã, Boleka,
Oregu, Kusibi) [des] 960 in Brazil (1995 SIL). Population
total all countries: 1,760. Northwestern Amazonas. Also
spoken in Colombia. *Class:* Tucanoan, Eastern Tucanoan,
Central, Desano. *Lg Use:* In Brazil speakers generally use
Tucano instead of Desano. *Lg Dev:* NT: 1984. *Other:*
Some form of whistle speech reported.

Enawené-Nawé (Eneuene-Mare, Salumã) [unk] 165
(1995). Mato Grosso within northeast Nambiquara reserve.
Class: Arawakan, Maipuran, Central Maipuran. *Dialects:*
Related to Parecís. *Other:* Another village of 30 to 50
people of totally different design is near this. Distinct from
Carib Salumá in Pará.

Fulniô (Furniô, Fornió, Carnijó, Iatê, Yatê) [fun] 2,788
(1995 SIL). Pernambuco. *Class:* Macro-Ge, Fulnio.
Dialects: Fulniô, Yatê. Lexical similarity 98% between
Fulniô and Yatê dialects. *Lg Use:* Fulniô language is
mainly used in 3-month annual religious retreat. Speakers
also use Portuguese. *Other:* Subsistence agriculturalists:
beans, cotton.

Gavião do Jiparaná (Gavião do Rondônia, Digüt,
Ikõro) [gvo] 472 (2002 SIL). Rondônia (Gavião). *Class:*
Tupi, Monde. *Dialect:* Gavião, Zoró (Panginey, Cabeça
Seca). Partially intelligible with Suruí. Rodrigues lists
Zoró and Cinta Larga as separate languages from Gavião
(1986). *Lg Dev:* Bible portions: 1988. *Other:* Different
from Gavião of Pará, which is Je.

Gavião, Pará (Parakatêjê, Pukobjê) [gvp] 180 (1995
SIL). State of Pará, in a new village called
'Kaikoturé', near Marabá. Some live scattered in or
near their original locations in Maranhão and Pará.
Class: Macro-Ge, Ge-Kaingang, Ge, Northwest,
Timbira. *Dialects:* Related to Krikati-Timbira, Canela,
Krahô. *Lg Use:* Positive language attitude. Increasing
use of regional Portuguese as second language.
Schools are in Portuguese. *Other:* They call
themselves 'Parakatêjê Indian Community'. 'Gavião',

meaning 'hawk', is used by outsiders. Not to be confused with the Gavião of Rondônia.

Guajá (Awá, Awá Guajá, Ayaya, Wazaizara, Guaxare) [gvj] 370 (1995 AMTB). Maranhão, babassu palm area near Gurupi and Upper Pindaré rivers, some in Serra Canastra, Tocantins, and Guamá Post in Pará. At least 6 isolated groups. *Class:* Tupi, Tupi-Guarani, Subgroup VIII. *Dialects:* Related to Guajajára. *Lg Use:* Speakers have low proficiency in Portuguese. *Other:* Hunter-gatherers.

Guajajára (Guazazzara, Tenetehar, Tenetehára) [gub] 15,000 (2000 SIL). Maranhco, Pindaré, Grajaú, Mearim, and Zutiua rivers, 81 villages. *Class:* Tupi, Tupi-Guarani, Subgroup IV. *Dialects:* Pindare, Zutiua, Mearim, Tembe of Gurupi. *Lg Use:* Speakers have some proficiency in Portuguese. *Lg Dev:* Literacy rate in first language: 30%. Literacy rate in second language: 30%. Grammar. NT: 1985.

Guana (Kinikinao, Chuala, Chana, East Paraná, Kinihinao, Equinao) [gqn] Extinct. Mato Grosso do Sul, near the Terêna. *Class:* Arawakan, Maipuran, Southern Maipuran, Bolivia-Parana. *Dialects:* Related to Terêna, Iranche.

Guanano (Wanána, Wanano, Uanana, Anana, Kótedia, Kótirya) [gvc] 550 in Brazil (1995 AMTB). Population total all countries: 1,000. Northwest Amazonas. Also spoken in Colombia. *Class:* Tucanoan, Eastern Tucanoan, Northern. *Lg Dev:* NT: 1982. *Other:* SOV.

Guaraní, Mbyá (Mbyá, Mbua, Mbiá, Bugre) [gun] 5,000 in Brazil (2000 Dooley). Population total all countries: 16,050. Southwestern Paraná, southeastern São Paulo, Santa Catarina, Rio Grande do Sul, Espíritu Santo, Minas Gerais. 35 villages in 7 states. Also spoken in Argentina, Paraguay, Uruguay. *Class:* Tupi, Tupi-Guarani, Subgroup I. *Dialects:* Tambéopé, Baticola. Lexical similarity 75% with Paraguayan Guaraní. *Lg Use:* Bilingual level estimates for Portuguese: Female: 0 30%, 1 50%, 2 18%, 3 2%, 4 0%, 5 0%; Male: 0 2%, 1 22%, 2 50%, 3 20%, 4 4%, 5 2%; Total: 0 16%, 1 36%, 2 34%, 3 11%, 4 2%, 5 1%. *Lg Dev:* Literacy rate in first language: 10% to 30%. Literacy rate in second language: 15% to 25%. NT: 1987. *Other:* SVO.

Guarequena (Urequema, Warekéna, Werekena, Uerequema, Werikena, Arequena) [gae] 338 in Brazil (1983 NTM). Amazonas, Rio Chié (Xié) and Içana near Venezuelan border. *Lg Use:* Spoken in remote areas. Positive language attitude. Many speak Nhengatu in Brazil. Those in centers are more bilingual. See main entry under Venezuela.

Guató [gta] 40 (1993 SIL). Ethnic population: 382 (1993 SIL). Mato Grosso do Sul and Bolivian border, banks of the Paraguai and going up the São Lourenço rivers. *Class:* Macro-Ge, Guato. *Other:* Nearly extinct.

Himarimã [hir] 40. Amazonas, Tapayá Valley, near the Jamamadi and Jarawara. *Class:* Unclassified. *Other:* Nearly extinct.

Hixkaryána (Hixkariana, Hishkaryana, Parukoto-Charuma, Parucutu, Chawiyana, Kumiyana, Sokaka, Wabui, Faruaru, Sherewyana, Xerewyana, Xereu, Hichkaryana) [hix] 600 (2000 SIL). Population includes 89 Xereuyana (1986 SIL). Ethnic population: 600 (2000). Amazonas, upper Nhamunda River to Mapuera and Jatapú rivers. *Class:* Carib, Southern, Southern Guiana. *Dialects:* Close to Waiwai. No dialectal variation. The Sherewyana speak the same language but some live with the Waiwai. *Lg Use:* Bilingual level estimates for Portuguese: 0 85%, 1 10%, 2 5%, 3 0%, 4 0%, 5 0%. *Lg Dev:* Literacy rate in first language: 30% to 60%. Literacy rate in second language: 25% to 50%. Grammar. NT: 1976. *Other:* In 1959 when linguists arrived, the population was about 100, with few children, high infant mortality, low will to live; by 1977 it was 237. Through modern medicine, intermarrying with the Waiwai, self-confidence through literature in Hixkaryana, 5 Hixkaryana teachers running a school for children ages 5 to 14, and government help in setting up a Brazil nut industry, they have continued to grow. OVS.

Hupdë ("Hupdá Makú," "Jupdá Macú," "Makú-Hupdá," "Macú de Tucano," Ubdé) [jup] 1,208 in Brazil (1995 SIL). Population total all countries: 1,358. Rio Auari, northwestern Amazonas. Also spoken in Colombia. *Class:* Maku. *Dialects:* Hupdë, Tuhup, Nëhup. Ruhlen and others classify it as Puinave, Macro-Tucanoan. Intelligibility among Yahup, Tuhup, and Nëhup needs investigation. Tuhup and Nëhup may be extinct. *Lg Use:* Possibly 50% also use Tucano or some other Tucanoan language. *Other:* They are subservient to the Tucano and other Tucanoan Indians. The name "Macú" is offensive. Some are nomadic between Brazil and Colombia. Tropical forest.

Iapama [iap] Border region of Pará and Amapá. *Class:* Unclassified. *Other:* Existence uncertain.

Ikpeng (Txikão, Txikân, Chicao, Tunuli, Tonore) [txi] 146 (1995). Xingú Park, Mato Grosso. *Class:* Carib, Northern, Northern Brazil. *Dialects:* Similar to Arara of Pará. *Lg Use:* Speakers have low proficiency in Portuguese. *Other:* Agriculturalists: maize, manioc, cotton, urucu, gourds; hunter-gatherers; fishermen.

Ingarikó (Acewaio, Akawai, Akawaio, Acahuayo) [ake] 500 in Brazil. Roraima and Rio Branco. *Lg Use:* Some speakers also use Portuguese. See main entry under Guyana (Akawaio).

Ipeka-Tapuia (Pato-Tapuya, Pato Tapuia, Cumata, Ipeca, Pacu, Paku-Tapuya, Payuliene, Payualiene, Palioariene) [paj] 135 (1976 RC). Içana, Amazonas. *Class:* Arawakan, Maipuran, Northern Maipuran, Inland. *Dialect:* Waliperi (Veliperi). Voegelin and Voegelin (1977) treat it as a dialect of Siuci (see Baniwa). *Other:* They may all speak Tucano.

Irántxe (Iranxe, Iranche, Münkü) [irn] 191 (1995 AMTB). Mato Grosso, headwaters of the Rio Cravari, tributary of the Rio Sangue, which is a tributary of the Rio Juruena. *Class:* Arawakan, Maipuran, Southern Maipuran, Unclassified. *Dialects:* Münkü (Mynky, Menku, Kenkü, Myy), Irántxe. *Lg Use:* Most also use Portuguese. *Other:* 'Münkü' is a self designation.

Jabutí (Yabutí, Jabotí, Djeoromitxi) [jbt] 5 (1990). Rio Branco Post, Rondônia. *Class:* Macro-Ge, Yabuti. *Other:* Nearly extinct.

Jamamadí (Yamamadí, Kanamanti, Canamanti) [jaa] 195 (1994 SIL). Population includes 12 Mamoria. Amazonas, scattered over 200,000 square miles. *Class:* Arauan. *Dialects:* Bom Futuro, Jurua, Pauini, Mamoria (Mamori), Cuchudua (Maima), Tukurina. Other groups are called 'Jamamadí' which are closer to Culina or Dení. Tukurina may be a separate language. Dialects or related languages: Araua, Pama, Sewacu, Sipo, Yuberi. *Lg Dev:* Literacy rate in first language: 60% to 100%. Literacy rate in second language: 75% to 100%. Bible portions: 1991. *Other:* People want a school. OSV. Christian, traditional religion.

Jaruára (Jarawara, Yarawara) [jap] 155 (2000 SIL). Amazonas, Lábrea Minicipality, near the Jamamadí, 7 villages. *Class:* Arauan. *Dialects:* Formerly considered a dialect of Jamamadí. *Lg Use:* Vigorous. Used in school, religious services, letters. All ages. Everyone speaks some Portuguese. *Lg Dev:* Literacy rate in first language: 30%. Literacy rate in second language: 5% to 15%. *Other:* Village locations change slightly every few years. Some Jaruára have moved to Brazilian settlements. OSV. Lowland. Rainforest. Subsistence agriculturalists; hunters; fishermen. Traditional religion, Christian.

Júma (Yumá, Katauixi, Arara, Kagwahiva, Kagwahibm, Kagwahiv, Kawahip, Kavahiva, Kagwahiph) [jua] 4 (1998). There were 300 in 1940. Amazonas, Rio

Açuã, tributary of the Mucuim. *Class:* Tupi, Tupi-Guaraní, Subgroup VI. *Other:* Call themselves 'Kagwahiva'. SVO. Tropical forest. Nearly extinct.

Jurúna (Yurúna, Iuruna, Jaruna, Yudya) [jur] 181 (1998 SIL). Xingú Park, northern Mato Grosso, near mouth of the Maritsauá-Mitau River, 2 villages. *Class:* Tupi, Yuruna. *Lg Use:* Some speakers also use Portuguese. *Other:* Agriculturalists: manioc; fishermen.

Kabixí (Cabichí, Cabishi) [xbx] 100 (1986 SIL). Slopes of Planalto dos Parecís, right bank of upper Guaporé, near Vila Bela, Mato Grosso. *Class:* Chapacura-Wanham, Guapore. *Dialects:* Related to Cujuna, Cumana, Mataua, Wanham, Urunumacan. *Lg Use:* Both people and language may be extinct. *Other:* The name is also used for Parecís or Nambikuára.

Kadiwéu (Mbaya-Guaikuru, Caduvéo, Ediu-Adig) [kbc] 1,200 (1995 SIL). Mato Grosso do Sul, around Serra da Bodoquena. 3 villages. *Class:* Mataco-Guaicuru, Guaicuruan. *Lg Dev:* Literacy rate in first language: 1% to 5%. Literacy rate in second language: 25% to 50%. NT: 1999. *Other:* 'Payagua' may be a term for 'enemy' applied to this group. SVO.

Kaimbé [xai] Extinct. Ethnic population: 1,100 to 1,400 (1986 SIL). Bahía. *Class:* Unclassified. *Lg Use:* Members of the ethnic group now speak Portuguese.

Kaingáng (Coroado, Coroados, Caingang, Bugre) [kgp] 18,000 (1989 SIL). São Paulo, Paraná, Santa Catarina, Rio Grande do Sul; 21 locations. Central Kaingang is in São Paulo and Santa Catarina. *Class:* Macro-Ge, Ge-Kaingang, Kaingang, Northern. *Dialects:* Paraná Kaingang, Central Kaingang, Southwest Kaingang, Southeast Kaingang. *Lg Use:* Speakers have some proficiency in Portuguese. *Lg Dev:* Dictionary. NT: 1977. *Other:* The name 'Bugre' is also used for Xokleng and Mbyá Guaraní. SOV.

Kaingáng, São Paulo [zkp] Extinct. São Paulo. *Class:* Macro-Ge, Ge-Kaingang, Kaingang, Northern.

Kaiwá (Caiwa, Caingua, Cayua, Caiua, Kayova, Kaiova) [kgk] 15,000 in Brazil (1994 SIL). Population total all countries: 15,512. Mato Grosso do Sul. Also spoken in Argentina. *Class:* Tupi, Tupi-Guaraní, Subgroup I. *Dialects:* Teüi, Tembekuá, Kaiwá. Somewhat intelligible with Paraguayan Guaraní. Lexical similarity 70% with Pai Tavytera of Paraguay. *Lg Dev:* Literacy rate in first language: 5% to 10%. Literacy rate in second language: 15% to 25%. NT: 1986.

Kamakan (Ezeshio) [vkm] Extinct. Bahia area. *Class:* Macro-Ge, Kamakan.

Kamayurá (Kamaiurá, Camaiura, Kamayirá) [kay] 279 (1995 AMTB). Xingú Park, Mato Grosso. *Class:* Tupi, Tupi-Guaraní, Subgroup VII. *Lg Use:* Some speakers also use Portuguese. *Other:* Hunters; fishermen; agriculturalists.

Kamba (Camba) [xba] Extinct. Ethnic population: 2,000 (1986 SIL). Mato Grosso do Sul, near Corumbá. *Class:* Unclassified. *Dialects:* May have been Tupí. *Lg Use:* Ethnic group came from Bolivia, and now speak Spanish.

Kambiwá [xbw] Extinct. Ethnic population: 1,108 (1995 SIL). Pernambuco. *Class:* Unclassified. *Lg Use:* Members of the ethnic group now speak Portuguese.

Kanamarí (Kanamaré, Canamarí) [knm] 647 (1995 SIL). Amazonas, upper regions of Jurua, Jutai, Itaquai rivers. *Class:* Katukinan. *Dialect:* Tshom-Djapa (Txunhuã-Djapá, Txunhuã Dyapá).

Kanoé (Canoé, Guarátégaya, Guarategaja, Koaratira, Guaratira, Amniapé, Mekem, Mekéns, Mequem, Mequen, Mequens, Muki) [kxo] Extinct. Ethnic population: 150 (2000 C. Jensen). Rondônia, Guaporé River, scattered locations. *Class:* Tupi, Monde. *Lg Use:* Members of the ethnic group now speak Portuguese. *Other:* Distinct from Ava (Canoeiros).

Kapinawá [xpn] Extinct. Ethnic population: 354 (1995 AMTB). Pernambuco. *Class:* Unclassified. *Lg Use:* Members of the ethnic group now speak Portuguese.

Karahawyana [xkh] 40 (1995 SIL). Amazonas, near the Waiwai. *Class:* Unclassified. *Dialects:* Probably Cariban. *Lg Use:* Today some live with the Waiwai and some near the Hixkaryana, and speak those languages. *Other:* Nearly extinct.

Karajá (Xambioá, Chamboa, Ynã) [kpj] 1,700 (1995 SIL). Population includes 383 Javaé (1986 SIL). Goiás, Pará, Mato Grosso, Araguaia River, Bananal Island, and Tocantins. *Class:* Macro-Ge, Karaja. *Dialect:* Javaé (Javahe). Men and women speak different dialects. *Lg Dev:* Literacy rate in second language: 70%. Grammar. NT: 1983. *Other:* Agriculturalists; hunters.

Karapanã (Carapana, Carapanã, Mextã) [cbc] 50 in Brazil (1986 SIL). São Gabriel and Pari-Cachoeira, Amazonas. See main entry under Colombia (Carapana).

Karipúna (Karipúna do Uaçá, Karipúna do Amapá) [kgm] Extinct. Territory of Amapá, on French Guiana border. *Class:* Tupi, Tupi-Guaraní, Subgroup VI. *Lg Use:* Members of the ethnic group now speak Karipúna Creole French.

Karipuná (Karipuná do Guaporé, Caripuna, Jau-Navo, Juanauo, Karipuná de Rondônia, Kagwahiva) [kuq] 12 to 15 (2000 SIL). Rondônia, Acre, banks of Jaru, Jamery, Urupa, Cabecciras, Candeias, and Jaciparana rivers. *Class:* Tupi, Tupi-Guaraní, Subgroup VI. *Dialect:* Jacaria, Pama (Pamana). Loukotka identified this as Panoan. *Lg Use:* They may be bilingual in Tenharim. *Other:* There may be more in the forest. Nearly extinct.

Karipúna Creole French (Crioulo) [kmv] 672 (1995 SIL). Amapá, on French Guiana border. *Class:* Creole, French based. *Dialects:* There are conflicting reports about how different it is from Guianese Creole French. It is different from Haitian Creole. *Lg Use:* Some speakers also use Portuguese. *Lg Dev:* Grammar. *Other:* Speakers formerly spoke Karipúna, an unclassified language, possibly formerly from Marajó Island at the mouth of the Amazon. SVO. Islands. Tropical forest, swamp. Fishermen; swidden agriculturalists: manioc. Traditional religion, Christian.

Kariri-Xocó (Karirí, Kariri Xucó, Kipeá, Xokó-Kariri, Xukuru Kariri, Xukurú, Xocó, Xokó) [kzw] Extinct. Ethnic population: 1,062 (1995 SIL). Alagoas. *Class:* Unclassified. *Dialects:* Kipeá (Quipea), Kamurú (Camuru), Dzubukuá (Dzubucua), Sabujá (Pedra Branca). Other dialects or languages are even less well attested. Classified as Equatorial (Greenberg 1959), Macro-Carib (Swadesh 1959), Macro-Ge (Rodrigues 1975), Isolate (Rivet and Loukotka 1952, Larsen 1984). *Lg Use:* Members of the ethnic group now speak Portuguese. *Lg Dev:* Grammar.

Karitiâna (Caritiana) [ktn] 200 (2000 SIL). Rondônia, Candeias River, tributary of the upper Madeira River. *Class:* Tupi, Arikem. *Lg Dev:* Dictionary. Grammar. Bible portions: 1981. *Other:* SVO.

Karo (Itogapúk, Itogapuc, Ntogapig, Ntogapid, Ramarama, Itanga, Arara-Karo, Uruku, Arára do Jiparaná, Arára) [arr] 150 (2000 SIL). Rondônia, and Mato Grosso. *Class:* Tupi, Ramarama. *Dialect:* Karo. *Lg Use:* Most speakers have low proficiency in Portuguese. *Other:* Different from Arára do Pará in Carib family.

Katawixi (Catawixi, Catauixi, Catawishi, Catauichi) [xat] 10 (1986 SIL). Amazonas. *Class:* Katukinan. *Other:* Nearly extinct.

Katukína (Katukina do Jutaí, Pidá-Djapá, Catuquina) [kav] 1 (1976 SIL). Ethnic population: 360. Acre. *Class:* Katukinan. *Dialect:* Cutiadapa (Kutia-Dyapa). *Other:* Different from Panoan Katukína in Amazonas and Acre. Nearly extinct.

Katukína, Panoan (Catuquina, Waninnawa, Kamanawa, Kamannaua, Katukina do Juruá) [knt] 196 (1995 AMTB). Amazonas, Acre. *Class:* Panoan, Southeastern. *Dialects:* Arara-Shawanawa (Shawanawa-Arara), Ararapina, Ararawa, Sanainawa (Saninawacana). Possibly intelligible with Marubo. *Other:* Different from other Katukína (Katukinan Family) in Acre.

Kaxararí (Kaxariri) [ktx] 220 (1995 AMTB). Alto Rio Marmelo, tributary of Rio Abuna, Acre, Rondônia, Amazonas. *Class:* Panoan, Eastern. *Lg Use:* Some speakers also use Portuguese. *Other:* Different from Arawakan Casharari (Cacharari; Voegelin and Voegelin 1977:215).

Kaxuiâna (Kashuyana, Kashujana, Kachuana, Warikyana, Warikiana, Kaxúyana) [kbb] 434 (1986 SIL). Population includes 300 Warikyana, 134 Kaxuiâna. Imabu River near perimetral norte, on Trombetes River near junction with Mapuwera, northwestern Para. A few are living with the Hixkaryána; most with the Trió. *Class:* Carib, Southern, Southern Guiana. *Dialect:* Pawiyana (Pawixi). *Lg Use:* Some speakers have routine proficiency in Trió.

Kayabí (Kajabí, Caiabi, Parua, Maquiri) [kyz] 800 (1994 SIL). Northern Mato Grosso, Xingú Park, and southern Para; Teles Pires River and Tatui, many villages. *Class:* Tupi, Tupi-Guarani, Subgroup V. *Lg Dev:* Literacy rate in first language: 1% to 5%. Literacy rate in second language: below 5%. Grammar. NT: 1999. *Other:* OSV.

Kayapó (Kokraimoro) [txu] 4,000 (1994 SIL). 3,950 monolinguals. Population includes 469 Xikrin (1986 SIL). Ethnic population: 4,000. Xingú Park, Mato Grosso, southern Pará, both sides of the Xingú River, on the west up to the Iriri and its tributaries, and on the west bank to the Fresco and Zinho rivers, 14 villages. *Class:* Macro-Ge, Ge-Kaingang, Ge, Northwest, Kayapo. *Dialects:* Xikrin (Xukru, Diore), Kararaó, Kayapó-Kradaú. Those listed as dialects are only slightly different. *Lg Use:* Vigorous. All domains. Spoken and written Kayapó used in religious services. Initial education is in Kayapó. Positive language attitude. 50 also speak some Portuguese. *Lg Dev:* Literacy rate in first language: 5% to 10%. Literacy rate in second language: 5% to 15%. 400 speakers can read Kayapó, 100 can write it. Taught in primary schools. Grammar. NT: 1996. *Other:* Village names sometimes listed as dialects are: Txukuhamai (Txucarramãe), Gorotire, Kube-Kran-Kenh (Cabeca Pelada), Kokraimoro, Menkragnotire (Mentuktire, Kuben-Kragnotire, Gente Preta, Kubenkrangnoti, Kubenkrankegn, Menkrangnoti), Pacajá, and others. SOV. Tropical forest, savannah. Hunter-gatherers traditionally. Traditional religion, Christian.

Kepkiriwát [kpn] Extinct. Rôndonia, formerly on the Pimenta Bueno River. *Class:* Tupi, Tupari.

Kohoroxitari [kob] 622 (1976 RC). Amazonas, Prelazia Rio Negro. *Class:* Unclassified. *Other:* Possibly Tucanoan. May be the same as Baniwa.

Korubo (Caceteiros) [xor] 500 (1995 AMTB). Amazonas. *Class:* Unclassified. *Dialects:* Possibly Panoan. May be the same as Marúbo, or related to Yanomámi.

Krahô (Craô, Kraô) [xra] 1,200 (1988 SIL). Maranhão, southeastern Pará, Tocantins, 5 villages. *Class:* Macro-Ge, Ge-Kaingang, Ge, Northwest, Timbira. *Dialects:* Different from Canela, but may be able to use literature adapted from Canela. *Lg Use:* Few speakers also use Portuguese. *Other:* The Krahô do not accept the name 'Canela'. SOV.

Kreen-Akarore (Kren Akarore, Panará) [kre] 122 (1995 AMTB). Xingú Park, northern Mato Grosso. *Class:* Macro-Ge, Ge-Kaingang, Ge, Northwest, Kreen-Akarore. *Dialects:* Not a dialect of Kayapó; possibly closer to Canela. *Lg Use:* Some speakers also use Portuguese. *Other:* Agriculturalists; hunter-gatherers.

Krenak [kqq] 80 (1989 SIL). Left margin of Doce River, on reservations in east São Paulo, Mato Grosso, Paraná.

Class: Macro-Ge, Botocudo. *Lg Use:* Speakers also use Portuguese.

Kreye (Krem-Ye, Crenge, Crange, Creye, Crenye, Taze, Tage) [xre] 30 (1995 SIL). Maranhão and Pará. *Class:* Macro-Ge, Ge-Kaingang, Ge, Northwest, Timbira. *Other:* Nearly extinct.

Krikati-Timbira [xri] 420 (1995). Maranhão, southeastern Pará, Tocantins. The Timbira are in Governador Village, Municipality of Amarante. *Class:* Macro-Ge, Ge-Kaingang, Ge, Northwest, Timbira. *Dialects:* Krinkati (Karakati), Timbira. The Krikati and Timbira are separate ethnic groups speaking related dialects. *Lg Use:* Few speakers also use Portuguese. *Other:* SOV.

Kuikúro-Kalapálo (Kuikuru, Guicurú, Kurkuro, Cuicutl, Kalapalo, Apalakiri, Apalaquiri) [kui] 526 (1995 AMTB). Population includes 277 Kuikúro and 249 Kalapálo. Xingú Park, Mato Grosso, three villages along the Culuene River. *Class:* Carib, Southern, Xingu Basin. *Dialects:* The Kuikúro and the Kalapálo speak the same language, but are separate ethnically. *Lg Use:* Some speakers also use Portuguese. *Other:* Fishermen; hunters; swidden agriculturalists: manioc, maize.

Kuruáya (Caravare, Curuaia, Kuruaia) [kyr] 52 to 147 (1998). Pará, tributaries of the lower Xingú River. *Class:* Tupi, Munduruku. *Lg Use:* There has been a major shift to Portuguese (1995).

Machinere (Manchinere, Manchineri, Manitenerí, Manitenére, Maxinéri) [mpd] 400 (1995 AMTB). Acre. May also be in Bolivia. *Class:* Arawakan, Maipuran, Southern Maipuran, Purus. *Dialects:* Distinct enough from Yine (Piro) in Peru to need separate literature. Manitenére may be different from Machinere. *Lg Dev:* Bible portions: 1960.

Macuna (Makuna, Buhagana, Baigana, Wuhána, Jepa-Matsi, Yepá-Mahsá, Yehpá Majsá, Yepá Maxsã, Yebamasã, Paneroa) [myy] 100 in Brazil (1973 RC). Rio Chié, Amazonas. See main entry under Colombia.

Macushi (Makusi, Makuxi, Macusi, Makushi, Teweya, Teueia) [mbc] 15,000 in Brazil. Population total all countries: 24,600. Contingo, Quino, Pium, and Mau rivers, northeast Roraima and Rio Branco. Also spoken in Guyana, Venezuela. *Class:* Carib, Northern, East-West Guiana, Macushi-Kapon, Macushi. *Dialects:* Not intelligible with Arecuna or Patamona. *Lg Use:* Bilingualism increasing in Portuguese. *Lg Dev:* NT: 1996. *Other:* OVS.

Makuráp (Makurápi, Macuráp, Macurapi, Massaka, Kurateg) [mpu] 114 (1995 AMTB). Ethnic population: 700 (2000 C. Jensen). Pororoca Post, Guaporé, and Mequéns rivers, Branco, Rondônia, and scattered locations. *Class:* Tupi, Tupari. *Lg Use:* Children speak Portuguese as first language. Young adults speak Portuguese as second language. *Other:* Intermarriage on same post with speakers of other languages. They call themselves 'Kurateg'.

Mandahuaca (Mandauaca, Mandawáka, Ihini, Maldavaca) [mht] 3 in Brazil (1993 ALEM). Amazonas, upper Cauaboris, tributary of the Rio Negro, Colombian border. *Other:* The name 'Baré' is also used as a cover term for separate languages: Baré, Mandahuaca, Guarekena, Baniwa, Piapoco. See main entry under Venezuela.

Mapidian (Maopityan, Maiopitian, Mawayana, Mahuayana) [mpw] 50 in Brazil (1986 Howard). Roraima, with the Waiwai. Also spoken in Guyana. *Class:* Arawakan, Maipuran, Northern Maipuran, Wapishanan. *Dialects:* Lexical similarity 10% with Wapishana and 20% with Atorada. *Lg Use:* They speak fluent Waiwai. *Other:* Nearly extinct.

Maquiritari (Mayongong, Maquiritare, Maquiritai, Makiritare, Pawana, Soto) [mch] 270 in Brazil (1986 SIL). Roraima. *Dialects:* Cunuana, De'cuana (Wainungomo),

Ihuruana, Maitsi, Mayongong (Ye'cuana, Yekuana). See main entry under Venezuela.

Maritsauá (Manitsawá, Mantizula) [msp] Extinct. Manitsaua-Missu, a tributary of the Upper Xingú, Xingú Park, Mato Grosso. *Class:* Tupi, Yuruna. *Dialect:* Arupai (Urupaya).

Marúbo (Maruba, Marova, Kaniuá) [mzr] 594 (1995 SIL). Amazonas, along the headwaters of the tributaries of the Curuçá, Ipixuna, and Javarí, near the Peru border. *Class:* Panoan, North-Central. *Dialects:* Speakers say they cannot understand Matsés (Mayoruna). Possibly intelligible with Panoan Katukína. *Other:* Korubo may be the same.

Matipuhy (Matipu, Mariape-Nahuqua) [mzo] 40 (1995 AMTB). Xingú Park, Mato Grosso. *Class:* Carib, Southern, Xingu Basin. *Dialect:* Matipuhy, Nahukuá (Nakukwa, Nafukwá, Nahuqua). Ruhlen says Kalapálo is a dialect of Nahukua. May also be intelligible with Kuikúro. *Other:* Fishermen; hunters; swidden agriculturalists: manioc, maize. Nearly extinct.

Matís [mpq] 120 (1995 SIL). Amazonas, Javari Valley, Municipality of Atalaia do Norte, on the border with Peru. *Class:* Panoan, Northern. *Dialects:* Seems to be different from Matsés, although similar.

Matsés (Matse, Mayoruna) [mcf] 1,000 in Brazil (2000 SIL). Amazonas. *Lg Use:* Some speak some Portuguese. Teachers are first-language Portuguese speakers. *Other:* Different from Mayo, Marubo, or Maya. Matís seems to be different. See main entry under Peru.

Maxakalí (Caposho, Cumanasho, Macuni, Monaxo, Monocho) [mbl] 728 (1994 SIL). Minas Gerais, 100 miles inland from coast, 14 villages. *Class:* Macro-Ge, Maxakali. *Lg Use:* The population is largely young. *Lg Dev:* Literacy rate in first language: 37%. Literacy rate in second language: 37%. NT: 1981. *Other:* SOV.

Mehináku (Mehinaco, Mahinaku, Minaco) [mmh] 121 (1995 AMTB). Xingú Park, Mato Grosso. *Class:* Arawakan, Maipuran, Central Maipuran. *Dialects:* Somewhat intelligible with Waurá. *Lg Use:* Speakers have low proficiency in Portuguese. *Other:* Fishermen; hunters; swidden agriculturalists: manioc, maize.

Miarrã [xmi] Xingú Park, Mato Grosso. *Class:* Unclassified.

Miraña (Boro, Bora) [boa] Amazonas near the Solimões, between the Tefé and Caiçara rivers, and along the Brazilian part of the Rio Içá. *Dialect:* Miranha (Miraña, Mirãnia). *Lg Use:* 457 Miranha in Brazil (1986 SIL) no longer speak the language. *Other:* Riverine. See main entry under Peru (Bora).

Miriti (Miriti-Tapuia, Miriti Tapuyo, Neenoá) [mmv] Extinct. Ethnic population: 55 (1995 AMTB). Pari-Cachoeira, Taracua, Amazonas. *Class:* Tucanoan, Miriti. *Lg Use:* Members of the ethnic group now speak Tucano. *Other:* 'Tapuya' comes from the Tupí word for 'enemy'.

Mondé (Sanamaiká, Sanamaykã, Sanamaica, Salamãi, Salamaikã) [mnd] 30 (1995 AMTB). Apidia River, tributary of Igarape Tanaru, near Pimenta Bueno, Rondônia. *Class:* Tupi, Monde. *Dialects:* Related to Arua, Gavião Do Jiparaná. *Lg Use:* May be extinct. *Other:* Nearly extinct.

Morerebi [xmo] 100 (2000). Amazonas, Rio Preto and Marmelos, 2 villages. *Class:* Tupi, Tupi-Guarani, Subgroup VI. *Dialects:* May be a Tenharim dialect. A family group that has not lived with the Tenharim for many years, and does not want contact with outside culture. *Other:* Existence not able to be confirmed in 1993.

Mundurukú (Mundurucu, Monjoroku, Weidyenye, Paiquize, Pari, Caras-Pretas) [myu] 7,000 (2000 SIL). Ethnic population: 7,000. Pará, Amazonas, middle and upper Tapajós and middle Madeira rivers, 22 villages. *Class:* Tupi, Munduruku. *Lg Use:* Vigorous. Most of the women and all of the children are monolingual. Those in

grasslands villages are also quite monolingual. Those in Jacareacanga have high proficiency in Portuguese. Those in Sai Cinza and those on the RC mission on the Cururu occasionally use Portuguese, men more than women. In many villages along the Cururu many men know trading vocabulary, many women know daily greetings. *Lg Dev:* Grammar. NT: 1980. *Other:* The population decreased by 10 times in size due to outsiders' diseases and malaria. They are presently growing in number. OV. Tropical forest, savannah. Traders: Brazil nuts, crude rubber, some gold, pelts. Traditional religion, Christian.

Nadëb (Nadeb Macu, Makú Nadëb, Makunadöbö, Nadöbö, Anodöub, Kabori, Kabari, Xiriwai, Xuriwai) [mbj] 300 (1986 SIL). Amazonas, three locations on the Uneiuxi River, a tributary of the Negro River, on the Japura and Negro rivers, and in other scattered places. *Class:* Maku. *Other:* Ruhlen and others classify it as Puinave in Macro-Tucanoan. The people are seminomadic. OSV. Hunter-gatherers.

Nambikuára, Northern (Mamaindé) [mbg] 136 (1999 SIL). Ethnic population: 136 (1999). Mato Grosso (Mamaindé), Rondônia (Latundê). *Class:* Nambiquaran. *Dialect:* Mamaindé, Negarotê, Tawanxte, Taxmainite, Taxwensite, Yalapmunxte (Lacondê, Latundê). *Lg Dev:* Bible portions: 1979–1980. *Other:* In 1900 the Mamaindé were 3,000 people, by 1965 the population was down to 50 because of intertribal wars and massacres in the 1930s and 1940s, several outbreaks of measles, encroaching Brazilians, and infant mortality. Modern medicine and Mamaindé literature have helped reverse the trend. The Latundê live with the Tubarão. Tropical forest. Rubber gatherers.

Nambikuára, Southern (Nambiquara, Nambikwara) [nab] 1,150 (2000 SIL). 950 monolinguals. Northwestern Mato Grosso, scattered along the Porto Velho-Cuiabá highway for about 300 km. 10 villages. *Class:* Nambiquaran. *Dialects:* Manduka, Khithaulhu, Halotesu, Saxwentesu, Wakalitesu, Serra Azul, Hahaintesu, Wasusu, Alatesu, Waikisu, Galera, Sarare. *Lg Use:* Vigorous. Positive language attitude. Some speakers also use Portuguese. *Lg Dev:* Literacy rate in first language: 10%. Some bilingual education. Dictionary. Grammar. NT: 1992. *Other:* The Manduca are semi-integrated. The Nambikuára were reduced from 10,000 to 600 in the 1920s, 1930s, and 1950s by measles and other epidemics. Settlers from outside are bringing in agriculture, lumber, and mining which threaten the Nambikuára way of life. Manairisu is a subgroup. SOV; tonal. Savannah, tropical forest. Hunter-gatherers: palm heart and other produce. Traditional religion, Christian.

Nhengatu (Yeral, Geral, Língua Geral, Nyengatú, Nheengatu, Nyengato, Ñeegatú, Waengatu, Coastal Tupian, Modern Tupí) [yrl] 3,000 in Brazil (1998). Population total all countries: 8,000. Lower Vaupés, Içana, and Negro River areas, Amazonas. Also spoken in Colombia, Venezuela. *Class:* Tupi, Tupi-Guarani, Subgroup III. *Dialects:* Based on Tupinambá, developed by the Portuguese during the 17th and 18th centuries as the language of communication. *Lg Use:* Trade language. All use Tucano as second language. *Lg Dev:* NT: 1973.

Ninam (Yanam, Xirianá, Shiriana Casapare, Kasrapai, Jawaperi, Crichana, Jawari) [shb] 466 in Brazil (1976 UFM). Most are monolingual. Population includes 236 in southern dialect, 230 in northern dialect. Population total all countries: 566. Mucajai, upper Uraricáa, and Paragua rivers, Roraima. Also spoken in Venezuela. *Class:* Yanomam. *Dialects:* Southern Ninam (Shirishana, Mukajai), Northern Ninam (Shiriana, Uraricaa-Paragua). *Lg Use:* All ages. A few children are beginning to learn Portuguese. *Lg Dev:* Bible portions: 1970. *Other:* Distinct from the Arawakan Xiriâna.

Nukuini (Nuquini) [nuc] Extinct. Acre, northwestern, from the upper Môa to the Rio Sungarú in Juruá. *Class:* Panoan, South-Central, Unclassified. *Dialect:* Cuyanawa. *Lg Use:* They have used mainly Portuguese for 3 generations. Some older people remember a little of the language.

Ofayé (Opaié-Shavante, Ofaié-Xavante, Opayé) [opy] 15 (2002). Ethnic population: 37 (1995 AMTB). Mato Grosso do Sul, along the Verde, Vacaris, and Ivinhema rivers, and area of Brazilândia. *Class:* Macro-Ge, Opaye. *Lg Use:* Members of the ethnic group now speak mainly Portuguese or Kaiwa. *Lg Dev:* Literacy rate in second language: 30%. *Other:* Language revival effort underway. Laborers. Christian. Nearly extinct.

Omagua (Canga-Peba, Agua, Janbeba, Compeva, Omagua-Yete, Ariana, Pariana, Anapia, Macanipa, Yhuata, Umaua, Cambeba, Campeba, Cambela) [omg] There may be none left in Brazil (1995). Amazonas. *Dialects:* Aizuare (Aissuari), Curacirari (Curazicari), Curucicuri (Curuzicari), Paguana (Paguara). *Other:* Nearly extinct. See main entry under Peru.

Oro Win [orw] 5 (1996 SIL). Ethnic population: 55 (1998). Headwaters of the Pacaas-Novos River, a tributary of the Mamoré River, along the Brazil-Bolivia border. *Class:* Chapacura-Wanham, Madeira. *Dialects:* Related to Tora, Itene (More), and Pakaasnovos (Wari), but not inherently intelligible with them. *Lg Use:* Speakers are older adults. Speakers also use Wari. *Other:* VOS. Nearly extinct.

Oti (Chavante, Euchavante) [oti] Extinct. São Paulo. *Class:* Macro-Ge, Oti.

Otuke (Otuque, Otuqui, Louxiru) [otu] Extinct. Mato Grosso lowlands into eastern Bolivia. *Class:* Macro-Ge, Bororo, Otuke. *Dialects:* Related dialects or languages: Covareca, Curuminaca, Coraveca (Curave), Curucaneca, Tapii; all are extinct.

Pakaásnovos (Jaru, Uomo, Pakaanovas, Pacaas-Novos, Pakaanova, Pacahanovo, Oro Wari, Wari) [pav] 1,833 (1994 SIL). Rondônia, 7 villages. *Class:* Chapacura-Wanham, Madeira. *Lg Dev:* Bible portions: 1975–1984.

Palikúr (Palikour, Palicur, Palijur) [plu] 800 in Brazil. Population total all countries: 1,300. Northern coastal tip along rivers, Amapá. Also spoken in French Guiana. *Class:* Arawakan, Maipuran, Eastern Maipuran. *Lg Use:* Speakers have some proficiency in Portuguese. *Lg Dev:* Literacy rate in second language: 25%. Grammar. NT: 1982. *Other:* Riverine, island. Hunters; agriculturalists.

Pankararé (Pankaré) [pax] Extinct. Ethnic population: 1,200 (1995 AMTB). Bahía. *Class:* Unclassified. *Lg Use:* Members of the ethnic group now speak Portuguese.

Pankararú (Pankarará, Pankarú, Pancaru, Pancaré, Pankaravu, Pankaroru) [paz] Extinct. Ethnic population: 3,676 (1995 AMTB). Pernambuco, Alagoas. *Class:* Language Isolate. *Dialects:* Possibly related to Kiriri. *Lg Use:* Members of the ethnic group now speak Portuguese.

Papavô [ppv] 170 (2000 WCD). Acre, Taramacá River. *Class:* Unclassified. *Lg Use:* Some speakers also use Portuguese.

Parakanã (Parakanân, Parocana, Awaeté) [pak] 451 (1995 AMTB). Pará, Xingú Park, lower Xingú River, near São Felix and Altamira towns. *Class:* Tupi, Tupi-Guarani, Subgroup IV. *Dialects:* A member of the Akwáwa cluster.

Paranawát (Paranauat, Pawaté, Majubim) [paf] Extinct. Ethnic population: 50 to 100 (1986 SIL). Rondônia, tributaries of the Jiparaná (Machado) River and Sono River. *Class:* Tupi, Tupi-Guarani, Subgroup VI.

Parecís (Paressí, Paresí, Haliti) [pab] 1,200 (1994 SIL). Mato Grosso, 6,000 square kilometers. 15 to 20 villages. *Class:* Arawakan, Maipuran, Central Maipuran. *Lg Use:* Speakers have some proficiency in Portuguese. *Lg Dev:* Dictionary. Grammar. NT: 1995. *Other:* There are public schools in 7 villages. SOV, OVS. Plateau. 650 meters.

Pataxó-Hãhaãi (Pataxi, Patashó, Patoxó, Pataxó-Hãhãhãe) [pth] Extinct. Ethnic population: 2,950 (1995 AMTB). Minas Gerais, Bahía, Pôsto Paraguassu in the municipality of Itabuna. *Class:* Unclassified. *Lg Use:* Members of the ethnic group now speak Portuguese.

Paumarí (Purupurú) [pad] 700 (1994 SIL). 3 villages, mainly on the Purus River. *Class:* Arauan. *Dialects:* Paumarm (Pammari), Kurukuru (Curucuru), Uaiai. 3 inherently intelligible dialects. *Lg Use:* Half the speakers are under 12 years of age (1984 SIL). Speakers also use Portuguese. *Lg Dev:* Literacy rate in first language: 10% to 30%. Literacy rate in second language: 15% to 25%. Grammar. NT: 1995. *Other:* In 1964 there were 96 Paumarí in 1 village. By 1994 they had increased to 700 in several villages. They now value their language and culture due to language development efforts.

Pemon (Pemong) [aoc] 679 in Brazil. 220 Taulipang dialect, 459 Ingarikó dialect. Rio Branco, near Guyana border, Roraima. *Dialects:* Taulipang (Taurepan), Camaracota (Ipuricoto), Arecuna (Aricuna, Arekuna, Jaricuna), Ingarikó (Ingaricó). See main entry under Venezuela.

Pirahã (Múra-Pirahã) [myp] 150 (1986 SIL). Ethnic population: 1,500 (1995 SIL). The Pirahã are small, the Múra larger. Amazonas, along the Maici and Autaces rivers. *Class:* Mura. *Dialect:* Múra. Probably related to Matanawi, which is extinct. *Lg Use:* Vigorous. The Pirahã are quite monolingual. The Múra are mostly integrated into Portuguese. *Lg Dev:* Grammar. Bible portions: 1987. *Other:* In the 1960s the population dwindled to 80 because of a viscious cycle of high infant mortality, death of mothers giving birth, and disease. The population has grown because of modern medicine. Some form of whistle speech reported. SOV. Riverine. Tropical forest. 10 to 40 meters. Hunter-gatherers.

Piratapuyo (Waikino, Pira-Tapuya, Uaikena, Uaicana, Waikhara, Waina, Uaiana, Uainana) [pir] 618 in Brazil (1986 SIL). Population total all countries: 1,068. Amazonas. Also spoken in Colombia. *Class:* Tucanoan, Eastern Tucanoan, Northern. *Dialects:* Close to Guanano linguistically; ethnically distinct, but the two groups do not intermarry. Lexical similarity 99% with Guanano (N. Waltz). *Lg Use:* Speakers also use Tucano. *Lg Dev:* NT: 1991.

Plautdietsch (Low German, Mennonite German) [pdt] 5,955 in Brazil (1985 SIL). Primarily in Canada. *Lg Use:* 110,735 or more in Latin America are fairly monolingual. Speakers also use Portuguese or Standard German. *Other:* Christian. See main entry under Canada.

Pokangá (Pakang, Pokangá-Tapuya, Bará, Barasano, Bara Sona) [pok] 100 (1983 SIL). Upper Tiquie, tributary of Vaupés, Amazonas. *Class:* Tucanoan, Eastern Tucanoan, Central, Bara. *Other:* It may be the same as Barasana or Waimaha (Northern Barasano, Bará).

Portuguese [por] 163,153,389 in Brazil (1998). Throughout the country. *Lg Use:* Official language. *Lg Dev:* Literacy rate in first language: 71%. *Other:* Christian, traditional religion. See main entry under Portugal.

Potiguára (Pitonara) [pog] Extinct. Ethnic population: 4,000 (2000 C. Jensen). Paraíba, Pôsto Nísia Brasileira on the Baía da Traição, in the municipality of Mamanguape. *Class:* Tupi, Tupi-Guarani, Subgroup III. *Lg Use:* Members of the ethnic group now speak Portuguese. *Other:* Descended from the Tupinambá.

Poyanáwa (Poianáua, Puinahua) [pyn] 310 (1995 AMTB). Acre, upper Rio Môa, tributary of the Jumá. *Class:* Panoan, South-Central, Yaminahua-Sharanahua.

Puri (Coroado) [prr] Extinct. Espíritu Santo, Minas Gerais, and adjacent areas. *Class:* Macro-Ge, Puri.

Puruborá (Puruba, Aurã, Pumbora, Puroborá, Burubora, Kuyubi, Cujubi, Migueleno, Miguelenho) [pur] 2 (2002 SIL). Rondônia, headwaters of the Rio São Miguel, tributary of the right bank of the Guaporé. *Class:* Tupi, Purubora. *Other:* Nearly extinct.

Rikbaktsa (Aripaktsa, Erikbatsa, Erikpatsa, Canoeiro) [rkb] 800 (1994 SIL). Mato Grosso, confluence of Sangue and Juruena rivers, Japuira on the east bank of the Juruena between the Arinos and Sangue rivers, and Posto Escondido on the west bank of the Juruena 700 km north. 9 villages and 14 settlements. *Class:* Macro-Ge, Rikbaktsa. *Lg Dev:* Literacy rate in first language: 5% to 10%. Literacy rate in second language: 15% to 25%. NT: 2000. *Other:* Distinct from Avá-Canoeiro and Kanoé. SOV. Tropical forest.

Sabanês (Sabones, Sabanê) [sae] 60 (1995 AMTB). Mato Grosso. *Class:* Nambiquaran. *Other:* Integrated into Brazilian culture. Men are trilingual, understanding Portuguese and Northern Nambikuára.

Sakirabiá (Sakirabiát, Sakirabiáp, Sakiriabar, Sakirabiák, Sakirap) [skf] 70 (2000 SIL). Rondônia, Municipality of Cerejeira and Colorado do Oeste, on the Mequens River. *Class:* Tupi, Tupari.

Salumá [slj] 239 (2000 WCD). Northwest Pará, on the upper Anamu, source of the Trombetas, along the Suriname border. *Class:* Carib, Northern, East-West Guiana, Waiwai, Sikiana. *Other:* Different from Salumã (Enawené-Nawé) in Mato Grosso.

Sanumá (Tsanuma, Sanema, Guaika, Samatari, Samatali, Xamatari) [xsu] 462 in Brazil (1976 UFM). Auaris River, Roraima. *Dialects:* Caura, Ervato-Ventuari, Auaris. *Lg Use:* In some areas up to 25% of the speakers also use Maquiritare. *Other:* Dialects are closely related. See main entry under Venezuela.

Sateré-Mawé (Maué, Mawé, Mabue, Maragua, Sataré, Andira, Arapium) [mav] 9,000 (1994 SIL). Pará, Amazonas, Andirá, and Maués rivers, between the lower Tapajós and lower Madeira rivers. More than 14 villages. *Class:* Tupi, Mawe-Satere. *Lg Use:* Some also use Portuguese. *Lg Dev:* Literacy rate in first language: 12%. Literacy rate in second language: below 5%. Grammar. NT: 1986.

Sharanahua (Acre Arara) [mcd] 500 in Brazil. Marináwa in Acre, along the upper Envira, tributary of the Tarauacá, municipality of Cruziero do Sul, on Rio Humaitá off the Juará River. *Dialects:* Marinahua (Marináwa), Chandinahua. *Lg Use:* The Marináwa are integrated into Brazilian society. There may be no speakers left. Speakers are shifting to Portuguese. See main entry under Peru.

Sikiana (Sikiâna, Shikiana, Sikïiyana, Chiquiana, Chikena, Chiquena, Xikujana, Xikiyana) [sik] 33 in Brazil (1986 SIL). Population total all countries: 48. Northwest Pará, between the Rio Cafuini and the headwaters of the Turuna and Itapi, near the Suriname border. Also spoken in Suriname, Venezuela. *Class:* Carib, Northern, East-West Guiana, Waiwai, Sikiana. *Dialects:* Close to Salumá. *Other:* Nearly extinct.

Siriano (Siriana, Siriane, Suryana, Surianá, Surirá, Sarirá) [sri] 10 in Brazil (1995 AMTB). São Gabriel, Amazonas. *Lg Use:* Second languages are Tucano and Nhengatu, but they are ethnically distinct. See main entry under Colombia.

Suruahá (Suruwahá, Zuruahá, Mndios do Coxodoá) [swx] 130 (1995 AMTB). Amazonas. *Class:* Arauan. *Other:* First contact with the outside was 1980. Tropical forest. Hunter-gatherers. Traditional religion.

Suruí (Suruí do Jiparaná, Suruí de Rondônia, Paiter) [sru] 800 (1994 SIL). A series of villages and scattered locations along the Rondônia-Mato Grosso border. 10 villages. *Class:* Tupi, Monde. *Dialects:* Related to Cinta Larga and Gavião do Jiparaná. *Lg Dev:* Literacy rate in first language: 10% to 30%. Literacy rate in second

language: 15% to 25%. Bible portions: 1991. *Other:* SOV. Agriculturalists: coffee.

Suruí do Pará (Akewere, Akewara, Aikewara, "Mudjétira," "Mudjetíre," "Mudjetíre-Suruí," Suruí) [mdz] 140 (1995 SIL). Pará, 110 km from Marabá, in municipio de São João Araguaia. *Class:* Tupi, Tupi-Guarani, Subgroup IV. *Dialects:* Member of Akwáwa cluster. Probably fairly close linguistic relationship to Asuriní and Parakanã. *Lg Dev:* Literacy rate in first language: below 1%. Literacy rate in second language: below 5%. *Other:* Different from Suruí do Jiparaná. The name "Mudjetire" is offensive to the people.

Suyá [suy] 196 (1995 AMTB). Population includes 31 Tapayuna. Xingú Park, Mato Grosso, headwaters of Rio Culuene. *Class:* Macro-Ge, Ge-Kaingang, Ge, Northwest, Suya. *Dialects:* Beiço de Pau (Tapayúna), Yaruma (Jarumá, Waiku). *Lg Use:* Few speakers also use Portuguese. *Other:* Yaruma may be extinct. Agriculturalists: manioc, maize; hunters; fishermen.

Tapeba (Tabeba) [tbb] Extinct. Ethnic population: 984 (1995 AMTB). On the Ceará River, in Caucaia, Ceará. *Class:* Unclassified. *Lg Use:* Members of the ethnic group now speak Portuguese.

Tapirapé [taf] 350 (2000 SIL). Mouth of the Tapirapé and Araguaia rivers, northeastern Mato Grosso. *Class:* Tupi, Tupi-Guarani, Subgroup IV. *Other:* Agriculturalists: manioc, maize, beans, pumpkins, peanuts, cotton; hunters; fishermen.

Tariano (Tarîna, Taliáseri) [tae] 100 in Brazil (1996 A. Aikhenvald). Ethnic population: 1,500 in Brazil (1985 Rodrigues). Middle Vaupés River, Santa Rosa (Juquira), Iauarete, Periquitos, and Ji-Ponta, Amazonas. Also spoken in Colombia. *Class:* Arawakan, Maipuran, Northern Maipuran, Inland. *Lg Use:* No one has been located who speaks Tariano in Colombia, but the group identity is still maintained. The first language is Tucano or Nhengatu. Speakers are older adults. *Other:* Nearly extinct.

Tembé (Tenetehara) [tqb] 150 to 200 (2000 SIL). Ethnic population: 700 (2000 C. Jensen). Maranhão, Gurupi, and Guamá rivers. None in Guamá speak Tembé, only Portuguese. In Gurupi about 100 of 170 speak Tembé. *Class:* Tupi, Tupi-Guarani, Subgroup IV. *Dialects:* The speech of most or all groups of this name is intelligible with Guajajára.

Tenharim (Tenharem, Tenharin, Kagwahiva, Kagwahiv, Kawaib) [pah] 493. Population includes 350 Tenharim (2000 SIL), 130 Parintintín (2000 SIL), 13 Diahói (1994 SIL). Amazonas. The Diahói are on the Rio Marmelos, Karipuna on Jaci Paraná River Post in Rondônia, Morerebi on Rio Preto and Marmelos. 2 villages. *Class:* Tupi, Tupi-Guarani, Subgroup VI. *Dialects:* Tenharim (Tenharem, Tenharin), Parintintín, Kagwahiv (Kawaib), Karipuna Jaci Paraná, Mialát, Diahói (Jahui, Giahoi). Boca Negra is a related ethnic group. Tenharim and Kagwahiv are nearly identical. Eru-eu-wau-wau (Uru-eu-wau-wau) and Morerebi may be dialects. The Tenharim consider the Diahói to be relatives; slight dialect difference. The Morerebi are a family group who have not lived with the Tenharim for many years, and do not want contact with outside culture. The Amundava, Kayabí, Parintintín, Tenharim, Júma, Karipuna, and Diahói all call themselves 'Kagwahiva' (Kagwahibm, Kagwahiv, Kawahip, Kavahiva, Kawaib, Kagwahiph). *Lg Use:* Speakers also use Portuguese. *Lg Dev:* Literacy rate in first language: 10% to 30%. Literacy rate in second language: 15% to 25%. Grammar. NT: 1996. *Other:* SVO. Fishermen; gatherers; agriculturalists.

Terêna (Tereno, Etelena) [ter] 15,000 (1991 SIL). Mato Grosso do Sul, in 20 villages and 2 cities. *Class:* Arawakan, Maipuran, Southern Maipuran, Bolivia-Parana. *Lg Use:* Many speakers have low proficiency in

Portuguese. *Lg Dev:* Literacy rate in first language: 20%. Literacy rate in second language: 80%. Dictionary. Grammar. NT: 1994. *Other:* VOS.

Ticuna (Tikuna, Tukuna, Magüta) [tca] 25,000 in Brazil (2000 SIL). Population total all countries: 41,000. West Amazonas. Also spoken in Colombia, Peru. *Class:* Language Isolate. *Lg Dev:* NT: 1986. *Other:* SVO.

Tingui-Boto (Tingui, Carapató, Karapató) [tgv] Extinct. Ethnic population: 800 (1986 SIL). Alagoas. *Class:* Unclassified. *Lg Use:* Members of the ethnic group now speak Portuguese.

Torá (Toraz) [trz] 40 (1990). Ethnic population: 120 (1990 YWAM). Amazonas, on the lower Rio Marmelos, tributary of the Rio Madeira. *Class:* Chapacura-Wanham, Madeira. *Other:* Nearly extinct.

Tremembé [tme] Almofa, la Ceará. *Class:* Unclassified. *Lg Use:* May be extinct (1995). Speakers also use Portuguese. *Other:* Nearly extinct.

Trió (Tirió, Tiriyó) [tri] 329 in Brazil (1995). Pará, Rio Mapari. *Dialect:* Pianocotó. *Other:* Pianokotó is probably extinct; no reports since 1957. See main entry under Suriname.

Truká [tka] Extinct. Ethnic population: 909 (1995 AMTB). Pernambuco, Bahía. *Class:* Unclassified. *Lg Use:* Members of the ethnic group now speak Portuguese.

Trumaí [tpy] 78 (1995). Xingú Park, source of Xingú River, villages along banks, Mato Grosso. *Class:* Language Isolate. *Dialects:* Ruhlen and others classify it as Equatorial. *Other:* Agriculturalists: manioc, peppers, beans.

Tubarão (Aikanã, Wari, Uari, Corumbiara, Kolumbiara, Huari) [tba] 90 (1986 SIL). Rondônia, west of Vilhena, near the Cuiabá-Porto Velho highway. *Class:* Arawakan, Maipuran, Northern Maipuran, Unclassified. *Dialect:* Masaká (Massaca).

Tucano (Tukána, Takuna, Daxsea) [tuo] 2,631 in Brazil (1986 SIL). Population total all countries: 4,631. Amazonas. Also spoken in Colombia. *Class:* Tucanoan, Eastern Tucanoan, Northern. *Dialects:* Yohoraa (Curaua), Wasona (Uasona). *Lg Use:* Trade language. Used as a second language by many neighboring groups. *Lg Dev:* Grammar. NT: 1988. *Other:* SOV.

Tukumanféd [tkf] Extinct. Rondônia, mouth of the Cacoal tributary of the Jiparaná. *Class:* Tupi, Tupi-Guarani, Subgroup VI.

Tuparí [tpr] 300 (2000). Rondônia, Branco River, tributary of the Guaporé, Pororoca Post. *Class:* Tupi, Tupari. *Other:* There are reported to be others upstream on the Rio Branco. Tropical forest.

Tupí [tpw] Extinct. Formerly along coast around what is now São Paulo. *Class:* Tupi, Tupi-Guarani, Subgroup III. *Other:* Its descendant, Tupí Austral, also called Lingua Geral of São Paulo, is also extinct.

Tupinambá (Tupí, Tupí Antigo, Old Tupí, Brasiliano, Brasilica) [tpn] Extinct. Formerly along coast from Rio de Janeiro north to the Amazon River. *Class:* Tupi, Tupi-Guarani, Subgroup III. *Lg Use:* Members of the ethnic group now speak Portuguese. *Other:* Modern descendant is Nhengatu. The last 2 alternate names were used in the 17th and 18th centuries.

Tupinikin (Tupinaki, Tupinikim, Tupiniquim) [tpk] Extinct. Ethnic population: 820 (1995 AMTB). Espirito Santo, Bahia. *Class:* Tupi, Tupi-Guarani, Subgroup III. *Lg Use:* Members of the ethnic group now speak Portuguese.

Turiwára (Turiuara) [twt] Extinct. Ethnic population: 30 (1995 SIL). Pará, live with the Tembé on the Acará-miri River. *Class:* Tupi, Tupi-Guarani, Subgroup VIII.

Tuxá (Tusha, Todela) [tud] Extinct. Ethnic population: 900 (1995 AMTB). Bahía, Pernambuco. *Class:* Language Isolate. *Lg Use:* Members of the ethnic group now speak Portuguese. *Other:* Ruhlen and others classify it as Equatorial.

Tuxináwa (Tuchinaua) [tux] Extinct. Acre. *Class:* Panoan, South-Central, Yaminahua-Sharanahua.

Tuyuca (Tuyuka, Tuiuca, Dochkafuara, Doka-Poara, Doxká-Poárá) [tue] 465 in Brazil (1995). Amazonas. *Dialect:* Tsola. *Lg Use:* Speakers also use Tucano or Waimaha. See main entry under Colombia.

Uamué (Aticum, Atikum, Huamuê) [uam] Extinct. Ethnic population: 3,900 (1995 AMTB). Pernambuco, vicinity of Floresta. *Class:* Unclassified. *Lg Use:* Members of the ethnic group now speak Portuguese.

Umotína (Umutina, Barbados) [umo] Extinct. Ethnic population: 160 (1993). Mato Grosso, along the Paraguay River. *Class:* Macro-Ge, Bororo, Bororo Proper. *Lg Use:* The last speaker died in 1988. Members of the ethnic group now speak Portuguese.

Uru-Eu-Wau-Wau (Uru-Eu-Uau-Uau, Eru-Eu-Wau-Wau, Uruewawau, Kagwahiva) [urz] 100 (1995). Rondônia, on the upper Jaciparaná, Cautário, and Jamari rivers. *Class:* Tupi, Tupi-Guarani, Subgroup VI.

Uru-Pa-In [urp] 200 (1995 SIL). Rondônia, Municipality of Ariquemes. *Class:* Unclassified. *Other:* No permanent contact.

Urubú-Kaapor (Urubú, Kaapor, Kaaporté, Caapor, Ka'apor) [urb] 500 (1988 SIL). Maranhão, Gurupi River, 8 to 10 villages scattered over 2,800 sq. mi. *Class:* Tupi, Tupi-Guarani, Subgroup VIII. *Lg Dev:* Literacy rate in first language: 6%. Literacy rate in second language: 6%. Dictionary. Grammar. NT: 1986. *Other:* Different from Urubu of Rondônia. SOV, OSV.

Urubú-Kaapor Sign Language (Urubú Sign Language) [uks] 7 users (1986 J. Kakumasu). Maranhão. *Class:* Deaf sign language. *Lg Use:* 500 second-language users. The deaf are monolingual in sign language. About one out of every 75 persons is deaf. Urubu hearing children grow up knowing both the verbal and the sign systems. *Other:* OSV.

Urumi [uru] Extinct. Formerly Rondônia, Marmelos River, tributary of the middle Madeira. *Class:* Tupi, Ramarama.

Waimaha (Waimaja, Northern Barasano, Barazana, "Bará") [bao] 100 in Brazil (1998). Prelazia Rio Negro, Amazonas. See main entry under Colombia.

Waiwai (Uaiuai, Uaieue, Ouayeone) [waw] 1,800 in Brazil (2003). Population total all countries: 2,000. Amazonas, Pará, Roraima. Also spoken in Guyana. *Class:* Carib, Northern, East-West Guiana, Waiwai. *Dialect:* Katawian (Katwena, Katawina, Catawian, Catauian, Parucutu, Parukutu, Katuena, Cachuena). Related to Salumá. Voegelin and Voegelin (1977) treat Katawian as a separate language. *Lg Dev:* Bible: 2002. *Other:* Hunters; fishermen.

Wakoná [waf] Extinct. Ethnic population: 500 to 1,000 (1995 SIL). Alagoas. *Class:* Unclassified. *Other:* They may not live together as a group.

Wapishana (Wapixiána, Wapisiana, Wapishiana, Wapixiana, Uapixana, Vapidiana) [wap] 1,500 in Brazil (1986 SIL). Roraima. *Dialects:* Amariba, Atorai. *Lg Use:* Amariba dialect may be extinct. Some also use Portuguese. *Other:* The dialect Atorai is not the same as the language Atroai (Atruahí). See main entry under Guyana.

Wasu (Waçu) [wsu] Extinct. Ethnic population: 1,024 (1995 AMTB). Alagoas. *Class:* Unclassified. *Lg Use:* Members of the ethnic group now speak Portuguese.

Waurá (Uaura, Aura) [wau] 240 (1994 SIL). Xingú Park, Mato Grosso. *Class:* Arawakan, Maipuran, Central Maipuran. *Dialects:* Partially intelligible with Mehináku. *Lg Dev:* Literacy rate in first language: 1% to 5%. Literacy rate in second language: 5% to 15%.

Wayampi (Guayapi, Guaiapi, Oyampí, Oiampí, Wajapae, Wayãpi, Waiãpi, Waiampi, Wayapae, Oyampík, Oyanpík, Wajapuku, "Oiampipucu," "Oyampipuku") [oym] 530 in

Brazil (2000 SIL). Population includes 520 speakers of Amapari in Brazil and 10 of Oiapoque. Along tributaries of the upper Amapari River, west central Amapá, and northern Pará. 8 villages. *Dialects:* Oiyapoque Wayampi, Amapari Wayampi, Jari. *Lg Use:* Language attitudes between speakers of the dialects have improved. Bilingual level estimates for Portuguese: 0 63%, 1 21%, 2 13%, 3 2.5%, 4 .5%, 5 0%. *Lg Dev:* Literacy rate in first language: 10% to 30%. Literacy rate in second language: below 5%. See main entry under French Guiana.

Wayana (Oayana, Oyana, Oiana, Uaiana, Wayâna, Upurui, Alukuyana) [way] 150 in Brazil. Amapá, among the Apalaí. *Dialects:* Rucuyen (Roucouyenne), Urucuiana (Urucena). See main entry under Suriname.

Wayoró (Wayurú, Ayurú, Ajurú, Uaiora, Wajaru) [wyr] 80 (2000 SIL). Rondônia, Pororoca Post, Guapore River. *Class:* Tupi, Tupari.

Wiraféd (Wiroféd, Uirafed) [wir] Extinct. Rondônia, on the Riosinho and Muquí tributaries of the Jiparaná. *Class:* Tupi, Tupi-Guarani, Subgroup VI. *Other:* Permanent contact reported in late 1950s.

Xakriabá (Chakriaba, Shacriaba, Chikriaba) [xkr] Extinct. Ethnic population: 4,643 (1995 AMTB). Minas Gerais. *Class:* Macro-Ge, Ge-Kaingang, Ge, Central, Acua. *Lg Use:* Members of the ethnic group now speak Portuguese.

Xavánte (A'uwe Uptabi, Akuên, Akwen, A'we, Chavante, Shavante, Crisca, Pusciti, Tapacua) [xav] 10,000 (2000 SIL). Mato Grosso, 6 noncontiguous reservations, 80 villages. *Class:* Macro-Ge, Ge-Kaingang, Ge, Central, Acua. *Lg Use:* Vigorous. 7,000 monolingual speakers. All domains. All ages. Positive language attitude. 3,000 speak some Portuguese with Brazilians only. *Lg Dev:* Literacy rate in first language: 10% to 30%. Literacy rate in second language: 25% to 50% (most men, few women). The Xavante teachers teach Xavante reading and writing. Dictionary. Grammar. Bible portions: 1970–1993. *Other:* During the first decade of contact with outsiders (1950s), outsider's diseases killed hundreds of Xavante. Being placed on reservations forced them to abandon seminomadic means of survival, and learn swidden agriculture. During the transition many died. OSV. Open scrub land, some tropical forest along rivers. Hunter-gatherers traditionally; swidden agriculturalists: rice, maize, squash, bananas. Traditional religion, Christian.

Xerénte (Sherenté) [xer] 1,552 (2002 SIL). Tocantins, between the Rio do Sono and Rio Tocantins. *Class:* Macro-Ge, Ge-Kaingang, Ge, Central, Acua. *Lg Use:* Some also use Portuguese. *Lg Dev:* Bible portions: 1970–1990.

Xetá (Aré, Seta, Sheta, Cheta) [xet] 3 (1990 SIL). Ethnic population: 100 to 250 (1986 SIL). Paraná, among the Kaingang. *Class:* Tupi, Tupi-Guarani, Subgroup I. *Other:* Nearly extinct.

Xipaya (Shipaja, Xipaia) [xiy] 2 (2000 SIL). Pará, lower Xingú River. *Class:* Tupi, Yuruna. *Other:* Nearly extinct.

Xipináwa (Shipinahua) [xip] Extinct. Southern Amazonas and Acre. *Class:* Panoan, South-Central, Yaminahua-Sharanahua. *Other:* Both people and language are thought to be extinct.

Xiriâna [xir] 903 (2000 WCD). Tributaries of Demeni and Rio Negro, Amazonas, near Venezuela border. *Class:* Arawakan, Unclassified. *Other:* Distinct from the Yanomam language, Ninam (Xirianá).

Xokleng (Aweikoma, Bugre, Botocudos) [xok] 250 (1975). Ethnic population: 784 (2000 WCD). Santa Catarina, along tributary of the Itajaí River. *Class:* Macro-Ge, Ge-Kaingang, Kaingang, Northern. *Lg Use:* Some also use Portuguese. *Other:* The name 'Bugre' is also used for Kaingang and Brazilian Guaraní. The name 'Kaingang' is sometimes used for Xokleng. SOV.

Xukurú (Kiriri, Kiriri-Xokó) [xoo] Extinct. Ethnic population: 1,800 (1995 SIL). Pernambuco, Serra de Urubá (Arobá) near the city of Cimbres, Bahía. *Class:* Unclassified. *Lg Use:* Members of the ethnic group now speak Portuguese.

Yabaâna (Jabaana, Yabarana) [ybn] Extinct. Ethnic population: 90 (1986 SIL). Amazonas, headwaters of the Marauia and Cauaboris, tributaries of the left bank of Rio Negro. *Class:* Arawakan, Maipuran, Northern Maipuran, Unclassified. *Lg Use:* Members of the ethnic group now speak Portuguese. *Other:* Distinct from Yabarana of Venezuela.

Yaminahua (Yamináwa, Jaminawá, Yamanawa) [yaa] 357 in Brazil (1986 SIL). Acre. *Other:* Same dialect as Bolivia, and the same as, or close to, that of Peru. See main entry under Peru.

Yanomámi (Waicá, Waiká, Yanoam, Yanomam, Yanomamé, Surara, Xurima, Parahuri) [wca] 9,000 (1994 SIL). Waicá post, Uraricuera River, Roraima, Toototobi post, Amazonas, Catrimani River, Roraima. *Class:* Yanomam. *Dialects:* Yanamam (Patimitheri, Waika), Yanomam (Naomam, Guadema, Wadema, Warema), Yanomay (Toototobi), Nanomam (Karime), Jauari (Joari, Yoari, Aica). Related to Yanomamö of Brazil and Venezuela. *Lg Use:* Most speakers are monolingual. *Other:* Seminomadic. SOV.

Yanomamö (Guaica, Guaharibo, Yanomami, Shamatri, Shaathari) [guu] 1,943 in Brazil. Amazonas, upper tributaries of Rio Negro. *Dialects:* Eastern Yanomami (Parima), Western Yanomami (Padamo-Orinoco). *Lg Use:* Most speakers monolingual. See main entry under Venezuela.

Yawalapití (Jaulapiti, Yaulapiti) [yaw] Extinct. Xingú Park, Mato Grosso. *Class:* Arawakan, Maipuran, Central Maipuran. *Dialects:* Related to Waurá and Mehináku.

Yawanawa (Iauanauá, Jawanaua, Yahuanahua) [ywn] 310 (1994 SIL). Acre. 1 village of 100 people, with the remainder living along a river. *Class:* Panoan, South-Central, Yaminahua-Sharanahua. *Lg Use:* Vigorous. Portuguese is used only with outsiders. *Lg Dev:* Bible portions.

Yuhup (Makú-Yahup, Yëhup, Yahup, Yahup Makú, "Maku") [yab] 360 in Brazil (1995). Amazonas, on a tributary of the Vaupés River. Also spoken in Colombia. *Class:* Maku. *Dialects:* Limited intelligibility of Hupdë. Ruhlen and other classify it as related to Puinave. *Other:* South of the Hupdë. The name "Maku" is offensive. OSV.

Yurutí (Juruti, Juruti-Tapuia, Luruty-Tapuya, Juriti, Yuriti, Yuriti-Tapuia) [yui] 50 in Brazil (1991 SIL). Iauarete, Amazonas. *Other:* Yuriti and Juriti are incorrect spellings. See main entry under Colombia.

Zo'é (Tupí of Cuminapanema, Poturu, Poturujara, Buré) [pto] 136 (1995 SIL). State of Pará, Municipality of Obidos, on the Cuminapanema River. *Class:* Tupi, Tupi-Guarani, Subgroup VIII. *Other:* Similar to Wayampi.

British Virgin Islands

British Virgin Islands. 22,187. National or official language: English. 60 islands, 15 are inhabited. Main islands: Tortola, Virgin Gorda, Anegada, Jost Van Dyke. Literacy rate: 98%. The number of languages listed for British Virgin Islands is 2. Of those, both are living languages. See map on page 740.

English [eng] 2,000 in British Virgin Islands (1998). *Lg Use:* Official language. See main entry under United Kingdom.

Virgin Islands Creole English [vic] 19,730 in British Virgin Islands (2003). *Lg Use:* Coexists with English in a fairly stable diglossic relationship (Holm 1989:455). See main entry under U.S. Virgin Islands.

Canada

Canada. 32,507,874. Indian 800,000 and Inuit 32,000 ethnic total (1993): 146,285 first-language speakers (1981 census). 4,120,770 non-English or French first language, or 15.3% (1991 census). National or official languages: English, French. Literacy rate: 96% to 99%. Also includes Afrikaans (2,353), Armenian (20,053), Assyrian Neo-Aramaic (5,000), Belarusan (2,280), Bulgarian (2,276), Central Khmer, Chaldean Neo-Aramaic, Corsican, Czech (27,038), Danish (29,807), Eastern Panjabi (214,530), Eastern Yiddish (49,890), Estonian (15,295), Finnish (39,069), Greek (143,892), Haitian Creole French (12,317), Hebrew, Hungarian (86,835), Icelandic, Irish Gaelic, Italian (514,410), Iu Mien (100), Japanese (43,000), Judeo-Moroccan Arabic, Kashubian, Korean (73,000), Lao, Latvian (15,000), Lithuanian, Macedonian (12,464), Maltese, Najdi Spoken Arabic (20,000), Northern Kurdish (6,000), Nung, Plains Indian Sign Language, Polish (222,355), Pontic, Portuguese (222,870), Romanian (16,356), Russian (31,745), Scottish Gaelic (3,525), Serbian (7,966), Sinhala (3,004), Slovak, Slovenian (6,415), Southwestern Caribbean Creole English, Spanish (228,580), Standard German (470,505), Swedish (21,591), Sylheti, Tagalog (158,210), Tongan, Turkish (5,179), Turoyo, Ukrainian (174,830), Vietnamese (60,000), Vlax Romani, Welsh (3,160), Western Farsi (15,000), Western Panjabi, Yue Chinese (250,000), India and Pakistan (280,000), speakers of many European languages. Information mainly from W. Chafe 1962, 1965; SIL 1951–2002. Blind population: 27,184. Deaf population: 1,704,551. Deaf institutions: Many. The number of languages listed for Canada is 89. Of those, 85 are living languages and 4 are extinct. See maps beginning on page 746.

Abnaki, Western (Abenaki, Abenaqui, St. Francis) [abe] 20 (1991 M. Krauss). Ethnic population: 1,800 including Eastern Abnaki in USA (1982 SIL). Quebec on St. Lawrence River between Montreal and Quebec City. *Class:* Algic, Algonquian, Eastern. *Lg Use:* Extinct in the USA. All speakers are older adults. Speakers also use French. *Lg Dev:* Dictionary. Grammar. Bible portions: 1844. *Other:* Nearly extinct.

Algonquin (Algonkin) [alq] 2,275 (1998 Statistics Canada). Less than 10% monolinguals. Ethnic population: 5,000 (1987 SIL). Southwestern Quebec, northwest of Ottawa and in adjacent areas of Maniwaki and Golden Lake, Ontario. *Class:* Algic, Algonquian, Central, Ojibwa. *Dialects:* Several dialects. The southern (Miniwaki) and northern varieties (several varieties) are very different. *Lg Use:* Some usage in religious services. Only used in administration and commerce at local community level. Some use of Algonquin as a teaching medium in kindergarten. In the east, Algonquin is the principal means of communication, and spoken by the majority of all ages. In the west, most adults speak Algonquin, young adults may prefer the national language, and children prefer the national language, although some may speak Algonquin. Positive language attitude. Most are bilingual with many (over 25%) multilingual. Speakers use English, French, or Southern East Cree. *Lg Dev:* Literacy rate in first language: 30% to 60%. Literacy rate in second language: 75% to 100%. Taught in primary schools. Spoken and written forms are studied some in secondary school. Roman script. NT: 1998. *Other:* Hills, plains. Boreal forest. Hunters; guides; community workers; miners; loggers; agriculturalists. Christian.

American Sign Language (ASL, Ameslan) [ase] English-speaking areas of Canada. *Lg Use:* Sign language interpreters are required for deaf people in court. Used for deaf college students, important public functions, job training, social service programs, sign language instruction for parents of deaf children, classes for hearing people, organization for sign language teachers, committee on national sign language. *Other:* Manual alphabet. See main entry under USA.

Assiniboine (Assiniboin) [asb] 250 in Canada (1997 D. Parks). Ethnic population: 5,000 (1997 Douglas Parks). West central and southeastern Saskatchewan (Mosquito-Grizzly Bear's Head) and southern Saskatchewan (part of Carry-the-Kettle and Whitebear). Also spoken in USA. *Class:* Siouan, Siouan Proper, Central, Mississippi Valley, Dakota. *Dialects:* Very close to the Assiniboine of Montana. Close to Stoney. Lexical similarity 94% with Dakota of Manitoba, 90% with Dakota of North Dakota, 89% with Lakota and Stoney. *Lg Use:* All speakers older than 40 years, most over 60 years. English is spoken extensively.

Atikamekw (Tête de Boule, Attimewk, Attikamek, Atihkamekw, Atikamek) [atj] 3,995 (1998 Statistics Canada). Three isolated communities on reservations of Manuane, Obedjiwan, Weymontachie, between La Tuque, Quebec, and Senneterre, Quebec, 200 to 400 km north of Montreal in south central Quebec, along the upper reaches of the St. Maurice River. *Class:* Algic, Algonquian, Central, Cree-Montagnais-Naskapi. *Dialects:* Nonpalatalized r-dialect within Cree-Montagnais-Naskapi language complex or dialect continuum. Very different from Montagnais and Naskapi in the nearby area. *Lg Use:* Vigorous. Speakers also use French. *Lg Dev:* Literacy rate in first language: 10% to 30%. Literacy rate in second language: 50% to 75%. Roman script. Dictionary. Grammar. Bible portions: 1980–1983. *Other:* Three subgroups: Manawan, Wemotaci, Opitciwan. Hunters; trappers.

Babine (Babine Carrier, Northern Carrier, Witsuwit'en) [bcr] 500 (1997 S. Hargus). Ethnic population: 2,200 (1982 SIL and 1997 S. Hargus). West central British Columbia, areas of Burns Lake, Babine Lake, Moricetown, towards the Takla Lake area. *Class:* Na-Dene, Nuclear Na-Dene, Athapaskan-Eyak, Athapaskan, Canadian, Carrier-Chilcotin, Babine-Carrier. *Lg Use:* Babine is still the principal means of communication among older adults. Children and young adults may speak Babine but prefer English. *Lg Dev:* Literacy rate in first language: 1% to 5%. Literacy rate in second language: 50% to 75%. Bible portions: 1978.

Beaver [bea] 300 (1991 M. Dale Kinkade). Ethnic population: 600 (1987 SIL). North eastern British Columbia and northwestern Alberta, Chateh (Assumption) on the Hay River, and Prophet River south of Fort Nelson. *Class:* Na-Dene, Nuclear Na-Dene, Athapaskan-Eyak, Athapaskan, Canadian, Beaver-Sekani. *Lg Use:* The remaining speakers are highly bilingual in English. *Lg Dev:* Literacy rate in first language: 5% to 15%. Literacy rate in second language: 25% to 50%. Bible portions: 1886–1989.

Bella Coola (Nuxalk) [blc] 20 (2002 Poser). Ethnic population: 700 (1991 Kinkade). Inlet on the central British Columbia coast at the mouth of Bella Coola River, on North Bentinck Arm at the head of Burke Channel. *Class:* Salishan, Bella Coola. *Lg Use:* Speakers are shifting to English. *Lg Dev:* Dictionary. Grammar. *Other:* There is a language course in Bella Coola (1991). Nearly extinct.

Beothuk (Beothuc, Bethuck, Bethuk, Newfoundland, Red Indians) [bue] Extinct. Newfoundland. *Class:* Unclassified. *Dialects:* The theory that it was an Algonquian language is not accepted by all Algonquianists. *Lg Use:* Became extinct in 1829.

Blackfoot (Pikanii, Blackfeet) [bla] 5,000 in Canada (2000 SIL). Possibly a few monolinguals. Population total all countries: 5,100. Ethnic population: 15,000. Blackfoot, Piegan, and Blood Reserves in southern Alberta. Also spoken in USA. *Class:* Algic, Algonquian, Plains. *Dialects:* Piegan (Peigan), Blood. *Lg Use:* Some efforts are under way in schools on the reserves to promote knowledge and use of the language. Used for some traditional ceremonies. In some places Blackfoot is the principal language for older adults. Positive language attitude. Younger speakers prefer to use English. Some also use Cree. *Lg Dev:* Roman script. Dictionary. Grammar. Bible portions: 1890–1980. *Other:* Foothills, plains. Christian, traditional religion.

Carrier (Central Carrier) [crx] 1,500 (1987 SIL). All Athapaskan language family first-language speakers in Canada 20,090 (1998 Statistics Canada). Ethnic population: 2,100 (1987 SIL). Central British Columbia, Stuart and Trembleur Lake area. *Class:* Na-Dene, Nuclear Na-Dene, Athapaskan-Eyak, Athapaskan, Canadian, Carrier-Chilcotin, Babine-Carrier. *Dialects:* Necoslie, Pinchie, Tachie, Grand Rapids, Middle River, Portage. *Lg Use:* Speakers are mainly adults. Bilingual literacy materials used in schools. Most children and young adults prefer English. *Lg Dev:* Literacy rate in first language: 5% to 10%. Literacy rate in second language: 50% to 75%. Taught in primary schools. Dictionary. Grammar. NT: 1995.

Carrier, Southern [caf] 500 (1987 SIL). Central British Columbia, west of Quesnel and south of Cheslatta Lake, towards the Fraser and its tributaries, and Anahim Lake-Ulkatcho. *Class:* Na-Dene, Nuclear Na-Dene, Athapaskan-Eyak, Athapaskan, Canadian, Carrier-Chilcotin, Babine-Carrier. *Dialects:* Cheslatta, Prince George, Stoney Creek, Nautley, Stellaquo. Can use literature adapted from Central Carrier. Lexical similarity 90% with Central Carrier. *Lg Use:* Vigorous. Speakers also use English. *Lg Dev:* Literacy rate in first language: below 1%. Literacy rate in second language: 50% to 75%. NT: 2002.

Cayuga [cay] 40 to 60 in Canada (2002 M. K. Foster). Population total all countries: 50 to 70. Ethnic population: 3,000 (1997 Mithun, Foster, Michelson). Six Nations, Ontario. Also spoken in USA. *Class:* Iroquoian, Northern Iroquoian, Five Nations, Seneca-Onondaga, Seneca-Cayuga. *Lg Use:* In Ontario most speakers are older adults. English is the first or second language for the ethnic group.

Chilcotin (Tzilkotin) [clc] 2,000 (2000). 100 monolinguals. Ethnic population: 2,500. West of Williams Lake, south central British Columbia. Seven reserve communities: Alexandria, Toosey, Anahim, Stone, Nemiah, Redstone, Ulkatcho. *Class:* Na-Dene, Nuclear Na-Dene, Athapaskan-Eyak, Athapaskan, Canadian, Carrier-Chilcotin, Chilcotin. *Lg Use:* Preferred by adults. Most children prefer English. Grandparents pass on the language to some children. Many people decry the perceived loss of Chilcotin among the younger generation. Speakers also use English or Carrier. *Lg Dev:* Literacy rate in first language: 25%. Literacy rate in second language: 25% to 50%. Taught in primary schools. Roman script. Bible portions: 1993. *Other:* SOV. Valleys. Boreal forest. Ranchers; government workers. Christian.

Chinook Wawa (Chinook Jargon, Chinook Pidgin) [chn] 83 in Canada (1962 Chafe). Population total all countries: 100. British Columbia. Also spoken in USA. *Class:* Pidgin, Amerindian. *Dialects:* Consists mainly of words from Chinook, with a large admixture of words from Nootka, Canadian French, and English. *Lg Use:* Formerly used along the Pacific coast from Oregon to Alaska, between Indian and White, and between speakers of different languages. All speakers are now probably scattered. Speakers are shifting to English. All speakers older than 50 years. *Lg Dev:* Dictionary. Bible portions: 1912. *Other:* Nearly extinct.

Chipewyan (Dene) [chp] 4,000 (1995 M. Krauss). Ethnic population: 6,000 (1995 M. Krauss). Northern Alberta, Saskatchewan, Manitoba, southeastern Northwest Territories (Snowdrift and Fort Resolution). Communities of Fort Smith, Fort Chipewyan, Wolliston Post, Buffalo Narrows, Brochet, and Reindeer Lake are some of the communities. *Class:* Na-Dene, Nuclear Na-Dene, Athapaskan-Eyak, Athapaskan, Canadian, Hare-Chipewyan, Chipewyan. *Dialect:* Yellowknife. *Lg Use:* Speakers include children in some places (1995). *Lg Dev:* Literacy rate in first language: 1% to 5%. Literacy rate in second language: 25% to 50%. Dictionary. Grammar. NT: 1881.

Comox (Comox-Sliammon) [coo] 400. Population includes 1 speaker of Island Comox, fewer than 400 of Sliammon (mainland) (1991 M. Dale Kinkade). Ethnic population: 850 (1983). British Columbia, Vancouver Island, and the coast north of Powell River. *Class:* Salishan, Central Salish, Northern. *Dialects:* Island Comox, Sliammon. Speakers all speak the Sliammon (mainland) dialect. No speakers of Island Comox left. *Lg Use:* All speakers are older adults. Speakers are highly bilingual in English. Some members of the ethnic group speak English as first language. *Lg Dev:* Grammar.

Cree, Moose (York Cree, West Shore Cree, West Main Cree) [crm] 4,500. All Cree first-language speakers in Canada 87,555 (1998 Statistics Canada). Ethnic population: 5,000 (1982 SIL). Southern tip of James Bay, Moosonee, Ontario. This community and surrounding area (Moose Factory, Ontario). Has speakers of Moose Cree, East Cree, and Swampy Cree in it. *Class:* Algic, Algonquian, Central, Cree-Montagnais-Naskapi. *Dialects:* Nonpalatalized l-dialect within Cree-Montagnais-Naskapi language complex or dialect cluster. *Lg Use:* Vigorous. Speakers also use English. *Lg Dev:* Literacy rate in first language: 5% to 10%. Literacy rate in second language: 75% to 100%. Cree syllabary, eastern finals. Grammar. NT: 1876.

Cree, Plains (Western Cree) [crk] 34,000 in Canada (1982 SIL). Population total all countries: 34,100. Ethnic population: 53,000. North central Manitoba westward across Saskatchewan and central Alberta to the foot of the Rocky Mountains. Also spoken in USA. *Class:* Algic, Algonquian, Central, Cree-Montagnais-Naskapi. *Dialects:* Plains Cree, Western York Cree, Northern Alberta Cree. Nonpalatalized y-dialect within Cree-Montagnais-Naskapi language complex or dialect cluster. *Lg Use:* Vigorous in many communities mainly in the north. All ages. Speakers also use English. *Lg Dev:* Literacy rate in first language: 1% to 5%. Literacy rate in second language: 50% to 75%. Cree syllabary. Grammar. Bible: 1861–1908.

Cree, Swampy (York Cree, West Shore Cree, West Main Cree) [csw] 4,500 (1982 SIL). All Cree first-language speakers in Canada 60,000 (1991 M. Dale Kinkade). Ethnic population: 5,000. Ontario, along the coast of Hudson Bay and northern west coast of James Bay, and inland into Saskatchewan. *Class:* Algic, Algonquian, Central, Cree-Montagnais-Naskapi. *Dialects:* Eastern Swampy Cree, Western Swampy Cree. Both nonpalatalized n-dialect and l-dialect within Cree-Montagnais-Naskapi language complex or dialect cluster. *Lg Use:* Vigorous. Speakers also use English. *Lg Dev:* Literacy rate in first language: 5% to 10%. Literacy rate in second language: 50% to 75%. Cree syllabary, western finals. Dictionary. Grammar. NT: 1976.

Cree, Woods [cwd] 35,000 (1982 SIL). Ethnic population: 53,000 (1982 SIL). Far north Manitoba and Saskatchewan, inland southwest from Churchill, Manitoba into Saskatchewan. *Class:* Algic, Algonquian, Central, Cree-Montagnais-Naskapi. *Dialects:* Nonpalatalized th-dialect within Cree-Montagnais-Naskapi language complex or dialect cluster. *Lg Use:* Vigorous. All ages.

Speakers also use English. *Lg Dev:* Literacy rate in first language: 1% to 5%. Literacy rate in second language: 50% to 75%. Cree syllabary, western finals.

Dakota (Sioux) [dak] 5,000 in Canada (1991 M. Dale Kinkade). Southern Manitoba and Saskatchewan, Oak River and Oak Lake, Long Plain west of Winnipeg, Standing Buffalo, Birdtail, Stony Wahpeton, and Moose Woods. May be at Wood Mountain. *Dialects:* Dakota (Santee), Nakota (Yankton). *Lg Use:* In some communities children and young adults may not speak Dakota or may prefer English. *Lg Dev:* Literacy rate in first language: below 1%. Literacy rate in second language: 50% to 75%. See main entry under USA.

Dogrib [dgr] 2,110 (2001 SIL). Ethnic population: 3,220. Between Great Slave Lake and Great Bear Lake, Northwest Territories, 6 communities (Rae-Edzo, Whati (formerly Lac la Martre), Rae Lakes, Snare Lake, Detah and Ndilo (a subcommunity of Yellowknife)). Rae is the center. *Class:* Na-Dene, Nuclear Na-Dene, Athapaskan-Eyak, Athapaskan, Canadian, Hare-Chipewyan, Hare-Slavey. *Dialect:* Detah-Ndilo. The Detah-Ndilo dialect developed from intermarriage between the Yellowknife subdivision of the Chipewyan and the Dogrib. Lexical similarity 84% with Southern Slavey, 82% with Northern Slavey. *Lg Use:* Adults prefer to use Dogrib in most contexts. All ages. Monolinguals include children and older adults. 16% speak a little English; 37% speak both Dogrib and English, but speak Dogrib better; 14% speak both languages equally; 9% speak both, but speak English better; 7% speak English and a little Dogrib; 3% are monolingual in English (children), 12% are monolingual in Dogrib. *Lg Dev:* Literacy rate in first language: 1% to 5%. Literacy rate in second language: 25% to 50%. Taught in primary schools. Dictionary. Grammar. NT: 2003. *Other:* SOV. Canadian shield. 100 meters. Hunters; trappers.

East Cree, Northern (Northern James Bay Cree, Northern Eastern James Bay Cree) [crl] 5,308 (1997 Quebec Ministere de la Sante et des Services Sociaux). West central Quebec, east coast of lower Hudson Bay and James Bay, communities of Whapmagoostui, Chisasibi, Wemindji, and most people in Eastmain. *Class:* Algic, Algonquian, Central, Cree-Montagnais-Naskapi. *Dialects:* Palatalized y-dialect within Cree-Montagnais-Naskapi language complex or dialect cluster. Sometimes classified as Montagnais. *Lg Use:* Vigorous. All domains. Language of instruction in lower grades, taught as a subject in upper grades. Speakers also use English. *Lg Dev:* Literacy rate in first language: 20% to 25%. Literacy rate in second language: 50%. Taught in primary schools. Cree syllabary, eastern finals. Dictionary. Grammar. Bible portions: 1921.

East Cree, Southern (James Bay Cree Southern Dialect, Eastern James Bay Cree Southern Dialect) [crj] 7,306 (1997 Quebec Ministere de la Sante et des Services Sociaux). Quebec, southeastward from James Bay, inland to the height of land (watershed) east of Lake Mistissini. Coastal communities of Waskaganish, some speakers in Eastmain. Inland, in Mistissini, Waswanipi, Nemaska, and Ouje-Bougoumo. *Class:* Algic, Algonquian, Central, Cree-Montagnais-Naskapi. *Dialects:* Palatalized y-dialect within Cree-Montagnais-Naskapi language complex or dialect cluster. Sometimes classified as Montagnais. *Lg Use:* Vigorous. All domains. Speakers also use English. *Lg Dev:* Literacy rate in first language: 15% to 20%. Literacy rate in second language: 50%. Language of instruction in lower grades, taught as a subject in upper grades. Cree syllabary, eastern finals. Dictionary. Grammar. NT: 2001.

English [eng] 17,100,000 in Canada (1998 Statistics Canada). 820,000 first-language speakers in Quebec (1995 Statistics Canada); plus another 1,500,000 in Quebec whose first or second language is English (1995 Statistics Canada). *Dialect:* Newfoundland English. *Lg Use:* Official language. See main entry under United Kingdom.

French (Français) [fra] 6,700,000 in Canada (1998 Statistics Canada). 300,000 speak Acadien, 500,000 speak Franco-Ontariens. Québécois is in Quebec, Franco-Ontariens in Ontario, Acadian is in Caraquet, Shippagan, the east coast of New Brunswick, pockets in Nova Scotia and Prince Edward Island. Some Québécois speakers in Manitoba and Newfoundland. *Dialect:* Québécois, Franco-Ontarien, Acadian (Acadien). *Lg Use:* Official language. All domains. English partly used in public contexts such as commerce, technology, government, or public discourse such as sports, rock and roll music, dialogue with English speakers. *Other:* Difficult intelligibility between speakers of Québécois and Acadian for speakers not fluent in Standard French. Québécois is used more vigorously than Acadian. Christian. See main entry under France.

German, Hutterite (Tyrolese, Tirolean, Hutterian German) [geh] 29,200 in Canada (2003 SIL). Population total all countries: 34,200. 333 colonies in Canada, and Japan 1. There are about 90 people in each colony. Also spoken in USA. *Class:* Indo-European, Germanic, West, High German, German, Upper German, Bavarian-Austrian. *Dialects:* About 50% intelligible to a speaker of Pennsylvania German, Plautdietsch, and Standard German. Although it is called 'Tirolean', it is not a Tirolean dialect. *Lg Use:* Used in the home. All ages. In addition to attendance at public schools, children attend supplemental private schools with instruction in religion and Biblical German. Most have limited comprehension of English and even less comprehension of Standard German. All speakers use Biblical German for all religious activities. *Lg Dev:* Almost all adults are literate in English and Biblical German. *Other:* Intensive agriculturalists. Christian.

German, Pennsylvania (Pennsylvanisch, Pennsylvania Dutch) [pdc] 15,000 in Canada (1995). Kitchener-Waterloo area, Ontario. *Dialect:* Amish Pennsylvania German, Non-Amish Pennsylvania German (Pennsylvanisch Deitsch). *Other:* Christian. See main entry under USA.

Gitxsan (Gitksan, Gityskyan, Giklsan) [git] 400 (1999 Jay Powell). Population includes 220 in the west, 180 in the east. Gitxsan on middle Skeena River in west central British Columbia. *Class:* Penutian, Tsimshian. *Dialects:* Gitxsan (Eastern Gitxsan), Gitsken (Western Gitsken). High degree of inherent intelligibility between Nisga'a and Gitxsan. *Lg Use:* About 1,500 speak Nisga'a as second or third language. Speakers consider Nisga'a and Gitxsan to be politically distinct. *Lg Dev:* Dictionary. Bible portions: 1906. *Other:* VSO; prepositions; genitives after noun heads; articles, adjectives, numerals before noun heads; relatives without noun heads; question word initial in sentence; 3 or 4 prefixes, 1 inflectional suffix; word order distinguishes subjects, objects, indirect objects, given and new information, topic and comment; verb affixes mark person and number of subject and object unless obscured by phonological rule; pronominal system is fully ergative; morphological passives, but not by construction; direct causatives indicated by suffixes, indirect (jussive) by prefix; CVC; nontonal. Riverine. Pine and cedar forest with some deciduous trees. Sea level to 300 meters. Fishermen; hunters; gatherers. Christian.

Gwich'in (Kutchin, Loucheux, Tukudh) [gwi] 430 in Canada (1998 Statistics Canada). Population includes 300 in Northwest Territories, and 100 in Yukon (1995 M. Krauss). Population total all countries: 730. Ethnic population: 1,900 including 1,500 in Northwest Territories, 400 in Yukon (1995 M. Krauss). Northwest Territories:

Aklavik, Inuvik, Tsiigehtchic, and Fort McPherson. Also spoken in USA. *Class:* Na-Dene, Nuclear Na-Dene, Athapaskan-Eyak, Athapaskan, Canadian, Han-Kutchin. *Dialects:* Fort Yukon Gwich'in, Arctic Village Gwich'in, Western Canada Gwich'in (Takudh, Tukudh, Loucheux), Arctic Red River. *Lg Use:* Vigorous in a few communities. Most adults speak the language. In a few communities used by all ages. Elsewhere younger tend to prefer English. *Lg Dev:* Literacy rate in first language: 1% to 5%. Literacy rate in second language: 50% to 75%. Dictionary. Grammar. Bible: 1898.

Haida, Northern (Masset) [hdn] 30 in Canada (1995 M. Krauss). Population total all countries: 45. Ethnic population: 1,100 in Canada (1995 M. Krauss). Queen Charlotte Islands, British Columbia. Also spoken in USA. *Class:* Na-Dene, Haida. *Dialects:* Borderline inherent intelligibility of Southern Haida. *Lg Use:* Speakers are shifting to English. Speakers are older adults. *Lg Dev:* Dictionary. Grammar. Bible portions: 1891–1899. *Other:* There are language courses in Haida (1991). Nearly extinct.

Haida, Southern (Skidegate) [hax] 10 (1995 M. Krauss). Ethnic population: 500 (1995 M. Krauss). Queen Charlotte Islands, Skidegate. *Class:* Na-Dene, Haida. *Dialects:* Borderline intelligibility of Northern Haida. *Lg Dev:* Grammar. *Other:* Nearly extinct.

Haisla [has] 25 (1991 M. Dale Kinkade). Ethnic population: 1,000 (1977 SIL). Inlet on central British Columbia coast at the head of Douglas Channel, near Kitimat. *Class:* Wakashan, Northern. *Dialect:* Kitimat (Kitamat). Related to Heiltsuk and Kwakiutl. *Lg Use:* Speakers are shifting to English. Most or all speakers are older adults. *Lg Dev:* Dictionary. *Other:* Nearly extinct.

Halkomelem (Holkomelem) [hur] 200 in Canada (2002 Poser). Population total all countries: 225. Ethnic population: 6,700 (1977 SIL). Southwestern British Columbia. Also spoken in USA. *Class:* Salishan, Central Salish, Halkomelem. *Dialects:* Chiliwack, Cowichan, Musqueam, Nanaimo. *Lg Use:* Speakers are older adults. Speakers also use English. *Lg Dev:* Dictionary. Grammar. *Other:* Language courses in Halkomelem (1991).

Han (Han-Kutchin, Moosehide, Dawson) [haa] 7 or 8 in Canada (1997 Krauss). Ethnic population: 300. Yukon River area in Alaska-Canada border, Dawson. *Lg Use:* Speakers are shifting to English. All speakers are older adults (1995). *Other:* Nearly extinct. See main entry under USA.

Heiltsuk [hei] 300 (1991 M. Dale Kinkade). Ethnic population: 1,200 (1977 SIL). Central British Columbia coast including Ooweekeeno on Rivers Inlet. *Class:* Wakashan, Northern. *Dialects:* Bella Bella (Northern Heiltsuk), Ooweekeeno (Southern Heiltsuk). Related to Haisla and Kwakiutl. *Lg Use:* Speakers are older adults. Speakers also use English. *Lg Dev:* Dictionary.

Inuktitut, Eastern Canadian (Eastern Canadian "Eskimo," "Eastern Arctic Eskimo," Inuit) [ike] 14,000 (1991 L. Kaplan). Ethnic population: 17,500 (1991 L. Kaplan). West of Hudson Bay and east through Baffin Island, Quebec, and Labrador. *Class:* Eskimo-Aleut, Eskimo, Inuit. *Dialects:* "Baffinland Eskimo," "Labrador Eskimo," "Quebec Eskimo." *Lg Use:* Vigorous except in Labrador, where less than half are speakers. In Labrador the youngest speakers average over 20 years old, except for possibly a few children at Nain. *Lg Dev:* Literacy rate in first language: 10% to 30%. Literacy rate in second language: 75% to 100%. Bible: 1826–1871. *Other:* In Northern Quebec and the Northwest Territories to the Central Arctic, it is spoken by over 90% of the population. Inuit is the name of the people, Inuktitut of the language.

Inuktitut, Western Canadian (Inuvialuktun) [ikt] 4,000 (1981). All Inuit first-language speakers in Canada 18,840 (1981 census). Ethnic population: 7,500 (1981

census). Central Canadian Arctic, and west to the Mackenzie Delta and coastal area, including Tuktoyaktuk on the Arctic coast north of Inuvik (but not Inuvik and Aklavik, and coastal area). *Class:* Eskimo-Aleut, Eskimo, Inuit. *Dialects:* Copper Inuktitut ("Copper Eskimo," Copper Inuit), "Caribou Eskimo" (Keewatin), Netsilik, Siglit. Caribou dialect may need separate literature. *Lg Use:* Vigorous in Caribou and Netsilik. In Commer and farther west, parent and grandparent generations speak the language (M. Krauss 1995). *Lg Dev:* Literacy rate in first language: 25% to 50%. Literacy rate in second language: 50% to 75%. NT: 1983.

Inupiatun, North Alaskan (North Alaskan Inupiat, Inupiat, Inupiaq, "Eskimo") [esi] Mackenzie delta region including Aklavik and Inuvik, into Alaska, USA. *Dialects:* West Arctic Inupiatun (Mackenzie Inupiatun, Mackenzie Delta Inupiatun), North Slope Inupiatun. *Lg Use:* Most speakers older than 30 years. Younger speakers prefer English. *Lg Dev:* Literacy rate in first language: below 1%. Literacy rate in second language: 50% to 75%. See main entry under USA.

Kaska (Caska, Eastern Nahane, Nahane, Nahani) [kkz] 400 (1995 M. Krauss). Ethnic population: 900 (1995 M. Krauss). Southeastern Yukon Territory Watson Lake, Ross River, and Lower Post, and northern British Columbia border area, Lower Post, Fireside, Good Hope Lake, Dease Lake, and Muncho Lake. *Class:* Na-Dene, Nuclear Na-Dene, Athapaskan-Eyak, Athapaskan, Tahltan-Kaska. *Dialects:* Close to Tahltan. *Lg Use:* Speakers are nearly middle aged, except at Ross River, where there may be younger speakers. Speakers also use English. *Lg Dev:* Taught in primary schools.

Kutenai (Ktunaxa, Kootenai, Kootenay) [kut] 6 in Canada (2002 Poser). Population total all countries: 12. Southeastern British Columbia, Columbia Lake, Lower Kootenay, St Mary's, and Tobacco Plains. Also spoken in USA. *Class:* Language Isolate. *Lg Use:* Speakers are shifting to English. Kutenai is offered as a second language course (1991). All speakers are middle aged or older adults. *Lg Dev:* Dictionary. Grammar. *Other:* Nearly extinct.

Kwakiutl (Kwagiutl, Kwak'wala) [kwk] 190 in Canada (2002 Poser). Population total all countries: 235. Ethnic population: 3,300 (1977 SIL). Northern Vancouver Island and adjacent mainland, British Columbia. Also spoken in USA. *Class:* Wakashan, Northern. *Dialects:* Related to Haisla and Heiltsuk. *Lg Use:* Speakers are shifting to English. Speakers are older adults. *Lg Dev:* Dictionary. Grammar. Bible portions: 1882–1900.

Lakota (Lakhota, Teton) [lkt] Wood Mountain. Those at Wood Mountain may be Dakota. See main entry under USA.

Laurentian (St. Lawrence Iroquoian) [lre] Extinct. Along the St. Lawrence River. *Class:* Iroquoian, Northern Iroquoian. *Other:* A group of languages; no modern descendants. Encountered by Jacques Cartier in 1534 and 1535.

Lillooet (St'at'imcets) [lil] 200 (2002 Poser). Ethnic population: 2,800 (1977 SIL). Southern British Columbia, area of Lillooet and middle Fraser rivers. *Class:* Salishan, Interior Salish, Northern. *Lg Use:* Speakers are older adults. Extensive bilingualism in English. *Lg Dev:* Dictionary. Grammar. *Other:* Language courses in Lillooet (1991).

Malecite-Passamaquoddy (Maliseet-Passamaquoddy) [pqm] 655 in Canada (1998 Statistics Canada). Population total all countries: 1,655. Ethnic population: 3,000 to 4,000 (1998 SIL). New Brunswick, villages along the Saint John River. Malecite mainly in Canada, Passamaquoddy in Maine, USA. Also spoken in USA. *Class:* Algic, Algonquian, Eastern. *Dialects:* Malecite

(Maliseet), Passamaquoddy. *Lg Use:* Most speakers are older adults, but in some communities younger ones may speak it. Interest in the language is increasing in some places. English is preferred by most younger ones. *Lg Dev:* Dictionary. Grammar. Bible portions: 1870.

Maritime Sign Language (Nova Scotian Sign Language) [nsr] Nova Scotia, New Brunswick, and Prince Edward Island. *Class:* Deaf sign language. *Lg Use:* Remembered only by older deaf people. *Other:* Based on British Sign Language. Distinct from American and Quebec sign languages. Nearly extinct.

Michif (French Cree, Metis) [crg] 600 in Canada (1998). Scattered locations in Canada. *Lg Use:* Most or all speakers are older adults. Speakers also use English. *Other:* Formerly buffalo hunters. See main entry under USA.

Micmac (Mi'gmaq, Miigmao, Mi'kmaq, Restigouche) [mic] 7,310 in Canada (1998 Statistics Canada). Population total all countries: 8,510. Ethnic population: 14,200 in Canada (1998 SIL). In Canada, 1,500 are in mainland Nova Scotia, 4,000 on Cape Breton Island, Nova Scotia, 800 on Prince Edward Island and Lennox Island, 4,550 on the east coast of New Brunswick, 3,150 on the Gaspe Peninsula, Quebec, 200 in Newfoundland. Central and northern Nova Scotia. The mainland has 6 major villages: Afton, Picto, Truro, Shubanakati, Bear River, and Yarmouth, and some small communities; Cape Breton Island of Nova Scotia with 5 major villages: Memberto, Eskasoni, Chapel Island, Wakmatkug, and Waikoqomaq; and one small village: Prince Edward Island; the east coast of New Brunswick: Fort Folly, Big Cove, Indian Island, Burnt Church, Eel Ground, Red Bank, Pabino Falls, and Eel River Bar; and eastern Gaspe Peninsula, Quebec, with 3 villages: Gespe'q, Gesgapeqiaq, and Listuguj; and Newfoundland with 1 major village: Conn River. Also spoken in USA. *Class:* Algic, Algonquian, Eastern. *Dialects:* Northern Micmac, Southern Micmac. Generally speakers of dialects have intelligibility between them, but there are lexical, inflectional, word order, and spelling differences. *Lg Use:* There are some communities where only older adults speak Micmac. In 5 communities the language has virtually ceased being used, 4 in English areas (Shubenagadie, Truro, Eel River Bar, Pabineo) and the fifth in Gaspe, Quebec where the second language is French. In larger areas children tend to begin speaking some Micmac, except in Listuguj, where some families are educating their children in French. In some communities, such as Gesgapegiaq, usage is more vigorous. Used in prayers, songs, and readings. Most adults speak Micmac. Many adults below 35 do not speak it. Younger ones may prefer English. Most children learn English first, but there is an effort in many communities to teach children Micmac. The people express the desire to maintain Micmac. There are no monolinguals. In Gesgapegiaq a good number speak Micmac, English, and French. *Lg Dev:* Literacy rate in first language: 1% to 5%. Literacy rate in second language: 50% to 75%. 800 or more readers, 200 who can write it. Oral and written courses exist in most schools in the primary grades. Radio programs. Dictionary. Grammar. NT: 1874–1998. *Other:* Forest. Fishermen; lumbermen. Christian, traditional religion.

Mohawk [moh] 350 in Canada (1998 Statistics Canada). Population total all countries: 3,350. Ethnic population: 24,000 in Canada, 30,000 including USA (1999 SIL). Southwestern Quebec, southern Ontario. Also spoken in USA. *Class:* Iroquoian, Northern Iroquoian, Five Nations, Mohawk-Oneida. *Lg Use:* Most speakers are older adults. In some areas younger ones may speak the language. Speakers also use English. *Lg Dev:* Literacy rate in second language:

75% to 100%. Dictionary. Grammar. Bible portions: 1787–1991.

Montagnais (Innu Aimun, Innu) [moe] 8,483 (1987 Quebec Ministere de la Sante el des Services Sociaux). Population includes 5,866 in Western Montagnais, and 2,617 in Eastern Montagnais. 9,070 first-language speakers of Montagnais and Naskapi (1998 Statistics Canada). Ethnic population: 10,000 (1996 D. Myers SIL). 11 communities in Quebec and Labrador, from Lake St. John eastward along the Saguenay Valley to the north shore of the St. Lawrence River and Gulf of St. Lawrence eastward to St. Augustin, northward to the height of land at Schefferville and inland Labrador (Goose Bay, Lake Melville). Western Montagnais is in 4 communities: Mashteuiatsh (near Roberval, Quebec), Betsiamites, Uashat-Maliotenam (near Sept-Iles, Quebec), and Matimekosh (near Schefferville, Quebec). The others speak Eastern Montagnais: Mingan, Natashquan, La Romaine, Pakuashipi (St. Augustine, Quebec, sometimes called Pakuashipu), and Sheshatshiu (North-West River, Labrador). *Class:* Algic, Algonquian, Central, Cree-Montagnais-Naskapi. *Dialects:* Western Montagnais, Eastern Montagnais. Palatalized l-dialect and palatalized n-dialect within Cree-Montagnais-Naskapi language complex or dialect cluster. There are possibly 3 dialects based on the shifting of Proto-Algonquian *l within Western Montagnais to 'n'. Two Western Montagnais communities (Mashteuiatsh, Betsiamites) use 'l' as the reflex of Proto-Algonquian *l, and the other Western Montagnais (Uashat-Maliotenam, Matimekosh) use 'n'. Uashat-Maliotenam and Matimekosh could be classified as Central Montagnais. All Eastern Montagnais speakers use 'n'. *Lg Use:* Vigorous in all but 2 communities. Rapid shift occurring in communities close to national language cities. Strong use in lower north shore communities and Schefferville. Montagnais has been used as language of instruction in Betsiamites in recent past, and is taught as a subject in other classes. Taught as second language in 2 communities. All ages. Women of all ages and men over 55 are mainly not fluent in national languages: 3,000 people. Mashteuiatsh nearly all French-speaking. Many speakers are fluent in Quebec English (Sheshatshiu in Labrador) or French (other communities in Quebec). *Lg Dev:* Literacy rate in first language: 5%. Literacy rate in second language: 50% to 75% in French or English. Taught in primary schools. Roman script. Dictionary. Grammar. NT: 1990. *Other:* The language is also called 'Innu' in northeast Quebec and Labrador. Culture was and is for the most part based on designated family hunting grounds visited seasonally. Hunting exploited a large variety of animals and fish, including extensive salt-water fishing. Traditionally hunters; trappers; fishermen.

Munsee (Delaware, Ontario Delaware) [umu] 7 or 8 (1991 M. Dale Kinkade). Ethnic population: 400 (1991 M. Dale Kinkade). Southern Ontario, Moraviantown Reserve. *Class:* Algic, Algonquian, Eastern. *Dialects:* Close to Unami in USA. *Lg Use:* Speakers have shifted to English. Speakers are older adults. *Lg Dev:* Dictionary. Grammar. Bible portions: 1818–1821. *Other:* Nearly extinct.

Naskapi (Innu Aimuun, Iyuw Imuun) [nsk] 1,177. Population includes 677 Western Naskapi, 500 Eastern Naskapi (1996 Ministere de la Sante el des Services Sociaux). 9,070 first-language speakers of Naskapi and Montagnais (1998 Statistics Canada). Ethnic population: 1,177 (1996). 2 communities in Quebec and Labrador. Those in Kawawachikamach are about 10 km northeast of Schefferville in northeastern Quebec at the height of land (watershed). On December 15, 2002 most of the Mushuau Innu moved from Utshimassits (Davis Inlet) to Natuashish on the mainland. Natuashish is an isolated community in

Labrador. *Class:* Algic, Algonquian, Central, Cree-Montagnais-Naskapi. *Dialect:* Western Naskapi, Eastern Naskapi (Mushuau Innu). *Lg Use:* Vigorous in both dialects. Slow shift occurring to English. Western Naskapi as language of instruction in school at Kawawachikamach, elsewhere as a subject in school in lower grades, taught as a subject up to secondary level. *Lg Dev:* Literacy rate in first language: 1% to 5%. Literacy rate in second language: 50%. Taught in primary schools. Cree syllabary. Dictionary. Grammar. *Other:* Naskapi culture was nomadic and completely dependent on the migratory habits of the caribou. Caribou hunting and land use still seen as important. Hunting in the bush in watersheds north from Schefferville, west from Davis Inlet.

Nisga'a (Nass, Niska, Nishka, Nisk'a, Nishga) [ncg] 700. Possibly 5 scattered speakers in Alaska (1997). Ethnic population: 5,400 (1997 M. Krauss). Lower Nass River Valley, villages of Aiyansh (Ay'ans), Canyon City (Gitwinksihlkw), Greenville (Laxtalts'ap or Gitxat'in), Kincolith (Gingolx), British Columbia. *Class:* Penutian, Tsimshian. *Dialects:* Variation within Nass not great enough to be considered dialects. High degree of inherent intelligibility between Nisga'a and Gitxsan. *Lg Use:* About 1,500 speak Nisga'a as second or third language. Speakers are from ages 22 to 95. Children learn Nisga'a in School District #92. Many young adults prefer English. Some children speak the language but most prefer English. Speakers consider Nisga'a and Gitxsan to be ethnically distinct. Some older Nisga'a speak Tsimshian as second language; English mostly used. *Lg Dev:* Dictionary. Grammar. Bible portions: 1906. *Other:* Schools try to teach oral and written Nisga'a. VSO; prepositions; genitives after noun heads; articles, adjectives, numerals before noun heads; relatives without noun heads; question word initial in sentence; 3 or 4 prefixes, 1 inflectional suffix; word order distinguishes subjects, objects, indirect objects, given and new information, topic and comment; verb affixes mark person and number of subject and object unless obscured by phonological rule; pronominal system is fully ergative; morphological passives, but not by construction; direct causatives indicated by suffixes, indirect (jussive) by prefix; CVC; nontonal. Riverine. Pine and cedar forest with some deciduous trees. Sea level to 300 meters. Fishermen; hunters; gatherers. Christian.

Nootka (Nutka, Nuuchahnulth) [noo] 200 (2002 Poser). Population includes Nitinat 30 (1991 M. Dale Kinkade). Ethnic population: 3,500 (1977 SIL). Southwestern British Columbia, Nitinat along Pacific side of Vancouver Island and on Nitinat Lake. *Class:* Wakashan, Southern. *Dialect:* Nitinat (Ditinat, Didinaht, Nitinaht). *Lg Use:* Speakers are older adults. Speakers also use English. *Lg Dev:* Dictionary. Grammar. *Other:* People are called 'West Coast People'.

Ojibwa, Central (Central Ojibwe, Ojibway, Ojibwe) [ojc] Central Ontario from Lake Nipigon in the west to Lake Nipissing in the east. *Class:* Algic, Algonquian, Central, Ojibwa. *Dialects:* An area of transitional dialects (see Lisa Valentine, 1995, Making it their own: Severn Ojibwe communicative practices, Univ. of Toronto Press, p. 22).

Ojibwa, Eastern (Ojibwe, Ojibway) [ojg] 25,885 (1998 Statistics Canada). Southern Ontario, north of Lake Ontario and east of Georgian Bay. East of a north-south line through the base of Bruce Peninsula (Rhodes 1976:131). *Class:* Algic, Algonquian, Central, Ojibwa. *Lg Use:* Dying out in many areas. Concerted effort via language teaching in public schools and other efforts to reverse the decline. Probably all speakers also use English; some use other Ojibwa varieties. *Lg Dev:* Taught in primary schools. Dictionary. Grammar.

Ojibwa, Northwestern (Northern Ojibwa, Ojibway, Ojibwe) [ojb] 20,000 (2000 UBS). Southern northwest Ontario into Manitoba. *Class:* Algic, Algonquian, Central, Ojibwa. *Dialects:* Berens River Ojibwa (Saulteaux), Lac Seul Ojibwa, Albany River Ojibwa, Lake of the Woods Ojibwa, Rainy River Ojibwa. *Lg Use:* Concerted effort via language teaching in public schools and other efforts to reverse decline in use. *Lg Dev:* Literacy rate in first language: 50% to 75%. Taught in primary schools. Grammar. NT: 1988.

Ojibwa, Severn (Northern Ojibwa, Ojibway, Ojibwe, Ojicree, Oji-Cree, Cree) [ojs] 8,000 (1989 SIL). Ethnic population: 8,000 or fewer, possibly including some Northwestern Ojibwa (1999 SIL). Northern northwest Ontario into Manitoba. *Class:* Algic, Algonquian, Central, Ojibwa. *Dialects:* Winisk River Ojibwa, Severn River Ojibwa. *Lg Use:* Concerted effort via language teaching in public schools and other efforts to reverse decline in use. Speakers are older adults. *Lg Dev:* Literacy rate in first language: 50% to 75%. Grammar. NT: 1988.

Ojibwa, Western (Saulteaux, Plains Ojibway, Ojibway, Ojibwe) [ojw] 10,000 (2002 Poser). Ethnic population: 60,000 (1997 SIL). Westward from Lake Winnipeg into Saskatchewan with outlying groups as far west as British Colombia. *Class:* Algic, Algonquian, Central, Ojibwa. *Lg Use:* Vigorous in most areas. In some areas young people and children prefer English. All ages in many areas. *Lg Dev:* Literacy rate in first language: 30% to 60%.

Okanagan (Okanagan-Colville, Okanagon, Okanogan) [oka] 400 in Canada (1977 SIL). Population total all countries: 512. Ethnic population: 3,000 (1977 SIL). Another source says 10,000 in the ethnic group (1996 Peter Stark). Colville has fewer than 200 (1999 R. McDonald). South central British Columbia, east of the Fraser Valley and to the west of Kootenai. Also spoken in USA. *Class:* Salishan, Interior Salish, Southern. *Dialects:* Southern Okanagan, Sanpoil. *Lg Use:* Speakers are older adults. Speakers also use English. *Lg Dev:* Dictionary. Grammar. *Other:* Language courses in Okanagan (1991).

Oneida [one] 200 in Canada (1991 M. Dale Kincade). Population total all countries: 250. Ethnic population: 1,500 to 2,000 (1997 K. Michelson). Southern Ontario, Six Nations Reserve. Also spoken in USA. *Class:* Iroquoian, Northern Iroquoian, Five Nations, Mohawk-Oneida. *Lg Use:* Speakers are older adults. Speakers also use English. *Lg Dev:* Grammar. Bible portions: 1880–1942.

Onondaga (Onandaga) [ono] 50 to 100 in Canada (1991 M. Dale Kinkade). Population total all countries: 65 to 115. Ethnic population: 18,173 (1997 H. Woodbury). Southern Ontario: Six Nations Reserve. Also spoken in USA. *Class:* Iroquoian, Northern Iroquoian, Five Nations, Seneca-Onondaga, Onondaga. *Lg Use:* Speakers are older adults. Speakers also use English. *Lg Dev:* Grammar.

Ottawa (Odawa, Ojibwe, Ojibway) [otw] Including Ottawa, Eastern and Central Ojibwa in USA: 8,000 speakers. Including Ottawa and all Ojibwa in Canada: 30,000 (1999 C. Fiero SIL). All Ojibwa first-language speakers in Canada: 25,885 (1998 Statistics Canada). Total of 35,000 in all Ojibwa, Chippewa, and Ottawa in Canada and USA (1999 C. Fiero). Ethnic population: 60,000. Islands in, and areas surrounding, Lake Huron, from the region of Manitoulin Island to southern Ontario north of Lake Erie. Walople Island Reserve. West of a north south line through the base of Bruce Peninsula (Rhodes 1976:131). Also spoken in USA. *Class:* Algic, Algonquian, Central, Ojibwa. *Lg Use:* Vigorous on Manitoulin Island. Dying out in many areas. Concerted effort via language teaching in public schools and other efforts to reverse the decline. Most adults and some younger ones. All speakers also use English, some use other Ojibwa varieties. *Lg Dev:* Taught in primary schools. Dictionary. Grammar. Bible portions: 1841–1844.

Other: Called Eastern Ojibwa in Bloomfield's grammar. In southern Ontario also called Chippewa.

Pentlatch (Puntlatch) [ptw] Extinct. Ethnic population: 40 (1977 SIL). South Vancouver Island, British Columbia. *Class:* Salishan, Central Salish, Northern. *Lg Use:* Extinct since about 1940.

Plautdietsch (Low German, Mennonite German, Mennoniten Platt) [pdt] 80,000 in Canada (1978 Kloss and McConnell). Total German first-language speakers in Canada including standard German, 561,000 (1986 Hawkins in B. Comrie). 110,735 in Latin America are fairly monolingual. Population total all countries: 401,699. Southern Canada; Ontario, Saskatchewan, Manitoba, Alberta, British Columbia. Also spoken in Argentina, Belize, Bolivia, Brazil, Costa Rica, Germany, Kazakhstan, Mexico, Paraguay, Russia (Asia), Uruguay, USA. *Class:* Indo-European, Germanic, West, Low Saxon-Low Franconian, Low Saxon. *Dialects:* 50% intelligible with other Low German languages, Standard German, Pennsylvania German, or Hutterite German. *Lg Use:* 20,000 second-language speakers. 110,735 or more speakers in Latin America are mainly monolingual in Plautdietsch. 50% of speakers in Canada speak Standard German and 95% speak English as second language. *Lg Dev:* Literacy rate in second language: 95%. Bible: 2003. *Other:* SVO; prepositions; genitives after noun heads; question word initial; 5 prefixes; 2 suffixes; nontonal. Christian.

Potawatomi (Pottawottomi) [pot] Southern Ontario, Walpole Island Reserve. *Lg Use:* Speakers are shifting to English. Speakers are older adults. See main entry under USA.

Quebec Sign Language (Langue Signe Quebecars, Langue des Signes Québécoise, LSQ, Langue des Signes du Québec) [fcs] 50,000 to 60,000 (2000 SIL). Quebec, except northern Quebec, Ottawa, Northern Ontario, Bathurst New Brunswick, and a few in Vancouver and Edmonton. *Class:* Deaf sign language. *Dialects:* Related to French Sign Language (LSF). *Lg Use:* In northern Quebec, deaf people use ASL, with English the second language. Some use Signed French. Segregated deaf education by sex resulted in some lexical differences between the sexes; female use more influenced by ASL and LSQ; male by Signed French and LSQ. It is rare for a deaf child to learn both LSQ and ASL. A few adults have a working knowledge of both. *Other:* Christian.

Salish, Straits (Straits) [str] 20 in Canada (2002 Poser). Ethnic population: 3,000 (1977 SIL). Southeastern tip of Vancouver Island, British Columbia. Also spoken in USA. *Class:* Salishan, Central Salish, Straits. *Dialects:* Saanich, Samish, Lummi, Ts'ooke, Semiahmoo, Songish. Most speakers are of the Saanich dialect. *Lg Use:* Ts'ooke, Semiahmoo, Songish dialects are extinct. Speakers are shifting to English. Speakers are older adults. *Lg Dev:* Dictionary. Grammar. *Other:* Nearly extinct.

Sarsi (Sarcee, Tsuu T'ina) [srs] 50 (1991 M. Dale Kinkade). Ethnic population: 600 (1977 SIL). Alberta, near Calgary. *Class:* Na-Dene, Nuclear Na-Dene, Athapaskan-Eyak, Athapaskan, Canadian, Sarcee. *Lg Use:* Speakers are shifting to English. Speakers are older adults. *Lg Dev:* Grammar.

Sechelt [sec] 40 (1990 M.D. Kinkade). Ethnic population: 550 (1977 SIL). British Columbia coast north of Vancouver. *Class:* Salishan, Central Salish, Northern. *Lg Use:* Speakers are shifting to English. *Lg Dev:* Dictionary. Grammar. *Other:* Nearly extinct.

Sekani [sek] 30 to 40 (1997 Sharon Hargus). Ethnic population: 600 (1982 SIL and 1997 S. Hargus). North central British Columbia, McLeod Lake, Ware (Finlay River), Ingenika. *Class:* Na-Dene, Nuclear Na-Dene, Athapaskan-Eyak, Athapaskan, Canadian, Beaver-Sekani.

Lg Use: Speakers are older adults. The majority also use English. *Lg Dev:* Bible portions: 1969. *Other:* Nearly extinct.

Seneca [see] 25 in Canada (1991 M. Dale Kinkade). Six Nations Reserve, Ontario. *Lg Use:* Speakers are shifting to English. Speakers are older adults. See main entry under USA.

Shuswap (Secwepemc) [shs] 500 (2002 Poser). Ethnic population: 6,500 (1990 M.D. Kinkade). British Columbia, east central. *Class:* Salishan, Interior Salish, Northern. *Dialects:* Eastern Shuswap, Western Shuswap. *Lg Use:* Speakers are shifting to English. Speakers are older adults. *Lg Dev:* Dictionary. Grammar. *Other:* Language courses in Shuswap (1991).

Slavey, North (Slavi, Dené, Mackenzian, "Slave") [scs] 790 (2001 SIL). Ethnic population: 1,600 (1995 Michael Krauss). Mackenzie District, along the middle Mackenzie River from Fort Norman north, around Great Bear Lake, Northwest Territories, and in the Mackenzie Mountains In the isolated communities of Deline, Fort Good Hope, Tulita, Colville Lake, Norman Wells, and Yellowknife. *Class:* Na-Dene, Nuclear Na-Dene, Athapaskan-Eyak, Athapaskan, Canadian, Hare-Chipewyan, Hare-Slavey. *Dialects:* Hare, Bearlake, Mountain. Distinct from South Slavey. *Lg Use:* 4 or 5 communities have vigorous language use. All ages in some communities. *Lg Dev:* Dictionary.

Slavey, South (Slavi, "Slave," Dené, Mackenzian) [xsl] 1,410 (2001 SIL). Ethnic population: 3,600 (1995 M. Krauss). Great Slave Lake, upper Mackenzie River and drainage in Mackenzie District, northeast Alberta, northwest British Columbia in the communities of Fort Liard, Fort Providence, Fort Simpson, Fort Smith, Hay River, Hay River Dene (reserve), Jean Marie River, Nahanni Butte, Trout Lake, Wrigley and Yellowknife. *Class:* Na-Dene, Nuclear Na-Dene, Athapaskan-Eyak, Athapaskan, Canadian, Hare-Chipewyan, Hare-Slavey. *Dialects:* North and South Slavey are separate languages. *Lg Use:* People older than young people still use South Slavey in smaller, isolated communities, but serious attrition among children and young people. *Lg Dev:* Literacy rate in first language: below 1%. Literacy rate in second language: 25% to 50%. Dictionary. Grammar. NT: 1891.

Squamish [squ] 15 (2002 Poser). Ethnic population: 2,300. Southwestern British Columbia, north of Vancouver. *Class:* Salishan, Central Salish, Squamish. *Lg Use:* Speakers are shifting to English. Speakers are older adults. *Lg Dev:* Dictionary. Grammar. *Other:* VSO. Nearly extinct.

Stoney (Stony, Nakoda) [sto] 1,000 to 1,500 (1987 SIL). Ethnic population: 3,200 (1987 SIL). Southern Alberta, west and northwest of Calgary, and central Alberta, west of Edmonton. Southern Stoney occupy 3 reserves represented on the Stoney Tribal Council at Morley, Alberta: Eden Valley, west of Longview, Alberta, the southernmost reserve and principally Bearspaw Band members (about 400 speakers); Morley, west of Calgary, the main administrative center of Stoney Country, with about 2,700 people of all three southern bands: the Bearspaw, Chiniki, and Wesley Bands; Big Horn Reserve west of Rocky Mountain House, the most northerly of the 3, with about 100 people, mostly Wesley Band. *Class:* Siouan, Siouan Proper, Central, Mississippi Valley, Dakota. *Dialects:* Southern Stoney, Northern Stoney. Dialects nearly 100% intelligible with each other. The northern dialect is spoken at Duffield (Paul Band) and Lac St. Anne (Alexis Band). Lexical similarity 89% with Assiniboine, 86% with Dakota of Manitoba, 85% with Dakota of North Dakota, 83% with Lakota. *Lg Use:* Speakers are adults. *Lg Dev:* Literacy rate in first language: below 1%. Literacy rate in second language: 75% to 100%. Bible portions: 1970.

Tagish [tgx] 2 (1995 M. Krauss). Ethnic population: 400 possibly (1995 M. Krauss). Southern Yukon, west or west-northwest of the Tlingit, with some at Carcross. *Class:* Na-Dene, Nuclear Na-Dene, Athapaskan-Eyak, Athapaskan, Tahltan-Kaska. *Lg Use:* Speakers are also fluent in Tlingit and speak English as second language. *Other:* Tagish label was also applied to inland Tlingit. Nearly extinct.

Tahltan [tht] 35 (2002 Poser). Ethnic population: 750 (1977 SIL). Telegraph Creek, northwest British Columbia. *Class:* Na-Dene, Nuclear Na-Dene, Athapaskan-Eyak, Athapaskan, Tahltan-Kaska. *Dialects:* Close to Kaska. *Lg Use:* Speakers are shifting to English. Speakers are older adults. *Other:* Nearly extinct.

Tanana, Upper (Nabesna) [tau] 10 in Canada (1995 M. Krauss). Ethnic population: 40 (1995 M. Krauss). Southwestern Yukon Territory, Beaver Creek. *Lg Use:* Speakers are shifting to English. See main entry under USA.

Thompson (Ntlakapmuk, Nklapmx) [thp] 595 (1998 Statistics Canada). Ethnic population: 3,000 (1977 SIL). British Columbia, south central. Fraser River north of Yale, and the lower Thompson River and tributaries. *Class:* Salishan, Interior Salish, Northern. *Lg Use:* Speakers are older adults. Speakers also use English. *Lg Dev:* Dictionary. Grammar. *Other:* Language courses in Thompson (1991). Nicola and Coldwater are tribal bands.

Tlingit (Thlinget, Tlinkit) [tli] 145 in Canada (1998 Statistics Canada). Ethnic population: 1,000 in Canada (1995 M. Krauss). Northwestern British Columbia: Atlin, and southern Yukon: Carcross and Teslin. *Lg Use:* Speakers are older adults, but many in the 40 to 55 range understand a certain amount of Tlingit. English is the first or second language of the ethnic group. *Lg Dev:* In Teslin. See main entry under USA.

Tsetsaut [txc] Extinct. Portland Canal area, borderline to southwest Alaska and British Columbia. *Class:* Na-Dene, Nuclear Na-Dene, Athapaskan-Eyak, Athapaskan. *Lg Use:* Became extinct about 1930.

Tsimshian (Tsimpshean, Zimshian, Chimmezyan) [tsi] 750 in Canada (2002 Poser). Population includes 1 Southern Tsimshian. Population total all countries: 800. Ethnic population: 3,200 in Canada (1995 M. Krauss). Northern coast of British Columbia. Southern Tsimshian is at the southern end on the coast at Klemtu. Also spoken in USA. *Class:* Penutian, Tsimshian. *Dialects:* Southern Tsimshian (Sguxs, Old Klemtu), Coast Tsimshian (Sm'algyax). *Lg Use:* Speakers are older adults. Speakers also use English. *Lg Dev:* Dictionary. Grammar. Bible portions: 1885–1898. *Other:* Southern Tsimshian is very divergent. SOV; prepositions; genitives, adjectives before noun heads.

Tuscarora [tus] 7 or 8 in Canada (1991 Kinkade). Population total all countries: 11 to 13. Six Nations Reserve, Ontario. Also spoken in USA. *Class:* Iroquoian, Northern Iroquoian, Tuscarora-Nottoway. *Lg Use:* Speakers are shifting to English. Speakers are older adults. *Lg Dev:* Dictionary. Grammar. *Other:* Nearly extinct.

Tutchone, Northern (Selkirk) [ttm] 200 (1995 M. Krauss). Ethnic population: 1,000 (1995 M. Krauss). Central Yukon, Mayo-Stewart, Selkirk-Pelly, Carmacks, Whitehorse, and White River areas. *Class:* Na-Dene, Nuclear Na-Dene, Athapaskan-Eyak, Athapaskan, Tutchone. *Lg Use:* Speakers are shifting to English. Speakers are older adults. *Lg Dev:* Taught in primary schools.

Tutchone, Southern [tce] 200 (1995 M. Krauss). Ethnic population: 1,400 (1995 M. Krauss). Southwestern Yukon Territory, Whitehorse, Aishihik-Champagne, and Kluane-Burwash areas. *Class:* Na-Dene, Nuclear Na-

Dene, Athapaskan-Eyak, Athapaskan, Tutchone. *Lg Use:* Speakers are shifting to English. Speakers are older adults. *Lg Dev:* Taught in primary schools.

Cayman Islands

Cayman Islands. 43,103. National or official language: English. Literacy rate: 97.5% over age 15. Also includes Haitian Creole French (20,762), Spanish (2,212). Deaf institutions: 1. The number of languages listed for Cayman Islands is 1. See map on page 739.

English [eng] 20,000 in Cayman Islands (2002). *Dialect:* Cayman Islands English. *Lg Use:* National language. *Other:* The colloquial English seems to have borrowed creole features similar to Jamaica and Central America without having undergone creolization (John Holm 1989:479–480). Structurally similar to a creole language. May be close to Belize Kriol. Agriculturalists: cotton. See main entry under United Kingdom.

Chile

Republic of Chile, República de Chile. 15,823,957. National or official language: Spanish. Literacy rate: 92% to 95%. Also includes Catalan-Valencian-Balear, Standard German (35,000), Vlax Romani. Information mainly from A. Tovar 1961, 1966; Grete Mostny 1965; S. Wurm and S. Hattori 1981; N. Besnier OIEL 1992; SIL 1969–2003. Blind population: 100,000. Deaf population: 845,849. Deaf institutions: 7. The number of languages listed for Chile is 11. Of those, 9 are living languages and 2 are extinct. See map on page 741.

Aymara, Central [ayr] 899 in Chile (1994 Hans Gundermann K.). Ethnic population: 20,000 in Chile (1983 SIL). Mountains of extreme north, first region Tarapacá; Arica, Parinacota, Iquique. *Lg Use:* Speakers also use Spanish. See main entry under Bolivia.

Chilean Sign Language [csg] *Class:* Deaf sign language.

Huilliche (Veliche, Huiliche) [huh] 2,000 (1982 SIL). South of the Mapuche, Tenth Region, from Valdivia to Chiloé. *Class:* Araucanian. *Dialect:* Tsesungún. Related to Mapudungun, but barely intelligible with it. *Lg Use:* Few domains. Speakers are older adults. Most of the ethnic group speaks Spanish as first language. *Other:* Mountain valleys.

Kakauhua (Kaukaue, Cacahue) [kbf] Extinct. *Class:* Alacalufan.

Kunza (Likanantaí, Lipe, Ulipe, Atacameño) [kuz] Extinct. A few speakers were located in 1949 and since by anthropologists. Ethnic population: 2,000 (2000 W. Adelaar). Peine, Socaire (Salar de Atacama), and Caspana. *Class:* Unclassified. *Dialects:* Greenberg places it in Macro-Chibchan. *Lg Use:* Members of the ethnic group now speak Spanish. *Lg Dev:* Dictionary.

Mapudungun (Mapudungu, "Araucano," Mapuche) [arn] 200,000 in Chile (1982 SIL). Population total all countries: 300,000. Ethnic population: 928,000 (1992 census). Between the Itata and Tolten rivers. Also spoken in Argentina. *Class:* Araucanian. *Dialects:* Moluche (Ngoluche, Manzanero), Picunche, Pehuenche. Easy intelligibility among all dialects. Pehuenche and Moluche are very close. *Lg Use:* All ages. Bilingual level estimates for Spanish: 0 0%, 1 8%, 2 50%, 3 30%, 4 10%, 5 2%. *Lg Dev:* Literacy rate in first language: below 1%. Literacy rate in second language: 21%. 85,000 are literate in Spanish. NT: 1997. *Other:* The people name is 'Mapuche'. SVO. Mountain slope, coastal plain, riverine. Deciduous forest, rolling farm land. Sea level to 2,000 meters. Peasant agriculturalists. Traditional religion, Christian.

Qawasqar (Kaweskar, Kawesqar, Alacalufe, Alacaluf, Halakwulup) [alc] 20 (1996 Oscar Aguilera). Population includes 10 in Puerto Edin. Channel Region, western Patagonia, Isle of Wellington off south Chilean coast, 49 degrees south with center in Puerto Edin. Speakers of the extinct Aksanás dialect also lived in Puerto Edén. *Class:* Alacalufan. *Dialect:* Aksanás (Aksana). *Lg Use:* The youngest speakers are from 3 to 20 years old (1996). Positive language attitude. Reports are that speakers are not bilingual in Spanish (Christos Clairis, M. Ruhlen 1987, personal communication). *Lg Dev:* Dictionary. Grammar. *Other:* J. Suarez says Aksanás vocabulary differences might be explained by word taboo. Fishermen. Nearly extinct.

Quechua, Chilean [cqu] Ethnic population: 4,563 (2000 WCD). Northern second region. *Class:* Quechuan, Quechua II, C. *Dialects:* May be intelligible with, or the same as, South Bolivian Quechua. *Lg Use:* There may be no Quechua speakers in Chile.

Rapa Nui (Easter Island, Pascuense) [rap] 3,392 in Chile (2000 WCD). Population includes 2,200 on Easter Island; 200 to 300 on Chile mainland, Tahiti, and USA. Ethnic population: 3,500. Easter Island, 3,800 km from Chile, 4,000 km from Tahiti. Also spoken in French Polynesia, USA. *Class:* Austronesian, Malayo-Polynesian, Central-Eastern, Eastern Malayo-Polynesian, Oceanic, Central-Eastern Oceanic, Remote Oceanic, Central Pacific, East Fijian-Polynesian, Polynesian, Nuclear, East, Rapanui. *Dialects:* Lexical similarity 64% with Hawaiian, Mangareva, Rarotonga, 63% with Marquesan; 62% with Tahitian, Paumotu. *Lg Use:* Speakers also use Spanish. *Lg Dev:* Literacy rate in first language: below 1%. Literacy rate in second language: 25% to 50%. Grammar. *Other:* Difficult cultivation. VSO. Volcanic island. Tropical. Fishermen; craftsmen.

Spanish (Español, Castellano) [spa] 13,800,000 in Chile (1995). Population includes 25% Spanish, 66% mestizo. *Lg Use:* National language. See main entry under Spain.

Yámana (Yaghan, Yagán, Tequenica, Háusi Kúta) [yag] 1 (2003). Ethnic population: 100 (2000 W. Adelaar). Patagonia, Isla Navarino, Puerto Williams, Ukika hamlet. Extinct in Argentina. *Class:* Language Isolate. *Dialects:* Tovar (1961) says it was closest to Qawasqar, and had some relationship to Ona. Earlier there were up to five dialects. *Lg Use:* One report says that there are still speakers near the Beagle Canal Naval Base in Chile. Members of the ethnic group now speak Spanish. *Lg Dev:* Dictionary. Bible portions: 1881–1886. *Other:* Their name for their language is 'Háusi Kúta'. Nearly extinct.

Colombia

Republic of Colombia, República de Colombia. 42,310,775. 500,000 speakers of American Indian languages (1997 Centro Colombiano de Estudios de Lenguas Aborígenes). National or official language: Spanish. Literacy rate: 70% to 80%. Also includes Catalan-Valencian-Balear, Yagua, Yuhup. Information mainly from S. H. Levinsohn 1976 a, b, c; Arango and Sánchez 1998; SIL 1964–2003. Blind population: 30,000 (1982 WCE). Deaf population: 300,000 to 2,157,094 in Colombia (1998), 50,000 in Bogotá, half school-aged (1992). Deaf institutions: 8. The number of languages listed for Colombia is 101. Of those, 80 are living languages and 21 are extinct. See maps beginning on page 750.

Achagua (Ajagua, Xagua) [aca] 400 (1994 SIL). Rio Meta near Puerto Gaitan. Not in Venezuela. *Class:* Arawakan, Maipuran, Northern Maipuran, Inland. *Dialects:* Close to Piapoco. *Lg Use:* Used in the home. Speakers are trilingual in Achagua, Spanish, and Piapoco. *Lg Dev:*

Literacy rate in first language: 1% to 5%. Literacy rate in second language: 5% to 25%. *Other:* Fair degree of acculturation. Agriculturalists.

Andaqui (Andaki) [ana] Extinct. Southern highlands. *Class:* Barbacoan, Andaqui. *Other:* Not the same as Andoque, which is in Amazonas.

Andoque (Andoke) [ano] 619 (2000 WCD). 50 monolinguals. Extinct in Peru (1992 SIL). There were 10,000 in 1908 (Landaburu 1979). Aduche River (tributary of Caquetá) 15 km downriver from Araracuara, Amazonas. *Class:* Language Isolate. *Dialects:* Mason (1950:246 with disclaimer), Tax (1960:433), and Kaufman (1990:43 tentatively) say this is Witotoan. Tovar (1961:150), Witte (1981:1), and Aschmann (1993:2) say it is an isolate. *Lg Use:* 80% have routine proficiency in Spanish. *Other:* People are somewhat acculturated. Tropical forest. Rubber gatherers.

Anserma (Anserna) [ans] Extinct. *Class:* Choco. *Dialects:* Related to Cauca, Arma (both extinct), and Caramanta.

Arhuaco (Aruaco, Bintuk, Bíntukua, Bintucua, Ica, Ijca, Ijka, Ika, Ike) [arh] 14,301 (1998 Arango and Sánchez). 90% are monolingual. Ethnic population: 14,301. Southern slopes of Sierra Nevada de Santa Marta. *Class:* Chibchan, Aruak. *Lg Use:* All ages. A few use Spanish as second language. *Lg Dev:* Literacy rate in first language: 1% to 5%. Literacy rate in second language: 15% to 25%. Grammar. *Other:* The people use the name 'Ika'. Strong traditional culture. SOV.

Arma [aoh] Extinct. *Class:* Choco. *Lg Use:* People spoke either Cenu or Cauca (both extinct).

Awa-Cuaiquer (Coaiquer, Quaiquer, Kwaiker, Awa, Awa Pit, Cuaiquer) [kwi] 20,000 in Colombia (1986 SIL). Population total all countries: 21,000. Pacific slopes of the Andes, Nariño, from Ecuador border north, near Barbacoas. Also spoken in Ecuador. *Class:* Barbacoan, Pasto. *Dialects:* More distantly related to Chachi and Colorado. *Lg Use:* Bilingual level estimates for Spanish: 0 55%, 1 30%, 2 10%, 3 5%, 4 0%, 5 0%. Most men also use Spanish. It is mainly women and children that are monolingual. *Lg Dev:* Literacy rate in first language: below 1%. Literacy rate in second language: below 5%. Grammar. NT: 2002. *Other:* SOV. Mountain slope. Tropical forest. 200 to 300 meters. Swidden agriculturalists.

Barasana (Southern Barasano, Paneroa, Eduria, Edulia) [bsn] 350 (1990 SIL). Pira-Paraná River and tributaries, southern Vaupés Region. Jepa Matsi in Brazil may be a dialect. *Class:* Tucanoan, Eastern Tucanoan, Central, Southern. *Dialects:* Taiwano (Taibano, Taiwaeno), Janera, Comematsa. *Lg Use:* Taiwano is treated culturally as a separate language. *Lg Dev:* Literacy rate in first language: 1% to 5%. Literacy rate in second language: 5% to 15%. Dictionary. Grammar. NT: 2001. *Other:* OVS. Interfluvial. Tropical forest. 200 meters. Swidden agriculturalists.

Barbacoas [bpb] Extinct. Near the coastal town of Barbacoas, Nariño. *Class:* Barbacoan, Pasto.

Barí (Motilone, Motilón) [mot] 850 in Colombia (2000 WCD). Population total all countries: 1,700. Oro River and Catatumbo River Region. Also spoken in Venezuela. *Class:* Chibchan, Motilon. *Dialects:* M. Durbin questions its classification as Chibchan; Voegelin and Voegelin (1977) classify it as Arawakan. *Lg Dev:* Bible portions.

Bora (Boro) [boa] 500 in Colombia. Population includes 100 or more Miraña and 400 other Bora. Bora are in Providencia on the Igaraparana (tributary of the Putumayo). Miraña are on the lower Caquetá River, near the mouth of the Cabinari River, Amazonas. *Dialects:* Miraña (Miranha), Bora. *Other:* The Miraña want a school. Riverine. See main entry under Peru.

Cabiyarí (Cabiuarí, Cauyarí, Kauyarí, Cuyare, Kawillary) [cbb] 50 (1976 Bourgue). Cananarí River (tributary of the

Apaporis and Vaupés). *Class:* Arawakan, Maipuran, Northern Maipuran, Inland. *Other:* High degree of intermarriage with Barasana. Nearly extinct.

Cacua (Macu de Cubeo, Macu de Guanano, Macu de Desano, Báda, Kákwa) [cbv] 150 (1982 SIL). Many are monolingual, especially children. Wacará, 30 kilometers east of Mitú, Lower Vaupés Region. *Class:* Maku. *Dialects:* Vaupés Cacua, Macú-Paraná Cacua. Related to Jupda and Nukak. *Lg Use:* Vigorous. Some bilingualism in Cubeo, Desano, and Guanano, but none in Spanish. *Lg Dev:* Literacy rate in first language: 10%. Literacy rate in second language: below 5% in Spanish. Bible portions: 1975. *Other:* SOV, OSV. Interfluvial. Tropical forest. 200 meters. Hunters; gatherers (nomadic); swidden agriculturalists.

Cagua [cbh] Extinct. *Class:* Unclassified.

Camsá (Kamsa, Coche, Sibundoy, Kamemtxa, Kamse, Camëntsëá) [kbh] 4,022 (1998 Arango and Sánchez). Ethnic population: 4,020. Sibundoy Valley, Putumayo Region. *Class:* Language Isolate. *Lg Dev:* Literacy rate in first language: 40%. Literacy rate in second language: 85%. NT: 1990. *Other:* Ruhlen and others classify it as Equatorial. Mountain slope.

Carabayo ("Amazonas Macusa") [cby] 150. Amazonas Department, halfway between the San Bernardo and Pure rivers. 3 long houses, at least. *Class:* Unclassified. *Other:* The name "Macusa" or "Macú" means 'savage', and is arbitrarily applied to uncontacted groups.

Caramanta [crf] Extinct. Near city of Andes, Christiania, Municipio de Jardín, Antioquía region. *Class:* Choco.

Carapana (Mochda, Moxdoa, Karapaná, Karapano, Carapana-Tapuya, Mextã) [cbc] 600 in Colombia (1990 SIL). Population total all countries: 650. Caño Tí (tributary of the middle Vaupés River) and upper Papurí and Pirá-Paraná rivers, Vaupés Region. Also spoken in Brazil. *Class:* Tucanoan, Eastern Tucanoan, Central, Tatuyo. *Lg Use:* Due to intermarriage with neighboring groups, almost all Tatuyo and Waimaha speak Carapana as well as their first language. *Lg Dev:* Literacy rate in first language: 50%. Literacy rate in second language: 50%. Grammar. NT: 1992. *Other:* Riverine, interfluvial. Tropical forest. Swidden agriculturalists.

Carijona (Karijona, Carihona, Omagua, Umawa, Hianacoto-Umaua) [cbd] 140 (1993 SIL). Upper Vaupés, Yarí, and lower Caquetá rivers, 1 hour by motorized canoe; 2 to 3 hours by canoe south of Miraflores, around Puerto Nare. *Class:* Carib, Southern, Southeastern Colombia. *Dialects:* M. Durbin says there are possibly two separate languages, Hianacoto-Umaua and Carijona. The two groups have not had contact for many years. *Lg Use:* Inter-marrying with other tribes. Some bilingualism in Spanish. *Lg Dev:* Some interest in literacy. *Other:* All worked for one rubber hunter. Reported to have come from the Yarí Indian area originally. Male descent groups, exogamous. OVS. Hunters; fishermen; agriculturalists: manioc. Formerly rubber hunters.

Cauca [cca] Extinct. *Class:* Choco. *Dialects:* Related to Anserma.

Chibcha (Muisca, Mosca) [chb] Extinct. Central highlands. *Class:* Chibchan, Chibchan Proper. *Lg Use:* The Chibcha people are still located near the towns of Tocancipa, Cota, Gachancipa and Tenjo. No speakers are left. *Other:* Almost one million before extinction in the 18th century. SOV.

Chimila (Caca Weranos, San Jorge, Shimizya) [cbg] 2,000 (1993 census). Lowlands south and west of Fundación, and scattered in the central part of Magdalena Department. *Class:* Chibchan, Unclassified. *Lg Use:* Vigorous. Speakers have low proficiency in Spanish. *Lg Dev:* Literacy rate in first language: 1% to 2%. Literacy rate in second language: 5%. *Other:* Its classification as Aruak is

questionable. There are two major separated groups. Work for local settlers.

Chipiajes [cbe] Extinct. *Class:* Unclassified. *Other:* A Sáliba last name. Many Guahibo have that last name.

Cocama-Cocamilla (Cocama, Kokama) [cod] Ethnic population: 20 in Colombia. Lower Putumayo. *Lg Use:* Speakers in Colombia are trilingual in Spanish, Portuguese, and Cocama. See main entry under Peru.

Cofán (Kofan, Kofane, A'i) [con] 600 in Colombia (2000 SIL). Many monolinguals. Ethnic population: 600 to 700 in Colombia (2000 Borman). Colombia-Ecuador border area, Putumayo Province. *Dialects:* Aguarico, Santa Rosa. *Lg Use:* Some children not learning Cofán. *Other:* Chibchan with Western Tucanoan features (Ferndon, Borman), Barbacoan (Mason), or Jivaroan (Ruhlen 1987). Traditional religion, Christian. See main entry under Ecuador.

Cogui (Kogui, Coghui, Kogi, Kagaba, Kaggaba) [kog] 9,770 (2000 SIL). Nearly all are monolingual. Ethnic population: 11,000 (1998 census). Northern, eastern, and western slopes of Sierra Nevada de Santa Marta. *Class:* Chibchan, Aruak. *Lg Use:* Bilingual level estimates for Spanish: 0 92%, 1 7%, 2 1%, 3 0%, 4 0%, 5 0%. A few also speak Malayo. *Lg Dev:* Literacy rate in first language: below 1%. Literacy rate in second language: below 5%. Bible portions. *Other:* SOV. Mountain slope. Tropical forest. 750 to 1,750 meters. Swidden agriculturalists.

Colombian Sign Language [csn] 50,000 deaf in Bogotá in 1992. *Class:* Deaf sign language. *Dialects:* Some signs are similar to those in sign languages of El Salvador, Spain, and the USA. *Lg Use:* There are at least 4 deaf schools (begun in 1924); 2 in Bogotá and 2 in Medellín, and 3 other deaf institutions. Some schools use sign language in the classroom. Interpreters are provided at important public events, and for college students. Many sign language classes for hearing people. There is a committee on the national sign language, and an organization for sign language teachers. Little research. It is not clear how many deaf persons know a sign language. Half of school age children are speakers. *Lg Dev:* TV. Dictionary. Grammar. *Other:* Begun in 1929. There is a manual alphabet for spelling.

Coxima (Koxima) [kox] Extinct. *Class:* Unclassified.

Coyaima [coy] Extinct. Tolima Region. *Class:* Carib, Northern, Coastal. *Dialects:* Ruhlen says it was a Yukpa variety. *Lg Use:* The tribe still exists as an entity, but has not spoken the language for several generations. Spanish is now spoken.

Cubeo (Cuveo, Kobeua, Kubwa, Kobewa, Pamiwa, Hehenawa) [cub] 6,000 in Colombia (1994 SIL). 10% monolinguals. Population total all countries: 6,150. Vaupés, Cuduyari, Querarí rivers and tributaries, Vaupés Region. Also spoken in Brazil, Venezuela. *Class:* Tucanoan, Central Tucanoan. *Lg Use:* Trade language. Vigorous. Cubeo is the lingua franca for the northwest Vaupés area. All domains, home, religion, commerce. About 5% of the population are 5 years old or younger. Positive language attitude. Most speakers also use other Tucanoan languages, Spanish, Portuguese. *Lg Dev:* Literacy rate in first language: 35%. Literacy rate in second language: 60%. Written form used for religion and commerce. Both oral and written in primary school. Roman script. Newspapers. NT: 1970–1989. *Other:* Exogamous marriage pattern with speakers of other languages. SOV. Riverine. Tropical forest. 200 to 500 meters. Swidden agriculturalists. Traditional religion, Christian, syncretism.

Cuiba (Cuiva, Cuiba-Wámonae) [cui] 2,343 in Colombia (1993 census). 50% monolingual. Population total all countries: 2,993. Meta Casanare and Capanapara rivers and tributaries. Also spoken in Venezuela. *Class:*

Guahiban. *Dialects:* Chiricoa, Masiware (Masiguare), Chiripo (Wupiwi, Siripu), Yarahuuraxi-Capanapara, Mayayero, Mochuelo-Casanare-Cuiba, Tampiwi (Mariposas), Amaruwa (Amorua). 8 dialects; 2 in Venezuela, 7 in Colombia. *Lg Dev:* Literacy rate in first language: 45%. Literacy rate in second language: 45%. Grammar. NT: 1988. *Other:* Seminomadic bands. Savannah. Hunters; gatherers; swidden agriculturalists.

Cumeral [cum] Extinct. *Class:* Arawakan, Unclassified.

Curripaco (Curipaco, Kuripaco, Kurripaco, Koripako) [kpc] 2,699 in Colombia (2000 WCD). 6,943 in Colombia including Baniwa. Population total all countries: 3,719. Guainia, Isana, and Inirida rivers. Also spoken in Brazil, Venezuela. *Class:* Arawakan, Maipuran, Northern Maipuran, Inland. *Dialects:* Close to Baniwa and Carutana. *Lg Dev:* NT: 1959. *Other:* Agriculturalists.

Desano (Desána, Dessana, Wina, Boleka, Oregu, Kusibi) [des] 800 in Colombia (1995 SIL). Papurí and Abiyu rivers (tributary of the Vaupés), Pacá River (tributary of the Papurí), and Macú Parana River (tributary of the Papurí), plus other tributaries of the Papurí. *Lg Use:* All speak at least one other Tucanoan language. Spanish is also used. Desano in Brazil generally speak Tucano instead of Desano. *Lg Dev:* Literacy rate in first language: 30%. Literacy rate in second language: 25% to 35%. See main entry under Brazil.

Emberá, Northern (Emperã, Eberã Bed'ea, Eperã Pedea, Atrato, Darién, Dariena, Panama Embera, Eberã, Cholo) [emp] 13,000 in Colombia (1988 Aguirre and Pardo-Rojas). Atrato River basin in Chocó Department, Pacific coastal rivers from Cabo Corrientes, to Antioquia (Rio Verde) Department. *Other:* 'Embena' (Embera, Epena), meaning 'people' is used by all Choco peoples except Waunana to refer to themselves. Traditional religion, Christian. See main entry under Panama.

Emberá-Baudó (Baudó, Catrú) [bdc] 5,000 (1995 SIL). Ethnic population: Total Embera in Colombia: 71,000 (1998 Arango and Sánchez). Baudó River basin and Pacific (north) coastal rivers between cabo corrientes and the south of the San Juan River, near Northern Emberá. *Class:* Choco, Embera, Southern. *Dialects:* Somewhat intelligible with Northern Embera and Epena.

Emberá-Catío (Catio, Katio, Embena, Eyabida) [cto] 15,000 in Colombia (1992 SIL). 90% to 95% are monolingual. Population total all countries: 15,040. Upper Sinu, San Jorge, San Pedro, Murri rivers. Also spoken in Panama. *Class:* Choco, Embera, Northern. *Lg Use:* A few use Spanish as second language. *Lg Dev:* Literacy rate in first language: below 1%. Literacy rate in second language: 5% to 15%. *Other:* The term 'Catio' is sometimes used for other Choco groups.

Emberá-Chamí (Chami) [cmi] 11,000 (1995 SIL). Departments of Risaralda, Caldas, Antioquía, Valle, including the Municipio of Caramanta. *Class:* Choco, Embera, Southern. *Lg Dev:* Literacy rate in first language: below 1%. Literacy rate in second language: 5% to 15%. Bible portions: 1989. *Other:* Fairly monolingual. Mountain slope.

Emberá-Tadó (Embená Tadó) [tdc] 1,000 (1991 SIL). Upper San Juan River Region, Andes, Risaralda Region, near the Chamí. *Class:* Choco, Embera, Southern. *Lg Dev:* Literacy rate in first language: below 1%. Literacy rate in second language: below 5%. *Other:* Secluded.

Epena (Emberá-Saija, Saija, Epená Saija, Epéna Pedée, Southern Embera, Southern Empera, Cholo) [sja] 8,000 in Colombia (2000 SIL). Population total all countries: 8,050. Southern Pacific coast, Caucá, Nariño, Chocó departments. Also spoken in Ecuador, Panama. *Class:* Choco, Embera, Southern. *Dialect:* Basurudó. *Lg Use:* Vigorous. Used in the home, religion, fiestas, ceremonies, commerce. Positive language attitude. Bilingual level estimates for Spanish: 0

0%, 1 20%, 2 30%, 3 50%, 4 0%, 5 0%. No speakers are monolingual. All speak Spanish, and some speak Won Meu. There is intermarriage with speakers of Won Meu. *Lg Dev:* Literacy rate in first language: 1% to 5%. Literacy rate in second language: 25% to 50%. 400 read Epena, 50 write it. Movement toward using the language in primary schools. Roman script. Grammar. Bible portions: 1991. *Other:* SOV. Coastal, riverine. Tropical forest. Sea level to 70 meters. Fishermen; lumbermen; agriculturalists. Traditional religion, Christian.

Guahibo (Guajibo, Goahibo, Guaigua, Guayba, Wahibo, Goahiva, "Sicuani," "Sikuani") [guh] 18,772 in Colombia (1993 census). 40% monolingual. Population total all countries: 23,772. Ethnic population: 21,425 in Colombia (1998 Arango and Sánchez). Casanare, eastern Meta, Vichada, Guaviare, Guainia states, plains regions. Also spoken in Venezuela. *Class:* Guahiban. *Dialects:* Guahibo (Sikuani), Amorua (Rio Tomo Guahibo), Tigrero. The Guahiban languages may not be within Arawakan. *Lg Dev:* Literacy rate in first language: 45%. Literacy rate in second language: 45%. Primary schools in most areas. Secondary schools in some areas. Newspapers. Dictionary. Grammar. NT: 1982. *Other:* Rio Tomo Guahibo are nomadic. The name "Sicuani" is derogatory, and is disliked by most Guahibo. SOV, SVO. Plains, riverine, interfluvial. Savannah, gallery forest. 200 meters. Swidden agriculturalists; fishermen; hunters; gatherers; animal husbandry. Traditional religion, Christian, secular.

Guambiano (Guambia, Moguex, Namdrik) [gum] 15,596 (2000 WCD). Less than 10% monolinguals. Ethnic population: 12,000 to 15,000 (2000). Central Andes Range near Popayán, Cauca, in concentrated areas. *Class:* Barbacoan, Coconucan. *Lg Use:* Vigorous. All domains. Administration, commerce, labor relations. Positive language attitude. Over 90% also use some Spanish. *Lg Dev:* Literacy rate in first language: 10% to 20%. Literacy rate in second language: 50% to 75%. 2,000 or more read Guambiano, a few can write it. The orthography lacks agreement. It is taught in the schools to some degree. Roman script. Grammar. NT: 2000. *Other:* Mountain slope. Agriculturalists: potatoes, onions. Christian, traditional religion.

Guanano (Wanana, Uanano, Kotiria, Anana, Kótedia) [gvc] 450 in Colombia (1983 SIL). Lower Vaupés River region. *Lg Dev:* Literacy rate in first language: 5% to 10%. Literacy rate in second language: 25% to 50%. *Other:* Riverine. Tropical forest. Fishermen; swidden agriculturalists. See main entry under Brazil.

Guayabero (Jiw, Cunimía, Mítus, Mítua) [guo] 1,237 (1993 census). Ethnic population: 1,237 (1993). Upper Guaviaré River, Metá and Guaviaré states. *Class:* Guahiban. *Lg Use:* Young children and older women are monolingual in Guayabero. Others know varying degrees of Spanish. Bilingual level estimates for Spanish: 0 33%, 1 50%, 2 15%, 3 2%, 4 0%, 5 0%. *Lg Dev:* Literacy rate in first language: Few. Literacy rate in second language: 15% to 20%. Available in most villages. Bible portions: 1961–1995. *Other:* SOV. Riverine. Savannah, tropical forest. Hunters; gatherers; swidden agriculturalists. Traditional religion.

Huitoto, Minica (Minica, Meneca) [hto] 1,700 in Colombia (1995 SIL). Population total all countries: 1,705. Upper Igara-Parana. Caquetá River at Isla de los Monos, Caguan River near Sanvicente del Caguan. Also spoken in Peru. *Class:* Witotoan, Witoto, Witoto Proper, Minica-Murui. *Lg Dev:* Literacy rate in first language: 75%. Literacy rate in second language: 85%. Dictionary. Grammar. NT: 1985.

Huitoto, Murui (Bue, Witoto) [huu] 1,900 in Colombia (1995 SIL). Caraparana, Putumayo, and Leticia rivers. None left in Brazil. See main entry under Peru.

Hupdë (Ubdé, "Hupdá Makú," "Jupdá Macú," "Macú de Tucano," "Makú-Hupdá") [jup] 150 in Colombia (1991 SIL). Papurí and Tiquié river systems. *Lg Use:* Possibly half the speakers use Tucano or another Tucano language as second language. *Other:* Subservient to the Tucano and other Tucanoan Indians. The name "Macú" is offensive. Some are nomadic between Colombia and Brazil. Tropical forest. See main entry under Brazil.

Inga (Highland Inga) [inb] 12,000 in Colombia (2000 SIL). Population total all countries: 16,000. Ethnic population: 17,860. Sibundoy Valley, in and around Santiago, San Andrés, and Colón; Aponte, Department of Nariño. 1,000 in Bogotá, small numbers in regional capitals. None in Ecuador. Also spoken in Venezuela. *Class:* Quechuan, Quechua II, B. *Dialects:* Santiago Inga, San Andrés Inga, Aponte Inga. Partially intelligible with Imbabura Quichua of Ecuador. Aponte Inga may need separate literature. *Lg Use:* Bilingual level estimates for Spanish: 0 0%, 1 10%, 2 10%, 3 20%, 4 40%, 5 20%. *Lg Dev:* Literacy rate in first language: 10% to 60%. Literacy rate in second language: 25% to 50%. Dictionary. Grammar. NT: 1996. *Other:* SOV. Mountain mesa. Deciduous forest. 2,100 to 2,500 meters. Intensive agriculturalists; craftsmen.

Inga, Jungle (Lowland Inga, Mocoa, Ingano) [inj] 9,141 (2000 WCD). Upper Caquetá and Putumayo rivers. *Class:* Quechuan, Quechua II, B. *Dialects:* Yunguillo-Condagua, Guayuyaco. Closest to Highland Inga. Distinct from Napo Quechua. *Lg Use:* Speakers also use Spanish. *Lg Dev:* Literacy rate in first language: 10% to 30%. Literacy rate in second language: 25% to 50%. *Other:* SOV. Hills, riverine. Tropical forest. 200 to 1,000 meters. Intensive agriculturalists.

Islander Creole English (San Andrés Creole, Bende) [icr] 12,000 to 18,000 (1981 SIL). San Andrés and Providencia Islands. *Class:* Creole, English based, Atlantic, Western. *Dialects:* There is reported to be a 'deep Creole'. Very close to Belize Creole English. *Lg Use:* Probably the first language of the majority of the Islanders. Creole is considered appropriate for oral purposes only in popular thinking. Standard English is used among the most highly educated. *Lg Dev:* Literacy rate in second language: 90% Spanish, 80% English. Bible portions: 1999. *Other:* Mountain slope, plains.

Koreguaje (Coreguaje, Correguaje, Ko'reuaju, Caquetá, Chaocha Pai) [coe] 2,000 (1995 SIL). Orteguaza and Caquetá rivers and tributaries, Caquetá Region. *Class:* Tucanoan, Western Tucanoan, Northern, Coreguaje. *Lg Use:* Members of the Tama ethnic group now speak Koreguaje. 90% use Spanish as second language. *Lg Dev:* Literacy rate in first language: 10% to 30%. Literacy rate in second language: 25% to 40%. NT: 1991. *Other:* 'Caquetá' is the name of the river, not the people. Agriculturalists.

Kuna, Border (Colombia Cuna, Caiman Nuevo, Cuna, Paya-Pucuro) [kvn] 876 in Colombia (2000 WCD). Population total all countries: 1,576. North coastal region near the Panama isthmus. Also spoken in Panama. *Class:* Chibchan, Kuna. *Dialects:* Classification of Kuna is uncertain; it may be an isolate with certain Chibchan features. *Lg Dev:* NT: 1993. *Other:* SOV.

Macaguaje [mcl] Extinct. Ethnic population: 50 (1998 Arango and Sánchez). Lower Putumayo, tributaries of Caquetá River. *Class:* Tucanoan, Western Tucanoan, Northern, Siona-Secoya. *Lg Use:* Members of the ethnic group now speak Siona or Coreguaje. *Other:* A few still maintain group identity.

Macaguán (Macaguane, Agualinda Guahibo, Hitnü) [mbn] 405 (1993 census). Most are monolingual. Ethnic population: 542 (1998 Arango and Sánchez). Arauca, Agualinda, and San José de Lipa between the Lipa, Ele, and Cuiloto rivers and Caño Colorado, and other scattered locations. *Class:* Guahiban. *Dialects:* Unintelligible to

speakers of other Guahibo varieties. *Lg Use:* Vigorous. *Lg Dev:* Dictionary. Grammar. *Other:* Small groups. Seminomadic. Hunters; gatherers; agriculturalists.

Macuna (Makuna, Buhagana, Roea, Emoa, Ide, Yeba, Suroa, Tabotiro Jejea, Umua, Wuhána, Paneroa, Jepa-Matsi, Yepá-Mahsá) [myy] 450 in Colombia (1991 SIL). Population total all countries: 550. Lower Pira-Parana, Vaupés Region; Apaporis tributaries and Miriti-Parana. Also spoken in Brazil. *Class:* Tucanoan, Eastern Tucanoan, Central, Southern. *Lg Dev:* Literacy rate in first language: 5% to 10%. Literacy rate in second language: 15% to 25%. Dictionary. NT: 1989. *Other:* OVS. Interfluvial. Tropical forest. Swidden agriculturalists.

Malayo (Marocasero, Maracasero, Sanja, Sanka, Sancá, Arosario, Arsario, Guamaka, Guamaca, Wiwa) [mbp] 3,225 (1993 Organizacósn Gonawindu Tayrona). Southern and eastern slopes of Sierra Nevada de Santa Marta. *Class:* Chibchan, Aruak. *Lg Dev:* Literacy rate in first language: below 1%. Literacy rate in second language: below 5%.

Muinane (Muinana, Muinani, Muename) [bmr] 150 (1982 SIL). Upper Cahuinarí, (tributary Caquetá) Amazonas. *Class:* Witotoan, Boran. *Lg Use:* All also use Bora or Huitotoan languages. *Lg Dev:* Literacy rate in first language: 1% to 5%. Literacy rate in second language: below 5%. NT: 1981. *Other:* Not to be confused with Muinane Huitoto.

Natagaimas [nts] Extinct. Tolima Region. *Class:* Unclassified. *Lg Use:* Has not been spoken for several generations. Members of the ethnic group now speak Spanish.

Nhengatu (Yeral, Geral, Nheengatu, Nyengato, Waengatu, Modern Tupi) [yrl] 3,000 in Colombia. Vaupés. See main entry under Brazil.

Nukak Makú (Maczsa, Guaviare) [mbr] 300. Jungle region between Guaviare and Inirida rivers, up to Maparipan. Near Charco Caimán. *Class:* Maku. *Other:* Evasive hunters.

Ocaina (Okaina) [oca] 12 in Colombia (1982 SIL). Upper Igara-Paraná and tributaries, Amazonas Region. *Dialects:* Dukaiya, Ibo'tsa. *Lg Use:* Speakers also use Murui Huitoto, Bora, or Spanish. See main entry under Peru.

Omejes [ome] Extinct. *Class:* Arawakan, Unclassified.

Páez (Nasa Yuwe) [pbb] 71,400 to 83,300 (2000 SIL). 35,700 to 41,650 monolinguals. Ethnic population: 122,638 (2000 WCD). Central Andes Range near Popayán, Cauca. *Class:* Language Isolate. *Dialect:* Pitayo, Paniquita (Panikita). *Lg Use:* Many are passing the language on, but some prefer to have children use only Spanish. Some oral and written use in religious services, commerce. Earlier, people were embarrassed because of negative attitudes from nonspeakers. Attitudes toward the language have improved since development of the written form. Bilingual level estimates for Spanish: 0 50%, 1 25%, 2 13%, 3 10%, 4 2%, 5 0%. 25% speak Páez and some Spanish, 25% speak Páez and are fluent in Spanish. Spanish is the predominant language of instruction in schools. *Lg Dev:* Literacy rate in first language: 10% to 30%. Literacy rate in second language: 25% to 50%. Some attempts have been made to promote the language, mainly literacy courses. Some private primary schools teach reading and writing in Páez along with Spanish. Roman script. Radio programs. Dictionary. Grammar. NT: 1980. *Other:* SOV. Mountain mesa, mountain slope. Scrub forest. 2,500 to 3,000 meters. Peasant agriculturalists. Christian, syncretism.

Palenquero (Palenque, Lengua) [pln] 500 (1989 J. Holm). Ethnic population: 2,500 (1989 J. Holm). Village of San Basilio de Palenque southeast of Cartagena, and 2 neighborhoods in Barranquilla. *Class:* Creole, Spanish based. *Dialects:* Entirely unintelligible to Spanish speakers. Linguistic influences from Kongo in Democratic Republic of the Congo (I. Hancock 1987). *Lg Use:* 10% of those under 25 speak it (1998 Armin Schwegler). Most speakers are older. Positive language attitude. Most members of the ethnic group speak Spanish as first language, but some older adults have low proficiency in Spanish. *Lg Dev:* Grammar. *Other:* People are culturally distinct from nearby Spanish speakers.

Piapoco [pio] 4,542 in Colombia (1993 census). Population total all countries: 4,641. Tributaries and lower Vichada River region, and Meta and Guaviare rivers. Also spoken in Venezuela. *Class:* Arawakan, Maipuran, Northern Maipuran, Inland. *Lg Use:* Bilingual level estimates for Spanish: 0 60%, 1 20%, 2 10%, 3 10%, 4 0%, 5 0%. *Lg Dev:* Literacy rate in first language: 30% to 40%. Literacy rate in second language: 20% to 40%. Dictionary. NT: 1966–1987. *Other:* SVO. Plains. Savannah. 250 to 300 meters. Hunter-gatherers; swidden agriculturalists.

Piaroa (Kuakua, Guagua, Quaqua) [pid] 80 in Colombia (1991 Adelaar). Near the Sáliba. *Other:* 'Ature' (Adole) may be an alternate name. Agriculturalists. See main entry under Venezuela.

Pijao (Piajao) [pij] Extinct. Tolima Region. *Class:* Unclassified. *Dialects:* M. Durbin said there is not enough data to classify it linguistically. *Lg Use:* There have been no speakers since the 1950s. Members of the ethnic group now speak Spanish.

Piratapuyo (Waikino, Urubu-Tapuya, Uaikena) [pir] 450 in Colombia. Papurí River and lower Vaupés, Amazonas. Most near RC mission at Teresita. Others in small groups. *Lg Use:* Distinct ethnically from the Guanano, but the exogamy system does not permit the two groups to intermarry. All also use at least one other Tucanoan language, especially Desano or Tucano. Spanish also used. *Lg Dev:* Literacy rate in first language: 5% to 10%. Literacy rate in second language: 40% to 60%. *Other:* 75% intelligibility of Guanano (N. Waltz). See main entry under Brazil.

Playero (Rio Arauca Guahibo) [gob] 244 (2000 WCD). Arauca River, Venezuela border, Arauca Division, on the banks of the Arauca River from Gaviotas Island to Arauca. *Class:* Guahiban. *Dialects:* Low intelligibility of other Guahibo. *Lg Use:* Somewhat acculturated and bilingual in Spanish for trading purposes. *Lg Dev:* Interest in literacy. *Other:* Many have fields in Venezuela.

Ponares [pod] Extinct. *Class:* Arawakan, Unclassified. *Other:* A Sáliba last name. Might have been a Piapoco or Achagua subgroup.

Providencia Sign Language [prz] Known by most people on the Island including 19 born deaf out of 2,500 to 3,000 population (1986 W. Washabaugh). Providencia Island off the coast of Nicaragua. *Class:* Deaf sign language. *Dialects:* They have not been exposed to other sign languages. East differs from west with some variation between villages. *Lg Dev:* Untutored and do not use finger spelling. *Other:* The high deaf population is probably caused by in-breeding. The deaf are fairly well integrated into daily activities. The system is about 100 years old.

Puinave (Puinabe) [pui] 2,000 in Colombia (1977 NTM). Population total all countries: 2,240. Inírida River and tributaries, Territory of Guainia. Also spoken in Venezuela. *Class:* Language Isolate. *Dialects:* Ruhlen and others classify it as related to Macú. *Lg Dev:* NT: 1964. *Other:* Plains.

Quichua, Napo Lowland (Lowland Napo Quechua) [qvo] Undetermined number in Colombia. Putumayo River. See main entry under Peru (Quechua, Napo Lowland).

Romani, Vlax [rmy] 79,000 Gypsies in Colombia (2001 Johnstone and Mandryk). Several hundred thousand in Latin America (1984 Ian Hancock). *Other:* Christian. See main entry under Romania.

Runa [rna] Extinct. *Class:* Choco.

Sáliba (Sáliva) [slc] 1,305 in Colombia (1993 census). Population total all countries: 1,555. Meta and Casanare rivers. Also spoken in Venezuela. *Class:* Salivan. *Lg Use:* Most families not passing on Sáliba to their children, but they are beginning to rethink that practice (2000). Speakers are older adults. *Lg Dev:* Literacy rate in first language: 1% to 5%. Literacy rate in second language: 15% to 25%. *Other:* SOV. Plains, interfluvial. Tropical forest. Lower than 200 meters. Swidden agriculturalists.

Siona (Sioni, Pioje, Pioche-Sioni) [snn] 300 in Colombia (1982 SIL). Population total all countries: 550. Live on both sides of the Putumayo River. Also spoken in Ecuador. *Class:* Tucanoan, Western Tucanoan, Northern, Siona-Secoya. *Lg Use:* Bilingual level estimates for Spanish: 0 0%, 1 5%, 2 20%, 3 60%, 4 10%, 5 5%. *Lg Dev:* Literacy rate in first language: 5% to 10%. Literacy rate in second language: 15% to 25%. NT: 1982. *Other:* Those in Ecuador consider themselves Colombians. Distinct from Secoya (Siona-Secoya). SOV. Interfluvial. Tropical forest. 320 meters. Swidden agriculturalists.

Siriano [sri] 337 in Colombia (2001 WCD). Population total all countries: 347. Paca and Vina rivers, Vaupés Region. Also spoken in Brazil. *Class:* Tucanoan, Eastern Tucanoan, Central, Desano. *Dialects:* Different from Desano. *Lg Use:* Ethnic differences are important because of the system of exogamy, and persons are identified by first language of father. All speak at least one other Tucanoan language. Spanish is also used. *Lg Dev:* Literacy rate in first language: 5% to 30%. Literacy rate in second language: 15% to 25%. NT: 1998. *Other:* SOV. Riverine. Tropical forest. 100 to 200 meters. Swidden agriculturalists. Traditional religion, Christian.

Spanish [spa] 34,000,000 in Colombia (1995). *Lg Use:* National language. See main entry under Spain.

Tama [ten] Extinct. Vicente, Orteguaza River, Caquetá Region. *Class:* Tucanoan, Western Tucanoan, Northern, Tama. *Dialects:* Ruhlen says it is a Koreguaje dialect. *Lg Use:* Those living on the Orteguaza River have completely integrated with the Coreguaje.

Tanimuca-Retuarã (Retuama, Retuarã, Letuama, Letuhama, Ufaina, Uairã) [tnc] 300 (1976 SIL). Population includes 180 Tanimuca. Guacayá, Oiyaka rivers (tributaries of the Mirití-Parana), Mirití-Parana, Apaporis, and Popeyaka rivers near the mouth of the Pira River below Popeyaca, Amazonas Region. *Class:* Tucanoan, Western Tucanoan, Tanimuca. *Dialects:* Tanimuca, Retuarã. The Tanimuca and Retuarã are two ethnic groups living close together who speak the same language. Possibly Eastern Tucanoan. *Lg Use:* Quite a few from the Apaporis and Popeyaka understand Macuna; those in other areas are often fluent in Yucuna. The Retuarã are more monolingual than the Tanimuca. *Lg Dev:* Literacy rate in first language: 1% to 5%. Literacy rate in second language: below 5%. Grammar. Bible portions. *Other:* All work for one rubber hunter. Tropical forest. Swidden agriculturalists.

Tariano (Tariána) [tae] Ethnic population: 332 in Colombia (1998 Arango and Sánchez). Lower Papurí, Vaupés Region. *Lg Use:* No one has been located who speaks Tariano in Colombia, but the group identity is still maintained. All speak Tucano. *Other:* Nearly extinct. See main entry under Brazil.

Tatuyo (Pamoa, Oa, Tatutapuyo, Juna) [tav] 350 (1983 SIL). Pira-Paraná headwaters and Upper Papurí, Vaupés Region. *Class:* Tucanoan, Eastern Tucanoan, Central, Tatuyo. *Lg Use:* All speak at least one other Tucanoan language. *Lg Dev:* Literacy rate in first language: 1% to 5%. Literacy rate in second language: below 5%. NT: 1987. *Other:* The majority marry Carapana, Northern

Barasano, or Barasana women. Interfluvial. Tropical forest. 235 to 245 meters. Swidden agriculturalists.

Ticuna (Tikuna, Tukúna, Tucuna) [tca] 8,000 in Colombia (2000 SIL). Amazon River. See main entry under Brazil.

Tinigua (Tiniguas) [tit] 2 (2000). Ethnic population: 2. Sierra de la Macarena, Metá Department. Formerly they were in the Llanos de Yarí, Caquetá Department. *Class:* Language Isolate. *Other:* Nearly extinct.

Tomedes (Tamudes) [toe] Extinct. *Class:* Arawakan, Unclassified.

Totoro [ttk] 4 (1998 Arango and Sánchez). Ethnic population: 3,650 (1998 Arango and Sánchez). 17 km west of Silvia, Cauca, in town of Totoro. *Class:* Barbacoan, Coconucan. *Other:* Nearly extinct.

Tucano (Daxsea, Dachsea, Dasea, Betoya, Betaya, Tukana) [tuo] 2,000 in Colombia. Upper Papurí River and tributaries. *Lg Use:* Trade language. Tucano is the second language of many neighboring groups, especially south and east of Mitú. All speak at least one other Tucanoan language or Spanish as second language. *Lg Dev:* Literacy rate in first language: 30% to 40%. Literacy rate in second language: 30% to 40%. *Other:* 6 regional dialects. Riverine, hills. Tropical forest. 200 to 250 meters. Swidden agriculturalists. See main entry under Brazil.

Tunebo, Angosturas [tnd] 50. *Class:* Chibchan, Chibchan Proper, Tunebo. *Dialects:* 71% intelligibility between Eastern and Angosturas Tunebo. *Lg Use:* Speakers are shifting to Spanish. *Other:* Nearly extinct.

Tunebo, Barro Negro (Eastern Tunebo) [tbn] 300 (1981 SIL). Isolated, on the edge of the eastern plains in the Andes foothills above Paz de Ariporo, in Barro Negro, San Lope (Casanare), and Tabías (Casanare), south of Tame Arauca. *Class:* Chibchan, Chibchan Proper, Tunebo. *Dialects:* 62% intelligibility of Cobaría Tunebo. *Lg Use:* Used in the home. Partly bilingual, somewhat acculturated. *Other:* 1,200 to 1,600 meters. Swidden agriculturalists: maize; hunters; gatherers; fishermen.

Tunebo, Central (Cobaría Tunebo, U'wa) [tuf] 2,500 in Colombia (2000 SIL). North slopes of Sierra Nevada de Cocuy, Boyaca and Arauca regions; Satocá, Calafita, Tegría (Boyaca), Cobaría (Boyacá). Also spoken in Venezuela. *Class:* Chibchan, Chibchan Proper, Tunebo. *Lg Use:* All ages. Bilingual level estimates for Spanish: 0 65%, 1 20%, 2 10%, 3 4%, 4 .5%, 5 .5%. *Lg Dev:* Literacy rate in first language: 1% to 5%. Literacy rate in second language: 5% to 25%. Dictionary. NT: 1987. *Other:* They have had a taboo on the use of paper. SOV. Mountain slope. Tropical forest. 500 to 1,500 meters. Swidden agriculturalists; gatherers; some hunting.

Tunebo, Western (Aguas Blancas, U'wa) [tnb] 700 (1998). Santander del Sur. *Class:* Chibchan, Chibchan Proper, Tunebo. *Dialects:* The most divergent of the Tunebo languages. *Lg Use:* Speakers have low proficiency in Spanish. *Lg Dev:* Bible portions. *Other:* Swidden agriculturalists: maize; hunters; gatherers; fishermen.

Tuyuca (Dochkafuara, Tejuca, Tuyuka) [tue] 350 in Colombia (1995 SIL). Population total all countries: 815. Inambu, Tiquie, and Papurí rivers. Also spoken in Brazil. *Class:* Tucanoan, Eastern Tucanoan, Central, Bara. *Lg Use:* All speak at least one other Tucanoan language. Second language is Tucano or Waimaha. Spanish used in schools in the area. *Lg Dev:* Literacy rate in first language: 10%. Literacy rate in second language: 60%. Dictionary. Grammar. Bible portions: 1991–1994.

Waimaha (Waimaja, "Bará," Northern Barasano, Barasano) [bao] 600 in Colombia (1995 SIL). Almost no monolinguals. Population total all countries: 700. Tributaries of mid and upper Pira-Paraná, upper Papurí and Tiquié, in and around the capital of the Vaupés, Mitú, southeastern Vaupés region. Also spoken in Brazil. *Class:* Tucanoan, Eastern Tucanoan, Central, Bara. *Dialects:*

Eastern Waimaha, Pamoa Bara. *Lg Use:* Waimaha is passed on as children become speakers of father's language. Most domains, home, family, religion, local commerce, community. All ages. Positive language attitude. 40% to 50% speak Spanish as second language. Spanish is used in school and with government officials. All speak 2 to 4 of these: Tucano, Tatuyo, Tuyuca, Taiwano, Barasana, Yuruti, Macuna, Carapana, because of marriage patterns across language boundaries. Children speak the language of each parent, but identify with the father's language. *Lg Dev:* Literacy rate in first language: 25%. Literacy rate in second language: 25% to 40%. Letter writing between communities. Written form used in religious services. Roman script. Bible portions: 1975–1994. *Other:* The name "Bará" has derogatory connotations to some speakers. SOV. Riverine, interfluvial. Tropical forest. Swidden agriculturalists. Christian, traditional religion.

Wayuu (Guajiro, Goajiro, Guajira) [guc] 135,000 in Colombia (1995 SIL). Population total all countries: 305,000. Guajira Peninsula on the Caribbean coast. Also spoken in Venezuela. *Class:* Arawakan, Maipuran, Northern Maipuran, Caribbean. *Lg Dev:* Literacy rate in first language: below 1%. Literacy rate in second language: 5% to 15%. NT: 2002. *Other:* VSO. Coastal. Desert. Sea level. Pastoralists.

Woun Meu (Waun Meo, Waumeo) [noa] 3,000 in Colombia. San Juan River basin. *Other:* The people's name for themselves is 'Wounaan', and for their language 'Woun Meo'. See main entry under Panama.

Yahuna (Yaúna, Yayuna) [ynu] Extinct. Ethnic population: Fewer than 23 in ethnic group, fewer than 20 on Umana River, 3 on Apaporis River (1988). Umuqa River, a tributary of the Piraparana River. *Class:* Tucanoan, Eastern Tucanoan, Unclassified. *Dialects:* Opaina, Datuana. *Lg Use:* Members of the ethnic group now speak Macuna.

Yarí [yri] 758 (2000 WCD). Yarí River, Caquetá Region, above El Capitán waterfalls near the Yarí River. About 50 years ago 140 of them migrated to the Apaporis River, and settled on the upper Vaupés River near Puerto Nare. *Class:* Unclassified. *Dialects:* Possibly a dialect of Carijona (Carib), a Western Tucanoan language, or Huitoto. *Other:* They were given the name 'Yarí' by outsiders because of their location on the Yarí River.

Yucuna (Matapi, Yukuna) [ycn] 1,800 (2001 SIL). 10 to 20 monolinguals. Ethnic population: 1,800. Miriti-Parana (tributary Caquetá), Amazonas Region. Some have moved to La Pedrera on the lower Caquetá, Ararcuara, some to Leticia. *Class:* Arawakan, Maipuran, Northern Maipuran, Inland. *Dialects:* In some traditional ceremonies they use a ritual language which is mostly unintelligible even to those who have learned it. *Lg Use:* Vigorous. All domains. Oral and written Yucuna is sometimes used in religious services, and oral Yucuna in the traditional religion. Yucuna is used for letter writing. Positive language attitude. 1,500 have varying proficiency in Spanish. Nearly all formal education is in Spanish. Spanish is used with outsiders. Some who have married Tanimuca speakers also speak Tanimuca. *Lg Dev:* Literacy rate in first language: 5% to 10%. Literacy rate in second language: 15% to 25%. 500 read Yucuna, 300 can write it. Roman script. NT: 1982. *Other:* Over 100 years ago the Yucuna fought about 10 ethnic groups in the area, and assimilated them. The Matap'i were not their enemies, intermarried with them, and lost their language except for a few words. Subversive activity in the area has caused some Yucuna to move to other areas. SVO. Riverine. Tropical forest. 300 meters. Swidden agriculturalists. Traditional religion, Christian.

Yukpa (Yuko, Yuco, Yupa, Yucpa, Northern Motilón, Carib Motilón) [yup] 2,500 in Colombia (1976 SIL). Population total all countries: 3,000. Ethnic population: 3,530 (1998

Arango and Sánchez). Serranía de Perijá, Cesar Department, Municipio of Augustín Codazzi and neighboring municipios north and south, Colombia-Venezuela border. Río Cascará dialect is in the Municipio of Agustín Codassi along the Casacará River and the Caño Iroka. Caqo Padilla-La Laguna is small and farther north. Río Maracas is to the south in the Municipio of Becerril. Also spoken in Venezuela. *Class:* Carib, Northern, Coastal. *Dialects:* Río Casacará (Iroka), Río Maracas, Caño Padilla-La Laguna, Coyaima. At least five extant dialects including two in Venezuela. Ruhlen says Coyaima was a dialect. Río Cascará and Río Maracas dialects are probably the largest ones, and different enough to probably be separate languages. Venezuela dialects seem more similar to Río Maracas. Relations between speakers of different dialects have sometimes been hostile in the past. Presently they have little contact with each other. Unrelated to Bari. Low lexical similarity with Japreira of Venezuela (Luis Oquendo, U. of Zulia-Venezuela). *Lg Use:* Vigorous. Men can use Spanish for buying and selling only.

Yurutí (Juruti, Yuruti-Tapuya, Luruty-Tapuya, Yuriti, Juriti, Juriti-Tapuia, Wayhara, Patsoka, Wajiaraye) [yui] 300 in Colombia (1991 SIL). Population total all countries: 350. Ethnic population: 300. Upper Pacá River (tributary of Papurí) and Caño Yi River, Vaupés. Also spoken in Brazil. *Class:* Tucanoan, Eastern Tucanoan, Central, Bara. *Lg Use:* Vigorous. Positive language attitude. Eastern Tucanoan languages within the region are learned. Tucano is the lingua franca along the Pacá and Caño Yi rivers. Spanish used in schools and government contexts. *Lg Dev:* Literacy rate in first language: 10%. Literacy rate in second language: 15% to 25%. 5% can write Yuruti. Bible portions: 1985. *Other:* Marriage pattern requires that spouses be from different language groups. Children speak the languages of both parents, but identify with the father's language. Their own name is 'Wajiaraye'. Yuriti and Juriti are incorrect spellings. Riverine. Tropical forest. 300 meters. Agriculturalists: manioc; fishermen; hunters; gatherers.

Costa Rica

Republic of Costa Rica, República de Costa Rica. 3,956,507. National or official language: Spanish. Literacy rate: 93% (1989 WA). Also includes Basque, Eastern Yiddish, Ngäbere (5,092), Yue Chinese (4,500). Information mainly from SIL 1967–2002. Blind population: 2,500. Deaf population: 202,625. Deaf institutions: 9. The number of languages listed for Costa Rica is 10. Of those, 9 are living languages and 1 is extinct. See map on page 749.

Boruca (Borunca, Burunca, Brunca, Brunka) [brn] 5 women (1986 SIL). 30 to 35 nonfluent speakers. Ethnic population: 1,000 (1991). Southern coast between Playa Bonita and Golfito. *Class:* Chibchan, Talamanca. *Lg Use:* Nearly all speak only Spanish. *Other:* SOV. Agriculturalists: maize, beans, vegetables; hunters; gatherers. Nearly extinct.

Bribri (Talamanca) [bzd] 11,000 (2002). Ethnic population: 12,172 (2000). Southern, along Lari, Telire, and Uren rivers, Canton of Talamanca, Limón Province; Canton of Buenos Aires, Puntarenas Province. *Class:* Chibchan, Talamanca. *Dialects:* Salitre-Cabagra, Amubre-Katsi, Coroma. Closest to, but unintelligible to speakers of Cabécar, Guatuso, and Teribe. At least 3 major dialects which are inherently intelligible to each other's speakers. *Lg Use:* 75% of the ethnic group are speakers. Used in the home. All ages. Speakers also use Spanish. *Lg Dev:* Literacy rate in first language: 2% to 3%. Literacy rate in second language: 50% read halting Spanish. Bible portions: 1905–1994. *Other:* SOV.

Cabécar (Chirripó) [cjp] 8,840 (2000). 7,072 monolinguals (80%). Ethnic population: 9,308 (2000). Turrialba Region. *Class:* Chibchan, Talamanca. *Dialects:* Chirripó, Telire, Estrella, Ujarrás. *Lg Use:* 95% of the ethnic group are speakers. Bilingual level estimates for Spanish: 0 80%, 1–5 20%. *Lg Dev:* Dictionary. Grammar. NT: 1993. *Other:* Identified historically with the Huetares. SOV.

Chorotega (Choluteca, Mangue, Diria, Orotina) [cjr] Extinct. Ethnic population: 795 (2000). Some from the ethnic group live near Tuturrialba. They were originally from the Guanacaste Region near the Nicaraguan border. Some were also in El Salvador and Honduras. *Class:* Oto-Manguean, Chiapanec-Mangue. *Dialect:* Chorotega, Diria, Nagrandan, Nicoya, Orisi, Orotinya (Orotina). *Lg Use:* Became extinct in Costa Rica the end of the 18th century, in Nicaragua in the 19th century. *Other:* Reported to have been quite similar to Chiapanec of Mexico.

Costa Rican Sign Language [csr] *Class:* Deaf sign language. *Dialects:* May be related to Providencia Sign Language. Lexical similarity 60% with ASL.

Limón Creole English (Southwestern Caribbean Creole English) [jam] 55,100 in Costa Rica (1986). East of San José, principally along the railroad between Siquirres and Limón, and south of Limón along the road. *Lg Use:* Vigorous. All ages. Creole is not considered proper for literary purposes. They consider Jamaican Creole to be more 'broken' than their own. Most speakers have limited comprehension of Standard English. *Other:* Jamaican migrants settled in Limón about the middle of the 19th century, as they also did in Panama, so those varieties are close. Some say they do not understand Islander Creole English of San Andrés. See main entry under Jamaica (Jamaican Creole English).

Maléku Jaíka (Guatuso) [gut] 750 (2000). Ethnic population: 1,074 (2000). Northern. *Class:* Chibchan, Rama. *Lg Use:* 70% of the ethnic group are speakers. Bilingual level estimates for Spanish: 0 0%, 1 0%, 2 4%, 3 58%, 4 37%, 5 1%. *Other:* Agriculturalists: tubers, bananas, white cacao; hunters.

Plautdietsch (Low German, Mennonite German) [pdt] 100 in Costa Rica (1974 Minnich). Sarapiqui area. *Lg Use:* Used in the home. Speakers also use Spanish. *Other:* Christian. See main entry under Canada.

Spanish (Español, Castellano) [spa] 3,300,000 in Costa Rica (1995). *Lg Use:* Official language. See main entry under Spain.

Teribe (Terraba) [tfr] 5 in Costa Rica (1991 SIL). Ethnic population: 35 to 300 in Costa Rica (1991 SIL). Southeastern, north coast. *Lg Use:* Terraba in Costa Rica who know only a little Teribe want to relearn the language and culture (1991). See main entry under Panama.

Cuba

Republic of Cuba, República de Cuba. 11,308,764. National or official language: Spanish. Literacy rate: 94% (1991 National Geographic). Also includes Catalan-Valencian-Balear (3,500), Corsican. Deaf population: 670,810. Deaf institutions: 4. The number of languages listed for Cuba is 3. Of those, 2 are living languages and 1 is a second language without mother-tongue speakers. See map on page 739.

Cuba Sign Language [csf] *Class:* Deaf sign language.

Lucumi [luq] *Class:* Niger-Congo, Atlantic-Congo, Volta-Congo, Benue-Congo, Defoid, Yoruboid, Edekiri. *Lg Use:* A secret language used for ritual by the Santeria religion. *Other:* The people are sometimes called 'Yoruba'. Santeria. Second language only.

Spanish [spa] 10,000,000 in Cuba (1995). *Lg Use:* National language. See main entry under Spain.

Dominica

Commonwealth of Dominica. 69,278. National or official language: English. Self governing part of British West Indies. Literacy rate: 80% to 94%. Deaf population: 5,335. The number of languages listed for Dominica is 4. Of those, 3 are living languages and 1 is extinct. See map on page 740.

Carib, Island [crb] Extinct. Formerly also in Lesser Antilles, excluding Trinidad. Also spoken in Saint Vincent and the Grenadines. *Class:* Arawakan, Maipuran, Northern Maipuran, Caribbean. *Dialects:* Was not intelligible with Black Carib (D. Taylor 1959). Vincentian on Saint Vincent may have been closer to Black Carib than to Island Carib. Not inherently intelligible with Garífuna (D. Taylor IJAL 1959:67). *Lg Use:* Became extinct in Dominica about 1920. Used as a special language of Cariban origin to address men (Berend Hoff).
Dominican Creole French (Lesser Antillean Creole French, Patwa, Patois, Kwèyòl) [acf] 42,600 in Dominica (1998). *Lg Use:* Most use English, especially the youth. Standard French understood by no more than 10% of the population (Adler 1977). *Other:* Loanwords from Island Carib and Arawak. Christian. See main entry under Saint Lucia (Saint Lucian Creole French).
English [eng] 10,000 in Dominica (2004). *Dialect:* Dominican English. *Lg Use:* Official language. See main entry under United Kingdom.
Kokoy Creole English (Leeward Caribbean Creole English) [aig] 200 in Dominica (2004). Kokoy dialect is in 2 villages: Marigot and Wesley in northeast Dominica. *Lg Use:* People use it with Jamaicans and some other Caribbean people, but not with non-Caribbean people. See main entry under Antigua and Barbuda (Antigua and Barbuda Creole English).

Dominican Republic

República Dominicana. 8,833,634. National or official language: Spanish. Literacy rate: 68% to 94%. Also includes Catalan-Valencian-Balear, Japanese (1,500), North Levantine Spoken Arabic (3,000), Southwestern Caribbean Creole English (22,000), Chinese (25,000). Blind population: 5,000. Deaf population: 474,490. Deaf institutions: 3. The number of languages listed for Dominican Republic is 4. Of those, all are living languages. See map on page 739.

Dominican Sign Language [doq] *Class:* Deaf sign language. *Dialects:* Lexical similarity 85% to 90% with ASL, and uses most of the features of ASL, such as absent referent and reduplication. *Lg Use:* Many are not fluent or use home sign.
English [eng] 8,000 in Dominican Republic (1989 J. Holm). Samaná Peninsula, northeastern Dominican Republic. *Dialect:* Samaná English. *Lg Use:* Spanish is used as second language. Some use Haitian Creole. *Other:* A community of descendants of ex-USA slaves settled in 1824. It is reported that there was a settlement of African slaves here in the early 1500s. There are features of creolization and archaic Black English. See main entry under United Kingdom.
Haitian Creole French (Kreyol, Aiysyen) [hat] 159,000 in Dominican Republic (1987). See main entry under Haiti.
Spanish [spa] 6,886,000 in Dominican Republic (1995). *Lg Use:* National language. See main entry under Spain.

Ecuador

Republic of Ecuador, República del Ecuador. 13,212,742. 2,300,000 speakers of American Indian languages (Adelaar 1991). National or official languages: Spanish, Cofan, Quichua. Literacy rate: 70% to 90%. Also includes English (65,000), Standard German (32,000), Arabic (1,800), Chinese (7,000). Information mainly from SIL 1955–2003. Blind population: 10,000 (1982 WCE). Deaf population: 64,692 to 150,000 or more (1986 Gallaudet University). Deaf institutions: 3. The number of languages listed for Ecuador is 24. Of those, 23 are living languages and 1 is extinct. See map on page 752.

Achuar-Shiwiar (Achuar, Achual, Achuara, Achuale, Jivaro, Maina) [acu] 2,000 in Ecuador. Ethnic population: 5,000 (2000). Pastaza and Bobonaza river areas, 7 villages. *Lg Use:* Bilingual level estimates for Spanish: 0 60%, 1 20%, 2 10%, 3 7%, 4 3%, 5 0%. Many in the Ecuador group seem to have routine proficiency in Shuar, but their comprehension is limited. *Other:* Interfluvial. Tropical forest. 150 to 500 meters. Swidden agriculturalists; hunter-gatherers; fishermen. Traditional religion. See main entry under Peru.
Awa-Cuaiquer (Awa, Awapit, Cuaiquer) [kwi] 1,000 in Ecuador (1991 Adelaar). Ethnic population: 2,000 in Ecuador (2000). Extreme north, on the western slopes of the Andes, Colombia-Ecuador border, Carchi Province. *Other:* Speakers call themselves 'Awa' in Ecuador. See main entry under Colombia.
Chachi (Cayapa, Cha' Palaachi) [cbi] 3,450 (2000 SIL). Ethnic population: 3,500 to 5,000. North coastal jungle, Esmeraldas Province, Cayapas River and its tributaries (Onzole, Canandé, Sucio, Cojimíes, and others). *Class:* Barbacoan, Cayapa-Colorado. *Lg Use:* Bilingual level estimates for Spanish: 0 6%, 1 25.5%, 2 26.5%, 3 34.5%, 4 6%, 5 1.5%. Women, older adults, and those living in the isolated headwaters of the river are less bilingual in Spanish. *Lg Dev:* Dictionary. Bible portions: 1964–1980. *Other:* The name of the people is 'Chachilla'. SOV. Coastal, riverine. Tropical forest. 10 to 400 meters. Swidden agriculturalists: plantain; fishermen: shrimp, fish; hunters. Traditional religion, Christian.
Cofán (Kofán, A'i, Kofane, A'ingae) [con] 800 in Ecuador (2000 Juncosa). 800 monolinguals. Population total all countries: 1,400. Ethnic population: 1,500. Both sides of the Colombia and Ecuador border, Napo Province near Santa Rosa de Sucumbios, and down the Aguarico River about 80 miles. Sucumbios Province. 5 centers in Ecuador, and scattered places between. Also spoken in Colombia. *Class:* Chibchan, Cofan. *Dialects:* Chibchan with Western Tucanoan features (Ferndon, Borman), Barbacoan (J.A. Mason), or Jivaroan (Ruhlen 1987). *Lg Use:* Official language. Vigorous. Some Siona and Secoya have learned Cofán because of intermarriage, and their children learn Cofán. All domains. Used in religious services. All ages. Positive language attitude. Bilingual level estimates for Spanish: 0 1%, 1 33%, 2 28%, 3 25%, 4 12%, 5 1%. Some speakers also use Siona, Secoya, or Napo Lowland Quichua. Schools are in Spanish, except for early grades which provide bilingual education. *Lg Dev:* Literacy rate in first language: 60%. Taught in primary schools. Roman script. Radio programs. Dictionary. NT: 1980–2002. *Other:* SOV. Riverine. Tropical forest. 200 to 1,000 meters. Swidden agriculturalists; crafts for tourists. Traditional religion, Christian.
Colorado (Tsachila, Tsafiki) [cof] 2,300 (2000 SIL). Ethnic population: 2,300 (2000 SIL). Northwestern jungle west of Quito, around Santo Domingo de los Colorados. *Class:* Barbacoan, Cayapa-Colorado. *Lg Use:* All are

bilingual. *Lg Dev:* Dictionary. Grammar. NT: 1980–1990. *Other:* SOV. Interfluvial. Tropical forest. 550 to 600 meters. Peasant agriculturalists. Traditional religion, Christian.

Ecuadorian Sign Language [ecs] 188,000 (1986 Gallaudet Univ.). *Class:* Deaf sign language. *Dialects:* Slight regional variants in sign languages. Some influences from USA Peace Corps, others from people educated in Spain or Argentina. *Lg Use:* Some deaf schools use total communication; speaking and signing.

Epena (Emberá-Saija, Epená, Saija, Epená Saija, Epéna Pedée, Southern Embera, Southern Empera, Cholo) [sja] 50 in Ecuador (2000 Wiebe). Town of Borbón. Northern Pacific Coast. *Dialect:* Basurudo. See main entry under Colombia.

Media Lengua [mue] 1,000 (1999 Peter Bakker). Population includes first- and second-language speakers. A few villages. *Class:* Mixed Language, Spanish-Quechua. *Other:* Has a Quechua grammatical system and a Spanish vocabulary.

Quichua, Calderón Highland (Calderón Quichua, Pichincha Quichua, Cayambe Quichua) [qud] 25,000 (1987 SIL). Ethnic population: 35,049 (2000 WCD). Calderón and Cayambe areas of Pichincha Province around Quito. *Class:* Quechuan, Quechua II, B. *Dialects:* Distinct from Chimborazo, Imbabura, Salasaca. *Lg Use:* Speakers are shifting to Spanish. Used in the home. All ages. *Other:* All Quichua are called 'Quechua' in most other countries. SOV.

Quichua, Cañar Highland [qxr] 100,000 (1991 UBS). Southern highlands, Cañar Province. *Class:* Quechuan, Quechua II, B. *Dialects:* Lexical differences and a strong sense of linguistic and cultural identity make separate literature necessary. *Lg Use:* Strong use of Quichua away from the road. They consider Chimborazo to be a separate language. *Lg Dev:* NT: 1996. *Other:* SOV. Traditional religion, Christian.

Quichua, Chimborazo Highland [qug] 1,000,000 (1990 UBS). Central highlands, Chimborazo and Bolivar provinces. Dialects of Cotopaxi and the rest of Tungurahua, large towns around Ambato not called Salasaca. *Class:* Quechuan, Quechua II, B. *Lg Use:* High percentage of monolinguals. *Lg Dev:* Bible: 1989. *Other:* SOV. Traditional religion, Christian.

Quichua, Imbabura Highland (Otavalo Quichua) [qvi] 300,000 (1977 SIL). Many monolinguals. Northern highlands, Imbabura Province. *Class:* Quechuan, Quechua II, B. *Lg Use:* Vigorous. All ages. *Lg Dev:* Bible: 1994. *Other:* SOV. Traditional religion, Christian.

Quichua, Loja Highland (Saraguro Quichua, Loja Quichua) [qvj] 30,524 (2000 WCD). Northern area of Loja Province in southern highlands. *Class:* Quechuan, Quechua II, B. *Dialects:* Close to Cañar Highland Quichua. *Lg Use:* Speakers prefer to use Chimborazo Highland Quichua and are shifting to it. *Other:* SOV. Traditional religion, Christian.

Quichua, Napo Lowland (Ingano, Lowland Napo Quichua, Napo Quichua, Runa Shimi) [qvo] 4,000 in Ecuador (2000 SIL). Ethnic population: 5,000 in Ecuador. Eastern jungle along the Napo, Aguarico, and Putomayo rivers, concentrated near schools. *Dialect:* Santa Rosa Quechua. *Lg Use:* Official language. Language use stable in completely Quichua areas, more bilingual where Spanish is needed. Outside landowners and their families, priests, and nuns learn Quichua. Used in religious services. Bilingual level estimates for Spanish: 0 15%, 1 21%, 2 50%, 3 10%, 4 3%, 5 1%. *Lg Dev:* Literacy rate in first language: 20%. The orthography differs from that used in Peru. *Other:* 'Ingano' is a name for all lowland Quichua. Schools use Spanish. Locations along the Putomayo River are not confirmed. Riverine. Tropical forest. 280 meters.

Swidden agriculturalists. Traditional religion, Christian. See main entry under Peru (Quechua, Napo Lowland).

Quichua, Northern Pastaza (Bobonaza Quichua, Pastaza Quichua, Alama, Canelos Quichua, Sarayacu Quichua) [qvz] 4,000 in Ecuador. Population total all countries: 6,000. Eastern jungle along Bobonaza and Conambo rivers, Pastaza Province. Tigre Quechua is in Peru. Also spoken in Peru. *Class:* Quechuan, Quechua II, B. *Dialect:* Tigre Quechua. *Lg Dev:* NT: 1992. *Other:* Distinct from Southern Pastaza Quechua of Peru. SOV. Riverine. Tropical forest. 300 to 600 meters. Swidden agriculturalists. Traditional religion, Christian.

Quichua, Salasaca Highland (Salasaca Quichua, Tungurahua Quichua, Tungurahua Highland Quichua) [qxl] 14,331 (2000 WCD). South and east of Ambato in Tungurahua Province. At least 15 towns in the Salasaca area, not counting other varieties of Quichua. *Class:* Quechuan, Quechua II, B. *Other:* Lexically distinct from Chimborazo, Imbabura, and Calderón. SOV. Traditional religion, Christian.

Quichua, Tena Lowland (Yumbo) [quw] 5,000 (1976 SIL). Eastern jungle, Tena, Arajuno, Shandia area. *Class:* Quechuan, Quechua II, B. *Dialects:* Napo, Pastaza and Tena Quichua understand each other's spoken language, but not written texts. *Lg Dev:* NT: 1972. *Other:* SOV. Interfluvial. Tropical forest. 600 meters. Swidden agriculturalists. Traditional religion, Christian.

Secoya [sey] 290 in Ecuador. Population includes 170 Secoya Angotero, 120 Ecuadorian Siona. Population total all countries: 434. Ethnic population: 297 (1987 Vickers). Northeastern jungle Aguarico, Cuyabeno, and Eno rivers, near Colombian border. Also spoken in Peru. *Class:* Tucanoan, Western Tucanoan, Northern, Siona-Secoya. *Dialects:* Ecuadorian Siona, Angotero. Identical to Secoya in Peru. Ecuadorian Siona is distinct from Siona of Colombia. *Lg Use:* Once used as a wider contact language by the Spanish colonial administration. Bilingual level estimates for Spanish: 0 55%, 1 23%, 2 15%, 3 36%, 4 1%, 5 0%. *Lg Dev:* NT: 1990. *Other:* SOV. Riverine. Tropical forest. 300 to 350 meters. Swidden agriculturalists. Traditional religion, Christian.

Shuar (Jivaro, Xivaro, Jibaro, Chiwaro, Shuara) [jiv] 46,669 (2000 WCD). Ethnic population: 15,000 to 50,000 (Montaluisa). Southeastern jungle, Morona-Santiago Province. *Class:* Jivaroan. *Lg Use:* Bilingual level estimates for Spanish: 0 14%, 1 30%, 2 25%, 3 20%, 4 10%, 5 1%. *Lg Dev:* NT: 1976–1983. *Other:* Different from Achuar Jivaro of Peru. The people prefer to be called 'Shuar'. SOV. Mountain slope, plains, interfluvial. Tropical forest. 500 to 1,000 meters. Swidden, peasant agriculturalists. Traditional religion, Christian.

Siona [snn] 250 in Ecuador (2000 Juncosa). Putumayo River. *Other:* Distinct from Secoya (Siona-Secoya). Riverine. Tropical forest. 300 to 350 meters. Swidden agriculturalists. See main entry under Colombia.

Spanish (Castellano, Español) [spa] 9,500,000 in Ecuador (1995). *Lg Use:* Official language. *Other:* Christian. See main entry under Spain.

Tetete [teb] Extinct. Ethnic population: 3 (1969 SIL). Near the Colombian border, eastern jungle in Cofán area. *Class:* Tucanoan, Western Tucanoan, Northern, Tetete. *Dialects:* Close to Secoya but intelligible only with difficulty.

Waorani ("Auca," Huaorani, Waodani, Huao, Sabela) [auc] 1,650 (2004). Ethnic population: 1,400 (2000 SIL). Eastern jungle between the Napo and Curaray rivers. *Class:* Language Isolate. *Lg Use:* All ages. Bilingual level estimates for Spanish: 0 94%, 1 5%, 2 1%, 3 0%, 4 0%, 5 0%. Speakers also use Quichua. *Lg Dev:* NT: 1992. *Other:* "Auca" means 'savage' in Quichua. SOV. Riverine. Tropical forest. 300 to 400 meters. Swidden agriculturalists. Traditional religion, Christian.

Záparo (Zápara, Kayapwe) [zro] 1 (2000 SIL). Ethnic population: 170 (2000 M. R. Wise SIL). Pastaza Province, Peru border, between the Curaray and Bobonaza rivers. *Class:* Zaparoan. *Lg Use:* Extinct in Peru. Members of the ethnic group now speak Quichua. May be extinct. Language revival effort; classes in 2 schools. *Other:* Distinct from Andoa (Shimagae) of Peru. SOV. Riverine. Tropical forest. 300 to 400 meters. Swidden agriculturalists. Nearly extinct.

El Salvador

Republic of El Salvador, República de El Salvador. 6,587,541. National or official language: Spanish. Literacy rate: 55% to 63%. Also includes Central Pokomam, Turkish (500), Chinese (1,300). Blind population: 8,000. Deaf population: 150,000 to 348,804 (1998). Deaf institutions: 4. The number of languages listed for El Salvador is 6. Of those, 5 are living languages and 1 is extinct. See map on page 753.

Cacaopera [ccr] Extinct. Department of Morazán. *Class:* Misumalpan. *Dialects:* Close to Matagalpa. *Lg Use:* In 1974 several older adult men could remember a few words and fixed phrases, but none had been native speakers.
Kekchí (Quecchí, Cacché) [kek] 12,286 in El Salvador. See main entry under Guatemala (Q'eqchi').
Lenca [len] Ethnic population: 36,858 in El Salvador (1987). Town of Chilango. *Lg Use:* Speakers are shifting to Spanish. *Other:* Nearly extinct. See main entry under Honduras.
Pipil (Nahuat, Nawat) [ppl] 20 (1987). Ethnic population: 196,576 (1987). Municipio of Dolores, Ocotepeque Department, near the El Salvador border. Extinct in Honduras. *Class:* Uto-Aztecan, Southern Uto-Aztecan, Aztecan, General Aztec, Pipil. *Dialects:* Not intelligible with Isthmus Nahuatl of Mexico. *Lg Use:* Speakers are older adults. *Lg Dev:* Has been taught in some schools for several years (D. Stewart 1994). Grammar. *Other:* Nearly extinct.
Salvadoran Sign Language (El Salvadoran Sign Language) [esn] *Class:* Deaf sign language. *Other:* Different from French or Spanish sign languages.
Spanish (Español, Castellano) [spa] 5,900,000 in El Salvador (1995). *Lg Use:* National language. See main entry under Spain.

Falkland Islands

Islas Malvinas. 2,000 (1998 UN). National or official language: English. A British dependency. About 200 islands. The number of languages listed for Falkland Islands is 1.

English [eng] 1,991 in Falkland Islands (1993 Johnstone). *Lg Use:* National language. See main entry under United Kingdom.

French Guiana

French Guiana. 191,309. National or official language: French. Literacy rate: 78% to 82%. Also includes Aukan (6,592), Haitian Creole French, Hmong Njua (2,000), North Levantine Spoken Arabic (800), Saramaccan (3,000). Information mainly from A. Butt 1966; SIL 1965–2003. The number of languages listed for French Guiana is 10. Of those, all are living languages. See map on page 754.

Arawak (Lokono) [arw] 150 in French Guiana. Coastal areas. *Lg Use:* All speakers are older adults. See main entry under Suriname.
Carib (Caribe, Cariña, Kalihna, Kalinya, Galibi) [car] 1,200 in French Guiana. Coastal areas. *Dialect:* Tyrewuju (Eastern Carib). See main entry under Venezuela.

Chinese, Hakka [hak] 5,000 in French Guiana. *Lg Use:* Use of Hakka Chinese is being maintained. See main entry under China.
Emerillon (Emerilon, Melejo, Mereo, Mereyo, Emereñon, Teco) [eme] 400 (2001). Southern border area, Ouaqui, Camopi and Oiapoque rivers. None in Brazil. *Class:* Tupi, Tupi-Guarani, Subgroup VIII. *Dialects:* Probably not intelligible with Wayampi. *Other:* Heavy borrowing from Wayana.
French [fra] *Lg Use:* National language. See main entry under France.
Guianese Creole French (Guyanais, Guyane, Guyane Creole, Patois, Patwa, French Guianese Creole French) [gcr] 50,000 (1977 SIL). *Class:* Creole, French based. *Dialects:* Intelligibility of Saint Lucia Creole is 78%, of Karipúna Creole of Brazil 77%. *Lg Use:* Trade language. Over 30% of the population in the capital speaks Creole as first language. It is the most important rural language. Educated people can all speak it, but try to avoid it. Low status. Not taught in schools. Some decreolization is taking place. Most speakers also use French to some degree. *Lg Dev:* Dictionary. Grammar.
Javanese, Caribbean [jvn] Coastal area. *Lg Use:* Most are bilingual. *Other:* Muslim. See main entry under Suriname.
Palikúr (Palikour, Palicur) [plu] 500 in French Guiana. Eastern border area. See main entry under Brazil.
Wayampi (Oiampí, Oyapí, Oyampí, Wayãpi, Wayapi, Wajapi, Oiumpian) [oym] 650 in French Guiana (2000 SIL). Population includes 120 Camopí and Masikilí on the middle Oyapock River, and 180 in 3 villages on upper Oyapock around Trois-Sauts (1980 Frangoise Grenand). Population total all countries: 1,180. Southern border area. Also spoken in Brazil. *Class:* Tupi, Tupi-Guarani, Subgroup VIII. *Dialects:* Oiyapoque, Wajapuku. Inherently intelligible with Oiapoque Wayampi. Not intelligible with Emerillon. *Lg Use:* 20 on the upper Oyapock River speak imperfect Wayana. Monolinguals include children under 6, more than half the women, most men over 45, and all of those recently from Brazil. All ages. Everyone on the middle Oyapock and a few on the upper Oyapock can understand Emerillon, but no one will speak it. 7 people on upper Oyapock and 8 on middle Oyapock speak French well. Half can partially understand Guianese Creole French; 30 speak it well around Camopí. A few speak Portuguese passably. *Lg Dev:* Dictionary. Grammar. NT: 2003. *Other:* 2 schools since 1956 and 1971. SOV.
Wayana (Oayana, Guayana, Uaiana, Alukuyana, Upurui) [way] 200 in French Guiana. Ethnic population: 1,000 in French Guiana. Southwestern border area. See main entry under Suriname.

Greenland

Kalaallit Nunaat. 56,384. National or official languages: Greenlandic Inuktitut, Danish. Affiliated with Denmark; home rule since 1979. Literacy rate: 93%. The number of languages listed for Greenland is 2. Of those, both are living languages.

Danish [dan] 7,830 in Greenland (1986). *Lg Use:* National language. See main entry under Denmark.
Inuktitut, Greenlandic (Greenlandic, Kalaallisut) [kal] 47,800 in Greenland (1995 Krauss). Population includes 3,000 East Greenlandic, 44,000 West Greenlandic, 800 North Greenlandic. Population total all countries: 54,800. Greenland. About 80 communities of populations over 10. Also spoken in Denmark. *Class:* Eskimo-Aleut, Eskimo, Inuit. *Dialect:* West Greenlandic, East Greenlandic, "Polar Eskimo" (North Greenlandic, Thule Inuit). Dialects border on being different languages (M. Krauss 1995). *Lg Use:*

National language. Vigorous in Greenland. Speakers also use Danish. *Lg Dev:* Taught in primary schools. Radio programs. Bible: 1900. *Other:* Fishermen; fur export.

Grenada

Grenada. 89,211. National or official language: English. Grenada, Carriacou, and Petit Martinique Islands. Literacy rate: 95% (1991 WA). Also includes East Indian (3,300). Deaf population: 5,699. Deaf institutions: 1. The number of languages listed for Grenada is 3. Of those, all are living languages. See map on page 740.

English [eng] 750 in Grenada (2004). *Dialect:* Grenadian English. *Lg Use:* Official language. *Other:* Post-creole English with French Creole influences (M. Alleyne). See main entry under United Kingdom.

Grenadian Creole English [gcl] 89,227 (2001). *Class:* Creole, English based, Atlantic, Eastern, Southern. *Dialect:* Carriacou Creole English. Closest to Trinidad and Barbados. *Lg Use:* M. Alleyne says it is a post-creole English with French creole influence, no longer a creole. R. Kephart says Carriacou is a creole English. J. Holm says the creole predominates in Grenada (1989:458). *Lg Dev:* Grammar.

Grenadian Creole French (Lesser Antillean Creole French) [acf] 2,300 in Grenada (2004). Carriacou Island. On northern Grenada Island it is in scattered pockets, mainly in rural areas. *Dialects:* Patwa, Patois. *Lg Use:* All speakers older than 50 years. *Other:* The same as, or similar to, that spoken in Saint Lucia (M. Alleyne). See main entry under Saint Lucia (Saint Lucian Creole French).

Guadeloupe

Guadeloupe. 444,515. National or official language: French. A French department in the Leeward Islands. Two large islands: Basse Terre, Grande Terre; also Marie Galante, the Saintes group, Desirade, St. Barthélemy, most of St. Martin. Literacy rate: 89% to 90%. The number of languages listed for Guadeloupe is 4. Of those, all are living languages. See map on page 740.

English [eng] 200 in Guadeloupe (2002). St. Barthélemy Island. *Dialect:* Gustavia English (St. Barth English). *Lg Use:* All are fluent in French. *Other:* English with some creole influence. See main entry under United Kingdom.

French [fra] 7,300 in Guadeloupe (2004). *Lg Use:* Official language. *Other:* There is a variety on the northwest end of St. Barthélemy, west of but not including Gustavia, similar to Cajun French of the USA (Julianne Maher 1997). See main entry under France.

Guadeloupean Creole French (Patwa, Patois, Kreyol) [gcf] 430,000 in Guadeloupe (2001). Population total all countries: 848,454. Eastern St. Barthélemy, Marie Galante islands. Also spoken in Martinique. *Class:* Creole, French based. *Dialects:* Marie Galante Creole French, St. Barth Creole French. St. Barth Creole is distinct in grammatical, phonological, and lexical features, and may not be a dialect (J. Maher 1989). Comprehension of Saint Lucia Creole is 89%. *Lg Dev:* Dictionary. Grammar.

Haitian Creole French (Kreyol, Aiysyen) [hat] 12,000 in Guadeloupe (2004). St. Maartin, St. Barths, and Guadeloupe. See main entry under Haiti.

Guatemala

Republic of Guatemala, República de Guatemala. 14,280,596. Indian 55%, Mestizo 44% (1990 WA). National or official language: Spanish. Literacy rate: 48% to 55%; Indian 0% to 25%, Mestizo 75% to 85%. Information

mainly from M. K. Mayers 1965a, b; SIL 1952–1999. Blind population: 6,000 (1982 WCE). Deaf population: 100,000 to 650,014 (1998). Deaf institutions: 5. The number of languages listed for Guatemala is 56. Of those, 54 are living languages and 2 are extinct. See map on page 755.

Achi', Cubulco [acc] 48,252 (2000 WCD). Central area west of Rabinal, Baja Verapaz Department. *Class:* Mayan, Quichean-Mamean, Greater Quichean, Quichean, Quiche-Achi. *Lg Dev:* Literacy rate in first language: 1% to 5%. Literacy rate in second language: 11%. Taught in primary schools. Dictionary. Grammar. NT: 1984. *Other:* SVO.

Achi', Rabinal (Rabinal K'iche') [acr] 37,300 (1990 SIL). Central Rabinal area, Baja Verapaz Department. *Class:* Mayan, Quichean-Mamean, Greater Quichean, Quichean, Quiche-Achi. *Dialects:* Closest linguistically to Cubulco Achi'. *Lg Use:* All ages. Possibly 20% of speakers can discuss more than common topics in Spanish. *Lg Dev:* Literacy rate in first language: 15% to 20%. Literacy rate in second language: 25% to 40%. Taught in primary schools. Dictionary. Bible portions: 1966–1993. *Other:* SVO.

Akateko (Acateco, Acatec, San Miguel Acatán Kanjobal, Conob, Western Kanjobal, Western Q'anjob'al) [knj] 48,500 in Guatemala (1998). Population total all countries: 58,600. San Miguel Acatán. Also spoken in Mexico, USA. *Class:* Mayan, Kanjobalan-Chujean, Kanjobalan, Kanjobal-Jacaltec. *Lg Use:* All ages. Few speakers also use Spanish. *Lg Dev:* Literacy rate in first language: 5% to 10%. Literacy rate in second language: 20%. Taught in primary schools. NT: 1981. *Other:* VOS.

American Sign Language (ASL, Ameslan) [ase] *Other:* There may be other sign languages besides ASL. See main entry under USA.

Awakateko (Aguacateco, Aguacatec) [agu] 18,000 (1998 SIL). Western Huehuetenango Department. *Class:* Mayan, Quichean-Mamean, Greater Mamean, Ixilan. *Lg Use:* All ages. *Lg Dev:* Literacy rate in first language: 10%. Literacy rate in second language: 29%. Taught in primary schools. Dictionary. Grammar. NT: 1971–1993. *Other:* VSO.

Chicomuceltec (Cakchiquel Mam) [cob] Extinct. Ethnic population: 100 in Guatemala (1982 GR). *Lg Use:* Members of the ethnic group now speak Spanish. See main entry under Mexico.

Ch'orti' [caa] 30,000 in Guatemala (2000 Lubeck). Population total all countries: 30,010. Eastern border with Honduras, and into Honduras. Also spoken in Honduras. *Class:* Mayan, Cholan-Tzeltalan, Cholan, Chorti. *Lg Use:* All ages. *Lg Dev:* Literacy rate in first language: 15%. Literacy rate in second language: 30%. Taught in primary schools. Dictionary. Grammar. NT: 1997. *Other:* Not the same as the extinct language called 'Choltí' formerly spoken in the Quiriguá and Izabal area. Nearly extinct in Honduras. VOS.

Chuj, Ixtatán (Chuh, Chuje, Chuhe, Chuj de San Mateo Ixtatán) [cnm] 22,130 in Guatemala (1991 SIL). Population total all countries: 31,630. Western Huehuetenango Department. Also spoken in Mexico. *Class:* Mayan, Kanjobalan-Chujean, Chujean. *Lg Dev:* Literacy rate in first language: 20% to 40%. Literacy rate in second language: 25%. NT: 1970–1994. *Other:* VOS.

Chuj, San Sebastián Coatán [cac] 19,458 (1991 SIL). Central western Coatán River area, western Huehuetenango Department. *Class:* Mayan, Kanjobalan-Chujean, Chujean. *Lg Dev:* Literacy rate in first language: 30% to 60%. Literacy rate in second language: 25%. NT: 1969. *Other:* VSO.

Garifuna (Garífuna, Black Carib, Caribe, Central American Carib) [cab] 16,700 in Guatemala. Two villages on the northeast coast: Livingston and Puerto Barrios.

Lg Use: Speakers also use Spanish. *Lg Dev:* Literacy rate in first language: 1% to 5%. Literacy rate in second language: 15% to 20%. *Other:* Ancestors brought from Saint Vincent Island in 1796–1797, and taken to Roatan Island. Most went to Trujillo in 1937. About 35 years later political troubles threatened their existence, and they fled further east in Honduras and Belize. Later they emigrated to other countries. See main entry under Honduras.

Guatemalan Sign Language [gsm] *Class:* Deaf sign language.

Itza' (Petén Itzá Maya, Yucatec Maya, Icaiche Maya, Maya) [itz] 12 (1986 SIL). Ethnic population: 1,800 (2001). North central, north of Lake Petén Itzá in San José Petén, 15 minutes by auto from Flores. The language is extinct in Belize. *Class:* Mayan, Yucatecan, Mopan-Itza. *Lg Use:* The language is nearly extinct in Guatemala, but the ethnic group retains the Indian culture. 60 bilingual nonfluent speakers (1991 A. Hofling). The ethnic group in Belize now speaks Spanish. Speakers are older adults. *Other:* Nearly extinct.

Ixil, Chajul [ixj] 18,000 (1998 SIL). Quiché Department. *Class:* Mayan, Quichean-Mamean, Greater Mamean, Ixilan. *Dialect:* Ilom. *Lg Use:* All ages. *Lg Dev:* Literacy rate in first language: 10% to 30%. Literacy rate in second language: 16%. Taught in primary schools. Dictionary. Grammar. Bible portions: 1981–1999. *Other:* VSO.

Ixil, Nebaj [ixi] 35,000 (1991 SIL). Nebaj area, Quiché Department. *Class:* Mayan, Quichean-Mamean, Greater Mamean, Ixilan. *Lg Use:* All ages. *Lg Dev:* Literacy rate in first language: 10%. Literacy rate in second language: 7%. Dictionary. Grammar. Bible portions: 1960–1997. *Other:* VSO.

Ixil, San Juan Cotzal [ixl] 16,000 (1998 SIL). Quiché Department. *Class:* Mayan, Quichean-Mamean, Greater Mamean, Ixilan. *Dialects:* 70% to 75% intelligibility among the three Ixil languages. *Lg Use:* All ages. Little bilingualism in Spanish. *Lg Dev:* Literacy rate in first language: 10% to 30%. Literacy rate in second language: 15% to 25%. Taught in primary schools. NT: 2001. *Other:* VOS.

Jakalteko, Eastern (Jacalteco, Eastern) [jac] 11,000 (1998 SIL). Huehuetenango Department near Mexico border, Concepción Huista area. *Class:* Mayan, Kanjobalan-Chujean, Kanjobalan, Kanjobal-Jacaltec. *Lg Use:* All ages. *Lg Dev:* Literacy rate in first language: 5% to 10%. Literacy rate in second language: 15% to 28%. NT: 1997. *Other:* VSO.

Jakalteko, Western (Western Jacalteco, Popti') [jai] 77,700 in Guatemala (1998). Population total all countries: 88,000. Huehuetenango Department, around Jakaltenango. Also spoken in Mexico. *Class:* Mayan, Kanjobalan-Chujean, Kanjobalan, Kanjobal-Jacaltec. *Dialects:* Eastern and Western Jakalteko understand each other's spoken languages, but not written text. *Lg Dev:* Literacy rate in first language: 5% to 10%. Literacy rate in second language: 52%. NT: 1979. *Other:* VSO.

Kaqchikel, Akatenango Southwestern (Acatenango Southwestern Cakchiquel) [ckk] 500 (1997 SIL). Municipio of Akatenango, town of Akatenango. *Class:* Mayan, Quichean-Mamean, Greater Quichean, Quichean, Cakchiquel. *Lg Use:* Speakers are shifting to Spanish. *Lg Dev:* Literacy rate in second language: 38%. *Other:* Agriculturalists: maize, beans, squash, coffee.

Kaqchikel, Central (Cakchiquel, Kaqchiquel) [cak] 132,200 (1990 SIL). Southern Guatemala, Chimaltenango Department. *Class:* Mayan, Quichean-Mamean, Greater Quichean, Quichean, Cakchiquel. *Lg Use:* All ages. *Lg Dev:* Literacy rate in first language: 5% to 10%. Literacy rate in second language: 25% to 39%. Dictionary. Grammar. NT: 1931–1980. *Other:* SVO.

Kaqchikel, Eastern (Eastern Cakchiquel) [cke] 100,000 (1998 SIL). Northwest of and near Guatemala City, San Juan Sacatepéquez. *Class:* Mayan, Quichean-Mamean, Greater Quichean, Quichean, Cakchiquel. *Lg Use:* All ages. *Lg Dev:* Literacy rate in first language: 3%. Literacy rate in second language: 45%. Taught in primary schools. NT: 1986. *Other:* SVO.

Kaqchikel, Northern (Northern Cakchiquel) [ckc] 24,000 (2000 SIL). Ethnic population: 40,000. Central highlands, northeastern Chimaltenango Department, San Martín Jilotepeque Municipality in rural areas and towns of San Martín and Santa Ana Chimaltenango. *Class:* Mayan, Quichean-Mamean, Greater Quichean, Quichean, Cakchiquel. *Lg Use:* There are efforts toward producing a standardized Kaqchikel. All speakers are older than 45 years. Spanish is used with outsiders. In border areas, some people also speak Quiché. *Lg Dev:* Literacy rate in first language: below 1%. Literacy rate in second language: 30% of those under 25. Bible portions: 1982–1991. *Other:* SVO. Mountain mesa, mountain slope, valleys. Agriculturalists; farm workers for landowners; merchants; craftsmen. Traditional religion, Christian.

Kaqchikel, Santa María de Jesús (Kach'ab'al, Santa María de Jesús Cakchiquel) [cki] 18,000 (2000 SIL). Southeast of Antigua, Sacatepéquez Department, Santa María de Jesus Municipality. *Class:* Mayan, Quichean-Mamean, Greater Quichean, Quichean, Cakchiquel. *Lg Use:* Vigorous. Nearly all parents pass Kaqchikel on to children. Most domains, home, local administration and commerce; used in traditional religious services, some religious services have the sermon in Kaqchikel, announcements in Kaqchikel. Few are monolingual, nearly all have moderate fluency in Spanish, less than 100 speak some English. *Lg Dev:* Literacy rate in first language: below 1%. Literacy rate in second language: 54%. 200 people read Kaqchikel, 50 write it. Roman script. *Other:* Mountain slope, volcanic. 2,000 meters. Agriculturalists: Chinese peas. Traditional religion, Christian.

Kaqchikel, Santo Domingo Xenacoj (Santo Domingo Xenacoj Cakchiquel, Xenacoj) [ckj] 5,200 (1991 SIL). West of Guatemala City on the Pan American highway. *Class:* Mayan, Quichean-Mamean, Greater Quichean, Quichean, Cakchiquel. *Lg Use:* All ages. *Lg Dev:* Literacy rate in first language: 2%. Literacy rate in second language: 50%. Taught in secondary schools. Bible portions: 1982–1998. *Other:* SVO.

Kaqchikel, South Central (South Central Cakchiquel) [ckd] 43,000 (1998 SIL). Pan American highway west of Guatemala City. *Class:* Mayan, Quichean-Mamean, Greater Quichean, Quichean, Cakchiquel. *Lg Use:* All ages. *Lg Dev:* Literacy rate in first language: 1% to 5%. Literacy rate in second language: 25% to 63%. Taught in secondary schools. Bible portions: 1982–1997. *Other:* SVO.

Kaqchikel, Southern (Southern Cakchiquel) [ckf] 43,000 (1993 SIL). Area south of Antigua. *Class:* Mayan, Quichean-Mamean, Greater Quichean, Quichean, Cakchiquel. *Lg Use:* All speakers are older than 30 years. Some speakers are shifting to Spanish. *Lg Dev:* Literacy rate in first language: 30%. Literacy rate in second language: 73%. Taught in primary schools. NT: 1993. *Other:* SVO.

Kaqchikel, Western (Western Cakchiquel) [ckw] 77,000 (1998 SIL). Northern and eastern shores of Lake Atitlán, Departamento de Sololá. *Class:* Mayan, Quichean-Mamean, Greater Quichean, Quichean, Cakchiquel. *Lg Use:* All speakers are older than 25 years. *Lg Dev:* Literacy rate in first language: 1% to 5%. Literacy rate in second language: 25% to 43%. Dictionary. Grammar. NT: 1996. *Other:* SVO. Swidden agriculturalists: maize, beans, squash.

Kaqkchikel, Yepocapa Southwestern (Yepocapa
Southwestern Cakchiquel) [cbm] 8,000 (1991 SIL). Ethnic
population: 15,000 (1991 SIL). Municipio of Yepocapa.
Class: Mayan, Quichean-Mamean, Greater Quichean,
Quichean, Cakchiquel. *Lg Use:* All speakers are older
than 40 years. *Lg Dev:* Literacy rate in first language: 1%
to 5%. Literacy rate in second language: 25%. NT: 1990.
Other: SVO.

Kaqkchikel-K'iche' Mixed Language (Cauque
Mixed Language) [ckz] 2,000 (1998 SIL). Santiago,
Sacatepéquez, Santa María Cauque aldea. *Class:* Mixed
Language, Cakchiquel-Quiché. *Dialects:* Speakers came
from the K'iche' area in the colonial period. Older
speakers show a base of K'iche'. *Lg Use:* The language is
changing to become more like South Central Kaqkchikel.
All speakers are older than 30 years. Speakers are fully
bilingual in South Central Cakchiquel and becoming
bilingual in Spanish.

K'iche', Central (Quiché, Central Quiché, Chiquel,
Cachabel) [quc] 1,900,000 (2000 SIL). Central highlands,
Totonicapan, southern El Quiché, eastern Sololá, eastern
Quezaltenango departments. *Class:* Mayan, Quichean-
Mamean, Greater Quichean, Quichean, Quiche-Achi.
Lg Use: Vigorous. All domains, interpreters required in
courts, some bilingual schools, oral use in religious services.
Positive language attitude. 300,000 are monolingual in
K'iche', 400,000 have varying proficiency in Spanish, about
100,000 know Kaqkchikel or Tzutujil, a few speak Q'eqchi'
or Mam. *Lg Dev:* Literacy rate in first language: below 1%.
Literacy rate in second language: 25% to 35%. 40,000 can
read K'iche', 20,000 can write it. Taught in primary
schools. Roman script. Radio programs. Videos. Dictionary.
Grammar. Bible: 1995. *Other:* SVO. Hills, valleys.
Agriculturalists. Traditional religion, Christian.

K'iche', Cunén (Cunén Quiché, Northern Quiché, Chuil
Quiché, Cunenteco Quiché, Cunenteco K'iche') [cun]
9,000 (2000 Marhenke). Ethnic population: 9,000
including 7,000 and growing in the municipio plus 2,000
in Guatemala City (1993 Marhenke). K'iche' Department.
Class: Mayan, Quichean-Mamean, Greater Quichean,
Quichean, Quiche-Achi. *Lg Use:* There are 2 other
K'iche' languages in the municipio, but Cunenteco, not
Spanish, is the predominant language in the market. There
is significant monolingualism among men in the aldeas,
and even more among women. Very gradual language shift
toward Spanish. Most children. *Lg Dev:* Literacy rate in
second language: 24%. *Other:* Swidden agriculturalists:
maize, beans, squash.

K'iche', Eastern (East Central Quiché, Chichicastenango
Eastern Quiché, Eastern Quiché) [quu] 100,000 (1991
SIL). Includes Chichicastenango and Chiché. *Class:*
Mayan, Quichean-Mamean, Greater Quichean, Quichean,
Quiche-Achi. *Lg Use:* All ages. *Lg Dev:* Literacy rate in
first language: 5% to 10%. Literacy rate in second
language: 15% to 25%. Taught in primary schools.
Dictionary.

K'iche', Joyabaj (Joyabaj Quiché) [quj] 54,298 (1991
SIL). Quiché Department. *Class:* Mayan, Quichean-
Mamean, Greater Quichean, Quichean, Quiche-Achi.
Lg Dev: Literacy rate in first language: below 1%. Literacy
rate in second language: 12%. NT: 1984. *Other:* SVO.

K'iche', San Andrés (San Andrés Sajcabajá Quiché)
[qxi] 19,728 (1991 SIL). Quiché Department. *Class:*
Mayan, Quichean-Mamean, Greater Quichean, Quichean,
Quiche-Achi. *Lg Use:* All ages. *Lg Dev:* Literacy rate in
first language: 5%. Literacy rate in second language: 10%
to 15%. Taught in primary schools. Bible portions: 1997.
Other: Swidden agriculturalists: maize, beans, squash.

K'iche', West Central (Southwestern Quiché, Cantel
Quiché) [qut] 250,000 (1994 SIL). Southwest of Lake
Atitlán, Quezaltenango, and Totonicapan departments.

Class: Mayan, Quichean-Mamean, Greater Quichean,
Quichean, Quiche-Achi. *Dialects:* Coastal K'iche',
Western K'iche'. *Lg Use:* All ages. *Lg Dev:* Literacy rate
in first language: 5% to 10%. Literacy rate in second
language: 25% to 55%. Dictionary. Grammar. NT: 1997.
Other: SVO.

Mam, Central (Comitancillo Mam, Western Mam, Mam
Occidental, Mam Marquense, San Marcos Comitancillas
Mam) [mvc] 100,000 (1992 SIL). San Marcos Department
(10 towns). The towns of San Miguel Ixtahuacán (18,000)
and Concepción Tutapa (30,000) could be considered
dialects of Northern Mam. *Class:* Mayan, Quichean-
Mamean, Greater Mamean, Mamean. *Dialects:* Lexical
similarity 77% between Tajumulco and Comitancillo.
Lg Use: All ages. *Lg Dev:* Literacy rate in first language:
1% to 5%. Literacy rate in second language: 25% to 32%
Spanish. Taught in primary schools. Dictionary. Grammar.
NT: 1998.

Mam, Northern (Huehuetenango Mam) [mam] 200,279
in Guatemala (2000 WCD). Population total all countries:
201,279. Western Huehuetenango Department (San
Sebastián and other towns) and San Marcos Department;
17 towns. Also spoken in Mexico. *Class:* Mayan,
Quichean-Mamean, Greater Mamean, Mamean. *Lg Dev:*
Literacy rate in first language: 1% to 5%. Literacy rate in
second language: 21%. Bible: 1993. *Other:* VSO.

Mam, Southern (San Juan Ostuncalco Mam, Ostuncalco
Mam, Quetzaltenango Mam, Mam Quetzalteco) [mms]
125,000 (1991 SIL). Quetzaltenango Department (9
towns), Retalhuleu Department (1 town); Western
Ostuncalco area (San Juan Ostuncalco, San Martín
Sacatepéquez, and other towns). *Class:* Mayan, Quichean-
Mamean, Greater Mamean, Mamean. *Dialect:* San Martín
Sacatepéquez Mam (San Martín Chile Verde Mam).
Lg Dev: Literacy rate in first language: 1% to 5%.
Literacy rate in second language: 37%. NT: 1939–1980.
Other: VSO.

Mam, Tajumulco [mpf] 35,000 (1992 SIL). San Marcos
Department, Tajumulco and Ixchiguán towns. *Class:*
Mayan, Quichean-Mamean, Greater Mamean, Mamean.
Dialects: Very different from Central Mam, although
close geographically. Lexical similarity 77% with
Comitancillo. *Lg Use:* Positive language attitude.
Lg Dev: Literacy rate in first language: below 1%.
Literacy rate in second language: 5% to 15%.

Mam, Todos Santos Cuchumatán [mvj] 50,000 in
Guatemala (1998 SIL). Population total all countries:
60,000. Huehuetenango Department, town of Todos
Santos Cuchumatán. Also spoken in Mexico. *Class:*
Mayan, Quichean-Mamean, Greater Mamean, Mamean.
Lg Dev: Literacy rate in first language: below 1%.
Literacy rate in second language: 15% to 21%. NT: 1997.
Other: VSO.

Maya, Mopán (Maya Mopán, Mopane) [mop] 2,600 in
Guatemala (1990 SIL). Petén Department. *Lg Dev:*
Literacy rate in first language: below 1%. Literacy rate in
second language: 5% to 15%. See main entry under Belize.

Poqomam, Central (Central Pocoman, Pokomam,
Pocomán) [poc] 8,600 in Guatemala (1990 SIL). 9
kilometers northwest of Guatemala City, Chinautla. Also
spoken in El Salvador. *Class:* Mayan, Quichean-Mamean,
Greater Quichean, Pocom. *Lg Use:* Speakers are shifting
to Spanish. *Lg Dev:* Literacy rate in first language: below
1%. Literacy rate in second language: 25% to 32%. Bible
portions: 1981–1982. *Other:* SVO.

Poqomam, Eastern (Pocomam Oriental, Eastern
Pokomam) [poa] 12,500 (1990 SIL). Eastern Guatemala,
Jalapa Department, San Luis Jilotepeque. *Class:* Mayan,
Quichean-Mamean, Greater Quichean, Pocom. *Dialects:*
Possibly 50% intelligibility of Central Poqomam. *Lg Use:*
Speakers are shifting to Spanish. *Lg Dev:* Literacy rate in

first language: below 1%. Literacy rate in second language: 27%. Bible portions: 1966–1982. *Other:* SVO.

Poqomam, Southern (Palín Pocomam, Southern Pokomam) [pou] 27,910 (1991 SIL). 20 kilometers south of Guatemala City. *Class:* Mayan, Quichean-Mamean, Greater Quichean, Pocom. *Lg Use:* Speakers are shifting to Spanish. *Lg Dev:* Literacy rate in first language: below 1%. Literacy rate in second language: 25% to 30%.

Poqomchi', Eastern (Tactic Pokomchí, Pocomchí, Poconchí, Pokonchí, Eastern Pokomchí) [poh] 42,164 (2000 WCD). Atla Verapaz Department. *Class:* Mayan, Quichean-Mamean, Greater Quichean, Pocom. *Lg Use:* Speakers also use Spanish or Q'eqchi'. *Lg Dev:* Literacy rate in first language: below 1%. Literacy rate in second language: 21%. NT: 1983.

Poqomchi', Western (Western Pocomchí, Pocomchí, Poqomchi', Western Pokomchí) [pob] 50,000 (1998 SIL). Around San Cristobal. *Class:* Mayan, Quichean-Mamean, Greater Quichean, Pocom. *Dialect:* Santa Cruz Verapaz Poqomchi'. *Lg Use:* All ages. *Lg Dev:* Literacy rate in first language: 5% to 10%. Literacy rate in second language: 35%. Taught in primary schools. Dictionary. Grammar. Bible portions: 1957–1979. *Other:* SVO. Swidden agriculturalists: maize, black beans, bananas; rope makers.

Q'anjob'al, Eastern (Santa Eulalia Kanjobal, Kanhobal, Qanjobal, Conob, Eastern Kanjobal) [kjb] 77,700 in Guatemala (1998). Huehuetenango Department, Santa Eulalia. Also spoken in USA. *Class:* Mayan, Kanjobalan-Chujean, Kanjobalan, Kanjobal-Jacaltec. *Lg Use:* Few speakers also use Spanish. *Lg Dev:* Literacy rate in first language: 5% to 10%. Literacy rate in second language: 26%. Bible: 1989. *Other:* VSO.

Q'eqchi' (Quecchi', Cacche', Ketchi', Kekchi') [kek] 400,000 in Guatemala (1998 SIL). Population total all countries: 421,286. Northern Alta Verapaz, southern Petén departments in Guatemala. Also spoken in Belize, El Salvador. *Class:* Mayan, Quichean-Mamean, Greater Quichean, Kekchi. *Dialects:* Only slight dialect differences. Prestige dialect is Cobán, Alta Verapaz. *Lg Use:* All ages. *Lg Dev:* Literacy rate in first language: 10% to 30%. Literacy rate in second language: 22%. Taught in primary and secondary schools. Dictionary. Grammar. Bible: 1988–2001. *Other:* SVO. Traditional religion, Christian.

Sakapulteko (Sacapulas K'iche', Sacapulteco) [quv] 36,823 (1991 SIL). Quiché Department, and some speakers in Guatemala City. *Class:* Mayan, Quichean-Mamean, Greater Quichean, Sacapulteco. *Lg Use:* Speakers are shifting to Spanish. *Lg Dev:* Literacy rate in first language: below 1%. Literacy rate in second language: 16%. Bible portions: 1980.

Sipakapense (Sipacapeño, Sipacapa Quiché, Sipacapense) [qum] 8,000 (2000 SIL). Ethnic population: 12,000 or more (2000 E. Kindberg SIL). San Marcos Department. *Class:* Mayan, Quichean-Mamean, Greater Quichean, Sipacapeno. *Lg Use:* Vigorous. All ages. In a survey of 80 people in 2000, many children were actively using Sipakapense. People prefer Sipakapense. Some speakers have negative attitudes toward Sipakapense. People want to be bilingual in Spanish. Some also use Spanish. *Lg Dev:* Literacy rate in first language: 1%. Literacy rate in second language: 20%. Dictionary. Grammar. Bible portions: 1992–1998. *Other:* Mountain slope. 2,000 to 3,000 meters. Agriculturalists. Traditional religion, Christian.

Spanish (Español, Castellano) [spa] 4,673,000 in Guatemala (1995). *Lg Use:* National language. See main entry under Spain.

Tacanec (Tacaná Mam, Western Mam, Tiló, Mamé) [mtz] 20,000 in Guatemala (1991 SIL). Population total all countries: 21,200. Western San Marcos Department; rural areas west of the town of Tacaná, western Guatemala border, and in Sibinal and Tectitán. Also spoken in Mexico. *Class:* Mayan, Quichean-Mamean, Greater Mamean, Mamean. *Dialects:* The most distinctive of all the Mam varieties. *Lg Use:* Speakers are shifting to Spanish. Very few speakers under 25 years old. *Lg Dev:* Literacy rate in second language: 25%. *Other:* VSO. Mountain slope. 2,400 meters. Agriculturalists: maize, beans, potatoes, cabbage, wheat.

Tektiteko (Teco, "Teko," Tectitán Mam, Maya-Tekiteko, Tectiteco) [ttc] 1,265 in Guatemala (2000 WCD). Population total all countries: 2,265. Area of Tectitán, western Guatemala border. Also spoken in Mexico. *Class:* Mayan, Quichean-Mamean, Greater Mamean, Mamean. *Dialects:* Close to Mam. *Lg Use:* Within the municipality of Tectitán, there is a resurgence of language use. Vitality stronger than 20 years ago (2000). All ages. In the largest villages, Tektiteko is commonly used by children. In some areas, parents desire their children to speak only Spanish. Some parents tend to discourage younger children from Tektiteko usage. *Lg Dev:* Literacy rate in first language: 10% to 20%. Literacy rate in second language: 15% to 20%. Dictionary. Grammar. NT: 2003. *Other:* VSO.

Tz'utujil, Eastern (Tzutujil Oriental, Santiago Atitlán Tzutujil, Tzutuhil) [tzj] 50,000 (1998 SIL). 17,000 monolinguals. Southern shore of Lake Atitlán, Sololá Department. *Class:* Mayan, Quichean-Mamean, Greater Quichean, Quichean, Tzutujil. *Dialects:* 99% of the people understand and speak Eastern Tz'utujil. *Lg Use:* Vigorous. All domains, letters, local commerce. All ages. 25% are fairly fluent in Spanish, 65% are less fluent. *Lg Dev:* Literacy rate in first language: 10%. Literacy rate in second language: 25%. 25% of the people read Eastern Tz'utujil, 5% write it. Taught in primary schools. Radio programs. Grammar. NT: 1992. *Other:* Coastal, mountain slope, volcanic. Agriculturalists.

Tz'utujil, Western [tzt] 33,800 (1990 SIL). Southern Sololá area, southwestern shore of Lake Atitlán. *Class:* Mayan, Quichean-Mamean, Greater Quichean, Quichean, Tzutujil. *Lg Use:* All ages. *Lg Dev:* Literacy rate in first language: 3% to 4%. Literacy rate in second language: 50%. Grammar. NT: 1981–1989. *Other:* SVO. Agriculturalists.

Uspanteko (Uspanteco) [usp] 3,000 (1998 SIL). Quiché Department. The center is Las Pacayas. *Class:* Mayan, Quichean-Mamean, Greater Quichean, Uspantec. *Lg Use:* The Mayan Academy is actively promoting language use. All ages. *Lg Dev:* Literacy rate in first language: below 1%. Literacy rate in second language: 16%. Radio programs. Grammar. NT: 1999. *Other:* SVO.

Xinca (Szinca) [xin] Extinct. Southeastern. *Class:* Unclassified. *Dialects:* Language may be related to Lenca. *Lg Use:* Members of the ethnic group now speak Spanish.

Guyana

Co-operative Republic of Guyana. Formerly British Guiana. 705,803. 43,000 Amerindians (1990 Janette Forte). National or official language: English. Literacy rate: 91%. Also includes Portuguese, Saint Lucian Creole French (250), Urdu, Chinese (1,500). Information mainly from J. Forte 1990; SIL 1965–2003. Blind population: 1,300 (1982 WCE). Deaf population: 44,199. Deaf institutions: 6. The number of languages listed for Guyana is 17. Of those, 16 are living languages and 1 is extinct. See map on page 756.

Akawaio (Acewaio, Akawai, Acahuayo, Kapon) [ake] 4,500 in Guyana, (2002 SIL). Population total all countries: 5,000. West central, north of Patamona. Also spoken in Brazil, Venezuela. *Class:* Carib, Northern, East-West Guiana, Macushi-Kapon, Kapon. *Dialects:*

Close to Macushi, marginally intelligible with Arecuna. *Lg Dev:* Bible portions: 1873. *Other:* Important differences in vocabulary from Patamona. Language attitudes indicate separate literature is needed. They and the Patamona call themselves 'Kapon'. Tropical forest. Hunter-gatherers; fishermen. Traditional religion.

Arawak (Arowak, Lokono) [arw] 1,500 in Guyana (2000 Forte). Ethnic population: 15,500 in Guyana. West coast and northeast along the Corantyne River. *Lg Use:* All speakers are older adults in Guyana and Suriname. *Other:* The ethnic group in Guyana represents 33% of the Amerindians. See main entry under Suriname.

Atorada (Ator'ti, Dauri, Atorai) [aox] Few speakers in Guyana. Southwest Guyana, near the Wapishana. Also spoken in Brazil. *Class:* Arawakan, Maipuran, Northern Maipuran, Wapishanan. *Dialects:* Lexical similarity 50% with Wapishana, 20% with Mapidian. *Lg Use:* All speakers older than 50 years. Speakers also use Wapishana. *Other:* Savannah. Swidden agriculturalists: cassava. Traditional religion, Christian.

Berbice Creole Dutch [brc] 4 or 5 (1993 S. Kouwenberg). 15 with limited competence (1989 J. Holm). Berbice River area. *Class:* Creole, Dutch based. *Dialects:* Speakers claim it is not inherently intelligible with Skepi or Rupununi. About 30% of the basic lexicon and most of the productive morphology is from Eastern Ijo in Nigeria; most of the rest of the lexicon is from Dutch, 10% loans from Arawak and Guyanese Creole English. *Lg Use:* Speakers also use Guyanese, which has influenced Berbice considerably. *Lg Dev:* Grammar. *Other:* SVO. Nearly extinct.

Carib (Caribe, Cariña, Kalihna, Kalinya, Galibi) [car] 475 in Guyana (1991). Ethnic population: 3,000 in Guyana (2000 J. Forte). West coast and northwest. *Dialect:* Murato (Myrato, Western Carib). *Other:* The ethnic group in Guyana represents 6% of the Amerindians. See main entry under Venezuela.

English [eng] *Dialect:* Guyanese English. *Lg Use:* National language. *Other:* Spoken as first language by some Blacks and some Hindustanis. See main entry under United Kingdom.

Guyanese Creole English (Creolese, Guyanese Creole) [gyn] 650,000 in Guyana. Population includes 250,000 Blacks and 400,000 Hindustanis. Population total all countries: 700,000. Georgetown, coast, and Rupununi River area. There may be some in French Guiana. Also spoken in Suriname, USA. *Class:* Creole, English based, Atlantic, Eastern, Southern. *Dialects:* Afro-Guyanese Creole, Rupununi, Indo-Guyanese Creole. It may be intelligible with other English-based creoles of the Caribbean. Closest to creoles of Saint Vincent and Tobago. Rupununi may be a separate language. Speakers of Rupununi, Berbice Creole Dutch, and Skepi Creole Dutch claim they are not inherently intelligible with each other. *Lg Use:* The first or second language of most people, but it has no official status. Creole is the home language and used alongside Standard English (M. Adler 1977). There is a creole continuum with Standard English. *Lg Dev:* Grammar.

Hindustani, Caribbean (Aili Gaili) [hns] Ethnic population: 538,500 in Guyana. *Lg Use:* Many of the ethnic group in Guyana speak Guyanese as first language. Only a few older people of Guyanese origin in Guyana speak Caribbean Hindustani. Those closer to Georgetown use a more standard English than Guyanese. A few are learning Hindi for religious purposes. *Other:* Coastal. Agriculturalists. Hindu. See main entry under Suriname.

Macushi (Makushi, Makusi, Makuxi, Macusi, Macussi, Teweya, Teueia) [mbc] 9,000 in Guyana (2003 SIL). Ethnic population: 9,000. Southwestern border area, Rupununi north savannahs. Spread out in small settlements up to the foothills of the Pakaraima Mountains. *Lg Use:* The second

language is English in Guyana, Portuguese in Brazil, Spanish in Venezuela. See main entry under Brazil.

Mapidian (Maopityan, Maiopitian) [mpw] Southwest Guyana, with the Waiwai. *Lg Use:* Members of the ethnic group probably speak Waiwai. *Other:* Most if not all speakers moved to Brazil in the 1960s. Probably extinct in Guyana. Savannah. Nearly extinct. See main entry under Brazil.

Mawayana (Mahuayana) [mzx] 50 (1986 Howard). Southwest Guyana, living with the Waiwai. *Class:* Arawakan, Maipuran. *Dialects:* Mawayana shows no semantic similarity with Wapishana, Atorada, or Mapidian (Richard Hicks 2002). *Lg Use:* Speakers are also fluent in Waiwai. *Other:* Savannah. Swidden agriculturalists: cassava. Traditional religion, Christian. Nearly extinct.

Patamona (Ingariko, Eremagok, Kapon) [pbc] 4,700 (1990 J. Forte). Ethnic population: 5,000 (2000 Forte). West central, about 13 villages. *Class:* Carib, Northern, East-West Guiana, Macushi-Kapon, Kapon. *Dialects:* Close to Macushi but not inherently intelligible. Marginally intelligible with Arecuna. Closest to Akawaio, but vocabulary differences and language attitudes make separate literature necessary. *Lg Dev:* People in the village of Paramakatoi are literate in English and Patamona. Some in other villages are literate in English. NT: 1974. *Other:* The Akawaio are less acculturated than Patamona. 'Ingariko' is the Macushi term for 'bush people'.

Pemon (Pemong) [aoc] 475 Arekuna in Guyana, (1990 J. Forte). Ethnic population: 500. Paruima Settlement. *Dialects:* Camaracoto, Taurepan (Taulipang), Arecuna (Aricuna, Arekuna, Jaricuna). See main entry under Venezuela.

Skepi Creole Dutch [skw] Extinct. Essequibo Region. *Class:* Creole, Dutch based. *Dialect:* Essequibo. Speakers said it was not inherently intelligible with Berbice or Rupununi. Lexical similarity 52% with Berbice. *Lg Use:* Became extinct by 1998.

Waiwai (Uaiuai, Uaieue, Ouayeone, Parukota) [waw] 200 in Guyana (1990 J. Forte). Southwest Guyana, headwaters of the Essequibo River. *Dialect:* Katawian (Katwena, Katawina). *Other:* Tropical forest. See main entry under Brazil.

Wapishana (Wapichana, Wapichan, Wapitxana, Wapishshiana, Wapisiana, Vapidiana, Wapixana, Wapisana, Uapixana) [wap] 6,000 in Guyana (2000 J. Forte). Population total all countries: 7,500. Southwest Guyana, south of the Kanuku Mountains, northwest of the Waiwai; a few villages. Also spoken in Brazil. *Class:* Arawakan, Maipuran, Northern Maipuran, Wapishanan. *Dialect:* Amariba. Lexical similarity 10% with Mapidian. *Lg Use:* Amariba dialect may be extinct. English is taught in school. *Lg Dev:* Bible portions: 1975–1994. *Other:* Their own name for the people is 'Wapichana' or 'Wapichan'. Savannah. Swidden agriculturalists: cassava. Traditional religion, Christian.

Warao (Warau, Warrau, Guarao, Guarauno) [wba] Few speakers in Guyana (1990 J. Forte). Ethnic population: 5,000 in Guyana (2000 J. Forte). Northwestern, at Oreala, Guyana near coast, mixed with Arawak and Carib speakers. *Lg Use:* Speakers are older adults. Speakers also use Guyanese. See main entry under Venezuela.

Haiti

Republic of Haiti, République d'Haiti. 7,656,166. National or official languages: Haitian Creole French, French. Literacy rate: 23% to 33%. Blind population: 60,000. Deaf population: 93,549. Deaf institutions: 4. The number of languages listed for Haiti is 3. Of those, 2 are living languages and 1 is a second language without mother-tongue speakers. See map on page 739.

French [fra] 600 in Haiti (2004). *Lg Use:* Official language. 400,000 second-language speakers. See main entry under France.

Haitian Creole French (Kreyol, Aiysyen) [hat] 6,964,549 in Haiti (2001). Population total all countries: 7,389,066. Throughout the country. Also spoken in Bahamas, Canada, Cayman Islands, Dominican Republic, French Guiana, Guadeloupe, Puerto Rico, USA. *Class:* Creole, French based. *Dialects:* Fablas, Plateau Haitian Creole. Linguistic influences from Wolof (Benjamin 1956), Fon, and Éwé (C. Lefebvre) of West Africa. *Lg Use:* Official language. Vigorous. Speakers also use French. *Lg Dev:* Newspapers. Radio programs. TV. Dictionary. Grammar. Bible: 1985. *Other:* In 1961 it was granted legal and educational status in Haiti. A growing literature, including poetry. Lower social status than Standard French. SVO; prepositions; articles after noun heads.

Haitian Vodoun Culture Language (Langay, Langaj) [hvc] *Class:* Unclassified. *Lg Use:* Used for religion, song, dance. *Other:* It uses some Haitian creole words, and others which may have African or American Indian influence. Second language only.

Honduras

Republic of Honduras, República de Honduras. 6,823,568. National or official language: Spanish. Literacy rate: 56% to 60%. Also includes Armenian (1,300), Turkish (900), Yue Chinese (1,000), Arabic (42,000), Chinese (2,000). Information mainly from D. Oltrogge 1977; L. Campbell and D. Oltrogge 1980. Blind population: 1,000 (1982 WCE). Deaf population: 322,248. Deaf institutions: 2. The number of languages listed for Honduras is 10. Of those, all are living languages. See map on page 753.

Ch'orti' [caa] 10 in Honduras (1997 Reeck). Ethnic population: 4,200 in Honduras (1997 Reeck). Copan Department, along the Guatemala border. See main entry under Guatemala.

English [eng] 31,500 in Honduras (2001). Population includes 22,500 Bay Islands English speakers on the north coast. Bay Islands (Guanaja, Roatán, Utila), and large cities along north coast of mainland. *Dialect:* Bay Islands English. *Other:* Some creole influence. See main entry under United Kingdom.

Garifuna (Caribe, Central American Carib, Black Carib, Garífuna) [cab] 98,000 in Honduras (1993 Ramon D. Rivas). 100 monolinguals. Population total all countries: 191,974. Mainly of the north coast between Masca, Cortés Department and Plaplaya, Gracias a Dios Department. 37 villages in Honduras, 46 in Central America (plus cities La Ceiba, San Pedro Sula, Tegucigalpa, and Puerto Cortés). Also spoken in Belize, Guatemala, Nicaragua, USA. *Class:* Arawakan, Maipuran, Northern Maipuran, Caribbean. *Dialects:* Eastern Garifuna, Western Garifuna. Eastern Garifuna is in Honduras and Nicaragua (leaves out 'r' and tends to shorten words), Western Garifuna in Guatemala and Belize. Related to Island Carib, with Spanish, English, and French borrowings. *Lg Use:* In some villages in Honduras speakers are shifting to Spanish. All domains, family, friends, local administration, some religious services. In about half of the villages the people are proud of Garifuna. 5% trilingual with English. *Lg Dev:* Literacy rate in first language: 1% to 5%. Literacy rate in second language: 5% to 15%. English-oriented orthography used for Belize, Spanish-oriented in Guatemala. The Western dialect is used as the written standard, and the orthography is being standardized. Roman script. Radio programs. Dictionary. Bible: 2002. *Other:* VSO. Coastal. Agriculturalists; fishermen; sailors on merchant and cruise ships; city jobs. Christian, traditional religion.

Honduras Sign Language [hds] *Class:* Deaf sign language.

Lenca [len] Only a few speakers in Honduras (1993 Ramon D. Rivas). Ethnic population: 100,000. La Paz, Intibucá, Lempira, Comayagua, Santa Bárbara, Valle and Francisco Morozan departments. Also spoken in El Salvador. *Class:* Unclassified. *Dialects:* Some consider it to be Macro-Chibchan. The dialect in El Salvador is different from Honduras. *Lg Use:* Speakers are shifting to Spanish. *Other:* Nearly extinct.

Mískito (Mísquito, Marquito, Mískitu, Mosquito) [miq] 29,000 in Honduras (1993 Ramon D. Rivas). Gracias a Dios Department. *Lg Use:* Trade language. All ages. *Lg Dev:* Literacy rate in first language: 1% to 10%. Literacy rate in second language: 5% to 25%. See main entry under Nicaragua.

Pech (Paya, Seco) [pay] 994 (1993 Ramon D. Rivas). Ethnic population: 2,586 (1993 Ramon D. Rivas). North central coast, Municipio Dulce Nombre de Culmí, Olancho Department,Santa María del Carbón. Speakers also in Las Marias, Gracias a Dios, Silin, Colon. *Class:* Chibchan, Paya. *Lg Use:* More active in using Pech in Agua Amarilla and La Laguna in El Carbón. Speakers are older adults. Speakers are shifting to Spanish. *Other:* There is a lot of interest in the community in preserving the Pech language, and some work is being done to preserve it. SOV.

Spanish (Español, Castellano) [spa] 5,600,000 in Honduras (1996). *Lg Use:* National language. See main entry under Spain.

Sumo Tawahka (Sumo, Sumu, Soumo, Sumoo) [sum] 700 in Honduras (1997 SIL). Ethnic population: 800 to 1,000 in Honduras (1993 Ramon D. Rivas). Banks of the Patuca River, Gracias a Dios and parts of Olancho departments. *Lg Use:* All ages. *Lg Dev:* Literacy rate in first language: 10% to 30%. Literacy rate in second language: 25% to 50%. *Other:* The name 'Sumo' is not used by speakers in Honduras. In Honduras the Sumo are increasingly using Mískito and rapidly becoming culturally intigrated into the Mískito community. See main entry under Nicaragua (Sumo-Mayangna).

Tol (Tolpan, Jicaque, Xicaque) [jic] 350 (1997). Ethnic population: 593 (1990 Educación Comunitaria para la Salud-Honduras). Also 19,000 ethnic Tolpan in the Department of Yoro. Montaña de la Flor, northern Francisco Morazán Department, north central Honduras, some in Yoro. *Class:* Language Isolate. *Dialects:* No distinct dialects. It may be distantly related to Subtiaba of Nicaragua (extinct linguistically), Malinaltepec Tlapanec of Mexico, and the Hokan languages. *Lg Use:* All ages. Varying degrees of proficiency in Spanish; adult male leaders are more fluent, women and children have low proficiency. Ethnic Tolpan who do not speak Tol speak Spanish. *Lg Dev:* Literacy rate in first language: 5% to 10%. Literacy rate in second language: 5% to 15%. NT: 1993. *Other:* SOV. Christian, traditional religion.

Jamaica

Jamaica. 2,713,130. National or official language: English. Literacy rate: 82% to 89%. Also includes North Levantine Spoken Arabic (2,000), Portuguese (5,000), Spanish (8,000), Chinese (31,000). Deaf population: 154,909. Deaf institutions: 26. The number of languages listed for Jamaica is 3. Of those, all are living languages. See map on page 739.

English [eng] *Lg Use:* National language. See main entry under United Kingdom.

Jamaican Country Sign Language (Country Sign) [jcs] *Class:* Deaf sign language. *Dialects:* There is no standardized sign language, but 'Country Sign' differs from region to region. *Lg Use:* It is used for all communication needs outside the classroom. Signed English is used in at least one deaf school, but students do not understand many of the function words. *Other:* Many deaf children do not attend school.

Jamaican Creole English (Patwa, Patois, Bongo Talk, Quashie Talk, Southwestern Caribbean Creole English) [jam] 2,665,636 in Jamaica (2001). Population total all countries: 3,181,171. Also spoken in Canada, Costa Rica, Dominican Republic, Panama, United Kingdom, USA. *Class:* Creole, English based, Atlantic, Western. *Dialects:* The basilect (extreme varieties) and Standard English are inherently unintelligible to each other's speakers (Voegelin and Voegelin, LePage, Adler). It may be partly intelligible to speakers of Cameroon Pidgin and Krio of Sierra Leone, spoken by descendants of Jamaicans repatriated between 1787 and 1860. Inherently intelligible to speakers of creoles in Panama and Costa Rica. Reported to be very close to Belize Creole, close to Grenada, Saint Vincent, different from Tobago, very different from Guyana, Barbados, Leeward and Windward islands. Lexical similarity 25% with Guyanese, 13% with Belizean, 9% with Trinidadian, 8% with Barbadian, 5% with Nicaraguan. *Lg Use:* Vigorous. Creole is the dominant language and gaining in prestige. Continuum of speech from the distinct creole to provincial Standard English of town dwellers. Most speakers believe that they speak Standard English. Most speakers have some competence in Standard English. Education is in Standard English. *Lg Dev:* Literacy rate in second language: High in English. Dictionary. Grammar. *Other:* Linguistic influences from Akan in Ghana and Bantu (I. Hancock 1988).

Martinique

Martinique. 429,510. National or official language: French. A French department in the Windward Islands. Literacy rate: 89% to 93%. Also includes Vietnamese (330), Arabic (500), Chinese (500). The number of languages listed for Martinique is 2. Of those, both are living languages. See map on page 740.

French [fra] 9,000 in Martinique (2004). *Lg Use:* National language. See main entry under France.

Martiniquan Creole French (Patwa, Patois, Guadeloupean Creole French) [gcf] 418,454 in Martinique (2001). See main entry under Guadeloupe (Guadeloupean Creole French).

Mexico

Estados Unidos Mexicanos. 104,959,594. Speakers of American Indian languages 8%. National or official language: Spanish. Literacy rate: 87% to 88%. Also includes Basque, Catalan-Valencian-Balear, English (350,000), Japanese (35,000), Tohono O'odham, Vlax Romani (5,000), Arabic (400,000), Chinese (31,000). Information mainly from S. Gudschinsky 1953, 1959; R. Longacre 1957; A. Wares 1965; D. Bartholomew 1965; C. Rensch 1966, 1968; C. H. Bradley 1968; P. Kirk 1970; E. Casad 1974; W. R. Miller 1975; S. Egland, D. Bartholomew, and S. Ramos 1983; SIL 1951–2003. Blind population: 200,000. Deaf population: 1,300,000 to 5,590,207 (1998). Deaf institutions: 30. The number of languages listed for Mexico is 298. Of those, 291 are living languages and 7 are extinct. See maps beginning on page 757.

Afro-Seminole Creole (Afro-Seminole, Afro-Seminol Criollo) [afs] 200 in Mexico (1990). Nacimiento de los Negros, Coahuila, Mexico. *Dialect:* Mexico Afro-Seminole. *Lg Use:* All speakers are older adults in Nacimiento. Speakers also use Spanish. See main entry under USA.

Amuzgo, Guerrero (Nomndaa) [amu] 23,000 (1990 census). 10,000 monolinguals (1990 census). Southeastern Guerrero, Xochistlahuaca municipio, Zacoalpan, Cochoapa, Huehuetonoc, Tlacoachistlahuaca, Guadalupe Victoria, Cozoyoapan, Huistepec, and Rancho del Cura. The Santa Catarina River separates the Guerrero variety from the Oaxaca varieties. *Class:* Oto-Manguean, Amuzgoan. *Dialects:* 67% intelligibility of San Pedro Amuzgos Amuzgo. *Lg Use:* Vigorous. Spanish, Nahuatl, and Mixtec speakers living among them learn to speak it. All domains. Oral use in local administration, commerce. Oral and written use in religion. All ages. Positive language attitude. Bilingual level estimates for Spanish: 0 50%, 1 37%, 2 10%, 3 2.5%, 4 .5%, 5 0%. *Lg Dev:* Literacy rate in first language: 10% adults, 15% children. Literacy rate in second language: 30% adults, 40% children. 5,000 read it and 500 write it. Bilingual school system grades 1 to 6. Radio programs. Videos. Dictionary. Grammar. NT: 1973–2001. *Other:* Very few speakers leave the area. VSO; short word; affixes; clitics; tonal. Mountain slope. Subtropical deciduous. 400 to 1,600 meters. Peasant agriculturalists. Christian.

Amuzgo, Ipalapa (Amuzgo de Santa María Ipalapa) [azm] 2,000 (1992 SIL). Monolinguals over 60 (1992 SIL). Oaxaca, Putla District, about 8 to 10 miles northeast of San Pedro Amuzgos; five locations around Santa María Ipalapa. Just off the highway from Tlaxiaco to the coast. *Class:* Oto-Manguean, Amuzgoan. *Dialects:* Not intelligible with other Amuzgo. *Lg Use:* All ages. Some speakers also use Spanish. *Other:* Primary and secondary education available. Tonal. Mountain slope, coastal. Savannah, scrub, or gallery forest. 600 meters. Swidden agriculturalists: maize, beans, squash, chili peppers, tomatoes.

Amuzgo, San Pedro Amuzgos (Oaxaca Amuzgo, Amuzgo de San Pedro Amuzgos) [azg] 4,000 (1990 census). Southwestern Oaxaca, Putla District, San Pedro Amuzgos. One town with outlying settlements. *Class:* Oto-Manguean, Amuzgoan. *Dialects:* 76% comprehension of Amuzgo of Guerrero. *Lg Use:* Bilingual level estimates for Spanish: 0 50%, 1 35%, 2 15%, 3 0%, 4 0%, 5 0%. *Lg Dev:* Dictionary. Grammar. NT: 1992. *Other:* VSO; affixes; tonal. Mountain slope. Gallery forest. 350 to 500 meters. Peasant agriculturalists.

Chatino, Eastern Highland (Chatino de la Zona Alta Oriental, Lachao-Yolotepec Chatino, Sierra Oriental Chatino) [cly] 2,000 (1993 SIL). Southeastern Oaxaca, villages of Lachao Pueblo Nuevo and Santa María Yolotepec. *Class:* Oto-Manguean, Zapotecan, Chatino. *Dialects:* One dialect. Uses lengthened word forms similar to Zenzontepec Chatino. Similar to Zacatepec, but geographically and socioeconomically separated. 87% intelligibility of Yaitepec, 83% of Nopala, 77% of Panixtlahuaca, 21% of Tataltepec. *Lg Use:* 30% to 40% of the speakers have low to routine proficiency in Spanish. *Other:* VSO; long words; affixes, clitics, tonal. Mountain slope, coastal. 1,800 to 2,400 meters. Subsistence agriculturalists: coffee; timber.

Chatino, Nopala [cya] 11,000 (1990 census). 2,300 monolinguals. Southeastern Oaxaca, Juquila District, Santos Reyes Nopala, Santa María Texmaxcaltepec, San María Magdalena Tiltepec, Teotepec, Cerro el Aire, Santiago Cuixtla, Atotonilco, San Gabriel Mixtepec. *Class:* Oto-Manguean, Zapotecan, Chatino. *Dialects:* 59% intelligibility of Panixtlahuaca, 73% of Yaitepec, 13% of Tataltepec. *Lg Use:* Speakers also use Spanish. *Lg Dev:* NT: 2001. *Other:* VSO; short words; affixes; clitics; tonal. Coastal, mountain slope. Tropical forest. 480 to 1,600 meters. Peasant agriculturalists; craftsmen.

Chatino, Tataltepec (Lowland Chatino) [cta] 4,000 (1990 census). 470 monolinguals. Southeastern Oaxaca, Juquila District, extreme west lowland Chatino area, in the towns of Tataltepec de Valdez and San Pedro Tututepec, and a few speakers in nearby Spanish population centers. *Class:* Oto-Manguean, Zapotecan, Chatino. *Dialects:* 38% intelligibility of Yaitepec, 35% of Panixtlahuaca, 33% of Nopala, 27% of Zacatepec. *Lg Use:* Bilingual level estimates for Spanish: 0 1%, 1 9%, 2 65%, 3 20%, 4 5%, 5 0%. *Lg Dev:* Dictionary. Grammar. NT: 1981. *Other:* VSO; long words; affixes; clitics; tonal. Coastal, foothills. Scrub forest, tropical forest. 300 to 500 meters. Swidden agriculturalists.

Chatino, Western Highland (Chatino de la Zona Alta Occidental, Cha't-An, Sierra Occidental Chatino) [ctp] 12,000 (2000 SIL). 6,000 monolinguals (1990 census). Southwestern Oaxaca, Juquila District, towns of Panixtlahuaca, San Juan Quiahije, and Yaitepec; villages of Ixtapan, Tepenixtelahuaca, Ixpantepec, and Amialtepec, plus various rancherías. *Class:* Oto-Manguean, Zapotecan, Chatino. *Dialects:* Panixtlahuaca Chatino, San Juan Quiahije Chatino, Yaitepec Chatino. 71% intelligibility of Yaitepec, 66% of Nopala, 46% of Zacatepec, 32% of Tataltepec. Yaitepec has 80% intelligibility of Nopala, 78% of Panixtlahuaca, 20% of Tataltepec. *Lg Use:* Vigorous. 1 or 2 speakers of other languages speak Chatino. All domains. Oral use in local administration, commerce, religious services, some in elementary and secondary education. All ages. Positive language attitude. Bilingual level estimates for Spanish: 0 60%, 1 30%, 2 9.95%, 3 .05%, 4 0%, 5 0%. Yaitepec is one of the most monolingual Chatino towns. 10 can also speak English, 10 to 20 speak either Tataltepec Chatino or Zenzontepec Chatino. *Lg Dev:* 500 can read it, 50 can write it. Radio programs. Dictionary. Grammar. NT: 1992. *Other:* The economic situation varies from poor in Ixtapan to some wealthy families in Panixtlahuaca and San Juan Quiahije. Some annual migration to work in coastal coffee growing areas. VSO; short words; affixes; clitics; tonal. Mountain slope. Tropical, pine forest. 650 to 2,335 meters. Swidden agriculturalists, coffee culture; loggers; animal husbandry: cattle. Traditional religion, syncretism, Christian.

Chatino, Zacatepec (Chatino de San Marcos Zacatepec) [ctz] 1,000 (1990 census). Southeastern Oaxaca, village of San Marcos Zacatepec and Juquila. *Class:* Oto-Manguean, Zapotecan, Chatino. *Dialects:* 66% intelligibility of Nopala, 61% of Panixtlahuaca, 57% of Yaitepec, 6% of Tataltepec. Lengthened word forms are like Zenzontepec Chatino. Similar to Lachao-Yolotepec Chatino in some respects, but geographically and socioeconomically separated. *Lg Use:* Spoken in Zacatepec. Virtually extinct in Juquila with 2 older adult men speakers. *Other:* Mountain slope. Tropical forest. 500 to 600 meters. Agriculturalists: maize, coffee, palm nuts, fruit.

Chatino, Zenzontepec (Northern Chatino) [czn] 8,000 (1990 census). 2,000 monolinguals. Southeastern Oaxaca, Juquila District, various sectors in the municipios of Santa Cruz Zenzontepec and San Jacinto Tlacotepec, and parts of the former municipio of Santa María Tlapanalquiahuitl. It does not include the adjacent Zapotec areas of Texmelucan or Zaniza. *Class:* Oto-Manguean, Zapotecan, Chatino. *Dialects:* Some dialect differences in Santa María Tlapanalquiahuitl area. One of the most isolated and conservative groups in Oaxaca. *Lg Use:* Bilingual level estimates for Spanish: 0 50%, 1 20%, 2 20%, 3 10%, 4 0%, 5 0%. *Other:* Economically marginal. SVO; long words; affixes; tonal. Mountain slope. Scrub forest. 1,000 to 1,500 meters. Swidden agriculturalists.

Chiapanec (Chiapaneco) [cip] 17 (1990 census). Ethnic population: 32. State of Chiapas, El Bosque (2), Las Margaritas (2), Ocosingo (4), Palenque (2), Sabanilla (7).

Class: Oto-Manguean, Chiapanec-Mangue. *Dialects:* Reported to be quite similar to Chorotega of Costa Rica. *Other:* Nearly extinct.

Chichimeca-Jonaz (Pame de Chichimeca-Jonaz, Meco) [pei] 200 (1993 K. Olson Instituto Betania). State of Guanajuato, San Luís de la Paz, Jonáz village. *Class:* Oto-Manguean, Otopamean, Chichimec. *Lg Use:* Speakers also use Spanish.

Chicomuceltec (Cac'chiquel Mam, Cakchiquel Mam, Chicomulcelteco) [cob] Extinct. Ethnic population: 1,500 in Mexico. Chiapas, towns of Mazapa de Madero, Amatenango, and Chicomuselo. Also spoken in Guatemala. *Class:* Mayan, Huastecan. *Lg Use:* Reported to be extinct in recent Mayanist literature.

Chinantec, Chiltepec [csa] 1,000 (1994). 4,000 in Chiltepec municipio with 250 monolinguals (1990 census). Oaxaca, San José Chiltepec. *Class:* Oto-Manguean, Chinantecan. *Dialects:* 76% intelligibility of Tlacoatzintepec (closest), 20% of Usila and Ojitlán, 13% of Valle Nacional. *Lg Use:* Speakers use Spanish as second language, but outlying towns are not as bilingual as the center. *Other:* Riverine. Below 900 meters.

Chinantec, Comaltepec (Jmii') [cco] 2,000 (1990 census). 145 monolinguals. Ethnic population: 2,000. North Oaxaca, Santiago Comaltepec, Soledad Tectitlán, La Esperanza, San Martín Soyolapan, Vista Hermosa (Quiotepec), San Pedro Yolox, Rosario Temextitlán, Maninaltepec. *Class:* Oto-Manguean, Chinantecan. *Dialects:* 69% intelligibility of Quiotepec (closest), 7% of Tepetotutla. *Lg Use:* Vigorous. All domains, local administration, preschool, religion. Written use to record customs, traditions, history. All ages. Positive language attitude. Bilingual level estimates for Spanish: 0 5%, 1 15%, 2 30%, 3 30%, 4 19%, 5 1%. 80 can also speak English. *Lg Dev:* Literacy rate in first language: 1.5%. Literacy rate in second language: 75%. 1,5% can read it, 0.8% can write it. Radio programs. Videos. NT: 2002. *Other:* People leave the area for jobs. VSO; short words; affixes; tonal. Mountain slope. Pine forest. 1,300 to 1,500 meters. Swidden agriculturalists.

Chinantec, Lalana (Chinanteco de San Juan Lalana) [cnl] 10,500 (1998). 2,500 monolinguals. Oaxaca-Veracruz border, 25 towns. *Class:* Oto-Manguean, Chinantecan. *Dialects:* 87% intelligibility of Tepinapa (closest, but lower in outlying areas), 43% of Ozumacín, 24% of Lealao. *Lg Use:* Bilingual level estimates for Spanish: 0 50%, 1 29%, 2 10%, 3 10%, 4 1%, 5 0%. *Lg Dev:* NT: 1974–1994. *Other:* VOS; short words; affixes, clitics; tonal. Mountain slope, interfluvial. Tropical. 100 to 2,000 meters. Peasant agriculturalists.

Chinantec, Lealao (Chinanteco de San Juan Lealao) [cle] 2,000 (1990 census). 500 monolinguals. Northeastern Oaxaca, San Juan Lealao, Latani, Tres Arroyos, and La Hondura. *Class:* Oto-Manguean, Chinantecan. *Dialects:* Considered the most divergent of the Chinantec languages. *Lg Use:* Vigorous. All domains. Oral and written use in religious services. Oral use in local commerce. All ages. Speakers consider it to be inferior to Spanish, but they continue to use it. Bilingual level estimates for Spanish: 0 5%, 1 45%, 2 50%, 3 0%, 4 0%, 5 0%. There is also some bilingualism in Zapotec. *Lg Dev:* 50 can read it, 5 can write it. Dictionary. NT: 1980. *Other:* Immunizations in the 1970s and since have reduced child deaths. VOS; short words; affixes; tonal. Mountain slope. Tropical. 400 to 1, 500 meters. Swidden agriculturalists. Christian, syncretism with traditional religion.

Chinantec, Ojitlán [chj] 22,000 (1990 census). 2,800 monolinguals. Northern Oaxaca, San Lucas Ojitlán, including 4 towns and 15 rancherías, and Veracruz, Hidalgotitlán and Minatitlán municipios. Most speakers have been relocated because a dam flooded their land in

1991. *Class:* Oto-Manguean, Chinantecan. *Dialects:* 49% intelligibility of Sochiapan (closest), 43% of Usila, 39% of Palantla, 31% of Chiltepec. *Lg Dev:* NT: 1968.

Chinantec, Ozumacín (Chinanteco de Ayotzintepec, Juujmii) [chz] 5,000 (2000 SIL). 260 monolinguals (1990 census). Northeast Oaxaca, 3 towns: San Pedro Ozumacín, Ayotzintepec, Santiago Progreso. *Class:* Oto-Manguean, Chinantecan. *Dialect:* Ayotzintepec. Ozumacín town has slight dialect difference from others. 63% intelligibility of Palantla (closest), 22% of Lalana and Valle Nacional. *Lg Use:* Half of parents pass it on to children. Most domains, local administration, commerce, some in religious services. All ages. Speakers view Chinantec as inferior to Spanish, but continue to use it. 3,500 speak some Spanish. Some speak some Palantla Chinantec. *Lg Dev:* Literacy rate in first language: below 1%. Literacy rate in second language: 50% to 75%. 15 can read it, 4 can write it. NT: 2003. *Other:* Mountain slope. Forests. 400 to 800 meters. Agriculturalists: maize; animal husbandry: pigs, poultry. Christian.

Chinantec, Palantla (Chinanteco de Santiago Tlatepusco) [cpa] 12,000 (1990 census). 1,500 monolinguals. Oaxaca, San Juan Palantla plus 13 towns. *Class:* Oto-Manguean, Chinantecan. *Dialects:* 78% intelligibility of Tepetotutla (closest), 72% of Valle Nacional, 69% of Usila, 54% of Ozumacín. *Lg Use:* Bilingual level estimates for Spanish: 0 10%, 1 25%, 2 35%, 3 25%, 4 5%, 5 0%. *Lg Dev:* Literacy rate in first language: below 1%. Literacy rate in second language: 50%. Dictionary. NT: 1973. *Other:* VSO; short words; tonal. Mountain slope. Tropical. 50 to 500 meters. Swidden agriculturalists.

Chinantec, Quiotepec (Highland Chinantec) [chq] 8,000 (1998). 1,750 monolinguals. Oaxaca, Ixtlán District: San Juan Quiotepec, Reforma, Maninaltepec, San Pedro Yolox, Rosario Temextitlán; Oaxaca, Etla District: San Juan Bautista Atatlah. *Class:* Oto-Manguean, Chinantecan. *Dialect:* Yolox Chinanteco. 87% intelligibility of Comaltepec (closest, lower in outlying areas), 7% of Tepetotutla. The highland Chinantec languages share a complexity of vowel length and tone extensions that Tepetotutla and Palantla do not have. *Lg Use:* Bilingual level estimates for Spanish: 0 35%, 1 20%, 2 15%, 3 15%, 4 10%, 5 5%. *Lg Dev:* NT: 1983. *Other:* VSO; short words; affixes; tonal. Mountain slope. Deciduous forest, pine forest. 1,000 to 2,400 meters. Peasant agriculturalists.

Chinantec, Sochiapan [cso] 5,800 (2000 SIL). 725 monolinguals (1990 census). Ethnic population: 6,000. North Oaxaca, Cuicatlán: San Pedro Sochiapan, Retumbadero, San Juan Zautla, Santiago Quetzalapa, San Juan Zapotitlán. *Class:* Oto-Manguean, Chinantecan. *Dialects:* 66% intelligibility of Tlacoatzintepec (closest), 56% of Chiltepec, 45% of Usila, 11% of Tepetotutla. *Lg Use:* Vigorous. All domains. Oral use in local administration, commerce. A few teachers try to teach it in school. Oral and written use in church. All ages. Positive language attitude. Bilingual level estimates for Spanish: 0 15%, 1 15%, 2 30%, 3 30%, 4 9%, 5 1%. 10 to 20 know some English. *Lg Dev:* 10% can read it, 5% can write it. Dictionary. Grammar. NT: 1986. *Other:* Transients go to Mexico City to work as maids, gardeners, or laborers, but the majority return and settle down in the villages. VSO; short words; affixes, clitics; tonal. Mountain slope. Cloud forest. 800 to 2,000 meters. Swidden agriculturalists. Christian, traditional religion.

Chinantec, Tepetotutla [cnt] 2,000 (1990 census). North Oaxaca, Santa Cruz Tepetotutla, San Antonio del Barrio, San Pedro Tlatepusco, Santo Tomás Texas, Vega del Sol, El Naranjal. *Class:* Oto-Manguean, Chinantecan. *Dialects:* 60% intelligibility of Quiotepec, 59% of Palantla, 48% of Yolox. *Lg Dev:* Grammar. NT: 1994. *Other:*

VSO; short words; affixes, clitics; tonal. Tropical forest, mountain slope. 1,200 meters. Agriculturalists: coffee.

Chinantec, Tepinapa [cte] 8,000 (1990 census). 2,500 monolinguals. Oaxaca, Choapan District, Santiago Jocotepec Municipio: San Pedro Tepinapa; San Juan Petlapa Municipio: Santa María Lovani, San Juan Toavela, and Santa Isabel Cajonos. Very remote area. *Class:* Oto-Manguean, Chinantecan. *Dialects:* 79% intelligibility of Comaltepec, 87% to 68% of Lalana, 24% of Lealao, 23% of Ozumacín. *Lg Use:* Vigorous. Most children are monolingual when they start school. Some speakers also use Spanish. *Other:* Most villages have less than 6 grades of primary school. Mountain slope. 300 to 900 meters. Agriculturalists: maize, coffee, ixtle.

Chinantec, Tlacoatzintepec [ctl] 2,000 (1990 census). 550 monolinguals. Oaxaca, San Juan Bautista Tlacoatzintepec, San Pedro Alianza, Santiago Quetzalapa, San Juan Zapotitlán. *Class:* Oto-Manguean, Chinantecan. *Dialects:* 85% intelligibility of Chiltepec (closest, lower in outlying areas), 84% of Usila, 74% of Sochiapan, 15% of Tepetotutla. *Lg Use:* Bilingual level estimates for Spanish: 0 50%, 1 40%, 2 9%, 3 1%, 4 0%, 5 0%. *Other:* VSO; short words; affixes, clitics; tonal. Mountain slope. Tropical forest. 1,000 meters. Swidden agriculturalists.

Chinantec, Usila [cuc] 9,000 (1990 census). 2,200 monolinguals. Oaxaca, San Felipe Usila plus 12 towns, and 1 in Veracruz (Pueblo Doce). *Class:* Oto-Manguean, Chinantecan. *Dialects:* 48% intelligibility of Tlacoatzintepec (closest), 33% of Palantla, 32% of Sochiapan, 31% of Ojitlán. *Lg Use:* Bilingual level estimates for Spanish: 0 50%, 1 30%, 2 10%, 3 7%, 4 2%, 5 1%. *Lg Dev:* Literacy rate in first language: 1%. Literacy rate in second language: 20%. Dictionary. Grammar. NT: 1983. *Other:* VSO; short words; affixes, clitics; tonal. Riverine. Tropical. 100 to 400 meters. Swidden agriculturalists.

Chinantec, Valle Nacional [cvn] 1,000 to 2,000 (1990 census). North Oaxaca, San Juan Bautista Valle Nacional and mainly in San Mateo Yetla. *Class:* Oto-Manguean, Chinantecan. *Dialects:* 71% intelligibility of Chiltepec (closest), 70% of Palantla, 53% of Ozumacín, 40% of Tepetotutla. *Lg Use:* Speakers also use Spanish.

Chochotec (Chocho) [coz] 770 (1998). Oaxaca, Nochixtlán District, Santa María Nativitas (428 out of 764 population), San Juan Bautista Coixtlahuaca (272 out of 3,111 population), San Martín Toxpalán (207 out of 2,462 population), San Miguel Tulancingo (72 out of 553 population). *Class:* Oto-Manguean, Popolocan, Chocho-Popolocan, Chocho. *Lg Use:* Speakers also use Spanish. *Other:* 'Chocho' speakers were also reported in the 1990 census in Puebla and other parts of Mexico, apparently referring to Popoloca speakers.

Chol, Tila [cti] 43,870 (2000 WCD). 10,000 monolinguals. Chiapas, Tila, Vicente Guerrero, Chivalito, Limar. *Class:* Mayan, Cholan-Tzeltalan, Cholan, Chol-Chontal. *Dialects:* 86% intelligibility of Sabanilla, 82% of Tumbalá. *Lg Dev:* Dictionary. Grammar. NT: 1976.

Chol, Tumbalá (Ch'ol de Sabanilla) [ctu] 90,000 (1992). 30,000 monolinguals. Population includes 10,000 in Sabanilla. North central Chiapas, Tumbalá, Sabanilla, Misijá, Limar, Chivalita, Vicente Guerrero. *Class:* Mayan, Cholan-Tzeltalan, Cholan, Chol-Chontal. *Lg Use:* Bilingual level estimates for Spanish: 0 50%, 1 25%, 2 20%, 3 3%, 4 1%, 5 1%. *Lg Dev:* Dictionary. Grammar. Bible: 1977–1992. *Other:* SVO; VOS; long words; affixes, clitics; nontonal. Mountain slope, interfluvial. Tropical, deciduous forest. 100 to 1,600 meters. Peasant agriculturalists. Christian, traditional religion.

Chontal, Highland Oaxaca (Chontal de la Sierra de Oaxaca, Tequistlatec) [chd] 3,600 (1990 census). Southernmost part of Oaxaca, west of the Isthmus of

Tehuantepec, San José Chiltepec, San Lucas Ixcatepec, plus 15 towns. *Class:* Hokan, Tequistlatecan. *Lg Use:* Bilingual level estimates for Spanish: 0 1%, 1 2%, 2 70%, 3 22%, 4 5%, 5 0%. *Lg Dev:* Literacy rate in first language: 60% to 100%. Literacy rate in second language: 75% to 100%. NT: 1991. *Other:* 'Tequistlateco' has been used in publications, but the true Tequistlateco was spoken in the town of Tequisistlán, and is now extinct. VS, SV, or VO; medium long words; affixes; nontonal. Mountain slope. Tropical, deciduous forest, pine forest. 1,500 to 2,300 meters. Swidden agriculturalists.

Chontal, Lowland Oaxaca (Huamelula Chontal, Chontal de la Costa de Oaxaca, Huamelulteco) [clo] 950 (1990 census). Southern Oaxaca, Tehuantepec District, San Pedro Huamelula and Santiago Astata. *Class:* Hokan, Tequistlatecan. *Lg Use:* Bilingual level estimates for Spanish: 0 0%, 1 0%, 2 0%, 3 40%, 4 30%, 5 30%. *Lg Dev:* Bible portions: 1955. *Other:* VSO; medium long words; affixes; clitics; nontonal. Coastal. Scrub forest. 300 meters. Swidden agriculturalists.

Chontal, Tabasco (Yocot'an) [chf] 55,000 (1995 census). North central and southern Tabasco, 21 towns. *Class:* Mayan, Cholan-Tzeltalan, Cholan, Chol-Chontal. *Dialects:* Tamulté de las Sábanas Chontal, Buena Vista Chontal, Miramar Chontal. Speakers of all dialects understand San Carlos Macuspana 80% to 94%. *Lg Dev:* Dictionary. NT: 1977.

Chuj, Ixtatán (Chapai, Chuj de San Mateo Ixtatán) [cnm] 9,500 in Mexico (1991 Schumann). Population includes 8,000 refugees. Municipio of Trinitaria, Chiapas; villages of Tziscau and Cuauhtémoc. *Lg Use:* The Mexican group is reported to be bilingual in Spanish. See main entry under Guatemala.

Cochimi (Cochimtee, Cochetimi, Cochima, Cadegomo, Cadegomeño, Didiu, Laimon, Laymonem, Laymon-Cochimi, San Javier, San Xavier, San Joaquín, San Francesco Saverio Mission, San Francisco Xavier de Viggé-Biaundo Mission) [coj] Extinct. Baja California Norte, north of Loreto to the northern part of the peninsula. *Class:* Hokan, Esselen-Yuman, Yuman, Cochimi. *Dialects:* Troike (1970) regards it as two distinct languages. Kumiai (Tipai) in La Huerta now call themselves 'Cochimí'. *Lg Use:* Old Cochimí is extinct (Mixco 1978).

Cocopa (Cocopá, Cocopah, Cucupá, Cucapá, Kwikapá, Kikimá) [coc] 200 in Mexico (1998 Peter Larson). Population total all countries: 350. Ethnic population: 200 in Mexico (1998). Baja California, El Mayor, San Poza de Aroizú (to the south of Río San Luis Colorado). Also spoken in USA. *Class:* Hokan, Esselen-Yuman, Yuman, Delta-Californian. *Lg Dev:* Bible portions: 1972. *Other:* Hunter-gatherers; agriculturalists: maize.

Cora, El Nayar (Cora de el Nayar) [crn] 8,000 in Mexico (1993 SIL). North central Nayarit. Also spoken in USA. *Class:* Uto-Aztecan, Southern Uto-Aztecan, Sonoran, Corachol. *Dialects:* Jesús María Cora (El Nayar), La Mesa del Nayar Cora (Mesa del Nayar), San Francisco Cora, Presidio de los Reyes Cora. Santa Teresa Cora is distinct enough to need separate literature. *Lg Use:* Bilingual level estimates for Spanish: 0 5%, 1 10%, 2 25%, 3 35%, 4 15%, 5 10%. *Lg Dev:* Grammar. NT: 1999. *Other:* VSO, VOS; short nouns; long verbs; affixes, clitics; tonal. Mountain mesa, mountain slope. Scrub forest, tropical forest, pine forest. 100 to 2,300 meters. Swidden agriculturalists: maize, beans, squash.

Cora, Santa Teresa [cok] 7,000 (1993 SIL). North central Nayarit, Santa Teresa, Dolores, San Blasito. *Class:* Uto-Aztecan, Southern Uto-Aztecan, Sonoran, Corachol. *Dialects:* Santa Teresa Cora, Dolores Cora, San Blasito Cora, San Juan Corapan Cora, Rosarito Cora. Difficult intelligibility of other Cora varieties. *Lg Dev:* Bible portions: 2000.

Cuicatec, Tepeuxila [cux] 8,500 (1990 census). 850 monolinguals. Northwestern Oaxaca, 16 towns. *Class:* Oto-Manguean, Mixtecan, Mixtec-Cuicatec, Mixtec. *Dialect:* Santa María Pápalo. 88% intelligibility of Teutila. *Lg Use:* Bilingual level estimates for Spanish: 0 1%, 1 1%, 2 9%, 3 9%, 4 80%, 5 0%. *Lg Dev:* NT: 1974. *Other:* VSO; short words; affixes, clitics; tonal. Mountain slope. Pine forest. 2,000 to 2,500 meters. Swidden agriculturalists.

Cuicatec, Teutila [cut] 10,000 (1990 census). 260 monolinguals. Teutila, Oaxaca, 8 towns. *Class:* Oto-Manguean, Mixtecan, Mixtec-Cuicatec, Cuicatec. *Dialects:* 79% intelligibility of Tepeuxila. *Lg Use:* Bilingual level estimates for Spanish: 0 3%, 1 22%, 2 5%, 3 10%, 4 50%, 5 10%. *Lg Dev:* NT: 1972. *Other:* VSO; short words; affixes; tonal. Mountain slope. Pine forest. 1,700 to 2,300 meters. Peasant agriculturalists.

Huarijio (Guarijío, Warihío, Varihío) [var] 5,000 (1994 SIL). Nearly all are monolingual. Western Sierra Madre Mountains, west central Chihuahua, from Río Chinipas on the east to the Sonora border, to the headwaters of the Río Mayo in Sonora, more than 17 villages. *Class:* Uto-Aztecan, Southern Uto-Aztecan, Sonoran, Tarahumaran, Guarijio. *Dialects:* Highland Huarijío, Lowland Huarijío. Intelligibility of Tarahumara is less than 50%. 'Maculai' (Macurawe, Macuyawe) is used by the upriver Huarijio to refer to the downriver Huarijio, who may have inter-married with the Mayo in the past. There are old town ruins called Macoyawi, now under Lake Mocutzari, which also refer to them. *Lg Use:* Bilingual level estimates for Spanish: 0 50%, 1 20%, 2 19%, 3 10%, 4 1%, 5 0%. *Lg Dev:* Literacy rate in first language: below 1%. Literacy rate in second language: 5% adults. Bible portions: 1995. *Other:* OVS; long words, affixes, clitics; nontonal. Riverine. Scrub forest. 300 to 800 meters. Swidden agriculturalists.

Huastec, San Luís Potosí (Potosino Huastec) [hva] 70,000 (1990 census). San Luís Potosí, 12 villages. *Class:* Mayan, Huastecan. *Dialects:* Intelligibility tests indicate one Huasteco language, but sociological factors require literature in the Veracruz variety. *Lg Use:* Bilingual level estimates for Spanish: 0 25%, 1 40%, 2 15%, 3 10%, 4 6%, 5 4%. *Lg Dev:* Newspapers. NT: 1971. *Other:* SVO; short words, affixes; nontonal. Coastal, mountain slope. Semitropical. 93 meters. Peasant agriculturalists.

Huastec, Southeastern (Huasteco de San Francisco Chontla) [hsf] 1,749 (1990 census). Northern Veracruz, directly east of Huasteco Veracruz, including Cerro Azul on the southeastern edge, Tepetzintla on the southern edge, Tantima on the northern edge, Santa María Ixcatepec on the western edge, San Francisco Chontla, Tancoco, Amatlán Tuxpan, Galeana y Zaragoza Vieja, Tamiahua. *Class:* Mayan, Huastecan. *Dialects:* 80% intelligibility of Veracruz Huastec. *Lg Use:* Children do not speak the language. Speakers also use Spanish or Eastern Huasteca Nahuatl. *Other:* Mountain slope. Scrub forest. 500 to 700 meters. Peasant agriculturalists.

Huastec, Veracruz (Huasteco de Tantoyuca) [hus] 50,000 (1990 census). Northern Veracruz, 60 villages. *Class:* Mayan, Huastecan. *Dialects:* 84% intelligibility of San Luís Potosí Huastec. *Lg Use:* Bilingual level estimates for Spanish: 0 5%, 1 25%, 2 30%, 3 40%, 4 0%, 5 0%. Speakers also use Spanish or Eastern Huasteca Nahuatl. *Lg Dev:* Literacy rate in first language: below 1%. Literacy rate in second language: 52%. Bible portions: 1994–2000. *Other:* SVO; short words, affixes, clitics; nontonal. Mountain slope. Scrub forest. 500 to 700 meters. Peasant agriculturalists.

Huave, San Dionisio del Mar [hve] 4,944 (2000 WCD). Southeastern coast, Oaxaca, Juchitán District, San Dionisio del Mar. *Class:* Huavean. *Dialects:* 98%

intelligibility of Santa María del Mar Huave, 88% of San Mateo del Mar Huave. *Lg Use:* Speakers also use Spanish. *Other:* Nontonal. Coastal. Desert. Sea level to 60 meters. Fishermen.

Huave, San Francisco del Mar [hue] 900 (1990 census). 30% to 40% monolingual in the old village. Ethnic population: 3,900 (1990 census). Southeastern coast, Oaxaca, Juchitán District, San Francisco del Mar, old town and new town. *Class:* Huavean. *Dialects:* 38% intelligibility of San Mateo del Mar Huave. The most divergent variety of Huave. Only fishermen were tested, and they are familiar with the other varieties. *Lg Use:* Younger speakers use Spanish as second language. 2,000 to 3,000 in the new San Francisco town have shifted from Huave to Spanish. *Other:* Nontonal. Coastal. Desert. Sea level to 60 meters. Fishermen.

Huave, San Mateo del Mar [huv] 12,000 (1990 census). 1,800 monolinguals. Southeastern coast, Oaxaca, San Mateo del Mar. *Class:* Huavean. *Dialects:* Only very limited intelligibility of other Huave varieties; 88% of San Dionisio del Mar. *Lg Use:* Bilingual level estimates for Spanish: 0 1%, 1 14%, 2 40%, 3 35%, 4 10%, 5 0%. *Lg Dev:* Literacy rate in first language: 60%. Literacy rate in second language: 40%. Dictionary. NT: 1972–1996. *Other:* Their legend says they came from Central America. SVO; short words; affixes; nontonal. Coastal. Desert. Sea level. Fishermen; agriculturalists.

Huave, Santa María del Mar [hvv] 500 (1993 SIL). Southeastern coast, Oaxaca, Santa María del Mar. *Class:* Huavean. *Dialects:* Very limited intelligibility of other Huave, although closest to San Dionisio. *Lg Use:* Children learn Spanish first, but learn Huave by adulthood, because adults speak Huave. *Other:* Nontonal. Coastal. Desert. Sea level to 60 meters. Fishermen.

Huichol (Vixaritari Vaniuqui, Vizaritari Vaniuki) [hch] 20,000 (1990 census). Ethnic population: 20,000. Northeastern Nayarit and northwestern Jalisco. The main centers are Guadalupe Ocotán, Nayarit, San Andrés Cohamiata, Jal., San Sebastián, Jal., Santa Catarina, Jal., Tuxpan de Bolaños, Jal. *Class:* Uto-Aztecan, Southern Uto-Aztecan, Sonoran, Corachol. *Dialects:* San Andrés Cohamiata (Western Huichol), San Sebastián-Santa Catarina (Eastern Huichol), Coyultita. 58% cognate with El Nayar Cora, closest (Wick Miller 1984). *Lg Use:* Vigorous. All domains. Oral and written use in religious services, oral use in local commerce, administration, oral literature, songs. Letter writing. All ages. Positive language attitude. Bilingual level estimates for Spanish: 0 10%, 1 50%, 2 30%, 3 9%, 4 1%, 5 0%. A very few also know El Nayar Cora. Spanish used in schools. *Lg Dev:* Literacy rate in first language: 5% to 10%. Literacy rate in second language: 5% to 15%. Roman script. Dictionary. Grammar. NT: 1967. *Other:* Few schools, clinics. They go to the Pacific coast for temporary labor in the spring. They make their own violins and guitars. Their music is unique. SOV; long words; prefixes; suffixes; clitics; CV, CVV; tonal. Mountain slope. Scrub forest. 500 to 2,500 meters. Swidden agriculturalists: maize, beans, squash, vegetables; animal husbandry: chickens, pigs, donkeys, horses, cattle. Traditional religion, Christian.

Ixcatec [ixc] 119 (1983 Jorge Suárez). Santa María Ixcatlán, Oaxaca is the original town, surrounded by Mixtec speakers. *Class:* Oto-Manguean, Popolocan, Ixcatecan. *Dialects:* Different from San Pedro Ixcatlán Mazatec. *Lg Dev:* Dictionary. *Other:* Primer, description of phonology, tone.

Jacaltec, Western (Jacalteco del Oeste) [jai] 10,300 in Mexico (1991 Schumann). Population includes 1,300 long-term residents (1990 census) and 10,000 refugees. Concepción Saravia near the municipio of Comalapa de la Frontera, and Amatenango de la Frontera, Chiapas.

Lg Use: Mexican group is bilingual in Spanish. See main entry under Guatemala (Jakalteko, Western).

Kanjobal, Western (Acateco, Acatec, Kanjobal de San Miguel Acatán, Conob) [knj] 10,100 in Mexico (1991 Schumann). 100 Western Kanjobal native to Mexico; 10,000 refugees. Trinitaria, Comalapa, and Mazapa de Madero, Chiapas, and Quintana Roo. See main entry under Guatemala (Akateko).

Kickapoo (Kikapú, Kicapus, Kikapaux, Kicapoux, Kikabeeux, Quicapause) [kic] 300 in Mexico (1992 SIL). Coahuila: Nacimiento de Kikapú, 25 miles northeast of Muzquiz. *Lg Use:* Vigorous in Mexico. *Lg Dev:* Literacy rate in first language: 5%. Literacy rate in second language: 1% Spanish, 45% English. *Other:* Most speakers spend part of the year in the USA working. See main entry under USA.

Kiliwa (Kiliwi, Quiligua) [klb] 24 to 32 (1994 SIL). Arroyo León (4 or 5 houses), Agua Escondida (1 house), La Parra (1 or 2 houses) southeast of Ensenada, Baja California Norte. South of the Paipai, Tipai, and Cocopa. *Class:* Hokan, Esselen-Yuman, Yuman, Kiliwa. *Dialects:* Linguistically distinct from Paipai, Tipai, Cocopa (A. Wares). *Lg Use:* A Kiliwa population sample understood Paipai at 87%, but a Paipai sample understood no Kiliwa. *Other:* Nearly extinct.

Kumiai (Diegueño, Tipái, Tipai', Tipéi, Cochimí, Cuchimí, Kamia, Kamiai, Quemayá, Comeya, Kumeyaai, Kamiyai, Kamiyahi, Ki-Miai, Kumia, Kumeyaay, Campo, Ko'al, Ku'ahl, Kw'aal) [dih] 220 in Mexico (1991 Garza and Lastra). Population total all countries: 295. Baja California, Rancho Nejí, in the mountains southeast of Tecate, 60 km east of Ensenada, in La Huerta de los Indios, San Antonio Nécua, San José de la Zorra, Cañon de los Encinos, and Ja'áa. Also spoken in USA. *Class:* Hokan, Esselen-Yuman, Yuman, Delta-Californian. *Dialects:* It is not clear how the above names group into different dialects. Speakers in Neji call themselves 'Kumiai', in La Huerta call themselves 'Cochimí'. *Lg Use:* Speakers also use Spanish. *Lg Dev:* Grammar. *Other:* Different from the extinct language called 'Cochimí'.

Lacandon [lac] 1,000 (2000 SIL). 178 monolinguals (1942). Population includes 69 at Lake Metzaboc, Chiapas. Ethnic population: 1,000 (2000). Southeastern Chiapas, Najá, Lacanjá San Quintín, Metzaboc, Betel. *Class:* Mayan, Yucatecan, Yucatec-Lacandon. *Dialects:* Lacanjá, Najá. *Lg Use:* All ages. Bilingual level estimates for Tzeltal: 0 49%, 1 20%, 2 20%, 3 10%, 4 1%, 5 0%. Speakers also use Chol, Spanish. *Lg Dev:* Dictionary. NT: 1978. *Other:* SVO; short words, affixes, clitics; nontonal. Interfluvial. Tropical forest. 500 to 1,200 meters. Swidden agriculturalists.

Mam, Northern [mam] 1,000 in Mexico (1980 census). Total Mam in Mexico: 28,000. Chiapas, outside of Pacayal near La Mesilla border, and in Ojo de Agua near Guadalupe. *Other:* These are two colonies of Northern Mam Indians from Guatemala. Most are native of either Cuilco or San Ildefonso Ixtahuacan. See main entry under Guatemala.

Mam, Todos Santos (Mam de Todos Santos Cuchumatán) [mvj] 10,000 in Mexico (1991 SIL). Cacahuatán and Tapachula, Chiapas. See main entry under Guatemala (Mam, Todos Santos Cuchumatán).

Matlatzinca, Atzingo (Ocuilteco, Ocuiltec, Atzinteco, Tlahura, Tlahuica) [ocu] 50 to 100 (1993 SIL). Ethnic population: 642 (1990 census). State of Mexico, Ocuilan municipio, San Juan Atzingo, Santa Lucía del Progreso. *Class:* Oto-Manguean, Otopamean, Matlatzincan. *Dialects:* Close to San Francisco Matlatzinca, but not inherently intelligible. *Lg Use:* Speakers also use Spanish. *Other:* Mountain slope. Nearly extinct.

Matlatzinca, San Francisco (Matlatzinca, Matlatzinca de San Francisco de los Ranchos) [mat] Ethnic population: 1,167 (2000 WCD). State of Mexico, 1 village: San Francisco de los Ranchos. *Class:* Oto-Manguean, Otopamean, Matlatzincan. *Lg Use:* Most or all speakers are older adults. Speakers also use Spanish. *Other:* About half the people are working in Mexico City or elsewhere most of the time. Nearly extinct.

Maya, Chan Santa Cruz [yus] 40,000 (1990 census). East central Quintana Roo. *Class:* Mayan, Yucatecan, Yucatec-Lacandon. *Lg Use:* Speakers also use Maya of Yucatán.

Maya, Yucatán (Peninsular Maya) [yua] 700,000 in Mexico (1990 census). Population total all countries: 700,000 (1990). Campeche, Quintana Roo, Yucatán. Also spoken in Belize. *Class:* Mayan, Yucatecan, Yucatec-Lacandon. *Lg Dev:* Bible: 1992. *Other:* SVO.

Mayo [mfy] 40,000 (1995 census). 113 monolinguals (1995 census). Ethnic population: 100,000 (1983). Southern Sonora around Navojoa along the coast (Huatabampo), and a few in northern Sinaloa (Los Mochis, Guasave, San José Ríos, north of Guamuchil). At least 100 villages. *Class:* Uto-Aztecan, Southern Uto-Aztecan, Sonoran, Cahita. *Dialects:* 90% intelligibility of Yaqui. *Lg Use:* The government is offering scholarships to young people who demonstrate proficiency in Mayo. In the majority of villages, speakers are over 40 years of age. In at least 6 villages, children are learning Mayo as first language. Many in the range from age 30 to 50 grew up hearing Mayo in the home but were forbidden to speak it. They have a degree of comprehension but rarely if ever use it themselves (2000 L. Hagberg). Mayo people are reticent to identify as Mayo. The more monolingual speakers avoid contact with outsiders. Speakers prefer Mayo. Bilingual level estimates for Spanish: 0 2%, 1 10%, 2 40%, 3 35%, 4 8%, 5 5%. *Lg Dev:* Literacy rate in first language: 1%. Literacy rate in second language: 10%. Radio programs. Dictionary. Bible portions: 1962–2000. *Other:* SOV; medium word length, clitics, affixes; nontonal. Coastal. Desert, gallery forest. Sea level to 100 meters. Peasant agriculturalists; pastoralists; fishermen. Traditional religion, Christian.

Mazahua Central [maz] 350,000 (1993 SIL). Western and northwestern State of Mexico and some in D. F. *Class:* Oto-Manguean, Otopamean, Otomian, Mazahua. *Dialects:* Atlacomulco-Temascalcingo, Santa María Citendejé-Banos, San Miguel Tenoxtitlán. The Atlacomulco-Temascalcingo dialect uses different kinship terms, has phonological differences, grammatical variation among towns, and may need further adaptation of literature. 85% to 100% intelligibility among dialects. *Lg Use:* Bilingual level estimates for Spanish: 0 7%, 1 40%, 2 37%, 3 12%, 4 3%, 5 1%. *Lg Dev:* Literacy rate in first language: below 1%. Literacy rate in second language: 35%. NT: 1970. *Other:* VSO, (usually VS or VO); short words, affixes, clitics; tonal. Mountain mesa, mountain slope, riverine. Savannah, gallery forest, deciduous forest, pine forest. 1,500 to 2,750 meters. Pastoralists; peasant agriculturalists. Traditional religion, Christian.

Mazahua, Michoacán [mmc] 15,000 to 20,000 (1993 SIL). Eastern Michoacán. *Class:* Oto-Manguean, Otopamean, Otomian, Mazahua. *Lg Use:* Speakers also use Spanish. *Lg Dev:* Bible portions: 1987. *Other:* VSO, (usually VS or VO); short words, affixes, clitics; tonal. Mountain mesa, mountain slope, riverine. Savannah, gallery forest, deciduous forest, pine forest. 1,500 to 2,750 meters. Pastoralists; peasant agriculturalists. Traditional religion, Christian.

Mazatec, Ayautla [vmy] 3,500 (1994 SIL). 2,800 are monolingual. Oaxaca, southeastern Teotitlán District, San Bartolomé Ayautla. *Class:* Oto-Manguean, Popolocan,

Mazatecan. *Dialects:* 80% intelligibility of Huautla, 79% of San Miguel Hualtepec, 40% of Soyaltepec, 37% of Jalapa, 24% of Ixcatlán. *Lg Use:* A prestige variety. Vigorous. All domains. All ages. *Lg Dev:* There is a secondary school. People are interested in literature. There is a bilingual school. *Other:* 600 meters. Agriculturalists: maize, beans, chili, coffee, vanilla.

Mazatec, Chiquihuitlán (Mazateco de San Juan Chiquihuitlán) [maq] 2,500 (1990 census). 340 monolinguals. Oaxaca. *Class:* Oto-Manguean, Popolocan, Mazatecan. *Dialects:* 47% intelligibility of Huautla (closest), 37% of Ayautla, 29% of Soyaltepec, 20% of Ixcatlán. *Lg Use:* Bilingual level estimates for Spanish: 0 3%, 1 3%, 2 23.5%, 3 60%, 4 10%, 5 .5%. *Lg Dev:* Dictionary. Grammar. NT: 1991. *Other:* VSO, (with fronting of S or O for focus); clitics, affixes; tonal. Mountain slope. Tropical forest. 1,300 meters. Swidden, peasant agriculturalists.

Mazatec, Huautla (Mazateco de Huautla de Jimenez, Mazateco de la Sierra, Highland Mazatec) [mau] 72,000 (1990 census). 27,000 monolinguals. Northern Oaxaca, Huautla and vicinity. *Class:* Oto-Manguean, Popolocan, Mazatecan. *Dialects:* San Mateo, San Miguel. 90% intelligibility of San Jerónimo Tecóatl (closest, lower in outlying areas), 60% of Mazatlán, 35% of Jalapa. Lexical similarity 94% with San Miguel, 93% with San Mateo, 80% with Soyaltepec, 78% with San Pedro Ixcatlán, 74% with Jalapa de Díaz. *Lg Use:* Vigorous. All domains. Oral use in local administration, commerce, oral and written use in elementary schools, some use in religion. Letter writing. Speakers feel Mazatec is needed, and serves locally, but they recognize Spanish for prestige. Spanish is the second language, increasing in use in the city of Huautla. *Lg Dev:* Dictionary. NT: 1961. *Other:* They use a whistle speech, which distinguishes tones of the spoken language, described by G. Cowan (1948, 1952). Short words; tonal. Mountain slope, valleys. Agriculturalists: maize, coffee. Traditional religion, Christian.

Mazatec, Ixcatlán (Mazateco de San Pedro Ixcatlán) [mzi] 11,000 (1990 census). 3,150 monolinguals. Oaxaca, towns of Chichicazapa, Nuevo Ixcatlán, San Pedro Ixcatlán. *Class:* Oto-Manguean, Popolocan, Mazatecan. *Dialects:* 76% intelligibility of Huautla (closest). Different from Ixcatec. Lexical similarity 78% with Huautla, 86% with San Mateo Eloxochitlán, 85% with San Miguel Hualtepec and Soyaltepec, 82% with Jalapa de Díaz. *Lg Use:* Most speakers also use Spanish.

Mazatec, Jalapa de Díaz (Mazateco de San Felipe Jalapa de Díaz, Lowland Mazatec) [maj] 15,500 (1990 census). 4,600 monolinguals. Northern Oaxaca and Veracruz, 13 towns. *Class:* Oto-Manguean, Popolocan, Mazatecan. *Dialects:* 73% intelligibility of Huautla (closest), 62% of Ixcatlán, 51% of Soyaltepec, 46% of San Jerónimo Tecóatl, 35% of Mazatlán. Lexical similarity 82% with Ixcatlán, San Mateo Eloxochitlán, and San Miguel Hualtepec; 80% with Soyaltepec, 74% with Huautla. *Lg Use:* Bilingual level estimates for Spanish: 0 75%, 1–5 25%. *Lg Dev:* Literacy rate in first language: below 1%. Literacy rate in second language: 5%. Bible portions: 1968–2002. *Other:* VSO; short words, affixes, clitics; tonal. Coastal, mountain slope. Tropical. 150 meters. Swidden, peasant agriculturalists.

Mazatec, Mazatlán (Mazateco de Mazatlán Villa de Flores) [vmz] 13,000 (1990 census). 2,200 monolinguals. Oaxaca, southern Teotitlán District, Mazatlán Villa de Flores, plus 32 towns and villages, and others in D.F. *Class:* Oto-Manguean, Popolocan, Mazatecan. *Dialects:* Loma Grande, Zoyaltitla. 80% intelligibility of San Jerónimo Tecóatl, 78% of Huautla, 16% of Jalapa de Díaz, 8% of Chiquihuitlán. *Lg Use:* A significant number of monolinguals are 5 to 9 years old. Over half the children do not know Spanish when entering school. *Other:* Every village has a primary school, and some have secondary schools. 1,200 meters. Agriculturalists: maize, coffee, mango, zapote, banana.

Mazatec, San Jerónimo Tecóatl (Mazateco de San Jerónimo Tecóatl, Mazateco de San Antonio Eloxochitlán, Northern Highland Mazatec) [maa] 34,000 (1990 census). Population includes 8,000 in Puebla. Oaxaca, San Jerónimo Tecóatl, San Lucas Zoquiapan, Santa Cruz Acatepec, San Antonio Eloxochitlán, San Pedro Ocopetatillo, San Lorenzo, Santa Ana municipios, and a few in Puebla. 12 towns. *Class:* Oto-Manguean, Popolocan, Mazatecan. *Dialects:* San Jerónimo Tecóatl Mazatec, San Antonio Eloxochitlán Mazatec, San Lucas Zoquiapan Mazatec, Santa Cruz Ocopetatillo Mazatec, San Lorenzo Cuanecuiltitla Mazatec, Santa Ana Ateixtlahuaca Mazatec, San Francisco Huehuetlán Mazatec. 76% intelligibility of Huautla (closest), 26% of Jalapa. *Lg Use:* Bilingual level estimates for Spanish: 0 30%, 1 30%, 2 25%, 3 5%, 4 5%, 5 5%. *Lg Dev:* Taught in primary schools. Videos. Dictionary. Grammar. Bible portions: 1995–1999. *Other:* VSO; nouns up to 2 syllables; verbs long, affixes, clitics; tonal. Mountain slope. Mixed forest. 1,700 to 2,700 meters. Peasant agriculturalists.

Mazatec, Soyaltepec (Mazateco de San Miguel Soyaltepec, Mazateco de Temascal) [vmp] 23,000 (1990 census). 6,000 monolinguals. The original Soyaltepec variety may only be 900 speakers, most of whom are monolingual. Oaxaca, northwestern Tuxtepec District, part of Soyaltepec Municipio, towns of Santa María Jacatepec and San Miguel Soyaltepec, Soyaltepec Island. *Class:* Oto-Manguean, Popolocan, Mazatecan. *Dialects:* 5% intelligibility of Chiquihuitlán. A separate language from other Mazatec. *Lg Use:* Speakers also use Spanish. *Lg Dev:* A bilingual primary school and a secondary school on the Island. *Other:* Description of phonology, tone, primers. A dam built in 1954, so this Municipio includes many speakers of other Mazatec varieties. Soyaltepec Island has the least mixture of dialects. Below 300 meters. Agriculturalists: maize, beans, bananas, squash; fishermen; embroidery.

Mexican Sign Language (Lenguaje de Signos Mexicano, LSM, Lenguaje de las Manos, Lenguaje Manual Mexicana) [mfs] 87,000 to 100,000 mainly monolingual users (1986 T. C. Smith-Stark), out of 1,300,000 deaf persons in Mexico (1986 Gallaudet University). Used throughout Mexico, except in some American Indian areas (see Yucatec Mayan Sign Language): Mexico D.F. Guadalajara, Monterrey, Hermosillo, Morelia, Veracruz, Oaxaca, San Luis Potosí, Querétaro, Puebla, Cuernavaca, Torreón, Saltillo, Toluca. *Class:* Deaf sign language. *Dialects:* Influence from French Sign Language. Users of ASL have 14% intelligibility of LSM. Preliminary investigation indicates lexical similarities from 85% to 100% among regional dialects, nearly all above 90% (A. Bickford SIL 1989). *Lg Use:* Most deaf schools use the oralist method, but some use signs. At least 3 deaf churches in Mexico City, 3 in Guadalajara. 19 schools for the deaf in Saltillo, Torreón, Guadalajara (3), Mexico City (6), Morelia, Cuernavaca, Monterrey, Ciudad Obregón, Hermosillo, Villahermosa, Matamoros, Veracruz; athletic clubs, craft schools, rehabilitation institutions. *Lg Dev:* Dictionary. *Other:* It does not follow Spanish grammar. The deaf are called 'sordos, sordomudos, los silentes'.

Mixe, Coatlán (Southeastern Mixe) [mco] 5,000 (1993 SIL). Speakers of all Mixe languages: 90,000 (1993 SIL). East central Oaxaca, including Coatlán, Camotlán, San José, Santa Isabel, Ixcuintepec. *Class:* Mixe-Zoque, Mixe, Eastern Mixe. *Dialects:* Coatlán Mixe, Camotlán Mixe. *Lg Use:* Bilingual level estimates for Spanish: 0 10%, 1

50%, 2 25%, 3 10%, 4 5%, 5 0%. *Lg Dev:* Literacy rate in first language: 25%. Videos. Dictionary. NT: 1976. *Other:* Long words, affixes, clitics; nontonal. Mountain slope. Tropical forest, deciduous forest, pine forest. 500 to 2,500 meters. Swidden agriculturalists.

Mixe, Isthmus (Mixe del Istmo, Eastern Mixe, Guichicovi Mixe) [mir] 20,000 (1990 SIL). Northeastern Oaxaca, throughout the Municipio of San Juan Guichicovi, near the border of Veracruz, on the Isthmus of Tehuantepec, 3 towns. *Class:* Mixe-Zoque, Mixe, Eastern Mixe. *Lg Dev:* Literacy rate in first language: 10%. Literacy rate in second language: 30%. NT: 1988. *Other:* SOV; long words, affixes, clitics; prepositions; genitives and demonstratives before noun heads; relative clauses after noun head; question words initial; nontonal. Traditional religion, Christian.

Mixe, Juquila (South Central Mixe) [mxq] 8,000 (2002 SIL). East central Oaxaca, including the municipios of Juquila, Quetzaltepec, Ocotepec, and 1 or 2 other towns. *Class:* Mixe-Zoque, Mixe, Eastern Mixe. *Dialects:* Juquila Mixe, Ocotepec Mixe. *Lg Dev:* NT: 1980–2003.

Mixe, Mazatlán (East Central Mixe, Tutla Mixe) [mzl] 19,211 (2000 WCD). Eastern Oaxaca, including 7 towns. *Class:* Mixe-Zoque, Mixe, Eastern Mixe.

Mixe, North Central (Mixe de Atitlán, Northeastern Mixe, Atitlán Mixe) [neq] 13,000 (2002 SIL). Ethnic population: 13,000 (2002 SIL). Northeastern Oaxaca, several towns in the northeastern part of the Mixe District, including those listed as dialects. *Class:* Mixe-Zoque, Mixe, Eastern Mixe. *Dialects:* Mixe de San Juan Cotzocón, Zacatepec, Puxmetecán, Olotepec, Mixistlan, Cotzocón Mixe, Atitlán Mixe. *Lg Dev:* Bible portions: 1994–2001. *Other:* Mountain slope. Tropical forest. Swidden agriculturalists, some cash crops.

Mixe, Quetzaltepec (Central Mixe) [pxm] 6,700 (2000 census). Northeastern Oaxaca, several towns in the northeastern part of the Mixe District, including those listed as dialects. *Class:* Mixe-Zoque, Mixe, Eastern Mixe. *Lg Dev:* Bible portions: 1999–2002. *Other:* Foothills. Tropical forest. Swidden agriculturalists, some cash crops.

Mixe, Tlahuitoltepec (West Central Mixe) [mxp] 5,000 (1991 SIL). Northeastern Oaxaca. Some have moved into central Oaxaca, in the area of Albarradas Zapoteco, 3 towns. *Class:* Mixe-Zoque, Mixe, Western Mixe. *Lg Use:* Bilingual level estimates for Spanish: 0 10%, 1 50%, 2 30%, 3 9%, 4 1%, 5 0%. *Lg Dev:* NT: 1988. *Other:* SOV, VOS; long words, affixes; nontonal. Mountain slope. Pine forest. 1,845 to 3,380 meters. Swidden agriculturalists.

Mixe, Totontepec (Northwestern Mixe, Ayuk) [mto] 5,200 (1990 census). 870 monolinguals. Northeastern Oaxaca, north of Zacatepec, 10 towns. *Class:* Mixe-Zoque, Mixe, Western Mixe. *Dialects:* The most distinct of the Mixe varieties. 89% intelligibility of Acatepec, 79% of Alotepec, 72% of Tlahuitoltepec, 70% of Mixistlán. *Lg Use:* Vigorous. All domains. Used in education, religion. All ages. Speakers accept continued use of Mixe. Bilingual level estimates for Spanish: 0 15%, 1 15%, 2 20%, 3 25%, 4 20%, 5 5%. Some also speak Zapotec, or Chinantec in Chinantequilla. *Lg Dev:* Literacy rate in first language: below 1%. Literacy rate in second language: 50%. 40 to 50 people read it, very few write it. Dictionary. NT: 1989. *Other:* SOV; long words, affixes, clitics; nontonal. Mountain slope. Forest. 1,200 to 2,300 meters. Peasant agriculturalists. Christian.

Mixtec, Alacatlatzala (Highland Guerrero Mixtec, Mixteco de Alacatlatzala, To'on Savi) [mim] 22,226 (2000 WCD). 60% monolingual. Over 300,000 speakers in all Mixtecan languages (1995). Eastern Guerrero, towns of Alacatlatzala, Tenaztalcingo, Ocuapa, Potoichan, and more. There are tiny communities in Acapulco, Guerrero;

Cuautla, Morelos; and Culiacán, Sinaloa, also near San Quintín, Baja California. An area southwest to south of Tlapa, from 20 to 80 km from Tlapa del Comonfort. Also scattered emigration to the USA, especially New York. *Class:* Oto-Manguean, Mixtecan, Mixtec-Cuicatec, Mixtec. *Dialects:* Potoichan (Ocuapa), Atlamajalcingo del Monte, Tototepec, Cuatzoquitengo, Plan de Guadalupe. 65% to 85% intelligibility of Metlatonoc. Some had 70% intelligibility of Silacayoapan. *Lg Use:* Vigorous. Parents who have left the area have children who understand Mixtec, but speak only Spanish. Very few speakers of other languages use this Mixtec language. Nearly all domains; home, local shops, among officials in the town hall for commerce, for teaching in the classroom even though materials are in Spanish. Some use in religion. All ages, but young people speak somewhat more Spanish than others. High appreciation for Mixtec among speakers. Spanish is viewed as appropriate for reading and writing, and the prestige language. Bilingual level estimates for Spanish: 0 60%, 1 20%, 2 19%, 3 1%, 4 0%, 5 0%. They use Spanish when trying to communicate with people from Silacayoapan. About 20% (nearly all men) speak some Spanish for trade, travel, or work outside the area. Less than 5% also use Tlapanec or Nahuatl resulting from intermarriage. *Lg Dev:* Literacy rate in first language: 5%. Literacy rate in second language: 30%. Desire for literacy in either language is somewhat limited. Some adaptation of materials for Potoichan may be needed. Radio programs. Dictionary. Bible portions: 1990–1998. *Other:* The land is not enough to support everyone, so many leave to find jobs elsewhere. VSO; short words, clitics; tonal. Mountain slope. Scrub and pine forest. 1,076 to 2,153 meters. Peasant agriculturalists. Traditional religion, syncretism, Christian.

Mixtec, Alcozauca (Mixteco de Alocozauca, Mixteco de Xochapa) [xta] 10,000 (1994 SIL). 4,000 monolinguals. Eastern Guerrero, near Metlatonoc, 14 villages. *Class:* Oto-Manguean, Mixtecan, Mixtec-Cuicatec, Mixtec. *Dialects:* Xochapa Mixtec, Petlacalancingo Mixtec. 92% intelligibility of Metlatonoc. Metlatonoc has 70% intelligibility of Xochapa. A separate language from Metlatonoc. *Lg Dev:* Dictionary. Bible portions: 1997–2001. *Other:* Mountain slope.

Mixtec, Amoltepec (Western Sola de Vega Mixtec, Mixteco de Amoltepec) [mbz] 6,091 (2000 WCD). 1,200 monolinguals (1990 census). Ethnic population: 8,000 to 9,000. Oaxaca, western edge of Sola de Vega District, Santiago Amoltepec Municipio, and settlements (Las Cuevas, La Mesilla, El Armadillo, El Mamey, El Zapote, Colonia de Jesús, Barranca Oscura, Llano Tigre, Llano Conejo, El Cocal, El Laurel, La Tortuga). 20 villages in the southern part of Santiago Amoltepec Municipio. *Class:* Oto-Manguean, Mixtecan, Mixtec-Cuicatec, Mixtec. *Dialects:* 63% intelligibility of Ixtayutla, 52% of Pinotepa Nacional, 46% of Yosondúa, 42% of Nuyoo, 32% of Zacatepec, 25% of San Juan Colorado, 20% of Jamiltepec, 15% of Chayuco. *Lg Use:* Functionally monolingual parents do pass Mixtec on to children. Used in local administration, commerce. Many children speak Spanish more than Mixtec, but they know Mixtec. The language has low prestige. Older adults want to preserve the language. Speakers in Amoltepec center know some very basic Spanish, but those in the outlying rancherías are quite monolingual. A few know some English words. *Lg Dev:* Literacy rate in first language: 0%. *Other:* Schools through 6th grade. Many men work outside the area temporarily. 300 to 1,800 meters. Agriculturalists. Traditional religion, Christian.

Mixtec, Apasco-Apoala (Northern Nochixtlán Mixtec, Mixteco de Santiago Apoala, Mixteco de Chocho, Apoala Mixtec, Apasco Mixtec) [mip] 7,866 (1990 census). 6,728

monolinguals. Oaxaca, 40 km north northwest of Nochixtlán. Includes towns of Santa Catarina Ocotlán, San Miguel Chicagua, San Miguel Chicahuastepec, Jocotepec, Santa María Apasco, San Miguel Huautla, Nduayaco, and 2 others. *Class:* Oto-Manguean, Mixtecan, Mixtec-Cuicatec, Mixtec. *Dialects:* 26% intelligibility of Southern Puebla Mixtec (closest). *Lg Use:* Positive language attitude. *Lg Dev:* Bible portions: 1966.

Mixtec, Atatláhuca (Mixteco de San Esteban Atatláhuca, South Central Tlaxiaco Mixtec) [mib] 8,300 (1995 census). 435 monolinguals. West central Oaxaca, towns of San Esteban Atatláhuca, Santa Lucía Monteverde, and Santa Catarina Yosonotú. *Class:* Oto-Manguean, Mixtecan, Mixtec-Cuicatec, Mixtec. *Dialects:* 68% intelligibility of Yosondúa. San Agustín Tlacotepec may need separate literature (69% intelligibility of San Esteban; closest). Santa Lucía Monteverde Mixtec may also need separate literature. *Lg Use:* Bilingual level estimates for Spanish: 0 50%, 1 30%, 2 15%, 3 5%, 4 0%, 5 0%. *Lg Dev:* NT: 1973. *Other:* VSO; tonal; short words, clitics. Mountain slope. Pine forest. 3,000 meters. Peasant agriculturalists.

Mixtec, Ayutla (Coastal Guerrero Mixtec, Mixteco de Ayutla) [miy] 8,500 (1990 census). 3,000 monolinguals. Guerrero, Ayutla. *Class:* Oto-Manguean, Mixtecan, Mixtec-Cuicatec, Mixtec. *Lg Dev:* Literacy rate in first language: below 1%. Literacy rate in second language: 75% to 100%. Bible portions: 1970–2002. *Other:* Coastal.

Mixtec, Cacaloxtepec (Huajuapan Mixtec, Mixteco de Cacaloxtepec) [miu] 848 (1990 census). 100 monolinguals. Ethnic population: 1,254. Oaxaca, town of Santiago Cacaloxtepec. *Class:* Oto-Manguean, Mixtecan, Mixtec-Cuicatec, Mixtec. *Dialects:* 59% intelligibility of Silacayoapan (closest). *Lg Use:* Most monolinguals are older adults. Speakers also use Spanish.

Mixtec, Chayuco (Mixteco de Chayucu, Eastern Jamiltepec-Chayuco Mixtec) [mih] 30,000 (1977 SIL). Southwest Oaxaca. *Class:* Oto-Manguean, Mixtecan, Mixtec-Cuicatec, Mixtec. *Dialects:* 69% intelligibility of Western Jamiltepec. *Lg Dev:* NT: 1979.

Mixtec, Chazumba (Mixteco de Chazumba, Northern Oaxaca Mixtec) [xtb] 2,477 (1995 census). 32 monolinguals. Oaxaca, close to the Puebla border, with a few in Puebla. Near Southern Puebla Mixtec. The largest group speaking Mixtec is in Santiago Chazumba. Some other villages with speakers are San Pedro y San Pablo Tequixtepec (in Oaxaca), Zapotitlán, Petlalcingo, and Tototltepec de Guerrero (in Puebla). *Class:* Oto-Manguean, Mixtecan, Mixtec-Cuicatec, Mixtec. *Dialects:* 65% inherent intelligibility of Xayacatlán, 53% of Cacaloxtepec, 24% of Chigmecatitlán, 19% of Cuyamecalco (Coatzospan). *Lg Use:* 75% of the speakers are scattered over a large area, with most villages having fewer than 15% of the population able to speak Mixtec. A large percentage of the populations of each village no longer speak Mixtec, but speak Spanish. Most speakers older than 50 years.

Mixtec, Chigmecatitlán (Mixteco de Santa María Chigmecatitlán, Central Puebla Mixtec) [mii] 1,600 (1990 census). Puebla, straight south of Puebla city, about halfway to Oaxaca border. Includes Santa Catarina Tlaltemplan. *Class:* Oto-Manguean, Mixtecan, Mixtec-Cuicatec, Mixtec. *Dialects:* 23% intelligibility of Chazumba (Southern Puebla; closest). An 'island' of Mixtec surrounded by Popoloca and Nahuatl. Low intelligibility of all Mixtec; very different. *Lg Use:* 217 speakers over 50 years old, 273 monolinguals (1990). Most speakers also use Spanish. *Other:* 1,200 to 1,600 meters.

Mixtec, Coatzospan (Teotitlan Mixtec, Mixteco de San Juan Coatzospan) [miz] 5,000 (1994 SIL). 500 monolinguals. Oaxaca. *Class:* Oto-Manguean, Mixtecan,

Mixtec-Cuicatec, Mixtec. *Dialects:* 25% intelligibility of Chazumba. Cuyamecalco is close, but inherent intelligibility is inadequate. *Lg Use:* Bilingual level estimates for Spanish: Women: 0 90%, 1 5%, 2 2%, 3 1%, 4 1%, 5 1%; Men: 0 10%, 1 61%, 2 25%, 3 2%, 4 1%, 5 1%. Some speakers also use Mazatec. *Lg Dev:* Literacy rate in first language: 5%. Literacy rate in second language: 60%. Dictionary. NT: 2003. *Other:* VSO; short words, affixes, clitics; tonal. Mountain slope. Scrub forest. 1,000 to 2,000 meters. Pastoralists; swidden, peasant agriculturalists.

Mixtec, Cuyamecalco (Mixteco de Cuyamecalco, Cuicatlán Mixtec) [xtu] 2,600 (1994 SIL). 72 monolinguals in San Miguel. Oaxaca, Cuyamecalco, San Miguel Santa Flor. *Class:* Oto-Manguean, Mixtecan, Mixtec-Cuicatec, Mixtec. *Dialects:* Close to San Juan Coatzospan. *Lg Use:* Speakers also use Spanish. *Other:* Mountain slope. Scrub forest. 1,000 to 2,000 meters. Pastoralists; swidden, peasant agriculturalists.

Mixtec, Diuxi-Tilantongo (Central Nochistlán Mixtec, Mixteco de Diuxi-Tilantongo) [xtd] 8,500 (1990 census). 300 monolinguals (1990 census). Oaxaca, 20 towns and villages in the Diuxi and Tilantongo area, Oaxaca City, Puebla City, Mexico City. *Class:* Oto-Manguean, Mixtecan, Mixtec-Cuicatec, Mixtec. *Dialects:* 37% intelligibility of Peñoles (Eastern); closer to Nuxaá. *Lg Use:* All ages. Bilingual level estimates for Spanish: 0 20–30%, 1 20–30%, 2 20–30%, 3 15–30%, 4 0–3%, 5 0–1%. *Lg Dev:* NT: 2001. *Other:* VSO; short words, affixes, clitics; stems are CVCV or CVV; tonal. Mountain mesa, mountain slope. Savannah, scrub forest. 2,000 to 3,200 meters. Peasant agriculturalists: wheat; pastoralists: goats, sheep.

Mixtec, Huitepec (Mixteco de Zaachila, Mixteco de Huitepec, Mixteco de San Antonio Huitepec) [mxs] 4,000 (1990 census). 200 monolinguals. Population includes 2,000 in the town of Huitepec. Oaxaca, 60 km west of Zaachila, 25 km southwest of Peñoles, Huitepec Municipio, towns of San Antonio Huitepec, San Francisco Yucucundo, and San Francisco Infiernillo. *Class:* Oto-Manguean, Mixtecan, Mixtec-Cuicatec, Mixtec. *Dialects:* 77% intelligibility of Estetla (Eastern), 75% of Chalcatongo, 52% of Peñoles, 20% of Yosondúa, 8% of Tilantongo. *Lg Use:* Spoken in most homes in Huitepec town; more so in rural areas. *Other:* Secondary school. Mountain slope. Pine forest. 2,000 to 2,400 meters.

Mixtec, Itundujia (Mixteco de Santa Cruz Itundujia, Eastern Putla Mixtec) [mce] 1,082 (1990 census). 33 monolinguals. Oaxaca, Putla District, 10 km southwest of Yosondúa, 40 km southeast of Putla. Most in Morelos and Guerrero villages. *Class:* Oto-Manguean, Mixtecan, Mixtec-Cuicatec, Mixtec. *Dialects:* 60% intelligibility of Yosondúa, 59% of Chalcatongo, 25% of San Martín Peras, 15% of Amoltepec, 12% of Zacatepec, 10% of San Esteban Atatláhuca, Nuyoo, 0% of Ixtayutla. *Lg Use:* Nearly all of the monolinguals and over half of the speakers are over 50 years old. Speakers also use Spanish.

Mixtec, Ixtayutla (Mixteco de Santiago Ixtayutla, Northeastern Jamiltepec Mixtec) [vmj] 5,500 (1990 census). 2,800 monolinguals. Oaxaca, Jamiltepec District, Santiago Ixtayutla and about 15 settlements (Nuyuku, Xiniyuva, La Humedad, Pueblo Viejo, Musko, Yukuyaa, Llano Verde, Yomuche, Carasul, Frutillo). *Class:* Oto-Manguean, Mixtecan, Mixtec-Cuicatec, Mixtec. *Dialects:* 79% intelligibility of Amoltepec, 59% of Chayuco, 49% of Jamiltepec, 40% of San Juan Colorado, 30% of Zacatepec. *Other:* School through 6th grade in Ixtayutla. Some settlements have schools. 550 meters. Agriculturalists: bananas, beans, maize; sell rope, animal husbandry: goats. Christian, traditional religion.

Mixtec, Jamiltepec (Mixteco de Jamiltepec, Eastern Jamiltepec-San Cristobal Mixtec) [mxt] 10,000 (1983 SIL). Southwest Oaxaca. *Class:* Oto-Manguean, Mixtecan,

Mixtec-Cuicatec, Mixtec. *Dialects:* Intelligibility and sociolinguistic attitudes make separate literature from Chayuco advisable. *Lg Use:* Bilingual level estimates for Spanish: 0 25%, 1 50%, 2 20%, 3 3%, 4 2%, 5 0%. *Lg Dev:* NT: 1983. *Other:* VSO; short words, affixes, clitics; tonal. Mountain slope. Semitropical. 200 to 300 meters. Peasant agriculturalists.

Mixtec, Juxtlahuaca (Mixteco de Juxtlahuaca, Central Juxtlahuaca Mixtec) [vmc] 16,000 (1990 census). 5,500 monolinguals. Oaxaca, central Santiago Juxtlahuaca, towns of San Sebastián Tecomaxtlahuaca, San Miguel Tlacotepec, Santos Reyes Tepejillo, Santa María Tindú, and Santa María Yucunicoco, San Quintín valley, Baja California. *Class:* Oto-Manguean, Mixtecan, Mixtec-Cuicatec, Mixtec. *Dialects:* 84% intelligibility of Silacayoapan, 80% of Yucucani and San Miguel Peras, 63% of Santa Cruz Mixtepec, 48% of Coicoyán (Western Juxtlahuaca), 37% of Tezoatlán, 18% of Zacatepec, 10% of Ñumí. *Other:* Secondary school. Many work in Culiacán or the Usa. Little tillable land. Mountain slope. Desert. 1,200 to 2,000 meters.

Mixtec, Magdalena Peñasco [xtm] 4,200 (1990 census). 1,050 monolinguals. Oaxaca, Tlaxiaco District, municipios de Santa María, Magdalena Peñasco, San Cristobal Amoltepec, and San Agustín Tlacotepec. Also includes the town of San Mateo Peñasco. *Class:* Oto-Manguean, Mixtecan, Mixtec-Cuicatec, Mixtec. *Dialects:* San Agustín Tlacotepec, San Cristóbal Amoltepec Mixtec, San Mateo Peñasco Mixtec, Santo Domingo Heundío Mixtec, San Miguel Achiutla Mixtec. Speakers have 89% intelligibility of San Cristóbal Amoltepec, 76% of Tijaltepec and Sinicahua, 73% of San Miguel el Grande, 72% of Tlacotepec, 68% of Ocotepec, 64% of Nduaxico, 58% of Yucuañe. A distinct language, different from Santiago Amoltepec Mixtec. *Lg Use:* Positive language attitude. *Lg Dev:* Bilingual primary school. Bible portions: 2002. *Other:* Secondary school. 2,000 meters. Agriculturalists: maize, weavers: tenates, hats.

Mixtec, Metlatónoc (Mixteco de San Rafael) [mxv] 46,648 (2000 WCD). 14,000 monolinguals. Eastern Guerrero, Metlatonoc, San Rafael, and towns further south. *Class:* Oto-Manguean, Mixtecan, Mixtec-Cuicatec, Mixtec. *Dialects:* 90% or higher intelligibility among nearby towns, but only 50% with most in the Alacatlatzala area. Alcozauca Mixtec is a separate language. Investigation needed to determine if Chilistlahuaca and Ojo de Pescado are different. *Lg Dev:* Bible portions: 1959–1998. *Other:* Mountain slope.

Mixtec, Mitlatongo (Mixteco de Mitlatongo) [vmm] 1,800 (1994 SIL). Oaxaca, Nochixtlán, Santiago Mitlatongo, Santa Cruz Mitlatongo. *Class:* Oto-Manguean, Mixtecan, Mixtec-Cuicatec, Mixtec. *Dialects:* 70% intelligibility of Yutanduchi, 56% of Peñoles, 54% of San Juan Tamazola, 43% of Teita, 10% of Nuxaá, 8% of Diuxi. *Lg Use:* All ages. Children are learning Spanish, but it is limited. *Other:* Secondary school. Some men work outside, and a few in the USA. Mountain slope. 2,200 meters. Agriculturalists: maize, beans, anona (chirimoya, ice cream fruit), lima beans, dates.

Mixtec, Mixtepec (Eastern Juxtlahuaca Mixtec, Mixteco de San Juan Mixtepec) [mix] 12,000 in Mexico (1990 census). 2,600 monolinguals (1990 census). Oaxaca, San Juan Mixtepec, about 2000 located in Tlaxiaco (district head), San Quintín valley, Baja California. Also spoken in USA. *Class:* Oto-Manguean, Mixtecan, Mixtec-Cuicatec, Mixtec. *Dialects:* Distinct from other Mixtec. *Lg Use:* Some speakers also use Spanish. *Lg Dev:* Bible portions: 1974.

Mixtec, Northern Tlaxiaco (Mixteco de San Juan Ñumí, Ñumí Mixtec) [xtn] 14,000 (1990 census). Oaxaca, Tlaxiaco District, San Juan Ñumí and Santiago Nundichi municipios; Teposcolula District, San Antonino Monte Verde and San Sebastián Nicananduta municipios. *Class:* Oto-Manguean, Mixtecan, Mixtec-Cuicatec, Mixtec. *Dialects:* Monte Verde Mixtec, Yosoñama. *Lg Dev:* Literacy rate in first language: 20%. Literacy rate in second language: 40%. Grammar. Bible portions: 1995–2000.

Mixtec, Northwest Oaxaca (Mixteco del Noroeste de Oaxaca, Mixteco de Yucuná) [mxa] 2,500 (1990 census). 2,195 monolinguals. Northwest Oaxaca, towns of Santos Reyes Yucuná, Guadalupe Portezuelo, and San Simón Zahuatlán. *Class:* Oto-Manguean, Mixtecan, Mixtec-Cuicatec, Mixtec. *Lg Use:* Bilingual level estimates for Spanish: 0 20%, 1 40%, 2 40%, 3 0%, 4 0%, 5 0%. *Other:* SVO; short words, clitics; tonal. Mountain slope. Sparse to barren scrub or deciduous forest. 1,500 to 1,800 meters. Peasant agriculturalists.

Mixtec, Ocotepec (Mixteco de Santo Tomás Ocotepec, Ocotepec Mixtec) [mie] 5,000 to 8,000 (1982 SIL). West central Oaxaca. *Class:* Oto-Manguean, Mixtecan, Mixtec-Cuicatec, Mixtec. *Dialect:* Santa Catarina Yosonotu. 80% intelligibility of Ñumí (Northwestern Tlaxiaco). *Lg Use:* Bilingual level estimates for Spanish: 0 40%, 1 30%, 2 25%, 3 5%, 4 0%, 5 0%. *Lg Dev:* NT: 1977. *Other:* VSO; short words, clitics; tonal. Mountain slope. Pine forest. 2,500 meters. Peasant agriculturalists.

Mixtec, Peñoles (Eastern Mixtec, Mixteco de San Mateo Tepantepec) [mil] 13,417 in Mexico (2000 WCD). 2,000 monolinguals (1990 census). West central Oaxaca. Santa María Peñoles municipio, Monteflor, San Mateo Tepantepec, Estetla and Cholula agencias; Santiago Tlazoyaltepec municipio; and Huazolotipac agencia in Huitepec municipio, Zaachila District, and San Mateo Sindihui town. Also spoken in USA. *Class:* Oto-Manguean, Mixtecan, Mixtec-Cuicatec, Mixtec. *Dialects:* Santa María Peñoles (Peñoles), Santiago Tlazoyaltepec (Tlazoyaltepec), San Mateo Tepantepec (Tepantepec). 14% intelligibility of Chalcatongo. Nuxaá has 30% intelligibility of Peñoles. *Lg Use:* Bilingual level estimates for Spanish: 0 25%, 1 20%, 2 30%, 3 20%, 4 4%, 5 1%. *Lg Dev:* Literacy rate in first language: 5%. Literacy rate in second language: 40%. NT: 1979–2002. *Other:* VSO; short words, clitics; tonal. Mountain slope. Deciduous, pine forest. 1,500 to 2,600 meters. Peasant agriculturalists; pastoralists.

Mixtec, Pinotepa Nacional (Western Jamiltepec Mixtec, Coastal Mixtec, Lowland Jicaltepec Mixtec, Mixteco de Pinotepa Nacional) [mio] 20,000 (1990 census). 2,200 monolinguals. Oaxaca, around Jamiltepec. *Class:* Oto-Manguean, Mixtecan, Mixtec-Cuicatec, Mixtec. *Dialects:* Investigation needed to determine how different Huazolititlán and Don Luís Pinotepa are. *Lg Use:* Bilingual level estimates for Spanish: 0 23%, 1 24%, 2 22%, 3 13%, 4 10%, 5 8%. *Lg Dev:* NT: 1980. *Other:* VSO; short words, affixes, clitics; tonal. Coastal. Scrub forest. 300 to 500 meters. Swidden agriculturalists.

Mixtec, San Juan Colorado (Mixteco de San Juan Colorado) [mjc] 13,500 (1990 census). 3,100 monolinguals. Oaxaca. *Class:* Oto-Manguean, Mixtecan, Mixtec-Cuicatec, Mixtec. *Lg Use:* Bilingual level estimates for Spanish: 0 60%, 1 35%, 2 5%, 3 0%, 4 0%, 5 0%. *Lg Dev:* NT: 1994. *Other:* VSO; short words, clitics, affixes; tonal. Mountain slope. Semitropical. 150 to 220 meters. Peasant agriculturalists.

Mixtec, San Juan Teíta (Teita Mixtec) [xtj] 550 to 650 (2002 SIL). Oaxaca, Tlaxiaco District, 30 km southeast of Tlaxiaco, town of San Juan Teíta. *Class:* Oto-Manguean, Mixtecan, Mixtec-Cuicatec, Mixtec. *Dialect:* Santa Maria Tataltepec. May be closest to Diuxi Mixtec, but not close enough to any other Mixtec for adequate comprehension. *Lg Use:* Most prefer Mixtec for family and informal usage. All ages. Positive language attitude. All ages and sexes speak some Spanish; some

women have only basic knowledge, and some young people and men are very fluent. Many children now prefer Spanish. *Lg Dev:* Literacy rate in second language: Possibly 40% in Spanish. They have a bilingual primary school. Bible portions: 1998. *Other:* Mountain valley. Scrub forest desert; good water supply for irrigation due to river system of canals. 1,500 to 2,000 meters. Peasant agriculturalists: maize, export of palm leaf, bananas, mamey, zapote; weavers: palm leaf tenates, hats.

Mixtec, San Miguel Piedras [xtp] 448 (1990 census). Ethnic population: 1,123 (1990 census). Oaxaca, Nochixtlán District, Yutanduchi de Guerrero. *Class:* Oto-Manguean, Mixtecan, Mixtec-Cuicatec, Mixtec. *Dialects:* 49% intelligibility of Estetla (Eastern), 29% of Soyaltepec, Yosondúa, 18% of Peñoles, 15% of Chalcatongo, 13% of Tilantongo, 11% of Chicahua. *Lg Use:* A few younger speakers, but most are older adults. Speakers also use Spanish.

Mixtec, San Miguel el Grande [mig] 14,453 (1990 census). 226 monolinguals in Chalcatongo, 800 in other dialects. Population includes 4,453 in Chalcatongo. West central Oaxaca. *Class:* Oto-Manguean, Mixtecan, Mixtec-Cuicatec, Mixtec. *Dialects:* San Pedro Molinos, Santa María Yosoyúa, Santa Catarina Ticuá, San Miguel Chalcatongo. 86% intelligibility of Yosondúa (closest). *Lg Dev:* NT: 1951. *Other:* VSO; short words, clitics; tonal. Mountain slope. Pine forest. 1,846 to 3,077 meters. Peasant agriculturalists.

Mixtec, Santa Lucía Monteverde [mdv] 4,000 (2001 Williams). 203 monolinguals (1995 census). Ethnic population: 6,000 (1995 census). West central Oaxaca, northeastern Putla District, town of Santa Lucía Monteverde. *Class:* Oto-Manguean, Mixtecan, Mixtec-Cuicatec, Mixtec. *Dialects:* Intelligibility is 83% of San Esteban Atatláhuca; people had difficulty understanding written materials in it. Santa Catarina Yosonotu Mixtec may be closer to this than to Atatláhuca. *Lg Use:* 2,300 people between 5 to 14 years old, of whom 1,200 speak Mixtec, including 4 monolinguals (1995 census). Speakers also use Spanish. *Other:* Mountain slope. Pine forest. Peasant agriculturalists.

Mixtec, Santa María Zacatepec (Zacatepec Mixtec, Mixteco de Santa María Zacatepec, Southern Putla Mixtec, "Tacuate," Tu'un Va'a) [mza] 6,000 (1992 SIL). Less than 20% monolingual. Population includes 3,000 in Zacatepec and 3,000 in surrounding rancherías and villages. Oaxaca, 45 km south of Putla, on paved road from Tlaxiaco to Pinotepa Nacional. Towns of Tapanco, Nejapa, Atotonilco, San Miguel, San Juan Viejo, Rancho de la Virgen, Las Palmas. *Class:* Oto-Manguean, Mixtecan, Mixtec-Cuicatec, Mixtec. *Dialects:* 64% intelligibility of Ixtayutla, 63% of Jicaltepec (Pinotepa Nacional Mixtec), 40% to 50% of Metlatonoc, 25% to 30% of Yoloxochitl. *Lg Use:* Vigorous. Some Spanish-speaking merchants can understand Mixtec. All domains. Oral use in local administration, commerce. Some use in elementary schools, churches. All ages. Speakers continue to use it, but are ashamed to use it in front of outsiders. About 100 can speak some English. *Lg Dev:* Literacy rate in first language: 1%. Literacy rate in second language: 30%. Bible portions: 1995. *Other:* About 1,000 speakers working in the USA. Called "Tacuates" by people in the area including Indians, which can be offensive depending on context and other signals. 1,200 meters. Agriculturalists. Christian.

Mixtec, Silacayoapan [mks] 18,717 in Mexico (2000 WCD). 1,500 monolinguals (1990 census). Oaxaca, including towns of Santo Domingo Tonala (5,704 in 1990 census) and San Jorge Nuchita (3,052), and Tijuana. Also spoken in USA. *Class:* Oto-Manguean, Mixtecan, Mixtec-Cuicatec, Mixtec. *Dialect:* San Simón Zahuatlán. 70%

intelligibility of Metlatonoc, 68% of Santa María Peras. Cuatzoquitengo may need separate literature; testing incomplete; also Guadalupe Portezuelo (65% intelligibility of Silacayoapan). *Lg Use:* Bilingual level estimates for Spanish: 0 20%, 1 40%, 2 28%, 3 10%, 4 2%, 5 0%. *Lg Dev:* Grammar. NT: 1999. *Other:* VSO; short words, affixes, clitics; tonal. Mountain mesa. Desert, scrub forest. 2,100 to 3,000 meters. Swidden, peasant agriculturalists.

Mixtec, Sindihui [xts] 138 (1990 census). West central Oaxaca. *Class:* Oto-Manguean, Mixtecan, Mixtec-Cuicatec, Mixtec. *Dialects:* Distinct from Yutanduchi. *Lg Use:* Speakers are older adults.

Mixtec, Sinicahua (Mixteco de San Antonio Sinicahua) [xti] 1,300 (1990 census). 400 monolinguals. Oaxaca, Tlaxiaco District, San Antonio Sinicahua, Siniyucu, and settlements of Sinicahua Municipio. *Class:* Oto-Manguean, Mixtecan, Mixtec-Cuicatec, Mixtec. *Dialects:* Speakers have 75% intelligibility of Yosoyúa, 73% of Ocotepec, 72% of San Miguel el Grande, and 51% of Nduaxico (Northern Tlaxiaco Mixtec). *Lg Use:* Speakers have low proficiency in Spanish. *Other:* Primary and secondary schools. 2,700 meters. Agriculturalists: maize, wheat, peas.

Mixtec, Southeastern Nochixtlán (Mixteco de Santo Domingo Nuxaá, Mixteco de Nuxaá, Mixteco del Sureste de Nochixtlán) [mxy] 7,000 (1990 census). 4,075 monolinguals. Oaxaca, Nochixtlán District, 30 km along highway 190, starting 20 km southeast of Nochixtlán, four turn-offs from highway 190. Well-graded gravel road. Main towns are Santo Domingo Nuxaá, San Andrés Nuxiño, Santa Inez Zaragoza. Also Ojo de Agua Nuxaá, El Oro, La Herradura, La Unión Zaragoza, Reforma, La Paz, and other hamlets. *Class:* Oto-Manguean, Mixtecan, Mixtec-Cuicatec, Mixtec. *Dialects:* 60% to 70% intelligibility of Peñoles Mixtec. Speakers understand little of San Miguel Piedras or San Pedro Tidaá Mixtec. *Lg Use:* Used in the home. Spanish is preferred in Santa Inez Zaragoza; elsewhere Mixtec is preferred. *Lg Dev:* Literacy rate in first language: 5% to 10%. Literacy rate in second language: 75% to 100%. Dictionary. Bible portions: 2002. *Other:* VSO; tonal. Mountain slope. Pine forest in highest areas, mixed deciduous forest, scrub in lower areas. 1,800 to 2,500 meters. Peasant agriculturalists.

Mixtec, Southern Puebla (Mixteco del Sur de Puebla, Acatlán Mixtec) [mit] 1,330 (1990 census). 386 monolinguals. Oaxaca, southwestern Puebla, town of Zapotitlán Palmas. *Class:* Oto-Manguean, Mixtecan, Mixtec-Cuicatec, Mixtec. *Dialects:* 53% intelligibility of Cacaloxtepec (Huajuapan; closest). *Lg Use:* Most children under 16 have little or no proficiency in Mixtec and are monolingual in Spanish. Bilingual level estimates for Spanish: 0 0%, 1 5%, 2 20%, 3 60%, 4 10%, 5 5%. *Lg Dev:* NT: 1978. *Other:* VSO; short words, clitics; tonal. Mountain slope. 1,800 to 2,000 meters. Pastoralists; peasant agriculturalists.

Mixtec, Southwestern Tlaxiaco (Mixteco de Santiago Nuyoo, Nuyoo Mixtec, Southeastern Ocotepec Mixtec) [meh] 6,000 (1990 census). 1,000 monolinguals. Oaxaca. *Class:* Oto-Manguean, Mixtecan, Mixtec-Cuicatec, Mixtec. *Dialects:* Nuyoo, Yucuhiti. 54% intelligibility of Atatláhuca (closest). *Lg Dev:* Literacy rate in first language: 5%. Literacy rate in second language: 60%. Bible portions: 1999–2003.

Mixtec, Soyaltepec (Mixteco de San Bartolo Soyaltepec) [vmq] 322 (1990 census). Ethnic population: 926 (1990 census). Oaxaca, Teposcolula District, villages of San Bartolo Soyaltepec and Guadalupe Gabilera. *Class:* Oto-Manguean, Mixtecan, Mixtec-Cuicatec, Mixtec. *Dialects:* 28% intelligibility of Tilantongo, 25% of Ñumí, 23% of Apoala. *Lg Use:* All ages in some places. Children are learning Mixtec in Guadalupe. Speakers also use Spanish.

Mixtec, Tacahua (Mixteco de Santa Cruz Tacahua) [xtt] 585 (1990 census). 78 monolinguals. Oaxaca, Tlaxiaco District, east of Yosondúa, southeast of San Miguel el Grande. *Class:* Oto-Manguean, Mixtecan, Mixtec-Cuicatec, Mixtec. *Lg Use:* 70% of the monolinguals are older adults, none under 35.

Mixtec, Tamazola (Mixteco de San Juan Tamazola) [vmx] 2,500 (1990 census). Oaxaca, Nochixtlán, San Juan Tamazola. *Class:* Oto-Manguean, Mixtecan, Mixtec-Cuicatec, Mixtec. *Lg Use:* Speakers also use Spanish.

Mixtec, Tezoatlán (Mixteco de Tezoatlán de Segura y Luna) [mxb] 6,200 (1990 census). 850 monolinguals. Oaxaca, Tezoatlán area, southwest of Huajuapan, about 40 to 50 km off the highway by gravel road; 25 miles south of Cacaloxtepec; towns of Yucuquimi de Ocampo, San Andrés Yutatío, Yucuñuti de Benito Juárez, San Juan Diquiyú, San Marcos de Garzón, San Martín del Río, Santa Catarina Yotandu, San Isidro de Zaragoza, San Valentín. *Class:* Oto-Manguean, Mixtecan, Mixtec-Cuicatec, Mixtec. *Dialects:* Tezoatlán, Yucu Ñuti. Speakers in each town speak a little differently. 70% to 80% intelligibility of Silacayoapan and Atenango. *Lg Use:* Vigorous except in 2 towns. Some speak Mixtec to their children, but those in Yucuñuti and Huajuapan speak Spanish to them. All domains. Oral use in local administration, commerce. Some use in kindergarten. Some oral and written use in church. All ages. Young people sometimes speak more Spanish than others. Speakers view Mixtec as appropriate for their villages, but are ashamed to speak it in front of outsiders. Some also use Spanish. A few speak some English. *Lg Dev:* Radio programs. Grammar. Bible portions: 1992–2003. *Other:* Mountain slope. Few trees except on the tops of mountains. Swidden agriculturalists: maize; basket and hat weavers; merchants. Christian, traditional religion.

Mixtec, Tidaá (Mixteco de Tidaá, North Central Nochixtlán Mixtec) [mtx] 550 (1990 census). Ethnic population: 900 (1990 census). Oaxaca. *Class:* Oto-Manguean, Mixtecan, Mixtec-Cuicatec, Mixtec. *Dialects:* 60% intelligibility of Peñoles (Eastern); closest. Nuxaá is close. *Lg Use:* 2 monolinguals are over 50 years of age. Most speakers are over age 40. 13% of children 5 to 15 years of age are speakers (1990). Other children are not learning Mixtec. Speakers also use Spanish.

Mixtec, Tijaltepec (Mixteco de San Pablo Tijaltepec) [xtl] 3,559 (2000 WCD). 800 monolinguals. Oaxaca, southeastern Tlaxiaco District, towns of San Pablo Tijaltepec, Santa María Yosoyúa, and all their communities. *Class:* Oto-Manguean, Mixtecan, Mixtec-Cuicatec, Mixtec. *Dialects:* Speakers have 89% intelligibility of San Miguel el Grande and Yosoyúa, 82% of San Mateo Peñasco, 81% of Sinicahua and 66% of Teita. *Other:* Primary schools, 1 secondary school. Some work outside in Veracruz or the USA. 2,300 meters. Agriculturalists: maize, wheat, beans, chilacayote squash.

Mixtec, Tlazoyaltepec (Mixteco de Santiago Tlazoyaltepec) [mqh] West central Oaxaca, Santiago Tlazoyaltepec municipio. *Class:* Oto-Manguean, Mixtecan, Mixtec-Cuicatec, Mixtec. *Lg Use:* Speakers also use Spanish. *Other:* VSO; short words, clitics; tonal. Mountain slope. Deciduous, pine forest. 1,500 to 2,600 meters. Peasant agriculturalists; pastoralists.

Mixtec, Tututepec (Mixteco de San Pedro Tututepec) [mtu] 817 (1990 census). Ethnic population: 30,046 (1990 census). Oaxaca, 10 km north of coastal highway, on dirt road that turns off pavement 40 km southeast of Jamiltepec. Includes San Pedro Tututepec, Santa María Acatepec, Santa Cruz Tututepec, other towns and villages. *Class:* Oto-Manguean, Mixtecan, Mixtec-Cuicatec, Mixtec. *Dialect:* Santa María Acatepec. 61% intelligibility of Ixtayutla (closest), 50% of Pinotepa.

Lg Use: Most vigorous in Acatepec, but young people not using Mixtec. Most speakers older than 50 years (1990). Speakers also use Spanish. *Other:* Below 700 meters.

Mixtec, Western Juxtlahuaca (Mixteco del Oeste de Juxtlahuaca, Coicoyán Mixtec) [jmx] 25,000 (1992 SIL). 7,000 monolinguals (1990 census). Population includes 7,000 in San Martín Peras, 2,000 in Santa Cruz Yucucani, 2,000 in San José Yoxocaño. Oaxaca-Guerrero border due west of Juxtlahuaca. In Oaxaca: San Martín Peras. Other municipios: Río Frijol, Santa Cruz Yucucani, San José Yoxocaño (all towns in these municipios). In Guerrero: Malvabisco, Rancho Limón, Río Aguacate, Boca de Mamey. *Class:* Oto-Manguean, Mixtecan, Mixtec-Cuicatec, Mixtec. *Dialects:* San Martín Peras, Coicoyán, San Juan Piñas. 82% intelligibility of Metlatonoc, 80% of Silacayoapan, 65% of Juxtlahuaca, 19% of Cuatzoquitengo, 16% of Zacatepec. *Lg Use:* Very little comprehension or use of Spanish. *Other:* There is a primary school in San Martín. Many work in Culiacán during the cold months. Mountain slope. Pine forest. 2,000 meters. Agriculturalists. Traditional religion, Christian.

Mixtec, Yoloxochitl [xty] 2,540 (1994 SIL). Southeastern Guerrero, San Luís Acatlán Municipio, just south of Tlapanec, and about halfway between Metlatonoc and Ayutla Mixtec; town of Yoloxochitl and possibly a few speakers in Cuanacastitlán. *Class:* Oto-Manguean, Mixtecan, Mixtec-Cuicatec, Mixtec. *Dialects:* Metlatonoc has 35% intelligibility of Yoloxochitl, and Ayutla has 30% intelligibility of it. *Lg Use:* All domains. There is a bilingual primary school using Spanish. *Other:* Coastal. 500 meters. Agriculturalists: maize, beans, tropical fruits, jamaica; embroidery.

Mixtec, Yosondúa (Mixteco de Santiago Yosondúa, Southern Tlaxiaco Mixtec) [mpm] 5,000 (1990 census). 240 monolinguals. Oaxaca. *Class:* Oto-Manguean, Mixtecan, Mixtec-Cuicatec, Mixtec. *Dialects:* 70% intelligibility of San Miguel el Grande and Chalcatongo (closest). San Mateo Sindihui has 19% intelligibility of Yosondúa. *Lg Use:* Bilingual level estimates for Spanish: 0 15%, 1 20%, 2 35%, 3 20%, 4 5%, 5 5%. *Lg Dev:* Dictionary. NT: 1988. *Other:* Mountain mesa, mountain slope. Gallery, pine forest. Peasant agriculturalists.

Mixtec, Yucuañe (Mixteco de San Bartolomé Yucuañe) [mvg] 515 (1990 census). 88 monolinguals. Oaxaca, northeastern Tlaxiaco District, 30 km southeast of Tlaxiaco, town of San Bartolomé Yucuañe. Many work in D.F. and USA. *Class:* Oto-Manguean, Mixtecan, Mixtec-Cuicatec, Mixtec. *Dialects:* May be closest to Diuxi Mixtec, but not close enough to any other Mixtec for adequate comprehension. Speakers have 87% intelligibility of San Cristobal Amoltepec, 86% of Yosoyúa, 85% of Magdalena Peñasco, 64% of Teita, 60% of Nduaxico (Northern Tlaxiaco Mixtec), 56% of Tlacotepec. 2 dialects in different halves of San Agustín Tlacotepec. *Lg Use:* Used in the home. All ages. All also use Spanish; some women have only basic knowledge, and some young people and men are very fluent. *Lg Dev:* Literacy rate in second language: Possibly 40% in Spanish. *Other:* Primary and secondary schools. Mountain valley. Tropical forest, scrub forest desert. 1,800 meters. Peasant agriculturalists: maize; palm and cactus fiber gathering.

Mixtec, Yutanduchi (Southern Nochixtlan Mixtec, Mixteco de Yutanduchi) [mab] 1,800 (1990 census). 38 monolinguals. Oaxaca, Nochixtlán District, Yutanduchi de Guerrero. *Class:* Oto-Manguean, Mixtecan, Mixtec-Cuicatec, Mixtec. *Dialects:* 49% intelligibility of Estetla (Eastern), 48% of San Juan Tamazola, 20% of Yosondúa and Soyaltepec, 36% to 18% of Peñoles, 15% of Chalcatongo, 13% of Tilantongo. *Lg Use:* Speakers also use Spanish. *Other:* Primary and secondary school.

Mountain slope. 1,600 meters. Agriculturalists; export palm leaf; make rope, woven mats.

Mocho (Motozintleco) [mhc] 168 (1990 census). Chiapas, on border of Guatemala and Mexico (area of Tuzantán and Motozintla). *Class:* Mayan, Kanjobalan-Chujean, Kanjobalan, Mocho. *Dialects:* Motozintleco, Tuzanteco. Not intelligible with Mam dialects (Paul Townsend SIL 1973). Tuzanteco and Mocho are two distinct dialects of the same language (Terrence Kaufman 1967). *Lg Use:* Only a few speakers still use the language in the home. Speakers are older adults. Speakers also use Spanish.

Nahuatl, Central (Náhuatl del Centro, Central Aztec, Tlaxcala-Puebla Nahuatl) [nhn] 40,000 (1980 census). 1,000 monolinguals (1990 census). Speakers of all Nahuatl varieties: 1,376,898. Ethnic population: 63,000 (1986). States of Tlaxcala and Puebla. *Class:* Uto-Aztecan, Southern Uto-Aztecan, Aztecan, General Aztec, Aztec. *Lg Use:* There are some monolingual children. The most monolingual location is northeast of Puebla City about 15 km. Spanish is used by a few.

Nahuatl, Central Huasteca [nch] 200,000 (2000 census). States of Hidalgo, Veracruz, and San Louis Potosi. *Class:* Uto-Aztecan, Southern Uto-Aztecan, Aztecan, General Aztec, Aztec. *Lg Use:* Speakers also use Spanish. *Lg Dev:* Bible portions: 2003. *Other:* SVO; long words, affixes; nontonal. Mountain mesa. Scrub forest. Sea level to 2,000 meters. Swidden agriculturalists.

Nahuatl, Central Puebla (Central Puebla Nahuatl, Southwestern Puebla Nahuatl, Náhuatl del Suroeste de Puebla) [ncx] 16,000 (1998 SIL). 1,430 monolinguals. Population includes 800 in Teopantlán, 600 in Huatlatlauca. South of Puebla City (97" 08' 56 W Long, 17" 10' 27 N Lat), Teopantlán, Tepatlaxco de Hidalgo, Tochimilco, Atoyatempan, Huatlathauca, Huehuetlán (near Molcaxac). *Class:* Uto-Aztecan, Southern Uto-Aztecan, Aztecan, General Aztec, Aztec. *Lg Use:* 70% to 80% of children entering school in some towns do not speak Spanish. In other towns the younger generation are not learning Nahuatl. Speakers also use Spanish. *Other:* There are schools in most towns. 1,700 meters. Agriculturalists; mat makers, laborers.

Nahuatl, Classical (Classical Aztec) [nci] Extinct. Central Mexico, Tenochtitlán, Aztec Empire. *Class:* Uto-Aztecan, Southern Uto-Aztecan, Aztecan, General Aztec, Aztec. *Lg Dev:* Grammar. NT: 1833.

Nahuatl, Coatepec (Náhuatl de Coatepec, Coatepec Aztec) [naz] 1,400 (1990 census). 15 monolinguals. State of Mexico, Coatepec Costales, Tlacultlapa, Texcalco, Tonalapa, Maxela, Machito de las Flores, Chilacachapa, Miacacsingo, Los Sabinos, and Acapetlahuaya, all west of Iguala, Guerrero. The language has strongest usage in Coatepec Costales and Chilacachapa. *Class:* Uto-Aztecan, Southern Uto-Aztecan, Aztecan, General Aztec, Aztec. *Dialects:* 54% intelligibility of Santa Catarina (Morelos), 48% of Atliaca (Guerrero), 35% of Copalillo Guerrero, 28% of Zongolica (Orizaba). *Lg Use:* Speakers are older adults. Speakers also use Spanish.

Nahuatl, Durango (Mexicanero, Durango Aztec, Náhuat de Durango) [nln] 1,000 (1990 census). Southern Durango, Mezquital Municipio, San Pedro de la Jicoras and San Juan de Buenaventura. San Pedro is 30-minute walk from the nearest air strip, one-day trail from nearest highway. *Class:* Uto-Aztecan, Southern Uto-Aztecan, Aztecan, General Aztec, Aztec. *Dialects:* Vocabulary and phonological differences between San Pedro Jicoras and San Agustín Buenaventura. 76% intelligibility of Michoacán Nahuatl (closest). *Lg Use:* Vigorous. Some Tepehuans intermarry with them and speak Nahuatl. All domains. Oral use in elementary education, religion, local commerce. All ages. Positive language attitude. Moderate bilingualism in Spanish. 5% to 10% understand some

Southeastern Tepehuan. Lg Dev: Radio programs. *Other:* 'Mexicanero' is the local name. Valleys, mountain slope. Agriculturalists: maize, squash, beans; animal husbandry: cattle, goats, pigs. Traditional religion, Christian.

Nahuatl, Eastern Huasteca (Eastern Huasteca Aztec, Náhuatl de Hidalgo, Náhuatl de la Huasteca Oriental) [nhe] 410,000 (1991 SIL). Huautla, Hidalgo is the center; also in Puebla and Veracruz. 1,500 villages. *Class:* Uto-Aztecan, Southern Uto-Aztecan, Aztecan, General Aztec, Aztec. *Dialect:* Southeastern Huasteca Nahuatl. 85% intelligibility between Eastern and Western Huasteca Nahuatl. Survey of other dialects needed. Southeastern Huasteca Nahuatl may need separate materials. *Lg Use:* Bilingual level estimates for Spanish: 0 50%, 1 10%, 2 10%, 3 10%, 4 19%, 5 1%. *Lg Dev:* Radio programs. NT: 1984. *Other:* SVO; long words, affixes; nontonal. Mountain mesa. Scrub forest. Sea level to 2,000 meters. Swidden agriculturalists.

Nahuatl, Guerrero (Guerrero Aztec, Náhuatl de Guerrero) [ngu] 150,000 (1998 SIL). Balsas River, Guerrero. *Class:* Uto-Aztecan, Southern Uto-Aztecan, Aztecan, General Aztec, Aztec. *Lg Use:* Bilingual level estimates for Spanish: 0 5%, 1 20%, 2 40%, 3 20%, 4 10%, 5 5%. *Lg Dev:* Videos. Dictionary. NT: 1987. *Other:* SVO; long words, affixes, clitics; nontonal. Mountain mesa. Desert. 600 to 2,200 meters. Peasant agriculturalists. Traditional religion, Christian.

Nahuatl, Highland Puebla (Náhuat de la Sierra de Puebla, Sierra Puebla Náhuatl, Sierra Aztec, Zacapoaxtla Náhuat, Mejicano de Zacapoaxtla) [azz] 125,000 (1983). Northeast Puebla. *Class:* Uto-Aztecan, Southern Uto-Aztecan, Aztecan, General Aztec, Aztec. *Lg Use:* Bilingual level estimates for Spanish: 0 20%, 1 30%, 2 30%, 3 10%, 4 5%, 5 5%. Speakers also use Totonac. *Lg Dev:* NT: 1979. *Other:* VSO, long words, affixes, nontonal. Mountain slope. Tropical forest. 1,000 to 1,500 meters. Pastoralists; peasant agriculturalists.

Nahuatl, Huaxcaleca (Huaxcaleca Aztec, Náhuatl de Chichiquila) [nhq] 7,000 (1990 census). 55 monolinguals. Puebla, towns of Chichiquila and Chilchotla. *Class:* Uto-Aztecan, Southern Uto-Aztecan, Aztecan, General Aztec, Aztec. *Dialects:* 87% intelligibility of Highland Puebla Nahuatl, 85% on Orizaba Nahuatl. *Lg Use:* The population in about 12 municipios no longer speak Nahuatl. 800 speakers are over 50. 2% under 20 speak Nahuatl.

Nahuatl, Isthmus-Cosoleacaque (Náhuatl del Istmo-Cosoleacaque, Cosoleacaque Aztec) [nhk] 5,144 (1990 census). 12 monolinguals. Veracruz, Cosoleacaque, Oteapan, Jáltipan de Morelos, Hidalgotitlán, Soconusco. *Class:* Uto-Aztecan, Southern Uto-Aztecan, Aztecan, General Aztec, Aztec. *Dialects:* 84% intelligibility of Pajapan, 83% of Mecayapan, 46% on Xoteapan. Not intelligible with Pipil of El Salvador. *Lg Use:* Most of the monolinguals are older adults. Speakers also use Spanish.

Nahuatl, Isthmus-Mecayapan (Isthmus Aztec-Mecayapan, Náhuat de Mecayapan) [nhx] 20,000 (1994 SIL). Southern Veracruz, Mecayapan Municipio, Mecayapan and Tatahuicapan towns. *Class:* Uto-Aztecan, Southern Uto-Aztecan, Aztecan, General Aztec, Aztec. *Dialects:* Not intelligible with Pipil of El Salvador. *Lg Use:* All ages. *Lg Dev:* Dictionary. Grammar. Bible portions: 1952.

Nahuatl, Isthmus-Pajapan (Náhuat de Pajapan) [nhp] 7,000 (1990 census). 500 monolinguals. Veracruz, towns of Pajapan, San Juan Volador, Santanón, Sayultepec, Jicacal. *Class:* Uto-Aztecan, Southern Uto-Aztecan, Aztecan, General Aztec, Aztec. *Dialects:* 83% intelligibility of Mecayapan (Isthmus Nahuatl), 94% of Oteapan (Cosoleacaque). *Lg Use:* Some young families use Nahuatl, others are not teaching it to their children. All domains for older speakers. Oral use in early elementary education, local

commerce. All ages. Older adults use it more than others. Low interest in preserving the language. Others have varying fluency in Spanish. A few also speak Popoluca. *Lg Dev:* Bible portions: 1990. *Other:* People leave the area to find better jobs or for trade. Coastal. Agriculturalists.

Nahuatl, Michoacán (Nahual de Michoacán, Michoacan Aztec) [ncl] 3,000 (1990 census). Michoacán near the coast around Pómaro. *Class:* Uto-Aztecan, Southern Uto-Aztecan, Aztecan, General Aztec, Aztec. *Lg Use:* Bilingual level estimates for Spanish: 0 0%, 1 0%, 2 0%, 3 45%, 4 50%, 5 5%. *Lg Dev:* Literacy rate in first language: 5% to 10% (mainly children). Literacy rate in second language: 35%. NT: 1998. *Other:* SVO, VSO; long words, affixes. Mountain slope. Scrub forest. 200 meters. Pastoralists; swidden agriculturalists.

Nahuatl, Morelos (Náhuatl de Cuentepec) [nhm] 15,000 (1990 census). 300 monolinguals. Morelos, towns of Cuentepec, Santa Catarina Tepoztlán, Tetela del Volcán, Hueyapan, Temixco, Xocotitlán, Tepetlapa, Puente de Ixtla. *Class:* Uto-Aztecan, Southern Uto-Aztecan, Aztecan, General Aztec, Aztec. *Dialects:* 72% inherent intelligibility of Cuaohueyalta (Northern Puebla), 69% of Atliaca (Guerrero), 54% of Macuilocatl (Western Huasteca), 40% of Yahualica (Eastern Huasteca), 36% of Pómaro (Michoacán), 34% of Tetelcingo, 27% of Chilac (Southeast Puebla), 19% of Tatóscac (Highland Puebla), 0% of Mecayapan (Isthmus). Dialects in Canoa, Tlaxcala, and northern Puebla need to be compared with this. *Lg Use:* Cuentepec has the most vigorous language use. Only a few children do not speak Nahuatl. Bilingual level estimates for Spanish: 0 0%, 1 5%, 2 10%, 3 45%, 4 30%, 5 10%. *Lg Dev:* There is a bilingual primary school. *Other:* There is a secondary school. SVO; long words, affixes; nontonal. Mountain mesa. Deciduous forest. 1,200 meters. Peasant agriculturalists.

Nahuatl, Northern Oaxaca (Náhuatl del Norte de Oaxaca) [nhy] 9,000 (1990 census). 1,400 monolinguals. Northwestern Oaxaca, near Southeast Puebla Náhuatl, towns of Santa María Teopoxco, San Antonio Nanahuatipan, San Gabriel Casa Blanca, Teotitlán del Camino, San Martín Toxpalan, Ignacio Zaragosa, Apixtepec, El Manzano de Mazatlán, Cosolapa, Tesonapa (one of the last 2 towns is in Veracruz). In Puebla: Coxcatlán. *Class:* Uto-Aztecan, Southern Uto-Aztecan, Aztecan, General Aztec, Aztec. *Dialects:* 80% intelligibility of Orizaba Nahuatl, 76% of Southeast Puebla and Canoa, 75% of North Puebla, 48% of Tatóscac. *Lg Dev:* Bible portions: 1999–2002.

Nahuatl, Northern Puebla (North Puebla Aztec, Náhuatl del Norte de Puebla) [ncj] 60,000 (1990 census). Naupan, northern Puebla. *Class:* Uto-Aztecan, Southern Uto-Aztecan, Aztecan, General Aztec, Aztec. *Lg Use:* Bilingual level estimates for Spanish: 0 20%, 1 30%, 2 30%, 3 15%, 4 5%, 5 0%. *Lg Dev:* Dictionary. NT: 1979. *Other:* SVO; long words, affixes, clitics; nontonal. Mountain slope. Pine forest. 2,000 meters. Swidden, peasant agriculturalists.

Nahuatl, Ometepec (Ometepec Aztec) [nht] 433 (1990 census). Southern Guerrero, Arcelia, Acatepec, Quetzalapa de Azoyú, Rancho de Cuananchinicha, and El Carmen; and some in Oaxaca, Juxtlahuaca District, Cruz Alta and San Vicente Piñas towns; and Putla District, Concepción Guerrero town. *Class:* Uto-Aztecan, Southern Uto-Aztecan, Aztecan, General Aztec, Aztec. *Dialects:* May be 3 languages. *Lg Use:* Speakers also use Spanish.

Nahuatl, Orizaba (Orizaba Aztec, Náhuatl de la Sierra de Zongolica) [nlv] 120,000 (1991 SIL). Veracruz, Orizaba area. *Class:* Uto-Aztecan, Southern Uto-Aztecan, Aztecan, General Aztec, Aztec. *Dialect:* Ixhuatlancillo Nahuatl. 79% intelligibility of closest Nahuatl (Morelos). *Lg Dev:* Bible portions: 1995. *Other:* There are primary schools and 1 secondary. 1,300 meters. Animal husbandry: cattle; agriculturalists: sugarcane; merchants.

Nahuatl, Santa María la Alta (Náhuatl de Santa María la Alta) [nhz] 2,472 (2000 WCD). 9 monolinguals. Puebla, Santa María la Alta, Atenayuca. A pocket northwest of Tehuacán, off the Puebla-Tehuacán highway. *Class:* Uto-Aztecan, Southern Uto-Aztecan, Aztecan, General Aztec, Aztec. *Dialects:* 60% intelligibility of Pómaro (Michoacán), 53% of Huatlatlauca, Puebla; 50% of Zautla (Highland Puebla), Chilac (Southeastern Puebla); 40% of Zongolica (Orizaba); 33% of Mecayapan, Veracruz (Isthmus); 30% of Canoa, Puebla. *Lg Use:* Reported to be bilingual in Spanish.

Nahuatl, Southeastern Puebla (Náhuatl del Sureste de Puebla, Tehuacán Náhuatl) [nhs] 130,000 (1991 SIL). Southeast Puebla, Tehuacán Region, Chilac and San Sebastián Zinacatepec area. *Class:* Uto-Aztecan, Southern Uto-Aztecan, Aztecan, General Aztec, Aztec. *Dialects:* Approximately 60% intelligibility of Morelos Nahuatl. *Lg Use:* Bilingual level estimates for Spanish: 0 30%, 1 20%, 2 20%, 3 20%, 4 10%, 5 0%. *Lg Dev:* Bible portions: 1992–1995. *Other:* Long words, affixes; nontonal. Mountain slope, plains. Desert. Peasant, intensive agriculturalists with irrigation.

Nahuatl, Tabasco (Tabasco Aztec) [nhc] Extinct. State of Tabasco, towns of Cupilco and Tecominoacan. *Class:* Uto-Aztecan, Southern Uto-Aztecan, Aztecan, General Aztec, Aztec.

Nahuatl, Temascaltepec (Temascaltepec Aztec, Almomoloya Náhuatl) [nhv] 311 (1990 census). State of Mexico, towns of San Mateo Almomoloa, Santa Ana, La Comunidad, and Potrero de San José, southwest of Toluca. *Class:* Uto-Aztecan, Southern Uto-Aztecan, Aztecan, General Aztec, Aztec. *Dialects:* 53% intelligibility of Coatepec, Guerrero; 45% of Pómaro, Michoacán; 40% of Santa Catarina, Morelos; 10% of Tlaxpanaloya, Puebla. *Lg Use:* Reported to be bilingual in Spanish.

Nahuatl, Tenango (San Miguel Tenango Náhuatl, Tenango Aztec) [nhi] 1,977 (2000 WCD). North of Puebla City, just south of Zacatlán, Puebla, 8 km on a road which branches to the east. 6 towns: San Miguel Tenango, Yehuala, Cuacuila, Tetelatzingo, Zonotla, Zoquitla. *Class:* Uto-Aztecan, Southern Uto-Aztecan, Aztecan, General Aztec, Aztec. *Dialects:* Close to Southeastern Puebla Nahuatl, but first-language speakers of both discovered many differences over a 2-day period. About 50% to 60% intelligibility of Sierra Nahuatl and Northern Puebla Nahuatl, about 80% to 90% of Southeastern Puebla Nahuatl. *Lg Use:* Children play in Nahuatl. Positive language attitude. Most speakers can apparently speak some Spanish, but are more comfortable in Nahuatl. *Other:* 2,000 meters. Agriculturalists: maize, peas, chilacayotes. Christian.

Nahuatl, Tetelcingo (Tetelcingo Aztec) [nhg] 3,500 (1990 census). State of Morelos, town of Tetelcingo. *Class:* Uto-Aztecan, Southern Uto-Aztecan, Aztecan, General Aztec, Aztec. *Dialects:* Distinct from Morelos Nahuatl. *Lg Use:* Bilingual level estimates for Spanish: 0 1%, 1 5%, 2 30%, 3 24%, 4 30%, 5 10%. *Lg Dev:* Grammar. NT: 1980. *Other:* SVO, VSO, VOS (order of frequency); long words, affixes, clitics; nontonal. Mountain slope, plains. Savannah. 1,500 to 1,800 meters. Agriculturalists.

Nahuatl, Tlalitzlipa [nhj] 108 (1990 census). Near Zacatlán, Puebla, 1 village. *Class:* Uto-Aztecan, Southern Uto-Aztecan, Aztecan, General Aztec, Aztec. *Dialects:* 77% inherent intelligibility of Tlaxpanaloya (North Puebla), 58% of Macuilocatl (Western Huasteca Nahuatl), 41% of Tatóscac (Highland Puebla).

Nahuatl, Tlamacazapa [nuz] 1,548 (1990 census). 12 monolinguals. Tlamacazapa, 1 hour from Taxco on a good road. *Class:* Uto-Aztecan, Southern Uto-Aztecan, Aztecan,

General Aztec, Aztec. *Dialects:* Different from Morelos Nahuatl and Guerrero Nahuatl. 79% inherent intelligibility of Guerrero. *Lg Use:* Some young children are speakers.

Nahuatl, Western Huasteca (Western Huasteca Aztec, Náhuatl de Tamazunchale, Náhuatl de la Huasteca Occidental) [nhw] 400,000 (1991 SIL). Tamazunchale, San Luis Potosí is the center; also in Hidalgo. 1,500 villages. *Class:* Uto-Aztecan, Southern Uto-Aztecan, Aztecan, General Aztec, Aztec. *Dialect:* Western Huasteca Náhuatl. 85% intelligibility between Eastern and Western Huasteca Nahuatl. Separate literature needed for 100,000 speakers of a Central dialect. *Lg Use:* Bilingual level estimates for Spanish: 0 50%, 1 10%, 2 10%, 3 10%, 4 19%, 5 1%. *Lg Dev:* Radio programs. Bible: 2004. *Other:* SVO; long words, affixes; nontonal. Mountain mesa. Scrub forest. Sea level to 2,000 meters. Swidden agriculturalists.

Opata (Endeve) [opt] 15. Population includes 11 in Distrito Federal, 4 in State of Mexico (1993 Instituto Nacional Indigenista). Sonora: Nacori, Bacahora, Suaqui, Sahuaripa, Arivechi, Onavas, Tecoripa is the traditional area. *Class:* Uto-Aztecan, Southern Uto-Aztecan, Sonoran, Cahita. *Other:* The last speakers had been reported to have died about 1930. Nearly extinct.

Otomi, Eastern Highland (Eastern Otomi, Otomí de la Sierra, Yuhu, Otomí de Huehuetla, Otomí del Oriente, Sierra Oriental Otomi) [otm] 20,000 (1990 census). 4,700 monolinguals. Vicinity of Huehuetla and San Bartolo, Hidalgo; Tlachichilco and Ixhuatlán, Veracruz. *Class:* Oto-Manguean, Otopamean, Otomian, Otomi. *Dialects:* 81% intelligibility of Tenango (closest), 50% of Mezquital. *Lg Use:* Bilingual level estimates for Spanish: 0 16%, 1 59%, 2 20%, 3 3%, 4 1%, 5 1%. *Lg Dev:* Literacy rate in first language: 1%. Literacy rate in second language: 40%. Dictionary. NT: 1974–2000. *Other:* VOS; short words, affixes, clitics; tonal. Mountain slope. Semitropical. 555 to 770 meters. Peasant agriculturalists.

Otomi, Estado de México (Hñatho, Otomí del Estado de México, Otomí de San Felipe Santiago, State of Mexico Otomi) [ots] 10,000 (1990 census). 400 monolinguals. State of Mexico. *Class:* Oto-Manguean, Otopamean, Otomian, Otomi. *Dialect:* San Felipe Santiago Otomí. 73% intelligibility of Mezquital Otomi (closest), lower in outlying areas. *Lg Use:* Bilingual level estimates for Spanish: Women: 0 0%, 1 20%, 2 40%, 3 40%, 4 0%, 5 0%; Men: 0 0%, 1 20%, 2 30%, 3 50%, 4 0%, 5 0%. *Lg Dev:* NT: 1975. *Other:* VOS; short words, affixes, clitics; tonal. Mountain mesa. Savannah. 2,500 to 2,600 meters. Peasant agriculturalists: maize. Traditional religion, Christian.

Otomi, Ixtenco (Southeastern Otomí) [otz] 736 (1990 census). 4 monolinguals (1990 census). Ethnic population: 5,356 (1990 census). Tlaxcala, San Juan Bautista Ixtenco. *Class:* Oto-Manguean, Otopamean, Otomian, Otomi. *Dialects:* 41% intelligibility of Estado De México Otomi (closest), 23% of Mezquital, and Eastern Highland Otomi, 22% of Tenango Otomi. *Lg Use:* Speakers are older adults. Speakers also use Spanish.

Otomi, Mezquital (Hñahñu, Otomí del Valle del Mezquital) [ote] 100,000 in Mexico (1990 census). Population includes 100 in North Carolina, USA. Mezquital Valley, Hidalgo. Some in Florida, USA. Also spoken in USA. *Class:* Oto-Manguean, Otopamean, Otomian, Otomi. *Lg Dev:* Dictionary. Grammar. NT: 1970. *Other:* Plains, mountain slope. Desert, semiarid. 1,600 meters. Pastoralists: sheep, goats; swidden agriculturalists: maize. Traditional religion, Christian.

Otomi, Querétaro (Hñohño, Otomí de Querétaro, Western Otomi, Northwestern Otomi) [otq] 33,000 (1990 census). Amealco Municipio: towns of San Ildefonso, Santiago Mexquititlán; Acambay Municipio; Tolimán

Municipio. *Class:* Oto-Manguean, Otopamean, Otomian, Otomi. *Dialects:* 78% intelligibility of Mezquital (closest), lower in outlying areas. *Lg Dev:* NT: 2003. *Other:* Mountain mesa. Semiarid, savannah. 2,000 meters. Pastoralists: sheep, goats, cattle; agriculturalists: maize. Traditional religion, Christian.

Otomi, Temoaya [ott] 37,000 (1990 census). 850 monolinguals. State of Mexico Temoyaya Municipio and 16 barrios, including San Pedro Arriba, San Pedro Abajo, Enthavi, Solalpan, and Jiquipilco el Viejo. *Class:* Oto-Manguean, Otopamean, Otomian, Otomi. *Lg Use:* It is mainly those over 40 years old who have difficulty with Spanish (1999). Bilingual level estimates for Spanish: Women: 0 0%, 1 0%, 2 20%, 3 40%, 4 30%, 5 10%; Men: 0 0%, 1 0%, 2 5%, 3 15%, 4 40%, 5 40%. *Other:* VOS; short words, affixes, clitics; tonal. Mountain slope. Deciduous forest. 2,700 to 2,850 meters. Peasant agriculturalists; laborers in city (men). Christian.

Otomi, Tenango (Otomí de Tenango) [otn] 10,000 (1990 census). San Nicolás, Hidalgo, and Puebla. *Class:* Oto-Manguean, Otopamean, Otomian, Otomi. *Dialects:* 53% intelligibility of Eastern Highland Otomi (closest). *Lg Dev:* NT: 1975.

Otomi, Texcatepec (Northeastern Otomí, Otomí de Texcatepec) [otx] 12,000 (1990 census). 3,000 monolinguals. Northwestern Veracruz, Texcatepec Municipio: Texcatepec, Ayotuxtla, Zontecomatlán Municipio: Hueytepec, Amajac, Tzicatlán. *Class:* Oto-Manguean, Otopamean, Otomian, Otomi. *Dialects:* 70% to 79% intelligibility of Eastern Otomi, 57% of Ixmiquilpan, 44% of Tolimán, 40% of San Felipe, 20% of Ixtenco. *Lg Use:* Speakers have low proficiency in Spanish. *Other:* 1,800 meters. Pastoralists: sheep. Christian, traditional religion.

Otomi, Tilapa [otl] 400 (1990 census). Santiago Tilapa town between Mexico, D. F. and Toluca, State of Mexico. *Class:* Oto-Manguean, Otopamean, Otomian, Otomi. *Lg Use:* Speakers are older adults. Speakers also use Spanish.

Paipai (Akwa'ala) [ppi] 300 (1990 census). Santa Catarina (about 300 people), and some near Valle de la Trinidad in Los Pocitos, Estado Valle de la Trinidad (1 or 2 houses), and Rancho Aguascalientes or La Palmita (2 to 3 families), Ensenada, Baja California Norte, south of the Diegueño. *Class:* Hokan, Esselen-Yuman, Yuman, Pai. *Lg Use:* Speakers are shifting to Spanish. A Kiliwa speaker sample understood Paipai at 87%, but Paipai speakers understood no Kiliwa. *Other:* Mountain slope.

Pame, Central (Pame del Centro, Pame de Santa María Acapulco, Chichimeca) [pbs] 4,350 (1990 census). San Luis Potosí, Santa María Acapulco. *Class:* Oto-Manguean, Otopamean, Pamean. *Lg Use:* Most children still speak Central Pame. Bilingual level estimates for Spanish: 0 10%, 1 70%, 2 15%, 3 5%, 4 0%, 5 0%. *Lg Dev:* Bible portions: 1953–1998. *Other:* SVO; pitch-accent; short words, affixes. Mountain slope, valleys. Desert, forest. 600 to 1,200 meters. Pastoralists; peasant agriculturalists.

Pame, Northern (Pame del Norte) [pmq] 5,616 (2000 WCD). San Luis Potosí, north of Río Verde to the border with Tamaulipas. Includes Alaquines, Morales, Pasito de San Francisco, Las Crucitas, La Palma, Santa Catarina, Tamasopo, Rayón, Cuesta Blanca. Most speakers are in a natural corridor from the base of the Sierra del Mezquital along La Cañada River. *Class:* Oto-Manguean, Otopamean, Pamean. *Dialects:* 10% to 15% intelligibility of Santa María Acapulco; 87% intelligibility of Alaquines by La Palma speakers. *Lg Use:* Speakers have low proficiency in Spanish. *Other:* 2 to 6 years of primary school in the 2 towns. Semiarid. 800 meters. Agriculturalists: banana.

Pame, Southern [pmz] Extinct. Jiliapan. *Class:* Oto-Manguean, Otopamean, Pamean.

Pima Bajo (Nebome, Mountain Pima, Lower Piman) [pia] 1,000 (1989 SIL). Central Sonora-Chihuahua border, scattered. *Class:* Uto-Aztecan, Southern Uto-Aztecan, Sonoran, Tepiman. *Dialects:* Chihuahua Pima Bajo (Lower Piman), Sonora Pima Bajo. Sonora, Pima Bajo and Pima of the USA are close. Lexical similarity 85% with Pima (Tohono O'odham) of USA and Northern Tepehuán. *Lg Use:* Speakers have some proficiency in Spanish. *Lg Dev:* Bible portions: 1994. *Other:* Agriculturalists: maize, lumber mill workers.

Plautdietsch (Low German, Mennonite German) [pdt] 40,000 in Mexico (1996). Chihuahua (Cuauhtemoc, Virginias, Buenos Aires, Capulín), Durango (Nuevo Ideal, Canatlán), Campeche (Chávez, Progreso, Yalnon), Zacatecas (La Honda, La Batea). *Lg Use:* 22% speak Standard German, 5% speak English, 30% speak Spanish, 5% speak Russian as second language. *Lg Dev:* Literacy rate in second language: 60%. *Other:* Intensive agriculturalists; cheese production. Christian. See main entry under Canada.

Popoloca, Coyotepec [pbf] 500 (1990 census). Ethnic population: 7,000. State of Puebla, west of Tehuacán city, east of Ahuatempan, towns of Coyotepec and San Mateo (2 miles from Coyotepec). *Class:* Oto-Manguean, Popolocan, Chocho-Popolocan, Popolocan. *Dialects:* San Vicente Coyotepec Popoloca, San Mateo Zoyamazalco Popoloca. 41% intelligibility of Otlaltepec, 23% of Atzingo, 15% of Tlacoyalco Northern Popoloca. San Mateo may be intelligible with Coyotepec, San Felipe, or may be a separate language. *Lg Use:* Speakers also use Spanish.

Popoloca, Mezontla (Los Reyes Metzontla Popoloca, Southern Popoloca) [pbe] 2,000 (1993 SIL). State of Puebla, 1 town. *Class:* Oto-Manguean, Popolocan, Chocho-Popolocan, Popolocan. *Dialects:* 52% intelligibility of Atzingo Popoloca, 35% of Tlacoyalco (Northern Popoloca), 11% of Otlaltepec. *Lg Dev:* Grammar.

Popoloca, San Felipe Otlaltepec (Popoloca de San Felipe Otlaltepec, Western Popoloca, Popoloca del Poniente) [pow] 3,000 (2000 SIL). 100 monolinguals. Ethnic population: 6,585 (2000 WCD). State of Puebla, 3 towns: San Felipe Otlaltepec (5,000), Santa María Nativitas (500), Huejonapan (500). *Class:* Oto-Manguean, Popolocan, Chocho-Popolocan, Popolocan. *Dialects:* Santa María Nativitas, Huejonapan. *Lg Use:* Parents are not passing it on to children. All domains among adults. Oral use 50% of the time in local administration, commerce, 20% of the time in religious services. All ages. Children speak Spanish to each other. Older people want to use Popoloca, but it has low prestige among younger people. The average level of bilingual proficiency is about 2 + (routine topics) in Spanish. *Lg Dev:* Literacy rate in first language: 1% to 5%. Literacy rate in second language: 25% to 50%. Bible portions: 1955–1980. *Other:* People leave the area for schooling and jobs. SVO; long words, affixes; nontonal. Mountain slope. Desert, deciduous forest. 2,000 meters. Swidden agriculturalists.

Popoloca, San Juan Atzingo (Atzingo Popoloca, Eastern Popoloca, Southern Popoloca, Ngigua, Popoloca del Oriente, Popoloca de San Juan Atzingo) [poe] 5,000 (1991 SIL). San Juan Atzingo, Puebla: 1 town. *Class:* Oto-Manguean, Popolocan, Chocho-Popolocan, Popolocan. *Dialects:* 76% intelligibility of Metzontla Popoloca (closest), 26% of San Felipe Popoloca. *Lg Use:* Vigorous. Some Nahuatl speakers in Chilac speak some Popoloca. Some temporary migration for jobs, but speakers retain the language. All domains. Oral use in local administration, commerce. Oral and written use in elementary and secondary school, religious services. All ages. Strong pride in culture and language. Bilingual level estimates for Spanish: 0 50%, 1 50%, 2 0%, 3 0%, 4 0%, 5 0%. Most women over 50 are functionally monolingual; perhaps 500 people. Most men also speak elementary Spanish. Many women who cannot speak Spanish speak Nahuatl for trading in San Gabriel Chilac. Onyx and sugarcane workers have team leaders who speak Spanish for them. *Lg Dev:* Literacy rate in first language: 20%. Literacy rate in second language: 30%. 1,000 read it, 200 write it. Dictionary. NT: 1982. *Other:* VSO; short words, affixes, clitics; tonal. Mountain slope. Desert. 1,538 meters. Pastoralists: goats; onyx miners; potters; sewing factory workers.

Popoloca, San Luís Temalacayuca (Popoloca de San Luis Temalacayuca) [pps] 4,729 (1994 SIL). San Luís Temalacayuca, Puebla. *Class:* Oto-Manguean, Popolocan, Chocho-Popolocan, Popolocan. *Dialects:* San Luís has 84% intelligibility of San Marcos, 22% of Atzingo, 8% of Otlaltepec. *Lg Use:* Vigorous. All children speak Popoloca. All children know a little Spanish when they enter school. Most speak limited Spanish. *Other:* Kindergarten, primary, and secondary schools. About 25% of the men work part of the year in the D.F. or USA. Mountain mesa. Desert, plains. 1,800 meters. Peasant agriculturalists.

Popoloca, San Marcos Tlalcoyalco (Northern Popoloca, Popoloca de San Marcos Tlalcoyalco) [pls] 5,000 (1993 SIL). San Marcos Tlacoyalco, Puebla. *Class:* Oto-Manguean, Popolocan, Chocho-Popolocan, Popolocan. *Dialects:* San Luis has 90% intelligibility of San Marcos. *Lg Use:* Bilingual level estimates for Spanish: 0 5%, 1 30%, 2 60%, 3 5%, 4 0%, 5 0%. *Lg Dev:* NT: 1983. *Other:* VSO; long words, affixes, clitics; tonal. Mountain mesa. Desert, plains. 2,100 meters. Peasant agriculturalists.

Popoloca, Santa Inés Ahuatempan (Ngigua, Popoloca de Santa Inés Ahuatempan) [pca] 4,000 to 5,000 (2000 SIL). Few monolinguals. State of Puebla, west of Coyotepec and Tehuacán city, 2 towns. *Class:* Oto-Manguean, Popolocan, Chocho-Popolocan, Popolocan. *Dialects:* Ahuatempan Popoloca, Todos Santos Almolonga Popoloca. 75% intelligibility of San Felipe Popoloca (closest). *Lg Use:* All domains among older adults. Popoloca used half the time in local commerce, administration. Most children under 15 speak only Spanish. Negative language attitude. Spanish is the second language. *Lg Dev:* Literacy rate in first language: below 1%. Literacy rate in second language: 55%. 500 can read it, 5 can write it. Bible portions: 1994. *Other:* Many leave area to find jobs. Desert. High altitude. Agriculturalists: maize, black beans, avocados, oranges, lemons, papaya. Traditional religion, Christian.

Popoluca, Highland (Highland Popoluca, Popoluca de la Sierra) [poi] 30,000 (1991 SIL). Soteapan, Veracruz. *Class:* Mixe-Zoque, Zoque, Veracruz Zoque. *Dialects:* Closer to Zoque than to Mixe. *Lg Use:* Bilingual level estimates for Spanish: 0 5%, 1 40%, 2 20%, 3 15%, 4 10%, 5 10%. Some speakers also use Nahuatl. *Lg Dev:* Dictionary. Grammar. NT: 1977–1996. *Other:* VOS, short words, affixes; nontonal. Mountain slope, coastal. Tropical, pine forest. 10 to 600 meters. Swidden agriculturalists.

Popoluca, Oluta [plo] 102 (1990 census). Ethnic population: 10,000 (1990 census). Southeastern Veracruz, Oluta, inland, west of Texistepec. *Class:* Mixe-Zoque, Mixe, Veracruz Mixe. *Lg Use:* Speakers are older adults. Speakers are shifting to Spanish. *Lg Dev:* Dictionary.

Popoluca, Sayula [pos] 4,000 (1990 census). 14 monolinguals. Sayula, Veracruz. *Class:* Mixe-Zoque, Mixe, Veracruz Mixe. *Lg Use:* Bilingual level estimates for Spanish: 0 5%, 1 10%, 2 10%, 3 15%, 4 55%, 5 5%. *Lg Dev:* Dictionary. NT: 1969. *Other:* Some form of whistle speech reported. SOV, VOS; long words, affixes,

clitics; nontonal. Coastal. Tropical. 10 to 600 meters. Peasant agriculturalists.

Popoluca, Texistepec [poq] 427 (1990 census). Ethnic population: 15,779 (1990 census). Southeastern Veracruz, Texistepec, east of Oluta. *Class:* Mixe-Zoque, Zoque, Veracruz Zoque. *Lg Use:* Speakers are shifting to Spanish. Speakers are older adults.

Purepecha (Tarasco, Tarascan, Phorhépecha, Porhé) [tsz] 120,000 (1990 census). Michoacán. *Class:* Tarascan. *Dialects:* Several varieties do not have functional intelligibility of each other. *Lg Dev:* Dictionary. Grammar. NT: 1969.

Purepecha, Western Highland (Western Highland Purépecha, Purépecha del Oeste de las Sierras, Tarasco, Tarascan, Sierra Occidental Purépecha) [pua] Michoacán, western mountains, Zamora on the northern edge, Los Reyes de Salgado on the southwestern corner, Paracho on the eastern edge, including Pamatácuaro. *Class:* Tarascan. *Dialects:* All Purépecha varieties lack functional intelligibility of some other Purépecha: the western mountain variety has 60% intelligibility of Pátzcuaro.

Seri [sei] 800 (2000 SIL). The population was 215 in 1951. Sonora coast, 2 villages. *Class:* Hokan, Salinan-Seri. *Lg Use:* Bilingual level estimates for Spanish: 0 6%, 1 70%, 2 10%, 3 10%, 4 3%, 5 1%. *Lg Dev:* Dictionary. Grammar. NT: 1982. *Other:* SOV; long words, affixes, clitics; nontonal. Coastal. Desert. Sea level. Fishermen; hunter-gatherers (traditionally); craftsmen (ironwood carvings, basketry, necklaces).

Spanish (Español, Castellano) [spa] 86,211,000 in Mexico (1995). *Lg Use:* National language. *Other:* Some form of whistle speech reported. See main entry under Spain.

Tacanec (Tacaneco, Tacana Mam, Mame) [mtz] 1,200 in Mexico (1990 census). Buenos Aires, hills above Motozintla, and Mazapa, eastern Chiapas. *Lg Use:* Speakers are adults. Speakers are highly bilingual in Spanish in Mexico. *Other:* Widespread seasonal migration to the Pacific coast for labor. See main entry under Guatemala.

Tarahumara, Central (Tarahumara del Centro, Samachique Tarahumara) [tar] 55,000 (2000 SIL). 10,000 are monolingual. Southwestern Chihuahua. Most live west and south of Chihuahua, from Cuautemoc, southwest to Creel, down the River Urique, east up the Sinforosa Canyon, southeast to Chinantu, north to Balleza. Many have migrated to Chihuahua City for jobs. *Class:* Uto-Aztecan, Southern Uto-Aztecan, Sonoran, Tarahumaran, Tarahumara. *Lg Use:* Parents pass it on to children in the rural areas. Some older Spanish speakers who live there speak Tarahumara for work or trade. All domains. Use in schools in rural areas, local use in administration, oral use in traditional religion, local commerce. All ages. Positive language attitude. 45,000 also use some Spanish. *Lg Dev:* Literacy rate in first language: 1%. Literacy rate in second language: 20%. 5,000 can read, 1,000 can write it. Radio programs. NT: 1972. *Other:* Mountain slope. Pine and oak forests, poor soil. 2,300 meters. Agriculturalists. Traditional religion, Christian.

Tarahumara, Lowland (Western Tarahumara, Tarahumara del Poniente, Ralámuli de la Tarahumara Baja, Rocoroibo, Baja Tarahumara) [tac] 15,000 (1990 census). Chihuahua. *Class:* Uto-Aztecan, Southern Uto-Aztecan, Sonoran, Tarahumaran, Tarahumara. *Dialects:* Closest to Tai Dam. *Lg Use:* Bilingual level estimates for Spanish: 0 5%, 1 15%, 2 30%, 3 30%, 4 15%, 5 5%. *Lg Dev:* Bible portions: 1975–1985. *Other:* SOV; long words, affixes; nontonal. Mountain slope. Pine forest. 600 to 3,000 meters. Seminomadic pastoralists; swidden or peasant agriculturalists.

Tarahumara, Northern (Tarahumara del Norte, Ariseachi Tarahumara) [thh] 300 (1993 SIL). Ethnic

population: 1,500 (1993 SIL). Chihuahua, towns of Santa
Rosa Ariseachi, Agua Caliente Ariseachi, Bilaguchi,
Tomochi, La Nopalera. *Class:* Uto-Aztecan, Southern
Uto-Aztecan, Sonoran, Tarahumaran, Tarahumara.
Dialects: 45% intelligibility of Central Tarahumara, 25%
of Tarahumara Baja. *Lg Use:* May be extinct. Speakers
are older adults. Speakers also use Spanish. *Other:*
Mountain slope. Agriculturalists: maize, beans, squash,
potatoes; pastoralists: goats, sheep, cattle; hunters.
Tarahumara, Southeastern (Tarahumara del Sureste,
Tarahumara de Chinatú) [tcu] Chinatú, Chihuahua. *Class:*
Uto-Aztecan, Southern Uto-Aztecan, Sonoran,
Tarahumaran, Tarahumara. *Dialect:* Chinatú Tarahumara.
Tarahumara, Southwestern (Tarahumara del
Suroeste, Tubare) [twr] 100 (1983 SIL). Chihuahua, town
of Tubare. *Class:* Uto-Aztecan, Southern Uto-Aztecan,
Sonoran, Tarahumaran, Tarahumara. *Lg Use:* Speakers
also use Tarahumara or Spanish. *Other:* May be the
original town of the extinct Tubar language. Nontonal.
Mountain slope. Scrub forest. 350 to 1,600 meters. Hunter-
gatherers; agriculturalists.
Tectitec (Teco, Tectitán Mame) [ttc] 1,000 in Mexico.
Amatenango de la Frontera and Mazapa de Madero,
Chiapas. *Lg Use:* Speakers are older adults. The Mexican
group is highly bilingual in Spanish, but not the Guatemalan
group. See main entry under Guatemala (Tektiteko).
Tepecano [tep] Extinct. Northwestern Jalisco near Bolaños.
Class: Uto-Aztecan, Southern Uto-Aztecan, Sonoran,
Tepiman, Southern Tepehuan. *Lg Use:* Extinct before 1972.
Tepehua, Huehuetla (Tepehua de Hidalgo, Tepehua de
Huehuetla) [tee] 3,000 (1982 SIL). Northeastern Hidalgo,
Huehuetla, and half the town of Mecapalapa in Puebla.
Class: Totonacan, Tepehua. *Dialects:* 70% intelligibility
of Pisa Flores (closest). *Lg Use:* Bilingual level estimates
for Spanish: 0 10%, 1 37%, 2 25%, 3 10%, 4 10%, 5 8%.
Lg Dev: NT: 1976. *Other:* They use a whistle speech (G.
Cowan 1952, 1972), which distinguishes consonants and
vowels of the spoken language. SVO; long words, affixes;
nontonal. Mountain slope. Tropical. 300 meters. Swidden,
peasant agriculturalists.
Tepehua, Pisaflores [tpp] 4,000 (1990 census).
Veracruz, towns of Pisaflores, Ixhuatlán de Madero, and
one other town. Not in Puebla. *Class:* Totonacan, Tepehua.
Dialects: 59% intelligibility of Huehuetla (closest), 40% or
less of Tlachichilco. *Lg Use:* Speakers have low proficiency
in Spanish. *Lg Dev:* Bible portions: 1998.
Tepehua, Tlachichilco [tpt] 3,000 (1990 SIL).
Tlachichilco, Veracruz. *Class:* Totonacan, Tepehua.
Dialects: 37% intelligibility of Pisa Flores (closest).
Lg Use: Bilingual level estimates for Spanish: 0 5%, 1
20%, 2 50%, 3 20%, 4 4%, 5 1%. Some speakers also use
Otomi or Nahuatl. *Lg Dev:* Literacy rate in first language:
2%. Literacy rate in second language: 10%. NT: 2003.
Other: SVO; long words, affixes, clitics; nontonal.
Mountain slope. Tropical. 500 to 900 meters. Swidden,
peasant agriculturalists.
Tepehuan, Northern (Tepehuán del Norte) [ntp] 8,000
(1990 census). Southern Chihuahua, Baborigame area.
Class: Uto-Aztecan, Southern Uto-Aztecan, Sonoran,
Tepiman. *Dialects:* Related to Pima Bajo, Tohono
O'odham, Southern Tepehuán. *Lg Use:* Bilingual level
estimates for Spanish: 0 15%, 1 15%, 2 20%, 3 35%, 4
10%, 5 5%. Some speakers also use Tarahumara. *Lg Dev:*
Literacy rate in first language: 25%. Literacy rate in
second language: 35%. Dictionary. NT: 1982. *Other:* VSO;
long words, affixes, clitics; tonal. Mountain mesa,
mountain slope. Tropical, deciduous, pine forest. 700 to
4,000 meters. Pastoralists.
Tepehuan, Southeastern (Tepehuán del Sureste,
Tepehuano) [stp] 9,937 (2000 WCD). Southeastern
Durango, Mezquital Municipio. Santa María Ocotán is the

cultural and religious center. *Class:* Uto-Aztecan,
Southern Uto-Aztecan, Sonoran, Tepiman, Southern
Tepehuan. *Dialects:* 78% intelligibility of Southwestern
Tepehuán. *Lg Use:* Vigorous. Speakers of Durango
Nahuatl who marry Tepehuan speakers learn it. Their
children usually speak both languages. All domains. Used
in the first 2 grades of elementary education. All ages.
Positive language attitude. Bilingual level estimates for
Spanish: 0 50%, 1 30%, 2 15%, 3 4%, 4 1%, 5 0%. Very
few speak anything other than Tepehuan and Spanish.
Lg Dev: Literacy rate in first language: 5% to 7%.
Literacy rate in second language: 25%. 500 to 1,000 can
read and write it. Roman script. Videos. Bible portions:
1991–2003. *Other:* They go to the Pacific coast for
temporary labor in the spring. VSO, VOS; long words,
affixes, clitics; nontonal. Mountain slope. Deciduous, pine
forest. 1,500 to 3,000 meters. Pastoralists; peasant
agriculturalists. Christian, traditional religion.
Tepehuan, Southwestern (Tepehuán del Suroeste)
[tla] 8,187 (2000 WCD). Southwestern Durango, Lajas,
Taxicaringa, Teneraca. *Class:* Uto-Aztecan, Southern
Uto-Aztecan, Sonoran, Tepiman, Southern Tepehuan.
Dialects: 55% intelligibility of Southeastern Tepehuán.
Lg Use: Speakers have low proficiency in Spanish. *Other:*
Swidden agriculturalists: maize, beans, squash;
pastoralists. Traditional religion.
Tlapanec, Acatepec (Western Tlapanec, Me'pa,
Me'phaa, Me'pa Wì'ìn) [tpx] 33,000 (1994 SIL). 10,000
monolinguals. Acatepec, Guerrero, Zapotitlán Tablas
Municipio: Huitzapula, Ayotoxtla, Excalerilla,
Huiztlatzala; Acatepec Municipio: Acatepec, Apetzuca,
Tenamazapa, Barranca Pobre, Mezcalapa, Metlapilapa,
Tres Cruces, El Salto, Zochitepec, Caxitepec; Platanillo
municipio: Nanzintla, Teocuitlapa. *Class:* Subtiaba-
Tlapanec. *Dialects:* Acatepec, Zapotitlán Tablas,
Platanillo. 83% intelligibility of Malinaltepec, 79% of
Tlacoapa. *Lg Use:* Many bilingual school teachers from
Malinaltepec. *Other:* Primary schools in most villages,
secondary schools in major centers. Mountain slope. 1,600
to 2,000 meters. Swidden agriculturalists.
Tlapanec, Azoyú (Tlapaneco de Azoyú, Me'phaa,
Tsíndíí) [tpc] 682. No monolinguals. Ethnic population:
17,000 in the Municipio. East and a little south of
Chilpancingo, Guerrero, Azoyú, Maxnadi, Toxnene,
Zapotitlán del Puente, San Isidro del Puente, El Carrizo.
Class: Subtiaba-Tlapanec. *Dialects:* 50% intelligible of
Malinaltepec. *Lg Use:* Speakers are older adults. Speakers
also use Spanish.
Tlapanec, Malinaltepec (Me'phaa, Mi'pha, Eastern
Tlapanec, Tlapaneco de Malinaltepec, Mañuwîîn) [tcf]
33,000 (1994 SIL). 6,000 monolinguals (1994 SIL). East
and a little south of Chilpancingo, Guerrero. *Class:*
Subtiaba-Tlapanec. *Dialects:* Malinaltepec (Huizapula),
Huizapula-Zapotitlán Tablas (Águàá-Xìrágáá),
Zilacayotitlán (Tsírà'khàmájíín). Malinaltepec speakers
have 50% intelligibility of Tlacoapa. Speakers define 8
varieties of Tlapanec. Linguistically closest to Subtiaba of
Nicaragua (extinct). It may be distantly related to Tol of
Honduras. *Lg Dev:* Radio programs. Grammar. Bible
portions: 1994.
Tlapanec, Tlacoapa (Mínguíín, Tlapaneco de Tlacoapa)
[tpl] 3,461 (2000 WCD). East and a little south of
Chilpancingo, Guerrero. *Class:* Subtiaba-Tlapanec.
Dialects: Malinaltepec speakers have 50% intelligibility of
Tlacoapa. *Lg Use:* Speakers recognize Tlacoapa as
different from Malinaltepec. Tlacoapa Tlapanec speakers
can understand Malinaltepec because of learning. *Lg Dev:*
NT: 1975.
Tojolabal (Chañabal, Comiteco) [toj] 36,000 (1990
census). 7,700 monolinguals. Ethnic population: 36,000.
Chiapas, Margaritas, and Altamirano. *Class:* Mayan,

Kanjobalan-Chujean, Chujean. *Lg Use:* All domains. Used in religious services. Spanish is used as second language. *Lg Dev:* NT: 1972–1994. *Other:* Mountain slope. Tropical forest. Agriculturalists: maize, coffee; truck drivers. Christian.

Totonac, Coyutla (Totonaco de Coyutla) [toc] 48,062 (2000 WCD). Speakers of all Totonac languages: 196,003 (1980 census). Puebla, foot of the mountains north of the 'Sierra Totonaca' and the Olintla River. *Class:* Totonacan, Totonac. *Dialect:* Cerro Grande Totonac. Closest to Highland Totonac with many similarities to Papantla. *Lg Dev:* NT: 1987.

Totonac, Filomena Mata-Coahuitlán (Totonaco de Filomena Mata-Coahuitlán, Santo Domingo Totonac) [tlp] 15,108 (2000 WCD). Veracruz, highlands, in the middle of the main highlands dialect. *Class:* Totonacan, Totonac. *Dialects:* 93% intelligibility of speakers in Nonacatlán. Linguistically between Highland and Northern Totonac. *Lg Use:* Speakers also use Coyutla Totonac.

Totonac, Highland (Totonaco de la Sierra, Sierra Totonac) [tos] 120,000 (1982 SIL). Zacatlán, Puebla area, and Veracruz. *Class:* Totonacan, Totonac. *Lg Use:* Bilingual level estimates for Spanish: 0 10%, 1 50%, 2 34%, 3 10%, 4 5%, 5 1%. Some speakers also use Nahuatl. *Lg Dev:* Dictionary. NT: 1959–2000. *Other:* VSO; long words, affixes, clitics; nontonal. Mountain slope, interfluvial. Tropical. 300 to 2,500 meters. Peasant agriculturalists.

Totonac, Ozumatlán (Totonaco de Ozumatlán) [tqt] 4,000 (1990 census). Puebla, Ozumatlán, Tepetzintla, Tlapehuala, San Agustín. *Class:* Totonacan, Totonac. *Dialects:* 79% intelligibility of Highland Totonac, 75% of Northern Totonac, 67% of Zihuateutla, Puebla, 43% of Papantla. *Lg Use:* Speakers are not bilingual in Spanish. *Other:* 1,700 meters. Agriculturalists: maize, squash; animal husbandry: poultry, pigs.

Totonac, Papantla (Lowland Totonaca, Totonaco de Papantla) [top] 80,000 (1982 SIL). Veracruz. *Class:* Totonacan, Totonac. *Dialects:* 40% intelligibility of Highland Totonac (closest). *Lg Use:* Bilingual level estimates for Spanish: 0 5%, 1 10%, 2 50%, 3 15%, 4 10%, 5 10%. *Lg Dev:* Dictionary. NT: 1979. *Other:* VSO; long words, affixes, clitics; nontonal. Mountain slope, coastal, interfluvial. Savannah, tropical. Sea level to 300 meters. Peasant agriculturalists. Traditional religion, Christian.

Totonac, Patla-Chicontla (Totonaco de Patla y Chicontla) [tot] 6,000 (1990 census). 20% to 30% are monolingual. Northeastern Puebla, Patla, Chicontla, Tecpatlán, and 2 other villages. *Class:* Totonacan, Totonac. *Dialects:* It is difficult for speakers to understand Northern Totonac materials. *Lg Use:* Moderate use. Not all parents pass it on to children. Oral use in local administration, commerce, some in religion. Older adults use it more often, adults use both, children use more Spanish than Totonac. Speakers do not depreciate Totonac. 70% to 80% use Spanish as second language. A few may also speak Nahuatl. Education is all in Spanish. *Lg Dev:* Literacy rate in first language: 5%. Literacy rate in second language: 30%. NT: 1999. *Other:* They have electricity, TV, telephone. Young people must leave to find jobs. Mountain valley, mountain slope. Just above sea level to 600 meters. Agriculturalists: coffee.

Totonac, Xicotepec de Juárez (Northern Totonac, Totonaco de Villa Juárez) [too] 3,000 (2000 SIL). 500 monolinguals. Ethnic population: 13,733 (2000 WCD). Northeastern Puebla, Xicotepec de Juárez, and Veracruz; 30 towns. *Class:* Totonacan, Totonac. *Dialect:* Zihuateutla Totonac. 87% intelligibility of Ozumatlán (closest). *Lg Use:* Older adults use Totonac more than Spanish. Others use Spanish more than Totonac. Children not learning it. Negative language attitude. Bilingual level

estimates for Spanish: 0 3%, 1 7%, 2 35%, 3 40%, 4 10%, 5 5%. Possibly 200 can also speak some Tepehua, Nahuatl, Otomi. *Lg Dev:* Literacy rate in first language: 20%. Literacy rate in second language: 60%. NT: 1978. *Other:* They have electricity, TV. Young people must leave area for jobs. SVO; long words, affixes, clitics; nontonal. Mountain slope. Tropical. 215 to 1,230 meters. Peasant agriculturalists: coffee.

Totonac, Yecuatla [tlc] 500 (1994 SIL). Near southern coast, Veracruz, towns of Yecuatla (293 speakers out of 11,541 population) and Misantla (126 speakers out of 50,000 population). *Class:* Totonacan, Totonac. *Lg Use:* Speakers are older adults. Speakers also use Spanish.

Triqui, Chicahuaxtla (Triqui de San Andrés Chicahuaxtla, Chicahuaxtla Trique) [trs] 6,000 (1982). Tlaxiaco area, Oaxaca. *Class:* Oto-Manguean, Mixtecan, Trique. *Dialect:* Laguna. 74% intelligibility of Copala. Lexical similarity 100% with Laguna, 87% with Itunyoso, 78% with Sabana. *Lg Use:* Bilingual level estimates for Spanish: 0 15%, 1 40%, 2 20%, 3 14%, 4 10%, 5 1%. *Lg Dev:* Dictionary. Grammar. NT: 1968. *Other:* VSO; short words, affixes, clitics; tonal. Mountain slope. Scrub forest. 1,200 to 2,500 meters. Peasant agriculturalists.

Triqui, Copala (Triqui de San Juan Copala, Copala Trique) [trc] 15,000 (1990 census). Oaxaca, San Juan Copala, San Quintín valley, Baja California. *Class:* Oto-Manguean, Mixtecan, Trique. *Dialects:* 56% intelligibility of Chicahuaxtla. *Lg Use:* Bilingual level estimates for Spanish: 0 40%, 1 30%, 2 15%, 3 10%, 4 5%, 5 0%. *Lg Dev:* Literacy rate in first language: 1%. Literacy rate in second language: 20%. Grammar. NT: 1988. *Other:* VSO; short words, affixes, clitics; tonal. Mountain slope. Pine forest. 1,000 to 2,200 meters. Swidden agriculturalists.

Triqui, San Martín Itunyoso (Triqui de San Martín Itunyoso, San Martín Itunyoso Trique) [trq] 2,000 (1983). Oaxaca. *Class:* Oto-Manguean, Mixtecan, Trique. *Dialects:* Lexical similarity 87% with Laguna, Chicahuaxtla; 84% with Sabana, San Miguel. *Lg Use:* Bilingual level estimates for Spanish: 0 50%, 1 40%, 2 4%, 3 3%, 4 2%, 5 1%. *Lg Dev:* NT: 1996. *Other:* VSO; short words, affixes; tonal. Mountain slope. Scrub forest. Sedentary pastoralists; peasant agriculturalists.

Tubar (Tubare) [tbu] Extinct. Chihuahua, where the Río San Ignacio (Verde) and Río Urique meet in the southwest near the Sinaloa and Sonora borders. *Class:* Uto-Aztecan, Southern Uto-Aztecan, Sonoran, Tubar. *Other:* There may have been as many as 100 in 1970.

Tzeltal, Bachajón (Lowland Tzeltal, Tzeltal de Ocosingo) [tzb] 100,000 (1993 SIL). 50,000 are monolingual. Speakers of all Tzeltal varieties: 215,145 (1980 census). East central Chiapas, Chilon and Ocosingo municipalities. *Class:* Mayan, Cholan-Tzeltalan, Tzeltalan. *Dialect:* Amatenango del Valle. *Lg Use:* Vigorous. Some families now use Spanish. Some Ch'ol in the northern border area and lowland have learned Tzeltal. All domains. Minimal use in government schools. Oral use in local commerce. Oral and written use in religion. All ages. Spanish use increasing among young people. Positive language attitude. 50,000 use Spanish as second language, 500 also speak some Ch'ol. *Lg Dev:* 50,000 can read it, 40,000 can write it. Radio programs. Dictionary. NT: 1964. *Other:* Hills, lowland. Tropical forest. 150 to 1,200 meters. Agriculturalists: maize, coffee; animal husbandry: cattle.

Tzeltal, Oxchuc (Highland Tzeltal, Tenejapa, Chanal, Cancuc, Tenango) [tzh] 90,000 (2000 S. Hoffman REF). 50,000 are monolingual. East central Chiapas, Oxchuc area. *Class:* Mayan, Cholan-Tzeltalan, Tzeltalan. *Dialects:* Chanal Cancuc, Tenango. *Lg Use:* Vigorous. Some Tzotzil speakers also speak Tzeltal. All domains. Oral use in administration, commerce, some oral and written use in education, religion. All ages. Young people are increasing use of Spanish. Positive language attitude. 40,000 use Spanish as second language. 100 can also speak Tojolabal. *Lg Dev:* 50,000 can read it, 40,000 can write it. Radio programs. TV. Dictionary. Bible: 2002. *Other:* VOS. Hills. 300 to 2,000 meters. Agriculturalists: maize, coffee. Christian.

Tzotzil, Chamula (Chamula) [tzc] 130,000 (1990 census). Speakers of all Tzotzil languages: 265,000 (1990 census). West central Chiapas, San Juan Chamula, Huitiupan, Simojovel, San Juan del Bosque, San Cristóbal Las Casas, Bochil, Pueblo Nuevo Solistahuacan, Ocozocoautla, Ixtapa (Nibak), Jitotol, Teopisca, Amatan, Ishuatan. *Class:* Mayan, Cholan-Tzeltalan, Tzeltalan. *Lg Dev:* Bible: 2001.

Tzotzil, Chenalhó (Chenaló) [tze] 35,000 (1990 census). Chenalhó Region, Chiapas. *Class:* Mayan, Cholan-Tzeltalan, Tzeltalan. *Dialects:* San Pedro Chenalhó, San Pablo Chalchihuitan, Santa Catarina Pantelho, San Miguel Mitontic. Partially intelligible with San Andrés Larrainzar Chamula. *Lg Use:* Bilingual level estimates for Spanish: 0 95%, 1 1%, 2 1%, 3 2%, 4 .5%, 5 0%. *Lg Dev:* Bible: 1997. *Other:* SVO or VOS; short and long words, affixes; nontonal. Mountain slope. Scrub forest. Swidden agriculturalists.

Tzotzil, Huixtán (Huixteco, Tzotzil de Huixtán) [tzu] 20,000 (1990 census). Huixtán Region, Chiapas. *Class:* Mayan, Cholan-Tzeltalan, Tzeltalan. *Dialects:* Huixtán, Angel Albino Corzo, La Concordia, Villa Corzo. *Lg Use:* Bilingual level estimates for Spanish: 0 98%, 1 .5%, 2 .5%, 3 .5%, 4 .3%, 5 .2%. *Lg Dev:* NT: 1975–1995. *Other:* SVO, VOS; short words, affixes; nontonal. Mountain slope. Pine forest. 2,185 meters. Sedentary pastoralists; swidden agriculturalists.

Tzotzil, San Andrés Larrainzar (Tzotzil de San Andrés Larrainzar) [tzs] 50,000 (1990 census). West central Chiapas. *Class:* Mayan, Cholan-Tzeltalan, Tzeltalan. *Lg Dev:* Dictionary. NT: 1983. *Other:* Mountain slope, plains. Pine forest. 1,500 to 3,000 meters. Swidden agriculturalists.

Tzotzil, Venustiano Carranza (San Bartolomé Venustiano Carranza Tzotzil) [tzo] 4,226 (1990 census). 58 monolinguals. Ethnic population: 60,000 (1990 census). Central Chiapas, Venustiano Carranza Municipio, towns of Venustiano Carranza, El Puerto, and El Paraiso de Grijalva. *Class:* Mayan, Cholan-Tzeltalan, Tzeltalan. *Dialects:* 66% intelligibility of Chenalhó Tzotzil, 65% of Zinacantán, 57% of Chamula, 56% of Huixtán. *Lg Use:* Spanish proficiency is low. *Other:* Primary schools and a secondary school. 450 meters. Agriculturalists: maize, beans; fishermen.

Tzotzil, Zinacantán (Zinacanteco Tzotzil) [tzz] 25,000 (1990 census). West central Chiapas. *Class:* Mayan, Cholan-Tzeltalan, Tzeltalan. *Lg Use:* Bilingual level estimates for Spanish: 0 94%, 1 3%, 2 2%, 3 1%, 4 0%, 5 0%. *Lg Dev:* NT: 1987. *Other:* SVO or VOS; short and long words, affixes; nontonal. Mountain slope. Scrub forest. Pastoralists; swidden agriculturalists.

Yaqui [yaq] 16,000 in Mexico (1993 SIL). Population total all countries: 16,406. Sonora. Also spoken in USA. *Class:* Uto-Aztecan, Southern Uto-Aztecan, Sonoran, Cahita. *Dialects:* Partially intelligible with Mayo. *Lg Use:* Bilingual level estimates for Spanish: 0 0%, 1 0%, 2 1%, 3 55%, 4 40%, 5 4%. Some speakers also use English. *Lg Dev:* Literacy rate in first language: 1%. Literacy rate in second language: 5% to 10%. Grammar. NT: 1977–2003. *Other:* SOV; long words, affixes, clitics; tonal. Coastal, riverine. Desert, gallery forest. Sea level to 100 meters. Pastoralists; hunters; fishermen; agriculturalists.

Yucatec Maya Sign Language (Nohya Sign Language) [msd] 16 deaf people out of a village of 500 in the primary location (1999 H. Smith). All use sign (1989 Sacks), including hearing people in the village. Concentrated population in south central Yucatán and in smaller groups in the same region, and a sizeable concentration in northern Quintana Roo (1999 H. Smith). Chican, formerly called 'Nohya', Yucatán. An isolated village plus other villages (at least 2 in Oxkutzcab, 4 in Xyatil, 1 in Carillo Puerto) throughout a wide portion of the lowland Mayan Region. Kinil is also mentioned (1997 H. Smith). *Class:* Deaf sign language. *Dialects:* Dialects of Yucatán and Quintana Roo probably differ, but users have no contact with each other. There is a report of a person in Guatemala who uses related signs. Not intelligible with Mexican Sign Language used elsewhere in Mexico, or other sign languages. *Lg Use:* 400 to 500 who use it as a second or third language (1999 H. Smith). 3 years old to 70 years old (1999 H. Smith). 13 adults and 3 children under 5 (1997 H. Smith), plus all hearing people (1989 Sacks). 100% monolingual. *Lg Dev:* Literacy rate in second language: 0%. *Other:* Congenital deafness. It is of some antiquity. Lowland.

Zapotec, Aloápam (Zapoteco de Aloápam) [zaq] 2,100 (2004). Northern Oaxaca, San Miguel Aloápam, San Isidro Aloápam. *Class:* Oto-Manguean, Zapotecan, Zapotec. *Dialects:* Distinct from Teococuilco Zapotec. *Lg Dev:* Bible portions: 1996–2001. *Other:* VSO; affixes, clitics. Pine forest. Pastoralists; peasant agriculturalists.

Zapotec, Amatlán (Zapoteco del Noreste de Miahuatlán, Zapoteco de San Cristóbal Amatlán, Dizhe) [zpo] 6,000 (2000 SIL). 30% are monolingual. Southern Oaxaca, east of Miahuatlán, 3 towns. *Class:* Oto-Manguean, Zapotecan, Zapotec. *Dialects:* Closest to Loxicha. *Lg Use:* Vigorous. A few Spanish speakers who live there can speak it. All domains. Oral use in local administration, commerce, oral literature. Some oral and written use in religious services. Written use in stories. All ages. Fluency in Spanish has increased, but people still prefer Zapotec. Bilingual level estimates for Spanish: 0 60%, 1 20%, 2 15%, 3 4%, 4 1%, 5 0%. A few can also speak other forms of Zapotec. *Lg Dev:* Literacy rate in first language: 0.08%. Literacy rate in second language: 35%. 500 can read and write it. NT: 2002. *Other:* Speakers leave the area to find work. Some return. VSO; short words; tonal. Mountain slope. Gallery forest. 1,690 meters. Pastoralists; peasant agriculturalists.

Zapotec, Asunción Mixtepec (North Central Zimatlan Zapotec, Zapoteco de Asunción Mixtepec) [zoo] 100 (1990 census). Ethnic population: 2,476 (1990 census). Southwest of Oaxaca City in central Oaxaca, Asunción Mixtepec and another town. *Class:* Oto-Manguean, Zapotecan, Zapotec. *Dialects:* 22% intelligibility of Ayoquesco (closest), and 3% of San Pedro el Alto. *Lg Use:* Speakers also use Spanish. *Other:* Nearly extinct.

Zapotec, Ayoquesco (Western Ejutla Zapotec, Zapoteco de Santa María Ayoquesco) [zaf] 876 (1990 census). 9 monolinguals. Oaxaca, Santa María Ayoquesco, Santa Cruz Nexila, San Andrés Zabache, and San Martín Lachila. *Class:* Oto-Manguean, Zapotecan, Zapotec. *Dialects:* Closest to Ocotlán Zapotec (23% intelligibility). *Lg Use:* Most vigorous in Nexila where 52% of the population speak Zapotec. All ages in Santa Cruz Nexila. Positive language attitude. Speakers also use Spanish.

Zapotec, Cajonos (Zapoteco de San Pedro Cajonos, Southern Villa Alta Zapotec) [zad] 5,000 in Mexico (1993 SIL). Northern Oaxaca, towns of San Pedro Cajonos, San Francisco Cajonos, San Mateo Cajonos, San Miguel Cajonos, San Pablo Yaganiza, Xagacía. Also spoken in USA. *Class:* Oto-Manguean, Zapotecan, Zapotec. *Dialects:* Cajonos Zapotec, Yaganiza-Xagacía Zapotec. Yaganiza and Xagacía are similar. Major differences between those two towns and the other four towns; adaptation of literature will probably be needed. 73% intelligibility of San Pedro Cajonos with Zoogocho (closest other Zapotec). *Lg Use:* Bilingual level estimates for Spanish: 0 10%, 1 20%, 2 20%, 3 30%, 4 10%, 5 10%. Many nearly monolingual speakers in Yaganiza. *Lg Dev:* The school is bilingual. Dictionary. Bible portions: 1982–2002. *Other:* VSO; long words, affixes, clitics; tonal. Mountain slope. Deciduous, pine forests. 1,800 meters. Agriculturalists; craftsmen; merchants.

Zapotec, Chichicapan (Zapoteco de San Baltazar Chichicapan, Eastern Ocotlán Zapotec) [zpv] 4,000 (1993 SIL). Central Oaxaca. *Class:* Oto-Manguean, Zapotecan, Zapotec. *Dialects:* 59% intelligibility of Ocotlán Zapotec (closest). *Lg Use:* Monolinguals are mainly women and older people. Bilingual level estimates for Spanish: 0 30%, 1 5%, 2 60%, 3 4%, 4 1%, 5 0%. *Lg Dev:* Literacy rate in first language: below 5%. Literacy rate in second language: 30% to 50%. NT: 1990. *Other:* VSO; short words, affixes, clitics; tonal. Mountain slope. Desert, scrub, gallery forest. 1,666 to 3,030 meters. Peasant agriculturalists; pastoralists.

Zapotec, Choapan (Zapoteco de Choapan) [zpc] 24,000 (1991 SIL). North central Oaxaca and Veracruz, including Comaltepec. *Class:* Oto-Manguean, Zapotecan, Zapotec. *Dialects:* 60% intelligibility of Zoogocho (closest). *Lg Use:* Bilingual level estimates for Spanish: 0 10%, 1 25%, 2 30%, 3 20%, 4 12%, 5 3%. *Lg Dev:* Dictionary. Grammar. NT: 1986. *Other:* VSO; short words, affixes, clitics; tonal. Mountain slope. Tropical. 840 meters. Swidden agriculturalists.

Zapotec, Coatecas Altas (Zapoteco de San Juan Coatecas Altas) [zca] 5,000 (1993 SIL). 100 monolinguals. Ejutla, Oaxaca. *Class:* Oto-Manguean, Zapotecan, Zapotec. *Dialects:* Closest to San Gregorio Ozolotepec (83% intelligibility) and Miahuatlán (Cuitla). *Lg Dev:* Literacy rate in first language: below 1%. Literacy rate in second language: 20% to 30%.

Zapotec, Coatlán (Western Miahuatlán Zapotec, Zapoteco de Santa María Coatlán, San Miguel Zapotec) [zps] 500 (1992 SIL). Southern Oaxaca near Chatino Region, about 7 towns, but mainly in Santo Domingo Coatlán. *Class:* Oto-Manguean, Zapotecan, Zapotec. *Dialects:* 54% intelligibility of Loxicha (closest), 51% of San Gregorio Ozolotepec, 44% of Cuixtla, 29% of Logueche, 16% of San Juan Mixtepec, 1% of Santa Catalina Quierí. *Lg Use:* Speakers are reported to be bilingual in Spanish.

Zapotec, El Alto (South Central Zimatlan Zapotec, Zapoteco de San Pedro el Alto) [zpp] 900 (1990 census). 29 monolinguals. Western Oaxaca, San Pedro el Alto, San Antonino el Alto, San Andrés el Alto. *Class:* Oto-Manguean, Zapotecan, Zapotec. *Dialects:* 20% intelligibility of Totomachapan (closest). *Lg Use:* Speakers also use Spanish.

Zapotec, Elotepec (Zapoteco de San Juan Elotepec, Papabuco) [zte] 200 (1990 census). Western Oaxaca, west of Zimatlán, 1 village. *Class:* Oto-Manguean, Zapotecan, Zapotec. *Dialects:* 68% intelligibility of Santa María Zaniza (closest), 10% of Texmelucan. *Lg Use:* Speakers are older adults. Speakers also use Spanish. *Other:* Mountain slope.

Zapotec, Guevea de Humboldt (Northern Isthmus Zapotec, Zapoteco de Guevea de Humboldt) [zpg] 7,000 (1977 SIL). Eastern Oaxaca. *Class:* Oto-Manguean, Zapotecan, Zapotec. *Dialects:* 49% intelligibility of Lachiguiri (Northwestern Tehuantepec; closest). *Lg Dev:* Literacy rate in first language: 2%. Literacy rate in second language: 20% to 30%. Bible portions: 1982. *Other:* VSO; short words, clitics, affixes; tonal. 500 to 800 meters.

Zapotec, Güilá (Zapoteco de San Pablo Güilá, Zapoteco de San Dionisio Ocotepec) [ztu] 9,500 (1990 census). 2,300 monolinguals. San Pablo Güilá and San Dionisio Ocotepec municipios, Oaxaca. *Class:* Oto-Manguean, Zapotecan, Zapotec. *Dialects:* San Dionisio has 80%

inherent intelligibility of Mitla. Güilá has 83% inherent intelligibility of San Juan Guelavía, 80% of Chichicapan, 69% of Tilquiapan, 41% of Mitla, 35% of Ocotlán, 5% of Santa María Albarradas.

Zapotec, Isthmus (Zapoteco del Istmo) [zai] 85,000 (1990 census). Tehuantepec and Juchitán, Oaxaca. *Class:* Oto-Manguean, Zapotecan, Zapotec. *Dialects:* 18% intelligibility of Santa María Petapa (closest). *Lg Use:* Bilingual level estimates for Spanish: 0 10%, 1 40%, 2 20%, 3 10%, 4 10%, 5 10%. *Lg Dev:* Dictionary. Grammar. NT: 1972–2002. *Other:* VSO; short words, affixes, clitics; tonal. Coastal. Sea level. Fishermen; peasant agriculturalists; merchants.

Zapotec, Lachiguiri (Northwestern Tehuantepec Zapotec, Zapoteco de Santiago Lachiguiri) [zpa] 5,000 (1977 SIL). Oaxaca, north of Isthmus, 15 km southwest of Guevea de Humboldt. Includes towns in neighboring municipios, such as Santa María Totolapilla, Jalapa, and Magdalena. *Class:* Oto-Manguean, Zapotecan, Zapotec. *Dialects:* 62% intelligibility in Lachixila (Northeastern Yautepec) and Juchitán (Isthmus; closest). *Lg Use:* Although speakers have routine proficiency in Spanish, there is a strong preference for Zapotec. *Other:* Mountain slope. 1,000 to 1,200 meters.

Zapotec, Lachirioag (Lachiruaj Zapotec, San Cristóbal Lachiruaj Zapotec) [ztc] 2,000 (1999 SIL). Oaxaca, San Cristóbal Lachiruáj. *Class:* Oto-Manguean, Zapotecan, Zapotec. *Dialects:* Closest to Villa Alta Zapotec and Yalálag Zapotec. Distinct from Yatee. *Lg Use:* Speakers have low proficiency in Spanish.

Zapotec, Lachixío (Eastern Sola de Vega Zapotec, Zapoteco de Lachixío, Dialu) [zpl] 6,500 (1990 census). 50% are monolingual. Western Oaxaca, eastern Sola de Vega, towns of Santa Marma Lachixío, San Vicente Lachixío. *Class:* Oto-Manguean, Zapotecan, Zapotec. *Dialects:* Southwestern Zimatlán dialect speakers need separate literature. 73% intelligibility of San Pedro el Alto, 80% of San Miguel Mixtepec and San Mateo Mixtepec, 99% of San Vicente Lachixío. *Lg Use:* Vigorous. All domains. Oral and written use in administration. Some oral use in religion. Oral use in local commerce. Positive language attitude. Bilingual level estimates for Spanish: 0 50–60%, 1 20–30%, 2 5–15%, 3 3–8%, 4 2–5%, 5 0%. Spanish used to communicate with outsiders. *Lg Dev:* Literacy rate in first language: 5%. Literacy rate in second language: 60%. Dictionary. Grammar. Bible portions: 1984–1989. *Other:* Some go to the city looking for work. VSO; short words, affixes, clitics; tonal. Mountain slope. Pine forest. 1,846 to 2,460 meters. Peasant agriculturalists; carpenters. Christian.

Zapotec, Loxicha (Western Pochutla Zapotec, Zapoteco de Loxicha, Copalita Zapotec) [ztp] 50,000 (1990 census). In many towns perhaps 70% of the men and 90% of the women are monolingual. Oaxaca, 120 km south of Oaxaca city, west of highway 175, halfway between Miahuatlán and Pochutla. Includes Candelaria Loxicha, Buena Vista, and San Bartolomé Loxicha. *Class:* Oto-Manguean, Zapotecan, Zapotec. *Dialects:* San Agustín Loxicha Zapotec, Candelaria Loxicha Zapotec. Distinct from San Baltázar Loxicha and Santa Catarina Loxicha. *Lg Use:* Those in town centers also use Spanish. *Lg Dev:* Bible portions.

Zapotec, Mazaltepec (Zapoteco de Santo Tomás Mazaltepec, Etla Zapotec) [zpy] 2,200 (1990 census). 24 monolinguals. Western Oaxaca Valley, Etla District, 20 km northwest of Oaxaca city; Santo Tomás Mazaltepec, San Pedro y San Pablo Etla, and a few in San Andrés Zautla. *Class:* Oto-Manguean, Zapotecan, Zapotec. *Dialects:* 10% intelligibility of San Juan Guelavía, none of other Zapotec varieties. *Lg Use:* Approximately 58% are speakers. Used in the home. 25% of children do not speak Spanish when entering school. Positive language attitude. Most speakers also use Spanish. *Other:* Kindergarten and primary school. 1,700 meters. Agriculturalists; adobe brick makers.

Zapotec, Miahuatlán (Zapoteco de Miahuatlán) [zam] 80,000 (1982 SIL). South central Oaxaca, Cuixtla. *Class:* Oto-Manguean, Zapotecan, Zapotec. *Lg Use:* Bilingual level estimates for Spanish: 0 10%, 1 5%, 2 30%, 3 4%, 4 1%, 5 50%. *Lg Dev:* Dictionary. NT: 1971. *Other:* SVO; short words, affixes, clitics; tonal. Mountain slope. Desert, scrub forest. 1,800 meters. Swidden, peasant agriculturalists.

Zapotec, Mitla (East Central Tlacolula Zapotec, East Valley Zapotec, Didxsaj) [zaw] 19,500 (1983 SIL). Less than 1% monolingual. Population includes 4,500 in Matatlán (1983 SIL). Mitla Valley, Oaxaca. *Class:* Oto-Manguean, Zapotecan, Zapotec. *Dialect:* Santiago Matatlán Zapotec (Matatlán Zapotec). 75% intelligibility of San Juan Guelavía (closest). *Lg Use:* Vigorous in some families. All domains among most adults. Oral use in local administration, commerce, some in media, in religious services. Young adults use Zapotec half the time, most children use more Spanish than Zapotec. Positive language attitude. Bilingual level estimates for Spanish: 0 5%, 1 30%, 2 30%, 3 15%, 4 15%, 5 5%. Speakers are shifting to Spanish. Maybe 10% can speak some English. *Lg Dev:* Literacy rate in first language: 40%. Literacy rate in second language: 80% to 90%. 10% can write it. Dictionary. NT: 1981. *Other:* SVO or VSO; short and long words, clitics and affixes; tonal. Mountain slope, plains. Desert, gallery, scrub, deciduous, and pine forests. 1,500 meters. Pastoralists; peasant agriculturalists; craftsmen; merchants. Traditional religion, Christian.

Zapotec, Mixtepec (Eastern Miahuatlán Zapotec, Zapoteco de San Juan Mixtepec) [zpm] 7,000 (1991 SIL). Southern Oaxaca. *Class:* Oto-Manguean, Zapotecan, Zapotec. *Dialects:* 80% intelligibility of Santiago Lapaguía (closest). A separate language from San Agustín Mixtepec Zapotec. *Lg Use:* Bilingual level estimates for Spanish: 0 40%, 1 15%, 2 30%, 3 15%, 4 0%, 5 0%. *Lg Dev:* Videos. NT: 1998. *Other:* VSO; short words, clitics; tonal. Mountain slope. Pine forest. Pastoralists; peasant agriculturalists; merchants.

Zapotec, Ocotlán (Zapoteco del Poniente de Ocotlán, Ocotlán Oeste Zapotec) [zac] 15,000 (1993 SIL). Ocotlán, central Oaxaca around Santiago Apóstol. *Class:* Oto-Manguean, Zapotecan, Zapotec. *Dialects:* 67% intelligibility of Tilquiapan (closest). *Lg Use:* Bilingual level estimates for Spanish: 0 10%, 1 30%, 2 40%, 3 10%, 4 6%, 5 4%. *Lg Dev:* Literacy rate in first language: below 1%. Literacy rate in second language: 50%. NT: 1983. *Other:* VSO; short words, affixes; tonal. Plains. Deciduous forest. 1,385 meters. Peasant agriculturalists; merchants.

Zapotec, Ozolotepec (Zapoteco de Ozolotepec) [zao] 6,500 (1990 census). People in the towns of San Marcial, San Gregorio, San Esteban, and Santo Domingo are monolingual. Oaxaca, southeastern Miahuatlán, east side of highway 175, about halfway between Miahuatlán and coast. The majority of towns with 'Ozolotepec' in the name are included, however, not San Francisco Ozolotepec. *Class:* Oto-Manguean, Zapotecan, Zapotec. *Dialects:* San Marcial Ozolotepec Zapotec, San Gregorio Ozolotepec Zapotec. 87% intelligibility of Cuixtla (Central Miahuatlán), 84% of Candelaria Loxicha (Northeastern Pochutla). Cuixtla literature not acceptable here. *Lg Dev:* Bible portions: 2000. *Other:* 2,000 meters.

Zapotec, Petapa (Zapoteco de Santa María Petapa) [zpe] 8,000 (1990 census). 220 monolinguals. Oaxaca, north of the Isthmus, Juchitán District, Santa María Petapa and Santo Domingo Petapa. *Class:* Oto-Manguean, Zapotecan, Zapotec. *Dialects:* 55% intelligibility of Guevea (closest), 34% of Lachiguiri. *Lg Use:* Speakers also use Spanish.

Zapotec, Quiavicuzas (Zapoteco de Quiavicuzas, Zapoteco de San Juan Lachixila O, Northeastern Yautepec

Zapotec) [zpj] 4,000 (1990 census). 180 monolinguals. Oaxaca, northeast corner of Yautepec District, 45 km northeast of Pan American highway, 75 km east of Mitla. San Carlos Yautepec Municipio: Santiago Quiavicuzas; Nejapa de Madero Municipio: San Juan Lachixila, Corral de Piedra, Carrizal; Guevea de Humboldt Municipio: Guadalupe Guevea. *Class:* Oto-Manguean, Zapotecan, Zapotec. *Dialects:* 59% intelligibility of Lachiguiri (Northwestern Tehuantepec; closest). *Lg Use:* 40 of the 180 monolinguals are between ages 5 to 9. Speakers also use Spanish. *Other:* Primary schools. 600 to 1,600 meters. Agriculturalists.

Zapotec, Quioquitani-Quierí (Zapoteco de Quioquitani Y Quierí) [ztq] 4,000 (1991 SIL). Yautepec, Oaxaca, Quioquitani and Quierí municipios, and including Leapi. *Class:* Oto-Manguean, Zapotecan, Zapotec. *Dialects:* Quioquitani Zapotec (Santa Catarina Quioquitani Zapotec), Quierí Zapotec (Santa Catarina Quierí Zapotec). Closest to Eastern Miahuatlán. *Lg Dev:* NT: 2000.

Zapotec, Rincón (Zapoteco del Rincón, Zapoteco de Yagallo, Northern Villa Alta Zapotec) [zar] 29,246 (2000 WCD). Northern Oaxaca. *Class:* Oto-Manguean, Zapotecan, Zapotec. *Dialects:* 64% intelligibility of Choapan (closest). Temaxcalapan may not be part of this language. *Lg Use:* Bilingual level estimates for Spanish: 0 50%, 1 35%, 2 10%, 3 3%, 4 2%, 5 0%. *Lg Dev:* NT: 1971. *Other:* VOS; short words, affixes, clitics; nontonal. Mountain slope. Deciduous forest. 400 to 1,000 meters. Peasant agriculturalists.

Zapotec, San Agustín Mixtepec [ztm] 59 (1994 SIL). Oaxaca, Miahuatlán, town of San Agustín Mixtepec. *Class:* Oto-Manguean, Zapotecan, Zapotec. *Dialects:* Distinct from San Juan Mixtepec Zapotec. *Other:* Nearly extinct.

Zapotec, San Baltazar Loxicha (Northwestern Pochutla Zapotec, Zapoteco de San Baltázar Loxicha, San Baltázar Loxicha Zapotec) [zpx] 1,500 (1990 census). 19 monolinguals. Oaxaca, 115 km south of Oaxaca city. San Baltázar Loxicha and Santa Catarina Loxicha. *Class:* Oto-Manguean, Zapotecan, Zapotec. *Dialects:* 71% intelligibility of Santa María Coatlán (closest), 63% of Cuixtla (Central Miahuatlán), 46.5% of San Vicente Coatlán. *Lg Use:* Speakers also use Spanish. *Other:* Mountain slope. 1,200 meters.

Zapotec, San Juan Guelavía (Western Tlacolula Zapotec, Zapoteco de San Juan Guelavía) [zab] 28,000 in Mexico (1990 census). Population total all countries: 28,500. Central Oaxaca. Also spoken in USA. *Class:* Oto-Manguean, Zapotecan, Zapotec. *Dialects:* Jalieza Zapotec, Teotitlán del Valle Zapotec, San Martín Tilcajete Zapotec. 20% intelligibility of Zegache (closest). Jalieza has 99% intelligibility of San Juan Guelavía. Teotitlán del Valle has 100% intelligibility of San Juan Guelavía, but San Juan Guelavía only 59% of Teotitlán del Valle. *Lg Use:* Bilingual level estimates for Spanish: 0 40%, 1 10%, 2 10%, 3 20%, 4 10%, 5 10%. *Lg Dev:* Literacy rate in second language: 10%. Dictionary. NT: 1995. *Other:* VSO; affixes, clitics; tonal. Mountain valley. Desert, scrub forest. 1,650 meters. Peasant agriculturalists.

Zapotec, San Pedro Quiatoni (Zapoteco de San Pedro Quiatoni, Quiatoni Zapotec, Eastern Tlacolula Zapotec) [zpf] 14,821 (2000 WCD). Central Oaxaca, San Pedro Quiatoni, Salinas, Unión Juárez, and nearby settlements. *Class:* Oto-Manguean, Zapotecan, Zapotec. *Dialects:* 76% intelligibility of Mitla; closest. *Lg Dev:* Literacy rate in first language: 1%. Literacy rate in second language: 75%. Bible portions: 2000. *Other:* Traditional religion.

Zapotec, San Vicente Coatlán (Southern Ejutla Zapotec, Zapoteco de San Vicente Coatlán, Coatlán Zapotec) [zpt] 2,430 (1990 census). 584 monolinguals.

Oaxaca, Ejutla District, 90 km south of Oaxaca city. San Vicente Coatlán, a municipio town. *Class:* Oto-Manguean, Zapotecan, Zapotec. *Dialects:* 75% intelligibility of San Baltázar Loxicha (closest, Northwestern Pochutla), 45% of Santa María Coatlán. *Lg Use:* Vigorous. *Other:* Primary school. Agriculturalists; mezcal makers.

Zapotec, Santa Catarina Albarradas (Zapoteco de Santa Catarina Albarradas) [ztn] 1,000 (1990 census). Oaxaca, Santa Catarina Albarradas. *Class:* Oto-Manguean, Zapotecan, Zapotec. *Dialects:* 80% intelligibility of Santo Domingo Albarradas; Santo Domingo 52% of Santa Catarina. Differences in phonology and grammar between them. *Lg Use:* About half the population can understand San Pedro Cajonos Zapotec reasonably well because of trading with them.

Zapotec, Santa Inés Yatzechi (Zapoteco de Zegache, Zapoteco de Santa Inés Yatzechi, Southeastern Zimatlán Zapotec) [zpn] 2,235 (1990 census). Central Oaxaca, Zimatlán District, 40 km south of Oaxaca city, west of Ocotlán de Morelos. *Class:* Oto-Manguean, Zapotecan, Zapotec. *Dialect:* Zaachila. 75% intelligibility of San Antonino Ocotlán (closest). Zaachila may need some separate literature. San Miguel Tilquiapan may be a dialect. *Lg Use:* Zapotec is apparently no longer spoken in Santa Ana Zegache, and going out of use in Zaachila. Vigorous use among children in Santa Inés, some of whom are monolinguals (1990). 176 monolinguals. *Lg Dev:* Bible portions: 1989–1991.

Zapotec, Santa María Quiegolani (Zapoteco de Santa María Quiegolani, Quiegolani Zapotec, Western Yautepec Zapotec) [zpi] 3,000 (1990 census). Central Oaxaca. *Class:* Oto-Manguean, Zapotecan, Zapotec. *Dialects:* 60% intelligibility of San Juan Mixtepec (closest). *Lg Dev:* Grammar. *Other:* Traditional religion, Christian.

Zapotec, Santiago Lapaguía (Zapoteco de Santiago Lapaguía) [ztl] 4,200 (1983 SIL). Oaxaca, southeastern Miahuatlán, including four towns: Lapaguía (700, monolingual), San Felipe Lachillo (500, settled from Lapaguía), La Merced del Potrero (2,500, bilingual), San Juan Guivini (500, monolingual). *Class:* Oto-Manguean, Zapotecan, Zapotec. *Dialects:* 80% intelligibility of San Juan Mixtepec Zapotec. *Lg Use:* Speakers have low proficiency in Spanish.

Zapotec, Santiago Xanica (Xanica Zapotec) [zpr] 2,500 (1990 census). Oaxaca, southeastern Miahuatlán, including four towns: Santiago Xanica, Santa María Coixtepec, San Andrés Lovene, San Antonio Ozolotepec. *Class:* Oto-Manguean, Zapotecan, Zapotec. *Dialects:* 72% intelligibility of San Gregorio Ozolotepec, 70% of Cuixtla (Central Miahuatlán). *Lg Use:* Speakers also use Spanish. *Other:* 1,000 to 1,200 meters. Agriculturalists: coffee.

Zapotec, Santo Domingo Albarradas (Albarradas Zapotec, Zapoteco de Santo Domingo Albarradas) [zas] 5,500 (1980 census). Population includes 1,500 to 2,000 in Santo Domingo (1993 SIL). All Zapotec languages: 422,937. Central Oaxaca, Santa María Albarradas, Santo Domingo Albarradas, San Miguel Albarradas. *Class:* Oto-Manguean, Zapotecan, Zapotec. *Dialects:* 39% intelligibility of Mitla (closest). Santa Catarina Albarradas may need separate literature. *Lg Use:* Since 1979 speakers in Santo Domingo have shown increasing preference for Zapotec, but in Santa María it is reported to be diminishing in use. Some immigrant Mixe have learned the local Zapotec, but few Zapotec have learned Mixe. Bilingual level estimates for Spanish: 0 3%, 1 17%, 2 40%, 3 30%, 4 9%, 5 1%. Speakers use Spanish for communication with Mitla Zapotec speakers. Spanish is generally used between them and the Mixe in mixed marriages. *Lg Dev:* Literacy rate in first language: 1%. Literacy rate in second language: 80%. Videos. Bible portions: 2000. *Other:* VSO, varying word length, clitics

and affixes; tonal. Mountain slope. Gallery forest. 1,200 to 2,000 meters. Swidden agriculturalists.

Zapotec, Sierra de Juárez (Zapoteco de Atepec, Ixtlán Zapoteco) [zaa] 4,000 (1990 census). 150 monolinguals. Northern Oaxaca. *Class:* Oto-Manguean, Zapotecan, Zapotec. *Lg Use:* Bilingual level estimates for Spanish: 0 25%, 1 25%, 2 25%, 3 18%, 4 5%, 5 2%. *Lg Dev:* Dictionary. NT: 1970. *Other:* Some form of whistle speech reported. VSO; long words, affixes, clitics; tonal. Mountain slope. Scrub, pine forests. 1,540 to 2,770 meters. Pastoralists; swidden, peasant agriculturalists.

Zapotec, Southeastern Ixtlán (Zapoteco del Sureste de Ixtlán, Yavesía Zapotec, Latuvi Zapotec) [zpd] 6,000 (1992 SIL). Northern Oaxaca, Santa María Yavesía (center), Carrizal, Latuvi, Benito Juárez, Ixtlán de Juárez, Santa Catarina Lachatao, Llano Grande, La Trinidad, Nevería, San Miguel Amatlán, Capulalpan de Morelos, Santiago Xiacui, Natividad, Guelatao de Juárez. *Class:* Oto-Manguean, Zapotecan, Zapotec. *Dialects:* 63% intelligibility of Atepec (Sierra de Juárez), 43% of Teococuilco. *Lg Use:* Speakers also use Spanish.

Zapotec, Southern Rincon (Zapoteco de Rincón Sur) [zsr] 12,000 (1990 census). Oaxaca. *Class:* Oto-Manguean, Zapotecan, Zapotec. *Lg Dev:* NT: 1992.

Zapotec, Tabaa (Central Villa Alta Zapotec, Zapoteco de Tabaa) [zat] 2,000 (1992 SIL). Oaxaca. *Class:* Oto-Manguean, Zapotecan, Zapotec. *Lg Use:* Bilingual level estimates for Spanish: 0 50%, 1 30%, 2 13%, 3 5%, 4 2%, 5 0%. *Lg Dev:* NT: 1981. *Other:* VSO; long words, affixes, clitics; tonal. Mountain slope. Scrub, pine forest. 300 to 800 meters. Pastoralists; swidden, peasant agriculturalists.

Zapotec, Tejalapan (Zapoteco de San Felipe Tejalapan, Zapoteco de Tejalápam) [ztt] 124 (1990 census). Ethnic population: 4,656. Oaxaca, Etla District, town of San Felipe Tejalapan. *Class:* Oto-Manguean, Zapotecan, Zapotec. *Dialects:* Distinct from Santo Tomás Mazaltepec Zapotec. *Lg Use:* 92 speakers are older than 50 years, including the 2 monolinguals. Speakers also use Spanish. *Other:* They came from Ixtepeji area 300 years ago.

Zapotec, Texmelucan (Central Sola de Vega Zapotec, Zapoteco de San Lorenzo Texmelucan, Papabuco) [zpz] 4,100 (1992 SIL). Western Oaxaca. *Class:* Oto-Manguean, Zapotecan, Zapotec. *Dialects:* Closest to Western Sola de Vega (Zaniza). *Lg Use:* Bilingual level estimates for Spanish: 0 70%, 1 20%, 2 8%, 3 2%, 4 0%, 5 0%. *Lg Dev:* NT: 1989. *Other:* Zaniza and Elotepec Zapotec are also called 'Papabuco'. VSO; short words, affixes, clitics; tonal. Mountain slope. Pine, tropical forest. 1,365 to 1,846 meters. Swidden, peasant agriculturalists.

Zapotec, Tilquiapan (Zapoteco de San Miguel Tilquiapan) [zts] 2,700 (1990 census). 900 monolinguals. Central Oaxaca, Ocotlán, San Miguel Tilquiapan town. *Class:* Oto-Manguean, Zapotecan, Zapotec. *Dialects:* 87% intelligibility of Santa Inés Yatzechi, 65% of Chichicapan, 59% of Ocotlán, 45% of San Juan Guelavía. *Lg Use:* Sociolinguistic differences with nearest Zapotec. Speakers also use Spanish. *Lg Dev:* Primary school with bilingual teachers. *Other:* Semiarid, rocky. 1,600 meters. Agriculturalists.

Zapotec, Tlacolulita (Southeastern Yautepec Zapotec, Zapoteco de Asunción Tlacolulita) [zpk] 135 (1990 census). Ethnic population: 904 (1990 census). Eastern Oaxaca, Asunción Tlacolulita and San Juan Alotepec. *Class:* Oto-Manguean, Zapotecan, Zapotec. *Dialects:* 15% intelligibility of Lachixila (closest), 10% on Mitla and San Juan Guelavía, 0% on Lachiguiri, Juchitán, Guevea de Humboldt, Petapa, San Juan Mixtepec, and Quiegolani. *Lg Use:* 111 speakers are 50 years of age or older (1990). Speakers also use Spanish.

Zapotec, Totomachapan (Western Zimatlán Zapotec, Zapoteco de San Pedro Totomachapan) [zph] 259 (1990 census). Ethnic population: 1,009 (1990 census). Western Oaxaca, 2 towns. *Class:* Oto-Manguean, Zapotecan, Zapotec. *Dialects:* No intelligibility of other Zapotec. *Lg Use:* Speakers are older adults. Speakers also use Spanish.

Zapotec, Xadani (Zapoteco de Santa María Xadani, Eastern Pochutla Zapotec) [zax] 338 (1990 census). Oaxaca, Pochutla District, San Miguel del Puerto Municipio, Santa María Xadani, 16 towns or villages. *Class:* Oto-Manguean, Zapotecan, Zapotec. *Lg Use:* 122 speakers older than 50 years, 90 between 35 and 50, 1 monolingual (1990). Speakers also use Spanish. *Other:* Coastal.

Zapotec, Xanaguía (Zapoteco de Santa Catarina Xanaguía, Diidz Zë) [ztg] 2,500 (1990 census). 35% monolingual, mainly older women. Oaxaca, southeastern Miahuatlán, including three towns: Santa Catarina Xanaguía, San Francisco Ozolotepec, and San José Ozolotepec. *Class:* Oto-Manguean, Zapotecan, Zapotec. *Dialects:* A few phonological and lexical differences between San Francisco and San José. *Lg Use:* Vigorous. A very few speakers of other languages have married into it and speak it. Used in the home. Oral use in local administration, commerce, religion. All ages. Positive language attitude. 20% have some degree of fluency in Spanish. 6th grade education in Spanish available in Xanaguía. Most children finish third or fourth grade. Those finishing 6th grade, the highest available locally, still have limited Spanish proficiency. San Francisco reported to be more monolingual than Santa Catarina, and San José the most bilingual. Some speakers can speak other varieties of Zapotec. *Lg Dev:* Literacy rate in first language: 1%. Literacy rate in second language: 10%. Bible portions: 1996. *Other:* Many women over 40 and some men have no education. People leave the area for jobs. VSO. Mountain slope. 2,000 meters. Swidden agriculturalists: maize, beans, herbs, coffee. Christian, traditional religion.

Zapotec, Yalálag (Zapoteco de Yalálag) [zpu] 5,000 in Mexico (1990 census). 2,000 are in Yalálag, others are in D. F., Oaxaca City, Veracruz. Also in Los Angeles, California, USA. Oaxaca. Also spoken in USA. *Class:* Oto-Manguean, Zapotecan, Zapotec. *Lg Use:* Bilingual level estimates for Spanish: 0 10%, 1 10%, 2 30%, 3 30%, 4 10%, 5 10%. *Lg Dev:* Literacy rate in first language: 1%. Literacy rate in second language: 60%. NT: 2000. *Other:* VSO; short words, affixes, clitics; tonal. Mountain slope. Pine, scrub forests. 1,400 meters. Peasant agriculturalists; craftsmen.

Zapotec, Yareni (Western Ixtlán Zapotec, Zapoteco de Teococuilco de Marcos Pérez, Zapoteco de Santa Ana Yareni, Etla Zapotec) [zae] 6,000 (1982 SIL). Northern Oaxaca. *Class:* Oto-Manguean, Zapotecan, Zapotec. *Dialects:* 80% intelligibility of Sierra de Juárez Zapotec. Different from Aloapam Zapotec. *Lg Use:* Bilingual level estimates for Spanish: 0 20%, 1 40%, 2 25%, 3 10%, 4 5%, 5 0%. *Lg Dev:* Literacy rate in first language: below 1%. Literacy rate in second language: 60% to 75%. Bible portions: 1966–1990. *Other:* VSO; affixes, clitics; tonal. Pine forest. 1,900 to 2,300 meters. Pastoralists; peasant agriculturalists.

Zapotec, Yatee (Zapoteco de Yatee) [zty] 3,000 (1999 SIL). Oaxaca, San Francisco Yatee, 4 towns. *Class:* Oto-Manguean, Zapotecan, Zapotec. *Dialects:* Closest to Villa Alta Zapotec and Yalálag Zapotec. Distinct from Lachiruaj. *Lg Use:* Most speakers have low proficiency in Spanish. *Lg Dev:* NT: 2002.

Zapotec, Yatzachi (Zapoteco de Yatzachi, Villa Alta Zapotec) [zav] 2,500 in Mexico (1990 census). Villages of Yatzachi el Bajo, Yatzachi el Alto, Xoochixtepec, Yohueche, Zoochina, Zoochila, Yalina, north central Oaxaca. Also spoken in USA. *Class:* Oto-Manguean,

Zapotecan, Zapotec. *Dialects:* 90% intelligibility of Zoogocho on narrative, 85% of Cajonos (Southern Villa Alta) and Yalálag, and somewhat intelligible with Solaga and Tabaa. *Lg Use:* Bilingual level estimates for Spanish: 0 10%, 1 10%, 2 40%, 3 25%, 4 14%, 5 1%. *Lg Dev:* Literacy rate in first language: 30%. Literacy rate in second language: 60%. Dictionary. Grammar. NT: 1971. *Other:* VSO; long words, affixes, clitics; tonal. Mountain slope. Scrub forest. 615 to 1,690 meters. Peasant agriculturalists in Oaxaca, wage laborers outside.

Zapotec, Yautepec (Zapoteco de San Bartolo Yautepec, Northwestern Yautepec Zapotec) [zpb] 314 (1990 census). Eastern Oaxaca, San Bartolo Yautepec. *Class:* Oto-Manguean, Zapotecan, Zapotec. *Dialects:* 10% intelligibility of Tlacolulita (closest), no intelligibility of other Zapotec. *Lg Use:* 126 speakers between 35 and 50 years of age, 138 over 50, 4 monolinguals over 50 (1990). Speakers also use Spanish.

Zapotec, Zaachila (San Raymundo Jalpan Zapotec) [ztx] 550 (1990 census). Ethnic population: 10,000 or more (1990 census). Oaxaca, 15 km south of the city of Oaxaca, past Xoxo, town of Zaachila (416 speakers out of 10,601 population) and San Raymundo Jalpan (116 speakers out of 1,270 population). A few in San Bartolo Coyotepec, San Pablo Cuatro Venados, and Santa María Coyotepec. *Class:* Oto-Manguean, Zapotecan, Zapotec. *Dialects:* 85% intelligibility of Zegache, 75% of Tilquiapan, 72% of San Juan Guelavía, 10% of Ocotlán. *Lg Use:* Only those older than 50 years understand but do not normally speak it, but this includes 3 women monolinguals (1990). No children speak it. Speakers also use Spanish.

Zapotec, Zaniza (Zapoteco de Santa María Zaniza, Western Sola de Vega Zapotec, Papabuco) [zpw] 770 (1990 census). 4 monolinguals. Western Oaxaca, Santa María Zaniza, Santiago Textitlán, Santiago Xochiltepec, El Frijol, Buenavista. *Class:* Oto-Manguean, Zapotecan, Zapotec. *Dialects:* 10% intelligibility of Texmelucan (closest). *Lg Use:* 35% of speakers are under 40. Speakers also use Spanish. *Other:* Texmelucan is also called 'Papabuco'.

Zapotec, Zoogocho (Zapoteco de San Bartolomé Zoogocho) [zpq] 1,000 in Mexico (1991 SIL). Population total all countries: 1,400. Zoogocho, Yalina, Tabehua, and Oaxaca City, Oaxaca, and Mexico City. Also spoken in USA. *Class:* Oto-Manguean, Zapotecan, Zapotec. *Dialects:* Zoogocho, Yalina, Tabehua. 57% intelligibility of Comaltepec (Choapan; closest). Zoogocho is the market town, so most Yatzachi people go there weekly, but Zoogocho people do not understand Yatzachi as well (80%). *Lg Use:* Bilingual level estimates for Spanish: 0 10%, 1 10%, 2 45%, 3 20%, 4 14%, 5 1%. *Lg Dev:* Literacy rate in first language: 30%. Literacy rate in second language: 60%. Dictionary. NT: 1988. *Other:* The local economy is supported to a large extent by those working outside the area. VSO; long words, affixes, clitics; tonal. Mountain slope. Scrub forest. 900 to 1,800 meters. Peasant agriculturalists in Zoogocho, wage laborers outside.

Zoque, Chimalapa [zoh] 4,500 (1990 census). 15 monolinguals. Oaxaca, Santa María Chimalapa and San Miguel Chimalapa. *Class:* Mixe-Zoque, Zoque, Oaxaca Zoque. *Lg Use:* Speakers also use Spanish. *Lg Dev:* Bible portions.

Zoque, Copainalá (Zoque de Copainalá) [zoc] 10,000 (1990 census). Copainalá, Chiapas. *Class:* Mixe-Zoque, Zoque, Chiapas Zoque. *Dialects:* Ocotepec, Ostuacán. 83% intelligibility of Francisco León (closest). *Lg Use:* Bilingual level estimates for Spanish: 0 0%, 1 5%, 2 5%, 3 30%, 4 50%, 5 10%. *Lg Dev:* Dictionary. Grammar. NT: 1967. *Other:* VSO; long words, affixes, clitics; non-tonal. Mountain slope, riverine. Tropical. 215 to 1,845 meters. Agriculturalists.

Zoque, Francisco León (Zoque de Francisco León, Santa Magdalena Zoque) [zos] 20,000 (1990 census). Mezcalapa, Chiapas. *Class:* Mixe-Zoque, Zoque, Chiapas Zoque. *Dialects:* Chapultenango, San Pedro Yaspac. Close to Copainalá. *Lg Use:* Bilingual level estimates for Spanish: 0 40%, 1 35%, 2 10%, 3 10%, 4 3%, 5 2%. *Lg Dev:* Dictionary. NT: 1978. *Other:* The eruption of El Chicón volcano in 1982 has necessitated relocation; the original town of Francisco León is buried. Long words, affixes; nontonal. Mountain slope. Tropical. 200 to 800 meters. Peasant agriculturalists.

Zoque, Rayón (Zoque de Rayón) [zor] 2,000 to 2,300 (1990 census). 20 monolinguals (1990 census). Ethnic population: 10,400 (1990 census). Northwest Chiapas, Rayón and Tapilula. *Class:* Mixe-Zoque, Zoque, Chiapas Zoque. *Dialects:* Distinct from other Zoque. *Lg Use:* Bilingual level estimates for Spanish: 0 25%, 1 25%, 2 50%, 3 0%, 4 0%, 5 0%. *Lg Dev:* Dictionary. *Other:* VOS; short and long words, clitics, affixes; nontonal. Mountain mesa. Scrub forest. 1,337 meters. Swidden or peasant agriculturalists.

Zoque, Tabasco (Zoque de Tabasco, Zoque de Ayapanec) [zoq] 40 (1971 García de León). Ethnic population: 367 (1960 census). Municipio of Jalapa de Méndez, Ayapa, Tabasco. *Class:* Mixe-Zoque, Zoque, Veracruz Zoque. *Lg Use:* Speakers are shifting to Spanish. *Other:* Nearly extinct.

Montserrat

Montserrat. 9,245. National or official language: English. Literacy rate: 97%. Also includes Arabic 500, Chinese 500. The number of languages listed for Montserrat is 2. Of those, both are living languages. See map on page 740.

English [eng] 100 in Montserrat (2004). *Lg Use:* National language. See main entry under United Kingdom.

Montserrat Creole English (Leeward Caribbean Creole English) [aig] 7,574 in Montserrat (2001). *Other:* Many people have recently left the island due to volcanic activity. Agriculturalists: cotton. See main entry under Antigua and Barbuda (Antigua and Barbuda Creole English).

Netherlands Antilles

Netherlands Antilles. 218,126. Population includes St. Eustatius 1,000, Saba 1,000, St. Maarten 10,000 (1995). National or official language: Dutch. Self-governing part of the Netherlands. By agreement of all parties, it remains in the Kingdom of the Netherlands (1996). Leeward islands: Curaçao, Bonaire; Windward islands: St. Maarten, Saba, St. Eustatius. Literacy rate: 95%. Also includes Spanish (2,100), Sranan (6,400), Arabic, Chinese. Blind population: 500 (1982 WCE). Deaf institutions: 3. The number of languages listed for Netherlands Antilles is 4. Of those, all are living languages. See map on page 740.

Dutch [nld] 4,000 in Netherlands Antilles. *Lg Use:* Official language. *Other:* Its use is decreasing in importance. See main entry under Netherlands.

English [eng] 1,800 in Netherlands Antilles (2004). More use on Saba and Statia than other islands. *Lg Use:* Gaining importance in Netherlands Antilles. *Other:* Post-creole English is the dialect used (Alleyne). See main entry under United Kingdom.

Netherlands Antilles Creole English (Virgin Islands Creole English) [vic] 16,700 in Netherlands Antilles (2002 SIL). Population includes 14,000 on St. Maarten, 1,100 on Saba, 1,600 on St. Eustatius. Southern St. Maarten, Saba, St. Eustatius. *Dialects:* St. Maarten Creole English, Saba

Creole English, Statia Creole English. See main entry under U.S. Virgin Islands (Virgin Islands Creole English).

Papiamentu (Papiamento, Papiam, Papiamentoe, Papiamen, Curaçoleño, Curassese) [pap] 179,000 in Netherlands Antilles (1998). Population total all countries: 319,400. Curaçao, St. Maarten, Bonaire Islands off Venezuela coast, and islands off Netherlands Antilles. Also spoken in Aruba, Netherlands, Puerto Rico, U.S. Virgin Islands. *Class:* Creole, Iberian based. *Dialects:* The language is becoming more like Spanish, which is prestigious. *Lg Use:* About 20,000 speak it as second language. Importance is different on each island. Not used as widely on St. Maarten, and even less on Saba and Statia. All domains. All ages. Using both Papiamentu and Dutch is not considered an indication of lack of education. However, inability to use Dutch hinders social and political mobility, and leads to discontent. On Curaçao and Bonaire they use Dutch at school, Spanish with Spanish-speaking persons, English and Dutch with tourists. *Lg Dev:* Taught in first 2 years of primary school on Curaçao and Bonaire. Newspapers. Dictionary. Grammar. Bible: 1997. *Other:* Christian.

Nicaragua

Republic of Nicaragua, República de Nicaragua. 5,359,759. National or official language: Spanish. Literacy rate: 66% to 74%. Also includes Arabic (400), Chinese (7,000). Blind population: 1,800 (1982 WCE). Deaf population: 248,401. The number of languages listed for Nicaragua is 10. Of those, 7 are living languages and 3 are extinct. See map on page 764.

Garifuna (Garífuna, Caribe, Black Carib, Central American Carib, "Moreno") [cab] A few speakers in Nicaragua (2001 Elias Velásquez). Ethnic population: 1,500 in Nicaragua (1982 Meso-America). Región Atlántica Autónoma del Sur, Orinoco village, far from speakers in other countries. *Lg Use:* All speakers are older adults in Nicaragua. Speakers also use Creole. See main entry under Honduras.

Matagalpa (Pantasmas) [mtn] Extinct. Ethnic population: 18,000 to 20,000 (1981 MARC). The ethnic group is in the Central highlands, Matagalpa and Jinotega departments, and in Honduras, El Paraíso department. *Class:* Misumalpan. *Lg Use:* Members of the ethnic group now speak Spanish. *Other:* Agriculturalists.

Mískito (Mísquito, Mískitu, Mosquito, Marquito) [miq] 154,400 in Nicaragua (1993 census). Population total all countries: 183,400. Ethnic population: 154,400 (1993). From Pearl Lagoon to Black River, coast and lowlands. Zalaya Department, North Atlantic Autonomous Region (RAAN) with a concentration in the city of Puerto Cabeza, and towns and villages of Prinzapolka, Tronquera, San Carlos (Río Coco), Waspam, Leimus, Bocana de Paiwas, Karawala, Sangnilaya, Wasla, Sisin, Rosita, Bonanza, Siuna, Bihmuna, and all along the Río Coco area. Also in South Atlantic Autonomous Region (RAAS). Also spoken in Honduras. *Class:* Misumalpan. *Dialects:* Honduran Mískito (Mam), Tawira (Tauira), Baymuna (Baymunana, Baldam), Wanki (Wangki), Cabo (Kabo). The language is closest to Sumo Mayangna. Wangki is spoken around Puerto Cabeza. The other dialects are in settlements to the southwest. *Lg Use:* Trade language. Many Hispanic people have learned Mískito. Educational materials are in Wangki. All Mískito understand the language. Widespread use among older adults. Bilingual level estimates for Spanish: 0 0%, 1 2%, 2 3%, 3 15%, 4 70%, 5 10%. Secondary school children are taught in Spanish, Some English is known. *Lg Dev:* Literacy rate in first language: 52% to 58%. Widespread in primary shools. Bible: 1999.

Other: SOV; articles, relatives after noun heads; word order distinguishes subject, object; verb affixes mark person, number; ergative; passive; CVC; nontonal. Coastal. Semitropical to tropical. Just above sea level. Agriculturalists; fishermen; government workers; education workers. Christian.

Monimbo [mom] Extinct. Ethnic population: 10,000 (1981 MARC). *Class:* Unclassified. *Other:* Few traits of their pre-conquest American Indian culture remain.

Nicaragua Creole English (Mískito Coast Creole English) [bzk] 30,000 (1986 Carrier Pidgin). Includes 625 speakers of Rama Cay Creole (1989 Holm). Bluefields Region including Rama Cay Island, Pearl Lagoon, Prinzapolka, Puerto Cabezas, Corn Islands. *Class:* Creole, English based, Atlantic, Western. *Dialects:* Rama Cay Creole English, Bluefields Creole English. *Lg Use:* The first language of the Creole people and most Garifuna; the second language of most Mískito and some Spanish speakers. Positive language attitude. Speakers also use English or Spanish. *Lg Dev:* Bible portions: 1999.

Nicaraguan Sign Language (Idioma de Senas de Nicaragua) [ncs] 3,000 (1997 Asociación Nacional de Sordos de Nicaragua). Population includes hearing people. Managua and throughout the nation. *Class:* Deaf sign language. *Dialects:* There are two sign languages in Nicaragua. Unrelated to El Salvadoran, Costa Rican, or other sign languages. *Lg Use:* Officially used in school since 1992, and used outside the classroom. Users know little Spanish. *Lg Dev:* Dictionary.

Rama [rma] 24 (1989 J. Holm). Ethnic population: 900 (2000 C. Grinevald). Rama Cay, 30-mile radius. *Class:* Chibchan, Rama. *Lg Use:* Speakers on Rama Key use Nicaragua Creole English. *Lg Dev:* Dictionary. *Other:* Nearly extinct.

Spanish (Español, Castellano) [spa] 4,347,000 in Nicaragua (1995). *Lg Use:* Official language. See main entry under Spain.

Subtiaba [sut] Extinct. Ethnic population: 5,000 (1981 MARC). Plains of León, Pacific slope. *Class:* Subtiaba-Tlapanec. *Other:* Few traits of their pre-conquest culture remain.

Sumo-Mayangna (Sumo, Sumu, Soumo, Sumoo, Woolwa, Sumo Tawahka, Taguaca) [sum] 6,700 in Nicaragua (1982 Mesoamerica). Population total all countries: 7,400. Upriver locations from Prinzapolka River in the south into Honduras in the north. Also spoken in Honduras. *Class:* Misumalpan. *Dialects:* Panamahka, Nicaraguan Tawahka, Ulwa, Bawihka, Kukra. A distinct dialect is spoken in Honduras. *Lg Use:* Speakers also use Mískito or Spanish. *Lg Dev:* Literary development has been in the Tawahka dialect. Bible: 1999. *Other:* SOV. Hunter-gatherers; fishermen; swidden agriculturalists: manioc.

Panama

Republic of Panama, República de Panamá. 3,000,463. National or official language: Spanish. Literacy rate: 87% to 88%. Also includes Eastern Yiddish, Hebrew, Japanese (1,200), Korean, Arabic (15,000). Information mainly from P. Cohen 1976; SIL 1970–1998. Blind population: 2,000 (1982 WCE). Deaf population: 159,456. The number of languages listed for Panama is 14. Of those, all are living languages. See map on page 765.

Buglere (Bokota, Bogota, Bofota, Bobota, Bocota, Bukueta, Nortenyo, Murire, Veraguas Sabanero) [sab] 2,500 (1986 SIL). Mountains of western Panama. *Class:* Chibchan, Guaymi. *Dialects:* Sabanero, Bokotá. *Lg Use:* Speakers of Sabanero are few and integrated among the Guaymí. *Lg Dev:* NT: 1988.

Chinese, Hakka [hak] 6,000 in Panama (1981 MARC). Ethnic population: 30,000 to 60,000 including Cantonese (1981 MARC). Panama City, Colón, larger towns of interior. *Lg Use:* Speakers also use Spanish. *Other:* Merchants. See main entry under China.

Chinese, Yue (Yue, Yueh, Cantonese) [yue] Panama City, Colón, larger towns of interior. *Lg Use:* Speakers also use Spanish. *Other:* Merchants. See main entry under China.

Emberá, Northern (Empera, Ebera Bedea, Atrato, Darien, Dariena, Panama Embera, Cholo, Eerã) [emp] 10,480 in Panama (2000 WCD). Population total all countries: 23,480. Southeastern Panama, Darién area, lowland jungle. Also spoken in Colombia. *Class:* Choco, Embera, Northern. *Dialects:* Related languages in order of closeness: Emberá-Catío, Emberá-Baudó, Emberá-Tadó, Epena, Emberá-Chamí, and Wounmeu. Panama and Colombia dialects are inherently intelligible. Northern Embera of the Upper Baudó area and downriver Emberá-Baudó are inherently intelligible. *Lg Use:* Bilingual level estimates for Spanish: 0 40%, 1 32%, 2 25%, 3 2.5%, 4 .5%, 5 0%. *Lg Dev:* Dictionary. Grammar. NT: 1993. *Other:* SOV. Interfluvial. Tropical forest. 100 to 400 meters. Swidden agriculturalists. Traditional religion, Christian.

Emberá-Catío (Catío, Katio, Embena, Epera) [cto] 40 in Panama (1982 SIL). See main entry under Colombia.

Epena (Emberá-Saija, Saija, Epena Saija, Epéna Pedée, Southern Embera, Southern Empera, Cholo) [sja] Southeastern Panama. *Dialect:* Basurudo. *Lg Use:* Bilingual level estimates for Spanish: 0 0%, 1 20%, 2 30%, 3 50%, 4 0%, 5 0%. *Other:* Coastal, riverine. Tropical forest. Sea level to 70 meters. Fishermen; agriculturalists. See main entry under Colombia.

Kuna, Border (Paya-Pucuro Kuna, Kuna de la Frontera, Colombia Cuna, Caiman Nuevo, Long Hair Cuna, Cuna) [kvn] 700 in Panama (1991 SIL). Southeastern Panama, villages of Paya and Pucuro. *Lg Use:* Bilingual level estimates for Spanish: 0 20%, 1 70%, 2 7%, 3 3%, 4 0%, 5 0%. *Other:* Riverine. Tropical forest. 90 to 120 meters. Swidden agriculturalists. See main entry under Colombia.

Kuna, San Blas (San Blas Cuna) [cuk] 57,114 (2000 WCD). Population includes 10,000 in Panama City, Colón, and on banana plantations (1991 SIL). San Blas Islands and on the mainland. *Class:* Chibchan, Kuna. *Dialect:* Chuana, Cueva, Bayano (Alto Bayano, Maje). *Lg Use:* Bilingual level estimates for Spanish: 0 60%, 1 20%, 2 12%, 3 2%, 4 3%, 5 3%. Speakers also use English. *Lg Dev:* NT: 1970–1995. *Other:* SOV. Island, riverine. Tropical forest. Sea level to 70 meters. Swidden agriculturalists; fishermen. Christian.

Ngäbere (Valiente, Chiriqui, Ngobere, Guaymí) [gym] 128,000 in Panama (1990 census). Population total all countries: 133,092. Northeastern Chiriqui, Bocas del Toro, western Veraguas, western provinces. Also spoken in Costa Rica. *Class:* Chibchan, Guaymi. *Dialect:* Valiente, Eastern Guaymí (Tolé, Chiriquí). *Lg Use:* Bilingual level estimates for Spanish: 0 30%, 1 40%, 2 15%, 3 10%, 4 4.5%, 5 .5%. Some speakers also use English creole. *Lg Dev:* NT: 1977. *Other:* 'Ngäbere' is name preferred by speakers for the language, 'Ngäbe' for themselves. SOV. Mountain slope, coastal. Tropical forest. 30 to 2,000 meters. Swidden agriculturalists; hunters; fishermen.

Panamanian Creole English (Southwestern Caribbean Creole English) [jam] 268,435 in Panama (2000 WCD). Bocas del Toro, Colón, and Rio Abajo in Panama City. *Lg Use:* Formerly education was in English, but is now in Spanish. *Other:* Ancestors came from Barbados and Jamaica in mid-19th century to work in fruit plantations, and later to build the railway and canal. Influences from both eastern and western Caribbean Creole English. See main entry under Jamaica (Jamaican Creole English).

284

San Miguel Creole French [scf] 3 (1999 SIL). *Class:* Creole, French based. *Other:* Ancestors came from Saint Lucia in mid-19th century as laborers. The Creole had Spanish influences. Nearly extinct.

Spanish (Español, Castellano) [spa] 2,100,000 in Panama (1995). Enclaves of speakers. *Lg Use:* Official language. See main entry under Spain.

Teribe (Terraba, Tiribi, Tirribi, Nortenyo, Quequexque, Naso) [tfr] 3,000 in Panama (1996 SIL). Population total all countries: 3,005. Northwestern area, Changuinola, Teribe River. Also spoken in Costa Rica. *Class:* Chibchan, Talamanca. *Lg Use:* Speakers also use Spanish. *Lg Dev:* Bible portions: 1979–1984. *Other:* 'Naso' is the name preferred by speakers. OVS. Interfluvial. Tropical forest. 70 meters. Swidden agriculturalists.

Woun Meu (Waun Meo, Waunana, Waumeo, Wounmeu, Wounaan, Noanama, Noenama, Nonama, Chocama, Chanco) [noa] 3,000 in Panama. Population total all countries: 6,000. Southeastern Panama, lowlands. Also spoken in Colombia. *Class:* Choco. *Lg Use:* Bilingual level estimates for Spanish: 0 10%, 1 50%, 2 25%, 3 13.5%, 4 1.0%, 5 0.5%. *Lg Dev:* NT: 1988. *Other:* The people call themselves 'Wounaan'. SOV. Riverine. Tropical forest. 15 meters. Swidden agriculturalists.

Paraguay

Republic of Paraguay, República del Paraguay. 6,191,368. 50,000 speakers of American Indian languages not counting Paraguayan Guaraní (Adelaar 1991). National or official languages: Paraguayan Guaraní, Spanish. Literacy rate: 81% to 90%. Also includes Greek (2,473), Italian (26,000), Japanese (12,000), Korean (6,000), Portuguese (636,000), Ukrainian (26,000), Chinese (7,500). Information mainly from SIL 1969–2002. Blind population: 4,000 (1982 WCE). Deaf population: 316,214. Deaf institutions: 3. The number of languages listed for Paraguay is 22. Of those, 20 are living languages, 1 is a second language without mother-tongue speakers, and 1 is extinct. See map on page 768.

Aché ("Guaiaqui," "Guayakí," "Guoyagui," Guayaki-Ache, Axe) [guq] 1,500 (2002). Eastern, Alto Paraná, Caaguazú, Chopa Pou, Cerro Moroti, and Puerto Barra reservations, and Tupa Renda. *Class:* Tupi, Tupi-Guarani, Subgroup I. *Dialects:* Reported to be four dialects, one of which is nearly extinct. *Lg Use:* Speakers are becoming bilingual in Paraguayan Guaraní. *Lg Dev:* Dictionary. Bible portions: 1978. *Other:* Scattered and nomadic. The name "Guayakí" is derogatory. Hunter-gatherers.

Ayoreo (Morotoco, Moro, Ayoré, Pyeta Yovai) [ayo] 3,000 in Paraguay (1991). Population total all countries: 3,771. Chaco and northern Alto Paraguay departments. Also spoken in Bolivia. *Class:* Zamucoan. *Dialect:* Tsiracua. *Lg Use:* All ages. *Lg Dev:* Grammar. NT: 1982. *Other:* Partially nomadic.

Chamacoco (Ishiro, Jeywo) [ceg] 1,800 (1991 SIL). Northeastern Chaco, eastern Alto Paraguay Department, Puerto Bahia Negra, Puerto Diana, Puerto Esperanza, Dos Estrellas, Potrerito, Fuerte Olimpo, along the Paraguay River. There may be some in Brazil. *Class:* Zamucoan. *Dialects:* Chamacoco Bravo (Tomaraho, Tomaraxa), Ebitoso (Ishiro). *Lg Use:* Vigorous. All ages. Speakers have low proficiency in Spanish and Guaraní. *Lg Dev:* NT: 2001. *Other:* Traditionally hunter-gatherers. Presently agriculturalists; animal husbandry: sheep, goats, pigs, cows, horses, poultry; ranch hands; day laborers; maids; basketry; wood carvers; selling alligator skins.

Chiripá (Tsiripá, Txiripá, Ava, Ava Guaraní, Apytare, Nhandeva, Ñandeva) [nhd] 7,000 in Paraguay (1991). Population total all countries: 11,900. Eastern Paraguay. Also spoken in Argentina, Brazil. *Class:* Tupi, Tupi-Guarani, Subgroup I. *Dialect:* Apapocuva. Close to Paraguayan Guaraní. *Lg Use:* Speakers are shifting to Guaraní. All ages. *Lg Dev:* Bible. *Other:* Most speakers are of the Apapocuva group, which has been described by ethnographers. Fewer Spanish loanwords than Guaraní. Called 'Chiripá' in Paraguay, 'Nhandeva' in Brazil. 'Ñandeva' is used in the Chaco in Paraguay to refer to Tapiete, a different but related language.

Chorote, Iyo'wujwa (Manjuy, Manjui, Choroti) [crq] 500 in Paraguay (1991 SIL). 100% monolingual. Pilcomayo, Boquerón, Chaco. *Lg Use:* Vigorous. All ages. See main entry under Argentina.

Emok (Toba-Emok, Toba, Paraguayan Toba) [emo] Extinct. Ethnic population: 630 (1981 census). Near Asunción. Eastern Chaco. *Class:* Mascoian. *Other:* Agriculturalists; fishermen; hunters.

German, Standard [deu] 166,000 in Paraguay. Population includes 19,000 who are also first-language speakers of Plautdietsch. See main entry under Germany.

Guana (Kaskihá, Cashquiha) [gva] 55 (2002 Adelaar). Ethnic population: 406 to 3,000 (2000 Adelaar). Boquerón, Salado River, south of Chamacoco, north of Sanapaná, Loma Plata. *Class:* Mascoian. *Dialects:* Layana (Niguecactemigi), Echoaldi (Echonoana, Chararana). Close to Sanapaná. *Lg Use:* Increasing use of Paraguayan Guaraní as second language. *Other:* A separate Guana (Kinikinao) is in Mato Grosso, Brazil, related to Chané of Argentina and Terena of Brazil (Arawakan; Voegelin and Voegelin 1977:216, 284; Ruhlen 1987:374, 375; Branislava Susnik). Unconfirmed reports of some Guana in Bolivia. Many live in large villages divided into two sections based on kinship; others live in scattered groups. Some intermarriage with other language groups. Agriculturalists: maize; hunters; fishermen.

Guaraní, Eastern Bolivian (Guasurango, Guarayo, "Chawuncu," "Chiriguano") [gui] 304 in Paraguay (2000 W. Adelaar). Ethnic population: 1,006 to 1,707 (2000 W. Adelaar). Chaco. *Other:* Called 'Guasurango', 'Guarayo', or "Chiriguano" in Paraguay. Different from Guarayo of Bolivia or Huarayo (Ese Ejja) of Peru and Bolivia. "Chawuncu" and "Chiriguano" are derogatory names. See main entry under Bolivia.

Guaraní, Mbyá (Mbyá, Mbua) [gun] 8,000 in Paraguay (2000 Dooley). Departamentos de Caaguazú, Guairá, Caazapá, San Pedro, Concepción, Canindeyú, Itapúa, and other scattered locations. *Lg Use:* All ages. *Other:* Some Chiripá may live among them. They use a special vocabulary, 'ayvu porã', for ritual purposes. Traditionally hunter-gatherers. See main entry under Brazil.

Guaraní, Paraguayan (Avañe'e) [gug] 4,648,000 in Paraguay (1995). Population total all countries: 4,848,000. Also spoken in Argentina. *Class:* Tupi, Tupi-Guarani, Subgroup I. *Dialect:* Jopará (Yopará). One speaker of Chiripá indicated it was bilingualism rather than linguistic closeness that made Paraguayan Guaraní intelligible to him. Jopará is the colloquial form mixed with Spanish loanwords, used by 90% of the population in and around Asunción. Lexical similarity 80% with Chiriguano and 75% lexical similarity with Mbyá. *Lg Use:* Official language. 52% of rural Paraguayans are monolingual in Guaraní. Used some in education. All ages. *Lg Dev:* Bible: 1997. *Other:* SVO.

Lengua (Enxet) [leg] 6,705 (2000 Adelaar). Ethnic population: 8,485 (2000 Adelaar). Chaco, Presidente Hayes Department, Boquerón. *Class:* Mascoian. *Dialects:* Northern Lengua (Eenthlit, Vowak, Lengua Norte), Southern Lengua (Lengua Sur). Differences between the two dialects are reported to be mainly phonological and orthographic. Southern Lengua are seminomadic. *Lg Use:* Southern Lengua women are less bilingual in Paraguayan Guaraní. *Lg Dev:* Different orthography between Southern and Northern Lengua. Roman script. Bible: 1995. *Other:* Southern Lengua: agriculturalists; animal husbandry: cattle, sheep, horses; hunters; gatherers; fishermen.

Maca (Towolhi, Maka, Mak'á, Maká, Macá, Enimaca, Enimaga) [mca] 1,500 (2000 Chief Andrés Chemhey). Ethnic population: 1,500 (2000). Southwestern, Presidente Hayes Department, Colonia Juan Belaieff Island in Paraguay River west of Asunción. Many were taken to Asunción. *Class:* Mataco-Guaicuru, Mataco. *Lg Use:* Vigorous. Older adults and preschool children are monolingual. Used in the home, village, church. All ages. Strongly supportive toward Macá. Language and identity are closely linked by the Macá. Strong cultural cohesion. Men are more proficient in Spanish than women. *Lg Dev:* Bible portions: 1985. *Other:* Alternate names may be 'Nynaka', 'Toothle'. Artifact craftsmen, hunters; agriculturalists. Christian, traditional religion.

Maskoy Pidgin [mhh] Puerto Victoria. *Class:* Pidgin, Mascoian based. *Lg Use:* A mixed language formerly used in a tannin factory with Lengua, Sanapana, Angaite, Guana, and Toba-Maskoy influences. Speakers are reported to have returned to former areas and languages, or to Guaraní-speaking rural areas. Speakers also use Paraguayan Guaraní. *Other:* Different from Toba-Maskoy. Second language only.

Nivaclé ("Chulupí," "Churupí," "Chulupie," "Chulupe," Nivaklé, Ashlushlay, Axluslay) [cag] 18,000 in Paraguay (1991 SIL). Population total all countries: 18,200. Chaco, Presidente Hayes Department, Boquerón. Also spoken in Argentina. *Class:* Mataco-Guaicuru, Mataco. *Dialects:* Forest Nivaclé, River Nivaclé. Mataguayo languages in Paraguay are less similar than Mascoi languages in Paraguay (Fasold 1984). *Lg Use:* Vigorous by all Nivaclé. Nivaclé is the language of the home. All ages. *Lg Dev:* Taught in primary schools. Radio programs. Dictionary. Bible: 1995. *Other:* "Chulupí" is a derogatory name.

Pai Tavytera (Pai, Tavytera, Ava) [pta] 10,000 to 12,000 (1991 SIL). Eastern, Colonia Juan Carlos. *Class:* Tupi, Tupi-Guarani, Guarani I. *Dialects:* Lexical similarity 70% with Kaiwá of Brazil. *Lg Use:* Speakers are shifting to Guaraní. All ages.

Plautdietsch (Low German) [pdt] 38,000 in Paraguay. Population includes 19,000 who speak Plautdietsch and Standard German both as first language. Chaco and eastern Paraguay; towns of Filadelfia, Menno Colony, Loma Plata, Neuland. *Lg Use:* Speakers also use Spanish or German. *Other:* Agriculturalists: dairy, grain, cotton, peanuts. Christian. See main entry under Canada.

Sanapaná (Quiativis, Quilyacmoc, Lanapsua, Saapa, Sanam) [sap] 6,900 (1991 SIL). Population includes 2,900 Sanapana and 4,000 Angaite. Chaco. Sanapana are north of Angaite and Lengua; Boquerón, Presidente Hayes Department, Galbán River. Large concentrations at Salazar Ranch, La Patria, and Esperanza. Angaite are in the southeast Chaco, Presidente Hayes Department, Boquerón, San Carlos. *Class:* Mascoian. *Dialect:* Sanapana, Angaite (Angate, Enlit, Covavitis, Covahloc). Lexical similarity 85% with Northern Lengua. *Lg Use:* Vigorous. All ages. Some of the older people are monolingual. Very limited comprehension of Lengua and Paraguayan Guaraní. Some older adults are monolingual. Many young people speak only Guaraní, but comprehend Angaite. *Lg Dev:* Bible portions: 1994–1995. *Other:* Children do not go to school. An alternate name may be 'Kasnatan'. Agriculturalists; plantation laborers; tannin factory workers; cattle hands.

Spanish [spa] 186,880 in Paraguay (2000 WCD). Mainly Asunción, urban areas. *Lg Use:* Official language. Used in education and government. See main entry under Spain.

Tapieté (Guasurango, Guasurangue, Tirumbae, Yanaigua, Ñanagua, Nandeva) [tpj] 33 in Paraguay (1991 Adelaar). Population total all countries: 203. Ethnic population: 513

to 1,519 (2000 Adelaar). Chaco, northwestern border area, Laguna Negra reservation. Also spoken in Argentina, Bolivia. *Class:* Tupi, Tupi-Guarani, Guarani I. *Dialects:* Linguistically between Chiriguano and Paraguayan Guaraní. *Lg Use:* Speakers have reservations about use of their language outside their culture area. Reported to use Paraguayan Guaraní. Some also use Spanish.

Toba (Toba-Qom, Qom) [tob] 700 in Paraguay (1991 SIL). 60 km northwest of Asunción, Franciscan mission. *Other:* Different from Toba-Maskoy and Toba-Pilagá. See main entry under Argentina.

Toba-Maskoy (Toba of Paraguay, Quilyilhrayrom, Cabanatit, Machicui, Enenlhit) [tmf] 2,500 (1991 SIL). Reserve of 30,000 hectares near Puerto Victoria and Puerto Guaraní, eastern Chaco. *Class:* Mascoian. *Lg Use:* Men 40 years and older speak Paraguayan Guaraní, others use it as second language, and it is used as the church language. They are reported to speak a 'poor' variety of Paraguayan Guaraní. Young people speak Toba-Maskoy and learn some Spanish in school. *Other:* Different from Toba Qom, Toba-Pilagá of Argentina, Maskoy of Paraguay, or Maskoy Pidgin.

Peru

Republic of Peru, República del Perú. 27,544,305. National or official language: Spanish. All languages are official languages in Peru. Literacy rate: 67% to 79%. Also includes North Bolivian Quechua, Chinese (100,000). Information mainly from E. Loos 1973; M. R. Wise 1983; D. Payne 1988, 1991; SIL 1951–2003. Blind population: 30,000. Deaf population: 1,433,960. Deaf institutions: 73 or more. The number of languages listed for Peru is 108. Of those, 93 are living languages and 15 are extinct. See maps beginning on page 766.

Abishira (Abiquira, Auishiri, Agouisiri, Avirxiri, Abigira, Ixignor, Vacacocha, Tequraca) [ash] Extinct. Puerto Elvira on Lake Vacacocha on the Napo River. *Class:* Unclassified. *Lg Use:* Official language. *Other:* Distinct from Aushiri (Wise 1987). In 1925 there were 55 to 75 speakers.

Achuar-Shiwiar (Achuar, Achual, Achuara, Achuale, Jivaro, Maina) [acu] 3,000 in Peru. Population total all countries: 5,000. Morona, Macusari, Tigre, Huasaga, and Corrientes rivers. Also spoken in Ecuador. *Class:* Jivaroan. *Dialects:* Different from Shuar (Jivaro) of Ecuador. *Lg Use:* Official language. Bilingual level estimates for Spanish: 0 90%, 1 6%, 2 3%, 3 1%, 4 0%, 5 0%. *Lg Dev:* Literacy rate in first language: 10% to 30%. Literacy rate in second language: 1%. Dictionary. Grammar. NT: 1981–1994. *Other:* SOV.

Aguano (Uguano, Aguanu, Awano, Santa Crucino) [aga] Extinct. Ethnic population: 40 families in Santa Cruz de Huallaga who did not use Aguano but were members of the ethnic group (1959). Lower Huallaga and upper Samiria rivers, the right bank tributary of the Marañon River. *Class:* Unclassified. *Other:* Ruhlen says this is the same as Chamicuro (1987, personal communication). Chamicuro speakers say they were not the same, but the Aguano spoke Quechua (Wise 1987, personal communication).

Aguaruna (Aguajun, Ahuajun) [agr] 38,290 (2000 WCD). Almost no monolinguals. Western upper Marañon River area, Potro, Mayo, and Cahuapanas rivers. *Class:* Jivaroan. *Dialects:* Close to Huambisa, Achuar-Shiwiar. *Lg Use:* Official language. Vigorous. Spanish speakers and Quechuas in the area also use Aguaruna. All domains. Oral and written use in commerce. Letters. Positive toward bilingualism. Bilingual level estimates for Spanish: 0 35%, 1 20%, 2 20%, 3 15%, 4 9.9%, 5 .1%. Primary education begins in Aguaruna and Spanish is gradually added. *Lg Dev:* Literacy rate in first language: 60% to 100%. Literacy rate in second language: 50% to 75%. Taught in primary schools. Roman script. Dictionary. Grammar. NT: 1973. *Other:* SOV. Mountain slope. Tropical forest. 200 to 1,000 meters. Swidden agriculturalists: manioc, bananas, peanuts, wild potatoes; hunting and fishing. Christian, traditional religion.

Ajyíninka Apurucayali (Ashaninca, Ashéninca Apurucayali, "Apurucayali Campa," Ajyéninka, "Campa," "Axininka Campa") [cpc] 4,000 (2000 SIL). Apurucayali tributary of the Pachitea River. *Class:* Arawakan, Maipuran, Southern Maipuran, Pre-Andine. *Dialects:* Not intelligible with other varieties of Ashéninka. *Lg Use:* Official language. Bilingual level estimates for Spanish: 0 20%, 1 40%, 2 30%, 3 10%, 4 0%, 5 0%. *Lg Dev:* Literacy rate in first language: 20%. Literacy rate in second language: 30%. Dictionary. Grammar. NT: 2000. *Other:* "Campa" is a derogatory name. VSO.

Amahuaca (Amawaka, Amaguaco, Ameuhaque, Ipitineri, Sayaco) [amc] 90 to 130 in Peru (2000 SIL). 20 monolinguals. Population total all countries: 310. Ethnic population: 500 (300 in Peru and 200 in Brazil). Perhaps 50 in the border areas have not been contacted. Widely scattered in the southeastern Amazon Basin in Ucayali and Madre de Dios states on the following rivers: Sepahua, Curiuja, Curanja, Upper Ucayali, Inuya, Mapuya, Purus, Aguaytía, Yuruá, and Las Piedras. Also spoken in Brazil. *Class:* Panoan, South-Central, Amahuaca. *Dialects:* Closest to Cashinahua and Shipibo. *Lg Use:* Official language. The group is disintegrating and losing its identity due to intermarriage with non-Amahuaca speakers. Used in the home and with neighbors. Children not learning Amahuaca (1999). Some speakers over 50 and some former students in bilingual schools. Negative language attitude. 60% can speak Spanish fairly well. Most speak some Spanish, Yaminahua, or Sharanahua. *Lg Dev:* Literacy rate in first language: 30%. Literacy rate in second language: 50%. Roman script. Dictionary. Grammar. Bible portions: 1963–1997. *Other:* SOV. Plains, hills. Hunters; fishermen; swidden agriculturalists; lumber workers; oil company workers; maids in cities; on the Piedres River only, harvesting and processing Brazil nuts. Christian, traditional religion.

Amarakaeri (Amarakaire, Amaracaire, "Mashco") [amr] 500 (1987 SIL). Madre de Dios and Colorado rivers. *Class:* Harakmbet. *Dialect:* Kisambaeri. The Harakmbet languages are not Arawakan. *Lg Use:* Official language. Bilingual level estimates for Spanish: 0 20%, 1 30%, 2 40%, 3 5%, 4 5%, 5 0%. *Lg Dev:* Literacy rate in first language: below 1%. Literacy rate in second language: 5% to 15%. Dictionary. NT: 1986. *Other:* "Mashco" is a derogatory term. Ethnic subgroups: Kochimberi, Küpondirideri, Wíntaperi, Wakitaneri, Kareneri. SOV. Gold panners.

Andoa (Shimigae, Semigae, Gae, Gaye) [anb] Extinct. Pastaza River. None in Ecuador. *Class:* Zaparoan. *Dialects:* A distinct language from Záparo (Kayapwe) of Ecuador, which is now extinct in Peru. *Lg Use:* The ethnic group speaks Pastaza Quechua. Integrated with the Quechua. Some also use Spanish. Last known speaker died 1993.

Arabela (Chiripuno, Chiripunu) [arl] 50 (2002 SIL). Ethnic population: 500 (2002 SIL). Arabela River, tributary of Napo, two villages. *Class:* Zaparoan. *Lg Use:* Official language. Some members of the ethnic group understand Arabela but do not speak it. Seriously endangered. Bilingual level estimates for Quechua: 0 0%, 1 0%, 2 20%, 3 60%, 4 20%, 5 0%; Spanish: 0 0%, 1 20%, 2 40%, 3 30%, 4 10%, 5 0%. Quechua and Spanish are used as second language by speakers and by members of the ethnic group who do not speak Arabela. *Lg Dev:* Literacy rate in first language: 10%

to 30%. Literacy rate in second language: 50% to 75%. NT: 1986. *Other:* Pananuyuri is a division of the Arabela. SOV. Tropical forest.

Asháninka (Asháninca, "Campa") [cni] 23,750 to 28,500 (2000 SIL). Ethnic population: 25,000 to 30,000 (2000 SIL). Apurimac, Ene, Perene, Tambo rivers and tributaries. *Class:* Arawakan, Maipuran, Southern Maipuran, Pre-Andine. *Dialects:* Close to Ashéninka, Caquinte, Machiguenga. *Lg Use:* Official language. Vigorous. *Lg Dev:* Literacy rate in first language: 10% to 30%. Literacy rate in second language: 15% to 25%. Dictionary. NT: 1972. *Other:* "Campa" is a derogatory name. VSO. Foothills. Tropical forest. Swidden agriculturalists: manioc; hunting; fishing.

Ashéninka Pajonal (Ashéninca, Atsiri, Pajonal, "Campa") [cjo] 12,000 (2002 SIL). Ethnic population: 12,000 (2002 SIL). Central Gran Pajonal area. *Class:* Arawakan, Maipuran, Southern Maipuran, Pre-Andine. *Lg Use:* Official language. All but a handful in Pajonal Ashéninka speak the language. Bilingual level estimates for Spanish: 0 79%, 1 15%, 2 5%, 3 .5%, 4 .5%, 5 0%. *Lg Dev:* Literacy rate in first language: 20%. Literacy rate in second language: 15%. NT: 2002. *Other:* "Campa" is a derogatory name. VSO.

Ashéninka Perené ("Perené Campa," Ashéninca Perené) [prq] 5,500 (2001 SIL). Upper Perené River (tributary of the Pachitea River). *Class:* Arawakan, Maipuran, Southern Maipuran, Pre-Andine. *Dialects:* Somewhat intelligible with other varieties of Ashéninka. *Lg Use:* Official language. 30% of speakers have routine proficiency in Spanish. 40% have higher than routine proficiency. *Lg Dev:* Literacy rate in first language: 30%. Literacy rate in second language: 55%. Grammar. *Other:* "Campa" is a derogatory name. VSO.

Ashéninka, Pichis (Pichis Ashéninca, "Pichis Campa") [cpu] 12,000 (2001 SIL). Pichis and its tributaries except Apurucayali. *Class:* Arawakan, Maipuran, Southern Maipuran, Pre-Andine. *Dialects:* Somewhat intelligible with other varieties of Ashéninka. *Lg Use:* Official language. 35% of speakers have routine proficiency in Spanish. 15% have higher than routine proficiency. *Lg Dev:* Literacy rate in first language: 30%. Literacy rate in second language: 35%. Dictionary. NT: 1996. *Other:* "Campa" is a derogatory name. VSO.

Ashéninka, South Ucayali [cpy] 13,000 (2002 SIL). Ethnic population: 14,000 (2002 SIL). Upper Ucayali River and tributaries (Southernmost part of Ucayali Department). *Class:* Arawakan, Maipuran, Southern Maipuran, Pre-Andine. *Dialects:* Most closely related to Pajanol Ashéninka. *Lg Use:* Official language. Speakers also use Spanish. *Lg Dev:* Literacy rate in first language: 15%. Literacy rate in second language: 35%. Bible portions: 1976–1986. *Other:* VSO.

Ashéninka, Ucayali-Yurúa (Ucayali Ashéninca) [cpb] 7,000 in Peru (2001 SIL). Population total all countries: 7,212. Tributaries of the Ucayali River (Pachitea, Arruya, Shahuaya, Sheshea, Cohengua, Inuya) and Yurúa River. Also spoken in Brazil. *Class:* Arawakan, Maipuran, Southern Maipuran, Pre-Andine. *Dialects:* Somewhat intelligible with other varieties of Ashéninka. *Lg Use:* Official language. Bilingual level estimates for Spanish: 0 20%, 1 30%, 2 25%, 3 15%, 4 5%, 5 5%. *Lg Dev:* Literacy rate in first language: 15%. Literacy rate in second language: 20%. Dictionary. Grammar. NT: 2000. *Other:* VSO.

Atsahuaca (Yamiaca) [atc] Extinct. Carama River, tributary of Tambopata, and Chaspa River, tributary of Inambari. *Class:* Panoan, North-Central. *Other:* In 1904 there were 20 speakers.

Aushiri (Auxira) [avs] Extinct. Tributaries of the right bank of the Napo River, Escuelacocha. *Class:* Zaparoan.

Other: Similar to Arabela. Distinct from Abishira (Wise 1987).

Aymara, Central [ayr] 441,743 in Peru (2000 WCD). Lake Titicaca area, Puno. *Lg Use:* Official language. All ages. *Other:* Lupaca is the main literary dialect. See main entry under Bolivia.

Aymara, Southern [ayc] From Lake Titicaca toward ocean. *Class:* Aymaran. *Dialects:* Some important verb forms and vocabulary differences from Central Aymara. Dialect intelligibility needs investigation in Tacna and Moquegua (Landerman 1984). *Lg Use:* Official language. Most speakers have low proficiency in Spanish.

Bora [boa] 2,328 in Peru (2000 WCD). Population total all countries: 2,828. Northeast Yaguasyacu, Putumayo, Ampiyacu River area, five villages in Peru. Also spoken in Brazil, Colombia. *Class:* Witotoan, Boran. *Dialect:* Miraña. A distinct language from Bora Muinane but related. 94% intelligibility of Miraña. *Lg Use:* Official language. *Lg Dev:* Literacy rate in first language: 10% to 30%. Literacy rate in second language: 25% to 50%. Dictionary. Grammar. NT: 1982. *Other:* SOV.

Cahuarano [cah] 5 (1976 SIL). Nanay River. *Class:* Zaparoan. *Lg Use:* Official language. It may be extinct. Speakers have shifted to Spanish. *Other:* Nearly extinct.

Candoshi-Shapra (Kandoshi, Candoshi, Candoxi, Murato) [cbu] 3,000 (1981 SIL). Morona, Pastaza, Huitoyacu, and Chapuli rivers. *Class:* Language Isolate. *Dialects:* Chapara (Shapra), Kandoashi. May be distantly related to Arawakan; probably not Jivaroan. *Lg Use:* Official language. Positive language attitude. Bilingual level estimates for Spanish: 0 88.5%, 1 10%, 2 1%, 3 .5%, 4 0%, 5 0%. *Lg Dev:* Literacy rate in first language: 10% to 30%. Literacy rate in second language: 15% to 25%. Dictionary. Grammar. NT: 1979–1993. *Other:* SOV.

Capanahua (Kapanawa) [kaq] 387 (2000 WCD). No monolinguals. Ethnic population: 400 (2000 W. Adelaar). Tapiche-Buncuya rivers area. *Class:* Panoan, North-Central. *Dialect:* Pahenbaquebo. Closest language is Shipibo. Lexical similarity 50% to 60% with Shipibo. *Lg Use:* Official language. Almost no children speak the language. Used by adults in the home. Use of Spanish to a Capanahua by a Capanahua can be interpreted as rejecting the other person as an outsider. Bilingual level estimates for Spanish: 0 0%, 1 0%, 2 15%, 3 50%, 4 30%, 5 5%. Capanahua is used to some degree in two bilingual schools. *Lg Dev:* Literacy rate in first language: below 10%. Literacy rate in second language: 5% to 15%. Taught in primary schools. Roman script. Dictionary. Grammar. NT: 1978. *Other:* "Capacho" is a pejorative term. SOV. Tropical forest. 115 meters. Swidden agriculturalists. Christian, traditional religion.

Caquinte (Caquinte Campa, Poyenisati, "Cachomashiri") [cot] 300 (2000 SIL). Ethnic population: 300. Poyeni, Mayapo, and Picha rivers. Along the upper Poyeni River, which flows into the Tambo; along the Yori and Agueni rivers which become the Mipaya River flowing into the Urubamba. A few speakers also live on the Sensa and Vitiricaya rivers, affluents of the Urubamba. *Class:* Arawakan, Maipuran, Southern Maipuran, Pre-Andine. *Dialects:* Closest to Asháninka. *Lg Use:* Official language. Vigorous. Oral and written Caquinte is used in religious services. The language is mostly spoken in the local community. Letters are sometimes exchanged between Caquinte villages. All ages. Positive language attitude. Bilingual level estimates for Machiguenga: 0 85%, 1 5%, 2 8%, 3 2%, 4 0%, 5 0%. Almost none can converse in Spanish. Some use Asháninka as second language. Some are borrowing words from Asháninka or Machiguenga. *Lg Dev:* Literacy rate in first language: 33%. Literacy rate in second language: below 5%. 100 people can read and write Caquinte. Oral and written in primary school. Roman

script. Grammar. Bible portions: 1984–1991. *Other:* "Cachomashiri" and "Campa" are derogatory names. VSO. Valleys, hills. Tropical forest. Agriculturalists; hunters; fishermen. Very little cash income.

Cashibo-Cacataibo (Caxibo, Cacibo, Cachibo, Cahivo, Managua, Hagueti) [cbr] 5,000 (1999). Some women over 50 are monolingual. Aguaytía, San Alejandro, and Súngaro rivers. *Class:* Panoan, Western. *Dialects:* Cacataibo de Mariscal, Cacataibo de Sinchi Roca, Cashibo. *Lg Use:* Official language. Vigorous. All domains. Used in schools up to third grade. All ages. Bilingual level estimates for Spanish: 0 34%, 1 24%, 2 22%, 3 12%, 4 6%, 5 2%. *Lg Dev:* Literacy rate in first language: 5% to 10%. Literacy rate in second language: 15% to 25%. Taught in primary schools. Poetry. Dictionary. NT: 1978. *Other:* SOV. Traditional religion, Christian.

Cashinahua (Kaxinawá, Kaxynawa, Caxinawa, Caxinawá) [cbs] 1,600 in Peru (2003). Population total all countries: 2,000. Ethnic population: 5,000. Curanja and Purus rivers. Also spoken in Brazil. *Class:* Panoan, Southeastern. *Dialects:* It may be closest to Sharanahua. *Lg Use:* Official language. All ages. 5% to 10% have routine proficiency in Spanish. *Lg Dev:* Literacy rate in first language: 40%. Literacy rate in second language: 20% to 30%. Roman script. Dictionary. NT: 1980. *Other:* SOV; postpositions; genitives before noun heads; articles, adjectives after noun heads; question word initial; 7 prefixes, 3 suffixes; ergative; lexical tone. Riverine. Tropical forest. Swidden agriculturalists; hunters. Christian, traditional religion.

Chamicuro (Chamicura, Chamicolo) [ccc] 2 (2000 Adelaar). Ethnic population: 10 to 20 (2000 Adelaar). Pampa Hermosa on a tributary of Huallaga. *Class:* Arawakan, Maipuran, Western Maipuran. *Lg Use:* Official language. Speakers have shifted to Spanish. No children. *Lg Dev:* Dictionary. *Other:* Ruhlen says Aguano is the same as this (1987, personal communication). Chamicuro speakers say it was different (Wise 1987). Nearly extinct.

Chayahuita (Chayawita, Chawi, Tshaahui, Chayhuita, Chayabita, Shayabit, Balsapuertino, Paranapura, Cahuapa) [cbt] 11,384 (2000 WCD). Paranapura, Cahuapanas, Sillay, and Shanusi rivers. *Class:* Cahuapanan. *Dialects:* Chayahuita, Cahuapana. Not intelligible with Jebero. *Lg Use:* Official language. All ages. Bilingual level estimates for Spanish: 0 60%, 1 20%, 2 10%, 3 6%, 4 3%, 5 1%. *Lg Dev:* Literacy rate in first language: 1% to 5%. Literacy rate in second language: 5% to 15%. Dictionary. NT: 1978. *Other:* SOV.

Cholón (Tinganeses, Seeptsa) [cht] Extinct. Valley of the Huallaga River from Tingo María to Valle. *Class:* Hibito-Cholon. *Dialects:* Ruhlen says it is Andean. Adelaar says it is in the Hibito-Cholon family. *Lg Use:* Extinct in 2000 (2000 Wise). Members of the ethnic group now speak Quechua.

Cocama-Cocamilla (Cocama, Kokama, Ucayali, Xibitaoan, Huallaga, Pampadeque, Pandequebo) [cod] 2,000 in Peru (2000 W. Adelaar). Few monolinguals. Population total all countries: 2,050. Ethnic population: 15,000 in Peru (2000 W. Adelaar). Northeastern lower Ucayali, lower Marañon, and Huallaga rivers area. Also spoken in Brazil, Colombia. *Class:* Tupi, Tupi-Guarani, Subgroup III. *Dialects:* Cocamilla, Cocama. Closest to Omagua. *Lg Use:* Official language. All speakers are older adults (1981). Bilingual level estimates for Spanish: 0 0%, 1 0%, 2 2%, 3 28%, 4 60%, 5 10%. *Lg Dev:* Literacy rate in first language: 3%. Literacy rate in second language: 50%. Grammar. Bible portions: 1961–1967. *Other:* SOV. Traditional religion, Christian.

Culina (Kulina, Kulino, Kulyna, Kurina, Kollina, Madija, Madihá) [cul] 400 in Peru (2002 Boyer). Primarily monolingual. Ethnic population: 400. Southeast, near Brazilian border, upper Purus and Santa Rosa rivers. *Lg Use:* Official language. Vigorous. All ages. Bilingual level estimates for Spanish: 0 78%, 1 10%, 2 5%, 3 5%, 4 1.5%, 5 .5%. *Lg Dev:* Literacy rate in first language: Over 50%. Literacy rate in second language: 1% to 5%. Mostly in Spanish, a little in Culina. *Other:* 200 meters. Christian. See main entry under Brazil.

Ese Ejja (Ese Exa, Ese Eja, Ese'ejja, Tiatinagua, Tambopata-Guarayo, Huarayo, "Chama") [ese] 472 in Peru (2000 WCD). Ethnic population: 400 to 500 in Peru (2000 SIL). Tambopata and Heath rivers around Maldonado. *Lg Use:* Official language. Most ages. Almost all in Peru also use Spanish. *Other:* "Chama" is a derogatory name. Swidden agriculturalists; fishermen. See main entry under Bolivia.

Hibito (Jibito, Chibito, Zibito, Ibito, Xibita) [hib] Extinct. Bobonaje River, tributary of Jelache, tributary of Huayabamba, coming into Huallaga on the west side. *Class:* Hibito-Cholon. *Other:* In 1851 there were 500.

Huachipaeri (Huachipaire, Wacipaire, "Mashco") [hug] 311 (2000 WCD). Population includes 12 Sapiteri, 10 Toyeri, 20 Arasairi, 50 Manuquiari, 36 to 50 Pukirieri (Puncuri). Upper Madre de Dios and Keros rivers. *Class:* Harakmbet. *Dialects:* Huachipaire, Sapiteri, Toyeri (Toyoeri, Tuyuneri), Arasairi. Close to Amarakaeri but they probably cannot use the same literature. The Sapiteri are integrating with the Amarakaeri. Toyeri is similar to Sapiteri. Some Kisambaeri (Amarakaeri dialect) have integrated with the Toyeri and others with the Sapiteri. Manuquiari may be a subgroup of Toyeri or Huachipaeri. Pukirieri may be a subgroup of Toyeri or Arasairi. Arasairi is distinct from Amarakaeri or Huachipaeri; similar to Sapiteri. *Lg Use:* Official language. Speakers have some proficiency in Spanish. *Other:* "Mashco" is a derogatory name. SOV.

Huambisa (Huambiza, Wambisa) [hub] 9,333 (2000 WCD). Morona and Santiago rivers. *Class:* Jivaroan. *Dialects:* Close to Aguaruna and Achuar-Shiwiar. *Lg Use:* Official language. Trade language. All domains. All ages. Positive language attitude. Bilingual level estimates for Spanish: 0 20%, 1 25%, 2 25%, 3 20%, 4 9%, 5 1%. *Lg Dev:* Literacy rate in first language: 50%. Literacy rate in second language: 50%. Dictionary. NT: 1975–1997. *Other:* SOV. Tropical forest. Swidden agriculturalists. Christian, traditional religion.

Huitoto, Minica (Minica Huitoto) [hto] 5 in Peru (1995 SIL). *Lg Use:* Official language. See main entry under Colombia.

Huitoto, Murui (Bue, Witoto) [huu] 1,000 in Peru (1995 SIL). Very few monolinguals. Population total all countries: 2,900. Ampiyacu, Putumayo, and Napo rivers. None left in Brazil. Northeastern Peru, southwestern Colombia. Generally north of Amazon River between Iquitos, Peru and Leticia, Colombia on the south, to the Caquetá River on the north. Also spoken in Colombia. *Class:* Witotoan, Witoto, Witoto Proper, Minica-Murui. *Dialect:* Mica. *Lg Use:* Official language. Speakers are shifting to Spanish. Recognized by Peruvian government for use in schools. Used in written and oral forms for religious services. Huitoto has more prestige in Colombia than in Peru. Bilingual level estimates for Spanish: 0 1%, 1 9%, 2 45%, 3 35%, 4 9%, 5 1%. 90% of those under 50 have routine proficiency in Spanish. Very few are monolingual. A few speak Bora. *Lg Dev:* Literacy rate in first language: below 1%. Literacy rate in second language: 15% to 25%. 95% of those under 40 are literate. Roman script. Dictionary. Grammar. NT: 1978. *Other:* SOV. Tropical forest. Low altitude. Christian, traditional religion.

Huitoto, Nüpode (Nipode Witoto, Muinane Huitoto) [hux] 100 (1991 SIL). *Class:* Witotoan, Witoto, Witoto

Proper, Nipode. *Lg Use:* Official language. Speakers also use Minica Huitoto or Murui Huitoto. *Lg Dev:* Dictionary. Grammar. Bible portions: 1961.

Iñapari (Inamari) [inp] 4 (1999 SIL). Piedras River, at the mouth of Sabaluyo, near Puerto Maldonado. Extinct in Bolivia. *Class:* Arawakan, Maipuran, Southern Maipuran, Purus. *Lg Use:* Official language. No children. All are reported to be bilingual in Spanish. *Lg Dev:* Dictionary. *Other:* Nearly extinct.

Iquito (Iquita, Ikito, Amacacore, Hamacore, Quiturran, Puca-Uma) [iqu] 35 (2002 SIL). 1 monolingual. Ethnic population: 500. Loreto Province, Pintoyacu, Nanay, and Chambira rivers, villages of San Antonia and Atalaya. *Class:* Zaparoan. *Dialect:* Pintuyacu. Was close to Cahuarano. *Lg Use:* Official language. Speakers are older adults. Negative language attitude. Widespread use of Spanish. *Lg Dev:* Literacy rate in second language: 75%. Roman script. Bible portions: 1963. *Other:* About 350 years ago they were a large group living where the city of Iquitos now is. By 1958–1966 they had 100 speakers on the verge of extinction and acculturation to Spanish-speaking society. Children understood but did not speak Iquito, adults were bilingual with Spanish, older people understood Spanish, but only spoke Iquito. Speakers died from measles, whooping cough, and pneumonia. The rubber boom and landowner (patron) system had devastating effects. Tropical forest. Swidden agri-culturalists: yucca; fishermen; hunters; chicle and rubber gatherers; traders. Christian. Nearly extinct.

Isconahua (Iscobaquebu) [isc] 82 (2000 WCD). Callaria River. *Class:* Panoan, North-Central. *Dialects:* Most closely related to Shipibo. *Lg Use:* Official language. They live close to the Shipibo and also use Shipibo. *Other:* Nearly extinct.

Jaqaru (Haqearu, Haqaru, Haq'aru, Aru) [jqr] 736 (2000 W. Adelaar). Population includes 725 Jaqaru, 11 Kawki. Ethnic population: 2,000 (2000 W. Adelaar). Lima Department, Yauyos Province, Tupe village (Jaqaru) and Cachuy village (Cauqui). *Class:* Aymaran. *Dialect:* Cauqui (Kawki, Cachuy). Lexical similarity 73% with Aymara, 79% between Kawki and Aymara. *Lg Use:* Official language. Cauqui dialect is nearly extinct. Adult speakers. Most or all use Spanish as second language. There may still be a few monolinguals, all women.

Jebero (Xebero, Chebero, Xihuila) [jeb] Ethnic population: 2,000 to 3,000 (2000 W. Adelaar). District of Jebero. *Class:* Cahuapanan. *Lg Use:* Official language. Speakers are older adults. Interest in language revival. Widespread use of Spanish. *Lg Dev:* Bible portions: 1959. *Other:* Nearly extinct.

Machiguenga (Matsiganga, Matsigenka, Mañaries) [mcb] 10,149 (2000 WCD). Urubamba, Camisea, Picha, Manu, Timpia, Tigompinia, Kompiroshiato, and Mishagua rivers. *Class:* Arawakan, Maipuran, Southern Maipuran, Pre-Andine. *Dialects:* Closest to Nomatsiguenga. There are minor dialects. *Lg Use:* Official language. All ages. Bilingual level estimates for Spanish: 0 60%, 1 25%, 2 8.3%, 3 4.6%, 4 1.6%, 5 .5%. *Lg Dev:* Literacy rate in first language: 30% to 60%. Literacy rate in second language: 25% to 50%. Dictionary. NT: 1976–1997. *Other:* VSO.

Mashco Piro (Cujareno, Cujareño, "Mashco") [cuj] 20 to 100 (1976 SIL). All are completely monolingual. Manu Park, Dept. of Madre de Dios. Cujar, Purus, Tahuamanu, Mishagua, and Piedras rivers. Extinct in Bolivia. *Class:* Arawakan, Maipuran, Southern Maipuran, Purus. *Dialects:* About 60% inherent intelligibility of Yine. "Mashco" is a derogatory name. *Lg Use:* Official language. *Other:* Highly nomadic. Hunter-gatherers. Nearly extinct.

Matsés (Mayoruna, Maxuruna, Majuruna, Mayiruna, Maxirona, Magirona, Mayuzuna) [mcf] 2,000 in Peru (2003 SIL). Population total all countries: 3,000 to 3,500.

Yaquerana. Also spoken in Brazil. *Class:* Panoan, Northern. *Dialects:* Different from Mayo, or Maya and Marubo of Brazil. *Lg Use:* Official language. Vigorous. Schools are taught by Matsés teachers in communities in Peru. All ages. Bilingual level estimates for Spanish: 0 97%, 1 3%, 2 0%, 3 0%, 4 0%, 5 0%. *Lg Dev:* Literacy rate in first language: 1% to 5%. Literacy rate in second language: 5% to 15%. Grammar. NT: 1993. *Other:* SOV.

Muniche (Otanave, Otanabe, Munichino, Munichi) [myr] 3 (1988 SIL). Town of Muniches on the Paranapura River. *Class:* Language Isolate. *Lg Use:* Official language. Speakers are shifting to Spanish. May be extinct. *Lg Dev:* Dictionary. Grammar. *Other:* Nearly extinct.

Nanti ("Cogapacori," "Kogapakori") [cox] 350 to 600 (2002 Michael). Headwaters of the Camisea and Timpia rivers. *Class:* Arawakan, Maipuran, Southern Maipuran, Pre-Andine. *Dialects:* Language is most closely related to Machiguenga, but they have remained separate. *Lg Use:* Official language. Speakers also use Spanish or Machiguenga. *Lg Dev:* Literacy rate in first language: 0.5%. Literacy rate in second language: 0%. Bible portions: 2000. *Other:* Need literature adapted from Machiguenga. VSO. Traditional religion.

Nocamán (Nocomán) [nom] Extinct. Headwaters of the Inuya River, Amueya River, Tamaya River. *Class:* Panoan, Western. *Dialects:* May have been a dialect of Cashibo. *Other:* In 1925 there were 3 speakers.

Nomatsiguenga ("Nomatsiguenga Campa," Atiri) [not] 6,500 (2003 SIL). 5,500 to 6,000 monolinguals. Departamento de Junín, between the rivers Ene and Perene, and Anapati River system in the foothills. *Class:* Arawakan, Maipuran, Southern Maipuran, Pre-Andine. *Dialects:* Closest to Machiguenga. *Lg Use:* Official language. All ages. Bilingual level estimates for Spanish: 0 5%, 1 15%, 2 30%, 3 25%, 4 20%, 5 5%; Asháninca: 0 5%, 1 10%, 2 15%, 3 20%, 4 25%, 5 25%. *Lg Dev:* Literacy rate in first language: 50%. Literacy rate in second language: 35% to 40%. Videos. Dictionary. Grammar. NT: 1980. *Other:* VSO. Traditional religion, Christian, syncretism.

Ocaina (Okaina) [oca] 54 in Peru (2000). Population total all countries: 66. Ethnic population: 150 in Peru (2000 W. Adelaar). Yaguasyacu, Ampuyacu, and Putumayo rivers, northeastern Peru. Also spoken in Colombia. *Class:* Witotoan, Witoto, Ocaina. *Dialects:* Dukaiya, Ibo'tsa. *Lg Use:* Official language. Few children speakers. Speakers also use Bora, Murui Huitoto, or Spanish. *Lg Dev:* Dictionary. Bible portions: 1964–1971.

Omagua (Omagua-Yete, Ariana, Pariana, Anapia, Macanipa, Kambeba, Yhuata, Umaua, Cambeba, Campeba, Cambela, Cambeeba, Compeva, Canga-Peba, Agua) [omg] 10 to 100 in Peru (1976 SIL). Population total all countries: 10 to 100. Ethnic population: 627 (1976). Omaguas near Iquitos. There may be none left in Brazil (1995). Also spoken in Brazil. *Class:* Tupi, Tupi-Guarani, Subgroup III. *Dialects:* Closest to Cocama. *Lg Use:* Official language. No child speakers. In Peru all also use Spanish or Cocama. *Other:* Nearly extinct.

Omurano (Humurana, Roamaina, Numurana, Umurano, Mayna) [omu] Extinct. *Class:* Zaparoan. *Lg Use:* Became extinct by 1958.

Orejón (Coto, Koto, Payagua, Mai Ja, Oregon, Orechon, Tutapi) [ore] 190 (1976 SIL). Ethnic population: 405 (2000 WCD). Yanayacu, Sucusari, Algodon, and Putumayo rivers. *Class:* Tucanoan, Western Tucanoan, Southern. *Dialect:* Nebaji. *Lg Use:* Official language. Some children speakers. Speakers also use Spanish. *Lg Dev:* Dictionary. Bible portions: 1967–1976.

Panobo (Manoa, Pano, Pana, Pelado, Wariapano, Huariapano) [pno] Extinct. Along the Ucayali River and mixed with the Shetebo. *Class:* Panoan, Unclassified.

Other: Data obtained January 1991. Not a Shipibo-Conibo dialect. The last speaker died in March 1991; 100 to 200 in 1925.

Peruvian Sign Language [prl] *Class:* Deaf sign language. *Lg Use:* There are over 70 deaf schools, but the oralist method is used by most in the classroom. The majority of students use sign language outside the classroom. The sign language used in the schools is different from what adults use outside. *Lg Dev:* TV. Dictionary. *Other:* There is a manual alphabet for spelling.

Pisabo (Pisagua, Pisahua) [pig] 513 (2000 WCD). Between the Tapíche and Blanco rivers. *Class:* Panoan, Northern. *Lg Use:* Official language.

Puquina [puq] Extinct. South shore of Lake Titicaca, town of Puquina. *Class:* Unclassified. *Lg Use:* Extinct for at least 200 years. *Other:* Proposals for its classification are inconclusive.

Quechua, Ambo-Pasco (San Rafael-Huariaca Quechua) [qva] 90,000 (1998 SIL). 20% monolinguals. Ethnic population: 90,000. In province of Ambo (department of Huánuco), districts of Huacar, San Francisco de Mosca, and San Rafael. In province of Pasco (department of Pasco), districts of Chaupimarca, Huachón, Huariaca, Ninacaca, Pallanchacra, San Francisco de Asís de Yarusyacán, Simón Bolívar, Ticlacayán, Tinyahuarca, Vicco, and Yanacancha. *Class:* Quechuan, Quechua I. *Lg Use:* Official language. Vigorous in isolated communities; used by very few as a second language. Used in the home, fields, community. All ages. Low prestige. Speakers also use Spanish. *Lg Dev:* Literacy rate in first language: below 1%. Literacy rate in second language: 25% to 50%. Roman script. Radio programs. Dictionary. Bible portions: 1993–1997. *Other:* SOV. 2,200 to 4,400 meters. Agriculturalists; animal husbandry. Christian, traditional religion.

Quechua, Arequipa-La Unión (Arequipa Quechua, Cotahuasi Quechua) [qxu] 18,628 (2000 WCD). 10,000 monolinguals. Ethnic population: 32,000. Arequipa Department, La Unión Province, Cotahuasi District; Apurímac Department, Antabamba Province. *Class:* Quechuan, Quechua II, C. *Dialect:* Cotahuasi, Northern Arequipa, Highland Arequipa, Antabamba (Apurimac). Closer linguistically to Cuzco than to Ayacucho. Very close to eastern Apurímac. *Lg Use:* Official language. Vigorous. It is used in some schools. Some families are switching to Spanish. Speakers of other languages use Quechua in order to talk to monolinguals. Spoken form is used for administration, commerce, and labor relations, and occasionally in religious services. All ages. The language is considered inferior to Spanish. Fluent speakers of Spanish usually leave the area. Those who return do not like Quechua speakers to use Spanish loans. Spanish is the second language. Many monolinguals. Cusco Quechua used in schools. *Lg Dev:* Literacy rate in first language: 5%. Literacy rate in second language: 30%. 600 can read Quechua, 200 can write it. Taught in primary schools. Roman script. Radio programs. Videos. Dictionary. Bible portions: 1993. *Other:* SOV. Mountain slope, plateau. 2,000 to 4,900 meters. Agriculturalists. Christian.

Quechua, Ayacucho (Runasimi, Chanka) [quy] 900,000 (2000 SIL). 300,000 monolinguals. Southwestern Ayacucho Region and Lima. *Class:* Quechuan, Quechua II, C. *Dialects:* Andahuaylas, Huancavelica. Lexical similarity 96% with Surcubamba, Puquio, and Cuzco. *Lg Use:* Official language. Vigorous. Used in the home, family, administration, religion, commerce. Oral and written Quechua used in some schools, more than one university. Written form used in religious services. The language is considered inferior to Spanish. Bilingual level estimates for Spanish: 0 31%, 1 20%, 2 20%, 3 20%, 4 8%, 5 1%. Some families are shifting to Spanish. *Lg Dev:*

Literacy rate in first language: 5% to 10%. Literacy rate in second language: 25% to 50%. Perhaps 10,000 read it, 2,000 can write it. Some oral and written in primary education. Roman script. Radio programs. Dictionary. Grammar. Bible: 1987. *Other:* SOV. Low valleys, mountain slope, plateau. Tropical vegetation in lowlands. Agriculturalists. Christian, traditional religion.

Quechua, Cajamarca [qvc] 30,000 (2000 D. Coombs). Cajamarca, Chetilla, and Los Baños districts. The western dialect in the district of Chetilla. The eastern variety in Porcon and in several areas around the valley of Cajamarca. *Class:* Quechuan, Quechua II, A. *Dialects:* Western Cajamarca, Eastern Cajamarca. Dialect differences are relatively minor. Lexical similarity 94% with Lambayeque (closest), 92% with Pacaraos. *Lg Use:* Official language. Relatively strong Quechua use in 8 to 10 communities. Strong pressure from Spanish in all communities because of secondary schools and gold mining in the area. Many deny the existence of Quechua (D. Coombs 2000). Used in the home. Very young children in some areas are still learning to speak Quechua, but in the majority of Quechua-speaking communities the language is losing ground among the young. Low prestige. Bilingual level estimates for Standard Spanish: 0 30%, 1 10%, 2 15%, 3 25%, 4 15%, 5 5%; Peasant Spanish: 0 15%, 1 20%, 2 10%, 3 15%, 4 30%, 5 10%. At least 20,000 to 25,000 are able to speak a country dialect of Spanish. *Lg Dev:* Literacy rate in first language: 5% to 10%. Literacy rate in second language: 25% to 35%. There is a series of basic primers and graded readers in Quechua. Some Quechua reading classes are taught in a few rural schools. A few Quechua reading and grammar classes in rural secondary schools. Roman script. Radio programs. Dictionary. Grammar. NT: 2004. *Other:* SOV. Layered sedimentary ridges, extruded igneous formations. In the western dialect area the ecozones include a small amount of intermontane valley land, below 2,500 meters, but most Quechua speakers live at the upper edge or above the corn belt in the upper parts of the valleys (2,800 to 3,600 meters) and a smaller number in the Jalca (Puna), the subalpine grasslands above 3,600 meters. 2,000 to 4,000 meters, but most live between 2,800 and 3,500 meters. Agriculturalists; animal husbandry; handcrafts production; seasonal manual labor. Christian.

Quechua, Cajatambo North Lima [qvl] 7,000 (2000 SIL). 2,800 monolinguals. Northeast Lima Department: districts of Copa, Cajatambo, Huancapón, northern Manas, and northeastern Gogor and Southeast Ancash Department: districts of Pacllón, La Primavera, and Mangas (south of the Llamac River and east of the Pativilca River). *Class:* Quechuan, Quechua I. *Dialects:* 74% intelligibility of Huamalíes Quechua. *Lg Use:* Official language. Used in the family, community. Most speakers older than 25 years. Rural areas are predominately monolingual or barely functionally bilingual. A portion of the population seems fluent in Spanish, but most are not. *Lg Dev:* Literacy rate in first language: below 1%. Literacy rate in second language: 25%. *Other:* SOV. 2,000 to 4,000 meters. Christian.

Quechua, Chachapoyas (Amazonas) [quk] 7,000 (2003 SIL). 100 to 300 monolinguals (2003). Ethnic population: 7,000. Chachapoyas and Luya provinces, Amazonas Department. *Class:* Quechuan, Quechua II, B. *Dialects:* Lamud (West Chachapoyas), Grenada-Mendoza (East Chachapoyas), La Jalca (South Chachapoyas), Llakwash Chachapoyas. Closest to San Martín Quechua. *Lg Use:* Official language. All ages in Conila, elsewhere older adults. Speakers also use Spanish. *Lg Dev:* Literacy rate in first language: below 1%. Literacy rate in second language: 15% to 25%. Taught in primary and secondary schools. *Other:* SOV. Traditional religion, Christian.

Quechua, Chincha [qxc] 6,000 (2000 SIL). Northeastern Chincha Province, Ica; northwestern Castrovirreyna Province, Huancavelica; southeastern Yauyos Province, Lima. *Class:* Quechuan, Quechua II, A. *Lg Use:* Official language. Many of those in their 20s and 30s speak Quechua and varying levels of Spanish. Separate identity from Wanka, Junin, and Ayacucho Quechua. A segment of the population are predominantly Quechua speakers, especially women over 40 with little or no formal education. Little or no contact with other varieties of Quechua in surrounding areas. Some contact with Jaqaru. *Lg Dev:* Literacy rate in first language: below 1%. Literacy rate in second language: below 5%. *Other:* A highly differentiated linguistic area with many one-village varieties. SOV.

Quechua, Chiquián Ancash [qxa] 10,000 (2000 SIL). 4,000 monolinguals. Southeast Ancash Department, Bolognesi Province, Chiquián District, Western Bolognesi west of the Pativilca River and north of the Llamac River, and eastern Ocros, those areas that border the Corpanqui Valley. Western Ocros may be included, but the dialect is somewhat different. *Class:* Quechuan, Quechua I. *Dialects:* Possibly intelligible with Cajatambo Quechua. Some contact with Cajatambo and very little with Huamalíes. 73% intelligibility of Huamalíes. *Lg Use:* Official language. Used in the home, work, community. Most speakers older than 25 years. They have a different identity from Huamalíes and Huaraz. Rural areas are predominately monolingual or barely functional bilingual. Spanish is not well understood nor well spoken. *Lg Dev:* Literacy rate in first language: below 1%. Literacy rate in second language: 25%. *Other:* SOV. 2,000 to 4,000 meters. Christian.

Quechua, Classical [qwc] Extinct. Central Peru. *Class:* Quechuan, Quechua II, C. *Lg Dev:* Bible portions: 1880.

Quechua, Corongo Ancash [qwa] 4,000 (2000 SIL). 1,700 monolinguals (2000 SIL). Northern Ancash Department, Corongo Province, Aco, Corongo, Cusca, La Pampa, and Yanac districts. Most prevalent in Aco and Cusca. *Class:* Quechuan, Quechua I. *Dialects:* Most closely related to Huaylas and Sihuas Quechua. Some contact with Sihuas, Northern Conchucos, and Huaylas by road. *Lg Use:* Official language. Used in the family, community. Predominantly those older than 40 years, especially women with little or no formal education. Corongo has separate identity from Sihuas, Northern Conchucos, and Huaylas. Those in their 20s and 30s speak both Quechua and varying levels of Spanish. *Lg Dev:* Literacy rate in first language: below 1%. Literacy rate in second language: 30%. *Other:* SOV. 2,000 to 4,000 meters. Christian.

Quechua, Cusco (Cuzco Quechua, Quechua Qosqo-Qollaw, Runasimi Qusqu Qullaw, Quechua de Cusco-Collao, Qheswa, Quechua Cusco, Quechua de Cuzco) [quz] 1,500,000 (1989 UBS). 300,000 to 500,000 monolinguals. Total Quechua speakers in Peru 3,500,000 to 4,400,000 including Quechua I 750,000, Quechua II 2,675,000 (2000 Adelaar). Ethnic population: 1,500,000. Departments of Cusco, half of Puno, and northeast Arequipa. *Class:* Quechuan, Quechua II, C. *Dialects:* Caylloma Quechua, Eastern Apurímac Quechua, Puno Quechua. Some dialect differences, but not as distinct as elsewhere. Substantial phonological and morphological differences with Ayacucho Quechua. *Lg Use:* Official language. All ages. People in towns and cities generally want their children to primarily speak Spanish. In rural areas 65% may be bilingual, and in urban areas it might be 90% to 95%. *Lg Dev:* Literacy rate in first language: 1% to 5%. Literacy rate in second language: 62%. Taught in primary schools. Poetry. Radio programs. Dictionary.

Grammar. Bible: 1988. *Other:* SOV. 100 to 5,000 meters. Christian, traditional religion.

Quechua, Eastern Apurímac (Quechua del Este de Apurímac, Apurímac Quechua) [qve] 200,000 (2002 SIL). 80,000 monolinguals (30% in towns, 60% to 70% in remote areas, especially at high altitudes). Ethnic population: 200,000. Abancay, Grau, Cotabambas, Aymaraes and Antabamba Ayamaraes, Chuquibambilla, and Anda provinces of the department of Apurímac. The province of La Unión, Arequipa. *Class:* Quechuan, Quechua II, C. *Dialects:* Abancay, Antabamba, Cotabambas. La Unión Quechua (Arequipa) is very similar to Antabamba. *Lg Use:* Official language. All ages. *Lg Dev:* Literacy rate in first language: 1% to 3%. Literacy rate in second language: 40% to 50% (According to census: 65%). Census figure: 40,000 nonliterate adults. 35% of adults, or 20% of total population. In rural areas 47.5% of the adults are nonliterate. Taught in primary schools. Bible portions: 1974. *Other:* Different from Cuzco Quechua and Ayacucho Quechua. SOV. 500 to 5,000 meters. Christian, traditional religion.

Quechua, Huallaga Huánuco [qub] 40,000 (1993 SIL). 66% monolingual. Northeast Huánuco Department, including the city of Huánuco. *Class:* Quechuan, Quechua I. *Lg Use:* Official language. *Lg Dev:* Literacy rate in first language: below 1%. Literacy rate in second language: 15% to 25%. Radio programs. Dictionary. Grammar. Bible portions: 1917–1995. *Other:* SOV.

Quechua, Huamalíes-Dos de Mayo Huánuco [qvh] 72,440 (2000 WCD). 20,000 to 30,000 monolinguals. Ethnic population: 80,000 to 110,000. Northwest Huánuco Department. *Class:* Quechuan, Quechua I. *Dialects:* Monzón, Huamalíes, Northern Dos de Mayo. Lexical similarity 96% with Margos-Yarowilca-Lauricocha Quechua. *Lg Use:* Official language. *Lg Dev:* Literacy rate in first language: below 1%. Literacy rate in second language: below 5%. Dictionary. Grammar. NT: 2003. *Other:* SOV.

Quechua, Huaylas Ancash (Huaraz Quechua) [qwh] 336,332 (2000 WCD). Less than 20,000 monolinguals. Ethnic population: 300,000. Central Ancash Department, provinces of Huaraz, Carhuaz, Caraz; in the Callejón de Huaylas. *Class:* Quechuan, Quechua I. *Dialect:* Huaraz, Yungay, Huailas (Huaylas). Parker says it is not intelligible with Cuzco, Ayacucho, Southern Junín (Huanca), Cajamarca, Amazonas (Chachapoyas), or San Martín Quechua. *Lg Use:* Official language. Vigorous. Used in the home, work, market, social gatherings. All ages. Positive language attitude. Bilingual level estimates for Spanish: 1 10%, 2 50%, 3 30%, 4 8%, 5 2%. Bilingualism is more developed in men than in women. *Lg Dev:* Literacy rate in first language: below 5%. Literacy rate in second language: 25% to 50%. Bilingual education in some Quechua areas. Roman script. Poetry. Radio programs. TV. Dictionary. Grammar. NT: 1993. *Other:* SOV. Sea level to 4,000 meters. Christian.

Quechua, Huaylla Wanca (Southern Huancayo Quechua, Huanca Huaylla Quechua) [qvw] 250,000 (2002 SIL). Southern Junín Department, Huancayo and Concepción provinces. *Class:* Quechuan, Quechua I. *Dialects:* Waycha (Huaycha, Central Huancayo), East Waylla, West Waylla. *Lg Use:* Official language. Waycha dialect is nearly extinct in Concepción. All ages, but first language of those 25 and up in particular. *Lg Dev:* Literacy rate in first language: below 1%. Literacy rate in second language: below 5%. Radio programs. Dictionary. Grammar. Bible portions: 1991–1992. *Other:* SOV.

Quechua, Jauja Wanca (Shausha Wanka Quechua, Huanca Jauja Quechua) [qxw] 14,550 to 31,500 (1962 census). Ethnic population: 77,727 (2000 WCD). Central Junín Department, Jauja Province. *Class:* Quechuan,

Quechua I. *Dialects:* Considerable phonological differences with Tarma. *Lg Use:* Official language. Speakers also use Spanish. *Lg Dev:* Grammar. *Other:* SOV.

Quechua, Lambayeque (Ferreñafe) [quf] 20,000 (1998 SIL). Lambayeque Region, Inkawasi, Kañaris, and Miracosta districts, and the communities of Penachí and Santa Lucía, and in adjacent areas of other departments (Cajamarca, Piura). *Class:* Quechuan, Quechua II, A. *Dialects:* Incahuasi, Cañaris. Lexical similarity 94% with Cajamarca Quechua. *Lg Use:* Official language. *Lg Dev:* Literacy rate in first language: below 1%. Literacy rate in second language: below 5%. Dictionary. Grammar. Bible portions: 1992. *Other:* SOV.

Quechua, Margos-Yarowilca-Lauricocha [qvm] 83,395 (1993 census). 14,000 monolinguals. Ethnic population: 114,000 (1993 census). Southwest and south central Huánuco Department, districts of Obas, Aparicio Pomares, Cahuac, Chavinillo, Chacabamba, Jacas Chico, Rondos, San Francisco de Asis, Jivia, Baños, Queropalca, Jesús, San Miguel de Cauri, Yarumayo, Margos, and Chaulán. *Class:* Quechuan, Quechua I. *Dialects:* Literature can be adapted from Huamalíes-Dos de Mayo. Lexical similarity 90% with Panao, 85% with Corongo (Ancash), Sihuas, Monzón, Tarma, Ulcumayo Quechua. *Lg Use:* Official language. Vigorous. Speakers also use Spanish. *Lg Dev:* Literacy rate in first language: 10%. Literacy rate in second language: 62%. Radio programs. Dictionary. NT: 2003. *Other:* SOV.

Quechua, Napo Lowland (Runa Shimi, Santa Rosa Quechua, Santarrosino, Quixo, Kicho, Quijo, Napo, Yumbo, Lowland Napo Quichua, Napo Kichua) [qvo] 8,000 in Peru. Population total all countries: 12,000. Napo River Region. Also communities on the Putumayo. Some were moved to Madre de Dios. Also spoken in Colombia, Ecuador. *Class:* Quechuan, Quechua II, B. *Lg Use:* Official language. Speakers also use Spanish. *Lg Dev:* The orthography differs from that used in Ecuador. Roman script in Ecuador. Radio programs. Dictionary. NT: 1988. *Other:* SOV. Tropical forest. Christian.

Quechua, North Junín (Tarma-Junín Quechua, Junín Quechua) [qvn] 60,000 (1998). 7,000 monolinguals (1972 census). Northern Junín Department, districts of Junín, Carhuamayo, Ondores, San Pedro de Cajas, southeast of Pasco. *Class:* Quechuan, Quechua I. *Dialects:* There are two dialects in Tarma Province which differ from the town of Junín. Lexical similarity 97% with Cajatambo, 96% with La Unión Quechua. *Lg Use:* Official language. Bilingual level estimates for Spanish: 0 30%, 1 20%, 2 10%, 3 10%, 4 25%, 5 5%. *Lg Dev:* Literacy rate in first language: below 1%. Literacy rate in second language: below 5%. Dictionary. Grammar. NT: 1997. *Other:* SOV. Mountain slope. Pastoralists; peasant agriculturalists.

Quechua, Northern Conchucos Ancash (Conchucos Quechua, Northern Conchucos Quechua) [qxn] 250,000 (2002 SIL). 65,000 monolinguals (1994 census). East Ancash Department, Pomabamba to San Luis, and Huacrachuco in northwest Huánuco Department. May include a small part of the northern Marañon area. *Class:* Quechuan, Quechua I. *Dialects:* Related to Southern Conchucos, Huamalíes, Sihuas. *Lg Use:* Official language. Vigorous. Used in the home, work, play. All ages. Positive language attitude. Speakers also use Spanish. *Lg Dev:* Literacy rate in first language: below 15%. Literacy rate in second language: 15% to 25%. Roman script. Radio programs. NT: 2002. *Other:* SOV. Mountain slope. 2,400 to 4,000 meters. Agriculturalists; animal husbandry. Christian, traditional religion.

Quechua, Pacaraos [qvp] 250 (1984 W. Adelaar). Ethnic population: 900. East central Lima Department, Pacaraos village. *Class:* Quechuan, Quechua II, A. *Dialects:* Divergent lexically, morphologically, and phonologically from other Quechua. By its archaic features it occupies an important position relative to the reconstruction of Proto-Quechua. Lexical similarity 94% with Huarí, Cajatambo, Tarma, and Carás Quechua. *Lg Use:* Official language. Speakers are older adults. *Other:* SOV.

Quechua, Panao Huánuco (Pachitea Quechua) [qxh] 50,000 (2002 SIL). 10,000 monolinguals. East central Huánuco Department. *Class:* Quechuan, Quechua I. *Dialects:* Lexical similarity 98% with La Unión, 96% with Cajatambo Quechua. *Lg Use:* Official language. *Lg Dev:* Literacy rate in first language: below 1%. Literacy rate in second language: 15% to 25%. Dictionary. Grammar. Bible portions: 1994–1995. *Other:* SOV.

Quechua, Puno (Quechua Qollaw, Quechua Collao) [qxp] 500,000. 100,000 monolinguals (2002). Puno Department and adjacent areas: northeast Arequipa, highland area of Moquegua. *Class:* Quechuan, Quechua II, C. *Dialects:* North Bolivian Quechua, Cailloma Quechua. Mutually intelligible with Cusco Quechua and North Bolivian Quechua: possibly sufficient to understand complex and abstract discourse. *Lg Use:* Official language. All ages. People in towns and cities mostly want their children to speak Spanish. *Lg Dev:* Literacy rate in first language: below 1% to 5%. Literacy rate in second language: 71% (official figure for rural areas). Taught in primary schools. Radio programs. Dictionary. Grammar. Bible: 1988. *Other:* Differs from Cuzco Quechua in its borrowing of lexicon and morphology from Aymara. SOV. 100 to 5,500 meters. Christian, traditional religion.

Quechua, San Martín (Ucayali, Lamista, Lamisto, Lama, Lamano, Motilón) [qvs] 15,000 (2000 SIL). 2,000 monolinguals. Ethnic population: 43,982 (2000 WCD). Loreto Department, San Martín Region, Sisa, Lamas, and other districts, and along parts of the Ucayali River. Lamas town is "the cradle of the culture" and 22 km from Tarapota. *Class:* Quechuan, Quechua II, B. *Dialects:* Several minor dialects. *Lg Use:* Official language. Few parents pass the language on to children. Bilingual parents want their children to learn Spanish. Shamans use the language in chants. Protestants use it in singing with published hymnbook. Few use printed Scripture; scattered occasional use in religious services apart from singing. Speakers are embarrassed to be heard using the language. Parents want their children to speak Spanish. Bilingual level estimates for Spanish: 0 1%, 1 9%, 2 10%, 3 40%, 4 40%, 5 0%. Most parents teach Spanish to their children first. The bilingual education program is designed to teach Quechua to Spanish-speaking ethnic Quechua children who do not speak Quechua. *Lg Dev:* Literacy rate in first language: 10%. Literacy rate in second language: 50% to 75%. 1,500 can read it, 400 can write it. Some oral and a little written Quechua taught in schools. Roman script. Dictionary. Grammar. NT: 1992. *Other:* SOV. Mountain valleys. Agriculturalists. Traditional religion, Christian.

Quechua, Santa Ana de Tusi Pasco [qxt] 10,000 (1993 SIL). Pasco Department, southeastern part of District Daniel Carrion. *Class:* Quechuan, Quechua I. *Dialects:* Probably a dialect of Chaupihuaranga Quecha. *Lg Use:* Official language. *Other:* SOV.

Quechua, Sihuas Ancash [qws] 6,500 (2002 SIL). 3,000 monolinguals. Ancash Department, Sihuas Province, districts west of Sihuas River and north of Rupac River: southern Quiches, Alfonso Ugarte, Huayllabamba, Sihuas, and western Ragash. *Class:* Quechuan, Quechua I. *Dialects:* Most closely related to Northern Conchucos and Corongo Quechuas. Intelligibility testing has been conducted with these two language groups and initial results show intelligibility of Corongo Quechua to be on the high end of marginal. Intelligibility of Northern Conchucos appears to be lower. *Lg Use:* Official

language. Used in rural daily life primarily among women over 40 years old. Predominantly those over 40 years of age, especially women with little or no formal education. Those in their 20s and 30s speak both Quechua and varying levels of Spanish. Fluency among those who speak Spanish is limited. *Lg Dev:* Literacy rate in first language: below 1%. Literacy rate in second language: 28%. *Other:* 2,000 to 3,900 meters.

Quechua, Southern Conchucos Ancash (Conchucos Quechua, Southern Conchucos Quechua) [qxo] 250,000 (1994 census). 80,000 monolinguals. East Ancash Department, Chavín to San Luis to Llamellín in East Ancash Department, and Huacaybamba, Huacrachuco, San Buenaventura, and Pinra in northwest Huánuco Department. Includes much of southern Marañon. *Class:* Quechuan, Quechua I. *Dialects:* Related to Northern Conchucos, Huamalíes, Huaylas. *Lg Use:* Official language. Vigorous in most but not all communities. Spanish-speaking health workers and teachers learn Quechua in order to communicate. All domains, local administration, written and oral interpretation of Spanish used in church, oral use in commerce and labor relations, used at health centers. Positive language attitude. Rural areas are predominantly monolingual. 170,000 speak some Spanish, possibly 20 speak some English. *Lg Dev:* Literacy rate in first language: below 1%. Literacy rate in second language: 15% to 25%. Taught in primary and secondary schools. Roman script. Radio programs. TV. NT: 2002. *Other:* SOV. Mountain slope. Agriculturalists. Christian, syncretism, traditional religion.

Quechua, Southern Pastaza (Inga) [qup] 1,553 (2000 WCD). 20% monolinguals. Northern jungle, Anatico Lake, Pastaza and Huasaga rivers, along the Ñucuray River and Manchari. *Class:* Quechuan, Quechua II, B. *Lg Use:* Official language. Used in the home, work, play, church. All ages. Bilingual level estimates for Spanish: 0 60%, 1 20%, 2 10%, 3 10%, 4 0%, 5 0%. *Lg Dev:* Literacy rate in first language: below 1%. Literacy rate in second language: 5% to 15%. Dictionary. Grammar. NT: 1997. *Other:* Distinct from Northern Pastaza Quechua of Peru and Ecuador. SOV. Tropical forest, riverine. 300 meters.

Quechua, Yanahuanca Pasco (Daniel Carrion) [qur] 20,500 (1972 census). 8,200 monolinguals. Western Pasco Department, sparsely populated high country, and more densely populated valleys, districts of Yanahuanca, Villcabamba, Tapoc, Chacayan, Paucar, San Pedro de Pillao, Goyllarisquizqa, Chinche. *Class:* Quechuan, Quechua I. *Dialects:* Many related Quechua dialects intersect here: Junín, Ambo-Pasco, Santa Ana de Tusi, Cajatambo, Dos de Mayo. Further intelligibility studies may be needed. *Lg Use:* Official language. Used in the home and community. Most speakers older than 25 years. Rural areas are predominately monolingual or barely functional bilingual. Spanish is not well understood nor well spoken. *Lg Dev:* Literacy rate in first language: below 1%. Literacy rate in second language: below 20%. *Other:* SOV. 2,400 to 4,200 meters.

Quechua, Yauyos [qux] 6,500 (2003 SIL). Lima Department, Yauyos Province; Ica Department, northern section of Chincha Province; Huancavelica Department, northeastern corner of Castrovirreyna Province. *Class:* Quechuan, Quechua II, A. *Dialects:* San Pedro de Huacarpana, Apurí, Madean-Viñac (Madeán), Azángaro-Huangáscar-Chocos (Huangáscar), Cacra-Hongos, Tana-Lincha (Lincha), Tomás-Alis (Alis), Huancaya-Vitis, Laraos. Not a single language, but a cover term for a highly differentiated linguistic area with many one-village varieties. *Lg Use:* Official language. There are monolinguals in the Chincha area, primarily older women. High bilingualism with Spanish throughout the area (2000 SIL). There may be 1,200 older adult speakers. Reported to be high proficiency in Spanish. *Lg Dev:* Literacy rate in first language: below 1%. Literacy rate in second language: below 5%. *Other:* SOV.

Quichua, Northern Pastaza (Tigre Quechua, Alama, Bobonaza) [qvz] 2,000 in Peru. Alamas, Tigre River. *Lg Use:* Official language. *Other:* Distinct from Southern Pastaza Quechua. Tropical forest. See main entry under Ecuador.

Remo (Rheno) [rem] Extinct. Between the Tapiche and Calleria rivers. If they exist, they are in Brazil at the headwaters of the Moa River; but there is no evidence of their existence in Brazil. *Class:* Panoan, North-Central.

Resígaro (Resígero) [rgr] 14 (1976 SIL). Northeastern Peru, Loreto Department, in Bora and Ocaina villages. *Class:* Arawakan, Maipuran, Northern Maipuran, Inland. *Lg Use:* Official language. Speakers also use Ocaina, Bora, Murui Huitoto, or Spanish. *Lg Dev:* Dictionary. *Other:* Nearly extinct.

Secoya (Angotero, Encabellao) [sey] 144 in Peru. Northern Peru, Boca de Angusilla and Santa Marta, a small river off the Napo River near the Ecuador border. *Dialects:* Angotero, Piojé. *Lg Use:* Official language. All ages. See main entry under Ecuador.

Sensi (Senti, Tenti, Mananahua) [sni] Extinct. Right bank of the Ucayali River. *Class:* Panoan, North-Central. *Other:* In 1925 there were 100. Subgroups: Ynubu (Inubu), Runubu, Casca.

Sharanahua [mcd] 450 in Peru (2000 SIL). 70% monolinguals. Population includes 200 to 300 Mastanahua. Population total all countries: 950. Upper Purus River area. Also spoken in Brazil. *Class:* Panoan, South-Central, Yaminahua-Sharanahua. *Dialects:* Marinahua (Marinawa), Chandinahua, Mastanahua. Close to Yaminahua, Chitonahua, Yora. *Lg Use:* Official language. On the Purus River used in the home. All ages. Bilingual level estimates for Spanish: 0 7%, 1 67%, 2 25%, 3 1%, 4 0%, 5 0%. Some intermarry with Spanish speakers and use Spanish in the home. Those who have been to school can use varying degrees of Spanish. *Lg Dev:* Literacy rate in first language: 10% to 30%. Literacy rate in second language: 5% to 10%. Taught in primary schools. TV. Dictionary. NT: 1996. *Other:* SOV. Tropical forest. Below 300 meters. Agriculturalists; animal husbandry: cattle, sheep; fishermen; hunters. Christian, traditional religion.

Shipibo-Conibo [shp] 26,000 (2003 SIL). Northeastern middle Ucayali River area, Painaco, Requena, Sur Bolognesi, Pisqui (on the other side of Contamana). *Class:* Panoan, North-Central. *Dialects:* Shipibo (Alto Ucayali), Conibo (Coniba), Pisquibo, Shetebo (Setebo, Setibo, Xitibo, Manoita), Shipibo del Madre de Dios. *Lg Use:* Official language. All ages. Positive language attitude. Bilingual level estimates for Spanish: 0 10%, 1 20%, 2 23%, 3 30%, 4 15%, 5 2%. Eager to learn and use Spanish. *Lg Dev:* Literacy rate in first language: 1% to 5%. Literacy rate in second language: 15% to 25%. Dictionary. Grammar. NT: 1983. *Other:* Agriculturalists; fishermen; animal husbandry. Christian, traditional religion.

Spanish (Español, Castellano) [spa] 20,000,000 in Peru (1995). *Lg Use:* Official language. See main entry under Spain.

Spanish, Loreto-Ucayali (Jungle Spanish) [spq] Loreto and Ucayali river areas. *Class:* Indo-European, Italic, Romance, Italo-Western, Western, Gallo-Iberian, Ibero-Romance, West Iberian, Castilian. *Dialects:* Some other speakers have limited comprehension of colloquial standard Spanish. *Lg Use:* Official language. There are monolingual speakers.

Taushiro (Pinchi, Pinche) [trr] 1 (2002 SIL). Ethnic population: 20. Off the Tigre River, Aucayacu River,

tributary of the Ahuaruna River. *Class:* Language Isolate. *Dialects:* Possibly Zaparoan. Ruhlen says it is related to Candoshi. *Lg Use:* Official language. *Other:* VSO. Nearly extinct.

Ticuna (Tikuna, Tukuna) [tca] 8,000 in Peru (2000 SIL). Northeastern Amazon River Region, from Chimbote in Peru to San Antonio do Iça in Brazil. *Lg Use:* Official language. All ages. *Lg Dev:* Literacy rate in first language: 30% to 60%. Literacy rate in second language: 25% to 50%. *Other:* Christian, traditional religion. See main entry under Brazil.

Urarina (Shimacu, Simacu, Itucali) [ura] 3,000 (2002 SIL). Urarinas District, Pucayacu, Chambira, and Urituyacu rivers. *Class:* Language Isolate. *Dialects:* There are several dialects with minor differences. Ruhlen and others classify it as Andean. *Lg Use:* Official language. All ages. Bilingual level estimates for Spanish: 0 60%, 1 20%, 2 10%, 3 7%, 4 3%, 5 0%. Women are monolingual. Men range from monolingual to routine proficiency in Spanish, with the majority able to handle commercial matters. *Lg Dev:* Literacy rate in first language: below 1%. Literacy rate in second language: below 5%. Grammar. Bible portions: 1973–1990. *Other:* OVS.

Yagua (Nijyamïí Nikyejaada, Yahua, Llagua, Yava, Yegua) [yad] 5,692 in Peru (2000 WCD). 2,000 monolinguals. Ethnic population: 6,000. Loreto, northeastern Amazon River Region, from Iquitos to the Brazil border. Some go to urban centers like Iquitos for economic reasons. Some occasionally go into Brazil. Also spoken in Colombia. *Class:* Peba-Yaguan. *Dialects:* 2 dialects. *Lg Use:* Official language. All domains. Some use of Yagua in religious ceremonies and services. Eight bilingual Spanish-Yagua schools. Most people along the main rivers are apathetic about Yagua, preferring their children to learn Spanish. Many are monolingual in isolated areas. Bilingual level estimates for Spanish: 0 54%, 1 20%, 2 15%, 3 9%, 4 1%, 5 1%. *Lg Dev:* Literacy rate in first language: below 1%. Literacy rate in second language: 25% to 50%. Taught in primary schools. Roman script. Dictionary. Grammar. NT: 1994. *Other:* VSO. Tropical forest. Swidden agriculturalists; hunters; fishermen. Christian, traditional religion.

Yameo [yme] Extinct. Marañon and Amazon rivers from the mouth of the Tigre to the Nanay River. *Class:* Peba-Yaguan.

Yaminahua (Yaminawa, Jaminawá, Yuminahua, Yamanawa) [yaa] 750 in Peru (2003 SIL). Population includes 400 Yaminahua (1998 SIL), 200 Mastanahua (1981 SIL), 150 Chitonahua. Population total all countries: 1,244. Huacapishtea and Mapuya. Chitonahua at the headwaters of the Embira River. Also spoken in Bolivia, Brazil. *Class:* Panoan, South-Central, Yaminahua-Sharanahua. *Dialect:* Yaminahua, Chitonahua (Morunahua, Moronahua, Foredafa, Horudahua, Horunahua). Closest to Sharanahua. *Lg Use:* Official language. All ages. Bilingual level estimates for Spanish: 0 50%, 1 15%, 2 25%, 3 8%, 4 2%, 5 0%. *Lg Dev:* Literacy rate in first language: below 1%. Literacy rate in second language: below 5%. Grammar. NT: 2003. *Other:* Subgroups: Masronahua (Masrodawa), Nishinahua (Nishidawa), Chitonahua (Chitodawa), Shaonahua (Shaodawa). SOV.

Yanesha' (Amuesha, Amuese, Amueixa, Amoishe, Amagues, Amage, Omage, Amajo, Lorenzo, Amuetamo, Amaje) [ame] 9,831 (2000 WCD). Ethnic population: 10,000 (2000 W. Adelaar). Central and eastern Pasco Region and Junín, western jungle, headwaters of the Pachitea and Perene rivers. *Class:* Arawakan, Maipuran, Western Maipuran. *Lg Use:* Official language. Bilingual level estimates for Spanish: 0 5%, 1 15%, 2 40%, 3 20%, 4 10%, 5 10%. *Lg Dev:* Literacy rate in first language:

10% to 30%. Literacy rate in second language: 15% to 25%. Dictionary. Grammar. NT: 1978. *Other:* The people prefer to be called 'Yanesha''. VSO.

Yine ("Piro," Pirro, Pira, "Simirinche," Simiranch, Contaquiro) [pib] 4,000 (2000 SIL). Ethnic population: 4,000 to 5,000. Departments of Ucayali and Cusco, east central Urubamba River area; Department of Ucayali and Loreto, along the Ucayali River (Conatmana and Pucallpa); Department of Madre de Dios, Madre de Dios River. *Class:* Arawakan, Maipuran, Southern Maipuran, Purus. *Dialects:* Machinere in Brazil is different enough to need separate literature. *Lg Use:* Official language. Vigorous. All domains. Written form and many songs in the language used in religious services. All ages. Positive language attitude. Probably not more than 30% are fluent in Spanish. Nearly all are able to trade in Spanish. Those in the downriver area are more bilingual in Spanish than upriver Yine. Speakers may have some proficiency in Machiguenga (in Senza and Miaria), Ashaninka (in Miaria, Bufeo Pozo, and Senza), and Quechua. *Lg Dev:* Literacy rate in first language: 60%. Literacy rate in second language: 75% to 80%. They desire higher education in Yine. Bilingual education. There are secondary schools in Miaria (with a Yine director and 3 Yine teachers), Sepahua (all teaching done in Spanish), Puija, Rimac, Bufeo Pozo. Roman script. Dictionary. NT: 1960–2002. *Other:* SOV. Tropical forest. Agriculturalists; fishermen; animal husbandry: cattle; lumber work. Christian.

Yora (Yura, Yoranahua, Manu Park Panoan, Parquenahua, Nahua) [mts] 350 to 400 (1998 SIL). Manu Park, Panagua River. Some are outside of the Park on the Mishagua River. There may be more in Brazil. *Class:* Panoan, South-Central, Yora. *Dialects:* Close to Yaminahua and Sharanahua. *Lg Use:* Official language. Vigorous. All ages. A few speakers also use Spanish. *Lg Dev:* Literacy rate in first language: below 1%. Literacy rate in second language: below 5%. *Other:* SOV; postpositions; genitives, relatives, adjectives before noun head numerals after noun head; maximum prefix, 1; maximum suffix, 7 or 8; noun affixes indicate case; verb affixes mark person and number; ergative; CV, CVC, V, VC; tonal. Riverine, interfluvial. Tropical forest. 280 to 350 meters. Swidden agriculturalists. Christian, traditional religion.

Puerto Rico

Puerto Rico. 3,897,960. National or official languages: Spanish, English. Self governing, part of USA. Literacy rate: 89% to 90%. Also includes Corsican, Eastern Yiddish, French (2,624), Haitian Creole French (438), Italian (1,556), Ladino, North Levantine Spoken Arabic, Papiamentu (200), South Levantine Spoken Arabic, Standard German (1,453), Chinese (2,000). Deaf population: 8,000 to 40,000 (1986 Gallaudet University). Deaf institutions: 5. The number of languages listed for Puerto Rico is 3. Of those, all are living languages. See map on page 739.

English [eng] 82,000 in Puerto Rico (1995). *Lg Use:* National language. 376,371 second-language users (1970 census). See main entry under United Kingdom.

Puerto Rican Sign Language (PRSL) [psl] Ethnic population: 8,000 to 40,000 deaf persons (1986 Gallaudet Univ.). *Class:* Deaf sign language. *Dialects:* Related to American Sign Language. *Lg Use:* Signs were introduced in 1907 by nuns. Some home signs are also used. 4 varieties are used: Signed Spanish as a pidgin with hearing Spanish speakers, Signed English as a pidgin with deaf educated in USA and with hearing English speakers, American Sign Language with those who know only that, and PRSL. Some know only PRSL.

Spanish [spa] 3,437,120 in Puerto Rico (1996). *Lg Use:* National language. *Other:* Some dialects are considered to be archaic. See main entry under Spain.

Saint Kitts and Nevis

Federation of Saint Kitts and Nevis. 38,836. National or official language: English. Gained independence in 1983. Literacy rate: 88% to 90%. Deaf institutions: 1. The number of languages listed for Saint Kitts and Nevis is 2. Of those, both are living languages. See map on page 740.

English [eng] 200 in Saint Kitts and Nevis (2004). *Lg Use:* National language. See main entry under United Kingdom.

Saint Kitts Creole English (Kittitian Creole English, Leeward Caribbean Creole English) [aig] 39,000 in Saint Kitts. Throughout the islands. *Dialect:* Nevis Creole English. *Other:* Agriculturalists: sugarcane. See main entry under Antigua and Barbuda (Antigua and Barbuda Creole English).

Saint Lucia

Saint Lucia. 164,213. National or official language: English. Independent member of the British Commonwealth. 238 sq. miles. Literacy rate: 54%. Information mainly from L. Carrington 1984; H. Simmons-McDonald 1994. Blind population: 2,276 (1991 census). Deaf population: 800 to 8,791. Deaf institutions: 1. The number of languages listed for Saint Lucia is 2. Of those, both are living languages. See map on page 740.

English [eng] 1,600 in Saint Lucia (2004). *Dialect:* Saint Lucian English. *Lg Use:* Official language. *Other:* There is an emerging English vernacular on Saint Lucia in a certain rural area. It is significantly restructured, heavily French creole influenced, English lexicon (Paul Garrett 1998). See main entry under United Kingdom.

Saint Lucian Creole French (Patwa, Patois, Kwéyòl, Lesser Antillean Creole French) [acf] 158,178 in Saint Lucia (2001). Population total all countries: 357,128. Also spoken in Dominica, France, Grenada, Guyana, Trinidad and Tobago. *Class:* Creole, French based. *Dialects:* Not intelligible with Standard French. Saint Lucia Creole French is close to Dominican Creole French (97% to 99% intelligibility). Goodman (1964) says all French creoles of the Caribbean are somewhat inherently intelligible to each other's speakers. The dialect of Dominica is virtually the same as Saint Lucia. *Lg Use:* In the islands under French influence nearly all the population speaks creole as first language, although there is a local variety of Standard French. In those under English influence, the creole has less standing, and its speakers have a low literacy rate in the creole. All domains. Standard French is understood by no more than 10% of the population in Saint Lucia. Standard French is used in some religious services. English is also used. *Lg Dev:* Literacy rate in second language: 36%. Roman script. Newspapers. Radio programs. Dictionary. Grammar. NT: 1999. *Other:* Christian.

Saint Pierre and Miquelon

Saint Pierre and Miquelon. 6,995. National or official language: French. French Department; islands off the southwest coast of Newfoundland, Canada. Also includes Algerian Spoken Arabic (200). The number of languages listed for Saint Pierre and Miquelon is 2. Of those, both are living languages.

English [eng] 188 in Saint Pierre and Miquelon (1967 census). See main entry under United Kingdom.

French [fra] 5,114 in Saint Pierre and Miquelon (1967 census). Ethnic population: 5,235. *Lg Use:* Official language. See main entry under France.

Saint Vincent and the Grenadines

Saint Vincent and the Grenadines. 117,193. National or official language: English. Self governing, part of British West Indies. Literacy rate: 85%. Also includes Portuguese (200). The number of languages listed for Saint Vincent and the Grenadines is 3. Of those, 2 are living languages and 1 is extinct. See map on page 740.

Carib, Island [crb] Extinct. Formerly also in Dominica. *Dialect:* Vincentian. *Lg Use:* Became extinct in Dominica and Saint Vincent about 1920. See main entry under Dominica.

English [eng] 400 in Saint Vincent and the Grenadines (2004). *Lg Use:* National language. See main entry under United Kingdom.

Vincentian Creole English [svc] 138,000 (1989 J. Holm). Saint Vincent and the Grenadines. *Class:* Creole, English based, Atlantic, Eastern, Southern. *Dialects:* Closest to Guyana, Tobago. *Other:* May have some French influence, although the former French creole used here is virtually gone. J. Holm says it is the only folk language (1989:457).

Suriname

Republic of Suriname. 436,935. National or official language: Dutch. Literacy rate: 65% to 95%. Also includes English, Korean, North Levantine Spoken Arabic, Portuguese. Information mainly from SIL 1964–2003. Blind population: 1,300 (1982 WCE). Deaf population: 25,646. Deaf institutions: 1. The number of languages listed for Suriname is 17. Of those, 16 are living languages and 1 is a second language without mother-tongue speakers. See map on page 754.

Akurio (Akoerio, Akuri, Akurijo, Akuriyo, Akuliyo, Wama, Wayaricuri, Oyaricoulet, Triometesem, Triometesen) [ako] 10 (2000 E. B. Carlin). Ethnic population: 50. Southeast jungle. *Class:* Carib, Northern, East-West Guiana, Wama. *Dialects:* Related to, but not inherently intelligible with, Trió. Dialects or related languages: Urukuyana, Kumayena. *Lg Use:* All but one group is living with the Trió and bilingual in Trió. Children speak Trió. *Other:* Contacted in 1969. Hunter-gatherers. Nearly extinct.

Arawak (Lokono, Arowak) [arw] 700 in Suriname (1980 census). Population total all countries: 2,450. Ethnic population: 2,051 in Suriname (1980 census). Scattered locations across the north of Suriname. Also spoken in French Guiana, Guyana, Venezuela. *Class:* Arawakan, Maipuran, Northern Maipuran, Caribbean. *Lg Use:* All speakers are older adults in Suriname and Guyana. The young people use Sranan. *Lg Dev:* Literacy rate in first language: below 1%. Literacy rate in second language: 25% to 50%. Dictionary. Grammar. Bible portions: 1850–1978.

Aukan (Ndyuka, Ndjuká, Njuká, "Djuka," "Djoeka," Aukaans, Okanisi) [djk] 15,542 in Suriname. 10% to 20% monolingual. Population includes 14,353 Aukan, 33 Aluku, 1,156 Paramaccan (1980 census). Population total all countries: 22,134. Eastern along the Marowijne and Tapanahony rivers, northeastern along the Cottica River. Aluku are along the French Guiana border. Paramaccan are in northeast Suriname. In the 1980s and 1990s many went to Paramaribo. Also spoken in French Guiana. *Class:* Creole, English based, Atlantic, Suriname, Ndyuka. *Dialects:* Aukan, Aluku (Aloekoe, Boni), Paramaccan.

Kwinti is further removed from Aukan than are Aluku and Paramaccan. *Lg Use:* Vigorous. In Paramaribo some have shifted to Dutch, some younger ones to Sranan. All domains. Used in oral and written form in religious services. Positive language attitude. Most men can speak Sranan Tongo, and many women can understand it. Schools are in Dutch, so many younger ones can read and write it, but the majority are not fluent. Perhaps 30% to 50% can speak all 3 languages. *Lg Dev:* Literacy rate in first language: below 10%. Literacy rate in second language: 15% to 25%. Radio programs. Dictionary. Grammar. NT: 1999. *Other:* The society was formed by escaped slaves. Subsistence and economy is Amerindian; social culture and religion are West African. Aluku has more French influence than Paramaccan does. Any spelling of Ndyuka without the initial nasal is considered derogatory. 'Aukan' is English, 'Aukaans' is Dutch. In the early 1900s an Aukaner named Afaka developed a syllabic writing system, but few learned to read it, and it was not officially endorsed. 12 clans. Tonal. Coastal, mountain slope, riverine. Swampy, rainforest. Gold miners; river transport; lumbermen; agriculturalists; manual labor; government workers; manufacturing; politics. Traditional religion, Christian.

Carib (Caribe, Cariña, Kalihna, Kalinya, Kali'na, Galibí, Marawomo) [car] 1,200 in Suriname (2001 Carlin). Ethnic population: 3,000. Various locations along the north coast. The eastern dialect in Suriname is primarily in the Albina area and in French Guiana, Brazil, and Venezuela; the western dialect is in the central and western areas of Suriname and in Guyana. *Dialects:* Murato (Myrato, Western Carib), Tyrewuju (Eastern Carib). *Lg Use:* All ages in some areas. The eastern dialect is the prestige dialect in Suriname. Speakers of the central dialect are reported to be bilingual and shifting to Sranan. They also speak Dutch as second language. *Lg Dev:* Literacy rate in first language: below 1%. Literacy rate in second language: 25% to 50%. *Other:* Their own name for the language is 'Kari'na auran', 'Kari'na' for the people. The name in Dutch is 'Kara'ibs', in French 'Galibi', in Spanish 'Caribe', in English 'Carib'. See main entry under Venezuela.

Chinese, Hakka [hak] 7,008 in Suriname (2000 WCD). Ethnic population: 42,000 Chinese, including Yue (1971). See main entry under China.

Dutch [nld] 200,000 in Suriname (1997 Christa DeKleine). *Lg Use:* Official language. Many are native bilingual speakers of Sranan or Sarnami Hindustani. See main entry under Netherlands.

Guyanese Creole English (Creolese, Guyanese Creole) [gyn] 50,000 in Suriname (1986 SIL). *Lg Dev:* Literacy rate in second language: 25% to 50%. See main entry under Guyana.

Hindustani, Caribbean [hns] 150,000 in Suriname (1986). Population total all countries: 165,633. Coastal region. Also spoken in Guyana, Netherlands, Trinidad and Tobago. *Class:* Indo-European, Indo-Iranian, Indo-Aryan, Eastern zone, Bihari. *Dialect:* Trinidad Bhojpuri, Sarnami Hindustani (Sarnami Hindi, Aili Gaili). Closer to Bhojpuri than to Hindi. Similar dialect to Trinidad-Tobago. *Lg Use:* There are monolingual speakers. Some speakers use Sranan or Dutch as second language. *Lg Dev:* Literacy rate in first language: below 1%. Literacy rate in second language: 50% to 75%. NT: 1997. *Other:* Based on Bhojpuri, with influences from Awadhi. It has loans from Sranan, Dutch, and English. Hindu, Muslim.

Javanese, Caribbean (Suriname Javanese) [jvn] 60,000 in Suriname (1986). Coastal area. Also spoken in French Guiana. *Class:* Austronesian, Malayo-Polynesian, Javanese. *Dialects:* Significantly different from the Javanese of Indonesia. *Lg Dev:* Literacy rate in first language: below 1%. Literacy rate in second language: 50% to 75%. Dictionary. NT: 1999. *Other:* Descended from plantation workers brought from Java between 1890–1939. Muslim, traditional religion.

Kwinti [kww] 133 (1980 census). North central, along the Coppename River, upstream from Carib villages in Kaimanstan and Witagron. *Class:* Creole, English based, Atlantic, Suriname, Ndyuka. *Dialects:* Further removed from Ndyuka than Aluku and Paramaccan. Probably needs literature adapted from Ndyuka. *Lg Use:* Speakers also use Saramaccan or Sranan Tongo. *Other:* Traditional religion.

Ndyuka-Trio Pidgin [njt] Southern Suriname, upper Tapanahonij River. *Class:* Pidgin. *Lg Use:* Trade language. Formerly used until the 1960s by the Ndyuka and Trio and Wayana peoples for trading. Increasing travel by the Indians to the coast at that time cut back on that trade, and also gave some of them opportunity to use Sranan in contact with the Ndyuka. Many Ndyuka men in their 30s or older now do not know it. Scarcely used at all now. *Other:* Second language only.

Saramaccan [srm] 23,000 in Suriname (1995 SIL). Population includes 1,000 Matawari. Population total all countries: 26,000. Central, along Saramacca and upper Suriname rivers. Refugees are in Paramaribo. Also spoken in French Guiana. *Class:* Creole, English based. *Dialect:* Matawari (Matawai, Matuari, Matoewari). Ian Hancock classifies it as Portuguese based rather than English based. Linguistic influences from Kongo (Hancock 1988). 20% or more of the lexicon has an African component. *Lg Dev:* Literacy rate in first language: below 1%. Literacy rate in second language: 15% to 25%. Dictionary. Grammar. NT: 1991–1999. *Other:* A Bush Negro ethnic group with background similar to the Ndyuka. Tonal, one tone per vowel. Traditional religion.

Sikiana (Sikiyana, Chikena, Tshikiana) [sik] 15 in Suriname (2001 Carlin). Ethnic population: 50. On the Sipaliwini River in Kwamalasamutu. *Lg Use:* All speak Trió as second language. *Other:* Nearly extinct. See main entry under Brazil.

Sranan (Sranan Tongo, Taki-Taki, Surinaams, Surinamese, Suriname Creole English) [srn] 120,000 in Suriname (1993). Population total all countries: 126,400. Mainly in Paramaribo and along the coast. Also spoken in Aruba, Netherlands, Netherlands Antilles. *Class:* Creole, English based, Atlantic, Suriname. *Dialects:* Similar to Ndyuka, but there are cultural differences. Also has many similarities to Krio of Sierra Leone. *Lg Use:* Language of wider communication. 300,000 second-language speakers. Some literature. The lingua franca of 80% of the population of the country, including the Hindustanis, Javanese, Chinese, American Indians, and Bush Negroes. Speakers also use Dutch. *Lg Dev:* Literacy rate in first language: 10%. Literacy rate in second language: 50% to 75%. Bible: 1997. *Other:* Christian, traditional religion.

Trió (Tirió) [tri] 822 in Suriname villages (1980 census). Population total all countries: 1,151. South central, villages of Tepoe and Alalapadu. Also spoken in Brazil. *Class:* Carib, Northern, East-West Guiana, Wayana-Trio. *Lg Use:* All domains. Speakers have an attitude of pride toward Trió, but do not consider it to be appropriate for a subject or instruction in school. The purer Trió is considered to be spoken by the older men and storytellers, and not by most of the younger men, those who have lived in town, or children of mixed marriages (E. B. Carlin 1998). *Lg Dev:* Literacy rate in first language: 10% to 30%. Literacy rate in second language: 25% to 50%. NT: 1979.

Warao (Warrau, Guarao, Guarauno) [wba] Few speakers in Suriname. Near Guyana border. *Lg Use:* Speakers are older adults. Speakers also use Guyanese. See main entry under Venezuela.

Wayana (Oayana, Wajana, Uaiana, Oyana, Oiana, Alukuyana, Upurui, Roucouyenne) [way] 397 in Suriname (1980 census). Population total all countries: 747. Villages

in southeastern Suriname. Also spoken in Brazil, French Guiana. *Class:* Carib, Northern, East-West Guiana, Wayana-Trio. *Dialects:* Partially intelligible with Apalaí. *Lg Dev:* Literacy rate in first language: 10% to 30%. Literacy rate in second language: 25% to 50%. NT: 1979.

Trinidad and Tobago

Republic of Trinidad and Tobago. 1,096,585. Afro-Trinidadian 40%, East Indian 41%, mixed 14%, white 1%, Chinese 1%, other 1%. National or official language: English. Literacy rate: All 97%: male 98%, female 96%. Also includes North Levantine Spoken Arabic (2,600), Chinese (6,500). Information mainly from S. R. Sperl 1980; I. Hancock 1985; P. Mohan and P. Zador 1986; L. Winer 1993. Deaf institutions: 2. The number of languages listed for Trinidad and Tobago is 6. Of those, all are living languages. See map on page 740.

English [eng] 2,600 in Trinidad and Tobago (2004). *Lg Use:* Official language. See main entry under United Kingdom.

Hindustani, Caribbean (Trinidad Bhojpuri) [hns] 15,633 in Trinidad and Tobago (1996). Ethnic population: East Indians are 41% of the population. *Lg Use:* Speakers are older adults. 90% or more of the Hindustanis are reported to speak English or Trinidadian Creole English as first language. *Lg Dev:* Literacy rate in second language: 70%. *Other:* Hindu, Muslim, Christian. See main entry under Suriname.

Spanish [spa] 4,100 in Trinidad and Tobago (2004). Fishing villages and communities of the southern peninsula. *Lg Use:* Users seem to be second-language users only. Frequent contact with Venezuelan fishing communities that lie 9 miles off the coast of Trinidad. See main entry under Spain.

Tobagonian Creole English (Tobagonian Dialect) [tgh] 36,000 (1990). Tobago. *Class:* Creole, English based, Atlantic, Eastern, Southern. *Dialects:* Closest to Guyana and Saint Vincent. *Lg Dev:* Dictionary. *Other:* Plains, mountain slope.

Trinidadian Creole English [trf] 9,600 (2004). Trinidad. *Class:* Creole, English based, Atlantic, Eastern, Southern. *Lg Dev:* Dictionary. Grammar. *Other:* Plains, mountain slope.

Trinidadian Creole French (Patois, Patwa, Lesser Antillean Creole French) [acf] 3,800 in Trinidad and Tobago (2004). Trinidad, villages of the Northern Range, fishing communities in the islands, and coastal settlements along the peninsula to the west of the capital especially (I. Hancock, ms.). *Lg Use:* In settlements around Dragon Mouths children under 10 speak the language; elsewhere speakers are older adults (Hancock 1984). *Lg Dev:* Literacy, using Saint Lucian materials, is being taught to teachers and other adults in Paramin. *Other:* Fishermen. See main entry under Saint Lucia (Saint Lucian Creole French).

Turks and Caicos Islands

Turks and Caicos Islands. 19,956. National or official language: English. Literacy rate: Over age 15 86.7% (1985). The number of languages listed for Turks and Caicos Islands is 2. Of those, both are living languages. See map on page 739.

English [eng] 920 in Turks and Caicos Islands (2004). *Lg Use:* Official language. See main entry under United Kingdom.

Turks and Caicos Creole English [tch] 10,730 (1995). *Class:* Creole, English based, Atlantic, Eastern.

Other: This variety has not been studied, but it may be related to Bahamas Creole (Holm 1989:489). Agriculturalists: cotton.

U.S. Virgin Islands

U.S. Virgin Islands. 108,775. National or official language: English. U.S. Territory. 50 small islands plus St. John, St. Croix, St. Thomas. Literacy rate: 90% to 95%. Also includes Papiamentu (200), Spanish (4,444). Deaf institutions: 2. The number of languages listed for U.S. Virgin Islands is 3. Of those, 2 are living languages and 1 is extinct. See map on page 740.

English [eng] 8,414 in U.S. Virgin Islands (1970 census). *Lg Use:* Official language. See main entry under United Kingdom.
Negerhollands (Dutch Creole) [dcr] Extinct. Formerly in Leeward Islands, Puerto Rico, St. John, St. Thomas, U.S. Virgin Islands. *Class:* Creole, Dutch based. *Lg Use:* There may be some remaining second-language speakers. *Lg Dev:* NT: 1781–1833.
Virgin Islands Creole English [vic] 52,250 in U.S. Virgin Islands (1980 WA). Population total all countries: 88,680. Also spoken in British Virgin Islands, Netherlands Antilles. *Class:* Creole, English based, Atlantic, Eastern, Southern. *Dialect:* Cruzan. St. Croix, St. Eustatius, St. John, and Saba are closest. Alleyne says it is post-creole English. *Lg Dev:* Dictionary.

USA

United States of America. 293,027,571. Population includes 1,900,000 American Indians, Inuits, and Aleut, not all speaking indigenous languages (1990 census). National or official languages: Hawaiian (in Hawaii), Spanish (in New Mexico). Literacy rate: 95% to 99%. Also includes Adyghe (3,000), Armenian (1,100,000), Assyrian Neo-Aramaic (80,000), Bahamas Creole English, Bahnar, Balkan Romani, Basque (8,108), Belarusan (70,808), Belize Kriol English (40,000), Bengali, Breton (32,722), Bukharic (50,000), Bulgarian, Burmese (1,581), Cajonos Zapotec, Carpathian Romani (18,000), Catalan-Valencian-Balear (40,000), Cebuano, Central Khmer (50,000), Chaldean Neo-Aramaic (80,000), Chru, Corsican, Crimean Turkish, Czech (1,452,812), Danish (194,000), Eastern Cham, Eastern Frisian, Eastern Kanjobal, Eastern Mnong, Eastern Panjabi (100,000), Eastern Yiddish (1,250,000), El Nayar Cora, Estonian (26,610), Fijian Hindustani, Finnish (266,096), French (1,100,000), Garifuna (65,000), Georgian (757), Gheg Albanian (79,829), Greek (458,699), Gujarati, Guyanese Creole English, Haitian Creole French (200,000), Hakka Chinese, Hebrew, Hiligaynon, Hindi (26,253), Hmong Daw (70,000), Hmong Njua (100,000), Hulaulá, Hungarian (447,497), Icelandic (9,768), Ilocano, Indonesian, Irish Gaelic, Italian (906,000), Iu Mien (24,000), Japanese (804,000), Jarai, Judeo-Tunisian Arabic, Kabardian (2,000), Kabuverdianu (400,000), Kalmyk-Oirat, Karachay-Balkar, Khmu, Khuen, Klao, Koho, Korean (1,800,000), Ladin, Ladino, Lahu Shi (2,000), Lao (171,577), Latvian (50,000), Laven, Laz, Lithuanian, Lombard, Luxembourgeois (20,618), Mal, Malay (6,253), Maltese, Mandarin Chinese, Mezquital Otomi, Min Nan Chinese, Mixtepec Mixtec, Najdi Spoken Arabic (193,520), Northern Kurdish, Northern Uzbek, Nung, Parsi (75,000), Peñoles Mixtec, Phu Thai, Piemontese, Pingelapese (500), Polish (3,398,763), Pontic, Portuguese (1,313,424), Rade, Rapa Nui, Romanian (56,590), Samoan (63,104), San Juan Guelavía Zapotec (500), Scottish Gaelic, Senaya (400), Serbian (169,938), Shelta (50,000), Sherpa (500), Silacayoapan Mixtec, Sindhi, Slovak, Slovenian (82,321), South Azerbaijani,

Southwestern Caribbean Creole English, Standard German (6,093,054), Swahili (3,991), Swedish (626,102), Sylheti, Tagalog (377,000), Tai Daeng, Tai Dam (3,000), Tatar (7,000), Tày, Thai (14,416), Tibetan (3,000), Tokelauan, Tondano, Tongan (3,000), Tosk Albanian, Traveller Scottish, Turkish (24,123), Turkmen, Turoyo (5,000), Ukrainian (844,026), Upper Guinea Crioulo (156,000), Upper Ta'oih, Uyghur, Vietnamese (859,000), Vlax Romani (650,000), Western Bru, Western Cham (3,000), Western Farsi (900,000), Western Kanjobal, Western Panjabi, Yalálag Zapotec, Yatzachi Zapotec, Yoruba, Yue Chinese, Zoogocho Zapotec (400), Arabic (3,000,000), Chinese (1,645,000), from the Philippines (1,405,000), South Asians (634,000), speakers of other African, Asian, European, Latin American, and Pacific languages. Approximately (1,000,000) Gypsies use a variety of Romani as first or second language (1980 census). Information mainly from W. Chafe 1962, 1965; L. Campbell and M. Mithun 1979; C. A. Callaghan 1998; M-L Tarpent and D. Kendall 1998; SIL 1951–2003. Blind population: 500,000. Deaf population: nearly 2,000,000 (1988). Deaf institutions: Many. The number of languages listed for USA is 238. Of those, 162 are living languages, 3 are second language without mother-tongue speakers, and 73 are extinct. See maps beginning on page 769.

Abnaki, Eastern (Abenaki) [aaq] Extinct. Ethnic population: 1,800 including Western Abnaki in Canada (1982 SIL). Formerly near Bangor, Maine, 1 village (Penobscot). *Class:* Algic, Algonquian, Eastern. *Dialect:* Penobscot. *Lg Use:* The last speaker of Penobscot died in the 1990s. Other dialects also extinct.
Achumawi (Achomawi, Pitt River) [acv] 10 nonfluent speakers (1997 Nevin). Ethnic population: 1,000 (1997 Bruce Nevin). Northeastern California. *Class:* Hokan, Northern, Karok-Shasta, Shasta-Palaihnihan, Palaihnihan. *Dialects:* Originally there were nine dialects. *Lg Use:* All speakers are older adults. *Other:* Nearly extinct.
Afro-Seminole Creole (Afro-Seminole, Seminole, Black Seminole) [afs] Population total all countries: 200. Bracketville, Texas. Also spoken in Mexico. *Class:* Creole, English based, Atlantic, Eastern, Northern. *Dialects:* Texas, Mexico. Separated from coastal Sea Islands Creole between 1690 and 1760. Similar to Sea Islands Creole of USA and Bahamas Creole. Lexical similarity 90% with Sea Islands Creole. *Lg Use:* No speakers left in Oklahoma. Probably absorbed by Bahamian on Andros Island and by Spanish in Cuba. Speakers also use English or Spanish.
Ahtena (Atna, Ahtna, Copper River, Mednovskiy) [aht] 80 (1995 M. Krauss). Ethnic population: 500 (1995 M. Krauss). Alaska, Copper River above the Eyak River at its mouth, and upper Susitna and Nenana drainages. 8 communities. *Class:* Na-Dene, Nuclear Na-Dene, Athapaskan-Eyak, Athapaskan, Tanaina-Ahtna. *Lg Use:* All speakers older than 50 years. Speakers also use English. *Lg Dev:* Dictionary. *Other:* There is a growing interest in the language among the population. Nearly extinct.
Alabama (Alibamu) [akz] 100 (1997 Timothy Montler). Ethnic population: 500 to 600 (1990 Heather Hardy). Alabama-Coushatta Reservation near Livingston in southeastern Texas. No speakers left in Oklahoma. *Class:* Muskogean, Eastern. *Dialects:* Less than 50% cognate with Koasati. *Lg Use:* Speakers are shifting to English.
Aleut [ale] 300 in the USA (1995 M. Krauss). Population total all countries: 490. Ethnic population: 2,000 (1995 M. Krauss). Western Aleut on Atka Island (Aleutian Chain); Eastern Aleut on eastern Aleutian Islands, Pribilofs, and Alaskan Peninsula. Also spoken in Russia (Asia). *Class:* Eskimo-Aleut, Aleut. *Dialects:* Western Aleut (Atkan, Atka, Attuan, Unangany, Unangan), Eastern Aleut

(Unalaskan, Pribilof Aleut). *Lg Use:* All but 4 speakers can speak English well. *Lg Dev:* Dictionary. Grammar. Bible portions: 1840–1903. *Other:* Copper Island Aleut is a mixed Aleut-Russian language, or pidgin, spoken on Mednyj Island. Many school texts have been produced.

Alsea (Alséya) [aes] Extinct. Oregon, on Alsea River and Bay. *Class:* Penutian, Oregon Penutian, Coast Oregon, Yakonan. *Dialect:* Yaquina (Yakwina, Yakon, Yakona). *Other:* There were fewer than 10 in 1930 (1977 Voegelin and Voegelin).

Amerax [aex] *Class:* Unclassified. *Lg Use:* Spoken by Neo-Muslims in prisons. Reported to not have first-language speakers. *Other:* It may have Arabic influences (Cowan 1990). Muslim. Second language only.

American Sign Language (ASL, Ameslan) [ase] 100,000 to 500,000 primary users (1986 Gallaudet Univ.) out of nearly 2,000,000 profoundly deaf persons in the USA (1988), 0.8% of the USA population. 15,000,000 hard of hearing persons in the USA (1989 Sacks). Also used in varying degrees in Canada, Philippines, Ghana, Nigeria, Chad, Burkina Faso, Gabon, Democratic Republic of the Congo, Central African Republic, Côte d'Ivoire, Mauritania, Kenya, Madagascar, Benin, Togo, Zimbabwe, Singapore, China (Hong Kong). Also used in Canada, Guatemala. *Class:* Deaf sign language. *Dialects:* Black American Sign Language, Tactile Sign Language. In Canada there are dialect differences with USA ASL and regional differences from east to west. Structurally and grammatically distinct from Quebec Sign Language (LSQ). Has grammatical characteristics independent of English. A few adults know both ASL and LSQ. Most signers from eastern Canada use ASL with some British Sign Language vocabulary, a remnant from Maritime Sign Language, which came from British Sign Language. Black American Sign Language developed in segregated schools in the south. It contains much sign vocabulary not in ASL and some different grammatical structure. Tactile Sign Language is used by over 900 persons in Louisiana who know ASL, but have lost their sight from a generic cause: Usher's Syndrome. They communicate by touch on each other's wrists. Some have migrated to Seattle. Some have learned Braille. ASL has 43% lexical similarity with French Sign Language in an 872-word list. *Lg Use:* Sign language interpreters provided in court, for college students, at important public events, in job training, at social services programs, in mental health service programs, some instruction for parents of deaf children, many sign language classes for hearing people. There is an organization for sign language teachers. Many hearing people are learning ASL as second language. Reported to be the third largest language in the USA (1993 Honolulu Advertiser). Used since 1817. *Lg Dev:* The average deaf person graduates from high school with 3rd or 4th grade reading level in English. TV. Videos. Dictionary. Bible portions: 1982–1996. *Other:* ASL is different from 'English on the Hands' (Signed English, Siglish). There are several systems of manually coded English, including different ones in different countries. Also several systems called Pidgin Signed English. Pidgin Signed English is taught in schools in the USA rather than ASL. SOV; prepositions, genitives, articles, adjectives, numerals, relatives before noun heads; question word initial.

Angloromani (English Romani, Romani English, Romanichal, Romanis) [rme] 100,000 in North America. See main entry under United Kingdom.

Apache, Jicarilla [apj] 812 (1990 census). Ethnic population: 2,000 (1977 SIL). Northern New Mexico, area of Dulce. *Class:* Na-Dene, Nuclear Na-Dene, Athapaskan-Eyak, Athapaskan, Apachean, Navajo-Apache, Eastern Apache. *Lg Use:* Children and most young adults prefer English.

Apache, Kiowa [apk] 18 (1990 census). Ethnic population: 1,000 (1977 SIL). Western Oklahoma, Caddo County. *Class:* Na-Dene, Nuclear Na-Dene, Athapaskan-Eyak, Athapaskan, Apachean, Kiowa Apache. *Lg Use:* Speakers are shifting to English. *Other:* Nearly extinct.

Apache, Lipan [apl] 2 or 3 (1981 R. W. Young). Ethnic population: 100 (1977 SIL). New Mexico, Mescalero Reservation. *Class:* Na-Dene, Nuclear Na-Dene, Athapaskan-Eyak, Athapaskan, Apachean, Navajo-Apache, Eastern Apache. *Lg Use:* May be extinct. Speakers have shifted to English. All speakers were older adults in 1981. *Other:* Nearly extinct.

Apache, Mescalero-Chiricahua [apm] 1,800 (1977 SIL). Population includes 279 Chiricahua speakers (1990 census). Ethnic population: 2,395 (2000). Mescalero Reservation, New Mexico. A small number of Chiricahua at Ft. Sill, Oklahoma. *Class:* Na-Dene, Nuclear Na-Dene, Athapaskan-Eyak, Athapaskan, Apachean, Navajo-Apache, Eastern Apache. *Dialects:* Chiricahua, Mescalero. *Lg Use:* In Oklahoma most or all speakers are older adults. *Lg Dev:* Dictionary.

Apache, Western (Coyotero) [apw] 12,693 (1990 census). 303 in San Carlos. East central Arizona, several reservations. *Class:* Na-Dene, Nuclear Na-Dene, Athapaskan-Eyak, Athapaskan, Apachean, Navajo-Apache, Western Apache-Navajo. *Dialects:* White Mountain, San Carlos, Cibecue, Tonto. *Lg Use:* Vigorous. *Lg Dev:* Dictionary. NT: 1966.

Arapaho (Arrapahoe) [arp] 1,038 (1990 census). Ethnic population: 5,000 (1977 SIL). Wind River Reservation, Wyoming, and associated with the Cheyenne in western Oklahoma. *Class:* Algic, Algonquian, Plains, Arapaho. *Lg Use:* Speakers are shifting to English. Most or all speakers are older adults. *Lg Dev:* Bible portions: 1903.

Arikara (Arikari, Arikaris, Arikaree, Ree, Ris) [ari] 20 (1997 Parks). Ethnic population: 3,000. Fort Berthold Reservation, North Dakota. *Class:* Caddoan, Northern, Pawnee-Kitsai, Pawnee. *Lg Use:* Speakers are shifting to English. Most or all speakers are older adults. *Lg Dev:* Dictionary. Grammar. *Other:* Reported to be one of the groups Lewis and Clark met in 1804 in North Dakota. There had been 30,000 reduced to 6,000 because of smallpox. Arikara instructional material has been published for use in a language-teaching program. Nearly extinct.

Assiniboine (Assiniboin, Hohe) [asb] Ethnic population: 1,983 (2000). Fort Belknap and Fort Peck reservations, Montana. *Lg Use:* All speakers are over 50 years, most over 60 years (1986). English is spoken extensively. See main entry under Canada.

Atakapa [aqp] Extinct. Southwestern Louisiana and southeastern Texas. *Class:* Gulf. *Lg Dev:* Dictionary. Grammar.

Atsugewi [atw] 3 (1994 L. Hinton). Ethnic population: 200 (1977 SIL). 1,350 with Achumawi (2000 A. Yamamoto). Northeastern California. *Class:* Hokan, Northern, Karok-Shasta, Shasta-Palaihnihan, Palaihnihan. *Other:* Nearly extinct.

Barbareño [boi] Extinct. Southern California, near Santa Barbara. *Class:* Chumash. *Dialects:* Was not intelligible with other Chumash varieties.

Biloxi [bll] Extinct. Lower Mississippi Valley. *Class:* Siouan, Siouan Proper, Southeastern, Biloxi-Ofo.

Blackfoot (Pikanii, Blackfeet) [bla] 100 in the USA (2001 Goddard). Ethnic population: 5,000 to 8,000 in USA (2001 Ives Goddard). Blackfeet Reservation, Montana. *Dialect:* Piegan (Peigan). *Lg Use:* In USA most speakers are older adults. Speakers are shifting to English. *Other:* In Missoula, Montana, summer language classes are offered in Blackfoot. See main entry under Canada.

Caddo (Kado, Caddoe, Kadohadacho) [cad] 25 (1997 Chafe). Ethnic population: 3,371 (1997 W. Chafe). Western

Oklahoma, Caddo County. Formerly in northeastern Texas, extending into southwestern Arkansas. *Class:* Caddoan, Southern. *Dialects:* Related to Pawnee, Wichita, and two extinct languages: Kitsai and Adai. *Lg Use:* All speakers older than 70 years (2000). Speakers have shifted to English. No monolinguals (2000 Levy). *Other:* The tribes are Cahinnio, Hasinai, Kadohadacho, Nanatsoho, Upper Nasoni, Upper Natchitoches, Upper Yatasi. Nearly extinct.

Cahuilla [chl] 7 to 20 (1994 L. Hinton). Ethnic population: 35 (1990 census). Southern California, San Gorgonio Pass and Mohave Desert areas. *Class:* Uto-Aztecan, Northern Uto-Aztecan, Takic, Cupan, Cahuilla-Cupeno. *Lg Use:* Speakers have shifted to English. All speakers are older adults. *Other:* Nearly extinct.

Carolina Algonquian [crr] Extinct. Formerly spoken in northeastern North Carolina. *Class:* Algic, Algonquian.

Catawba [chc] Extinct. Ethnic population: 500 (1977 SIL). Near Rock Hill, northern South Carolina. *Class:* Siouan, Catawba. *Dialects:* There were several dialects. *Lg Use:* The last fluent speaker died prior to 1960. Members of the ethnic group now speak English.

Cayuga [cay] 10 in the USA (1991 M. Dale Kinkade). Cattaraugus Reservation, western New York, and formerly in northeastern Oklahoma. *Lg Use:* Speakers have shifted to English. All speakers are older adults. See main entry under Canada.

Chehalis, Lower [cea] Extinct. Southwestern coast of Washington. *Class:* Salishan, Tsamosan, Inland.

Chehalis, Upper (Chehalis, Kwaiailk) [cjh] Extinct. Ethnic population: 200 (1977 SIL). Washington, south of Puget Sound. *Class:* Salishan, Tsamosan, Inland. *Dialects:* A separate language from Lower Chehalis. Not to be confused with Halkomelem on the Chehalis River in British Columbia. *Lg Dev:* Dictionary.

Cherokee (Tsalagi, Tslagi) [chr] 15,000 to 22,500. 130 monolinguals. Population includes 14,000 speakers on Oklahoma rolls (1986 Durbin Feeling, Cherokee Nation, OK), 1,000 in North Carolina (1997 Robin Sabino). Ethnic population: 308,132 (1990 census) including 70,000 on Oklahoma rolls (1986 D. Feeling), 9,800 in Eastern Band (1997 Robin Sabino). Eastern and northeastern Oklahoma and Cherokee Reservation, Great Smokey Mountains, western North Carolina. *Class:* Iroquoian, Southern Iroquoian. *Dialects:* Elati (Lower Cherokee, Eastern Cherokee), Kituhwa (Middle Cherokee), Otali (Upper Cherokee, Western Cherokee, Overhill Cherokee), Overhill-Middle Cherokee. *Lg Use:* Vigorous in some Oklahoma communities. Elsewhere most younger speakers prefer English. The Elati dialect is extinct. *Lg Dev:* Literacy rate in first language: 15% to 20% can read it, 5% can write it (1986 Cherokee Heritage Center). Now being taught in schools, churches, and other classes (1986 Cherokee Advocate). Sequoyah syllabary. Dictionary. Grammar. NT: 1850–1951. *Other:* Christian, traditional religion.

Chetco [ctc] 5 (1962 Chafe). Ethnic population: 100 possibly (1977 SIL). Southern coast, Oregon. *Class:* Na-Dene, Nuclear Na-Dene, Athapaskan-Eyak, Athapaskan, Pacific Coast, Oregon, Tolowa-Galice. *Lg Use:* Speakers have shifted to English. *Other:* Possibly extinct. Nearly extinct.

Cheyenne [chy] 1,721 (1990 census). Ethnic population: 5,000 (1987 SIL). Northern Cheyenne Reservation, southeastern Montana; associated with Arapaho in western Oklahoma. *Class:* Algic, Algonquian, Plains. *Lg Use:* Northern Cheyenne in Montana have a summer camp for children, where 5 fluent speakers teach the language (1998). In Montana many parents and older adults speak the language but younger ones use English. In Oklahoma most speakers are older adults. *Lg Dev:* Literacy rate in first language: 1% to 5%. Literacy rate in second language: 50% to 100%. Grammar. NT: 1934.

Chickasaw [cic] 1,000 (1987 Munro and Willmond). Ethnic population: 35,000 to 37,000 (1999 Chickasaw nation). Principally in south central Oklahoma, from Byng or Happyland (near Ada) in the north, and from Davis or Ardmore in the west to Fillmore and Wapanucka in the east. Some in Los Angeles, California. *Class:* Muskogean, Western. *Dialects:* Choctaw speakers find Chickasaw to be unintelligible. *Lg Use:* Speakers are shifting to English. Most speakers older than 50 years. *Lg Dev:* Dictionary.

Chimakum (Chemakum) [cmk] Extinct. Washington State, Puget Sound side of Olympic Peninsula. *Class:* Chimakuan.

Chimariko [cid] Extinct. Ethnic population: No members of the ethnic group left (1997 K. Turner). Northwest California. *Class:* Hokan, Northern.

Chinook (Lower Chinook) [chh] 12 speakers of Kiksht dialect (1996). Ethnic population: 300 possibly (1977 SIL). Lower Columbia River, Oregon, and Washington. *Class:* Penutian, Chinookan. *Dialects:* Klatsop (Tlatsop), Clackama, Kiksht. *Lg Use:* Speakers have shifted to English. *Other:* SVO, VSO. Nearly extinct.

Chinook Wawa (Chinook Jargon, Chinook Pidgin, Tsinuk Wawa) [chn] 17 in the USA (1990 census). Formerly used along the Pacific coast from Oregon to Alaska. All speakers are probably now scattered. *Lg Use:* Trade language. Speakers are shifting to English. Formerly used widely during the 19th century between Indian and White, and between speakers of different languages. *Other:* Nearly extinct. See main entry under Canada.

Chippewa (Southwestern Ojibwa, Ojibwe, Ojibway) [ciw] 5,000. Ethnic population: 103,826 in USA (1990 Census Bureau). Upper Michigan westward to North Dakota. *Class:* Algic, Algonquian, Central, Ojibwa. *Dialects:* Upper Michian-Wisconsin Chippewa, Central Minnesota Chippewa, Red Lake Chippewa, Minnesota Border Chippewa. Turtle Mountain in North Dakota shares features with Central Minnesota. Red Lake includes Northwest Angle on shore of Lake of the Woods. Nett Lake on the Minnesota border is closely related to Lac la Croix (Rainy River Ojibwa of Northwestern Ojibwa) in Ontario. *Lg Use:* Concerted effort via language teaching in public schools and other efforts to reverse decline. Most or all speakers are older adults. *Lg Dev:* Taught in primary schools. Dictionary. Grammar. NT: 1833–1854.

Chitimacha [ctm] Extinct. Ethnic population: 300 (1977 SIL). Southern Louisiana. *Class:* Gulf.

Choctaw [cho] 9,211 (2000). Ethnic population: 120,400 including 111,400 in Oklahoma (1998 Choctaw Language Department, Choctaw Nation of Oklahoma). Principally in southeastern Oklahoma (McCurtain County) and east central Mississippi. Some in Louisiana and Tennessee. *Class:* Muskogean, Western. *Dialects:* Recent reports indicate that Choctaw speakers find Chickasaw to be unintelligible. *Lg Use:* Most children prefer English. All speakers older than 45 years. Some children are being raised speaking Choctaw in Mississippi. *Lg Dev:* Literacy rate in first language: 5% to 10%. Literacy rate in second language: 75% to 100%. NT: 1848. *Other:* The Houma are 12,000 racially mixed descendants of a Choctaw subgroup in southern Louisiana who speak a dialect of Cajun French, and no longer speak Choctaw.

Chumash [chs] Extinct. Ethnic population: 156 (2000 A. Yamamoto). Southern California coast near Santa Barbara. *Class:* Chumash. *Dialects:* Inherently unintelligible Chumash varieties formerly spoken included Obispeño, Ineseño, Purisimeño, Barbareño, Ventureño, and Cruzeño (Island Chumash, Isleño), named after the missions to which they were brought. Marianne Mithun says it is not Hokan. *Lg Use:* Extinct since 1965.

Clallam (Klallam, S'klallam, Na'klallam) [clm] 10 (1997 Timothy Montler). Ethnic population: Several thousands (1997 T. Montler). Washington, northeastern Olympic Peninsula, Port Angeles. *Class:* Salishan, Central Salish, Straits. *Dialects:* Close to Saanich. *Lg Use:* All speakers are older adults. *Other:* Nearly extinct.

Cocopa (Kikima, Cucapá, Cocopah, Kwikapa, Delta River Yuman) [coc] 150 in the USA (1994 L. Hinton). 6 monolinguals. Ethnic population: 321 in the USA (1990). Lower Colorado River south of Yuma, Arizona. The majority live in Baja California, Mexico. *Lg Use:* Passed on to some children. Course on Cocopa taught at nearby college. See main entry under Mexico.

Coeur d'Alene [crd] 5 (1999 R. McDonald). Ethnic population: 800 (1977 SIL). Northern Idaho, Coeur d'Alene Reservation. *Class:* Salishan, Interior Salish, Southern. *Lg Use:* There are language lessons in the school curriculum for children and classes for adults. *Other:* Nearly extinct.

Columbia-Wenatchi (Wenatchi-Columbia) [col] 75 (1990 M. D. Kinkade). Population includes 39 Columbia speakers (1990 census). Ethnic population: 500 possibly (1977 SIL). North central Washington, Colville Reservation. *Class:* Salishan, Interior Salish, Southern. *Dialects:* Columbia (Sinkiuse, Columbian), Wenatchi (Wenatchee, Entiat, Chelan). *Lg Use:* All speakers are older adults.

Comanche [com] 200 (2000). Ethnic population: 10,000 (2000). Western Oklahoma. *Class:* Uto-Aztecan, Northern Uto-Aztecan, Numic, Central. *Dialects:* Close to Shoshoni, Panamint. *Lg Use:* Speakers are shifting to English. Most or all speakers are older adults (1998). *Lg Dev:* Dictionary. Grammar. Bible portions: 1958.

Coos (Hanis) [csz] 1 or 2 (1962 Chafe). Ethnic population: 250 (1977 SIL). Southern Oregon coast. *Class:* Penutian, Oregon Penutian, Coast Oregon, Coosan. *Lg Use:* Speakers have shifted to English. Possibly extinct. *Other:* Nearly extinct.

Coquille (Upper Coquille, Mishikhwutmetunee) [coq] Extinct. Southwestern Oregon, formerly on upper Coquille River. *Class:* Na-Dene, Nuclear Na-Dene, Athapaskan-Eyak, Athapaskan, Pacific Coast, Oregon, Tolowa-Galice.

Cowlitz (Lower Cowlitz) [cow] Extinct. Ethnic population: 200 (1990 M. D. Kinkade). Southwestern Washington. *Class:* Salishan, Tsamosan, Inland.

Cree, Plains (Western Cree) [crk] 100 in the USA (2001 I. Goddard). North central Montana, Rocky Boy Reservation. *Lg Use:* Most or all speakers are older adults. Speakers also use English. *Lg Dev:* Literacy rate in first language: 1% to 10%. Literacy rate in second language: 50% to 75%. See main entry under Canada.

Crow (Apsaalooke) [cro] 4,280 (1990 census). Ethnic population: 9,840 enrolled in the nation (1999 BIA). Southern Montana. *Class:* Siouan, Siouan Proper, Missouri Valley. *Dialects:* Close to Hidatsa. *Lg Use:* 77% of Crow people over 66 years old speak the language; no preschoolers do. 80% prefer to use English (1998). Spoken by some parents and older adults (1998). Few high school students speak Crow. *Lg Dev:* Literacy rate in first language: 1% to 5%. Literacy rate in second language: 75% to 100%. Bible portions: 1980–1998.

Cruzeño (Island Chumash, Isleño) [crz] Extinct. Formerly in Southern California, near Santa Barbara. *Class:* Chumash. *Dialects:* Was not intelligible with other Chumash varieties. Had multiple dialects.

Cupeño (cup) Extinct. Ethnic population: 700 (2000 A. Yamamoto). Southern California, near the Pala Reservation, north of Valley Center. *Class:* Uto-Aztecan, Northern Uto-Aztecan, Takic, Cupan, Cahuilla-Cupeno. *Lg Use:* Members of the ethnic group now speak English.

Dakota (Sioux) [dak] 15,355 in the USA (1990 census). 31 monolinguals (1990 census). Population includes 250 speakers of Yanktonais (1997 Douglas Parks). Population total all countries: 20,355. Ethnic population: Includes 5,000 Yanktonais (1997 D. Parks). Northern Nebraska, southern Minnesota, North and South Dakota, northeastern Montana. Also spoken in Canada. *Class:* Siouan, Siouan Proper, Central, Mississippi Valley, Dakota. *Dialects:* Dakota (Dakhota, Santee, Santee-Sisseton), Nakota (Nakoda, Yankton, Yankton-Yanktonais). Lexical similarity 83% to 86% with Stoney, 89% to 94% with Assiniboine, 90% to 95% among dialects. *Lg Use:* Most younger ones prefer English or do not speak the language. A few children are being raised speaking the language in the northern Plains (1998). *Lg Dev:* Grammar. Bible: 1879.

Degexit'an ("Ingalik," "Ingalit," Deg Xinag, Deg Xit'an) [ing] 20 to 30 (1997 Sharon Hargus). Ethnic population: 250 to 300 (1997 M. Krauss). Alaska, Shageluk, Anvik, and Athapaskans at Holy Cross, below Grayling on the Yukon River. *Class:* Na-Dene, Nuclear Na-Dene, Athapaskan-Eyak, Athapaskan, Ingalik-Koyukon, Ingalik. *Lg Use:* Speakers are shifting to English. Speakers are older adults. *Other:* The names "Ingalik" and "Ingalit" formerly applied to this language are unacceptable to its speakers. Nearly extinct.

Delaware, Pidgin [dep] Extinct. Formerly in the Middle Atlantic region. *Class:* Pidgin, Amerindian. *Lg Use:* Widely used in the 17th century between Algonquians and Europeans as a second language.

English [eng] 210,000,000 in the USA (1984). 8,400,000 USA residents 14 years old or older who do not speak fluent English; 38% or 7,700,000 households headed by immigrants. *Dialect:* Black English. *Other:* Many regional dialects. See main entry under United Kingdom.

Esselen [esq] Extinct. Ethnic population: 80 (2000 A. Yamamoto). Formerly on central California coast near Carmel. *Class:* Hokan, Esselen-Yuman, Esselen. *Lg Use:* There is a language revival effort.

Eyak [eya] 1 (1996 N. Barnes). Ethnic population: 50 (1995 M. Krauss). Mouth of the Copper River, Alaska. Last speaker lives in Anchorage. *Class:* Na-Dene, Nuclear Na-Dene, Athapaskan-Eyak, Eyak. *Lg Use:* Speakers have shifted to English. *Other:* Nearly extinct.

French, Cajun (Français Acadien, Acadian, Cajun, Cajan, Cadien) [frc] 1,000,000 (1988 Harris). Southern Louisiana west of the Mississippi as far north as Avoyelles, Evangeline, Allen, and Calcasieu parishes. *Class:* Indo-European, Italic, Romance, Italo-Western, Western, Gallo-Iberian, Gallo-Romance, Gallo-Rhaetian, Oïl, French. *Dialects:* Marsh French, Prairie French, Big Woods French. Ancestors came from French Canada in the 18th century. It is reported that Cajun speakers can partially understand Standard French. Different from the variety of 'Broken French' used by 8,000 African Americans, or the 'Napoleanic Era French' (located around Houma and north of Theriot on Hwy. 315, speaking an archaic French and English). *Lg Use:* Most under 50 speak English as first language, Cajun as second. There are children actively speaking Cajun to friends and family. Many speakers have low proficiency in English. Some use Cajun English. *Lg Dev:* Literacy rate in second language: 60% English, 0% French. Radio programs. Dictionary. Grammar. *Other:* Textbooks on Cajun; translations of some classics. Swamps. Fishermen; fur trappers. Christian.

Galice [gce] Extinct. Formerly in southwestern Oregon. *Class:* Na-Dene, Nuclear Na-Dene, Athapaskan-Eyak, Athapaskan, Pacific Coast, Oregon, Tolowa-Galice.

German, Hutterite (Tyrolese, Tirolean, Hutterian German) [geh] 5,000 in the USA (1981 SIL). 123 colonies in USA (South Dakota 53, North Dakota 6, Minnesota 9,

Montana 34, Washington State 6, and Oregon 1). *Lg Use:* Speakers use Standard German in church and for Scriptures. They are partly bilingual in English and Standard German. *Other:* Have their own schools. Strict communal living. Communal groups in New York, Connecticut, Pennsylvania, and Japan have affiliated recently with Hutterians but are not ethnically Hutterian. Intensive agriculturalists. Christian. See main entry under Canada.

German, Pennsylvania (Pennsylvania Deitsh, Pennsylvanish, Pennsylvania Dutch) [pdc] 85,000 in the USA (2000 SIL). Population total all countries: 100,000. Ethnic population: 200,000 (1978 Kloss and McConnell). Pennsylvania, Ohio, Indiana, Iowa, Kansas, Oklahoma, Virginia, West Virginia, and Florida, and new communities in other states. Also spoken in Canada. *Class:* Indo-European, Germanic, West, High German, German, Middle German, West Middle German. *Dialects:* Amish Pennsylvania German (Plain Pennsylvania German), Non-Amish Pennsylvania German (Pensylvanisch Deitsch, Non-Plain Pennsylvania German). Blending of several German dialects, primarily Rhenish Palatinate (Pfalzer) German, with syntactic elements of High German and English. Mostly incomprehensible now to a person from the Palatinate (Kloss 1978). *Lg Use:* Plain community not shifting to English, but maintains stable bilingualism (Louden 1987). All domains. Preaching in Pennsylvania German, Scripture in High German in Amish religious services. Nonplain community: youngest fluent speakers 40 to 50 years of age (Louden 1987). Only preschoolers are monolingual. School children and adults also speak English. *Lg Dev:* Roman script. NT: 1994–2002. *Other:* Separate orthographies for Pennsylvania and Ohio dialects. Agriculturalists. Christian.

Gros Ventre (Gros Ventres, Atsina, White Clay People, Ahahnelin, Ahe, Fall Indians, Ananin) [ats] 10 (1977 SIL). Very few semispeakers in 2000 (2001 Goddard). Ethnic population: 1,200 (1977 SIL). Fort Belknap Reservation, Milk River, north central Montana. *Class:* Algic, Algonquian, Plains, Arapaho. *Lg Use:* Speakers have shifted to English. *Other:* Closely related to Arapaho. Nearly extinct.

Gwich'in (Kutchin) [gwi] 300 in the USA (1995 M. Krauss). Ethnic population: 1,100 (1995 M. Krauss). Northeastern Alaska on Yukon River and tributaries. 5 villages: Fort Yukon, Chalkyitsik, Birch Creek, Venetie, and Arctic Village. *Dialects:* Fort Yukon Gwich'in, Arctic Village Gwich'in, Western Canada Gwich'in (Takudh, Tukudh, Loucheux), Arctic Red River. *Lg Use:* Greater use in isolated communities. Most speakers are older adults. Most children only speak English. *Lg Dev:* Literacy rate in first language: 1% to 5%. Literacy rate in second language: 75% to 100%. See main entry under Canada.

Haida, Northern (Masset) [hdn] 15 in the USA (1995 M. Krauss). Ethnic population: 600 in the USA (1995 M. Krauss). Southern tip of Alaska panhandle, southern half of Prince of Wales Island, Hydaburg, Kasaan, Craig, and Ketchikan. *Lg Use:* Speakers have shifted to English. Speakers are older adults. There is interest in reviving the language. *Other:* Nearly extinct. See main entry under Canada.

Halkomelem (Holkomelem) [hur] 25 in the USA (1997 Galloway). Ethnic population: 5,267 (1997 Galloway). Washington. *Dialects:* Chiliwack, Cowichan, Musqueam, Nanaimo. *Lg Use:* Speakers have shifted to English. See main entry under Canada.

Han (Han-Kutchin, Moosehide, Dawson) [haa] 7 or 8 in Alaska (1995 M. Krauss). Population total all countries: 14. Ethnic population: 300. Yukon River in area of Alaska-Canada border, Eagle, Alaska. Also spoken in Canada. *Class:* Na-Dene, Nuclear Na-Dene, Athapaskan-Eyak, Athapaskan, Canadian, Han-Kutchin. *Lg Use:*

Speakers have shifted to English. Being taught in bush schools as an elective to native and nonnative children. *Lg Dev:* Taught in primary schools. Grammar. *Other:* There is a Han textbook with tapes for teaching the language. Nearly extinct.

Havasupai-Walapai-Yavapai (Upper Colorado River Yuman, Upland Yuman) [yuf] 2,693 (1990 census). Population includes 530 Havasupai speakers (2000 Yamamoto), 1,000 Walapai speakers (2000 Yamamoto), 163 Yavapai speakers. Ethnic population: 3,857 including 565 Havasupai, 1,872 Walapai, 1,420 Yavapai (2000). Central and northwestern Arizona. The Walapai are on top of the south rim of the Grand Canyon, the Havasupai at the bottom. *Class:* Hokan, Esselen-Yuman, Yuman, Upland Yuman. *Dialects:* Walapai (Hualpai, Hwalbáy), Havasupai, Yavapai. 78% to 98% intelligibility among the dialects. Lexical similarity 91% to 95% among the dialects. *Lg Use:* Vigorous in Havasupai. All ages in Havasupai. Most or all Yavapai speakers are older adults. Many younger Walapai prefer English and some do not speak Walapai. Children being raised speaking Havasupai and Walapai (1998). *Lg Dev:* Literacy rate in first language: 1% to 5%. Literacy rate in second language: 75% to 100%. Grammar. Bible portions: 1980.

Hawai'i Creole English (Pidgin, Hawai'i Pidgin, HCE) [hwc] 600,000 (1986 Forman). Population includes 100,000 to 200,000 who have low proficiency in Standard English and near Standard English (1986 Forman). Another 100,000 speakers on the USA mainland. All the Hawaiian Islands, USA mainland (especially the west coast, Las Vegas, and Orlando). *Class:* Creole, English based, Pacific. *Dialects:* The basilect (heavy creole) is barely intelligible with Standard English (H. McKaughan and M. Forman 1982). *Lg Use:* Vigorous use by 100,000 to 200,000. The native speech of a large number of those born or brought up in Hawaii, regardless of racial origin. There is a continuum of speech from the distinct creole to Standard English of Hawaii. Different speakers control different spans along the continuum; there are those whose only form of verbal communication is the creole. There are some communication problems at university level. Many second-language speakers. Used in courts by officers, jurors, plaintiffs, defendants, witnesses. Creative writing in it in some schools. A growing body of serious literature. Used in schools, personal letters, local commerce, a few songs. All ages. It is accepted by many as an important part of the local culture, a distinctive local language, but looked down on by others. Some official acknowledgement of it in print and public discussion, Miranda rights. 50% of children in Hawaii do not speak English as first language when entering school. Most of these speak HCE as first language. English is used in school. Most songs are in Hawaiian or English. Other languages used are Hakka, Cantonese, Japanese, Korean, Tagalog, Ilocano, Cebuano, Hiligaynon, Portuguese, Spanish, or Samoan. *Lg Dev:* Literacy rate in first language: 66% to 75%. Literacy rate in second language: 66% to 75%. Roman script. Radio programs. TV. Grammar. NT: 2000. *Other:* Volcanic islands, coral reefs, coastal, mountain slope, valleys, plains. Tropical forest to desert, savannah, scrub, evergreens. Sea level to 1,200 meters. Fishermen; agriculturalists; animal husbandry; white and blue collar workers; tourism; military; construction and maintenance workers. Christian, Hawaiian traditional religion, Buddhist, syncretism.

Hawai'i Pidgin Sign Language (Pidgin Sign Language) [hps] A few users out of about 6,000 profoundly deaf people in Hawaii (1987 Honolulu Star-Bulletin), 72,000 deaf or hard-of-hearing people in Hawaii (1998 Honolulu Advertiser). Hawaiian Islands. *Class:* Deaf sign language. *Lg Use:* 9,600 deaf people in Hawaii now use American Sign Language with a few local signs for place names and cultural items (1998 Honolulu Advertiser). Speakers are older adults. American Sign Language is also used. *Other:* This is not a pidgin sign language in the regular sense of that term, but is the name given it by others. Nearly extinct.

Hawaiian ('Olelo Hawai'i, 'Olelo Hawai'i Makuahine) [haw] 1,000. 500 with Ni'ihau Island connections, another 500 in their 70s or 80s (1995 Laina Wong Univ. of Hawaii). 8,000 can speak and understand it (1993 Keith Haugen). In 1900 there were 37,000 first-language speakers (1995 Honolulu Advertiser). Ethnic population: 400,000 in Hawaii (2003 Office of Hawaiian Affairs), 18.8% of the population (1990 Hawaii State Dept. of Health), and 99,269 ethnic Hawaiians on the USA mainland (1990 census), including 24,245 in California. Ethnic Hawaiians include 8,244 pure Hawaiian, 72,809 between 50% and 99% Hawaiian, 127,523 less than 50% Hawaiian in Hawaii (1984 Office of Hawaiian Affairs). In 1778 there were believed to have been more than 500,000 pure Hawaiians (1995 Wayne Harada). Hawaiian Islands, mainly Ni'ihau Island and the Big Island of Hawai'i, some on all the other islands. *Class:* Austronesian, Malayo-Polynesian, Central-Eastern, Eastern Malayo-Polynesian, Oceanic, Central-Eastern Oceanic, Remote Oceanic, Central Pacific, East Fijian-Polynesian, Polynesian, Nuclear, East, Central, Marquesic. *Dialects:* Lexical similarity 79% with Rarotongan, 77% with Tuamotuan, 76% with Tahitian (Elbert), 71% with Maori (Schütz), 70% with Marquesan, 64% with Rapa Nui. *Lg Use:* Official language in the state of Hawaii. All domains. Oral literature, songs, religion. 500 first-language speakers are all older adults. People 2 years old and older are learning it as second language: 1,000 up to age 15. 350 from ages 15 to 25 (1997 Rosemary Henze). Speakers use Hawaii Creole English (Pidgin) or English as second language. *Lg Dev:* Punana Leo private schools offer Hawaiian immersion programs (as a second language) for about 800 from 2-year-old ethnic Hawaiians up to high school. The University of Hawaii offers a BA in the Hawaiian language. Roman script. Dictionary. Grammar. Bible: 1838. *Other:* VSO. Christian, traditional religion.

Hidatsa (Minitari, Hiraca, Hinatsa) [hid] 100 (1986 SIL). 6 monolinguals. 25 to 50 semifluent speakers. Ethnic population: 1,200 (1986 SIL). Fort Berthold Reservation, North Dakota. *Class:* Siouan, Siouan Proper, Missouri Valley. *Dialects:* Close to Crow. *Lg Use:* Speakers are shifting to English. Most speakers are older adults (1998).

Ho-Chunk (Winnebago, Hocak Wazijaci, Hocák, Hocank, Hochank) [win] 230 (1997 Valdis J. Zeps). Ethnic population: 6,000 (1995 V. Zeps). 822 enrolled in Nebraska (1968 USA BIA). Scattered locations in central Wisconsin and Winnebago Reservation in eastern Nebraska. *Class:* Siouan, Siouan Proper, Central, Mississippi Valley, Winnebago. *Dialects:* Wisconsin, Nebraska. *Lg Use:* In Wisconsin, most adults speak the language. In Nebraska, most are older adults (1998). In 1968, 10% were limited in their use of English. Now reported to be proficient in English. *Lg Dev:* There is a Language Program which plans a full-immersion Hocák school system, grades preschool through community college. Bible portions: 1907. *Other:* The name is written with a hook under the 'a' of 'Hocák', representing a nasalized vowel. The official name for the people is Hocák Nation. 'Winnebago' is the Algonquin name.

Holikachuk [hoi] 12 (1995 M. Krauss). Ethnic population: 200 (1995 M. Krauss). Village of Grayling on lower Yukon River, Alaska. *Class:* Na-Dene, Nuclear Na-Dene, Athapaskan-Eyak, Athapaskan, Ingalik-Koyukon, Koyukon-Holikachuk. *Lg Use:* Speakers are shifting to English. All speakers are older adults. *Other:* Nearly extinct.

Hopi [hop] 5,264 (1990 census). 40 monolinguals. Ethnic population: 6,500 (1977 SIL). Several villages in northeast Arizona, with small numbers in Utah and New Mexico. *Class:* Uto-Aztecan, Northern Uto-Aztecan, Hopi. *Lg Use:* Vigorous. Young speakers prefer English. All ages, 5,264 were over 5 years old, 989 of those were 5 to 17, 3,390 were 18 to 54, 388 were 55 to 64, 578 were 65 and older (1990). *Lg Dev:* Dictionary. NT: 1972.

Hupa (Hoopa) [hup] 8 (1998 Brook). Ethnic population: 2,000. Hoopa Valley Reservation, northwestern California. *Class:* Na-Dene, Nuclear Na-Dene, Athapaskan-Eyak, Athapaskan, Pacific Coast, California, Hupa. *Dialect:* Whilkut. *Lg Use:* Speakers have shifted to English. Language revitalization effort is in progress. Adult classes, language immersion camps. Speakers are older adults. *Lg Dev:* Taught in primary schools. Dictionary. Grammar. *Other:* Nearly extinct.

Ineseño [inz] Extinct. Formerly in southern California, near Santa Barbara. *Class:* Chumash. *Dialects:* Was not intelligible with other Chumash varieties.

Inupiatun, North Alaskan (North Alaskan Inupiat, Inupiat, "Eskimo") [esi] Ethnic population: 8,000. Norton Sound and Point Hope, Alaska. Also spoken in Canada. *Class:* Eskimo-Aleut, Eskimo, Inuit. *Dialects:* North Slope Inupiatun (Point Barrow Inupiatun), West Arctic Inupiatun, Point Hope Inupiatun, Anaktuvik Pass Inupiatun. *Lg Use:* Most speakers older than 40 years. Younger speakers prefer English. *Lg Dev:* Dictionary. Grammar. NT: 1968.

Inupiatun, Northwest Alaska (Northwest Alaska Inupiat, Inupiatun, "Eskimo") [esk] 4,000 (1978 SIL). Speakers of all Inuit languages: 75,000 out of 91,000 in the ethnic group (1995 M. Krauss). Ethnic population: 8,000 (1978 SIL). Alaska, Kobuk River, Noatak River, Seward Peninsula, and Bering Strait. *Class:* Eskimo-Aleut, Eskimo, Inuit. *Dialect:* Northern Malimiut Inupiatun, Southern Malimiut Inupiatun, Kobuk River Inupiatun, Coastal Inupiatun, Kotzebue Sound Inupiatun, Seward Peninsula Inupiatun, King Island Inupiatun (Bering Strait Inupiatun). *Lg Use:* Most speakers of Seward Peninsula older than 40 years (1990). *Lg Dev:* Literacy rate in first language: 1% to 5%. NT: 1997.

Iowa-Oto [iow] Extinct. Ethnic population: 2,400, including 1,000 Iowa, 1,400 Oto (1986 SIL). Formerly in north central Oklahoma and Iowa Reservation, northeast Kansas. *Class:* Siouan, Siouan Proper, Central, Mississippi Valley, Chiwere. *Dialects:* Iowa (Baxoje, Ioway), Oto (Jiwere, Otoe, Jiwele, Chiwere), Niutaji (Nyut'chi, Missouri, Missouria). *Lg Use:* Iowa and Oto were a single language, with some family variations cross-cutting the tribal affiliations. Missouri dialect has been extinct for many years. *Other:* Last fluent speakers of Iowa and Oto died the end of 1996. There are others who have some degree of knowledge of the language (1997 Jimm G. GoodTracks).

Jemez (Towa) [tow] 1,301 (1990 census). 6 monolinguals (1990). Ethnic population: 1,488 (1980 census). North central New Mexico. *Class:* Kiowa Tanoan, Kiowa-Towa, Towa. *Lg Use:* Vigorous. 95% of the population under 18 years of age are speakers (1980). *Lg Dev:* Literacy rate in first language: below 1%. Literacy rate in second language: 50% to 75%. *Other:* Traditional religion, Christian.

Kalapuya (Santiam, Lukamiute, Wapatu) [kyl] 1 or 2 (1962 Chafe). Northwest Oregon. *Class:* Penutian, Oregon Penutian, Kalapuyan. *Lg Use:* May be extinct. Speakers have shifted to English. *Other:* Nearly extinct.

Kalispel-Pend D'Oreille (Kalispel-"Flathead," "Flathead"-Kalispel, Salish) [fla] 200 (1997). Ethnic population: 6,800 (1997). Kalispel Reservation, northeast Washington, Flathead Reservation, northwest Montana. *Class:* Salishan, Interior Salish, Southern. *Dialects:* Pend

D'oreille, Kalispel. *Lg Use:* Speakers are shifting to English. All speakers are older adults. *Other:* Spokane is a coordinate language variety.

Kansa (Kaw, Konze, Kanze) [ksk] 19 (1990 census). Ethnic population: 250 (1986 SIL). Oklahoma, north central. *Class:* Siouan, Siouan Proper, Central, Mississippi Valley, Dhegiha. *Dialects:* Close to Omaha, Osage, Ponca, Quapaw. *Lg Use:* Speakers have shifted to English. *Other:* Nearly extinct.

Karkin [krb] Extinct. Formerly in north Central California. *Class:* Penutian, Yok-Utian, Utian, Costanoan. *Lg Use:* Became extinct in the 1950s.

Karok (Karuk) [kyh] 10 (1997 William Bright). Ethnic population: 1,900 (2000 A. Yamamoto). Northwestern California, along the banks of the Klamath River. *Class:* Hokan, Northern, Karok-Shasta. *Dialects:* No significant dialect differences. *Lg Use:* Speakers are shifting to English. Most or all speakers are older adults. *Other:* Nearly extinct.

Kashaya (Southwestern Pomo) [kju] 45 (1994 L. Hinton). *Class:* Hokan, Northern, Pomo, Russian River and Eastern, Russian River, Southern. *Lg Use:* Speakers are shifting to English. *Other:* A separate language from other Pomo varieties. Some teaching materials. Nearly extinct.

Kato (Cahto, Batem-Da-Kai-Ee, Kai Po-Mo, Tlokeang) [ktw] Extinct. Ethnic population: 92 (1982 SIL). Formerly on the Laytonville Reservation, northwestern California. *Class:* Na-Dene, Nuclear Na-Dene, Athapaskan-Eyak, Athapaskan, Pacific Coast, California, Mattole-Wailaki.

Kawaiisu [xaw] 8 to 10 (2000 L. Hinton). Ethnic population: 35 (2000 A. Yamamoto). California, south, Tehachapi-Mojave area of the Mojave Desert. *Class:* Uto-Aztecan, Northern Uto-Aztecan, Numic, Southern. *Lg Use:* Speakers have shifted to English. *Lg Dev:* Dictionary. Grammar. *Other:* Nearly extinct.

Keres, Eastern (Eastern Keres Pueblo) [kee] 4,580. Population includes 463 Zia, 229 Santa Ana, 1,560 San Felipe, 1,888 Santo Domingo, 384 Cochiti. Ethnic population: 5,701 including 602 Zia, 374 Santa Ana, 1,789 San Felipe, 2,140 Santo Domingo, 796 Cochiti. North central New Mexico. *Class:* Keres. *Dialects:* Zia, Santa Ana, San Felipe, Santo Domingo, Cochiti. *Lg Use:* Vigorous in some pueblos; in others some younger people prefer English. Percentage of persons under 18 who are speakers: 47.7%, including Laguna 32.3%, Acoma 67.9%; above 18: 75.1%. *Lg Dev:* Literacy rate in first language: below 1%. Literacy rate in second language: 75% to 100%. Bible portions: 1933–1936.

Keres, Western (Western Keres Pueblo) [kjq] 3,391 (1980 census). Population includes 1,695 Laguna, 1,696 Acoma. Ethnic population: 5,880, including 3,526 Laguna, 2,354 Acoma (1980 census). New Mexico, north central. *Class:* Keres. *Dialect:* Acoma (Laguna). *Lg Use:* In Acoma most adults speak the language but some younger people prefer English and many children do not speak the language. In Laguna most or all speakers are middle aged or over. Percentage under 18 years old who are speakers: 47.7%, including Laguna 32.3%, Acoma 67.9%; above 18: 75.1% (1998). *Lg Dev:* Literacy rate in first language: below 1%. Literacy rate in second language: 50% to 75%. Grammar. Bible portions: 1966–1997.

Kickapoo (Kikapoo, Kikapú) [kic] 539 in the USA (1990 census). 6 monolinguals. Population total all countries: 839. Northeastern Kansas: Horton; central Oklahoma: McCloud, Jones; Texas: Nuevo Nacimiento. Also spoken in Mexico. *Class:* Algic, Algonquian, Central. *Dialects:* Possibly intelligible with Sac and Fox (Mesquakie). *Lg Use:* In Oklahoma some younger people prefer English, and in Kansas most or all speakers are older adults. *Lg Dev:* Dictionary.

Kiowa [kio] 1,092 (1990 census). Ethnic population: 6,000 (1977 SIL). Oklahoma, west central. *Class:* Kiowa Tanoan, Kiowa-Towa, Kiowa. *Lg Use:* Speakers are shifting to English. Speakers are older adults. *Lg Dev:* Dictionary.

Kitsai (Kichai) [kii] Extinct. Ethnic population: 2,000 (1997 Scott DeLancey). Formerly in west central Oklahoma among the Caddo, Caddo County. *Class:* Caddoan, Northern, Pawnee-Kitsai, Kitsai. *Dialects:* Closer to Pawnee than to Wichita.

Klamath-Modoc [kla] 1 (1998 N.Y. Times, April 9, p. A20). Ethnic population: 2,000 (1997 Scott DeLancey). Oregon, south central, around and to the east and north of Klamath and Agency lakes; Modoc directly to the south. *Class:* Penutian, Plateau Penutian, Klamath-Modoc. *Dialects:* Closest to Molala and Sahaptian. *Lg Use:* Speakers have shifted to English. *Lg Dev:* Dictionary. Grammar. *Other:* Active language programs and materials development in Modoc. Nearly extinct.

Koasati (Coushatta) [cku] 200 (2000 SIL). Ethnic population: 600, including 100 in Texas. Koasati Reservation near Elton, Louisiana, and Alabama-Koasati Reservation near Livingston, Texas. Others elsewhere; 1 family in Oregon. The language is no longer used in Oklahoma. *Class:* Muskogean, Eastern. *Dialects:* The grammars of Koasati and Alabama are significantly different. Less than 50% cognate with Alabama. *Lg Use:* More speakers in Louisiana than Texas. The language was being passed down until the last decade. Less than 10 elementary school-age children speak the language. In Louisiana, the people use Koasati in some homes and for some religious services. Young people invariably speak English to all but older adults. Positive language attitude. 30 speakers have limited English proficiency (1992 Rising). Others have high proficiency in English. A few are better speakers of Cajun French than of English. Some also use Alabama or Choctaw. *Lg Dev:* Written usage is minimal. Roman script. Dictionary. *Other:* Pine forest. Christian.

Koyukon (Ten'a) [koy] 300 (1995 Krauss). Ethnic population: 2,300 (1995 Krauss). Alaska, Koyukuk and middle Yukon rivers. *Class:* Na-Dene, Nuclear Na-Dene, Athapaskan-Eyak, Athapaskan, Ingalik-Koyukon, Koyukon-Holikachuk. *Lg Use:* Speakers are older adults. Speakers also use English. *Lg Dev:* Dictionary. Bible portions: 1974–1980.

Kumiai (Kumeyaay, Diegueño, Digueño, Campo, Kamia) [dih] 75 in the USA (1994 L. Hinton). Population includes 50 Kumiai, 25 Ipai. Southern California east of San Diego, including some in Imperial Valley. *Dialects:* Kimiai, Ipai, Tipai. *Lg Use:* Speakers in California are proficient in English. Spanish is the second language in Mexico. See main entry under Mexico.

Kuskokwim, Upper (Mcgrath Ingalik, Kolchan) [kuu] 40 (1995 Krauss). 3 households (1997). Ethnic population: 160 (1995 Krauss). Nikolai, Telida, McGrath, Upper Kuskokwim River, central Alaska. *Class:* Na-Dene, Nuclear Na-Dene, Athapaskan-Eyak, Athapaskan, Tanana-Upper Kuskokwim, Upper Kuskokwim. *Lg Use:* Speakers are shifting to English. Youngest speakers, average age 30. *Other:* At one time the people were regarded as part of the Ingalik tribe. Nearly extinct.

Kutenai (Ktunaxa, Kootenai) [kut] 6 in the USA (2002). Northern Idaho, Flathead Reservation, Montana. *Lg Use:* Speakers are shifting to English. Kutenai is offered as a second language course (1991). All speakers are older adults. *Other:* Nearly extinct. See main entry under Canada.

Lakota (Lakhota, Teton) [lkt] 6,000 in the USA (1987 SIL and 1997 Pustet). Ethnic population: 20,000 (1987 SIL and 1997 Pustet). 103,255 ethnic Sioux in USA (1990 Census Bureau). Northern Nebraska, southern Minnesota, North and South Dakota, northeastern Montana. Also spoken in Canada. *Class:* Siouan, Siouan Proper, Central, Mississippi Valley, Dakota. *Dialect:* Brulé. *Lg Use:* Vigorous in some Lakota communities. *Lg Dev:* Grammar.

Louisiana Creole French [lou] 60,000 to 80,000 (1985 Neumann). Ethnic population: 4,000,000 (1997 M. Melançon). Predominantly in St. Martin parish (St. Martinville, Breaux Bridge, Cecilia), New Roads and Edgard, Louisiana, parts of east Texas, small community in Sacramento, California. *Class:* Creole, French based. *Dialects:* Different from Standard French, the Cajun French also spoken in Louisiana, Haitian Creole French, and others of the Caribbean. "No slaves (and few if any of the slaveowners) appear to have come from the French Antilles....What we now need is a careful comparison between Louisiana Creole and other French Caribbean creoles, detailing the similarities and differences" (D. Bickerton, Carrier Pidgin 1995 23(2):2). *Lg Use:* Those over 60 prefer Creole, and those under 30 prefer English. 4.6% in the older group are monolingual in Creole. Some in the younger group are monolingual in English. Reported to have high proficiency in English. *Lg Dev:* Dictionary. Grammar.

Luiseño [lui] 30 to 40 (2000 L. Hinton). Ethnic population: 2,000 (2000 A. Yamamoto). Southern California. *Class:* Uto-Aztecan, Northern Uto-Aztecan, Takic, Cupan, Luiseno. *Dialects:* Juaneño (Ajachema, Ajachemem, Agachemem, Acgachemem), Luiseño. *Lg Use:* Juaneño dialect is extinct. Speakers are shifting to English. There are language preservation efforts. Speakers are older adults. *Lg Dev:* Grammar. *Other:* Nearly extinct.

Lumbee (Croatan) [lmz] Extinct. Ethnic population: 30,000 (1977 SIL). Formerly in southern North Carolina and into South Carolina and Maryland. *Class:* Algic, Algonquian, Unclassified. *Other:* Racially mixed descendants of a Pamlico group. Still a distinct ethnic group.

Lushootseed [lut] 60 (1990 M. D. Kinkade). Population evenly divided between the northern and southern dialects. Ethnic population: 2,000 (1990 M. D. Kinkade). Washington, Puget Sound area. *Class:* Salishan, Central Salish, Twana. *Dialects:* Northern Lushootseed (Northern Puget Sound Salish), Southern Lushootseed (Southern Puget Sound Salish). Northern Lushootseed includes subdialects Skagit, Snohomish, and Swinomish; southern Lushootseed includes Duwamish, Nisqually, Puyallup, and Suquamish. *Lg Use:* There are numerous programs starting up around Puget Sound teaching Lushootseed, in which children, parents, and elders are taking part. It is also being introduced as a language available at local colleges. *Other:* Nearly extinct.

Mahican [mjy] Extinct. Formerly on the Upper Hudson River and later in Wisconsin. *Class:* Algic, Algonquian.

Maidu, Northeast (Mountain Maidu) [nmu] 1 to 2 (1994 L. Hinton). Ethnic population: 108 (1990 census). California, northern Sierras, Plumas and Lassen counties. *Class:* Penutian, Maiduan. *Lg Use:* Members of the ethnic group now speak English. *Other:* Nearly extinct.

Maidu, Northwest (Hololupai, Maiduan, Meidoo, Michopdo, Nákum, Secumne, Sekumne, Tsamak, Yuba, Konkow, Konkau, Concow, "Digger") [mjd] 3 to 6 (1994 L. Hinton). Ethnic population: 200 (1977 SIL). Lower foothills of the Sierras, central California. The ethnic group is scattered. *Class:* Penutian, Maiduan. *Dialects:* A separate language from other Maidu varieties. *Lg Use:* Speakers are older adults. Members of the ethnic group now speak English. *Lg Dev:* Dictionary. *Other:* Alternate names listed apply to all Maidu except the last four. Nearly extinct.

Maidu, Valley [vmv] Extinct. Formerly in California, between Sacramento and the Sierra foothills. *Class:* Penutian, Maiduan. *Lg Dev:* Dictionary.

Makah (Kwe-Nee-Chee-Aht, Kweedishchaaht) [myh] Extinct. Formerly on the northern tip of Olympic Peninsula, opposite Vancouver Island, Washington. *Class:* Wakashan, Southern. *Lg Use:* Makah is taught bilingually in preschool on the reservation and is ongoing throughout grade school. *Lg Dev:* Taught in primary schools. *Other:* No first-language speakers. Became extinct 2002.

Malecite-Passamaquoddy (Maliseet-Passamaquoddy) [pqm] 1,000 in the USA (1997 Teeter). Ethnic population: 2,500 to 3,000 (1997 Teeter). Maine, New Brunswick border area. Malecite mainly in Canada, Passamaquoddy mainly in Maine. *Dialects:* Malecite (Maliseet), Passamaquoddy. *Lg Use:* Most speakers of Passamaquoddy are older adults (1998) with younger speakers in a few areas. English is preferred by most younger ones. See main entry under Canada.

Mandan [mhq] 6 (1992 M. Krauss). Ethnic population: 400 (1986 SIL and 1997 M. Mixco). Fort Berthold Reservation, North Dakota. *Class:* Siouan, Siouan Proper, Central, Mandan. *Lg Use:* Speakers have shifted to English. Speakers are older adults (1992), 2 semifluent over 60 (1986). *Lg Dev:* Grammar. *Other:* Nearly extinct.

Maricopa (Cocomaricopa) [mrc] 181 (1990 census). Ethnic population: 400 (1977 SIL). Associated with the Pima on the Gila River and Salt River reservations near Phoenix, Arizona. *Class:* Hokan, Esselen-Yuman, Yuman, River Yuman. *Dialects:* Lexical similarity 85% with Mohave, 58% with Havasupai, 57% with Walapai and Yavapai. *Lg Use:* Speakers are older adults. Speakers also use English.

Martha's Vineyard Sign Language (MVSL) [mre] Extinct. Formerly in Martha's Vineyard, Massachusetts. *Class:* Deaf sign language. *Dialects:* The early sign language was based on a regional one in Weald, England, where the deaf persons' ancestors had lived. French Sign Language was introduced to Martha's Vineyard in 1817. MVSL was later combined with American Sign Language (ASL), but never became identical to ASL. *Lg Use:* From 1692 to 1910 nearly all hearers on Martha's Vineyard were bilingual in English and sign language. *Other:* The first deaf person arrived in 1692. From 1692 to 1950 there was a high rate of hereditary deafness. In the 19th century, 1 in 5700 Americans were deaf, 1 in 155 in Martha's Vineyard, 1 in 25 in one town, 1 in 4 in one neighborhood.

Mattole [mvb] Extinct. Formerly in northern California. *Class:* Na-Dene, Nuclear Na-Dene, Athapaskan-Eyak, Athapaskan, Pacific Coast, California, Mattole-Wailaki.

Menominee (Menomini) [mez] 39. Ethnic population: 3,500 (1977 SIL). Northeastern Wisconsin, on what was formerly the Menomini Reservation. *Class:* Algic, Algonquian, Central. *Lg Use:* Speakers have shifted to English. Speakers are older adults. *Lg Dev:* Grammar. *Other:* Nearly extinct.

Mesquakie (Meskwakie, Sac And Fox, Sauk-Fox) [sac] 200 to 300 (2001 Goddard). A handful of Sauk speakers (2000 Ives Goddard). Ethnic population: 1,200. Mesquakie at Tama, Iowa; Sac and Fox at Sac and Fox Reservation on eastern Kansas-Nebraska border and central Oklahoma. *Class:* Algic, Algonquian, Central. *Dialects:* Fox, Sac, Mesquakie. Kansas and Oklahoma groups are closely related to Kickapoo of Oklahoma and Mexico. *Lg Use:* Speakers are shifting to English. Most speakers are older adults. *Lg Dev:* Literacy rate in first language: below 1%. Literacy rate in second language: 75% to 100%. Bible portions: 1986–1996.

Miami (Miami-Illinois, Miami-Myaamia, Illinois) [mia] Extinct. Ethnic population: 2,000 (1977 SIL). Formerly in Miami in north central Indiana, Miami and Peoria in northeast Oklahoma, Illinois in Illinois and Iowa. *Class:* Algic, Algonquian, Central. *Dialects:* Miami, Peoria. *Lg Use:* There are some who know a few words and phrases. A revitalization program is in progress. *Other:* Extinct before 1996.

Michif (French Cree, Mitchif) [crg] 390 in the USA (1990 census). Population total all countries: 990. Turtle Mountain Reservation, North Dakota. Also spoken in Canada. *Class:* Mixed Language, French-Cree. *Dialects:* Closest to Plains Cree. Several varieties in Canada. *Lg Use:* Most or all speakers are older adults. Speakers also use English. *Lg Dev:* Dictionary. Grammar.

Micmac (Mi'gmaw, Miigmao, Mi'kmaw, Restigouche) [mic] 1,200 in the USA. Population includes 200 in Maine, and 1,000 largely in Boston. Northern Maine near Fort Fairfield, Boston, Massachusetts, and small scattered places elsewhere in the USA. *Lg Dev:* Literacy rate in first language: 1% to 5%. Literacy rate in second language: 50% to 75%. See main entry under Canada.

Mikasuki (Hitchiti, Mikasuki Seminole, Miccosukee) [mik] 496 (1990 census). 33 monolinguals. Ethnic population: 1,200 (1977 SIL). Southern Florida. *Class:* Muskogean, Eastern. *Dialects:* Hitchiti, Mikasuki. Not intelligible with Creek, Alabama, or Koasati. *Lg Use:* There are monolinguals only among older adult women. Others also use English. *Lg Dev:* Bible portions: 1980–1985.

Miwok, Bay (Saclan, Saklan) [mkq] Extinct. Formerly in northern California, San Francisco Bay. *Class:* Penutian, Yok-Utian, Utian, Miwokan, Eastern.

Miwok, Central Sierra [csm] 12. Population includes 6 Eastern Central Sierra, 6 Western Central Sierra (1994 L. Hinton). Ethnic population: Possibly 5,000 all Miwok (2000 Yamamoto). California, upper valleys of the Stanislause and Tuolumne. *Class:* Penutian, Yok-Utian, Utian, Miwokan, Eastern, Sierra. *Dialects:* Eastern Central Sierra Miwok, Western Central Sierra Miwok. A separate language from other Miwok varieties. *Lg Use:* Speakers are shifting to English. *Other:* Nearly extinct.

Miwok, Coast [csi] Extinct. Formerly in California, coast from San Francisco Bay to Bodega Bay. *Class:* Penutian, Yok-Utian, Utian, Miwokan, Western. *Dialects:* Bodega, Huimen, Marin Miwok. *Lg Use:* Members of the ethnic group now speak English. *Other:* A separate language from other Miwok varieties. Became extinct in 1960s or 1970s. Bodega and Marin Miwok were possibly separate languages.

Miwok, Lake [lmw] 1 to 2 (1994 L. Hinton). California, Clear Lake basin. *Class:* Penutian, Yok-Utian, Utian, Miwokan, Western. *Dialects:* A separate language from other Miwok varieties. *Lg Use:* Speakers have shifted to English. *Other:* Nearly extinct.

Miwok, Northern Sierra [nsq] 6 (1994 L. Hinton). California, upper valleys of Mokelumne and Calaveras rivers. *Class:* Penutian, Yok-Utian, Utian, Miwokan, Eastern, Sierra. *Dialects:* A separate language from other Miwok varieties. *Lg Use:* Members of the ethnic group now speak English. *Other:* Nearly extinct.

Miwok, Plains (Valley Miwok) [pmw] 1 (1962 H. Landar in Sebeok 1977). California, deltas of the San Joaquin and Cosumnes rivers. *Class:* Penutian, Yok-Utian, Utian, Miwokan, Eastern. *Lg Use:* Members of the ethnic group now speak English. *Other:* Nearly extinct.

Miwok, Southern Sierra (Meewoc, Mewoc, Me-Wuk, Miwoc, Miwokan, Mokélumne, Moquelumnan, San Raphael, Talatui, Talutui, Yosemite) [skd] 7 Southern Central Sierra Miwok (1994 L. Hinton). California, along headwaters of the Merced and Chowchilla rivers and on Mariposa Creek. *Class:* Penutian, Yok-Utian, Utian, Miwokan, Eastern, Sierra. *Lg Use:* Speakers are shifting to English. *Other:* Alternate names listed refer to all Miwok except last three. Nearly extinct.

Mobilian (Mobilian Jargon) [mod] Extinct. Formerly in the lower Mississippi River valley area, south central USA. *Class:* Pidgin, Amerindian. *Dialects:* Muskogean-based pidgin, formerly used as lingua franca. Loanwords from Spanish, English, French, Creek, Alabama-Koasati, Choctaw, Chickasaw. *Lg Use:* Became extinct about 1900. *Other:* OSV.

Mohave (Mojave) [mov] 65 to 85 (1994 L. Hinton). Population includes 30 to 35 at Fort Mohave, 35 to 50 at Colorado River. Ethnic population: 767 (2000 A. Yamamoto). Fort Mohave and Colorado River reservations on the California-Arizona border. *Class:* Hokan, Esselen-Yuman, Yuman, River Yuman. *Dialects:* Lexical similarity 85% with Maricopa, 63% with Walapai and Havasupai, 62% with Yavapai. *Lg Use:* Most adults speak the language but many younger ones do not. Speakers also use English. *Other:* Language materials, programs for children. Both communities have writing systems.

Mohawk (Kanien'kehaka) [moh] 3,000 in the USA (1990 census and 1997 N. Bonvillain). Ethnic population: 6,000 in the USA (1997 Bonvillain, Mithun, Michelson). St. Regis Reservation, northern New York. *Lg Use:* Most speakers are older adults. In some areas the younger ones may speak the language. Speakers also use English. See main entry under Canada.

Mohegan-Montauk-Narragansett [mof] Extinct. Ethnic population: 1,400 population (1977 SIL). Formerly in Connecticut, Rhode Island, Long Island, New York, Wisconsin. *Class:* Algic, Algonquian, Eastern. *Dialects:* Pequot-Mohegan, Narrangansett, Montauk (Shinnecock-Poosepatuck), Stockbridge.

Molale (Molele, Molala, Molalla) [mbe] Extinct. Formerly in Washington and Oregon in the valley of the Deschutes River, later west into the Molala and Santiam River valleys, and to the headwaters of the Umpqua and Rogue rivers. *Class:* Penutian, Unclassified. *Dialects:* Not close to Cayuse as formerly thought.

Mono (Monachi) [mnr] 37 to 41 (1994 L. Hinton). Population includes 10 to 12 North Fork, 15 Auberry, 7 to 8 Big Sandy, 5 to 6 Dunlap, no Waksachi. Ethnic population: 600 (2000 A. Yamamoto). East central California. *Class:* Uto-Aztecan, Northern Uto-Aztecan, Numic, Western. *Dialects:* Related to Northern Paiute. *Lg Use:* Speakers have shifted to English. North Fork: informal language classes, dictionary under development; Big Sandy: language classes, wordlists. Speakers are older adults. *Other:* Nearly extinct.

Muskogee (Creek) [mus] 4,300 (1997 Pye). 43 monolinguals. Ethnic population: 52,000 (1997 Pye). Creek and Seminole of east central Oklahoma, Creek of southern Alabama, Seminole of Brighton Reservation, Florida. *Class:* Muskogean, Eastern. *Dialects:* Creek, Seminole. Close to Mikasuki in Florida. The dialects are very similar. *Lg Use:* Many adults in Muskogee speak the language. Most younger ones prefer English and many do not speak the language. A dozen speakers in Florida. *Lg Dev:* NT: 1886–1891.

Nanticoke [nnt] Extinct. Ethnic population: 400 (1977 SIL). Formerly in southern Delaware and eastern Maryland. *Class:* Algic, Algonquian, Eastern.

Natchez [ncz] Extinct. Formerly in Oklahoma. *Class:* Gulf. *Other:* There are some individuals of Natchez descent among the Creek and Cherokee in Oklahoma.

Navajo (Diné, Navaho) [nav] 148,530 (1990 census). 7,616 monolinguals. Ethnic population: 219,198 (1990 USA Census Bureau). Northeastern Arizona, northwestern New Mexico, southeastern Utah, and a few in Colorado. *Class:* Na-Dene, Nuclear Na-Dene, Athapaskan-Eyak, Athapaskan, Apachean, Navajo-Apache, Western Apache-Navajo. *Lg Use:* Vigorous in some families. First-language speakers among first graders are 30% versus 90% in 1968 (1998). *Lg Dev:* Bible: 1985–2000. *Other:* The people prefer the name 'Diné'.

Nawathinehena [nwa] Extinct. Formerly spoken among the Arapaho. *Class:* Algic, Algonquian, Plains, Arapaho.

Nez Perce [nez] 100 to 300 (1997 Haruo Aoki). Ethnic population: 2,700 (1997 Haruo Aoki). Northern Idaho. *Class:* Penutian, Plateau Penutian, Sahaptin. *Lg Use:* Speakers are shifting to English. Speakers are older adults. *Lg Dev:* Dictionary. Bible portions: 1845–1876. *Other:* Conversational Nez Perce taught in Nespelem, Washington.

Nisenan (Southern Maidu, Neeshenam, Nishinam, Pujuni, Wapumni) [nsz] 1 (1994 L. Hinton). Central California, scattered, foothills of the Sierras. *Class:* Penutian, Maiduan. *Dialects:* A separate language from other Maidu varieties. *Lg Use:* One older adult speaker. Members of the ethnic group now speak English. *Other:* Nearly extinct.

Nooksack (Nootsack) [nok] Extinct. Ethnic population: 1,600 (1997 B. Galloway). Formerly in the northwest corner of Washington. *Class:* Salishan, Central Salish, Nooksack. *Lg Use:* Extinct since about 1988. There are 2 or 3 older adults who each know less than 30 or 40 words (1998).

Nottoway [ntw] Extinct. Formerly in Southampton County, Virginia. *Class:* Iroquoian, Northern Iroquoian, Tuscarora-Nottoway. *Lg Use:* Extinct around 1958. Members of the ethnic group now speak English.

Obispeño [obi] Extinct. Formerly in California, near Santa Barbara. *Class:* Chumash. *Dialects:* Not inherently intelligible with other Chumash varieties.

Ofo [ofo] Extinct. Formerly in the lower Mississippi Valley. *Class:* Siouan, Siouan Proper, Southeastern, Biloxi-Ofo.

Ohlone, Northern ("Costanoan") [cst] Extinct. Formerly in north central California, Monterrey and San Benito counties. *Class:* Penutian, Yok-Utian, Utian, Costanoan. *Dialects:* East Bay, San Francisco, Santa Clara, Santa Cruz, Soledad. *Lg Use:* Some Ohlones are collecting and studying language materials. Lost its fluent speakers in the 18th or early 19th centuries. Subdialects of East Bay were Huchiun (Juichun), Niles (Chocheño), San José, San Lorenzo. Soledad may be transitional between Northern and Southern Ohlone. *Other:* The name "Costanoan" is derogatory. Coastal, valleys.

Ohlone, Southern ("Costanoan") [css] Extinct. Formerly in north central California, Monterrey and San Benito counties. *Class:* Penutian, Yok-Utian, Utian, Costanoan. *Dialects:* Monterey, Mutsun (San Juan Bautista), Rumsen (Runsien, San Carlos, Carmel). *Lg Use:* Became extinct in the 1950s. *Other:* The name "Costanoan" is reported to be disliked by the people. Coastal, valleys.

Okanagan (Okanagan-Colville, Okanagon, Okanogan) [oka] 112 in the USA (1990 census). Colville Reservation, Washington. *Dialects:* Southern Okanogan, Sanpoil, Colville, Lake. *Lg Use:* Speakers are older adults. Speakers also use English. See main entry under Canada.

Omaha-Ponca (Mahairi, Ponka, Umanhan, Ppankka) [oma] 85 (1986 SIL). Population includes 60 speakers of Omaha (1993 V. Zeps), and 25 fluent speakers over 60 and a few semifluent speakers of Ponca. Ethnic population: 5,000 including 3,000 of Omaha (1993 C. Rudin), and 2,000 of Ponca (1986 SIL). Omaha Reservation, eastern Nebraska (Omaha), and north central Oklahoma (Ponca). *Class:* Siouan, Siouan Proper, Central, Mississippi Valley, Dhegiha. *Dialects:* Omaha, Ponca. Ponca and Omaha are completely inherently intelligible to each other's speakers, Close to Osage, Quapaw, and Kansa. *Lg Use:* Omaha is used formally for prayers, especially at funerals, for songs, powwow announcements, but usually translated into English for nonspeakers present. Many adults speak the language. Most young adults may prefer English. Children tend to prefer English, but many can understand Omaha and some may speak it. In 1985 only a few older women seemed

less than fully fluent in at least the regional English. *Lg Dev:* Grammar. *Other:* Christian, Native American Church, Mormon, Baha'i.

Oneida [one] 50 in the USA (1991 M. Dale Kincade). 6 monolinguals. Central New York, eastern Wisconsin. *Lg Use:* Speakers are shifting to English. Only a few older adult speakers in New York. See main entry under Canada.

Onondaga (Onandaga) [ono] 15 in the USA (1993 V. Zeps). Ethnic population: 1,000 in USA (1993 V. Zeps). Central New York south of Syracuse. *Lg Use:* Speakers are shifting to English. Speakers are older adults. See main entry under Canada.

Osage (Wazhazhe) [osa] 5 (1991 M. Krauss). Ethnic population: 15,000 (1997 Carolyn Quintero). North central Oklahoma. *Class:* Siouan, Siouan Proper, Central, Mississippi Valley, Dhegiha. *Dialects:* Close to Omaha, Ponca, Quapaw, and Kansa. *Lg Use:* Speakers have shifted to English. A few semifluent speakers. Speakers are older adults. *Lg Dev:* Bible portions. *Other:* Nearly extinct.

Ottawa (Odawa, Chippewa, Eastern Ojibwa, Ojibwe) [otw] 10 monolinguals. Population includes 330 Ottawa, 5,065 Ojibwa in USA (1990 census). Ethnic population: 20,000 (Ottawa and Chippewa) in USA (1991 M. Dale Kincade). Lower Michigan and upper Michigan near Sault Ste. Marie. *Lg Use:* Ottawa is dying out in many areas. Concerted effort via language teaching in public schools and other efforts to reverse the decline. Probably all speakers also use English, some use other Ojibwa varieties. *Lg Dev:* Taught in primary schools. See main entry under Canada.

Paiute, Northern (Paviotso) [pao] 1,631 (1999 SIL). Ethnic population: 6,000 (1999 SIL). Northern Nevada and adjacent areas of Oregon, California, and Idaho. Spoken on about twenty reservations spread out over 1,000 miles. *Class:* Uto-Aztecan, Northern Uto-Aztecan, Numic, Western. *Dialects:* Bannock, North Northern Paiute (Mcdermitt), South Northern Paiute (Yerington-Schurz). Related to Mono. Almost every reservation has its own dialect. All dialects are inherently intelligible. *Lg Use:* Greatest use in McDermitt. Informal language programs in Owens Valley Paiute, language classes, written materials for Gidutikad band. Many adults speak the language but most younger ones do not. *Lg Dev:* NT: 1985.

Panamint (Panamint Shoshone, Tümpisa Shoshoni, Koso, Coso, Koso Shoshone) [par] 20. Ethnic population: 100 (1998 John E. McLaughlin). The Panamint are in southeastern California, in and around southern Owens Valley around Owens Lake Coso Range, southwest of Darwin, and Little Lake area, southern Eureka Valley, southwest of Lida in Nevada, Saline Valley and eastern slopes of Inyo Mountains, Argus Range south of Darwin, northern Panamint Valley and Panamint Mountains north and central Death Valley, Grapevine Mountains and Funeral Range on California-Nevada border, west and southwest of Beatty, Nevada, Amargosa Desert, and area around Beatty. *Class:* Uto-Aztecan, Northern Uto-Aztecan, Numic, Central. *Dialects:* Close to Shoshoni and Comanche. Not inherently intelligible with them. *Lg Use:* Only used among oldest speakers to each other. They lament the shift to English by younger people. Younger speakers attempting to revive interest in Panamint among the younger generations, but with little success. Speakers are older adults. English is used in nearly all situations. *Lg Dev:* Literacy rate in second language: 90%. Grammar. *Other:* Nearly extinct.

Pawnee [paw] 20 (1997 Parks). Ethnic population: 2,500 (1997 Parks). North central Oklahoma. *Class:* Caddoan, Northern, Pawnee-Kitsai, Pawnee. *Dialect:* South Band, Skiri (Skidi). Close to Arikara, but not inherently intelligible with it. Kitsai is between Pawnee and Wichita, but closer to Pawnee. *Lg Use:* Speakers are shifting to

English. All speakers are older adults. *Other:* Nearly extinct.

Piro (Tompiro) [pie] Extinct. Formerly in Socorro, left bank of Rio Grande, USA, and Senecu, right bank, Mexico. *Class:* Kiowa Tanoan, Tewa-Tiwa, Tiwa.

Piscataway (Conoy) [psy] Extinct. Formerly spoken in Maryland. *Class:* Algic, Algonquian.

Plains Indian Sign Language (Plains Sign Language) [psd] Great Plains of the USA. Also spoken in Canada. *Class:* Sign language. *Dialects:* Some variation by ethnic group and region. *Lg Use:* Formerly used between nations in hunting, trade, by deaf people, and at every level of social interaction, and with non-Indians. Today used within nations in storytelling, rituals, legends, prayers, and by deaf people. *Other:* Second language only.

Plautdietsch (Low German, Mennonite German) [pdt] 11,974 in the USA (2000). Hillsboro, Kansas; Reedley, California; and Corn, Oklahoma. *Lg Use:* 5% speak Standard German, 98% speak English as second language. *Lg Dev:* Literacy rate in second language: 95%. *Other:* Christian. See main entry under Canada.

Pomo, Central (Ballo-Kai-Pomo, Cabanapo, Habenapo, H'hana, Kábinapek, Khabenapo, Khana, Kulanapan, Kulanapo, Venaambakaia, Venambakaiia, Yokaia) [poo] 2 to 5 (1997 Mithun). Ethnic population: 4,766 (1997 Mithun). Clear Lake area, northern California. *Class:* Hokan, Northern, Pomo, Russian River and Eastern, Russian River, Southern. *Dialects:* Point Arena, Hopland, Ukiah. *Lg Use:* Intermittent teaching at Hopland. Members of the ethnic group now speak English. *Other:* Nearly extinct.

Pomo, Eastern (Clear Lake Pomo) [peb] Extinct. Formerly in California, Clear Lake area. *Class:* Hokan, Northern, Pomo, Russian River and Eastern, Eastern.

Pomo, Northeastern (Salt Pomo) [pef] Extinct. Formerly in California, Coast Range Valley of Story Creek; a tributary of the Sacramento River. *Class:* Hokan, Northern, Pomo, Russian River and Eastern, Russian River, Northeastern.

Pomo, Northern [pej] Extinct. Formerly in California, Sherwood Valley area. *Class:* Hokan, Northern, Pomo, Russian River and Eastern, Russian River, Northern. *Dialects:* Guidiville, Sherwood Valley. *Lg Use:* Became extinct in 1994 (M. Krauss).

Pomo, Southeastern (Lower Lake Pomo) [pom] 5 (1994 L. Hinton). California, eastern shores of Clear Lake. *Class:* Hokan, Northern, Pomo, Southeastern. *Lg Use:* Speakers have shifted to English. *Other:* Nearly extinct.

Pomo, Southern (Gallinoméro) [peq] 1 (1994 L. Hinton). California. *Class:* Hokan, Northern, Pomo, Russian River and Eastern, Russian River, Southern. *Lg Use:* Members of the ethnic group now speak English. *Other:* Nearly extinct.

Potawatomi (Pottawotomi) [pot] 50 in the USA (1995 Potawatomi Language Institute). Ethnic population: 25,000 (1997 Laura Buszard-Welcher). Southwestern and northern Michigan, northern Wisconsin and northeastern Kansas. Also spoken in Canada. *Class:* Algic, Algonquian, Central. *Lg Use:* Speakers are shifting to English. *Lg Dev:* Grammar. Bible portions: 1844. *Other:* 85% have varying degrees of language retention.

Powhatan (Virginia Algonkian, Virginia Algonquian) [pim] Extinct. Ethnic population: 3,000 (1977 SIL). Formerly scattered in eastern Virginia and Powhatan Renape Nation, Rankokus Indian Reservation, Rancocas, New Jersey. *Class:* Algic, Algonquian, Eastern.

Purisimeño [puy] Extinct. Formerly in southern California, near Santa Barbara. *Class:* Chumash. *Dialects:* Was not intelligible with other Chumash varieties.

Quapaw (Arkansas, Alkansea, Capa, Ogxpa) [qua] 34 (1990 census). Ethnic population: 2,000 (1986 SIL).

Northeastern corner of Oklahoma. *Class:* Siouan, Siouan Proper, Central, Mississippi Valley, Dhegiha. *Dialects:* Close to Kansa, Omaha, Osage, and Ponca, all called 'Dhegiha'. *Lg Use:* Speakers are shifting to English. *Other:* Nearly extinct.

Quechan (Kechan, Yuma, Quecl) [yum] 150 (1994 L. Hinton). Ethnic population: 3,000 (2000 A. Yamamoto). Ft. Yuma Reservation, southeastern corner of California. *Class:* Hokan, Esselen-Yuman, Yuman, River Yuman. *Dialects:* Close to Maricopa and Mohave. *Lg Use:* Speakers are shifting to English. Speakers are older adults.

Quileute [qui] 10 (1977 SIL). Ethnic population: 300 (1977 SIL). Pacific side of Olympic Peninsula in Washington. *Class:* Chimakuan. *Dialects:* Quileute, Hoh. *Lg Use:* Speakers are shifting to English. *Other:* Nearly extinct.

Quinault [qun] Extinct. Ethnic population: 1,500 (1977 SIL). Formerly on the Pacific side of the Olympic Peninsula in Washington. *Class:* Salishan, Tsamosan, Maritime. *Dialect:* Lower Chehalis. *Lg Use:* Members of the ethnic group now speak English. *Other:* Some who heard it as children have good pronunciation.

Russian (Russki) [rus] 334,615 in the USA (1970 census). *Lg Use:* The Doukhobors and Molokans are conservative religious groups who speak Standard Russian. Other Russian speakers in the USA have long-standing residence; still others have come more recently. See main entry under Russia (Europe).

Salinan [sln] Extinct. Ethnic population: Hundreds (1997 K. Turner). Formerly in California, central coast. *Class:* Hokan, Salinan-Seri. *Dialects:* There were two dialects. *Other:* Interest in language revival.

Salish, Southern Puget Sound [slh] 107 (1990 census). 5 monolinguals. Ethnic population: 2,000 (1977 SIL). Southern end of Puget Sound, Washington. *Class:* Salishan, Central Salish, Twana. *Dialects:* Duwamish, Muckleshoot, Nisqually, Puyallup, Snoqualmie, Suquh. *Lg Use:* Speakers are shifting to English. Speakers are older adults.

Salish, Straits (Straits) [str] Southeastern Vancouver Island, British Columbia and adjoining portions of Washington, including the islands in between. *Dialects:* Saanich, Lummi, Samish, Sooke, Songish. *Lg Use:* The Semiahmoo, Ts'ooke, and Songish dialects are extinct. Speakers are older adults. *Lg Dev:* Conversational Salish is taught in Nespelem, Washington, but it is not known which Salish dialect. *Other:* Nearly extinct. See main entry under Canada.

Sea Island Creole English (Gullah, Geechee) [gul] 250,000 (2000). 7,000 to 10,000 monolinguals. Population includes 10,000 in New York City (1989 Holm). Ethnic population: 250,000. Coastal region from Jacksonville, North Carolina to Jacksonville, Florida, and especially on the Sea Islands off the Georgia coast. Small clusters in New York City and Detroit. *Class:* Creole, English based, Atlantic, Eastern, Northern. *Dialects:* Northeast Florida Coast, Georgia, South Carolina. Intelligibility of other English-based creoles is undetermined. Very close to Bahamas Creole and Afro-Seminole. Lexical similarity 90% with Afro-Seminole. *Lg Use:* Vigorous. Barely understandable with Standard English. Government bilingual education program begun. *Lg Dev:* Literacy rate in first language: 1% to 5%. Literacy rate in second language: 75% to 100%. Dictionary. Bible portions: 1994. *Other:* Linguistic influences from Fula, Mende, upper Guinea coast, Gambia River area (Hancock 1987). Coastal. Swamp. Agriculturalists: rice, cotton.

Seneca [see] 150 in the USA (1997 Wallace Chafe). Population total all countries: 175. Ethnic population: 6,241 (1997 W. Chafe). Tonawanda, Cattaraugus, and Allegheny reservations in western New York, and mixed with Cayuga in northeastern Oklahoma. Also spoken in Canada. *Class:* Iroquoian, Northern Iroquoian, Five Nations, Seneca-Onondaga, Seneca-Cayuga. *Lg Use:* Speakers are older adults in New York (1998). Speakers are shifting to English. *Lg Dev:* Dictionary. Grammar. Bible portions: 1829–1874.

Serrano [ser] 1 (1994 Coker). Southern California, San Bernardino and San Gorgonio Pass area. *Class:* Uto-Aztecan, Northern Uto-Aztecan, Takic, Serrano-Gabrielino. *Lg Use:* The speaker is an older adult (1994). Members of the ethnic group now speak English. *Other:* Nearly extinct.

Shasta (Sastean, Shastan) [sht] Extinct. Ethnic population: 12 (1990 census). Formerly in northern California. *Class:* Hokan, Northern, Karok-Shasta, Shasta-Palaihnihan, Shastan. *Dialects:* Formerly there were four dialects. *Lg Use:* Members of the ethnic group now speak English.

Shawnee [sjw] 200 (2002 Pearson). Ethnic population: 2,500. Central and northeastern Oklahoma. *Class:* Algic, Algonquian, Central. *Lg Use:* Speakers are shifting to English. Speakers are older adults. *Lg Dev:* Dictionary. Bible portions: 1842–1929.

Shoshoni (Shoshone) [shh] 2,284 (1990 census). Ethnic population: 7,000 (1977 SIL). The Western Shoshoni are in central to northeastern Nevada and Fort Hall Reservation in Idaho; Northern Shoshoni in Wind River Reservation, Wyoming, Goshute in western Utah. *Class:* Uto-Aztecan, Northern Uto-Aztecan, Numic, Central. *Dialects:* Gosiute (Goshute), Western Shoshoni, Northern Shoshoni. Wind River Shoshoni is a subdialect of Northern Shoshoni, spoken at Wind River Reservation. Close to Comanche and Panamint, which are not inherently intelligible with Shoshoni. *Lg Use:* Vigorous in a few families. In most locations only the older ones speak the language. Speakers also use English. *Lg Dev:* Bible portions: 1986.

Siuslaw [sis] Extinct. Formerly on the southern Oregon coast. *Class:* Penutian, Oregon Penutian, Coast Oregon, Siuslawan. *Other:* "There have been no speakers of Siuslaw for many years" (M. Dale Kinkade 1998).

Skagit (Swinomish) [ska] 100 (1977 SIL). Ethnic population: 350 (1977 SIL). East side of Puget Sound, Washington. *Class:* Salishan, Central Salish, Twana. *Lg Use:* Speakers are shifting to English. Speakers are older adults.

Snohomish [sno] 10 (1998 J. Brooke). Ethnic population: 800 (1977 SIL). Tulalip Reservation, northwestern Washington. *Class:* Salishan, Central Salish, Twana. *Lg Use:* Speakers are shifting to English. Speakers are older adults. *Other:* Nearly extinct.

Spanish (Español, Castellano) [spa] 22,400,000 in the USA (1990 census). San Antonio, Texas to Los Angeles; Miami, Florida area; New York City; Illinois; Denver; other areas. *Lg Use:* Official status in New Mexico. *Other:* Population has increased 61% or more since 1970. See main entry under Spain.

Spokane (Spokan) [spo] 50 (1990). Ethnic population: 1,000 (1977 SIL). Northeastern Washington. *Class:* Salishan, Interior Salish, Southern. *Dialects:* Close to Kalispel-Pend d'Oreille. *Lg Use:* Speakers are shifting to English. Some revival efforts. Speakers are older adults. *Lg Dev:* Dictionary.

Susquehannock (Susquehanna, Conestoga, Andaste, Minqua) [sqn] Extinct. Formerly along the Susquehanna River. *Class:* Iroquoian. *Lg Use:* Became extinct about 1763.

Takelma (Takilma, Lowland Takelma) [tkm] Extinct. Formerly on the middle course of the Rogue River, Oregon. *Class:* Penutian, Oregon Penutian, Takelma. *Dialects:* May be in a Takelma-Kalapuyan subgroup, but not conclusive.

Tanacross [tcb] 35 (1997 G. Holton). Population includes 3 in the Healy Lake dialect, 32 in Mansfield-Ketchumstuck.

Ethnic population: 120 (1997 G. Holton). Eastern Alaska, near the Upper Tanana, Tanacross, Healy Lake, Dot Lake, Tok. *Class:* Na-Dene, Nuclear Na-Dene, Athapaskan-Eyak, Athapaskan, Tanana-Upper Kuskokwim, Tanana. *Dialects:* Healy Lake, Mansfield-Ketchumstuck. Little dialect variation. Mansfield-Ketchumstuck is the most important politically and numerically. Closest to Upper Tanana, but they have different tone systems. *Lg Use:* Tanacross spoken only between older adults in the home. Speakers are fluent in English and Upper Tanana. *Lg Dev:* Grammar. *Other:* Recognized as a distinct language in the 1970s. Tonal. Nearly extinct.

Tanaina (Dena'ina, Kinayskiy) [tfn] 75 (1997 M. Krauss). Ethnic population: 900 (1997 M. Krauss). Around Cook Inlet and adjacent area of southern Alaska. *Class:* Na-Dene, Nuclear Na-Dene, Athapaskan-Eyak, Athapaskan, Tanaina-Ahtna. *Dialects:* Kenai Peninsula, Upper Inlet, Coastal-Inland, Stoney River. *Lg Use:* Speakers are shifting to English. Kenai dialect is nearly extinct. Youngest speakers in their 20s at Lime Village, but elsewhere in their 50s and older. *Other:* Nearly extinct.

Tanana, Lower (Tanana) [taa] 30 (1995 M. Krauss). Ethnic population: 380 (1995 M. Krauss). Tanana River below Fairbanks, Nenana, and Minto, central Alaska. *Class:* Na-Dene, Nuclear Na-Dene, Athapaskan-Eyak, Atha-paskan, Tanana-Upper Kuskokwim, Tanana. *Dialects:* Chena, Salcha-Goodpaster. *Lg Use:* Speakers are shifting to English. Chena River dialect became extinct in 1976 and Salcha-Goodpaster Rivers in 1993. Speakers are older adults. *Other:* Nearly extinct.

Tanana, Upper (Nabesna) [tau] 105 in the USA (1995 M. Krauss). Population total all countries: 115. Ethnic population: 300 in the USA (1995). Area of upper Tanana River, east central Alaska. Also spoken in Canada. *Class:* Na-Dene, Nuclear Na-Dene, Athapaskan-Eyak, Atha-paskan, Tanana-Upper Kuskokwim, Tanana. *Lg Use:* Speakers are shifting to English. Youngest speakers are in their 20s at Tetlin, older elsewhere. *Lg Dev:* Bible portions: 1970–1982.

Tenino (Warm Springs) [tqn] 200 (1977 SIL). Ethnic population: 1,000 (1977 SIL). Warm Springs Reservation, Oregon. *Class:* Penutian, Plateau Penutian, Sahaptin. *Lg Use:* Speakers are older adults. Speakers are shifting to English.

Tewa [tew] 1,298 (1980 census). 18 monolinguals (1990 census). Population includes 50 Nambe speakers, 25 Pojoaque, 349 San Ildefonso, 495 San Juan, 207 Santa Clara, 172 Tesuque (1980 census). Ethnic population: 2,383 including 175 Nambe, 37 Pojoaque, 478 San Ildefonso, 1,146 San Juan, 318 Santa Clara, 229 Tesuque (1980 census). North of Santa Fe, New Mexico and at Hano on the Hopi Reservation, Arizona. *Class:* Kiowa Tanoan, Tewa-Tiwa, Tewa. *Dialects:* Hano, San Juan, Nambe, Pojoaque, Santa Clara, San Ildefonso, Tesuque. *Lg Use:* Speakers are shifting to English. 49.8% of the population below 18 years are speakers, 70% above 18 (1980 census). Most adults speak the language. Many younger ones prefer English and some do not speak the language. *Lg Dev:* Dictionary. Bible portions: 1969–1984.

Tillamook [til] Extinct. Formerly in northwestern Oregon. *Class:* Salishan, Tillamook. *Lg Use:* The last speaker died in 1970. Members of the ethnic group now speak English.

Tiwa, Northern [twf] 927 (1980 census). Population includes 803 Taos speakers, 101 Picuris speakers (1990 census). Ethnic population: 1,166 (1980 census), including 1,042 Taos, 124 Picuris (1990 census). North central New Mexico. *Class:* Kiowa Tanoan, Tewa-Tiwa, Tiwa. *Dialects:* Taos, Picuris. *Lg Use:* Vigorous at Taos. 67.3% of the Taos under 18 are speakers, 92.9% over 18 are speakers (1980 census). Speakers are older adults. Most speakers also use English. *Lg Dev:* Literacy rate in first language: 1% to 5%. Literacy rate in second language: 50% to 75%. Bible portions: 1976–1992.

Tiwa, Southern [tix] 1,631 (1980 census). Population includes 1,588 Isleta speakers (1980 census). 43 Sandia speakers (1990 census) out of 220 population. Ethnic population: 2,469 (1980 census) including 2,249 Isleta, 220 Sandia (1990 census). New Mexico, pueblos of Isleta and Sandia, north and south of Albuquerque. *Class:* Kiowa Tanoan, Tewa-Tiwa, Tiwa. *Dialect:* Sandia, Isleta (Isleta Pueblo). *Lg Use:* Vigorous in a few families. Diminishing vigor at Isleta among adults, except older adults. There is an attempt to reestablish use of Southern Tiwa at Sandia Pueblo and Ysleta del Sur, El Paso, Texas. Oral form is used for commerce on tribal land. Southern Tiwa is considered the only language of traditional ceremonial life. Most speakers are older adults. There is regret at apparent demise of the language. People are apprehensive about losing their culture if the language is not revived. Speakers range from being fluent in English to low proficiency. *Lg Dev:* Roman script. Bible portions: 1981–1987. *Other:* Riverine, plateau, foothills. Christian, traditional religion.

Tlingit (Thlinget, Tlinkit) [tli] 700 in the USA (1995 M. Krauss). Population total all countries: 845. Ethnic population: 10,000 in the USA (1995 M. Krauss). Southeastern Alaska from Yakutat south to the Canadian border at Portland Canal. Also spoken in Canada. *Class:* Na-Dene, Nuclear Na-Dene, Tlingit. *Lg Use:* Speakers are older adults, but many in the 40 to 55 range understand a certain amount of Tlingit. English is the first or second language of the ethnic group. *Lg Dev:* Dictionary. Grammar. Bible portions: 1969. *Other:* There is growing interest in the language among the population. SOV. Coastal. Fishermen; lumbermen.

Tohono O'odham (Papago-Pima, O'othham, Nevome, Nebome, O'odham, Upper Piman) [ood] 11,819 in the USA(1990 census). 181 monolinguals (1990 census). Ethnic population: 20,000 (1977 SIL). South central Arizona. 60 villages on 7 reservations. Also spoken in Mexico. *Class:* Uto-Aztecan, Southern Uto-Aztecan, Sonoran, Tepiman. *Dialects:* Tohono O'odam ("Papago"), Akimel O'odham (Pima). *Lg Use:* Vigorous in the west and south. In the north and east some younger ones do not speak it or they prefer English. Most speakers are 25 years of age or older. *Lg Dev:* From primary school on, schools on the Tohono O'Odham Nation teach the language. Grammar. NT: 1975. *Other:* Different from Pima Bajo of Mexico.

Tolowa (Smith River) [tol] 4 to 5 (1994 Hinton). Ethnic population: 1,000 (2000 Yamamoto). Southwestern Oregon. *Class:* Na-Dene, Nuclear Na-Dene, Athapaskan-Eyak, Athapaskan, Pacific Coast, Oregon, Tolowa-Galice. *Lg Use:* Chasta Costa was a separate tribe in Oregon; now extinct. There are some language revival efforts. *Other:* Nearly extinct.

Tonkawa [tqw] Extinct. North central Oklahoma. *Class:* Coahuiltecan. *Lg Use:* Members of the ethnic group now speak English. *Other:* No fluent speakers left out of a population of 90 (1977 SIL).

Tsimshian (Sm'algyax, Tsimshean, Zimshian, Chimmezyan, Coast Tsimshian) [tsi] 50 in the USA (2002). Ethnic population: 1,300 in USA (1995 M. Krauss). Tip of Alaska panhandle, (New) Metlakatla on Annette Island, some in Ketchikan. *Lg Use:* Speakers are shifting to English. Speakers are older adults. See main entry under Canada.

Tübatulabal [tub] 6. Ethnic population: 900 (2000 Yamamoto). South central California. *Class:* Uto-Aztecan, Northern Uto-Aztecan, Tubatulabal. *Lg Use:* May be extinct (1987), Speakers are older adults. *Other:* Nearly extinct.

Tunica [tun] Extinct. Central Louisiana. *Class:* Gulf. *Other:* No speakers left out of a population of 150 (1977 SIL).

Tuscarora (Skarohreh) [tus] 4 to 5 in the USA (1997 Mithun). Ethnic population: 1,200 in the USA (1997 Mithun). Tuscarora Reservation near Niagara Falls, New York, eastern North Carolina. *Lg Use:* Speakers have shifted to English. Speakers are older adults. Children are being taught the Tuscarora language in eastern North Carolina. *Other:* Nearly extinct. See main entry under Canada.

Tutelo (Saponi) [tta] Extinct. Formerly in the lower Mississippi Valley. *Class:* Siouan, Siouan Proper, Southeastern, Tutelo. *Other:* Saponi was either the same or very similar to Tutelo.

Tututni [tuu] 10 (1962 Chafe). Southwestern Oregon. *Class:* Na-Dene, Nuclear Na-Dene, Athapaskan-Eyak, Athapaskan, Pacific Coast, Oregon, Tolowa-Galice. *Lg Use:* Speakers are older adults. *Other:* Nearly extinct.

Twana (Skokomish) [twa] Extinct. Ethnic population: 350 (1977 SIL). East of Puget Sound, Washington. *Class:* Salishan, Central Salish, Twana. *Dialects:* Skokomish, Quilcene. *Lg Use:* Extinct since 1980. Members of the ethnic group now speak English.

Umatilla (Columbia River Sahaptin) [uma] 50 (1977 SIL). Ethnic population: 120 (1977 SIL). Umatilla Reservation, Oregon. *Class:* Penutian, Plateau Penutian, Sahaptin. *Lg Use:* Speakers are older adults. Speakers are shifting to English.

Unami (Delaware, Lenni-Lenape, Lenape, Tla Wilano) [unm] Extinct. Ethnic population: 13,500 (1997 J. Rementer). Formerly in northeastern and west central Oklahoma, northern New Jersey, and lower Delaware Valley. *Class:* Algic, Algonquian, Eastern. *Dialects:* Related to Munsee in Ontario. *Lg Dev:* Grammar.

Ute-Southern Paiute [ute] 1,984 (1990 census). 20 monolinguals (1990 census). Population includes 3 Chemehuevi on Chemehuevi Reservation, 10 on Colorado River Reservation (1994 L. Hinton). Ethnic population: 5,000 (1977 SIL). Ute in southwestern Colorado and southeastern and northeastern Utah; Southern Paiute in southwestern Utah, northern Arizona, and southern Nevada; Chemehuevi on lower Colorado River, California. *Class:* Uto-Aztecan, Northern Uto-Aztecan, Numic, Southern. *Dialects:* Southern Paiute, Ute, Chemehuevi. *Lg Use:* Most speakers are adults. *Lg Dev:* Literacy rate in first language: below 1%. Literacy rate in second language: 75% to 100%.

Ventureño [veo] Extinct. Formerly in southern California, near Santa Barbara. *Class:* Chumash. *Dialects:* Was not intelligible with other Chumash varieties. Had multiple dialects.

Wailaki [wlk] Extinct. Formerly on the Round Valley Reservation, northern California. *Class:* Na-Dene, Nuclear Na-Dene, Athapaskan-Eyak, Athapaskan, Pacific Coast, California, Mattole-Wailaki.

Walla Walla (Northeast Sahaptin) [waa] 100 (1977 SIL). Ethnic population: 700 (1977 SIL). Umatilla Reservation, Oregon. *Class:* Penutian, Plateau Penutian, Sahaptin. *Lg Use:* Speakers are older adults. Speakers are shifting to English.

Wampanoag (Massachusett, Massachusetts, Natick) [wam] Extinct. Ethnic population: 1,200 (1977 SIL). Southeastern Massachusetts. *Class:* Algic, Algonquian, Eastern. *Lg Use:* Members of the ethnic group now speak English. *Lg Dev:* Dictionary. Bible: 1663–1685.

Wappo [wao] Extinct. Ethnic population: 50 (1977 SIL). California, north of the San Francisco Bay area. *Class:* Yuki. *Lg Use:* Members of the ethnic group now speak English. *Lg Dev:* Grammar.

Wasco-Wishram (Upper Chinook) [wac] 69 (1990 census). 7 monolinguals. Ethnic population: 750 possibly (1977 SIL). North central Oregon, south central Washington. *Class:* Penutian, Chinookan. *Lg Use:* Speakers are shifting to English. *Other:* Nearly extinct.

Washo (Washoe) [was] 10 (1998 J. Brooke). Ethnic population: 1,500 (2000 A. Yamamoto). California-Nevada border southeast of Lake Tahoe. *Class:* Hokan, Washo. *Lg Use:* Speakers are shifting to English. Informal language classes taught by elder, plans for a preschool. Speakers are older adults. *Other:* Nearly extinct.

Wichita [wic] 3 (2000 Brian Levy). Ethnic population: 1,400 (2000 David S. Rood). West central Oklahoma. *Class:* Caddoan, Northern, Wichita. *Dialects:* Waco, Tawakoni. Close to Kitsai and Pawnee. *Lg Use:* Speakers have shifted to English. Speakers are older adults. *Other:* Nearly extinct.

Wintu (Wintun) [wit] 5 or 6 (1997 Shepherd). Ethnic population: 2,244 (1997 Shepherd). California, Clear Lake and Colusa area and northward. *Class:* Penutian, California Penutian, Wintuan. *Dialects:* Wintu, Patwin, Nomlaki. *Lg Use:* Speakers have shifted to English. *Other:* Nearly extinct.

Wiyot [wiy] Extinct. Ethnic population: 450 (2000 Yamamoto) to 800 (1997 Teeter). Formerly in northwestern California. *Class:* Algic, Wiyot. *Lg Use:* Last speaker died in 1962 (Teeter 1975). *Lg Dev:* Dictionary. Grammar.

Wyandot (Wendat, Wyendat, Wyandotte) [wya] Extinct. Ethnic population: 3,200 (1997 Bruce L. Pearson). Formerly in northeastern Oklahoma. *Class:* Iroquoian, Northern Iroquoian, Huron. *Dialects:* Huron, Wyandot. *Lg Use:* Wyandot was spoken until quite recently near Sandwich, Ontario, and Wyandotte, Oklahoma. There were 2 older adult speakers in 1961. Huron was last spoken at Lorette, near Quebec City, in the mid-19th century, or 1912. *Lg Dev:* The language is being taught to children in school (1999). Dictionary.

Yakima [yak] 3,000 (1977 SIL). Ethnic population: 8,000 (1977 SIL). Yakima Valley, south central Washington. *Class:* Penutian, Plateau Penutian, Sahaptin. *Dialects:* Yakima, Klikitat. *Lg Use:* Speakers are older adults. Speakers also use English. *Other:* Together with Cowlitz and Klikitat, sometimes called 'Northwest Sahaptin'.

Yana [ynn] Extinct. Formerly in the Upper Sacramento Valley, California. *Class:* Hokan, Northern, Yana. *Dialects:* Northern Yana, Central Yana, Southern Yana, Yahi. *Lg Use:* An extinct group of varieties, including Yahi. Extinct since 1917.

Yaqui [yaq] 406 in the USA (1990 census). 2 monolinguals. Tucson and Phoenix, Arizona area. *Lg Use:* Speakers also use English or Spanish. See main entry under Mexico.

Yinglish (Ameridish) [yib] Also spoken in United Kingdom. *Class:* Indo-European, Germanic, West, English. *Lg Use:* Speakers also use English. *Other:* Professor Joshua A. Fishman says, "'Yinglish' is a variety of English influenced by Yiddish (lexically, particularly, but also grammatically and phonetically). Any good English dictionary will now include 50–100 (or more) 'borrowings from Yiddish' (Yinglish)....These forms are now used not only by Jews but by others, inversely proportionally to their distance from NYC. In the case of non-Jews the original Yiddish meaning may no longer be known and a related metaphoric or contextual meaning is intended....Since the variety is only used... (by speakers who can always speak 'proper English') Yinglish is never a first language acquired by the usual process of intergenerational transmission. French, Spanish, and Russian counterparts (also a Hebrew counterpart) also exist, but are more restricted in nature, both in size as well as in availability to non-Jews." Jewish. Second language only.

Yokuts [yok] 78 speakers of Northern Foothill Yokuts (1990 census). Ethnic population: 2,500 (2000 A. Yamamoto). California, San Joaquin River and the slopes of the Sierra Nevada, San Joaquin Valley. *Class:* Penutian, Yok-Utian, Yokuts. *Dialects:* Northern Foothill Yokuts, Southern Foothill Yokuts, Valley Yokuts. Many subdialects. *Lg Use:* Speakers are shifting to English. Southern Foothill and Valley Yokuts are extinct. Chukchansi trying to start language programs. Tachi has headstart language program. *Lg Dev:* Grammar. *Other:* Nearly extinct.

Yuchi (Uchean) [yuc] 10 to 12 (1997 Mary Linn). Ethnic population: 1,500 (1977 SIL). Among Creek people in east central Oklahoma. *Class:* Language Isolate. *Lg Use:* Speakers are shifting to English. Speakers are older adults. *Lg Dev:* Dictionary. *Other:* Nearly extinct.

Yuki [yuk] Extinct. Ethnic population: 1,200 (2000 A. Yamamoto). Formerly on the Round Valley Reservation, northern California. *Class:* Yuki. *Lg Use:* Members of the ethnic group now speak English.

Yupik, Central (Central Alaskan Yupik) [esu] 10,000 (1995 M. Krauss). Ethnic population: 21,000 (1995 M. Krauss). Nunivak Island, Alaska coast from Bristol Bay to Unalakleet on Norton Sound and inland along Nushagak, Kuskokwim, and Yukon rivers. *Class:* Eskimo-Aleut, Eskimo, Yupik, Alaskan. *Dialect:* Kuskokwim Yupik (Bethel Yupik). There are 3 dialects, which are quite different. *Lg Use:* All ages along the central coast and up the Kuskokwim River. In Bristol Bay, Yukon Delta, Bethel, and on Nunivak Island, the average age of youngest speakers is from 20 to 40. Speakers also use English. *Lg Dev:* Grammar. NT: 1956.

Yupik, Central Siberian (St. Lawrence Island "Eskimo," Bering Strait Yupik) [ess] 1,050 in the USA (1995 Krauss). Population total all countries: 1,350. Ethnic population: 1,050 in USA (1995 Krauss). St. Lawrence Island, Alaska; Gambell and Savonga villages, Alaska. Also spoken in Russia (Asia). *Class:* Eskimo-Aleut, Eskimo, Yupik, Siberian. *Dialect:* Chaplino. *Lg Use:* Vigorous in Alaska. Some children prefer English. In Alaska, children are being raised speaking the language (1998). In Siberia, only older adults speak the language. *Lg Dev:* Literacy rate in first language: 1% to 10%. Literacy rate in second language: 40% to 50%. Dictionary. Grammar. Bible portions: 1974–1998.

Yupik, Pacific Gulf (Alutiiq, Sugpiak "Eskimo," Sugpiaq "Eskimo," Chugach "Eskimo," Koniag-Chugach, Suk, Sugcestun, Aleut, Pacific Yupik, South Alaska "Eskimo") [ems] 400 (1995 M. Krauss). Ethnic population: 3,000 (1995 M. Krauss). Alaska Peninsula, Kodiak Island (Koniag dialect), Alaskan coast from Cook Inlet to Prince William Sound (Chugach dialect). 20 villages. *Class:* Eskimo-Aleut, Eskimo, Yupik, Alaskan. *Dialects:* Chugach, Koniag. *Lg Use:* Most speakers are older adults. The youngest are in the late 20s at the tip of the Kenai Peninsula and the 50s or 60s on Kodiak Island. Speakers also use English. *Lg Dev:* Dictionary. Grammar. Bible portions: 1848. *Other:* They call themselves 'Aleut'.

Yurok [yur] 12 (2002 Goddard). Ethnic population: 3,000 to 4,500 possibly (1982 SIL). Northwestern California. *Class:* Algic, Yurok. *Lg Use:* Speakers are shifting to English. Speakers are older adults (Ives Goddard 2002). Few if any full bloods younger than 20 years old. *Other:* Nearly extinct.

Zuni (Zuñi, Shiwi'ma) [zun] 9,651 (2000 SIL). Ethnic population: 9,651. New Mexico, reservation in southern McKinley County, south of Gallup. *Class:* Language Isolate. *Lg Use:* Some children are being raised speaking the language (1998). Speakers are slowly shifting to English. Oral language is used in traditional tribal council meetings. Zuni is used exclusively in all Zuni religious ceremonies, occasionally in religious services. Speakers were 85.5% of the population below 18 years of age, 6.2% above 18 (1980). Positive language attitude. Few, if any, monolinguals (2000). Schools are in English. *Lg Dev:* Literacy rate in first language: below 1%. Literacy rate in second language: 75% to 100%. Some study of oral and written Zuni in primary school. Roman script. Radio programs. Bible portions: 1941–1970. *Other:* Mountain mesa, valleys. Village at 2,000 meters. Jewelry making; government workers. Traditional religion.

Uruguay

Republic of Uruguay, República Oriental del Uruguay. 3,399,237. National or official language: Spanish. Literacy rate: 95% to 96%. Also includes Catalan-Valencian-Balear, Corsican, Eastern Yiddish, Italian (79,000), Lithuanian, Plautdietsch (1,200), Portuguese (28,000), Russian (14,000), Standard German (28,000). Deaf institutions: 4. The number of languages listed for Uruguay is 2. Of those, both are living languages.

Spanish [spa] 3,000,000 in Uruguay (1995). *Lg Use:* National language. See main entry under Spain.

Uruguayan Sign Language [ugy] *Class:* Deaf sign language. *Lg Use:* The sign language has been used since 1910. Used in schools. Sign language interpreters are required in court. Instruction for parents of deaf children. A committee on national sign language, and an organization for sign language teachers. *Lg Dev:* TV. Videos. Dictionary. *Other:* There is a manual alphabet for spelling.

Venezuela

Bolivarian Republic of Venezuela, República Bolivariana de Venezuela. 25,017,387. Population includes 145,230 American Indians (Mosonyi 1987). National or official language: Spanish. Literacy rate: 88% (1991 WA). Also includes Catalan-Valencian-Balear, Corsican, Cubeo, English (20,000), Inga (4,000), Latvian, Arabic (110,000), Chinese (400,000). Information mainly from M. Durbin and H. Seijas 1973; E. Migliazza 1977. Deaf population: 1,246,674. Deaf institutions: 3. The number of languages listed for Venezuela is 46. Of those, 40 are living languages and 6 are extinct. See map on page 776.

Akawaio (Acewaio, Akawai, Acawayo, Acahuayo, Waicá) [ake] Few speakers in Venezuela. Bolivar State. *Lg Use:* Positive language attitude. Some speakers also use Spanish. *Other:* The Akawaio and Patamona call themselves 'Kapon'. See main entry under Guyana.

Arawak (Arowak, Lokono) [arw] 100 in Venezuela (2002 SIL). Coastal area near Guyana, Delta Amacuro. *Lg Use:* Most also use Arawak, Spanish, or English. *Other:* Came to Venezuela from Guyana. See main entry under Suriname.

Arutani (Auaqué, Auake, Awaké, Uruak, Urutani, Aoaqui, Oewaku) [atx] 2 in Venezuela (2002 SIL). Ethnic population: 39 in Venezuela (2002 SIL). Below the Sape of the Karum River area, Bolivar State, headwaters of the Paraqua and Uraricáa rivers. *Lg Use:* The remaining speakers also use Ninam. Most are intermarried with the Ninam, some with the Pemon (Arecuna), a few with the Sape, and they do not speak Arutani fluently. *Other:* Nearly extinct. See main entry under Brazil.

Baniva (Avani, Ayane, Abane) [bvv] Extinct. Colombian border area. *Class:* Arawakan, Maipuran, Northern Maipuran, Inland. *Dialects:* Baniva, Quirruba. *Other:* Distinct from Baniwa in Rio Negro region.

Baniwa (Baniua do Içana, Maniba, Baniva, Baniba) [bwi] 433 in Venezuela (2002 SIL). Ethnic population: 1,150 (2002 SIL). Amazonas, between the Curipaco and the

Guarequena, along the Colombian border. *Lg Use:* Nearly all speakers also use Spanish. See main entry under Brazil.

Baré (Barawana, Barauna, Barauana, Ihini, Arihini, Maldavaca, Cunipusana, Yavita, Mitua) [bae] Extinct. Ethnic population: Perhaps 238 (1975 Gaceta Indigenista). Colombian border in extreme southwest, Amazonas, along the upper Rio Negro from Brazil-Venezuela border to the Casiquiare Canal, Maroa. *Class:* Arawakan, Maipuran, Northern Maipuran, Inland. *Lg Use:* Members of the ethnic group now speak Spanish or Nhengatu. *Other:* The name 'Baré' is also used as a cover term for separate languages: Baré, Mandahuaca, Guarekena, Baniwa, Piapoco.

Barí (Motilone, Motilón) [mot] 850 in Venezuela (1980 Seely). Venezuelan and Colombian border, Zulia State. *Other:* Unrelated to Carib Motilón (Yukpa). Tropical forest. See main entry under Colombia.

Carib (Caribe, Cariña, Kalihna, Kalinya, Galibi) [car] 7,251 in Venezuela (2000 WCD). Population total all countries: 10,226. Monagas and Anzoategui states, northeast near Orinoco River mouth, plus a few communities in Bolivar State, just south of Orinoco. Also spoken in Brazil, French Guiana, Guyana, Suriname. *Class:* Carib, Northern, Galibi. *Dialect:* Tabajari. *Lg Use:* Quite well integrated into Venezuelan culture, though they do speak their own language among themselves. Older adults and very young are monolingual. *Lg Dev:* Dictionary. Grammar. NT: 2003.

Chaima (Chayma, Sayma, Warapiche, Guaga-Tagare) [ciy] Eastern Venezuela coastal region. *Class:* Carib, Northern, Coastal. *Lg Use:* All speakers also use Spanish.

Cuiba (Cuiva) [cui] 650 in Venezuela (1995 SIL). Nearly all are monolingual. Apure Division. *Dialects:* Chiricoa, Amaruwa (Amorua), Masiguare, Siripu, Yarahuuraxi-Capanapara, Mella, Ptamo, Sicuane (Sicuari). *Lg Dev:* Literacy rate in second language: 1%. *Other:* Seminomadic bands. Hunter-gatherers. See main entry under Colombia.

Cumanagoto [cuo] Extinct. Eastern Venezuela coastal region. *Class:* Carib, Northern, Coastal.

Curripaco (Curipaco, Kuripako, Kurripako) [kpc] 210 in Venezuela (1970 census). Amazonas. *Other:* An alternate name may be 'Yaverete-Tapuya'. See main entry under Colombia.

Eñepa (Panare, Panari, Abira, Eye) [pbh] 1,200. Nearly all are monolingual. 150 mile perimeter south of Caicaro de Orinoco basin of the Cuchivero River; Bolivar State. Two groups: jungle and highland. 20 or more villages. *Class:* Carib, Northern, Western Guiana. *Lg Dev:* Grammar. Bible portions: 1984–1991. *Other:* SVO, OVS. Tropical forest, mountain slope.

German, Colonia Tovar (Alemán Coloneiro) [gct] *Class:* Indo-European, Germanic, West, High German, German, Upper German, Alemannic. *Dialects:* Developed from the Alemannisch (Oberdeutsch) of 1843 under the influence of many other dialects of south Germany, Austria, and Switzerland. Not intelligible with Standard German. *Lg Use:* Speakers also use Spanish. *Lg Dev:* Newspapers.

Guahibo (Guajibo, Wahibo) [guh] 5,000 in Venezuela. Orinoco River from Caicaro de Orinoco on the upper Orinoco, Amazonas, and Apure states. *Other:* The Guahiban languages may not be within Arawakan. Plains. See main entry under Colombia.

Guarequena (Guarekena, Arequena, Urequema, Uerequema, Warekena) [gae] 367 in Venezuela. Population total all countries: 705. Village of Guzmán Blanco, half an hour below Maroa. San Miguel River, Amazonas. Also possibly in Colombia. Also spoken in Brazil. *Class:* Arawakan, Maipuran, Northern Maipuran, Inland. *Lg Use:* Speakers are shifting to Spanish in Venezuela. Speakers are older adults.

Japrería (Yaprería) [jru] 90 to 100 (2002 SIL). Ethnic population: 152 (2000 WCD). Northern region of Sierra de Perija, Zulia State. *Class:* Carib, Northern, Coastal. *Dialects:* Not inherently intelligible with other Carib languages of the area (M. Durbin). Low lexical similarity with Yukpa (Luis Oquendo: U. of Zulia).

Maco (Mako, Itoto, Wotuja, Jojod) [wpc] 2,500 (2002 Miller). Tributaries of the Ventuari River, Wapuchi, Paru, Yureba, and Marueta rivers, in the villages of Marueta, Wapuchi, Porvenir, Tavi-Tavi, Mariche, Morocoto. *Class:* Salivan. *Lg Use:* Possibly 50% of the men also use Spanish. Some also speak Piaroa. *Other:* Agriculturalists; hunters; fishermen.

Macushi (Makusi, Makuxi, Makushi, Teweya) [mbc] 600 in Venezuela. Eastern border area. *Lg Use:* Some from Guyana in Bolivar State speak English as second language. See main entry under Brazil.

Mandahuaca (Mandauaca, Mandawaka, Ihini, Arihini, Maldavaca, Cunipusana, Yavita, Mitua) [mht] 3,000 in Venezuela (1975 Gaceta Indigenista). Population total all countries: 3,003. Colombian border in extreme southwest, Amazonas, east of the Baré on the Baria River and Casiquiare Canal. Also spoken in Brazil. *Class:* Arawakan, Maipuran, Northern Maipuran, Inland. *Dialects:* Related to Adzaneni, Yabaana, Masaca. *Lg Use:* Nearly extinct in Brazil. *Other:* The name 'Baré' is also used as a cover term for separate languages: Baré, Mandahuaca, Guarekena, Baniwa, Piapoco.

Mapoyo (Mapayo, Mapoye, Mopoi, Nepoye, Wanai) [mcg] 3 (2000 Muller). Ethnic population: 120. Suapure River, 100 kilometers north of La Urbana, Amazonas. *Class:* Carib, Northern, Western Guiana. *Dialects:* Close to Yawarana. *Lg Use:* Members of the ethnic group now speak Spanish. May be extinct. *Other:* Ergative. Nearly extinct.

Maquiritari (Maiongong, Maquiritare, Yekuana, De'cuana, Ye'cuana, Maquiritai, Soto, Cunuana, Pawana) [mch] 4,970 in Venezuela (1975 Gaceta Indigenista). Population total all countries: 5,240. Bolivar State and Amazonas, near the Brazilian border on the mid-Paragua, Caura, Erebato, upper Ventuari, upper Auaris, Matacuni, Cuntinano, Padamo, and Cunucunuma rivers. Also spoken in Brazil. *Class:* Carib, Southern, Southern Guiana. *Lg Dev:* Literacy rate in second language: 15%. NT: 1970.

Nhengatu (Yeral, Geral, Waengatu, Modern Tupi) [yrl] 2,000 in Venezuela (1987 Mosonyi). *Lg Use:* Trade language. See main entry under Brazil.

Ninam (Yanam, Xiriana) [shb] 100 in Venezuela. Karun and Paragua rivers, Bolivar State. *Dialects:* Northern Ninam, Southern Ninam. *Lg Use:* In Venezuela all speakers also use Spanish or Arecuna or both. See main entry under Brazil.

Paraujano (Parahujano, Añú) [pbg] Extinct. Ethnic population: 4,306 (1975 Gaceta Indigenista). Lake Maracaibo, near Guajiro, Zulia State. *Class:* Arawakan, Maipuran, Northern Maipuran, Caribbean. *Dialects:* Alile, Toa.

Pemon (Pemong) [aoc] 5,000 in Venezuela (2001 Becsky). Many are monolingual. Population total all countries: 6,154. Ethnic population: 18,871 in Venezuela (1993 census, may include Macushi). Bolivar State, Gran Sabana and adjacent areas, southeastern Venezuela. Also spoken in Brazil, Guyana. *Class:* Carib, Northern, East-West Guiana, Macushi-Kapon, Kapon. *Dialects:* Camaracoto, Taurepan (Taulipang), Arecuna (Aricuna, Arekuna, Jaricuna, Pemon, Daigok, Potsawugok, Pishauco, Purucoto, Kamaragakok). Marginally intelligible with Akawaio and Patamona. The Camaracoto dialect may be a distinct language. *Lg Use:* In some areas most children have Spanish as first language. Some children can understand Pemon but do not speak it. *Lg Dev:* Dictionary. Grammar. Bible portions: 1990. *Other:* OVS.

Pémono [pev] 1 (2000 M-C Mattei Muller). Lives with the Yabarana in an Upper Majagua village. *Class:* Carib, Northern, Western Guiana. *Dialects:* Close to Mapoyo and Yawarana. *Lg Use:* Members of the ethnic group now speak Spanish. May be extinct. 80-year-old woman in 1998. *Other:* Not the same as Pemon of Venezuela, Brazil, and Guyana. Unknown until 1998. Ergative. Nearly extinct.

Piapoco (Dzaze, Piapoko) [pio] 99 in Venezuela (1975 Gaceta Indigenista). Area of San Fernando de Atapapo, Amazonas along the Orinoco. See main entry under Colombia.

Piaroa (Kuakua, Guagua, Quaqua) [pid] 12,000 in Venezuela (1987 UBS). Population includes 130 Maco. Population total all countries: 12,080. South bank of the Orinoco River, inland from the Paguasa River to Manipiari, Amazonas. Large area. Also spoken in Colombia. *Class:* Salivan. *Lg Use:* Possibly 50% of the men also use Maquiritare, Yabarana, or Spanish. *Lg Dev:* NT: 1986–2001. *Other:* 'Ature' (Adole) may be an alternate name.

Puinave (Puinare, Wanse) [pui] 240 in Venezuela (1975 Gaceta Indigenista). Amazonas. See main entry under Colombia.

Pumé (Llaruro, Yaruro, Yaruru, Yuapín) [yae] 3,396 (2000 WCD). Orinoco, Sinaruco, Meta, and Apure rivers, Amazonas and Apure states. *Class:* Unclassified. *Lg Dev:* Bible portions: 1999. *Other:* Plains.

Sáliba (Sáliva) [slc] 250 in Venezuela (1991 Adelaar). Cedoño Department. *Lg Use:* Speakers are shifting to Spanish. *Other:* Very acculturated in Venezuela. See main entry under Colombia.

Sanumá (Tsanuma, Sanema, Sanima, Guaika, Samatari, Samatali, Xamatari, Chirichano) [xsu] 4,612 in Venezuela (2000 WCD). Population includes 500 Yanoma. Population total all countries: 5,074. Caura and Ervato-Ventuari rivers. Also spoken in Brazil. *Class:* Yanomam. *Dialect:* Yanoma, Cobari (Kobali, Cobariwa). *Lg Use:* Nearly all are monolingual.

Sapé (Kariana, Kaliána, Caliana, Chirichano) [spc] 5 (1977 E. Migliazza). Ethnic population: 25 or fewer (1977 Migliazza). 3 small settlements on Paragua and Karuna rivers. *Class:* Arutani-Sape. *Dialects:* Some lexical correspondences Warao (Language Isolate). Greenberg classified it provisionally as Macro-Tucanoan. *Lg Use:* Most have intermarried with Arecuna (Pemon) and a few with Arutani and Ninam. There are conflicting reports on the number of speakers and degree of bilingualism. *Lg Dev:* Bible portions. *Other:* Nearly extinct.

Sikiana (Sikiána, Shikiana, Chiquiana, Chikena, Chiquena) [sik] *Other:* Possibly extinct in Venezuela. Nearly extinct. See main entry under Brazil.

Spanish [spa] 21,480,000 in Venezuela (1995). *Lg Use:* Official language. See main entry under Spain.

Tamanaku [tmz] Extinct. Near Mapoyo and Yawarana. *Class:* Carib, Northern, Western Guiana. *Dialects:* Similar to Eñepa. *Other:* Incipient syllabic reduction and complex verbal morphology.

Tunebo, Central [tuf] Apure State. *Lg Use:* A few speakers in Venezuela. See main entry under Colombia.

Venezuelan Sign Language [vsl] *Class:* Deaf sign language. *Dialects:* The sign language used in the classroom is different from the one used by adults outside. *Lg Use:* There have been schools for the deaf since 1937, and they use sign language. Deaf people can attend college with a sign language interpreter. There is a national bilingual education program for Venezuelan Sign Language and Spanish. *Lg Dev:* Dictionary. Grammar. *Other:* There is a manual alphabet for spelling.

Warao (Guarauno, Guarao, Warrau) [wba] 18,000 in Venezuela (1993 UBS). 10,000 monolinguals. Ethnic population: 27,000. On the delta of the Orinoco River,

Delta Amacuro, Sucre, Monagas. Also spoken in Guyana, Suriname. *Class:* Language Isolate. *Lg Use:* All ages. *Lg Dev:* NT: 1974.

Wayuu (Guajiro, Guajira, Goajiro) [guc] 170,000 in Venezuela (1995 SIL). Zulia State, Guajira Peninsula. See main entry under Colombia.

Yabarana (Yauarana, Yawarana) [yar] 20 to 50 (1977 Migliazza). North central, Nueva Esparta, area of the Manapiare River basin above the village of San Juan de Manapiare, Amazonas. *Class:* Carib, Northern, Western Guiana. *Dialect:* Curasicana, Wokiare (Uaiquiare, Guayqueri). Close to Mapoyo and Pémono. *Other:* Distinct from Yabaana of Brazil. Ergative. Nearly extinct.

Yanomamö (Yanomame, Yanomami, Guaica, Guaharibo, Guajaribo, Shamatari, Cobari Kobali, Cobariwa) [guu] 15,710 in Venezuela (2000 WCD). Population total all countries: 17,653. Orinoco-Mavaca area. The Eastern dialect is in the Parima Mountains, east of Batau River, Western dialect in Padamo River basin; Ocamo, Manaviche, and upper Orinoco rivers; and south of the Orinoco River up to headwaters of Marania and Cauaburi rivers, and a number of large villages in the Siapa River area in southern Venezuela. Also spoken in Brazil. *Class:* Yanomam.

Dialects: Eastern Yanomami (Parima), Western Yanomami (Padamo-Orinoco). Related to Yanomámi (Waiká) of Brazil. The Cobari dialect is easily intelligible with the others. *Lg Dev:* NT: 1984. *Other:* Tropical forest. Hunters; agriculturalists: bananas, tubers, tobacco.

Yavitero (Paraene) [yvt] Extinct. *Class:* Arawakan, Maipuran, Northern Maipuran, Inland. *Lg Use:* The last known speaker died in 1984.

Yukpa (Yuko, Yucpa, Yupa, Northern Motilón) [yup] 500 in Venezuela. Areas adjacent to Colombia border, Zulia State. *Dialects:* Yrapa, Río Negro. *Other:* Possible alternate name: 'Manso'. See main entry under Colombia.

Yuwana (Yoana, Yuana, Waruwaru, Chicano, Chikano, Joti, Jodi, Hoti) [yau] 300 (1970 census). Central Venezuela. A northern group is in Bolivar Division on the Kaima River, a tributary of the Cuchivero River; an isolated southern group is in Amazonas on the Iguana, a tributary of the Asita River, and on the Parucito, a tributary of the Manapiare River. *Class:* Unclassified. *Dialects:* There are linguistic similarities to Yanomamö and Piaroa (Salivan). *Lg Use:* The southern group is monolingual; the northern group is partially bilingual in Eñepa. *Lg Dev:* Bible portions: 1999.

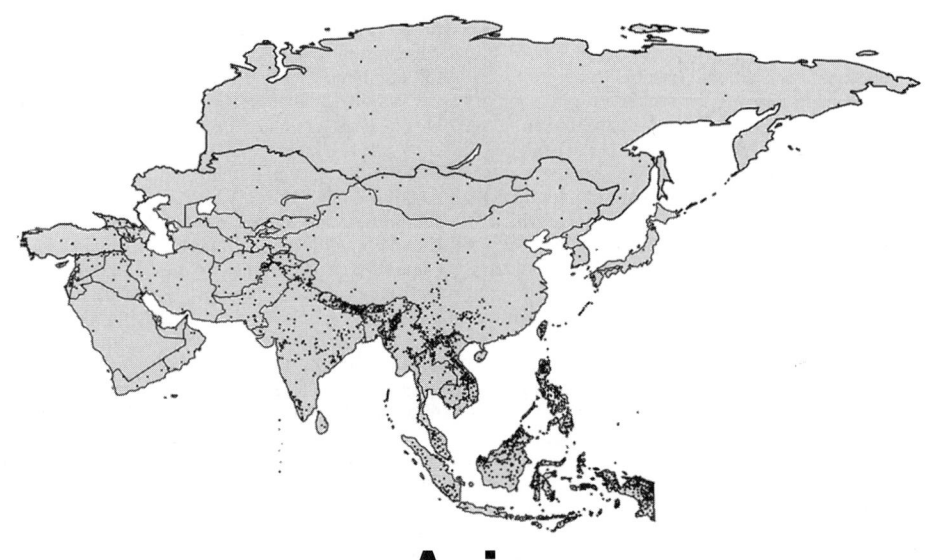

Asia

Afghanistan

Republic of Afghanistan. De Afghanistan Jamhuriat.
28,513,677. Population includes an estimated 2,500,000
nomads. National or official languages: Eastern Farsi,
Southern Pashto. Literacy rate: 31.5% 15 years and older:
male 47.2%, female 15%. Also includes Parsi-Dari (350,000),
Tatar (350), Urdu, Western Panjabi (35,000). Information
mainly from G. Buddress 1960; A. Farhadi 1967; A.
Grjunberg 1968, 1971; T. Sebeok 1970; R. Strand 1973; G.
Morgenstierne 1974; L. Dupree 1980; J. R. Payne 1987. Blind
population: 200,000 (1982 WCE). The number of languages
listed for Afghanistan is 47. Of those, all are living languages.

Aimaq (Barbari, Berberi, Chahar-Aimaq, Char Aimaq)
[aiq] 480,000 in Afghanistan (1993). Population includes
1,000 Jamshidi (1978 MARC). Population total all
countries: 650,000. West of the Hazara, central northwest
Afghanistan, eastern Iran, and Tajikistan (Jamshidi and
Khazara). Also spoken in Iran, Tajikistan. *Class:* Indo-
European, Indo-Iranian, Iranian, Western, Southwestern,
Persian. *Dialects:* Taimuri (Teimuri, Timuri, Taimouri),
Taimani, Zohri (Zuri), Jamshidi (Jamshedi, Djamchidi,
Yemchidi, Dzhemshid), Firozkohi, Maliki, Mizmast,
Chinghizi, Zainal. Dialect names listed may be ethnic
names. Dari Persian dialects with some Turkic and
Mongolian elements, possibly quite distinct. *Lg Dev:*
Literacy rate in second language: 5% to 15%. *Other:*
'Barbari' and 'Berberi' are also applied to Hazara people
in and around Mashad, Iran. Agriculturalists; pastoralists.
Muslim (Hanafi Sunni).
Arabic, Tajiki Spoken [abh] 5,000 in Afghanistan (1967
Farhadi). Population total all countries: 6,000. Spoken in a
few villages west of Daulatabad (Khushalabad), near Balkh
(Yakhdan), Aq Chah (Sultan Aregh), Shibarghan
(Hassanabad), and south of Talukan in Takhar Province; 4
northern provinces. Some in Uzbekistan. Also spoken in
Tajikistan, Uzbekistan. *Class:* Afro-Asiatic, Semitic,
Central, South, Arabic. *Dialect:* Balkh Arabic. May be a
mixed language. The language is close to Mesopotamian
Spoken Arabic. Sharp dialect differences between Bukhara
and Kashkadarya regions in Tajikistan. Bukhara is strongly
influenced by Tajiki; Kashkadarya by Uzbek and other

Turkic languages. *Lg Use:* Use is declining. Speakers are
reported to be bilingual in Tajiki. *Other:* A form of
Persianized Arabic. Muslim.
Ashkun (Ashkund, Ashkuni, Wamayi, Wamais) [ask]
1,200 (2000). Pech Valley around Wama, northwest of
Asadabad in Kunar Province. *Class:* Indo-European,
Indo-Iranian, Indo-Aryan, Nuristani. *Dialects:* Ashuruveri
(Kolata, Titin Bajaygul), Gramsukraviri, Suruviri
(Wamai). *Lg Dev:* Literacy rate in second language: 5%
to 15%. *Other:* Not written. Muslim.
Azerbaijani, South (Azeri) [azb] Afshari dialect spoken
in small groups north of Kabul, Chandaul quarter of
Kabul City, also some in Herat city. *Dialect:* Afshari
(Afshar, Afsar). *Lg Use:* Those under 35 do not know any
Azerbaijani. Part of the Qizilbash speak Dari. All speakers
also use Persian or Pashto. *Other:* Muslim. See main
entry under Iran.
Balochi, Western (Baluchi, Baluci, Baloci) [bgn]
200,000 in Afghanistan (1979). Along Helmand River and
Zaranj area, in the southwest desert region. *Dialect:*
Rakhshani (Raxshani). *Lg Dev:* Literacy rate in first
language: 5% to 10%. Literacy rate in second language:
15% to 25%. *Other:* Largely nomadic. Muslim (Sunni).
See main entry under Pakistan.
Brahui (Brahuiki, Birahui, Kur Galli) [brh] 200,000 in
Afghanistan (1980 Dupree). Among the Baluchi in the
south, from Shorawak to Chakhansoor. *Lg Dev:* Literacy
rate in first language: below 1%. Literacy rate in second
language: 15% to 25%. *Other:* Pastoralists. Muslim. See
main entry under Pakistan.
Darwazi [drw] 10,000 (1983). Town of Darwaz on the
Amu Darya River, in the northernmost tip of Afghanistan.
May also be in Tajikistan. *Class:* Indo-European, Indo-
Iranian, Iranian, Western, Southwestern, Persian. *Lg Dev:*
Literacy rate in first language: below 1%. Literacy rate in
second language: 15% to 25%. *Other:* May be called
Badakhshani. Muslim.
Domari [rmt] *Dialect:* Churi-Wali. *Lg Dev:* Literacy rate
in first language: below 1%. Literacy rate in second
language: below 5%. *Other:* Muslim. See main entry
under Iran.
Farsi, Eastern (Persian, Dari, Parsi) [prs] 5,600,000 in
Afghanistan (1996). Population total all countries:

315

7,600,000. Various Dari dialects in Khorasan Province (Iran), and provinces of Herat, Hazarajat, Balkh, Ghor, Ghazni, Budaksham, Panjsher, and Galcha-Pamir Mountains and Kabul regions. Also spoken in Iran, Pakistan. *Class:* Indo-European, Indo-Iranian, Iranian, Western, Southwestern, Persian. *Dialects:* Dari (Afghan Farsi, Herati, Tajiki, Kaboli, Kabuli, Khorasani), Parsiwan. Radio Afghanistan broadcasts are promoting a standardized pronunciation of the literary language which is based on the old dictional tradition of the country, with its archaic phonetic characteristics. Formal style is closer to Tehrani Persian (Farsi); informal style in some parts of Afghanistan is closer to Tajiki of Tajikistan. Phonological and lexical differences between Iran and Afghanistan cause little difficulty in comprehension. Most Afghan dialects are closer to literary Persian than Iranian dialects are to literary Persian. Zargari (Morghuli) is a secret language used among goldsmiths and perhaps others, based on a dialect of Persian. See also Balkan Romani in Iran. *Lg Use:* National language. *Lg Dev:* Taught in schools. Arabic script. Radio programs. NT: 1982–1985. *Other:* Muslim (Sunni and Shi'a).

Gawar-Bati (Gowari, Narsati, Narisati, Arandui, Satre) [gwt] 8,000 in Afghanistan. Population total all countries: 9,500 (1992). 8 or 9 villages in the Kunar Valley. Also spoken in Pakistan. *Class:* Indo-European, Indo-Iranian, Indo-Aryan, Northwestern zone, Dardic, Kunar. *Dialects:* Lexical similarity 47% with Shumashti, 44% with Dameli, 42% with Savi and Grangali. *Lg Use:* Some bilingualism in Pashto. *Lg Dev:* Literacy rate in first language: below 1%. Literacy rate in second language: 5% to 15%. *Other:* Mountain valleys. Muslim (Sunni).

Grangali (Gelangali, Jumiaki) [nli] 5,000 (1994). Grangali and Zemiaki in 2 small valleys on the south side of the Pech River at Kandai. Nangalami was in Ningalam village where the Waigal River meets the Pech River, but there may be no speakers left. *Class:* Indo-European, Indo-Iranian, Indo-Aryan, Northwestern zone, Dardic, Kunar. *Dialects:* Nangalami (Ningalami), Grangali, Zemiaki (Zamyaki). Zemiaki may be related to Waigali. Nangalami had 63% lexical similarity with Shumashti, 42% with Gawar-Bati. *Lg Dev:* Literacy rate in first language: below 1%. Literacy rate in second language: 5% to 15%. *Other:* Mountain valleys. Muslim.

Gujari (Gujuri Rajasthani, Gojri, Gojari) [gju] 2,000 in Afghanistan (1994). Nomads travelling in the summer in the valleys of eastern Afghanistan. *Lg Dev:* Literacy rate in first language: below 1%. Literacy rate in second language: below 5%. *Other:* Pastoralists. Muslim. See main entry under India.

Hazaragi (Azargi, Hazara, Hezareh) [haz] 1,770,000 in Afghanistan (2000). Population total all countries: 2,209,794. Central Afghanistan mountains between Kabul and Herat (Hazarajat), in Kabul, in area between Maimana and Sari-Pul, in settlements in north Afghanistan and from immediately south of the IKoh i Baba mountain range almost all the way to Mazar e Sharif, and in the area of Qunduz, in Baluchistan and near Quetta in Pakistan. Some have moved to northern Iran. Many are refugees. Also spoken in Iran, Pakistan, Tajikistan. *Class:* Indo-European, Indo-Iranian, Iranian, Western, Southwestern, Persian. *Dialects:* They speak a variety related to Dari; possibly distinct. *Lg Dev:* Literacy rate in first language: below 1%. Literacy rate in second language: Possibly 10% to 20%. Radio programs. *Other:* Ethnic group names are (Central) Dai Kundi, Dai Zangi, Behsud, Yekaulang, (Southern) Polada, Urusgani, Jaguri, Ghazni Hazaras, Dai Miradad. In Hazarajat: agriculturalists; semisedentary pastoralists; in cities like Kabul and Mazar e Sharif they are laborers; traders; shopkeepers; tradesmen; transportation workers. Muslim.

Jakati (Jati, Jatu, Jat, Jataki, Kayani, Musali) [jat] 1,365 in Afghanistan (2000 WCD). Kabul (25 families); Jalalabad (50 families); Charikar (15 families). *Other:* Spoken by the Jats of Afghanistan. Different from Jadgali of Pakistan. Nomadic. Ironsmiths; fortune tellers. Muslim. See main entry under Ukraine.

Kamviri (Kamdeshi, Lamertiviri, Shekhani, Kamik) [xvi] 4,000 in Afghanistan (1973 R. Strand). Population total all countries: 5,500. Lower Bashgal Valley, mainly around Kamdesh and Kishtoz villages. Also spoken in Pakistan. *Class:* Indo-European, Indo-Iranian, Indo-Aryan, Nuristani. *Dialects:* Kamviri, Shekhani. Shekhani in Pakistan may be a separate language. Related to Kati. *Lg Use:* Speakers also use Pashto. *Lg Dev:* Literacy rate in first language: below 1%. Literacy rate in second language: 15% to 25%. *Other:* Mountain valleys.

Karakalpak (Qaraqulpaqs) [kaa] 2,000 in Afghanistan. North of Jalalabad, also some south of Mazar-i Sharif. *Dialects:* Northeast Karakalpak, Southwest Karakalpak. *Lg Use:* Speakers also use Eastern Farsi. *Lg Dev:* Literacy rate in first language: below 1%. Literacy rate in second language: 5% to 15%. *Other:* There may be none now in Afghanistan; the reference to them is from many years ago. They may now speak closely related Uzbek, or have been absorbed into Farsi or Pashto. Muslim. See main entry under Uzbekistan.

Kati (Bashgali, Kativiri, Nuristani) [bsh] 15,000 in Afghanistan (1994). Population total all countries: 18,700. Western Kativiri is in Ramgal, Kulam, Ktivi, or Kantiwo, and Paruk or Papruk valleys. Mumviri is in Mangul, Sasku, Gabalgrom villages in the Bashgal Valley. Eastern Kativiri is in the upper Bashgal Valley. Also spoken in Pakistan. *Class:* Indo-European, Indo-Iranian, Indo-Aryan, Nuristani. *Dialects:* Eastern Kativiri (Shekhani), Western Kativiri, Mumviri. Mumviri may be a separate language. *Lg Use:* Bilingual level estimates for Pashto: Western Kati Men: 0 50%, 1 3–5%, 2 3–5%, 3 35–40%, 4 0%, 5 0%; Western Kati Women: 0–1 100%, 2–5 0%. Speakers also use Eastern Farsi as a second language. *Lg Dev:* Literacy rate in first language: below 1%. Literacy rate in second language: 15% to 25%. Radio programs. *Other:* Shekhani is different from the Kamviri which is also called 'Shekhani' in Pakistan. Men take turns 20 days, taking goats to high summer pastures. CVC, CCVC, CV. Mountain valley. Savannah, scrub forest. 2,400 to 4,200 meters. Pastoralists: goats. Muslim.

Kazakh (Kazakhi, Qazaqi, Qazaq) [kaz] 2,000 in Afghanistan (2000). Northern Afghanistan, especially Chahar Dara District west of Kunduz, and around Khanabad and Andkhoi. 500 in Herat city. *Dialects:* Northeastern Kazakh, Southern Kazakh, Western Kazakh. *Lg Dev:* Literacy rate in first language: below 1%. *Other:* Muslim. See main entry under Kazakhstan.

Kirghiz (Kirghizi, Kirgiz) [kir] 750 in Afghanistan (2000). 445 in the Great Pamir, plus a few in Badakhshan. Great Pamir Valley east of 73E, in the very northeast. It is spoken by a few Kirghiz who wander across the Chinese and Kyrgyzstan frontiers. All from the Little Pamir went to Pakistan and then Turkey in 1982. *Lg Dev:* Literacy rate in first language: below 1%. Afghan Kirghiz do not read Cyrillic. *Other:* Muslim (Sunni). See main entry under Kyrgyzstan.

Malakhel [mld] 2,860 (2000). Southwest of Kabul in Logar, north of Baraki. *Class:* Unclassified. *Lg Dev:* Literacy rate in first language: below 1%. Literacy rate in second language: 5% to 15%. *Other:* May be the same as Ormuru. Muslim.

Mogholi (Moghol, Mogul, Mogol, Mongul) [mhj] 200. Ethnic population: A few thousand. Two villages near Herat: Kundur and Karez-i-Mulla. *Class:* Altaic, Mongolian, Western. *Dialects:* Kundur, Karez-I-Mulla.

Unintelligible to remaining body of Mongol speakers; linguistically relatively well explored. *Lg Use:* Speakers are older adults. In the two villages Farsi is the common language and is rapidly replacing Mogholi. Moghol people in northern Afghanistan now speak Pashto. *Other:* Muslim (Sunni).

Munji (Munjani, Munjhan, Munjiwar) [mnj] 3,768 (2000 WCD). Northeastern Afghanistan in the Munjan and Mamalgha Valleys. *Class:* Indo-European, Indo-Iranian, Iranian, Eastern, Southeastern, Pamir. *Dialects:* Northern Munji, Central Munji, Southern Munji, Mamalgha Munji. Lexical similarity 68% among 'dialects', 56% to 80% with Yidgha in Pakistan. *Lg Use:* Speakers also use Eastern Farsi. *Lg Dev:* Literacy rate in first language: below 1%. Literacy rate in second language: 15% to 25%. *Other:* Little contact with Yidgha. Muslim.

Ormuri (Bargista, Baraks, Ormui, Oormuri) [oru] 50 in Afghanistan. Ethnic population: 2,000 to 5,000 in Afghanistan. Spoken by a few families in Baraki-Barak in Logar. *Dialects:* Kanigurami, Logar. *Lg Dev:* Literacy rate in first language: below 1%. Literacy rate in second language: 5% to 15%. *Other:* Muslim. See main entry under Pakistan.

Pahlavani [phv] 2,100 (2000 WCD). Spoken in village Haji Hamza Khan of Karim Kushta in Chakhansoor Province. *Class:* Indo-European, Indo-Iranian, Iranian, Western, Southwestern, Persian. *Dialects:* Similar to Dari Persian. *Lg Dev:* Literacy rate in first language: below 1%. *Other:* Muslim.

Parachi [prc] 600. Ethnic population: 5,000 to 6,000. Villages in Nijrau and Tagau (600 families), Pachaghan, Shutul (400 families), Ghujulan (100 families), Hindu Kush Valley near Kabul. *Class:* Indo-European, Indo-Iranian, Iranian, Western, Northwestern, Ormuri-Parachi. *Dialects:* Shutul, Ghujulan, Nijrau. Close affinity to Ormuri. Dialect diversity seems to be slight. *Lg Dev:* Literacy rate in first language: below 1%. Literacy rate in second language: 5% to 15%. *Other:* Muslim.

Parya (Afghana-Yi Nasfurush, Afghana-Yi Siyarui, Laghmani) [paq] 1,300 in Afghanistan (2000). *Lg Use:* Used in the home. Speakers also use Tajiki. *Lg Dev:* Literacy rate in first language: below 1%. Literacy rate in second language: 5% to 15%. See main entry under Tajikistan.

Pashayi, Northeast [aee] 54,412 (2000 WCD). Side valleys between the Kunar and Pech rivers, in Kunar Province, west of Asadabad. *Class:* Indo-European, Indo-Iranian, Indo-Aryan, Northwestern zone, Dardic, Kunar, Pashayi. *Dialects:* Aret, Chalas (Chilas), Kandak, Kurangal, Kurdar. Unintelligible to other Pashayi language speakers. *Lg Dev:* Literacy rate in first language: below 1%. Literacy rate in second language: 5% to 15%. *Other:* The villages of Kandak, Shemul, Aret, Shumasht, and Kordar belong to the Chugani people; Chalas and Kurangal are separate. Muslim.

Pashayi, Northwest [glh] From Gulbahar across Kapisa and Laghman provinces to Nuristan on the Alingar River, especially the Alisheng Valley and valleys north of Sarobi. *Class:* Indo-European, Indo-Iranian, Indo-Aryan, Northwestern zone, Dardic, Kunar, Pashayi. *Dialects:* Gulbahar, Kohnadeh, Laurowan, Sanjan, Shutul, Bolaghain, Pachagan, Alasai, Shamakot, Uzbin, Pandau, Najil, Parazhghan, Pashagar, Wadau, Nangarach. Unintelligible to other Pashayi language speakers. *Lg Dev:* Literacy rate in first language: below 1%. Literacy rate in second language: 5% to 15%. *Other:* Muslim.

Pashayi, Southeast (Pashai) [psi] 54,412 (2000 WCD). Upper and Lower Darrai Nur Valley, Damench, Shale (Shari). North of Shewa in Nangarhar Province, and adjacent regions of the Alingar Valley in southern Laghman Province. *Class:* Indo-European, Indo-Iranian, Indo-Aryan, Northwestern zone, Dardic, Kunar, Pashayi. *Dialects:* Darrai Nur, Wegal, Laghman, Alingar, Kunar. Unintelligible to other Pashayi language speakers. In the upper Darrai Nur there are ten villages (including Bamba Kot, Lamatek, and Sutan) which form a single people group with their own dialect. Residents of the lower Darrai Nur (Nur River) are separate and perhaps not ethnically an organized people. *Lg Dev:* Literacy rate in first language: below 1%. Literacy rate in second language: 5% to 15%. *Other:* Muslim.

Pashayi, Southwest [psh] 108,000 (1982). Population includes all Pashayi languages or dialects. Tagau (Tagab) Valley, north of Sarobi, northeast of Kabul. *Class:* Indo-European, Indo-Iranian, Indo-Aryan, Northwestern zone, Dardic, Kunar, Pashayi. *Dialects:* Tagau, Ishpi, Isken. Not intelligible with other Pashayi languages. *Lg Dev:* Literacy rate in first language: below 1%. Literacy rate in second language: 5% to 15%. *Other:* All Pashayi peoples have rich folklore and songs preserved by oral tradition. Muslim.

Pashto, Northern (Paktu, Pakhtu, Pakhtoo, Afghan) [pbu] Central Ghilzai area. *Dialects:* Northwestern Pashto, Ghilzai, Durani. *Lg Use:* One of the two official languages taught in schools. The Ghilzai speakers are nomadic and 24% of the national population. The Durani, 16%, live in permanent settlements. Speakers also use Farsi. *Lg Dev:* Literacy rate in first language: 5% to 10%. Literacy rate in second language: 15% to 25%. *Other:* The people are called 'Pakhtoon' in the north, 'Pashtoon' in the south. Pashto clans are: Mohmandi, Ghilzai, Durani, Yusufzai, Afridi, Kandahari (Qandahari), Waziri, Chinwari (Shinwari), Mangal, Wenetsi. Muslim (Hanafi Sunni). See main entry under Pakistan.

Pashto, Southern [pbt] 1,088,248 in Afghanistan (2000 WCD). 8,000,000 all Pashto in Afghanistan. Kandahar area. *Dialect:* Southwestern Pashto, Kandahar Pashto (Qandahar Pashto). *Lg Use:* National language. Since the early 1930s the Afghan government has been exerting considerable effort to standardize and publicize the language. *Other:* Muslim. See main entry under Pakistan.

Prasuni (Prasun, Veruni, Parun, Wasi-Veri, Veron, Verou) [prn] 1,000 (2000). Prasun (Parun) Valley on the upper reaches of Pech River in Nuristan; villages of Shupu (Ishtivi, Shtevgrom), Sech, Ucu, Ushut, Zumu. *Class:* Indo-European, Indo-Iranian, Indo-Aryan, Nuristani. *Dialect:* Upper Wasi-Weri, Central Prasun, Lower Prasun (Ushut). Very closely related to Bashgali but more archaic. The most aberrant of the Nuristani languages. *Lg Dev:* Literacy rate in first language: below 1%. Literacy rate in second language: 5% to 15%. *Other:* Muslim.

Sanglechi-Ishkashimi [sgl] 1,000 in Afghanistan. Population total all countries: 1,500. Ethnic population: 1,000 in Afghanistan (1990 A. E. Kibrik). Sanglech Valley, Ishkashim area. Ishkashimi spoken in 17 villages; Sanglechi in 2. Also spoken in Tajikistan. *Class:* Indo-European, Indo-Iranian, Iranian, Eastern, Southeastern, Pamir. *Dialects:* Zebak (Zebaki), Sanglechi, Ishkashimi (Ishkashmi, Ishkashim, Eshkashimi). Dialects listed may be separate languages. *Lg Use:* Spoken mainly in villages; formerly used more widely. Speakers also use Western Farsi. *Lg Dev:* Literacy rate in first language: below 1%. Literacy rate in second language: 15% to 25%. *Other:* Muslim.

Savi (Sawi, Sauji, Sau) [sdg] 3,000 in Afghanistan (1983). Sau village on the Kunar River. Some might still live in refugee camps in Pakistan. Also spoken in Pakistan. *Class:* Indo-European, Indo-Iranian, Indo-Aryan, Northwestern zone, Dardic, Shina. *Dialects:* Lexical similarity 56% to 58% with Phalura. *Lg Use:* Speakers also use Pashto. *Lg Dev:* Literacy rate in first language: below 1%. Literacy rate in second language: 5% to 15%. *Other:* Muslim.

Shughni [sgh] 20,000 in Afghanistan (1994). Both sides of Afghan-Tajikistan border, some 30 miles north of Ishkashim, Pamir Mountains. *Dialects:* Roshani (Rushani, Rushan, Oroshani), Shughni (Shugni, Shighni, Shughnani, Shugan, Khugni, Kushani, Saighani, Ghorani), Bartangi (Bartang), Oroshor (Oroshori). *Lg Dev:* Literacy rate in first language: below 1%. Literacy rate in second language: 5% to 15%. *Other:* Pastoralists. Muslim. See main entry under Tajikistan.

Shumashti (Shumasht) [sts] 1,000 (1994). Chitral frontier, 60 miles up the Kunar River from Gawar-Bati, on the west side, Darrai Mazar Valley. Shumast village has two languages: Shumashti and a Northeast Pashayi dialect. *Class:* Indo-European, Indo-Iranian, Indo-Aryan, Northwestern zone, Dardic, Kunar. *Dialects:* Lexical similarity 63% with Nangalami (Grangali), 47% with Gawar-Bati. Heavily influenced by Pashayi. *Lg Dev:* Literacy rate in first language: below 1%. Literacy rate in second language: 5% to 15%. *Other:* Muslim.

Tangshewi (Tangshuri) [tnf] 10,000 (1994). East of Darwazi on the Amu Darya, far northeast of Badakhshan. May also be in Turkmenistan. *Class:* Indo-European, Indo-Iranian, Iranian, Unclassified. *Dialects:* May be Eastern Iranian. Probably closely related to Darwazi. *Lg Dev:* Literacy rate in first language: below 1%. Literacy rate in second language: 5% to 15%. *Other:* May be called 'Tajiki'. Muslim.

Tirahi [tra] 100. Ethnic population: Possibly 5,000. Southeast of Jalalabad, and west of the Khyber Pass; village of Nangarhar. Not in Pakistan. *Class:* Indo-European, Indo-Iranian, Indo-Aryan, Northwestern zone, Dardic, Kohistani. *Dialects:* Most closely related to Kohistani languages of Pakistan. *Lg Use:* Most members of the ethnic group now speak Pashtu. Speakers are older adults. *Other:* Muslim. Nearly extinct.

Tregami (Trigami) [trm] 1,000 (1994). Nuristan, Tregam Valley, villages of Katar and Gambir. *Class:* Indo-European, Indo-Iranian, Indo-Aryan, Nuristani. *Dialects:* Lexical similarity 76% to 80% with Waigali. *Lg Dev:* Literacy rate in first language: below 1%. Literacy rate in second language: 5% to 15%. *Other:* Muslim.

Turkmen (Turkoman, Trukmen, Turkman) [tuk] 500,000 in Afghanistan (1995). Along the border of Turkmenistan, especially the border regions of Fariab and Badghis provinces. Some in Andkhoi town and Herat city. *Dialects:* Salor, Teke (Tekke, Chagatai, Jagatai), Ersari, Sariq, Yomut. *Lg Use:* Speakers also use Pashtu. *Lg Dev:* Literacy rate in second language: 15% to 25%. *Other:* Refugee group in Kabul. People called 'Turkomen' in Syria are Azerbaijani speakers. Sharp dialect differences. Probably mainly Ersari dialect in Afghanistan. Nomadic, cultivators, pastoralists; Persian lamb export, Persian rugs. Muslim (Hanafi Sunni), traditional religion. See main entry under Turkmenistan.

Uyghur (Uighur, Uighuri, Wighor, Uighor, Uiguir) [uig] 3,000 in Afghanistan. Spoken in a few villages in Badakshan and Abi-i-Barik. Also possibly in Iran and Taiwan. *Dialects:* Kashgar-Yarkand (Yarkandi), Taranchi. *Lg Dev:* Literacy rate in first language: below 1%. Literacy rate in second language: 5% to 15%. *Other:* Muslim (Sunni). See main entry under China.

Uzbek, Southern (Uzbeki, Usbeki, Uzbak) [uzs] 1,403,000 in Afghanistan (1991 WA). Population total all countries: 1,454,981. Many places in north Afghanistan, especially Fariab Province. Maimana town is largely Uzbek. Also possibly in Germany. Also spoken in Pakistan, Turkey (Asia). *Class:* Altaic, Turkic, Eastern. *Dialects:* Limited comprehension of Northern Uzbek. Differences in grammar and loanwords from Western Farsi. *Lg Use:* City dwellers also use Dari; village dwellers have limited ability in Dari. 20% use Dari as

second language. Pashto is also used. *Lg Dev:* Literacy rate in first language: 10% to 30%. Literacy rate in second language: 15% to 25% in Dari. Arabic script. Dictionary. Grammar. *Other:* The only literature is 2 journals, circulation 400. Mainly settled agriculturalists; some nomads, some craftsmen: gold, jewels, pottery, leather. Muslim (Hanafi Sunni).

Waigali (Waigeli, Waigalii, Waigala, Zhonjigali, Suki, Wai-Ala, Wai, Kalasha-Ala) [wbk] 1,500 (2000 Van Driem). Southeast Nuristan, north of Pech in central Kunar Province. Varjan is in north Waigal Valley, villages of Waigal, Zonchigal, Jamach, Ameshdesh, and eastward in the Veligal Valley and villages there. Chima-Nishey is in villages in the lower valley. *Class:* Indo-European, Indo-Iranian, Indo-Aryan, Nuristani. *Dialects:* Varjan, Chima-Nishey. Lexical similarity 76% to 80% with Tregami. *Lg Dev:* Literacy rate in first language: below 1%. Literacy rate in second language: 15% to 25%. *Other:* Muslim.

Wakhi (Wakhani, Wakhigi, Vakhan, Khik, Guhjali) [wbl] 9,566 in Afghanistan (2000 WCD). Ethnic population: 18,000 in Afghanistan (1990 A. E. Kibrik). East of Ishkashim, Pamir Mountains, in 64 villages on the left bank of the Panj River in the Wakhan Corridor, as far as Sarhad village (about 73E). Center is Khandud. Most have scattered as refugees in Afghanistan or Pakistan. *Lg Dev:* Literacy rate in first language: below 1%. *Other:* People are called 'Guhjali'. There may be none in Afghanistan now. Muslim. See main entry under Pakistan.

Warduji [wrd] 5,000 (1994). Werdoge River area west of Ishkashim, northeast Afghanistan. *Class:* Unclassified. *Dialects:* Probably a Western Farsi dialect. May be Pamir. *Lg Dev:* Literacy rate in first language: below 1%. Literacy rate in second language: 5% to 15%. *Other:* Muslim.

Wotapuri-Katarqalai [wsv] 2,000 (1994). South of Waigali area in Nuristan in the towns of Wotapuri and Katarqalai. *Class:* Indo-European, Indo-Iranian, Indo-Aryan, Northwestern zone, Dardic, Kohistani. *Lg Dev:* Literacy rate in first language: below 1%. Literacy rate in second language: 15% to 25%. *Other:* Muslim.

Armenia

Armenia. 2,991,360. National or official language: Armenian. Capital: Erevan. 11,306 square miles. Literacy rate: 99%. Also includes Georgian (1,563), Greek (4,700), Karachay-Balkar (323), Russian (70,000), Ukrainian (8,000). The number of languages listed for Armenia is 6. Of those, all are living languages.

Armenian (Haieren, Somkhuri, Ermenice, Ermeni Dili, Armjanski Yazyk) [hye] 3,399,903 in Armenia (2001 Johnstone and Mandryk). Population total all countries: 6,723,840. Throughout the country. Also spoken in Azerbaijan, Bulgaria, Canada, Cyprus, Egypt, Estonia, France, Georgia, Greece, Honduras, Hungary, India, Iran, Iraq, Israel, Jordan, Kazakhstan, Kyrgyzstan, Lebanon, Palestinian West Bank and Gaza, Romania, Russia (Europe), Syria, Tajikistan, Turkey (Europe), Turkmenistan, Ukraine, USA, Uzbekistan. *Class:* Indo-European, Armenian. *Dialects:* Eastern Armenian, Erevan (Eriwan), Tbilisi (Tiflis), Karabagh, Shamakhi (Schamachi), Astrakhan (Astrachan), Dzhulfa (Dschugha, Dschulfa), Agulis, Khvoy-Salmst (Choi-Salmst), Urmia-Maragheh (Urmia-Maragha), Artvin (Artwin), Karin (Erzurum, Erzerum), Mus (Musch), Van (Wan), Tigranakert (Diyarbakir, Diarbekir), Kharberd (Charberd, Erzincan, Erzenka), Shabin-Karahissar (Schabin-Karahissar), Trabzon (Trapezunt), Hamshen (Hamschen), Malatya (Malatia), Kilikien, Syria (Syrien), Arabkir, Akn, Sebaste, Ewdokia (Tokat), Smyrna (Izmir), North Komedia, Constantinople (Konstantinopel, Istanbul),

Rodosto, Crimea (Krim), Ashkharik. All dialects in all countries usually reported to be inherently intelligible. Eastern Armenian (4,341,000) is spoken in Armenia and its Turkish and Iranian borderlands; Western Armenian (879,612) is spoken elsewhere. Western Armenian is understood only by some in Iran. In Syria, people in Kessaberen (northeastern mountain village of Kessab) and the village of Musa Dagh (now relocated to Lebanon) speak related varieties which other Western Armenian speakers do not understand. Most speakers of Kessaberen have now learned Western Armenian. Western (Turkish) Armenian and Ararat (Russian) are easily intelligible. *Lg Use:* National language. 91% of the ethnic group in the former USSR spoke it as first language (1979 census). All ages. About 30% of speakers also use Russian. *Lg Dev:* Unique script. Dictionary. Grammar. Bible: 1883–1994. *Other:* Speakers refer to this language as Haieren. SVO. National Armenian Christian Church.

Armenian Sign Language [aen] *Class:* Deaf sign language.

Assyrian Neo-Aramaic (Aisorski, Sooreth) [aii] 3,000 in Armenia (1999). Ethnic population: 15,000. Erevan and scattered throughout Transcaucasia. *Lg Use:* Most speakers in Armenia are older adults. Many speakers use Russian as primary language. *Other:* 'Aisor' is the Russian name for the people. The Assyrian and Chaldean separated denominationally during the 16th century. Christian (Nestorian). See main entry under Iraq.

Azerbaijani, North (Azeri Turk, Turkler, Azerbaydzhani) [azj] 161,000 in Armenia (1993 Johnstone). In southern Dagestan, along the Caspian coast and beyond the Caucasus Mountains. *Dialects:* Kuba, Derbent, Baku, Semakha, Saliany, Lenkoran, Kazakh, Airym, Borcala, Terekeme, Kyzylbash, Nukha, Zakataly (Mugaly), Kutkasen, Erevan, Nakhichevan, Ordubad, Kirovabad, Susa (Karabakh), Karapapak. *Lg Use:* Used in schools, publications. *Lg Dev:* Literacy rate in second language: High. *Other:* Muslim (Shi'a). See main entry under Azerbaijan.

Kurdish, Northern (Kurmanji, Kurmancî, Êzdîkî) [kmr] 100,000 in Armenia (2004). *Lg Use:* Language of wider communication. Used in schools, texts. Positive language attitude. *Lg Dev:* Well-developed literary standard and much literature. Some classes in schools. *Other:* Yezidi. See main entry under Turkey (Asia).

Lomavren (Armenian Bosha, Armenian Bosa, Bosha, Bosa) [rmi] 50 in Armenia (2004). Armenia, southern Caucasus. Also spoken in Azerbaijan, Russia (Asia), Syria. *Class:* Mixed Language, Armenian-Romani. *Dialects:* Gramatically restructured to be like Armenian with phonology and lexicon also influenced by Armenian.

Azerbaijan

Azerbaijan. 7,868,385. National or official language: North Azerbaijani. Capital: Baku. 33,400 square miles. Literacy rate: 98%. Also includes Assyrian Neo-Aramaic (1,231), Belarusan (5,208), Dargwa (863), Erzya (1,150), Georgian (16,259), Karachay-Balkar (184), Lak (1,205), Lishán Didán (100), Lomavren, Osetin (2,521), Polish (1,264), Pontic, Romanian (1,397), Russian (475,000), Rutul (111), South Azerbaijani, Tabassaran (279), Tatar (31,787), Turkish (18,000), Ukrainian (32,000), Western Farsi. Information mainly from T. Sebeok 1963; A. Grjunberg 1963; Q. Voroshil 1972; A. Kibrik 1991. The number of languages listed for Azerbaijan is 14. Of those, all are living languages. See map on page 778.

Armenian (Haieren, Somkhuri, Ermenice, Armjanski) [hye] Nagorno-Karabakh Region. *Dialect:* Western Armenian. *Other:* Christian, Monophysite. See main entry under Armenia.

Avar (Avaro, Dagestani) [ava] 44,000 in Azerbaijan (1989 census). Northwest, Zaqatala and Balakan regions. *Dialect:* Zaqatala (Zakataly, Char). *Other:* Muslim (Sunni). See main entry under Russia (Europe).

Azerbaijani, North (Azerbaijan, Azeri Turk, Azerbaydzhani) [azj] 6,069,453 in Azerbaijan (1989 census). 4,000,000 monolinguals. Population total all countries: 7,059,529. Azerbaijan, and southern Dagestan, along the Caspian coast in the southern Caucasus Mountains. Also spoken in Armenia, Estonia, Georgia, Kazakhstan, Kyrgyzstan, Russia (Asia), Turkmenistan, Uzbekistan. *Class:* Altaic, Turkic, Southern, Azerbaijani. *Dialects:* Quba, Derbend, Baku, Shamakhi, Salyan, Lenkaran, Qazakh, Airym, Borcala, Terekeme, Qyzylbash, Nukha, Zaqatala (Mugaly), Qabala, Yerevan, Nakhchivan, Ordubad, Ganja, Shusha (Karabakh), Karapapak. Dialect differences are slight. The Qazakh dialect is not related to the Kazakh language. Significant differences from South Azerbaijani in phonology, lexicon, morphology, syntax, and loanwords. *Lg Use:* National language. In the republics of the former USSR, 98% of the ethnic group speak Azerbaijani as first language. 8,000,000 second-language speakers. Used in publications. Everyone is familiar with the standardized written and spoken forms. Taught as a second language in Russian language schools. *Lg Dev:* Literacy rate in second language: High. Roman script official, but Cyrillic script widely used; Cyrillic script in Armenia. Radio programs. TV. Dictionary. Grammar. Bible: 1891. *Other:* North and South Azerbaijani are spoken by one ethnic group. Each language group is reluctant to accept the written form of the other. Muslim (Shi'a and Sunni).

Budukh (Budux, Budug, Bukukhi, Budugi) [bdk] 1,000 (1990). Ethnic population: 1,000 (1990 A. E. Kibrik). Quba Region. *Class:* North Caucasian, East Caucasian, Lezgic, Nuclear Lezgic, South Lezgic. *Dialects:* Budukh, Yerguych. *Lg Use:* All domains. 30% to 50% of children speak Budukh. Positive language attitude. Azerbaijani is used as the literary language. *Other:* Not a written language. Muslim (Sunni).

Judeo-Tat (Judeo-Tatic, Jewish Tat, Bik, Dzhuhuric, Juwri, Juhuri) [jdt] 24,000 in Azerbaijan (1989 census). Northeast, especially Quba Region Baku, and Derbent (Russia). None in Iran. *Lg Use:* Tats holding to the Gregorian (Armenian) church used to live in Madrasa village until the late 1980s, and spoke a variety of Tat similar to Judeo-Tat. They may have gone to Armenia or Russia. *Other:* Jewish. See main entry under Israel.

Khalaj [kjf] *Other:* Pronounced with 2 short or front a's. Different from Turkic Khalaj in Iran. See main entry under Iran.

Khinalugh (Khinalug, Xinalug, Khinalugi) [kjj] 1,500. Quba. *Class:* North Caucasian, East Caucasian, Khinalugh. *Dialects:* The most divergent Lezgian language. *Lg Use:* All domains. 30% to 50% of children speak Khinalugh. Positive language attitude. Azerbaijani is used as the literary language. *Other:* Not a written language. Muslim.

Kryts (Kryz, Kryc, Kryzy, Katsy, Dzek, Dzhek, Dzheki) [kry] 6,000 (1975 SIL). Quba. *Class:* North Caucasian, East Caucasian, Lezgic, Nuclear Lezgic, South Lezgic. *Dialects:* Kryts, Dzhek, Xaput (Khaput), Yerguydzh, Alyk. Dialects are quite distinct; perhaps separate languages. *Lg Use:* All domains. 30% to 50% of children speak Kryts. Positive language attitude. Azerbaijani is used as the literary language. *Other:* Not a written language. Muslim (Sunni).

Kurdish, Northern (Kurmanji, Kurmancî, Kurdî) [kmr] 20,000 in Azerbaijan (1989 census). Originally around Basargechar, Minkend, Kubatly, Zangelan, especially

Kelbajar and Lachin. Many have been displaced. *Other:* Muslim (Sunni). See main entry under Turkey (Asia).

Lezgi (Lezgian, Lezghi, Lezgin, Kiurinty) [lez] 171,400 in Azerbaijan (1996). Near the northeastern border with Russia and on the southern slopes of the main Caucasus chain. *Dialect:* Quba. *Lg Use:* Speakers also use Azerbaijani. *Other:* Muslim. See main entry under Russia (Europe).

Talysh (Talish, Talesh, Talyshi) [tly] 800,000 in Azerbaijan (1996). Population total all countries: 912,000. Along the Caspian coast south of the Viliazh-Chai River. There may be speakers in Central Asia and Siberia. Also spoken in Iran. *Class:* Indo-European, Indo-Iranian, Iranian, Western, Northwestern, Talysh. *Dialects:* Astara, Lenkoran, Lerik, Massali. Northern Talyshi is in Azerbaijan and Iran. Dialects in Azerbaijan are close. Dialects in Iran may be separate languages. Close to Harzani. Agajani and Sasani may be dialects. *Lg Use:* Azerbaijani is used as literary language. Speakers also use Azerbaijani. *Lg Dev:* Taught in primary schools. Arabic script. Newspapers. Dictionary. Grammar. *Other:* Muslim (Shi'a and Sunni).

Tat, Muslim (Mussulman Tati, Muslim Tat, Tati) [ttt] 18,000 in Azerbaijan (1989 census). Population total all countries: 26,000. Ethnic population: 22,041 in Azerbaijan (1990 A. E. Kibrik). It may be declining around Baku, but still widely used in the mountainous area around Qonaqkend. Also spoken in Iran, Russia (Europe). *Class:* Indo-European, Indo-Iranian, Iranian, Western, Southwestern, Tat. *Dialects:* Quba, Devechi, Qonaqkend, Qyzyl Qazma, Aruskush-Daqqushchu (Khyzy), Absheron, Balakhani, Surakhani, Lahyj, Malham. Difficult intelligibility of Judeo-Tat. Close to Farsi. It has vowel harmony like Azerbaijani. Balakhani are recent exiles from Iran, and their language is very close to Farsi. Lahyj may be a separate language. *Lg Use:* Used in the home. A few children speak Tat. Positive language attitude. Lahyi use Azerbaijani as a literary language. *Lg Dev:* Taught in primary schools. Dictionary. Grammar. *Other:* Different from Takestani of Iran. Muslim (Shi'a).

Tsakhur (Sakhur, Tsaxur, Tsakhury, Caxur) [tkr] 13,000 in Azerbaijan (1989 census). Population total all countries: 20,073. Ethnic population: 13,318 in Azerbaijan (1989 census). Northwest. Also spoken in Russia (Europe), Uzbekistan. *Class:* North Caucasian, East Caucasian, Lezgic, Nuclear Lezgic, West Lezgic. *Other:* Muslim.

Udi (Udin, Uti) [udi] 4,200 in Azerbaijan (1995). Population total all countries: 5,720. Qabala, Nic, and Mirzabeyli villages, and Oghuz, Oghuz town. Most Udi are reported to have left Oghuz. Also spoken in Georgia, Russia (Asia), Turkmenistan. *Class:* North Caucasian, East Caucasian, Lezgic, Udi. *Dialects:* Oghuz (Vartashen), Nidzh (Nij, Nic, Nizh), Oktomberi. Oktomberi is more different from Nic Udi than Oghuz Udi is. One of the most divergent of the Lesgian languages. *Lg Use:* Up to 1954 schooling was in Azerbaijani. New primers and folk tales have been prepared for publication. Udi is used for intragroup communication. 30% to 50% of children speak Udi. Russian and sometimes Azerbaijani used as literary languages; in some areas they use Armenian or Georgian. In Nic the children attend Russian language schools. *Lg Dev:* Cyrillic script. Dictionary. Grammar. Bible portions: 1902. *Other:* Plains. Deciduous forest. Peasant agriculturalists: horticulture; animal husbandry: hogs, cattle. Christian.

Bahrain

State of Bahrain. Dawlat al-Bahrayn. 677,886. National or official language: Standard Arabic. Literacy rate: 49% to 75%. Also includes Kerinci (25,000), Korean (1,200), Malayalam (23,600), Northern Kurdish, Tamil (18,000),

Telugu (13,000), Urdu (28,789), Western Farsi (48,000), people from the Philippines (22,000). Information mainly from T. M. Johnstone 1967; W. Fischer and O. Jastrow 1980; M. Al-Tajir 1982; C. Holes 1990. Blind population: 62. Deaf population: 35,529. The number of languages listed for Bahrain is 3. Of those, all are living languages.

Arabic, Baharna Spoken (Bahraini Shi'ite Arabic, Baharnah, Baharna) [abv] 300,000 in Bahrain (1995). Population total all countries: 310,000. Also spoken in Oman. *Class:* Afro-Asiatic, Semitic, Central, South, Arabic. *Lg Use:* Negative language attitude. Speakers also use Gulf Spoken Arabic. *Other:* Muslim (Shi'a).

Arabic, Gulf Spoken (Khaliji, Gulf Arabic) [afb] 100,000 in Bahrain (1995). *Dialect:* Bahraini Gulf Arabic. *Other:* Muslim (Sunni). See main entry under Iraq.

Arabic, Standard (Modern Literary Arabic, Fasih, High Arabic) [arb] Middle East, North Africa. *Lg Use:* National language. Used for education, official purposes. See main entry under Saudi Arabia.

Bangladesh

People's Republic of Bangladesh. GaNa Prajãtantrï Bangladesh. Formerly East Pakistan. 141,340,476. Population density 2.026 per square mile. 531,000 speakers of Tibeto-Burman languages, 125,000 speakers of Austro-Asiatic languages (1991 J. Matisoff). National or official language: Bengali. Literacy rate: 24% to 25%. Also includes Eastern Panjabi (23,674), Gujarati, Hindi (346,000), Oriya (32,534), Sadri (200,000), Sauria Paharia (12,000), Urdu (600,000). Information mainly from B. Comrie 1987; J. Matisoff et al. 1996. Blind population: 1,085. Deaf population: 7,596,511. Deaf institutions: 14. The number of languages listed for Bangladesh is 39. Of those, all are living languages. See maps beginning on page 780.

Arakanese (Marama, "Maghi," "Mogh," "Magh," Mash, Marma) [mhv] 200,000 in Bangladesh (2001 Johnstone and Mandryk). Population includes 150,000 Marmar, 35,000 Rakhain (SIL 2002). Southeast, Chittagong Hills area. Marma is in the hills and Rakhine along the coast. *Dialects:* Marma (Morma), Rakhine (Rakhain, Yakhain). *Lg Use:* Educated speakers know and read standard Burmese. Many men can speak Bengali. *Lg Dev:* Literacy rate in first language: 80%. Literacy rate in second language: 60% Rakhain; 30% Marmar. Literacy rate in Arakanese decreasing with Bengali emphasis. *Other:* People came to Bangladesh over a period of time. The Marma and Rakhine are ethnic Arakanese Buddhists who speak a dialect of Arakanese Burmese, but were born in southeastern Bangladesh. Tropical forest. Agriculturalists. Buddhist, Muslim, Christian. See main entry under Myanmar.

Assamese (Asambe, Asami) [asm] See main entry under India.

Bengali (Banga-Bhasa, Bangala, Bangla) [ben] 100,000,000 in Bangladesh (1994 UBS). 211,000,000 including second-language speakers (1999 WA). Population total all countries: 171,070,202. Western. Also spoken in India, Malawi, Nepal, Saudi Arabia, Singapore, United Arab Emirates, United Kingdom, USA. *Class:* Indo-European, Indo-Iranian, Indo-Aryan, Eastern zone, Bengali-Assamese. *Dialects:* Languages or dialects in the Bengali group according to Grierson: Central (Standard) Bengali, Western Bengali (Kharia Thar, Mal Paharia, Saraki), Southwestern Bengali, Northern Bengali (Koch, Siripuria), Rajbanshi, Bahe, Eastern Bengali (East Central, including Sylhetti), Haijong, Southeastern Bengali (Chakma), Ganda, Vanga, Chittagonian (possible dialect of Southeastern Bengali). *Lg Use:* Official language.

Lg Dev: Taught in primary schools. Bengali script. Bible: 1809–2000. *Other:* Muslim.

Bishnupriya (Bishnupuriya, Bisna Puriya, Bishnupria Manipuri) [bpy] 40,000 in Bangladesh (2003). *Dialects:* Rajar Gang, Madoi Gang. *Lg Use:* Bengali used with Meitei speakers. See main entry under India.

Burmese (Bama, Bamachaka, Myen) [mya] 300,000 in Bangladesh (2001 Johnstone and Mandryk). Area bordering Myanmar. *Dialect:* Bomang. *Other:* Buddhist. See main entry under Myanmar.

Chak (Sak) [ckh] 5,500 in Bangladesh (2002). Most in Arakan Blue Mountains, Baishari, Banderbon, South, Nrrkhinsorithan, Bishar Chokpra. *Lg Use:* Most Chak living near Banderbon can speak Marma (dialect of Arakanese). *Lg Dev:* Literacy rate in second language: 25% Bengali. *Other:* Distinct from Chakma. Ancient script supposed to exist but not now known. Tropical forest. Agriculturalists. Traditional religion. See main entry under Myanmar.

Chakma (Takam) [ccp] 312,207 in Bangladesh (2000 WCD). Population total all countries: 612,207. Southeast, Chittagong Hills area, and Chittagong City. Also spoken in India. *Class:* Indo-European, Indo-Iranian, Indo-Aryan, Eastern zone, Bengali-Assamese. *Dialects:* 6 dialects. Chakma of India understood with difficulty. *Lg Use:* Educated speakers know Bengali. Many men can speak Bengali. *Lg Dev:* Literacy rate in first language: 2.5%. Literacy rate in second language: 70%. Roman, Bengali scripts. NT: 1926–1991. *Other:* Hills. Tropical forest. Agriculturalists: paddy rice; fishermen. Buddhist, Christian.

Chin, Asho (Sho, Shoa, Khyang, Khyeng, Qin) [csh] 1,422 in Bangladesh (1981 census). Chittagong Hills. *Dialects:* Chittagong, Lemyo, Minbu, Saingbaun, Sandoway, Thayetmyo. *Other:* Tropical forest. Agriculturalists. See main entry under Myanmar.

Chin, Bawm (Bawn, Bawng, Bom, Bawm) [bgr] 5,773 in Bangladesh (1981 census). Chittagong Hills. *Other:* Tropical forest. Agriculturalists. See main entry under India.

Chin, Falam (Hallam Chin, Halam, Fallam, Falam) [flm] *Dialects:* Chorei, Zanniat. See main entry under Myanmar.

Chin, Haka (Haka, Baungshe, Lai) [cnh] 1,264 in Bangladesh (2000 WCD). *Dialects:* Klangklang (Thlantlang), Zokhua, Shonshe. *Other:* Shonshe may be a separate language. See main entry under Myanmar.

Chin, Khumi (Khumi, Khami, Kami, Kumi, Khweymi, Khuni) [cnk] 1,188 in Bangladesh (1981 census). *Dialects:* Khimi, Yindi (Yindu), Khami, Ngala. *Other:* Khami and Ngala may be separate languages. Tropical forest. Agriculturalists. See main entry under Myanmar.

Chittagonian (Chittagonian Bengali) [cit] 14,000,000 in Bangladesh (1998 H. Ebersole). Chittagong Region. Also spoken in Myanmar. *Class:* Indo-European, Indo-Iranian, Indo-Aryan, Eastern zone, Bengali-Assamese. *Dialect:* Rohinga (Akyab). Not inherently intelligible with Bengali, although considered to be a nonstandard Bengali dialect. A continuum of dialects from north to south, with a larger religious distinction between Muslim and others. An ethnic Bengali Muslim who speaks the Muslim variety of Chittagonian Bengali and was born in Arakan state, Myanmar, is called a 'Rohinga'. The dialect is intelligible to those born in southeastern Bangladesh. *Lg Use:* Used for religious instruction in village mosques. Village women without access to TV do not understand Bengali. Many educated people understand some Bengali, but are not comfortable using it. All education is in Standard Bengali. *Lg Dev:* Lower literacy rate than most of the country. TV. *Other:* Muslim, Hindu, Christian.

Darlong (Dalong) [dln] 9,000 in Bangladesh. Population total all countries: 15,000. Also spoken in India. *Class:*

Sino-Tibetan, Tibeto-Burman, Kuki-Chin-Naga, Kuki-Chin, Central. *Dialects:* Also reported to be related to Tipura. *Lg Dev:* Roman script in India. NT: 1995.

Garo (Garrow, Mande) [grt] 102,000 in Bangladesh (1993). Northeastern, Mymensingh plains, Tangail Shripur, Jamelpur, Netrakara, Sylhet, Dhaka. *Dialects:* Abeng, Achik. *Lg Use:* All ages. Parents want their children to read and write Garo. *Lg Dev:* Literacy rate in second language: 90% in Bengali. *Other:* They speak in Abeng but write in Achik. See main entry under India.

Hajong (Haijong) [haj] See main entry under India.

Ho (Lanka Kol) [hoc] *Other:* Distinct from Ho (Hani) of Myanmar, China, Viet Nam, Laos. See main entry under India.

Indian Sign Language [ins] *Other:* The Indian manual English system is hardly understandable to American Signed English. See main entry under India.

Khasi (Kahasi, Khasiyas, Khuchia, Kyi, Cossyah, Khassee, Khasie) [kha] Very few speakers of standard Khasi. Moulvibazar District, near Fenchuganj, Madhabkunda, Barlekha, Goalbari, Fultala, Alinagar, Islampur, Khajori, Rashidpur, Satgoan, Kamalganj, and Alinagar; Sylhet District, near Jaflong, Tamabil, Jaintiapur and north of Raipur; Hobiganj District. *Dialects:* Khasi (Cherrapunji), Lyngngam (Lngngam). *Lg Use:* Speakers also use Bengali. See main entry under India.

Koch (Koc, Kocch, Koce, Kochboli, Konch) [kdq] *Dialects:* Banai, Harigaya, Satpariya, Tintekiya, Wanang. See main entry under India.

Kok Borok (Tripuri, Tripura, Tipura, Mrung, Usipi) [trp] 100,000 in Bangladesh (2001). *Dialects:* Jamatia, Noatia, Riang (Tipra), Halam, Debbarma. See main entry under India.

Kurux (Kurukh, Uraon, Oraoan) [kru] See main entry under India.

Megam (Migam) [mef] 6,872 (2000 WCD). Northeastern Bangladesh. *Class:* Sino-Tibetan, Tibeto-Burman, Jingpho-Konyak-Bodo, Konyak-Bodo-Garo, Bodo-Garo, Garo. *Dialects:* Called a dialect of Garo, but may be a separate language.

Meitei (Meithei, Meithe, Mitei, Mithe, Meiteiron, Manipuri, Kathe, Kathi, Ponna) [mni] 15,000 in Bangladesh (2003). Sylhet. *Lg Dev:* Literacy rate in first language: 30%. *Other:* Hindu, traditional religion, Muslim, Christian. See main entry under India.

Mizo (Lusai, Lushai, Lushei, Sailau, Hualngo, Whelngo, Lei) [lus] 1,041 in Bangladesh (1981 census). Mizo Hills, Chittagong, Sylhet. *Dialects:* Ralte, Dulien, Ngente, Mizo, Le. *Lg Use:* Vigorous. *Other:* Tropical forest. Agriculturalists. Christian. See main entry under India.

Mru (Murung, Mrung, Maru, Niopreng) [mro] 80,000 in Bangladesh (2002 SIL). Population total all countries: 81,231. Southeastern, Chittagong Hills; 200 villages. Also spoken in India. *Class:* Sino-Tibetan, Tibeto-Burman, Mru. *Dialects:* Lexical similarity 13% with Mro Chin. *Lg Dev:* Literacy rate in second language: 10%. 70% of young people know orthography. NT: 1994. *Other:* Ethnically related to the Khumi. Divided into 5 linguistically distinct groups: the Anok and Tshungma in the north, Domrong in the lowlands north of the Matamuri, Dopreng and Rumma in the far south and into Arakan (Brauns and Loffler 1990). A distinctive script under development. SOV. Tropical forest. Agriculturalists. Buddhist, syncretism with traditional religion.

Mundari (Munda, Mandari, Munari, Horo, Mondari, Colh) [muw] *Dialects:* Hasada', Latar, Naguri, Kera'. See main entry under India.

Pankhu (Pankho, Panko, Pangkhu) [pkh] 2,278 in Bangladesh (1981 census). Population total all countries: 2,512. Bandarban, Rangamati, Kagrachori, and some in Malumghat and Chittagong. Also spoken in India,

Myanmar. *Class:* Sino-Tibetan, Tibeto-Burman, Kuki-Chin-Naga, Kuki-Chin, Central. *Lg Use:* Education for the few in school is in Bengali and English. *Lg Dev:* Roman and Devanagari scripts in India. *Other:* Tropical forest. Agriculturalists.

Pnar [pbv] 4,000 in Bangladesh (2002). Along the India border in the northeast; Sylhet Division, Sylhet District, near Jaflong, Tamabil, Jaintiapur, and north of Raipur; Moulavi Bazar District, near Fenchuganj, Madhabkunda, Barlekha, Goalbari, Fultala, Alinagar, Islampur, Khajori, Rashidpur, Satgoan, Kamalganj. *Lg Use:* Most speakers have high proficiency in War. See main entry under India.

Rajbanshi (Rajbangsi, Rajbansi, Tajpuri) [rjb] 12,916 in Bangladesh (2000). Northwest regions of Bangladesh. *Dialect:* Bahe. See main entry under India.

Riang (Reang, Kau Bru) [ria] 1,011 in Bangladesh (2000). Chittagong Hills. *Other:* Not the same as Riang of Myanmar, a Mon Khmer language. See main entry under India.

Sadri, Oraon [sdr] 165,683 (2000 WCD). Throughout Rajshahi Division; in Chittagong Division, Moulvibazar and Hobigani districts; and Khulna Division, Jhenaidah District (Jhenaidah Thana, Moheshpur Thana), Kushtia District (Mirpur Thana), Magura District (Magura Thana). *Class:* Indo-European, Indo-Iranian, Indo-Aryan, Eastern zone, Bihari. *Dialects:* Borail Sadri, Nurpur Sadri, Uchai Sadri, Mokkan Tila Sadri. The dialects listed may need separate literature. Inherent intelligibility of 7 Sadri varieties on Borail ranges from 70% to 93%; of 8 varieties on Nurpur from 78% to 94%. Lexical similarity of 14 Sadri varieties with Borail Sadri ranges from 88% to 97%. *Lg Use:* Vigorous but some educated people do not use Oraon with their children. Bangladesh Oraon Foundation was set up to make a commitment to language revitalization. Speakers have low proficiency in Bengali. *Lg Dev:* Literacy rate in second language: 30%. NT: 2003. *Other:* The Oraon people came from India over 100 years ago. Sometime in the past some Oraon shifted from Kurukh, a Dravidian language, to Sadri, which is Indo-Aryan. Some Oraon people still speak Kurukh. Agriculturalists. Traditional religion, Hindu.

Santali (Hor, Satar, Santhali, Sandal, Sangtal, Santal, Har, Sonthal) [sat] 157,000 in Bangladesh (2001 Johnstone and Mandryk). Ethnic population: 42,698. *Dialects:* Karmali (Khole), Kamari-Santali, Lohari-Santali, Paharia, Mahali (Mahle) Manjhi. *Lg Use:* Positive language attitude. *Lg Dev:* Literacy rate in first language: 50%. See main entry under India.

Shendu (Khyen, Khyeng, Khieng, Shandu, Sandu) [shl] 1,000 in Bangladesh (1980 UBS). Chittagong Hills. Also spoken in India. *Class:* Sino-Tibetan, Tibeto-Burman, Kuki-Chin-Naga, Kuki-Chin, Southern, Sho. *Dialects:* Close to Asho, Khyang, Thayetmo, Minbu, Chinbon, Lemyo, Mara Chin (Lakher).

Sylheti (Sylhetti, Sylhetti Bangla, Sileti, Siloti, Syloti, Syloty) [syl] 7,000,000 in Bangladesh. Population total all countries: 10,300,000. Ethnic population: 8,000,000 or more. District of Sylhet, Sunamgani, Habigani, Moulvibazar. Sylhet is about 100 miles north of Dacca. Also spoken in Australia, Canada, India, Italy, Malaysia, Myanmar, Singapore, United Kingdom, USA. *Class:* Indo-European, Indo-Iranian, Indo-Aryan, Eastern zone, Bengali-Assamese. *Dialects:* Close to Bengali, Assamese. Lexical similarity 70% with Bengali. *Lg Use:* 1,500,000 second-language speakers. All ages. Speakers also use Bengali, primarily men. Bengali is used for education and the media. *Lg Dev:* Literacy rate in second language: 10%. Educated speakers can read Bengali. Few women are educated. Bengali and Roman scripts. Bible portions: 1993. *Other:* Muslim, Hindu.

Tangchangya (Tanchangya) [tnv] 17,695 (1981 census). Chittagong Hills. *Class:* Indo-European, Indo-Iranian, Indo-Aryan, Eastern zone, Bengali-Assamese. *Dialects:* Close to Chakma. *Other:* Tropical forest. Agriculturalists.

Tippera (Tippera-Bengali, Tipperah, Tipra, Tipura, Triperah, Tippurah, Tripura) [tpe] 100,000 (2001 Johnstone and Mandryk). Chittagong Hills. *Class:* Indo-European, Indo-Iranian, Indo-Aryan, Unclassified. *Dialects:* 36 dialects. *Lg Use:* Many men can speak Bengali. *Lg Dev:* NT: 1995. *Other:* Tropical forest. Agriculturalists. Traditional religion, syncretism with Hindu.

Usui (Unshoi, Unsuiy, Ushoi) [usi] 4,010 (1981 census). Chittagong Hills. *Class:* Indo-European, Indo-Iranian, Indo-Aryan, Unclassified. *Dialects:* Close to Tippera. *Other:* Tropical forest. Agriculturalists. Hindu, traditional religion.

War (Amwi, Waar) [aml] 16,000 in Bangladesh (2003 SIL). Population total all countries: 28,000. Along the India border in the northeast; Sylhet Division, Sylhet District, near Jaflong, Tamabil, Jaintiapur, and north of Raipur; Moulavi Bazar District, near Fenchuganj, Madhabkunda, Barlekha, Goalbari, Fultala, Alinagar, Islampur, Khajori, Rashidpur, Satgoan, Kamalganj, Alinagar. Also spoken in India. *Class:* Austro-Asiatic, Mon-Khmer, Northern Mon-Khmer, Khasian. *Dialects:* War-Jaintia, War-Khasi. Probably distinct from War, a dialect of Khasi in India. 75% intelligibility of Khasi by War-Jaintia. Jirang is similar, and may be a dialect. Lexical similarity 70% to 75% between War-Jaintia and War-Khasi; War-Jaintia dialect 41% to 45% with Pnar (from scant data), 35% with standard Khasi. *Lg Use:* Speakers also use Khasi, Bengali, Sylheti, or English. *Lg Dev:* Literacy rate in second language: 25% Bengali; many are literate in standard Khasi. Grammar. *Other:* Hills. Christian.

Bhutan

Kingdom of Bhutan, Druk-Yul. 2,185,569. National or official language: Dzongkha. Literacy rate: 15% to 18%. Also includes Assamese (40,000), Eastern Magar, Eastern Tamang, Limbu, Santali, Sherpa, Western Gurung. Information mainly from V. H. Coelho 1967; J. C. White 1971; N. Singh 1972; J. Matisoff 1991; Matisoff et al. 1996; G. Van Driem 1993; E. Andvic 1993. Deaf population: 105,435. The number of languages listed for Bhutan is 24. Of those, all are living languages.

Adap [adp] South central, between Damphu and Shemgang, Ada village, Wangdue Phodrang District. *Class:* Sino-Tibetan, Tibeto-Burman, Himalayish, Tibeto-Kanauri, Tibetic, Tibetan, Southern. *Dialects:* Lexical similarity 77% with Dzongkha, 62% to 65% with Bumthangkha, 41% with Tshangla. *Other:* May be the same as Tapadamteng (see Dzongkha).

Brokkat (Brokskad, Jokay) [bro] 300 (1993 Van Driem). Dur in central Bumthang District. *Class:* Sino-Tibetan, Tibeto-Burman, Himalayish, Tibeto-Kanauri, Tibetic, Tibetan, Southern. *Other:* A different language from Brokpake (1993 Van Driem).

Brokpake (Mira Sagtengpa, Dakpa, Brokpa, Dap, Mera Sagtengpa, Sagtengpa, Meragsagstengkha, Jobikha, Drokpakay, Damilo) [sgt] 5,000 (1993 Van Driem). Population includes 2,000 in and around Mera, 3,000 in and around Sagteng. Sakteng Valley east of Trashigang District, mainly in Merak and Sakteng villages. *Class:* Sino-Tibetan, Tibeto-Burman, Himalayish, Tibeto-Kanauri, Tibetic, Tibetan, Southern. *Dialects:* Related to Monpa of Tawang in Arunachal Pradesh, India. *Other:* Speakers are called 'Dakpa'. 3,000 meters. Agriculturalists: corn, barley, beets; butter producers. Buddhist.

Bumthangkha (Bumtanp, Bumthapkha, Bumtang, Kebumtamp, Bhumtam, Bumthang, Bumtangkha) [kjz] 30,000 (1993 Van Driem). Central. Bumthang and in the whole of central Bhutan. Mangdikha is in Mangdi District around Tongsa. Tsamangkha is on the east northeast border of Kurto. Salabekha is in the Yangtse District and Tawang and southeast Tibet. *Class:* Sino-Tibetan, Tibeto-Burman, Himalayish, Tibeto-Kanauri, Tibetic, Tibetan, Eastern. *Dialects:* Ura, Tang, Chogor, Chunmat. Khengkha and Bumthangkha are reported by one source to be intelligible with each other. Cuona Monpa is the same as, or closely related to, Bumthangkha (see Moinba in India and China). Lexical similarity 92% with Khengkha. 47% to 52% with Dzongkha, 62% to 65% with Adap, 40% to 50% with Sharchagpakha. *Lg Dev:* Uchen script. Bible portions: 1938. *Other:* Gungdekha is an archaic language today reluctantly joined politically to the Khen or Bhumtam group. Buddhist.

Chalikha (Chali, Tshali, Chalipkha, Tshalingpa) [tgf] 1,000 (1993 Van Driem). In and around Chali area, Mongar District, east Bhutan, north of Monggar. *Class:* Sino-Tibetan, Tibeto-Burman, Himalayish, Tibeto-Kanauri, Tibetic, Tibetan, Eastern. *Dialects:* Related to Bumthangkha and Kurtopakha.

Chocangacakha (Maphekha, Rtsamangpa'ikha, Tsagkaglingpa'ikha, Kursmadkha) [cgk] 20,000 (1993 Van Driem). East of Dzongkha, in lower areas of Monggar District, Tsamang and Tsakaling villages, and Lhuntsi District, Kurmet village. *Class:* Sino-Tibetan, Tibeto-Burman, Himalayish, Tibeto-Kanauri, Tibetic, Tibetan, Southern. *Dialects:* Related to Dzongkha.

Dakpakha [dka] 1,000 (1993 Van Driem). Near Brokpake. *Class:* Sino-Tibetan, Tibeto-Burman, Himalayish, Tibeto-Kanauri, Tibetic, Tibetan, Eastern. *Dialects:* May be a dialect of Brokpake. Has been influenced by Dzalakha, and Brokpake has not.

Dzalakha (Dzalamat, Yangtsebikha) [dzl] 15,000 (1993 Van Driem). Northeastern in Lhüntsi, Kurto District. *Class:* Sino-Tibetan, Tibeto-Burman, Himalayish, Tibeto-Kanauri, Unclassified. *Dialect:* Khomakha.

Dzongkha (Drukke, Drukha, Dukpa, Bhutanese, Jonkha, Bhotia of Bhutan, Bhotia of Dukpa, Zongkhar, Rdzongkha) [dzo] 130,000 in Bhutan (2003). Population total all countries: 133,009. Ha, Paru, Punakha districts. Also spoken in India, Nepal. *Class:* Sino-Tibetan, Tibeto-Burman, Himalayish, Tibeto-Kanauri, Tibetic, Tibetan, Southern. *Dialects:* Wang-The (Thimphu-Punakha), Ha, Northern Thimphu. As different from Lhasa Tibetan as Nepali is from Hindi. Partially intelligible with Sikkimese (Drenjoke). Names listed as dialects may be separate languages. Lexical similarity 48% with Sharchagpakha, 47% to 52% with Kebumtamp, 77% with Adap. *Lg Use:* Official language. *Lg Dev:* Literacy rate in first language: 54%. Literacy rate in second language: below 5%. Common school language. Uchen script. Grammar. Bible portions: 1970. *Other:* Buddhist.

Gongduk (Gongdubikha) [goe] 2,000 (1993 Van Driem). Eastern Bhutan, Mongar District, Gongdu Gewog, villages of Dagsa, Damkhar, Pangthang, Pam, Yangbari, Bala. *Class:* Sino-Tibetan, Tibeto-Burman, Himalayish, Tibeto-Kanauri, Tibetic, Tibetan. *Other:* Retain the complex verbal agreement system of Proto-Tibeto-Burman. Said to belong to one of the ancient populations of Bhutan.

Khengkha (Khenkha, Khen, Keng, Ken, Kyengkha, Kenkha) [xkf] 40,000 (1993 Van Driem). 60% monolinguals. Zhemgang, Mongar districts; near Bumthangkha. Middle dialect in northwest part of Zhemgang. Upper dialect is northeast of Zhemgang; also Mongar District. Lower Kheng is in southern Zhemgang. *Class:* Sino-Tibetan, Tibeto-Burman, Himalayish, Tibeto-Kanauri, Tibetic, Tibetan, Eastern. *Dialects:* Middle Kheng, Upper Kheng, Lower Kheng. Bumthangkha is closest related language. Intelligibility of Bumthangkha not sufficient for complex discourse. Intelligibility of Kurtokha only with difficulty. Lexical similarity 75% to 85% with Bumthangkha, 70% with Kurtokha and Nyengkha, 65% with Adap, 34% with Dzongkha, 40% with Sharchagpakha, and Chacangacakha, 28% with Tibetan, 22% with Tshangla, 75% to 100% between dialects. *Lg Use:* Vigorous. 15,000 second-language speakers. Used in the home, commerce, local politics, traditional religion domains, but not allowed in school. All ages. Negative attitude toward Gonphu village speaking style. Lower Kheng considered the most backward. Middle Kheng is the most prestigious. Negative towards Nepali. English spoken by educated young people (10%). Nepali spoken by those who live near the road (20%), Dzongkha spoken well only by educated and some elder males. Bumthangkha, Kurtokha, Nyengkha spoken by those who travel or have intermarried. Tshangla spoken by those who travel on eastern side of Kheng area. *Lg Dev:* Literacy rate in second language: 20% in Dzongkha. Uchen script. *Other:* Middle Kheng region is economically most strong and has the most development. Lower Kheng is the least developed. SOV; postpositions; genitives, relatives before noun heads, articles, adjective after noun heads; maximum prefixes 1; maximum suffixes 4; affixes indicate case; ergative; passives; causatives; some comparatives; CCVC; tonal. Mountain slope. Forest. 100 to 2,500 meters. Swidden agriculturalists. Buddhist.

Kurtokha (Gurtü, Kurtopakha, Kürthöpka, Kurteopkha, Kurthopkha, Kurtobikha) [xkz] 10,000 (1993 Van Driem). Northeastern, especially in Kurto. The dialect around Tangmachu is more divergent. *Class:* Sino-Tibetan, Tibeto-Burman, Himalayish, Tibeto-Kanauri, Tibetic, Tibetan, Eastern. *Dialects:* Related to Bumthangkha and Khengkha.

Lakha (Tshangkha) [lkh] 8,000 (1993 Van Driem). *Class:* Sino-Tibetan, Tibeto-Burman, Himalayish, Tibeto-Kanauri, Tibetic, Tibetan, Southern. *Other:* Mountain slope.

Layakha [lya] 1,100 (2003). Northern Punakha District, around Laya; Gasa District; Thimphu District, Lingzhi gewog. *Class:* Sino-Tibetan, Tibeto-Burman, Himalayish, Tibeto-Kanauri, Tibetic, Tibetan, Southern. *Dialects:* Close to Dzongkha, but many divergent grammatical features significantly limit intelligibility between them. Spoken by Layabs, alpine yakherds in northern Bhutan, and Lingzhibs in Western Bhutan.

Lepcha (Lapcha, Rong, Rongke, Rongpa, Nünpa) [lep] 35,000 in Bhutan (Johnstone and Mandryk). Lower valleys in the west and south. *Dialects:* Ilammu, Tamsangmu, Rengjongmu. *Other:* Agriculturalists; pastoralists. Traditional religion, Buddhist (Lamaist). See main entry under India.

Lhokpu (Lhobikha, Taba-Damey-Bikha) [lhp] 2,500 (1993 Van Driem). South western Bhutan, between Samtsi and Phuntsoling in Samtsi District, in 2 villages of Taba and Damtey. Also in Loto Kuchu, Sanglong, Sataka, and Lotu villages. *Class:* Sino-Tibetan, Tibeto-Burman, Himalayish, Tibeto-Kanauri, Tibetic, Tibetan. *Other:* Said to be one of the ancient populations of Bhutan.

Lunanakha [luk] 700 (1998). North, northeastern quadrant of Punakha District, community of Lunana, on the Pho Chhu River north from Punakha, on the right fork about halfway up the valley. *Class:* Sino-Tibetan, Tibeto-Burman, Himalayish, Tibeto-Kanauri, Tibetic, Tibetan, Southern. *Dialects:* Close to Dzongkha, but many divergent grammatical features limit intelligibility between them. *Other:* Speakers are called 'Lunape'. They often take their herds over to Gasa District, north from Punakha up the Mo Chhu River. Alpine yak herdsmen.

Nepali (Nepalese, Gorkhali, Gurkhali, Khaskura, Parbatiya, Eastern Pahari, Lhotshammikha) [nep] 156,000 in Bhutan (1993 Van Driem). In the foothills the entire length of Bhutan, especially south central. *Other:* People are called 'Paharia'. May be the majority language of the south. Many are Bhutanese citizens. Hindu, Christian. See main entry under Nepal.

Nupbikha [npb] Around Trongsa town. *Class:* Sino-Tibetan, Tibeto-Burman, Himalayish, Tibeto-Kanauri, Tibetic, Tibetan, Eastern. *Dialects:* Related to Bumthangkha. Has phonological similarities to Khengkha. *Lg Use:* Speakers view their language as different from Bumthangkha.

Nyenkha (Henkha, Lap, Mangsdekha) [neh] 10,000 (1993 Van Driem). Sephu Geo. The Black River passes below their villages. *Class:* Sino-Tibetan, Tibeto-Burman, Himalayish, Tibeto-Kanauri, Tibetic, Tibetan, Eastern. *Dialects:* Phobjikha, Chutobikha. Related to Bumthangkha. *Other:* Mountain slope.

Olekha (Monpa, Ole Mönpa) [ole] 1,000 (1993 Van Driem). The 2 dialects have the Black Mountains between them, central Bhutan. *Class:* Sino-Tibetan, Tibeto-Burman, Himalayish, Tibeto-Kanauri, Tibetic, Tibetan, Eastern. *Dialects:* Retained complex verbal system of Proto-Tibeto-Burman. 2 main dialects. *Lg Dev:* Grammar. *Other:* Said to be one of the ancient populations of Bhutan.

Tibetan (Bhokha) [bod] 4,673 in Bhutan (2000). *Other:* Refugees from Tibet since 1959. People of Tibetan origin are referred to as 'Bhotia'. Buddhist (Lamaist). See main entry under China (Tibetan, Central).

Tseku (Tsuku, Tzuku) [tsk] 6,255 in Bhutan (2000 WCD). *Other:* This may be an alternate name for a language variety listed under another name, or it may only be in Tibet. See main entry under China.

Tshangla (Sangla, Sharchagpakha, Sarchapkkha, Shachopkha, Shachobiikha, Sharchhopkha, Tsangla, Menba, Monpa) [tsj] 138,000 in Bhutan (1993 Van Driem). Population total all countries: 143,000. Eastern and southeastern Bhutan, especially in Tashigang and Dungsam. Also spoken in China, India. *Class:* Sino-Tibetan, Tibeto-Burman, Himalayish, Tibeto-Kanauri, Tibetic, Bodish, Tshangla. *Dialects:* Standard variety in Tashigang. Lexical similarity 40% to 50% with Bumthangkha, 48% with Dzongkha, 41% with Adap. *Lg Dev:* Literacy rate in first language: below 1%. Literacy rate in second language: below 5%. Uchen script; Tibetan script in India. Grammar. Bible portions: 2000. *Other:* A speaker is called 'Schachop' in Dzongkha, 'Sharchhokpa' (pl.). Not the same as Tsanglo (Angami Naga) of Assam, India. It may also be classified as North Assam, Monpa. SOV; numbers and adjectives follow noun head; singular-dual-plural personal pronouns; nontonal. Buddhist.

Brunei

State of Brunei Darussalam. Negara Brunei Darussalam. 365,251. National or official languages: English, Malay. Literacy rate: 85% to 95%. Also includes Korean, Nepali, people from South Asia (4,200), others from the Philippines. Information mainly from R. Needham 1954; S. Wurm and S. Hattori 1981; K. Purnama 1991; P. Martin 1991; P. Martin, C. Oxog, and G. Poedjosoedarmo 1996. The number of languages listed for Brunei is 17. Of those, all are living languages.

Belait (Balait Jati, Lemeting, Meting) [beg] 700 (1995 Martin). Scattered areas in Belait District, Kampung Kiudang, in Tutong District. *Class:* Austronesian, Malayo-Polynesian, Northwest, North Sarawakan, Berawan-Lower Baram, Lower Baram, Central, A. *Dialects:* Related to Kiput, Baram, Tinjar. Lexical similarity 54% with Tutong 2. *Lg Use:* Speakers are

shifting to Brunei. Used more among those above 19 years old. *Other:* Recognized by the government as an indigenous group. The Muslim Belait are Malay in orientation. The non-Muslims retain their Belait identity more. Heavy intermarriage with Tutong 1, Bisaya, and Chinese. Muslim.

Bisaya, Brunei (Bisayah, Bisaya Bukit, Visayak, Bekiau, Lorang Bukit, Basaya, Besaya, Bisaia, Jilama Bawang, Jilama Sungai, Southern Bisaya) [bsb] 600 (1984 Dunn). East of Tutong 1 and east to the coast, west of Seria, a few villages near the Sarawak border. *Class:* Austronesian, Malayo-Polynesian, Northwest, Sabahan, Dusunic, Bisaya, Southern. *Dialects:* Lexical similarity 78% to 79% with Sarawak Bisaya, 57% to 59% with Sabah Bisaya, and 50% with other Dusunic languages. *Other:* Recognized by the government as an indigenous group.

Brunei (Brunei-Kadaian, Orang Bukit) [kxd] 250,000 in Brunei (1984 SIL). Population total all countries: 304,000. Brunei is in the capital, Brunei-Muara District, and the coastal strip. Kedayan is in West Brunei-Muara District and Tutong District. Also spoken in Malaysia (Sabah). *Class:* Austronesian, Malayo-Polynesian, Malayic, Malayan, Local Malay. *Dialects:* Brunei Malay, Kedayan (Kadaian, Kadayan, Kadian, Kadien, Kadyan, Karayan, Kedyan, Kedien. Kerayan), Kampong Ayer. Brunei, Kadayan, and Kampong Ayer have 94% to 95% lexical similarity with each other, 80% to 82% lexical similarity with Standard Malay. *Lg Use:* The de facto national language. Vigorous. Brunei is used by those in Bandar Seri Begawan and surroundings, and by young people and educated older people from different language or dialect backgrounds. All ages. Speakers also use Malay. *Other:* Brunei and Kadayan are both recognized by the government as indigenous groups. 'Orang Bukit' is the name of the people. Kadayan: agriculturalists; Kampong Ayer: fishermen and craftsmen in Water Village. Muslim.

Chinese, Hakka (Hakka) [hak] 5,253 in Brunei (2000 WCD). 44,400 speakers of all Chinese languages (1989). See main entry under China.

Chinese, Mandarin [cmn] 9,848 in Brunei (2000 WCD). See main entry under China.

Chinese, Min Dong [cdo] 6,566 in Brunei (2000 WCD). 11.88% of ethnic Chinese. *Dialect:* Foochow. *Other:* Buddhist, Daoist, Christian. See main entry under China.

Chinese, Min Nan (Min Nan, Minnan) [nan] 12,147 in Brunei (2000 WCD). *Dialects:* Chaochow (Tiuchiu, Teochow), Hainan, Fujian (Hokkien). See main entry under China.

Chinese, Yue (Yue, Yueh, Cantonese) [yue] 5,909 in Brunei (2000 WCD). See main entry under China.

English [eng] 8,000 in Brunei. *Lg Use:* National language. Used in government, education, and by educated speakers as first or second language. See main entry under United Kingdom.

Iban (Sea Dayak) [iba] 15,000 in Brunei (1995 Martin). Rural areas of Belait and Tutong districts, and Temburong District. *Dialects:* Batang Lupar, Bugau. See main entry under Malaysia (Sarawak).

Lundayeh (Lun Bawang, Lun Daye, Brunei Murut, Southern Murut, Murut) [lnd] 300 in Brunei (1987 Langub). 7 villages in Temburong District. *Dialect:* Trusan. *Other:* Not Murutic, although sometimes called Southern Murut. 'Murut' is recognized by the government as an indigenous group. Christian (Lunbawang, Lundayeh), traditional religion. See main entry under Indonesia (Kalimantan).

Malay (Standard Malay) [mly] *Lg Use:* Official language since 1959. Used only in formal domains, like religion, government. *Lg Dev:* Taught through third grade; used in the classroom through the final year. *Other:* Muslim (Sunni). See main entry under Malaysia (Peninsular).

Melanau (Milanau, Milano, Belana'u) [mel] 200 in Brunei (1995 Martin). Around Kuala Belait town. *Dialect:* Mukah-Oya (Mukah, Muka, Oya, Oya', Oga). *Lg Use:* Speakers also use Malay. *Other:* Mukah is spoken in Brunei. Tropical forest. Agriculturalists: sago, rice, coconut, rubber; fishermen; loggers; animal husbandry: poultry, goats, water buffaloes; traders with Iban. Muslim. See main entry under Malaysia (Sarawak).

Penan, Eastern ("Punan") [pez] East of the Baram River, Apoh River District. *Dialect:* Penan Apoh. See main entry under Malaysia (Sarawak).

Penan, Western [pne] 50 in Brunei (1988 Lian). West of the Baram River. *Dialects:* Nibong (Nibon, Penan Nibong), Bok Penan (Bok), Penan Silat, Penan Gang (Gang), Penan Lusong (Lusong), Sipeng (Speng), Penan Lanying, Jelalong Penan. *Lg Use:* Speakers also use Iban. *Other:* They consider "Punan," meaning 'to quarrel' to be derogatory. Traditionalists are nomadic and seminomadic; Muslims are settled. Schools. Tropical forest. Agriculturalists; hunter-gatherers. Muslim, traditional religion. See main entry under Malaysia (Sarawak).

Tutong 1 (Dusun) [ttx] 15,000 in Brunei (1995 Martin). Population total all countries: 25,000. Central and interior Belait and Tutong districts, east of Bisaya, south of Tutong 2. Also spoken in Malaysia (Sarawak). *Class:* Austronesian, Malayo-Polynesian, Northwest, Sabahan, Dusunic, Bisaya, Southern. *Lg Use:* 72% of parents below 40 years of age use Tutong with their children. In mixed marriages, 57% of parents use Brunei Malay with children. *Other:* Distinct from Tutong 2 in Baram-Tinjar Subgroup. 'Dusun' is recognized by the government as an indigenous group. Muslim.

Tutong 2 (Tutung) [ttg] 12,000 (1996 Martin, Ozog, and Poedjosoedarmo). Around Tutong town on the coast and central Tutong District. *Class:* Austronesian, Malayo-Polynesian, Northwest, North Sarawakan, Berawan-Lower Baram, Lower Baram, Central, B. *Dialects:* Lexical similarity 54% with Belait. *Lg Use:* Used with other ethnic groups. 63% of parents below 40 years old use Tutong 2 with their children. In mixed marriages, 48% use Brunei Malay with their children. Positive language attitude. *Lg Dev:* Dictionary. *Other:* Different from Tutong 1 in Dusunic, Bisaya Group. Tutong 2 is recognized by the government as an indigenous group. Muslim.

Cambodia

State of Cambodia. Formerly Kampuchea, Khmer Republic. 13,363,421. 12,601,706 or 94.3% speakers of Austro-Asiatic languages, 235,000 or 1.76% speakers of Austronesian languages. National or official language: Central Khmer. Literacy rate: 48% to 50%. Also includes Lao (17,000), Mandarin Chinese (350,000), Vietnamese (393,121). Information mainly from F. Lebar, G. Hickey, J. Musgrave 1964; D. Thomas and R. Headley 1970; S. Wurm and S. Hattori 1981. Blind population: 40,000 (1982 WCE). Deaf population: 622,366. The number of languages listed for Cambodia is 21. Of those, all are living languages. See map on page 779.

Brao (Braou, Proue, Brou, Love, Lave, Laveh) [brb] 5,286 in Cambodia (1980 Diffloth). Northeastern Cambodia on the Laos border, Ratanakiri Province. See main entry under Laos (Lave).

Cham, Western (Cambodian Cham, Tjam, Cham, New Cham) [cja] 220,000 in Cambodia (1992 govt. figure). Population total all countries: 253,100. Near the major cities and along the Mekong. Also spoken in Australia, France, Indonesia, Libya, Malaysia, Saudi Arabia, Thailand, USA, Viet Nam, Yemen. *Class:* Austronesian, Malayo-Polynesian, Malayic, Achinese-Chamic, Chamic,

South, Coastal, Cham-Chru. *Dialects:* The language differs somewhat from Eastern Cham of central Viet Nam. *Lg Dev:* Devanagari script. *Other:* Roman script under discussion in USA and elsewhere. Muslim (Sunni).

Chong (Chawng, Shong, Xong) [cog] 5,000 in Cambodia. Population total all countries: 5,500. Thai-Cambodia border southeast of Chantaburi, Pursat Province. Also spoken in Thailand. *Class:* Austro-Asiatic, Mon-Khmer, Eastern Mon-Khmer, Pearic, Western, Chong. *Dialects:* Somray in Cambodia is a separate but related language.

English [eng] *Lg Use:* Replacing French as second language, especially in Phnom Penh. See main entry under United Kingdom.

French [fra] *Lg Use:* Still a second language for older Cambodians. See main entry under France.

Jarai (Djarai, Gia-Rai, Jorai, Cho-Rai, Chor, Mthur, Chrai, Gio-Rai) [jra] 15,000 in Cambodia (1998). Ratanakiri Province, principally the districts of Bokeo, Andons, Meas, O Yadou, along northeast border near Viet Nam. *Dialects:* Puan, Hodrung (Hdrung), Jhue, Aráp, Habau (Ho-Bau), To-Buan, Sesan, Chuty, Pleikly, Golar. *Other:* A different script is used in Cambodia and Viet Nam. See main entry under Viet Nam.

Kaco' (Kachah') [xkk] 2,000 (1992 G. Diffloth). Ratanakiri Province. *Class:* Austro-Asiatic, Mon-Khmer, Eastern Mon-Khmer, Bahnaric, Central Bahnaric. *Dialects:* Not intelligible to Tampuan speakers. *Lg Use:* Speakers are not bilingual.

Khmer, Central (Khmer, Cambodian) [khm] 12,110,065 in Cambodia (2004). Population total all countries: 13,276,639. Throughout the country. Also spoken in Canada, China, France, Laos, USA, Viet Nam. *Class:* Austro-Asiatic, Mon-Khmer, Eastern Mon-Khmer, Khmer. *Dialects:* Distinct from Northern Khmer of Thailand. *Lg Use:* Official language. 1,000,000 second-language speakers. *Lg Dev:* 35% of the population over 15 cannot read or write Khmer. Script derived from a southern Indian alphabet. First written during the period of Indian influence. Grammar. Bible: 1954–1998. *Other:* SVO.

Kraol [rka] 2,600 (1992 G. Diffloth). Kratie Province. *Class:* Austro-Asiatic, Mon-Khmer, Eastern Mon-Khmer, Bahnaric, South Bahnaric, Sre-Mnong, Mnong, Southern-Central Mnong. *Dialects:* Not intelligible to Mnong speakers. *Lg Use:* Not bilingual. *Other:* Different from the Kraol dialect of Kuy.

Kravet (Kowet, Khvek, Kavet) [krv] 3,012 (1988 govt. figure). Northeastern Cambodia. *Class:* Austro-Asiatic, Mon-Khmer, Eastern Mon-Khmer, Bahnaric, West Bahnaric, Brao-Kravet.

Kru'ng 2 (Krueng) [krr] 9,368 (1982 G. Diffloth). Northeastern, Ratanakiri Province and eastern Stung Treng. *Class:* Austro-Asiatic, Mon-Khmer, Eastern Mon-Khmer, Bahnaric, West Bahnaric, Brao-Kravet. *Dialects:* Brao, Kravet, Krung 2 in Cambodia are inherently intelligible with each other. *Lg Use:* Central Khmer was formerly known to a lesser extent than Lao for second-language use. *Other:* Different from Krung 1 dialect of Rade in Viet Nam.

Kuy (Kuay) [kdt] 15,495 in Cambodia (1989). Northeastern Cambodia, most districts of Preah Vihear, eastern Siem Reap, northern Kampong Thom, western Stung Traeng, and several areas of Kratie Province. *Dialects:* Kuy Antra, Kuy Anthua, Kuy May (Kuy Ma'ay), Kuy Mlor. *Lg Use:* Speakers also use Central Khmer. *Lg Dev:* Literacy rate in second language: 50%. *Other:* Central Khmer is used in the schools. See main entry under Thailand.

Lamam (Lmam) [lmm] 1,000 (1981 Wurm and Hattori). Near northeast corner on the Viet Nam border. *Class:* Austro-Asiatic, Mon-Khmer, Eastern Mon-Khmer, Bahnaric, Central Bahnaric. *Dialects:* Related to Bahnar, Tampuan, Alak 1.

Mnong, Central (Phong, Phnong, Bunong, Budong, Phanong) [cmo] 20,000 in Cambodia (2002). Northeastern, 80% of Mondolkiri Province, all districts. *Dialects:* Biat, Preh, Bu Nar, Bu Rung, Dih Bri, Bu Dang. *Lg Use:* Central Khmer only spoken well by a few individuals. Most have low proficiency. *Lg Dev:* Literacy rate in second language: Low. *Other:* Biat is the main dialect of Cambodian Mnong. See main entry under Viet Nam.

Pear (Por, Kompong Thom) [pcb] 1,300 (1988 govt.). Southwestern, Kompong Thom. *Class:* Austro-Asiatic, Mon-Khmer, Eastern Mon-Khmer, Pearic, Eastern.

Samre [sxm] 50 (2000 D. Bradley). Ethnic population: 200 (2000 D. Bradley). Just north of Siemreap. *Class:* Austro-Asiatic, Mon-Khmer, Eastern Mon-Khmer, Pearic, Western, Samre. *Dialects:* Related to Sa'och, Suoy, Pear.

Sa'och (Sauch, Saotch) [scq] 500 (1981 Wurm and Hattori). Southwest near Kompong Som on the coast. *Class:* Austro-Asiatic, Mon-Khmer, Eastern Mon-Khmer, Pearic, Western, Chong. *Dialects:* Related to Samre, Suoy, Pear.

Somray [smu] 2,000 (1981 Wurm and Hattori). West; north, east, and west of Phum Tasanh, and Tanyong River around Phum Pra Moi; 2 areas. *Class:* Austro-Asiatic, Mon-Khmer, Eastern Mon-Khmer, Pearic, Western, Samre. *Dialects:* Related to Chong.

Stieng, Bulo (Kajiang) [sti] 6,059 in Cambodia (2000 WCD). Eastern, Kratie Province, Snuol District, and southern Mondolkiri. *Dialects:* Budip, Bulo. *Lg Use:* Speakers also use Mnong or Khmer. *Lg Dev:* Literacy rate in second language: Low. See main entry under Viet Nam.

Suoy [syo] 200 (1981 Wurm and Hattori). Central, northwest of Phnom Penh. *Class:* Austro-Asiatic, Mon-Khmer, Eastern Mon-Khmer, Pearic, Western, Suoy. *Dialects:* Related to Sa'och, Samre, Pear.

Tampuan (Tamphuan, Tampuen, Tampuon, Kha Tampuon, Campuon, Proon, Proons) [tpu] 25,000 (1998). Northeast border area, south of Brao, west of Jarai, Central Ratanakiri Province. *Class:* Austro-Asiatic, Mon-Khmer, Eastern Mon-Khmer, Bahnaric, Central Bahnaric. *Dialects:* Related to Bahnar, Lamam, Alak 1, but geographically separated. *Lg Use:* Central Khmer is known by some individuals, Lao by some. *Other:* Exogamous clans, together with Kaco' and Jarai, that override ethnic and linguistic boundaries.

China

People's Republic of China. Zhonghua Renmin Gongheguo. 1,298,847,624. 55 official minority nationalities total 91,200,314 or 6.5% of the population (1990). Han Chinese 1,033,057,000 or 93.5% (J. Matisoff). National or official languages: Mandarin Chinese, regional languages: Daur, Kalmyk-Oirat, Lu, Peripheral Mongolian, Central Tibetan, Uyghur, Xibe, Northern Zhuang. Literacy rate: 73% to 76.5%. Also includes Central Khmer (1,000), Parsi (5,000), Portuguese (2,000), Shan, Tai Dam (10,000), Tai Dón (10,000). Information mainly from J. Dreyer 1976; S. Wurm et al. 1987; J-O Svantesson 1989, 1995; J. Janhunen 1989; J. Matisoff et al. 1996; J. Evans 1999; Ostapirat 2000. Blind population: 2,000,000. Deaf population: 3,000,000 (1986 Gallaudet University). Deaf institutions: 7. The number of languages listed for China is 236. Of those, 235 are living languages and 1 is extinct. See maps beginning on page 782.

Achang (Ngochang, Achung, Atsang, Ach'ang, Acang, Ahchan, Ngacang, Ngatsang, Ngachang, Ngac'ang, Ngo Chang, Mönghsa, Maingtha) [acn] 27,708 in China (1990 census). Population total all countries: 29,408. Dehong Dai-Jingpo Autonomous Prefecture and Baoshan District, western Yunnan Province, along the Myanmar border, Longchuan, Lingbe, and Luxi counties. Also spoken in Myanmar. *Class:* Sino-Tibetan, Tibeto-Burman, Lolo-Burmese, Burmish, Northern. *Dialects:* Longchuan, Lianghe, Luxi. The 3 dialects are reported to not be inherently intelligible to one another's speakers. Longchuan differs more from the other dialects, and has more Dai loanwords. Lianghe and Luxi use many Chinese loanwords. There are also Burmese loanwords. Related to Phun, Maru, Lashi, Zaiwa. *Lg Use:* Speakers are mainly adults. The Longchuan dialect is stable, but speakers of other dialects are shifting to Chinese. Many Han people in Longchuan County use Achang in informal situations. All domains. Spoken Chinese and Dai are in common use as second languages. Written Chinese is also in use. *Lg Dev:* Literacy rate in second language: 39%. Roman script. NT: 1992. *Other:* Part of the Achang nationality. Unidentified ethnic groups in the area: Ben Ren, Hknong. Mingled with Lashi. SOV; tonal, 4 tones. Plains, mountain slope. Agriculturalists: rice; craftsmen; transportation; metal workers. Polytheist, Buddhist (Hinayana).

Ai-Cham (Jiamuhua, Jinhua, Atsam) [aih] 2,700 (2000). 13 villages in Di'e and Boyao townships in Libo County of the Qiannan Buyi-Miao Autonomous Prefecture in southern Guizhou Province. *Class:* Tai-Kadai, Kam-Tai, Kam-Sui. *Dialects:* Di'e, Boyao. The two dialects listed have phonological differences, but are largely intelligible to each other's speakers. Similar to Mak. *Other:* Part of the Bouyei nationality. SVO; tonal, 6 tones. Polytheist.

Ainu (Aynu, Aini, Abdal) [aib] 6,570 (2000). Yengixar (Shule) town, Hanalik and Paynap villages in the Kashgar area, and Gewoz village near Hoban; Hetian, Luopu, Moyu, Shache, Yingjisha and Shulekuche counties of southwestern Xinjiang Autonomous Region. *Class:* Altaic, Turkic, Eastern. *Dialects:* The language has the same grammar as Uyghur but much Persian vocabulary. Some consider it to be a dialect of Uyghur, others to be an Iranian language heavily influenced by Uyghur. The government counts them as Uyghur. *Lg Use:* Used in the home. Uyghur spoken to outsiders. *Other:* Part of the Uyghur nationality. They do not intermarry with the Uyghur. Different from the Ainu spoken in Russia and Japan. Caste of circumcisers. Muslim (Sunni).

Akha (Kaw, Ekaw, Ko, Aka, Ikaw, Ak'a, Ahka, Khako, Kha Ko, Khao Kha Ko, Ikor, Aini, Yani) [ahk] 130,000 in China (1990). Southwest Yunnan, Xishuangbanna Prefecture. *Other:* Part of the Hani nationality. Traditional religion, Christian. See main entry under Myanmar.

Atuence (Atuentse, Anshuenkuan Nyarong, Nyarong, Nganshuenkuan) [atf] 590,000. Yunnan-Tibet border. *Class:* Sino-Tibetan, Tibeto-Burman, Himalayish, Tibeto-Kanauri, Tibetic, Tibetan, Central. *Dialects:* It has been identified as Central Bodish (Shafer 1955, 1966), Archaic Nomad Dialect of Tibetan (Roerich 1931), or Central Tibetan (Voegelin and Voegelin 1977). *Other:* Probably part of the Tibetan nationality. This may be the same as the Rgalthangwas language in Yunnan on the Tibet Autonomous Region border. There is a town named 'Atuentze' in Dechen Tibetan Autonomous Prefecture, Yunnan, on the border of the Tibet Autonomous Region. Buddhist (Lamaist), Christian.

Ayi [ayx] 2,200 (2004). Fugong and Gongshan counties, Nujiang Nu-Lisu Autonomous Prefecture of northwestern Yunnan. *Class:* Sino-Tibetan, Tibeto-Burman, Unclassified. *Other:* Part of the Nu nationality. Subclassification unknown, perhaps Lolo. SOV; 3-way obstruent distinction (voiced-voiceless-aspirated); voiced and voiceless nasals and liquids, inflecting. Loanwords from Chinese, Lisu, Bai, Burmese, and Tibetan; tonal, 4 tones. Polytheist, Christian.

Bai, Central (Pai, Minjia, Minchia, Minkia, Labbu, Nama, Leme) [bca] 800,000 (2003). Northwest Yunnan, Jianchuan, Heqing, Lanping, Eryuan, and Yunlong. *Class:*

Sino-Tibetan, Tibeto-Burman, Bai. *Dialects:* Jianchuan, Heqing, Lanping, Eryuan, Yunlong. *Lg Use:* Vigorous. All domains. All ages. Positive language attitude. Some others also speak Chinese. A few also speak Lisu, Nu, and Naxi. *Lg Dev:* Literacy rate in second language: 70%. Roman script. Poetry. Radio programs. Dictionary. Grammar. *Other:* Part of the Bai nationality. Classification difficult because of heavy borrowing (60% to 70%) from Chinese. It is considered to be genetically related to Chinese, or a mixed language with Chinese, or related to Yi, or an independent branch of Tibeto-Burman. An old script dates from the 8th century, called 'Bowen' or 'Lao Baiwen', based on Chinese characters, but this was never standardized. SVO; attributives precede noun heads; number classifier constructions follow noun heads; tense-lax vowel distinction; tonal, 5 to 8 tones. Mountain slope, valleys, plateau. 2,000 meters and higher. Agriculturalists: wet rice, maize, broad bean, wheat; traders; craftsmen. Polytheist, Buddhist, Daoist.

Bai, Northern (Bijang Bai) [bfc] 40,000 (2003). Northwest Yunnan, Nujiang, and Lanping. *Class:* Sino-Tibetan, Tibeto-Burman, Bai. *Dialects:* Nujiang, Lanping. *Other:* Part of the Bai nationality. Classification difficult because of heavy borrowing (60% to 70%) from Chinese. It is considered to be genetically related to Chinese, or a mixed language with Chinese, or related to Yi, or an independent branch of Tibeto-Burman. Polytheist, Buddhist, Daoist.

Bai, Southern [bfs] 400,000 (2003). Northwest Yunnan, Dali, and Xiangyun provinces. *Class:* Sino-Tibetan, Tibeto-Burman, Bai. *Dialects:* Dali, Xiangyun. *Lg Dev:* Roman script. *Other:* Part of the Bai nationality. Classification difficult because of heavy borrowing (60% to 70%) from Chinese. It is considered to be genetically related to Chinese, or a mixed language with Chinese, or related to Yi, or an independent branch of Tibeto-Burman. An old script dates from the 8th century, called 'Bowen' or 'Lao Baiwen', based on Chinese characters, but this was never standardized. SVO; attributives precede noun heads; number classifier constructions follow noun heads; tense-lax vowel distinction tonal, 5 to 8 tones. Polytheist, Buddhist, Daoist.

Baima (Bai Ma, Pe) [bqh] 11,000 (1999 Sun Hongkai). Older adults and a few middle aged are monolingual. Ethnic population: 110,000 (1995 EDCL). Pingwu, Nanping, and Songpan counties in north central Sichuan Province, and Wen County of Gansu Province. *Class:* Sino-Tibetan, Tibeto-Burman, Himalayish, Unclassified. *Dialects:* Southern Baima (Pingwu Baima), Northern Baima (Wen Baima), Western Baima (Nanping Baima). Considered to be an independent language or related to Khams Tibetan. *Lg Use:* Vigorous among adults in Pingwu and Nanping counties. All domains among adults. Most are indifferent, but some leaders want to preserve it. Schools use Chinese. About 1,000 Baima people speak only Chinese. *Other:* Part of the Tibetan nationality. The Baima clan is distinct. SOV; initial consonant clusters; no consonantal codas; mostly monosyllabic morphemes; loans from Chinese and Tibetan; tonal, 4 tones. Plateau, foot-hills, mountain slope. Agriculturalists; animal husbandry: chickens, pigs, sheep, cattle; beekeepers; forest conservation. Traditional religion.

Biao [byk] 50,000 (1999 Liang Min and Zhang Junru). 10,000 women and small children are monolingual. Villages in western Huaji County and neighboring areas in Fengkai County, Guangdong Province. *Class:* Tai-Kadai, Kam-Tai, Kam-Sui. *Lg Use:* Vigorous. All domains. All ages. Children and young people use it about half the time. Positive language attitude. 30,000 also speak Yue Chinese. 10,000 can also speak Cantonese, Mandarin, or Zhuang. *Lg Dev:* Radio programs. Grammar. *Other:* Hills.

Agriculturalists; washing gold. Traditional religion, Daoist, Chinese Buddhist.

Biao Mon (Biaoman, Biao Mien, Min Yao, Sida Min Yao, Changping) [bmt] 20,000 (1995 Wang and Mao). Guangxi Zhuang Autonomous Region, Mengshan, Zhaoping, Pingle, Lipu, and Gongcheng counties. *Class:* Hmong-Mien, Mienic, Mian-Jin. *Dialects:* Biao Mon (Min Yao), Shi Mun (Sida Min Yao). May be intelligible with some dialects of Iu Mien. Quite different from and unintelligible with Biao Jiao or its dialect Biaomin, also called 'Biao Mien'. *Other:* Part of the Yao nationality. Mountain slope. Swidden agriculturalists: paddy rice. Daoist, secular.

Biao-Jiao Mien (Biao Chao, Byau Min) [bje] 43,000 (1995 Wang and Mao). Northeastern Guangxi Zhuang Autonomous Region, Quanzhou, Guanyang, and Gongcheng Yao Autonomous counties; southern Hunan Province, Shuangpai, and Daoxian counties. *Class:* Hmong-Mien, Mienic, Biao-Jiao. *Dialects:* Biao Min (Biaomin, Biao Mien, Dongshan Yao), Jiaogong Mian (Chao Kong Meng, Shikou). The two dialects are reported to be unintelligible. Quite different from and unintelligible with Biao Mon (Biaoman). Lexical similarity 70% with Iu Mien, 67% with Kim Mun, 58% with Dzao Min. *Lg Dev:* Grammar. *Other:* Part of the Yao nationality. Daoist.

Bisu (Mbisu, Misu, Mibisu, Mbi, Laomian, Laopin, Lawa, Lua) [bii] 2,000 in China (1999 Xu Shixuan). 500 monolinguals. Population total all countries: 3,000. Xishuangbanna area of southwestern Yunnan Province: in Mengzhe village of Menghai County, in the villages of Zhutang, Laba, Donglang, and Fubang in Lancang County, in the villages of Jingxin, Fuyan, and Nanya in Menglian County, and in parts of Ximeng County. Possibly also in Laos and Myanmar. Also spoken in Thailand. *Class:* Sino-Tibetan, Tibeto-Burman, Lolo-Burmese, Loloish, Southern, Phunoi. *Dialects:* Lanmeng, Huaipa, Dakao. Close to Mpi, Pyen, and Phunoi. There are some dialect differences based on Dai versus Lahu loanwords. Lexical similarity 36% with Hani, 32% with Lahu, 31% with Lisu. *Lg Use:* Speakers are shifting to Lahu or Dai. Adults use mainly Bisu with each other. Young people and children use Bisu to adults. Speakers view Bisu as an important link to their culture and hope to preserve it. 80% in China can also speak Dai, Lahu, or Chinese. 10% can speak all of those and Hani. *Lg Dev:* Grammar. *Other:* Part of the Hani nationality. Bisu in Menghai County are called 'Laopin' or 'Pin'; they call themselves 'Mbisu'; those in Lancang and Menglian are called 'Laomian'; those in Thailand call themselves 'Bisu', 'Misu', or 'Mbi'. SVO; simple syllable structure; certain obstruent onsets may be prenasalized, aspirated, or palatalized, but otherwise no consonant clusters; syllables may be closed by stop or nasal; 3 tones, tone sandhi; words have 1 or 2 syllables; modifiers follow heads; loanwords from Dai and Chinese. Mountain slope. High altitude. Agriculturalists. Traditional religion.

Bit (Khabit, Phsing, Phsin) [bgk] 500 in China (1990 Svantesson). Southern Yunnan Province. See main entry under Laos.

Biyo (Bio, Biyue) [byo] 100,000 (1990 J-O Svantesson). Yunnan, near the Hani. *Class:* Sino-Tibetan, Tibeto-Burman, Lolo-Burmese, Loloish, Southern, Akha, Hani, Bi-Ka. *Other:* Part of the Hani nationality. A distinct language from Akha and Kaduo. Traditional religion, Christian.

Blang (Bulang, Pulang, Pula, Plang, Kawa, K'ala, Kontoi) [blr] 24,000 in China (1990 J-O Svantesson). Population total all countries: 37,200. Southwestern Yunnan Province, Xishuangbanna Dai Autonomous Prefecture, and the Simao and Lincang regions. Most live in Menghai and Shuangjiang counties. Some are scattered, living among Va (Wa). May also be in Laos. Also spoken in Myanmar, Thailand. *Class:* Austro-Asiatic, Mon-Khmer, Northern

Mon-Khmer, Palaungic, Western Palaungic, Waic, Bulang. *Dialects:* Phang, Kem Degne. Dialects listed may be separate languages. Chinese sources list two dialects: Bulang (Blang Proper), and Awa (A'erwa). It is not known how these relate to the dialects listed above. Close to Wa. In Thailand, the group from Mae Sai came from Sipsongpanna, Yunnan, China, stayed in Myanmar for a while, and have been in Thailand since 1974. There are 6 to 10 dialects represented in one refugee village in Thailand. Samtao of Myanmar and China is not intelligible with Blang, but is closely related to Blang and Wa. *Lg Use:* Vigorous. All domains. All ages. Positive language attitude. Dai, Wa, and Chinese are in common use. *Lg Dev:* 2 alphabetic scripts used: 'Totham' in the Xishuangbanna area and 'Tolek' from Dehong to Lincang. Grammar. *Other:* Part of the Bulang nationality. The nationality includes Blang, Lawa, and Angkuic languages, Puman, U, and 3 to 7 others. SVO; modifiers follow noun heads; voiceless nasal initials; singular-dual-plural pronoun distinction; rich in morphophonemic processes; tonal, 4 tones. Mountain slope, foothills, valleys. 1,500 meters and over. Agriculturalists. Buddhist (Hinayana), Christian.

Bogan (Bengan) [bgh] 6,000 (2001). Yunnan. *Class:* Austro-Asiatic, Mon-Khmer, Palyu. *Other:* Part of the Yi nationality. Traditional religion.

Bolyu (Lai, Palju, Palyu, Polyu) [ply] 10,000 (1993). Far western Guangxi on the Guizhou border, Xilin and Longlin counties, in 2 groups. There may be some in Yunnan. *Class:* Austro-Asiatic, Mon-Khmer, Palyu. *Other:* Part of the Gelao nationality. Called 'Lai' in Chinese. SVO; modifiers follow heads; grammatical relations marked mainly by word order and particles; reported to have long and half long versus short vowel distinction; uvular stops; 6 tone categories in unchecked syllables plus 5 in checked syllables. Shows similarities to Kadai languages. Traditional religion.

Bonan (Bao'an, Boan, Paoan, Paongan, Baonan) [peh] 6,000 (1999 Junast). Ethnic population: 10,000 (1999 Junast), including 6,000 Jishishan, 4,000 Tongren. Southwestern Gansu Province in the Jishishan Bao'an-Dongxiang-Sala Autonomous County of the Linxia Hui Autonomous Prefecture, and Bonan-speaking Tu in Tongren, eastern Qinghai Province. *Class:* Altaic, Mongolian, Eastern, Mongour. *Dialects:* Jishishan (Dahejia, Dajiahe, Dakheczjha), Tongren (Tungyen). Jishishan subdialects are Ganhetan and Dadun; Tongren subdialects are Nianduhu, Guomari, Gajiuri, and Lower Bao'an village. Jishishan has been influenced by Chinese, Tongren by Tibetan. There are phonological and grammatical differences between the two, and inherent intelligibility may be low. *Lg Use:* Oral use in religion, local administration. Positive language attitude. Written Chinese is in common use. *Lg Dev:* Literacy rate in second language: 24%. Dictionary. Grammar. *Other:* An official nationality. They moved into Jishishan from Tongren in 1858–1863. SOV; stress on final syllable; modifiers precede noun heads; Tongren variety allows onset consonant clusters which resemble Tibetan; Jishishan variety has Chinese-type syllable structure. Agriculturalists; forestry; crafts. Muslim (Sunni), Buddhist (Lamaist).

Bouyei (Buyi, Bui, Bo-I, Buyei, Buyui, Puyi, Pui, Pu-I, Pu-Jui, Pujai, Puyoi, Dioi, Tujia, Shuihu, Zhongjia, Chung-Chia) [pcc] 2,000,000 in China (1990 census). Population total all countries: 2,049,203. Guizhou-Yunnan plateau, mainly Buyi-Miao and Miao-Dong autonomous prefectures, Zhenning and Guanling counties, south and southwest Guizhou, and some in Yunnan Province, Luoping County, and Sichuan Province, Ningnan and Huidong counties. Also spoken in France, USA, Viet Nam. *Class:* Tai-Kadai, Kam-Tai, Be-Tai, Tai-Sek, Tai, Northern. *Dialects:* Qiannan (Southern Guizhou, Bouyei

1), Qianzhong (Central Guizhou, Bouyei 2), Qianxi (Western Guizhou, Bouyei 3). Dialect continuum to Northern Zhuang. *Lg Use:* Vigorous. Rare oral use in local administration, commerce, education. All ages. Chinese is the second language of all bilingual speakers. Written Chinese is in common use. *Lg Dev:* Literacy rate in second language: 46%. Roman script. Poetry. Newspapers. Dictionary. *Other:* Part of the Bouyei nationality. The name 'Quinnan hua' (Quinnan speech) also refers to a dialect of southwestern Mandarin spoken in Guizhou, and should not be confused with Qiannan Bouyei. An official nationality in Viet Nam. SVO; modifiers follow heads; highly monosyllabic; tonal, 6 tone categories in open syllables and 4 in closed syllables. Mountain slope, karst. Agriculturalists: oranges; batik dyers; textiles; tung oil; kapok. Polytheist, Daoist, Buddhist.

Bugan (Pukan, Hualo, Huazu) [bbh] 3,000 (1996 Edmondson). Southern Guangnan and northern Xichou counties in southeastern Yunnan Province, Laowalong, Xinwalong, Jiuping, Shibeipo, Xinzhai, Manlong, and Nala villages. *Class:* Austro-Asiatic, Mon-Khmer, Unclassified. *Dialects:* 1 dialect. *Other:* They live with Han Chinese in 3 villages, by themselves in 4. Traditionally endogamous. Colorful printed dresses. Prenasalized and plain stop and affricate initials; tense and lax vowel contrast; nasal and stop variation word final; tone sandhi, 6 tones. Mountain slope. Traditional religion.

Bunu, Bu-Nao (Punu, Bunao, Po-Nau) [bwx] 258,000 (1995 McConnell). 97,000 are monolingual. Ethnic population: 439,000 (1982 census). 100,000 ethnic Bunu speak Zhuang as first language. Western Guangxi Zhuang Autonomous Region (Du'an, Bama, Dahua, Lingyun, Nandan, Tiandong, Tianyang, Pingguo, Fengshan, Donglan, Hechi, Mashan, Bose, Tianlin, Leye, Tiandeng, Xincheng, Shanglin, Long'an, Debao, Laibin, Luocheng counties), Guizhou Province (Libo County), and Yunnan Province (Funing County). *Class:* Hmong-Mien, Hmongic, Bunu. *Dialects:* Dongnu (Tung Nu), Nunu, Bunuo (Pu No), Naogelao (Nao Klao), Numao (Nu Mhou, Hong Yao). The dialects listed may be 5 languages (D. Strecker 1987), communication is difficult (McConnell 1995). *Lg Use:* Vigorous. All domains. All ages. Positive language attitude. Speakers also use Zhuang, Chinese, or Bouyei. Mandarin used in schools. *Lg Dev:* Dictionary. Grammar. *Other:* Part of the Yao nationality. SVO; modifiers follow heads; the greatest number is 11; complex set of initials including prenasalized stops; relatively simple rhymes; tonal, most dialects have 8 tones. Mountain slope, plateau, valleys. 1,500 meters. Agriculturalists; trading. Daoist.

Bunu, Jiongnai (Punu, Qiungnai, Kiong Nai, Jiongnai, Jiongnaihua, Hualan Yao) [pnu] 1,078 (1999 Mao Zongwu). 269 monolinguals. Eastern Guangxi Zhuang Autonomous Region, Jinxiu Yao Autonomous County. *Class:* Hmong-Mien, Hmongic, Bunu. *Dialects:* Very different from and unintelligible to speakers of surrounding Yao and other Bunu languages. Lexical similarity 52% with Bu-Nao Bunu. *Lg Use:* Vigorous in most families. All domains. All ages. Indifferent language attitude. Speakers also use Mandarin, Zhuang, Iu Mien, Lakkia or Hmong. *Lg Dev:* Grammar. *Other:* Part of the Yao nationality. The Han call them 'Hualan Yao' which means 'Flowery Blue Yao'. 'Bunu' is a cover term for separate languages. Mountain slope, valleys, riverine. Agriculturalists: wet rice. Daoist, polytheist.

Bunu, Wunai (Punu, Wunai, Ngnai, Hm Nai) [bwn] 18,442 (1995 McConnell). Western Hunan Province, Longhui, Xupu, Tongdao, Chenxi, Dongkou, Cengbu, and Xinning counties. *Class:* Hmong-Mien, Hmongic, Bunu. *Lg Use:* Speakers also use Zhuang, Chinese. *Other:* Part of the Yao nationality. 'Bunu' is a cover term for separate languages. SVO; has uvular onsets; only final nasal is velar. Daoist.

Bunu, Younuo (Punu, Pu No, Younuo, Yunuo, Yuno) [buh] 9,716 (1995 McConnell). Northeastern Guangxi Zhuang Autonomous Region, Xing'an and Longsheng counties. *Class:* Hmong-Mien, Hmongic, Bunu. *Lg Use:* Speakers also use Zhuang or Mandarin. *Other:* Part of the Yao nationality. 'Bunu' is a cover term for separate languages (D. Strecker 1989). SVO; relatively simple set of initials; many Chinese loans; tonal, 6 tones. Daoist.

Buriat, China (Buryat, Buriat-Mongolian, Northern Mongolian, Northeastern Mongolian, Bargu Buriat) [bxu] 65,000 (1982 census). Population includes 47,000 New Bargu, 14,000 Old Bargu, 4,500 Buriat. Hulun-Buyr District of Inner Mongolia, near Russian (Siberian) and Mongolian borders. *Class:* Altaic, Mongolian, Eastern, Oirat-Khalkha, Khalkha-Buriat, Buriat. *Dialects:* Bargu (Old Bargu, New Bargu), Khori, Aga. Officially included under Mongolian in China. Differs from Buriat of Mongolia and Russia because of influences from different languages. *Other:* Part of the Mongolian nationality. Buddhist (Lamaist), traditional religion.

Buxinhua [bxt] 200 (1994). Mengla County, Xishuangbanna Dai Autonomous Prefecture, southwestern Yunnan Province. *Class:* Austro-Asiatic, Mon-Khmer, Unclassified. *Other:* SVO; complex morphology (prefixing); attributives follow noun heads; adverbials precede verb heads; simple syllable structure; nontonal. Traditional religion.

Buyang [byu] 2,772 (2000 WCD). Ethnic population: 3,000 (2000 D. Bradley). Yunnan Province, Wenshan Zhuang-Miao Autonomous District, Guangnan County, one location, and Funing County, Gula Township. *Class:* Tai-Kadai, Kadai, Yang-Biao. *Dialects:* Yalang, Ecun, Langjia. A number of dialects. Some similarities grammatically with Kam-Sui. Lexical similarity 38% with Pubiao, 34% with Lati, 32% with Northern Zhuang, 31% with Gelo, 28% with Dong, 24% with Laka, 23% with Hlai, 10% with Hmong, 6% with Mien. *Lg Use:* Most speakers can use Southwest Mandarin, except for children and older adults. Those from 15 to 50 can speak the local kind of Zhuang. About half can speak Yerong. *Lg Dev:* Grammar. *Other:* Part of the Zhuang nationality. SVO; adjectives follow nouns; tonal, 6 tones (combining categories in checked and unchecked syllables). Polytheist.

Cao Lan (Caolan, San Chay, San Chi, "Man Cao-Lan," Sán-Chi, "Mán," Cao Lan-Sán Chi) [mlc] 40,000 in China (2002). *Other:* "Man" is derogatory. Traditional religion. See main entry under Viet Nam.

Cao Miao (Mjiuniang, Grass Miao) [cov] 63,632 (2000 WCD). Liping county of southeastern Guizhou Province, Tongdao Dong Autonomous County of southwestern Hunan Province, and Sanjiang Dong Autonomous County of northeastern Guangxi, near Southern Dong, in small villages. *Class:* Tai-Kadai, Kam-Tai, Kam-Sui. *Dialects:* Close to Northern Dong and sometimes referred to as a special dialect of Dong. *Lg Use:* Used in daily communication. Speakers also use Mandarin. *Other:* Part of the Miao nationality. Chinese used in singing. Members of the Miao nationality. Tonal, 6 tones. Mountain slope. Traditional religion.

Chinese Sign Language [csl] Ethnic population: 3,000,000 deaf persons in China (1986 Gallaudet Univ.). Also used in Malaysia, Taiwan. *Class:* Deaf sign language. *Dialect:* Shanghai Sign Language. There are several dialects, of which Shanghai is the most influential. Few signs of foreign origin. The varieties used in Hong Kong, Taiwan, and Malaysia may have changed. *Lg Use:* Schools and workshops or farms for the deaf are channels of dissemination. *Lg Dev:* TV. Dictionary. Grammar. *Other:* Developed since the late 1950s. There are also

Chinese character signs. Others use home sign languages. The first deaf school was begun by missionary C. R. Mills and wife in 1887, but American Sign Language did not influence Chinese Sign Language.

Chinese, Gan (Gan, Kan) [gan] 20,580,000 (1984). Jiangxi and southeastern corner of Hubei including Dachi, Xianning, Jiayu, Chongyang, and parts of Anhui, Hunan, and Fujian provinces. Chang-Jing dialect includes the speech of Nanchang City, Xiuhui, and Jing'an; Yi-Liu includes Yichun (Ichun) in Jiangxi to Liuyang in Hunan. *Class:* Sino-Tibetan, Chinese. *Dialects:* Chang-Jing, Yi-Liu, Ji-Cha, Fu-Guang, Ying-Yi. Marginally intelligible with Mandarin and Wu Chinese. *Lg Use:* Speakers are reported to be sufficiently bilingual in Standard Chinese (Mandarin) to use that literature. *Lg Dev:* Chinese script. *Other:* Part of the Han nationality.

Chinese, Hakka (Hakka, Hokka, Kejia, Kechia, Ke, Xinminhua, Majiahua, Tu Guangdonghua) [hak] 25,725,000 in mainland China (1984). Population total all countries: 29,937,959. Spoken in many parts of mainland China side by side with other dialects. Greatest concentration of speakers in eastern and northeastern Guangdong, otherwise especially in Fujian, Jiangxi, Guangxi, Hunan, and Sichuan. Also spoken in Brunei, French Guiana, French Polynesia, Indonesia (Java and Bali), Malaysia (Peninsular), Mauritius, New Zealand, Panama, Singapore, South Africa, Suriname, Taiwan, Thailand, United Kingdom, USA. *Class:* Sino-Tibetan, Chinese. *Dialects:* Yue-Tai (Meixian, Raoping, Taiwan Kejia), Yuezhong (Central Guangdong), Huizhou, Yuebei (Northern Guangdong), Tingzhou (Min-Ke), Ning-Long (Longnan), Yugui, Tonggu. Yue-Tai is now the standard dialect. *Lg Dev:* Roman script in Taiwan. Bible: 1916. *Other:* Part of the Han nationality.

Chinese, Huizhou (Huizhou) [czh] South Anhui Province and north Zhejiang Province. *Class:* Sino-Tibetan, Chinese. *Dialects:* Jixi, Xiuyi, Qide, Yanzhou, Jingzhan. Formerly considered to be part of the Jianghuai dialect of Mandarin, but now considered by many to be a separate major variety of Chinese. Dialects are reported to differ greatly from each other. Different from the Huizhou dialect of Hakka. *Lg Use:* Speakers are reported to be sufficiently bilingual in Standard Chinese to use that literature. *Lg Dev:* Chinese script. *Other:* Part of the Han nationality.

Chinese, Jinyu (Jinyu) [cjy] 45,000,000 (1995). Mainly in Shanxi Province, with some in Shaanxi and Henan provinces. *Class:* Sino-Tibetan, Chinese. *Dialects:* Formerly considered to be part of the Xibei Guanhua dialect of Mandarin, but now considered by many to be a separate major variety of Chinese. Unlike Mandarin in having contrastive glottal checked syllables and other distinctive features. *Lg Use:* Speakers are reported to be sufficiently bilingual in Standard Chinese to use that literature. *Lg Dev:* Chinese script. *Other:* Part of the Han nationality.

Chinese, Mandarin (Mandarin, Guanhua, Beifang Fangyan, Northern Chinese, Guoyu, Standard Chinese, Putonghua, Hanyu) [cmn] 867,200,000 in mainland China (1999). 70% of the population, including 8,602,978 Hui (1990 census). Other estimates for Hui are 20,000,000 or more. 1,042,482,187 all Han in China (1990 census). Population total all countries: 873,014,298. Covers all of mainland China north of the Changjiang River, a belt south of the Changjiang from Qiujiang (Jiangxi) to Zhenjiang (Jiangsu), Hubei except the southeastern corner, Sichuan, Yunnan, Guizhou, the northwestern part of Guangxi, and the northwestern corner of Hunan. Also spoken in Brunei, Cambodia, Indonesia (Java and Bali), Laos, Malaysia (Peninsular), Mauritius, Mongolia, Philippines, Russia (Asia), Singapore, Taiwan, Thailand,

United Kingdom, USA, Viet Nam. *Class:* Sino-Tibetan, Chinese. *Dialects:* Huabei Guanhua (Northern Mandarin), Xibei Guanhua (Northwestern Mandarin), Xinan Guanhua (Southwestern Mandarin), Jinghuai Guanhua (Jiangxia Guanhua, Lower Yangze Mandarin). Wenli is a literary form. Written Chinese is based on the Beijing dialect, but has been heavily influenced by other varieties of Northern Mandarin. Putonghua is the official form taught in schools. Hezhouhoua is spoken in the Linxia Hui Autonomous Prefecture and Gannan Tibetan Autonomous Prefecture of southern Gansu Province, and in neighboring areas in Qinghai Province. The grammar is basically Altaic or Tibetan, while the vocabulary and phonology is basically Northwestern Mandarin, or a relexified variety of Tibetan. Putonghua is inherently intelligible with the Beijing dialect, and other Mandarin varieties in the northeast. Mandarin varieties in the Lower Plateau in Shaanxi are not readily intelligible with Putonghua. Mandarin varieties of Guilin and Kunming are inherently unintelligible to speakers of Putonghua. Taibei Mandarin and Beijing Mandarin are fully inherently intelligible to each other's speakers. Nearly all first-language speakers in Taiwan speak with Min-influenced grammar and various degrees of Min-influenced pronunciation. Many of the educated strive to cultivate standard pronunciation. Grammatical differences of the Taiwan variety often appear in writing. *Lg Use:* National language. Vigorous. Many speakers of other languages use it as second language. 178,000,000 second-language speakers. All domains. All ages. Most speakers live in monolingual areas, so are not conscious of other languages. They do recognize the difference between standard Mandarin (Putonghua), and approve its use, especially in northern areas. Few speakers are bilingual. *Lg Dev:* If literate, they read Chinese. A few read Arabic. Official language taught in all schools in Han China and Taiwan. Chinese script. Magazines. Newspapers. Radio programs. TV. Dictionary. Grammar. Bible: 1874–1983. *Other:* SVO, SOV. Mountain slope, plateau, plains, hills. Agriculturalists (rural); traders (urban); businessmen; industry; herders; fishermen; construction; transport; telecommunications; teachers; government workers. Traditional Chinese religion, Confucianist, Daoist, Buddhist, Muslim (Hui), Jewish, Christian, secular.

Chinese, Min Bei (Northern Min, Min Pei) [mnp] 10,290,000 in China (1984). Population total all countries: 10,294,000. Northern Fujian Province in 7 counties around Jian'ou. Also spoken in Singapore. *Class:* Sino-Tibetan, Chinese. *Dialects:* The Chinese now divide Chinese Min into 5 major varieties: Min Nan, Min Bei, Min Dong, Min Zhong, and Pu-Xian. Others say there are at least 9 varieties which are inherently unintelligible to one another's speakers. *Lg Dev:* NT: 1934. *Other:* Part of the Han nationality. Buddhist, Daoist, Christian.

Chinese, Min Dong (Eastern Min) [cdo] 8,820,252 in China (2000 WCD). Population total all countries: 9,103,157. Area from Fu'an in northeastern Fujian to Fuzhou in east central Fujian. Also spoken in Brunei, Indonesia (Java and Bali), Malaysia (Peninsular), Singapore, Thailand. *Class:* Sino-Tibetan, Chinese. *Dialect:* Fuzhou (Fuchow, Foochow, Guxhou). The prestige variety is that spoken in Fujian. *Lg Use:* Speakers are adequately bilingual in Standard Chinese. *Lg Dev:* Highly literate in Chinese, and they use that literature. Bible: 1884–1905. *Other:* Part of the Han nationality.

Chinese, Min Nan (Southern Min, Minnan) [nan] 25,725,000 in mainland China (1984). 2.5% of the population, including 1,000,000 Xiamen dialect (1988 census), 6,000,000 Quanzhou dialect (Quanzhoushi Fangyan Zhi). Population total all countries: 46,227,965. Southern Fujian, Guangdong, south Hainan Island,

southern Zhejiang, southern Jiangxi provinces. Xiamen is spoken in southern Fujian, Jiangxi, and Taiwan; Hainan dialect in Hainan; Leizhou on the Leizhou peninsula of southwestern Guangdong; Chao-Shan in the far eastern corner of Guangdong in the Chaozhou-Shantou area; Longdu is a dialect island in the area around Zhongshan City and Shaxi in Guangdong south of Guangzhou; Zhenan Min in southeastern Zhejiang Province around Pingyang and Cangnan and on the Zhoushan archipelago of northeastern Zhejiang. Also spoken in Brunei, Indonesia (Java and Bali), Malaysia (Peninsular), Philippines, Singapore, Taiwan, Thailand, USA. *Class:* Sino-Tibetan, Chinese. *Dialects:* Xiamen (Amoy), Leizhou (Lei Hua, Li Hua), Chao-Shan (Choushan, Chaozhou), Hainan (Hainanese, Qiongwen Hua, Wenchang), Longdu, Zhenan Min. Xiamen has subdialects Amoy, Fujian (Fukien, Hokkian, Taiwanese). Amoy is the prestige dialect. Amoy and Taiwanese are easily intelligible to each other. Chao-Shan has subdialects Chaoshou (Chaochow, Chaochow, Teochow, Teochew) and Shantou (Swatow). Chao-Shan, including Swatow, has very difficult intelligibility of Amoy. Sanjiang is somewhat difficult for other dialect speakers. Hainan is quite different from other dialects. Min Nan is the most widely distributed and influential Min variety. There are two subdialects in Taiwan: Sanso and Chaenzo. Most Min Nan speakers in Thailand speak the Chaoshou dialect. *Lg Use:* Speakers of other languages use for commerce. Most domains. All ages. Shantou and Chenhai varieties of the Chao-shan dialect are considered to be cultured. Chao-shan speakers may speak Mandarin, Cantonese, or English for buying and selling, Mandarin to outside Chinese and government purposes, English to foreigners. Those under 30 are more bilingual. *Lg Dev:* Literacy rate in first language: 30% literate in Chao-shan. Many older people cannot read Chinese, but all young people can read standard Mandarin Chinese. Roman script in Taiwan. Poetry. Dictionary. Grammar. Bible: 1884–1933. *Other:* Part of the Han nationality. Traditional Chinese religion, Buddhist, Christian, Daoist.

Chinese, Min Zhong (Central Min) [czo] Area around Yong'an, Sanming, and Shaxian in central Fujian Province. *Class:* Sino-Tibetan, Chinese. *Lg Use:* Speakers are adequately bilingual in Standard Chinese to use that literature. *Lg Dev:* Highly literate in Chinese and they use that literature. *Other:* Part of the Han nationality.

Chinese, Pu-Xian [cpx] 2,520,072 in China (2000 WCD). Population total all countries: 2,600,810. Putian and Xianyou counties of east central Fujian Province. Also spoken in Malaysia (Peninsular), Singapore. *Class:* Sino-Tibetan, Chinese. *Dialects:* Putian (Putten, Xinghua, Hinghua, Henghua, Hsinghua), Xianyou (Hsienyu). *Lg Use:* Speakers are adequately bilingual in Standard Chinese. *Lg Dev:* Highly literate in Chinese, and they use that literature. Bible: 1912. *Other:* Part of the Han nationality.

Chinese, Wu (Wu) [wuu] 77,175,000 (1984). Jiangsu south of the Changjiang River, east of Zhenjiang, on Chongming Island in the mouth of the Changjiang, and north of the Changjiang in the area around Nantong, Haimen, Qidong, and Qingjiang, and in Zhejiang Province as far south as Quzhou, Jinhua, and Wenzhou. *Class:* Sino-Tibetan, Chinese. *Dialects:* Taihu, Jinhua (Kinhwa), Taizhou, Oujiang, Wuzhou, Chuqu, Xuanzhou. Subdialects of the Taihu dialect are Piling, Su-Hu-Jia, Tiaoxi, Hangzhou, Lin-Shao, Yongjiang. Chuqu subdialects are Chuzhou, Longqu. Xuanzhou subdialects are Tongjing, Taigao, Shiling. *Lg Use:* Mandarin is used for news and official broadcasts. *Lg Dev:* Radio programs. TV. Bible: 1908–1914. *Other:* Part of the Han nationality.

Chinese, Xiang (Hunan, Hunanese, Xiang, Hsiang) [hsn] 36,015,000 (1984). Hunan Province, over 20 counties in Sichuan, and parts of Guangxi and Guangdong provinces. *Class:* Sino-Tibetan, Chinese. *Dialects:* Changyi, Luoshao, Jishu. Linguistically between Mandarin and Wu Chinese and marginally intelligible with them. *Lg Use:* Sufficiently bilingual in Standard Chinese to use that literature. *Lg Dev:* Chinese script. *Other:* Part of the Han nationality.

Chinese, Yue (Yuet Yue, Gwong Dung Waa, Cantonese, Yue, Yueh, Yueyu, Baihua) [yue] 52,000,000 in mainland China (1984). Population includes 498,000 in Macau. Population total all countries: 54,810,598. Spoken in Guangdong (except for the Hakka speaking areas especially in the northeast, the Min Nan speaking areas of the east, at points along the coast as well as Hainan Island), Macau, and in the southern part of Guangxi. Also possibly in Laos. Also spoken in Australia, Brunei, Canada, Costa Rica, Honduras, Indonesia (Java and Bali), Malaysia (Peninsular), Mauritius, Nauru, Netherlands, New Zealand, Panama, Philippines, Singapore, South Africa, Thailand, United Kingdom, USA, Viet Nam. *Class:* Sino-Tibetan, Chinese. *Dialects:* Yuehai (Guangfu, Hong Kong Cantonese, Macau Cantonese, Shatou, Shiqi, Wancheng), Siyi (Seiyap, Taishan, Toisan, Hoisan, Schleiyip), Gaolei (Gaoyang), Qinlian, Guinan. The Guangzhou variety is considered the standard. Subdialects of Yuehai are Xiangshan, spoken around Zhongshan and Shuhai, and Wanbao around Dong Guan City and Bao'an County. *Lg Dev:* Chinese script in Viet Nam. TV. Grammar. Bible: 1894–1981. *Other:* Part of the Han nationality. Outside of mainland China, many Cantonese-specific characters are used in the writing system. SVO; prepositions; genitives, relatives after noun heads; articles, adjectives, numerals before noun heads; word order mainly distinguishes subjects, objectives, indirect objects; passives usually indicated by adding a word in front of the verb; tonal.

Choni (Chona, Chone, Cone, Jone) [cda] 24,000 (2002). Yunnan-Tibet border. *Class:* Sino-Tibetan, Tibeto-Burman, Himalayish, Tibeto-Kanauri, Tibetic, Tibetan, Northern. *Dialect:* Hbrugchu. Related to Amdo Tibetan, Golog, and Kham. Possible dialects or related languages: Dpari (Dpalri, Dparus), Rebkong, Wayen, Horke. *Other:* Part of the Tibetan nationality.

Cun (Ngao Fon, Cunhua, Cun-Hua) [cuq] 80,000 (1999 Ouyang Jueya). 59% are monolingual, mainly children, elders, and some women. South bank of Changhua River in north Dongfang county and north bank in Changjiang county, Hainan Island. *Class:* Tai-Kadai, Kadai, Yang-Biao. *Dialects:* Lexical similarity 40% with Hlai. Many loanwords from Chinese. *Lg Use:* Vigorous. All domains. All ages. Positive language attitude. 41% can use Chinese as second language. Very few can also speak Hlai. *Lg Dev:* Grammar. *Other:* Part of the Han nationality. SVO; tonal, 10 tones (5 in checked syllables and 5 in unchecked syllables). Coastal, mountain slope. Agriculturalists; fishermen; fish breeding. Traditional religion.

Darang Deng (Darang, Digaro, Darang Dengyu) [dat] 850 (1999 Sun Hongkai). 750 are monolingual. Chayu (Zayü) County along the Dulai River valley in southeastern Tibet Autonomous Region, Xiazayu, Qu'antong, and Gayao townships, Nyingchi Prefecture. *Class:* Sino-Tibetan, Tibeto-Burman, North Assam, Deng. *Lg Use:* Vigorous. A few Geman Deng speak it as second language. All domains. All ages. Positive language attitude. About 20 can also speak Chinese and Tibetan, 70 can also speak Chinese, 10 Tibetan, 1 Geman Deng. *Lg Dev:* Grammar. *Other:* Some believe them to be in the Jingpo branch. May be in the Tibetan nationality in China. SOV; tonal, 4 tones which are reported to vary considerably among speakers. Mountain slope. Thickly forested. Traditionally hunter-gatherers; agriculturalists: wet rice, maize, yams, vegetables. Traditional religion.

Daur (Dagur, Daguor, Dawar, Dawo'er, Tahur, Tahuerh) [dta] 96,085 in China (1999 Dong Ying). About 24,270 are monolingual. Ethnic population: 121,357 (1990 census). Inner Mongolia, Hailar Prefecture, and border of Heilongjiang Province, Qiqihar Prefecture, and northwest Xinjiang, Tacheng Prefecture. Also spoken in Mongolia. *Class:* Altaic, Mongolian, Eastern, Dagur. *Dialects:* Buteha (Bataxan), Haila'er (Hailar), Qiqiha'er (Qiqihar, Tsitsikhar). Definitely distinct from other Mongolian languages (Voegelin and Voegelin 1977). Some sources list Tacheng (spoken in Xinjiang) as a dialect. Some list Haila'er as a dialect of Evenki. *Lg Use:* Official regional language. All domains. It has moderately vigorous use among adults, but decreasing use among young people and children. Speakers seem indifferent toward preservation of Daur. Speakers also use Chinese or Mongolian. A few also speak Ewenki, Kazakh, Oroqen, or Manchu. Speakers are reported to have high and widespread levels of bilingualism in Chinese. Chinese is the language of schools. *Lg Dev:* Literacy rate in second language: 81%. Some literacy in Mongolian among those 30 to 50 years of age in Hala'er. Radio programs. Films. Dictionary. Grammar. *Other:* An official nationality. A Daur script was used during the Qing dynasty, then experimental Cyrillic script in 1957, then Latin based on Chinese orthography, but scholars are experimenting with a Latin orthography based on Pinyin. Written Manchu once used, now written Chinese used. SOV; grammatical funcion marked mainly by suffixes; vowel harmony but not very strict; many consonant clusters; palatalized and labialized consonants; rich vocabulary related to hunting, fishing, animal husbandry; loans from Chinese, Manchu, Evenki. Plain. Agriculturalists; pastoralists; hunters. Shamanist, Buddhist (Lamaist), Christian.

Dong, Northern (Kam, Gam, Tong, Tung, Tung-Chia) [doc] 463,000 in China (2003). Area where southeastern Guizhou (Yuping Autonomous County), western Hunan, and northern Guangxi provinces meet, and Guangxi Zhuang Autonomous Region, 20 contiguous counties. Also spoken in Viet Nam. *Class:* Tai-Kadai, Kam-Tai, Kam-Sui. *Dialects:* Zhanglu speech in Rongjiang County, Guizhou Province is the standard variety. Reported to be close to Mulam. Lexical similarity 80% within Northern Dong, 71% between Northern Dong and Southern Dong. Lexical similarity 49% with Northern Zhuang, 46% with Laka, 29% with Laqua, 28% with Buyang, 26% with Hlai, 24% with Gelo, 22% with Lati, 6% with Hmong, 4% with Mien. *Lg Use:* Vigorous. All domains. All ages. Speakers of Northern Dong are more bilingual than are those in Southern Dong. Speakers use Mandarin for literature. *Lg Dev:* Literacy rate in second language: 55%. Dictionary. Grammar. *Other:* Part of the Dong nationality. 'Kam' is their own name, 'Dong' is the Chinese name. Traditional way of life is relatively undisturbed. Tonal, 9 tones. Mountain slope. 500 to 1,000 meters. Agriculturalists: rice, tung oil, tea oil; forestry. Polytheist.

Dong, Southern (Kam, Gam, Tong, Tung, Tung-Chia) [kmc] 1,000,000. 68% of the 1,463,000 Dong speakers speak Southern Dong. Area where southeastern Guizhou (Yuping Autonomous County), western Hunan, and northern Guangxi provinces meet, and Guangxi Zhuang Autonomous Region, 20 contiguous counties. *Class:* Tai-Kadai, Kam-Tai, Kam-Sui. *Dialects:* Close to Mulam. Lexical similarity 93% within Southern Dong, 71% between Northern Dong and Southern Dong. Lexical similarity 49% with Northern Zhuang, 46% with Laka, 29% with Laqua, 28% with Buyang, 26% with Hlai, 24% with Gelo, 22% with Lati, 6% with Hmong, 4% with Mien. *Lg Use:* Vigorous. All domains. All ages. Speakers view it as superior to Hmong, but inferior to Chinese. Speakers of Northern Dong are more bilingual than those of Southern Dong. Speakers use Mandarin for literature. *Lg Dev:* Magazines. Dictionary. *Other:* Part of the Dong nationality. 'Kam' is their own name, 'Dong' is the Chinese name. Traditional way of life is relatively undisturbed. Tonal, 9 tones. Agriculturalists: wet rice, rape, wheat, maize, tung oil, tea oil; forestry. Polytheist.

Dongxiang (Tunghsiang, Santa, Tung) [sce] 250,000 (1999 Junast). About 80,000 monolinguals. Half in the Suonanba dialect. Ethnic population: 373,872 (1990 census). Southwest Gansu Province, mainly in Linxia Hui Autonomous Prefecture, 7 counties and a city, and in Yining and Huocheng counties in Ili Kazak Autonomous Prefecture in Xinjiang Uygur Autonomous Region. *Class:* Altaic, Mongolian, Eastern, Mongour. *Dialects:* Suonanba (Xiaonan), Wangjiaji, Sijiaji. Some intelligibility of Bonan. Minor dialect differences in pronunciation and borrowed words. Suonanba is considered to be the standard. *Lg Use:* Use in religion, local commerce, oral tradition. Positive language attitude. Written Chinese is in common use. *Lg Dev:* Literacy rate in second language: 12%. Radio programs. Dictionary. Grammar. *Other:* An official nationality. 30% of vocabulary borrowed from Chinese. The people call themselves 'Santa'. SOV; no vowel harmony or vowel length distinction; rich in consonants including uvulars; case marking. Plain. Agriculturalists; pastoralists. Muslim (Sunni).

Drung (Trung, Tulung, Dulong, Qiu, Rawang) [duu] 11,300. 95% monolingual. Population includes 5,816 Drung (1990 census) and 5,500 ethnic Nung in the Nu nationality (1990 J-O Svantesson). About 6,000 in Nu River dialect, about 4,000 in Dulong River dialect. Dulong River dialect is spoken along both sides of the Dulong River in Gongshan Dulong-Nu Autonomous County in far northwestern Yunnan. Nu River dialect is spoken from Gongshan Dulong-Nu Autonomous County west to Chayu (Zayü) County in Tibet. *Class:* Sino-Tibetan, Tibeto-Burman, Nungish. *Dialects:* Dulong River (Derung River), Nu River. The dialects are reported to be inherently intelligible. The Nu River Drung is not the same as the Tibeto-Burman 'Nung', which are also in Myanmar. Not the same as Rawang in Myanmar. Other possible dialect names are Melam, Metu, Tamalu, Tukiumu. *Lg Use:* Vigorous. Speakers of other languages living among them use Drung as second language. All domains. All ages. Positive language attitude. Speakers also use Chinese, Burmese, or Lisu. *Lg Dev:* Very few can read or write. Roman script. *Other:* An official nationality, called 'Dulong'. 'Qiuzu' is an old term for the people. Not a written language. SOV; tonal, 3 tones. Mountain slope. Agriculturalists; fishermen. Polytheist, Christian.

Dzao Min (Yao Min, Zaomin, Yau Min, Ba Pai Yao) [bpn] 60,000 (1995 Wang and Mao). Northern Guangdong Province, Liannan and Yangshan counties; southern Hunan Province, Yizhang County. *Class:* Hmong-Mien, Mienic, Zaomin. *Dialects:* Not intelligible with other Mienic languages. Lexical similarity 61% with Iu Mien, 59% with Kim Mun, 58% with Biao-Jiao Mien. *Other:* Part of the Yao nationality. Mountain slope. Swidden agriculturalists: paddy rice. Daoist.

E (Kjang E, "Wuse Hua," "Wusehua") [eee] 30,000 (1992 Edmondson). Northern Guangxi-Zhuang Autonomous Region, Rongshui Hmong Autonomous County, Yongle Township, and neighboring border areas of Luocheng Mulam Autonomous County. Yongle and nineteen surrounding villages. *Class:* Tai-Kadai, Kam-Tai, Be-Tai, Tai-Sek, Tai, Central. *Lg Use:* Chinese is the second language (especially the Tuguai Hua variety of Cantonese) or Yue. *Other:* A mixed language, with large amounts of Tuguai Hua (Chinese) vocabulary, tone category, voice

quality, and some word structure. The grammar has been more resistant to Chinese influence. Officially under the Zhuang nationality in China, but the speakers do not speak Zhuang. "Wuse" is the Chinese name, with derogatory connotations. 'E' is their name for themselves. Tonal. Plains. Agriculturalists: paddy rice; skilled labor. Traditional religion.

English [eng] 59,000 in China (1993). Mainly in Hong Kong. See main entry under United Kingdom.

Ersu (Duoxu, Erhsu) [ers] 9,000 (1999 Sun Hongkai). About 500 older adults are monolingual. Ethnic population: 20,000 (2000 D. Bradley). South central Sichuan in the lower reaches of the Dadu River; Ganluo, Yuexi, Mianning, and Muli counties of Liangshan Yi Autonomous Prefecture, Shimian and Hanyuan counties of Ya'an Prefecture, Jiulong County of Ganzi Tibetan Autonomous Prefecture in their own villages, and dispersed among the Yi, Chinese, and Tibetan peoples. *Class:* Sino-Tibetan, Tibeto-Burman, Tangut-Qiang, Qiangic. *Dialects:* Ersu (Eastern Ersu), Duoxu (Central Ersu), Lisu (Western Ersu, Lüzü, Liru). Menia (Menya) is reported to be a dialect, but it is unclear how it relates to the other dialects. Dialect differences are reported to be great, so speakers do not understand each other. *Lg Use:* All domains by older adults. In the eastern area: vigorous use among older adults. Adults use Ersu with each other about half the time, young people and children know it, but mainly use Chinese or Yi. Indifferent language attitude. About 8,000 also use Chinese, 400 also use Yi. *Lg Dev:* About 10 people can read the Shaba script. *Other:* Part of the Tibetan nationality. A Shaba is a professional religious practitioner who recites their scriptures at weddings, funerals, when treating the sick, in divination and fortune-telling, oral literature, songs. Has a pictographic script, Ersu Shaba Picture Writing, in which the color used is reported to play a role in expressing meaning, used in religious ceremonies. SOV; adjectives and number-classifier constructions follow noun heads; consonant cluster onsets; most morphemes monosyllabic; tonal, 3 tones. Mountain slope. Sparse forest cover. Raising silkworms; animal husbandry: chickens, pigs, cattle, sheep. Traditional Shaba religion.

Evenki (Ewenke, Ewenki, Owenke, Solon, Suolun, Khamnigan) [evn] 19,000 in China (1999 Chaoke). 3,000 monolinguals. Population total all countries: 29,000. Ethnic population: 34,000 in China (1995 M. Krauss). Hulunbuir Banners Ewenki, Moriadawa, Oronchon, Chen Bargu, Arong, Ergune East, and Huisuomu in Inner Mongolia; Nale Prefecture in Heilongjiang Province; and a few in Xinjiang. Also spoken in Mongolia, Russia (Asia). *Class:* Altaic, Tungus, Northern, Evenki. *Dialects:* Haila'er, Aoluguya (Olguya), Chenba'erhu, Morigele (Mergel), Huihe (Hoy). Huihe is the standard dialect. Significant dialect differences from Russia. *Lg Use:* Vigorous. They maintain native language and customs. It has official regional recognition in China. Speakers of other languages in the area use Evenki as second language. All domains. All ages. Positive language attitude. Bilinguals use Mongolian, Daur, Chinese, or Oroqen as second language. Written Mongolian and Chinese used as literary languages. Herdsmen use Mongolian as second language, farmers use Chinese. *Lg Dev:* Literacy rate in second language: 81%. Radio programs. TV. Dictionary. Grammar. *Other:* An official nationality. 'Solon' is their name for themselves in China, but they also now use the official name 'Ewenke'. 'Sulong' and 'Solong' may be alternate spellings. Mountain forests, marshlands. Nomadic pastoralists: reindeer; hunters; agriculturalists; forestry. Shamanist, Buddhist (Lamaist).

Gahri (Bunan, Lahuli of Bunan) [bfu] See main entry under India.

Gelao (Gelo, Kelao, Keleo, Kehlao, Klau, Klo, Ilao, Khi, Chilao, Lao) [gio] 3,000 (1999 Li Jinfang). About 500 monolinguals. Ethnic population: 579,357. Daozhen and Wuchuan counties, Anshun and Bijie prefectures of southwest Guizhou Province, southern Yunnan (Zhuang-Miao Autonomous District at Maguan, Malipo, and nearby counties), Guangxi (Longlin Pan-Nationalities Autonomous County), and Hunan. *Class:* Tai-Kadai, Kadai, Ge-Chi. *Dialects:* Qau (Gao, Aqao), A'ou (A'uo), Hagei (Hakei, Hakhi), Duoluo (Toluo). The 'dialects' are reported to be 4 languages (2000 D. Bradley). Phonologically close to Hmong, grammatically to Northern Zhuang and Bouyei. Lexical similarity 45% with Southern Zhuang and Dai, 40% with Dong, 36% with Lati, 32% with Laqua, 29% with Buyang, 24% with Northern Zhuang, 24% with Dong, 22% with Laka, 27% to 40% with Hlai, 10% to 15% with Hmong, 5% to 15% with Mien. *Lg Use:* Most domains by older adults. Used in traditional religion. Most speakers are older adults, only used about half time by younger adults, young people use more Chinese, and children may not speak it. Positive language attitude. About 2,500 also speak Hmong, Chinese, or Vietnamese. *Other:* An official nationality. Called 'Gelo' in China. SVO; adjectives follow noun head; negative follows predicate but other adverbials precede predicate; only final consonants are alveolar and velar nasals; nasal-stop and some obstruent-lateral onset clusters; tonal, 6 tones. Mountain slope. Agriculturalists. Polytheist.

Geman Deng [gen] 200 in China (1999 Sun Hongkai). About 180 monolinguals. Several townships in Chayu (Zayü) County, Nyingchi Prefecture, on the tablelands on either side of the lower reaches of the Chayu (Zayü) River in the southeastern corner of Tibet Autonomous Region, in their own small villages. Also spoken in India, Myanmar. *Class:* Sino-Tibetan, Tibeto-Burman, North Assam, Deng. *Lg Use:* Vigorous. All domains. All ages. Some also use Chinese or Tibetan, and a few Darang Deng. *Lg Dev:* Grammar. *Other:* 'Kuman' may be an alternate name. Some believe them to be in the Jingpo branch. May be in the Tibetan official nationality in China. SOV; tonal, 4 tones which are reported to have a low functional load. Mountain slope. Thickly forested. Traditionally hunter-gatherers; now agriculturalists. Traditional religion.

Groma (Tromowa) [gro] 12,840 in China (1993). Chambi Valley, between Sikkim and Bhutan, Tibet. Also spoken in India. *Class:* Sino-Tibetan, Tibeto-Burman, Himalayish, Tibeto-Kanauri, Tibetic, Tibetan, Southern. *Dialects:* Upper Groma, Lower Groma. Possible dialects or related languages: Spiti, Tomo (Chumbi). *Other:* Part of the Tibetan nationality. Traditional religion, Buddhist (Lamaist).

Guanyinqiao (Zhongzhai, Western Jiarong) [jiq] 50,000 (1993 Lin). North central Sichuan, along the tributaries of the Jinchuan River in the southwestern tip of Maerkang County, northwestern Jinchuan County, and southeastern Rangtang County. *Class:* Sino-Tibetan, Tibeto-Burman, Tangut-Qiang, rGyarong. *Dialects:* Xiaoyili, Siyaowu, Muerzong, Guanyinqiao, Ergali, Taiyanghe, Ere, Yelong. Phonologically Western and Northern are fairly similar and differ greatly from Eastern. Western and Northern Jiarong have 60% lexical similarity. *Other:* Part of the Tibetan nationality. SOV; phonologically and lexically similar to Tibetan, grammatically more similar to Pumi and Qiang; complex consonant clusters; limited pitch contrast. Buddhist (Lamaist), polytheist.

Guiqiong (Guichong) [gqi] 6,000 (2000 Sun Hongkai). Fewer than 1,000 monolinguals, mainly older adults. Ethnic population: 7,000 (2000 D. Bradley). Plateaus on both sides of the Dadu River north from Luding County in the Ganzi (Garzê) Tibetan Autonomous Prefecture in west central Sichuan, and nearby in northwest Tianquan

County. One town is Wasigou. *Class:* Sino-Tibetan, Tibeto-Burman, Tangut-Qiang, Qiangic. *Dialects:* Phonological dialect differences, but communication is possible. There are 2 or 3 varieties whose speakers find it difficult to understand each other. *Lg Use:* Vigorous. All domains. All ages. Some intellectuals are worried about losing Guiqiong. About 5,000 also speak Chinese. About 1,000 ethnic Guiqiong are reported to understand it, but not speak it. *Lg Dev:* Dictionary. Grammar. *Other:* Part of the Tibetan nationality. SOV; adjectives and number-classifier constructions follow noun heads; tonal, 4 tones. Riverine, mountain slope. 2,000 meters. Agriculturalists; animal husbandry: chickens, pigs, sheep, cattle; manual workers; soldiers; teachers. Traditional religion.

Hani (Hanhi, Haw, Hani Proper) [hni] 500,000 in China (1990 Svantesson). 60% of the official nationality are monolingual. Population total all countries: 518,657. Jingdong and Jinggu counties, Yuanjiang and Lancang (Mekong) River basins, Ailao Mountains, south Yunnan. None in Thailand. Also spoken in Laos, Viet Nam. *Class:* Sino-Tibetan, Tibeto-Burman, Lolo-Burmese, Loloish, Southern, Akha, Hani, Ha-Ya. *Dialects:* Haya, Haohai, Bika. Divided into three dialect groups depending on whether and to what degree they have vowels with 'clear-muddy' vowel contrasts (P. B. Denlinger 1974). Sang Kong (Sangkong; 2,000) in Jing Hong Xishuangbanna Dai Autonomous State, Yunnan, is officially under Hani, and may be a separate language. Kaduo is reported to be a separate language. Haya is the standard dialect. *Lg Use:* Vigorous. Some speakers of nearby languages also speak Hani. Taught at Kunming Institute. All domains. All ages. Positive language attitude. 40% of the others can also use Chinese. A few can also speak Yi or Lü. Written Chinese is in common use. *Lg Dev:* 40,000 who can read and write it. Roman script. Newspapers. Radio programs. Films. TV. Dictionary. Grammar. *Other:* Hani ethnic groups include Pudu (Putu). Part of the Hani nationality. The official nationality probably includes Kado, Mahei, Sansu, Akha, Biyo (Bio, Biyue), Honi, possibly Menghua and others. The term 'Hani' has been applied to South, Central, and North Lolo languages. In Honghe Prefecture Hani writing is used, in Xishuangbanna Prefecture another form of Hani writing is used which is closer to the 1958 version. SOV; tonal, 3 tones. Mountain slope, plateau. Subtropical mountains. 800 to 2,600 meters. Swidden agriculturalists: rice, millet, maize, cotton, buckwheat, peanuts, tea, indigo; small businessmen. Polytheist, traditional religion.

Hlai (Li, Dai, Day, Lai, La, Loi, Le, Dli, Bli, Klai, Slai) [lic] 667,000 (1999 Ouyang Jueya). 160,000 monolinguals (24% of population—10% children and 14% adults). 432,000 Ha, 178,000 Qi, 52,000 Jiamao, 44,000 Bendi, 30,000 Meifu (1990 census). Mountains in central and south central Hainan Province, southern China. *Class:* Tai-Kadai, Hlai. *Dialects:* Ha (Luohua-Hayan-Baoxian), Qi (Gei, Tongshi-Qiandui-Baocheng), Meifu (Moifau), Bendi (Zwn, Baisha-Yuanmen). Divided into 5 groups: Ha Li, Meifu Li, Qi Li, Local Li, Detou Li. Some varieties listed as dialects may be separate languages. J. Matisoff lists 8 varieties: Baoding, Xifang, Tongshi, Baisha, Qiandiu, Heitu, Yuanmen, Baocheng. Luowo speech of Ha dialect is considered to be the standard. Lexical similarity 30% with Northern Zhuang, 27% with Gelo, 26% with Dong and Laqua, 25% with Lati, 23% with Buyang. *Lg Use:* Vigorous. Some Chinese living in the area can also speak Hlai. All domains. All ages. Positive language attitude. Bilinguals use Chinese as second language. A few also speak Mien or Zhuang. Spoken and written Chinese in common use. Mandarin used in secondary schools. *Lg Dev:* Literacy rate in second language: 54%. Roman script. Dictionary. *Other:* Part of the Li nationality. Traditional culture. Mountain slope, coastal. Tropical forest. Agriculturalists: rice, coconut, betel nut, sisal, hemp, lemon grass, cocoa, coffee, rubber, palm oil; textiles; traditionally hunters. Polytheist.

Hmong Daw (White Meo, White Miao, Meo Kao, White Lum, Peh Miao, Pe Miao, Chuan Miao, Bai Miao) [mww] 232,700 in China (2004). All Hmong in China: 7,000,000 (1999 Li Yunbing). Population total all countries: 514,895. Central and western Guizhou, southern Sichuan, and Yunnan. Also spoken in France, Laos, Thailand, USA, Viet Nam. *Class:* Hmong-Mien, Hmongic, Chuan-qiandian. *Dialects:* Hmong Gu Mba (Hmong Qua Mba, Striped Hmong), Mong Leng, Petchabun Miao. In Thailand, also spoken by the Hmong Qua Mba people, an ethnic subgroup who live in Hmong Daw or Hmong Njua villages, except possibly in Nan Province, with no significant dialect differences. Largely intelligible with Hmong Njua. Mong Leng is intelligible with Hmong Daw, but sociolinguistic factors require separate literature. Probably the same as Peh Miao (White Miao). *Lg Use:* Sociolinguistic factors require separate literature for Mong Leng. *Lg Dev:* Literacy rate in second language: 42%. Dictionary. Bible: 2000. *Other:* Part of the Miao nationality. Traditional religion, Christian.

Hmong Njua (Chuanqiandian Miao, Chuanchientien Miao, Sichuan-Guizhou-Yunnan Hmong, Tak Miao, Meo, Miao, Western Miao, Western Hmong) [blu] 1,000,000 in China (1982). Population includes 29,000 Bunu of the Yao nationality who speak it as first language. Population total all countries: 1,290,600. The area where Guizhou, Sichuan, and Yunnan provinces meet. Also spoken in French Guiana, Laos, Myanmar, Thailand, USA, Viet Nam. *Class:* Hmong-Mien, Hmongic, Chuanqiandian. *Dialects:* Xiao Hua Miao (Atse, Small Flowery Miao), Tak Miao (Ching Miao, Green Miao, Blue Miao). Corresponds more or less to Ma's Western and Northern groups, and Purnell's Central and Western groups. Hua, the Miao (Hmongic) group, consists of 30 to 40 varieties which are inherently unintelligible to one another's speakers (Joakim Enwall 1993:12). A distinct variety called 'Gejiahua' with 50,000 speakers in Huangping County and Kaili City is believed to belong to Hmong Njua. It has 6 tones. Another distinct variety called 'Xijiahua' or 'Haiba Miano' with 50,000 speakers in Huangping, Fuquan, Weng'an, Longli, and Guiding counties and Kaili City, is believed to belong to Hmong Njua. Another distinct variety called 'Dongjiahua' in Majiang, Longli, and Xiuwen counties and Kaili City is believed to belong to Hmong Njua. Speakers are called 'Dongjian', 'Duck-Raising Miano', or 'Duck-Raising Gedou'. It shares many characteristics with Gejiahua. Largely intelligible with Hmong Daw. *Lg Dev:* Dictionary. Bible: 2000. *Other:* Part of the Miao nationality. Village centered. SOV; tonal, 3 tones. Agriculturalists. Traditional religion, Christian.

Hmong, Central Huishui (Central Huishui Miao, Miao) [hmc] 30,000 (1987 Wurm et al.). Gaopa, Huishui, Guiding, Changshun, Ziyun, and Pingba counties, Guiyang City Region, central portion. *Class:* Hmong-Mien, Hmongic, Chuanqiandian. *Dialects:* Inherently unintelligible to speakers of other Hmong varieties. 30 to 40 different Hmong (Miao) languages in China. Linguistic differences are great (Joakim Enwall 1993). *Lg Use:* All domains. *Other:* Part of the Miao nationality. Agriculturalists. Polytheist, Christian.

Hmong, Central Mashan (Central Mashan Miao, Miao) [hmm] 50,000 (1987 Wurm et al.). Southwestern Guizhou, Ziyun, Changshun, Luodian, Huishui, and Wangmo counties, central portion. *Class:* Hmong-Mien, Hmongic, Chuanqiandian. *Dialects:* Not inherently intelligible with other varieties of Hmong. *Lg Use:* All

domains. *Other:* Part of the Miao nationality. Tonal, 13 tones. Traditional religion.

Hmong, Chonganjiang (Chong'anjiang Miao) [hmj] 70,000 (1982). Kaili City, Chong'an township, Huangping county, east central Guizhou. *Class:* Hmong-Mien, Hmongic, Chuanqiandian. *Dialect:* Gejiahua (Ge, Gedou Miao, Keh-Deo, Getou, Gedang, Huadou Miao). Not inherently intelligible with other varieties of Hmong. Gedou may be separate from Chong'anjiang. *Lg Use:* All domains. *Lg Dev:* Bible portions: 1937. *Other:* Part of the Miao nationality. Traditional religion.

Hmong, Eastern Huishui (Eastern Huishui Miao, Miao) [hme] 20,000 (1987 Wurm et al.). Gaopa, Huishui, Guiding, Changshun, Ziyun, and Pingba counties, Guiyang City Region, eastern portion. *Class:* Hmong-Mien, Hmongic, Chuanqiandian. *Dialects:* Inherently unintelligible to speakers of other Hmong varieties. *Lg Use:* All domains. *Other:* Part of the Miao nationality. Agriculturalists. Polytheist, Christian.

Hmong, Eastern Qiandong (Eastern Qiandong Miao, Hmu, Miao, Black Miao, Central Miao, Eastern East-Guizhou Miao) [hmq] 200,000 (1987 Zhang and Cao). Qiandongnan Miao Dong Autonomous Prefecture, Guizhou, and eastward into Hunan Province. *Class:* Hmong-Mien, Hmongic, Qiandong. *Dialects:* Not intelligible with other varieties of Hmong. Corresponds more or less to Ma's Central Miao and Purnell's Eastern Miao. *Lg Dev:* Dictionary. Bible portions: 1928. *Other:* Part of the Miao nationality. Agriculturalists. Polytheist, Christian.

Hmong, Eastern Xiangxi (Eastern Xiangxi Miao, Hsianghsi Miao, Red Miao, Meo Do, Red Meo, Ghao-Xong, Eastern West-Hunan Miao) [muq] 70,000 (1987 Zhang and Cao). Western Hunan, Xiangxi Tujia Miao Autonomous Prefecture, and some places in Hubei. *Class:* Hmong-Mien, Hmongic, Xiangxi. *Dialects:* Not inherently intelligible with other varieties of Hmong (Miao). *Other:* Part of the Miao nationality. 'Maojiahua' is a variety of Chinese spoken by about 20,000 members of the Miao nationality in southwestern Hunan, Chengbu Miao Autonomous County, Xining and Suining, and in northeastern Guangxi, Longshen Pan-nationalities Autonomous County and the area around Ziyuan, with 7 tones. Polytheist, Christian.

Hmong, Luopohe (Luobohe Miao, Ximahe Miao, Xijia Miao) [hml] 40,000 (1987 Wurm et al.). Fuquan, Guiding, Longli, Kaiyang, and Kaili counties east of Guiyang, central Guizhou. *Class:* Hmong-Mien, Hmongic, Chuanqiandian. *Dialects:* Not inherently intelligible with other varieties of Hmong. *Lg Use:* All domains. *Other:* Part of the Miao nationality. Polytheist.

Hmong, Northeastern Dian (A-Hmao, Diandongbei, Variegated Miao, Ta Hua Miao, Ta Hwa Miao, Big Flowery Miao, Hua Miao, Hwa Miao, Flowery Miao, Northeastern Yunnan Miao) [hmd] 200,000 (1987 Wurm et al.). Northwestern Guizhou, northeast and central Yunnan provinces. *Class:* Hmong-Mien, Hmongic, Chuanqiandian. *Dialects:* Inherently unintelligible to speakers of other Hmong varieties. *Lg Use:* All domains. *Lg Dev:* Dictionary. NT: 1917–1936. *Other:* Part of the Miao nationality. Agriculturalists. Polytheist, Christian.

Hmong, Northern Guiyang (Northern Guiyang Miao, Miao) [huj] 60,000 (1987 Wurm et al.). Suburbs of Guiyang City, Pingba, Zhenning, Kaiyang, Guiding, Qingzhen, and Anshun counties or towns, northern portion. *Class:* Hmong-Mien, Hmongic, Chuanqiandian. *Dialects:* Inherently unintelligible to speakers of other Hmong varieties. *Lg Use:* All domains. *Other:* Part of the Miao nationality. Agriculturalists. Polytheist, Christian.

Hmong, Northern Huishui (Northern Huishui Miao, Miao) [hmi] 50,000 (1987 Wurm et al.). Gaopa, Huishui, Guiding, Changshun, Ziyun, and Pingba counties, Guiyang

City Region, northern portion. *Class:* Hmong-Mien, Hmongic, Chuanqiandian. *Dialects:* Inherently unintelligible to speakers of other Hmong varieties. *Lg Use:* All domains. *Other:* Part of the Miao nationality. Agriculturalists. Polytheist, Christian.

Hmong, Northern Mashan (Northern Mashan Miao) [hmp] 25,000 (1987 Wurm et al.). Southwestern Guizhou, Ziyun, northern portions of Changshun, Luodian, Huishui, and Wangmo counties. *Class:* Hmong-Mien, Hmongic, Chuanqiandian. *Dialects:* Not inherently intelligible with other varieties of Hmong. *Other:* Part of the Miao nationality. Tonal, 13 tones. Traditional religion.

Hmong, Northern Qiandong (Northern Qiandong Miao, Chientung Miao, East Guizhou Miao, Hmu, Miao, Black Miao, Heh Miao, Hei Miao, Central Miao, Northern East-Guizhou Miao) [hea] 900,000 (1987 Zhang and Cao). Northeast Yunnan and upper Cingshuiho River area of southeast Guizhou (southeast, south, and southwest Guizhou Autonomous areas, Songtao County, Guanling County, Ziyun County). *Class:* Hmong-Mien, Hmongic, Qiandong. *Dialects:* Not intelligible with other varieties of Hmong. Corresponds more or less to Ma's Central Miao and Purnell's Eastern Miao. Hmu was chosen by the government as the standard variety. It is based on Yanghao, but with some similarities to other varieties. *Lg Dev:* Dictionary. NT: 1934. *Other:* Part of the Miao nationality. Agriculturalists. Polytheist, Christian.

Hmong, Southern Guiyang (Southern Guiyang Miao, Miao) [hmy] 20,000 (1987 Wurm et al.). Suburbs of Guiyang City, Pingba, Zhenning, Kaiyang, Guiding, Qingzhen, and Anshun counties or towns, southern portion. *Class:* Hmong-Mien, Hmongic, Chuanqiandian. *Dialects:* Inherently unintelligible to speakers of other Hmong varieties. *Lg Use:* All domains. *Other:* Part of the Miao nationality. Agriculturalists. Polytheist, Christian.

Hmong, Southern Mashan (Southern Mashan Miao, Miao) [hma] 7,000 (1987 Wurm et al.). Southwestern Guizhou, southern portions of Ziyun, Changshun, Luodian, Huishui, and Wangmo counties. *Class:* Hmong-Mien, Hmongic, Chuanqiandian. *Dialects:* Not inherently intelligible with other varieties of Hmong. *Lg Use:* All domains. *Other:* Part of the Miao nationality. Tonal, 13 tones. Traditional religion.

Hmong, Southern Qiandong (Southern Qiandong Miao, Hmu, Miao, Black Miao, Central Miao, Southern East-Guizhou Miao) [hms] 300,000 (1987 Zhang and Cao). Qiandongnan Miao Dong Autonomous Prefecture, Guizhou Province, and southward into Guangxi Province. *Class:* Hmong-Mien, Hmongic, Qiandong. *Dialects:* Not intelligible with other varieties of Hmong. Corresponds more or less to Ma's Central Miao and Purnell's Eastern Miao. *Lg Dev:* Dictionary. *Other:* Part of the Miao nationality. Agriculturalists. Polytheist, Christian.

Hmong, Southwestern Guiyang (Southwestern Guiyang Miao, Miao) [hmg] 50,000 (1987 Wurm et al.). Suburbs of Guiyang City, Pingba, Zhenning, Kaiyang, Guiding, Qingzhen, and Anshun counties or towns, southwestern portion. *Class:* Hmong-Mien, Hmongic, Chuanqiandian. *Dialects:* Inherently unintelligible to speakers of other Hmong varieties. *Lg Use:* All domains. *Other:* Part of the Miao nationality. Agriculturalists. Polytheist, Christian.

Hmong, Southwestern Huishui (Southwestern Huishui Miao, Miao) [hmh] 40,000 (1987 Wurm et al.). Gaopa, Huishui, Guiding, Changshun, Ziyun, and Pingba counties, Guiyang City Region, southwestern portion. *Class:* Hmong-Mien, Hmongic, Chuanqiandian. *Dialects:* Inherently unintelligible to speakers of other Hmong varieties. *Lg Use:* All domains. *Other:* Part of the Miao nationality. Agriculturalists. Polytheist, Christian.

Hmong, Western Mashan (Western Mashan Miao, Miao) [hmw] 10,000 (1987 Wurm et al.). Southwestern Guizhou, Ziyun, Changshun, Luodian, Huishui, and Wangmo counties, western portion. *Class:* Hmong-Mien, Hmongic, Chuanqiandian. *Dialects:* Not inherently intelligible with other varieties of Hmong. *Lg Use:* All domains. *Other:* Part of the Miao nationality. Tonal, 13 tones. Traditional religion.

Hmong, Western Xiangxi (Red Miao, Meo Do, Red Meo, Western Xiangsi Miao, Ghao-Xong, Huayuan Miao, Hsianghsi Miao, West Hunan Miao, Western West-Hunan Miao) [mmr] 700,000 (1987 Zhang and Cao). Western Hunan, Xiangxi Tujia Miao Autonomous Prefecture, Songtao County in Guizhou, Xiushan County in Sichuan, and some places in Guangxi. Possibly also in Ha Tuyen Province, northern Viet Nam and in Thailand. *Class:* Hmong-Mien, Hmongic, Xiangxi. *Dialects:* Not inherently intelligible with other varieties of Hmong (Miao). *Lg Use:* Vigorous, strong sense of ethnic identity. Most domains except education. Positive language attitude. *Lg Dev:* Literacy rate in second language: 40% or more. Dictionary. *Other:* Part of the Miao nationality. Polytheist, Christian.

Honi (Woni, Ouni, Uni, Ho, Haoni) [how] 100,000 (1990 Svantesson). Yunnan, near the Hani. May also be in Viet Nam. *Class:* Sino-Tibetan, Tibeto-Burman, Lolo-Burmese, Loloish, Southern, Akha, Hani, Hao-Bai. *Dialect:* Baihong. *Other:* Part of the Hani nationality, but it is a distinct language. Baihong may be a separate language. Polytheist, Christian.

Horpa (Hor, Hórsók, Ergong, Danba, Western Jiarong, Pawang, Bawang) [ero] 38,000 (1999 Sun Hongkai). 15,000 monolinguals. Danba (= Rongzhag), Daofu (Dawu), Luhuo, Xinlong (Nyagrong) counties of the Ganzi (Garzê) Tibetan Autonomous Prefecture of western Sichuan, and Jinchua (Quqên) County of the Aba (Ngawa) Tibetan-Qiang Autonomous Prefecture of northwestern Sichuan. Central and eastern Daofu County, Chengguan District, Wari, Xiajia, and Muru townships of Wari District, and Shazhong township of Bamei District; and central and northwestern Danba County, in Geshiza, Bianer, and Dandong townships of Dasang District, Donggu township in Chuangu District, Bawang and Jinchuan townships of Jinchuan District; of Ganzi Prefecture, an area traditionally known as the five parts of Horpa territory. Scattered communities are also in adjacent Luhuo (in Renda township of Xialatuo District, and Xinlong in Manqing, Zhuwo, and Duoshan townships of Hexi District). *Class:* Sino-Tibetan, Tibeto-Burman, Tangut-Qiang, rGyarong. *Dialects:* Daofu (Daofuhua, Taofu, Western Horpa, Western Ergong), Geshiza (Geshitsa). Hongkai Sun (1999) lists 4 dialects: Western as above, Central (Danba), Eastern (Jinchuan, Lawurong), Northern (Rangtang). Huang Bufan and Sun Tianxin suggest that the eastern variety is a separate language. *Lg Use:* All domains. All ages. Greater use by adults than young people. Children are mainly using Chinese. Indifferent language attitude. 2,000 can also use both Chinese and Tibetan. 20,000 use Chinese, 1,000 use Tibetan. *Lg Dev:* Dictionary. Grammar. *Other:* Part of the Tibetan nationality. SOV; adjectives and number-classifier constructions follow noun heads; affixation; compounding; reduplication; complex consonant cluster onsets; nontonal. Mountain slope, riverine. Forests. Agriculturalists; animal husbandry: chickens, pigs, sheep. Buddhist (Lamaist), traditional religion.

Hu [huo] 1,000 (1984 Svantesson). Southwestern Yunnan Province, Mengla, Jinghong, 5 villages. *Class:* Austro-Asiatic, Mon-Khmer, Northern Mon-Khmer, Palaungic, Western Palaungic, Angkuic. *Other:* Counted separately in 1982 census and combined into a group of

'Undetermined Minorities'. Affixes; tonal. Traditional religion.

Ili Turki (T'urk, Tuerke) [ili] 120 in China (1980 R. F. Hahn). Ili Valley near Kuldja, Xinjiang. Probably some in Kazakhstan. Also spoken in Kazakhstan. *Class:* Altaic, Turkic, Eastern. *Lg Use:* Speakers are older adults. Younger people are intermarrying with neighboring groups. Speakers also use Kazakh or Uyghur. *Other:* Ethnically and linguistically distinct, discovered in 1956. Their oral history says they came from the Ferghana Valley (Uzbekistan and Kyrgyzstan) about 200 years ago. SOV; vowel harmony; influenced greatly by Kazakh and Uyghur; has Arabic, Persian, Chinese, and Russian loans. Mulsim (Sunni).

Iu Mien (Youmian, Yiu Mien, Yao, Mien, Mian, Myen, Highland Yao, Pan Yao, Ban Yao) [ium] 383,000 in China (1995 Wang and Mao). Population total all countries: 818,685. Dayao Mountains, Guangxi Zhuang Autonomous Region, Guangdong, Yunnan, Hunan, and Guizhou provinces. In Guizhou Province Mien are in Rongjiang, Congjiang, and Libo counties; in Guangdong Province, in Ruyuan County. Also spoken in Belgium, Canada, Denmark, France, Laos, Myanmar, New Zealand, Switzerland, Thailand, USA, Viet Nam. *Class:* Hmong-Mien, Mienic, Mian-Jin. *Dialects:* The different dialects may not be intelligible. Biao Mon may be a dialect of Iu Mien. Differences from other Mienic languages are in the tone system, consonants, vowel quality, vowel length. Chinese linguists consider the Iu Mien spoken in Changdong, Jinxiu Yao Autonomous County, Guangxi to be the standard. May be closest to Mandarin. Lexical similarity 78% with Kim Mun, 70% with Biao-Jiao Mien, 61% with Dzao Min. *Lg Use:* Vigorous. All domains. All ages. Positive language attitude. Children tend to be monolingual. Spoken and written Chinese are also in use. *Lg Dev:* Roman script. Radio programs. Dictionary. Grammar. NT: 1975–1991. *Other:* The largest language in the Yao nationality. Ethnic groups: Hua Lan, Hua, Hung, Cao Long, Coc, Khoc, Quan Coc, Quan Trang, Son Trang, Sung, Tien (Tiao Tchaine), Yaya. The Laka, Mun, Bunu languages, plus speakers of other Mienic and Hmongic languages, and ethnic Yao who speak Chinese, are officially included under the Yao nationality in China. 'Pingdi Yao' (Piongtuojo, Piongtoajeu) is a variety of Chinese with 1,000,000 speakers, half of whom are members of the Yao nationality, in Hunan-Guangxi border and Guangdong Province. Tonal, 7 tones. Mountain slope, plains. Peasant agriculturalists: paddy rice; hunters; lumbermen; weavers; embroiderers. Daoist, traditional religion.

Jiamao (Kamau, Tai) [jio] 52,300 (1987 Wurm et al.). Near Wuzhi Mountain in southern Hainan Province, Baoting, Lingshui, and Qiongzhong counties. *Class:* Tai-Kadai, Hlai. *Dialects:* Very different from Hlai dialects in phonology, grammar, and vocabulary. *Other:* Part of the Li nationality. Polytheist.

Jiarong (Jyarung, Gyarong, Gyarung, Rgyarong, Chiarong, Jarong) [jya] 83,000 (1999 Sun Hongkai). 25,000 monolinguals. Ethnic population: 151,377 including 139,000 in Situ Jiarong, 12,197 in Chabao and Sidaba (1993 Lin). North central Sichuan. Situ is in the traditional territory of four chieftaincies: Zhuokeji, Suomo, Songgang, Dangba. Chabao is in the northeastern corner of Maerkang county, at Longerjia, Dazang, and Shaerzong townships in Chabao District. Sidaba is in Caodeng, Kangshan, and Ribu townships in Sidaba District of Maerkang County. Some outlying Sidaba communities are to the north in certain villages of Kehe and Rongan townships, at the southwesten corner of the Aba County, and to the west along the middle Duke River between Wuyi and Shili townships in Rangtang County, spilling over to a small area near the confluence of the Seda and Duke rivers in Seda County. *Class:* Sino-Tibetan, Tibeto-Burman, Tangut-Qiang, rGyarong. *Dialects:* Chabao (Dazang, Northeastern Jiarong), Sidaba (Caodeng, Northwestern Jiarong), Situ (Eastern Jiarong). Subdialects of Situ are: Maerkang, Lixian, Jinchuan, Xiaojin; of Sidaba Caodeng and Ribu. Phonologically Western and Northern are fairly similar and differ greatly from Eastern. Lexical similarity 75% between Eastern and Northern Jiarong, 60% between Western and Northern 60%, 13% between Situ and Horpa. *Lg Use:* Vigorous. All domains. All ages. Positive language attitude, but intellectuals are worried about diminishing use of the language. 56,000 use Chinese, 950 Tibetan, 50 Qiang as second language. *Lg Dev:* Radio programs. Dictionary. *Other:* Part of the Tibetan nationality. SOV; phonologically and lexically similar to Tibetan, grammatically more similar to Pumi and Qiang; complex consonant clusters; limited pitch contrast. Mountain slope, plains, riverine. Agriculturalists: apples, pears; lumbermen. Traditional religion, Buddhist (Lamaist).

Jingpho (Jingpo, Jinghpaw, Chingpaw, Chingp'o, Kachin, Marip, Dashanhua) [kac] 40,000 in China (1999 Xu Xijian). 50% monolingual. Ethnic population: 119,209 in China (1990 census). Western Yunnan, Dehong Dai-Jingpo Autonomous Prefecture, Yingjiang County (Shidan dialect; Enkun dialect elsewhere in Dehong Dai-Jingpo Autonomous Prefecture). *Dialects:* Enkun, Shidan, Hkaku (Hka-Hku), Kauri (Hkauri, Gauri), Dzili (Jili), Dulong. *Lg Use:* Vigorous. Speakers of other languages in the area speak Jingpho as second language. Taught at Kunming Institute. All domains. Positive language attitude. Speakers also use Zaiwa, Lashi, Maru, or Chinese. Chinese is used in some secondary schools. *Other:* Part of the Jingpo nationality. 'Kachin' refers to the cultural rather than the linguistic group. An official nationality in China; includes 70,000 Atsi, and Maru and Lashi officially. Has a Pinyin alphabet in China. Orthography at Kunming Institute is based on Enkun dialect. Mountain slope. Pastoralists; agriculturalists. Polytheist, Buddhist, Christian. See main entry under Myanmar.

Jinuo, Buyuan (Jino, Buyuan) [jiy] 1,000 (1994). Most are monolingual. Ethnic population: 18,021 (1990 census). South Yunnan, Xishuangbanna Dai Autonomous Pre-fecture, near Laos and Myanmar borders, 53 kilometers east of Jinghong. Youle Mountains. 40 villages. Over 3,000 square kilometers. *Class:* Sino-Tibetan, Tibeto-Burman, Lolo-Burmese, Loloish, Southern. *Dialects:* The two 'dialects' (Buyuan and Youle) are not inherently intelligible with each other. Their speakers use Chinese for communication. *Lg Use:* Vigorous. All domains. All ages. Some speakers also use Dai or Chinese. *Lg Dev:* Literacy rate in second language: 49%. Roman script. *Other:* Part of the Jino nationality. SOV; 6 tones; initial consonant clusters (stop or nasal plus 'r'); no syllable-final consonants; mostly monosyllabic words. Mountain slope. Forests. Agriculturalists: rice; hunter-gatherers traditionally. Worship of Kong Ming (a Chinese hero).

Jinuo, Youle (Jino, Youle) [jiu] 13,000 (2000). Most speakers are monolingual. South Yunnan, Xishuangbanna Dai Autonomous Prefecture, near Laos and Myanmar borders, 53 kilometers east of Jinghong. Youle Mountains. 40 villages. Over 3,000 square kilometers. *Class:* Sino-Tibetan, Tibeto-Burman, Lolo-Burmese, Loloish, Southern. *Dialects:* The two 'dialects' (Youle and Buyuan) are not inherently intelligible with each other. Their speakers use Chinese to communicate with each other. *Lg Use:* Vigorous. All domains. All ages. Positive language attitude. Some speakers also use Dai or Chinese. Chinese is used in education. *Lg Dev:* Literacy rate in second language: 49%. Roman script. Films. *Other:* Part of the Jino nationality. SOV; initial consonant clusters (stop or nasal plus 'r'); no syllable-final consonants; mostly monosyllabic words; tonal, 6 tones. Mountain slope. Forests. Agriculturalists: rice; hunter-gatherers traditionally. Worship of Kong Ming (a Chinese hero).

Jurchen (Nuzhen, Nuchen) [juc] Extinct. *Class:* Altaic, Tungus, Southern, Southwest. *Dialects:* Related to Manchu. *Other:* It was spoken by the Nuzhen people.

Kado (Kadu, Katu, Kato, Kudo, Gado, Asak, Sak, Thet, That, Mawteik, Puteik) [kdv] 100,000 in China (1990 Svantesson). South Yunnan. *Dialects:* Kadu, Ganaan (Ganan), Andro, Sengmai, Chakpa, Phayeng. *Other:* Part of the Hani nationality. Different from Katu, a Mon-Khmer language of Viet Nam and Laos. See main entry under Myanmar.

Kaduo (Gazhuo, Kado, Kadu) [ktp] 5,292 in China (2000 WCD). South central Yunnan Province, Hexi District of Tonghai County. *Other:* Part of the Mongolian nationality. Remnants of an outpost dating back to the Yuan Dynasty. See main entry under Laos.

Kalmyk-Oirat (Oirat, Weilate, Xinjiang Mongolian, Western Mongol) [xal] 139,000 in China (1989 Wurm et al.). Population includes 106,000 Torgut, 60,000 Kok Nur. Bayan Gool Autonomous Prefecture and Bortala Autonomous Prefecture. *Dialects:* Jakhachin, Bayit, Mingat, Olot (Ööld, Elyut, Eleuth), Khoshut (Khoshuud), Dorbot. *Lg Use:* Official regional language. Since 1982 schooling has been in Chahar Mongolian. Speakers have high bilingualism in Chahar Mongolian in China. *Other:* Part of the Mongolian nationality. See main entry under Russia (Europe).

Kang [kyp] 34,065 in China (1993). Southwest Yunnan. *Other:* Part of the Dai nationality. Related ethnic groups, dialects, or languages in the area: Chang Teo Fah, Kentse, Mengka (Mengkah). See main entry under Laos.

Kangjia (Kangyang Hui) [kxs] 377 to 487 (1999 Sechenchogt). Ethnic population: 487. Shalimu, Zongzila, and Hangdao villages, Jainca County, Huangnan Tibetan Autonomous Prefecture, Qinghai Province. *Class:* Altaic, Mongolian, Eastern, Mongour. *Lg Use:* Used in local commerce, some oral traditional literature. Older adults speak Kangjia half the time, adults less, and younger ones do not speak it. Indifferent language attitude. Others can also speak Chinese or Tibetan. *Lg Dev:* Dictionary. Grammar. *Other:* Part of the Hui nationality. Riverine. Below 2,048 meters. Agriculturalists; forestry; animal husbandry; businessmen. Muslim (Jahaliyah).

Kazakh (Kazak, Kazax, Hazake) [kaz] 1,111,718 in China (1990 census). 85% are monolingual. Population includes 830,000 Northeastern Kazakh, 70,000 Southwestern Kazakh (1982). North Xinjiang (Yili Kazakh Autonomous Prefecture), east Xinjiang (Mulei Kazakh Autonomous County and Balikun Kazakh Autonomous County), northwest Gansu (Akesai Kazakh Autonomous County), and northwest Qinghai provinces. *Dialects:* Northeastern Kazakh, Southwestern Kazakh. *Lg Use:* Vigorous. Speakers of nearby languages use Kazakh as second language. All domains. All ages. Positive language attitude. 15% can also use Chinese. *Lg Dev:* Literacy rate in second language: 72%. *Other:* An official nationality in China. Plains. Desert. Pastoralists; some agriculturalists. Muslim (Sunni), Shamanist. See main entry under Kazakhstan.

Kemiehua [kfj] 1,000 (1991). Jinghong County, Xishuangbanna Dai Autonomous Prefecture, southwestern Yunnan Province. *Class:* Austro-Asiatic, Mon-Khmer, Unclassified. *Other:* SVO; most modifiers follow heads, although adverbial phrases precede heads; simple syllable structure; tonal. Traditional religion.

Khakas (Khakhas, Khakhass, Abakan Tatar, Yenisei Tatar) [kjh] 10 in China (1982 census). Ethnic population: 875 in ethnic group in China (1982 census). Fuyu County, north of Qiqihar, in Heilongjiang Province. *Dialects:* Sagai,

Beltir, Kacha, Kyzyl, Shor, Kamassian. *Lg Use:* Only about 10 very old people speak fluently, others use some words, but mainly Mongolian. The young people are monolingual in Chinese. Speakers also use Mongolian or Chinese. *Other:* Part of the Kirghiz nationality. People came from the Altay Mountains in Russia in 1761. Buddhist (Lamaist), traditional religion. See main entry under Russia (Asia).

Khmu (Kammu, Khamu, Khmu', Khamuk, Kamhmu, Kamu, Kemu, Khomu, Mou, Lao Terng, Pouteng, Theng) [kjg] 1,600 in China (1990). Mengla and Jinghong counties of Xishuangbanna Prefecture, southwestern Yunnan. *Other:* Khmu was counted separately in the 1982 census and combined into a group of 'Undetermined Minorities'. It may soon be recognized as an official nationality. Phsing (Bit) is regarded as Khmu in China, but is in the Palaungic branch (Svantesson 1990). See main entry under Laos.

Khuen (Kween, Khween, Khouen) [khf] 1,000 in China (1993). See main entry under Laos.

Kim Mun (Mun, Kem Mun, Gem Mun, Jim Mun, Jinmen, Kimmun, Men, Man Lantien, Lanten, Lan Tin, Lowland Yao, Chasan Yao, Shanzi Yao, Hainan Miao) [mji] 200,000 in China (1995 Wang and Mao). Population includes 61,000 in Hainan Province (2000 census). Population total all countries: 374,500. Yunnan Province, seventeen counties; Guangxi Zhuang Autonomous Region, thirteen counties; Hainan Province, seven counties. Also spoken in Laos, Viet Nam. *Class:* Hmong-Mien, Mienic, Mian-Jin. *Dialects:* Dao Quan Trang, Dao Ho. Not intelligible with Iu Mien. Lexical similarity 78% with Iu Mien, 67% with Biao-Jiao Mien, 59% with Dzao Min. *Lg Dev:* Roman script. Dictionary. *Other:* Part of the Yao nationality, except for those on Hainan Island, who are included in the Miao nationality. The largest Yao group after Iu Mien. Daoist.

Kirghiz (Kirgiz, Kara, Ke'erkez) [kir] 437,238 in China (1999 Hu Zhenhua). Older adults are monolingual. West and southwest Xinjiang, in Wuqia, Akqi, Akto, Tekes, Zhaosu, Baicheng, Wushi counties. *Dialects:* Southern Kirghiz, Northern Kirghiz. *Lg Use:* Vigorous. All domains. All ages. Positive language attitude. Speakers also use Uyghur or Chinese. *Lg Dev:* Literacy rate in first language: 80% to 85%. Literacy rate in second language: 59%. Taught in primary and secondary schools. *Other:* Part of the Kirghiz nationality. 2 dialects, divided by Kyzyl Su (Kizil) River. Northern Kirghiz is the standard one. Mountain slope. Animal husbandry; agriculturalists. Muslim (Sunni), Shamanist. See main entry under Kyrgyzstan.

Kon Keu [kkn] 6,300 (2000 WCD). *Class:* Austro-Asiatic, Mon-Khmer, Northern Mon-Khmer, Palaungic, Western Palaungic, Angkuic. *Other:* Part of the Bulang nationality. May be in Myanmar or Laos. Traditional religion.

Korean (Chaoxian) [kor] 1,920,597 in China (1990 census). 1,200,000 are monolingual. Inner Mongolia. 46% of Koreans in China live in Hyanbian Korean Auton-omous District along Tumen River, Jilin (Kirin), and Heilongjiang, and Liaoning. *Lg Use:* Used mainly among adults. All domains. All ages. Positive language attitude. 700,000 also use Chinese. A few can speak Russian. Those who finished secondary school by 1945 can speak Japanese. Chinese speakers living among them also speak Korean as second language. *Other:* An official nationality called Chaoxian. High level of education. Mountain slope, foothills, plains. 500 to 1,000 meters. Agriculturalists: wet rice; industrial workers; businessmen. Buddhist, Christian. See main entry under Korea, South.

Kuanhua [xnh] 1,000 (1991). Jinghong County, Xishuangbanna Dai Autonomous Prefecture, southwestern

Yunnan Province. *Class:* Austro-Asiatic, Mon-Khmer, Unclassified. *Other:* SVO. Traditional religion.

Kyerung [kgy] 100 in China (2002). Tibet. *Other:* Part of the Tibetan nationality. Apparently distinct from Jiarong (Gyarung). Buddhist (Lamaist). See main entry under Nepal.

Lachi (La Chi, Lati, Tai Lati, Laji, Lipulio, I To, Y To, Y Poong, Y Mia, Ku Te) [lbt] 1,153 in China (1990 Liang Min). Population includes 193 Bag Lachi in 37 households, 852 Han Lachi in 179 households, 157 Red Lachi in 27 households, 432 Flowery Lachi in 72 households. Ethnic population: 1,634. Yunnan Province, Wenshan Zhuang-Miao Autonomous Prefecture, southern Maguan County, several villages: Bag Lachi in Nanlao Township, Han Lachi in Renhe and Jiahanqing townships, Red Lachi in Xiaobazi Township, and Flowery Lachi in Jinchang. *Dialects:* Lipute (Bag Lachi), Liputcio (Han Lachi), Lipuke (Red Lachi), Lipuliongtco (Flowery Lachi), Liputiõ (Black Lachi), Lipupi (Long-Haired Lachi). *Lg Use:* Used in the home. Speakers are adults. Those who do not speak Lachi speak Chinese. The Flowery Lachi also speak Chinese, most can speak Southern Zhuang, and some can speak Miao and Dai. Mixed families speak Chinese. *Other:* Part of the Yi nationality, but their language is unrelated to most Yi languages. See main entry under Viet Nam.

Ladakhi (Ladaphi, Ladhakhi, Ladak, Ladwags) [lbj] 12,000 in China (1995). Western Tibet. *Dialects:* Leh (Central Ladakhi), Shamma (Sham, Shamskat, Lower Ladakhi), Nubra Ladakhi. *Other:* Part of the Tibetan nationality. Mountain valleys. 2,400 to 5,000 meters. Agriculturalists: wheat, barley; pastoralists: yaks, goats, sheep (cashmere wool). Buddhist (Lamaist). See main entry under India.

Lahu (Lohei, Lahuna, Laku, Kaixien, Namen, Mussuh, Muhso, Musso, Mussar, Moso) [lhu] 411,476 in China (1990 census). 360,000 are monolingual. Population includes 240,000 Na, probably including Kutsung and Laopang. Population total all countries: 577,178. Ethnic population: 417,000. Lancang Lahu Autonomous County, Gengma, and Menglian counties, southwestern Yunnan. Also spoken in Laos, Myanmar, Thailand, Viet Nam. *Class:* Sino-Tibetan, Tibeto-Burman, Lolo-Burmese, Loloish, Southern, Akha, Lahu. *Dialects:* Na (Black Lahu, Musser Dam, Northern Lahu, Loheirn), Nyi (Red Lahu, Southern Lahu, Musseh Daeng, Luhishi, Luhushi), Shehleh. Na is the standard dialect. Black Lahu and Lahu Shi (Yellow Lahu, Kutsung) have difficult intelligibility. (See separate entry for Lahu Shi.) Mossu is in Laos. Lahu Shi (Yellow Lahu, Kutsung) is distinct. *Lg Use:* Vigorous. Some speakers of other languages use Lahu as second language for commerce. Taught at Kunming Institute. All domains. All ages. Positive language attitude. 20% to 30% also use Chinese fluently, 50% to 60% use simple Chinese, 10% can understand but not speak it. 1,000 also use Lü, Hani, Blang, Va, or Yi as second languages. *Lg Dev:* Literacy rate in first language: 62.5%. Taught in primary schools. Roman script. Newspapers. Radio programs. Dictionary. Grammar. Bible: 1989. *Other:* Part of the Lahu nationality. SOV; Lü and Hani loanwords. Mountain slope, riverine. Subtropical forest. Low altitude. Agriculturalists: rice, maize; hunters. Traditional religion, Buddhist, Christian.

Lahu Shi (Lahu Xi, Kutsung, Kucong, Kur, Shi, Yellow Lahu, Kwi) [kds] 5,000 in China (1984). Southern Yunnan. *Other:* Part of the Lahu nationality. See main entry under Laos.

Lakkia (Lakkja, Lakja, Lakia, Lajia, Tai Laka, Laka, Chashan Yao, Tea Mountain Yao) [lbc] 12,000 (1999 Liu Baoyuan). 4,000 monolinguals. Ethnic population: 12,000. Eastern Guangxi Zhuang Autonomous Region, Jinxiu Yao Autonomous County. *Class:* Tai-Kadai, Kam-Tai, Lakkja. *Dialects:* Officially under the Yao (Mien) nationality, but the language is Tai-Kadai (Svantesson). Phonetically similar to Mien, word order to Bunu. Not intelligible with Hmong or Bunu. Minimal variation within Lakkia. All varieties are inherently intelligible to each other's speakers. Lexical similarity 45% with Dong, 44% with Northern Zhuang, 24% with Buyang, 23% with Lati and Laqua, 22% with Gelo. *Lg Use:* Vigorous. Some speakers of other languages use Lakkia for trade. All domains. All ages. Positive language attitude. Speakers also use Mandarin Chinese, Mien, or Zhuang. *Lg Dev:* Dictionary. Grammar. *Other:* Part of the Yao nationality. Different from Lashi, which is also called Chashan(hua). 'Lajia' is the same name used for the Yayao variety of the Siyi dialect of Cantonese spoken in Heshan County, Guangdong. SVO; modifiers follow heads; consonant clusters and palatalized and labialized onsets; voiced and voiceless nasal onsets; long-short vowel distinction; 6 basic tone categories in unchecked syllables and 2 in checked with further split in checked syllables according to vowel length. Mountain slope, riverine. Forest. 115 to 1,979 meters. Agriculturalists. Daoist, polytheist.

Laqua (Pubiao, Pupeo, Pu Péo, Ka Biao, Ka Bao, Ka Beo, Kabeo, Qabiao) [laq] 307 in China (1990 Zhang Junru). 58 households. Yunnan Province, Wenshan Zhuang-Miao Autonomous Prefecture, Malipo County, Tiechang, Matong, Punong, Pucha, and Pufeng towns. *Lg Use:* Nearly 30% of the younger generation speak Laqua. Generally everyone can also speak Southwestern Mandarin. Those at Pialong can speak Southern Zhuang. Those near Matong can speak Hmong. *Other:* Part of the Yi nationality. Ka Biao is their name for themselves. See main entry under Viet Nam (Qabiao).

Lashi (Lasi, Leqi, Letsi, Lachikwaw, Chashanhua, Acye) [lsi] 1,800 (1997). Luxi, Longchuan, Yingjiang, and Ruili counties, Dehong Dai-Jingpo Autonomous Prefecture, western Yunnan. *Other:* Part of the Jingpo nationality. See main entry under Myanmar.

Lawa, Western (Wa, Wa Proper, Lava, Luwa, Lua, L'wa, Lavua, Lavüa, Mountain Lawa) [lcp] 75,000 in China. Population includes 30,000 in the Blang nationality, 45,000 in the Va nationality (1990 Svantesson). Population total all countries: 82,000. Southwest Yunnan Province. Also spoken in Thailand. *Class:* Austro-Asiatic, Mon-Khmer, Northern Mon-Khmer, Palaungic, Western Palaungic, Waic, Lawa. *Dialects:* Unintelligible to speakers of Eastern Lawa in Thailand. Some dialects are unintelligible to each other's speakers. Related to Wa and Parauk in Myanmar and China. *Lg Dev:* Dictionary. NT: 1972. *Other:* Part of the Wa nationality. Traditional religion, Buddhist, Christian.

Lhomi (Lhoket, Shing Saapa) [lhm] 1,000 in Tibet. Tibet. *Other:* Probably part of the Tibetan nationality. Agriculturalists; pastoralists. Traditional religion, Buddhist (Lamaist). See main entry under Nepal.

Lingao (Vo Limkou, Limkow, Linkow, Ongbe, Ong-Be, Bê) [onb] 600,000 (2000 Liang Min). 100,000 monolinguals. Population includes 350,000 Lincheng, 170,000 Qiongshan. North central coast of Hainan, entire Lingao county, parts of Danxian, Chengmai, and Qiongshan counties, and suburbs of Haikou city. *Class:* Tai-Kadai, Kam-Tai, Be-Tai, Be. *Dialects:* Lincheng (Lingao Proper-Dengmai), Qiongshan. *Lg Use:* Vigorous. Speakers of other languages in the area speak it. All domains. All ages. Positive language attitude. Urban members also use Hainan dialect of Min Nan Chinese. 300,000 speak Chinese as second language, 200,000 speaking Hainan dialect, 100,000 speaking Jun or Danzhou dialects. Chinese used in secondary schools. *Lg Dev:* Taught in primary schools. Radio programs.

Dictionary. Grammar. *Other:* Part of the Han nationality. SVO; linguistically similar to Zhuang and Dai. Lincheng reported to have 7 tone categories, Qiongshan 13. Loans from Cantonese and Hainan variety of Min Nan Chinese. Coastal, foothills. Agriculturalists; fishermen. Traditional religion, Daoist, Buddhist.

Lipo (Eastern Lisu, Taku Lisu, He Lisu, Black Lisu, Taku) [lpo] 60,068 (1993). Around Taku, east Yunnan, highland areas. *Class:* Sino-Tibetan, Tibeto-Burman, Lolo-Burmese, Loloish, Northern, Lisu. *Dialects:* Not intelligible with Lisu. *Lg Dev:* NT: 1951. *Other:* Part of the Lisu nationality. Use a different script from Lisu. Christian, traditional religion.

Lisu (Lissu, Lisaw, Li-Shaw, Li-Hsaw, Lu-Tzu, Lesuo, Li, Lishu, Liso, Leisu, Leshuoopa, Loisu, Southern Lisu, Yao Yen, Yaw-Yen, Yaw Yin, Yeh-Jen, Chung, Cheli, Chedi, Lip'a, Lusu, Khae) [lis] 580,000 in China (1999 Mu Yuzhang). 467,869 are monolingual. Population total all countries: 723,000. West Yunnan Province, 11 prefectures, 63 counties, upper reaches of the Salween and Mekong rivers, and Sichuan Province, Xichang Prefecture. Also spoken in India, Myanmar, Thailand. *Class:* Sino-Tibetan, Tibeto-Burman, Lolo-Burmese, Loloish, Northern, Lisu. *Dialects:* Hua Lisu (Flowery Lisu), Pai Lisu (White Lisu), Lu Shi Lisu. Dialect differences are not great. Dialect variation across country borders. *Lg Use:* Vigorous. Speakers of other languages in the area use Lisu for administration, religion, and bilingual education in schools. In Drung and Nu areas, oral and written Lisu are used for Christian activities. Taught at Kumning Institute. All domains. All ages. Positive language attitude. Speakers also use Chinese. 150,000 can also speak Bai, Tibetan, Naxi, Lü, or Jingpho. Chinese is used in secondary schools. *Lg Dev:* 150,000 can read it, 30,000 can write it. Roman script. Newspapers. Radio programs. Dictionary. Bible: 1968–1986. *Other:* Part of the Lisu nationality. There are 2 older alphabetic orthographies and 1 indigenous script. Tonal, 4 tones. Mountain slope, valleys, riverine. Agriculturalists; animal husbandry. Polytheist, Christian.

Lü (Tai Lu, Lue, Ly, Lu, Dai, Dai Le, Xishuangbanna Dai, Sipsongpanna Dai, Pai-I, Pai'i', Shui-Pai-I) [khb] 250,000 in China (1990 Svantesson). 50% monolingual. Population total all countries: 672,064. South Yunnan, Jinghong (Chiang Hung, Chien Rung), Xishuangbanna Dai Autonomous Prefecture, west of the Lixianjiang (Black) River. Also spoken in Laos, Myanmar, Thailand, Viet Nam. *Class:* Tai-Kadai, Kam-Tai, Be-Tai, Tai-Sek, Tai, Southwestern, Northwest. *Dialects:* Mu'ang Yong and dialects in the Lanna area may converge phonologically with Lanna (Diller 1990). Low intelligibility of Shan (Dehong). Different from Tai Nüa, each having their own traditions. Most closely related to Khun. Lexical similarity 88% with Northern Thai, 74% with Central Thai. *Lg Use:* Official regional language. Vigorous. Some speakers of other languages use Lü as second language for trade. All domains. All ages. Positive language attitude. Speakers also use Chinese or Jingpho. Some schools only teach in Chinese. *Lg Dev:* Old Lü script. Magazines. Newspapers. Radio programs. TV. Dictionary. Grammar. NT: 1933. *Other:* Part of the Dai nationality. An official nationality in Viet Nam. SVO; modifiers follow noun heads. Valleys, plateaus, plains. Agriculturalists: wet rice; merchants; small businessmen. Traditional religion, Buddhist.

Luoba, Boga'er (Lhoba, Lho-Pa, Boga'er, Bengni-Boga'er, Bokar, Adi-Bokar, Adi, Abor) [adi] 1,088 in China (1999 Ouyang Jueya). 400 monolinguals. Lhunze and Mainling counties in southeast Tibet, south of the Yaluzangjiang River in the Luoyu area. *Lg Use:* Vigorous. All domains. All ages. 55% use Tibetan or Cona Monba as second language. 23% can also speak Tibetan and Chinese in Mainling and Lhunze counties, and Tibetan, Chinese,

and Monba in Medog County. Elementary schools use Tibetan, Chinese, or Monba. *Lg Dev:* 27% attended school, 31% have some degree of literacy, 0.8% have a university degree. *Other:* Part of the Lhoba nationality. Different from Lowa (Loba) in Nepal. Not a written language. Mountain slope, plateau. Evergreen and bamboo forest. Swidden agriculturalists: rice, maize, barley, cotton; hunters; forestry; animal husbandry; fishermen. Traditional religion, Buddhist (Lamaist). See main entry under India (Adi).

Luoba, Yidu (Lhoba, Lho-Pa, Yidu, Idu Mishmi, Idu Lhoba, Chulikata) [clk] 80 in China (1999 Sun Hongkai). 50 are monolingual. Townships of Xia Chayu (Zayu) and Ba'antong of the Xia Chayu (Zayu) Zone, Chayu County of Nyingchi Prefecture, in southeast Tibet, in the Danba River valley and adjoining mountain slopes, near the Bhutan border. *Lg Use:* Vigorous. All domains. All ages. Indifferent language attitude. 25 can also speak Chinese or Tibetan. *Lg Dev:* 27% attended primary school, 31% have some degree of literacy, 0.8% have a university degree. *Other:* Part of the Lhoba nationality. Different from Lowa (Loba) in Nepal. Not a written language. Mountain valley, mountain slope. Evergreen and bamboo (subtropical) forest. Swidden agriculturalists: rice, maize, barley, cotton; forestry; animal husbandry; hunters; fishermen. Traditional religion, Buddhist (Lamaist). See main entry under India (Idu-Mishmi).

Macanese (Macao Creole Portuguese, Macaense) [mzs] 4,000 (1977 Voegelin and Voegelin). Ethnic population: 8,500 (1985). Hong Kong. Possibly in USA. *Class:* Creole, Portuguese based. *Lg Use:* A small number of older adult women in Macau speak it as first language (1996).

Mak (Mo, Mohua, Mo-Hua, Ching, Mojiahua, Mochiahua) [mkg] 10,000 (1982 census). Ethnic population: 10,000 (2000 D. Bradley). Yangfeng, Fangcun, Jialiang, and Di'e villages in northwestern Libo County in Guizhou Province, and some in neighboring Dushan County, Guizhou. *Class:* Tai-Kadai, Kam-Tai, Kam-Sui. *Dialects:* Mak, Chi, Ching (Cham), Hwa, Lyo. Dialect differences are minor. Similar to Ai-Cham. *Lg Use:* Local Chinese and Bouyei are used as second languages. *Other:* Part of the Bouyei nationality. Traditional religion.

Man Met (Manmit, Manmi) [mml] 900 (1984 Svantesson). Southwestern Yunnan Province, 5 communities in Xishuangbanna near the Hu. *Class:* Austro-Asiatic, Mon-Khmer, Northern Mon-Khmer, Palaungic, Western Palaungic, Angkuic. *Other:* Counted separately in 1982 census and combined into a group of 'Undetermined Minorities'. Reported to be similar to Hu. Tonal; affixes. Mountain slope. Buddhist, traditional religion.

Manchu (Man) [mnc] 60 (1999 Zhao Aping). Ethnic population: 1,821,180 (1990 census). Heilongjiang, a few Manchu-speaking villages in Aihui and Fuyu counties. The ethnic group is in Heilongjiang, Jilin, and Liaoning provinces. There may also be members of the ethnic group in North Korea and Siberia. *Class:* Altaic, Tungus, Southern, Southwest. *Dialects:* Bala, Alechuxa, Jing, Lalin. *Lg Use:* Speakers are older adults. Positive language attitude. All are bilingual. The nonspeakers of Manchu in the ethnic group speak Mandarin. Written Chinese in common use. *Lg Dev:* Literacy rate in second language: 82%. About 50 speakers can read and write it. Dictionary. NT: 1835. *Other:* An official nationality called Man. Scholars are involved in studying the history, language, and literature. Written Manchu adopted in 1599 was once in use with old Manchu script. Agriculturalists; fishermen. Chinese traditional religion, Shamanist, Buddhist.

Mang (Mang U, Xamang, Chaman, Manbu, Ba'e) [zng] 500 in China. Yunnan, Jinping County, Hani-Yi Autonomous Prefecture. *Other:* Counted separately in 1982 census and combined into a group of 'Undetermined

Minorities'. Dai, Hani, and Kutsung call them 'Chaman', 'Manbu', 'Ba'e'. An official ethnic community in Viet Nam. Mountain slope. Thick forests. Agriculturalists: maize, rice; hunters. Polytheist. See main entry under Viet Nam.

Maonan (Ai Nan) [mmd] 20,000 (2000 Liang Min). A few thousand women and children are monolingual. Ethnic population: 71,968 (1990 census). Xianan area of Huanjiang Maonan Autonomous County in north central Guangxi Zhuang Autonomous Region. A few in nearby Hechi, Yishan, Nandan, and Du'an counties. *Class:* Tai-Kadai, Kam-Tai, Kam-Sui. *Lg Use:* Vigorous. Speakers of other languages living in the area can speak Maonan. All domains. All ages. Used less by young people and children. Positive language attitude. About 10,000 also use Chinese or Zhuang. Written Chinese in use. *Lg Dev:* Taught in primary schools. Chinese script. Radio programs. Grammar. *Other:* Part of the Maonan nationality. SVO; numbers and adjectives follow nouns; reduplication; glottalized prenasalized, palatalized, and labialized onsets; nasal and stop finals; many Chinese loans; tonal, 6 tone categories in unchecked syllables, 2 in checked (split into 4 according to vowel length). Mountain slope. Agriculturalists: rice, maize, sweet potatoes; animal husbandry: pigs, cattle. Daoist, Christian.

Maru (Matu, Malu, Lawng, Laungwaw, Laungaw, Langsu, Lang'e, Nyky, Diso, Zi, Lhao Vo) [mhx] 3,500 in China (1997). Over 10,000 households (1999). Western Yunnan, Luxi, Longchuan, Yingjiang, Ruili, and Lianghe counties of the Dehong Dai-Jingpo Autonomous Prefecture. *Other:* Part of the Jingpo nationality. Different from the Matu variety of Khumi Chin. See main entry under Myanmar.

Moinba (Menba, Cuona Menba, Cuona Monpa, Cona Monba, Menpa, Monpa, Monba, Mompa, Momba) [mob] 36,000 in China (1999 Shaozun Lu). 20,000 are mono-lingual. To the east of Bhutan, partly in southeastern Tibet, mainly on the Yarlung-Zanbo River, Medog, Nyinchi, Cuona counties. There may be speakers in Bhutan. *Dialects:* Northern Cuona, Southern Cuona. *Lg Use:* Vigorous. Tibetans and some Chinese speakers who live among them speak Moinba as second language. All domains. All ages. Positive language attitude. 16,000 can also use Tibetan, 2,000 can also use Tshangla. 5,000 can also use Chinese, mainly young people. Written Tibetan is used. *Other:* Part of the Monba nationality. Tshangla (7,000) is also officially included in the Moinba nationality. There are more speakers of Southern Cuona. More Chinese loans in Southern Cuona, and a different number of tones from Northern Cuona. Cuona differs from Tshangla in phonology, vocabulary, and grammar. Cuona is the same as, or closely related to, Bumthangkha of Bhutan. May also be classified as North Assam, Monpa. Plains, mountain slope. 6,500 meters. Agriculturalists: rice, maize, bananas, peppers, leeks, ginger, millet; animal husbandry: cattle. Buddhist (Lamaist). See main entry under India.

Mongolian, Peripheral (Mongol, Monggol, Menggu, Southern-Eastern Mongolian, Inner Mongolian) [mvf] 3,381,000 in China (1982). 2,500,000 are monolingual. Population includes 4,806,849 Buriat and Tuvin (1990 census). 299,000 Chakhar, 317,000 Bairin, 1,347,000 Khorain, 593,00 Karachin, 123,000 Ordos, 34,000 Ejine (1982 census). Inner Mongolia, Liaoning, Jilin, and Heilongjiang provinces, Urumchi to Hailar. Also spoken in Mongolia. *Class:* Altaic, Mongolian, Eastern, Oirat-Khalkha, Khalkha-Buriat, Mongolian Proper. *Dialects:* Chahar (Chaha'er, Chakhar, Qahar), Ordos (E'erduosite), Tumut (Tumet), Shilingol (Ujumchin), Ulanchab (Urat, Mingan), Jo-Uda (Bairin, Balin, Naiman, Keshikten), Jostu (Ke'erqin, Kharchin, Kharachin, Kharchin-Tumut, Eastern Tumut), Jirim (Kalaqin, Khorchin, Jalait, Gorlos), Ejine.

Largely intelligible with Halh standard dialect of Mongolia, but there are phonological and important loan differences. *Lg Use:* Official regional language. Language of wider communication. Vigorous. Chinese speakers living in the area can also speak it. All domains. All ages. Positive language attitude. Speakers also use Chinese. About 70,000 can also speak Uyghur or Kazakh. Written Chinese is in use. *Lg Dev:* Literacy rate in second language: 71%. Taught in primary and secondary schools. Standard Inner Mongolian script. Magazines. Newspapers. Radio programs. TV. Grammar. NT: 1952–2003. *Other:* Part of the Mongolian nationality. One of the five main official nationalities. The government includes Buriat, Tuvin, Oirat, and other varieties under the Mongolian official nationality. In Xinjiang, the Torgut, Oold, Korbet, and Hoshut peoples are known as the 'Four tribes of Oirat'. SOV. Mountain mesa, plains. Desert. Agriculturalists; pastoralists; animal husbandry. Buddhist (Lamaist), Shamanist.

Mulam (Mulao, Molao, Mulou, Muliao, Mulao Miao, Abo, Ayo) [mlm] 50,000 to 60,000 (2000 Liang Min). 10,000 monolinguals (including women and preschool children). Ethnic population: 159,328 (1990 census). Luocheng Mulam Autonomous County (90% in Dongmen and Siba communes), and adjacent counties in north central Guizhou Province; and in Majiang and Kaili City in Guizhou Province. *Class:* Tai-Kadai, Kam-Tai, Kam-Sui. *Dialects:* Close to Dong. Lexical similarity 65% with Dong (probably Southern Dong), 53% with Zhuang (probably Northern Zhuang). *Lg Use:* Vigorous. Many Han Chinese and Zhuang also speak Mulam. All domains. Used mainly among older adults, and less among young people and children. Positive language attitude. Chinese is used as second language. Written Chinese in common use. Bilinguals use various Chinese varieties or Zhuang as second language. Many also use Northern Zhuang and some use Maonan. Chinese is used in secondary schools, in Daoist and Buddhist services. *Lg Dev:* Literacy rate in second language: 65%. Radio programs. Grammar. *Other:* An official nationality. They live close to the Han, Zhuang, Dong, Hmong, and Mien. They call themselves 'Mulam'. Some around Luocheng call themselves 'Kyam'. SVO; reduplication; aspirated, palatalized, labialized, voiceless nasal, lateral onsets; nasal and stop finals; many Chinese loans; tonal, 6 tone categories in unchecked syllables, 2 in checked (split into 4 according to vowel length). Plains, mountain slope. Agriculturalists: wet rice, maize; miners. Polytheist, Daoist, Buddhist.

Muya (Miyao, Minyak, Manyak) [mvm] 13,000 (2000 Sun Hongkai). About 2,000 are monolingual. West central Sichuan, Kangbo (Kangding) and Jiulong (Gyaisi) in the Ganzi (Garzê) Tibetan Autonomous Prefecture, and Simian (Shimian) County in the Ya'an District. *Class:* Sino-Tibetan, Tibeto-Burman, Tangut-Qiang, Qiangic. *Dialects:* Eastern Muya, Western Muya. The 'dialects' listed are reported to not be inherently intelligible to each other's speakers. *Lg Use:* All domains. Eastern Muya: all ages. Used mainly among older adults, moderately use among adults, used half the time by young people, sometimes by children. Indifferent language attitude. About 7,000 also speak Chinese, 3,000 also speak Khams Tibetan. In the west they tend to be more fluent in Tibetan, in the east in Chinese. *Lg Dev:* Dictionary. Grammar. *Other:* Part of the Tibetan nationality. 'Muyak' may be an alternate name. Speakers belong to the Tibetan nationality. SOV; adjectives and number-classifier con-structions follow noun heads; compounding; affixation; reduplication; consonant cluster onsets; tense-lax vowel distinction; nasalized vowels; tonal, 4 tones. Mountain slope. 3,000 meters. Animal husbandry: pigs, chickens, sheep, cattle; agriculturalists. Lamaist, traditional religion.

Namuyi (Namuzi) [nmy] 4,000 (2000 Sun Hongkai). 200 monolingual speakers, mainly older adults. Mianning, Muli, Xichang, and Yanyuan counties of the Liangshan Yi Autonomous Prefecture, and Jiulong (Gyaisi) County in the Ganzi (Garzê) Tibetan Autonomous Prefecture of southwestern Sichuan. _Class:_ Sino-Tibetan, Tibeto-Burman, Tangut-Qiang, Qiangic. _Dialects:_ Eastern Namuyi, Western Namuyi. Some intelligibility between the dialects, with lexical and phonological differences. Their speakers use Chinese when communicating with speakers of the other dialect. _Lg Use:_ Vigorous. All domains. All ages. Positive language attitude. About 2,000 can also speak Chinese, 500 Yi, 500 Pumi, a few Tibetan or Ersu. _Lg Dev:_ Speakers are generally better educated than the Yi or Tibetan peoples. Dictionary. Grammar. _Other:_ Part of the Tibetan nationality. They call themselves 'Namuzi'. SOV; adjectives and number-classifier constructions follow noun heads; compounding; affixation; consonant cluster onsets but no consonantal codas; tense-lax vowel distinction; nasalized and retroflexed vowels; tonal, 4 tones. Mountain slope, riverine. Not many trees. Agriculturalists; animal husbandry: poultry, pigs, cattle; beekeepers. Traditional religion, Daoist, Buddhist, syncretism.

Nanai (Goldi, Gold, Sushen, Juchen) [gld] 12 in China (1999 Chaoke). Ethnic population: 4,245 in China (1990 census). Sanjiang plain in the northeastern corner of Heilongjiang Province, near where the Heilong, Songhua, and Wusuli rivers merge, with most in Tongjiang county, Bacha and Jiejinkou villages, and in Sipai village in Raohe County. _Dialects:_ Hezhen (Hezhe, Heche), Qileng (Qile'en, Kili, Kilen, Kirin). _Lg Use:_ 47 can understand Nanai. Used in religion, traditional literature. All speakers are older adults. Younger generation in China speaks Chinese. People have lost hope that it will survive. All are first- or second-language speakers of Chinese. Written Chinese in common use. _Lg Dev:_ Literacy rate in second language: 84%. _Other:_ An official nationality, called Hezhen. Formerly called 'Sushen'. Mountain slope, riverine. Forests. Agriculturalists; fishermen; hunters; forestry. Shamanist, Buddhist. See main entry under Russia (Asia).

Naxi (Nahsi, Nasi, Nakhi, Lomi, Mu, "Moso," "Mosso," "Mo-Su") [nbf] 308,839 (2000 census). 100,000 monolinguals. Most (200,000) in Lijiang Naxi Autonomous County, northwestern Yunnan. Some scattered through Weixi, Zhongdian, Ninglang, Deqing, Yongsheng, Heqing, Jianchuan, and Lanping counties. Some in Yanyuan, Yanbian, and Muli counties of Sichuan Province. A few in Mangkang county, southeastern Tibet. Possibly also in Myanmar. _Class:_ Sino-Tibetan, Tibeto-Burman, Lolo-Burmese, Naxi. _Dialects:_ Lichiang (Lijiang), Lapao, Lutien. The western dialect is reported to be fairly uniform and is considered to be the standard (from Dayan town in Lijiang County). Eastern has some internal differences, and intelligibility may be low within it. _Lg Use:_ Vigorous. Some speakers of other languages in the area use Naxi in local government offices, markets, gatherings, and when visiting Naxi families. All domains. All ages. Positive language attitude. 170,000 use Chinese, Tibetan, Bai, or English as second language. Written Chinese in common use. _Lg Dev:_ Literacy rate in second language: 62%. 75,000 can read and write it. Taught in primary schools. Poetry. Newspapers. Radio programs. TV. Dictionary. Grammar. Bible portions: 1932. _Other:_ An official nationality. People resent the older term "Moso." The 8,000 or so 'Eastern' Naxi in the Lugu Lake area are matriarchal. Most Naxi are patriarchal. Roman alphabet developed in the 1950s and revised in 1984. An ideographic writing system called 'Dongba' ('Domba') is not practical for everyday use, but is a system of prompt-illustrations for reciting classic texts. 2 syllabary scripts

called 'Geba' and 'Malimasa' are also used in Weixi County. SOV; no checked syllables; tonal, 4 tones. Mountain slope, plains. Semitropical; scrub forest; pine forest; spruce forest; Alpine. High altitude. Agriculturalists; animal husbandry; hunters. Buddhist (Lamaist), Chinese Buddhist, Daoist, Confucianist, traditional religion, Christian.

Nung (Anung, Anong, Anoong, Anu, Nu, Lutzu, Lutze, Kiutze, Khanung, Kwinp'ang, Khupang, Kwingsang, Fuch'ye) [nun] 390 in China (1999 Sun Hongkai). Almost no monolinguals. Ethnic population: 500 in China (1999 Sun Hongkai). Middle reaches of Nu (Salween) River, Yunnan. Along the border region of Fugong County in the Nujiang Lisu Autonomous Prefecture in Yunnan, 7 hamlets: Mugujia, Hashi, Muleng, Lagagong, Ani, Qia, Lahaigong in Mugujia village, administrative region of Shangpa Township. _Dialects:_ Cholo, Gwaza, Miko. _Lg Use:_ Used in the home. Used in all domains among the older adults. Speakers are older adults. Indifferent language attitude. A few leaders are concerned about its loss. Most also speak Lisu. About 100 speak Nung, Lisu, or Chinese. _Other:_ Part of the Nu nationality. Different from Nung (Tai family) of Viet Nam, Laos, and China, and from Chinese Nung (Cantonese) of Viet Nam. Slopes between Biluo Mt. and Gaoligong Mt. Agriculturalists; gatherers; fishermen. Polytheist, Christian, Buddhist (Lamaist). See main entry under Myanmar.

Nusu [nuf] 7,500 (1999 Sun Hongkai). 1,000 monolinguals (mainly older adults). Population includes 2,000 in Northern Nusu, 3,000 in Southern Nusu, and 4,000 in Central Nusu. Lushui and Fugong counties in Nujiang Lusu Autonomous Prefecture of northwestern Yunnan. _Class:_ Sino-Tibetan, Tibeto-Burman, Lolo-Burmese, Loloish, Unclassified. _Dialects:_ Northern Nusu (Wawa-Kongtong), Southern Nusu (Guoke-Puluo), Central Nusu (Zhizhiluo-Laomudeng). May be Nungish or a variety of Yi (Matisoff et al. 1996:74). The 3 'dialects' listed above are not inherently intelligible to one another's speakers. _Lg Use:_ Vigorous. All domains. All ages. Intellectuals want to preserve it. About 7,000 use Lisu or Chinese as second languages, mainly Lisu. _Other:_ Part of the Nu nationality. A separate language officially under the Nu nationality with Ayi, Zauzou (1,500), and 5,500 speakers of Drung. SOV; grammatical relations indicated mainly by word order and particles; tonal, 4 tones with relatively complex sandhi; loans from Lisu, Chinese, and a few from Burmese. Mountain slope, riverine. Agriculturalists; animal husbandry: poultry, pigs, sheep, cattle; beekeepers. Traditional religion.

Oroqen (Orochon, Oronchon, Olunchun, Elunchun, Ulunchun) [orh] 1,200 (2002 Whaley). 800 are monolingual. Ethnic population: 7,004 (2000 D. Bradley). Huma, Aihui, Sunko districts, Great Xingan Ridge, Heilongjiang Province and Inner Mongolia. Possibly eastern Siberia. _Class:_ Altaic, Tungus, Northern, Evenki. _Dialects:_ Gankui, Heilongjiang Oroqen. Gankui in Inner Mongolia is the standard dialect. _Lg Use:_ Some Daur and Chinese people speak Oroqen as second language. All domains. Speakers hope to preserve the language. Speakers also use Chinese, Mongolian, Russian, Ewenki, or Daur. _Lg Dev:_ Literacy rate in second language: 84%. Radio programs. _Other:_ An official nationality. Maintain native language and customs. Not a written language. They came to China from Russia in the recent past. Mountain slope. Dense mountain forests. Lumbermen; agriculturalists. Shamanist, traditional religion.

Pa Di (Padi) [pdi] 1,000 in China. Population total all countries: 1,300. Also spoken in Viet Nam. _Class:_ Tai-Kadai, Kam-Tai, Be-Tai, Tai-Sek, Tai, Southwestern. _Other:_ Tonal. Traditional religion.

Pa-Hng (Pa Hng, Pa Ngng, Paheng, Baheng, Bahengmai, Pa Then, Tóng, Meo Lai, Man Pa Seng) [pha] 26,815 in China (1995 McConnell). 10,000 monolinguals. Population total all countries: 32,384. Ethnic population: 26,815 in China. Guizhou Province (Liping and Congjiang counties), northeastern Guangxi Zhuang Autonomous Region (Rongshui, Sanjiang, Longsheng, Rong'an, and Lingui counties). Also spoken in Viet Nam. *Class:* Hmong-Mien, Hmongic, Pa-hng. *Lg Use:* Vigorous. All domains. Positive language attitude. Speakers also use Hmong, Dong, Chinese, Zhuang, or Dai. *Lg Dev:* Grammar. *Other:* Part of the Yao nationality. An official ethnic community in Viet Nam, although the variety spoken there may be a separate language. Those in Viet Nam may have migrated there from 1368–1644. SVO; uvular onsets; no nasal-final syllables but has nasalized vowels. Mountain slope. Forests. Agriculturalists. Daoist.

Palaung, Pale (Dlang, Ngwe Palaung, Silver Palaung, Pale, Palay, Bulai, Bulei, Pulei, Southern Ta'ang) [pce] 5,000 in China (1995). Western Yunnan, Luxi County, just east of Rumai. *Dialects:* Bulei, Raojin. *Lg Use:* Vigorous. 50% of the De'ang speak Pale. Some speakers of other languages use it as second language. All domains. All ages. Some also speak Lü, Jingpho, or Chinese. *Other:* Part of the De'ang nationality. Agriculturalists; weavers; metal workers; potters; construction workers. Buddhist (Hinayana). See main entry under Myanmar.

Palaung, Rumai (Rumai, Ruomai, Humai) [rbb] 2,000 in China (1995). Far western Yunnan, Longchuan, and Ruili counties. *Lg Use:* 20% of the De'ang speak Rumai. *Other:* Part of the De'ang nationality. See main entry under Myanmar.

Palaung, Shwe (Ta-Ang Palaung, Golden Palaung, Shwe) [pll] 2,000 in China (1995 SIL). Total De'ang in China 15,462 (1990 census). Yunnan. *Other:* Officially included under De'ang in China. Foothills, plains. Buddhist (Hinayana). See main entry under Myanmar.

Panang (Panags, Panakha, Pananag, Banag, Banang, Sbanag, Sbranag) [pcr] 12,000 (2002). Tibet. *Class:* Sino-Tibetan, Tibeto-Burman, Himalayish, Tibeto-Kanauri, Tibetic, Tibetan, Central. *Other:* Probably part of the Tibetan nationality. May not be a separate language.

Parauk (Wa, Praok, Baraog, Baroke) [prk] 180,000 in China (1990 census). Awa Mountains, southwest Yunnan as far east as the Lancang (Mekong) River. *Other:* Part of the Wa official nationality, which includes 3 languages: Parauk, Wa, and Western Lawa. Parauk is the largest and the standard. A large and powerful group. Traditional culture. Taught at Kunming Institute. Mountain slope. Agriculturalists: potatoes, cotton, hemp, tobacco, sugarcane, tea, rice, beans, buckwheat, maize; some hunters. Buddhist (Hinayana), Christian. See main entry under Myanmar.

Pela (Bela, Bola, Pala, Polo) [bxd] 400 (2000 D. Bradley). Ethnic population: 1,000 (2001 J. Edmondson). Yunnan Province, Dehong Prefecture, Luxi County, Santaishan Township, and Yingjiang and Lianghe counties. May also be in Myanmar. *Class:* Sino-Tibetan, Tibeto-Burman, Lolo-Burmese, Burmish, Northern. *Dialects:* Close to Zaiwa. *Lg Use:* Used in the home. Half of children speak it. Neutral language attitude. *Other:* Part of the Jingpo nationality. The first vowel in the name is a schwa. Live among the Jingpo majority and wear Jingpo clothing. They regard themselves as different from Zaiwa and Jingpo and have different traditions. SOV; only voiceless affricates and stops; no consonant clusters; palatalized and non-alatalized series of labials and velars; nasal and stop codas; tense-lax and nasal unnasalized vowels; Chinese, Jingpo, Dai, and Burmese loans; tonal, 4 tones, tone sandhi. Agriculturalists: long grain rice. Polytheist.

Phula (Phù Lá, Phu Khla, Fu Khla, Phù Lá Hán) [phh] 4,200 in China (2002). *Lg Use:* Part of the Yi nationality.

Endangered. Most have shifted to Vietnamese. See main entry under Viet Nam.

Pumi, Northern (P'umi, Pimi, Primmi, Pruumi, P'ömi, P'rome, Ch'rame) [pmi] 35,000 (1999). Perhaps 1/3 are monolingual. 24,000 in the Pumi nationality, 30,000 in the Tibetan nationality (1994). Southwestern Sichuan, Muli, Yanyuan, and Kiulong counties; and northwestern Yunnan, Yongning District of Ninglang County. *Class:* Sino-Tibetan, Tibeto-Burman, Tangut-Qiang, Qiangic. *Dialect:* Taoba. Northern Pumi has 5 subdialects. Intelligibility of Southern Pumi is difficult. Lexical similarity between Northern and Southern is 60%, grammatical differences minor. *Lg Use:* Vigorous. All domains. All ages. Positive language attitude. Speakers also use Chinese, Tibetan, Lisu, Bai, Naxi, or Yi. *Lg Dev:* Literacy rate in second language: 39%. Taught in primary schools. *Other:* Part of the Tibetan nationality rather than the Pumi nationality. No written form. SOV; adjectives and numbers follow noun heads; no uvular obstruents; no initial 's' or consonant clusters; different vowels from S. Pumi; loans mainly from Tibetan (10% of the vocabulary); tonal, 3 tones. Mountain slope, plateau, riverine. 2,200 to 3,000 meters. Agriculturalists; animal husbandry. Buddhist (Lamaist).

Pumi, Southern (P'umi, Pimi, Primmi, Pruumi, P'ömi, P'rome) [pmj] 19,000 (1999). About 1/3 are monolingual. 24,000 in the Pumi nationality, 30,000 in the Tibetan nationality (1994). Northwestern Yunnan Province, Lanping, Weixi, Yongsheng, and Lijiang counties, and Xinyingpan District of Ninglang County. *Class:* Sino-Tibetan, Tibeto-Burman, Tangut-Qiang, Qiangic. *Dialect:* Qinghua. Southern Pumi has 5 subdialects. Intelligibility of Northern Pumi is difficult. Lexical similarity 60% between Northern and Southern. *Lg Use:* Vigorous. All domains. Positive language attitude. Speakers also use Mandarin Chinese, Tibetan, Lisu, Bai, Naxi, or Yi. *Lg Dev:* Literacy rate in second language: 39%. Taught in primary schools. Grammar. *Other:* Part of the Pumi nationality. No written form. SOV; adjectives and numbers follow noun heads; uvular obstruents; initial 's' + consonant clusters; different vowels from N. Pumi; loans mainly from Chinese (making up 15% of the vocabulary); tonal, 2 tones. Mountain slope, plateau, riverine. 2,200 to 3,000 meters. Agriculturalists; animal husbandry; lumbermen. Buddhist (Lamaist).

Qiang, Northern (Ch'iang) [cng] 57,800 (1999). 130,000 in all Qiang languages, including 80,000 in the Qiang nationality and 50,000 in the Tibetan nationality (1990 J-O Svantesson). 198,252 ethnic population in the Qiang nationality (1990 census). North central Sichuan Province, Mao, Songpan, Heishui, and Beichuan counties. *Class:* Sino-Tibetan, Tibeto-Burman, Tangut-Qiang, Qiangic. *Dialects:* Yadu, Weigu, Cimulin, Luhua. *Lg Use:* Language in decline. Parents are encouraging children to speak Mandarin Chinese. Used in the home. All speakers older than 25 years. Negative language attitude. No monolinguals. Speakers use Chinese or Tibetan as second language. Written Chinese is in use. *Lg Dev:* Men are more literate than women. Those under 30 are fairly literate in Chinese. Roman script. Radio programs. Grammar. *Other:* Part of the Qiang nationality and the Tibetan nationality. SOV; more consonants than Southern Qiang; heavy phonemic inventory; consonant clusters in syllable onsets; nontonal. Mountain slope. Pine forest, but largely deforested. 2,200 to 3,000 meters. Agriculturalists; some animal husbandry. Buddhist (Lamaist), Daoist, polytheist.

Qiang, Southern (Ch'iang) [qxs] 81,300 (1999 Jonathan Evans). No monolinguals. North central Sichuan Province, along the Minjiang River basin between Zhenjiangguan in Songpan County to the north and Wenchuan and Li counties to the south, as far east as Beichuan County.

Class: Sino-Tibetan, Tibeto-Burman, Tangut-Qiang, Qiangic. *Dialects:* Dajishan (Daqishan), Taoping, Longxi, Mianchi, Heihu, Sanlong, Jiaochang. Related to Manyak, Menia, Muli. *Lg Use:* Language in decline. Used in the home. Speakers are older adults. Negative language attitude. Many also speak Chinese or Tibetan. Written Chinese is in use in the education system. *Lg Dev:* Those under 35 are functionally literate in Chinese. *Other:* Part of the Qiang nationality and the Tibetan nationality. SOV; heavy phonemic inventory; consonant clusters in syllable onsets; tonal, 6 tones. Mountain slope. 1,800 to 2,800 meters. Agriculturalists; animal husbandry. Buddhist (Lamaist), polytheist, Daoist.

Queyu (Zhaba) [qvy] 7,000 (1995). Xinlong (Nyagrong), Yajiang (Nyagquka) and Litang counties in the Ganzi (Garzê) Tibetan Autonomous Prefecture of western Sichuan. *Class:* Sino-Tibetan, Tibeto-Burman, Tangut-Qiang, Qiangic. *Dialects:* Close to Zhaba. *Other:* Part of the Tibetan nationality. The term 'Zhaba' is used in Tuanjie township of Yajiang county. Different from the Zhaba language in Zhamai District. SOV; adjectives and number-classifier constructions follow noun heads; consonant cluster initials; tonal, 4 tones. Buddhist (Lamaist), polytheist.

Riang (Riang-Lang, Liang, Yang Sek, Yang Wan Kun, Yin, Yanglam) [ril] 3,000 in China (1995). Western Yunnan, vicinities of Zhenkang and Baoshan. *Other:* Part of the De'ang nationality. Traditional religion. See main entry under Myanmar.

Russian (Olossu, Eluosi, Russ, Russki) [rus] 13,504 in China (1990 census). North Xinjiang, including Urumqi, and Heilongjiang. *Lg Use:* All domains. It may not be used by children. Most of the speakers in China have an indifferent attitude toward Russian. Second languages are Chinese and Uyghur. *Other:* An official nationality in China. Agriculturalists; animal husbandry; beekeepers; repair shops; craftsmen; transport services. Christian, secular. See main entry under Russia (Europe).

Salar (Sala) [slr] 60,000 (2002). Under 20,000 monolinguals. Ethnic population: 113,000. Xunhua Salar Autonomous County and Hualong Hui Autonomous County in Qinghai Province, Jishishan Autonomous County in Gansu Province, and Yining in Xinjiang. *Class:* Altaic, Turkic, Southern. *Dialects:* Jiezi, Mengda. Reinhard F. Hahn says Salar is spoken by descendants of an Oghuz-Turkic-speaking subtribe that, in the 15th century area of Samarkand, split off a main tribe and 'returned eastward', eventually settling in Western China. Their language has an Oghuz Turkic base, has taken on a medieval Chaghatay Turkic stratum through Central Asian contacts and finally acquired a stratum of features from local languages. Jiezi is often taken as the standard dialect. *Lg Use:* Some speakers of other languages in the area use Salar, especially men. All domains. All ages, but children use Salar less. Negative or indifferent language attitude. Speakers use Chinese as literary language. Reported high proficiency in Mandarin Chinese, Uyghur, and Tibetan. *Lg Dev:* Literacy rate in second language: 27%. Dictionary. Grammar. *Other:* An official nationality. SOV; Plateau, riverine. Average 3,000 meters. Agriculturalists; animal husbandry; commerce. Sufi, Sunni, Ikhwan.

Samei [smh] 10,000 (2000 D. Bradley). Ethnic population: 28,200. Yunnan, Dabanqiao District, 13 villages. *Class:* Sino-Tibetan, Tibeto-Burman, Lolo-Burmese, Loloish, Northern. *Lg Use:* Children do not speak Samei. *Other:* Part of the Yi nationality. Traditional religion.

Samtao (Samtau, Samtuan) [stu] 100 in China (1993). Southwest Yunnan, Xishuangbanna Prefecture. *Other:* Part of the Bulang nationality. Different from Blang. Buddhist (Theravada), traditional religion. See main entry under Myanmar.

Sarikoli (Sarykoly, Salikur, Tajik, Tadzik, Tajiki) [srh] 16,000 (2000 Gao Erqing). Monolinguals include preschool children, and those who have not been to school. Ethnic population: 20,412 (2000 Gao Erqing). Southwest Xinjiang, in and around Taxkorgan (Tashkurghan), Sarikol Valley. *Class:* Indo-European, Indo-Iranian, Iranian, Eastern, Southeastern, Pamir, Shugni-Yazgulami. *Dialects:* Not intelligible with Shughni of Russia and Afghanistan. *Lg Use:* Vigorous. The majority of Tajiks in China speak Sarikoli, the remainder speak Wakhi. All domains. All ages. Positive language attitude. 10,000 also speak Uyghur. Written Uyghur is used. Chinese is also used, Kirghiz, and some varieties of Persian. *Lg Dev:* Literacy rate in second language: 15% to 52%. Taught in primary schools. Dictionary. Grammar. *Other:* Part of the Tajik nationality. Different from Tajiki of Tajikistan, Afghanistan, and Iran. The label 'Tajik' is used in different ways in different countries. SOV. Mountain slope, plateau. Pastoralists; agriculturalists: wheat, barley, peas. Ismaili Muslim.

Shangzhai (Western Jiarong) [jih] 4,100 (2004). North central Sichuan, near the confluence of the Duke River and its tributary Zhongke River in Shili, Zongke, and Puxi townships, Shangzhai District, southern Rangthang County. *Class:* Sino-Tibetan, Tibeto-Burman, Tangut-Qiang, rGyarong. *Dialects:* Dayili, Zongke, Puxi. Phonologically Western and Northern are fairly similar and differ greatly from Eastern. Lexical similarity 75% between Eastern and Northern Jiarong, 60% between Western and Northern. *Other:* Part of the Tibetan nationality. SOV; phonologically and lexically similar to Tibetan, grammatically more similar to Pumi and Qiang; complex consonant clusters; limited pitch contrast. Buddhist (Lamaist), polytheist.

She (Huo Nte, Ho Nte) [shx] 911 (1999 Mao Zongwu). 197 monolinguals. Population includes 579 Luofu, 386 Lianhua (1995 McConnell). Ethnic population: 630,378 (1990 census) in the official nationality, including 270,000 in Fujian and a smaller group in Guangdong. Southeastern Guangdong Province, (Lianhua dialect in Haifeng and Huidong counties; Luofu dialect in Boluo and Zengcheng counties), more than 10 villages. *Class:* Hmong-Mien, Ho Nte. *Dialects:* Luofu (Eastern She), Lianhua (Western She). Major linguistic differences with Mien. Closest to Jiongnai Bunu. Dialects are inherently intelligible. Classification within Hmong-Mien is in dispute (McConnell 1995:1320). *Lg Use:* Used mainly by adults. All domains by some speakers. Children were predominantly monolingual in She, but now they speak Chinese. Indifferent language attitude. Bilinguals use Hakka or Min or Mandarin Chinese as first or second language. Written Chinese is in common use. 'Shehua' refers to the variety of Hakka spoken by the She. *Lg Dev:* Grammar. *Other:* An official nationality. SVO; modifiers precede noun heads; mainly monosyllabic roots, but mainly compound words; loans from Hakka and Cantonese Chinese; tonal, 8 tones. Mountain slope, riverine, foothills, hills. Agriculturalists: wet rice. Daoist.

Sherpa (Sharpa, Sharpa Bhotia, Xiaerba, Serwa) [xsr] 800 in China (1994). Tibet. *Other:* Part of the Tibetan nationality. Buddhist (Lamaist). See main entry under Nepal.

Shixing [sxg] 1,800 (2000 D. Bradley). 1,200 are monolingual. Ethnic population: 2,000 (2000 D. Bradley). Muli Tibetan Autonomous County in the Liangshan Yi Autonomous Prefecture of southwestern Sichuan. *Class:* Sino-Tibetan, Tibeto-Burman, Tangut-Qiang, Qiangic. *Lg Use:* Vigorous. All domains. All ages. About 500 also use Chinese, about 100 Naxi, about 100 Tibetan. Tibetan is used in the temples. *Lg Dev:* Dictionary. *Other:* Part of the Tibetan nationality. SOV; adjectives and number-classifier constructions follow noun heads; consonant cluster initials; tonal, 4 tones. Riverine, mountain slope. Agriculturalists: wet rice; animal husbandry: poultry, pigs, cattle, sheep. Buddhist (Lamaist), traditional religion.

Sui (Shui, Ai Sui, Sui Li, Suipo) [swi] 200,000 in China (1999 Zeng Xiaoyu). 100,000 monolinguals. Population total all countries: 200,120. Ethnic population: 200,000 or more (1999 Zeng Xiaoyu). Districts of Sandu and Libo in Guizhou and District of Nandan in Guangxi, dispersed in Guangxi and northeastern Yunnan. Also spoken in Viet Nam. *Class:* Tai-Kadai, Kam-Tai, Kam-Sui. *Dialects:* Sandong (San Tung), Anyang (Yang'an), Pandong. Dialect differences are minor. That spoken in Yunnan is reported to be more different. Sandong is the standard. *Lg Use:* Vigorous. All domains. All ages. Positive language attitude. About 200,000 use Chinese as second language. Bilingualism is low in the main areas. Written Chinese is in use. *Lg Dev:* Literacy rate in second language: 37%. Taught in primary schools. Radio programs. Films. *Other:* An official nationality. 70 syllable-initial consonants. Mountain slope, plateau. Agriculturalists. Polytheist, Daoist, traditional religion.

Tai Hongjin [tiz] 150,000 (1995 Luo Meizhen). Scattered communities in Honghe, Jinshajiang, Yuanyang, Yuanjiang, Xinping, Maguan, Wuting, and Sichuan north of the Yangtze at Huili and Takou. *Class:* Tai-Kadai, Kam-Tai, Be-Tai, Tai-Sek, Tai, Southwestern, Unclassified. *Other:* Part of the Dai nationality. Traditional religion.

Tai Nüa (Dai Nuea, Tai Neua, Tai Nue, Tai Nü, Dai Na, Dehong Dai, Dehong, Tai Dehong, Tai Le, Tai-Le, Dai Kong, Tai-Kong, Tai Mao, Chinese Shan, Chinese Tai, Yunannese Shan, Yunnan Shant'ou) [tdd] 250,000 in China (1990 Svantesson). Population total all countries: 357,400. Ethnic population: 1,025,128 in the official nationality (1990 census). Dehong Prefecture, southwest of Dali near the Lancang (Mekong) River in south central Yunnan. Also possibly in northern Viet Nam. Also spoken in France, Laos, Myanmar, Switzerland, Thailand. *Class:* Tai-Kadai, Kam-Tai, Be-Tai, Tai-Sek, Tai, Southwestern, Northwest. *Dialects:* Dehong, Tai Pong (La, You, Ya, Ka, Tai Ka, Sai), Yongren. Lexical similarity 65% with Northern Zhuang, 29% with Laqua, 27% with Buyang and Lati, 22% with Gelo. *Lg Dev:* Liek script. Dictionary. Bible portions: 1931–1948. *Other:* Part of the Dai nationality and the Zhuang nationality. Northern Shan-like varieties referred to collectively as 'Tai Nüa'. Officially included under Dai in China; called 'Dehong Dai'. Language taught at Kunming Institute. SVO; modifiers follow heads. Agriculturalists: paddy rice, sugar, Pu'er tea, bananas, coconuts, papayas, rubber. Buddhist (Theravada), polytheist.

Tai Ya (Tai-Cung, Tai-Chung, Tai Cung, Cung, Daiya, Ya) [cuu] 34,000 (1982). Central Yunnan Province, Xinping Yi-Dai Autonomous County, Mosha District. *Class:* Tai-Kadai, Kam-Tai, Be-Tai, Tai-Sek, Tai, Southwestern. *Dialects:* Probably not intelligible with other varieties of Dai. Close to Tai Nüa. *Lg Dev:* Dictionary. Grammar. Bible portions: 1922. *Other:* Part of the Dai nationality. Called 'Daiya' in China. SVO; tonal, 6 tone categories in unchecked syllables, 2 (split into 4 according to vowel length) in checked syllables; nasal and stop finals. Traditional religion.

Takpa (Dwags, Dakpa) [tkk] *Class:* Sino-Tibetan, Tibeto-Burman, Himalayish, Tibeto-Kanauri, Tibetic, Tibetan, Western, Ladakhi. *Other:* Part of the Tibetan nationality.

Tatar (Tartar, Tata'er) [tat] 800 in China (1999 Chen Zongzhen). No monolinguals. Ethnic population: 4,873 in the official nationality in China (1990 census). North Xinjiang, mainly in Yining (Ghulja, Kulja), Qvqek, and Üümqi. *Lg Use:* Used for oral tradition, songs. Speakers are older adults. Written Uyghur and Kazakh are used as literary languages; nearly all use them. *Other:* An official

nationality. They moved into China only 200 years ago. Some members of the nationality speak only Kazakh. Speech in different areas is influenced by Uyghur and Kazakh. Traders; craftsmen; agriculturalists. Muslim (Sunni). See main entry under Russia (Europe).

T'en (Then, Yanghuang, Rau) [tct] 15,000 (1999 Bo Wenze). No monolinguals. Ethnic population: 25,000 (2000 D. Bradley). Guizhou Province, east part of Pingtang county; some villages in Dushan county; a few villages in Huishui, just south of Guiyang. *Class:* Tai-Kadai, Kam-Tai, Kam-Sui. *Dialects:* Hedong, Hexi, Huishui. Close to Sui. *Lg Use:* Moderately vigorous. Chinese and Bouyei speakers in the area also speak T'en. Used in religion. All ages. Children and young people do not use it as often as adults. Local Chinese and Bouyei are used as second languages. *Lg Dev:* Grammar. *Other:* Part of the Bouyei nationality. Mountain slope, riverine. Agriculturalists; craftsmen. Traditional religion.

Thangmi (Thami, Dolakha) [thf] 300 in China (2002). Tibet. See main entry under Nepal.

Tibetan, Amdo (Amdo, Anduo, Ngambo) [adx] 809,500 (1987 Wurm et al.). Population includes 538,500 Hbrogpa, 97,600 Rongba, 112,800 Rongmahbrogpa, 60,600 Rtahu. Huangnan, Hainan, Haibei, and Guoluo (Golog) Tibetan Autonomous prefectures and the Haixi Mongolian-Tibetan-Kazakh Autonomous Prefecture of Qinghai Province; in the Gannan Tibetan Autonomous Prefecture and Tianzhu Autonomous County of southwestern Gansu Province, and in parts of the Ganzi and Aba (Ngawa) Tibetan Autonomous prefectures of western and northern Sichuan Province. *Class:* Sino-Tibetan, Tibeto-Burman, Himalayish, Tibeto-Kanauri, Tibetic, Tibetan, Northern. *Dialects:* Hbrogpa, Rongba, Rongmahbrogpa, Rtahu. Speakers do not find Central Tibetan or Kham varieties intelligible. Those listed as dialects may not be intelligible with each other. Lexical similarity 70% with Central Tibetan and Kham. *Lg Use:* All ages. *Lg Dev:* Dictionary. *Other:* Part of the Tibetan nationality. Speakers in 'Golog' are called 'Golog', 'Ngolok', 'Mgolog', 'Ggolo'. SOV; many onset clusters. Pastoral: yak, sheep; wool. Buddhist (Lamaist).

Tibetan, Central (Wei, Weizang, Bhotia, Zang, Phoke, Dbus, Dbusgtsang, U, Tibetan) [bod] 1,066,200 in China (1990 census). About 86% are monolingual. Population includes 570,000 Dbus, 460,000 Gtsang, 40,000 Mngahris out of 4,593,000 in the official nationality. Population total all countries: 1,261,587. Tibet, Sichuan, Qinghai. Also spoken in Bhutan, India, Nepal, Norway, Switzerland, Taiwan, USA. *Class:* Sino-Tibetan, Tibeto-Burman, Himalayish, Tibeto-Kanauri, Tibetic, Tibetan, Central. *Dialects:* Gtsang (Tsang, Lhasa), Dbus, Mngahris (Ngari). In the exile community a so-called diaspora Tibetan has developed. This is based on Central Tibetan. *Lg Use:* Official regional language. Vigorous. Speakers of other languages in the area can also speak Tibetan. All domains. All ages. Positive language attitude. *Lg Dev:* Literacy rate in second language: 30%. Motivation for literacy is high. Taught in primary and secondary schools. Magazines. Newspapers. Radio programs. Dictionary. Grammar. Bible: 1948. *Other:* Part of the Tibetan nationality called Zang. Xifan (Hsifan) and Bhotia are general terms for Tibetan. Probably officially includes many separate languages: Atuence, Choni, Groma, Niarong, Lhomi, Panang, Sherpa, Tseku, Tinan Lahul, Khams Tibetan. Nomads in central and northern Tibet in Phala on the 15,000 foot Chang Tang plateau are known as 'Drokba'. They number around 500,000. Written Tibetan is reported to be based on a southern dialect. 2 scripts are known: U-chan is a common script used by all, the other is a less-widely known and more priestly script. SOV; tonal, 4 tones. Plateau. Very high altitude. Agriculturalists;

pastoralists: yak, sheep, goats; weavers; salt traders (Drokba). Buddhist (Lamaist), Muslim.

Tibetan, Khams (Khams, Khams-Yal, Khams Bhotia, Kam, Khamba, Khampa, Kang) [khg] 1,487,000 (1994). Population includes 996,000 Eastern, 135,000 Southern, 158,000 Western, 91,000 Northern, 77,000 Jone, 30,000 Hbrugchu. Northeastern Tibet, Changdu (Qamdo) and Naqu (Nagqu) districts; Ganzi (Garzê) Tibetan Autonomous Prefecture in western Sichuan; Diqing (Dêqên) Tibetan Autonomous Prefecture in northwestern Yunnan Province; and Yushu Tibetan Autonomous Prefecture in southwestern Qinghai Province. *Class:* Sino-Tibetan, Tibeto-Burman, Himalayish, Tibeto-Kanauri, Tibetic, Tibetan, Northern. *Dialects:* Eastern Khams, Southern Khams, Western Khams, Northern Khams, Hbrugchu, Jone. Dialects listed may be separate languages; differences are reported to be large. Lexical similarity 80% with Dbusgtsang (Central Tibetan). *Other:* Part of the Tibetan nationality. Different from Western Parbate, Eastern Parbate, Sheshi, Maikoti, and Gamale Kham of Nepal. SOV; tonal, 4 tones. Pastoralists; agriculturalists. Traditional religion.

Tinani (Lahuli Tinan, Bhotia of Lahul, Lahauli, Lahouli, Rangloi, Gondla) [lbf] 450 to 1,600 in China (1977 Voegelin and Voegelin). Western Tibet border. *Other:* Probably part of the Tibetan nationality. Different from Bunan and Pattani in India. See main entry under India.

Tsat (Utsat, Utset, Huihui, Hui, Hainan Cham) [huq] 3,800 (1999 Zheng Yiqing). Ethnic population: 5,000 (2000 D. Bradley). Southern Hainan, villages of Huixin and Huihui in the Yanglan suburban district of Sanya City. *Class:* Austronesian, Malayo-Polynesian, Malayic, Achinese-Chamic, Chamic, North. *Dialects:* Closest to Northern Roglai, but very different. Tsat is structurally changed to be like Chinese. *Lg Use:* Vigorous. All domains. All ages. Positive language attitude. Others speak second-languages Fukienese or Cantonese Chinese for commerce, or Mandarin Chinese for school. *Other:* Part of the Hui nationality. The phonology suggests a history of some independence from other Chamic languages (Maddieson). Their name for themselves is 'Utsat', for their language 'Tsat'. 'Huihui' or 'Hui' is the Chinese name. Tonal. Coastal. Fishermen; agriculturalists: vegetables. Muslim.

Tseku (Tsuku, Tzuku) [tsk] 12,600 in China (2000 WCD). Population total all countries: 23,641. Tibet. Possibly only in Tibet. Also spoken in Bhutan, Nepal. *Class:* Sino-Tibetan, Tibeto-Burman, Himalayish, Tibeto-Kanauri, Tibetic, Tibetan, Central. *Other:* Probably part of the Tibetan nationality.

Tshangla (Sangla, Tsangla, Tsanglo, Cangluo Menba, Canglo Monba, Motuo Menba, Menba, Monba, Monpa, Central Monpa) [tsj] 5,000 in China (1997). Southeastern Tibet, Motuo (Medoz, Medog) and Linzhi (Ngingchi) counties, including Padma-bkot (Pemak), just north of (and possibly on both sides of) the McMahon line, and clustered near the Tshangpo (Siang) River. *Lg Use:* Vigorous. All domains. Positive language attitude. *Other:* Part of the Moinba nationality. Not the same as Tsanglo (Angami Naga) of India. Their speech is nearly identical to that of eastern Bhutan, except for the loss of initial voicing and tonogenesis in Tibet. Differs from Cuona Menba in phonology, vocabulary, and grammar. Mountain slope. Agriculturalists: rice. Buddhist (Lamaist). See main entry under Bhutan.

Tu (Mongour, Monguor, Mongor) [mjg] 152,000 (1999 Li Keyu). Very few monolinguals. Ethnic population: 190,000. East Qinghai Province, Huzhu Tu Autonomous County; Gansu Province. *Class:* Altaic, Mongolian, Eastern, Mongour. *Dialects:* Huzhu (Mongghul, Halchighol, Naringhol), Minhe (Mangghuer). Said to be the most divergent of all the Mongolian languages.

Intelligibility is reported to be low between dialects. Dongren speech of Huzhu is considered to be the standard. *Lg Use:* Positive language attitude. Most can also speak Chinese or Tibetan. Written Chinese or Tibetan are used. 30,000 people have shifted to Chinese. *Lg Dev:* Literacy rate in second language: 42%. About 2,000 can read it, 200 can write it. Roman script. Magazines. Films. Dictionary. Grammar. *Other:* Part of the Tu nationality. An unwritten language. SOV; postpositions; genitives, adjectives, numerals and relative clauses precede head noun; question word appears in the position of the thing being questioned; verbs may bear up to three or four suffixes; word order distinguishes subject and direct object; topicalized noun phrases are often fronted; case is marked by enclitic postpositions; verbs are marked for the pragmatic category of perspective (a binary distinction between the perspective of the speaker and that of anyone else); causatives are extremely common; syllables (C)(C)V(C) (clusters must involve a glide in Mangghuer, while Mongghul allows a wider range of onset clusters); stress falls on the final syllable of a phonological word; no vowel harmony (in Mangghuer). Mountain slope, riverine. Agriculturalists. Buddhist (Lamaist), traditional religion.

Tujia, Northern (Tuchia, Tudja) [tji] 70,000 (2002 Brassett). 100 monolinguals. Ethnic population: 7,353,300. Northwest Hunan, Hubei, Guizhou in Yingjiang and Yanhe counties, Wuling Mt. range. *Class:* Sino-Tibetan, Tibeto-Burman, Tujia. *Dialects:* Longshan, Baojing. There are also phonological and grammatical differences with Southern Tujia. Not intelligible to each other's speakers. Lexical similarity 40% with Southern Tujia. *Lg Use:* Regularly used but increasingly younger speakers prefer Chinese and are encouraged to do so by their parents. In most areas children acquire a passive knowledge only. All domains. 60% of speakers older than 50 years, 30% between 20 and 50, 10% under 25. Positive language attitude. Speakers also use Chinese or Hmong. Written Chinese is in use. Chinese is used in schools. *Lg Dev:* Grammar. *Other:* An official nationality. SOV; no voiced stops or affricates; tonal, 4 tones. Limestone mountain slope, valleys. Agriculturalists; light industry. Traditional religion, Buddhist.

Tujia, Southern (Tuchia) [tjs] 1,500 (2002 Brassett). Monolingual speakers are mainly women, children, and older adults. Ethnic population: 7,353,300. Northwest Hunan Province, Luxi county, 3 villages. *Class:* Sino-Tibetan, Tibeto-Burman, Tujia. *Dialects:* There are phonological and grammatical differences with Northern Tujia. Lexical similarity 40% with Northern Tujia. *Lg Use:* Used in the home and village. Positive language attitude. Spoken and written Chinese are in use. Chinese is used in schools. *Lg Dev:* Literacy rate in second language: Probably 50%, basic literacy approaching 100% in children. *Other:* Part of the Tujia nationality. SOV; voiced stops and affricates; tonal, 5 tones. Limestone mountain slope, valleys. Agriculturalists. Traditional religion, Buddhist.

Tuvin (Diba, Kök, Mungak, Tuwa) [tyv] 2,400 in China (1999 Wu Hongwei). No monolinguals. Burjin, Habahe, Fuyun, and Altay counties of Altay Prefecture, Yinjiang Autonomous Region. *Lg Use:* Vigorous. Used in religious services. All ages. Younger ones use it less. Positive language attitude. Chahar Mongolian used in education. More than 90% also use Kazakh, 30% also know Kalmyk-Oirat. Some speak Chinese. *Other:* Part of the Mongolian nationality. Mountain slope. Animal husbandry; agriculturalists; hunters. Buddhist (Lamaist), syncretism with shamanism. See main entry under Russia (Asia).

U (Puman, P'uman) [uuu] 3,000 (1990 Svantesson). Southwestern Yunnan Province. *Class:* Austro-Asiatic, Mon-Khmer, Northern Mon-Khmer, Palaungic, Western

Palaungic, Angkuic. *Dialects:* Not closely related to Blang (Svantesson). *Other:* Part of the Blang nationality. Buddhist (Theravada), traditional religion.

Uyghur (Uighur, Uygur, Uigur, Uighuir, Uiguir, Weiwuer, Wiga) [uig] 7,214,431 in China (1990 census). Most are monolingual. Population includes 4,700,000 Central Uyghur, 1,150,000 Hotan, 25,000 Lop. Population total all countries: 7,601,431. Throughout the Xinjiang Autonomous Region. Also spoken in Afghanistan, Australia, Germany, India, Indonesia, Kazakhstan, Kyrgyzstan, Mongolia, Pakistan, Saudi Arabia, Taiwan, Tajikistan, Turkey (Asia), USA, Uzbekistan. *Class:* Altaic, Turkic, Eastern. *Dialects:* Central Uyghur, Hotan (Hetian), Lop (Luobu). The Akto Türkmen speak a dialect of Uyghur with 500 different seldom-used words. There are 2,000 in two villages, Kösarap and Oytak in Akto County, south of Kashgar, Xinjiang. Dolan is a dialect spoken around the fringes of the Taklimakan Desert in Xinjiang. Chinese linguists recognize 3 dialects. Others have used the following dialect names: Kashgar-Yarkand (Kashi-Shac he), Yengi Hissar (Yengisar), Khotan-Kerya (Hotan-Yutian), Charchan (Qarqan, Qiemo), Aksu (Aqsu), Qarashahr (Karaxahar), Kucha (Kuqa), Turfan (Turpan), Kumul (Hami), Ili (Kulja, Yining, Taranchi), Urumqi (Urumchi), Lopnor (Lopnur), Dolan, Akto Türkmen. There are significant dialect differences between China, Kazakhstan, Kyrgyzstan, and Uzbekistan. *Lg Use:* Official regional language. Widely used in print media in Kashgar. Vigorous. All domains. All ages. Positive language attitude. Young people and intellectuals can also speak Chinese, a few can also speak English, Japanese, or Russian. *Lg Dev:* Literacy rate in second language: 56%. Literacy based on Central Uyghur as spoken in the area between Yili (Ili) and Urumqi. Roman, Arabic, and Cyrillic scripts; Cyrillic script in Kazakhstan; Roman script in Turkey; Arabic script in Afghanistan. Newspapers. Radio programs. TV. Grammar. Bible: 1950. *Other:* Part of the Uyghur nationality. One of the five main official nationalities in China. Those in the north are more influenced by modern Chinese culture. SOV; postpositions; genitives, adjectives, numerals, relatives before noun heads; question words initial; a few prefixes; 3 suffixes on nouns; 6 suffixes on verbs; word order distinguishes subjects and indirect objects, topic and comment; eight noun cases shown by suffixes; verb suffixes mark subject person, number, 2nd person marks plural and 3 levels of respect; passive, reflexive, reciprocal and causative; comparatives; CV, CVC, CVCC syllables; nontonal. Valleys, mountain slope. Desert, oases. Agriculturalists: grain, fruit, grapes, vegetables, cotton; traders; craftsmen; animal husbandry. Muslim (Sunni).

Uzbek, Northern (Ozbek, Ouzbek, Usbeki, Usbaki) [uzn] 5,000 in China (2000 Aixinjueluo Chentgshiliang). North and west Xinjiang; Urumqi, Kashgar, and Yining (Ghulja) cities, especially Ili. *Dialects:* Andizhan, Tashkent, Samarkand, Fergana. *Lg Use:* Vigorous. Some speakers of other languages in the area can also speak Uzbek. All domains. All ages. Positive language attitude. They use Uyghur and Kazakh as literary languages. Some also speak Chinese. *Lg Dev:* Literacy rate in second language: 79%. *Other:* An official nationality. Desert, oases. Agriculturalists; some traders; merchants; animal husbandry; government workers; teachers; medical doctors. Muslim (Sunni). See main entry under Uzbekistan.

Vietnamese (Jing, Gin, Kinh, Ching, Annamese) [vie] 7,200 in China (1999 Ouyag Jueya). 14,000 monolinguals (half older adults and half children). On the Shanxin, Wanwei, and Wutou peninsulas in the Jiangping Region of the Fangcheng Pan-Nationality Autonomous County on the south coast of Guangxi Province. *Lg Use:* Vigorous. A few Chinese living in the area speak Vietnamese as

second language. All domains. All ages. Speakers are accustomed to using their language locally and Yue outside. Bilinguals use Chinese as a written language. Bilingualism in Yue Chinese of Guanxi is reported to be high. About 100 can also speak Zhuang. Yue or Mandarin used in secondary education. *Other:* An official nationality in China, called 'Jing'. Not written in China. Coastal plain reclaimed from islands in 1955. Fishermen; agriculturalists; aquatic breeding; small businessmen. Christian, Daoist. See main entry under Viet Nam.

Wa (Va, Awa, K'awa, Kawa, Vo, Wa Pwi, Wakut) [wbm] 280,000 in China (1999 Chen Guoqing). Many are monolingual. Awa Mountains, southwest Yunnan as far east as the Lancang (Mekong) River. *Dialects:* Baraoke, Va, Ava. *Lg Use:* Vigorous. All domains. All ages. Positive language attitude. Speakers also use Chinese, Lü or Lahu. *Lg Dev:* Literacy rate in first language: 1%. *Other:* Part of the Wa nationality. Traditional culture. Mountain slope, riverine, plains. 1,500 to 2,000 meters. Agriculturalists: potatoes, cotton, hemp, tobacco, sugarcane, tea, rice, beans, buckwheat, maize; ironsmiths; weavers; bamboo craftsmen; brewers; animal husbandry. Traditional religion, Buddhist, Christian. See main entry under Myanmar.

Wakhi (Vakhan, Wakhani, Wakhigi, Khik) [wbl] 6,000 in China. Ethnic population: 15,000 in China (A. E. Kibrik). Taxkorgan Tajik Autonomous County (especially Daftar), and in the mountains south of Pishan, Xinjiang. *Dialect:* Eastern Wakhi. *Lg Use:* Speakers also use Mandarin Chinese. *Other:* Part of the Tajik nationality. Pastoralists: sheep, cattle; agriculturalists: barley, wheat, peas. Ismaili Muslim. See main entry under Pakistan.

Waxianghua (Xianghua, Wogang) [wxa] 300,000 (1995). A 6,000 square km area in western Hunan Province, Wuling Mountains, including Yuanling, Chunxi, Jishou, Guzhang, and Dayong. *Class:* Unclassified. *Dialects:* Part of the Han nationality. It differs greatly from both Southwestern Mandarin (Xinan Guanhua) and Xiang Chinese (Hunanese), but is relatively uniform within itself. Neighboring Han Chinese, Miao, and Tujia people do not understand it. Some view it as a special variety of Chinese, others as a minority language, perhaps related to Miao. *Other:* Mountain slope.

Wutunhua (Wutun) [wuh] 2,000 (1995). Eastern Qinghai Province, Huangnan Tibetan Autonomous Prefecture, Tongren County, Longwu township, Upper and Lower Wutun villages and Jiangchama village. *Class:* Mixed Language, Chinese-Tibetan-Mongolian. *Other:* Part of the Tu nationality. Reported to be a variety of Chinese heavily influenced by Tibetan or perhaps a Tibetan language undergoing relexification with Chinese forms. Also described as Chinese which converged to an agglutinative language, using only Chinese material, towards Tibetan-Mongolian. Neighboring Tibetans refer to the Wutun people as 'Sanggaixiong', meaning 'center of the lion'. Known for their paintings of Buddha. Some consider themselves members of the Tu nationality, others Han Chinese. SOV; adjectives follow nouns; adverbials precede predicate; case and number marked on nouns; prenasalized consonants; 11 different syllable-final consonants; tone and stress have low functional load; most words polysyllabic; 60% Chinese, 20% Tibetan vocabulary with the rest having mixed Chinese and Tibetan elements. Agriculturalists. Buddhist (Lamaist).

Xiandao (Xiandaohua) [xia] 100 (1994). Xiandao and Meng'e villages, Manmian Township, Jiemao District, Yingjiang County in the Dehong Dai-Jingpo Autonomous Prefecture in extreme western Yunnan. *Class:* Sino-Tibetan, Tibeto-Burman, Lolo-Burmese, Burmish, Unclassified. *Dialects:* Spoken by members of the Achang nationality, and some consider it to be a dialect of Achang. *Other:* Part of the Achang nationality. SOV;

voiced and voiceless nasals and laterals; loanwords from Chinese, Jingpo, Dai, and Burmese; tonal, 4 tones. Christian.

Xibe (Sibo, Xibo, Sibe, Sibin) [sjo] 30,000 (2000 An Jun). Few monolinguals. Ethnic population: 33,082 in Xinjiang Province, 172,847 in the nationality (1990 census). 50,000 ethnic Xibe in northeast China speak Chinese as first language. Mainly in Ili Region of Xinjiang Province, and some in Ürümqi City and Tacheng Region of Xinjiang Province. *Class:* Altaic, Tungus, Southern, Southwest. *Dialects:* Colloquial Manchu. Reported to be inherently intelligible with Manchu. *Lg Use:* Official regional language. Vigorous. Speakers of Chinese, Uyghur, or Kazakh in the area can also speak Xibe. All domains. All ages in rural areas. Positive language attitude. Many prefer Chinese as a literary language. Some can speak or write Uyghur, Kazakh, English, or Russian. *Lg Dev:* Literacy rate in first language: 50%. Literacy rate in second language: 52%. About 15,000 can read and write it. Taught in primary schools. Manchu script. Newspapers. Radio programs. Dictionary. Grammar. *Other:* An official nationality. Descendants of an 18th century Qing dynasty military garrison. Loans from Uyghur, Kazakh, and Chinese. SOV; genitives, articles, adjectives, numerals precede noun heads; question word initial; complex vowel harmony. Plains between mountain slope, riverine. Desert, savannah. 1,000 to 3,000 meters. Peasant agriculturalists; animal husbandry; commerce. Atheist, polytheist.

Yerong (Daban Yao) [yrn] 378 (2000 WCD). Western Guangxi Zhuang Autonomous Region, Napo County, Longhe Township and Pohe Township, just northeast of where Yunnan, Guangxi, and Viet Nam meet. *Class:* Tai-Kadai, Kadai, Bu-Rong. *Other:* Part of the Yao nationality. 'Yeyong' may refer to this. Traditional religion.

Yi, Ache [yif] 35,000 (2003). Yunnan, in Shuangbo, Yimen, Eshan, and Lufeng counties. *Class:* Sino-Tibetan, Tibeto-Burman, Lolo-Burmese, Loloish. *Other:* Part of the Yi nationality. Polytheist.

Yi, Awu (Luowu, Luwu) [yiu] 20,000 (2002). Southeastern Yunnan in Mile County and Qujing Prefecture. *Class:* Sino-Tibetan, Tibeto-Burman, Lolo-Burmese, Loloish, Northern, Yi, Southeastern Yi. *Dialects:* Northern Awu Yi, Southern Awu Yi. *Other:* Part of the Yi nationality. Traditional religion, Christian.

Yi, Axi (Axibo, Axipo, Ahi) [yix] 60,000 (2002). Southeastern Yunnan in Mile, Luxi and Shilin counties. *Class:* Sino-Tibetan, Tibeto-Burman, Lolo-Burmese, Loloish, Northern, Yi, Southeastern Yi. *Lg Use:* Speakers also use Mandarin Chinese. *Lg Dev:* A phonetic script. Dictionary. *Other:* Part of the Yi nationality. SOV. Traditional religion, Christian.

Yi, Azhe [yiz] 40,000 (2002). Southeastern Yunnan in Mile County. *Class:* Sino-Tibetan, Tibeto-Burman, Lolo-Burmese, Loloish, Northern, Yi, Southeastern Yi. *Lg Use:* Speakers also use Mandarin Chinese. *Other:* Part of the Yi nationality. Traditional religion.

Yi, Central (Lolopho) [ycl] 380,000 (1991 Encyclopedic Dictionary of Chinese Linguistics). Central Yunnan, including Nanhua, Xiangyun, Yao'an, Jingdong, Chuxiong, Shuangbo, Mouding, Yanxing, Weishan, and Lufeng counties. *Class:* Sino-Tibetan, Tibeto-Burman, Lolo-Burmese, Loloish, Northern, Yi, Central Yi. *Dialects:* Nanhua Lolopho, Shuangbo Lolopho, Yao'an Lolopho. *Lg Use:* Vigorous. All ages. Positive language attitude. *Lg Dev:* Newspapers. Radio programs. Films. *Other:* Part of the Yi nationality. SOV; tonal, 4 tones; tonal splits. Mountain slope. Agriculturalists. Traditional religion, Christian.

Yi, Dayao (Dayao Lipo) [yio] 170,000 (2002). Yunnan, in Dayao, Yongren, Yao'an, Mouding, and Jingdong

counties. *Class:* Sino-Tibetan, Tibeto-Burman, Lolo-Burmese, Loloish, Northern, Yi, Central Yi. *Other:* Part of the Yi nationality.

Yi, Eastern Lalu [yit] 38,000 (2002). Yunnan, in Xinping, Zhenyuan, Mojiang, and Yuanjiang counties. *Class:* Sino-Tibetan, Tibeto-Burman, Lolo-Burmese, Loloish, Northern, Yi, Western Yi. *Other:* Part of the Yi nationality.

Yi, Eshan-Xinping (E-Xin Yi) [yiv] 300,000 (2002). Yunnan, in Eshan, Xinping, Yimen, Yuxi, Jiangchuan, Shuangbo, Puning, Dengjiang, and Yuanjiang counties. *Class:* Sino-Tibetan, Tibeto-Burman, Lolo-Burmese, Loloish, Northern, Yi, Southern Yi. *Dialects:* Eshan Nasu, Xinping Nisu. *Other:* Part of the Yi nationality.

Yi, Guizhou (Eastern Yi, Southeastern Yi) [yig] 905,000 (2002 Chenmin). Guizhou Province, Weining Yi-Hui-Miao Autonomous County, Dafang Autonomous County, Hezhang County, Pan County; some in the Baise District of western Guangxi. *Class:* Sino-Tibetan, Tibeto-Burman, Lolo-Burmese, Loloish, Northern, Yi. *Dialects:* Qian Xi, Bijie, Dafang. Distinct from other Yi. Intelligibility between dialects is reported to be low. *Lg Dev:* There is a traditional orthography for Guizhou Yi, related to but distinct from the traditional orthographies used by some other Yi languages. Dictionary. *Other:* Part of the Yi nationality. SOV.

Yi, Limi (Liumi) [ylm] 29,000 (2002). Yunnan, in Yongde, Fengqing, and Yunxian counties. *Class:* Sino-Tibetan, Tibeto-Burman, Lolo-Burmese, Loloish. *Lg Use:* Vigorous. *Other:* Part of the Yi nationality. Polytheist.

Yi, Mili [ymh] 23,000 (2002). Yunnan, in Jingdong, Yunxian, Zhenyuan, and Xinping counties. *Class:* Sino-Tibetan, Tibeto-Burman, Lolo-Burmese, Loloish. *Lg Use:* Vigorous. *Other:* Part of the Yi nationality. Polytheist.

Yi, Miqie (Micha, Minqi) [yiq] 13,000 (2002). Yunnan, in Wuding, Fumin, Lufeng, Luquan, Yimen, and Anning counties. *Class:* Sino-Tibetan, Tibeto-Burman, Lolo-Burmese, Loloish, Northern, Yi, Central Yi. *Other:* Part of the Yi nationality.

Yi, Muji [ymj] 52,000. Southeastern Yunnan, in Gejiu, Mengzi, Pingbian, Hekou, and Jinping counties. *Class:* Sino-Tibetan, Tibeto-Burman, Lolo-Burmese, Loloish. *Other:* Part of the Yi nationality. Polytheist.

Yi, Naluo (Qiaojia-Wuding Yi, Qiao-Wu Yi) [ylo] 40,000. Yunnan, in Qiaojia, Wuding, Luquan, Yuanmou, and Huize counties. *Class:* Sino-Tibetan, Tibeto-Burman, Lolo-Burmese, Loloish, Northern, Yi, Eastern Yi. *Other:* Part of the Yi nationality. Polytheist, Christian.

Yi, Poluo (Pola) [yip] 230,000 (2002). Southeastern Yunnan, in Yanshan, Wenshan, Qiubei, Maguan, Pingbian, Guangnan, Xichou, and Hekou counties. *Class:* Sino-Tibetan, Tibeto-Burman, Lolo-Burmese, Loloish. *Other:* Part of the Yi nationality. Polytheist.

Yi, Pula (Pula) [ypl] 20,000 (2002). Yunnan, in Honghe, Yuanyang, Yuanjiang, Gejiu, Shiping, and Jianshui counties. *Class:* Sino-Tibetan, Tibeto-Burman, Lolo-Burmese, Loloish. *Other:* Part of the Yi nationality. Polytheist.

Yi, Puwa [ypw] 29,000 (2002). Yunnan, in Mengzi, Yanshan, and Kaiyuan counties. *Class:* Sino-Tibetan, Tibeto-Burman, Lolo-Burmese, Loloish. *Other:* Part of the Yi nationality. Polytheist.

Yi, Sani [ysn] 90,000 (1991 EDCL). Southeastern Yunnan in Shilin, Yilang, Mile, Luxi, and Qiubei Counties. *Class:* Sino-Tibetan, Tibeto-Burman, Lolo-Burmese, Loloish, Northern, Yi, Southeastern Yi. *Dialects:* Northern Sani, Southern Sani. *Lg Use:* Speakers also use Mandarin Chinese. *Lg Dev:* There is a traditional orthography for Sani, related to but distinct from the traditional orthographies used by some other Yi languages. Dictionary. *Other:* Part of the Yi nationality (population

7,762,272; 2000 census). The Samei, an Eastern Yi group east of Kunming in the Guandu region call themselves Sani, but are not part of the Sani in Shilin. Tones differ on the two names, [sa21 ni53] versus [sa21 ni21]. An Eastern Yi group with a similar name call themselves Sanyie, immediately to the west of Kunming in the Xishan region and in Anning County. In case of the Samei, Sani is their autonym. In case of the Sani in Shilin, Sani is an exonym. The Sani of Shilin call themselves [ni21], but outsiders know them by the Chinese name Sani, the Chinese tones being [sa1-ni2]. SOV. Plains. Agriculturalists; animal husbandry: goats, cattle. Polytheist, traditional Yi religion, Christian.

Yi, Sichuan (Liangshan Yi, Liangshan Nosu, Northern Yi) [iii] 1,600,000 (1991 EDCL). Mainly in Greater and Lesser Liangshan Mountains, southern Sichuan, northwestern Yunnan. Spoken in over 40 counties. *Class:* Sino-Tibetan, Tibeto-Burman, Lolo-Burmese, Loloish, Northern, Yi. *Dialects:* Yishengzha Yi, Yinuo Yi, Butuo Yi, Huili Yi. *Lg Use:* Written Chinese is also used. *Lg Dev:* Has an official script, the Yi syllabary based on the traditional Sichuan Yi script and on the syllable inventory of a variety of Shengzha Yi spoken in Xide county, used in the Liangshan area both in southern Sichuan and northwestern Yunnan. The traditional writing system for Sichuan Yi is related to but distinct from the traditional orthographies used by some other Yi languages. Scholars disagree on whether traditional Yi orthographies are more phonetic or more ideographic. Perhaps they can be described as inconsistent syllabaries that fit the ancient syllable inventories better than they fit the present day syllable inventories. The traditional orthography is still in use in many villages, passed from father to son by certain priestly clans. Individual priests invent symbols of their own, so that the traditional orthography varies from village to village. However, there is a core of symbols that all the priests are likely to know. Dictionary. *Other:* Part of the Yi nationality. When applied to the Sichuan Yi, the terms 'Black Yi' (Hei Yi) and 'White Yi' (Bai Yi) refer to caste distinctions rather than to ethnic or linguistic distinctions. However, the same terms often do refer to ethnic and linguistic distinctions when applied to many of the Yi groups in Yunnan. Also, some outsiders refer to all Sichuan Yi as 'Black Yi'. The term "Lolo" is often considered derogatory when applied to the Sichuan Yi. Plains. Swidden agriculturalists; some animal husbandry. Polytheist, Christian.

Yi, Southeastern Lolo [yso] 36,000 (2002). Southeastern Yunnan, in Maguan, Funing, Xichou, Malipo, and Honghe counties. *Class:* Sino-Tibetan, Tibeto-Burman, Lolo-Burmese, Loloish, Northern, Yi. *Other:* Part of the Yi nationality. May be the same language as is called Lolo in Vietnam. Polytheist.

Yi, Southern (Nisu, Shiping-Jianshui Nisu, Shiping-Jianshui Yi) [nos] 470,000 (2002). Yunnan, in Shiping, Jianshui, Tonghai, Gejiu, Kaiyuan, Mengzi, Pingbian, and Hekou counties. *Class:* Sino-Tibetan, Tibeto-Burman, Lolo-Burmese, Loloish, Northern, Yi. *Dialects:* Degree of similarity with Eshan-Xinping Yi and Yuanjiang-Mojiang Yi may warrant investigation. *Lg Dev:* There is a traditional orthography for Southern Yi, related to but distinct from the traditional orthographies used by some other Yi languages. Few people nowadays can read this orthography. *Other:* Part of the Yi nationality. Mountain slope. Swidden agriculturalists; animal husbandry. Polytheist.

Yi, Southern Lolopho [ysp] 190,000 (2002). Yunnan, in Jingdong, Jinggu, Lancang, Zhenyuan, Simao, and Pu'er counties. *Class:* Sino-Tibetan, Tibeto-Burman, Lolo-Burmese, Loloish, Northern, Yi, Central Yi. *Other:* Part of the Yi nationality. Polytheist.

Yi, Western (Dongshan Lalu Yi, Lalo, Lalopa, Misaba) [ywt] 300,000 (1991 EDCL). Western Yunnan, in Weishan, Fengqing, Midu, Changning, Lincang, Yunxian, Jingdong, Jinggu, Yongde, Shidian, Nanjian, Yangbi, Zhenkang, Yunlong, Zhenyuan, Binchuan, Eryuan, and Heqing counties. *Class:* Sino-Tibetan, Tibeto-Burman, Lolo-Burmese, Loloish, Northern, Yi, Western Yi. *Lg Use:* Bilingualism in Chinese is reported to be high, especially among young people. *Lg Dev:* Yi syllabary not used. *Other:* Part of the Yi nationality. Traditional religion.

Yi, Western Lalu [ywl] 38,000 (2002). Western Yunnan, in Baoshan, Shidian, Zhenkang, Longling, and Luxi counties. *Class:* Sino-Tibetan, Tibeto-Burman, Lolo-Burmese, Loloish, Northern, Yi, Western Yi. *Other:* Part of the Yi nationality. Traditional religion.

Yi, Wuding-Luquan (Wu-Lu Yi, Dian Dongbei Yi) [ywq] 210,000 (2002). Yunnan, in Luquan, Wuding, Yongren, Lufeng, Yuanmou, Qujing, Xundian, and Huize counties, and in Huili county of southern Sichuan. *Class:* Sino-Tibetan, Tibeto-Burman, Lolo-Burmese, Loloish, Northern, Yi, Eastern Yi. *Dialects:* Luquan Naso, Wuding Naisu. Degree of similarity between dialects may need investigation. Also, degree of similarity with Naluo Yi needs investigation. *Lg Dev:* Pollard script is still in use, though many speakers, especially younger ones, have not learned to read it. There is also a traditional orthography for Wuding-Luquan Yi, related to but distinct from the traditional orthographies used by some other Yi languages. Few people can read the traditional orthography. NT: 1948. *Other:* Part of the Yi nationality. Christian, Polytheist.

Yi, Wumeng [ywm] 40,000 (2002). Northwestern Yunnan, in Zhaotong, Yongshan, Daguan, and Ludian counties. *Class:* Sino-Tibetan, Tibeto-Burman, Lolo-Burmese, Loloish, Northern, Yi, Eastern Yi. *Other:* Part of the Yi nationality. Polytherist, Christian.

Yi, Wusa (Yuan-Mo Yi) [ywu] 200,000. Western Guizhou and Eastern Yunnan, in Weining, Shuicheng, Hezhang, Nayong, Xuanwei, Huize, and Yiliang counties. *Class:* Sino-Tibetan, Tibeto-Burman, Lolo-Burmese, Loloish, Northern, Yi, Eastern Yi. *Dialects:* Weining Yi, Hezhang Yi, Hen-Ke Yi. *Other:* Part of the Yi nationality. Polytheist, Christian.

Yi, Xishan Lalu (Lalu, Lalupa) [yik] 320,000 (2002). Western Yunnan, in Weishan, Yangbi, Midu, Xiaguan, Yongping, Baoshan, and Lancang counties. *Class:* Sino-Tibetan, Tibeto-Burman, Lolo-Burmese, Loloish, Northern, Yi, Western Yi. *Other:* Part of the Yi nationality. Daoist, traditional religion.

Yi, Yuanjiang-Mojiang (Yuan-Mo Yi) [yym] 230,000 (2002). Yunnan, in Yuanyang, Mojiang, Jiangcheng, Simao, Honghe, Lüchun, Jinping, Pu'er, Yuanjiang, and Xinping counties. *Class:* Sino-Tibetan, Tibeto-Burman, Lolo-Burmese, Loloish, Northern, Yi, Southern Yi. *Dialects:* Yuanyang Nisu, Mojiang Nisu. *Other:* Part of the Yi nationality.

Yugur, East (Enger, Shira Yugur, Shera Yogur, Eastern Yogor, Yogor, Yögur, Yugu, Yugar) [yuy] 3,000 (1999 Junast). Ethnic population: 6,000 (2000 D. Bradley). Northwest Gansu Province, eastern Sunan Yugur Autonomous County, Kangle, Mati, and Dahe districts. *Class:* Altaic, Mongolian, Eastern, Mongour. *Lg Use:* Speakers also use Mandarin Chinese. *Lg Dev:* Literacy rate in second language: 59%. Written Chinese is in use. Dictionary. Grammar. *Other:* Part of the Yugur nationality. Pastoralists. Shamanist, Buddhist (Lamaist).

Yugur, West (Sarygh Uygur, Sarig, Ya Lu, Yellow Uighur, Sari Yogur, Yuku, Yugu, Sary-Uighur) [ybe] 2,600 (1999 Zhong Jinwen). Ethnic population: 6,000 (2000 D. Bradley). Sunan Yugur Autonomous County near Zhangye (Kanchow) in northwest Gansu Province. *Class:* Altaic, Turkic, Eastern. *Lg Use:* Decreasing use.

Used in religion, some commerce, oral literature. Positive language attitude. Speakers also use Mandarin Chinese. *Lg Dev:* Literacy rate in second language: 59%. Written Chinese is in use. *Other:* Part of the Yugur nationality. SOV. Mountain slope, plains. Animal husbandry; agriculturalists. Buddhist (Lamaist), Shamanist.

Zaiwa (Tsaiwa, Atsi, Atzi, Aji, Atshi, Aci, Azi, Atsi-Maru, Szi, Xiaoshanhua) [atb] 80,000 in China (1999 Xu Xijian). 20,000 monolinguals. Population total all countries: 110,000. Yunnan Province, Luxi, Ruili, Longchuan, Yingjiang, Bangwa districts in Dehong Dai-Jingpo Autonomous Prefecture. Also spoken in Myanmar. *Class:* Sino-Tibetan, Tibeto-Burman, Lolo-Burmese, Burmish, Northern. *Dialects:* Zaiwa, Langwa, Polo. Close to Maru, Lashi, and Pela. Related to Phun, Achang. Dialects have only minor phonological differences. *Lg Use:* Vigorous. Speakers of other languages in the area also speak Zaiwa. All domains. All ages. Used less by young people and children. Positive language attitude. Intellectuals are concerned about preservation of Zaiwa. Most speakers are trilingual in Chinese, Lisu, or Bai. Others can speak Lachi, Maru, Jingpho, or Chinese as second language. *Lg Dev:* Literacy rate in first language: 60%. 50,000 can read and write it. A Roman script orthography was developed in 1957, based on the speech of Longzhun in the Xishan District of Luxi County. Both oral and written in some primary schools. Newspapers. Radio programs. TV. Dictionary. Bible portions: 1939–1951. *Other:* Part of the Jingpo nationality. They call themselves 'Tsaiva'. Distinct from the Ahi group under Yi. SOV; 3 tone categories in unchecked syllables and 2 in checked; tense-lax vowel contrast. Valley, riverine. Agriculturalists; beekeepers; animal husbandry: chickens, pigs, sheep, cattle. Polytheist, Daoist, Christian.

Zauzou (Rourou, Raorou, Jaojo) [zal] 2,300 (1999 Sun Hongkai). About 10% are monolingual, mainly older adults. Ethnic population: 2,500 (1999 Sun Hongkai). Northwestern Yunnan Province, Lanping and Lushui counties. *Class:* Sino-Tibetan, Tibeto-Burman, Lolo-Burmese, Loloish, Unclassified. *Dialects:* Bijilan, Wupijiang. *Lg Use:* Vigorous. All domains. All ages. Used less by young people and children. Concern about possible loss. About 75% also speak Chinese, about 40% Lisu, about 9% Bai. *Lg Dev:* Grammar. *Other:* Part of the Nu nationality with Ayi, Nusu, and 5,500 ethnic Nung who are Drung speakers. SOV; no consonant clusters; no checked syllables; tense-lax and nasalized-unnasalized vowel distinctions; tonal, 6 tones. Valleys, riverine. Agriculturalists; beekeepers; animal husbandry: poultry, pigs, sheep, cattle. Polytheist, traditional religion, Daoist.

Zhaba (Zaba) [zhb] 7,700 (1995). Zhamai District of Yajiang (Nyagquka) County and Zhaba District of Daofu (Dawu) County, which are in the Ganzi (Garzê) Tibetan Autonomous Prefecture of western Sichuan. *Class:* Sino-Tibetan, Tibeto-Burman, Tangut-Qiang, Qiangic. *Dialects:* Close to Queyu. *Other:* Part of the Tibetan nationality. Different from Queyu, also called 'Zhaba'. Buddhist (Lamaist), traditional religion.

Zhuang, Northern (Chuang, Tai Chuang, Vah Cuengh, Cangva) [ccx] 10,000,000 (1992 Edmondson). 50% are monolingual. Population includes Yongbei 1,600,000, Youjiang 732,000, Guibian 522,000, Liujiang 1,300,000, Guibei 1,300,000, Hongshuihe 2,700,000, Qiubei (not available). Northern Guangxi Zhuang Autonomous Region, Wenshan Zhuang-Miao Autonomous Prefecture. Guizhou Province, Congjiang County, southwestern Hunan and northeastern Guangdong in Lianshan Zhuang-Yao Autonomous County. Yongbei is north of the Yongjiang and Youjiang rivers in the area from Hengxian to Pingguo; Hongshuihe is along the Red Water River; Liujiang around the town of Liujiang west of Liuzhou city; Youjiang

straddles the Youjiang River in the area from Tiandong to Baise; Guibian in the northwesternmost region of Guangxi (Guibian lies across north central Guangxi); and Quibei around the town of Qiubei in Yunnan. *Class:* Tai-Kadai, Kam-Tai, Be-Tai, Tai-Sek, Tai, Northern. *Dialects:* Yongbei (Yungpei), Liujiang (Liuchiang), Youjiang (Yuchiang), Guibian (Kueipien), Qiubei (Chiupei), Hongshuihe, Guibei, Lianshan. Dialect continuum to Bouyei. 'Biao' (Pumen) is a special variety spoken in Lianshan area of northwestern Guangdong and in eastern Guangxi around He Xian. Lexical similarity 75% to 86% among the dialects, average 65% between Northern and Southern Zhuang, Northern Zhuang 49% with Dong, 44% with Laka, 32% with Buyang, 30% with Laqua and Hlai, 28% with Lati, 25% with Gelo. *Lg Use:* Official regional language. Vigorous. Some speakers of other languages also speak it. All domains. All ages. Positive language attitude. In a Mandarin-speaking area, but some also speak Cantonese. Many in more developed locations control a variety of Chinese to some useful degree, but the majority in the countryside do not. Chinese used in secondary schools. *Lg Dev:* Literacy rate in second language: 67%. Literacy generally low except in major towns and cities. Roman script based on the pronunciation of the Yongbei dialect spoken in Wuming County. May be difficult for some dialect speakers to use. Traditional ideographic script based on Chinese characters. Not standardized or widely used for general purposes. Taught in primary schools. Newspapers. Radio programs. TV. Dictionary. Grammar. Bible portions: 1904. *Other:* Part of the Zhuang nationality. SVO; modifiers follow heads; Wuming dialect has 6 tone categories in unchecked syllables and 2 (split into 4 according to vowel length) in checked syllables; most dialects lack aspirated stop series; rich in reduplicating modifiers and sound symbolism employing vowel gradation; several historical layers of borrowing from Chinese. Mountain slope. Agriculturalists: paddy rice; animal husbandry; small commerce; transport. Polytheist, Daoist, Buddhist.

Zhuang, Southern [ccy] 4,000,000 (1990 Svantesson). About 50% monolingual. Population includes Yongnan 1,400,000, Zuojiang 1,400,000, De-Jing 980,000, Yan-Guang (not available), Wen-Ma 100,000. Southwest Guangxi and southern Wenshan Zhuang-Miao Autonomous Prefecture of southeastern Yunnan Province. Yongnan is south of the Yongjiang River from Yongning in the east to Long'an in the west; Zuojiang is in southwestern Guangxi around Tiandeng, Daxin, Chongzuo, Longzhou, Pingxiang, and Ningming, down to the Viet Nam border; De-Jing is in southwestern Guangxi around Debao, Jingxi, and Napo, down to the Yunnan and Viet Nam borders; Wen-Ma is in southeastern Yunnan Province south of Wenshan and Malipo, but excluding an area west of Maguan; Yan-Guang is in southeastern Yunnan Province north of Wenshan and Malipo, including Yanshan and north to Guangnan, and west of Maguan along the Viet Nam border. *Class:* Tai-Kadai, Kam-Tai, Be-Tai, Tai-Sek, Tai, Central. *Dialects:* Yongnan (Yungnan), Zuojiang (Tsochiang), De-Jing (Teching), Yan-Guang (Yenkuang), Wen-Ma (Wenma). Dialect continuum into Viet Nam. Speakers of the varieties between the Youjiang River and the Viet Nam border (particularly Zuojiang and De-Jing) refer to the language as 'Tho', share many regional characteristics, and are intelligible with the Tay ("Tho") of Viet Nam. The Yan-Guang and De-Jing varieties are intelligible with Nung (and Tay) of Viet Nam, and refer to their language as 'Nong'. Cao Lan may be close to the Yan-Guang dialect (if found in China—that name is not used) of Viet Nam. Lexical similarity 70% between dialects, 65% with Northern Zhuang. *Lg Use:* Vigorous. Speakers of other languages in the area can speak it. All domains. All ages. Speakers also use Chinese, Hmong, Mien, or Dong. *Other:* Part of the Zhuang nationality. Similar to Northern Zhuang, but has aspirated stop series. Plains. Agriculturalists; animal husbandry. Traditional religion, Daoist.

Cyprus

Cyprus. 775,927. National or official languages: Greek, Turkish. Republic of Cyprus, Kypriaki Dimokratia, Kibris Cumhuriyeti. Literacy rate: 95% to 99%. Also includes Assyrian Neo-Aramaic, North Levantine Spoken Arabic. Information mainly from A. Borg 1985. Deaf population: 49,259. Deaf institutions: 2. The number of languages listed for Cyprus is 4. Of those, all are living languages. See map on page 787.

Arabic, Cypriot Spoken (Cypriot Maronite Arabic, Maronite, Sanna) [acy] 1,300 (1995). Ethnic population: 6,000 in the Cypriot Maronite ethnic group, 140 Maronites in Kormatiki, 80 to 100 in Limassol, the rest in the Maronite community in Nicosia. Kormakiti, one of 4 Maronite villages in the mountains of northern Cyprus, and in refugee communities in Nicosia and Limassol. *Class:* Afro-Asiatic, Semitic, Central, South, Arabic. *Lg Use:* All speakers older than 30 years. 140 mainly older adults in Kormatiki. No diglossia with Standard Arabic. Those in Kormatiki use Greek or possibly Turkish; those in southern Cyprus use Greek. *Other:* A hybrid language with roots in the Arabic of both the Anatolia and the Levant. Many borrowings from Syriac and Greek. People are called 'Maronites'. Christian.
Armenian (Haieren, Somkhuri, Ermenice, Armjanski) [hye] 2,740 in Cyprus (1987). *Dialect:* Western Armenian. *Lg Use:* Most speak Greek. The older ones speak Turkish. *Other:* Urban population. Christian. See main entry under Armenia.
Greek [ell] 578,000 in Cyprus (1995). Nearly all in southern Cyprus. *Dialect:* Cypriot Greek. *Lg Use:* National language. *Other:* Christian. See main entry under Greece.
Turkish (Osmanli) [tur] 177,000 in Cyprus (1995). Nearly all in northern Cyprus. *Lg Use:* National language. *Other:* Muslim. See main entry under Turkey (Asia).

East Timor

Democratic Republic of East Timor, Timor Timus, Timor L'este, Timor Lorosae. 1,019,252. National or official languages: Tetun, Portuguese. Literacy rate: below 30%. Information mainly from C. Grimes, T. Therik, B. D. Grimes, and M. Jacob 1997. The number of languages listed for East Timor is 20. Of those, 19 are living languages and 1 is extinct. See map on page 788.

Adabe (Ataura, Atauru, Atauro, Raklu-Un, Raklu Un) [adb] 1,000 (1981 Wurm and Hattori). Ethnic population: 1,000. Atauro Island, north of Dili on Timor Island. *Class:* Trans-New Guinea, South Bird's Head-Timor-Alor-Pantar, Timor-Alor-Pantar. *Dialect:* Munaseli Pandai. Reported to be different from Galoli dialects on Atauro. No relationship to Kolana.
Baikeno (Baikenu, Vaikenu, Vaikino, Biqueno, Ambeno, Ambenu, Uab Meto, Uab Pah Meto, Oecussi, Oe Cusi, Oekusi) [bkx] 20,000 (2003 UKAW). Many are monolingual. Population includes several thousand refugees in west Timor. Ethnic population: 20,000. Oekusi enclave separated from the rest of East Timor. Traditional kingship of Ambeno on north coast of west Timor. The Kais Metan dialect is spoken in the Pantai Makasar and Oesilu districts. Tai Boko is spoken in the Nitib District. The two dialects together take up most of the northern part of Ambeno. Uis Tasae is spoken in the Pasab District, taking up the southern

third. Kais Metan has two subdialects: Kais Metan in the north, and Bob Meto in the south. *Class:* Austronesian, Malayo-Polynesian, Central-Eastern, Central Malayo-Polynesian, Timor, Nuclear Timor, West. *Dialects:* Kais Metan (East Baikeno, Bob Meto), Tai Boko (West Baikeno), Uis Tasae (South Baikeno). Baikeno is linguistically a dialect of Uab Meto, but for political reasons has to be treated as a separate language for vernacular literature. It is intelligible with the Uab Meto dialects of Amfo'an, northern Mollo, and Insana. Significant differences with Amarasi block intelligibility. They see themselves as part of the wider Atoni cultural, linguistic, political, and historical network, in contrast to being Tetun, Helong, or Rote. They refer to themselves as 'atoni' (person), speaking 'uab meto' (the language of the dry). The Kais Metan dialect is the most populous and most influential, being around the town of Oekusi, the seat of the former king, and the commercial and government center. *Lg Use:* Vigorous. All domains. All ages. Less than 1% can perform job related functions in Portuguese. Many have difficulty with low levels of Indonesian. Only those who have studied or worked in Dili can function in Tetun Dili. Baikeno as a whole has a different political and contact history from other dialects of Uab Meto, having been under Portuguese domination, rather than Dutch. Nevertheless, there are surprisingly few Portuguese loans (sentilu, turisti). There is almost no influence from Tetun Dili. *Other:* Baikeno and Uab Meto refer to the language. Ambeno refers to the traditional kingship. Oekusi is the main town in Ambeno, but people in other parts of East Timor tend to use it in a part-whole relationship to refer to the whole enclave. Locals object to this usage. Agriculturalists: wet rice on flats, swidden agriculturalists; animal husbandry: cattle. Traditional religion.
Bunak (Buna', Bunake, Bunaq) [bfn] 50,000 in East Timor (1977 Voegelin and Voegelin). Population total all countries: 100,000. Ethnic population: 50,000. Central interior Timor Island, south coast. Also spoken in Indonesia (Nusa Tenggara). *Class:* Trans-New Guinea, South Bird's Head-Timor-Alor-Pantar, Timor-Alor-Pantar, Bunak. *Dialects:* Not closely related to other languages. *Lg Use:* Many speakers bilingual in Tetun. *Lg Dev:* Grammar. *Other:* Some small groups are scattered among other languages. Traditional religion.
Fataluku (Dagaga, Dagoda', Dagada) [ddg] 30,000 (1989). Ethnic population: 30,000. Eastern tip of Timor Island around Los Palos. *Class:* Trans-New Guinea, South Bird's Head-Timor-Alor-Pantar, Timor-Alor-Pantar, Fataluku. *Dialects:* May be related to Oirata on nearby Kisar Island. Significant dialect variation. May turn out to be several languages. *Lg Use:* Some speakers cannot function at all in Indonesian, Portuguese, or Tetun Dili. *Other:* Verb final. Traditional religion, Christian.
Galoli (Galole) [gal] 50,000 (1981 Wurm and Hattori). Ethnic population: 50,000. North coast between Mambae and Makasae, regions of Laklo, Manatutu, Laleia, and We-Masin, Wetar Island. *Class:* Austronesian, Malayo-Polynesian, Central-Eastern, Central Malayo-Polynesian, Timor, Nuclear Timor, East. *Dialects:* Na Nahek, Edi, Dadua, Galoli, Baba, Hahak. Talur on Wetar Island in Maluku may be inherently intelligible.
Habu [hbu] 1,260 (2000 WCD). Northeast of Laclubar and the Idate language. *Class:* Austronesian, Malayo-Polynesian, Central-Eastern, Central Malayo-Polynesian, Timor, Nuclear Timor, Waima'a. *Dialects:* Many loanwords from Trans-New Guinea languages similar to Makasae, but with Austronesian structure. Related to Waima'a and Kairui. Classification needs further investigation.
Idaté [idt] 5,000 (1981 Wurm and Hattori). Ethnic population: 5,000. Central East Timor, mountains of part

of the Laclubar area, surrounded by the Mambae, Galoli, Kairui, and Tetun. *Class:* Austronesian, Malayo-Polynesian, Central-Eastern, Central Malayo-Polynesian, Timor, Nuclear Timor, East. *Dialects:* Closest to Lakalei and Galoli. *Other:* Mountain slope.

Kairui-Midiki (Cairui, Midiki) [krd] 2,000 (2001). Ethnic population: 2,000. Central small mountainous area surrounded by Makasai, Waima'a, Tetun, Galoli. *Class:* Austronesian, Malayo-Polynesian, Central-Eastern, Central Malayo-Polynesian, Timor, Nuclear Timor, Waima'a. *Dialect:* Kairui, Midiki (Midik). Vocabulary is predominantly Trans-New Guinea, structure is Austronesian. Related to Waima'a and Habu. Classification needs further investigation. May be a co-dialect with Waima'a. *Other:* Mountain slope.

Kemak (Ema) [kem] 50,000 in East Timor (1981 Wurm and Hattori). Population total all countries: 100,000. Ethnic population: 50,000. North central Timor Island, border area between East Timor and West Timor, mostly on eastern side. Also spoken in Indonesia (Nusa Tenggara). *Class:* Austronesian, Malayo-Polynesian, Central-Eastern, Central Malayo-Polynesian, Timor, Nuclear Timor, East. *Dialects:* Nogo (Nogo-Nogo), Kemak. Close to Tetun. Most closely related to Mambae and Tukudede. Also related to Uab Meto. Morris 1992 counts Nogo as a separate language from Kemak. *Other:* OSV. Traditional religion, Christian.

Lakalei [lka] 5,000 (1981 Wurm and Hattori). Ethnic population: 5,000. Central Timor Island, north of Same, northeast of Ainaro. *Class:* Austronesian, Malayo-Polynesian, Central-Eastern, Central Malayo-Polynesian, Timor, Nuclear Timor, East. *Dialects:* Close to Idate, Tetun, Galoli. *Other:* Many loanwords from Tetun, Mambae, and Idate.

Makasae (Makassai, Macassai, Ma'asae, Makasai) [mkz] 70,000 (1989). Ethnic population: 70,000. Timor Island, eastern end around Baucau and inland, west of Fataluku, from northern to southern coast in a dialect chain. *Class:* Trans-New Guinea, South Bird's Head-Timor-Alor-Pantar, Timor-Alor-Pantar, Makasai-Alor-Pantar, Makasai. *Dialects:* Maklere, Makasai. Not closely related to other languages. Non-Austronesian. *Lg Use:* Some speakers cannot function at all in Indonesian, Portuguese, or Tetun Dili. *Other:* Traditional religion, Christian.

Maku'a (Lovaea, Lovaia) [lva] 50 (1981 Wurm and Hattori). Ethnic population: 50. Northeast tip of Timor Island, around Tutuala. *Class:* Trans-New Guinea, South Bird's Head-Timor-Alor-Pantar, Timor-Alor-Pantar, Maku'a. *Lg Use:* Younger generation uses Fataluku as first or second language.

Mambae (Mambai, Manbae) [mgm] 80,000 in East Timor (1981 Wurm and Hattori). Ethnic population: 80,000. Mountains of central Timor, around Ermera, Aileu, and Ainaro. One of the dominant groups among Timorese communities in Australia. Also spoken in Australia. *Class:* Austronesian, Malayo-Polynesian, Central-Eastern, Central Malayo-Polynesian, Timor, Nuclear Timor, East. *Dialects:* Damata, Lolei, Manua, Mambai. *Lg Use:* Second most widely spoken language of East Timor. Some speakers cannot function at all in Indonesian, Portuguese, or Tetun Dili. *Other:* Mountain slope. Traditional religion, Christian.

Nauete (Nauhete, Naueti, Naóti, Nauote, Nauoti) [nxa] 1,000 (1981 Wurm and Hattori). Ethnic population: 1,000. South coast, eastern tip of Timor Island, west of Tiomar. The main town is Uato Lari. *Class:* Austronesian, Malayo-Polynesian, Central-Eastern, Central Malayo-Polynesian, Timor, Nuclear Timor. *Dialects:* Naumik, Oso Moko. Not closely related to any other language. Many loanwords from Trans-New Guinea languages like Makasae. *Lg Use:* Vigorous.

Pidgin, Timor (Timor Creole Portuguese) [tvy] Extinct. Timor Island, around Bidau, Dili, and Lifan. *Class:* Creole, Portuguese based. *Dialects:* Português de Bidau, Macaísta.

Portuguese (Português) [por] *Lg Use:* Official language. Probably 2% of the population from East Timor worldwide can function in it, including about 9,000 people living overseas. *Other:* Christian. See main entry under Portugal.

Tetun (Tetum, Tettum, Teto, Tetu, Tetung, Belu, Belo, Fehan, Tetun Belu) [tet] 50,000 in East Timor (2004). Western East Timor on the south coast from Suai to Viqueque. East of Atoni, west of Bunak (in Batagude) around Batibo, and in from the south coast around Viqueque and Soibada. *Dialects:* Eastern Tetun (Soibada, Natarbora, Lakluta, Tetun Loos, Tetun Los), Southern Tetun (Lia Fehan, Plain Tetun, Tasi Mane, Belu Selatan, South Belu, South Tetun), Northern Tetun (Lia Foho, Hill Tetun, Tasi Feto, Belu Utara, North Belu, Tetun Terik, Tetun Therik). *Lg Use:* Official language. Spoken by some Bunak around Suai as second language. *Other:* Christian, traditional religion. See main entry under Indonesia (Nusa Tenggara).

Tetun Dili (Tetun, Tetum, Tetum Prasa, Tetum Praça, Dili Tetum, Tetum Dili) [tdt] 50,000 (1995). First-language speakers concentrated in and around Dili on the north coast of East Timor. Second-language speakers scattered widely throughout the western part of East Timor. *Class:* Creole, Tetun based. *Dialects:* There are important differences with Tetun in parts of the grammar, morphology, functors, and much of the lexicon. There is heavy influence of Portuguese and some Indonesian or Malay loans in Tetun Dili. *Lg Use:* Language of wider communication. Growing in its role as a language of wider communication, predominantly in urban areas. There are 3 second-language varieties spoken by different people: (1) fluent Tetun Dili spoken throughout the western part of East Timor, primarily by those who have lived in Dili for one or more years, (2) occasional Dili residents with significant influence from their own first languages, and (3) people originally from East Timor who are overseas residents in Portugal or Australia, with higher portion of inflected Portuguese vocabulary and almost complete lack of Indonesian or Malay loans. There is also 'Tetum Ibadat' or 'liturgical Tetum' which is not spoken by anyone for everyday communication, nor as first language, with a lot of vocabulary and some grammar that is not understood widely. All domains. All ages. Speakers of North and South Tetun have significant difficulty understanding it in many speech domains, and vice versa. Some first-language speakers of Tetun Dili consider themselves to be bilingual in Tetun because of contact, but when pressed, admit there are domains in which communication is completely blocked. *Lg Dev:* Grammar. Bible portions: 1996–2002. *Other:* Cultural rituals and themes in Tetun are not as deeply rooted in Tetun Prasa. Heavy Portuguese and Mambae influence. Compared to Tetun: many more Portuguese loanwords; does not inflect V-initial verb roots for person or number; uses more periphrastic constructions than morphological constructions (e.g., causatives); differences in possessive constructions and negatives. Christian.

Tukudede (Tukude, Tokodede, Tokodé, Tocod) [tkd] 63,170 (2000 WCD). Timor Island, north coast, regions of Maubara and Liquisa from the banks of the Lois River to Dili. *Class:* Austronesian, Malayo-Polynesian, Central-Eastern, Central Malayo-Polynesian, Timor, Nuclear Timor, East. *Dialects:* Keha (Keia), Tukudede. *Other:* Christian.

Waima'a (Uai Ma'a, Waimaha, Waimoa, Uaimo'a) [wmh] 3,000 (2001). Ethnic population: 3,000 or more. Northeast coast Timor Island, enclave within Makasae-speaking area. *Class:* Austronesian, Malayo-Polynesian, Central-Eastern, Central Malayo-Polynesian, Timor, Nuclear

Timor, Waima'a. *Dialects:* Many Trans-New Guinea loanwords similar to Makasae. Related to Habu and Kairui. Classification needs further investigation. May be a co-dialect with Kairui-Midiki.

Georgia

Georgia. 4,693,892. National or official language: Georgian. Capital: Tbilisi. 26,911 square miles. Literacy rate: 99%. Also includes Armenian (448,000), Chechen, Greek (38,000), Judeo-Crimean Tatar, Lak (246), Lezgi (3,650), North Azerbaijani (308,000), Pontic (120,000), Russian (372,000), Tatar (3,102), Turkish (3,102), Udi (500), Ukrainian (52,000). Information mainly from T. Sebeok 1963; E. Haby 1975, A. Kibrik 1991. The number of languages listed for Georgia is 12. Of those, all are living languages.

Abkhaz (Abxazo) [abk] 101,000 in Georgia (1993). Population total all countries: 105,952. Abkhaz Republic within Georgia, Black Sea coast. Also spoken in Turkey (Asia), Ukraine. *Class:* North Caucasian, West Caucasian, Abkhaz-Abazin. *Dialects:* Bzyb, Abzhui, Samurzakan. *Lg Use:* 94% speak it as first language. *Lg Dev:* Bible portions: 1912–1981. *Other:* Mountain slope, coastal. Forest. Agriculturalists: maize, tobacco, tea; animal husbandry: sheep, goats, horses; forestry. Christian, Muslim.

Assyrian Neo-Aramaic (Aisorski) [aii] 3,000 in Georgia (1999). Ethnic population: 14,000. Erevan and scattered throughout Transcaucasia. *Lg Use:* Most speakers are older adults. Many use Russian as primary language. *Other:* 'Aisor' is the Russian name for the people. Christian (Nestorian). See main entry under Iraq.

Bats (Batsi, Batsaw, Tsova-Tush, Tush, Batsbi, Bac, Batsbiitsy) [bbl] 3,420 (2000 WCD). Georgia, spoken by about half the inhabitants of Zemo-Alvani. *Class:* North Caucasian, East Caucasian, Nakh, Batsi. *Lg Use:* Few key domains, home. A few children speak Bats. Neutral language attitude. Georgian is used as the literary language. *Lg Dev:* Grammar. *Other:* Traditional territory and way of life. Muslim (Sunni).

Bohtan Neo-Aramaic [bhn] 1,000 in Georgia (1999 Fox). Mainly in Garbadani village, Georgia. Also spoken in Russia (Asia). *Class:* Afro-Asiatic, Semitic, Central, Aramaic, Eastern, Central, Northeastern. *Lg Use:* Most over 60. Younger generations tend to shift to Georgian or Russian. *Other:* Originally spoken by villagers in Anatolia, Ottoman Empire, east of the Tigris River (present-day southeastern Turkey). They fled to Russia during World War I. Christian.

Georgian (Kartuli, Gruzinski, Common Kartvelian) [kat] 3,901,380 in Georgia (1993 UBS). Population total all countries: 4,178,604. Ethnic population: 3,981,000 (1993 UBS). 69,700 square miles. Also spoken in Armenia, Azerbaijan, Iran, Kazakhstan, Kyrgyzstan, Russia (Asia), Tajikistan, Turkey (Asia), Turkmenistan, Ukraine, USA, Uzbekistan. *Class:* Kartvelian, Georgian. *Dialects:* Imeretian, Racha-Lexchxum (Lechkhum), Gurian, Adzhar (Acharian), Imerxev Kartlian, Kaxetian (Kakhetian), Ingilo, Tush, Xevsur (Kheysur), Moxev (Mokhev), Pshav, Mtiul, Ferejdan, Meskhur-Javakhuri. Imerxev is in Turkey, Ferejdan may no longer be spoken in Iran. *Lg Use:* Official language. The Meskhi are ethnically Georgian, speak Georgian, are Eastern Orthodox, and live in southwestern Georgia. *Lg Dev:* Mkhedruli script. Grammar. Bible: 1743–1989. *Other:* Adzhai Muslims are in Armenia. South Caucasian is also called 'Kartvelian'. 'Gruzinski' is the Russian name. SVO. Christian (Georgian Orthodox), Muslim (Sunni and Shi'a).

Judeo-Georgian [jge] 20,000 in Georgia (1995). Some have gone elsewhere in the former USSR and to other countries. *Other:* Oriental and Ashkenazic Jews in Georgia live separately. Judeo-Georgian speakers live separately from non-Jewish Georgian speakers. Jewish. See main entry under Israel.

Kurdish, Northern (Kurmanji, Kurmancî, Kurdî) [kmr] 40,000 in Georgia (1991). Around Tblisi. *Other:* Yezidi. See main entry under Turkey (Asia).

Laz (Laze, Chan, Chanzan, Zan, Chanuri) [lzz] 2,000 in Georgia (1982). Adjar, Georgia, a couple of villages. *Dialects:* Xopa (Hopa), Chxala (Ckhala), Vice-Arxava (Vital-Arkhava), Atina, Samurzakan-Zugdidi, Senaki. *Lg Use:* Georgian used as literary language. *Other:* Their name for their language is 'Lazuri'. Not a written language in Georgia or Turkey. Muslim. See main entry under Turkey (Asia).

Mingrelian (Margaluri, Megrel, Megruli) [xmf] 500,000 (1989 Hewitt). Lowland west Georgia. *Class:* Kartvelian, Zan. *Dialects:* Officially considered to be a single language with Laz, called Zan, but linguists recognize that they are not inherently intelligible with each other. *Lg Use:* Georgian used as a literary language. *Other:* Their name for themselves is 'Margaluri'. Not a written language. Christian.

Osetin (Ossete, Ossetian) [oss] 100,000 in Georgia (2001 Johnstone and Mandryk). Population total all countries: 526,453. Also spoken in Azerbaijan, Germany, Kazakhstan, Russia (Asia), Tajikistan, Turkey (Asia), Turkmenistan, Ukraine, Uzbekistan. *Class:* Indo-European, Indo-Iranian, Iranian, Eastern, Northeastern. *Dialects:* Digor, Tagaur, Kurtat, Allagir, Tual, Iron. *Lg Dev:* Cyrillic script. NT: 1993. *Other:* Muslim (Sunni), Christian.

Svan (Lushnu, Svanuri) [sva] 15,000 (2000 A. E. Kibrik). Ethnic population: 15,000 (2000 A. E. Kibrik). Svantetia Region. *Class:* Kartvelian, Svan. *Dialects:* Upper Bal, Lower Bal, Lashx, Lentex. *Lg Use:* Not a written language. All domains. A few children speak Svan. Proficiency limited among young people. People are neutral toward Svan. Reports indicate that speakers want to remain separate from Georgian. Georgian and Russian are used as literary languages. *Other:* Traditional territory and way of life. Their name for their language is 'Lushnu'. Christian (Lakhamul).

Urum [uum] 97,746 in Georgia (2000 WCD). Population total all countries: 192,729. Caucasus. In recent years there has been emigration of Urum speakers from Georgia to Greece. Also spoken in Greece, Ukraine. *Class:* Altaic, Turkic. *Dialects:* Related to Crimean Tatar. A number of inherently intelligible dialects. *Other:* Spoken by ethnic 'Greeks'.

India

Republic of India, Bharat. 1,065,070,607. Indo-Aryan 777,361,000, 76%; Dravidian 216,635,000, 21.6%; Austro-Asiatic 12,250,000, 1.2%; Tibeto-Burman 10,350,000, 1%; Other 2,468,600, 0.2%. National or official languages: Hindi and English. There are 22 official 'scheduled' languages: Assamese, Bengali, Bodo, Dogri, Gujarati, Hindi, Kannada, Kashmiri, Konkani, Maithili, Malayalam, Marathi, Meitei, Nepali, Oriya, Eastern Panjabi, Sanskrit, Santali, Sindhi, Tamil, Telugu, Urdu. Literacy rate: 36% to 52%. Also includes Armenian (560), Burushaski, Chitwania Tharu, Geman Deng, Judeo-Iraqi Arabic, Kathoriya Tharu, Northern Pashto (15,000), Portuguese (250,000), Russian (1,036), Uyghur, Walungge, Western Farsi (18,000), Arabic, Chinese. Information mainly from G. Marrison 1967; R. Hugoniot 1970; C. Masica 1991; K. S. Singh 1994, 1995; J. Matisoff, S. Baron, and J. Lowe 1996; R. Breton 1997; R. Burling ms 1998. Blind population: 9,000,000. Deaf population: 9,400,000 to 14,000,000 (2001). Deaf institutions: 850. The number of languages listed for India is 428. Of those, 415 are living languages and 13 are extinct.

A-Pucikwar (Pucikwar, Puchikwar) [apq] 24 (2000 Verma). Andaman Islands, Boratang Island, south coast of Middle Andaman Island, northeast coast of South Andaman Island. *Class:* Andamanese, Great Andamanese, Central. *Lg Use:* Speakers are shifting to Hindi. *Lg Dev:* Literacy rate in first language: below 1%. Grammar. *Other:* Other languages in the Central Andamanese group are extinct. Great Andamanese is classified as a Scheduled Tribe in India. Puchikwar is a subtribe. Nearly extinct.

Aariya [aay] Madhya Pradesh, Chhatarpur, Datia, Panna, Rewa, Satna, Shahdol, Sidhi, Tikamgarh districts. *Class:* Unclassified.

Adi (Abhor, Abor, Boga'er Luoba, Lhoba, Luoba) [adi] 110,000 in India (1997 BSI). Population includes 1,200 Palibo. Population total all countries: 111,088. Arunachal Pradesh, East, West, and Upper Siang districts, Upper Subansiri and Dibang Valley districts; Assam, north hills of Assam Valley, between Bhutan and the Buruli River. Also spoken in China. *Class:* Sino-Tibetan, Tibeto-Burman, North Assam, Tani. *Dialects:* Ashing, Bokar (Boga'er Luoba), Bori, Karko, Komkar, Milang, Minyong, Padam (Standard Adi), Pailibo, Pangi, Pasi, Ramo, Shimong, Tangam. Sun (1993) lists Tani languages and dialects as Apatani, Milang, Bokar, Damu, Mising, Padam, Bangni, Tagin, Sagli, south Aya, Leli, and perhaps Pailibo, Ramo, Asing, Bori, Pasi, Panggi, Simong, Minyong, Karok, Hill Miri, and some northern and western dialects of Nisi. Intelligible with Adi Galo but they are sociolinguistically distinct. A different language from Yidu Lhoba. *Lg Use:* Speakers also use Assamese, Hindi, or Nepali. *Lg Dev:* Literacy rate in second language in China. Grammar. NT: 1988. *Other:* Adi is a Scheduled Tribe in India with several subgroups. 'Adi', meaning 'hillman', has been used as a cover term for the eastern Tani group of languages. SOV; particles indicate grammatical relations; long-short vowel distinction; most words polysyllabic; loans mainly from Tibetan. Agriculturalists: rice, grain, beans, fruit, eggs; hunters. Traditional religion, Christian.

Adi, Galo (Adi, Adi-Gallong, Adi-Galo, Gallong, Galong) [adl] 150,000 (2004). A few older adult monolinguals. Arunachal Pradesh, West Siang, East Siang, Dibang Valley (south), Lohit (east), Changlang (northeast), and some in Upper Subansiri (west) districts. *Class:* Sino-Tibetan, Tibeto-Burman, North Assam, Tani. *Dialects:* Reportedly intelligible with other Adi dialects but they are sociolinguistically distinct. *Lg Use:* Used in the village, home. All ages. Padam has not been accepted as the standard Adi dialect by the Galo or other groups. Nearly all speak some Hindi and Assamese. Hindi is used with the military. English is spoken by the educated and the young. *Lg Dev:* Literacy rate in second language: 40%. Roman script. Radio programs. *Other:* A Scheduled Tribe in India. SOV; postpositions; genitives after noun heads; articles, adjectives, numerals before and after noun heads; relatives after noun heads or without; question word initial; maximum prefixes 2, maximum suffixes 4–5; affixes indicate case of noun phrase; there are causatives and comparatives; CV, CVC, CVV patterns; nontonal. Agriculturalists. Traditional religion, Hindu, Christian.

Agariya (Agaria, Agharia, Agoria) [agi] 55,757 (1981 census). Madhya Pradesh, Mandla, Bilaspur, Rewa districts, Maikal hills; Chhattisgarh, Bilaspur District Uttar Pradesh, Agra, Mathura, Mirzapur districts. *Class:* Austro-Asiatic, Munda, North Munda, Kherwari. *Lg Use:* Speakers also use Hindi. *Lg Dev:* Literacy rate in second language: 5%. *Other:* A Scheduled Caste in Uttar Pradesh. Singh reports Chhattisgarhi as first language of tribe. Traditional religion, Hindu.

Ahirani (Ahiri) [ahr] 779,000 (1997). Maharashtra, Dhule, Jalgaon districts; Gujarat. *Class:* Indo-European, Indo-Iranian, Indo-Aryan, Central zone, Khandesi. *Dialects:* Preliminary findings are that it is distinct from Khandesi. *Lg Use:* Speakers also use Hindi or Marathi. *Other:* Hindu.

Ahom (Tai Ahom) [aho] Extinct. Assam. *Class:* Tai-Kadai, Kam-Tai, Be-Tai, Tai-Sek, Tai, Southwestern, Northwest. *Lg Use:* No longer spoken in daily life, but used in religious chants and literary materials. *Other:* Former language of the Tai-Ahom King. Possibly 8,000,000 Assamese speakers claim to be of Ahom descent (A. Diller 1990).

Aimol [aim] 2,643 in Manipur (2001 census). Assam; Manipur; Chandel District, Unapal, Satu, Kumirei, Chingunghut, Aimol Tampak, Khodamphai, Ngairong Aimol, Chandonpokpi, Soibong (Khudengthabi); Senapati District, Tuikhong; Churachandpur District, Kha-Aimol, Luichungbum. *Class:* Sino-Tibetan, Tibeto-Burman, Kuki-Chin-Naga, Kuki-Chin, Northern. *Dialect:* Langrong. Langrong may be a separate language. Related to Chiru, Purum. Reportedly intelligible to Koireng. *Lg Use:* Used in the home, church. Most speakers highly proficient in Meitei. *Lg Dev:* Literacy rate in second language: 60% to 70%. Roman script. *Other:* A Scheduled Tribe in India. Plains, foothills. Swidden agriculturalists. Christian.

Aiton (Aitonia) [aio] 5,000 (1990 Diller). Assam, Jorhat, Karbi Anglong districts, Doboroni, Banlung, Ahomoni, Balipathar, Kaliyani, Chakihula, Tengani, Barhula villages. *Class:* Tai-Kadai, Kam-Tai, Be-Tai, Tai-Sek, Tai, Southwestern, Northwest. *Dialects:* Close to Phake. Related to Shan of Myanmar. *Lg Use:* Some speakers use Assamese, Hindi, or English. *Lg Dev:* Literacy rate in first language: below 1%. Tai script. *Other:* Agriculturalists. Buddhist.

Aka-Bea (Bea, Beada, Biada, Aka-Beada, Bojigniji, Bogijiab, Bojigyab) [abj] Extinct. Andaman Islands, coasts of South Andaman Island except northeast coast, and north and east interiors; coastal Rutland Island except south coast; small islands southeast of Rutland; and Labyrinth Islands. *Class:* Andamanese, Great Andamanese, Central.

Aka-Bo (Bo, Ba) [akm] Extinct. Andaman Islands, east central coast of North Andaman Island, and North Reef Island. *Class:* Andamanese, Great Andamanese, Northern.

Aka-Cari (Cari, Chariar) [aci] Extinct. Andaman Islands, north coast of North Andaman Island, Landfall Island, and other nearby small islands. *Class:* Andamanese, Great Andamanese, Northern.

Aka-Jeru (Jeru, Yerawa) [akj] Extinct. Andaman Islands, interior and south North Andaman Island, and Sound Island. *Class:* Andamanese, Great Andamanese, Northern.

Aka-Kede (Kede) [akx] Extinct. Andaman Islands, central and north central Middle Andaman Island. *Class:* Andamanese, Great Andamanese, Central.

Aka-Kol (Kol) [aky] Extinct. Andaman Islands, southeast Middle Andaman Island. *Class:* Andamanese, Great Andamanese, Central.

Aka-Kora (Kora) [ack] Extinct. Andaman Islands, northeast and north central coasts of North Andaman Island, and Smith Island. *Class:* Andamanese, Great Andamanese, Northern.

Akar-Bale (Bale, Balwa) [acl] Extinct. Andaman Islands, Ritchie's Archipelago, Havelock Island, Neill Island. *Class:* Andamanese, Great Andamanese, Central.

Allar (Alan, Alanmar, Alar, Allan, Chatans) [all] 350. Kerala, Palakkad, Malappuram districts. *Class:* Dravidian, Unclassified. *Lg Dev:* Literacy rate in first language: below 1%. *Other:* Animal husbandry; laborers. Traditional religion.

Amri (Amri Karbi) [ajz] 125,000 (2003). Assam, Kamrup District, south of the Brahmaputra River including Chandubi, Loharghat, Rani block, Jalukbari, Pandu,

Basbistha, Panikhaith, Jorabat, Sonapur, Khetri, Kahi Kusi; Meghalaya; East Khasi Hills District, Nongpoh area, including Barni Hat and Umling. *Class:* Sino-Tibetan, Tibeto-Burman, Mikir. *Dialects:* Reported to be unintelligible with Karbi. Lexical similarity 75% with Rengkhang and Chingthang, 90% with the Karbi spoken in West Bengal. *Lg Use:* Positive language attitude. Strong feelings of separateness from the dominant Karbi group in Karbi, Anglong District. Speakers of all ages use Assamese as second language. *Lg Dev:* Literacy rate in second language: 20%. Roman script. Newspapers. Radio programs. *Other:* Hindu, traditional religion, Christian.

Anal (Namfau) [anm] 13,853 in India (2001 census). Southeast Manipur, Chandel District, Chandel, Chakpikarong, Tengnoupal subdivisions, on banks of Chakpi River. Possibly in Bangladesh. Also spoken in Myanmar. *Class:* Sino-Tibetan, Tibeto-Burman, Kuki-Chin-Naga, Kuki-Chin, Northern. *Dialects:* Laizo, Mulsom. Closest to Lamgang (Kuki Naga). *Lg Use:* Speakers also use Meitei. *Lg Dev:* Literacy rate in first language: below 1%. Roman script. NT: 1983. *Other:* A Scheduled Tribe in India. Declared themselves Nagas (ethnically) 1963. SOV. Forest. Christian.

Andaman Creole Hindi (Andaman Hindi) [hca] 10,000 to 31,000 (2002). Andaman and Nicobar Islands, Port Blair and 40 villages south of Port Blair. *Class:* Creole, Hindi based. *Dialects:* A creolization of Hindustani, Bengali, Malayalam. *Lg Use:* Used in the home. All ages. Use standard Hindi with outsiders. A diglossic situation exists. *Other:* Spoken as first language by mixed generations of communities who refer to themselves as 'locals'. Contains elements of Indo-Aryan and Dravidian grammar. No literature exists in the creole. Standard Hindi literature is used.

Andh (Andha, Andhi) [anr] 80,000 (1991). Maharashtra, Akola, Aurangabad, Buldana, Nanded, Parbhani, Yeotmal districts; Andhra Pradesh, Adilabad, Hyderabad; Madhya Pradesh. *Class:* Unclassified. *Lg Dev:* Literacy rate in first language: below 1%. *Other:* A Scheduled Tribe in India. Singh reports they speak Marathi as first language. Agriculturalists. Hindu, Christian.

Angika (Anga, Angikar, Chhika-Chhiki) [anp] 725,000 in India (1997). Population total all countries: 740,892. Northern Bihar. Also spoken in Nepal. *Class:* Indo-European, Indo-Iranian, Indo-Aryan, Eastern zone, Bihari. *Dialects:* 79% inherent intelligibility of Brahmin Maithili. Lexical similarity 81% (Brahmin) to 87% (non-Brahmin) with Darbhanga Maithili. *Lg Use:* Used in the home, community. All ages. Negative language attitude. Hindi is used for trading, government, praying. *Lg Dev:* Radio programs. *Other:* Hindu, Christian.

Apatani (Apa) [apt] 23,000 (1997). Assam; Arunachal Pradesh, Subansiri District, 7 villages in and around Hapoli and Zirol; Nagaland. *Class:* Sino-Tibetan, Tibeto-Burman, North Assam, Tani. *Dialects:* It may be intelligible with Nisi. *Lg Use:* Speakers also use Assamese, Hindi, or Nefamese. *Lg Dev:* Literacy rate in first language: below 1%. Literacy rate in second language: 6%; 11% Male, 1% Female (1997). *Other:* A Scheduled Tribe in India. Hills. 1,700 meters. Agriculturalists: wet rice; hunters. Traditional religion, Christian.

Arakanese (Mogh, Mog, "Magh," "Maghi," Morma, Yakan, Yakhaing, Rakhain, Marma) [mhv] 24,000 in India (1997). Assam; Tripura; Mizoram, Mombusu, Dungjangtalang, Mowthimambrow villages; West Bengal. *Lg Use:* Speakers also use Bengali. *Lg Dev:* Literacy rate in first language: 10% to 30%. *Other:* Mag is a Scheduled Tribe in India. "Magh" is a derogatory term. Few Arakanese in Mizoram or Tripura attend school. No one has attained higher education in Mizoram (Singh).

Agriculturalists. Buddhist syncretism with traditional religion, Christian. See main entry under Myanmar.

Aranadan (Aranatan, Eranadans) [aaf] 236 (1981 census). Kerala, Kozhihkode District, Ernad taluk; Palghat District; Tamil Nadu, Karnataka. *Class:* Dravidian, Southern, Tamil-Kannada, Tamil-Kodagu, Tamil-Malayalam, Malayalam. *Lg Use:* Speakers also use Malayalam. *Lg Dev:* Literacy rate in first language: below 1%. Literacy rate in second language: 20% in Kerala (1981 census). *Other:* A Scheduled Tribe in India. Speak a mixture of Tamil, Malayalam and Tulu (Shashi). Wage laborers; animal husbandry. Hindu.

Assamese (Asambe, Asami, Asamiya) [asm] 15,334,000 in India (1997). Population total all countries: 15,374,000. Assam; West Bengal; Meghalaya; Arunachal Pradesh. Also spoken in Bangladesh, Bhutan. *Class:* Indo-European, Indo-Iranian, Indo-Aryan, Eastern zone, Bengali-Assamese. *Dialects:* Jharwa (Pidgin), Mayang, Standard Assamese, Western Assamese. *Lg Use:* State language of Assam. *Lg Dev:* Bengali script. Bible: 1833.

Asuri (Ashree, Asura, Assur, Maleta) [asr] 16,596 (2001). Jharkhand, Gumla and Lohardaga districts of Chotanagpur Plateau; Chhattisgarh, Raigarh District, Jashpur area; Maharashtra; Orissa, Sambalpur District; West Bengal. *Class:* Austro-Asiatic, Munda, North Munda, Kherwari, Mundari. *Dialects:* Brijia (Birjia, Koranti), Manjhi. *Lg Use:* Speakers also use Sadri or Bengali. *Lg Dev:* Literacy rate in first language: below 1%. *Other:* Asur and Birjia are both Scheduled Tribes in India. Hindu, traditional religion, Christian.

A'tong [aot] Assam. *Class:* Sino-Tibetan, Tibeto-Burman, Jingpho-Konyak-Bodo, Konyak-Bodo-Garo, Bodo-Garo, Koch. *Dialects:* Most closely related to Koch and Rabha. *Lg Use:* Not inherently intelligible with Garo, but many A'tong speak Garo as second language.

Awadhi (Abadi, Abohi, Ambodhi, Avdhi, Baiswari, Kojali, Kosali) [awa] 20,000,000 in India (1999). Population total all countries: 20,560,744. Bihar; Madhya Pradesh; Uttar Pradesh, Kheri, Sitapur, Lucknow, Unnao, Rae-Bareli, Bahraich, Bara-Banki, Pratapgarh, Sultanpur, Gonda, Faizabad, Allahabad districts; Delhi. Also spoken in Nepal. *Class:* Indo-European, Indo-Iranian, Indo-Aryan, East Central zone. *Dialects:* Gangapari, Mirzapuri, Pardesi, Uttari. Awadhi in Banke, Bardiya districts in Nepal may not be intelligible with Awadhi in India. *Lg Use:* Education is in Hindi. *Lg Dev:* Literacy rate in first language: 50% to 75%. Devanagari script. Bible: 2000. *Other:* Awadhi is the standard for literature. There is considerable epic literature. 'Kosali' is a name used for the Eastern Hindi group. Hindu holy book is in Awadhi: Tulsi Das author, Ramcharitmanas title. Hindu, Muslim, Christian.

Badaga (Badag, Badagu, Badugu, Baduga, Vadagu) [bfq] 245,374 (2000 WCD). Tamil Nadu, Madras-Nilgiri, Kunda hills. 200 villages. *Class:* Dravidian, Southern, Tamil-Kannada, Kannada. *Lg Dev:* Tamil script. NT: 1999.

Bagheli (Bagelkhandi, Bhugelkhud, Mannadi, Riwai, Gangai, Mandal, Kewot, Kewat, Kawathi, Kenat, Kevat Boli, Kevati, Kewani, Kewati) [bfy] 396,000 in India (1997). Northeast Madhya Pradesh, Satna, Rewa, Shahdol, Sidhi, Jabalpur, Mandla, Chhindwara districts; Maharashtra; Uttar Pradesh, Banda District. Also spoken in Nepal. *Class:* Indo-European, Indo-Iranian, Indo-Aryan, East Central zone. *Dialects:* Ojhi (Ojaboli, Ojha, Ojhe, Oza, Ozha), Powari, Banapari, Gahore, Tirhari, Godwani (Mandlaha), Sonpari. *Lg Dev:* Devanagari script. NT: 1821. *Other:* The Ojhi are seminomadic. Has had literature since the 16th century. Hindu, traditional religion (Ojhi).

Bagri (Bagari, Bagria, Bagris, Baorias, Bahgri) [bgq] 1,899,100 in India (2000). Population total all countries: 2,099,100. Punjab, Firozepur, Muktsar districts; Rajasthan,

Hanumangarh, Sriganganagar districts; Haryana, Sirsa, Hissar districts; Madhya Pradesh. Also spoken in Pakistan. *Class:* Indo-European, Indo-Iranian, Indo-Aryan, Central zone, Rajasthani, Unclassified. *Dialects:* Lexical similarity 62% with Hindi, 65% with Haryanvi, 51% to 66% with Marwari, 58% to 69% with Merwari, 69% to 76% with Shekhawati, 47% to 63% with Godwari, 63% to 65% with Dhundari, 60% to 66% with Mewati, 74% with Jandavra. *Lg Dev:* Grammar. *Other:* A Scheduled Caste in India. Singh (1993) reports they speak Malvi in Madhya Pradesh, Bagri in Rajasthan. SOV; tonal, 3 tones. Desert. Traditional religion, Christian.

Balochi, Eastern (Balochi, Baluci, Baloci) [bgp] 5,000 in India (1977 Voegelin and Voegelin). Uttar Pradesh; Gujarat. *Lg Use:* Speakers also use Urdu. *Other:* Distinct from Western Balochi of Pakistan, Afghanistan, Iran, Turkmenistan; and Southern Balochi of Pakistan, Iran, Oman, United Arab Emirates. Muslim (Sunni). See main entry under Pakistan.

Balti (Sbalt, Baltistani, Bhoti of Baltistan) [bft] 67,000 in India (1997). Jammu and Kashmir. *Lg Use:* Some Shina is used as second language. Urdu proficiency is reported to be high in some places. Women and the uneducated have little knowledge of Urdu. Many Purik have shifted to Balti. *Other:* A Scheduled Tribe in India. Muslim (Shi'a), Christian. See main entry under Pakistan.

Bareli, Palya (Pali, Palodi, Palya Bareli) [bpx] 10,000 to 25,000 (2000 Varkey). Madhya Pradesh, Barwani District: Rajpur, Barwani tahsils; Khargone District: Jhirniya tahsil; Maharashtra, Jalgaon District: Yawal, Raver tahsils; Dhule District: Shirpur tahsil. *Class:* Indo-European, Indo-Iranian, Indo-Aryan, Central zone, Bhil. *Dialects:* Dialect center is MP, Barwani District, Choutharya village of Rajpur tahsil. Lexical similarity is 62 to 66% with Pauri Bareli; 67 to 73% with Rathwi Bareli. *Lg Use:* Vigorous. All domains except education. Positive language attitude. Most speakers have low proficiency in regional (Nimadi, Ahirani) and state (Hindi, Marathi) languages. *Lg Dev:* Literacy rate in second language: below 10%.

Bareli, Pauri (Barewali, Barli, Bareli) [bfb] 150,000 to 200,000 (2000). Maharashtra; Nandurbar District, Dhadgaon, Shahada, Taloda tahsils; Dhule District; Shirpur tahsil; Madhya Pradesh; Barwani District; Pansemal tahsil; Nivali and Pati blocks. *Class:* Indo-European, Indo-Iranian, Indo-Aryan, Central zone, Bhil. *Dialects:* Pauri Bareli not intelligible with Rathwi Bareli or Palya Bareli. Dialect center is in Maharashtra, Nandurbar District, Dhadgaon tahsil. Lexical similarity 81 to 88% among varieties of Pauri Bareli; 68 to 79% with Rathwi Bareli; 62 to 66% with Palya Bareli. *Lg Use:* Vigorous. All domains except education. Positive language attitude. Most speakers have low proficiency in regional (Nimadi, Ahirani) and state (Hindi, Marathi) langauges. *Lg Dev:* Literacy rate in second language: below 10%.

Bareli, Rathwi (Barel, Pauri, Pawri, Pawari, Rathwi Pauri, Rathi, Rathia) [bgd] 63,700 (2000). Madhya Pradesh; Barwani District; Barwani, Sendhwa, Rajpur tahsils; Khargone District; Bhagawanpura, Jhirniya, Bhikangaon tahsils; Dewas District; Bagli tahsil; Khandwa District; Burhanpur tahsil; Dhar District; Dahi block; Rathia Bhilala in South Jhabua District; Maharashtra northern Dhule District; Shirpur tahsil; Jalgaon District; Chopda, Raver, Yawal tahsils. *Class:* Indo-European, Indo-Iranian, Indo-Aryan, Central zone, Bhil. *Dialects:* Pauri Bareli and Rathwi Pauri not intelligible with Vasavi or Bhilori. Dialect center is Madhya Pradesh, Barwani District, Chiklia. Not intelligible with Palya Bareli or Pauri Bareli. Understood by Rathia Bhilala of Nimad, Bhilala of Sondhwa block of Jhabua District and Bhils of south Dhar District. Lexical similarity 81% to 93% among Rathwi Bareli dialects; 67 to 73% with Palya Bareli; 68 to 79%

with Pauri Bareli. *Lg Use:* Vigorous. All domains except education. Positive language attitude. Most speakers have low proficiency in regional (Nimadi, Ahirani) and state (Hindi, Marathi) languages. *Lg Dev:* Literacy rate in second language: below 10%. Devanagari script. Bible portions: 1986. *Other:* Bareli is a Scheduled Tribe in India. Speakers are called 'Barela' and 'Paura'. Traditional religion, Hindu, Christian.

Bateri [btv] 800 in India. 200 families. Jammu and Kashmir, near Srinagar. See main entry under Pakistan.

Bauria (Badak, Babri, Basria, Bawari, Bawaria, Bhoria, Vaghri, Baori) [bge] 247,872 (1999). Punjab; Himachal Pradesh; Delhi; Haryana; Chandigarh; Rajasthan; Uttar Pradesh. *Class:* Indo-European, Indo-Iranian, Indo-Aryan, Central zone, Bhil. *Lg Use:* Speakers also use Panjabi. *Lg Dev:* Literacy rate in first language: below 1%. *Other:* A Scheduled Caste in India. In Punjab (only) they speak "a particular dialect named after the community" with population 62,624 (Singh 1993). Traditional religion, Hindu, Christian.

Bazigar [bfr] 58,236 (1981 census). Haryana; Chandigarh; Delhi; Gujarat; Himachal Pradesh; Punjab; Jammu and Kashmir; Madhya Pradesh; Karnataka. *Class:* Dravidian, Unclassified. *Lg Dev:* Literacy rate in first language: below 1%. *Other:* Bazigar is a Scheduled Caste noted for juggling and acrobatics. Those in Himachal Pradesh and Punjab speak Punjabi (Singh 1993). Hindu.

Bellari [brw] 1,352 (1981 census). Karnataka; Kerala; Tamil Nadu. *Class:* Dravidian, Southern, Tulu. *Dialects:* Related to Tulu, Koraga. *Lg Dev:* Literacy rate in first language: below 1%. *Other:* Bellara is a Scheduled Caste in Karnataka, Kerala, Tamil Nadu. Singh reports they speak a dialect of Kannada.

Bengali (Bangala, Bangla, Bangla-Bhasa) [ben] 70,561,000 in India (1997). West Bengal; Jharkhand, Dhanbad, Manbhum, Singhbhum, Santal Parganas; Bihar; Assam, Goalpara District; Meghalaya, Garo Hills; Mizoram; Nagaland. *Dialect:* Barik, Bhatiari, Chirmar, Kachari-Bengali, Lohari-Malpaharia, Musselmani, Rajshahi, Samaria, Saraki, Siripuria (Kishanganjia). *Lg Use:* State language of West Bengal. Spoken by some Koda as first language. *Lg Dev:* Literacy rate in first language: 85%. *Other:* Muslim, Hindu, Christian. See main entry under Bangladesh.

Bhadrawahi (Baderwali, Badrohi, Bhaderbhai Jamu, Bhaderwali Pahari, Bhadrava, Bhadri, Bahi) [bhd] 69,000 (1997). Jammu and Kashmir. *Class:* Indo-European, Indo-Iranian, Indo-Aryan, Northern zone, Western Pahari. *Dialects:* Bhalesi, Padar, Padari. *Other:* Pangwali is reported to be nearly the same as Bhadrawahi. Hindu, Muslim.

Bhalay [bhx] 8,672 (1981 census). Maharashtra, Amravati District. *Class:* Indo-European, Indo-Iranian, Indo-Aryan, Southern zone, Unclassified. *Lg Use:* Some speakers also use Hindi. Singh says the Balahi of Maharashtra speak Marathi in addition to their first language. *Other:* Bhalay probably an alternate spelling of Balahi (Balai), a Scheduled Caste found in Madhya Pradesh, Maharashtra, Rajasthan, and Uttar Pradesh. Hugoniot lists Balai as Tibeto-Burman.

Bharia (Bhar, Bharat, Bhumia, Bhumiya, Paliha) [bha] 196,512 (1981 census). Madhya Pradesh, Chhatarpur, Chhindwara, Datia, Jabalpur, Mandla, Panna, Rewa, Sidhi, Tikamgarh districts; Chhattisgarh, Bilaspur, Durg, Surguja districts; Uttar Pradesh; West Bengal. *Class:* Dravidian, Unclassified. *Dialects:* Singh 1993 reports they speak a variety of Hindi. *Lg Dev:* Devanagari script. *Other:* A Scheduled Tribe in India. Forest. Hindu.

Bhatola [btl] 5,045 (2000 WCD). Madhya Pradesh. *Class:* Unclassified. *Other:* Hugoniot (Tribes of Madhya Pradesh 1964) lists Bhatola as a Scheduled Tribe but Singh does not.

Bhatri (Bhattri, Bhattra, Bhatra, Basturia, Bhottada, Bhottara) [bgw] 600,000 (2000). Andhra Pradesh; Chhattisgarh, Bastar District, Jagdalpur tahsil; Maharashtra; Orissa, Koraput District, Kotpad tahsil. *Class:* Indo-European, Indo-Iranian, Indo-Aryan, Eastern zone, Oriya. *Dialects:* All dialects understand each other at 88%. Close to Halbi. Lexical similarity 70% to 90% between dialects, 58% with Adivasi Oriya. *Lg Use:* Vigorous. Bhatri is preferred in home and religious domains. Positive language attitude. Communities in Madhya Pradesh have low proficiency in Hindi. Those in Orissa have low proficiency in Oriya. One-third of the speakers have enhanced comprehension of Halbi because of closeness to the Halbi-speaking area. *Lg Dev:* Literacy rate in second language: 7.5% (1981 census). Oriya script. *Other:* A Scheduled Tribe in India. Plains. Agriculturalists. Hindu syncretism with traditional religion.

Bhattiyali (Bhateali, Bhatiali Pahari, Bhatiyali) [bht] 102,252 (1991 census). Himachal Pradesh, Chamba District, Bhattiyat tahsil, Sihunta Sub-tahsil. *Class:* Indo-European, Indo-Iranian, Indo-Aryan, Northern zone, Western Pahari. *Dialects:* Lexical similarity 86% with Chambeali, 83% with Palampuri Kangri, 76% with Bilaspuri. *Lg Use:* All ages. Speakers also use Hindi, Panjabi, or Urdu. *Lg Dev:* Literacy rate in first language: below 1%. *Other:* SOV. Mountain slope, valley. 300 to 1,350 meters. Agriculturalists: rice, maize, millet. Hindu, Muslim, Sikh, Buddhist, Christian.

Bhilali (Bhilala) [bhi] 1,000,000 to 1,300,000 (2000). Population includes 25,000 to 50,000 Parya Bhilali. Madhya Pradesh, Khargone (Segaon), Barwani (Rajpur), southern Jhabua and southern Dhar districts; Maharashtra, Dhule District; some in Gujarat; Karnataka; Rajasthan. *Class:* Indo-European, Indo-Iranian, Indo-Aryan, Central zone, Bhil. *Dialect:* Parya Bhilali. Lexical similarity 61 to 79% between Parya Bhilali and other Bhilali varieties. *Other:* A Scheduled Tribe in India. They call the language 'Bhili' in some areas, but it is a different language from Bhili. Agriculturalists; wage laborers. Traditional religion.

Bhili (Bhilbari, Bhilboli, Bhilla, Bhil, Bhilodi, Vil, Bhagoria, Lengotia) [bhb] 1,300,000 (1994). Population includes 1,000,000 Bhil plus 300,000 Patelia in Madhya Pradesh. 12,688 Kotvali (1994), 5,624,000 in languages in the Bhil family. Madhya Pradesh, Jhabua, Char, Ratlam districts; Gujarat, Panchmahals, and Dahod districts; Rajasthan; Maharashtra; some in Jammu and Kashmir; Andhra Pradesh; Karnataka; Punjab; Bihar; Tripura; mountainous areas. *Class:* Indo-European, Indo-Iranian, Indo-Aryan, Central zone, Bhil. *Dialects:* Ahiri, Anarya (Pahadi), Bhilodi, Bhim, Charani, Habura, Konkani, Kotali (Kotvali, Kotwalia), Magra Ki Boli, Nahari (Baglani), Naikdi, Panchali, Patelia, Ranawat, Rani Bhil, Siyalgir. Bhili of Ratlam District in Madhya Pradesh is inherently intelligible with Wagdi and a connecting link between Gujarati and Rajasthani (Marwari). Bhili highly intelligible to Bhilodi. *Lg Use:* Spoken as first language by the Patelia in Madhya Pradesh. Most speakers have low proficiency in Hindi. *Lg Dev:* Literacy rate in first language: 1% to 5%. Literacy rate in second language: 10%. Devanagari script. TV. Videos. Grammar. NT: 1930. *Other:* 'Bhil' is an ethnic designation (caste or tribe). Bhili is a Scheduled Tribe in Rajasthan, Gujarat, Maharashtra, Madhya Pradesh, Tripura; Kotwalia a Scheduled Tribe in Gujarat and Maharashtra. Dewali (Dehawali) is a cover term for Vasavi and Kotali, among others. Traditional religion.

Bhojpuri (Bhojapuri, Bhozpuri, Bajpuri, Bihari, Deswali, Khotla, Piscimas) [bho] 24,544,000 in India (1997). Population total all countries: 26,592,536. Bihar, Champaran, Saran, Shahabad districts; Jharkhand, Palamu, Ranchi districts; Uttar Pradesh, Gorakhpur, Basti, Deoria, Azamgarh, Ghazipur, Varanasi, Mirzapur, Ballia districts;

Assam; Delhi; Madhya Pradesh; West Bengal. Also spoken in Mauritius, Nepal. *Class:* Indo-European, Indo-Iranian, Indo-Aryan, Eastern zone, Bihari. *Dialects:* Northern Standard Bhojpuri (Gorakhpuri, Sarawaria, Basti), Western Standard Bhojpuri (Purbi, Benarsi), Southern Standard Bhojpuri (Kharwari), Tharu, Madhesi, Domra, Musahari. May be more than one language. Extent of dialect variation in India and Nepal not yet determined. The cover term 'Bihari' (Behari) is used for Bhojpuri, Maithili, and Magahi. Tharu is a dialect of Bhojpuri spoken by the Tharu caste in Nepal. It is distinct from Chitwan and other Tharu. *Lg Dev:* Literacy rate in first language: 5% to 30%. Literacy rate in second language: 50% to 75%. Kaithi and Devanagari script. NT: 1999. *Other:* Agriculturalists. Hindu, Muslim, Christian.

Bhunjia (Bunjia, Bhumjiya, Bhunjiya) [bhu] 18,601 (1981 census). Madhya Pradesh, Hoshangabad District; Chhattisgarh, Raipur District; Orissa, Nuapada, Koraput, Dhenkanal, Balasore (Baleshwar), Keonjhar Sambalpur districts, Sunabera Plateau area; Maharashtra. *Class:* Indo-European, Indo-Iranian, Indo-Aryan, Eastern zone, Oriya. *Dialects:* Called a more divergent dialect of Halbi. *Lg Use:* Some also use Chhattisgarhi or Hindi for intergroup communication (Singh). *Lg Dev:* Literacy rate in second language: 8.5% (1981). Devanagari script. *Other:* A Scheduled Tribe in India. Agriculturalists. Hindu.

Biete (Baite, Bete, Biate) [biu] 19,000 (1997). Meghalaya, Jaintia Hills District; Mizoram northeast, Aizawl District, Darlawn, Ratu, New Vervek villages; Assam; Cachar Hills; Manipur. *Class:* Sino-Tibetan, Tibeto-Burman, Kuki-Chin-Naga, Kuki-Chin, Northern. *Dialects:* Closest to Hrangkhol. *Lg Use:* Speakers also use Mizo. *Lg Dev:* Literacy rate in first language: 56%. Roman script. NT: 1985–1991. *Other:* A Scheduled Tribe in India. An ethnic subgroup of the Mizo. Not the same as Biate, dialect of Chin Thado (Roland Breton). Swidden agriculturalists; hunter-gatherers. Christian.

Bijori (Binjhia, Birijia, Brijia, Burja, Birjia) [bix] 2,391 (1961 census). Jharkhand, Cowerdaga, and Ranchi districts; West Bengal, Darjeeling, and Jalpaiguri districts; Madhya Pradesh; Orissa. *Class:* Austro-Asiatic, Munda, North Munda, Kherwari. *Lg Dev:* Literacy rate in second language: 10% Hindi. *Other:* A Scheduled Tribe in India. The ethnic group is called 'Birjia'. Swidden agriculturalists. Hindu, Christian.

Bilaspuri (Bilaspuri Pahari, Pacchmi, Kahluri, Kehluri, Kehloori Pahari) [kfs] 295,387 (1991 census). Himachal Pradesh, Bilaspur District. *Class:* Indo-European, Indo-Iranian, Indo-Aryan, Northern zone, Western Pahari. *Dialects:* 95% intelligibility of Mandeali, 94% of Kangri. Lexical similarity 90% with Kangri of Palampur, 86% with Mandeali, 84% with Chambeali. *Lg Use:* Used in the home, community, agricultural and religious domains. All ages. Hindi is used for instruction in school and politics. Middle aged and older women have limited comprehension of Hindi. Some speak Panjabi as second language. Urdu is also spoken by older educated people. *Lg Dev:* Radio programs. *Other:* 'Kahluri' is based on the old name for the princely state. SOV. Mountain slope, valley. 300 to 1,350 meters. Agriculturalists: rice, maize, millet. Hindu, Christian.

Birhor (Bihor, Birhar, Birhore, Mankidi, Mankidia) [biy] 10,000 (1998 GR). Jharkhand, Hazaribagh, Singbhum, and Ranchi districts; Chhattisgarh, Raigarh District; Orissa, Sundargarh, Kalahandi, Keonjhar, Mayurbhanj, Sambalpur districts; West Bengal; Maharashtra. *Class:* Austro-Asiatic, Munda, North Munda, Kherwari, Mundari. *Dialects:* Lexical similarity 55% to 72% with Santhali, Ho, Mundari. *Lg Use:* Vigorous. No indication of language shift. Most domains. Positive language attitude. Speakers also use Sadri, Santhali, Ho, Mundari, Hindi,

Oriya in market. *Lg Dev:* Literacy rate in first language: 0.02% (1971 census). Literacy rate in second language: 10% Hindi. *Other:* A Scheduled Tribe in India. Traditionally nomadic. Rope makers; hunter-gatherers; fishermen; agriculturalists. Hindu, traditional religion.

Bishnupriya (Bishnupuriya, Bisna Puriya, Bishnupria Manipuri) [bpy] 75,000 in India (1997). Population total all countries: 115,000. Assam, Cachar, Hailakandi, Karimganj districts; Tripura, North. Also spoken in Bangladesh. *Class:* Indo-European, Indo-Iranian, Indo-Aryan, Eastern zone, Bengali-Assamese. *Dialects:* Madai Gang (Leimanai), Rajar Gang (Ningthaunai). Related to Bengali and Assamese. Though once regarded as a Bengali-Meitei creole, it retains pre-Bengali features (Masica 1991). *Lg Use:* Speakers also use Bengali. *Lg Dev:* Literacy rate in second language: High. Bengali script. Bible portions: 1995. *Other:* Valley. Agriculturalists. Hindu.

Bodo (Boro, Bodi, Bara, Boroni, Mechi, Meche, Mech, Meci, Kachari) [brx] 600,000 in India (1997). Population total all countries: 603,301. Assam, South Bank; West Bengal, Darjeeling, Jalpaiguri, Coch-Behar districts; Manipur, Chandel (Tengnoupal) District; Meghalaya, West Garo Hills District, 7 villages in the Tikrikilla block. Also spoken in Nepal. *Class:* Sino-Tibetan, Tibeto-Burman, Jingpho-Konyak-Bodo, Konyak-Bodo-Garo, Bodo-Garo, Bodo. *Dialects:* Chote, Mech. Related to Dimasa, Tripuri, Lalunga. The dialect of West Bengal is reportedly different from Assam. *Lg Use:* Official language. Vigorous Bodo language and culture. Most Mech in Assam speak Assamese as first language (R. Breton 1997:24). *Lg Dev:* Literacy rate in second language: 40% Assamese. Devanagari, Assamese, and Roman script. Magazines. Dictionary. Grammar. Bible: 1981. *Other:* 3 Scheduled Tribes: Mech, Boro-Kachari, Plains Kachari. Agriculturalists. Traditional religion, Christian.

Bodo Parja (Bodo Paraja, Parji, Parja, Paroja, Poroja, Jhodia Parja, Sodia Parja, Parjhi, Parajhi, Harja, Jharia, Jhaliya) [bdv] 50,000 (2001). Orissa, Koraput District. *Class:* Indo-European, Indo-Iranian, Indo-Aryan, Eastern zone, Oriya. *Dialects:* Phonology and grammar show Indo-European relationship, not related to Dravidian Duruwa Parji. 86% to 96% intelligibility between Bodo and Jhodia caste varieties. Lexical similarity 76% to 86% between Bodo and Jhodia caste varieties, 70% to 89% with Desia. *Lg Use:* Bodo is higher caste than Jhodia, showing some signs of negative attitudes, despite high intelligibility. Most speakers have low proficiency in Adivasi Oriya, which is used in the market. *Lg Dev:* Oriya script. *Other:* Paroja is a Scheduled Tribe in India. Paroja comes from the Sanskrit word for 'subjects'. It is used for a variety of ethnic groups from different language families. Mountain valley. Scrub forest. 200 to 1,000 meters. Peasant agriculturalists; laborers. Hindu, traditional religion, Christian.

Bondo (Poraja Katha, Bhonda Bhasha, Bondo-Poraja, Remo, Remosum, Bonda, Nanqa Poroja) [bfw] 9,000 (2002 SIL). Few Lower Bondo are monolingual. Population includes 5,565 Upper Bondo and 3,500 Lower Bondo. Orissa, Malkangiri District, Khoirput Block, Bondo Hills. *Class:* Austro-Asiatic, Munda, South Munda, Koraput Munda, Gutob-Remo-Geta', Gutob-Remo. *Dialects:* Upper Bondo, Lower Bondo. Closest to Didayi, Gutob Gadaba, Parenga. 88% comprehension of Upper Bondo by Lower Bondo. Lexical similarity 70% to 94% with other Bondo varieties, 45% to 51% with Gadaba Gutob, 22% to 32% with Upper Gata' (Didayi). *Lg Use:* Positive language attitude. Many speak Adivasi Oriya for trade and interactions with surrounding communities. Few Upper Bondo are bilingual. *Lg Dev:* Literacy rate in second language: 0.7% female, 6.8% male, 3.6% total (1981 census). Oriya script. *Other:* A Scheduled Tribe in

India. Nonvegetarians who occasionally eat meat. Hills. 900 meters. Swidden agriculturalists; hunter-gatherers. Traditional religion, Hindu.

Braj Bhasha (Braj, Braj Bhakha, Brij Bhasha, Antarbedi, Antarvedi, Bijbhasha, Bri, Briju, Bruj) [bra] 44,000 (1997). Uttar Pradesh, Agra Region; Rajasthan, Bharatpur, Sawai Madhopur districts; Haryana, Gurgaon District; Bihar; Madhya Pradesh; Delhi. *Class:* Indo-European, Indo-Iranian, Indo-Aryan, Central zone, Western Hindi, Unclassified. *Dialects:* Braj Bhasha, Antarbedi, Bhuksa, Sikarwari, Jadobafi, Dangi. Bhuksa is sometimes mentioned as a dialect of Kanauji. *Lg Dev:* NT: 1824–1999. *Other:* Hindu, Muslim, Christian.

Brokskat (Brokpa, Brokpa of Dah-Hanu, Dokskat, Kyango) [bkk] 3,000 (1981 census). Jammu and Kashmir, along the Indus River in Ladakh and Kargil districts, northern Kashmir, villages around Garkhon, including Darchiks, Chulichan, Gurgurdo, Batalik, Dah, and formerly in Hanu. *Class:* Indo-European, Indo-Iranian, Indo-Aryan, Northwestern zone, Dardic, Shina. *Lg Use:* Many are fluent in Ladakhi. *Lg Dev:* Literacy rate in first language: below 1%. Balti script. Dictionary. Grammar. *Other:* Broq-pa is a Scheduled Tribe in India. A very divergent variety of Shina. Minaro is an alternate ethnic name. 'Brokpa' is the name given by the Ladakhi for the people. 'Brokskat' is the language. This is the oldest surviving member of the ancient Dardic language. 2,750 meters. Buddhist, traditional religion, Muslim.

Bugun (Khowa, Kho, Khoa) [bgg] 1,046 (1991 census). Arunachal Pradesh; West Kameng District, in 7 or 8 villages on the mountains on both sides of the Rupa River, interspersed among the Hruso. *Class:* Sino-Tibetan, Tibeto-Burman, North Assam, Tani. *Dialects:* Mutually intelligible with Sulung (Chowdhury). *Lg Use:* Speakers also use Nefamese, Sherdukpen, Hruso, Monpa, or Hindi. *Lg Dev:* Literacy rate in second language: 24% (1981 census), 35% for men, 12% for women. *Other:* Spoken by the Khoa (Khowa) ethnic group. They are culturally like the Hruso, but speak a different language. Mountain slope. Pine and oak forests. High altitude. Agriculturalists. Traditional religion.

Buksa [tkb] 43,000 (1999). Uttaranchal, southwestern Nainital District, along a diagonal from Ramnagar to Keneshpur. 130 villages in Kichha and Kashipur tahsils, and small numbers in Bijnor and Garhwal districts. *Class:* Indo-European, Indo-Iranian, Indo-Aryan, Eastern zone, Unclassified. *Dialects:* 95% intelligibility of Rana Tharu. Lexical similarity 58% to 79% with western Tharu varieties, 58% with Chitwania Tharu, 83% with Hindi. *Other:* Agriculturalists; pastoralists. Traditional religion.

Bundeli (Bondili, Bundelkhandi) [bns] 644,000 (1997). Uttar Pradesh, Jalaun, Jhansi, Hamirpur, Banda districts; Madhya Pradesh, Balaghat, Chhindwara, Hoshangabad, Sagar, Sehore, Panna, Satna, Chhatarpur, Tikamgarh, Shivpuri, Guna, Bhind, Morena, Gwalior, Lalitpur, Narsinghpur, Seoni, Datia districts; Maharashtra, Bhandara, Nagpur districts; Rajasthan; Gujarat; Andhra Pradesh. *Class:* Indo-European, Indo-Iranian, Indo-Aryan, Central zone, Western Hindi, Bundeli. *Dialects:* Standard Bundeli, Pawari (Powari), Lodhanti (Rathora), Khatola, Banaphari, Kundri, Nibhatta, Tirhari, Bhadauri (Towargarhi), Gaoli, Kirari, Raghobansi, Nagpuri Hindi, Chhindwara Bundeli. Intelligibility testing of Standard varieties gave 83%, 92%, and 98%. Chhatapur dialect is widely understood. Other dialects listed by Grierson are Standard Braj of Mathura, Aligarh, western Agra; Standard Braj of Bulandshahr; Standard Braj of eastern Agra, southern Morena, southern Bharatpur; Braj merging into Kanauji in Etah, Mainpuri, Budaun, and Bareilly; Braj merging into the Bhadauri subdialect in northern Morena; Braj merging into Jaipuri (Rajasthani) in northern Bharatpur and Sawai Uradhopur;

Bhuksa in southern Nainital. Lexical similarity 65% to 85% between Chhindwara and Standard Bundeli, 41% with Nagpuri Hindi. *Lg Use:* Used in the home. Favorable attitudes toward Chhatapur dialect. The uneducated have low proficiency in Hindi. *Lg Dev:* Radio programs. *Other:* Plains. Agriculturalists. Hindu, Buddhist, Muslim, Christian.

Byangsi (Byangkho Lwo, Byanshi, Byansi, Bhotia, Byangkhopa, Jaba, Saukas, Shaukas, Rang) [bee] 2,829 in India (2000). Population total all countries: 4,563. Uttaranchal, Pithoragarh District, Darchula and Munsyari tahsils, in the Kuthi Yangti River valley high in the Himalayas on the border with Tibet and Nepal. In Byangs Patti from Budi in the south to Kuti village in the north including Nabi, Gunji, Napalchyu, Rongkang, and Garbyang villages. Also spoken in Nepal. *Class:* Sino-Tibetan, Tibeto-Burman, Himalayish, Tibeto-Kanauri, Western Himalayish, Almora. *Dialects:* Pangjungkho Boli, Yerjungkhu Boli, Kuti. Related to Rangkas, Darmiya, Chaudangsi. Devidatta Sharma 1989 suggests that Chaudangsi and Byangsi are varieties of one language. Considered to be dialects of one language with Chaudangsi and dialects in Chhanguru and Tinker districts of Nepal. *Lg Use:* Some domains, home, friends. High level of bilingualism in Kumauni or Hindi. Some also use Tibetan or Nepali. Hindi is the medium of education at all levels. *Lg Dev:* Grammar. *Other:* Cultural center seems to be India. 'Ranglo' or 'Rang' often used as a cover term for Byangs, Chaudangs, Darmiya and Rongpo. Some borrowing from Indo-Aryan. Mountain slope. Hindu.

Chakma (Takam, Chakama, Tsakma) [ccp] 300,000 in India (1987). Mizoram, southwestern part along Karnafuli River; Tripura, North Tripura District, Kailashahar Subdivision, South Tripura District; Assam, Karbi, Anglong, North Cachar, Cachar districts; Arunachal Pradesh, Tirap District, Changlang District, Miao Subdivision; Lohit District, Chowkham Circle; West Bengal; Manipur. *Lg Use:* Speakers also use Bengali or Mizo. *Other:* A Scheduled Tribe in India. Forest. Swidden agriculturalists. Buddhist syncretism traditional religion. See main entry under Bangladesh.

Chamari (Chamar, Chambhar Boli, Chambhari) [cdg] 5,324 (1971 census). Madhya Pradesh; Uttar Pradesh, Lucknow; Maharashtra. *Class:* Indo-European, Indo-Iranian, Indo-Aryan, Central zone, Western Hindi, Unclassified. *Lg Dev:* Literacy rate in first language: below 1%. *Other:* Chamar is a caste name meaning 'skin and hide worker'. They are found in many states throughout India speaking regional languages (Singh).

Chambeali (Chamaya, Chambiali, Chambiyali, Chamiyali Pahari, Chamya, Cameali) [cdh] 129,654 (1991 census). Himachal Pradesh, Chamba District, Chamba Tahsil; Jammu and Kashmir. *Class:* Indo-European, Indo-Iranian, Indo-Aryan, Northern zone, Western Pahari. *Dialects:* Bansbali, Bansyari, Gadi Chameali. 91% intelligibility of Mandeali, 87% of Kangri. Lexical similarity 90% with Palampuri Kangri, 86% with Bhattiyali, 84% with Bilaspuri, 83% with Mandeali, 79% with Gaddi, 78% with Churahi. *Lg Use:* All ages. Speakers also use Hindi, Panjabi, or Urdu. *Lg Dev:* Radio programs. Bible portions: 1883–1979. *Other:* SOV. Mountain slope, valley. 900 to 3,000 meters. Agriculturalists: rice, maize millet, fruit. Hindu, Christian.

Changthang (Changtang, Changtang Ladakhi, Changs-Skat, Byangskat, Byanskat, Rong, Rupshu, Stotpa, Upper Ladakhi) [cna] 10,089 (2000 WCD). Jammu and Kashmir, Tibetan border area, Changthang Region east and southeast of Leh. *Class:* Sino-Tibetan, Tibeto-Burman, Himalayish, Tibeto-Kanauri, Tibetic, Tibetan, Western, Ladakhi. *Dialects:* May be intelligible with Ladakhi. *Lg Use:* Some multilingualism in Ladakhi, Urdu, Kashmiri, Hindi, or English. *Lg Dev:* Bodhi script.

Other: Champa is a Scheduled Tribe. People are called 'Champas'. Nomadic. They barter for grain from the Zangskari. Noted for music and dance. Plateau. 4,000 to 5,000 meters. Pastoralists: sheep (cashmere wool), goats; traders: wool, salt. Buddhist.

Chaudangsi (Chaudans Lo, Chanpa Lo, Bangba Lo, Tsaudangsi, Bangbani, Saukas, Shaukas) [cdn] 1,825 in India (2000). Population total all countries: 3,022. Uttaranchal, Pithoragarh District, Darchula and Munsyari tahsils, Chaudangs Patti, in 14 villages along the west bank of the Kali River facing the Nepal border along the Mahakali Valley. Villages include Panggu, Rongto, Rimzhim, Waiku, Monggong, Chilla, Song, Sosa, Sirdang, Sirkha, Rung, Zipti, Gala, Tangkul, SyangKhola. Also spoken in Nepal. *Class:* Sino-Tibetan, Tibeto-Burman, Himalayish, Tibeto-Kanauri, Western Himalayish, Almora. *Dialects:* Related to Rangkas, Darmiya, Byangsi. *Lg Use:* Used mainly in the home and with friends. Negative language attitude. High level of bilingualism in Kumauni and Hindi. Some also use Tibetan or Nepali. *Lg Dev:* Literacy rate in first language: below 1%. Hindi is used for written communication. Grammar. *Other:* 'Ranglo' or 'Rang' often used as a cover term for Byangs, Chaudangs, Darmiya, and Rongpo. Low altitude. Hindu.

Chaura (Chowra, Tutet) [crv] 2,018 (2000 WCD). Nicobar Islands, Chaura Island. *Class:* Austro-Asiatic, Mon-Khmer, Nicobar, Chowra-Teressa.

Chenchu (Chenchucoolam, Chenchwar, Chenswar, Choncharu) [cde] 28,754 (1981 census). Andhra Pradesh, highest concentration in Kurnool District, Nallamalla Hills; Karnataka; Orissa. *Class:* Dravidian, South-Central, Telugu. *Lg Dev:* Literacy rate in second language: 9.7% (1981 census). Telugu script. *Other:* A Scheduled Tribe in India. Tropical forest. Agriculturalists. Hindu, Christian.

Chhattisgarhi (Laria, Khaltahi) [hne] 11,535,000. Population includes 11,456,000 Chhattisgarhi (1997), 79,000 Laria (1997). Chhattisgarh; Bihar; Orissa; and possibly in Maharashtra, Uttar Pradesh, and Tripura. *Class:* Indo-European, Indo-Iranian, Indo-Aryan, East Central zone. *Dialects:* Surgujia, Sadri Korwa, Baigani (Baiga, Bega, Bhumia, Gowro), Binjhwari, Kalanga, Bhulia, Chhattisgarhi Proper, Kavardi, Khairagarhi. Most closely related to Awadhi and Bagheli. Surgujia in the Surguja and Raigarh districts of Chhattisgarh; Sadri Korwa spoken by Korwa people of Jashpur tahsil of Raigarh District; Baigani in Balaghat, Raipur, and Bilaspur districts of Chhattisgarh, and Sambalpur District of Orissa; Binjhwari is spoken in Raipur and Raigarh districts of Chhattisgarh; Kalanga and Bhulia are spoken in Patna District of Bihar; Chhattisgarhi Proper is spoken in Raipur, Durg, Bilaspur, and other districts of Chhattisgarh. *Lg Use:* Spoken as first language by the Kawari. Nearly all domains. Positive language attitude. Speakers have low proficiency in Hindi. Oriya also used. *Lg Dev:* Devanagari script. Poetry. Newspapers. Radio programs. TV. Bible portions: 1904–1952. *Other:* Spoken by the Kawar people, among others. Desert. Traditional religion, Hindu, Muslim.

Chin, Bawm (Bawm, Bawng, Bawn, Bom) [bgr] 4,439 in India (2004). Population total all countries: 13,793. Mizoram, Chhimtuipui, Lunglei, and Aizawl districts; Tripura; Assam. Also spoken in Bangladesh, Myanmar. *Class:* Sino-Tibetan, Tibeto-Burman, Kuki-Chin-Naga, Kuki-Chin, Central. *Dialects:* Regard themselves correctly as a subgroup of the Laizou (Anal) (Matisoff et al. 1996:8). *Lg Use:* Speakers also use Mizo. *Lg Dev:* Bible: 1989. *Other:* A Scheduled Tribe in India. SOV. Swidden agriculturalists. Christian.

Chin, Falam (Halam Chin, Hallam, Fallam, Tipura) [flm] 25,367 in India (1994). Population includes 7,000 Ranglong. Assam, Karimganj District, south, a few villages in Cachar and North Hills districts; Tripura;

Mizoram; West Bengal. *Dialects:* Chorei, Chari Chong, Halam, Kaipang, Kalai (Koloi), Mursum (Molsom), Rupini, Ranglong, Tapong. *Lg Dev:* Literacy among Kaipeng in Tripura is low. *Other:* Halam is a Scheduled Tribe in India. Many ethnic Halam speak Kokborok as first language. Halam is a generic term under which nine subgroups, each having a separate dialect, are grouped together (Sakachep, Chorei, Rupini, Ranglong, Marcephang (Khochung), Molsom, Keipang, Bondcher, Rangkhol). Hindu, traditional religion, Christian. See main entry under Myanmar.

Chin, Haka (Haka, Baungshe, Lai, Lai Pawi, Lai Hawlh) [cnh] 345,000 Lai in India (1996 UBS). Mizoram, Chhimtuipui and Aizawi District, southernmost tip; Assam; Meghalaya. *Dialects:* Klangklang (Thlantlang), Zokhua, Shonshe. *Lg Dev:* Most young people can read in Haka. Taught in primary schools. *Other:* Lai Pawi is a Scheduled Tribe in India. Hills. Forest. Swidden agriculturalists. Christian. See main entry under Myanmar.

Chin, Khumi (Kami, Khami, Khumi, Khuni, Khweymi, Kumi) [cnk] Assam. *Dialects:* Khami, Khimi. *Other:* Called Khami Chin in India. Tropical forest. Traditional religion, Christian. See main entry under Myanmar.

Chin, Mara (Lakher, Zao, Maram, Mira, Mara) [mrh] 22,000 in India (1997). Population total all countries: 42,000. Mizoram, Chhimtuipui District, 60 villages. Also spoken in Myanmar. *Class:* Sino-Tibetan, Tibeto-Burman, Kuki-Chin-Naga, Kuki-Chin, Southern. *Dialects:* Tlongsai (Tlosai-Siaha), Hlawthai. Close to Shendu. Reported to be affiliated with Lai (Haka Chin). Tlosai-Siaha dialect is the lingua franca of all Mara (Singh). *Lg Use:* Speakers also use Mizo or English. *Lg Dev:* Taught in primary schools since 1978. Roman script. Bible: 1956–2002. *Other:* A Scheduled Tribe in India. A subgroup of Mizo (Lushai). SOV. Christian.

Chin, Matu (Matupi, Ngala) [hlt] 20,000 in India (2000). Mizoram. *Dialects:* Haltu, Thui Phum. *Lg Use:* Many are bilingual in Chin Haka. *Lg Dev:* Literacy rate in second language: 70%. *Other:* Christian. See main entry under Myanmar (Nga La).

Chin, Paite (Paite, Paithe, Parte, Haithe, Zoukam) [pck] 45,000 in India (1997). Population total all countries: 53,900. Assam; Manipur, Churachandpur District, Khuga Valley, Copur Bazar; Mizoram, Aizawl District, Champhai Subdivision, 20 villages; Tripura. Also spoken in Myanmar. *Class:* Sino-Tibetan, Tibeto-Burman, Kuki-Chin-Naga, Kuki-Chin, Northern. *Dialects:* Bukpi (Bukpui), Dapzal (Dapzar), Dim, Dimpi, Lamzang, Lousau, Saizang, Sizhang, Telzang (Teizang), Tuichiap. Related to Thado Chin, Tedim Chin, Ralte, Zomi. *Lg Use:* Speakers also use Mizo. *Lg Dev:* Roman script. Dictionary. Grammar. Bible: 1971. *Other:* A Scheduled Tribe in India. Paites in Mizoram speak Mizo (Go 1996). Teizang and Dapzal dialects are spoken by the majority. (Singh 95). SOV. Hills. Swidden agriculturalists. Christian.

Chin, Tedim (Tedim, Tiddim) [ctd] 155,000 in India (1990 BAP). Mizoram (north), Manipur (south). *Dialect:* Sokte, Kamhau (Kamhow, Kamhao). *Lg Use:* Trade language of Tiddim political subdivision. *Other:* Christian, traditional religion. See main entry under Myanmar.

Chin, Thado (Thadou, Thado-Ubiphei, Thado-Pao, Kuki, Kuki-Thado, Thaadou Kuki) [tcz] 125,100 in India. Population total all countries: 151,300. Assam; Manipur, Chandel District; Nagaland, Kohima District; Mizoram, northeast; Tripura. Also spoken in Myanmar. *Class:* Sino-Tibetan, Tibeto-Burman, Kuki-Chin-Naga, Kuki-Chin, Northern. *Dialect:* Baite, Changsen, Jangshen, Kaokeep, Khongzai, Kipgen, Langiung, Sairang, Thangngen, Hawkip, Shithlou, Singson (Shingsol). Related to Kamhau, Ralte, Paite, Zo. *Lg Use:* Speakers also use Meitei or Nepali. *Lg Dev:* Literacy rate in second language: 24% (1971).

Literacy low among older people and in villages. Taught in schools in Manipur. Magazines. Radio programs. Dictionary. Grammar. Bible: 1971–1994. *Other:* A Scheduled Tribe in India. Some of those listed as dialects are separate languages. SOV. Agriculturalists. Christian.

Chinali (Chinal, Chana, Dagi, Shipi, Harijan, Channali) [cih] 500 to 1,000 (1996). Himachal Pradesh, throughout Lahul Valley, especially in Pattan Valley, Gushal village. *Class:* Indo-European, Indo-Iranian, Indo-Aryan, Unclassified. *Dialects:* Speakers say Chinali is closely related to Sanskrit. *Lg Dev:* Devanagari script. *Other:* Spoken by the Chinal caste. Many are well educated. Hindu.

Chiru (Chhori) [cdf] 7,000 (2000 Khorong). Manipur, Tamenglong District, Lamdangmei, Dolang villages; Senapati, Kangchup, Thangzing, Sadu, Bungte, Nungshai, Dolang Khunou, Uram villages; Churachandpur District, Charoi Khullen village; Thoubal District, Vaithou; Bishnupur District; Assam, Cachar District, one village near Jirbom; Nagaland. Scattered. *Class:* Sino-Tibetan, Tibeto-Burman, Kuki-Chin-Naga, Kuki-Chin, Northern. *Dialects:* Closest language linguistically is Chin Mizo. *Lg Use:* All ages. Educated youths are more interested in developing first language and preserving culture than the elders. Speakers have high proficiency in Meitei. *Lg Dev:* Literacy rate in second language: 56% in English and Meitei (Khorong 2000). Older people read Meitei in Bengali script. Younger people read English in Roman script. Roman, Bengali scripts. *Other:* A Scheduled Tribe in India. Mountain slope, plains. Scrub forest and tropical forest. Agriculturalists: swidden and wet cultivation. Christian.

Chodri (Chaudri, Chodhari, Chaudhari, Choudhary, Choudhara, Chowdhary) [cdi] 226,534 (1994). Mainly in Gujarat, Surat, Broach and Dangs districts. Some in Maharashtra, Karnataka, Rajasthan. *Class:* Indo-European, Indo-Iranian, Indo-Aryan, Central zone, Bhil. *Lg Dev:* Literacy rate in second language: 20% Gujarati, Hindi (1977). Gujarati script. Bible portions: 1991. *Other:* A Scheduled Tribe in India. Ethnically Bhil. Traditional religion, Hindu, Christian.

Churahi (Churahi Pahari, Chaurahi, Churai Pahari) [cdj] 110,552 (1991 census). Himachal Pradesh, Chamba District, Chaurah and Saluni tahsils, Bhalai Sub-tahsil. *Class:* Indo-European, Indo-Iranian, Indo-Aryan, Northern zone, Western Pahari. *Dialects:* 90% intelligibility of Mandeali, 83% of Kangri, 85% of Chambeali. Lexical similarity 78% with Chambeali (closest), 70% with Palampuri Kangri and Bhattiyali, 67% to 69% with Gaddi, 65% with Mandeali and Bilaspuri, 64% with Pangi. *Lg Use:* All ages. Speakers also use Hindi, Panjabi, or Urdu. *Other:* SOV; postpositions; genitives after noun heads; adjectives, numerals before noun heads; question word initial; verb suffixes mark person, number, gender of subject. Mountain slope, valley. 1,500 to 3,000 meters. Agriculturalists: rice, maize millet, wheat, barley. Hindu, traditional religion, Christian.

Darlong (Dalong) [dln] 6,000 in India (1998 Thanglura Darlong). Tripura, North Tripura District, Kailashahar and Kamalpur subdivisions. *Lg Dev:* Literacy rate in first language: below 1%. Literacy rate in second language: 45%. See main entry under Bangladesh.

Darmiya (Darimiya, Darmani, Saukas, Shaukas) [drd] 2,027 in India (2000). Population total all countries: 3,224. Uttaranchal, Pithoragarh District, Darchula and Munsyari tahsils, Dhauli Valley, from Tawaghat near Dharchula in the south to Sipoo in the north along the river Dhauli. Dar, Bongling, Selachal, Nanglin, Baling, Dugtu, Saung, Baun, Philam, Datu, Gwo, Marchha, Dhakar, Sobla, Sipoo villages. Also spoken in Nepal. *Class:* Sino-Tibetan, Tibeto-Burman, Himalayish, Tibeto-Kanauri, Western Himalayish, Almora. *Dialects:* Related to Rangkas, Chaudangsi, Byangsi. *Lg Use:* Used in the home and with friends. Low prestige. High level of bilingualism in Kumauni or Hindi. Some also use Tibetan or Nepali. Hindi is the medium of education at all levels. *Lg Dev:* Literacy rate in first language: below 1%. Grammar. *Other:* 'Ranglo' or 'Rang' often used as a cover term for Byangs, Chaudangs, Darmiya, and Rongpo. Agriculturalists; weavers. Hindu.

Deccan (Desi, Dekini, Deccani) [dcc] 10,709,800 (1990). Central Maharashtra, Deccan Plateau; Karnataka, Belgaum, Bijapur districts; Madhya Pradesh, Raisen, Sehore districts; Gujarat. *Class:* Indo-European, Indo-Iranian, Indo-Aryan, Southern zone, Unclassified. *Dialects:* Kalvadi (Dharwar), Bijapuri. *Other:* Distinct from Deccan (Dakhini, Mirgan) dialect of Urdu. Plateau. Arid. Muslim (Sunni and Shi'a).

Degaru (Dhekaru) [dgu] 10,089 (2000 WCD). Bihar; West Bengal. *Class:* Indo-European, Indo-Iranian, Indo-Aryan, Eastern zone, Unclassified.

Deori (Chutiya, Deuri, Dewri, Drori, Dari) [der] 26,900 (2000). Ethnic population: 50,000. Assam, Lakhimpur, Demaji, Tinsukia, Jorhat districts. *Class:* Sino-Tibetan, Tibeto-Burman, Jingpho-Konyak-Bodo, Konyak-Bodo-Garo, Bodo-Garo, Bodo. *Dialects:* Deori may constitute its own subgroup under Bodo-Garo. Not close to other languages. Dialect of Lakhimpur District is regarded as purest. Lexical similarity 77% to 93% among Deori varieties, 11% to 16% with Bodo. *Lg Use:* Used in the home, village, religion, work. Positive language attitude. Widespread bilingualism in Assamese but women, older adults and uneducated are observed to have less proficiency. *Lg Dev:* Literacy rate in second language: 71%. Assamese and Roman scripts. Poetry. *Other:* A Scheduled Tribe in India. Deori means 'the temple guard'. Deori Chutiya is one of four Chutiya subgroups. They do not refer to themselves as Chutiya. Plains. Agriculturalists. Traditional religion syncretism with Hindu, Christian.

Dhanki (Dhanka, Dangi, Dangri, Dangs Bhil, Tadavi, Tadvi Bhil, Kakachhu-Ki Boli) [dhn] 138,000 (1997). Gujarat, Dangs District; Maharashtra, Jalgaon District; Karnataka; Rajasthan. *Class:* Indo-European, Indo-Iranian, Indo-Aryan, Central zone, Khandesi. *Lg Use:* Trade language. Speakers also use Gujarati. *Other:* Dhankia and Tadvi Bhil are both Scheduled Tribes. Dhanka of Rajasthan reportedly speak Hindi as first language. Dhanka of Maharashtra reportedly speak Gujarati as first language. The Tadvi Bhil reportedly speak Bhil as first language. The people are called 'Dhanka'. Agriculturalists. Hindu, Muslim, traditional religion.

Dhanwar (Dhanvar, Danuwar) [dha] 104,195 (1981 census). Chhattisgarh, Bilaspur, Raigarh, Surguja districts; Maharashtra, Akola, Amravati, Yavatmal, Nagpur, Wardha, Chandrapur, Buldana, Satara districts. *Class:* Indo-European, Indo-Iranian, Indo-Aryan, East Central zone. *Other:* A Scheduled Tribe in India. In Chhattisgarh they are reported to speak Chhattisgarhi as first language, and in Maharashtra Marathi. A distinct language from Danuwar Rai in Nepal. Pastgoralists; animal husbandry: cattle; marketers; blanket weavers. Hindu, traditional religion.

Dhatki (Thar) [mki] 16,400 in India (2000). Western Rajasthan. *Other:* A Scheduled Tribe in India. Muslim, Hindu, traditional religion. See main entry under Pakistan.

Dhimal [dhi] 450 in India (2000 Cooper). West Bengal, 16 villages. *Dialect:* Eastern Dhimal. See main entry under Nepal.

Dhodia (Dhobi, Dhori, Dhore, Dhowari, Doria) [dho] 139,000 (1997). Gujarat, Surat and Valsad districts, Daman and Diu, Dadra and Nagar Haveli; Madhya Pradesh; Maharashtra; Karnataka; Rajasthan. *Class:* Indo-European, Indo-Iranian, Indo-Aryan, Central zone, Bhil. *Lg Use:* Speakers also use Gujarati. *Other:* A Scheduled

Tribe in India. Not the same as Dori in Pakistan. Agriculturalists; fishermen. Traditional religion, Christian.

Dhundari (Dhundari-Marwari, Jaipuri) [dhd] 9,000,000 (2002 Gusain). Rajasthan, Jaipur, Dausa, Tonk, Karauli, Sawai Madhopur districts. *Class:* Indo-European, Indo-Iranian, Indo-Aryan, Central zone, Rajasthani, Marwari. *Dialects:* 54% intelligibility with Marwari. Lexical similarity 77% between dialects; 62% to 70% with Merwari, 66 to 73% with Shekhawati, 46% to 66% with Godwari, 56% to 64% with Mewari, 64% to 73% with Harauti, 62% to 67% with Mewati. *Lg Use:* Speakers also use Hindi. *Other:* SOV.

Digaro-Mishmi (Digaro, Digaru, Taaon, Taraon, Taying, Mishmi) [mhu] 8,622 (2001 census). Arunachal Pradesh, Lohit District, Hayuliang, Changlagam, Goiliang circles, Dibang Valley District; Assam. *Class:* Sino-Tibetan, Tibeto-Burman, North Assam, Tani. *Dialects:* They may not be in the Tani group, but are related to the Tani group. Lexical similarity 25% with Idu-Mishmi, 10% with Miju-Mishmi. *Lg Use:* Some speakers have routine proficiency in English or Assamese. *Lg Dev:* Dictionary. *Other:* A Scheduled Tribe in India. Mountain slope. Forest. Agriculturalists. Buddhist, syncretism with traditional religion, Christian.

Dimasa (Dimasa Kachari) [dis] 106,000 (1997). Assam, North Cachar District and Cachar Hills, Karbi Anglong, Nowgong districts; Nagaland, Haflong District. *Class:* Sino-Tibetan, Tibeto-Burman, Jingpho-Konyak-Bodo, Konyak-Bodo-Garo, Bodo-Garo, Bodo. *Dialects:* Dimasa, Hariamba. Related to Kachari. *Lg Use:* Kachar Barman and Kachar Hoja speak Dimasa as first language. *Lg Dev:* Literacy rate in second language: 19% (1981 census). Bengali, Roman, and Assamese scripts. Dictionary. Grammar. Bible portions: 1905–1908. *Other:* A Scheduled Tribe in India. Some Dimasa speak other languages as first language: Mikir, Bengali, Assamese. 3 scripts. Swidden agriculturalists. Hindu mixed with traditional religion, Christian.

Dogri (Dhogaryali, Dogari, Dogri Jammu, Dogri-Kangri, Dogri Pahari, Dongari, Hindi Dogri, Tokkaru) [dgo] 2,105,000 (1997). Jammu and Kashmir, between the Ravi and Chenab rivers; Chandigarh; West Bengal. *Class:* Indo-European, Indo-Iranian, Indo-Aryan, Northern zone, Western Pahari. *Dialects:* Bhatbali, Dogri, East Dogri, Kandiali, North Dogri. *Lg Use:* Official language. All ages. Urdu (older adults), Hindi (school, shops. cities), and Panjabi (shops) are spoken as second languages. *Lg Dev:* Literacy rate in second language: 18% to 19%. Nastaliq script. Radio programs. Films. NT: 1826. *Other:* Dogri formerly considered a Panjabi dialect, but now promoted as a written language in India. Dhogri is a Scheduled Caste in Himachal Pradesh and Punjab. They reportedly speak Chambeali in Himachal and Dogri in Jammu. SOV. Mountain slope, valley. 300 to 1,350 meters. Agriculturalists: rice, maize, millet, fruit. Hindu, Muslim, Sikh, Buddhist, Christian.

Domari (Dom, Domra Magu Hiya) [rmt] 201,787 in India (2000 WCD). Bihar, Saran and Champaran districts; Assam; West Bengal; Uttar Pradesh; Punjab; Madhya Pradesh; Jammu and Kashmir; Orissa. *Dialects:* Domaki, Wogri-Boli. *Lg Use:* A Gypsy language partly used for in-group identification. *Other:* Efforts made to hide meaning of words from outsiders. Similar to Bhojpuri. Muslim, Christian. See main entry under Iran.

Dubli (Dubala, Dubla, Rathod, Talavia) [dub] 202,000 (1991). Gujarat, Surat, Valsad, Bharuch, Vadodara districts; Maharashtra, Thana District, Talasari and Dahanu areas; Dadra and Nagar Haveli; Daman and Diu; Karnataka: Rajasthan. *Class:* Indo-European, Indo-Iranian, Indo-Aryan, Central zone, Bhil. *Lg Dev:* Literacy rate in second language: 10%. *Other:* A Scheduled Tribe in India. Language name is 'Dubli', people's name 'Dubla'. Reports they speak Gujarati have not been confirmed. Hindu, Christian, Muslim.

Dungra Bhil [duh] 100,000 (2000). Gujarat, Baroda District; Madhya Pradesh; Maharashtra. *Class:* Indo-European, Indo-Iranian, Indo-Aryan, Central zone, Bhil. *Dialects:* 84% to 89% intelligibility of Bhilori of Maharashtra. Lexical similarity 86% between subgroups, 71% to 87% with Bhilori and Noiri Bhili, below 53% with Girasia. *Other:* A Scheduled Tribe in Gujarat. A Bhil subgroup. 'Dungra Bhil' is sometimes used as an alternate name for Adivasi Girasia and Rajput Girasia but probably refers to more than one group living in the hills ('Dungra' means 'hill'). Agriculturalists.

Duruwa (Dhurwa, Dhruva, Durva, Parji, Parjhi, Paraja, Parajhi, Thakara, Tagara, Tugara) [pci] 75,000 (2000). Ethnic population: 100,000 in the ethnic group (1986), 65% in Bastar, 35% in Koraput. Chhattisgarh, Bastar Disctrict, southeast Jagdalpur Tahsil; Orissa, Koraput District. *Class:* Dravidian, Central, Parji-Gadaba. *Dialects:* Tiriya, Nethanar, Dharba, Kukanar. Nethanar dialect is central. Lexical similarity 90% to 96% between dialects, 70% to 82% lexical similarity with Halbi. *Lg Use:* 90% of the ethnic group speaks Parji as first language. Parji is spoken by the Madiya for communicating with the Dhurwa people. Halbi is the second language. Part of the ethnic group speaks Halbi as first language (around Jagdalpur, Bastar District); 1% speak Oriya; less than 2% use Bhatri (northern Bastar District). Hindi is the state language, but it is not well known except by the educated. *Lg Dev:* Literacy rate in first language: below 1%. Literacy rate in second language: 15% to 25%. Devanagari and Oriya scripts. *Other:* A Scheduled Tribe in India. Name of the people is 'Dhurwa', the language 'Parji'. Plains. Forest. Lumbermen; hunter-gatherers; agriculturalists. Traditional.

Dzongkha (Lhoskad, Hloka) [dzo] 3,000 in India (1996). Sikkim, Kalimpong, Darjeeling; West Bengal, just inside the Indo-Bhutan border. See main entry under Bhutan.

English [eng] *Lg Use:* National language. Second-language speakers in India: 11,021,610 (1961 census). See main entry under United Kingdom.

Gadaba, Bodo (Gadba, Gutob, Gutop, Gudwa, Godwa, Gadwa, Boi Gadaba) [gbj] 8,000 (2000). Andhra Pradesh, Vishakhapatnam District; Orissa, Koraput District. Lamtaput block in Koraput is the largest concentration. *Class:* Austro-Asiatic, Munda, South Munda, Koraput Munda, Gutob-Remo-Geta', Gutob-Remo. *Dialects:* Munda Orissa Gadaba, Munda Andhra Pradesh Gadaba. Lexical similarity 69% to 89% among 7 varieties of Orissa, between 2 in Andhra Pradesh 73%, others 30% to 37%. *Lg Use:* Few children. Adivasi Oriya is used as second language. Low bilingualism in Oriya in Orissa. Speakers use Telugu in Andhra Pradesh as second language. *Lg Dev:* Literacy rate in second language: 6.5%. Literacy classes in progress. Oriya script. *Other:* A Scheduled Tribe in India. Some ethnic Gadaba in Madhya Pradesh speak Bhatri as first language. Different from Dravidian Gadaba. Nonvegetarian. Hills. Swidden agriculturalists; gatherers. Hindu, traditional religion.

Gadaba, Mudhili (Gadaba, Gol Gadaba, Salur Ollar Gadaba, Kondekar, Kondkor) [gau] 8,000 (2000). Andhra Pradesh, Vizianagaram, Vishakhapatnam, Salur, Pachipenta Mandals,and Srikakulam districts. *Class:* Dravidian, Central, Parji-Gadaba. *Dialects:* 93% to 98% intelligibility among dialects. Lexical similarity 84% to 94% between dialects, 42% to 47% with Dravidian Gadaba in Pottangi, Orissa. *Lg Use:* All domains, home, village, religion. Positive language attitude. Speakers have low proficiency in Telugu. *Lg Dev:* Literacy rate in second language: 6.5%. Telugu script. *Other:* A

Scheduled Tribe in India. Nonvegetarian. Plains. Swidden agriculturalists.

Gadaba, Pottangi Ollar (Ollar Gadaba, Ollari, Ollaro, Hallari, Allar, Hollar Gadbas, San Gadaba, Gadba, Sano, Kondekar, Kondkor) [gdb] 15,000 (2000). 4,000 to 7,000 in Pottangi Block, Koraput District (1995). Orissa, Koraput District, Pottangi and Nandapur blocks. *Class:* Dravidian, Central, Parji-Gadaba. *Dialects:* 4 varieties investigated in Orissa had 69% to 80% lexical similarity, and with one in Andhra Pradesh 42% to 47%; 52% to 62% with Gadaba Salur in Andhra Pradesh. *Lg Use:* Positive language attitude. Adivasi Oriya is the main second language. Speakers have low proficiency in Oriya. Telugu is also used. *Lg Dev:* Literacy rate in second language: 6.5%. Oriya script in Orissa and Telugu script in Andhra Pradesh. *Other:* Gabada is a Scheduled Tribe. Different from Gadaba in Munda family, also spoken in Koraput. Hills. Hindu, traditional religion.

Gaddi (Bharmauri Bhadi, Pahari Bharmauri, Panchi Brahmauri Rajput, Gaddyali, Gadiali, Gadi) [gbk] 120,000 (1997). Himachal Pradesh, Chamba District, Brahmaur Tahsil and Holi sub-tahsils; Uttar Pradesh; Jammu and Kashmir. Higher elevations in summer, lower in winter. *Class:* Indo-European, Indo-Iranian, Indo-Aryan, Northern zone, Western Pahari. *Dialects:* Bharmauri, Macleod Ganj. 93% intelligibility of Mandeali, 97% of Kangri, 83% of Chambeali. Lexical similarity 74% to 80% with Palamur Kangri, 79% with Chambeali, 67% to 73% with Mandeali. *Lg Use:* Hindi is used for instruction in school, shops, and cities. *Lg Dev:* Radio programs. *Other:* A Scheduled Tribe in India. SOV. Mountain slope. 1,340 to 5,882 meters. Nomadic pastoralists. Hindu.

Gahri (Ghara, Lahuli of Bunan, Boonan, Punan, Poonan, Erankad, Keylong Boli, Bunan) [bfu] 4,000 in India (1997). Himachal Pradesh, Gahr Valley along the Bhaga River from its confluence with the Chandra and upstream about 25 km, Biling, Kardang, Kyelang, Guskyar, Yurnad, Gumrang, Barbog, Paspara, Pyukar, Styering villages. Also spoken in China. *Class:* Sino-Tibetan, Tibeto-Burman, Himalayish, Tibeto-Kanauri, Western Himalayish, Kanauri. *Dialects:* Related to Tukpa, Kanashi, Thebor, Kanam, Lippa, Sumtsu (Sumchu), Sungnam (Sungam), Zangram. Lexical Similarity 39% with Sunam, 26% to 39% with varieties of Chamba Lahuli (Pattani), 37% with Tinani, 26% to 34% with varieties of central Tibetan, 34% with Jangshung and Shumcho, 31% with Kinnaur Bhoti, 30% with Chitkuli and Nesang (Tukpa), 24% with Lhasa Tibetan, 23% with Kanauri. *Lg Use:* All domains, home. *Lg Dev:* Literacy rate in first language: below 1%. Formerly Takari, then Tibetan script. Bible portions: 1911–1923. *Other:* Speakers are called 'Gahri', and call themselves 'Lahuli'. Bodh caste, but they speak a different language from the Bodhs of Mayar, Khoksar, and Stod valleys. They consider themselves to be different from Bodhs of the north, whom they call Tibetans. Only singular and plural number; no gender indicated in verbs or pronouns. Agriculturalists: cultivators. Buddhist.

Gamit (Gamati, Gamti, Gamta, Gavit, Gamith, Gameti) [gbl] 400,000 (2000). Gujarat, mainly Surat District, some in Bharuch, Dangs, and Valsad districts. *Class:* Indo-European, Indo-Iranian, Indo-Aryan, Central zone, Bhil. *Dialects:* Similar to Mawchi. *Lg Dev:* Most speakers have high school or college education. Barati script. NT: 1982. *Other:* A Scheduled Tribe in India. Traditional religion, Christian.

Gangte (Gante) [gnb] 15,100 in Manipur (2001 census). Manipur, concentrated in southern Churachandpur District, 37 villages; Megalaya; Assam. Also spoken in Myanmar. *Class:* Sino-Tibetan, Tibeto-Burman, Kuki-Chin-Naga, Kuki-Chin, Northern. *Dialects:* Related to

Thado Chin. Differs little from Vaiphei, Paite, or Zou (Singh). *Lg Use:* Speakers also use Meitei or English. *Lg Dev:* Literacy high among young people and lower among older people. Roman script. Magazines. Newspapers. Bible: 1991. *Other:* A Scheduled Tribe in India. Agriculturalists. Christian.

Garasia, Adiwasi (Adiwasi Girasia, Girasia, Adiwasi Gujarati) [gas] 100,000 (1988 Williams). Northern Gujarat, Banaskantha District, Danta taluk; Sabarkantha District, Poshina taluk. *Class:* Indo-European, Indo-Iranian, Indo-Aryan, Central zone, Bhil. *Dialects:* Understand Rajput Garasia very well. Could probably use same reading materials. Lexical similarity 89% to 96% between dialects, 75% to 93% with dialects of Rajput Garasia; 79% to 92% with dialects of Patelia; 79% to 93% with Wagdi; 76% to 87% with Marwari dialects. *Lg Use:* Speakers have low proficiency in Gujarati. *Lg Dev:* Literacy rate in second language: 15% to 25%. Bible portions. *Other:* Speakers are Bhils. Traditional religion, Hindu, Christian.

Garasia, Rajput (Rajput Garasia, Girasia, Grasia, Dungri Grasia, Dhungri Garasia, Dungari Garasia) [gra] 100,000 (IEM 1999). Rajasthan, Sirchi, Pali, and Udaipur districts; Gujarat, Banaskantha District. *Class:* Indo-European, Indo-Iranian, Indo-Aryan, Central zone, Bhil. *Dialects:* Not intelligible with Adiwasi Garasia. Lexical similarity 94% to 99% with Gujarat and Rajasthan dialects, 75% to 93% with Adiwasi Garasia dialects; 76% to 84% with Patelia dialects; 79% to 86% with Wagdi; 67% to 84% with Marwari dialects. *Lg Use:* Positive attitude toward Garasia. Some negative attitudes toward Adiwasi Garasia and Bhil. Speakers have low proficiency in Hindi and Gujarati. *Lg Dev:* Literacy rate in second language: 15% to 25%. Gujarati and Devanagari scripts. Bible portions: 1998. *Other:* A Scheduled Tribe in Rajasthan. Speakers are of the warrior caste. Separate language from Dungra Bhil. 'Dungra Bhil' is sometimes used as an alternate name for Adiwasi Garasia and Rajput Garasia but probably refers to more than one group living in the hills ('Dungra' means 'hill'). Agriculturalists: maize, wheat, sesame seed, aniseed, mustard seed, lentils; laborers during dry season. Traditional religion, Christian.

Garhwali (Gadhavali, Gadhawala, Gadwahi, Gashwali, Godauli, Gorwali, Gurvali, Pahari Garhwali, Girwali) [gbm] 2,920,000 (2000). Uttaranchal; Tehri Garhwal, Pauri Garhwal, Uttarkashi, Chamoli, Dehra Dun, Rudraprayag districts; Himachal Pradesh. Jaunpuri and Ravai in Tehri and Uttarkashi. *Class:* Indo-European, Indo-Iranian, Indo-Aryan, Northern zone, Garhwali. *Dialects:* Srinagaria, Tehri (Gangapariya), Badhani, Dessaulya, Lohbya, Majh-Kumaiya, Bhattiani, Nagpuriya, Rathi, Salani (Pauri), Ravai, Bangani, Parvati, Jaunpuri, Gangadi (Uttarkashi), Chandpuri. Kumauni is closest language; Jaunsari is sometimes referred to as a dialect of Garhwali, but most say they can't understand it. Parvati also reportedly not intelligible. Bangani more similar to Pahari dialects of Himachal. Srinagari is the literary standard. Pauri generally regarded as the 'sweetest'. Srinagari and Pauri are very similar. Lexical similarity is 53 to 84% among dialects; 54 to 69% with Hindi, 55 to 66% with Kumauni. *Lg Use:* Vigorous. Home and village domains. All ages. Positive language attitude. Almost everyone speaks some Hindi. Men, educated, and the youth are more fluent. Hindi used in market. *Lg Dev:* Literacy rate in first language: 30% to 60%. Literacy rate in second language: 61.4%; female 45%, male 78% (1991 census). Village censuses from 2000 survey show the literacy rate has risen 12 to 18%. Literacy needed for older women. Uttaranchal becoming a state may have a positive influence on first-language literacy and use in the school system. Devanagari script. Poetry. Magazines.

Radio programs. NT: 1827–1994. *Other:* Jaunpuri and Ravai are culturally similar to Jaunsari and distinct from Garhwali. Castes are Brahmin, Rajput, Harijan. SOV. Mountain slope. Agriculturalists. Hindu, syncretism with traditional religion.

Garo (Garrow, Mande) [grt] 575,000 in India (1997). Population total all countries: 677,000. Meghalaya, Garo Hills District; West Assam, Goalpara, Kamrup, Karbi Anglong districts; Nagaland, Kohima District; Tripura, South Tripura District, Udaipur subdivision; North Tripura District, Kamalpur, Kailasahar subdivisions; West Tripura District, Sadar subdivision; West Bengal, Jalpaiguri and Cooch Behar districts. Also spoken in Bangladesh. *Class:* Sino-Tibetan, Tibeto-Burman, Jingpho-Konyak-Bodo, Konyak-Bodo-Garo, Bodo-Garo, Garo. *Dialects:* A'beng (A'bengya, Am'beng), A'chick (A'chik), A'we, Chisak, Dacca, Ganching, Kamrup, Matchi. The Achik dialect predominates among several inherently intelligible dialects. The Abeng dialect is in Bangladesh. Closest to Koch. *Lg Use:* Awe dialect, spoken by Garo of Assam, is nearly obsolete. Most use standard Garo. *Lg Dev:* Literacy rate in second language: 23% (1971). General level of education is low compared to Khasi. Taught in primary schools. Roman script. Films. Dictionary. Grammar. Bible: 1924–1994. *Other:* A Scheduled Tribe in India. Christian.

Gata' (Gataq, Getaq, Geta', Gta', Gta Asa, Didei, Didayi, Dire) [gaq] 3,055 (1991 census). Orissa, Koraput, and Malkangiri districts, Kudumulgumma and Chitrakonda blocks, south of the Bondo Hills. Some communities in the Khairput block. 47 villages. *Class:* Austro-Asiatic, Munda, South Munda, Koraput Munda, Gutob-Remo-Geta', Geta'. *Dialects:* Plains Geta', Hill Geta'. Ruhlen treats Plains Geta' and Hill Geta' as separate languages. Lexical similarity 68% to 93% with other Gata' varieties, 27% to 37% with Bondo varieties, 22% to 28% with Gadaba Gutob. *Lg Use:* Many speak Desiya in the market. *Lg Dev:* Literacy rate in second language: 0.5% female, 5.99% male, 3.19% total. *Other:* A Scheduled Tribe in India. They are occasional nonvegetarians. Swidden agriculturalists; hunter-gatherers. Traditional religion, Hindu.

Godwari [gdx] Rajasthan, Jhalor, Sirohi, Pali districts. *Class:* Indo-European, Indo-Iranian, Indo-Aryan, Central zone, Rajasthani, Marwari. *Dialects:* Balvi, Khuni, Madahaddi, Sirohi. 61% intelligibility of Marwari. Lexical similarity 58% to 70% between dialects; 50% to 72% with Marwari, 44% to 70% with Merwari, 45% to 69% with Shekhawati, 51% to 73% with Mewari, 46% to 66% with Dhundari, 44% to 67% with Harauti. *Lg Use:* Speakers also use Hindi.

Gondi, Northern (Gondi, Gaudi, Gondiva, Gondwadi, Goondile, Goudwal, Ghond, Godi, Gondu, Goudi) [gno] 1,954,000 Betul (1997). 2,632,000 all Gondi. Madhya Pradesh, Betul, Chhindwara, Seoni, Mandla, Balaghat districts; Maharashtra State, Amravati, Wardha, Nagpur, Bhandara, Yavatmal districts. *Class:* Dravidian, South-Central, Gondi-Kui, Gondi. *Dialects:* Betul, Chhindwara, Mandla, Seoni, Amravati, Bhandara, Nagpur, Yavatmal. Inherent intelligibility between dialects 94% to 97%. Speakers tested in some other dialects understood Amravati 94% to 97%; Betul 83% to 96%, and Seoni 82% to 97%. 58% to 78% intelligibility of Southern Gondi. A separate language from Muria, Maria of Garhichiroli, Dandami Maria, and Koya. Lexical similarity 58% to 90% among dialects. *Lg Use:* All ages. Positive language attitude. Some bilingualism in Hindi in Madhya Pradesh and Marathi in Maharashtra, but proficiency is not very high. *Lg Dev:* Literacy rate in first language: 1% to 5%. Literacy rate in second language: 25% to 50%. Devanagari script. Radio programs. Films. NT: 1996.

Other: The people are called 'Gond'. Forest. Agriculturalists; city dwellers. Traditional religion, Hindu.

Gondi, Southern (Koi Gondi, Telugu Gondi) [ggo] 250,000 (2000). Andhra Pradesh, Adilabad District; Maharashtra, southern Yavatmal, southern Chandrapur and southeastern Garhchiroli districts. *Class:* Dravidian, South-Central, Gondi-Kui, Gondi. *Dialects:* Sironcha, Nirmal (Adilabad), Bhamragarh, Utnoor, Aheri, Rajura, Etapally Gondi. Sironcha is the dialect understood best by the others, with 90% to 98% intelligibility. 49% to 58% intelligibility of Northern Gondi. Lexical similarity 64% to 90% among dialects. *Lg Dev:* Literacy rate in second language: 25% to 50%. Telugu script. Bible portions: 1962. *Other:* Speakers are called 'Gond'. Plains, hills. Tropical forests, deforested agricultural lands. Swidden agriculturalists; hunters; fishermen. Traditional religion, Hindu.

Gowlan [goj] 20,179 (2000 WCD). Maharashtra, Amravati District, and in some cases in the same communities as Korku people. Also in Hoshangabad District. Some reported in northern Karnataka. *Class:* Indo-European, Indo-Iranian, Indo-Aryan, Southern zone, Unclassified. *Dialects:* Dialects in Maharashtra and Karnataka reported to be different. May be closer to Hindi (Central zone) than to Marathi (Southern zone). *Lg Use:* Positive language attitudes toward Gowlan and Hindi. Only some want their children to learn Marathi. Bilingualism in Hindi is low in at least the Chikli area. *Other:* Surrounded by Korku. Belong to Gowli caste. Pastoralists: cattle. Traditional religion, Christian.

Gowli (Nand) [gok] 35,000 (1997). Madhya Pradesh; Maharashtra, Amravati District. *Class:* Indo-European, Indo-Iranian, Indo-Aryan, Central zone, Western Hindi, Unclassified. *Dialects:* Nand, Ranya, Lingaayat, Khamla. Nand subdialects have 93% or higher intelligibility of the Khamla dialect. Dialect used in Madhya Pradesh appears closer to Marathi (Southern zone) than to Hindi (Central zone). Ranya has 84% to 92% lexical similarity with Nand. *Lg Use:* Used in the home. Many have some comprehension of Marathi and Hindi. *Lg Dev:* Literacy rate in first language: below 1%. Literacy rate in second language: 5% to 15%. *Other:* Speakers belong to Gowli caste. There are 12 and a half subgroups; Nand Gowli the highest, Musalman (the 'half tribe') the lowest. Surrounded by Korku. Mountain slope. Tropical forest. Agriculturalists; laborers. Hindu, traditional religion.

Groma (Tromowa) [gro] Sikkim. *Dialects:* Upper Groma, Lower Groma. *Other:* Buddhist (Lamaist), Christian. See main entry under China.

Gujarati (Gujrathi, Gujerati, Gujerathi) [guj] 45,479,000 in India (1997). Population total all countries: 46,106,136. Gujarat; Maharashtra; Rajasthan; Karnataka; Madhya Pradesh. Also spoken in Bangladesh, Fiji, Kenya, Malawi, Mauritius, Oman, Pakistan, Réunion, Singapore, South Africa, Tanzania, Uganda, United Kingdom, USA, Zambia, Zimbabwe. *Class:* Indo-European, Indo-Iranian, Indo-Aryan, Central zone, Gujarati. *Dialects:* Standard Gujarati (Saurashtra Standard, Nagari, Bombay Gujarati, Patnuli), Gamadia (Gramya, Surati, Anawla, Brathela, Eastern Broach Gujarati, Charotari, Patidari, Vadodari, Ahmedabad Gamadia, Patani), Parsi, Kathiyawadi (Jhalawadi, Sorathi, Holadi, Gohilwadi, Bhawnagari), Kharwa, Kakari, Tarimuki (Ghisadi). Some Pakistani dialects are closer to standard Gujarati than others. Pakistani Gujarati is probably a subdialect of Patani (Voegelin and Voegelin 1977). The Memoni ethnic group in Karachi, Hyderabad, Sukkur, and other parts of Pakistan are reported to speak a variety closer to Gujarati, while those in India are reported to speak a variety of Kachchi. *Lg Use:* State language of Gujarat. Spoken as first language by the Keer. *Lg Dev:* Literacy rate in second language: 30% (1974). Gujarati script. Newspapers. Radio programs. Grammar. Bible: 1823–2002. *Other:* Hindu, Muslim (Sunni), Christian.

Gujari (Gujuri, Gujer, Gujar, Gujjari, Gurjar, Gojri, Gogri, Kashmir Gujuri, Rajasthani Gujuri, Gojari) [gju] 690,315 in India (2000 WCD). Population total all countries: 992,315. Ethnic population: 1,600,000 (2002) in Uttar Pradesh, Haryana, Madhya Pradesh, Rajasthan, Maharashtra, Gujarat, Punjab, Delhi. Jammu, border tahsils along the Line of Control; Kashmir, Kukernag, Kangan, Tral, Doru, Pahalgam, Shopian, Kulgam, Handwara, Karnah, Kupwara, Uri tahsils; Himachal Pradesh; Uttaranchal. Also spoken in Afghanistan, Pakistan. *Class:* Indo-European, Indo-Iranian, Indo-Aryan, Central zone, Rajasthani, Unclassified. *Dialect:* Ajiri of Hazara. Poonch may be understood by others and form the basis for a standard dialect. In Pakistan, Eastern Gujari appears closer to Northern Hindko or Pahari-Potwari. Western Gujari speakers appear to understand the Eastern dialect better than vice versa. Comparison with India varieties is needed. Lexical similarity between Uttar Pradesh and Pakistan average 60%, with Poonch 76%. *Lg Use:* In general, the Hindu agriculturalists have not retained the Gujari language and culture, whereas the Muslim Gujari have. Gujars outside of Jammu-Kashmir and Himachal Pradesh do not speak Gujari, but regional languages. All domains, home, about 50% for religion. They perceive Gujari as one people and one language. Positive language attitude toward Gujari, and toward second languages if it is advantageous to use them. Speakers also use Hindi, Urdu, Kumauni, Garwhali, Kullu, Jaunsari, Kashmiri, or Dogri. *Lg Dev:* Literacy rate in second language: 5% to 15%. Nastaliq and Devanagari scripts. Poetry. Magazines. Radio programs. TV. *Other:* A Scheduled Tribe in India. Mountain slope, hills. Muslim Gujari are transhumant pastoralists: Bakarwal goats, sheep, Dodhi buffalo. Hindu Gujari are agriculturalists. Hindu, Muslim.

Gurung, Western (Gurung Kura) [gvr] 82 in India (1961 census). West Bengal, Darjeeling. Also possibly in Myanmar. See main entry under Nepal.

Hajong (Haijong, Hazong) [haj] 19,000 in India (1997). Meghalaya, West Garo Hills District, western side, West and East Khasi Hills; Assam, Goalpara and Nowgong districts; Arunachal Pradesh; West Bengal. Also spoken in Bangladesh. *Class:* Indo-European, Indo-Iranian, Indo-Aryan, Eastern zone, Bengali-Assamese. *Dialects:* Formerly a Tibeto-Burman language, but culturally and linguistically Hinduized and Bengalized (Breton 1997). *Lg Use:* Speakers are shifting to Assamese. *Lg Dev:* Assamese script. *Other:* A Scheduled Tribe in India. Agriculturalists. Traditional religion, Hindu.

Halbi (Bastari, Halba, Halvas, Halabi, Halvi, Mahari, Mehari) [hlb] 500,000 (2000). Madhya Pradesh, Balaghat District; Chhattisgarh, open plains in Bastar District; Maharashtra; Orissa, Koraput District; Andhra Pradesh. *Class:* Indo-European, Indo-Iranian, Indo-Aryan, Eastern zone, Bengali-Assamese. *Dialects:* Adkuri, Bastari, Bhunjia, Chandari, Gachikolo, Kawari, Mehari, Muri (Muria), Sundi. Bhunjia, Kawari are considered to be more divergent dialects. Reported to be a creole language. Grierson called it a dialect of Marathi for convenience, but noted similarities to Bhatri, a dialect of Oriya. Mehari intelligible only with difficulty. *Lg Use:* Trade language. 200,000 second-language speakers (Thomas 2001). Men who have been to school use Hindi as second language for trading and common topics. Some use Bhatri as second language. *Lg Dev:* Literacy rate in second language: 8% or less. Government literacy program using Hindi primers. Devanagari script. Bible portions: 1989. *Other:* A Scheduled Tribe in India. SOV; postpositions; genitives, articles, adjectives, numerals before noun heads; 2 or 3 affixes per word; word order distinguishes given and new information; noun affixes indicate case; verb affixes mark person, number, gender of subject; passives; causatives; comparatives; CV, CVC, CVV; nontonal. Plains. Scrub forest, semitropical. 600 meters. Pastoralists; peasant agriculturalists. Traditional religion, Hindu, Christian.

Harauti (Hadauti, Hadoti, Hadothi, Piploda) [hoj] 886,000 (2002). Rajasthan, Kota, Jhalawar, Bundi, Baran districts; Madhya Pradesh. *Class:* Indo-European, Indo-Iranian, Indo-Aryan, Central zone, Rajasthani, Unclassified. *Dialects:* Sipari, Harauti. 45% of standard Marwari. Lexical similarity 73% to 81% between dialects, 57% to 67% with Merwari, 58% to 66% with Shekhawati, 44% to 67% with Godwari, 61% to 71% with Mewari, 64% to 73% with Dhundari, 52% to 70% with Mewati, 55% to 62% with Bagri. *Lg Use:* First language of the ethnic Saharia and Aheri of Rajasthan. *Lg Dev:* Devanagari script. NT: 1822. *Other:* Saharia is a Scheduled Tribe in India. SOV. Hindu, Muslim, Jain, Christian.

Haryanvi (Bangaru, Banger, Bangri, Bangru, Haryani, Hariyani, Hariani, Desari, Chamarwa, Jatu) [bgc] 13,000,000 (1992 SIL). Population includes 107,000 Haryanvi proper (1997). Ethnic population: 16,000,000 (1992 SIL). Haryana; Punjab; Karnataka; Delhi; Himachal Pradesh; Uttar Pradesh. *Class:* Indo-European, Indo-Iranian, Indo-Aryan, Central zone, Western Hindi, Unclassified. *Dialects:* Bangaru Proper, Deswali, Bagdi, Khadar, Mewati. 'Bagdi' is the variety used around Fatehabad and Sirsa, and south of Bhiwani (distinct from the Wagdi language in southern Rajasthan). Needs comparison with Bagri. Intelligibility among dialects is good, but Haryanvi is not intelligible with Hindi, the closest language. Closest to Braj Bhasha. Lexical similarity 92% among dialects. *Lg Use:* Some domains, home, religion. All ages. Positive language attitude. Hindi is used as second language; proficiency higher among educated speakers than uneducated ones. Some bilingual ability in all social groups for education and contact with non-Haryanvi speakers. *Lg Dev:* Literacy rate in second language: 55% Hindi. Dictionary. Bible portions: 2001. *Other:* 'Bangru' now used for speakers in Jind area. 'Khadar' is used by speakers in Jind to refer to the speech of Rohtak and Sonipat. Plains. Hindu, Muslim.

Hindi (Khari Boli, Khadi Boli) [hin] 180,000,000 in India (1991 UBS). Population total all countries: 180,764,791. Ethnic population: 363,839,000 (1997 IMA). Throughout northern India: Delhi; Uttar Pradesh; Uttaranchal; Rajasthan; Punjab; Madhya Pradesh; northern Bihar; Himachal Pradesh. Also spoken in Bangladesh, Belize, Botswana, Germany, Kenya, Nepal, New Zealand, Philippines, Singapore, South Africa, Uganda, United Arab Emirates, United Kingdom, USA, Yemen, Zambia. *Class:* Indo-European, Indo-Iranian, Indo-Aryan, Central zone, Western Hindi, Hindustani. *Dialects:* Formal vocabulary is borrowed from Sanskrit, de-Persianized, de-Arabicized. Literary Hindi, or Hindi-Urdu, has four varieties: Hindi (High Hindi, Nagari Hindi, Literary Hindi, Standard Hindi); Urdu; Dakhini; Rekhta. State language of Delhi, Uttar Pradesh, Rajasthan, Madhya Pradesh, Bihar, Himachal Pradesh. Languages and dialects in the Western Hindi group are Hindustani, Haryanvi, Braj Bhasha, Kanauji, Bundeli; see separate entries. *Lg Use:* Official language. Spoken as first language by the Saharia in Madhya Pradesh. Hindi, Hindustani, Urdu could be considered co-dialects, but have important sociolinguistic differences. 120,000,000 second-language speakers (1999 WA). *Lg Dev:* Devanagari script. Radio programs. Grammar. Bible: 1818–2000. *Other:* SOV. Hindu.

Hinduri (Handuri) [hii] 138 (1961 census). Himachal Pradesh, Shimla and Solan districts. *Class:* Indo-European, Indo-Iranian, Indo-Aryan, Northern zone, Western Pahari. *Dialects:* May be a dialect of Mahasu Pahari. Masica (1991:429) says it is "transitional between Panjabi and West Pahari of Mahasui type."

Hmar (Hamar, Mhar, Hmari) [hmr] 50,000 (1997). Assam, North Cachar and Cachar districts; Manipur, south, Tipaimukh, Churachandpur, 35 villages; Mizoram, Aizawl, Cachar, North Cachar districts; Tripura. *Class:* Sino-Tibetan, Tibeto-Burman, Kuki-Chin-Naga, Kuki-Chin, Central. *Dialects:* Close to Zomi. *Lg Use:* Speakers also use Assamese. *Lg Dev:* Literacy rate in second language: 90%. Taught in primary schools. Roman script. Dictionary. Grammar. Bible: 1968–1987. *Other:* A Scheduled Tribe in India. Ethnic Hmar living in Mizoram speak Mizo as first language. Christian.

Ho (Lanka Kol, Bihar Ho) [hoc] 1,077,000 in India (1997). Population includes 444,000 in Singhbhum, 200,000 in Oriya (1990 UBS). Jharkhand, mainly in Singhbhum District; Orissa, Mayurbhanj and Koenjhar districts; West Bengal. Also spoken in Bangladesh. *Class:* Austro-Asiatic, Munda, North Munda, Kherwari, Mundari. *Dialects:* Lohara, Chaibasa-Thakurmunda. Most speakers understand the Chaibasa and Thakurmunda dialects well, at 90% to 92% on narrative discourse. 'Kherwari' (Khanwar, Kharar, Kharoali, Kharwari) is a group name for Ho, Mundari, and Santali, which are closely related languages, and some other smaller languages or dialects. Lexical similarity 85% between most dialects, except for three on the southern and eastern edges of the Ho area. *Lg Use:* Vigorous. Positive language attitude. Oriya, Santali, or Hindi are used in limited domains. *Lg Dev:* Literacy rate in first language: 1% to 5%. Literacy rate in second language: 25% to 50%. Literacy program in progress. Devanagari script used in Bihar; Oriya script in Orissa. Dictionary. Grammar. NT: 1997. *Other:* A Scheduled Tribe in India. Different from Ho (Hani) of Myanmar, China, Viet Nam, Laos. Forest. Agriculturalists; hunters. Traditional religion, Hindu, Christian.

Holiya (Holar, Holari, Hole, Holian, Holu, Golari-Kannada, Gohllaru) [hoy] 8,000 (1984 GR). Madhya Pradesh; Maharashtra; Karnataka. *Class:* Dravidian, Southern, Tamil-Kannada, Kannada. *Lg Dev:* Literacy rate in first language: below 1%. Literacy rate in second language: 5% Kannada. *Other:* A Scheduled Caste in Madhya Pradesh. Singh reports they speak Hindi as first language. Hunter-gatherers; mixed commerce. Hindu, traditional religion.

Hrangkhol (Rangkhol) [hra] 18,665 in India (2000 WCD). Manipur; Assam; Tripura. *Dialect:* Hadem. *Lg Dev:* Literacy rate in first language: below 1%. See main entry under Myanmar.

Hruso (Aka, Hrusso, Angka, Angkae, Tenae) [hru] 4,000 (1997 Breton). Arunachal Pradesh, Kameng District, Thrizino circle, 15 villages, mainly in villages of Dijungania, Jamiri, Puragaon; between Monpa on the west and the Tani languages on the east. *Class:* Sino-Tibetan, Tibeto-Burman, Unclassified. *Dialect:* Hruso, Levai (Bangru). No wider affiliation within Tibeto-Burman is apparent. These varieties are sometimes grouped under Tibeto-Burman as 'Hruish'. The names listed as dialects may be separate languages. *Lg Use:* Many are fluent in Miji, Monpa, Assamese, Hindi (Singh). *Other:* Aka means 'painted'. Aka has 2 ethnic groups, Kavatsun and Kutsun, and an additional subdivision called Miri-Akas on the other side of the Kaya River, known as 'Khrome'. They speak Miri, not Hruso. Probably not the same as plains Miri or Hill Miri (Sinha 62). Mountain slope. Forest. 947 to 1,893 meters. Swidden agriculturalists. Traditional religion, syncretism, Buddhist.

Idu-Mishmi ("Chulikata," "Chulikotta," Ida, Idu, Midhi, Midu, Yidu Luoba) [clk] 11,041 in India (2001 census). Population total all countries: 11,121. Arunachal Pradesh,

Dibang Valley District; Assam; West Bengal. Also spoken in China. *Class:* Sino-Tibetan, Tibeto-Burman, North Assam, Tani. *Dialects:* Closest to Digaro-Mishmi. A different language from Boga'er Lhoba. May be a dialect of Miri. Lexical similarity 7% with Miju-Mishmi, 25% with Digaro-Mishmi (IICCC). *Lg Use:* Few domains, home, family, friends. All ages. Positive language attitude. Everyone speaks Assamese, Hindi or Nepali which are used in the market. Only the educated speak English. *Lg Dev:* Literacy rate in first language: below 1%. Literacy rate in second language: 3.63%, 6.4% male, 0.4% female (Muanthanga 1997). Tibetan script in China. Radio programs. Grammar. *Other:* Mishmi Idu is a Scheduled Tribe in India. "Chulikota" is derogatory, therefore Idu is preferred. May not be in the Tani group, but is related to the Tani group. SOV; postpositions; genitives, adjective, relatives before noun heads; numerals after noun heads; affixes indicate case of noun phrase; comparatives; open syllables; tonal. Mountain slope. 1500 meters. Hunter-gatherers; swidden agriculturalists: millet, maize, rice, wheat, sweet potatoes; fishermen; animal husbandry: pigs, chicken, goats, mithun (high altitude cattle); weavers. Traditional religion, Buddhist, Hindu, Christian.

Indian Sign Language (Indo-Pakistani Sign Language, Urban Indian Sign Language) [ins] 2,680,000 in India (2003). All over the country. Also used in Bangladesh, Pakistan. *Class:* Deaf sign language. *Dialects:* Delhi Sign Language, Calcutta Sign Language, Bangalore-Madras Sign Language, Bombay Sign Language, Bangalore-Chennai-Hyderabad Sign Language, Mumbai-Delhi Sign Language. Over 75% of signs from all regions are related. Mumbai-Delhi dialect is the most influential. Some influence from British Sign Language in the fingerspelling system and a few other signs. Developed indigenously in India. Related to Nepalese Sign Language. *Lg Use:* Deaf schools mainly do not use ISL, but vocational programs often do. Over 1,000,000 deaf adults, and about 500,000 deaf children (1986). Nearly all educated deaf are bilingual in a wider community language to some degree. *Lg Dev:* Literacy rate in second language: below 2%. Male literacy rate is higher than female as men are more likely to attend school. TV. Videos. Dictionary. *Other:* 2% or less of deaf children attend deaf schools. In 2001, interpretive training courses were initiated in Mumbai by the Ali Yavar Jung National Institute for Hearing Handicapped.

Indo-Portuguese [idb] 700 monolinguals in Korlai (1977 Theban). Maharashtra, Korlai near Bombay, Daman and Diu; Vypeen Island, and Cochin area. *Lg Use:* Active use among Catholic citizens in Daman (1982 Jackson). Some communities in India have become extinct. See main entry under Sri Lanka.

Irula (Eravallan, Erukala, Irava, Irulan, Irular, Irular Mozhi, Irulavan, Iruliga, Iruligar, Kad Chensu, Korava) [iru] 200,000 (2003). Tamil Nadu, Nilgiri, Coimbatore, Periyar, Salem, Chengai Anna districts; Karnataka; Kerala, Palakkad District; Andhra Pradesh. *Class:* Dravidian, Southern, Tamil-Kannada, Tamil-Kodagu, Tamil-Malayalam, Tamil. *Dialects:* Irula Pallar (Urali Irula), Mele Nadu Irula (Southern Irula), Northern Irula (Kasaba, Kasava, Kasuba), Vette Kada Irula. Vette Kada had 73% intelligibility of Mele Nadu, Northern Irula had 83% intelligibility of Mele Nadu. Irula is not inherently intelligible with Tamil. Lexical similarity 78% to 86% between Mele Nadu varieties, 67% to 70% with Northern Irula, 64% to 66% with Vette Kada, 47% to 50% with Tamil. *Lg Use:* All domains, home, village, market, politics, prayers. Positive language attitude. Nearly all speak some Tamil, 44% Kannada, 32% Badaga. Proficiency in Tamil is low. *Lg Dev:* Literacy rate in first language: below 1%. Literacy rate in second language: 20% among adults, 50% among younger generation. Bible

portions: 2001–2002. *Other:* A Scheduled Tribe in India. Called 'Kad Chensu' in Andhra Pradesh. Some people called 'Irula' speak Tamil as first language. SOV; postpositions; nontonal. Mountain slope, plains. Subtropical forest. 300 to 1,900 meters. Peasant agriculturalists: coffee; tea laborers. Hindu, traditional religion, Christian.

Jad (Bhotia, Dzad) [jda] 300 (2001 Roland-Breton). Uttaranchal, Uttarkashi district, Jadang and Nilang villages in Harsil subdivision in the gorges of the Jad Ganga. *Class:* Sino-Tibetan, Tibeto-Burman, Himalayish, Tibeto-Kanauri, Tibetic, Tibetan, Central. *Dialects:* Close to Spiti Bhoti. *Lg Use:* Used in the home and with friends. All ages. Low prestige. High degree of bilingualism in Garhwali. Some speakers also use Hindi or Tibetan. *Lg Dev:* Hindi is used for all written communication. *Other:* Some borrowing of vocabulary from Hindi and Garhwali. Does not have pronominalization found in other languages of the area. Mountain slope. 3,300 meters. Agriculturalists; animal husbandry: sheep, goats; weavers. Buddhist.

Jangshung (Jangrami, Zangram, Zhang-Zhung, Jangiam, Thebor, Thebör Skadd, Thebarskad, Central Kinnauri) [jna] 1,990 (1998). Himachal Pradesh, Kinnaur District, Jangi, Lippa, and Asrang villages in Morang Tahsil. *Class:* Sino-Tibetan, Tibeto-Burman, Himalayish, Tibeto-Kanauri, Western Himalayish, Kanauri. *Dialects:* Closest to Shumcho and Sunam. Lexical similarity 70% with Shumcho, 65% with Sunam, 51% with Chitkuli, 49% with Lower Kinnauri. *Other:* Mountain slope, valleys. 5,000 to 6,770 meters. Pastoralists; peasant agriculturalists. Traditional religion, Hindu, Buddhist (Lamaist).

Jarawa [anq] 300 (2001 CIIL). 300 monolinguals. Ethnic population: 300 (1999 report). Andaman Islands, interior and south central Rutland Island, central interior and south interior South Andaman Island, Middle Andaman Island, west coast, 70 square km reserve. *Class:* Andamanese, South Andamanese. *Dialects:* Different from Önge and Sentinel. *Lg Dev:* Literacy rate in first language: below 1%. Dictionary. Grammar. *Other:* They are seminomadic. Forest. Hunter-gatherers. Traditional religion.

Jaunsari (Jaunsauri, Jansauri, Pahari) [jns] 97,000 (1997). Uttaranchal, Dehra Dun District, Chakrata tahsil, Jaunsar-Bawar Division; Himachal Pradesh. *Class:* Indo-European, Indo-Iranian, Indo-Aryan, Northern zone, Western Pahari. *Dialects:* Srinagar dialect is considered to be the standard by a community organization. May be intelligible with Mahasu Pahari or Garhwali. Grierson said it was also close to western Hindi. It is perceived by some as a dialect of Garhwali. Lexical similarity 63% to 70% with Garhwali dialects, 64% with Kumauni, 66% with Hindi. *Lg Dev:* Literacy rate in first language: below 1%. Literacy rate in second language: 15% to 25%. Bible portions: 1895–1904. *Other:* A Scheduled Tribe in India. Hindu.

Juang (Puttooas, Patua, Patra-Saara, Juango) [jun] 50,000 (2000). Orissa, southern Keonjhar, northern Angul, and eastern Dhenkanal districts. *Class:* Austro-Asiatic, Munda, South Munda, Kharia-Juang. *Dialects:* Not closely related to other languages. Lexical similarity 20% to 22% with Kharia. *Lg Use:* Used in the home, community. Positive language attitude. Comprehension and use of Oriya is limited. Proficiency is higher among men and the educated. *Lg Dev:* Literacy rate in second language: 8% (14.5% males, 1.7% females). Grammar. *Other:* A Scheduled Tribe in India. Mountain slope, plateau, plain. Forest. Agricultural laborers; basket makers; firewood traders. Traditional religion.

Juray [juy] 801,096 (2000 WCD). Orissa. *Class:* Austro-Asiatic, Munda, South Munda, Koraput Munda, Sora-Juray-Gorum, Sora-Juray. *Dialects:* Closest to Sora.

Kachari (Cachari) [xac] 59,000 (1997). Assam, North Cachar District and the Cachar Hills; Nagaland, Kohima District, Dimapur, Dhansiri administrative circles, 16 villages. *Class:* Sino-Tibetan, Tibeto-Burman, Jingpho-Konyak-Bodo, Konyak-Bodo-Garo, Bodo-Garo, Bodo. *Lg Use:* Fewer than 30% of ethnic Kachari speak it as first language. Most Kachari speak Assamese as first language. *Other:* A Scheduled Tribe in India. Mountain slope.

Kachchi (Kachchhi, Kutchchi, Cuchi, Cutch, Kutchie, Kachi, Katch, Kautchy, Katchi) [kfr] 806,000 in India (1997). Population total all countries: 866,000. Gujarat, Rann of Kachchh Area; Andhra Pradesh; Madhya Pradesh; Uttar Pradesh; Assam; Kerala; Tamil Nadu; Maharashtra; Karnataka; Orissa. Also spoken in Kenya, Malawi, Pakistan, Tanzania. *Class:* Indo-European, Indo-Iranian, Indo-Aryan, Northwestern zone, Sindhi. *Dialect:* Jadeji. Close to Sindhi. *Lg Use:* Most Kachchi do not understand Gujarati. *Lg Dev:* Devanagari script. Bible portions: 1834. *Other:* Agriculturalists; mixed commerce. Hindu, Muslim.

Kadar (Kada, Kadir) [kej] 2,265 (1981 census). Kerala, Ernakulam, Palakkad, and Trichur districts; Andhra Pradesh; Tamil Nadu, Coimbatore, Tiruchchirappalli and Thanjavur districts. *Class:* Dravidian, Southern, Tamil-Kannada, Tamil-Kodagu, Tamil-Malayalam, Malayalam. *Dialects:* Close to Malayalam (Thundyil 1975:246). Close to Tamil (Singh 1994). A variant form of Tamil, mixed with Malayalam elements (Shashi). *Lg Use:* They speak Malayalam or Tamil with outsiders. *Lg Dev:* Literacy rate in first language: below 1%. *Other:* A Scheduled Tribe in India. Hills. Forest. 600 meters. Hunter-gatherers traditionally, now some settled cultivators, agricultural laborers. Hindu.

Kaikadi (Kokadi, Kaikai, Kaikadia) [kep] 11,846 (1971 census). Maharashtra, Jalgaon District; Karnataka. *Class:* Dravidian, Southern, Tamil-Kannada, Tamil-Kodagu, Tamil-Malayalam, Tamil. *Other:* Nomadic. Mountain slope. Hunter-gatherers; mixed commerce. Traditional religion, Christian.

Kamar [keq] 23,456 (1981 census). Madhya Pradesh, Rewa District; Chhattisgarh, Raipur District; Maharashtra. *Class:* Dravidian, Unclassified. *Lg Use:* Singh 1994 reports they speak Chhattisgarhi among themselves and Hindi with others. *Other:* A Scheduled Tribe in India. No relationship between the Kamar caste of iron workers in Bengal and Chota Nagpur and this ethnic group. Swidden agriculturalists. Traditional religion.

Kanashi (Kanasi) [xns] 1,400 (2002 Chauhan). Himachal Pradesh, Kullu District, Kullu Tahsil, glen of the Bios Valley, around the village of Malana (Malani). *Class:* Sino-Tibetan, Tibeto-Burman, Himalayish, Tibeto-Kanauri, Western Himalayish, Kanauri. *Dialects:* No intelligibility of any Tibeto-Burman languages of Lahul-Spiti and Kinnaur (Chauhan). *Other:* Surrounded by speakers of Indo-Aryan languages. Malana village has the oldest surviving democracy in the world. They practice their own parliamentary form of government (Sharma). 3,000 meters.

Kanauji (Bhakha, Braj, Braj Kanauji, Kannauji) [bjj] 6,000,000 (1977 Voegelin and Voegelin). Uttar Pradesh, Kanpur, Farrukhabad, Etawah, Hardoi, Shahjahanpur, Pilibhit, Mainpuri, Auraiya districts. *Class:* Indo-European, Indo-Iranian, Indo-Aryan, Central zone, Western Hindi, Unclassified. *Dialects:* Kanauji Proper, Tirhari, Transitional Kanauji. Transitional Kanauji dialect is between Kanauji and Awadhi. Grierson calls it a form of Braj Bhasha. The variety spoken in Kannauj and Farrukhabad is considered the pure form. Lexical similarity 84% to 97% between all varieties of Kanauji, 72% to 76% with Bundeli, 70% to 78% with Braj Bhasha, 83% to 94% with Hindi. *Lg Use:* Kanauji being used in various domains of daily life but there is a shift towards

Hindi. Nobody refers to their language as Kanauji. The language has a very low identity. They regard their own language as being Hindi. However, a small group in the region is interested in promoting Kanauji before it dies out. Most are bilingual in Hindi. The less-educated have lower proficiency in Hindi. *Lg Dev:* Literacy rate in first language: below 1%. Literacy rate in second language: 60% (2001 census). Devanagari script. NT: 1821. *Other:* Kanauji may be only a name given by scholars. Plains. 140 meters. Agriculturalists. Hindu.

Kangri (Kangra-Dogri, Pahari Kangri, Pahari) [xnr] 1,700,000. Himachal Pradesh, Kangra, Hamirpur, Una districts. *Class:* Indo-European, Indo-Iranian, Indo-Aryan, Northern zone, Western Pahari. *Dialects:* Hamirpuri, Palampuri. Palampuri Kangri has lexical similarity 90% with Bilaspuri and Chambeali, 89% with Mandeali, 83% with Bhattiyali, 80% with MacLeod Ganj Gaddi. *Lg Use:* Vigorous. Used at home, work, market. All ages. Educators promote Kangri. Speakers are proud of their language and show interest in reading anything in first language. Acceptability of other Pahari dialects is high. Speakers also use Urdu or Panjabi. Hindi used for communicating with outsiders. Most urban people know Hindi quite well. Very few are fluent in English. *Lg Dev:* Literacy rate in second language: 70.5%. Devanagari script. Poetry. Radio programs. *Other:* Mountain slope, valley. 300 to 1,350 meters. Agriculturalists: tea, rice, maize, millet, fruit. Hindu.

Kanikkaran (Kanikkar, Kannikan, Kannikaran, Kannikharan, Malampashi) [kev] 25,000 (1982 GR). Kerala, Kozhikode, Ernakulam, Koliam, Trivandrum districts, Neyyattinkara and Nedumangadu taluks; Tamil Nadu, Kanniyakumari, and Tirunelveli districts, Tirunelveli District. *Class:* Dravidian, Unclassified. *Lg Use:* 90% also use Malayalam. 10% also use Tamil. *Lg Dev:* Literacy rate in second language: 20% Malayalam. *Other:* A Scheduled Tribe in India. Malaryan may be the same. Hills. Hunter-gatherers; agriculturalists. Hindu, traditional religion.

Kanjari (Kagari, Kangar Bhat, Kangri, Kanjri) [kft] 55,386 (1971 census). Andhra Pradesh; Madhya Pradesh; Uttar Pradesh, Aligarh, Farrukhabad, Etawah, Sitapur, Kheri districts; Rajasthan. *Class:* Indo-European, Indo-Iranian, Indo-Aryan, Unclassified. *Dialect:* Kuchbandhi. It may be in the Panjabi group. *Other:* Sometimes called a 'Gypsy' language. They are reported to use certain linguistic means of disguising their language to make it unintelligible to outsiders. Kanjar is a Scheduled Caste reportedly speaking a dialect of Hindi in Uttar Pradesh, a dialect of Mewari in Rajasthan and Hindi in Bihar and Madhya Pradesh. (Singh). Hunters; mat making of Sirki reed, ropes, brushes.

Kannada (Kanarese, Canarese, Banglori, Madrassi) [kan] 35,346,000 (1997). Karnataka; Andhra Pradesh; Tamil Nadu; Maharashtra. *Class:* Dravidian, Southern, Tamil-Kannada, Kannada. *Dialects:* Bijapur, Jeinu Kuruba, Aine Kuruba. About 20 dialects; Badaga may be one. *Lg Use:* State language of Karnataka. 9,000,000 second-language speakers. *Lg Dev:* Literacy rate in first language: 60%. Literacy rate in second language: 60%. Kannada script. Bible: 1831–2000. *Other:* sov. Hindu, Muslim, Christian.

Karbi (Manchati, Karbi Karbak, Arleng Alam, "Mikir," "Mikiri," Nihang, Puta) [mjw] 478,000. Population includes 341,000 Karbi (1997), 137,000 Amri (1997). Assam, Karbi Anglong District, Mikir and Rengma hills, Kamrup, Nowgong districts; Arunachal Pradesh, Papumpare District, Balijan circle; Meghalaya, Jaintia, and East Khasi Hills districts; Nagaland, foothills around Dimapur. *Class:* Sino-Tibetan, Tibeto-Burman, Mikir. *Dialects:* Rong Kethang, Chingthang, Mirlong. *Lg Use:* Some other groups speak Karbi as first language, including some Dimasa. Speakers of all ages use

Assamese as second language. *Lg Dev:* Literacy rate in second language: 17% (1971). Roman script. Grammar. Bible: 1952. *Other:* A Scheduled Tribe in India. 'Mikir' is derogatory. Agriculturalists: wet rice. Hindu, traditional religion, Christian.

Kashmiri (Keshur, Kaschemiri, Cashmiri, Cashmeeree, Kacmiri) [kas] 4,391,000 in India. Population includes including 4,370,000 Kashmiri, 21,000 Kishtwari (1997). Population total all countries: 4,611,000. Jammu and Kashmir; Punjab; Uttar Pradesh; Delhi; Kashmir Valley. Also spoken in Pakistan, United Kingdom. *Class:* Indo-European, Indo-Iranian, Indo-Aryan, Northwestern zone, Dardic, Kashmiri. *Dialects:* Bakawali, Bunjwali, Standard Kashmiri, Kishtwari (Kashtawari, Kistwali, Kashtwari, Kathiawari), Miraski, Poguli, Rambani, Riasi, Shah-Mansuri, Siraji of Doda, Siraji-Kashmiri, Zayoli, Zirak-Boli. Transitional dialects to Panjabi. Kashtawari dialect is standard, other dialects are influenced by Dogri. *Lg Use:* Official language. 80% in Urdu (85% male, 12% female over 35 years) (Koul and Schmidt). 83% prefer use of Kashmiri as medium in primary school, 48% in middle school (Koul and Schmidt). Some use English or Hindi as a second language. *Lg Dev:* Literacy rate in first language: 88% male 12% female over 35 years of age (Koul and Schmidt). Literacy rate in second language: Men 36.3%, women 15.9%; rural 21.6%, urban 45.5% (1981 census). Persian-based script. Newspapers. Radio programs. Films. Grammar. Bible: 1899. *Other:* Literature can be traced to the 1400s, and poetry is important. Not used in primary education. SVO. Mountain slope, valleys. 1,800 meters. Agriculturalists: rice, wheat, maize; craftsmen: weaving, carpets, carving, furniture, papier-mâché. Muslim, Hindu, Sikh.

Katkari (Katari, Katakari, Kathodi, Katvadi) [kfu] 4,951 (1961 census). Maharashtra, Raigad and Thane districts, along the foothills of the Sahayadri Range; Rajasthan, northwest, Onga, Samicha Parebati, Mubusha, Jhadol police station areas; Gujarat, Surat, Bharuch, Sabarkantha, Dang districts; Dadra and Nagar Haveli, Amboli and Dapada Panchayat areas. *Class:* Indo-European, Indo-Iranian, Indo-Aryan, Southern zone, Konkani. *Dialects:* Northern Katkari, Central Katkari, Southern Katkari. Referred to as a dialect of Marathi. 89% to 96% intelligibility between dialects. Lexical similarity 67% to 75% with Marathi, 77% to 90% among dialects. *Lg Use:* Vigorous. Used in the home and within the community. Majority also use Marathi. *Other:* A Scheduled Tribe. Singh (1994:475–479) reports their first language in Maharashtra is Marathi, in Dadra and Nagar Haveli is Kokni, in Gujarat is a variety of Marathi, in Rajasthan is Kathodi, a variety of Marathi. Agriculturalists. Hindu syncretism with traditional religion.

Khaling (Khalinge Rai, Khael Bra, Khael Baat) [klr] Darjeeling and Sikkim, scattered. *Lg Use:* Not used in Sikkim. They speak Nepali amongst themselves and with others. See main entry under Nepal.

Khamba (Khamba Khaadi) [kbg] 1,333 (1991). Arunachal Pradesh, West Siang District, Singa circle, Yang Sang Chu valley, Nyering, Nuykkang, Yortung, Mankota, Tashigong villages. *Class:* Sino-Tibetan, Tibeto-Burman, Unclassified. *Lg Dev:* Hingna script. *Other:* Primary schools in Singa circle headquarters and Nuykkang village. Valley. Forest. 1,056 meters. Agriculturalists. Buddhist.

Khamti (Kham-Tai, Hkamti, Khampti, Khamti Shan, Khantis, Tai Kham Ti) [kht] 8,879 in India (2000 WCD). Assam, Lakimpur District; Arunachal Pradesh, Siang and Lohit districts, Chakham, Memong, Barpathar, Mime, Kheram, M.Pong, Man Khao villages within the Namsai subdivision. Also possibly in China. *Dialects:* Assam Khamti, North Burma Khamti, Sinkaling Hkamti. *Lg Dev:* Literacy rate in second language: 16.1%; 24% male, 7.8%

female (1997). *Other:* A Scheduled Tribe in India. Plains. Agriculturalists. Buddhist, Hinayana sect. See main entry under Myanmar.

Khamyang (Khamjang, Khamiyang, Shyam, Tai Khamyang) [ksu] 50 (2003). Assam, Tinsukia District, Pawaimukh village. *Class:* Tai-Kadai, Kam-Tai, Be-Tai, Tai-Sek, Tai, Southwestern, Northwest. *Dialects:* Similar to Phake of Assam and Shan of Myanmar. *Lg Use:* Speakers are shifting to the Assamese language and script. Old people still read and write Tai language which is mainly used for religion. *Lg Dev:* Literacy rate in second language: 58% Assamese (1981 census). *Other:* A Scheduled Tribe in India. Close affinity to the Khampti of Arunachal. Several thousand Assamese speakers may still use the name for their ethnic group. Buddhist. Nearly extinct.

Khandesi (Khandeshi, Khandish, Dhed Gujari) [khn] 1,579,000 (1997). Maharashtra, Dhule District, Sakri tahsil, Nasik District, Satna tahsil, Nandurbar district, Nandurbar and Shahada tahsils; Gujarat. *Class:* Indo-European, Indo-Iranian, Indo-Aryan, Central zone, Khandesi. *Dialects:* Dangri, Kunbi (Kunbau), Rangari, Khandesi, Kotali Bhil. All varieties of Khandesi tested at 90% or higher intelligibility of each other. *Lg Use:* Vigorous. A group of Kukna in Dhule district speak Khandesi. Positive language attitude. Speakers also use Kukna and Marathi. *Other:* See also Dhanki. Traditional religion, Hindu, Christian.

Kharia (Haria, Kharvi, Khatria, Kheria, Khadia, Khariya) [khr] 292,000 in India (1997). Population total all countries: 293,575. Primarily Jharkhand, Ranchi District, Simdega subdivision, Thethaitangar Anchal and Kolebira Anchal in Khunti subdivision; West Singhbhum, East Singhbhum; also Chhattisgarh, Raigarh, Jashpur, Durg, Bilaspur, Raipur districts; Orissa, Sundargarh, Sambalpur, Mayurbhanj districts; Assam; Tripura; West Bengal; Andaman and Nicobar Islands. Dhelki Kharia are centered in Raigarh district. Hill Kharia are centered in Singhbhum districts. Also spoken in Nepal. *Class:* Austro-Asiatic, Munda, South Munda, Kharia-Juang. *Dialects:* Dhelki Kharia, Dudh Kharia, Mirdha-Kharia. *Lg Dev:* Literacy rate in second language: 15% Hindi. Devanagari and Roman scripts. Dictionary. Grammar. NT. *Other:* A Scheduled Tribe in Bihar, Madhya Pradesh, Orissa, West Bengal. A Scheduled Caste in Tripura. Christian, Hindu.

Kharia Thar [ksy] Jharkhand; Orissa, Mayurbhanj District; West Bengal, Bankura, Medinipur districts. *Class:* Indo-European, Indo-Iranian, Indo-Aryan, Eastern zone, Bengali-Assamese. *Dialects:* Grierson classifies it as Western subdialect of Bengali. *Other:* Spoken by the Hill Kharia. The ethnic group is also referred to as Kheria, Erenga, or Pahari.

Khasi (Kahasi, Khasiyas, Khuchia, Kassi, Khasa, Khashi) [kha] 865,000 in India (1997). Assam, Cachar, Nowgong, North Cachar Hills, Lakhimpur, Kamrup districts; Meghalaya, East and West Khasi Hills, Jaintia Hills districts; Manipur; West Bengal; Tripura. Also spoken in Bangladesh. *Class:* Austro-Asiatic, Mon-Khmer, Northern Mon-Khmer, Khasian. *Dialects:* Bhoi-Khasi, Lyngngam (Megam), Khasi, War, Cherrapunji (Sohra), Khynrium. Bhoi in East Khasi Hills, Nongpoh block, and Nonglung in East Khasi Hills, Umksning block are very different from standard Khasi, with different word order. Lyngngam dialect in West Khasi Hills, Mawshynrut block is divergent, and may not be a dialect (Abbi 1997). Many varieties called dialects have only partial inherent intelligibility of each other by their speakers. War (Amwi) is a separate language (B. Comrie 1989). *Lg Use:* Official regional language of Meghalaya. Used in government, courts, mass media in Meghalaya. *Lg Dev:* Literacy rate in second language: 29% (1971). Taught in primary schools. Roman script. Radio programs. TV. Dictionary. Grammar. Bible: 1891. *Other:* A Scheduled Tribe in India. Lyngngam is a former Garo clan, but do not mix with the Garo, and consider themselves to be Khasi (R. Breton 1997). SVO. Traditional religion, Christian.

Khirwar (Khirwara, Kherwari) [kwx] 34,251. Madhya Pradesh, Bhind, Guna, Morena, Vidisha districts; Chhattisgarh, Surguja District. *Class:* Dravidian, South-Central, Gondi-Kui, Gondi. *Other:* Hindu, traditional religion.

Khowar [khw] 19,200 in India (2000). *Other:* Muslim. See main entry under Pakistan.

Kinnauri (Kinnaura Yanuskad, Kanoreunu Skad, Kanorug Skadd, Lower Kinnauri, Kinori, Kinner, Kanauri, Kanawari, Kanawi, Kunawari, Kunawur, Tibas Skad, Kanorin Skad, Kanaury Anuskad, Koonawure, Malhesti, Milchanang, Milchan, Milchang) [kfk] 48,778 in Kinnaur District in India. Himachal Pradesh, Kinnaur, and Lahul-Spiti districts, from Chauhra to Sangla and north along the Satluj River to Morang and several villages of the upper Ropa River Valley; Uttar Pradesh; Punjab; Kashmir. *Class:* Sino-Tibetan, Tibeto-Burman, Himalayish, Tibeto-Kanauri, Western Himalayish, Kanauri. *Dialects:* Nichar has 79% inherent intelligibility of Sangla. All other varieties have functional intelligibility of each other. Related languages: Kanashi, Chitkuli, Tukpa, Jangshung. Lexical similarity 76% to 90% among varieties. *Lg Use:* Trade language. Vigorous. 15,000 to 20,000 second-language speakers in Kinnaur District. Speakers have low proficiency in Hindi. *Lg Dev:* Literacy rate in second language: 37%: men 51.5%, women 21.8%. Devanagari script. Dictionary. Grammar. Bible portions: 1909–1917. *Other:* In 1981 there were 14 high schools, 19 middle schools, 134 primary schools. A Scheduled Tribe in India. Mountain slope, valley. 5,000 to 6,770 meters. Peasant agriculturalists; pastoralists. Hindu, Buddhist (Lamaist), traditional religion.

Kinnauri, Bhoti (Nyamskad, Mnyam, Myamskad, Myamkat, Nyamkat, Bud-Kat, Bod-Skad, Sangyas, Sangs-Rgyas, Bhotea of Upper Kinnauri) [nes] 6,000 (1998). Himachal Pradesh, Kinnaur District, Morang Tahsil, upper Kinnauri Sutlej River basin where it turns into the Spiti River, Nesang village in Morang Tahsil, Puh village in Puh Tahsil. It may also be spoken in Kuno and Charang villages. *Class:* Sino-Tibetan, Tibeto-Burman, Himalayish, Tibeto-Kanauri, Western Himalayish, Kanauri. *Dialects:* May constitute more than one language. Lexical similarity 71% with Tukpa, 63% with Mane village, 59% with Darcha village, 54% with Lhasa Tibetan. *Lg Dev:* Grammar. *Other:* Kinnaura is a Scheduled Tribe. Mountain slope, valleys. 5,000 to 6,770 meters. Pastoralists; peasant agriculturalists. Traditional religion, Hindu, Buddhist (Lamaist).

Kinnauri, Chitkuli (Chitkuli, Chitkhuli, Tsíhuli, Tsitkhuli, Kinnauri, Kanauri, Thebarskad) [cik] 1,060 (1998). Himachal Pradesh, Kinnaur District, Chitkul and Rakchham villages along the Baspa River in the Sangla Valley. *Class:* Sino-Tibetan, Tibeto-Burman, Himalayish, Tibeto-Kanauri, Western Himalayish, Kanauri. *Dialects:* Lexical similarity 46% with Kinnauri, 51% with Jangshung, 43% with Shumcho, 38% with Sunam. *Lg Use:* Speakers also use Kinnauri. *Lg Dev:* Literacy rate in first language: below 1%. Grammar. *Other:* Kinnaura is a Scheduled Tribe in India. Mountain slope, valleys. 5,000 to 6,770 meters. Pastoralists; peasant agriculturalists. Traditional religion, Hindu, Buddhist (Lamaist).

Kinnauri, Harijan (Harijan Boli, Ores Boli Chamang Boli, Sonar Boli) [kjo] 6,331 (1998). Himachal Pradesh, spoken by Scheduled Caste communities in villages throughout Kinnaur District. *Class:* Indo-European, Indo-Iranian, Indo-Aryan, Northern zone, Western Pahari.

Other: Spoken by different scheduled castes. Not spoken by all Harijans in India.

Koch (Koc, Kocch, Koce, Kochboli, Konch) [kdq] 23,000 in India (1997). Meghalaya, West Garo Hills District; Assam; Tripura; Manipur; West Bengal; Bihar. Also spoken in Bangladesh. *Class:* Sino-Tibetan, Tibeto-Burman, Jingpho-Konyak-Bodo, Konyak-Bodo-Garo, Bodo-Garo, Koch. *Dialects:* Banai, Harigaya, Satpariya, Tintekiya, Wanang. *Lg Use:* Koch of Meghalaya can speak Bengali, Assamese, Garo; educated speak English and Hindi. *Lg Dev:* Show a growing interest toward education (Singh). Assamese script. *Other:* A Scheduled Tribe in India. Plains. Agriculturalists. Hindu, traditional religion.

Koda (Kaora, Korali, Korati, Kore, Kora, Mudi, Mudikora) [cdz] 300 (1991 Parkin). Ethnic population: 28,200 (1991 census). West Bengal, Burdwan and Bankura. *Class:* Austro-Asiatic, Munda, North Munda, Kherwari, Mundari. *Lg Use:* Most of the ethnic group (also in Jharkhand, Chhattisgarh, and Orissa) speaks Bengali, Oriya, or Kurux as a first language.

Kodagu (Coorge, Kadagi, Khurgi, Kotagu, Kurja, Kurug, Kodava Thak) [kfa] 122,000 (1997). Karnataka, Coorg (Kodagu) District, around Mercara, bordering on Malayalam to the south. *Class:* Dravidian, Southern, Tamil-Kannada, Tamil-Kodagu, Kodagu. *Dialects:* May be more than one language. 66% intelligibility of Malappuram Paniya. Lexical similarity 72% with Malappuram Paniya. *Lg Use:* Vigorous. First language of the Airi, Male-Kudiya, Meda, Kembatti, Kapal, Maringi, Heggade, Kavadi, Kolla, Thatta, Koleya, Koyava, Banna, Golla, Kanya, Ganiga, Malaya. Used in the home and for community gatherings. First language used as a symbol of identity. 80% of speakers also use Kannada. Some also use Malayalam, Hindi, or English. *Lg Dev:* Kannada script. Newspapers. Radio programs. Films. TV. *Other:* Kodagu means 'situated to the west'. Northern variety of Kodava has emerged as a standard variety by the use of it in Kodava literature (Rajyashree). Agriculturalists. Hindu, traditional religion.

Koireng (Kwoireng, Koirng, Kolren, Koren, Quoireng, Liyang, Liyangmai, Liangmai, Liangmei, Lyengmai) [nkd] 3,000 (2002). 1,056 in Manipur (2001 census). Manipur, Senapati District, 5 villages in Saikul and Kangpokpi subdivisions; Bishnupur District, 3 villages south of Moirang; Chandel District, 2 villages near Palel; Nagaland. *Class:* Sino-Tibetan, Tibeto-Burman, Kuki-Chin-Naga, Naga, Zeme. *Dialects:* Not intelligible with any related speech varieties (Khasung). Lexical similarity 62% to 68% with Aimol, 60% to 66% with Purum, 64% with Kharam. *Lg Use:* Purest Koireng spoken in Satu and Utonglo (Shiekshel). All ages, although children mix Meitei in when speaking Koireng. Proficiency in Meitei is limited (Khasung). All speak Meitei, 50% speak it well. Young people speak English. 15% speak Kom (Shiekshel). *Lg Dev:* Literacy rate in first language: below 1%. Literacy rate in second language: 70% to 80%. Older adults read Meitei in Bengali script, Young speakers read English in Roman Script. *Other:* Different than Liangmai Naga. A Scheduled Tribe. Assigned to be under three different Naga groups politically. Plains, mountain slope. Scrub forest. Swidden agriculturalists, wet cultivation. Christian, traditional religion.

Kok Borok (Tripuri, Tipura, Usipi Mrung, Tripura, Kakbarak, Kokbarak) [trp] 691,000 in India (1997). Population total all countries: 791,000. Assam; eastern Tripura. Also spoken in Bangladesh. *Class:* Sino-Tibetan, Tibeto-Burman, Jingpho-Konyak-Bodo, Konyak-Bodo-Garo, Bodo-Garo, Bodo. *Dialects:* Jamatia, Noatia, Halam, Debbarma. 13 dialects. Debbarma is spoken by the royal family and is the medium of communication with the other dialects. It is understood by all, but not vice versa.

Lg Dev: Literacy rate in second language: 18% (1971). Bengali and Roman scripts. Newspapers. Dictionary. Grammar. Bible: 1998. *Other:* Jamatia, Noatia, Halam, and Tripuri are Scheduled Tribes in India. Traditional religion, Muslim, Hindu, Christian.

Kolami, Northwestern (Kolamboli, Kulme, Kolam, Kolmi, Kolamy) [kfb] 50,000 (1989 F. Blair). All Kolami 115,000 (1997). Maharashtra, Yavatmal, Wardha, and Nanded districts; Andhra Pradesh; Madhya Pradesh. *Class:* Dravidian, Central, Kolami-Naiki. *Dialects:* Madka-Kinwat, Pulgaon, Wani, Maregaon. Northwestern and Southeastern Kolami are not inherently intelligible. Kolami is probably not intelligible with Parji, Gadaba, or Pottangi Ollar. Lexical similarity 61% to 68% with Southeastern Kolami. *Lg Use:* Kolami is used within the caste; the state language for outside communication. Nearly all adults have some proficiency in Marathi, Telugu, or Gondi. Proficiency is very limited in Marathi; actually a nonstandard Marathi, also used by first-language Marathi speakers in the region. *Lg Dev:* Literacy rate in first language: 4.2%. *Other:* People are called 'Kolavar' or 'Kolam'. Kolam is a Scheduled Tribe in India. Hills, plains. Agriculturalists; forest laborers. Traditional religion, Hindu.

Kolami, Southeastern [nit] 10,000 (1989 F. Blair). Andhra Pradesh, Adilabad District; Maharashtra, Chandrapur, and Nanded districts. *Class:* Dravidian, Central, Kolami-Naiki. *Dialects:* Metla-Kinwat, Utnur, Asifabad, Naiki. Not intelligible with Northwestern Kolami. Rao (1950) reports another dialect in Chinnoor and Sirpur taluks of Adilabad District. Naiki is different from Naikri (Zvelebil 1970:13). Lexical similarity 85% to 88% between Naiki and other Southeastern Kolami dialects; 83% between Metla-Kinwat and Utnur; 86% between Asifabad and Utnur; 60% to 74% with Northwestern Kolami. *Lg Use:* The Arakh speak the Naiki dialect as first language. Speakers also use Telugu or Marathi except in Maharashtra District. *Lg Dev:* Literacy rate in second language: Low.

Koli, Kachi (Bajania, Kuchi, Kachi, Katchi, Koli, Kohli, Kolhi, Kori, Kuchikoli, Vagari, Vagaria, Vaghri, Kachi Gujarati) [gjk] 400,000 in India (1998). Population includes 100,000 Kachi Koli, 250,000 Rabari, 50,000 or more Vagri Meghwar, Katai Meghwar, and Zalavaria Koli. There may be a group in India, concentrated in their ancestral homeland centered around Bhuj, in the Rann of Kachchh, Gujarat. *Dialects:* Kachi, Rabari (Rahabari), Kachi Bhil, Vagri (Kachi Meghwar), Katai Meghwar, Zalavaria Koli. *Other:* Hindu. See main entry under Pakistan.

Koli, Wadiyara (Wadaria, Wadhiara) [kxp] 403,575 in India (2000 WCD). Population total all countries: 578,575. Also spoken in Pakistan. *Class:* Indo-European, Indo-Iranian, Indo-Aryan, Central zone, Gujarati. *Dialects:* Mewasi and Wadiyara are almost the same linguistically and are coming together as a caste. Dialects listed are distinct sociolinguistic endogamous ethnic groups. Lexical similarity 78% with Kachi Koli.

Kom (Kom Rem) [kmm] 5,000 (2003). East and central Manipur, Churachandandpur, Tamenglong, and Senapati districts, 22 villages. *Class:* Sino-Tibetan, Tibeto-Burman, Kuki-Chin-Naga, Kuki-Chin, Northern. *Dialect:* Kolhreng. Kolhreng may be a separate language. *Lg Use:* Speakers of Aimol, Koireng, and Chiru also understand Kom. Fluent in Meitei (Singh). *Lg Dev:* Literacy rate in second language: 42% (1981 census). Roman script. Newspapers. Dictionary. Bible: 1996. *Other:* A Scheduled Tribe in India. Foothills, plains. Agriculturalists. Christian.

Konda-Dora (Porja) [kfc] 15,000 (2000). Konda-Dora in Andhra Pradesh, Visianagaram, Srikakulam, East Godavari districts; Kubi in Orissa, Koraput District; Assam. *Class:* Dravidian, South-Central, Gondi-Kui, Konda-Kui, Konda.

Dialects: Konda-Dora (Konda), Kubi. Lexical similarity 83% between Konda and Kubi, 28% to 36% with Telugu. *Lg Use:* A few speakers also use Telugu. Many speakers along roads through Araku are competent in Adivasi Oriya, others are more limited. *Lg Dev:* Literacy rate in second language: 10% (1981 census). *Other:* A Scheduled Tribe in India. Language is called 'Konda-Dora', people are 'Porja'. Many ethnic Konda-Kora have adopted Telugu as first language. 900 meters. Agriculturalists: settled cultivation. Hindu.

Konkani (Konkan Standard, Bankoti, Kunabi, North Konkan, Central Konkan, Concorinum, Cugani, Konkanese) [knn] 4,000,000 (1999 WA). Population includes 99,000 Thakuri (1991). North and central coastal strip of Maharashtra; Karnataka; Dadra and Nagar Haveli; Kerala. *Class:* Indo-European, Indo-Iranian, Indo-Aryan, Southern zone, Konkani. *Dialects:* Agari of Kolaba, Parabhi (Kayasthi, Damani), Koli, Kiristav, Dhanagari, Bhandari, Thakuri (Thakari, Thakri, Thakua, Thakura), Karhadi, Sangamesvari (Bakoti, Bankoti), Ghati (Maoli), Mahari (Dhed, Holia, Parvari). The dialects listed are closely related. Related to Katkari (Kathodi, Katvadi), Varli, Phudagi, Samvedi, Mangelas. *Lg Use:* Official language. Some speak nonstandard Konkani. *Lg Dev:* Kannada script. Newspapers. Films. Dictionary. Grammar. NT: 1970. *Other:* Hindu, Christian.

Konkani, Goanese (Gomataki, Goan) [gom] 3,632,174 in India (2000). Population total all countries: 3,636,074. Southern coastal strip of Maharashtra, primarily in the districts of Ratnagari and Goa; Karnataka; Kerala. Also spoken in Kenya, United Arab Emirates. *Class:* Indo-European, Indo-Iranian, Indo-Aryan, Southern zone, Konkani. *Dialects:* Standard Konkani (Goanese), Bardeskari (Gomantaki), Sarasvat Brahmin, Kudali (Malvani), Daldi (Nawaits), Chitpavani (Konkanasths), Mangalore. Daldi and Chitapavani are transitional dialects between Goanese and Standard Konkani. *Lg Dev:* Kannada, Roman script. NT: 1818–1999. *Other:* Agriculturalists; mixed commerce.

Koraga, Korra (Koragar, Koragara, Korangi, Korra) [kfd] 15,000 (1981 census). Ethnic population: Total ethnic Koraga: 16,665 (1981 census). Karnataka, Dakshina Kannada District; Kerala, Kannur, and Kasargod districts; Tamil Nadu. *Class:* Dravidian, Southern, Tulu, Koraga. *Dialects:* Ande, Mudu, Onti, Tappu. Related to Tulu and Bellari. Not intelligible with Mudu Koraga, Tulu, or Kannada. Structural differences in phonology with Mudu Koraga. According to Bhat there are 4 dialects, Onti (spoken in Udipi), Tappu (spoken in Hebri), Mudu (spoken in Coondapur), Ande (spoken in Mangalore). *Lg Use:* Speakers also use Tulu. *Other:* Koraga is a Scheduled Tribe. Hindu.

Koraga, Mudu (Mu:du) [vmd] 15,000. Ethnic population: 16,665 (1981 census). Kerala. *Class:* Dravidian, Southern, Tulu, Koraga. *Dialects:* Distinct from Korra Koraga, Tulu, or Kannada. Structural differences in phonology with Korra Koraga. *Lg Use:* Speakers also use Kannada. *Other:* Koraga is a Scheduled Tribe. Hindu.

Koraku (Kodaku, Korku) [ksz] Chhattisgarh, Surguja District; some in Jharkhand, Palamau District. *Class:* Austro-Asiatic, Munda, North Munda, Kherwari. *Dialects:* A subgroup of the Korwa (Parkin). *Lg Use:* Men also speak Hindi or Kurux. Women are monolingual (Parkin). *Other:* Separate dialect or language from Korku. Hugoniot (1970) lists Kodaku as an alternate name for Korku.

Korku (Bondeya, Bopchi, Korki, Kurku, Kuri, Ramekhera, Kurku-Ruma) [kfq] 478,000 (1997). Southern Madhya Pradesh, southern Betul District, north of and around Betul city, Hoshangabad District, East Nimar (Khandwa) District; northern Maharashtra, Amravati, Buldana, Akola districts. *Class:* Austro-Asiatic, Munda, North Munda,

Korku. _Dialect:_ Bouriya, Bondoy, Ruma, Mawasi (Muwasi, Muasi). Dialects in northern Maharashtra and south central Madhya Pradesh constitute one language; 82% to 97% intelligibility among them. Bouriya is most widely understood. Lexical similarity of dialects with Laki Bouriya is 76% to 82%. _Lg Use:_ Positive language attitude. Bilingualism in Hindi and Marathi is low. _Lg Dev:_ Literacy rate in first language: 1% to 5%. Literacy program in some villages in Chikaldara field. 50 literates reported. Devanagari script. Bible portions: 1900–1981. _Other:_ Different from Koraku. A Scheduled Tribe in India. Hills, plains. Traditional religion, Hindu.

Korlai Creole Portuguese [vkp] 750 (1998 J.C. Clements). Maharashtra, Korlai, 200 km south of Bombay, west coast. _Class:_ Creole, Portuguese based. _Dialects:_ A blend of Portuguese and Marathi. _Lg Use:_ First language of the Christian farming community in upper Korlai. Originated around 1520. Originally cut off from Hindu and Muslim neighbors by social and religious barriers, lost virtually all Portuguese contact as well after 1740. Situation now rapidly changing, with intense cultural pressure from the surrounding Marathi-speaking population. Used in the home. Speak Marathi fluently with outsiders. _Lg Dev:_ Devanagari and Roman scripts. _Other:_ Christian.

Korwa (Ernga, Singli) [kfp] 66,000 (1997). Jharkhand, Palamau and Gumla districts; Chhattisgarh, Surguja, Raigarh, Bilaspur districts; Orissa, Mayurbhanj and Sundargarh districts; Uttar Pradesh, Mirzapur District; West Bengal; Andhra Pradesh; Maharashtra. _Class:_ Austro-Asiatic, Munda, North Munda, Kherwari, Mundari. _Dialect:_ Majhi-Korwa. _Lg Use:_ Ethnic Kodaku speak Korwa as first language. Some ethnic Korwa speak Sadri or Chhattisgarhi as first language. Rapid shift to Sadri. _Lg Dev:_ Literacy rate in first language: below 1%. _Other:_ A Scheduled Tribe in Madhya Pradesh, Bihar, Orissa, West Bengal. Also a Scheduled Caste in Uttar Pradesh reportedly speaking Hindi as first language (Singh). Hindu, Muslim.

Kota (Kotta, Kowe-Adiwasi, Kother-Tamil) [kfe] 2,000 (1992). Tamil Nadu, Madras; Nilgiri Hills, Trichikadi village and a few others around Kokkal Kotagiri. _Class:_ Dravidian, Southern, Tamil-Kannada, Tamil-Kodagu, Toda-Kota. _Dialect:_ Ko Bashai. _Lg Dev:_ Literacy rate in first language: below 1%. Tamil script. _Other:_ A Scheduled Tribe in India. Endogamous within the ethnic group. Mountain slope. Agriculturalists. Hindu.

Koya (Koi, Koi Gondi, Kavor, Koa, Koitar, Koyato, Kaya, Koyi, Raj Koya) [kff] 330,000 (1997). Population includes 24,320 Dorli (1972 census). Estimates up to 10,000,000 speakers. Andhra Pradesh, south of the Godavari River and in adjoining districts north of the river; Maharashtra; Chhattisgarh, Bastar District; Orissa, Koraput District, Malkangiri Subdivision; 300 km east to west, 200 km north to south. _Class:_ Dravidian, South-Central, Gondi-Kui, Konda-Kui, Manda-Kui, Kui-Kuvi. _Dialects:_ Malakanagiri Koya, Podia Koya (Gotte Koya), Jaganathapuram Koya (Gommu Koya, Godavari Koya), Dorli (Chintoor Koya, Korla, Dora, Dor Koi, Dora Koi, Dorla Koitur, Dorla Koya). Chintoor is the linguistic center. The Malkangiri and Podia varieties are more divergent. A separate language from Gondi. _Lg Use:_ Telugu is their second language but proficiency is low. _Lg Dev:_ Literacy rate in second language: 7%. Literacy centers. Some Telugu materials available. Literacy classes. Telugu, Oriya, and Devanagari scripts. Roman script reportedly preferred by Koya leaders. NT: 1997. _Other:_ Different from Kui and Kuvi. A Scheduled Tribe in India. Swidden agriculturalists; peasant agriculturalists. Traditional religion, Hindu, Christian.

Kudiya (Male Kudiya) [kfg] 2,462 (1981 census). Kerala, Kannur, Kasargod districts; Karnataka, Coorg and Dakshina Kannada districts; Tamil Nadu. _Class:_ Dravidian, Southern, Tulu. _Lg Use:_ Tulu, Kodagu, Kannada, Malayalam spoken with outsiders. _Lg Dev:_ Literacy rate in second language: 30% (1981 census). Kannada and Malayalam scripts. _Other:_ A Scheduled Tribe in India. Traditional religion mixed with Hindu.

Kudmali (Kurmali, Kurumali, Kurmali Thar, Bedia, Dharua) [kyw] 37,000 (1997). Bihar; West Bengal; Orissa, Assam, Darrang, Sonitpur, Golaghat, Jorhat districts. _Class:_ Indo-European, Indo-Iranian, Indo-Aryan, Eastern zone, Bihari. _Dialects:_ Related to Sadri. Possibly the same as Panchpargania. _Lg Use:_ Spoken by some Scheduled Tribes and Castes, including Bedia of West Bengal and Dharua. _Other:_ 'Mahato' could be an alternate name. Kudmali is spoken by the Kurmi people of Assam who were brought to the tea gardens from Bihar, Orissa, and West Bengal. Hindu.

Kui (Kandh, Khondi, Khond, Khondo, Kanda, Kodu, Kodulu, Kuinga, Kuy) [kxu] 717,000 (1997). Orissa, Phulbani, Koraput, Ganjam districts, Udayagiri area in Ganjam; Andhra Pradesh; Madhya Pradesh; Tamil Nadu. _Class:_ Dravidian, South-Central, Gondi-Kui, Konda-Kui, Manda-Kui, Kui-Kuvi. _Dialects:_ Khondi, Gumsai. _Lg Use:_ Spoken by the Dal and Sitha Kandha as first language. _Lg Dev:_ Oriya script. NT: 1954–1975. _Other:_ Different from Kuvi and Koya (Koi). Kondh is a Scheduled Tribe. Christian, traditional religion, Hindu.

Kukna (Kanara, Kanara Konkani, Kokna, Kokni) [kex] 570,419 (1981 census). Gujarat, Dangs, and Valsad districts; Maharashtra, Dhule, Nasik, and Thane districts; Dadra and Nagar Haveli; Karnataka, Dakshina Kannada (Kanara) District; Rajasthan. _Class:_ Indo-European, Indo-Iranian, Indo-Aryan, Southern zone, Konkani. _Lg Use:_ Trade language. 100,000 second-language speakers (1998). _Lg Dev:_ Literacy rate in first language: 10% to 30%. Some literacy work being done. Gujarati and Devanagari scripts. Radio programs. NT: 1977–2002. _Other:_ May be the same as Dhanki. Agriculturalists. Hindu, Christian.

Kulung (Khulunge Rai, Kulu Ring, Khulung, Kholung) [kle] Sikkim; West Bengal, Jalpaiguri District; Uttaranchal, Dehradun. See main entry under Nepal.

Kumarbhag Paharia (Malto, Malti, Maltu, Maler, Mal, Mad, Paharia, Pahariya, Kumar) [kmj] 20,179 (2000 WCD). Population includes several thousand in West Bengal. Jharkhand, central part of former Santhal Pargana District, Sundar Pahari Block of Godda District, and all but southernmost block of Pakaur District. Reported in at least Bankura, Barddhaman, and Murshidabad districts of West Bengal; Orissa, Mayurbhanj. _Class:_ Dravidian, Northern. _Dialects:_ Low comprehension of Mal Paharia. Related to Kurux. Lexical similarity 80% with Mal Paharia. _Lg Use:_ Vigorous. All domains. Positive language attitude. Low bilingualism in Hindi and Bengali. _Other:_ Part of the Malto ethnic group. Hills, plains. Forest. 300 to 600 meters. Agriculturalists: rice, maize, wheat, sugarcane, lentils, vegetables; firewood gatherers; fishermen; hunters. Traditional religion.

Kumauni (Kamaoni, Kumaoni, Kumau, Kumawani, Kumgoni, Kumman, Kunayaoni) [kfy] 2,360,000 in India (1998). Uttaranchal, Almora, Nainital, Pithoragarh, Bageshwar, Champawat, Udhamsingh Nagar districts; Assam; Bihar; Delhi; Madhya Pradesh; Maharashtra; Nagaland. Central Kumauni is in Almora and northern Nainital, Northeastern Kumauni is in Pithoragarh, Southeastern Kumauni is in Southeastern Nainital, Western Kumauni is west of Almora and Nainital. Also spoken in Nepal. _Class:_ Indo-European, Indo-Iranian, Indo-Aryan, Northern zone, Central Pahari. _Dialects:_ Central Kumauni, Northeastern Kumauni, Southeastern Kumauni, Western Kumauni. People report the eastern dialects to be different. Names sometimes listed for dialects or subgroups are: Askoti, Bhabari of Rampur, Chaugarkhiya, Danpuriya, Gangola, Johari, Khasparjiya, Kumaiya Pachhai, Pashchimi, Phaldakotiya, Kumaoni, Rau-Chaubhaisi, Sirali, Soriyali. Most closely related to Garwhali and Nepali. _Lg Use:_ Used in the home and villages. All ages. The Southeast dialect is reported to be 'sweet'. The Central one is the most accepted. Hindi valued as the language of education and progress. English valued as the gateway to success. Hindi used in towns and markets. Spoken by most men, the few women who have been to school, and school-aged children. Men can converse about common topics, some women only about trade. _Lg Dev:_ Literacy rate in second language: 58% (73% men, 41% women). Motivation not high. Kumauni script. Poetry. Magazines. Radio programs. Dictionary. Grammar. Bible portions: 1825–1876. _Other:_ Mountain slope. 1,500 to 2,500 meters. Hindu.

Kupia (Valmiki) [key] 4,000 (1983 SIL). Andhra Pradesh, Vishakhapatnam and East Godavari districts. _Class:_ Indo-European, Indo-Iranian, Indo-Aryan, Eastern zone, Oriya. _Lg Use:_ Used only in the home. Speakers use Telegu in the market, work, travel. _Lg Dev:_ NT: 1983. _Other:_ A Scheduled Tribe in India. People called 'Valmiki'. Ethnic Valmiki are not the same as first-language Kupia speakers. Agriculturalists. Traditional religion, Christian.

Kurichiya (Kurichia, Kurichchia, Kowohans, Kurichiyars, Kuruchans) [kfh] 29,375 (1981 census). Kerala, Wynad, Kannur, Kozhikode districts; Tamil Nadu, Dharampuri District. _Class:_ Dravidian, Unclassified. _Lg Use:_ Speakers are shifting to Malayalam in Kerala and Kannada in Tamil Nadu. The Central Institute of Indian Languages lists this as an endangered language. Further study is being done at Annamalai University. _Lg Dev:_ Grammar. _Other:_ A Scheduled Tribe in India. Consider themselves higher caste than Brahmin. Forest. Agriculturalists. Hindu, traditional religion, Christian.

Kurmukar (Karmakar, Kamar, Kumar, Kumhar, Kumbhakar) [kfv] 3,000 in India (2000). Assam, Barpeta, Goalpara, Dhubri districts; Tripura, West Bengal, Bihar, a few in Madhya Pradesh. Also spoken in Nepal. _Class:_ Indo-European, Indo-Iranian, Indo-Aryan, Eastern zone, Bengali-Assamese. _Lg Use:_ Speakers have high proficiency in Assamese; educated speak Hindi and English. _Other:_ A dialect of Bengali "which differs a lot from the standard" (Singh). Hindu.

Kurumba (Korambar, Kuramwari, Kurumar, Kuremban, Kuruba, Kurubas Kuruban, Kurubar, Kuruma, Kuruman, Kurumans, Kurumbas, Kurumban, Palu Kurumba, Southern Kannada, Canarese) [kfi] 179,793 (2000 WCD). Tamil Nadu, Coimbatore District, Pollachi, Western Fields, Western Gate Hills; Dharmapuri, South Arcot, and Chingalpattu districts; in pockets in Salem and North Arcot districts; Theni District, Cumbari Valley; Dindukat District, Sirumalai, Senkuruchi Hillocks, Palani; Karnataka; Andhra Pradesh. _Class:_ Dravidian, Southern, Tamil-Kannada, Tamil-Kodagu, Kodagu. _Lg Use:_ Low bilingual proficiency in Tamil and Standard Kannada. _Lg Dev:_ Younger generation over 50% literate, older generation less. Tamil script. _Other:_ There are reported to be 3 groups of Gowda: Okkili, Anuppa, and Kurumba. These may be languages or dialects of one language. Sometimes referred to as Alu or Palu Kurumba, but it is a different language from Alu Kurumba in the hills. Kurumba and Kuruman are different Scheduled Tribes. Plains. Agriculturalists; pastoralists; urban workers. Hindu, traditional religion, Christian.

Kurumba, Alu (Alu Kurumba Nonstandard Kannada, Pal Kurumba, Hal Kurumba) [xua] 2,500 (1997). Tamil Nadu, eastern side of Nilgiri Hills. _Class:_ Dravidian, Southern, Tamil-Kannada, Tamil-Kodagu, Kodagu. _Dialects:_ Lexical similarity 80% between Alu and Pal. _Lg Use:_ Vigorous. Some speakers also use Tamil, Standard Kannada, or Southern Nonstandard Kannada. _Lg Dev:_ Literacy rate in first language: below 1%. Literacy rate in second language: 15% to 25%. _Other:_ A Scheduled Tribe in India. Hunter-gatherers; tea and coffee laborers; beekeepers; horticulturalists. Traditional religion, Hindu, Christian.

Kurumba, Betta (Betta Kurumba Nonstandard Tamil, Kadu Kurumba, Urali Kurumba) [xub] 32,000 (2003). Tamil Nadu, Nilgiri District; Karnataka, Mysore District, north side of Nilgiri Hills, just east of Kerala border; Kerala, Wynad District. _Class:_ Dravidian, Southern, Tamil-Kannada, Tamil-Kodagu, Tamil-Malayalam, Tamil. _Dialects:_ A nonstandard variety of Tamil or Kannada. May be the same as Betta Kuruba in Coorg District. Lexical similarity 59% to 77% among groups that are called 'Betta Kurumba'. _Lg Use:_ The Central Institute of Indian Languages lists Urali Kurumba as endangered. It is being studied by Annamalai University. _Lg Dev:_ Literacy rate in second language: 15% to 25%. Favorable attitude toward literacy. Grammar. _Other:_ 'Kadu Kurumba' means 'Jungle Shepherds'. 'Betta Kurumba' means 'Hill Shepherds'. There are 3 subdivisions: Ane (elephant) Kurumba, Bevina (neem tree) Kurumba, and Kolli (firebrand) Kurumba. A Scheduled Tribe in India. Tropical forest. Swidden agriculturalists; basket makers; laborers. Traditional religion, Hindu, Christian.

Kurumba, Jennu (Jennu Kurumba Nonstandard Kannada, Jen Kurumba, Ten Kurumba, Jennu Nudi, Naikan, Kattu Nayaka, Naik Kurumba) [xuj] 35,000 (1997). North side of Nilgiri Hills on the border between Tamil Nadu and Karnataka, just east of the Kerala border, Mysore and Kodagu districts of Karnataka; Kerala, Wynad District. _Class:_ Dravidian, Southern, Tamil-Kannada, Tamil-Kodagu, Kodagu. _Dialects:_ May or may not be the same as Jeinu Kuruba, a variety of Kannada. Lexical similarity 61% to 83% among varieties called 'Jennu Kurumba', less than 60% lexical similarity with Betta Kurumba dialects. _Lg Use:_ Positive language attitude. Speakers have low proficiency in Kannada, Malayalam, or Tamil. _Lg Dev:_ Literacy rate in second language: Low. Attitudes favorable toward literacy. _Other:_ Jennu Kurumba means 'Honey Shepherds'. A Scheduled Tribe in India. Tropical forest. Hunter-gatherers; day laborers, agriculturalists. Traditional religion, Hindu, Christian.

Kurumba, Mullu [kpb] 6,000 (1994 Singh). Tamil Nadu, Nilgiri District; Kerala, Wynad District. _Class:_ Dravidian, Southern, Tamil-Kannada, Tamil-Kodagu, Kodagu. _Dialects:_ Lexical similarity 34% to 41% with other Kurumba languages. _Lg Dev:_ Favorable motivation toward literacy. _Other:_ A Scheduled Tribe in India. Hunters; agriculturalists; field laborers. Traditional religion, Hindu, Christian.

Kurux (Uraon, Kurukh, Kunrukh, Kadukali, Kurka, Oraon, Urang, Kisan, Kunha, Kunhar, Kunuk, Kunna, Kuda, Kora, Koda, Kola, Morva, Birhor) [kru] 2,053,000 in India (1997). Population includes 1,834,000 Oraon, 219,000 Kisan. Bihar; Chhattisgarh, Raigarh, Surguja districts; Jharkhand Ranchi District; West Bengal, Jalpaigiri District; Orissa, Sundargarh District; Assam; Tripura. Also spoken in Bangladesh. _Class:_ Dravidian, Northern. _Dialects:_ Oraon, Kisan. Kisan and Oraon have 73% intelligibility. Oraon becoming standardized. Related to Malto. Different from Nepali Kurux. _Lg Dev:_ Literacy rate in first language: 23% Oraon, 17% Kisan. Devanagari script. Dictionary. Grammar. Bible: 2000. _Other:_ Kisan and Oraon are Scheduled Tribes in India.

Kuvi (Kuwi, Kuvinga, Kuvi Kond, Kond, Khondi, Khondh, Jatapu) [kxv] 300,000 (1990 UBS). Orissa, mainly

Koraput District, also Kalahandi, Ganjam, and Phulbani districts; Andhra Pradesh, Vishakhapatnam, Vizianagaram, Srikakulam districts. *Class:* Dravidian, South-Central, Gondi-Kui, Konda-Kui, Manda-Kui, Kui-Kuvi. *Lg Use:* The Dongria and Kuvi subgroups speak Kuvi as first language. *Lg Dev:* Oriya script. NT: 1987. *Other:* Kondh is a Scheduled Tribe in India. Distinct from Kui and Koi (Koya). Hindu.

Ladakhi (Ladaphi, Ladhakhi, Ladak, Ladwags) [lbj] 102,000 in India (1997). Population includes 29,800 to 33,300 Shamma (Voegelin and Voegelin 1977.328). Population total all countries: 114,000. Jammu and Kashmir, Ladakh District, 250 villages and hamlets. Also spoken in China. *Class:* Sino-Tibetan, Tibeto-Burman, Himalayish, Tibeto-Kanauri, Tibetic, Tibetan, Western, Ladakhi. *Dialects:* Leh (Central Ladakhi), Shamma (Sham, Shamskat, Lower Ladakhi), Nubra Ladakhi. Perhaps 30% to 40% intelligibility of Tibetan. Leh is used as the medium of communication. Leh speakers understand Zangskari and Changthang at more than 90% on recorded text tests. Not known if speakers of all dialects understand Leh well. Leh is in Leh and surrounding areas. Shamma is west of Leh along the Indus Valley and to the south of Khaltse. Nubra is in Nubra Tahsil north of Leh. Lexical similarity 71% to 83% with Purik, 53% to 60% with Tibetan, 84% to 94% among 5 main dialects. *Lg Use:* All ages. Many speakers in urban areas use Urdu, Hindi, or English, but rural speakers are mainly monolingual in Ladakhi. *Lg Dev:* Literacy rate in second language: Men: 36%, women: 12% in Hindi, Urdu, Tibetan, or English (1991). Tibetan script. Grammar. Bible: 1948. *Other:* Written Ladakhi is distinct from the spoken forms. The dialect of Leh has been acknowledged as standard spoken Ladakhi. It is the medium of Leh radio broadcasts and the standard medium of communication among all Ladakh dialects, including Changthang and Zangskari (Paldan 2002). SOV; postpositions; genitives, relatives before noun heads; articles, adjectives numerals after noun heads; suffixes indicate case of noun phrase; ergative; causatives; comparative; CCVCC or CCCVV maximum; nontonal. Mountain valleys. 2,400 to 5,000 meters. Agriculturalists: wheat, barley; pastoralists: yaks, goats, sheep (cashmere wool); cottage industries: weaving, jewelry making, religious artifact production. Buddhist, Muslim, Christian.

Lambadi (Lamani, Lamadi, Lambani, Labhani, Lambara, Lavani, Lemadi, Lumadale, Labhani Muka, Banjara, Banjari, Bangala, Banjori, Banjuri, Brinjari, Gohar-Herkeri, Goola, Gurmarti, Gormati, Kora, Singali, Sugali, Sukali, Tanda, Vanjari, Wanji) [lmn] 2,867,000 (1994). Population includes 1,961,000 Lambadi (1994), plus 769,120 Banjari. Andhra Pradesh; Madhra Pradesh; Himachal Pradesh; Gujarat; Tamil Nadu; Maharashtra; Karnataka; Orissa; West Bengal. *Class:* Indo-European, Indo-Iranian, Indo-Aryan, Central zone, Rajasthani, Unclassified. *Dialects:* Maharashtra Lamani, Karnataka Lamani (Mysore Lamani), Andhra Pradesh Lamani (Telugu Lamani). *Lg Use:* Speakers also use Telugu, Kannada, or Marathi. *Lg Dev:* Literacy rate in second language: 18% Marathi. Each of the three dialects needs a different script: Maharashtra uses Devanagari script, Karnataka uses Kannada script, Andhra Pradesh uses Telugu script. NT: 1999. *Other:* A Scheduled Tribe in Orissa, a Scheduled Caste in Karnataka, Haryana, Punjab, Himachal Pradesh. 'Gormati' is self name. SOV. Agriculturalists; laborers. Traditional religion, Hindu, Christian.

Lamkang ("Lamgang," "Hiroi-Lamgang," Lamkaang, Lamkang Naga) [lmk] 10,000 in India (1999 village govt. census). Southeast Manipur, Chandel District, 6 villages in West of Chandel District east of Shuganu, 6 villages on the road between Chalong and Mombi New, 18 villages

on roads between Palel and Chandel town and Palel and Sibong; Nagaland; Dimapur, Thamlakhuren; 1 village in Myanmar: Betukshangreng, 20 km from the border with Southeast Manipur. Also spoken in Myanmar. *Class:* Sino-Tibetan, Tibeto-Burman, Kuki-Chin-Naga, Kuki-Chin, Northern. *Dialects:* Closest to Anal Naga. *Lg Use:* All ages. All understand Meitei. Some also speak Hindi or English. *Lg Dev:* Literacy rate in second language: 40% Meitei: 10 to 40 year olds (Towar 2000). Literacy help requested, only 2% can read Roman script. Roman script; Burmese script in Myanmar. NT: 2002. *Other:* A Scheduled Tribe in India. "Lamgang" and "Hiroi-Lamgang" are not correct names. SOV; postpositions; genitives before head nouns; adjectives and numerals after noun heads; noun prefixes mark person, number of possessor; VC, CV, CVC, CCCVC. Mountain slope. Scrub forest. Agriculturalists. Christian.

Lepcha (Lapche, Rong, Rongke, Rongpa, Nünpa) [lep] 38,000 in India (1997). Population total all countries: 75,826. Sikkim, Dzongu District; West Bengal, Darjeeling District, Kalimpong. Also spoken in Bhutan, Nepal. *Class:* Sino-Tibetan, Tibeto-Burman, Himalayish, Tibeto-Kanauri, Lepcha. *Dialects:* Ilammu, Tamsangmu, Rengjongmu. Has been classified both in Himalayan and Naga groups. Classification still uncertain. *Lg Use:* Vigorous in Sikkim. In Sikkim, all ages. *Lg Dev:* Literacy rate in second language: 26% (1971). Taught in primary schools. Has own script. Dictionary. Grammar. NT: 1989. *Other:* A Scheduled Tribe in India. 'Lepcha' is the name of both people and language. Language of instruction in some schools in Sikkim. Up to 1,200 meters. Agriculturalists; pastoralists. Buddhist.

Lhomi (Lhoket, Shing Saapa) [lhm] 1,000 in India. West Bengal, Darjeeling. *Lg Dev:* Literacy rate in first language: below 1%. Literacy rate in second language: 5% to 25% (men). *Other:* Traditional religion, Buddhist (Lamaist). See main entry under Nepal.

Limbu (Limbo, Lumbu) [lif] 28,000 in India (1997). Sikkim, mainly West District; West Bengal, Darjeeling District. *Other:* Buddhist, traditional religion, Hindu. See main entry under Nepal.

Lisu (Yobin, Yawyin) [lis] 1,000 in India (2000 J.R.L. Breton). Arunachal Pradesh, Changlang District, Miao and Vijaynagar circles. *Lg Dev:* Literacy rate is low. *Other:* Script is consistent across country borders. Agriculturalists. Christian, Buddhist. See main entry under China.

Lodhi (Lodha, Lodi, Lohi, Lozi) [lbm] 75,000 (1997). Orissa, Mayurbhanj and Baleshwar districts; West Bengal, Medinipur District. *Class:* Austro-Asiatic, Munda, South Munda, Koraput Munda, Sora-Juray-Gorum, Sora-Juray. *Dialects:* Related to Sora. *Lg Use:* They are reported to be fluent in Bengali. *Lg Dev:* Literacy rate in second language: 9% (1981 census). *Other:* Lodha is a Scheduled Tribe in India. Hindu, Christian.

Lohar, Gade (Gaduliya Lohar, Lohpitta, Rajput Lohar, Bagri Lohar, Bhubaliya Lohar, Lohari, Gara, Domba, Dombiali, Chitodi Lohar, Panchal Lohar, Belani, Dhunkuria, Kanwar Khati, Chittoriya Lohar, Gadia Lohar) [gda] 1,009 (2000 WCD). Rajasthan; Gujarat; Madhya Pradesh; Maharashtra; Uttar Pradesh; Delhi; Haryana; Punjab. *Class:* Indo-European, Indo-Iranian, Indo-Aryan, Central zone, Rajasthani, Unclassified. *Dialects:* No significant dialect differences. May be the same as Loarki listed in Pakistan. *Lg Dev:* Literacy rate in second language: 40% (1981 census). Devanagari script. *Other:* 'Gade Lohar' refers to people who travel in bullock carts and are blacksmiths. Nomadic blacksmiths; carpentry; construction; agriculturalists; animal husbandry. Hindu.

Lohar, Lahul (Garas, Lohar) [lhl] 750 (1996). Himachal Pradesh, Lahul Valley. *Class:* Indo-European, Indo-Iranian, Indo-Aryan, Unclassified. *Dialects:* A different language from Gade Lohar. *Lg Use:* Speakers also use Hindi. *Lg Dev:* Devanagari script. *Other:* Lohar is a Scheduled Caste in Himachal Pradesh, all of whom do not speak this language. Similar name, occupation to 'Gade Lohar'. Metalsmiths.

Magahi (Magadhi, Magaya, Maghai, Maghaya, Maghori, Magi, Magodhi, Bihari, Megahi) [mag] 13,000,000 (2002). Bihar, Gaya, Bhagalpur, eastern Patna districts; Jharkhand, northern Chotanagpur Division, Hazaribagh District; West Bengal, Maldah District. *Class:* Indo-European, Indo-Iranian, Indo-Aryan, Eastern zone, Bihari. *Dialects:* Southern Magahi, Northern Magahi, Central Magahi. *Lg Use:* Used as a religious language. Positive language attitude. Educated people, city dwellers, and those who travel know Hindi well. Much Hindi exposure through TV and radio. *Lg Dev:* Literacy rate in first language: 30%. Literacy rate in second language: 30% Hindi. Bhojpuri can use Magahi materials. Devanagari script. Magazines. Newspapers. Radio programs. Grammar. NT: 1826. *Other:* Hindu, traditional religion, Jainism.

Magar, Eastern (Magari, Manggar, Mangari, Magarkura) [mgp] 67,691 in India (2000). Sikkim, concentrated in South District, scattered in East District. *Lg Use:* Used in the home. Speakers also use Nepali. *Other:* Mountain slope. 1,262 to 1,899 meters. Agri-culturalists: rice, corn, wheat; hunters. See main entry under Nepal.

Mahali (Mahili, Mahli, Mahle) [mjx] 66,000 (1991). Jharkhand, Chotanagpur Region; Orissa, Balasore, Mayurbhanj, Keonjhar districts; West Bengal; Assam. *Class:* Austro-Asiatic, Munda, North Munda, Kherwari, Santali. *Dialects:* Possible dialect of Santali. *Lg Use:* Speakers also use Oriya. *Other:* Mahli is a Scheduled Tribe, reported speaking Sadri as first language in Jharkhand, Thar in Orissa, and Bengali in West Bengal. Christian.

Maithili (Maitli, Maitili, Methli, Tirahutia, Bihari, Tirhuti, Tirhutia, Apabhramsa) [mai] 22,000,000 in India (1981). Population total all countries: 24,797,582. Bihar, from Muzaffarpur on the west, past the Kosi on the east to western Purnia District, to the districts of Munger and Bhagalpur in the south, and the Himalayan foothills on the north. Cultural and linguistic centers are the towns of Madhubani and Darbhanga. Janakpur also important culturally and religiously. Delhi, Calcutta, Bombay have thousands. Many have settled abroad. Also spoken in Nepal. *Class:* Indo-European, Indo-Iranian, Indo-Aryan, Eastern zone, Bihari. *Dialects:* Standard Maithili, Southern Standard Maithili, Eastern Maithili (Khotta, Kortha, Kortha Bihari), Western Maithili, Jolaha, Central Colloquial Maithili (Sotipura), Kisan, Dehati. Caste variation more than geographic variation in dialects. Functional intelligibility among all dialects, including those in Nepal. Closest to Magahi. Brahmin and non-Brahmin dialects average 91% lexical similarity. *Lg Use:* Official language. Spoken by Brahmin and other high caste or educated Hindus, who influence the culture and language, and other castes. There is a Maithili Academy. Linguistics and literature are taught at the L. N. Mithila University in Darbhanga and Patna University. Used in the home, village, town, or cities. Language attitudes are influenced by caste, ranging from superiority to resentment. Non-Brahmin speech viewed as inferior. Hindi considered superior, Nepali generally accepted. Hindi, Nepali, English, Bhojpuri, Bengali used mainly for commerce or social interaction outside the home by men or working women with various degrees of proficiency from marketing only to fluency. In cities some may use Hindi, Nepali, or English in the home. *Lg Dev:* Literacy rate in first language: 25% to 50%. Literacy rate in second language: 25% to 50%. If they can read Nepali or Hindi, they can read Maithili. The educated read Hindi,

Nepali, or English books for pleasure. Literacy effort needed. Some literacy work in India. Devanagari script. Poetry. Magazines. Newspapers. Radio programs. Films. TV. Dictionary. Grammar. *Other:* SOV; postpositions; genitives, articles, numerals before noun heads, adjectives before and after noun heads; 1 prefix, 1 suffix; object marked by position; person, gender, animate distinguished, obligatory for subject; transitives; passives; causatives; comparatives; V, VC, VCC, CV, CVC, CVV, CCV, CVCC, CCVCC; nontonal. Plains. Tropical forest, gallery forest. 80 meters. Peasant agriculturalists: rice. Hindu, Muslim.

Majhi (Manjhi) [mjz] 246 in Sikkim (1981 census). Jharkhand, Gumla District; Sikkim, South District, Majhigaon near Jorethang, East District, Majhitar near Rangpo; West Bengal; Assam. *Lg Use:* Majhi used rarely at home; younger generation uses Nepali in Sikkim. *Lg Dev:* Literacy rate in second language: below 7%. Girls not sent to school at all. *Other:* Distinct from Majhi dialect of Panjabi or Bote-Majhi of Nepal. Commerce, contract workers (Sikkim), agriculturalists (plains). Hindu. See main entry under Nepal.

Majhwar (Majhvar, Manjhi, Manjhia) [mmj] 27,958. Chhattisgarh, Bilaspur District, Katghora tahsil, Raigarh and Surguja districts; Uttar Pradesh, Allahabad, Varanasi, Mirzapur districts; Sikkim. *Class:* Unclassified. *Dialects:* Possibly a dialect of Asuri. *Other:* A Scheduled Tribe in Chhattisgarh, reportedly speaking Chhattisgarhi as first language. Hindu.

Mal Paharia (Malto, Malti, Maltu, Maler, Malpaharia, Marpaharia, Mal Pahariya, Mal, Manlati, Mar, Maw, Mawdo, Mawer, Mawer Nondi, Mad, Mader, Dehri, Paharia, Parsi) [mkb] 51,000 to 71,000 (1994). Possibly 40,000 in West Bengal. Ethnic population: 110,983 (2000 WCD). Jharkhand southern part of former Santal Pargana District, Ramgarh Hills. Mainly in Dumka District, but many villages are in Pakaur, southern Godda, and Deoghar districts, and a few as far north as Depart village north of Borio in Sahibganj District. Reported in at least Bankura, Barddhaman, and Murshidabad districts of West Bengal. Possibly in Bangladesh. *Class:* Indo-European, Indo-Iranian, Indo-Aryan, Eastern zone, Bengali-Assamese. *Dialects:* Not inherently intelligible with Kumarbhag Paharia, Sauria Paharia, Bengali, or Hindi. Part of the Malto ethnic group. Speak a variety similar to Kharia Thar of Manbhum (Bihar). Dialects have 85% or higher lexical similarity with each other, but 59% with Mal Paharia Barmasiya and 55% with Khorta Babudoha. *Lg Use:* Vigorous. All domains. Positive language attitude. Some have shifted to Bengali or Khorta. *Lg Dev:* Literacy rate in second language: 12.8% male, 2.3% female, average 7.6% (1981). Bible portions: 1994. *Other:* A Scheduled Tribe in India. Hills, plains. Forest. 300 to 700 meters. Firewood gatherers; agriculturalists. Traditional religion, Christian.

Malankuravan (Malaikuravan, Malakkuravan, Mala Koravanm, Male Kuravan) [mjo] 7,339 (1981 census). Tamil Nadu, Kanniyakumari District; Kerala, Trivandrum, Kollam, Kottayam districts, Chittar, Kattachira, Rajanpara in the Ranni Range, Pathanamthitta Taluk, Nottakal in the Pathanapuram Taluk, on the banks of the Pampa River and in the forest tracts of Neduvanged Taluk. *Class:* Dravidian, Unclassified. *Dialect:* Malayadiars. *Lg Use:* Speakers also use Tamil. *Other:* A Scheduled Tribe in India. Reported to speak Malayalam as first language. Agriculturalists; hunters and gatherers. Traditional religion, Hindu.

Malapandaram (Malapantaram, Malepantaram, Hill Pantaram, Pandaram Basha) [mjp] 3,147 (1981 census). Kerala, Kottayam, Ernakulam, Pathanamthitta and Koliam districts; Tamil Nadu. *Class:* Dravidian, Southern, Tamil-Kannada, Tamil-Kodagu, Tamil-Malayalam, Malayalam. *Lg Use:* Speakers also use Malayalam. *Lg Dev:* Literacy rate in second language: 37% (44% males, 31% females) (1991 census). *Other:* A Scheduled Tribe in India. Hindu, traditional religion.

Malaryan (Arayans, Karingal, Malai Arayan, Malayarayan, Malayarayar, Male Arayans, Maley Arayan, Vazhiyammar) [mjq] 16,068 (1991 census). Kerala, Ernakulam, Idukki, Kottayam, and Trichur districts; Tamil Nadu. *Class:* Dravidian, Southern, Tamil-Kannada, Tamil-Kodagu, Tamil-Malayalam, Malayalam. *Lg Use:* May be in process of language shift to Malayalam. *Lg Dev:* Literacy rate in second language: 76% Malayalam. Grammar. *Other:* A Scheduled Tribe in India. They are reported to speak a variety of Malayalam as first language. Possibly the same as Kanikkaran. Agriculturalists. Hindu, Christian.

Malavedan (Malai Vedan, Malavetan, Towetan, Vedans) [mjr] 15,241 (1991 census). Kerala, Ernakulam, Kottayam, Koliam, Trivandrum districts; Tamil Nadu, Kanniyakumari and Tirunelveli districts. *Class:* Dravidian, Southern, Tamil-Kannada, Tamil-Kodagu, Tamil-Malayalam, Malayalam. *Dialects:* Vetan, Vettuvan. *Lg Use:* First language dying out in Idukki district, being replaced by Malayalam. Speakers in other districts may be retaining the language. Speakers also use Tamil. *Lg Dev:* Literacy rate in second language: 32% (1981 census). *Other:* A Scheduled Tribe in India. Nomadic. Hunter-gatherers. Traditional religion.

Malayalam (Alealum, Malayalani, Malayali, Malean, Maliyad, Mallealle, Mopla) [mal] 35,351,000 in India (1997). Population total all countries: 35,757,100. Kerala, Laccadive Islands, and neighboring states. Also spoken in Bahrain, Fiji, Israel, Malaysia, Qatar, Singapore, United Arab Emirates, United Kingdom. *Class:* Dravidian, Southern, Tamil-Kannada, Tamil-Kodagu, Tamil-Malayalam, Malayalam. *Dialects:* Malabar, Nagari-Malayalam, Malayalam, South Kerala, Central Kerala, North Kerala, Kayavar, Namboodiri, Moplah, Pulaya, Nasrani, Nayar. Caste and communal dialects: Namboodiri, Nayar, Moplah, Pulaya, Nasrani. *Lg Use:* State language of Kerala. The Cochin Jews in Kerala speak Malayalam. *Lg Dev:* Malayalam script. Bible: 1841–2002. *Other:* State language of Kerala. Saivite Hindu, Muslim, Christian, Jewish.

Maldivian (Malikh, Mahl, Malki, Devehi, Divehli, Divehi Bas) [div] 4,500 in India (1997). Minicoy Island in the Laccadive Islands in India. *Lg Use:* Speakers also use Arabic. *Lg Dev:* Literacy rate in first language: 60% to 100%. Literacy rate in second language: 75% to 100%. *Other:* Fishermen. Muslim (Sunni), traditional religion. See main entry under Maldives.

Malvi (Malavi, Mallow, Malwada, Malwi, Ujjaini) [mup] 1,102,000 (1997). Madhya Pradesh, Ujjain, Indore, Rathlam, Mandsaur, Rajgarh districts; Rajasthan, Chittaurgarh, Jhalawar districts; Maharashtra; Gujarat. Sondwari dialect geographically isolated from the others. *Class:* Indo-European, Indo-Iranian, Indo-Aryan, Central zone, Rajasthani, Unclassified. *Dialect:* Bachadi, Bhoyari, Dholewari, Hoshangabad, Jamral, Katiyai, Malvi Proper, Patvi, Rangari, Rangri, Sondwari (Soudhwari). Considered the standard dialect of Southeastern Rajasthani. Nimadi is closest language linguistically with 70% intelligibility. 88% to 99% intelligibility of Ujjaini dialect by other dialects. Lexical similarity 65% to 89% among dialects. *Lg Use:* Speakers of dialects have positive attitudes toward other dialects. About 55% are reported to have high proficiency in Hindi, and 20% to have routine proficiency. *Lg Dev:* Literacy rate in second language: 40%. Government project discontinued due to low response. Devanagari script. Poetry. Radio programs. Dictionary. NT: 1826. *Other:* A survey in 2001 found only 4 dialects: Ujjaini (spoken by Balai and Malvi in Ujjain, Indore, Dewas, Sehore districts), Rajawadi (spoken by Rajputs in

Rathlam, Mandsaur, Nimuch districts), Umadwadi (spoken by Umads in Rajghargh District), Sondhwadi (spoken by Sondhiyas in Jhalawar District, Rajasthan). SOV; nontonal. Plains. Savannah. Agriculturalists. Hindu, Muslim.

Manda [mha] 4,036 (2000 WCD). Orissa, Kalahandi District, Thuamul Rampur Subdivision. *Class:* Dravidian, South-Central, Gondi-Kui, Konda-Kui, Manda-Kui, Manda-Pengo. *Other:* Discovered in 1964.

Mandeali (Mandi, Pahari Mandiyali, Mandiali, Himachali) [mjl] 776,372 (1991 census). Himachal Pradesh, Mandi District. *Class:* Indo-European, Indo-Iranian, Indo-Aryan, Northern zone, Western Pahari. *Dialects:* Preliminary survey suggests Mandeali speakers have functional intelligibility of Dogri-Kangri. Lexical similarity 89% with Palampuri Kangri, 83% with Chambeali. *Lg Use:* All ages. Speakers use Hindi for instruction in school, shops, in cities; Panjabi, shops; or Urdu, middle aged or older. *Lg Dev:* Devanagari script. Radio programs. Grammar. Bible portions: 1970. *Other:* SOV. Mountain slope, valley. 300 to 3,000 meters. Agriculturalists: rice, maize, millet, fruit. Hindu.

Manna-Dora [mju] 18,964 (1981 census). Andhra Pradesh, East Godavari, Srikakulam, Vishakhapatnam, Vizianagaram districts; Tamil Nadu. *Class:* Dravidian, South-Central, Telugu. *Lg Dev:* Literacy rate in second language: 6.8% Telugu (1981 census). Telugu script. *Other:* A Scheduled Tribe in India. Reported to speak Telugu as first language. Agriculturalists.

Mannan (Manne, Mannyod) [mjv] 7,289 (1991 census). Kerala, Idukki District, Udumpanchola, Devikulam, Pirmed tahsils; Tamil Nadu, Madurai district. *Class:* Dravidian, Southern, Tamil-Kannada, Tamil-Kodagu, Tamil-Malayalam. *Dialects:* Little variation between varieties of Mannan with 92% intelligibility, 70% intelligibility of Malayalam. Lexical similarity 86% to 96% between varieties of Mannan, 57% to 61% with Tamil, 56% to 64% with Malayalam. *Lg Use:* Speakers are shifting slowly to Malayalam; used by some children. Used in the home, village, and religious domains. All ages. Positive. Interest in language development. Self-reported good comprehension of Malayalam. Educated and those having contact with outsiders are more bilingual. *Lg Dev:* Literacy rate in second language: 35% Malayalam (41% men, 30% women) (1991 census). Grammar. *Other:* A Scheduled Tribe in Kerala and Tamil Nadu. Not the same as the Scheduled Caste, Mannan in Trivandrum and other adjoining districts of Kerala and Tamil Nadu who speak Malayalam. Romanized spelling is the same but the Scheduled Caste name is pronounced with retroflex double 'n'. Mountain slope. Tropical forest. Agricultural laborers; settled cultivation; animal husbandry; mat weavers. Hindu syncretism with traditional religion.

Marathi (Maharashtra, Maharathi, Malhatee, Marthi, Muruthu) [mar] 68,030,000 in India (1997). Population total all countries: 68,049,787. Maharashtra and adjacent states. Also spoken in Israel, Mauritius. *Class:* Indo-European, Indo-Iranian, Indo-Aryan, Southern zone. *Dialects:* Cochin, Gawdi of Goa, Kasargod, Kosti, Kudali, Nagpuri Marati. 42 dialects. The dialect situation throughout the greater Marathi speaking area is complex. Dialects bordering other major language areas share many features with those languages. See separate entries for dialects or closely related languages: Konkani, Goanese, Deccan, Varhadi-Nagpuri, Gowlan. There is a dialect in Thanjavur District and elsewhere in Tamil Nadu, which has been influenced by Tamil and Kannada words, with at least 100,000 speakers. *Lg Use:* State language of Maharashtra. Spoken by the Mangelas as first language. The Bene Israel are a Marathi-speaking Jewish group of Bombay. 3,00,000 second-language speakers. *Lg Dev:* Literacy rate in first language: 34%. Literacy rate in second language: 34%. Devanagari script. Bible: 1821–2002. *Other:* The Habshi are descended from East African slaves brought to western India, and are Muslim. 'Are' is a synonym for a Marathi caste name. 'Are' also used to refer to Marathi-speaking communities in south India. SOV. Hindu, Muslim, Sikh, Christian, Jain, Jewish (Bene Israel).

Maria (Hill Maria, Madi, Madia, Madiya, Modh, Modi) [mrr] 134,000 (1997). Maharashtra, Garhchiroli (Chanda) District, Etapalli, Bhamragad, and Sironcha tahsils; Madhya Pradesh, Bastar District, Narayanpur and Bijapur tahsils. In Narayanpur, an administrative block of 200 villages is known as 'Abujhmar block'. *Class:* Dravidian, South-Central, Gondi-Kui, Gondi. *Dialects:* Abujmaria (Abujhmadia, Abujhmaria, Abujmariya, Abujmar Maria, Hill Maria), Adewada, Bhamani Maria (Bhamani), Etapally Maria. Etapally Maria is apparently understood by all. A separate language from Muria, Dandami Maria, Northern Gondi, Southern Gondi, and Koya. 76% to 77% intelligibility of other Gondi varieties. Muria Gondi is intelligible to Abujmaria around Narainpur area but not elsewhere. "Distinct from Maria dialect of Chanda District MH" (Natarajan). Intelligibility 90% to 100% of Bhamragarh dialect by other Maria speakers. Maria is intelligible with the speech of the Gatte Maria, an ethnic group. Lexical similarity 59% to 80% among dialects (Beine), 65% to 98% (Vaz). *Lg Use:* All domains. Speakers have negative attitudes toward the varieties mentioned above. Most men can speak some Muria, Halbi or Hindi. *Lg Dev:* Literacy rate in first language: Men 5%, women 0%. Literacy rate in second language: 25% to 50%. Literacy help urgently requested. High interest in literacy. Dictionary. Grammar. *Other:* A Scheduled Tribe in India. Gatte Maria is an ethnic group that seems to not be distinctive linguistically from Abujmaria. Hills. Swidden agriculturalists. Hindu, traditional religion, Christian.

Maria, Dandami (Bison Horn Maria, Maria Gond, Madiya, Dhuru, Dandami Madiya) [daq] 200,000 (2000). Chhattisgarh, central and southern Bastar District, Dantewara tahsil; Maharashtra, Garhichiroli District. *Class:* Dravidian, South-Central, Gondi-Kui, Gondi. *Dialect:* Geedam, Sukma (Suka). Geedam and Bailadila have 95% to 98% intelligibility of each other, 81% of Sukma, but 18% to 21% of Maria, 18% to 45% of Muria. Speakers in Sukma understood Geedam at 81% or lower; those in Bailadila understood Sukma at 92%. May be more than one language. A separate language from Northern Gondi, Southern Gondi, Maria of Garhichiroli, and Koya. *Lg Use:* All ages. *Lg Dev:* Literacy program in progress. Grammar. *Other:* A Scheduled Tribe in India. Speakers are called 'Maria'. Plains, hills. Degraded forests, tropical forest. Swidden agriculturalists; peasant agriculturalists; hunter-gatherers. Hindu, Traditional religion.

Marwari (Marvari, Rajasthani) [rwr] 13,000,000 in India (2002 Gusain). Population total all countries: 13,022,637. Rajasthan, Jodhpur, Jaisalmer, Barmer, Bikaner, Churu, Pali, Jalore districts; Gujarat; Madhya Pradesh; Punjab; Delhi; Haryana; Uttar Pradesh; throughout India. Also spoken in Nepal, Pakistan. *Class:* Indo-European, Indo-Iranian, Indo-Aryan, Central zone, Rajasthani, Marwari. *Dialect:* Barmeri, Bikaneri, Jaisalmeri, Standard Marwari (Jodhpuri). The standard form of Rajasthani. May or may not be different from Marwari of Pakistan. 67% intel- ligibility by Shekhawati, 61% by Godwari, 54% by Mewari, 54% by Dhundari, 45% by Harauti, 45% by Mewati. Lexical similarity 57% to 69% between dialects; 49% to 74% with Merwari, 51% to 68% with Shekhawati, 50% to 72% with Godwari, 56% to 70% with Mewari, 53% to 60% with Dhundari, 50% to 60% with Harauti, 50% to 61% with Mewati; 80% to 85% among some Gujarat and Rajasthan Marwari Bhil dialects; 75% to 80% with Wagdi; 75% to 83% with Patelia; 67% to 87% with

Adiwasi Girasia; 67% to 84% with Rajput Girasia. *Lg Use:* National language. Speakers also use Hindi. *Lg Dev:* Literacy rate in first language: 5% to 10%. Literacy rate in second language: 50% to 75%. Devanagari script. NT: 1820–1821. *Other:* Desert. Hindu, Jain, Muslim.

Mawchi (Mauchi, Mavchi, Mawachi, Mowchi, Mawchi Bhil) [mke] 76,000 (1997). Southwest Gujarat; Maharashtra, Dhule District. *Class:* Indo-European, Indo-Iranian, Indo-Aryan, Central zone, Bhil. *Dialects:* Gamti, Mawchi, Padvi. *Lg Use:* Speakers also use Marathi. *Lg Dev:* Literacy rate in first language: 5% to 10%. Literacy rate in second language: 25% to 50%. NT: 1989. *Other:* A Scheduled Tribe in Maharashtra. Agriculturalists. Traditional religion.

Meitei (Meithei, Meithe, Mithe, Mitei, Meiteilon, Meiteiron, Manipuri, Menipuri, Kathe, Kathi, Ponna) [mni] 1,240,000 in India (1997). Population total all countries: 1,261,000. Manipur (most); Assam, Cachar, Karimganji; Nagaland; Tripura, West and North Tripura districts; Uttar Pradesh; West Bengal. Also spoken in Bangladesh, Myanmar. *Class:* Sino-Tibetan, Tibeto-Burman, Meitei. *Dialects:* Meitei, Loi (Chakpa), Pangal (Manipuri Muslim). Intelligibility of Meitei in Bangladesh is difficult. *Lg Use:* Official language. Trade language. Speakers also use Hindi. *Lg Dev:* Literacy rate in second language: 24%. Bengali script; Meitei Mayak script in Bangladesh. Dictionary. Grammar. Bible: 1984. *Other:* Mainly rural. 7 clans (Ningthonia, Luwang, Angom, Moirang, Khabanaganba, Chonglei). They had an earlier script called 'Meitei Mayek'. Valley. Agriculturalists: rice, vegetables; fishermen 60%; government workers 20%; technicians 10% businessmen 10%; weavers; wood craftsmen. Hindu, traditional religion (Sana Mahi), Muslim, Christian.

Merwari (Ajmeri) [wry] 1,312 (2000 WCD). Rajasthan, Ajmer, Nagaur districts. *Class:* Indo-European, Indo-Iranian, Indo-Aryan, Central zone, Rajasthani, Marwari. *Dialects:* Lexical similarity 60% to 73% between varieties of Merwari in Ajmer and Nagaur districts; 49% to 74% with Marwari, 58% to 80% with Shekhawati, 44% to 70% with Godwari, 54% to 72% with Mewari, 62% to 70% with Dhundari, 57% to 67% with Harauti. *Lg Use:* Speakers also use Hindi.

Mewari (Mewadi) [mtr] 1,058,000 (1997). Rajasthan, Udaipur, Bhilwara, Chittoaurgarh districts; Gujarat; Haryana; Delhi; Madhya Pradesh; Uttar Pradesh. *Class:* Indo-European, Indo-Iranian, Indo-Aryan, Central zone, Rajasthani, Marwari. *Dialects:* Gorawati, Sarwari, Khairari. 54% intelligibility of Marwari. Lexical similarity 69% to 81% between dialects, 56% to 70% with Marwari, 54% to 72% with Merwari, 57% to 66% with Shekhawati, 51% to 73% with Godwari, 56% to 64% with Dhundari, 61% to 71% with Harauti. *Lg Use:* Mewari is spoken as first language by Scheduled Tribe Bhil Gametia and 7 Scheduled Castes. Speakers also use Hindi. *Lg Dev:* Devanagari script. Bible portions: 1815. *Other:* Different from Mewati, dialect of Haryanvi. SOV. Hindu, traditional religion.

Mewati (Mewathi) [wtm] 5,000,000 (2002 Gusain). Rajasthan, Alwar, Bharatpur, Dholpur districts; Uttar Pradesh, Madhura District; Haryana, Gurgaon, Faridabad districts. *Class:* Indo-European, Indo-Iranian, Indo-Aryan, Central zone, Unclassified. *Dialects:* 45% intelligibility of Marwari. Lexical similarity 72% to 77% with Hindi, 63% to 68% with Haryanvi, 57% to 70% with Shekhawati, 62% to 67% with Dhundari, 52% to 70% with Harauti, 68% to 71% with Braj Bhasha. *Lg Use:* Speakers also use Hindi. *Other:* Many Urdu loanwords. Muslim.

Miju-Mishmi (Kaman, Mishmi, Miji, Miju) [mxj] 6,500 (2001). Assam; Arunachal Pradesh, Lohit District, 25

villages, high altitudes of eastern part, including upper Lohit and Dau valleys, the area to the east of the Haguliang, Billong, and Tilai valleys. *Class:* Sino-Tibetan, Tibeto-Burman, North Assam, Tani. *Dialects:* Conflicting reports about Miju-Mishmi closeness to Idu-Mishmi and Digaro-Mishmi. They are ethnically related, but may not be linguistically close. Related to Kachin, Chin and Lepcha languages (Chowdhury). Idu-Mishmi can understand Miju-Mishmi and Digaro-Mishmi. Lexical similarity 7% with Idu-Mishmi, 10% with Digaro-Mishmi (IICCC). *Lg Use:* Some speakers also use Digaru, Assamese, Hindi, Nepali, or English. *Lg Dev:* Roman script. *Other:* A Scheduled Tribe in India, subgroup of Mishmi. Different from the Miji who speak Sajalong. Hills. Forest. Swidden agriculturalists. Buddhist, syncretism with traditional religion.

Mina [myi] 900,000 (1991). Madhya Pradesh, Gwalior, Shivpuri, Guna, Rajgarh districts, Vidisha District, Sironj Subdivision; Rajasthan, Jaipur, Alwar, Bharatpur, Sawai Madhopur, Tonk, Bundi, Ajmer districts. *Class:* Indo-European, Indo-Iranian, Indo-Aryan, Unclassified. *Other:* A Scheduled Tribe in India. It is reported that their first language is Dhundhari in Rajasthjan and Braj Bhasha in Madhya Pradesh. Agriculturalists; animal husbandry. Hindu, Christian.

Mirgan (Panika, Panka, Mirkan, Mirgami) [zrg] 12,000 (1992). Population includes 10,000 in Orissa, 2,000 in Madhya Pradesh. Chhattisgarh, Bastar District; Orissa, Koraput District. *Class:* Indo-European, Indo-Iranian, Indo-Aryan, Eastern zone, Bengali-Assamese. *Dialects:* Dialects have good intelligibility. Not functionally intelligible with Halbi. Lexical similarity 83% to 95% among dialects. *Lg Use:* Vigorous. Used in the home, religion. Positive language attitude. Speakers have low proficiency in Oriya. Oriya and Adivasi Oriya are used in Orissa, Hindi and Halbi in Madhya Pradesh. *Lg Dev:* Literacy rate in second language: 10% Oriya. Oriya and Telugu scripts. *Other:* Declared a General Caste by the government. Divided into 2 groups, the larger Kabirpanthi and the smaller, less advanced Sakta. Hills, plains. Scrub forest, semitropical. 200 to 1,000 meters. Traditionally weavers, now peasant agriculturalists; pastoralists; city workers. Hindu, Kabirpanthi.

Miri (Mishing, Mising, Takam) [mrg] 400,000 (1998). Population includes 10,050 Hill Miri. Assam, North Lakhimpur, Sonitput, Dhemaji, Dibrugarh, Sibsagar, Jorhat, Golaghat, Tinsukia districts; Arunachal Pradesh, Lower Subansiri District, Ziro subdivision, a few villages near Pasighat, on both sides of the Kamla River; Upper Subansiri District, Daporizo subdivision. The Hill Miri are in Arunachal Pradesh, the Plain Miri are in Assam. *Class:* Sino-Tibetan, Tibeto-Burman, North Assam, Tani. *Dialects:* Idu may be a dialect. *Lg Use:* Speakers also use Assamese. *Lg Dev:* Assamese and Devanagari scripts. NT: 2001. *Other:* A Scheduled Tribe in India. Mountain slope, plains. 914 to 1,219 meters for Hill Miri. Swidden agriculturalists. Hindu, traditional religion.

Mizo (Dulien, Duhlian Twang, Lusai, Lushai, Lusei, Lushei, Lukhai, Lusago, Sailau, Hualngo, Whelngo) [lus] 529,000 in India (1997). Population total all countries: 542,541. Mizoram; Assam; Manipur, Churachandpur District; Nagaland; Tripura, Jampui Hill range. Also spoken in Bangladesh, Myanmar. *Class:* Sino-Tibetan, Tibeto-Burman, Kuki-Chin-Naga, Kuki-Chin, Central. *Dialects:* Fannai, Mizo, Ngente, Tlau, Le. Related to Hmar, Pankhu, Zahao (Falam Chin). *Lg Dev:* Literacy rate in second language: 60% (1971). Taught in primary schools. Roman script. Magazines. Dictionary. Grammar. Bible: 1959–1995. *Other:* Mizo is a Scheduled Tribe in India with subgroups listed as dialects. SOV. Christian.

Moinba (Monba, Mompa, Monpa, Momba, Menba, Men-Pa) [mob] 46,000 in India (1997). Population total all countries: 82,000. Arunachal Pradesh, Tawang, and West Kameng districts. Also spoken in China. *Class:* Sino-Tibetan, Tibeto-Burman, Himalayish, Mahakiranti, Kiranti, Eastern. *Dialects:* Matchopa Nagnoo (But), Chug, Sangla (Dirang), Kalaktang (Southern Monpa), Kishpignag (Lish), Monkit (Northern Monpa, Tawang). The Lish, But, and Chug dialects differ from the others, resembling Aka, Miji, and Sherdukpen languages (Singh). Chowdhury says Lish and Chug dialects are "markedly different and distinct from Monpa." Identical or closely related to Cuona Monpa in Tibet and Brokpa and Brami of Bhutan (Andvik 2002). *Lg Dev:* Devanagari script. Radio programs. Dictionary. Grammar. *Other:* Officially recognized nationality in China. A Scheduled Tribe in India. Tonal, 2 tones (Northern), 4 tones (Southern). Mountain slope. 914 to 3,658 meters. Agriculturalists. Buddhist (Lamaist) mixed with traditional religion.

Mru (Mro, Murung, Niopheng, Mrung) [mro] 1,231 in India (1981 census). West Bengal, Nadia and Hoogly districts. *Other:* Traditional religion with some Buddhist elements. See main entry under Bangladesh.

Mugom [muk] 100 families in India. Himachal Pradesh, Kullu, Manali mainly; also Kinnaur, Dharmshala, Ladakh. *Lg Use:* Younger Mugom people born in India still use their own language at home but may not necessarily know it very well. *Other:* Many migrate from Nepal temporarily for work but many stay 20 to 30 years. See main entry under Nepal.

Mukha-Dora (Conta-Reddi, Mukha Dhora, Nooka Dora, Nuka-Dora, Reddi, Reddi-Dora, Riddi) [mmk] 17,456 (1981 census). Andhra Pradesh, Vishakhapatnam, Srikakulam, Vizianagaram districts. *Class:* Unclassified. *Lg Use:* Speakers also use Adivasi Oriya. *Other:* A Scheduled Tribe in India. Reported that they speak Telugu as first language (Singh). Speakers live scattered throughout the Adivasi Oriya area. Swidden agriculturalists. Hindu, syncretism with traditional religion, Christian.

Mundari (Mandari, Munari, Munda, Mondari, Horo, Colh, Killi) [muw] 2,069,000 in India (1997). Population includes 1,022,000 Mundari, 519,000 Munda, 528,000 Bhumij. Population total all countries: 2,074,700. Assam; Jharkhand, mainly in southern and western parts of Ranchi District; Himachal Pradesh; Madhya Pradesh; Orissa; Tripura; West Bengal; Andaman and Nicobar Islands. Also spoken in Bangladesh, Nepal. *Class:* Austro-Asiatic, Munda, North Munda, Kherwari, Mundari. *Dialect:* Hasada', Latar, Naguri, Kera', Bhumij (Sadar Bhumij, Bhumij Munda, Bhumij Thar). Related to Ho and Santali, but a separate language. 75% intelligibility of Ho. Lexical similarity 70% to 84% with Bhumij. *Lg Dev:* Literacy rate in first language: 10% to 30%. Literacy rate in second language: 50% to 75%. Dictionary. Grammar. Bible: 1910–1932. *Other:* A Scheduled Tribe in India. There is Bhumij literature. Plateau. 600 meters. Agriculturalists. Traditional religion, Hindu.

Muria, Eastern [emu] 10,089 (2000 WCD). Chhattisgarh, Northeastern Bastar District; Orissa, northwestern Koraput District. *Class:* Dravidian, South-Central, Gondi-Kui, Gondi. *Dialects:* Raigarh, Lanjoda. 95% intelligibility between dialects; 73% to 83% of Western Muria; 19% to 34% of Northern Gondi; 35% of Dandami Maria. *Lg Use:* All domains. All ages. *Other:* Speakers are called 'Muria'. A Scheduled Tribe in India. Plains, hills. Degraded forest, tropical forest. Swidden agriculturalists; peasant agriculturalists; hunter-gatherers. Traditional religion, Hindu.

Muria, Far Western [fmu] 10,089 (2000 WCD). Maharashtra, northern Garhchiroli District, Kurkhed

Taluk. *Class:* Dravidian, South-Central, Gondi-Kui, Gondi. *Dialects:* 79% to 88% intelligibility of other Muria languages; 74% of Dandami Maria, 0% to 34% of Northern Gondi, 6% to 50% of Southern Gondi, 2% to 70% of Maria. *Lg Use:* All domains. All ages. *Other:* Speakers are called 'Muria' or 'Gond'. A Scheduled Tribe in India. Plains, hills. Degraded forest, tropical forest. Swidden agriculturalists; hunter-gatherers. Traditional religion, Hindu.

Muria, Western (Jhoria, Mudia, Muria Gondi) [mut] 12,898 (1971 census). Chhattisgarh, northern and western Bastar District. *Class:* Dravidian, South-Central, Gondi-Kui, Gondi. *Dialects:* Sonapal, Banchapai, Dhanora. 80% to 96% intelligibility among dialects, 69% to 73% of Eastern Muria, 51% to 78% of Far Western Muria. Not inherently intelligible with Dandami Maria, Northern Gondi, Southern Gondi, or Maria. *Lg Use:* All domains. All ages. *Other:* Speakers are called 'Muria'. A Scheduled Tribe in India. Plains, hills. Degraded forest, tropical forest. Swidden agriculturalists; hunter-gatherers. Traditional religion, Hindu.

Muthuvan (Mudavan, Muduvar, Mudugar, Mutuvar, Muduvan) [muv] 12,219 (1981 census). Kerala, Idukki district, Devikulam tahsil, Devikulam and Adimali blocks; Kozhikode, Kannur, Ernakulam, Kottayam, and Trichur districts; Tamil Nadu, Coimbatore District, Udumalpet and Valparai tahsils, Anaimalai Hills; Madurai district, Cardamom hills; Andhra Pradesh. *Class:* Dravidian, Southern, Tamil-Kannada, Tamil-Kodagu, Tamil-Malayalam, Tamil. *Dialects:* Western (Malayalam Muthuvan, Nattu Muthuvan), Eastern (Tamil Muthuvan, Pandi Muthuvan). 82% to 87% between dialects, eastern dialect more intelligible to western than vice versa, 80% intelligibility of Malayalam. Lexical similarity 77% to 88% between dialects, 62% to 67% with Tamil, 58% to 68% with Malayalam. *Lg Use:* Vigorous. Used in the home, village, and religious domains. All ages. Positive language attitude. The young understand Malayalam better than Tamil while the older people understand Tamil better. *Lg Dev:* Literacy rate in second language: 24% (31% males, 17% females) (1991 census). *Other:* A Scheduled Tribe in India. The Mudugar are reportedly an entirely different group, not an alternate name. Mountain slope. Tropical forest. 900 to 1,800 meters. Hunter-gatherers; agriculturalists. Hindu.

Na [nbt] 1,500 (est. for year 2000 by Roland-Breton 1997). Arunachal Pradesh, Upper Subansiri District; Taksing circle, Gumsing, Taying, Esnaya, Lingbing, Tongla, Yeja, Reding, Redi, Dadu villages. *Class:* Sino-Tibetan, Tibeto-Burman, North Assam, Tani. *Dialects:* Has an affinity with Tagin (dialect of Nisi) (Singh 95). *Lg Use:* Speakers also use Hindi or English. *Lg Dev:* Literacy rate in second language: 30% (Singh 95). Devanagari and Roman scripts. *Other:* A Scheduled Tribe in India. 2,250 meters. Agriculturalists: terrace cultivation; hunter-gatherers. Buddhist (Mahayana), traditional religion.

Naga Pidgin (Nagamese, Naga-Assamese, Naga Creole Assamese, Kachari Bengali, Bodo) [nag] 30,000 (1989 J. Holm). Nagaland, especially Kohima District, Dimapur Subdivision; bordering areas of Arunachal Pradesh. *Class:* Creole, Assamese based. *Dialects:* A variety farthest from Assamese is spoken by the Yimchenger Naga, and varieties closest to Assamese by the Angami Naga, and around Dimapur and Kohima. *Lg Use:* Trade language. First language for the Kachari in and around Dimapur, a small community, and among children of interethnic marriages. Used by most of the 500,000 speakers of 29 Naga languages as second language. An official medium of instruction in schools. *Lg Dev:* Taught in primary schools. Grammar. *Other:* Mountain slope.

Naga, Angami (Gnamei, Ngami, Angamis, Tsoghami, Tsugumi, Monr, Tsanglo, Tendydie) [njm] 109,000 (1997). Western Nagaland, Kohima District; Manipur; Maharashtra. *Class:* Sino-Tibetan, Tibeto-Burman, Kuki-Chin-Naga, Naga, Angami-Pochuri. *Dialects:* Kohima, Dzuna, Kehena, Khonoma, Chakroma (Western Angami), Mima, Nali, Mozome, Tengima, Tenyidie (Tenyidye). Kohima dialect is now standard Angami. Naga Chokri and Naga Kezhama are eastern Angami groups with their own dialects. Tenyidye is the standard dialect and is understood by all. There are 2 southern varieties (Viswemal, Jakhama) that are not intelligible with these. *Lg Use:* Trade language for about 30,000 Naga of other groups. Speakers also use English, Assamese, Naga Pidgin, or Hindi. *Lg Dev:* Most young people read Angami. Literacy among older people is lower. Roman script. Magazines. Dictionary. Grammar. Bible: 1970. *Other:* A Scheduled Tribe in India. SOV; numerals after noun heads; postpositions; tonal. Christian.

Naga, Ao (Aorr, Paimi, Cholimi, Nowgong, Hatigoria, Uri, Ao) [njo] 141,000 (1997). Northeastern Nagaland, central Mokokchung District; Assam. *Class:* Sino-Tibetan, Tibeto-Burman, Kuki-Chin-Naga, Naga, Ao. *Dialects:* Mongsen Khari, Changki, Chongli (Chungli), Dordar (Yacham), Longla. *Lg Use:* Speakers also use Assamese, English, or Hindi. *Lg Dev:* Literacy rate in second language: 12% (1971). Roman script. Dictionary. Grammar. Bible: 1964. *Other:* A Scheduled Tribe in India. Christian.

Naga, Chang (Chang, Mojung, Machongrr, Mochumi, Mochungrr, Changyanguh) [nbc] 31,000 (1997). Assam; east central Nagaland, Tuensang District, 36 villages. *Class:* Sino-Tibetan, Tibeto-Burman, Jingpho-Konyak-Bodo, Konyak-Bodo-Garo, Konyak. *Dialects:* Close to Wancho Naga. Dialect of Tuensang village is central dialect and intelligible to all. *Lg Use:* Speakers also use Naga Pidgin, Ao, Assamese, English, or Hindi. *Lg Dev:* Roman script. Dictionary. NT: 1982. *Other:* Agriculturalists. Christian, traditional religion.

Naga, Chokri (Eastern Angami, Chakrima Naga, Chakru, Chokri, Chakhesang) [nri] 24,000 (2001). Ethnic population: 24,000. Nagaland, Phek District, Cheswezumi is the main village. *Class:* Sino-Tibetan, Tibeto-Burman, Kuki-Chin-Naga, Naga, Angami-Pochuri. *Lg Use:* Some bilingual ability in Angami Naga and English. *Lg Dev:* Literacy rate in second language: 27% English or Angami Naga. Roman script. *Other:* An eastern Angami tribe with its own language. Chokri, Khezha, and Sangtam-Pochuri make up the Chakhesang Naga community (see separate entries). Chakhesang Naga is a Scheduled Tribe in India. Mountain slope. Tropical forest. Agriculturalists; mixed commerce. Christian, traditional religion.

Naga, Chothe (Chothe, Chowte, Chawte) [nct] 3,600 (2001). Ethnic population: 3,600. Southeast Manipur, Chandel District, 15 villages, Khongkhang, Chandolpokpi, Lunghu, Lirungtabi, Zeonthang, Ajouhu, Pumthapokpi, Laininghu, Chandrapoto, Tampokhu, Lamlanghupi, Purumchumbang, Old Wangparal, New Wangparal, Lungle; Nagaland, near Myanmar border. *Class:* Sino-Tibetan, Tibeto-Burman, Kuki-Chin-Naga, Kuki-Chin, Northern. *Dialects:* Closest to Tarao Naga. Reported intelligibility of Aimol. Lexical similarity less than 60% with any neighboring languages. *Lg Use:* Purest Chothe is spoken in Purum Khullen. Positive language attitude. Speakers also use Meitei or English. *Lg Dev:* Literacy rate in second language: 90% in Meitei (Bengali script) (Yoktel Chothe 2000). Roman and Bengali scripts. *Other:* A Scheduled Tribe in India. Plains, mountain slope. Scrub forest. Agriculturalists. Christian.

Naga, Inpui (Inpui, Kabui, Kapwi, Koboi, Kubai, Kabui Naga) [nkf] 10,000 (2000 Bapt Assn). Manipur, Senapati,

Tamenglong, Imphal districts, 16 villages; Nagaland, 4 villages near Dimapur including New Zaluke, Mahei Namchi, Peren; Assam. *Class:* Sino-Tibetan, Tibeto-Burman, Kuki-Chin-Naga, Naga, Zeme. *Dialects:* Considered by some to be the same language as Puimei Naga. Lexical similarity 68% with Puimei Naga. *Lg Use:* Used in the home. All ages; children speak it as their first language. Negative toward Kuki. Speakers want Inpui Naga to be written. 80% speak Meitei, old and young. Educated speak it fluently. Some speakers also use English or Rongmei. *Lg Dev:* Literacy rate in second language: 70% in English and in Meitei (Bengali script) (Kujinang 2000). Young people want to use Roman script. Meitei is in Bengali script. Some older people read Meitei, few read English. Literacy high among young people in Meitei and English. Roman script. *Other:* Speakers are known as 'Inpui'. 'Kabui' is the name used by others, and is the government name for Inpui plus Rongmei. Kabui recognized as Scheduled Tribe combining Inpui and Rongmei. Tropical and scrub forest. Agriculturalists; hunters: trappers. Christian.

Naga, Kharam (Thinglong, Duisalongmei) [kfw] 1,400 (2000 SIL). Manipur, Senapati District, Phaijol, Laikot, Thuisenpai villages (15–22 km northeast of Imphal), Kharam Pallen village (37 km northwest of Imphal). *Class:* Sino-Tibetan, Tibeto-Burman, Kuki-Chin-Naga, Kuki-Chin, Northern. *Dialects:* Lexical similarity 71% to 73% with Purum, 58% to 60% with Kom, 64% with Koireng. *Lg Use:* All ages. Would not use materials written in Purum. All speak Meitei. Can read and understand Purum. *Lg Dev:* Literacy rate in second language: 30% Meitei, English, Hindi. Some can read Bengali and Devanagari script. Older people would like to learn to read. Most 5- to 20-year-olds have learned to read in school. Roman script. *Other:* Mountain slope. Forest. Agriculturalists. Christian.

Naga, Khezha (Kezami, Khezhama, Khezha) [nkh] 23,000 (1997). Eastern Nagaland, Kohima District, Khezhakhonoma, Phek District. *Class:* Sino-Tibetan, Tibeto-Burman, Kuki-Chin-Naga, Naga, Angami-Pochuri. *Dialects:* An eastern Angami group with its own language. *Lg Use:* Speakers also use Angami Naga. *Lg Dev:* Grammar. *Other:* The speakers of Khezha belong to the Chakhesang Naga community.

Naga, Khiamniungan (Khiamngan, Khiamniungan, Khienmungan, Khemungan, Kemmungam, Kalyokengnyu, Makware, Nokaw, Para, Ponyo, Aoshedd, Welam) [nky] 25,000 in India (1997). Nagaland, east central part of Tuensang District. Also spoken in Myanmar. *Class:* Sino-Tibetan, Tibeto-Burman, Jingpho-Konyak-Bodo, Konyak-Bodo-Garo, Konyak. *Dialects:* A divergent member of the Konyak subgroup. *Lg Dev:* Roman script. NT: 1981. *Other:* In Myanmar the alternate names are Makware, Nokaw, Para, Ponyo, and Welam. A Scheduled Tribe in India. SOV. Christian.

Naga, Khoibu (Khoibu, Khoibu Maring, Khoibu Maring Naga) [nkb] 25,600 (2001). Ethnic population: 25,600. Manipur, southeast, Laiching; mountainous regions along the northern border of Chandel District, Khoibu, Narum, Yangkhul, Saibol villages. *Class:* Sino-Tibetan, Tibeto-Burman, Kuki-Chin-Naga, Naga, Tangkhul. *Lg Dev:* NT: 1988.

Naga, Konyak (Kanyak, Konyak) [nbe] 105,000 (1997). Assam, Sibsagar District, Nagagaon, Bortol villages near Simulguri township; northeast Nagaland, Mon and Tuensang districts. *Class:* Sino-Tibetan, Tibeto-Burman, Jingpho-Konyak-Bodo, Konyak-Bodo-Garo, Konyak. *Dialects:* Angphang, Hopao, Changnyu, Chen, Chingkao, Chinglang, Choha, Gelekidoria, Jakphang, Kongon, Longching, Longkhai, Longmein, Longwa, Mohung, Tableng, Mon, Mulung, Ngangching, Sang, Shanlang,

Shunyuo, Shengha, Sima, Sowa, Shamnyuyanga, Tabu, Tamkhungnyuo, Tang, Tobunyuo, Tolamleinyua, Totok. Tableng is standard dialect spoken in Wanching and Wakching. Close to Phom Naga. *Lg Use:* Speakers also use Naga Pidgin, English, or Hindi. *Lg Dev:* Literacy rate in first language: 13% (1994 Singh). Taught in primary schools. Roman script. Bible: 1992. *Other:* A Scheduled Tribe in India. Hunter-gatherers; agriculturalists. Christian.

Naga, Liangmai (Kacha, Liyang, Liangmai, Lyengmai, Liangmei, Lyangmay) [njn] 20,000 (1997 BSI). Nagaland, Kohima District, Jhaluke, Paren, Medzephima blocks, upper Barak Valley. *Class:* Sino-Tibetan, Tibeto-Burman, Kuki-Chin-Naga, Naga, Zeme. *Lg Dev:* Roman script. Bible: 2001. *Other:* Now merged ethnically with the Zeme and Rongmei Naga to form the Zeliang (or Zeliangrong) community.

Naga, Lotha (Chizima, Choimi, Hlota, Kyong, Lhota, Miklai, Tsindir, Lutha, Lotha, Tsontsii) [njh] 80,000 (1997). Nagaland, west central, Workha District. *Class:* Sino-Tibetan, Tibeto-Burman, Kuki-Chin-Naga, Naga, Ao. *Dialects:* Live, Tsontsu, Ndreng, Kyong, Kyo, Kyon, Kyou. *Lg Use:* Speakers also use Naga Pidgin. *Lg Dev:* Literacy rate is high. Taught in primary schools. Roman script. Grammar. Bible: 1967–2000. *Other:* A Scheduled Tribe in India. 1,200 meters. Christian.

Naga, Mao (Mao, Spowama, Sopvoma, Maikel, Memi, Sopfomo, Emela) [nbi] 81,000 (1997). Northwest Manipur, Senapati District; Nagaland. *Class:* Sino-Tibetan, Tibeto-Burman, Kuki-Chin-Naga, Naga, Angami-Pochuri. *Dialect:* Paomata. Related to Angami. Breton says Paomata and Pome (alt. name for Poumei) are the same. *Lg Use:* Speakers also use Meitei. *Lg Dev:* Literacy rate in second language: 25% Meitei, English. Literacy rate is high. Roman script. Dictionary. Bible: 2001. *Other:* Mao is a Scheduled Tribe in India. Mountain slope. Hunter-gatherers; agriculturalists. Christian.

Naga, Maram (Maram) [nma] 25,000 (2000). Ethnic population: 25,000. Assam; north Manipur, Senapati District, 5 villages near Senapati, 26 villages near Maram; Imphal District. *Class:* Sino-Tibetan, Tibeto-Burman, Kuki-Chin-Naga, Naga, Zeme. *Dialects:* Willong Circle, Maram Khullen Circle, T. Khullen, Ngatan. *Lg Use:* All ages. Men are more bilingual in Meitei than women. *Lg Dev:* Literacy rate in first language: 60% (2003). Literacy rate in second language: 20% (Chema 2000) or 40% to 50% (2003). All young people can read Roman script. Writing system does not indicate tone. Literacy among older people is lower. Roman script. Grammar. Bible portions: 1998. *Other:* A Scheduled Tribe in India. Hills. Scrub and tropical forest. Agriculturalists. Christian, traditional religion.

Naga, Maring (Maring) [nng] 17,361 (2001 census). Manipur, southeast, Laiching; mountainous regions along the northern border of Chandel District, Tengnoupal subdivision. *Class:* Sino-Tibetan, Tibeto-Burman, Kuki-Chin-Naga, Naga, Tangkhul. *Lg Dev:* Bengali script. NT: 2001. *Other:* A Scheduled Tribe in India. Mountain slope. Tropical forest. Swidden agriculturalists. Christian, traditional religion.

Naga, Monsang (Moshang, Monshang, Mushang, Mawshang) [nmh] 3,200 (2001). Ethnic population: 3,200. Manipur, Chandel District, Chandel subdivision, Liwchangning, Heibunglok, Liwa Sarei, Japhou, Monsang Pantha villages; Northern Nagaland, near Myanmar border. *Class:* Sino-Tibetan, Tibeto-Burman, Kuki-Chin-Naga, Kuki-Chin, Northern. *Dialects:* Closest to Moyon Naga and Anal. *Lg Use:* Speakers also use Meitei, English, Hindi, or Naga Pidgin. *Lg Dev:* Literacy rate in second language: 80% (Kotha 1988). Literacy program in progress by government and church. (Kotha 88) All can read and write Meitei (Singh 1998). Roman script. *Other:*

A Scheduled Tribe in India. Hills. Swidden agriculturalists. Christian.

Naga, Moyon (Moyon, Mayon Naga, Mayol) [nmo] 3,700 (2001). Ethnic population: 3,700. Nagaland, near Myanmar border; Manipur State, Chandel District, 14 villages including Moyon Khullen, Khongjom, Mitong, Komlathabi, Penaching, Heigru Tampak. *Class:* Sino-Tibetan, Tibeto-Burman, Kuki-Chin-Naga, Kuki-Chin, Northern. *Dialects:* Related to Monsang Naga and Anal. *Lg Use:* Can read, speak, and write Meitei quite fluently. Conversant with Monsang and Anal (Singh 98). *Lg Dev:* Literacy program in progress (Roel 1988). Bengali and Roman scripts. *Other:* A Scheduled Tribe in India. Hills. Swidden agriculturalists. Christian.

Naga, Mzieme (Mzieme, Northern Zeme) [nme] 29,000 (1997). Southwestern Nagaland, northeast of Zeme. *Class:* Sino-Tibetan, Tibeto-Burman, Kuki-Chin-Naga, Naga, Zeme. *Dialects:* Different from Zeme Naga. *Lg Dev:* Roman script. Bible: 1992. *Other:* Has adopted the designation of 'Northern Zeme' because Zeme has government recognition while Mzieme does not. The peoples are closely related.

Naga, Nocte (Borduria, Jaipuria, Mohongia, Namsangia, Nocte, Nokte, Paniduria) [njb] 35,000 (2001 Mema). Southeastern Arunachal Pradesh, Tirap District, Khonsa, Namsang, Laju circles; Changlang District; Assam, Lakhimpur District, Jaipur; Northern Nagaland, Mon District, Namsang. *Class:* Sino-Tibetan, Tibeto-Burman, Jingpho-Konyak-Bodo, Konyak-Bodo-Garo, Konyak. *Dialect:* Khapa, Laju, Ponthai (Lamlak). Close to Tase Naga. Ponthai may be the name of an ethnic group, not a dialect. 50% intelligible with Wancho Naga. *Lg Use:* All domains. All ages. Assamese or Hindi also used mostly by men, young people and educated people. Others speak Assamese only for trade. English is used by educated office workers. People want to learn English. *Lg Dev:* Literacy rate in second language: 5.4% (10% male, 0.7% female) (1997 Muanthanga) or 25% (Mema 2001). Radio programs. *Other:* A Scheduled Tribe in India. Tutsa, Wancho, Laju, Lamlak are considered ethnic subgroups of Nocte although Tutsa consider themselves never to have been related to Nocte. SOV; postpositions; genitives before noun heads; articles, adjectives, numerals after noun heads; affixes indicate case of noun phrase; causatives; comparatives; CV, CVC, CVV, CVVC, V; tonal, at least 3 tones. Hills. Agriculturalists: millet, paddy, yams. Christian, traditional religion, Hindu, syncretism.

Naga, Northern Rengma (Ntenyi, Ntenyi Naga, Nthenyi, Northern Rengma) [nnl] 13,000 (1997). Nagaland; Kohima District, northern section of Rengma. Kotsenyu is chief village of Ntenyi. *Class:* Sino-Tibetan, Tibeto-Burman, Kuki-Chin-Naga, Naga, Angami-Pochuri. *Lg Dev:* Roman script. NT: 1979–2002.

Naga, Phom (Phom, Phon, Tamlu Naga, Chingmengu, Tamlu) [nph] 34,000 (1997). Northeastern Nagaland, Tuensang District, Longleng Subdivision, 36 villages. *Class:* Sino-Tibetan, Tibeto-Burman, Jingpho-Konyak-Bodo, Konyak-Bodo-Garo, Konyak. *Dialect:* Yongyasha. Close to Konyak. *Lg Use:* Speakers also use Naga Pidgin. *Lg Dev:* Literacy rate in second language: 35% adults. Roman script. Dictionary. Grammar. NT: 1978. *Other:* A Scheduled Tribe in India. Tonal. Mountain slope. 650 to 2,000 meters. Agriculturalists; hunter-gatherers. Christian.

Naga, Pochuri (Pochuri, Pochury) [npo] 13,000 (1997). Southeast Nagaland. All 27 villages are in the Meluri Subdivision of Phek District. *Class:* Sino-Tibetan, Tibeto-Burman, Kuki-Chin-Naga, Naga, Angami-Pochuri. *Lg Use:* Speakers also use Naga Pidgin. *Lg Dev:* Literacy rate in second language: 39% (Singh). Roman script. NT: 1994. *Other:* A Scheduled Tribe in India. Meluri is a place-name in this region. Pochury is an amalgamation of

3 place-names: Sapo, Kechuri, Khury. Mountain slope. Swidden agriculturalists. Christian, traditional religion.

Naga, Poumei (Poumei, Paumei, Pomai, Pome) [pmx] 51,000 (1997). Manipur. *Class:* Sino-Tibetan, Tibeto-Burman, Kuki-Chin-Naga, Naga, Angami-Pochuri. *Dialects:* Close to Mao. Not the same as Puimei (Breton 1997:217). *Lg Dev:* Roman script. NT: 1992.

Naga, Puimei (Puimei) [npu] 3,000 in Manipur (2001). Ethnic population: 3,000. Manipur; Assam. *Class:* Sino-Tibetan, Tibeto-Burman, Kuki-Chin-Naga, Naga, Unclassified. *Dialects:* Different from Poumei (Breton 1997:217). Not functionally intelligible with any related language (Khasung). Lexical similarity 68% with Inpui Naga. *Other:* Were assigned to be under the Rongmei. Christian, traditional religion.

Naga, Purum [puz] 503 (2001 census). Manipur, Senapati District, Purumlikli, Purumkhulen, Purumkhunou, Waicheiphai, Moibunglikli villages; Chandel District, Lamlang Huipi, Chandanpokpi, Khongkhang Chothe, Loirang Talsi, Salemthar, Zat'lang, New Wangparan. *Class:* Sino-Tibetan, Tibeto-Burman, Kuki-Chin-Naga, Kuki-Chin, Northern. *Dialects:* 95% intelligibility of Kharam, a nearby language. Lexical similarity 60% to 65% with Kom, 60% to 66% with Koireng, 57% to 60% with Aimol, 71% to 73% with Kharam. *Lg Use:* All ages. Positive towards development of first language. Meitei used in market with Meitei, Thangkul, Kuki, and Kom. *Lg Dev:* Literacy rate in second language: 30% to 40% (2000). *Other:* Scheduled Tribe in India. SOV; postpositions; numerals, adjectives, articles after noun head; question word between subject and object; word order distinguishes subject, object, indirect object; V, CV, CVC, CVV; nontonal. Plains. Christian, traditional religion.

Naga, Rongmei (Maruongmai, Nruanghmei, Rongmei, Rongmai, Kabui) [nbu] 59,000 (1997). Northwest Manipur; Nagaland; Assam, Cachar District. *Class:* Sino-Tibetan, Tibeto-Burman, Kuki-Chin-Naga, Naga, Zeme. *Dialect:* Songbu. *Lg Dev:* Literacy rate in first language: High. Magazines. Radio programs. Bible: 1989. *Other:* Songbu is the principal division of Rongmei. Merged with Zeme and Liangmai Naga to form the Zeliang community. The government calls Inpui and Rongmei 'Kabui'. Traditional religion, Christian.

Naga, Sangtam (Sangtam, Isachanure, Lophomi) [nsa] 39,000 (1997). Southeast Nagaland, Tuensang District, Kiphire Subdivision and Chare Circle. *Class:* Sino-Tibetan, Tibeto-Burman, Kuki-Chin-Naga, Naga, Ao. *Dialects:* Kizare, Pirr (Northern Sangtam), Phelongre, Thukumi (Central Sangtam), Photsimi, Purr (Southern Sangtam). Standard is based on Tsadanger village dialect (Singh). Kizare spoken north of Meluri. It is not known how much it differs from other Sangtam. *Lg Use:* Speakers also use Naga Pidgin, Ao, Hindi, or English. *Lg Dev:* Literacy rate in second language: 20% Assamese, English. Bible: 1995. *Other:* Chokri, Khezha, and a small section of Sangtam make up the Chakhesang Naga community. A Scheduled Tribe in India. Kizare: woodwork. Christian, traditional religion.

Naga, Southern Rengma (Rengma, Rengma Naga, Mozhumi, Moiyui, Mon, Unza, Nzong, Nzonyu, Injang, Southern Rengma) [nre] 21,000 (1997). West central Nagaland, Kohima District, Tseminyu subdivision; Assam; Manipur. Tseminyu is the main center for the principal dialect. *Class:* Sino-Tibetan, Tibeto-Burman, Kuki-Chin-Naga, Naga, Angami-Pochuri. *Dialect:* Keteneneyu, Azonyu (Nzonyu, Southern Rengma). Tseminyu is the main center for the principal dialect. Southern Rengma and Northern Rengma are reported to be inherently unintelligible to each other's speakers. *Lg Use:* Speakers also use Naga Pidgin or English.

Lg Dev: Literacy in Rengma is higher among older people. Young people are learning English. Roman script. Bible: 2000. *Other:* A Scheduled Tribe in India. Christian.

Naga, Sumi (Sema, Simi, Sumi) [nsm] 132,000 (1997). Central and southern Nagaland, Zunheboto, Kohima, Mokokchung, Tuensang districts; Assam, Tinsukia District, seven villages. Dayang is spoken near the Dayang River. *Class:* Sino-Tibetan, Tibeto-Burman, Kuki-Chin-Naga, Naga, Angami-Pochuri. *Dialects:* Dayang (Western Sumi), Lazemi, Zhimomi, Zumomi. *Lg Use:* Speakers also use Naga Pidgin, Angami, Ao, Lotha, English, or Hindi. *Lg Dev:* Literacy rate in second language: 50% Assamese, English. Roman script. Dictionary. Grammar. Bible: 2000. *Other:* A Scheduled Tribe in India. 1,500 to 2,000 meters. Agriculturalists, seminomadic. Christian, traditional religion.

Naga, Tangkhul (Tangkhul, Tagkhul, Thangkhulm, Champhung, Luhuppa, Luppa, Somra) [nmf] 110,000 (1997). Manipur, Ukhrul District; Nagaland; Tripura. *Class:* Sino-Tibetan, Tibeto-Burman, Kuki-Chin-Naga, Naga, Tangkhul. *Dialects:* Ukhrul, Khunggoi, Khangoi, Kupome, Phadang. Ukhrul is principal dialect. *Lg Dev:* Literacy rate in first language: High among young people, lower among older people. Literacy rate in second language: 70% Meitei, English. Taught in primary schools. Roman script. Magazines. Newspapers. Radio programs. Dictionary. Grammar. Bible: 1976. *Other:* A Scheduled Tribe in India. The most educated group of Manipur. Mountain slope, plains. Agriculturalists. Christian.

Naga, Tarao (Tarao, Tarau, Taraotrong) [tro] 870 (2000). Manipur: Chandel District, 3 villages near Palel (Heikakpokpi, Leishokching, Khuringmul), Laiminei village; Ukhrul District, Sinakeithei village. *Class:* Sino-Tibetan, Tibeto-Burman, Kuki-Chin-Naga, Kuki-Chin, Northern. *Dialects:* Closest to Chothe Naga, 70% intelligibility. Lexical similarity less than 60% with any neighboring languages; 43% to 46% with Chothe. *Lg Use:* All ages. Speakers have low proficiency in Meitei or English. *Lg Dev:* Literacy rate in second language: 75% Meitei, English. Literacy program in progress. Older people can read Meitei in Bengali script. Young people prefer Roman script. Most villages have primary and junior schools; attendance is irregular. *Other:* Not recognized as a separate Scheduled Tribe by the government because of its small size. Postpositions; genitives, articles, adjectives, numerals, relatives before noun heads; maximum affixes 2; word order distinguishes subjects, objects and indirect objects; noun affix marks case; verb affixes mark number; no passive; causatives and comparatives; CVC. Hills. Scrub and tropical forest. Swidden agriculturalists; some work as sharecroppers for the Moyon, Monsang, and Maring. Christian.

Naga, Tase (Cham Chang, Rangpan, Tangsa, Tasey) [nst] 45,000 in India (2001 Chamchang). Southeastern Arunachal Pradesh, Changlang District, Eastern Hills, Tirap River valley and Namchik area; Assam. *Dialects:* Have (Havoy), Higsho, Higtsii, Kimsing (Khemsing, Chamchang), Longphi (Longkhi), Lungchang, Lungri, Miti, Moklum, Mosang, Mungray (Morang), Ngemu, Ponthai, Rongrang, Ronrang (Poerah), Sangche, Sangwal, Sanke (Shangge, Sechu), Taipi, Tikhak, Tonglim, Yogli (Jugli), Yongkuk (Yukok). *Lg Use:* Tase Naga is the language of the home, village. All ages. Positive language attitude. Most know market Hindi and Assamese. Assamese is preferred over Hindi. Only educated can speak Burmese, English, or Singpho fluently. *Lg Dev:* Literacy rate in second language: 8.8% (male 14.8%, female 3.2%) (Muanthanga 1997) or 70% (Chamchang 2001). *Other:* 'Tase' is the name of the language; 'Tangsa' of the people. 'Tangsa' means 'hill people'. A Scheduled Tribe in India. There may be up to 36 subtribes

of Tangsa (Rai 2000). Interview with Chamchang indicated that 'Tangsa' is used for both people and language. Kimsing dialect speakers can understand all dialects well, possibly sufficient to understand complex discourse. Kimsing is similar to Tutsa. Higsho is similar to Nocte. Kimsing has most speakers and is most influential. (Chamchang 2001). Hills. Agriculturalists: rice, maize, oil rape seed, potatoes. Traditional religion, Christian, Buddhist. See main entry under Myanmar.

Naga, Thangal (Khoirao, Khoirao Naga, Koirao, Kolya, Mayangkhang, Miyang-Khang, Ngari, Thangal, Thanggal, Tukaimi) [nki] 23,600 (2001). Ethnic population: 23,600. North Manipur, Senapati District, hill ranges of East and West Sadar Hills subdivisions, 9 villages along National Highway #39, Mapao Thangal, Thangal Surung, Makeng Thangal, Tumnoupokpi, Yaikangpou, Tikhulen, Ningthoubam, Mayangkhang, and Gailongde. Most are east of Barak Valley groups. 250 square miles. *Class:* Sino-Tibetan, Tibeto-Burman, Kuki-Chin-Naga, Naga, Zeme. *Dialects:* Close to Maram. *Lg Use:* Speakers also use Meitei. *Lg Dev:* Literacy rate in second language: 90% Meitei, English. Roman and Bengali scripts. Dictionary. *Other:* A Scheduled Tribe in India. Postpositions; genitives, relatives before noun head; articles, adjectives, numerals after noun head; question word initial; case marked by postpositional clitics; comparatives; CV, CVC, CVV, VC, V syllables; nontonal. Mountain slope. Agriculturalists. Christian.

Naga, Tutsa (Totcha, Tutsa) [tvt] 25,000 (2001). Arunachal Pradesh, south Changlang and east Tirap districts. *Class:* Sino-Tibetan, Tibeto-Burman, Jingpho-Konyak-Bodo, Konyak-Bodo-Garo, Konyak. *Dialects:* Close to Nocte and Tase, but intelligible only with difficulty. *Lg Use:* Used in the home and village. All ages. Consider themselves separate from Nocte and Tase. Assamese spoken by young people; Hindi by young and slightly educated people; English by educated young people. English has prestige as international language. *Lg Dev:* Literacy rate in second language: 5%. *Other:* Very few people with higher education. SOV; postpositions; genitives and articles before noun heads; adjectives and numerals after noun heads; maximum affixes 2; affixes indicate case of noun phrase; ergativity; CV, CVC, VC; may be tonal but it does not carry much functional load. Agriculturalists: millet, maize, tapioca, yams, rice. Traditional religion, Christian.

Naga, Wancho (Wancho, Banpara Naga, Joboka) [nnp] 45,000 (1997). Assam; Nagaland; southeastern Arunachal Pradesh, Tirap District, 36 villages on the southwestern side. *Class:* Sino-Tibetan, Tibeto-Burman, Jingpho-Konyak-Bodo, Konyak-Bodo-Garo, Konyak. *Dialects:* Changnoi, Bor Muthun (Bor Mutonia), Horu Muthun, Kulung Muthun (Mithan). There is a significant variation between the language spoken in the upper regions and that in the lower ones. (Singh) Close to Chang Naga and Konyak Naga. *Lg Use:* The younger generation speaks Hindi or Assamese as second language. *Lg Dev:* Literacy rate in second language: 1.2% (2.5% male, 0.03% female) (1997). Roman and Devanagari scripts. NT: 2002. *Other:* A Scheduled Tribe in India. Mountain slope. Forest. Swidden agriculturalists. Traditional religion.

Naga, Yimchungru (Yanchunger, Yimchungru, Yimchunger, Yimchungre, Tozhuma, Yachumi) [yim] 37,000 (1997). Nagaland, northern between Namchik and Patkoi, Tuensang District. *Class:* Sino-Tibetan, Tibeto-Burman, Kuki-Chin-Naga, Naga, Ao. *Dialects:* Tikhir, Wai, Chirr, Minir, Pherrongre, Yimchungru. The last three dialects listed are southern. *Lg Use:* Speakers also use Naga Pidgin, Hindi, or English. *Lg Dev:* Roman script. NT: 1981–1989. *Other:* A Scheduled Tribe in India. 800 to 3,840 meters. Swidden agriculturalists. Christian.

Naga, Zeme (Kachcha, Kacha, Kutcha, Mezama, Sangrima, Sengima, Arung, Empui, Jeme, Zemi) [nzm] 30,800 (2001). Ethnic population: 30,800. Manipur, Tamenglong District; Nagaland, Kohima District, Jhaluke, Paren, Medzephima blocks; Assam, large upper Barak Valley. *Class:* Sino-Tibetan, Tibeto-Burman, Kuki-Chin-Naga, Naga, Zeme. *Dialects:* Paren, Njauna. *Lg Dev:* Roman script. NT: 1978–1992. *Other:* Called 'Zeliang' or 'Zeliangrong' together with Liangmai and Rongmei. A Scheduled Tribe in India. Christian, traditional religion.

Nagarchal (Nagar, Nagarchi) [nbg] 7,090 (1971 census). Madhya Pradesh, Balaghat, Chhindwara, Mandla, Seoni districts; Chhattisgarh, Durg District; Maharashtra, Bhandara District; Rajasthan. *Class:* Dravidian, South-Central, Gondi-Kui, Gondi. *Other:* Nagarchi is the name of a people group living in Seoni, Jabalpur and Mandla districts of Madhya Pradesh. They reportedly speak Hindi (Singh).

Nahali (Kalto, Nahal, Nahale) [nlx] 15,000 (2003). Maharashtra, Nandurbar District, Dhadgaon tahsil, 12 villages around Toranmal, Jalgaon district; Chopda tahsil, north of Amalwadi. *Class:* Indo-European, Indo-Iranian, Indo-Aryan, Central zone, Bhil. *Dialects:* Lexical similarity 58% to 68% with Noiri varieties, 60% to 61% with Dungra Bhil, 69% to 73% with Bareli Pauri. *Other:* 96% intelligibility of Bareli Pauri. This may be acquired rather than inherent (S. Watters). Nihali and Nahali are different languages. Forest.

Nahari (Nahali) [nhh] 108 (1961 census). Chhattisgarh, Raipur, Bilaspur districts; Orissa, Sambalpur District. *Class:* Indo-European, Indo-Iranian, Indo-Aryan, Eastern zone, Bengali-Assamese. *Dialects:* A more divergent variety, related to Halbi. *Other:* A Scheduled Tribe in India. Singh 1994 reports they speak Nimadi as first language. Hindu.

Nefamese (Arunamese) [nef] Arunachal Pradesh. *Class:* Pidgin, Assamese based. *Dialects:* Most closely related to Adi Galo. *Lg Use:* A lingua franca of Arunachal Pradesh. Spoken as second language by Zakhring, Apatani, Bugun, and other minority peoples.

Nepali (Nepalese, Gorkhali, Gurkhali, Khaskura, Parbatiya, Eastern Pahari) [nep] 6,000,000 in India (1984 Far Eastern Economic Review). West Bengal, Darjeeling area; Sikkim; Assam; Arunachal Pradesh; Bihar; Haryana; Himachal Pradesh; Uttar Pradesh; Uttaranchal; Manipur; Mizoram; Nagaland; Meghalaya, Tripura. *Dialects:* Gorkhali, Palpa, Nepali. *Lg Use:* Official language. *Lg Dev:* Literacy rate in first language: 30% to 100%. Literacy rate in second language: 25% to 75%. *Other:* People are called 'Paharia'. Hindu. See main entry under Nepal.

Newar ("Newari") [new] Sikkim; West Bengal; Some in Bettiah, Bihar; Andamans. *Other:* "Newari" considered offensive to Newars. See main entry under Nepal.

Nicobarese, Car (Pu, Car) [caq] 30,000 (1997). North Nicobar Islands, Car Island. *Class:* Austro-Asiatic, Mon-Khmer, Nicobar, Car. *Lg Dev:* Literacy rate in second language: 18% (1971). Roman script. Dictionary. Grammar. Bible: 1969. *Other:* A Scheduled Tribe in India.

Nicobarese, Central (Nicobar) [ncb] 2,200 (1981). Population includes 800 Nancowry, 1,400 closely related dialects (1981 Radhakrishnan). 22,100 in all six Nicobarese languages (1981 Wurm and Hattori). Nicobar Islands, Katchal, Camorta, Nancowry, and Trinket islands. *Class:* Austro-Asiatic, Mon-Khmer, Nicobar, Nancowry. *Dialects:* Camorta (Kamorta), Katchal (Kachel, Tehnu), Nancowry (Nancoury), Trinkut (Trinkat). Related to Car, Chaura, Shom Peng, Southern Nicobarese, Teressa. *Lg Dev:* Devanagari and Roman scripts. Bible portions: 1884–1890.

Nicobarese, Southern (Nicobara) [nik] 5,045 (2000 WCD). Nicobar Islands, Little Nicobar and outer Great Nicobar islands. *Class:* Austro-Asiatic, Mon-Khmer, Nicobar, Great Nicobar. *Dialects:* Condul (Kondul), Great Nicobar, Little Nicobar, Milo, Sambelong, Tafwap.

Nihali (Nihal) [nll] 2,000 (1991 Parkin). Ethnic population: 5,000 (1987). Maharashtra, Buldana District, Jamod Jalgaon tahsil. *Class:* Language Isolate. *Dialects:* Nihal in Chikaldara taluk and Akola District have 25% lexical similarity with Korku (Munda). *Lg Use:* Speakers also use Korku, Hindi, or Marathi. *Other:* They live in or near Korku villages in a position of subordination to the Korku people. Possibly belonged to a now extinct speech family of India. Has been influenced significantly by Munda and Dravidian languages. 60% to 70% of vocabulary has been borrowed. Nihali and Nahali are different languages. Mountain slope. Tropical forest.

Nimadi (Nemadi, Nimari, Nimiadi) [noe] 1,359,000 (1997). Madhya Pradesh, Khandwa, Khargone, Barwani, and southern Dhar districts; Uttar Pradesh; Maharashtra. *Class:* Indo-European, Indo-Iranian, Indo-Aryan, Central zone, Rajasthani, Unclassified. *Dialect:* Bhuani. Dialects have 90 to 100% inherent intelligibility among speakers. Lexical similarity 74% to 94% among dialects, 64% to 75% with Malvi, 62% to 77% with Hindi, 56% to 64% with Gujarati, 49% to 58% with Marathi. *Lg Use:* Vigorous. All key domains except with government officials. Positive language attitude. Speakers have low proficiency in Hindi. Hindi used in education. *Lg Dev:* Literacy rate in second language: 40%. Radio programs. TV. *Other:* Hindu syncretism, Muslim, Christian.

Nisi ("Dafla," "Daphla," Nissi, Nishi, Nyising, Nyishi, Bangni, Lel) [dap] 261,000 (1997). Population includes 37,300 Tagin. Assam, Darrang District; Arunachal Pradesh, Lower Subansiri and East Kameng districts. *Class:* Sino-Tibetan, Tibeto-Burman, North Assam, Tani. *Dialects:* Aka Lel, Bangni, Tagin, Nishang. Related to Apatani, Adi, Yano, possibly Lepcha. Tagin may be a separate language. Apatani may be a dialect of Nisi. *Lg Dev:* Literacy rate in second language: 10% Assamese. Assamese script. NT: 2002. *Other:* Nisi and Tagin are both Scheduled Tribes in India. 'Nisi' has been used as a cover term for the western Tani languages. The name "Dafla" means 'wild man' and is considered derogatory. 300 meters. Swidden agriculturalists. Traditional religion, Christian, Hindu.

Noiri (Bhilori, Mathwadi) [noi] 100,000 (2003 Varghese). Maharashtra, Nandurbar District, Dhadgaon, Akkalkua, and Shahada tahsils; Dhule District, Shirpur Tahsil; Jalgaon District, Chopda Tahsil; Madhya Pradesh, Badwani District, Pansemal Tahsil. *Class:* Indo-European, Indo-Iranian, Indo-Aryan, Central zone, Bhil. *Dialect:* Barutiya. Highly intelligible with Dungra Bhili. Barutiya have high acquired intelligibility of Vasavi and Bareli Pauri. Lexical similarity 77% to 87% with Dungra Bhili, 60% to 71% with different Vasavi varieties, 58% to 68% with Nahali of Toranmal, 47% to 54% with Kotali; Barutiya lexical similarity 64% to 70% with Bareli Pauri. Noiri-Barutiya falls between Vasavi and Bareli on a dialect continuum. *Lg Use:* Vigorous. Used in the home, village. Positive language attitude to the west. Less positive to the east. Low proficiency in Marathi and Hindi. *Lg Dev:* Literacy rate in second language: 1% in Marathi. Devanagari script. *Other:* A Scheduled Tribe in Maharashtra and Madhya Pradesh. A Bhil subgroup. "Noira" means people who speak through the nose. Traditional religion, Christian, Hindu.

Oko-Juwoi (Oku-Juwoi, Juwoi, Junoi) [okj] Extinct. Andaman Islands, west central and southwest interior Middle Andaman Island. *Class:* Andamanese, Great Andamanese, Central.

Önge (Ong) [oon] 96 (1997 CIIL). Speakers are mainly monolingual. Ethnic population: 110 (1999 report). Southern Andaman Islands, Dugong Creek and South Bay islands. *Class:* Andamanese, South Andamanese. *Dialects:* A distinct language from Sentinelese. *Lg Use:* Reserved toward outsiders. *Lg Dev:* Dictionary. *Other:* A Scheduled Tribe in India. Hunter-gatherers; fishermen. Traditional religion.

Oriya (Uriya, Utkali, Odri, Odrum, Oliya, Orissa, Vadiya, Yudhia) [ori] 31,666,000 in India (1997). Population total all countries: 31,698,534. Orissa; Jharkhand, Singhbhum, Ranchi districts; Chhattisgarh, Raigarh, Raipur, Bastar districts; West Bengal, Medinipur (Midnapore) District; Assam; Andhra Pradesh, Vishakhapatnam District. Also spoken in Bangladesh. *Class:* Indo-European, Indo-Iranian, Indo-Aryan, Eastern zone, Oriya. *Dialects:* Mughalbandi (Oriya Proper, Standard Oriya), Southern Oriya, Northwestern Oriya, Western Oriya (Sambalpuri), North Balasore Oriya, Midnapore Oriya, Halbi. Some of the larger dialects have many subdialects. Sambalpuri around Sambalpur and Sundargh needs intelligibility testing with Standard Oriya. *Lg Use:* State language of Orissa. Spoken as first language by the Bathudi, Bhuiya, Chakali, some Koda, and the Mali. *Lg Dev:* Literacy rate in first language: 30% to 60%. Literacy rate in second language: 25% to 50%. Oriya script. Bible: 1815–2002. *Other:* Hindu, Muslim, Christian.

Oriya, Adivasi (Adiwasi Oriya, Tribal Oriya, Kotia Oriya, Kotiya) [ort] 150,000 (1991 U. Gustafsson). Andhra Pradesh, Vishakhapatnam District, Araku Valley. *Class:* Indo-European, Indo-Iranian, Indo-Aryan, Eastern zone, Oriya. *Dialects:* Lexical similarity 38% to 42% between Andhra Pradesh varieties and Standard Oriya, 80% to 85% with Desiya dialects in Orissa. *Lg Use:* Trade language. 200,000 second-language users (1998 U. Gustafsson). *Lg Dev:* Literacy rate in first language: 7.3%. Telugu script. Dictionary. Bible portions: 1977–1982. *Other:* Kotia is a Scheduled Tribe in India. The people are called 'Kotia'. Agriculturalists; mixed commerce. Traditional religion, Hindu, Christian.

Oriya, Desiya (Desiya, Desia, Deshia, Koraput Oriya) [dso] 50,000 (2003). Orissa, Koraput district, Lamtaput block, Nowrangpur District. *Class:* Indo-European, Indo-Iranian, Indo-Aryan, Eastern zone, Oriya. *Dialects:* Intelligible with Adivasi Oriya but uses different scripts. Lexical similarity 80% to 85% with Adivasi Oriya dialects in Andhra Pradesh. *Lg Dev:* Oriya script. *Other:* Agriculturalists; mixed commerce. Traditional religion, Christian.

Pahari, Kullu (Kului, Kullui, Kauli, Kulu Boli, Kulu Pahari, Pahari, Pahari Kullu, Phari Kulu, Kulvi, Kulwali) [kfx] 109,000 (1997). All Pahari 2,173,000 (1997). Himachal Pradesh, Kullu District. *Class:* Indo-European, Indo-Iranian, Indo-Aryan, Northern zone, Western Pahari. *Dialects:* Inner Siragi (Inner Seraji, Siragi, Siraji, Saraji), Kllui, Outer Seraji. Inner Siraji is apparently different from Siraji-Kashmiri. Lexical similarity 85% or higher among dialects. *Lg Use:* Some speakers also use Hindi. Panjabi, Urdu, Lahuli, or Nepali. *Lg Dev:* Devanagari script. Radio programs. Dictionary. Bible portions: 1932–1980. *Other:* Literacy program needed. Mountain slope. Hindu.

Pahari, Mahasu (Mahasui) [bfz] 500,000 (1992). Population includes 3,976 Baghati (1961 census). Himachal Pradesh, Shimla (Simla) and Solan districts. *Class:* Indo-European, Indo-Iranian, Indo-Aryan, Northern zone, Western Pahari. *Dialects:* Lower Mahasu Pahari (Kiunthali, Baghati, Baghliani), Upper Mahasu Pahari (Shimla Siraji, Sodochi, Rampuri, Rohruri). The Kiunthali subdialect appears to be understood by speakers of the other varieties, and their attitude toward it is favorable. The Rampuri subdialect is also called 'Kochi'; the Rohruri subdialect also called 'Soracholi'. Intelligibility among dialects is above 85%. Lexical similarity 74% to 82% with upper dialects, 74% to 95% with lower dialects. *Lg Use:*

Some domains, home, religion. All ages. Bilingual level estimates for Hindi: 0 0%, 1 40%, 2 30%, 3 15%, 4 10%, 5 5%. Those with more than 5 years of schooling are more proficient in Hindi. *Lg Dev:* Literacy rate in second language: below 40% in Hindi. Radio programs. Dictionary. *Other:* Speakers are called 'Pahari'. SOV; postpositions, genitives after noun heads, nontonal. Mountain slope, valleys. Peasant agriculturalists. Hindu, Muslim, Christian.

Pali [pli] Extinct. Also spoken in Myanmar, Sri Lanka. *Class:* Indo-European, Indo-Iranian, Indo-Aryan, Unclassified. *Lg Use:* Used as the literary language of the Buddhist scriptures. *Lg Dev:* NT: 1835. *Other:* Buddhist.

Paliyan (Palaya, Palayan, Paliyar, Malai Paliyar, Palliyar, Poliyar, Palleyan, Palani, Makkal, Seramar) [pcf] 8,615 (1991 census). Kerala, Idukki district, Pirmed tahsil, Kumily, Vandanmedu, Chakkupallam panchayats; Ernakulam, Kottayam districts; Tamil Nadu, Madurai, Ramanathapuram, Thanjavur, Pudukkottai, Tirunelveli, Coimbatore districts; Karnataka. *Class:* Dravidian, Southern, Tamil-Kannada, Tamil-Kodagu, Tamil-Malayalam, Malayalam. *Dialect:* Mala Pulayan (Hill Pulaya, Karavazhi). Lexical similarity 75% with Tamil, 62% with Malayalam, 85% with Mala Pulayan. *Lg Use:* Speakers have high proficiency in Tamil. Some are becoming literate in Malayalam. *Other:* A Scheduled Tribe in India. Agriculturalists; plantation laborers. Traditional religion, syncretism, Hindu, Christian.

Panchpargania (Tamaria, Tair, Tamara, Temoral, Tumariya, Tanti, Chik Barik, Bedia, Pan, Pan Sawasi) [tdb] 274,000 (1997). Jharkhand, Ranchi, Singhbhum districts; West Bengal; Assam, tea gardens of upper Assam. *Class:* Indo-European, Indo-Iranian, Indo-Aryan, Eastern zone, Oriya. *Dialects:* Related to Sadri. Possibly the same as Kudmali. *Lg Use:* Spoken by the Bedia and Pan Sawasi of Bihar, Pan of Assam (who migrated from Ranchi, Nagpur and Sambalpur), and Chik Barik of West Bengal. *Other:* Panchpargania means '5 districts', namely Silli, Bundu, Rahe, Baranda, and Tamar parganas of Ranchi (Singh, The Scheduled Castes 1993:1038). Hindu, traditional religion.

Pangwali (Pahari, Pangi, Pangwali Pahari) [pgg] 17,000 (1997). Himachal Pradesh, Lahul-Spiti District, Udaipur down the Chenab (Chandra-Bhaga) River to the Chamba border at Purthi, and possibly from Tandi to the Sanch Pass. Another dialect over the pass; Chamba District, Pangi Tahsil. *Class:* Indo-European, Indo-Iranian, Indo-Aryan, Northern zone, Western Pahari. *Dialects:* Reported to be nearly the same as Bhadrawahi. 64% inherent intelligibility of Mandeali, 52% of Kangri, 44% of Chambeali. Lexical similarity 55% with Hindi, 77% with Kullui Pahari. *Lg Use:* Hindi is the language of education and government; it is used as second language by men who have traveled, anyone with 5th grade education or higher, some women who have an educated person in the home. Second-language Hindi speakers can handle marketing in Hindi, and some men can discuss common topics. Those with a college education have learned English, and speak it outside Pangi and in educated circles. *Lg Dev:* Literacy rate in second language: 9% men, 1% women. In 1981 9% of the men had a 5th grade education, 1% of the women; 3% of the men had an 8th grade education, 0.3% of the women. *Other:* Speakers are called 'Pangwala' or 'Pangi'. A Scheduled Tribe in India. Mountain slope. Alpine forest. 1,600 to 3,600 meters. Agriculturalists: wheat, barley, maize, ragi, millet, potatoes, pulses; animal husbandry: cattle, yaks, sheep, goats. Hindu.

Paniya (Pania, Paniyan, Panyah, Nil) [pcg] 63,827 (1981 census). Population includes 56,952 in Kerala, 6,393 in Tamil Nadu, 482 in Karnataka. Kerala, Wynad,

Kozhikode, Kannur, Malappuram districts; Tamil Nadu, west of Nilgiris Hillls; Karnataka. *Class:* Dravidian, Southern, Tamil-Kannada, Tamil-Kodagu, Tamil-Malayalam, Malayalam. *Dialects:* Intelligibility of Malappura Paniya by Kodagu is 66%. Dialects have 79% to 88% lexical similarity with Malappura Paniya, Kodagu has 71%. *Lg Use:* Used in the home and religion. Christians pray in Malayalam. State languages: Malayalam, Tamil, or Kannada used with non-Paniya speakers. *Lg Dev:* Literacy rate in second language: 11% (1981 census). Malayalam in Kerala, Tamil in Tamil Nadu, and Kannada in Karnataka. *Other:* A Scheduled Tribe in India. Mountain slope, hills, coastal. Forest. Agricultural workers; woodcutters; fishermen. Hindu, traditional religion, Christian.

Panjabi, Eastern (Punjabi, Gurmukhi, Gurumukhi) [pan] 27,109,000 in India. Population includes 26,975,000 Panjabi, 134,000 Bhatneri (1991). Population total all countries: 28,006,704. Punjab, Majhi in Gurdaspur and Amritsar districts, Bhatyiana in South Firozpur District; Rajasthan, Bhatyiana in north Ganganagar District; Haryana; Delhi; Jammu and Kashmir. Also spoken in Bangladesh, Canada, Fiji, Kenya, Malaysia, Mauritius, Singapore, United Arab Emirates, United Kingdom, USA. *Class:* Indo-European, Indo-Iranian, Indo-Aryan, Central zone, Panjabi. *Dialects:* Panjabi Proper, Majhi, Doab, Bhatyiana (Bhatneri, Bhatti), Powadhi, Malwa, Bathi. Western Panjabi is distinct from Eastern Panjabi, although there is a chain of dialects to Western Hindi (Urdu). Bhatyiana considered to be a mixture of Panjabi and Rajasthani. See separate entry for Dogri-Kangri. *Lg Use:* State language of Punjab. *Lg Dev:* Gurmukhi and Devanagari scripts. Grammar. Bible: 1959–2002. *Other:* Gurumukhi is associated with Sikhs. Different from Majhi in India and Nepal. Sikh, Muslim (Bhatneri).

Panjabi, Mirpur (Mirpuri) [pmu] 1,022,000 in India (2000). Population total all countries: 1,042,000. Kashmir, Mirpur area, near Pakistan border. Also possibly in Pakistan. Also spoken in United Kingdom. *Class:* Indo-European, Indo-Iranian, Indo-Aryan, Northwestern zone, Lahnda. *Dialects:* Distinct from Western Panjabi, although closely related. *Other:* Agriculturalists. Hindu, Sikh, Christian.

Panjabi, Western (Hindki, Western Punjabi, Lahnda, Lahanda, Lahndi) [pnb] 27,386 in India (1991 census). Jammu and Kashmir; Delhi; Haryana. *Other:* Muslim, Christian. See main entry under Pakistan.

Pankhu (Pankho, Panko, Pangkhu, Pankhua, Pang Khua, Pankua, Paang, Pang) [pkh] 234 in India (1971). Mizoram, Chhimtuipui, Lunglei districts, 12 villages. *Lg Use:* Speakers also use Mizo, Chin Bawm, or English. *Other:* Scheduled Tribe in India. A subgroup of the Mizo. Tropical forest. Agriculturalists. Christian. See main entry under Bangladesh.

Pao (Pabra) [ppa] 7,223 (1981 census). Madhya Pradesh, Satna, Chhatarpur, Datia, Panna, Rewa, Shahdol, Sidhi, Tikamgarh districts. *Class:* Sino-Tibetan, Tibeto-Burman, Unclassified. *Dialects:* May not be Tibeto-Burman. *Lg Use:* Speakers also use Hindi. *Other:* A Scheduled Tribe in India. Singh (1994) reports they speak Bagheli as first language. Agriculturalists. Hindu.

Pardhan (Pradhan, Pradhani) [pch] 116,919 (1981 census). Andhra Pradesh, Adilbad District; Madhya Pradesh, Seoni, Mandla, Chhindawara, Hoshangabad, Betul, Balaghat, Jabalpur districts; Chhattisgarh, Raipur, Bilaspur districts; Maharashtra, Bhandara, Garhchiroli, Nagpur, Wardha,Yavatmal districts. *Class:* Dravidian, South-Central, Gondi-Kui, Gondi. *Dialects:* Probably more than 1 language. *Lg Use:* Most speak Hindi in Madhya Pradesh, Marathi in Maharashtra. *Other:* Singh (1994) says Gondi is their first language. Agriculturalists. Hindu.

Pardhi (Bahelia, Chita Pardhi, Lango Pardhi, Paidia, Paradi, Paria, Phans Pardhi, Takankar, Takia) [pcl] 119,700 (2000). Andhra Pradesh; Madhya Pradesh; Gujarat; Maharashtra; scattered over wide area. *Class:* Indo-European, Indo-Iranian, Indo-Aryan, Central zone, Bhil. *Dialects:* Neelishikari, Pittala Bhasha, Takari. Probably more than 1 language (Lango). Possibly a dialect of Bhili. *Other:* Reported they speak Gujarati and Hindi as first language in Madhya Pradesh. A Scheduled Tribe in India, Scheduled Caste in Madhya Pradesh. Different than Paradhi, who speak Kachchi. Plains. Hunter-gatherers; mixed commerce; agriculturalists. Traditional religion, Hindu, Christian.

Parenga (Parengi, Pareng, Parenga Parja, Parenji, Poroja, Gorum, Gorum Sama) [pcj] Ethnic population: 767 (2002). Orissa, Koraput District; Andhra Pradesh. *Class:* Austro-Asiatic, Munda, South Munda, Koraput Munda, Sora-Juray-Gorum, Gorum. *Lg Use:* Study being done at Telugu University. Remembered only by a few older adults and is not actively spoken by anyone (Chamberlain 1997). Probably extinct. Speakers are shifting to Adivasi Oriya. *Lg Dev:* Literacy rate in second language: 11.5% (1981 census). *Other:* A Scheduled Tribe in India. Erroneously called Gadaba. Nearly extinct.

Parsi (Parsee) [prp] 151,341 in India (2000 WCD). Population total all countries: 326,341. Gujarat; Maharashtra. Also reported to be in Australia, Bangladesh, Canada, Germany, Hong Kong, Kazakhstan, Kyrgyzstan, Malaysia, New Zealand, Singapore, Switzerland, Tajikistan, Uzbekistan, southern and western Africa, elsewhere in Europe. Also spoken in China, Pakistan, United Kingdom, USA. *Class:* Indo-European, Indo-Iranian, Iranian, Western, Northwestern, Central Iran. *Dialects:* Parsi is reported to not be inherently intelligible with Parsi-Dari, from whom they separated 600 to 700 years ago or more. Other reports say they came to India 1300 years ago. Related to Dari in Iran. *Lg Dev:* Literacy rate in second language: 90% in English. Most speakers are well educated. *Other:* 'Parsee' is the name of the ethnic group. Distinct from Parsi, a dialect of Gujarati. Zoroastrian.

Pattani (Manchati, Manchad, Patni, Chamba, Chamba Lahuli, Lahuli, Swangla, Changsapa Boli) [lae] 11,000 (1997). Himachal Pradesh, Lahul Valley, Pattan, Chamba-Lahul, and lower Mayar valleys. *Class:* Sino-Tibetan, Tibeto-Burman, Himalayish, Tibeto-Kanauri, Western Himalayish, Kanauri. *Dialects:* Chamba-Lahuli (Western Pattani), Eastern Pattani, Central Pattani. Western Pattani has 63% to 55% lexical similarity with Tinani, 39% to 26% with Bunan, 37% with Shumcho, 35% with Jangshung, 33% with Sunam, 31% with Chitkuli and Kanauri, 25% with Puh and Kinnaur District varieties (Kinnaur Bhoti) of Tibetan, 22% with Nesang, 18% with Lhasa Tibetan, 14% to 15% with the Spiti and Stod varieties of Tibetan. *Lg Use:* Language of wider communication. 5,000 second-language speakers (1997). Used in the home, village, religion. Positive language attitude. Hindi is used in education and trade. *Lg Dev:* Literacy rate in second language: High. Poetry. Bible portions: 1907–1914. *Other:* Lahaula and Swangla are both Scheduled Tribes in India. Hindu.

Pengo (Pengu, Hengo, Hengo Poraja, Jani, Muddali, Paraja, Pango, Pengua, Pango Paraja) [peg] 350,000 (2000). Orissa, Koraput District, Kashipur, Pappadahandi, Nowrangapur, Dasamantapur and Nandapur tahsils, Kalahandi District. *Class:* Dravidian, South-Central, Gondi-Kui, Konda-Kui, Manda-Kui, Manda-Pengo. *Dialects:* Indi, Awe. *Lg Use:* Many Pengo outside the area speak only Oriya (Burrow). Most are fluent in Oriya (Burrow). *Lg Dev:* Dictionary. *Other:* They consider themselves to be separate from Jhodia Poraja. Swidden agriculturalists. Traditional religion, Hindu.

Phake (Phakial, Phakey, Faake) [phk] 5,000 (1990 Diller). Assam, Dibrugarh District, Bor-phake, Nam-phake, Tipam-phake, Man-long, Man-po-mung, Pha-neng, Ning-gam, Nong-lai, Mung-lang villages along the Dihing River; Arunachal Pradesh. *Class:* Tai-Kadai, Kam-Tai, Be-Tai, Tai-Sek, Tai, Southwestern, Northwest. *Dialects:* Close to Aiton. Similar to Shan of Myanmar. *Lg Use:* Speakers also use Assamese. Tai language is taught to children in village schools. *Lg Dev:* Tai script.

Phudagi (Vadval) [phd] 1,009 (2000 WCD). Maharashtra, Thane District. *Class:* Indo-European, Indo-Iranian, Indo-Aryan, Southern zone, Konkani. *Dialects:* A more divergent dialect of, or closely related language to, Konkani.

Pnar [pbv] 84,000 in India (1991). Population total all countries: 88,000. Meghalaya, Khasi and Jaintia Hills, north of the War Jaintia; Mizoram, Aizawl District, north; Assam, North Cachar Hills, Jatinga, Borolokha, Dibruchera; Karbi Anglong District, Ulukunchi. Also spoken in Bangladesh. *Class:* Austro-Asiatic, Mon-Khmer, Northern Mon-Khmer, Khasian. *Dialects:* Jaintia (Synteng), Nongtung. Formerly considered to be a dialect of Khasi. Jaintia dialect has 12 spoken forms: Jowai, Shangpung, Batau, Raliang, Sutnga, Sumer, Martiang, Barato, Rymbai, Lakadong, Mynso, Nongtalang. All are intelligible except for Nongtalang which is akin to Khmer. Jowai is the standard spoken form. *Lg Use:* Speakers also use Bengali, Hindi, or Mizo. *Lg Dev:* Roman script. Radio programs. *Other:* A Scheduled Tribe in India. Agriculturalists; hunter-gatherers. Christian.

Powari [pwr] 213,874 (1991 census). Ethnic population: 2,000,000 (1986 All India Powar council). Madhya Pradesh, Balaghat, Seoni, Chindwara, Betul districts; Maharashtra, Wardha, Bhandara, Gondia districts. *Class:* Indo-European, Indo-Iranian, Indo-Aryan, Central zone. *Dialects:* Bhoyar Powari (Bhoyari, Bhomiyari, Bhoyaroo, Bhuiyar, Bhuria, Bohoyeri), Vyneganga Powari, Govari of Seoni, Khalari, Koshti, Kumbhari, Lodhi, Marari. Reported intelligibility between Bhoyar and Vyneganga. Balaghat district dialect is considered central among Bhoyar and Vyneganga varieties. Lexical similarity 60% to 87% among dialects; Koshti, Kumbhari, and Khalari cluster at 80% to 83%; 49% to 65% with Bagheli, 46% to 64% with Bundeli. *Lg Use:* Powari use is decreasing in the Bhoyar and Vyneganga dialect areas. Half the children learn Hindi or Marathi first. Used mainly in the home except by a very few older adult women. Neutral or negative language attitude to first language. For education and community development many prefer Hindi or Marathi. About 50% of those in Madhya Pradesh are adequately bilingual in Hindi or Marathi. *Lg Dev:* Literacy rate in second language: 72% in the Powari-speaking districts (2001 census). *Other:* Younger generation is getting education. Hills. Forest. Agriculturalists. Hindu.

Purik (Purigskad, Burig, Purig, Purki, Purik Bhotia, Burigskat) [prx] 132,000 (1991). North Kashmir, Kargil District. Suru Valley is the main population center. It is the dominant group in Suru, a sizeable minority is in Dras Valley, and a minority is in the western Himalayas. *Class:* Sino-Tibetan, Tibeto-Burman, Himalayish, Tibeto-Kanauri, Tibetic, Tibetan, Western. *Dialects:* Close to Balti. *Lg Use:* Dominant language in Kargil District. Level of education and bilingual proficiency in Urdu is low. Uneducated men speak little Urdu. Women tend to speak only Purik. *Lg Dev:* Persian-Arabic script. NT: 1950. *Other:* People are called 'Purig-pa'. 'Purig' means 'of Tibetan origin'. People prefer to be culturally and linguistically identified with Tibet, although religiously with Islam. A Scheduled Tribe in India. Muslim (Shi'a), Christian.

Rabha (Rava) [rah] 139,365 (2004). Ethnic population: 200,000 (2002). West Assam, Darrang, Goalpara, Kamrup districts; Nagaland; West Bengal, Jalpaiguri, Alipurduar Subdivision, Cooch Behar District, Tafangunj Subdivision; Meghalaya, East Garo Hills District. *Class:* Sino-Tibetan, Tibeto-Burman, Jingpho-Konyak-Bodo, Konyak-Bodo-Garo, Bodo-Garo, Koch. *Dialects:* Maitaria (Maituri, Maitoria), Rangdania (Rongdani). Maituri and Rongdania have inherent intelligibility to each other's speakers. There is a third dialect called Koch Rabha, spoken in Assam close to West Bengal border. It is not intelligible with Rongdania (Fr. Jose 2002). Possibly as many as 7 dialects. *Lg Use:* The majority of the ethnic group speak Assamese as first language; the rest speak Rabha as first language. Rongdani is the standard dialect but is almost dying out. Assamese and Bengali spoken by many. *Lg Dev:* Literacy rate in second language: 25%. Assamese script. Radio programs. TV. Dictionary. Grammar. NT: 2000. *Other:* A Scheduled Tribe in India. Agriculturalists. Traditional religion, Hindu, Christian.

Rajbanshi (Kamtapuri, Rajbangsi, Rajbansi, Rajbongshi, Tajpuri) [rjb] 2,839,481 in India (1991 census). Population total all countries: 2,982,280. West Bengal, Jalpaiguri, Cooch Behar, Darjeeling, Maldah, Murshidabad districts; Assam, Goalpara District; Bihar, Purnia District. Also spoken in Bangladesh, Nepal. *Class:* Indo-European, Indo-Iranian, Indo-Aryan, Eastern zone, Bengali-Assamese. *Dialects:* Western Rajbanshi, Central Rajbanshi, Eastern Rajbanshi. Central dialect has majority of speakers and is quite uniform; it is used in publications. Western dialect has more diversity. Lexical similarity 77% to 89% between dialects, 48% to 55% with Hindi, 43% to 49% with Nepali. *Lg Use:* Assamese is spoken by the Rajbanshi in Assam. *Lg Dev:* Devanagari script in Nepal. Poetry. Magazines. Videos. Dictionary. Grammar. *Other:* A Scheduled Caste in India. SOV; passive voice is occasionally used; nontonal. Agriculturalists. Hindu syncretism with traditional religion.

Ralte [ral] 303 in India (2000 WCD). Mizoram, mainly Aizawl District, scattered in Lunglei and Chhimtuipui districts; Manipur; Tripura, a few villages in the Jampui Hills. *Lg Use:* Speakers also use Mizo. *Lg Dev:* Though literacy is high, formal education level is low (in Tripura). *Other:* A Scheduled Tribe in India. A subgroup of the Mizo. Spoken only in villages of northern Mizoram (Singh 95). Agriculturalists. Christian. See main entry under Myanmar.

Rangkas (Johari, Saukiya Khun, Saukas, Shaukas, Chyanam, Kyonam, Canpa) [rgk] Extinct. Ethnic population: 1,014 in India, 1,421 all countries (2000). Uttaranchal, Pithoragarh District, Johar Valley, Darchula and Munsyari tahsils, facing the Nepal border along the Mahakali Valley. *Class:* Sino-Tibetan, Tibeto-Burman, Himalayish, Tibeto-Kanauri, Western Himalayish, Almora. *Other:* Rangkas people have merged their identity with the dominant Kumauni people and the language has been replaced by Kumauni. 'Rangkas' sometimes used to refer to the whole group of Darmiya, Chaudangsi, Byangsi and the now extinct Johari.

Rathawi (Kohelia, Bal-La) [rtw] 308,640 (1981 census). Gujarat, Baroda and Panchmahals districts. *Class:* Indo-European, Indo-Iranian, Indo-Aryan, Central zone, Bhil. *Dialects:* 76% intelligibility of Bhilali. There is a dialect continuum from Bhilali to Rathawa, but the extremes have limited intelligibility of each other. Lexical similarity 83% with Bhilali. *Lg Dev:* Literacy rate in second language: 12%, 21% males, 3% females. *Other:* A Scheduled Tribe in India. Distinct from Rathwi Bareli in Madhya Pradesh. Agriculturalists. Hindu.

Ravula (Adiya, Adiyan, Yoruba, Yerava, Panjiri Yerava, Iryavula) [yea] 27,413 (1981). Population includes 19,261 Yerava in Karnataka (1981 census), and 8,152 Adiya in Kerala (1981 census). Karnataka, Coorg (Kodagu) District; Kerala, Wayanad and Kannur districts. *Class:*

Dravidian, Southern, Tamil-Kannada, Tamil-Kodagu, Tamil-Malayalam, Malayalam. *Dialects:* Adiya, Pani Yerava, Panjiri Yerava. 93% to 94% dialect intelligibility between Yerava and Adiya. Relationship of Pani Yerava is uncertain. May be a dialect of Ravula or of Paniya. Lexical similarity 83% to 98% among Yerava and Adiya varieties, 53% to 61% with Standard Malayalam, 35% to 40% with Badaga, 32% to 42% with Colloquial Kannada, 66% to 74% Pani Yerava with Adiya and Yerava. *Lg Use:* Vigorous. Positive language attitude. Proficiency in Kannada (in Karnataka) and Malayalam (in Kerala) is low. *Lg Dev:* Literacy rate in second language: In Karnataka, 6.4%; male 8.6%, female 4%; in Kerala, 15%; male 21%, female 9.3%. High motivation for literature, literacy. Kannada and Malayalam scripts. *Other:* Speakers are called 'Ravula' or 'Panjiri Yerava' in Karnataka, and 'Ravula' or 'Adiya' in Kerala. They prefer 'Ravula' in both places. Adiyan is a Scheduled Tribe in Karnataka and Tamil Nadu. Yerava is a Scheduled Tribe in Karnataka. Pani Yeravas are not the same as the Paniya of Wynad District. Hills. Tropical forest. 700 to 2,100 meters. Agricultural workers. Hindu, Muslim, Buddhist, Christian.

Rawang (Nung Rawang, Ganung-Rawang, Hkanung, Numg, Krangku, Taron, Kiutze, Ch'opa, Chiutse) [raw] 60,536 in India (2000 WCD). *Dialect:* Kunlang. *Other:* The Chinese name is 'Kiutze' or 'Qiuze'. The Lisu name is 'Ch'opa'. See main entry under Myanmar.

Rawat (Dzanggali, Janggali, Jangali, Jhangar, Raut, Raji, Ban Rauts, Ban Manus, Bhulla) [jnl] 2,926 in India (2000 WCD). Uttaranchal, Pithoragarh District, north of Askot Maila, 9 villages. *Lg Use:* Speakers also use Kumauni. *Lg Dev:* Literacy rate in first language: below 1%. Younger generation taking interest in literacy. *Other:* Raji is a Scheduled Tribe in India. The name Raji used by the government. Contains a lot of Indo-Aryan loans. Raute are found in Kumaon where they are known as Raji (Gurung). Forest dwellers. 900 to 1,600 meters. Hunter-gatherers; recently agriculturalists. Hindu, traditional religion. See main entry under Nepal.

Reli (Relli) [rei] 19,000 (1997). Andhra Pradesh, near Adiwasi Oriya; Orissa, Koraput District. *Class:* Indo-European, Indo-Iranian, Indo-Aryan, Eastern zone, Oriya. *Dialects:* Possibly a dialect of Oriya. *Other:* Speakers known by Adiwasi Oriya people. A Scheduled Caste in India. Hindu.

Riang (Reang, Kau Bru, Tipra) [ria] 139,000 in India (1997). Population total all countries: 140,011. Assam, Karimganj District; central Tripura; Mizoram, Aizawl, Lunglei, Chhimtuipui districts, mostly along bank of Karnafuli River, 30 villages. Also spoken in Bangladesh. *Class:* Sino-Tibetan, Tibeto-Burman, Jingpho-Konyak-Bodo, Konyak-Bodo-Garo, Bodo-Garo, Bodo. *Dialects:* Considered to be a dialect of Kok Borok. *Lg Dev:* Literacy rate in second language: Very low. School attendance is low. Roman script. NT: 1990. *Other:* A Scheduled Tribe in India. Different from Riang of Myanmar, a Mon-Khmer language. Muanthanga says they speak a dialect of Kokborok called "Polong-O." Forest. Traditional religion, Muslim, Christian.

Rongpo ("Manchhi Bhassa," "Marchha," "Marchha Pahari," Rangkas, Rangpa, Rang Po Bhasa, "Tolchha") [rnp] 7,500 (2001 D. Bradley). Uttaranchal, Chamoli district, Joshimath Tahsel, Niti valley, Niti, Gamshali, Bampa, Malari villages; Mana valley, Mana, Indradhara, Gajkoti, Pathiya-Dhantoli, Hanuman Chatti, Benakuli, Aut; Marchha dialect in Mana and Niti valleys, Tolchha in Niti valley (very few in number). *Class:* Sino-Tibetan, Tibeto-Burman, Himalayish, Tibeto-Kanauri, Western Himalayish. *Dialects:* "Marchha," "Tolchha." A Himalayan language distinct from Tibetan. Differences between Marchha and Tolchha dialects are phonetic only. *Lg Use:* Rongpo

speakers learn Garhwali simultaneously with Rongpo. Code switching and code mixing are very common. Used in the home and with friends from same group. Not used in any type of written domain. All ages. There is a history of stable bilingualism in Garhwali or Hindi. Some speakers also use Kumauni. *Lg Dev:* Hindi is used for all written communication. *Grammar. Other:* Contains a large number of Indo-Aryan loanwords. Grierson referred to this as the "Garhwal dialect of Tibetan." Marchha and Tolchha names are not very acceptable to the people. 'Ranglo' or 'Rang' often used as a cover term for Byangs, Chaudangs, Darma, and Rongpo. Hindu.

Ruga [ruh] Meghalaya, near the Garo. *Class:* Sino-Tibetan, Tibeto-Burman, Jingpho-Konyak-Bodo, Konyak-Bodo-Garo, Bodo-Garo, Koch. *Dialects:* Most closely related to A'tong, Koch, Rabha. Not inherently intelligible with Garo. *Lg Use:* Speakers are older adults. Most Ruga are more fluent in Garo than Ruga. *Other:* Nearly extinct.

Sadri (Sadani, Sadana, Sadati, Sadari, Sadhan, Sadna, Sadrik, Santri, Siddri, Sradri, Sadhari, Sadan, Nagpuria, Nagpuri, Chota Nagpuri, Dikku Kaji, Gawari, Ganwari, Goari, Gauuari, Jharkhandhi) [sck] 1,965,000 in India (1997). Population includes 1,381,000 Sadani, 574,000 Nagpuria. Population total all countries: 2,165,000. Jharkhand, Ranchi, Palamu districts; Assam; Madhya Pradesh; West Bengal; Orissa; Andaman Islands; Nagaland. Also spoken in Bangladesh. *Class:* Indo-European, Indo-Iranian, Indo-Aryan, Eastern zone, Bihari. *Dialects:* Intelligibility of all dialects with each other is high, except for Sadri of Bangladesh, where it is 77%. Speakers name 3 kinds of Sadri: Sadani (finer, respectful, formal), Common Sadri (Nagpuri), and Lower Sadri (rough). Dialects have 77% to 96% lexical similarity, 58% to 71% with Hindi, 47% to 54% with Oriya, 45% to 61% with Bengali. *Lg Use:* Spoken by Scheduled Tribes, Scheduled Castes, and other communities. Spoken by the Chero as first language. Positive language attitude. Speakers also use Hindi, Oriya, and Bengali. Hindi used in market, with leaders, for prayer and worship, but proficiency is low. *Lg Dev:* Literacy rate in second language: 15% to 25%. Devanagari script. Magazines. Radio programs. Dictionary. NT: 1931–1986. *Other:* Agriculturalists; laborers: tea estates, rice. Hindu, traditional religion, Christian, Muslim.

Sajalong (Miji, Dammai) [sjl] 4,000 (1999 Breton). Arunachal Pradesh, West Kemang District, Bichom and Pakesa River valley, 25 villages including Debbing, Dichik, Rurang, Nachinghom, Upper Dzang, Naku, Khellong, Dibrick, Nizong, Najang, Zangnaching, Chalang, Nafra, Lower Dzang; East Kameng District including villages of Wakke, Nabolong, Kojo, Rojo, Sekong, Panker, Zarkam, Drackchi, Besai, Naschgzang, Sachung, Gerangzing, Kampaa, Salang, Lada Circle, Pego, Dongko. *Class:* Sino-Tibetan, Tibeto-Burman, Unclassified. *Dialects:* Generally considered to be in the Mirish subgroup. *Lg Use:* All ages. Speakers also use Aka, Nisi, Moinba, Assamese, English, or Hindi. Educated speak Hindi more fluently than uneducated, but all speakers know some Hindi. *Lg Dev:* Literacy rate in second language: 3%. Roman script. *Other:* A Scheduled Tribe in India. Hills, mountain slope. Forest. Swidden agriculturalists. Traditional religion (Phong kelum), Christian.

Sakechep (Sankechep) [sch] 20,000 to 30,000 (2003). Assam, Karbi Anglong, N. Cachar Hills, Cachar Hills districts; Nagaland, Kohima District, Khelma village; Meghalaya, Jaintia Hills District, Saithsma, Rumphung, Mongor villages; Tripura. *Class:* Sino-Tibetan, Tibeto-Burman, Kuki-Chin-Naga, Kuki-Chin, Northern. *Dialects:* Khelma, Thangkachep, Sakechep. Dialects are intelligible and are maybe just alternate names for Sakechep depending on the region. Closely related to

Biete, Hrangkhol. *Lg Use:* Sakechep spoken at home. All ages. Bilingualism varies according to which state they live in. Some speak Hindi, Bengali, Khasi, Karbi, Hmar, Chin Thado. *Lg Dev:* Literacy rate in second language: 25%. Roman script. Radio programs. Bible portions: 2002. *Other:* Hindu, Christian.

Samvedi [smv] Maharashtra. *Class:* Indo-European, Indo-Iranian, Indo-Aryan, Southern zone, Konkani. *Dialects:* A more divergent dialect of, or closely related language to Konkani. Shares many features with Gujarati.

Sansi (Bhilki, Sansiboli) [ssi] 60,000 in India (2002 Gusain). Population total all countries: 76,200. Punjab; Rajasthan; Haryana; Delhi; Jammu and Kashmir; Madhya Pradesh; Karnataka; Uttar Pradesh. Also spoken in Pakistan. *Class:* Indo-European, Indo-Iranian, Indo-Aryan, Central zone, Western Hindi, Hindustani, Sansi. *Dialects:* Intermediate between Punjabi and Hindustani. They sometimes identify themselves as Marwari. Lexical similarity 71% with Urdu, 83% with the Sochi language variety. Numerous phonological and morphological borrowings from Punjabi, Hindi, and Gujarati (Gusain). *Lg Use:* Not being passed on to the next generation and is on the verge of extinction. Much mixing of Hindi, Punjabi, or Gujarati into the language (Gusain). Few people below the age of forty are fully competent in the language and probably none of them will become active speakers (Gusain). Second language is Sindhi, followed by Urdu, Panjabi, and Saraiki. *Lg Dev:* Literacy rate in first language: below 1%. Literacy rate in second language: below 5%. *Other:* Related to Rajasthani, Sindhi, Punjabi. Bhils by caste. Called a 'Gypsy' language. They have an argot called 'Farsi'. Gusain classifies this as a Rajasthani dialect. They are socially separate from surrounding groups and are governed by their own social norms and economy. They are in the process of losing their tribal characteristics but are not yet integrated into the national mainstream (Gusain). Sharecroppers; cobblers (Sochi). Hindu.

Sanskrit [san] 6,106 (1981 census). *Class:* Indo-European, Indo-Iranian, Indo-Aryan. *Lg Use:* Official language. 194,433 second-language speakers. *Lg Dev:* Literacy rate in first language: 60% to 100%. Literacy rate in second language: 15% to 25% literate. Bible: 1822. *Other:* Literary and liturgical language.

Santali (Hor, Har, Satar, Santhali, Sandal, Sangtal, Santal, Sentali, Samtali, Santhiali, Sonthal) [sat] 5,959,000 in India (1997). Population total all countries: 6,156,260. Assam; Bihar; Orissa; Tripura; West Bengal; Mizoram. Also spoken in Bangladesh, Bhutan, Nepal. *Class:* Austro-Asiatic, Munda, North Munda, Kherwari, Santali. *Dialects:* Karmali (Khole), Kamari-Santali, Lohari-Santali, Manjhi, Paharia, Mahali (Mahili, Mahli). Close to Ho and Mundari. *Lg Use:* Official language. *Lg Dev:* Literacy rate in first language: 10% to 30%. Literacy rate in second language: 25% to 50%. Taught in primary schools. Roman and Oriya scripts; Roman script in Bangladesh. Magazines. Dictionary. Grammar. Bible: 1914–2001. *Other:* Santali is a Scheduled Tribe in India. Agriculturalists; laborers. Hindu, traditional religion, Christian.

Saurashtra (Saurashtri, Sourashtra, Sowrashtra, Patnuli) [saz] 310,000 (1997). The districts mentioned each have communities of at least 5,000 speakers. Tamil Nadu, Madurai, Thanjavur, Dindugul Quaid-E. Milleth, Ramanathapuram, Chengai-Annai, Salem, Tiruchchirappalli, Tirunelveli, North Arcot districts; Madras, Deccan, Madurai, Thanjavur, Salem cities; Karnataka; Andhra Pradesh. *Class:* Indo-European, Indo-Iranian, Indo-Aryan, Central zone, Gujarati. *Dialects:* Southern Saurashtra, Northern Saurashtra. Indo-Aryan elements in its deep structure reveal Gujarati relationship. Has borrowed some structure from Dravidian, lexicon from Telugu and Tamil. An Indo-European island surrounded by Dravidian languages. The 3 main populations in Salem, Thanjavur, and Madurai cities had between 67% and 97% inherent intelligibility. All varieties sampled had 77% to 96% lexical similarity. The 3 main populations in Salem, Thanjavur, and Madurai cities 84% to 96%. Southern dialects have 83% or higher lexical similarity with Thanjavur dialect. *Lg Use:* Vigorous. Used at home and in prayer. Most adults speak Saurashtra in private. Most adults speak Tamil in public. *Lg Dev:* Dictionary. NT: 2001. *Other:* The nonweavers are generally better educated. System of exogamous clans. Has had its own script for centuries. A modern version developed in the late 1800s. Since the end of the 19th century, books have been printed using Telugu, Tamil, Devanagari, and Saurashtra scripts. Currently an adapted Tamil script is most commonly employed, using superscript numbers and a colon to show sounds not used in Tamil. Traditionally silk weavers 40% to 70%; commerce; professions. Hindu (Brahmin).

Sauria Paharia (Malto, Malti, Maltu, Maler, Sawriya Malto, Malatri) [mjt] 110,000 in India (2000). Population total all countries: 122,000. Jharkhand, northern part of former Santhal Pargana District, Rajmahal hills proper, mainly in Sahibganj and Godda districts, Litipara Block of Pakaur District; West Bengal, Bankura, Barddhaman, and Murshidabad districts. Also spoken in Bangladesh. *Class:* Dravidian, Northern. *Dialect:* Sahibganj, Godda, Hiranpur, Litipara (Chatgam). Inherent intelligibility with Kumarbhag Paharis is inadequate. Related to Kurux. Lexical similarity 80% with Kumarbhag Paharia. *Lg Dev:* Literacy rate in second language: 6.9%. Literacy classes. Magazines. Newspapers. NT: 1999. *Other:* Part of the Malto ethnic group. A Scheduled Tribe in India. Hills, plains. Forest. 300 to 700 meters. Swidden agriculturalists: rice, maize, wheat, sugarcane, lentils, vegetables; animal husbandry: dairy cattle, goats, pigs, poultry; fishermen; hunters; firewood gatherers. Traditional religion, Christian.

Savara [svr] 20,179 (2000 WCD). Andhra Pradesh; Orissa. *Class:* Dravidian, South-Central, Telugu. *Lg Dev:* Savara indigenous, Oriya and Telugu scripts. *Other:* Distinct from Sora (Savara).

Sentinel (Sentinelese) [std] 101 (2000 WCD). Southeastern Andaman Islands, Sentinel Island. *Class:* Andamanese, South Andamanese. *Dialects:* Similar to Önge. *Other:* A Scheduled Tribe in India. Reserved toward outsiders. Hills. Forest. Hunter-gatherers; fishermen. Traditional religion.

Seraiki (Saraiki, Multani, Mutani, Siraiki, Southern Panjabi, Reasati, Riasati, Bahawalpuri) [skr] 20,000 in India (2000). Punjab; Maharashtra; Andhra Pradesh; Madhya Pradesh; Uttar Pradesh; Rajasthan; Delhi; Gujarat. *Dialect:* Jafri, Siraiki Hindki, Thali, Jatki, Bahawalpuri (Bhawalpuri, Riasati, Reasati). *Lg Dev:* Literacy rate in first language: below 1%. Literacy rate in second language: 15% Urdu, Marathi. *Other:* A new literary language based on south Lahnda dialects, especially Multani and Bahawalpuri. Mountain slope. Tropical forest. Muslim (Hanafite), Christian. See main entry under Pakistan.

Shekhawati (Shekhawati-Marwari) [swv] 3,000,000 (2002 Gusain). Rajasthan, Sikar, Jhunjhunun, Churu districts. *Class:* Indo-European, Indo-Iranian, Indo-Aryan, Central zone, Rajasthani, Marwari. *Dialects:* Jhunjhunu-Churu, Sikar. 67% comprehension of Marwari. Lexical similarity 74% to 77% between dialects; 51% to 68% with Marwari, 58% to 80% with Merwari, 45% to 69% with Godwari, 57% to 66% with Mewari, 66% to 73% with Dhundari, 58% to 66% with Harauti, 57% to 70% with Mewati, 69% to 76% with Bagri, 61% to 73% with Haryanvi. *Lg Use:* Speakers also use Hindi.

Shendu (Khyen, Khieng, Shandu, Sandu) [shl] Mizoram. See main entry under Bangladesh.

Sherdukpen (Ngnok) [sdp] 3,100 (2001). Assam; Arunachal Pradesh, West Kameng District, south of the Bomdi La Range, in the valleys of the Tengapani River, mainly Rupa (Kupa), Shargang (Shergaon), Jigang (Jigaon), and Thungrao villages. *Class:* Sino-Tibetan, Tibeto-Burman, Himalayish, Tibeto-Kanauri, Tibetic, Tibetan, Unclassified. *Dialects:* Bugun (Khoa), Lishpa, and Butpa might be related, but are little-known languages (Sun Tianshin Jackson 1993). Sulung may also be related. *Lg Use:* Speakers also use Assamese, Hindi, or Tshangla. *Lg Dev:* Literacy rate in second language: 14.6% (20.4% male, 7.2% female) (1997 Muanthanga). *Other:* A Scheduled Tribe in India. Forest. 1,450 to 2,051 meters. Swidden agriculturalists. Buddhist (Lamaist), syncretism with traditional religion.

Sherpa (Sharpa, Sharpa Bhotia, Xiaerba, Serwa) [xsr] 20,000 in India (1997). West Bengal, Darjeeling District; Sikkim; Arunachal Pradesh. *Other:* A Scheduled Tribe in India. 'Sharpa' means 'easterner', so the term used in different countries may not always refer to this language. Buddhist (Lamaist). See main entry under Nepal.

Shina (Shinaki, Sina) [scl] 21,000 in India (1997). Northern Kashmir, Dras Valley and Gurais area in Kishenganga Valley near the cease fire line. *Dialects:* Drasi, Gurezi. *Lg Use:* Many in Dras Valley also speak Purik, but there are villages in Dras Valley that are pure Shina speaking. *Other:* Speakers are called 'Shin'. People are open to education and jobs outside the area. Distinct from Brokskat. Buddhist, traditional religion, Muslim (Sunni and Shi'a). See main entry under Pakistan.

Sholaga (Kadu Sholigar, Sholiga, Sholigar, Solaga, Soliga, Soligar, Solanayakkans, Sholanayika) [sle] 24,000 (1984 GR). Karnataka, Mysore District, Biligiri Rangana Hills; Tamil Nadu. *Class:* Dravidian, Southern, Tamil-Kannada, Tamil-Kodagu, Tamil-Malayalam, Tamil. *Dialects:* Lexical similarity 65% with Kannada. *Other:* A Scheduled Tribe in India. May be in the Kannada group. Tropical forest. Hunter-gatherers; agriculturalists: cultivators. Hindu, traditional religion.

Shom Peng (Shom Pen, Shompeng, Shompen, Shobang) [sii] 223 (1981 census). Nicobar Islands, interior Great Nicobar Island. *Class:* Austro-Asiatic, Mon-Khmer, Nicobar, Shom Peng. *Dialects:* Distinct from other Nicobarese languages. *Lg Use:* Speakers are mainly monolingual. *Lg Dev:* Dictionary. *Other:* A Scheduled Tribe in India. Seminomadic. Hunter-gatherers; fishermen. Traditional religion.

Shumcho (Sumchu, Sumtsu, Shumcu, Thebor, Thebör Skadd, Thebarskad, Central Kinnauri, Sumcho) [scu] 2,174 (1998). Himachal Pradesh, Kinnaur District, Kanam, Labrang, Spilo, Shyaso, Taling, and Rushkaling villages of Puh Tahsil. *Class:* Sino-Tibetan, Tibeto-Burman, Himalayish, Tibeto-Kanauri, Western Himalayish, Kanauri. *Dialects:* Lexical similarity 70% with Jangshung, 67% with Sunam, 45% with Lower Kinnauri, 43% with Chitkuli. *Other:* Mountain slope, valleys. 5,000 to 6,770 meters. Pastoralists, peasant agriculturalists. Traditional religion, Hindu, Buddhist (Lamaist).

Sikkimese (Sikkim Bhotia, Sikkim Bhutia, Dandzongka, Danjongka, Danyouka, Denjong, Denjongkha, Denjongpa, Denjonke, Denjonka, Lachengpa, Lachungpa, Sikami) [sip] 28,600 (1996). Sikkim, all districts; West Bengal, Darjeeling. Possibly also in Tibet. *Class:* Sino-Tibetan, Tibeto-Burman, Himalayish, Tibeto-Kanauri, Tibetic, Tibetan, Southern. *Dialects:* Partially intelligible with Dzongkha of Bhutan. Lexical similarity 65% with Dzongkha of Bhutan, 42% with Tebetan. *Lg Use:* Vigorous. Positive language attitude. Nepali used for education and trade. A few can speak Tibetan, which is

viewed as appropriate for religion. *Other:* Agriculturalists; pastoralists. Buddhist, Christian.

Simte [smt] 7,150 (2001 census). Southwest Manipur, Churachandpur District, Mingjang, Tubuong, Simveng, New Bazar, Thanlon, Leikangpai, Zouthang, Shumtuk, Monjon, Pamjal, Sasinoujang, Tallian, Dumsao, Khungung, Lungthul, Singhat, Moijin, Maokot, Suangdai, Suangpuhmun. *Class:* Sino-Tibetan, Tibeto-Burman, Kuki-Chin-Naga, Kuki-Chin, Northern. *Dialects:* Related to Thado and Zome. Singh (1994) says this is an alternate name for Paite. *Lg Dev:* Bible: 1992. *Other:* A Scheduled Tribe in India. Christian.

Sindhi [snd] 2,812,000 in India (1997). Gujarat; Maharashtra; Rajasthan; Andhra Pradesh; Bihar; Delhi; Madhya Pradesh; Orissa; Tamil Nadu; Uttar Pradesh. *Dialects:* Bhatia, Jadeji, Kayasthi, Lari, Lasi, Thareli, Thari, Viccholi, Visholi. *Lg Use:* Official language. Many Sindhi do not learn their traditional ethnic language. Used mainly by women and older adults. *Other:* Hindu, Sikh, Muslim, Christian. See main entry under Pakistan.

Singpho (Sing-Fo, Kachin, Jingphaw) [sgp] 3,000 (1997 R. Breton). Assam, Tinsukia District, Margherita Subdivision; Arunachal Pradesh, Lohit, and Changlang districts. *Class:* Sino-Tibetan, Tibeto-Burman, Jingpho-Konyak-Bodo, Jingpho-Luish, Jingpho. *Dialects:* Lexical similarity 50% with Jingpho of Myanmar. *Lg Use:* Speakers also use Hindi or Assamese. *Lg Dev:* Roman script. Bible portions: 1907. *Other:* Many loans from Khamti. 'Kachin' refers to a cultural rather than a linguistic group. A Scheduled Tribe in India. Agriculturalists. Buddhist, syncretism.

Sirmauri (Sirmouri, Sirmuri) [srx] 25,000 (1997). Himachal Pradesh, Shimla (Simla) and Solan districts. *Class:* Indo-European, Indo-Iranian, Indo-Aryan, Northern zone, Western Pahari. *Dialects:* Giripari, Dharthi. May be a dialect of Mahasu Pahari. Dharthi dialect more influenced by Hindi. *Lg Dev:* Takri script. Grammar. *Other:* Dharthi is spoken in Giriwar area, Giripari in Giripar area. Mountain slope.

Sora (Saora, Saonras, Shabari, Sabar, Saura, Savara, Sawaria, Swara, Sabara) [srb] 288,000 (1997). South Orissa, mainly in the Ganjam District, also in the Koraput and Phulbani districts; Andhra Pradesh, Srikakulam District; Madhya Pradesh; Bihar; Tamil Nadu; West Bengal; the Plains Division of Assam. *Class:* Austro-Asiatic, Munda, South Munda, Koraput Munda, Sora-Juray-Gorum, Sora-Juray. *Lg Dev:* Roman and Telugu scripts. Bible: 1992–2000. *Other:* A Scheduled Tribe in India. Hindu, Christian.

Spiti Bhoti (Piti Bhoti) [spt] 10,000 (2000). Himachal Pradesh, Lahul-Spiti District, Spiti subdistrict. *Class:* Sino-Tibetan, Tibeto-Burman, Himalayish, Tibeto-Kanauri, Tibetic, Tibetan, Central. *Dialects:* Not intelligible with Ladakhi, intelligible only with difficulty with Stod Bhoti. All areas of Spiti understand each other. Lexical similarity 41% with Lhasa Tibetan, 57% with Ladakhi (Leh), 57% with Stod Bhoti from Darcha. *Lg Use:* All ages. Positive attitude toward speakers of Ladakhi and Stod Bhoti. Some younger people, educated people, and leaders speak Hindi or English well enough to cover most common topics. Hindi and English seen as avenues to economic advancement. *Lg Dev:* Most literates read Hindi. Some older people and Buddhist monks and nuns read Tibetan. Literacy effort needed. Radio programs. *Other:* Mountain valley. Desert. 3,000 to 4,270 meters (Gete village at 4,270 meters is the highest year-round inhabited village in the world). Pastoralists. Buddhist.

Stod Bhoti (Stod, Tod, Tod-Kad, Stod-Kad, Lahul Bhoti) [sbu] 2,500 (1996). Himachal Pradesh, Lahul Region, Stod, Khoksar, and upper Mayar valleys. *Class:* Sino-Tibetan, Tibeto-Burman, Himalayish, Tibeto-Kanauri,

Tibetic, Tibetan, Central. *Dialects:* Stod (Kolong), Khoksar (Khoksar Bhoti), Mayar (Mayar Bhoti, Mayari). 85% intelligibility of Stod Bhoti by Khoksar, 75% by Mayar, 62% of Khoksar by Mayar, 95% of Khoksar by Stod Bhoti. Lexical similarity 74% with Spiti. *Lg Use:* Used in the home, community, and religion. Attitudes good among speakers toward dialects and with Ladakhi. Many speak Hindi, but their comprehension is lower than that of other Lahul communities. Hindi is used for trade and education. *Lg Dev:* Desire for literacy in Stod Bhoti. Devanagari and Tibetan scripts. *Other:* Buddhist.

Sulung (Puroik) [suv] 5,443 (1991 census). Arunachal Pradesh, East Kameng and Lower Subansiri districts, along the Par River, 53 villages. *Class:* Sino-Tibetan, Tibeto-Burman, North Assam, Tani. *Dialect:* Bugun. A divergent language which some suggest is not Sino-Tibetan but possibly Austro-Asiatic. Chowdhury says intelligible with Bugun. *Lg Use:* Speakers also use Nefamese. *Lg Dev:* Literacy rate in second language: 2%. Devanagari, Assamese, and Roman scripts. Dictionary. *Other:* A 'satellite relationship' to the Nisi and Bangni, 'bonded economically'. A Scheduled Tribe in India. Claim kinship with the Khoa or Bugun. Mountain slope. 914 to 2,134 meters. Transitional between hunter-gatherer and agriculturalists. Traditional religion, Christian, Hindu.

Sunam (Sungam, Sungnam, Thebor, Thebör Skadd, Thebarshad, Central Kinnauri, Sangnaur) [ssk] 558 (1998). Himachal pradesh, Kinnaur District, Sunam village in Puh Tahsil. *Class:* Sino-Tibetan, Tibeto-Burman, Himalayish, Tibeto-Kanauri, Western Himalayish, Kanauri. *Dialects:* Lexical similarity 67% with Shumcho, 65% with Jangshung, 38% with Lower Kinnauri and Chitkuli Kinnauri. *Other:* Mountain slope, valleys. 5,000 to 6,770 meters. Pastoralists, peasant agriculturalists. Traditional religion, Hindu, Buddhist (Lamaist).

Surajpuri (Suraji, Choupal, Chaupal) [sjp] 273,000 (1997). Bihar. *Class:* Indo-European, Indo-Iranian, Indo-Aryan, Eastern zone, Bihari. *Dialects:* May be a dialect of Maithili.

Sylheti (Sylhetti, Sileti, Siloti, Syloti, Syloty, Srihattia, Bengali of Cachar, Sylheti Bangla, Sylheti Bengali) [syl] 3,000,000 in India (2003). South Assam: Surma Valley Region; Karimgani, Karimganj, Cachar, Hailakandi districts; Meghalaya, (Shillong, Jawai); Tripura, (Agartala); Nagaland, (Dimapur); Delhi, Calcutta, Hyderabad, Bombay, other cities. *Lg Dev:* Literacy rate in second language: 10%. Educated speakers can read Bengali. Few women are educated. *Other:* Muslim, Hindu. See main entry under Bangladesh.

Tamang, Eastern [taj] 14,000 in India (1997). West Bengal, Darjeeling; Sikkim, concentrated in lower Teesta valley and Rangit valley; Arunachal Pradesh. *Other:* They migrate from Nepal. See main entry under Nepal.

Tamil (Tamalsan, Tambul, Tamili, Tamal, Damulian) [tam] 61,527,000 in India (1997). Population total all countries: 66,020,200. Tamil Nadu and neighboring states. Also spoken in Bahrain, Fiji, Germany, Malaysia (Peninsular), Mauritius, Netherlands, Qatar, Réunion, Singapore, South Africa, Sri Lanka, Thailand, United Arab Emirates, United Kingdom. *Class:* Dravidian, Southern, Tamil-Kannada, Tamil-Kodagu, Tamil-Malayalam, Tamil. *Dialects:* Adi Dravida, Aiyar, Aiyangar, Arava, Burgandi, Kongar, Madrasi, Pattapu Bhasha, Tamil, Sri Lanka Tamil, Malaya Tamil, Burma Tamil, South Africa Tamil, Tigalu, Harijan, Sanketi, Hebbar, Mandyam Brahmin, Secunderabad Brahmin. Kasuva is a jungle group dialect and may not be intelligible with Tamil. Burgandi speakers are nomadic. Aiyar and Aiyangar are Brahmin dialects. *Lg Use:* State language of Tamil Nadu. 8,000,000 second-language speakers. *Lg Dev:* Tamil script. Films. Bible: 1727–2002. *Other:* SOV. Hindu, Muslim.

Telugu (Telegu, Andhra, Gentoo, Tailangi, Telangire, Telgi, Tengu, Terangi, Tolangan) [tel] 69,634,000 in India (1997). Population total all countries: 69,688,278. Andhra Pradesh and neighboring states. Also spoken in Bahrain, Fiji, Malaysia, Mauritius, Singapore, United Arab Emirates. *Class:* Dravidian, South-Central, Telugu. *Dialect:* Berad, Dasari, Dommara, Golari, Kamathi, Komtao, Konda-Reddi, Salewari, Telangana, Telugu, Vadaga, Srikakula, Vishakhapatnam, East Godaveri, Rayalseema, Nellore, Guntur, Vadari, Yanadi (Yenadi). *Lg Use:* State language of Andhra Pradesh. Yanadi and Bagata are ethnic groups speaking Telugu as first language. 5,000,000 second language speakers. *Lg Dev:* Telugu script. Films. Bible: 1854–2002. *Other:* SOV.

Teressa (Taih-Long) [tef] 2,767 (1999 Hackworth). Nicobar Islands, Teressa and Bompoka islands. *Class:* Austro-Asiatic, Mon-Khmer, Nicobar, Chowra-Teressa. *Dialect:* Bompoka (Bompaka, Pauhut).

Tharu, Dangaura (Chaudary, Chaudhuri, Chaudhari, Dang, Dangora, Dangura, Dangali, Dangha) [thl] 31,000 in India (1981 census). Uttar Pradesh, along the border in Nighasan tahsil of Kheri District and Tulsipur tahsil of Gonda District, also Bahraich District. *Lg Use:* Hindi bilingual proficiency is limited among the 70% to 90% who are uneducated. *Lg Dev:* Literacy rate in second language: 20% to 25% (census). *Other:* Tharu is a Scheduled Tribe in India. Hindu, traditional religion. See main entry under Nepal.

Tharu, Kochila (Saptari) [thq] *Dialect:* Morangia. *Other:* Traditional religion with Hindu overlay. See main entry under Nepal.

Tharu, Rana (Rana Thakur) [thr] 64,000 in India (1981 census). Border with Nepal, Uttar Pradesh: near Nighasan Tahsil of Kheri District and Pilibhit District; Uttaranchal: Khatima, Sitargani, Kiccha, and Haldwani tahsils of Nainital District. *Lg Use:* Among the 70% to 90% who are uneducated, proficiency in Hindi is low. *Lg Dev:* Literacy rate in second language: 20% to 25% (census). *Other:* Tharu is a Scheduled Tribe in India. Hindu, traditional religion. See main entry under Nepal.

Thulung (Thulunge Rai) [tdh] 3,313 in India (1961 census). Sikkim; Uttar Pradesh. *Other:* Agriculturalists; pastoralists. Hindu. See main entry under Nepal.

Tibetan (Central Tibetan, Bhotia, Pohbetian, Tebilian, Tibate, Bod Skad, Poke, Phoke) [bod] 124,280 in India (1994). Tibet border, Himachal Pradesh; Uttaranchal; Arunachal Pradesh; Assam; Delhi; Sikkim. The Darjeeling-Kalimpong area of West Bengal has been heavily settled by Tibetans since at least 1900. *Dialects:* Aba (Batang), Dartsemdo (Tatsienlu), Dru, Gtsang, Hanniu, Jad (Dzad), Kongbo, Marchha, Nganshuenkuan (Anshuenkuan Nyarong), Panakha-Panags, Paurong, Takpa (Dwags). *Other:* Tibetan is a Scheduled Tribe in India. In Himalayan countries 'Bhotiya' means 'people of Tibetan origin' and is applied to those speaking various languages. Buddhist (Lamaist), Christian. See main entry under China (Tibetan, Central).

Tinani (Lahauli, Lahouli, Rangloi, Tinan Lahuli, Lahuli, Teenan, Gondla, Gondhla) [lbf] 2,000 in India (1996). Population total all countries: 2,450 to 3,600. Himachal Pradesh, Lahul and Spiti Subdivision, lower Chandra Valley (Tinan or Rangloi Valley). Gondhla is the main village. Also spoken in China. *Class:* Sino-Tibetan, Tibeto-Burman, Himalayish, Tibeto-Kanauri, Western Himalayish, Kanauri. *Dialects:* Close to Pattani. Lexical similarity 63% to 56% with Chamba Lahuli (Pattani), 32% to 37% with Bunan, 21% with the Spiti and Stod varieties of central Tibetan, 62% with Tandi village, 34% with Shumcho, 32% with Jangshung, 31% with Kanauri and Sunam, 13% with Lhasa Tibetan. *Lg Use:* Used in the home and village, infrequently in religion. Speakers also use Hindi or Pattani.

Lg Dev: Literacy rate in second language: High. Bible portions: 1908–1915. *Other:* 'Lahuli' as applied to the inhabitants of Lahul and Spiti refers primarily to the language of a place. It is not a tight linguistic designation. Speakers are well educated. Mountain slope, valleys. 3,700 to 7,000 meters. Buddhist, Hindu.

Tiwa (Dowyan, Lalung) [lax] 23,000 (1997). Assam, Nowgong, Karbi Anglong, Kamrup, Sibsagar, Lakhimpur districts; Meghalaya, Khasi Hills District. *Class:* Sino-Tibetan, Tibeto-Burman, Jingpho-Konyak-Bodo, Konyak-Bodo-Garo, Bodo-Garo, Bodo. *Lg Use:* In the plains Assamese is used. *Lg Dev:* Literacy rate in second language: 21.5% (31.5% males, 11.2% females). Assamese, Roman scripts. Dictionary. Grammar. NT. *Other:* A Scheduled Tribe in India. Agriculturalists. Buddhist (Tantrayana), syncretism, Hindu, Christian.

Toda (Todi, Tuda) [tcx] 600 (2000). Ethnic population: 1,413 (2000 WCD). Orissa; Tamil Nadu, Nilgiri Hills, Kunda hills. *Class:* Dravidian, Southern, Tamil-Kannada, Tamil-Kodagu, Toda-Kota. *Lg Dev:* Tamil script. Dictionary. Grammar. Bible portions: 1897–1910. *Other:* Toda is a Scheduled Tribe in India. Traditional religion, Christian.

Toto [txo] 20,000 (1994 King). West Bengal, Subhapara, Dhunchipara, Panchayatpara hillocks on the Indo-Bhutan border. *Class:* Sino-Tibetan, Tibeto-Burman, Himalayish, Tibeto-Kanauri, Tibetic, Dhimal. *Dialects:* Not inherently intelligible with Dhimal of Nepal. Low lexical similarity with Dhimal. *Lg Use:* Hindi is also used. The Toto can converse in Bengali and Nepali. *Lg Dev:* Devanagari and Bengali scripts. *Other:* Toto is a Scheduled Tribe in India. SOV; postpositions; genitives, demonstratives, relatives before noun heads; nontonal. Agriculturalists; animal husbandry: poultry, pigs. Traditional religion, Hindu.

Tshangla (Tsangla, Sangla, Cangluo Menba, Memba, Menba, Monba, Monpa, Motuo, Central Monpa) [tsj] Western Arunachal Pradesh, Kameng District, in and around Dirang, Bishing, and several other villages; West Siang District, former Padma-bkod Region, Tuting, Mechuka circles, Mechuka, Opu, Bona, Galling, Korfu, Dorgling Halung, Tuting villages. *Lg Use:* Adi Bokar, Adi Ramo, Hindi and English spoken by some (West Siang). *Other:* A Scheduled Tribe in India. Chowdhury separates Memba (Tshangla-speakers) and Khamba as different tribes in Siang District, both separate from Monpa, in Kameng District. Breton says not the same as Moinba. They claim to have come from Bhutan. Many young people attend school. Sparse forest. Swidden agriculturalists: rice, wet cultivation. Buddhist. See main entry under Bhutan.

Tukpa (Nesang) [tpq] 723 (1998). Himachal Pradesh, Kinnaur District, Nesang, Charang, and Kunnu villages. *Class:* Sino-Tibetan, Tibeto-Burman, Himalayish, Tibeto-Kanauri, Western Himalayish, Kanauri. *Dialects:* Related to Bhoti Kinnauri, Chitkuli Kinnauri, Kanashi.

Tulu (Tal, Tallu, Thalu, Tilu, Tuluva Bhasa, Tullu, Thulu) [tcy] 1,949,000 (1997). 636,123 monolinguals (1981). Andhra Pradesh; Kerala, Kasargod District; Tamil Nadu; Maharashtra; Karnataka, South Kanara (Dakshina Kannada) and Udipi districts; Meghalaya. *Class:* Dravidian, Southern, Tulu. *Lg Use:* Speakers also use Kannada, Hindi, English, or Marathi. *Lg Dev:* Literacy rate in second language: 20% Kannada, Malayalam. Kannada script. Magazines. Films. Dictionary. Grammar. NT: 1847–1892. *Other:* There is also an ancient Tulu script and philosophical texts and religious verses are sometimes written in Tulu script. Mixed commerce; fishermen. Hindu, traditional religion, Christian.

Turi [trd] 6,054 (2000 WCD). Ethnic population: 150,000 (1981 census). Jharkhand, Ranchi, Gumla, Lohardaga districts, Chotanagpur area; Chhattisgarh, Raigarh District;

Orissa, Sambalpur and Sundargarh districts; West Bengal, Birbhum, Nadia, Murshidabad, Bankura districts. *Class:* Austro-Asiatic, Munda, North Munda, Kherwari, Santali. *Other:* A Scheduled Caste in India. Singh (1993) reports they speak Sadri as first language in Jharkhand, Mundari in West Bengal, Oriya in Orissa. Breton refers to the Turi language spoken only in Chotanagpur. There is a Turi caste in Gujarat that is not related linguistically to this group.

Turung (Tai Turung, Tairong, Tailung) [try] Extinct. Assam, Golaghat District, Titabar; Karbi Anglong. *Class:* Tai-Kadai, Kam-Tai, Be-Tai, Tai-Sek, Tai, East Central, Northwest. *Other:* Members of the ethnic group now speak a dialect of Singpho with borrowed Tai words.

Ullatan (Katan, Kattalan, Kochuvelan, Ulladan) [ull] 14,846 (1991 census). Kerala, Palakkad, Trichur, Ernakulam, Kottayam, Idukki, Koliam, Pathanamthitta, Alleppey, Trivandrum districts. *Class:* Dravidian, Southern, Unclassified. *Lg Use:* Ullatan people report they only use Malayalam. Prefer to be considered Malayalis rather than Ullatan. *Lg Dev:* Literacy rate in second language: 67% (70% males, 64% females) (1991 census). *Other:* Ulladan and Kochu Velan are both Scheduled Tribes in India. Singh reports their first language is Malayalam. Animal husbandry; salaried jobs; wage labor. Traditional religion, Hindu.

Urali (Oorazhi, Uraly, Urli) [url] 5,843 (2003). Kerala, Idukki District, Upputhara, Kanchiyar, Vannappuram, Velliyamattom, Ayyappankovil panchayats. *Class:* Dravidian, Southern, Tamil-Kannada, Kannada. *Dialects:* A distinct speech variety, sharing features with Tamil, Irula, and Kannada (Mohan Lal 1991). Lexical similarity 60% with Malayalam, 54% with Tamil. *Lg Use:* May be dying out and being replaced by Malayalam. *Lg Dev:* Literacy rate in second language: 56% in Kerala (49% males, 42% females) (1991 census). *Other:* A Scheduled Tribe in India. Singh (1994) reports they speak Malayalam as first language. Separate linguistically from both Urali Irula in Tamil Nadu and Urali Kurumba in Wynad District, Kerala. 900 meters. Hunter-gatherers; agriculturalists. Hindu, Christian.

Urdu (Islami, Undri, Urudu) [urd] 48,062,000 in India (1997). Jammu and Kashmir and by Muslims in many parts of India; Dakhini dialect spoken around Hyderabad and in Maharashtra. *Dialects:* Dakhini (Dakani, Deccan, Desia, Mirgan), Pinjari, Rekhta (Rekhti). *Lg Use:* State language of Jammu and Kashmir, medium of instruction in government schools. *Lg Dev:* Taught in primary schools. *Other:* Muslim. See main entry under Pakistan.

Vaagri Booli (Narakureavar, Narikkorava, Kuruvikkaran, Karikkorava, Hakkipikkaru, Haki Piki, Guvvalollu, Shikarijanam, Rattiyan, Marattiyan, Wogri Boli) [vaa] 10,000 (1970 Varma). Tamil Nadu, Arcot District. *Class:* Indo-European, Indo-Iranian, Indo-Aryan, Unclassified. *Lg Dev:* Tamil script. Bible portions: 1975. *Other:* Hakkipikki is a Scheduled Tribe in India. The name of the language means 'bird catchers'. Hindu, Christian.

Vaiphei (Bhaipei, Vaipei, Veiphei) [vap] 27,791 in Manipur (2001 census). Assam; south Manipur: Churachandpur District, 30+ villages; Meghalaya; Tripura. *Class:* Sino-Tibetan, Tibeto-Burman, Kuki-Chin-Naga, Kuki-Chin, Northern. *Lg Dev:* Roman script. NT: 1957–1989. *Other:* A Scheduled Tribe in India. Reported to be a subgroup of Zomi. Mountain slope. Agriculturalists; mixed commerce. Christian.

Varhadi-Nagpuri (Madhya Pradesh Marathi, Berari, Berar Marathi, Dhanagari, Kumbhari) [vah] 463 (1961 census). Population includes 186 Dahngari, 271 Kumbhari, 6 Warhadi. Maharashtra, Amravati, Buldana, Akola districts; Madhya Pradesh, Chhindwara and Balaghat districts; Andhra Pradesh, Adilabad and Nizamabad districts. *Class:* Indo-European, Indo-Iranian,

Indo-Aryan, Southern zone, Unclassified. *Dialects:* Brahmani, Kunbi, Raipur, Jhadpi, Govari, Kosti (Rangari), Kunban (Kohli), Mahari (Dhedi). Regarded by some as a dialect of Marathi. More distinct dialects or languages are Marheti, Natakani, Katia (Katiyai). *Lg Dev:* Bible portions: 1834.

Varli (Warli) [vav] 600,000 (2003). Maharashtra, northern Thane District, especially Dahanu and Talasari taluks, and some in Nasik and Dhule districts; Gujarat, Valsad District, especially Dharampur taluk; Dadra and Nagar Haveli. Davari dialect in far north Thane District and southern Gujarat; Nihiri elsewhere. *Class:* Indo-European, Indo-Iranian, Indo-Aryan, Southern zone, Konkani. *Dialects:* Davari, Western Nihiri, Eastern Nihiri. Some classify this as a dialect of Gujarati or Bhili. Lexical similarity 61% to 93% among dialects. *Lg Use:* Speakers have low proficiency in Marathi or Gujarati. *Lg Dev:* Radio programs. *Other:* Each dialect group is endogamous. Patrilocal. A Scheduled Tribe in India. Hills. Forest. 1,604 meters. Agriculturalists: rice; animal husbandry; fishermen. Traditional religion, Hindu influences, Christian.

Vasavi (Vasave, Vasava, Vasava Bhil) [vas] 900,000 (1997 BSI). Maharashtra, small villages and hamlets around the Tapti River; Gujarat, Surat and Bharuch districts, north of the Tapti River in the southern areas of Akkalkuwa and Akrani tahsils on a narrow belt of land between the Satpudas and the Tapti banks; some in the Satpudas; south of the Tapti in the central and northern Nandurbar and Nawapur tahsils. *Class:* Indo-European, Indo-Iranian, Indo-Aryan, Central zone, Gujarati. *Dialects:* Dehvali, Ambodi (Ambodia), Dogri (Dungri, Dhogri), Khatalia, Kotni. Not intelligible with Pauri or Bhili. 77% to 93% intelligibility between Dogri, Khatali, Dehwali, Dubli, and Kotni varieties. *Lg Use:* Speakers have low proficiency in Marathi. *Lg Dev:* Literacy rate in second language: Low. Gujarati and Marathi scripts. Bible portions: 1998. *Other:* Subgroup of Bhil ethnic group. 'Vasava' is the name of the people. Speakers in different locations are known as Adiwasi Bhil, Dhogri Bhil, Keski Bhil, Bhilori, Padwi Bhilori, Ambodia Bhil, Vasave Bhil. A Scheduled Tribe in India. Agriculturalists. Traditional religion.

Vishavan (Malankudi, Malarkuti) [vis] 150 (Shashi 1994). Kerala, Ernakulam, Kottayam, Trichur districts, Parana and Perumuzhi on Idamala River, Idyara Range, Moovatupuzha Taluk; groups on Chalakudi River near Ittyani. *Class:* Dravidian, Unclassified. *Other:* Forest. Traditional religion.

Waddar (Od, Orh, Vadari, Vadda Beldar, Werders, Wodde) [wbq] 1,930,000 (2003 IMA). Ethnic population: Population of India, Pakistan, Nepal, and Sri Lanka is 3.2 million (IMA 2003). Andhra Pradesh; Karnataka; Maharashtra, Jalgaon District. *Class:* Dravidian, South-Central, Telugu. *Lg Use:* Some speak Telugu, Marathi, Hindi. *Lg Dev:* Some are literate in Telugu or Marathi. *Other:* Known as 'Od' in North India and Pakistan. Traditional religion, Hindu.

Wagdi (Wagadi, Vagdi, Vagadi, Vagari, Vageri, Vaged, Vagi, Wagari, Waghari, Wagri, Wagholi, Mina Bhil, Bhili, Bhilodi) [wbr] 1,621,000 (1997). Rajasthan, southern Udaipur, Dungarpur and Banswara districts; Gujarat, Sabarkantha and Panchmahals; Andhra Pradesh, Hyderabad. *Class:* Indo-European, Indo-Iranian, Indo-Aryan, Central zone, Bhil. *Dialects:* Kherwara, Sagwara, Adivasi Wagdi. Intelligibility among dialects is above 95%. Wagdi Banswara highly intelligible to Bhilodi of Gujarat. Wagdi highly intelligible to Patelia of Gujarat. Lexical similarity 84% with Patelia dialects; 75% to 80% with Marwari dialects; 79% to 93% with Adiwasi Girasia dialects; 79% to 87% with Rajput Girasia dialects. *Lg Use:* Language of wider communication. A regional language in Vagad Desh. Merchants and government workers use it as second language. No feeling of inferiority attached to Wagdi. Some also use Hindi; proficiency is adequate for market and other common topics. *Lg Dev:* Literacy rate in first language: below 1%. Literacy rate in second language: 25% to 50%. Devanagari script. Radio programs. *Other:* Speakers are called 'Bhil'. Vagri is a Scheduled Tribe in Gujarat. SOV; postpositions; genitives after noun heads; nontonal. Plains, hills. Desert. Peasant agriculturalists. Traditional religion.

War (Amwi) [aml] 12,000 in India (2000 SIL). Meghalaya, Jaintia Hills, in and around Amlarem Block. *Dialects:* War-Jaintia (Amwi), War-Khasi. *Lg Use:* Vigorous. Used in the home, community. All ages. Age and gender are not significant factors in ability to understand standard Khasi. Education is a slight factor but some uneducated understand some standard Khasi. *Other:* Separate from War dialect of Khasi. War-Jaintia spoken in Meghalaya, India. War-Khasi spoken primarily in Bangladesh. Christian, traditional religion. See main entry under Bangladesh.

Yakha (Yakkha, Yakkhaba) [ybh] 1,000 in India (2002). Among British Gurkhas in Sikkim. *Lg Use:* Younger generation is using Nepali (Singh). *Other:* Terrace cultivation; animal husbandry. Buddhist, Hindu. See main entry under Nepal.

Yerukula (Yerukala, Yarukula, Yerkula, Yerukla, Erukala, Korava, Yerukala-Korava, Yerukula-Bhasha, Eruku Bhasha, Korchi, Kurutha, Kurru Bhasha) [yeu] 300,000 (1997). Andhra Pradesh, Rayalseema, Telengana and Andhra regions; Tamil Nadu, Nilgiri, Coimbatore, Periyar, Salem, Chengai Anna; Karnataka; Kerala; Maharashtra. *Class:* Dravidian, Southern, Tamil-Kannada, Tamil-Kodagu, Tamil-Malayalam, Tamil. *Dialects:* Parikala, Sankara-Yerukala. Close to Ravula and Irula. Lexical similarity among varieties ranges from 53% to 81%, with Irula from 33% to 38%, with Ravula from 28% to 45%, with Tamil from 27% to 45%. *Lg Use:* Fairly vigorous language use. In Andhra Pradesh, increasing use in home, friends, religion. In Rayalseema and Telengana regions it is even greater. Positive language attitude. Some regions have low bilingual proficiency in Telugu, higher in Andhra Pradesh and among educated adults. *Lg Dev:* Literacy rate in second language: 14.5%. Most want Yerukula books, but script decision is sensitive. Telugu script. *Other:* Some people called 'Yerukula' speak Telugu as first language. Traditionally nomadic. A Scheduled Tribe in India. Mountain slope, plains. Subtropical forest. 300 to 2,000 meters. Basketmakers; animal husbandry: pigs. Hindu, Christian.

Zakhring (Charumba, Meyor, Zaiwa) [zkr] 300 (2002). Arunachal Pradesh, Lohit District, hilly terrain and banks of the Lohit River in the Walong and Kibithoo area. *Class:* Sino-Tibetan, Tibeto-Burman, Unclassified. *Dialects:* Close to Tibetan (Singh) and Miju-Mishmi. Not related to Zaiwa in Yunnan. *Lg Use:* Speakers also use Hindi, Nefamese, or Tibetan. *Other:* A Scheduled Tribe in India. Speakers call themselves 'Charumba'. Agriculturalists. Buddhist (Lamaist), syncretism.

Zangskari (Zanskari, Zaskari) [zau] 12,006 (2000 WCD). Jammu and Kashmir, Ladakh district, Zanskar tahsil, south of Leh in the Zaskar Mountains, between Himalayas and Indus River Valley. Possibly Tibet. *Class:* Sino-Tibetan, Tibeto-Burman, Himalayish, Tibeto-Kanauri, Tibetic, Tibetan, Western. *Dialects:* Closer to Changthang than to Ladakhi. *Lg Use:* Some also use the Leh dialect of Ladakhi. *Lg Dev:* Literacy rate in second language: Speakers in Ladakh have the highest rate. Tibetan script. Bible portions: 1945–1951. *Other:* Small primary schools throughout Zanskar, lower high schools in Karsha and Zangla, high school in Padum. 90% of students are male.

Nearly all teachers are from outside the area. People trade grain with Changthang to acquire wool and salt. Buddhist.

Zome (Zorni, Zomi, Zoli, Zo, Zou) [zom] 9,112 in Manipur (2001 census). Manipur, Chandel, Singngat subdivision and Sungnu area; Churachandpur districts; Assam. *Lg Dev:* Literacy rate in second language: 33%: males 42%, females 24% (1981 census). *Other:* 'Zome' is the general name for all Chin, but also refers to this specific group. Zou is a Scheduled Tribe in India. Agriculturalists: shifting cultivation. Christian. See main entry under Myanmar.

Zyphe (Zophei, Zoptei, Vawngtu) [zyp] 3,000 in India (2000). Mizoram, Lakher District. *Dialects:* Lower Zyphe, Upper Zyphe. *Lg Use:* Many also use Haka Chin, Lakher, or Mara, depending on location. See main entry under Myanmar.

Indonesia

Republic of Indonesia, Republik Indonesia. 238,452,952. National or official language: Indonesian. Literacy rate: 78% to 85%. Also includes Dutch, Portuguese, Tringgus, Uyghur, Western Cham, Arabic, people from India, Europe. Information mainly from R. Blust 1983–1984; S. Wurm and S. Hattori 1981; D. T. Tryon 1995. Blind population: 1,000,000. Deaf population: 2,000,000 or more (1993). Deaf institutions: 94. The number of languages listed for Indonesia is 742. Of those, 737 are living languages, 2 are second language without mother-tongue speakers, and 3 are extinct. See map on page 789.

Indonesia (Java and Bali)

Indonesia (Java and Bali). 120,000,000 in Java (2003), 3,151,162 in Bali (2000 census). The number of languages listed for Indonesia (Java and Bali) is 20. Of those, all are living languages. See map on page 790.

Badui [bac] 5,000 (1989). West Java, Mount Kendeng, Kabupaten Rangkasbitung, Pandeglang, and Sukabumi. *Class:* Austronesian, Malayo-Polynesian, Sundanese. *Dialects:* Sometimes considered a dialect of Sunda. *Other:* A separate socio-religious group. 'Inner' and 'outer' Badui refer to location and status within the group religion. Traditional religion with Hindu or Buddhist influences.

Bali (Balinese) [ban] 3,900,000 (2001 Johnstone and Mandryk). Island of Bali, northern Nusa Penida, western Lombok Islands, and east Java. 7,000 in South Sulawesi. *Class:* Austronesian, Malayo-Polynesian, Bali-Sasak. *Dialects:* Lowland Bali (Klungkung, Karangasem, Buleleng, Gianyar, Tabanan, Jembrana, Badung), Highland Bali ("Bali Aga"), Nusa Penida. Reported to be two distinct dialects: High Balinese is used in religion, but those who can handle it are diminishing. There are speech strata in several lowland varieties (Clynes 1989, personal communication). *Lg Dev:* Bible: 1990. *Other:* The term "Bali Aga" is considered derogatory by those who are called that. The variety spoken on Nusa Penida Island is associated with Bali Aga. It is a scattering of villages with minimal influence from the former Majapahit Empire. Hindu.

Bali Sign Language [bqy] 2,200 in the village, out of 50 deaf people and 2,150 hearing people (1995 T. Friedman). 1 village in Bali. *Class:* Deaf sign language. *Lg Use:* The majority of the hearing people learn and use the sign language.

Betawi (Jakarta Malay, Betawi Malay, Batavi, Batawi, Melayu Jakarte) [bew] 2,700,000 (1993 Johnstone). Jakarta, Java. *Class:* Creole, Malay based. *Dialects:* 'A Malay-based creole which is quite distinct from both standard Indonesian and from other Malay-based pidgins and creoles'. It evolved by the mid-19th century. Unique phonological, morphological, and lexical traits. There are also influences from Peranakan Chinese and Bali. Often not intelligible to Indonesian speakers not familiar with it (R. B. Allen, Jr. 1989). *Lg Use:* Functions as a 'low' variety in a diglossic situation, but is a prestige variety when used by the upper class. *Lg Dev:* Grammar. *Other:* The people are called 'Betawi Asli' or 'Betawi'.

Chinese, Hakka [hak] 640,000 in Indonesia (1982). See main entry under China.

Chinese, Mandarin [cmn] 460,000 in Indonesia (1982). Scattered throughout Indonesia. *Lg Use:* Of the five to six million ethnic Chinese in Indonesia (5,500,000 in 1976, or 4% of total population according to United Nations), 65% (3,500,000 to 4,000,000) speak Indonesian in the home, 35% (2,000,000) speak 5 Chinese languages in the home. See main entry under China.

Chinese, Min Dong (Min Dong) [cdo] 20,000 in Indonesia (1982). *Dialect:* Xinghua (Hsinghua). See main entry under China.

Chinese, Min Nan (Minnan, Min Nan) [nan] 700,000 in Indonesia (1982). Pontianak (West Borneo) and elsewhere. *Dialects:* Fujian (Hokkien), Chaochow (Tiu Chiu). See main entry under China.

Chinese, Yue (Cantonese, Yue, Yueh) [yue] 180,000 in Indonesia (1982). See main entry under China.

Indonesian (Bahasa Indonesia) [ind] 22,803,774 in Indonesia (2000 WCD). Population total all countries: 23,143,354. Used in all regions of Indonesia. Also spoken in Netherlands, Philippines, Saudi Arabia, Singapore, USA. *Class:* Austronesian, Malayo-Polynesian, Malayic, Malayan, Local Malay. *Lg Use:* Official language. Over 140,000,000 second-language speakers. *Lg Dev:* Roman and Arabic scripts. Grammar. Bible: 1974–2000. *Other:* Reported to be modeled on Riau Malay of northeast Sumatra. Has regional variants. Over 80% cognate with Standard Malay. Muslim.

Indonesian Sign Language [inl] Ethnic population: 2,000,000 deaf people (1993). *Class:* Deaf sign language. *Lg Use:* 94 schools for the deaf use the oral method for instruction. *Other:* A blend of Malaysian Sign Language and indigenous signs. ASL not used.

Indonesian, Peranakan (Chinese Indonesian, Baba Indonesian, Peranakan) [pea] 20,000 (1981 Wurm and Hattori). East and central Java. *Class:* Creole, Indonesian based. *Dialects:* It is based in Indonesian and Javanese. It has Mandarin elements in contrast to Baba Malay, which has Hokkien elements. *Lg Use:* Monolinguals are older adults. *Other:* Developed at the beginning of the 17th century among Low Malay-speaking Chinese traders from Fukien who married Javanese women.

Javanese (Jawa, Djawa) [jav] 75,200,000 in Indonesia (1989). Population includes 500,000 Banten, 2,500,000 Cirebon. About 25,000 in South Sulawesi. Population total all countries: 75,508,300. Central Java, eastern third of west Java, southwestern half of east Java. Also resettlements in Papua, Sulawesi, Maluku, Kalimantan, and Sumatra. Also spoken in Malaysia (Sabah), Netherlands, Singapore. *Class:* Austronesian, Malayo-Polynesian, Javanese. *Dialects:* Jawa Halus, Cirebon (Tjirebon, Cheribon), Tegal, Indramayu, Solo, Tembung, Pasisir, Surabaya, Malang-Pasuruan, Banten, Manuk. West Javanese dialects: Banten, Cirebon, Tegal; central Javanese dialect: Solo in Yogyakarta; East Javanese dialects: Surabaya, Malang-Pasuruan. High Javanese (Jawa Halus) is the language of religion, but the number of people that can control that form is diminishing. The Javanese in Suriname and in New Caledonia have changed sufficiently to be only partially intelligible with difficulty. Javanese in New Caledonia are reported to not be able to use High Javanese (Koentjaraninggrat). Several dialects in

Sabah. *Lg Dev:* Traditional Javanese script. Bible: 1854–1994. *Other:* SVO. Muslim, Christian.

Kangean [kkv] 21,209 (2000 WCD). Eastern Madura area. *Class:* Austronesian, Malayo-Polynesian, Madurese. *Dialects:* Barely intelligible with East Madura. A separate language (Stevens 1968). Lexical similarity 75% with Madura.

Madura (Madurese, Madhura, Basa Mathura) [mad] 13,694,000 in Indonesia (1995). Population includes 70,000 Bawean. Population total all countries: 13,694,900. Island of Madura, Sapudi Islands, northern coastal area of eastern Java. Also spoken in Singapore. *Class:* Austronesian, Malayo-Polynesian, Madurese. *Dialects:* Bawean (Boyanese), Bangkalan (Bangkalon), Pamekesan (Pamekasan), Sampang, Sapudi, Sumenep. There is a dialect continuum. Reports differ about inherent intelligibility among dialects, but some speakers of Sumenep and Sampang report that they cannot understand Pamekasan or Sumenep. Difficult intelligibility of Kangean. Lexical similarity 75% with Kangean. *Lg Use:* All domains. East Madurese, especially Sumenep, is considered 'high', or 'standard Madurese'. Sumenep is isolated culturally and geographically. Bangkalon, spoken in Surabaya, is important economically because that is the city with the greatest outside contact and commerce. It is highly urbanized and affected by Bahasa Indonesia. About 60% of men and 40% of women speak 'passable' Indonesian to outsiders. *Lg Dev:* Literacy rate in second language: 40%. Literacy higher among Bangkalan speakers. Grammar. Bible: 1994. *Other:* Mainly rural. Muslim, Christian.

Malay, Balinese [mhp] 3,151,162 (2000 census). Bali. *Class:* Austronesian, Malayo-Polynesian, Malayic, Malayan, Local Malay. *Lg Use:* Trade language.

Osing (Banyuwangi) [osi] 481,852 (2000 WCD). East and northeast coast of east Java. *Class:* Austronesian, Malayo-Polynesian, Javanese. *Dialects:* Related to East Javanese. *Lg Dev:* Javanese script. *Other:* Muslim.

Petjo (Petjoh, Pecok) [pey] Djakarta (Batavia), Java. *Class:* Creole, Dutch based. *Dialects:* Influences from Dutch, Javanese, and Betawi. *Other:* Little is known of this language. May be a pidgin or mixed language, rather than a creole.

Sunda (Sundanese, Priangan) [sun] 27,000,000 (1990 Clynes). Western third of Java Island. *Class:* Austronesian, Malayo-Polynesian, Sundanese. *Dialects:* Banten, Bogor (Krawang), Pringan, Cirebon. *Lg Use:* 60% use Indonesian and 5% use Dutch as second language. *Lg Dev:* Bible: 1891–1991. *Other:* Muslim, Christian, traditional religion.

Tengger (Tenggerese) [tes] 500,000 (1989). East Java, on the Tengger-Semeru massif and the slopes of Mt. Bromo. *Class:* Austronesian, Malayo-Polynesian, Javanese. *Dialects:* May be marginally intelligible with Javanese. *Lg Use:* Javanese is used as second language. 20% use Indonesian. *Lg Dev:* Literacy rate in second language: 20%. *Other:* Ethnically distinct. Mountain slope, volcanic. Agriculturalists: vegetables. Hindu, Muslim, Christian.

Indonesia (Kalimantan)

Indonesia (Kalimantan). 11,331,558 (2000 census). 4 provinces. Information mainly from A. A. Cense and E. M. Uhlenbeck 1958; R. Blust 1974. The number of languages listed for Indonesia (Kalimantan) is 83. Of those, all are living languages. See maps beginning on page 791.

Ahe (Ahe Dayak, Dayak Ahe) [ahe] 30,000 (1990 UBS). *Class:* Austronesian, Malayo-Polynesian, Land Dayak.

Ampanang [apg] 30,000 (1981 Wurm and Hattori). East central, southeast of Tunjung, around Jambu and Lamper. *Class:* Austronesian, Malayo-Polynesian, Barito, Mahakam.

Aoheng (Penihing) [pni] 2,630 (1981 Wurm and Hattori). North central near Sarawak border. *Class:* Austronesian, Malayo-Polynesian, Kayan-Murik, Muller-Schwaner 'Punan'. *Dialects:* Lexical similarity 69% with Kereho, 67% with Hovongan.

Bahau [bhv] 3,200 (1981 Wurm and Hattori). Northeast, north, and southeast of Busang. *Class:* Austronesian, Malayo-Polynesian, Kayan-Murik, Kayan.

Bakumpai (Bara-Jida) [bkr] 100,000 (2003). Kapuas and Barito rivers, northeast of Kualakapuas. *Class:* Austronesian, Malayo-Polynesian, Barito, West, South. *Dialect:* Bakumpai, Mengkatip (Mangkatip, Oloh Mengkatip). Related to Ngaju, Kahayan, Katingan. Lexical similarity 75% with Ngaju, 45% with Banjar. *Lg Use:* Language of wider communication. *Lg Dev:* Dictionary. *Other:* Muslim.

Banjar (Banjarese, Bandjarese, Banjar Malay) [bjn] 5,000,000 in Indonesia (2001 Johnstone and Mandryk). Population total all countries: 5,900,000. Around Banjarmasin in the south and east, and one pocket on east coast south of the Kelai River mouth. Also spoken in Malaysia (Sabah). *Class:* Austronesian, Malayo-Polynesian, Malayic, Malayan, Local Malay. *Dialects:* Kuala, Hulu. Lexical similarity 45% with Bakumpai, 35% with Ngaju. *Lg Use:* Language of wider communication. *Lg Dev:* Dictionary. *Other:* Strongly influenced by Javanese. Settled 800 to 1000 A.D. Muslim.

Basap [bdb] 17,000 (1981 Wurm and Hattori). Eastern Kalimantan, scattered throughout Bulungan, Sangkulirang, and Kutai. *Class:* Austronesian, Malayo-Polynesian, Northwest, Rejang-Sajau. *Dialects:* Jembayan, Bulungan, Berau, Dumaring, Binatang, Karangan. *Other:* Cave-dwellers. Traditional religion, Christian.

Bekati' (Bakatiq) [bei] 4,000 (1986 UBS). Northwestern near Sarawak border, around Sambas and Selvas. *Class:* Austronesian, Malayo-Polynesian, Land Dayak. *Lg Dev:* Bible portions: 1986.

Benyadu' [byd] 45,000 (1981 Wurm and Hattori). Northwestern near Sarawak border, around Tan, Darit. *Class:* Austronesian, Malayo-Polynesian, Land Dayak.

Biatah (Bideyu, Siburan, Lundu, Landu, Pueh) [bth] 8,484 in Indonesia (2000 WCD). Northwest Kalimantan, on Sarawak border. Mainly in Sarawak. *Other:* May be distinct from Biatah of Sarawak. Christian, traditional religion. See main entry under Malaysia (Sarawak).

Bolongan (Bulungan) [blj] 15,000 (1989). Northeast, around Tanjungselor, lower Kayan River. *Class:* Austronesian, Malayo-Polynesian, Northwest, North Sarawakan, Dayic, Murutic, Tidong. *Dialects:* May be a dialect of Tidong or Segai. Classification uncertain. *Other:* Traditional religion.

Bukar Sadong (Sadong, Tebakang, Buka, Bukar, Serian, Sabutan) [sdo] *Dialect:* Bukar Sadong, Bukar Bidayuh (Bidayuh, Bidayah). See main entry under Malaysia (Sarawak).

Bukat [bvk] 400 (1981 Wurm and Hattori). North central near Sarawak border, Kapuas River, southeast of Mendalam, 3 areas. *Class:* Austronesian, Malayo-Polynesian, Kayan-Murik, Muller-Schwaner 'Punan'.

Bukitan (Bakitan, Bakatan, Beketan, Mangkettan, Manketa, Pakatan) [bkn] 573 in Indonesia (2000 WCD). Population total all countries: 862. Iwan River, on the Sarawak border. Also spoken in Malaysia (Sarawak). *Class:* Austronesian, Malayo-Polynesian, Northwest, Melanau-Kajang, Kajang. *Dialects:* Punan Ukit, Punan Busang. *Other:* Christian.

Burusu [bqr] 6,000 (1981 Wurm and Hattori). Northeast, around Sekatakbunyi, north of Sajau Basap language.

Class: Austronesian, Malayo-Polynesian, Northwest, Rejang-Sajau.

Dayak, Land [dyk] 57,619 (1981). Western Kalimantan. *Class:* Austronesian, Malayo-Polynesian, Land Dayak. *Dialects:* Karagan (Karangan), Sidin (Siding, Sinding), Meratei (Meretei), Sau (Sauh, Biratak), Sermah (Bionah), Berang, Sabungo, Santan, Gurgo, Sinan, Sumpo, Budanoh, Sering, Gugu, Matan, Temila, Behe, Ipoh, Manyukai (Menjuke, Menyukai, Manyuke, Manukai), Punan (Bunan, Murang Punan, Penyabung Punan, Busang, Djuloi), Kati, Beta. There may be several languages represented among the dialects listed. All Land Dayak in Sarawak are covered by separate listings. *Lg Dev:* Bible portions: 1935.

Djongkang [djo] 45,000 (1981 Wurm and Hattori). Northwest, south of Balai Sebut. *Class:* Austronesian, Malayo-Polynesian, Land Dayak.

Dohoi (Ot Danum, Uut Danum, Uud Danum, Malahoi) [otd] 25,000 (2003). Extensive area south of the Schwaner Range on the upper reaches of south Borneo rivers. The Ulu Ai' are on the Mandai River with 7 villages. *Class:* Austronesian, Malayo-Polynesian, Barito, West, North. *Dialects:* Ot Balawan, Ot Banu'u, Ot Murung 1 (Murung 1, Punan Ratah), Ot Olang, Ot Tuhup, Sarawai (Melawi), Dohoi, Ulu Ai' (Da'an), Sebaung, Kadorih. Lexical similarity 70% with Siang, 65% with Kohin, 60% with Katingan, 50% with Ngaju. *Lg Dev:* NT: 1998. *Other:* Dohoi and Murung 1 may be separate languages. Traditional religion, Christian.

Dusun Deyah (Deah, Dejah) [dun] 20,000 (1981 Wurm and Hattori). Southeast, Tabalong River northeast of Bongkang. *Class:* Austronesian, Malayo-Polynesian, Barito, East, Central-South, Central. *Dialects:* Lexical similarity 53% with Lawangan, 52% with Tawoyan.

Dusun Malang [duq] 4,500 (2003). Population includes 2,000 Bayan. East central, west of Muarainu, northeast of Muarateweh. *Class:* Austronesian, Malayo-Polynesian, Barito, East, Central-South, South. *Dialects:* Bayan, Dusun Malang. Closest to Ma'anyan, Paku, Dusun Witu, Malagasy. Lexical similarity 90% between Dusun Malang and Bayan.

Dusun Witu [duw] 5,000 (2003). Southeast, regions of Pendang and Buntokecil; south of Muarateweh. *Class:* Austronesian, Malayo-Polynesian, Barito, East, Central-South, South. *Dialects:* Dusun Pepas, Dusun Witu. Closest to Ma'anyan, Paku, Dusun Malang, Malagasy. Lexical similarity 75% with Ma'anyan, 73% with Paku.

Embaloh (Mbaloh, Maloh, Malo, Memaloh, Matoh, Pari, Palin, Sangau, Sanggau) [emb] 10,000 (1991 NTM). West central, Hulu Kapuas Regency, just south of the Sarawak border, upper Kapuas River: Embaloh, Leboyan, Lauh, Palin, Nyabau, Mandai, and Kalis tributaries. *Class:* Austronesian, Malayo-Polynesian, Sulawesi, South Sulawesi, Bugis, Tamanic. *Dialect:* Kalis (Kalis Maloh, Kalis Dayak). Kalis may be a separate language. *Lg Dev:* NT: 1998. *Other:* Complex mix of ethnic groups: Taman of upper Kapuas Riiver, Suai, Taman Mendalem, Taman Sibau, Palin, Lauk, Leboyan, Kalis Dayak. Traditional religion, Christian.

Hovongan (Punan Bungan) [hov] 1,000 (1991 NTM). North central near Sarawak border, 2 areas. *Class:* Austronesian, Malayo-Polynesian, Kayan-Murik, Muller-Schwaner 'Punan'. *Dialects:* Hovongan, Semukung Uheng. Lexical similarity 69% with Kereho, 67% with Aoheng. *Other:* Traditional religion, Christian.

Iban (Sea Dayak) [iba] Western and northern Kalimantan. *Dialect:* Batang Lupar, Bugau, Seberuang, Kantu', Desa, Ketungau (Air Tabun, Sigarau, Sekalau, Sekapat, Banjur, Sebaru', Demam, Maung). *Other:* Seberuang (20,000 speakers on the Kapuas River) may be a separate language. Traditional religion, Christian. See main entry under Malaysia (Sarawak).

Kahayan (Kahaian, Kahajan) [xah] 45,000 (1981 Wurm and Hattori). Kapuas and Kahayan rivers, south central, northeast of Ngaju. *Class:* Austronesian, Malayo-Polynesian, Barito, West, South. *Dialect:* Kapuas. Related to Ngaju, Bakumpai. Lexical similarity 73% with Katingan. *Lg Dev:* Bible portions: 1990.

Katingan [kxg] 45,000 (1981 Wurm and Hattori). Katingan River, south central. *Class:* Austronesian, Malayo-Polynesian, Barito, West, South. *Dialects:* Katingan Ngawa, Katingan Ngaju. Related to Bakumpai. Lexical similarity 72% with Ngaju, 69% with Kohin, 65% with Dohoi. *Lg Dev:* Grammar.

Kayan Mahakam [xay] 1,300 (1981 Wurm and Hattori). North central, Mahakam River, 2 areas. *Class:* Austronesian, Malayo-Polynesian, Kayan-Murik, Kayan. *Other:* A mixture of Kayan and Ot Danum (Dohoi).

Kayan, Busang (Kajan, Kajang, Busang) [bfg] 3,000 (1981 Wurm and Hattori). On the upper Mahakam, Oga, and Belayan rivers. *Class:* Austronesian, Malayo-Polynesian, Kayan-Murik, Kayan. *Dialects:* Mahakam Busang, Belayan, Long Bleh. *Other:* Christian, traditional religion.

Kayan, Kayan River (Kayan River Kajan, Kajang) [xkn] 2,000 (1981 Wurm and Hattori). Northeast, Kayan River, 2 areas. *Class:* Austronesian, Malayo-Polynesian, Kayan-Murik, Kayan. *Dialects:* Uma Lakan, Kayaniyut Kayan.

Kayan, Mendalam (Mendalam Kajan) [xkd] 1,500 (1981 Wurm and Hattori). North central, northeast of Putus Sibau, Mendalam River. *Class:* Austronesian, Malayo-Polynesian, Kayan-Murik, Kayan.

Kayan, Wahau (Wahau Kajan) [whu] 500 (1981 Wurm and Hattori). Northeast, north of Muara Wahau. *Class:* Austronesian, Malayo-Polynesian, Kayan-Murik, Kayan.

Kelabit (Kalabit, Kerabit) [kzi] 636 in Indonesia (2000 WCD). Remote mountains, on Sarawak border, northwest of Longkemuat. Mainly in Sarawak. *Dialect:* Lon Bangag. *Other:* Mountain slope. Agriculturalists: paddy and hill rice. Christian. See main entry under Malaysia (Sarawak).

Kembayan [xem] 45,000 (1981 Wurm and Hattori). Northwest, near Sarawak border, around Balaikarangan, Kembayan, Landak River. *Class:* Austronesian, Malayo-Polynesian, Land Dayak.

Kendayan (Baicit, Kendayan-Ambawang, Kendayan Dayak) [knx] 150,000 (1981 Wurm and Hattori). Kalimantan Barat, northeast of Bengkayang in the Ledo area, extending into the jungle area of Madi and Papan. *Class:* Austronesian, Malayo-Polynesian, Malayic, Malayic-Dayak. *Dialects:* Ambawang, Kendayan. *Other:* Indonesian is well understood only by the few who have had at least a 6th grade education.

Keninjal (Kaninjal Dayak, Dayak Kaninjal, Kaninjal) [knl] 35,000 (1990 UBS). West central, Sayan and Melawi rivers, around Nangapinoh, Nangaella, Nangasayan, Gelalak. *Class:* Austronesian, Malayo-Polynesian, Malayic, Malayic-Dayak.

Kenyah, Bahau River (Bahau River Kenya) [bwv] 1,500 (1981 Wurm and Hattori). Northeast, on Sarawak border, around Longkemuat, Iwan River. *Class:* Austronesian, Malayo-Polynesian, Northwest, North Sarawakan, Kenyah, Main Kenyah. *Dialects:* Long Atau, Long Bena, Long Puyungan.

Kenyah, Bakung (Bakung, Bakung Kenya, Bakong) [boc] 1,485 in Indonesia (2000 WCD). Northeast, near the Sarawak border, Oga River and southeast of Datadian, and around Kubumesaai. Also spoken in Malaysia (Sarawak). *Class:* Austronesian, Malayo-Polynesian, Northwest, North Sarawakan, Kenyah. *Dialects:* Boh Bakung, Oga Bakung, Kayan River Bakung. *Other:* Muslim.

Kenyah, Kayan River (Kayan River Kenya, Kenya, Kenja, Kenyah, Kinjin, Kindjin, Kehja) [knh] 6,000 (1981 Wurm and Hattori). Northeast, Apo Kayan highlands where Kayan River begins, Iwan River, and around Longbia. *Class:* Austronesian, Malayo-Polynesian, Northwest, North Sarawakan, Kenyah, Main Kenyah. *Dialects:* Lower Kayan Kenyah, Longbia, Kayaniyut Kenyah, Long Nawan, Long Kelawit. *Lg Dev:* NT: 1978. *Other:* Christian.

Kenyah, Kelinyau (Kelinyau, Kelinjau, Kenja, Kenyah, Kenya, Kinjin, Kindjin, Kehja) [xkl] 1,200 (1981 Wurm and Hattori). Northeast, Kinjau River, around Long Laes, and Telen River. *Class:* Austronesian, Malayo-Polynesian, Northwest, North Sarawakan, Kenyah, Main Kenyah. *Dialects:* Uma Bem, Uma Tau, Lepo' Kulit, Uma Jalam.

Kenyah, Mahakam (Mahakam Kenya, Kenya, Kenja, Kenyah, Kinjin, Kindjin, Kehja) [xkm] 7,000 (1981 Wurm and Hattori). Northeast, east of Bahau, and on Mahakam River, 5 areas. *Class:* Austronesian, Malayo-Polynesian, Northwest, North Sarawakan, Kenyah, Main Kenyah. *Dialects:* Mahakam Kenyah, Boh.

Kenyah, Upper Baram (Upper Baram Kenja, Kenja, Kenyah, Kinjin, Kanyay, Kindjin) [ubm] 636 in Indonesia (2000 WCD). Border with Sarawak, northwest of Longkemuat. See main entry under Malaysia (Sarawak).

Kenyah, Wahau (Wahau Kenya) [whk] 1,000 (1981 Wurm and Hattori). Northeast, north of Muara Wahau and Wahau Kayan. *Class:* Austronesian, Malayo-Polynesian, Northwest, North Sarawakan, Kenyah. *Dialect:* Uma Timai.

Kereho-Uheng (Keriau Punan) [xke] 500 (2003). North central near Sarawak border, south of Bukat and Hovongan. *Class:* Austronesian, Malayo-Polynesian, Kayan-Murik, Muller-Schwaner 'Punan'. *Dialect:* Seputan. Lexical similarity 69% with Hovongan, 69% with Aoheng.

Kohin (Seruyan, Bahasa Seruyan) [kkx] 8,000 (2003). Central Kalimantan, Kotawaringin Timur District, along the central and northern Seruyan River. 10 villages. *Class:* Austronesian, Malayo-Polynesian, Barito, West, North. *Dialects:* Lexical similarity 69% with Katingan, 60% to 65% with Dohoi, 50% to 62% with Ngaju.

Lara' (Luru) [lra] 8,272 in Indonesia (2000 WCD). Upper Lundu and Sambas rivers, around Bengkayang east of Gunung Pendering, and farther north, Pejampi and two other villages. *Other:* Traditional religion. See main entry under Malaysia (Sarawak).

Lawangan (Luwangan, Northeast Barito) [lbx] 100,000 (1981 Wurm and Hattori). Around the Karau River in east central Kalimantan. *Class:* Austronesian, Malayo-Polynesian, Barito, East, North. *Dialects:* Ajuh, Bakoi (Lampung), Bantian (Bentian), Banuwang, Bawu (Bawo), Kali, Karau (Beloh), Lawa, Lolang, Mantararen, Njumit, Purai, Purung, Tuwang, Pasir, Benua. At least 17 dialects. Tawoyan may be inherently intelligible. Lexical similarity 77% with Tawoyan, 53% with Dusun Deyah.

Lengilu [lgi] 3 to 4 (2000 Wurm). Northeast, between Sa'ban and Lundayeh. *Class:* Austronesian, Malayo-Polynesian, Northwest, North Sarawakan, Dayic, Kelabitic. *Other:* Nearly extinct.

Lundayeh (Southern Murut, Lun Daye, Lun Dayah, Lun Daya, Lun Dayoh, Lundaya) [lnd] 25,000 in Indonesia (1987). Population total all countries: 38,100. Interior about 4 degrees north from Brunei Bay to headwaters of Padas River, to headwaters of Baram, and into Kalimantan, Indonesian mountains where tributaries of Sesayap River arise. Also spoken in Brunei, Malaysia (Sarawak). *Class:* Austronesian, Malayo-Polynesian, Northwest, North Sarawakan, Dayic, Kelabitic. *Dialect:* Lun Daye, Papadi, Lun Bawang (Long Bawan, Sarawak Murut). *Lg Dev:* Radio programs. Bible: 1982. *Other:* Not Murutic, although sometimes called Southern Murut. Christian (Lunbawang, Lundayeh), traditional religion.

Ma'anyan (Maanyak Dayak, Ma'anjan) [mhy] 150,000 (2003). South around Tamianglayang area of the drainage of Patai River. *Class:* Austronesian, Malayo-Polynesian, Barito, East, Central-South, South. *Dialects:* Samihim (Buluh Kuning), Sihong (Siong), Dusun Balangan. Related to Malagasy in Madagascar. Lexical similarity 77% with Paku, 75% with Dusun Witu. *Lg Dev:* NT: 1999. *Other:* Traditional religion.

Malay, Berau (Berau, Merau Malay) [bve] 20,000 (1981 Wurm and Hattori). East central coastal area, Tanjungreder and Muaramalinau in the north to Sepinang in the south. *Class:* Austronesian, Malayo-Polynesian, Malayic, Malayan, Local Malay. *Other:* Shares phonological innovations with Kutai Malay, Banjar, and Brunei.

Malay, Bukit (Bukit, Meratus) [bvu] 50,000 (1981 Wurm and Hattori). Southeastern, Sampanahan River, northwest of Limbungan. *Class:* Austronesian, Malayo-Polynesian, Malayic, Malayan, Local Malay. *Other:* Traditional religion.

Malay, Kota Bangun Kutai [mqg] 80,000 (1981 Wurm and Hattori). Central Mahakam River basin. *Class:* Austronesian, Malayo-Polynesian, Malayic, Malayan, Local Malay. *Dialects:* Not intelligible with Tenggarong Kutai Malay. May be intelligible with Northern Kutai.

Malay, Tenggarong Kutai (Kutai, Tenggarong) [vkt] 210,000 (1981 Wurm and Hattori). Population includes 100,000 in Tenggarong, 60,000 in Ancalong, 50,000 in Northern Kutai. Mahakam River basin, east central coastal area, from Sepinang and Tg. Mangkalihat in the north to Muarabadak and Samarinda in the south. *Class:* Austronesian, Malayo-Polynesian, Malayic, Malayan, Local Malay. *Dialects:* Tenggarong Kutai, Ancalong Kutai, Northern Kutai. Many dialects. Tenggarong and Kota Bangun are not inherently intelligible. Shares phonological innovations with Berau Malay, Banjar, and Brunei.

Malayic Dayak [xdy] 520,000 (1981 Wurm and Hattori). Population includes 300 Tapitn, 100,000 Banana', 100,000 Kayung, 200,000 Delang, 10,000 Semitau, 10,000 Suhaid, 20,000 Mentebah-Suruk. Western Kalteng and much of KalBar. Banana' and Tapitn are western, between Singkawang, Bengkayang, Darit, and Sungairaya; Kayung and Delang are southern, between Sandai, Muarakayang, Pembuanghulu, Sukamara, and Sukaraja; Semitau, Suhaid, and Mentebah-Suruk are eastern, southeast of Kapuas River from Sintang to Putus Sibau. *Class:* Austronesian, Malayo-Polynesian, Malayic, Malayic-Dayak. *Dialects:* Tapitn, Banana', Kayung (Kayong), Delang, Semitau, Suhaid, Mentebah-Suruk, Arut (Sukarame), Lamandau (Landau Kantu), Sukamara (Kerta Mulya), Riam (Nibung Terjung), Belantikan (Sungkup). The listed dialects form a chain and may constitute 3 or more languages. Related to Selako, Kendaya, and Keninjal. *Other:* Muslim, Christian.

Modang [mxd] 15,300 (1981 Wurm and Hattori). Around Segah, Kelinjau, and Belayan rivers in northeast Kalimantan, 5 areas. *Class:* Austronesian, Malayo-Polynesian, Kayan-Murik, Modang. *Dialects:* Kelingan (Long Wai, Long We), Long Glat, Long Bento', Benhes, Nahes, Liah Bing.

Mualang [mtd] 10,000 (1981 Wurm and Hattori). Along the Ayak and Belitang rivers, about 200 miles upstream from Pontianak. *Class:* Austronesian, Malayo-Polynesian, Malayic, Malayic-Dayak, Ibanic. *Dialects:* Close to Iban.

Ngaju (Ngadju, Ngaju Dayak, Biadju, Southwest Barito) [nij] 800,000 (2003). Kapuas, Kahayan, Katingan, and Mentaya rivers, south. *Class:* Austronesian, Malayo-Polynesian, Barito, West, South. *Dialects:* Pulopetak, Ba'amang (Bara-Bare, Sampit), Mantangai (Oloh Mangtangai). Related to Katingan, Kahayan, Bakumpai. Lexical similarity 75% with Bakumpai, 72% with Katingan, 62% with Kohin, 50% with Dohoi, 35% with

Banjar. *Lg Use:* Trade language. Trade language for most of Kalimantan, from the Barito to the Sampit rivers, east of the Barito languages, and north in the Malawi River region. *Lg Dev:* Dictionary. Grammar. Bible: 1858–1955.

Nyadu (Njadu, Balantiang, Balantian) [nxj] 9,000. West and north Kalimantan, Landak, tributary of Sambas River. *Class:* Austronesian, Malayo-Polynesian, Land Dayak. *Lg Dev:* Bible portions: 1952. *Other:* Similar to Lara' spoken along upper Lundu and Sambas rivers.

Okolod (Kolod, Kolour, Kolur, Okolod Murut) [kqv] 3,393 in Indonesia (2000 WCD). Population total all countries: 4,971. Northeast along Sabah border, east of Lumbis, north of Lundayeh. Primarily Kalimantan and Sarawak, some in Sabah. Also spoken in Malaysia (Sarawak). *Class:* Austronesian, Malayo-Polynesian, Northwest, North Sarawakan, Dayic, Murutic, Murut. *Dialects:* Lexical similarity 82% with Okolod of Sabah, 70% with Pensiangan Murut (Tagal), 34% with Lundayeh. *Other:* Traditional religion, Christian.

Paku [pku] 3,500 (2003). Southeast, south of Ampah. *Class:* Austronesian, Malayo-Polynesian, Barito, East, Central-South, South. *Dialects:* Closest to Ma'anyan, Malagasy, Dusun Malang, Dusun Witu. Lexical similarity 77% with Ma'anyan, 73% with Dusun Witu.

Punan Aput (Aput) [pud] 370 (1981 Wurm and Hattori). Northeast, west, and north of Mt. Menyapa. *Class:* Austronesian, Malayo-Polynesian, Kayan-Murik, Muller-Schwaner 'Punan'.

Punan Merah [puf] 137 (1981 Wurm and Hattori). Northeast, Mahakam River, east of Ujohhilang. *Class:* Austronesian, Malayo-Polynesian, Kayan-Murik, Muller-Schwaner 'Punan'. *Other:* Distinct from Punan Merap.

Punan Merap [puc] 200 (1981 Wurm and Hattori). Northeast, east of Longkemuat. *Class:* Austronesian, Malayo-Polynesian, Northwest, Rejang-Sajau. *Other:* Distinct from Punan Merah.

Punan Tubu [puj] 2,000 (1981 Wurm and Hattori). Northeast, Malinau, Mentarang, and Sembakung rivers, 8 locations. *Class:* Austronesian, Malayo-Polynesian, Northwest, North Sarawakan, Kenyah. *Other:* May not be a Kenyah language. Blust 1974, 'penan' is a generic term for nonagricultural peoples. It does not reflect language differences; there are no 'Penan' languages as a distinguishable subgrouping.

Putoh [put] 6,000 (1981 Wurm and Hattori). Northeast, east of Lundayeh and Sa'ban, Mentarang River, around Longberang, Mensalong, and Bangalan. *Class:* Austronesian, Malayo-Polynesian, Northwest, North Sarawakan, Dayic, Kelabitic. *Dialects:* Pa Kembaloh, Abai.

Ribun [rir] 45,000 (1981 Wurm and Hattori). Northwest, south of Kembayan. *Class:* Austronesian, Malayo-Polynesian, Land Dayak.

Sa'ban [snv] 848 in Indonesia (2000 WCD). Northeast on Sarawak border, south of Lundayeh. See main entry under Malaysia (Sarawak).

Sajau Basap (Sajau, Sujau) [sjb] 6,000 (1981 Wurm and Hattori). Northeast, northeast of Muaramalinau. *Class:* Austronesian, Malayo-Polynesian, Northwest, Rejang-Sajau. *Dialects:* Punan Sajau, Punan Basap, Punan Batu 2. Related to Basap.

Sanggau [scg] 45,000 (1981 Wurm and Hattori). Northwestern, around Sanggau, Kapuas River. *Class:* Austronesian, Malayo-Polynesian, Land Dayak.

Sara [sre] 200. Near Sanggau-Ledo northeast of Ledo. *Class:* Austronesian, Malayo-Polynesian, Land Dayak. *Dialects:* Some dialect differences, but one written form can serve. *Lg Dev:* Bible portions: 1986.

Seberuang [sbx] 20,000 (1993 UBS). Kapuas River. *Class:* Austronesian, Malayo-Polynesian, Malayic, Malayic-Dayak, Ibanic. *Other:* SVO. Traditional religion, Christian.

Segai [sge] 2,000 (1981 Wurm and Hattori). Northeast, Kelai River and around Longlaai. *Class:* Austronesian, Malayo-Polynesian, Kayan-Murik, Modang. *Dialects:* Kelai, Segah. Bolongan may be a dialect.

Selako (Selako Dayak, Salakau, Silakau) [skl] 100,000 in Indonesia (1981 Wurm and Hattori). Population total all countries: 103,800. Northwest, around Pemangkat. Also spoken in Malaysia (Sarawak). *Class:* Austronesian, Malayo-Polynesian, Malayic, Malayic-Dayak. *Other:* Traditional religion.

Selungai Murut [slg] 636 in Indonesia (2000 WCD). Population total all countries: 1,009. Along the upper reaches of the Sembakung River, east of Lumbis. Also spoken in Malaysia (Sabah). *Class:* Austronesian, Malayo-Polynesian, Northwest, North Sarawakan, Dayic, Murutic, Murut.

Semandang [sdm] 30,000 (1981 Wurm and Hattori). West central, around Balaiberkuwak, north of Sandai. *Class:* Austronesian, Malayo-Polynesian, Land Dayak. *Dialects:* Semandang, Gerai, Beginci, Bihak. *Lg Dev:* Bible portions: 1982. *Other:* Traditional religion, Christian.

Sembakung Murut (Simbakong, Sembakoeng, Sembakong, Tinggalan, Tinggalum, Tingalun) [sbr] 3,181 in Indonesia (2000 WCD). Along the Sembakung River in northern Kalimantan, from the mouth, into Sabah. See main entry under Malaysia (Sabah).

Siang (Ot Siang) [sya] 60,000 (1981 Wurm and Hattori). Central, east of Dohoi. *Class:* Austronesian, Malayo-Polynesian, Barito, West, North. *Dialects:* Siang, Murung 2. Related to Dohoi.

Tagal Murut (Sumambu-Tagal, Sumambu, Sumambuq, Semembu, Semambu) [mvv] 2,000 Alumbis in Indonesia. Along the Pegalan Valley, Alumbis River. *Dialects:* Rundum (Arundum), Tagal (Tagol, North Borneo Murut, Sabah Murut), Sumambu (Semembu, Sumambuq), Tolokoson (Telekoson), Sapulot Murut (Sapulut Murut), Pensiangan Murut (Pentjangan, Tagul, Taggal, Lagunan Murut), Alumbis (Lumbis, Loembis), Tawan, Tomani (Tumaniq), Maligan (Mauligan, Meligan, Bol Murut, Bole Murut). See main entry under Malaysia (Sabah).

Taman (Taman Dayak, Dayak Taman) [tmn] 6,214 (2000 WCD). North central, Kapuas River in the area directly upriver from Putussibau, and the Mendalam and Sibau tributaries. *Class:* Austronesian, Malayo-Polynesian, Sulawesi, South Sulawesi, Bugis, Tamanic. *Other:* Traditional religion, Christian.

Tausug (Taw Sug, Sulu, Suluk, Tausog, Moro Joloano, Sooloo, Taosug, Joloano Sulu) [tsg] 12,000 in Indonesia (1981 Wurm and Hattori). Settlements along the coast of northeastern Kalimantan, immigrants from the Sulu Archipelago in the Philippines. *Other:* Fishermen. Muslim. See main entry under Philippines.

Tawoyan (Tawoyan Dayak, Tewoyan, Taboyan, Tabuyan, Tabojan, Tabojan Tongka) [twy] 20,000 (1981 Wurm and Hattori). East Central around Palori. *Class:* Austronesian, Malayo-Polynesian, Barito, East, North. *Dialects:* Lexical similarity 77% with Lawangan, 52% with Dusun Deyah. *Lg Dev:* Grammar. Bible portions: 1985.

Tidong (Camucones, Tidung, Tedong, Tidoeng, Tiran, Tirones, Tiroon, Zedong) [tid] 15,082 in Indonesia (2000 WCD). Population total all countries: 24,882. Population center is along Sembakung and Sibuka rivers of eastern Kalimantan, coast and islands around Tarakan and interior, Malinau River. Also spoken in Malaysia (Sabah). *Class:* Austronesian, Malayo-Polynesian, Northwest, North Sarawakan, Dayic, Murutic, Tidong. *Dialects:* Nonukan (Nunukan), Penchangan, Sedalir (Salalir, Sadalir, Saralir, Selalir), Tidung, Tarakan (Terakan), Sesayap (Sesajap), Sibuku.

Tunjung (Tunjung Dayak) [tjg] 50,000 (1981 Wurm and Hattori). East central, between Adas, Dempar, Melak, and east around the lake; south around Muntaiwan. *Class:* Austronesian, Malayo-Polynesian, Barito, Mahakam. *Dialects:* Tunjung (Tunjung Tengah), Tunjung Londong, Tunjung Linggang, Pahu.

Indonesia (Maluku)

Indonesia (Maluku). 2,549,454 (2000 census). Information mainly from K. Whinnom 1956; K. Polman 1981; J. Collins 1983; C. and B. D. Grimes 1983; B. D. Grimes 1994; C. Grimes 1995, 2000; E. Travis 1986; R. Bolton 1989, 1990; P. Taylor 1991; M. Taber 1993. The number of languages listed for Indonesia (Maluku) is 132. Of those, 129 are living languages and 3 are extinct. See maps beginning on page 793.

Alune (Sapalewa, Patasiwa Alfoeren) [alp] 17,243 (2000 WCD). 5 villages in Seram Barat District, and 22 villages in Kairatu and Taniwel districts, west Seram, central Maluku. 27 villages total. *Class:* Austronesian, Malayo-Polynesian, Central-Eastern, Central Malayo-Polynesian, Central Maluku, East, Seram, Nunusaku, Three Rivers, Amalumute, Northwest Seram, Ulat Inai. *Dialects:* Kairatu, Central West Alune (Niniari-Piru-Riring-Lumoli), South Alune (Rambatu-Manussa-Rumberu), North Coastal Alune (Nikulkan-Murnaten-Wakolo), Central East Alune (Buriah-Weth-Laturake). Rambatu dialect is reported to be prestigious. Kawe may be a dialect. Related to Nakaela and Lisabata-Nuniali. Lexical similarity 77% to 91% among dialects, 64% with Lisabata-Nuniali, 63% with Hulung and Naka'ela. *Lg Use:* The largest language in west Seram. The people in the interior, who are the majority, use the language daily. Usage in the coastal villages is not as vigorous. The southern dialect in Kairatu village is nearly extinct. *Lg Dev:* Literacy rate in first language: 50% to 65%. Literacy rate in second language: 40% to 55%. Bible portions: 1991–1997. *Other:* Christian.
Amahai (Amahei) [amq] 50 (1987 SIL). Central Maluku, southwest Seram, 4 villages near Masohi. *Class:* Austronesian, Malayo-Polynesian, Central-Eastern, Central Malayo-Polynesian, Central Maluku, East, Seram, Nunusaku, Piru Bay, East, Seram Straits, Uliase, Hatuhaha, Elpaputi. *Dialects:* Makariki, Rutah, Soahuku. Language cluster with Iha and Kaibobo. Also related to Elpaputih and Nusa Laut. Lexical similarity 87% between the villages of Makariki and Rutah; probably two languages, 59% to 69% with Saparua, 59% with Kamarian, 58% with Kaibobo, 52% with Piru, Luhu, and Hulung, 50% with Alune, 49% with Naka'ela, 47% with Lisabata-Nuniali and South Wemale, 45% with North Wemale and Nuaulu, 44% with Buano and Saleman. *Other:* Muslim, Christian. Nearly extinct.
Ambelau (Amblau) [amv] 5,700 (1989 SIL). Ethnic population: 5,700. Ambelau Island off the southeastern coast of Buru Island. Wae Tawa village on the coast of Buru, opposite Ambelau. 8 villages. Central Maluku. *Class:* Austronesian, Malayo-Polynesian, Central-Eastern, Central Malayo-Polynesian, Central Maluku, Ambelau. *Dialects:* Not intelligible with Buru. *Lg Dev:* Literacy rate in first language: below 1%. *Other:* Schools through junior high on the island. Wild pigs and rocky terrain on Ambelau make cultivation impossible; that is done in Wae Tawa village on Buru Island. Island, plains. Clove cultivation; agriculturalists: vegetables, tubers; copra production. Muslim.
Aputai (Ilputih, Opotai, Tutunohan) [apx] 150 (1990 Hinton). Wetar Island coast, Ilputih village, south central Wetar coast, and Lurang village, north central Wetar coast, southwest Maluku. *Class:* Austronesian, Malayo-Polynesian, Central-Eastern, Central Malayo-Polynesian, Timor, Southwest Maluku, Wetar. *Dialects:* Ilputih, Lurang, Welemur. Lexical similarity 79% with Perai, 74%

with Tugun, 69% with Ili'uun, 57% with Talur. Lexical similarity 93% among dialects. *Lg Use:* Welemur dialect is extinct. Ilputih speakers use Talur as second language. All Aputai speakers are bilingual to some extent in regional Malay. *Lg Dev:* Literacy rate in first language: below 1%. *Other:* Mountain slope, coastal. Swidden agriculturalists: maize. Christian.
Asilulu [asl] 8,756 (1987 SIL). Asilulu, Ureng, Negeri Lima villages, northwest Ambon Island, and some families in villages on the south coast of the Hoamoal Peninsula in West Seram. Spoken as second language in northwest Ambon, north and west Seram, Manipa, Boano, Kelang islands. *Class:* Austronesian, Malayo-Polynesian, Central-Eastern, Central Malayo-Polynesian, Central Maluku, East, Seram, Nunusaku, Piru Bay, West, Asilulu. *Dialect:* Asilulu, Ureng, Negeri Lima (Lima, Henalima). Lexical similarity 88% between Asilulu and Negeri Lima, 78% to 82% with Hila-Kaitetu, 72% to 73% with the Wakal dialect of Hitu, 67% to 72% with Larike-Wakasihu, 71% to 73% with Luhu on Seram. *Lg Use:* Trade language. *Lg Dev:* Literacy rate in first language: below 1%. Literacy rate in second language: 15% to 25%. *Other:* Coastal. Muslim.
Babar, North [bcd] 1,500 (1989 SIL). North Babar Islands, east of Timor, south Maluku. 6 villages. *Class:* Austronesian, Malayo-Polynesian, Central-Eastern, Central Malayo-Polynesian, Babar, North. *Dialects:* Reported dialect variation. *Lg Use:* Vigorous. Speakers also use Malay. *Lg Dev:* Literacy rate in first language: below 1%. *Other:* Coastal. Agriculturalists: maize, cassava; fishermen. Christian.
Babar, Southeast [vbb] 3,325 (1989 SIL). Southeast Babar Island, south Maluku. *Class:* Austronesian, Malayo-Polynesian, Central-Eastern, Central Malayo-Polynesian, Babar, South, Masela-South Babar. *Lg Dev:* Literacy rate in first language: below 1%.
Banda [bnd] 3,000 (1987 SIL). West and northeastern side of Kei Besar Island in Kei Islands, villages of Banda-Eli and Banda-Elat, south Maluku. There may be a third village. The people originally came from the Banda Islands, but the language is no longer spoken there. *Class:* Austronesian, Malayo-Polynesian, Central-Eastern, Central Malayo-Polynesian, Central Maluku, East, Banda-Geser. *Dialects:* Eli, Elat. Different from other languages of south Maluku. *Lg Use:* All domains. Speakers also use Kei. *Lg Dev:* Literacy rate in first language: below 1%. *Other:* Muslim.
Barakai (Workai) [baj] 4,300 (1995 SIL). Barakai Island, southeast Aru Islands; 4 villages on Barakai Island (Longgar, Apara, Bemun, and Mesiang) and one on Gomo-Gomo Island northeast of Barakai, south Maluku. *Class:* Austronesian, Malayo-Polynesian, Central-Eastern, Central Malayo-Polynesian, Aru. *Dialects:* Barakai, Mesiang. Close to Karey. Lexical similarity 70% with Batuley. *Lg Use:* Vigorous. *Lg Dev:* Literacy rate in first language: below 1%. *Other:* Christian, Muslim, traditional religion.
Bati (Gah) [bvt] 3,500 (1989 Loski). Eastern Seram Island along the coast between Kian Darat and Keleser, and in the interior. *Class:* Austronesian, Malayo-Polynesian, Central-Eastern, Central Malayo-Polynesian, Central Maluku, East, Banda-Geser, Geser-Gorom. *Dialects:* Related to Geser and Watubela. *Lg Use:* Strong separation of ethnolinguistic identity with Geser. Many claim to be bilingual in Geser. *Lg Dev:* Literacy rate in first language: below 1%. *Other:* Muslim.
Batuley (Watulai, Gwataley) [bay] 3,840 (1995 SIL). 7 villages in Aru on small islands off the east coast of Wokam Island, south Maluku. *Class:* Austronesian, Malayo-Polynesian, Central-Eastern, Central Malayo-Polynesian, Aru. *Dialects:* Fairly closely related to

Kompane to the north and Lola to the south, slightly more distant from Dobel. Lexical similarity 70% with Barakai and Karey, 81% with Mariri. *Lg Use:* Vigorous. *Lg Dev:* Literacy rate in first language: below 1%. *Other:* Muslim, Christian.

Benggoi (Bengoi, Kobi-Benggoi, Uhei-Kaclakin, Uhei Kachlakan, Uhei-Kahlakim, Isal) [bgy] 350 (1989 SIL). North coast, Werinama and Bula districts, east Seram, central Maluku, 3 villages (Benggoi, Balakeo, Lesa). *Class:* Austronesian, Malayo-Polynesian, Central-Eastern, Central Malayo-Polynesian, Central Maluku, East, Seram, Manusela-Seti. *Dialects:* Lesa, Benggoi, Balakeo. Lexical similarity 70% among 'dialects'; 54% to 66% with Liana-Seti, 46% to 50% with Salas Gunung, 32% to 46% with Manusela. *Lg Dev:* Literacy rate in first language: below 1%. *Other:* 'Isal' was given by Salzner in the area where Benggoi is located; the name is not used now. Christian, Muslim.

Boano (Buano) [bzn] 3,240 (1982). Boano Island west of Seram, mainly in North Buano village, central Maluku. *Class:* Austronesian, Malayo-Polynesian, Central-Eastern, Central Malayo-Polynesian, Central Maluku, East, Seram, Nunusaku, Piru Bay, West, Hoamoal, East. *Dialects:* Related to Larike-Wakasihu. Lexical similarity 60% with Luhu, 61% with Lisabata-Nuniali (closest). *Lg Use:* Vigorous in north Boano. South Boano may be extinct. *Other:* Different from Boano in Sulawesi. Muslim, Christian.

Bobot (Werinama, Hatumeten, Atiahu, Ahtiago, Ntau) [bty] 4,500 (1989 SIL). Southeast Seram, Werinama District, from the village of Atiahu to Kota Baru, and Tunsai village in the Liana area, central Maluku. *Class:* Austronesian, Malayo-Polynesian, Central-Eastern, Central Malayo-Polynesian, Central Maluku, East, Seram, Bobot. *Dialects:* Lexical similarity 44% with Sepa and Teluti, 42% with Atamanu. *Lg Dev:* Literacy rate in first language: below 1%. *Other:* Atiahu is a village name, not a dialect. Coastal. Muslim.

Buli [bzq] 2,524 (2000 WCD). North Maluku, central Halmahera, east coast, three villages. *Class:* Austronesian, Malayo-Polynesian, Central-Eastern, Eastern Malayo-Polynesian, South Halmahera-West New Guinea, South Halmahera, Southeast. *Dialect:* Buli, Wayamli (Wajamli, Jawanli). *Lg Dev:* Literacy rate in first language: below 1%. *Other:* Several communities of over 100 dwellings. Coconut plantations. Muslim, Christian.

Buru (Boeroe, Buruese) [mhs] 32,980 in Indonesia (1989 SIL). Population includes 6,622 Wae Sama, 9,600 Masarete, 14,258 Rana, 500 Fogi, and 2,000 in Ambon. South, southeast, and central Buru Island, central Maluku, Ambon, Jakarta, and the Netherlands, 70 villages. Also spoken in Netherlands. *Class:* Austronesian, Malayo-Polynesian, Central-Eastern, Central Malayo-Polynesian, Central Maluku, Buru. *Dialects:* Masarete (South Buru), Wae Sama (Waesama), Central Buru (Rana, Wae Geren, Wae Kabo), Fogi (Li Emteban, Tomahu). Li Garan is a special taboo dialect spoken by the Rana people (3,000 to 5,000 users). Fogi dialect 500 ethnic population, but no speakers. Lexical similarity 90% between Masarete and Wae Sama, 88% between Masarete and Rana, 80% between Wae Sama and Rana, 68% between Li Enyorot (Lisela) and Masarete, 48% between Liliali and Masarete, 45% between Kayeli and Masarete, 44% between Ambelau and Masarete, 27% to 33% between Buru and the languages of Sula. *Lg Use:* Vigorous in most areas. Fogi has apparently undergone complete shift to Ambonese Malay. All domains. All ages. Bilingual level estimates for Ambonese Malay: 0 15%, 1 20%, 2 50%, 3 10%, 4 5%, 5 0%; Indonesian: 0 15%, 1 40%, 2 35%, 3 7%, 4 3%, 5 0%. *Lg Dev:* Roman script. Grammar. Bible portions: 1904–1997. *Other:* There are word taboos and

complex intermarriage patterns on the island. Exogamous. 10 clans. SVO; prepositions; genitives before nouns; predominantly head marking; CV, CVC, V, VC; nontonal. Coastal, mountain slope. Tropical forest, savannah. Sea level to 1,500 meters. Swidden agriculturalists: cloves, tuber crops; sago gatherers; copra production. Traditional religion, Muslim, Christian.

Dai [dij] 808 (1981 Wurm and Hattori). South, Dai and Babar islands. Dai is 15 miles north of Babar. 3 villages. *Class:* Austronesian, Malayo-Polynesian, Central-Eastern, Central Malayo-Polynesian, Babar, North. *Dialects:* No dialect variation. Lexical similarity 72% with Dawera-DawELoor (closest), 71% with Nakarahamto, 49% with Masela-South Babar, 48% with Tepa (Luang). *Lg Use:* Vigorous. Speakers also use Malay. *Lg Dev:* Literacy rate in first language: below 1%. *Other:* Mountain slope. Sea level. Agriculturalists: maize, cassava; fishermen. Christian.

Damar, East (South Damar) [dmr] 2,800 (1990 SIL). Six villages along the east side of Damar Island, north and east of Roma Island, north of the eastern tip of Timor Island, south Maluku. *Class:* Austronesian, Malayo-Polynesian, Central-Eastern, Central Malayo-Polynesian, Timor, Southwest Maluku, East Damar. *Dialects:* Not intelligible with West Damar. *Lg Dev:* Literacy rate in first language: below 1%.

Damar, West (North Damar) [drn] 800 (1987 SIL). Two villages on the north side of Damar Island, north of the eastern tip of Timor Island, south Maluku, Indonesia. *Class:* Austronesian, Malayo-Polynesian, Central-Eastern, Central Malayo-Polynesian, West Damar. *Dialects:* Not intelligible with East Damar. *Lg Dev:* Literacy rate in first language: below 1%.

Dawera-Daweloor (Davelor) [ddw] 1,500 (1989 SIL). South Maluku, six villages on Dawera and Daweloor islands. The islands are 11 miles northeast of Babar Island. *Class:* Austronesian, Malayo-Polynesian, Central-Eastern, Central Malayo-Polynesian, Babar, North. *Dialects:* Minor dialect differences. *Lg Use:* Vigorous. Speakers also use Malay. *Lg Dev:* Literacy rate in first language: below 1%. *Other:* Coastal. Sea level. Agriculturalists: maize, cassava; fishermen. Christian.

Dobel (Doibel, Sersifar Tannin, Kobro'or, Kobroor) [kvo] 8,000 (2000 SIL). Population includes 6,500 plus 1,000 outside the area; 2,700 in Northern Dobel, 1,800 in Straits Dobel, 1,400 in Southeast Dobel. Aru Islands, along the whole east coast of Kobror Island, one village in southeast Wokam Island, 4 villages on both sides of the eastern half of Barakai Strait (on both Kobror Islands and Koba Island), and 2 villages in central Kobror Island. 18 villages. Southeast Maluku. Also in Dobo and Ambon. *Class:* Austronesian, Malayo-Polynesian, Central-Eastern, Central Malayo-Polynesian, Aru. *Dialects:* Northern Dobel, Straits Dobel, Southeast Dobel. At least three dialects. Related to Lola and Lorang. Lexical similarity 78% to 86% with Koba. *Lg Use:* Vigorous. All Lorang speakers use Dobel as second language. Some Chinese merchants who are speakers of Dobo Malay and the older ones of Hokkien learn Dobel. All domains, family, social interaction, local activities, talking to local Chinese, traditional and political village meetings. Children play and interact in Dobel, a little use in some religious services. Some letters written in it. Some speakers have written stories. Oral literature. All ages. Positive language attitude. Dobo Malay, a dialect of Ambonese Malay, is used with outsiders and in the classroom. Some preschool children do not know Dobo Malay. Dobo Malay-flavored Indonesian used for speaking to non-Maluku people, opening and closing local political meetings, school classrooms, religious services, and formal religious activities. Stable bilingualism with Dobo Malay and Indonesian used for certain domains, Dobel for others.

Few can speak Standard Indonesian. Some also speak Manombai. *Lg Dev:* Literacy rate in first language: 30%. Literacy rate in second language: 25% to 50%. Bible portions: 1991–2004. *Other:* Flat coral, riverine. Tropical forest, mangrove swamp. Low altitude. Diving for oysters (for oyster farms and mother-of-pearl); fishermen; agriculturalists. Christian, Muslim.

Elpaputih (Elpaputi) [elp] 424 (2000 WCD). West Seram, central Maluku. *Class:* Austronesian, Malayo-Polynesian, Central-Eastern, Central Malayo-Polynesian, Central Maluku, East, Seram, Nunusaku, Piru Bay, East, Seram Straits, Uliase, Hatuhaha, Elpaputi. *Dialects:* Closest to Nusalaut, Amahai.

Emplawas [emw] 250 (1989 SIL). Emplawas village, southwest Babar Island, south Maluku. *Class:* Austronesian, Malayo-Polynesian, Central-Eastern, Central Malayo-Polynesian, Babar, South, Southwest Babar. *Lg Dev:* Literacy rate in first language: below 1%.

Fordata (Larat, Vai Tnebar, Vaidida, Vai Fordata) [frd] 50,000. Population includes 25,000 in the language area and 25,000 elsewhere (2000 C. Marshall). Southeast Maluku, northern Tanimbar Islands of the Fordata, Larat, the Molu-Maru group, a few villages on the northwest part of Yamdena, and on Seira off the west coast of Yamdena. 30 villages. Also in Saumlaki, Ambon, Tual, Sorong, Hayapura, Jakarta. *Class:* Austronesian, Malayo-Polynesian, Central-Eastern, Central Malayo-Polynesian, Southeast Maluku, Kei-Tanimbar, Kei-Fordata. *Dialects:* Fordata-Larat I, Fordata-Larat II, Molo (Molo-Maru), Sera (Seira). Sera is the most divergent dialect. Lexical similarity 68% with Kei. *Lg Use:* Trade language formerly of the Tanimbar Islands and the language of ritual. It is now not well known by speakers of the other 3 languages, except for some older people who use it for ritual. Vigorous. 2 villages of mainly Muslim Geser and Bugis use Fordata as second language. All domains, home, fields, trails, traditional law, local administration and commerce, traditional religious ceremonies. Positive language attitude. Nearly everyone is bilingual to some degree in Ambonese Malay, the trade language. They are less bilingual in Standard Indonesian, usually the third language learned. Less than 1% monolingual. Indonesian and Ambonese Malay used in schools, government, most churches. Most parents speak mixed Fordata and Malay to their children. *Lg Dev:* Literacy rate in first language: 1% to 5%. Literacy rate in second language: 50% to 75%. 2,500 read, 1,500 can write. Dictionary. Grammar. Bible portions: 1996. *Other:* Elementary schools in nearly every village, secondary schools for every 3 or 4 villages. Coastal. Reef ecosystems. Swidden agriculturalists with diversification of crops and planting cycles: dry field rice, maize, tubers, beans; cash crop is copra; palm brandy; fishermen. Christian, Muslim.

Galela [gbi] 79,000 (1990 SIL). Population includes 41,000 Kadai, 10,000 Kadina, 24,000 Morotai, and 4,000 Sopi. North Maluku, Galela Bay, and north of Tobelo to the northern tip of Halmahera, Morotai Island except southeast quadrant, islands of Gunage and Moari near Kayoa, Bacan, Obi, scattered along the southwest coast of Halmahera. *Class:* West Papuan, North Halmahera, North, Galela-Loloda. *Dialects:* Kadai, Kadina, Morotai, Sopi. Laba may be a dialect. Speakers have 65% intelligibility of Loloda, Loloda 85% of Galela. *Lg Use:* Vigorous. Speakers also use Indonesian. *Lg Dev:* Literacy rate in first language: 5% to 10%. Literacy rate in second language: 50% to 75%. Dictionary. Grammar. NT: 2002. *Other:* Agriculturalists; fishermen. Christian, Muslim.

Gamkonora [gak] 1,500 (1987 Voorhoeve and Visser). North Halmahera, a few villages along the coast to the south of the Ibu area, north Maluku. *Class:* West Papuan, North Halmahera, North, Sahu. *Dialects:* Lexical

similarity 81% with Waioli. *Lg Dev:* Literacy rate in first language: below 1%. *Other:* Muslim, Christian.

Gane (Gani, Giman) [gzn] 2,900 (1982 Teljeur). North Maluku, Halmahera Island, south part of southern peninsula. *Class:* Austronesian, Malayo-Polynesian, Central-Eastern, Eastern Malayo-Polynesian, South Halmahera-West New Guinea, South Halmahera, East Makian-Gane. *Dialects:* Close to East Makian and Kayoa. *Lg Use:* Positive language attitude. *Lg Dev:* Literacy rate in first language: below 1%. *Other:* Muslim.

Gebe (Gebi) [gei] 2,651 (2000 WCD). North Maluku, Gebe, Yoi'umiyal, and Gag islands between southern Halmahera and Waigeo Island (Papua), 4 villages. *Class:* Austronesian, Malayo-Polynesian, Central-Eastern, Eastern Malayo-Polynesian, South Halmahera-West New Guinea, West New Guinea, Cenderawasih Bay, Raja Ampat. *Dialect:* Umera. Lexical similarity 44% with Patani. *Lg Use:* All domains. Bilingualism in Indonesian increasing because of mining operation and schools. *Lg Dev:* Literacy rate in first language: below 1%. *Other:* A school in each village. Muslim.

Geser-Gorom (Geser, Gesa, Gorom, Goram, Goran, Gorong, Seram, Seran, Seran Laut) [ges] 36,500 (1989 SIL). Eastern end of Seram, and the Gorom Islands. *Class:* Austronesian, Malayo-Polynesian, Central-Eastern, Central Malayo-Polynesian, Central Maluku, East, Banda-Geser, Geser-Gorom. *Dialects:* Goram Laut, Mina Mina Gorong, Kelimuri. Lexical similarity 73% to 93% among dialects, 51% to 61% with Watubela. *Lg Use:* Watubela speakers use this as second language. *Lg Dev:* Literacy rate in first language: below 1%. Literacy rate in second language: 50% to 75%. *Other:* Muslim.

Gorap [goq] 1,000 (1992 SIL). North Maluku, Morotai Island, Pilowo and Waringin villages; Central Halmahera, Bobane and Igo villages. *Class:* Austronesian, Malayo-Polynesian, Unclassified. *Dialects:* Reported to be a mixed language, including Ternate and Malay words, with different word order from other languages of north Halmahera or the Austronesian languages. Lexical similarity 85% with Indonesian, but comprehension is limited. *Lg Use:* All domains. *Other:* Speakers consider Sulawesi to be their ancestral homeland.

Haruku [hrk] 18,219 (1989 SIL). Haruku Island, Lease Islands, central Maluku. *Class:* Austronesian, Malayo-Polynesian, Central-Eastern, Central Malayo-Polynesian, Central Maluku, East, Seram, Nunusaku, Piru Bay. *Dialects:* Hulaliu, Pelauw, Kailolo, Rohomoni. Each village is a separate dialect. Lexical similarity 81% to 92% among dialects. Lexical similarity 74% to 76% with Tulehu, 67% to 71% with Saparua. *Lg Use:* Speakers also use Ambonese Malay. *Lg Dev:* Literacy rate in first language: below 1%. *Other:* Muslim, Christian.

Hitu [htu] 15,965 (1987 SIL). 5 villages: Wakal, Hitu, Mamala, Morela, and Hila; Hitu Peninsula, Ambon Island. *Class:* Austronesian, Malayo-Polynesian, Central-Eastern, Central Malayo-Polynesian, Central Maluku, East, Seram, Nunusaku, Piru Bay, East, Seram Straits, Ambon. *Dialects:* Wakal, Morela, Mamala, Hitu, Hila. Lexical similarity 67% to 82% with Seit-Kaitetu, 74% to 82% with Tulehu. *Lg Use:* Moderate to vigorous. *Lg Dev:* Literacy rate in first language: below 1%. *Other:* Muslim, Christian.

Horuru [hrr] 4,242 (2000 WCD). Seram, central Maluku. *Class:* Austronesian, Malayo-Polynesian, Central-Eastern, Central Malayo-Polynesian, Central Maluku, East, Seram, Nunusaku, Three Rivers, Amalumute, Northwest Seram. *Dialects:* Hulung may be related. This may be an alternate name for another language.

Hoti [hti] 10 (1987 SIL). East Seram, central Maluku. *Class:* Austronesian, Malayo-Polynesian, Central-Eastern, Central Malayo-Polynesian, Central Maluku, East, Seram,

East Seram. *Lg Use:* All speakers are older adults (1987). *Other:* Nearly extinct.

Huaulu (Alakamat, Bahasa Asli) [hud] 300 (1987 SIL). East Seram, central Maluku, northwest of Manusela, 10 villages. *Class:* Austronesian, Malayo-Polynesian, Central-Eastern, Central Malayo-Polynesian, Central Maluku, East, Seram, Manusela-Seti. *Dialects:* Lexical similarity 64% to 72% with Manusela dialects. *Other:* Culturally distinct from Manusela. Traditional religion.

Hukumina (Bambaa) [huw] 1 (1989 SIL). Formerly spoken in Hukumina, Palumata, and Tomahu districts of northwest Buru Island. The present speaker is from the former village of Hukumina that used to be located behind the present village of Masarete, near the fort at Kayeli in northeast Buru. *Class:* Austronesian, Malayo-Polynesian, Unclassified. *Lg Use:* The one speaker was 80 years old in 1989. *Other:* 'Bambaa' in Hukumina means 'there isn't any'. Nearly extinct.

Hulung [huk] 10 (1991 SIL). Hulung village, and Sauweli hamlet, west Seram, central Maluku. *Class:* Austronesian, Malayo-Polynesian, Central-Eastern, Central Malayo-Polynesian, Central Maluku, East, Seram, Nunusaku, Three Rivers, Amalumute, Northwest Seram, Hulung. *Dialects:* Lexical similarity 67% with Lisabata-Nuniali, 66% with Naka'ela and South Wemale, 63% with Alune, 59% with North Wemale. *Other:* Christian. Nearly extinct.

Ibu [ibu] 35 (1987 Voorhoeve and Visser). Ethnic population: 50 to 200 in the ethnic group (1984). North Maluku, northern Halmahera Island, mouth of Ibu River, villages of Gamlamo and Gamici. *Class:* West Papuan, North Halmahera, North, Sahu. *Dialects:* May be inherently intelligible with Sahu. *Lg Use:* Speakers are older adults (1987). *Other:* Nearly extinct.

Ili'uun (Iliun, Hahutau, Hahutan, Limera, Ilmaumau, Erai) [ilu] 1,400 (1990 SIL). Wetar Island coast, villages of Telemar, Karbubu, Klishatu, Ilmaumau, Erai (Eray), Nabar, and Esulit on the west end of Wetar, and Istutun village on Lirang Island off the southwest tip of Wetar, southwest Maluku. *Class:* Austronesian, Malayo-Polynesian, Central-Eastern, Central Malayo-Polynesian, Timor, Southwest Maluku, Wetar. *Dialects:* Telemar, Karbubu, Ustutun, Klishatu, Ilmaumau, Eray, Nabar, Esulit. All speakers now speak the Ili'uun dialect. Lexical similarity 93% to 97% among dialects. Lexical similarity 73% with Tugun, 69% with Aputai, 67% with Perai, 51% with Talur. *Lg Use:* Jeh and Juru are extinct. Many also use regional Malay. *Lg Dev:* Literacy rate in first language: below 1%. *Other:* Mountain slope, coastal. Swidden agriculturalists: maize. Christian.

Imroing (Imroin) [imr] 450 (1989 SIL). Village of Imroing, southwest Babar Island, south Maluku. *Class:* Austronesian, Malayo-Polynesian, Central-Eastern, Central Malayo-Polynesian, Babar, South, Southwest Babar. *Lg Dev:* Literacy rate in first language: below 1%.

Kadai [kzd] 350 (2000 WCD). North Maluku, Sula Islands, Taliabu Island, interior mountains. Possibly also in the mountains of Mangole Island. *Class:* Austronesian, Malayo-Polynesian, Central-Eastern, Central Malayo-Polynesian, Central Maluku, Sula, Taliabo. *Dialects:* May be intelligible with Taliabu. *Other:* The government wants to resettle them along the coast. Traditional religion.

Kaibobo (Kaibubu) [kzb] 500 (1983 Collins and Voorhoeve). Kaibobo, Hatusua, Waisamu, Kamarian, Seruawan, Tihulale, and Rumahkay villages in Kairatu District; 8 villages total, Piru Bay, west Seram, central Maluku. *Class:* Austronesian, Malayo-Polynesian, Central-Eastern, Central Malayo-Polynesian, Central Maluku, East, Seram, Nunusaku, Piru Bay, East. *Dialects:* Kaibobo, Hatusua. Related to Lisabata-Nuniali. Lexical similarity 82% to 88% between Kaibobo and Hatusua, 75% with Kamarian, 62% to 65% with Saparua, 62% with

Piru, 58% to 62% with Luhu, 61% with Naka'ela. *Lg Use:* Language use may be shifting to Ambonese Malay in some villages. *Other:* Christian.

Kamarian (Kamariang, Seruawan) [kzx] 10 (1987 SIL). Ethnic population: 6,000 in the village (1987 SIL). West Seram, central Maluku, Kamarian village on the south coast of Seram, at the eastern end of Piru Bay. *Class:* Austronesian, Malayo-Polynesian, Central-Eastern, Central Malayo-Polynesian, Central Maluku, East, Seram, Nunusaku, Piru Bay, East, Seram Straits, Uliase, Kamarian. *Dialects:* Lexical similarity 75% with Kaibobo, 67% with Saparua, 60% with Lisabata-Nuniali, 59% with Amahai, Piru, Naka'ela, and Hulung. *Other:* Nearly extinct.

Kao (Kau, Ka'u) [kax] 403 (2000 WCD). North Maluku, interior North Halmahera, around the town of Kao, near the mouth of the Kao River. *Class:* West Papuan, North Halmahera, North, Kao River. *Dialects:* Could be a marginal dialect of Pagu, but relates uniquely to other languages in the Kao River subbranch. *Lg Use:* Membership in the ethnic group is expressed by knowing the language. Children learn Kao when they become teenagers. *Lg Dev:* Literacy rate in first language: below 1%. Literacy rate in second language: 50% to 75%. *Other:* Muslim.

Karey (Kerei, Krei) [kyd] 950 (1995 SIL). Village of Karey, east coast of Tarangan Island, southern Aru Islands, south Maluku. *Class:* Austronesian, Malayo-Polynesian, Central-Eastern, Central Malayo-Polynesian, Aru. *Dialects:* Lexical similarity 70% with East Tarangan and Batuley. *Lg Use:* Vigorous. *Lg Dev:* Literacy rate in first language: below 1%. *Other:* Christian, Muslim.

Kayeli (Kajeli, Cajeli, Caeli, Gaeli) [kzl] 3 (1995). Not used for 3 decades by the speakers (1989 C. Grimes SIL). Ethnic population: 800 (1995). Southern Namlea Bay, north Buru Island, central Maluku. *Class:* Austronesian, Malayo-Polynesian, Central-Eastern, Central Malayo-Polynesian, Central Maluku, East, Seram, Nunusaku, Kayeli. *Dialects:* Kayeli, Leliali (Liliali), Lumaete (Lumaiti, Mumaite, Lumara). *Lg Use:* Lumaete became extinct in the 1990s and Leliali became extinct in March 1989. Speakers are older adults. Others have completely shifted to Ambonese Malay as first language. *Other:* The ethnic group continues to function. Muslim. Nearly extinct.

Kei (Veveu Evav, Kai) [kei] 85,000 (2000 Ed Travis). 4,500 monolinguals. Kei Kecil, Kei Besar, and surrounding islands, except the villages of Banda Eli and Banda Elat on Kei Besar, and the Kur Islands, where Kei is used as a lingua franca. About 207 villages in the major part of 10 islands. Southeast Maluku. *Class:* Austronesian, Malayo-Polynesian, Central-Eastern, Central Malayo-Polynesian, Southeast Maluku, Kei-Tanimbar, Kei-Fordata. *Dialects:* Kei Kecil, Kei Besar, Tayando, Tanimbar Kei (Atnebar), Ta'am. Kei Kecil is the city dialect that has prestige. Kei Besar people usually know the Kei Kecil dialect, but not vice versa. Kei Besar is closer to Fordata than the other Kei dialects. Tanimbar Kei is spoken in only one village. Lexical similarity 60% with Fordata. *Lg Use:* Trade language of speakers of Banda and Kur, and outsiders like the ethnic Chinese and Butonese who live in Kei. Fairly vigorous. Banda and Kur speakers use Kei as second language. All domains, songs in church, local commerce, oral literature. Children usually use a second language, but they also speak Kei. Positive language attitude. 95% speak Indonesian at some level. About 2,000 speak Kei, Indonesian, and Banda. *Lg Dev:* Literacy rate in first language: below 1%. Literacy rate in second language: 50% to 75%. 100 can read it, 10 can write it. Used informally in school for explanations. Dictionary. Grammar. *Other:* Coral Islands, mountain slope. Little remaining forest. Low to 30 meters

(Kei Kecil), to 240 meters (Kei Besar, Tanimbar-Kei). Agriculturalists: millet, tapioca, corn; copra production; fishermen. Muslim, Christian, traditional religion.

Kisar (Meher, Yotowawa) [kje] 20,000 (1995 SIL). Kisar Island northeast of Timor Island, 19 villages, villages of Hila and Likagraha (Solath) on Roma Island, 3 villages on Wetar Island (Amau, Naumatan, Hi'ai), and several hundred in Ambon city, Dili, and Kupang. Used as a second language by a handful of Oirata speakers on Kisar. South Maluku. *Class:* Austronesian, Malayo-Polynesian, Central-Eastern, Central Malayo-Polynesian, Timor, Southwest Maluku, Kisar-Roma. *Dialects:* Not related to Oirata, which has sometimes been called a dialect. *Lg Use:* Trade language. *Lg Dev:* Literacy rate in first language: below 1%. Literacy rate in second language: 25% to 50%. Bible portions: 1997. *Other:* Called Yotowawa or Meher locally. Christian.

Koba [kpd] 600 (2000 J. Hughes). Aru Islands, southeast Maluku, 3 villages on Baun and Fukarel islands bordering Dobel. The islands where Koba is spoken are to the southeast of Kobror Island, at the mouth of the Barakai Strait. *Class:* Austronesian, Malayo-Polynesian, Central-Eastern, Central Malayo-Polynesian, Aru. *Dialect:* Southeast Koba. Low comprehension of Dobel. Lexical similarity 78% to 86% with Dobel.

Kola (Warilau, Kulaha, Marlasi) [kvv] 7,700 (1995 SIL). North Aru Islands, all around the coast of Kola Island and adjacent islands, south Maluku. 22 villages. *Class:* Austronesian, Malayo-Polynesian, Central-Eastern, Central Malayo-Polynesian, Aru. *Dialects:* Intelligibility testing showed Marlasi is intelligible to Kompane speakers, but with some possible adaptation of literature needed. Lexical similarity 77% with Kompane, 70% with Ujir. *Lg Use:* Vigorous. Outsiders want to learn it. *Lg Dev:* Literacy rate in first language: below 1%. Literacy rate in second language: 25% to 50%. Bible portions: 2004.

Kompane (Komfana, Kongampani) [kvp] 330 (1995 SIL). Northeast Aru in Kompane village on the east coast of Kongan Island, south of Kola and north of Wokam islands, south Maluku. *Class:* Austronesian, Malayo-Polynesian, Central-Eastern, Central Malayo-Polynesian, Aru. *Dialects:* Close to Kola, linguistically between Kola and Batuley. Intelligibility of Kola is good, but some adaptation of literature may be needed. *Lg Use:* Vigorous. *Other:* Muslim.

Kur [kuv] 3,181 (2000 WCD). Kur Island and nearby islands, western Kei Kecil District, south Maluku. *Class:* Austronesian, Malayo-Polynesian, Central-Eastern, Central Malayo-Polynesian, Teor-Kur. *Dialects:* Separate language from Kei. Survey needed to determine boundaries of intelligibility of dialects to the north and the central dialect, and of Teor. Lexical similarity 47% to 50% with Kei, 71% to 83% with Teor, 41% with Watubela, 38% with Geser. *Lg Use:* Vigorous. *Other:* Muslim.

Laba (South Loloda, Kedi) [lau] 2,000 (1991 SIL). North Maluku, 4 villages to the interior of the south end of Loloda District. *Class:* West Papuan, North Halmahera, North, Galela-Loloda. *Dialects:* Phonology like Galela, 70% intelligibility, 75% of Loloda. Lexical similarity 75% with Galela, 78% with Loloda. *Other:* Christian.

Laha (Central Ambon) [lhh] 3,894 (1987 SIL). Laha village and several nearby smaller villages, south central coast of Ambon Island, central Maluku. *Class:* Austronesian, Malayo-Polynesian, Central-Eastern, Central Malayo-Polynesian, Central Maluku, East, Seram, Nunusaku, Piru Bay, East, Seram Straits, Ambon. *Dialects:* Related to Seram languages, but distinct from Manusela. Lexical similarity 64% to 66% with Asilulu and Hila-Kaitetu (closest). *Lg Use:* Parents encourage children to speak Laha. All ages. Speakers also use Ambonese Malay. *Other:* Muslim, Christian.

Larike-Wakasihu [alo] 12,557 (1987 SIL). Larike, Wakasihu, Tapi, Allang, and Lai villages, southwest Hitu Peninsula, Ambon Island. *Class:* Austronesian, Malayo-Polynesian, Central-Eastern, Central Malayo-Polynesian, Central Maluku, East, Seram, Nunusaku, Piru Bay, West, Hoamoal, East. *Dialects:* Allang, Wakasihu, Larike. Wakasihu may need separate literature from Larike. The western end of the Ambon dialect cluster. Lexical similarity 81% among Allang and Larike and Wakasihu, 92% between Larike and Wakasihu. 68% to 71% with Asilulu, 67% to 72% with Negeri Lima. *Lg Use:* Vigorous use in Larike and Wakasihu, weak in Allang. Only older adults in Allang, Allang Asaude, Uraur, and Urusana still know Allang, but apparently do not use it. *Lg Dev:* Literacy rate in first language: 1% to 5%. Literacy rate in second language: 50% to 75%. *Other:* Muslim, Christian.

Latu [ltu] 2,134 (1982 SIL). Latu village, Elpaputih Bay, southwest Seram Island, central Maluku. *Class:* Austronesian, Malayo-Polynesian, Central-Eastern, Central Malayo-Polynesian, Central Maluku, East, Seram, Nunusaku, Piru Bay, East, Seram Straits, Uliase, Hatuhaha, Saparua. *Dialects:* Lexical similarity 82% to 84% with Saparua dialects.

Leti [lti] 7,500 (1995 SIL). Leti Island. *Class:* Austronesian, Malayo-Polynesian, Central-Eastern, Central Malayo-Polynesian, Timor, Southwest Maluku, Luang. *Dialects:* Marginal intelligibility of Luang. They have difficulty with written Luang. Lexical similarity 89% with Luang. *Lg Use:* They share a historical and cultural heritage with Luang, but maintain their own identity and local pride. *Lg Dev:* Literacy rate in first language: below 1%. Literacy rate in second language: 25% to 50%. *Other:* Matrilineal. Christian.

Liana-Seti (Liana, Lianan, Uhei Kaclakin, Uhei Kachlakan, Uhei Kahlakim, Teula, Liambata-Kobi) [ste] 3,000 (1989 SIL). Eastern Teluti Bay to the north coast, districts of Seram, Bula, Werinama, and Tehoru, central Maluku, 8 villages. *Class:* Austronesian, Malayo-Polynesian, Central-Eastern, Central Malayo-Polynesian, Central Maluku, East, Seram, Manusela-Seti. *Dialects:* "Seti," Wahakaim, Kobi. Lexical similarity 66% to 74% between Seti (westernmost and interior) and Wahakaim (near coast), 69% to 78% between Kobi and Seti, 70% between Kobi and Wahakaim, 42% to 61% between Kobi and Manusela, 54% to 66% between Kobi and Benggoi, 48% to 58% between Kobi and Salas Gunung. *Lg Use:* Vigorous. Seti use Teluti as second language. *Lg Dev:* Literacy rate in first language: below 1%. Literacy rate in second language: 25% to 50%. *Other:* Speakers use the name 'Liana'; "Seti" is derogatory. Christian.

Lisabata-Nuniali (Lisabata, Nuniali, Noniali) [lcs] 1,830 (1982). Spread across the north coast of West and North Seram, 5 villages, central Maluku. *Class:* Austronesian, Malayo-Polynesian, Central-Eastern, Central Malayo-Polynesian, Central Maluku, East, Seram, Nunusaku, Three Rivers, Amalumute, Northwest Seram. *Dialects:* Lisabata-Timur, Nuniali, Sukaraja, Kawa. Lexical similarity between Kawa (far western) and Lisabata Timur (far eastern) is 85%, 72% with Naka'ela, 67% with Hulung, 63% with Alune. *Lg Use:* Vigorous except in Kawa. Speakers also use Ambonese Malay. *Other:* Muslim, Christian (Nuniali).

Lisela (Buru, North Buru, Li Enyorot, Liet Enjorot, Wayapo) [lcl] 11,922 (1989 SIL). Northern, northeastern, north central coastal strips, and northwestern Buru Island, lower Wae Geren and Vae Apo valleys of Buru Island, central Maluku. Some in Ambon. *Class:* Austronesian, Malayo-Polynesian, Central-Eastern, Central Malayo-Polynesian, Central Maluku, Buru. *Dialects:* Lisela (Licela, Licella), Tagalisa. *Lg Use:* Speakers are shifting to Ambonese Malay. *Other:* Coastal, mountain slope. Tropical forest, savannah. Sea level to 500 meters. Swidden agriculturalists; eucalyptus oil. Muslim, traditional religion.

Lola [lcd] 830 (1995 SIL). 3 villages of Lola, Warabal, and Jambuair on 3 islands east of Kobroor and Baun islands, Aru Islands, southeast Maluku. *Class:* Austronesian, Malayo-Polynesian, Central-Eastern, Central Malayo-Polynesian, Aru. *Dialects:* Lola, Warabal. Linguistically between Batuley and Dobel; close to Koba. *Lg Use:* Most vigorous in Warabal. In Lola some young people use Ambonese Malay among themselves. In Jambuair there are many non-Aru people, so Ambonese Malay is in common use. *Other:* Muslim.

Loloda (Loda, North Loloda) [loa] 15,000 (1991 SIL). Population includes 2,000 Bakun. North Maluku, northwest coast of Halmahera. *Class:* West Papuan, North Halmahera, North, Galela-Loloda. *Dialect:* Bakun. Intelligibility with Laba is very limited. Speakers have 85% intelligibility of Galela, Galela has 65% of Loloda. *Lg Use:* Vigorous. *Lg Dev:* Literacy rate in first language: below 1%. Literacy rate in second language: 50% to 75%. Grammar. Bible portions: 1915. *Other:* Christian, Muslim.

Lorang [lrn] 325 (1995 SIL). Village of Lorang, center of Aru, on Koba Island. Southeast Maluku. *Class:* Austronesian, Malayo-Polynesian, Central-Eastern, Central Malayo-Polynesian, Aru. *Dialects:* Close to Koba, and to a lesser extent to Dobel. Some similarities with Manombai, but intelligibility is lower than might be expected. *Lg Use:* Vigorous. Speakers use several local languages to some degree and speak Dobel from childhood. *Other:* Christian.

Loun [lox] 20. North central Seram, central Maluku. *Class:* Austronesian, Malayo-Polynesian, Central-Eastern, Central Malayo-Polynesian, Central Maluku, East, Seram, Nunusaku, Three Rivers, Amalumute, Northwest Seram, Loun. *Other:* Nearly extinct.

Luang (Letri Lgona, Literi Lagona, Lgona) [lex] 18,000 (1995 SIL). 200 monolinguals. Moa, Lakor, Luang, Sermata, Wetan, northwest Babar Islands east of Timor, south Maluku. *Class:* Austronesian, Malayo-Polynesian, Central-Eastern, Central Malayo-Polynesian, Timor, Southwest Maluku, Luang. *Dialects:* Luang, Wetan (Wetang), Moa, Lakor. Low comprehension of Leti. Lexical similarity 89% with Leti. *Lg Use:* Positive language attitude. Speakers also use Ambonese Malay, Bahasa Indonesia, Leti, or Kisar. *Lg Dev:* Literacy rate in first language: 15%. Literacy rate in second language: 15% to 25%. Bible portions: 1995–1997. *Other:* Matrilineal. Fishermen; harvesting sea shells, seaweed, sea cucumbers; copra production; animal husbandry: goats, water buffalo. Christian.

Luhu [lcq] 6,500 (1983 Collins and Voorhoeve). Luhu village on Hoamoal Peninsula, west Seram Island, and Boano and Kelang islands, off of west Seram. *Class:* Austronesian, Malayo-Polynesian, Central-Eastern, Central Malayo-Polynesian, Central Maluku, East, Seram, Nunusaku, Piru Bay, West, Hoamoal, West. *Dialects:* Luhu, Batu Merah, Kelang. Related to Manipa. Lexical similarity 77% with Piru, 71% to 73% with Asilulu. *Lg Use:* Vigorous. Batu Merah dialect spoken on Ambon Island is nearly extinct. *Other:* Historically one language with Piru. Muslim.

Maba (Bitjoli, Bicoli, Ingli) [mqa] 6,617 (2000 WCD). North Maluku, northern coast of southeastern peninsula of Halmahera, and in Wasilei area. *Class:* Austronesian, Malayo-Polynesian, Central-Eastern, Eastern Malayo-Polynesian, South Halmahera-West New Guinea, South Halmahera, Southeast. *Lg Dev:* Literacy rate in first language: below 1%. Literacy rate in second language: 25% to 50%. *Other:* Muslim.

Makian, East (Makian Timur, Makian Dalam) [mky] 20,000. Population includes 18,000 or more in East Makian, 2,000 or more in Kayoa (1983 SIL). Eastern Makian Island, southern Mori Island, Kayoa islands, west coast of south Halmahera, Bacan and Obi islands, north Maluku. Transmigration project near Kao. *Class:* Austronesian, Malayo-Polynesian, Central-Eastern, Eastern Malayo-Polynesian, South Halmahera-West New Guinea, South Halmahera, East Makian-Gane. *Dialect:* East Makian, Kayoa (Kajoa). Close to Gane. *Lg Use:* Positive language attitude. *Lg Dev:* Literacy rate in first language: below 1%. Literacy rate in second language: 25% to 50%. *Other:* Muslim.

Makian, West (Makian Barat, Makian Luar) [mqs] 12,000 (1977 Voegelin and Voegelin). Population includes 7,000 on Makian Island, 5,000 on Kayoa Islands. Western Makian Island, some of the Kayoa Islands, areas along the west coast of southern Halmahera, north Maluku. *Class:* West Papuan, North Halmahera, North, West Makian. *Dialects:* Language isolate within north Halmahera. Formerly classified as Austronesian. *Lg Dev:* Literacy rate in first language: below 1%. Literacy rate in second language: 25% to 50%. *Other:* Muslim.

Malay, Ambonese (Malayu Ambon, Ambonese, Ambong) [abs] 200,000 in Indonesia (1987 J. Collins). Population total all countries: 245,020. Central Maluku, Ambon, Haruku, Nusa Laut, Saparua Islands, along the coastal areas of Seram, and southern Maluku. Also spoken in Netherlands, USA. *Class:* Creole, Malay based. *Dialect:* Dobo Malay. Marginal intelligibility of Indonesian. Difficult intelligibility of Ternate Malay; speakers switch to Indonesian. Lexical similarity 81% with Standard Malay. *Lg Use:* Trade language. Many second-language speakers. Bilingualism in Indonesian is high around Ambon city, Some Dutch is known. *Lg Dev:* Literacy rate in first language: 1% to 5%. Literacy rate in second language: 50% to 75%. Grammar. NT: 1877–1883. *Other:* Developed from Bazaar Malay and still reflects some archaic forms. Further diverged by adapting to the vernaculars of central Maluku. Considered to be a Malay-based creole by B. D. Grimes (1988, 1991) and J. Holm (1989:581–583). Christian, Muslim.

Malay, Bacanese (Bacan, Batjan) [btj] 2,500 (1991 H. Shelden SIL). Over 1,000 in Labuha (1987 J. Collins). North Maluku, Bacan Island west of southern Halmahera. Centered around the site of the former palace in Labuha, 1 village within about 5 km walking distance from Labuha, another hour by dugout (Indomut), and half the population of Waya and Lele villages on Mandioli Island. *Class:* Austronesian, Malayo-Polynesian, Malayic, Malayan, Local Malay. *Lg Use:* No second-language speakers of Bacanese Malay. *Lg Dev:* Literacy rate in first language: 1% to 5%. Literacy rate in second language: 50% to 75%. *Other:* No evidence of an earlier indigenous language (J. Collins). The Portuguese cut off Bacan from other Malay in 1515. No historic connection with Borneo since. Junior high school in Labuha. Agriculturalists. Muslim.

Malay, Banda [bpq] 3,690 (2000 WCD). Banda Islands. *Class:* Creole, Malay based. *Other:* Muslim.

Malay, North Moluccan (Ternate Malay) [max] 700,000 (2001 R. Whisler). 100,000 monolinguals. North Maluku, Halmahera, Sula, and Obi islands. First-language speakers in one neighborhood of Labuha (Christian), and some other families with parents of different ethnic origins. *Class:* Austronesian, Malayo-Polynesian, Malayic, Malayan, Local Malay. *Dialects:* Different meaning of particles from Manado Malay. Closer to Manado Malay than to Ambonese Malay. *Lg Use:* Trade language. A few small communities speak it as first language. Used orally between speakers of different languages. Not written. 300,000 second-language users

(2001 R. Whisler). *Lg Dev:* Literacy rate in first language: 1% to 5%. Literacy rate in second language: 50% to 75%. *Other:* Muslim, Christian.

Mangole (Mangoli, Sula Mangoli) [mqc] 7,275 (2000 WCD). North Maluku, southern coast of Mangole Island and northern tip of Sulabesi of the Sula Islands. *Class:* Austronesian, Malayo-Polynesian, Central-Eastern, Central Malayo-Polynesian, Central Maluku, Sula. *Other:* Muslim.

Manipa (Soow Huhelia) [mqp] 1,500 (1983 Collins and Voorhoeve). Manipa Island west of Seram, central Maluku, 4 villages. *Class:* Austronesian, Malayo-Polynesian, Central-Eastern, Central Malayo-Polynesian, Central Maluku, East. *Dialects:* Lexical similarity 72% with Luhu, 64% with Piru, 60% to 62% with Hitu, 60% to 61% with Tulehu and Asilulu, 58% to 61% with Hila-Kaitetu, 55% to 60% with Larike-Wakasihu, 56% with Boano and Kaibobo. *Other:* Muslim.

Manombai (Manobai, Wokam, Wamar) [woo] 7,475 (1995 J. Hughes). West coast of Wokam Island, from Wokam village southwards, in 21 villages along both sides of Manombai Strait (Sungai) as far as Wakua, and in Benjina on Kobror Island, and Gardakau on Maikor Island at the western end of Barakai Strait, and small village of Kobamar on east coast of Wokam Island. It may be no longer spoken on Wamar Island. Aru Islands, Southeast Maluku. *Class:* Austronesian, Malayo-Polynesian, Central-Eastern, Central Malayo-Polynesian, Aru. *Dialects:* Not inherently intelligible with Dobel. Lexical similarity 76% with Lorang. *Lg Use:* Vigorous. *Other:* Christian, Muslim.

Manusela (Wahai, Wahinama) [wha] 7,000 (1989 SIL). 30 villages, Manusela mountains of north Seram and along Teluti Bay in south Seram, central Maluku. *Class:* Austronesian, Malayo-Polynesian, Central-Eastern, Central Malayo-Polynesian, Central Maluku, East, Seram, Manusela-Seti. *Dialects:* Kanikeh, Hatuolu, Maneo, South Manusela. Kanikeh has 66% to 74% lexical similarity with other varieties, Hatuolo 67% to 75%, Maneo 64% to 86%, Maneoratu 66% to 86%, South Manusela 67% to 80%, dialects have 64% to 72% with Huaulu, 42% to 61% with Liana, 45% with Saleman. *Lg Use:* Vigorous. Speakers also use Teluti. *Lg Dev:* Grammar. *Other:* Mountain slope. Traditional religion, Christian, Hindu.

Mariri (Mairiri) [mqi] 390 (1995 SIL). Eastern Aru on Mariri Island east of Kobroor Island, 1 village, south Maluku. *Class:* Austronesian, Malayo-Polynesian, Central-Eastern, Central Malayo-Polynesian, Aru. *Dialects:* Lexical similarity 81% with Batuley. *Lg Use:* Vigorous. *Other:* Muslim.

Masela, Central (Central Marsela, Marsela-South Babar) [mxz] 511 (1980 de Jonge). 3 villages on Marsela Island, south Maluku. *Class:* Austronesian, Malayo-Polynesian, Central-Eastern, Central Malayo-Polynesian, Babar, South, Masela-South Babar. *Lg Dev:* Literacy rate in first language: below 1%. *Other:* Christian.

Masela, East (East Marsela) [vme] 519 (1980 de Jonge). 3 villages on Marsela Island, south Maluku. *Class:* Austronesian, Malayo-Polynesian, Central-Eastern, Central Malayo-Polynesian, Babar, South, Masela-South Babar. *Lg Dev:* Literacy rate in first language: below 1%. *Other:* Christian.

Masela, West (West Marsela) [mss] 850 (1980 de Jonge). 5 villages on Marsela Island, south Maluku. *Class:* Austronesian, Malayo-Polynesian, Central-Eastern, Central Malayo-Polynesian, Babar, South, Masela-South Babar. *Lg Dev:* Literacy rate in first language: below 1%. *Other:* Christian.

Masiwang (Bonfia) [bnf] 1,000 (1989 SIL). Seram Island, Waru Bay area, Bula District, central Maluku. *Class:* Austronesian, Malayo-Polynesian, Central-Eastern, Central Malayo-Polynesian, Central Maluku, East, Seram,

Masiwang. *Dialects:* Lexical similarity 44% with Bobot, 43% with Salas Gunung, 39% with Sepa and Teluti, 36% with Liana and Atamanu. *Lg Use:* Used by Salas as second language. Some use Geser as second language. *Lg Dev:* Grammar.

Modole (Madole) [mqo] 2,000 (1983 SIL). North Maluku, interior north Halmahera Island, headwaters of Kao River. *Class:* West Papuan, North Halmahera, North, Kao River. *Dialects:* North Modole, South Modole. Minimal differences between north and south Modole. *Lg Use:* Positive language attitude. *Other:* Some intermarriage with the Tobaru. Christian.

Moksela (Maksela, Opselan) [vms] Extinct. Central Maluku, possibly east Buru Island, near Kayeli. *Class:* Austronesian, Malayo-Polynesian, Central-Eastern, Central Malayo-Polynesian, Central Maluku, Buru. *Lg Use:* Last speaker died in 1974.

Naka'ela [nae] 5 (1985 SIL). Kairatu village, northwest Seram, central Maluku. *Class:* Austronesian, Malayo-Polynesian, Central-Eastern, Central Malayo-Polynesian, Central Maluku, East, Seram, Nunusaku, Three Rivers, Amalumute, Northwest Seram, Ulat Inai. *Dialects:* Lexical similarity 71% with Lisabata-Nuniali, 66% with Hulung, 63% with Alune. *Other:* Formerly lived in mountains. Reportedly decreased in number after moving down to Kairatu. Christian. Nearly extinct.

Nila [nil] 1,800 (1989 SIL). Transmigration area on south central Seram Island, central Maluku. 6 villages. (Originally Nila Island in south central Maluku). *Class:* Austronesian, Malayo-Polynesian, Central-Eastern, Central Malayo-Polynesian, Timor, Southwest Maluku, Teun-Nila-Serua, Nila-Serua. *Dialects:* Close to Serua. Not intelligible with Teun. *Lg Dev:* Literacy rate in first language: below 1%. *Other:* They have been moved to Seram because of volcanic activity on their island.

Nuaulu, North (Nuaulu, Patakai, Fatakai) [nni] 500 (1990 SIL). Two villages on the north coast of central Seram Island, central Maluku. *Class:* Austronesian, Malayo-Polynesian, Central-Eastern, Central Malayo-Polynesian, Central Maluku, East, Seram, Sawai-Nuaulu. *Dialects:* Lexical similarity 67% with South Nuaulu, 64% with Saleman. *Other:* A distinct language from Huaulu.

Nuaulu, South (Nuaulu, Patakai, Fatakai) [nxl] 1,500 (1995 SIL). 6 villages on the south coast and interior of Amahai District, Seram Island, central Maluku. *Class:* Austronesian, Malayo-Polynesian, Central-Eastern, Central Malayo-Polynesian, Central Maluku, East, Seram, Sawai-Nuaulu. *Dialects:* Lexical similarity 67% with North Nuaulu, 50% with South Wemale, Hulung, and Naka'ela, 48% with Saleman. *Lg Use:* Vigorous. Many also use Sepa. Some do not speak Indonesian. *Lg Dev:* Literacy rate in first language: below 1%. Literacy rate in second language: 5% to 15%. Bible portions: 1991–1995. *Other:* Different from Huaulu. Christian, traditional religion.

Nusa Laut (Nusalaut) [nul] 10. Ethnic population: 2,226 (1989 SIL). Titawai village, Nusa Laut Island, Lease Islands, central Maluku. *Class:* Austronesian, Malayo-Polynesian, Central-Eastern, Central Malayo-Polynesian, Central Maluku, East, Seram, Nunusaku, Piru Bay, East, Seram Straits, Uliase, Hatuhaha, Elpaputi. *Dialects:* Lexical similarity 69% with Saparua, 65% with Amahai. *Lg Use:* Speakers are older adults. *Other:* Christian. Nearly extinct.

Oirata (Maaro) [oia] 1,221 (1987 SIL). 2 villages in east and west Oirata in southeast Kisar Island, south Maluku, and in Ambon city (several hundred). *Class:* Trans-New Guinea, South Bird's Head-Timor-Alor-Pantar, Timor-Alor-Pantar, Oirata. *Dialects:* Not related to other languages on Oirata or central Maluku languages. Related to languages in East Timor, but not closely. *Lg Dev:* Literacy rate in first language: below 1%. *Other:* SOV. Christian.

Pagu (Pago, Pagoe) [pgu] 3,309 (2000 WCD). North Maluku, interior North Halmahera south of the Modole language area out to the mouth of the Kao River. *Class:* West Papuan, North Halmahera, North, Kao River. *Dialect:* Isam, Pagu, Toliwiku (Toliliko). *Lg Dev:* Literacy rate in first language: below 1%. Literacy rate in second language: 25% to 50%. *Other:* Muslim, Christian.

Palumata (Palamata, Balamata) [pmc] Extinct. Central Maluku, northwest Buru Island. *Class:* Austronesian, Malayo-Polynesian, Central-Eastern, Central Malayo-Polynesian, Central Maluku, Buru.

Patani [ptn] 10,583 (2000 WCD). North Maluku, the entire narrow tip of the southeastern peninsula of Halmahera, extending west along coast of peninsula. Nine villages: Patani, Peniti, Tepeleu, Gemya, Kipai, Wailegi, Yeisowo, Banemo, Moreala, Sibenpopu (with some Tobelo speakers). *Class:* Austronesian, Malayo-Polynesian, Central-Eastern, Eastern Malayo-Polynesian, South Halmahera-West New Guinea, South Halmahera, Southeast. *Lg Use:* Vigorous. *Lg Dev:* Literacy rate in first language: below 1%. Literacy rate in second language: 25% to 50%. *Other:* Schools. Swidden agriculturalists; lumbermen. Muslim.

Paulohi [plh] 50 (1982). Central Maluku, West Seram, western shore of Elpaputih Bay in south central Seram Island, 2 villages, Kecamatan Amahai. *Class:* Austronesian, Malayo-Polynesian, Central-Eastern, Central Malayo-Polynesian, Central Maluku, East, Seram, Nunusaku, Piru Bay, East, Seram Straits, Solehua. *Other:* Experienced a severe earthquake and tidal wave. Nearly extinct.

Perai (Tutunohan) [wet] 278 (1990 Hinton). Wetar Island coast, north of Timor, southwest Maluku, Uhak and Moning villages on the northeast coast. *Class:* Austronesian, Malayo-Polynesian, Central-Eastern, Central Malayo-Polynesian, Timor, Southwest Maluku, Wetar. *Dialects:* Moning, Uhak. Lexical similarity 93% among dialects, 79% with Aputai, 76% with Tugun, 67% with Ili'uun, 51% with Talur. *Lg Use:* Most also use regional Malay. *Lg Dev:* Literacy rate in first language: below 1%. *Other:* They intermarry with the Kisar. Coastal. Swidden agriculturalists: maize. Christian.

Piru [ppr] 10 (1985 Y. Taguchi SIL). 1 village, west Seram Island, central Maluku. *Class:* Austronesian, Malayo-Polynesian, Central-Eastern, Central Malayo-Polynesian, Central Maluku, East, Seram, Nunusaku, Three Rivers, Amalumute, Northwest Seram. *Dialects:* Lexical similarity 72% with Luhu. *Lg Use:* All also use Ambonese Malay. *Other:* Christian. Nearly extinct.

Roma (Romang) [rmm] 1,700 (1991 SIL). Jerusu village, Roma Island, north of Timor Island, south Maluku. *Class:* Austronesian, Malayo-Polynesian, Central-Eastern, Central Malayo-Polynesian, Timor, Southwest Maluku, Kisar-Roma. *Lg Dev:* Literacy rate in first language: below 1%. Literacy rate in second language: 25% to 50%. *Other:* Christian.

Sahu (Sa'u, Sau, Sahu'u) [saj] 7,500 (1987 Voorhoeve and Visser). Population includes 3,500 in Tala'i, 4,000 in Pa'disua. North Maluku, southwestern north Halmahera Island. *Class:* West Papuan, North Halmahera, North, Sahu. *Dialects:* Pa'disua (Palisua), Tala'i. Close to Waioli and Gamkonora. *Lg Use:* Vigorous. *Lg Dev:* Literacy rate in first language: below 1%. Literacy rate in second language: 25% to 50%. Dictionary. Grammar. *Other:* Christian, Muslim.

Salas (Liambata, Lenkaitahe, Salas Gunung) [sgu] 50 (1989 SIL). Salas Gunung village, Seram Island, Waru Bay, central Maluku. *Class:* Austronesian, Malayo-Polynesian, Central-Eastern, Central Malayo-Polynesian, Central Maluku, East, Seram, Manusela-Seti. *Dialects:* Lexical similarity 48% to 58% with Liana, 46% to 50%

with Benggoi, 35% to 46% with Manusela. *Lg Use:* Most use Masiwang as second language. *Other:* Christian.

Saleman (Sawai, Seleman, Hatue, Wahai) [sau] 4,800 (1989 SIL). 5 villages (Saleman, Pasanea, Sawai, Besi, Wahai), north central Seram, central Maluku. *Class:* Austronesian, Malayo-Polynesian, Central-Eastern, Central Malayo-Polynesian, Central Maluku, East, Seram, Sawai-Nuaulu. *Dialects:* Lexical similarity 64% with North Nuaulu, 48% with South Nuaulu. *Lg Use:* Vigorous except in Wahai. *Other:* Muslim.

Saparua [spr] 10,216 (1989 SIL). Population includes 4,519 in Iha. Kulur, Iha, and Siri-Sori villages on Saparua Island and Iha, Kulur, Latu, Hualoy, and Tomalehu villages on Seram Island, Lease Islands, central Maluku. Also spoken by hundreds of Latu people in Kairatu village. *Class:* Austronesian, Malayo-Polynesian, Central-Eastern, Central Malayo-Polynesian, Central Maluku, East, Seram, Nunusaku, Piru Bay, East, Seram Straits, Uliase, Hatuhaha, Saparua. *Dialects:* Kulur, Iha-Saparua, Iha-Seram, Siri-Sori. Each village is a dialect. Lexical similarity 86% to 89% among dialects; 82% to 84% with Latu, 69% with Amahai, 67% with Kamarian, 68% to 71% with Haruku, 65% with Kaibobo, 62% to 66% with Tulehu, 54% to 62% with Luhu, 49% with Piru, 54% with Naka'ela. *Lg Dev:* Literacy rate in first language: below 1%. *Other:* Muslim, Christian.

Sawai (Weda, Were, Weda-Sawai) [szw] 12,000 (2000 R. Whisler). Few monolinguals. North Maluku, Gane Timur and Weda districts, coastal area between southern and southeastern peninsulas of Halmahera. 13 villages (Mafa, Foya, Weda, Kobe Tanjung, Kobe Gunung, Kobi Peplis, Lelilef Sawai, Lelilef Woebulan, Gemaf, Sagea, Wale, Messa, Dote). A few families dispersed in 4 or 5 cities in Indonesia. *Class:* Austronesian, Malayo-Polynesian, Central-Eastern, Eastern Malayo-Polynesian, South Halmahera-West New Guinea, South Halmahera, Southeast. *Dialects:* Weda, Sawai, Kobe, Faya-Mafa, Messa-Dote. Lexical similarity 64% with North Nuaulu. *Lg Use:* In some domains North Moluccan Malay is replacing it. Used in local commerce. The younger generation is taught Indonesian first and learns to understand Sawai. Positive language attitude. Nearly all speak North Moluccan Malay. Maybe 35% also speak some Tidore, Ternate, Tobelo, Patani, Buli, Maba, Gane Timur. A few speak Indonesian. *Lg Dev:* Literacy rate in first language: 10%. Literacy rate in second language: 25% to 50%. 5,000 can read it, 1,000 can write it. Bible portions: 1994. *Other:* Different from Saleman (Sawai). Coastal, hills, plains. Sago swamp. Agriculturalists: cocoa; growing coconut; fishermen. Muslim, Christian.

Seit-Kaitetu (Hila-Kaitetu) [hik] 10,171 (1987 SIL). Seit (Seith) and Kaitetu villages, north coast of Ambon Island, central Maluku. *Class:* Austronesian, Malayo-Polynesian, Central-Eastern, Central Malayo-Polynesian, Central Maluku, East, Seram, Nunusaku, Piru Bay, West, Asilulu. *Dialects:* Seit (Seith), Kaitetu. Lexical similarity 85% between Kaitetu and Seit. Lexical similarity 78% to 82% with Asilulu, 67% to 74% with Tulehu. *Lg Use:* Vigorous. Speakers also use Ambonese Malay. *Other:* Muslim, Christian.

Selaru (Salaru) [slu] 8,000 (2001 SIL). Tanimbar, six of seven villages on Selaru Island, half of the village of Latdalam on Yamdena Island, and Lingada village on Nus-Wotar Island off the west coast of Yamdena. 8 villages. South Maluku. Sizeable communities in Saumlake and Ambon. *Class:* Austronesian, Malayo-Polynesian, Central-Eastern, Central Malayo-Polynesian, Southeast Maluku, Southern. *Dialect:* Kandar. Slight dialect differences. Not closely related to other nearby languages. Lexical similarity 56% with Seluwasan. *Lg Use:* Vigorous. *Lg Dev:* Literacy rate in first language:

below 1%. Literacy rate in second language: 25% to 50%. Grammar. Bible portions: 1997. *Other:* Christian.

Seluwasan (Selvasa, Selwasa) [sws] 2,839 (1980 government report). Population includes 739 in Makatian, 2,100 in Seluwasan. Southwest coast of Yamdena Island, south Maluku. Three villages: Wermatang, Batu Putih, and Marantutul. *Class:* Austronesian, Malayo-Polynesian, Central-Eastern, Central Malayo-Polynesian, Southeast Maluku, Southern. *Dialects:* Seluwasan, Makatian. Makatian is quite different from other dialects. *Other:* Hunters. Christian.

Sepa (Tamilouw) [spb] 2,600 (1989 SIL). Sepa village, Seram Island, central Maluku. *Class:* Austronesian, Malayo-Polynesian, Central-Eastern, Central Malayo-Polynesian, Central Maluku, East, Seram, Nunusaku, Piru Bay, East. *Dialects:* Lexical similarity 79% between Sepa and Tamilouw, 69% to 78% with Teluti, 50% with Atamanu. *Lg Use:* Trade language. Used as a second language by South Nuaulu speakers.

Serili [sve] 328 (1980 de Jonge). Northeast Marsela Island, south Maluku. *Class:* Austronesian, Malayo-Polynesian, Central-Eastern, Central Malayo-Polynesian, Babar, South, Masela-South Babar. *Lg Dev:* Literacy rate in first language: below 1%. *Other:* Christian.

Serua [srw] 2,000 (1990 SIL). Transmigration area in south central Seram Island, central Maluku. 4 villages. Originally Serua Island in south central Maluku. *Class:* Austronesian, Malayo-Polynesian, Central-Eastern, Central Malayo-Polynesian, Timor, Southwest Maluku, Teun-Nila-Serua, Nila-Serua. *Dialects:* Close to Nila. Not intelligible with Teun. *Lg Dev:* Literacy rate in first language: below 1%. *Other:* Moved by the government to Seram because of volcanic activity on their island.

Sula (Sanana) [szn] 20,000 (1983 SIL). North Maluku, Sula Islands, Sulabesi Island, and scattered communities on the eastern and western ends and north coast of Mangole Island, and northeast coast of Buru Island. *Class:* Austronesian, Malayo-Polynesian, Central-Eastern, Central Malayo-Polynesian, Central Maluku, Sula. *Dialect:* Fagudu, Falahu, Facei (Facé). Close to Mangole. *Lg Use:* Vigorous. *Lg Dev:* Literacy rate in first language: below 1%. *Other:* Muslim.

Tabaru (Tobaru) [tby] 15,000 (1991 SIL). North Maluku, Ibu, Jailolo, and Oba districts. *Class:* West Papuan, North Halmahera, North, Tobaru. *Dialects:* Adu, Nyeku. The northern dialect is the main one. The two dialects are inherently intelligible with each other. *Lg Dev:* Literacy rate in first language: below 1%. Literacy rate in second language: 25% to 50%. Bible portions: 1998. *Other:* Christian.

Taliabu (Taliabo) [tlv] 4,518 (2000 WCD). Population includes 500 to 1,500 in Mangei. North Maluku, Taliabu Island, northwestern Mangole, Sula Islands. *Class:* Austronesian, Malayo-Polynesian, Central-Eastern, Central Malayo-Polynesian, Central Maluku, Sula, Taliabo. *Dialects:* Padang (Samada), Mananga, Mangei (Mange'e, Mange, Mang, Soboyo, Sobojo). Dialects share lexical similarities in the upper 90% range. *Lg Use:* Positive language attitude. *Other:* Talo, Seho, Biha, Bono (Mbono) are place names. Traditional religion, Christian.

Talur (Ilwaki, Iliwaki, Galoleng, Lir Talo, Ilmedu) [ilw] 675 (1990 SIL). Hiay, Ilputih (a), and Ilwaki villages in south central Wetar Island, 60 km north of East Timor, in southwest Maluku. *Class:* Austronesian, Malayo-Polynesian, Central-Eastern, Central Malayo-Polynesian, Timor, Southwest Maluku, Wetar. *Dialects:* Ilputih, Ilwaki (Iliwaki), Hiay. Lexical similarity 94% to 98% between dialects. Lexical similarity 86% with Galoli in East Timor, 57% with Aputai, 52% with Tugun, 51% with Perai and Ili'uun. *Lg Use:* Most also use regional Malay. *Lg Dev:* Literacy rate in first language: below 1%. *Other:*

Immigrants from Kisar learned Talur. Mountain slope, coastal. Up to 1,430 meters. Swidden agriculturalists: maize. Christian.

Tarangan, East (East Trangan, Tarangan Timur) [tre] 3,784 (1987 Maluku Dalam Angka). East coast of Tarangan Island, south Aru Islands, and villages in Maikor Strait (Sungai Maikor), 13 villages. South Maluku. *Class:* Austronesian, Malayo-Polynesian, Central-Eastern, Central Malayo-Polynesian, Aru. *Dialects:* Lexical similarity 71% with West Tarangan. *Lg Use:* Vigorous. *Lg Dev:* Literacy rate in first language: below 1%. *Other:* Christian, Muslim.

Tarangan, West (West Trangan, Tarangan Barat) [txn] 6,478 (1987 Maluku Dalam Angka). West coast of Tarangan Island, southern Aru Islands, south Maluku. Largest language in the Aru Islands. *Class:* Austronesian, Malayo-Polynesian, Central-Eastern, Central Malayo-Polynesian, Aru. *Dialects:* Southwestern Tarangan, North Central Tarangan. 2 sharply distinct dialect groups, with minor variation within them. Lexical similarity 70% with East Tarangan and Wokam. *Lg Use:* Trade language of Aru Islands, especially in the south. Vigorous. *Lg Dev:* Literacy rate in first language: 10% to 70%. Literacy rate in second language: 60% to 70%. Bible portions: 1997–2004. *Other:* Christian, Muslim.

Tela-Masbuar (Tela'a, Masbuar-Tela) [tvm] 1,050 (1990 SIL). Villages of Tela and Masbuar, southwest Babar Island, south Maluku. *Class:* Austronesian, Malayo-Polynesian, Central-Eastern, Central Malayo-Polynesian, Babar, South, Southwest Babar. *Lg Dev:* Literacy rate in first language: below 1%.

Teluti (Taluti, Tihoru, Tehoru, Silen, Wolu) [tlt] 17,000 (1989 SIL). Central Maluku, south Seram Island, Teluti Bay. *Class:* Austronesian, Malayo-Polynesian, Central-Eastern, Central Malayo-Polynesian, Central Maluku, East, Seram, Nunusaku, Piru Bay, East. *Dialects:* West Teluti (Haya, Wolu, Tehoru, Tehua), Laha Serani. Lexical similarity 74% to 89% among dialects, 69% to 78% with Sepa, 50% with Atamanu. *Lg Use:* Trade language. Used as second language by many Manusela and Seti speakers in the area. *Other:* Muslim, Christian.

Teor (Tio'or) [tev] 1,100 (1986 SIL). Teor and Ut islands, South Maluku. *Class:* Austronesian, Malayo-Polynesian, Central-Eastern, Central Malayo-Polynesian, Teor-Kur. *Dialects:* Gaur Kristen, Ut. Speakers say they understand Kur. Lexical similarity 79% between Gaur Kristen and Ut, 71% to 83% with Kur, 41% with Watubela, 38% with Geser. *Other:* Muslim, Christian.

Ternate [tft] 42,000 (1981 Wurm and Hattori). North Maluku, islands of Ternate, Kayoa, Bacan, Obi, and coastal communities on western north Halmahera. Lingua franca in northern and northeastern Halmahera. *Class:* West Papuan, North Halmahera, South. *Dialects:* Close to Tidore. *Lg Use:* Trade language. Vigorous. 20,000 second-language speakers. *Lg Dev:* Literacy rate in first language: 1% to 5%. Literacy rate in second language: 25% to 50%. *Other:* Muslim.

Ternateño (Ternatenyo) [tmg] Extinct. North Maluku, Ternate Island, west of Halmahera Island. Varieties of Portuguese creole were also spoken in Banda and Ambon. *Class:* Creole, Portuguese based. *Dialects:* Spanish relexification. Historical relationship with Chavacano and dialects, which are still spoken in the Philippines. *Lg Use:* The Jakarta variety of creole Portuguese survived in Tugu until recent times (1981 Wurm and Hattori). Varieties of creole Portuguese were also spoken in Larantuka, Flores; Adonara (Vure), Solor; as well as Sumatra, Kalimantan, Sulawesi, and Maluku. Varieties of creole Portuguese were also spoken in Banda and Ambon.

Te'un [tve] 1,200 (1990 SIL). Transmigration area in south central Seram Island, central Maluku. 4 villages. Originally Teun Island in south central Maluku. *Class:*

Austronesian, Malayo-Polynesian, Central-Eastern, Central Malayo-Polynesian, Timor, Southwest Maluku, Teun-Nila-Serua, Teun. *Lg Dev:* Literacy rate in first language: below 1%. *Other:* Moved by the government because of volcanic activity on their island.

Tidore [tvo] 26,000 (1981 Wurm and Hattori). North Maluku, islands of Tidore, Maitara, Mare, northern half of Moti, and some areas of west coast of Halmahera. *Class:* West Papuan, North Halmahera, South. *Dialects:* Close to Ternate. *Lg Use:* 20,000 second-language speakers. Positive language attitude. *Lg Dev:* Literacy rate in first language: 1% to 5%. Literacy rate in second language: 25% to 50%. *Other:* Muslim.

Tobelo [tlb] 27,720 (2000 WCD). North Maluku, north Halmahera Island, Tobelo, Kao, and Jailolo districts, and Maba and Wasile districts, Halmahera Tengah; northern half of Morotai, all coastal areas of Kao Bay and inland, Patani, Weda, Gane, Bacan, Obi, Ambon, Raja Ampat islands of Papua, Sorong, Papua. *Class:* West Papuan, North Halmahera, North, Tobelo. *Dialect:* Dodinga, Boëng, Tobelo (Heleworuru). *Lg Use:* Positive language attitude. Speakers also use Indonesian. *Lg Dev:* Literacy rate in first language: 1% to 5%. Literacy rate in second language: 25% to 50%. Dictionary. Grammar. NT: 1993. *Other:* Tobelo taught in middle school in Tobelo town. Traditional religion, Christian.

Tugun (Tutunohan, Mahuan) [tzn] 1,200 (1990 SIL). 1% monolinguals. Wetar Island, north of Timor, southwest Maluku; Mahuan, Masapun, Tomliapat, Ilpokil, Kahailin, Ilway, Arwala villages, on the southeast end of Wetar. *Class:* Austronesian, Malayo-Polynesian, Central-Eastern, Central Malayo-Polynesian, Timor, Southwest Maluku, Wetar. *Dialects:* Mahuan, Masapua, Tomliapat, Ilpokil, Kahailin Ilway, Arwala. Lexical similarity 92% to 97% among dialects, 76% with Perai, 74% with Aputai, 73% with Ili'uun, 52% with Talur. *Lg Use:* Vigorous. Used in the home, local commerce, oral tradition. Positive language attitude. Most also use Indonesian or Ambonese Malay. *Lg Dev:* Literacy rate in first language: below 1%. Literacy rate in second language: 15% to 25%. *Other:* Mountain slope, coastal. Swidden agriculturalists: maize. Christian.

Tugutil [tuj] 2,588 (2000 WCD). North Maluku, north Halmahera Island, inland around Kusuri, inland in Kecamatan Tobelo, around Taboulamo in Kecamatan Kao, in the pass between Lolobata and Buli in Kecamatan Wasilei, along the Dodaga and Tutuling rivers, and along the Akelamo and Mabulan rivers in Kecamatan Maba, Tanjung Lili, villages of Miaf, Bebseli, and Marasibno. A few along the Lili, Waisango, and Afu rivers, and reports of other places. *Class:* West Papuan, North Halmahera, North, Tobelo. *Dialects:* Teluk Lili, Kusuri. Possibly several dialects separated by large distances. Intelligibility of Tobelo dialects is inadequate. *Lg Use:* Positive language attitude. Speakers also use Indonesian. *Lg Dev:* Literacy rate in first language: below 1%. Literacy rate in second language: 5% to 15%. *Other:* A group of forest people who have contact with village people for selling copra and purchasing supplies. Traditional religion, Christian.

Tulehu (Northeast Ambon) [tlu] 18,843 (1987 SIL). 4 villages on the coast of northeast Ambon Island, central Maluku. *Class:* Austronesian, Malayo-Polynesian, Central-Eastern, Central Malayo-Polynesian, Central Maluku, East, Seram, Nunusaku, Piru Bay, East, Seram Straits, Ambon. *Dialects:* Tulehu, Liang, Tengah-Tengah, Tial. Each dialect is in a separate village. Eastern end of Ambon dialect chain. Lexical similarity 84% to 90% among dialects, 74% to 82% with Hitu, 72% to 76% with Haruku. *Lg Use:* Vigorous. *Other:* Muslim, Christian.

Ujir (Udjir) [udj] 975 (1995 J. Hughes). 2 villages, Ujir on Ujir Island and Samang on the end of western peninsula on Wokam Island, in northwest Aru Islands, south

Maluku. *Class:* Austronesian, Malayo-Polynesian, Central-Eastern, Central Malayo-Polynesian, Aru. *Dialects:* Lexical similarity 75% with Kola in north Aru, and slightly less with Kulaha on the west coast of Kola Island. *Lg Use:* Language use is declining in Ujir because of the influence of Malay used by an increasing number of outsiders. Use is reported to be less in Samang than in Ujir. *Other:* Muslim.

Waioli (Wajoli, Wayoli) [wli] 3,000 (1987 Voorhoeve and Visser). North Halmahera, between Sahu and Ibu languages, north Maluku. *Class:* West Papuan, North Halmahera, North, Sahu. *Dialects:* Lexical similarity 81% with Gamkonora. *Other:* Christian, Muslim.

Watubela (Snabi Watubela, Kasiui, Kesui, Kasui, Wesi, Esiriun, Matabello) [wah] 4,000 (1990 SIL). Watubela Islands, east central Maluku, north of Kur Island. *Class:* Austronesian, Malayo-Polynesian, Central-Eastern, Central Malayo-Polynesian, Central Maluku, East, Banda-Geser, Geser-Gorom. *Dialects:* Tamher Timur, Sulmelang. Lexical similarity 77% between dialects, 51% to 61% with Geser-Gorom, 41% with Teor and Kur, 37% with Bobot, 34% with Masiwang. *Lg Use:* Many claim to use Geser-Gorom as second language. *Other:* Muslim, Christian.

Wemale, North [weo] 4,929 (1982). Spread along the north coast of Taniwel District, east of Taniwel, and in the westernmost part of East Seram District, 24 villages. *Class:* Austronesian, Malayo-Polynesian, Central-Eastern, Central Malayo-Polynesian, Central Maluku, East, Seram, Nunusaku, Three Rivers, Wemale. *Dialects:* Horale, Kasieh, Uwenpantai. Kawe may be a dialect. Lexical similarity between east and central dialects is 80%, 72% with South Wemale, 59% with Hulung. *Lg Use:* Vigorous. Used in religious services. *Lg Dev:* Literacy rate in first language: below 1%. *Other:* Christian, Muslim.

Wemale, South (Tala, Honitetu) [tlw] 3,726 (1987 SIL). Central Maluku, west Seram, 15 villages; 13 in Kairatu, mainly in the interior, and two westernmost coastal villages of Amahai District. *Class:* Austronesian, Malayo-Polynesian, Central-Eastern, Central Malayo-Polynesian, Central Maluku, East, Seram, Nunusaku, Three Rivers, Wemale. *Dialects:* Dialect chain between Horale, Kasieh, Uwenpantai, and Honitetu. Kawe may be a dialect. Lexical similarity between Horale and Kasieh, and between Uwenpantai and Honitetu is 80%, 72% with North Wemale, 66% with Hulung, 47% with Atamanu. *Lg Use:* Vigorous. *Lg Dev:* Literacy rate in first language: below 1%. *Other:* Christian.

Yalahatan (Atamanu, Jahalatan, Jahalatane, Awaiya) [jal] 1,700 (2004 SIL). Population includes approximately 850 in each village. West Seram, villages of Yalahatan and Haruru, central Maluku. *Class:* Austronesian, Malayo-Polynesian, Central-Eastern, Central Malayo-Polynesian, Central Maluku, East, Seram, Nunusaku, Three Rivers. *Dialects:* Slight dialect differences reported between the two villages. Lexical similarity 50% to 52% with Sepa, 49% to 50% with Teluti. *Lg Dev:* Literacy rate in first language: below 1%. Literacy rate in second language: 15% to 25%. *Other:* Speakers are not familiar with the name 'Atamanu'.

Yamdena (Jamdena, Jamden) [jmd] 25,000 (1991 SIL). Ethnic population: 35,000 to 40,000 (1991 SIL). Southeast Maluku, eastern coast of Yamdena, Adaut village on northern tip of Selaru, and one of the two languages spoken in Latdalam village, southwest Yamdena. 35 villages. *Class:* Austronesian, Malayo-Polynesian, Central-Eastern, Central Malayo-Polynesian, Southeast Maluku, Kei-Tanimbar, Yamdena. *Dialects:* North Yamdena, South Yamdena. Dialect chaining from north to south, but with considerable morphological and phonological differences. The southern dialect is more prestigious. Lexical similarity 90% between the north and south dialects, 47% with

Fordata. *Lg Use:* Vigorous except for some villages, especially in the north. Speakers also use Ambonese Malay, or Indonesian. *Lg Dev:* Literacy rate in first language: 2% to 5%. Literacy rate in second language: 80%. Dictionary. Grammar. *Other:* Christian.

Indonesia (Nusa Tenggara)

Indonesia (Nusa Tenggara). 7,961,540 (2000 census). Population includes 3,370,000 in West Nusa Tenggara (1993), 3,269,000 in East Nusa Tenggara (1993). Information mainly from C. Grimes, T. Therik, B. D. Grimes, and M. Jacob 1997. The number of languages listed for Indonesia (Nusa Tenggara) is 73. Of those, all are living languages. See maps beginning on page 796.

Abui (Barue, "Barawahing," Namatalaki) [abz] 16,000. Ethnic population: 16,000 (1981 Wurm and Hattori). Central and western Alor in the Lesser Sundas. *Class:* Trans-New Guinea, South Bird's Head-Timor-Alor-Pantar, Timor-Alor-Pantar, Makasai-Alor-Pantar, Alor. *Dialects:* Atimelang, Kobola, Alakaman. Much dialect diversity. The Alakaman dialect may be a dialect of Kamang (Woisika). May be more than one language. *Other:* "Barawahing" is a derogatory name.

Adang (Alor) [adn] 31,814 (2000 WCD). Northwestern (Bird's Head) Alor Island in the Lesser Sundas. *Class:* Trans-New Guinea, South Bird's Head-Timor-Alor-Pantar, Timor-Alor-Pantar, Makasai-Alor-Pantar, Alor. *Dialect:* Aimoli. On the basis of linguistic differences and social identity, it is considered a separate language from Kabola. *Other:* Christian.

Adonara (Nusa Tadon, Waiwerang, Vaiverang, Sagu) [adr] 16,967 (2000 WCD). Adonara Island, and eastern Solor Island, between Flores and Lembata. *Class:* Austronesian, Malayo-Polynesian, Central-Eastern, Central Malayo-Polynesian, Timor, Flores-Lembata. *Dialects:* West Adonara, East Adonara, East Solor. *Lg Use:* Lamaholot is used as a language of wider communication. *Other:* Muslim, Christian.

Alor (Alorese) [aol] 25,000 (1997 Grimes, Therik, Grimes, Jacob). West and south of Bird's Head of Alor, north Ternate Island, pockets along northern Pantar and adjacent islands. *Class:* Austronesian, Malayo-Polynesian, Central-Eastern, Central Malayo-Polynesian, Timor, Flores-Lembata. *Dialects:* Speakers oriented toward Lembata and Adonara, but Alor is not inherently intelligible with those languages. *Lg Use:* Speakers use Lamaholot as language of wider communication, so it was formerly thought to be a dialect of Lamaholot. *Other:* Muslim, Christian.

Amarasi (Timor Amarasi) [aaz] 50,000 (1997 C. Grimes, Therik, B. D. Grimes, Jacob). Ethnic population: 60,000 (2001 C. Grimes). Southwestern tip, Timor Island. Kotos is central and east, Ro'is is west, Ro'is Tais Nonof is southern, Ro'is Hero is surrounded by the Helong. 24 townships. *Class:* Austronesian, Malayo-Polynesian, Central-Eastern, Central Malayo-Polynesian, Timor, Nuclear Timor, West. *Dialect:* Kotos, Ro'is, Ro'is Tais Nonof, Ro'is Hero (Kopa). Closest to Uab Meto, but a separate language with differences in phonology, vocabulary, and discourse, with semantic shifts, structural differences, intelligibility problems. Ro'is Tais Nonof has intonation like Ro'is, vocabulary like Kotos. There are differences in speech in speaking to a king, nobility, or commoner. *Lg Use:* Some speakers also use Indonesian. *Other:* They live interspersed with Helong speakers. Part of Atoni ethnically. Literature is in Kotos. Christian.

Anakalangu (Anakalang) [akg] 14,000. Ethnic population: 14,000 (1981 Wurm and Hattori). Sumba Island, southwest coast, east of Wanukaka. *Class:* Austronesian, Malayo-Polynesian, Central-Eastern, Central Malayo-Polynesian, Bima-Sumba. *Dialects:* Close to, but unintelligible to speakers of Wejewa, Mamboru, Wanukaka, and Lamboya.

Bilba (Rote, Roti, Rotinese, Rote Timur, Eastern Rote, Belubaa, Bilbaa) [bpz] 7,000 (2002 UKAW). Ethnic population: 7,000. Rote Island east, domains of Bilba, Diu, and Lelenuk. West of Ringgou. Communities on Semau Island and Timor mainland near Kupang. *Class:* Austronesian, Malayo-Polynesian, Central-Eastern, Central Malayo-Polynesian, Timor, Nuclear Timor, West. *Dialects:* Bilba, Diu, Lelenuk. *Lg Use:* Vigorous. All domains. All ages. Speakers also use Kupang, Indonesian. *Other:* Christian.

Bima (Bimanese) [bhp] 500,000 (1989). Sunda Islands, eastern Sumbawa Island, east of the isthmus. *Class:* Austronesian, Malayo-Polynesian, Central-Eastern, Central Malayo-Polynesian, Bima-Sumba. *Dialects:* Kolo, Sangar (Sanggar), Toloweri, Bima, Mbojo. *Other:* Muslim, Christian.

Blagar (Belagar, Tarang) [beu] 11,000 (1981 Wurm and Hattori). Ethnic population: 11,000. Eastern Pantar, northern Pura, southern Ternate islands, Lesser Sundas. *Class:* Trans-New Guinea, South Bird's Head-Timor-Alor-Pantar, Timor-Alor-Pantar, Makasai-Alor-Pantar, Pantar. *Dialects:* Apuri, Limarahing, Bakalang, Pura. The Retta variety on south Pura is thought to be a separate language by 2 Alorese.

Bunak (Buna', Bunake, Bunaq) [bfn] 50,000 in Indonesia (1977 Voegelin and Voegelin). Ethnic population: 50,000. Central interior Timor Island, south coast. *Lg Use:* Many speakers bilingual with Tetun. *Other:* Some small groups are scattered among other languages. Traditional religion. See main entry under East Timor.

Dela-Oenale (Rote, Roti, Rotinese, Rote Barat, Western Rote, Delha, Oe Nale) [row] 7,000 (2002 UKAW). Ethnic population: 7,000. Rote Island west coast, domains of Dela and Oe Nale. *Class:* Austronesian, Malayo-Polynesian, Central-Eastern, Central Malayo-Polynesian, Timor, Nuclear Timor, West. *Dialects:* Dela (Delha), Oenale (Oe Nale). Dela-Oenale seems to be between Dengka and Dhao. *Lg Use:* Vigorous. All domains. All ages. Speakers also use Kupang, Indonesian. *Other:* Christian, traditional religion.

Dengka (Rote, Roti, Rotinese, Rote Barat, Western Rote) [dnk] 20,000 (2002 UKAW). Ethnic population: 20,000. Rote Island northwest, domains of Dengka and Lelain, east of Dela-Oenale, west of Lole (Ba'a). *Class:* Austronesian, Malayo-Polynesian, Central-Eastern, Central Malayo-Polynesian, Timor, Nuclear Timor, West. *Dialects:* Western Dengka, Eastern Dengka, Lelain. Western Dengka has marked intonation; some 'ngg' in Eastern Dengka becomes 'nd' in Western Dengka. Some vocabulary of Western Dengka is like Dhao. Dengka and Dela-Oenale are more divergent from other languages on Rote. *Lg Use:* Vigorous. All domains. All ages. Speakers also use Kupang or Indonesian. *Other:* Christian, traditional religion.

Dhao (Ndao, Dao, Ndaonese, Ndaundau) [nfa] 5,000 (1997 Ranoh). Island of Ndao, scattered on Rote, and Timor. *Class:* Austronesian, Malayo-Polynesian, Central-Eastern, Central Malayo-Polynesian, Bima-Sumba. *Dialects:* Related to Sabu. Difficult phonology. *Lg Dev:* Bible portions: 2000–2001. *Other:* 'Dhao' is how they refer to themselves. 'Ndao' is how their Rote neighbors refer to them. Silversmiths. Men leave the island for long periods of seasonal work. Women are well known as weavers of traditional cloth. Christian.

Ende (Endeh) [end] 87,000 (1981 Wurm and Hattori). Population includes 78,000 Ende, 9,000 Nga'o. South central Flores, west of Sikka, Lesser Sundas. *Class:* Austronesian, Malayo-Polynesian, Central-Eastern, Central Malayo-Polynesian, Bima-Sumba, Ende-Lio. *Dialects:* Ende (Endeh, Ja'o, Djau), Nga'o (Ngao, West Ende).

Dialect cluster. Li'o is on the border between a separate language or dialect of Ende. *Other:* Christian.

Hamap [hmu] 1,294 (2000 WCD). Kalabahi Bay, across from Kalabahi city, around Moru town. 2 villages. Migration in 1947 from Mo'eng, a few kilometers to the south. Still on their traditional land, but now in an interethnic community with Kui speakers. 18 km by road from Kalabahi. *Class:* Trans-New Guinea, South Bird's Head-Timor-Alor-Pantar, Timor-Alor-Pantar, Makasai-Alor-Pantar, Alor. *Dialects:* Said to be intelligible with the Adang-Aimoli dialect of Kabola, but 'Kabola' is associated with the Bird's Head area of Alor. Structural and lexical differences with Kabola. *Other:* Separate sociopolitical history from Kabola. Some intermarriage. Verb final contrast between close and open [e]; vowel-initial and glottal-initial words. Christian.

Helong (Helon, Semau, Kupang) [heg] 14,000 (1997 Grimes, Therik, Grimes, Jacob). Ethnic population: 15,000 to 20,000. Western tip of Timor Island near the port of Tenau (4 villages), in and around Kupang, extending across the island to the Amarasi Region, and most villages on Semau Island. *Class:* Austronesian, Malayo-Polynesian, Central-Eastern, Central Malayo-Polynesian, Timor, Helong. *Dialects:* Helong Pulau (Semau, Island Helong), Helong Darat (Bolok), Funai (Land Helong). 2 groups which have minor dialect differences: Helong Darat on the Timor mainland and Helong Pulau on Semau Island. *Lg Use:* Helong Darat speakers are shifting to Kupang Malay under the influence of people from Rote and Savu. Funai dialect is endangered, with many speakers having married spouses from other ethnic groups and youth having shifted to Kupang Malay. Used for daily domestic and rural routine and traditional ceremonies. Speakers are in contact with Rote, Sabu, Dhao, Uab Meto, Kupang Malay, and Standard Indonesian. *Lg Dev:* Dictionary. Bible portions: 2002. *Other:* Unlike many surrounding languages, does not inflect V-initial verb roots for person or number; has long and short vowels; glottal stop, metathesis. Christian, traditional religion.

Ile Ape (Nusa Tadon) [ila] North Lembata (Lomblen Island), including Ile Ape volcanic peninsula and nearby mainland Lembata. North Ile Ape is on the peninsula, South Ile Ape is on the mainland. *Class:* Austronesian, Malayo-Polynesian, Central-Eastern, Central Malayo-Polynesian, Timor, Flores-Lembata. *Dialects:* North Ile Ape, South Ile Ape. *Lg Use:* Speakers also use Lamaholot.

Kabola [klz] 3,900 (1995 N. Johnston). Northwestern (Bird's Head) Alor Island in the Lesser Sundas. *Class:* Trans-New Guinea, South Bird's Head-Timor-Alor-Pantar, Timor-Alor-Pantar, Makasai-Alor-Pantar, Alor. *Dialects:* Pintumbang, Tang'ala, Meibuil, Otvai, Kebun Kopi. The names and locations of the dialect in Wurm and Hattori (1981) are disputed by native speakers. May be more than one language. On the basis of linguistic differences and social identity, is best considered a separate language from Adang. *Other:* Christian, Muslim.

Kafoa (Jafoo, Ruilak, Aikoli, Fanating, Pailelang) [kpu] 1,000 (1981 Wurm and Hattori). Ethnic population: 1,000. Southwest Alor Island, north of Aluben, between Abui and Kelong languages. *Class:* Trans-New Guinea, South Bird's Head-Timor-Alor-Pantar, Timor-Alor-Pantar, Makasai-Alor-Pantar, Alor. *Other:* The name 'Jafoo' is suggested by some Alorese. The name 'Kafoa' is not known locally.

Kamang (Woisika, Waisika) [woi] 16,522 (2000 WCD). Alor Island, east central, between Abui and Tanglapui. 'Woisika' is the name of 1 village. The Kamang dialect is spoken there and in 2 other villages. Apui is reported as a place name, not a dialect. *Class:* Trans-New Guinea, South Bird's Head-Timor-Alor-Pantar, Timor-Alor-Pantar, Makasai-Alor-Pantar, Alor. *Dialects:* Lembur (Limbur, Kawel), Sibo, Kamang, Tiayai, Watang, Kamana-Kamang.

Probably more than one language. *Other:* It is reported that 'Kamang' is preferred by speakers as the language name.

Kambera (Sumbanese, East Sumbanese, Oost-Sumbaas, Humba, Hilu Humba, East Sumba, Sumba) [xbr] 234,574 (2000 WCD). Eastern half of Sumba Island, south of Flores, Lesser Sundas. *Class:* Austronesian, Malayo-Polynesian, Central-Eastern, Central Malayo-Polynesian, Bima-Sumba. *Dialects:* Kambera, Melolo, Uma Ratu Nggai (Umbu Ratu Nggai), Lewa, Kanatang, Mangili-Waijelo (Wai Jilu, Waidjelu, Rindi, Waijelo), Southern Sumba. Dialect network. Kambera dialect is widely understood. Speakers of Lewa and Uma Taru Nggai have difficulty understanding those from Mangili in many speech domains. *Lg Dev:* Dictionary. Grammar. Bible: 1995. *Other:* Distinct from Sumbawa in the Bali-Sasak group. Christian, traditional religion.

Kedang (Dang, Kdang, Kédang, Kedangese) [ksx] 30,000 (1997 N. Johnston). Northeast Lembata (Lomblen) Island, Lesser Sundas. All modern villages located on a ring road around the base of a volcano. *Class:* Austronesian, Malayo-Polynesian, Central-Eastern, Central Malayo-Polynesian, Timor, Flores-Lembata. *Other:* Christian, Muslim.

Kelon (Kelong, Kalong) [kyo] 6,000 (1997 Grimes, Therik, Grimes, Jacob). Southwestern Alor Island, Lesser Sundas. *Class:* Trans-New Guinea, South Bird's Head-Timor-Alor-Pantar, Timor-Alor-Pantar, Makasai-Alor-Pantar, Alor. *Dialects:* Probur, Halerman, Gendok, Panggar.

Kemak (Ema) [kem] 50,000 in Indonesia (1981 Wurm and Hattori). Ethnic population: 50,000. North central Timor Island, border area between West Timor and East Timor, mostly on eastern side. *Dialects:* Nogo (Nogo-Nogo), Kemak. *Other:* Traditional religion, Christian. See main entry under East Timor.

Ke'o (Nage-Keo) [xxk] 40,000 (2001 L. Baird). Ethnic population: 40,000. South central Flores, east of Ngad'a, south of Nage, south and southeast of the volcano Ebu Lobo. Kecamatans Mauponggo and Nangaroro, Kabupaten Ngada. Bordered to the north by the Nage, to the west by the Ngada, and to the east by the Ende. *Class:* Austronesian, Malayo-Polynesian, Central-Eastern, Central Malayo-Polynesian, Bima-Sumba, Ende-Lio. *Dialects:* Distinct from Nage. Close to Nage, Ngad'a, Ende, Lio, Palu'e, Riung. Closest to Nage. *Lg Use:* All domains with Ke'o speakers. Ceremonies, personal letter writing in Ke'o, but Indonesian viewed as the proper language for writing and using with outsiders. All ages. Speakers view Indonesian as the prestige language that children need to speak to get better jobs. They view Nage and Ngada as superior to Ke'o because of a cultural belief that mountain languages are more refined. English is viewed as a very prestigious language. 0.02% are fluent in Indonesian. Ke'o migrants in towns and cities are tending to teach children Indonesian instead of Ke'o. *Lg Dev:* Literacy rate in second language: 20% Indonesian. Literacy program by government for adults and in schools. Grammar. *Other:* People and language are both called Ke'o. SVO; isolating language; 4-way phonemic stop distinction. Muslim, Christian, traditional religion.

Kepo' (Kepoq) [kuk] 10,605 (2000 WCD). Central Flores, between Manggarai and Rembong, with a separate enclave between Manggarai and Wae Rana. *Class:* Austronesian, Malayo-Polynesian, Central-Eastern, Central Malayo-Polynesian, Bima-Sumba. *Dialects:* May be intelligible with one of the surrounding languages.

Kodi (Kudi) [kod] 40,000 (1987 UBS). West Sumba, Lesser Sundas. *Class:* Austronesian, Malayo-Polynesian, Central-Eastern, Central Malayo-Polynesian, Bima-Sumba. *Dialect:* Kodi Bokol, Kodi Bangedo, Nggaro (Nggaura). May be closest to Wejewa. *Lg Dev:* Bible portions: 1977. *Other:* Traditional religion, Christian.

Komodo [kvh] 700 (2000 WCD). Komodo Island and west coast of Flores. Not on Timor. *Class:* Austronesian, Malayo-Polynesian, Central-Eastern, Central Malayo-Polynesian, Bima-Sumba. *Dialects:* Considered a separate language from Manggarai by Verheijen.

Kui (Lerabain, Masin-Lak) [kvd] 4,242 (2000 WCD). Ethnic population: 5,000 (1981 Wurm and Hattori). Alor Island in scattered enclaves. Kui dialect is on the south coast in Lerabaing and Buraga; Batulolong dialect is in Sibera and Kapebang. Kui is also in Moru in Kalabahi Bay, interspersed with Hamap speakers. *Class:* Trans-New Guinea, South Bird's Head-Timor-Alor-Pantar, Timor-Alor-Pantar, Makasai-Alor-Pantar, Alor. *Dialects:* Kui (Lerabaing, Buraga), Kiramang (Kramang), Batulolong. *Other:* 'Masin-Lak' is speakers' own name for their language. Muslim, Christian.

Kula (Lantoka, Tanglapui, Lamtoka, Kola) [tpg] 5,000 (1997 Grimes, Therik, Grimes, Jacob). Eastern quarter of Alor Island, between Kamang and Sawila. Naumang is an old village. Other villages are the result of recent migrations from older locations. Most are in higher elevations, but the villagers of Maukuru, Takala, Koilela, Peisaka, and Kiralela on the north coast also speak Kula. *Class:* Trans-New Guinea, South Bird's Head-Timor-Alor-Pantar, Timor-Alor-Pantar, Tanglapui. *Dialects:* Iramang, Kula, Kulatela, Watena, Larena, Kula Watena, Sumang, Arumala. Structurally similar to Sawila. Intelligibility of Sawila is marginal. *Other:* Mountain slope, coastal. Christian, traditional religion.

Lamaholot (Solor, Solorese) [slp] 150,000 (1997 Grimes, Therik, Grimes, Jacob). Lesser Sundas. Used as first language on the eastern tip of Flores, east of the Sika language, and on western Solor. Used as language of wider communication on all of Solor. Adonara Lembata (except the Kedang area) and in enclaves on the northern coast of Pantar, northwest Alor, and surrounding islands. *Class:* Austronesian, Malayo-Polynesian, Central-Eastern, Central Malayo-Polynesian, Timor, Flores-Lembata. *Dialects:* West Lamaholot (Muhang, Pukaunu), Lamaholot (Taka, Lewolaga, Ile Mandiri, Tanjung Bunda, Larantuka, Ritaebang), West Solor. Wide variation among dialects. Possibly up to 10 languages. Keraf (1978) reports 18 distinct languages. *Lg Use:* Language of wider communication. The area around Larantuka is multiethnic and some people have shifted to Malay. *Lg Dev:* Grammar. *Other:* 'Lamaholot-Alor' is used to refer to (1) a lingua franca, (2) any of several Austronesian varieties spoken from eastern Flores to Alor. Traditional religion, Muslim, Christian.

Lamalera (Mulan, Kawela, Lebatukan) [lmr] South coastal Lembata (Lomblen) Island, about 4 villages. *Class:* Austronesian, Malayo-Polynesian, Central-Eastern, Central Malayo-Polynesian, Timor, Flores-Lembata. *Lg Use:* Speakers also use Lamaholot. *Lg Dev:* Grammar. *Other:* Traditionally whale hunters.

Lamatuka (Lamatoka) [lmq] Central Lembata (Lomblen) Island, between Ile Ape and Lewo Eleng. Several villages. Villages near the north coast are the result of recent government-induced migrations. *Class:* Austronesian, Malayo-Polynesian, Central-Eastern, Central Malayo-Polynesian, Timor, Flores-Lembata. *Dialects:* Lewo Eleng is probably the most closely related language. *Lg Use:* Speakers also use Lamaholot. *Other:* Mountain slope. Candlenut harvesters. Christian, traditional religion.

Lamboya [lmy] 25,000 (1997 Grimes, Therik, Grimes, Jacob). Sumba Island, southwest coast, southwest of Waikabubak. *Class:* Austronesian, Malayo-Polynesian, Central-Eastern, Central Malayo-Polynesian, Bima-Sumba. *Dialects:* Lamboya, Nggaura. Close to Wejewa, Mamboru, Wanukaka, Anakalangu.

Lamma (Lemma, Lamma', Mauta) [lev] 10,000. Ethnic population: 10,000. Southwestern and western Pantar, Lesser Sundas. *Class:* Trans-New Guinea, South Bird's Head-Timor-Alor-Pantar, Timor-Alor-Pantar, Makasai-Alor-Pantar, Pantar. *Dialects:* Kalondama, Tubal (Tube, Mauta), Biangwala.

Laura (Laora) [lur] 10,000 (1997 Grimes, Therik, Grimes, Jacob). Northwest Sumba, between Kodi and Mamboru. *Class:* Austronesian, Malayo-Polynesian, Central-Eastern, Central Malayo-Polynesian, Bima-Sumba. *Dialect:* Laura, Mbukambero (Bukambero). Not intelligible with Kodi.

Lembata, South [lmf] South Lembata (Lomblen) Island, between Lamalera and Lamatuka. *Class:* Austronesian, Malayo-Polynesian, Central-Eastern, Central Malayo-Polynesian, Timor, Flores-Lembata. *Lg Use:* Speakers also use Lamaholot.

Lembata, West (Mingar, Labalekan) [lmj] Western end of Lembata (Lomblen) Island, west of Levuka. Both mountain and coastal villages around the base of a volcano. *Class:* Austronesian, Malayo-Polynesian, Central-Eastern, Central Malayo-Polynesian, Timor, Flores-Lembata. *Lg Use:* Speakers also use Lamaholot.

Levuka (Lewuka, Lembata, Painara, Lewokukun) [lvu] West central Lembata (Lomblen) Island, between Ile Ape and Lamalera. *Class:* Austronesian, Malayo-Polynesian, Central-Eastern, Central Malayo-Polynesian, Timor, Flores-Lembata. *Dialects:* Levuka, Kalikasa. *Lg Use:* Speakers also use Lamaholot. *Other:* Recent road to Lamalera. Mountain slope. Christian, traditional religion.

Lewo Eleng [lwe] East central Lembata (Lomblen) Island, between Lamatuka and Kedang. Several villages. Villages near the north coast are the result of recent government-induced migrations. *Class:* Austronesian, Malayo-Polynesian, Central-Eastern, Central Malayo-Polynesian, Timor, Flores-Lembata. *Dialects:* Lamatuka is probably the most closely related language. *Lg Use:* Speakers also use Lamaholot. *Other:* Mountain slope. Candlenut harvesters. Christian, traditional religion.

Lewotobi (Southwest Lamaholot) [lwt] 289,357 (2000 WCD). Eastern Flores, south of Lamaholot and east of Sika. *Class:* Austronesian, Malayo-Polynesian, Central-Eastern, Central Malayo-Polynesian, Timor, Flores-Lembata. *Lg Use:* Speakers also use Lamaholot.

Li'o (Lio, Aku, Tanah Kunu, Lionese) [ljl] 130,000 (1981 Wurm and Hattori). Central Flores, west of Sikka around Paga and Dondo, Lesser Sundas. *Class:* Austronesian, Malayo-Polynesian, Central-Eastern, Central Malayo-Polynesian, Bima-Sumba, Ende-Lio. *Dialects:* Dialect cluster with Ende. Palu'e is borderline between language and dialect with Li'o. *Other:* Christian.

Lole (Rote, Roti, Rotinese, Rote Tengah, Central Rote, Loleh, Ba'a, Baä) [llg] 20,000 (2002 UKAW). Ethnic population: 20,000. Rote Island west central, domains of Lole and Ba'a. North Lole dialect covers north and central regions of Lole domain. *Class:* Austronesian, Malayo-Polynesian, Central-Eastern, Central Malayo-Polynesian, Timor, Nuclear Timor, West. *Dialects:* North Lole, South Lole, Ba'a. North Lole 'na-hina' becomes South Lole 'ni-hina'. *Lg Use:* Vigorous. All domains. All ages. Speakers also use Kupang, Indonesian. *Other:* Christian.

Malay, Kupang (Kupang, Basa Kupang) [mkn] 200,000 (1997 Max Jacob). Kupang and surrounding towns, West Timor. *Class:* Creole, Malay based. *Dialect:* Air Mata. 2 dialects. *Lg Use:* Vigorous. Second-language speakers. All domains. Used in religious services, radio, daily newspaper column. All ages. *Lg Dev:* Newspapers. Radio programs. Dictionary. Bible portions: 1999–2002. *Other:* Loanwords from Rote, Portuguese, Chinese, Uab Meto (Atoni), Sabu, Spanish, Dutch, English. Christian.

Mamboru (Memboro) [mvd] 16,000 (1981 Wurm and Hattori). Northwest Sumba Island, coast around Memboro.

Class: Austronesian, Malayo-Polynesian, Central-Eastern, Central Malayo-Polynesian, Bima-Sumba. *Dialects:* Related to Wejewa, Wanukaka, Lamboya, Anakalangu.

Manggarai [mqy] 500,000 (1989). Western third of Flores Island, Lesser Sundas. *Class:* Austronesian, Malayo-Polynesian, Central-Eastern, Central Malayo-Polynesian, Bima-Sumba. *Dialects:* Western Manggarai, Central Manggarai (Ruteng), West-Central Manggarai, Eastern Manggarai. Around 43 subdialects. Close to Riung. *Lg Dev:* Dictionary. *Other:* Christian, Muslim.

Nage (Nagé, Nage-Keo) [nxe] 50,000 (1993 Forth). Central Flores, northeast of Ngad'a, on the northern and western slopes of Ebu Lobo volcano. *Class:* Austronesian, Malayo-Polynesian, Central-Eastern, Central Malayo-Polynesian, Bima-Sumba, Ende-Lio.

Nedebang (Balungada, Nédebang) [nec] 1,379 (2000 WCD). North central Pantar, south and southwest of Kabir. *Class:* Trans-New Guinea, South Bird's Head-Timor-Alor-Pantar, Timor-Alor-Pantar, Makasai-Alor-Pantar, Pantar.

Ngad'a (Ngadha, Ngada, Nad'a, Nga'da, Bajava, Badjava, Bajawa, Rokka) [nxg] 60,000 (1995). South central Flores, between Manggarai and Ende and Li'o. *Class:* Austronesian, Malayo-Polynesian, Central-Eastern, Central Malayo-Polynesian, Bima-Sumba. *Dialects:* Central Ngada, Bajawa, South Ngada. Dialect diversity. *Lg Dev:* Grammar. *Other:* Christian.

Ngad'a, Eastern (Southeast Ngada) [nea] 5,000 (1994). South central Flores, between Ngad'a and Nage in Kecamatan Golewa in the administrative villages of Sara Sedu, Taka Tunga, Sanga Deto, and in Kecamatan Boawae in desa Rowa, all in Kabupaten Ngada. *Class:* Austronesian, Malayo-Polynesian, Central-Eastern, Central Malayo-Polynesian, Bima-Sumba. *Dialects:* Minor dialect variation. *Other:* Christian.

Palu'e (Palue, Lu'a, Paluqe) [ple] 10,000 (1997 Grimes, Therik, Grimes, Jacob). Palu Island, north of central Flores. Also the village of Nangahure on the north coast of the Flores mainland northwest of Maumere. *Class:* Austronesian, Malayo-Polynesian, Central-Eastern, Central Malayo-Polynesian, Bima-Sumba. *Dialects:* Dialect cluster with Ende-Lio; marginal intelligibility of Li'o. *Other:* Christian, traditional religion.

Rajong (Razong) [rjg] 4,242 (2000 WCD). Central Flores, 2 enclaves between Manggarai, Wae Rana, Ngad'a, and Rembong. *Class:* Austronesian, Malayo-Polynesian, Central-Eastern, Central Malayo-Polynesian, Bima-Sumba.

Rembong [reb] 2,121 (2000 WCD). North central Flores, between Eastern Manggarai and Riung. *Class:* Austronesian, Malayo-Polynesian, Central-Eastern, Central Malayo-Polynesian, Bima-Sumba. *Dialects:* Rembong, Wangka, Namu.

Retta [ret] Southern Pura Island at mouth of Kalabahi Bay, and southern part of Ternate Island. *Class:* Trans-New Guinea, South Bird's Head-Timor-Alor-Pantar, Timor-Alor-Pantar, Makasai-Alor-Pantar, Pantar. *Dialects:* Not intelligible with languages on north Pura.

Ringgou (Rote, Roti, Rotinese, Rote Timur, Eastern Rote, Rikou) [rgu] 10,000 (2002 UKAW). Ethnic population: 10,000. Rote Island eastern tip, domains of Ringgou, Landu and Oepao. *Class:* Austronesian, Malayo-Polynesian, Central-Eastern, Central Malayo-Polynesian, Timor, Nuclear Timor, West. *Dialect:* Ringgou, Landu, Oe Pao (Oepao). *Lg Use:* Vigorous. All domains. All ages. Speakers also use Kupang, Indonesian. *Other:* 'Ringgou' is the pronunciation from other Rote languages. 'Rikou' is how they pronounce it themselves. Christian.

Riung (Far Eastern Manggarai) [riu] 14,000 (1981 Wurm and Hattori). North central Flores Island, Kecamatan Riung in Kabupaten Ngada, Lesser Sundas. *Class:* Austronesian, Malayo-Polynesian, Central-Eastern, Central

Malayo-Polynesian, Bima-Sumba. *Dialects:* Close to Manggarai, but marginal intelligibility.

Rongga [ror] 2,121 (2000 WCD). South central Flores, between Manggarai and Ngad'a, and south of Wae Rana. *Class:* Austronesian, Malayo-Polynesian, Central-Eastern, Central Malayo-Polynesian, Bima-Sumba.

Sabu (Hawu, Havunese, Savu, Sawu, Sawunese, Savunese) [hvn] 110,000 (1997). Population includes 15,000 to 25,000 outside of Sabu (1981 Wurm and Hattori). Islands of Sawu and Raijua south of Flores and west of Timor, and in Sumba (especially in Waingapu and Melolo), in Ende on Flores, and the Kupang area of Timor. Administratively in Kabupaten Kupang. Airstrip is served irregularly. *Class:* Austronesian, Malayo-Polynesian, Central-Eastern, Central Malayo-Polynesian, Bima-Sumba. *Dialects:* Seba (Heba), Timu (Dimu), Liae, Mesara (Mehara), Raijua (Raidjua). Related to Dhao. *Lg Dev:* Grammar. NT: 2000. *Other:* Complex phonetics with implosives, glottal, long and short vowels, diphthongs, long and short consonants. Christian, traditional religion (Jengetiu).

Sasak (Lombok) [sas] 2,100,000 (1989). Lombok Island. *Class:* Austronesian, Malayo-Polynesian, Bali-Sasak. *Dialects:* Kuto-Kute (North Sasak), Ngeto-Ngete (Northeast Sasak), Meno-Mene (Central Sasak), Ngeno-Ngene (Central East Sasak, Central West Sasak), Mriak-Mriku (Central South Sasak). Complex dialect network. Some 'dialects' have difficult intelligibility with each other. Related to Sumbawa and Balinese. *Lg Dev:* Bible portions: 1948. *Other:* Subgroups: Waktu Lima, Waktu Telu. Most Waktu Telu own farms; most Waktu Lima are landless, travel more, and have diverse occupations. Many Balinese also on Lombok Island, especially in the west. Waktu Telu: agriculturalists. Muslim, Christian, traditional religion (Waktu Telu).

Sawila (Tanglapui) [swt] 3,000 (1997 Grimes, Therik, Grimes, Jacob). Eastern Alor Island, between Kula and Wersing. Many current village locations are the result of recent migrations from older locations. *Class:* Trans-New Guinea, South Bird's Head-Timor-Alor-Pantar, Timor-Alor-Pantar, Tanglapui. *Dialects:* Sawila, Lona, Salimana, Lalamana, Sileba. Intelligibility of Kula is marginal, and the historical ethnic identities are distinct. Structurally similar to Kula. *Other:* Mountain slope, coastal. Christian, traditional religion.

Sika (Sara Sikka, Sikkanese, Sikka, Krowe, Maumere) [ski] 175,000 (1990 E.D. Lewis). Eastern Flores Island, between Li'o and Lamaholot, Lesser Sundas. *Class:* Austronesian, Malayo-Polynesian, Central-Eastern, Central Malayo-Polynesian, Timor, Flores-Lembata. *Dialects:* Sara Krowe (Central Sikka), Sikka Natar (South Coast Sikka, Kangaé), Tana Ai. Wide variation within language and culture. *Lg Dev:* Grammar. *Other:* Christian.

So'a (Soa) [ssq] 10,000 (1994). Central Flores, central Kabupaten Ngada, between Ngad'a and Riung. *Class:* Austronesian, Malayo-Polynesian, Central-Eastern, Central Malayo-Polynesian, Bima-Sumba. *Dialects:* Close to Ngad'a. *Other:* Christian.

Sumbawa (Semawa, Sumbawarese) [smw] 300,000 (1989). Western end of Sumbawa Island, west of the isthmus. *Class:* Austronesian, Malayo-Polynesian, Bali-Sasak. *Other:* Different from Sumba (Kambera).

Tereweng [twg] 800 (1997). Ethnic population: 800 (1997 Grimes, Therik, Grimes, Jacob). Tereweng Island off southeast Pantar. 2 villages on the northern side of the island and one on Pantar mainland. Water and gardens on Pantar. *Class:* Trans-New Guinea, South Bird's Head-Timor-Alor-Pantar, Timor-Alor-Pantar, Makasai-Alor-Pantar, Pantar. *Dialects:* There is disagreement over whether this is a dialect of Blagar or a separate language. Grouped by Stokhof (1975) with Blagar, by Vatter (1932) with Kelong, and by van Gaalen (1945) as distinct. *Lg Use:* Distinct ethnic identity from Blagar.

Termanu (Rote, Roti, Rotinese, Rote Tengah, Central Rote, Pa'da) [twu] 30,000 (2002 UKAW). Ethnic population: 30,000. Central Rote Island, domains of Termanu, Keka, Talae, Korbafo, and Bokai. Speakers also in Kupang, West Timor, and Jakarta. *Class:* Austronesian, Malayo-Polynesian, Central-Eastern, Central Malayo-Polynesian, Timor, Nuclear Timor, West. *Dialects:* Pa'da (Termanu), Pa'da Kona (Keka-Talae, Southern Termanu), Korbafo (Korbaffo), Bokai. Seems closer to Lole than to other varieties on Rote. Korbafo and Bokai may need to be separated for sociolinguistic reasons. *Lg Use:* Vigorous. All domains. All ages. Speakers also use Kupang, Indonesian. Generally educated in Indonesian, some older people in Dutch. *Lg Dev:* Dictionary. Grammar. Bible portions: 1895–2002. *Other:* Christian.

Tetun (Tetum, Tettum, Teto, Tetu, Tetung, Belu, Belo, Fehan, Tetun Belu) [tet] 400,000 in Indonesia (2004). Population total all countries: 450,000. Central Timor corridor from the north to the south coasts, east of Atoni, west of Bunak (in Batagude) around Batibo and in from the south coast around Viqueque and Soibada. Also spoken in East Timor. *Class:* Austronesian, Malayo-Polynesian, Central-Eastern, Central Malayo-Polynesian, Timor, Nuclear Timor, East. *Dialects:* Eastern Tetun (Soibada, Natarbora, Lakluta, Tetun Loos, Tetun Los), Southern Tetun (Lia Fehan, Plain Tetun, Tasi Mane, Belu Selatan, South Belu, South Tetun), Northern Tetun (Lia Foho, Hill Tetun, Tasi Feto, Belu Utara, North Belu, Tetun Terik, Tetun Therik). Wide variation in morphology and syntax among major dialects, and variation in social structure. *Lg Dev:* Grammar. Bible portions: 1983–1997. *Other:* Christian, traditional religion.

Tewa [twe] 5,000 (1981 Wurm and Hattori). Central Pantar. *Class:* Trans-New Guinea, South Bird's Head-Timor-Alor-Pantar, Timor-Alor-Pantar, Makasai-Alor-Pantar, Pantar. *Dialects:* Deing, Madar, Lebang.

Tii (Rote, Roti, Rotinese, Rote Barat, Western Rote, Thie, Ti) [txq] 20,000 (2002 UKAW). Ethnic population: 20,000. Rote Island southwest, domain of Tii, east of Dela-Oenale, west of Lole, south of Dengka. *Class:* Austronesian, Malayo-Polynesian, Central-Eastern, Central Malayo-Polynesian, Timor, Nuclear Timor, West. *Dialects:* Minor variation, third singular verb prefix 'na-fa'da' varies with 'i-fa'da'. *Lg Use:* Vigorous. All domains. All ages. Speakers also use Kupang, Indonesian. *Other:* Christian.

Uab Meto (Atoni, Meto, Uab Atoni Pah Meto, Uab Pah Meto, Timor, Timorese, Timol, Timoreesch, Timoreezen, "Dawan," "Timor Dawan," "Rawan," Orang Gunung) [aoz] 586,000 (1997 Grimes, Therik, Grimes, Jacob). Western Timor Island. *Class:* Austronesian, Malayo-Polynesian, Central-Eastern, Central Malayo-Polynesian, Timor, Nuclear Timor, West. *Dialects:* Amfoan-Fatule'u-Amabi (Amfoan, Amfuang, Fatule'u, Amabi), Amanuban-Amanatun (Amanuban, Amanubang, Amanatun), Mollo-Miomafo (Mollo, Miomafo), Biboki-Insana (Biboki, Insanao), Kusa-Manlea (Kusa, Manlea). Much dialect variation. Ethnological and linguistic differences in nearly every valley. Close to Amarasi. *Lg Dev:* Bible: 2000. *Other:* The people are called 'Atoni'. Christian.

Wae Rana (Waerana) [wrx] 4,242 (2000 WCD). South central Flores, between Manggarai and Ngad'a. *Class:* Austronesian, Malayo-Polynesian, Central-Eastern, Central Malayo-Polynesian, Bima-Sumba.

Wanukaka (Wanokaka) [wnk] 10,000 (1981 Wurm and Hattori). Sumba Island, southwest coast, east of Lamboya. *Class:* Austronesian, Malayo-Polynesian, Central-Eastern, Central Malayo-Polynesian, Bima-Sumba. *Dialects:* Wanukaka, Rua. Close to, but unintelligible to speakers of

Wejewa, Mamboru, Lamboya, and Anakalangu. Intelligibility of varieties in east Sumba and Kambera uncertain.

Wejewa (Wewewa, Wajewa, Wewjewa, Waidjewa, West Sumbanese, Weyewa, Veveva) [wew] 65,000 (1997 Grimes, Therik, Grimes, Jacob). Interior of western Sumba Island, Lesser Sundas. *Class:* Austronesian, Malayo-Polynesian, Central-Eastern, Central Malayo-Polynesian, Bima-Sumba. *Dialects:* Weyewa, Lauli (Loli), Tana Righu. *Lg Dev:* NT: 1971. *Other:* Traditional religion.

Wersing (Kolana-Wersin, Kolana, Wersin, Warsina) [kvw] 3,700 (1997 Grimes, Therik, Grimes, Jacob). Alor Island, east coast around Kolana, southeast coast at Pietoko and Pureman, 2 enclaves on north central north coast. *Class:* Trans-New Guinea, South Bird's Head-Timor-Alor-Pantar, Timor-Alor-Pantar, Kolana. *Dialect:* Kolana, Maneta, Langkuru (Pureman, Mademang). Close to Kamang. *Other:* Cultural and historical relationship with Liquisa area in East Timor. Said to have migrated from Timor mainland prior to 1500, first to Pureman on the south coast, then Kolana on the east coast, then on the north coast near Taramana. The former king was at Kolana. Coastal. Christian, traditional religion.

Indonesia (Papua)

Indonesia (Papua). 2,220,934 (2000 census). Information mainly from C. Roesler 1972; C. L. Voorhoeve 1975; M. Donohue 1998–1999; SIL 1975–2003. The number of languages listed for Indonesia (Papua) is 271. Of those, 269 are living languages and 2 are second language without mother-tongue speakers. See maps beginning on page 798.

Abinomn (Avinomen, "Baso," Foya, Foja) [bsa] 300 (1999 Clouse and Donohue). Lakes Plain area, from the mouth of the Baso River just east of Dabra at the Idenburg River to its headwaters in the Foya Mountains, Jayapura Kabupaten, Mamberamo Hulu Kecamatan. *Class:* Language Isolate. *Dialects:* Close to Warembori. *Lg Use:* Positive language attitude. *Lg Dev:* Literacy rate in first language: 10%. Low level of schooling. *Other:* They strongly dislike the name "Baso." SOV. 100 to 600 meters. Christian, traditional religion.

Abun (Yimbun, A Nden, Manif, Karon) [kgr] 3,000 (1995 SIL). North coast and interior of central Bird's Head, north and south of Tamberau ranges. Sorong Kabupaten, Ayamaru, Sausapor, and Moraid kecamatans. About 20 villages. *Class:* West Papuan, Bird's Head, North-Central Bird's Head, North Bird's Head. *Dialects:* Abun Tat (Karon Pantai), Abun Ji (Madik), Abun Je. *Lg Dev:* Literacy rate in first language: 5% to 15%. Bible portions: 1991–1995. *Other:* Christian, traditional religion.

Aghu (Djair, Dyair) [ahh] 3,000 (1987 SIL). South coast area along the Digul River west of the Mandobo language, Merauke Kabupaten, Jair Kecamatan. *Class:* Trans-New Guinea, Main Section, Central and Western, Central and South New Guinea-Kutubuan, Central and South New Guinea, Awyu-Dumut, Awyu, Aghu. *Lg Dev:* Grammar. *Other:* Different from Aghu of Australia. Swamp. Below 100 meters. Sago gatherers; fishermen. Christian, traditional religion.

Airoran (Aeroran, Adora, Iriemkena) [air] 1,000 (1998 SIL). North coast area on the lower Apauwer River. Subu, Motobiak, Isirania and other villages, Jayapura Kabupaten, Mamberamo Hilir, and Pantai Barat kecamatans. *Class:* Trans-New Guinea, Main Section, Central and Western, Dani-Kwerba, Northern, Kwerba. *Lg Use:* Used in religious services. *Other:* Coastal, river. Sea level to 400 meters. Fishermen. Christian, traditional religion.

Ambai (Ambai-Menawi) [amk] 10,053 (2000 WCD). On Ambai Island in Cenderawasih Bay, south of Serui Island, along the south coast of Serui Island from 136.20' to 136.45', Yapen Waropen Kabupaten, Yapen Selatan, and Yapen Timur kecamatans. 10 villages. *Class:* Austronesian, Malayo-Polynesian, Central-Eastern, Eastern Malayo-Polynesian, South Halmahera-West New Guinea, West New Guinea, Cenderawasih Bay, Yapen, Central-Western. *Dialects:* Randawaya, Ambai (Wadapi-Laut), Manawi. Lexical similarity 77% with Serui-Laut, 71% with Wandamen. Closely related to Ansus, Woi, Pom, Wabo, Marau, Papuma, Munggui, Kurudu. *Lg Use:* Children use Indonesian. *Lg Dev:* Literacy rate in first language: 25% to 50%. Literacy rate in second language: 50% to 75%. Bible portions: 1991–2000. *Other:* Serial verbs; complex directional demonstrative system. Muslim, Christian.

Anasi (Bapu) [bpo] 2,000 (1993 Doriot). North coast area along the west bank of the lower Mamberamo River. Jayapura Kabupaten, Mamberamo Hilir Kecamatan. *Class:* Geelvink Bay, East Geelvink Bay. *Other:* 100 meters. Fishermen; hunter-gatherers. Christian, traditional religion.

Ansus [and] 4,600 (1987 SIL). Miosnum Island and the south coast of Serui Island, from 135.35' to 135.50', Yapen Waropen Kabupaten, Yapen Barat Kecamatan, Ansus, Kairawi, Aibondeni, and Yenusi villages. *Class:* Austronesian, Malayo-Polynesian, Central-Eastern, Eastern Malayo-Polynesian, South Halmahera-West New Guinea, West New Guinea, Cenderawasih Bay, Yapen, Central-Western. *Dialects:* Lexical similarity 82% with Marau Papuma, 77% with Wandamen. *Other:* Coastal. Sea level to 350 meters. Sago gatherers. Christian, traditional religion.

Anus [auq] 70 (2000 Wurm). Island off north coast east of the Tor River, Jayapura Kabupaten, Bonggo Kecamatan. *Class:* Austronesian, Malayo-Polynesian, Central-Eastern, Eastern Malayo-Polynesian, Oceanic, Western Oceanic, North New Guinea, Sarmi-Jayapura Bay, Sarmi. *Lg Use:* 40% to 60% of the ethnic group speaks Anus. Most domains, family. A few children speak Anus. *Other:* Coastal. Below 100 meters. Fishermen.

Arandai (Yaban, Jaban, Dombano, Sebyar) [jbj] 1,000 (1987 SIL). Southern Bird's Head, east and west of the Wariaga River and around the Sebyar (Timoforo) River, Manokwari Kabupaten, Bintuni Kecamatan. *Class:* Trans-New Guinea, South Bird's Head-Timor-Alor-Pantar, South Bird's Head, South Bird's Head Proper, Eastern. *Dialects:* Kemberano (Tomu), Dombano (Arandai). Related to Kampong Baru. Kemberano and Dombano appear to have 71% lexical similarity with each other in preliminary wordlists; probably 2 separate languages. *Other:* Below 100 meters. Fishermen; agriculturalists. Christian, traditional religion.

Arguni (Argoeni) [agf] 150 (2000 Wurm). Northwest coast of Bomberai Peninsula on an island in the Maccluer Gulf. *Class:* Austronesian, Malayo-Polynesian, Central-Eastern, Central Malayo-Polynesian, North Bomberai. *Other:* Coastal. Below 100 meters. Traditional religion, Christian.

As [asz] 230 (2000 Wurm). West Bird's Head, north coast, villages of Asbakin (main center), Maklaumkarta, and Mega. *Class:* Austronesian, Malayo-Polynesian, Central-Eastern, Eastern Malayo-Polynesian, South Halmahera-West New Guinea, West New Guinea, Cenderawasih Bay, Raja Ampat. *Dialects:* Lexical similarity 90% with some dialects on Misool Island. *Lg Use:* Speakers also use Moi or Indonesian. *Other:* Reported to originate from Gag Island, west of Waigeo Island. Coastal. Below 100 meters. Traditional religion, Christian.

Asmat, Casuarina Coast (Kaweinag) [asc] 9,000 (1991 SIL). Population includes 5,200 in Matia and 3,400 in Sapan. Casuarina coast from the Ewta River in the north to the Kuti River in the south, inland as far as 25 km from the coast in some places. Merauke Kabupaten, Pantai Kasuari Kecamatan. *Class:* Trans-New Guinea, Main Section, Central and Western, Central and South New

Guinea-Kutubuan, Central and South New Guinea, Asmat-Kamoro. *Dialect:* Matia, Sapan (Safan). *Lg Use:* Used in the home and with friends. *Other:* Coastal. Swamp. Below 100 meters. Agriculturalists; fishermen. Traditional religion, Christian.

Asmat, Central (Manowee, Jas, Yas) [cns] 7,000 (1972 Roesler TEAM). On the south coast from the Owap River in the northwest to the Farec River in the southwest, inland toward the foothills to 210 kilometers from the coast in some areas. Merauke Kabupaten, Sawa-Erma, Agats, Atsy, and Pantai Kasuari kecamatans. Between the Kamoro and Sawi languages. *Class:* Trans-New Guinea, Main Section, Central and Western, Central and South New Guinea-Kutubuan, Central and South New Guinea, Asmat-Kamoro. *Dialects:* Simai (Simay), Misman, Ajam (Ayam). North Asmat is the most distinct dialect. Related to the Sempan language north of the rivers. Close to Kamoro and Citak. *Lg Use:* Many are becoming bilingual in Indonesian; some in neighboring languages. *Lg Dev:* NT: 1985. *Other:* Christian, traditional religion.

Asmat, North (Keenok) [nks] 1,000 (1991 SIL). Near the headwaters of the Paterle Cocq River to the west, to the Unir River to the east, to the foothills in some places, Merauke Kabupaten, Sawa-Erma Kecamatan. *Class:* Trans-New Guinea, Main Section, Central and Western, Central and South New Guinea-Kutubuan, Central and South New Guinea, Asmat-Kamoro. *Other:* Riverine. Swamp. 100 to 200 meters. Agriculturalists; hunter-gatherers. Christian, traditional religion.

Asmat, Yaosakor (Yaosakor) [asy] 2,000 (1991 SIL). South coast along the Sirac River, Merauke Kabupaten, Agats, and Atsy kecamatans. *Class:* Trans-New Guinea, Main Section, Central and Western, Central and South New Guinea-Kutubuan, Central and South New Guinea, Asmat-Kamoro. *Lg Dev:* NT: 1995. *Other:* Riverine. Swamp. Fishermen; agriculturalists; government workers. Christian, traditional religion.

Atohwaim (Kaugat) [aqm] 1,000 (1987 SIL). South coast on the Cook and Kronkel rivers, between the Sawi and Kaygir languages. Merauke Kabupaten, Pantai Kasuari Kecamatan. *Class:* Trans-New Guinea, Main Section, Central and Western, Kayagar. *Lg Use:* About 50% are bilingual in Indonesian, Sawi, or Kaygir. *Other:* Swamp. Below 100 meters. Sago gatherers. Christian, traditional religion.

Auye (Auwje) [auu] 350 (1995 SIL). Ethnic population: 350 (2000 Moxness SIL). Central Highlands, Siriwo River, mountains southeast of Cenderawasih Bay. Paniai Kabupaten, Napan Kecamatan. *Class:* Trans-New Guinea, Main Section, Central and Western, Wissel Lakes-Kemandoga, Ekari-Wolani-Moni. *Dialects:* Related to Ekari. *Lg Use:* Vigorous. All domains, family, friends, church, home. All ages. Most speakers do not know Indonesian (2000 Moxness). *Lg Dev:* Literacy rate in first language: 25%. Bible portions: 1993. *Other:* Distinct from Awyi (Awye) in Taikat group. Mountain slope. 400 to 4,000 meters. Agriculturalists; hunter-gatherers. Christian, traditional religion.

Awbono (Kvolyab) [awh] 100 (1999 SIL). 100% monolinguals. South of Tokuni on the Modera River. Kvolyab is on the south coast, northwest of Korowai. *Class:* Bayono-Awbono. *Dialects:* Not related to Ok, Asmat, Awyu-Dumut, Momuna, or highland languages like Dani or Mek. Lexical similarity 55% with Bayono. *Other:* The Awbono are frequently at war with the Kopkaka and Korowai. SOV. Below 100 meters. Agriculturalists; hunter-gatherers.

Awera [awr] 70 (2000 Wurm). Village at the mouth of the Wapoga River, east side of Cenderawasih Bay, Yapen Waropen Kabupaten, Waropen Bawah Kecamatan. Same community with 100 Ansus-speaking people. *Class:*

Geelvink Bay, Lakes Plain, Awera. _Lg Use:_ Some domains, home, community. Ansus and Indonesian are used widely in the community. _Other:_ Below 100 meters. Loggers; fishermen. Christian, traditional religion.

Awyi (Awye, Awje, Awji, Nyao, Njao) [auw] 350 (2000 Wurm). Northeast near Papua New Guinea border, just south of Jayapura, Jayapura Kabupaten, Arso Kecamatan. _Class:_ Trans-New Guinea, Northern, Border, Taikat. _Other:_ Distinct from Auye in Ekari-Wolani-Moni group. 350 to 600 meters. Agriculturalists; hunter-gatherers. Christian, traditional religion.

Awyu, Asue (Miaro, Pisa, Miaro Awyu) [psa] 6,500 (2002 SIL). South coast area, southwest of Wildeman River and east of Kampong River, inland from Pirimapun. _Class:_ Trans-New Guinea, Main Section, Central and Western, Central and South New Guinea-Kutubuan, Central and South New Guinea, Awyu-Dumut, Awyu. _Dialects:_ Close to Edera Awyu and South Awyu. A separate language from Central Awyu and Jair Awyu. _Lg Use:_ All domains. Used in religious services. _Lg Dev:_ Bible portions: 1985. _Other:_ Below 100 meters. Fishermen; agriculturalists; hunter-gatherers. Christian, traditional religion.

Awyu, Central (Auyu, Awya, Awju, Ajau, Avio, Nohon) [awu] 7,500 (2002 Sohn, Myo-sook). South coast east of Bipim, northwest of Yaqay, west of Tanamerah, southwest of Boma. Merauke Kabupaten, Edera, Pantai Kasuari, Kouh, Mandobo, Asgon, and Kepi kecamatans. _Class:_ Trans-New Guinea, Main Section, Central and Western, Central and South New Guinea-Kutubuan, Central and South New Guinea, Awyu-Dumut, Awyu. _Dialects:_ About 9 dialects. _Lg Use:_ Most domains, home. Many becoming bilingual in Indonesian. _Lg Dev:_ Bible portions: 1985. _Other:_ Swamp. Below 100 meters. Hunter-gatherers. Traditional religion.

Awyu, Edera (Siagha, Syiagha, Sjiagha, Oser, Yenimu, Jenimu) [awy] 3,870 (2002 SIL). Southeast near coast, north of lower Digul River. _Class:_ Trans-New Guinea, Main Section, Central and Western, Central and South New Guinea-Kutubuan, Central and South New Guinea, Awyu-Dumut, Awyu. _Lg Use:_ All domains, home, religious services. _Other:_ Swamp. 1 to 100 meters. Agriculturalists; hunters. Christian, traditional religion.

Awyu, Jair [awv] 2,300 (2002 SIL). _Class:_ Trans-New Guinea, Main Section, Central and Western, Central and South New Guinea-Kutubuan, Central and South New Guinea, Awyu-Dumut, Awyu. _Lg Use:_ Used with family, friends. _Other:_ 1 to 100 meters. Fishermen. Christian, traditional religion, Muslim.

Awyu, North (Dyair, Djair, Yair, Awyu, Jair) [yir] 1,500 (1987 SIL). South coast west side of Digul River, south of Kombai, east of Awyu. _Class:_ Trans-New Guinea, Main Section, Central and Western, Central and South New Guinea-Kutubuan, Central and South New Guinea, Awyu-Dumut, Awyu. _Other:_ Swamp. Below 100 meters. Fishermen; agriculturalists. Christian, traditional religion.

Awyu, South (Siagha, Syiagha, Sjiagha, Oser, Yenimu, Jenimu) [aws] 9,340 (2002 SIL). Southeast near coast, north of lower Digul River. _Class:_ Trans-New Guinea, Main Section, Central and Western, Central and South New Guinea-Kutubuan, Central and South New Guinea, Awyu-Dumut, Awyu. _Lg Use:_ All domains, family, friends, religious services. _Other:_ Swamp. 1 to 100 meters. Hunter-gatherers; agriculturalists. Christian, traditional religion.

Bagusa (Kapeso, Suaseso) [bqb] 300 (1987 SIL). East of Mamberamo, Lake Rombebai, north of Kauwera language. Jayapura Kabupaten, Mamberamo Tengah Kecamatan. _Class:_ Trans-New Guinea, Main Section, Central and Western, Dani-Kwerba, Northern, Kwerba. _Dialects:_ Lexical similarity 64% with Kwerba. _Lg Use:_ Vigorous.

All ages. _Other:_ Tropical forest, swamp. Sea level to 200 meters. Hunter-gatherers; fishermen. Traditional religion, Christian.

Baham (Patimuni) [bdw] 1,100 (1987 SIL). West Bomberai Peninsula east of the Iha language. Fakfak Kabupaten, Kaimana, Fakfak, and Kokas kecamatans. _Class:_ Trans-New Guinea, Main Section, Central and Western, West Bomberai, West Bomberai Proper. _Dialects:_ Close to Iha. _Other:_ Coastal. Sea level to 1,600 meters. Fishermen; agriculturalists. Christian, traditional religion.

Barapasi (Baropasi) [brp] 2,500 (1995 SIL). East side of Cenderawasih Bay just east of the Waropen language, along the Barapasi River and its tributaries. Yapen Waropen Kabupaten, Waropen Atas Kecamatan. _Class:_ Geelvink Bay, East Geelvink Bay. _Dialects:_ Sipisi, Marikai. Lexical similarity 67% with Kofei, 71% with Sauri, 61% with Tefaro, 64% with Woria. _Lg Use:_ All domains, home. _Lg Dev:_ Literacy rate in second language: 15% to 25%. _Other:_ Riverine. 1 to 600 meters. Fishermen. Traditional religion, Christian.

Bauzi (Baudi, Bauri, Baudji, Baudzi) [bvz] 1,500 (1991 SIL). 1,350 monolinguals. Around Lake Holmes near the mid-Mamberamo River, Danau Bira area, northeast, Kasonoweja north of Kustera. Jayapura and Yapen Waropen kabupatens, Mamberamo Tengah and Waropen Atas kecamatans; Vakiadi, Noiadi, Danau Bira, Solom, Kustera, Neao, Itaba villages. _Class:_ Geelvink Bay, East Geelvink Bay. _Dialects:_ Gesda Dae, Neao, Aumenefa. _Lg Use:_ Vigorous. Some Aliki speak Bauzi because of intermarriage and trading. All domains. Oral and written use in religious services, local commerce. Oral literature. Positive language attitude. Bilingual level estimates for Eritai: 0 90%, 1 5%, 2 5%, 3 0%, 4 0%, 5 0%. 10% are bilingual with Aliki, 2% can speak some Indonesian. _Lg Dev:_ Literacy rate in first language: 10% to 25%. 230 can read and write it. Bible portions: 1985–1994. _Other:_ Some form of whistle speech reported. Swamp, tropical forest. Agriculturalists: bananas, papaya. Christian, traditional religion.

Bayono [byl] 100 (1999 SIL). South of Tokuni on the Steenboom River. _Class:_ Bayono-Awbono. _Dialects:_ Not related to Ok, Asmat, Awyu-Dumut, Momuna, or highlands languages like Dani or Mek. Lexical similarity 55% with Awbono. _Other:_ SOV. Below 100 meters. Agriculturalists.

Bedoanas [bed] 180 (2000 Wurm). Northwest coast, Bomberai Peninsula, Fakfak Kabupaten, Kokas Kecamatan. _Class:_ Austronesian, Malayo-Polynesian, Central-Eastern, Eastern Malayo-Polynesian, South Halmahera-West New Guinea, West New Guinea, Bomberai. _Other:_ Coastal. Sea level to 200 meters. Christian, traditional religion.

Berik (Berrik, Berick, Upper Tor) [bkl] 1,200 (1994 SIL). North coast area along the mid and upper Tor River, inland from Sarmi. Jayapura Kabupaten, Tor Atas Kecamatan; Bora Bora, Waf, Doronta, Beu, Togonfo, Dangken, Kondirjan, Somanente, Tenwer, Sewan, Safrontani, and Taminambor villages. _Class:_ Trans-New Guinea, Northern, Tor, Tor. _Dialects:_ Lexical similarity 45% with Keder, 13% with Orya. _Lg Use:_ Bilingual level estimates for Papuan Malay: 0 10%, 1 30%, 2 25%, 3 20%, 4 10%, 5 5%. _Lg Dev:_ NT: 1993. _Other:_ Formerly the trade language of the Tor area. Christian, traditional religion.

Betaf [bfe] 500 (2000). North coast area east of Sarmi, Jayapura Kabupaten, Pantai Timur Kecamatan. _Class:_ Unclassified. _Other:_ Coastal. Below 100 meters. Fishermen; agriculturalists. Christian, traditional religion.

Biak (Biak-Numfor, Noefoor, Mafoor, Mefoor, Nufoor, Mafoorsch, Myfoorsch, Noefoorsch) [bhw] 30,000 (2000

Wurm). Islands of Biak and Numfor to the north and on numerous small islands east and west of the Bird's Head, including Mapia Island. Biak Numfor Kabupaten. *Class:* Austronesian, Malayo-Polynesian, Central-Eastern, Eastern Malayo-Polynesian, South Halmahera-West New Guinea, West New Guinea, Cenderawasih Bay, Biakic. *Dialects:* Ariom, Bo'o, Dwar, Fairi, Jenures, Korim, Mandusir, Mofu, Opif, Padoa, Penasifu, Samberi, Sampori (Mokmer), Sor, Sorendidori, Sundei, Wari, Wadibu, Sorido, Bosnik, Korido, Warsa, Wardo, Kamer, Mapia, Mios Num, Rumberpon, Monoarfu, Vogelkop. Some consider Biak and Numfor to be two languages. *Lg Use:* Vigorous. A few thousand second-language users. *Lg Dev:* NT: 1990. *Other:* Island. Sea level to 600 meters. Christian, traditional religion.

Biga [bhc] 300 (2001 Remijsen). Misool Island, Biga village. *Class:* Austronesian, Malayo-Polynesian, Central-Eastern, Eastern Malayo-Polynesian, South Halmahera-West New Guinea, West New Guinea, Cenderawasih Bay, Raja Ampat. *Other:* Island. Sea level to 300 meters. Sago gatherers.

Biritai (Ati, Aliki, Biri) [bqq] 250 (1988 SIL). Lakes Plain just north of mid-Rouffaer River, village of Biri. *Class:* Geelvink Bay, Lakes Plain, Tariku, East. *Dialects:* Lexical similarity 69% with Obokuitai, 61% with Eritai, 60% with Kwerisa, 69% with Kai. *Other:* SOV; tonal. Sea level to 500 meters. Agriculturalists. Christian, traditional religion.

Bonerif (Beneraf) [bnv] 4 (1994 SIL). North coast area on east side of the upper Tor River, north of Mander and south of Berik and Kwesten languages, village of Beneraf. Jayapura Kabupaten, Pantai Timur Kecamatan. *Class:* Trans-New Guinea, Northern, Tor, Tor. *Lg Use:* 20% to 30% of the ethnic group speaks Bonerif. Used in the home. A few children speak Bonerif. Speakers intermarry with the Berik and use Berik as second language. *Other:* Christian, traditional religion. Nearly extinct.

Bonggo (Armopa, Bgu, Bogu, Bongo) [bpg] 600 (2000). Northeast coast east of Sarmi and west of Demta near Betaf; villages of Taronta, Tarawasi, Armopa. Jayapura Kabupaten, Bonggo Kecamatan. *Class:* Austronesian, Malayo-Polynesian, Central-Eastern, Eastern Malayo-Polynesian, Oceanic, Western Oceanic, North New Guinea, Sarmi-Jayapura Bay, Sarmi. *Other:* Coastal. Below 100 meters. Agriculturalists: sago; copra production. Christian, traditional religion.

Burate [bti] 100 (2000 Wurm). Near mouth of the Wapoga River, Yapen Waropen Kabupaten, Waropen Bawah Kecamatan, 1 village. *Class:* Geelvink Bay, East Geelvink Bay. *Dialects:* Lexical similarity 69% with Demisa, 75% with Tunggare. *Other:* Seminomadic. Hunter-gatherers; loggers. Traditional religion, Christian.

Burmeso (Taurap, Boromeso, Borumesso, Burumeso, Monau, Monao, Manau) [bzu] 250 (1998 Donohue). Burmeso village and isolated temporary houses along nearby rivers, mid-Mamberamo River between Trimuris and Sikari northeast of Danau Bira (Lake Holmes). Jayapura Kabupaten, Mamberamo Tengah Kecamatan. *Class:* Language Isolate. *Dialects:* Less than 5% lexical similarity with any other languages. *Lg Use:* Vigorous. Not spoken by outsiders. All domains. All ages. Positive language attitude. Many proficient in Indonesian, more than surrounding groups. Many understand nearby languages. *Lg Dev:* Dictionary. *Other:* 150 to 600 meters. Fishermen; hunters; sago horticulturalists; animal husbandry: chickens, ducks. Christian, traditional religion.

Burumakok [aip] 40 (1994 Kroneman). Lowlands area south of the main ranges, southeast of Sumo and Dekai, south of Langda and Bomela, Jayawijaya Kabupaten, Kurima Kecamatan, village of Burumakok, south of Sumtanon, east of Siradala. *Class:* Trans-New Guinea, Main Section, Central and Western, Central and South New Guinea-Kutubuan, Central and South New Guinea,

Ok, Western. *Lg Use:* All ages. *Other:* 350 to 3,000 meters. Agriculturalists. Nearly extinct.

Buruwai (Asienara, Asianara, Karufa, Madidwana, Sabakor) [asi] 1,000 (2000). South Bomberai Peninsula along the southwest part of Kamrau Bay, Fakfak Kabupaten, Kaimana Kecamatan; Yarona, Kuna, Esania, Marobia, Guriasa, Tairi, Hia, and Gaka villages. *Class:* Trans-New Guinea, Main Section, Central and Western, Central and South New Guinea-Kutubuan, Central and South New Guinea, Asmat-Kamoro. *Dialects:* Lexical similarity 60% with Kamberau. *Other:* Coastland. Below 100 meters. Fishermen; gatherers. Christian, traditional religion.

Busami [bsm] 700 (1993 Doriot). South and north coast, Serui Island near 136', villages of Kamanap, Masiaroti, Kaonda. Yapen Waropen Kabupaten, Yapen Barat and Yapen Selatan kecamatans. *Class:* Austronesian, Malayo-Polynesian, Central-Eastern, Eastern Malayo-Polynesian, South Halmahera-West New Guinea, West New Guinea, Cenderawasih Bay, Yapen, Central-Western. *Dialects:* 3 dialects. Lexical similarity 71% with Ansus, 63% with Serui-Laut. *Other:* Fishermen; agriculturalists. Traditional religion, Christian.

Citak (Cicak, Tjitak, Tjitjak, Kaunak, Asmat Darat) [txt] 8,000 (1985 M. Stringer TEAM). South coast area, west of the upper Digul River, north of Awyu, east of Asmat, Senggo, and north, 19 villages. Merauke Kabupaten, Citak-Mitak Kecamatan. *Class:* Trans-New Guinea, Main Section, Central and Western, Central and South New Guinea-Kutubuan, Central and South New Guinea, Asmat-Kamoro. *Dialects:* Senggo, Komasma, Bubis, Esaun, Pirabanak, Vakam, Tiau. Close to Asmat. *Lg Use:* Vigorous. Bilingual level estimates for Indonesian: 0 90%, 1 10%, 2 0%, 3 0%, 4 0%, 5 0%. *Lg Dev:* NT: 1995. *Other:* Agriculturalists. Christian, traditional religion.

Citak, Tamnim (Tamnim, Asmat Darat) [tml] 290 (1993 Doriot). Near Senggo, villages of Tamnim, Epem, Zinak, Wowi. Merauke Kabupaten, Citak-Mitak Kecamatan. *Class:* Trans-New Guinea, Main Section, Central and Western, Central and South New Guinea-Kutubuan, Central and South New Guinea, Asmat-Kamoro. *Dialects:* May be linguistically closer to Asmat, but the speakers want to be called Citak, not Asmat. *Lg Use:* Vigorous. *Other:* Christian, traditional religion.

Dabe (Mangambilis) [dbe] 200 (1993). Upper Tor River area, north coast east of Sarmi, village of Dabe. Jayapura Kabupaten, Pantai Timur Kecamatan. *Class:* Trans-New Guinea, Northern, Tor, Tor. *Other:* Coastal. Below 100 meters. Fishermen. Christian, traditional religion.

Damal (Uhunduni, Amung, Amung Kal, Amungme, Amuy, Enggipiloe, Hamung, Oehoendoeni) [uhn] 14,000 (1991 UBS and 2000 Wurm). Central highlands west of the Western Dani, east of Ekari, southeast of the source of the Kemandoga River, all around Puncak Jaya, northern and southern Carstens Mountains, Paniai Kabupaten, Ilaga and Beoga kecamatans. *Class:* Trans-New Guinea, Main Section, Central and Western, Wissel Lakes-Kemandoga, Uhunduni. *Dialects:* Damal, Amung, Amongme, Enggipilu. Related to Ekari, Moni, Wolani. *Lg Dev:* NT: 1988. *Other:* Tonal. Mountain slope. 100 to 5,000 meters. Agriculturalists. Christian.

Dani, Lower Grand Valley [dni] 20,000 (SIL 1996). Central highlands, Baliem Grand Valley, and upper gorge. *Class:* Trans-New Guinea, Main Section, Central and Western, Dani-Kwerba, Southern, Dani. *Dialects:* Lower Grand Valley Hitigima (Dani-Kurima, Kurima), Upper Bele, Lower Bele, Lower Kimbin (Kibin), Upper Pyramid. *Lg Dev:* NT: 1988–1994. *Other:* Mountain slope. Agriculturalists. Traditional religion, Christian.

Dani, Mid Grand Valley (Tulem, Central Grand Valley Dani, Baliem Valley Dani) [dnt] 50,000 (1990 UBS).

Baliem Valley. *Class:* Trans-New Guinea, Main Section, Central and Western, Dani-Kwerba, Southern, Dani. *Lg Dev:* NT: 1990. *Other:* Mountain slope. Agriculturalists: sweet potatoes; animal husbandry: pigs. Christian, traditional religion.

Dani, Upper Grand Valley [dna] 20,000 (1996). Central highlands, Baliem Grand Valley, and upper gorge. *Class:* Trans-New Guinea, Main Section, Central and Western, Dani-Kwerba, Southern, Dani. *Lg Dev:* NT: 1992. *Other:* Christian, traditional religion.

Dani, Western (Dani Barat, Ilaga Western Dani, Lani, Laany, Oeringoep, Timorini) [dnw] 180,000 (1993 census). Central highlands, west of Baliem Grand Valley, and east from upper Kemandoga Valley. *Class:* Trans-New Guinea, Main Section, Central and Western, Dani-Kwerba, Southern, Dani. *Dialects:* Western Dani of Pyramid, Western Dani of Bokondini. Many other dialects are not as distinct as those listed. Lexical similarity 65% with Obokuitai, 60% with Wano. *Lg Dev:* Literacy rate in second language: 10% semiliterate. NT: 1981. *Other:* Mountain slope. Agriculturalists. Christian, traditional religion.

Dao (Maniwo, "X-Ray") [daz] 250 (1991 SIL). West central highlands, Paniai Kabupaten, Napan Kecamatan, east of Cenderawasih Bay along the Dao River. *Class:* Trans-New Guinea, Main Section, Central and Western, Wissel Lakes-Kemandoga, Ekari-Wolani-Moni. *Dialects:* Lexical similarity 75% with Auye. *Lg Use:* Used in the home with family and friends. *Other:* Mountain slope. 350 to 5,000 meters. Agriculturalists; hunter-gatherers. Traditional religion.

Dem (Lem, Ndem) [dem] 1,000 (1987 SIL). Western highlands along upper Rouffaer River north of Damal, northeast of Western Dani. *Class:* Trans-New Guinea, Main Section, Central and Western, Dem. *Other:* Mountain slope. Agriculturalists. Christian, traditional religion.

Demisa [dei] 400 to 500 (2000 Wurm). First language in Desawa and Muyere villages along the coast in Waropen Bawah District and Botawa village in the interior along the Wonoi River. Reported to be the lingua franca of most of the eastern side of Cenderawasih Bay and of seminomadic people in interior Waropen Bawah. *Class:* Geelvink Bay, East Geelvink Bay. *Dialects:* Lexical similarity 69% with Burate, 64% with Kofei, 60% with Sauri, 65% with Tunggare, 64% with Woria. *Lg Use:* Used in the home and religious services. *Other:* Lowland. 100 to 900 meters. Agriculturalists; hunter-gatherers. Christian, traditional religion.

Demta (Muris) [dmy] 1,300 (2000). North coast west of Tanamerah Bay, villages of Demta, Muris Besar, Muris Kecil, Ambora, Yougafsa. *Class:* Trans-New Guinea, Main Section, Central and Western, Sentani. *Other:* Sea level to 600 meters. Fishermen; agriculturalists. Christian, traditional religion.

Dera (Kamberataro, Mangguar, Dra) [kbv] 1,000 in Indonesia (1987 SIL). Population total all countries: 1,687. Northeast Papua, south of Jayapura, near Waris; 13 villages. Also spoken in Papua New Guinea. *Class:* Trans-New Guinea, Senagi. *Other:* 350 to 500 meters. Agriculturalists. Christian, traditional religion.

Diuwe [diy] 100 (1999 SIL). 12 miles southwest of Sumo, east of the Catalina River. *Class:* Trans-New Guinea, Main Section, Central and Western, Central and South New Guinea-Kutubuan, Central and South New Guinea, Asmat-Kamoro. *Other:* Below 100 meters.

Doutai (Taori-So, Taori, Tolitai) [tds] 70 to 100 (2000 Wurm). Ethnic population: 335 (1993 R. Doriot UFM). Lakes Plain area at Toli-Dou village, west and south of Taiyeve. *Class:* Geelvink Bay, Lakes Plain, Tariku, East. *Other:* Riverine. Fishermen; hunter-gatherers. Christian, traditional religion.

Dubu [dmu] 110 (2000 Wurm). Border area south of Jayapura, south of Waris, east of Emumu, north of Towei languages, villages of Affi, Dobu, Yambe. *Class:* Trans-New Guinea, Pauwasi, Western. *Other:* 600 to 800 meters. Agriculturalists. Christian, traditional religion.

Duriankere (Esaro, Sailen, Duriankari) [dbn] 30 (2000 Wurm). On a small island in the Raja Ampat Islands in the strait between Salawati Island and the west end of Bird's Head. *Class:* Trans-New Guinea, South Bird's Head-Timor-Alor-Pantar, South Bird's Head, Inanwatan. *Lg Use:* 40% to 60% of the ethnic group speak Duriankere. Speakers are older adults. *Other:* Below 100 meters. Christian, traditional religion. Nearly extinct.

Dusner (Dusnir) [dsn] 20 (2000). Around the town of Dusner, west coast of Cenderawasih Bay, Wandamen Bay area. Only one village. *Class:* Austronesian, Malayo-Polynesian, Central-Eastern, Eastern Malayo-Polynesian, South Halmahera-West New Guinea, West New Guinea, Cenderawasih Bay, Biakic. *Other:* Traditional religion, Christian. Nearly extinct.

Duvle (Duvele, Wiri, Duvde, Duvre, Duve) [duv] 933 (2000 WCD). Lakes Plain area south of Van Daalen River and north of Mulia, Paniai. Eastern dialect along Dagai River, western dialect along Fedide and Wedi rivers. *Class:* Geelvink Bay, Lakes Plain, Tariku, Duvle. *Dialects:* Eastern Duvle, Western Duvle. Closest to Kaiy. Little difference between dialects. *Lg Use:* Vigorous. Wano is the trade language. *Other:* 150 to 2,300 meters. Christian, traditional religion.

Edopi (Elopi, Dou, Doufou, Dosobou, Turu, Iau, Yau, Foi, Ururi, Urundi) [dbf] 1,000 (1995 SIL). Around the juncture of the Tariku (Rouffaer) and Kliki (Fou) rivers. *Class:* Geelvink Bay, Lakes Plain, Tariku, Central. *Lg Dev:* Literacy rate in first language: below 5%. Literacy rate in second language: below 5%. Bible portions: 1997. *Other:* SOV; tonal. Riverine. Fishermen; hunter-gatherers. Christian, traditional religion.

Eipomek (Eipo, T-Valley) [eip] 3,000 (1987 SIL). Eastern highlands area, Eipo River, east of Nalca. *Class:* Trans-New Guinea, Mek, Eastern. *Dialects:* Lexical similarity 75% with Una. *Other:* 850 to 2,850 meters. Hunters; agriculturalists. Christian, traditional religion.

Ekari (Kapauku, Ekagi, Mee Mana, Tapiro, Me Mana) [ekg] 100,000 (1985 Doble). West central highlands, Paniai. *Class:* Trans-New Guinea, Main Section, Central and Western, Wissel Lakes-Kemandoga, Ekari-Wolani-Moni. *Dialects:* Simori, Yabi (Jabi), Mapiya-Kegata, Mee. Closest to Wolani. Slight dialect difference with Mapiya-Kegata. *Lg Use:* Bilingual level estimates for Indonesian: 0 10%, 1 40%, 2 20%, 3 15%, 4 10%, 5 5%. *Lg Dev:* NT: 1963–1985. *Other:* They call themselves 'Me'. The Moni call them 'Ekari'. 'Kapauku' is used for them by their southern neighbors. Mountain chains, valleys. Tropical forest, pine forest, savannah, swamps. 1,500 meters. Agriculturalists; government workers. Christian.

Elseng ("Morwap," Janggu, Djanggu, Tabu, Sawa) [mrf] 300 (1991 SIL). Jayapura Kabupaten, Arso, Abepura, Kemtuk Gresi, Senggi kecamatans, south of Jayapura, northeast of the Kaure. *Class:* Trans-New Guinea, Morwap. *Dialects:* Not closely related to any other language. *Lg Use:* Vigorous. Used in religious services. Reported minimal ability in Indonesian. *Other:* Almost no influence from outside. "Morwap" means 'what is that?' and is vigorously rejected by speakers and government officials. Mountain slope, valley. Lowland sago palm. 700 to 3,000 meters. Horticulturalists and gatherers: sago. Christian, traditional religion.

Emumu (Kiamerop, Imimkal) [enr] 1,100 (1987 SIL). Border area south of Jayapura, 11 villages. *Class:* Trans-New Guinea, Pauwasi, Eastern. *Other:* 600 to 1,350 meters. Agriculturalists. Christian, traditional religion.

Eritai (Editode Edai, Erai, Eri, Barua, Baburiwa, Babiruwa, Babruwa, Babrua, Aliki, Haya) [ert] 530 (2000 WCD). West of the Mamberamo River, Lakes Plain area in low mountains just south of Danau Bira (Lake Holmes), around the Kustera airstrip, to the villages of Erai to the east, Kustera, and Haya to the south. Jayapura Kabupaten, Mamberamo Tengah and Mamberamo Hulu kecamatans. *Class:* Geelvink Bay, Lakes Plain, Tariku, East. *Dialects:* The dialect in Obogwi village is close, but not the same. Also related to Kaiy, Doutai, Biritai. Lexical similarity 76% with Obokuitai, 50% with Sikaritai. *Lg Use:* Vigorous. Some at Kustera also use Bauzi, but not those in other villages. *Lg Dev:* Literacy rate in first language: 0% to 10%. *Other:* SOV; tonal. 150 to 800 meters. Hunter-gatherers. Christian, traditional religion.

Erokwanas [erw] 200 (2000 Wurm). Northwest coast of Bomberai Peninsula, north of Baham language. *Class:* Austronesian, Malayo-Polynesian, Central-Eastern, Eastern Malayo-Polynesian, South Halmahera-West New Guinea, West New Guinea, Bomberai. *Other:* Coastal. Traditional religion, Christian.

Fayu (Sehudate) [fau] 350 (2000 Wurm). West of juncture of Tariku (Rouffaer) and Kliki (Fou) rivers, west of the Kirikiri language. *Class:* Geelvink Bay, Lakes Plain, Tariku, West. *Other:* 4 nomadic groups. Lowland, riverine. 100 to 200 meters. Hunter-gatherers; fishermen. Traditional religion, Christian.

Foau (Doa) [flh] 232 (1975 SIL). Foa and Mudiay village, east Lakes Plain area just north of lower Idenburg River. *Class:* Geelvink Bay, Lakes Plain, East Lakes Plain. *Dialects:* Close to Taworta. *Other:* Swamp. 100 to 700 meters. Agriculturalists: sago, vegetables; hunters: pigs, crocodiles. Christian, traditional religion.

Gresi (Gresik, Klesi, Glesi) [grs] 2,500 (1987 SIL). West of Lake Sentani, southeast of Genyem, in villages of Hawa, Bring, Tabangkwari, Yansu, Ibub, Sunna, Klaysu. *Class:* Trans-New Guinea, Nimboran. *Dialects:* Lexical similarity 80% with Kemtuik. *Lg Use:* Speakers also use Indonesian. *Other:* Hunter-gatherers; agriculturalists. Traditional religion, Christian.

Hatam (Hattam, Atam, Tinam, Miriei, Moi, Adihup, Uran, Borai, Mansim) [had] 16,000 (1993 TEAM). Eastern Bird's Head, northeast of Manikion, south and southwest of Manokwari. Manokwari Kabupaten; Warmare, Ransiki, and Oransbari kecamatans. *Class:* West Papuan, Hattam. *Dialects:* Moi (Moire), Tinam, Miriei, Adihup, Uran. *Lg Dev:* NT: 1993. *Other:* Mountain slope. Christian, traditional religion.

Hupla (Soba) [hap] 3,000 (1982 WT). Central highlands area near east side of Baliem gorge. *Class:* Trans-New Guinea, Main Section, Central and Western, Dani-Kwerba, Southern, Dani. *Dialects:* Close to Lower Grand Valley Dani. *Lg Dev:* NT: 1994. *Other:* Christian, traditional religion.

Iau (Foi, Urundi, Ururi, Yau, Turu, Iaw) [tmu] 600 (2000 J. Bateman). 500 monolinguals. Ethnic population: 600 or more. Kabupaten Puncak Jaya, Faui, Lakes Plain area between Rouffaer and upper Van Daalen rivers, villages of Barere, Fawi, and Taiyai. Poi dialect on Rouffaer River, Turu dialect on Van Daalen River. *Class:* Geelvink Bay, Lakes Plain, Tariku, Central. *Dialects:* Foi, Turu, Iau. Close to Edopi. Distinct from Turu (Yawa). The varieties listed as dialects above may be separate languages. *Lg Use:* Vigorous. Speakers of other languages in the western Lakees Plains area speak basic Iau. All domains. All ages. Positive language attitude. Bilingual level estimates for Indonesian: 0 98%, 1 2%, 2 0%, 3 0%, 4 0%, 5 0%. Speakers school age to about 35 years know varying degrees of Indonesian. A few speak Duvle or Dani. *Lg Dev:* Literacy rate in first language: 5% to 15%. 200 or more can read and write it. Bible portions: 1985–

1993. *Other:* Riverine, mountain slope. Swamp. Agriculturalists; fishermen; hunter-gatherers. Christian.

Iha (Kapaur) [ihp] 5,500 (1987 SIL). Bomberai Peninsula, far west end around Fak Fak and north. *Class:* Trans-New Guinea, Main Section, Central and Western, West Bomberai, West Bomberai Proper. *Dialects:* Close to Baham. *Other:* Coastal. Below 100 meters. Fishermen; agriculturalists. Christian, traditional religion.

Iha Based Pidgin [ihb] Bomberai Peninsula, far west end around Fak Fak and north. *Class:* Pidgin, Iha based. *Lg Use:* Trade language. *Other:* Muslim, Christian. Second language only.

Irarutu (Irahutu, Irutu, Kasira, Arguni Bay, Kaitero) [irh] 4,000 (1987 SIL). East Bomberai Peninsula southwest from Arguni Bay north to Bintuni Bay, 44 villages. *Class:* Austronesian, Malayo-Polynesian, Central-Eastern, Eastern Malayo-Polynesian, South Halmahera-West New Guinea, South Halmahera. *Dialects:* 6 or 7 dialects. Lexical similarity 90% with Kuri. *Lg Use:* Used in the home and with friends. *Lg Dev:* Literacy rate in second language: 15% to 25%. Bible portions: 1992–2000. *Other:* Coastal, hills. Tropical forest, swamp. Fishermen; agriculturalists. Christian, Muslim.

Iresim (Beduba, Yerisiam) [ire] 70 (2000 Wurm). South Cenderawasih Bay, west of Nabire and around Yamur Lake. *Class:* Austronesian, Malayo-Polynesian, Central-Eastern, Eastern Malayo-Polynesian, South Halmahera-West New Guinea, West New Guinea, Cenderawasih Bay, Iresim. *Other:* Coastal. Sea level to 1,000 meters. Hunters; fishermen. Traditional religion, Christian.

Isirawa (Saweri, Saberi, Okwasar) [srl] 1,800 (2000 Wurm). Jayapura, north coast, around Sarmi and to the west, the villages of Mararena, Kamenawari, Amsira, Siaratesa, Perkami, Martewar, Arsania, Nisero, Arabais, Webro, Wari, Nuerawar, and Waim. *Class:* Trans-New Guinea, Main Section, Central and Western, Dani-Kwerba, Northern, Isirawa. *Dialects:* Western Isirawa, Eastern Isirawa. Close to Kwerba. The dialects are very close. *Lg Use:* Trade language. Vigorous. Bilingual level estimates for Indonesian: 0 0%, 1 30%, 2 40%, 3 30%, 4 0%, 5 0%. *Lg Dev:* Literacy rate in first language: 5% to 15%. NT: 2002. *Other:* Fishermen; agriculturalists. Christian, traditional religion.

Itik (Ittik, Betef, Ittik-Tor, Borto) [itx] 80 (2000 Wurm). North coast east of Tor River, along upper Biri River. *Class:* Trans-New Guinea, Northern, Tor, Tor. *Dialects:* Ittik, Ittik-Tor. *Lg Use:* 40% of the ethnic group speaks Itik. *Other:* Ethnic group: Borto. Fishermen. Christian, traditional religion.

Iwur (Iwoer) [iwo] 1,000 (1987 SIL). Border area in valley of Iwur River, Ok Iwur, and east to Ok Denom. *Class:* Trans-New Guinea, Main Section, Central and Western, Central and South New Guinea-Kutubuan, Central and South New Guinea, Ok, Lowland. *Other:* 400 to 4,000 meters. Hunters; agriculturalists. Christian, traditional religion.

Kaburi [uka] 600 (1986 SIL). Southern Bird's Head, east of Kemberano and Arandai languages, north of Kokoda and Fakfak, Manokwari Kabupaten, Merdei and Inanwatan kecamatans. *Class:* Trans-New Guinea, South Bird's Head-Timor-Alor-Pantar, South Bird's Head, South Bird's Head Proper, Western. *Lg Use:* Used in the home. *Other:* Below 100 meters. Sago-gatherers; hunters: crocodiles; oil company workers; fishermen. Christian, traditional religion.

Kais (Aiso, Atori, Mintamani, Kampung Baru) [kzm] 700 (1993 Doriot). South Bird's Head area inland along Kais River, 8 villages. *Class:* Trans-New Guinea, South Bird's Head-Timor-Alor-Pantar, South Bird's Head, South Bird's Head Proper, Western. *Other:* Below 100 meters. Sago-gatherers; fishermen. Christian, traditional religion.

Kaiy (Taori-Kaiy, Taori-Kei, Kai, Todi) [tcq] 220 (2000 Wurm). Lakes Plain area around airstrip of Kaiy on lower Rouffaer River, villages of Kaiy and Kokou. *Class:* Geelvink Bay, Lakes Plain, Tariku, East. *Dialects:* Lexical similarity 69% with Biritai. *Other:* 100 to 200 meters. Fishermen; gatherers. Christian, traditional religion.

Kalabra (Beraur) [kzz] 3,287 (2000 WCD). West Bird's Head, south of Madik language, east of Moi. *Class:* West Papuan, Bird's Head, West Bird's Head. *Dialects:* Closest to Tehit. Lexical similarity 60% with Tehit. *Lg Use:* Used in religious services. *Other:* Coastal. Below 100 meters. Fishermen. Christian, traditional religion.

Kamberau (Kamrau, Iria) [irx] 1,570 (1993 Doriot). Southeast Bomberai Peninsula around Kamrau Bay, villages of Ubia-Seramuku, Bahomia, Waho, Wamoma, Inari, Tanggaromi, Koi, Wamesa, Coa. *Class:* Trans-New Guinea, Main Section, Central and Western, Central and South New Guinea-Kutubuan, Central and South New Guinea, Asmat-Kamoro. *Dialects:* Close to Buruwai. Lexical similarity 60% with Buruwai. *Other:* Coastal. Sea level to 1,000 meters. Fishermen; hunters: crocodile; agriculturalists. Christian, traditional religion.

Kamoro (Kamora, Mimika, Lakahia, Nagramadu, Umari, Mukamuga, Neferipi, Nefarpi, Nafarpi, Kaokonau, Umar) [kgq] 8,000 (1987 SIL). South coast from Etna Bay to Mukamuga River. *Class:* Trans-New Guinea, Main Section, Central and Western, Central and South New Guinea-Kutubuan, Central and South New Guinea, Asmat-Kamoro. *Dialects:* Tarya, Yamur, Nanesa. 4 other dialects. *Lg Use:* Many becoming bilingual in Indonesian. *Other:* Different from Yeretuar (Umari). Island, coastal. Sea level to 2,600 meters. Fishermen; marketing; sago-processing; hunters. Christian, traditional religion.

Kanum, Bädi (Enkelembu, Knwne, Kenume) [khd] 10 (1996 Mark Donohue). South coast border area, east of Merauke, bordering Southeast Marind on the east: Yanggandur, Tomer, Tomerau, Sota, Kondo, Onggaya, north and west of Smärky language. *Class:* Trans-New Guinea, Trans-Fly-Bulaka River, Trans-Fly, Morehead and Upper Maro rivers, Tonda. *Dialects:* Intelligible to other Kanum variety speakers only with difficulty. Close to Yei. It has also been classified as Australian, Pama-Nyungan. *Lg Use:* Used in the home and in hunting camps. All ages. They use Moraori or Indonesian as trade languages, Indonesian for official purposes. *Lg Dev:* Literacy rate in second language: 5%. *Other:* One ethnic group with other Kanum varieties. Clan marriages common and much ritual exchange. Swamp. Below 100 meters. Fishermen; agriculturalists. Christian, traditional religion. Nearly extinct.

Kanum, Ngkâlmpw (Enkelembu, Knwne, Kenume) [kcd] 150 (1996 Mark Donohue). South coast border area, east of Merauke, bordering Southeast Marind on the east: Yanggandur, Tomer, Tomerau, Sota, Kondo, Onggaya to the north and west of Smärky language. *Class:* Trans-New Guinea, Trans-Fly-Bulaka River, Trans-Fly, Morehead and Upper Maro rivers, Tonda. *Dialects:* The Kanum varieties are separate languages, intelligible to each other's speakers only with difficulty. Close to Yei. It has also been classified as Australian, Pama-Nyungan. *Lg Use:* Used in the home and in hunting camps. All ages. They use Moraori or Indonesian as trade languages, Indonesian for official purposes. *Lg Dev:* Literacy rate in second language: 5%. *Other:* One ethnic group with the other Kanum varieties. Clan marriages common, and much ritual exchange. Swamp. Below 100 meters. Fishermen; agriculturalists. Christian.

Kanum, Smärky (Enkelembu, Knwne, Kenume) [kxq] 80 (1996 Mark Donohue). South coast border area, east of Merauke, bordering Southeast Marind on the east: Yanggandur, Tomer, Tomerau, Sota, Kondo, Onggaya,

bordering Papua New Guinea. *Class:* Trans-New Guinea, Trans-Fly-Bulaka River, Trans-Fly, Morehead and Upper Maro rivers, Tonda. *Dialects:* Intelligible to other speakers Kanum varieties only with difficulty. Close to Yei. It has also been classified as Australian, Pama-Nyungan. *Lg Use:* Used in the home and in hunting camps. All ages. Moraori or Indonesian are used as trade languages, Indonesian for official purposes. *Lg Dev:* Literacy rate in second language: 5%. *Other:* One ethnic group with other Kanum varieties. Clan marriages common, and much ritual exchange. Swamp. Below 100 meters. Fishermen; agriculturalists. Christian.

Kanum, Sota (Enkelembu, Knwne, Kenume) [krz] 100 (1996 Mark Donohue). South coast border area, east of Merauke, bordering Southeast Marind on the east: Yanggandur, Tomer, Tomerau, Sota, Kondo, Onggaya, north and west of Smärky language. *Class:* Trans-New Guinea, Trans-Fly-Bulaka River, Trans-Fly, Morehead and Upper Maro rivers, Tonda. *Dialects:* Intelligible to other Kanum variety speakers only with difficulty. Close to Yei. It has also been classified as Australian, Pama-Nyungan. *Lg Use:* Used in the home and in hunting camps. All ages. They use Moraori or Indonesian as trade languages, Indonesian for official purposes. *Lg Dev:* Literacy rate in second language: 5%. *Other:* One ethnic group with other Kanum varieties. Clan marriages common, and much ritual exchange. Not spoken in Papua New Guinea. Swamp. Below 100 meters. Fishermen; agriculturalists. Christian.

Kapori (Kapauri) [khp] 30 to 40 (2000 Wurm). Village of Pagai on north bank of upper Idenburg River. *Class:* Trans-New Guinea, Kaure. *Other:* 150 meters. Fishermen. Christian, traditional religion. Nearly extinct.

Karas [kgv] 100 (2000 Wurm). Karas Island, off southwest coast of Bomberai Peninsula, southeast from Fak Fak. *Class:* Trans-New Guinea, Main Section, Central and Western, West Bomberai, Karas. *Other:* Island. Sea level to 500 meters. Agriculturalists: spice; fishermen; copra production; lumbermen; oil workers. Christian, traditional religion.

Karon Dori (Maiyach, Meon, Mari) [kgw] 5,000 (1987 SIL). Central Bird's Head north of Brat, villages of Pef, Asses, Sunopi, Siakwa. *Class:* West Papuan, Bird's Head, North-Central Bird's Head, Central Bird's Head. *Dialects:* Close to Mai Brat. *Other:* Fishermen; agriculturalists: peanuts, onions, corn, taro, manioc, potatoes, greens, bananas, pineapples, citrus, papaya; animal husbandry: pigs. Christian, traditional religion.

Kaure (Kaureh) [bpp] 450 (1995 SIL). Southwest of Lake Sentani along Nawa River, in villages of Lereh, Harna, Wes, Masta, Aurina. *Class:* Trans-New Guinea, Kaure, Kaure Proper. *Lg Use:* Used in religious services. *Lg Dev:* Literacy rate in first language: 10%. Bible portions: 1990. *Other:* SOV. Hills. Swamp. 200 to 850 meters. Agriculturalists; hunter-gatherers. Christian, traditional religion.

Kauwera (Kauwerawec, Kauwerawetj, Kaowerawedj, Kawera, Kabera, Koassa, Tekutameso) [xau] 400 (1987 SIL). East of mid-Mamberamo, north and south of Kasonaweja. *Class:* Trans-New Guinea, Main Section, Central and Western, Dani-Kwerba, Northern, Kwerba. *Lg Use:* Vigorous. *Other:* Tropical forest. 100 to 400 meters. Hunters; horticulturalists; fishermen. Traditional religion, Christian.

Kawe [kgb] 600 (2001 Remijsen). West end of Waigeo Island off west coast of Bird's Head, Raja Ampat Islands, villages of Salio, Selepele, Bianci, Menyefun. *Class:* Austronesian, Malayo-Polynesian, Central-Eastern, Eastern Malayo-Polynesian, South Halmahera-West New Guinea, West New Guinea, Cenderawasih Bay, Raja Ampat. *Dialects:* Related to Maya, Maden, Palamul, Matbat.

Other: Coastal. Below 100 meters. Fishermen; agriculturalists. Traditional religion, Christian.

Kayagar (Kaygir, Kajagar, Kaygi, Wiyagar) [kyt] 10,000 (1993 WT). South coast near Pirimapun and Sawi, Merauke area. *Class:* Trans-New Guinea, Main Section, Central and Western, Kayagar. *Lg Use:* Used in religious services. *Lg Dev:* Literacy rate in second language: 10% semiliterate in Indonesian. *Other:* Swamp. Below 100 meters. Agriculturalists: garden and fruit trees; hunter-gatherers. Traditional religion, Christian.

Kayupulau (Kajupulau) [kzu] 50 (2000 Wurm). Ethnic population: 573 (1978 SIL). Villages of Kayubatu and Kayupulau in Jayapura harbor. *Class:* Austronesian, Malayo-Polynesian, Central-Eastern, Eastern Malayo-Polynesian, Oceanic, Western Oceanic, North New Guinea, Sarmi-Jayapura Bay, Jayapura Bay. *Dialects:* Not a dialect of Tobati (Yotafa). *Lg Use:* Under 10% of the ethnic group speaks Kayupulau. Declining in use. Speakers are adults. *Other:* Christian.

Keder [kdy] 180 (2000 Wurm). Ethnic population: 600 (1973 SIL). North coast east of Tor River mouth. *Class:* Trans-New Guinea, Northern, Tor, Tor. *Dialects:* Lexical similarity 45% with Berik. *Other:* Coastal. Below 100 meters. Fishermen. Christian, traditional religion.

Kehu [khh] 25 (2002 SIL). Area between Auye and Dao who live in the foothills, and the Wapoga River. *Class:* Unclassified. *Other:* Lowland. Swamp. 100 to 1,000 meters. Hunters; agriculturalists; fishermen. Nearly extinct.

Kemberano (Kalitami, Wariagar, Barau, Arandai) [bzp] 1,500 (1987 SIL). Southern Bird's Head along the coast, east of Komundan River, south of Arandai language. Several villages also northwest Bomberai Peninsula, south from Kalitami across Bintuni Bay. *Class:* Trans-New Guinea, South Bird's Head-Timor-Alor-Pantar, South Bird's Head, South Bird's Head Proper, Eastern. *Dialects:* Barau, Weriagar. Lexical similarity 85% with Arandai, 60% with Kokoda. *Other:* Coastal. Below 100 meters. Sago marketing. Christian, traditional religion.

Kembra [xkw] 20 (2000 Wurm). Jayawijaya Kabupaten, Okbibab Kecamatan, east of the Sogber River. *Class:* Unclassified. *Lg Use:* 20% to 60% of the ethnic group speaks Kembra. Used in the home. A few children speak Kembra. *Other:* Agriculturalists. Nearly extinct.

Kemtuik (Kemtuk, Kamtuk) [kmt] 2,500 (1987 SIL). West of Lake Sentani, villages of Mamdayawang, Meikari, Merem, Yanim, Braso, Aib, Sabransamon, Mamda, Sabeyap, Sabeyap Kecil, Sekorup, Aimbe, Sabron Yaru. East of Gresi language. *Class:* Trans-New Guinea, Nimboran. *Dialects:* Lexical similarity 80% between Kemtuik and Gresi. *Lg Use:* All ages. Speakers also use Indonesian. *Lg Dev:* Literacy rate in first language: 25% to 50%. Literacy rate in second language: 25% to 50%. Bible portions: 1980–1993. *Other:* Hunters; agriculturalists. Traditional religion, Christian.

Ketengban (Kupel, Oktengban) [xte] 9,968 (2000 WCD). Scattered slopes in eastern highlands area east of Eipomek and west of Ngalum language near Papua New Guinea border. *Class:* Trans-New Guinea, Mek, Eastern. *Dialects:* Okbap, Omban, Bime, Onya. Lexical similarity 69% with Una. *Lg Use:* All domains, church. *Lg Dev:* Literacy rate in first language: 30% to 40%. Dictionary. NT: 1997. *Other:* Tropical forest. 600 to 7,000 meters. Agriculturalists; some hunter-gatherers. Christian, traditional religion.

Ketum [ktt] 100 (2001 SIL). 99% monolinguals. Arimbit village, plus some in forest. *Class:* Trans-New Guinea, Main Section, Central and Western, Central and South New Guinea-Kutubuan, Central and South New Guinea, Awyu-Dumut, Unclassified. *Dialects:* Lexical similarity 49% with Wambon. *Lg Use:* Used in the home with family and friends.

Other: Foothills. 200 to 500 meters. Agriculturalists; hunters. Traditional religion, Christian.

Kimaama (Kimaghama, Kaladdarsch, Teri-Kalwasch) [kig] 3,000 (1987 SIL). Kolopom (Frederik Hendrik) Island west of southeast Papua. Ngolar II, village 10 km east of Marauke, is all Kimaama. *Class:* Trans-New Guinea, Kolopom. *Lg Use:* Used in the home. *Other:* Coastal. Swamp. Below 100 meters. Hunters; agriculturalists; fishermen. Christian, traditional religion.

Kimki (Aipki, Kimgi, Sukubatom, Sukubatong) [sbt] 350 (1978 UFM). Border area where Sepik River enters Papua. *Class:* Sepik-Ramu, Sepik, Biksi. *Other:* 200 to 500 meters. Fishermen; agriculturalists; hunters. Christian, traditional religion.

Kirikiri (Kirira) [kiy] 250 (1982 SIL). Most are monolingual. West of juncture of the Tariku (Rouffaer) and Kliki (Fou) rivers, villages at Dofu Wahuka, Paniai. *Class:* Geelvink Bay, Lakes Plain, Tariku, West. *Dialects:* Kirikiri, Faia. *Lg Use:* Vigorous. All ages. Most are functionally bilingual in Fayu or Edopi. No Indonesian spoken. 5% functional in Irian Malay. *Lg Dev:* Literacy rate in first language: below 5%. Literacy rate in second language: below 5%. Dictionary. *Other:* No schools in the area. SOV; tonal. Lowland swamp. Hunter-gatherers, sago. Traditional religion, Christian.

Kofei [kpi] 100 (2000 Wurm). East side of Geelvink Bay, recently moved to Sauri-Sirami village. There may be more living seminomadically in the interior. *Class:* Geelvink Bay, East Geelvink Bay. *Dialects:* Lexical similarity 67% with Barapasi, 64% with Demisa, 76% with Sauri, 63% with Woria. *Other:* 100 to 200 meters. Hunter-gatherers. Christian, traditional religion.

Kokoda (Samalek, Oderago, Komudago, Nebes, Tarof, Kasuweri) [xod] 3,700 (1991 SIL). Bird's Head, south coast on Maccluer Gulf, east of Inanwatan. *Class:* Trans-New Guinea, South Bird's Head-Timor-Alor-Pantar, South Bird's Head, South Bird's Head Proper, Central. *Dialects:* Kasuweri (Komudago), Negri Besar (Negeri Besar), Tarof. Wurm and Hattori 1981 list Kasuweri and Tarof as separate languages. Komudago and Tarof are closest. Lexical similarity 60% with Kemberano. Kasuweri lexical similarity 86% with Tarof, Negri Besar 82% with Tarof. *Lg Use:* Used in the home. *Other:* Coastal. Below 100 meters. Hunters; sago marketers; fishermen.

Kombai (Komboy) [tyn] 4,000 (1991 SIL). South coast area east of Senggo around Boma. *Class:* Trans-New Guinea, Main Section, Central and Western, Central and South New Guinea-Kutubuan, Central and South New Guinea, Awyu-Dumut, Dumut. *Dialects:* Central Kombai, Tayan. Close to Wambon, Mandobo Atas, Mandobo Bawah, Wanggom. *Other:* Lowland. Below 100 meters. Agriculturalists; hunters; lumbermen. Christian, traditional religion.

Komyandaret [kzv] 300 (2000 SIL). East of Korowai and north of Tsaukambo, Wanggom language areas. *Class:* Trans-New Guinea, Main Section, Central and Western, Central and South New Guinea-Kutubuan, Unclassified. *Other:* Lowland. 100 to 200 meters. Agriculturalists; lumbermen. Traditional religion.

Konda (Ogit, Yabin-Konda, Yabin) [knd] 500 (1988 SIL). Southwest Bird's Head along lower Waromge River south of Teminabuan, villages of Konda and Teminabuan District. *Class:* Trans-New Guinea, South Bird's Head-Timor-Alor-Pantar, South Bird's Head, Konda-Yahadian. *Dialects:* Lexical similarity 61% with Yahadian. *Other:* Coastal. Below 100 meters. Christian, traditional religion.

Koneraw (Konorau) [kdw] 200 (2000 Wurm). South coast of Frederik Hendrik Island. *Class:* Trans-New Guinea, Main Section, Central and Western, Central and South New Guinea-Kutubuan, Central and South New Guinea, Mombum. *Other:* Coastal. Swamp. Below 100 meters.

Agriculturalists; hunters; fishermen. Christian, traditional religion.

Kopkaka (Kopka) [opk] 400 (2002 SIL). Lowlands area south of the main ranges, southeast of Sumo and Dekai, south of Langda and Bomela, Jayawijaya Kabupaten, Kurima Kecamatan, villages of Siradala and Burungmakok. *Class:* Trans-New Guinea, Main Section, Central and Western, Central and South New Guinea-Kutubuan, Central and South New Guinea, Ok, Western. *Dialects:* Marub, Tokuni. Close to Kwer. *Lg Use:* No bilingual speakers. *Other:* 350 to 1,800 meters. Agriculturalists; hunters. Christian, traditional religion.

Korowai (Kolufaup) [khe] 700 (1998 M. Donohue). South coast area, north of Boma, east of Senggo. *Class:* Trans-New Guinea, Main Section, Central and Western, Central and South New Guinea-Kutubuan, Central and South New Guinea, Awyu-Dumut, Unclassified. *Lg Use:* Used in the home. Younger speakers use Indonesian as second language. *Other:* Lowland swamp. Below 100 meters. Christian, traditional religion.

Korowai, North [krg] 100 (1998 M. Donohue). North of Korowai area, southeast of Siradala, west of Awimbon. *Class:* Trans-New Guinea, Main Section, Central and Western, Central and South New Guinea-Kutubuan, Central and South New Guinea, Awyu-Dumut, Unclassified. *Other:* 300 to 1,000 meters.

Korupun-Sela (Korapun, Kimyal of Korupun) [kpq] 8,000 (1996 E. Young). Eastern highlands on upper reaches of Erok River, southwest of Nalca, east of Yali of Ninia, Jayawijaya District, Kurima Region. *Class:* Trans-New Guinea, Mek, Western. *Dialects:* Korupun (Duram), Dagi, Sisibna (Gobugdua), Deibula, Sela. Related to Nalca. Lexical similarity 60% to Nipsan. *Lg Use:* Used in religious services. Bilingual level estimates for Nipsan: 0 98%, 1 0%, 2 0%, 3 0%, 4 1.5%, 5 .5%. *Lg Dev:* Bible portions: 1980–1985. *Other:* 600 to 5,000 meters. Agriculturalists. Traditional religion, Christian.

Kosadle (Kosare) [kiq] 250 (1993 Doriot). Hulu Atas just west of juncture of Nawa and Idenburg rivers. *Class:* Trans-New Guinea, Kaure, Kaure Proper. *Other:* 200 to 500 meters. Agriculturalists; hunters. Christian, traditional religion.

Kowiai (Koiwai, Kaiwai, Kuiwai, Aiduma, Kayumerah, Kajumerah, Adi, Namatota, Namatote) [kwh] 600 (2000 SIL). Bomberai Peninsula; southwest coast at Kaimana and in Kamrau Bay on several islands, villages of Keroi, Adijaya, Namatota, Waikala, Kayumerah. *Class:* Austronesian, Malayo-Polynesian, Central-Eastern, Central Malayo-Polynesian, South Bomberai. *Dialects:* Keroi, Adijaya, Namatota, Waikala. Blust says this is Central Malayo-Polynesian. *Lg Use:* 70% are speakers. The language is passed on to 60% of the children. Most domains. Positive language attitude. Bilingual level estimates for Indonesian: 0 0%, 1 0%, 2 60%, 3 34%, 4 5%, 5 1%; Papuan Malay: 0 0%, 1 0%, 2 1%, 3 99%, 4 0%, 5 0%. *Other:* Mountain slope, coral islands. Tropical forest. Sea level to 200 meters. Fishermen; some hunters; nutmeg sales; shell divers; collectors. Muslim, Christian.

Kuri (Modan, Nabi) [nbn] 500 (1982 SIL). Southwest Bomberai Peninsula, along Nabi (Kuri) River west from Wandamen Bay, 16 villages. *Class:* Austronesian, Malayo-Polynesian, Central-Eastern, Unclassified. *Dialects:* Close to Irarutu. Lexical similarity 90% with Irarutu. *Lg Use:* Used in the home. *Other:* 'Nabi' is a name used by outsiders, 'Kuri' by insiders. Sea level to 1,100 meters. Traditional religion, Christian.

Kurudu [kjr] 2,180 (1993 Doriot). Kurudu Island between eastern tip of Serui Island and mainland of Papua to east, villages of Kaipuri, Poiwai. *Class:* Austronesian, Malayo-Polynesian, Central-Eastern, Eastern Malayo-Polynesian, South Halmahera-West New Guinea, West New Guinea,

Cenderawasih Bay, Yapen, East. *Dialects:* Kaipuri dialect has highest lexical similarity with Yapen group. Lexical similarity 71% with Wabo, 46% with Western Serui. *Lg Use:* Vigorous. Used in religious services. *Other:* Island. Below 100 meters. Fishermen. Christian.

Kwer [kwr] 100 (1998 M. Donohue). Lowlands area south of the main ranges, southeast of Sumo and Dekai, south of Langda and Bomela, Jayawijaya Kabupaten, Kurima Kecamatan, village of Kwer. *Class:* Trans-New Guinea, Main Section, Central and Western, Central and South New Guinea-Kutubuan, Central and South New Guinea, Ok, Western. *Dialects:* Close to Kopkaka. *Lg Use:* All ages. *Other:* 100 to 200 meters. Agriculturalists; hunters.

Kwerba (Airmati, Naibedj, Tekutameso, Armati, Matawega, Segar Tor, Serikenam, Koassa) [kwe] 2,500 (1996 SIL). Upper Tor River area, northeast, headwaters of Apauwer River inland from Sarmi east to Berik language, villages of Aurime, Munukania, Wamariri, Tatsewalem around Apiaweti. *Class:* Trans-New Guinea, Main Section, Central and Western, Dani-Kwerba, Northern, Kwerba. *Dialects:* Serikenam, Sasawa, Nogukwabai. Lexical similarity 64% with Bagusa. *Lg Dev:* Literacy rate in first language: below 5%. Bible portions: 1986–1991. *Other:* Tropical forest. Hunter-gatherers; some agriculturalists. Traditional religion, Christian.

Kwerba Mamberamo (Nopukw, Nopuk, Nobuk, Napok, Tatsewalem, Nogukwabai) [xwr] 300 (1993 Doriot). East of Mamberamo River, in the mountains between the villages of Kwerba, Edifalen, and Marinafalen, south of Kasonaweja. *Class:* Trans-New Guinea, Main Section, Central and Western, Dani-Kwerba, Northern, Kwerba. *Lg Use:* Vigorous. All ages. *Other:* 'Nopukw' means 'language' in the Kwerba family, and does not distinguish a particular variety. Mountain slope. Tropical forest. 150 to 1,600 meters. Hunter-gatherers; fishermen. Traditional religion, Christian.

Kwerisa (Taogwe) [kkb] 15 to 50 (2000 Wurm). At village of Kaiy on lower Rouffaer River. *Class:* Geelvink Bay, Lakes Plain, Tariku, East. *Dialects:* Lexical similarity 60% with Biritai. *Lg Use:* About 20% to 30% of the ethnic group speaks Kwerisa. Used in the home. There may be a few older adult speakers (1987). Most or all now speak Kaiy. *Other:* Fishermen; hunters. Traditional religion, Christian. Nearly extinct.

Kwesten [kwt] 2,000 (1987 SIL). Lower Tor River, north coast area inland east of Sarmi, villages of Holmhaven, Mafenter, Arare, Omte. *Class:* Trans-New Guinea, Northern, Tor, Tor. *Dialects:* Lexical similarity 40% with Berik. *Other:* Sea level to 500 meters. Agriculturalists; copra production; pitsawing. Christian, traditional religion.

Legenyem (Laganyan) [lcc] 250 (2000 Wurm). Raja Ampat Islands, Waigeo Island in northwest end of main bay and on south coast, villages of Beo, Lempintol, and Wawiai. *Class:* Austronesian, Malayo-Polynesian, Central-Eastern, Eastern Malayo-Polynesian, South Halmahera-West New Guinea, West New Guinea, Cenderawasih Bay, Raja Ampat. *Other:* Sea level to 500 meters. Fishermen; agriculturalists. Muslim, traditional religion, Christian.

Lepki [lpe] 530 (1991 SIL). Jayawijaya Kabupaten, Okbibab Kecamatan, on the Sogber River, east and north of the Ketengban. *Class:* Unclassified. *Lg Use:* Used in the home, religious services, and market. Some speakers at Luban have some ability in Ketengban. *Other:* SOV; head and dependent marking; tonal. Hills, plains. Tropical forest. 200 to 1,200 meters. Hunter-gatherers; agriculturalists. Traditional religion, Christian.

Liki (Moar) [lio] 100 (1998 M. Donohue). Islands off north coast of Sarmi, Jayapura Kabupaten, Sarmi Kecamatan. *Class:* Austronesian, Malayo-Polynesian, Central-Eastern,

Eastern Malayo-Polynesian, Oceanic, Western Oceanic, North New Guinea, Sarmi-Jayapura Bay, Sarmi. *Lg Use:* Used in church by local leaders. *Other:* Reported to be the same as Sobei. Sea level to 200 meters. Fishermen.

Maden (Sapran, Saparan, Palamul) [xmx] 600 (2001 Remijsen). Raja Ampat Islands, western Salawati Island. *Class:* Austronesian, Malayo-Polynesian, Central-Eastern, Eastern Malayo-Polynesian, South Halmahera-West New Guinea, West New Guinea, Cenderawasih Bay, Raja Ampat. *Dialect:* Kawait. *Other:* Possibly the same as Maya. Island. Below 100 meters. Christian, traditional religion.

Mai Brat (Ayamaru, Ajamaru, Brat, Maibrat, Mey Brat, Atinjo, Majbrat, Maite) [ayz] 20,000 (1987 SIL). Central Bird's Head around Ayamaru Lakes, about 40 villages. *Class:* West Papuan, Bird's Head, North-Central Bird's Head, Central Bird's Head. *Dialects:* Maisawiet, Maiyah, Maimaka, Maite, Maisefa. Lexical similarity 10% with Tehit, Mpur, Abun, its closest neighbors. *Lg Use:* Used in religious services. All ages. 5,000 to 7,000 are in cities and are very bilingual, some highly educated. *Lg Dev:* Literacy rate in first language: 25% to 50%. Literacy rate in second language: 25% to 50%. Bible portions: 1990–2000. *Other:* 'Ayamaru' is name of the people. SVO; heavy verb serialization. Traditional religion, Christian.

Mairasi (Faranyao, Kaniran) [zrs] 3,300 (1996 SIL). Bomberai Peninsula, southwest coast of neck, east and northeast from Kaimana, Wasior, Triton Bay. *Class:* Trans-New Guinea, Main Section, Central and Western, Mairasi-Tanahmerah, Mairasi. *Dialect:* Northeastern Mairasi. Close to Semimi. Northeastern Mairasi may be a separate language. Lexical similarity 69% with Semimi, 61% with Mer. *Lg Use:* Bilingual level estimates for Indonesian: 0 5%, 1 20%, 2 30%, 3 20%, 4 23%, 5 2%. Some also speak Kowiai. *Lg Dev:* Literacy rate in second language: 15% to 25%. Bible portions: 1986–1999. *Other:* Hunters; agriculturalists. Christian, traditional religion.

Maklew (Makleu) [mgf] 120. South coast area, east side of Marianne strait, west of Marind and east of Yelmek languages. *Class:* Trans-New Guinea, Trans-Fly-Bulaka River, Bulaka River. *Lg Use:* Used in the home, friends. *Other:* Swamp. Below 100 meters. Fishermen; agriculturalists. Christian, traditional religion.

Mander [mqr] 20 (1991 SIL). North coast area on the upper Bu River, a tributary of the Upper Tor River. *Class:* Trans-New Guinea, Northern, Tor, Tor. *Lg Use:* Used in the home. No children speak Mander. Speakers intermarry with the Berik and speak Berik as second language. *Other:* Nomadic. Fishermen; agriculturalists. Christian, traditional religion. Nearly extinct.

Mandobo Atas (Nub, Dumut, "Kaeti," Kwem, Mandobbo, Kambon, Wambon) [aax] 1,000 (2002 SIL). Border area near Fly River on east side of Digul River between Tanahmerah and Mindiptanah. *Class:* Trans-New Guinea, Main Section, Central and Western, Central and South New Guinea-Kutubuan, Central and South New Guinea, Awyu-Dumut, Dumut. *Other:* "Kaeti" is considered derogatory. Swamp. Below 100 meters. Agriculturalists. Christian, traditional religion.

Mandobo Bawah (Nub, Dumut, "Kaeti," Mandobbo, Kambon) [bwp] 2,000 (2002 SIL). Border area near Fly River on east side of Digul River between Tanahmerah and Mindiptanah, villages of Getentiri, Anggai, Butiptiri, Subur, Aiwat, Kaisah. *Class:* Trans-New Guinea, Main Section, Central and Western, Central and South New Guinea-Kutubuan, Central and South New Guinea, Awyu-Dumut, Dumut. *Other:* "Kaeti" is an offensive name. Lowland. Below 100 meters. Agriculturalists. Christian, traditional religion.

Manem (Yeti, Jeti, Wembi, Skofro) [jet] 400 in Indonesia (1978 SIL). Northeast border area south of Jayapura, villages of Wembi, Yeti, Kiba. *Lg Use:* Speakers also use

Indonesian. *Lg Dev:* Literacy rate in second language: Significant level. *Other:* 200 to 300 meters. Agriculturalists; hunters. Christian, traditional religion. See main entry under Papua New Guinea.

Manikion (Mantion, Sougb, Sogh) [mnx] 12,000 (1987 SIL). East Bird's Head, east of Meyah, south of Manokwari, about 50 villages. *Class:* East Bird's Head. *Dialects:* 4 dialects. *Lg Dev:* NT: 1997. *Other:* Fishermen; agriculturalists. Christian, traditional religion.

Mapia (Mapian) [mpy] 1. Mapia Islands, about 180 miles north of Manokwari. *Class:* Austronesian, Malayo-Polynesian, Central-Eastern, Eastern Malayo-Polynesian, Oceanic, Central-Eastern Oceanic, Remote Oceanic, Micronesian, Micronesian Proper, Ponapeic-Trukic, Trukic. *Lg Use:* Ethnic group went to Micronesia and presumably speak a language from there, probably either Palauan, Sonsorol, or Tobian. Speaker is older adult. *Other:* Traditional religion, Christian. Nearly extinct.

Marau [mvr] 1,700 (1987 SIL). South coast of Serui Island, 5 villages. *Class:* Austronesian, Malayo-Polynesian, Central-Eastern, Eastern Malayo-Polynesian, South Halmahera-West New Guinea, West New Guinea, Cenderawasih Bay, Yapen, Central-Western. *Dialect:* Warabori (Natabui, Warembori). Lexical similarity 82% with Pom, Munggui, Papuma, Ansus. *Other:* Island, coastal. Sea level to 350 meters. Fishermen; agriculturalists. Christian.

Maremgi (Marengge) [mrx] 40 (2000 Wurm). North coast inland from Bonggo language, village of Marengge. *Class:* Trans-New Guinea, Northern, Tor, Tor. *Dialects:* Unintelligible to speakers in neighboring settlements including Bonggo. *Lg Use:* 20% to 40% of the ethnic group speaks Maremgi. Used in the home. A few children speak Maremgi. *Other:* Coastal. Below 100 meters. Fishermen. Christian, traditional religion. Nearly extinct.

Marind (Southeast Marind, Holifoersch, Tugeri, Gawir) [mrz] 7,000 (1987 SIL). South coast around Merauke, 2 villages. *Class:* Trans-New Guinea, Main Section, Central and Western, Marind, Marind Proper. *Dialects:* Gawir, Southeast Marind, Tugeri, Halifoersch. 4 or more dialects. Significant differences between inland and coastal dialects, but speakers report intelligibility. *Lg Use:* Vigorous. Used in the home and market. Children in towns have passive ability. Positive language attitude. *Lg Dev:* Dictionary. Grammar. Bible portions. *Other:* Seasonal savannah, swamp. Below 100 meters. Hunters (sellers of game), agriculturalists; gatherers, lumbermen. Christian, traditional religion.

Marind, Bian (Boven-Mbian, Bian, Northwest Marind) [bpv] 2,900 (2002 Sohn, Myo-sook). Bian River area near Merauke, Merauke Kabupaten, Muting Kecamatan, and Sanayu village on Maro River. *Class:* Trans-New Guinea, Main Section, Central and Western, Marind, Marind Proper. *Dialects:* Not inherently intelligible with Marind. *Lg Use:* Used in the home. *Other:* Swamp. Sea level to 100 meters. Hunters: deer, pig; fishermen; agriculturalists: coconut-sago planting. Traditional religion, Christian.

Masimasi [ism] 200 (1973 SIL). Island off north coast east of the Tor River mouth, Jayapura Kabupaten, Pantai Timur Kecamatan. *Class:* Austronesian, Malayo-Polynesian, Central-Eastern, Eastern Malayo-Polynesian, Oceanic, Western Oceanic, North New Guinea, Sarmi-Jayapura Bay, Sarmi. *Other:* Island, coastal. Below 100 meters. Fishermen. Christian, traditional religion.

Massep (Masep, Wotaf, Potafa) [mvs] 25 (2000 Wurm). North coast east of Mamberamo River mouth and west of Sarmi, near Apauwer River. *Class:* Trans-New Guinea, Main Section, Central and Western, Dani-Kwerba, Northern, Massep. *Lg Use:* 30% or less of the ethnic group speaks Massep. Used in the home and religious services. *Other:* Below 100 meters. Fishermen;

agriculturalists. Christian, traditional religion. Nearly extinct.

Matbat (Me) [xmt] 1,250 (2001 Remijsen). Raja Ampat Islands, Misool Island, Segaf Islands. *Class:* Austronesian, Malayo-Polynesian, Central-Eastern, Eastern Malayo-Polynesian, South Halmahera-West New Guinea, West New Guinea, Cenderawasih Bay, Raja Ampat. *Other:* Tonal, 5 tones. Island. Sea level to 300 meters. Fishermen; agriculturalists. Traditional religion, Christian.

Mawes [mgk] 693 (1975 SIL). Northeast coast east of Sarmi near mouth of Wirowai River, villages of Mawes, Mawesweres, Mawesdai. *Class:* Trans-New Guinea, Northern, Tor, Mawes. *Other:* Coastal. Below 100 meters. Fishermen. Christian, traditional religion.

Ma'ya (Salawati, Samate, Sailolof) [slz] 4,000 (2001 Remijsen). Raja Ampat Islands, central Waigeo Island and central Salawati Island. *Class:* Austronesian, Malayo-Polynesian, Central-Eastern, Eastern Malayo-Polynesian, South Halmahera-West New Guinea, West New Guinea, Cenderawasih Bay, Raja Ampat. *Dialects:* Ma'ya, Banlol, Batanta Island. *Other:* Fishermen; agriculturalists. Christian, traditional religion.

Mekwei (Menggei, Munggai, Mungge, Demenggong-Waibron-Bano, Menggwei, Munkei, Mooi, Moi, Waipu) [msf] 1,200 (1987 SIL). West of Lake Sentani, villages of Maribu, Waibrong, Kendate, Sabron Dosay. *Class:* Trans-New Guinea, Nimboran. *Dialects:* Lexical similarity 60% with Kemtuik. *Lg Use:* Speakers also use Indonesian. *Other:* Different from Moi (Mosana). 100 to 500 meters. Agriculturalists; hunters. Christian, traditional religion.

Meoswar (War) [mvx] 250 (1993 Doriot). Meoswar Island, west Cenderawasih Bay. *Class:* Austronesian, Malayo-Polynesian, Central-Eastern, Eastern Malayo-Polynesian, South Halmahera-West New Guinea, West New Guinea, Cenderawasih Bay, Biakic. *Other:* Island. Sea level to 500 meters. Traditional religion, Christian.

Mer (Muri, Miere) [mnu] 85 (2000 WCD). Central Bird's Head, headwaters of Wosimi and Uremo rivers. *Class:* Trans-New Guinea, Main Section, Central and Western, Mairasi-Tanahmerah, Mairasi. *Dialects:* Lexical similarity 63% with Semimi, 61% with Mairasi. *Other:* Hunters; agriculturalists. Christian, traditional religion.

Meyah (Meax, Meyach, Meah, Mejah, Mejach, Arfak, Mansibaber) [mej] 14,783 (2000 WCD). East Bird's Head, north coast, west of Manokwari, north of Hattam language, and scattered locations. *Class:* East Bird's Head, Meax. *Dialects:* Closest to Manikion. *Lg Use:* Many are becoming bilingual in Indonesian. *Lg Dev:* Literacy rate in first language: 25% to 50%. Literacy rate in second language: 25% to 50%. NT: 1997. *Other:* Hunters; agriculturalists. Christian, traditional religion.

Mlap (Kwansu, Kwansu-Bonggrang, Kuangsu-Bonggrang, Kwangsu-Bonggrang) [kja] 300 (2000 Wurm). West of Lake Sentani, just north of Gresi language. *Class:* Trans-New Guinea, Nimboran. *Dialects:* Lexical similarity 60% with Kemtuik. *Lg Use:* Most speakers use Indonesian as second language. Many or most speak or understand Kemtuik. There is a lot of intermarriage with Kemtuik speakers. *Other:* 'Kwansu' is an obsolete village name. Agriculturalists; hunters. Christian, traditional religion.

Moi (Mosana, Mooi, Mekwei) [mxn] 4,600 (1993 Doriot). Salawati Island, west Bird's Head around Sorong, 9 villages. *Class:* West Papuan, Bird's Head, West Bird's Head. *Other:* Different from Mekwei (Moi). Coastal. Below 100 meters. Fishermen; agriculturalists; traders; lumbermen; collect Lawan tree oil; sell pigs, casuari, tree kangeroo. Christian, traditional religion.

Molof (Ampas) [msl] 200 (1978 SIL). South of Jayapura, west of Waris. *Class:* Trans-New Guinea, Molof. *Dialects:* Not closely related to any other language. *Other:* Agriculturalists. Christian, traditional religion.

Mombum (Kemelom, Kemelomsch, Komolom) [mso] 250 (1993 Doriot). Island next to southeast coast of Fredrik Hendrik Island. *Class:* Trans-New Guinea, Main Section, Central and Western, Central and South New Guinea-Kutubuan, Central and South New Guinea, Mombum. *Dialects:* Closest to Koneraw. *Other:* Swamp. Sea level to 100 meters. Fishermen. Christian, traditional religion.

Momina [mmb] 200 (1998 M. Donohue). Lowlands just south of main ranges extending from south of Silimo east to south of Una language, Samboka village. *Class:* Trans-New Guinea, Main Section, Central and Western, Central and South New Guinea-Kutubuan, Central and South New Guinea, Momuna. *Other:* 350 to 1,900 meters. Hunters; agriculturalists; fishermen.

Momuna (Somahai, Somage, Sumohai) [mqf] 2,000 (2000 Wurm). 2,000 monolinguals. Lowlands just south of main ranges extending from south of Silimo east to south of Una language. *Class:* Trans-New Guinea, Main Section, Central and Western, Central and South New Guinea-Kutubuan, Central and South New Guinea, Momuna. *Lg Dev:* Literacy rate in first language: 5% to 15%. Bible portions: 1985–1987. *Other:* They have contact with Dani who are learning Momuna. Christian, traditional religion.

Moni (Migani, Djonggunu, Jonggunu) [mnz] 20,000 (1991 SIL). Central highlands, 10 to 70 miles northeast of Lake Paniai. *Class:* Trans-New Guinea, Main Section, Central and Western, Wissel Lakes-Kemandoga, Ekari-Wolani-Moni. *Dialect:* Awembak (Awembiak). *Lg Dev:* NT: 1990. *Other:* Mountain slope. Agriculturalists. Traditional religion, Christian.

Mor (Austronesian Mor) [mhz] 700 (1987 SIL). Mor Islands in east Cenderawasih Bay near Nabire. *Class:* Austronesian, Malayo-Polynesian, Central-Eastern, Eastern Malayo-Polynesian, South Halmahera-West New Guinea, West New Guinea, Cenderawasih Bay, Mor. *Other:* Different from Trans-New Guinea Mor. Tonal. Island, coastal. Below 100 meters. Fishermen; agriculturalists. Traditional religion, Christian.

Mor (Mor2) [moq] 20 to 30 (2000 Wurm). Northwest Bomberai Peninsula, coast of Bintuni Bay. *Class:* Trans-New Guinea, Main Section, Central and Western, Mor. *Lg Use:* Used in the home. Few or no children speak Mor. *Other:* Distinct from Austronesian Mor. Christian, traditional religion. Nearly extinct.

Moraid [msg] 1,000 (1988 SIL). West Bird's Head, east of Moi and south of Madik languages, villages of Sailala, Makbon, Luwelala, Seni. *Class:* West Papuan, Bird's Head, West Bird's Head. *Lg Use:* Used in religious services. *Other:* 1 to 500 meters. Agriculturalists; hunters; lawan tree oil marketers. Christian, traditional religion.

Morori (Moraori, Moaraeri, Morari, Marori) [mok] 50 (1998 M. Donohue). Ethnic population: 250 (1998 M. Donohue). South coast border area 20 km east of Merauke, east of Marind, west of Kanum. *Class:* Trans-New Guinea, Trans-Fly-Bulaka River, Trans-Fly, Moraori. *Dialects:* Menge dialect remembered as the language of ceremony, though the last Menge speaker died in 1997. *Lg Use:* Speakers are older adults. All use Papuan Malay or Indonesian as second language. Many proficient in Marind. *Other:* Coastal. Rainforest, swamp. Below 100 meters. Fishermen; gatherers. Christian, traditional religion.

Moskona (Sabena, Meninggo, Meningo, Meyah) [mtj] 8,000 (1996 SIL). Southeast Bird's Head, south of Meyah and west of Manikion. *Class:* East Bird's Head, Meax. *Dialects:* Lexical similarity 85% with Meyah. Also related to Manikion. *Lg Dev:* NT: 2001. *Other:* Christian, traditional religion.

Mpur (Kebar, Amberbaken, Ekware, Dekwambre) [akc] 7,000 (1993). North coast of Bird's Head, west of

Manokwari, and Kebar Valley. *Class:* West Papuan, Kebar. *Dialects:* Sirir, Ajiw. *Lg Dev:* Literacy rate in second language: 15% to 25%. Bible portions: 1998. *Other:* Agriculturalists; hunters; animal husbandry: pigs. Christian, traditional religion.

Munggui (Natabui) [mth] 800 (1982 SIL). North coast of Serui Island near 135.50', villages of Munggui, Windesi, Murui, Asei Puramati. *Class:* Austronesian, Malayo-Polynesian, Central-Eastern, Eastern Malayo-Polynesian, South Halmahera-West New Guinea, West New Guinea, Cenderawasih Bay, Yapen, Central-Western. *Dialects:* Lexical similarity 82% with Marau, Papuma. *Other:* Island, coastal. Sea level to 500 meters. Fishermen; agriculturalists. Traditional religion, Christian.

Murkim [rmh] Jayawijaya Kabupaten, Kiwirok Kecamatan, border area around the Mot airstrip, near the headwaters of the Sepik River. *Class:* Unclassified. *Other:* 350 to 600 meters. Agriculturalists.

Muyu, North (Yongom, Yonggom, Yongkom, North Kati, North Moejoe, Niinati, Ninatie, Kati-Ninanti, Kataut) [kti] 8,000 (2002 SIL). South coast border area just north of where Fly River forms border between Papua, Indonesia, and Papua New Guinea. *Class:* Trans-New Guinea, Main Section, Central and Western, Central and South New Guinea-Kutubuan, Central and South New Guinea, Ok, Lowland. *Dialect:* Kanggewot, Toemoetoe (Are).

Muyu, South (Yongom, Yonggom, Yongkom, South Kati, South Moejoe, Digoel, Digul, Metomka, Kati Metomka, Ok Bari) [kts] 4,000 (2002 SIL). South coast border area just north of where Fly River forms border between Papua, Indonesia, and Papua New Guinea. *Class:* Trans-New Guinea, Main Section, Central and Western, Central and South New Guinea-Kutubuan, Central and South New Guinea, Ok, Lowland. *Dialect:* Metomka.

Nafri [nxx] 1,630 (1975 SIL). Nafri village, southeast end of Yotafa Bay, Jayapura area. *Class:* Trans-New Guinea, Main Section, Central and Western, Sentani, Sentani Proper. *Other:* Sea level to 200 meters. Agriculturalists; fishermen; hunters: pig, casuri, deer; traders. Christian, traditional religion.

Nakai (Nagai, Na'i, Na'ai) [nkj] 700 (1999 Mark Donohue). East of the upper Digul River, Awimbom village in the center of 5 other villages extending toward Ok Sibil to the northeast, and a little way to the southwest toward Iwur. No settlement on the west side of the Digul River, with a large unpopulated area between Nakai and Burumakok. *Class:* Trans-New Guinea, Main Section, Central and Western, Central and South New Guinea-Kutubuan, Central and South New Guinea, Ok, Mountain. *Lg Use:* Used in the home and by local government. They report difficulty in understanding Indonesian or Malay. *Other:* Lowland. 350 to 1,850 meters. Agriculturalists: sago, bananas; hunters. Traditional religion.

Nalca (Hmanggona, Naltje, Naltya, Hmonono, Kimyal, Kimjal) [nlc] 11,092 (2000 WCD). Eastern highlands area on north slopes of ranges northeast of Korupun and southeast of Nipsan. *Class:* Trans-New Guinea, Mek, Western. *Dialects:* Lexical similarity 59% with Yale, Kosarek. *Lg Dev:* Literacy rate in second language: below 1% semiliterate. NT: 2001. *Other:* Distinct from Korupun (Kimyal). Christian, traditional religion.

Narau [nxu] 80 to 90 (2000 Wurm). Kecamatan Kaureh, Jayapura area. *Class:* Trans-New Guinea, Kaure, Kaure Proper. *Other:* 200 to 300 meters. Fishermen. Christian, traditional religion.

Ndom [nqm] 1,200 (2002 SIL). Kolopom (Frederik Hendrik) Island. *Class:* Trans-New Guinea, Kolopom. *Dialects:* Closest to Kimaama, Riantana. *Other:* Coastal. Swamp. Below 100 meters. Agriculturalists; hunters; fishermen. Christian, traditional religion.

Nduga (Ndugwa, Ndauwa, Dauwa, Dawa, Pesechem, Pesecham, Pesegem) [ndx] 10,000 (1985 Mary Owen CMA). Jayawijaya, Tiom, central highlands, south of high ranges, south of Western Dani, north of Asmat. Widely scattered. *Class:* Trans-New Guinea, Main Section, Central and Western, Dani-Kwerba, Southern, Ngalik-Nduga. *Dialects:* Sinak Nduga, Hitadipa Nduga. *Lg Use:* Bilingual level estimates for Dani: 0 60%, 1 10%, 2 20%, 3 0%, 4 0%, 5 10%. Some also speak Damal, Moni, or Indonesian. *Lg Dev:* NT: 1984. *Other:* Mountain slope. Swidden agriculturalists. Christian, traditional religion.

Ngalum (Sibil) [szb] 10,000 in Indonesia (1987 SIL). Population total all countries: 18,000. Valleys of Ok Sibil, Ok Tsop, and perhaps Ok Bon, border area in main range north of Muyu (Yongkom) and Iwur languages, northeast of Nakai. Also spoken in Papua New Guinea. *Class:* Trans-New Guinea, Main Section, Central and Western, Central and South New Guinea-Kutubuan, Central and South New Guinea, Ok, Mountain. *Dialects:* Ngalum, Apmisibil, Sibil. *Lg Dev:* NT: 1992. *Other:* Hunters; agriculturalists. Christian, traditional religion.

Nggem [nbq] 3,000 (1991 SIL). Along the middle Haflifoeri River, north of Wamena. *Class:* Trans-New Guinea, Main Section, Central and Western, Dani-Kwerba, Southern, Dani. *Dialects:* Close to Walak. Lexical similarity 50% with Western Dani. *Lg Dev:* Bible portions: 1982. *Other:* SOV; clause chaining. Mountain slope. 1,100 to 3,000 meters. Agriculturalists. Christian, traditional religion.

Nimboran (Nambrong) [nir] 2,000 (1987 SIL). Ethnic population: 3,500 (1987 SIL). North Papua, due west of Lake Sentani, about 26 villages. *Class:* Trans-New Guinea, Nimboran. *Dialects:* Lexical similarity 40% with Kemtuik. *Lg Use:* Restricted to older people. Children learn Papuan Malay exclusively. Speakers also use Papuan Malay. *Lg Dev:* Bible portions: 1982–1985. *Other:* 300 to 600 meters. Hunters; agriculturalists.

Ninggerum (Ninggrum, Ninggirum, Ninggeroem, Kativa, Kasiwa, Orgwo, Muyu) [nxr] 1,000 in Indonesia. Border area and in Papua New Guinea between the Ok Birim and Ok Tedi rivers. *Other:* Speakers are called 'Muyu'. 300 to 600 meters. Agriculturalists; hunters. Christian, traditional religion. See main entry under Papua New Guinea.

Nipsan (Southern Jale, Yale-Nipsan) [nps] 2,500 (1993 Doriot). Jayawijaya, Kurima, just west of Hmanggona. *Class:* Trans-New Guinea, Mek, Western. *Dialects:* Lexical similarity 78% with Yale, Kosarek, 59% with Nalca. *Lg Use:* Used in religious services. *Lg Dev:* NT: 1975. *Other:* Distinct from Yali of Ninia, Yali of Angguruk, and Yali of Pass Valley. 1,600 to 3,600 meters. Agriculturalists. Christian, traditional religion.

Nisa (Bonefa, Kerema) [njs] 500 (1987 SIL). Inland from east side of Geelvink Bay around Danau Nisa. *Class:* Geelvink Bay, East Geelvink Bay. *Lg Use:* Vigorous. *Other:* Lowland. 100 to 200 meters. Agriculturalists: tubers, greens, sago; fishermen. Christian, traditional religion.

Obokuitai (Obogwitai, Ati, Aliki) [afz] 120 (2000 Wurm). Lakes Plain just north of mid-Rouffaer River, village of Obogwi. *Class:* Geelvink Bay, Lakes Plain, Tariku, East. *Dialects:* Related to Doutai, Biritai, Sikaritai. Lexical similarity 78% with Eritai, 69% with Biritai. *Lg Dev:* Literacy rate in first language: 15%. Bible portions: 1994. *Other:* Ati means 'language'. SOV; tonal.

Onin (Onim, Sepa) [oni] 500 (2000 Wurm). North and northwest Bomberai Peninsula. *Class:* Austronesian, Malayo-Polynesian, Central-Eastern, Central Malayo-Polynesian, North Bomberai. *Dialects:* Nikuda, Ogar, Patipi, Sepa. *Other:* Coastal. Sea level to 200 meters. Fishermen; agriculturalists. Traditional religion, Christian.

Onin Based Pidgin [onx] Onin Peninsula. *Class:* Pidgin, Onin based. *Other:* Second language only.

Ormu [orz] 500 (2000 Wurm). North coast area just west of Jayapura, villages of Ormu Besar and Ormu Kecil, north of the Cyclops Mountains. *Class:* Austronesian, Malayo-Polynesian, Central-Eastern, Eastern Malayo-Polynesian, Oceanic, Western Oceanic, North New Guinea, Sarmi-Jayapura Bay, Jayapura Bay. *Lg Use:* May use Indonesian as second language. *Other:* Sea level to 1,400 meters. Fishermen; agriculturalists. Traditional religion, Christian.

Orya (Uria, Warpok, Warpu, Oria) [ury] 1,600 (1985 Philip Fields SIL). Population includes 900 in Unurum-Guay, 100 in Kecamatan Bonggo, 600 in Kecamatan Lereh. Kecamatan District, Unurum-Guay, Kecamatan Bonggo, Kecamatan Lereh in the villages of Taja, Witi, and Wamho (formerly of Orya). *Class:* Trans-New Guinea, Northern, Tor, Orya. *Dialects:* Barat (West Orya), Timur (East Orya), Yapsi-Taja. Slight dialect differences. *Lg Use:* Children learn Orya in most cases. All domains, adult literacy classes, religion, commerce, letters. Positive language attitude. Bilingual level estimates for Indonesian: 0 0%, 1 55%, 2 23%, 3 19%, 4 2%, 5 1%. All Orya can speak Indonesian or Papuan Malay. A very few (perhaps 9) speak Sause. Indonesian used with outsiders, in church, especially when outsiders are present, for discipline, for discussion of government issues, some commerce. *Lg Dev:* Literacy rate in first language: 5% to 15%. Some adult literacy classes. Roman script. Bible portions: 1987–1995. *Other:* 'Uria' is a misspelling used earlier. 'Warpok' is the Nimboran name. Interfluvial. Tropical forest. 100 to 400 meters. Swidden agriculturalists: papaya, bananas, kankong; hunters: pig, wallaby, cassowary. Traditional religion, Christian.

Papasena [pas] 400 (1982 SIL). Lakes Plain area on lower Idenburg River just east of juncture with Rouffaer River. *Class:* Geelvink Bay, Lakes Plain, Tariku, East. *Dialects:* Lexical similarity 23% with Sikaritai. *Other:* 100 to 500 meters. Fishermen; agriculturalists. Christian, traditional religion.

Papuma [ppm] 600 (1982 SIL). South coast of Serui Island near 135.50', village of Papuma. *Class:* Austronesian, Malayo-Polynesian, Central-Eastern, Eastern Malayo-Polynesian, South Halmahera-West New Guinea, West New Guinea, Cenderawasih Bay, Yapen, Central-Western. *Dialects:* Lexical similarity 82% with Munggui, Marau, Ansus. *Lg Use:* Vigorous. *Other:* Island, coastal. Sea level to 400 meters. Fishermen. Christian, traditional religion.

Podena [pdn] 200 (1954 A. C. van der Leeden ms.). Island off north coast of Biri River, Jayapura Kabupaten, Bonggo Kecamatan. *Class:* Austronesian, Malayo-Polynesian, Central-Eastern, Eastern Malayo-Polynesian, Oceanic, Western Oceanic, North New Guinea, Sarmi-Jayapura Bay, Sarmi. *Other:* Island. Below 100 meters. Fishermen; agriculturalists.

Pom [pmo] 2,000 (1987 SIL). Miosnum Island and west Serui Island, villages of Pom, Serewen, Mias Endi. *Class:* Austronesian, Malayo-Polynesian, Central-Eastern, Eastern Malayo-Polynesian, South Halmahera-West New Guinea, West New Guinea, Cenderawasih Bay, Yapen, Central-Western. *Dialect:* Jobi. *Other:* Island, coastal. Sea level to 200 meters. Fishermen; agriculturalists. Christian, traditional religion.

Puragi (Mogao) [pru] 700 (1991 SIL). Southwest Bird's Head along Maccluer Gulf, inland around Matamani River. *Class:* Trans-New Guinea, South Bird's Head-Timor-Alor-Pantar, South Bird's Head, South Bird's Head Proper, Western. *Other:* Below 100 meters. Oil company workers, agriculturalists. Christian, traditional religion.

Rasawa [rac] 200 (1987 SIL). Two villages near the southern coast of Waropen Bawah District. *Class:* Geelvink Bay, Lakes Plain, Rasawa-Saponi. *Lg Use:* Used in the home. *Other:* Coastal. Below 100 meters. Fishermen; gatherers. Christian, traditional religion.

Riantana (Kimaam) [ran] 1,100 (1977 Voegelin and Voegelin). Frederik Hendrik Island. *Class:* Trans-New Guinea, Kolopom. *Lg Use:* Used in the home. *Other:* Coastal. Swamp. Sea level to 100 meters. Agriculturalists; hunters; fishermen. Christian, traditional religion.

Roon (Ron) [rnn] 1,100 (1993 Doriot). Roon Island west of Cenderawasih Bay, north of Wandamen Peninsula. *Class:* Austronesian, Malayo-Polynesian, Central-Eastern, Eastern Malayo-Polynesian, South Halmahera-West New Guinea, West New Guinea, Cenderawasih Bay, Yapen, Central-Western. *Other:* Island. Sea level to 350 meters. Fishermen; agriculturalists. Traditional religion, Christian.

Samarokena (Samarkena, Karfasia, Tamaya, Tamaja) [tmj] 400 (1982 SIL). North coast inland just east of Apawar River, west of Sarmi, villages of Karfasia, Samarkena, Maseb, Tamaya. *Class:* Trans-New Guinea, Main Section, Central and Western, Dani-Kwerba, Northern, Samarokena. *Lg Use:* Speakers bilingual in Airoran, Isirawa, and some in Kwerba. *Other:* Coastal. Below 100 meters. Fishermen; agriculturalists. Christian, traditional religion.

Saponi [spi] 4 to 5 (2000 Wurm). Botawa village, interior Waropen Bawah District. *Class:* Geelvink Bay, Lakes Plain, Rasawa-Saponi. *Other:* Christian. Nearly extinct.

Sauri [srt] 100 (1987 SIL). East side of Cenderawasih Bay near Waropen language, in Sauri-Sirami village, near Sirami River. *Class:* Geelvink Bay, East Geelvink Bay. *Dialects:* Lexical similarity 71% with Barapasi, 60% with Demisa, 76% with Kofei, 63% with Tefaro. *Other:* Christian, traditional religion.

Sause (Seuce) [sao] 250 (2000 Wurm). Southwest of Sentani, northwest of Lereh, villages of Ures, Mubararon, Sause-Bokoko, Witti-Yadow, Lidya, Puaral. *Class:* Trans-New Guinea, Northern, Tor, Unclassified. *Other:* 100 to 900 meters. Hunter-gatherers; agriculturalists; lumbermen. Traditional religion, Christian.

Saweru [swr] 300 (1991 SIL). Central Serui Island, Serui Waropen Kabupaten, Yapen Selatan Kecamatan, on an island south of Yapen Island near Serui. *Class:* Geelvink Bay, Yawa. *Other:* Island coastal. Coastal. Below 100 meters. Fishermen. Christian, traditional religion.

Sawi (Sawuy, Aejauroh) [saw] 3,500 (1993 Doriot). Merauke, Atsy, near south coastal lowland, between Kronkel and Ayip rivers and upper Fayit River area, villages of Kamur, Esebor, Wiagas, Minahai, Comoro. *Class:* Trans-New Guinea, Main Section, Central and Western, Central and South New Guinea-Kutubuan, Central and South New Guinea, Awyu-Dumut, Sawi. *Dialects:* Closest to Awyu. *Lg Use:* Bilingual level estimates for Indonesian: 0 75%, 1 25%, 2 0%, 3 0%, 4 0%, 5 0%. *Lg Dev:* Literacy rate in second language: 5% semiliterate. NT: 1973–1994. *Other:* Christian, traditional religion.

Seget [sbg] 1,200 (1988 SIL). West Bird's Head southwest of Sorong, west and southwest of Moi language, villages of Walian, Sailolof, Segum, Seget. *Class:* West Papuan, Bird's Head, West Bird's Head. *Other:* Coastal. Below 100 meters. Christian, traditional religion.

Sekar (Seka) [skz] 450 (1977 Voegelin and Voegelin). Northwest Bomberai Peninsula on coast and one small island. *Class:* Austronesian, Malayo-Polynesian, Central-Eastern, Central Malayo-Polynesian, North Bomberai. *Dialects:* Arguni has the highest percentage of lexical similarity with Sekar. *Other:* Coastal. Below 100 meters. Christian, traditional religion.

Semimi (Etna Bay, Wesrau, Muri) [etz] 1,000 (1991 SIL). Bomberai Peninsula close to Kaniran, south part of neck extending west to Triton Bay. *Class:* Trans-New Guinea, Main Section, Central and Western, Mairasi-Tanahmerah, Mairasi. *Dialects:* Lexical similarity 69% with Mairasi,

63% with Mer. *Other:* Sea level to 1,000 meters. Fishermen; lumbermen. Christian, traditional religion.

Sempan (Nararapi) [xse] 1,000 (1987 SIL). Middle south coast, between Kokonao and Agats, east of Kamoro and west of Asmat languages. *Class:* Trans-New Guinea, Main Section, Central and Western, Central and South New Guinea-Kutubuan, Central and South New Guinea, Asmat-Kamoro. *Dialects:* Close to Kamoro and Nefarpi. *Other:* Coastal. Below 100 meters. Fishermen; sago-gatherers. Christian, traditional religion.

Senggi [snu] 100 (2000 Wurm). Border area south of Jayapura, villages of Senggi and Tomfor. *Class:* Trans-New Guinea, Northern, Border, Waris. *Other:* 300 meters. Christian, traditional religion.

Sentani (Buyaka) [set] 30,000 (1996 SIL). Few monolinguals. Around Lake Sentani, about 30 villages. Also scattered in the rest of Papua and a few other parts of Indonesia. *Class:* Trans-New Guinea, Main Section, Central and Western, Sentani, Sentani Proper. *Dialects:* East Sentani, West Sentani, Central Sentani. Lexical similarity 30% with Tabla. *Lg Use:* Vigorous in most families. All domains. Sometimes used in church. Oral use in commerce, oral literature. Schools are beginning to use Sentani in grades 1 to 6. Positive language attitude. Most speak some degree of Indonesian. Parents want their children to be prepared for school in Indonesian. *Lg Dev:* Literacy rate in first language: 16%. Literacy rate in second language: 50% to 75%. About 5,000 can read and write it. Dictionary. Grammar. NT: 1997. *Other:* 'Buyaka' is their name for themselves. Lake shore, hills. Fishermen; agriculturalists. Traditional religion, Christian.

Serui-Laut (Arui) [seu] 1,200 (1987 SIL). South central Serui Island and Nau Island south of Serui, 5 villages. *Class:* Austronesian, Malayo-Polynesian, Central-Eastern, Eastern Malayo-Polynesian, South Halmahera-West New Guinea, West New Guinea, Cenderawasih Bay, Yapen, Central-Western. *Dialects:* Lexical similarity 82% with Ansus, 77% with Ambai. *Lg Use:* Vigorous. *Other:* Island, coastal. Below 100 meters. Fishermen; agriculturalists. Christian.

Sikaritai (Aikwakai, Tori Aikwakai, Sikari, Ati, Tori, Araikurioko) [tty] 800 (1993 Doriot). Lakes Plain area just north of junction of Idenburg and Rouffaer rivers, along Mamberamo River, and west 15 miles, south 10 miles, villages of Sikari, Haya, Iri. *Class:* Geelvink Bay, Lakes Plain, Tariku, East. *Dialects:* Lexical similarity 86% with Eritai. *Lg Use:* Vigorous. *Lg Dev:* Bible portions: 1992. *Other:* 100 to 200 meters. Christian, traditional religion.

Silimo (South Ngalik, Paiyage, Usak, Wulik) [wul] 5,000 (1987 SIL). 50% monolinguals. Central highlands south of the range immediately west of the Baliem River, Amo, Kiniage valleys. *Class:* Trans-New Guinea, Main Section, Central and Western, Dani-Kwerba, Southern, Ngalik-Nduga. *Dialect:* Lower Samenage. *Lg Dev:* NT: 1992. *Other:* Mountain slope. Agriculturalists. Traditional religion, Christian.

Skou (Sko, Skouw, Skow, Sekou, Tumawo, Te Mawo, Sekol, Sukou) [skv] 700 (1999 M. Donohue). North coast border area east of Jayapura, at the mouth of the Tami River, villages of Sko-Yambe, Sko-Mabu, Sko-Sai. *Class:* Sko, Vanimo. *Dialects:* Related to Vanimo, Wutung, Yako. *Lg Use:* Some older Wutung people use Sko as their second or third language. All domains. All ages. They have reservations about Indonesian. Most use Papuan Malay, Indonesian, Wutung of Papua New Guinea, or Vanimo to speakers of those languages. Comprehension is limited. *Lg Dev:* Literacy rate in first language: 10%. Literacy rate in second language: 10% Indonesian. Literacy motivation high, program in progress. Dictionary. *Other:* Coastal. Sago swamp. Fishermen; agriculturalists. Christian, traditional religion.

Sobei (Biga, Imasi, Liki) [sob] 1,000 (2000 Wurm). Ethnic population: 1,850 (2000 D. Tryon). North coast area east of Sarmi, Jayapura Kabupaten, Sarmi Kecamatan. *Class:* Austronesian, Malayo-Polynesian, Central-Eastern, Eastern Malayo-Polynesian, Oceanic, Western Oceanic, North New Guinea, Sarmi-Jayapura Bay, Sarmi. *Dialects:* Reported to be the same as, or intelligible with, Liki. *Lg Use:* Children bilingual in Indonesian. Many also use Papuan Malay. *Lg Dev:* Grammar. *Other:* Government schools through entire area. Intermarriage with other language groups increasing. Fishermen; agriculturalists. Christian.

Sowanda (Waina, Wina, Wanya, Wanja, Waina-Sowanda) [sow] 212 in Indonesia (2002 SIL). Northeast border area south of Jayapura. *Other:* 350 to 500 meters. Agriculturalists; hunters. Christian, traditional religion. See main entry under Papua New Guinea.

Suabo (Suabau, Inanwatan, Mirabo, Iagu) [szp] 1,100 (1987 SIL). South Bird's Head along Maccluer Gulf, 15 villages. *Class:* Trans-New Guinea, South Bird's Head-Timor-Alor-Pantar, South Bird's Head, Inanwatan. *Dialects:* Closest to Duriankere. *Other:* Coastal. Below 100 meters. Fishermen. Christian, traditional religion.

Tabla (Tepera, Tanah Merah, Tabi, Tanahmerah 2, Jakari) [tnm] 3,750 (1990 UBS). Jayapura, Demta, Depapre, 13 villages on north coast east and west of Tanahmerah Bay. *Class:* Trans-New Guinea, Main Section, Central and Western, Sentani, Sentani Proper. *Dialects:* Yokari, Tepera, Yewena-Yongsu. Yokari dialect understood by other dialects at 80% to 95%, others have 95% to 100% intelligibility of each other. Tabla has 30% lexical similarity with Sentani (closest). *Lg Use:* Bilingual level estimates for Indonesian: 0 1%, 1 1%, 2 8%, 3 85%, 4 5%, 5 0%. *Lg Dev:* Bible portions: 1986. *Other:* Distinct from Tanahmerah (Sumeri) of Bomberai Peninsula. 'Tepera' is their name for themselves. Sea level to 200 meters. Hunters; fishermen; agriculturalists; lumbermen. Christian, traditional religion.

Taikat (Tajkat, Arso) [aos] 500 (2000 Wurm). Northeast border area, straight south of Jayapura. *Class:* Trans-New Guinea, Northern, Border, Taikat. *Dialects:* Closest to Awyi. *Other:* Agriculturalists; hunters. Christian, traditional religion.

Tamagario (Buru, Tamaraw, Wagow) [tcg] 3,500 (1987 SIL). South coast area between Gondu and Bapai rivers. *Class:* Trans-New Guinea, Main Section, Central and Western, Kayagar. *Other:* Swamp. 1 to 100 meters. Fishermen; sago-gatherers. Christian, traditional religion.

Tanahmerah (Sumeri, Sumerine) [tcm] 500 (1978 SIL). North Bomberai Peninsula along the Gondu and Bapai rivers. *Class:* Trans-New Guinea, Main Section, Central and Western, Mairasi-Tanahmerah, Tanahmerah. *Other:* Distinct from Tanahmerah (Tabla) of Sentani branch. Coastal. Below 100 meters. Fishermen; agriculturalists. Christian, traditional religion.

Tandia [tni] 2 (1991 SIL). Bird's Head neck area just south of Wandamen Peninsula along Wohsimi River. *Class:* Austronesian, Malayo-Polynesian, Central-Eastern, Eastern Malayo-Polynesian, South Halmahera-West New Guinea, West New Guinea, Cenderawasih Bay, Tandia. *Lg Use:* Most Tandia people speak Wandamen. *Other:* Traditional religion, Christian. Nearly extinct.

Tangko [tkx] 85 (2000 WCD). *Class:* Trans-New Guinea, Main Section, Central and Western, Central and South New Guinea-Kutubuan, Central and South New Guinea, Ok. *Other:* Foothills. 500 to 1,600 meters. Agriculturalists; hunters. Christian, traditional religion.

Tarpia (Kaptiauw, Kapitiauw, Tarfia, Sufrai) [suf] 300 (2000 Wurm). North coast area near Demta, villages of Tarfia and Kaptiau, Jayapura Kabupaten, Demta and

Bonggo kecamatans. *Class:* Austronesian, Malayo-Polynesian, Central-Eastern, Eastern Malayo-Polynesian, Oceanic, Western Oceanic, North New Guinea, Sarmi-Jayapura Bay, Sarmi. *Dialect:* Sufrai, Tarpia (Tarfia). Closest to Bonggo. *Other:* Sea level to 500 meters. Fishermen. Christian.

Tause (Doa, Darha) [tad] 300 (2000 Wurm). Around Deraposi, southwest of Danau Bira, northeast of Fayu language, northwest of Edopi language, western Lakes Plain (Paniai). *Class:* Geelvink Bay, Lakes Plain, Tariku, West. *Dialects:* Tause, Weirate, Deirate. Related to Fayu and Kirikiri. *Lg Use:* Bilingual level estimates for Fayu: 0 75%, 1 15%, 2 7%, 3 2%, 4 0%, 5 1%. No Indonesian spoken. Fayu is spoken with nearby language speakers. *Other:* First contact with outside world in 1982. Lowland. 100 to 500 meters. Hunter-gatherers. Christian, traditional religion.

Taworta (Taworta-Aero, Taria, Dabra, Bok) [tbp] 140 (2000 Wurm). Lakes Plain area on the south side of the Idenburg River east of Taiyeve, Jayapura Kabupaten, Mamberamo Hulu Kecamatan. *Class:* Geelvink Bay, Lakes Plain, East Lakes Plain. *Other:* Lowland. Swamp. Hunters: crocodile hides; lumbermen; agriculturalists. Christian, traditional religion.

Tefaro (Demba) [tfo] 100 (1987 SIL). East side of Cenderawasih Bay, in villages of Tefaro and Demba. *Class:* Geelvink Bay, East Geelvink Bay. *Dialects:* Lexical similarity 61% with Barapasi, 63% with Sauri, 70% with Tunggare. *Lg Use:* Used in the home. *Other:* Lowland. 100 to 200 meters. Agriculturalists. Traditional religion, Christian.

Tehit (Tehid, Kaibus, Teminabuan, Tahit) [kps] 10,000 (2000 R. Hesse). 500 monolinguals. Southwest Bird's Head, Kabupaten Sorong, most of Kecamatan Teminabuan and half of Kecamatan Sawiat, about 31 villages. *Class:* West Papuan, Bird's Head, West Bird's Head. *Dialects:* Tehit Jit, Mbol Fle, Saifi, Imyan, Sfa Riere, Fkar, Sawiat Salmeit. Closest to Kalabra. Lexical similarity 60% with Kalabra. *Lg Use:* Vigorous. In interior villages parents pass Tehit on to children. For villages bordering town, they speak Indonesian to children. People from bordering languages that interact in both languages learn Tehit. All domains. Some oral use in schools, religious services, labor relations, traditional oral literature. Positive language attitude. 5% monolingual. Others speak Indonesian or Maibrat. 1% speak Dutch or English. Schools are taught in Indonesian, although most teachers speak Tehit. Indonesian is the trade language. *Lg Dev:* Literacy rate in first language: 5%. Literacy rate in second language: 15% to 25%. Taught in primary schools. *Other:* Hills, lowland, riverine. Tropical forest, swamp. Agriculturalists: oil extract. Christian, traditional religion.

Tobati (Jotafa, Yotafa, Yautefa, Humboldt Jotafa, Jayapura, Enggros, Tobwadic) [tti] 350 (1998 M. Donohue). Jayapura Bay, close to Jayapura, villages of Tobati, Enggros, Entrop, Kota Raja, Tanah Hitam. *Class:* Austronesian, Malayo-Polynesian, Central-Eastern, Eastern Malayo-Polynesian, Oceanic, Western Oceanic, North New Guinea, Sarmi-Jayapura Bay, Jayapura Bay. *Dialects:* Formerly classified as Papuan. *Lg Use:* Tobati villagers have mainly assimilated to Indonesian culture and language. Enggros maintains stronger language use, but speakers are completely bilingual in Papuan Malay. *Other:* Coastal. Sea level to 150 meters. Christian.

Tofanma (Tofamna) [tlg] 90 (2000 Wurm). Tofanma village, south of Jayapura just east of Nawa River. *Class:* Trans-New Guinea, Tofanma. *Dialects:* Not closely related to any other language. *Other:* 600 to 1,850 meters. Hunter-gatherers; agriculturalists. Christian, traditional religion.

Towei (Towe) [ttn] 115 (1975 SIL). Border area south of Jayapura, south of Dubu, west of Emumu languages, in and around Towe. *Class:* Trans-New Guinea, Pauwasi,

Western. *Other:* 600 to 1,400 meters. Agriculturalists. Christian, traditional religion.

Trimuris [tip] 300 (1999 SIL). East bank of the Mamberamo River between Kauwera and Bagusa languages, Jayapura Kabupaten, Mamberamo Tengah Kecamatan. *Class:* Trans-New Guinea, Main Section, Central and Western, Dani-Kwerba, Northern, Kwerba. *Dialects:* They do not understand Kwerba very well. Lexical similarity 70% with Kauwera and 60% with Kwerba. *Lg Use:* Vigorous. All ages. *Other:* Tropical forest, swamp. 100 to 350 meters. Hunter-gatherers; fishermen. Traditional religion, Christian.

Tsakwambo (Kotogüt, Tsokwambo) [kvz] 500 (1991 SIL). South coast area on upper Digul River north of Mandobo language area. *Class:* Trans-New Guinea, Main Section, Central and Western, Central and South New Guinea-Kutubuan, Central and South New Guinea, Awyu-Dumut, Awyu, Aghu. *Dialects:* Related to Ederah, Kia, Upper Digul, Upper Kaeme. *Lg Use:* Used in the home. *Other:* Lowland. Below 100 meters. Hunter-gatherers; fishermen; lumbermen. Traditional religion, Christian.

Tunggare (Tarunggare, Turunggare) [trt] 500 (1993 Doriot). North central, inland from Waropen group, west of Mamberamo River, east Geelvink Bay near Nabire. *Class:* Geelvink Bay, East Geelvink Bay. *Dialects:* Most closely related to Bauzi. Lexical similarity 70% with Bauzi, 75% with Burate, 65% with Demisa, 70% with Tefaro, 69% with Woria. *Other:* Coastal. Sea level to 350 meters. Hunters; fishermen. Christian, traditional religion.

Una (Goliath, Mt. Goliath, Oranje-Gebergte, Langda) [mtg] 4,000 (1991 SIL). Eastern highlands on south slopes of main ranges east of Sela Valley, west of Ngalum, Bidabuh, east Weip Valley, Yay Valley, around Langda, Bomela, Sumtamon. *Class:* Trans-New Guinea, Mek, Eastern. *Dialects:* Lexical similarity 75% with Eipomek, 69% with Ketengban. *Lg Use:* Used in religious services. *Lg Dev:* Literacy rate in first language: 5% to 15%. Bible portions: 1999. *Other:* SOV; clause chaining; switch reference; split ergative. River valleys. Christian, traditional religion.

Uruangnirin (Faur, Tubiruasa) [urn] 250 (1977 Voegelin and Voegelin). Two small islands between Karas Island and mainland of southwest Bomberai Peninsula. *Class:* Austronesian, Malayo-Polynesian, Central-Eastern, Central Malayo-Polynesian, North Bomberai. *Other:* Blust says this appears to be Central Malayo-Polynesian. Islands. Below 100 meters. Fishermen; lumbermen; oil workers; cocoa; spice. Traditional religion, Christian.

Usku [ulf] 20 (2000 Wurm). Usku village, south of Jayapura, just south of Pauwasi. *Class:* Trans-New Guinea, Usku. *Dialects:* Not closely related to any other language. *Other:* 350 to 1,100 meters. Agriculturalists. Nearly extinct.

Wabo (Woriasi, Nusari) [wbb] 1,500 (1987 SIL). North and south coast of east end of Serui Island, near 136.45' to 136.55', 6 villages. *Class:* Austronesian, Malayo-Polynesian, Central-Eastern, Eastern Malayo-Polynesian, South Halmahera-West New Guinea, West New Guinea, Cenderawasih Bay, Yapen, East. *Dialects:* Lexical similarity 71% with Kurudu, 46% with Western Serui. *Other:* Island. Sea level to 700 meters. Fishermen. Traditional religion, Christian.

Waigeo (Ambel, Amber, Amberi, Waigiu) [wgo] 300 (1978 SIL). North central Waigeo Island off western Bird's Head, Sorong Kabupaten, Waigeo Selatan Kecamatan, Warsanbin, Selegop, Waifoi, Go, Kabilol, Kabare, and Nyandesawai villages. *Class:* Austronesian, Malayo-Polynesian, Central-Eastern, Eastern Malayo-Polynesian, South Halmahera-West New Guinea, West New Guinea, Cenderawasih Bay, Raja Ampat. *Dialects:* Metnyo, Metsam. *Other:* Limestone island. Sea level to 800 meters. Christian, traditional religion.

Wakde [wkd] 400 (1980 SIL). Wakde Islands off the north coast just east of the Tor River, Jayapura Kabupaten, Pantai Timur Kecamatan. *Class:* Austronesian, Malayo-Polynesian, Central-Eastern, Eastern Malayo-Polynesian, Oceanic, Western Oceanic, North New Guinea, Sarmi-Jayapura Bay, Sarmi. *Other:* Island. Fishermen. Christian, traditional religion.

Walak (Lower Pyramid, Wodo) [wlw] 1,500 (1993 Doriot). Villages of Ilugwa, Wodo, Bugi, Mogonik, Wurigelebut. *Class:* Trans-New Guinea, Main Section, Central and Western, Dani-Kwerba, Southern, Dani. *Other:* Traditional religion, Christian.

Wambon [wms] 3,000 (1987 SIL). South coast area northeast of Mandobo language area. *Class:* Trans-New Guinea, Main Section, Central and Western, Central and South New Guinea-Kutubuan, Central and South New Guinea, Awyu-Dumut, Dumut. *Lg Use:* Used in the home. *Other:* Foothills. Below 100 meters. Agriculturalists; fishermen; hunters; lumbermen. Christian, traditional religion.

Wandamen (Wandamen-Windesi, Windesi, Windessi, Bintuni, Bentuni, Bentoeni, Wamesa) [wad] 5,000 (1993 Doriot). Wasior, Manokwari, west Cenderawasih Bay along Wandamen Bay extending west to east end of Bintuni Bay. *Class:* Austronesian, Malayo-Polynesian, Central-Eastern, Eastern Malayo-Polynesian, South Halmahera-West New Guinea, West New Guinea, Cenderawasih Bay, Yapen, Central-Western. *Dialects:* Windesi, Bintuni, Wamesa, Wasior, Ambumi, Dasener, Aibondeni. *Lg Use:* Speakers also use Indonesian. *Lg Dev:* Literacy rate in first language: 25%. Literacy rate in second language: 50%. Bible portions: 1937–1994. *Other:* Coastal. Sea level to 1,000 meters. Agriculturalists: coffee, hunters; fishermen. Christian.

Wanggom (Wanggo, Wangom) [wng] 875 (2002 SIL). Biwage II village. *Class:* Trans-New Guinea, Main Section, Central and Western, Central and South New Guinea-Kutubuan, Central and South New Guinea, Awyu-Dumut, Dumut. *Dialects:* Close to Wambon, Mandobo Atas, Mandobo Bawah, Kombai. *Lg Use:* Used in the home. *Other:* Swamp. Sea level to 100 meters. Fishermen; hunter-gatherers; lumbermen.

Wano (Waano) [wno] 7,000 (2001 Burung). Central highlands area on upper Rouffaer River basin north of Damal, northwest of Dem, south of Kirikiri. Places are Kiagai, Lumo, Weiga, Puduk (Puluk), Yamo River, Wodegoduk, Kendo-Kendo River, Dukibeci (Lukibesi), Mui River, Fawi, Nggweri, Dagai, Acodi, Wuduma, Tigit, Dumo (Lumo), Kirudomo, Puduk, Mburumuome, Biricare, Mbomban, Yedome (Yei), Acodi, Wanggiva, Kawaimu, Damuk, Anevawi, Ambogobak, Tumbwi, Nggibaga, Nggubugani, Wandini. Partial villages are Iratoi, Turumo, Fawi. *Class:* Trans-New Guinea, Main Section, Central and Western, Dani-Kwerba, Southern, Wano. *Dialects:* Close to Western Dani, Nggem, Walak. Lexical similarity 65% with Western Dani. *Lg Use:* Used in religious services. Western Dani, Dem, Moni, or Indonesian spoken by leaders, men, adults, young people who have been to school and who have intermarried. *Lg Dev:* Grammar. Bible portions: 1979–1989. *Other:* SOV; postpositions; genitives before noun head; articles, adjectives, numerals, and relatives after noun head; question word initial; two prefixes, 5 suffixes; switch reference; CVC; nontonal. Mountain slope. Tropical forest. 85 to 2,000 meters. Hunter-gatherers; seminomadic. Traditional religion, Christian.

Warembori (Warenbori, Waremboivoro) [wsa] 600 (1998 SIL). North coast, mouth of Mamberamo River and west to Poiwai, villages of Warembori, Tamakuri, and Bonoi. *Class:* Lower Mamberamo. *Dialects:* Close to Yoke. Lexical similarity 33% with Yoke and 30% with Austronesian. *Lg Use:* About 20 people use it as their second or third language. Used in the home. Most are 20 and older, but there are speakers below 20. Most are proficient in Papuan Malay. Indonesian and Yoke also spoken. *Lg Dev:* Literacy rate in second language: 30% in Indonesian. Dictionary. Grammar. *Other:* Much typology resembles Austronesian. SVO; prepositions; genitives before noun heads; articles, adjectives, numerals, relatives after noun heads; 1 prefix, 6 or more suffixes on a word; word order distinguishes subject, object, indirect object; topic (SVO) is for pragmatic salience; affixes do not indicate case of noun phrase; obligatory subject agreement, optional object agreement shown by verb affixes; the scope of a serialized quantifier shows a trace of ergativity; causative shown by verbs 'make' and 'give'; CV; nontonal. Riverine, coastal. Swamp. Sea level. Swidden agriculturalists; hunters; fishermen: crabbing. Traditional religion, Christian.

Wares [wai] 200 (1993 Doriot). North coast area inland from Kwesten language on upper Biri River, south side, village of Mauswares. *Class:* Trans-New Guinea, Northern, Tor, Tor. *Other:* Distinct from Waris or Wari. 100 to 200 meters. Fishermen. Christian, traditional religion.

Waris (Walsa) [wrs] 1,500 in Indonesia. Northeast Papua south of Jayapura. *Other:* Hunters; agriculturalists. Christian, traditional religion. See main entry under Papua New Guinea.

Waritai (Weretai, Wari) [wbe] 150 (2000 Wurm). Lakes Plain area around Taiyeve. *Class:* Geelvink Bay, Lakes Plain, Tariku, East. *Dialects:* Related to Doutai. *Other:* Different from Waris or Wares. 200 to 500 meters. Forest hunter-gatherers; agriculturalists. Christian, traditional religion.

Warkay-Bipim (Bipim As-So, Bipim) [bgv] 300 (1993). South coast area bordering Asmat to east and Sawi to west, lower Eilanden River, 3 villages. *Class:* Trans-New Guinea, Main Section, Central and Western, Marind, Yaqay. *Lg Use:* 50% of speakers have some proficiency in Indonesian or Asmat. *Other:* Swamp. Below 100 meters. Fishermen; sago-gatherers. Traditional religion, Christian.

Waropen (Wonti, Worpen, Aropen) [wrp] 6,000 (1987 SIL). East Cenderawasih Bay, south coast of Serui Island. *Class:* Austronesian, Malayo-Polynesian, Central-Eastern, Eastern Malayo-Polynesian, South Halmahera-West New Guinea, West New Guinea, Cenderawasih Bay, Waropen. *Dialects:* Waropen Kai, Napan, Mo'or. *Lg Dev:* Literacy rate in second language: 25%. *Other:* Coastal. Below 100 meters. Fishermen: crabbing; sago gatherers. Christian.

Wauyai [wuy] 300 (2001 B. Remijsen). Southwest Waigeo Island, Wauyai village. *Class:* Austronesian, Malayo-Polynesian, Central-Eastern, Eastern Malayo-Polynesian, South Halmahera-West New Guinea, West New Guinea, Cenderawasih Bay, Raja Ampat. *Other:* Limestone island. Christian, traditional religion.

Woi (Wo'oi) [wbw] 1,300 (1987 SIL). Miosnum and west Serui Islands, villages of Wooi and Wainap. *Class:* Austronesian, Malayo-Polynesian, Central-Eastern, Eastern Malayo-Polynesian, South Halmahera-West New Guinea, West New Guinea, Cenderawasih Bay, Yapen, Central-Western. *Dialects:* Lexical similarity 77% with Pom, Marau, Ansus. *Other:* Island, coastal. Sea level to 200 meters. Fishermen; agriculturalists. Christian.

Wolani (Wodani, Woda, Woda-Mo) [wod] 5,000 (1992 UBS). Western central highlands along Kemandoga and Mbiyandogo rivers, north of Ekari language 75 miles northeast of Lake Paniai, north of Wissel Lakes and northwest of the Moni. *Class:* Trans-New Guinea, Main Section, Central and Western, Wissel Lakes-Kemandoga, Ekari-Wolani-Moni. *Lg Dev:* Bible portions: 1984–1995. *Other:* Mountain slope. 850 to 2,600 meters. Agriculturalists; hunters: pigs, birds. Traditional religion, Christian.

Woria [wor] 5 to 6 (2000 Wurm). Interior Waropen Bawah, Botawa village. *Class:* Geelvink Bay, East Geelvink Bay. *Dialects:* Lexical similarity 64% with Barapasi, 64% with Demisa, 63% with Kofei, 69% with Tunggare. *Other:* Botawa is a Demisa and Waropen-speaking village. Nearly extinct.

Yafi (Jafi, Yaffi, Wagarindem, Wargarindem, Jafi Wagarindem) [wfg] 175 (1975 SIL). Northeast Papua, border area south of Jayapura near Ampas, villages of Yaffri, Sungguar, Tainda, Abiu, Tokondo. *Class:* Trans-New Guinea, Pauwasi, Eastern. *Other:* 300 to 400 meters. Agriculturalists. Christian, traditional religion.

Yahadian (Nerigo, Jahadian, Yabin Yahadian) [ner] 500 (1991 SIL). South Bird's Head, between lower Mintamani River and Sekak River along Maccluer Gulf. *Class:* Trans-New Guinea, South Bird's Head-Timor-Alor-Pantar, South Bird's Head, Konda-Yahadian. *Dialects:* Lexical similarity 60% with Konda. *Other:* Coastal. Below 100 meters. Sell sago, fishermen. Christian, traditional religion.

Yale, Kosarek (Kosarek, Yale-Kosarek, Wanam, In-lom) [kkl] 2,300 (1993 Doriot). Nearly 100% are monolingual. Ethnic population: 2,300. Eastern highlands, just east of Yali of Ninia, northwest of Nipsan, east of Dani, a little north of Yali of Angguruk. *Class:* Trans-New Guinea, Mek, Western. *Dialects:* Kosarek, Gilika (Kilika), Tiple. Close to Nipsan, Nalca, and Gilika. Lexical similarity 78% with Nipsan, 59% with Nalca. *Lg Use:* Vigorous. All domains, home, sermons and songs in church, local commerce. Speakers think it is inferior to Indonesian. Some speakers also use Indonesian with outsiders, in school, and in church. *Lg Dev:* Literacy rate in second language: below 5%. Bible portions: 1992–1996. *Other:* The term 'In-lom' refers to only half the group. Hills. Agriculturalists. Christian, traditional religion.

Yali, Angguruk (Northern Yali, Angguruk, Yalimo) [yli] 15,000 (1991 UBS). Central highlands area northwest of Nalca, east of Grand Valley Dani. *Class:* Trans-New Guinea, Main Section, Central and Western, Dani-Kwerba, Southern, Ngalik-Nduga. *Dialects:* Related to Yali of Ninia and Yali of Pass Valley. *Lg Dev:* NT: 1988. *Other:* Christian, traditional religion.

Yali, Ninia (Ninia, Yali Selatan, Jaly, Jalè, North Ngalik, Southern Yali) [nlk] 10,500 (1999 Wilson). Central highlands area south of Angguruk, east of Soba, west of Korupun, including Ninia, Holuwon, and Lolat villages. Several hundred at Elelim, transmigrated by government in 1989 following earthquake. More than 50 villages. *Class:* Trans-New Guinea, Main Section, Central and Western, Dani-Kwerba, Southern, Ngalik-Nduga. *Dialects:* Different from Yali of Pass Valley, Yali of Angguruk, and Hupla, but closely related. *Lg Dev:* Literacy rate in first language: 20% to 25%. Literacy rate in second language: 15% to 20%. Approximately 10% read haltingly. Bible: 2000. *Other:* Plains. Christian, traditional religion.

Yali, Pass Valley (Western Yali, Pass Valley, Abendago, Yaly, North Ngalik) [yac] 5,000 (1988 SIL). Central highlands, east of Angguruk and northwest of Naltya, Jayawijaya, Kurulu, and Kurima. *Class:* Trans-New Guinea, Main Section, Central and Western, Dani-Kwerba, Southern, Ngalik-Nduga. *Dialects:* Pass Valley, Landikma, Apahapsili. Related to Yali of Ninia and Yali of Angguruk. *Lg Dev:* NT: 1977. *Other:* Christian, traditional religion.

Yamna [ymn] 250 (1980 SIL). Island off the north coast east of the Tor River, Jayapura Kabupaten, Pantai Timur Kecamatan. *Class:* Austronesian, Malayo-Polynesian, Central-Eastern, Eastern Malayo-Polynesian, Oceanic, Western Oceanic, North New Guinea, Sarmi-Jayapura Bay, Sarmi. *Other:* Island. Below 100 meters. Fishermen. Christian, traditional religion.

Yaqay (Yaqai, Jakai, Sohur, Mapi, Jaqai) [jaq] 10,000 (1987 SIL). South coast area north of Odamun River and along Miwamon River southeast of Sawuy and Kaygir languages. *Class:* Trans-New Guinea, Main Section, Central and Western, Marind, Yaqay. *Dialects:* Oba-Miwamon, Nambiomon-Mabur, Bapai. *Lg Use:* Used in the home, religious services. Many becoming bilingual in Indonesian. *Other:* Swamp. Below 100 meters. Hunter-gatherers; fishermen; plant trees; gather sandalwood, gaharu, and frankincense. Traditional religion, Christian, Muslim.

Yarsun [yrs] 200 (1991 SIL). Island off the north coast east of the Biri River, Jayapura Kabupaten, Bonggo Kecamatan. *Class:* Austronesian, Malayo-Polynesian, Central-Eastern, Eastern Malayo-Polynesian, Oceanic, Western Oceanic, North New Guinea, Sarmi-Jayapura Bay, Sarmi. *Other:* Island. Below 100 meters. Fishermen; agriculturalists. Christian, traditional religion.

Yaur (Jaur) [jau] 350 (1978 SIL). Lower end of Cenderawasih Bay, west of Iresim. *Class:* Austronesian, Malayo-Polynesian, Central-Eastern, Eastern Malayo-Polynesian, South Halmahera-West New Guinea, West New Guinea, Cenderawasih Bay, Yaur. *Other:* Coastal. Sea level to 1,000 meters. Fishermen; agriculturalists. Traditional religion, Christian.

Yawa (Yapanani, Mora, Turu, Mantembu, Yava, Iau) [yva] 6,000 (1987 SIL). Central Serui Island, Serui Waropen, Serui Selatan, Timur Barat, 8 north coast villages, 2 interior villages, 18 south coast villages. *Class:* Geelvink Bay, Yawa. *Dialects:* Central Yawa (Mora), West Yawa, South Yawa, North Yawa, East Yawa. *Lg Use:* Used in the home, market, and religious services. *Lg Dev:* Literacy rate in first language: 15% to 25%. Bible portions: 1989–1999. *Other:* Distinct from Iau in Lakes Plain area. Agriculturalists; fishermen. Christian, traditional religion.

Yei (Yey, Jei, Je, Yei-Nan) [jei] 900 (1996 M. Donohue). Ethnic population: 1,100 (1996 M. Donohue). Border area of south coast, east of Marind along Maro River, 6 villages. *Class:* Trans-New Guinea, Trans-Fly-Bulaka River, Trans-Fly, Morehead and Upper Maro rivers, Yey. *Dialects:* Upper Yei, Lower Yei. The dialects are inherently intelligible with each other only with difficulty. *Lg Use:* Used in the home. Most are proficient in Papuan Malay or Marind. *Other:* Different cultural group from Marind. Not spoken in Papua New Guinea. Lowland. Below 100 meters. Hunters; fishermen; agriculturalists. Christian, traditional religion.

Yelmek (Jelmek, Jab, Jabsch, Jelmik) [jel] 400 (1978 SIL). South coast area on east side of Marianne Strait between Kolopom (Frederik Hendrik) Island and mainland. *Class:* Trans-New Guinea, Trans-Fly-Bulaka River, Bulaka River. *Dialects:* Closest to Maklew. *Other:* Swamp. Below 100 meters. Fishermen; sago-gatherers. Christian, traditional religion.

Yeretuar (Goni, Umar, Umari) [gop] 350 (2000). Lower Cenderawasih Bay, south of Wandamen language. *Class:* Austronesian, Malayo-Polynesian, Central-Eastern, Eastern Malayo-Polynesian, South Halmahera-West New Guinea, West New Guinea, Cenderawasih Bay, Yeretuar. *Other:* Distinct from Kamoro. Coastal. Sea level to 1,000 meters. Fishermen; agriculturalists. Christian, traditional religion.

Yetfa (Biksi, Biaksi, Inisine) [yet] 1,000 in Indonesia (1996). Population total all countries: 1,200. Jayawijaya Kabupaten, Okbibab Kecamatan, border area east and north of the Sogber River, many villages south of Gunung. Also spoken in Papua New Guinea. *Class:* Sepik-Ramu, Sepik, Biksi. *Dialects:* Yetfa and Biksi are 2 ethnic groups, speaking the same language. *Lg Use:* Trade language in the area, extending to Papua New Guinea border. Used in the home, market, and religious services.

Other: Foothills. Tropical forest. 400 to 1,200 meters. Agriculturalists; hunters. Christian, traditional religion.

Yoke (Yoki, Yauke, Jauke, Pauwi) [yki] 200 (1998 Donohue). East of Warembori east of the Mamberamo River, Jayapura Kabupaten, Mantarbori village. Recently moved to coastal location from the interior. *Class:* Lower Mamberamo. *Dialects:* Lexical similarity 33% with Warembori. *Lg Use:* Vigorous. Used in religious services. All ages. Almost no ability in Indonesian. Some ability in Warembori, though more Warembori speak Yoke than vice versa. *Other:* Coastal plain. Below 100 meters. Marketers: sirup hiu, crocodile skins, bananas, sago, clams. Traditional religion, Christian.

Indonesia (Sulawesi)

Indonesia (Sulawesi). 14,111,444 (2000 census). 4 provinces. Information mainly from T. Sebeok 1971; J. C. Anceaux 1978; S. Kaseng 1978, ms (1983); B. H. Bhurhanuddin ms (1979); J. N. Sneddon 1983, 1989, 1993; C. E. and B. D. Grimes 1987; T. Friberg 1987; T. Friberg and T. Laskowske 1988; R. van den Berg 1988, 1996; M. Martens 1989; N. P. Himmelmann 1990; R. Blust 1991; Noorduyn 1991a; D. E. Mead 1998. The number of languages listed for Indonesia (Sulawesi) is 114. Of those, all are living languages. See maps beginning on page 802.

Andio (Masama, Andio'o, Imbao'o) [bzb] 1,700 (1991 SIL). Central Sulawesi, Banggai District, Lamala Subdistrict, eastern peninsula, Taugi and Tangeban villages. *Class:* Austronesian, Malayo-Polynesian, Sulawesi, Saluan-Banggai, Western. *Dialects:* Related to Balantak, Saluan. Lexical similarity 44% with Bobongko, 62% with Coastal Saluan, 66% with Balantak. *Other:* 'Masama' is the preferred local name. Muslim.

Aralle-Tabulahan [atq] 12,000 (1984 SIL). South Sulawesi, Mambi Subdistrict, between Mandar and Kalumpang. *Class:* Austronesian, Malayo-Polynesian, Sulawesi, South Sulawesi, Northern, Pitu Ulunna Salu. *Dialects:* Aralle, Tabulahan, Mambi. Aralle has 84% to 89% lexical similarity with other dialects listed, 75% to 80% with dialects of Pitu Ulunna Salu, Pannei, Ulumandak. *Lg Dev:* Bible portions: 1999. *Other:* Christian, Muslim.

Bada (Bada', Tobada') [bhz] 10,000 (1991 SIL). South central portion of central Sulawesi, in 14 villages of Lore Selatan Subdistrict, two mixed villages of Pamona Selatan Subdistrict, four mixed villages of Poso Pesisir Subdistrict, part of Lemusa village in Parigi Subdistrict, and Ampibabo Subdistrict. Ako village is in northern Mamuju District, Pasangkayu Subdistrict. 23 villages or parts of villages. Members of the ethnic group in south Sulawesi, headwaters of the Budong-Budong River in Budong-Budong Subdistrict, Mamuju District, no longer speak the language. One speaker spoke some, with influences from other languages. *Class:* Austronesian, Malayo-Polynesian, Sulawesi, Kaili-Pamona, Southern, Badaic. *Dialects:* Bada, Ako. The Hanggira dialect is no longer distinguished from Bada. Lexical similarity 85% between Bada and Besoa, 91% between Besoa and Napu, 80% between Bada and Napu. The three are geographically, politically, culturally distinct. *Lg Use:* All domains, home, work. Speakers use Indonesian as second language with varying proficiency. *Other:* 'Tobada' means 'Bada person'. 800 meters. Agriculturalists: rice. Christian, Muslim.

Bahonsuai [bsu] 200 (1991 SIL). Central Sulawesi, Bungku Tengah Subdistrict, Bahonsuai village on the east coast. *Class:* Austronesian, Malayo-Polynesian, Sulawesi, Bungku-Tolaki, Eastern, East Coast. *Dialects:* Lexical similarity 71% with Tomadino, 68% with Mori Atas, Mori Bawah, and Padoe. *Other:* Coastal. Muslim.

Bajau, Indonesian (Badjaw, Badjo, Bajo, Bajao, Bayo, Gaj, Luaan, Lutaos, Lutayaos, Sama, Orang Laut, Turije'ne') [bdl] 90,000 (2000). Population includes 25,000 in central Sulawesi (1979 D. Barr), 8,000 to 10,000 in south Sulawesi (1983 C. Grimes), 5,000 or more in north Maluku (1982 C. Grimes), several thousand in Nusa Tenggara (1981 Wurm and Hattori). In south Sulawesi in Selayar, Bone, and Pangkep districts. On the east coast of southeast Sulawesi on Wowonii, Muna, northern Buton, Kabaena, and northern Tukang Besi islands. Widely distributed throughout Sulawesi, north Maluku (Bacan, Obi, Kayoa, and Sula Islands), Kalimantan, and the islands of the East Sunda Sea. Other Bajau languages are in Sabah, Malaysia, and the southern Philippines. *Class:* Austronesian, Malayo-Polynesian, Sama-Bajaw, Sulu-Borneo, Borneo Coast Bajaw. *Dialects:* Jampea, Same', Matalaang, Sulamu, Kajoa, Roti, Jaya Bakti, Poso, Tongian 1, Tongian 2, Wallace. *Lg Use:* Vigorous in north Maluku. *Other:* Known as Bayo and Turijene in the language of Macassar. Known as Bajo in Buginese. It may include several languages. There are schools in some villages. They live in houses on stilts over water. Coastal, islands. Seamen. Muslim, traditional religion.

Balaesang (Balaesan, Balaisang, Pajo) [bls] 3,200 (2001 Himmelmann). Central Sulawesi, Balaesang Subdistrict, 5 villages on the Manimbayu Peninsula. *Class:* Austronesian, Malayo-Polynesian, Sulawesi, Tomini-Tolitoli, Tomini, Southern. *Dialects:* Not closely related to other languages. *Other:* Muslim.

Balantak (Kosian) [blz] 30,000 (2000 R. Busenitz). 3,000 are monolingual. East central Sulawesi; Banggai District, Luwuk, Balantak, Tinangkung, and Lamala subdistricts, eastern peninsula; 49 villages, or parts of villages. *Class:* Austronesian, Malayo-Polynesian, Sulawesi, Saluan-Banggai, Eastern. *Dialects:* Related to Andio, Saluan. Lexical similarity 66% with Andio, 51% with Coastal Saluan, 39% with Bobongko. *Lg Use:* Vigorous. Speakers of other languages in the area also speak Balantak as second language. All domains. Oral and written use in some churches, oral use in local commerce. Medium of oral instruction in earliest education. Positive language attitude. 27,000 can speak Indonesian. A handful know some neighboring languages. *Lg Dev:* Literacy rate in first language: 10%. 3,000 can read it, 300 can write it. Taught in primary schools. Radio programs. Dictionary. Bible portions: 1991. *Other:* Coastal, mountain slope. Sea level to 600 meters. Agriculturalists; coconut production. Muslim, Christian, traditional religion.

Bambam [Pitu-Ulunna-Salu) [ptu] 22,000 (1988 SIL). South Sulawesi, watershed of the Maloso and Mapilli rivers in Mambi Subdistrict of western Polmas District, overlapping into Majene and Mamuju districts. *Class:* Austronesian, Malayo-Polynesian, Sulawesi, South Sulawesi, Northern, Pitu Ulunna Salu. *Dialects:* Bambam Hulu, Salu Mokanam, Bumal, Mehalaan, Pattae', Matangnga, Issilita', Pakkau. Complex dialect chain. Bumal has 83% to 94% lexical similarity with all dialects listed. Lexical similarity 85% to 80% with dialects of Aralle-Tabulahan, Pannei, and Ulumandak. *Lg Use:* Vigorous. All ages. *Lg Dev:* Grammar. Bible portions: 1994–1999. *Other:* Mountain slope, riverine. Agriculturalists: wet rice, coffee, cacao. Christian, Muslim, traditional religion.

Banggai (Aki) [bgz] 100,000 (1995 SIL). Central Sulawesi; Banggai, Liang, Bulagi, Buko, Totikum, Tinangkum, Labobo Bangkurung subdistricts; Banggai Islands off the eastern peninsula; 157 villages, or parts of villages. *Class:* Austronesian, Malayo-Polynesian, Sulawesi, Saluan-Banggai, Western. *Dialects:* East Banggai, West Banggai. *Lg Dev:* Dictionary. Grammar. NT: 1993. *Other:* Muslim, Christian.

Bantik [bnq] 11,000 (1981 Wurm and Hattori). Northeast section of the northern peninsula of Sulawesi; 11 villages around Manado. *Class:* Austronesian, Malayo-Polynesian, Sulawesi, Sangiric, Southern. *Lg Use:* Speakers also use Manado Malay. *Other:* Christian.

Baras (Ende) [brs] 250 (1987 SIL). 50 households. South Sulawesi, Mamuju District, south Pasangkayu and north Budong-Budong subdistricts, a few villages, mainly in Desa Baras, between the Lariang and Budong-Budong rivers. *Class:* Austronesian, Malayo-Polynesian, Sulawesi, Kaili-Pamona, Northern, Kaili. *Dialects:* Lexical similarity 84% with Da'a, 85% with Inde, 80% or more with other Kaili varieties, 64% with Uma. *Other:* Some think the language will die out. Muslim.

Bentong (Dentong) [bnu] 25,000 (1987 SIL). South Sulawesi, northwest corner of the southern tip of the peninsula; inland parts of Maros, Bone, Pangkep, and Barru districts. *Class:* Austronesian, Malayo-Polynesian, Sulawesi, South Sulawesi, Makassar. *Dialects:* Closest to Konjo. *Other:* Muslim, Christian.

Besoa (Behoa) [bep] 8,000 (2000 SIL). Central Sulawesi, Lore Utara Subdistrict, Napu Valley, 8 villages. *Class:* Austronesian, Malayo-Polynesian, Sulawesi, Kaili-Pamona, Pamona. *Dialects:* Geographically, politically, culturally, and lexically distinct from Bada and Napu. *Lg Use:* 70% are speakers. The language is passed on to more than 60% of the children. Most domains. Positive language attitude. Nearly everyone can speak Indonesian at some level. *Other:* 1,100 meters. Agriculturalists: rice. Christian, Muslim.

Bintauna [bne] 6,000 (1981 Wurm and Hattori). Northeast Sulawesi, around Bintauna. *Class:* Austronesian, Malayo-Polynesian, Sulawesi, Gorontalo-Mongondow, Gorontalic. *Other:* Muslim.

Boano (Bolano, Djidja) [bzl] 2,700 (2001 N. Himmelmann). Central Sulawesi, Montong Subdistrict, Bolano village, on the south coast. *Class:* Austronesian, Malayo-Polynesian, Sulawesi, Tomini-Tolitoli, Tolitoli. *Dialects:* Lexical similarity 83% with Totoli. *Other:* Different from Boano in Maluku. Muslim.

Bobongko [bgb] 1,500 (2001 SIL). Population includes 1,100 in Lembanato and 400 in Tumbulawa. Central Sulawesi, Togian Islands, Lembanato village, on Kilat Bay on the north side, and Tumbulawa village on the northwest coast of Batu Daka Island. *Class:* Austronesian, Malayo-Polynesian, Sulawesi, Saluan-Banggai, Western, Saluanic. *Dialects:* Related to Saluan. Not the same as Andio. Lexical similarity is 53% with Coastal Saluan, 44% with Andio, and 30% with Gorontalo, 25% to 30% with Gorontalo-Mongondow languages. *Other:* The name 'Bobongko' is not derogatory to its speakers, but it is to the Andio. Muslim, Christian.

Bolango (Bulanga, Bulanga-Uki, Diu) [bld] 20,000 (1981 Wurm and Hattori). Population includes 5,000 in Bolango, 15,000 in Atinggola. Northeastern Sulawesi. Bolango is on the south coast of the peninsula around Molibagu and Atinggola on the north central coast around Atinggola, between Kaidipang and Gorontalo. *Class:* Austronesian, Malayo-Polynesian, Sulawesi, Gorontalo-Mongondow, Gorontalic. *Dialects:* Bolango, Atinggola. *Other:* Separate language from Gorontalo (J. Little). Muslim.

Bonerate [bna] 9,500 (1987 SIL). South Sulawesi, Bonerate, Madu, Kalaotoa, and Karompa islands. *Class:* Austronesian, Malayo-Polynesian, Sulawesi, Muna-Buton, Tukangbesi-Bonerate. *Dialects:* Bonerate, Karompa. Lexical similarity 79% to 81% with Tukang Besi South, 31% with Kalao, 25% with Laiyolo. *Other:* Muslim.

Budong-Budong (Tangkou, Tongkou) [bdx] 70 (1988). Tongkou village, Mamuju District, Budong-Budong Subdistrict, on the Budong-Budong River. *Class:* Austronesian, Malayo-Polynesian, Sulawesi, South Sulawesi, Seko. *Dialects:* Closer to Aralle-Tabulahan and Ulumandak. Lexical similarity 56% with Mamuju and Seko Padang, 61% with Seko Tengah, 72% with Panasuan. *Lg Use:* Some speakers are becoming bilingual in Topoiyo through intermarriage and geographical proximity. *Other:* Muslim.

Bugis (Buginese, Bugi, Boegineesche, Boeginezen, Ugi, De', Rappang Buginese) [bug] 3,500,000 in Indonesia (1991 SIL). South Sulawesi, 3.5' to 5' South, other areas of the coastal swamp such as Bulukumba, Luwu, Polewali in Polmas, Pasangkayu in Mamuju districts. On the western coast of southeast Sulawesi in Kolaka, Wundulako, Rumbia, and Poleang districts. Also in major towns of Sulawesi. Large enclaves also in other provinces of Sulawesi, Kalimantan, Maluku, Papua, and Sumatra. Also spoken in Malaysia (Sabah). *Class:* Austronesian, Malayo-Polynesian, Sulawesi, South Sulawesi, Bugis. *Dialects:* Bone (Palakka, Dua Boccoe, Mare), Pangkep (Pangkajene), Camba, Sidrap (Sidenrang, Pinrang Utara, Alitta), Pasangkayu (Ugi Riawa), Sinjai (Enna, Palattae, Bulukumba), Soppeng (Kessi), Wajo, Barru (Pare-Pare, Nepo, Soppeng Riaja, Tompo, Tanete), Sawitto (Pinrang), Luwu (Luwu', Bua Ponrang, Wara, Malangke-Ussu). The Bone or Soppeng dialects are central. *Lg Use:* Vigorous. 500,000 second-language speakers. *Lg Dev:* Bugis Lontara syllabary. Dictionary. Grammar. Bible: 1900–1997. *Other:* Coastal, hills. Swamp. Agriculturalists: wet rice; famous as seafarers; merchants. Muslim, Christian.

Bungku (Nahine) [bkz] 21,500 (1995 SIL). Population includes 100 Routa, 16,400 Bungku, 2,500 Torete, 1,000 Tulambatu, 800 Landawe, 650 Waia. Central Sulawesi, Bungku Utara, Bungku Tengah, and Bungku Selatan subdistricts, along east coast; 45 villages or parts of villages. Also Tulambatu dialect in northern Southeast Sulawesi, Kendari District, Asera, Soropia, and Lasolo subdistricts, where there is difficult access. *Class:* Austronesian, Malayo-Polynesian, Sulawesi, Bungku-Tolaki, Eastern, East Coast. *Dialects:* Bungku, Routa, Tulambatu, Torete (To Rete), Landawe, Waia. Lexical similarity 81% with Torete, Waia, Tulambatu, and Landawe, 38% with Pamona dialects, Tulambatu 88% lexical similarity with Landawe, 84% with Waia, 82% with Torete, 74% with Wawonii, 66% with Taloki, Kulisusu, and Koroni, 65% with Moronene, 54% with the Mori and Tolaki groups. Lexical similarity 82% between Bungku and Routa. *Lg Use:* Bungku was a language of wider communication before independence. The Torete dialect is not becoming extinct, as reported earlier. *Other:* Muslim.

Buol (Bual, Bwo'ol, Dia) [blf] 75,000 (1989). Central Sulawesi; Paleleh, Bunobogu, Bokat, Momunu, Biau, Baolan subdistricts; north coast near the border with north Sulawesi, 68 villages. *Class:* Austronesian, Malayo-Polynesian, Sulawesi, Gorontalo-Mongondow, Gorontalic. *Dialects:* Lexical similarity 61% with Totoli. *Other:* Muslim.

Busoa (Bosoa) [bup] 500 (1991 SIL). Southeast Sulawesi, Batauga Subdistrict, southwest coast of Buton Island, south of the Katobengke-Topa-Sulaa-Lawela area. *Class:* Austronesian, Malayo-Polynesian, Sulawesi, Muna-Buton, Munan. *Dialects:* Kambe-Kambero shares some innovations with Kaimbulawa and may not be a Busoa dialect. Lexical similarity 84% with Kambe-Kambero, 70% to 79% with Muna dialects, 71% with Muna, 76% with Lantoi. *Other:* Muslim.

Campalagian (Tallumpanuae, Tjampalagian, Tasing) [cml] 30,000 (1986 SIL). South Sulawesi, Majene Kabupaten, Polmas, south coast. *Class:* Austronesian, Malayo-Polynesian, Sulawesi, South Sulawesi, Bugis. *Dialects:* Campalagian, Buku. Lexical similarity 50% to 58% with Mandar, 50% to 62% with Bugis, 55% with Bugis Bone, 62% with Bugis Pangkajene, Bugis Sidrap.

Lg Use: Vigorous. *Other:* Coastal. Merchants, fishermen; agriculturalists. Muslim.

Cia-Cia (South Buton, Southern Butung, Buton, Butung, Butonese, Boetoneezen) [cia] 15,000 (1986 SIL). Southeast Sulawesi, south Buton Island. *Class:* Austronesian, Malayo-Polynesian, Sulawesi, Muna-Buton, Buton, West Buton. *Dialects:* Kaesabu, Sampolawa (Mambulu-Laporo), Wabula, Masiri. Wabula dialect has subdialects Wabula, Burangasi, Wali, Takimpo, Kondowa, Holimombo. Lexical similarity 93% with Masiri, 74% with Kambe-Kambero, 69% with Busoa, 67% with Lantoi, 66% with Liabuku, 61% with Wolio, 60% with Muna. *Lg Use:* Speakers also use Wolio. *Other:* "Cia-Cia" is the generally used name, although it is a negative term. Muslim.

Dakka [dkk] 1,500 (1986 SIL). South Sulawesi, Polewali-Mamasa District, Wonomulyo Subdistrict. *Class:* Austronesian, Malayo-Polynesian, Sulawesi, South Sulawesi, Northern, Pitu Ulunna Salu. *Dialects:* Lexical similarity 72% to 77% with Pannei and Pitu Ulunna Salu. *Other:* Muslim.

Dampelas (Dian, Dampal, Dampelasa) [dms] 10,300 (2001 N. Himmelmann). Central Sulawesi; Dampelas Sojol and Balaesang subdistricts, 8 villages. *Class:* Austronesian, Malayo-Polynesian, Sulawesi, Tomini-Tolitoli, Tomini, Southern. *Other:* Muslim.

Dondo [dok] 13,000 (2001 N. Himmelmann). Central Sulawesi; Tolitoli Buol District, Tolitoli Utara, Baolan, Dondo, Galang, and Dampal Utara subdistricts on the north coast; 25 villages, or parts of villages. *Class:* Austronesian, Malayo-Polynesian, Sulawesi, Tomini-Tolitoli, Tomini, Northern. *Dialects:* Speakers consider Dondo a separate language from Totoli. It is probably separate from Tomini. *Other:* Muslim, Christian.

Duri (Masenrempulu, Massenrempulu) [mvp] 95,000 (1991 SIL). Population includes 90,000 in Enrekang District. South Sulawesi, northern Enrekang District, and in Ujung Pandang and elsewhere in South Sulawesi. *Class:* Austronesian, Malayo-Polynesian, Sulawesi, South Sulawesi, Northern, Masenrempulu. *Dialects:* Cakke, Kalosi. *Lg Use:* Vigorous. Duri is the prestige language of the Masenrempulu group. *Lg Dev:* Bible portions: 1998. *Other:* VSO, split ergative. Mountain slope. Agriculturalists: vegetables, coffee, wet rice. Muslim, Christian.

Enrekang (Endekan, Endekan Timur) [ptt] 50,000 (1991 SIL). South Sulawesi, Enrekang, and Pinrang districts. *Class:* Austronesian, Malayo-Polynesian, Sulawesi, South Sulawesi, Northern, Masenrempulu. *Dialect:* Enrekang, Ranga, Pattinjo (Letta-Batulappa-Kassa). *Other:* Foothills, plains. Agriculturalists: maize, wet rice, cassava, vegetables. Muslim.

Gorontalo (Hulontalo) [gor] 900,000 (1989). Northwestern Sulawesi, southern coast of northern peninsula. *Class:* Austronesian, Malayo-Polynesian, Sulawesi, Gorontalo-Mongondow, Gorontalic. *Dialects:* East Gorontalo, Gorontalo Kota, West Gorontalo (Kwandang), Tilamuta, Limboto (Limbotto). The Gorontalo-Mongondow subgroup may relate more closely to a Greater Central Philippines subgroup than to the Sulawesi subgroup (Blust 1991). *Lg Dev:* NT: 2000. *Other:* Muslim, Christian.

Kaidipang (Kaidipan, Dio) [kzp] 22,000 (1981 Wurm and Hattori). Northern Sulawesi, northern coast on both sides of Bolang Itang. *Class:* Austronesian, Malayo-Polynesian, Sulawesi, Gorontalo-Mongondow, Gorontalic. *Dialect:* Kaidipan, Bolaang Itang (Bolang Itang). *Other:* Muslim.

Kaili, Da'a (Da'a, Bunggu) [kzf] 35,000. Population includes Da'a and Inde. 3,000 to 5,000 Da'a and Inde are in south Sulawesi. Central Sulawesi and South Sulawesi provinces in the Marawola, Dolo, Sigi-Biromaru, Palolo, and Banawa subdistricts. 'Bunggu' is the name used for Da'a and Inde in south Sulawesi, Mamuju District, Pasangkayu Subdistrict, near Palu. *Class:* Austronesian, Malayo-Polynesian, Sulawesi, Kaili-Pamona, Northern, Kaili. *Dialects:* Da'a (Pekawa, Pekava, Pakawa), Inde. There is some intelligibility with Ledo and other Kaili varieties, but with major sociolinguistic differences. Da'a and Inde have 98% lexical similarity. *Lg Use:* Vigorous. All domains. Oral use in local administration, commerce, school. Some oral and written use in church, along with Indonesian. All ages. Positive language attitude. Most children know little Indonesian when entering school. *Lg Dev:* Literacy rate in first language: 45%. 16,000 read and write it. NT: 1998. *Other:* Mountain slope, mountain valley. Up to 2,200 meters. Agriculturalists. Christian.

Kaili, Ledo (Ledo, Palu, Paloesch) [lew] 233,500. Population includes 128,000 Ledo, Doi, Ado, and Edo together, 7,500 Ija and Taa together, 55,000 Rai and Raio together, 43,000 Tara (1979 Barr, Barr, and Salombe). 8,000 to 10,000 are in south. Central and south Sulawesi. *Class:* Austronesian, Malayo-Polynesian, Sulawesi, Kaili-Pamona, Northern, Kaili. *Dialects:* Ledo (Palu), Doi, Ado, Edo, Tado, Tara (Parigi), Rai (Sindue-Tawaili, Tawaili-Sindue), Raio (Kori), Ija (Sigi), Taa. Doi is intelligible with Ledo, Edo; Ado the next most intelligible; Tado a little less. Some intelligibility of Da'a, but there are major sociolinguistic differences. Ledo has 80% to 88% lexical similarity with Ado, Edo, Doi, and Lindu. *Lg Use:* Trade language. Ledo is the lingua franca throughout the West Toraja area; the largest and most prestigious of the Kaili varieties in Sulawesi. *Lg Dev:* NT: 1999. *Other:* The Tado dialect is different from 'Tado', used as an alternate name for Lindu. Coastal, mountain slope. Swidden and peasant agriculturalists: wet rice; copra production. Muslim, Christian.

Kaili, Unde (Banawa, Banava) [unz] 20,000 (1979 Barr, Barr, and Salombe). Central Sulawesi in the Banawa, Palu and Tawaeli subdistricts, and South Sulawesi in the Pasangkayu Subdistrict. *Class:* Austronesian, Malayo-Polynesian, Sulawesi, Kaili-Pamona, Northern, Kaili. *Other:* Muslim.

Kaimbulawa [zka] 1,500 (1991 SIL). Southeast Sulawesi, part of Siompu Island. *Class:* Austronesian, Malayo-Polynesian, Sulawesi, Muna-Buton, Munan, Munic. *Dialects:* Lantoi, Kambe-Kambero. Not a dialect of Muna or Cia-Cia. Lexical similarity 96% with Lantoi, 75% with Busoa, 64% to 74% with Muna dialects, 64% with Muna, 70% with Liabuku, 66% with Cia-Cia, 58% with Wolio, 45% with Kaledupa. *Other:* Muslim.

Kalao (Kalaotoa) [kly] 500 (1988 SIL). South Sulawesi, eastern Kalao Island, south of Selayar Island. *Class:* Austronesian, Malayo-Polynesian, Sulawesi, Wotu-Wolio, Kalao. *Dialects:* Related to Laiyolo (lexical similarity 76%) and Wotu. *Other:* Muslim.

Kalumpang (Makki, Mangki, Maki, Ma'ki, Mangkir, Galumpang) [kli] 12,000 (1991 SIL). South Sulawesi, southeast Mamuju District, Kalumpang Subdistrict. *Class:* Austronesian, Malayo-Polynesian, Sulawesi, South Sulawesi, Northern, Toraja-Sa'dan. *Dialects:* Karataun, Mablei, Mangki (E'da), Bone Hau (Ta'da). There are other small dialects not listed. Lexical similarity 78% with Mamasa, 78% with Rongkong, 74% with Toraja-Sa'dan. Between Karataun and Bone Hau dialects: average 82%. *Lg Use:* Vigorous. *Other:* Mountain slope, riverine. Agriculturalists: rice; coffee. Christian, Muslim.

Kamaru [kgx] 2,000 (1979 Bhurhanuddin). Southeastern Buton Island, southeast Sulawesi. *Class:* Austronesian, Malayo-Polynesian, Sulawesi, Wotu-Wolio, Wolio-Kamaru. *Dialects:* Lexical similarity 68% with Lasalimu, 67% with Wolio, 54% with Cia-Cia, 51% with Pancana, 49% with Tukang Besi, 45% with Muna. *Other:* Muslim.

Kioko [ues] 1,000 (1991 SIL). Southeast Sulawesi, Kulisusu Subdistrict on Buton Island. *Class:*

Austronesian, Malayo-Polynesian, Sulawesi, Muna-Buton, Munan, Munic, Western. *Dialects:* Kioko, Kambowa. Possibly dialect of the Pancana language. Lexical similarity 82% with Kambowa, 81% with Laompo dialect of Muna, 74% with Muna, 75% with Liabuku and Busoa. *Other:* Muslim.

Kodeoha (Kondeha) [vko] 1,500 (1991 SIL). Southeast Sulawesi, Kolaka District, Lasusua Subdistrict, west coast of Kolaka. 4 villages. *Class:* Austronesian, Malayo-Polynesian, Sulawesi, Bungku-Tolaki, Western, West Coast. *Dialects:* Lexical similarity 75% with Rahambuu; 70% with Tolaki, Mekongga, and Waru; 54% with the Mori and Bungku groups. *Lg Use:* Speakers also use Bugis. *Other:* Muslim.

Konjo, Coastal (Kondjo, Tiro) [kjc] 125,000 (1991 SIL). Population includes 50,000 Kajang, 10,000 Tiro. South Sulawesi, southeast corner of the southern tip of the peninsula; parts of Sinjai, Bulukumba, and Bantaeng districts. *Class:* Austronesian, Malayo-Polynesian, Sulawesi, South Sulawesi, Makassar. *Dialects:* Konjo Pesisir (Ara, Bira), Tana Toa (Tana Towa, Black Konjo, Kajang, Kadjang), Bantaeng (Bonthain). Tana Toa is at the northern end of the dialect cluster. Lexical similarity 76% with Makassar. Tana Toa is within 10% lexical similarity of the other coastal dialects. *Lg Use:* Vigorous. *Other:* Tana Towa resist modern ways, contact with outsiders. Coastal. Agriculturalists; fishermen; boat builders. Muslim, traditional religion (Tana Towa).

Konjo, Highland (Konjo Pegunungan, Konyo) [kjk] 150,000 (1991 SIL). South Sulawesi, central mountain area, Sinjai, Bone, Gowa, Bulukumba districts. *Class:* Austronesian, Malayo-Polynesian, Sulawesi, South Sulawesi, Makassar. *Dialects:* Lexical similarity 75% with Coastal Konjo. *Other:* Mountain slope. Agriculturalists: wet rice, fruit, vegetables, coffee. Muslim, Christian.

Koroni [xkq] 500 (1991 SIL). Central Sulawesi, Bungku Tengah Subdistrict, Unsongi village on the east coast 12 km south of Bungku town. *Class:* Austronesian, Malayo-Polynesian, Sulawesi, Bungku-Tolaki, Eastern, East Coast, Kulisusu. *Dialects:* Lexical similarity 75% with Taloki and Kulisusu, 66% with Wawonii, Bungku, Tulambatu; 65% with Moronene. *Other:* Coastal. Muslim.

Kulisusu (Kalisusu, Kolinsusu, Kolensusu) [vkl] 22,000 (1995 SIL). Southeast Sulawesi, Kulisusu and Bonegunu subdistricts on the northeast corner of Buton Island. *Class:* Austronesian, Malayo-Polynesian, Sulawesi, Bungku-Tolaki, Eastern, East Coast, Kulisusu. *Dialects:* Lexical similarity 81% between dialects, 77% with Taloki, 75% with Koroni, 66% with Wawonii and the Bungku group, 65% with Moronene, 54% with the Mori and Tolaki groups. *Other:* Muslim.

Kumbewaha (Umbewaha) [xks] 250 (1993 Mark Donohue). Sulawesi Tenggara Province, Buton District, Lasalimu Subdistrict in southeast Buton Island, Kumbewaha village. *Class:* Austronesian, Malayo-Polynesian, Sulawesi, Muna-Buton, Buton, East Buton. *Lg Use:* All domains. All ages. They use Indonesian for school, official purposes, Lasilimu if they have family ties, Tukang Basi for trade or family. *Lg Dev:* Literacy rate in second language: 20%. *Other:* Muslim.

Laiyolo (Da'ang, Barang-Barang) [lji] 800 (1997 SIL). Population includes 250 Laiyolo, 550 Barang-Barang. South Sulawesi, Laiyolo in villages of Lembang Mate'ne in Desa Laiyolo, and a few in Kilotepo' and Sangkeha'. Barang-Barang in Barang-Barang village in Desa Lowa, southern tip of Selayar Island. *Class:* Austronesian, Malayo-Polynesian, Sulawesi, Wotu-Wolio, Kalao. *Dialects:* Barang-Barang (Loa, Loa', Lowa), Laiyolo (Lajolo, Layolo). Barang-Barang may need separate literature. Lexical similarity 86% between Laiyolo and

Barang-Barang, 76% with Kalao, 65% with Buton, 53% with Wotu, 39% with Muna. *Lg Use:* Vigorous in Barang-Barang dialect. Children in Laiyolo villages are reported to not be using Laiyolo. Selayar is second language used. Indonesian used little. *Other:* Coastal, hills. Agriculturalists: maize, cassava cultivation; copra production. Muslim, Christian.

Lasalimu [llm] 2,000 (1979 Bhurhanuddin). Southeastern part of Buton Island, Lasalimu Subdistrict, southeast Sulawesi. *Class:* Austronesian, Malayo-Polynesian, Sulawesi, Muna-Buton, Buton, East Buton. *Dialects:* Lexical similarity 68% with Kamaru, 64% with Cia-Cia, 57% with Tukang Besi, 51% with Pancana, 50% with Wolio and Muna. *Other:* Muslim.

Lauje (Laudje, Tinombo, Ampibabo-Lauje) [law] 44,000 (2001 N. Himmelmann). Central Sulawesi, Dampelas Sojol, Dondo, Tinombo, Tomini, and Ampibabo subdistricts, along Tomini Bay, Sidoan River area. *Class:* Austronesian, Malayo-Polynesian, Sulawesi, Tomini-Tolitoli, Tomini, Northern. *Dialect:* Ampibabo. Ampibabo may be a separate language. *Lg Dev:* Bible portions. *Other:* Muslim, Christian, traditional religion.

Lemolang (Baebunta) [ley] 2,000 (1995 SIL). South Sulawesi, Luwu District, inland from the northeast coast, centered in the villages of Sassa and Salassa, with other scattered speakers in Sabbang Subdistrict, and possibly Baebunta. *Class:* Austronesian, Malayo-Polynesian, Sulawesi, South Sulawesi, Lemolang. *Dialects:* Lexical similarity 41% with Mori Bawah, 39% with Mori Atas, 38% with Bungku, 39% with Buton, 31% with Seko Padang, 30% with Rampi, 29% with Toraja-Sa'dan, 26% with Muna, 25% with Wotu, 24% with Bugis. *Lg Use:* Some children do not speak Lemolang; however, of 25 children questioned in 1990, 76% said they spoke it well. Bilingual level estimates for Indonesian: 0 0%, 1 3%, 2 75%, 3 22%, 4 0%, 5 0%. Tae' Luwu is the dominant language of the area. *Other:* Foothills. Muslim.

Liabuku (Liabuka) [lix] 75 (2004 SIL). Southeast Sulawesi, one village north of Bau-Bau in Bungi and Kapontori districts, south Buton Island. *Class:* Austronesian, Malayo-Polynesian, Sulawesi, Muna-Buton, Munan, Munic, Western. *Dialects:* Quite divergent from other Muna varieties. Lexical similarity 82% with the Burukene dialect of Muna, 72% to 76% with other Muna dialects, 72% with Muna, 75% with Kioko. *Lg Use:* Use is in decline. *Other:* Muslim.

Lindu (Linduan, Tado) [klw] 2,000 (1990 SIL). Central Sulawesi, Kulawi Subdistrict; villages of Anca, Tomado, Langko, near Lake Lindu. *Class:* Austronesian, Malayo-Polynesian, Sulawesi, Kaili-Pamona, Northern, Kaili. *Other:* 'Tado' as an alternate name for Lindu is different from the Tado dialect of Ledo Kaili. Christian.

Lolak [llq] 5,000 (1983 J. N. Sneddon). Northeastern Sulawesi, villages of Lolak, Mongkoinit, and Motabang. *Class:* Austronesian, Malayo-Polynesian, Sulawesi, Gorontalo-Mongondow, Gorontalic. *Dialects:* Structurally related to Gorontalo, but with heavy lexical borrowing from Mongondow. Lexical similarity 79% with Mongondow, 66% with Ponosakan, 63% with Kaidipang. *Lg Use:* Surrounded by Mongondow, which is the second language of speakers. *Other:* Muslim.

Maiwa (Masenrempulu) [wmm] 50,000 (1990 SIL). South Sulawesi, Enrekang and Sidenrang districts. *Class:* Austronesian, Malayo-Polynesian, Sulawesi, South Sulawesi, Northern, Masenrempulu. *Other:* Lowland. Pastoralists; agriculturalists: fruit, palm sugar. Muslim.

Makasar (Makassar, Macassarese, Macassar, Makassa, Makassarese, Taena, Tena, Goa, Mengkasara, Mangasara, Makassaarsche) [mak] 1,600,000 (1989). South Sulawesi, southwest corner of the peninsula, most of Pangkep, Maros, Gowa, Bantaeng, Jeneponto, and Takalar districts.

Class: Austronesian, Malayo-Polynesian, Sulawesi, South Sulawesi, Makassar. *Dialects:* Gowa (Goa, Lakiung), Turatea (Jeneponto), Maros-Pangkep. The Gowa dialect is prestigious. Dialects form a chain. *Lg Use:* Trade language. Vigorous. Many ethnic Chinese speak Makassar as first language. 400,000 second-language speakers. *Lg Dev:* Lontara script is a Bugis-Makasar syllabary still in use. Dictionary. Grammar. Bible: 1900–1999. *Other:* Coastal, foothills. Fishermen; agriculturalists: wet rice, corn, cassava, vegetables; salt harvest. Muslim, Christian.

Malay, Makassar [mfp] 1,876,548 (2000 WCD). Makassar Region. *Class:* Austronesian, Malayo-Polynesian, Malayic, Malayan, Local Malay. *Lg Use:* Trade language.

Malay, Manado (Manadonese Malay, Minahasan Malay) [xmm] 850,000 (2001). North Sulawesi, Minahasa District, west coast around the port of Manado. Used as second language by many in North Sulawesi. *Class:* Creole, Malay based. *Dialects:* Closest to North Moluccan Malay. Also close to Sri Lankan Malay. *Lg Use:* Trade language. An important, growing lingua franca in many parts of Sulawesi. 1,500,000 second-language speakers. Speakers also use Indonesian. *Lg Dev:* Dictionary. *Other:* Influences from Portuguese and Ternate. Christian, Muslim.

Malimpung [mli] 5,000 (1995 SIL). South Sulawesi, Pinrang District, Patampanua Subdistrict, Malimpung area. *Class:* Austronesian, Malayo-Polynesian, Sulawesi, South Sulawesi, Northern, Masenrempulu. *Dialects:* Lexical similarity 80% with Maiwa, 70% with Enrekang. *Lg Use:* They view themselves as distinct from Bugis and Enrekang. *Other:* Muslim.

Mamasa [mqj] 100,000 (1991 SIL). South Sulawesi, Polmas District, Polewali Subdistrict, along the Mamasa River. *Class:* Austronesian, Malayo-Polynesian, Sulawesi, South Sulawesi, Northern, Toraja-Sa'dan. *Dialect:* Northern Mamasa, Central Mamasa, Pattae' (Southern Mamasa, Patta' Binuang, Binuang, Tae', Binuang-Paki-Batetanga-Anteapi). Lexical similarity 78% with Toraja-Sa'dan. *Lg Use:* Vigorous. *Lg Dev:* Bible portions: 1995. *Other:* River valleys. Wet rice cultivation, coffee. Christian, Muslim (Pattae'), traditional religion.

Mamuju (Mamudju, Udai, Mamoedjoe, Mamoedjoesch) [mqx] 60,000 (1991 SIL). Population includes 50,000 in Mamuju dialect. South Sulawesi, Mamuju District, on the coast of Mamuju, Kalukku, and Budong-Budong subdistricts. *Class:* Austronesian, Malayo-Polynesian, Sulawesi, South Sulawesi, Northern, Mamuju. *Dialects:* Mamuju, Sumare-Rangas, Padang, Sinyonyoi. The Mamuju dialect is prestigious. *Lg Use:* Trade language. Positive language attitude. *Other:* Coastal, foothills. Agriculturalists: cloves, maize, cassava, rattan; cocoa and copra production; fishermen. Muslim.

Mandar (Andian, Manjar, Mandharsche) [mdr] 200,000 (1985). South Sulawesi, Majene and Polewali-Mamasa districts, a few settlements in Mamuju District, on the islands of Pangkep District, and at Ujung Lero near Pare-Pare. *Class:* Austronesian, Malayo-Polynesian, Sulawesi, South Sulawesi, Northern, Mandar. *Dialects:* Majene, Balanipa (Napo-Tinambung), Malunda, Pamboang, Sendana (Cenrana, Tjendana). Mandar is a complex dialect grouping; there may be more dialects than those listed. Balanipa and Sendana may each be more than one dialect. Balanipa is the prestige dialect. Mandar, Mamuju, and Pitu Ulunna Salu are separate languages in a language chain. *Lg Dev:* Lontara syllabary script. Dictionary. *Other:* Coastal plain, hills. Fishermen; agriculturalists: cacao, maize, cassava; copra production. Muslim.

Moma (Kulawi) [myl] 5,500 (1985 SIL). Central Sulawesi, northern Kulawi Subdistrict, primarily around Kulawi and Toro towns. *Class:* Austronesian, Malayo-Polynesian, Sulawesi, Kaili-Pamona, Northern, Kaili. *Dialects:*

Historically a 'dialect' of Kaili, but strong influences from Uma. Lexically similar to Uma, but grammatically similar to Lindu. *Lg Dev:* Bible portions: 1939. *Other:* Christian, Muslim.

Mongondow (Bolaang Mongondow, Mongondou, Minahassa) [mog] 900,000 (1989). Northeast Sulawesi, between Tontemboan and Gorontalo. *Class:* Austronesian, Malayo-Polynesian, Sulawesi, Gorontalo-Mongondow, Mongondowic. *Dialects:* Lolayan, Dumoga, Pasi. *Lg Dev:* Dictionary. Grammar. Bible portions: 1932–1939. *Other:* Traditional religion, Muslim, Christian.

Mori Atas (West Mori, Upper Mori) [mzq] 16,098 (2000 WCD). Central Sulawesi at the neck of the southeastern peninsula, Mori Atas, Lembo, and Petasia subdistricts. Also in south Sulawesi. 25 villages or parts of villages. *Class:* Austronesian, Malayo-Polynesian, Sulawesi, Bungku-Tolaki, Western, Interior. *Dialect:* Aikoa. Lexical similarity 73% to 86% with Mori Bawah and Padoe. *Lg Dev:* NT: 1948. *Other:* Christian, Muslim.

Mori Bawah (East Mori, Lower Mori, Nahina) [xmz] 16,098 (2000 WCD). Central Sulawesi at the neck of the southeastern peninsula; Petasia and Lembo subdistricts; 24 villages, or parts of villages. Also in south Sulawesi. *Class:* Austronesian, Malayo-Polynesian, Sulawesi, Bungku-Tolaki, Eastern, East Coast. *Dialects:* Tambe'e, Nahina, Petasia, Soroako, Karonsie. Lexical similarity 73% to 86% with Mori Atas, 75% with Padoe. *Lg Dev:* Grammar. *Other:* Christian, Muslim.

Moronene (Maronene) [mqn] 37,000 (2000 D. Andersen). 5% are monolingual. Population includes 23,000 in Moronene, 14,000 in Tokotu'a. This includes about 3,500 now living in cities. The second or third generations no longer speak Moronene. Southeast Sulawesi, Buton District. Tokotu'a dialect is on Kabaena Island, Wita Ea is on the mainland portion of Buton District opposite Kabaena, with Rumbia subdialect in Rumbia Subdistrict, and Poleang subdialect in Poleang, Poleang Timur, and Watubangga Subdistrict of Kolaka District. *Class:* Austronesian, Malayo-Polynesian, Sulawesi, Bungku-Tolaki, Eastern, Southwest. *Dialects:* Wita Ea (Rumbia, Poleang, Moronene), Tokotu'a (Kabaena). Moronene dialect has 80% lexical similarity with Tokotu'a; 68% with Wawonii-Menui, 66% with Kulisusu, 65% with Taloki, Koroni, Tulambatu, 64% with Bungku, and 57% with Tolaki. *Lg Use:* Vigorous. Many Bugis and Muna speakers living in Moronene villages can speak Moronene with varying degrees of fluency. All domains. Oral use in local administration, occasional oral use in church, letter writing. Positive language attitude. Bilingual level estimates for Indonesian: 0 5%, 1 15%, 2 67%, 3 12.5%, 4 .5%, 5 0%. Some also speak Bugis. *Lg Dev:* Taught as an oral and written subject. Radio programs. *Other:* Formerly a kingdom. Mountain slope, valleys. Agriculturalists. Muslim, Christian.

Muna (Wuna, Mounan) [mnb] 227,000 (1989 van den Berg). Population includes 600 in Ambon (1985 SIL). 150,000 Standard Muna, 10,000 Tiworo, 7,000 Siompu, 60,000 Gulamas (1989 van den Berg). Muna Island off southeast Sulawesi, northwest coast of Buton Island, and Ambon, central Maluku. *Class:* Austronesian, Malayo-Polynesian, Sulawesi, Muna-Buton, Munan, Munic, Western. *Dialects:* Standard Muna (Northern Muna), Gulamas (Southern Muna), Siompu, Tiworo (Eastern Muna). Subdialects of Standard Muna are: Tungkuno, Kabawo, Lawa, Katobu, Tobea Besar; of Gulamas are: Gu, Mawasangka, Lakudo, Wale-Ale, Lawama, Kadatua, Lowu-Lowu, Kalia-Lia, Katobengke, Topa, Salaa, Lawela, Laompo, Burukene. Lexical similarity 71% with Pancana, 62% with Cia-Cia, 52% with Wolio, 50% with Lasalimu, 47% with Tukang Besi, 45% with Kamaru. *Lg Dev:*

Dictionary. Grammar. Bible portions: 1993. *Other:* 'Wuna' is their self-name. Muslim, Christian.

Napu (Pekurehua) [npy] 6,000 (1995). Central Sulawesi, Lore Utara Subdistrict, Napu Valley, 10 villages. *Class:* Austronesian, Malayo-Polynesian, Sulawesi, Kaili-Pamona, Southern, Badaic. *Dialects:* Closest to Besoa. *Lg Use:* 60% of parents pass it on to the children. Some or most domains. Napu hymns, work announcements. Napu people are at least mildly supportive of the Napu language. Nearly all speakers use Indonesian as second language with varying proficiency. Indonesian is used for writing, at government offices, for town meetings, for religious services, but Napu is also used for these purposes. *Lg Dev:* Interest in Napu literature is high. NT: 2000. *Other:* 1,000 meters. Agriculturalists: rice. Christian, Muslim.

Padoe (South Mori, Padoé, Alalao) [pdo] 6,000 (1991 D. Andersen). South Sulawesi, eastern Luwu District in Nuha, Malili, and Mangkutana subdistricts; Central Sulawesi, Banggai District, 2 villages in Mori Atas Subdistrict and 1 village in Pamona Utara Subdistrict. *Class:* Austronesian, Malayo-Polynesian, Sulawesi, Bungku-Tolaki, Western, Interior. *Dialects:* 2 dialects. Lexical similarity 73% to 86% with Mori Atas, 75% with Mori Bawah. *Lg Use:* Vigorous. Bilingual level estimates for Indonesian: 0 0%, 1–2 82%, 2+ 33%, 3 17%, 4 1%, 5 0%. *Other:* Christian, Muslim.

Pamona (Bare'e, Baree, Poso, Taa, Wana) [bcx] 106,000 (1979 Barr). Population includes 100,000 in Central Sulawesi, 6,000 to 10,000 in South Sulawesi. Central Sulawesi; Poso District, Poso Kota, Poso Pesisir, Parigi, Lage, Pamona Utara, Pamona Selatan, Tojo, Ulubongko, Ampana Kota, Ampanatete, Una-Una, Mori Atas, Petasia, Bungku Utara, Bungku Tengah subdistricts; 193 villages. South Sulawesi in Mangkutana Subdistrict and north Wotu and Bone-Bone subdistricts in Luwu District. *Class:* Austronesian, Malayo-Polynesian, Sulawesi, Kaili-Pamona, Northern, Pamona. *Dialects:* Pamona, Laiwonu (Iba), Batui, Sinohoan (Daido, Ido, Idore'e), Mbelala (Baria, Bela, Belala), Rapangkaka (Aria), Tomoni, Tobau (Tobao, Tobalo, Bare'e), Tokondindi, Topada, Taa (Wana, Topotaa). Laiwonu, Batui, Sinohoan, Mbelala, and Rapangkaka may be separate languages. Pamona speakers in Bungku Utara recognize 5 ethnic groups with minor dialect differences: Pusangke, Kajumorangka, Tokasiala, Burangas, Topotaa. The first 4 are mountain dwellers in the interior; the Topotaa live along the coast. Speakers in Bungku Tengah recognize 5 varieties: Topotaa (the same as Taa), Tobau, Tokondindi, Topada, and Tombelala. Lexical similarity 76% (Taa) to 90% among dialects, except for Tombelala, which has 66% to 76% lexical similarity with other Bungku Tengah dialects, and is considered to be a separate language. *Lg Use:* Speakers also use Indonesian. *Lg Dev:* Dictionary. Grammar. NT: 1933–1992. *Other:* They call themselves 'Taa' or 'Wana'. Mountain slope, foothills, coastal. Swidden agriculturalists; copra production. Christian.

Panasuan (To Panasean, To Pamosean) [psn] 900 (1988 T. Laskowske). Ethnic population: 900 or more. South Sulawesi, northeast of Kalumpang-speaking area and west of Seko area merging into Kalumpang area in Mamuju District. 2 villages. *Class:* Austronesian, Malayo-Polynesian, Sulawesi, South Sulawesi, Seko. *Dialects:* Lexical similarity 67% with Seko Tengah, 63% with Seko Padang, 72% with Tangkou. *Lg Use:* Used in the home, church announcements, sermons, village government, school, trade. All ages. Highly positive language attitude. *Other:* Christian.

Pancana (Pantjana) [pnp] 15,000 (1979 Bhurhanuddin). Southeast Sulawesi, near Muna, central Buton Island. *Class:* Austronesian, Malayo-Polynesian, Sulawesi, Muna-Buton, Munan, Munic, Western. *Dialects:* Kapontori,

Kalende (Lawele), Labuandiri. Dialect names are also place names. May be more than one language. Lexical similarity 71% with Muna, 57% with Cia-Cia. *Lg Use:* Speakers also use Wolio. *Other:* Muslim.

Pannei (Tapango) [pnc] 9,000 (1986 SIL). South Sulawesi, Polewali-Mamasa District, Wonomulyo Subdistrict. *Class:* Austronesian, Malayo-Polynesian, Sulawesi, South Sulawesi, Northern, Pitu Ulunna Salu. *Dialects:* Tapango, Bulo. Bulo has 87% to 93% lexical similarity with all dialects. Lexical similarity 75% to 80% with dialects of Ulumandak, Pitu Ulunna Salu, Aralle-Tabulahan. *Other:* Muslim.

Pendau (Ndau, Ndaoe, Umalasa) [ums] 3,200 (2001 Himmelmann). Central Sulawesi, Balaesang Subdistrict, villages of Walandano and part of Sibayu, and Simatang Island; and Dampelas Sojol, Ampibabo, Sirenja, Tinombo subdistricts, close to and north of Tajio. *Class:* Austronesian, Malayo-Polynesian, Sulawesi, Tomini-Tolitoli, Tomini, Southern. *Other:* Muslim, Christian.

Ponosakan (Ponasakan) [pns] 3,000 (1981 Wurm and Hattori). Northeast Sulawesi around Belang. *Class:* Austronesian, Malayo-Polynesian, Sulawesi, Gorontalo-Mongondow, Mongondowic. *Dialects:* Lexical similarity 75% with Mongondow, 66% with Lolak. *Other:* Muslim.

Rahambuu (Wiau, Wiaoe) [raz] 5,000 (1991 SIL). Southeast Sulawesi, Kolaka District, Pakue Subdistrict, west coast north of the Kodeoha. *Class:* Austronesian, Malayo-Polynesian, Sulawesi, Bungku-Tolaki, Western, West Coast. *Dialects:* Lexical similarity 87% between dialects, 75% with Kodeoha, 70% with Tolaki, Mekongga, and Waru; 54% with the Mori and Bungku groups. *Other:* Muslim.

Rampi (Leboni, Rampi-Leboni, Ha'uwa) [lje] 8,000 (1991 SIL). 2,300 in South Sulawesi, 5,700 in Central Sulawesi. South Sulawesi, 6 villages in an isolated mountain area of Masamba Subdistrict in Luwu District; also in Sabbang Limbong, Wotu, and Mangkutana subdistricts; and about 15 villages in Poso and Donggala districts of Central Sulawesi. Rato speakers have moved elsewhere. *Class:* Austronesian, Malayo-Polynesian, Sulawesi, Kaili-Pamona, Southern. *Dialects:* Rampi (Lambu), Rato. Leboni is the prestige dialect. *Lg Use:* Vigorous. *Other:* Mountain slope. Swidden agriculturalists. Christian, Muslim.

Ratahan (Bentenan, Pasan) [rth] 30,000 (1989). Northeastern section of the northern peninsula of Sulawesi, around Ratahan and to the southeast coast of the northern peninsula. *Class:* Austronesian, Malayo-Polynesian, Sulawesi, Sangiric, Southern. *Lg Dev:* Grammar. *Other:* Traditional religion, Christian.

Saluan, Coastal (Loinang, Loindang, Madi) [loe] 74,000 (1979 Barr). East central Sulawesi; Luwuk, Balantak, Lamala, Buko, Totikum, Kintom, Batui, Pagimana, Bunta subdistricts; 136 villages. Loinang dialect is in the mountains. *Class:* Austronesian, Malayo-Polynesian, Sulawesi, Saluan-Banggai, Western, Saluanic. *Dialects:* Related to Kahumamahon Saluan, Balantak, Andio. Lexical similarity 53% with Bobongko, 62% with Andio, 51% with Balantak. *Other:* The name 'Saluan' is preferred over 'Loinang' by the speakers. Muslim, traditional religion, Christian.

Saluan, Kahumamahon (Interior Saluan, Kahumamahon) [slb] 2,142 (2000 WCD). East central Sulawesi. *Class:* Austronesian, Malayo-Polynesian, Sulawesi, Saluan-Banggai, Western, Saluanic. *Dialects:* Related to Coastal Saluan, Balantak, Andio. *Lg Dev:* Bible portions. *Other:* Traditional religion, Christian.

Sangir (Sangihé, Sangirese, Sangi, Sangih) [sxn] 200,000 in Indonesia (1995 Indonesian Consul, Davao, Philippines). Population includes 50,000 Siau. Population total all countries: 255,000. North Sulawesi, Great Sangir Island, and north Maluku. Also spoken in Philippines. *Class:* Austronesian, Malayo-Polynesian, Sulawesi,

Sangiric, Northern. *Dialects:* Siau, Manganitu, Tamako, North Tabukang (Tabukang, Tabukan), South Tabukang, Central Tabukang, Kandar, Taruna, Tagulandang (Tahulandang). *Lg Dev:* Dictionary. Grammar. NT: 1883–1994. *Other:* Christian, Muslim.

Sarudu (Doda') [sdu] 4,000 (1990 SIL). South Sulawesi, south Pasangkayu District, Mamuju Subdistrict. *Class:* Austronesian, Malayo-Polynesian, Sulawesi, Kaili-Pamona, Southern. *Dialect:* Nunu', Kulu (Lariang). Lexical similarity 75% with Uma, 80% with Benggaulu. *Other:* They have contact with Bugis and Kaili speakers. Lowland, coastal. Swamp. Sago palm; fishermen. Muslim.

Sedoa (Tawaelia) [tvw] 600 (1979 Barr). East central Sulawesi, Lore Utara, and Poso Pesisir subdistricts; villages of Sedoa and parts of Tambarona and Pinedapa. *Class:* Austronesian, Malayo-Polynesian, Sulawesi, Kaili-Pamona, Northern, Kaili. *Dialects:* Not a dialect of nearby Napu or Kaili. *Lg Use:* Vigorous. *Other:* Christian.

Seko Padang (Seko, Wono, Sua Tu Padang) [skx] 5,000 (1991 SIL). Population includes 2,300 in the Seko area. South Sulawesi, northeast section of Limbong Subdistrict in Luwu District. About half the speakers have resettled in Palolo Valley of Central Sulawesi. *Class:* Austronesian, Malayo-Polynesian, Sulawesi, South Sulawesi, Seko. *Dialect:* Lodang, Hono' (Wono). *Lg Use:* Vigorous. Speakers also use Indonesian. *Other:* Many primary schools. 'Sua Tu Padang' is self name. Plains. 1,150 meters. Agriculturalists: coffee, wet rice, corn, cassava. They provide their own meat and fish. Christian, Muslim.

Seko Tengah (Seko, Pohoneang, Pewanean, Pewaneang) [sko] 2,500 (1995 SIL). Northern south Sulawesi, western part of Limbong Subdistrict along the Betue River. *Class:* Austronesian, Malayo-Polynesian, Sulawesi, South Sulawesi, Seko. *Dialects:* Lexical similarity 71% with Seko Padang, 67% with Panasuan. *Lg Use:* Speakers also use Indonesian. *Other:* Mountain slope, mountain mesa. Agriculturalists: dry rice, coffee, corn, cassava. Christian, Muslim.

Selayar (Salayar, Salajar, Salayer, Silajara, Siladja, Saleier) [sly] 90,000 (1983 SIL). South Sulawesi, Selayar Island. *Class:* Austronesian, Malayo-Polynesian, Sulawesi, South Sulawesi, Makassar. *Dialects:* Lexical similarity 69% with Makassar. *Lg Use:* Vigorous. Bilingual level estimates for Bugis: 0 28%, 1–2 51%, 3 17%, 4 4%, 5 0%. Speakers also use Indonesian. *Other:* Mountain slope, coastal. Agriculturalists: copra plantations, maize, cassava. Muslim, Christian.

Suwawa (Bune, Bonda, Bunda, Suwawa-Bunda) [swu] 10,000 (1981 Wurm and Hattori). Northeastern Sulawesi, around Suwawa and Pinogu, east of Gorontalo town and Lake Limboto. *Class:* Austronesian, Malayo-Polynesian, Sulawesi, Gorontalo-Mongondow, Gorontalic. *Dialect:* Bunda. *Other:* Separate language from Gorontalo. Muslim.

Tae' (Rongkong, Rongkong Kanandede, To Rongkong, Luwu, Toraja Timur, East Toraja, Sada, Toware, Sangangalla', Taeq, Tae' Tae') [rob] 250,000 (1992 SIL). South Sulawesi, Kabupaten Luwu from the Larompong District through Sabbang, with some other scattered pockets. Rongkong dialect is in southeast Limbong and Sabbang subdistricts of Luwu District. Also an enclave in Wasuponda, Nuha Subdistrict near the town of Soroako. Rongkong Atas is the upper river system in Limbong and in Seko Lemo. Rongkong Bawah is the lower river system in Sabbang. *Class:* Austronesian, Malayo-Polynesian, Sulawesi, South Sulawesi, Northern, Toraja-Sa'dan. *Dialects:* Rongkong, Northeast Luwu, South Luwu, Bua. Lexical similarity 92% among dialects, over 86% with the northern dialects, 80% with Toraja-Sa'dan. *Lg Use:* Vigorous. Lemolang and some Bugis, Torajans speak Tae'. Written use for ancestral stories. All domains. Positive language attitude. Indonesian used in school. *Lg Dev:*

Literacy rate in first language: 20% to 30%. About 10% to 20% write it. *Other:* Coastal, valleys. Agriculturalists: wet rice, coffee, vegetables. Muslim, Christian.

Taje (Petapa) [pee] 350 (2001 N. Himmelmann). Central Sulawesi, village of Tanampedagi in Ampibabo Subdistrict; also near Sipeso in Sindue Subdistrict. *Class:* Austronesian, Malayo-Polynesian, Sulawesi, Tomini-Tolitoli, Tomini, Southern. *Other:* Muslim.

Tajio (Kasimbar, Tadjio, Ta'adjio, Adjio) [tdj] 12,000 (2001 N. Himmelmann). Central Sulawesi; Ampibabo, Tinombo, and Sindue subdistricts; 21 villages, or parts of villages. *Class:* Austronesian, Malayo-Polynesian, Sulawesi, Tomini-Tolitoli, Tomini, Southern. *Other:* Self name is 'Tajio'. Kasimbar is the name of the main town. Muslim, Christian.

Talaud (Talaut, Talodda) [tld] 60,000 (1981 UBS). North Sulawesi, Talaud Islands northeast of the Sangihe Islands. *Class:* Austronesian, Malayo-Polynesian, Sulawesi, Sangiric, Southern. *Dialects:* Kaburuang, South Karakelong (Karakelong, Karakelang), Nenusa-Maingas, Essang, Arangka'a, Dapalan (Riung), Awit, Beo, Lirang (Salibabu, Salebabu). *Lg Dev:* NT: 1993. *Other:* Christian.

Taloki (Taluki) [tlk] 500 (1995 SIL). Southeast Sulawesi, northwest coast Buton Island, Wakorumba Subdistrict, Maligano village, and possibly some on south Buton Island, Kapontori Subdistrict, Wakalambe village. *Class:* Austronesian, Malayo-Polynesian, Sulawesi, Bungku-Tolaki, Eastern, East Coast, Kulisusu. *Dialects:* Lexical similarity 77% with Kulisusu; 75% with Koroni; 66% with Wawonii, Bungku, Tulambatu; 65% with Moronene. *Lg Use:* Speakers are reported to have a high bilingualism in Muna. *Other:* Muslim.

Talondo' [tln] 500 (1986 SIL). Ethnic population: 500. Talondo and Pedasi villages, Mamuju District, Kalumpang Subdistrict, 1 village. *Class:* Austronesian, Malayo-Polynesian, Sulawesi, South Sulawesi, Northern, Toraja-Sa'dan. *Dialects:* May be in the Seko subgroup. Lexical similarity 80% with Kalumpang. *Lg Use:* Used in the home, playing field. All ages. Very small children know only Talondo'. They claim to understand the Bone Hau dialect of Kalumpang, but Kalumpang speakers cannot understand Talondo'. They use Kalumpang with the Kalumpang. Indonesian used for trade because sellers are Bugis. Talondo' not used in school because teachers are not Talondo'. *Other:* Agriculturalists: cacao. Christian, Muslim.

Toala' (Toala, Toala-Palili, Luwu', Toraja Timur, East Toraja, Sada, Toware, Sangangalla') [tlz] 30,000 (1983 SIL). South Sulawesi, Luwu District from Masamba to the southern tip of the district. Toala' dialect is from the foothills up to the divide. Palili' dialect is on a narrow coastal strip overlapping with Bugis Luwu. *Class:* Austronesian, Malayo-Polynesian, Sulawesi, South Sulawesi, Northern, Toraja-Sa'dan. *Dialects:* Toala', Palili'. Probably at least 4 dialects. Lexical similarity 74% with Toraja-Sa'dan. *Lg Use:* Vigorous. *Other:* Coastal, mountain slope. Copra plantations; swidden agriculturalists. Muslim.

Tolaki (To'olaki, Lolaki, Lalaki, Laki, Kolaka, "Noie," "Noihe," "Nehina," "Nohina," "Nahina," "Akido") [lbw] 281,000 (1991 SIL). Population includes 230,000 Konawe, 50,000 Mekongga, 650 Asera, fewer than 100 Wiwirano, 200 Laiwui. Southeast Sulawesi, Kendari and Kolaka districts. Mekongga are in the Mekongga Mountains on the western edge of the group near Soroako. *Class:* Austronesian, Malayo-Polynesian, Sulawesi, Bungku-Tolaki, Western, West Coast. *Dialects:* Wiwirano, Asera, Konawe (Kendari), Mekongga (Bingkokak), Norio, Konio, Tamboki (Tambbuoki), Laiwui (Kioki). Wiwirano has 88% lexical similarity with Asera, 84% with Konawe, 85% with Mekongga, 81%

with Laiwui, 78% with Waru, 70% with Rahambuu and Kodeoha, 54% with the Mori and Bungku groups. Mekongga has 86% with Konawe, 80% with Laiwui. *Lg Use:* Wiwirano dialect is spoken only by older adults. *Lg Dev:* Dictionary. Grammar. *Other:* Negative names are no longer in use. Muslim, Christian.

Tomadino [tdi] 600 (1991 SIL). Central Sulawesi, Bungku Tengah Subdistrict, Sakita village on the east coast, outskirts of Bungku town. *Class:* Austronesian, Malayo-Polynesian, Sulawesi, Bungku-Tolaki, Western, Interior. *Dialects:* Lexical similarity 71% with Bahonsuai, 68% with Mori Atas, Mori Bawah, and Padoe. *Lg Use:* Speakers also use Bungku. *Other:* Coastal. Muslim.

Tombelala [ttp] 1,100 (1995 SIL). Central Sulawesi, Bungku Tengah Subdistrict, 4 villages. *Class:* Austronesian, Malayo-Polynesian, Sulawesi, Kaili-Pamona, Northern, Pamona. *Dialects:* Lexical similarity 66% to 76% with Pamona varieties and 38% with Bungku. *Lg Use:* Speakers consider themselves part of Pamona. Speakers also use Indonesian. *Other:* Muslim.

Tombulu (Tombulu', Tombula, Toumbulu, Tombalu, Minahasa, Minhasa) [tom] 60,000 (1981 Wurm and Hattori). Northeastern Sulawesi, around Tanawangko and Tomohon. *Class:* Austronesian, Malayo-Polynesian, Sulawesi, Minahasan, North, Northeast. *Dialects:* Taratara, Tomohon. Closest to Toulour and Tonsea. *Lg Dev:* Bible portions: 1933. *Other:* Traditional religion, Christian.

Tomini (Tiadje, Tialo, Mouton) [txm] 30,000 (2001 N. Himmelmann). Central Sulawesi; Moutong, Tomini, Tinombo subdistricts along Tomini Bay; 42 villages. *Class:* Austronesian, Malayo-Polynesian, Sulawesi, Tomini-Tolitoli, Tomini, Northern. *Other:* Muslim.

Tondano (Tondanou, Tolou, Tolour, Toulour) [tdn] 80,000 in Indonesia (1991 Noorduyn). Northeastern Sulawesi around Tondano and to the southeast coast of the northern peninsula, Toulour District. Also spoken in USA. *Class:* Austronesian, Malayo-Polynesian, Sulawesi, Minahasan, North, Northeast. *Dialects:* Tondano, Kakas (Ka'kas), Remboken. Closest to Tombulu and Tonsea. *Lg Dev:* Grammar. NT: 1996. *Other:* Christian.

Tonsawang (Tombatu) [tnw] 20,000 (1981 Wurm and Hattori). Northeastern Sulawesi around Tombatu. *Class:* Austronesian, Malayo-Polynesian, Sulawesi, Minahasan. *Lg Use:* Speakers also use Manado Malay. *Other:* Christian.

Tonsea (Tonsea') [txs] 90,000 (1989). Northeastern tip of Sulawesi. *Class:* Austronesian, Malayo-Polynesian, Sulawesi, Minahasan, North, Northeast. *Dialects:* Maumbi, Airmadidi, Likupang, Kauditan, Kalabat Atas. *Other:* Traditional religion, Christian.

Tontemboan (Tompakewa, Tountemboan, Pakewa) [tnt] 150,000 (1990). Northeastern coast of Minahasa Peninsula from Sonder to around Motoling and Tompasobaru. *Class:* Austronesian, Malayo-Polynesian, Sulawesi, Minahasan, North. *Dialects:* Langoan, Tompaso (Makelai, Makela'i-Maotow), Sonder (Matanai, Matana'i-Maore'). *Lg Dev:* Dictionary. Grammar. NT: 1933. *Other:* Christian.

Topoiyo [toy] 2,000 (1988 T. Laskowske). South Sulawesi, Budong-Budong Subdistrict in Mamuju District, inland along Budong-Budong River. *Class:* Austronesian, Malayo-Polynesian, Sulawesi, Kaili-Pamona, Northern, Kaili. *Dialects:* Lexical similarity 66% with Sarudu and Da'a, 56% with Ledo, 54% with the Parigi dialect of Kaili. *Lg Use:* Vigorous. *Other:* Recent settlers from elsewhere and rubber plantation development have brought new language contacts. Riverine. Swidden agriculturalists; rubber plantation workers. Muslim.

Toraja-Sa'dan (Sa'dan, Sadan, Sadang, Toraja, Toradja, Tae', Ta'e, South Toraja, Sa'dansche) [sda] 500,000 (1990 UBS). South Sulawesi, Tana Toraja District with large enclaves in Luwu District. Several thousand also in Ujung

Pandang city. Also on west coast of southeast Sulawesi in Kolaka and Wundulako districts. *Class:* Austronesian, Malayo-Polynesian, Sulawesi, South Sulawesi, Northern, Toraja-Sa'dan. *Dialects:* Makale (Tallulembangna), Rantepao (Kesu'), Toraja Barat (West Toraja, Mappa-Pana). Rantepao is prestige dialect. *Lg Dev:* Dictionary. Bible: 1960–1995. *Other:* River valleys. Agriculturalists: wet rice, coffee. Christian, traditional religion, Muslim.

Totoli (Tontoli, Tolitoli, Gage) [txe] 25,000 (2001 N. Himmelmann). Central Sulawesi, Tolitoli Utara, Galang, Baolan, Dondo, subdistricts on the north coast; 29 villages, or parts of villages. *Class:* Austronesian, Malayo-Polynesian, Sulawesi, Tomini-Tolitoli, Tolitoli. *Other:* Muslim.

Tukang Besi North (Wakatobi, Buton) [khc] 120,000 in Indonesia (1995 SIL). Population includes 60,000 in Maluku. Northern islands of Tukang Besi Archipelago, Kaledupa and Wanci, off Southeast Sulawesi; several hundreds in Singapore and Baubau city; on Bacan, Taliabu, Mongole, Buru, Sulabesi, Seram, and Ambon islands in Maluku; Papua; and Sumbawa. Most speakers in Nusa Tenggara and Maluku have a lot of movement and are mixed with Tukang Besi South. Also spoken in Singapore. *Class:* Austronesian, Malayo-Polynesian, Sulawesi, Muna-Buton, Tukangbesi-Bonerate. *Dialects:* Kaledupa (Kahedupa), Wanci (Wanji, Wantji, Wanje, Wangi- Wangi). Lexical similarity 80% between Kaledupa and Wanci; they may be separate languages. 70% to 75% with Tukang Besi South, 48% with Lasalimu, 47% with Cia-Cia, 40% with Kamaru, an average of 35% with other nearby languages. *Lg Dev:* Grammar. *Other:* Muslim.

Tukang Besi South (Tukang-Besi, Wakatobi, Buton) [bhq] 130,000 (1995 SIL). Population includes 100,000 in Maluku. Southern islands of Tukang Besi archipelago, (Binongko and Tomea islands) off Southeast Sulawesi; Taliabu, Mongole, Sulabesi, Buru, Seram, Ambon, and Alor islands in Maluku; Bonerate dialect in Bonerate, Madu, Kalaotoa, and Karompa islands in Selayar District, South Sulawesi; numerous settlements throughout western Papua. *Class:* Austronesian, Malayo-Polynesian, Sulawesi, Muna-Buton, Tukangbesi-Bonerate. *Dialect:* Binongko, Tomea (Tomia). Lexical similarity 70% to 75% with Tukang Besi North, 48% with Cia-Cia, 49% with Lasalimu, average of 35% with other nearby languages. Lexical similarity 85% between Binongko and Tomea, 81% with Bonerate, 79% between Tomea and Bonerate. *Lg Use:* Speakers also use Wolio. *Lg Dev:* Grammar. *Other:* Pronominal indexing, grammatical status of subject, morphological case, causative, Philippine and Oceanic type language features. Muslim.

Ulumanda' (Ulumandak, Oeloemanda, Ulunda, Tubbi, Botteng-Tappalang, Awo-Sumakuyu, Kado) [ulm] 30,000 (1986 SIL). Population includes 18,000 in Polmas and Majene. South Sulawesi, Majene, Mamuju, and Polewali-Mamasa districts. *Class:* Austronesian, Malayo-Polynesian, Sulawesi, South Sulawesi, Northern, Pitu Ulunna Salu. *Dialects:* Sondoang, Tappalang, Botteng. About 6 dialects. Lexical similarity 75% to 80% with dialects of Pitu Ulunna Salu, Aralle-Tabulahan, Pannei. *Other:* Muslim.

Uma (Pipikoro, Oema) [ppk] 20,000 (1990 SIL). Population includes 15,000 in the region, 5,000 outside (1990 M. Martens SIL), 500 in Benggaulu. The Uma homeland is Pipikoro, 'banks of the Koro', along the Lariang, 'Koro' River in central Sulawesi, Donggala District, southern half of Kulawi Subdistrict. 32 villages. Bana dialect is in South Sulawesi, enclave within the Seko Padang dialect area, Kabupaten Luwu. Benggaulu is in South Sulawesi, south Pasangkayu District, Mamuju Subdistrict. Other Uma have migrated to Gimpu and Palolo valleys, Palu and Pani'i, about 120 km north of Palu. *Class:* Austronesian, Malayo-Polynesian, Sulawesi, Kaili-Pamona, Southern. *Dialects:* Winatu (Northern Uma), Tobaku (Western Uma, Dompa, Ompa), Tolee' (Eastern Uma), Kantewu (Central Uma), Southern Uma (Aria), Benggaulu (Bingkolu), Bana. Literature is in Kantewu dialect, but many would prefer to read their own dialect. *Lg Use:* Kantewu is the prestige dialect. Use of Uma is vigorous in the Uma homeland. Among those living outside (e.g., in Palu, Palolo, Gimpu), use of Uma is vigorous among adults. For those who move away as adults, Uma remains language of the home. For those who move away as children, half retain Uma as home language. Used in daily work and local adminstrative activities, and in some religious services in homeland. Oral teaching medium in early primary grades. In Uma homeland children grow up speaking Uma as first language but are bilingual in Indonesian by end of elementary school. Most children living outside the homeland learn Indonesian as first language. Positive language attitude. Most Uma speak Indonesian fluently. In addition approximately 5,000 speak Kaili, 500 Seko Padang, 500 Rampi (2000 SIL). *Lg Dev:* Taught in primary schools. Roman script. Grammar. NT: 1996. *Other:* 600 to 1,000 meters. Swidden agriculturalists: coffee as cash crop. Christian, Muslim.

Waru (Mopute, Mapute) [wru] 350 (1991 SIL). Southeast Sulawesi, Kendari District, Asera Subdistrict, Mopute village by the Lindu River. *Class:* Austronesian, Malayo-Polynesian, Sulawesi, Bungku-Tolaki, Western, West Coast. *Dialects:* Waru, Lalomerui. Waru dialect has 86% lexical similarity with Lalomerui, 79% with Tolaki dialects and Mekongga, 70% with Rahambuu and Kodeoha, 54% with the Mori and Bungku groups. *Other:* Muslim.

Wawonii (Wowonii) [wow] 22,000 (1991 SIL). Population includes 14,000 Wawonii, 7,500 Menui. Southeast Sulawesi, Wawonii and Menui islands near Kendari. *Class:* Austronesian, Malayo-Polynesian, Sulawesi, Bungku-Tolaki, Eastern, East Coast. *Dialects:* Wawonii, Menui. Lexical similarity 75% with Bungku and Tulambatu, 66% with Taloki, Kulisusu, and Koroni, 65% with Moronene. *Other:* Muslim.

Wolio (Baubau) [wlo] 34,529 in Indonesia (2000 WCD). Southwestern Buton Island in Bau-Bau, Southeast Sulawesi. Also spoken in Malaysia (Sabah). *Class:* Austronesian, Malayo-Polynesian, Sulawesi, Wotu-Wolio, Wolio-Kamaru. *Dialects:* Lexical similarity 61% with Cia-Cia, 60% with Masiri and Lantoi. *Lg Use:* Trade language. Wolio is the former court language of the Sultan at Baubau and a few surrounding communities, and formerly used by the nobility in the region. Official regional language. *Lg Dev:* Arabic script. Dictionary. Grammar. *Other:* The name 'Buton' is usually used generically inside Southeast Sulawesi to refer to Wolio; outside Southeast Sulawesi it refers to people from Southeast Sulawesi, or is sometimes confused with Bajau people as sailors. Muslim.

Wotu [wtw] 5,000 (1987 SIL). South Sulawesi, town of Wotu, Wotu Subdistrict, Luwu District. *Class:* Austronesian, Malayo-Polynesian, Sulawesi, Wotu-Wolio. *Dialects:* Lexical similarity 58% with Wolio, 53% with Barang-Barang (Laiyolo), average 43% with South Sulawesi Group, 43% with Kaili-Pamona Subgroup, 41% with Seko Padang, 39% with Tae' Luwu, 36% to 43% with Bungku-Tolaki Subgroup, 37% with Toraja-Sa'dan, 33% with Bugis, 31% with Rampi, 25% with Lemolang. *Lg Use:* Bilingual level estimates for Indonesian: 0 0%, 1 8%, 2 83%, 3 9%, 4 0%, 5 0%. Bugis-Luwu is the dominant second language. *Other:* Muslim.

Indonesia (Sumatra)

Indonesia (Sumatra). 43,309,707 (2000 census). 7 provinces. Information mainly from P. Voerhoeve 1955; D. Walker 1976. The number of languages listed for Indonesia (Sumatra) is 49. Of those, all are living languages. See maps beginning on page 804.

Abung [abl] 700,000 (2000). South. *Class:* Austronesian, Malayo-Polynesian, Lampungic, Abung. *Dialects:* Jabung, Menggala (Northeast Lampung), Kota Bumi (Northwest Lampung). Many differences in vocabulary and phonology with Pesisir. Menggala has 72% lexical similarity with Kalianda, a dialect of Southern Pesisir. Lexical similarity 77% among dialects. *Other:* Muslim.

Aceh (Atjeh, Atjehnese, Achinese, Achehnese) [ace] 3,000,000 (1999 WA). Northern, Aceh Province, northern and southern coasts around the tip of Sumatra. *Class:* Austronesian, Malayo-Polynesian, Malayic, Achinese-Chamic, Achinese. *Dialects:* Banda Aceh, Baruh, Bueng, Daja, Pase, Pidie (Pedir, Timu), Tunong. *Lg Use:* Language of wider communication. Speakers also use Indonesian. *Lg Dev:* Dictionary. Grammar. Bible: 1997. *Other:* SVO. Coastal. Muslim, Christian.

Batak Alas-Kluet (Alas-Kluet Batak) [btz] 80,000 (1989). Northern, northeast of Tapaktuan and around Kutacane. *Class:* Austronesian, Malayo-Polynesian, Sumatra, Batak, Northern. *Dialect:* Alas. *Other:* Reported to not be Batak. Muslim.

Batak Angkola (Anakola, Angkola) [akb] 750,000 (1991 UBS). North central, Sipirok area. *Class:* Austronesian, Malayo-Polynesian, Sumatra, Batak, Southern. *Dialects:* Close to Mandailing Batak, but distinct sociolinguistically. *Lg Dev:* Bible: 1991. *Other:* Christian, Muslim.

Batak Dairi (Dairi, Pakpak, Pakpak Dairi) [btd] 1,200,000 (1991 UBS). Northern, southwest of Lake Toba around Sidikalang. *Class:* Austronesian, Malayo-Polynesian, Sumatra, Batak, Northern. *Lg Use:* Diari and Pakpak are sociolinguistically distinct. *Lg Dev:* Bible: 1998. *Other:* Christian.

Batak Karo (Karo Batak) [btx] 600,000 (1991 UBS). Central and northern, west and northwest of Lake Toba. *Class:* Austronesian, Malayo-Polynesian, Sumatra, Batak, Northern. *Dialect:* Singkil. *Lg Dev:* Grammar. Bible: 1987–1995. *Other:* Christian, traditional religion.

Batak Mandailing (Mandailing Batak, Batta) [btm] 400,000 (1989). Northern. *Class:* Austronesian, Malayo-Polynesian, Sumatra, Batak, Southern. *Lg Use:* Sociolinguistically different from Angkola. *Other:* A general form of Batak common to a wider area than Angkola. Muslim.

Batak Simalungun (Timur, Simelungan) [bts] 1,200,000 (2000). Northern, northeast of Lake Toba. *Class:* Austronesian, Malayo-Polynesian, Sumatra, Batak, Simalungan. *Lg Dev:* Bible: 1976.

Batak Toba (Toba Batak, Batta) [bbc] 2,000,000 (1991 UBS). Samosir Island and east, south, and west of Toba Lake in north Sumatra. *Class:* Austronesian, Malayo-Polynesian, Sumatra, Batak, Southern. *Dialects:* Close to Angkola Batak. *Lg Dev:* Traditional Batak script. Bible: 1894–1989. *Other:* Christian.

Bengkulu (Benkulan, Bencoolen) [bke] 55,000 (1989). Small area around Benkulu city, western end of southern Sumatra. *Class:* Austronesian, Malayo-Polynesian, Malayic, Malayan, Local Malay. *Other:* Muslim.

Enggano (Engganese) [eno] 700 (2000 Wurm). Enggano Island, southwest of Sumatra and on four smaller nearby islands. *Class:* Austronesian, Malayo-Polynesian, Sumatra, Enggano. *Dialects:* Not closely related to other languages.

Enim [eni] 70,000 (1989). Southern Sumatra, south of Muaraenim, east and southeast of Lahat. *Class:*

Austronesian, Malayo-Polynesian, Malayic, Malayan, Local Malay. *Other:* Muslim.

Gayo (Gajo) [gay] 180,000 (1989). Mountain region of north Sumatra around Takengon, Genteng, and Lokon. *Class:* Austronesian, Malayo-Polynesian, Gayo. *Dialects:* Dorot, Bobasan, Serbodjadi, Tampur. Not closely related to other languages. *Other:* Muslim, traditional religion.

Kaur (Ka'ur, Bintuhan) [vkk] 20,000 (1989). Southwestern Sumatra, South Bengkulu, Southern Kaur area, and Northern Kaur area. *Class:* Austronesian, Malayo-Polynesian, Malayic, Malayan, Local Malay. *Dialects:* Related to Serawai. *Other:* Muslim, traditional religion.

Kayu Agung [vky] 45,000 (1989). Southern Sumatra, around Kayuagung. *Class:* Austronesian, Malayo-Polynesian, Lampungic, Abung. *Other:* Muslim.

Kerinci (Kerinchi, Kerintji, Kinchai) [kvr] 300,000 in Indonesia (1989). Population total all countries: 325,000. Western mountains of Jambi Province around Sungaipenuh and north and west. Also spoken in Bahrain. *Class:* Austronesian, Malayo-Polynesian, Malayic, Malayan, Local Malay. *Dialects:* Ulu, Mamaq, Akit, Talang, Sakei. *Lg Dev:* Traditional script. *Other:* Distinct from Kerinci-Minangkabau dialect of Minangkabau. Muslim.

Komering (Komerin, Njo) [kge] 700,000 (1989). Population includes 20,000 in Jakarta (1992). Southeastern Sumatra, Martapura, Kangkung, nearly to Kayuagung, and east to the coast. *Class:* Austronesian, Malayo-Polynesian, Lampungic, Pesisir. *Dialects:* Lexical similarity 70% with Kalianda, 74% with Sungkai (closest). *Lg Use:* Speakers also use Indonesian. *Other:* Called 'Njo' together with Krui. Lowland. Swamp. Agriculturalists: wet rice. Muslim (Shafi Sunni).

Krui (Kroe, Kru'i, Western Lampung, Njo) [krq] 31,687 (2000 WCD). Southern, south Benkulu Province around Krui, Sanggi, Kotajawa, and possibly into Lampung Province. *Class:* Austronesian, Malayo-Polynesian, Lampungic, Pesisir. *Dialects:* Related to Komering. Lexical similarity 84% with Ranau. Vocabulary differences with other Pesisir languages. *Other:* Called 'Njo' together with Komering. Muslim.

Kubu [kvb] 10,000 (1989). Spread across Jambi, Riau and south Sumatra, eastern swamp region. *Class:* Austronesian, Malayo-Polynesian, Malayic, Malayan, Local Malay. *Dialects:* Lalang, Bajat, Ulu Lako, Tungkal, Tungkal Ilir, Dawas, Supat, Djambi, Ridan, Nomadic Kubu. Related to Lubu. *Other:* Forest dwellers. Swamp forest. Traditional religion, Muslim, Christian.

Lampung (Api, Lampong) [ljp] 1,500,000 (1981 Wurm and Hattori). Southern Sumatra, entire province of Lampung. *Class:* Austronesian, Malayo-Polynesian, Lampungic, Pesisir. *Lg Use:* Outside of the city, Lampung is used daily in home and village. Teachers must use Lampung to communicate with children, especially in lower grades. The majority can speak some Indonesian, which is used in schools, and increasingly in the city as first language by Lampung people. *Lg Dev:* Roman and Lampung scripts. Grammar. Bible portions: 1999–2000. *Other:* Muslim.

Lematang (Lemantang) [lmt] 150,000 (1989). Southern Sumatra, around Muaraenim and another pocket southeast of Sarolangun. *Class:* Austronesian, Malayo-Polynesian, Malayic, Malayan, Local Malay. *Other:* Muslim.

Lembak (Linggau) [liw] 50,000 (1989). Interior south Sumatra around Lubuklinggau and east of Bengkulu; 2 areas. *Class:* Austronesian, Malayo-Polynesian, Malayic, Malayan, Local Malay. *Dialects:* Lembak Bliti (Bliti), Lembak Sindang. *Other:* Muslim.

Lintang [lnt] 70,000 (1989). Southern Sumatra, between Lahat and Kapahiang. *Class:* Austronesian, Malayo-Polynesian, Malayic, Malayan, Local Malay. *Other:* Muslim.

Lom (Belom, Mapor, Maporese) [mfb] 2 to 10 (2000 Wurm). Sumatra, northeast Bangka Island, Belinyu District. *Class:* Austronesian, Malayo-Polynesian, Malayic, Malay, Lom. *Dialects:* Not closely related to other languages. *Other:* The people are called 'Lom' or 'Mapur'. Nearly extinct.

Loncong (Lontjong, Lonchong, Orang Laut, Seka, Sekah) [lce] 424 (2000 WCD). East coast on both sides of the mouths of the Kampat and Inderagiri rivers, nearby islands, and coasts of Bangka and Belitung islands. *Class:* Austronesian, Malayo-Polynesian, Malayic, Malayan, Local Malay. *Other:* It may be two languages. Other languages have been called Orang Laut: Lawta of Myanmar and Indonesian Bajau (see Sulawesi).

Lubu [lcf] 30,000 (1981 Wurm and Hattori). Central region of east Sumatra. *Class:* Austronesian, Malayo-Polynesian, Malayic, Malayan, Local Malay. *Dialects:* Related to Kubu. *Other:* Lubu people consider the name "Kerinci" an insult. Muslim.

Malay (Melayu, Malayu, Melaju, Bahasa Melayu, Bahasa Malay, Standard Malay) [mly] 10,000,000 in Indonesia (1981 Wurm and Hattori). Population includes 2,000,000 in Riau, 40,000 in Bangka, 170,000 in Belitung. Also in Kalimantan, Java, Maluku, Sulawesi, Papua, Nusa Tenggara. *Dialects:* Riau (Riouw-Lingga, Johor), Jakarta, Sambas, Deli, Melayu Pasar (Bazaar Malay, Pasir), Borneo (Sintang), Kota-Waringin, Sukadana, Makakau, Makassarese, Manadonese (Menadonese), Labu (Lebu, Labu Basap), Papuan Malay (Irianese), Ritok (Siantan, Pontianak), Balikpapan, Sampit, Bakumpai, West Borneo Coast Malay, Belide, Lengkayap, Aji, Daya, Mulak, Bangka, Belitung, Larantuka (Ende Malay), Peranakan, Basa Kupang (Kupang). *Other:* See separate entries for Kalimantan: Kutai Malay, Berau Malay, Bukit; Maluku: Ambonese Malay, Bacan Malay, North Moluccan Malay; Nusa Tenggara: Kupang Malay; Sumatra: Enim, Kaur, Kayu Agung, Lematang, Lembak, Jambi Malay, Lintang, Penesak, Rawas, Sindang Kelingi. Some listed as dialects are probably not inherently intelligible with Standard Malay or Indonesian. Kupang Malay and Larantuka Malay in Nusa Tenggara are very similar to each other. Muslim (Sunni). See main entry under Malaysia (Peninsular).

Malay, Jambi [jax] 890,000 (1989). Southeastern Sumatra, Jambi Province. *Class:* Austronesian, Malayo-Polynesian, Malayic, Malayan, Local Malay. *Dialects:* Suku Batin (Batin), Ilir, Ulu. *Other:* Muslim.

Mentawai (Mentawei, Mentawi) [mwv] 50,000 (1992 UBS). Mentawai Islands off the west coast of Sumatra. *Class:* Austronesian, Malayo-Polynesian, Sumatra, Mentawai. *Dialects:* Simalegi, Sakalagan, Silabu, Taikaku, Saumanganja, North Siberut, South Siberut, Sipura, Pagai. *Lg Dev:* NT: 1987–1996. *Other:* Christian, traditional religion.

Minangkabau (Minang, Padang) [min] 6,500,000 (1981 Moussay). Population includes 500,000 in Jakarta. West central Sumatra around Padang and throughout the Indonesian Archipelago. Nearly half live outside of central Sumatra. *Class:* Austronesian, Malayo-Polynesian, Malayic, Malayan, Para-Malay. *Dialects:* Agam, Pajokumbuh, Tanah, Si Junjung, Batu Sangkar-Pariangan, Singkarak, Orang Mamak, Ulu, Kerinci-Minangkabau, Aneuk Jamee (Jamee), Penghulu. Not intelligible with Indonesian. Muko-Muko and Pekal may be intelligible with Minang. *Lg Dev:* Taught in primary schools. Newspapers. Radio programs. NT: 1996. *Other:* Instruction in Minang in grades 1 and 2. SVO. Muslim (Sunni).

Muko-Muko (Mokomoko) [vmo] 30,000 (1989). Southern Sumatra, west coast around Mukomuko. *Class:* Austronesian, Malayo-Polynesian, Malayic, Malayan, Para-Malay. *Dialects:* Related to Minangkabau with strong influences from Rejang. *Other:* Muslim.

Musi [mui] 403,000 (2001). South Sumatra Province, Musi Banyuasin Regency, both sides of the Musi River west and upstream of Palembang. *Class:* Austronesian, Malayo-Polynesian, Malayic, Malayan, Local Malay. *Dialect:* Sekayu Malay. *Lg Use:* 75% of the Sekayu Malay speakers have varying proficiency in Indonesian, 5% in English, 10% in other languages. *Other:* Muslim.

Nias (Batu) [nia] 480,000 (1989). Nias and Batu islands off the west coast of Sumatra. *Class:* Austronesian, Malayo-Polynesian, Sumatra, Northern. *Dialects:* Nias, Batu. *Lg Dev:* Bible: 1911. *Other:* Christian.

Ogan [ogn] 300,000 (1989). South Sumatra around Baturaja, Pagerdewa, and north and west of Kayuagung. *Class:* Austronesian, Malayo-Polynesian, Malayic, Malayan, Local Malay. *Other:* Muslim.

Palembang (Palembang Malay) [plm] 500,000 (1989). Southeast Sumatra, Palembang area, Musi River. *Class:* Austronesian, Malayo-Polynesian, Malayic, Malayan, Local Malay. *Other:* Coastal. Swamp. Muslim.

Pasemah (Besemah) [pse] 400,000 (1989). Central Bukit Barisan highlands. *Class:* Austronesian, Malayo-Polynesian, Malayic, Malayan, Local Malay. *Other:* Mountain slope. Muslim.

Pekal [pel] 30,000 (1989). Southern Sumatra, west coast from north of Ipuh to Tembesi River, to near Argamakmur in the south. *Class:* Austronesian, Malayo-Polynesian, Malayic, Malayan, Para-Malay. *Dialects:* Related to Minangkabau with strong Rejang influences. *Other:* Muslim.

Penesak (Penasak) [pen] 20,000 (1989). Southern Sumatra, around Prabumulih. *Class:* Austronesian, Malayo-Polynesian, Malayic, Malayan, Local Malay. *Other:* Muslim.

Pesisir, Southern [pec] 400,000 (1976 D. Walker). South Sumatra. *Class:* Austronesian, Malayo-Polynesian, Lampungic, Pesisir. *Dialects:* Kota Agung (Southwest Lampung), Way Lima, Kalianda (Southeast Lampung), Telukbetung, Talang Padang. Lexical similarity 79% between Kota Agung and Kalianda, 70% between Kalianda and Komering, 78% between Kota Agung and Pubian, 78% between Kota Agung and Krui, 78% between Way Lima and Kalianda, 72% between Kalianda and Menggala (Abung). *Other:* Muslim.

Pubian [pun] 400,000 (1976 D. Walker). South Sumatra. *Class:* Austronesian, Malayo-Polynesian, Lampungic, Pesisir. *Dialects:* Lexical similarity 76% to 81% with other Pesisir languages.

Ranau [rae] 60,000 (1989). Southern Sumatra, south of Muaradua, near headwaters of Kanan River. *Class:* Austronesian, Malayo-Polynesian, Lampungic, Abung. *Dialects:* Lexical similarity 84% with Krui. *Other:* Distinct from Ranau dialect of Central Dusun in Sabah, Malaysia. Muslim.

Rawas [rws] 150,000 (1989). South Sumatra Province, Musi Rawas Regency, around Ambacang and along Musi River. *Class:* Austronesian, Malayo-Polynesian, Malayic, Malayan, Local Malay. *Dialects:* Rupit, Rawas Ulu, Rawas Ilir. *Other:* Muslim.

Rejang (Redjang, Rejang-Lebong, Jang, Djang, Djang Bele Tebo) [rej] 1,000,000 (1989 Wurm and Hattori). Southwest highlands, north Bengkulu Province, around Argamakmur, Muaraaman, Curuo, and Kapahiang. *Class:* Austronesian, Malayo-Polynesian, Unclassified. *Dialects:* Lebong (Djang Lebong), Kebanagung, Pasisir, Musi, Rawas. *Lg Dev:* Literacy rate in second language: 45%. Traditional script. Grammar. *Other:* Subgroups: Jang Lebong, Jang Musai, Jang Lai, Jang Bekulau, Abeus. 85% live in remote rural areas. Very different from Serawai. Different from Rejang-Baram group of languages on Borneo. Musi and Rawasi dialects are not to be confused with Malay varieties of the same name. Muslim.

Semendo [sdd] 105,000 (1989). Interior south Sumatra; two areas: west of Baturaja and south of Pajarbulan. *Class:* Austronesian, Malayo-Polynesian, Malayic, Malayan, Local Malay. *Other:* Muslim.

Serawai (Serawaj, Serawi) [srj] 225,000 (1989). South Bengkulu coast. *Class:* Austronesian, Malayo-Polynesian, Malayic, Malayan, Local Malay. *Dialects:* The two dialects may not be very different. Related to Pasemah. *Lg Dev:* NT: 1995. *Other:* Muslim, traditional religion, Christian.

Sikule (Sichule, Wali Banuah, Sikhule) [skh] 20,000. Central Simeulue Island. *Class:* Austronesian, Malayo-Polynesian, Sumatra, Northern. *Dialects:* Lekon, Tapah. Close to Nias.

Simeulue (Simalur, Simulul, Simeuloë, Long Bano) [smr] 100,000 (1981 Wurm and Hattori). West and east ends of Simeulue Island, Babi and Banjak islands. *Class:* Austronesian, Malayo-Polynesian, Sumatra, Northern. *Dialects:* Related to Sikule and Nias. *Other:* Muslim.

Sindang Kelingi (Kelingi) [sdi] 50,000 (1989). Southern Sumatra, around Muaraklingi, south, east, and north. *Class:* Austronesian, Malayo-Polynesian, Malayic, Malayan, Local Malay. *Other:* Muslim.

Sungkai [suu] 6,363 (2000 WCD). South Sumatra, northeast of Krui, west of Abung. *Class:* Austronesian, Malayo-Polynesian, Lampungic, Pesisir. *Dialects:* Lexical similarity 76% with Pubian (closest), 74% with Komering.

Iran

Islamic Republic of Iran, Jomhouri-e-Eslami-e-Irân. 67,503,205. National or official language: Western Farsi. Literacy rate: 70% to 75% among those 6 years old and over (1995–1996 Iran Statistical Center). Also includes Eastern Farsi (1,000,000), Hulaulá (300), Tajiki, Turkish (2,570), people from Afghanistan (3,000,000), Kurds from Iraq (120,000), Shi'a Arabs from Iraq. Information mainly from E. Drower 1939; R. Macuch 1965; I. Garbell 1965; T. Sebeok 1969, 1970; G. Doerfer et al. 1971; R. Oberling 1974; D. L. Stilo 1981; R. D. Hoberman 1988a, b. Blind population: 200,000 (1982 WCE). Deaf population: 3,978,055. Deaf institutions: 50. The number of languages listed for Iran is 77. Of those, 75 are living languages and 2 are extinct.

Aimaq [aiq] 170,000 in Iran (1993 Johnstone). Mazanderan Province. *Dialect:* Teimuri (Teimurtash). See main entry under Afghanistan.

Alviri-Vidari [avd] Near Saveh, Markazi Province. *Class:* Indo-European, Indo-Iranian, Iranian, Western, Northwestern, Talysh. *Dialects:* Alvir (Alviri), Vidar (Vidari). Related to Gozarkhâni and Vafsi. *Other:* Muslim.

Arabic, Gulf Spoken (Khaliji, Gulf Arabic) [afb] 200,000 in Iran (1993). Southern coast; Khamseh nomads live in eastern Fars Province; other Arab nomadic groups in several southcentral provinces of Iran. *Dialects:* Al-Hasâ, Khamseh. *Lg Use:* The largest of five Khamseh clans now uses Western Farsi as a first language. Speakers also use Western Farsi. See main entry under Iraq.

Arabic, Mesopotamian Spoken (Mesopotamian Gelet Arabic, 'Arabi, Arabi) [acm] 1,200,000 in Iran. Khuzestan Province, southwest side of Zagros Mountains, along the bank of the Shatt al Arab. *Other:* Muslim (Shi'a). See main entry under Iraq.

Armenian (Haieren, Somekhuri, Ermenice, Armjanski, Armani, Erâmani) [hye] 170,800 in Iran (1993). Northern Iran, Azerbaijan Provinces around Khoi, Shahpur, Ahar, Tabriz, Tehran, Esfahan, Shiraz. *Dialects:* Eastern Armenian, Agulis, Astrakhân, Jolfâ (Dzhulfa), Karabagh Shamakhi, Khoi-Salmst (Khvoy), Urmia-Maragheh. *Lg Use:* Vigorous. Used in the home, church, school. All ages. Speakers also use Western Farsi or South

Azerbaijani. *Lg Dev:* Literacy rate in second language: 80%. Taught in Armenian private schools. *Other:* Merchants. Christian. See main entry under Armenia.

Ashtiani (Astiani, Ashtiyani) [atn] 21,099 (2000 WCD). Ashtiyan and Tafresh, Markazi Province. *Class:* Indo-European, Indo-Iranian, Iranian, Western, Northwestern, Central Iran. *Dialects:* Ashtiani, Tafresh. Transitional between central Iranian dialects and Talysh. Dialects may be separate languages. Very close to Vafsi. *Lg Use:* Speakers also use Western Farsi. *Other:* Muslim.

Assyrian Neo-Aramaic [aii] 10,000 to 20,000 in Iran (1994). Ethnic population: 80,000 (1994). Reza'iyeh (Rizaiye, Urmia, Urmi). Most in TehranTehran. *Dialect:* Iranian Koine (General Urmi). *Other:* The Assyrian separated denominationally from the Chaldean in the 16th century. Christian (Nestorian). See main entry under Iraq.

Avestan (Pazend, Avesta) [ave] Extinct. *Class:* Indo-European, Indo-Iranian, Iranian, Eastern, Northeastern. *Lg Use:* The language of the Zoroastrian scriptures, from 600 B.C. *Other:* Zoroastrian.

Azerbaijani, South (Azeri, Torki) [azb] 23,500,000 in Iran (1997). Population includes 290,000 Afshar, 5,000 Aynallu, 7,500 Baharlu, 1,000 Moqaddam, 3,500 Nafar 1,000 Pishagchi, 3,000 Qajar, 2,000 Qaragozlu, 130,000 Shahsavani (1993). Population total all countries: 24,364,000. East and West Azerbaijan, Ardebil, Zanjan, and part of Markazi provinces. Many in a few districts of TehranTehran. Some Azerbaijani-speaking groups are in Fars Province and other parts of Iran. Also spoken in Afghanistan, Azerbaijan, Iraq, Jordan, Syria, Turkey (Asia), USA. *Class:* Altaic, Turkic, Southern, Azerbaijani. *Dialects:* Aynallu (Inallu, Inanlu), Karapapakh, Tabriz, Afshari (Afshar, Afsar), Shahsavani (Shahseven), Moqaddam, Baharlu (Kamesh), Nafar, Qaragozlu, Pishagchi, Bayat, Qajar. Distinctive linguistic differences between the Azerbaijani of the former USSR (North) and Iranian Azerbaijani (South) in phonology, lexicon, morphology, syntax, and loanwords. Teimurtash (7,000 in Mazanderan; possibly the same as Teimuri, Timuri, Taimouri) and Salchug (in Kerman Province) may be dialects. Qashqa'i may be a dialect. Part of the Qizilbash merchant group speak the Afshari dialect, which is strongly influenced by Persian. The dialect spoken in Syria is different from Kirkuk of Iraq, and may be closer to Turkish (Osmanli) than to Azerbaijani. There is a gradual transition of dialects from Turkish to Azerbaijani from central to western Turkey. *Lg Use:* Language of wider communication. Vigorous. All ages. Speakers also use Western Farsi. *Lg Dev:* Arabo-Persian script, Roman-based script and Cyrillic script; Cyrillic script in Afghanistan; Arabic script in Iraq. Poetry. Newspapers. *Other:* Agriculturalists; pastoralists. Muslim (Shi'a).

Bakhtiari (Lori-ye Khaveri, Luri, Lori) [bqi] 1,000,000 (2001). 350,000 monolinguals. Ethnic population: 1,000,000 (2001). Southwestern Iran: western Chahar-Mahal va Bakhtiari, eastern Khuzestan, eastern Lorestan, and western Esfahan. Masjed-e Soleiman, Shahr-e Kord, Dorud. *Class:* Indo-European, Indo-Iranian, Iranian, Western, Southwestern, Luri. *Dialect:* Haft-Lang, Charlang, Chelgerd, Kuhrang (Kohrang). Bakhtiari is on a dialect continuum between Northern Luri and Southern Luri. Farsi dialects in Chaharmahal va Bakhtiari Province are mutually intelligible with Bakhtiari. Close to Kumzari. Lexical similarity 75% with Southern Luri (Mamasani), 86% with Southern Luri (Boyerahmadi), 73% with Northern Luri (rural), 78% with Northern Luri (Khorramabadi), 76% with Western Farsi. *Lg Use:* Vigorous. Used in the home, commerce. All ages. Positive language attitude. Some speakers use Western Farsi or English. Older speakers and women have lower levels of bilingualism. *Lg Dev:* A few native authors have

attempted to use an Arabo-Persian script for Bakhtiari. Poetry. Dictionary. Grammar. *Other:* Speakers have little contact with Southern Luri, some contact with Northern Luri. 200 to 3000 meters. Haflang: nomadic pastoralists (sheep), Charlang: settled. Muslim (Shi'a).

Balochi, Southern (Baluchi, Baluci, Baloci) [bcc] 405,000 in Iran. Southern Sistan va Baluchistan Province. *Dialect:* Makrani (Lotuni). *Other:* Muslim (Sunni). See main entry under Pakistan.

Balochi, Western (Baluchi, Baluci, Baloci) [bgn] 451,000 in Iran (1986). Northern Sistan va Baluchistan Province. Half are settled in cities and villages, half are nomadic. *Dialects:* Rakhshani (Raxshani), Sarawani. *Lg Use:* Few speak Farsi. *Other:* Distinct from Eastern and Southern Balochi. Ethnic group: Yarahmadza. Muslim (Sunni and Shi'a). See main entry under Pakistan.

Bashkardi (Bashaka) [bsg] 7,033 (2000 WCD). Eastern Hormozgan, Southern Kerman, and possibly southwestern Sistan va Baluchistan provinces. *Class:* Indo-European, Indo-Iranian, Iranian, Western, Northwestern, Balochi. *Dialects:* Northern Bashaka, Southern Bashaka. *Other:* Muslim.

Brahui (Brahudi, Birahui, Kur Galli) [brh] 10,000 in Iran (1983). Central Sistan and Baluchistan provinces, including Zahedan. *Dialects:* Jharawan, Kalat, Sarawan. *Lg Use:* Brahui in Iran are reported to speak Western Balochi now. *Other:* In Iran, they work for the Baloch. Pastoralists; merchants; tailors. Muslim. See main entry under Pakistan.

Dari, Zoroastrian (Dari, "Gabri," "Gabar," "Yazdi") [gbz] 8,000 to 15,000 (1999). Yezd and Kerman areas. *Class:* Indo-European, Indo-Iranian, Iranian, Western, Northwestern, Central Iran. *Dialects:* Related to Parsi-Dari and Nâyini. *Lg Use:* Spoken by Persian Zoroastrians in their personal communications as a private language. Speakers also use Western Farsi. *Other:* A different language from Dari (Eastern Farsi) of Afghanistan, although both names come from Darius, the ancient Emperor, whom they both relate to ("dar" is also Classical Persian for 'court'). Many Zoroastrians speak Parsi-Dari and do not know Zoroastrian Dari. "Gabri," "Gabar" and "Yazdi" are derogatory names. Zoroastrian.

Dezfuli (Dezhfili, Dizfuli) [def] Dezful, northern Khuzestan Province. *Class:* Indo-European, Indo-Iranian, Iranian, Western, Northwestern, Unclassified. *Lg Use:* Speakers also use Western Farsi or Bakhtiari. *Lg Dev:* Grammar. *Other:* Muslim.

Domari (Middle Eastern Romani, Tsigene, Gypsy, Luti, Mehtar) [rmt] 1,338,271 in Iran (2000 WCD). Population total all countries: 1,876,116. Kurbat and Luli are in western Iran. Mehtar is in Fars and Kohgiluyeh va Boyerahmad Province. Karachi is in northern Iran. Also spoken in Afghanistan, Egypt, India, Iraq, Israel, Jordan, Libya, Palestinian West Bank and Gaza, Russia (Europe), Sudan, Syria, Turkey (Europe), Uzbekistan. *Class:* Indo-European, Indo-Iranian, Indo-Aryan, Central zone, Dom. *Dialects:* Kurbati (Ghorbati), Qinati, Yürük, Koli, Karachi, Luli, Maznoug, Nawar. A number of the dialects in Iran may be highly divergent from one another. Not intelligible to Romani speakers. *Lg Use:* Vigorous. Used only as a private language for communication with other Gypsies. All ages. Speakers also use Western Farsi, Luristani, Bakhtiari, Southern Luri, Qashqa'i. *Lg Dev:* Grammar. *Other:* Influenced by Arabic, as well as the languages of the host ethnic groups with which any gypsy group is associated. Blacksmiths; haircutters; musicians; carpenters; butchers. Muslim.

Dzhidi (Judeo-Persian, Djudi, Judi) [jpr] *Other:* Jewish. See main entry under Israel.

Eshtehardi [esh] Eshtehard and environs, Karaj District, Markazi Province. *Class:* Indo-European, Indo-Iranian,

Iranian, Western, Northwestern, Talysh. *Dialects:* Close to Takestani. Eshtehardi may be the same language as some other dialects spoken to the southwest of Qazvin. *Other:* Muslim.

Fars, Northwestern [faz] Scattered in isolated pockets of Fars Province. *Class:* Indo-European, Indo-Iranian, Iranian, Western, Northwestern, Central Iran. *Dialects:* Close to Sivandi. *Other:* Distinct from Farsi. Muslim.

Fars, Southwestern ("Tajik") [fay] Central Fars Province: Somghun, Papun, Masarm, Buringun, Kondazi, Davâni, others. *Class:* Indo-European, Indo-Iranian, Iranian, Western, Southwestern, Fars. *Dialects:* Related to Lari. *Other:* Distinct from Farsi. Muslim.

Farsi, Western (Persian, New Persian, Parsi, Irani) [pes] 22,000,000 in Iran (1997). Population includes 800,000 Eastern Farsi in Khorasan, Gilan, Tat, Bakhtiari, Lur. Population total all countries: 24,316,121. Throughout Iran. Most heavily concentrated in central, south central, and northeastern Iran. Also spoken in Australia, Austria, Azerbaijan, Bahrain, Canada, Denmark, France, Germany, Greece, India, Iraq, Israel, Netherlands, Oman, Qatar, Saudi Arabia, Spain, Sweden, Tajikistan, Turkey (Asia), Turkmenistan, United Arab Emirates, United Kingdom, USA, Uzbekistan. *Class:* Indo-European, Indo-Iranian, Iranian, Western, Southwestern, Persian. *Dialects:* Ketabi, Tehrani, Shirazi, Old Shirazi, Qazvini, Mahalhamadani, Kashani, Esfahani, Sedehi, Kermani, Araki, Shirazjahromi, Shahrudi Kazeruni, Mashadi (Meshed), Basseri, Yazdi, Bandari. The literary language is virtually identical in Iran and Afghanistan, with very minor lexical differences. Zargari may be a dialect used by goldsmiths (also see Balkan Romani in Iran). Dialect shading into Dari in Afghanistan and Tajiki in Tajikistan. Many of the dialects may be separate languages. *Lg Use:* National language. Vigorous. All domains. All ages. Many study English, but proficiency is low. Speakers also use Azerbaijani. *Lg Dev:* Taught in primary and secondary schools. Poetry. Magazines. Newspapers. Radio programs. Films. TV. Videos. Dictionary. Grammar. Bible: 1838–1995. *Other:* SOV. Muslim (Shi'a), Baha'i, Christian.

Gazi [gzi] 7,033 (2000). Gaz. *Class:* Indo-European, Indo-Iranian, Iranian, Western, Northwestern, Central Iran. *Other:* Muslim.

Georgian (Kartuli, Gruzin) [kat] 50,000 in Iran. Fereydan and Fereydunshahr provinces, Esfahan, Najaf Abad, Shahin Shahr, Yazdanshahr. *Dialect:* Fereydan (Ferejdan). *Other:* Ferejdan may no longer be spoken in Iran. Muslim (Shi'a). See main entry under Georgia.

Gilaki (Gelaki, Gilani, Guilaki, Guilani) [glk] 3,265,000 (1993). Population includes 2,000 Galeshi. Gilan Region, coastal plain, south of Talish. Galeshi is a mountain dialect. *Class:* Indo-European, Indo-Iranian, Iranian, Western, Northwestern, Caspian. *Dialects:* Galeshi, Rashti. Close to Mâzanderâni. *Lg Use:* Speakers use Western Farsi as second language. The educated can read Farsi well. *Lg Dev:* Dictionary. Grammar. *Other:* Heavy influence from Farsi. Agriculturalists; fishermen. Muslim (Shi'a), Christian.

Gozarkhani [goz] Gozarkhan (northwest of Qazvin); Tajrish, north of Tehran; Alamut area. *Class:* Indo-European, Indo-Iranian, Iranian, Western, Northwestern, Talysh. *Dialects:* Close to Maraghei, as well as Semnani languages. *Other:* Muslim.

Harzani [hrz] 28,132 (2000 WCD). West Azerbaijan Province: Qalingie, between Marand and Jolfa, northwest of Tabriz; related varieties in Galin Qaya, Babra, and Dizmar. *Class:* Indo-European, Indo-Iranian, Iranian, Western, Northwestern, Talysh. *Dialects:* Close to Karingani and Talysh. *Other:* Muslim.

Hawrami (Hewrami, Howrami, Hawramani, Awromani, Gurani, Gorani) [hac] 22,948 in Iran (2000 WCD). For all speakers of Gurani group, several million; Hawrami dialect: 20,000 (Blau 1989). Western part of Kordestan province, near Iraqi border, in Hewraman, east of Sanandaj, also north of Kermanshah. *Dialects:* Kakai (Macho), Hawraman-I Luhon, Hawraman-I Taxt, Kandula, Gawhara, Gurani (Gorani). *Lg Use:* Speakers also use Farsi or Central Kurdish. *Other:* Muslim, Ahl-e Haqq. See main entry under Iraq (Gurani).

Hazaragi (Hazara, Hezareh, Hezare'i) [haz] 283,000 in Iran (1993). Population has increased significantly due to the influx of Hazaragi-speaking refugees from Afghanistan. Throughout Iran, especially urban centers. *Lg Use:* Men are bilingual in Western Farsi. *Other:* Ethnic group names are (Central) Dai Kundi, Dai Zangi, Behsud, Yekaulang, (Southern) Polada, Urusgani, Jaguri, Ghazni Hazaras, Dai Miradad. Laborers. Muslim (Imami Shi'a, Ismaili, and Sunni). See main entry under Afghanistan.

Jadgali (Jatgali, Jatki, Jat) [jdg] *Other:* People called 'Jats'. Different from Jakati of Afghanistan and Ukraine, and Russian Central Asia. Muslim. See main entry under Pakistan.

Kabatei [xkp] Rudbar District, Gilan Province. *Class:* Indo-European, Indo-Iranian, Iranian, Western, Northwestern, Talysh. *Dialects:* Kalas, Kabate. Close to Upper Taromi. *Other:* Muslim.

Kajali [xkj] Khalkhal District in Eastern Azerbaijan Province, Kaqazkonan District, Kajal. *Class:* Indo-European, Indo-Iranian, Iranian, Western, Northwestern, Talysh. *Dialects:* Close to Shahrudi and Koresh-e Rostam. *Other:* Muslim.

Karingani (Keringani) [kgn] 17,583 (2000 WCD). East Azerbaijan Province, Dizmar District, Keringan village, and Hasanu District, northeast of Tabriz. *Class:* Indo-European, Indo-Iranian, Iranian, Western, Northwestern, Talysh. *Dialects:* Various dialects. Very close to Harzani. *Other:* Muslim.

Kazakh (Kazak, Kazakhi, Gazaqi) [kaz] 3,000 in Iran (1982). Gorgan City, Mazanderan Province. *Other:* Muslim. See main entry under Kazakhstan.

Khalaj [kjf] 42,107 in Iran (2000 WCD). Also spoken in Azerbaijan. *Class:* Indo-European, Indo-Iranian, Iranian, Western, Northwestern. *Dialects:* Related to Kurdish and Talysh. *Other:* Pronounced with 2 short or front a's. Different from Turkic Khalaj in Iran.

Khalaj, Turkic (Khalaj) [klj] 42,107 (2000 WCD). Northeast of Arak in Central Province. *Class:* Altaic, Turkic, Southern, Azerbaijani. *Dialects:* Not a dialect of Azerbaijani, as previously supposed. An independent language distinct from other extant Turkish languages (Doerfer 1971). *Lg Use:* Some children know only Farsi. Most also use Farsi. *Other:* Different from Indo-Iranian Khalaj. Muslim.

Kho'ini [xkc] Kho'in District, Zanjan Province. *Class:* Indo-European, Indo-Iranian, Iranian, Western, Northwestern, Talysh. *Dialects:* Various dialects. Related to Kabatei and Takestani. Closely related varieties spoken in the nearby villages of Balbavin, Sefidkamar, Halab, Sa'dabad, and other villages. *Other:* Muslim.

Khorasani Turkish (Quchani) [kmz] 400,000 (1977 Doerfer). Northeast Iran, in the northern part of Khorasan Province, especially northwest of Mashhad. West dialect in Bojnurd Region; north dialect in Quchan Region (probably the largest), south dialect around Soltanabad near Sabzevar. *Class:* Altaic, Turkic, Southern, Turkish. *Dialects:* West Quchani (Northwest Quchani), North Quchani (Northeast Quchani), South Quchani. Midway linguistically between Azerbaijani and Turkmen, but not a dialect of either. Oghuz-Uzbek in Uzbekistan is reported to be a dialect. *Lg Use:* Speakers also use Farsi. *Lg Dev:* Radio programs. *Other:* Different from Khorasani, a local Persian dialect in Khorasan. Muslim.

Khunsari [kfm] 21,099 (2000 WCD). Esfahan Province, Kashan and Esfahan areas. *Class:* Indo-European, Indo-Iranian, Iranian, Western, Northwestern, Central Iran. *Dialects:* Khunsari may be only one of a large complex of dialects in Esfahan Province. Other Northwestern dialects that have been described in the same area and which may be very closely related include those of Vonishun, Qohrud, Keshe, Zefre, Sedeh, Gaz, Kafran, Mahallat, So, Mejme, and Djaushaqan. *Other:* Distinct from Kumzari of Oman. Muslim.

Koresh-e Rostam [okh] Eastern Azerbaijan Province, Koresh-e Rostam District. *Class:* Indo-European, Indo-Iranian, Iranian, Western, Northwestern, Talysh. *Dialects:* Related to Shahrudi and Kajali. *Other:* Muslim.

Koroshi [ktl] 160 to 200 (1992 Mohamedi). 40 to 50 families. Fars Province. *Class:* Indo-European, Indo-Iranian, Iranian, Western, Northwestern, Balochi. *Other:* Appears to be Baluchi with some features of Farsi. They work for the Qashqa'i people. Camel keepers.

Kurdish, Central (Kordi, Korkora, Kurdi, Kurdy, Sorani, Mukri, Mokri, Sine'i, Wawa) [ckb] 3,250,000 in Iran. Northwest Iran, primarily Kordestan, West Azerbaijan provinces, areas north of Kermanshah. Mukri is spoken around Mahabad, and Sineyi (Sine'i) is spoken around Sanandaj (Sine). *Dialects:* Mukri, Sanandaji (Sine'i, Sina'i, Sineyi), Southern Jafi, Pijdari. *Lg Use:* Language of wider communication. *Lg Dev:* Literacy rate in second language: All people: 1%, boys: 15%. Mukri is also used as a literary language. It is close to the literary language of Central Kurdish (Sorani) used in Iraqi Kurdistan (Hajo 1994). *Other:* 90% are settled in cities or villages, 10% are nomadic. Jafi may be a separate language. Taught at 2 universities. The name Kordi may also sometimes be used to refer generally to Northern Kurdish varieties (such as in Khorasan province), and for varieties of Southern Kurdish, such as Kermanshahi. Muslim (Sunni). See main entry under Iraq.

Kurdish, Northern (Kurmanji, Kurmancî, Eastern Kurmanji, Kordi, Kurdi) [kmr] 350,000 in Iran (1988 Stanzer). North and west of Lake Urmia, extending to border with Azerbaijan. Some small communities live in the Caspian region (Mazandaran, Kalardasht [Fattah 2000]). Khorasani Kurmanji speakers live east of the Caspian Sea, in northern Khorasan Province, bordering Turkmenistan. Centers include Quchan and Bojnurd. *Dialect:* Khorasani Kurmanji. *Other:* Teaching Kurmanji is prohibited in Iranian schools. Muslim (Sunni and Shi'a), Yezidi. See main entry under Turkey (Asia).

Kurdish, Southern [sdh] 3,000,000 in Iran (2000 Fattah). Western Iran, Kermanshah, Ilam provinces; Eastern Iraq bordering these provinces including Xanaqin. Also spoken in Iraq. *Class:* Indo-European, Indo-Iranian, Iranian, Western, Northwestern, Kurdish. *Dialects:* Kolyai, Kermanshahi (Kermanshani), Kalhori, Garrusi (Bijari) Sanjabi, Malekshahi (Maleksh ay), Bayray, Kordali, Feyli, Luri. *Lg Use:* Used in the home. Speakers also use Farsi. *Other:* Muslim (Shi'a).

Laki (Leki, Alaki) [lki] 1,000,000 (2002 Fattah). 150,000 monolinguals. Population includes 10,000 Nahavand Lurs. Western Iran, Ilam, Lorestan provinces, cities of Aleshtar, Kuhdesht, Nurabad-e Dolfan, Khorramabad. *Class:* Indo-European, Indo-Iranian, Iranian, Western, Northwestern, Kurdish. *Dialects:* Lexical similarity 70% with Western Farsi, 78% with Luristani (Khorramabadi), 69% with Northern Luri (central rural dialects). *Lg Use:* Vigorous. Used in the home. All ages. A few young people whose parents speak Laki have learned only Northern Luri or Western Farsi. Positive language attitude. Speakers also use Northern Luri or Western Farsi. *Lg Dev:* Poetry. Dictionary. *Other:* Agriculturalists. Muslim (Shi'a), Ahl-e Haqq.

Lari (Larestani, Achomi) [lrl] 80,000. Ethnic population: 100,000. Throughout Lar District, South Fars Province; Shiraz; United Arab Emirates. *Class:* Indo-European, Indo-Iranian, Iranian, Western, Southwestern, Fars. *Dialect:* Lari. Verbal system is quite distinct from Western Farsi. *Lg Use:* Vigorous. Used in home, commerce. Speakers also use Western Farsi or Gulf Spoken Arabic. *Lg Dev:* Dictionary. *Other:* 400 to 1,200 meters. Agriculturalists; merchants. Muslim (Sunni and Shi'a).

Lasgerdi [lsa] In Lasjerd, Semnan Province (40 km southwest of Semnan). *Class:* Indo-European, Indo-Iranian, Iranian, Western, Northwestern, Semnani. *Dialects:* Related to Sorkhei. *Lg Dev:* Dictionary. *Other:* Muslim.

Luri, Northern (Lori, Luri) [lrc] 1,500,000 (2001). Ethnic population: 1,700,000 (2001). Western Iran: Central and Southern Lorestan, Northern Khuzestan, Southern Hamadan Province, the southern edge of Markazi Province, some regions of Ilam, and possibly a small population in eastern Iraq. Populations also in Khorramabad, Borujerd, Andimeshk. *Class:* Indo-European, Indo-Iranian, Iranian, Western, Southwestern, Luri. *Dialects:* Khorramabadi, Borujerdi, Nahavandi, Andimeshki, Bala-Gariva'i, Mahali (Rural), Cagani. The major Northern Luri dialects (Khorramabadi, Borujerdi, etc.) are found in Lorestan and Khuzestan. Some local regions in Ilam Province (Posht-e Kuh) are said to speak Northern Luri dialects. Mainly south Kurdish dialects are spoken in Ilam Province (Fattah 2000). Also, according to Fattah, there are a small number of villages in Iraq, where a dialect of Northern Luri may be spoken. Close to Kumzari. Lexical similarity of Mahali dialect 80% with Western Farsi, 69% with Laki, and 73% with Bakhtiari (Haflang); Khorramabadi dialect 85% with Western Farsi, 78% with Laki, and 75% with Bakhtiari (Haflang). Similarity to Western Farsi is due to language shift, but also to lexical borrowing. *Lg Use:* Vigorous. Used in the home, commerce. All ages. Speakers also use Western Farsi or Laki. *Lg Dev:* Poetry. Radio programs. TV. Dictionary. Grammar. *Other:* Ethnic groups: Pish-e Kuh, some parts of Posht-e Kuh. 100 to 3000 meters. Posht-e Kuh: nomadic; Pish-e Kuh: agriculturalists. Muslim (Shi'a).

Luri, Southern (Ruliy, Lori-ye Jonubi, Luri, Lur, Lor, Lori) [luz] 875,000 (1999). 300,000 monolinguals. Ethnic population: 900,000. Kohgiluyeh va Boyerahmad Province (Yasuj is center of Boyerahmadi, Dehdasht is center of Kohgiluyeh), eastern Khuzestan Province (Kohgiluyeh), Northwestern Fars Province (Nurabad is center of Mamasani, Shul is center of Shuli), Shiraz. *Class:* Indo-European, Indo-Iranian, Iranian, Western, Southwestern, Luri. *Dialects:* Boyerahmadi, Yasuji (Yasichi), Kohgiluyeh, Mamasani, Shuli. Southern Luri is on a continuum between Bakhtiari and Western Farsi "dialects" such as Bushehri and Fars Province varieties. There is a non-Lur tribe in Fars Province called Kurdshuli, which is reported to speak a Southern Luri dialect. Their winter quarters are at Qasr-e Dasht near Sivand, which is 70 km from Sharaz on the Shiraz-Esfahan road (Ivanow 1959, unpublished). Close to Kumzari. Lexical similarity 75% with Western Farsi, 80% with Bushehri dialect of Western Farsi; Mamasani dialect 75% with Bakhtiari, Boyerahmadi dialect 86% with Bakhtiari. *Lg Use:* Vigorous. Used in the home, commerce, some media. All ages. Bilingual level estimates for Western Farsi: 1 25%, 2 35%, 3 35%, 4 5%, 5 0%. Older people and women are much less bilingual. *Lg Dev:* Literacy rate in first language: 0%. Literacy rate in second language: 60%. Poetry. Radio programs. Dictionary. Grammar. *Other:* SOV. Open forest, mountains. 1,000 to 3,000 meters. Agriculturalists; seminomadic pastoralists; hunters; industrial workers. Muslim (Shi'a).

Mandaic (Mandaean, Neo-Mandaic, Modern Mandaic, Manda:yi, Mandi, Subbi, Sabean, Sabe'in) [mid] 500 (2001). Ethnic population: 23,000. Hoveiseh and other towns, Khuzestan. *Class:* Afro-Asiatic, Semitic, Central, Aramaic, Eastern, Mandaic. *Dialects:* Ahwaz (Ahvaz), Shushtar, Iraqi Neo-Mandaic. Little dialect variation. *Lg Use:* Ethnic group of 5,000 in Khuzistan, Iran, speak Western Farsi (1994 H. Mutzafi). Iraqi Neo-Mandaic extinct during the 20th century. Shustar may be extinct. Speakers are older bilingual adults. Speakers also use Mesopotaman Spoken Arabic or Western Farsi. *Lg Dev:* Mandaic script. *Other:* Ethnic Mandaeans in Iraq now speak Arabic (H. Mutzafi 1994). Assyrians in the USA report Mandaic speakers there, whom they call 'Yokhananaye'. Riverine. Goldsmiths. Mandaism (Gnostic).

Mandaic, Classical (Classical Mandaean) [myz] Extinct. Also used in Iraq (Basrah) and small communities in the USA (New York) and Australia (300 Mandaeans in Sydney in 1995). *Class:* Afro-Asiatic, Semitic, Central, Aramaic, Eastern, Mandaic. *Dialects:* Appears to be the direct ancestor of Modern Mandaic. *Lg Use:* The liturgical language used by followers of the Mandaean religion. *Lg Dev:* Mandaic script. *Other:* Mandaism.

Maraghei [vmh] Upper Rudbar area (Rudbar-e Alamut). *Class:* Indo-European, Indo-Iranian, Iranian, Western, Northwestern, Talysh. *Dialect:* Dikini. Various dialects. Close to Gozarkhani. Dialect in Kuhpayeh may be the same language. *Other:* Muslim.

Mazanderani (Tabri, Mazandarani) [mzn] 3,265,000 (1993). Northern Iran near Caspian Sea, southern half of Mazanderan Province. *Class:* Indo-European, Indo-Iranian, Iranian, Western, Northwestern, Caspian. *Dialects:* Mazanderani, Gorgani. Related to Gilaki. Qadikolahi (Ghadikolahi) and Palani may be dialects. *Lg Use:* Speakers also use Western Farsi. *Lg Dev:* The educated can read Farsi well. Grammar. *Other:* Agriculturalists; fishermen. Muslim (Shi'a).

Natanzi [ntz] 7,033 (2000 WCD). Esfahan Province: Natanz, on the Esfahan-Kashan Road. *Class:* Indo-European, Indo-Iranian, Iranian, Western, Northwestern, Central Iran. *Dialects:* Natanzi may be part of a larger complex of Esfahan Province dialects including Yarani (Yarandi) and Farizandi. *Other:* Muslim.

Nayini (Biyabanak) [nyq] 7,033 (2000 WCD). Esfahan Province: Nayin and Anarak, 100 km east of Esfahan; Khuri is spoken in Khur (Khvor) and Mehrjan, 250 km northeast of Esfahan. *Class:* Indo-European, Indo-Iranian, Iranian, Western, Northwestern, Central Iran. *Dialects:* Nayini, Anarak, Khuri. Dialects listed may be separate languages. Khuri is distinct from other dialects. Related to Zoroastrian Dari. *Other:* Muslim.

Parsi-Dari (Parsee-Dari) [prd] 350,000 in Iran. Population total all countries: 700,000. Also spoken in Afghanistan. *Class:* Indo-European, Indo-Iranian, Iranian, Western, Northwestern, Central Iran. *Dialects:* Parsi-Dari is reported to not be inherently intelligible with Parsi of India, Pakistan, and other countries, but linguistically and ethnically related. They diverged 600 to 700 years ago or more. It is related to Dari. *Lg Use:* Many are reported to not speak other languages well. *Other:* 'Parsee' is the name of the ethnic group. Zoroastrian.

Pashto, Southern (Pashtu, Paktu, "Afghani") [pbt] 113,000 in Iran (1993). Population does not include refugees. Khorasan on Afghanistan border east of Qa'en. *Lg Use:* Men are bilingual in Western Farsi. *Other:* Different from Northern Pashto of Pakistan and India. Laborers. Muslim (Sunni). See main entry under Pakistan.

Persian Sign Language [psc] *Class:* Deaf sign language. *Lg Dev:* Dictionary.

Qashqa'i (Qashqay, Qashqai, Kashkai) [qxq] 1,500,000 (1997). Southwestern Iran, Fars Province and Southern

Kohgiluyeh va Boyerahmad Province. Shiraz, Gachsaran, and Firuzabad are centers. *Class:* Altaic, Turkic, Southern, Azerbaijani. *Dialects:* Very close to Azerbaijani. *Lg Use:* Vigorous. Used in the home, commerce. All ages. Many also use Western Farsi. *Lg Dev:* Many can read Farsi well. *Other:* Nomadic. Desert. Rug weavers; pastoralists: sheep, donkeys, camels. Muslim (Shi'a).

Razajerdi [rat] Qazvin and Kuhpayeh area, Razajerd. *Class:* Indo-European, Indo-Iranian, Iranian, Western, Northwestern, Talysh. *Dialects:* Various dialects. Related to Takestani. *Other:* Muslim.

Romani, Balkan [rmn] *Dialect:* Zargari. *Other:* Also see Western Farsi in Iran concerning Zargari. Muslim. See main entry under Serbia and Montenegro.

Rudbari [rdb] Sefid Rud Valley. *Class:* Indo-European, Indo-Iranian, Iranian, Western, Northwestern, Talysh. *Dialects:* Various dialects. Transitional to Caspian languages and related to Vafsi. *Other:* Muslim.

Salchuq [slq] *Class:* Altaic, Turkic, Southern, Azerbaijani. *Dialects:* Probably a dialect of Azerbaijani. *Other:* Muslim.

Sangisari (Sangesari) [sgr] Semnân Province. *Class:* Indo-European, Indo-Iranian, Iranian, Western, Northwestern, Semnani. *Lg Dev:* Dictionary. *Other:* Muslim.

Semnani [smy] 21,099 (2000 WCD). Semnan Province. *Class:* Indo-European, Indo-Iranian, Iranian, Western, Northwestern, Semnani. *Lg Dev:* Dictionary. *Other:* Muslim.

Senaya (Sena:ya, Christian Neo-Aramaic, Shan Sray, Lshan Sray, Soray, Sray, Shan Gyanan) [syn] 60 in Iran (1997 H. Mutzafi). Population total all countries: 460. Tehran and Qazvin. Originally in Sanandaj, Kordestan Province. Some in western Europe. Also spoken in Australia, USA. *Class:* Afro-Asiatic, Semitic, Central, Aramaic, Eastern, Central, Northeastern. *Dialects:* The variety in Qazvin is slightly different from that spoken by Sanandaj-born people. *Lg Use:* Speakers are shifting to Assyrian Neo-Aramaic. *Lg Dev:* Syriac script. *Other:* Christian (Chaldean).

Shahmirzadi [srz] Shahmirzad, Semnan Province. *Class:* Indo-European, Indo-Iranian, Iranian, Western, Northwestern, Caspian. *Dialects:* Close to Mazanderani and Gilaki. *Lg Dev:* Dictionary.

Shahrudi [shm] Khalkhal District in Eastern Azerbaijan Province, Shahrud District, Shal, Kolur, Lerd. *Class:* Indo-European, Indo-Iranian, Iranian, Western, Northwestern, Talysh. *Dialects:* Close to Kajali and Koresh-e Rostam. Different from Sharudi, a Western Farsi dialect. *Other:* Muslim.

Sivandi [siy] 7,033 (2000 WCD). Sivand, Fars Province (70 km northwest of Shiraz on the Shiraz-Esfahan Road). *Class:* Indo-European, Indo-Iranian, Iranian, Western, Northwestern, Central Iran. *Dialects:* Related to Northwestern Fars varieties. *Other:* Muslim.

Soi [soj] 7,033 (2000 WCD). *Class:* Indo-European, Indo-Iranian, Iranian, Western, Northwestern, Central Iran. *Other:* Muslim.

Sorkhei [sqo] Semnan Province: Sorkheh, 19 km southwest of Semnan. *Class:* Indo-European, Indo-Iranian, Iranian, Western, Northwestern, Semnani. *Dialects:* Related to Lasgerdi. *Lg Dev:* Dictionary. *Other:* Muslim.

Takestani (Takistani) [tks] 220,000. Zanjan, Qazvin and Markazi provinces: various towns and villages in the mainly Azerbaijani-speaking region from Khalkhal to Saveh, especially in Takestan and villages to the south and southeast. *Class:* Indo-European, Indo-Iranian, Iranian, Western, Northwestern, Talysh. *Dialect:* Khalkhal, Tarom, Zanjan, Kharaqan, Ramand (Takestan). Close to Talysh, especially Khalkhal dialect. Transitional between Talysh and Semnani languages. Close to Eshtehardi.

Lg Use: Speakers also use Farsi. *Other:* Different from Tat of Russia, Azerbaijan, and Iran. Muslim.

Talysh (Talyshi, Talish, Talishi, Talesh, Taleshi) [tly] 112,000 in Iran (1993). Northwest Gilan Province along Caspian coastal plain and adjacent mountainous areas from Masuleh, Masal, and Kapur-Chal (Kepri-Chal) (each about 50 km east of Rasht) to the Azerbaijan border. Northern Talyshi is centered around Astara and the Caspian littoral in Azerbaijan; Central Talyshi is centered in the Asalem-Hashtpar area along the Caspian littoral in Gilan Province; Southern Talyshi is centered around Shandermen, Masal, Masuleh, and surrounding mountainous areas in Gilan Province. *Dialects:* Northern Talyshi, Central Talyshi, Southern Talyshi. *Lg Use:* Speakers also use Western Farsi. *Other:* Muslim. See main entry under Azerbaijan.

Taromi, Upper [tov] Upper Tarom of Zanjan Province, Hazarrud, Siavarud. *Class:* Indo-European, Indo-Iranian, Iranian, Western, Northwestern, Talysh. *Dialects:* Various dialects. Close to Kabatei. *Other:* Muslim.

Tat, Muslim (Mussulman Tati) [ttt] 8,000 in Iran. *Lg Use:* Speakers use Azerbaijani as a literary language in Azerbaijan. *Other:* Not written. Different from Takestani of Iran. Muslim (Shi'a). See main entry under Azerbaijan.

Turkmen (Torkomani) [tuk] 2,000,000 in Iran (1997). Northeast, mainly in Mazanderan Province, along the Turkmenistan border; important centers are Gonbad-e Kavus and Pahlavi Dezh. *Dialects:* Anauli, Khasarli, Nerezim, Nokhurli (Nohur), Chavdur, Esari (Esary), Goklen (Goklan), Salyr, Saryq, Teke (Tekke), Yomud (Yomut), Trukmen. *Lg Use:* Speakers also use Farsi. *Other:* Not a literary language in Iran. Many are seminomadic. Ethnic groups: Yomut, Goklan. Agriculturalists: cotton, wheat, barley; animal husbandry: cattle. Muslim (Hanafi Sunni and Shi'a). See main entry under Turkmenistan.

Vafsi [vaf] 18,000 (2003). Markazi Province, Arak District, Vafs, near Tafresh. *Class:* Indo-European, Indo-Iranian, Iranian, Western, Northwestern, Central Iran. *Dialects:* Various dialects. Transitional between central Iranian dialects and Talysh; very close to Ashtiani. *Lg Use:* Speakers also use Western Farsi. *Other:* Muslim.

Iraq

Republic of Iraq, al Jumhouriya al'Iraqia. 25,374,691. National or official languages: Standard Arabic, Kurdi. Literacy rate: 60% to 70%. Also includes Egyptian Spoken Arabic (450,000), Syriac, Turkish (3,000), Turkmen (227,000), Turoyo (3,000). Information mainly from A. M. Maclean 1893; T. Sebeok 1963; T. M. Johnstone 1967; H. Kloss and G. McConnell 1974; O. Jastrow 1978; W. Fischer and O. Jastrow 1980; B. Ingham 1982; R. D. Hoberman 1988a, b; M. Izadi 1993. Blind population: 75,000 (1982 WCE). Deaf population: 1,205,930. Deaf institutions: 5. The number of languages listed for Iraq is 22. Of those, 21 are living languages and 1 is extinct. See map on page 806.

Adyghe (West Circassian, Adygey) [ady] 19,000 in Iraq (1993). *Other:* Muslim (Sunni). See main entry under Russia (Europe).

Arabic, Gulf Spoken (Khaliji, Gulf Arabic) [afb] 40,000 in Iraq. Population total all countries: 2,338,600. In and around Zubair and on the Fau Peninsula. Also spoken in Bahrain, Iran, Kuwait, Oman, Qatar, Saudi Arabia, United Arab Emirates, Yemen. *Class:* Afro-Asiatic, Semitic, Central, South, Arabic. *Dialect:* Zubair-Faau Arabic.

Arabic, Judeo-Iraqi (Iraqi Judeo-Arabic, Jewish Iraqi-Baghdadi Arabic, Arabi, Yahudic) [yhd] 100 to 150 in Iraq (1992 H. Mutzafi). Most in Israel. *Lg Use:* Speakers are older adults. *Other:* Jewish. See main entry under Israel.

Arabic, Mesopotamian Spoken (Mesopotamian Qeltu Arabic, Mesopotamian Gelet Arabic, Baghdadi

Arabic, Iraqi Arabic, Furati) [acm] 11,500,000 in Iraq. Population total all countries: 15,100,000. Tigris and Euphrates clusters are in Iraq. Also spoken in Iran, Jordan, Syria, Turkey (Asia). *Class:* Afro-Asiatic, Semitic, Central, South, Arabic. *Dialects:* Anatolian Cluster, Tigris Cluster, Euphrates Cluster. Geographical and sectarian divisions correlate with Iraqi dialects. The vernacular standard is forming based on Baghdad speech. There are also Bedouin dialects. Nearly unintelligible to speakers of certain other vernacular Arabic varieties. *Lg Use:* National language. *Lg Dev:* Radio programs. TV. *Other:* SVO. Muslim (Shi'a, Sunni), Christian, Jewish, Yezidi.

Arabic, Najdi Spoken [ars] 900,000 in Iraq. Central Najdi is spoken by Bedouin in the western desert, North Najdi by Bedouin in the south between the rivers up to the Syrian border. *Dialects:* North Najdi (Shammar), Central Najdi. See main entry under Saudi Arabia.

Arabic, North Mesopotamian Spoken (Syro-Mesopotamian Vernacular Arabic, Moslawi, Mesopotamian Qeltu Arabic) [ayp] 5,400,000 in Iraq (1992). Population total all countries: 6,300,000. Along most of the Tigris and part of the Euphrates valleys north of Baghdad. Also spoken in Jordan, Syria, Turkey (Asia). *Class:* Afro-Asiatic, Semitic, Central, South, Arabic. *Dialects:* Very close to Judeo-Iraqi Arabic, but there are important sociolinguistic differences. *Other:* Muslim, Christian.

Arabic, Standard [arb] Middle East, North Africa. *Lg Use:* National language. Used for education, official purposes. See main entry under Saudi Arabia.

Armenian [hye] 60,000 in Iraq. *Dialect:* Western Armenian. *Other:* Christian. See main entry under Armenia.

Assyrian Neo-Aramaic (Lishana Aturaya, Suret, Sooreth, Sureth, Suryaya Swadaya, Assyrian, Neo-Syriac, Assyriski, Aisorski, Assyrianci) [aii] 30,000 in Iraq (1994). Population total all countries: 210,231. Ethnic population: 4,250,000 (1994). Northern Iraq, Baghdad, Basrah, Karkuk, Arbil. Also spoken in Armenia, Australia, Austria, Azerbaijan, Belgium, Brazil, Canada, Cyprus, France, Georgia, Germany, Greece, Iran, Italy, Lebanon, Netherlands, New Zealand, Russia (Europe), Sweden, Switzerland, Syria, Turkey (Asia), United Kingdom, USA. *Class:* Afro-Asiatic, Semitic, Central, Aramaic, Eastern, Central, Northeastern. *Dialects:* Close linguistically to other Northeastern Aramaic varieties. Inherent intelligibility is hard to estimate due to intense exposure of most speakers throughout the Assyrian diaspora to many dialects, especially to Urmi and Iraqi Koine. Only because of this exposure is actual intelligibility between different dialects as high as 80% to 90%. Subdialects of the Urmian group: Urmi, Sipurghan, Solduz; of the Northern Group: Salamas, Van, Jilu, Gavar, Qudshanis, Upper Barwari, Dez, Baz; of the Central Group: Mar Bishu, Nochiya (Shamezdin), Tergawar, Anhar; of the Western Group: Tkhuma, Lower Barwari, Tal, Lewin. The Sapna cluster includes Aradhin, Tina, Daudiya, Inishke, Benatha. Standard literary Assyrian is based on Urmi. Many speakers have left the original areas and have developed a common spoken and written form based on the prestigious Urmi dialect as spoken by those from Iraq living in Baghdad, Chicago, and elsewhere (Iraqi Koine). Most Christians understand it. The Urmi subdialect of this language is different from the Urmi subdialect of Lishán Didán. All dialects of Western, Northern, and Central Assyrian are spoken in Syria. *Lg Use:* In some countries, young people speak the language of that country, not Assyrian Neo-Aramaic. *Lg Dev:* Syriac script. Radio programs. Bible: 1852–1919. *Other:* The Assyrian and Chaldean separated denominationally in the 16th century. Christian (Nestorian and other).

Azerbaijani, South [azb] 300,000 to 900,000 in Iraq (1982). Kirkuk City, Arbil, Rowanduz, towns and villages southeast from Kirkuk as far as Al Miqdadiyah, Khanaqin, and Mandali; also several places in the Mosul Region. *Dialect:* Kirkuk. *Lg Use:* They speak South Azerbaijani at home. *Lg Dev:* Many read Arabic or Kurdish. Low literacy rate in South Azerbaijani. *Other:* They are called 'Turkmen', or 'Turks', in Iraq and Syria. There is little literature. Muslim. See main entry under Iran.

Bajelani (Bajalani, Gurani, Chichamachu, Bajoran, Bejwan) [bjm] 20,000 (1976 Sara). Qasr-e Shirin, Zohab, Bin Qudra, Quratu, north of Khanaqin, also in Mosul Province. Since late 1980s, many have become displaced. *Class:* Indo-European, Indo-Iranian, Iranian, Western, Northwestern, Zaza-Gorani. *Dialects:* In the Gurani and Zaza group. *Other:* Muslim.

Chaldean Neo-Aramaic (Chaldean, Kildani, Kaldaya, Neo-Chaldean, Modern Chaldean, Sureth, Soorith, Soorath, Suras, Lishana Kaldaya, Fellihi, Fallani) [cld] 100,000 to 120,000 in Iraq (1994 Mutzafi). Population total all countries: 206,000. Originally in central western and northern Iraqi Kurdistan and some in bordering Turkey. Now in Mosul, Baghdad, Basrah, southeastern Iraqi Kurdistan. Also spoken in Australia, Belgium, Canada, Germany, Lebanon, Netherlands, Sweden, Syria, Turkey (Asia), USA. *Class:* Afro-Asiatic, Semitic, Central, Aramaic, Eastern, Central, Northeastern. *Dialects:* Mangesh, Alqosh, Tel Kepe, Tisqopa, Bartille, Shirnak-Chizre (Bohtan), Dihok. High intelligibility of Lishana Deni and Ashirat (western dialect group of Assyrian Neo-Aramaic); little or no intelligibilty with other Northeastern Aramaic varieties. Comprehension among all of these improves with contact. *Lg Dev:* Syriac script. Bible portions: 1992. *Other:* The ethnic group is distinct denominationally from speakers of other Northeastern Aramaic varieties; separated from the Assyrian during the 16th century. The names 'Chaldean' and 'Assyrian' are sometimes each used in a popular sense to include both groups. A Syriac script is basically the 22-letter alphabet of Classical Syriac. It can be compatible to Sooreth by adding diacritics. Christian (Chaldean, Uniate Catholic, Syrian Orthodox).

Domari (Middle Eastern Romani) [rmt] 22,946 in Iraq (2000 WCD). *Other:* People called 'Zott'. Muslim. See main entry under Iran.

Farsi, Western (Persian) [pes] 227,000 in Iraq (1993). *Other:* Muslim. See main entry under Iran.

Gurani (Hawrami, Hewrami, Hawramani, Gorani, Macho) [hac] 21,099 in Iraq (2000 WCD). Several hundred thousand for group of Gurani speakers in both Iraq and Iran (Blau 1989). Population total all countries: 44,047. Near Halabja, east of Suleimaniye, Topzawa near Tawuq, pockets ('islands') from Mosul to Khanaqin. Also spoken in Iran. *Class:* Indo-European, Indo-Iranian, Iranian, Western, Northwestern, Zaza-Gorani. *Lg Use:* Some speakers also use Central Kurdish (Sorani) or Arabic. *Lg Dev:* Modified Arabic script. *Other:* There is a very old literary tradition. Muslim, Ahl-e Haq.

Jewish Babylonian Aramaic (Babylonian Talmudic Aramaic) [tmr] Extinct. *Class:* Afro-Asiatic, Semitic, Central, Aramaic, Eastern, Central, Northeastern. *Lg Use:* The language of the Babylonian Talmud and other sacred Jewish works. Familiar among students of Judaism in both religious and scholarly realms, and studied diligently by most Orthodox Jewish young men. Used widely in Jewish culture and life. *Other:* Extinct around 11th or 12th century.

Koy Sanjaq Surat (Koi Sanjaq Soorit, Koy Sanjaq Soorit, Koi-Sanjaq Sooret, Koy Sanjaq Sooret) [kqd] 800 to 1,000 (1995 H. Mutzafi). Northern Iraq, town of Koi-Sanjaq, and nearby village of Armota. *Class:* Afro-Asiatic, Semitic, Central, Aramaic, Eastern, Central,

Northeastern. *Dialects:* Related in certain morphological and lexical respects to Senaya. *Lg Dev:* Syriac script. *Other:* Speakers call their language 'Surat'. Christian (Chaldean, Uniate Catholic).

Kurdish, Central (Kurdi, Sorani) [ckb] 462,000 in Iraq (2004). Population total all countries: 3,712,000. South of the Great Zab River, in Suleimaniye, Arbil, Kirkuk, and Khanaqin and Mandali provinces. Speakers have also been displaced. Diaspora communities in other areas, including western Europe, USA. Also spoken in Iran. *Class:* Indo-European, Indo-Iranian, Iranian, Western, Northwestern, Kurdish. *Dialects:* Hewleri (Arbili), Xoshnaw, Pizhdar, Suleimani (Silemani) Warmawa, Rewandiz, Bingird, Mukri, Kerkuki, Garmiyani. *Lg Use:* Official language. Language of wider communication. Positive language attitude. *Lg Dev:* Literary standard is based on Sorani (from Suleimaniye). Modified Arabic script. NT: 1994. *Other:* Muslim (Sunni).

Kurdish, Northern (Behdini, Bahdini, Badinani, Kirmanciya Jori, Kurmanji) [kmr] 2,800,000 in Iraq (2004). Northern Kurdish is spoken north of the Great Zab River, in Dohuk and Mosul provinces. Speech varieties, such as Surchi, sharing elements of both Northern and Central Kurdish, are spoken near the Great Zab River. Many speakers have been displaced since the late 1980s. *Dialects:* Surchi, Akre, Amadiye, Barwari Jor, Gulli, Zakho, Sheikhan. *Lg Use:* Language of wider communication. Positive language attitude. *Other:* Muslim (Sunni), Yezidi. See main entry under Turkey (Asia).

Kurdish, Southern [sdh] South of Xanaqin, Kirind, and Qorwaq. *Dialects:* Kolyai, Kermanshahi (Kermanshani), Kalhori, Sanjabi, Maleksh ahi (Maleksh ay), Bayray, Kordali, Feyli, Luri. *Lg Use:* Official language. Used in the home. Speakers also use Arabic. *Other:* Muslim (Shi'a). See main entry under Iran.

Sarli (Sarliya) [sdf] Fewer than 20,000. North of Mosul, also in Kirkuk Province, many are displaced. *Class:* Indo-European, Indo-Iranian, Iranian, Western, Northwestern, Zaza-Gorani. *Dialects:* In the Gurani (Gorani) and Zaza group. *Other:* Muslim.

Shabak [sdb] 10,000 to 20,000 (1989 Blau). In villages of Ali Rach, Yangija, Khazna, Talara, north of Mosul, but since late 1980s, many have become displaced. *Class:* Indo-European, Indo-Iranian, Iranian, Western, Northwestern, Zaza-Gorani. *Dialects:* In the Gurani (Gorani) and Zaza group. *Other:* Muslim.

Israel

State of Israel, Medinat Israel. 6,199,008. Population includes 4,700,000 Jewish (1997), 805,000 Muslim, 160,000 Christian, 95,000 Druze, 300 Samaritan (1995 Central Statistics Dept., Israel). National or official languages: Hebrew, Standard Arabic, English. About half the Jewish people are Sephardi and half Ashkenazi. Literacy rate: 88% to 92% (Jewish), 70% (Arab). Also includes Bulgarian, Czech, Egyptian Spoken Arabic (25,000), French (40,000), Italian (7,249), Levantine Bedawi Spoken Arabic (50,000), Malayalam (8,000), Marathi (8,000), North Levantine Spoken Arabic (100,000), Northern Uzbek, Samaritan, Samaritan Aramaic, Spanish (60,000), Standard German (30,000), Turkish (30,000), Western Farsi, Western Yiddish, many other languages. Information mainly from D. Gold 1974; H. Kloss and G. McConnell 1974; H. Paper 1978; W. Fischer and O. Jastrow 1980; T. K. Harris 1994; J. Fishman 1985, 1991; J. Chetrit 1985; D. Cohen 1985; B. Comrie 1987; A. Saenz-Badillos 1993; P. E. Miller 1993; Y. Mutzafi 1992–2004. Blind population: 5,285. Deaf population: 4,500 to 306,242 (1998). Deaf institutions: 31. The number of languages listed for Israel is 34. Of those, 33 are living languages and 1 is extinct.

Adyghe (West Circassian, Adygey) [ady] 3,000 in Israel (1987). Kafr Kama and Rehaniya, small border villages. *Lg Use:* Speakers also use South Levantine Arabic. *Other:* They came about 100 years ago from the Caucasus (now Russia). They call themselves 'Circassian'. Very slight dialect differences between the two villages. They understand radio programs in Adyghe from Jordan. Muslim (Sunni). See main entry under Russia (Europe).

Amharic [amh] 40,000 in Israel (1994 H. Mutzafi). *Lg Use:* Speakers also use Hebrew. *Other:* Spoken by Jews of Ethiopian origin. They call themselves 'Beta Israel', and consider "Falasha" pejorative. Jewish. See main entry under Ethiopia.

Arabic, Judeo-Iraqi (Iraqi Judeo-Arabic, Jewish Iraqi-Baghdadi Arabic, Arabi, Yahudic) [yhd] 100,000 in Israel (1994). Population total all countries: 100,100. Originally from Iraq. Also spoken in India, Iraq, United Kingdom. *Class:* Afro-Asiatic, Semitic, Central, South, Arabic. *Dialects:* Not intelligible with Judeo-Tripolitanian Arabic, Judeo-Tunisian Arabic, or Judeo-Moroccan Arabic. Close to Baghdadi Arabic and North Mesopotamian Arabic. *Lg Use:* Speakers are older adults. Speakers in Israel are reported to be bilingual in Hebrew. *Lg Dev:* Hebrew script. *Other:* The term 'Yahudic' is used by a few scholars to denote all Judeo-Arabic languages. Jewish.

Arabic, Judeo-Moroccan [aju] 250,000 in Israel (1992 H. Mutzafi). Population total all countries: 258,925. Also spoken in Canada, France, Morocco. *Class:* Afro-Asiatic, Semitic, Central, South, Arabic. *Dialects:* Many dialects. Much intelligibility with Tunisian Judeo-Arabic, some with Judeo-Tripolitanian Arabic, but none with Judeo-Iraqi Arabic. May be inherently intelligible with Moroccan Arabic. *Lg Use:* Speakers in Israel are reported to be bilingual in Hebrew. *Lg Dev:* Hebrew script. Radio programs. *Other:* Large number of borrowings from Spanish, Ladino, French. Jewish.

Arabic, Judeo-Tripolitanian (Tripolitanian Judeo-Arabic, Jewish Tripolitanian-Libyan Arabic, Tripolita'it, Yudi) [yud] 30,000 in Israel (1994 H. Mutzafi). Population total all countries: 35,000. Originally from Tripolitania, Libya. None left in Libya. Also spoken in Italy. *Class:* Afro-Asiatic, Semitic, Central, South, Arabic. *Dialects:* Not intelligible with Judeo-Iraqi Arabic. Medium intelligibility with Judeo-Tunisian Arabic and Judeo-Morocco Arabic. *Lg Use:* Most speakers older than 40 years. Speakers in Israel are reported to be bilingual in Hebrew. *Lg Dev:* Hebrew script. *Other:* Jewish.

Arabic, Judeo-Tunisian [ajt] 45,000 in Israel (1995 H. Mutzafi). Population total all countries: 45,500. Also spoken in France, Italy, Spain, Tunisia, USA. *Class:* Afro-Asiatic, Semitic, Central, South, Arabic. *Dialects:* Medium intelligibility with Judeo-Moroccan Arabic and Judeo-Tripolitanian Arabic, but none with Judeo-Iraqi Arabic. A lexicon of 5,000 words in 1950 had 79% words of Arabic origin, 15% Romance loanwords, 4.4% Hebrew loanwords, 1.6% others (D. Cohen 1985:254). *Lg Use:* Speakers are older adults. Younger generation has only passive knowledge of Judeo-Tunisian Arabic. In Israel the generation of immigrants is reported to be bilingual in Hebrew. *Lg Dev:* Hebrew script. Bible portions: 1897–1937. *Other:* Jewish.

Arabic, Judeo-Yemeni (Judeo-Yemeni, Yemenite Judeo-Arabic) [jye] 50,000 in Israel (1995 Y. Kara). Population total all countries: 51,000. Also spoken in Yemen. *Class:* Afro-Asiatic, Semitic, Central, South, Arabic. *Dialects:* San'a, 'Aden, Be:da, Habban. Language varieties are all markedly different from their coterritorial Muslim ones. *Lg Dev:* Hebrew script. *Other:* Jewish.

Arabic, South Levantine Spoken (Levantine, Palestanian-Jordanian Arabic) [ajp] 910,000 in Israel. *Dialects:* Madani, Fellahi. *Lg Use:* Speakers also use

Hebrew. *Lg Dev:* Literacy rate in second language: 90% in Arabic, 60% in Hebrew. *Other:* A few hundred speakers are of Gypsy origin. Muslim, Christian, Jewish, Druze. See main entry under Jordan.

Arabic, Standard [arb] Middle East, North Africa. *Lg Use:* National language. Used for education and communication among Arabic-speaking countries. See main entry under Saudi Arabia.

Armenian (Haieren, Somkhuri, Ermenice, Armjanski) [hye] 3,000 in Israel (1971 The Armenian Review). Jerusalem. *Dialect:* Western Armenian. *Lg Use:* Speakers also use South Levantine Arabic. *Other:* Eastern Armenian is spoken in Armenia, Turkey, and Iran; Western in other countries, including Israel. Christian. See main entry under Armenia.

Barzani Jewish Neo-Aramaic (Lishan Didan, Lishan Dideni, Bijil Neo-Aramaic) [bjf] 20 (2004 Mutzafi). In Israel since 1951. *Class:* Afro-Asiatic, Semitic, Central, Aramaic, Eastern, Central, Northeastern. *Dialects:* Barzan, Shahe, Bijil. Sandu is a Jewish Neo-Aramaic dialect closely related to Barzani, but evinces several isoglosses binding it with Lishana Deni. *Lg Use:* The last speaker of the Bijil dialect died in 1998, age over 80. She learned it from one parent, while the other parent was a Kurdish or Arabic native speaker. In 1951, it was spoken among the 8 Jewish families of Bijil, a village in Iraqi Kurdistan. (1998 Hezy Mutzafi). All speakers older than 70 years. Some passive speakers in their 50s. Speakers are all competent in Hebrew and Kurdish, which they speak as their primary languages, and some speak other Neo-Aramaic languages. *Other:* Originally spoken in 3 villages near Aqra, Iraq. It was also spoken in the village of Nerim, perhaps as a separate dialect, probably extinct. Nearly extinct.

Bukharic (Bokharic, Bukharian, Bokharan, Bukharan, Judeo-Tajik) [bhh] 50,000 in Israel (1995 H. Mutzafi). Population total all countries: 110,000. Also spoken in USA, Uzbekistan. *Class:* Indo-European, Indo-Iranian, Iranian, Western, Southwestern, Persian. *Dialects:* Related to Tajiki Persian. May be easily intelligible with Tajiki or Farsi. Also close to Judeo-Persian. *Lg Dev:* Hebrew script. Radio programs. *Other:* Many are recent immigrants (1995). Jewish.

Domari (Nawari, Dom, Near-Eastern Gypsy) [rmt] 2,000 in Israel (1997 Yaron Matras). Population includes Palestinian West Bank and Gaza. Mainly Jerusalem (Old City), Bir Zeit near Ramallah, and Gaza. *Dialect:* Nawari. *Lg Use:* The first language of children in some places. Speakers also use South Levantine Spoken Arabic. *Other:* They call themselves 'Dom'. A large number of loanwords from Arabic, Kurdish, and some other Iranian languages. Muslim. See main entry under Iran.

Dzhidi (Judeo-Persian) [jpr] 60,000 in Israel (1995). Also spoken in Iran. *Class:* Indo-European, Indo-Iranian, Iranian, Western, Southwestern, Persian. *Dialects:* Close to Bukharic, Western Farsi. *Lg Use:* Many are speakers of Western Farsi. *Other:* Jewish.

English (Anglit) [eng] 100,000 in Israel (1993). *Lg Use:* Auxiliary official language. See main entry under United Kingdom.

Hebrew (Ivrit) [heb] 4,847,000 in Israel (1998). Population total all countries: 5,055,000. Also spoken in Australia, Canada, Germany, Palestinian West Bank and Gaza, Panama, United Kingdom, USA. *Class:* Afro-Asiatic, Semitic, Central, South, Canaanite. *Dialects:* Standard Hebrew (General Israeli, Europeanized Hebrew), Oriental Hebrew (Arabized Hebrew, Yemenite Hebrew). Not a direct offspring from Biblical or other varieties of Ancient Hebrew, but an amalgamation of different Hebrew strata plus intrinsic evolution within the living speech. *Lg Use:* Official language. Some who use it as primary language now in Israel learned it as their second language originally. Spoken by all Israelis as first or second language. There is a Hebrew Language Academy. _Lg Dev:_ Dictionary. Grammar. Bible: 1599–1877. _Other:_ SVO. Jewish.

Hebrew, Ancient (Old Hebrew) [hbo] Extinct. _Class:_ Afro-Asiatic, Semitic, Central, South, Canaanite. _Lg Use:_ Used as a liturgical language and for the text of the Jewish Bible. _Lg Dev:_ OT: c. 2000–400 B.C. _Other:_ Jewish.

Hulaulá (Judeo-Aramaic, Lishana Noshan, Lishana Axni, Jabali, Kurdit, Galiglu, 'Aramit, Hula Hula) [huy] 10,000 in Israel (1999 H. Mutzafi). Population total all countries: 10,300. Also spoken in Iran, USA. _Class:_ Afro-Asiatic, Semitic, Central, Aramaic, Eastern, Central, Northeastern. _Dialects:_ Saqiz, Kerend, Sanandaj, Suleimaniya. Very different and not intelligible with the Christian Aramaic languages or Lishana Deni. 60% to 70% intelligibility of Lishanan and Lishanid Noshan. _Lg Use:_ Many speakers use Hebrew as second language. The older speakers use Kurdish as second language. _Lg Dev:_ Hebrew script. _Other:_ Originally from Iranian Kurdistan and adjoining areas of Iraq. Jewish.

Hungarian [hun] 70,000 in Israel (1998 H. Mutzafi). _Lg Use:_ Older adults speakers use Hebrew as second language but prefer Hungarian. _Other:_ Jewish. See main entry under Hungary.

Israeli Sign Language (ISL) [isr] 5,000 users including some hearing persons (1986 Gallaudet Univ.). _Class:_ Deaf sign language. _Dialects:_ Not derived from and relatively little influence from other sign languages. No special signs have been introduced from outside by educators. Minor dialect variation. _Lg Use:_ Not all deaf use ISL. Interpreters are provided in courts. Some interpretation for college students. Sign language instruction for parents of deaf children. Many sign language classes for hearing people. There is a committee on national sign language, and an organization for sign language teachers. The sign language used in classrooms and that by deaf adults outside is different. _Lg Dev:_ Employs the Eshkol-Wachmann movement notation system. Films. TV. Videos. Dictionary. Grammar. _Other:_ The first deaf school was established in Jerusalem in 1934. A fingerspelling system was developed in 1976. Jewish.

Judeo-Berber [jbe] 2,000 (1992 Podolsky). Formerly High Atlas range, Tifnut, and other communities. Speakers went to Israel from 1950 to 1960. _Class:_ Afro-Asiatic, Berber, Northern, Atlas. _Lg Use:_ Speakers are older adults. Monolingual communities may have disappeared before 1930 in Morocco. Speakers also formerly used Judeo-Arabic (J. Chetrit 1985). _Lg Dev:_ Hebrew script. _Other:_ Jewish.

Judeo-Georgian [jge] 59,800 in Israel (2000 WCD). Population total all countries: 79,800. Some have gone elsewhere in the former USSR and to other countries. Also spoken in Georgia. _Class:_ Kartvelian, Georgian. _Dialects:_ Oriental and Ashkenazic Jews in Georgia live separately. Judeo-Georgian speakers live separately from non-Jewish Georgian speakers. May not be a separate language from Georgian, but a dialect using various Hebrew loanwords. _Other:_ Jewish.

Judeo-Tat (Judeo-Tatic, Jewish Tat, Bik, Dzhuhuric, Juwri, Juhuri) [jdt] 70,000 in Israel (1998). Population total all countries: 101,000. Sderot, Haderah, and Or Akiva, Israel. None in Iran. They are emigrating from the Caucasus Mountains to Israel at the rate of 2,000 a year. Also spoken in Azerbaijan, Russia (Europe). _Class:_ Indo-European, Indo-Iranian, Iranian, Western, Southwestern, Tat. _Dialect:_ Derbend. Several dialects. Difficult intelligibility of Mussulman Tat. There may also be a Christian dialect. _Lg Dev:_ Hebrew, Cyrillic, and Roman scripts. Bible portions: 1980. _Other:_ Speakers of Judeo-Tat are called 'Bik'. They call their language 'Juwri' or

'Juhuri'. They are called 'Gorskiye Yevreyi', or 'Mountain Jews' in the Caucasus. Speakers consider the label "Tati" to be pejorative. Tradition says that they have lived in the Caucasus since 722 B.C. Different from Takestani of Iran. Agriculturalists: marena grass for dyeing (traditionally); merchants. Jewish.

Ladino (Judeo Spanish, Sefardi, Dzhudezmo, Judezmo, Spanyol, Haquetiya) [lad] 100,000 in Israel (1985). Population total all countries: 110,000. Ethnic group members also in Salonica, Greece; Sofia, Bulgaria. Formerly also in Morocco. Also spoken in Greece, Puerto Rico, Turkey (Europe), USA. _Class:_ Indo-European, Italic, Romance, Italo-Western, Western, Gallo-Iberian, Ibero-Romance, West Iberian, Castilian. _Dialects:_ Judezmo (Judyo, Jidyo), Ladino, Haquetiya (Haketia, Haketiya, Hakitia). The Balkan dialect is more influenced by Turkish and Greek. The North African dialect is more influenced by Arabic and French. _Lg Use:_ It is not the dominant language for most speakers. Formerly the main language of Sefardic Jewry. There are no monolinguals. _Lg Dev:_ Roman script in Turkey. Newspapers. Radio programs. Bible: 1829. _Other:_ The name 'Dzhudezmo' is used by Jewish linguists and Turkish Jews; 'Judeo-Spanish' by Romance philologists; 'Ladino' by laymen, especially in Israel; 'Hakitia' by Moroccan Jews; 'Spanyol' by some others. Different from Ladin in the Rhaeto-Romansch group. The Hebrew (Rashi) alphabet does not work well because of the need to differentiate vowels. Yet there are texts in Hebrew script. Jewish.

Lishán Didán (Lishanán, Lishanid Nash Didán, Persian Azerbaijan Jewish Aramaic, Lakhlokhi, Galihalu) [trg] 4,228 in Israel (2001 WCD). Population total all countries: 4,378. Jerusalem and Tel-Aviv area mainly. Originally Iranian Azerbaijan and southeast Turkey. Also spoken in Azerbaijan, Georgia. _Class:_ Afro-Asiatic, Semitic, Central, Aramaic, Eastern, Central, Northeastern. _Dialects:_ Northern Cluster Lishán Didán, Southern Cluster Lishán Didán. 60% to 70% intelligibility of Hulaulá and Lishanid Noshan, but not of other Aramaic languages. Northern cluster subdialects are Urmi, Salmas, Anatolia; southern cluster dialects are Naghada, Ushno, Mahabad. The Urmi subdialect of Lishán Didán is different from the Urmi subdialect of Assyrian Neo-Aramaic. _Lg Use:_ Speakers are older adults. Hebrew is the second language. Some are multilingual. Many are married to nonspeakers. _Lg Dev:_ Hebrew script. OT: 1950s. _Other:_ Many loanwords from Kurdish, Turkish, Arabic, Persian, Hebrew, and several other European languages. Sometimes erroneously called 'Judeo-Kurdish' or 'Azerbaijani Kurdish'. Jewish.

Lishana Deni (Judeo-Aramaic, Lishan Hudaye, Lishan Hozaye, Kurdit) [lsd] 7,000 to 8,000 (1999 H. Mutzafi). Ethnic population: 9,061 (2000 WCD). Jerusalem and vicinity, including Maoz Tsiyon. Originally from northwest Iraqi Kurdistan. _Class:_ Afro-Asiatic, Semitic, Central, Aramaic, Eastern, Central, Northeastern. _Dialects:_ Zakho, Amadiya, Barashe, Shukho, Nerwa, Dohuk, Atrush, Bétanure. Resembles Chaldean Neo-Aramaic, but there are differences in morphology and other features. Inherent intelligibility is high between them. Low intelligibility of Ashirat dialects of Assyrian New-Aramaic; not intelligible with other Neo-Aramaic varieties. _Lg Use:_ The Shukho dialect probably extinct. Speakers are older adults. _Lg Dev:_ Hebrew script. Bible portions. _Other:_ Jewish.

Lishanid Noshan (Lishana Didán, Hulani, Kurdit, Galigalu, Jbeli, Hula'ula) [aij] 2,000 to 2,500 (1994 H. Mutzafi). Originally eastern and southern Iraqi Kurdistan. _Class:_ Afro-Asiatic, Semitic, Central, Aramaic, Eastern, Central, Northeastern. _Dialects:_ Arbel (Arbil), Dobe, Koy Sanjaq, Rwanduz, Rustaqa, Shaqlawa, Ranye, Qaladze.

60% to 70% inherent intelligibility of Lishanan and Hulaulá. Very different and not inherently intelligible with the Christian Aramaic languages and Lishana Deni. Western cluster subdialects are Arbil, Dobe. Eastern cluster subdialects are Southeastern varieties: Koy Sanjaq, Qaladze. Northeastern varieties: Rwanduz, Rustaqa. *Lg Use:* Speakers are older adults. *Lg Dev:* Hebrew script. *Other:* Jewish.

Polish (Polski) [pol] 100,000 in Israel (1992 H. Mutzafi). *Lg Use:* All speakers also use Hebrew but prefer Polish. *Other:* Jewish. See main entry under Poland.

Romanian [ron] 250,000 in Israel (1993 Statistical Abstract of Israel). *Lg Use:* Older adult speakers use Hebrew as second language, but prefer Romanian. *Other:* Jewish. See main entry under Romania.

Russian (Russit, Russki) [rus] 750,000 in Israel (1999 H. Mutzafi). *Lg Use:* Most speakers use Hebrew as second language, but prefer Russian. *Other:* Jewish. See main entry under Russia (Europe).

Tigrigna (Tigrinya) [tir] 10,000 in Israel (1994 H. Mutzafi). *Lg Use:* Speakers also use Amharic or Hebrew. *Other:* Called "Falashas," which they consider to be pejorative. They call themselves 'Beta Israel'. Their liturgy is written in Geez. Jewish. See main entry under Ethiopia.

Yevanic (Judeo-Greek, Yevanitika) [yej] 35 in Israel. There were a few semispeakers left in 1987 and may be none now. Population total all countries: 50. There may be a handful of older adult speakers still in Turkey. Also spoken in USA. *Class:* Indo-European, Greek, Attic. *Other:* Jews gave it up in Rome by 4th century, Spain by 6th-7th centuries, Crimea by 8th century. After 1000 A.D. almost entirely in Greece, some in the Balkans (Wexler 1985). Jewish. Nearly extinct.

Yiddish Sign Language [yds] *Class:* Deaf sign language. *Other:* Apparently distinct from Israeli Sign Language. Jewish.

Yiddish, Eastern (Judeo-German, Yiddish) [ydd] 215,000 in Israel (1986). Population total all countries: 3,142,560. Southeastern dialect in Ukraine and Romania, Mideastern dialect in Poland and Hungary, Northeastern dialect in Lithuania and Belarus. Also spoken in Argentina, Australia, Belarus, Belgium, Canada, Costa Rica, Estonia, Hungary, Latvia, Lithuania, Moldova, Panama, Poland, Puerto Rico, Romania, Russia (Europe), South Africa, Ukraine, Uruguay, USA. *Class:* Indo-European, Germanic, West, High German, Yiddish. *Dialects:* Southeastern Yiddish, Mideastern Yiddish, Northeastern Yiddish. Has many loans from Hebrew and local languages where spoken. Eastern Yiddish originated east of the Oder River through Poland, extending into Belarus, Russia (to Smolensk), Lithuania, Latvia, Hungary, Rumania, Ukraine, and pre-state British-Mandate Palestine (Jerusalem and Safed). Western Yiddish originated in Germany, Holland, Switzerland, Alsace (France), Czechoslovakia, western Hungary, and is nearing extinction. It branched off medieval High German (mainly Rhenish dialects) and received Modern German influences during the 19th and early 20th centuries. Eastern and Western Yiddish have difficult inherent intelligibility because of differing histories and influences from other languages. There are some Western Yiddish speakers in Israel (M. Herzog 1977). *Lg Use:* The vast majority speak Eastern Yiddish. *Lg Dev:* Hebrew script. Magazines. Radio programs. Bible: 1821–1936. *Other:* SVO. Jewish.

Japan

Nippon. 127,333,002. National or official language: Japanese. Also includes English (70,000), , Chinese (150,000), from the Philippines (36,000), from Pakistan, Iran, Bangladesh, Thailand, Malaysia over (300,000). Information mainly from S. Wurm and S. Hattori 1981; M. Shibatani 1990. Blind population: 256,700. Deaf population: 317,000 to 7,585,237 (1998). Deaf institutions: 131. The number of languages listed for Japan is 15. Of those, all are living languages. See map on page 807.

Ainu (Ainu Itak) [ain] 15 in Japan (1996 Alexander Vovin). Ethnic population: 15,000 in Japan. Kuril Islands (Tsishima), Hokkaido. Formerly also on south Sakhalin Island, Russia. Also spoken in Russia (Asia). *Class:* Language Isolate. *Dialects:* Sakhalin (Saghilin), Taraika, Hokkaido (Ezo, Yezo), Kuril (Shikotan, Tsishima). The last speaker of Sakhalin dialect died in 1994. There were at least 19 dialects. *Lg Use:* Most of the people speak only Japanese and are integrated into Japanese culture. *Lg Dev:* NT: 1897. *Other:* The Ainu in China is a different, unrelated language. SOV. Nearly extinct.

Amami-Oshima, Northern (Northern Amami-Osima, Oshima, Osima, Oosima) [ryn] 10,000 (2004). Northwestern Okinawa; northern Amami-oshima Island. *Class:* Japanese, Ryukyuan, Amami-Okinawan, Northern Amami-Okinawan. *Dialects:* Naze, Sani. Inherent intelligibility is generally impossible, or very difficult, with other Ryukyuan languages and Japanese. *Lg Use:* Only adult speakers, but understand and use Standard Japanese. The younger the generation, the more fluently they speak Japanese (Hattori in Wurm and Hattori 1981). Those under 20 are mainly monolingual in Japanese (T. Fukuda SIL 1989).

Amami-Oshima, Southern (Southern Amami-Osima) [ams] 1,800 (2004). Northern Okinawa; southern Amami-oshima, Kakeroma, Yoro, and Uke islands. *Class:* Japanese, Ryukyuan, Amami-Okinawan, Northern Amami-Okinawan. *Dialects:* Inherent intelligibility is low with other Ryukyuan languages and Japanese. *Lg Use:* Those over 50 use the vernacular at home among themselves, but understand and use Standard Japanese. Those 20 to 50 understand the vernacular, but mainly speak Japanese. The younger the generation, the more fluently they speak Japanese (Hattori in Wurm and Hattori 1981). Those under 20 are monolingual in Japanese.

Japanese [jpn] 121,050,000 in Japan (1985). Population total all countries: 122,433,899. Throughout the country. Also spoken in American Samoa, Argentina, Australia, Belize, Brazil, Canada, Dominican Republic, Germany, Guam, Mexico, Micronesia, Mongolia, New Zealand, Northern Mariana Islands, Palau, Panama, Paraguay, Philippines, Singapore, Taiwan, Thailand, United Arab Emirates, United Kingdom, USA. *Class:* Japanese. *Dialects:* Western Japanese, Eastern Japanese. Possibly related to Korean. The Kagoshima dialect is 84% cognate with Tokyo dialect. *Lg Use:* National language. 1,000,000 second-language speakers. *Lg Dev:* Hiragana, Katakana, and Kanji (Chinese character) writing systems. Grammar. Bible: 1883–1987. *Other:* SOV; postpositions; demonstrative, numeral, adjective, possessive, relative clause, proper noun precede noun head; adverb precedes verb; sentence final question particle; CV. Buddhist, Shintoist.

Japanese Sign Language (Shuwa, Temane) [jsl] 317,000 (1986 Gallaudet Univ.). *Class:* Deaf sign language. *Dialects:* Related to Taiwanese and Korean sign languages. *Lg Use:* Over 95% of the deaf understand Japanese Sign Language. 107 deaf schools. The first school was in Kyoto in 1878. *Lg Dev:* TV. *Other:* 'Temane' is the former name. Pidgin Signed Japanese is used often in formal situations, lectures, speeches. 80% of the deaf understand finger spelling.

Kikai [kzg] Ethnic population: 13,066 (2000 WCD). Northeastern Okinawa; Kikai Island. *Class:* Japanese,

Ryukyuan, Amami-Okinawan, Northern Amami-Okinawan. *Dialect:* Onotsu. Inherent intelligibility is generally impossible or very difficult of other Ryukyuan languages and Japanese. *Lg Use:* Speakers are older adults. Those 20 to 50 can understand Kikai, but mainly speak Japanese. The younger the generation, the more fluently they speak Japanese (Hattori in Wurm and Hattori 1981). Those under 20 are mainly monolingual in Japanese (T. Fukuda SIL 1989).

Korean [kor] 670,000 in Japan (1988). *Lg Use:* Speakers also use Japanese. *Other:* Buddhist, Christian. See main entry under Korea, South.

Kunigami [xug] 5,000 (2004). Central Okinawa; central and northern Okinawa Island, Iheya, Izena, Ie-jima, Sesoko islands. *Class:* Japanese, Ryukyuan, Amami-Okinawan, Southern Amami-Okinawan. *Dialect:* Nago. Inherent intelligibility is generally impossible, or very difficult, of other Ryukyuan languages and Japanese. Ryukyu languages are 62% to 70% cognate with Tokyo dialect of Japanese. *Lg Use:* Older adult speakers can understand and use Japanese. Those 20 to 50 can understand Kunigami, but mainly use Japanese at home and work. The younger the generation, the more fluently they speak Japanese (1981 Hattori in Wurm and Hattori). Those under 20 are mainly monolingual in Japanese (T. Fukuda SIL 1989).

Miyako [mvi] Ethnic population: 67,653 (2000 WCD). Southern Okinawa; Miyako, Ogami, Ikema, Kurima, Irabu, Tarama, Minna islands. *Class:* Japanese, Ryukyuan, Sakishima. *Dialects:* Miyako-Jima (Hirara, Ogami), Irabu-Jima, Tarama-Minna. Not intelligible with other Ryukyuan languages and Japanese. The dialects listed have noticeable differences, but not impossible communication. *Lg Use:* Those over 50 years of age use Miyako at home, but can understand and speak Japanese. Those age 20 to 50 can understand Miyako, but mainly use Japanese at home and work. The younger the generation, the more fluently they speak Japanese (Hattori in Wurm and Hattori 1981). Those under 20 are mainly monolingual in Japanese (T. Fukuda SIL 1989). *Lg Dev:* Dictionary. Grammar.

Oki-No-Erabu [okn] 3,200 (2004). North central Okinawa; Oki-no-erabu Island. *Class:* Japanese, Ryukyuan, Amami-Okinawan, Southern Amami-Okinawan. *Dialects:* East Oki-No-Erabu, West Oki-No-Erabu. Inherent intelligibility is generally impossible, or very difficult, with other Ryukyuan languages and Japanese. Dialect differences are noticeable, but communication is not impossible. Ryukyu languages are 62% to 70% cognate with Tokyo dialect of Japanese. *Lg Use:* Those over 50 use the vernacular at home among themselves, but can understand and use Standard Japanese. Those 20 to 50 can understand the vernacular, but use Japanese at home and work. The younger the generation, the more fluently they speak Japanese (1981 Hattori in Wurm and Hattori). Those under 20 are monolingual in Japanese (T. Fukuda SIL 1989).

Okinawan, Central (Okinawan, Luchu) [ryu] 984,285 (2000 WCD). Ethnic population: The total ethnic population of Okinawan is 120,000,000 (2000 Yukio Uemura). Central Okinawa; southern Okinawa Island, Kerama Islands, Kume-jima, Tonaki, Aguna islands, and islands east of Okinawa Island. *Class:* Japanese, Ryukyuan, Amami-Okinawan, Southern Amami-Okinawan. *Dialects:* Shuri, Naha, Torishima, Kudaka. Inherent intelligibility is generally impossible, or very difficult, with other Ryukyuan languages and Japanese. Ryukyu languages are 62% to 70% cognate with Tokyo dialect of Japanese. *Lg Use:* Adult speakers can also understand and use Standard Japanese. Those 20 to 50 can understand Okinawan, but use Japanese at home and work. The younger the generation, the more fluently they speak

Japanese (Wurm and Hattori 1981). Those under 20 are mainly monolingual in Japanese (T. Fukuda SIL 1989). *Lg Dev:* Dictionary. Bible portions: 1855–1858.

Toku-No-Shima [tkn] 5,100 (2004). Northern Okinawa; Toku-no-shima Island. *Class:* Japanese, Ryukyuan, Amami-Okinawan, Northern Amami-Okinawan. *Dialect:* Kametsu. Inherent intelligibility is generally impossible, or very difficult, of other Ryukyuan languages and Japanese. *Lg Use:* Adult speakers understand and use Standard Japanese. Those 20 to 50 understand the vernacular, but use Japanese at home and work. The younger the generation, the more fluently they speak Japanese (Hattori in Wurm and Hattori 1981). Those under 20 are monolingual in Japanese (T. Fukuda SIL 1989).

Yaeyama (Yayeyama) [rys] Ethnic population: 47,636 (2000 WCD). Southern Okinawa; Ishigaki, Iriomote, Hatoma, Kohama, Taketomi, Kuroshima, Hateruma, Aregusuku islands. *Class:* Japanese, Ryukyuan, Sakishima. *Dialects:* Ishigaki, Kabira, Shiraho, Taketomi, Kohama, Hatoma, Sonai, Kuroshima, Hateruma. Inherent intelligibility is generally impossible, or very difficult, with other Ryukyuan languages and Japanese. *Lg Use:* Adult speakers can also understand and use Standard Japanese. Those 20 to 50 can understand Yaeyama, but mainly use Japanese at home and work. The younger the generation, the more fluently they speak Japanese (Hattori in Wurm and Hattori 1981). Those under 20 are monolingual in Japanese (T. Fukuda SIL 1989).

Yonaguni [yoi] 800 (2004). Southern Okinawa; Yonaguni Island. *Class:* Japanese, Ryukyuan, Sakishima. *Dialects:* Inherent intelligibility is generally impossible, or very difficult, with other Ryukyuan languages and Japanese. *Lg Use:* Older adult speakers can understand Japanese. Those 20 to 50 can understand Yonaguni, but mainly use Japanese at home and work (T. Fukuda SIL 1989). The younger the generation, the more fluently they speak Japanese (Hattori in Wurm and Hattori 1981). Those under 20 are monolingual in Japanese (T. Fukuda SIL 1989).

Yoron [yox] 950 (2004). North central Okinawa; Yoron Island. *Class:* Japanese, Ryukyuan, Amami-Okinawan, Southern Amami-Okinawan. *Dialects:* Inherent intelligibility is generally impossible, or very difficult, with other Ryukyuan languages and Japanese. Ryukyu languages are 62% to 70% cognate with Tokyo dialect of Japanese. *Lg Use:* Older adult speakers can also understand and use Standard Japanese. Those from 20 to 50 understand Yoron, but mainly speak Standard Japanese at home and work. The younger the generation, the more fluently they speak Japanese (Wurm and Hattori 1981). Those under 20 are monolingual in Japanese (T. Fukuda SIL 1989).

Jordan

Hashemite Kingdom of Jordan, al Mamlaka al Urduniya al Hashemiyah. 5,611,202. National or official language: Standard Arabic. Literacy rate: 71% to 80%. Also includes Egyptian Spoken Arabic (10,000), Greek, Mesopotamian Spoken Arabic (500,000), North Mesopotamian Spoken Arabic (200,000), Northern Kurdish (4,000), South Azerbaijani (4,000), people from Pakistan, Philippines (5,000). Information mainly from T. Sebeok 1963; T. M. Johnstone 1967; W. Fischer and O. Jastrow 1980; B. Ingham 1982. Blind population: 9,000 (1982 WCE). Deaf population: 240,155. Deaf institutions: 2. The number of languages listed for Jordan is 9. Of those, all are living languages. See map on page 808.

Adyghe (West Circassian, Adygey) [ady] 44,280 in Jordan (1986). *Other:* City dwellers. Muslim (Sunni). See main entry under Russia (Europe).

Arabic, Levantine Bedawi Spoken (Bedawi) [avl] 700,000 in Jordan. Throughout Jordan, but especially in the east. *Dialects:* South Levantine Bedawi Arabic, North Levantine Bedawi Arabic, Eastern Egyptian Bedawi Arabic. *Other:* The language of Jordan before Palestinian refugees arrived. It remains the language of the army. Muslim (Sunni), Christian. See main entry under Egypt (Arabic, Eastern Egyptian Bedawi Spoken).

Arabic, Najdi Spoken [ars] 50,000 in Jordan. Far eastern Jordan. See main entry under Saudi Arabia.

Arabic, South Levantine Spoken (Levantine Arabic, South Levantine Arabic, Palestinian-Jordanian Arabic) [ajp] 3,500,000 in Jordan (1996). Population total all countries: 6,145,000. Also spoken in Argentina, Egypt, Israel, Kuwait, Palestinian West Bank and Gaza, Puerto Rico, Syria. *Class:* Afro-Asiatic, Semitic, Central, South, Arabic. *Dialects:* Madani, Fellahi. There are differences from village to village of which speakers are aware. There is a newly emerging urban standard dialect based on Amman. *Lg Use:* Used in drama. *Lg Dev:* Radio programs. TV. Bible portions: 1940–1973. *Other:* Muslim, Christian.

Arabic, Standard [arb] Middle East, North Africa. *Lg Use:* Official language. Used for education, official purposes, communication among Arabic-speaking countries. Education officials promoting this variety among students. Regional varieties have been used in classrooms, but this is changing. See main entry under Saudi Arabia.

Armenian [hye] 8,000 in Jordan (1971 The Armenian Review). *Dialect:* Western Armenian. *Other:* Christian. See main entry under Armenia.

Chechen [che] 3,000 in Jordan (1993 Johnstone). In 2 or 3 villages mixed among Adygey and Arabic speakers. *Other:* Muslim (Sunni, Sufi). See main entry under Russia (Europe).

Domari (Middle Eastern Romani, Tsigene, Gypsy, Nawar, Kurbat, Barake) [rmt] 4,913 in Jordan (2000 WCD). *Dialects:* Nawar, Kurbat, Barake. *Other:* Arabic influence. Muslim. See main entry under Iran.

Jordanian Sign Language [jos] *Class:* Deaf sign language.

Kazakhstan

Kazakhstan. 15,143,704. National or official languages: Kazakh, Russian. 1,000,000 square miles. Also includes Armenian (19,000), Avar (959), Bashkir (21,442), Belarusan (183,000), Chechen, Chuvash (22,871), Dargwa (636), Eastern Mari (9,089), Erzya (34,371), Gagauz, Georgian (7,700), Greek (47,000), Judeo-Crimean Tatar, Karachay-Balkar (1,456), Karakalpak, Kirghiz (9,612), Korean (103,000), Kumyk (554), Lak (617), Lezgi (2,570), Lithuanian (10,964), Nogai (155), North Azerbaijani (90,000), Northern Kurdish (25,000), Northern Uzbek (332,000), Osetin (3,491), Polish (61,445), Pontic, Romanian (33,000), Russian (6,227,000), Tabassaran (225), Tajiki (26,000), Tatar (328,000), Turkish, Turkmen (3,265), Udmurt (15,786), Ukrainian (898,000). Information mainly from T. Sebeok 1963; Z. Xiangru and R.F. Hahn 1989. The number of languages listed for Kazakhstan is 7. Of those, all are living languages. See map on page 809.

Dungan [dng] *Dialect:* Shaanxi. *Other:* They came from China over 100 years ago. See main entry under Kyrgyzstan.

German, Standard [deu] 958,000 in Kazakhstan. Population excludes Plautdietsch. See main entry under Germany.

Ili Turki (T'urk, Tuerke) [ili] Ili Valley near Kuldja, Xinjiang, China. There may be none in Kazakhstan.

Lg Use: Speakers are older adults. Younger people understand Ili Turki, but are adopting Kazakh or Uyghur and intermarrying with neighboring groups. See main entry under China.

Kazakh (Kazak, Kaisak, Kosach, Qazaq) [kaz] 5,293,400 in Kazakhstan (1979 census). Population total all countries: 8,178,879. Kazakhstan, northern Soviet Middle Asia and into western Siberia. Also spoken in Afghanistan, China, Germany, Iran, Kyrgyzstan, Mongolia, Russia (Asia), Tajikistan, Turkey (Asia), Turkmenistan, Ukraine, Uzbekistan. *Class:* Altaic, Turkic, Western, Aralo-Caspian. *Dialects:* Northeastern Kazakh, Southern Kazakh, Western Kazakh. Minor dialect differences. *Lg Use:* National language. 98% speak Kazakh as first language. Increasing ethnic pride and feelings of Islamic brotherhood. Many speakers also use Russian or Uzbek. *Lg Dev:* Increasing education in Kazakh. Cyrillic script; also in Mongolia; Arabic script in China and Iran; Roman script in Turkey. Newspapers. Radio programs. TV. NT: 1820–1910. *Other:* Semi-nomadic. The names 'Eastern Kirghiz' and 'Western Kirghiz' have been erroneously applied to Kazakh. SOV. Traditionally pastoralists, now agriculturalists; industrial workers. Muslim (Sunni).

Plautdietsch (Low German) [pdt] 100,000 in Russia and Kazakhstan (1986). Various locations including Alma Ata near the China border, beyond Tashkent, and Kazakhstan. *Lg Use:* 50% speak Russian as second language. *Other:* Christian. See main entry under Canada.

Romani, Sinte (Sinti, Tsigane, Manuche, Manouche) [rmo] Kazakhstan (formerly Volga area until 1941). *Other:* Ethnic group: Sasítka Romá. Christian. See main entry under Serbia and Montenegro.

Uyghur (Uighur, Uiguir, Uygur, Novouygur) [uig] 300,000 in Kazakhstan (1993). Taranchi dialect in Kazakhstan, Kashgar-Yarkand dialect in Uzbekistan. *Dialects:* Taranchi (Kulja), Kashgar-Yarkand. *Lg Use:* 86% speak it as first language. *Other:* Agriculturalists. Muslim (Sunni). See main entry under China.

Korea, North

Democratic People's Republic of Korea, Chosun Minchu-chui Inmin Konghwa-guk. 22,697,553. National or official language: Korean. Literacy rate: 91% to 99%. Also includes Chinese (51,000). Information mainly from B. Comrie 1987. Blind population: 110,000 (1982 WCE). The number of languages listed for Korea, North is 1.

Korean [kor] 20,000,000 in North Korea (1986). *Dialects:* Hamgyongdo (North Hamgyongdo, South Hamgyongdo), P'yong'ando (North P'yong'ando, South P'yong'ando), Hwanghaedo. *Lg Use:* National language. *Other:* Buddhist-Confucianist, Christian. See main entry under Korea, South.

Korea, South

Republic of Korea, Taehan Min'guk. 48,598,175. National or official language: Korean. Literacy rate: 92%. Also includes English (63,600), Sherpa, Chinese (24,000). Information mainly from B. Comrie 1987. Blind population: 48,000 (1982 WCE). Deaf institutions: 28. The number of languages listed for Korea, South is 2. Of those, both are living languages.

Korean (Hanguohua, Hanguk Mal) [kor] 42,000,000 in South Korea (1986). Population total all countries: 67,019,690. Also spoken in American Samoa, Australia, Bahrain, Belize, Brazil, Brunei, Canada, China, Germany, Guam, Japan, Kazakhstan, North Korea, Kyrgyzstan,

Mauritania, Mongolia, New Zealand, Northern Mariana Islands, Panama, Paraguay, Philippines, Russia (Asia), Saudi Arabia, Singapore, Suriname, Tajikistan, Thailand, Turkmenistan, USA, Uzbekistan. *Class:* Language Isolate. *Dialects:* Seoul (Kangwondo, Kyonggido), Ch'ungch'ongdo (North Ch'ungch'ong, South Ch'ungch'ong), Kyongsangdo (North Kyongsangdo, South Kyongsangdo), Chollado (North Chollado, South Chollado), Cheju Island. There is a difference of opinion among scholars as to whether or not Korean is related to Japanese. Some scholars suggest that both languages are possibly distantly related to Altaic. Dialect boundaries generally correspond to provincial boundaries. Some dialects are not easily intelligible with others (Voegelin and Voegelin 1977). The suffix '-do' on dialect names means 'province'. Comprehension of Standard Korean may be lower on Cheju Island. *Lg Use:* National language. *Lg Dev:* Literacy rate in first language: 98% (1995 est.). Higher adult illiteracy is reported on Cheju Island. Korean script (Hangul). Newspapers. Radio programs. TV. Dictionary. Grammar. Bible: 1911–1993. *Other:* The McCune-Reischauer system is the official Roman orthography in South Korea used for maps and signs. SOV. Buddhist, Christian.

Korean Sign Language [kvk] *Class:* Deaf sign language. *Dialects:* Related to Japanese and Taiwanese sign languages. *Lg Use:* Used since 1889. Signed interpretation required in court, used at important public events, in social services programs. There is sign language instruction for parents of deaf children. Many sign language classes for hearing people. *Lg Dev:* Primary schools for deaf children using sign language since 1908. TV. Dictionary. *Other:* There is a manual system for spelling.

Kuwait

State of Kuwait, Dowlat al-Kuwait. 2,257,549. National or official language: Standard Arabic. Literacy rate: 71% to 79%. Also includes Egyptian Spoken Arabic (20,000), Najdi Spoken Arabic (200,000), Northern Kurdish, South Levantine Spoken Arabic (85,000), Balochi, people from India, Pakistan, the Philippines (50,000). Information mainly from T. M. Johnstone 1967; B. Ingham 1982; C. Holes 1990. Deaf population: 110,285. Deaf institutions: 1. The number of languages listed for Kuwait is 3. Of those, all are living languages.

Arabic, Gulf Spoken (Khaliji) [afb] 500,000 in Kuwait (1986). *Dialect:* Kuwaiti Hadari Arabic. *Other:* Muslim. See main entry under Iraq.

Arabic, Standard [arb] Middle East, North Africa. *Lg Use:* Official language. Used for education, official purposes. See main entry under Saudi Arabia.

Mehri (Mahri) [gdq] 14,358 in Kuwait (2000 WCD). Scattered individuals in Kuwait. *Other:* Muslim. See main entry under Yemen.

Kyrgyzstan

Kyrgyz Republic. 5,081,429. National or official languages: Kirghiz, Russian. 76,642 square miles. Literacy rate: 99%. Also includes Armenian (3,285), Bashkir (3,250), Belarusan (7,676), Chechen, Chuvash (2,092), Crimean Turkish (38,000), Dargwa (1,419), Erzya (5,390), Georgian (1,002), Halh Mongolian, Kalmyk-Oirat, Karachay-Balkar (2,463), Karakalpak, Kazakh (37,000), Korean (18,000), Lak (257), Lezgi (1,599), Lithuanian (430), North Azerbaijani (17,207), Northern Kurdish (14,000), Northern Uzbek (657,440), Romanian (1,375), Standard German (101,057), Tajiki (34,000), Tatar (70,000), Turkish, Turkmen (352), Ukrainian (109,000), Uyghur (37,000). Information mainly from T.

Sebeok 1963. The number of languages listed for Kyrgyzstan is 3. Of those, all are living languages. See map on page 812.

Dungan (Dzhunyan, Tungan, Huizu, Zwn'jan, Kwuizwu) [dng] 40,000 in Kyrgyzstan (2001 Johnstone and Mandryk). Population total all countries: 41,400. Ethnic population: 100,000. The Gansu dialect is mainly in Prschewalsk and Osh, Kyrgyzstan, the Shaanxi dialect in Kazakhstan, and in Fergana, Uzbekistan. Also spoken in Kazakhstan, Tajikistan, Turkmenistan, Uzbekistan. *Class:* Sino-Tibetan, Chinese. *Dialects:* Ganzu (Gansu), Shaanxi (Shensi), Yage. Speakers of the Shaanxi and Ganzu varieties have difficult inherent intelligibility of each other. There is a debate regarding whether Dungan has three tones (a merging of two Standard Mandarin tones) or four tones (with only a partial merging of the two Standard Mandarin tones). Also different from Mandarin in phonology and lexicon. *Lg Use:* Those under 50 to 55 speak Russian as first language. *Lg Dev:* Cyrillic script. *Other:* The people call themselves 'Huizu'. They came from China over 100 years ago. Muslim (Sunni).

Kirghiz (Kara-Kirgiz, Kirgiz) [kir] 2,448,220 in the former USSR (1993 UBS). Population total all countries: 3,136,733. Throughout the country. Also spoken in Afghanistan, China, Kazakhstan, Tajikistan, Turkey (Asia), Uzbekistan. *Class:* Altaic, Turkic, Western, Aralo-Caspian. *Dialects:* Northern Kirghiz, Southern Kirghiz. *Lg Use:* Official language. 98% of the 2,539,000 Kirghiz speak it as first language. The Ichkilik are a Kirghiz-speaking people of non-Kirghiz origin. 29% also speak Russian. *Lg Dev:* Schools in Kirghiz. Cyrillic script; Arabic script in China and Roman script in Turkey. Newspapers. Radio programs. Films. TV. NT: 1991. *Other:* The names 'Eastern Kirghiz' and 'Western Kirghiz' have been erroneously applied to Kazakh. Increasing education. Increasing feelings of Islamic brotherhood. SOV. Mountain slope. Muslim (Sunni), Buddhist (Lamaist).

Russian [rus] 1,408,800 in Kyrgyzstan (1996). *Lg Use:* Official language. *Other:* Christian. See main entry under Russia (Europe).

Laos

Lao People's Democratic Republic, Sathanalat Paxathipatai Paxaxon Lao. 6,068,117. Population includes 2,769,000, or 71% speakers Daic languages, 1,100,000, or 24.1% Austro-Asiatic languages, 175,000, or 4% Miao-Yao languages, 42,500, or 1% Tibeto-Burman languages (1991 J. Matisoff). National or official language: Lao. Literacy rate: 43% to 45%. Also includes Central Khmer (10,400), Mandarin Chinese, Sedang (786), Vietnamese (76,000). Information mainly from F. Lebar, G. Hickey, J. Musgrave 1964; D. Thomas and R. Headley 1970; S. Wurm and S. Hattori 1981; J. Matisoff et al. 1996; J. Edmondson and D. Solnit 1997; R. Burling ms. (1998). Blind population: 10,000 (1982 WCE). The number of languages listed for Laos is 82. Of those, all are living languages. See maps beginning on page 810.

Aheu (Kha Tong Luang, Thavung, Phon Soung, Phonsung, So) [thm] 1,770 in Laos (2000). Pak Sane Province, Khamkeut District, near Lak Sao. *Other:* Traditional religion. See main entry under Thailand.

Akha (Kaw, Ekaw, Ko, Aka, Ikaw, Ak'a, Ahka, Khako, Hka Ko, Khao Kha Ko, Ikor, Aini, Yani) [ahk] 58,000 in Laos (1995 Nguyen Duy Thieu). Luang Namtha, Phongsali provinces. *Other:* Traditional religion, Christian. See main entry under Myanmar.

Alak (Hrlak) [alk] 4,000 (2000 Bradley). Southern Laos, mainly in Saravan and Sekong provinces. *Class:* Austro-Asiatic, Mon-Khmer, Eastern Mon-Khmer, Bahnaric,

Central Bahnaric. *Dialects:* Included under Bahnaric as closest to Bahnar, Tampuan, Lamam. Also included under Katuic. *Other:* Traditional religion.

Arem (Chomrau, Chombrau, Umo) [aem] 20 in Laos. Ethnic population: 500 (1995). West central, both sides of the Viet Nam-Laos border, west of Phuc Trach. *Other:* Nearly extinct. See main entry under Viet Nam.

Bit (Khabit, Khbit, Phsing, Phsin) [bgk] 1,530 in Laos (1985 Proschan). Population total all countries: 2,030. Near the northern border with China, northeast of Namtha, Luang Namtha Province, and south of Boun Neua; Phongsali Province, Boun-Tai, Samphan, and Khoa districts, 8 villages. Also spoken in China. *Class:* Austro-Asiatic, Mon-Khmer, Northern Mon-Khmer, Khmuic, Khao. *Dialects:* Not Khmuic, but Palaungic (J-O Svantesson 1990). Related to Khao in Viet Nam. *Other:* 400 to 1,000 meters. Traditional religion.

Bo [bgl] 2,950 (2000). Central Laos inland from the bend of the Mekong, Nhang River, around Nape, Kammouan Province and Lak Sao, Bolikhamxay Province, Hinboun District. *Class:* Austro-Asiatic, Mon-Khmer, Viet-Muong, Muong. *Other:* Traditional religion.

Bru, Eastern [bru] 69,000 in Laos (1999). Population total all countries: 129,559. Eastern Savannehkhet Province, Sepone District. Also spoken in Thailand, Viet Nam. *Class:* Austro-Asiatic, Mon-Khmer, Eastern Mon-Khmer, Katuic, West Katuic, Brou-So. *Dialect:* Tri (So Tri, So Trii, Chali). It is partially intelligible with Western Bru of Thailand. Related to Khua. Mangkong in Viet Nam and eastern Laos is a dialect of Eastern Bru, different linguistically from the Mangkong that are the same as So of Thailand. Mangkong is an ethnic group. *Lg Dev:* Literacy rate in first language: 1% to 5%. Literacy rate in second language: 15% to 25%. Dictionary. NT: 1981. *Other:* Traditional religion.

Chut (May, Ruc, Sach, Salang) [scb] 450 in Laos (1995 census). Khammouan Province, Bouarapha District, near the Viet Nam border at about the latitude of the Mu Gia Pass. *Dialects:* May, Ruc. *Other:* Seminomadic. 2,000 meters. Traditional religion. See main entry under Viet Nam.

Con [cno] 1,000 (1981 Wurm and Hattori). Luang Namtha Province, southwest of Vieng Pou Kha. *Class:* Austro-Asiatic, Mon-Khmer, Northern Mon-Khmer, Palaungic, Western Palaungic, Lametic.

Halang Doan (Halang Duan, Duan, Doan) [hld] 2,346 in Laos (2000). Attopeu Province, Kasseng Plateau, Sanxai District, on the left banks of the Kamane and Dak Robay rivers, near the Viet Nam border. *Other:* Traditional religion. See main entry under Viet Nam.

Hani (Hanhi, Haw) [hni] 1,122 in Laos (1995). Phongsali Province, along the Yunnan border. None in Thailand. *Other:* An official nationality in China. Polytheist, traditional religion. See main entry under China.

Hmong Daw (White Meo, White Miao, Meo Kao, White Lum, Bai Miao) [mww] 169,800 in Laos (1995 census). Northern Laos. *Dialects:* Hmong Gu Mba (Hmong Qua Mba, Striped Hmong), Mong Leng. *Other:* Traditional religion. See main entry under China.

Hmong Njua (Blue Meo, Blue Miao, Tak Meo, Hmong Njwa, Hmong Leng, Miao, Meo) [blu] 145,600 in Laos (1995). Northern Laos. *Other:* Traditional religion. See main entry under China.

Hung [hnu] 2,000 in Laos (1996 Ferlus). Population total all countries: 2,700 to 3,700. Bolikhamsay, Khammouan provinces. The Toum live northeast of Nape and south of the Phong. Also spoken in Viet Nam. *Class:* Austro-Asiatic, Mon-Khmer, Viet-Muong, Cuoi. *Dialects:* Toum (Tum), Phong (Pong, Poong, Pong 1, Pong 2). *Other:* Traditional religion.

Ir (In, Yir) [irr] 4,420 (2000). Saravan Province, east of Saravan town. *Class:* Austro-Asiatic, Mon-Khmer,

Eastern Mon-Khmer, Katuic, Central Katuic, Ta'oih. *Dialects:* Closest to Ong. *Other:* Traditional religion.

Iu Mien (Mien, Man, Yao, Myen, Highland Yao) [ium] 20,250 in Laos (2000). *Lg Use:* Some language shift. *Other:* Almost all refugees in the West have come from Laos. 600 to 1,500 meters. Daoist, traditional religion. See main entry under China.

Jeh (Die, Yeh, Gie) [jeh] 8,013 in Laos (1995 census). Southern Laos, Xekong Province, Dakchung District; Attopeu Province, Sanxai District, basin of Poko, Kamane, and Dak Main rivers. *Dialects:* Jeh Bri La, Jeh Mang Ram. *Lg Dev:* Literacy rate in first language: 1% to 5%. Literacy rate in second language: 15% to 25%. *Other:* Traditional religion. See main entry under Viet Nam.

Jeng (Cheng, Chiengceng) [jeg] 7,320 (2000). Attopeu Province, Samakkhixai and Sanamxai districts, 6 villages north of Attopeu town. *Class:* Austro-Asiatic, Mon-Khmer, Eastern Mon-Khmer, Bahnaric, West Bahnaric, Oi-The. *Dialects:* Related to Oy, Sapuan, Sok. *Other:* Traditional religion.

Kado (Kadu, Katu, Asak, Sak, Gadu, Thet) [kdv] 225 in Laos (2000). Phongsali Province. *Dialects:* Kadu, Ganaan (Ganan), Andro, Sengmai, Chakpa, Phayeng. *Other:* Distinct from Katu, a Mon-Khmer language of Viet Nam and Laos. Traditional religion. See main entry under Myanmar.

Kaduo (Gazhuo) [ktp] 5,000 in Laos (1981 Wurm and Hattori). Population total all countries: 10,292. North central on the China border, north of Mong Ou Tay. Also spoken in China. *Class:* Sino-Tibetan, Tibeto-Burman, Lolo-Burmese, Loloish, Southern, Akha, Hani, Bi-Ka. *Dialects:* No information on intelligibility of other Lolo languages. No significant dialect differences. *Other:* Different from Kado and Katu. SOV; CV(V); a voiced-voiceless distinction only for fricatives; no tense or nasalized vowels; nouns mostly polysyllabic, other words mostly monosyllabic; many loanwords from Chinese; tonal, 8 tones.

Kang (Tai Khang) [kyp] 47,636 in Laos (1995 census). Population total all countries: 81,701. Houaphan Province, Xam-Tai District; Xiangkhoang Province, Nonghet District. Also spoken in China. *Class:* Tai-Kadai, Kam-Tai, Kam-Sui.

Kasseng (Koseng, Kaseng, Kraseng) [kgc] 1,200 (2000 D. Bradley). Ethnic population: 6,000 (2000). Southern Laos near Viet Nam border, Boloven Plateau area north of Attopeu, and between the Jeh, Alak, Laven, and Tareng peoples. *Class:* Austro-Asiatic, Mon-Khmer, Eastern Mon-Khmer, Katuic, East Katuic, Kaseng. *Other:* Also classified as West Bahnaric. Traditional religion.

Kataang (Katang) [kgd] 107,350 (2000). Southern Laos near the Ta'oih and Bru people, around Muong Nong, in Saravan, Savannakhet, Sekong, and Champassak provinces, around Toumlanh District, 2 villages in Khong Chiem, Ubon Ratachatani District, Thailand. *Class:* Austro-Asiatic, Mon-Khmer, Eastern Mon-Khmer, Katuic, Central Katuic, Ta'oih. *Lg Dev:* Literacy rate in first language: below 1%. Literacy rate in second language: 25% to 50%. Dictionary.

Katu, Western [kuf] 14,700 (1998). Upper Xe Kong River, high basin of Song Boung River watershed along the Vietnamese border, Sekong, Saravan, and Champassak provinces. *Class:* Austro-Asiatic, Mon-Khmer, Eastern Mon-Khmer, Katuic, East Katuic, Katu-Pacoh. *Dialects:* A different language variety and orthography from Viet Nam. *Lg Dev:* 'Liek' script. *Other:* Traditional religion.

Khlor (Klor, Lor) [llo] 6,000 (1981 Wurm and Hattori). Saravan Province, Laongam District, south of Ir and Ong. *Class:* Austro-Asiatic, Mon-Khmer, Eastern Mon-Khmer, Katuic, East Katuic, Ngeq-Nkriang. *Dialects:* Closest to Ngeq. *Other:* Traditional religion.

Khmu (Kmhmu, Khmu', Khamu, Kamu, Kammu, Khamuk, Kamhmu, Khomu, Mou, Pouteng, Pu Thenh, Tenh, Theng, Lao Terng) [kjg] 389,694 in Laos (1985 F. Proschan). Population total all countries: 479,739. Scattered through northern Laos. Also spoken in China, France, Myanmar, Thailand, USA, Viet Nam. *Class:* Austro-Asiatic, Mon-Khmer, Northern Mon-Khmer, Khmuic, Mal-Khmu', Khmu'. *Dialects:* Yuan, Khroong (Krong), Luang Prabang, Sayabury, Lyy, Rok, U, Hat. *Lg Dev:* Duota script in China. Bible portions: 1918. *Other:* SVO. Traditional religion.

Khua [xhv] 2,000 in Laos (1981). Khammouan Province, Bouarapha District, northwest of Boualapha. *Other:* Different from Cua. Traditional religion. See main entry under Viet Nam.

Khuen (Kween, Khween, Khouen) [khf] 8,000 in Laos (1995 Chazee). Population total all countries: 9,000. Luang Namtha Province, Nale, Sing, and Viangphoukha districts. Near the Lamet people. Also spoken in China, USA. *Class:* Austro-Asiatic, Mon-Khmer, Northern Mon-Khmer, Khmuic, Mal-Khmu', Khmu'. *Other:* Distinct from Kuan, Tai Kouanne, and Khmu Keun. Buddhist.

Kim Mun (Mun, Lan Tin, Lanten, Man Lan-Tien, Lowland Yao, Jim Mun) [mji] 4,500 in Laos (1995 Chazee). Northwestern Laos, Luang Namtha Province, Long, Namtha districts; Huay Sai Province; Nam Moh District, Udom Sai Province, Nam Moh District; Bokeo Province. *Lg Use:* A few know Lahu, Mien, Lao. *Other:* Included in the Yao nationality in Laos. Daoist. See main entry under China.

Kiorr (Saamtaav, Samtao, Samtao 2, Con, Col) [xko] 2,359 in Laos (1985 F. Proschan). Louang Nam Tha and Bokeo provinces, 6 villages. Also spoken in Myanmar. *Class:* Austro-Asiatic, Mon-Khmer, Northern Mon-Khmer, Palaungic, Western Palaungic, Angkuic. *Other:* Buddhist.

Kuan [uan] 2,500 (1995 census). Bolikhamxay Province, Viangthong District, near the Mouan River. *Class:* Tai-Kadai, Kam-Tai, Be-Tai, Tai-Sek, Tai, Unclassified. *Dialects:* Some classification problems, possibly because of migration. *Other:* Traditional religion.

Kuy (Sui, Suai, Suay, Suoi, Soai, Suei, Aouei, Kuoy, Kui, Dui, Khamen-Boran, Old Khmer, Cuoi) [kdt] 51,180 in Laos (2000). 80% monolingual. Savannakhet, Saravan, Sedone provinces. A large group on both sides of the Mekong in southern Laos. *Dialects:* Antra, Na Nhyang. *Lg Dev:* Literacy rate in first language: 1% to 5%. Literacy rate in second language: 37%. *Other:* A different script is used in Laos. Traditional religion. See main entry under Thailand.

Lahu (Museu, Mussuh, Muhso, Musso) [lhu] 8,702 in Laos (1995 census). Bokeo Province, Peung, Tonpheung, Houayxay districts. *Dialects:* Na (Black Lahu, Musser Dam, Northern Lahu, Loheirn), Nyi (Red Lahu, Southern Lahu, Musseh Daeng, Luhishi, Luhushi), Shehleh. *Other:* 1,400 meters. Traditional religion, Christian. See main entry under China.

Lahu Shi (Kutsung, Kucong, Yellow Lahu, Shi, Kui, Kwi) [kds] 3,240 in Laos (2000). Population total all countries: 40,240. Bokeo Province, Kentung District. Also spoken in China, Myanmar, Thailand, USA, Viet Nam. *Class:* Sino-Tibetan, Tibeto-Burman, Lolo-Burmese, Loloish, Southern, Akha, Lahu. *Dialects:* Difficult intelligibility of Black Lahu. A distinct language from Nyi (Red Lahu). *Other:* SOV. Traditional religion.

Lamet (Lemet, Kha Lamet, Khamet, Khamed, Rmeet) [lbn] 16,740 in Laos (1995 census). Population total all countries: 16,864. Northwestern Laos, Luang Namtha, Bokeo provinces. Also spoken in Thailand, USA. *Class:* Austro-Asiatic, Mon-Khmer, Northern Mon-Khmer, Palaungic, Western Palaungic, Lametic. *Dialects:* Upper Lamet, Lower Lamet. *Lg Dev:* Literacy rate in first language: below 1%. Literacy rate in second language:

25% to 50%. *Other:* Called 'Lamet' in Laos and 'Khamet' in Thailand. Traditional religion.

Lao (Laotian Tai, Laotian, Phou Lao, Eastern Thai, Lum Lao, Lao Wiang, Lao Kao, Rong Kong, Tai Lao, Lao-Tai, Làо, Lao-Lum, Lao-Noi) [lao] 3,000,000 in Laos (1991 UBS). Population total all countries: 3,188,577. Mekong River Valley from Luang Prabang south to the Cambodian border. The Lao Kao went to Thailand and are in Nan, Loei, Saraburi, and elsewhere; the Lao-Khrang are in the Nakhonsawan and Nakhon Pathom area. May also be in Viet Nam. Also spoken in Australia, Cambodia, Canada, France, Thailand, USA. *Class:* Tai-Kadai, Kam-Tai, Be-Tai, Tai-Sek, Tai, Southwestern, Lao-Phutai. *Dialects:* Luang Prabang, Vientiane (Wiang Jan), Savannakhet (Suwannakhet), Pakse, Lao-Kao, Lao-Khrang. Dialect cluster with Northeastern Tai of Thailand. *Lg Use:* Official language. 800,000 second-language speakers. *Lg Dev:* Literacy rate in first language: 30% to 60%. Literacy rate in second language: 50% to 75%. Bible: 1932. *Other:* SOV. Buddhist, traditional religion, Christian.

Laos Sign Language [lso] *Class:* Deaf sign language. *Dialects:* Related to sign languages in Viet Nam and earlier ones in Thailand. *Other:* May be more than one sign language.

Lave (Brao, Braou, Brau, Proue, Brou, Love, Laveh, Rawe) [brb] 12,750 in Laos (1984). Population total all countries: 18,444. Attopeu Province, Laos-Cambodian border. Also spoken in Cambodia, France, USA, Viet Nam. *Class:* Austro-Asiatic, Mon-Khmer, Eastern Mon-Khmer, Bahnaric, West Bahnaric, Brao-Kravet. *Dialect:* Palau. Close to Krung 2, Kravet, Sou. *Other:* Called 'Lave' in Laos. Traditional religion.

Laven (Loven, Boloven, Boriwen, Laweenjru, Jaru, Jru', Jruq) [lbo] 40,519 in Laos (1995 census). Southwestern Laos, Champassak, Attopeu provinces, Boloven Plateau, near the Alak. Also spoken in USA. *Class:* Austro-Asiatic, Mon-Khmer, Eastern Mon-Khmer, Bahnaric, West Bahnaric, Laven. *Other:* Different from Brao. Traditional religion.

Lü (Lue, Lu, Pai-I, Shui-Pai-I) [khb] 134,100 in Laos (2000). Western Phongsali, Luang Namtha, Bokeo, Udomxay, Xanyabouli, Luang Prabang provinces. *Other:* Traditional religion, Buddhist. See main entry under China.

Mal (Khatin, T'in, Htin, Thin, Tin) [mlf] 23,193 in Laos (1995 census). Population total all countries: 26,193. Xaignabouli Province, Phiang District, west of the Mekong River. Also spoken in Thailand, USA. *Class:* Austro-Asiatic, Mon-Khmer, Northern Mon-Khmer, Khmuic, Mal-Khmu', Mal-Phrai. *Dialects:* Not intelligible with Lua, Phai, or Pray 3. *Lg Dev:* NT: 1994. *Other:* 'Mal' and 'Madl' are self names. 'T'in' is an ethnic name used in Thailand. Traditional religion.

Maleng (Malieng, Malang) [pkt] 800 in Laos (1996 Ferlus). Population total all countries: 1,000. Khammouan Province, Nakay District, Nam Theun Valley, near the banks of the Theun River. Also spoken in Viet Nam. *Class:* Austro-Asiatic, Mon-Khmer, Viet-Muong, Chut. *Dialects:* Maleng, Pakatan (Kha Pakatan), Malang, Hareme. *Other:* Agriculturalists. Traditional religion.

Mlabri (Mla, Mla-Bri, Mabri, Mrabri, Yumbri, Ma Ku, Yellow Leaf) [mra] 24 in Laos (1985 F. Proschan). Xaignabouli Province, Phiang District, near Thailand border. *Other:* Nomadic. Mlabri are different from Kha Tong Luang (Phi Tong Luang, Yellow Leaf), which are Western Viet-Muong (Wurm and Hattori 1981). Forest. Traditional religion. See main entry under Thailand.

Ngeq (Ngeh, Nge', Ngae, Kriang, Nkriang) [ngt] 12,189 (1995 census). 70% monolingual. Southern Laos, Sekong, Saravan, Champassak provinces, 25 villages. *Class:* Austro-Asiatic, Mon-Khmer, Eastern Mon-Khmer, Katuic, East Katuic, Ngeq-Nkriang. *Dialects:* Closest to Khlor.

Related to Alak 2. *Lg Dev:* Literacy rate in first language: below 1%. Literacy rate in second language: 15% to 25%. Dictionary. *Other:* "Kha Koh" means '(derogatory) mountain people'. 'Nkriang' is their name for themselves. Traditional religion, Christian.

Nung (Nong) [nut] A few in Laos. *Other:* Different from Chinese Nung (Cantonese in Viet Nam) and Tibeto-Burman Nung. An official ethnic community in Viet Nam. See main entry under Viet Nam.

Nyaheun (Nha Heun, Nyah Heuny, Hoen, Nia Hoen, Hun, Hin, Niahon, Nyahön, Yaheun) [nev] 5,152 (1995 census). Eastern part of Boloven Plateau near Sekong and Paksong. *Class:* Austro-Asiatic, Mon-Khmer, Eastern Mon-Khmer, Bahnaric, West Bahnaric, Nyaheun. *Lg Dev:* Literacy rate in first language: below 1%. Literacy rate in second language: 15% to 25%. *Other:* Traditional religion.

O'du (O Du, Iduh, 'Iduh, "Tay Hat," "Hat," "Haat") [tyh] 194 in Laos (1996 F. Proschan). Xiang Khoang Province, Nonghet District. *Other:* An official ethnic community in Viet Nam. Speakers call themselves 'O Du'. Traditional religion. See main entry under Viet Nam.

Ong (Tong, Hantong) [oog] 10,300 (2000). Saravan Province, north of Saravan town. *Class:* Austro-Asiatic, Mon-Khmer, Eastern Mon-Khmer, Katuic, Central Katuic, Ta'oih. *Dialects:* Closest to Ir. *Other:* Traditional religion.

Oy (Huei, Oi) [oyb] 14,947 (1995 census). 80% monolingual. Attopeu Province, at the foot of the Bolaven Plateau near Pakse. *Class:* Austro-Asiatic, Mon-Khmer, Eastern Mon-Khmer, Bahnaric, West Bahnaric, Oi-The. *Dialects:* Riyao, Tamal Euy, Inn Tea, Kranyeu. Related to Jeng, Sapuan, Sok, The. *Other:* Traditional religion.

Pacoh (Bo River Van Kieu, Pokoh) [pac] 13,224 in Laos (1995 census). 70% monolingual. Saravan Province, Samouay District; Savannakhet Province, Nong District. *Dialect:* Pahi. *Lg Dev:* Literacy rate in first language: below 1%. Literacy rate in second language: 15% to 25%. *Other:* Swidden agriculturalists. Traditional religion. See main entry under Viet Nam.

Phai (Thung Chan Pray, Phay, Kha Pray, Pray 1, Prai) [prt] 15,000 in Laos (1995 census). Phongsali Province, Boun-Tai, Boun-Nua, Phongsali, Samphan districts; Xaignabouli Province, Hongsa, Xaignabouli, Phiang districts. *Other:* Distinct from Lua, Mal, and Pray 3. Traditional religion. See main entry under Thailand.

Phana' (Pana', Bana') [phq] 350 (1995 census). Luang Namtha Province, Luang Namtha District, Bopiet and Namtoung villages; Bokeo Province, Houayxay District, one village. *Class:* Sino-Tibetan, Tibeto-Burman, Lolo-Burmese, Loloish, Southern, Akha. *Lg Use:* Adults speak some Lahu. *Other:* Larger population may be in China under the Han nationality.

Phong-Kniang (Pong 3, Khaniang, Kenieng, Keneng, Lao Phong) [pnx] 1,000 (1981 Wurm and Hattori). Southern Houaphan Province, Viangthong and Houamuang districts, near the Neun River; northern Xieng Khouang Province. *Class:* Austro-Asiatic, Mon-Khmer, Northern Mon-Khmer, Khmuic, Xinh Mul. *Dialects:* Related to Puoc and Khang. *Lg Dev:* Many are educated. *Other:* Phong is the exonym of the Kenieng and is not to be confused with Kha Phong, a dialect of Maleng, nor with the autonym Pong as applied to one of the dialects of Hung (Ferlus 1996:16, 19). Traditional religion.

Phu Thai (Putai, Phutai, Puthay) [pht] 154,400 in Laos (2001 Johnstone and Mandryk). Khammouan, Savannakhet, Saravan, Champassak provinces; some found in Oudomxai and Luang Prabang provinces. *Lg Use:* Speakers also use Laotian. *Other:* Agriculturalists. Traditional religion. See main entry under Thailand.

Phuan (Lao Phuan, Phu Un) [phu] 106,099 in Laos (2000 WCD). Bolikhamxai, Vientiane, Xiangkhoang, and Houaphan. *Other:* The name is also used for Lao speakers in Thailand. Buddhist. See main entry under Thailand.

Phunoi (Phounoy, Phu Noi, Punoi) [pho] 35,635 in Laos (1995 census). North central, around Phony Saly. Also spoken in Thailand. *Class:* Sino-Tibetan, Tibeto-Burman, Lolo-Burmese, Loloish, Southern, Phunoi. *Dialects:* Black Khoany, White Khoany, Mung, Hwethom, Khaskhong. Close to Bisu, Pyen, and Mpi. Those listed as dialects may be separate languages. *Other:* Called 'Phunoi' or 'Phounoy' in Laos, 'Côông' in Viet Nam. "Kha Punoi" is derogatory. Traditional religion, Buddhist.

Pu Ko (Poko) [puk] 2 villages. *Class:* Tai-Kadai, Kam-Tai, Be-Tai, Tai-Sek, Tai, Southwestern.

Puoc (Kha Puhoc, Puhoc, Puok, Pou Hok, Xinh Mul, Xin Mul, Xing Mun, Ksing Mul, Lao Muh, Kha Niang) [puo] 2,164 in Laos (1985 F. Proschan). Northeast, Houaphan Province, Xiangkho District; Xieng Khouang Province, Het River, along the Viet Nam border. *Other:* Buddhist. See main entry under Viet Nam.

Rien [rie] 5,279 (2000 WCD). *Class:* Tai-Kadai, Kam-Tai, Be-Tai, Tai-Sek, Tai.

Saek (Sek, Tai Sek, Set) [skb] 14,000 in Laos (1990 Diller). Population total all countries: 25,000. Central Laos near the Viet Nam border. Upper Nam Noy and Nam Pheo areas in Khammouan Province and the village of Na Kadok in Khamkeut District, Borikhamxay Province. Also spoken in Thailand. *Class:* Tai-Kadai, Kam-Tai, Be-Tai, Tai-Sek, Sek. *Dialects:* Na Kadok, Khammouan. Close to Tai Mène. *Lg Use:* Speakers also use Lao. *Other:* The Saek of Na Kadok claim to have come originally from Phu Quan, Ban Pho Quang, Duc Tho District, in what is now Ha Tinh Province, Viet Nam. The Khammouan dialect speakers are originally from Nakai District, and it is still spoken in Toeng, Nam Meo, Na Moey, and Beuk. Traditional religion.

Salang (Halang) [hal] 4,000 in Laos. Southern Laos, Attopeu Province. *Lg Dev:* Literacy rate in first language: 5% to 10%. Literacy rate in second language: 25% to 50%. *Other:* Traditional religion. See main entry under Viet Nam (Halang).

Sapuan (Sapouan) [spu] 2,400 (1981). Southern Laos, Attopeu Province, banks of the Se Kong and Se Kamane rivers. *Class:* Austro-Asiatic, Mon-Khmer, Eastern Mon-Khmer, Bahnaric, West Bahnaric, Oi-The. *Dialects:* Related to Oy, Sok, Jeng. *Other:* Traditional religion.

Sila [slt] 1,772 in Laos (1995 census). Population total all countries: 2,612. North central, north of Muong Hai. Also spoken in Viet Nam. *Class:* Sino-Tibetan, Tibeto-Burman, Lolo-Burmese, Loloish, Southern, Akha, Hani. *Other:* Traditional religion.

Sô (Mangkong, Mang-Koong, Makong, So Makon, Mankoong, Mang Cong, Bru, Kah So, Thro) [sss] 102,000 in Laos (1993). Population total all countries: 160,000. Khammouan, Thakhek, Savannakhet provinces, both sides of the Mekong River. Also spoken in Thailand. *Class:* Austro-Asiatic, Mon-Khmer, Eastern Mon-Khmer, Katuic, West Katuic, Brou-So. *Dialects:* So Trong, So Slouy, So Phong. Close to Bru. *Lg Dev:* Literacy rate in first language: below 1%. Literacy rate in second language: 15% to 25%. Dictionary. Bible portions: 1980. *Other:* Called 'Mangkong' and 'Bru' in Laos. The name 'So' is not used in Laos. Traditional religion.

Sok (Sork, Sawk) [skk] 1,600 (1981). Attopeu Province. *Class:* Austro-Asiatic, Mon-Khmer, Eastern Mon-Khmer, Bahnaric, West Bahnaric, Oi-The. *Dialects:* Related to Oy, Sapuan, Jeng.

Sou (Suq, Souk, Su, Su', Sawk) [sqq] 2,360 (2000). Southern Laos, Attopeu Province, Phouvong and Sanamxai districts. *Class:* Austro-Asiatic, Mon-Khmer, Eastern Mon-Khmer, Bahnaric, West Bahnaric, Brao-Kravet. *Other:* Traditional religion.

Tai Daeng (Red Thai, Thai Do, Thai Dang, Tai Deng, Daeng) [tyr] 25,000 in Laos (1991). Northeastern Laos, near the Viet Nam border. *Other:* Part of the official Thai ethnic community in Viet Nam. Traditional religion. See main entry under Viet Nam.

Tai Dam (Black Tai, Tai Noir, Thai Den) [blt] 50,000 in Laos (1995). Khammouan Province. *Dialect:* Tai Muoi (Tai Muei, Tay Mueai, Meuay). *Other:* Part of the Dai official nationality in China and the Thai official nationality in Viet Nam. See main entry under Viet Nam.

Tai Dón (Tai Blanc, Thái Tráng, Tai Lai, Tai Kao, White Tai) [twh] 200,000 in Laos (1995 census). Northeastern Laos. *Lg Use:* A large influential group. Those who have had prolonged contact with Tai Dam have become bilingual in it. Many have not had that contact. *Other:* Part of the Thai official ethnic community in Viet Nam. Traditional religion. See main entry under Viet Nam.

Tai Loi (Loi, Tailoi, Wakut, Monglwe) [tlq] 500 in Laos (1995 census). Luang Namtha Province, Long District. Tai Loi is across the border in Myanmar. Tai Loi may also be in China. *Dialects:* Tai Loi, Doi. *Other:* Traditional religion. See main entry under Myanmar.

Tai Long [thi] 4,800 (2004). *Class:* Tai-Kadai, Kam-Tai, Be-Tai, Tai-Sek, Tai, Southwestern. *Other:* May be the same as Mao (Tai-Long, Tai-Mao, Maw, Mau) on the Burma-Yunnan border, a variety of Dai in China.

Tai Mène (Tai Maen, Tai-Maen, Tay Mènè, Tai Mene, Tai Man, Tai Men) [tmp] 7,200 (1995 census). Borikhamxay Province, Vieng Thong District, several villages; Khamkeut District, many villages: Lak Xao, Khamkeut, Na Heuang, Nam Sak, Sop Chat, Ka'ane, Phon Thoen, Sop Pone, and Tha Veng. *Class:* Tai-Kadai, Kam-Tai, Be-Tai, Tai-Sek, Tai, Northern. *Dialects:* Close to Saek. *Other:* They claim to have come from Xieng Lip and Ban Pot in Nghe An, Viet Nam.

Tai Nüa (Chinese Shan, Tai Neua, Tai Nuea) [tdd] 35,000 in Laos (1995 Chazee). Northwestern Laos. Also possibly in north Viet Nam. *Other:* Called 'Dehong Dai' or 'Shan' in China. A different dialect from that in China. Traditional religion. See main entry under China.

Tai Pao [tpo] 3,300 (1995 census). Bolikhamxay Province, Viangthong, Khamkeut, Pakkading districts. *Class:* Tai-Kadai, Kam-Tai, Be-Tai, Tai-Sek, Tai. *Other:* Classification problems, possibly due to migration. Traditional religion.

Talieng (Taliang, Tariang) [tdf] 23,091 (1995 census). Muong Phine-Bung Sai area, Savannakhet Province. *Class:* Austro-Asiatic, Mon-Khmer, Eastern Mon-Khmer, Bahnaric, North Bahnaric, West. *Dialects:* Related to Trieng or Hre in Viet Nam; may be the same as Trieng. *Other:* Apparently different from Tareng, which is East Katuic. 'Tariang' means 'headhunters'. 1,500 meters. Traditional religion.

Ta'oih, Lower (Tong) [tto] 15,836 (2000 WCD). Saravan Province, northwest of Saravan town. *Class:* Austro-Asiatic, Mon-Khmer, Eastern Mon-Khmer, Katuic, Central Katuic, Ta'oih. *Dialects:* Tong, Hantong'. Not intelligible with Upper Ta'oih. *Lg Use:* Some also use Upper Ta'oih.

Ta'oih, Upper (Ta-Oy, Ta-Oi, Tau Oi, Ta Hoi, Kantua) [tth] 30,876 in Laos (1995 census). 70% monolingual. Population total all countries: 49,876. Saravan Province, mainly in Ta-Oy District. Also spoken in USA, Viet Nam. *Class:* Austro-Asiatic, Mon-Khmer, Eastern Mon-Khmer, Katuic, Central Katuic, Ta'oih. *Dialect:* Pasoom, Kamuan', Palee'n, Leem, Ha'aang (Sa'ang). Not intelligible with Lower Ta'oih until speakers have had at least 2 weeks' contact. *Other:* Traditional religion.

Tareng (Tariang) [tgr] 5,000 (1981 Wurm and Hattori). Just west of Viet Nam border, east of Kayong, north of Chavane and Thia. *Class:* Austro-Asiatic, Mon-

Khmer, Eastern Mon-Khmer, Katuic, East Katuic, Katu-Pacoh. *Other:* Distinct from Talieng, which is North Bahnaric.

Tay Khang [tnu] 200. Khammouan Province. Possibly also in Viet Nam. *Class:* Tai-Kadai, Kam-Tai, Be-Tai, Tai-Sek, Tai. *Other:* Some problem in classification and confusion with Khang of Viet Nam.

Thai, Northern (Lanna, Lan Na, Lanatai, Lannatai, "Yuan," "Youon," "Youanne," Myang, Muang) [nod] 9,396 in Laos (2000 WCD). Haut Mekong and Sayaboury provinces, Laos. *Dialect:* Nan. See main entry under Thailand.

The (Thae) [thx] 2,920 (2000). Attopeu Province. *Class:* Austro-Asiatic, Mon-Khmer, Eastern Mon-Khmer, Bahnaric, West Bahnaric, Oi-The.

Yoy (Yoi, Yooi, Yooy, Dioi, Jui) [yoy] 1,000 in Laos (1995 census). *Lg Use:* All also use Lao. *Other:* May be the same as Tai Yo of Khamouan Province, a Northern Tai language. Buddhist. See main entry under Thailand.

Lebanon

Republic of Lebanon, al-Jumhouriya al-Lubnaniya. 3,777,218. National or official languages: Standard Arabic, French. Literacy rate: 70% to 75%. Also includes Assyrian Neo-Aramaic (1,000), Chaldean Neo-Aramaic (18,000), Turoyo (18,000). Information mainly from T. Sebeok 1963; H. Fleisch 1974; W. Fischer and O. Jastrow 1980. Blind population: 5,000. Deaf population: 219,480. Deaf institutions: 13. The number of languages listed for Lebanon is 6. Of those, all are living languages.

Arabic, North Levantine Spoken (Levantine Arabic, Lebanese-Syrian Arabic, Syro-Lebanese Arabic) [apc] 3,900,000 in Lebanon (1991). Throughout Lebanon. *Dialects:* North Lebanese Arabic, South Lebanese Arabic (Shii, Metuali), North-Central Lebanese Arabic (Mount Lebanon Arabic), South-Central Lebanese Arabic (Druze Arabic), Standard Lebanese Arabic, Beqaa Arabic, Sunni Beiruti Arabic, Saida Sunni Arabic, Iqlim-Al-Kharrub Sunni Arabic, Jdaideh Arabic. *Lg Use:* National language. *Other:* Muslim, Christian, Druze. See main entry under Syria.

Arabic, Standard [arb] Middle East, North Africa. *Lg Use:* Official language. Used for education, official purposes, communication among Arabic speaking countries. See main entry under Saudi Arabia.

Armenian (Ermenice, Armanski, Haieren, Somkhuri) [hye] 234,600 in Lebanon (1986). *Dialect:* Western Armenian. *Lg Use:* Language of wider communication. *Other:* 'Haieren' is their own name. Christian. See main entry under Armenia.

English [eng] 3,300 in Lebanon (2004). *Lg Use:* Has been used to some extent since the founding of the American University of Beirut in 1866. Many English language publications. Not spoken on the street or in Lebanese homes. See main entry under United Kingdom.

French [fra] 16,600 in Lebanon (2004). *Lg Use:* Official language. An estimated 20% of the population speak French in their daily lives, and up to 65% of the population can read and converse in French. A number of government and private universities teach in French. The language of instruction in most schools. *Lg Dev:* Taught in primary and secondary schools. See main entry under France.

Kurdish, Northern [kmr] 75,000 in Lebanon (2002 Meho). Ethnic population: 215,384 (2000 WCD). Beirut, also Sidon, Tripoli, and Biqa Valley. *Dialect:* Mhallami (Mardinli). *Lg Dev:* Literacy rate in first language: 40%. *Other:* Muslim (Sunni). See main entry under Turkey (Asia).

Malaysia

Malaysia. 23,522,482. National or official language: Malay. Also includes Burmese, Chinese Sign Language, Eastern Panjabi (43,000), Malayalam (37,000), Sylheti, Telugu (30,000), Western Cham, people from Indonesia, Pakistan, the Philippines, Sri Lanka, Thailand, United Kingdom. Information mainly from S. Wurm and S. Hattori 1981. Deaf population: 31,000 (1980). Deaf institutions: 5. The number of languages listed for Malaysia is 141. Of those, 140 are living languages and 1 is extinct.

Malaysia (Peninsular)

Malaysia (Peninsular). 10,115,000 (1979). 6,396,790 speakers of Austronesian languages, 3,399,000 speakers of Chinese languages, 44,610 speakers of Austro-Asiatic languages (1991 J. Matisoff), 1,090,000 speakers of Dravidian languages. Information mainly from W. G. Shellabear 1913; F. Lebar, G. Hickey, J. Musgrave 1964; R. K. Dentan 1968; I. Hancock 1969; S. Lim 1981; B. Comrie 1987; A. Baxter 1988; J. Holm 1989. Blind population: 22,300. The number of languages listed for Malaysia (Peninsular) is 40. Of those, all are living languages.

Batek (Bateq, Bateg, Batok, Kleb, Tomo, Nong) [btq] 700 (2000 D. Bradley). Ethnic population: 700 (2000 D. Bradley). Northern Pahang, Kelantan, Trengganu. *Class:* Austro-Asiatic, Mon-Khmer, Aslian, North Aslian, Eastern. *Dialects:* Batek Teq (Teq), Batek De' (Deq), Batek Iga, Batek Nong (Nong). Deq and Nong may be separate languages.
Besisi (Mah Meri, Cellate) [mhe] 1,356 (2000 D. Bradley). Ethnic population: 1,356 (2000 D. Bradley). Selangor coast, Malacca. *Class:* Austro-Asiatic, Mon-Khmer, Aslian, South Aslian. *Dialects:* Kuala Langot Besisi, Malakka Besisi, Ulu Langat Orang Bukit, Selangor Sakai, Betise' (Betisek), Sisi. *Lg Use:* One other dialect became extinct in late 19th century. *Lg Dev:* NT: 1933.
Chewong (Cheq Wong, Che'wong, Siwang, Beri, Chuba) [cwg] 200 (2000 D. Bradley). Ethnic population: 200 (2000 D. Bradley). Just south of Semai, Pahang. *Class:* Austro-Asiatic, Mon-Khmer, Aslian, North Aslian, Chewong.
Chinese, Hakka [hak] 985,635 in Malaysia (1980 census). Population includes 786,097 in Peninsular Malaysia, 109,060 in Sarawak, 90,478 in Sabah. See main entry under China.
Chinese, Mandarin [cmn] 417,070 in Malaysia (1970 census). Peninsular Malaysia, Sabah, and Sarawak. *Other:* Speakers are primarily urban, in commerce. See main entry under China.
Chinese, Min Dong [cdo] 222,185 in Malaysia (2000 WCD). Population includes 85,368 in Peninsular Malaysia, 120,645 in Sarawak (1979, including Pu-Xian Chinese). *Dialect:* Foochow (Fuzhou). See main entry under China.
Chinese, Min Nan (Min Nan, Minnan) [nan] 1,946,698 in Malaysia. Population includes 1,824,741 in Peninsular Malaysia, 7,990 Teochew, 5,083 Hainanese, 24,604 Hokkien in Sabah (1980 census) 84,280 in Sarawak (1979). *Dialects:* Fukienese (Amoy, Fujianese, Hokkien), Hainanese, Chaochow (Teochow, Teochew). See main entry under China.
Chinese, Pu-Xian [cpx] 66,655 in Malaysia (2000 WCD). Peninsular Malaysia and Sarawak. *Dialect:* Xinghua (Hsinghua, Hinghua). See main entry under China.
Chinese, Yue (Cantonese, Yue, Yueh) [yue] 748,010 in Malaysia (1980 census). Population includes 704,286 in Peninsular Malaysia, 24,640 in Sarawak, 19,184 in Sabah.

Dialects: Cantonese, Toishanese. See main entry under China.
Duano' (Orang Kuala, Desin Dola') [dup] 1,922 (1981 Wurm and Hattori). Ethnic population: 2,000 (2000 D. Bradley). South coast around Pontian Kecil and northwest. *Class:* Austronesian, Malayo-Polynesian, Malayic, Malayan, Para-Malay.
English [eng] See main entry under United Kingdom.
Jah Hut (Jah Het) [jah] 2,442 (2000 D. Bradley). Ethnic population: 2,442 (2000 D. Bradley). Just south of main body of Semai, Kuala Krau, Pahang. *Class:* Austro-Asiatic, Mon-Khmer, Aslian, Jah Hut. *Dialects:* Kerdau, Krau, Ketiar Krau (Tengganu), Kuala Tembeling, Pulau Guai, Ulu Ceres (Cheres), Ulu Tembeling.
Jakun (Jaku'd, Jakud'n, Jakoon, Djakun, Orang Hulu) [jak] 9,799 (1981 Wurm and Hattori). East coast and inland, Pairang River, Pekan to Sri Gading, east to Benut, northwest to around middle Muat River. *Class:* Austronesian, Malayo-Polynesian, Malayic, Malayan, Aboriginal Malay.
Jehai (Jahai, Pangan) [jhi] 1,250 (1981 Wurm and Hattori). Ethnic population: 1,375 (2000 D. Bradley). Northeastern Perak and western Kelantan. *Class:* Austro-Asiatic, Mon-Khmer, Aslian, North Aslian, Eastern. *Dialects:* Jehai, Batek Teh.
Kensiu (Kenseu, Kensieu, Kensiw, Moniq, Monik, Mendi, Ngok Pa, Orang Bukit, Orang Liar) [kns] 3,000 in Malaysia (1984 D. Hogan). Population total all countries: 3,300. Northeast Kedah, near Thai border. Overlaps slightly into southern Yala Province of Thailand. Also spoken in Thailand. *Class:* Austro-Asiatic, Mon-Khmer, Aslian, North Aslian, Western. *Dialects:* Ijoh (Ijok), Jarum, Jeher (Sakai Tanjong of Temongoh), Kedah (Quedah), Plus, Ulu Selama, Kensiu Batu, Kensiu Siong, Kentaq Nakil. *Other:* Negrito. 'Semang' means 'debt slave' in Khmer, used more for primitive Negritos. 'Semang' is used to differentiate western groups from eastern ones, called Pangan. Orang Asli means 'aborigine' in Malay. Tropical forest. Nomadic.
Kintaq (Kenta, Kintak, Kintaq Bong, Bong) [knq] 220 in Malaysia (2003 SIL). Kedah-Perak border area, Thai border. Overlaps slightly into Southern Yala Province of Thailand. Also spoken in Thailand. *Class:* Austro-Asiatic, Mon-Khmer, Aslian, North Aslian, Western.
Lanoh (Jengjeng) [lnh] 224 (2000 D. Bradley). Ethnic population: 224 (2000 D. Bradley). North central Perak. *Class:* Austro-Asiatic, Mon-Khmer, Aslian, Senoic.
Malaccan Creole Malay (Chitties Creole Malay) [ccm] Malacca Straits. *Class:* Creole, Malay based. *Dialects:* May be historically related to Sri Lankan Creole Malay. *Lg Use:* Spoken since the 16th century by descendants of Tamil merchants who intermarried with other groups. The speakers are called 'Chitties' (Lim 1981:126–128; Holm 1989:580). *Other:* Has not been studied in detail.
Malaccan Creole Portuguese (Malaysian Creole Portuguese, Malaccan, Papia Kristang, Kristang, Portuguese Patois, Serani, Bahasa Serani, Bahasa Geragau, Malaqueiro, Malaquense, Malaquês, Malaquenho, Português de Malaca, Malayo-Portuguese) [mcm] 5,000 in Malaysia (1997 Col. Timothy D'Souza, Eurasian Association). Population total all countries: 5,000 (1997). Trankera and Hilir, Melaka, Straits of Malacca. Related varieties in parts of Kuala Lumpur and Singapore. Variety in Pulau Tikus spoken more in 1997 than in 1987. Also spoken in Singapore. *Class:* Creole, Portuguese based. *Lg Use:* Trade language. Also spoken as second language by some Chinese shopkeepers in Hilir. Most people over 20 years of age speak Kristang, and less than half of those under 20. Most speakers also know local varieties of Bazaar Malay and Malaysian English. Some older women speakers have low proficiency in English. *Lg Dev:*

Dictionary. Grammar. Bible portions: 1884. *Other:* 'Kristang' is their name for the language, people, and religion. Fishermen.

Malay (Bahasa Malaysia, Bahasa Malayu, Malayu, Melaju, Melayu, Standard Malay) [mly] 7,181,000 in Malaysia (1986). Population includes 248,757 in Sarawak (1980 census), 2,000,000 in Kelantan and Trengganu, and 1,000,000 in other parts of Malaysia. Population total all countries: 17,604,253. All districts of Peninsular Malaysia, Sabah, and Sarawak. Also spoken in Brunei, Indonesia (Sumatra), Myanmar, Singapore, Thailand, United Arab Emirates, USA. *Class:* Austronesian, Malayo-Polynesian, Malayic, Malayan, Local Malay. *Dialects:* Trengganu, Kelantan, Kedah, Perak (Southern Malay), Sarawak Malay, Bazaar Malay (Low Malay, Pasar Malay, Pasir Malay, Trade Malay). 'Bazaar Malay' is used to refer to many regional nonstandard dialects. Over 80% cognate with Indonesian. *Lg Use:* Official language. 3,000,000 second-language speakers. Speakers also use English, Chinese, or Tamil. *Lg Dev:* Roman and Arabic (Jawi) scripts. Newspapers. Radio programs. TV. Grammar. Bible: 1733–1993. *Other:* SVO. Agriculturalists: wet and dry rice, rubber, fruits, vegetables; fishermen.

Malay, Baba (Straits Malay, Chinese Malay) [mbf] 5,000 in Malacca (1979 Tan Chee Beng). Melaka Tengah, Malacca Straits, Peninsular Malaysia. *Lg Use:* The only monolinguals are over 70 years old. *Other:* It developed since the 15th century from Low Malay with many Hokkien Chinese borrowings. Lim (1981) and Holm (1989) treat it as a Malay-based creole. See main entry under Singapore.

Malay, Kedah (Satun Malay) [meo] Kedah, Penang, and Perlis states. Also spoken in Thailand. *Class:* Austronesian, Malayo-Polynesian, Malayic, Malayan, Local Malay. *Dialects:* Distinct from Pattani Malay or Standard Malay. *Lg Use:* Speakers also use Central Thai. *Other:* More people in the area speak Thai than Pattani. Most outside contacts are with centers of Thai population in Songkhla, Phattalung, and Haad Yai; with west coast Malay states of Perlis and Kedah. Culturally Malay. Tropical forest.

Malaysian Sign Language (Bahasa Isyarat Malaysia) [xml] *Class:* Deaf sign language. *Lg Use:* Under development by the Ministry of Education since 1978 and used in government programs.

Minriq (Menriq, Menrik, Mendriq, Menraq) [mnq] 125 (1981 Wurm and Hattori). Southeast Kelantan. *Class:* Austro-Asiatic, Mon-Khmer, Aslian, North Aslian, Eastern.

Mintil (Mitil) [mzt] 40 (1975 SIL). Tamun River, Pahang. *Class:* Austro-Asiatic, Mon-Khmer, Aslian, North Aslian, Eastern. *Other:* Nearly extinct.

Negeri Sembilan Malay (Malaysian Minangkabau, Ulu Muar Malay, Orang Negeri) [zmi] 300,000 (1981 Wurm and Hattori). Southeast of Kuala Lumpur, Ulu Muar District. *Class:* Austronesian, Malayo-Polynesian, Malayic, Malayan, Para-Malay. *Dialects:* Related to Minangkabau in Sumatra, Indonesia. *Other:* People call themselves 'Orang Negeri', or use their district name, and call Minangkabau immigrants, who have come during the last 60 to 80 years, 'Minang'.

Orang Kanaq [orn] 34 (1981 Wurm and Hattori). Southeast and northeast of Mawai. *Class:* Austronesian, Malayo-Polynesian, Malayic, Malayan, Aboriginal Malay. *Other:* Nearly extinct.

Orang Seletar [ors] 853 in Malaysia (2000 WCD). Population total all countries: 1,737. Southeast coast around Kukuo, Jahore Bahru, east and north, and the north coast of Singapore. Also spoken in Singapore. *Class:* Austronesian, Malayo-Polynesian, Malayic, Malayan, Aboriginal Malay. *Other:* Coastal.

Penang Sign Language [psg] Penang. *Class:* Deaf sign language. *Lg Use:* Users are also able to communicate in Malaysian Sign Language. *Other:* Deaf school established in 1954, where only oral method was used. Sign language evolved outside the classroom. Use declined in the late 1970s due to spread of other sign languages, but there are still users.

Sabüm [sbo] 889 (2000 WCD). North central Perak. *Class:* Austro-Asiatic, Mon-Khmer, Aslian, Senoic. *Dialects:* Closest to Lanoh and Semnam, but not the same as Lanoh.

Selangor Sign Language (Kuala Lumpur Sign Language, KLSL) [kgi] Selangor and elsewhere in Peninsular Malaysia. *Class:* Deaf sign language. *Lg Use:* American signs were introduced in the late 1960s to a class for deaf children. They were promoted by the club for deaf adults which was started at the YMCA in 1973. Many former users of Penang Sign Language now use Selangor Sign Language. Uses predominantly American signs in a mixture of English and Malay word order.

Semai (Central "Sakai," Senoi, Sengoi) [sea] 18,327 (2000 D. Bradley). Ethnic population: 18,327 (2000 D. Bradley). Northwest Pahang and southern Perak, Selangor, Negri Sembilan, central mountain area. *Class:* Austro-Asiatic, Mon-Khmer, Aslian, Senoic. *Dialect:* Jelai, Orang Tanjong of Ulu Langat, Sungkai, Perak I, Perak II, Cameron, Telom, Bidor, Betau, Lipis, Bil, Ulu Kampar (Kampar). *Lg Use:* Speakers also use Malay. *Lg Dev:* Bible portions: 1951–1962. *Other:* Sakai means 'slave'. The west Semai are more acculturated to Malay society than the east Semai. Mountain slope. Tropical forest. 800 to 900 meters. Agriculturalists: rice, sweet potatoes, bananas, fruit, rubber.

Semaq Beri (Semaq Bri, Semoq Beri) [szc] 2,078 (2000 D. Bradley). Ethnic population: 2,078. Pahang, Trengganu, Kelantan. *Class:* Austro-Asiatic, Mon-Khmer, Aslian, South Aslian. *Dialects:* 2 dialects.

Semelai [sza] 2,932 (2000 D. Bradley). Ethnic population: 2,932 (2000 D. Bradley). Between Segamat (Johore) and the Pahang River. *Class:* Austro-Asiatic, Mon-Khmer, Aslian, South Aslian. *Lg Use:* Two dialects became extinct in the early 20th century.

Semnam [ssm] 667 (2000 WCD). North central Perak. *Class:* Austro-Asiatic, Mon-Khmer, Aslian, Senoic. *Dialects:* Close to Lanoh and Sabüm.

Tamil [tam] 1,060,000 in Malaysia (1993). *Lg Use:* Speakers also use Malay or English. *Other:* Together with speakers of Hindi, Telugu, Malayalam, Urdu, Gujarati, Sindhi, Panjabi, they total 10% of the population, or 1,528,000. Plantation workers. See main entry under India.

Temiar (Temer, Northern Sakai, Seroq, Pie) [tea] 11,593 (2000 D. Bradley). Ethnic population: 11,593 (2000 D. Bradley). Mostly in Perak and Kelantan; also Pahang. *Class:* Austro-Asiatic, Mon-Khmer, Aslian, Senoic. *Dialects:* Grik, Kenderong, Kenering, Po-Klo (Sakai Bukit of Temongoh), Sakai of Plus Korbu, Sungai Piah, Tanjong Rambutan, Tembe' (Tembi), Ulu Kinta (Kinta Sakai), Lanoh Kobak. *Lg Dev:* Grammar. *Other:* Seminomadic.

Temoq [tmo] 350 (1981 Wurm and Hattori). Jeram River, southeast Pahang. *Class:* Austro-Asiatic, Mon-Khmer, Aslian, South Aslian.

Temuan (Benua, Niap) [tmw] 9,312 (1981 Wurm and Hattori). Southern extension of the main range in the southern half of the peninsula, Selangor, Pahang, Johore, Negri Sembilan, Kuala Langat, scattered settlements. *Class:* Austronesian, Malayo-Polynesian, Malayic, Malayan, Aboriginal Malay. *Dialects:* Beduanda (Biduanda), Belanda (Belana, Blanda, Landa, Belanas, Belandas), Berembun (Birmun), Mantra (Mentera, Mintra), Temuan, Udai. *Other:* Also classified as Malacca group of Austro-Asiatic phylum. Beduanda is sometimes considered to be a separate language.

Tonga (Mos) [tnz] Northwest tip north of Kaki. *Dialect:* Satun. *Lg Use:* May be extinct (2000 D. Bradley). See main entry under Thailand.

Malaysia (Sabah)

Malaysia (Sabah). 1,002,608 (1980). Literacy rate: 58%. Information mainly from C. P. Miller 1981–1982, 1987; J. K. King and J. W. King 1984; A. K. Pallesen 1984; J. Walton and D. Moody 1984; P. R. Kroeger 1985, 1986; M. and A. Boutin 1985; M. Boutin 1986; C. Sather 1997. The number of languages listed for Malaysia (Sabah) is 54. Of those, all are living languages.

Abai Sungai [abf] 400 (2000 Wurm). Lower reaches of the Kinabatangan River. *Class:* Austronesian, Malayo-Polynesian, Northwest, Sabahan, Paitanic. *Lg Use:* 40% to 60% of the ethnic group speaks Abai Sungai. Used in the home. About 30% to 50% of the children speak it. Neutral language attitude. *Other:* Distinct from other Paitanic languages (Upper Kinabatangan, Tombonuwo). Fishermen.

Bajau, West Coast (Land Bajaw, West Coast Bajao) [bdr] 40,000 (1982). Kuala Penyu to Kudat, northern and some eastern areas, west coast of Sabah. *Class:* Austronesian, Malayo-Polynesian, Sama-Bajaw, Sulu-Borneo, Borneo Coast Bajaw. *Dialects:* Kota Belud, Kawang, Putatan, Papar, Banggi, Sandakan Bajau, Pitas Bajau. Diversified in structure more than other Borneo languages. Related to, but a distinct language from Sama (East Coast Bajau) groups of Malaysia and Philippines, and Indonesian Bajau (K. Pallesen 1977). 60% intelligibility of Sama. Papar dialect used in national broadcasting. May be more than one language. *Lg Dev:* Radio programs. *Other:* Fishermen; agriculturalists: rice, fruit, vegetables; animal husbandry: chickens, goats, water buffaloes, ponies.

Balangingi (Balangingi Bajau, Baangingi', Northern Sinama, Balanian, Balagnini, Balanini, Balignini, Binadan, Banadan, Sama) [sse] 30,000 in Malaysia (1977 SIL). Population includes all East Coast Bajau (Sama), including Kagayan (Sama Mapun) and Southern Sama. East coast of Sabah. See main entry under Philippines.

Banjar (Banjarese, Bandjarese, Banjar Malay) [bjn] 900,000 in Malaysia (1993). Tawau. *Other:* Separated from Brunei-Kedayan for at least 400 years. See main entry under Indonesia (Kalimantan).

Bisaya, Sabah (Basaya, Besaya, Bisaia, Bisayah, Jilama Bawang, Jilama Sungai) [bsy] 15,822 (2000 WCD). On the coast north of and around Brunei Bay, mainly in west Beaufort along Padas River, south of Weston, and south Kuala Penyu District to coast. *Class:* Austronesian, Malayo-Polynesian, Northwest, Sabahan, Dusunic, Bisaya. *Dialects:* 90% intelligibility of Tatana. Lexical similarity 58% with Sarawak Bisaya, 57% to 59% with Brunei Bisaya ('Dusun'). *Lg Dev:* Bible portions: 1938. *Other:* Both North and South Bisaya are in Sabah (Wurm and Hattori 1981). Most people are educated to primary level, not many to secondary.

Bonggi (Banggi, Bangay, Banggi Dusun) [bdg] 1,400 (1990 UBS). Banggi Island in Kudat District, 15 villages. *Class:* Austronesian, Malayo-Polynesian, Meso Philippine, Palawano. *Dialects:* Closest to Molbog of the Philippines. *Lg Use:* Speakers also use Sabah Malay. *Lg Dev:* Bible portions: 1992.

Bookan (Baukan, Baukan Murut) [bnb] 2,764 (2000 WCD). Population includes 300 or more Tengara. Keningau and Kinabatangan districts around the headwaters of the Sook and Kinabatangan rivers. *Class:* Austronesian, Malayo-Polynesian, Northwest, North

Sarawakan, Dayic, Murutic, Northern. *Dialects:* Baukan (Baokan, Bokan, Bookan, Boken, Bokun, Bukun, Bokon, Ulun-No-Bokon, Ulun-No-Bokan, Pingas), Kokoroton Murut, Tengara (Tungara, Tingara, Tenggaraq, Tangara', Tanggaraq, Kinabatangan Murut). Close to Keningau Murut, Timugon, Tagal.

Brunei (Brunei-Kadaian, Orang Bukit) [kxd] 54,000 in Malaysia. Population includes 46,500 in Sabah, 7,500 in Sarawak. Upper Balait and Tutau rivers, northern coast, 4th and 5th divisions, Sarawak; Sabah in Beaufort, Kuala Penyu, Labuan, Labuk-Sugut, Papar, Sipitang, Sandakan, and Tenom districts. *Dialect:* Brunei, Kadaian (Kadayan, Kadian, Kadien, Kadyan, Karayan, Kedyan, Kedayan, Kedien, Kerayan). *Lg Use:* Speakers also use Malay. *Other:* Dialect variations are regional, not ethnic. Agriculturalists (Kedayan); fishermen (Brunei). See main entry under Brunei.

Bugis (Buginese) [bug] See main entry under Indonesia (Sulawesi).

Chavacano [cbk] One village in Semporna. See main entry under Philippines.

Dumpas (Doompas) [dmv] 1,078 (2000 WCD). Perancangan village in Labuk-Sugut District. *Class:* Austronesian, Malayo-Polynesian, Northwest, Sabahan, Dusunic, Unclassified. *Dialects:* May be Paitanic. Comprehension of Tombonuo 87%, Eastern Kadazan 57%, Coastal Kadazan 44%. *Lg Use:* Language dying out as a result of intermarriage with other groups. Speakers also use Tambanua.

Dusun, Central (Dusun, Dusan, Dusum, Dusur, Kadayan, Kedayan, Kadasan, Central Kadazan) [dtp] 140,500 (1991 SIL). Population includes 50,000 Ranau (1989 UBS), 70,000 Bundu (1990 UBS), 500 (?) Kuala Monsok Dusun (1981 Wurm and Hattori). Beaufort, Kota Belud, Kota Kinabalu, Kota Marudu, Kinabatangan, Keningau, Labuk-Sugut, Penampang, Papar, Ranau, Tambunan, Tenom, Tuaran, and Tawau districts. *Class:* Austronesian, Malayo-Polynesian, Northwest, Sabahan, Dusunic, Dusun, Central. *Dialects:* Dusun Sinulihan (Sinulihan), Kadazan-Tagaro (Tagaro), Kiundu, Pahu', Sokid, Tindal, Menggatal (Kiulu, Telipok), Ranau, Bundu (Taginambur), Beaufort, Luba, Kuala Monsok Dusun. Ranau dialect is different from Ranau in Sumatra, Indonesia. *Lg Dev:* Dictionary. Bible: 2000.

Dusun, Sugut (Dusun, Sugut, Sugut Kadazan, Kadayan, Tanggal, Tilau-Ilau) [kzs] 12,225 (2000 WCD). Headwaters of the Sugut River, Labuk-Sugut District. *Class:* Austronesian, Malayo-Polynesian, Northwest, Sabahan, Dusunic, Dusun, Central. *Dialects:* Tinagas, Talantang. *Lg Use:* Speakers also use Central Dusun. *Other:* Comprehension testing needed with Central Dusun, Minokok, and Kimaragang.

Dusun, Tambunan (Tambunan) [kzt] 15,553 (2000 WCD). Throughout Tambunan District and parts of Keningau. *Class:* Austronesian, Malayo-Polynesian, Northwest, Sabahan, Dusunic, Dusun, Central. *Other:* Agriculturalists: rice.

Dusun, Tempasuk (Tindal, Kedamaian Dusun, Tampasuk, Tampassuk, Tampasok, Tempasok) [tdu] 6,000 (1981 Wurm and Hattori). Area around Tempasuk village, Kota Belud. *Class:* Austronesian, Malayo-Polynesian, Northwest, Sabahan, Dusunic, Dusun, Central.

Gana (Ganaq, Gana', Minansut, Keningau Dusun) [gnq] 2,000 (1985 SIL). Minusut and Kuangoh, Keningau District along the Baiaya River, a tributary of the Pegalan River, north of Keningau town. *Class:* Austronesian, Malayo-Polynesian, Northwest, Sabahan, Dusunic, Dusun. *Lg Use:* People seldom use Gana. Speakers also use Sabah Malay, Central Dusun, or Bahasa Malaysia.

Ida'an (Eraans, Bulud Upi, Idaan, Idahan, Idan, Idayan) [dbj] 6,000 (1987 SIL). Population includes 1,500

Begahak. East coast of Sabah, Lahad Datu, Kinabatangan, and Sandakan districts. *Class:* Austronesian, Malayo-Polynesian, Northwest, Sabahan, Ida'an. *Dialects:* Begak (Begahak, Bagahak), Subpan (Supan, Sungai), Ida'an. Not closely related to other languages. *Lg Dev:* Bible portions: 1987–1997.

Iranun ("Ilanun," Illanun, Illanoan, Illanoon, Iranon Maranao, Iranum, Lanoon, Ylanos, Lanun, Illanos) [ill] 12,000 (2003). 17 villages around Lahad Datu and Kota Belud districts; also reported to be in Kudat and Marudu. *Class:* Austronesian, Malayo-Polynesian, Southern Philippine, Danao, Maranao-Iranon. *Dialects:* Most closely related to Maranao of the Philippines (85% intelligibility). Related to, but distinct from, Iranun and Maguindanao of the Philippines. *Other:* They claim to have come from Mindanao, Philippines, in 1850. Different from Lahanan (Lanun) of Sarawak. Fishermen; agriculturalists: rice, fruit trees.

Javanese (Jawa) [jav] 300,000 in Malaysia (1981 Wurm and Hattori). See main entry under Indonesia (Java and Bali).

Kadazan, Coastal (Penampang Kadazan, Papar Kadazan, Membakut Kadazan, Kadazan Tangaa') [kzj] 60,000 (1986 SIL). West coast of Sabah, Penampang, and Papar districts. *Class:* Austronesian, Malayo-Polynesian, Northwest, Sabahan, Dusunic, Dusun. *Lg Dev:* Dictionary. Bible portions: 1986. *Other:* VSO.

Kadazan, Klias River [kqt] 1,000 (1984 SIL). Klias River area, Beaufort District. *Class:* Austronesian, Malayo-Polynesian, Northwest, Sabahan, Dusunic, Dusun. *Dialects:* Low intelligibility of Coastal Kadazan. Lexical similarity 77% with Tatana. *Other:* Agriculturalists.

Kadazan, Labuk-Kinabatangan (Eastern Kadazan, Labuk Kadazan, Sogilitan, Tindakon, Tompulung) [dtb] 20,583 (2000 SIL). Population includes 14,000 to 16,000 Labuk (1987 SIL), 7,000 to 8,000 Sungai (1982 SIL). Northeast Sabah, Sandakan, Labuk-Sugut, and Kinabatangan districts. *Class:* Austronesian, Malayo-Polynesian, Northwest, Sabahan, Dusunic, Dusun, Eastern. *Dialects:* Mangkaak (Mangkahak, Mangkok, Mangkak), Sukang, Labuk, Lamag Sungai (Sungei). *Lg Use:* Speakers also use Sabah Malay. *Lg Dev:* NT: 1996. *Other:* VSO, prepositions; genitives after nouns; question word initial; nontonal.

Kalabakan (Kalabakan Murut, Tawau Murut, Tidung) [kve] 2,229 (2000 WCD). Tawau District along the Kalabakan River. *Class:* Austronesian, Malayo-Polynesian, Northwest, North Sarawakan, Dayic, Murutic, Tidong.

Keningau Murut (Central Murut) [kxi] 7,001 (2000 WCD). Population includes 1,000 to 1,200 Dusun Murut (1985 SIL). All Murut in Sabah 34,282 (1980 census). Keningau District within a 10-mile radius to the north of Keningau town along the Pegalan River. *Class:* Austronesian, Malayo-Polynesian, Northwest, North Sarawakan, Dayic, Murutic, Murut. *Dialects:* Nabay (Nabai, Nebee, Dabay, Dabai, Rabay, Rabai), Ambual, Dusun Murut. Close to Bookan and Timugon. *Lg Use:* No one under 20 uses Nabay as first language.

Kimaragang (Kimaragan, Kimaragangan, Maragang, Marigang) [kqr] 10,000 (1987 SIL). Population includes 6,000 Tandek, 2,000 Sonsogon. Kota Marudu and Pitas districts. *Class:* Austronesian, Malayo-Polynesian, Northwest, Sabahan, Dusunic, Dusun. *Dialects:* Tandek (Garo), Pitas Kimaragang, Sandayo, Sonsogon. Dandun is somewhat different. Intelligibility of Sandayo with other dialects needs testing. *Lg Dev:* Bible portions: 1996. *Other:* Agriculturalists: paddy rice, cocoa, cash crops.

Kinabatangan, Upper [dmg] 7,856 (2000 WCD). Population includes 500 Dusun Segama and 800 to 900 Sinabu' (1985 SIL). Primarily the upper reaches of the Kinabatangan River, also Lahad Datu and Sandakan districts, Maligatan, Minusu, and Tongud. *Class:* Austronesian, Malayo-Polynesian, Northwest, Sabahan, Paitanic, Upper Kinabatangan. *Dialects:* Kalabuan (Kolobuan), Makiang, Dusun Segama (Saga-I, Soghai, Segai), Sinabu' (Sinabu). Dialects have approximately 87% intelligibility between them. Lexical similarity over 90% among all dialects, except Makiang and Sinabu' with 80%. *Lg Dev:* Bible portions: 1984–1995. *Other:* Agriculturalists; rattan gatherers; lumbermen.

Kota Marudu Talantang [grm] 1,797 (2000 WCD). Kota Marudu District, in Talantang 1 and Talantang 2. *Class:* Austronesian, Malayo-Polynesian, Northwest, Sabahan, Dusunic, Dusun. *Lg Use:* Speakers also use Kimaragang. *Other:* Agriculturalists: wet rice.

Kota Marudu Tinagas [ktr] 1,250 (1985 SIL). Southern Kota Marudu and Parong, a migrant village in northern Kota Marudu. *Class:* Austronesian, Malayo-Polynesian, Northwest, Sabahan, Dusunic, Dusun, Central.

Kuijau (Kijau, Kujau, Kwijau, Minansut, Kuliow, Kuiyow, Kuriyo, Koijoe, Menindal, Tindal, Menindaq, Tidung, Hill Dusun) [dkr] 7,910 (2000 WCD). Keningau District to the west and north of Keningau town within a 12-mile radius. *Class:* Austronesian, Malayo-Polynesian, Northwest, Sabahan, Dusunic, Dusun. *Lg Use:* Speakers also use Central Dusun.

Lobu, Lanas [ruu] 2,800 (1986 SIL). Population includes 2,000 in Lobu, 800 in Rumanau. Lobu in Keningau District near Lanas, Rumanau in Masaum, Mangkawagu, Minusu, Kinabatangan District. *Class:* Austronesian, Malayo-Polynesian, Northwest, Sabahan, Paitanic, Upper Kinabatangan. *Dialect:* Lobu, Rumanau (Rumanau Alab, Romanau, Roomarrows). *Other:* Agriculturalists.

Lobu, Tampias [low] 1,800 (1985 SIL). 3 villages in Ranau around Tampias. *Class:* Austronesian, Malayo-Polynesian, Northwest, Sabahan, Paitanic, Upper Kinabatangan. *Dialects:* High intelligibility of Upper Kinabatangan. Lexical similarity 73% with Lanas Lobu. *Lg Use:* High bilingualism in Central Dusun. *Other:* Plantation agriculturalists.

Lotud (Latod, Latud, Suang Lotud, Tuaran Dusun) [dtr] 5,000 (1985 SIL). Tuaran District, just north of Kota Kinabalu, a 10-mile radius around Tuaran town. *Class:* Austronesian, Malayo-Polynesian, Northwest, Sabahan, Dusunic, Dusun. *Lg Dev:* Bible portions: 1992. *Other:* Agriculturalists: rice.

Malay, Cocos Islands (Cocos, Kokos, Kukus) [coa] 5,443 in Malaysia (2000). Population total all countries: 6,443. Tawau and Lahad Datu. From the Cocos Islands (Keeling Islands), an Australian territory. Also spoken in Australia. *Class:* Austronesian, Malayo-Polynesian, Malayic, Malayan, Local Malay.

Malay, Sabah (Bazaar Malay, Pasar Malay) [msi] *Class:* Austronesian, Malayo-Polynesian, Malayic, Malayan, Local Malay. *Lg Use:* Trade language of Sabah. A few first-language speakers in urban areas, especially children of parents who have other first languages. Used mainly as a contact language, so it is not yet fully developed. Speakers shift to various other languages they know to fill in expressions in domains where Sabah Malay is lacking. For at least this reason, if the only form of Malay a person knows is Sabah Malay, he will have difficulty understanding Standard Malay in other domains. *Lg Dev:* Dictionary. *Other:* 'Bazaar Malay' is used to refer to many regional nonstandard varieties of Malay. SVO. Agriculturalists: wet and dry rice, rubber, fruits, vegetables; fishermen; shopkeepers; small traders.

Mapun (Sama Mapun, Jama Mapun, Cagayan de Sulu, Cagayanon, Bajau Kagayan, Orang Cagayan, Kagayan) [sjm] East coast of Sabah, concentrated in Sandakan, west coast of Sabah: Banggi, Marudu, Kudat, Kota Kinabalu. See main entry under Philippines.

Minokok [mqq] 2,000 (1981 Wurm and Hattori). Headwaters of Kinabatangan River. *Class:* Austronesian, Malayo-Polynesian, Northwest, Sabahan, Dusunic, Dusun, Central. *Dialects:* Closest to Labuk-Kinabatangan Kadazan and Kimaragang.

Molbog [pwm] Banggi Island. See main entry under Philippines.

Paluan [plz] 3,677 (2000 WCD). Population includes 3,000 Paluan, 1,000 to 2,000 Pandewan. Sabah, Tenom, Keningau, and Pensiangan districts along some tributaries of the Padas River, and along the Dalit, Keramatoi, Nabawan, Pamentarian, and Mesopo rivers, and the lower Sook River valley, and the headwaters of the Talankai and Sapulut rivers. *Class:* Austronesian, Malayo-Polynesian, Northwest, North Sarawakan, Dayic, Murutic, Murut. *Dialects:* Paluan (Peluan), Dalit Murut, Sook Murut, Takapan, Makaheeliga (Makialiga), Pandewan (Pandewan Murut). Closest to Tagal Murut. *Lg Use:* Speakers are also fluent in Tagal.

Papar (Bajau Bukit) [dpp] 1,000 (2000 WCD). Kuala Penyu District. *Class:* Austronesian, Malayo-Polynesian, Northwest, Sabahan, Dusunic, Dusun. *Lg Use:* High comprehension of Tatana. Much intermarriage with Tatana, Bisaya, Bajau, Brunei Kedayan speakers.

Rungus (Dusun Dayak, Melobong Rungus, Memagun, Memogun, Momogun, Roongas, Rungus Dusun) [drg] 15,000 (1991 UBS). Kudat, Pitas, and Labuk-Sugut districts. *Class:* Austronesian, Malayo-Polynesian, Northwest, Sabahan, Dusunic, Dusun. *Dialects:* Nulu, Gonsomon, Rungus. *Lg Dev:* Dictionary. NT: 1981.

Sama, Central (Siasi Sama, Central Sinama, Samal, Sinama) [sml] Southeastern Sabah, especially Semporna District. See main entry under Philippines.

Sama, Southern (Sama Sibutu', Southern Bajau) [ssb] 20,000 in Malaysia. East, north, and west coasts: Banggi, Kota Belud, Gaya Island, Kuala Penyu. *Dialects:* Bajau Banaran, Bajau Darat, Bajau Laut (Mandelaut, Pala'au, Sama Laut, Sama Mandelaut, Sea Bajau, Sea Gypsies), Bajau Semporna (Bajau Asli, Kubang, Sama Kubang), Laminusa (Laminusa Sinama), Sibutu (Sibutuq, Sama Sibutu, Samah-Samah, Samah Lumbuh), Simunul (Sama Simunul), Sikubung (Kubung, Sama Kubung), Sama (A'a Sama, Sama', Samah, Samal, Samar), Ubian (Obian, Sama Ubian, Tau Ubian). *Lg Use:* Speakers also use Malay, Tausug, or other Sama languages. See main entry under Philippines.

Selungai Murut [slg] 373 in Malaysia (2000 WCD). Pensiangan District, 1 village, along the Sapulut River from the confluence with the Pensiangan River south to the Indonesian border. See main entry under Indonesia (Kalimantan).

Sembakung Murut (Tinggalan, Tinggalum, Tingalun, Simbakong, Sembakoeng, Sembakong, Tidong, Tidoeng, Tidung) [sbr] 6,666 in Malaysia (2000 WCD). Population total all countries: 9,847. Along the Sembakung River in northern Kalimantan, Indonesia, from the mouth upstream possibly as far as Sabah. Also spoken in Indonesia (Kalimantan). *Class:* Austronesian, Malayo-Polynesian, Northwest, North Sarawakan, Dayic, Murutic, Tidong.

Serudung Murut (Serudong, Tawau Murut, Tidung) [srk] 1,000 (1989 SIL). Tawau District along the Serudung River and one village 12 miles from Tawau town. *Class:* Austronesian, Malayo-Polynesian, Northwest, North Sarawakan, Dayic, Murutic, Tidong.

Tagal Murut [mvv] 46,054 in Malaysia (2000 WCD). Population total all countries: 48,054. Pensiangan, Keningau, Tenom, Sipitang districts over the whole southwestern portion of Sabah, south into Kalimantan, Indonesia. Also spoken in Indonesia (Kalimantan). *Class:* Austronesian, Malayo-Polynesian, Northwest, North Sarawakan, Dayic, Murutic, Murut. *Dialects:* Rundum

(Arundum), Tagal (Taggal, Tagul, Tagol, North Borneo Murut, Sabah Murut), Sumambu (Semembu, Semambu, Sumambuq), Tolokoson (Telekoson), Sapulot Murut (Sapulut Murut), Pensiangan Murut (Pentjangan, Lagunan Murut), Salalir (Sadalir, Sedálir, Saralir), Alumbis (Lumbis, Loembis), Tawan, Tomani (Tumaniq), Maligan (Mauligan, Meligan, Bol Murut, Bole Murut). Closest to Paluan. *Lg Dev:* Literacy rate in second language: 20%. NT: 1984–1991.

Tatana (Tatana', Tatanaq) [txx] 5,500 (1982 SIL). Kuala Penyu District. *Class:* Austronesian, Malayo-Polynesian, Northwest, Sabahan, Dusunic, Bisaya.

Tausug (Taw Sug, Sulu, Suluk, Sooloo, Tausog, Taosug, Moro, Joloano, Joloano Sulu) [tsg] 110,000 in Malaysia (1982 SIL). Sempurna, Sandakan, Tawau, Lahad Datu, Labuk-Sugut, Kudat districts. *Other:* Immigrants from the Sulu Archipelago in the Philippines. Known as 'Suluk' in Sabah. Agriculturalists: dry and wet rice, maize, millet, cassava, yam, bananas, fruit, coconuts; fishermen; animal husbandry: goats, cattle, water buffaloes, poultry. See main entry under Philippines.

Tebilung (Tabilong, Tobilang, Tobilung) [tgb] 2,000 (1984 SIL). Kota Marudu District, on the road from Kota Belud to Kudat, and in Kota Belud. *Class:* Austronesian, Malayo-Polynesian, Northwest, Sabahan, Dusunic, Dusun. *Dialects:* Low intelligibility of Central Kadazan, Kimaragang.

Tidong (Camucones, Nonukan, Tedong, Tidoeng, Tiran, Tirones, Tiroon, Zedong) [tid] 9,800 in Malaysia (1982 SIL). Sabah, Labuk-Sugut, Sandakan, and Tawau districts. Population center is along northeast coast of Kalimantan, Indonesia. *Dialects:* Tarakan (Terakan), Sesayap (Sesajap). See main entry under Indonesia (Kalimantan).

Timugon Murut (Timugon, Timogun, Timigan, Timigun, Timogon, Tumugun, Tenom Murut) [tih] 12,098 (2000 WCD). Population includes 1,200 to 1,700 in Beaufort Murut (1982 SIL). Tenom District along the Padas River from Melalap to Batu, and Beaufort District along the Bukau and lower Padas rivers. *Class:* Austronesian, Malayo-Polynesian, Northwest, North Sarawakan, Dayic, Murutic, Murut. *Dialects:* Kapagalan, Poros, Beaufort Murut (Binta'), Timugon, Sandiwar (Sandewar), Dabugus, Lower Murut, Murut Padas, Bukau (Bukow). *Lg Dev:* NT: 1998.

Tombonuwo (Tombonuo, Tombonuva, Tambanuo, Tambanua, Tambanuva, Tambanwas, Tambenua, Tambunwas, Tembenua, Tunbumohas, Tumbunwha, Paitan, Sungai, Sungei, Lobu) [txa] 20,000 (1991 UBS). Population includes 3,000 Lingkabau. Labuk-Sugut, Kota Marudu, and Pitas districts. *Class:* Austronesian, Malayo-Polynesian, Northwest, Sabahan, Paitanic. *Dialect:* Lingkabau Sugut (Linkabau). *Lg Dev:* NT: 2002.

Wolio (Buton, Butung, Butonese) [wlo] *Other:* The name 'Buton' is often used generically outside southeast Sulawesi for people from southeast Sulawesi, or is confused with Bajau people as sailors. The varieties spoken in Sabah may be Cia-Cia, Tukang Besi, Indonesian Bajau, or some other. See main entry under Indonesia (Sulawesi).

Yakan (Yacan) [yka] 10,787 in Malaysia (2000 WCD). *Other:* Mainly temporary workers. See main entry under Philippines.

Malaysia (Sarawak)

Malaysia (Sarawak). 1,294,000 (1979). Information mainly from A. A. Cense and E. M. Uhlenbeck 1958; R. Blust 1974; P. Sercombe 1997. The number of languages listed for Malaysia (Sarawak) is 47. Of those, 46 are living languages and 1 is extinct.

Balau (Bala'u) [blg] 5,000 (1981 Wurm and Hattori). Southwest Sarawak, southeast of Simunjan. *Class:*

Austronesian, Malayo-Polynesian, Malayic, Malayic-Dayak, Ibanic.

Berawan [lod] 870 (1981 Wurm and Hattori). Tutoh and Baram rivers in the north. *Class:* Austronesian, Malayo-Polynesian, Northwest, North Sarawakan, Berawan-Lower Baram, Berawan. *Dialects:* Batu Bla (Batu Belah), Long Pata, Long Jegan, West Berawan, Long Terawan. It may be two languages: West Berawan and Long Terawan, versus East-Central Berawang: Batu Belah, Long Teru, and Long Jegan (Blust 1974).

Biatah (Kuap, Quop, Bikuab, Sentah) [bth] 21,219 in Malaysia (2000 WCD). Population total all countries: 29,703. Sarawak, 1st Division, Kuching District, 10 villages. Also spoken in Indonesia (Kalimantan). *Class:* Austronesian, Malayo-Polynesian, Land Dayak. *Dialects:* Siburan, Stang (Sitaang, Bisitaang), Tibia. Speakers cannot understand Bukar Sadong, Silakau, or Bidayuh from Indonesia. Lexical similarity 71% with Singgi. *Lg Use:* Siburan is the prestige dialect. *Lg Dev:* Literacy rate in second language: 45%. Radio programs. NT: 1963–2003. *Other:* 'Bidayuh' is a cover term for all Sarawak Land Dayak groups, plus Selako. 'Siburan' is the speakers' name for themselves. Agriculturalists: sago, wet rice, vegetables, fruit, rubber, pepper; animal husbandry: pigs, poultry; government employees.

Bintulu [bny] 4,200 (1981 Wurm and Hattori). Northeast coast around Sibuti, west of Niah, around Bintulu, and two enclaves west. *Class:* Austronesian, Malayo-Polynesian, Northwest, North Sarawakan, Bintulu. *Dialects:* Could also be classified as a Baram-Tinjar Subgroup or as an isolate within the Rejang-Baram Group. Blust classifies as an isolate with North Sarawakan. Not close to other languages. *Other:* Coastal.

Bisaya, Sarawak (Bisayah, Bisaya Bukit, Visayak, Bekiau, Lorang Bukit) [bsd] 7,000 (1984 SIL). Southeast of Marudi, 5th Division. *Class:* Austronesian, Malayo-Polynesian, Northwest, Sabahan, Dusunic, Bisaya, Southern. *Dialects:* Lower Bisaya, Mid Bisaya, Upper Bisaya. Lexical similarity 58% with Sabah Bisaya, 78% to 79% with Brunei Bisaya, and lower with other Dusunic languages. *Lg Dev:* Radio programs. Bible portions: 1938. *Other:* Agriculturalists: hill and wet rice, fruit, vegetables, rubber; sago palm; animal husbandry: water buffalo; fishermen.

Bukar Sadong (Sadong, Buka, Bukar, Tebakang, Serian, Sabutan, Seputan, Saputan) [sdo] 34,600 in Malaysia (1981 Wurm and Hattori). Serian 1st Division, Sarawak, 30 or more villages. Also spoken in Indonesia (Kalimantan). *Class:* Austronesian, Malayo-Polynesian, Land Dayak. *Dialects:* Bukar Bidayuh (Bidayuh, Bidayah, Bideyu), Bukar Sadong, Mentuh Tapuh. Lexical similarity 86% with Kereho, 80% with Aoheng, 75% with Hovongan, 57% with Bahasa Malaysia. *Lg Dev:* Radio programs.

Bukitan (Bakitan, Bakatan, Beketan, Mangkettan, Manketa, Pakatan) [bkn] 289 in Malaysia (2000 WCD). Kapit, 7th Division. See main entry under Indonesia (Kalimantan).

Daro-Matu [dro] 7,600 (1981 Wurm and Hattori). Population includes 4,800 Matu, 2,800 Daro. Matu River from north channel of Rejang River to the sea, around Daro and Matu. *Class:* Austronesian, Malayo-Polynesian, Northwest, Melanau-Kajang, Melanau. *Dialects:* Daro, Matu.

Iban (Sea Dayak) [iba] 400,000 in Malaysia (1995 Martin). Population total all countries: 415,000. From Sadong River north to Bintulu, Sibu, one village in Tawau District of Sabah. Also spoken in Brunei, Indonesia (Kalimantan). *Class:* Austronesian, Malayo-Polynesian, Malayic, Malayic-Dayak, Ibanic. *Dialects:* Batang Lupar, Bugau, Skrang, Dau, Lemanak, Ulu Ai, Undup. Dialect of Second Division is the norm for literature. *Lg Use:* 600,000 second-language speakers. *Lg Dev:* Iban taught in some primary schools. Radio programs. Dictionary. Grammar.

Bible: 1988. *Other:* Largest language group in Sarawak. SVO. Agriculturalists: dry and wet rice, fruit, rubber; fishermen.

Jagoi (Sarawak Dayak, Jaggoi, Bau-Jagoi) [sne] 19,000 (1981 Wurm and Hattori). Bau, 1st Division, Sadong, Samarahan and Lundu rivers, about 50 villages. *Class:* Austronesian, Malayo-Polynesian, Land Dayak. *Dialects:* Grogo (Grogoh), Stenggang Jagoi, Krokong, Gumbang, Serambau (Serambu, Serambo), Empawa, Assem, Singge (Singgai, Singgi, Singgie, Singhi, Bisingai), Suti, Tengoh, Dongay, Taup (Tahup). Gumbang may not be a Jagoi dialect, but closer to Tringus. Related to Tringus. Lexical similarity 69% with Bukar Sadong, 53% between Bukar Sadong and Singgai. *Lg Dev:* Radio programs.

Kajaman (Kayaman, Kejaman) [kag] 500 (1981 Wurm and Hattori). Near Belaga on the Baloi River in central Sarawak, 7th Division. *Class:* Austronesian, Malayo-Polynesian, Northwest, Melanau-Kajang, Kajang. *Lg Use:* Limited comprehension of Iban.

Kanowit [kxn] 100 (2000 Wurm). Middle Rejang River, below Tanjong language, 3rd Division. *Class:* Austronesian, Malayo-Polynesian, Northwest, Melanau-Kajang, Melanau. *Lg Use:* 20% to 60% of the ethnic group speaks Kanowit. Used in the home. Few or no children speak Kanowit. People negative or neutral toward Kanowit. Being absorbed by Iban.

Kayan, Baram (Baram Kajan) [kys] 4,150 (1981 Wurm and Hattori). Baram River area, Upper Sarawak. Not in Brunei. *Class:* Austronesian, Malayo-Polynesian, Kayan-Murik, Kayan. *Dialects:* Long Atip, Long Akahsemuka. *Lg Use:* Trade language. *Lg Dev:* Bible: 1990. *Other:* Agriculturalists: wet and dry rice, sweet potatoes, bananas, tobacco, sugarcane, maize, rubber; hunters; fishermen; rattan sellers; beeswax; camphor.

Kayan, Murik [mxr] 1,120 (1981 Wurm and Hattori). Below Long Miri (Banyuq) and below Lio Mato (Semiang) on the Baram River. *Class:* Austronesian, Malayo-Polynesian, Kayan-Murik, Murik. *Dialects:* Long Banyuq (Banyuq), Long Semiang (Semiang). Not closely related to other languages.

Kayan, Rejang (Rejang Kajan) [ree] 3,030 (1981 Wurm and Hattori). Rejang, Balui river areas. *Class:* Austronesian, Malayo-Polynesian, Kayan-Murik, Kayan. *Dialects:* Ma'aging, Long Badan, Uma Daro, Long Kehobo (Uma Poh), Uma Juman, Long Murun, Long Geng, Lemena, Lisum. Limited comprehension of Baram Kayan. *Other:* Different from Rejang in Sumatra.

Kelabit (Kalabit, Kerabit) [kzi] 1,111 in Malaysia (2000 WCD). Population total all countries: 1,747. Northern Sarawak, in the remotest and highest of Borneo mountains. Also spoken in Indonesia (Kalimantan). *Class:* Austronesian, Malayo-Polynesian, Northwest, North Sarawakan, Dayic, Kelabitic. *Dialects:* Brung, Libbung, Lepu Potong, Bario, Lon Bangag. Long Napir, Long Seridan, Pa'Dalih, Long Leilang, Bruang may also be dialects (Blust 1974). *Lg Dev:* Bible portions: 1965. *Other:* Speakers strongly independent. Agriculturalists: paddy and hill rice, maize, tapioca, pineapple, pumpkin, cucumber, beans, fruits; hunters; fishermen.

Kenyah, Bakung (Bakung, Bakong, Bakung Kenya) [boc] South central, near Kalimantan border. *Dialect:* Oga Bakung. See main entry under Indonesia (Kalimantan).

Kenyah, Sebob (Sibop, Sebop, Sebob, Sabup, Sambup) [sib] 1,730 (1981 Wurm and Hattori). On the upper Tinjar River in northern Sarawak, 4th Division, between the Rejang and Baram rivers, several large villages. *Class:* Austronesian, Malayo-Polynesian, Northwest, North Sarawakan, Kenyah, Sebob. *Dialects:* Tinjar Sibop, Lirong, Long Pokun, Bah Malei (Ba Mali), Long Atun, Long Ekang (Long Ikang), Long Luyang. Not closely related to other languages.

Kenyah, Tutoh (Tutoh Kenya) [ttw] 600 (1981 Wurm and Hattori). Northeast, Tutoh River. *Class:* Austronesian, Malayo-Polynesian, Northwest, North Sarawakan, Kenyah. *Dialects:* Long Wat, Long Labid, Lugat. Not closely related to other languages.

Kenyah, Upper Baram (Upper Baram Kenja, Kenja, Kenyah, Kinjin, Kindjin, Kanyay) [ubm] 2,222 in Malaysia (2000 WCD). Population total all countries: 2,858. Upper Baram River near the Kalimantan border. Not in Brunei. Also spoken in Indonesia (Kalimantan). *Class:* Austronesian, Malayo-Polynesian, Northwest, North Sarawakan, Kenyah, Main Kenyah. *Dialects:* Long Anap may be a dialect (Blust 1974).

Kenyah, Western (Western Kenya, Kenja, Kinjin, Kindjin, Kanyay) [xky] 1,250 (1981 Wurm and Hattori). Balui, Belaga, Kalua, and Kemena rivers. *Class:* Austronesian, Malayo-Polynesian, Northwest, North Sarawakan, Kenyah, Main Kenyah. *Dialects:* Long Bangan, Kemena Penan, Kakus Penan, Uma Bakah (Long Bulan), Lunan. Madang may be a dialect. Lexical similarity 80% between Madang and Lepu Kulit. *Other:* Agriculturalists: wet and dry rice, sweet potatoes, bananas, tobacco, sugarcane, maize, rubber; hunters; fishermen.

Kiput [kyi] 2,460 (1981 Wurm and Hattori). Northeast around Marudi. Not in Brunei. *Class:* Austronesian, Malayo-Polynesian, Northwest, North Sarawakan, Berawan-Lower Baram, Lower Baram, Central, A. *Dialects:* Long Kiput, Long Tutoh (Kuala Tutoh), Lemiting. Related to Narom, Lelak, Tutong 2, Belait, Berawan.

Lahanan (Lanun, Lanan) [lhn] 350 (1981 Wurm and Hattori). Central, east of Belaga, southwest of Long Murum. *Class:* Austronesian, Malayo-Polynesian, Northwest, Melanau-Kajang, Kajang. *Dialects:* Closest to Kayaman. *Other:* Not the same as Illanun of Sabah or Iranun of the Philippines.

Lara' (Luru) [lra] 11,331 in Malaysia (2000 WCD). Population total all countries: 19,603. Two small villages on Pasir River, Lundu, 1st Division. Also spoken in Indonesia (Kalimantan). *Class:* Austronesian, Malayo-Polynesian, Land Dayak. *Dialects:* Related to Bukar-Sadong.

Lelak [llk] 220 (1981 Wurm and Hattori). Northeast, east of Sibuti (Dali) and the Tinjar River (Lelak). *Class:* Austronesian, Malayo-Polynesian, Northwest, North Sarawakan, Berawan-Lower Baram, Lower Baram, Central, B. *Dialects:* Lelak, Dali. Related to Narom, Kiput, Tutong 2, Berawan. *Lg Use:* They may now speak only Belait.

Lundayeh (Lun Dayah, Lun Daye, Lun Dayeh, Lun Daya, Lun Dayoh, Lundaya, Lun Lod, Southern Murut) [lnd] 12,800 in Malaysia (1982 SIL). Population includes 10,000 in Lun Bawang dialect in Sarawak (1987), 2,800 in Lun Daye in Sabah. Southwestern border of Sabah and Sarawak. *Dialects:* Lun Bawang (Sarawak Murut), Lun Dayah, Adang, Balait (Tabun, Treng), Kolur, Padas, Trusan (Lawas, Limbang), Lepu Potong. *Other:* Not Murutic, although sometimes called Southern Murut. Agriculturalists: wet and dry rice, coffee, sugarcane, maize, cucumber, pumpkin, tapioca, coconut, banana, pomelo, papaya, durian, mango; animal husbandry: poultry, pigs, buffaloes; hunters; fishermen. See main entry under Indonesia (Kalimantan).

Madang (Badang, Medang, Malang, Lepo Tau Kenyah, Lepo Tau Kenya, Lepu Tau) [mqd] 2,222 (2000 WCD). Tinjar River, 4th Division. *Class:* Austronesian, Malayo-Polynesian, Northwest, North Sarawakan, Kenyah, Sebob. *Lg Dev:* Literacy rate in second language: 25%. NT: 1978.

Melanau (Milanau, Milano, Belana'u) [mel] 29,899 in Malaysia (2000 WCD). Population total all countries: 30,099. Coastal area of the Rejang delta up to the Balingian River, 3rd Division. Also spoken in Brunei. *Class:* Austronesian, Malayo-Polynesian, Northwest,

Melanau-Kajang, Melanau. *Dialects:* Mukah-Oya (Mukah, Muka, Oya, Oya', Oga), Balingian, Bruit, Dalat (Dalad), Igan, Sarikei, Segahan, Prehan, Segalang, Siteng. *Lg Use:* Speakers also use Malay. *Lg Dev:* Literacy rate in second language: 52%. *Other:* Tropical forest. Agriculturalists: sago, rice, coconut, rubber; fishermen; lumbermen; animal husbandry: poultry, goats, water buffaloes; traders with Iban.

Narom (Narum) [nrm] 2,420 (1981 Wurm and Hattori). South of the mouth of the Baram River around Miri and to the south. *Class:* Austronesian, Malayo-Polynesian, Northwest, North Sarawakan, Berawan-Lower Baram, Lower Baram, Central, B. *Dialects:* Narom, Miri.

Okolod (Kolour, Kolur, Kolod, Okolod Murut) [kqv] 1,578 in Malaysia (2000 WCD). Population includes 1,000 in Sarawak, 100 to 200 in Sabah. Sabah southwest of Tenom and Sipitang districts on some of the plantation estates and some along the headwaters of the Padas River. Primarily in Sarawak and Kalimantan, Indonesia. See main entry under Indonesia (Kalimantan).

Penan, Eastern ("Punan") [pez] 2,100 in Malaysia (2004). East of the Baram River, Apoh River District. Also spoken in Brunei. *Class:* Austronesian, Malayo-Polynesian, Punan-Nibong. *Dialect:* Penan Apoh. Related to Western Penan and Kenyah, but not inherently intelligible to each other's speakers.

Penan, Western (Nibong, Nibon, "Punan") [pne] 9,000 in Malaysia (1988 Lian). Population total all countries: 9,050. Upper Baram and Balui rivers around Mt. Dulit, 3 villages, 4th to 7th divisions, and Nibong branch of the Lobong River, a tributary of the Tinjar River. Also spoken in Brunei. *Class:* Austronesian, Malayo-Polynesian, Punan-Nibong. *Dialects:* Nibong, Bok Penan (Bok), Penan Silat, Penan Gang (Gang), Penan Lusong (Lusong), Penan Apo, Sipeng (Speng), Penan Lanying, Jelalong Penan. Not closely related to other languages. *Lg Dev:* NT: 1974. *Other:* Traditionalists are nomadic and seminomadic. Tropical forest. Agriculturalists; hunter-gatherers.

Punan Bah-Biau [pna] 450 (1981 Wurm and Hattori). Central, around Merit, Rejang River, 7th Division. *Class:* Austronesian, Malayo-Polynesian, Northwest, Rejang-Sajau. *Dialects:* Punan Bah (Punan Ba), Punan Biau. *Other:* Nomadic. They get salt from the Kayan. Hunter-gatherers.

Punan Batu 1 [pnm] 30 (2000 Wurm). Central, west of Long Geng, southeast of Belaga. *Class:* Austronesian, Malayo-Polynesian, Northwest, Melanau-Kajang, Kajang. *Other:* Different from Punan Batu 2, a dialect of Sajau Basap in Kalimantan. Nomadic. They get salt from the Kayan. Hunter-gatherers. Nearly extinct.

Remun (Milikin, Millikin) [lkj] 3,500 (2000 SIL). Serian District, Kuching Division, 13 villages southeast of Serian to Balai Ringin. *Class:* Austronesian, Malayo-Polynesian, Malayic, Malayic-Dayak, Ibanic. *Lg Use:* All ages. Attitudes toward Iban and Malay go from indifferent to unfriendly. Strong sense of identity centered around the Remun isolect. Speakers also use Iban, Sawawak Malay, Bahasa Malaysia, English, Bidayuh. *Other:* The people's name for their language is 'Remun', and for themselves is 'Remun Iban'.

Sa'ban [snv] 1,111 in Malaysia (2000 WCD). Population total all countries: 1,959. Northeast on the Kalimantan border, northeast of Ramudu, Upper Baram, 4th Division, including Long Banga'. Also spoken in Indonesia (Kalimantan). *Class:* Austronesian, Malayo-Polynesian, Northwest, North Sarawakan, Dayic, Kelabitic. *Lg Dev:* Bible portions: 1969.

Sebuyau (Sibuyau, Sabuyau, Sibuian, Sibuyan, Sabuyan) [snb] 9,000 (1981 Wurm and Hattori). Lundu, 1st Division, mouth of the Lupa River, west bank around

Sebuyau. *Class:* Austronesian, Malayo-Polynesian, Malayic, Malayic-Dayak, Ibanic.

Sekapan (Sekepan) [skp] 750 (1981 Wurm and Hattori). Belaga, 7th Division. *Class:* Austronesian, Malayo-Polynesian, Northwest, Melanau-Kajang, Kajang.

Selako (Selakau, Salakau, Silakau) [skl] 3,800 in Malaysia (1981 Wurm and Hattori). Saak, Lundu, 1st Division, 22 villages. *Lg Use:* Gradually being adopted by the younger speakers of Lara'. See main entry under Indonesia (Kalimantan).

Seru [szd] Extinct. Kabong, 2nd Division. *Class:* Austronesian, Malayo-Polynesian, Northwest, Melanau-Kajang, Melanau.

Sian (Sihan) [spg] 50 (2000 Wurm). Belaga, 7th Division. *Class:* Austronesian, Malayo-Polynesian, Northwest, Melanau-Kajang, Kajang. *Dialects:* May be intelligible with Bukitan, Ukit, Punan Batu 1.

Sibu (Siduan, Siduani, Seduan-Banyok) [sdx] 420 (1981 Wurm and Hattori). Sibu, 3rd Division, Rejang River. *Class:* Austronesian, Malayo-Polynesian, Northwest, Melanau-Kajang, Melanau. *Dialects:* Seduan, Banyok. May be intelligible with Melanau.

Tanjong [tnj] 100 (1981 Wurm and Hattori). Rejang River above the Kanowit language area, below Song village, Kapit, 7th Division. *Class:* Austronesian, Malayo-Polynesian, Northwest, Melanau-Kajang, Melanau.

Tring [tgq] 551 (2000 WCD). Long Terawan village, lower Tutoh River. *Class:* Austronesian, Malayo-Polynesian, Northwest, North Sarawakan, Dayic, Kelabitic. *Other:* Not the same as Tringgus.

Tringgus (Tringus) [trx] 350 in Malaysia (1981 Wurm and Hattori). Southwest of Kuching, south of the Jagoi, on the Kalimantan border. Also spoken in Indonesia. *Class:* Austronesian, Malayo-Polynesian, Land Dayak. *Dialect:* Tringgus, Mbaan (Sembaan, Bimbaan). Each dialect has a few villages. Closer to Biatah than to Jagoi. Gumbang may be a Tringgus dialect rather than a Jagoi dialect. *Other:* A different language from Tring.

Tutong 1 [ttx] 10,000 in Malaysia. Along the lower Limbang River. *Other:* Distinct from Tutong 2 in Baram-Tinjar Subgroup. May not be in Sarawak. See main entry under Brunei.

Ukit [umi] 120 (1981 Wurm and Hattori). Upper Rajom and Tatau rivers, Baleh, 7th Division. *Class:* Austronesian, Malayo-Polynesian, Northwest, Melanau-Kajang, Kajang. *Other:* Different from the Punan Ukit dialect of Bukitan.

Maldives

Republic of Maldives. 339,330. National or official language: Maldivian. 1,200 islands; 203 inhabited. Literacy rate: 93% to 95.4%. Also includes Sinhala (1,400), Arabic (300), people from India (1,000). Information mainly from J. Gair 1980. Deaf population: 15,278. The number of languages listed for Maldives is 1.

Maldivian (Malikh, Mahl, Malki, Divehi, Divehli, Divehi Bas) [div] 282,696 in Maldives (2000 WCD). Population total all countries: 287,196. Throughout the country. Also spoken in India. *Class:* Indo-European, Indo-Iranian, Indo-Aryan, Sinhalese-Maldivian. *Dialects:* Extensive dialect variation. Some dialects may not be mutually intelligible with each other. *Lg Use:* National language. Speakers also use Arabic or English. English is the medium of education in most schools. *Lg Dev:* Literacy rate in second language: 98%. Thaana script. *Other:* Coral island. Tropical forest. Sea level. Fishermen; tourist industry. Muslim (Sunni), traditional religion.

Mongolia

Mongolian People's Republic, Bügd Nayramdakh Mongol Ard Uls. 2,751,314. National or official language: Halh Mongolian. Literacy rate: 89% to 90%. Also includes Japanese, Korean. Information mainly from T. Sebeok 1967; N. Poppe 1970. Blind population: 10,000 to 40,000 visually handicapped (1997). Deaf population: 10,000 to 147,330. The number of languages listed for Mongolia is 13. Of those, all are living languages.

Buriat, Mongolia (Buryat, Buriat-Mongolian, Northern Mongolian, Mongolian Buriat, Bur:aad) [bxm] 64,900 (1995). Northeast, especially bordering Buryat ASSR. *Class:* Altaic, Mongolian, Eastern, Oirat-Khalkha, Khalkha-Buriat, Buriat. *Dialects:* Khori, Aga. Buriat in Mongolia is a variety of Khori and differs considerably from Buriat of China and Russia. The language has been influenced by Standard (Halh) Mongolian. *Lg Use:* Halh Mongolian is used as a literary language. *Lg Dev:* Literacy rate in second language: High in Halh. *Other:* There are some books in Buriat. Not a literary language in Mongolia. Traditional religion, Buddhist (Lamaist).

Chinese, Mandarin (Hoton, Qotong, Hui-Zu, Hui, Xui, Northern Chinese, Mandarin, Hytad) [cmn] 35,000 in Mongolia (1993 Johnstone). Population includes 2,000 Qotong. Northwestern Mongolia, Uvs Aimag. *Lg Use:* Speakers also use Halh or Mongolian. *Lg Dev:* Literacy rate in second language: high in Halh, or Mandarin. *Other:* Traditional religion, Maoist, Confucianist, Muslim. See main entry under China.

Darkhat [drh] 20,350 (2000). Hövsgöl Aimag, north Mongolia, around Lake Khubsugul. *Class:* Altaic, Mongolian, Eastern, Oirat-Khalkha, Oirat-Kalmyk-Darkhat. *Lg Use:* Speakers are fully bilingual in Halh Mongolian. *Lg Dev:* Literacy rate in second language: High in Halh. *Other:* One of the Oirat peoples. Influences from Oirat and possibly the Buriat languages. Distinct from Darkhan, which refers to southern Khalkha people in Ulanchab League, Inner Mongolia, China, and to Khorchin people in eastern Inner Mongolia.

Daur (Dagur, Daguor, Dawar, Dawo'er, Tahur, Tahuerh) [dta] *Dialects:* Buteha (Bataxan), Haila'er (Hailar), Qiqiha'er (Qiqihar, Tsitsikhar). See main entry under China.

Evenki (Khamnigan, Tungus, Solon) [evn] 1,000 in Mongolia (1995 M. Krauss). Selenge Aimag, north Mongolia. *Lg Use:* Speakers also use Halh Mongolian. *Other:* Shamanist, Buddhist (Lamaist). See main entry under China.

Kalmyk-Oirat (Oirat, Western Mongol) [xal] 205,500 in Mongolia. Population includes 139,000 Oirat, 55,100 Dorbot, 11,400 Torgut. *Dialects:* Jakhachin, Bayit, Mingat, Olot (Ööld, Elyut, Eleuth), Khoshut (Khoshuud), Uriankhai, Khoton (Hoton). *Other:* Khoton (Hoton) were originally of Turkic origin (G. Kara). They were once Muslim. Different from the Chinese-speaking Qotong (Hoton). See main entry under Russia (Europe).

Kazakh (Kazakhi, Qazaq, Qazaqi, Kazax, Kaisak, Kosach) [kaz] 182,000 in Mongolia (2001 Johnstone and Mandryk). Bayan-Olgiy Aimag, northwest Mongolia, mining communities east of the capital, and in far east around Choibalsan. *Other:* Traditional religion, Muslim. See main entry under Kazakhstan.

Mongolian Sign Language [msr] Unknown number of users out of 10,000 to 147,330 deaf (1998). *Class:* Deaf sign language. *Other:* Different from Russian Sign Language and other sign languages.

Mongolian, Halh (Halh, Khalkha Mongolian, Mongol, Central Mongolian) [khk] 2,329,000 in Mongolia (1995).

Population includes 32,300 Dariganga. Population total all countries: 2,337,095. Buryat ASSR of Russia and Issyk-Kul Oblast of Kyrgyzstan. Also spoken in Kyrgyzstan, Russia (Asia), Taiwan. *Class:* Altaic, Mongolian, Eastern, Oirat-Khalkha, Khalkha-Buriat, Mongolian Proper. *Dialects:* Halh (Khalkha), Dariganga, Khotogoit, Sartul, Tsongol. *Lg Use:* National language. Ethnic Zahchin (Dzakhachin, Jakhachin, 24,700 or 1.3%), Mingat (possibly 4,000; 1984), Bayad (Bayit, Bait, 39,900 or 2.1%), Oold (Oolet, Olot, 11,400 or .6%) are bilingual in Halh Mongolian. *Lg Dev:* Ethnic Zahchin, Mingat, Bayad, Oold are literate in Halh. Cyrillic script. NT: 1990. *Other:* Traditionally pastoralists, now many industrial workers.

Mongolian, Peripheral (Southern-Eastern Mongolian) [mvf] *Dialects:* Ujumchin (Uzemchin, Ujumuchin), Jostu (Kharchin, Kharachin), Tumut (Tumet), Jirim (Khorchin), Urat, Ordos. *Lg Use:* Speakers also use Halh Mongolian. *Lg Dev:* Literacy rate in second language: In Halh Mongolian. See main entry under China.

Russian (Russki) [rus] 4,000 in Mongolia (1993 Johnstone). *Other:* Russians who are permanent residents are called 'Mectny Oros'. Widely taught in schools and for higher education. Atheist. See main entry under Russia (Europe).

Tuvin (Uriankhai, Uryankhai-Monchak, Tuvinian, Tuva, Tuba, Tannu-Tuva, Soyon, Soyod, Soyot, Tuvan, Tuvia, Diba, Kök, Mungak, Tuva-Uriankhai, Tuwa-Uriankhai) [tyv] 27,000 in Mongolia (1993 Johnstone). Hövsgöl and Hovd Aimags, north and west Mongolia. *Dialects:* Kokchulutan, Khöwsögöl Uigur. *Lg Use:* Speakers also use Halh Mongolian. *Lg Dev:* Literacy rate in second language: In Halh Mongolian. *Other:* Buddhist. See main entry under Russia (Asia).

Uyghur (Uygur, Uighur, Uigur, Uighuir, Uiguir) [uig] 1,000 in Mongolia (1982). Hövsgöl Aimag, north Mongolia. *Lg Dev:* Literacy is in Halh in Mongolia; the Uyghur are generally assimilated to Halh culture. *Other:* Muslim (Sunni). See main entry under China.

Myanmar

Union of Myanmar, Pyeidaungzu Myanma Naingngandaw. Formerly Burma. 42,720,196. Speakers of Tibeto-Burman languages: 28,877,000 or 78% of the population, Daic languages 2,778,900 or 9.6%, Austro-Asiatic languages 1,934,900 or 6.7%, Hmong-Mien languages 6,000 (1991 J. Matisoff). National or official language: Burmese. Literacy rate: 66% to 78%; 78.5% over 15 years old (1991). Also includes Eastern Tamang, Geman Deng, Iu Mien, Malay (21,000), Sylheti, Chinese (1,015,000), people from Bangladesh and India (500,000). Information mainly from F. Lebar, G. Hickey, J. Musgrave 1964; A. Hale 1982; B. Comrie 1987; R. B. Jones 1988; J. Matisoff et al. 1996; D. Bradley 1997; R. Burling ms. (1998). Blind population: 214,440. Deaf population: 2,684,514. Deaf institutions: 1. The number of languages listed for Myanmar is 109. Of those, 108 are living languages and 1 is extinct.

Achang (Anchan, Chung, Atsang, Acang, Ngac'ang, Ngachang, Ngochang, Mönghsa, Tai Sa') [acn] 1,700 in Myanmar (1983). West of the Irrawaddy River in Katha District, near Banmauk, scattered among the Lashi. Along the China border. *Dialect:* Maingtha. *Lg Use:* Also spoken by the Tai Sa blacksmiths among the northern Shan. *Lg Dev:* Literacy rate in first language: below 1%. Literacy rate in second language: 5% to 15%. *Other:* Their own name is Ngochang, the Burmese name Maingtha, the Chinese name Achang. Not a literary language. Polytheist, Buddhist (Hinayana). See main entry under China.

Akha (Kaw, Ekaw, Ko, Aka, Ikaw, Ak'a, Ahka, Khako, Kha Ko, Khao Kha Ko, Ikor, Aini, Yani) [ahk] 200,000 in

Myanmar (1991 UBS). Population total all countries: 449,261. Eastern part of Kengtung Shan State. Also spoken in China, Laos, Thailand, Viet Nam. *Class:* Sino-Tibetan, Tibeto-Burman, Lolo-Burmese, Loloish, Southern, Akha, Hani, Ha-Ya. *Dialects:* Ako, Asong. *Lg Dev:* Dictionary. Bible: 2001. *Other:* SOV. Traditional religion, Christian, Buddhist.

Anal (Namfau) [anm] Also possibly in Bangladesh. See main entry under India.

Anu [anl] 700. *Class:* Sino-Tibetan, Tibeto-Burman, Unclassified. *Other:* May be the same as Anal, Nung of Rawang, or some other language. SOV.

Arakanese (Maghi, Morma, Yakan, Yakhaing, Rakhain, Mogh, Magh, Marma, Mash, Rakhine) [mhv] 730,000 in Myanmar (2001 Johnstone and Mandryk). Population total all countries: 954,000. Southwest, Arakan Province. Also possibly in China. Also spoken in Bangladesh, India. *Class:* Sino-Tibetan, Tibeto-Burman, Lolo-Burmese, Burmish, Southern. *Dialects:* One of the better known varieties of nonstandard Burmese with profound pronunciation and vocabulary differences from Burmese. *Lg Dev:* Burmese script in India. Bible portions: 1914. *Other:* The people wear Burmese dress. SOV. Buddhist, Muslim, Hindu.

Blang (Bulang, Pulang, Pula, Kawa, K'ala, Plang, Kontoi) [blr] 12,000 in Myanmar (1994). Eastern Shan State, Mong Yang area, and Kengtung. *Other:* Some are becoming urbanized in Myanmar, Thailand, and China. An official nationality in China. Agriculturalists. Buddhist (Hinayana), Christian. See main entry under China.

Burmese (Bama, Bamachaka, Myen, Myanmar) [mya] 32,000,000 in Myanmar (2000 D. Bradley). Population total all countries: 32,301,581. South, central, and adjacent areas. Also spoken in Bangladesh, Malaysia, Thailand, USA. *Class:* Sino-Tibetan, Tibeto-Burman, Lolo-Burmese, Burmish, Southern. *Dialects:* Merguese (Mergui, Beik), Yaw, Danu (Taruw), Burmese, Palaw. There are diglossic high and low varieties. The preferred variety is spoken in Mandalay. Merguese (250,000 speakers), Danu (100,000 speakers), and Yaw (20,000) may be separate languages. They are distinct varieties (1997 D. Bradley). Speakers in Bangladesh speak Bomang, not Standard Burmese. *Lg Use:* National language. 10 million second-language speakers. Many Mon and some Shan are monolingual in Burmese. Native speakers of Burmese seldom speak a second indigenous language. If they have one, it is usually English. *Lg Dev:* Burmese script. Bible: 1835. *Other:* Burmese dominates the nation's publishing production. Myanma is the largest ethnic group; another is Baramagyi (Barua). Educated speech has many Pali borrowings. The Rawang people call them 'Myen'. SOV. Alluvial plains. Scrub forest. Sea level and higher. Peasant agriculturalists; fishermen; craftsmen; industrialists. Buddhist.

Chak [ckh] 20,000 in Myanmar (2002). Population total all countries: 25,500. Most in Arakan Blue Mountains, Myanmar. Also spoken in Bangladesh. *Class:* Unclassified. *Other:* Distinct from Chakma. Tropical forest. Agriculturalists. Traditional religion.

Chaungtha [ccq] 121,700 (1983). *Class:* Sino-Tibetan, Tibeto-Burman, Lolo-Burmese, Burmish, Southern. *Dialects:* Related to Burmese. *Other:* Their name means 'People of the valley', or 'People of the stream'. SOV.

Chin, Asho (Qin, Asho, Ashu, Shoa, Sho, Khyang, Kyang) [csh] 10,000 in Myanmar (1991 UBS). Population total all countries: 11,422. Irrawaddy River, lowlands. Also spoken in Bangladesh. *Class:* Sino-Tibetan, Tibeto-Burman, Kuki-Chin-Naga, Kuki-Chin, Southern, Sho. *Dialects:* Thayetmyo (Thayetmo), Minbu, Lemyo, Khyang. Close to Saingbaung Chin. Also related to Shendu and Chinbon. Lemyo, Thayetmo, Minbu, and Khyang may be separate languages. *Lg Use:* Speakers are quite bilingual in Burmese. *Lg Dev:* NT: 1954. *Other:* SOV.

Chin, Bawm (Bawm, Bawn, Bawng, Bom) [bgr] 3,581 in Myanmar (2000 WCD). Falam area, Chin Hills. See main entry under India.

Chin, Bualkhaw [cbl] Chin State, Falam Township. *Class:* Sino-Tibetan, Tibeto-Burman, Kuki-Chin-Naga, Kuki-Chin, Southern, Sho. *Dialects:* Closest to Zanniet Chin.

Chin, Chinbon (Ütbü, Chindwin Chin, Sho, Chinbon) [cnb] 19,600 (1983). Kanpetlet, Yaw, Seidoutia, and Paletwa townships. *Class:* Sino-Tibetan, Tibeto-Burman, Kuki-Chin-Naga, Kuki-Chin, Southern, Sho. *Dialects:* Lexical similarity 50% with Asho Chin. *Other:* Buddhist.

Chin, Daai (Daai, Dai, M'kaang) [dao] 30,000 (1994 UBS). Matupi, Paletwa, Kanpetiet townships. *Class:* Sino-Tibetan, Tibeto-Burman, Kuki-Chin-Naga, Kuki-Chin, Southern. *Dialects:* Matupi Daai, Paletwa Daai, Kanpetiet Daai. Two subgroups: one of them Tuishiip, or Shiip. Daai is reported to have 6 main subgroups. *Lg Dev:* NT: 1996. *Other:* Sometimes called 'Mün', or 'Ütbü' ethnically, but those groups are linguistically distinct. In the past, they called themselves 'Mün', 'Ütbü', and 'Khyo' (Hyo, Sho, Zo) for higher status. Matupi Daai may be a separate language. SOV. Mountain slope. Tropical forest. 800 to 1,700 meters. Swidden agriculturalists.

Chin, Falam (Hallam Chin, Halam, Fallam, Falam) [flm] 100,000 in Myanmar (1991 UBS). Population includes 9,000 Tashon, 16,000 Zanniat, 7,000 Khualshim, 4,000 Lente, 14,400 Zahao 18,600 in Laizao (1983). Population total all countries: 125,367. Falam District, Chin Hills. Also spoken in Bangladesh, India. *Class:* Sino-Tibetan, Tibeto-Burman, Kuki-Chin-Naga, Kuki-Chin, Northern. *Dialects:* Zanniat, Tashon (Tashom, Shunkla, Sunkhla), Laizo (Laiso, Laizao, Laizo-Shimhrin), Zahao (Zahau, Yahow, Zahau-Shimhrin, Lyen-Lyem), Khualshim (Kwelshin), Lente (Lyente), Chorei. Chorei may be a separate language. In India, other dialect or clan names are: Choral, Dap, Eauglong, Ranjkho, Bong, Bongcher, Kaljang, Korbong, Langkai, Moosephang (Machaphang), Migli, Mitahar. They are collectively called 'Baro Halam'. Rupini and Koloi are said to be quite different from the others. Tapong is reported to have difficult intelligibility for speakers of other dialects. *Lg Dev:* Most young people and some older people, if educated, can read Falam (Myanmar). Roman script in India. Bible: 1991. *Other:* SOV. Christian.

Chin, Haka (Haka, Hakha, Baungshe, Lai) [cnh] 100,000 in Myanmar (1991 UBS). Population includes 2,000 Zokhua, 60,100 Lai (1983). Population total all countries: 446,264. Chin Hills, Haka area. Also spoken in Bangladesh, India. *Class:* Sino-Tibetan, Tibeto-Burman, Kuki-Chin-Naga, Kuki-Chin, Central. *Dialects:* Klangklang (Thlantlang), Zokhua, Shonshe. Shonshe may be a separate language. *Lg Dev:* Literacy rate lower for older people. Roman script in India. Bible: 1978–1999.

Chin, Khumi (Khumi, Khami, Khweymi, Khimi, Khuni) [cnk] 36,700 in Myanmar (1983). Population total all countries: 37,888. Arakan Hills, Akyab area. Matu are in Southern Chin State, Matupi, Mindat, and Paletwa townships, western Myanmar. Also spoken in Bangladesh, India. *Class:* Sino-Tibetan, Tibeto-Burman, Kuki-Chin-Naga, Kuki-Chin, Southern, Khumi. *Dialects:* Khimi, Yindi (Yindu), Khami, Ngala. *Lg Use:* Speakers also use Burmese. *Lg Dev:* Literacy rate in second language: 60%. Roman script in India. NT: 1959–1999. *Other:* Khami and Ngala may be separate languages. SOV; genitives, articles, adjectives, numerals after noun heads. Mountain slope. Tropical forest. 1,200 meters. Peasant agriculturalists. Christian, traditional religion, Buddhist.

Chin, Khumi Awa [cka] 40,900 (2003). Arakan Hills, coast areas. *Class:* Sino-Tibetan, Tibeto-Burman, Kuki-

Chin-Naga, Kuki-Chin, Southern, Khumi. *Dialects:* The coastal dialect differs from the inland Khumi. *Lg Dev:* Bible portions: 1939. *Other:* SOV.

Chin, Mara (Mara, Lakher, Zao, Maram, Mira) [mrh] 20,000 in Myanmar (1994). Lushai Hills. *Dialects:* Tlongsai, Hlawthai, Sabeu. See main entry under India.

Chin, Mro [cmr] 137,765 (2000 WCD). Arakan State. *Class:* Sino-Tibetan, Tibeto-Burman, Kuki-Chin-Naga, Kuki-Chin, Southern. *Dialects:* Lexical similarity 13% with Mru of Bangladesh and Myanmar.

Chin, Mün (Mün, Ng'men, Cho, Yawdwin, Mindat, "Chinbok") [mwq] 30,000 (1991 UBS). Chin Hills, western. *Class:* Sino-Tibetan, Tibeto-Burman, Kuki-Chin-Naga, Kuki-Chin, Southern. *Dialect:* Nitu. Related to Daai Chin. *Lg Dev:* NT: 1999. *Other:* "Chinbok," "Tsinbok," "Chinme," "Chinbe" are derogatory names for this group and not separate languages. SOV.

Chin, Ngawn (Ngawn, Ngorn, Ngon) [cnw] 15,000 (1984). Chin Hills, Falam area. *Class:* Sino-Tibetan, Tibeto-Burman, Kuki-Chin-Naga, Kuki-Chin, Central. *Lg Dev:* Bible portions: 1951. *Other:* SOV.

Chin, Paite (Paite, Paithe, Oarte, Hainte, Vuite) [pck] 8,900 in Myanmar (1983). Tiddim District, Chin Hills. See main entry under India.

Chin, Senthang (Senthang, Hsemtang) [sez] 18,200 (1983). Haka, Chin Hills. *Class:* Sino-Tibetan, Tibeto-Burman, Kuki-Chin-Naga, Kuki-Chin, Central. *Dialects:* Very different from other Chin languages. *Other:* SOV.

Chin, Siyin (Siyin, Siyang, Sizang) [csy] 10,000 (1991 UBS). Chin Hills. *Class:* Sino-Tibetan, Tibeto-Burman, Kuki-Chin-Naga, Kuki-Chin, Northern. *Dialects:* Close to Paite Chin. *Lg Dev:* NT: 1995. *Other:* SOV.

Chin, Tawr (Tawr, Torr) [tcp] 700 (1996 D. Van Bik). Falam, Haka, Chin Hills. *Class:* Sino-Tibetan, Tibeto-Burman, Kuki-Chin-Naga, Kuki-Chin, Central. *Other:* SOV.

Chin, Tedim (Tedim, Tiddim) [ctd] 189,100 in Myanmar (1990 BAP). Population total all countries: 344,100. Chin Hills State, Upper Chindwin, Tiddim area. Also spoken in India. *Class:* Sino-Tibetan, Tibeto-Burman, Kuki-Chin-Naga, Kuki-Chin, Northern. *Dialect:* Sokte, Kamhau (Kamhow, Kamhao). Other Chin languages or dialects of this area are Saizang, Teizang, Zo (Zome). *Lg Use:* Trade language of the Tiddim political subdivision. *Lg Dev:* Poetry. Bible: 1983. *Other:* SOV.

Chin, Thado (Thadou, Thado-Ubiphei, Thado-Pao, Kuki, Kuki-Thado) [tcz] 26,200 in Myanmar (1983). *Dialects:* Baite, Changsen, Jangshen, Kaokeep, Khongzai, Kipgen, Langiung, Sairang, Thangngen, Hawkip. See main entry under India.

Chin, Zotung (Zotung, Banjogi, Bandzhogi, Zobya) [czt] 40,000 (1990 UBS). Chin Hills, Haka area. *Class:* Sino-Tibetan, Tibeto-Burman, Kuki-Chin-Naga, Kuki-Chin, Central. *Dialects:* Zotung is reported to be intelligible with Haka. *Lg Dev:* Bible portions: 1951.

Chittagonian [cit] Arakan State. *Dialect:* Rohinga (Akyab). *Other:* They migrated from Bangladesh several generations ago. 250,000 refugees went back to Bangladesh recently, but most have been repatriated back to Myanmar by UNHCR. Muslim, Hindu, Christian. See main entry under Bangladesh.

Danau (Danaw) [dnu] 10,000 (1984). *Class:* Austro-Asiatic, Mon-Khmer, Northern Mon-Khmer, Palaungic, Eastern Palaungic, Danau. *Dialects:* Closest to Riang-Lang and Pale Palaung. *Other:* It may be in Thailand or China rather than, or in addition to, Myanmar.

Gangte (Gante) [gnb] See main entry under India.

Hmong Njua (Blue Meo, Green Miao, Tak Meo, Hmong Njwa, Hmong Leng) [blu] 10,000 in Myanmar (1987 Haiv Hmoob). See main entry under China.

Hpon (Hpön, Phun, Phön, Phon, Megyaw, Samong) [hpo] A few hundred speakers (1997 D. Bradley). Ethnic population: 2,254 (2000 WCD). Gorges of the upper Irrawaddy, north of Bhamo. *Class:* Sino-Tibetan, Tibeto-Burman, Lolo-Burmese, Burmish, Northern. *Dialects:* North Hpon, South Hpon. *Lg Use:* Both dialects are moribund (no children speaking them) and may be nearly extinct. All speakers are older adults.

Hrangkhol (Rangkhol) [hra] 8,117 in Myanmar (2000 WCD). Population total all countries: 26,782. Also spoken in India. *Class:* Sino-Tibetan, Tibeto-Burman, Kuki-Chin-Naga, Kuki-Chin, Northern. *Dialects:* Closest to Biete. *Lg Dev:* Roman script in India. NT: 1997. *Other:* SOV.

Intha (Inntha) [int] 90,000 (2000 D. Bradley). Near Inle Lake in the southern Shan state. *Class:* Sino-Tibetan, Tibeto-Burman, Lolo-Burmese, Burmish, Southern. *Dialects:* One of the better-known varieties of nonstandard Burmese with profound pronunciation and vocabulary differences from Burmese. *Other:* SOV. Fishermen; agriculturalists. Buddhist, traditional religion.

Jingpho (Kachin, Jinghpaw, Chingpaw, Chingp'o, Marip) [kac] 900,000 in Myanmar (2001 Johnstone and Mandryk). Population total all countries: 940,000. Kachin State. Also spoken in China. *Class:* Sino-Tibetan, Tibeto-Burman, Jingpho-Konyak-Bodo, Jingpho-Luish, Jingpho. *Dialects:* Hkaku (Hka-Hku), Kauri (Hkauri, Gauri), Dzili (Jili), Dulong. Dzili may be a separate language. Hkaku and Kauri are only slightly different than Jingpho. Lexical similarity 50% with Singhpo of India. *Lg Use:* Serves as lingua franca for Zaiwa, Lashi, and Maru. *Lg Dev:* Literacy rate in first language: 60% to 100%. Literacy rate in second language: 50% to 75%. Newspapers. Radio programs. Films. Dictionary. Bible: 1927. *Other:* 'Kachin' refers to the cultural rather than the linguistic group. Called 'Aphu' or 'Phu' by the Rawang people. SOV; tonal, 4 tones. Pastoralists; agriculturalists. Polytheist, Buddhist, Christian.

Kado (Kadu, Katu, Kato, Kudo, Asak, Sak, Gadu, Thet, That, Mawteik, Puteik, Woni, Kadu-Ganaan) [kdv] 128,500 in Myanmar (1983). Population includes 90,300 Kado, 38,200 Ganaan. Population total all countries: 228,725. The Kado are found in Ban Mauk Township, Sagaing Division (a region west of the railway midway between Mandalay and Myitkyina). The Ganaan are found just west of the Kadu people. The Thet are found in Rakhine State. Also spoken in China, Laos. *Class:* Sino-Tibetan, Tibeto-Burman, Jingpho-Konyak-Bodo, Jingpho-Luish, Luish. *Dialects:* Kadu, Ganaan (Ganan), Andro, Sengmai, Chakpa, Phayeng. Kadu, Ganaan, Andro, Sengmai, Chakpa, and Phayeng may be separate languages. *Lg Dev:* Bible portions: 1939. *Other:* Different from Katu, a Mon-Khmer language of Viet Nam, China, and Laos. Some Kadu report Ganan is a distinct language from Kado.

Karen, Brek (Brek, Brec, Bre, Pramano, Pre, Laku) [kvl] 16,600 (1983). All Karen languages in Myanmar 2,600,000. Southwestern Kayah State. *Class:* Sino-Tibetan, Tibeto-Burman, Karen, Sgaw-Bghai, Brek. *Other:* 'Brek' and 'Bwe' are variant names of a dialect cluster that extends from southwest Kayah State to northeast Karen State. 'Brek' or 'Bre' usually refers to varieties in Kayah State. Christian.

Karen, Bwe (Bghai Karen, Baghi, Bwe) [bwe] 15,700 (1983). Kyèbogyi area of Kayah State. A few in Thailand. *Class:* Sino-Tibetan, Tibeto-Burman, Karen, Sgaw-Bghai, Bghai, Unclassified. *Lg Dev:* Literacy rate in first language: below 1%. Bible portions: 1857–1862. *Other:* 'Kayin' is Burmese for all Karen, 'Yang' is Thai for all Karen. SOV.

Karen, Geba (Geba, Kaba, Karenbyu, Kayinbyu, White Karen, Eastern Bwe) [kvq] 10,000 (2000 D. Bradley).

Ethnic population: 10,000 (2000 D. Bradley). Northern Kayah State and southern Shan State. *Class:* Sino-Tibetan, Tibeto-Burman, Karen, Sgaw-Bghai, Bghai, Western. *Dialects:* May be part of the same dialect cluster with Bwe and Brek. *Other:* There is some literature in Geba. Christian.

Karen, Geko (Gek'o, Gheko, Gekho, Ghekhol, Ghekhu, Keku, Kekhong, Kekaungdu, Gaikho, Padaung) [ghk] 9,500 (1983). Yamethin, Toungoo districts, Mobyè State of the southern Shan States. *Class:* Sino-Tibetan, Tibeto-Burman, Karen, Sgaw-Bghai, Bghai, Unclassified. *Other:* SVO. Christian.

Karen, Lahta (Lahta, Taru, Tarulakhi, Khahta, Peu) [kvt] 9,550 (2000 WCD). Southern Shan State. *Class:* Sino-Tibetan, Tibeto-Burman, Karen, Sgaw-Bghai, Bghai, Eastern.

Karen, Manumanaw (Manumanaw, Manu, Monu, Manö) [kxf] 10,000 (2000 D. Bradley). Ethnic population: 10,000 (2000 D. Bradley). Western Kyèbogyi part of Kayah State. *Class:* Sino-Tibetan, Tibeto-Burman, Karen, Sgaw-Bghai, Kayah. *Other:* Christian.

Karen, Paku (Paku, Pagu, Monnepwa, Monebwa, Mopwa, Mopha, Mopaga, Mogpha, Mogwa, Thalwepwe) [kpp] 5,300 (1983). Southern hills east of Taungoo in Kayah State. *Class:* Sino-Tibetan, Tibeto-Burman, Karen, Sgaw-Bghai, Sgaw. *Dialects:* Bilichi, Dermuha. Close to S'gaw. Some reports indicate Paku and Mopwa are separate languages. *Other:* SVO.

Karen, Pa'o (Northern Taungthu, Black Karen, Pa-U, Pa'o, Pa Oh, Pa-O) [blk] 560,000 in Myanmar (1983). Population total all countries: 560,743. Southwestern Shan State and east of the Gulf of Martaban in Tenasserim. Also spoken in Thailand. *Class:* Sino-Tibetan, Tibeto-Burman, Karen, Pa'o. *Dialects:* Southern Pa'o, Northern Pa'o. Southern Pa'o is in Myanmar, Northern Pa'o in Thailand. *Lg Dev:* Bible portions: 1912–1964. *Other:* SVO. Buddhist, traditional religion.

Karen, Pwo Eastern (Phlou, Moulmein Pwo Karen) [kjp] 1,000,000 in Myanmar (1998). Population total all countries: 1,050,000. Karen State, Mon State, Tennserim Division. Also spoken in Thailand. *Class:* Sino-Tibetan, Tibeto-Burman, Karen, Pwo. *Dialects:* Pa'an (Moulmein, Inland Pwo Eastern Karen), Kawkareik (Eastern Border Pwo Karen), Tavoy (Southern Pwo Karen). Not intelligible with other Pwo Karen varieties. Lexical similarity 91% to 97% among dialects, 63% to 65% with other Pwo Karen varieties. *Lg Dev:* Monastic Burmese script, Mon-based script being developed for Myanmar and Thailand; Christian script Burmese based; Leke script; Thai-based script in Thailand. Bible portions: 2002. *Other:* SVO.

Karen, Pwo Western (Mutheit, Delta Pwo Karen, Bassein Pwo Karen, Phlong Sho) [pwo] 210,000. Irrawaddy Delta. *Class:* Sino-Tibetan, Tibeto-Burman, Karen, Pwo. *Dialects:* Bassein, Tuan Tet, Maubin. *Lg Dev:* Burmese-based script. Bible: 1883–1885. *Other:* SVO. Traditional religion, Christian, Buddhist.

Karen, S'gaw (S'gaw, S'gau, S'gaw Kayin, Kanyaw, Paganyaw, Pwakanyaw, White Karen, Burmese Karen, Yang Khao, Pchcknya, Kyetho) [ksw] 1,284,700 in Myanmar (1983). Population total all countries: 1,584,700. Irrawaddy delta area, Tenasserim, the Pegu range between the Irrawaddy and Sittang, the eastern hills. Also spoken in Thailand. *Class:* Sino-Tibetan, Tibeto-Burman, Karen, Sgaw-Bghai, Sgaw. *Dialect:* Panapu, Palakhi (Palachi). Close to Paku. *Lg Dev:* Bible: 1853–1995. *Other:* SVO.

Karen, Yinbaw (Yinbaw, Yeinbaw) [kvu] 7,300 (1983). Shan Plateau of eastern Shan State. *Class:* Sino-Tibetan, Tibeto-Burman, Karen, Sgaw-Bghai, Kayah. *Dialects:* Reported to be a variety of Padaung. *Other:* Buddhist, Christian, traditional religion.

Karen, Yintale (Yintale, Yintalet, Yangatalet, Yangtadai, Taliak) [kvy] 10,000 (2000 D. Bradley). Ethnic population: 10,000 (2000 D. Bradley). Bawlakhè part of Kayah State. *Class:* Sino-Tibetan, Tibeto-Burman, Karen, Sgaw-Bghai, Kayah. *Dialects:* Reported to be a variety of Kayah. *Other:* Buddhist, traditional religion.

Karen, Zayein (Zayein, Khaungtou, Gaungtou) [kxk] 9,300 (1983). Between the towns of Mobyè and Phekon in the southern Shan State. *Class:* Sino-Tibetan, Tibeto-Burman, Karen, Unclassified. *Dialects:* Close to Sawntung, Padang, Banyang.

Kayah, Eastern (Red Karen, Karenni, Kayay, Kayah) [eky] 261,578 in Myanmar (2000 WCD). Population total all countries: 360,220. Maehongson, east of the Salween River. Also spoken in Thailand. *Class:* Sino-Tibetan, Tibeto-Burman, Karen, Sgaw-Bghai, Kayah. *Dialects:* Distinct from but related to Bwe Karen (Bghai), forming a dialect cluster. Speakers have difficulty understanding Western Kayah of Myanmar. *Lg Dev:* Literacy rate in first language: 1% to 5%. Literacy rate in second language: 50% to 75%.

Kayah, Western (Kayah Li, Karenni, Karennyi, Red Karen, Yang Daeng, Karieng Daeng) [kyu] 210,000 (1987). Kayah and Karen states, west of the Pong River. *Class:* Sino-Tibetan, Tibeto-Burman, Karen, Sgaw-Bghai, Kayah. *Dialects:* Distinct from but related to Bwe Karen, forming a dialect continuum from Thailand (Eastern Kayah) to western Kayah State. *Lg Dev:* Literacy rate in first language: 1% to 5%. Dictionary. *Other:* Christian, traditional religion.

Kayan (Padaung, Kayang, Padaung Karen) [pdu] 40,900 in Myanmar (1983). Population total all countries: 41,050. Kayah State, Mobyè State, town of Phekon in the southern Shan States, and hills east of Toungoo. A few villages in Thailand. Also spoken in Thailand. *Class:* Sino-Tibetan, Tibeto-Burman, Karen, Sgaw-Bghai, Bghai, Eastern. *Lg Dev:* Literacy rate in first language: below 1%. Literacy rate in second language: below 5%. *Other:* Traditional religion, Buddhist, Christian.

Khamti (Hkamti, Khampti, Khamti Shan, Khampti Shan, Khandi Shan, Kam Ti, Tai Kam Ti, Tai-Khamti) [kht] 4,235 in Myanmar (2000 WCD). Population total all countries: 13,114. Northwestern Myanmar. Also possibly in China. Also spoken in India. *Class:* Tai-Kadai, Kam-Tai, Be-Tai, Tai-Sek, Tai, Southwestern, Northwest. *Dialects:* Assam Khamti, North Burma Khamti, Sinkaling Hkamti. Related to Shan. Some similarities to northern Shan. In India, related to Phakaes, Aiton, Khamjang, Turung. *Lg Use:* Speakers also use Burmese or Jingpho. *Lg Dev:* Lik-Tai script; resembles Mon script in India. *Other:* SOV; postpositional case-marking particle. Buddhist.

Khmu (Kmhmu, Khmu', Kamu, Kammu, Khamuk, Kamhmu, Khomu, Mou, Pouteng, Pu Thenh, Tenh, Theng, Lao Terng) [kjg] See main entry under Laos.

Khün (Hkun, Khun Shan, Khyn, Gon Shan, Tai Khun, Khuen, Tai-Khuen) [kkh] 114,574 in Myanmar (2000 WCD). Population total all countries: 120,855. Main Kentung Valley in the center of Shan State. Also spoken in Thailand. *Class:* Tai-Kadai, Kam-Tai, Be-Tai, Tai-Sek, Tai, Southwestern, Northwest. *Dialects:* Close to Lü and Northern Tai or southern Shan. Lanna and Khun dialects are considered close by their speakers. *Lg Dev:* Script close to that of the Lanna. Bible portions: 1938. *Other:* Different from Khouen (Khuen), a Mon-Khmer language of Laos. Buddhist.

Kiorr (Saamtaav, Con, Col) [xko] See main entry under Laos.

Lahu (Lohei, Lahuna, Launa, Museu, Mussuh, Muhso, Musso) [lhu] 125,000 in Myanmar (1993 Johnstone). Shan State, Kentung area. *Dialects:* Na (Black Lahu, Musser Dam, Northern Lahu, Loheirn), Nyi (Red Lahu, Southern

Lahu, Musseh Daeng, Luhishi, Luhushi), Shehleh. *Other:* Mountain slope. Tropical forest, scrub forest. Swidden agriculturalists. Christian. See main entry under China.

Lahu Shi (Kutsung, Kucong, Yellow Lahu, Shi, Kui, Kwi) [kds] 10,000 in Myanmar (1998). Kentung District. See main entry under Laos.

Lama [lay] 3,000 (1977 Voegelin and Voegelin). *Class:* Sino-Tibetan, Tibeto-Burman, Nungish. *Dialects:* Dialect or closely related language to Norra. *Other:* SOV.

Lamkang ("Lamgang," "Hiroi-Lamgang," Lamkaang, Lamkang Naga) [lmk] Betukshangreng village, 20 km from the border with southeast Manipur, India. See main entry under India.

Laopang (Laopa) [lbg] 9,550 (2000 WCD). *Class:* Sino-Tibetan, Tibeto-Burman, Lolo-Burmese, Loloish, Unclassified. *Other:* Possibly same as Laba, a group of Lahu near Lao-Thai border (Mundhenk 1973). SOV.

Lashi (Lachik, Lasi, Letsi, Lechi, Leqi, Lashi-Maru, Chashan, Lachikwaw, Ac'ye, Lacik, Lacid) [lsi] 30,000 in Myanmar (2000 D. Bradley). Population total all countries: 31,800. Htawgaw Subdivision, Kachin State. Also spoken in China. *Class:* Sino-Tibetan, Tibeto-Burman, Lolo-Burmese, Burmish, Northern. *Lg Dev:* Literacy rate in first language: below 1%. Literacy rate in second language: 5% to 15%. *Other:* Their own name is Lachik, the Jingpho and Burmese name is Lashi, the Chinese name Lachi. SOV.

Lisu (Lisaw, Li-Shaw, Li-Hsaw, Lu-Tzu, Southern Lisu, Yao Yen, Yaw-Yen, Yaw Yin, Yeh-Jeh, Central Lisu) [lis] 126,000 in Myanmar (1987). Around Lashio, in Wa State, around Myitkyina and Bhamo, around Putar towards Assam border, around Loilem area in Shan States. *Dialects:* Hwa Lisu (Flowery Lisu), Black Lisu, White Lisu, Lu Shi Lisu. *Lg Dev:* Literacy rate in first language: 30% to 60%. Literacy rate in second language: 50% to 75%. *Other:* All four dialects are in Myanmar. Black Lisu is the most distinct. Burmese and Thai Lisu have difficulties in communicating because of dialect differences. Yawgin, Tangsir, Hkwinhpang are dialects or ethnic groups. Polytheist, Christian. See main entry under China.

Lopi [lov] 4,775 (2000 WCD). Possibly also in China. *Class:* Sino-Tibetan, Tibeto-Burman, Lolo-Burmese, Loloish, Unclassified. *Other:* SOV.

Lü (Pai-I, Shu-Ai-I, Lue, Tai Lu) [khb] 200,000 in Myanmar (1981). Kengtung District. *Other:* Traditional religion, Buddhist. See main entry under China.

Lui (Loi) [lba] 200. *Class:* Sino-Tibetan, Tibeto-Burman, Unclassified. *Other:* 'Loi' means 'mountain' in Shan, and many groups are called that.

Mahei (Mahe, Mabe) [mja] 12,000. *Class:* Sino-Tibetan, Tibeto-Burman, Lolo-Burmese, Loloish, Southern, Akha. *Dialects:* Ethnic group or dialect of Hani or Akha. *Other:* SOV.

Maru (Matu, Malu, Lawng, Laungwaw, Laungaw, Langsu, Lang, Mulu, Diso, Zi, Lhao Vo) [mhx] 100,000 in Myanmar (1997 D. Bradley). Population total all countries: 103,500. Kachin State, eastern border area, widely dispersed, north Myanmar. Also spoken in China. *Class:* Sino-Tibetan, Tibeto-Burman, Lolo-Burmese, Burmish, Northern. *Dialects:* Dago' Lawng Bit, Zagaran Mran, Gawan Naw', Hlo'lan, Laking, Wa Khawk, Lawng Hsu. Lawng Hsu may have difficult intelligibility of the other dialects. *Lg Dev:* Literacy rate in first language: below 1%. Literacy rate in second language: 25% to 50%. Roman script. NT: 1985–1994. *Other:* Different from the Matu variety of Khumi Chin. Culture similar to Kachin. Self name is 'Lawngwaw'. Jingpho name and Burmese name is 'Maru'. Chinese name is 'Langsu'. SOV.

Meitei (Meithei, Meithe, Mithe, Mitei, Meiteiron, Manipuri, Menipuri, Kathe, Kathi, Ponna) [mni] 6,000

in Myanmar (1931). *Other:* Hindu, traditional religion, Muslim, Christian. See main entry under India.

Mizo (Hualngo, Whelngo, Le, Lushei, Lusai, Lushai) [lus] 12,500 in Myanmar (1983). Western Myanmar. *Dialects:* Dulien, Ngente, Mizo. See main entry under India.

Moken (Mawken, Basing, Selung, Selong, Salong, Salon, Chau Ko') [mwt] 7,000 in Myanmar (1993 Johnstone). Mergui Archipelago, Dung, and other islands in south Myanmar. Also spoken in Thailand. *Class:* Austronesian, Malayo-Polynesian, Malayic, Moklen. *Dialects:* Dung, Ja-It, L'be. Closest to Moklen. Related to Urak Lawoi. *Lg Dev:* NT: 2002. *Other:* They live primarily on boats, but occasionally settle on islands in the area. SVO. Islands. Tropical forest. Sea level. Fishermen: marine products. Traditional religion, Muslim.

Mon (Talaing, Mun, Peguan) [mnw] 742,900 in Myanmar (2004). Population total all countries: 850,530. Eastern delta region from east of Rangoon as far as Ye and Thailand; south Martaban, adjacent area. Also spoken in Thailand. *Class:* Austro-Asiatic, Mon-Khmer, Monic. *Dialects:* Mataban-Moulmein (Central Mon, Mon Te), Pegu (Northern Mon, Mon Tang), Ye (Southern Mon, Mon Nya). *Lg Use:* Many young people use only Burmese. The Mon can read Burmese and are generally bilingual in Burmese. *Lg Dev:* Ancient script, Indic-based derived from Pali. Bible: 1928. *Other:* Remnants of a nation that once spread over southern Myanmar and western Thailand. SVO.

Naga, Khiamniungan (Khiamngan, Khiamniungan, Kalyokengnyu, Makware, Nokaw, Para, Ponyo, Welam) [nky] Northwestern. See main entry under India.

Naga, Tase (Cham Chang, Rangpan, Tase, Tangsa, Tasey) [nst] 55,389 in Myanmar (2000). Population total all countries: 100,389. Northwestern Myanmar. Also spoken in India. *Class:* Sino-Tibetan, Tibeto-Burman, Jingpho-Konyak-Bodo, Konyak-Bodo-Garo, Konyak. *Dialects:* Gashan, Hkaluk, Sangche, Saukrang, Langshin, Mawrang, Myimu, Sangtai, Tulim, Longri. Some dialects are widely divergent. Close to Nocte Naga. *Lg Dev:* Roman script in India. Radio programs. TV. NT: 1992. *Other:* SOV.

Nga La (Matu Chin, Thlan Tan) [hlt] 40,000 in Myanmar (2000). Population total all countries: 60,000. Also spoken in India. *Class:* Sino-Tibetan, Tibeto-Burman, Kuki-Chin-Naga, Kuki-Chin, Southern. *Dialects:* Va Lang (Warang), Tlam Tlaih. Not intelligible with Chin Haka. *Lg Dev:* NT: 1999–2000.

Norra (Nora, Noza, Nurra) [nrr] 6,207 (2000 WCD). Myanmar-Tibet border. *Class:* Sino-Tibetan, Tibeto-Burman, Nungish. *Dialects:* Nora, Byabe, Kizolo. Lama (3,000) may be a dialect. *Other:* SOV.

Nung (Anung, Anong, Anoong, Anu, Nu, Lu, Lutzu, Lutze, Kiutze, Khanung, Kwinp'ang, Khupang, Kwingsang, Fuch'ye) [nun] 400 in Myanmar (2000 D. Bradley). Population total all countries: 790. Ethnic population: 6,000 in Myanmar (2000 D. Bradley). North Myanmar. Salween (Nu) River. Also spoken in China. *Class:* Sino-Tibetan, Tibeto-Burman, Nungish. *Dialects:* Cholo, Gwaza, Miko. 15 or 16 dialects, mostly inherently intelligible with each other. They understand the Mutwang dialect of Rawang. They may be the same as the Nu River Drung in China. May be related to Jingpho. Lexical similarity 70% with Rawang. *Lg Dev:* Grammar. *Other:* Different from Nung (Tai family) of Viet Nam, Laos, and China, and from Chinese Nung (Cantonese) of Viet Nam. SOV. Agriculturalists. Polytheist, Christian, Buddhist (Lamaist).

Palaung, Pale (Di-Ang, Ngwe Palaung, Silver Palaung, Pale, Palay) [pce] 257,539 in Myanmar (2000 WCD). Total Palaung and Riang in Myanmar: 250,000. Population total all countries: 267,539. Southern Shan State area near Kalaw. 10,000 square mile area. Also spoken in China, Thailand. *Class:* Austro-Asiatic, Mon-Khmer, Northern Mon-Khmer, Palaungic, Eastern Palaungic, Palaung. *Dialects:* Close to Shwe Palaung and Rumai Palaung. *Lg Dev:* Literacy rate in first language: below 1%. Literacy rate in second language: below 5%. Grammar. *Other:* SVO. Mountain slope. Evergreen forest. 1,200 meters. Peasant agriculturalists. Buddhist.

Palaung, Rumai (Rumai) [rbb] 137,000 in Myanmar. Population total all countries: 139,000. Northern Shan State. Also spoken in China. *Class:* Austro-Asiatic, Mon-Khmer, Northern Mon-Khmer, Palaungic, Eastern Palaungic, Palaung. *Dialects:* Close to Shwe Palaung and Pale Palaung. Officially included De'ang nationality in China. *Other:* SVO.

Palaung, Shwe (Ta-Ang Palaung, Golden Palaung, Shwe) [pll] 148,000 in Myanmar (1982). Population total all countries: 150,000. Northern Shan State, centered in Nam Hsan. Also spoken in China. *Class:* Austro-Asiatic, Mon-Khmer, Northern Mon-Khmer, Palaungic, Eastern Palaungic, Palaung. *Dialects:* 15 Palaung dialects in Myanmar. Pale Palaung and Rumai are closely related, but distinct languages. *Lg Use:* Shan is the lingua franca for intercommunication among Palaung groups with marked dialect differences and between Palaung and Shan, Kachin, and smaller groups such as Lisu. *Other:* Included under De'ang official nationality in China. SVO. Buddhist.

Pali [pli] Extinct. *Lg Use:* Used as the literary language of the Buddhist Scriptures. *Other:* Buddhist. See main entry under India.

Palu [pbz] 4,775 (2000 WCD). *Class:* Sino-Tibetan, Tibeto-Burman, Unclassified. *Other:* SOV.

Pankhu (Pankho, Panko, Pangkhu) [pkh] Falam area, Chin Hills. *Other:* Tropical forest. Agriculturalists. See main entry under Bangladesh.

Parauk (Wa, Praok, Phalok, Baraog) [prk] 348,400 in Myanmar (1983). Population total all countries: 528,400. Shan State, upper Salween River area. Also spoken in China. *Class:* Austro-Asiatic, Mon-Khmer, Northern Mon-Khmer, Palaungic, Western Palaungic, Waic, Wa. *Dialects:* Related to Lawa and Wa in Thailand and China. *Lg Use:* A large and powerful group. The standard form for the Wa official nationality in China. *Lg Dev:* NT: 1938. *Other:* Traditional culture. Mountain slope. Buddhist (Hinayana), Christian.

Purum (Puram) [pub] 300 (1977 Voegelin and Voegelin). *Class:* Sino-Tibetan, Tibeto-Burman, Kuki-Chin-Naga, Kuki-Chin, Northern. *Dialects:* Related to Chiru, Aimol, Langrong. *Other:* SOV.

Pyen (Hpyin) [pyy] 800 (1981 Wurm and Hattori). East central, 2 enclaves very near the Laos border, near the Kha River. *Class:* Sino-Tibetan, Tibeto-Burman, Lolo-Burmese, Loloish, Southern, Phunoi. *Dialects:* Close to Phunoi, Bisu, Mpi.

Ralte [ral] 24,801 in Myanmar (2000 WCD). Population total all countries: 25,104. Also spoken in India. *Class:* Sino-Tibetan, Tibeto-Burman, Kuki-Chin-Naga, Kuki-Chin, Northern. *Dialects:* Related to Tiddim, Paite, Thado, Zo. *Other:* SOV.

Rawang (Nung Rawang, Ganung-Rawang, Hkanung, Nung, Krangku, Taron, Kiutze, Ch'opa, Chiutse) [raw] 62,074 in Myanmar (2000 WCD). Population total all countries: 122,610. Kachin State, highlands. Serwang is close to the Tibet border. Wadamkong is in Myanmar. Also spoken in India. *Class:* Sino-Tibetan, Tibeto-Burman, Nungish. *Dialects:* Rawang, Agu, Hpungsi, Htiselwang, Matwanly, Mutwang, Serhta, Serwang, Wadamkong, Wahke, Taron, Tangsarr, Longmi (Lungmi), Zithung, Kunlang. 75 to 100 dialects, some of which are inherently unintelligible to each other's speakers. Five major divisions: Longmi, Mutwang, Serwang, Tangsarr, Kwinpang (Nung); each has 20 to 30 subdialects. Dialect continuum with Nu nationality in China. Dialects near the Tibet border are harder to understand. Kunglang in India; communication cut off in 1950s. Most dialects understand Mutwang, the central, written dialect. Related, but not the same as Drung in China. *Lg Use:* All domains. Oral and written use in religion. Their second language is Burmese, third is English. Some also speak Lisu and Kachin. *Lg Dev:* Literacy rate in first language: 30% to 60%. Literacy rate in second language: 75% to 100%. Bible: 1986. *Other:* The Chinese name is 'Kiutze' or 'Qiuze'. The Lisu name is 'Ch'opa'. 'Krangku' is a regional name of Rawang. SOV. Plateau.

Riang (Black Karen, Yanglam, Black Yang, Riang-Lang, Yin, Yang, Liang Sek, Yang Wan Kun) [ril] 48,819 in Myanmar (2000 WCD). Population total all countries: 51,819. Shan State, southeastern Myanmar. Also spoken in China. *Class:* Austro-Asiatic, Mon-Khmer, Northern Mon-Khmer, Palaungic, Eastern Palaungic, Riang. *Dialects:* Close to Pale Palaung. May be the same as Shwe Palaung. *Lg Use:* Speakers also use Shan. *Lg Dev:* Bible portions: 1950. *Other:* Not related to the Tripuri-speaking Riang of India and Bangladesh. Not related to Black (Pa'o) Karen, which is Sino-Tibetan. Officially included under De'ang nationality in China. SVO.

Samtao (Samtau, Samtuan) [stu] 9,550 in Myanmar (2000 WCD). Population total all countries: 9,650. Eastern Shan State. Also spoken in China. *Class:* Austro-Asiatic, Mon-Khmer, Northern Mon-Khmer, Palaungic, Western Palaungic, Angkuic. *Other:* Different from Blang.

Sansu [sca] 4,775 (2000 WCD). *Class:* Sino-Tibetan, Tibeto-Burman, Lolo-Burmese, Loloish, Southern, Akha, Hani. *Dialects:* May not be a distinct language. In China, included with the Hani. *Other:* SOV.

Shan (Sha, Tai Shan, Sam, Thai Yai, Tai Yai, Great Thai, Tai Luang, Mau, "Ngio," "Ngiow," "Ngiaw," "Ngiao," "Ngeo") [shn] 3,200,000 in Myanmar (2001 Johnstone and Mandryk). Population includes 350,000 Tai Mao (1990 A. Diller ANU). Population total all countries: 3,260,000. Shan States, southeast Myanmar. Kokant Shan is in the Kokant area in northern Wa State in the Shan States. Tai Mao is on the Burma-Yunnan border, centered at Mu'ang Mao Long or Namkham, Myanmar. Also spoken in China, Thailand. *Class:* Tai-Kadai, Kam-Tai, Be-Tai, Tai-Sek, Tai, Southwestern, Northwest. *Dialect:* Kokant Shan, Tai Mao (Mao, Maw, Mau, Tai Long, Northern Shan). Burmese Shan is spoken with regional dialect differences, but dialects are close linguistically. Tai-Khae (Khe) may be a dialect. Low intelligibility of Lü. *Lg Dev:* Bible: 1892. *Other:* Tai Mao have own script. Southern Shan traditionally written with a Burmese-like script which does not distinguish tone or some vowels. Plains. Agriculturalists: paddy rice; artisans (gold, silver, blacksmiths); shopkeepers. Buddhist.

Tai Loi (Loi, Tailoi, Wakut, Monglwe) [tlq] 1,432 in Myanmar (2000 WCD). Population total all countries: 1,932. Namkham, in the northeast corner near the Laos and Chinese borders. Doi is across the border in Laos. Also spoken in Laos. *Class:* Austro-Asiatic, Mon-Khmer, Northern Mon-Khmer, Palaungic, Western Palaungic, Angkuic. *Dialects:* Tai Loi, Doi. Closest to Pale Palaung, but with a lot of sound changes, also separating it from Palaung in China. *Other:* Nontonal. Mountain slope.

Tai Nüa (Tai Neua, Chinese Shan, Tai Kong) [tdd] 72,400 in Myanmar (1983). Also possibly in northern Viet Nam. *Other:* Called 'Dehong Dai' in China. The Laos dialect is different from China. See main entry under China.

Taman [tcl] 10,000. *Class:* Sino-Tibetan, Tibeto-Burman, Jingpho-Konyak-Bodo, Jingpho-Luish, Jingpho. *Other:* SOV.

Taungyo (Taru, Tavoya, Tavoyan, Dawe, Dawai, Tawe-Tavoy, Toru) [tco] 40,000 (2000 D. Bradley). East central;

vicinity of Taunggyi, Shan State southward to Tavoy, Tenasserim State. *Class:* Sino-Tibetan, Tibeto-Burman, Lolo-Burmese, Burmish, Southern. *Dialects:* Related to Burmese. *Other:* SOV.

Tavoyan [tvn] 400,000 (2000 D. Bradley). Southeast. *Class:* Sino-Tibetan, Tibeto-Burman, Lolo-Burmese, Burmish, Southern. *Dialects:* One of the better known varieties of nonstandard Burmese with profound pronunciation and vocabulary differences from Burmese. *Other:* SOV. Buddhist.

Wa (K'awa, Kawa, Va, Vo, Wa Pwi, Wakut) [wbm] 558,000 in Myanmar (1993 Johnstone). Population total all countries: 838,000. Shan State, upper Salween River area. Kentung Wa are in or around Kentung City in southern Wa area. Also spoken in China. *Class:* Austro-Asiatic, Mon-Khmer, Northern Mon-Khmer, Palaungic, Western Palaungic, Waic, Wa. *Dialects:* Wa Lon, Wu, Kentung Wa, Son, En, La. Related to Lawa and Parauk in Thailand and China. Kentung Wa is more closely related to Lawa than are the northern dialects. En and Son are very different from each other. Son, En, and La may be separate languages. *Lg Dev:* Magazines. Radio programs. TV. Dictionary. Grammar. NT: 1938. *Other:* 'Kawa' may refer to Blang. An official nationality in China. 'Wa pwi' means 'Wa people'. SVO. Mountain slope, plateau. Defoliated into scrub forest. 1,000 to 2,000 meters. Swidden agriculturalists. Traditional religion, Christian, Buddhist.

Welaung [weu] 9,550 (2000 WCD). *Class:* Sino-Tibetan, Tibeto-Burman, Kuki-Chin-Naga, Kuki-Chin, Southern. *Other:* SOV.

Wewaw (Wewau) [wea] 23,874 (2000 WCD). Toungoo District. *Class:* Sino-Tibetan, Tibeto-Burman, Karen, Sgaw-Bghai, Sgaw. *Other:* SOV.

Yangbye (Yanbe, Yangye, Yanbye) [ybd] 810,300 (1983). *Class:* Sino-Tibetan, Tibeto-Burman, Lolo-Burmese, Burmish, Southern. *Other:* SOV.

Yinchia (Striped Karen, Yinnet, Black Riang, Ranei) [yin] 4,000 (1974 Hackett). Shan State south. *Class:* Austro-Asiatic, Mon-Khmer, Northern Mon-Khmer, Palaungic, Eastern Palaungic, Riang. *Dialects:* Related to Riang Lang and Wa. Not Karen. *Other:* SVO.

Yos (Yo, Yote) [yos] 3,400 (1983). *Class:* Sino-Tibetan, Tibeto-Burman, Kuki-Chin-Naga, Kuki-Chin, Northern. *Other:* Different from Mizo Chin. SOV.

Zaiwa (Zi, Tsaiwa, Atsi, Atshi, Atzi, Azi, Aci) [atb] 30,000 in Myanmar (1997). Kachin State, Sedan, Kentung. *Lg Use:* They use Jingpho as lingua franca. *Lg Dev:* Literacy rate in first language: below 1%. Literacy rate in second language: 50% to 75%. *Other:* Their name and the Chinese name is Tsaiwa, the Jingpho name is Atsi, the Burmese name is Zi. Mountain slope, interfluvial. Tropical forest. Peasant agriculturalists. See main entry under China.

Zome (Zorni, Zomi, Zou, Zo, Kuki Chin) [zom] 30,000 in Myanmar. Population total all countries: 39,112. Chin State, Tiddim, Chin Hills. Also spoken in India. *Class:* Sino-Tibetan, Tibeto-Burman, Kuki-Chin-Naga, Kuki-Chin, Northern. *Dialects:* Paite Chin, Zome, and Simte are almost identical. *Lg Dev:* Roman script in India. Bible: 1992. *Other:* 'Zomi' is a general name for all Chin, but is also used for this specific group. SOV.

Zyphe (Zophei, Zoptei) [zyp] 17,000 in Myanmar (1994). Population total all countries: 20,000. Chin State, Thantlang Township. Also spoken in India. *Class:* Sino-Tibetan, Tibeto-Burman, Kuki-Chin-Naga, Kuki-Chin, Southern. *Dialects:* Lower Zyphe, Upper Zyphe. Close to Mara Chin. Myanmar and India varieties reported intelligible to each other's speakers (Davis 01). *Lg Use:* Many also use Haka Chin, Lakher, or Mara, depending on location.

Nepal

Kingdom of Nepal, Sri Nepala Sarkar. 27,070,666. 2,423,840 speakers of Tibeto-Burman languages (1991 J. Matisoff). National or official language: Nepali. Literacy rate: 20% to 29%. Also includes Kharia (1,575), Urdu (174,840). Information mainly from R. Hugoniot 1970; D. B. Bista 1972; S. Toba 1976, 1983, 1991; A. Hale 1982; W. Winter 1991; K. Ebert 1994; J. Matisoff et al. 1996; R. Burling ms (1998). Blind population: 100,000. Deaf population: 1,275,776. Deaf institutions: 3. The number of languages listed for Nepal is 126. Of those, 123 are living languages and 3 are extinct. See maps beginning on page 813.

Angika (Anga, Angikar, Chhika-Chhiki) [anp] 15,892 in Nepal (2001 census). Terai. See main entry under India.

Athpariya (Athapre, Ath Paharia Rai, Athpare, Athpre, Arthare, Arthare-Khesang, Jamindar Rai) [aph] 2,000 (1995 Ebert). 439,312 all Rai languages (1991 census). Kosi Zone, Dhankuta District, north of the Tamur, between the Dhankutakhola in the west and the Tangkhuwa in the east; Dhankuta and Bhirgaon panchayats. *Class:* Sino-Tibetan, Tibeto-Burman, Himalayish, Mahakiranti, Kiranti, Eastern. *Dialects:* Athpare from Dhankuta and Belhara are very similar, but not inherently intelligible to each other's speakers (Bickel 1996:21). Reported to be close to Limbu, but not inherently intelligible with it. The term 'Kiranti' covers about 21 speech varieties, of which fewer than half are even partially intelligible to each other. *Lg Use:* Used by all, including educated speakers. Low bilingualism in Nepali. Some speakers also use Chhilinge or Limbu. *Lg Dev:* Literacy rate in second language: 2%. Devanagari script. Grammar. *Other:* 'Athpare' refers to the ethnic unit formed by close cultural ties between the Belhare and the autochthonous inhabitants of neighboring Dhankuta bazaar. People from each recognize the linguistic difference and distinguish them by calling the Dhankuta people 'Noupagari' and the Belhare people 'Athpagari' (Bickel 1996:21). 'Rai' and 'Kiranti' are partially overlapping terms and subject to many interpretations. SOV; postpositions; genitives, adjectives, numerals before noun heads; polar questions marked with a suffix attached to the verb sentence final; content questions can have the same word order as assertive sentences, or the question word occurs directly before the verb; maximum number of suffixes 9; affixes indicate case of noun phrase; verb affixes mark person, number, object—obligatory; split ergative; comparatives with Nepali 'Bhanda'; CV, CVC, CVCC; nontonal. Mountainous. 1,000 to 2,000 meters. Agriculturalists; animal husbandry; petty trade; labor. Hindu, Buddhist, syncretism with traditional religion.

Awadhi (Abadi, Abadhi, Abohi, Ambodhi, Avadhi, Baiswari, Kojali, Kosali) [awa] 560,744 in Nepal (2001 census). Lumbini Zone, Kapilbastu District; Bheri Zone, Banke and Bardiya districts. *Dialects:* Bagheli, Gangapari, Mirzapuri, Pardesi, Tharu, Uttari. *Lg Use:* 19,996 second-language speakers in Nepal (1991 census, under Abadhi). *Lg Dev:* Literacy rate in second language: 50% to 75%. *Other:* Hindu. See main entry under India.

Bagheli (Bagelkhandi, Bhugelkhud, Mannadi, Riwai, Gangai, Mandal, Kewot, Kewat, Kawathi, Kenat, Kevat Boli, Kevati, Kewani, Kewati) [bfy] Ethnic population: 136,953 Kewat. Koshi Zone, Morang District. *Dialects:* Ojhi, Powari, Banapari, Gahore, Tirhari, Godwani (Mandlaha), Sonpari. *Lg Use:* Trade language. *Other:* Gangai recognized as an official nationality by the Government of Nepal. See main entry under India.

Bahing (Rumdali, Bainge Rai, Baing, Baying, Bayung, Bahing Lo, Bayung Lo) [bhj] 2,765 (2001 census).

Sagarmatha Zone, Okhaldunga District, south of the Solu River in the Nachedanda ranges, east of the Melung River to the Thatan River and its tributaries in the west. *Class:* Sino-Tibetan, Tibeto-Burman, Himalayish, Mahakiranti, Kham-Magar-Chepang-Sunwari, Sunwari. *Dialects:* Namber Sacha, Rokhung, Khaling, Banenge, Dobo Lo, Proca Lo. The Khaling dialect of Bahing is distinct from the Khaling language. More homogeneous than most Kiranti languages. Related to Sunwar. *Lg Use:* The language still in use by the younger generation. Degree of Nepalization is relatively low (Winter 1991). *Other:* Agriculturalists; pastoralists.

Bantawa (Bantawa Rai, Bantaba, Bontawa, Bantawa Yüng, Bantawa Yong, Bantawa Dum, Kiranti) [bap] 371,056 (2001 census). Less than 5% monolinguals. Koshi Zone, Morang, Dhankuta, Bhojpur, western Dhankuta, and Khotang districts. Amchoke is in Limbuwan, especially in Ilam District; Sagarmatha Zone, Udayapur District; Mechi Zone, Japa District. Many villages. *Class:* Sino-Tibetan, Tibeto-Burman, Himalayish, Mahakiranti, Kiranti, Eastern. *Dialects:* Northern Bantawa (Dilpali), Southern Bantawa (Hatuwali, Hangkhim), Eastern Bantawa (Dhankuta), Western Bantawa (Amchoke, Amchauke). Southern and Northern Bantawa are the most similar and could be united as 'Intermediate Bantawa'. Dialects reported to be inherently intelligible with each other. Sorung and Saharaja are Amchoke subdialects. Rungchenbung and Yangma are Northern subdialects. Eastern dialect is most divergent. Most closely related to Dungmali. Also related to Puma, Sampang, and Chhintange. *Lg Use:* Some shift to Nepali evident, especially among Northern dialect speakers. Some varieties are used as the traditional lingua franca among Rai minorities in Limbuwan, Sikkim India, and Bhutan, and as first language among Rai of other origin. This is true for the Lambichong, Mugu, and Chhintange (Bradley 1996). Positive language attitude. Most speak some Nepali. There is a wide range of proficiency. In some regions, young people prefer Nepali. Hindi common among ex-soldiers. *Lg Dev:* Literacy rate in second language: 54% in Bhojpur District. Devanagari script. Poetry. Magazines. Films. Dictionary. Grammar. *Other:* SOV; postpositions; genitives, adjectives, numerals before noun heads; polar questions marked only with rising intonation; content questions same word order as assertive sentences or question word directly before the verb; affixes indicate case of noun phrases; verb affixes mark person, number, object—obligatory; split ergative; comparatives use Nepali word, 'bhanda'; CV, CVC, CVCC; nontonal. Mountain slope, plains. Scrub forest. 500 to 2,800 meters. Agriculturalists; pastoralists. Traditional religion, Hindu, Christian.

Baraamu (Barhamu, Brahmu, Bhramu, Bramu, Baram) [brd] 2,000 (1998). Ethnic population: 7,383. Gandaki Zone, North Gorkha District, Takhu village up the Doraundi Khola on the east side above Chorgate, near Kumhali, about 7 villages. They may be in Dhading District. *Class:* Sino-Tibetan, Tibeto-Burman, Himalayish, Tibeto-Kanauri, Western Himalayish, Eastern. *Dialects:* Related to Thangmi (Grierson-Konow). *Lg Use:* Speakers are shifting to Nepali. Spoken mainly by those older than 40 years. *Other:* 'Baramo' recognized as an official nationality by the Government of Nepal. OV (Subject position varies); postpositions; genitives, articles, adjectives, numerals before noun heads; maximum number of suffixes 3; word order does not distinguish subjects, objects, or indirect objects; affixes indicate case of noun phrase; verb affixes mark person, number—obligatory; ergative; passives, causatives, comparatives; simple syllable patterns; nontonal. Mountain slope. 500 to 1,500 meters. Peasant agriculturalists. Traditional religion, Hindu.

Belhariya (Belhare, Athpariya, Athpahariya, Athpare, Athpagari) [byw] 500 (1995 Ebert). Kosi Zone, Dhankuta District, Belhara village and hill west of Dhankuta Bajar. *Class:* Sino-Tibetan, Tibeto-Burman, Himalayish, Mahakiranti, Kiranti, Eastern. *Dialects:* Different from Athpariya, although also called that, and closely related to it (Winter 1991). Not intelligible with Athpariya (Bickel 1996:21). Appears to be between Athpariya, Yakkha, and Chhilling linguistically. *Lg Use:* Belhare is preferred and the standard means of communication in most households. All speakers also use Nepali (Bickel 1996). *Other:* 'Athpare' refers to the ethnic group made up of Belhare and Athpariya. They have close cultural ties, but recognize their linguistic differences. They can clarify by calling the Dhankuta people 'Noupagari' and the Belhare people 'Athpagari' (Bickel 1996:21). 1,150 meters.

Bengali (Bangala, Bangla, Bangla-Bhasa) [ben] 23,602 in Nepal (2001 census). Mechi Zone, Jhapa District; Koshi Zone, Morang and Sunsari districts; Sagarmatha Zone, Saptari District. *Dialects:* Barik, Bhatiari, Chirmar, Kachari-Bengali, Lohari-Malpaharia, Musselmani, Rajshahi, Samaria, Saraki, Siripuria. *Lg Dev:* Literacy rate in second language: 51.2%. *Other:* Hindu, Christian. See main entry under Bangladesh.

Bhojpuri (Bhojapuri, Bhozpuri, Bajpuri) [bho] 1,712,536 in Nepal (2001 census). Main concentration in Narayani Zone, Rautahat, Para, and Parsa districts. Also near the India border in Lumbini Zone, Nawalparasi District; Janakpur Zone, Sarlahi District; Koshi Zone, Morang District; Mechi Zone, Jhapa District. *Dialects:* Bhojpuri Tharu, Teli. *Lg Use:* 74,148 second-language speakers in Nepal (1991 census). Speakers also use Hindi, Maithili, Nepali, or Awadhi. *Lg Dev:* Literacy rate in first language: 5% to 30%. Literacy rate in second language: 50% to 75%. 40% literate in Nepali, Hindi. *Other:* Hindu, Muslim, Christian. See main entry under India.

Bodo (Boro, Bodi, Bara, Boroni, Meche, Mechi, Meci, Mech, Mache) [brx] 3,301 in Nepal (2001 census). Ethnic population: 3,763. Mechi Zone, Jhapa District. *Other:* Meche recognized as an official nationality by the Government of Nepal. Hindu, traditional religion, Christian. See main entry under India.

Bote-Majhi (Kushar) [bmj] 11,000 (1991 census). Narayani Zone, mainly Chitawan District, near Kumhali. *Class:* Indo-European, Indo-Iranian, Indo-Aryan, Eastern zone, Unclassified. *Other:* Bote recognized as an official nationality by the Government of Nepal. Boatmen along various rivers, fishermen. Hindu syncretism with traditional religion.

Bujhyal (Gharti, Bujhel, Bujal, Western Chepang) [byh] 5,000 (1998). Ethnic population: 117,568. Gandaki Zone, East Tanahun District, south side of Chimkesori Peak, behind Yangchok, near the Magar. Separated from the Chepang by the Trisuli (Narayani) River. *Class:* Sino-Tibetan, Tibeto-Burman, Himalayish, Mahakiranti, Kham-Magar-Chepang-Sunwari, Chepang. *Dialects:* Pronominal affix differences hinder intelligibility. More like the East Himalayish languages. Lexical similarity 98% with Chepang. *Lg Use:* Used in the home. All ages. Not a high view of Bujhyal. Chepang viewed as superior. Nepali valued for education. Bilingual level estimates for Nepali: 0 5%, 1 30%, 2 40%, 3 15%, 4 10%, 5 0%. Young people sometimes speak Nepali to each other. Speakers over 5 know some Nepali, which is learned in school. Men can talk about most common and political topics. Women know greetings and how to trade in Nepali. *Lg Dev:* Literacy rate in second language: 15% in Nepal. *Other:* Distinct from slave Gharti. Similar culturally to Chepang. Recognized as an official nationality by the Government of Nepal. OV (S varies); postpositions; genitives, articles, adjectives, numerals, before noun heads; relatives before or without noun heads; question word final; maximum number of suffixes 8; word order does not distinguish subjects, objects, indirect objects; affixes indicate case of noun phrase; verb affixes mark person, number, subject, object—obligatory; passives; causatives; comparatives; CV to CCCVCCC with certain restrictions, semitonal. Mountain slope. Tropical to subtropical. 450 to 1,500 meters. Swidden agriculturalists. Traditional religion, Hindu.

Byangsi (Byanshi, Byansi, Byangkho Lwo, Byasi, Sauka, Shauka) [bee] 1,734 in Nepal (2001 census). Ethnic population: 2,103. Mahakali Zone, Darchula District, 9 villages in Byas Valley. *Lg Use:* 161 second langauge speakers in Nepal (1991 census, under Byanshi). Nepali, Hindi, Kumauni are widely used. *Other:* Recognized as an official nationality by the Government of Nepal. Buddhist. See main entry under India.

Camling (Chamling, Chamlinge Rai, Rodong) [rab] 10,000 (1995 Karen Ebert). Sagarmatha Zone, Khotang District, from Durchhim in W. Khotang all the way east across Diktel to the border of Bhojpur District. From there, south to the Sawa Khola, scattered in Udayapur District. Also spread throughout more districts of eastern Nepal. Sikkim and Darjeeling and Bhutan. *Class:* Sino-Tibetan, Tibeto-Burman, Himalayish, Mahakiranti, Kiranti, Eastern. *Dialects:* Closest to Bantawa and Puma linguistically. Many people speak a variety mixed with Nepali. *Lg Use:* Many ethnic Camling are not fluent in Camling. Learned by children only in a remote area of Udayapur. *Other:* Many ethnic subgroups, but linguistically homogeneous. 'Rodong' means 'Kiranti', not 'Camling'. Some Bantawa call their language 'Camling'. Hindu, traditional religion.

Chantyal (Chentel, Chantel, Chhantel) [chx] 2,000 (1997 Michael Noonan). Ethnic population: 9,814. Dhaulagiri Zone, Myagdi District, Kali Gandaki River valley. Ethnic Chantel also in Baglung District. *Class:* Sino-Tibetan, Tibeto-Burman, Himalayish, Tibeto-Kanauri, Tibetic, Tamangic. *Dialects:* Related to Gurung, Manang, Tamang, Thakali (Noonan). *Lg Use:* Chantel appears to be decreasing in use and Nepali increasing. In Baglung, Chantel ceased to be spoken in the 19th century, and only Nepali is used (Noonan 1997). Used in the home villages (Noonan 1997). Chantel not used for singing. Some speakers believe Chantel will be replaced soon (Noonan 1995:257, 260). Everyone also speaks Nepali. *Lg Dev:* Dictionary. *Other:* Outsiders often regard it as Magar, but they claim a Thakuri origin, (Anne de Sales in G. I. Toffin 1993). A lot of lexical borrowing from Nepali. Recognized as an official nationality by the Government of Nepal. Traditional religion.

Chaudangsi (Tsaudangsi, Bangba Lwo, Sauka, Shauka) [cdn] 1,197 in Nepal (2000). Mahakali Zone, Darchula District, Chaudas Valley, 10 villages. *Other:* May only be in India (Bradley 1997:14). Buddhist. See main entry under India.

Chepang (Tsepang) [cdm] 36,807 (2001 census). Ethnic population: 52,237. Inner Terai; Narayani Zone, Makwanpur, Chitawan, and South Dhading districts; Gandaki Zone, South Gorkha District. *Class:* Sino-Tibetan, Tibeto-Burman, Himalayish, Mahakiranti, Kham-Magar-Chepang-Sunwari, Chepang. *Dialects:* Eastern Chepang, Western Chepang. Bujhel can be considered a dialect close to Western Chepang, but has difficult intelligibility of Chepang, different morphology. Dialects differ in verb forms. Similar in morphology to Kiranti languages. Lexical similarity 98% with Bujhel. *Lg Use:* Used in the home. All ages. Negative language attitude. Bilingual level estimates for Nepali: 0 5%, 1 30%, 2 40%, 3 15%, 4 10%, 5 0%. Speakers over 5 know some Nepali. It is often learned in school. Men can talk about most common topics and political affairs. Women know greetings and vocabulary for trade. Young people may sometimes speak Nepali to each other. *Lg Dev:* Literacy rate in first language: 1% to 5%. Literacy rate in second language: 40% men, 15% women in Nepali; 13.9% ethnic group (1991 census). Difficulties in reading Chepang: long words, consonant clusters. They do not know how to write it. Written Chepang has lower prestige than Nepali. Motivation high for Nepali. Devanagari script. Newspapers. Radio programs. Dictionary. Grammar. *Other:* Recognized as an official nationality by the Government of Nepal. Some form of whistle speech reported. OV (Subject position varies); postpositions; genitives, articles, adjectives, numerals before noun heads; relatives before or without noun heads; question word final; maximum number of suffixes 8; word order does not distinguish subjects, objects, or indirect objects; affixes indicate case of noun phrase; verb affixes mark person, number, subject, object—obligatory; ergative; passives; causatives; comparatives; CV to CCCVCCC with certain restrictions; semitonal. Mountain slope. Tropical to subtropical. 450 to 1,500 meters, especially 600 to 1,500. Swidden agriculturalists. Traditional religion, Hindu syncretism, Christian.

Chhintange (Chhintang, Teli, Chintang Rûng, Chintang) [ctn] 1,500 (2003). Koshi Zone, Lower Arun Region, Dhankuta District, Chhintang Panchayat, Sambhung and Pokhare, and Ankhisalla Panchayat, Dandagaon. *Class:* Sino-Tibetan, Tibeto-Burman, Himalayish, Mahakiranti, Kiranti, Eastern. *Dialects:* Probably not intelligible with Bantawa, although sometimes considered a dialect of it because of ethnic similarities. *Lg Use:* The ethnic group has largely shifted to Bantawa or Nepali (Bradley 1996); UNESCO reports there may be more vitality than formerly supposed. *Other:* 'Chimtan' recognized as an official nationality by the Government of Nepal.

Chhulung (Chulung, Chüling, Chhûlûng Rûng, Chholung, Chhilling) [cur] 1,314 (2001 census). Koshi Zone, Ankhisalla Panchayat, Dhankuta District, end of Chhintang Panchayat. *Class:* Sino-Tibetan, Tibeto-Burman, Himalayish, Mahakiranti, Kiranti, Eastern. *Lg Use:* Speakers know a moderate amount of Nepali. *Other:* Traditional religion.

Chukwa (Cukwa Ring, Pohing, Pohing Kha) [cuw] 100 (1991 W. Winter). Koshi Zone, Bhojpur District, Kulung Panchayat. *Class:* Sino-Tibetan, Tibeto-Burman, Himalayish, Mahakiranti, Kiranti, Eastern. *Lg Use:* Speakers also use Nepali. *Other:* Linguistically between Kulung-Nachering-Sangpang and Meohang-Saam. Nearly extinct.

Darai [dry] 10,210 (2001 census). Ethnic population: 14,859. Inner Terai, Narayani Zone, Chitawan District; Gandaki Zone, Tanahu District. *Class:* Indo-European, Indo-Iranian, Indo-Aryan, Unclassified. *Lg Use:* Speakers also use Nepali. *Lg Dev:* Literacy rate in second language: 36.5% (1991 census). *Other:* Typological affinities with Northwestern Zone, Dardic group. Recognized as an official nationality by the Government of Nepal. The Darai do not have any of the social subdivisions found in the majority of other Nepali groups. They do not organize their communities into social, religious, economic, or political organizations (Bista). Hindu mixed with traditional religion.

Darmiya (Darimiya, Sauka, Shauka) [drd] 1,197 in Nepal (2000). Mahakali Zone, Darchula District, Dhauli or Darma Valley, 16 villages. *Other:* May only be in India; for example, in Bradley (1997) it is said to be only in India and in Sharma (1989) there is no reference to speakers in Nepal, but Rana mentions Shaukas in Darma Valley. Hindu. See main entry under India.

Dhanwar (Dhanvar, Danuwar Rai, Danuwar, Denwar) [dhw] 31,849 (2001 census). 70% to 75% monolingual.

Ethnic population: 53,229. Janakpur Zone, Sindhuli District; Eastern hills and plain, inner Terai and Terai south of Kathmandu, Makwanpur District, Narayani Zone. *Class:* Indo-European, Indo-Iranian, Indo-Aryan, Unclassified. *Dialects:* Danuwar Done in Makwanpur and India and Danuwar Kachariya in Rautahat and elsewhere are probably distinct languages from Danuwar Rai. Typological affinities with Northwestern Zone, Dardic group. *Lg Use:* Others use Nepali as second language. *Lg Dev:* Literacy rate in second language: 24.5% (1991 census). *Other:* Hindu, syncretism with traditional religion, traditional religion, Christian.

Dhimal [dhi] 17,308 in Nepal (2001 census). Population total all countries: 17,758. Ethnic population: 19,537. Mechi Zone, Jhapa District, 24 villages; Koshi Zone, Morang District, 51 villages; East and West dialects are separated by the Kankai River in Jhapa. Also spoken in India. *Class:* Sino-Tibetan, Tibeto-Burman, Himalayish, Tibeto-Kanauri, Tibetic, Dhimal. *Dialects:* Eastern Dhimal, Western Dhimal. Toto in India is a separate language with no inherent intelligibility between them. 75% to 80% intelligibility between eastern and western dialect speakers. Low lexical similarity with Toto. 80% to 82% between dialects. *Lg Use:* 405 second-language speakers (1991 census). Used in the home, community. All ages. No strong attitudes as to what is 'pure' Dhimal. No negative feelings between speakers of different dialects. Positive language attitude toward Nepali. Most are partially bilingual in Nepali, but very few are fluent. Men are more fluent than women, educated people more than uneducated. Hindi, Rajbansi also used. *Lg Dev:* Literacy rate in second language: 39.2% (1991 census). Devanagari script. Dictionary. *Other:* Recognized as an official nationality by the Government of Nepal. SOV; postpositions; genitives, demonstratives, relatives before noun heads; nontonal. Plains. Forest. Peasant agriculturalists.

Dolpo (Phoke Dolpa, Dolpa Tibetan, Dolpike) [dre] 9,000 (2003). 5,000 monolinguals (2003). Karnali Zone, northern Dolpo District, villages of Goomatara, Kola, Tachel, Kani, Bajebara, Laun, Chilpara, Bantari, Byas, above Dolpa up to Tibet. It is beyond the mountains west of the upper Kali Gandaki River Valley. Confined by the Dhaulagire Himal on the south and Tibet on the north. Includes the headwaters of the Karnali River. About 24 small villages scattered over 500 square miles in Namgang, Panzgang, Tarap, and Chharbung subdistricts. *Class:* Sino-Tibetan, Tibeto-Burman, Himalayish, Tibeto-Kanauri, Tibetic, Tibetan, Central. *Dialects:* Dho Tarap, Phoksumdo Lake, Barbung River, and Charka-Dolpo Chu River areas are slightly different, but inherent intelligibility is very good. Closest language is Lowa. Dho Tarap reportedly understood best by all speakers. Reported to be close to Tichurong. Lexical similarity 78% with Lowa; 69% with Lhomi; 68% with Lhasa Tibetan, Walungge, and Kyerung; 67% with Kutang Bhotia; 66% with Helambu Sherpa; 62% with Jirel and Sherpa. *Lg Use:* Used in the home. Dho Tarap speech may have highest prestige. Tibetan is spoken in trade with Tibetan neighbors across the border and with Tibetans that are encountered in Nepal and other areas. Tibetan is spoken by men who have traveled to Kathmandu or other locations in South Asia where Tibetan is used as a language of wider communication. Few women know Tibetan. 2,000 to 3,000 speak Tibetan. To Nepali officials, shopkeepers, when conducting commerce, trade, etc., Nepali is spoken. Men who travel, traders, and younger children who have attended some school will speak some Nepali in certain domains. Women know little or no Nepali. About 2,000 are fluent in Nepali. Lowa is also used. *Other:* Recognized as an official nationality by the Government of Nepal. Speakers call themselves and their language 'Dolpo'. SOV. Mountain valley. 2,500 to 4,500 meters. Agriculturalists: local consumption only; pastoralists: local homes, but some members may be away tending herds 10 months every year. Buddhist, Bonpo.

Dumi (Dumi Bo'o, Dumi Bro, Ro'do Bo', Lsi Rai, Sotmali) [dus] 3 (2000 Van Driem). Ethnic population: 1,000 to 2,000 (1991 W. Winter). Sagarmatha Zone, Northern Khotang District, hills near the middle of the Rawakhola Valley, Baksila, Saptesvara abutting Rava and Tap rivers near the confluence and upriver. *Class:* Sino-Tibetan, Tibeto-Burman, Himalayish, Mahakiranti, Kiranti, Western. *Dialects:* Brasmi, Kharbari, Lamdija, Makpa. Closest to Khaling and Koi. *Lg Use:* Speakers are shifting to Nepali. All speakers are older adults. *Lg Dev:* Grammar. *Other:* Nearly extinct.

Dungmali (Dungmali Pûk, Dungmali-Bantawa, Arthare, Arthare-Khesang) [raa] 4,609 (2000 SIL). East of central Bhojpur District, northeast of the Singtang Lekh, bend of the Arun River between its confluence with the Piukhuwa and the first confluence with the Piluwa River. *Class:* Sino-Tibetan, Tibeto-Burman, Himalayish, Mahakiranti, Kiranti, Eastern. *Dialect:* Khesang (Khesange). The term 'Kiranti' covers about 21 dialects, of which fewer than half are even partially intelligible. *Other:* Local names which may not be dialects: Chhinamkhang, Hangbang, Khandung, Pungwai, Roktulung, Tuncha, Waitpang.

Dura [drq] Extinct. Ethnic population: 3,397 (2001 census). Gandaki Zone, Lamjung District, Dura Danda. *Class:* Sino-Tibetan, Tibeto-Burman, West Bodish. *Lg Use:* Members of the ethnic group now speak Nepali.

Dzongkha (Jonkha, Bhotia of Bhutan, Zongkhar, Drukke, Drukha, Bhutanese) [dzo] 9 in Nepal (2001 census). Some in Kathmandu. *Other:* 'Lhoke' means 'southern language'. Traders; shopkeepers. See main entry under Bhutan.

Ghale, Kutang (Bhotte) [ght] 1,300 (1992). Gandaki Zone, Northern Gorkha District, Buri Gandaki Valley from Nyak, up to and including Prok. *Class:* Sino-Tibetan, Tibeto-Burman, Himalayish, Tibeto-Kanauri, Tibetic, Tamangic. *Dialects:* Bihi, Chak, Rana. Barpak Ghale is understood fairly well farther north. There is a smaller difference between Uiya and Philim than between Barpak and either Uiya or Philim. Lexical similarity 62% to 76% among dialects. Rana is the most diverse. Lexical similarity 39% to 49% with Southern Ghale, 45% to 61% with Northern Ghale, 18% with Banspur Gurung, 16% to 23% with Tamang varieties, 13% to 31% with Nubri, 23% to 27% with Tsum, 22% to 27% with Kyerung, 19% to 24% with Tibetan. *Lg Use:* Vigorous. Some Tibetan religious books have been translated into Kutang Ghale by priests who speak the language. Nearly every domain. Attitude toward their language is positive and strong. Tibetan viewed favorably for religious use, Nepali for education and advancement. Speakers in Bihi village have minimal bilingual proficiency in Tibetan and Nepali. Nepali used for communicating with Northern and Southern Ghale speakers. *Lg Dev:* Literacy rate in first language: Some can read Kutang Ghale in Tibetan script. Literacy rate in second language: 5%. Because literacy in the Tibetan script is currently so low, it is recommended that initial literature development be done in Devanagari script to assist the people in making the transition to Nepali literature as well (Webster 1992:29). Tibetan script. *Other:* They call their language 'thieves language' because they think of it as a mixture of nearby languages. Mountain slope. Gallery forest. 2,000 to 4,100 meters. Swidden and peasant agriculturalists. Buddhist (Lamaist).

Ghale, Northern [ghh] 2,500 (1991 Smith). Gandaki Zone, Gorkha District, Buri Gandaki Valley. *Class:* Sino-Tibetan, Tibeto-Burman, Himalayish, Tibeto-Kanauri, Tibetic, Tamangic. *Dialects:* Khorla, Uiya, Jagat, Philim, Nyak. Nyak is the most diverse dialect. Philim people have 94% intelligibility of Uiya. Speakers have 75% to 79% intelligibility of Barpak in Southern Ghale. Dialect chain runs north and south. Lexical similarity 73% to 89% among dialects. Lexical similarity 65% to 81% with Southern Ghale, 45% to 61% with Kutang Ghale, 29% to 37% with Western Tamang, 21% to 27% with Nubri, 22% to 25% with Tsum, 19% to 23% with Kyerung, 19% to 21% with Tibetan. *Lg Use:* Vigorous. All domains. Positive attitudes toward N. Ghale. Nepali seen as good for use with government and other groups. Uiya and Barpak are the centers, Barpak has the most prestige. Speakers in Philim, Lho, and Bihi have no more than basic bilingual proficiency in Nepali. *Other:* Mountain slope, valley. Gallery forest. 2,000 to 4,100 meters. Swidden and peasant agriculturalists. Buddhist.

Ghale, Southern (Galle Gurung) [ghe] 25,189 (2000). Gandaki Zone, Gorkha District, hills south of Macha Khola. *Class:* Sino-Tibetan, Tibeto-Burman, Himalayish, Tibeto-Kanauri, Tibetic, Tamangic. *Dialects:* Barpak, Kyaura, Laprak. Some intelligibility between N. and S. Ghale. Dialect cluster. Glover (1974:8–12) has a Ghale branch under Bodish intermediate between the Tibetan and Gurung branches. Lexical similarity 75% to 78% among dialects. Lexical similarity 65% to 81% with Northern Ghale, 39% to 49% with Kutang Ghale, 27% to 30% with Banspur Gurung, 31% with Western Tamang, 20% with Nubri and Tsum, 18% with Tibetan. *Lg Use:* Vigorous. All domains. Positive attitudes toward Southern Ghale. Barpak is the most prestigious center. Nepali is viewed as useful for intergroup commerce and government. 30% to 40% monolingual. Others use Nepali, Hindi, or English as second languages. Nepali used with Kutang Ghale and other groups. *Lg Dev:* Literacy rate in second language: 5% to 15%. Dictionary. NT: 1992. *Other:* Mountain slope, valley. Gallery forest. 600 to 1,800 meters. Swidden and peasant agriculturalists. Hindu, Buddhist.

Gurung, Eastern [ggn] 105,000 (1991 census). 227,918 all Gurung languages in Nepal (1991 census). Western Dev. Region, Gandaki Zone, mainly Lamjung, Tanahu, and western Gorkha districts. Possibly some in Manang District. *Class:* Sino-Tibetan, Tibeto-Burman, Himalayish, Tibeto-Kanauri, Tibetic, Tamangic. *Dialects:* Lamjung Gurung, Gorkha Gurung, Tamu Kyi. Eastern and Western Gurung do not have adequate intelligibility to handle complex and abstract discourse. Daduwa town seems central linguistically. *Lg Use:* Used in the home. All ages. Language reinforces ethnic membership. Nepali viewed as essential, English as economically advantageous. All also use Nepali. School graduates use some English. *Lg Dev:* Literacy rate in first language: 30%. Literacy rate in second language: 30%. Devanagari script. Radio programs. *Other:* Gurung recognized as an official nationality by the Government of Nepal. SOV; postpositions; genitives, adjectives relatives before noun heads; numerals after noun heads; rising intonation in bipolar questions; 1 prefix on negative verbs; maximum number of suffixes 3; case of noun phrase shown by preposition; no subject or object referencing in verbs; split ergative system according to tense; causatives; benefactives; CV, CCV, CCCV; tonal. Mountain slope, foothills. 1,500 to 3,000 meters. Peasant agriculturalists; pastoralists. Buddhist, Hindu.

Gurung, Western (Gurung, Tamu Kyi) [gvr] 72,000 in Nepal (1991 census). Population total all countries: 72,082. Gandaki Zone, Kaski, Syangja districts; Dhaulagiri Zone, Parbat District. Also possibly in Myanmar. Also spoken in Bhutan, India. *Class:* Sino-Tibetan, Tibeto-Burman, Himalayish, Tibeto-Kanauri, Tibetic, Tamangic. *Dialects:* Southern Gurung (Syangja Gurung), Northwestern Gurung (Kaski Gurung). Dialect speakers may have enough inherent intelligibility of each other to understand complex and abstract discourse. Not enough with Eastern Gurung. Related to Thakali. *Lg Use:* 18,918 second-language speakers on all Gurung languages (1991 census). Used in the home. All ages. Positive language attitude. All ages and sexes use Nepali. Most can talk about common topics in Nepali. Nepali is viewed as necessary. School graduates speak some English, which is viewed as economically advantageous. *Lg Dev:* Literacy rate in first language: 30%. Literacy rate in second language: 30%. Devanagari script. Radio programs. Dictionary. Grammar. NT: 1982. *Other:* Recognized as an official nationality by the Government of Nepal. SOV; postpositions; genitives, adjectives, relatives before noun heads; numerals after noun heads; rising intonation marks bipolar questions; one negative prefix on verbs; maximum number of suffixes is 3; case of noun phrases is indicated by postpositions; no subject or object referencing in verbs; split ergative system according to tense; causatives; benefactives; CV, CCV, CCCV; tonal. Mountain slope, foothills. 1,500 to 3,000 meters. Peasant agriculturalists; pastoralists. Traditional religion, Hindu.

Helambu Sherpa (Yholmo, Yohlmu Tam) [scp] 7,565 (2000 WCD). Bagmati Zone, Nuwakot and Sindhupalchok districts, Helambu area. *Class:* Sino-Tibetan, Tibeto-Burman, Himalayish, Tibeto-Kanauri, Tibetic, Tibetan, Central. *Dialects:* Eastern Helambu Sherpa, Western Helambu Sherpa. Melamchi River divides the dialects. Speakers understand other dialects even for abstract and complex subjects, including possibly Tarke Ghyang, Khang-Kharka, Pahndang, but not Kagate. Lexical similarity 66% with Dolpo and Walungge, 65% with Lhasa Tibetan, Jirel, and Kyerung, 63% with Lowa and Sherpa, 61% with Nubri, 60% with Lhomi. *Lg Use:* Used in the home. All ages in homeland. In Kathmandu, parents tend to speak Nepali to children. Helambu Sherpa is more prestigious than Kagate, has more of the original culture preserved. Shermathang-Chhimi area in the east is prestigious. Many lamas live there. Not much contact with Kagate; attitudes are indifferent toward it. Nepali is viewed as useful. Most can talk about common topics in Nepali. Men know more than women. In Kathmandu, some people pick up Tibetan quite quickly; also Hindi (through TV). *Lg Dev:* Literacy rate in first language: below 1%. Literacy rate in second language: 15% to 25%. Literacy motivation not high, except in English. Devanagari script. Radio programs. Dictionary. NT: 2000. *Other:* They go to India as laborers. SOV; postpositions; genitives, relatives before noun heads; articles, adjectives, numerals mostly after noun heads; maximum number of prefixes 1; maximum number of suffixes 2–3; word order distinguishes subject, object, indirect object some, but normally marked by postpositions; case of noun phrase indicated by postposition; split ergativity; impersonal voice; causatives; comparatives; CV, CVC, CVV, CCV, CCVV, CVVC; tonal. Mountain slope. 2,000 to 3,000 meters. Peasant agriculturalists. Buddhist (Lamaist), traditional religion.

Hindi [hin] 105,765 in Nepal (2001 census). Southern strip of low country. *Lg Use:* Language of wider communication. 489,578 second-language speakers in Nepal (1991 census). *Other:* Hindu. See main entry under India.

Humla (Dangali, Phoke, Humla "Bhotia") [hut] 2,393 (2000). Seti Zone, Bajura District; Karnali Zone, Humla District. *Class:* Sino-Tibetan, Tibeto-Burman, Himalayish, Tibeto-Kanauri, Tibetic, Tibetan, Central. *Dialects:* Probably a separate language from Tibetan. *Lg Dev:* Literacy rate in second language: Low in Tibetan. *Other:* Buddhist.

Jerung (Jero, Jerum, Jerunge, Jherung, Jero Mala, Zero, Zerum, Zero Mala) [jee] 1,914 (2000). Janakpur Zone,

Sindhuli District, around and above the mouth of the Melungkhola River. *Class:* Sino-Tibetan, Tibeto-Burman, Himalayish, Mahakiranti, Kiranti, Western. *Dialect:* Madhavpur, Balkhu-Sisneri, Ratnawati (Sindhuli). Linguistically closest to Wambule. *Lg Use:* Use is declining. (Winter 1991). Used mainly by older adults. Young people appear to not speak Jerung. Speakers also use Nepali. *Other:* Hindu.

Jirel (Ziral, Jiri, Jirial) [jul] 4,919 (2001 census). Janakpur Zone, Dolakha District, Jiri and Sikri valleys, eastern hills. Jiri is the main area. Others include Chhyatrapa; Lumbini and Nawalparasi districts. *Class:* Sino-Tibetan, Tibeto-Burman, Himalayish, Tibeto-Kanauri, Tibetic, Tibetan, Southern. *Dialects:* Accent differences, but not real dialects. Some comprehension of Lhasa Tibetan and some Tibetan dialects. Lexical similarity 67% with Sherpa, 65% with Helambu Sherpa, 62% with Dolpo and Lowa, 60% with Kyerung, 57% with Nubri, Lhomi, and Walungge, 54% with Lhasa Tibetan. *Lg Use:* All ages. Karsa and Kharok accents are more prestigious, more educated. Nepali viewed as prestigious, needed for education, work, talking to non-Jirel people. Bilingual level estimates for Nepali: 0 few%, 1 5%, 2 40%, 3 40–50%, 4 5–10%, 5 0%. A few know some Sherpa, very few some Tamang and Sunwar. Some know enough Nepali only for trade (mainly women). *Lg Dev:* Literacy rate in first language: 25% to 30% adults, 60% younger people. Literacy rate in second language: 25% to 30% adults, 60% younger people (1991 census). People literate in Nepali can read Jirel. Devanagari script. Dictionary. NT: 1992. *Other:* Recognized as an official nationality by the Government of Nepal. SOV; postpositions; genitives, demonstratives, adjectives before noun heads; numerals after noun heads; relatives before and without noun heads; content question word initial or medial; polar question word final; maximum number of prefixes 1, maximum number of suffixes 4; subjects, objects, indirect objects distinguished by case marker; affixes indicate case of noun phrases; verb affixes mark person; ergative; causatives; CV, CVC, V, VC; tonal. Mountain slope. 1,700 to 2,000 meters. Peasant agriculturalists. Hindu, Buddhist, syncretism with traditional religion.

Jumli (Jumeli, Jumleli, Jumla, Khas Nepali, Sijali, Singja) [jml] 800,000 (2003). Karnali Zone, Jumla District. *Class:* Indo-European, Indo-Iranian, Indo-Aryan, Northern Zone, Eastern Pahari. *Dialects:* Assi, Chaudhabis, Paachsai, Sinja. 73% to 89% intelligible with standard Nepali. Not sufficient to understand complex and abstract discourse. Lexical similarity 73% to 80% with standard Nepali. *Lg Use:* Used in the home. Positive language attitude. Some are embarrassed by their own speech. Men who travel and those who are educated speak more Nepali. Lamas speak Bhote. Some use Hindi as a second language. *Lg Dev:* Literacy rate in second language: 22% to 32%. *Other:* Mountain slope. Forest. 3,500 meters. Peasant agriculturalists. Hindu, Buddhist (Lamaist), syncretism with traditional religion.

Kagate (Shuba, Shyuba, Syuba, Kagate Bhote) [syw] 1,273 (2000). Janakpur Zone, Ramechhap District, on one of the ridges of Likhu Khola. *Class:* Sino-Tibetan, Tibeto-Burman, Himalayish, Tibeto-Kanauri, Tibetic, Tibetan, Central. *Dialects:* Differs from Helambu Sherpa by using less the honorific system in verbs. *Lg Use:* All domains. All ages. Attitude toward Helambu Sherpa is indifferent—not much contact because of distance. Reserved attitude toward Nepali people, but positive toward Nepali language. Some also use Nepali. More Nepali used in Kathmandu. *Lg Dev:* Literacy rate in second language: Few. Devanagari script. Bible portions: 1977. *Other:* SOV; postpositions; genitives, adjectives, relatives before noun heads; numerals after noun heads; maximum number of prefixes 1; maximum number of suffixes 3; subject, object, indirect object, case of noun phrase indicated by postpositions; split ergativity; impersonal voice; causatives; comparatives; CV, CVC, CVV, CCV, CCVV, CVVC; tonal. Mountain slope. 2,000 meters. Peasant agriculturalists. Buddhist (Lamaist), syncretism with traditional religion.

Kaike (Tarali Kham) [kzq] 794 (2001 census). Karnali Zone, Dolpa District; Dhaulagiri Zone. *Class:* Sino-Tibetan, Tibeto-Burman, Himalayish, Tibeto-Kanauri, Western Himalayish, Kanauri. *Lg Use:* They view Kaike in low regard because it is felt to be unsophisticated and unexpressive, very low cultural self-esteem (Fisher 1987:130). Speakers also use Nepali. *Other:* Kaike is also sometimes known as 'Tarali Kham', though it is quite different from Kham, a Himalayan language of western Nepal. (Bradley 1997:11). Sometimes called 'Khamkura'. This can have a general meaning of "local non-Nepali dialect." Hunter-gatherers.

Kayort [kyv] 22,000 (2002). Koshi Zone, Morang District, Dakuwa Danga, near Rajbanshi language. *Class:* Indo-European, Indo-Iranian, Indo-Aryan, Eastern zone, Bengali-Assamese. *Dialects:* Related to Bengali.

Khaling (Kaling, Khalinge Rai, Khael Bra, Khael Baat) [klr] 9,288 in Nepal (2001 census). Sagarmatha Zone, SoluKhumbu, Khotang districts; Koshi Zone, Bhojpur, Sankhuwasawa, Terhathum districts; Mechi Zone, Panchthar and Ilam districts. Also spoken in India. *Class:* Sino-Tibetan, Tibeto-Burman, Himalayish, Mahakiranti, Kiranti, Western. *Dialects:* Closest to Dumi and Koi. *Lg Use:* All ages. Bilingual level estimates for Nepali: 0 0%, 1 1%, 2 5%, 3 50%, 4 30%, 5 14%. Older women are less bilingual and many have only minimal comprehension of Nepali. *Lg Dev:* Literacy rate in first language: below 1%. Literacy rate in second language: 5% to 15%. Dictionary. NT: 1994. *Other:* SOV; postpositions; articles, adjectives, numerals, relatives before noun heads; question word initial; maximum number of prefixes 1; word order distinguishes subject, object, indirect object; affixes indicate case of noun phrase; verb affixes mark person and number of subject—obligatory; ergative; causatives; comparatives; C, V, CCCV; tonal. Mountain valley. Scrub forest: dwarf, or stunted trees and shrubs. 1,300 to 2,300 meters. Peasant agriculturalists: adapted marginally to market system. Traditional religion.

Kham, Gamale (Gamale) [kgj] 10,000 (1988). Rapti Zone, Rukum and Rolpa districts, western hills, Gam Khola. *Class:* Sino-Tibetan, Tibeto-Burman, Himalayish, Mahakiranti, Kham-Magar-Chepang-Sunwari, Kham. *Dialects:* Tamali, Ghusbanggi. Lexical similarity 71% with Western Parbate (closest), 55% with Eastern Parbate and Sheshi, 45% with Bhujel. *Lg Use:* Vigorous. Most have limited bilingualism in Nepali. *Lg Dev:* Literacy rate in first language: 1% to 5%. Literacy rate in second language: 5% to 15%. *Other:* Hindu, traditional religion, Buddhist.

Kham, Sheshi (Sheshi) [kip] 20,000 (2003). Rapti Zone, Rukum and Rolpa districts, western hills, Jangkot, Kotgaon (Tapnang), Rimsek, Korcabang, Dangdung, Hwama, Dhangsi, Bhabang, and Ghapa villages. *Class:* Sino-Tibetan, Tibeto-Burman, Himalayish, Mahakiranti, Kham-Magar-Chepang-Sunwari, Kham. *Dialects:* Tapnanggi, Jangkoti. Lexical similarity 55% with Gamale Kham (closest), 51% with Western Parbate, 46% with Bhujel, 44% with Eastern Parbate. *Lg Use:* Vigorous. Some speakers also use Nepali. *Lg Dev:* Literacy rate in first language: below 1%. Literacy rate in second language: below 5%.

Koi (Koyu, Kohi, Koyi, Koi Bo'o, Koyu Bo') [kkt] 2,641 (2001 census). Sagarmatha Zone, northeastern Khotang District, Sungdel Panchayat near the headwaters of the Rawakhola, 2 villages. *Class:* Sino-Tibetan, Tibeto-Burman, Himalayish, Mahakiranti, Kiranti, Western. *Dialects:* Sungdel, Behere. Closest to Dumi and Khaling. *Lg Use:* Speakers also use Nepali. *Other:* Some people called 'Koi' who live scattered in other language areas speak only Nepali.

Kulung (Khulunge Rai, Kulu Ring, Khulung, Kholung) [kle] 18,686 in Nepal (2001 census). Sagarmatha Zone, Solu Khumbu District, eastern hills, Hongu Valley, Mahakulung Region; Koshi Zone, Sankhuwasawa, Terhathum, Panchthar, Ilam districts. In Solu Khumbu, they live primarily along the Hongu Khola in villages of Bumng (Bung), Pilmu, Cheskam Sadhi, Gudel, and Namlu. In Sankhuwasawa District in villages of Baliyamnang, Phedi Khola, Wasepla, Mangtewa, Yaphu, Chayeng, Walung, and Sheduwa. These areas are mainly in the drainages of the Sangkhuwa and Siswa rivers, which flow into the Arun River. Also spoken in some Terai areas. Also spoken in India. *Class:* Sino-Tibetan, Tibeto-Burman, Himalayish, Mahakiranti, Kiranti, Eastern. *Dialects:* Sotang (Sotaring, Sottaring), Mahakulung, Tamachhang, Pidisoi, Chhapkoa, Pelmung, Namlung, Khambu. Intelligibility between Kulung and Sota Ring is 100% because only some words are pronounced differently. Related to Sangpang and Nachereng. *Lg Use:* Attitudes among dialects from positive to unfriendly. Up to 50% of the population can understand some Nepali at a basic level. Only Kulung who live on the border with other language groups speak the other language. *Lg Dev:* Literacy rate in second language: 10% to 50% adults, 10% women. High motivation for literacy. Devanagari script. Dictionary. Grammar. *Other:* Exogamous clan marriage. The high number of Kulung reflect the tendency of smaller groups to consider themselves Kulung, but they are by origin not Kulung. The Kulung possibly absorb smaller groups. Case, ergative. Mountain valley. Scrub forest: dwarf or stunted trees and shrubs. 1,400 to 3,300 meters. Agriculturalists: millet, maize; hunters; fishermen. Traditional religion, Hindu, Buddhist.

Kumauni (Kumaon) [kfy] Mahakali Zone, Kanchanpur District. See main entry under India.

Kumhali (Kumhale, Kumbale, Kumkale, Kumali) [kra] 6,533 (2001 census). Ethnic population: 99,389. Lumbini Zone, Nawalparasi District, south of the Darai. *Class:* Indo-European, Indo-Iranian, Indo-Aryan, Unclassified. *Lg Use:* Some are partially bilingual in Nepali. *Other:* 'Kumal' recognized as an official nationality by the Government of Nepal. Lowland, riverine. Agriculturalists; pastoralists; fishermen. Hindu, traditional religion.

Kurmukar [kfv] See main entry under India.

Kurux, Nepali (Dhangar, Jhanger, Janghard, Jangad, Uraon, Orau, Oraon) [kxl] 28,615 (2001 census). Ethnic population: 41,764 Dhagar and Jhagar. Eastern Terai, Janakpur Zone, Dhanusa District, may be scattered as far as from Sarlahi to Moran districts. *Class:* Dravidian, Northern. *Dialects:* Different from Kurux of India and Bangladesh. *Lg Use:* Speakers also use Maithili, Nagpuri, Bhojpuri, or Assamese. *Lg Dev:* Literacy rate in second language: 10%. Bible portions: 1977. *Other:* The alternate names are used for the people. Jangad recognized as an official nationality by the Government of Nepal. Agriculturalists. Hindu, Christian.

Kusunda (Kusanda) [kgg] Extinct. Ethnic population: 164. Gandaki Zone, Tanahu District, western hills, Satto Bhatti west of Chepetar, and possibly jungle south of Ambhu. Kireni, near Kumhali. *Class:* Sino-Tibetan, Tibeto-Burman, Himalayish, Mahakiranti, Kham-Magar-Chepang-Sunwari, Chepang. *Lg Use:* 3 speakers reported in 2001. Their descendants do not speak the language. In 2001, a second-hand report of a speaker in Surket. *Other:* Recognized as an official nationality by the Government of Nepal. Caughley suggests it is not a Tibeto-Burman language. Verb pronominalization with subject agreement. Hunters.

Kyerung (Kyirong, Gyirong) [kgy] 4,786 in Nepal (2000). Population total all countries: 4,886. Bagmati Zone, Rasuwa District, Langtang Region, Rasua Garbi, Birdim, Thangjet, Syabru, and Syabrubensi villages; and large concentrations in Kathmandu. Also spoken in China. *Class:* Sino-Tibetan, Tibeto-Burman, Himalayish, Tibeto-Kanauri, Tibetic, Tibetan, Central. *Dialects:* Close to Lhasa Tibetan. Lexical similarity 68% with Dolpo, Walungge, Lhomi, and Lowa, 65% with Nubri and Lhasa Tibetan, 63% with Helambu Sherpa, 60% with Jirel, 57% with Sherpa. *Other:* Buddhist.

Lambichhong (Lambichong, Lambicchong, Lambitshong) [lmh] 500 (1991 W. Winter). Eastern bank of the Arun River, in a strip between Mugakhola and Sinuwakhola; Koshi Zone, Dhankuta District, Muga and Pakhribas panchayats. *Class:* Sino-Tibetan, Tibeto-Burman, Himalayish, Mahakiranti, Kiranti, Eastern. *Dialects:* Ethnically related to the Bantawa. *Lg Use:* Speakers are shifting to Bantawa (D. Bradley 1996). *Other:* Sometimes incorrectly called 'Mugali' or 'Yakkha'.

Lepcha (Rong, Rongke, Lapche, Rongpa, Nünpa) [lep] 2,826 in Nepal (2001 census). Ethnic population: 3,660. Mechi Zone, Ilam District. *Dialects:* Ilammu, Tamsangmu, Rengjongmu. *Lg Use:* Many of the younger generation in Nepal speak Nepali as first language and do not speak Lepcha. *Other:* Linguistic position within Tibeto-Burman still under discussion. Recognized as an official nationality by the Government of Nepal. Agriculturalists; pastoralists. Buddhist. See main entry under India.

Lhomi (Lhoket, Shing Saapa, Kath Bhote, Kar Bhote) [lhm] 4,000 in Nepal. Population total all countries: 6,000. Koshi Zone, Sankhuwasawa District, Chepuwa VDC, Chepuwa, Chyamtang, Gumba, Chhumusur, Rukuma (or Ridak) villages; Hatiya VDC, Hatiya, Hungung, Pharang, Syaksila, Simbung (or Shembung), Namase (or Namuchhe), Shiprung villages; some in Kathmandu. Also spoken in China, India. *Class:* Sino-Tibetan, Tibeto-Burman, Himalayish, Tibeto-Kanauri, Tibetic, Tibetan, Central. *Dialects:* The dialect may be different across the Tibet border. Lexical similarity 69% with Dolpo, 68% with Lowa, 66% with Walungge, 65% with Lhasa Tibetan and Kyerung, 64% with Nubri, 60% with Helambu Sherpa, 58% with Sherpa, 57% with Jirel. *Lg Use:* Speakers also use Nepali. *Lg Dev:* Literacy rate in first language: below 1%. Literacy rate in second language: 5% to 25% (men). NT: 1995. *Other:* Recognized as an official nationality by the Government of Nepal. Village Development Committee (VDC) is a body with authority over "4 to 7" villages. SOV. Agriculturalists; pastoralists. Traditional religion, Buddhist (Lamaist).

Limbu (Yakthung Pan) [lif] 333,633 in Nepal (2001 census). Population total all countries: 361,633. Limbuwan (preferred term for the Limbu area), Eastern hills, east of the Arun River; Koshi Zone, Dhankuta, Sankhuwasawa, Terhathum, Dhankuta, and Morang districts; Mechi Zone, Taplejung, Panchthar, Ilam, and Jhapa districts. There may be migrant workers in Myanmar. Also spoken in Bhutan, India. *Class:* Sino-Tibetan, Tibeto-Burman, Himalayish, Mahakiranti, Kiranti, Eastern. *Dialects:* Taplejunge (Tamorkhole, Taplejung), Panthare (Pantharey, Panchthare, Panchthar, Panthare-Yanggrokke-Chaubise-Charkhole), Phedappe, Chattare (Chhattare, Chhathar, Chatthare, Chatthare Yakthungba Pan, Yakthung Pan). Related to Lohorong and Yakha. Chaubise dialect is similar to Panthare, and Phedappe to Taplejunge. Chattare is poorly understood by speakers of the other dialects. Inherent intelligibility among the dialect speakers is 80% to 90%. Lexical similarity above 80% among the dialects.

Lg Use: Vigorous. One of the main groups in eastern Nepal. Used in the home and worship. All ages. Positive language attitude. Panthare dialect is dominant in size, prestige, and language development. People prefer their own dialect, but are not negative toward others. 28% of adult speakers (48% of men and 6% of women) have completed 5 years of school, and have good general proficiency in Nepali. 62% of the Limbu have no more than basic proficiency. There is a trend toward more use of Nepali, especially among young people, but it is not replacing Limbu in any domain. *Lg Dev:* Literacy rate in first language: 1% in Sirijangga script, 40% in Devanagari. Literacy rate in second language: 46.8% among the Limbu ethnic group (1991 census). Extensive literacy effort needed. Motivation high among all. It would be easier to read Limbu in Devanagari, but attitudes strongly positive toward Sirijannga script being taught. Local script; Roman, Devanagari, and Limbu scripts in India. Poetry. Magazines. Newspapers. Radio programs. TV. Dictionary. Grammar. *Other:* Common Limbu is called 'Tajengpan'. The priestly high language, also known by some older people, is called 'Mundumban'. Limbu recognized as an official nationality by the Government of Nepal. SOV; postpositions; genitives, articles, adjectives, numerals before noun heads; content question word initial; bipolar question word final; maximum of 3 prefixes, 6 suffixes; affixes indicate case of noun phrases; verb affixes mark subjects, objects, indirect objects—obligatory; split ergativity; reflexes conjugated intrasitively can be used as a kind of passive; antipassives; causatives; comparatives; V, CV, CVC, CCV, CCVC; nontonal. Mountain slope. Gallery forest. 800 to 1,600 meters. Peasant agriculturalists. Kiranti traditional religion.

Lingkhim (Limkhim, Linkhim, Lingkhim Rai) [lii] 1 (1991 W. Winter). Mechi Zone, Ilam District, Sumbek Panchayat Yokpi. Original homeland was apparently near the lower Dudhkosi River. *Class:* Sino-Tibetan, Tibeto-Burman, Himalayish, Mahakiranti, Kiranti, Western. *Lg Use:* Speakers have shifted to Bantawa. *Other:* Little information available. Nearly extinct.

Lorung, Northern (Lohorong, Lohrung, Lohrung Khanawa) [lbr] 11,521 (2000 WCD). Koshi Zone, middle Sankhuwasawa District, between the middle Arun Valley and the Sabhakhola. *Class:* Sino-Tibetan, Tibeto-Burman, Himalayish, Mahakiranti, Kiranti, Eastern. *Dialect:* Biksit (Bikshi). A Rai group. Related to Yamphu, Yamphe, Southern Lorung, and Yakkha, but a separate language. Ethnic subgroups are Kipa and Loke Lorung, but they do not appear to speak different dialects. *Lg Use:* Medium or high degree of retention of first language can be assumed with some certainty in all areas except Biksit (Winter 1991). *Other:* Agriculturalists; pastoralists. Hindu, traditional religion.

Lorung, Southern (Lohorong, Lohrung, Lohrung Khap, Lohrung Khate, Yakkhaba Lorung) [lrr] 5,761 (2000 WCD). Koshi Zone, Dhankuta District, in a small strip south of the Tamorkhola, between the Jaruwakhola in the east and the Raghuwkhola in the west, Bodhe, Maunabuduke, and Rajarani panchayats. *Class:* Sino-Tibetan, Tibeto-Burman, Himalayish, Mahakiranti, Kiranti, Eastern. *Dialect:* Gess. A Rai group. Related to Yamphu, Yamphe, Northern Lorung, and Yakkha, but a separate language. *Other:* Sometimes incorrectly called 'Yakkha'. Agriculturalists; pastoralists. Hindu, traditional religion.

Lowa (Lopa, Loyu, Loba, Lo Ke, Mustangi, Lo Montang) [loy] 7,500 (2001 census). Population includes 5,000 Upper Mustang and 2,500 Baragaunle. Dhaulagiri Zone, Mustang District, north central along the upper Kali Gandaki River and in surrounding high valleys north of the middle-range Thakali, Gurung and Magar areas - Bahragaun dialect spoken in Kagbeni, Muktinath, Dzong

VDCs; Upper Mustang spoken in Ghimi, Tsarang, Lo Monthang, Surkhang, Chhosher, Chunnup VDCs, and the Village of Samar in Chuksang VDC; very few in Karnali Zone, Dolpa District. _Class:_ Sino-Tibetan, Tibeto-Burman, Himalayish, Tibeto-Kanauri, Tibetic, Tibetan, Central. _Dialects:_ Baragaunle (Baragaun, Baragaon, Bhoti Gurung), Upper Mustang (Lowa). Close to Dolpo. Reported high intelligibility between dialects. Lexical similarity 80% to 90% between dialects, 59% to 71% with Dolpo, 54% to 57% with Lhasa Tibetan, 58% to 67% with Mugom. _Lg Use:_ Some young people have had whole education outside of language area and may not be able to speak the first language. Used in the home, religion. Lowa spoken with Seke and Dolpo speakers. All ages. Language variety in the capital, Lo Monthang, has highest prestige. No strong negative attitudes between dialects. Positive attitudes toward own language and want children to marry within language group. Use Nepali with Thakali and Nepali speakers. Tibetan and Drokpa (a dialect of western Tibet) are also spoken. _Lg Dev:_ Literacy rate in second language: 41% for whole district, includes Thakalis, Nepalis, etc. (males 57%, females 28%). _Other:_ Distinct from Lhoba in China and India, a Mirish language. The inhabitants of Lo are called 'Lopa'. Their capital is Manthang, called Mustang by outsiders. Manthang has 200 houses, many gombas. Lhopa is recognized as an official nationality by the Government of Nepal. Village Development Committee (VDC) is a body with authority over several (4 to 7) villages. Desert. 3,000 to 4,000 meters. Salt traders, agriculturalists; pastoralists. Buddhist, traditional religion.

Lumba-Yakkha (Yakkhaba Cea) [luu] 1,197 (2000). Koshi Zone, North Dhankuta District, Arkhaule Jitpur and Marek Katahare panchayats, around Lakhshmikhola. _Class:_ Sino-Tibetan, Tibeto-Burman, Himalayish, Mahakiranti, Kiranti, Eastern. _Dialects:_ Related to Yakkha, Chhulung, Chhintange, and Lambichhong. _Lg Use:_ There appears to be retention of language use at least among some members of the younger generation (Winter 1991). _Other:_ Buddhist.

Magar, Eastern (Magari, Manggar) [mgp] 288,383 in Nepal (1994). Population total all countries: 356,074. Gandaki Zone, Tanahu District, east of Bagmati River, central mountains. A few main centers are Okhaldhunga, Taplejung, Bhojpur, Dhankuta, Chainpur, Terhathum, Ilam, and Letang. Also spoken in Bhutan, India. _Class:_ Sino-Tibetan, Tibeto-Burman, Himalayish, Mahakiranti, Kham-Magar-Chepang-Sunwari, Magar. _Lg Use:_ One of the main groups in the central mountains. All domains. Nepali bilingualism in the Nawalparasi Hills is quite low; among the 70% to 80% who are uneducated, there is only a basic proficiency. _Lg Dev:_ Literacy rate in first language: 1% to 5%. Literacy rate in second language: 25% to 50%. Devanagari script in India. NT: 1991. _Other:_ Magar recognized as an official nationality by the Government of Nepal. Mountain slope. Agriculturalists: rice, corn, wheat; hunters; pastoralists; army. Hindu, traditional religion.

Magar, Western (Magar, Magari, Manggar, Magar Nuwakot) [mrd] 210,000 (1994). Bheri Zone, Surkhet, Banke, and Dialekh districts, West of Pokhara, Tansen highway; Gandaki Zone, Pokhara (Kaski) and Syangja districts; Koshi Zone, Morang and Dhankuta districts; Lumbini Zone, Nawalparasi District. The center is Surkhet District. _Class:_ Sino-Tibetan, Tibeto-Burman, Himalayish, Mahakiranti, Kham-Magar-Chepang-Sunwari, Magar. _Lg Use:_ Partially bilingual in Nepali. _Lg Dev:_ Literacy rate in first language: below 1%. Literacy rate in second language: 5% to 15%. _Other:_ Magar recognized as an official nationality by the Government of Nepal. Agriculturalists; pastoralists. Traditional religion, Hindu.

Maithili (Apabhramsa, Bihari, Maitli, Maitili, Methli, Tirahutia, Tirhuti, Tirhutia) [mai] 2,797,582 in Nepal (2001 census). Population includes 489 Kisan. Narayani Zone, Rautahat District; Janakpur Zone, Sarlahi, Mahottari, Dhanusa districts; Sagarmatha Zone, Siraha, Saptari districts; Koshi Zone, Sunsari District. _Dialects:_ Bantar, Barei, Barmeli, Kawar, Kisan, Kyabrat, Makrana, Musar, Sadri, Tati, Dehati. _Lg Use:_ Spoken by a wide variety of castes, both 'high' and 'low'. There is a Maithili Academy in Patna. Bihar Maithili is taught at several universities including L. N. Mithila University in Darbhanga, Patna University, and Janakpur Campus of Tribhuvan University. Used in the home, village, towns, cities. All ages. Brahmin speech considered to be standard. Brahmins consider themselves superior, varying from friendly to domineering. Others vary toward Brahmins from friendly to resentment. Hindi and its speakers considered close, culturally similar; Nepali accepted. Second languages used by men or working women mostly only for commerce, social interaction outside the home. In cities some may use Hindi, Nepali, or English even at home and with other Maithili. Bhojpuri or Bengali are used with friends from those groups. Bilingual ability varies greatly, from being limited to using them for trade, to being highly fluent. _Lg Dev:_ Literacy rate in first language: 20%. Literacy rate in second language: 25% to 50%. The educated read Hindi, Nepali, or English. If they can read Hindi or Nepali, they can read Maithili. _Other:_ Plains. Tropical forest, gallery forest. Peasant agriculturalists. Hindu, Muslim. See main entry under India.

Majhi (Manjhi) [mjz] 21,841 in Nepal (2001 census). Population total all countries: 22,087. Ethnic population: 72,614. Janakpur Zone, Sindhuli and Ramechhap districts; Narayani Zone; Lumbini Zone. Also spoken in India. _Class:_ Indo-European, Indo-Iranian, Indo-Aryan, Eastern zone, Bihari. _Lg Dev:_ Literacy rate in second language: 22.2% (Census 1991). Devanagari script in India. _Other:_ Distinct from Majhi in Panjabi group or Bote-Majhi. 'Majhi', 'Bote', and 'Kushar' all are used by hill peoples. Recognized as an official nationality by the Government of Nepal. Traditional religion.

Manangba (Manang, Manangi, Nyeshang, Nyishang, Northern Gurung, Manangbolt, Manangbhot, Nyeshangba) [nmm] 3,736 (1988 Pohle). Gandaki Zone, Manang District, Nyeshang area, 7 villages, Marsyangdi River. _Class:_ Sino-Tibetan, Tibeto-Burman, Himalayish, Tibeto-Kanauri, Tibetic, Tamangic. _Dialect:_ Prakaa. Manangba may be distinct from Northern Gurung, which is spoken in Manang District. Very different from Eastern Gurung. _Other:_ Language has Tibetan influence. They claim to be Gurung but are not accepted as such by their proper Gurung neighbors to the south. (Bista 1996:199) Recognized as an official nationality by the Government of Nepal. Mountain slope. 3,200 to 3,700 meters. Traders. Buddhist.

Marwari (Marwadi) [rwr] 22,637 in Nepal (2001 census). Ethnic population: 43,971. Mechi Zone, Jhapa District; Koshi Zone, Morang and Sunsari districts; Narayani Zone, Parsa District, some in Kathmandu; Eastern upper Sindh Province. _Lg Use:_ 933 second-language speakers in Nepal (1991 census, under Marwari). _Lg Dev:_ Literacy rate in second language: 88%. _Other:_ Hindu. See main entry under India.

Meohang, Eastern (Newang, Newahang, Newange Rai, Newahang Jimi, Mewahang) [emg] Koshi Zone, Sankhuwasawa District, upper Arun Valley east of the river, eastern Nepal. One dialect is in Sunsari District, Bhaludhunga, Bishnupaduka Panchayat; Dibum (Dibung) in Mangtewa Panchayat, Mulgaon-Wangtang in Yaphu Panchayat. _Class:_ Sino-Tibetan, Tibeto-Burman, Himalayish, Mahakiranti, Kiranti, Eastern. _Dialects:_

Sunsari, Dibum, Mulgaon-Wangtang. Structurally different from Western Meohang. *Lg Use:* May be extinct or nearly extinct, being replaced by Nepali. *Other:* Mountain slope. Agriculturalists; pastoralists.

Meohang, Western (Newang, Newahang, Newange Rai, Newahang Jimi, Mewahang) [raf] 2,000 to 5,000 (1991 W. Winter). Koshi Zone, Sankhuwasawa District, upper Arun Valley west of the river, eastern Nepal. Bala is in Bala village, Sankhuwasawa Panchayat; Bumdemba in Sishuwakhola Panchayat. 2 villages. *Class:* Sino-Tibetan, Tibeto-Burman, Himalayish, Mahakiranti, Kiranti, Eastern. *Dialects:* Bala (Balali), Bumdemba. Structurally different from Eastern Meohang. *Lg Use:* Many speakers use Kulung as a second language. *Other:* Mountain slope. Agriculturalists; pastoralists.

Mugom (Mugali, Mugu, Mugum) [muk] 3,558 in Nepal (2000 WCD). Karnali Zone, Mugu, Jumla districts; some in Kathmandu. Also spoken in India. *Class:* Sino-Tibetan, Tibeto-Burman, Himalayish, Tibeto-Kanauri, Tibetic, Tibetan, Central. *Dialects:* Karani, Mugali. Intelligibility 89% to 93% between speakers of dialects (possibly even higher). Definitely sufficient to understand complex and abstract discourse. Close to Humla, Dolpo, Loba. Not closely related to Western Parbate, Eastern Parbate, Maikoti, Sheshi, or Gamale Kham. Lexical similarity 85% between dialects, 56% to 57% with Tibetan. *Lg Use:* Less than 50 second-language speakers. Used in the home and village. All ages. Mugalis may not accept materials written in Karani. Mugom value Nepali and English as a way to higher education. Mugalis see themselves a little higher than Karanis. Mugalis are more influential as they travel and trade more. Nepali used for outside contacts such as trading, communicating with officials, and in school. Basic or limited Nepali ability for uneducated people, routine or good ability for the educated. Tibetan rarely used, though sometimes by Lamas in religious ceremonies. Those who have worked in India know Hindi. *Lg Dev:* Literacy rate in second language: Up to 21.65% Nepali; men 30%, women 5%. Mugu District ranks very low in literacy among Nepal districts, especially among children and women. Tibetan script. *Other:* Mountain slope. 1,500 to 3,000 meters. Agriculturalists; pastoralists; traders. Buddhist, syncretism with traditional religion.

Mundari (Munda, Mandari, Mondari, Munari, Horo) [muw] 5,700 in Nepal (1993 Johnstone). Ethnic population: 660 Munda. Mechi Zone, Jhapa District; Koshi Zone, Morang District. *Dialects:* Hasada, Latar, Naguri, Kera. See main entry under India.

Musasa (Musahar, Rishaidep) [smm] 50,000 (2003). Population includes 20,000 Musasa and 30,000 Musasa Bantar. Ethnic population: 172,434 in Nepal. Koshi Zone, Morang District; Janakpur Zone, Sindhuli, Dolakha districts, Sagarmatha Zone, Siraha District. *Class:* Indo-European, Indo-Iranian, Indo-Aryan, Eastern zone, Bihari. *Dialect:* Bantar. Close to Tharu, Saptari. *Lg Use:* Speakers have high proficiency in Nepali. *Other:* Landless, bonded laborers. Considered to be among the lowest of the untouchables. Plains. Agricultural laborers. Hindu.

Naaba (Nawa Sherpa, Naba, Naapa, Naapaa) [nao] 500 (1985). Koshi Zone, Sankhuwasawa District. Kimathanka village in Kimathanka VDC and villages of Dangok and Pharang in Hatiya VDC. *Class:* Sino-Tibetan, Tibeto-Burman, Himalayish, Tibeto-Kanauri, Tibetic, Tibetan, Unclassified. *Lg Use:* All ages. The Lhomi consider the Naaba people a distinct group. Inhabitants of Pharang and Dangok can fully understand Lhomi, most in Kimathanka can understand Lhomi. Little intermarriage. *Other:* Village Development Committee (VDC) is a body with authority over several (4 to 7) villages. Buddhist.

Nachering (Nacering Ra, Nachering Tûm, Mathsereng, Nacchhering, Nasring, Bangdale, Bangdel Tûm, Bangdile)

[ncd] 3,553 (2001 census). Sagarmatha Zone, upper northeastern Khotang District near the Rawakhola Valley, on the slopes around the Lidim Khola River from the headwaters and its tributaries down to Aiselukharke to the south. *Class:* Sino-Tibetan, Tibeto-Burman, Himalayish, Mahakiranti, Kiranti, Eastern. *Dialects:* Dimali, Parali, Hedangpa (Sangpang), Bangdale (Hachero, Achero, Hangkula), Kharlali, Rakheli. Related to Kulung and Sangpang. *Lg Use:* The Hedangpa dialect is nearly extinct. *Other:* It is not the same as the Sangpang language, although it is sometimes called 'Sangpang'.

Nar Phu (Nar-Phu) [npa] 533 (1988 Pohle). Gandaki Zone, Manang District, Nar Valley north of Manang Valley, Nar (Nargaon) and Phu (Phugaon) villages. *Class:* Sino-Tibetan, Tibeto-Burman, Himalayish, Tibeto-Kanauri, Tibetic, Tamangic. *Dialects:* Nar (Nar-Mä, Lower Nar), Phu (Nar-Tö, Upper Nar). *Lg Use:* Many men are fluent in Tibetan. *Lg Dev:* Many men are literate in Classical Tibetan. *Other:* 4,000 to 4,200 meters.

Nepalese Sign Language [nsp] 5,743 (2001 census). *Class:* Deaf sign language. *Dialects:* Developed from local signs and introduced signs. Related to Indian and Pakistan Sign Languages. *Lg Use:* Used by USA Peace Corps.

Nepali (Nepalese, Gorkhali, Gurkhali, Khaskura, Parbatiya, Eastern Pahari) [nep] 11,053,255 in Nepal (2001 census). Population total all countries: 17,209,255. Eastern region and adjacent south central region. Also spoken in Bhutan, Brunei, India. *Class:* Indo-European, Indo-Iranian, Indo-Aryan, Northern zone, Eastern Pahari. *Dialects:* Baitadi, Bajhangi, Bajurali (Bajura), Doteli (Dotali, Gaunle), Soradi, Acchami, Darjula. Dialects listed may be quite distinct from Standard Nepali. *Lg Use:* National language. *Lg Dev:* Bible: 1914–2000. *Other:* 4 castes: Brahmin (highest or priestly), Chhetri (warrior), Vaishya (trader and farmer), Shudra (untouchable or lowest). People are called 'Paharia'. Hindu, Buddhist, Muslim, Christian.

Newar (Nepal Bhasa, "Newari") [new] 825,458 in Nepal (2001 census). Many women are monolingual. Ethnic population: 1,256,737 including 1,245,232 Newar plus 11,505 Pahari. Kathmandu Valley and in all towns and bigger villages thoughout Nepal. Fewer in the far west. Also spoken in India. *Class:* Sino-Tibetan, Tibeto-Burman, Himalayish, Mahakiranti, Newari. *Dialects:* Dolkhali (Dolakha), Sindhupalchok Pahri (Pahri, Pahari), Totali, Citlang, Kathmandu-Pathan-Kirtipur, Baktapur, Baglung. Dolkhali of Dolakha and Pahri of Sindhupalchok may be separate languages (Genetti 1994:2–3). Dolakha, Totali, and Pahari are conservative linguistically. Kirtipur is close to Kathmandu. Baktapur people can mostly understand Kathmandu. There are some vocabulary differences between Hindus and Buddhists. *Lg Use:* Language shift is greater among Hindus than among Buddhists. All ages. Dolakha and Totali people are reserved toward outsiders. Kathmandu is the prestige dialect; most published materials are in this dialect. Many attitudes are linked with political groupings. English is highly valued; there are mixed feelings about Hindi; Tibetan does not have high prestige. People learn whichever language will help them economically: Nepali, English, Hindi, and others. *Lg Dev:* Literacy rate in first language: 60.4% (1991 census). Literacy rate in second language: 60.4% (1991 census). There are enough Newari teachers to teach their own people, no need for outside help. Young people are more literate than old people; men are more literate than women. Devanagari script. Magazines. Newspapers. Radio programs. Films. Dictionary. Grammar. NT: 1986. *Other:* Recognized as an official nationality by the Government of Nepal. "Newari" considered offensive to Newars. Pracalit lipi script was in common use by Newars during the Malla period and earlier. There have been attempts to revive it recently. Newari has a complex history of scripts. SOV; postpositions; genitives, adjectives, demonstratives before noun heads; relatives before and without noun heads; in polar questions there is a particle sentence finally; maximum number of prefixes 2; maximum number of suffixes 4; affixes or clitics indicate case of noun phrases; ergative; causatives; comparatives; CVC; nontonal. Mountain valley. Urban. 300 to 2,000 meters. Jyapu intensive agriculturalists (farming caste); full range of occupations. Buddhist, Hindu, syncretism with traditional religion.

Nubri (Kutang Bhotia, Larkye) [kte] 3,776 (2000). Gandaki Zone, North Gorkha District, along the upper reaches of the Buri Gandaki River, west of and including Prok village, between Himal Chuli and Manaslu Himal on the west and Ganesh Himal on the east. The local people view Sama as regional center. *Class:* Sino-Tibetan, Tibeto-Burman, Himalayish, Tibeto-Kanauri, Tibetic, Tibetan, Central. *Dialects:* Sama, Lho, Namrung, Prok. Only moderately intelligible with Kyirong Tibetan (74%) and Tsum (32%). Lexical similarity 78% to 93% among dialects. Prok is more distinct. 71% to 78% with Tsum, 66% to 74% with Kyirong Tibetan; 67% with Dolpo; 65% with Lowa, 59% to 64% with Lhasa Tibetan; 64% with Olangchung Gola (Walungge) and Lhomi; 61% with Helambu Sherpa; 57% with Jirel; 55% with Sherpa, 21% to 27% with Northern Ghale, 20% to 23% with Southern Ghale, 14% to 31% with Kutang Ghale, 14% with Eastern Gorkha Tamang, Western Gurung, and Banspur Tamang. *Lg Use:* Vigorous. Nearly every domain. Positive attitudes toward Nubri. Tibetan viewed favorably in the religious domain, Nepali for education and potential advancement. Speakers have minimal bilingual proficiency in Nepali and Tibetan. Nepali is used to outsiders. *Lg Dev:* Literacy rate in second language: below 10%. *Other:* Women from Prok marry men from Nubri area primarily and some from Kutang area. People trade with Gorkha District and Tibet. Most villages have primary schools. "Bhotia" or "Bhote" refers to people of Tibetan origin; in at least some contexts it is derogatory. 'Larke' recognized as an official nationality by the Government of Nepal. Mountain slope, valley. Gallery forest. 2,000 to 4,000 meters. Swidden and peasant agriculturalists. Buddhist (Lamaist).

Palpa (Pahari-Palpa) [plp] 7,562 (2000). Lumbini Zone, town of Palpa. *Class:* Indo-European, Indo-Iranian, Indo-Aryan, Northern zone, Eastern Pahari. *Dialects:* This language stands midway between Nepali (Eastern Pahari) and Kumauni (Central Pahari). Sometimes considered a Kumauni or Nepali dialect. *Lg Dev:* NT: 1827. *Other:* There is also a dialect of Newar called Pahari. The term literally means 'of the hills'.

Parbate, Eastern (Nisi, Nisel, Nishel Kham, Nisi Kham) [kif] 3,000 (1988). Dhaulagiri Zone, Baglung District, Nishel in 3 villages of Nisi, Bhalkot, Budhathok; Bhujel live in villages Kuku, Diza, Kang, Masbang, Musuri, and Sukurdung. *Class:* Sino-Tibetan, Tibeto-Burman, Himalayish, Mahakiranti, Kham-Magar-Chepang-Sunwari, Kham. *Dialect:* Bhujel Kham. Partially intelligible with Western Parbate dialects. Lexical similarity 79% with Bhujel Kham (closest), 71% with Western Parbate, 55% with Gamale, 44% with Sheshi. *Lg Use:* Vigorous. Some speakers also use Nepali. *Lg Dev:* Literacy rate in first language: below 1%. Literacy rate in second language: below 5%.

Parbate, Western (Kham-Magar, Takale, Takale Kham, Maikoti Kham) [kjl] 46,466 (2000 WCD). Rapti Zone, Rukum, Rolpa districts, west central Nepal. Taka-Shera is the center. Some in Dhaulagiri Zone, Baglung District. *Class:* Sino-Tibetan, Tibeto-Burman, Himalayish, Mahakiranti, Kham-Magar-Chepang-Sunwari, Kham. *Dialects:* Takale, Lukumel, Wale, Thabanggi. Greatest similarities between Takale Kham and Nisi Kham. The

Parbate, Sheshi, and Gamale groups are all inherently unintelligible. Mahatale and Miruli are 2 dialects whose position within the Kham linguistic group has not been decided. Lexical similarity 71% with Gamale Kham, Eastern Parbate; 58% with Bhujel Kham, 51% with Sheshi. 25% lexical similarity with Magar and Gurung, slightly below 25% with the Tibetan group, 15% with the Rai and Limbu groups. *Lg Use:* Trade language for Kham area. All domains. All ages. Speakers use Nepali only when outside their homeland. Young men are most proficient, older adult women the least. Most can discuss common topics in Nepali. *Lg Dev:* Literacy rate in first language: Some. Literacy rate in second language: Some. Devanagari script. *Other:* Different from the Khams of eastern Tibet as spoken by the Khampa. People migrate in summer to the foot of glaciers on the western end of the Dhaulagiri massif, and in winter to the southern hills of Rolpa District. SOV; postposition; genitives, adjectives, numerals, relatives before noun heads; maximum number for nouns: 1 prefix, 8 suffixes; for verbs: 5 prefixes, 7 suffixes; objects and indirect objects partially marked by word order; case marked on NPs by affixes; verb affixes mark person and number of subject and object—obligatory; split ergative; detransitivization common, some of which is passive-like; a kind of semantic inverse marked in verb morphology; causatives; applicatives; (C)V(V)(C) where the second V is a dipthong or long vowel; tonal. Mountain slope, alpine. Northern type forests on north facing slopes, savannah on south facing slopes. 1,800 to 2,500 meters. Seminomadic pastoralists: sheep, goats; agriculturalists; peasants. Traditional religion, Buddhist (Tantrayana), Hindu.

Phangduwali (Phangduwali Poti, Phangduvali) [phw] Directly above the headwaters of the Mugakhola, Koshi Zone, Dhankuta District, Pakhribas Panchayat, Phangduwa village (W. Winter 1991:79). *Class:* Sino-Tibetan, Tibeto-Burman, Himalayish, Mahakiranti, Kiranti, Eastern. *Dialects:* Linguistically between Yakkha and Belhariya. *Lg Use:* It may be nearly extinct.

Pongyong (Ponyon Kulung, Samakulung, Kulung Pun) [pgy] Mechi Zone, Ilam District, Kannyam Panchayat, Ambikau. *Class:* Sino-Tibetan, Tibeto-Burman, Himalayish, Mahakiranti, Kiranti, Eastern. *Dialects:* Closest to Kulung and Sangpang. *Other:* Nearly extinct.

Puma (Puma Pima, Puma La, Puma Kala) [pum] 4,310 (2001 census). Sagarmatha Zone, Khotang District, Diplung, Chisapani, Devisthan, Manwabote, Panwasera, Rila; Udayapur District, Beltar, Basaha, Chandandi, Apraha villages; Northwestern slopes of the Rapcha Range from the highest peaks to the Sawa Khola Valley, directly south of the Khotang Bajar. *Class:* Sino-Tibetan, Tibeto-Burman, Himalayish, Mahakiranti, Kiranti, Eastern. *Lg Use:* The language appears to be still alive among most members of the younger generation (Winter 1991). Still spoken by most young people. *Other:* Buddhist.

Rajbanshi (Rajbangsi, Rajbansi, Tajpuria, Koch, Koche) [rjb] 129,883 in Nepal (2001 census). Population includes 54 Koche. Mechi Zone, Jhapa District; Koshi Zone, Morang District. Western dialect spoken from Morang's west border to Bakraha River, Eastern dialect from Kankai River to eastern border with India, Central dialect from Bakraha River to Kankai River. *Dialects:* Western Rajbanshi, Eastern Rajbanshi, Central Rajbanshi. *Lg Use:* Vigorous. 3,217 second-language speakers in Nepal (1991 census, under Rajbansi). Used in the home, village, market, religion, songs. Positive attitude to first language and to language development and literacy. Attitude between dialects and towards Nepali is indifferent. 30% of the population use Nepali as second language, 30% Hindi, 60% Khavas Tharu. Maithili and Bengali also used. *Lg Dev:* Literacy rate in second language: 37.7% (1991 census). Different scripts in both countries will require separate materials. *Other:* Rajbanshi (Koch) and Tajpuria are recognized as official nationalities by the Government of Nepal. Eastern dialect has more speakers than Western. 94% intelligibility of Eastern dialect in the west; 75% of Western dialect in the east. Tajpuria may be a distinct language. Plains. Forest. 70 to 140 meters. Agriculturalists; pastoralists. Hindu, Muslim, traditional religion. See main entry under India.

Raji (Rajibar) [rji] 2,413 (2001 census). Bheri Zone, Surkhet and Bardiya districts; Seti Zone, Kailali District. *Class:* Sino-Tibetan, Tibeto-Burman, Himalayish, Mahakiranti, Kham-Magar-Chepang-Sunwari, Magar. *Dialects:* Close to Rawat and Raute. Devidatta Sharma (1990) concludes that Raji in India is a Munda language with borrowing from Tibeto-Burman and Indo-Aryan. *Lg Use:* Vigorous in some homes. 1,210 second-language speakers (1991 census). Used in the home. Nepali is used with outsiders. *Lg Dev:* Literacy rate in second language: 21.5% (1991 census). Grammar. *Other:* Has been a nomadic group, but has now settled. Recognized as an official nationality by the Government of Nepal. Riverine. Swidden agriculturalists. Traditional religion, Hindu.

Raute (Rautye, Harka Gurung, Khamchi) [rau] 518 (2001 census). Population includes 130 nomadic Raute. Ethnic population: 658. Mainly in western Nepal, Seti Zone, Achham, Doti districts; Bheri Zone, Surkhet, Jajarkot, Banke districts; Rapti Zone, Pyuthan District; Karnali Zone, Jumla, Dolpa. *Class:* Sino-Tibetan, Tibeto-Burman, Himalayish, Mahakiranti, Kiranti, Western. *Dialects:* May be a dialect of Rawat. *Lg Use:* All ages. The nomadic Raute are secretive about their language; the settled Raute are not. Some youth in Nepal speak Nepali or Hindi among themselves in front of outsiders. The Raute are viewed as low caste by others. The settled Raute also use Nepali. Among the nomadic Raute, only the leaders have contact with outsiders. *Lg Dev:* Literacy rate in second language: 25.5% (1991 census). *Other:* Migratory cycle is reported to be about 2 years. They may have been joined to the Rawat and Raji, but those groups are now settled. Singh 1997 reports they communicate with the Rawat in the 'Khamchi' language. Recognized as an official nationality by the Government of Nepal. 125 to 3,000 meters. Hunter-gatherers. Traditional religion.

Rawat (Janggali, Jangali, Jhangar, Dzanggali) [jnl] 23,024 in Nepal (2000). Population total all countries: 25,950. Mainly in 2 or 3 resettlement villages in the Nepal lowlands, and some in Mahakali Zone, Darchula, Baitadi, and Dadeldhura districts. Also spoken in India. *Class:* Sino-Tibetan, Tibeto-Burman, Himalayish, Tibeto-Kanauri, Western Himalayish, Janggali. *Dialects:* Very close to Raute and Raji. Related to Rongpo. Gurung says it is Indo-aryan but vocabulary includes Tibetan elements. *Lg Use:* 192 second-language speakers (1991 census, under Jhangar). *Lg Dev:* Grammar. *Other:* Called 'Rawat' in India. OV (S varies); postpositions; genitives, articles, adjectives, numerals before noun heads; maximum number of suffixes 3; affixes indicate case of noun phrases; verb affixes mark person, number— obligatory; passives; causatives; comparatives; CV, CVC; nontonal. Mountain slope. 300 to 1,500 meters. Swidden agriculturalists. Traditional religion, Hindu.

Saam (Saam Rai, Samakha, Saama Kha) [raq] 23 (2001 census). Mechi Zone, Southern Ilam District. *Class:* Sino-Tibetan, Tibeto-Burman, Himalayish, Mahakiranti, Kiranti, Eastern. *Dialects:* Bungla, Sambya. *Lg Use:* Speakers are shifting to Nepali or Bantawa. A few older adult speakers. Speakers also use Nepali or Bantawa. *Other:* Other groups called 'Saam' may be Kulung, Limkhim, or Pongyong speakers. Hindu, traditional religion. Nearly extinct.

Sampang (Sampange Rai, Sangpang, Sangpang Kha, Sangpang Gun, Sangpang Gîn) [rav] 10,810 (2001 census). Sagarmatha Zone, Khotang District, Khartamchha, Baspani, Patekha, Phedi Village District Councils; Koshi Zone, Bhojpur District; from Dingla in the northeast to Kharpa in the southwest. The upper ridges south and east of the Rawakhola Valley and adjoining ridges in the northeast at the headwaters of the main tributaries of the lower and middle Arun River. Also scattered throughout Dharan, Ilam, Kathmandu and the Terai. *Class:* Sino-Tibetan, Tibeto-Burman, Himalayish, Mahakiranti, Kiranti, Eastern. *Dialects:* Tana, Halumbung (Wakchali), Samarung, Bhalu, Tongeccha, Phali, Khartamche, Khotang. *Lg Use:* Used in the home and village. All ages. Positive language attitude. Most speak some Nepali but men, educated and younger people have higher proficiency. Some younger educated people know Nepali well enough to understand complex discourse. Some older people know hardly any Nepali. Nepali valued as language of education. *Lg Dev:* Literacy rate in second language: 80%. *Other:* Mountain slope, valley. Forest. 1,500 to 2,500 meters. Peasants. Hindu, traditional religion.

Santali (Satar, Santhali, Santhal, Sonthal, Sandal, Sangtal, Santal, Sentali, Sainti, Hor, Har) [sat] 40,260 in Nepal (2001 census). Ethnic population: 42,698. Koshi Zone, Morang District; Mechi Zone, Jhapa District. *Lg Use:* 1,339 second-language Satar speakers and 559 second-language Santhal speakers (1991 census). Some bilingualism in Maithili and Nepali. *Lg Dev:* Literacy rate in first language: Few. Literacy rate in second language: Few. *Other:* Recognized as an official nationality by the Government of Nepal. Hunter-gatherers; agriculturalists. Hindu, Christian. See main entry under India.

Seke [skj] 500 (2001 census). Dhaulagiri Zone, Mustang District, Chuksang, Tsaile, Tangbe, Tetang, Gyakar villages. *Class:* Sino-Tibetan, Tibeto-Burman, Himalayish, Tibeto-Kanauri, Tibetic, Tamangic. *Dialects:* Tangbe, Tetang, Chuksang. Related to Gurung. Some similarities with Thakali and Manangba. Very different from Lowa. Tangbe people do not understand Chuksang very well, but Chuksang understand Tangbe. They are reported to understand Gurung but Gurung speakers do not understand Seke. *Lg Use:* All ages. Use Nepali with the Gurung. A few also speak Lowa. *Other:* Desert. Buddhist.

Sherpa (Sharpa, Sharpa Bhotia, Xiaerba, Serwa) [xsr] 129,771 in Nepal (2001 census). Population total all countries: 151,071. Ethnic population: 154,622 (2001 census). Sagarmatha Zone, Solu Khumbu District, northern mountains. Khumbu extends north from Namche Bazaar. Solu is the southern region including the villages of Gumdi, Sete, Junbesi, Phaplu, and Sallery. Around Rolwaling, northern border of Janakpur District, and Taplejung, Mechi Zone. There may be some around Lukla. Also spoken in Bhutan, China, India, South Korea, USA. *Class:* Sino-Tibetan, Tibeto-Burman, Himalayish, Tibeto-Kanauri, Tibetic, Tibetan, Southern. *Dialect:* Solu, Khumbu, Ramechap (Western). 95% comprehension of Solu dialect by Western and Khumbu speakers. Lexical similarity 77% to 92% between Solu and Khumbu dialects; 67% with Jirel; 65% with Helambu Sherpa; 62% with Lowa and Dolpo; 58% with Lhomi and Baraguanle; 57% with Kyerung; 55% with Kutang Bhotia (Nubri) and Walungge; 30% to 35% with Lhasa Tibetan. *Lg Use:* Vigorous in villages but not in towns. Use is diminishing. All ages, but children use it infrequently. They are proud of their language, but ashamed that it isn't developed more. In schools children are teased if they use Sherpa. In Kathmandu parents use Nepali with school-age children. Some use Nepali, Tibetan, English, as second language. Lamas are fluent in Tibetan. Guides (men) learn trekkers' languages: German, Korean, French, etc. (SIL 1998). At

Ethnologue

least 90% speak Nepali (UNESCO). *Lg Dev:* Literacy rate in first language: 8% to 9%. Literacy rate in second language: 35% (1991 census). In Kathmandu people are about 20% more literate than in Sherpa country. Devanagari and Tibetan scripts; Tibetan script in India. Radio programs. Grammar. *Other:* Recognized as an official nationality by the Government of Nepal. Tibetan carries tones in the script. SOV. 1,000 to 4,000 meters. Buddhist (Lamaist).

Sonha (Sonahaa) [soi] 14,700 (2000). Seti Zone, Kailali District, along Karnali River; Bheri Zone, Surkhet District along the Bheri River; Mahakali Zone, along the Mahakali River; Kanchanpur District, Mahendranagar tahsil. *Class:* Indo-European, Indo-Iranian, Indo-Aryan, Central zone, Unclassified. *Dialects:* Close to Dangura Tharu; 80% intelligibility. Lexical similarity 69% with Rana Tharu, 73% with Kathoriya Tharu, 72% with Dangaura Tharu. Sonha and Kathoriya form a lexical bridge between Rana and Dangaura varieties of Tharu. *Other:* A Tharu clan. Gold panners; agriculturalists. Traditional religion, Hindu.

Sunwar (Sunuwar, Sunbar, Sunwari, Sonowar, Sonowal, Mukhiya, Kwoico Lo) [suz] 26,611 (2001 census). Ethnic population: 95,254. Janakpur Zone, Ramechhap District, eastern hills, and Sagarmatha Zone, northwestern Okhaldhunga District. *Class:* Sino-Tibetan, Tibeto-Burman, Himalayish, Mahakiranti, Kham-Magar-Chepang-Sunwari, Sunwari. *Dialect:* Surel. Related to Bahing, and more distantly to Thulung, Wambule, Jerung. Hayu is closest to Sunwar. *Lg Use:* Younger people speak Nepali for trade, official purposes with low proficiency. *Lg Dev:* Literacy rate in first language: Young people 90%. Literacy rate in second language: Males 15% in villages, 20% in Kathmandu. Poetry. Dictionary. *Other:* Sunwar and Surel are recognized as official nationalities by the Government of Nepal. SOV; portpositions; genitives after noun heads; relatives before noun heads; question word initial; maximum number of prefixes 1; suffixes 3; verb affixes mark person, number; causatives; comparatives; CV, CVC CVV, CCV, CCVC, V, VC; tonal. Mountain slope. Subtropical savannah, valley. 1,500 meters. Pastoralists; hunter-gatherers; peasant agriculturalists. Traditional religion, Hindu.

Tamang, Eastern [taj] 759,257 in Nepal (2000 WCD). Population total all countries: 773,257. Kathmandu and to the northeast, east, and south. Outer-Eastern Tamang is in Janakpur Zone, eastern Sindhupalchowk, Ramechhap, Dolakha districts, and in most districts in eastern Nepal and parts of northeastern India. Central-Eastern Tamang is in Bagmati Zone, most of Kabhre District, western Sindhupalchowk, Lalitpur, Bhaktapur, Kathmandu, eastern Nuwakot districts, and districts south of those. Southwestern Tamang is in Narayani Zone, western Makwanpur and Chitawan districts, and districts. Also spoken in Bhutan, India, Myanmar. *Class:* Sino-Tibetan, Tibeto-Burman, Himalayish, Tibeto-Kanauri, Tibetic, Tamangic. *Dialects:* Outer-Eastern Tamang, Central-Eastern Tamang, Southwestern Tamang. Central-Eastern Tamang is the most widely understood variety among all those tested to date: 85% by both Trisuli and Rasuwa Western Tamang, 93% to 98% by Outer-Eastern, 87% by Southwestern Tamang. Comprehension of Outer-Eastern Tamang was 58% by Western Rasuwa Tamang, 64% to 75% by Western Trisuli Tamang, 67% to 54% by Southwestern Tamang, 88% to 93% by Central-Eastern Tamang, and 90% to 98% among its own varieties. Southwestern Tamang may be a bridge between Eastern and Western Tamang. Outer-Eastern Tamang varieties have 88% to 99% lexical similarity with each other; Central-Eastern varieties have 89% to 100% with each other. Outer-Eastern varieties have 79% to 93% with Central-Eastern varieties, and 77% to 82% with

Southwestern Tamang. Southwestern has 86% to 93% with Central-Eastern. All Eastern varieties have 74% to 80% with Western Trisuli Tamang, 69% to 81% with Western Rasuwa Tamang, 72% to 80% with Northwestern Dhading Tamang, 63% to 77% with Eastern Gorkha Tamang. *Lg Use:* Vigorous. There is a Tamang Language and Literature Council, and a Nepal Tamang Student Group. 23,645 second-language speakers of all Tamang (1991 census). Used in the home, indigenous religion, social gatherings, market, officials who understand, local literature. All ages. Attitudes correlate with understanding, but none are negative toward other Tamang varieties. Those who have been to school or traveled often speak routine to good Nepali, others have limited proficiency, especially women, older adults, children. *Lg Dev:* Literacy rate in first language: 1% to 5%. Literacy rate in second language: 25% to 50%. Some literacy materials and classes conducted. Devanagari and Tibetan scripts. Poetry. Magazines. Radio programs. Films. Videos. Dictionary. Grammar. *Other:* Tamang recognized as an official nationality by the Government of Nepal. Tamang is the largest Tibeto-Burman language in Nepal. SOV; postpositions; genitives after nouns; question word medial; ergative; CV, CVC, CCV, V, CCVC; tonal. Mountain slope, valley. Gallery forest. Swidden and peasant agriculturalists. Traditional religion, Buddhist, Hindu.

Tamang, Eastern Gorkha [tge] 3,977 (2000 WCD). Gandaki Zone, North Gorkha District, south and east of Jagat. *Class:* Sino-Tibetan, Tibeto-Burman, Himalayish, Tibeto-Kanauri, Tibetic, Tamangic. *Dialects:* Kasigaon, Kerounja. Dialects have 89% lexical similarity with each other, 76% to 77% with Northwestern (Dhading) Tamang, 77% to 79% with Western (Trisuli) Tamang, 72% to 73% with Western (Rasuwa) Tamang, 70% to 73% with Southwestern Tamang, 63% to 73% with Eastern Tamang dialects, (Varenkamp 96), 50% with Banspur Gurung, 31% to 37% with Northern and Southern Ghale, 18% to 23% with Kutang Ghale, 14% to 16% with Nubri, Tsum, and Kyerung, 12% to 14% with Tibetan (Webster 92). *Lg Dev:* Literacy rate in second language: below 10%. *Other:* Speakers refer to themselves as 'Gurung', but recognize that their language is different. A few primary schools. The nearest middle and secondary schools are in Arughat. Tamang recognized as an official nationality by the Government of Nepal. Mountain slope, valley. Gallery forest. 600 to 1,800 meters. Swidden and peasant agriculturalists. Traditional religion, Buddhist, Hindu.

Tamang, Northwestern [tmk] 55,000 (1991 census). Bagmati Zone, Nuwakot District, central mountainous strip. Migrations to the Terai. *Class:* Sino-Tibetan, Tibeto-Burman, Himalayish, Tibeto-Kanauri, Tibetic, Tamangic. *Dialect:* Dhading. Lexical similarity 94% with Western Trisuli Tamang, 82% to 83% with Western Rasuwa Tamang, 76% to 78% with Southwestern Tamang, 76% to 77% with Eastern Gorkha Tamang, 72% to 80% with Eastern Tamang. *Lg Dev:* Literacy rate in first language: 1% to 10%. Literacy rate in second language: 25% to 75%. *Other:* Tamang recognized as an official nationality by the Government of Nepal. SOV; postpositions; genitives after noun head; relatives before noun head; question word medial; CV, CVC, CCV, V, CCVC, CVCCC; tonal. Mountain slope, valley. Gallery forest. Swidden and peasant agriculturalists. Traditional religion, Buddhist, Hindu.

Tamang, Southwestern [tsf] 109,051 (1991 census). Narayani Zone, Western Makwanpur and Chitawan districts, and south and southwest of those districts. It may extend to the western and northwestern parts of Kathmandu District in Bagmati Zone. Migrations to Terai. *Class:* Sino-Tibetan, Tibeto-Burman, Himalayish, Tibeto-Kanauri, Tibetic, Tamangic. *Dialects:* Preliminary results:

86% intelligibility by Western Trisuli Tamang, 87% by Central-Eastern Tamang, 54% to 67% by Outer-Eastern Tamang. Relationship within Tamang still needs evaluation. Southwestern Tamang has 80% lexical similarity with Western Trisuli Tamang, 76% to 78% with Western Rasuwa dialect, 78% with Northwestern Tamang, 70% to 73% with Eastern Gorkha Tamang, 77% to 93% with Eastern Tamang. *Lg Dev:* Literacy rate in first language: 1% to 10%. Literacy rate in second language: 25% to 75%. *Other:* Tamang recognized as an official nationality by the Government of Nepal. SOV; postpositions; genitives after nouns; relatives before nouns; question word medial; CV, CVC, CCV, V, CCVC, CVCCC; tonal. Mountain slope, valley. Gallery forest. Swidden and peasant agriculturalists.

Tamang, Western (Murmi) [tdg] 322,598 (2000 WCD). Bagmati Zone, western Nuwakot, Rasuwa, Dhading, and parts of Gorkha District in Gandaki Zone, and other districts to the west and possibly southwest, central mountainous strip. Migrations to the Terai. *Class:* Sino-Tibetan, Tibeto-Burman, Himalayish, Tibeto-Kanauri, Tibetic, Tamangic. *Dialects:* Trisuli (Nuwakot), Rasuwa, Northwestern (Dhading), Southwestern. Preliminary results showed 86% intelligibility of Western by Rasuwa, 81% to 88% by Central-Eastern, 78% to 88% by Outer-Eastern, 86% by Southwestern; 80% of Rasuwa by Trisuli, 13% by Outer-Eastern. Trisuli has 94% lexical similarity with Northwestern Tamang, 82% to 83% with Rasuwa Tamang, 80% with Southwestern Tamang, 77% to 79% with Eastern Gorkha Tamang. Rasuwa has 82% to 83% with Northwestern, 78% with Southwestern, 72% with Eastern Gorkha Tamang. All Western varieties have 69% to 81% with Eastern Tamang varieties. *Lg Dev:* Literacy rate in first language: 1% to 10%. Literacy rate in second language: 25% to 75%. Devanagari and Tibetan scripts. NT: 1990. *Other:* 'Murmi' is an archaic term used only in old British writings. No one uses it now. Tamang recognized as an official nationality by the Government of Nepal. SOV; postpositions; genitives after nouns, relatives before nouns, question word medial, CV, CVC, CCV, V, CCVC, CVCCC; tonal. Mountain slope, valley. Gallery forest. Swidden and peasant agriculturalists. Traditional religion, Buddhist, Hindu.

Thakali (Tapaang, Thaksya, Panchgaunle) [ths] 6,441 (2001 census). Ethnic population: 12,973 (2001 census). Dhaulagiri Zone, Mustang District, Thak Khola, the mid Kali Gandaki Valley, with Annapurna Himal on one side and Dhaulagiri Himal on the other, from Tatopani village in the south to Jomosom in the north. Many live outside the area. Tukche is the cultural center. Tukche dialect is in Tukche and all the villages south to Ghasa, also in Jomsom. Syang dialect in Syang, Thini, Chhairo and Chimang. *Class:* Sino-Tibetan, Tibeto-Burman, Himalayish, Tibeto-Kanauri, Tibetic, Tamangic. *Dialects:* Tukche (Thaksatsae, Thaksaatsaye), Marpha, Syang (Yhulkasom). Thakali dialects have 91% to 97% inherent intelligibility. Tukche is most easily understood by others. Lexical similarity 41% to 46% with Gurung, 46% to 51% with Tamang (Webster 1994). Thakali dialects in 4 villages have 75% to 86% lexical similarity with each other. *Lg Use:* The younger generation in Tukche is maintaining Thakali more strongly than in other areas. Elsewhere the younger generation uses less Thakali, but will develop it more fully as they grow older (Webster 1994). 1,056 second-language speakers (1991 census). All ages except some educated ones under 30 who will probably speak it more fluently later. Tukche is the prestige dialect. 43% of the adult population (45% of men and 33% of women) have good, general proficiency in Nepali; others are less proficient. *Lg Dev:* Literacy rate in second language: 62.2% (1991 census). *Other:* Marpha

dialect is in an endogamous village. Thakali, Marphali and Syangtan recognized as official nationalities by the Government of Nepal. The people of Marpha, Syang, Thini, Chhairo and Chimang villages are sometimes collectively known as Panchgaunle (5 villages). This name used for both ethnic group and language. Traders. Buddhist, Jhankrism, Bonpo, Hindu.

Thangmi (Thami, Dolakha) [thf] 18,991 in Nepal (2001 census). Population total all countries: 19,291. Ethnic population: 22,999. Most in Janakpur Zone, Dolakha District; villages in Bagmati Zone, Sindhupalchok District, west of the Sun Kosi; a few villages in Ramechaap along the Sailung Khola. Also spoken in China. *Class:* Sino-Tibetan, Tibeto-Burman, Himalayish, Tibeto-Kanauri, Western Himalayish, Eastern. *Dialects:* Eastern Thami, Western Thami, Sindhupalcok. Related to Baraamu (Grierson-Konow). *Lg Use:* Speakers also use Nepali. *Lg Dev:* Literacy rate in second language: 22.3% (1991 census). Poetry. Dictionary. *Other:* Recognized as an official nationality by the Government of Nepal. Extinct in India. Slate miners; transporters; hunters; agriculturalists; pastoralists; road builders. Traditional religion, Hindu.

Tharu, Chitwania (Chituan Tharu, Chitawan Tharu) [the] 80,000 in Nepal (based on 1991 census). 993,388 all Tharu. Narayani Zone, Chitawan District; Lumbini Zone, Nawalparasi District. Also spoken in India. *Class:* Indo-European, Indo-Iranian, Indo-Aryan, Eastern zone, Unclassified. *Lg Use:* Speakers also use Nepali, Hindi, or Bhojpuri Tharu. *Lg Dev:* Literacy rate in first language: below 1%. Literacy rate in second language: 27.7% (1991 census). Bible portions: 1977. *Other:* Tharu recognized as an official nationality by the Government of Nepal. Plains. Traditional religion syncretism with Hindu, Hindu.

Tharu, Dangaura (Chaudary Tharu, Chaudhari Tharu, Dangora, Dangura, Dangauli, Dangha) [thl] 500,000 in Nepal (2003). 10% to 15% monolingual. Population total all countries: 531,000. Rapti Zone, Dang-Deokhuri District. Also in other areas of the Tarai, Bheri Zone, Bardiya, Banke districts; Seti Zone, Kailali District; Mahakali Zone, Kanchanpur District; Surkhet District. Also spoken in India. *Class:* Indo-European, Indo-Iranian, Indo-Aryan, Central zone, Unclassified. *Dialects:* Kailali (Malhora), Deokhuri (Deokhar, Deokri), Dang, Banke, Bardiya, Surkhet, Kanchanpur. 68% to 91% intelligibility of Rana, 95% to 97% of Kathoriya. Some intelligibility difficulty with speakers from India. Possibly Eastern Hindi Group. Lexical similarity 74% to 79% with Kathoriya, 72% to 74% with Sunha, 63% to 72% with Rana Thakur, 61% to 67% with Chitwania, 58% to 65% with Hindi. *Lg Use:* High vitality but with an increase in Nepali loanwords. Used in the family. All ages. Educated people tend to use more Nepali, men more than women, young people more than older people. Hindi and Maithili are also used. *Lg Dev:* Literacy rate in second language: 27.7% all Tharu. Devanagari script. Magazines. Radio programs. Dictionary. Grammar. *Other:* Tharu recognized as an official nationality by the Government of Nepal. SOV; postpositions; genitives after noun heads; adjectives, numerals before noun heads; CV, CVC, CCV; nontonal. Hills, valleys. Subtropical. 400 to 900 meters. Agriculturalists. Traditional religion syncretism with Hindu, Hindu.

Tharu, Kathoriya (Kathariya) [tkt] 60,000 in Nepal (1981). Seti Zone, Kailali District. Also spoken in India. *Class:* Indo-European, Indo-Iranian, Indo-Aryan, Central zone, Unclassified. *Dialects:* There appear to be differences in speech between Nepal and India dialects. Possibly Eastern Hindi Group. Lexical similarity 79% with Dangaura and Rana, 66% with Hindi, 66% to 69% with Buksa, 63% with Chitwania. *Lg Use:* Speakers also use Nepali or Hindi. *Lg Dev:* Literacy rate in second language: 27.7% (1991 census). *Other:* Tharu recognized as an official nationality by the Government of Nepal. Hindu, syncretism with traditional religion.

Tharu, Kochila [thq] 258,211 in Nepal (2003). Koshi Zone, Morang and Sunsari districts; Sagarmatha Zone, Saptari, Udayapur, and Siraha districts; Janakpur Zone, Mahottari, Sarlahi, Dhanusa districts. Also spoken in India. *Class:* Indo-European, Indo-Iranian, Indo-Aryan, Eastern zone, Unclassified. *Dialects:* Saptari, Morangiya, Udayapur, Sunsari, Siraha, Mahottari, Sarlahi, Dhanusa. Speakers in each district speak a different variety. *Lg Use:* Vigorous. Used among family, older people, children, village leaders. Speakers also use Nepali or Maithili. *Lg Dev:* Literacy rate in first language: below 1%. Literacy rate in second language: 27.7% (all Tharu as an ethnic group). *Other:* Tharu recognized as an official nationality by the Government of Nepal. The Tharu from each district usually take the district name as a more specific name or identity. Other Tharu in Siraha, Udayapur, and Saparti districts who call themselves 'Kochila' but do not speak Kochila can be distinguished by dress, customs, and language. They have adopted Maithili culture. Traditional religion syncretism with Hindu, Hindu.

Tharu, Rana (Rana Thakur) [thr] 303,853 in Nepal (2000). Population total all countries: 367,853. Mahakali Zone, Kanchanpur District; Seti Zone, Kailali District. Also spoken in India. *Class:* Indo-European, Indo-Iranian, Indo-Aryan, Eastern zone, Unclassified. *Dialects:* Speakers appear to have 96% to 99% intelligibility among dialects, 90% of Kathoriya, 51% to 88% reported of Dangaura. Differences with India dialects. Lexical similarity 83% to 97% among dialects, 73% to 79% with Buksa, 74% to 79% with Kathoriya, 70% to 73% with Sunha, 63% to 71% with Dangaura, 56% to 60% with Chitwania, 68% to 72% with Hindi. *Lg Use:* Vigorous. Used among family, older people, children, mainly in village. Speakers also use Nepali or Hindi. *Lg Dev:* Literacy rate in first language: below 1%. Literacy rate in second language: 27.7% (1991 census). Dictionary. *Other:* Tharu recognized as an official nationality by the Government of Nepal. Agriculturalists; pastoralists. Traditional religion with Hindu overlay.

Thudam (Thudam "Bhote") [thw] 1,800 (2000). Koshi Zone, Sankhuwasawa District, Chepuwa VDC, Thudam village (only one village). *Class:* Sino-Tibetan, Tibeto-Burman, Himalayish, Tibeto-Kanauri, Tibetic, Tibetan, Unclassified. *Dialects:* Reportedly very close to Tibetan. *Other:* Recognized as an official nationality by the Government of Nepal. Culturally akin to the Walungs. Village Development Committee (VDC) is a body with authority over several (4 to 7) villages. Tenant farmers for the Lhomi and Walungge. Buddhist.

Thulung (Thulunge Rai, Thulu Luwa, Thululoa, Thulung La, Tholong Lo, Thulung Jemu, Toaku Lwa) [tdh] 30,000 in Nepal (2003). Population total all countries: 33,313. Sagarmatha Zone, southeast Solukhumbu District, eastern hills; 6 to 7 villages in Okhaldhunga District and 1 in Bhojpur District of Koshi Zone. West of the highest ridges of the slopes to Dudhkosi, north of the Nechedanda and Halesidanda ranges, east of the upper Solu River, and south of the Kakukhola and the confluence of Ingkhukhola and Dudhkosi. Also spoken in India. *Class:* Sino-Tibetan, Tibeto-Burman, Himalayish, Mahakiranti, Kiranti, Western. *Dialects:* Lannachyo, Northern Thulung, Southern Thulung, Central Thulung, Eastern Thulung. Related to Lingkhim. Related to Bahing, Wambule, Jerung. High degree of cognancy with Khaling. All listed dialects are mutually intelligible although the people themselves don't refer to these dialect names. *Lg Use:* The degree of language retention high compared to other Rai languages (Winter 1991). All ages. They do not

believe each other's dialect is 'pure' Thulung. Women speak less Nepali than men. Most men speak Nepali well. *Other:* Village Development Committee (VDC) is a body with authority over several (4 to 7) villages. Mountain slope. 1,000 to 2,000 meters. Agriculturalists; pastoralists. Kiranti traditional religion, Hindu.

Tibetan (Bhotia, Zang Wen, Bod Skad, Poke, Phoke, Central Tibetan) [bod] 60,000 in Nepal (1973 SIL). Mainly Kathmandu and Pokhara. Some scattered refugee communities in few districts along the China border. *Dialect:* Utsang. *Other:* Agriculturalists; pastoralists; weavers. Buddhist (Lamaist). See main entry under China (Tibetan, Central).

Tichurong (Ticherong) [tcn] 2,417 (2000). Karnali Zone, Dolpa District, in the basin of the Bheri River. *Class:* Sino-Tibetan, Tibeto-Burman, Himalayish, Tibeto-Kanauri, Tibetic, Tibetan, Central. *Dialects:* Close to Dolpa Tibetan. *Other:* Culturally distinct from Dolpo. Buddhist.

Tilung (Tiling, Tilling, Tilung Blama) [tij] 310 (2001 census). Sagarmatha Zone, Halesidanda Range in the outer west of Khotang District, between Dudhkosi and Sunkosi. *Class:* Sino-Tibetan, Tibeto-Burman, Himalayish, Mahakiranti, Kiranti, Western. *Dialects:* Choskule, Dorunkecha. Choskule and Dorungkecha may be dialects or related languages; no linguistic data available. *Other:* Little information available. Mountain slope. Traditional religion.

Tomyang (Chongka, Tomyang Rai) [tmx] 20 villages in Ibadeviar of Num Village Development Committee (VDC). Koshi Zone, Sankhuwasawa District. *Class:* Sino-Tibetan, Tibeto-Burman, Himalayish, Mahakiranti, Kiranti. *Dialects:* Newly discovered in 2000 by a team of Nepali linguists.

Tseku (Tsuku, Tzuku) [tsk] 4,786 in Nepal (2000). Mechi Zone, Panchthar District. *Other:* Buddhist. See main entry under China.

Tsum (Tsumge) [ttz] 4,786 (2000). Gandaki Zone, northern Gorkha District, Tsum area, the region drained by the Shiar Khola north of Ganesh Himal. Chekampar (Chokong) is the prestige village. *Class:* Sino-Tibetan, Tibeto-Burman, Himalayish, Tibeto-Kanauri, Tibetic, Tibetan, Central. *Dialects:* 71% to 78% intelligibility of Nubri, 66% of Kyerung; 60% to 66% of Lhasa Tibetan; 22% to 25% of Northern Ghale, 22% of Southern Ghale, 23% to 27% of Kutang Ghale, 14% to 16% of Eastern Gorkha Tamang, 14% of Western Gurung, 15% of Banspur Tamang. Divided into upper region, 'Yarba', and lower region, 'Ushug'. *Lg Use:* Vigorous. Nearly every domain. Highly positive language attitude. Speakers have minimal bilingualism in Nepali. Nepali used only with those who do not understand Tsum. Tibetan is viewed very favorably in the religious domain, and Nepali is viewed fairly positively as a language of education and potential advancement. *Lg Dev:* Literacy rate in second language: 10% or less. *Other:* A few primary schools. Tibetans in Kathmandu call the people 'Tsumba' and the language 'Tsumge'. Mountain slope, valley. Gallery forest. Agriculturalists; traders. Buddhist (Lamaist).

Waling (Walung, Walüng) [wly] Extinct. Koshi Zone, Bhojpur District, Khairang Panchayat. *Class:* Sino-Tibetan, Tibeto-Burman, Himalayish, Mahakiranti, Kiranti, Eastern. *Dialects:* Related to Dungmali. *Lg Use:* Members of the ethnic group now speak Bantawa.

Walungge (Olangchung Gola, Walungchung Gola, Walung, Walunggi Keccya) [ola] 10,000 to 15,000 in Nepal. Population includes 3,500 in the original area. Population total all countries: 10,000 to 15,000. Mechi Zone, Taplejung District, Tamar valley, 5 main villages: Walungchung, Yangma, Gunsa, Lilip, and Lungtung, and 6 or 7 smaller villages. Speakers also in Lungthung, Amjilesa, and Kambachen. Also spoken in India. *Class:*

Sino-Tibetan, Tibeto-Burman, Himalayish, Tibeto-Kanauri, Tibetic, Tibetan, Central. *Dialects:* Similar to Tibetan dialect in Tingay district of Tibet. Lexical similarity 71% with Lhasa Tibetan, 68% with Dolpo, Lowa, and Kyerung, 66% with Lhomi and Helambu Sherpa, 64% with Nubri, 57% with Jirel, 55% with Sherpa. *Lg Use:* Young people in Kathmandu losing the language. In all areas except Kathmandu there is a strong sense of cultural identity revolving around their religion and language. *Lg Dev:* Tibetan script. *Other:* The people are called 'Walungba'. Each of the main villages has a school. Cut off from the Lhomi, more links to Tibet. Some intermarriage with Lhomi and Tibetan speakers. Recognized as an official nationality by the Government of Nepal. Animal husbandry; traders. Buddhist.

Wambule (Tsaurasya, Chaurasia, Chaurasya, Chourase, Chourasia, Ambule, Ombule, Umbule) [wme] 4,471 (2001 census). Sagarmatha Zone, Udayapur and Okhaldhunga districts. *Class:* Sino-Tibetan, Tibeto-Burman, Himalayish, Mahakiranti, Kiranti, Western. *Dialects:* Bonu, Ubu. Closest to Jerung. *Lg Use:* Vigorous. All ages. Nepali is used. Some bilingualism in Bahing resulting from intermarriage. *Lg Dev:* Literacy rate in second language: 10%. Dictionary. *Other:* Mountain slope. Agriculturalists.

Wayu (Hayu, Vayu, Wayo) [vay] 1,743 (2001 census). Ethnic population: 1,821 (2001 census) to 2,826 (2000). Janakpur Zone, Ramechhap and Sindhuli districts, on the hills on both sides of the Sun Kosi River. *Class:* Sino-Tibetan, Tibeto-Burman, Himalayish, Mahakiranti, Kham-Magar-Chepang-Sunwari, Chepang. *Dialects:* Distinct from Chepang. *Lg Use:* Hodgson said it was becoming extinct in the mid-19th century, but it has survived until the end of the 20th century (Michailovsky 1988). No monolingual children (Matisoff 1991). *Other:* Now strong Nepali influences in phonology, lexicon, and grammar (J. Matisoff 1991). Recognized as an official nationality by the Government of Nepal. 1,000 to 1,500 meters. Traditional religion.

Yakha (Yakkha, Yakkhaba, Yakkhaba Cea, Yakkhaba Sala, Dewansala) [ybh] 14,648 in Nepal (2001 census). Population total all countries: 15,648. Ethnic population: 17,003. Koshi Zone, Terhathum District, Sankhuwasawa District, Dhankuta District. East of the middle Arun River between the Hinuwankhola in the north and the Legu-wakhola in the south. Northern Yakha is in the south of Sankhuwasawa District, and the adjoining strip of land in extreme northern Dhankuta District. Southern Yakha is in Dhankuta District. Eastern Yakha is in Mechi Zone, Ilam and Panchthar districts. Also spoken in India. *Class:* Sino-Tibetan, Tibeto-Burman, Himalayish, Mahakiranti, Kiranti, Eastern. *Dialects:* Northern Yakha, Southern Yakha, Eastern Yakha. Dialects have minimum diversity. Related to Lumba-Yakkha, Phangduwali, Mugali, Chhintange, Chhulung, Belhariya, Lohorong, Limbu and Athpahariya. *Lg Use:* Less use among the younger generation. *Other:* Yakhas are considered by many to be a distinct group of Kiranti not fitting neatly into either the Rai or the Limbu groups. (Bista 1996:39) Recognized as an official nationality by the Government of Nepal. Agriculturalists; pastoralists. Buddhist, Hindu.

Yamphe (Yamphu, Newahang Yamphe, Yamphe Kha) [yma] 1,722 (2001 census). Koshi Zone, northern Sankhuwasawa District, both sides of the upper Arun River, Makalu Panchayat. To the south, the Jaljale Himal east of the Arun and the Apsuwakhola west of the Arun; to the north as far as the Leksuwakhola and Barun rivers. *Class:* Sino-Tibetan, Tibeto-Burman, Himalayish, Mahakiranti, Kiranti, Eastern. *Dialects:* Sibao-Yamphe, Pa-O. Related to Yamphu, but distinct in grammar and phonology. *Lg Use:* Still spoken by many people.

Other: Sometimes called 'Yakkha' or 'Yamphu', but it is a distinct language. Mountain slope.

Yamphu (Yamphu Rai, Yamphu Kha, Yanphu, Yamphe) [ybi] 1,722 (2001 census). Many are monolingual. Koshi, Mechi zones, directly southwest of the Jaljale Mountains, extreme north of the Northern Lorung area, Sankhu-wasawa District, Matsayapokhari Panchayat, upper Arun Valley, eastern hills. *Class:* Sino-Tibetan, Tibeto-Burman, Himalayish, Mahakiranti, Kiranti, Eastern. *Dialects:* Related to Yamphe but different grammatically and phonologically. *Lg Use:* Most are uncomfortable in Nepali (GR). *Other:* Dialects of Southern Lorung and the Yamphe language are also called 'Yamphu'. Mountain slope. Hindu.

Oman

Sultanate of Oman, Saltanat 'Uman. 2,903,165. 535,000 are expatriates (1993 census). National or official language: Standard Arabic. Literacy rate: 59.75% (1993 census). Also includes Baharna Spoken Arabic (10,000), Gujarati, Portuguese, Shihhi Spoken Arabic (22,000), Sindhi, Somali, Swahili (22,000), Urdu (30,000), people from Bangladesh (88,000), Egypt (33,000), India (268,000), Jordan (8,000), Pakistan (63,000), Philippines (10,000), Sri Lanka (25,000), Sudan (9,000), other Gulf States (6,000), other Arab (10,000), United Kingdom (7,000). Information mainly from T. M. Johnstone 1967; C. Holes 1988, 1990. Deaf population: 103,131. The number of languages listed for Oman is 13. Of those, all are living languages. See map on page 817.

Arabic, Dhofari Spoken (Dhofari, Zofari) [adf] 70,000 (1996). In Salala and its nearby coastal regions. *Class:* Afro-Asiatic, Semitic, Central, South, Arabic. *Dialects:* Related to Hadromi Spoken Arabic and Gulf Spoken Arabic. *Other:* Different from Omani Spoken Arabic.

Arabic, Gulf Spoken (Omani Bedawi Arabic, Bedawi, Gulf Arabic, Khaliji) [afb] 441,000 in Oman (1995). Most coastal regions and most border regions with the United Arab Emirates. *Other:* Muslim. See main entry under Iraq.

Arabic, Omani Spoken (Omani Hadari Arabic) [acx] 720,000 in Oman (1996). Population total all countries: 815,000. Mainly in the Hajar Mountains highlands and a few coastal regions. Also spoken in Kenya, Tanzania, United Arab Emirates. *Class:* Afro-Asiatic, Semitic, Central, South, Arabic. *Other:* svo.

Arabic, Standard [arb] Middle East, North Africa. *Lg Use:* Official language. Used for education, official purposes, formal speeches. See main entry under Saudi Arabia.

Balochi, Southern (Baluchi, Baluci, Baloci) [bcc] 130,300 in Oman (1993). Ethnic population: 312,000 in Oman (1993). Most were in Mutrah, but have dispersed a bit up the coast. *Dialects:* Makrani (Lotuni, Zadgaali), Barahuwi, Bashgaadi, Huuti. *Lg Use:* Ethnic Baloch who immigrated long ago are Omani citizens, but no longer speak Balochi. *Other:* Speakers come from Pakistan. The majority are not Omani citizens. Muslim (Sunni). See main entry under Pakistan.

Bathari (Batahari, Bathara) [bhm] 200 in Oman. Dhofar Governorate, in coastal towns of Shuwaymiya and Sharbithat. *Other:* Muslim. See main entry under Yemen.

Farsi, Western (Persian) [pes] 25,000 in Oman (1993). Scattered in cities along the coast. Many in a community in Jabroo, on the way out of Mutrah, going toward Ruwi. *Lg Use:* Many women speak only Farsi. Men who go outside the community speak Arabic as second language, and many know 2 or 3 other languages. *Other:* Muslim (Shi'a). See main entry under Iran.

Harsusi (Hersyet, Harsi 'Aforit) [hss] 1,000 to 2,000 (1998 H. Mutzafi). Jiddat al-Harasis, Dhofar Province, south central Oman. *Class:* Afro-Asiatic, Semitic, South, South Arabian. *Dialects:* Close to Mehri, but usually considered to be a separate language. *Lg Use:* It is reported that they are increasing in use of Mehri and proficiency in it, and also bilingual in Arabic. *Other:* Spoken by the Harasis and 'Ifar ('Afar).

Hobyót (Hewbyót, Hobi) [hoh] 100 in Oman (1998 Hezy Mutzafi). Near the Yemen border. Also spoken in Yemen. *Class:* Afro-Asiatic, Semitic, South, South Arabian. *Dialects:* Related to Mehri and Jibbali. Possibly a mixed language from Shehri and Mehri. *Other:* They define themselves as belonging to the Mahra tribe. Muslim.

Kumzari (Kumzai) [zum] 1,700 (1993 census). Spoken only on the Musandam Peninsula of northern Oman. *Class:* Indo-European, Indo-Iranian, Iranian, Western, Southwestern, Luri. *Other:* Distinct from Khunsari of Iran. Fishermen. Muslim.

Luwati [luv] 5,000 (1996). In a walled quarter of Mutrah, facing the old harbor, and in Muscat and other cities. *Class:* Indo-European, Indo-Iranian, Unclassified. *Other:* The people are called 'Luwathiya'. Their ancestors are reported to have migrated from Iran to Hyderabad, then to Mutrah. Sometimes called 'Persians'. Businessmen. Muslim (Shi'a).

Mehri (Mahri) [gdq] 50,763 in Oman (2000 WCD). South Oman near Yemen border. *Dialect:* Nagdi. *Other:* Muslim. See main entry under Yemen.

Shehri (Geblet, Sheret, Sehri, Shahari, Jibali, Jibbali, Ehkili, Qarawi) [shv] 25,000 (1993 census). Dofar, in the mountains north of Al-Salala. *Class:* Afro-Asiatic, Semitic, South, South Arabian. *Dialects:* Central Jibbali, Eastern Jibbali, Western Jibbali. Eastern Jibbali includes Kuria Muria ('Baby' Jibbali). Speakers are reported to be increasingly bilingual in Dhofari Arabic. *Other:* Spoken by the Qara (Ehkeló, Ahkló), Shahra (Sheró, Shahara), Barahama, Bait Ash-Shaik, and some Batahira. Muslim.

Pakistan

Islamic Republic of Pakistan, Islam-i Jamhuriya-e Pakistan. 159,196,336. National or official languages: Urdu, Sindhi, English. Literacy rate: 26%. Also includes Indian Sign Language, Parsi (20,000), Southern Uzbek (50,000), Turkmen, Uyghur, Arabic (122,000), Chinese (6,000). Information mainly from R. F. Strand 1973; G. Morgenstierne 1974; C. Shackle 1979, 1980; J. C. Sharma 1982; J. S. Addleton 1986; J. R. Payne 1987; C. P. Masica 1991; C. O'Leary 1992. Blind population: 1,500,000. Deaf population: 7,398,329. Deaf institutions: 31. The number of languages listed for Pakistan is 72. Of those, all are living languages.

Aer [aeq] 100 to 200 (1998). Women are monolingual. Lower Sindh, Jikrio Goth near Kunri around Deh 333, Hyderabad, and at Jamesabad. Others are reported to have migrated to India at Partition in 1947, living in the Kach Bhuj area in Gujarat. *Class:* Indo-European, Indo-Iranian, Indo-Aryan, Central zone, Gujarati. *Dialects:* Jikrio Goth Aer, Jamesabad Aer. Lexical similarity 78% with Katai Meghwar and Kachi Bhil, 75% to 77% with Rabari, 76% with Kachi Koli. *Lg Use:* All ages. They also speak Sindhi (adult men only for common topics), Panjabi (adult men of Jikrio Goth only for common topics), and Gujarati. 100% of boys and 25% of girls attend Sindhi medium schools. *Lg Dev:* Literacy rate in second language: 15% in Sindhi. Sindhi-based script. *Other:* Unusual interrogative word suggests possible historical connection with Western Rajasthani group. Speakers in Pakistan are running out of marriage possibilities and may have to move to India. The group in India is the most influential. Other Aer people in Nawabshah, Sindh are reported to speak a different

language, dress differently, and do not intermarry with this group. Hindu.

Badeshi [bdz] Ethnic population: 2,825 (2000 WCD). Upper reaches of Bishigram (Chail) Valley, east of Madyan, Swat Kohistan. One village. *Class:* Indo-European, Indo-Iranian, Unclassified. *Lg Use:* Speakers also use Pashto. *Other:* Existence unconfirmed. The Torwali say they speak Ushojo, and the Ushojo say they speak Torwali. May be a family name of people who came from Badakhshan. Muslim (Sunni).

Bagri (Bagari, Bagria, Bagris, Baorias, Bahgri, Bawri) [bgq] 200,000 in Pakistan. 100,000 in Sind Province (1998). In the Sindh and Punjab. *Lg Use:* They speak some Sindhi and understand some Urdu. *Lg Dev:* Literacy rate in first language: below 1%. Literacy rate in second language: below 5%. *Other:* Distinct from Vaghri. Nomadic. See main entry under India.

Balochi, Eastern (Baluchi, Baluci, Baloci) [bgp] 1,800,000 in Pakistan (1998). 5,000,000 including second-language users of all Balochi languages. Population total all countries: 1,805,000. Northeastern Balochistan Province, northwestern Sind, southwestern Punjab. Also spoken in India. *Class:* Indo-European, Indo-Iranian, Iranian, Western, Northwestern, Balochi. *Lg Dev:* Literacy rate in first language: below 1%. Literacy rate in second language: 5% to 15%. Urdu script. Radio programs. Bible portions: 1815–1906. *Other:* One of the major languages in Pakistan. Distinct from Western Balochi and Southern Balochi. Balochi has a small body of literature. Muslim (Sunni).

Balochi, Southern (Baluchi, Baluci, Baloci, Makrani) [bcc] 2,765,000 in Pakistan (1998). Population total all countries: 3,400,300. Southern Balochistan, southern Sind, Karachi. Also spoken in Iran, Oman, United Arab Emirates. *Class:* Indo-European, Indo-Iranian, Iranian, Western, Northwestern, Balochi. *Dialect:* Coastal Balochi, Kechi, Makrani (Lotuni). Distinct from Eastern Balochi and fairly distinct from Western Balochi. *Lg Dev:* Literacy rate in first language: below 1%. Literacy rate in second language: 5% to 15%. Urdu script. Bible portions: 1992–1994. *Other:* Muslim (Sunni), Zigri (Zikri).

Balochi, Western (Baluchi, Baloci, Baluci) [bgn] 1,116,000 in Pakistan (1998). Population total all countries: 1,799,842. Northwestern Balochistan Province. Also spoken in Afghanistan, Iran, Tajikistan, Turkmenistan. *Class:* Indo-European, Indo-Iranian, Iranian, Western, Northwestern, Balochi. *Dialects:* Rakhshani (Raxshani), Sarawani. Strongly influenced by Fars, but not intelligible with Farsi. *Lg Dev:* Literacy rate in first language: 1% to 5%. Literacy rate in second language: 5% to 15%. Urdu script; Arabic script in Afghanistan. Newspapers. Radio programs. Bible portions: 1984. *Other:* Balochi is the official spelling in Pakistan. It has a small body of literature. Muslim (Sunni).

Balti (Sbalti, Baltistani, Bhotia of Baltistan) [bft] 270,000 in Pakistan (1992). Population total all countries: 337,000. Primarily northeastern Pakistan: Baltistan District, Skardu, Rondu, Shigar, Khapalu, Kharmang, and Gultari valleys. Also spoken in India. *Class:* Sino-Tibetan, Tibeto-Burman, Himalayish, Tibeto-Kanauri, Tibetic, Tibetan, Western. *Dialects:* Chorbat is the most divergent dialect. Lexical similarity 87% to 100% among dialects, 78% to 85% with Purik. *Lg Use:* Some Shina is used as second language. Urdu proficiency is reported to be high in some places. Women and the uneducated have little knowledge of Urdu. Many Purik have shifted to Balti. *Lg Dev:* Literacy rate in second language: 3% to 5% in Urdu. Perso-Arabic script. Bible portions: 1903–1940. *Other:* Muslim (Shi'a).

Bateri (Bateri Kohistani, Batera Kohistani, Baterawal, Baterawal Kohistani) [btv] 28,251 in Pakistan (2000

WCD). Population total all countries: 29,051. Extreme southern corner, Kohistan District, small pocket on the east bank of the Indus River, north of Besham; Batera area. Also spoken in India. *Class:* Indo-European, Indo-Iranian, Indo-Aryan, Northwestern zone, Dardic, Kohistani. *Dialects:* Closer to Indus Kohistani than to Shina, but distinct from both. Lexical similarity 58% to 61% with Indus Kohistani, 60% with Gowro, 54% with Chilisso, 29% with Shina and Torwali, 27% with Kalami. *Lg Use:* Vigorous. Speakers also use Pashto or Shina.

Bhaya [bhe] 70 to 700 (1998). Lower Sindh: Kapri Goth near Samaro, near Khipro, Jamesabad, Mir ke goth, Mirpurkhas, Phuladia, a few families in Hyderabad. There may be more in India. *Class:* Indo-European, Indo-Iranian, Indo-Aryan, Central zone, Western Hindi, Unclassified. *Dialects:* Similarity of key morphemes: The possessive postposition with 'g-' contrasts with all other languages in the area. Gender endings match Rajasthani. This might be the same as Bhoyari in India. It may be in the Western Hindi group. Lexical similarity 84% with Marwari sweeper, 75% with Malhi, 73% with Bhat, 72% to 73% with Goaria, 70% to 73% with Sindhi Meghwar, 63% to 72% with Mogi, 63% to 71% with Sindhi Bhil, 70% with Urdu.

Brahui (Brahuidi, Birahui, Brahuigi, Kur Galli) [brh] 2,000,000 in Pakistan (1998). Population total all countries: 2,210,000. South central, Quetta and Kalat Region, east Baluchistan and Sind provinces. Also spoken in Afghanistan, Iran, Turkmenistan. *Class:* Dravidian, Northern. *Dialects:* Jharawan, Kalat, Sarawan. Kalat is the standard dialect, Jharawan is lowland. *Lg Use:* Some speakers also use Western Balochi. *Lg Dev:* Literacy rate in first language: below 1%. Literacy rate in second language: below 5%. Nastaliq script. Bible portions: 1905–1978. *Other:* Pastoralists. Muslim.

Burushaski (Brushaski, Burushaki, Burucaki, Burushki, Burucaski, Biltum, Khajuna, Kunjut) [bsk] 87,049 in Pakistan (2000 WCD). Hunza-Nagar area and Yasin area in Gilgit District, Northern Areas. Scattered speakers also in Gilgit, Kashmir, and various cities. Also spoken in India. *Class:* Language Isolate. *Dialects:* Nagar (Nagir), Hunza, Yasin (Werchikwar). Yasin is geographically separated from other dialects. Lexical similarity 91% to 94% between Nagar and Hunza dialects, 67% to 72% between Yasin and Hunza, 66% to 71% between Yasin and Nagar, and may be a separate language. *Lg Use:* Yasin speakers have some proficiency in Khowar. Knowledge of Urdu is limited among women and others. *Lg Dev:* Literacy rate in second language: 20%. *Other:* People are called Burusho. SOV. Muslim (Ismaili and Shi'a).

Chilisso (Chiliss, Galos) [clh] 1,600 to 3,000 (1992 SIL). Scattered families in the Koli, Palas, Jalkot area of the Indus Kohistan, east bank of the Indus River. *Class:* Indo-European, Indo-Iranian, Indo-Aryan, Northwestern zone, Dardic, Kohistani. *Dialects:* Lexical similarity 70% with Indus Kohistani, 65% to 68% with Gowro, 54% with Bateri, 48% to 56% with Shina. 26% with Torwali, 25% with Kalami. *Lg Use:* Socially integrated with the Kohistani Shina, and most or all speak that as first or second language.

Dameli (Damel, Damedi, Damia, Gudoji) [dml] 5,000 (1992 SIL). In the Damel Valley, about 32 miles south of Drosh in southern Chitral District, on the east side of the Kunar River. 11 villages. *Class:* Indo-European, Indo-Iranian, Indo-Aryan, Northwestern zone, Dardic, Kunar. *Dialects:* Two groups: Shintari and Swati, but no significant dialect variation. Lexical similarity 44% with Gawar-Bati, Savi, and Phalura, 33% with Kamviiri, 29% with Kati. *Lg Use:* Vigorous. Used in the home and with friends. A few men use Urdu as second language. Few women know Pashto. *Other:* They are reported to have

come from Afghanistan several hundred years ago. The language has been influenced by Nuristani languages. Mountain valleys. Pastoralists. Muslim (Sunni).

Dehwari (Deghwari) [deh] 13,000 (1998). Central Balochistan, in Kalat and Mastung. *Class:* Indo-European, Indo-Iranian, Iranian, Western, Southwestern, Persian. *Lg Dev:* Literacy rate in first language: below 1%. Literacy rate in second language: below 5%. *Other:* Influenced by Brahui.

Dhatki (Dhati) [mki] 131,863 in Pakistan (2000 WCD). Population includes 100,000 in Sind (1987). Population total all countries: 148,263. Lower Sind in Tharparkar and Sanghar districts. Also spoken in India. *Class:* Indo-European, Indo-Iranian, Indo-Aryan, Central zone, Rajasthani, Marwari. *Dialects:* Eastern Dhatki, Southern Dhatki, Central Dhatki, Barage, Malhi. Varies considerably from northern Marwari, although they claim to understand one another. The Malhi are an ethnic group living in 3 main areas. Those in the Kunri-Pithoro-Noakot-Mithi area speak a dialect with 80% lexical similarity to Dhatki, 74% to Sindhi, and work as water-drawers. Lexical similarity 80% to 83% with Marwari dialects. Dhatki of Rajasthan and Dhatki of Thar are 88% lexically similar. *Lg Use:* Some also use Sindhi or Urdu. *Lg Dev:* Literacy rate in first language: below 5%. Literacy rate in second language: below 5%. Sindhi-based script. *Other:* Hindu, Muslim, Christian.

Domaaki (Dumaki, Doma) [dmk] 500 (1989). Gilgit District, Northern Areas, mainly in Hunza Valley, Mominabad village, a few households in Big Nagar, Shishkat (Gojal), Dumial in Gilgit, Oshkandas (east of Gilgit), and Bakor village in Punyal. *Class:* Indo-European, Indo-Iranian, Indo-Aryan, Northwestern zone, Dardic, Shina. *Dialects:* It has loanwords from Shina and Burushaski, but is not intelligible to speakers of those languages. Lexical similarity 40% with Gilgit Shina. *Lg Use:* Used in the home. Bilingualism in Burushaski is fairly high, especially among young people. Shina and Urdu also used as second languages. *Other:* The people are called 'Bericho', 'Dom', or 'Doma'. Musicians; blacksmiths. Muslim.

English [eng] *Lg Use:* Official language. Mainly second-language speakers in Pakistan. See main entry under United Kingdom.

Farsi, Eastern (Dari, Tajik, Madaglashti, Badakhshi) [prs] 1,000,000 in Pakistan. 1,400 in Madaglasht, and many refugees (1992 SIL). Southeast Chitral, Madaglasht village of Shishi Koh Valley, Peshawar, Rawalpindi, Lahore, Karachi, other large cities. *Other:* Madaglasht community came from Badakhshan, Afghanistan 200 years ago. Other communities have been in Pakistan for many generations. Muslim. See main entry under Afghanistan.

Gawar-Bati (Gowar-Bati, Gowari, Arandui, Satre, Narsati, Narisati) [gwt] 1,500 in Pakistan (1992). Southern Chitral, Arandu, and several villages along the Kunar River south of Arandu. *Lg Use:* Vigorous. All domains. Some use Pashto as second language. *Other:* Mountain valleys. Muslim (Sunni). See main entry under Afghanistan.

Ghera (Sindhi Ghera, Bara) [ghr] 10,000 (1998). A single colony in Hyderabad, between the main bus stop and the railway station. Speakers say more than 90% of the people remained in Surat and Ahmedabad, India. *Class:* Indo-European, Indo-Iranian, Indo-Aryan, Central zone, Western Hindi, Unclassified. *Dialects:* Quite different grammatically from Gurgula and similar to Urdu. Lexical similarity 87% with Gurgula, 70% with Urdu. *Lg Use:* Widespread multilingualism among both sexes with both Sindhi and Urdu. 25% of boys and some girls attend Sindhi medium schools. *Lg Dev:* Literacy rate in second language: 20% Sindhi. *Other:* Almost totally urbanized. Sellers of ceramic dishes, used clothing. Hindu.

Goaria [gig] 25,426 (2000 WCD). All towns in Sindh Province except Karachi: including Larkana, Sukkur, Moro, Badin, Umerkot. They claim to have come from Jodhpur Rajasthan, India, where there may be more. *Class:* Indo-European, Indo-Iranian, Indo-Aryan, Central zone, Rajasthani, Marwari. *Dialects:* This might be the same as Gawari in India. Lexical similarity 75% to 83% with Jogi, 76% to 80% with Marwari sweeper, 72% to 78% with Marwari Meghwar, 70% to 78% with Loarki. *Lg Use:* All domains except religion. All ages. Adults speak Sindhi and other local languages for trade, Hindi for worship. *Lg Dev:* Literacy rate in second language: below 1% in Sindhi. Sindhi-based script. *Other:* Plains. Desert. Sea level to 100 meters. Women sell trinkets, men transport people by horse cart and goods by donkey or donkey cart. Hindu.

Gowro (Gabaro, Gabar Khel) [gwf] 200 (1990). Indus Kohistan on the eastern bank, Kolai area, Mahrin village. *Class:* Indo-European, Indo-Iranian, Indo-Aryan, Northwestern zone, Dardic, Kohistani. *Dialects:* Lexical similarity 65% to 68% with Chilisso, 62% with Indus Kohistani, 60% with Bateri, 40% to 43% with Shina, 25% with Torwali, 24% with Kalami. *Lg Use:* Speakers also use Shina. *Other:* Different from Gawri, an alternate name for Kalami.

Gujarati [guj] Lower Punjab, Sindh. *Lg Use:* All Parsi (5,000), many Ismaili Muslims, and many Hindu sweepers (10,000 to 100,000) speak Gujarati. Many Parsi and Ismaili Muslims are literate in Gujarati. There seems to be a shift to Urdu among many Gujarati-speaking sweepers. See main entry under India.

Gujari (Gujuri, Gujuri Rajasthani, Gujer, Gojri, Gogri, Gojari, Gujjari, Kashmir Gujuri) [gju] 300,000 in Pakistan (1992). Population includes 2,910 in Chitral (1969), 20,000 in Swat Kohistan (1987), 200,000 to 700,000 in Azad Jammu and Kashmir (1989). Throughout northern Pakistan, mainly in the east in Hazara District, NWFP, in Kaghan Valley, Azad Jammu, and Kashmir. Scattered communities in southern Chitral, Swat Kohistan, and Dir Kohistan, NWFP, and Gilgit Agency, Northern Areas. *Dialects:* Western Gujari, Eastern Gujari. *Lg Use:* It is reported that most Gujars in Pakistani Punjab have shifted to Panjabi. Spoken in some pockets of Punjab by immigrants from elsewhere. *Other:* Some speakers move with herds up in summer, down in winter. Some unpublished literature. Some nomadic pastoralists; some settled agriculturalists. Muslim. See main entry under India.

Gurgula (Marwari Ghera) [ggg] 35,314 (2000 WCD). Sindh Province, largest concentration in Bhens Colony, Karachi, others in smaller urban centers through Sindh, including Mirpur Khas, Shahdadpur, Panj, Moro, Sabura and Tando Allahyar. *Class:* Indo-European, Indo-Iranian, Indo-Aryan, Central zone, Rajasthani, Unclassified. *Dialects:* Ghera is quite different gramatically. Lexical similarity 87% with Ghera. *Lg Use:* All domains. Positive language attitude. Widespread multilingualism in Sindhi, Urdu, some Gujarati among all ages and sexes as needed, with men being the most proficient. *Lg Dev:* Literacy rate in second language: 5% in Urdu. Sindhi-based script. *Other:* Plains. Desert with irrigation. Below 100 meters. Itinerant marketers. Hindu.

Hazaragi (Azargi, Hazara, Hezareh) [haz] 156,794 in Pakistan (2000 WCD). Population includes many recent refugees from Afghanistan. Quetta (100,000 to 200,000), Karachi and Islamabad (10,000), some villages in rural Sindh. *Lg Dev:* Literacy rate in first language: below 10%. Literacy rate in second language: 10% to 30% Urdu, Dari or Farsi. *Other:* The alternate names listed refer to the people. Group or regional names are (Central) Dai Kundi, Dai Zangi, Behsud, Yekaulang, (Southern) Polada, Urusgani, Jaguri, Ghazni Hazaras, Dai Miradad, Kabul.

Laborers; civil servants; tradesmen; shopkeepers; traders. Muslim (Imami Shi'a). See main entry under Afghanistan.

Hindko, Northern (Hazara Hindko, Hindki, Kaghani, Kagani) [hno] 1,875,000 (1981 census). Total Hindko in Pakistan 3,000,000 (1993). Hazara Division, Mansehra and Abbotabad districts, Indus and Kaghan valleys and valleys of Indus tributaries, NWFP. Rural and urban. *Class:* Indo-European, Indo-Iranian, Indo-Aryan, Northwestern zone, Lahnda. *Dialects:* Also related to Panjabi, Siraiki, and Pahari-Potwari; which have all been called 'Greater Panjabi', forming part of 'Lahnda'. Lexical similarities within Northern Hindko dialects are 82% to 92%, between Northern and Southern Hindko varieties 67% to 82%. *Lg Use:* Second languages are Urdu for the educated, with varied proficiency, and Pashto or Panjabi. For most speakers proficiency is low. *Lg Dev:* Literacy rate in second language: below 20%. Perso-Arabic script. Poetry. Radio programs. TV. NT: 1991. *Other:* Plains, hills. Muslim (Sunni).

Hindko, Southern [hnd] 625,000 (1981 census). Attock District, Punjab Province, and into the southernmost portion of Hazara Division, NWFP; Kohat and Peshawar districts, NWFP. Rural and urban. *Class:* Indo-European, Indo-Iranian, Indo-Aryan, Northwestern zone, Lahnda. *Dialects:* Peshawar Hindko (Peshawari), Attock Hindko (Attock-Haripur Hindko), Kohat Hindko (Kohati), Rural Peshawar Hindko. The dialect in Dera Ismail Khan, sometimes called 'Hindko', is apparently closer to Siraiki. *Lg Use:* Most have some proficiency in Urdu, Pashto, Panjabi, or other languages. Urdu is known by educated speakers. *Lg Dev:* Perso-Arabic script. Radio programs. TV. *Other:* Plains, hills. Muslim (Sunni).

Jadgali (Jatgali, Jatki, Jat) [jdg] 100,000 in Pakistan (1998). Southeast Balochistan Province, southwest Sind. Also spoken in Iran. *Class:* Indo-European, Indo-Iranian, Indo-Aryan, Northwestern zone, Sindhi. *Lg Dev:* Literacy rate in first language: below 1%. Literacy rate in second language: below 5%. *Other:* People called Jats. Different from Jakati of Afghanistan and Ukraine. Muslim.

Jandavra (Jhandoria) [jnd] 5,000 (1998). Southern Sindh Province from Hyderabad to east of Mirpur Khas. Reported to be many more in Jodhpur, Rajasthan, India. *Class:* Indo-European, Indo-Iranian, Indo-Aryan, Central zone, Gujarati. *Dialects:* Lexical similarity 74% with Bagri and Katai Meghwar, 68% with Kachi Koli. *Lg Use:* All ages. Men tend to be conversant in Sindhi and Urdu, at least on a basic level, but women are not. *Lg Dev:* Literacy rate in second language: No literates. *Other:* Plains. Desert. Sea level to 100 meters. Hindu.

Kabutra (Nat, Natra) [kbu] 1,000 (1998). Sindh, some concentrations around Umerkot, Kunri, and Nara Dhoro. Speakers say that 90% of the people remain in the Zal area of Marwar, India. *Class:* Indo-European, Indo-Iranian, Indo-Aryan, Central zone, Western Hindi, Hindustani, Sansi. *Dialects:* Speakers report they have inherent intelligibility of Sansi and Sochi, and use Kabutra when speaking to them. Lexical similarity 74% with the Sochi language variety. *Lg Use:* All ages and sexes speak Urdu for most common topics, some Sindhi. Women speak Urdu better than in most Hindu groups. *Lg Dev:* Literacy rate in second language: 5% in Urdu. *Other:* Entertainers, dancers. Hindu.

Kachchi (Kachchhi, Kutchchi, Cuchi, Cutch, Kutchie, Kachi, Katch, Kautchy, Katchi) [kfr] 50,000 in Pakistan (1998). Karachi. *Dialect:* Jadeji. *Lg Use:* Most Kachchi do not understand Gujarati. See main entry under India.

Kalami (Garwi, Gawri, Gowri, Garwa, Gaawro, Kalami Kohistani, Kohistani, Kohistana, Bashkarik, Bashgharik, Dir Kohistani, Diri, Dirwali) [gwc] 40,000 (1987). Upper Swat Kohistan from between Peshmal and Kalam north to upper valleys above Kalam, also in Dir Kohistan, in Thal,

Lamuti (Kinolam), Biar (Jiar), and Rajkot (Patrak) villages. People at Khata Khotan, China, are reported to be related, recognized by their clothing and language. *Class:* Indo-European, Indo-Iranian, Indo-Aryan, Northwestern zone, Dardic, Kohistani. *Dialects:* Kalam, Ushu, Thal, Lamuti (Lamti), Rajkoti (Patrak), Dashwa. Dialect differences do not hinder communication, except that speakers of other dialects have difficulty with Rajkot. Lexical similarity 90% to 93% among the main dialects; Rajkoti has 75% with Kalam; Dashwa has 77% with Kalami, and 74% with Rajkoti. *Lg Use:* There appear to be few speakers of Dashwa. Kalami and Ushu speakers indicate some negative attitudes toward each other's speech. The most widely understood indigenous language in northern Swat and Dir Kohistan. Men have routine proficiency in Pashto; women are more limited. Rajkoti men have high proficiency in Pashto. Uneducated men and women have low proficiency in Urdu. *Other:* Dashwa is a clan name of people originally from around Rajkot; little information available. About 30% migrate in winter to Mingora, Mardan, Peshawar, or the Punjab in search of work. Speakers of Pashto, Gujari, Khowar, and other Kohistani languages live among them, but they are generally in the majority. Patrilineal descent groups are: Drekhel, Nilor (Niliyor), Jaflor (Jafalor). The Drekhel are divided into the Kalamkhel, Akarkhel, and Chinorkhel. The Mullakhel are Pashtoons from Lower Swat who now speak Pashto as first language, but speak, understand, and identify with Kalami. Muslim.

Kalasha (Kalashamon, Kalash) [kls] 5,029 (2000 WCD). Southern Chitral District. The largest village is Balanguru in Rumbur Valley. Southern Kalasha is in Urtsun Valley; Northern Kalasha in Rumbur, Bumboret, and Birir valleys. *Class:* Indo-European, Indo-Iranian, Indo-Aryan, Northwestern zone, Dardic, Chitral. *Dialects:* Southern Kalasha (Urtsun), Northern Kalasha (Rumbur, Bumboret, Birir). There may be an eastern dialect on the east side of the Chitral River south of Drosh. Related to Khowar. Little contact between Northern and Southern dialects. The southern dialect has 75% lexical similarity with the northern dialects. *Lg Use:* Used in the home and for in-group communication in the north. In the south Khowar or Kati are sometimes used in the home and within the group. Speakers have low proficiency in Khowar; in Birir some men do not speak Khowar. Women are learning Khowar, and some learning Urdu. *Other:* SOV. Pastoralists: goats, sheep, cattle; agriculturalists: wheat, barley, corn, apples, mulberries, walnuts, grapes. Traditional religion, Muslim.

Kalkoti [xka] 4,000 (1990). Dir Kohistan, NWFP, in Kalkot village. A little more than half the people in the village are speakers. *Class:* Indo-European, Indo-Iranian, Indo-Aryan, Northwestern zone, Dardic, Kohistani. *Dialects:* Lexical similarity 69% with Kalami. *Lg Use:* Kalami is used as second language. Kalami do not understand Kalkoti. All men and most women are reported to speak Pashto as second language. *Other:* Muslim.

Kamviri (Kamdeshi, Kamik, Lamertiviri, Shekhani) [xvi] 1,500 to 2,000 in Pakistan plus refugees (1992). Southern Chitral District, Langorbat or Lamerot, Badrugal, and the Urtsun Valley. *Dialects:* Kamviri, Shekhani. *Lg Use:* Some bilingualism in Pashto. *Other:* This Shekhani is different from the Kati dialect also called 'Shekhani'. Mountain valley. See main entry under Afghanistan.

Kashmiri (Kaschemiri, Kacmiri, Keshuri, Cashmiri, Cashmeeree) [kas] 105,000 in Pakistan (1993). Jammu and Kashmir, south of Shina. *Lg Use:* Poor language attitude. See main entry under India.

Kati (Kativiri, Bashgali, Nuristani) [bsh] 3,700 to 5,100 Eastern Kativiri in Pakistan (1992). Eastern Kativiri is in the Chitral District; in Gobar in the Lutkuh Valley,

Kunisht in the Rumbur Valley, Shekhanan Deh in the Bumboret Valley, and in the Urtsun Valley. *Dialects:* Eastern Kativiri (Shekhani), Western Kativiri, Mumviri. *Other:* Eastern Kativiri is often called 'Shekhani' in Pakistan, but is different from the Kamviri which is also called 'Shekhani' in Southern Chitral. Mountain valleys. See main entry under Afghanistan.

Khetrani [xhe] 4,000. Northeast Balochistan Province. *Class:* Indo-European, Indo-Iranian, Indo-Aryan, Northwestern zone, Lahnda. *Dialects:* Related to Siraiki. *Lg Dev:* Literacy rate in first language: below 1%. Literacy rate in second language: below 5%. *Other:* Influenced by Balochi. Muslim.

Khowar (Khawar, Chitrali, Citrali, Chitrari, Arniya, Patu, Qashqari, Kashkari) [khw] 222,800 in Pakistan (1992). Population total all countries: 242,000. Chitral; Shandur Pass to Fupis in Ghizr Valley, Yasin and Ishkhoman valleys in Gilgit Agency, Ushu in northern Swat Valley, and large communities in Peshawar and Rawalpindi. Also spoken in India. *Class:* Indo-European, Indo-Iranian, Indo-Aryan, Northwestern zone, Dardic, Chitral. *Dialects:* North Khowar, South Khowar, East Khowar, Swat Khowar. The northern dialect is considered to be more 'pure'. Related to Kalasha, but different. Lexical similarity 86% to 98% among dialects. *Lg Use:* Trade language. The most important language of Chitral. Urdu schools; some girls go through fifth grade or higher. Different second languages used in different areas: Pashto in the south, Shina and Burushaski in the Gilgit Agency, Kalami and some Pashto in Swat, Urdu and English among the educated. *Lg Dev:* Literacy rate in second language: 15% to 20% men, 1% women. Radio programs. *Other:* 'Kho' means 'people', 'war' means 'language'. Monthly journal in Khowar. SOV. Mountain valleys. Muslim (Sunni and Ismali).

Kohistani, Indus (Kohistani, Kohiste, Khili, Maiyon, Mair, Maiyã, Shuthun) [mvy] 220,000 (1993). Indus Kohistan District on the western bank of the Indus River. *Class:* Indo-European, Indo-Iranian, Indo-Aryan, Northwestern zone, Dardic, Kohistani. *Dialects:* Indus (Mani, Seo, Pattan, Jijal), Duber-Kandia (Manzari, Khili). A separate language from nearby varieties (Bateri, Chilisso, Gowro, Shina, Torwali, Kalami). The names 'Mani' and 'Manzari' are not used by speakers for the dialects, but refer to legendary brothers whose descendants settled in the two dialect areas. Lexical similarity 90% among dialects, 70% with Chilisso, 61% with Gowro, 58% with Bateri, 49% with Shina, 28% with Kalami and Torwali.

Koli, Kachi (Kuchi, Kachi, Katchi, Koli, Kohli, Kolhi, Kori, Vagari, Vagaria, Kachi Gujarati) [gjk] 170,000 in Pakistan (1998). Population includes 80,000 to 100,000 Kachi Koli, 5,000 to 6,000 Rabari, 10,000 Kachi Bhil, 50,000 Vagri, 10,000 Katai Meghwar, 1,000 Zalavaria Koli. Population total all countries: 570,000. Lower Sindh in an area bordered by Sakrand and Nawabshah in the north, Matli in the south, and east beyond Mirpur Khas and Jamesabad. Concentrated in an area around the towns of Tando Allahyar and Tando Adam. There may be an equal number in India, concentrated in their ancestral homeland centered around Bhuj, in the Rann of Kach, Gujarat. Also spoken in India. *Class:* Indo-European, Indo-Iranian, Indo-Aryan, Central zone, Gujarati. *Dialects:* Kachi, Rabari (Rahabari), Kachi Bhil, Vagri (Kachi Meghwar), Katai Meghwar, Zalavaria Koli. Intermediate between Sindhi and Gujarati; it is becoming more like Sindhi. Kachi has 89% lexical similarity with Rabari, 96% with Kachi Bhil, 86% with Vagri, 92% with Katai Meghwar, 88% with Zalavaria Koli, lexical similarity 78% with Gujarati, 76% with Tharadari Koli. *Lg Use:* Complex situation: people with basically the same language are socially quite distinct. *Lg Dev:* Literacy rate in first language: below 1%. Literacy rate in second language: below 5%. Based on Sindhi, based in turn on Arabic. Some older people use Gujarati script, related to Devanagari. Bible portions: 1834–1995. *Other:* Sharecropper agriculturalists. Hindu, Christian.

Koli, Parkari (Parkari) [kvx] 250,000 (1995). Centered in Tharparkar District, especially the town of Nagar Parkar in the southeastern tip of Sindh bordering India. It covers most of the lower Thar Desert and west as far as the Indus River, bordered in the north and west by Hyderabad, and down to the south and west of Badin. An unknown (probably small) population in India. *Class:* Indo-European, Indo-Iranian, Indo-Aryan, Central zone, Gujarati. *Dialects:* Lexical similarity 77% to 83% with Marwari Bhil, 83% with Tharadari Koli. *Lg Dev:* Literacy rate in first language: below 1%. Literacy rate in second language: below 5%, mostly in Sindhi, a few in Urdu, very few in Gujarati. Based on Sindhi, based in turn on Arabic. NT: 1996. *Other:* Agriculturalists: sharecroppers in irrigated area, subsistence and stockbreeders in desert (east). Hindu, Christian.

Koli, Wadiyara (Wadaria, Wadhiara) [kxp] 175,000 in Pakistan (1998). Population includes 75,000 Wadiyara, 5,000 Mewasi and Nairya, 30,000 Tharadari, 45,000 Hasoria, 20,000 Rardro. Sind in an area bounded by Hyderabad, Tando Allahyar and Mirpur Khas in the north, and Matli and Jamesabad in the south. *Dialects:* Mewasi (Mayvasi Koli), Wadiyara Koli, Nairya Koli, Tharadari Koli, Tharadari Bhil, Hasoria Koli, Hasoria Bhil, Rardro Bhil. *Lg Use:* There is gradual beginning of breakdown of some strict caste rules concerning intermarriage and interdining: possibly 'lower' groups wishing to move 'up', and barriers in 'close' castes breaking down. *Lg Dev:* Literacy rate in first language: below 1%. Literacy rate in second language: below 5%. See main entry under India.

Lasi (Lassi) [lss] 15,000 (1998). Southeast Balochistan Province, Las Bela District, about 80 miles north northwest of Karachi. *Class:* Indo-European, Indo-Iranian, Indo-Aryan, Northwestern zone, Sindhi. *Lg Dev:* Literacy rate in first language: below 1%. Literacy rate in second language: below 5%. *Other:* Influenced by Balochi. Muslim.

Loarki [lrk] 20,000 (1998). Sindh Province, rural. 500 to 750 in India. *Class:* Indo-European, Indo-Iranian, Indo-Aryan, Central zone, Rajasthani, Marwari. *Dialects:* Probably the same as Gade Lohar in Rajasthan, India, a Rajasthani language. Lexical similarity 82% with Jogi, 80% with Marwari. *Lg Use:* All domains. All ages. All ages and sexes speak Sindhi, the educated or those working outside the community speak Urdu for most common topics. *Lg Dev:* Literacy rate in second language: 25% boys, some older men, no girls or women in Sindhi, some Urdu. *Other:* Alternate names for the people are: Loar, Lohar, Gadlia, Gadolia Rajput, Gadolia Rajput Loar, Karia, Sisudia Rajput, Sisudia Loar. Plains. Desert. Sea level to 100 meters. Craftsmen. Hindu.

Marwari [rwr] Eastern upper Sindh Province. See main entry under India.

Marwari (Merwari, Rajasthani, Marwari Meghwar, Jaiselmer, Marawar, Marwari Bhil) [mve] 220,000. Population includes 100,000 Northern Marwari, 120,000 or more Southern Marwari (1998). The latter includes 100,000 Marwari Bhil, 10,000 Marwari Meghwar, 12,000 to 13,000 Marwari Bhat. Northern Marwari: South Punjab and northern Sindh, north of Dadu and Nawabshah; Southern Marwari: Sindh and southern Punjab provinces, between Tando Mohammed Khan and Tando Ghulam Ali to the south, Dadu and Nawabshab to the north. *Class:* Indo-European, Indo-Iranian, Indo-Aryan, Central zone, Rajasthani, Marwari. *Dialects:* Northern Marwari, Southern Marwari, Marwari Bhil, Marwari Meghwar, Marwari Bhat. Northern and Southern Marwari are inherently intelligible to speakers. Lexical similarity 79%

to 83% with Dhatki, 87% between Southern and Northern Marwari, 78% with Marwari Meghwar and Marwari Bhat. *Lg Use:* One sweeper community of 10,000 to 100,000 identifies itself as Marwari, but is undergoing rapid shift to Urdu. Marwari is not usually written. Speakers are moderately bilingual in Sindhi. Educated speakers are trilingual in Urdu. The literary language of Rajasthan is Hindi. *Lg Dev:* Literacy rate in first language: below 1%. Literacy rate in second language: below 5% in Sindhi or Urdu. Sindhi and Urdu scripts. Newspapers. Bible portions: 1969–1991. *Other:* The name 'Rajasthani' is a linguistic cover term for a group of languages. Speakers tend to be urban and educated. Northern Bhil tribes: Marwari-Thori, Gulguli, Shikari, Jogi, Sochi. Hindu, Muslim, Christian.

Memoni [mby] Karachi. *Class:* Indo-European, Indo-Iranian, Indo-Aryan, Unclassified. *Dialects:* Memoni language appears to have similarities to Sindhi and Gujarati. *Lg Use:* The younger generation might not learn it as first language. They learn Urdu, Sindhi, or Gujarati as second language. *Lg Dev:* Most are highly educated. *Other:* All speakers in Pakistan came from India at the time of the partition. It is reported that 500 to 600 years ago they moved from a Sindhi-speaking area to a Gujarati-speaking area. Muslim.

Od (Oad, Odki) [odk] 50,000 (1998). Widely scattered in the Sindh and a few in southern Punjab. May also be in Rajasthan, India. *Class:* Indo-European, Indo-Iranian, Indo-Aryan, Unclassified. *Dialects:* Resembles Marathi with Gujarati features and borrowings from Marwari and Panjabi. Lexical similarity 86% to 88% among dialects in Dadu, Shikarpur, and Pithoro, 70% to 78% with Marwari, Dhatki, and Bagri. *Lg Use:* 80% also use Sindhi; 10% are trilingual in Urdu, Sindhi, and Odki. *Lg Dev:* Sindhi script. *Other:* Brickmakers, builders.

Ormuri (Urmuri, Ormur, Ormui, Bargista, Baraks, Baraki) [oru] 1,000 in Pakistan (2000 J. Owens). Population total all countries: 1,050. Kaniguram, a pocket in Mahsud Pashto area northwest of Dera Ismail Khan, Wazirstan. Also spoken in Afghanistan. *Class:* Indo-European, Indo-Iranian, Iranian, Western, Northwestern, Ormuri-Parachi. *Dialects:* Kanigurami, Logar. Lexical similarity 27% with Waneci, 25% to 33% with Pashto dialects. *Lg Use:* The Kanigurami retain the language.

Pahari-Potwari (Potwari, Pothohari, Potohari, Chibhali, Dhundi-Kairali) [phr] 49,440 (2000 WCD). Murree Hills north of Rawalpindi, and east to Azad Kashmir. To the north in the lower half of the Neelum Valley. Poonchi is east of Rawalakot. Potwari is in the plains around Rawalpindi. Punchhi and Chibhali are reported to be in Jammu and Kashmir. *Class:* Indo-European, Indo-Iranian, Indo-Aryan, Northern zone, Western Pahari. *Dialects:* Pahari (Dhundi-Kairali), Pothwari (Potwari), Chibhali, Punchhi (Poonchi), Mirpuri. Pahari means 'hill language' referring to a string of divergent dialects, some of which may be separate languages. A dialect chain with Panjabi and Hindko. Closeness to western Pahari is unknown. Lexical similarity 76% to 83% among varieties called 'Pahari', 'Potwari', and some called 'Hindko' in Mansehra, Muzzaffarabad, and Jammun. *Other:* Muslim.

Pakistan Sign Language (Isharon Ki Zubann) [pks] *Class:* Deaf sign language. *Dialects:* Related to Nepalese Sign Language; may be the same language as Indian Sign Language. *Lg Use:* Used in urban centers with some regional variation in vocabulary. The National Institute of Special Education encourages a total communication approach, including the teaching of PSL. *Lg Dev:* Dictionary. Grammar.

Panjabi, Western (Western Punjabi, Lahnda, Lahanda, Lahndi) [pnb] 60,647,207 in Pakistan (2000 WCD). Population total all countries: 60,812,093. Mainly in the

Punjab area of Pakistan. Also spoken in Afghanistan, Canada, India, United Arab Emirates, United Kingdom, USA. *Class:* Indo-European, Indo-Iranian, Indo-Aryan, Northwestern zone, Lahnda. *Dialects:* There is a continuum of varieties between Eastern and Western Panjabi, and with Western Hindi and Urdu. 'Lahnda' is a name given earlier for Western Panjabi; an attempt to cover the dialect continuum between Hindko, Pahari-Potwari, and Western Panjabi in the north and Sindhi in the south. Grierson said Majhi is the purest form of Panjabi. Several dozen dialects. The Balmiki (Valmiki) sweeper caste in Attock District speak a dialect of Panjabi. *Lg Dev:* Perso-Arabic script. Radio programs. Films. TV. NT: 1819–2000. *Other:* Muslim, Christian.

Pashto, Central (Mahsudi) [pst] 7,922,657. Wazirstan, Bannu, Karak, southern ethnic group territories and adjacent areas. *Class:* Indo-European, Indo-Iranian, Iranian, Eastern, Southeastern, Pashto. *Dialects:* Waciri (Waziri), Bannuchi (Bannochi, Bannu). Lexical comparison and interviews indicate this is distinct from Northern and Southern Pashto. *Lg Dev:* Dictionary. Grammar. *Other:* Muslim (Sunni).

Pashto, Northern (Pakhto, Pashtu, Pushto, Yusufzai Pashto) [pbu] 9,585,000 in Pakistan (1993). Population includes all Pashto. Population total all countries: 9,700,000. Ethnic population: 49,529,000 possibly total Pashto in all countries. Along Afghanistan border, most of NWFP, Yusufzai, and Peshawar. Also spoken in Afghanistan, India, United Arab Emirates, United Kingdom. *Class:* Indo-European, Indo-Iranian, Iranian, Eastern, Southeastern, Pashto. *Dialects:* Ningraharian Pashto, Northeastern Pashto. A good deal of similarity with Northwestern Pashto in Afghanistan. Subdialects of Northeastern Pashto are Kohat (Khatak), Yusufzai (Peshawar), Afridi, Shinwari, Mohmand, Shilmani. Lexical similarity 80% between Northeastern and Southwestern Pashto. *Lg Use:* Rich literary tradition. The Powinda are a nomadic Pashto-speaking group. *Lg Dev:* Literacy rate in second language: Low. Taught in primary schools. Perso-Arabic script; Urdu script in United Arab Emirates. Newspapers. Radio programs. Films. TV. Dictionary. Bible: 1895. *Other:* Muslim (Sunni and Shi'a).

Pashto, Southern (Pashtu, Pushto, Pushtu, Quetta-Kandahar Pashto) [pbt] 1,356,059 in Pakistan (2000 WCD). Population total all countries: 2,674,367. Balochistan, Quetta area. Also spoken in Afghanistan, Iran, Tajikistan, United Arab Emirates, United Kingdom. *Class:* Indo-European, Indo-Iranian, Iranian, Eastern, Southeastern, Pashto. *Dialects:* Southeastern Pashto, Quetta Pashto. There is generally an 80% lexical similarity between the northern and southern varieties of Pashto. *Lg Use:* Some Pashto speakers educated in Urdu medium schools mix Urdu into their Pashto speech. *Lg Dev:* Perso-Arabic script. Grammar. *Other:* Muslim.

Phalura (Palula, Palola, Phalulo, Dangarik, Biyori) [phl] 8,600 (1990). 7 villages on the east side of the lower Chitral Valley, possibly 1 village in Dir Kohistan; Purigal, Ghos, the Biori Valley, Kalkatak, and Ashret. *Class:* Indo-European, Indo-Iranian, Indo-Aryan, Northwestern zone, Dardic, Shina. *Dialects:* Ashreti, Northern Phalura. Ashreti has 92% lexical similarity with Northern Phalura. Lexical similarity 56% to 58% with Savi in Afghanistan, 38% to 42% with Shina. *Lg Use:* Speakers also use Khowar. *Other:* Speakers are called 'Phalulo'. Muslim (Sunni).

Sansi (Bhilki) [ssi] 16,200 in Pakistan (2000). Northern Sindh Province, main town, and some in Karachi. The Sochi live throughout Sindh. *Dialect:* Sochi. *Lg Use:* Second language is Sindhi, followed by Urdu, Panjabi, and Saraiki. *Lg Dev:* Literacy rate in first language: below 1%. Literacy rate in second language: below 5%. *Other:* Bhils by caste. Immigrated from India in 1947.

Sharecroppers; cobblers (Sochi). Hindu, Muslim. See main entry under India.

Savi (Sawi, Sauji, Sau) [sdg] Some might still live in refugee camps near Timargarha in Dir, Pakistan and near Drosh in Chitral, Pakistan. Probably most have returned to Afghanistan. *Lg Use:* Speakers also use Pashto. *Lg Dev:* Literacy rate in first language: below 1%. Literacy rate in second language: 5% to 15%. *Other:* Muslim. See main entry under Afghanistan.

Seraiki (Saraiki, Riasiti, Bahawalpuri, Multani, Southern Panjabi, Siraiki) [skr] 13,843,106 in Pakistan (2000 WCD). Population total all countries: 13,863,106. Southern Punjab and northern Sind, Indus River Valley, Jampur area. Derawali is in Dera Ismail Khan, Tank, Bannu, and Dera Ghazi Khan. Jangli is in Sahiwal area. Also spoken in India, United Kingdom. *Class:* Indo-European, Indo-Iranian, Indo-Aryan, Northwestern zone, Lahnda. *Dialects:* Derawali, Multani (Khatki), Bahawalpuri (Riasati, Reasati), Jangli, Jatki. Dialects blend into each other, into Panjabi to the east, and Sindhi to the south. Until recently it was considered to be a dialect of Panjabi. 80% intelligibility of Dogri. May be intelligible with Bahawalpuri. Lexical similarity 85% with Sindhi; 68% with Dhatki, Odki, and Sansi. *Lg Dev:* Literacy rate in first language: below 1%. Literacy rate in second language: 5% to 15%. Radio programs. TV. Dictionary. Grammar. NT: 1819. *Other:* Muslim, Hindu.

Shina (Sina, Shinaki, Brokpa) [scl] 300,000 in Pakistan (1981 census). Population total all countries: 321,000. Northern Areas including Gilgit District, scattered villages in Yasin and Ishkoman valleys, Punial, Gilgit, Haramosh, lower Hunza Valley; Diamer District, Chilas area, Darel and Tangir valleys, Astor Valley; scattered areas of Baltistan District, Satpara, Kharmang, Kachura, and other small valleys; NWFP, east part of Kohistan District, Sazin, Harban. Also spoken in India. *Class:* Indo-European, Indo-Iranian, Indo-Aryan, Northwestern zone, Dardic, Shina. *Dialects:* Gilgiti (Gilgit, Punial, Hunza-Nagar, Bagrote, Haramosh, Rondu, Bunji), Astori (Astor, Gurezi, Dras, Satpara, Kharmangi), Chilasi Kohistani (Chilas, Darel, Tangir, Sazin, Harban). Gilgit functions as the language standard. Shina is the primary language in Gilgit and Diamer districts. Lexical similarity 79% to 99% within the Gilgiti (Northern) dialect cluster, 81% to 96% among the Astori (Eastern) cluster, 84% to 98% among the Chilas (Diamer) cluster. *Lg Dev:* Bible portions: 1929. *Other:* 'Brokpa' is the name used for Shina speakers in Baltistan and Ladakh. 'Brokskat' refers to their language. 'Brokskat' is used semiofficially in India to refer to a highly divergent variety of Shina spoken by Buddhists. Muslim (Shi'a and Sunni).

Shina, Kohistani (Palasi-Kohistani, Kohistani, Kohistyo) [plk] 200,000 (1981 census). East bank of the Indus in Kohistan District, NWFP, in the Jalkot, Palas, and Kolai valleys and surrounding areas. *Class:* Indo-European, Indo-Iranian, Indo-Aryan, Northwestern zone, Dardic, Shina. *Dialects:* Palasi, Jalkoti, Kolai. A somewhat divergent variety of Shina linguistically and socially. Closer to Shina of Chilas, but more distant from Gilgit. *Other:* Muslim (Sunni).

Sindhi [snd] 18,500,000 in Pakistan (2001 Johnstone and Mandryk). Population includes 1,200,000 Hindu Sindhi (1986). Population total all countries: 21,362,000. Sindh. Also possibly United Arab Emirates. Also spoken in India, Oman, Philippines, Singapore, United Kingdom, USA. *Class:* Indo-European, Indo-Iranian, Indo-Aryan, Northwestern zone, Sindhi. *Dialects:* Kachchi, Lari, Lasi, Thareli, Vicholo (Vicholi, Viccholi, Central Sindhi), Macharia, Dukslinu (Hindu Sindhi), Sindhi Musalmani (Muslim Sindhi). Some southern Bhil groups speak dialects of Sindhi. 100,000 speakers in rural Sindh came originally from the Kathiawar Peninsula in India. They are solidly Muslim, have widespread bilingualism in Sindh, and are almost completely assimilated with the Sindhi people. Lexical similarity 77% with Katiavari Kachi. *Lg Use:* Official regional language. Some Hindu speakers are first-language speakers, most are second-language speakers. Shikari (hunter) Bhils are a nomadic group of 2,000 to 3,000 who live in southern Sindh Province, centered around Badin, and have adopted the Sindhi language. Some are Hindu, others are Muslim. They are not literate. *Lg Dev:* Arabic script; Arabic and Gurumukhi scripts in India. Dictionary. Grammar. Bible: 1954. *Other:* Muslim, Hindu, Christian.

Sindhi Bhil [sbn] 56,502 (2000 WCD). Sindh Province, Mohrano, Badin-Matli-Thatta, Ghorabari (on west). Sindhi Meghwar are scattered in an area from Badin-Matli to Tando Allahyar. *Class:* Indo-European, Indo-Iranian, Indo-Aryan, Northwestern zone, Sindhi. *Dialects:* Sindhi Bhil, Mohrano, Badin, Sindhi Meghwar. Badin is close to Sindhi. Lexical similarity 82% between Mohrani and Sindhi; 89% between Sindhi Bhil and Sindhi Meghwar. *Lg Use:* Speakers consider the Mohrano dialect to be different from Sindhi and Dhatki. There is a positive attitude toward its use in traditional ceremonies. The Sindhi Bhil look with favor on the idea of literature in their language. They can converse in Sindhi, those in Mohrano area also in Dhatki. Women use Sindhi Bhil when talking to Sindhi and Dhatki speakers. *Other:* Sindhi or Dhatki orthographies acceptable. Hindu, Muslim.

Torwali (Turvali) [trw] 60,000 (1987). Swat Kohistan, on both sides of Swat River from just beyond Madyan north to Asrit (between Mankjal and Peshmal), and in Chail Valley east of Madyan, Bahrain and Chail are centers. *Class:* Indo-European, Indo-Iranian, Indo-Aryan, Northwestern zone, Dardic, Kohistani. *Dialects:* Bahrain, Chail. Lexical similarity 44% with Kalkoti and Kalami, 89% between Behrain and Chail. *Lg Use:* Men have routine proficiency in Pashto, more limited in Urdu. Women are limited in use of Pashto, and know almost no Urdu. *Other:* Muslim (Sunni).

Urdu [urd] 10,719,000 in Pakistan (1993). Population total all countries: 60,503,579. Also spoken in Afghanistan, Bahrain, Bangladesh, Botswana, Fiji, Germany, Guyana, India, Malawi, Mauritius, Nepal, Norway, Oman, Qatar, Saudi Arabia, South Africa, Thailand, United Arab Emirates, United Kingdom, Zambia. *Class:* Indo-European, Indo-Iranian, Indo-Aryan, Central zone, Western Hindi, Hindustani. *Dialects:* Intelligible with Hindi, but has formal vocabulary borrowed from Arabic and Persian. Dakhini is freer of Persian and Arabic loans than Urdu. Rekhta is a form of Urdu used in poetry. *Lg Use:* Official language. Including second-language speakers: 104,000,000 (1999 WA). The second or third language of most Pakistanis for whom it is not the first language. *Lg Dev:* Arabic script. Grammar. Bible: 1843–1998. *Other:* Muslim.

Ushojo (Ushuji) [ush] 2,000 (1992). Upper reaches of Bishigram (Chail) Valley, east of Madyan, Swat Kohistan. 12 villages. *Class:* Indo-European, Indo-Iranian, Indo-Aryan, Northwestern zone, Dardic, Shina. *Dialects:* Lexical similarity 50% with Kolai Shina, 48% with Palas Shina, 42% with Gilgiti Shina, 35% with Chail Torwali, 31% with Biori Phalura, 27% with Bateri, 23% with Kalami, 22% with Kalkoti. *Lg Use:* Children are learning Ushojo in the home. Pashto seems to be influencing some adult speech. Pashto appears to be the main second language used. Education in Urdu is limited. Torwali is also used. *Other:* Not known by linguists until 1989. Reportedly came from Kolai, Indus Kohistan several hundred years ago. SOV. Mountain valleys. Muslim (Sunni).

Vaghri (Vaghri Koli, Salavta, Bavri) [vgr] 10,000 in Pakistan (1998). Sindh, in Sukkur, Karachi (Bhes Colony), Nawabshah, Sakrand, Hala, Sanghar, Tando Adam, Tando Mohammed Khan, Badin, Matli, Tando Ghulam Ali, Digri, Noakot, Jang Sai, Mirpur Khas, and Tando Allahyar. Possibly 90,000 in India. *Class:* Indo-European, Indo-Iranian, Indo-Aryan, Central zone, Gujarati. *Dialects:* Related to the language spoken by the Kukar people living near Chanesar Halt, Mehmoodabad in Karachi. Lexical similarity 78% with Wadiyari Koli. *Lg Use:* They speak some Sindhi, Urdu, and Gujarati. *Lg Dev:* Literacy rate in first language: below 1%. Literacy rate in second language: below 5%. *Other:* People are urbanized. Masons; fruit vendors. Hindu.

Wakhi (Wakhani, Wakhigi, Vakhan, Khik) [wbl] 9,100 in Pakistan. Population includes 4,500 to 6,000 Gojal, 2,000 Ishkoman, 200 Yasin, 900 Yarkhun (1992), plus refugees. Population total all countries: 31,666. Northeasternmost part of Chitral, called Baroghil area; in glacier neighborhood. Gojal is in the upper Hunza valley from Gulmit to the Chinese and Afghanistan borders, and the Shimshal and Chupursan valleys; also in upper Yarkhun valley of Chitral, and upper Ishkoman valley. Also spoken in Afghanistan, China, Tajikistan. *Class:* Indo-European, Indo-Iranian, Iranian, Eastern, Southeastern, Pamir. *Dialects:* Gojal, Ishkoman, Yasin, Yarkhun. Dialect intelligibility is reported to not be a problem even of those in other countries. Lexical similarity 84% between Ishkoman and Gojal, 89% between Yasin and Gojal, 91% between Ishkoman and Yasin. *Lg Use:* Positive language attitude. Men and young people have routine proficiency in Urdu. Fewer than half the women, and few older people in remote areas speak Urdu. Older people and those who live in mixed villages in Gojal can use Burushaski. *Other:* The people are called 'Guhjali' in upper Hunza, but call themselves 'Khik'. SOV. Valleys. Pastoralists: sheep, goats, cattle, yak, camels; agriculturalists: barley. Ismaili Muslim.

Waneci (Wanechi, Wanetsi, Vanechi, Tarino, Chalgari) [wne] 95,000 (1998). Northeastern Balochistan Province, Harnai area. *Class:* Indo-European, Indo-Iranian, Iranian, Eastern, Southeastern, Pashto. *Dialects:* Lexical similarity 71% to 75% with Southern Pashto, 63% to 72% with other Pashto varieties, 27% with Ormuri. *Lg Dev:* Literacy rate in first language: below 1%. Literacy rate in second language: below 5%. *Other:* Muslim.

Yidgha (Yudgha, Yudga, Yidga, Lutkuhwar) [ydg] 6,145 (2000 WCD). Upper Lutkuh Valley of Chitral, west of Garam Chishma. *Class:* Indo-European, Indo-Iranian, Iranian, Eastern, Southeastern, Pamir. *Dialects:* No significant dialect variation within Yidgha. Lexical similarity 56% to 80% with Munji in Afghanistan. *Lg Use:* Yidgha is used in many homes and for much in-group communication, and speakers have positive attitudes toward it. Khowar is the main second language used, although with much Yidgha language influence, and proficiency among women is low. *Other:* Mountain valleys. 2,200 meters. Ismaili Muslim.

Palestinian West Bank and Gaza

Palestinian West Bank and Gaza. 2,311,204. National or official language: Standard Arabic. Recognized by the United Nations during the interim period, based on the Israeli-Palestinian Declaration of Principles of 1993. Also includes Armenian, Hebrew (200,000). Information mainly from W. Fischer and O. Jastrow 1980. The number of languages listed for Palestinian West Bank and Gaza is 6. Of those, 4 are living languages and 2 are extinct.

Arabic, Levantine Bedawi Spoken (Bedawi) [avl] 10,000 in Palestinian West Bank and Gaza (1996). Judean desert and along the Jordan River. *Dialects:* South Levantine Bedawi Arabic, North Levantine Bedawi Arabic, Eastern Egyptian Bedawi Arabic. *Other:* Muslim (Sunni). See main entry under Egypt (Arabic, Eastern Egyptian Spoken).

Arabic, South Levantine Spoken (Bedawi) [ajp] 1,600,000 in Palestinian West Bank and Gaza (1996). *Dialects:* Madani, Fellahi. *Lg Use:* Speakers also use Hebrew. *Other:* Distinct from North Levantine (Lebanese-Syrian) Arabic. Muslim, Christian. See main entry under Jordan.

Arabic, Standard [arb] Middle East, North Africa. *Lg Use:* National language. Used for education, official purpose, formal speeches. See main entry under Saudi Arabia.

Domari (Nawari, Dom, Near-Eastern Gypsy) [rmt] 2,000 in Palestinian West Bank and Gaza (1997). Population includes Israel. Gaza and Bir Zeit near Ramallah. *Dialect:* Nawari. *Lg Use:* The first language of children in some places. Speakers also use South Levantine Spoken Arabic. *Other:* They call themselves 'Dom'. A large number of loanwords from Arabic, Kurdish, and some other Iranian languages. Muslim. See main entry under Iran.

Samaritan (Samaritan Hebrew) [smp] Extinct. Ethnic population: 620 (1999 H. Mutzafi). West bank near Nablus and in Tel Aviv, Israel. Also spoken in Israel. *Class:* Afro-Asiatic, Semitic, Central, South, Canaanite. *Lg Use:* They use Samaritan Hebrew mainly and Samaritan Aramaic secondarily as liturgical languages. About 30% live near Nablus and speak Palestinian Arabic as first language. Others live near Tel Aviv and speak Hebrew as first language. Liturgy. *Lg Dev:* Samaritan-Hebrew script. Bible: 1853. *Other:* They call themselves 'Shamerim'. Samaritan religion, related to Judaism.

Samaritan Aramaic [sam] Extinct. Ethnic population: 620 (1999 H. Mutzafi). West Bank near Nablus and in Tel Aviv, Israel. Also spoken in Israel. *Class:* Afro-Asiatic, Semitic, Central, Aramaic, Western. *Lg Use:* The language ceased to be spoken as first language in the 10th to 12th centuries A.D. They use Samaritan Hebrew mainly and Samaritan Aramaic secondarily as liturgical languages. About 30% live near Nablus and speak Palestinian Arabic as first language. Others live near Tel Aviv and speak Hebrew as first language. Liturgy. *Lg Dev:* Syriac script. *Other:* They call themselves 'Shamerim'. Samaritan religion, related to Judaism.

Philippines

Republic of the Philippines. 86,241,697. National or official languages: Filipino, English. Literacy rate: 88% to 89%. Also includes Basque, French (698), Hindi (2,415), Indonesian (2,580), Japanese (2,899), Korean, Sindhi (20,000), Standard German (961), Vietnamese, Arabic. Information mainly from L. A. Reid 1971; SIL 1954–2003. Blind population: 1,144,500. Deaf population: 100,000 to 4,232,519 (1998). Deaf institutions: 17. The number of languages listed for Philippines is 175. Of those, 171 are living languages and 4 are extinct. See maps beginning on page 818.

Agta, Alabat Island (Alabat Island Dumagat) [dul] 30 (2000 Wurm). East of Quezon Province, Luzon. *Class:* Austronesian, Malayo-Polynesian, Northern Philippine, Northern Luzon, Northern Cordilleran, Dumagat, Southern. *Lg Use:* 20% to 60% of the ethnic group speaks Agta. Used in the home. A few children speak Agta. Neutral language attitude. Speakers also use Tagalog. *Other:* Nearly extinct.

Agta, Camarines Norte (Manide, Agiyan) [abd] 150 (2000 Wurm). Luzon, Santa Elena and Labo, Camarines Norte. *Class:* Austronesian, Malayo-Polynesian, Northern

Philippine, Northern Luzon, Northern Cordilleran, Dumagat, Southern. *Dialects:* Lexical similarity 67% with Alabat Agta, 35% with Mt. Iriga Agta. *Lg Use:* 40% to 60% of the ethnic group speaks Agta. Used in the home. A few children speak Agta. People mildly supportive toward Agta.

Agta, Casiguran Dumagat (Casiguran Dumagat) [dgc] 606 (2000 T. Headland). East coast of Luzon, Aurora Province. *Class:* Austronesian, Malayo-Polynesian, Northern Philippine, Northern Luzon, Northern Cordilleran, Dumagat, Northern. *Dialects:* Intelligibility of Paranan 83%. *Lg Use:* All ages. Children are learning Tagalog before becoming teenagers. *Lg Dev:* Literacy rate in first language: 2.4%. Literacy rate in second language: 2.4%. NT: 1979. *Other:* Negrito. There is pressure on them from Filipino homesteaders moving into the area. Traditional lands now being used by homesteaders for agriculture. Hunter-gatherers.

Agta, Central Cagayan [agt] 779 (2000 WCD). Northeast Luzon. *Class:* Austronesian, Malayo-Polynesian, Northern Philippine, Northern Luzon, Northern Cordilleran, Dumagat, Northern. *Lg Use:* 95% of the ethnic group speaks Agta. All domains. All or nearly all the children speak Agta. Positive language attitude. They use Ilocano with all non-Agta who do not know Agta. Tagalog is the instructional language in school. *Lg Dev:* Literacy rate in first language: 6%. Literacy rate in second language: 6%. NT: 1992. *Other:* Negrito. Christian.

Agta, Dicamay (Dicamay Dumagat) [duy] Extinct. Luzon, Isabela Province, near Jones. *Class:* Austronesian, Malayo-Polynesian, Northern Philippine, Northern Luzon, Northern Cordilleran, Dumagat, Northern.

Agta, Dupaninan (Eastern Cagayan Agta) [duo] 1,200 (1986 SIL). Northeast Luzon, from below Divilacan Bay in the south to Palaui Island in the north. *Class:* Austronesian, Malayo-Polynesian, Northern Philippine, Northern Luzon, Northern Cordilleran, Dumagat, Northern. *Dialects:* Yaga, Tanglagan, Santa Ana-Gonzaga, Barongagunay, Palaui Island, Camonayan, Valley Cove, Bolos Point, Peñablanca, Roso (Southeast Cagayan), Santa Margarita. Yaga and Central Cagayan Agta are 63% intelligible. Lexical similarity 51% between Central Cagayan Agta and Tanglagan, 66% between Yaga and Central Cagayan Agta. *Lg Use:* A small sample of speakers of Yaga had 70% comprehension of Ilocano. *Lg Dev:* Literacy rate in first language: below 1%. Literacy rate in second language: below 1%. NT: 2001. *Other:* Hunter-gatherers.

Agta, Isarog [agk] 5 to 6 (2000 Wurm). Ethnic population: 1,000 (1984 SIL). Mt. Isarog east of Naga City, Bicol Province, Luzon. *Class:* Austronesian, Malayo-Polynesian, Meso Philippine, Central Philippine, Bikol, Coastal, Naga. *Lg Use:* Under 10% of the ethnic group speaks Agta. Used in the home. Negative language attitude. Speakers also use Central Bicolano. *Other:* Nearly extinct.

Agta, Mt. Iraya (Inagta of Mt. Iraya, Rugnot of Lake Buhi East, Lake Buhi East, Itbeg Rugnot) [atl] 150 (2000 Wurm). East of Lake Buhi, Bicol Province, Luzon. *Class:* Austronesian, Malayo-Polynesian, Meso Philippine, Central Philippine, Bikol, Coastal, Naga. *Dialects:* 54% to 86% comprehension of Naga (Central) Bicolano, 94% comprehension of Mt. Iriga Agta, Iriga City dialect. Lexical similarity 85% to 90% with Bicolano; 70% with Mt. Iriga Agta, Iriga City dialect. Lexical similarity 93% among four dialects. *Lg Use:* 20% to 60% of the ethnic group speaks Agta. Used in the home. A few children speak Agta. Negative language attitude. A population sample had 45% comprehension of Tagalog narrative. *Other:* Heavy borrowing from Legaspi (Central) Bicolano.

Agta, Mt. Iriga (San Ramon Inagta, Lake Buhi West, Mt. Iriga Negrito) [agz] 1,500 (1979 SIL). East of Iriga City, west of Lake Buhi, Bicol Province, Luzon. *Class:* Austronesian, Malayo-Polynesian, Meso Philippine, Central Philippine, Bikol, Inland. *Dialects:* 86% intelligibility of Iriga City Bicolano, 82% of Mt. Iraya, 72% of Central Bicolano (Naga). It is doubtful whether Naga Bicolano is adequately understandable to Mt. Iriga Agta speakers. Lexical similarity 76% with Iriga City Bicolano, 66% with Mt. Iraya, 66% with Central Bicolano (Naga). *Lg Use:* Iriga City Bicolano has higher prestige. Iriga City inhabitants regard Naga as true Bicolano. Moderate comprehension of Tagalog.

Agta, Remontado (Hatang-Kayey, Sinauna) [agv] 2,527 (2000 WCD). Luzon; Santa Inez, Rizal Province; Paimohuan, General Nakar, Quezon Province. *Class:* Austronesian, Malayo-Polynesian, Northern Philippine, Bashiic-Central Luzon-Northern Mindoro, Central Luzon, Sinauna. *Dialects:* Lexical similarity 73% with Tagalog, 37% with Umiray Dumaget. *Lg Use:* Speakers also use Tagalog. *Other:* No schools.

Agta, Umiray Dumaget (Umirey Dumagat, Umiray Agta) [due] 3,000 (1994 SIL). Quezon Province, Luzon. *Class:* Austronesian, Malayo-Polynesian, Northern Philippine, Northern Luzon, Northern Cordilleran, Dumagat, Southern. *Dialects:* Palaui Island Agta, Anglat Agta. *Lg Use:* Some parents pass it on to children, Used mainly among adults. All domains, home, religion, commerce. Some are proud of their culture and language but many seem indifferent to them. Most speakers are also fluent in Tagalog or Ilocano. *Lg Dev:* Literacy rate in first language: 5% to 10%. Literacy rate in second language: 5% to 10%. Roman script. NT: 1977. *Other:* Mountain slope, coastal. Hunter-gatherers.

Agta, Villa Viciosa [dyg] Extinct. Luzon, Abra Province. *Class:* Austronesian, Malayo-Polynesian, Northern Philippine, Northern Luzon, Northern Cordilleran, Ibanagic, Ibanag. *Lg Use:* Members of the ethnic group now speak Ilocano.

Agutaynen (Agutaynon, Agutayno) [agn] 10,384 (1990 census). Agutaya Island, five smaller surrounding islands, and the municipalities of Roxas, San Vicente, and Brooke's Point, Palawan. A few also in Taytay, Linapacan, on Mindoro, and in Manila. *Class:* Austronesian, Malayo-Polynesian, Meso Philippine, Kalamian. *Dialects:* Lexical similarity 52% with Cuyonon; 71% with Calamian Tagbanwa. *Lg Use:* Most speakers have low proficiency in Cuyonon, Tagalog, or English. *Lg Dev:* Literacy rate in first language: 90%. Literacy rate in second language: 90%. Bible portions: 1989–1993. *Other:* Culturally lowland. Subsistence agriculturalists: rice; fishermen.

Aklanon (Aklan, Aklano, Panay, Aklanon-Bisayan) [akl] 394,545 (1990 census). Aklan Province, northern Panay. *Class:* Austronesian, Malayo-Polynesian, Meso Philippine, Bisayan, West, Aklan. *Dialects:* 66% intelligibility of Hiligaynon. Lexical similarity 68% with Hiligaynon. *Lg Use:* Speakers also use Hiligaynon. *Lg Dev:* Literacy rate in first language: 69.7%. Literacy rate in second language: 69.7%. Bible portions: 1990–1993.

Alangan [alj] 7,694 (2000 WCD). North central Mindoro. *Class:* Austronesian, Malayo-Polynesian, Northern Philippine, Bashiic-Central Luzon-Northern Mindoro, Northern Mindoro. *Lg Dev:* NT: 1989.

Alta, Northern (Edimala, Baler Negrito, Ditaylin Alta, Ditaylin Dumagat) [aqn] 200 (2000 Wurm). Eastern Luzon, Aurora Province, Bayanihan, San Luis; Diteki, the first settlement along the road after coming through the mountains from Cabanatuan. *Class:* Austronesian, Malayo-Polynesian, Northern Philippine, Northern Luzon, South-Central Cordilleran, Alta. *Dialects:* Not close to other languages (Lawrence Reid). Lexical similarity 34% with Southern Alta. *Lg Use:* 40% to 60% of the ethnic group speaks Alta. Used in the home. A few children speak Alta. Neutral language attitude.

Alta, Southern (Kabuluen, Kabuluwen, Kabuluwan, Kabulowan, Kaboloan, Baluga, Pugot, Ita) [agy] 1,000 (1982 SIL). Eastern Nueva Ecija, Sierra Madre and coast areas of Quezon Province, town of San Miguel, and a large community in a remote part of San Miguel, Bulacan Province. North of the Umiray Dumaget. *Class:* Austronesian, Malayo-Polynesian, Northern Philippine, Northern Luzon, South-Central Cordilleran, Alta. *Dialects:* Not close to other languages. Lexical similarity 34% with Northern Alta. *Lg Use:* Speakers also use Tagalog. *Lg Dev:* Bible portions: 1970. *Other:* Speakers at Angat Dam in Bulacan are mixed with Umiray Dumaget Agta and call themselves 'Kaboloan'. Agriculturalists: maize.

Arta [atz] 15 (2000 Wurm). Population includes 12 in Villa Santiago, 1 in Villa Gracia, 3 or 4 in Nagtipunan (1992 L. Reid). Quirino Province, town of Aglipay, Villa Santiago and Villa Gracia, and town of Nagtipunan. *Class:* Austronesian, Malayo-Polynesian, Northern Philippine, Northern Luzon, Arta. *Dialects:* Not linguistically close to any other language (Lawrence Reid). *Lg Use:* Under 10% of the ethnic group speaks Arta. Three families speak Arta in the home (1992 L. Reid). Negative or neutral language attitude. Other families are intermarried with Ilocano speakers or also use Casiguran Dumagat Agta. Negrito. *Other:* Nearly extinct.

Ata [atm] 2 to 5 (2000 Wurm). Mabinay, Negros Oriental. *Class:* Austronesian, Malayo-Polynesian, Meso Philippine, Central Philippine. *Lg Use:* Negative language attitude. Speakers have high proficiency in Cebuano. *Other:* Different from Ata Manobo or the Atta languages. Nearly extinct.

Ati (Inati) [atk] 1,500 (1980 SIL). Panay Island, small groups in all provinces. *Class:* Austronesian, Malayo-Polynesian, Meso Philippine, Central Philippine, Bisayan, Central, Peripheral. *Dialects:* Malay, Barotac Viejo Nagpana. *Lg Use:* Used in the home and with friends. Barotac Viejo Nagpana is the prestige dialect. Bilingual level estimates for Hiligaynon: 1–3 5%, 3+ 11%, 4 50%, 4+ 32%, 5 2%; Kinaray-a: 1–3 9%, 3+ 30%, 4 61%, 5 0%. Hiligaynon is used for school, contact with outsiders, outside culture topics, jobs, religion. The Malay people mainly speak Malaynon. *Other:* Negrito.

Atta, Faire (Southern Atta) [azt] 300 (2000 Wurm). Near Faire-Rizal, Cagayan Province, Luzon. *Class:* Austronesian, Malayo-Polynesian, Northern Philippine, Northern Luzon, Northern Cordilleran, Ibanagic, Ibanag. *Dialects:* Lexical similarity 81% with Pudtol Atta; 60% with Isnag; 66% with Central Cagayan Agta; 82% with Pamplona Atta; 90% with Rizal Atta; 72% with Ibanag. *Lg Use:* 40% to 60% of the ethnic group speaks Atta. Used in the home. A few children speak Atta. Neutral language attitude. Speakers also use Ibanag or Pamplona Atta. *Lg Dev:* Literacy work needed for Sinundungan Valley: 100 families. *Other:* Negrito.

Atta, Pamplona (Northern Cagayan Negrito) [att] 1,000 (1998 SIL). Ethnic population: 1,000. Northwestern Cagayan Province, Luzon. *Class:* Austronesian, Malayo-Polynesian, Northern Philippine, Northern Luzon, Northern Cordilleran, Ibanagic, Ibanag. *Dialects:* Comprehension of Ibanag North 97%, of Itawit 52%. Lexical similarity 91% with Ibanag North; 63% with Ilocano; 69% with Itawit. *Lg Use:* Speakers also use Ilocano. *Lg Dev:* Literacy rate in first language: 20% to 25%. Literacy rate in second language: 20% to 25%. NT: 1996.

Atta, Pudtol [atp] 711 (2000 WCD). Luzon, Kalinga-Apayao Province, Pudtol, on the Abulog River south of Pamplona. *Class:* Austronesian, Malayo-Polynesian,

Northern Philippine, Northern Luzon, Northern Cordilleran, Ibanagic, Ibanag. *Dialects:* Lexical similarity 86% with Pamplona Atta; 75% with Ibanag; 63% with Isnag; 81% with Faire Atta; 42% with Ilocano. *Lg Use:* Speakers also use Ibanag or Pamplona Atta. *Other:* Negrito.

Ayta, Abenlen (Abenlen, Ayta Abenlen Sambal, Aburlin Negrito) [abp] 6,850 (1985 SIL). Luzon, Tarlac Province, Maontoc, Labnay, Maamot, San Pedro, Dalayap, Pilyen, Tangan-Tangan. *Class:* Austronesian, Malayo-Polynesian, Northern Philippine, Bashiic-Central Luzon-Northern Mindoro, Central Luzon, Sambalic. *Dialects:* Abenlen Ayta speakers' comprehension of Botolan Sambal is 28%, of Tina Sambal is 48%. Lexical similarity 66% with Botolan Sambal, 49% with Tina Sambal, 38% to 44% with Ilocano, Pangasinan, Tagalog, Pampangan. *Lg Use:* Some in remote areas are nearly monolingual. *Lg Dev:* Literacy rate in first language: 3%. Literacy rate in second language: 3%. *Other:* Mountain slope.

Ayta, Ambala (Ambala Agta, Ambala Sambal) [abc] 1,657 (1986 SIL). A few barrios of San Marcelino, Zambales, several of Subic City, Zambales, a few of Olongapa, Zambales, a few of Castillejos, Zambales, a few of Dinalupinan, Bataan Province, Luzon. Affected by Mt. Pinatubo eruption. *Class:* Austronesian, Malayo-Polynesian, Northern Philippine, Bashiic-Central Luzon-Northern Mindoro, Central Luzon, Sambalic. *Dialects:* Ambala Ayta speakers' comprehension of Botolan Sambal is 60%, of Ayta Indi Sambal is 54%, of Ayta Anchi Sambal is 60%, of Bataan Sambal is 70%. Lexical similarity 70% with Botolan Sambal, 55% with Tagalog. *Lg Use:* Speakers also use Tagalog. *Lg Dev:* Literacy rate in first language: 25%. Literacy rate in second language: 25%. *Other:* They do not mix with other Ayta groups. Traditional religion, Christian.

Ayta, Bataan (Mariveles Ayta, Bataan Sambal, Bataan Ayta) [ayt] 500 (2000 Wurm). Mariveles, Bataan Province, Luzon. *Class:* Austronesian, Malayo-Polynesian, Northern Philippine, Bashiic-Central Luzon-Northern Mindoro, Central Luzon, Sambalic. *Dialects:* Lexical similarity 63% with Botolan Sambal and Tagalog. *Lg Use:* 40% to 60% of the ethnic group speaks Ayta. Few key domains. 30% to 50% of children speak Ayta. Mildly supportive language attitude. Speakers also use Tagalog. *Other:* Negrito.

Ayta, Mag-Anchi (Mag-Anchi Sambal) [sgb] 8,200 (1992 SIL). East side of mountain, Botolan Sambal area, close to Tarlac-Pampanga border, several barrios of Capas, Tarlac, several of Bamban, Tarlac, several of San Marcelino, Zambales, 2 of Castillejos, Zambales, 2 of Mabalacat, Pampanga, several of Sapang Bato, Angeles City, central Luzon. People affected by Mt. Pinatubo eruption. *Class:* Austronesian, Malayo-Polynesian, Northern Philippine, Bashiic-Central Luzon-Northern Mindoro, Central Luzon, Sambalic. *Dialects:* 77% intelligibility of Ayta Indi Sambal, 65% of Ayta Ambala Sambal, 46% of Pampangan. Lexical similarity 76% with Botolan Sambal, 50% with Tagalog, 46% with Pampangan. *Lg Dev:* Literacy rate in first language: 10%. Literacy rate in second language: 10%. Bible portions: 1995–2000. *Other:* People scattered because of Mt. Pinatubo eruption.

Ayta, Mag-Indi (Baloga, Mag-Indi Sambal, Indi Ayta) [blx] 5,000 (1998 SIL). A few barrios of Florida Blanca, several of Porac, Pampanga Province, several of San Marcelino, Zambales, Luzon. People affected by Mt. Pinatubo eruption. *Class:* Austronesian, Malayo-Polynesian, Northern Philippine, Bashiic-Central Luzon-Northern Mindoro, Central Luzon, Sambalic. *Dialects:* 46% comprehension of Botolan Sambal, 50% of Ayta Ambala Sambal, 59% of Pampangan, 32% of Ayta Anchi Sambal. Lexical similarity 66% to 73% with Botolan

Sambal, 44% with Tagalog, 73% to 81% with Ayta Anchi Sambal. *Lg Dev:* Literacy rate in first language: below 10%. Literacy rate in second language: below 10%. Bible portions: 2002. *Other:* Mountain slope.

Ayta, Sorsogon [ays] 15 to 20 (2000 Wurm). Prieto Diaz, Sorsogon Province. *Class:* Austronesian, Malayo-Polynesian, Meso Philippine, Central Philippine. *Lg Use:* Under 10% of the ethnic group speaks Ayta. Used in the home. No children speak Ayta. Negative language attitude. *Other:* Frequent intermarriage with other groups. Nearly extinct.

Ayta, Tayabas [ayy] Extinct. Tayabas, Quezon Province, Luzon. *Class:* Austronesian, Malayo-Polynesian, Meso Philippine, Central Philippine. *Lg Use:* Members of the ethnic group now speak Tagalog. *Other:* Negrito.

Balangao (Balangao Bontoc, Balangaw, Farangao) [blw] 21,271 (2000). Eastern Bontoc Province, Luzon. *Class:* Austronesian, Malayo-Polynesian, Northern Philippine, Northern Luzon, South-Central Cordilleran, Central Cordilleran, Nuclear Cordilleran, Balangao. *Lg Dev:* Literacy rate in first language: 42.2%. Literacy rate in second language: 42.2%. NT: 1982. *Other:* Agriculturalists: rice. Traditional religion, Christian.

Balangingi (Baangingi', Bangingi Sama, Northern Sama, Northern Sinama, Sama, Sama Bangingih, Balanguingui) [sse] 10,000 in the Philippines (2002 SIL). Population total all countries: 40,000. Sulu Archipelago northeast of Jolo, islands and coastal areas of Zamboanga coast peninsula and Basilan Island, western Mindanao. Some Balangingi may be on Luzon and Palawan. Northern Sama speakers are at White Beach on Luzon near Subic Bay on Luzon. Also spoken in Malaysia (Sabah). *Class:* Austronesian, Malayo-Polynesian, Sama-Bajaw, Sulu-Borneo, Inner Sulu Sama. *Dialects:* Lutangan (Lutango), Sibuco-Vitali (Sibuku), Sibuguey (Batuan), Balangingi, Daongdung, Kabinga'an. Most Lutangan speakers (2,000 to 3,000, Olutangga Island, western Mindanao) understand Balangingi, the prestige dialect. Intelligibility of Central Sama is 71%, of Lutangan is 83%, of Sibuco-Vitali is 85%. Lexical similarity 77% of Lutangan, 75% of Sibuco-Vitali. *Lg Use:* Vigorous. Used in the home, community. All ages. Positive language attitude. People have good comprehension of Tausug. Some also use Chavacano, English, or Tagalog. *Lg Dev:* Literacy rate in first language: 40% to 45%. Literacy rate in second language: 40% to 45%. Most urban men are literate. Grammar. Bible portions: 1979–1988. *Other:* Coastal. Sea level. Fishermen; traders; agriculturalists; professional. Muslim.

Bantoanon (Asiq) [bno] 200,000 (2002 SIL). 500 to 1,000 monolinguals. Western Visayas (Romblon Province). *Class:* Austronesian, Malayo-Polynesian, Meso Philippine, Central Philippine, Bisayan, Banton. *Dialects:* Banton, Calatravanhon, Odionganon, Sibalenhon (Sibale), Simaranhon. 63% intelligibility of Hiligaynon; 92% of Loocnon. Odionganon dialect is preferred for literature. Lexical similarity 83% with Romblomanon (Zorc 1977). *Lg Use:* Most domains, home, community. All ages. Tagalog is used for some politics, education, and with non-Bantuanon speakers. Some use English, Romblomanon, or Loocnon. *Lg Dev:* Literacy rate in first language: 80% to 90%. Literacy rate in second language: 80% to 90%. Bible portions: 1992–1996. *Other:* Sea level. Agriculturalists; forestry; fishermen. Christian.

Batak (Babuyan, Tinitianes, Palawan Batak) [bya] 200 (2000 Wurm). Ethnic population: 2,041 (1990 census). North central Palawan. *Class:* Austronesian, Malayo-Polynesian, Meso Philippine, Palawano. *Lg Use:* 40% to 60% of the ethnic group speaks Batak. Few key domains. 30% to 50% of the children speak Batak. Mildly supportive language attitude. Speakers also use Tagalog. *Lg Dev:* Bible portions: 1972. *Other:* Negrito. VOS.

Bicolano, Albay [bhk] 1,900,907 (2000). Western Albay Province and Buhi, Camarines Sur, Luzon. *Class:* Austronesian, Malayo-Polynesian, Meso Philippine, Central Philippine, Bikol, Inland, Buhi-Daraga. *Dialects:* Buhi (Buhi'non), Daraga, Libon, Oas, Ligao. *Lg Use:* Speakers have some proficiency in Central Bicolano.

Bicolano, Central (Bikol) [bcl] 2,500,000 (1990 census). 3,519,236 includes all Bikol languages. Southern Catanduanes, Northern Sorsogon, Albay, Camarines Norte and Sur, Luzon. Naga City and Legaspi City are centers. *Class:* Austronesian, Malayo-Polynesian, Meso Philippine, Central Philippine, Bikol, Coastal, Naga. *Dialects:* Naga, Legaspi. *Lg Use:* Trade language. *Lg Dev:* Bible: 1915.

Bicolano, Iriga (Rinconada Bicolano) [bto] 234,361 (2000). Iriga City, Baao, Nabua, Bato, Camarines Sur, Luzon. *Class:* Austronesian, Malayo-Polynesian, Meso Philippine, Central Philippine, Bikol, Inland, Iriga.

Bicolano, Northern Catanduanes (Pandan) [cts] 122,035 (2000). Luzon, Northern Catanduanes, east of Bicol. *Class:* Austronesian, Malayo-Polynesian, Meso Philippine, Central Philippine, Bikol, Pandan. *Dialects:* Comprehension of Naga 68%. *Lg Use:* A population sample had 66% comprehension of Tagalog narrative.

Bicolano, Southern Catanduanes (Virac) [bln] 85,000 (1981 SIL). Luzon, Southern Catanduanes, east of Bicol. *Class:* Austronesian, Malayo-Polynesian, Meso Philippine, Central Philippine, Bikol, Coastal, Virac. *Dialects:* Northern Catanduanes intelligibility 91%. Virac dialect is preferable for literature. *Lg Use:* Population samples had 85% comprehension of Central Bicolano and Tagalog narrative.

Binukid (Binukid Manobo, Binokid, Bukidnon) [bkd] 100,000 (1987 SIL). North central Mindanao, southern Bukidnon, northeastern Cotabato, Agusan del Sur. *Class:* Austronesian, Malayo-Polynesian, Southern Philippine, Manobo, North. *Dialects:* Literature should serve Kalabugao, Bukidnon, Minalowang, Esperanza, and Agusan del Sur. Close to Higaonon. *Lg Dev:* Literacy rate in first language: 63%. Literacy rate in second language: 63%. NT: 1986. *Other:* Lowland, mountain slope.

Blaan, Koronadal (Koronadal Bilaan, Bilanes, Biraan, Baraan, Tagalagad) [bpr] 100,000 (1981 SIL). South Cotabato Province, Mindanao. *Class:* Austronesian, Malayo-Polynesian, South Mindanao, Bilic, Blaan. *Lg Use:* Speakers have low proficiency in Cebuano. *Lg Dev:* Literacy rate in first language: 20%. Literacy rate in second language: 20%. NT: 1995. *Other:* Traditional religion, Christian.

Blaan, Sarangani (Bilaan, Balud, Tumanao) [bps] 90,754 (2000 WCD). South Cotabato Province, Sarangani, Davao Del Sur Province, Mindanao. *Class:* Austronesian, Malayo-Polynesian, South Mindanao, Bilic, Blaan. *Lg Dev:* Literacy rate in first language: 28%. Literacy rate in second language: 28%. Videos. NT: 1981. *Other:* Traditional religion, Christian.

Bolinao (Binobolinao, Bolinao Sambal, Bolinao Zambal) [smk] 50,000 (1990). 500 monolinguals. West Pangasinan Province, Luzon. Primarily municipalities of Bolinao and Anda. *Class:* Austronesian, Malayo-Polynesian, Northern Philippine, Bashiic-Central Luzon-Northern Mindoro, Central Luzon, Sambalic. *Lg Use:* Speakers are shifting to Tagalog. Taught as a course of study in higher education. Speakers of other languages use it in trade and politics. All domains by some ages, administration, commerce, religion. Written form used for administration and personal written communication. Speakers are older adults. Use among young people and children is diminishing. The people hold protective, preserving attitude toward Bolinao. 500 monolinguals. Nearly all also use Tagalog or Ilocano, some Pangasinan. *Lg Dev:* Literacy rate in first language: 86.8%. Literacy rate in second language: 86.8%. High literacy rate in Ilocano and Tagalog. Taught as a course. Roman script. Bible portions: 1963–1984. *Other:* Coastal, island, upland. Fishermen. Christian, traditional religion.

Bontoc, Central (Bontok, Igorot) [bnc] 40,000 (1994 SIL). Central Mountain Province, Luzon. *Class:* Austronesian, Malayo-Polynesian, Northern Philippine, Northern Luzon, South-Central Cordilleran, Central Cordilleran, Nuclear Cordilleran, Bontok-Kankanay, Bontok. *Dialects:* Sadanga, Guinaang Bontoc, Bayyu. Intelligibility of Ilocano 58%, Finallig 56%. *Lg Use:* Speakers also use Ilocano. *Lg Dev:* Literacy rate in first language: 35%. Literacy rate in second language: 35%. NT: 1992.

Buhid (Bukil, Bangon, Batangan) [bku] 8,000 (1991 OMF). Southern Mindoro. *Class:* Austronesian, Malayo-Polynesian, Meso Philippine, South Mangyan, Buhid-Taubuid. *Lg Dev:* NT: 1988.

Butuanon [btw] 34,547 (1990 census). Butuan City, Mindanao. *Class:* Austronesian, Malayo-Polynesian, Meso Philippine, Central Philippine, Bisayan, South, Butuan-Tausug. *Dialects:* Lexical similarity 70% with Kamayo; 69% with Surigaonon. *Lg Use:* Speakers also use Cebuano.

Caluyanun (Caluyanen, Caluyanhon) [clu] 30,000 (1994 SIL). Caluya Islands, Antique. *Class:* Austronesian, Malayo-Polynesian, Meso Philippine, Central Philippine, Bisayan, West. *Dialect:* Semirara. A sample of speakers scored 69% on Hiligaynon narrative comprehension; 62% on Cuyonon. *Lg Use:* Speakers also use Hiligaynon. *Lg Dev:* Literacy rate in first language: 67%. Literacy rate in second language: 67%. NT: 1990.

Capiznon (Capisano, Capiseño) [cps] 638,653 (2000). Northeast Panay. *Class:* Austronesian, Malayo-Polynesian, Meso Philippine, Central Philippine, Bisayan, Central, Peripheral. *Lg Use:* A population sample had 91% comprehension of Hiligaynon narrative. Tagalog is also used.

Cebuano (Sugbuhanon, Sugbuanon, Visayan, Bisayan, Binisaya, Sebuano) [ceb] 20,043,502 in the Philippines (1995 census). Negros, Cebu, Bohol, Visayas and parts of Mindanao. Also spoken in USA. *Class:* Austronesian, Malayo-Polynesian, Meso Philippine, Central Philippine, Bisayan, Cebuan. *Dialects:* Cebu, Boholano, Leyte, Mindanao Visayan. Boholano is sometimes considered a separate language. *Lg Use:* Language of wider communication. Speakers also use Tagalog. *Lg Dev:* Dictionary. Grammar. Bible: 1917–1981. *Other:* Christian.

Chavacano (Zamboangueño, Chabakano) [cbk] 292,630 in the Philippines (1990 census). Population includes 155,000 Zamboangueño (1989 J. Holm), 27,841 Caviten, 3,750 Ternateño (1975 census), 5,473 Cotabato Chavacano (1981 Wurm and Hattori). Zamboanga, Basilan, Kabasalan, Siay, Margosatubig, Ipil, Malangas, Lapuyan, Buug, Tungawa, Alicia, Isabela, Lamitan, Maluso, Malamawi, Cotabato City, Mindanao; Cavite, Ternate, and Ermita near Manila. The 1970 census listed speakers in 60 of the 66 provinces. Also spoken in Malaysia (Sabah). *Class:* Creole, Spanish based. *Dialects:* Caviteño, Ternateño (Ternateño Chavacano), Ermitaño (Ermiteño), Davawenyo Zamboanguenyo (Abakay Spanish, Davao Chavacano, Davaoeño, Davaweño), Cotobato Chavacano (Cotabateño), Zamboangueño (Chavacano). A creole with predominantly Spanish vocabulary and Philippine-type grammatical structure. *Lg Use:* Davawen Zamboangueño may be extinct. Nearly all Caviten speak Tagalog, but many still speak Caviteño. The major language of Zamboanga City. Ermiteño is extinct. *Lg Dev:* Literacy rate in first language: 80%. Literacy rate in second language: 80%. Taught in primary schools. Newspapers. Radio programs. NT: 1981.

Chinese, Mandarin [cmn] 500 to 600 in the Philippines. All ethnic Chinese are 53,273 (1990 census). See main entry under China.

Chinese, Min Nan (Min Nan) [nan] 592,200 in the Philippines. 98.7% of Chinese population in Philippines (1982). See main entry under China.

Chinese, Yue [yue] 9,782 in the Philippines (2000 WCD). See main entry under China.

Cuyonon (Cuyono, Cuyunon, Cuyo, Kuyunon, Kuyonon) [cyo] 123,384 (1990 census). Palawan coast, Cuyo Islands between Palawan and Panay. *Class:* Austronesian, Malayo-Polynesian, Meso Philippine, Central Philippine, Bisayan, West, Kuyan. *Dialects:* Close to Ratagnon. *Lg Use:* Trade language. *Lg Dev:* NT: 1982.

Davawenyo (Matino, Davaoeño, Davaweño) [daw] 147,279 (1990 census). Davao Oriental, Davao del Sur, Mindanao. *Class:* Austronesian, Malayo-Polynesian, Meso Philippine, Central Philippine, Mansakan, Davawenyo. *Dialects:* Synthesis of Tagalog, Cebuano, other Visayan dialects. Some Spanish words. Not a Spanish Creole. Different from Davaweño which is dialect of Chavacano. Two dialects: East Coast with 90% of speakers, and Davao City and environs (Whinnom 1956). Speakers of Lowland Davaweño have 89% intelligibility of Kamayo. *Lg Use:* Speakers of Lowland Davawenyo also use Cebuano 91% to 97%. Of Highland Davawenyo, they have much lower comprehension of Cebuano.

English [eng] 32,802 in the Philippines (1990 census). *Lg Use:* Official language. 52% of the population said they could speak it as a second language (1980 census). See main entry under United Kingdom.

Filipino (Pilipino) [fil] Throughout the country. *Class:* Austronesian, Malayo-Polynesian, Meso Philippine, Central Philippine, Tagalog. *Lg Use:* Official language. Widely spoken as a second language. *Lg Dev:* Taught in primary and secondary schools. Bible: 1905. *Other:* Based on Tagalog with the inclusion of terms from other regional languages. Christian.

Finallig (Southern Bontoc, Kadaklan-Barlig Bontoc, Eastern Bontoc) [bkb] 5,000 (1998 SIL). Central Mountain Province, Luzon. *Class:* Austronesian, Malayo-Polynesian, Northern Philippine, Northern Luzon, South-Central Cordilleran, Central Cordilleran, Nuclear Cordilleran, Bontok-Kankanay, Bontok. *Dialects:* Lias, Barlig, Kadaklan. Intelligibility of Ilocano 53%; Balangao 49%. *Lg Use:* Speakers also use Ilocano. *Lg Dev:* Literacy rate in first language: 67%. Literacy rate in second language: 67%. Bible portions: 1977–1999. *Other:* Traditional religion.

Ga'dang (Baliwon, Gaddang, Ginabwal) [gdg] 6,000 (2002 SIL). Very few monolinguals. Paracelis, Mt. Province, Luzon; Poña, Ifugao. *Class:* Austronesian, Malayo-Polynesian, Northern Philippine, Northern Luzon, Northern Cordilleran, Ibanagic, Gaddang. *Dialects:* Related to Gaddang, Itawit, Yogad, Gaddang, Ibanag, Isnag. Lexical similarity 80% with Gaddang. *Lg Use:* Most speakers are bilingual. *Lg Dev:* Literacy rate in first language: 60% to 80%. Literacy rate in second language: 60% to 80%. NT: 2000. *Other:* Traditional religion, Christian.

Gaddang (Cagayan) [gad] 30,000 (1984 SIL). Central Isabela, and Bagabag, Solano, and Bayombong in Nueva Vizcaya, Luzon. *Class:* Austronesian, Malayo-Polynesian, Northern Philippine, Northern Luzon, Northern Cordilleran, Ibanagic, Gaddang. *Dialects:* Less than 80% intelligibility of Ga'dang. Lexical similarity 80% with Ga'dang. *Lg Use:* Speakers also use Ilocano. *Lg Dev:* Dictionary. Grammar. *Other:* A lowland group. 'Gaddang' refers to those in Nueva Vizcaya, 'Cagayan' to those in central Isabela. Christian.

Giangan (Bagobo, Jangan, Guanga, Gulanga, Clata, Eto, Atto) [bgi] 55,040 (1990 census). Davao City, Mindanao; eastern slopes of Mt. Apo, Davao del Sur. *Class:* Austronesian, Malayo-Polynesian, South Mindanao, Bagobo. *Dialects:* 69% comprehension of Tagabawa; 79% of Obo Manobo. Lexical similarity 34% with Tagabawa, 35% with Obo Manobo; 43% with Blaan. *Lg Use:* Marginally bilingual in Cebuano. *Other:* Different from Manobo.

Hanunoo (Hanonoo) [hnn] 13,020 (2000 WCD). Southern Oriental Mindoro. *Class:* Austronesian, Malayo-Polynesian, Meso Philippine, South Mangyan, Hanunoo. *Dialects:* Gubatnon (Gubat, Sorsogonon), Binli, Kagankan, Waigan, Wawan, Bulalakawnon. *Lg Dev:* NT: 1985.

Higaonon (Misamis Higaonon Manobo) [mba] 30,000 (1996 NTM). Misamis Oriental, south of Ginoog City, north central Mindanao. *Class:* Austronesian, Malayo-Polynesian, Southern Philippine, Manobo, North. *Dialects:* Related to Binukid; 77% to 81% intelligibility. *Lg Use:* Comprehension of Cebuano is limited. *Lg Dev:* Bible portions: 1987.

Hiligaynon (Ilonggo, Illogo, Hiligainon) [hil] 7,000,000 in the Philippines (1995). Iloilo and Capiz provinces, Panay, Negros Occidental, Visayas. Also spoken in USA. *Class:* Austronesian, Malayo-Polynesian, Meso Philippine, Central Philippine, Bisayan, Central, Peripheral. *Dialects:* Hiligaynon, Kawayan, Bantayan, Kari. *Lg Use:* Language of wider communication. Speakers also use Tagalog. *Lg Dev:* Bible: 1912–2002. *Other:* Christian.

I-Wak (Iwaak) [iwk] 3,261 (2000 WCD). Reported to live in the following villages: Tojongan, Bakes, Lebeng, Domolpos, Bujasjas, Kayo-ko, Salaksak (in Kayapa), extreme eastern Itogon, Benguet Province, Luzon. I-wak people also live in Capintalan in Nueva Ecija, but speak only Kallahan. *Class:* Austronesian, Malayo-Polynesian, Northern Philippine, Northern Luzon, South-Central Cordilleran, Southern Cordilleran, Pangasinic, Benguet, Iwaak. *Dialects:* Related to Karao, Ibaloi, Kallahan. *Other:* Less acculturated to outside culture than other mountain groups. Mountain slope.

Ibaloi (Ibaloy, Ibadoy, Inibaloi, Nabaloi, Benguet-Igorot, Igodor) [ibl] 111,449 (1990 census). Central and southern Benguet Province, western Nueva Vizcaya Province, Luzon. *Class:* Austronesian, Malayo-Polynesian, Northern Philippine, Northern Luzon, South-Central Cordilleran, Southern Cordilleran, Pangasinic, Benguet, Ibaloi-Karao. *Dialects:* Daklan, Kabayan, Bokod. *Lg Dev:* Literacy rate in first language: 75% to 100%. Literacy rate in second language: 75% to 100%. NT: 1978.

Ibanag (Ybanag) [ibg] 500,000 (1990 SIL). Isabela and Cagayan provinces, Luzon. *Class:* Austronesian, Malayo-Polynesian, Northern Philippine, Northern Luzon, Northern Cordilleran, Ibanagic, Ibanag. *Dialects:* North Ibanag, South Ibanag. 69% intelligibility of Itawit. *Lg Use:* Positive language attitude. Bilingual level estimates for Ilocano: 0 5%, 1 25%, 2 30%, 3 25%, 4 10%, 5 5%. Speakers also use Tagalog as second language. *Lg Dev:* Literacy rate in first language: 75% to 100%. Literacy rate in second language: 75% to 100%. NT: 1911–1989. *Other:* VSO; genitives after noun heads; adjectives and numerals before noun heads; CV, CVC; nontonal.

Ibatan (Babuyan, Ibataan, Ivatan) [ivb] 1,350 (2000 SIL). Babuyan Island, north of Luzon; Northern Luzon (a few students). *Class:* Austronesian, Malayo-Polynesian, Northern Philippine, Bashiic-Central Luzon-Northern Mindoro, Bashiic, Ivatan. *Dialects:* Intelligibility of Itbayaten Ivatan 64%; Basco Ivatan 31%. Lexical similarity 72% with Itbayaten Ivatan, 74% with Basco Ivatan. *Lg Use:* Speakers are shifting to Ilocano. All domains. Used in religious services and ceremonies, local commerce. All ages. Positive language attitude. All speakers use Ilocano as second language. 10% also use Pilipino (Tagalog) or Chinese (Taiwanese or Mandarin).

Schooling is in Tagalog or English, but Ibatan is used periodically to ensure student comprehension. *Lg Dev:* Literacy rate in first language: 77%. Literacy rate in second language: 60%. 1,000 can read and write it. Taught in primary schools. Roman script. NT: 1996. *Other:* In 1975 many died from measles and polio. Since 1978 the population has increased from 450 to 1,350 because of medicine. Volcanic island 5 miles in diameter. Sea level to over 1,000 meters. Agriculturalists: dry and wet rice; fishermen. Christian.

Ifugao, Amganad (Amganad) [ifa] 27,100 (2000 SIL). 8,000 monolinguals. 167,503 all Ifugao (1990 census). Central Ifugao Province, Luzon. *Class:* Austronesian, Malayo-Polynesian, Northern Philippine, Northern Luzon, South-Central Cordilleran, Central Cordilleran, Nuclear Cordilleran, Ifugao. *Dialects:* Burnay Ifugao, Banaue Ifugao. Burnay has 81% intelligibility of Amganad. Burnay has 83% lexical similarity of Amganad. *Lg Use:* Vigorous. All domains. Used in religious services and traditional ceremonies. Used in administration, commerce relations and traditional ceremonies. All ages. Positive language attitude. 10,000 use Ilocano or English as second language. 8,000 others also use a little Tagalog. *Lg Dev:* Literacy rate in first language: 20%. Literacy rate in second language: 65%. 17,550 read it, 16,000 write it. Oral in lower grades. Roman script. Radio programs. TV. Videos. NT: 1980. *Other:* Mountain slope. Semitropical. Sea level to 1,300 meters. Agriculturalists; government workers. Traditional religion, Christian.

Ifugao, Batad (Batad) [ifb] 43,000 (1987 SIL). Ifugao Province, Luzon. *Class:* Austronesian, Malayo-Polynesian, Northern Philippine, Northern Luzon, South-Central Cordilleran, Central Cordilleran, Nuclear Cordilleran, Ifugao. *Dialects:* Ayangan Ifugao, Batad Ifugao, Ducligan Ifugao. Intelligibility of Batad: Ayangan 87%; Mayoyao 86% to 94%. Lexical similarity with Batad, with Ayangan 81%, with Ducligan 89%, with Mayoyao 79%. *Lg Dev:* Literacy rate in first language: 55% to 60%. Literacy rate in second language: 55% to 60%. Dictionary. NT: 1977. *Other:* Traditional religion, Christian.

Ifugao, Mayoyao (Mayoyao, Mayaoyaw) [ifu] 40,000 (1998 SIL). Ifugao Province, Luzon. *Class:* Austronesian, Malayo-Polynesian, Northern Philippine, Northern Luzon, South-Central Cordilleran, Central Cordilleran, Nuclear Cordilleran, Ifugao. *Dialects:* 86% to 94% intelligibility of Batad. Grammatical markers are different. Lexical similarity 79% with Batad Ifugao, 85% with Ayangan. *Lg Dev:* Literacy rate in first language: 50% to 60%. Literacy rate in second language: 50% to 60%. Bible portions: 1994–1999. *Other:* Secondary schools. Mountain slope. Agriculturalists: wet rice. Traditional religion, Christian.

Ifugao, Tuwali (Kiangan Ifugao, Quiangan, Gilipanes, Tuwali) [ifk] 30,000 (2000 SIL). Southern Ifugao Province, Luzon. *Class:* Austronesian, Malayo-Polynesian, Northern Philippine, Northern Luzon, South-Central Cordilleran, Central Cordilleran, Nuclear Cordilleran, Ifugao. *Dialects:* Hapao Ifugao, Hungduan Ifugao, Lagawe Ifugao. 77% intelligibility of Amganad Ifugao, 78% of Batad. Hapao has 88% intelligibility of Kiangan, Hungduan has 85% of Kiangan. Lexical similarity 80% with Amganad Ifugao, 72% with Batad Ifugao, 78% with Hapao, 86% with Hungduan. *Lg Use:* Vigorous. Speakers of other languages use it in trading and if married to a speaker. All domains. Court, religion, commerce. All ages. Positive toward Tuwali use in home and market, preferring English for school and church. All speakers also use English, Ilocano, Tagalog, or Amganad Ifugao. Those over 40 use more English than others. All members of the community are multilingual by high school. Tuwali used in grade school as transition to English, Ilocano, or Tagalog. *Lg Dev:* Literacy rate in first

language: 83%. Literacy rate in second language: 60%. Taught in primary schools. Roman script. NT: 1991. *Other:* Kiangan is the place, Tuwali is the language. 25,000 can read and write it. Some traditional stories and fables have been recorded. VSO; prepositions; genitives, relatives after noun heads; articles, adjectives, numerals before noun heads; question word initial; one suffix, two infixes; passives; causatives; comparatives; V, CV, CVC. Mountain slope. Tropical forest. 500 to 900 meters. Peasant agriculturalists; rice; shopkeepers. Traditional religion, Christian.

Ilocano (Iloko, Ilokano) [ilo] 8,000,000 in the Philippines (1991 UBS). Northwestern Luzon, La Union and Ilocos provinces, Cagayan Valley, Babuyan, Mindoro, Mindanao. Also spoken in USA. *Class:* Austronesian, Malayo-Polynesian, Northern Philippine, Northern Luzon, Ilocano. *Dialects:* There is a Pidgin Ilocano used in northern Luzon highlands. *Lg Use:* Language of wider communication. *Lg Dev:* Roman script. Bible: 1909–1996. *Other:* Christian.

Ilongot (Bugkalut, Bukalot, Lingotes) [ilk] 50,786 (1990 census). Eastern Nueva Vizcaya, Western Quirino, Luzon. *Class:* Austronesian, Malayo-Polynesian, Northern Philippine, Northern Luzon, South-Central Cordilleran, Southern Cordilleran, Ilongot. *Dialects:* Abaka (Abaca), Egongot, Ibalao (Ibilao), Italon, Iyongut. *Lg Dev:* NT: 1982.

Inabaknon (Abaknon, Capul, Capuleño, Kapul, Sama, Abaknon Sama) [abx] 21,400 (2000 M. Jacobson SIL). 4,000 monolinguals (almost all children). Population includes 13,400 on Capul, 8,000 elsewhere. Capul Island in the San Bernardino Strait, Northwest Samar and in communities along the western Samar coast facing the island; Manila. *Class:* Austronesian, Malayo-Polynesian, Sama-Bajaw, Abaknon. *Lg Use:* Vigorous. All domains, religion, commerce. All ages. Positive language attitude. 14,000 multilingual in combinations of Tagalog, English, Samareño, Bikolano, Cebuano. *Lg Dev:* Literacy rate in first language: 90% to 95%. Literacy rate in second language: 90% to 95%. Taught in primary schools. NT: 1996. *Other:* 'Abaknon' is the name of the people, 'Capul' of the island, and 'Sama' of the language family. The population has increased by 300 to 500 per year. About 500 per year leave to find opportunities elsewhere. 11,000 can read and write. Written form in village health education, song books, some event programs, and religious ceremonies. Volcanic island, reef. Agriculturalists: rice; copra production; fishermen, exporting fish. Christian.

Inonhan (Loocnon, Looknon, "Unhan") [loc] 85,829 (2000 WCD). Southern Tablas Island, Romblon Province, Mindoro Oriental and Mindoro Occidental. *Class:* Austronesian, Malayo-Polynesian, Meso Philippine, Central Philippine, Bisayan, West, North Central. *Dialects:* Bulalakaw, Dispoholnon, Looknon, Alcantaranon. Lexical similarity with 70% Odionganon (Bantuanon), 93% with Aklanon, 86% with Caluyanun. *Lg Use:* Speakers also use Hiligaynon. *Lg Dev:* NT: 2000. *Other:* Loocnon is the name of a town. "Unhan" is derogatory.

Iraya [iry] 10,000 (1991 OMF). Northern Mindoro. *Class:* Austronesian, Malayo-Polynesian, Northern Philippine, Bashiic-Central Luzon-Northern Mindoro, Northern Mindoro. *Dialects:* Abra-De-Ilog, Alag-Bako, Pagbahan, Palauan-Calavite, Pambuhan, Santa Cruz. *Lg Use:* Many speak Tagalog in the home. *Lg Dev:* NT: 1991.

Isinai (Insinai, Isinay, Isnay, Inmeas) [inn] 5,524 (1990 census). Luzon: Bambang, Dupax, and Aritao, Nueva Vizcaya. *Class:* Austronesian, Malayo-Polynesian, Northern Philippine, Northern Luzon, South-Central Cordilleran, Central Cordilleran, Isinai. *Dialects:* Not close to other languages. Lexical similarity 47% with

Ilocano. *Lg Use:* Positive language attitude. Speakers have routine proficiency in Ilocano.

Isnag (Dibagat-Kabugao-Isneg, Isneg, Maragat) [isd] 30,000 (1994 SIL). Northern Apayao, Luzon. *Class:* Austronesian, Malayo-Polynesian, Northern Philippine, Northern Luzon, Northern Cordilleran, Ibanagic, Isnag. *Dialects:* Bayag, Dibagat-Kabugao, Calanasan, Karagawan (Daragawan), Talifugu-Ripang (Tawini). Intelligibility testing: Calanasan: 94% of Dibagat, 88% of Ilocano; Talifugu-Ripang: 89% of Dibagat, 71% of Ilocano. *Lg Use:* Speakers also use Ilocano. *Lg Dev:* Literacy rate in first language: 50%. Literacy rate in second language: 50%. NT: 1980.

Itawit (Itawis, Tawit, Itawes) [itv] 134,126 (1990 census). Population includes 119,584 Itawit, 14,542 Malaweg. Luzon, southern Cagayan. *Class:* Austronesian, Malayo-Polynesian, Northern Philippine, Northern Luzon, Northern Cordilleran, Ibanagic, Ibanag. *Dialects:* Malaweg (Malaueg), Itawis. Related to Ibanag. 72% intelligibility of South Ibanag; 68% of Ilocano. Lexical similarity 53% with Ilocano. *Lg Use:* Speakers also use Ilocano. *Lg Dev:* NT: 1992.

Itneg, Adasen (Adasen, Addasen Tinguian, Addasen) [tiu] 4,000 (NTM). Luzon, northeastern Abra Province. *Class:* Austronesian, Malayo-Polynesian, Northern Philippine, Northern Luzon, Northern Cordilleran, Ibanagic, Isnag. *Dialects:* Eastern Addasen, Western Addasen. Comprehension of Isnag 74%. *Lg Use:* 70% of the ethnic group speaks Adasen. Most domains. 30% of the children speak Adasen. Mildly supportive. Speakers have high proficiency in Ilocano. Second language used for most key domains. *Lg Dev:* NT: 1990.

Itneg, Banao (Banao, Timggian, Tinguian) [bjx] 3,500 (2003 SIL). Unknown number in the Malibcong dialect area. Eastern Abra Province, Luzon. *Class:* Austronesian, Malayo-Polynesian, Northern Philippine, Northern Luzon, South-Central Cordilleran, Central Cordilleran, Kalinga-Itneg, Kalinga. *Dialects:* Malibcong Banao, Banao Pikekj, Gubang Itneg. Lexical similarity Banao of Malibcong 58% with Ilocano, 81% with Lubuagan Kalinga, 79% with Limos Kalinga. Banao Pikek (Daguioman) 62% with Ilocano, 83% with Masadiit Itneg of Boliney, 79% with Masadiit Itneg of Sallapadan, 78% with Banao of Malibcong, and 73% with Binongan Itneg. *Lg Use:* Moderate vitality. Used in the home and community. All ages. Positive language attitude. Most speakers have high proficiency in Ilocano. Speakers also use Tagalog or English. *Other:* High value placed on education. Mountain slope. Rainforest. 700 too 900 meters. Agriculturalists: rice. Traditional religion, Christian.

Itneg, Binongan (Tinguian, Tingguian) [itb] 7,500 (2003 SIL). 46,405 in all Itneg varieties (1990 census). Ba-ay Valley and Licuan Abra Province, Luzon. *Class:* Austronesian, Malayo-Polynesian, Northern Philippine, Northern Luzon, South-Central Cordilleran, Central Cordilleran, Kalinga-Itneg, Itneg. *Dialects:* Lexical similarity 69% with Ilocano, 79% with Masadiit Itneg. *Lg Use:* Vigorous. Used in the home and community. All ages. Most speakers have high proficiency in Ilocano. Speakers also use Tagalog and English. *Lg Dev:* Grammar. Bible portions: 1967. *Other:* 1,200 meters. Agriculturalists: rice, fruit. Christian.

Itneg, Inlaod (Tinguian, Tinggian, Inlaod) [iti] 9,000 (2003 SIL). Northern Luzon, southwest of Binongan Itneg, northwest of Masadiit Itneg; Abra Province, a few barangays of Penarubia, Lagangilang, Danglas, and Langiden. *Class:* Austronesian, Malayo-Polynesian, Northern Philippine, Northern Luzon, South-Central Cordilleran, Central Cordilleran, Kalinga-Itneg, Itneg. *Dialects:* Lexical similarity Inlaod of Langiden 73% with Ilocano; Inlaod of Danglas 71% with Ilocano, 75% to 77%

with Binongan Itneg, 75% to 76% with Masadiit of Sallapadan, 74% to 75% with Moyadan Itneg. Inlaod of Langiden and Inlaod of Danglas 86% with each other. *Lg Use:* Vigorous in some communities. Used in the home and community. Use among children is decreasing. Most speakers have high proficiency in Ilocano. Some speakers also use Tagalog or English. *Other:* Agriculturalists: rice; fishermen. Christian.

Itneg, Maeng (Luba-Tiempo Itneg, Southern Itneg) [itt] 18,000 (2003 SIL). Ethnic population: 18,000. Luzon, southern Abra Province, Luba, Tubo, Villavisciosa municipalities. *Class:* Austronesian, Malayo-Polynesian, Northern Philippine, Northern Luzon, South-Central Cordilleran, Central Cordilleran, Kalinga-Itneg, Itneg. *Dialects:* Lexical similarity Tubo 60% with Ilocano, 68% with Northern Kankanaey; Villavisciosa 76% with Ilocano, 61% with Northern Kankanaey. *Lg Use:* Vigorous. Used in the home and community. All ages. Most speakers have high proficiency in Ilocano. Some speakers use Tagalog or English. *Other:* Swidden agriculturalists: rice, tobacco, mango-tree orchards, vegetables; animal husbandry. Christian.

Itneg, Masadiit [tis] 7,500. 45,000 all Itnegs in province of Abra. Luzon, Abra Province, Sallapadan and Bucloc, Boliney. *Class:* Austronesian, Malayo-Polynesian, Northern Philippine, Northern Luzon, South-Central Cordilleran, Central Cordilleran, Kalinga-Itneg, Itneg. *Dialects:* Masadiit Boliney, Masadiit Sallapadan. Lexical similarity 62% with Ilocano, 70% with Guinaang Kalinga, 86% with Binongan Itneg. *Lg Use:* Vigorous. Used in the home and community. All ages. Most speakers have high proficiency in Ilocano. Some speakers use Tagalog or English. *Other:* Agriculturalists: rice. Christian.

Itneg, Moyadan (Tinggian, Tinguian) [ity] 12,000 (2003 SIL). Luzon, Abra Province. *Class:* Austronesian, Malayo-Polynesian, Northern Philippine, Northern Luzon, Northern Cordilleran, Ibanagic. *Dialects:* Lexical similarity 68% with Ilocano, 85% with Masadiit Sallapadan, 80% with Masadiit Boliney, 76% with Binongan, 75% with Inlaod Danglas, 74% with Inlaod Langiden, 73% with Maeng of Tubo. *Lg Use:* Moderately vigorous. Used in the home and community. All ages. Positive language attitude. Most speakers have high proficiency in Ilocano. Speakers also use Tagalog or Spanish. *Other:* Agriculturalists: rice. Christian.

Ivatan [ivv] 35,000 (1998 SIL). Population includes 3,448 Itbayatan (1996 census). Batanes Islands. Many relocated on Mindanao near boundary of Bukidnon, Lanao del Sur, and Cotabato; some in Manila, Luzon, Palawan, other countries. *Class:* Austronesian, Malayo-Polynesian, Northern Philippine, Bashiic-Central Luzon-Northern Mindoro, Bashiic, Ivatan. *Dialects:* Itbayaten, Basco Ivatan, Southern Ivatan. *Lg Use:* Vigorous. The very young and very old use only Ivatan. Not used in schools. All domains, home, administration, religion, commerce, labor relations, letters. All ages. Positive language attitude. Only preschool children are monolingual. 90% use Tagalog as second language. Some can use English. *Lg Dev:* Literacy rate in first language: 91.8%. Literacy rate in second language: 91.8%. Roman script. Radio programs. Dictionary. Grammar. NT: 1984. *Other:* Literary tradition of laji (old songs) and folklore. Letters, hymnbooks. Mountain slope. Animal husbandry: cattle; fishermen. Christian.

Kagayanen (Cagayano Cillo, Cagayancillo) [cgc] 25,000 (2000 SIL). Few monolinguals. Ethnic population: 25,000. Palawan Province, Cagayan Island, between Negros and Palawan, and communities on the coast of Palawan, and in Coron Municipality in the Busuanga Region of northern Palawan. Also clusters in Iloilo Province, Silay, Negros and Manila. *Class:* Austronesian, Malayo-Polynesian,

Southern Philippine, Manobo, North. *Lg Use:* Speakers are shifting to Tagalog. All domains. Some oral use in local administration, commerce, religion, some schools. Letters, oral literature. Most speak Tagalog and some English. Many speak Cuyonon and one or more Visayan languages as well. Tagalog considered appropriate for school, market, church, reading. *Lg Dev:* Literacy rate in first language: 85%. Literacy rate in second language: 75%. Roman script. Bible portions: 1983–1994. *Other:* There is a growing number moving to cities for economic improvement, education. Islands, coastal. Sea level. Agriculturalists; fishermen; seaweed farmers. Christian, traditional religion.

Kalagan [kqe] 21,402 (1990 census). Along east and west shores of Davao Gulf in Davao del Sur and Davao Oriental. *Class:* Austronesian, Malayo-Polynesian, Meso Philippine, Central Philippine, Mansakan, Western. *Dialects:* Isamal, Piso, Tumuaong, Lactan. Piso dialect may be the prestige dialect. Piso has 91% intelligibility of Kagan; 65% intelligibility of Tagakaulu, 92% intelligibility of Mansaka. Piso has 72% lexical similarity with Kagan, 74% lexical similarity with Mansaka; 83% lexical similarity with Sangab Mandaya. *Lg Use:* A population sample scored 87% on Cebuano narrative text. *Lg Dev:* Literacy rate in first language: 80%. Literacy rate in second language: 80%. *Other:* VSO. Muslim.

Kalagan, Kagan (Kaagan, Kagan Kalagan) [kll] 6,000 (1981 SIL). Davao City, Mindanao. *Class:* Austronesian, Malayo-Polynesian, Meso Philippine, Central Philippine, Mansakan, Western. *Dialects:* Related to Kalagan; 82% intelligibility of Piso dialect. *Lg Use:* Positive language attitude. Speakers also use Cebuano. *Lg Dev:* Literacy rate in second language: Perhaps 60%. Bible portions: 1980.

Kalagan, Tagakaulu (Tagakaolo) [klg] 71,356 (2000 WCD). 40,000 monolinguals. Ethnic population: 100,000. Southern Mindanao, Sarangani Province and Davao Del Sur. *Class:* Austronesian, Malayo-Polynesian, Meso Philippine, Central Philippine, Mansakan, Western. *Dialects:* Related to Mandaya, Kalagan, and Kamayo. About 85% intelligibility of Mansaka. *Lg Use:* All ages. Speakers also use Cebuano or Hiligaynon. *Lg Dev:* Literacy rate in first language: 20% to 30%. Literacy rate in second language: 20% to 30%. Radio programs. Bible portions: 1964–2002. *Other:* Mountain slope. Gallery forests. 30 to 1,000 meters. Swidden agriculturalists; peasants. Christian, traditional religion.

Kalinga, Butbut (Butbut) [kyb] 8,000 (1998). Luzon, Butbut, Tinglayan, Kalinga-Apayao Province. *Class:* Austronesian, Malayo-Polynesian, Northern Philippine, Northern Luzon, South-Central Cordilleran, Central Cordilleran, Kalinga-Itneg, Kalinga. *Dialects:* 72% intelligibility of Limos Kalinga; 44% of Ilocano; 70% of Guinaang, 47% of Tanudan, 74% of Bangad (Southern) Kalinga. Lexical similarity 82% with Bangan Kalinga, 78% of Guinaang and Tanudan.

Kalinga, Limos (Limos-Liwan Kalinga, Northern Kalinga) [kmk] 20,000 (1977 SIL). Luzon, Kalinga-Apayao Province. *Class:* Austronesian, Malayo-Polynesian, Northern Philippine, Northern Luzon, South-Central Cordilleran, Central Cordilleran, Kalinga-Itneg, Kalinga. *Lg Dev:* Literacy rate in first language: 55%. Literacy rate in second language: 80%. Bible portions: 1977–1985.

Kalinga, Lower Tanudan (Lower Tanudan) [kml] 11,243 (1998 SIL). Under 10% monolinguals. Luzon, southern Kalinga Province. *Class:* Austronesian, Malayo-Polynesian, Northern Philippine, Northern Luzon, South-Central Cordilleran, Central Cordilleran, Kalinga-Itneg, Kalinga. *Dialects:* Minangali, Tinaloctoc, Pinangol. Intelligibility of Limos Kalinga 79%, Guinaang 66%. Lexical similarity 97% with Pangul, 80% with Madukayang. *Lg Use:* Positive language attitude. Speakers

also use Ilocano, English, or Tagalog. *Lg Dev:* Literacy rate in first language: 82%. Literacy rate in second language: 82%. Roman script. Bible portions: 1980. *Other:* Swidden agriculturalists. Christian.

Kalinga, Lubuagan [knb] 14,003 (2000 WCD). Ethnic population: 15,000. Eastern Abra and Kalinga-Apayao provinces, Luzon. *Class:* Austronesian, Malayo-Polynesian, Northern Philippine, Northern Luzon, South-Central Cordilleran, Central Cordilleran, Kalinga-Itneg, Kalinga. *Dialect:* Guinaang, Balbalasang, Lubuagan, Ableg-Salegseg, Balatok-Kalinga (Balatok-Itneg). Intelligibility of Balbalasang 81%, Sumadel 82%, Limos 70%. Lexical similarity 81% with Balbalasang and Limos. *Lg Use:* All domains except church. All ages. A population sample averaged 48% comprehension on Ilocano narrative. Educated people prefer English or Ilocano. *Lg Dev:* Literacy rate in first language: 50%. Literacy rate in second language: 40%. Taught in primary schools. Dictionary. Grammar. Bible portions: 1970–1984. *Other:* Mountain slope. Rainforest. 750 to 1,000 meters. Traditional religion, Christian.

Kalinga, Mabaka Valley (Mabaka Itneg, Kal-Uwan, Mabaka) [kkg] Luzon, southeastern Kalinga-Apayao Province. *Class:* Austronesian, Malayo-Polynesian, Northern Philippine, Northern Luzon, South-Central Cordilleran, Central Cordilleran, Kalinga-Itneg, Kalinga. *Lg Use:* Bilingual in Limos Kalinga. 79% average comprehension among the speakers tested.

Kalinga, Madukayang (Majukayong) [kmd] 1,500 (1990 SIL). Southern Mountain Province, Luzon. *Class:* Austronesian, Malayo-Polynesian, Northern Philippine, Northern Luzon, South-Central Cordilleran, Central Cordilleran, Kalinga-Itneg, Kalinga. *Dialects:* 83% intelligibility of Limos and Balangao, 86% of Mangali. Lexical similarity 80% with Tanudan Kalinga, 68% with Limos, 65% with Balangao, 80% with Mangali. *Lg Use:* A population sample averaged 68% comprehension on an Ilocano narrative test.

Kalinga, Southern (Tinglayan Kalinga) [ksc] 13,000 (2000 SIL). 58% are monolingual. Kalinga Province, Luzon. 13 villages. Some are in Tabuk, the provincial capital. *Class:* Austronesian, Malayo-Polynesian, Northern Philippine, Northern Luzon, South-Central Cordilleran, Central Cordilleran, Kalinga-Itneg, Kalinga. *Dialects:* Mallango, Sumadel, Bangad, Tinglayan. Intelligibility of Guinaang Kalinga 63%, Mangali 51%. *Lg Use:* Vigorous. All domains. Written use in religious services. All ages. Positive language attitude. Speakers also use Ilocano or English. *Lg Dev:* Literacy rate in first language: 65%. Literacy rate in second language: 65%. Language of instruction. Roman script. Grammar. NT: 1986. *Other:* Mountain slope. Agriculturalists. Traditional religion, Christian.

Kalinga, Upper Tanudan (Upper Tanudan) [kgh] 3,000 (1991 SIL). Luzon, Kalinga-Apayao Province, southern end of the Tanudan Valley. *Class:* Austronesian, Malayo-Polynesian, Northern Philippine, Northern Luzon, South-Central Cordilleran, Central Cordilleran, Kalinga-Itneg, Kalinga. *Lg Use:* Language attitudes require separate literature from Lower Tanudan Kalinga. *Lg Dev:* Literacy rate in first language: 52%. Literacy rate in second language: 70% to 75%.

Kallahan, Kayapa (Kayapa, Kalangoya, Kalanguya, Kalkali, Ikalahan, Kalangoya-Ikalahan, Akab) [kak] 15,000 (1991 UBS). Western Nueva Vizcaya, northeastern Pangasinan, western Ifugao, Luzon. *Class:* Austronesian, Malayo-Polynesian, Northern Philippine, Northern Luzon, South-Central Cordilleran, Southern Cordilleran, Pangasinic, Benguet, Kallahan. *Lg Dev:* NT: 1983.

Kallahan, Keley-I (Antipolo Ifugao, Keleyqiq Ifugao, Keley-I, Hanalulo, Keley-I Kalanguya) [ify] 8,000 (2000

SIL). Napayo, Kiangan Ifugao Province, northwest of Aritao, Nueva Vizcaya, Luzon. *Class:* Austronesian, Malayo-Polynesian, Northern Philippine, Northern Luzon, South-Central Cordilleran, Southern Cordilleran, Pangasinic, Benguet, Kallahan. *Dialects:* Bayninan, Ya-Tuka. *Lg Use:* Vigorous. All domains. Used as a teaching medium in early grades of education. Oral and written Keley-I used in court cases and religious services. Oral use in commerce. Personal letters. All ages. Positive language attitude. Only children under 5 years old are monolingual. All of high school age and above use Tuwali Ifugao, Ilocano, and English as second languages. *Lg Dev:* Literacy rate in second language: 70% to 75%. 4,000 to 5,000 can read and write it. NT: 1980. *Other:* Mountain slope. Agriculturalists: rice. Traditional religion, Christian.

Kallahan, Tinoc (Tinoc Kalangoya) [tne] Tinoc, a barrio of Hungduan in Luzon. *Class:* Austronesian, Malayo-Polynesian, Northern Philippine, Northern Luzon, South-Central Cordilleran, Southern Cordilleran, Pangasinic, Benguet, Kallahan. *Dialects:* Intelligibility of Akab 95%, Tinoc 89%. *Lg Use:* Literature from other areas is probably not acceptable to the people.

Kamayo [kyk] 7,565 (2000 WCD). Surigao del Sur between Marihatag and Lingig, Mindanao. *Class:* Austronesian, Malayo-Polynesian, Meso Philippine, Central Philippine, Mansakan, Northern. *Dialects:* North Kamayo, South Kamayo. Intelligibility of Surigaonon 92%, of Butuanon 87%, of Mansaka 82%. Lexical similarity 66% with Surigaonon, 70% with Butuanon. *Lg Use:* Speakers also use Cebuano.

Kankanaey (Central Kankanaey, Kankanai, Kankanay) [kne] 150,000 (1991 SIL). All Kankanai 218,279 (1990 census). Northern Benguet Province, southwestern Mountain Province, southeastern Ilocos Sur, northeastern La Union, Luzon. *Class:* Austronesian, Malayo-Polynesian, Northern Philippine, Northern Luzon, South-Central Cordilleran, Central Cordilleran, Nuclear Cordilleran, Bontok-Kankanay, Kankanay. *Dialects:* Mankayan-Buguias, Kapangan, Bakun-Kibungan, Guinzadan. *Lg Dev:* Literacy rate in first language: 75%. Literacy rate in second language: 78%. NT: 1990. *Other:* Mountain slope. Agriculturalists: rice, vegetables. Traditional religion, Christian.

Kankanay, Northern (Sagada Igorot, Western Bontoc) [xnn] 70,000 (1987 SIL). Western Mountain Province, southeastern Ilocos Sur, Luzon. *Class:* Austronesian, Malayo-Polynesian, Northern Philippine, Northern Luzon, South-Central Cordilleran, Central Cordilleran, Nuclear Cordilleran, Bontok-Kankanay, Kankanay. *Lg Dev:* Literacy rate in first language: 65% to 70%. Literacy rate in second language: 65% to 70%. Grammar. NT: 1984.

Karao (Karaw) [kyj] 1,400 (1998 SIL). Karao and Ekip, Bokod, eastern Benguet Province, Luzon. *Class:* Austronesian, Malayo-Polynesian, Northern Philippine, Northern Luzon, South-Central Cordilleran, Southern Cordilleran, Pangasinic, Benguet, Ibaloi-Karao. *Dialects:* Limited comprehension testing showed Kayapa Kallahan 85%; Ilocano 78%. Lexical similarity 90% with Ibaloi. *Lg Use:* Vigorous. All domains. All ages. Bilingual level estimates for Ibaloi: 1–2 47%, 3 18%, 3 + 22%, 4 13%, 5 0%. Speakers also use Kalangoya, Ilocano, or English. *Lg Dev:* Literacy rate in first language: 80% to 90%. Literacy rate in second language: 80% to 90%.

Karolanos [kyn] 15,131 (2000 WCD). Mid-central Negros, Kabankalan. *Class:* Austronesian, Malayo-Polynesian, Meso Philippine, Central Philippine. *Dialects:* Close to Magahat.

Kasiguranin (Casiguranin) [ksn] 10,000 (1975 SIL). Casiguran, Aurora Province, Luzon. *Class:* Austronesian, Malayo-Polynesian, Northern Philippine, Northern Luzon, Northern Cordilleran, Dumagat, Northern. *Dialects:* 82% intelligibility of Paranan. Lexical similarity 52% with Tagalog, 75% with Paranan. *Lg Use:* Speakers also use Tagalog.

Katabaga [ktq] Extinct. Bondoc Peninsula, Luzon. *Class:* Austronesian, Malayo-Polynesian, Unclassified. *Lg Use:* Members of the ethnic group now speak Tagalog. *Other:* Negrito.

Kinaray-A (Hinaray-A, Kiniray-A, Karay-A, Antiqueño, Hamtiknon, Sulud, Ati, Panayano) [krj] 377,529 (1994 SIL). Iloilo and Antique provinces, western Panay. *Class:* Austronesian, Malayo-Polynesian, Meso Philippine, Central Philippine, Bisayan, West, Kinarayan. *Dialect:* Pandan, Hamtik, Anini-Y, Pototan, Lambunao, Miag-Ao, Guimaras Island (Gimaras). Antique has 67% comprehension of Tagalog; 61% of Hiligaynon; Iloilo has 78% of Hiligaynon; 85% of Antique. *Lg Use:* Speakers also use Hiligaynon. *Lg Dev:* Bible portions: 1982–1985.

Magahat (Bukidnon, Ata-Man) [mtw] 7,565 (2000 WCD). Southwestern Negros, Mt. Arniyo near Bayawan, upper Tayaban, Bayawan (Tolong), Tanjag, Santa Catalina, and Siaton provinces. *Class:* Austronesian, Malayo-Polynesian, Meso Philippine, Central Philippine. *Dialects:* Close to Karolanos. Reported to include a heavy mixture of Cebuano and Hiligaynon. *Other:* Magahat tend to live in high elevations.

Maguindanao (Magindanaon, Magindanaw) [mdh] 1,000,000 (1999 WA). Population includes 766,565 Magindanaon (1990 census), 241,000 Iranun (1981 SIL). Maguindanao, North Cotabato, South Cotabato, Sultan Kuderat, and Zamboanga del Sur provinces; Iranun also in Bukidnon, Mindanao. *Class:* Austronesian, Malayo-Polynesian, Southern Philippine, Danao, Magindanao. *Dialects:* Laya, Ilud, Biwangan, Sibugay, Iranun (Ilanon, Illanon, Ilanum, Iranon), Tagakawanan. 84% intelligibility of Iranun, 60% of Maranao. Iranun has 98% intelligibility of Maguindanao; 96% of Illanun of Sabah, Malaysia and 95% of Maranao. Subdialects of Iranun: Iranun and Ise-banganen. *Lg Use:* Trade language. Comprehension of Tagalog is low. *Lg Dev:* Literacy rate in first language: 60%. Literacy rate in second language: 60%. Dictionary. Bible portions: 1946–1995. *Other:* Muslim, Christian.

Malaynon [mlz] 8,500 (1973 SIL). Malay, northwest Aklan Province, lowland, Panay. *Class:* Austronesian, Malayo-Polynesian, Meso Philippine, Central Philippine, Bisayan, West, Aklan. *Dialects:* Lexical similarity 93% with Aklanon. *Lg Use:* Vigorous.

Mamanwa (Mamanwa Negrito, Minamanwa) [mmn] 5,152 (1990 census). Agusan del Norte and Surigao provinces, Mindanao. *Class:* Austronesian, Malayo-Polynesian, Meso Philippine, Central Philippine, Mamanwa. *Lg Dev:* Literacy rate in first language: 7%. Literacy rate in second language: 7%. NT: 1982.

Mandaya, Cataelano (Cateelenyo) [mst] 19,000 (1980 census). 34,317 all Mandaya (1990 census). Town of Cateel, Davao Oriental, Mindanao. *Class:* Austronesian, Malayo-Polynesian, Meso Philippine, Central Philippine, Mansakan, Eastern, Mandayan. *Lg Use:* Speakers also use Mansaka.

Mandaya, Karaga (Carraga Mandaya, Manay Mandayan, Mangaragan Mandaya) [mry] 3,000 (1982 SIL). Lamiyawan area, Davao Oriental, Mindanao. *Class:* Austronesian, Malayo-Polynesian, Meso Philippine, Central Philippine, Mansakan, Eastern, Caraga. *Dialects:* Lexical similarity 89% with Mansaka. *Lg Use:* Speakers also use Mansaka.

Mandaya, Sangab (Sangab) [myt] 7,565 (2000 WCD). Head of Carraga River, Banlalaysan area, highland, Davao del Norte, Mindanao. *Class:* Austronesian, Malayo-Polynesian, Meso Philippine, Central Philippine, Mansakan, Eastern, Mandayan. *Dialects:* 77% intelligibility of Mansaka. Lexical similarity 83% with

Tumuwaong (Kalagan), 79% with Boston, 72% with Boso. *Lg Use:* Some speakers also use Cebuano.

Manobo, Agusan (Agusan) [msm] 60,000 (2002 SIL). 157,408 all Manobo (1990 census). Agusan del Norte, Agusan del Sur, Surigao del Sur, Mindanao. *Class:* Austronesian, Malayo-Polynesian, Southern Philippine, Manobo, Central, East. *Dialects:* Umayam, Adgawan, Surigao. 83% intelligibility of Dibabawon. Omayamnon has 80% lexical similarity with the other dialects, 85% with Dibabawon. *Lg Dev:* Literacy rate in first language: 54.3%. Literacy rate in second language: 55% to 60%. Dictionary. NT: 1999. *Other:* The people call themselves 'Manobo' and the language 'Minanubu'. Christian, traditional religion.

Manobo, Ata (Atao Manobo, Ata of Davao, Langilan) [atd] 26,653 (2000 WCD). Mindanao, northwestern Davao. *Class:* Austronesian, Malayo-Polynesian, Southern Philippine, Manobo, Central, South, Ata-Tigwa. *Lg Dev:* Literacy rate in first language: 25%. Literacy rate in second language: 25% to 30%. NT: 2000. *Other:* Different from Ata of Mabinay, Negros Oriental, and Atta languages. A Negrito people.

Manobo, Cinamiguin (Cinamiguin, Kinamigin, Kamigin) [mkx] 60,000 (1973 SIL). Camiguin Island, north of Mindanao. *Class:* Austronesian, Malayo-Polynesian, Southern Philippine, Manobo, North. *Lg Use:* Speakers also use Cebuano.

Manobo, Cotabato (Dulangan Manobo) [mta] 30,000 (2002 SIL). 5,000 monolinguals. Ethnic population: 30,000. Sultan Kudarat Province, Mindanao. *Class:* Austronesian, Malayo-Polynesian, Southern Philippine, Manobo, South. *Dialects:* Tasaday, Blit. *Lg Use:* Vigorous. All ages. Some speakers also use Cebuano, Filipino, or Ilongo. *Lg Dev:* Literacy rate in first language: 20% to 25%. Literacy rate in second language: 20% to 25%. Dictionary. NT: 1988. *Other:* 150 to 1,000 meters. Swidden agriculturalists. Traditional religion, Christian.

Manobo, Dibabawon (Mandaya, Dibabaon, Debabaon) [mbd] 10,000 (1978 SIL). Manguagan, Davao del Norte, Mindanao. *Class:* Austronesian, Malayo-Polynesian, Southern Philippine, Manobo, Central, East. *Lg Dev:* Literacy rate in first language: 23%. Literacy rate in second language: 23%. NT: 1978.

Manobo, Ilianen (Ilianen) [mbi] 14,609 (2000 WCD). Few monolinguals. Northern Cotabato, Mindanao. Being pushed more north and east up to Obo Manobo country. *Class:* Austronesian, Malayo-Polynesian, Southern Philippine, Manobo, Central, West. *Dialects:* Livunganen, Puleniyan, Arkan Valley. *Lg Use:* Vigorous. All domains. Positive language attitude. Most use Cebuano and Magaindanaon. Some also speak Tagalog. *Lg Dev:* Literacy rate in first language: 15% to 20%. Literacy rate in second language: 15% to 20%. Roman script. NT: 1989. *Other:* They could not enforce their traditional land claims. Hills. Formerly forest. Swidden agriculturalists: maize, horticulture; hunter-gatherers; fishermen. Corn as cash crop. Traditional religion, Christian, Muslim.

Manobo, Matigsalug (Matig-Salug Manobo) [mbt] 30,000 (2002 SIL). 5,000 monolinguals. Ethnic population: 30,000. Davao del Norte, southeast Bukidnon, Mindanao. *Class:* Austronesian, Malayo-Polynesian, Southern Philippine, Manobo, Central, South, Ata-Tigwa. *Dialects:* Kulamanen, Tigwa, Tala Ingod, Matig-Salud. Tigwa has marginal intelligibility of Matigsalug. Tala Ingod may have adequate intelligibility of Matigsalug. *Lg Use:* Speakers increasingly use Cebuano. *Lg Dev:* Literacy rate in first language: 10%. Literacy rate in second language: 25%. Bible portions: 1972-2002. *Other:* Mountain slope.

Manobo, Obo (Obo Bagobo, Bagobo, Kidapawan Manobo) [obo] 93,341 (2000 WCD). 35,000 monolinguals. Northeastern slope of Mt. Apo, between Davao del Sur and North Cotabato, Mindanao. *Class:* Austronesian, Malayo-Polynesian, Southern Philippine, Manobo, Central, South, Obo. *Dialects:* Kidapawan Manobo, Magpet Manobo, Arakan Manobo. 69% intelligibility of Tigwa (Matig-Salug Manobo; closest), 60% of Tagabawa, 13% of Ilianen Manobo. Lexical similarity 63% with Tagabawa and Ilianen Manobo; lexical similarity 35% with Cebuano. *Lg Use:* All ages. Positive language attitude. Speakers have low proficiency in Cebuano. Cebuano is the trade language used in the market place and in the church. Tagabawa or Diangan are used by those living in the area who have married someone of Obo Manobo background. *Lg Dev:* Literacy rate in second language: 40% (1994). Literacy work is ongoing. Roman script. Radio programs. Bible portions: 1941-1999. *Other:* 750 to 900 meters. Swidden agriculturalists. Christian, traditional religion.

Manobo, Rajah Kabunsuwan (Rajah Kabungsuan Manobo) [mqk] 7,565 (2000 WCD). Southern Surigao del Sur. *Class:* Austronesian, Malayo-Polynesian, Southern Philippine, Manobo, Central, East. *Dialects:* Intelligibility of Dibabawon Manobo 80%, San Miguel Calatugan Agusan 81% intelligibility. Lexical similarity 82% with Dibabawon Manobo, 76% with Sagunto Agusan Manobo and San Miguel Calatugan Agusan Manobo. *Lg Use:* Low bilingualism in Cebuano, some in Dibabawon and Agusan Manobo.

Manobo, Sarangani [mbs] 35,000 (1987 SIL). Southern and eastern Davao, Mindanao. *Class:* Austronesian, Malayo-Polynesian, Southern Philippine, Manobo, South. *Dialect:* Governor Generoso Manobo. *Lg Dev:* Literacy rate in first language: 44%. Literacy rate in second language: 44%. NT: 1982.

Manobo, Western Bukidnon [mbb] 19,034 (2000 WCD). Mindanao, southern Bukidnon Province. *Class:* Austronesian, Malayo-Polynesian, Southern Philippine, Manobo, Central, West. *Dialects:* Ilentungen, Kiriyenteken, Pulangiyen. *Lg Dev:* Literacy rate in first language: 45%. Literacy rate in second language: 45%. NT: 1978. *Other:* Mountain slope. Tropical forest. Formerly swidden agriculturalists: upland rice; hunter-gatherers. Presently peasant agriculturalists: maize.

Mansaka (Mandaya Mansaka) [msk] 57,761 (2000 WCD). Eastern Davao and Davao Oriental provinces, Mindanao. *Class:* Austronesian, Malayo-Polynesian, Meso Philippine, Central Philippine, Mansakan, Eastern, Mandayan. *Dialects:* Lexical similarity 80% with Bislig-Mati, 89% with Karaga Mandaya, 84% with Mati, 74% with Piso (Kalagan). *Lg Dev:* NT: 1975.

Mapun (Sama Mapun, Jama Mapun, Cagayan de Sulu, Cagayanon, Kagayan, Bajau Kagayan, Orang Cagayan, Cagayano) [sjm] 40,588 in the Philippines (2000 WCD). Cagayan de Sulu and Palawan islands. Also spoken in Malaysia (Sabah). *Class:* Austronesian, Malayo-Polynesian, Sama-Bajaw, Sulu-Borneo, Borneo Coast Bajaw. *Dialects:* 59% intelligibility of Central Sama. *Lg Use:* Speakers have some proficiency in Tausug. *Lg Dev:* Literacy rate in first language: 65% to 70%. Literacy rate in second language: 65% to 70%. Bible portions: 1979-1985. *Other:* Muslim.

Maranao (Ranao, Maranaw) [mrw] 776,169 (1990 census). Mindanao, Lanao del Norte and Lanao del Sur provinces. *Class:* Austronesian, Malayo-Polynesian, Southern Philippine, Danao, Maranao-Iranon. *Dialects:* 87% intelligibility of Iranun (see Magindanaon); 52% of Maguindanao. *Lg Dev:* Literacy rate in second language: 20%. Dictionary. NT: 1981. *Other:* Muslim, Christian.

Masbatenyo (Minasbate, Masbateño) [msb] 350,000 (2002 SIL). 50,000 monolinguals, mostly children. Ethnic population: 700,000. Masbate Province, three islands. *Class:* Austronesian, Malayo-Polynesian, Meso Philippine,

Central Philippine, Bisayan, Central, Peripheral. *Dialects:* Related to Hiligaynon and Capiznon. Lexical similarity 79% with Capiznon, 76% with Hiligaynon. *Lg Use:* Language of wider communication. 250,000 second-language speakers (2002 SIL). Used in the home, market, work. All ages. *Lg Dev:* Literacy rate in first language: 65%. Literacy rate in second language: 50%. Taught in primary and secondary schools. Roman script. Newspapers. Radio programs. Dictionary. Grammar. NT: 1993. *Other:* Volcanic islands. Sea level to 550 meters. Agriculturalists; fishermen. Christian.

Molbog (Molbog Palawan) [pwm] 6,680 in the Philippines (1990 census). Balabac Island, southern Palawan. Also spoken in Malaysia (Sabah). *Class:* Austronesian, Malayo-Polynesian, Meso Philippine, Palawano. *Dialects:* Brooke's Point Palawano has 27% intelligibility; South Palawano 55% intelligibility. Lexical similarity 69% with Quezon Palawano (Central). *Lg Use:* Sama Mapun is used as second language, and 20% use Tagalog. *Lg Dev:* Literacy rate in first language: 5%. Literacy rate in second language: 7%. Bible portions: 1977.

Palawano, Brooke's Point (Palawan, Brooke's Point Palawan, Palaweño, Palawanun) [plw] 14,367 (2000 WCD). Southeastern Palawan. *Class:* Austronesian, Malayo-Polynesian, Meso Philippine, Palawano. *Dialect:* South Palawano (Bugsuk Palawano). Of Quezon Palawano (Central) 76% intelligibility, of Southwest Palawano 68%, of South Palawano 87% intelligibility. Lexical similarity 82% with Quezon Palawano (Central), 85% with Southwest Palawano, 83% with South Palawano. *Lg Use:* Comprehension of Tagalog is low. *Lg Dev:* Literacy rate in first language: 10%. Literacy rate in second language: 10%. Bible portions: 1992.

Palawano, Central (Quezon Palawano, Palawanen, Palaweño) [plc] 12,000 (1981 UBS). 40,549 all Palawano (1990 census). Central Palawan. *Class:* Austronesian, Malayo-Polynesian, Meso Philippine, Palawano. *Dialects:* Of Brooke's Point Palawano 95% intelligibility, of Southwest Palawano 46% intelligibility. Lexical similarity 82% with Brooke's Point Palawano, 78% of Southwest Palawano. *Lg Use:* Comprehension of Tagalog low. *Lg Dev:* NT: 1964.

Palawano, Southwest [plv] 3,000 (1985 UBS). Southwest Palawan from Rizal to the north to the southern tip of Palawan, from Canipaan to Canduaga. *Class:* Austronesian, Malayo-Polynesian, Meso Philippine, Palawano. *Dialects:* Intelligibility of Quezon Palawano (Central) 75%, Brooke's Point 76% intelligibility. Lexical similarity 85% with Brooke's Point Palawano, 78% with Quezon Palawano (Central). *Lg Use:* Low comprehension of Tagalog.

Pampangan (Pampango, Pampangueño, Kapampangan) [pam] 1,897,378 (1990 census). Pampanga, Tarlac, and Bataan provinces, Luzon. *Class:* Austronesian, Malayo-Polynesian, Northern Philippine, Bashiic-Central Luzon-Northern Mindoro, Central Luzon, Pampangan. *Lg Use:* Language of wider communication. Dominant language in Pampanga Province. *Lg Dev:* Bible: 1917–1994.

Pangasinan [pag] 1,164,586 (1990 census). Pangasinan Province, Luzon. *Class:* Austronesian, Malayo-Polynesian, Northern Philippine, Northern Luzon, South-Central Cordilleran, Southern Cordilleran, Pangasinic. *Lg Dev:* Grammar. Bible: 1915–1983.

Paranan (Palanenyo, Planan) [agp] 15,789 (2000 WCD). Population includes 13,220 Lowland Paranan, 1,000 to 2,000 Palanan Agta. East coast, Isabela Province, Luzon; surrounded by hills. Isolated. *Class:* Austronesian, Malayo-Polynesian, Northern Philippine, Northern Luzon, Northern Cordilleran, Dumagat, Northern. *Dialect:* Palanan Dumagat (Palanan Valley Agta, Palanan Valley Dumagat). Intelligibility of Casiguran Dumagat 76%.

Palanan Dumagat intelligibility of Paranan 98%, of Casiguran Dumagat 94%. Lexical similarity 85% with Palanan Dumagat, 87% with Casiguran Dumagat. *Lg Use:* Paranan speakers have moderate comprehension of Tagalog, low of Ilocano. Palanan Dumagat speakers have low comprehension of Tagalog and Ilocano. *Lg Dev:* Literacy rate in first language: 75% (lowlanders), 1% to 3% (Negritos). Literacy rate in second language: 75% (lowlanders), 1% to 3% (Negritos). Bible portions: 1988. *Other:* Lowland. Negrito. Coastal. Tropical forest.

Philippine Sign Language (Local Sign Language, Filipino Sign Language, FSL) [psp] 100,000 deaf persons (1986 Gallaudet Univ). *Class:* Deaf sign language. *Dialects:* Reported to be very similar to ASL. *Lg Use:* Total communication is used in deaf schools, with teachers both speaking and signing. Used by USA Peace Corps. American Sign Language is well known as a second language.

Porohanon (Camotes) [prh] 23,000. Camotes Islands. *Class:* Austronesian, Malayo-Polynesian, Meso Philippine, Central Philippine, Bisayan, Central, Peripheral. *Dialects:* Barely intelligible with Cebuano (J. Wolff 1967). Closer to Masbatenyo and Hiligaynon. Lexical similarity 87% with Cebuano (J. Wolff 1967). *Lg Use:* Bilingual level estimates for Cebuano: 1–3 25%, 3+ 29%, 4 46%, 5 0%.

Ratagnon (Datagnon, Latagnun, Latan, Lactan, Aradigi) [btn] 2 to 3 (2000 Wurm). Ethnic population: 2,000 (1997 SIL). Southern tip of western Mindoro. *Class:* Austronesian, Malayo-Polynesian, Meso Philippine, Central Philippine, Bisayan, West, Kuyan. *Dialects:* Ratagnon, Santa Teresa. Close to Cuyonon. *Lg Use:* Speakers are shifting to Tagalog. No children speak Ratagnon. Negative language attitude. *Other:* Nearly extinct.

Romblomanon (Romblon) [rol] 200,000 (1987 SIL). Romblon and Sibuyan Islands, parts of eastern Tablas Island, north of Panay. *Class:* Austronesian, Malayo-Polynesian, Meso Philippine, Central Philippine, Bisayan, Central, Romblon. *Dialects:* Sibuyan, Romblon, Basiq. Sibuyan Island has 70% intelligibility of Aklanon, 73% of Hiligaynon, 94% of Romblon. *Lg Use:* Speakers also use Tagalog. *Lg Dev:* Bible portions: 1999–2002.

Sama, Central (Siasi Sama, Central Sinama, Samal, Sinama) [sml] 90,027 in the Philippines (2000 WCD). Sulu Province. Also spoken in Malaysia (Sabah). *Class:* Austronesian, Malayo-Polynesian, Sama-Bajaw, Sulu-Borneo, Inner Sulu Sama. *Dialect:* Dilaut-Badjao. 59% intelligibility of Tausug; 79% of Balangingi. *Lg Dev:* Literacy rate in first language: 15%. Literacy rate in second language: 15%. NT: 1987. *Other:* Muslim, Christian.

Sama, Pangutaran (Siyama) [slm] 35,171 (2000 WCD). West central Sulu, Pangutaran Island, west of Jolo, Mindanao. Also southern Palawan, Cagayan de Tawi-Tawi. Reported that there are also 145 in Sabah, Malaysia, Look Banga village of 620, Lahad Datu. *Class:* Austronesian, Malayo-Polynesian, Sama-Bajaw, Sulu-Borneo, Western Sulu Sama. *Dialects:* 65% intelligibility of Central Sama. *Lg Use:* Vigorous. All domains. Oral use in education for explanations, market. Some written use in communications. Positive language attitude. Moderate bilingualism in Tausug by 80% of speakers, and 20% use Tagalog. Some who have been to Malaysia also speak Malay. *Lg Dev:* Literacy rate in first language: 25% to 30%. Literacy rate in second language: 25% to 35%. NT: 1994. *Other:* Coral island. Formerly forest. Low altitude. Agriculturalists: casava, maize, cocopalm cultivation. Muslim.

Sama, Southern (Sinama, Sinama Tawi-Tawi, Sama Sibutu', Sama Tawi-Tawi) [ssb] 120,000 in the Philippines (2000). 5,000 to 10,000 monolinguals. Population total all countries: 140,000. Archipelago northeast of Borneo, southern Sulu. Tawi-Tawi Island group includes Tawi-

Tawi, Simunul, Sibutu, and other major islands. Also spoken in Malaysia (Sabah). *Class:* Austronesian, Malayo-Polynesian, Sama-Bajaw, Sulu-Borneo, Inner Sulu Sama. *Dialects:* Sibutu' (Sibutu), Simunul, Tandubas, Obian, Balimbing, Bongao, Sitangkai, Languyan, Sapa-Sapa. Sibutu intelligibility: 77% of Sama Central; 89% of Simunul. Simunul intelligibility: 77% of Sama Central; 80% of Sibutu. *Lg Use:* Vigorous. Used in the home, local level official functions, religious services, commerce, and labor relations. Literature may not be acceptable to other dialect speakers because of marginal intelligibility. Proud of their language. Moderate bilingualism in Tausug by 40,000 to 45,000 Sibutu and Simunul speakers. About 70,000 speak Tausug, Malay, Mapun, Pangutaran Sama, Central Sama, or Tagalog with varying fluency. Men are more bilingual than women. *Lg Dev:* Literacy rate in first language: 65% to 70%. Literacy rate in second language: 65% to 70%. 65,000 can read it, 50,000 can write it. Taught in primary schools. Roman script. Radio programs. Bible portions: 1979–2000. *Other:* Simunul is central, prestige dialect. Bongao dialect from political, economic center of Southern Sama. Islands, mountain slope. Low altitude. Agriculturalists; seaweed; fishermen; copra production; tourist guides. Muslim.

Sambal, Botolan (Aeta Negrito, Botolan Zambal, Ayta Hambali) [sbl] 32,867 (2000 SIL). Central Luzon, Zambales Province, Botolan and Cabangan municipalities. People were affected by Mt. Pinatubo eruption. *Class:* Austronesian, Malayo-Polynesian, Northern Philippine, Bashiic-Central Luzon-Northern Mindoro, Central Luzon, Sambalic. *Dialects:* Ayta Hambali (Hambali Botolan), Sambali Botolan. The Ayta Hambali use some words like Ayta Mag-anchi among themselves. *Lg Use:* Vigorous. All domains. Local administration, commerce, religion, letters. All ages. Small children are monolingual. *Lg Dev:* Literacy rate in first language: 100%. Literacy rate in second language: 100%. All can read and write it. Roman script. Radio programs. Dictionary. NT: 1982. *Other:* Hills, coastal. Sea level and higher. Agriculturalists; fishermen; charcoal makers.

Sambal, Tinà (Tina, Sambali) [xsb] 70,000 (2000 SIL). Ethnic population: 70,000. Luzon, northern Zambales Province, 5 towns, 2 villages in Pangasinan Province, and village of Panitian, Quezon on Palawan Island. *Class:* Austronesian, Malayo-Polynesian, Northern Philippine, Bashiic-Central Luzon-Northern Mindoro, Central Luzon, Sambalic. *Dialects:* Santa Cruz, Masinloc, Iba. 70% intelligibility of Botolan. *Lg Use:* Young people start using it in work situations if they do not go on to higher education; little use among children. All domains among adults. Oral use in local commerce, occasional use in religion and political campaigning. Some letter writing. Speakers are adults. They do not use Sambal around outsiders, but they like it when a few outsiders learn Sambal. All have moderate comprehension of Filipino. Possibly 30% speak some Ilocano. Only Filipino and English taught in school. *Lg Dev:* Literacy rate in first language: 98%. Literacy rate in second language: 98%. Orthography close to Filipino. Roman script. Poetry. Newspapers. Radio programs. Videos. Dictionary. Grammar. NT: 1999. *Other:* There is migration to cities for economic improvement. Coastal. Sea level. Agriculturalists: rice; fishermen. Christian, syncretism.

Sangil (Sangiré, Sanggil) [snl] 15,000 (1996 SIL). Balut Island, Sarangani Island, Mindanao. *Class:* Austronesian, Malayo-Polynesian, Sulawesi, Sangiric, Northern. *Dialects:* Sarangani, Mindanao. Lexical similarity 90% with Sangir. *Lg Use:* Speakers have low proficiency in Cebuano. *Lg Dev:* Literacy rate in first language: 50%. Literacy rate in second language: 50%. Bible portions: 1989. *Other:* Muslim, Christian.

Sangir (Sangihé, Sangirese) [sxn] 55,000 in the Philippines (1981 SIL). Balut and Sarangani islands off of Mindanao. See main entry under Indonesia (Sulawesi).

Sorsogon, Masbate (Northern Sorsogon, Sorsogon Bicolano) [bks] 85,000 (1975 census). Luzon, Sorsogon, Casiguran and Juban, Sorsogon Province. *Class:* Austronesian, Malayo-Polynesian, Meso Philippine, Central Philippine, Bisayan, Central, Warayan. *Lg Use:* Those with less than high school education are highly bilingual in Tagalog and Naga Bicolano.

Sorsogon, Waray (Southern Sorsogon, Bikol Sorsogon, Gubat) [srv] 185,000 (1975 census). Southern Sorsogon Province. *Class:* Austronesian, Malayo-Polynesian, Meso Philippine, Central Philippine, Bisayan, Central, Warayan, Gubat. *Dialects:* Comprehension of Masbaten: 63% to 91%; Central Bicolano (Naga): 71% to 82%; Tagalog 85% to 91%. Close to Waray-Waray. *Lg Use:* Bilingual in Tagalog, Central Bicolano, or Masbatenyo.

Spanish [spa] 2,658 in the Philippines (1990 census). Mainly in Manila. *Lg Use:* Formerly the official language. Used by a few families as first language. *Other:* Christian. See main entry under Spain.

Subanen, Central (Sindangan Subanun) [syb] 140,011 (2000 WCD). Eastern Zamboanga Peninsula, Mindanao, Sulu Archipelago. *Class:* Austronesian, Malayo-Polynesian, Southern Philippine, Subanun, Eastern. *Dialect:* Eastern Kolibugan (Eastern Kalibugan). 71% intelligibility of Lapuyan. Lexical similarity 79% with Siocon. *Lg Use:* High comprehension of Cebuano. *Lg Dev:* Literacy rate in first language: 50%. Literacy rate in second language: 50%. NT: 1992. *Other:* Traditional religion, Christian, Muslim.

Subanen, Northern (Tuboy Subanon) [stb] 10,000 (1985 SIL). Tuboy: Sergio Osmeña, Mutia; Zamboanga del Norte; Salog: Misamis Occidental, Mindanao. *Class:* Austronesian, Malayo-Polynesian, Southern Philippine, Subanun, Eastern. *Dialects:* Dapitan, Salog (Salug), Dikayu. 63% intelligibility of Sindanga, 40% of Lapuyan. Lexical similarity 87% of Sindanga. *Lg Use:* Limited comprehension of Cebuano.

Subanon, Kolibugan (Kolibugan, Calibugan, Kalibugan) [skn] 20,000 (1998 SIL). Mindanao, Zamboanga Peninsula, southern Zamboanga del Norte and Zamboanga del Sur provinces. *Class:* Austronesian, Malayo-Polynesian, Southern Philippine, Subanun, Kalibugan. *Dialects:* Close to Western Subanon, but there are limitations on inherent intelligibility between the two. Lexical and grammatical differences. *Lg Use:* Culture and attitudes require Kolibugan to be viewed as separate from Western Subanon. *Lg Dev:* Literacy rate in first language: 39%. Literacy rate in second language: 39%. *Other:* Muslim, traditional religion.

Subanon, Western (Siocon) [suc] 75,000 (1997 SIL). Mindanao, Zamboanga Peninsula. *Class:* Austronesian, Malayo-Polynesian, Southern Philippine, Subanun, Kalibugan. *Dialect:* Western Kolibugan (Western Kalibugan). Lexical similarity 89% between Siocon and Western Kolibugan. *Lg Dev:* Literacy rate in first language: 39%. Literacy rate in second language: 39%. NT: 1996. *Other:* Christian.

Subanun, Lapuyan (Lapuyen, Margosatubig, Subanen) [laa] 25,000 (1978 SIL). Subpeninsulas of eastern Zamboanga del Sur, Mindanao. *Class:* Austronesian, Malayo-Polynesian, Southern Philippine, Subanun, Eastern. *Dialects:* Lapuyan Subanun speakers understand Sindangan (85%), but not vice versa. *Lg Use:* Low comprehension of Cebuano. *Lg Dev:* NT: 1982.

Sulod (Bukidnon, Mondo) [srg] 14,000 (1980 SIL). Tapaz, Capiz Province; Lambunao, Iloilo Province; Valderrama, Antique Province, Panay. *Class:* Austronesian, Malayo-Polynesian, Meso Philippine, Central Philippine.

Surigaonon [sul] 344,974 (1990 census). Surigao, Carrascal, Cantilan, Madrid, Lanusa. *Class:* Austronesian, Malayo-Polynesian, Meso Philippine, Central Philippine, Bisayan, South, Surigao. *Dialects:* Jaun-Jaun, Cantilan (Kantilan), Naturalis, Surigaonon. Lexical similarity 82% with Dibabawon Manobo, 81% with Agusan Manobo, 69% with Butuanon. *Lg Use:* Speakers have high proficiency in Cebuano.

Tadyawan (Pula, Tadianan, Balaban) [tdy] 4,146 (2000 WCD). East central Mindoro. *Class:* Austronesian, Malayo-Polynesian, Northern Philippine, Bashiic-Central Luzon-Northern Mindoro, Northern Mindoro. *Lg Use:* Most Tadyawan understand Tawbuid. A lot of intermarriage with the Tawbuid.

Tagabawa (Tagabawa Bagobo, Tagabawa Manobo) [bgs] 43,000 (1998 SIL). Mindanao, Davao City, slopes of Mt. Apo. *Class:* Austronesian, Malayo-Polynesian, Southern Philippine, Manobo, South. *Dialects:* 45% comprehension of Tigwa Manobo; low comprehension of Cebuano. Lexical similarity 62% with Sarangani Manobo; 34% with Bagobo (Giangan). *Lg Dev:* Literacy rate in second language: 90%. Radio programs. Bible portions: 1952–1992. *Other:* The official name is Tagabawa.

Tagalog [tgl] 14,486,888 in the Philippines (1995 census). Population total all countries: 15,900,098. Manila, most of Luzon, and Mindoro. Also spoken in Canada, Guam, Saudi Arabia, United Arab Emirates, United Kingdom, USA. *Class:* Austronesian, Malayo-Polynesian, Meso Philippine, Central Philippine, Tagalog. *Dialects:* Lubang, Manila, Marinduque, Bataan, Batangas, Bulacan, Tanay-Paete, Tayabas. *Lg Dev:* Taught in primary and secondary schools. Roman script. Grammar. Bible: 1905. *Other:* Used as the basis for the development of Filipino. Christian.

Tagbanwa (Tagbanua, Apurawnon, Aborlan Tagbanwa) [tbw] 10,000 (2002 SIL). 5% monolinguals. Palawan, in scattered communities ranging from about 120 km south to 60 km north of Puerto Princesa, on both sides of the island. *Class:* Austronesian, Malayo-Polynesian, Meso Philippine, Palawano. *Dialects:* Intelligibility of Quezon Palawano (Central) 66%, of Cuyonon 77%. Lexical similarity 65% with Quezon Palawano, 71% with Batak, 54% with Cuyonon. *Lg Use:* Used exclusively with other Tagbanwa in all situations. All ages. In the presence of non-Tagbanwa Filipinos, Tagbanwas are somewhat ashamed of being Tagbanwa, and speak Tagalog as they are able. Most also speak Tagalog to varying degrees. Very few would be highly bilingual. On the West coast, which is more isolated and less developed than the East coast, Tagalog comprehension and speaking ability are fairly low. *Lg Dev:* Literacy rate in first language: 36%. Literacy rate in second language: 36%. Syllabary formerly used by Tagbanwa and Palawano. NT: 1992. *Other:* Sea level to 300 meters. Fishermen; agriculturalists. Traditional religion, Christian.

Tagbanwa, Calamian (Kalamian, Calamiano, Kalamianon, Karamiananen) [tbk] 8,472 (1990 census). Coron Island, north of Palawan, northern Palawan and Busuanga. Baras is on eastern coast of Palawan opposite Dumaran Island. *Class:* Austronesian, Malayo-Polynesian, Meso Philippine, Kalamian. *Dialect:* Baras. Baras has 94% intelligibility of Calamian. Lexical similarity 80% between Calamian and Baras. *Lg Dev:* Literacy rate in first language: 40% to 50%. Literacy rate in second language: 40% to 50%. NT: 2002.

Tagbanwa, Central [tgt] 2,000 (1985 SIL). Northern Palawan. *Class:* Austronesian, Malayo-Polynesian, Meso Philippine, Kalamian. *Dialects:* Intelligibility of Tagbanwa (Lamane) 29%, 56% of Calamian Tagbanwa, 61% of Cuyonon. Lexical similarity 56% with Tagbanwa (Lamane), 57% with Calamian Tagbanwa, 48% with Cuyonon, 40% with Tagalog. *Lg Use:* Low comprehension of Tagalog.

Tausug (Taw Sug, Sulu, Suluk, Tausog, Moro Joloano, Jolohano, Sinug Tausug) [tsg] 900,000 in the Philippines (2000 SIL). 250,000 monolinguals. Population total all countries: 1,022,000. Jolo, Sulu Archipelago. Palawan Island, Basilan Island, Zamboanga City and environs. Also spoken in Indonesia (Kalimantan), Malaysia (Sabah). *Class:* Austronesian, Malayo-Polynesian, Meso Philippine, Central Philippine, Bisayan, South, Butuan-Tausug. *Lg Use:* Language of wider communication. Vigorous. Mapun, Central Sama, Balangingi Sama, Pangutaran Sama, Southern Sama, and Yakan speakers speak it as second language. All domains, local administration, commerce, religion, letters. All ages. Older people feel that young people do not know the 'deep' Tausug. Positive language attitude. *Lg Dev:* Literacy rate in first language: 50%. Literacy rate in second language: 50%. Roman, Arabic, Malay-Arabic scripts; Malay-Arabic script in Malaysia. Radio programs. Dictionary. NT: 1985–1998. *Other:* Agriculturalists; fishermen; traders. Muslim, Christian.

Tawbuid, Eastern (Bangon, Batangan, Tabuid, Taubuid, Tiron, Suri, Barangan, Binatangan, Fanawbuid) [bnj] 7,187 (2000 WCD). Central Mindoro. *Class:* Austronesian, Malayo-Polynesian, Meso Philippine, South Mangyan, Buhid-Taubuid. *Dialects:* Western Tawbuid is different enough to need separate literature. *Lg Dev:* Bible portions: 1980.

Tawbuid, Western (Batangan Taubuid, Fanawbuid, Western Taubuid) [twb] 6,809 (2000 WCD). Central Mindoro; Occidental Mindor, mainly Sablayan and Calintaan municipalities; Oriental Mindoro, Bongabon Municipality. *Class:* Austronesian, Malayo-Polynesian, Meso Philippine, South Mangyan, Buhid-Taubuid. *Dialects:* Different enough from Eastern Tawbuid to need separate literature. Closest to Buhid. *Lg Use:* All ages. Speakers also use Tagalog. *Lg Dev:* NT: 2001. *Other:* Christian, traditional religion.

Tboli (Tiboli, T'boli, "Tagabili") [tbl] 95,323 (2000 WCD). 10,000 monolinguals. Ethnic population: 100,000 to 120,000. South Cotabato Province, Southwestern Mindanao. *Class:* Austronesian, Malayo-Polynesian, South Mindanao, Bilic, Tboli. *Dialects:* Central Tboli, Western Tboli, Southern Tboli. *Lg Use:* All ages. They are speaking their language to each other more freely in buses, surrounding towns, etc. Tboli learn Ilongo easily. *Lg Dev:* Literacy rate in first language: Perhaps 50% to 60%. Literacy rate in second language: Perhaps 50% to 60%. Literacy program in heretofore unreached coastal mountain range. They operate their own government school. Roman script. Poetry. Grammar. NT: 1979–1992. *Other:* Isolating. Mountain slope. 300 to 1,600 meters. Swidden agriculturalists; hunter-gatherers. Christian, traditional religion.

Tiruray (Tirurai, Teduray) [tiy] 50,000 (2002 SIL). Ethnic population: 50,000. Upi, Cotabato, Mindanao. *Class:* Austronesian, Malayo-Polynesian, South Mindanao, Tiruray. *Lg Dev:* Literacy rate in first language: 49%. Literacy rate in second language: 49%. NT: 1983.

Waray-Waray (Samareño, Samaran, Samar-Leyte, Waray, Binisaya) [war] 2,437,688 (1990 census). Northern and eastern Samar-Leyte. *Class:* Austronesian, Malayo-Polynesian, Meso Philippine, Central Philippine, Bisayan, Central, Warayan, Samar-Waray. *Dialects:* Waray, Samar-Leyte, Northern Samar. Several dialects. *Lg Use:* Language of wider communication. *Lg Dev:* Bible: 1937–1984.

Yakan (Yacan) [yka] 105,545 in the Philippines (1990 census). 33% monolinguals. Population includes 86,926 in Basilan Province. Population total all countries: 116,332. Sulu Archipelago, Basilan Island and small surrounding islands, Sakol Island, east coast of Zamboanga peninsula, western Mindanao. They live more concentrated away from the coast. Also spoken in Malaysia (Sabah). *Class:*

Austronesian, Malayo-Polynesian, Sama-Bajaw, Yakan. *Lg Use:* Vigorous. All domains. Local administration, commerce, religion, oral traditional literature. Positive language attitude. Percentage of monolinguals higher among older population, especially women. Younger people and men tend to be multilingual. 60% speak Tausug, 10% Chavacano (1990 census). Educated persons can communicate in Tagalog and English to some extent as well. Pilipino (Tagalog) is the medium of instruction in elementary school, English in secondary school. *Lg Dev:* Literacy rate in first language: 35%. Literacy rate in second language: 25%. Roman script. Newspapers. Radio programs. Dictionary. NT: 1984. *Other:* Land division in families and increasing population pushes young people to seek employment in cities or other countries. Islands, mountain slope, riverine. Little virgin forest left. Coconut palms, rubber trees. Sea level to 1,000 meters. Agriculturalists. Muslim.

Yogad [yog] 16,043 (1990 census). Echague and several nearby towns, Isabela Province, Luzon. *Class:* Austronesian, Malayo-Polynesian, Northern Philippine, Northern Luzon, Northern Cordilleran, Ibanagic, Ibanag. *Dialects:* Related to Ibanag and Gaddang. Lexical similarity 52% with Ilocano, 66% with Itawit, 63% with Ibanag. *Lg Use:* Highly bilingual in Ilocano. *Lg Dev:* 77% literacy in Isabela in 1955. Dictionary. Grammar. *Other:* VSO.

Qatar

State of Qatar, Dawlet al-Qatar. 840,290. National or official language: Standard Arabic. Literacy rate: 60% to 76%. Also includes Malayalam (6,500), Tamil (2,200), Urdu (19,950), Balochi, people from the Philippines (25,000), Sri Lanka. Deaf population: 31,103. The number of languages listed for Qatar is 3. Of those, all are living languages.

Arabic, Gulf Spoken (Khaliji, Qatari, Gulf Arabic) [afb] 103,600 in Qatar (1986). *Dialects:* North Qatari Arabic, South Qatari Arabic. *Other:* Muslim. See main entry under Iraq.

Arabic, Standard [arb] Middle East, North Africa. *Lg Use:* Official language. Used for education, official purposes, formal speeches. See main entry under Saudi Arabia.

Farsi, Western (Persian) [pes] 73,000 in Qatar (1993). *Other:* Muslim. See main entry under Iran.

Russia (Asia)

Also see Russia in Europe for a listing of languages in Europe. See Russia in Europe for the list of languages in Europe. Also includes Baltic Romani (20,000), Georgian (130,000), Kazakh (636,000), Korean, Lomavren, Mandarin Chinese, North Azerbaijani (336,000), Northern Uzbek (61,588), Osetin (400,000), Plautdietsch, Tajiki (38,000), Turkish, Turkmen, Udi (1,000), Ukrainian (4,363,000). The number of languages listed for Russia (Asia) is 45. Of those, 42 are living languages and 3 are extinct. See maps beginning on page 822.

Ainu [ain] South Sakhalin Island and southern Kuril Islands. *Dialects:* Sakhalin (Saghilin), Taraika, Hokkaido (Ezo, Yezo), Kuril (Shikotan). *Lg Use:* The last speaker of Sakhalin dialect died in 1994. Except for 15 speakers (1996), the Ainu in Japan speak Japanese. *Other:* The Ainu spoken in China is a different, unrelated language. Nearly extinct. See main entry under Japan.

Aleut (Unangany, Unangan, Unanghan) [ale] 190 in Russia (2002 K. Matsumura). 5 on Bering Island Atkan (1995 M. Krauss). Ethnic population: 702 (1989 census). Nikolskoye

settlement, Bering Island, Commander (Komandor) Islands. *Dialect:* Beringov (Bering, Atkan). *Lg Use:* All speakers of Bering Island Atkan are 60 years and older (1995 M. Krauss). Neutral language attitude to mild support. Most ethnic group members in Russia speak Russian as first language. *Lg Dev:* Aleut is taught in school until the fourth grade. *Other:* From 1820 to 1840 dozens of Aleut families were brought from various islands to the Komandor Islands. Until the 1960s there were two villages on Bering and Medny islands. From the 1950s to the 1980s children were sent by the state to boarding schools. Christian. See main entry under USA.

Aleut, Mednyj (Medny, Copper, Copper Island Aleut, Attuan, Copper Island Attuan, Creolized Attuan) [mud] 10 (1995 M. Krauss). Copper Island, Komandor Islands. *Class:* Mixed Language, Russian-Aleut. *Lg Use:* Aleut is taught in school until the fourth grade. Most ethnic group members in Russia speak Russian as first language. *Lg Dev:* Grammar. *Other:* From 1820 to 1840 dozens of Aleut families were brought from various islands to the Komandor Islands. Until the 1960s there were two villages on Bering and Medny islands. From the 1950s to the 1980s children were sent by the state to boarding schools. Christian. Nearly extinct.

Altai, Northern (Teleut, Telengut, Telengit) [atv] 29,098 (2000 WCD). Gorno-Altai Ao mountains, bordering on Mongolia and China. *Class:* Altaic, Turkic, Northern. *Dialects:* No comprehension of Southern Altai. Considered a separate language outside the region. Teleut may be a separate language. *Lg Use:* Southern Altai is rejected by children. Speakers also use Russian. *Other:* Traditional religion, secularist.

Altai, Southern (Oirot, Oyrot, Altai) [alt] 20,000 (1993 Janhunen). Ethnic population: 68,686. Gorno-Altai Ao mountains, bordering on Mongolia and China. *Class:* Altaic, Turkic, Northern. *Dialects:* Altai Proper (Altai-Kizhi, Altaj Kizi, Maina-Kizhi, Southern Altai), Talangit (Talangit-Tolos, Chuy). Northern Altai and Southern Altai are not inherently intelligible, although there is a dialect cluster between them. *Lg Use:* Traditional domains. Written Altai is based on Southern Altai, but is rejected by Northern Altai children. Russian is used as the second language by all except older adults as a contact language, for literature, and urban professional and cultural life. *Lg Dev:* Cyrillic script. Bible portions: 1910–1996. *Other:* Different from Oirat (Kalmyk-Oirat), a Mongolian language. Mountain slope. Animal husbandry: cattle; agriculturalists; hunters. Traditional religion, secularist.

Alutor (Alyutor, Aliutor, Olyutor) [alr] 100 to 200 (2000 A. E. Kibrik). Ethnic population: 2,000 (1997 M. Krauss). Koryak National District, northeast Kamchatka Peninsula, many in Vyvenka village, 2 families in Rekinniki, and individual families in Tilichiki and Tymlyt. Some speakers are separated at considerable distances and without regular contact. *Class:* Chukotko-Kamchatkan, Northern, Koryak-Alyutor. *Dialects:* Alutorskij (Alutor Proper), Karaginskij (Karaga), Palanskij (Palana). Considered a dialect of Koryak until recently. *Lg Use:* Speakers are shifting to Russian. Used in the home. Older adults speak Alutor actively and some are monolinguals; the middle aged know it passively; those younger than 35 know only Russian (1997). *Lg Dev:* Dictionary. Grammar. *Other:* Children were sent to boarding schools during the 1950s to the 1970s.

Bohtan Neo-Aramaic [bhn] *Lg Use:* Most over 60. Younger generations tend to shift to Georgian or Russian. *Other:* Originally spoken by villagers in Anatolia, Ottoman Empire, east of the Tigris River (present-day southeastern Turkey). They fled to Russia during World War I. Christian. See main entry under Georgia.

Buriat, Russia (Buryat, Buriat-Mongolian, Northern Mongolian) [bxr] 318,000 (1990 National Geographic). Ethnic population: 422,000. East of Lake Baikal, Siberia, bordering on Mongolia. Ulan Ude is the capital. *Class:* Altaic, Mongolian, Eastern, Oirat-Khalkha, Khalkha-Buriat, Buriat. *Dialects:* Ekhirit, Unga, Ninzne-Udinsk, Barguzin, Tunka, Oka, Alar, Bohaan (Bokhan), Bulagat. The Buriat in newspapers is that of the area around Irkutsk, west of Lake Baikal. The Buriat east of the lake is less influenced by Russian and is more like that in Mongolia. The literary dialect differs considerably from those spoken in Mongolia and China, which are influenced by other languages. Khori is the main dialect in Russia. Speakers in Russia apparently understand each other well. *Lg Use:* The younger generation in cities are fluent in Russian, which is the contact language with the outside world. 72% speak Russian as second language. *Lg Dev:* Literacy rate in second language: Those on both sides of the lake are fully literate in the literary style. Cyrillic script. Newspapers. Bible: 1846. *Other:* Heavily influenced by Russian. East: pastoralists: cattle, horses, sheep, goats, camels; west: agriculturalists. Buddhist (Lamaist), traditional religion.

Chukot (Chukcha, Chuchee, Chukchee, Luoravetlan, Chukchi) [ckt] 10,000 (1997 M. Krauss). Ethnic population: 15,000. Chukchi Peninsula, Chukot and Koryak National Okrug, northeastern Siberia. *Class:* Chukotko-Kamchatkan, Northern, Chukot. *Dialects:* Uellanskij, Pevekskij, Enmylinskij, Nunligranskij, Xatyrskij, Chaun, Enurmin, Yanrakinot. *Lg Use:* 60% of the Chuckchi speak Chukot. Few domains except perhaps family. Nomadic groups have adult and some children speakers. Settled groups have few or no children speakers. Although those under 50 speak Russian with varying proficiency, nomadic groups resist Russian language and culture. People are mildly to strongly supportive toward Chukot. Speakers also use Russian, Yakut, Lamut, or Yukaghir. *Lg Dev:* Dictionary. Grammar. *Other:* School at Anadyr. Chukchi in Magadan area are nomadic. Reindeer herdsmen. Shamanist.

Chulym (Chulym-Turkish, Chulim, Melets Tatar, Chulym Tatar) [clw] 500 (1990). Ethnic population: 500 (1990 A. E. Kibrik). Basin of the Chulym River north of the Altay Mountains, a tributary of the Ob River. *Class:* Altaic, Turkic, Western, Uralian. *Dialects:* Lower Chulym, Middle Chulym. Close to Shor; some consider them one language. The government considers them separate. *Lg Use:* Speakers also use Russian. *Other:* Spoken in villages. Also spoken by the Kacik (Kazik, Kuarik).

Dolgan [dlg] 5,000 (1994 UBS). Ethnic population: 6,945 (1989 census). Yakut ASSR. *Class:* Altaic, Turkic, Northern. *Lg Use:* 82% of the ethnic group speaks Dolgan. Few key domains. A few to half the children speak Dolgan. Positive language attitude. Speakers also use Russian. *Lg Dev:* Cyrillic script. *Other:* A separate language from Yakut. Dolgan is the contact language on the Tajmyr Peninsula, and is spoken also by Evenki, Nganasan, and long-term Russian residents. Several publications in Dolgan. Traditional religion, Shamanist.

Enets, Forest (Yenisei Samoyedic, Bay Enets, Pe-Bae) [enf] 40 (1995 M. Krauss). Ethnic population: 209 with Tundra Enets (1989 census). Taimyr National Okrug. Along the Yenisei River's lower course, upstream from Dudinka. The Forest variety is in the Potapovo settlement of the Dudinka Region. *Class:* Uralic, Samoyed. *Dialects:* Forest and Tundra Enets are barely intelligible to each other's speakers. It is transitional between Yura and Nganasan. For a time it was officially considered part of Nenets. *Lg Use:* Under 10% of the ethnic group speaks Enets. Used in the home. All speakers older than 40 years. About half of the ethnic middle aged speak Enets, but no

children or adolescents. People are neutral to mildly supportive towards Enets. All speakers are bilingual or trilingual. *Lg Dev:* Taught in school. Dictionary. Grammar. *Other:* In summer they wander between the left bank of the Yenisei River and the Yenisei Gulf; in winter in the grove tundras between the left tributaries of the Yenisei and Pyasino Lake on the Kheta River on the Taimyr Peninsula. Russian and Nenets people also live in some settlements. Those who assimilate with the Nenets keep the traditional way of life, those with the Russians are acculturating to modern ways. Intermarriage with other ethnic groups is uncommon. Nearly extinct.

Enets, Tundra (Yenisei Samoyedic, Madu, Somatu) [enh] 30 (1995 M. Krauss). Ethnic population: 209 together with Forest Enets (1990 census). Taimyr National Okrug. Along the Yenisei River's lower course, upstream from Dudinka. 'Tundra' in the Vorontzovo settlement of the Ust-Yenisei Region. *Class:* Uralic, Samoyed. *Dialects:* Tundra and Forest Enets barely intelligible to each other's speaker. It is transitional between Yura and Nganasan. For a time it was officially considered part of Nenets. *Lg Use:* Under 10% of the ethnic groups speaks Enets. Used in the home. All speakers older than 40 years. About half of the ethnic middle aged speak Enets, but no children or adolescents. Neutral language attitude. All speakers are bilingual or trilingual. *Lg Dev:* Taught in school. Dictionary. Grammar. *Other:* In summer they wander between the left bank of the Yenisei River and the Yenisei Gulf; in winter in the grove tundras between the left tributaries of the Yenisei and Pyasino Lake on the Kheta River on the Taimyr Peninsula. Russian and Nenets people also live in some settlements. Those who assimilate with the Nenets keep the traditional way of life, those with the Russians are acculturating to modern ways. Intermarriage with other ethnic groups is uncommon. Nearly extinct.

Even (Lamut, Ewen, Eben, Orich, Ilqan) [eve] 7,543 (1989 census). Ethnic population: 17,199 (1989 census). Yakutia and the Kamchatka Peninsula, widely scattered over the entire Okhotsk Arctic coast. *Class:* Altaic, Tungus, Northern, Even. *Dialects:* Arman, Indigirka, Kamchatka, Kolyma-Omolon, Okhotsk, Ola, Tompon, Upper Kolyma, Sakkyryr, Lamunkhin. Ola dialect is not accepted by speakers of other dialects. A dialect cluster. It was incorrectly reported to be a Yukaghir dialect. *Lg Use:* 30% to 50% of the ethnic group speaks Even. Few key domains. Most speakers older than 30 years. Positive language attitude. Speakers also use Russian, Yakut. *Lg Dev:* Dictionary. Grammar. Bible portions: 1880. *Other:* Some literature available. Reindeer herdsmen, hunters. Christian (Russian Orthodox).

Evenki (Ewenki, Tungus, Chapogir, Avanki, Avankil, Solon, Khamnigan) [evn] 9,000 in Russia (1997 M. Krauss). Ethnic population: 30,000 in Russia (1997 M. Krauss). Evenki National Okrug, Sakhalin Island. Capital is Ture. *Dialects:* Manegir, Yerbogocen, Nakanna, Ilimpeya, Tutoncana, Podkamennaya Tunguska, Cemdalsk, Vanavara, Baykit, Poligus, Uchama, Cis-Baikalia, Sym, Tokmo-Upper Lena, Nepa, Lower Nepa Tungir, Kalar, Tokko, Aldan Timpton, Tommot, Jeltulak, Uchur, Ayan-Maya, Kur-Urmi, Tuguro-Chumikan, Sakhalin, Zeya-Bureya. *Lg Use:* Half or fewer of the ethnic group speaks Evenki. Used in the home. A few to none of the children. Positive language attitude. Speakers also use Russian, Yakut, or Buriat. *Lg Dev:* Literacy rate in second language: Nearly all. *Other:* Shamanist, Buddhist (Lamaist), Christian. See main entry under China.

Gilyak (Nivkh, Nivkhi) [niv] 1,089 (1989 census). Population includes 100 Amur, 300 Sakhalin (1995 M. Krauss). Ethnic population: 4,673 (1989 census), including

2,000 Amur, 2,700 Sakhalin (1995 M. Krauss). Sakhalin Island, many in Nekrasovka and Nogliki villages, small numbers in Rybnoe, Moskalvo, Chir-Unvd, Viakhtu, and other villages, and along the Amur River in Aleevka village. *Class:* Language Isolate. *Dialects:* Amur, East Sakhalin Gilyak, North Sakhalin Gilyak. The Amur and East Sakhalin dialects have difficult inherent intelligibility of each other. North Sakhalin is between them linguistically. *Lg Use:* Forced resettlement has weakened language use. Some are scattered and without regular contact with other speakers. Under 10% of the ethnic group speaks Gilyak. Used in the home. Most speakers are older adults. People neutral to mildly supportive toward Gilyak. All members of the ethnic group are reported to be bilingual or monolingual in Russian. *Lg Dev:* Taught through second grade in settlements at Nogliki and Nekrasovka. Not taught at Amur. Roman and Cyrillic scripts. Dictionary. Grammar. *Other:* Fishermen; agriculturalists.

Itelmen (Itelymem, Western Itelmen, Kamchadal, Kamchatka) [itl] 60 (2000). Ethnic population: 2,481 (1989 census). Southern Kamchatka Peninsula, Koryak Autonomous District, Tigil Region, primarily in Kovran and Upper Khairiuzovo villages, west coast of the Kamchatka River. *Class:* Chukotko-Kamchatkan, Southern. *Dialects:* Sedanka, Kharyuz, Itelmen, Xajrjuzovskij, Napanskij, Sopocnovskij. *Lg Use:* Speakers are shifting to Russian. Used in the home. Taught in school through fourth grade. Speakers are primarily older adults. People are neutral to mildly supportive. *Lg Dev:* Taught in primary schools. Dictionary. Bible portions: 1996. *Other:* From the 1950s to the 1980s the state sent all children to boarding schools. All are reported to be acculturated. Shamanist.

Kamas (Kamassian) [xas] Extinct. Sayan Mountains, Abalakovo village. *Class:* Uralic, Samoyed. *Dialects:* Kamassian, Koibal. *Lg Dev:* Grammar. *Other:* Originally spoken in Siberia. Different from the Kamassian dialect of Khakas.

Karagas (Tofa, Tofalar, Sayan Samoyed, Kamas, Karagass) [kim] 25 to 30 (2001). Ethnic population: 730 (1989 census). Siberia, Irkutsk Region. *Class:* Altaic, Turkic, Northern. *Lg Use:* 20% to 40% of the ethnic group speaks Karagas. Used in the home. Speakers are older adults. People neutral to mildly supportive toward Karagas. Speakers also use Russian. *Lg Dev:* Dictionary. Grammar. *Other:* The official name is 'Tofa' or 'Tofalar'. Christian (Russian Orthodox). Nearly extinct.

Kerek [krk] 2 (1997 M. Krauss). There were 200 to 400 speakers in 1900. Ethnic population: 400. Cape Navarin, in Chukot villages. *Class:* Chukotko-Kamchatkan, Northern, Koryak-Alyutor. *Dialects:* Mainypilgino (Majna-Pil'ginskij), Khatyrka (Xatyrskij). Previously considered a dialect of Chukot. *Lg Use:* Speakers are now assimilated into Chukot. *Other:* Nearly extinct.

Ket (Yenisei Ostyak, Yenisey Ostiak, Imbatski-Ket) [ket] 550 to 990 (1995 M. Krauss). Ethnic population: 1,222 (2000). Upper Yenisei Valley, Krasnoyarski krai, Turukhansk, and Baikitsk regions, Sulomai, Bakhta, Verkhneimbatsk, Kellog, Kangatovo, Surgutikha, Vereshchagino, Baklanikha, Farkovo, Goroshikha, and Maiduka villages. Between the Khanti and Mansi, eastern Siberia. *Class:* Yeniseian. *Lg Use:* Under 10% of the ethnic group speaks Ket. No other extant related languages: the Arin, Assan, and Kott peoples became extinct in the 19th century. Used in the home. All speakers are older adults. People are negative to mildly supportive toward Ket. Speakers also use Russian. *Lg Dev:* Taught in 5 schools. Dictionary. Grammar. *Other:* Traditional way of life has changed. Traditional religion.

Khakas (Khakhas, Khakhass, Abakan Tatar, Yenisei Tatar) [kjh] 64,800 in Russia (1993 UBS). Population total all countries: 64,810. Ethnic population: 80,000 in Russia. Khakassia, north of the Altai Mountains, and a few north of the Oblast. Ababan is the capital. Also spoken in China. *Class:* Altaic, Turkic, Northern. *Dialects:* Sagai (Sagaj), Beltir, Kacha (Kaca), Kyzyl, Shor, Kamassian. *Lg Use:* Speakers also use Russian. *Lg Dev:* Cyrillic script. Bible portions: 1995. *Other:* Animal husbandry: sheep, goats, cattle, horses; industrial workers. Traditional religion, Christian (Russian Orthodox).

Khanty (Khanti, Hanty, Xanty, Ostyak) [kca] 12,000 (1994 Salminen, 1994 Janhunen). Ethnic population: 21,000. Khanty-Mansi National Okrug. Farther east than the Mansi, along the Ob River. *Class:* Uralic. *Dialect:* Northern Khanti, Eastern Khanti, Southern Khanti, Vach (Vasyugan). Intelligibility is difficult between geographically distant dialects. Three dialect groups. Vach is an 'archaic' dialect. The dialect used in writing is rejected by many speakers. *Lg Use:* 20% to 60% of the ethnic group speaks Khanty. Northern Khanty has 9,000 speakers out of 15,000, Eastern Khanty has 3,000 speakers out of 5,000, Southern Khanty has few or no speakers out of 1,000. Few key domains. Few children speak Khanty. Positive language attitude. Russian is used in school. *Lg Dev:* Dictionary. Grammar. Bible portions: 1868. *Other:* Hunters; fishermen; animal husbandry: cattle. Traditional religion.

Koryak (Nymylan) [kpy] 3,500 (1997 M. Krauss). Ethnic population: 7,000. Koryak National Okrug, south of the Chukot; northern half of Kamchatka Peninsula and adjacent continent. *Class:* Chukotko-Kamchatkan, Northern, Koryak-Alyutor. *Dialects:* Cavcuvenskij (Chavchuven), Apokinskij (Apukin), Kamenskij (Kamen), Xatyrskij, Paren, Itkan, Palan, Gin. Chavchuven, Palan, and Kamen are apparently not inherently intelligible. *Lg Use:* 30% to 50% of the ethnic group speaks Koryak. Few key domains. A few children speak Koryak. Neutral to mildly supportive attitude toward Koryak. Speakers also use Russian. *Lg Dev:* Taught in school. Dictionary. Grammar. *Other:* Coast: fishermen; hunters; inland: animal husbandry: cattle. Traditional religion, Christian.

Mansi (Vogul, Vogulich, Mansiy, Voguly) [mns] 3,184 (1990 census). Northern Mansi has 3,000 speakers out of 7,000, Eastern Mansi has 100 speakers out of 1,000 population. Ethnic population: 8,500 including Northern Mansi 7,000, Eastern Mansi 1,000 (1989 census). Western Siberia between Komi-Zyrian and west of the Urals, between Urals and Ob River. *Class:* Uralic. *Dialects:* Northern Vogul (Sos'va, Sosyvin, Upper Lozyvin), Southern Vogul (Tavdin), Western Vogul (Pelym, Vagily, Middle Lozyvin, Lower Lozyvin), Eastern Vogul (Kondin). Intelligibility between geographically distant dialects is difficult. May be 4 languages. Closest to Hungarian. *Lg Use:* 50% or less of the ethnic group speaks Mansi. Southern Mansi has been extinct since about 1950. Western Mansi is nearly extinct or extinct. Few domains. Few to half of the children speak Mansi. Eastern Mansi is used only by older adults. People are neutral to strongly supportive toward Mansi. Russian is used in education. *Lg Dev:* Dictionary. Grammar. Bible portions: 1868–1882. *Other:* Hunters; fishermen; animal husbandry: cattle. Traditional religion.

Mator [mtm] Extinct. Sayan Mountains Region. *Class:* Uralic, Samoyed. *Dialects:* Mator, Taigi, Karagas. *Lg Use:* Became extinct at the beginning of the 19th century.

Mongolian, Halh (Halh, Khalkha Mongolian, Mongol, Central Mongolian) [khk] 2,095 in Russia (2000 WCD). Buryat. *Dialects:* Khalkha (Halh), Dariganga, Urat, Ujumuchin. *Other:* Halh serves as the basis for modern literary Mongolian. Buddhist. See main entry under Mongolia.

Nanai (Nanaj, Gold, Goldi, Hezhen, Hezhe, Heche) [gld] 5,760 in Russia (1990 census). Population total all countries: 5,772. Ethnic population: 11,877 in Russia. In the extreme Soviet far east, confluence of the Amur and Ussuri rivers, scattered in Ussuri Valley and Sikhote-Alin, settled more densely in the Amur Valley below Khabarovsk. Also spoken in China. *Class:* Altaic, Tungus, Southern, Southeast, Nanaj. *Dialects:* Sunggari, Torgon, Kuro-Urmi, Ussuri, Akani, Birar, Kila, Samagir. The dialects are quite distinct. *Lg Use:* 48.4% or less of the ethnic group speaks Nanai. Used in the home. Youngest speakers are over 30, with most over 50. Older adults use Chinese. People neutral to mildly supportive toward Nanai. Speakers also use Russian. *Lg Dev:* Dictionary. Bible portions: 1884. *Other:* Shamanist.

Negidal (Negidaly, Neghidal) [neg] 100 to 170 (1995 M. Krauss). Ethnic population: 500 (1995 M. Krauss). Lower reaches of the Amur River, in two regions of the Khabarovsk Krai (Kamenka settlement and Im, and in the Paulina Osipenko Region). *Class:* Altaic, Tungus, Northern, Negidal. *Dialects:* Nizovsk, Verkhovsk. *Lg Use:* Under 10% of the ethnic group speaks Negidal. Older adults have a good command of the language, younger adults can understand it, children speak and understand only Russian. Russian used for most domains. *Lg Dev:* Dictionary. Grammar. *Other:* From the 1950s to the 1980s the state sent all children to boarding schools. Traditional way of life. Contacts and intermarriage with the Ulch, Nanai, and Nivkh in the Amur area. Traditional religion.

Nenets (Nenec, Nentse, Nenetsy, Yurak, Yurak Samoyed) [yrk] 26,730 (1989 census). Population includes 1,300 Forest Nenets, 25,000 Tundra Nenets. Ethnic population: 34,665 (1989 census) including 2,000 Forest Enets. Northwest Siberia, tundra area from the mouth of the northern Dvina River in northeastern Europe to the delta of the Yenisei in Asia, and a scattering on the Kola Peninsula; Nenets, Yamalo-Nenets, and Taimyr national okrugs. *Class:* Uralic, Samoyed. *Dialects:* Forest Yurak, Tundra Yurak. *Lg Use:* 80% use Nenets in daily life. Few domains. A few to half the children speak Nenets. Positive language attitude. Speakers also use Russian. *Lg Dev:* Most have attended school and read Russian. Dictionary. Grammar. *Other:* Speakers are mainly nomadic. Reindeer herdsmen. Christian, traditional religion.

Nganasan (Tavgi Samoyed) [nio] 500 (1995 M. Krauss). Ethnic population: 1,300. Taimyr National Okrug, Taimyr Peninsula, Siberia, Ust-Avam village in the Dudinka Region; Volochanka and Novaya villages in the Khatang Region. They are the northernmost people in Russia, near the Yakut, Dolgan, and Evenki peoples. *Class:* Uralic, Samoyed. *Dialects:* Avam, Khatang. *Lg Use:* 20% to 60% of the ethnic group speaks Nganasan. Used in the home. The older and middle and a third of the younger generations have full command of the language. It is even more so in Volochanka. Few children are speakers. Ethnic pride is expressed. Status is enhanced by knowledge of the Nganasan language. People are neutral to mildly supportive toward Nganasan. Russian is used as second language. Dolgan is a separate language, but is also used by Nganasan speakers. They formerly had passive bilingualism or trilingualism with Tundra Enets and Nenets. *Lg Dev:* Taught in school as a second language. Dictionary. Grammar. *Other:* Two ethnic groups: Avam and Vadeyev. They were resettled in several villages they had formerly used as winter quarters or trading posts along their migratory routes in the 1940s. Before that they had intermittent contact with the Tundra Enets and the Nenets. They were formerly officially considered to be part of Nenets. Resettlement has brought close contact with Russian, Ukrainian, Belorussian, and Tatar peoples. Traditional religion, Shamanist.

Oroch (Orochi) [oac] 100 to 150 (1995 M. Krauss). Ethnic population: 900 (1990 census). Eastern Siberia in the Khabarovsk Krai along the rivers that empty into the Tatar Channel, on Amur River not far from the city of Komsomolsk-na-Amure. Many live in the Vanino Region in Datta and Uska-Orochskaya settlements. Some live among the Nanai. *Class:* Altaic, Tungus, Southern, Southeast, Udihe. *Dialects:* Kjakela (Kjakar, Kekar), Namunka, Orichen, Tez. *Lg Use:* 10% or fewer of the ethnic group speak Oroch. Older adults speak Oroch, but not those up to 20 years old, who speak Russian. Russian used for most key domains. *Lg Dev:* Dictionary. Grammar. *Other:* The larger of the two groups lives in the region of Sovetskaja Gavan' on the rivers flowing into the Tatar Strait separating Sakhalin Island from the mainland. Not taught in school. Russians, Ukrainians, and Evenki live among them. For a time it was officially considered part of Udihe. Different from Orok. Traditional religion, Buddhist, Christian.

Orok (Oroc, Ulta, Ujlta, Uilta) [oaa] 30 to 82 in Russia (1995 M. Krauss). Population total all countries: 33 to 85. Ethnic population: 250 to 300 (1995 M. Krauss). Sakhalin Island, Poronajsk District, Poronajsk town, Gastello and Vakhrushev settlements; Nogliki District, Val village, Nogliki settlement. Also spoken in Japan. *Class:* Altaic, Tungus, Southern, Southeast, Nanaj. *Dialects:* Poronaisk (Southern Orok), Val-Nogliki (Nogliki-Val, Northern Orok). Significant differences between dialects. For a while Orok was officially considered part of Nanai. *Lg Use:* Under 10% of the ethnic group speaks Orok. Used in the home. Older adults have high proficiency, the middle generation partial proficiency, children and adolescents no ability in Orok. Youngest fluent speakers are over 50 years of age. Prevalent intermarriage with Russians, Nivkh, Nanai, Evenksi, Negidal, and Korean people. *Lg Dev:* Dictionary. Grammar. *Other:* Speakers have been scattered and have relinquished their traditional way of life. Different from Oroch. Nearly extinct.

Selkup (Ostyak Samoyed) [sel] 1,570 (1994 Salminen, 1994 Janhunen). Northern Sel'kup has 1,400 speakers out of 1,700, Central Sel'kup has 150 speakers out of 1,700, Southern Sel'kup has 20 speakers out of 200. Ethnic population: 3,600. Tom Oblast, Yamalo-Nenets Autonomous District, Krasnoyarski Krai and Tomskaya Oblast. The northern dialect is spoken in Krasnoselkup Region, Krasnoselkup, Sidorovsk, Tolka, Ratta, and Kikiyakki villages; part of the Purovsk Region, Tolka Purovskaya village; adjacent regions of the Krasnoyarski Krai; Kureika village, Kellog, and Turukhan River basin and Baikha. The southern dialect (Tym) is spoken in a range of villages in the northern part of the Tomskaya Oblast. *Class:* Uralic, Samoyed. *Dialects:* Taz (Northern Sel'kup, Tazov-Baishyan), Tym (Central Selk'up, Kety), Narym (Central Sel'kup), Srednyaya Ob-Ket (Southern Sel'kup). A dialect continuum with difficult or impossible intelligibility between the extremes. Speakers in the south are separated from others. *Lg Use:* 20% to 50% of the ethnic group speaks Selkup. Selkup was formerly used as lingua franca by the Ket, Evenki, Nenets, and Khanty. Northern dialect: spoken by 90% of the Selkup, with young adults and younger not having mastered it. Southern dialect: spoken by 30% of the Selkup, with 10% speaking it fluently. Up to half the children speak Selkup. Positive language attitude. Russian used for most key domains except perhaps family. *Lg Dev:* The northern dialect is taught in the schools through fourth grade. Grammar. *Other:* Christian, Shamanist.

Shor (Shortsy, Aba, Kondoma Tatar, Mras Tatar, Kuznets Tatar, Tom-Kuznets Tatar) [cjs] 9,446 (1989 census). Ethnic population: 16,652 (1989 census). Altai Krai, Khakass Ao and Gorno-Altai Ao, on the River Tomy.

Class: Altaic, Turkic, Northern. *Dialects:* Mrassa (Mrasu), Kondoma. Some sources combine Shor and Chulym. *Lg Use:* There is now a revival of study (I. A. Nevskaya 1996). A language association has been formed, and a chair of Shor was formed at the Pedagogical Institute in Novokuzneck. Few domains except perhaps family. Few or no children speakers. Neutral to strongly supportive language attitude. *Lg Dev:* Grammar. *Other:* Shor is different from the Shor dialect of Khakas. Altai missionaries worked out the first alphabet in the middle of the 19th century. Mountain slope. Christian (Russian Orthodox).

Tuvin (Tuva, Tuvan, Tuvia, Tyva, Tofa, Tokha, Soyot, Soyon, Soyod, Tannu-Tuva, Tuba, Tuvinian, Uriankhai, Uriankhai-Monchak, Uryankhai, Diba, Kök Mungak) [tyv] 180,000 in Russia (2001). Population total all countries: 209,400. Tuvin Ao. Capital is Kyzl. Also spoken in China, Mongolia. *Class:* Altaic, Turkic, Northern. *Dialects:* Central Tuvin, Western Tuvin, Northeastern Tuvin (Todzhin), Southeastern Tuvin, Tuba-Kizhi. Sharp dialect differences. *Lg Use:* Speakers use Russian as second language, and Mongolian near the border. *Lg Dev:* Cyrillic script. NT: 2002. *Other:* Until 1944 Tuva was a formally independent state. Hunters; animal husbandry: cattle, horses, sheep, goats, camels, reindeer. Buddhist (Lamaist).

Udihe (Udekhe, Udegeis, Udehe) [ude] 100 (1991 Kibrik). Ethnic population: 1,600 (1991 Kibrik). Siberian far east; Khabarovsk Krai, Gvasiugi settlement, Lazo Region; Arsenievo settlement, Nanai Region; Primorski Krai, Krasny Yar settlement in the Pozharsk Region, Agzu settlement in the Terneisk Region. *Class:* Altaic, Tungus, Southern, Southeast, Udihe. *Dialects:* Khungari, Khor, Anjuski, Samargin, Bikin, Iman, Sikhota Alin. Dialect differences are not great. *Lg Use:* 10% or less of the ethnic group speaks Udihe. Used in the home. Speakers are older adults. *Lg Dev:* Dictionary. Grammar. *Other:* They were resettled into artificial villages, in a Russian-speaking region, with some Ukrainian and Nanai people. Children were sent to boarding schools. 'Hezhe' in China may refer to this. Shamanist. Nearly extinct.

Ulch (Ulchi, Ulcha, Ulych, Olch, Olcha, Olchis, Hoche, Hol-Chih) [ulc] 500 to 1,000 (1995 M. Krauss). Ethnic population: 3,200 (1990 census). Ulch Region of the Khabarovsk Krai along the Amur River and its tributaries, along the coast of the Tatar Channel. Bogorodskove is the capital. Also at Bulava, Dudi, Kalinovka, Mariinskoe, Nizhnaya Gavan, Savinskoe, Mongol, Solontsy, Kolchom, Sofiyskoe, Tur, and Ukhta. *Class:* Altaic, Tungus, Southern, Southeast, Nanaj. *Lg Use:* 40% or less of the ethnic group speak Ulch. Used in the home. The older generation knows the language, middle aged less well, adolescents and young adults passively, children under 20 do not speak it. Speakers also use Russian. *Lg Dev:* Taught in primary schools. Dictionary. *Other:* Close contact with Russian, Ukrainian, Nanai, Nivkh (Gilyak), Negidal, and others.

Yakut (Sakha, Yakut-Sakha) [sah] 363,000 (1993 UBS). Ethnic population: 382,000. Yakutia, near the Arctic Ocean, nearly the entire length of the basin of the middle Lena River and the Aldan and Kolyma rivers; 2,000 miles long. Jakutsk (Yakutsk) is the capital. *Class:* Altaic, Turkic, Northern. *Lg Use:* It is used as second language by some Evenki, Even, and Yukaghir people. A town koine has developed in Jakutsk, which older speakers rejected. A higher percentage of teachers and officials come from this group than from nearby languages. Positive language attitude. Russian is used in higher education. *Lg Dev:* Cyrillic script. Grammar. Bible portions: 1858–2000. *Other:* Nomadic. Fishermen; hunters; agriculturalists. Christian (Russian Orthodox), traditional religion, secular.

Yugh (Yug) [yuu] 2 or 3 (1991 G. K. Verner in Kibrik). Nonfluent speakers. Ethnic population: 10 to 15 (1991 G. K. Verner in Kibrik). Turukhan Region of the Krasnoyarsk Krai at the Vorogovo settlement. Previously they lived along the Yenisei River from Yeniseisk to the mouth of the Dupches. *Class:* Yeniseian. *Lg Dev:* Dictionary. *Other:* No published descriptions of the language (1991). Nearly extinct.

Yukaghir, Northern (Yukagir, Jukagir, Odul, Tundra, Tundre, Northern Yukagir) [ykg] 30 to 150 (1995 M. Krauss, 1989 census). Ethnic population: 230 to 1,100 (1995 M. Krauss, 1989 census). Yakutia and the Kamchatka Peninsula. *Class:* Yukaghir. *Dialects:* Distinct from Southern Yukaghir (Kolyma). It may be distantly related to Altaic or Uralic. *Lg Use:* Used in the home. Speakers are older adults. No sense of ethnic identity between speakers of the two Yukaghir varieties. People neutral or mildly supportive toward Yukaghir. Even is the literary language used. Speakers below 50 years use Russian as second language. All can speak Yakut. Reindeer herdsmen and some other families can speak Even. Chukot is also used. *Lg Dev:* Taught through fourth grade in the Adnriushkino settlement, and as an elective through eighth grade in Nelemnoye. Dictionary. Grammar. *Other:* In the 19th century their territory shrank because of merging clans, military clashes, assimilation with the Even, and later, collectivization. From the 1950s to the 1980s the state sent all children to boarding school. 'Odul' is their name for themselves. SOV; postpositions; genitives, articles, adjectives, numerals, relatives before noun heads; question word not initial or final; 2 prefixes, 6 suffixes; word order focus preverbal, subjects and topics tend to be initial; affixes indicate case of noun phrases; person and number of subject indicated by obligatory verb phrases; split-intransitivity: intransitive subjects encoded as transitive when nonfocus; focus marked the same way for intransitive subjects and direct objects, and only those, otherwise rather accusative; resultative; reflexive; reciprocal; causative; comparative; CV, CVCCVV; nontonal. Riverine. Pine and deciduous forest. Swidden agriculturalists. Christian, traditional religion. Nearly extinct.

Yukaghir, Southern (Yukagir, Jukagir, Odul, Kolyma, Kolym, Southern Yukagir) [yux] 10 to 50 (1995 M. Krauss, 1989 census). Ethnic population: 130 (1995 M. Krauss, 1989 census). Yakutia and the Kamchatka Peninsula. *Class:* Yukaghir. *Dialects:* Not inherently intelligible with Northern Yukaghir. *Lg Use:* Used in the home. Speakers are older adults. All can speak Russian as second language, especially those below 40. Those above 35 can speak Yakut, and those over 60 can speak Even. Russian is used as a literary language. *Lg Dev:* Dictionary. *Other:* SOV; postpositions; genitives, articles, adjectives, numerals, relatives before noun heads; question word not initial or final; 2 prefixes, 6 suffixes; focus is preverbal, subjects and topics tend to be initial; affixes indicate case of noun phrases; person and number of subject is obligatory; split intransitivity: intransitive subjects encode as transitive when nonfocus, focus marked the same for intransitive subjects and direct objects, and only for those; otherwise rather accusative; resultative; reflexive; reciprocal; causative; comparative; CV, CVCCVV; nontonal. Riverine. Pine and deciduous forest. Swidden agriculturalists. Christian, traditional religion. Nearly extinct.

Yupik, Central Siberian (Yoit, Yuk, Yuit, Siberian Yupik, "Eskimo," Bering Strait Yupik, Asiatic Yupik) [ess] 300 in Russia (1991 Kibrik). Ethnic population: 1,200 to 1,500 in Russia (1991 Kibrik). Chukchi National Okrug, coast of the Bering Sea, Wrangel Island. The Chaplino live in Providenie Region in Novo-Chaplino and Providenie villages. *Dialects:* Aiwanat, Noohalit (Peekit),

Wooteelit, Chaplino. *Lg Use:* 20% to 40% of the ethnic group speaks it. Resettlement has weakened language use, but recent contacts with Alaska have increased prestige. Chaplino is taught in schools through fourth grade. Older adults have active command of the language, those 35 to 50 have passive knowledge, children know what they have learned in school. Positive language attitude. *Lg Dev:* Taught in primary schools. *Other:* School at Anadyr. Chaplino and Naukan speakers have 60% to 70% inherent intelligibility with each other. Sirenik is a separate language. Shamanist. See main entry under USA.

Yupik, Naukan (Naukan, Naukanski) [ynk] 75 (1990 L.D. Kaplan). Ethnic population: 350. Chukota Region, Laurence, Lorino, and Whalen villages, scattered. Formerly spoken in Naukan village and the region surrounding East Cape, Chukot Peninsula, but they have been relocated. *Class:* Eskimo-Aleut, Eskimo, Yupik, Siberian. *Dialects:* 60% to 70% intelligibility of Chaplino.

Yupik, Sirenik (Sirenik, Sirenikski, Old Sirenik, Vuteen) [ysr] Extinct. Chukot Peninsula, Sireniki village. *Class:* Eskimo-Aleut, Eskimo, Yupik, Siberian. *Lg Use:* It became extinct in 1997. Inuit residents of Sirenik village now speak Central Siberian Yupik.

Saudi Arabia

Kingdom of Saudi Arabia, al-Mamlaka al-'Arabiya as-Sa'udiya. 25,795,938. National or official language: Standard Arabic. Literacy rate: 38%, 50% men. Also includes Bengali (15,000), Egyptian Spoken Arabic (300,000), English (60,000), French (22,000), Indonesian (37,000), Italian (22,000), Kabardian (17,000), Korean (66,000), Somali (42,727), Sudanese Spoken Arabic (86,000), Tagalog (700,000), Urdu (382,000), Uyghur (5,919), Western Cham (100), Western Farsi (102,000), Chinese (58,000), from India (120,000), from the Philippines (700,000), others from Nigeria. Information mainly from M. Bateson 1967; T. M. Johnstone 1987; B. Comrie 1987; A. S. Kaye 1988; C. Holes 1990; B. Ingham 1994. Blind population: 140,000. Deaf population: 1,103,284. The number of languages listed for Saudi Arabia is 5. Of those, all are living languages.

Arabic, Gulf Spoken (Gulf Spoken) [afb] 200,000 in Saudi Arabia. Northern and southern Eastern Province. *Dialect:* Al-Hasaa. See main entry under Iraq.

Arabic, Hijazi Spoken (Hijazi, West Arabian Colloquial Arabic) [acw] 6,000,000 in Saudi Arabia (1996). Red Sea coast and adjacent highlands. Also spoken in Eritrea. *Class:* Afro-Asiatic, Semitic, Central, South, Arabic. *Dialects:* North Hijazi, South Hijazi, Valley Tihaamah, Coastal Tihaamah. North Hijazi has 4 subdialects, South Hijazi has 16.

Arabic, Najdi Spoken [ars] 8,000,000 in Saudi Arabia. Population total all countries: 9,863,520. Also spoken in Canada, Iraq, Jordan, Kuwait, Syria, USA. *Class:* Afro-Asiatic, Semitic, Central, South, Arabic. *Dialects:* North Najdi (Shammari, Bani Khaalid, Dafiir), Central Najdi (Rwala, Haayil, Al-Qasiim, Sudair, Riyadh, Hofuf, Biishah, Najraan, Wild 'Ali, 'Awaazim, Rashaayda, Mutair, 'Utaiba, 'Ajmaan), South Anjdi (Aal Murrah, Najran). Some dialects are spoken by Bedouins. *Other:* SVO. Muslim.

Arabic, Standard (High Arabic, Al Fus-Ha, Al Arabiya) [arb] 206,000,000 first-language speakers of all Arabic varieties (1999 WA). Middle East, North Africa, other Muslim countries. Also spoken in Algeria, Bahrain, Chad, Comoros, Djibouti, Egypt, Eritrea, Iraq, Israel, Jordan, Kuwait, Lebanon, Libya, Morocco, Oman, Palestinian West Bank and Gaza, Qatar, Somalia, Sudan, Syria, Tanzania, Tunisia, United Arab Emirates, Yemen. *Class:*

Afro-Asiatic, Semitic, Central, South, Arabic. *Dialects:* Modern Standard Arabic (Modern Literary Arabic), Classical Arabic (Koranic Arabic, Quranic Arabic). Preserves the ancient grammar. *Lg Use:* National language. 246,000,000 second-language speakers of all Arabic varieties (1999 WA). Not a first language. Used for education, official purposes, written materials, and formal speeches. Classical Arabic is used for religion and ceremonial purposes, having archaic vocabulary. Modern Standard Arabic is a modernized variety of Classical Arabic. In most Arab countries only the well educated have adequate proficiency in Standard Arabic, while over 100,500,000 do not. *Lg Dev:* Arabic script in Algeria. Newspapers. Radio programs. Dictionary. Bible: 1984–1991. *Other:* VSO.

Saudi Arabian Sign Language [sdl] *Class:* Deaf sign language.

Singapore

Republic of Singapore. 4,353,893. National or official languages: Mandarin Chinese, Malay, Tamil, English. Literacy rate: 93% (2000 census). Also includes Hindi (5,000), Indonesian, Japanese (20,000), Korean (5,200), Sindhi (5,000), Sylheti, Telugu (603), Thai (30,000), Tukang Besi North, people from the Philippines (50,000). Blind population: 1,442. Deaf institutions: 3. The number of languages listed for Singapore is 21. Of those, all are living languages.

Bengali [ben] 600 in Singapore (1985). Ethnic population: 14,000 in Singapore (2001 Johnstone and Mandryk). *Other:* Hindu, Muslim. See main entry under Bangladesh.

Chinese, Hakka (Khek, Kek, Kehia, Kechia, Ke, Hokka) [hak] 69,000 in Singapore (1980). Ethnic population: 151,000 in Singapore (1993). See main entry under China.

Chinese, Mandarin (Huayu, Guoyu) [cmn] 201,000 in Singapore (1985). *Lg Use:* Official language. Increasing use. 880,000 second-language users. 44% also use other Chinese varieties at home; 12% use English at home. *Lg Dev:* Literacy rate in first language: 64.7% (2001 census). Taught in schools. *Other:* 2,505,209 ethnic Chinese (2000 census). See main entry under China.

Chinese, Min Bei (Min Pei) [mnp] 4,000 in Singapore (1985). Ethnic population: 11,000 in Singapore. *Dialect:* Hokchia (Hockchew). See main entry under China.

Chinese, Min Dong [cdo] 34,154 in Singapore (2000 WCD). Ethnic population: 31,391. Mainly in China. *Dialect:* Fuzhou (Fuchow, Foochow, Guxhou). See main entry under China.

Chinese, Min Nan (Min Nam, Southern Min) [nan] 1,170,000 in Singapore (1985). Population includes 736,000 speakers of Hokkien, 28.8% of the population (1993), 360,000 speakers of Teochew (1985), 14.2% of the population (1993); 74,000 speakers of Hainanese (1985), 2.9% of the population (1993). Ethnic population: 1,482,000 (1993) including 884,000 Hokkien (1993), 452,000 Teochew (1985), 146,000 Hainanese (1993). *Dialects:* Hokkien (Fukienese, Fujian, Amoy, Xiamen), Teochew (Chaochow, Chaozhou, Taechew), Hainanese. *Lg Use:* Trade language. The Hokkien dialect is the most widely understood in Singapore (Kuo 1979). Mandarin, English, and other Chinese varieties are also used at home. See main entry under China.

Chinese, Pu-Xian [cpx] 14,083 in Singapore (2000 WCD). *Dialect:* Henghua (Hinghua, Xinghua). See main entry under China.

Chinese, Yue (Cantonese, Yue, Yueh, Guangfu) [yue] 314,000 in Singapore (1985). Ethnic population: 338,000 (1993). See main entry under China.

English [eng] 227,000 in Singapore (1985). *Lg Use:* Official language. Second-language users (literate in English) are 71% of population (2000 census). Ethnic groups which use English: Chinese 154,000, 68%; European and Eurasian 34,000, 15%; Indian 32,000, 14%; Malay 6,000, 3%. Chinese varieties and Tamil also used at home. See main entry under United Kingdom.

Gujarati (Gujerathi, Gujerati) [guj] 800 in Singapore (1985). Ethnic population: 1,619 (1985). *Other:* Hindu. See main entry under India.

Javanese (Jawa, Djawa) [jav] 800 in Singapore (1985). Ethnic population: 21,230. *Other:* Muslim. See main entry under Indonesia (Java and Bali).

Madura (Madurese, Madhura) [mad] 900 in Singapore (1985). Ethnic population: 14,292 (1985). *Dialect:* Bawean (Boyanese). *Other:* Muslim. See main entry under Indonesia (Java and Bali).

Malaccan Creole Portuguese (Malaysian Creole Portuguese, Malaccan, Papia Kristang) [mcm] Trankera and Hilir, Melaka, Straits of Malacca. Related varieties in parts of Kuala Lumpur and Singapore. Variety in Pulau Tikus spoken more in 1997 than in 1987. *Lg Use:* Trade language. Also spoken as second language by some Chinese shopkeepers in Hilir. *Other:* Fishermen. Christian. See main entry under Malaysia (Peninsular).

Malay (Bahasa Malay, Melayu) [mly] 396,000 in Singapore (1985). *Lg Use:* Official language. Ethnic groups who speak Malay: Malay 339,000, 85%; Javanese 21,000, 5%; Indians 14,000, 3.5%; Bawean Madurese 14,000, 3.5%; Arabs 2,500, 0.6%; Bugis 500, 0.1%. English used at home by 7%. Mandarin and Hokkien are used as second languages by some, and 70% use English. *Lg Dev:* Literacy rate in second language: 85%. *Other:* Muslim (Sunni), Christian. See main entry under Malaysia (Peninsular).

Malay, Baba (Chinese Malay, Baba, Straits Malay) [mbf] 10,000 in Singapore (1986 Pakir). Population total all countries: 15,000. Ethnic population: 250,000 to 400,000 (1986). Mainly in the Katong District on the east coast and the surrounding districts of Geylang and Jao Chiat. Also spoken in Malaysia (Peninsular). *Class:* Creole, Malay based. *Dialects:* It developed since the 15th century from Low Malay with many Hokkien Chinese borrowings. Regional variants between Malacca and Singapore. Partially intelligible with Standard Malay. It is generally believed that the Baba of Malaysia is more 'refined', and that of Singapore more 'rough'. Most have learned Standard Malay and English in school. Lim (1981) and Holm (1989) treat it as a Malay-based creole. It is different from Peranakan Indonesian. *Lg Use:* Used mainly in the home. The only monolinguals are over 70 years old. Some who grew up with Chinese neighbors know Hokkien, Teochew, and Cantonese. Children now learn Mandarin in school rather than Standard Malay. *Lg Dev:* NT: 1913.

Malayalam (Alealum, Malayalani, Malayal, Malean, Maliyad, Mallealle, Mopla) [mal] 10,000 in Singapore. Ethnic population: 14,000 (1993). *Other:* Christian. See main entry under India.

Orang Seletar [ors] 884 in Singapore (2000 WCD). North coast of Singapore, and opposite coast of Malaysia. *Other:* Coastal. See main entry under Malaysia (Peninsular).

Panjabi, Eastern [pan] 9,500 in Singapore (1987). Ethnic population: 14,000 (1993). *Other:* Sikh. See main entry under India.

Singapore Sign Language [sls] *Class:* Deaf sign language. *Lg Dev:* Dictionary.

Sinhala (Sinhalese, Singhalese, Chingalese) [sin] 852 in Singapore (1987). Ethnic population: 12,000 (1993). *Other:* A great difference between the literary and colloquial language. Buddhist. See main entry under Sri Lanka.

Tamil [tam] 90,000 in Singapore (1985). Ethnic population: 111,000 (1993). *Lg Use:* Official language. 19% speak English at home. *Other:* Hindu. See main entry under India.

Sri Lanka

Democratic Socialist Republic of Sri Lanka. Sri Lanka Prajathanthrika Samajavadi Janarajaya. Formerly Ceylon. 19,905,165. National or official languages: Sinhala, Tamil. Literacy rate: 86% to 87%. Information mainly from J. Gair 1990; J. Holm 1989. Blind population: 13,800. Deaf population: 3,459 to 1,093,340 (1998). Deaf institutions: 14. The number of languages listed for Sri Lanka is 8. Of those, 7 are living languages and 1 is extinct. See map on page 828.

English [eng] 74,170 in Sri Lanka (2000 WCD). See main entry under United Kingdom.

Indo-Portuguese [idb] 3,406 in Sri Lanka (2000 WCD). Population includes 250 families in Batticaloa (1984 Ian Smith), but possibly only about 30 speakers left (1992 P. Baker). Colombo, Kandy, Trincomalee, Galle, Batticaloa. Also spoken in Australia, India. *Class:* Creole, Portuguese based. *Dialects:* Similar to Tamil in phonology and syntax. Varieties of creole Portuguese were also spoken in Myanmar, Bangladesh, Thailand, Indonesia, Malaysia, China. See also Malaccan Creole Portuguese (Peninsular Malaysia), Macao Creole Portuguese (Hongkong), Ternateño (Maluku, Indonesia), Timor Pidgin (East Timor). *Lg Use:* Many in the ethnic group may not know the creole well. Virtually no contact with Goa or Portugal since 1656. The creole is used at home only. Most of the Burgher caste speak it at home. Everyone is fluent in Tamil. Older speakers are also bilingual in English; some younger ones in Sinhalese. *Lg Dev:* NT: 1826–1852. *Other:* SOV.

Pali [pli] Extinct. *Lg Use:* The literary language of the Buddhist scriptures. Monks from different countries may speak Pali to each other. Sri Lankan history has been recorded in Pali. *Other:* Buddhist. See main entry under India.

Sinhala (Sinhalese, Singhalese, Singhala, Cingalese) [sin] 13,190,000 in Sri Lanka (1993). Population total all countries: 13,220,256. All parts of Sri Lanka except some districts in the north, east, and center. Also spoken in Canada, Maldives, Singapore, Thailand, United Arab Emirates. *Class:* Indo-European, Indo-Iranian, Indo-Aryan, Sinhalese-Maldivian. *Dialect:* Rodiya. There is a great difference between the literary and the colloquial language. The Rodiya dialect is spoken by low caste Rodiya people. *Lg Use:* Official language. 2,000,000 second-language speakers (1997). *Lg Dev:* Sinhalese script. Dictionary. Grammar. Bible: 1823–1982. *Other:* SOV; 7 long vowels, 7 short vowels, 24 consonants, including 4 which are prenasalized; gender, number, and case agreement between subject and verb in literary Sinhala. Buddhist, Christian.

Sri Lankan Creole Malay (Sri Lankan Malay, Melayu Bahasa, Java Jati) [sci] 50,000 (1986 Hussainmiya, Prentice 1994:411). Especially the cities of Colombo, Kandy, Badulla, Hambantota. *Class:* Creole, Malay based. *Dialects:* Not intelligible with standard Malay because of phonological and syntactic differences, and strong influence from Tamil. May be close to Malaccan Creole Malay (S. Lim 1981). *Lg Use:* There are current efforts to revive the older literature. Widely used. Used at home and among friends. All ages. Most or all may speak Tamil. *Lg Dev:* Roman script. Newspapers. Radio programs. *Other:* Malay vocabulary with grammatical structure based on Sri Lankan Moor Tamil. SOV; postpositions; case; adjectives and genitives precede noun heads. Muslim syncretism with traditional beliefs.

Sri Lankan Sign Language [sqs] 12,800 deaf persons (1986 Gallaudet Univ). *Class:* Deaf sign language. *Lg Use:* 14 deaf schools. Several sign languages used by different schools. *Other:* British English fingerspelling also used.

Tamil [tam] 3,000,000 in Sri Lanka (1993). North and northeast coasts, a few pockets in the south. *Lg Use:* National language. *Other:* Hindu, Muslim. See main entry under India.

Veddah (Veddha, Veda, Weda, Weddo, Beda, Bedda, Vaedda) [ved] 300 (1993 Johnstone). Ethnic population: 2,500 (2002). Eastern mountains, Badulla and Polonnaruwa districts. *Class:* Indo-European, Indo-Iranian, Indo-Aryan, Sinhalese-Maldivian. *Lg Use:* Speakers are shifting to Sinhalese. Breton 1997 says Veddah no longer used.

Syria

Syrian Arab Republic, al-jamhouriya al Arabia as-Souriya. 18,016,874. National or official language: Standard Arabic. Literacy rate: 65%, 78% males. Also includes Chaldean Neo-Aramaic (5,000), Chechen, South Levantine Spoken Arabic. Information mainly from T. Sebeok 1963; W. Fischer and O. Jastrow 1980; B. Ingham 1982. Blind population: 152. Deaf population: 902,598. Deaf institutions: 1. The number of languages listed for Syria is 16. Of those, 15 are living languages and 1 is extinct. See map on page 808.

Adyghe (West Circassian, Adygey) [ady] 25,000 in Syria. *Other:* Muslim (Sunni). See main entry under Russia (Europe).

Arabic, Levantine Bedawi Spoken (Bedawi) [avl] 70,000 in Syria. Southwest corner, Hawran Region, from the border to within 20 miles of Damascus. *Other:* Muslim (Sunni), Christian. See main entry under Egypt (Arabic, Eastern Egyptian Bedawi Spoken).

Arabic, Mesopotamian Spoken (North Syrian Arabic, Furati, Mesopotamian Gelet Arabic) [acm] 1,800,000 in Syria. Eastern Syria. *Dialect:* Euphrates Cluster. *Other:* Muslim, Christian, Jewish. See main entry under Iraq.

Arabic, Najdi Spoken (Bedawi) [ars] 500,000 in Syria. Population includes 100,000 North Najdi, 100,000 Central Najdi (1995). Syrian desert. *Lg Use:* Spoken by Bedouins. See main entry under Saudi Arabia.

Arabic, North Levantine Spoken (Levantine Arabic, North Levantine Arabic, Lebanese-Syrian Arabic, Syro-Lebanese Arabic) [apc] 8,800,000 in Syria (1991). Population includes 6,000,000 in Lebanese-Central Syrian, 1,000,000 in North Syrian. Population total all countries: 14,309,537. Also spoken in Antigua and Barbuda, Argentina, Belize, Cyprus, Dominican Republic, French Guiana, Israel, Jamaica, Lebanon, Mali, Puerto Rico, Suriname, Trinidad and Tobago, Turkey (Asia). *Class:* Afro-Asiatic, Semitic, Central, South, Arabic. *Dialects:* There is an urban standard dialect based on Damascus speech. Beiruti dialect is well accepted here. Aleppo dialect shows Mesopotamian (North Syrian) influence. *Lg Use:* Used in drama. *Lg Dev:* Radio programs. TV. *Other:* Muslim, Christian, Druze, Jewish.

Arabic, North Mesopotamian Spoken (Moslawi, Syro-Mesopotamian Arabic, Mesopotamian Qeltu Arabic) [ayp] 300,000 in Syria (1992). Far eastern Syria. *Other:* Muslim, Christian. See main entry under Iraq.

Arabic, Standard [arb] Middle East, North Africa. *Lg Use:* Official language. Used for education, official purposes, formal speeches. See main entry under Saudi Arabia.

Armenian (Haieren, Somkhuri, Ermenice, Armjanski) [hye] 320,000 in Syria (1993). *Dialect:* Western Armenian. *Lg Use:* Language of wider communication. *Other:* Christian. See main entry under Armenia.

Assyrian Neo-Aramaic (Lishana Aturaya, Suret, Sureth, Suryaya Swadaya, Assyrian, Neo-Syriac, Assyriski, Aisorski) [aii] 30,000 in Syria (1995). Ethnic population: 700,000. Over 30 villages on the banks of the Khabur River, northern Syria. *Other:* Christian (Nestorian). See main entry under Iraq.

Azerbaijani, South [azb] 30,000 in Syria (1961 census). Homs and Hama. *Lg Use:* Speakers also use Arabic. *Other:* They are called 'Turkmen' or 'Turkomen' in Syria and Iraq. Not a written language in Syria. Muslim. See main entry under Iran.

Domari (Middle Eastern Romani, Tsigene, Gypsy, Nawar, Kurbat, Barake) [rmt] 10,000 in Syria (1961). Turkey to India; Nawar is in Palestine, Syria, and Egypt; Kurbat in Syria and western Iran; Helebi in Egypt and Libya; Karachi in north Turkey, the Caucasus of Russia; and north Iran; Domaki and Wogri-Boli in India; Barake in Syria; Luli and Maznoug in Uzbekistan; other groups in Iran; Churi-Wali in Afghanistan. *Dialects:* Nawar, Kurbati, Beirut, Nablos, Barake. *Other:* Arabic influence. Muslim. See main entry under Iran.

Kurdish, Northern (Kurmanji, Kurmancî, Kurdi) [kmr] 938,000 in Syria (1993). Northern Syria: Northern Cizire (Qamishlok), Kurd-Dagh (Ciyayê Kurdî, Afrin), Ain-Arab, Allepo, Damascus. *Lg Use:* Language of wider communication. Speakers also use Arabic. *Other:* Agriculturalists. Muslim (Sunni), Yezidi. See main entry under Turkey (Asia).

Lomavren (Armenian Bosha, Arnebuab Bisa, Bosha, Bosa) [rmi] See main entry under Armenia.

Mlahsö (Suryoyo) [lhs] Extinct. Qamishli town. Originally in Mlahsó and 'Ansha villages, Diyarbakir Province, Turkey. *Class:* Afro-Asiatic, Semitic, Central, Aramaic, Eastern, Central, Northwestern. *Dialects:* Close to Turoyo. *Lg Use:* The last speaker died in 1998. His daughter knows Mlahsö well, but is nearly deaf and has no one to speak it to (1999). Mlahsö was still spoken by a handful of people during the 1970s. *Other:* 'Suryoyo' is their own name. A different language from Turoyo, also called 'Suryoyo'. Christian (Jacobite).

Turoyo (Suryoyo, Syryoyo, Turani) [tru] 7,000 in Syria (1994). Ethnic population: 20,000 (1994). *Lg Use:* Used in the home. Western Syriac used in church, Arabic in schools and trade. *Other:* Religious capital is in Damascus; formerly at Tur 'Abdin, Turkey. Christian (Jacobite). See main entry under Turkey (Asia).

Western Neo-Aramaic (Maalula, Siryon, Loghtha Siryanoytha, Neo-Western Aramaic) [amw] 15,000 (1996 Maalula Home Page, Internet). Population includes 8,000 in Maaloula. Qalamoun Mountains, 30 miles north of Damascus. Villages of Ma'lula, Bakh'a, and Jubb 'Adin. Only in Syria. *Class:* Afro-Asiatic, Semitic, Central, Aramaic, Western. *Dialects:* Ma'lula (Maalula, Maaloula, Ma'lu:la), Bakh'a (Bax'a), Jub-'adin (Jubb 'Adi:n). Little dialect variation. *Lg Use:* Used in the home and as a literary and religious language. Speakers also use Syrian Arabic. *Other:* There are members of the ethnic group in the USA who now speak Arabic. Mountain slope. 1,500 meters. Peasant agriculturalists: vineyards, orchards. Christian, Muslim (Sunni).

Taiwan

Republic of China, Chung-hua Min-kuo. Formerly Formosa. 22,749,838. Population includes 349,120 tribal people, or 2% of the population, Han Chinese 97.8%. National or official language: Mandarin Chinese. Literacy rate: 90% to 92%.

Also includes Chinese Sign Language, Halh Mongolian (6,000), Kalmyk-Oirat, Tibetan (2,000), Uyghur, people from the Philippines (50,000). Information mainly from T. Sebeok 1971; S. Tsuchida 1976; S. Wurm and S. Hattori 1981; P. Li 1987; D. T. Tryon 1995. Deaf population: 30,000 to 1,302,969 (1998). Deaf institutions: 8. The number of languages listed for Taiwan is 26. Of those, 22 are living languages and 4 are extinct. See map on page 829.

Amis (Ami, Amia, Pangcah, Pagcah, Pangtsah, Bakurut, Lam-Si-Hoan, Maran, Sabari, Tanah) [ami] 137,651 (2002 Council of Indigenous Peoples, Executive Yuan, ROC). Ethnic population: 137,651. Plains in the valley along the railroad between Hualien and Taitung, and on the east coast near the sea between Hualien and Taitung. *Class:* Austronesian, East Formosan, Central. *Dialects:* Central Amis (Haian Ami, Hsiukulan Ami), Tavalong-Vataan (Kwangfu, Kuangfu), Southern Amis (Peinan, Hengch'un Amis, Taitung), Chengkung-Kwangshan, Northern Amis (Nanshi Amis). The Chengkung-Kwangshan dialect is closest to Central Amis. *Lg Use:* Speakers also use Japanese or Mandarin. *Lg Dev:* Roman script. Dictionary. Grammar. Bible: 1997. *Other:* 'Amis' is their name for themselves; 'Ami' is the Chinese name. Traditionally matrilineal. Many are migrating to cities and industrial areas. Plains. Agriculturalists: rice.

Amis, Nataoran (Nataoran, Natawran, Tauran) [ais] 5 (2000 Wurm). Villages in the Hualien area and north of Fenglin. *Class:* Austronesian, East Formosan, Central. *Dialects:* Nataoran, Sakizaya (Sakiray, Sakiraya), Kaliyawan (Kaliyuawan), Natawran, Cikosowan, Pokpok, Ridaw. Not generally understood by other Amis. Sakizaya is even more divergent from Central Amis. In recent years the dialects have converged. Lexical similarity 50% with Central Amis. *Lg Use:* All speakers are older adults. *Lg Dev:* Dictionary. *Other:* In 1878 the Sakizaya were forcibly removed from their traditional land in the northern Amis area, and resettled in the southern Amis area, interspersed with other Amis. Later some returned (Tsuchida 1981). Nearly extinct.

Atayal (Tayal, Tyal, Taiyal, Ataiyal, Attayal, Taijyal, Bonotsek, Shabogala, Takonan, Tangao, Yukan) [tay] 84,330 (2002 Council of Indigenous Peoples, Executive Yuan, ROC). Ethnic population: 78,957 (1989 govt. figure), including 50 Mayrinax speakers left (2000 L. M. Huang). Mountains in the northeast, south of the Ketagalan area. *Class:* Austronesian, Atayalic. *Dialects:* Sqoleq (Squliq), Ts'ole' (Ci'uli'). Mayrinax is a Ci'uli' subdialect. *Lg Use:* In some areas Atayal is in active use. *Lg Dev:* Roman script. Dictionary. Grammar. Bible: 2002.

Babuza (Babusa, Favorlang, Favorlangsch, Jaborlang, Poavosa) [bzg] 3 to 4 (2000 S. Wurm). West central coast and inland, Tatu and Choshui rivers and beyond, around 24 degrees north. *Class:* Austronesian, Western Plains, Central Western Plains. *Dialects:* Poavosa, Taokas. Taokas dialect is extinct. *Lg Use:* Under 10% of the ethnic group speaks Babuza. Used in the home. No children speak Babuza. Neutral language attitude. *Lg Dev:* Bible portions. *Other:* Sinicized. Nearly extinct.

Basay (Kawanuwan, Basai) [byq] Extinct. North around Tam Shui to near Kungliao, Fengtzulin, Taipei, Sangchung, and northeast around Suao and east of Ilan. *Class:* Austronesian, East Formosan, Northern. *Dialects:* Trobiawan, Linaw-Qauqaul. *Lg Dev:* Grammar. *Other:* Sinicized. Older people can remember a few words.

Bunun (Bunti, Vonun, Bunan, Bubukun, Vunum, Vunun, Vunung, Bunum) [bnn] 37,989 (2002 Council of Indigenous Peoples, Executive Yuan, ROC). Ethnic population: 37,989. East central plain, south of the Sediq (Taroko). *Class:* Austronesian, Bunun. *Dialects:* Randai, Tondai, Shibukun (Sibukun, Sibukaun, Sibucoon,

Sivukun), North Bunun (Takitudu, Taketodo, Takebakha, Takibakha), Central Bunun (Takbanuao, Takivatan, Takevatan), South Bunun (Ishbukun), Takopulan. *Lg Use:* Also spoken by the Kanakanabu and the Saaroa in everyday life. *Lg Dev:* Roman script. Dictionary. Grammar. Bible: 2000.

Chinese, Hakka [hak] 2,366,000 in Taiwan (1993). Taoyuan, Hsinchu, Miaoli, Pingtung counties. Shi Xien is in northern and southern Taiwan, Hi-Lu is central and north central. *Dialects:* Hailu (Hoiluk, Hoilluk, Hi-Lu), Sanhsien (Shigen, Shixien, Shi Xien). *Other:* Settled in Taiwan for 200 years. Sanhsien closely resembles Yuetai of Mainland China. Hailu closely resembles Yong-Ting or Yuqui of Mainland China. See main entry under China.

Chinese, Mandarin (Kuoyu, Mandarin, Putonghua, Guoyu) [cmn] 4,323,000 in Taiwan (1993). Mainly in Taipei and 5 provincial cities. *Dialect:* Taibei Mandarin. *Lg Use:* Official language. 15,000,000 second-language speakers. Many of the 30- to 50-year-old generation in Taiwan are also fluent in Taiwan Min. *Lg Dev:* Kuoyu taught in all schools. *Other:* Traditional Chinese, Buddhist, Christian, Secular. See main entry under China.

Chinese, Min Nan (Min Nan, Minnan) [nan] 15,000,000 in Taiwan (1997 A. Chang). Tainan, Penghu Archipelago, cities on the east coast, western plain except for a few Hakka pockets. *Dialect:* Amoy (Taiwanese, Formosan). *Lg Use:* Mandarin is used as second language. Those over 60 also speak Japanese. *Other:* The Taiwanese people are called Hoklo or Holo. Chinese traditional religion, Buddhist, Christian, secular. See main entry under China.

Japanese [jpn] *Lg Use:* Trade language. 10,000 second-language users in Taiwan (1993). Used among a few older adult aboriginal speakers. See main entry under Japan.

Kanakanabu (Kanabu, Kanakanavu) [xnb] 6 to 8 (2000 Wurm). Ethnic population: 250 (UNESCO). Central Taiwan around Minchuan village, Sanmin Township, Kaohsiung County. *Class:* Austronesian, Tsouic. *Lg Use:* Members of the ethnic group now speak Bunun, Taiwanese, or Mandarin. *Lg Dev:* Grammar. *Other:* Nearly extinct.

Kavalan (Kuwarawan, Kiwarawa, Kuvarawan, Kibalan, Kiwaraw, Kuvalan, Kavarauan, Kvalan, Shekwan, Cabaran, Kabalan, Kabaran, Kamalan, Kavanan, Kbalan) [ckv] 24 (2000 Li). Northeast coast, above Toucheng to Ilan, nearly to Suao, and inland to Tayal language area. No longer spoken in the original area; a few migrants to the east coast, Hsishe village, Fengpin Township, Hualien County (1990). *Class:* Austronesian, East Formosan, Northern. *Dialect:* Kareovan (Kareowan). *Lg Use:* Under 10% of the ethnic group speaks Kavalan. Used only as a home language in 1930. Still spoken in Atayal territory (1987). Used in the home. No children speak Kavalan. Mainly older adult women. Neutral language attitude. They can speak Amis and Taiwanese fluently because they live among them, having migrated into the Amis region. *Lg Dev:* Roman script. Dictionary. Grammar. *Other:* Sinicized. Nearly extinct.

Ketangalan (Ketagalan, Tangalan) [kae] Extinct. North central, around Panchiao and to the northwest, west, and southeast. *Class:* Austronesian, Unclassified. *Other:* Sinicized.

Kulon-Pazeh (Kulon) [uun] 1 (2000 Paul Jen-Kuei Li). Near the west coast just north of 24 degrees north, east of Tayal, around Cholan, Houli, Fengyuan, Tantzu, Taichung, Tungshih. *Class:* Austronesian, Formosan, Paiwanic. *Lg Use:* Used only as a home language in 1930. One 86-year-old speaker (P. Li 2000). *Lg Dev:* Roman script. Dictionary. Grammar. *Other:* Sinicized. Nearly extinct.

Paiwan (Paiuan, Payowan, Li-Li-Sha, Samobi, Samohai, Saprek, Tamari, Kadas, Kale-Whan, Kapiangan, Katausan,

Butanglu, Stimul) [pwn] 66,084 (2002 Council of Indigenous Peoples, Executive Yuan, ROC). Ethnic population: 66,084. Southern, southeastern mountains. *Class:* Austronesian, Paiwan. *Lg Dev:* Roman script. Dictionary. Grammar. NT: 1973–1993.

Papora-Hoanya (Bupuran, Hinapavosa, Vupuran, Papola) [ppu] Extinct. North central coast around Lishui, Chingshui, Shalu, and inland to Taichung. *Class:* Austronesian, Formosan, Paiwanic. *Dialects:* Papora, Hoanya. *Other:* Sinicized.

Puyuma (Pyuma, Pilam, Pelam, Piyuma, Panapanayan, Kadas, Tipun) [pyu] 8,487 (2002 Council of Indigenous Peoples, Executive Yuan, ROC). Ethnic population: 8,487. Along the east coast south of Taitung and inland. *Class:* Austronesian, Puyuma. *Dialects:* Nanwang, Pinan. *Lg Use:* All domains. Most speakeres are older adults. *Lg Dev:* Dictionary. Grammar. Bible portions: 1990.

Rukai (Drukay, Drukai, Dyokay, Dukai, Rutkai, Tsarisen, Tsalisen, Sarisen, Banga, Bantalang, Bantaurang, Taloma, Kadas) [dru] 10,543 (2002 Council of Indigenous Peoples, Executive Yuan, ROC). Ethnic population: 10,543. South central mountains, west of the Pyuma, 11 villages around Ping Tung, and 2 or 3 villages near Taitung. *Class:* Austronesian, Rukai. *Dialects:* Budai, Labuan, Tanan, Maga, Tona, Mantauran. The Mantauran, Tona and Maga dialects are divergent. *Lg Use:* All domains. Some older adults are monolingual. Some speak Pyuma. Some older adults speak Japanese. Budai people speak Taiwanese. *Lg Dev:* Roman script. Dictionary. Grammar. NT: 2001. *Other:* Some linguists classify it as Paiwanic. There is Paiwanic influence. VSO.

Saaroa (Saroa, Saarua, Rarua, La'alua, La'arua, Pachien, Paichien, Sisyaban, Shishaban) [sxr] 5 to 6 (2000 Wurm). Ethnic population: 300 (2000 UNESCO Red Book). West central mountains, south and southeast of Minchuan, along the Laonung River. *Class:* Austronesian, Tsouic. *Dialects:* Close to Kanakanabu. *Lg Use:* On the verge of extinction in 1990. Speakers are shifting to Bunun. Older people speak Taiwanese. Used in the home. Some older people know Saaroa. No children speak it. The people have a neutral attitude toward Saaroa. There has been a major shift to Bunun since Bunun speakers migrated into the area. Older people speak Taiwanese. *Lg Dev:* Grammar. *Other:* Nearly extinct.

Saisiyat (Saiset, Seisirat, Saisett, Saisiat, Saisiett, Saisirat, Saisyet, Saisyett, Amutoura, Bouiok) [xsy] 4,750 (2002 Council of Indigenous Peoples, Executive Yuan, ROC). Western mountains, west of the Atayal, Nanchuang Township, Miaoli County and Wufong Township, Hsinchu County. *Class:* Austronesian, Northwest Formosan. *Dialects:* Taai (North Saiset), Tungho (South Saiset). The dialect differences are mainly phonological and lexical (Li 1978). *Lg Use:* 40% to 60% of the ethnic group speaks Saisiyat. Tungho: more active use. Taai: a few speakers, but nearly assimilated to Atayal. A few to half the children speak Saisiyat. Another report says a few children speak some lexical items. People have a mildly supportive attitude toward Saisiyat. Many young people speak Hakka Chinese. Atayal is also used. They live surrounded by the Atayal and the Hakka. Hakka Chinese used for most key domains. *Lg Dev:* Roman script.

Siraya (Formosan, Siraia, Siraiya, Sideia, Sideis, Sideisch, Baksa, Pepohoan, Pepo-Hwan) [fos] Extinct. South-western, around present-day Tainan, from Peimen to Hengchun to Tapu. *Class:* Austronesian, East Formosan, Southwest. *Dialects:* Siraya, Makatao (Makattao, Takaraya, Tta'o), Pangsoia-Dolatok, Taivoan (Tevorang), Lamai. *Lg Dev:* Dictionary. Bible portions: 1661. *Other:* It was still spoken in 1908. Sinicized.

Taiwan Sign Language (Taiwan Ziran Shouyu) [tss] 82,558 (2001). *Class:* Deaf sign language. *Dialects:*

Taipei, Tainan, Kaohsiung. 2 major dialects. The sources from which the sign language developed were indigenous sign systems before 1895, Japanese occupation and education 1895–1946, Mainland Chinese Sign Language brought by refugees in 1949 and some from Hongkong since. Lexical similarity 50% with Japanese Sign Language. *Other:* Quite different from (Mainland) Chinese Sign Language; only a few signs are the same or similar. Not related to Taiwanese languages. Some signs are borrowed from Mandarin through palmwriting. There is also a Signed Mandarin (Wenfa Shouyu).

Taroko (Sediq, Saediq, Seedik, Sejiq, Sedeq, Seedek, Seedeq, Shedekka, Sedek, Sediakk, Sedik, Sazek, Bu-Hwan, Che-Hwan, Daiya-Ataiyal, Hogo, Iboho, Paran, Taruku, Toroko, Truku, Toda) [trv] 4,750 (2002 Council of Indigenous Peoples, Executive Yuan, ROC). Ethnic population: 4,750. Central, eastern, and coastal; northern mountains in the Puli area and along the coast south of Hualien, south of the Atayal. *Class:* Austronesian, Atayalic. *Dialects:* Teruku (Truku), Te'uda (Tuuda), Tekedaya (Tkdaya, Paran). Dialects differ mainly in phonology and lexicon, and some in grammar. *Lg Use:* Chinese is used in schools. Older people also speak Japanese. *Lg Dev:* Roman script. Dictionary. Grammar. NT: 1963–1988.

Thao (Sau, Sao, Shao, Chuihwan, Chui-Huan, Suihwan, Vulung) [ssf] 5 to 6 (2000 Wurm). Ethnic population: 248 (1989). Central, southeastern shore of Sun Moon Lake, Te-hua village, and Ta-p'ing-lin 14 km away. *Class:* Austronesian, Western Plains, Thao. *Dialects:* Brawbaw, Shtafari. *Lg Use:* Members of the ethnic group now speak Mandarin. Used in the home. Negative language attitude. *Lg Dev:* Roman script. *Other:* There is cooperation with the Bunun, and intermarriage with Bunun women, loanwords from Bunun. Nearly extinct.

Tsou (Tsu-U, Tsoo, Tsuou, Tsu-Wo, Tzo, Tso, Namakaban, Niitaka, Tibola, Tibolah, Tibolak, Tibolal) [tsu] 2,127 (2002 Council of Indigenous Peoples, Executive Yuan, ROC). Ethnic population: 2,127. West central mountains southeast of Chiayi around Alishan (Mt. Ali). *Class:* Austronesian, Tsouic. *Dialects:* Duhtu, Luhtu, Tapangu, Tfuea, Iimutsu. *Lg Use:* Iimutsu is extinct (1981 Wurm and Hattori). The people speak Tsou in daily life. Young people speak Mandarin. Speakers also use Mandarin. *Lg Dev:* Roman script. Grammar. *Other:* Some linguistic work has been done.

Yami (Tao, Tawu, Botel Tabago, Botel Tobago, Lanyu) [tao] 3,384 (2002 Council of Indigenous Peoples, Executive Yuan, ROC). Ethnic population: 3,384. Orchid Island, Botel Tobago (Lanyu) Island, southeast coast. *Class:* Austronesian, Malayo-Polynesian, Northern Philippine, Bashiic-Central Luzon-Northern Mindoro, Bashiic, Yami. *Dialects:* Close to Ivatan of northern Philippines. *Lg Use:* Speakers also use Mandarin. *Lg Dev:* Roman script. Dictionary. Grammar. NT: 1994. *Other:* People prefer to be called 'Tao'. Traditional religion, Christian.

Tajikistan

Tajikistan. 7,011,556. National or official language: Tajiki. 54,019 square miles. Literacy rate: 99%. Also includes Aimaq, Armenian (6,000), Bashkir (5,412), Belarusan, Dungan, Georgian (808), Hazaragi, Kazakh (9,606), Kirghiz (64,000), Korean (13,000), Lak (861), Lithuanian (472), Northern Uzbek (873,000), Osetin (8,000), Romanian (580), Russian (237,000), Southern Pashto (4,000), Standard German, Tatar (80,000), Turkish, Turkmen (13,991), Ukrainian (41,000), Uyghur (3,581), Western Balochi (4,842). Information mainly from T. Sebeok 1963; S. Akiner 1983; B. Comrie 1987; A. Kibrik 1990. The number of languages listed for Tajikistan is 9. Of those, all are living languages. See map on page 812.

Arabic, Tajiki Spoken (Jugari, Bukhara Arabic, Buxara Arabic, Tajiji Arabic, Central Asian Arabic) [abh] 1,000 in Tajikistan. Villages in Vakhsh Valley of Khatlon Province, and communities in Kuliab and Leninabad cities. They mainly live in small villages. Some in Uzbekistan. *Lg Use:* Few members of the ethnic group now speak Arabic. Others speak Tajiki as first language. No diglossia with Modern Standard Arabic. Speakers use Tajiki to communicate with each other and as literary language. *Other:* They are endogamous and do not mix with speakers of other languages. Agriculturalists; animal husbandry: cattle. Muslim (Hanafi Sunni). See main entry under Afghanistan.

Farsi, Western (Persian) [pes] 50,000 in Tajikistan (2001 Johnstone and Mandryk). *Other:* Not a literary language in Tajikistan. Muslim (Shi'a). See main entry under Iran.

Parya (Afghana-Yi Nasfurush, Afghana-Yi Siyarui, Laghmani, Pbharya) [paq] 1,195 in Tajikistan (2000 WCD). Population total all countries: 2,495. Hissar Valley in Tajikistan and some in the upper part of the Surkhandarya Valley in Uzbekistan. Also spoken in Afghanistan, Uzbekistan. *Class:* Indo-European, Indo-Iranian, Indo-Aryan, Central zone, Unclassified. *Dialects:* It may be a dialect of Marwari, related to Panjabi, or the Laghman dialect of Southeast Pashayi of Afghanistan. Subgroups: Kalu, Jitain, Juni, Maggar, Bisiyan, Mussali, Shuiya. *Lg Use:* Uzbek and Tajiki men who marry Parya women learn Parya and become assimilated into the community. Used in the home. Speakers also use Tajiki. *Other:* They came to Tajikistan from Laghman, Afghanistan in 1880. They refer to themselves as 'Changgars'. Subgroup names are similar to those of the Changgars of Lahore, and to names used for groups mistakenly called 'Gypsies'. Collective farm workers. Muslim (Sunni).

Sanglechi-Ishkashimi [sgl] 500 in Tajikistan. Ethnic population: 1,000 in Tajikistan (1990 A. E. Kibrik). Tajikistan. *Dialects:* Ishkashimi (Ishkashim, Eshkashmi), Zebak (Zebaki), Sanglich. *Lg Use:* 70% of the ethnic group are speakers. Some key domains. 60% of children are speakers. Positive language attitude. Speakers also use Tajiki, which is used as literary language. *Other:* Not a written language. Ismaili Muslim. See main entry under Afghanistan.

Shughni (Shugnan-Rushan) [sgh] 40,000 in Tajikistan (1975 SIL). Population includes 20,000 Shugan, 1,500 to 2,000 Oroshor, 15,000 Rushan. Population total all countries: 60,000. Ethnic population: 73,000 (1990 A. E. Kibrik) including 50,000 Shugni, 2,000 Oroshor, 18,000 Rushan, 800 Khufi, 3,000 Bartang. Tajikistan, Gorno-Bagakhshan, Pamir Mountains. Also spoken in Afghanistan. *Class:* Indo-European, Indo-Iranian, Iranian, Eastern, Southeastern, Pamir, Shugni-Yazgulami. *Dialects:* Rushani (Rushan, Roshani, Oroshani), Bartangi (Bartang), Oroshor (Roshorvi), Khufi (Khuf, Chuf), Shughni (Shugan, Shugnan, Shighni, Khugni). Khufi and Bartangi may be separate languages. Oroshani may be separate from Rushani. Not intelligible of Sarikoli (called 'Tajiki' in China). *Lg Use:* 70% of the ethnic group speaks Shughni including dialects. Used in the home. 60% of children speak Shughni. Positive language attitude. Tajiki is used as a literary language. *Lg Dev:* Grammar. *Other:* Traditional territory and way of life. Mountain slope. Pastoralists. Ismaili Muslim.

Tajiki (Tadzhik, Tajiki Persian, Galcha) [tgk] 3,344,720 in Tajikistan (1991). Population total all countries: 4,380,212. Also spoken in Iran, Kazakhstan, Kyrgyzstan, Russia (Asia), Turkmenistan, Ukraine, Uzbekistan. *Class:* Indo-European, Indo-Iranian, Iranian, Western, Southwestern, Persian. *Dialects:* Four groups of small dialects; no distinct boundaries. Dialect blending into Dari Persian in Afghanistan. *Lg Use:* Official language. Most Tajiki are trilingual in Northern Uzbek, Russian, and Tajiki. *Lg Dev:* Cyrillic script. Bible: 1992. *Other:* Russian sources refer to all Persian dialects in Afghanistan as 'Tajiki'. So-called 'Tajiki' in China is actually Shugni or Wakhi. There are Tajiki-speaking Gypsy communities in Russian central Asia. There is some literature. Agriculturalists. Muslim (Sunni).

Wakhi (Vakhan, Wakhani, Wakhigi, Guhjali, Khik) [wbl] 7,000 in Tajikistan (1993 UBS). Ethnic population: 20,000 in Tajikistan (1990 Kibrik). Gorno-Badakhshan, Pamir Mountains. *Dialects:* Western Wakhi, Central Wakhi, Eastern Wakhi. *Lg Use:* 70% of the ethnic group speaks Wakhi. Not a written language. Some key domains. 60% of children speak Wakhi. Positive language attitude. Tajiki is used as a literary language. *Other:* Speakers are called 'Guhjali'. Ismaili Muslim. See main entry under Pakistan.

Yagnobi (Yagnob) [yai] 2,000 (1975 SIL). A high mountain valley of the Yagnob River. *Class:* Indo-European, Indo-Iranian, Iranian, Eastern, Northeastern. *Dialects:* Western Yagnobi, Eastern Yagnobi. *Lg Use:* Vigorous. Tajiki is used as literary language. Russian also used. *Other:* People were resettled in the 1960s to southern Tajikistan; a change from cool mountain valleys with water to irrigated desert plains. Muslim (Sunni).

Yazgulyam (Iazgulem, Yazgulam, Yazgulyami) [yah] 4,000 (1994 UBS). Along the Yazgulyam River, Gorno-Badakhshan Ao. *Class:* Indo-European, Indo-Iranian, Iranian, Eastern, Southeastern, Pamir, Shugni-Yazgulami. *Dialects:* Upper Yazgulyam, Lower Yazgulyam. Little dialect difference. *Lg Use:* 70% of the ethnic group speaks Yazgulyam. Used in the home. 60% of children speak Yazgulyam. Positive language attitude. Speakers also use Tajiki, which is used as literary language. *Other:* Not a written language. Ismaili Muslim.

Thailand

Kingdom of Thailand, Muang Thai or Prathet Thai. 64,865,523. Population includes 45,815,000 or 93.5% Daic languages, 1,037,650 or 2% Austro-Asiatic languages, 1,009,500 or 2% Austronesian languages, 533,500 or 1% Tibeto-Burman languages, 100,000 or 0.2% Hmong-Mien languages (1991 J. Matisoff). National or official language: Thai. Literacy rate: 89%. Also includes Burmese, Japanese, Kayan (150), Lao, Sinhala, Tai Daeng, Tamil, Urdu, Vietnamese. Information mainly from F. Lebar, G. Hickey, J. Musgrave 1964; H.C. Purnell 1970; W. Smalley 1976; S. Wurm and S. Hattori 1981; J. Matisoff 1991, J. Matisoff et al. 1996; P. Prachakij-karacak 1995. Blind population: 210,000 (1982 WCE). Deaf institutions: 22. The number of languages listed for Thailand is 74. Of those, all are living languages. See maps beginning on page 830.

Aheu (Phon Soung, So, Sotawueng) [thm] 750 in Thailand (1996 Ferlus). Population total all countries: 2,520. The Thavung live in Sakon Nakhon Province, Song Daw District, 3 villages. The Phon Soung live about 100 km south of the Thavung. Also spoken in Laos. *Class:* Austro-Asiatic, Mon-Khmer, Viet-Muong, Thavung. *Other:* Called 'So' in Thailand.

Akha (Kaw, Ekaw, Ko, Aka, Ikaw, Ak'a, Ahka, Khako, Kha Ko, Khao Kha Ko, Ikor, Aini, Yani) [ahk] 60,000 in Thailand (1998). Chiangmai, Chiangrai, Maehongson provinces. 250 villages. *Lg Dev:* Literacy rate in first language: 1% to 5%. Literacy rate in second language: 1% to 50%. *Other:* Traditional religion, Christian. See main entry under Myanmar.

Ban Khor Sign Language [bfk] Northeastern Thailand, a few villages. *Class:* Deaf sign language. *Dialects:* Not related to the original sign languages of Thailand, but there is some similarity.

Bisu (Mbisu, Mibisu) [bii] 1,000 in Thailand (1987 Purnell). Southwest Chiangrai, North Lampang. Two main villages, the largest with 100 houses. *Lg Use:* Vigorous. All ages. *Lg Dev:* Literacy rate in first language: below 1%. Literacy rate in second language: below 5%. *Other:* Mountain slope. Traditional religion. See main entry under China.

Blang (Sen Chun, Hkawa, Kawa, K'wa, K'ala, Bulang, Pulang, Pula, Plang, Wa, Khon Doi, Kontoi) [blr] 1,200 in Thailand (1998 SIL). Chiangrai; 1,000 live outside Mae Sai near the northern border, a village of 200 to 300 is near Mae Chan. About 200 live west of Bangkok and work in gardens. *Lg Dev:* Literacy rate in first language: below 1%. Literacy rate in second language: below 10%. *Other:* Horticulturalists. Buddhist (Hinayana), Christian. See main entry under China.

Bru, Eastern [bru] 5,000 in Thailand (1983 SIL). Sakon Nakhon Province. Tri are in Kusuman District, Kok Sa-at Bru are in Phanna Nikom and Phang Khon District, about 12 villages; one village in Amnat Charoen Province. *Dialects:* Tri, Bru Kok Sa-At, Bru Dong Sen Keo. *Lg Use:* Tri young people in Thailand do not speak the language. *Other:* Buddhist, traditional religion. See main entry under Laos.

Bru, Western (Bruu, B'ru, Baru) [brv] 20,000 in Thailand(1991). Dong Luang District of Mukdahan Province. Also spoken in USA. *Class:* Austro-Asiatic, Mon-Khmer, Eastern Mon-Khmer, Katuic, West Katuic, Brou-So. *Dialects:* It is partially intelligible with Eastern Bru. *Lg Dev:* Literacy rate in first language: 1% to 5%. Literacy rate in second language: 80%. *Other:* Buddhist, traditional religion, Christian.

Cham, Western (Cambodian Cham, Tjam, Cham, New Cham) [cja] 4,000 in Thailand. Ban Khrue, Bangkok, and possibly in refugee camps. *Lg Use:* There are conflicting reports about whether the people in Thailand still speak Cham or have shifted to Central Thai. *Other:* Austro-Asiatic influences. They are thought to be remnants of Cham who fought in the Thai army about 200 years ago. Muslim. See main entry under Cambodia.

Chiangmai Sign Language (Chiengmai Sign Language) [csd] Chiangmai. *Class:* Deaf sign language. *Dialects:* Related to present sign languages in Laos and Viet Nam (Haiphong, Hanoi, Ho Chi Minh City). A distinct language from Thai Sign Language. *Lg Use:* Still remembered by signers over 45 years old in Chiangmai. Younger signers use Modern Thai Sign Language.

Chinese, Hakka (Hakka) [hak] 58,800 in Thailand (1984). Cities. *Other:* Commerce class. See main entry under China.

Chinese, Mandarin [cmn] 5,880 in Thailand (1984). Bangkok, provincial towns, and Kra Peninsula in the south. *Dialect:* Ho (Haw, Cin Haw, Yunnanese, Western Mandarin, Hui, Hui-Tze, Hwei, Panghse, Pantha, Panthe, Pathee). *Other:* Chinese folk religion; Hui: Muslim. See main entry under China.

Chinese, Min Dong (Eastern Min) [cdo] *Dialect:* Fuzhou (Fuchow, Foochow). See main entry under China.

Chinese, Min Nan (Min Nan, Minnan) [nan] 1,081,920 in Thailand. Population includes 1,058,400 Chaochow (18%), 17,640 Fujian (.3%), 5,880 Hainanese (.1%) (1984). Cities. *Dialects:* Chaozhou (Chaochow, Tiuchiu, Teochow, Techu), Shantou (Swatow), Hainan, Fujian (Fukien, Hokkien). *Other:* Commerce; industrialists; clerks; sales; service; agriculturalists; professionals. Buddhist, Chinese folk religion, secular, Christian. See main entry under China.

Chinese, Yue (Cantonese, Yue, Yueh) [yue] 29,400 in Thailand (1984). See main entry under China.

Chong (Shong, Xong, Chawng) [cog] 500 in Thailand. Chantaburi, four villages, Trat Province, northwest of Par. See main entry under Cambodia.

Hmong Daw (White Meo, White Miao, Meo Kao, White Lum, Peh Miao, Pe Miao, Chuan Miao, Bai Miao) [mww] 32,395 in Thailand (2000 WCD). Petchabun, Tak, Maehongson, Chiangmai, Nan, Chiangrai, Pitsanalok, Loei, Sukhothai, Kamphaengphet, Prae, Phayao, Uttaradit, Lampang. *Dialects:* Hmong Gu Mba (Hmong Qua Mba, Striped Hmong, Miao Lai), Mong Leng, Petchabun Miao. *Other:* Traditional religion, Christian. See main entry under China.

Hmong Njua (Chuanqiandian Miao, Chuanchientien Miao, Sichuan-Guizhou-Yunnan Hmong, Tak Miao, Meo, Miao, Western Miao) [blu] 33,000 in Thailand (1987). Tak, Nan, Chiangmai, Maehongson, Petchabun, Chiangrai, Phayao, Phrae, Loei, Sukhothai, Kamphaengphet, Uthai provinces. *Other:* Agriculturalists. Traditional religion, Christian. See main entry under China.

Iu Mien (Mien, Yao, Mian, Myen, Yiu Mien, Youmian, Highland Yao, Pan Yao) [ium] 40,000 in Thailand (1999). Chiangmai, Chiangrai, Phayao, Lampang, Kampaengphet, Nan, and Sukhothai provinces, 159 villages. *Dialect:* Chiangrai. *Lg Use:* Speakers also use Northern Tai. *Other:* All 'Yao' and 'Mien' in Thailand are Iu Mien. Swidden agriculturalists: rice; hunters; weavers; embroiderers. Daoist, traditional religion. See main entry under China.

Karen, Pa'o (Taungtu, Black Karen, Pa-U, Pa'0, Pa Oh) [blk] 743 in Thailand (2000). Maehongson. See main entry under Myanmar.

Karen, Phrae Pwo (Pwo Phrae, Phrae, Prae, Northeastern Pwo Karen) [kjt] Northern Thailand, eastern provinces including Phrae Province. *Class:* Sino-Tibetan, Tibeto-Burman, Karen, Pwo. *Dialects:* Not intelligible with other Pwo Karen languages. Lexical similarity 87% with Northern Pwo Karen of Thailand, 67% to 71% with other Pwo Karen varieties. *Lg Use:* Most use Northern Thai and S'gaw Karen as second languages. *Lg Dev:* Literacy rate in first language: below 1%. Literacy rate in second language: 50% to 75%.

Karen, Pwo Northern (Phlong) [pww] 60,000 (1983 SIL). Mae Sarieng town in northwest Thailand, Mae Ngaw along the Salween River, 15 to 25 villages, Hot to Mae Sarieng (Highway 1099 which runs south to Omkoi). *Class:* Sino-Tibetan, Tibeto-Burman, Karen, Pwo. *Dialects:* Mae Ping, Omkoi (Hod), Mae Sarieng. Three dialects are intelligible with each other. The Pwo Karen of Phrae, Kanchanaburi, and Hua Hin are not intelligible with these. Lexical similarity 87% with Phrae Province Pwo Karen of Thailand, 68% to 73% with other Pwo Karen. *Lg Use:* Little knowledge of Thai in Hot to Mae Sarieng area. *Lg Dev:* Literacy rate in first language: below 1%. Literacy rate in second language: 25% to 50%. Thai-based script. NT: 2002. *Other:* SVO. Traditional religion, Christian.

Karen, Pwo Western Thailand (Phlou, Southern Pwo Karen) [kjp] 50,000 in Thailand (1998). Tak (Mae Sot south), Ulthaithani, Suphanburi, Kanchanaburi, Ratchaburi, Phetchaburi, and Prachuapkhirikhan (Huahin District) provinces. Kanchanaburi dialect is northern, Ratchaburi-Phetchaburi dialect is southern. *Dialect:* Kanchanaburi Pwo Karen, Ratchaburi Pwo Karen (Phetchaburi Pwo Karen). *Lg Dev:* Literacy rate in first language: below 1%. Literacy rate in second language: 15% to 50%. See main entry under Myanmar (Karen, Pwo Eastern).

Karen, S'gaw (S'gaw, S'gau, S'gaw Kayin, Kanyaw, Paganyaw, Pwakanyaw, White Karen, Burmese Karen, Yang Khao) [ksw] 300,000 in Thailand (1987 E. Hudspith). Tak, Maehongson, Chiangmai, and Chiangrai provinces, near the Myanmar border. *Dialect:* Panapu, Palakhi (Palachi). *Lg Dev:* Literacy rate in first language: 10% to 30%. Literacy rate in second language: 25% to 50%. *Other:* Traditional religion, Christian. See main entry under Myanmar.

Kayah, Eastern (Red Karen, Karennyi, Kayay, Kayah) [eky] 98,642 in Thailand (2000 WCD). Maehongson Province, east of the Salween River. *Lg Use:* They have a strong ethnic feeling that all Kayah are the same ethnic group. *Lg Dev:* Literacy rate in first language: 1% to 5%. Literacy rate in second language: 60% in Thai. See main entry under Myanmar.

Kensiu (Kense, Kensieu, Kenseu, Kensiw, Sakai, Moniq, Monik, Maniq, Moni, Menik, Meni, Ngok Pa, Orang Bukit, Orang Liar, Mos, Mengo, Tiong, Mawas, Belubn) [kns] 300 in Thailand. Southern Yala Province, Phattaloong, Satun, Narathiwat provinces, Thai-Malay border. Some in a resettlement camp in Yala. *Lg Dev:* Literacy rate in first language: below 1%. Literacy rate in second language: 5% to 15%. *Other:* Negrito pygmies, nomads, small bands. Tropical forest. Traditional religion. See main entry under Malaysia (Peninsular).

Khmer, Northern (Khmer Lue, Thailand Khmer) [kxm] 1,117,588 (2000 WCD). Very few are monolingual. Northeastern Thailand, mainly Surin, Sisaket, Buriram, Khorat provinces. *Class:* Austro-Asiatic, Mon-Khmer, Eastern Mon-Khmer, Khmer. *Dialects:* Buriram, Surin, Sisaket. Different from Central Khmer. Dialects are intelligible with each other. Many local varieties. *Lg Use:* Vigorous in towns. In cities it is being replaced by Isan and Thai. A few Chinese shopkeepers speak it. Informally used in education, media, religious services, commerce. Positive language attitude. Nearly all can speak Central Thai, most Isan (a dialect of Northeastern Thai), and some Central Khmer. *Lg Dev:* Literacy rate in first language: below 1%. Literacy rate in second language: 50% to 75%. 1,000 can read Northern Khmer, 100 can write it. NT: 1996. *Other:* SVO; prepositions; genitives, modifiers, relatives after noun heads; 1 prefix; CV, CVC, CCV; nontonal. Plains. Scrub forest. 500 meters. Peasant and intensive agriculturalists; craftsmen; educators; officials. Buddhist, Christian.

Khmu (Kmhmu, Khamu, Khmu', Khamuk, Kamhmu, Kamu, Kha Khmu, Kammu, Tmooy, Mou, Luu, Pouteng) [kjg] 31,403 in Thailand (2000 WCD). Scattered through Thailand, Chiangrai, Nan, Phayao. *Other:* Traditional religion, Christian. See main entry under Laos.

Khün (Hkun, Khun Shan, Gon Shan, Tai Khun, Khuen) [kkh] 6,281 in Thailand (2000 WCD). Chiangrai, Chiangmai. May not be in Thailand. *Other:* Different from Khouen (Khuen), a Mon-Khmer language of Laos. Buddhist. See main entry under Myanmar.

Kintaq (Kenta, Kintk, Kintaq Bong) [knq] Kedah-Perak border area, Thai border. Overlaps slightly into Southern Yala Province of Thailand. *Other:* Negrito pygmies, nomadic. Hunter-gatherers. Traditional religion. See main entry under Malaysia (Peninsular).

Korean [kor] Bangkok. *Other:* Buddhist, Christian. See main entry under Korea, South.

Kuy (Sui, Suai, Suay, Suoi, Soai, Suei, Cuoi, Kui Souei, Kui, Kuoy, Kuuy, Khamen-Boran) [kdt] 300,000 in Thailand (1992 Diffloth). Few monolinguals. Population total all countries: 366,675. East central Thailand, provinces of Buriram, Surin, Sisaket, Ubon, Roi Et. Also spoken in Cambodia, Laos. *Class:* Austro-Asiatic, Mon-Khmer, Eastern Mon-Khmer, Katuic, West Katuic, Kuay-Nheu. *Dialects:* Chang (Suai Chang), Nheu, Kuay. In Cambodia there are four Kuy dialects, based on the use of their word for 'what': Kuy Antra (northern Kompong Thom, southern Preah Vihear), Kuy Anthua (central Preah Vihear), Kuy May or Ma'ay (in Kratie), Kuy Mlor (one

village in northern Preah Vihear); only the older people still speak the last two dialects. *Lg Use:* Speakers have affection for Kuy and want to keep it, but want to also speak Lao or Isan (a dialect of Northeastern Thai) and Central Thai. About 99% can also speak Lao or Isan, 80% Central Thai, 40% Northern Khmer (mainly older adults). Kuy villages often intermingled with those of Lao and Northern Khmer speakers. *Lg Dev:* Literacy rate in first language: below 1%. Literacy rate in second language: 50%. Dictionary. NT: 1978. *Other:* A different script is used in Cambodia. Agriculturalists: rice. Traditional religion, Buddhist, Christian.

Lahu (Lohei, Muhsur, Mussuh, Muhso, Musso, Musser) [lhu] 32,000 in Thailand (2001 Johnstone and Mandryk). Chiangmai, Chiangrai, Maehongson, Lampang, Tak provinces, 119 known villages. There has been some migration from Myanmar and Laos. *Dialects:* Na (Black Lahu, Musser Dam, Northern Lahu, Loheirn), Nyi (Red Lahu, Southern Lahu, Musseh Daeng, Luhishi, Luhushi), Shehleh. *Lg Dev:* Literacy rate in first language: 30% to 60%. Literacy rate in second language: 5% to 15%. *Other:* Traditional religion, Christian. See main entry under China.

Lahu Shi (Kutsung, Kucong, Kui, Kwi, Shi, Yellow Lahu, Musseh Kwi, Musseh Lyang) [kds] 20,000 in Thailand (1998). In refugee camps near Laos border; formerly in Chiang Kham camp, but now in camps near Pua, Nan, or elsewhere. *Lg Dev:* Literacy rate in first language: below 1%. Literacy rate in second language: 5% to 15%. *Other:* Distinct from Kui (Kuy, Suoi), which is Mon-Khmer. See main entry under Laos.

Lamet (Kha Lamet, Khamet, Kamet, Lemet) [lbn] 100 in Thailand. Lampang, Chiangrai. *Dialects:* Upper Lamet, Lower Lamet. *Other:* Called 'Khamet' in Thailand and 'Lamet' in Laos. Traditional religion. See main entry under Laos.

Lawa, Eastern (Wiang Papao Lua, Northern Lawa) [lwl] 7,000 (1987 D. Schlatter). Northern; Chiangmai, Chiangrai, one village: Wiang Papao. *Class:* Austro-Asiatic, Mon-Khmer, Northern Mon-Khmer, Palaungic, Western Palaungic, Waic, Lawa. *Dialects:* Phalo, Phang. Not intelligible with Western Lawa. Phalo (100) and Phang (100) are treated as distinct languages in Wurm and Hattori 1981. *Lg Use:* Speakers also use Northern Tai. *Lg Dev:* Literacy rate in first language: below 1%. Literacy rate in second language: 25% to 50%. *Other:* Traditional religion, Buddhist.

Lawa, Western (Lava, Luwa, Lua, L'wa, Lavua, Lavüa, Mountain Lawa) [lcp] 7,000 in Thailand (1987 D. Schlatter). Numerous villages in Chiangmai and Maehongson provinces of northern Thailand. *Dialect:* La-Oor. *Lg Use:* Speakers also use Northern Tai. *Lg Dev:* Literacy rate in first language: 1% to 5%. Literacy rate in second language: 25% to 50%. *Other:* La-Oor is becoming the standard for literature. Traditional religion, Buddhist. See main entry under China.

Lisu (Lisaw, Li-Shaw, Li-Hsaw, Lu-Tzu, Southern Lisu, Yao Yen, Yaw-Yen, Yaw Yin, Yeh-Jen, Liso) [lis] 16,000 in Thailand (1993 Johnstone). Chiangmai, Chiangrai, Maehongson, Tak, Sukhothai, Kamphaeng Phet provinces. Some have migrated to northwest Thailand from Myanmar. *Dialect:* Lu Shi Lisu. *Lg Dev:* Literacy rate in first language: 5% to 10%. Literacy rate in second language: 50% to 75%. *Other:* Traditional religion, Christian. See main entry under China.

Lü (Lue, Tai Lue, Thai Lu, Tai Lu, Lu, Pai-I, Pai-Yi, Shui-Pai-I) [khb] 83,000 in Thailand (2001 Johnstone and Mandryk). Chiangrai, Payao, Lamphun, Nan, Chiang Kham, and throughout northern Thailand. *Lg Use:* All domains. All ages. Positive language attitude. Central Thai is used in schools and on the radio. Northern Thai is the language used in town for trade, employment, and with Northern Thai speakers. Many thousands of Lü speakers, including men and women, younger and older people understand very little Central Thai. *Lg Dev:* Literacy rate in first language: 1% to 5%. Literacy rate in second language: 50% to 75%. High in Central Thai in Thai script. *Other:* Valleys. Tropical forest. Agriculturalists: wet rice; fishermen. Traditional religion, Buddhist. See main entry under China.

Lua' (East Pua Pray, Pray 2) [prb] 6,281 (2000 WCD). East of Pua District in Nan Province. Also on Laos-Thailand border. *Class:* Austro-Asiatic, Mon-Khmer, Northern Mon-Khmer, Khmuic, Mal-Khmu', Mal-Phrai. *Lg Dev:* Bible portions: 1984. *Other:* Distinct from Mal, Phai, and Pray 3. Christian.

Mal (T'in, Ht'in, Thin, Tin, Khatin) [mlf] 3,000 to 4,000 in Thailand (1982 SIL). East of Pua District and Chiang Kam, valley near northern Laos border, Nan Province. *Lg Dev:* Literacy rate in first language: below 1% literate. Literacy rate in second language: 1% to 15%. *Other:* 'Mal' and 'Madl' are self names. 'T'in' is an ethnic name used in Thailand. See main entry under Laos.

Malay (Bahasa Malay, Melayu) [mly] Some villages in Ranong, south Thailand. *Other:* Shafi Muslim. See main entry under Malaysia (Peninsular).

Malay, Pattani (Thai Islam) [mfa] 3,100,000 (1998). Population includes 2,600,000 in southern Thailand, 500,000 in Bangkok and elsewhere. Chana (Chenok) Region of Songkhla (Singgora) Province in the north, traversing southward through Pattani, Narathiwat, Yala, Saiburi, Tak Bai. *Class:* Austronesian, Malayo-Polynesian, Malayic, Malayan, Local Malay. *Dialects:* Different from Kedah Malay and Standard Malay. *Lg Use:* Speakers also use Central Thai. *Lg Dev:* NT: 1981. *Other:* Muslim, Christian.

Malay, Satun (Kedah Malay) [meo] A few villages near Satun. Isolated. *Lg Use:* Speakers also use Central Thai. *Other:* More people in the area speak Thai than Pattani. Most outside contacts are with centers of Thai population in Songkhla, Phattalung, and Haad Yai; with west coast Malay states of Perlis and Kedah. Culturally Malay. Tropical forest. Muslim. See main entry under Malaysia (Peninsular) (Malay, Kedah).

Mlabri (Mla, Mla Bri, Mabri, Mrabri, Yumbri, Ma Ku, Yellow Leaf, Phi Thong Luang) [mra] 300 in Thailand (1982 E. R. Long). Population total all countries: 324. Laos border area. Phayao, Nan, Phrae, Utaradit, Phitsanuloke, Loey, and perhaps other provinces. Also spoken in Laos. *Class:* Austro-Asiatic, Mon-Khmer, Northern Mon-Khmer, Khmuic, Mlabri. *Lg Use:* They speak or understand some Hmong and Northern Thai. *Lg Dev:* Literacy rate in first language: below 1%. Literacy rate in second language: 0 to 1%. *Other:* Mlabri are different from the Kha Tong Luang (Phi Tong Luang, Yellow Leaf) in Laos, which are Western Viet-Muong (Wurm and Hattori 1981). Speakers are sometimes employed by the Hmong. Some are nomadic. Tropical forest. Agriculturalists: rice, maize; hunter-gatherers. Traditional religion.

Mok (Amok, Hsen-Hsum) [mqt] 7 (1981 Wurm and Hattori). Northwest; east northeast of Chiang Mai, on Wang River. *Class:* Austro-Asiatic, Mon-Khmer, Northern Mon-Khmer, Palaungic, Western Palaungic, Angkuic. *Other:* Nearly extinct.

Moken (Mawken, Basing, Selung, Selong, Salong, Salon, Chau Ko') [mwt] West coast of south Thailand, Phuket, Phangnga, Krabi, Ranong. *Dialects:* Dung, Ja-It, L'be. *Other:* They live primarily on boats, but occasionally settle on islands in the area. Fishermen. Traditional religion, Muslim. See main entry under Myanmar.

Moklen (Chau Pok) [mkm] 1,500 (1984 D. Hogan). Ethnic population: 4,000 (2000 D. Bradley). West coast of south Thailand, Phuket, Phangnga. *Class:* Austronesian, Malayo-Polynesian, Malayic, Moklen. *Other:* Heavy Thai and Mon-Khmer influence. Traditional religion, Muslim.

Mon (Talaing, Taleng, Aleng, Mun, Peguan, Takanoon) [mnw] 107,630 in Thailand (2000 WCD). On the Myanmar border, Kanchanaburi, Pathum Thani, Rat Buri, Surat Thani, Lopburi, Khorat; north and south of Bangkok. *Other:* In some areas they have apparently integrated with the Thai, in other areas they are separate. Traditional religion, Buddhist. See main entry under Myanmar.

Mpi (Mpi-Mi) [mpz] 900 (2000 D. Bradley). Ethnic population: 1,200 (2000 D. Bradley). Phrae, Phayao, two villages. *Class:* Sino-Tibetan, Tibeto-Burman, Lolo-Burmese, Loloish, Southern, Phunoi. *Dialects:* Close to Pyen, Phunoi. *Other:* Traditional religion.

Nyahkur (Nyah Kur, Nyakur, Niakuol, Niakuoll, "Chaobon," "Chaodon," Lawa) [cbn] 10,000 (2000 D. Bradley). Ethnic population: 20,000 (2000 D. Bradley). Central Thailand, Khorat, Petchabun, Chayaphum, a few villages, from north of B. Khum Chieo to south of Ban Kao, Thakhong and other rivers. *Class:* Austro-Asiatic, Mon-Khmer, Monic. *Lg Dev:* Literacy rate in first language: below 1%. Literacy rate in second language: 75% to 100%. *Other:* Their name for themselves is 'Nyahkur'. "Chaobon" is the Thai name and is derogatory. Buddhist.

Nyaw (Yo, Nyo, Nyoh, Jo) [nyw] 50,000 (1990 Diller). Sakorn Nakorn, Ta Bo', Nong Khai; Tha Uthen, Nakorn Panom. *Class:* Tai-Kadai, Kam-Tai, Be-Tai, Tai-Sek, Tai, Southwestern, Lao-Phutai. *Dialects:* Close to Isan (Northeastern Thai) and Luang Prabang Lao. *Lg Use:* Speakers also use Isan. *Other:* Maw may be an alternate name. Buddhist.

Nyeu (Yeu, Yoe) [nyl] 200. Sisaket. *Class:* Austro-Asiatic, Mon-Khmer, Eastern Mon-Khmer, Katuic, West Katuic, Kuay-Yoe. *Lg Dev:* Literacy rate in first language: below 1%. Literacy rate in second language: 25% to 50%.

Palaung, Pale (Di-Ang, Ngwe Palaung, Silver Palaung, Pale, Palay, Southern Ta-Ang) [pce] 5,000 in Thailand (1989). *Lg Dev:* Literacy rate in first language: below 1%. Literacy rate in second language: below 5%. *Other:* A distinct language from Shwe Palaung and Rumai Palaung. See main entry under Myanmar.

Phai (Phay, Thung Chan Pray, Kha Phay, Pray 1, Prai) [prt] 31,000 in Thailand (1993 Johnstone). Population total all countries: 46,000. Thung Chang District of Nan Province. Also spoken in Laos. *Class:* Austro-Asiatic, Mon-Khmer, Northern Mon-Khmer, Khmuic, Mal-Khmu', Mal-Phrai. *Dialects:* More Pray speakers have recently come from Laos to refugee camps, which could represent additional dialects. *Other:* Different from Lua, Mal, and Pray 3.

Phu Thai (Puthai, Putai, Phuu Thai, Phutai) [pht] 156,000 in Thailand (1993). Population total all countries: 519,400. Kham Chai, Nakorn Panom, Ubon, Kalasin, Sakorn Nakorn. Also possibly in China. Also spoken in Laos, USA, Viet Nam. *Class:* Tai-Kadai, Kam-Tai, Be-Tai, Tai-Sek, Tai, Southwestern, Lao-Phutai. *Dialects:* Little dialect differentiation. Close to Tai Dam and Tai Don. *Lg Use:* Speakers also use Isan (a dialect of Northeastern Thai). *Lg Dev:* Literacy rate in first language: below 1%. Literacy rate in second language: 75% to 100%. *Other:* Buddhist.

Phuan (Lao Phuan, Phu Un) [phu] 98,605 in Thailand (2000 WCD). Population total all countries: 204,704. Uthai Thani, Phichit, Petchabun, Lopburi, Singburi, Suphanburi, Saraburi, Nakorn Nayok, Phrachinburi, Udon, Loei, and one village south of Bangkok. Also spoken in Laos. *Class:* Tai-Kadai, Kam-Tai, Be-Tai, Tai-Sek, Tai,

Southwestern, East Central, Chiang Saeng. *Dialects:* Close to Northern Tai, Tai Dam, Song, Lao. *Lg Use:* Vigorous. Strong sense of identity. A socially prominent group. *Other:* They were relocated to Thailand from 1827 to 1890. The name is also used for Lao speakers in Thailand. There is an annual Phuan celebration in Bangkok. Buddhist.

Phunoi (Phu Noi, Punoi, Phounoy) [pho] Some in Chiangrai. *Dialects:* Black Khoany, White Khoany, Mung, Hwethom, Khaskhong. *Lg Dev:* Literacy rate in second language: 50% to 75%. *Other:* Known as 'Côông' in Viet Nam. See main entry under Laos.

Pray 3 [pry] 38,808 (2000 WCD). Interspersed in Thung Chang and Pua districts among the Mal. *Class:* Austro-Asiatic, Mon-Khmer, Northern Mon-Khmer, Khmuic, Mal-Khmu', Mal-Phrai. *Dialects:* One dialect is more distinct. Separate from Phai and Lua. *Lg Use:* Speakers also use Mal. *Lg Dev:* Literacy rate in first language: below 1%. Literacy rate in second language: 25% to 50%.

Saek (Sek, Tai Sek) [skb] 11,000 in Thailand (1993 Johnstone). Northeastern, Nakorn Panom. *Lg Use:* Speakers also use Lao. *Other:* Buddhist. See main entry under Laos.

Shan (Sha, Tai Shan, Sam, Tai Yay, Thai Yay, Great Thai, Tai Luang, "Ngio," "Ngiow," "Ngiaw," "Ngiao," "Ngeo") [shn] 60,000 in Thailand (2001 Johnstone and Mandryk). Maehongson, Myuang Haeng, Chiangrai, Chiangmai, Maesai, Tak, on northwestern border. *Other:* Plains. Agriculturalists: paddy rice; artisans (gold, silver, blacksmiths); shopkeepers. Buddhist, traditional religion, Christian. See main entry under Myanmar.

Sô (Kha So, Thro) [sss] 58,000 in Thailand (2001 Johnstone and Mandryk). Nakorn Panom, Sakorn Nakorn, Nong Kai, Kalasin. Both sides of Mekong River in northeastern Thailand. 53 villages in Thailand. *Dialects:* So Trong, So Slouy, So Phong, So Makon. *Lg Use:* Used in the home. All ages. They also speak Lao. They are adjusting to Thai culture and gradually becoming bilingual in Thai. *Lg Dev:* Literacy rate in first language: below 1%. Literacy rate in second language: 25% to 50%. *Other:* They came from Laos, and the same dialect is spoken there. Plains. Agriculturalists: wet rice. Buddhist, traditional religion, Christian. See main entry under Laos.

Tai Dam (Jinping Dai, Tai Noir, Thai Den, Black Tai) [blt] 700 in Thailand (2004). Loei Province, village of Ban Na Pa Nat. *Other:* Arrived in Thailand in 1885. See main entry under Viet Nam.

Tai Nüa (Chinese Shan, Tai Neua, Tai Man, Dehong Dai) [tdd] Also possibly in northern Viet Nam. See main entry under China.

Thai (Central Tai, Standard Thai, Thaiklang, Siamese) [tha] 20,182,571 in Thailand (2000 WCD). Population includes 400,000 Khorat (1984). 4,704,000 mother-tongue Thai speakers who are ethnic Chinese, or 80% of the Chinese (1984). Population total all countries: 20,229,987. Central Thailand, centered in Bangkok. Khorat dialect in Ratchasima. Also spoken in Singapore, United Arab Emirates, USA. *Class:* Tai-Kadai, Kam-Tai, Be-Tai, Tai-Sek, Tai, Southwestern, East Central, Chiang Saeng. *Dialect:* Khorat Thai (Korat, Thaikorat). *Lg Use:* Official language of the country and medium of education and most mass communication. 40,000,000 second-language speakers in Thailand (2001 A. Diller). *Lg Dev:* Thai script. Radio programs. Grammar. Bible: 1883–2000. *Other:* People sometimes called 'Siamese'. SVO. Buddhist, Christian.

Thai Sign Language [tsq] 51,000 profoundly, prelingually deaf people in Thailand (1997 Charles B. Reilly). 20% of deaf children go to school, where they get the opportunity to learn this language. Major regional centers and Bangkok. *Class:* Deaf sign language.

Dialects: The first deaf school was established in 1951, with influence from Gallaudet University in the USA. It uses a combination of indigenous signs and American Sign Language. Before 1950 Chiangmai and Bangkok had their own separate but related sign languages, and probably other 'urban' areas had their own sign languages, related to present sign languages in parts of Laos and Viet Nam, including Haiphong. The signs used at the deaf school at Tak are reported to be very different. *Lg Use:* Total communication used in school: speaking and signing. Reported to be high mobility among most deaf people today. The sign language used in the classroom and that by deaf adults outside is different. All deaf born since 1951, and some older ones. *Lg Dev:* Literacy rate in second language: Fewer than 10%. Educated deaf people have some Thai literacy skills, but limited. Taught in primary schools. TV. Dictionary. *Other:* There is a manual system for spelling. Buddhist.

Thai Song (Lao Song, Lao Song Dam, Song) [soa] 32,307 (2000 WCD). Kanchanaburi, Phetburi, Pitsanulok, Nakorn Sawaan, Nakorn Pathom, Suphanburi. *Class:* Tai-Kadai, Kam-Tai, Be-Tai, Tai-Sek, Tai, Southwestern, East Central, Chiang Saeng. *Dialects:* Only slight dialect differences. Close to Tai Dam. *Lg Dev:* Bible portions. *Other:* Traditional religion.

Thai, Northeastern (Isan, Isaan, Issan, Thai Isaan) [tts] 15,000,000 (1983 SIL). Population includes at least 1,000,000 in Bangkok. Kalerng has a few thousand speakers (1990 A. Diller ANU). Northeastern; 17 provinces. Kalerng is in Sakon Nakhon and Nakhon Phanom. *Class:* Tai-Kadai, Kam-Tai, Be-Tai, Tai-Sek, Tai, Southwestern, Lao-Phutai. *Dialects:* Northern Isan, Central Isan (Kalerng, Kaleung, Kaloeng), Southern Isan. Korat. The Korat dialect is quite different, and may be a separate language. *Lg Use:* 88% use Isan in the home, 1% use Central Thai, 11% use both. *Lg Dev:* Thai script. *Other:* The people are called 'Isan'. SVO. Buddhist.

Thai, Northern (Lanna, Lan Na, Lanatai, "Yuan," Phyap, Phayap, Payap, Kammüang, Kammyang, Myang, Kam Mu'ang, Mu'ang, Khon Mung, Khon Myang, Tai Nya, La Nya, Northern Thai, Western Laotian) [nod] 6,000,000 in Thailand (1983 SIL). Population total all countries: 6,009,396. Chiangmai, Chiangrai, Lamphun, Lampang, Maehongson, Hot, Nan, Phayao, Phrae, Uttaradit, Tak provinces. Also spoken in Laos. *Class:* Tai-Kadai, Kam-Tai, Be-Tai, Tai-Sek, Tai, Southwestern, East Central, Chiang Saeng. *Dialects:* Nan, Bandu, Tai Wang. The Nan dialect is more distinct. *Lg Use:* 87.5% use Northern Tai in the home, 3% use Central Thai, 9.5% use both. Rural or uneducated speakers have limited proficiency in Central Thai. *Lg Dev:* Newspapers. NT: 1914. *Other:* People are called 'Khon Mung', but do not like the name "Yuan." Has had Yuan script for a long time, in which are written Buddhist sermons, inscriptions, the Bible. Not used much now. Few can read it. Thai script has been used for literature in Northern Thai also, although it lacks some necessary contrasts. Buddhist.

Thai, Southern (Pak Thai, Pak Tai, Paktay, Dambro) [sou] 5,000,000 (1990 Diller). Population includes 1,500,000 to 3,000,000 or more Muslim Tai (2001). Chumphon, Nakorn Srithammarat; 14 provinces total. Muslim Tai in provinces of Chumporn, Nakorn Srithammarat, Phattalung, Songkhla, Ranong, Phanga, Phuket, Krabi, Trang, Satun. *Class:* Tai-Kadai, Kam-Tai, Be-Tai, Tai-Sek, Tai, Southwestern, Southern. *Dialects:* Tak Bai (Tai Tak Bai), Thai Malay (Tai Islam). A group of dialects more distantly related to other Tai languages. The border dialects are quite distinct from others. *Lg Use:* 81% use Southern Thai in the home, Muslim Tai ('Thai Malay') speak only Southern Thai. 8.5% use Central Tai.

Lg Dev: Speakers read Central Thai. Bible portions: 2000. *Other:* Buddhist, Muslim, Christian.

Tonga (Mos) [tnz] Ethnic population: 300 (2000 D. Bradley). Two areas in the south. Also spoken in Malaysia (Peninsular). *Class:* Austro-Asiatic, Mon-Khmer, Aslian, North Aslian, Tonga. *Dialect:* Satun. Probably close to Kensiu. *Lg Use:* May be extinct (2000 D. Bradley).

Ugong (Lawa, 'Ugong, Gong, Ugawng) [ugo] 80 (2000 D. Bradley). Ethnic population: 500. Kanchanaburi, Uthai Thani, Suphanburi. None in Myanmar. *Class:* Sino-Tibetan, Tibeto-Burman, Lolo-Burmese, Loloish, Southern. *Dialects:* Kok Chiang, Suphanburi. Not closely related to other languages. *Lg Use:* No longer spoken in most of its former locations. Children speak Thai as first language. Used by 80 adults as language of the home. Adult speakers, youngest in 50s. No children speakers since 1977. All speak some variety of Thai. *Other:* Distinct from Lawa in the Palaung-Wa branch of Mon-Khmer. They were relocated because of a dam.

Urak Lawoi' (Orak Lawoi', Lawta, Chaw Talay, Chawnam, Lawoi) [urk] 3,000 (1984 D. Hogan). Ethnic population: 3,000 (2000 D. Bradley). Phuket and Langta islands, west coast of southern Thailand. Not in Malaysia. *Class:* Austronesian, Malayo-Polynesian, Malayic, Malayan, Para-Malay. *Dialects:* Aboriginal Malays who speak a unique Malay language. *Lg Dev:* Grammar. NT: 1998. *Other:* Traditional religion, Christian.

Yong (Nyong) [yno] 12,561 (2000 WCD). Chiangrai, Chiangmai, Lamphun. May also be in Muang Yong, northern Myanmar. *Class:* Tai-Kadai, Kam-Tai, Be-Tai, Tai-Sek, Tai, Southwestern, Unclassified. *Dialects:* Phonology similar to Lü. *Lg Use:* Speakers also use Northern Tai. *Other:* Buddhist.

Yoy (Yoi, Yooi, Yooy, Dioi, Jui) [yoy] 5,000 in Thailand (1990 Diller). Population total all countries: 6,000. Sakorn Nakorn. Also spoken in Laos. *Class:* Tai-Kadai, Kam-Tai, Be-Tai, Tai-Sek, Tai, Northern. *Lg Use:* Speakers also use Northeastern Tai.

Turkey

Republic of Turkey, Turkiye Cumhuriyeti. 68,893,918. Population includes both Europe and Asia sections. National or official language: Turkish. Literacy rate: 76% to 90%. Also includes refugees from Central Asia (50,000). Information mainly from T. Sebeok 1963, 1970; O. Jastrow 1971, 1988; A. Nakano 1986; B. Comrie 1987; P. A. Andrews 1989; M. Izadi 1993. Blind population: 38,178. Deaf population: 316,839. Deaf institutions: 12. The number of languages listed for Turkey is 36. Of those, 34 are living languages and 2 are extinct.

Turkey (Asia)

Also see Turkey in Europe for a listing of languages in Europe. Also includes Assyrian Neo-Aramaic, Avar, Chaldean Neo-Aramaic, Chechen (8,000), Dargwa, Lak (300), Lezgi (1,200), Mesopotamian Spoken Arabic (100,000), North Levantine Spoken Arabic (500,000), Northern Uzbek, Western Farsi (500,000). The number of languages listed for Turkey (Asia) is 24. Of those, 23 are living languages and 1 is extinct.

Abaza (Abazin, Tapanta, Abazintsy, Ahuwa) [abq] 10,000 in Turkey (1995). *Dialects:* Tapanta, Ashkaraua (Ashkar), Bezshagh. *Lg Use:* Speakers also use Turkish. *Other:* Muslim. See main entry under Russia (Europe).

Abkhaz (Abxazo) [abk] 4,000 in Turkey (1980). Ethnic population: 39,000 in Turkey (2001 Johnstone and Mandryk). Coruh in northeast Turkey, and some in

northwest. Mainly villages in Bolu and Sakarya provinces. *Dialects:* Bzyb, Abzhui, Samurzakan. *Lg Use:* 96% bilingual in Turkish. *Other:* Agriculturalists. Muslim (Sunni). See main entry under Georgia.

Adyghe (Adygey, Circassian, Cherkes) [ady] 277,900 in Turkey (2000). 6,409 monolinguals (1965 census). Ethnic population: 130,000 in Turkey (1965 census). Villages in Kayseri, Tokat, Karaman Maras, and many other provinces in central and western Anatolia. *Lg Use:* 94% bilingual in Turkish. *Other:* Agriculturalists. Muslim (Sunni). See main entry under Russia (Europe).

Arabic, North Mesopotamian Spoken (Syro-Mesopotamian Vernacular Arabic) [ayp] 400,000 in Turkey (1992). Mardin and Siirt provinces. *Lg Use:* Men are quite bilingual in Turkish. *Other:* They do not read Arabic. Agriculturalists; small shops, businesses. Muslim, Christian. See main entry under Iraq.

Azerbaijani, South (Azeri) [azb] 530,000 in Turkey. Kars Province. *Dialect:* Kars. *Lg Use:* The people of Kars Province speak Azerbaijani but use Turkish as the literary language. *Other:* Muslim. See main entry under Iran.

Crimean Turkish (Crimean Tatar) [crh] It is not known how many still speak it in Turkey, though there are definitely some Crimean Tatar villages, such as Karakuyu in Polatli District of Ankara Province. *Dialects:* Northern Crimean (Crimean Nogai, Steppe Crimean), Central Crimean, Southern Crimean. *Other:* Muslim. See main entry under Uzbekistan.

Dimli (Dimili, Zazaki, Southern Zaza, Zaza) [diq] 1,000,000 in Turkey (1999 WA). Between 1.5 and 2.5 million speakers (including all dialects) (1998 Paul). East central, mainly in Elazig, Bingol, and Diyarbakir provinces, upper courses of the Euphrates, Kizilirmaq, and Murat rivers. Also spoken in Germany. *Class:* Indo-European, Indo-Iranian, Iranian, Western, Northwestern, Zaza-Gorani. *Dialects:* Sivereki, Kori, Hazzu (Hazo), Motki (Moti), Dumbuli (Dumbeli). Several dialects. Related to Gurani group. *Lg Use:* Some speakers know Kurmanji. *Lg Dev:* Magazines. *Other:* Mountain slope, plains. Agriculturalists; pastoralists; urban. Muslim (Sunni).

Georgian (Kartuli, Gruzin) [kat] 40,000 in Turkey (1980). 4,042 monolinguals (1965 census). Ethnic population: 91,000. Villages in Artvin, Ordu, Sakarya, and other provinces of north and northwest Anatolia. *Dialect:* Imerxev. *Lg Use:* 95% also use Turkish. *Other:* Muslim (Sunni). See main entry under Georgia.

Hértevin [hrt] 1,000 (1999 H. Mutzafi). Originally Siirt Province. They have left their villages, most emigrating to the West, but some may still be in Turkey. *Class:* Afro-Asiatic, Semitic, Central, Aramaic, Eastern, Central, Northeastern. *Dialects:* Hértevin Proper (Arton), Umraya, Jinet. Considerable differences from other Northeastern Aramaic varieties, and not intelligible with any or most of them. *Lg Use:* Speakers also use Kurdish, and some are multilingual. *Lg Dev:* Syriac script. *Other:* Christian (Chaldean).

Kabardian [kbd] 550,000 in Turkey (2001 Johnstone and Mandryk). Most around Kayseri. 1,000 villages of Kabardian and Adyghe in Turkey. *Other:* Muslim (Sunni). See main entry under Russia (Europe).

Kazakh (Kazakhi, Qazaqi, Kazax, Kosach, Kaisak) [kaz] 600 in Turkey (1982). Salihli town in Manisa Province, and an unknown number in Istanbul city; 308 in Kayseri Province; refugees from Afghanistan, now Turkish citizens. *Other:* Muslim. See main entry under Kazakhstan.

Kirghiz [kir] 1,137 in Turkey (1982). Van and Kars provinces. *Other:* Refugees from Afghanistan; now Turkish citizens. Muslim (Sunni). See main entry under Kyrgyzstan.

Kirmanjki (Zaza, Northern Zaza, Zazaki, Alevica, Dimilki, Dersimki, So-Bê, Zonê Ma) [kiu] 140,000 in Turkey. Population includes 100,000 in 182 villages in

Tunceli Province, 40,000 in 13 or more villages in Erzincan Province (1972). Tunceli Province, Tunceli Merkez, Hozat, Nazmiye, Pülümür, and Ovacik subprovinces; Erzincan Province, Erzincan and Cayirli subprovinces; 8 or more villages in Elazig Province, Elazig Merkez and Karakoqan subprovinces; 3 villages in Bingöl Province, Kigi and Karkiova subprovinces; 46 villages in Mush Province, Varto Subprovince; 15 or more villages in Sivas Province, Zara, Imranli, Kangal, and Divrigi subprovinces; 11 or more villages in Erzerum Province, Hinis and Tekman subprovinces; and in many major cities of Turkey. Also spoken in Austria, Denmark, France, Germany, Netherlands, Sweden, Switzerland, United Kingdom. *Class:* Indo-European, Indo-Iranian, Iranian, Western, Northwestern, Zaza-Gorani. *Dialects:* Tunceli, Varto. Closest to Dimli. Lexical similarity 70% with Dimli. *Lg Use:* Some Kurmanji know Kirmanjki as second language. Abroad they use Kirmanjki for close relationships. In Turkey Kirmanjki is used for conversations with family, friends, and neighbors. All ages, most between 20 and 50. Women over 50 in outlying villages in Tunceli Province and children under 7 are monolingual. Turkish is used for religious ceremonies and for official purposes. Most men know some Turkish. Abroad they use Turkish for religious ceremonies, wedding celebrations. All who live abroad learn the national languages to some degree and use them for communication with nationals. *Lg Dev:* Literacy rate in second language: School-age children to 30 years old, Turkish. Poetry. Magazines. *Other:* People from different ethnic groups or places call themselves 'Shar Ma', 'Sar Ma', 'Dimil' or 'Kirmandz'. SOV; pre- and postpositions; genitives, articles, adjectives relatives after noun heads; numerals before noun heads; question word replaces content word in content questions; 2 prefixes, 2 suffixes, word order distinguishes subject, object, indirect object; noun affixes indicate case; verb affixes indicate person, number, gender; ergativity; passives; causatives; comparatives; V, VC, VCC, CV, CVC, CVCC; nontonal. Mountain mesa, mountain slope, valleys. Deciduous forest. 1,000 to 3,000 meters. Pastoralists, peasant agriculturalists. Muslim (Alevi).

Kumyk (Kumuk, Kumuklar, Kumyki) [kum] A few villages. *Dialects:* Khasav-Yurt, Buinak, Khaidak. *Lg Use:* Language of wider communication. *Other:* Different from the Kumux dialect of Lak. Muslim. See main entry under Russia (Europe).

Kurdish, Northern (Kurmanji, Kurmancî, Kirmancî, Kermancî, Kurdi, Kurdî) [kmr] 3,950,000 in Turkey (1980). Population total all countries: 9,113,505. Ethnic population: 6,500,000 in Turkey (1993 Johnstone). The majority are in provinces of Hakkari, Siirt, Mardin, Agri, Diyarbakir, Bitlis, Bingol, Van, Adiyaman, and Mus. Also in Urfa, Kars, Tunceli, Malatya, Erzurum, Marash, Sivas, and other provinces. Communities in central Turkey (Cankiri, Cihanbeyli, near Konya). Many live in large cities in western Turkey (including Istanbul, Adana, Ankara, Izmir). Also spoken in Armenia, Australia, Austria, Azerbaijan, Bahrain, Belgium, Canada, Denmark, Finland, France, Georgia, Germany, Greece, Iran, Iraq, Italy, Jordan, Kazakhstan, Kuwait, Kyrgyzstan, Lebanon, Netherlands, Norway, Russia (Europe), Sweden, Switzerland, Syria, Turkmenistan, United Kingdom, USA. *Class:* Indo-European, Indo-Iranian, Iranian, Western, Northwestern, Kurdish. *Dialects:* Boti (Botani), Marashi, Ashiti, Bayezidi, Hekari, Shemdinani. Differences in speaking among dialects, but all use the same written form. *Lg Use:* Language of wider communication. Positive language attitude. Not many speakers use Turkish. *Lg Dev:* Literacy rate in second language: 28%. Much literature produced especially in twentieth century; Roman

alphabet developed in 1932; originally based on Boti (Botani, Ciziri) variety and more recently influenced by that which is used around Diyarbekir and other areas. There are literary works from 16th and 17th centuries and onward. Roman, Arabic, and Cyrillic scripts; also in Iran, Iraq, and Syria; Cyrillic script in Armenia. Newspapers. Radio programs. Dictionary. Grammar. NT: 1872–2000. *Other:* Mountain slope. Muslim (Sunni, Alevi), Yezidi.

Laz (Lazuri, Laze, Chan, Chanzan, Zan, Chanuri) [lzz] 30,000 in Turkey (1980). Population total all countries: 33,000. Ethnic population: 92,000 in Turkey (1980). Rize in northeast, towns of Kemer, Atin, Artasen, Vitse, Arkab, Hopa, Sarp; and villages in Artvin, Sakarya, Kocaeli, and Bolu provinces. Also spoken in Belgium, France, Georgia, Germany, USA. *Class:* Kartvelian, Zan. *Dialects:* Officially considered to be a single language with Mingrelian, called 'Zan', although linguists recognize that they are not inherently intelligible with each other. *Lg Use:* 95% reported to use Turkish. *Other:* Their name for their language is 'Lazuri'. Not a written language in Turkey. Fishermen. Muslim.

Osetin (Ossete) [oss] The Digor dialect is reported to be in Bitlis and another small town in the west. Iron dialect in cities or towns of Sarikamis and Erzerum. Also in Mugla, Kars, Antalya. May also be in Syria. *Dialects:* Digor, Tagaur, Kurtat, Allagir, Tual, Iron. *Other:* Christian (Russian Orthodox), Muslim (Sunni). See main entry under Georgia.

Syriac (Classical Syriac, Ancient Syriac, Suryaya, Suryoyo, Lishana Atiga) [syc] Extinct. Turkey, Iraq, and Syria. Also spoken in Iraq. *Class:* Afro-Asiatic, Semitic, Central, Aramaic, Eastern. *Dialects:* Western Syriac, Eastern Syriac. The Syrian churches: Eastern (Nestorian), Syrian Orthodox (Jacobite), Syrian Catholic (Melkite, Maronite) developed a vast literature based on the Edessa (currently Sanliurfa, southeastern Turkey) variety of the Syrian dialect. The Assyrian group (see Assyrian Neo-Aramaic in Iraq and elsewhere) separated denominationally from the Chaldean (see Chaldean Neo-Aramaic in Iraq) and Jacobite (see Turoyo in Turkey and Syria) in the Middle Ages. Neo-Eastern Aramaic languages spoken by Christians are often dubbed 'Neo-Syriac', although not directly descended from Syriac. *Lg Use:* Became extinct in the 10th to 12th centuries. Still used as a literary secular language among followers of the churches listed, although rarely. *Lg Dev:* Syriac script. Bible: 1645–1891. *Other:* Christian (Nestorian, Jacobite, Melkite, Maronite, Syrian Orthodox).

Turkish (Türkçe, Türkisch, Anatolian) [tur] 46,278,000 in Turkey (1987). Population total all countries: 50,625,794. Spoken throughout Turkey as first or second language. Also spoken in Australia, Austria, Azerbaijan, Belgium, Bosnia and Herzegovina, Bulgaria, Canada, Cyprus, Denmark, El Salvador, Finland, France, Georgia, Germany, Greece, Honduras, Iran, Iraq, Israel, Kazakhstan, Kyrgyzstan, Macedonia, Netherlands, Romania, Russia (Asia), Serbia and Montenegro, Sweden, Switzerland, Tajikistan, Ukraine, United Arab Emirates, United Kingdom, USA, Uzbekistan. *Class:* Altaic, Turkic, Southern, Turkish. *Dialects:* Danubian, Eskisehir, Razgrad, Dinler, Rumelian, Karamanli, Edirne, Gaziantep, Urfa. Danubian is western; other dialects are eastern. *Lg Use:* Official language. The Karamanli are Turkish-speaking Greeks. *Lg Dev:* Roman script. Dictionary. Grammar. Bible: 1827–1941. *Other:* SOV. Muslim.

Turkish Sign Language [tsm] *Class:* Deaf sign language.

Turkmen (Trukhmen) [tuk] 925 in Turkey (1982). Tokat Province. *Other:* Refugees from Afghanistan; now Turkish citizens. Muslim (Sunni). See main entry under Turkmenistan.

Turoyo (Suryoyo, Syryoyo, Turani, Süryani) [tru] 3,000 in Turkey (1994 Hezy Mutzafi). Population total all countries: 84,000. Ethnic population: 50,000 to 70,000 (1994). Southeastern Turkey, Mardin Province (originally). Also spoken in Argentina, Australia, Belgium, Brazil, Canada, Germany, Iraq, Lebanon, Netherlands, Sweden, Syria, USA. *Class:* Afro-Asiatic, Semitic, Central, Aramaic, Eastern, Central, Northwestern. *Dialects:* Midyat, Midin, Kfarze, 'Iwardo, Anhil, Raite. Related to Northeastern Aramaic varieties. Turoyo subdialects exhibit a cleavage between Town Turoyo (Midyat Turoyo), Village Turoyo, and Mixed (Village-Town) Turoyo. The latter is spoken mainly by the younger generation outside Tur 'Abdin, Turkey, the language's original location, and is gaining ground throughout the Jacobite diaspora in other countries. *Lg Use:* All speakers also use their national languages or local lingua francas, and some are multilingual. *Lg Dev:* Syriac script. Bible portions: 1983. *Other:* Known among scholars almost exclusively as 'Tûrôyo'. 'Suryoyo' is a popular name. 'Western Syriac' refers to the Classical Western Syriac liturgy and orthography used by Turoyo speakers. Christian (Jacobite).

Uyghur (Uighur, Uygur, Uigur) [uig] 500 in Turkey (1981). Kayseri city, and an unknown number in Istanbul. Possibly in Iran. *Other:* Muslim (Sunni). See main entry under China.

Uzbek, Southern [uzs] 1,981 in Turkey (1982). Hatay, Gaziantep, and Urfa provinces. Also possibly in Germany. *Other:* Refugees from Afghanistan; now Turkish citizens. Distinct from Northern Uzbek of Uzbekistan and China. Muslim (Sunni). See main entry under Afghanistan.

Turkmenistan

Turkmenistan. 4,863,169. National or official language: Turkmen. 188,417 square miles. Literacy rate: 98%. Also includes Armenian (32,000), Bashkir (2,607), Belarusan (5,289), Brahui, Dargwa (1,599), Dungan, Erzya (3,488), Georgian (1,047), Karakalpak (2,542), Kazakh (88,000), Korean (3,493), Lak (1,590), Lezgi (10,400), Lithuanian (224), North Azerbaijani (33,000), Northern Uzbek (317,000), Osetin (1,887), Romanian (1,561), Russian (349,000), Tabassaran (177), Tajiki (1,277), Tatar (40,434), Ukrainian (37,118), Western Farsi (8,000). Information mainly from T. Sebeok 1963. The number of languages listed for Turkmenistan is 4. Of those, 3 are living languages and 1 is extinct. See map on page 833.

Balochi, Western (Baloci, Baluchi, Balui) [bgn] 28,000 in Turkmenistan (1993). *Lg Use:* Turkmen is used as the literary language in Turkmenistan. *Other:* Distinct from Eastern and Southern Balochi. Muslim. See main entry under Pakistan.

Chagatai (Chaghatay, Jagatai) [chg] Extinct. *Class:* Altaic, Turkic, Eastern.

Kurmanji (Khorasani Kurmanji, Kurmancî, Khorasani) [kmr] 20,000 in Turkmenistan (1962 Bakaev). Around Ashkhabad. *Other:* Muslim (Shi'a). See main entry under Turkey (Asia) (Kurdish, Northern).

Turkmen (Turkomans, Turkmenler, Turkmanian, Trukhmen, Trukhmeny, Turkmani) [tuk] 3,430,000 in Turkmenistan (1995). Population total all countries: 6,403,533. Ethnic population: 3,465,000 (1995). Also spoken in Afghanistan, Germany, Iran, Iraq, Kazakhstan, Kyrgyzstan, Pakistan, Russia (Asia), Tajikistan, Turkey (Asia), USA, Uzbekistan. *Class:* Altaic, Turkic, Southern, Turkmenian. *Dialects:* Nokhurli, Anauli, Khasarli, Nerezim, Yomud, Teke (Tekke), Goklen, Salyr, Saryq, Esari, Cawdur. *Lg Use:* National language. 50% claim a good knowledge of Russian. *Lg Dev:* Roman script;

Arabic and Cyrillic scripts in Afghanistan; Arabic script in Iran. Newspapers. Radio programs. Dictionary. Grammar. Bible portions: 1880–1982. *Other:* The so-called 'Turkmen' in Syria, and possibly Iraq and Jordan, actually speak an ancient form of Turkmen; so-called 'Turkmen' in Tibet may speak a different Turkic language. Desert. Agriculturalists: cotton; animal husbandry: sheep; carpet weavers; gas, oil workers. Muslim (Sunni).

United Arab Emirates

Ittihad al-Imarat al-Arabiyah, UAE. Formerly called Trucial States. 2,523,915. National or official language: Standard Arabic. Literacy rate: 68% to 78%. Also includes Bengali (70,000), Danish (156), Eastern Panjabi, Egyptian Spoken Arabic (100,000), English (100), French (250), Goanese Konkani, Greek (100), Hindi, Italian (400), Japanese (1,300), Malay, Malayalam (300,000), Omani Spoken Arabic (80,000), Polish (100), Serbian (100), Sinhala (25,000), Somali (46,412), Soqotri (7,000), Standard German (1,300), Swahili (2,500), Swedish (113), Tagalog (80,000), Tamil, Telugu, Thai (3,000), Turkish (750), Urdu, Western Panjabi. Information mainly from T. Sebeok 1970. Deaf population: 109,218. The number of languages listed for United Arab Emirates is 7. Of those, all are living languages.

Arabic, Gulf Spoken (Khaliji, Gulf Arabic) [afb] 744,000 in United Arab Emirates. Gulf Bedu or village peoples. *Other:* Government officials; oil administration; commerce leaders; military; police; university professors; sports coaches. Muslim. See main entry under Iraq.

Arabic, Shihhi Spoken (Shihhi, Shihu, Shihuh, Al-Shihuh) [ssh] 5,000 in United Arab Emirates (1995). Population total all countries: 27,000. In the Musandam Peninsula in United Arab Emirates. Also spoken in Oman. *Class:* Afro-Asiatic, Semitic, Central, South, Arabic. *Lg Use:* Not a written language. Most Shihuh speak Shihhi, but the Kumazirah subdivision of Shihuh, like the Dhahuriyin tribe, speak Kumzari. *Lg Dev:* Some may be literate in Arabic. *Other:* Influenced by Farsi. 'Shihuh' is the name of the people. Muslim.

Arabic, Standard [arb] Middle East, North Africa. *Lg Use:* Official language. Used for education, official purposes, formal speeches. See main entry under Saudi Arabia.

Balochi, Southern (Baluchi, Baluci, Baloci) [bcc] 100,000 in United Arab Emirates. *Dialect:* Makrani (Lotuni). *Other:* Speakers come from Oman, Iran, and Pakistan. Unskilled laborers; police; military. Muslim (Sunni). See main entry under Pakistan.

Farsi, Western (Persian) [pes] 80,000 in United Arab Emirates (1986). *Other:* Merchants; traders. Muslim. See main entry under Iran.

Pashto, Northern (Pusto, Pashtu, Passtoo, Pakhtoo, Pushto) [pbu] 100,000 in United Arab Emirates (1986). *Other:* People called Pathans. Speakers have come from Pakistan. Unskilled laborers; drivers. Muslim. See main entry under Pakistan.

Pashto, Southern (Paktu, Pakhtu, Pakhtoo, Afghan) [pbt] 26,060 in United Arab Emirates (2000 WCD). *Other:* Speakers have come from Afghanistan. Unskilled laborers; drivers; shopkeepers. Muslim (Sunni). See main entry under Pakistan.

Uzbekistan

Uzbekistan. 26,410,416. National or official language: Northern Uzbek. 172,700 square miles. Literacy rate: 99%. Also includes Armenian (50,000), Bashkir (35,000), Belarusan (29,000), Chechen, Chuvash (8,868), Dargwa

(1,337), Domari, Dungan (1,400), Erzya (14,176), Georgian (4,088), Ingush, Karachay-Balkar (612), Kazakh (808,000), Kirghiz (175,776), Korean (183,000), Lak (1,762), Lezgi (1,585), Lithuanian (1,040), Nogai (151), North Azerbaijani (44,000), Osetin (6,000), Parya, Romanian (3,152), Russian (1,661,000), Standard German (40,000), Tabassaran (224), Tajiki (934,000), Tajiki Spoken Arabic, Tatar (468,000), Turkmen (228,000), Ukrainian (153,000), Uyghur (36,000), Western Farsi (31,121). Information mainly from T. Sebeok 1963; H. Paper 1978; S. Akiner 1983. The number of languages listed for Uzbekistan is 7. Of those, all are living languages. See map on page 833.

Arabic, Uzbeki Spoken (Jugari, Kashkadarya Arabic, Uzbeki Arabic, Central Asian Arabic) [auz] 700. Uzbekistan, Bukhara Province; middle and lower Zerafshan Valley in Samarkand Province, and a few in Katta-Kurgan town. They mainly live in small villages. *Class:* Afro-Asiatic, Semitic, Central, South, Arabic. *Dialects:* Close to North Mesopotamian Spoken Arabic. Sharp dialect differences between Bukhara and Kashkadarya regions. Bukhara is strongly influenced by Tajiki; Kashkadarya by Uzbek and other Turkic languages. May be a mixed language. *Lg Use:* Speakers use Northern Uzbek to communicate with each other, and as literary language. Few members of the ethnic group now speak Arabic. No diglossia with Modern Standard Arabic. *Other:* They are endogamous and do not mix with speakers of other languages. Agriculturalists; animal husbandry: cattle. Muslim (Hanafi Sunni).

Bukharic (Bukharan, Judeo-Tajik, Bokharic, Bukharin, Bokharian) [bhh] 10,000 in Uzbekistan (1995). Various parts of Uzbekistan. The cultural center is Bokhara (Buchara). *Other:* Jewish. See main entry under Israel.

Crimean Turkish (Crimean Tatar) [crh] 189,000 in Uzbekistan (1993). Population total all countries: 456,341. Removed from southern shore of Crimean Peninsula to Uzbekistan in 1944. Also spoken in Bulgaria, Kyrgyzstan, Moldova, Romania, Turkey (Asia), Ukraine, USA. *Class:* Altaic, Turkic, Southern. *Dialects:* Northern Crimean (Crimean Nogai, Steppe Crimean), Central Crimean, Southern Crimean. *Lg Dev:* Cyrillic script. NT: 1666–1825. *Other:* The census counted them with the Tatar, but the languages are distinct. Muslim.

Judeo-Crimean Tatar (Judeo-Crimean Turkish, Krimchak) [jct] Uzbekistan (most), Georgia, Kazakhstan. Also spoken in Georgia, Kazakhstan. *Class:* Altaic, Turkic, Western, Ponto-Caspian. *Lg Use:* There are few speakers left (T. Salminen 1993). *Other:* Jewish. Nearly extinct.

Karakalpak (Karaklobuk, Tchorny, Klobouki) [kaa] 407,000 in Uzbekistan (1993 UBS). Population total all countries: 411,542. Ethnic population: 424,000 in the former USSR. Along the lower Amu Darya and around the southern part of the Aral Sea. Also spoken in Afghanistan, Kazakhstan, Kyrgyzstan, Turkmenistan. *Class:* Altaic, Turkic, Western, Aralo-Caspian. *Dialects:* Northeastern Karakalpak, Southeastern Karakalpak. *Lg Use:* Speakers also use Uzbek or Russian. *Lg Dev:* Cyrillic script. Bible portions: 1996. *Other:* Some literature. Fishermen in Aral Sea, agriculturalists; craftsmen. Muslim (Sunni).

Turkish (Osmanli) [tur] 197,000 in Uzbekistan, Tajikistan, Kazakhstan, and Kyrgyzstan (based on 1979 census, not counting 56,000 'Turks of Fergana', who speak an Uzbek dialect). *Dialects:* Danubian, Eskisehir, Razgrad, Dinler, Rumelian, Karamanli, Edirne, Gaziantep, Urfa. *Lg Use:* Some speak Turkish; others Azerbaijani. Meskhetian Georgians, Khemshel Armenians, and Kurds in Uzbekistan speak Turkish. *Other:* Muslim (Sunni). See main entry under Turkey (Asia).

Uzbek, Northern (Özbek) [uzn] 16,539,000 in Uzbekistan (1995 UN). Population total all countries:

18,795,591. Uzbekistan and throughout Asian republics of the former USSR. East of the Amu Darya and around the southern Aral Sea. Possibly in Munich, Germany. Also spoken in Australia, China, Israel, Kazakhstan, Kyrgyzstan, Russia (Asia), Tajikistan, Turkey (Asia), Turkmenistan, Ukraine, USA. *Class:* Altaic, Turkic, Eastern. *Dialects:* Karluk (Qarlug), Kipchak (Kypchak), Oghuz. Distinct from Southern Uzbek of Afghanistan, Pakistan and Turkey. Russian influences in grammar, use of loanwords, script. Oghuz may be a dialect of Khorasani Turkish (see Turkey) rather than Uzbek. *Lg Use:* Official language. Vigorous. Turks of Fergana and Samarkand speak Uzbek. There are Uzbek-speaking Gypsy communities in Russian central Asia. All ages. Children speak Uzbek at home. Positive language attitude. 49% of speakers also use Russian, but rural people have low proficiency. *Lg Dev:* Literacy rate in second language: High. Taught in primary and secondary schools. Cyrillic script; Arabic, Sogdian, Roman, and Cyrillic scripts in China. Radio programs. TV. Dictionary. Grammar. NT: 1992–1995. *Other:* People are about one-third urbanized. Much Persian influence in language and culture. Patrilineal. 'Sart' is an obsolete name for sedentary Uzbek, possibly those who are ethnically Tajik. SOV; has lost its historical vowel harmony and its vowel system now resembles that of Tajiki. Valleys. Desert, semiarid. Agriculturalists: cotton, fruit, vegetables, grain; pastoralists: sheep; silk production; technicians, professionals, industrial workers, communications, medicine, educators, administrators. Muslim (Hanafi Sunni).

Viet Nam

Socialist Republic of Vietnam. Cong Hoa Xa Hoi Chu Nghia Viet Nam. 82,689,518. Population includes 54 official ethnic communities. 56,849,370 or 94% speakers of Austro-Asiatic languages, 2,255,450 or 3.7% speakers of Daic languages, 679,000 or 1.1% speakers of Miao-Yao languages, 492,000 or 0.8% speakers of Austronesian languages, 40,000 speakers of Tibeto-Burman languages (1991 J. Matisoff). National or official language: Vietnamese. Literacy rate: 78% to 88%. Also includes Mandarin Chinese, Northern Dong. Information mainly from C. P. Miller 1964, 1966; M. Barker 1966; D. Thomas 1966, 1969, 1976, 1980; D. Thomas and R. Headley, Jr. 1970; F. Lebar, G. Hickey, J. Musgrave 1964; K. Smith 1968; J. A. Edmondson and D. B. Solnit 1997. Blind population: 200,000 (1982 WCE). Deaf institutions: 1. The number of languages listed for Viet Nam is 103. Of those, 102 are living languages and 1 is extinct. See maps beginning on page 834.

Akha (Kaw, Ekaw, Ikaw, Aka, Ak'a, Ahka, Ko, Khako, Kha Ko, Khao Ikor, Aini, Yani) [ahk] 1,261 in Viet Nam (1995 Institute for Southeast Asian Studies, Hanoi). Quang Binh and Quang Tri Provinces both sides of the Viet Nam-Laos border, northeast of Phuc Trach. *Other:* Traditional religion, Christian. See main entry under Myanmar.

Arem (A-Rem, Chomrau, Chombrau, Umo) [aem] 20 in Viet Nam (1996 Ferlus). Population total all countries: 40. Ethnic population: 100 in Viet Nam (1996 Ferlus). Tan Trach and one or two families of Thuong Trach in Bo Trach District, Quang Binh Province. Also spoken in Laos. *Class:* Austro-Asiatic, Mon-Khmer, Viet-Muong, Chut. *Dialects:* Other dialects or ethnic names: Tu-vang, Pa-leng, Xo-lang, To-hung, Chà-cu, Tac-cui, Nhà Chút. *Lg Use:* Speakers also use Vietnamese. *Other:* Chút is an official ethnic community in Viet Nam, including Sách, Mày, Ruc, and Arem. Nearly extinct.

Bahnar (Bana) [bdq] 158,456 in Viet Nam (1999 census). Gia Lai, Kon Tum, Binh Dinh, Phu Yen provinces, central highlands. Also spoken in USA. *Class:* Austro-Asiatic,

Mon-Khmer, Eastern Mon-Khmer, Bahnaric, Central Bahnaric. *Dialects:* Tolo, Golar, Alakong (A-La Cong), Jolong (Gio-Lang, Y-Lang), Bahnar Bonom (Bomam), Kontum, Krem. Other dialects or ethnic names: Roh, Kpang Cong. Closest to Alak 1, Tampuan, and Lamam. *Lg Dev:* Literacy rate in first language: 10% to 30%. Literacy rate in second language: 50% to 75%. NT: 1977. *Other:* An official ethnic community in Viet Nam. Mountain slope. Traditional religion, Christian.

Brao (Brau, Braou, Proue, Brou, Love, Lave, Laveh, Rawe) [brb] 313 in Viet Nam (1999 census). Kon Tum Province, Cambodia-Laos border area. *Dialect:* Palau. *Other:* Traditional religion, Christian. See main entry under Laos (Lave).

Bru, Eastern (Bru, Brou, Van Kieu, Quang Tri Bru) [bru] 55,559 in Viet Nam (1999 census). Quang Binh, Quang Tri, and Dac Lac provinces. *Dialects:* Mangkong, Tri. *Lg Dev:* Literacy rate in first language: 1% to 5%. Literacy rate in second language: 15% to 25%. *Other:* The name 'Bru' means 'mountain people'. The So people in Laos call themselves 'Bru'. Traditional religion, Christian. See main entry under Laos.

Cao Lan (Caolan, San Chay, San Chi, "Man Cao-Lan," Sán-Chi, "Mán," Cao Lan-Sán Chi) [mlc] 147,315 in Viet Nam (1999 census). Population total all countries: 187,315. The San Chay are mainly concentrated in Tuyen Quang, Bac Can, and Thai Nguyen provinces. They are also found scattered in certain areas of Yen Bai, Vinh Phuc, Phu Tho, Bac Giang, and Quang Ninh provinces. Also spoken in China. *Class:* Tai-Kadai, Kam-Tai, Be-Tai, Tai-Sek, Tai, Central. *Dialects:* Maintains some features from Northern Tai. *Other:* The official San Chay nationality in Viet Nam. Speakers are said to have come from China in the 19th century. They may speak a form of Yue Chinese. "Man" is derogatory. Tonal. Traditional religion.

Cham, Eastern (Tjam, Chiem, Chiem Thành, Bhamam) [cjm] 72,873 in Viet Nam (2002). Binh Thuan, Ninh Thuan, Dong Nai provinces and Ho Chi Minh City. Also spoken in USA. *Class:* Austronesian, Malayo-Polynesian, Malayic, Achinese-Chamic, Chamic, South, Coastal, Cham-Chru. *Lg Dev:* Literacy rate in first language: 5% to 10%. Literacy rate in second language: 60%. Bible portions: 1973. *Other:* An official ethnic community in Viet Nam. Remnants of a once powerful kingdom. Austro-Asiatic influences. Agriculturalists. Traditional religion, Hindu, Christian.

Cham, Western (Cambodian Cham, Tjam, Cham, New Cham, Chiem) [cja] 25,000 in Viet Nam. Population includes 4,000 in Saigon. An Giang and Tay Ninh provinces and Ho Chi Minh City. *Other:* The language differs somewhat from Eastern Cham of central Viet Nam. Muslim. See main entry under Cambodia.

Chinese, Yue (Suòng Phóng, Quang Dong, Hai Nam, Ha Xa Phang, Minh Huong, Chinese Nung, Nung, Lowland Nung, Hoa, Han, Triều Chau, Phúc Kiến, Liem Chau, Samg Phang) [yue] 862,371 in Viet Nam (1999 census). Soc Trang, Can Tho, Vinh Long, Tra Vinh, Dong Nai, and Kieng Giang provinces and in the cities of Ho Chi Minh, Hanoi, and Haiphong, and along the northern Viet Nam-China border regions. *Other:* Renowned fighters. Came from Canton, China as railroad workers and soldiers several decades ago. They are not the same as the Nung in the Tai family or the Tibeto-Burman Nung (Nu) of China and Myanmar. Daoist, Christian. See main entry under China.

Chrau (Chauro, Choro, Ro, Tamun) [crw] 22,567 (1999 census). Few monolinguals. Dòng Nai Province. The Tamun group live in Tayninh and Binhlong provinces. *Class:* Austro-Asiatic, Mon-Khmer, Eastern Mon-Khmer, Bahnaric, South Bahnaric, Stieng-Chrau. *Dialects:* Jro, Dor (Doro), Prang, Mro, Voqtwaq, Vajieng, Chalah, Chalun, Tamun. *Lg Use:* Some parents pass on Chrau to

children. Informally used in education, oral and written use in religious services, oral literature. Positive language attitude. Nearly all speak Vietnamese as second language. *Lg Dev:* Literacy rate in first language: 30%. Literacy rate in second language: 50% to 75%. 5,000 can read Chrau, 500 can write it. Grammar. NT: 1982. *Other:* The name Chrau means 'mountain dweller'. Plains. Swidden agriculturalists. Traditional religion, Christian.

Chru (Churu, Choru, Chu Ru, Chu, Cru, Kru, Chrau Hma, Cadoe Loang, Seyu) [cje] 14,978 in Viet Nam (1999 census). Lam Dong and Binh Thuan provinces. Also spoken in France, USA. *Class:* Austronesian, Malayo-Polynesian, Malayic, Achinese-Chamic, Chamic, South, Coastal, Cham-Chru. *Dialect:* Rai, Noang (La-Dang). Close to Cham. *Lg Use:* Speakers also use Vietnamese. *Lg Dev:* Literacy rate in first language: 5% to 10%. Literacy rate in second language: 25% to 50%. Bible portions: 1955.

Chut (Sach, Salang, Ruc, May) [scb] 3,829 in Viet Nam (1999 census). Population total all countries: 4,279. Quang Binh Province, Thuong Hoa, Hoa Son, Dan Hoa communes, near the Laos border at the same latitude as Mu Gia Pass. Also spoken in Laos. *Class:* Austro-Asiatic, Mon-Khmer, Viet-Muong, Chut. *Dialect:* Sach, May, Ruc (Kha Mu Gia, Tac Cui). *Other:* Part of the Chut official ethnic community, together with Arem, May, and Ruc. Upland rice cultivation (Sach, Salang), seminomads (Ruc, May). Traditional religion.

Côông ("Xa Coong," "Xa Xam," Khoong, "Xa Xeng") [cnc] 2,000 (2002 Edmondson). Lai Chau Province, Muong Te District, east of Sila, south of Mang. 4 villages at Ban Nam Luong in Xa Can Ho, Bo Lech in Xa Can Ho, Nam Kha Co area at Ban Bo, Muong Tong at Nam Ke near the Lao border. *Class:* Sino-Tibetan, Tibeto-Burman, Lolo-Burmese, Loloish, Southern, Phunoi. *Dialects:* Quite different from Akha, Lahu, and Sila of this location. The northern and southern varieties in Viet Nam are different, but inherently intelligible to speakers. Bisu, Pyen, and Mpi are closely related. *Lg Use:* Few domains. Spoken by half the children. Mildly supportive language attitude. *Other:* No final consonants.

Cua (Bong Miew, Bòng Mieu) [cua] 27,766 (1999 census). Quang Ngai and Quang Nam provinces. *Class:* Austro-Asiatic, Mon-Khmer, Eastern Mon-Khmer, Bahnaric, North Bahnaric, East, Cua-Kayong. *Dialects:* Kol (Kor, Cor, Co, Col, Dot, Yot), Traw (Tràu, Dong). *Lg Dev:* Bible portions: 1973. *Other:* Traditional religion, Christian.

En (Nung Ven) [enc] 200 (1998 Edmondson). Cao Bang Province, Noi Thon village, about 20 km directly east on foot from Ho Quang City, Ho Quang District. *Class:* Tai-Kadai, Kadai, Yang-Biao. *Dialects:* Lexical similarity less than 50% with Laha, Qabiao (Laqua), Lachi, Gelao, Buyang, Hlai. *Other:* No uvular consonants; has its own number system.

Gelao, Green (Hoki Gelao, Cape Draping Gelao, Klau, Qau) [giq] 300 (2002 Edmondson). Yen Minh District, Pho La and Dong Van. *Class:* Tai-Kadai, Kadai, Ge-Chi. *Lg Use:* Many speakers are shifting to Hmong, Tay, or Chinese. *Other:* An official nationality in Viet Nam. Not mutually intelligible with Red Gelao (Edmondson). Agriculturalists: rice. Polytheist.

Gelao, Red (Voa Dê, Vandu Gelao) [gir] 20. Yen Minh District. *Class:* Tai-Kadai, Kadai, Ge-Chi. *Lg Use:* Speakers are shifting to Mandarin. *Other:* An official nationality in Viet Nam. Not mutually intelligible with White Gelao (Edmondson). Agriculturalists: rice. Polytheist. Nearly extinct.

Gelao, White (Tú Du, Telue, Southwestern Gelao) [giw] 20 (2002 Edmondson). Yen Minh District, Pho La and Dong Van. *Class:* Tai-Kadai, Kadai, Ge-Chi. *Other:* An official nationality in Viet Nam. Not mutually intelligible with Red Gelao (Edmondson). Agriculturalists: rice. Polytheist. Nearly extinct.

Giáy (Bouyei, Bo-Y, Bo-I, Buyi, Pu-I, Puyi, Pui, Chang Chá, Trong Ggia, Tu-Dìn, Nhaang, Nyang, Niang, Yai, Yay, Giai, Giang, Dang, Dioi, Pau Thin, Pú Nà, Pu-Nam, Cùi Chu, Xa Chung Chá, Chung Cha, Sa) [pcc] 49,098 in Viet Nam (1999 census). Lao Cai, Hà Giang, and Lai Chau provinces. *Dialects:* Tu-Dí, Nhang, Pú Nà. *Other:* An official nationality in Viet Nam and China. Polytheist, Daoist. See main entry under China (Bouyei).

Haiphong Sign Language [haf] Haiphong. *Class:* Deaf sign language. *Dialects:* Related to sign languages in Hanoi, Ho Chi Minh City, Laos, and earlier sign languages in Thailand.

Halang (Salang, Koyong) [hal] 13,500 in Viet Nam (2000). Population total all countries: 17,500. Kon Tum Province. Also spoken in Laos. *Class:* Austro-Asiatic, Mon-Khmer, Eastern Mon-Khmer, Bahnaric, North Bahnaric, West, Jeh-Halang. *Dialects:* Close to Jeh. Salang in Laos may be a different but related language. *Lg Dev:* Literacy rate in first language: 5% to 10%. Literacy rate in second language: 25% to 50%. Bible portions: 1970–1972. *Other:* Traditional religion.

Halang Doan (Halang Duan, Duan, Doan) [hld] 2,000 in Viet Nam (1981 Wurm and Hattori). Population total all countries: 4,346. Kon Tum Province, between the Sedang and the Cua. Also spoken in Laos. *Class:* Austro-Asiatic, Mon-Khmer, Eastern Mon-Khmer, Bahnaric, North Bahnaric, West, Duan. *Dialects:* May be intelligible with Takua, Kayong, Halang Daksut, or Rengao.

Hani (Hànhì, Haw, Uni, U Ní, Xauni, Xá U Ní) [hni] 17,535 in Viet Nam (1999 census). Lai Chau and Lao Cai provinces in northern Viet Nam. One variety is east, one west of Muong Te City. Not in Thailand. *Other:* An official nationality in Viet Nam and China. Speakers call themselves 'Hà Nhì'. Two close varieties in Viet Nam differ only in phonology and lexicon. Polytheist, traditional religion. See main entry under China.

Hanoi Sign Language [hab] Hanoi. *Class:* Deaf sign language. *Dialects:* Related to sign languages in Haiphong, Ho Chi Minh City, Laos, and earlier sign languages in Thailand.

Haroi (Hrway, Hroi, Hroy, Hoi, Aroi, Bahnar Cham) [hro] 35,000 (1998). Binh Dinh and Phu Yen provinces. *Class:* Austronesian, Malayo-Polynesian, Malayic, Achinese-Chamic, Chamic, South, Plateau.

Hmong Daw (White Meo, Meo Kao, White Lum, Mán Tráng, Bai Miao) [mww] All Hmong in Viet Nam: 787,604 (1999 census). Most live in several provinces of northern Viet Nam, now over 10,000 resettled in Dac Lac province in southern Viet Nam. *Dialect:* Hmong Xi (Meo Do). *Other:* Largely intelligible with Hmong Njua. No significant difference between White and Striped Hmong. Traditional religion, Christian. See main entry under China.

Hmong Dô [hmv] Ha Giang Province, Dong Van and Meo Vae districts; Lao Cai Province, Bac Ha District. *Class:* Hmong-Mien, Hmongic, Chuanqiandian. *Dialects:* Largely intelligible with Hmong Daw. Lexical similarity 80% with Hmong Daw. *Other:* Tonal, 8 tones. Traditional religion, Christian.

Hmong Don [hmf] Ha Giang Province, Hua Binh, YenBai, Nghia Lo. *Class:* Hmong-Mien, Hmongic, Chuanqiandian. *Other:* Tonal, 7 tones. Traditional religion, Christian.

Hmong Njua (Blue Meo, Green Miao, Tak Meo, Hmong Njwa, Hmong Leng) [blu] Living in many provinces of northern Viet Nam, probably some in Dac Lac Province in southern Viet Nam. *Dialect:* Hmong Hoa. *Other:* Traditional religion, Christian. See main entry under China.

Hmong Shua [hmz] 60 (2003). Ha Giang Province, 3 villages. *Class:* Hmong-Mien, Hmongic, Chuanqiandian.

Other: Likely most closely related to a Hmong group in China. SOV. Agriculturalists. Traditional religion.

Ho Chi Minh City Sign Language [hos] Ho Chi Minh City. *Class:* Deaf sign language. *Dialects:* Related to sign languages in Hanoi, Haiphong, Laos, and earlier sign languages in Thailand.

Hre (Davak, Davach, Moi Da Vach, Moi, Moi Luy, Cham-Re, Chom, Tachom) [hre] 113,111 (1999 census). Quang Ngai and Binh Dinh provinces. *Class:* Austro-Asiatic, Mon-Khmer, Eastern Mon-Khmer, Bahnaric, North Bahnaric, West, Sedang-Todrah, Sedang. *Dialects:* Rabah (Tava), Creq (Kare, Kre), Hre. Closest to Sedang. *Lg Dev:* Literacy rate in first language: 1% to 5%. Literacy rate in second language: 15% to 25%. Bible portions: 1967–1975. *Other:* An official ethnic community in Viet Nam. Traditional religion, Christian.

Hung (Cuói, K'katiam-Pong-Houk) [hnu] 700 in Viet Nam (1996 Ferlus). Pong dialect in Tam Thai commune, Tuong Duong District, Nghe An Province, and Dan Lai and Ly Ha dialects in Mon Son and Luc Da communes, Con Cuong District. *Dialects:* Pong (Poong, Phong, Tay Pong, Toum Phong, Khong Kheng, Xa La Vang, Pong 1, Pong 2), Dan Lai, Ly Ha. See main entry under Laos.

Iu Mien (Kim Mien, Yu Mien, Mien, "Mán," Yao, Myen, Highland Yao, Dao Do, Red Dao, "Dong," "Trai," "Xá," Dìu, Yao Kimmien, Yao Ogang, Dao Thanh Phan) [ium] 350,000 in Viet Nam (1999 H. Purnell). Throughout the highland regions of northern Viet Nam, about 16,000 in Dac Lak Province in the south. *Dialects:* Dao Do, Deo Tien, Dao Lan Tien, Dao Lo Gang, Cham, Quan Chet, Quan Trang. *Lg Use:* The language is the same as in Thailand and Laos. Not all ethnic Yao speak Mien; many speak Chinese. Part of the population figure given for Viet Nam may be for Kim Mun. *Other:* An official ethnic community in Viet Nam. Daoist, traditional religion. See main entry under China.

Jarai (Djarai, Gia-Rai, Jorai, Cho-Rai, Chor, Mthur, Chrai, Gio-Rai) [jra] 317,557 in Viet Nam (1999 census). Population total all countries: 332,557. Mainly in Gia Lai and Kon Tum Provinces, some in Dac Lac Province. Also spoken in Cambodia, USA. *Class:* Austronesian, Malayo-Polynesian, Malayic, Achinese-Chamic, Chamic, South, Plateau. *Dialects:* Puan, Hodrung (Hdrung), Jhue, Aráp, Habau (Ho-Bau), To-Buan, Sesan, Chuty, Pleikly, Golar. *Lg Dev:* Literacy rate in first language: 10% to 30%. Literacy rate in second language: 50% to 75%. NT: 1974. *Other:* An official ethnic community in Viet Nam. A different script used in Viet Nam and Cambodia. Mountain slope. Traditional religion, Christian.

Jeh (Die, Yeh, Gie) [jeh] 15,243 in Viet Nam (2002 SIL). Population total all countries: 23,256. Kon Tum and Quang Nam provinces. Also spoken in Laos. *Class:* Austro-Asiatic, Mon-Khmer, Eastern Mon-Khmer, Bahnaric, North Bahnaric, West, Jeh-Halang. *Dialects:* Jeh Bri La (Bri-La), Jeh Mang Ram. Related to Halang. *Lg Dev:* Literacy rate in first language: 1% to 5%. Literacy rate in second language: 15% to 25%. Bible portions: 1967–1978.

Katu, Eastern (High Katu) [ktv] 50,458 (1999 census). Quang Nam and Thua Thien provinces. *Class:* Austro-Asiatic, Mon-Khmer, Eastern Mon-Khmer, Katuic, East Katuic, Katu-Pacoh. *Dialects:* A different language variety and orthography in Laos. *Lg Dev:* Literacy rate in first language: below 1%. Literacy rate in second language: 5% to 15%. NT: 1978. *Other:* Traditional religion, Christian.

Katua (Ca Tua) [kta] 3,000 (1981 Wurm and Hattori). Gia Lai-Cong Tum Province, around Mang Buk, west of the Kayong language. *Class:* Austro-Asiatic, Mon-Khmer, Eastern Mon-Khmer, Bahnaric, North Bahnaric.

Kayong (Kagiuong, Ca Giong, Katang) [kxy] 2,000 (1981 Wurm and Hattori). Remote mountains of Cong Tum

Province. *Class:* Austro-Asiatic, Mon-Khmer, Eastern Mon-Khmer, Bahnaric, North Bahnaric, East, Cua-Kayong. *Dialects:* Close to Takua and Cua. *Other:* Mountain slope.

Kháng (Khaang, Tayhay, Tay Hay, Xa, Xá Khao, Xa Xua, Xa Don, Xa Dang, Xa Hoc, Xa Ai, Xa Bung, Quang Lam, Hang, Bren, Ksakautenh, Putenh, Pouteng, Teng, Theng) [kjm] 3,921 (1985 F. Proschan). Son La and Lai Chau provinces in northern Viet Nam. *Class:* Austro-Asiatic, Mon-Khmer, Northern Mon-Khmer, Khmuic, Xinh Mul. *Dialect:* Kháng Clau, Kháng Ai (Xa Khao, Xa Cau, Sakau). Related to Puoc and Phong-Kniang in Laos. *Other:* An official ethnic community. Traditional religion.

Khao [xao] 10,000 (1981 Wurm and Hattori). Northwest, near the Ma River, north of Pa Ma. *Class:* Austro-Asiatic, Mon-Khmer, Northern Mon-Khmer, Khmuic, Khao. *Dialects:* Related to Bit in Laos and China.

Khmer, Central (Cambodian, Kho Me, Cur Cul, Cu Tho, Viet Go Mien, Khome, Krom) [khm] 1,055,174 in Viet Nam (1999 census). Mainly in Hau Giang, Tra Vinh, Vinh Long, Kien Giang, An Giang, Bac Lieu, Ca Mau, Ba Ria-Vung Tau, Binh Phuoc, and Tay Ninh provinces and Ho Chi Minh City. *Dialects:* Central Khmer, Southern Khmer. *Other:* Buddhist, Christian. See main entry under Cambodia.

Khmu (Kmhmu, Khomu, Khamu, Mun Xen, Xa Cau, Kha Cau, Cam Mu) [kjg] 56,542 in Viet Nam (1999 census). Son La, Lai Chau, Nghe An, and Yen Bai provinces. *Other:* Traditional religion, Christian. See main entry under Laos.

Khua [xhv] 3,000 in Viet Nam (1981 Wurm and Hattori). Population total all countries: 5,000. West central; southeast of Giap Tam. Also spoken in Laos. *Class:* Austro-Asiatic, Mon-Khmer, Eastern Mon-Khmer, Katuic, West Katuic, Brou-So. *Dialects:* Related to Bru, Mangkong, Leun. *Other:* Distinct from Cua.

Kim Mun (Mun, Lanten, Lan Ten, Lantin, "Man Lan-Tien," Lowland Yao, Coc Mun, Jinmen, Dao Quan Trang, Red Trouser Yao, Dao Thanh Y, Dao Ao Dai, Great Tunic Yao, Dao Lam Dinh) [mji] 170,000 in Viet Nam (1999 J. Edmondson). *Other:* Included in the Dao nationality in Viet Nam. The variety at Lao Cai to the northwest of Lao City and Ha Giang at Na Khe village are very different phonetically. See main entry under China.

Koho (Coho, Caho, Kohor) [kpm] 128,723 in Viet Nam (1999 census). Lam Dòng, Binh Thuan, Ninh Thuan and Khanh Hoa provinces. Also spoken in USA. *Class:* Austro-Asiatic, Mon-Khmer, Eastern Mon-Khmer, Bahnaric, South Bahnaric, Sre-Mnong, Sre. *Dialects:* Chil (Kil), Tring (Trinh), Sre, Kalop, Sop, Laya, Rion, Nop (Xre Nop, Tu-Lop), Tala (To La), Kodu (Co-Don), Pru, Lac (Lat, Lach). *Lg Dev:* Literacy rate in first language: 10% to 30%. Literacy rate in second language: 50% to 75%. NT: 1967. *Other:* An official ethnic community. Christian, traditional religion.

Lachi (La Chi, Lachí, Laji, Lati, Tai Lati, Lipulio, Y To, Y Pí, Y Póng, Y Mia, Cù Te, Cu-Tê) [lbt] 7,863 in Viet Nam (1990 census). Population includes 3,990 women, in 1,450 households (1990 Liang Min), including Black Lachi 2,500 in 550 households, Long-Haired Lachi 4,500 in 900 households. 10,765 for all La Chi in Viet Nam (1999 census). Population total all countries: 9,016. Ethnic population: 9,600 (2000 D. Bradley). Hà Giang Province, mostly west of Hà Giang in the upper Clear River valley (Riviere Claire) on the China border: Black Lachi at Manyou, Long-Haired Lachi at Manpeng. Also spoken in China. *Class:* Tai-Kadai, Kadai, Ge-Chi. *Dialects:* Liputiõ (Black Lachi), Lipupi (Long-Haired Lachi). Related to Gelo. Long-Haired Lachi of Viet Nam (4,806 speakers) has 80% lexical similarity with Flowery Lachi of China; White Lachi of Viet Nam (1,602) has 30% to

40% similarity with the others, and should be considered a separate language. Lexical similarity 36% with Gelo, 33% with Laqua, 34% with Buyang, 28% with Northern Zhuang, 22% with Dong, 23% with Laka, 25% with Hlai. *Lg Use:* Those in Viet Nam continue to use the language. Speakers also use Zhuang, Miao, Chinese. *Other:* 'Red', 'Flowery', etc., refer to clothing color or other features of physical appearance. Agriculturalists: wet rice; animal husbandry. Traditional religion.

Lachi, White (White Lachi, Lipupõ) [lwh] 1,602 (1990 Liang Min). 300 households. Hà Giang Province, northern Viet Nam south of Maguan in China, Manbang and Manmei. *Class:* Tai-Kadai, Kadai, Ge-Chi. *Dialects:* Lexical similarity 30% to 40% with other Lachi. *Other:* Tonal.

Laghuu (Laopa, Xá Phó) [lgh] 300 (2002 Edmondson). Northwestern Viet Nam. Lao Cai Province, Sa Pa District, Nam Sa village. 15 km south and east of Sa Pa City, in the valley below the highest mountain in Viet Nam, Phan Si Pan (3,198 meters). *Class:* Sino-Tibetan, Tibeto-Burman, Lolo-Burmese, Loloish, Northern, Yi. *Dialects:* It is not known how this relates to Laopang (Laopa) of Myanmar, also in the Lolo group.

Laha (Xá Khao, Khlá Phlao, Klá Dong, Khlá Don, Khlá Dung, Khlá Liik, La Ha Ung, La Ha, Xá Chien, Xá Lay) [lha] 5,686 (1999 census). Lao Cai and Son La provinces, along the Red and Black rivers. *Class:* Tai-Kadai, Kadai, Yang-Biao. *Dialects:* Close to Qabiao. *Lg Use:* Those under 50 seldom speak Laha. Those under 50 speak Thái and dress like the Tai Dam. *Other:* An official nationality. They live together with the Thái and Kháng. Agriculturalists: wet and dry rice. Traditional religion.

Lahu (Lohei, Lahuna, Launa, Laku, Kaixien, Namen, Mussuh, Muhso, Musso, Mussar, Mooso) [lhu] 6,874 All Lahu (Yellow, Black, White) in Viet Nam (1999 census). Northwestern border of Viet Nam with Laos. Black Lahu are north of Muong Te City near the China border, at Ban Kiem Tra, Phu Nam Ma, Phu Nam Cau, Phu Nam Ha. White Lahu are in one village just to the east of Nha Ca in Muong Te. *Dialects:* Na (Black Lahu, Khucong, Musser Dam), Nyi (Red Lahu, Musseh Daeng), Shehleh, Lahu Phung (White Lahu). *Other:* An official ethnic community in Viet Nam. Distinct from Lahu Shi (Yellow Lahu). One source called them White Lahu. It is not clear if these are the same as Red Lahu, Black Lahu, or different. Traditional religion. See main entry under China.

Lahu Shi (Kutsung, Kucong, Khutsho, Yellow Lahu, Shi, Kui, Kwi, Ne Thu, La Hu Si) [kds] 6,874 all Lahu (Yellow, Black, White) in Viet Nam (1999 census). Lai Chau Province, just to the west of Muong Te City on the Son Da (Black River). See main entry under Laos.

Lü (Pai-I, Shui-Pai-I, Lue, Tai Lu, Nhuon, Duon) [khb] 4,964 in Viet Nam (1999 census). Lai Chau Province, northern Viet Nam in the Binh Lu area. *Other:* An official nationality in Viet Nam. Traditional religion, Buddhist. See main entry under China.

Maa (Maaq, Ma, Maa', Chauma, Ma Ngan, Che Ma, Ma Xop, Ma To, Ma Krung) [cma] 33,338 (1999 census). Lam Dong, Dong Nai provinces, spread over a wide area. *Class:* Austro-Asiatic, Mon-Khmer, Eastern Mon-Khmer, Bahnaric, South Bahnaric, Sre-Mnong, Sre. *Dialects:* Sometimes considered a Koho dialect. *Lg Dev:* Literacy rate in first language: 10% to 30%. Literacy rate in second language: 50% to 75%. *Other:* An official ethnic community. Traditional religion, Christian.

Maleng (Malieng, Malang) [pkt] 200 in Viet Nam (1996 Ferlus). Malieng in Thanh Hoa and Lam Hoa communes, Tuyen Hoa District, dan Hoa in Minh Hoa District, northern Quang Binh Province; Huong Lien commune in Huong Khe District, Ha Tinh Province, 2 or 3 villages bordering Laos, and another to the southeast. *Dialects:*

Malieng (Pa Leng), Kha Phong (Maleng Kari, Maleng Bro, Kha Nam Om). See main entry under Laos.

Mang (Mang U, Xá Mang, Xá Ó, Nieng Ó, Chaman, Manbu, Ba'e, Xá Lá Vàng) [zng] 2,663 in Viet Nam (1999 census). Population total all countries: 3,168. Ethnic population: 4,500 (2000 D. Bradley). Lai Chau Province, in villages in a triangle-shaped area between the Song Da (Black River) and the Nam Na at places such as Nam Nghe, Nam Xung, Nam Ban, Ban Nam Voi. Also spoken in China, Thailand. *Class:* Austro-Asiatic, Mon-Khmer, Northern Mon-Khmer, Mang. *Other:* An official ethnic community in Viet Nam. Traditional religion.

Mantsi (Lolo, Flowery Lolo, Black Lolo, Red Mantsi) [nty] 1,100 (2002 Edmondson). Hà Giang Province at Meo Vac and Dong Van districts. *Class:* Sino-Tibetan, Tibeto-Burman, Lolo-Burmese, Loloish, Northern, Yi. *Dialects:* Called 'Southeast Vernacular' type of Yi. May be related to what is called Southeastern Yi or Guizhou Yi in China. Not intelligible with Sichuan Yi (Nosu). *Lg Dev:* Yi script. *Other:* Many uvular consonants, tense-lax voice quality; tonal, 5 tones.

Mnong, Central (Pnong, Budong, Budang, Phanong) [cmo] 32,451 in Viet Nam (2002 SIL). Population total all countries: 52,451. Southwest of the Rade, mainly in Song Bé and western Dac Lac provinces. Also spoken in Cambodia. *Class:* Austro-Asiatic, Mon-Khmer, Eastern Mon-Khmer, Bahnaric, South Bahnaric, Sre-Mnong, Mnong, Southern-Central Mnong. *Dialects:* Préh (Pre), Biat (Bhiét), Bu Nar, Bu Rung, Dih Bri (Di-Pri), Bu Dang. Biat may be a separate language related to Eastern Mnong. *Lg Dev:* NT: 2001. *Other:* Mnong is an official ethnic community in Viet Nam. Mountain slope. Traditional religion, Christian.

Mnong, Eastern [mng] 30,000 in Viet Nam (2002 SIL). Southeast of the Rade in Dac Lac and Lam Dòng provinces. Also spoken in USA. *Class:* Austro-Asiatic, Mon-Khmer, Eastern Mon-Khmer, Bahnaric, South Bahnaric, Sre-Mnong, Mnong, Eastern Mnong. *Dialects:* Mnong Rolom (Rolom, Rolam, Rlam, Ralam), Mnong Gar (Gar), Mnong Kwanh, Chil. Biat may be closer to Eastern Mnong than to Central Mnong. *Lg Dev:* Bible portions: 1977.

Mnong, Southern [mnn] 30,000 (2002). Mostly in Binh Phuoc Province south of the Central Mnong and north of the Stieng. *Class:* Austro-Asiatic, Mon-Khmer, Eastern Mon-Khmer, Bahnaric, South Bahnaric, Sre-Mnong, Mnong, Southern-Central Mnong. *Dialects:* Bunong (Nong, Pnong), Prang (Po Rang). *Other:* Ra-Ong, Bu Sre, Bu Dip, and Kuenh are possibly subgroups. Probably the same as Pnong (Phnong) in Cambodia.

Monom (Bonom, Menam, Monam) [moo] 5,000 (1973 SIL). Eastern Gia Lai and Kon Tum provinces. *Class:* Austro-Asiatic, Mon-Khmer, Eastern Mon-Khmer, Bahnaric, North Bahnaric, West, Sedang-Todrah, Todrah-Monom.

Muong [mtq] 1,137,515 (1999 census). Hoa Bình, Thanh Hóa, Vinh Phú, Yen Bai, Son La, and Ninh Binh provinces, mostly in the mountains of north central Viet Nam. *Class:* Austro-Asiatic, Mon-Khmer, Viet-Muong, Muong. *Dialects:* Thang, Wang, Mol, Mual, Moi 1, Boi Bi (Moi Bi), Ao Tá (Au Tá). Related to Sach, May, Ruc, Arem, Thavung, Pakatan. *Lg Dev:* Literacy rate in first language: 1% to 5%. Literacy rate in second language: 50% to 70%. Bible portions: 1963. *Other:* An official ethnic community. Mountain slope. Traditional religion, Christian.

Ná-Meo [neo] 1,200 (2002). Northwest part of Lang Son Province, Trang Dinh District, Cao Minh Village and Khuoi Phu Dao Village, Khanh Long Hamlet; Thach An District, Ca Liec Village. *Class:* Unclassified. *Other:* Possible immigrants from Guangxi Province in China.

Nguôn (Ngouan) [nuo] 2,000 (1981 Wurm and Hattori). Minh Hoa District, northeastern Quang Binh Province.

Class: Austro-Asiatic, Mon-Khmer, Viet-Muong, Muong. *Dialects:* Diffloth (1992) groups Nguon as a separate language close to Vietnamese, but Doi (1996) and Ferlus (1996) group it with Muong.

Nung (Nong, Bu-Nong, Highland Nung, Tai Nung, Tay, Tày Nùng) [nut] 856,412 in Viet Nam (1999 census). Mainly in Cao Bang and Lang Son provinces. A number of Nung now live in Ho Chi Minh City, Dong Nai, Lam Dong, and Dac Lac. Also spoken in Australia, Canada, Laos, USA. *Class:* Tai-Kadai, Kam-Tai, Be-Tai, Tai-Sek, Tai, Central. *Dialects:* Xuòng, Giang, Nùng An, Nùng Phan Slình (Nùng Fan Slihng), Nùng Cháo, Nùng Lòi, Nùng Qúy Rin (Guiren), Khen Lài, Nùng Inh. Close to Tày and Southern Zhuang (Ningming, Longzhou varieties). Dialect cluster with Southern Zhuang in China. *Lg Use:* Members of the ethnic group have preserved the language and culture more than the Tày. *Lg Dev:* Literacy rate in first language: 1% to 5%. Literacy rate in second language: 50% to 75%. Dictionary. Bible portions: 1971–1975. *Other:* Different from Chinese Nung (Cantonese) and Tibeto-Burman Nung (Nu). An official nationality in Viet Nam.

O'du (O Du, Iduh, 'Iduh, "Tay Hat," Hat, Haat) [tyh] 301 in Viet Nam (1999 census). Population total all countries: 495. Nghe Tinh Province in northern Viet Nam. Also spoken in Laos. *Class:* Austro-Asiatic, Mon-Khmer, Northern Mon-Khmer, Khmuic, Mal-Khmu', Khmu'. *Other:* An official ethnic community in Viet Nam. Speakers call themselves 'O Du'. Traditional religion.

Pa Di (Padi) [pdi] 300 in Viet Nam. Lao Cai Province, Muong Khuong District. See main entry under China.

Pa-Hng (Pa Hng, Paheng, Baheng, Bahengmai, Pà Hung, Pà Then) [pha] 5,569 in Viet Nam (1999 census). Tuyên Quang and Hà Giang provinces. *Other:* An official ethnic community in Viet Nam. Mountain slope. Traditional religion. See main entry under China.

Pacoh (Paco, Pokoh, Bo River Van Kieu) [pac] 16,000 in Viet Nam (2002). Population total all countries: 29,224. Quang Tri Province. Also spoken in Laos. *Class:* Austro-Asiatic, Mon-Khmer, Eastern Mon-Khmer, Katuic, East Katuic, Katu-Pacoh. *Dialect:* Pahi (Ba-Hi). Related to Phuong. 'Koh' in 'Pacoh' means 'mountain'. *Lg Dev:* Literacy rate in first language: below 1%. Literacy rate in second language: 15% to 25%. Dictionary. Grammar. Bible portions: 1965–1969.

Phu Thai (Putai, Phutai, Puthay, Puthai) [pht] 209,000 in Viet Nam (2002). Northern. *Other:* Part of the Thái official ethnic community in Viet Nam. See main entry under Thailand.

Phula (Phu La, Phu Khla, Phu Kha, Fu Khla) [phh] 9,046 in Viet Nam (1999 census). Population total all countries: 13,246. Ethnic population: 13,246. Lao Cai Province, near Lao Cai City and one village in Xin Mun District of Hà Giang Province, also Lai Chau and Son La provinces. Also spoken in China. *Class:* Sino-Tibetan, Tibeto-Burman, Lolo-Burmese, Unclassified. *Dialects:* Related to Laghuu. *Lg Use:* An official minority nationality. Speakers are shifting to Vietnamese. *Other:* Tonal.

Phuong (Phuang, Phuong Catang) [phg] 15,112 (2000 WCD). Quang Nam-Da Nang and Gia Lai-Cong Tum provinces, southeast of the Pacoh language. *Class:* Austro-Asiatic, Mon-Khmer, Eastern Mon-Khmer, Katuic, East Katuic, Katu-Pacoh. *Other:* Part of the Katu official ethnic community.

Puoc (Kha Puhoc, Puhoc, Puok, Pua, Xinh Mul, Xinh-Mun, Xin Mul, Sing Mun, Ksing Mul) [puo] 18,018 in Viet Nam (1999 census). Population total all countries: 20,182. Lai Chau and Son La provinces in northern Viet Nam, along the Laos border. Also spoken in Laos. *Class:* Austro-Asiatic, Mon-Khmer, Northern Mon-Khmer, Khmuic, Xinh Mul. *Dialects:*

Related to Khang and Pong 3. *Other:* An official ethnic community in Viet Nam.

Qabiao (Ka Beo, Ka Bao, Ka Biao, Laqua, Pubiao, Pupeo, Pu Péo, Pen Ti Lolo, Bendi Lolo) [laq] 307 in Viet Nam (2002 Edmondson). Population total all countries: 614. Hà Giang Province, Viet Nam-Yunnan-Kwangsi border, upper Clear River valley, Dunshi, Pugao, Pula, Pubang, Manong; Yên Minh and Mèo Vac districts; Dông Van District, Phô Là and Sung Chang villages. Also spoken in China. *Class:* Tai-Kadai, Kadai, Yang-Biao. *Dialects:* Lexical similarity 38% with Gelo, 33% with Lati, 38% with Buyang, 30% with Northern Zhuang, 29% with Dong, 23% with Laka, 26% with Hlai, 10% with Hmong, 7% with Mien. *Other:* They call themselves 'Ka Beo' or 'Qa Beo'. An official ethnic community in Viet Nam. Sororate. Traditional religion.

Rade (Rhade, Raday, Rde, E-De, Edeh, De) [rad] 270,348 in Viet Nam (1999 census). Dac Lac and part of Phu Yen and Khanh Hoa provinces, centered around Banmethuot. Possibly also Cambodia. Also spoken in USA. *Class:* Austronesian, Malayo-Polynesian, Malayic, Achinese-Chamic, Chamic, South, Plateau. *Dialects:* Bih, Ndhur (Mdhur), Adham (A-Dham), Blo, Kodrao (Kdrao), Krung 1, Rde Kpa (Kpa). Bih (1,000) may be a separate language. The Krung 1 dialect is different from the Bahnaric language Krung 2, in Cambodia. Other names of dialects or ethnic groups: Ktul, Dlie, Rue, E-pan, Dong Kay, Arul, Kah. *Lg Dev:* Literacy rate in first language: 10% to 30%. Literacy rate in second language: 50% to 75%. NT: 1964. *Other:* An official ethnic community in Viet Nam. Christian, traditional religion.

Rengao (Ro-Ngao) [ren] 16,000 (2002). Kon Tum Province, from northwest of Dak To to southeast of Kontum city between Sedang and Bahnar. *Class:* Austro-Asiatic, Mon-Khmer, Eastern Mon-Khmer, Bahnaric, North Bahnaric, West, Rengao. *Dialects:* Western Rengao, Sedang-Rengao, Bahnar-Rengao. *Lg Dev:* Literacy rate in first language: 5% to 10%. Literacy rate in second language: 25% to 50%. Grammar. Bible portions: 1977.

Roglai, Cacgia (Ra-Glai) [roc] 3,000 (2002). Ninh Thuan Province, on the coast northeast of Phan Rang. *Class:* Austronesian, Malayo-Polynesian, Malayic, Achinese-Chamic, Chamic, South, Coastal, Roglai. *Dialects:* It is considerably different from other Roglai dialects.

Roglai, Northern (Radlai, Adlai, Rayglay, Ra-Glai, Rang Glai, Noang, La-Oang) [rog] 52,931 (2002). Ninh Thuan, Binh Thuan, Khanh Hoa and Lam Dong provinces, in the mountains west and south of Nhatrang, and some near Dalat. *Class:* Austronesian, Malayo-Polynesian, Malayic, Achinese-Chamic, Chamic, South, Coastal, Roglai. *Lg Dev:* Literacy rate in first language: 5% to 10%. Literacy rate in second language: 25% to 50%. Bible portions: 1966–1973. *Other:* Roglai is an official ethnic community. Traditional religion, Christian.

Roglai, Southern (Rai) [rgs] 41,000 (1999 census). Binh Thuan and Ninh Thuan provinces, southern Viet Nam. *Class:* Austronesian, Malayo-Polynesian, Malayic, Achinese-Chamic, Chamic, South, Coastal, Roglai. *Dialect:* Rai. Close to Chru and Northern Roglai. *Other:* Roglai is an official ethnic community. Traditional religion.

Romam [rmx] 250 (1993 Dang Nghiem Van). On the Viet Nam-Cambodian border. *Class:* Austro-Asiatic, Mon-Khmer, Eastern Mon-Khmer, Bahnaric, Central Bahnaric. *Other:* An official ethnic community. Traditional religion.

Sedang (Hadang, Hdang, Hoteang, Roteang, Rotea, Hotea, Xodang, Xa Dang, Cadong, Tang, Kmrang) [sed] 100,648 in Viet Nam (1999 census). Population total all countries: 101,434. Kon Tum, Quang Nam, Quang Ngai provinces. Also spoken in Laos. *Class:* Austro-Asiatic, Mon-Khmer, Eastern Mon-Khmer, Bahnaric, North Bahnaric, West, Sedang-Todrah, Sedang. *Dialects:*

Central Sedang, Greater Sedang, Dak Sut Sedang, Kotua Sedang, Kon Hring Sedang. Closest to Hre. *Lg Dev:* Literacy rate in first language: 5% to 10%. Literacy rate in second language: 25% to 50%. *Other:* Sakau or Xa Cau may be an alternate name. Traditional religion, Christian.

Sila (Sida) [slt] 840 in Viet Nam (1999 census). Lai Chau Province, Cú Dè Xù, Khá Pé. 3 villages: Ban Xeo Hai in Xa Can Ho, Xi Thao Chai of Pa Ha, Nam Xin of Muong Nhe. *Other:* An official ethnic community in Viet Nam. They say they came from Laos. Traditional religion. See main entry under Laos.

Stieng, Budeh (Lower Stieng, Southern Stieng) [stt] Southern Stieng area, Binh Phuoc and Tay Ninh provinces. *Class:* Austro-Asiatic, Mon-Khmer, Eastern Mon-Khmer, Bahnaric, South Bahnaric. *Dialects:* Different enough from Bulo Stieng that intelligibility is not functional.

Stieng, Bulo (Xtieng, Xa-Dieng, Budíp, Rangah, Upper Stieng, Northern Stieng) [sti] Population total all countries: 6,059. Binh Phuoc, Lam Dong, and Tay Ninh provinces. Also spoken in Cambodia. *Class:* Austro-Asiatic, Mon-Khmer, Eastern Mon-Khmer, Bahnaric, South Bahnaric, Stieng-Chrau. *Lg Dev:* Literacy rate in first language: below 1%. Literacy rate in second language: 15% to 25%. Bible portions: 1971. *Other:* Stieng is an official ethnic community in Viet Nam. Christian, traditional religion.

Sui [swi] 120 in Viet Nam (2002 Edmondson). Tuyen Quang, Chiem Hoa. *Other:* Have been in Viet Nam more than 150 years. See main entry under China.

Tai Daeng (Red Tai, Tai Rouge, Thai Do, Thai Dang, Tai Deng, Daeng, Táy-Môc-Châu, Môc-Châu) [tyr] 140,000 in Viet Nam (2002). Population total all countries: 165,000. North central Viet Nam in the area of Thanh Hoa Province, south of Sam Nuea. Also spoken in Laos, Thailand, USA. *Class:* Tai-Kadai, Kam-Tai, Be-Tai, Tai-Sek, Tai, Southwestern, East Central, Chiang Saeng. *Other:* Part of the Thái official nationality in Viet Nam. Speakers in Viet Nam tend to identify with Tai Dam, and deny they are 'Red Tai'.

Tai Dam (Tai Noir, Thái Den, Táy-Dam, Black Tai, Tai Do) [blt] 699,000 in Viet Nam (2002 SIL). Population total all countries: 763,700. Northern Viet Nam along the Red and Black rivers. Some moved south and are settled in Tung Nghia (Lam Dam),Tho Thanh (Dac Lac), Pleiku (Gia Lai), and elsewhere. Also spoken in Australia, China, France, Laos, Thailand, USA. *Class:* Tai-Kadai, Kam-Tai, Be-Tai, Tai-Sek, Tai, Southwestern, East Central, Chiang Saeng. *Dialect:* Táy Mu'ò'i (Tai Mueai, Meuay). Close to Song and Tai Dón, but not inherently intelligible with Tai Dón. *Lg Dev:* Literacy rate in first language: 1% to 5%. Literacy rate in second language: 50% to 75%. Bible portions: 1982–2000. *Other:* It is part of the Thái official nationality in Viet Nam (760,000 in 1984; official figure), which also includes Tai Dón and Tai Daeng. Officially included under Dai in China. Traditional religion.

Tai Do (Tay-Jo, Tay Yo, Tay Muoi, Tay Quy Chau) [tyj] 300 (2002). Northern Viet Nam. *Class:* Tai-Kadai, Kam-Tai, Be-Tai, Tai-Sek, Tai. *Other:* It may be the same as Tay Yo of Khamouan Province, Laos.

Tai Dón (Tai Blanc, Thái Tráng, Tai Lai, Tai Kao, Táy Khao, White Tai) [twh] 280,000 in Viet Nam (2002). Population total all countries: 490,000. North Viet Nam along the Red and Black rivers. Some are settled in southern Viet Nam, mainly in Tung Nghia (Lam Dong Province). Also spoken in China, France, Laos. *Class:* Tai-Kadai, Kam-Tai, Be-Tai, Tai-Sek, Tai, Southwestern, East Central, Chiang Saeng. *Dialects:* Not intelligible with Tai Dam. Lao has influenced the speech of some Tai Dón speakers. *Lg Use:* They have different customs from the Tai Dam. Tai Dón have strong ethnic pride. Those who have had prolonged contact with Tai Dam have become bilingual in it. Many have not had that contact. *Lg Dev:* Bible portions: 1969. *Other:* Part of the Thái official nationality in Viet Nam. Distinctive writing system. Traditional religion, Buddhist.

Tai Hang Tong (Hàng Tong, Tày Mường) [thc] 10,000 (2002). Northern Viet Nam. *Class:* Tai-Kadai, Kam-Tai, Be-Tai, Tai-Sek, Tai, Southwestern, East Central, Chiang Saeng. *Dialects:* Part of the Thái official ethnic community, related to White Thai, Tai Dam, Pu Thay, Tay Thanh, and Tho Da Bac.

Tai Thanh (Táy Thanh, Thanh, Tai Man Thanh) [tmm] 20,000 (2002). Northern Viet Nam, Thanh Hoa and Nghe An provinces. *Class:* Tai-Kadai, Kam-Tai, Be-Tai, Tai-Sek, Tai, Southwestern. *Dialects:* Part of the Thái official ethnic community, related to White Thai, Tai Dam, Tai Hang Tong, Pu Thay, and Tho Da Bac.

Takua (Quang Tin Katu, Langya) [tkz] 12,768 (2000 WCD). Quang Nam and Da Nang provinces. *Class:* Austro-Asiatic, Mon-Khmer, Eastern Mon-Khmer, Bahnaric, North Bahnaric, East, Takua. *Dialects:* Closest to Cua and Kayong.

Ta'oih, Upper (T-Oy, Tà-Oi, Tau Oi, Ta Hoi, Toi-Oi, Kantua) [tth] 19,000 in Viet Nam (2002). 70% monolingual. Thua Thien-Hue Province and Quang Tri Province. *Dialect:* Pasoom, Kamuan', Palee'n, Leem, Ha'aang (Sa'ang). *Lg Dev:* Literacy rate in first language: below 1%. Literacy rate in second language: 5% to 15%. *Other:* An official ethnic community in Viet Nam. Traditional religion, Christian. See main entry under Laos.

Tày ("Thô," Thu Lao, T'o, Tai Tho, Ngan, Phen) [tyz] 1,477,514 in Viet Nam (1999 census). Cao Bàng, Lang Son, Hà Giang, Tuye Quang, Bác Thái, Quang Ninh, Hà Bac, and Lam Dòng provinces, central and northeastern Viet Nam near the China border. Some moved south and settled in Tung Nghia and Song Mao. Also possibly in Laos. Also spoken in France, USA. *Class:* Tai-Kadai, Kam-Tai, Be-Tai, Tai-Sek, Tai, Central. *Dialects:* Central Tày, Eastern Tày, Southern Tày, Northern Tày, Tày Trung Khanh, Thu Lao, Tày Bao Lac. Dialect continuum to Southern Zhuang in China. Close to Nung. *Lg Use:* High degree of bilingualism and acculturation in Vietnamese. *Lg Dev:* Literacy rate in first language: 1% to 5%. Literacy rate in second language: 50% to 75%. Dictionary. Bible portions: 1938–1963. *Other:* There is also now another official nationality in Viet Nam, now called the 'Tho', which is a Viet-Muong language family group, not a Tai-based language group. Traditional religion, Christian.

Tay Boi (Tay Boy, Annamite French, Vietnamese Pidgin French) [tas] Extinct. Was used in the major ports of French Indo-China. *Class:* Pidgin, French based. *Lg Use:* Developed beginning in 1862. Influences from Vietnamese, French, English, Javanese, and Portuguese. It was used between French and Vietnamese until 1954, and in lower levels of administration, in the military, and by police. No longer spoken (1981 Wurm and Hattori).

Tày Sa Pa (Tai Sa Pa) [tys] 300 (2002 Edmondson). Lao Cai Province, Muong Khuong District. *Class:* Tai-Kadai, Kam-Tai, Be-Tai, Tai-Sek, Tai, Southwestern. *Other:* Tonal.

Tày Tac (Tai Tac) [tyt] Northwestern Viet Nam, Muong Tâc District in eastern Son La Province. *Class:* Tai-Kadai, Kam-Tai, Be-Tai, Tai-Sek, Tai, Southwestern, East Central, Chiang Saeng. *Dialects:* Related to Tai Dam, Tai Dón, Tai Daeng. *Other:* Part of the Thái official nationality in Viet Nam. The women's blouse is similar to that worn by White Tai women of Lai Châu, without the silver buttons. CN(C) in which N = V + tone, 22 consonants, 13 vowels, tonal, 6 tones on open syllables and those ending with a continuant, 3 tones on syllables ending with a stop.

Tho (Cuoi, Cuoi Cham, Keo, Ho Muong Meridional) [tou] 68,394 (1999 census). Northern Nghe An Province, highland areas. Cuoi Cham is in Tan Hop commune, Tan Ky District. *Class:* Austro-Asiatic, Mon-Khmer, Viet-Muong, Cuoi. *Dialects:* Cuoi Cham (Uy Lo), Mon. *Other:* An official ethnic community. Associated culturally with other principal local ethnonyms Keo, Mon, Cuoi, Ho, Dan, Lai-Ly Ha, and Tay Poong.

Thu Lao [tyl] 200 (2002 Edmondson). Cao Bàng, Lang Son, Hà Giang, Tuye Quang, Bác Thái, Quang Ninh, Hà Bac, and Lam Dòng provinces, central and northeastern Viet Nam near the China border. Some moved south and settled in Tung Nghia and Song Mao. Also possibly in Laos. *Class:* Tai-Kadai, Kam-Tai, Be-Tai, Tai-Sek, Tai, Southwestern, East Central, Chiang Saeng. *Other:* Traditional religion, Christian.

Todrah (Todrá, Didrah, Didra, Podra, Modra, Kodra) [tdr] 9,142 (2000 WCD). Kon Tum Province, northeast of Kon Tum City from Kon Hring to Kon Braih. *Class:* Austro-Asiatic, Mon-Khmer, Eastern Mon-Khmer, Bahnaric, North Bahnaric, West, Sedang-Todrah, Todrah-Monom. *Other:* Didra may be a separate language.

Trieng (Strieng, Gie-Trieng, Tareh, Treng, Ta-Rieng, Talieng, Dgiéh, Giang Ray, Pin) [stg] 15,000 (2002). Mainly in Kon Tum and Quang Nam provinces. *Class:* Austro-Asiatic, Mon-Khmer, Eastern Mon-Khmer, Bahnaric, North Bahnaric, West. *Dialects:* May be related to Jeh or Talieng in Laos. *Other:* An official ethnic community in Viet Nam. Traditional religion, Christian.

Ts'ün-Lao (Lao) [tsl] 10,000 (1993 Dang Nghiem Van). Lai Chau Province, northwestern Viet Nam. *Class:* Tai-Kadai, Kam-Tai, Be-Tai, Tai-Sek, Tai, Central. *Other:* Official ethnic community, with associated names Lào Bóc and Lào Noi. Traditional religion.

Vietnamese (Kinh, Gin, Jing, Ching, Viet, Annamese) [vie] 65,795,718 in VIet Nam (1999 census). Population total all countries: 67,439,139. The entire country. Also spoken in Australia, Cambodia, Canada, China, Côte d'Ivoire, Finland, France, Germany, Laos, Martinique, Netherlands, New Caledonia, Norway, Philippines, Senegal, Thailand, United Kingdom, USA, Vanuatu. *Class:* Austro-Asiatic, Mon-Khmer, Viet-Muong, Vietnamese. *Dialects:* Northern Vietnamese (Tonkinese, Hanoi), Central Vietnamese (Hue), Southern Vietnamese. Numerous dialects. *Lg Use:* Official language. *Lg Dev:* Literacy rate in first language: 65%. Literacy rate in second language: 80%. Roman script. Radio programs. Grammar. Bible: 1916–1994. *Other:* People are called 'Kinh'. SVO; prepositions; genitives, articles, adjectives, numerals, relatives before noun heads; question word initial. Buddhist, Christian.

Yemen

Republic of Yemen, al-Jumhurïyah al-Yamaniyah. 20,024,867. National or official language: Standard Arabic. Literacy rate: 25% to 39%. Also includes Egyptian Spoken Arabic (10,000), Gulf Spoken Arabic (10,000), Hindi (232,760), Hobyót, Somali (678,904), Western Cham, people from Africa (28,000), India and Pakistan (65,000). Information mainly from T. Sebeok 1970; R. F. Nyrop 1986; T. M. Johnstone 1987. Deaf population: 1,052,571. The number of languages listed for Yemen is 8. Of those, all are living languages. See map on page 839.

Arabic, Hadrami Spoken (Hadromi, Hadrami) [ayh] 300,000 in Yemen (1995). Population total all countries: 410,000. Hadramaut. Also spoken in Eritrea, Kenya. *Class:* Afro-Asiatic, Semitic, Central, South, Arabic.

Lg Dev: Literacy rate in second language: 10%. *Other:* Distinct from Ta'izzi-Adeni Spoken Arabic and Sanaani Spoken Arabic. Muslim.

Arabic, Judeo-Yemeni (Judeo-Yemeni, Yemenite Judeo-Arabic) [jye] 1,000 in Yemen (1995 H. Mutzafi). *Dialects:* San'a, 'Aden, Be:da, Habban. *Other:* Jewish. See main entry under Israel.

Arabic, Sanaani Spoken (Northern Yemeni Arabic) [ayn] 7,600,000 (1996). Extends as far south as Dhamar, about 14.4 degrees north. *Class:* Afro-Asiatic, Semitic, Central, South, Arabic. *Lg Dev:* Literacy rate in second language: 10%. *Other:* Distinct from Hadrami and Ta'izzi-Adeni Arabic. Zaydi Muslim.

Arabic, Standard [arb] *Lg Use:* National language. Used for education, official purposes, formal speeches. See main entry under Saudi Arabia.

Arabic, Ta'izzi-Adeni Spoken (Southern Yemeni Spoken Arabic) [acq] 6,760,000 in Yemen (1996). Population total all countries: 6,869,000. All provinces except 2 eastern and the northeastern ones. Probably a few in United Arab Emirates, Somalia, Egypt, and Saudi Arabia. Also spoken in Djibouti, Eritrea, Kenya, United Kingdom. *Class:* Afro-Asiatic, Semitic, Central, South, Arabic. *Dialects:* Ta'izzi, Adeni. Ta'izzi dialect is the one best-accepted throughout Yemen. *Lg Dev:* Literacy rate in second language:

10%. *Other:* Different from Hadromi and Sanaani Arabic Arabic. Zaydi Muslim.

Bathari (Bautahari, Botahari, Bathara) [bhm] Population total all countries: 200. Also spoken in Oman. *Class:* Afro-Asiatic, Semitic, South, South Arabian. *Dialects:* Close to Mehri. *Other:* Muslim.

Mehri (Mahri) [gdq] 70,643 in Yemen (2000). Population total all countries: 135,764. Mahrah Governorate. Also spoken in Kuwait, Oman. *Class:* Afro-Asiatic, Semitic, South, South Arabian. *Dialects:* Western Mehri (Mehriyet), Eastern Mehri (Mehriyot). Within the main dialects there are also differences between bedouin and city or village varieties. *Lg Dev:* Dictionary. Bible portions: 1902. *Other:* Spoken by the Mahra. Many ethnic Mehri in Yemen are Arabic first-language speakers. Muslim.

Soqotri (Saqatri, Sokotri, Suqutri, Socotri) [sqt] 57,000 in Yemen (1990 census). Population total all countries: 64,000. Mainly in Soqotra Island, hundreds in 'Abd al-Kuri island, and about a dozen in Samha Island in the Gulf of Aden. Also spoken in United Arab Emirates. *Class:* Afro-Asiatic, Semitic, South, South Arabian. *Dialects:* 'Abd Al-Kuri, Southern Soqotri, Northern Soqotri, Central Soqotri, Western Soqotri. *Lg Dev:* Bible portions: 1902. *Other:* North Soqotri includes North Central and Northwest Central (highland) Soqotri. Mostly monolingual in Soqotri. Muslim.

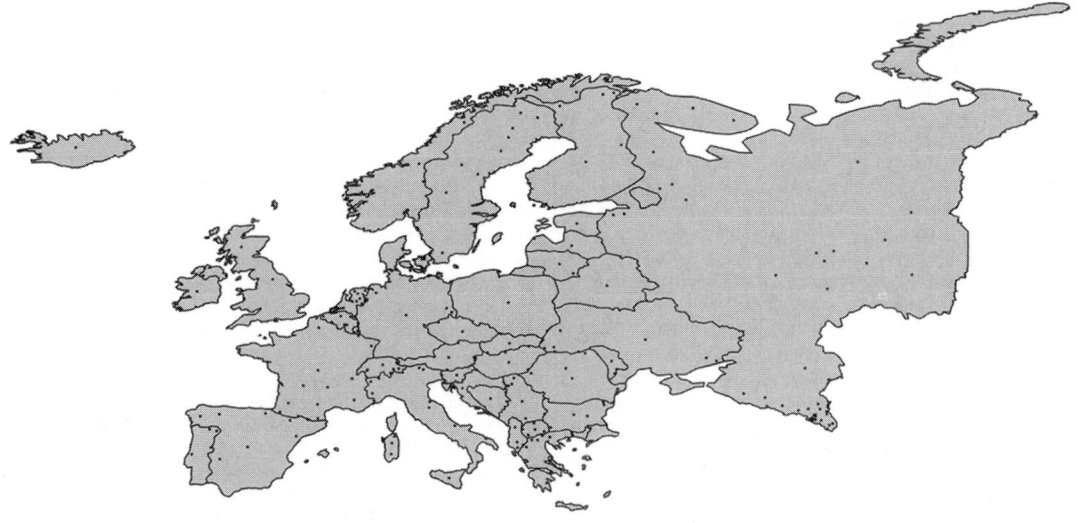

Europe

Albania

Republic of Albania. Republika e Shqipërisë. 3,544,808.
National or official language: Tosk Albanian. Literacy rate:
85% (1991 National Geographic). Information mainly from
G. Messing 1980; B. Comrie 1987; L. Newmark 1982. Blind
population: 2,000. Deaf population: 204,565 (1998). The
number of languages listed for Albania is 7. Of those, all are
living languages.

Albanian, Gheg (Geg, Gheg, Shopni, Guegue) [aln]
300,000 in Albania. Northern Albania. *Dialects:* Mandrica,
Ship (Kosove), Scutari, Elbasan-Tirana. *Lg Use:* Speakers
may be bilingual in Standard Albanian. *Other:* Muslim,
Christian. See main entry under Serbia and Montenegro.
Albanian, Tosk (Tosk, Arnaut, Shkip, Shqip, Skchip,
Shqiperë, Zhgabe) [als] 2,900,000 in Albania (1989).
Population total all countries: 2,980,000. Mainly south
Albania to the Shkumbi River. Also spoken in Belgium,
Egypt, Germany, Greece, Sweden, Turkey (Europe),
Ukraine, USA. *Class:* Indo-European, Albanian, Tosk.
Dialects: Arbanasi (Zadar), Srem (Syrmia), Camerija,
Korca. Reported to be inherently unintelligible with Gheg
Albanian and partially intelligible with Arvanitika
Albanian of Greece. Not intelligible with Arbëreshë of
Italy. Tosk has been the basis of the official language for
Standard Albanian since 1952. *Lg Use:* Official language.
It is used in schools. *Lg Dev:* Grammar. Bible: 1993.
Other: The Jevgjit claim to be Egyptians, but may be
assimilated Roma. SVO. Coastal, mountain slope.
Deciduous forest. Sea level to 800 meters. Peasant
agriculturalists; animal husbandry: sheep; petroleum
workers. Muslim, Christian (Orthodox).
Greek [ell] 60,000 in Albania (1989). Southern Albania.
See main entry under Greece.
Macedonian (Slavic, Macedonian Slavic) [mkd] 15,000
in Albania (2001 Johnstone and Mandryk). *Other:* Called
'Slavic' in Greece. See main entry under Macedonia.
Romani, Vlax [rmy] 60,000 in Albania (1991). *Dialect:*
Southern Vlax Romani. *Other:* Ethnic groups are
Mechkaria, Kurtofia, Chergaria, and Kabuzia. Christian.
See main entry under Romania.

Romanian, Macedo (Macedo-Rumanian, Arumanian,
Arumun, Aromunian, Armina, Vlach) [rup] 50,000 in
Albania (1995 T. J. Winnifrith). Ethnic population: Up to
400,000 in Albania. South Albania, especially in Korçë,
Lushnjë, Pernët, Gjirokastër, Sarandë, Berat, Durrës,
Kavajë, and Tiranë. *Lg Use:* A church in Korçë holds
services in Arumanian. *Other:* 'Armini' refers to the
people. See main entry under Greece.
Serbian (Montenegrin) [srp] Southwest Albania, 2 or 3
villages, and some in the city. *Other:* Muslim. See main
entry under Serbia and Montenegro.

Andorra

Principality of Andorra. Principat d'Andorra. 69,865.
National or official languages: Catalan-Valencian-Balear,
French. Literacy rate: 92% to 99%. Also includes English
(770), Portuguese (2,100). Deaf population: 3,880. The
number of languages listed for Andorra is 3. Of those, all
are living languages.

Catalan-Valencian-Balear (Català, Catalán, Bacavès)
[cat] 31,000 in Andorra (1990). *Lg Use:* Official
language. *Lg Dev:* Literacy rate in first language: 75% to
100%. Literacy rate in second language: 75% to 100%.
Other: Christian. See main entry under Spain.
French [fra] 2,400 in Andorra (1986). *Lg Use:* National
language. See main entry under France.
Spanish (Castilian) [spa] 24,600 in Andorra (1986). See
main entry under Spain.

Austria

Republic of Austria. Republik Österreich. 8,174,762.
National or official languages: Standard German, Slovenian
(regional). Literacy rate: 99% to 100%. Also includes
Assyrian Neo-Aramaic, Czech (7,100), French (15,000),
Greek (12,000), Kirmanjki, Northern Kurdish (23,000),
Polish (39,000), Turkish (68,000), Western Farsi (2,000),
Yeniche, Arabic (3,000), Chinese (1,200). Information
mainly from M. Stephens 1976; B. Comrie 1987. Blind
population: 11,005. Deaf population: 482,311. Deaf

institutions: 17. The number of languages listed for Austria is 9. Of those, all are living languages.

Alemannisch (Alemannic) [gsw] 300,000 in Austria (1991 Annemarie Schmidt). Western Austria, Vorarlberg. *Dialect:* High Alemannisch (Hochalemannisch). *Other:* Called 'Schwyzerdütsch' in Switzerland and 'Alsatian' in southeastern France. See main entry under Switzerland (Schwyzerdütsch).

Austrian Sign Language (Austro-Hungarian Sign Language) [asq] *Class:* Deaf sign language. *Dialects:* Partially intelligible with French Sign Language. Related to Russian Sign Language. The sign language used in class and that used by adults outside class are different. *Lg Use:* Deaf people go to different schools, each using a different sign language. Sign language interpreters are used some in court. Professionals are required to know sign language in job training and social services programs. There is little research. There are a few classes for hearing people. *Lg Dev:* Films. TV. Videos. Dictionary. *Other:* Originated 1870. There is a manual alphabet for spelling.

Bavarian (Bayerisch, Bairisch, Bavarian Austrian, Ost-Oberdeutsch) [bar] 6,983,298 in Austria (2000 WCD). Population total all countries: 7,667,478. Central Bavarian is in the Alps and Lower Austria and Salzburg; North Bavarian in the north of Regensburg, to Nuremburg and Western Bohemia, Czech Republic; South Bavarian in the Bavarian Alps, Tyrol, Styria, including the Heanzian dialect of Burgenland, Carinthia, northern Italy, and part of Gottschee. Also spoken in Czech Republic, Germany, Hungary, Italy. *Class:* Indo-European, Germanic, West, High German, German, Upper German, Bavarian-Austrian. *Dialects:* Central Bavarian, North Bavarian, South Bavarian. *Lg Use:* Vigorous. School is compulsory for 9 years, and is taught in Standard German. However, one report indicated that active competence in Standard German is limited for some speakers. News broadcasts in German are understood poorly by some of the population. *Lg Dev:* Bible: 1998. *Other:* SVO; prepositions; genitives; articles, adjectives, numerals, relatives before noun heads; question word initial; 2 prefixes, 3 to 4 suffixes on a word; word order distinguishes subjects, objects, indirect objects; affixes indicate case of noun phrase; obligatory verb affixes mark person and number of subject, other suffixes can mark gender of subject and person, number, and gender of object; causatives; comparatives; CV, CVC, CVV, CCV.

Croatian [hrv] 103,000 in Austria (1991). Burgenland and Vienna. *Dialect:* Burgenland Croatian. *Lg Use:* About 40 primary schools teach bilingually through Croatian and German. Rapid assimilation with the German-speaking population. *Lg Dev:* Literacy rate in first language: Few. *Other:* The form of Croatian spoken in Burgenland differs extensively from that spoken in the Republic of Croatia and intelligibility is difficult. Some dialects are heavily influenced by German. Christian. See main entry under Croatia.

German, Standard [deu] 7,500,000 in Austria (J. A. Hawkins in B. Comrie 1987). *Lg Use:* National language. See main entry under Germany.

Hungarian (Magyar) [hun] 22,000 in Austria (1995). Vienna, Lower Austria, Styria, Burgenland. *Dialect:* Oberwart. *Lg Use:* Taught at primary levels in schools where there are larger numbers of speakers in Burgenland. See main entry under Hungary.

Romani, Sinte (Rommanes, Sinte, Sinti) [rmo] 500 in Austria (1990 D. Holzinger). *Other:* Christian. See main entry under Serbia and Montenegro.

Slovenian (Slovene) [slv] 30,885 in Austria (2000 WCD). Population includes several thousand Windisch speakers (1995). Carinthia (Kärnten) and Steiermark (Styria), southwest Austria. *Dialect:* Windisch. *Lg Use:* Official

regional language in southern Carinthia. Some speakers speak Standard Slovene well; some use it only in church. Most do not consider themselves to be Slovenians, but Carinthians, belonging to the German culture. Speakers are bilingual or trilingual in the Slovenian dialect (Windisch), a German regional variety (Kärntnerisch or Steierisch), or Standard German. Most speakers educated since 1945 speak Standard German reasonably well. *Other:* Separated by the Karawanken Mountains from the larger group of Slovenes in Slovenia. They and their speech are called 'Windisch', an archaic form of Slovene, heavily influenced by German. Some of the ethnic group are able to speak the dialects, some are losing their command of them. Many speakers go to church, where they hear Standard Slovene. See main entry under Slovenia.

Walser (Walscher) [wae] 8,080 in Austria (2000 WCD). Vorarlberg (Grosses Walsertal: Blons, Fontanella, Raggal, St. Gerold, Sonntag, Thüringerberg); Kleinwalsertal (Mittleberg); Brandnertal (Brand); Montafon (Silbertal); Reintal (Laterns); Tannberg (Schricken, Lech, Warth); Tirol: Paznauntal (Galtnr). 14 communities in Austria. See main entry under Switzerland.

Belarus

Belarus. 10,310,520. National or official languages: Belarusan, Russian. Capital: Minsk. 80,200 square miles. Literacy rate: 99%. Also includes Baltic Romani, Eastern Yiddish (231,000), Latvian (1,000), Lithuanian (10,031), Polish (403,000), Russian (1,134,000), Tatar (12,000), Ukrainian (291,000). The number of languages listed for Belarus is 1.

Belarusan (Belarusian, Belorussian, Bielorussian, White Russian, White Ruthenian, Byelorussian) [bel] 6,715,000 in Belarus (2001 Johnstone and Mandryk). Population total all countries: 9,081,102. Also spoken in Azerbaijan, Canada, Estonia, Kazakhstan, Kyrgyzstan, Latvia, Lithuania, Moldova, Poland, Russia (Europe), Tajikistan, Turkmenistan, Ukraine, USA, Uzbekistan. *Class:* Indo-European, Slavic, East. *Dialects:* Northeast Belarusan (Polots, Viteb-Mogilev), Southwest Belarusan (Grodnen-Baranovich, Slutsko-Mozyr, Slutska-Mazyrski), Central Belarusan. Linguistically between Russian and Ukrainian, with transitional dialects to both. *Lg Use:* National language. 74% of the ethnic group from the former USSR speak it as first language. *Lg Dev:* Cyrillic script. Bible: 1973. *Other:* Christian, Muslim (Tatar).

Belgium

Kingdom of Belgium. Koninkrijk België. Royaume de Belgique. 10,348,276. National or official languages: Dutch, French, Standard German. Literacy rate: 98%. Also includes Algerian Spoken Arabic (10,800), Assyrian Neo-Aramaic, Catalan-Valencian-Balear, Chaldean Neo-Aramaic, Eastern Yiddish (20,000), Italian (280,000), Iu Mien (200), Kabyle (49,000), Laz, Moroccan Spoken Arabic (105,000), Northern Kurdish (22,000), Portuguese (80,000), Spanish (70,000), Tarifit, Tosk Albanian (3,000), Tunisian Spoken Arabic (8,900), Turkish (63,600), Turoyo (2,000), Western Yiddish, Chinese (14,000), people from Democratic Republic of the Congo (10,000). Information mainly from M. Stephens 1976; B. Comrie 1976. Blind population: 4,779. Deaf population: 610,119. Deaf institutions: 26. The number of languages listed for Belgium is 10. Of those, 9 are living languages and 1 is a second language without mother-tongue speakers. See map on page 841.

Belgian Sign Language [bvs] *Class:* Deaf sign language. *Dialects:* North Belgium Sign Language, South

Belgium Sign Language. A variety of regional dialects which have their roots in different deaf schools. The dialect in the Flemish region is closer to that in the Walloon region than it is to Dutch Sign Language. Adopted signs from the old French sign language directly and indirectly. It began in 1825. Different sign languages are used in the classroom and by adults outside the classroom. *Lg Use:* 3 deaf schools in Brussels have trained about 30% of the deaf in Belgium. There are 26 deaf institutions. Sign language interpreters are required in court. There is sign language instruction for parents of deaf children. There is a committee on national sign language. Little research on the language. There have been schools for deaf people since 1825. Limited influence from Signed Dutch and Signed French, which are used some for intercommunication with hearing people. *Lg Dev:* Films. TV. Videos. Dictionary.

Dutch (Nederlands) [nld] 4,620,150 in Belgium (1990 WA). The language of provinces of West Vlaanderen, Oost Vlaanderen, Antwerpen, Limburg, Vlaams-Brabant, and the bilingual part (10% to 20%) of Brussels. *Dialects:* Brabants, Oost-Vlaams. *Lg Use:* Official language. *Other:* Called 'Vlaams' in Belgium, even though it is different from the (West) Vlaams spoken there. In the Dutch linguistic area there are minority rights for French-speaking persons in Drogenbos, Kraainem, Linkebeek, Sint-Genesius-Rode, Wemmel, Wezembeek-Oppem, Mesen, Spiere-Helkijn, Ronse, Bever, Herstappe, Voeren. See main entry under Netherlands.

Europanto [eur] Brussels, European Union buildings. *Class:* Artificial language. *Lg Use:* A mixture of elements from some of the main European languages, for use among members of the European Union. *Other:* Second language only.

French (Français) [fra] 4,000,000 in Belgium (1988 M. Harris in B. Comrie). Official language in provinces of Hainaut, Namur, Liège, Luxembourg, Brabant-Walloon, southern hills, and the bilingual part of Brussels. Lorraine dialect, southern villages Luxembourg Province. *Dialect:* Lorraine. *Lg Use:* Official language. *Other:* The following municipalities have minority rights for Dutch-speaking persons: Comines-Warneton, Mouscron, Enghien, Floubecques; and for German-speaking persons: Malmèdy, Weismes, Welkenraedt. See main entry under France.

German, Standard [deu] 150,000 in Belgium (1988 Hawkins in B. Comrie). Official language in Liège Province, cantons of Eupen and Sankt-Vith, municipalities: Eupen, Kelmis, Lontzen, Raeren, Amel, Bnlingen, Bntchenbach, Sankt-Vith, and Burg-Reuland. *Lg Use:* Official language. See main entry under Germany.

Limburgisch (Limburgs Plat) [lim] 600,000 in Belgium (2001). Depending on the city in Belgium, 50% to 90% of the population speak it (2001 A. Schunck). Hasselt, Genk, Maaseik, Voeren, Eupen. *Lg Use:* Officially recognized in the Netherlands. Efforts are underway to have it officially recognized in Belgium. Promotion efforts are strong. It has more prestige in the Netherlands. All domains, songs. All ages. Speakers also use Dutch, French, or German. *Lg Dev:* Literacy rate in second language: 99% to 100%. *Other:* Laborers. Christian. See main entry under Netherlands.

Luxembourgeois (Letzburgisch) [ltz] 30,000 in Belgium (1998). Area of Arlon and Bastogne, Luxembourg Province. See main entry under Luxembourg.

Picard (Rouchi, Chtimi) [pcd] Most of Hainaut Province (Tournai, Mons, Ath). *Dialect:* Belgian Picard. *Lg Use:* The Belgian government recognizes Picard officially as an indigenous regional language. The European Bureau for Lesser Used Languages considers it as a language. Some reports used and edited by the French government consider it a separate language from French. Used in the home, family, friends, community. French is spoken at school, in court, for administration, with outsiders. See main entry under France.

Vlaams (Flamand, Vlaemsch) [vls] 1,070,000 in Belgium (1998 U. of Ghent). Population total all countries: 1,202,000. Large parts of the Province of West Flanders. Also spoken in France, Netherlands. *Class:* Indo-European, Germanic, West, Low Saxon-Low Franconian, Low Franconian. *Dialects:* Westvlaams (Vlaemsch), Oostvlaams, Antwerps, Limburgs, Brabants. Close to Dutch, English, Frisian. *Lg Use:* All ages. Speakers attitude toward French was hostile, but has normalized. Speakers also use French or English. *Lg Dev:* Magazines. Dictionary. *Other:* Speakers are called 'Vlamingen', language 'Vlaemsch'. The spelling systems in the 3 countries differ so as to make acceptance of written materials difficult among them. SOV. Christian.

Walloon (Wallon) [wln] 1,120,000 (1998). Few monolinguals. Population includes 320,000 young people (1998). 1,220,000 to 1,920,000 young people can understand it (1998). Wallonia. Central Walloon dialect, Namur, Wavre, and Dinant; Eastern Walloon dialect, Liège, Malmedy, Verviers, Huy, and Waremme; Western Walloon dialect, Charleroi, Nivelles, and Philippeville; Southern Walloon dialect, the Ardennes Region, Marche, and Neufchâteau. Also spoken in Luxembourg until recently. It is or was spoken in parts of northern France, and in Green Bay, Wisconsin, USA. *Class:* Indo-European, Italic, Romance, Italo-Western, Western, Gallo-Iberian, Gallo-Romance, Gallo-Rhaetian, Oïl, French. *Dialects:* Central Walloon, Eastern Walloon, Western Walloon, Southern Walloon. Walloon developed between the 8th and 12th centuries from remnants of Latin brought to the region by Roman soldiers, merchants, and settlers. The eastern subdialect of Walloon is considered to be the more difficult one to understand within Belgium. *Lg Use:* Many native authors. Used in theaters. Indigenous languages were recognized in Belgium in 1990. Usage began decreasing in the 20th century, but Walloon is increasingly recognized as valuable for informal purposes. More rural than urban. Not used in schools. There are some older adults whose main language is Walloon. *Lg Dev:* Magazines. Newspapers. Radio programs. TV. Dictionary. Grammar. Bible portions: 1934.

Bosnia and Herzegovina

Bosnia and Herzegovina. 4,007,608. National or official languages: Bosnian, Croatian, Serbian. Literacy rate: 92%. Also includes Italian (4,000), Macedo Romanian, Standard German, Turkish (50,000), Albanian. The number of languages listed for Bosnia and Herzegovina is 4. Of those, all are living languages.

Bosnian [bos] 4,000,000 (2004). *Class:* Indo-European, Slavic, South, Western. *Lg Use:* Official language. *Lg Dev:* Literacy rate in second language: 97%. Roman script. Dictionary. Bible: 1804–1968. *Other:* There are influences from Turkish and Arabic. SVO. Muslim, Christian, Jewish.

Croatian [hrv] 469,000 in Bosnia and Herzegovina (2004). *Dialects:* Croatian, Serbian. *Lg Use:* Official language. See main entry under Croatia.

Romani, Vlax (Tsigene, Danubian, Gypsy, Vlax) [rmy] 400,000 in Bosnia and Herzegovina (2004). *Dialects:* Serbo-Bosnian (Machwaya, Machvano), Kalderash, Southern Vlax. *Other:* Vlax and Kalderash are understood by the Lovari. Ethnic group: Gurbéti. Christian. See main entry under Romania.

Serbian (Montenegrin) [srp] 400,000 in Bosnia and Herzegovina (2004). *Lg Use:* Official language. See main entry under Serbia and Montenegro.

Bulgaria

Republic of Bulgaria. Narodna Republika Bulgaria.
7,517,973. National or official languages: Bulgarian,
Turkish. Literacy rate: 90% to 98%. Also includes
Armenian (27,000), Czech (9,000), Greek (11,000), Russian
(18,000), Serbian (9,000). Information mainly from B.
Comrie 1987. Blind population: 3,312. Deaf population:
533,544. Deaf institutions: 19. The number of languages
listed for Bulgaria is 11. Of those, all are living languages.

Albanian, Gheg [aln] 1,000 in Bulgaria (1963
Newmark). See main entry under Serbia and Montenegro.
Bulgarian (Balgarski) [bul] 7,986,000 in Bulgaria (1986).
Population total all countries: 8,954,811. Also spoken in
Canada, Greece, Hungary, Israel, Moldova, Romania,
Serbia and Montenegro, Turkey (Europe), Ukraine, USA.
Class: Indo-European, Slavic, South, Eastern. *Dialect:*
Palityan (Palitiani, Bogomil). Palityan is functionally
intelligible with Standard Bulgarian. The Pomak dialect
spoken in Greece is close to Serbian and Bulgarian;
geographical dialect shading toward each. *Lg Use:*
National language. The Sopa are of Petecheneg origin and
speak Bulgarian. *Lg Dev:* Grammar. Bible: 1864–1923.
Other: SVO. Christian.
Bulgarian Sign Language [bqn] *Class:* Deaf sign
language. *Dialects:* Different sign languages are used in
the classroom and by adults outside. *Lg Use:* Used since
1920. Elementary schools for deaf people since 1898.
Since 1945 sign language has been allowed in the
classroom. Sign language interpreters are required in
court. Some are available for college students. There is
sign language instruction for parents of deaf children.
There is a committee on national sign language. *Lg Dev:*
Films. TV. Videos. Dictionary. *Other:* There is a manual
alphabet for spelling.
Crimean Turkish (Crimean Tatar) [crh] 6,000 in
Bulgaria (1990). Northeast Bulgaria. *Dialects:* Northern
Crimean (Crimean Nogai, Steppe Crimean), Central
Crimean, Southern Crimean. *Other:* Muslim. See main
entry under Uzbekistan.
Gagauz (Gagauzi) [gag] 12,000 in Bulgaria (1982).
Varna coastal region. *Dialects:* Bulgar Gagauz,
Maritime Gagauz. *Other:* Christian. See main entry
under Moldova.
Macedonian [mkd] An undetermined number of
inhabitants of the Pirin Region in Bulgaria claim
Macedonian as first language, bordering the Former
Yugoslav Republic of Macedonia (Prof. Wayles Brown
1998, Cornell University). See main entry under
Macedonia.
Romani, Balkan (Gypsy) [rmn] 187,900 in Bulgaria.
Population includes 100,000 Arlija, 20,000 Dzambazi,
10,000 Tinsmiths, 10,000 East Bulgarian. Between Sofia
and the Black Sea (Central dialect). The Tinsmiths dialect
is in central and northwest Bulgaria; Arlija is in the Sofia
Region. *Dialects:* Arlija, Tinners Romani, Greek Romani,
Dzambazi, East Bulgarian Romani, Paspatian, Ironworker
Romani. *Lg Use:* 200,000 second-language speakers
(1985 Gunnemark and Kenrick). *Other:* Ethnic groups:
Jerlídes (western Bulgaria), Drindári (central Bulgaria).
Muslim. See main entry under Serbia and Montenegro.
Romani, Vlax [rmy] 500 Kalderash in Bulgaria. *Other:*
Christian. See main entry under Romania.
Romanian, Macedo (Macedo-Rumanian, Arumanian,
Aromanian, Armina) [rup] 4,770 in Bulgaria (2000 WCD).
Communities have associations in Peshtera, Velingrad,
Dupnitsa, Rakitovo, and Blagoevgrad. *Other:* 'Armini'
refers to the people. Their relatives emigrated from
Macedonia and northern Greece between 1850 and 1914.

The Romanian Cultural Institute has been closed since
1948. See main entry under Greece.
Russian Sign Language [rsl] *Other:* Originated 1806.
See main entry under Russia (Europe).
Turkish (Osmanli, Turki) [tur] 845,550 in Bulgaria (1986).
Kurdzhali Province and neighboring areas of South
Bulgaria, along the Danube, and various regions of East
Bulgaria. *Dialects:* Danubian, Razgrad, Dinler, Macedonian
Turkish. *Lg Use:* Official regional recognition. *Other:* The
Turkish language is gradually being replaced by Bulgarian,
although Islam and ethnic identity remain strong. Natural
growth has been balanced by emigration to Turkey.
Muslim. See main entry under Turkey (Asia).

Croatia

Croatia. 4,496,869. National or official languages: Croatian,
Italian. Literacy rate: 97%. Also includes Sinte Romani
(131,000), Slovenian (22,810). Information mainly from B.
Comrie 1987. The number of languages listed for Croatia is
7. Of those, 6 are living languages and 1 is extinct.

Croatia Sign Language [csq] *Class:* Deaf sign
language.
Croatian (Hrvatski) [hrv] 4,800,000 in Croatia (1995).
Population total all countries: 6,214,643. Also spoken in
Austria, Bosnia and Herzegovina, Germany, Hungary,
Italy, Slovakia, Slovenia. *Class:* Indo-European, Slavic,
South, Western. *Dialect:* Kaykavski, Chakavski,
Shtokavski (Ijekavski). Shtokavski is the official dialect,
but the others are recognized as valid dialects, with a large
body of literature. Other dialects in other countries, like
Burgenland Croatian in Austria, are less intelligible.
Lg Use: Official language. Speakers also use English or
German. *Lg Dev:* Literacy rate in second language: 90%.
Roman script. Bible: 1804–1968. *Other:* SVO. Christian.
Dalmatian (Ragusan, Vegliote) [dlm] Extinct. Coast near
Dubrovnik. *Class:* Indo-European, Italic, Romance, Italo-
Western, Italo-Dalmatian. *Lg Use:* Extinct late nineteenth
century. A dialect of Croatian is now spoken in the area.
Istriot [ist] 1,000 (2000 Salminen). Western coast of
Istrian Peninsula, now only in the towns of Rovinj
(Rovigno) and Vodnjan (Dignano). *Class:* Indo-European,
Italic, Romance, Italo-Western, Italo-Dalmatian. *Dialects:*
Reported to be an archaic Romance language, often
confused with Istro-Rumanian. Perhaps closer to Friulian
or Dalmatian than to Istro-Rumanian. *Lg Use:* Some
children speakers.
Italian [ita] 70,000 in Croatia whose first language is Italian
or Venetian (1998 Eugen Marinov). Population includes
30,000 ethnic Italian and 40,000 ethnic Croats and Istrian
people. Ethnic population: 30,000 (1998). Istria. *Lg Use:*
Official language. See main entry under Italy.
Romanian, Istro (Istro-Romanian) [ruo] 555 to 1,500
(1994). Northeast Istrian Peninsula, Zejane village and a
few villages to the south. *Class:* Indo-European, Italic,
Romance, Eastern. *Dialects:* Structurally a separate
language from Romanian (F. B. Agard). Split from the
other 3 Romanian languages between 500 and 1000 A.D.
Not the same as the Istriot language. *Lg Use:* Few
children speakers.
Venetian [vec] 100,000 in Croatia and Slovenia (1994
Tapani Salminen). See also Italian in Croatia. Istrian
Peninsula and Dalmatia. *Dialects:* Istrian, Tretine, Venetian
Proper. *Lg Use:* Vigorous. See main entry under Italy.

Czech Republic

Czech Republic. 10,246,178. National or official language:
Czech. Literacy rate: 99%. Also includes Russian (33,500).
Information mainly from B. Comrie 1987. Blind population:

10,000 in former Czechoslovakia. Deaf population: 63,037. Deaf institutions: 51 in former Czechoslovakia. The number of languages listed for Czech Republic is 9. Of those, 8 are living languages and 1 is extinct.

Bavarian (Bayerisch, Bavarian Austrian) [bar] 9,245 in Czech Republic (2000 WCD). North Bavarian is in Western Bohemia and in the north of Regensburg to Nuremburg; Central Bavarian is in the Alps and Lower Austria and Salzburg; South Bavarian is in the Bavarian Alps, Tyrol, Styria, including the Heanzian dialect of Burgenland, Carinthia, northern Italy, and part of Gottschee. *Dialects:* Central Bavarian, North Bavarian, South Bavarian. See main entry under Austria.
Czech (Cestina) [ces] 10,004,800 in Czech Republic (1990 WA). Population total all countries: 11,525,089. Western part, Bohemia, Moravia, Silesia. Also spoken in Austria, Bulgaria, Canada, Israel, Poland, Romania, Slovakia, Ukraine, USA. *Class:* Indo-European, Slavic, West, Czech-Slovak. *Dialects:* Central Bohemian, Czecho-Moravian, Hanak, Lach (Yalach), Northeast Bohemian, Southwest Bohemian. All Czech and Slovak dialects are inherently intelligible to each other's speakers. *Lg Use:* National language. *Lg Dev:* Grammar. Bible: 1380–1980. *Other:* SVO. Christian.
Czech Sign Language [cse] *Class:* Deaf sign language. *Dialects:* Partially intelligible with French Sign Language. *Lg Use:* Used since 1786 when deaf schools began. Sign language used in school different from that used by adults outside. Signed interpretation required in court. Some provided for college students and at important public events. There is sign language instruction for parents of deaf children. More than one sign language used in the country. There is a manual alphabet for spelling. *Lg Dev:* Films. TV. Videos. Dictionary.
German, Standard [deu] 50,000 in Czech Republic (1998). In the Erzgebirge, a mountain range along the border of Czech Republic. *Dialect:* Erzgebirgisch. *Lg Use:* Speakers also use Czech. See main entry under Germany.
Knaanic (Canaanic, Leshon Knaan, Judeo-Slavic) [czk] Extinct. *Class:* Indo-European, Slavic, West, Czech-Slovak. *Dialect:* Judeo-Czech. *Lg Use:* Became extinct in late Middle Ages. The name 'Knaanic' applied mainly to Judeo Czech, but also to other Judeo-Slavic varieties. *Other:* Jewish.
Polish (Polski) [pol] 50,000 in Czech Republic. *Other:* Christian. See main entry under Poland.
Romani, Carpathian (Bashaldo, Romungro, Hungarian-Slovak Romani) [rmc] 220,000 in Czech Republic (1980 UBS). Population includes Slovakia. Population total all countries: 461,000. Central, Bohemia, and Moravia. Also spoken in Hungary, Poland, Romania, Slovakia, Ukraine, USA. *Class:* Indo-European, Indo-Iranian, Indo-Aryan, Central zone, Romani, Northern. *Dialects:* Moravian Romani, East Slovakian Romani, West Slovakian Romani. Not intelligible with Vlax Romani or Angloromani. *Lg Use:* Speakers do not interact socially with speakers of Vlax Romani or Angloromani. *Lg Dev:* Dictionary. Grammar. Bible portions: 1936–1996. *Other:* Ethnic groups: Sárvika Romá (northern and eastern Slovakia), Ungrike Romá (southern Slovakia). The people are called 'Karpacki Roma'. Christian.
Romani, Sinte (Rommanes, Sinte, Sinti, Tsigane) [rmo] 5,100 in Czech Republic (2004). *Dialect:* Lallere. *Other:* The Lallere are those whose ancestors came from the Czech Republic. Ethnic group: Sasítka Romá. Christian. See main entry under Serbia and Montenegro.
Silesian, Lower (Lower Schlesisch) [sli] *Other:* Different from Upper Silesian, a dialect of Polish. Nearly extinct. See main entry under Poland.

Denmark

Kingdom of Denmark, Kongeriget Danmark. 5,413,392. Population includes 43,000 on Faroe Islands (1998 UN). National or official languages: Danish, Standard German (regional). Also see Greenland. Greenland and Faroe Islands both have home rule. Literacy rate: 99%. Also includes English (10,000), Iu Mien (200), Kirmanjki, Northern Kurdish (8,000), Turkish (30,000), Western Farsi (9,000), Romani (3,000), from the former Yugoslavia (10,000), from India or Pakistan (4,000). Information mainly from M. Stephens 1976; B. Comrie 1987; I. Hancock 1991. Blind population: 9,350. Deaf population: 3,500 to 314,548 (1998). Deaf institutions: 20. The number of languages listed for Denmark is 8. Of those, all are living languages. See map on page 842.

Danish (Dansk, Central Danish, Sjaelland) [dan] 5,000,000 in Denmark (1980). Population total all countries: 5,299,756. Also spoken in Canada, Germany, Greenland, Iceland, Norway, Sweden, United Arab Emirates, USA. *Class:* Indo-European, Germanic, North, East Scandinavian, Danish-Swedish, Danish-Riksmal, Danish. *Lg Use:* National language. *Lg Dev:* Newspapers. Dictionary. Grammar. Bible: 1550. *Other:* See separate entries for Scanian, often called 'Eastern Danish', and Jutish, often called 'Western Danish'. Also see Norwegian, Riksmal. SVO. Christian.
Danish Sign Language [dsl] 3,500 (1986 Gallaudet Univ.). *Class:* Deaf sign language. *Dialects:* Some signs are related to French Sign Language. Intelligible with Swedish and Norwegian sign languages with only moderate difficulty. Not intelligible with Finnish Sign Language. *Lg Use:* Used in all 5 state schools for the deaf. Signed interpretation required in court, college classes, at important public events, in job training, social services, and mental health programs. Instruction provided for parents of deaf children, for other hearing people. There is a committee on national sign language, an organization for sign language teachers. Signed Danish is distinct, but used in intercommunication with some hearing people. *Lg Dev:* Films. TV. Videos. Dictionary. Grammar. *Other:* The first school was begun in 1807.
Faroese (Føroyskt) [fao] 45,400 (2001). Faroe Islands. *Class:* Indo-European, Germanic, North, West Scandinavian. *Dialects:* Not inherently intelligible with Icelandic. *Lg Dev:* Bible: 1948–1961. *Other:* The Faroe Islands are self-governing in most matters.
German, Standard [deu] 23,000 in Denmark (1976 Stephens). North Slesvig (Sydjylland). *Lg Use:* Official regional language. *Other:* There are German schools. See main entry under Germany.
Inuktitut, Greenlandic (Greenlandic, Kalaallisut) [kal] 7,000 on Denmark mainland (1990 L. D. Kaplan). See main entry under Greenland.
Jutish (Jutlandish, Jysk, Western Danish) [jut] German-Danish border area, Southern Jutland on the Danish side, and in northern Schleswig, Schleswig-Holstein, Germany. Also spoken in Germany. *Class:* Indo-European, Germanic, North, East Scandinavian, Danish-Swedish, Danish-Riksmal, Danish. *Dialects:* The westernmost and southernmost dialects differ so much from Standard Danish that many people from the Eastern Islands have great difficulty understanding it. From the viewpoint of inherent intelligibility, it could be considered a separate language (Norbert Strade). *Lg Use:* All inhabitants in Rudbol village are reported to be able to speak 5 languages: Danish, Jutish, North Frisian, Low Saxon, and German.
Scanian (Skane, Skånska, Eastern Danish, Southern Swedish) [scy] Bornholm Island. *Dialects:* Hallaendska,

Skånska, Blekingska, Bornholm. *Lg Use:* Speakers are highly bilingual in Swedish or Danish. *Other:* The language has had no recognition since Sweden obtained Scånia from Denmark in 1658. It is called 'Southern Swedish' in Sweden, and 'Eastern Danish' in Denmark. See main entry under Sweden.

Traveller Danish (Rodi, Rotwelsch) [rmd] *Class:* Mixed Language, Danish-Romani. *Dialects:* An independent language based on Danish with heavy lexical borrowing from Northern Romani. Not inherently intelligible with Angloromani. It may be intelligible with Traveller Norwegian and Traveller Swedish. *Lg Use:* There are reported to be few speakers. It may be linguistically extinct (D. Kenrick 1986). *Other:* Romani people were transported to Denmark by James IV of Scotland in July 1505.

Estonia

Republic of Estonia, Eesti Vabariik. 1,341,664. National or official language: Estonian. 17,413 square miles. Capital Tallinn. Literacy rate: 99%. Also includes Armenian (837), Baltic Romani (465), Belarusan (8,841), Chuvash (563), Eastern Yiddish (570), Finnish (5,155), Latvian (1,794), Lithuanian (1,610), North Azerbaijani (869), Polish (601), Russian (468,216), Standard German (1,249), Tatar (2,248), Ukrainian (21,320). Information mainly from B. Comrie 1987. Deaf population: 1,600 (1998). The number of languages listed for Estonia is 2. Of those, both are living languages.

Estonian (Eesti, Viro) [est] 953,032 in Estonia (1989 census). Population total all countries: 1,075,497. Ethnic population: 963,281 (1989 census). Also spoken in Australia, Canada, Finland, Latvia, Russia (Europe), Sweden, United Kingdom, USA. *Class:* Uralic, Finnic. *Dialects:* Tallinn (Reval), Tartu (Dorpat), Mulgi, Vôru (Werro), Seto (Setu). Dialects are grouped into three: Northeastern Coastal Estonian (between Tallinn and Narva), North Estonian (island, western, central, and eastern dialects), and South Estonian (Mulgi, Tartu, Vôru). Vôru, Setu (a subdialect of Vôru), and Island are clearly distinct from standard Estonian. All the other dialects are assimilated into standard Estonian. North and South Estonian may be separate languages. *Lg Use:* Official language. Estonian has remained the language of education, including universities. Those over 60 and under 20 speak little Russian. It is spoken less in rural areas and in southern areas. 75% to 80% of the population in the northeast are Russian speakers. Those over 60 know some German. Most in the north speak Finnish for common topics. *Lg Dev:* Roman script. TV. Dictionary. Grammar. Bible: 1739–1995. *Other:* Some linguistic influences from Russian, German, Swedish, Latvian, Lithuanian, and Finnish. SVO; 14 cases: affixes indicate case of noun phrases; verb affixes mark person, number of subject, and agreement (obligatory); genitives, adjectives, numerals before noun heads; question word initial; 1 prefix maximum; 5–6 suffixes maximum; word order distinguishes given and new information; active and passive voice; 4 moods in both voices: indicative, imperative, conditional, oblique; 2 infinitives for all verbs; 4 tenses in both voices and all moods: present, past, perfect, pluperfect; 3 degrees of comparison: positive, comparative, superlative; V, CV, CVC, CVCCC, CVV, CVVC, VC, VCCC, VV, VVC, CCV, CCVV, CCVC, CCVCC, CCVVCC, CCVCCC; stress on first syllable; possible secondary stress on third syllable; nontonal. Christian.

Estonian Sign Language (Viipekeel) [eso] 4,500 users out of 1,600 deaf and 20,000 hearing impaired. 2,000 persons need regular help from interpreters (1998 Urmas Sutrop). Throughout Estonia, especially Tallinn and Pärnu.

Class: Deaf sign language. *Dialects:* Some local dialects. The dialect in Pärnu is the most archaic. Apparent influences from Finnish and Russian Sign Languages. *Lg Use:* Russian Sign Language is used in Tallinn by deaf Russians. In other regions Russians use some pidginized versions of Russian Sign Language mixed with Estonian Sign Language. Systematic teaching and research since 1990 at the Dept. of Special Education at Tartu University. Sign language instruction for parents of deaf children in Tallinn. Some can use both Estonian and Russian Sign Languages. *Lg Dev:* TV. Videos. Dictionary. Grammar.

Finland

Republic of Finland, Suomen Tasavalta. 5,214,512. National or official languages: Finnish, Swedish. Literacy rate: 100%. Also includes English (4,500), Northern Kurdish (1,293), Polish, Romanian (1,000), Russian (10,000), Somali (3,103), Spanish, Standard German, Tatar (1,000), Turkish (1,000), Vietnamese, Arabic, Chinese. Information mainly from M. Stephens 1976; B. Comrie 1987; T. Salminen 1987–1998. Blind population: 3,345. Deaf population: 8,000 to 307,333 (1986 Gallaudet University). Deaf institutions: 44. The number of languages listed for Finland is 13. Of those, 12 are living languages and 1 is extinct. See map on page 842.

Estonian (Viro, Eesti) [est] 6,000 in Finland (1993). Traditionally on the southern coast. *Dialects:* Tallinn (Reval, Northern Estonian), Tartu (Dorpat, Tatu, Southern Estonian), Setu, Muly (Mulgi), Vyrus (Voru). *Lg Use:* The traditional community was assimilated to the Swedish-speaking community. *Other:* Present speakers are refugees from World War II or recent immigrants. Christian. See main entry under Estonia.

Finnish (Suomi, Suomea) [fin] 4,700,000 in Finland (1993). Population includes 30,000 speakers of Tornedalen Finnish. Population total all countries: 5,232,728. Also spoken in Canada, Estonia, Norway, Russia (Europe), Sweden, USA. *Class:* Uralic, Finnic. *Dialects:* Southwestern Finnish, Häme (Tavast), South Pohjanmaa, Central and North Pohjanmaa, Peräpohja, Savo (Savolax), Southeastern Finnish (Finnish Karjala, Finnish Karelian). Southeastern dialects called 'Karelian' in colloquial Finnish are distinct from true Karelian (T. Salminen). Finnish is closely related to Karelian and Olonetsian. In Russia eastern dialects merge gradually into Karelian. *Lg Use:* Official language. About 300,000 also use Swedish. *Lg Dev:* Grammar. Bible: 1642–1991. *Other:* SVO. Christian.

Finnish Sign Language (Viittomakieli) [fse] 5,000 (1986 Gallaudet Univ.). Ethnic population: 8,000. *Class:* Deaf sign language. *Dialects:* 2 major dialects from the Finnish (17 schools) and Swedish (1 school) communities. Apparent influence from Swedish Sign Language merged with local indigenous varieties. Not intelligible with Danish Sign Language. *Lg Use:* The government pays interpreters to accompany the deaf to hospitals, college, church, etc. Signed interpretation required in court. Sign language instruction for parents of deaf children. Many classes for hearing people. There is a committee on national sign language. *Lg Dev:* Films. TV. Videos. Dictionary. Grammar. Bible portions: 1989. *Other:* The first deaf school was founded in the 1850s. Signed Finnish is distinct, but used by some teachers of the deaf.

Finnish, Tornedalen [fit] 30,000 in Finland (1997 Birger Winsa). See main entry under Sweden.

Finnish-Swedish Sign Language [fss] 150 (2001). *Class:* Deaf sign language. *Lg Use:* Private spheres only. Users are older adults. *Other:* Users attended a now closed Swedish school for the deaf.

Karelian (Karely, Karelian Proper) [krl] 10,000 in Finland (1994). There are two villages in Oulu Province, close to the Russian border (Northern Karelian), and others scattered around Finland (Southern Karelian). *Dialect:* Northern Karelian, Southern Karelian, Norgorod, Tver (Kalinin). *Lg Use:* Northern Karelian is traditionally spoken in Oulu, though decreasingly. Southern Karelian speakers were resettled from areas ceded to the former USSR from 1940 to 1944. All are now apparently completely competent in Finnish (T. Salminen). *Lg Dev:* Literacy rate in first language: 75% to 100%. Literacy rate in second language: 75% to 100%. See main entry under Russia (Europe).

Livvi (Olonetsian, Olonets, Livvikovian, Lívõnkél, Aunus) [olo] 5,172 in Finland (2000 WCD). Ethnic population: 140,000. Scattered around Finland. *Lg Use:* They now appear to be completely competent in Finnish (T. Salminen). *Lg Dev:* Literacy rate in first language: 75% to 100%. Literacy rate in second language: 75% to 100%. *Other:* Speakers were resettled from areas ceded to the former USSR from 1940 to 1944. See main entry under Russia (Europe).

Romani, Kalo Finnish (Fíntika Rómma, Gypsy) [rmf] 5,410 in Finland (2000 WCD). Population total all countries: 7,002. Ethnic population: 8,000 Gypsies in Finland (1980). Western and southern. Also spoken in Sweden. *Class:* Indo-European, Indo-Iranian, Indo-Aryan, Central zone, Romani, Northern. *Dialects:* Not inherently intelligible with Traveller Swedish, Traveller Norwegian, Traveller Danish, or Angloromani. *Lg Dev:* Literacy rate in first language: 10% to 30%. Literacy rate in second language: 50% to 100%. Bible portions: 1971. *Other:* Speakers originally came from Scotland. Christian.

Saami, Inari (Inari "Lappish," Anar, "Finnish Lapp," "Lapp," Sámi, Samic, Saam, Saame) [smn] 250 (1995 M. Krauss). 4,700 all Saami in Finland (1995). Ethnic population: 700 (1995 M. Krauss). Lapland, above 68.00N Lat., in an area about 15,400 square miles between Lake Inari and the Norway border. They are in the majority around the border town of Utsjoki. *Class:* Uralic, Sami, Eastern. *Lg Use:* Few children speakers. Finnish Saami all know Finnish and speak it for all purposes outside their work as reindeer herdsmen. Instruction in schools is in Finnish. *Lg Dev:* Literacy rate in first language: 30% to 100%. Literacy rate in second language: 75% to 100%. Bible portions: 1903–1980. *Other:* The name "Lapp" is derogatory. Some literature. Pastoralists: reindeer.

Saami, Kemi (Sámi, Sami, "Lapp") [sjk] Extinct. Lapland Province, Sodankyla and Kuolajarvi (Salla) counties. Formerly south as far as Kuusamo County. *Class:* Uralic, Sami, Eastern. *Lg Use:* Extinct since the 19th century.

Saami, North (Northern Lapp, Davvin, "Lapp," Saame, Same) [sme] 2,000 in Finland (1995 M. Krauss). Ethnic population: 3,500 (1995 M. Krauss). Utsjoki, Enontekio, and Sodankyla. *Dialects:* Ruija, Torne, Sea Lappish. *Lg Dev:* Literacy rate in first language: 30% to 100%. Literacy rate in second language: 75% to 100%. Some schools in Inari and Utsjoki. *Other:* The most widely spoken Saami language in Finland. See main entry under Norway.

Saami, Skolt (Skolt Lappish, Russian Lapp, "Lapp," Saame, Same, Lopar, Kolta, Koltta) [sms] 300 in Finland (1995 M. Krauss). Population total all countries: 320. Ethnic population: 500 in Finland (1995 M. Krauss). Northwest of Inari Saami. Also spoken in Russia (Europe). *Class:* Uralic, Sami, Eastern. *Lg Use:* Most or all speakers are older adults. Many use Finnish as second language. *Lg Dev:* Literacy rate in first language: 10% to 60%. Literacy rate in second language: 75% to 100%. Roman script. Dictionary. Bible portions: 1878–1988. *Other:* They moved here during World War II from what is now a part of Russia. Pastoralists: reindeer; fishermen; hunters. Christian.

Swedish [swe] 296,000 in Finland (1997). Coasts of the provinces of Central Österbotten (Ostrobothnia), Vasa (Vaasa), Southwest Finland, Nyland (Uusimaa) (Helsingfors), Åland Islands, Kymenlaakso. *Dialects:* Standard Swedish, Österbotten (Ostrobothnian), Åland Islands Swedish, Southwest Finland Swedish, Uusimaa Swedish, Nyland Swedish. *Lg Use:* Official language. Perhaps 75% of speakers are fluent in Finnish, 25% are totally bilingual. *Other:* Swedish Finns have a distinctive pronunciation compared to the dialect in Sweden, but no apparent difficulty in intelligibility. Some Österbotten dialects are intelligible to others with difficulty. See main entry under Sweden.

France

French Republic, République Francaise. 60,424,213. National or official language: French. Literacy rate: 99% (1991 WA). Also includes Adyghe, Algerian Spoken Arabic (660,000), Armenian (70,000), Assyrian Neo-Aramaic, Central Atlas Tamazight (150,000), Central Khmer (50,000), Chru, Giáy (100), Hmong Daw (10,000), Iu Mien (700), Judeo-Moroccan Arabic, Judeo-Tunisian Arabic, Kabuverdianu (8,000), Kabyle (537,000), Khmu (500), Kirmanjki, Lao, Laz, Lesser Antillean Creole French (150,000), Mandjak, Moroccan Spoken Arabic (492,700), Northern Kurdish, Standard German, Tachelhit, Tai Dam (1,000), Tai Dón, Tai Nüa, Tarifit, Tày, Tunisian Spoken Arabic (212,900), Turkish (135,000), Vietnamese (10,000), Western Cham (1,000), Western Farsi (40,000), Western Yiddish, Wolof (34,500), Yeniche. Information mainly from M. Stephens 1976; P. Blanchet 1986; B. Comrie 1987. Blind population: 43,000 (1982 WCE). Deaf population: 3,506,839. Deaf institutions: 99. The number of languages listed for France is 32. Of those, 29 are living languages, 1 is a second language without mother-tongue speakers, and 2 are extinct. See map on page 843.

Alemannisch (Alemannic) [gsw] 1,500,000 in France (1988 Hawkins in B. Comrie). Northeastern France, Alsace. *Dialect:* Alsatian (Alsacien, Elsaessisch). *Lg Use:* All ages. All speakers do not necessarily understand or read Standard German, but most also use French. Use of Standard French varies from 79% to 90% of the population in the different regions. Standard German is taught in some primary schools, and used in local newspapers. *Other:* Called 'Schwyzerdütsch' in Switzerland and 'Alemannisch' in Austria and parts of Germany. No standard form of Alsatian, but a variety of village dialects. Christian. See main entry under Switzerland (Schwyzerdütsch).

Auvergnat (Auvernhas, Auverne, Occitan) [auv] 1,315,000 (2004). Auvergne; Haut-Auvergnat in Cantal and south of Haute-Loire; Bas-Auvergnat in the north of Haute-Loire and in Puy-de-Dome. *Class:* Indo-European, Italic, Romance, Italo-Western, Western, Gallo-Iberian, Ibero-Romance, Oc. *Dialects:* Haut-Auvergnat, Bas-Auvergnat. Highly fragmented dialect situation, with limited intelligibility between northern and southern varieties. *Lg Use:* More vigorous use in the south. Attitudes are strong and differ about how different the Oc varieties are from each other. Speakers also use French. *Lg Dev:* Bible portions: 1831.

Basque, Navarro-Labourdin (Navarro-Labourdin) [bqe] 67,500 (1991). Population includes 45,000 Labourdin, 22,500 Lower Navarro. Total Basque speakers in France estimated at 80,000. Ethnic population: 730,000 (1993 Johnstone). French-Spanish border, 800 square miles surrounding Bayonne, Labourd (Lapurdi), and Basse-Navarre departments. *Class:* Basque. *Dialects:* Labourdin (Lapurdiera), Eastern Low Navarrese

(Benaffarera, Bajo Navarro Oriental), Western Low Navarrese (Bajo Navarro Occidental). Navarro-Labourdin is diverse from other Basque dialects, and needs separate literature. *Lg Use:* Basque has the status of a regional language in France. A few schools use Basque as an instructional language, others offer it as a subject. All domains. Home, school, work (agriculture, crafts, trade, commerce, advertising), drama, religion, music, cultural activities. All ages. Speakers also use French. *Lg Dev:* Newspapers. Radio programs. TV. Dictionary. Grammar. Bible: 1865. *Other:* Christian.

Basque, Souletin (Souletin, Souletino, Suletino, Xiberoera, Zuberoera, Suberoan) [bsz] 8,700 (1991). French-Spanish border, 800 square miles surrounding Bayonne, Soule, Pyrénées Atlantiques Province. *Class:* Basque. *Dialects:* Souletin is more diverse and speakers have difficulty understanding other varieties, especially for complex and abstract discourse. Separate literature desired and needed. *Lg Use:* Basque has the status of a regional language in France. *Lg Dev:* Dictionary. Grammar. Bible portions: 1856–1888. *Other:* Christian.

Breton (Brezhoneg) [bre] 500,000 in France (1989 ICDBL). 1,200,000 know Breton who do not regularly use it. Population total all countries: 532,722. Western Brittany, and dispersed in Eastern Brittany and Breton emigrant communities throughout the world. Also spoken in USA. *Class:* Indo-European, Celtic, Insular, Brythonic. *Dialects:* Leonais, Tregorrois, Vannetais, Cornouaillais. *Lg Use:* No official status. Strong nationalist movement demanding recognition, a place in the schools, media, and public life. 18,000 speakers are children under 14 years; 56,250 between 15 and 24; 423,000 between 25 and 64; 168,000 over 65 (1974). Some claim to be monolingual in Breton. *Lg Dev:* Literacy rate in first language: 25% can read and write Breton. Radio programs. TV. Grammar. Bible: 1866–1985. *Other:* VSO; prepositions; genitives, adjectives, relatives after noun heads; articles, numerals before noun heads; question word initial; probably 2 prefixes, 2 or 3 suffixes on a word; topic or focus first, verb second; verb affixes mark person, number of subject; passives; causatives and comparatives shown lexically; up to 3 consonants syllable initially, and 3 finally, one vowel; nontonal.

Caló (Gitano, Iberian Romani) [rmr] 21,580 in France (2000 WCD). Southern France. *Dialects:* Basque Calo, Catalonian Calo, Spanish Calo. *Lg Use:* Speakers also use Spanish or Portuguese. *Other:* Christian. See main entry under Spain.

Catalan-Valencian-Balear [cat] 100,000 in France (1996). Catalonian France. *Lg Use:* Many children speak the language. *Other:* Population given above may not all be first-language speakers. See main entry under Spain.

Corsican (Corsu, Corso, Corse, Corsi) [cos] 341,000 in Corsica (2001 Johnstone and Mandryk). Population total all countries: 402,000. Corsica, Paris, Marseilles. Also spoken in Bolivia, Canada, Cuba, Italy, Puerto Rico, Uruguay, USA, Venezuela. *Class:* Indo-European, Italic, Romance, Southern, Corsican. *Dialects:* Sartenais, Vico-Ajaccio, Northern Corsican (Cape Cors, Bastia), Venaco. Corsican is in the Tuscan group of Italian varieties. Southern Corsican is closer to Northern Sardinian or Gallurese than other Corsican dialects (R. A. Hall, Jr.). Lexical similarity 79% to 89% among dialects of Bastia, Venaco, Vico, and Sartene. Bonifacio on the southern tip of the island has 78% lexical similarity (highest) with Bastia at extreme north. Ajaccio dialect is central and prestigious. *Lg Use:* Vigorous. Corsican has been recognized as a language by the French government. All ages. Speakers also use French but many are not fluent in it. There is a movement for bilingual education. *Lg Dev:* Bible portions: 1861–1994.

Dutch [nld] 80,000 in Westhoek. Westhoek in the northeast corner of France between the Artois Hills and the Belgium border. *Lg Use:* Usage is declining. See main entry under Netherlands.

Esperanto (La Lingvo Internacia) [epo] 200 to 2,000 (1996). Speakers in about 115 countries, used most widely in central and eastern Europe, China and other countries in eastern Asia, certain areas of South America, and southwest Asia. *Class:* Artificial language. *Lg Use:* 2,000,000 second-language speakers (1999 WA). All ages. *Lg Dev:* Bible: 1900–1910. *Other:* Was developed from 1872 to 1885 by L. L. Zamenhof of Warsaw, Poland, for intercommunication by first-language speakers of other languages. SVO; prepositions; genitives, relatives after noun heads; articles, adjectives, numerals before noun heads; question word initial; accusative '-n', dative '-al'; affixes mark tense; passive with 'esti' passive participle; causative '-ig'; comparative word; nontonal.

Franco-Provençal (Patois, Arpitan) [frp] Population total all countries: 77,000. Savoie, Fribourg, and Valais, southeastern France, near the Italian and Switzerland borders. Also spoken in Italy, Switzerland. *Class:* Indo-European, Italic, Romance, Italo-Western, Western, Gallo-Iberian, Gallo-Romance, Gallo-Rhaetian, Oïl, Southeastern. *Dialects:* Dauphinois, Lyonnais, Neuchatelais, Savoyard. Structurally separate language from Provençal, French, Piemontese, and Lombard (F. B. Agard). In Switzerland, every canton has its own dialect, with no standardization. Difficult intelligibility among the dialects, and especially with Fribourg. *Lg Use:* Few speakers in France. Speakers also use French. *Lg Dev:* Literacy rate in second language: 100% in French. Dictionary. Grammar. Bible portions: 1830.

French (Français) [fra] 51,000,000 in France. Population total all countries: 64,858,311. Also spoken in Algeria, Andorra, Austria, Belgium, Benin, Burkina Faso, Burundi, Cambodia, Cameroon, Canada, Central African Republic, Chad, Comoros, Congo, Côte d'Ivoire, Democratic Republic of the Congo, Djibouti, Equatorial Guinea, French Guiana, French Polynesia, Gabon, Guadeloupe, Guinea, Haiti, Hungary, Israel, Italy, Lebanon, Luxembourg, Madagascar, Mali, Martinique, Mauritania, Mauritius, Mayotte, Monaco, Morocco, New Caledonia, Niger, Philippines, Puerto Rico, Réunion, Rwanda, Saint Pierre and Miquelon, Saudi Arabia, Senegal, Seychelles, Switzerland, Togo, Tunisia, United Arab Emirates, United Kingdom, USA, Vanuatu, Wallis and Futuna. *Class:* Indo-European, Italic, Romance, Italo-Western, Western, Gallo-Iberian, Gallo-Romance, Gallo-Rhaetian, Oïl, French. *Dialects:* Standard French, Norman (Normand), Angevin, Berrichon, Bourbonnais, Bourguignon, Franc-Comtois, Gallo, Poitevin, Santongeais, Lorraine. Lexical similarity 89% with Italian, 80% with Sardinian, 78% with Rheto-Romance, 75% with Portuguese, Romanian, and Spanish, 29% with German, 27% with English. *Lg Use:* National language. 50,000,000 second-language speakers. *Lg Dev:* Dictionary. Grammar. Bible: 1530–2000. *Other:* SVO. Deciduous forest. 80 meters. Intensive agriculturalists; industry workers, marketers. Christian.

French Sign Language (Langue des Signes Française, LSF, FSL) [fsl] 50,000 to 100,000 primary users in France (1986 Gallaudet Univ.). 1,000 users of Marseille Sign Language (1975 Sallagooty). Southern FSL is used in Marseille, Toulon, La Ciotat, and Salon de Provence. Also used in Togo. *Class:* Deaf sign language. *Dialect:* Marseille Sign Language (Southern French Sign Language). Many sign languages have been influenced by this, but are not necessarily intelligible with it. Reported to be partially intelligible with sign languages from Austria, Czech Republic, and Italy, at least. Lexical similarity 43% with American Sign Language in an 872-wordlist. *Other:*

First sign language in the western world to gain recognition as a language (1830). Originated in 1752. Sign languages were known in France in the 16th century, and probably earlier. Different from Signed French and Old French Sign Language.

Gascon (Occitan) [gsc] 250,000 in France (1990 P. Blanchet). Population total all countries: 253,814. Ethnic population: 400,000 (1982) in the Béarn region of southern Gasconha, France; 51% speak Gascon, 70% understand it, 85% are in favor of saving it. Gascogne Province, from Médoc to the Pyrénées, from the Atlantic to the Catalan area. Béarnese is spoken by a strong majority in the Béarn. Also spoken in Spain. *Class:* Indo-European, Italic, Romance, Italo-Western, Western, Gallo-Iberian, Ibero-Romance, Oc. *Dialects:* Landais, Béarnais (Biarnese), Ariégeois, Aranese. Gascon, Languedocien, and Limousin are structurally separate languages (F.B. Agard). Gascon speakers have some comprehension of Provençal; some or limited comprehension of Languedocien (reports differ). Inherently intelligible with Aranese Gascon in Spain, which is a dialect. *Lg Dev:* Literacy rate in first language: Much lower than in Spain. Newspapers. Radio programs. TV. Bible portions: 1583–1983.

Greek [ell] Cargese, Corsica. *Dialect:* Cargese. *Lg Use:* The last native speaker died about 1982 (Nick Nicholas 1997). Members of the ethnic group now speak French. See main entry under Greece.

Interlingua (Interlingua de Iala) [ina] *Class:* Artificial language. *Other:* A latinate language devised by Alexander Gode around 1950, and published by the International Auxiliary Language Association (IALA). Second language only.

Italian [ita] 1,000,000 in France (1977 Voegelin and Voegelin). *Lg Use:* Nearly all know French. See main entry under Italy.

Languedocien (Lengadoucian, Languedoc, Langadoc, Occitan, Occitani) [lnc] 5,000. Languedoc Province, from Montpellier to Toulouse, Bordeaux, Rodez, and Albi. *Class:* Indo-European, Italic, Romance, Italo-Western, Western, Gallo-Iberian, Ibero-Romance, Oc. *Dialects:* Bas-Languedocien, Languedocien Moyen, Haut-Languedocien, Guyennais. A separate language from Provençal (P. Blanchet 1990). Gascon speakers have limited intelligibility of Languedocien. *Lg Use:* Used with family and close friends. Mainly spoken in rural communities by all ages. Attempts to standardize Languedocien for all languages of southern France have not been accepted by speakers of those languages. Attitudes are strong and differ about how different the Oc varieties are from each other. Languedocien resembles most the literary variety of Middle Occitan used in the Troubadours of the Middle Ages. Everyone speaks French as first or second language. *Lg Dev:* Literacy rate in second language: 99%. Roman script. Poetry. Newspapers. Bible portions: 1888–1982.

Ligurian (Ligure) [lij] Bonifacio, Corsica, and between the Italian border and Monaco. *Dialect:* Genoese (Genoan, Genovese). See main entry under Italy.

Limousin (Lemosin, Occitan) [lms] 10,000. Limousin Province. Haut-Limousin around Limoges, Guéret, and Nontron in Charente; Bas-Limousin around Correze and Périgord. *Class:* Indo-European, Italic, Romance, Italo-Western, Western, Gallo-Iberian, Ibero-Romance, Oc. *Dialects:* Haut-Limousin, Bas-Limousin. Limousin, Languedocien, and Gascon are structurally separate languages (F. B. Agard). Partially intelligible to Provençal. In the north of the province people use a transition dialect with certain Oïl (north French) features. *Lg Use:* Few children speakers. Attitudes are strong and differ about how different the Oc varieties are from each other. Most also use French.

Luxembourgeois (Frankish, Platt) [ltz] 40,000 in France (2001 J. Nousse). Spoken along the border with Germany and Luxemburg in the Moselle Department, Thionville, France. *Lg Use:* The common language of French and German coal miners. See main entry under Luxembourg.

Lyons Sign Language [lsg] *Class:* Deaf sign language. *Dialects:* 250 miles from Paris, but difficult and little intelligibility of French Sign Language.

Picard (Rouchi, Chtimi) [pcd] Most of the Region de Picardie (Amiens, Abbeville, Beauvais, St. Quentin), the Region Nord-Pas-de-Calais (Lille, Douai, Cambrai, Arras, Valenciennes, Boulogne sur Mer, Calais), except the Dunkerque District, and a little eastern zone (border with Picardie of the Region de Haute Normandie near Dieppe). Also spoken in Belgium. *Class:* Indo-European, Italic, Romance, Italo-Western, Western, Gallo-Iberian, Gallo-Romance, Gallo-Rhaetian, Oïl, French. *Dialect:* Ponthieu, Vimeu, Hainaut, Artois, Lillois, Boulonnais, Santerre, Calaisis, Cambresis, Vermandois, Amienois (Amies). All dialects, including those in Belgium, are inherently intelligible to speakers. *Lg Use:* The Belgian government recognizes Picard officially as an indigenous regional language. The European Bureau for Lesser Used Languages considers it as a language. Some reports used and edited by the French government consider it a separate language from French. Boulonnais dialect has theater, poems, published grammar, dictionary. Used in the home, family, friends, community. French is spoken at school, in court, for administration, with outsiders. *Lg Dev:* Literacy rate in second language: 70%. Poetry. Bible portions: 1863. *Other:* Christian.

Portuguese [por] 750,000 in France (1989 National Geographic). *Lg Dev:* Literacy rate in second language: relatively low. See main entry under Portugal.

Provençal (Prouvençau, Mistralien) [prv] 250,000 in France (1990 P. Blanchet). Population total all countries: 354,500. Southeastern France, province of Provence, south of Dauphiné, region of Nimes in Languedoc. Also spoken in Italy, Monaco. *Class:* Indo-European, Italic, Romance, Italo-Western, Western, Gallo-Iberian, Ibero-Romance, Oc. *Dialects:* Transalpin, Niçard (Niçois), Maritime Provençal (Marseillais, Toulonnais, Varois), Gavot (Alpin, Valeien, Gapian, Forcalquieren), Rhodanien (Nimois), Dauphinois (Dromois). Gascon, Languedocien, and Limousin are structurally separate languages (F. Agard). Provençal and Languedocien (Occitan) are separate languages (P. Blanchet 1990). No Provençal variety is universally accepted as the standard literary form. Niçard and Northern Gavot (Valeien and Gapian) are more difficult for other dialect speakers to understand. *Lg Use:* 800,000 with some knowledge. There is regional pride and increasing status as a literary language. Strong demand for teaching in school and books in Provençal. Speakers are older adults. Attitudes are strong and differ about how different the Oc varieties are from each other. The Nobel Prize laureate Frederic Mistal wrote in Provençal. Through increased contact in army and school, most speakers are actively bilingual in French. Literary French is sometimes difficult for speakers with less school education. Regional French has a lot of Provençal influence. *Lg Dev:* Bible portions: 1824–1975.

Romani, Balkan [rmn] 10,500 in France. Population includes 10,000 Arlija, 500 Dzambazi. *Dialects:* Arlija, Dzambazi. *Other:* Muslim. See main entry under Serbia and Montenegro.

Romani, Sinte (Sinti, Rommanes, Tsigane) [rmo] 28,434 in France (2000 WCD). *Dialect:* Manouche (Manuche, Manush). *Other:* Ethnic group: Sasítka Romá. Christian. See main entry under Serbia and Montenegro.

Romani, Vlax (Romenes, Rom, Tsigane, Vlax) [rmy] 10,000 in France. Population includes 8,000 Kalderash,

2,000 Lovari. *Dialects:* Kalderash, Lovari. *Other:* Christian. See main entry under Romania.

Shuadit (Shuadi, Judeo-Provençal, Judeo-Comtadine) [sdt] Extinct. Department of Vaucluse in southern France, and city of Avignon. *Class:* Indo-European, Italic, Romance, Italo-Western, Western, Gallo-Iberian, Ibero-Romance, Oc. *Lg Use:* It became extinct in 1977. May still be used in Passover song. *Other:* Jewish.

Spanish (Castillan) [spa] See main entry under Spain.

Vlaams (Flamand, Flemish, Vlaemsch) [vls] 10,000 in France (1984 Menheere, 1993 Evenhuis). Westhoek (French Flanders). *Dialect:* Frans Vlaams (Vlaemsch). *Lg Use:* Used for informal situations. Speakers are older adults. Speakers view Dutch as a completely different, friendly language. Speakers also use French or English. *Other:* Speakers in France are called 'Vlamingen', the language called 'Vlaemsch'. Speakers sometimes refer to Dutch as 'Vlaams'. Different orthographies used in the 3 countries. Christian. See main entry under Belgium.

Zarphatic (Judeo-French) [zrp] Extinct. *Class:* Indo-European, Italic, Romance, Italo-Western, Western, Gallo-Iberian, Gallo-Romance, Gallo-Rhaetian, Oïl, French. *Other:* Jewish.

Germany

Federal Republic of Germany, Bundesrepublik Deutschland. 82,424,609. Population includes 5,241,801 without German citizenship (1990 official figures). National or official language: Standard German. Literacy rate: 99%. Also includes Adyghe (2,000), Algerian Spoken Arabic (26,000), Assyrian Neo-Aramaic, Catalan-Valencian-Balear, Chaldean Neo-Aramaic (3,000), Chechen, Croatian (652,000), Dimli, Dutch (101,000), English (110,000), Greek (314,000), Hausa, Hebrew, Hindi (24,500), Italian (548,000), Japanese (20,000), Jutish, Kabuverdianu (3,000), Kalmyk-Oirat, Kazakh, Kirmanjki, Korean (14,000), Latvian (8,000), Laz (1,000), Moroccan Spoken Arabic (44,200), Northern Kurdish (541,311), Osetin, Portuguese (78,000), Russian (360,000), Spanish (134,000), Tamil (35,000), Tarifit, Tigrigna (15,000), Tosk Albanian (25,000), Tunisian Spoken Arabic (26,000), Turkish (2,107,426), Turkmen, Turoyo (20,000), Urdu (23,000), Uyghur, Vietnamese (60,000), Western Farsi (90,000), Uyghur, Vietnamese 60,000, Chinese 40,000, from Afghanistan 29,000. Information mainly from M. Stephens 1976; B. Comrie 1987; S. Barbour and P. Stevenson 1990. Blind population: 82,000 in western Germany, including 51,000 blind, 31,000 severely visually handicapped (1989 SB). Deaf population: 50,000 to 8,000,000 (1986 Gallaudet University). Deaf institutions: 141. The number of languages listed for Germany is 29. Of those, 27 are living languages and 2 are extinct.

Alemannisch (Alemannic) [gsw] Southwestern, southern Baden-Wuerttemberg. *Dialects:* Low Alemannisch, High Alemannisch. *Lg Use:* Speakers also use Standard German. *Other:* Varieties in Germany include Low and High Alemannisch. Approximately 40% inherent intelligibility with Standard German. See main entry under Switzerland (Schwyzerdütsch).

Bavarian (Bairisch, Bayerisch, Bavarian Austrian) [bar] 246,050 in Germany (2000 WCD). North Bavarian is north of Regensburg, to Nuremburg and Western Bohemia, Czech Republic; Central Bavarian is in the Alps and Lower Austria and Salzburg; South Bavarian is in the Bavarian Alps, Tyrol, Styria, including the Heanzian dialect of Burgenland, Carinthia, northern Italy, and part of Gottschee in Slovenia. *Dialects:* Central Bavarian, North Bavarian, South Bavarian. *Lg Use:* Some speakers use Czech as a second language. School is taught in Standard German. See main entry under Austria.

Danish (Dänisch, Dansk) [dan] 20,963 in Germany (2000). South Schleswig. *Lg Use:* All speakers also use Standard German. *Other:* There are Danish schools. See main entry under Denmark.

Frankish (Fränkisch, Old Frankish) [frk] Extinct. *Class:* Indo-European, Germanic, West, High German, German. *Lg Dev:* Bible portions: 1758–1827. *Other:* Different from present day German language varieties.

Frisian, Eastern (Ostfriesisch, Saterlandic Frisian, Seeltersk Frisian) [frs] 11,000 in Germany (1976 Stephens). Schleswig-Holstein, Ostfriesland, the area around the towns of Emden and Oldenburg in Lower Saxony, and Saterland, Jeverland, and Butjadingen in 1976. Reported to be used only in Saterland, Eastern Frisia in 1998. Also spoken in USA. *Class:* Indo-European, Germanic, West, Low Saxon-Low Franconian. *Dialects:* Not intelligible with Western Frisian of the Netherlands or Northern Frisian (E. Matteson SIL 1978) or Saterfriesisch (Wolbert Smidt 2001). Lexical similarity 77% with Standard German, 74% with Western Frisian. *Lg Use:* Language of the home for 1,500 to 2,000 (1977 SIL). Most speakers are older adults (2001).

Frisian, Northern (Nordfriesisch) [frr] 10,000 (1976 Stephens). Ethnic population: 60,000 (1976 Stephens). Schleswig-Holstein, on the coastal strip between the rivers Eider in the south and Wiedau in the north, and adjacent islands of Föhr, Amrum, Sylt, Norstrand, Pellworm, the ten islands of the Halligen group, and Helgoland. *Class:* Indo-European, Germanic, West, Frisian. *Dialects:* Mooringer (Mooringa, Mainland Frisian), Ferring (Fohr-Amrum), Sölreng (Sylt), Helgoland. The first 3 dialects listed are different enough that more than one set of literature would be needed. Ferring dialect is actively used. Not intelligible to Eastern Frisian of Germany or Western Frisian of the Netherlands except to a few educated bilingual speakers of West Frisian. Mooringer has 70% lexical similarity with Standard German, 55% with English, 66% with Eastern Frisian; Föhr has 69% with Standard German, 62% with English, 68% with Western Frisian, 73% with Eastern Frisian, 86% with Mooringer, 91% with Amrum; Sylt has 64% with Standard German, 61% with English, 79% with Mooringer, 85% with Föhr. *Lg Use:* The Sölreng dialect is nearly extinct. Used in the home. Few children speakers. Positive language attitude. Speakers have some proficiency in Standard German, Low Saxon, or English. *Lg Dev:* Literacy rate in first language: Few read Frisian. Grammar. Bible portions: 1954. *Other:* Education is in Standard German only. Commerce and religious services in German.

German Sign Language (Deutsche Gebärdensprache, Dgs) [gsg] 50,000 (1986 Gallaudet Univ.). Population includes 22,000 members of German Deaf Association. Western Germany. *Class:* Deaf sign language. *Dialects:* Many regional lexical variations. Some similarity to French and other European sign languages. Relation to sign languages of eastern Germany, Austria, and Switzerland is not known. More than one sign language used in eastern Germany. *Lg Dev:* Bible portions: 1998.

German, Standard (Deutsch, Tedesco) [deu] 75,300,000 in Germany (1990). Population total all countries: 95,392,978. Also spoken in Argentina, Australia, Austria, Belgium, Bolivia, Bosnia and Herzegovina, Brazil, Canada, Chile, Czech Republic, Denmark, Ecuador, Estonia, Finland, France, Hungary, Israel, Italy, Kazakhstan, Kyrgyzstan, Liechtenstein, Luxembourg, Moldova, Namibia, Paraguay, Philippines, Poland, Puerto Rico, Romania, Russia (Europe), Slovakia, Slovenia, South Africa, Switzerland, Tajikistan, Ukraine, United Arab Emirates, Uruguay, USA, Uzbekistan. *Class:* Indo-European, Germanic, West, High German, German, Middle German, East Middle German. *Dialects:* Major related language areas are Bavarian, Schwäbisch, Allemannisch,

Mainfränkisch, Hessisch, Palatinian, Rheinfränkisch, Westfälisch, Saxonian, Thuringian, Brandenburgisch, and Low Saxon. Many varieties are not inherently intelligible with each other. Our present treatment in this edition is incomplete. Standard German is one High German variety, which developed from the chancery of Saxony, gaining acceptance as the written standard in the 16th and 17th centuries. High German refers to dialects and languages in the upper Rhine region. Lexical similarity 60% with English, 29% with French. *Lg Use:* National language. 28,000,000 second-language speakers. *Lg Dev:* Taught in primary and secondary schools. Poetry. Newspapers. Radio programs. Films. TV. Videos. Dictionary. Grammar. Bible: 1466–1982. *Other:* Christian.

Kölsch [ksh] 250,000 (1997 Holger Jakobs). Cologne (Köln) and surrounding areas. *Class:* Indo-European, Germanic, West, High German, German, Middle German, West Middle German, Ripuarian Franconian. *Lg Use:* Used in theaters, literature, and an academy for teaching it. All ages. Nearly all use Standard German as second language. *Lg Dev:* Literacy rate in second language: 99%. Bible portions: 1992. *Other:* Christian.

Limburgisch (Limburgs Plat) [lim] Depending on the city in Germany, 50% to 90% of the population speak it (2001 A. Schunck). German-administered Limburg: Cleves, Aachen, Viersen, Heinsberg. *Lg Use:* Officially recognized in the Netherlands. Efforts are underway to have it officially recognized in Belgium. Promotion efforts are strong. It has more prestige in the Netherlands. All domains, songs. All ages. Speakers also use German. *Lg Dev:* Literacy rate in second language: 99% to 100%. *Other:* Laborers. Christian. See main entry under Netherlands.

Luxembourgeois (Luxemburgian, Letzburgisch, Lëtzebuergesch, Moselle Franconian) [ltz] Few speakers in Germany. Bitburg area in western Germany. See main entry under Luxembourg.

Mainfränkisch (Franconian) [vmf] Spoken mostly along the River Main, including the city of Mainz, thus not far west of Frankfurt. *Class:* Indo-European, Germanic, West, High German, German, Middle German, West Middle German, Moselle Franconian. *Dialects:* Approximately 40% inherently intelligible with Standard German. *Lg Use:* Speakers also use Standard German.

Pfaelzisch (Pfälzische, Pfälzisch) [pfl] Southwest Palatinate, Rheinpfalz. *Class:* Indo-European, Germanic, West, High German, German, Middle German, West Middle German, Rhenish Franconian. *Dialects:* Various dialects. *Lg Use:* Speakers also use Standard German. *Lg Dev:* Dictionary. *Other:* Literature.

Plautdietsch [pdt] 90,000 in Germany (1996 Reuben Epp). See main entry under Canada.

Polabian [pox] Extinct. North of the Wend language area. *Class:* Indo-European, Slavic, West, Lechitic.

Polish (Polski, Polnisch) [pol] 241,000 in Germany. *Other:* Christian. See main entry under Poland.

Romani, Balkan [rmn] 3,500 in Germany. Population includes 2,000 Arlija and 1,500 Dzambazi. *Dialects:* Arlija (Erli), Dzambazi. *Other:* Muslim. See main entry under Serbia and Montenegro.

Romani, Sinte (Rommanes, Ziguener, Sintí, Sinte) [rmo] 80,000 in Germany (2000). Ethnic population: 200,000. Hamburg and colonies in the south. *Dialects:* Gadschkene, Estracharia, Krantiki, Kranaria, Eftawagaria, Praistiki. *Lg Use:* Vigorous. All ages. *Other:* Seminomadic. Christian. See main entry under Serbia and Montenegro.

Romani, Vlax [rmy] 1,699 in Germany (2000 WCD). Population includes 2,500 Lovari, 2,500 to 4,000 Kalderash. *Dialects:* Lovari, Kalderash. *Other:* Christian. See main entry under Romania.

Saterfriesisch (Saterfriesiesch, Saterländisch, Saterlandic Frisian) [stq] 5,000 (2001 Wolbert Smidt). Saterland, East

Frisia. *Class:* Indo-European, Germanic, West, Frisian. *Dialects:* Not intelligible with Eastern Frisian. Related to Western Frisian and Northern Frisian. *Lg Use:* Speakers are mainly older adults (2001). Saterfriesen or Friesen is the name of the ethnic group. Almost all also speak Eastern Frisian or Standard German for official purposes. *Lg Dev:* Literacy rate in second language: High in German. *Other:* Christian.

Saxon, Low (Neddersassisch, Niedersaechsisch, Nedersaksisch, Low German, Plattdütsch, Nedderdütsch) [nds] 1,000. 10,000,000 understand it in Germany, but few are native speakers (1996 Reinhard F. Hahn). Northern Germany. Lower Rhine Region below a line from Aachen to Witenberg. *Class:* Indo-European, Germanic, West, Low Saxon-Low Franconian, Low Saxon. *Dialects:* Northern Low Saxon, Eastphalian (Ostfaelisch, Ostfälisch), Mecklenburg-Anterior Pomerania (Mecklenburgisch-Vorpommersch), Mark-Brandenburg (Maerkisch-Brandenburgisch, Märkisch-Brandenburgisch, East Prussian). The dialects listed are in Germany. The first three dialects listed are Western Low Saxon, the other two are Eastern Low Saxon. Not intelligible to speakers of Standard German. A direct descendant of Old Saxon, related to English. 20 to 30 dialects with differing inherent intelligibility, depending on geographic distance. They did not experience the second consonant shift of the 8th and 9th centuries (J. Thiessen, U. of Winnipeg 1976). Its modern forms have been largely suppressed until recently and have received much German, Dutch, or Frisian influence, depending on the area. Low Saxon varieties listed as separate entries in the Netherlands, where they have official status. Pomerano is used in Latin America. Westphaelian and Plautdietsch also have separate entries. *Lg Use:* Officially recognized as a regional (separate) language in 8 states of Germany. Recognized as a regional (separate) language by the European Charta on Languages. Most speakers in Germany also use Standard German. *Lg Dev:* Dictionary. Bible: 1478–1534. *Other:* Printed fairly widely outside Europe, particularly in North and Latin America, Australia, Southern Africa, Eastern Europe (Siberia, Kazakhstan).

Saxon, Upper [sxu] 2,000,000 (1998 Andreas Thomsen). Eastern Germany, southeast, Sachsen with Dresden, Leipzig, Chemnitz, Halle in Sachsen-Anhalt. *Class:* Indo-European, Germanic, West, High German, German, Middle German, East Middle German. *Dialect:* Erzgebirgisch. *Lg Use:* Speakers also use Standard German. *Other:* Spoken by 'several millions'.

Silesian, Lower (Lower Schlesisch) [sli] Gorlitz, eastern Germany. *Lg Use:* There is literature by Gerhard Hauptmann. Spoken by younger people. Speakers also use Standard German. *Other:* Different from Upper Silesian, a dialect of Polish. Nearly extinct. See main entry under Poland.

Sorbian, Lower (Niedersorbisch, Bas Sorabe, Wendish, Lusatian, Lower Lusatian, Dolnoserbski, Delnoserbski) [dsb] 14,000 (1991 Elle). Ethnic population: 60,000. Niederlausitz (Dolna Luzica) in eastern Germany, Cottbus (Chósebuz) the main town. The ethnic group has over 60 towns and villages. *Class:* Indo-European, Slavic, West, Sorbian. *Lg Use:* Speakers are older adults. *Lg Dev:* Newspapers. Radio programs. TV. Bible: 1796–1824. *Other:* Their own name for the language is 'Dolnoserbski'. High school, Sorbian language school.

Sorbian, Upper (Obersorbisch, Haut Sorabe, Upper Lusatian, Wendish, Hornjoserbski, Hornoserbski) [hsb] 15,000 (1996). Ethnic population: 70,000 to 110,000 with Lower Sorbian (1999 Ken Sasahara). Upper Saxony, eastern Germany, principal towns Bautzen (Budysin, Catholic) and Kamenz (Protestant). Perhaps a few in

Texas, USA. _Class:_ Indo-European, Slavic, West, Sorbian. _Dialects:_ Bautzen, Kamenz. _Lg Use:_ Zgusta (1974) says Upper Sorbian and Lower Sorbian are two standard languages. Use of Sorbian is authorized in local government and schools. Increasing literature production. Now accepted as a minority language. 40,000 to 45,000 others have some knowledge of it. Most speakers are older adults. Most of the monolinguals are the very young (Stephens 1976). Nearly all also use German. _Lg Dev:_ Taught in primary schools. Newspapers. Radio programs. TV. Bible: 1728–1797.

Swabian (Schwäbisch, Suabian, Schwaebisch) [swg] Ethnic population: 820,168 (2000 WCD). Southwest, Wuerttemberg, the eastern part of Baden-Wuerttemberg, Schwaben, western Bavaria. _Class:_ Indo-European, Germanic, West, High German, German, Upper German, Alemannic. _Dialects:_ A variety of Highest Alemannisch. More distinct than Bavarian from Standard German. 40% inherently intelligible with Standard German (estimate). Swabian of the Black Forest is different from Swabian in the Alb (H. Kloss 1978). _Lg Use:_ Speakers also use Standard German. _Lg Dev:_ Dictionary. Bible portions.

Westphalien (Westfaelisch, Westfälisch) [wep] Northwestern, Westphalia. _Class:_ Indo-European, Germanic, West, Low Saxon-Low Franconian, Low Saxon. _Lg Use:_ Speakers also use Standard German. _Other:_ See also Low Saxon entry.

Yeniche (Jenisch, Yenishe, German Travellers) [yec] Also spoken in Austria, France, Netherlands, Switzerland. _Class:_ Mixed Language, German-Yiddish-Romani-Rotwelsch. _Dialects:_ German with a heavy cryptolectal lexical influsion from Rotwelsch, Yiddish, Romani, and Hebrew. _Lg Use:_ The first language of some (The Carrier Pidgin 1977). _Other:_ A blend language of certain urban nomadic groups. Not Gypsies. Possibly arose as a result of those who were dispossessed because of the Hanseatic laws (I. Hancock). They are a distinct ethnic group.

Yiddish, Western (Yiddish, Yidish, Judeo-German) [yih] Ethnic population: 49,210 in Germany (2000 WCD). Southwestern dialect in southern Germany, Switzerland, and Alsace (France), Midwestern dialect in central Germany and parts of the former Czechoslovakia, Northwestern dialect is northern Germany and the Netherlands. Also spoken in Belgium, France, Hungary, Israel, Netherlands, Switzerland. _Class:_ Indo-European, Germanic, West, High German, Yiddish. _Dialects:_ Southwestern Yiddish, Midwestern Yiddish, Northwestern Yiddish. Western Yiddish originated in Germany, Holland, Switzerland, Alsace (France), Czechoslovakia, western Hungary. "The variety of Western Yiddish in Hungary is probably the most readily intelligible to Yiddish speakers in Romania, the Baltic, and the Slavic countries in the East. The Western Yiddish variety in Holland less so; the Western Yiddish in Alsace (France) and Switzerland, least so" (M. Herzog 1997). _Lg Use:_ On the eve of the Holocaust it was spoken by several tens of thousands. _Lg Dev:_ Hebrew script. _Other:_ Jewish.

Gibraltar

Gibraltar. 27,833. National or official language: English. A British dependency. Literacy rate: 80%. Also includes Moroccan Spoken Arabic (2,900), India or Pakistan 360. The number of languages listed for Gibraltar is 2. Of those, both are living languages.

English [eng] 3,300 in Gibraltar (1993 Johnstone). _Dialect:_ Yanito. _Lg Use:_ Official language. _Other:_ Yanito is spoken by most Gibraltarians among themselves. It is a dialect of English with a strong Spanish influence, with over 500 words coming from Genoese (Ligurian) and Hebrew. See main entry under United Kingdom.

Spanish [spa] See main entry under Spain.

Greece

Hellenic Republic, Elliniki Dimokratia. 10,647,529. National or official language: Greek. Literacy rate: 94% to 96%. Also includes Armenian (20,000), Assyrian Neo-Aramaic (2,000), Balkan Gagauz Turkish, English (8,000), Ladino (2,000), Northern Kurdish (20,000), Russian, Serbian, Urum, Western Farsi (10,000), Arabic (28,000). Information mainly from R. Dawkins 1916; P. Trudgill and G. Tzavaras 1977; B. Comrie 1987; W. Browne 1989, 1998. Blind population: 13,000 (1982 WCE). Deaf population: 42,600 to 634,565 (1986 Gallaudet University). Deaf institutions: 17. The number of languages listed for Greece is 16. Of those, 14 are living languages and 2 are extinct. See map on page 844.

Albanian, Arvanitika (Arvanitika, Arvanitic, Arberichte) [aat] 150,000 (2000). Attica (Attiki), Boeotia (Viotia), southern Euboea (Evia), and the island of Salamis (Salamina); Thrace; Peloponiso Peninsula, Arkadia; Athens. Mainly rural. Also the Northwestern Peloponnese with enclaves elsewhere in the Peloponnese; north of the island of Andros, 300 villages. _Class:_ Indo-European, Albanian, Tosk. _Dialects:_ Thracean Arvanitika, Northwestern Arvanitika, South Central Arvanitika. Arvanitika is partially intelligible to speakers of Tosk. Dialects are perceived as unintelligible to speakers of other dialects. _Lg Use:_ Young people are migrating to Athens and assimilating as Greeks. Some cultural revival since the 1980s. Speakers are older adults. _Lg Dev:_ Greek script. Grammar. NT: 1827. _Other:_ Speakers are called 'Arvanites'. The language is heavily influenced by Greek. Christian.

Albanian, Tosk (Camerija, Arvanitika) [als] 10,000 in Greece (2002 Nicholas). Epyrus Region, village of Lehovo. _Other:_ In Greece, Tosk is called Arvanitika, Greek for 'Albanian'. Distinct from Arvanitika Albanian proper. See main entry under Albania.

Bulgarian [bul] 30,000 in Greece (1998 Greek Helsinki Monitor). Western Thrace, 3 departments, including Xanthi. _Dialect:_ Pomak (Pomakci, Pomakika). _Lg Use:_ Used in the home. Speakers also use Turkish or Greek. _Other:_ Also referred to locally as 'Macedonian' and 'Vlach'. The term 'Vlach' is applied variously to varieties of Bulgarian, Romani, and Romanian in Romania, Greece, Albania, and Serbia and Montenegro. Many Greek loanwords and others from the dead language, Thraco-Illyrian. Viewed as Turks in Greece. Muslim. See main entry under Bulgaria.

Cappadocian Greek [cpg] Extinct. Resettled to various locations in Greece in 1922. Formerly in central Turkey (Cappadocia). The Sille dialect was in Sille town near Konya, Western Cappadocian was in villages south of Kayseri, Pharasa was in Pharasa (Faràs) and surrounding villages. _Class:_ Indo-European, Greek, Attic. _Dialects:_ Sille, Western Cappadocian, Pharasa. Closest to Pontic. Even more distinct from Standard Greek than Pontic is. _Lg Use:_ Language was under extensive attrition from Turkish at the time of the population exchanges in 1922, and has now died out since the 1960s under pressure from Standard Greek (N. Nicholas 1997, Costakis). _Lg Dev:_ Dictionary. _Other:_ Different from the ancient Anatolian language spoken in Cappadocia. Christian.

Greek (Ellinika, Grec, Greco, Graecae, Romaic, Neo-Hellenic) [ell] 9,859,850 in Greece (1986). Population total all countries: 12,258,540. Throughout the country, concentrated in Greek Macedonia. Also spoken in Albania, Armenia, Australia, Austria, Bahamas, Bulgaria, Canada,

Congo, Cyprus, Democratic Republic of the Congo, Djibouti, Egypt, France, Georgia, Germany, Hungary, Italy, Jordan, Kazakhstan, Macedonia, Malawi, Paraguay, Poland, Romania, Russia (Europe), Sierra Leone, South Africa, Sweden, Tunisia, Turkey (Europe), Ukraine, United Arab Emirates, United Kingdom, USA. *Class:* Indo-European, Greek, Attic. *Dialects:* Katharevousa, Dimotiki, Saracatsan. Katharevousa is an archaic literary dialect, Dimotiki is the spoken literary dialect and now the official dialect. The Saracatsan are nomadic shepherds of northern Greece. The Greek of Italy and that of Corsica are probably separate languages (R. Zamponi 1992). In Cyprus, the dialect is reported to be closer to Classical Greek than that spoken in Greece in some vocabulary and grammar, and to have many Arabic and Turkish loanwords. Lexical similarity 84% to 93% with Standard Greek. *Lg Use:* Official language. *Lg Dev:* Cyrillic script in Ukraine. Dictionary. Grammar. Bible: 1840–1994. *Other:* Greeks in Russia and Ukraine speak either Greek or Turkish and are called 'Urums'. The Karamanli were Orthodox Christian Turks who came from central Turkey. SVO.

Greek Sign Language [gss] 42,600 (1986 Gallaudet Univ.). *Class:* Deaf sign language. *Lg Use:* 12,000 children and 30,000 active adult users (1996). *Other:* Roots in American and French sign languages and various indigenous sign languages, which came together in the 1950s.

Greek, Ancient [grc] Extinct. *Class:* Indo-European, Greek, Attic. *Dialects:* Koine Greek, Classical Greek. *Lg Use:* Koine Greek is used as a religious language by the Greek Orthodox Church. The language of the text of the Christian New Testament. *Lg Dev:* NT: c. 42–98 A.D.

Pontic (Pontic Greek) [pnt] 200,000 in Greece (2001 Johnstone and Mandryk). Population total all countries: 324,535. The majority of speakers live in Salonica, borough of Kalamaria, and the rest of Macedonia in Greece. Also spoken in Azerbaijan, Canada, Georgia, Kazakhstan, Russia (Europe), Turkey (Europe), USA. *Class:* Indo-European, Greek, Attic. *Dialects:* Speakers of Standard Greek cannot understand Pontic, and Pontic speakers are reported to not understand or speak Standard Greek. Pontic clubs and centers exist in the Athens-Peiraeus suburbs. *Lg Use:* Young people may speak Standard Greek as their first language. Speakers in North America are reported to maintain the use of Pontic more zealously than those in Greece. Ethnic Greeks in Georgia called 'Rumka' speak Pontic Greek. *Lg Dev:* Grammar. *Other:* Brought to Greece in the 1920s and 1930s by immigrants from the Black Sea coast, which had been inhabited by Greeks since antiquity.

Romani, Balkan [rmn] 40,000 in Greece (1996 Birgit Igla). Population includes 10,000 Arlija, 30,000 Greek Romani. About 500 families in Agia Varvara. Agia Varvara, a suburb of Athens. *Dialect:* Greek Romani, Arlija (Erli). *Lg Use:* Speakers also use Greek. *Other:* Christian, Muslim. See main entry under Serbia and Montenegro.

Romani, Vlax (Romanés, Tsingani, Rom) [rmy] 1,000 Lovari in Greece. *Dialect:* Lovari. *Lg Use:* Settled Gypsies are bilingual. *Other:* Speakers call themselves 'Rom'. Settled Gypsies accept being called 'Tsingani'. They call the nonsettled Gypsies 'Yifti'. Distinct from Rumanovlach, a variety of Rumanian. Christian. See main entry under Romania.

Romanian, Macedo (Macedo-Rumanian, Arumanian, Aromanian, Armina, Vlach) [rup] 200,000 in Greece (1995 Greek Monitor of Human and Minority Rights 1.3 Dec. 1995). Population total all countries: 306,237. Ethnic population: Possibly 700,000 in Greece (Association of French Aromanians). Northwest Salonika, and northern Greece, Pindus Mountains, around Trikala. Also spoken in Albania, Bosnia and Herzegovina, Bulgaria, Macedonia, Romania, Serbia and Montenegro. *Class:* Indo-European, Italic, Romance, Eastern. *Dialects:* Structurally a distinct language from Romanian (F. Agard). It split from the other 3 Rumanian languages between 500 and 1000 A.D. Many dialects. *Lg Use:* Rapid assimilation to Greek culture; children attend Greek schools. 20% live traditionally. No legal status in Greece. Not taught in school except for one course at the University of Salonica. Some revival of the culture in progress since the 1980s. People over 50 are fluent in Aromanian, many between 25 to 50 are passive speakers with limited knowledge of vocabulary and grammar. Some younger ones know the language. *Lg Dev:* Roman and Greek scripts. Newspapers. Radio programs. TV. Bible portions: 1881–1889. *Other:* 'Armini' refers to the people. Woodworkers. Christian.

Romanian, Megleno (Meglenitic, Meglenite) [ruq] 3,000 in Greece (2002 Nicholas). Population total all countries: 5,000. Kilkis prefecture, Meglen Region, north of Salonika. Also spoken in Macedonia. *Class:* Indo-European, Italic, Romance, Eastern. *Dialects:* Structurally a distinct language from Romanian, Macedo Romanian, and Istro Romanian (F. Agard). *Other:* The 4 Romanian languages split between 500 and 1000 A.D.

Romano-Greek (Hellenoromani, Romika) [rge] 30 (2000). *Class:* Mixed Language, Greek-Romani. *Dialects:* Structured on Greek with heavy Romani lexicon. *Lg Use:* Used only as a secrecy language in public. *Other:* Related variants are Dortika, a secret language spoken by wandering builders from Eurytania prefecture, and Kaliarda, spoken in Athens. Both may be extinct. Nearly extinct.

Slavic (Macedonian Slavic, Macedonian) [mkd] 180,180 in Greece (1986 census). Macedonia Region in Greece, Florina prefecture, northern Kastoria prefecture, and Thessalonica prefecture. *Lg Use:* Used in religion, education. Speakers also use Greek. *Other:* Called 'Slavic' in Greece, where 'Macedonian' refers only to people living in Macedonia, a region in Greece. See main entry under Macedonia (Macedonian).

Tsakonian (Tsakonia) [tsd] 1,200 (1981 J. Werner). 300 shepherds. Towns of Kastanitsa, Sitena, Prastos, Leonidi, Pramatefti, Sapounakeika, Tyros, Melana, possibly Korakovunio; eastern coast of Peloponnesos. Isolated in summer in the mountains west of Leonidi in the eastern Peloponnesus; in winter they descend to Leonidi and neighboring towns. *Class:* Indo-European, Greek, Doric. *Dialects:* Northern Tsakonian (Kastanista-Sitena), Southern Tsakonian (Leonidio-Prastos), Propontis Tsakonian (Vatka-Havoutsi). Derived from the Doric dialect spoken in Lakonia by ancient Spartans. Northern and Southern are reported to be intelligible to each other's speakers, but Propontis was more distinct, and closer to Standard Greek. Not inherently intelligible with modern Greek (Voegelin and Voegelin 1977). Lexical similarity 70% or less with Standard Greek. *Lg Use:* There were monolingual speakers in 1927. Few speakers of Northern Tsakonian. Speakers use Southern Tsakonian. Propontis Tsakonian has become extinct since 1970. All use Greek as second language. *Lg Dev:* Dictionary. Grammar. *Other:* Children attend Greek schools in winter, including kindergarten. Pastoralists. Christian.

Turkish (Osmanli) [tur] 128,380 in Greece (1976 WA). Thrace and Aegean regions. *Other:* The number of Turks in Greece remains fairly constant, because growth is offset by a steady flow of emigration to Turkey. Muslim, Christian. See main entry under Turkey (Asia).

Hungary

Republic of Hungary. Magyar Köztársaság. 10,032,375.
National or official language: Hungarian. Literacy rate: 98%
to 99%. Also includes Armenian, Bulgarian (1,100), Eastern
Yiddish, French (21,000), Greek, Macedonian, Polish
(21,000), Ukrainian (300,000), Western Yiddish.
Information mainly from I. Hancock 1979, 1987, 1988; B.
Comrie 1987. Blind population: 25,000 (1973 estimate);
10,000 (1982 WCE). Deaf population: 625,640. Deaf
institutions: 17. The number of languages listed for Hungary
is 12. Of those, all are living languages.

Bavarian (Bayerisch, Bavarian-Austrian) [bar] 170,000.
Lg Use: Most domains, home. Standard German used by
the educated. Hungarian, Standard German used in
professions. See main entry under Austria.
Croatian [hrv] 32,130 in Hungary (1986). Southern
border area. *Dialects:* Croatian, Serbian. *Other:*
Christian. See main entry under Croatia.
German, Standard [deu] 250,000 in Hungary (1988
Hawkins in B. Comrie). *Other:* Germans in Hungary
speak other Germanic varieties than Standard German at
home. See main entry under Germany.
Hungarian (Magyar) [hun] 10,298,820 in Hungary
(1995). Population total all countries: 13,611,600. Also
spoken in Australia, Austria, Canada, Israel, Romania,
Serbia and Montenegro, Slovakia, Slovenia, Ukraine,
USA. *Class:* Uralic, Finno-Ugric, Ugric, Hungarian.
Dialects: Alfold, West Danube, Danube-Tisza, King's
Pass Hungarian, Northeast Hungarian, Northwest
Hungarian, Székely, West Hungarian. Closest to Vogul
(Mansi) of Russia. Speakers of Standard Hungarian have
difficulty understanding Oberwart dialect. *Lg Use:*
National language. *Lg Dev:* Newspapers. Grammar. Bible:
1590–1991. *Other:* 'Magyar' is the Hungarian name. SVO.
Hungarian Sign Language (Magyar Jelnyelv) [hsh]
60,000 deaf (1999 National Association for Deaf and
Hard-of-Hearing). Used throughout Hungary. May also be
used in western Romania. *Class:* Deaf sign language.
Dialects: Budapest, Sopron, Miskolc, Debrecen, Szeged,
Eger. Related to Austrian Sign Language and German
Sign Language. May be related to Yugoslavian Sign
Language. Dialects have some different signs for lexical
items, similar or same grammar. *Lg Use:* 300,000 hard-
of-hearing people use it as second language. All ages.
Budapest dialect is viewed as the standard. *Lg Dev:*
Dictionary. *Other:* Extensive literacy effort needed.
Romani, Balkan (Cigány) [rmn] In Hungary, 150,000
Gypsies speak a variety of Romani as first language
(1995 Z. Réger). Ethnic population: 450,000 to
800,000 all Gypsies in Hungary. *Other:* This variety
may not be in Hungary. See main entry under Serbia
and Montenegro.
Romani, Carpathian (Cigány) [rmc] 3,000 in Hungary
(1980 UBS). Three divisions are recognized: Nograd
County north of Budapest, overlapping into Slovakia; in
Budapest and towns along the Danube such as Baja,
Dunaszekcso, Kalocsa, Mohacs, Pecs, and Versend as far
south as the Yugoslav border; and travelers with carnivals,
as knife grinders, horse dealers, and brick makers. One
dialect is in east Hungary, south Poland, and Galicia;
another in Transylvania, Romania; others in Czech
Republic and Slovakia; Ukraine, USA. *Dialects:* Galician,
Transylvanian. *Other:* Ethnic group: Ungrike Romá
(northern). Medicinal herb collectors and sellers; factory
workers; basketmakers; wood merchants; horse dealers;
rag-and-bone merchants; carnival workers; knife grinders;
brick makers; professionals. Christian. See main entry
under Czech Republic.

Romani, Sinte [rmo] Eastern Hungary. *Other:* Christian.
See main entry under Serbia and Montenegro.
Romani, Vlax (Gypsy, Tsigene, Cigány, Romungre)
[rmy] 20,932 in Hungary (2000 WCD). *Dialects:* Lovari,
Churari. *Other:* Vlax in Hungary and Slovakia are called
'Romungre'. Christian. See main entry under Romania.
Romanian (Rumanian, Daco-Romanian, Moldavian) [ron]
100,000 in Hungary (1995 Iosif Bena). *Dialect:* Bayash
Romanian. *Other:* Substantial literature. See main entry
under Romania.
Slovak [slk] 11,562 in Hungary (2000 WCD). See main
entry under Slovakia.
Slovenian (Slovene) [slv] 4,984 in Hungary (2000 WCD).
Near Slovenian border. *Dialect:* Prekmurski. See main
entry under Slovenia.

Iceland

Republic of Iceland, Lýdveldio Island. 293,966. National or
official language: Icelandic. Literacy rate: 100%. Blind
population: 43. Deaf population: 16,006. Deaf institutions:
2. The number of languages listed for Iceland is 3. Of those,
all are living languages.

Danish [dan] 2,250 (2001). *Other:* Christian. See main
entry under Denmark.
Icelandic (Íslenska) [isl] 230,000 in Iceland (1980 WA).
Population total all countries: 239,768. Also spoken in
Canada, USA. *Class:* Indo-European, Germanic, North,
West Scandinavian. *Dialects:* No appreciable dialect
differences (Nida 1972). Not inherently intelligible with
Faroese. *Lg Use:* National language. *Lg Dev:* Bible:
1584–1981. *Other:* SVO.
Icelandic Sign Language [icl] *Class:* Deaf sign
language. *Lg Dev:* TV. Dictionary. *Other:* Until 1910
Icelandic deaf people were sent to school in Denmark. The
sign language is based on Danish Sign Language, but has
changed and developed since then, so it is not the same
today. Signed interpretation provided for college students.
Instruction for parents of deaf children. There is a
committee on national sign language. There is a manual
spelling system.

Ireland

Éire. 3,969,558. National or official languages: Irish Gaelic,
English. Literacy rate: 99%. Information mainly from M.
Stephens 1976; R. McCrum, W. Cran, R. MacNeil 1986; J.
Fishman 1991. Deaf population: 214,569. Deaf institutions:
36. The number of languages listed for Ireland is 5. Of
those, all are living languages. See map on page 845.

English [eng] 2,600,000 in Ireland (1983). *Dialects:* South
Hiberno English, North Hiberno English. *Lg Use:*
National language. See main entry under United Kingdom.
Gaelic, Irish (Irish, Erse, Gaeilge) [gle] 260,000 in
Ireland (1983 census). Population total all countries:
355,000. Western isles northwest and southwest coasts;
Galway, part of Mayo, Kerry, Donegal, Meath, Cork,
Waterford, Scotland (Albain), Isle of Mann. Also spoken
in Brazil, Canada, United Kingdom, USA. *Class:* Indo-
European, Celtic, Insular, Goidelic. *Dialects:* Munster-
Leinster (Southern Irish), Connacht (Western Irish),
Donegal (Ulster, Northern Irish). *Lg Use:* National
language. Speakers also use English. *Lg Dev:* Radio
programs. Grammar. Bible: 1685–1989. *Other:* It is
taught as an official language in schools and encouraged
by the government. VSO.
Irish Sign Language [isg] Dublin and elsewhere.
Class: Deaf sign language. *Dialects:* In 1816 British signs
were brought in. In 1846 Irish signs developed in the girls'

school, in 1857 Irish signs brought into the boys' school. Related to French Sign Language. There are informal male and female sign systems. Females learn the male system during dating and marriage. The informal system is referred to as 'Deaf Sign Language'. Irish Sign Language is a new unified system, a manual code for English. It has structural features such as directional verbs. It has influenced sign languages in South Africa and Australia. *Lg Use:* It originated between 1846–1849. Several deaf schools with 750 to 800 students in each. There is a committee on national sign language and an organization for sign language teachers. *Lg Dev:* TV.

Scots [sco] 100,000 in Ireland (1999 Billy Kay). Population includes 60,000 in Lallans, 30,000 in Doric, 10,000 in Ulster. Donegal County. *Lg Use:* Used with family and friends. All ages. English is considered to be the language of education and religion. *Other:* Christian. See main entry under United Kingdom.

Shelta (The Cant, Cant, Irish Traveler Cant, Sheldru, Gammon) [sth] 6,000 in Ireland. Population total all countries: 86,000. Also spoken in United Kingdom, USA. *Class:* Mixed Language, Irish-undocumented. *Dialects:* Based largely on Irish with influence from an undocumented source. *Other:* The secret language, or cryptolect, of Travellers in the British Isles. Based largely on Irish. Not Gypsies.

Italy

Italian Republic, Repubblica Italiana. 58,057,477. National or official languages: Italian, regional languages: French, Standard German, Slovenian. Literacy rate: 97% to 98%. Also includes Assyrian Neo-Aramaic, English (29,000), Judeo-Tripolitanian Arabic (5,000), Judeo-Tunisian Arabic, Kabuverdianu (10,000), Maltese (28,000), Northern Kurdish (3,000), Somali (50,626), Sylheti, Chinese (40,000), people from Eritrea, the Philippines. Information mainly from R. A. Hall 1974; M. Stephens 1976; F. B. Agard 1984; B. Comrie 1987. Blind population: 100,000. Deaf population: 3,524,906. Deaf institutions: 80. The number of languages listed for Italy is 33. Of those, all are living languages.

Albanian, Arbëreshë (Arbëreshë) [aae] 80,000 (1963 L. Newmark). Ethnic population: 260,000 (1976 M. Stephens). Southern; Calabria, Apulia, Basilicata, Molise, Sicily. *Class:* Indo-European, Albanian, Tosk. *Dialects:* Sicilian Albanian, Calabrian Albanian, Central Mountain Albanian, Campo Marino Albanian. Speakers say the four Italian dialects are not inherently intelligible with each other. Lexical similarity 45% with Tosk Albanian. *Lg Use:* Strong position in some districts. Not used in schools. No official status. Used in the home. Speakers use Italian and regional Italian varieties in varying degrees; one report says they are highly bilingual. *Lg Dev:* Bible portions: 1868–1869. *Other:* Descendants of 15th century mercenaries and refugees from the Ottoman invasion. Some literature. Agriculturalists; animal husbandry: sheep. Christian.

Bavarian (Bayerisch, Bavarian Austrian) [bar] 258,885 in Italy (2000 WCD). South Bavarian is in the Bavarian Alps, Tyrol, Styria, including Heanzian dialect of Burgenland, Carinthia, northern Italy, and part of Gottschee; Central Bavarian is in the Alps and Lower Austria and Salzburg; North Bavarian in the north of Regensburg, to Nuremburg and Western Bohemia, Czech Republic. *Dialects:* Central Bavarian, North Bavarian, South Bavarian. *Lg Use:* School in South Tyrol is taught in Standard German. See main entry under Austria.

Catalan-Valencian-Balear [cat] 20,000 in Alghero (1996). Alghero, northwest coast on Sardinia. *Dialect:* Algherese. *Lg Use:* Italian or Logudorese Sardinian are

used as second language by many. See main entry under Spain.

Cimbrian (Tzimbro, Zimbrisch) [cim] 2,230. Population includes 500 in Lusernese Cimbrian in Trentino Alto Oolige 40 km southeast from Trento, plus 1,500 Sette Comuni Cimbrian (40% of Roana (Rowan), 70% of Messaselva di Roana Rotzo) in Veneto around 60 km north of Vicenza (1978 H. Kloss), and 230 or 65% of Giazza (Ijetzan) Veneto, 43 km northeast of Verona (1992 R. Zamponi). There were 22,700 speakers in Sieben Gemeinde and 12,400 in Dreizehn Gemeinde in 1854. Northeast Italy, Sette and Tredici Comuni (Sieben and Dreizehn Gemeinde) south of Trent, towns of Giazza (Glietzen, Ljetzen), Roana (Rabam), Lusern, some in Venetia Province. *Class:* Indo-European, Germanic, West, High German, German, Upper German, Bavarian-Austrian. *Dialects:* Lusernese Cimbrian, Tredici Communi Cimbrian (Tauch), Sette Comuni Cimbrian. Structural and intelligibility differences indicate that the 3 dialects listed could be considered separate languages. Lusernese Cimbrian is heavily influenced by Italian. Heavily influenced by Bajuwarisch dialects. It is sometimes considered to be a dialect of South Bavarian. Different from Bavarian, Walser, and Mocheno. No written influence from Standard German. *Lg Use:* Pastors preached in Cimbrian until the late 19th century. Attempts to promote it have been increasing in recent decades. It is taught in some classes. Speakers are all bilingual in Standard Italian and Venetian (Trentine), and many know Standard German.

Corsican (Corso, Corsu, Corse, Corsi) [cos] 1,000 in Italy (1990). Maddalena Island, northeast coast of Sardinia. See main entry under France.

Croatian [hrv] 3,500 in Italy (N. Vincent in B. Comrie 1987). Molise, southern, villages of Montemitro, San Felice del Molise, Acquaviva-Collecroce. *Dialect:* Croatian. *Lg Use:* Official language in one municipality. There are efforts to revive the use of Croatian literature. *Other:* Descendants of 15th and 16th century refugees. Christian. See main entry under Croatia.

Emiliano-Romagnolo (Emiliano, Emilian, Sammarinese) [eml] 2,000,000 in Emilia-Romagna (2003). Population total all countries: 2,020,112. Northwest Italy, region of Piacenza to that of Ravenna, and between the Po and the Adriatic and the Apennines, in the territories of Emilia and Romagna, southern Pianura Padana (all provinces), southern Lombardia (Provinces Mantova and Pavia), northern Toscana (Lunigiana), northern Marche (Province Pesaro). Also spoken in San Marino. *Class:* Indo-European, Italic, Romance, Italo-Western, Western, Gallo-Iberian, Gallo-Romance, Gallo-Italian. *Dialects:* Western Emiliano, Central Emiliano, Eastern Emiliano, Northern Romagnolo, Southern Romagnolo, Mantovano, Vogherese-Pavese, Lunigiano. A structurally separate language from Italian (F. B. Agard). Related to Lombard (R. A. Hall 1974:29, S. Fleischman 1992, OIEL 3:339). *Lg Use:* Few children speakers. Speakers are shifting to Italian. *Lg Dev:* Literacy rate in second language: 100%. Dictionary. Bible portions: 1862–1995. *Other:* svo. Christian.

Franco-Provençal [frp] 70,000 in Italy (1971 census). Population includes 700 Faetar speakers (1995 Naomi Nagy). Northwest Italy, Aosta Valley. A small speech community also in Faeto and Celle S. Vito in the Province of Foggia in Apulia, and Guardia Piemontese in Calabria, Cosenza. Covers a huge area. *Dialects:* Valle D'aosta (Patoé Valdoten, Valdotain, Valdostano), Faeto (Faetar), Celle San Vito. *Lg Use:* Most domains. Speakers also use Italian or Piemontese. See main entry under France.

French (Français) [fra] 100,000 in Italy (1987 Harris). Aosta Valley. *Lg Use:* Official regional language status. See main entry under France.

Friulian (Furlan, Frioulan, Frioulian, Priulian, Friulano) [fur] 794,000 (2000). Northeast and adjacent areas, northern Friuli-Venezia-Giulia on the borders of the Austrian Province of Corinthia and the Republic of Slovenia. *Class:* Indo-European, Italic, Romance, Italo-Western, Western, Gallo-Iberian, Gallo-Romance, Gallo-Rhaetian, Rhaetian. *Dialects:* East Central Friulian, Western Friulian, Carnico. Friulian, Ladin, and Romansch are separate languages (R. A. Hall, Jr. 1978, personal communication). F. B. Agard considers it to be structurally closer to Italian than to Romansch (personal communication 1981). *Lg Use:* Some are cultivating Friulian as a literary language. In the area of Gorizia all the Slovenes speak it as a second or third language. Germans in the area also speak it. Positive language attitude. Most speakers know Standard Italian. *Lg Dev:* NT: 1972.

German, Standard (Tedesco) [deu] 225,000 in Italy (1987 Vincent in B. Comrie). Northern, Trentino-Alto Adige, South Tyrol, Province of Bolzano. *Lg Use:* Official language in Alto-Adige region. Used in schools. See main entry under Germany.

Greek (Greco) [ell] 20,000 in Italy (1987 Vincent in B. Comrie). Southern, east of Reggio; Salento (Colimera, Sternatía, Zollino) and Aspromonte (Bova, Condofuri, Palizzi, Roccoforte, Roghudi). *Dialects:* Salento, Aspromonte. *Lg Use:* Most speakers are older adults. See main entry under Greece.

Italian (Italiano) [ita] 55,000,000 in Italy. Population includes some of whom are native bilinguals of Italian and regional varieties, and some of whom may use Italian as second language. Population total all countries: 61,489,984. Also spoken in Argentina, Australia, Belgium, Bosnia and Herzegovina, Brazil, Canada, Croatia, Egypt, Eritrea, France, Germany, Israel, Libya, Liechtenstein, Luxembourg, Paraguay, Philippines, Puerto Rico, Romania, San Marino, Saudi Arabia, Slovenia, Switzerland, Tunisia, United Arab Emirates, United Kingdom, Uruguay, USA, Vatican State. *Class:* Indo-European, Italic, Romance, Italo-Western, Italo-Dalmatian. *Dialects:* Tuscan, Abruzzese, Pugliese, Umbrian, Laziale, Central Marchigiano, Cicolano-Reatino-Aquilano, Molisano. Regional varieties coexist with the standard language; some are inherently unintelligible (Nida) to speakers of other varieties unless they have learned them. Aquilano, Molisano, and Pugliese are very different from the other Italian 'dialects'. Piemontese and Sicilian are distinct enough to be separate languages (F. B. Agard 1981, personal communication). Venetian and Lombard are also very different (Philippe Cousson 1981, personal communication). Neapolitan is reported to be unintelligible to speakers of Standard Italian. Northern varieties are closer to French and Occitan than to standard or southern varieties (Agard, N. Vincent). Lexical similarity 89% with French, 87% with Catalan, 85% with Sardinian, 82% with Spanish, 78% with Rheto-Romance, 77% with Rumanian. *Lg Use:* Official language. Most Italians use varieties along a continuum from standard to regional to local according to what is appropriate. Possibly nearly half the population do not use Standard Italian as first language. Only 2.5% of Italy's population could speak standard Italian when it became a unified nation in 1861. *Lg Dev:* Grammar. Bible: 1471–1985. *Other:* SVO.

Italian Sign Language (Lingua Italiana Dei Segni, Lis) [ise] *Class:* Deaf sign language. *Dialects:* Partially intelligible with French Sign Language. Not intelligible with American Sign Language. Regional differences, but signers from different regions seem to communicate fluently. *Lg Use:* All domains except school classroom.

Judeo-Italian (Italkian) [itk] 200. *Class:* Indo-European, Italic, Romance, Italo-Western, Italo-Dalmatian. *Lg Use:* More commonly spoken two generations ago. Used in Passover song. Perhaps 4,000 occasionally use elements of it in their speech (10% of Italy's 40,000 Jews). *Lg Dev:* Hebrew script. OT. *Other:* Jewish.

Ladin (Dolomite, Rhaeto-Romance) [lld] 30,000 in Italy (2001 census). Ethnic population: 38,000. Autonomous province of Bolzano or Southern Tyrol (German Südtirol, Italian Alto Adige), in the Valleys of Gherdëina (Italian Val Gardena, German Grödnertal) and of Badia (Italian Val Badia, German Gadertal); autonomous province of Trento (Trient) or Trentino, in the Valley of Fascia (Italian Val di Fassa, German Fassatal) and in the province of Belluno in Fodom (Italian Livinallongo, German Buchenstein) and in Anpezo (Italian Ampezzo, around Cortina d'Ampezzo). Also spoken in USA. *Class:* Indo-European, Italic, Romance, Italo-Western, Western, Gallo-Iberian, Gallo-Romance, Gallo-Rhaetian, Rhaetian. *Dialects:* Atesino, Cadorino, Nones (Nones Blot, Nonesh, Parlata Trentina, Nonese), Gardenese (Grüdno, Grödnerisch), Fassano, Badiotto (Gadertalisch), Marebbano (Ennebergisch), Livinallese, Ampezzano. Friulian, Ladin (in Italy), and Romansch (in Switzerland) are separate languages (R. A. Hall, Jr. 1978, personal communication). Seven dialects. The dialect of Val di Fassa is taught in schools. Distinct from Ladino (Dzhudezmo, Judeo-Spanish). *Lg Use:* Positive language attitude. Most speakers are trilingual (Ladin, German, Italian) in the two Ladin valleys of the South Tyrol and bilingual (Ladin, Italian) in Val di Fassa and Livinallongo. Mostly Italian only in Cortina d'Ampezzo. *Lg Dev:* Taught in primary schools. *Other:* Written since 1800 in Italy. Dialects of Gardenese, Badiotto, and Fassano are taught in school.

Ligurian (Líguru, Ligure) [lij] 1,915,749 in Italy (2000 WCD). Population total all countries: 1,920,849. Liguria, northern Italy; east and west of Genoa along the Riviera and mountain hinterland, St. Pietro and St. Antioch, islands off southwest coast of Sardinia, cities of Carloforte and Calasetta in Sardinia. Also spoken in France, Monaco. *Class:* Indo-European, Italic, Romance, Italo-Western, Western, Gallo-Iberian, Gallo-Romance, Gallo-Italian. *Dialect:* Genoese (Genoan, Genovese). Ligurian is closer to Piemontese, Lombard, and French than to Standard Italian. *Lg Use:* Speakers may all be adequately bilingual in Standard Italian. *Lg Dev:* Bible portions: 1860.

Lombard (Lombardo) [lmo] 8,830,855 in Italy (2000 WCD). Population total all countries: 9,133,855. Milan, Lombardy, 3 valleys of Graubünden (Val Mesolcina, Val Bregaglia, Val Poschiavo), northern Italy. Western Lombard varieties also in Sicily. Ticino is in Switzerland. Also spoken in Switzerland, USA. *Class:* Indo-European, Italic, Romance, Italo-Western, Western, Gallo-Iberian, Gallo-Romance, Gallo-Italian. *Dialects:* Milanese, Eastern Lombard, Western Lombard (Piazza Armerina, Novara, Nicosia, San Fratello), Alpine Lombard, Novarese Lombard, Trentino Western, Latin Fiamazzo, Latin Anaunico, Bergamasco, Ticinese (Ticino). A group of dialects, some of which may be separate languages. Western Lombard dialects (of Ticino and Graubnnden) are inherently intelligible to each other's speakers. Speakers in more conservative valleys may have to use some kind of 'standard' dialect to communicate with speakers of other dialects of Lombard. Very different from Standard Italian. *Lg Use:* Speakers may all be adequately bilingual in Standard Italian. *Lg Dev:* TV. Dictionary. Bible portions: 1859–1860.

Mócheno [mhn] 1,900 (1992 Raoul Zamponi). Population includes 400 Fierozzo, 1,000 Palú, 460 Gereut. Valle del Fersina (Trentino). *Class:* Indo-European, Germanic, West, High German, German, Upper German, Bavarian-Austrian. *Dialects:* Fierozzo (Florutz), Palú (Palai), Frassilongo (Gereut). Speakers can partially understand Bavarian, Cimbrian, or Standard German.

Napoletano-Calabrese (Neapolitan-Calabrese) [nap] 7,047,399 (1976). Campania and Calabria provinces, southern Italy. *Class:* Indo-European, Italic, Romance, Italo-Western, Italo-Dalmatian. *Dialects:* Napoletano (Neapolitan, Tirrenic), Northern Calabrese-Lucano (Lucanian, Basilicatan). Limited inherent intelligibility of Standard Italian. Neapolitan and Calabrese are reported to be very different from each other. Southern Calabrian is reported to be a dialect of Sicilian. *Lg Use:* Vigorous. Speakers also use Italian. *Lg Dev:* Bible portions: 1861–1862.

Piemontese (Piemontèis, Piedmontese) [pms] 3,106,620 in Italy (2000 WCD). Northwest Italy, Piedmont, except for the Provençal- and Franco-Provençal-speaking Alpine valleys. Also spoken in Australia, USA. *Class:* Indo-European, Italic, Romance, Italo-Western, Western, Gallo-Iberian, Gallo-Romance, Gallo-Italian. *Dialects:* High Piemontese (Alto Piemontese), Low Piemontese (Basso Piemontese). Distinct enough from Standard Italian to be considered a separate language. Considerable French influence. *Lg Use:* Speakers may all be highly bilingual in Standard Italian. *Lg Dev:* NT: 1834.

Provençal (Provenzale) [prv] 100,000 in Italy (1990 P. Blanchet). Upper valleys of the Italian Piedmont (Val Mairo, Val Varacho, Val d'Esturo, Entraigas, Limoun, Vinai, Pignerol, Sestriero), Guardia Piemontese in Calabria. *Dialect:* Transalpin. *Lg Use:* All ages. Speakers also use Piemontese or Italian. See main entry under France.

Romani, Balkan [rmn] 5,000 Arlija in Italy (1990). *Dialect:* Arlija (Erli). *Other:* Muslim. See main entry under Serbia and Montenegro.

Romani, Sinte [rmo] 14,000 in Italy (1980). Population includes 10,000 Manouche, 4,000 Slovenian-Croatian. North Italy. *Dialects:* Piedmont Sintí, Slovenian-Croatian, Manouche. *Other:* Christian. See main entry under Serbia and Montenegro.

Romani, Vlax [rmy] 4,000 in Italy. Population includes 1,000 to 3,000 Kalderash, 1,000 Lovari. *Dialects:* Kalderash, Lovari. *Other:* Christian. See main entry under Romania.

Sardinian, Campidanese (Sardu, Campidanese, Campidese, South Sardinian) [sro] 345,180 (2000 WCD). Southern Sardinia. *Class:* Indo-European, Italic, Romance, Southern, Sardinian. *Dialects:* Cagliare (Cagliari, Cagliaritan), Arborense, Sub-Barbaricino, Western Campidanese, Central Campidanese, Ogliastrino, Sulcitano, Meridionale, Sarrabense. Cagliaritan is the dialect of Cagliari, the capital of Sardinia. Campidanese is quite distinct from the other Sardinian languages. Lexical similarity 62% between Cagliare and Standard Italian, 73% with Logudorese, 66% with Gallurese. *Lg Use:* It is in general use in the south. A movement is growing to recognize Sard as an important part of their linguistic and cultural heritage. *Lg Dev:* Bible portions: 1860–1900.

Sardinian, Gallurese (Northeastern Sardinian, Gallurese) [sdn] Gallurese is in northeastern Sardinia. *Class:* Indo-European, Italic, Romance, Southern, Sardinian. *Dialects:* Lexical similarity 83% with Standard Italian, 81% with Sassarese, 70% with Logudorese, 66% with Cagliare. *Lg Use:* A growing movement to recognize Sard as an important part of their cultural and linguistic heritage. *Lg Dev:* Bible portions: 1861–1862. *Other:* Influenced by Corsican and Tuscan (Standard Italian). They call Campidanese and Logudorese 'Sard', and the people 'Sards', but do not include themselves or their language in those terms.

Sardinian, Logudorese (Sard, Sardarese, Logudorese, Central Sardinian) [src] 1,500,000 (1977 M. Ibba, Rutgers University). Population includes all Sardinian languages. Central Sardinia. *Class:* Indo-European, Italic, Romance, Southern, Sardinian. *Dialects:* Nuorese, Northern Logudorese, Barbaricino, Southwestern Logudorese. No one form of Sardinian is selected as standard for literary purposes. Logudorese is quite different from other Sardinian varieties. Lexical similarity 68% with Standard Italian, 73% with Sassarese and Cagliare, 70% with Gallurese. 'Sardinian' has 85% lexical similarity with Italian, 80% with French, 78% with Portuguese, 76% with Spanish, 74% with Rumanian and Rheto-Romance. *Lg Use:* Sardinian is in general use in central and southern areas. It has prestige equal to Italian in some contexts including writing. There is a growing movement to recognize Sard as an important part of their linguistic and cultural heritage. Italian is used for literary and teaching purposes. Farmers and housewives over 35 use almost no Italian. *Lg Dev:* Bible portions: 1858–1861. *Other:* Christian.

Sardinian, Sassarese (Northwestern Sardinian, Sassarese) [sdc] Northwestern Sardinia. *Class:* Indo-European, Italic, Romance, Southern, Sardinian. *Dialects:* Lexical similarity 81% with Gallurese, 76% with Standard Italian. *Lg Use:* There is a growing movement to recognize Sard as an important part of their cultural and linguistic heritage. *Lg Dev:* Bible portions: 1863–1866. *Other:* Influenced by Ligurian and Pisan (Pisa, northwest coast of Italy). They call Campidanese and Logudorese 'Sard', and the people 'Sards', but do not include themselves or their language in those terms.

Sicilian (Calabro-Sicilian, Sicilianu, Siculu) [scn] 4,832,520 (2000 WCD). Sicily, an island off the southern mainland. *Class:* Indo-European, Italic, Romance, Italo-Western, Italo-Dalmatian. *Dialects:* Western Sicilian (Palermo, Trapani, Central-Western Agrigentino), Central Metafonetica, Southeast Metafonetica, Eastern Nonmetafonetica, Messinese, Isole Eolie, Pantesco, Southern Calabro. Distinct enough from Standard Italian to be considered a separate language. Pugliese (see Italian) and Southern Calabrese are reported to be dialects of Sicilian. *Lg Use:* Vigorous. Speakers also use Italian. *Lg Dev:* Bible portions: 1860. *Other:* French influence. It may be Southern Romance instead of Italo-Western. Christian.

Slovenian (Slovene) [slv] 100,000 in Italy (N. Vincent in B. Comrie 1987). The provinces of Trieste and Gorizia in northeast near Slovenia border. *Dialects:* Primorski, Cividale, Resia. *Lg Use:* Official language. *Lg Dev:* The Slovene have their own schools. See main entry under Slovenia.

Venetian (Veneto, Venet) [vec] 2,180,387 in Italy (2000 WCD). Northern Italy, city of Venice, area of the Tre Venezie; Venezia Eugànea westward to Verona, southward to the Po, and eastward to the border of the Friuli; Venezia Tridentina, in the Adige valley and neighboring mountain regions to the north of Trent; and Venezia Giulia, east of the Friuli, and including Trieste. Bisiacco is spoken in Gorizia Province. Also spoken in Croatia, Slovenia. *Class:* Indo-European, Italic, Romance, Italo-Western, Western, Gallo-Iberian, Gallo-Romance, Gallo-Italian. *Dialects:* Istrian, Triestino, Venetian Proper, Bisiacco. Distinct from Standard Italian. *Lg Use:* Vigorous. Speakers also use Italian. *Lg Dev:* Bible portions: 1859.

Walser (Walscher) [wae] 3,400 in Italy (1978 Fazzini). Valle d'Aosta: Val Lesa (Gressoney, Issime, Gaby); Piemonte: Valsesie (Alagna, Rima S. Siuseppe, Rimelle), Novara: Valle Anzacxa (Macugnage); Val Formazza

(Formazza, Pomatt). 9 communities in Italy, and 4 former ones. *Lg Use:* Used in religious services. All ages. *Other:* In Valle d'Aosta it has been influenced by Franco-Provençal and Piemontese; elsewhere in Italy by Italian. See main entry under Switzerland.

Latvia

Republic of Latvia, Latvijas Republika. 2,306,306. 1,394,000 or 54.5% are Latvians (1994 V. Zeps). National or official language: Latvian. 24,695 square miles. Literacy rate: 99%. Also includes Belarusan (105,000), Estonian (3,000), Lithuanian (35,000), Polish (57,000), Russian (861,600), Tatar (5,000), Ukrainian (78,000). Information mainly from V. Zeps 1986–1995; A. E. Kibrik 1991; T. Salminen 1998. The number of languages listed for Latvia is 5. Of those, all are living languages.

Latvian ("Lettish," "Lettisch") [lav] 1,394,000 in Latvia. Population includes over 500,000 Latgalians. Population total all countries: 1,543,844. Also spoken in Australia, Belarus, Brazil, Canada, Estonia, Germany, Lithuania, New Zealand, Russia (Europe), Sweden, Ukraine, United Kingdom, USA, Venezuela. *Class:* Indo-European, Baltic, Eastern. *Dialects:* West Latvian (Central Latvian), East Latvian (High Latvian, Latgalian). Tamian is a subdialect of Central Latvian. *Lg Use:* Official language. *Lg Dev:* Roman script. Grammar. Bible: 1689–1995. *Other:* Latvians do not like the term "Lettish." Christian.
Latvian Sign Language [lsl] *Class:* Deaf sign language.
Liv (Livonian) [liv] 15 to 20 (1995 V. Zeps). 8 coastal villages west of Kolkasrags in Kurzeme and a dispersed population elsewhere, mostly in Riga. *Class:* Uralic, Finnic. *Dialects:* Western Livonian (Kurzeme, Raandalist), Eastern Livonian (Vidzeme). *Lg Use:* Eastern Livonian is now extinct. Speakers also use Latvian or Russian. *Lg Dev:* NT: 1942. *Other:* Christian. Nearly extinct.
Romani, Baltic [rml] 8,000 in Latvia (1995 V. Zeps). *Dialects:* Latvian Romani (Lettish Romani), North Russian Romani, White Russia Romani, Estonian Romani, Polish Romani. *Other:* Ethnic groups: Rúska Romá (northern Russian SFSR), Lotfítka Romá (western Latvia, Estonia), Lajenge Romá (eastern Estonia). Christian. See main entry under Poland.
Yiddish, Eastern (Judeo-German) [ydd] 40,000 in Latvia (1991). *Lg Use:* There may be no Yiddish speakers in Latvia now (1995). Of the 1,811,000 Jewish people listed in the 1979 USSR census, the majority spoke Russian as their first language and virtually all others spoke Russian as their second language. About 50,000 Jews spoke Georgian, Tat, or Tajiki as their first language. *Other:* Had literary status, but very little literature. Jewish. See main entry under Israel.

Liechtenstein

Principality of Liechtenstein, Fürstentum Liechtenstein. 33,436. National or official language: Standard German. Literacy rate: 100% (1989 WA). Also includes Italian (800). Deaf population: 1,818. The number of languages listed for Liechtenstein is 3. Of those, all are living languages. See map on page 846.

Alemannisch (Alemannic, Schwyzerdütsch, Schwytzertuetsch) [gsw] 29,000 in Liechtenstein. *Dialect:* High Alemannisch. *Lg Use:* Spoken by the majority of the people in the country. Speakers also use Standard German. See main entry under Switzerland (Schwyzerdütsch).
German, Standard [deu] *Lg Use:* Official language. See main entry under Germany.

Walser (Walscher) [wae] 1,300 in Liechtenstein (1995 C. Buchli). Triesenberg, including Saminatal and Malbun. 1 community in Liechtenstein. See main entry under Switzerland.

Lithuania

Republic of Lithuania, Lietuvos Respublika. 3,607,899. National or official language: Lithuanian. 26,173 square miles. Literacy rate: 99%. Also includes Belarusan (63,000), Eastern Yiddish, Latvian (5,000), Polish (258,000), Russian (344,000), Tatar (5,100), Ukrainian (45,000). The number of languages listed for Lithuania is 4. Of those, all are living languages.

Karaim (Karaite) [kdr] 3 (2000). Ethnic population: 5,000 in Lithuania. *Class:* Altaic, Turkic, Western, Ponto-Caspian. *Dialects:* Eastern Karaim, Northwestern Karaim, Trakay, Galits. Close to Karachay and Kumyk. *Lg Use:* National language of the Karaim. *Lg Dev:* Cyrillic and Hebrew scripts. OT: 1842. *Other:* Extinct in Israel and Ukraine. Karaim Jewish. Nearly extinct.
Lithuanian (Lietuviskai, Lietuvi, Litovskiy, Litewski, Litauische) [lit] 2,955,200 in Lithuania (1998). Population includes 3,460 Tatar. Population total all countries: 3,125,281. Throughout the country. Also spoken in Argentina, Australia, Belarus, Brazil, Canada, Estonia, Kazakhstan, Kyrgyzstan, Latvia, Poland, Russia (Europe), Sweden, Tajikistan, Turkmenistan, United Kingdom, Uruguay, USA, Uzbekistan. *Class:* Indo-European, Baltic, Eastern. *Dialects:* Aukshtaitish (Aukshtaichiai, Aukstaitiskai, Highland Lithuanian), Dzukish (Dzukiskai), Shamaitish (Samogitian, Zhemaitish, Zemaitis, Zemaitiskai, Zemachiai, Lowland Lithuanian), Suvalkietiskai. Aukstaitiskai speakers can understand Suvalkai easily, Dzukai with a little difficulty, and vice versa. Zemaitiskai is difficult for all others to understand. *Lg Use:* Official language. All domains. All ages. Some speakers have reserved attitudes toward Russian and Polish. Russian or English used with foreigners. *Lg Dev:* Literacy rate in first language: 99%. Roman script. Dictionary. Grammar. Bible: 1735–1998. *Other:* Postpositions; genitives, relatives after noun heads. Christian, Muslim (Tatar).
Lithuanian Sign Language [lls] *Class:* Deaf sign language. *Lg Dev:* Dictionary.
Romani, Baltic [rml] *Dialect:* Lithuanian Romani. See main entry under Poland.

Luxembourg

Grand Duchy of Luxembourg, Grand-Duché de Luxembourg. 462,690. National or official languages: French, Standard German, Luxembourgeois. Literacy rate: 100%. Also includes Italian (20,800), Kabuverdianu (3,000), Portuguese (100,000). Information mainly from M. Stephens 1976. Blind population: 204. Deaf population: 24,373. Deaf institutions: 1. The number of languages listed for Luxembourg is 3. Of those, all are living languages.

French [fra] 13,100 in Luxembourg (1993 Johnstone). *Lg Use:* National language. Used mainly by intellectuals, professionals, authorities. Taught in school as a third language. Used for streets, shops, travel tickets, hotel registries, menus. See main entry under France.
German, Standard [deu] 10,900 in Luxembourg (2001 Johnstone and Mandryk). *Lg Use:* National language. Taught in school as a second language. See main entry under Germany.
Luxembourgeois (Luxemburgish, Luxemburgian, Luxembourgish, Letzburgish, Lëtzebuergesch, Moselle

Franconian, Frankish) [ltz] 300,000 in Luxembourg, (2002). Population total all countries: 390,618. Also spoken in Belgium, France, Germany, USA. *Class:* Indo-European, Germanic, West, High German, German, Middle German, West Middle German, Moselle Franconian. *Dialects:* As distinct from Standard German as is Dutch (Stephens 1976), and not inherently intelligible with it. A Moselle variety of Frankish-German origin, related to varieties of Mitteldeutsch of Belgium. *Lg Use:* National language. Vigorous use. For most people it is the language of creativity. Literature flourishes at a modest level. Perhaps 50,000 second-language speakers. All domains, home, school for explanations, court, parliament. All ages. Pride in ethnic identity and language. West and Central varieties considered to be more sophisticated, North considered more rural, peasant-like. The variety used by older Belgian-border inhabitants is considered old fashioned and riddled with French words, but perfectly intelligible. German is considered to be a foreign language, not to be used with others who speak Luxembourgeois. Bilingual level estimates for French: 0 0%, 1 10%, 2 25%, 3 40%, 4 15%, 5 10%. Speakers learn French and German mainly in school. Younger well-educated people speak English. Most written statements are in French (official) or German (less official, TV, newspaper). French used in high school, for speaking to foreigners at work. German used in school for technical terms, speaking to tourists, commuters from Germany. *Lg Dev:* Literacy rate in second language: 99% German, French. Written Luxembourgeois taught in schools. Letters often written in it. Newspapers. Radio programs. TV. Dictionary. Grammar. Bible portions: 2000. *Other:* SVO; prepositions; genitives, articles, adjectives, numerals, relatives before noun heads; question word initial; 3 prefixes, 2 suffixes on a word; rigid word order; passives; nontonal. Christian.

Macedonia

The Former Yugoslav Republic of Macedonia (FYROM). 2,071,210. National or official language: Macedonian. Part of Yugoslavia until 1991. Different from the region of Greece with the name Macedonia. Also includes Greek. Information mainly from B. Comrie 1987; W. Browne 1989, 1996. The number of languages listed for Macedonia is 9. Of those, all are living languages. See map on page 844.

Adyghe (West Circassian, Adygey) [ady] A few villages in Macedonia. *Other:* Muslim (Sunni). See main entry under Russia (Europe).
Albanian, Gheg (Geg) [aln] 600,000 in Macedonia (2002). *Other:* Muslim (Sunni and Bektashi). See main entry under Serbia and Montenegro.
Balkan Gagauz Turkish (Balkan Turkic) [bgx] 4,000 in Macedonia and Greece. Macedonian Gagauz dialect in the Kumanovo area, Yuruk dialect in the Bitola area. *Dialect:* Macedonian Gagauz, Yuruk (Yoruk, Konyar). *Other:* A different language from Gagauz of Moldova, Bulgaria, and Romania. Nomadic shepherds (Yuruk). Christian, Muslim. See main entry under Turkey (Europe).
Macedonian (Makedonski, Slavic, Macedonian Slavic) [mkd] 1,386,000 in Macedonia (1986). Population total all countries: 1,598,247. The northern dialect is in Kumanovo-Kratovo Region; the southeastern dialect around Gevgelija, Strumica, and Lake Dojran; the western dialect has one subdialect in the Veles, Prilep, Kichevo, and Bitola Region, and another in the Debar-Galchnik Region. Also spoken in Albania, Bulgaria, Canada, Greece, Hungary, Slovenia. *Class:* Indo-European, Slavic, South, Eastern. *Dialects:* Northern Macedonian, Southeastern Macedonian, Western Macedonian. The standard dialect was recognized in 1944. *Lg Use:* National

language. Sociopolitical attitudes are strong: called 'Slavic' in Greece, considered to be a dialect of Bulgarian by some in Bulgaria. *Lg Dev:* Newspapers. Radio programs. Grammar. Bible: 1990.
Romani, Balkan [rmn] 120,000 in Macedonia and Serbia and Montenegro. Population includes 100,000 Arlija, 20,000 Dzambazi. Balkans. *Dialects:* Arlija, Dzambazi, Tinners Romani. *Other:* Ethnic group: Jerlídes (Macedonia, southern Serbia). Muslim. See main entry under Serbia and Montenegro.
Romanian, Macedo (Arumanian, Aromunian, Armina, Macedo-Rumanian) [rup] 8,467 in Macedonia (1994 official figures). Concentrated in the regions of Skopje, Stip, Bitola, Krusevo, and Struga, and in Ohrid, Kocani-Vinica, Sveti Nikole, Kumanovo, and Gevgelija. *Other:* Structurally a distinct language from Romanian (F. Agard). Split from the other 3 Romanian languages between 500 and 1000 A.D. 'Armini' refers to the people. See main entry under Greece.
Romanian, Megleno [ruq] 2,000 in Macedonia (2002 Nicholas). See main entry under Greece.
Serbian [srp] *Dialect:* Serbian. *Other:* Christian. See main entry under Serbia and Montenegro.
Turkish (Osmanli) [tur] 200,000 in Macedonia (1982). *Dialects:* Macedonian, Dinler. *Other:* Muslim (Sunni and Bektashi). See main entry under Turkey (Asia).

Malta

Repubblika Ta'Malta. 396,851. National or official languages: Maltese, English. Literacy rate: 90% to 96%. Also includes Arabic (250). Information mainly from M. Bateson 1967. Blind population: 565. Deaf population: 20,799. Deaf institutions: 3. The number of languages listed for Malta is 3. Of those, all are living languages.

English [eng] 2,400 in Malta (1993 Johnstone). *Lg Use:* Official language. See main entry under United Kingdom.
Maltese (Malti) [mlt] 300,000 in Malta (1975 Katzner). Population total all countries: 371,900. Also spoken in Australia, Canada, Italy, Tunisia, United Kingdom, USA. *Class:* Afro-Asiatic, Semitic, Central, South, Arabic. *Dialects:* Standard Maltese, Port Maltese, Rural West Maltese, Rural East Maltese, Rural Central Maltese, Zurrieq, Gozo. It is descended from Maghrebi Arabic but has borrowed heavily from Italian; it is a separately developed form with different syntax and phonology. *Lg Use:* Official language. Vigorous. No diglossia with Standard Arabic. *Lg Dev:* Roman script. Grammar. Bible: 1932–1984.
Maltese Sign Language [mdl] *Class:* Deaf sign language.

Moldova

Moldova. 4,446,455. National or official language: Romanian (Moldovan). Capital: Chisinau. 13,012 square miles. Literacy rate: 99%. Also includes Belarusan (20,000), Crimean Turkish (1,859), Eastern Yiddish, Russian (562,000), Standard German (7,000), Tatar, Ukrainian (600,000), Vlax Romani. Information mainly from T. Sebeok 1963. The number of languages listed for Moldova is 5. Of those, all are living languages.

Bulgarian [bul] 394,688 in Moldova. *Lg Use:* 68% speak it as first language. *Other:* Christian. See main entry under Bulgaria.
Gagauz (Gagauzi) [gag] 138,000 in Moldova (2000). Population total all countries: 150,000. Cultural center is Kishinev. Also spoken in Bulgaria, Kazakhstan, Romania, Ukraine. *Class:* Altaic, Turkic, Southern, Turkish.

Dialects: Bulgar Gagauzi, Maritime Gagauzi. Close to Turkish, but uses Russian Orthodox Christian religious vocabulary in contrast to the Islamic vocabulary of Turkish. *Lg Use:* 89% speak it as first language. *Lg Dev:* Cyrillic script. Bible portions: 1927–1996. *Other:* Speakers have proclaimed autonomy from Moldova and appealed to Turkey for protection. Christian.

Moldova Sign Language [vsi] *Class:* Deaf sign language.

Romani, Balkan (Gypsy) [rmn] 12,000 in Moldova (1993 Johnstone). Moldova; Crimean Peninsula, Ukraine. *Other:* Ethnic groups: Ursári (Moldova), Karamítika (Ukraine), Romá (Crimean Peninsula). Muslim. See main entry under Serbia and Montenegro.

Romanian (Moldavan, Roumanian, Rumanian) [ron] 2,664,000 in Moldova (1979 census). Moldova, and throughout the country. *Dialects:* Moldavan (Moldovian, Moldovean), Muntenian (Walachian, Muntean), Banat, Bayash, Chrishana, Maramuresh, Oltenia-Lesser Wallachia (Oltean). *Lg Use:* Official language. Many Gypsies in Moldova and southern Ukraine speak Moldavan as first language. *Other:* Called 'Moldavan' in Moldova. Christian. See main entry under Romania.

Monaco

Principality of Monaco. 32,270. National or official language: French. Literacy rate: 99%. Information mainly from R. Arveiller 1967. Deaf population: 1,879. The number of languages listed for Monaco is 3. Of those, all are living languages.

French (Français) [fra] 17,400 in Monaco (1988). *Lg Use:* Official language. See main entry under France.

Ligurian (Ligure) [lij] 5,100 in Monaco (1988). *Dialects:* Genoese (Genoan, Genovese), Monégasque (Munegasc, Ventimigliese). *Lg Use:* Monégasque was nearly extinct in the 1970s. *Lg Dev:* Compulsory learning in schools has revived it. See main entry under Italy.

Provençal [prv] 4,500 in Monaco (1988). *Dialect:* Niçard (Niçois). *Other:* Speakers come from Nice and Cannes. See main entry under France.

Netherlands

Kingdom of the Netherlands, Koninkrijk der Nederlanden. 16,318,199. National or official languages: Dutch, Achterhoeks, Drents, Western Frisian, Gronings, Limburgisch, Sinte Romani, Vlax Romani, Sallands, Stellingwerfs, Twents, Veluws, Western Yiddish. Literacy rate: 95% to 99%. Also includes Adyghe, Ambonese Malay (45,000), Assyrian Neo-Aramaic, Buru, Caribbean Hindustani, Chaldean Neo-Aramaic, Indonesian (300,000), Javanese (7,500), Kabuverdianu (20,000), Kirmanjki, Moroccan Spoken Arabic (30,000), Northern Kurdish (40,000), Papiamentu (80,000), Sranan, Tamil (7,000), Tarifit (200,000), Turkish (192,000), Turoyo (4,000), Vietnamese (16,000), Western Farsi (5,000), Western Yiddish, Yeniche, Yue Chinese (70,000). Information mainly from M. Stephens 1976; B. Comrie 1987; R. Hahn 1996–1998; D. Meijer 1996–1998; M. Evenhuis 1998. Blind population: 8,000 (1982 WCE). Deaf population: 28,000 to 931,761 (1998). Deaf institutions: 44. The number of languages listed for Netherlands is 15. Of those, all are living languages. See map on page 841.

Achterhoeks (Achterhoek, Aachterhoeks) [act] Northeastern, Gelderland Province. *Class:* Indo-European, Germanic, West, Low Saxon-Low Franconian, Low Saxon. *Lg Use:* Official language. Speakers also use Dutch. *Lg Dev:* Bible portions: 2002. *Other:* Implicitly recognized by the government in 1996 (being part of Low Saxonian).

Drents (Drente) [drt] Drenthe Province, northeastern Netherlands near German border. *Class:* Indo-European, Germanic, West, Low Saxon-Low Franconian, Low Saxon. *Dialects:* North Drente (Noord-Drents), South Drente (Zuid-Drents). *Lg Use:* Official language. Speakers also use Dutch. *Lg Dev:* Dictionary. Bible portions: 1981. *Other:* Implicitly recognized by the government in 1996 (being part of Low Saxonian).

Dutch (Nederlands, Hollands) [nld] 12,360,338 in the Netherlands (2000). Population total all countries: 17,370,777. Also spoken in Aruba, Belgium, France, Germany, Indonesia, Netherlands Antilles, Suriname. *Class:* Indo-European, Germanic, West, Low Saxon-Low Franconian, Low Franconian. *Dialect:* Northern North Hollandish (Westfries). The variety of Dutch (not Vlaams) spoken in Belgium is only slightly different from the variety spoken in the Netherlands. *Lg Use:* Official language. Practically all speakers of other languages in the Netherlands are also fluent in Dutch. *Lg Dev:* Radio programs. TV. Dictionary. Grammar. Bible: 1522–1995. *Other:* SOV.

Dutch Sign Language (Sign Language of the Netherlands, SLN) [dse] 20,000 (1986). There are 1,500,000 hearing impaired, 15,000 deaf. *Class:* Deaf sign language. *Lg Use:* All ages. *Lg Dev:* TV. Dictionary. *Other:* There are 5 varieties associated with 5 schools for the deaf, each with about 1,500 students. There have been elementary schools for the deaf since 1790. Developed from French Sign Language, some features similar to American and British sign languages. Currently in transition. Distinct from Signed Dutch. There is a manual system for spelling.

Frisian, Western (Frysk, Fries) [fri] 700,000 (1976 Stephens). Population includes 400,000 in Friesland, 300,000 elsewhere. Friesland, northern Netherlands. *Class:* Indo-European, Germanic, West, Frisian. *Dialects:* Westerlauwers Fries, Súdhoeksk, Wâldfrysk, Klaaifrysk. Linguistically between Dutch and English. Lexical similarity 71% with Standard German, 61% with English, 74% with Eastern Frisian. *Lg Use:* Official language. Over 70% of those in Friesland still speak Western Frisian. Positive language attitude. Most speakers also use Dutch. *Lg Dev:* Literacy rate in first language: Speakers not generally literate in Frisian. Radio programs. TV. Bible: 1943–1978. *Other:* Has an official orthography in the Netherlands.

Gronings (Groningen, Grunnings) [gos] 592,000 (2003). Groningen Province. *Class:* Indo-European, Germanic, West, Low Saxon-Low Franconian, Low Saxon. *Dialects:* West Groningen (West Gronings), Groningen-East Frisian (Gronings-Oostfries), Veenkoloniaals (Veen Colony), Westerwolds (Westerwold). *Lg Use:* Official language. The primary language of many rural people. Most use Dutch as second language. *Lg Dev:* Dictionary. Bible: 1987. *Other:* Implicitly recognized by the government in 1996 (being part of Low Saxonian).

Limburgisch (Limburgs Plat) [lim] 900,000 in the Netherlands (2001). Depending on the city in Netherlands, 50% to 90% of the population speak it (2001 A. Schunck). Population total all countries: 1,500,000. Maastricht, Heerlen, Roermond, Venlo. Also spoken in Belgium, Germany. *Class:* Indo-European, Germanic, West, High German, German, Middle German, West Middle German, Rhenisch Franconian. *Dialects:* A Rhenisch-Mass group of dialects, now often combined with the Cleves dialects (Kleverländisch) as 'Rheinmaasländisch'. Limburgisch straddles the borderline between 'Low Franconian' and 'Middle Franconian' varieties. They are more-or-less mutually intelligible with the Ripuarian dialects, but show fewer 'High German shifts' (R. Hahn 2001). *Lg Use:* Official language. Officially recognized in the Netherlands. Efforts are underway to have it officially recognized in Belgium. Promotion efforts are strong. It has more prestige in the Netherlands. All domains, songs. All ages. Speakers also use Dutch or German. *Lg Dev:* Literacy rate in second language: 99% to 100%. Dictionary. Bible portions: 2001. *Other:* Laborers. Christian.

Romani, Sinte [rmo] 1,222 in the Netherlands (2000 WCD). *Dialect:* Manouche. *Lg Use:* Official language. *Other:* Christian. See main entry under Serbia and Montenegro.

Romani, Vlax [rmy] 1,000 in the Netherlands. Population includes 500 Kalderash, 500 Lovari. *Dialects:* Kalderash, Lovari. *Lg Use:* Official language. *Other:* Christian. See main entry under Romania.

Sallands (Salland, Sallan) [sdz] Northeastern, Overijssels Province. Sallands in the Center. *Class:* Indo-European, Germanic, West, Low Saxon-Low Franconian, Low Saxon. *Lg Use:* Official language. Speakers also use Dutch. *Other:* Implicitly recognized by the government in 1996 as part of Low Saxonian.

Stellingwerfs (Stellingwerfstellingwarfs) [stl] Northeastern, Stellingwerven Region, Friesland Province. Centers are Oosterwoolde and Wolvege. *Class:* Indo-European, Germanic, West, Low Saxon-Low Franconian, Low Saxon. *Lg Use:* Official language. Speakers also use Dutch. *Other:* Implicitly recognized by the government in 1996 as part of Low Saxonian.

Twents (Twente) [twd] Northeastern, Overijssels Province. Twents is in the east. *Class:* Indo-European, Germanic, West, Low Saxon-Low Franconian, Low Saxon. *Lg Use:* Official language. Speakers also use Dutch. *Lg Dev:* NT: 1996. *Other:* Implicitly recognized by the government in 1996 as part of Low Saxonian.

Veluws (Veluwe) [vel] Northeastern, Gelderland Province. *Class:* Indo-European, Germanic, West, Low Saxon-Low Franconian, Low Saxon. *Dialects:* East Veluws, North Veluws. *Lg Use:* Official language. Speakers also use Dutch. *Other:* Implicitly recognized by the government in 1996 as part of Low Saxonian.

Vlaams (Flamand, Flemish) [vls] 122,000 in the Netherlands (1998 U. of Ghent). The Netherlands, southernmost island of the Province of Zeeland. *Dialect:* West Vlaams, Frans Vlaams (Vlaemsch). *Lg Use:* Speakers have Vlaams as first and sometimes only language. Used for informal situations. Varies locally from all ages to over 40. Speakers also use Dutch. *Lg Dev:* Literacy rate in second language: 99% Dutch. *Other:* Speakers sometimes refer to Dutch as 'Vlaams'. They view Dutch as the language of trade, tourism, school. Speakers have difficulty understanding nearby Brabant dialect of Dutch, perhaps due to the Scheldt River being a natural barrier. Christian. See main entry under Belgium.

Zeeuws (Zeaws) [zea] 220,000. The Netherlands: Province of Zeeland, Province of South Holland. (Every island in the Rhine-Scheldt Delta has its own dialect.). *Class:* Indo-European, Germanic, West, Low Saxon-Low Franconian, Low Franconian. *Dialects:* Goerees, Flakkees, Schouws, Duvelands, Fluplands, Bevelands, Walchers, Axels, Kezands. *Lg Use:* Speakers also use Dutch. *Lg Dev:* Literacy rate in second language: 99% Dutch. Bible portions: 1980–2003. *Other:* Recognition under Part 2 of the European Charter requested (2001). SOV. Christian.

Norway

Kingdom of Norway, Kongeriket Norge. 4,574,560. National or official language: Norwegian. Literacy rate: 96% to 100%. Also includes Danish (12,000), English, Finnish (5,358), Northern Kurdish (3,000), Russian (3,000), Spanish (6,500), Swedish (21,000), Tibetan, Urdu, Vietnamese (99,000), Chinese (3,000), from Africa (7,000), from Pakistan (17,000). Information mainly from M. Stephens 1976; B. Comrie 1987; I. Hancock 1991; J. Hupli 1998; B. Winsa 1998. Blind population: 4,000 (1982 WCE). Deaf population: 4,000 to 261,618 (1998). Deaf institutions: 12. The number of languages listed for Norway is 11. Of those, all are living languages. See map on page 842.

Finnish, Kven (Kven, North Finnish) [fkv] 5,000 to 8,000 (1998 The Federation of Norwegian Kven People). Northern Norway, Tromso and Finnmark counties, Ruija, Kveeniland; city of Tromso, and in Oteren, Skibotn, Storslett, Kvaenangsbotn, Nordreisa, Alta, Borselv, Neiden, Bygoynes, Vadso. *Class:* Uralic, Finnic. *Dialects:* Standard Finnish speakers generally understand most of it, except for some vocabulary. Closer to Tornedalen Finnish (see Sweden) than to Standard Finnish. Various dialects: northern west coast varieties differ from eastern ones. Kven has integrated Norwegian loans, whereas Tornedalen has integrated Swedish loans. *Lg Use:* Accepted from 1997 as a second language in Norway. It is now taught in schools 3 hours a week. Most speakers older than 70 years. Considered to be 'Old Finnish'. Speakers of Tornedalen and Kven recognize the differences between the two. Speakers also use Norwegian or Finnish. *Lg Dev:* Literacy rate in second language: Over 90% in Finnish. Newspapers. *Other:* Christian (Laestadian).

Norwegian Sign Language [nsl] 4,000 (1986 Gallaudet Univ.). *Class:* Deaf sign language. *Dialects:* Holmestrand, Oslo, Trondheim. Intelligible with Danish and Swedish sign languages with only moderate difficulty. Not intelligible with Finnish Sign Language. *Lg Use:* Used since 1815. The first deaf school was begun in 1825, first club in 1878. It is passed to the next generation mainly through the schools. 3 dialects are associated with 3 schools. Signed Norwegian is used by teachers; pupils use Norwegian Sign Language among themselves. Signed interpretation required in court, provided some for college students, in mental health programs. Sign language instruction provided for parents of deaf children. Many classes for hearing people. There is a committee on national sign language. There is a manual system for spelling. *Lg Dev:* Films. TV. Videos.

Norwegian, Bokmål (Bokmål, Bokmaal, Norwegian) [nob] *Class:* Indo-European, Germanic, North, East Scandinavian, Danish-Swedish, Danish-Bokmal. *Dialects:* Different from Riksmål in genders, lexicon, counting system, a tendency to permit concrete noun endings in abstract situations, diphthongs versus single vowels, and other features. It is an attempt to simplify written Norwegian. *Lg Use:* Official language. *Lg Dev:* Dictionary. Grammar. Bible: 1978. *Other:* A written standard only, not based on any one spoken dialect, drawing its lexicon and syntax from both West Scandinavian and East Scandinavian languages. A constructed language that replaced Riksmål as the official national language from 1938 onwards. 3 genders; diphthongs.

Norwegian, Nynorsk (New Norse, Nynorsk, Norwegian) [nno] *Class:* Indo-European, Germanic, North, West Scandinavian. *Dialects:* The linguist Ivar Aasen founded this written variety in the 1850s from spoken Norwegian and Old Norse. First official codification in 1901. Named Nynorsk in 1929. *Lg Use:* Official language. A written language only. Based on rural spoken varieties. Constructed to be used as one of the two norms for written Norwegian since 1938. In 1971 30% of the people use Nynorsk as their main written language. *Lg Dev:* Bible: 1938. *Other:* SVO.

Norwegian, Traveller (Rodi, Norwegian Traveller) [rmg] *Class:* Mixed Language, Norwegian-Romani. *Dialects:* An independent language based on Norwegian with heavy lexical borrowing from Northern Romani and German Rotwelsch. Not intelligible with Angloromani. *Lg Use:* Still very much alive (1997). *Other:* Spoken by the Fanter, who are not Gypsies, but have intermarried with Gypsies and Yeniche (German Travellers). The Romani influence comes from speakers who are descended from the first diaspora from India. Romani people were abandoned on the coast of Norway from British ships from 1544 onwards.

Romani, Tavringer (Rommani, Svensk Rommani, Traveller Swedish, "Tattare") [rmu] 6,000 in Norway (1998 Hallman). In eastern and northern Norway. *Lg Use:* Used mainly as a secret language by the speakers (D. Kenrick 1985). Speakers are fluent in Swedish or Norwegian. *Other:* Romani people arrived in Sweden via Denmark in 1512. A Gypsy group. See main entry under Sweden.

Romani, Vlax [rmy] 500 Lovari in Norway (1993 Johnstone). 3,500 Gypsies in Norway. *Dialect:* Lovari. *Lg Dev:* Literacy rate in first language: 30% to 60%. Literacy rate in second language: 75% to 100%. *Other:* Christian. See main entry under Romania.

Saami, Lule (Lule, Saame) [smj] 500 in Norway (1995 M. Krauss). Ethnic population: 1,000 to 2,000 in Norway (1995 M. Krauss). 31,600 to 42,600 ethnic Sámi in Norway (1995). Tysfjord, Hamaroy, and Folden, Norway. *Lg Use:* Few children speakers. *Lg Dev:* Literacy rate in first language: 30% to 60%. Literacy rate in second language: 75% to 100%. *Other:* Traditionally hunters; fishermen; reindeer herders. See main entry under Sweden.

Saami, North ("Northern Lappish," "Norwegian Lapp," Saami, Same, Samic, "Lapp," Northern Saami) [sme] 15,000 in Norway (1995 M. Krauss). Population total all countries: 21,000. Ethnic population: 30,000 to 40,000 in Norway (1995 M. Krauss). Finnmark, Troms, Nordland, Ofoten. Also spoken in Finland, Sweden. *Class:* Uralic, Sami, Western, Northern. *Dialects:* Ruija, Torne, Sea Lappish. *Lg Use:* Two-thirds of all Saami speak Ruija. *Lg Dev:* Literacy rate in first language: 30% to 60%. Literacy rate in second language: 75% to 100%. Taught in primary schools. Bible: 1895. *Other:* The people were formerly called "Finns," which they consider to be derogatory. The name "Lapp" is derogatory.

Saami, Pite ("Lapp," Pite) [sje] Between Saltenfjord and Ranenfjord in Norway. *Lg Use:* No speakers left in Norway (2000 T. Salminen). *Other:* Nearly extinct. See main entry under Sweden.

Saami, South ("Northern Lappish," "Norwegian Lapp," Saami, Same, Samic) [sma] 300 in Norway (1995 M. Krauss). Ethnic population: 600 in Norway. Hatfjelldal and Wefsen, south to Elga. *Lg Use:* Few children speakers. *Lg Dev:* Literacy rate in first language: 30% to 60%. Literacy rate in second language: 75% to 100%. See main entry under Sweden.

Poland

Republic of Poland. 38,626,349. National or official language: Polish. Literacy rate: 98% to 99%. Also includes Czech, Eastern Yiddish, Greek (114,000), Lithuanian (30,000), Russian (60,000), Slovak (38,000). Information mainly from A. Schenker and E. Stankiewicz 1980; B. Comrie 1987. Blind population: 21,523. Deaf population: 50,000 to 2,342,493 (1998). Deaf institutions: 11. The number of languages listed for Poland is 12. Of those, 11 are living languages and 1 is extinct.

Belarusan (Byelorussian, White Russian) [bel] 220,000 in Poland (2001 Johnstone and Mandryk). See main entry under Belarus.

German, Standard [deu] 500,000 in Poland (1998). Silesia and elsewhere. See main entry under Germany.

Kashubian (Kaszubski, Cashubian, Cassubian) [csb] 3,000 in Poland. Ethnic population: 100,000 or more (1993 T. Salminen). The left bank of the Lower Vistula in north central Poland, near the Baltic coast, west of the Bay of Gdansk, and a narrow strip inland, southwest from Gdynia. Also spoken in Canada. *Class:* Indo-European, Slavic, West, Lechitic. *Dialects:* Kashubian Proper, Slovincian. German influences in the language. There are transitional dialects between Kashubian Proper, Slovenian, and Polish. *Lg Use:* The Slovincian dialect is extinct. Few children speakers of Kashubian Proper. *Lg Dev:* NT: 1995. *Other:* Most of the ethnic group speak a regional variety of Polish (1993 Tapani Salminen).

Polish (Polski, Polnisch) [pol] 36,554,000 in Poland (1986). Population total all countries: 42,708,133. Also spoken in Australia, Austria, Azerbaijan, Belarus, Canada, Czech Republic, Estonia, Finland, Germany, Hungary, Israel, Kazakhstan, Latvia, Lithuania, Romania, Russia (Europe), Slovakia, Ukraine, United Arab Emirates, USA. *Class:* Indo-European, Slavic, West, Lechitic. *Dialect:* Upper Silesian. *Lg Use:* National language. *Lg Dev:* Roman script. Bible: 1561–1965. *Other:* Christian, Muslim.

Polish Sign Language [pso] 50,000 deaf, 25,000 members of Polish Association of the Deaf; 1986 Gallaudet Univ. *Class:* Deaf sign language. *Dialects:* Various regional dialects. Not intelligible with American Sign Language. *Lg Use:* 5,000 deaf children in deaf schools, plus 1,000 who attend school with hearing children. There is a committee for the unification of Polish Sign Language. Used since 1889. Elementary schools for deaf children since 1817. Signed interpretation required in court, provided for some college students and in important public events. Sign language instruction for parents of deaf children. Many sign language classes for hearing people. There is a committee on national sign language. There is a manual system for spelling. *Lg Dev:* Films. TV. Videos. Dictionary. Grammar.

Prussian (Old Prussian) [prg] Extinct. East Prussia, formerly in Germany, now in Poland and Russia. *Class:* Indo-European, Baltic, Western. *Dialects:* Among other extinct Baltic languages are: Selonian, Yotvingian, Semigallian, Curonian. *Lg Use:* Became extinct the end of the 17th or beginning of the 18th century.

Romani, Baltic [rml] 30,000 in Poland. Population total all countries: 58,465. Baltic Region, central and southern parts. Also spoken in Belarus, Estonia, Latvia, Lithuania, Russia (Asia), Ukraine. *Class:* Indo-European, Indo-Iranian, Indo-Aryan, Central zone, Romani, Northern. *Dialects:* Latvian Romani (Lettish Romani), North Russian Romani, White Russian Romani, Estonian Romani, Polish Romani. *Lg Dev:* Bible portions: 1933–1996. *Other:* Ethnic groups: Pólska Foldítka, Romá. Christian.

Romani, Carpathian [rmc] One dialect is in south Poland, east Hungary, and Galicia; another in Transylvania, Romania; others in Czech Republic and Slovakia; Ukraine, USA. *Dialects:* Galician, Transylvanian. *Other:* Christian. See main entry under Czech Republic.

Romani, Sinte (Sinti, Tsigane) [rmo] *Dialect:* Manuche (Manouche). *Other:* Ethnic group: Sasítka Romá. Christian. See main entry under Serbia and Montenegro.

Romani, Vlax [rmy] 5,000 Lovari in Poland. *Dialect:* Lovari. *Other:* Christian. See main entry under Romania.

Silesian, Lower (Lower Schlesisch) [sli] Dolny Slask (Lower Silesia). Also spoken in Czech Republic, Germany. *Class:* Indo-European, Germanic, West, High German, German, Middle German, East Middle German.

Lg Use: There is literature by Gerhard Hauptmann. Even spoken by younger people. Speakers also use Polish. *Other:* Different from Upper Silesian, a dialect of Polish. Nearly extinct.

Ukrainian [ukr] 150,000 in Poland. *Other:* The largest minority language group in Poland. Christian. See main entry under Ukraine.

Portugal

Republic of Portugal, República Portuguesa. 10,524,145. National or official languages: Portuguese, Miranda Do Douro (regional). Literacy rate: 83% to 84%. Also includes Kabuverdianu (50,000), Arabic (27,000), from Goa India (20,000), Timor Indonesia (3,000), Brazil (103,000), Angola or Mozambique (100,000), Cape Verde (3,000), elsewhere in Africa (800,000). Information mainly from André Du Nay 1977; F. B. Agard 1984; B. Comrie 1987. Blind population: 8,225. Deaf population: 8,000 to 638,070 (1998). Deaf institutions: 16. The number of languages listed for Portugal is 7. Of those, all are living languages. See map on page 847.

Asturian (Asturian-Leonese) [ast] 25,039 in Portugal. Miranda do Douro. *Dialect:* West Asturian, Central Asturian (Bable). *Lg Use:* Children 6 to 16 are required to study it in school. It is voluntary for those 16 to 19. They use Spanish in formal situations and with outsiders. The Vaqueros ethnic group speaks Western Asturian. *Other:* There is literature, both popular and literary, since the 17th century; poetry, traditional ballads, and chivalric novels of oral tradition. The Academy of the Asturian Language was formed in 1981, to revive the academy of the 18th century. Western Asturian may need orthography adaptation. See main entry under Spain.

Caló (Calão, Gitano, Iberian Romani) [rmr] 5,000 in Portugal. *Dialects:* Spanish Calo, Portuguese Calão (Calão, Lusitano-Romani), Catalonian Calo, Basque Calo, Brazilian Calão. *Lg Use:* Speakers also use Portuguese. *Other:* Christian. See main entry under Spain.

Galician (Galego, Gallego) [glg] 15,000 in Tras Os Montes (1994 SIL). Northern provinces of Entre-Minho-e-Douro and Trazoz-Montes (Tras Os Montes). *Lg Use:* There is an Academy of the Galician Language. There is tension between those in Tras Os Montes Portugal and Spain over dialect differences and identity. See main entry under Spain.

Miranda do Douro (Mirandesa, Mirandese) [mwl] 15,000 (2000). 10,000 who use it regularly, 5,000 use it when they return to the area. Northeast Portugal, southeastern tip of Tras Os Montes area, on the Spain border, at the latitude of Zamora, city of Miranda. *Class:* Indo-European, Italic, Romance, Italo-Western, Western, Gallo-Iberian, Ibero-Romance, West Iberian, Asturo-Leonese. *Dialects:* Related to Asturian and Leonés. Probably separated from them at the time of the invasion of the Moors. *Lg Use:* Official regional language. A folklore group is promoting the language and culture. The language has been introduced into the schools. It is sometimes used in court. *Other:* The people have a different style of dress from their neighbors (black, handwoven cloth). Agriculturalists: wheat, potatoes, oil; wine producers; animal husbandry: sheep, cattle; commerce.

Portuguese (Português) [por] 10,000,000 in Portugal. Population total all countries: 177,457,180. Iberia, Azores, Madeira. Also spoken in Andorra, Angola, Antigua and Barbuda, Belgium, Brazil, Canada, Cape Verde Islands, China, Congo, East Timor, France, Germany, Guinea-Bissau, Guyana, India, Indonesia, Jamaica, Luxembourg, Malawi, Mozambique, Namibia, Oman, Paraguay, Saint Vincent and the Grenadines, São Tomé e Príncipe, South Africa, Spain, Suriname, Switzerland, United Kingdom,

Uruguay, USA. *Class:* Indo-European, Italic, Romance, Italo-Western, Western, Gallo-Iberian, Ibero-Romance, West Iberian, Portuguese-Galician. *Dialects:* Beira, Galician, Madeira-Azores, Estremenho, Brazilian Portuguese. Standard Portuguese of Portugal is based on Southern or Estremenho dialect (Lisbon and Coimbra). *Lg Use:* Official language. 15,000,000 second-language speakers. *Lg Dev:* Literacy rate in second language: 83% to 84%. Dictionary. Grammar. Bible: 1751–1995. *Other:* SVO. Christian.

Portuguese Sign Language (Lingua Gestual Portuguesa) [psr] Used by a considerable portion of the 8,000 deaf persons; 1986 Gallaudet Univ. *Class:* Deaf sign language. *Dialects:* Lisbon, Oporto. Not derived from Portuguese. Different dialects in 2 different deaf schools in Lisbon and Oporto. Related to Swedish Sign Language. *Other:* Signed Portuguese has similar signs to Signed Swedish. It began in 1823.

Romani, Vlax [rmy] 500 Kalderash in Portugal. *Dialect:* Kalderash. *Other:* Christian. See main entry under Romania.

Romania

Romania. 22,355,551. National or official language: Romanian. Literacy rate: 96% to 98%. Also includes Armenian (762), Czech (3,339), Eastern Yiddish (1,100), Gheg Albanian (484), Italian (2,563), Russian (29,890), Slovak (16,108), Ukrainian (57,593). Information mainly from André Du Nay 1977; I. Hancock 1979, 1987, 1988; F. B. Agard 1984; B. Comrie 1987. Blind population: 15,918. Deaf population: 1,405,464. Deaf institutions: 20. The number of languages listed for Romania is 15. Of those, all are living languages.

Bulgarian [bul] 6,747 in Romania (2002 census). Romanian Banat. The Palitiyan dialect is also in Bulgaria and Hungary. *Dialect:* Palityan (Palitiani, Bogomil). *Lg Use:* In Romania it is a recognized minority language. *Other:* Christian. See main entry under Bulgaria.

Crimean Turkish (Crimean Tatar) [crh] 21,482 in Romania (2002 census). Eastern Romania. *Dialects:* Northern Crimean (Crimean Nogai, Steppe Crimean), Central Crimean, Southern Crimean. *Other:* Muslim. See main entry under Uzbekistan.

Gagauz (Gagauzi) [gag] *Dialects:* Bulgar Gagauz, Maritime Gagauz. *Other:* Christian. See main entry under Moldova.

German, Standard [deu] 45,129 in Romania (2002 census). Transylvania. *Dialect:* Transylvania. *Other:* Over 70% of the 500,000 1988 population has emigrated to Germany since 1988 (1993 Johnstone). The people are known as 'Saxons'. See main entry under Germany.

Greek [ell] 4,146 in Romania (2002 census). *Lg Use:* The Karakatchan are Romanian nomadic shepherds who speak Greek. See main entry under Greece.

Hungarian (Magyar) [hun] 1,447,544 in Romania (2002 census). Trans-Carpathian provinces. *Lg Use:* Speakers also use Romanian. See main entry under Hungary.

Polish (Polski) [pol] 2,755 in Romania (2002 census). *Other:* Christian. See main entry under Poland.

Romani, Balkan [rmn] Black sea region. *Dialect:* Ursári (Usari). *Other:* Many have gone to Germany since 1989. Muslim. See main entry under Serbia and Montenegro.

Romani, Carpathian [rmc] One dialect is in Transylvania. *Dialects:* Galician, Transylvanian. *Other:* Christian. See main entry under Czech Republic.

Romani, Vlax (Gypsy, Tsigene, Romanese, Vlax Romany, Danubian) [rmy] 241,617 in Romania (2002 census). 6,000,000 to 11,000,000 all Gypsies in the world (1987 Ian Hancock). Population total all countries:

1,497,846. Also spoken in Albania, Argentina, Bosnia and Herzegovina, Brazil, Bulgaria, Canada, Chile, Colombia, France, Germany, Greece, Hungary, Italy, Mexico, Moldova, Netherlands, Norway, Poland, Portugal, Russia (Europe), Slovakia, Spain, Sweden, Ukraine, United Kingdom, USA. *Class:* Indo-European, Indo-Iranian, Indo-Aryan, Central zone, Romani, Vlax. *Dialects:* Sedentary Romania, Kalderash (Kelderashícko, Coppersmith), Ukraine-Moldavia, Eastern, Churari (Churarícko, Sievemakers), Lovari (Lovarícko), Machvano (Machvanmcko), North Albanian, South Albanian, Serbo-Bosnian, Zagundzi, Sedentary Bulgaria, Ghagar, Grekurja (Greco). Vlax developed from the Romani spoken when they were slaves in Romania for 500 years. There were migrations out of Romania from the mid-14th to mid-19th centuries. Those who left earlier have less Romanian influence in their dialects. Kalderash, Ursari, Churari are occupational ethnonyms; Machvano is a geographical one. Other names are Argintari 'silversmith' and Lingurari 'spoonmakers'. Machvano and Serbian Kalderash have a south Slavic superstratum; Russian Kalderash is influenced by east Slavic, mainly Russian; Lovari is influenced by Hungarian; Grekurja is probably Turkish influenced and is distinct from the Greek Romani dialect of Balkan Romani. All 20 or more Vlax dialects are inherently intelligible; the differences are mainly lexical and sociolinguistic (I. Hancock). *Lg Dev:* Grammar. NT: 1984–1995. *Other:* Ethnic groups: Chache, Kaldarari, Lovári. The people are called 'Rroma'. Christian.

Romanian (Rumanian, Moldavian, Daco-Rumanian) [ron] 19,741,356 in Romania (2002 census). Population total all countries: 23,498,367. Moldavian is in Moldova to the northeast, and Muntenian in Muntenia, or Wallachia in the southeast, other dialects in the north and west, including much of Transylvania. Also spoken in Australia, Azerbaijan, Canada, Finland, Hungary, Israel, Kazakhstan, Kyrgyzstan, Moldova, Russia (Europe), Serbia and Montenegro, Tajikistan, Turkmenistan, Ukraine, USA, Uzbekistan. *Class:* Indo-European, Italic, Romance, Eastern. *Dialects:* Moldavian, Muntenian (Walachian), Transylvanian, Banat, Bayash. Little dialect variation. The Bayash are Gypsies who speak a dialect based on Banat, but influenced by Romani and Hungarian. Romanian has 77% lexical similarity with Italian, 75% with French, 74% with Sardinian, 73% with Catalan, 72% with Portuguese and Rheto-Romance, 71% with Spanish. *Lg Use:* Official language. *Lg Dev:* Roman script in Moldova. Radio programs. TV. Grammar. Bible: 1688–1989. *Other:* SVO. Mountain slope. Deciduous forest. Peasant agriculturalists. Christian.

Romanian Sign Language [rms] *Class:* Deaf sign language.

Romanian, Macedo (Aromanian) [rup] 28,000 in Romania (official). Southeastern Romania, especially Dobrudja (75%), but also in major cities such as Bucharest and Constanta, and other places. *Lg Use:* The educational structure is being set up to teach in Aromanian. *Other:* Speakers are officially related to the Romanians rather than classified as a minority. See main entry under Greece.

Serbian [srp] 27,001 in Romania (2002 census). *Other:* Christian, Muslim. See main entry under Serbia and Montenegro.

Turkish (Osmanli) [tur] 28,714 in Romania (2002 census). Along the Danube in southeast Romania. *Dialect:* Danubian. *Other:* Muslim. See main entry under Turkey (Asia).

Russia

Russia. 144,978,573. Population includes Europe and Asia regions. National or official language: Russian. See Russia,

Europe and Russia, Asia for languages in the European and Asian regions, respectively. Literacy rate: 98% to 99%. Information mainly from T. Sebeok 1963; B. Comrie 1987; A. E. Kibrik 1991. Blind population: 350,000 in the former USSR (1982 WCE). Deaf institutions: 22. The number of languages listed for Russia is 105. Of those, 101 are living languages and 4 are extinct.

Russia (Europe)

Also see Russia in Asia for a listing of languages in Asia. 143,782,338. See Russia in Asia for information about languages in Asia. Also includes Armenian (532,000), Assyrian Neo-Aramaic (10,000), Belarusan (1,206,000), Eastern Yiddish (701,000), Estonian (56,000), Greek (105,000), Latvian (29,000), Lithuanian (70,000), Northern Kurdish (30,000), Polish (94,000), Pontic, Romanian (178,000), Standard German (896,000). The number of languages listed for Russia (Europe) is 60. Of those, 59 are living languages and 1 is extinct. See maps beginning on page 848.

Abaza (Abazin, Abazintsy, Ashuwa) [abq] 34,800 in Russia (1989 census). Population total all countries: 44,895. Karachay-Cherkess Republic. Also spoken in Germany, Turkey (Asia). *Class:* North Caucasian, West Caucasian, Abkhaz-Abazin. *Dialects:* Tapanta, Ashkaraua (Ashkar), Bezshagh. Some dialects are partially intelligible with Abkhaz. *Lg Use:* More vigorous in Russia than Turkey. About 95% speak it as first language. 70% are fluent in Russian. *Lg Dev:* Modified Cyrillic script; Roman script in Turkey. Newspapers. Radio programs. TV. Dictionary. Grammar. *Other:* 'Abaza' is their name for themselves. 'Abazin, Abazintsy, Abazinskiy' are Russian names for them. SOV; ergative-absolutive agreement on the verb. Muslim.

Adyghe (Circassian, Lower Circassian, Kiakh, Kjax, West Circassian, Adygei, Adygey) [ady] 125,000 in Russia (1993 UBS). Population total all countries: 499,180. Adygea Republic. Maikop is the capital. Also spoken in Australia, Egypt, France, Germany, Iraq, Israel, Jordan, Macedonia, Netherlands, Syria, Turkey (Asia), USA. *Class:* North Caucasian, West Caucasian, Circassian. *Dialects:* Shapsug (Sapsug), Xakuchi, Bezhedukh (Bzedux, Bzhedug, Bzhedukh-Temirgoi, Temirgoj, Chemgui), Abadzex (Abadekh, Abadzeg), Natuzaj (Natukhai). Closest to Kabardian. *Lg Use:* 96% speak it as first language. *Lg Dev:* Taught in primary schools. Cyrillic script; Roman script in Turkey. Radio programs. Dictionary. Grammar. NT: 1992. *Other:* Some literature. SOV. Muslim (Sunni).

Aghul (Agul, Aghulshuy, Aguly) [agx] 17,373 in Russia (1989 census). Population total all countries: 17,405. Ethnic population: 17,728 in Russia (1989 census). Southern Dagestan ASSR. Also spoken in Azerbaijan. *Class:* North Caucasian, East Caucasian, Lezgic, Nuclear Lezgic, East Lezgic. *Dialects:* Koshan, Keren, Gekxun, Agul. *Lg Use:* 98% speak it as first language. Used in the home. 30% to 50% of children speak Aghul. Positive language attitude. Lezgi is used as the literary language. *Lg Dev:* Grammar. *Other:* Aminal husbandry. Muslim (Sunni).

Akhvakh (Axvax) [akv] 3,500 (1990). Ethnic population: 3,500 (1990 A. E. Kibrik). Southern Dagestan ASSR. *Class:* North Caucasian, East Caucasian, Avar-Andic, Andic. *Dialect:* Kaxib, Northern Akhvakh, Southern Akhvakh (Tlyanub, Tsegob). 'Dialects' are diverse; speakers communicate in Avar. *Lg Use:* Used in the home. 30% to 50% of children speak Akhvakh. Positive language attitude. Avar is used as the literary language. *Other:* Not a written language. Muslim.

Andi (Andii, Qwannab, Andiy) [ani] 10,000 (1993 UBS). Ethnic population: 20,000 (1990 A. E. Kibrik). Southern Dagestan ASSR. *Class:* North Caucasian, East Caucasian, Avar-Andic, Andic. *Dialects:* Munin, Rikvani, Kvanxidatl, Gagatl, Zilo. Dialects appear to be quite divergent. *Lg Use:* 30% to 50% of children speak Andi. Positive language attitude. Russian used for most key domains. Avar is used as the literary language. *Lg Dev:* Dictionary. Grammar. *Other:* Not a written language. Mountain slope. Agriculturalists: wheat, rye, potatoes; animal husbandry: sheep, oxen, horses. Muslim (Sunni).

Archi (Archin, Archintsy) [aqc] 1,000 (2000). Ethnic population: 1,000 (1990 A. E. Kibrik). Southern Dagestan. *Class:* North Caucasian, East Caucasian, Lezgic, Archi. *Dialects:* One of the most divergent of the Lezgian languages. *Lg Use:* Used in the home. Not a written language. 30% to 50% of children speak Archi. Positive language attitude. Avar is used as the literary language. *Lg Dev:* Dictionary. Grammar. *Other:* Muslim.

Avar (Avaro, Dagestani) [ava] 556,000 in Russia (1989 census). Population total all countries: 600,959. Southern Dagestan ASSR and Terek and Sulak river areas. Also spoken in Azerbaijan, Kazakhstan, Turkey (Asia). *Class:* North Caucasian, East Caucasian, Avar-Andic, Avar. *Dialects:* Salatav, Kunzakh (Xunzax, Northern Avar), Keleb, Bacadin, Untib, Shulanin, Kaxib, Hid, Andalal-Gxdatl, Karax (Karakh), Batlux, Ancux (Antsukh), Zakataly (Char). *Lg Use:* Trade language for Avar language group. Schools for the first two years, except in cities. Speakers also use Russian. *Lg Dev:* Taught in primary schools. Cyrillic script. Newspapers. Bible portions: 1979–1996. *Other:* North Caucasian is also called 'Caucasian'. Muslim (Sunni).

Bagvalal (Kvanadin, Kvanada, Bagwalal, Bagulal, Bagvalin, Barbalin) [kva] 2,000 (1990). Ethnic population: 2,000 (1990 A. E. Kibrik). Southern Dagestan ASSR. *Class:* North Caucasian, East Caucasian, Avar-Andic, Andic. *Dialect:* Tlisi. Close to Tindin. *Lg Use:* Used in the home. 30% to 50% of children speak Bagvalal. People are strongly supportive toward Bagvalal. Avar is used as a literary language. *Lg Dev:* Dictionary. Grammar. *Other:* Not a written language. Muslim.

Bashkir (Basquort, Bashkort) [bak] 1,800,000 in Russia (2001 Johnstone and Mandryk). Population total all countries: 1,871,383. Baskir ASSR, between the Volga River and Ural Mountains, and beyond the Urals. Ufa is the capital. Over 61% of the people live in cities. Also spoken in Kazakhstan, Kyrgyzstan, Tajikistan, Turkmenistan, Ukraine, Uzbekistan. *Class:* Altaic, Turkic, Western, Uralian. *Dialects:* Kuvakan (Mountain Bashkir), Yurmaty (Steppe Bashkir), Burzhan (Western Bashkir). Close to Tatar. *Lg Use:* 67% of the ethnic group are first-language speakers. Speakers also use Tatar. *Lg Dev:* Cyrillic script. Bible portions: 1899–1995. *Other:* The people call themselves 'Bashkort'. Oil workers; agriculturalists; traditionally cattle raisers. Muslim (Sunni).

Bezhta (Bezhita, Bezheta, Bezhti, Bexita, Bechitin, Kapucha, Kupuca, Kapuchin) [kap] 3,000 (1993 UBS). Ethnic population: 4,000 (1990 Kibrik). Southern Dagestan ASSR. *Class:* North Caucasian, East Caucasian, Tsezic, East Tsezic. *Dialects:* Bezhta, Tlyadaly, Khocharkhotin. A separate language from Hunzib (B. Comrie 1989). *Lg Use:* 50% to 60% of children speak Bezhta. Positive language attitude. Avar is used as the literary language; bilingual proficiency undetermined. *Other:* Not a written language. Muslim.

Botlikh (Botlix) [bph] 5,000 (1990). Ethnic population: 5,000 (1990 Kibrik). Southern Dagestan ASSR. *Class:* North Caucasian, East Caucasian, Avar-Andic, Andic. *Dialects:* Botlikh, Zibirkhalin. Close to Andi. Godoberi is a separate language (B. Comrie 1989). *Lg Use:* Few key

domains. 30% to 50% of children speak Botlikh. Positive language attitude. Avar is used as literary language; bilingual proficiency undetermined. *Other:* Not a written language. Muslim.

Chamalal (Camalal, Chamalin) [cji] 5,000 (1990). Ethnic population: 5,000 (1990 Kibrik). Southern Dagestan ASSR. *Class:* North Caucasian, East Caucasian, Avar-Andic, Andic. *Dialects:* Gadyri (Gachitl-Kvankhi), Gakvari (Agvali-Richaganik-Tsumada-Urukh), Gigatl. Dialects are quite distinct. *Lg Use:* Used in the home. 30% to 50% of children speak Chamalal. Strongly supportive language attitude. Avar is used as literary language. *Other:* Not a written language. Muslim.

Chechen (Nokhchiin, Nokchiin Muott, Galancho) [che] 944,600 in Russia (1989 census). Population total all countries: 955,600. Ethnic population: 956,879. Chechnya, north Caucasus. The capital is Syelzha Ghaala (Chechen name) or Grozny (Groznii; Russian name). 80% live in rural areas. Also spoken in Georgia, Germany, Jordan, Kazakhstan, Kyrgyzstan, Syria, Turkey (Asia), Uzbekistan. *Class:* North Caucasian, East Caucasian, Nakh, Chechen-Ingush. *Dialects:* Ploskost, Itumkala (Shatoi), Melkhin, Kistin, Cheberloi, Akkin (Aux). Melkhi is the transitional dialect to Ingush. Chechen is at least partially intelligible with Ingush, more so with contact. *Lg Use:* The largest Nakh-Daghestanian language. Used in publishing. Most speakers are quite fluent in Russian. *Lg Dev:* Taught in primary schools. Cyrillic script. Newspapers. Radio programs. Dictionary. Grammar. Bible portions: 1986–1995. *Other:* They call themselves 'Nakhchuo' (sg.) or 'Nokhchi' (pl.). There are many Russians, Ingush, Ossetins, and other peoples living among them. From 1944 to 1957 they were deported to Kazakhstan and Siberia, losing 25% to 50% of their population, and have lost much land, economic resources, and civil rights. They have been largely removed from the productive lowlands. Ergative case system; many consonants and vowels; extensive inflectional morphology, many nominal cases, several gender classes; complex sentences by chaining participial clauses; verbs have gender agreement with the direct object or intransitive subject, but no person agreement (Johanna Nichols). Mountain slope, foothills, plains. Alpine forest (highlands). Pastoralists; agriculturalists: grain. Muslim (Sunni, Sufi).

Chuvash (Bulgar) [chv] 1,800,000 in Russia (2001 Johnstone and Mandryk). Population total all countries: 1,834,394. Chuvashia, east of Moscow, near the Volga River. Cheboksary is their capital. About half live in towns (1995). Also spoken in Estonia, Kazakhstan, Kyrgyzstan, Uzbekistan. *Class:* Altaic, Turkic, Bolgar. *Dialects:* Anatri, Viryal. The only extant language in the Bolgar branch of Turkic. *Lg Use:* 200,000 second-language speakers. About 80% can use Russian as second language. *Lg Dev:* Cyrillic script. Newspapers. Radio programs. TV. NT: 1904–1911. *Other:* Agriculturalists. Christian (Russian Orthodox), traditional religion.

Dargwa (Dargin, Dargi, Dargintsy, Khiurkilinskii) [dar] 365,000 in the former USSR (1993 UBS). Population total all countries: 371,488. Southern Dagestan ASSR. Also spoken in Azerbaijan, Kazakhstan, Kyrgyzstan, Turkey (Asia), Turkmenistan, Ukraine, Uzbekistan. *Class:* North Caucasian, East Caucasian, Dargi. *Dialects:* Cudaxar (Tsudakhar), Akusha (Urkarax, Urakha-Akhush, Akkhusha), Uraxa-Axusha, Kajtak (Xajdak, Kaitak, Kaytak), Kubachi (Kubachin, Kubachintsy, Ughbug), Dejbuk, Xarbuk, Muirin, Sirxin, Itsari, Chirag. Kaytag, Kubachin, Itsari, and Chirag may be separate languages from Dargwa. *Lg Use:* 98% are first-language speakers. *Lg Dev:* Cyrillic script. Newspapers. Bible portions: 1996.

Other: Mountain slope. Agriculturalists. Muslim (Sunni and Shi'a).

Dido (Didoi, Tsez, Cez, Tsezy, Tsuntin) [ddo] 7,000 (1994 UBS). Ethnic population: 8,000 (1990 Kibrik). Southern Dagestan ASSR. *Class:* North Caucasian, East Caucasian, Tsezic, West Tsezic. *Dialect:* Sagadin. Sagadin dialect is most distinct. Slight dialect differences from village to village. *Lg Use:* Few key domains. Half the children speak Dido. Positive language attitude. Avar is used as the literary language. *Other:* Not a written language. Muslim.

Domari [rmt] Karachi dialect is in the Caucasus, Luli and Maznoug in Uzbekistan. *Dialects:* Karachi, Luli, Maznoug. *Other:* Muslim. See main entry under Iran.

Erzya (Mordvin-Erzya, Mordvin, Erzia) [myv] 440,000 in Russia. Population total all countries: 517,575. Mordovian Republic, northern and eastern. Also in the adjacent regions of Nizhni Novgorod, Ulyanovsk, Penza, Samara, Buguruslan, and the republics of Chuvassia, Tatarstan, and Bashkortostan. Also spoken in Azerbaijan, Kazakhstan, Kyrgyzstan, Turkmenistan, Ukraine, Uzbekistan. *Class:* Uralic, Mordvin. *Dialects:* Quite different from Moksha. *Lg Use:* Speakers are quite acculturated to national culture and the Russian language. *Lg Dev:* NT: 1824. *Other:* Christian (Russian Orthodox), traditional religion.

Finnish [fin] 17,050 in Russia (2000). Ethnic population: 77,000 in Russia (1979 census). St. Petersburg area, Ingria Region. *Lg Use:* Speakers also use Russian. *Other:* Christian. See main entry under Finland.

Ghodoberi (Godoberi, Godoberin) [gdo] 3,000 (1996). Ethnic population: 2,500 (1990 Kibrik). Southern Dagestan ASSR. *Class:* North Caucasian, East Caucasian, Avar-Andic, Andic. *Dialects:* Close to Andi. A separate language from Botlikh (B. Comrie 1989). *Lg Use:* All domains. 30% to 50% of children. Positive language attitude. Avar is used as literary language. *Other:* Traditional territory and way of life. Muslim.

Hinukh (Ginukh, Ginux, Ginukhtsy, Hinux) [gin] 200 (1991 Kibrik). Ethnic population: 300 (1990 Kibrik). Southern Dagestan ASSR. *Class:* North Caucasian, East Caucasian, Tsezic, West Tsezic. *Dialects:* Close to Tsez (Dido) but probably not inherently intelligible. *Lg Use:* Vigorous. Few key domains except family. 50% to 60% of children. Positive language attitude. Avar is used as the literary language. *Other:* Not a written language. Hinukh men marry Dido women. Hinukh women marry men from other ethnic groups. Muslim.

Hunzib (Gunzib, Xunzal, Khunzaly, Khunzal, Enzeb) [huz] 2,000 (1995 H. Ven den Berg). Ethnic population: 2,000. Southern Dagestan ASSR. *Class:* North Caucasian, East Caucasian, Tsezic, East Tsezic. *Dialects:* A separate language from Bezhta (B. Comrie 1989). *Lg Use:* Used in the home. 30% to 50% of children speak Hunzib. People are mildly supportive toward Hunzib. Avar is used as the literary language; bilingual proficiency undetermined. *Lg Dev:* Grammar. *Other:* Not a written language. 27 consonants, 16 vowels, word stress generally linked to prefinal vowel; 5 noun classes; agreement between nouns and coreferent adjectives, pronouns, verbs, and adverbs marked by prefixes; nominative-ergative system; demonstratives. Muslim.

Ingrian (Izhor) [izh] 302 (1989 census). Ethnic population: 820 (1989 census). Baltic area, Kingisepp and Lomonosov areas of St. Petersburg Oblast. *Class:* Uralic, Finnic. *Dialect:* Soykin, Khava, Lower Luzh, Oredezh (Upper Luzh). Close to Karelian but the government considers them separate languages. *Lg Use:* No children speakers. People neutral to mildly supportive. Russian is used for most domains. *Lg Dev:* Dictionary. Grammar. *Other:* Christian.

Ingush (Ghalghay, Ingus) [inh] 230,315 in Russia (1989 census). Ethnic population: 237,438. Chechen Ingushetia,

northern Caucasus, west of the Chechen. Vladikavkaz (Ordzhhonikidze) is the main city. Nazran in the lowlands is an important market town. 64.6% live in rural areas. Since 1992 up to 60,000 Ingush refugees are reported to be in Ingushetia. Also spoken in Uzbekistan. *Class:* North Caucasian, East Caucasian, Nakh, Chechen-Ingush. *Dialects:* Somewhat intelligible with Chechen, more so with contact. *Lg Use:* Many speak Russian as second language. *Lg Dev:* Cyrillic script. Grammar. *Other:* 'Ghalghay' is their name for themselves. From 1944 to 1957 they were deported to Kazakhstan and Siberia, losing 25% to 50% of their population, and have lost much land, economic resources, and civil rights. Many Russians, Ossetins, and Georgians live in Vladikavkaz; the Ingush were removed from there in late 1992. Mountain slope, foothills, lowland. Alpine highlands, plains. Muslim (Hanafi Sunni).

Judeo-Tat (Judeo-Tatic, Hebrew Tat, Jewish Tat, Bik, Dzhuhuric, Juwri, Juhuri) [jdt] 7,000 in Russia (1989 census). Dagestan ASSR, Nalchik in Kabardino-Balkar ASSR, in villages and ancient cities of the Caucasus mountains (Derbent, Makhachkale, Nalchik, Majalis, Pyatigorsk). Until recently they were in Grozny in Checheno-Ingush. None in Iran. *Dialect:* Derbend. *Other:* Speakers of Judeo-Tat are called 'Bik'. They are known as 'Mountain Jews'. They call their language 'Juwri' or 'Juhuri'. Tradition says that they have lived in the Caucasus since 722 B.C. Different from Takestani of Iran. Mountain slope. Agriculturalists: marena grass for dyeing (traditionally); fruit; hides; merchants; animal husbandry: cattle. Jewish. See main entry under Israel.

Kabardian (Beslenei, Upper Circassian, East Circassian, Kabardino-Cherkes, Kabardo-Cherkes) [kbd] 443,000 in Russia. Population includes 46,000 Cherkes in Russia (1993 UBS), 97% speak it as first language. Population total all countries: 1,012,000. Kabardino-Balkaria and Karachai-Cherkessia. Naltshik is the capital. Also spoken in Saudi Arabia, Turkey (Asia), USA. *Class:* North Caucasian, West Caucasian, Circassian. *Dialect:* Greater Kabardian, Baksan, Lesser Kabardian, Malka, Mozdok, Kuban, Cherkes, Beslenei (Beslenej). Close to Adygey. *Lg Dev:* Cyrillic script. Dictionary. Grammar. NT: 1993. *Other:* Muslim (Sunni).

Kalmyk-Oirat (Kalmuk, Kalmuck, Kalmack, Qalmaq, Kalmytskii Jazyk, Khal:mag, Oirat, Volga Oirat, European Oirat, Western Mongolian) [xal] 174,000 Kalmyk in Russia (1993 UBS). Population total all countries: 518,500. The Kalmyk are in Kalmykia, the steppes between the Don and Volga rivers, lower Volga Region, now the Astrakhan Province. The capital is Elista. The Dorbot and Torgut live between the Volga and the Don, west of the Caspian and north of the Caucasus, in the Republic of Kalmykia. Also spoken in China, Germany, Kyrgyzstan, Mongolia, Taiwan, USA. *Class:* Altaic, Mongolian, Eastern, Oirat-Khalkha, Oirat-Kalmyk-Darkhat. *Dialects:* Buzawa, Oirat, Torgut (Torguut, Torguud, Torghud, Torghoud), Dörböt (Dörböd, Derbet), Sart Qalmaq. Their language has diverged from other Mongolian languages and they are called 'Kalmyk' in Russia; 'Oirat' in China and Mongolia. In USA Kalmyk has not been heavily influenced by Russian as it has been in Russia. Different from other varieties in China called Oirat, which are sometimes called 'Asiatic Oirat'. *Lg Use:* 91% speak it as first language. Tibetan is used as religious language. Russian is used as second language for other purposes. *Lg Dev:* Cyrillic script. NT: 1827–2002. *Other:* In 1628 the Oirat moved from Dzungaria, Eastern Turkistan (Xinjiang, China) to the Volga, north and west of the Caspian Sea. Buddhist (Lamaist).

Karachay-Balkar (Karachay, Karachai, Karachayla, Karachaitsy, Karacaylar) [krc] 236,000 in Russia (1993

UBS). Population includes 156,000 Karachay, 85,000 Balkar. Population total all countries: 241,038. Karachi-Cherkessia and Kabardino-Balkaria. Karachaevsk-Cherkessk is the capital. The Balkar are isolated. Also spoken in Armenia, Azerbaijan, Kazakhstan, Kyrgyzstan, USA, Uzbekistan. *Class:* Altaic, Turkic, Western, Ponto-Caspian. *Dialects:* Balkar, Karachay. *Lg Use:* Used by 97% of the ethnic population. *Lg Dev:* Cyrillic script. NT: 1994. *Other:* Balkar and Karachay are almost identical. From 1944 to 1957 they were deported to Kazakhstan and Siberia, losing 25% to 50% of their population, and have lost much land, economic resources, and civil rights. Muslim (Sunni).

Karata (Karatin, Kirdi, Karatai) [kpt] 5,000 (1990). Ethnic population: 5,000 (1990 A. E. Kibrik). Southern Dagestan ASSR. *Class:* North Caucasian, East Caucasian, Avar-Andic, Andic. *Dialects:* Tokita (Tokitin), Anchix. Karatin and Tokitin are quite different. *Lg Use:* Used in the home. 30% to 50% of children speak Karata. Positive language attitude. Avar is used as the literary language. *Other:* Not a written language. Muslim.

Karelian (Karely, Karelian Proper, Sobstvenno-Karel'skij-Jazyk, Severno-Karel'skij, Karel'skiy Jazyk) [krl] 118,000 in Russia (1993 Johnstone). Population total all countries: 128,000. Ethnic population: 172,000 in Russia. Karelia, Tver (Kalinin), St. Petersburg, and Murmansk oblasts. Petrozavodsk is the capital. Also spoken in Finland. *Class:* Uralic, Finnic. *Dialect:* Northern Karelian, Southern Karelian, Novgorod, Tver (Kalinin). Ludic and Livvi are separate languages. *Lg Use:* Many also use Russian, but those over 50 have difficulty understanding Russian. Some use Finnish as second language. *Lg Dev:* Dictionary. Bible portions: 1820–1999. *Other:* A primer was recently produced in Tver Karelian. Agriculturalists; animal husbandry; wood industry.

Khvarshi (Xvarshi, Khvarshin) [khv] 500 (1990). Ethnic population: 500 (1990 A. E. Kibrik). Southern Dagestan ASSR. *Class:* North Caucasian, East Caucasian, Tsezic, West Tsezic. *Dialects:* Xvarshi, Inxokvari. Dialects are quite distinct. *Lg Use:* All domains. 50% to 60% of children speak Khvarshi. Positive language attitude. Avar is used as the literary language. *Other:* Traditional territory and way of life. Not a written language. Muslim.

Komi-Permyak (Permyak, Komi-Permyat, Kama Permyak, Komi-Perm) [koi] 116,000 (1979 census). Ethnic population: 151,000. Komi-Permyak National Okrug, west of the central Ural Mountains, south of Komi-Zyrian. *Class:* Uralic, Permian, Komi. *Dialects:* Zyudin, North Permyak (Kochin-Kam), South Permyak (Inyven). Possible difficulty in understanding among dialects. 80% cognate with Komi-Zyrian and Udmurt. *Lg Use:* Speakers also use Russian. *Lg Dev:* Bible portions: 1866–1882. *Other:* Some literature available. Ancient literary and cultural traditions. More densely populated and mixed, higher education, and more assimilated to national culture than Komi-Zyrian. Agriculturalists; some industrial workers. Christian (Russian Orthodox), traditional religion.

Komi-Zyrian (Komi) [kpv] 262,200 (1993 UBS). Ethnic population: 345,000. Komi ASSR, 60' N. Lat., nearly to the Arctic Ocean. South of Yurak, west of the Vogul (Mansi) peoples. Capital is Syktywkar. *Class:* Uralic, Permian, Komi. *Dialect:* Yazva. Lexical similarity 80% with Komi-Permyak and Udmurt. *Lg Use:* Komi is used in the Institute for Language and Literature of the Komi branch of the Academy of Science. Some use Nenets in the north. Russian is also used. *Lg Dev:* NT: 1979. *Other:* Pastoralists: reindeer; hunters; fishermen; lumbermen; traders. Christian (Russian Orthodox), traditional religion.

Kumyk (Kumuk, Kumuklar, Kumyki) [kum] 282,000 in Russia (1993 UBS). Population total all countries: 282,554. Southern Dagestan ASSR, northern and eastern Caucasian plain. Also spoken in Kazakhstan, Turkey (Asia). *Class:* Altaic, Turkic, Western, Ponto-Caspian. *Dialects:* Khasavyurt, Buinaksk, Khaikent. Dialects are apparently quite divergent. *Lg Use:* Most speakers use Russian as second language. Education is in Russian, with some in Kumyk in heavily populated Kumyk areas. *Lg Dev:* Literacy rate in first language: Higher in Kumyk where the majority speak Kumyk. Literacy rate in second language: High in Russian. Cyrillic script. Newspapers. Radio programs. Dictionary. Grammar. Bible portions: 1888–1996. *Other:* Different from the Kumux dialect of Lak. Plains. Muslim (Sunni).

Lak (Laki, Kazikumukhtsy) [lbe] 112,100 in Russia. Population total all countries: 119,512. Ethnic population: 118,000 in Russia. Southern Dagestan ASSR. Also spoken in Azerbaijan, Georgia, Kazakhstan, Kyrgyzstan, Tajikistan, Turkey (Asia), Turkmenistan, Ukraine, Uzbekistan. *Class:* North Caucasian, East Caucasian, Lak. *Dialects:* Kumux (Kumkh), Vicxin (Vitskhin), Vixlin (Vikhlin), Ashtikulin, Balxar-Calakan (Balkar-Tsalakan). Dialects are close. *Lg Dev:* Cyrillic script. Bible portions: 1996. *Other:* Muslim (Sunni).

Lezgi (Lezgian, Lezghi, Lezgin, Kiurinsty) [lez] 257,000 in Russia (1996). Population total all countries: 451,112. Southern Dagestan ASSR, the western Caspian Sea coast, central Caucasus. Also spoken in Azerbaijan, Georgia, Kazakhstan, Kyrgyzstan, Turkey (Asia), Turkmenistan, Ukraine, Uzbekistan. *Class:* North Caucasian, East Caucasian, Lezgic, Nuclear Lezgic, East Lezgic. *Dialects:* Kiuri, Akhty, Kuba, Gjunej, Garkin, Anyx, Stal. Some dialects are reported to not be inherently intelligible with others. Kuba is considerably different from the standard dialect. *Lg Dev:* Cyrillic script. Grammar. Bible portions: 1990–1996. *Other:* Mountain slope. Agriculturalists. Muslim (Sunni and Shi'a).

Livvi (Olonetsian, Olonets, Livvikovian, Livvikovskij Jazyk, Southern Karelian) [olo] 14,142 in Russia (2000 WCD). Population total all countries: 19,314. Ethnic population: 140,000. Karelian Republic. 'Olonets' is the Russian name of their capital, which they call 'Anus', or 'Aunus' in Finnish. Also spoken in Finland. *Class:* Uralic, Finnic. *Dialects:* Close to Karelian and Finnish. *Lg Use:* Since 1990 there has been a conscious attempt to revive use of the language. Spoken mostly by older adults. Proficiency among children is very low. All speakers also use Russian. *Lg Dev:* Taught in some primary schools but not as a compulsory subject. Poetry. Newspapers. Radio programs. TV. Dictionary. NT: 2003. *Other:* Ludic is transitional between Livvi and Veps. A distinct language from Karelian Proper and Ludic. Primers, textbooks, poetry.

Ludian (Lyudikovian, Lyudic, Ludic) [lud] 5,000 (2000 Salminen). Karelian ASSR. *Class:* Uralic, Finnic. *Dialects:* Ludian is transitional between Livvi and Veps. A separate language from Karelian (Juha Janhunen 1990). May be separate from Livvi. *Lg Use:* Some children speakers. Speakers also use Russian.

Mari, Eastern (Cheremis, Low Mari, Mari, Mari-Woods, Meadow Mari, Lugovo Mari) [mhr] 525,480 in Russia (1993 UBS). Population total all countries: 534,569. Ethnic population: 604,000. Mari ASSR, east of the Volga, Bashkir, Tatar, Udmurt ASSR, Perm, Sverov, Kirov Oblasts. Capital is Yoshkar-Ola, 500 km east of Moscow. Also spoken in Kazakhstan. *Class:* Uralic, Mari. *Dialect:* Grassland Mari (Meadow Mari, Sernur-Morkin, Yoshkar-Olin, Volga). *Lg Use:* Speakers also use Russian. *Lg Dev:* Taught in primary schools. Newspapers. Radio programs. NT: 1986. *Other:* Christian (Russian Orthodox), traditional religion.

Mari, Western (Cheremis, Gorno-Mariy, High Mari, Hill Mari, Mari-Hills) [mrj] 66,000 (1993 UBS). Mari ASSR, south of the Volga, Gorno-Mariy, and some in

Bashkortostan. Capital is Yoshkar-Ola. *Class:* Uralic, Mari. *Dialects:* Kozymodemyan, Yaran. Speakers have difficulty reading Eastern Mari because of lexical differences. There are also phonological and morphological differences. *Lg Use:* Speakers also use Russian or Eastern Mari. *Lg Dev:* NT: 1824. *Other:* Agriculturalists; lumbermen. Christian, traditional religion.

Moksha (Mordvin-Moksha, Mordov, Mordoff, Mokshan) [mdf] 296,904 (2000 WCD). Mordovia, southern. Saransk is the capital. *Class:* Uralic, Mordvin. *Dialects:* Considerable difference with Erzya. *Lg Use:* The Tengushen are Erzya ethnically, but speak Moksha. Speakers also use Russian. *Lg Dev:* Bible portions: 1879–1996. *Other:* Christian.

Nogai (Nogay, Noghay, Noghai, Noghaylar, Nogaitsy, Nogalar) [nog] 67,500 in Russia (1993 UBS). Population total all countries: 67,806. Ethnic population: 75,000. Northern Caucasus, Cherkes Ao. Also spoken in Kazakhstan, Uzbekistan. *Class:* Altaic, Turkic, Western, Aralo-Caspian. *Dialects:* White Nogai (Ak), Black Nogai (Kara), Central Nogai. Dialect differences are slight. *Lg Use:* Speakers also use Russian. *Lg Dev:* Cyrillic script. Bible portions: 1996. *Other:* Muslim (Sunni).

Romani, Vlax [rmy] 10,000 Kalderash in Russia, Ukraine, and Moldova. Russian SFSR, Odessa, Transcarpathia. *Dialects:* Central Vlax Romani, Kalderash. *Other:* Vlax from the former USSR are called 'Rusurja'. Ethnic groups: Sárvi (left-bank Ukraine), Volóxuja (right-bank Ukraine), Chache (Moldavia), Kalderari (Moldavia, Ukraine, Odessa, Transcarpathia), Lovári (Ukraine). About 300,000 Gypsies from the former USSR speak a variety of Romani, Lomavren, or Domari as first or second language (Gunnemark and Kenrick). Christian. See main entry under Romania.

Russian (Russki) [rus] 117,863,645 in Russia (2000 WCD). Population total all countries: 145,031,551. Also spoken in Armenia, Azerbaijan, Belarus, Bulgaria, Canada, China, Czech Republic, Estonia, Finland, Georgia, Germany, Greece, India, Israel, Kazakhstan, Kyrgyzstan, Latvia, Lithuania, Moldova, Mongolia, Norway, Poland, Romania, Slovakia, Tajikistan, Turkmenistan, Ukraine, Uruguay, USA, Uzbekistan. *Class:* Indo-European, Slavic, East. *Dialects:* North Russian, South Russian. *Lg Use:* National language. The Chuvan are a Yukagiric people now speaking Russian. The Meshcheryak are ethnically Erzya, but speak Russian. The Teryukhan are ethnically Erzya in Gorkiy, but speak Russian. 110,000,000 second-language speakers. *Lg Dev:* Dictionary. Grammar. Bible: 1680–1993. *Other:* SVO; prepositions; genitives after noun heads; articles, adjectives, numerals before noun heads; question word initial; 1 prefix on a word; recursive addition of suffixes allowed; nontonal. Christian.

Russian Sign Language [rsl] Moscow, Armavir, Gorky, Kazan, Kirov, Kolomna, Kujbyshev, St. Petersburg, Novosibirsk, Rostov on Don, Sverdlovsk have schools for the deaf. Also used in Bulgaria. *Class:* Deaf sign language. *Dialects:* Related to Austrian and French sign languages. *Lg Use:* There are deaf associations and athletic clubs. Signed interpretation required in court, and used at important public events. Many sign language classes for hearing people. There is an organization for sign language teachers. *Lg Dev:* Primary schools for deaf children since 1878. Films. TV. Videos. Dictionary. *Other:* Originated in 1806. There is a manual system for spelling.

Rutul (Rutal, Rutuly, Rututsy, Mykhanidy, Chal, Mukhad) [rut] 20,000 in Russia (1993 UBS). Population total all countries: 20,111. Ethnic population: 19,503 in Russia (1989 census). Southern Dagestan ASSR. Also spoken in Azerbaijan. *Class:* North Caucasian, East Caucasian, Lezgic, Nuclear Lezgic, West Lezgic. *Dialects:* Shina,

Borch, Ixreko-Muxrek. Dialects are not sharply defined. *Lg Use:* 99% speak it as first language. Used in the home. 30% to 50% of children speak Rutul. Positive language attitude. Lezgin is used as the literary language. *Lg Dev:* Grammar. *Other:* Not a literary language. Muslim (Sunni).

Saami, Akkala (Ahkkil, Babinsk, Babino) [sia] 8 (2000 T. Salminen). Ethnic population: 100 (1995 M. Krauss). Southwest Kola Peninsula. *Class:* Uralic, Sami, Eastern. *Dialects:* Closest to Skolt. *Other:* Nearly extinct.

Saami, Kildin ("Kildin Lappish," "Lapp," Saam, Saami) [sjd] 800 (2000 T. Salminen). 1,900 Saami in Russia (1995 M. Krauss). Ethnic population: 1,000 (1995 M. Krauss). *Class:* Uralic, Sami, Eastern. *Lg Use:* Few children speakers. Many also use Russian. *Lg Dev:* Local literacy effort. Roman script. *Other:* The name "Lapp" is derogatory; 'Saami' is preferred.

Saami, Skolt ("Skolt Lappish," "Russian Lapp," "Lapp," Saam, Lopar, Kolta, Skolt) [sms] 20 to 30 in Russia. Ethnic population: 400 in Russia (1995 M. Krauss). Northern and western Kola Peninsula around Petsamo. *Dialects:* Notozer, Yokan. *Lg Use:* Few children speakers. Many in Russia also use Russian. *Other:* The name "Lapp" is derogatory; 'Saami' is preferred. Christian. See main entry under Finland.

Saami, Ter ("Ter Lappish," "Lapp," Saam) [sjt] 6 (1995 M. Krauss). Ethnic population: 400 population (2000 Salminen). *Class:* Uralic, Sami, Eastern. *Lg Use:* Many also use Russian. *Other:* The name "Lapp" is derogatory; 'Saami' is preferred. Nearly extinct.

Serbian [srp] 5,000 in Russia (1959 census). *Other:* Christian, Muslim. See main entry under Serbia and Montenegro.

Slavonic, Old Church [chu] Extinct. *Class:* Indo-European, Slavic, South, Eastern. *Lg Use:* Used as liturgical language of various Orthodox and Byzantine Catholic churches. *Lg Dev:* Bible: 1581–1751. *Other:* Christian.

Tabassaran (Tabasaran, Tabasarantsy, Ghumghum) [tab] 95,000 in Russia (1993 UBS). Population total all countries: 95,905. Ethnic population: 98,000 in Russia. Southern Dagestan ASSR. Also spoken in Azerbaijan, Kazakhstan, Turkmenistan, Uzbekistan. *Class:* North Caucasian, East Caucasian, Lezgic, Nuclear Lezgic, East Lezgic. *Dialect:* South Tabasaran, North Tabasaran (Khanag). *Lg Dev:* Cyrillic script. Bible portions: 1996. *Other:* Muslim (Sunni).

Tat, Muslim (Mussulman Tati) [ttt] In Northern Caucasus (Dashestan) and a large community in Moscow. *Dialect:* Northern Tats. See main entry under Azerbaijan.

Tatar (Tartar) [tat] 464,669 in Russia (2000). Population total all countries: 1,610,032. Ethnic population: 6,645,588 in the former USSR (1989 census). Tatarstan, from Moscow to eastern Siberia. Capital is Kazan (Kasan), on the Volga River. Also spoken in Afghanistan, Azerbaijan, Belarus, China, Estonia, Finland, Georgia, Kazakhstan, Kyrgyzstan, Latvia, Lithuania, Moldova, Tajikistan, Turkey (Europe), Turkmenistan, Ukraine, USA, Uzbekistan. *Class:* Altaic, Turkic, Western, Uralian. *Dialects:* Middle Tatar (Kazan), Western Tatar (Misher), Eastern Tatar (Siberian Tatar). Eastern Tatar is divided into 3: Tobol-Irtysh, Baraba, and Tom. Tobol-Irtysh is divided into 5: Tyumen, Tobol, Zabolotny, Tevriz, and Tara (Tumasheva). Mixed dialects are: Astrakhan, Kasimov, Tepter, and Ural (Poppe). 43,000 Astrakhan have assimilated to the Middle dialect. Kasim (5,000) is between Middle and Western Tatar. Tepter (300,000) is reported to be between the Tatar and Bashkir languages. Uralic Tatar (110,000) is spoken by the Kerashen Tatar. *Lg Use:* The Karatai are ethnically Erzya, who speak Tatar. *Lg Dev:* Literacy rate in second language: High. Roman script. Grammar. Bible portions: 1864–2000.

Other: Different from Crimean Tatar (Crimean Turkish). SOV. Agriculturalists; oil workers; coal miners. Muslim (Sunni), Christian.

Tindi (Tindal, Tindin) [tin] 6,693 (2000 WCD). Southern Dagestan ASSR. *Class:* North Caucasian, East Caucasian, Avar-Andic, Andic. *Dialects:* Bagvalal is closely related, but probably not inherently intelligible. *Lg Use:* Used in family and community. 30% to 50% of children speak Tindi. Positive language attitude. Avar is used as the literary language. *Other:* Not a written language. Muslim.

Tsakhur (Tsaxur, Caxur, Tsakhury) [tkr] 7,000 in Russia. Southern Dagestan ASSR and Azerbaijan. *Dialects:* Kirmico-Lek, Mikik, Misles. *Lg Use:* Used in the home. 30% to 50% of children speak Tsakhur. Positive language attitude. Speakers also use Avar. *Other:* A written language. The most widely scattered of the smaller ethnic groups. Muslim. See main entry under Azerbaijan.

Udmurt (Votiak, Votyak) [udm] 550,000 in Russia (1989 census). Population total all countries: 565,786. Ethnic population: 750,000 in the former USSR. Udmurtia, 1,000 km northeast of Moscow, bounded by the Kama and Cheptsa rivers, near the Ural Mountains Izhyevsk (Ischewsk) is the capital. Also spoken in Kazakhstan. *Class:* Uralic, Permian. *Dialects:* North Udmurt (Besermyan, Udmurt), South Udmurt (Southwestern Udmurt). *Lg Use:* The Besermyan are Udmurt-speaking Tatar. Speakers also use Russian. *Lg Dev:* Bible portions: 1847–1995. *Other:* Agriculturalists. Christian, traditional religion, secular.

Veps (Vepsian, "Chudy," "Chuhari," "Chukhari") [vep] 6,355 (1990 A. Kibrik). Ethnic population: 13,500. Among Russian speakers, on the boundary between St. Petersburg and Vologda oblasts and in Karelian Republic. Half reportedly went to Finland during World War II. *Class:* Uralic, Finnic. *Dialect:* Southern Veps, Central Veps, Prionezh (North Veps). *Lg Use:* Few children speakers. Positive language attitude. Speakers also use Russian. *Lg Dev:* Taught in some primary schools, but not compulsory. Book of poems, school primers for grades 1 to 3. Poetry. Newspapers. Radio programs. TV. Dictionary. Grammar. Bible portions: 1992–1999. *Other:* Christian.

Vod (Votian, Vote, Vodian, Votish, Votic) [vot] 25 (1979 Valt). Ethnic population: 200 (1990 A. E. Kibrik). Kingisepp area of St. Petersburg. *Class:* Uralic, Finnic. *Dialects:* East Vod, West Vod. Intelligible with Estonian of the northeast coast. *Lg Use:* Used in the home. All speakers are adults. *Lg Dev:* Dictionary. *Other:* Nearly extinct.

San Marino

Most Serene Republic of San Marino, Serenissima Repubblica di San Marino. 28,503. National or official language: Italian. Literacy rate: 97% to 98%. Deaf population: 1,455. The number of languages listed for San Marino is 2. Of those, both are living languages.

Emiliano-Romagnolo [eml] 20,112 in San Marino (1993). *Dialect:* Sammarinese. See main entry under Italy.

Italian [ita] 25,000 in San Marino (2004). *Lg Use:* National language. See main entry under Italy.

Serbia and Montenegro

State Union of Serbia and Montenegro. 10,825,900. National or official languages: Serbian; regional languages: Hungarian, Gheg Albanian, Slovak. Literacy rate: 90% to 93%. Also includes Slovenian, Turkish (60,000), Ukrainian (2,955). Information mainly from M. Stephens 1976; B. Comrie 1987. Blind population: 23,000 in the former larger Yugoslavia (1982 WCE). Deaf population: 60,000 (1986 Gallaudet University). Deaf institutions: 56. The number of languages listed for Serbia and Montenegro is 11. Of those, all are living languages.

Albanian, Gheg (Geg, Shgip) [aln] 1,793,911 in Serbia and Montenegro (2000 WCD). Population includes 50,000 in Montenegro. Population total all countries: 2,779,246. Ethnic population: 2,000,000 (1998 Los Angeles Times). Kosova. Also spoken in Albania, Bulgaria, Macedonia, Romania, Slovenia, USA. *Class:* Indo-European, Albanian, Gheg. *Dialects:* Not intelligible with Tosk Albanian. *Lg Use:* Official regional language in Kossovo. Vigorous. Books are published in Gheg. Restrictions on Albanian at Kossovo's university since 1990. *Lg Dev:* Newspapers. NT: 1869–1990. *Other:* Speakers are called 'Kossovar'. Muslim, Christian.

Bulgarian [bul] Dmitrovgrad and Bosiljgrad districts. See main entry under Bulgaria.

Hungarian (Magyar) [hun] 450,500 in Serbia and Montenegro (1986). Vojvodine. *Lg Use:* Official regional status in Vojvodine. See main entry under Hungary.

Romani, Balkan [rmn] 120,000 in Serbia and Montenegro and Macedonia. Population includes 100,000 Arlija, 20,000 Dzambazi. Population total all countries: 523,900. Balkans, Kossovo. Also spoken in Bulgaria, France, Germany, Greece, Hungary, Iran, Italy, Macedonia, Moldova, Romania, Turkey (Europe), Ukraine, USA. *Class:* Indo-European, Indo-Iranian, Indo-Aryan, Central zone, Romani, Balkan. *Dialects:* Arlija, Dzambazi, Tinners Romani. The Arlija dialect (252,000 to 367,000 total) is understood by Greek Romani and Dzambazi speakers. *Lg Dev:* Dictionary. Grammar. Bible portions: 1912–1937. *Other:* Ethnic group: Jerlídes (Macedonia, southern Serbia). Muslim.

Romani, Sinte (Rommanes, Sinte, Sinti) [rmo] 31,000 in Serbia and Montenegro. Population includes 30,000 Serbian, 1,000 Manouche. Population total all countries: 315,103. Kossovo. Also spoken in Austria, Croatia, Czech Republic, France, Germany, Hungary, Italy, Kazakhstan, Netherlands, Poland, Slovenia, Switzerland. *Class:* Indo-European, Indo-Iranian, Indo-Aryan, Central zone, Romani, Northern. *Dialects:* Abbruzzesi, Slovenian-Croatian Romani, Serbian Romani. Croatian, Slovenian, and Serbian Romani speakers understand each other. Those varieties may be quite distinct from the German varieties. Sinte is characterized by German influence. Not intelligible with Vlax Romani. A Gypsy language. *Lg Dev:* Grammar. Bible portions: 1875–2001. *Other:* 'Rommanes' is the self-name. Ethnic group: Sasítka Romá. Christian.

Romanian (Rumanian, Moldavian, Daco-Rumanian) [ron] 200,000 to 300,000 in Serbia and Montenegro (1995 Iosif Bena). Vojvodina and the Timoc Valley. See main entry under Romania.

Romanian, Macedo [rup] 15,000 in Serbia and Montenegro (Society of Aromanians). Belgrade, Vojvodina and Kosovo. See main entry under Greece.

Romano-Serbian (Tent Gypsy) [rsb] Serbia. *Class:* Mixed Language, Serbian-Romani. *Dialects:* Related to Serbian with influences from Romani.

Serbian (Montenegrin) [srp] 10,200,000 in Serbia and Montenegro and Macedonia (1981 WA). Population total all countries: 11,144,758. Serbia and Montenegro. Also spoken in Albania, Australia, Bosnia and Herzegovina, Bulgaria, Canada, Greece, Macedonia, Romania, Russia (Europe), Sweden, Switzerland, Turkey (Europe), Ukraine, United Arab Emirates, USA. *Class:* Indo-European, Slavic, South, Western. *Dialect:* Shtokavski (Stokavian). *Lg Use:* National language. *Lg Dev:* Roman and Cyrillic scripts; Roman script in Macedonia. Dictionary. Grammar. Bible: 1804–1968. *Other:* Speakers are Serbs, Montenegrins. SVO; postpositions; genitives, articles, adjectives, numerals, relatives after noun heads;

question word initial; 1 suffix; case determines subject, object; obligatory verb affixes mark person, number, gender of subject, object, other noun phrase; passive for each tense, today not commonly used; causatives marked by separate words; comparatives marked by prefix; CCVCVC; nontonal. Christian.

Slovak [slk] 80,000 in Serbia and Montenegro (1996 W. Brown). Vojvodine. *Lg Use:* Official regional status in Vojvodine. See main entry under Slovakia.

Yugoslavian Sign Language [ysl] 30,000 users out of 60,000 deaf persons in the former larger Yugoslavia (1986 Gallaudet Univ.). Also used in Slovenia. *Class:* Deaf sign language. *Dialect:* Serbian Sign Language. Origin from deaf schools in Austria and Hungary. There are regional variants, but no problem in comprehension. Since 1979 there have been efforts to standardize. Slovenian Sign Language used in Slovenia is a dialect. *Lg Use:* First deaf school in 1840, but sign language is not used in schools. Interpreters are furnished in court. *Lg Dev:* TV.

Slovakia

Slovakia. 5,423,567. National or official language: Slovak. Officially separated from Czech Republic January 1, 1993. Literacy rate: 99%. Also includes Czech, Russian. Information mainly from B. Comrie 1987; I. Hancock 1990. Blind population: 10,000 in former Czechoslovakia. Deaf institutions: 51 in former Czechoslovakia. The number of languages listed for Slovakia is 10. Of those, all are living languages.

Croatian [hrv] *Dialect:* Croatian. *Other:* Christian. See main entry under Croatia.

German, Standard [deu] 15,000 in Czech Republic (1999). *Lg Use:* Speakers also use Slovakian or Hungarian. *Other:* Christian. See main entry under Germany.

Hungarian (Magyar) [hun] 597,400 in Slovakia (1993). In the south. See main entry under Hungary.

Polish (Polski) [pol] 50,000 in Slovakia. *Other:* Christian. See main entry under Poland.

Romani, Carpathian (Bashaldo, Romungro, Hungarian-Slovak Romani) [rmc] 220,000 in Slovakia (1980 UBS). Population includes Czech Republic. Northern, eastern, and southern Slovakia. *Dialects:* Moravian Romani, East Slovakian Romani, West Slovakian Romani. *Other:* Ethnic groups: Sárvika Romá (northern and eastern Slovakia), Ungrike Romá (southern Slovakia). The people are called 'Karpacki Rom'. Christian. See main entry under Czech Republic.

Romani, Vlax [rmy] 500 Lovari in Slovakia. *Dialect:* Lovari, Kalderash (Kaldarári). *Other:* Vlax from Hungary and Slovakia are called 'Romungre'. Christian. See main entry under Romania.

Rusyn (Ruthenian, Carpathian, Carpatho-Rusyn) [rue] 50,000 in Slovakia (1991 census). Northeast Slovakia, Preshov Region. *Dialect:* Lemko. *Lg Use:* Nearly 60% have assimilated culturally and linguistically with the Slovaks. Some ethnic Rusyns in Croatia are reported to speak Eastern Slovak, Sarish dialect, not Rusyn. In 1995 it was declared a normative, codified language in Slovakia, can formally be taught in schools, used for publications, school textbooks. *Other:* Christian. See main entry under Ukraine.

Slovak (Slovakian) [slk] 4,865,450 in Slovakia (1990 WA). Population total all countries: 5,011,120. Western upland country around Bratislava. Also spoken in Canada, Hungary, Poland, Romania, Serbia and Montenegro, Ukraine, USA. *Class:* Indo-European, Slavic, West, Czech-Slovak. *Dialects:* Western and central dialects of Slovak are inherently intelligible with Czech. *Lg Use:*

Official language. *Lg Dev:* Grammar. Bible: 1832–1999. *Other:* Christian.

Slovakian Sign Language [svk] *Class:* Deaf sign language. *Lg Dev:* Dictionary.

Ukrainian [ukr] 100,000 in Slovakia. *Other:* Christian. See main entry under Ukraine.

Slovenia

Slovenia. 1,954,033. National or official languages: Slovenian, Hungarian, Italian. Literacy rate: 98%. Also includes Croatian (155,013), Gheg Albanian (4,022), Macedonian (4,603), Sinte Romani (2,847), Standard German (1,543), Venetian. Information mainly from M. Stephens 1976: B. Comrie 1987; T. Priestley 1995; W. Browne 1996. The number of languages listed for Slovenia is 4. Of those, all are living languages.

Hungarian (Magyar) [hun] 9,240 in Slovenia (1991 census). Eastern Slovenia. *Lg Use:* Official language. *Other:* Acknowledged as autochthonous communities and protected by the constitution. See main entry under Hungary.

Italian [ita] 4,009 in Slovenia (1991 census). *Lg Use:* Official language. *Other:* Acknowledged as autochthonous communities and protected by the constitution. See main entry under Italy.

Slovenian (Slovenscina, Slovene) [slv] 1,727,360 in Slovenia (1991 census). Population total all countries: 1,984,775. Carniola and southern parts of Styria and Carinthia; Lower Carniola in Dolenjsko, Upper Carniola in Gorenjska, Primorski in West Slovenia, Stajerski in Styria. Also spoken in Argentina, Australia, Austria, Canada, Croatia, Hungary, Italy, Serbia and Montenegro, USA. *Class:* Indo-European, Slavic, South, Western. *Dialects:* Lower Carniola, Upper Carniola, Stajerski, Primorski, Prekmurski. The literary dialect is between the two main dialects, based on Dolenjsko. Dialects are diverse. *Lg Use:* National language. *Lg Dev:* Radio programs. Grammar. Bible: 1584–1996. *Other:* SVO.

Yugoslavian Sign Language [ysl] *Dialect:* Slovenian Sign Language. See main entry under Serbia and Montenegro.

Spain

España. 40,280,780. National or official languages: Spanish, regional languages: Aragonese, Asturian, Basque, Galician, Gascon (Aranese), Catalan. Literacy rate: 93% to 97%. Also includes Fa D'ambu (600), Judeo-Tunisian Arabic, Kabuverdianu (10,000), Portuguese, Tarifit, Vlax Romani (998), Western Farsi (25,000), Arabic (200,000), Chinese (20,000), from Latin America (150,000). Information mainly from M. Stephens 1976; P. Blanchet 1986; B. Comrie 1987; J. Fishman 1991. Blind population: 30,000 (1982 WCE). Deaf population: 120,000 to 2,383,940. Deaf institutions: 129. The number of languages listed for Spain is 15. Of those, 13 are living languages and 2 are extinct. See map on page 847.

Aragonese (Aragoieraz, Altoaragonés, Aragonés, Fabla Aragonesa, Patués, High Aragonese) [arg] 11,000. Ethnic population: 2,000,000 (1994). Zaragoza, Uesca Province. The northern limit is the Pyrenean border, separating Aragon from Occitania; the western limit is the border of Navarra; the eastern limit is north of Montsó. Western Aragonese includes the towns of Ansó, Echo, Chasa, Berdún, and Chaca; Central Aragonese the towns of Panticosa, Biescas, Torla, Broto, Bielsa, Yebra, and L'Ainsa; Eastern Aragonese the towns of Benás (Benasque, Benasc, Patués), Plan, Bisagorri, Campo,

Perarruga, Graus, Estadilla; Southern Aragonese the towns of Agüero, Ayerbe, Rasal, Bolea, Lierta, Uesca, Almudébar, Nozito, Labata, Alguezra, Angüés, Pertusa, Balbastro, Nabal. *Class:* Indo-European, Italic, Romance, Italo-Western, Western, Pyrenean-Mozarabic, Pyrenean. *Dialects:* Western Aragonese (Ansotano, Cheso), Central Aragonese (Belsetán, Tensino, Pandicuto, Bergotés), Eastern Aragonese (Benasqués, Grausino, Ribagorzano, Fobano, Chistabino), Southern Aragonese (Ayerbense, Semontanés). There are local varieties. Different from the local variety of Spanish (also called 'Aragonese', which is influenced by High Aragonese). Eastern Aragonese is transitional to Catalan. Similarities to Catalan, Occitan, and Gascon. *Lg Use:* Official language in Aragon. 20,000 people use it as second language (1993 Counsel of the Aragonese Language). There is an Aragonese Speakers' League (Ligallo de Fablans de l'Aragonés) in Zaragoza, and a Council of the Aragonese Language (Consello d'a Fabla Aragonesa) in Uesca. There are 5 magazines in Aragonese, and at least 6 organizations of first-language speakers working in the language. The written language is based on Central and Eastern Aragonese. Speakers include 500 older adult monolinguals (1993). Speakers use Spanish (Castilian) in varying degrees, depending on their education; generally they use it well. Used with outsiders. *Lg Dev:* Literacy rate in second language: Nearly 100%. Grammar. *Other:* Christian.

Asturian (Astur-Leonese, Asturian-Leonese, Asturianu) [ast] 100,000 in Spain (1994). Population includes 50,000 in Central Asturian, 30,000 in Western Asturian, 20,000 in Eastern Asturian. Population total all countries: 125,039. Ethnic population: 550,000 (1996). Princedom of Asturias except for the most western section where Galician is spoken, the western part of Cantabria and Leon, and northern Castilla-Leon. In Cantabria and Las Peñamelleras (Asturies) people speak Montañes, a Spanish dialect with Asturian influence. Leonese associations promote their language variety. There are Leonese minorities in Portugal. Also spoken in Portugal. *Class:* Indo-European, Italic, Romance, Italo-Western, Western, Gallo-Iberian, Ibero-Romance, West Iberian, Asturo-Leonese. *Dialects:* Leonese (Lleones), Western Asturian, Central Asturian (Bable), Eastern Asturian. As different from Spanish as Galician or Catalan; more different than Murcian and Andalusian. Close to Leonese. About 80% intelligibility of Spanish (R. A. Hall, Jr. 1989, personal communication); enough to cause disruption of communicative ability (T. Erickson SIL 1992). The Vaqueiros ethnic group speaks Western Asturian. Intelligibility among the three dialects is functional. Close to Mirandés in Portugal. Leonese may be a separate language. Central Asturian is considered the model, and has the most speakers. *Lg Use:* Official language in Asturias. 450,000 second-language speakers able to speak or understand it (1994 F. F. Botas). May be studied in school by ages 6 to 19 if teachers and books are available. Spanish is used in formal situations and with outsiders. *Lg Dev:* Dictionary. NT: 1997. *Other:* About 43% of the population in the region have immigrated into the region from the south since the 1950s, and they have not absorbed the Asturian culture or language. There is literature, both popular and literary, since the 17th century; poetry, traditional ballads, and chivalric novels of oral tradition. The Academy of the Asturian Language was formed in 1981 to revive the academy of the 18th century. Western Asturian may need orthography adaptation.

Basque (Vascuense, Euskera) [eus] 580,000 in Spain (1991 L. Trask U. of Sussex). There are 2,000,000 residents of the 3 provinces of Basque territory; 25% were born outside the territory, 40% in the territory were born to Basque parents. 4,400,000 in Spain have a Basque surname; 19% live in Basque country. Population total all

countries: 588,108. French-Spanish border, 3 Basque provinces: Alava (Araba), Biskaia (Biskay), and Gipuzkoa of the Autonomous Basque Community (CAV); in the northern area of the Autonomous Region of Navarra (Nafarroa) of north central Spain. Also spoken in Australia, Costa Rica, Mexico, Philippines, USA. *Class:* Basque. *Dialects:* Guipuzcoan (Guipuzcoano, Gipuzkoan), Alto Navarro Septentrional (High Navarrese, Upper Navarran), Alto Navarro Meridional, Biscayan (Vizcaino), Roncalese, Avalan. A degree of inherent intelligibility among all regional varieties except Souletin. Regional varieties are sometimes preferred for oral use, but in Spain there is also a fairly strong desire for the Batua unified standard. *Lg Use:* Official regional language. Ages 2 to 20 and over 50 as first language, all ages as first or second language in mainly Basque-speaking areas. Speakers also use Castilian or Catalan. *Lg Dev:* Dictionary. Grammar. Bible: 1855–1998. *Other:* 'Euzkadi' is the name of the Basque region, not for the language. Avalan is no longer spoken. Batua uses a unified orthography. SOV; prepositions; genitives, articles, adjectives, numerals, relatives after noun heads; question word initial; verb affix gender agreement obligatory; prefix marks causative; comparative shown lexically. Mountain slope, coastal, riverine. Deciduous forest. Sea level to 1,000 meters. Christian.

Caló (Gitano, Iberian Romani, Hispanoromani) [rmr] 40,000 in Spain. Population total all countries: 76,580. Also spoken in Brazil, France, Portugal. *Class:* Mixed Language, Iberian-Romani. *Dialects:* Spanish Caló, Portuguese Calão (Calão, Lusitano-Romani), Catalonian Calo, Basque Calo, Brazilian Calão. A Gypsy language very different from other Romani. A cryptological variety of Spanish (I. Hancock 1995). McLane found 300 to 400 words based on Romani, but no individual was acquainted with more than 100. The Iberian base for Calo is regional dialects, where the overlap is not distinct between Spanish and Portuguese. *Lg Use:* Speakers also use Spanish. *Lg Dev:* Grammar. Bible portions: 1837–1872. *Other:* There is a movement to revive the defunct inflected Spanish Romani, and a book has been printed in it (I. Hancock 1990). Christian.

Catalan-Valencian-Balear (Català, Catalán, Bacavès, Catalonian) [cat] 6,472,828 in Spain (1996). Population total all countries: 6,667,328. Northeastern Spain, around Barcelona; Catalonia, Valencia provinces, Balearic Islands, region of Carche, Murcia Province. Menorquin is on Menorca. Pallarese, a subdialect of Northwestern Catalan, is in Pallars. Ribagorçan, another subdialect extends from the Valley of Aran to the south of Tamarit, and from the Noguera Ribagorçana to the border with Aragonese. Also spoken in Algeria, Andorra, Argentina, Belgium, Brazil, Chile, Colombia, Cuba, Dominican Republic, France, Germany, Italy, Mexico, Switzerland, Uruguay, USA, Venezuela. *Class:* Indo-European, Italic, Romance, Italo-Western, Western, Gallo-Iberian, Ibero-Romance, East Iberian. *Dialects:* Catalan-Rousillonese (Northern Catalán), Valencian (Valenciano, Valencià), Balearic (Balear, Insular Catalan, Mallorqui, Menorqui, Eivissenc), Central Catalan, Algherese, Northwestern Catalan (Pallarese, Ribagorçan, Lleidatà, Aiguavivan). The standard variety is a literary composite which no one speaks, based on several dialects. Pallarese and Ribogorçan dialects are less similar to standard Catalan. Benasquese and Aiguavivan people live in isolated valleys and have a distinct phonology from their neighbors. Tortosin may be closer to Valencian. Central Catalan has about 90% to 95% inherent intelligibility to speakers of Valencian (R. A. Hall, Jr., 1989). Written Catalan is closest to Barcelona speech. Central Catalan has 87% lexical similarity with Italian, 85% with Portuguese and

Spanish, 76% with Rheto-Romance, 75% with Sardinian, 73% with Rumanian. *Lg Use:* Official regional language. 5,000,000 second- or third-language speakers in Spain (1994 La Generalitat de Catalunya). All domains. All ages. Speakers also use Spanish, French, Italian, Sard, or Occitan. *Lg Dev:* Literacy rate in first language: 60%. Literacy rate in second language: 96%. The high literacy in Catalan (60%) is recent. Pallarese and Ribogorçan speakers have less education, less contact with the standard, and live in high valleys of the Pyrenees. Some Valencian speakers desire separate literature. Radio programs. TV. Dictionary. Grammar. Bible: 1478–1993. *Other:* Christian, secular.

Catalonian Sign Language [csc] 18,000 (1994). Catalonia. *Class:* Deaf sign language. *Dialects:* An indigenous sign language, quite distinct from Spanish Sign Language. About 50% intelligibility by users of Spanish Sign Language.

Extremaduran (Extremeño, Ehtremeñu, Cahtúo, Cahtúö) [ext] 200,000. 500,000 able to use it, including some monolinguals (1994 T. Erickson). Most speakers are in the northern dialect. Ethnic population: 1,100,000 (1994). Autonomous region of Extremadura (except the Fala-speaking valley in the northwest, Portuguese dialect-speaking strips in the west, and Spanish-speaking strip in the east), and a few neighboring areas. *Class:* Indo-European, Italic, Romance, Italo-Western, Western, Gallo-Iberian, Ibero-Romance, West Iberian, Castilian. *Dialects:* Northern Extremaduran (Artu Ehtremeñu), Central Extremaduran (Meyu Ehtremeñu), Southern Extremaduran (Bahu Ehtremeñu). Related to the eastern dialect of Tur-Leonese. *Lg Use:* All domains. Most speakers older than 30 years (1994). Those who have gone to school speak Spanish in formal situations and to outsiders. *Lg Dev:* Literacy rate in second language: 90%. *Other:* 2 orthographies, one Castilian-like, developed around the turn of the 20th century by the famous poet José María Gabriel y Galán, the other more recent and more phonetic. SVO.

Fala (A Fala de Xálima, A Fala do Xãlima, Galaico-Extremaduran, "Chapurreáu") [fax] 10,500 (1994 T. Erickson). Population includes 5,500 active speakers in the language area; 5,000 outside, many of whom return each summer. Northwest corner of the autonomous region of Extremadura, an isolated valley on the Portuguese border called Val de Xalima or Val du riu Ellas, towns of Valverdi du Fresnu, Sa Ellas and Sa Martín de Trebellu. *Class:* Indo-European, Italic, Romance, Italo-Western, Western, Gallo-Iberian, Ibero-Romance, West Iberian, Portuguese-Galician. *Dialects:* Valvideiru, Mañegu, Lagarteiru. Not easily intelligible with the surrounding language varieties. Intelligible to speakers of Galician. *Lg Use:* Vigorous. All domains except school, church, and contacts with outsiders. All ages. The speakers do not identify with the Galicians. They speak Spanish in school, church, and with outsiders. *Lg Dev:* Literacy rate in second language: Nearly 100%. *Other:* Speakers do not want orthography to be like Galician.

Galician (Galego, Gallego) [glg] 3,173,400 in Spain (1986). Population total all countries: 3,188,400. Northwest Spain, Autonomous Region of Galicia. Also spoken in Portugal. *Class:* Indo-European, Italic, Romance, Italo-Western, Western, Gallo-Iberian, Ibero-Romance, West Iberian, Portuguese-Galician. *Dialects:* Galician is between Portuguese and Spanish, but closer to Portuguese. Portuguese has about 85% intelligibility to speakers of Galician (R. A. Hall, Jr., 1989). Many dialects. There is tension between those in Tras Os Montes Portugal and Spain over orthography. *Lg Use:* Official regional language. There is an Academy of the Galician Language. It has had many decades of development as a language of serious literature, including poetry, essays on

novel, ideological, philosophical, and sociological topics, and for all levels of education, including higher education. A growing sense of ethnic identity and of the Galician language. Speakers also use Spanish. *Lg Dev:* Bible: 1989–1992.

Gascon, Aranese (Aranés, Aranese, Arnais, Gascon, Aranese Occitan) [gsc] 3,814 in Spain (1991 linguistic census). Ethnic population: 5,552 (1991). Aran Valley, headwaters of the Garona River in the northwest corner of the autonomous region of Catalonia, Pyrenees Mountains The capital is Viella. *Dialects:* Baish Aranés, Mijaranés Aranés, Naut Aranés. *Lg Use:* Officially recognized in Spain. The Center of Linguistic Normalization is dedicated to the promotion of its use. It is an official language within the valley. The spelling has been standardized. 60% of the valley's inhabitants always or usually speak Aranese, over 10% speak it as a second language. 1,283 understand it, but do not speak it. Vigorous. Most domains. Speakers in Spain: 532 ages 2 to 14, 775 ages 15 to 29, 733 ages 30 to 44, 750 ages 45 to 64, 609 over 65, 9 without age indicated. Over half the speakers are fluent in French, Spanish, Catalan, or Occitan. Catalan and Spanish are taught in school. About half of those in Spain also speak French because of commercial traffic both ways across the border. 96.4% can understand Catalan, 73.3% can speak it. *Lg Dev:* Literacy rate in first language: 51% read Aranese; 18.6% write it (1991). Literacy rate in second language: Nearly 100% in Spanish, 50% in Catalan. Taught regularly in school since 1984. *Other:* Called 'Aranese' in France. Aranese is influenced by Catalan and Spanish more than French. The Aranese magazine 'Toti' is published monthly. Valley, plains. Forests, fields. See main entry under France (Gascon).

Guanche [gnc] Extinct. Canary Islands. *Class:* Afro-Asiatic, Berber, Guanche. *Dialects:* Its relation to Berber has been questioned. *Lg Use:* Extinct in the 16th century.

Mozarabic [mxi] Extinct. *Class:* Indo-European, Italic, Romance, Italo-Western, Western, Pyrenean-Mozarabic, Mozarabic. *Dialects:* A Romance language with Arabic influences. *Lg Use:* Used by Christians during the Moorish occupation of Spain in the Middle Ages. *Other:* Christian.

Quinqui [quq] Many live on the edge of towns. *Class:* Unclassified. *Lg Use:* A blend language of certain urban ex-nomadic groups. *Other:* It contains elements of Calo and Germania argot. They used to be tinsmiths—their name comes from 'quincalleria' meaning ironmongery. They prefer to be called 'mercheros'. Not Rom or Gypsies.

Spanish (Español, Castellano, Castilian) [spa] 28,173,600 in Spain (1986). Population total all countries: 322,299,171. Central and southern Spain and the Canary Islands. Also spoken in Andorra, Argentina, Aruba, Australia, Belgium, Belize, Bolivia, Canada, Cayman Islands, Chile, Colombia, Costa Rica, Cuba, Dominican Republic, Ecuador, El Salvador, Equatorial Guinea, Finland, France, Germany, Gibraltar, Guatemala, Honduras, Israel, Jamaica, Mexico, Morocco, Netherlands Antilles, Nicaragua, Norway, Panama, Paraguay, Peru, Philippines, Puerto Rico, Sweden, Switzerland, Trinidad and Tobago, U.S. Virgin Islands, Uruguay, USA, Venezuela. *Class:* Indo-European, Italic, Romance, Italo-Western, Western, Gallo-Iberian, Ibero-Romance, West Iberian, Castilian. *Dialects:* Andalusian (Andalú, Andaluz, Andalusí), Murcian, Aragonese, Navarrese, Castilian, Canary Islands Spanish, American Spanish. Leonese has similarities to Asturian, and may be extinct. Lexical similarity 89% with Portuguese, 85% with Catalan, 82% with Italian, 76% with Sardinian, 75% with French, 74% with Rheto-Romance, 71% with Rumanian. *Lg Use:* Official language. 60,000,000 second-language speakers. *Lg Dev:* Dictionary. Grammar. Bible: 1553–2000. *Other:* The Aragonese dialect of Spanish is different from the

Aragonese language. SVO; prepositions; genitives, relatives after noun heads; articles, numerals before noun heads; adjectives before or after noun heads depending on whether it is evaluative or descriptive; question word initial; (C(C))V(C); nontonal. Christian.

Spanish Sign Language (Mímica) [ssp] 102,000 (1994). 20,000 members of deaf associations (1986 Gallaudet University). *Class:* Deaf sign language. *Dialects:* Small differences throughout Spain with no difficulties in intercommunication, except in Catalonia. Origin unknown, but it is reported that there are influences from American, French, and Mexican sign languages. *Lg Use:* Some signed interpretation used in court, at important public events. There is sign language instruction for parents of deaf children. Many sign language classes for hearing people. There is a committee on national sign language. *Lg Dev:* Literacy rate in second language: 20% to 30%. Films. TV. Videos. Dictionary. *Other:* There is a manual system for spelling.

Sweden

Kingdom of Sweden, Konungariket Sverige. 8,986,400. National or official language: Swedish. Literacy rate: 99%. Also includes Amharic, Assyrian Neo-Aramaic, Chaldean Neo-Aramaic, Danish (35,000), Estonian (1,560), Greek (50,000), Kirmanjki, Latvian (450), Lithuanian (310), Northern Kurdish (10,000), Serbian (120,000), Somali, Spanish (35,000), Tosk Albanian (4,000), Turkish (20,000), Turoyo (20,000), Western Farsi (35,000), Chinese, people from Iraq (6,000), Eritrea, North Africa. Information mainly from B. Comrie 1987; I. Hancock 1991; E. Haugen 1992; O. Dahl 1996; B. Winsa 1998. Blind population: 15,716. Deaf population: 8,000 to 532,210 (1998). Deaf institutions: 72. The number of languages listed for Sweden is 15. Of those, all are living languages. See map on page 842.

Dalecarlian (Dalska, Dalmaal) [dlc] 1,500 (1996 Oesten Dahl). Upper Dalecarlia (Oevre Dalarna), especially Aelvdalen (Elfdal). *Class:* Indo-European, Germanic, North, East Scandinavian, Danish-Swedish, Swedish. *Dialects:* Quite deviant from other varieties. Various dialects, some of which are reported to be unintelligible to each other's speakers. *Lg Use:* Speakers also use Swedish.

Finnish (Suomi, Suomea) [fin] 200,000 in Sweden (1997 Birger Winsa). 'Swedish-Finns' were 446,134 in 1999, which counts those born in Finland and first generation born in Sweden, but not others, even if the first language is Finnish. *Other:* 1st to 3rd generation immigrants, apart from speakers of Tornedalen Finnish. Christian. See main entry under Finland.

Finnish, Tornedalen (Tornedalen, Meänkieli, Torne Valley Finnish, Tornedalsfinska, North Finnish) [fit] 79,579 in Sweden (2000 WCD). Population includes 40,000 to 70,000 in the main region (1997), and including 20,000 who speak it in the home (1996). Population total all countries: 109,579. Northeast Sweden, County of Norrbotten, municipalities of Gällivare, Kiruna, Pajala, Övertorneä, and Haparanda. Also spoken in Finland. *Class:* Uralic, Finnic. *Dialects:* Torne Valley Finnish, Vittangi Finnish, Gällivare Finnish. Standard Finnish is not entirely intelligible to speakers of Tornedalen, especially abstract and complex discourse. *Lg Use:* There is a Swedish Tornedalian Association with 5,000 members. Many Saami speak it as second language. The dominant first-language speakers are 30 years and older. Torne Valley dialect has the highest prestige. Gällivare dialect has the lowest prestige. Somewhat negative attitudes toward Standard Finnish, and weak motivation to learn it, although it is partially intelligible to Tornedalen speakers. Swedish is used as second language, and some speak Standard Finnish. *Lg Dev:* Literacy rate in first language: 20% to 30%. Dictionary. Grammar. Bible portions: 1993–1995. *Other:* Some speakers refer to it as 'Finnish'. It has influences from Swedish. Finnish speakers settled here in the 12th century. Quarterly magazine in Finnish, Tornedalen Finnish, and Swedish. 30 children's books. SVO; postpositions; genitives after noun heads; articles, adjectives, numerals before noun heads; question word initial. Christian (Lutheran, Laestadian).

Jamtska (Jamska) [jmk] 30,000 (2000 J. Persson). Jämtland and scattered elsewhere in Sweden. *Class:* Indo-European, Germanic, North, West Scandinavian. *Dialects:* Perhaps 95% lexical similarity to other Norwegian or Swedish dialects, other loans from German, Danish, and French. *Lg Use:* 60,000 or more second-language speakers. Many parents do not teach it to their children. *Lg Dev:* Bible portions: Christmas story. *Other:* Related to Norwegian and Swedish, a West Scandinavian language. It has a separate history from Swedish. Christian.

Romani, Kalo Finnish (Fíntika Rómma) [rmf] 1,592 in Sweden (2000 WCD). *Other:* Christian. See main entry under Finland.

Romani, Tavringer (Rommani, Svensk Rommani, Traveller Swedish, "Tattare") [rmu] 25,000 in Sweden (1998 Hallman). Population total all countries: 31,000. Scattered all over Sweden. Also spoken in Norway. *Class:* Mixed Language, Swedish-Romani. *Dialects:* An independent language based on Swedish with heavy lexical borrowing from Northern Romani. Not intelligible with Angloromani. *Lg Use:* Used mainly as a secret language by the speakers (D. Kenrick 1985), a Gypsy group in Sweden. Speakers are fluent in Swedish or Norwegian. *Other:* Romani people arrived in Sweden via Denmark in 1512. A Gypsy language.

Romani, Vlax (Zigenare) [rmy] 1,500 in Sweden. 500 Kalderash, 1,000 Lovari. *Dialects:* Kalderash, Lovari. *Other:* Christian. See main entry under Romania.

Saami, Lule (Lule, Saami, "Lapp") [smj] 1,500 in Sweden (1995 M. Krauss). Population total all countries: 2,000. Ethnic population: 6,000 in Sweden. Lapland along the Lule River in Gällivare and Jokkmokk. Also spoken in Norway. *Class:* Uralic, Sami, Western, Northern. *Dialects:* Lule Saami is quite distinct from other Saami. *Lg Use:* Few children speakers. *Lg Dev:* Literacy rate in first language: 1% to 5%. Literacy rate in second language: 75% to 100%. NT: 1903. *Other:* The name "Lapp" is derogatory.

Saami, North (Norwegian Saami, "Lapp," Saame, Same, Samic, Northern Lappish, Northern Saami) [sme] 4,000 in Sweden (1995 M. Krauss). Ethnic population: 5,000 in Sweden (1994 SIL). Karesuando and Jukkasjärvi. *Dialects:* Ruija, Torne, Sea Lappish. *Lg Dev:* Literacy rate in first language: 10% to 30%. Literacy rate in second language: 75% to 100%. See main entry under Norway.

Saami, Pite (Saami, "Lapp," Pite) [sje] 20 in Sweden (2000 T. Salminen). Ethnic population: 2,000 in Sweden (1995 M. Krauss). Lapland along Pite River in Arjeplog and Arvidsjaur. Also spoken in Norway. *Class:* Uralic, Sami, Western, Northern. *Lg Use:* More literary activity recently (2000). *Lg Dev:* Literacy rate in first language: below 1%. Literacy rate in second language: 75% to 100%. *Other:* Pite Saami is very distinct. Nearly extinct.

Saami, South ("Lapp," Southern Lapp) [sma] 300 in Sweden (1995 M. Krauss). Population total all countries: 600. Ethnic population: 600 in Sweden. Vilhelmina in Lapland, in Jämtland, Härjedalen, and Idre in Dalarna. Also spoken in Norway. *Class:* Uralic, Sami, Western, Southern. *Lg Use:* Few children speakers. *Lg Dev:* Literacy rate in first language: 1% to 5%. Literacy rate in second language: 75% to 100%. Bible portions.

Saami, Ume ("Lapp," Saami, Ume) [sju] 20 (2000 T. Salminen). Ethnic population: 1,000 (1995 M. Krauss). Lycksele, Mala, Tärna, and Sorsele, along the Ume River. Probably no speakers in Norway. *Class:* Uralic, Sami, Southern. *Lg Use:* Nearly extinct. *Lg Dev:* Literacy rate in first language: below 1%. Literacy rate in second language: 75% to 100%. Bible: 1811. *Other:* Nearly extinct.

Scanian (Skånska, Skånsk, Southern Swedish, Eastern Danish) [scy] 80,000 in Sweden (2002). Blekinge, Halland, Skåne in Sweden. The main regional city is Malmö. Also spoken in Denmark. *Class:* Indo-European, Germanic, North, East Scandinavian, Danish-Swedish, Swedish. *Dialects:* Halländska, Skånska, Blekingska, Bornholmsk. *Lg Use:* Speakers are highly bilingual in Swedish. *Lg Dev:* Literacy rate in second language: 100% Swedish. Dictionary. Bible: 1523. *Other:* The language has had no recognition since Sweden obtained Scania from Denmark in 1658. It is called 'Southern Swedish' in Sweden, and 'Eastern Danish' in Denmark. Today it is heavily influenced by Swedish in Sweden.

Swedish (Svenska, Ruotsi) [swe] 7,825,000 in Sweden (1986). Population includes 5,000 speakers of Gutniska (1998 Sven Håkansson). Population total all countries: 8,789,835. The Göta dialect group is southern, including parts of Småland, south Swedish provinces, Värmland, Västergvtland; the Svea dialect group is northern, including Hälsingland, parts of Östergötland and Uppland, and the Swedish-speaking parts of Finland. Southern Swedish is in Skåne, Blekinge, southern Småland, southern Halland. Northern Swedish is from northern Hälsingland and Jämtland and northwards. Eastern Swedish is in Finland, Estonia, and Gammalsvenskby, Ukraine. Gutnic is in southeastern Isle of Gotland and Fårö. Nearly extinct in Estonia. Also spoken in Canada, Estonia, Finland, Norway, United Arab Emirates, USA. *Class:* Indo-European, Germanic, North, East Scandinavian, Danish-Swedish, Swedish. *Dialects:* Northern Swedish (Norrland), Eastern Swedish (Finland Swedish, Estonian Swedish), Svea, Gutniska (Gutamal, Gotlandic, Gutnic). 'Proper' Swedish is considered to be spoken in Svealand. Dialect investigation is needed of diverse varieties Gutniska, Överkalixmål, Nörpes, Pitemål, provinces around the Bothnic Sea (Västerbotten and Norbotten in Sweden, and Oesterbotten in Finland), and the island of Gotland. Gutniska is descended from Forngutniska (Old Gotlandic), which is ranked as a separate language. A mixed variety, with Turkish influence, Rinkebysvenska, is used among immigrants. *Lg Use:* National language. Gutniska has 10,000 second-language speakers. There are, or were, Swedish varieties spoken in Estonia and Ukraine which are now more or less extinct. *Lg Dev:* Bible: 1541–1999. *Other:* See separate listing for Scanian, often called Southern Swedish.

Swedish Sign Language [swl] 8,000 deaf primary users, and the first language of many hearing children of deaf parents (1986 Gallaudet Univ.). *Class:* Deaf sign language. *Dialects:* No origins from other sign languages, but it has influenced Portuguese and Finnish sign languages. Intelligible with Norwegian and Danish sign languages with only moderate difficulty. Not intelligible with Finnish Sign Language. *Lg Use:* Sign language used since 1800. The first deaf school was established in 1809. There are 5 deaf schools, and they use Swedish Sign Language for instruction in all subjects. Also taught at the University of Stockholm. Many sign language classes for hearing people. Government interpreters assist the deaf in contacts with official and private institutions. There is an organization for sign language teachers. Signed Swedish is distinct. Much research. Today the deaf are regarded as a bilingual minority. *Lg Dev:* TV. Videos. Dictionary. Grammar.

Switzerland

Swiss Confederation. 7,450,867. National or official languages: French, Standard German, Italian, Romansch. Literacy rate: 99%. Also includes Assyrian Neo-Aramaic, Catalan-Valencian-Balear, English (73,000), Iu Mien (200), Kirmanjki, Northern Kurdish (35,135), Portuguese (86,000), Serbian (142,000), Spanish (117,000), Tai Nüa, Tibetan (1,434), Turkish (53,000), Western Yiddish, Yeniche. Information mainly from M. Stephens 1976; W. Moulton 1985; B. Comrie 1987; C. Buchli 1999. Blind population: 9,000. Deaf population: 7,200 to 426,835 (1998). Deaf institutions: 45. The number of languages listed for Switzerland is 12. Of those, all are living languages. See map on page 846.

Franco-Provençal (Patois) [frp] 7,000 in Valais Canton, Switzerland (1998). French cantons of Valais, Fribourg, and Vaud. *Dialects:* Savoyard, Neuch-Telois, Valaisan, Vaudois. *Lg Use:* Valais Canton: young and old in Evolène commune; communes of Hérémence, Vex, Saint-Martin, Savièse, Nendaz, Cermignon, Fully, Arbaz, Ayent, Vissole, and other smaller villages in the central Valais; persons in towns like Sion and Sierre; spoken by persons 50 and older, understood by persons 35 to 40. Fribourg Canton: rural areas as Gruyère. Speakers also use French. See main entry under France.

French (Français) [fra] 1,272,000 in Switzerland (1990 census). Western Switzerland. *Dialect:* Franche-Comtois (Jurassien, Fribourgois). *Lg Use:* Official language. 33% of the population of Switzerland speak French daily (1990 census). Used for education in French-speaking areas. See main entry under France.

German, Standard [deu] *Lg Use:* Official language. Not a first language for many. *Lg Dev:* Main language in education in Schwyzerdütsch (German) and Rheto-Romansch-speaking areas. See main entry under Germany.

Italian [ita] 195,000 in Switzerland (1990). *Lg Use:* Official language. People in all of the Italian cantons speak Italian as first or second language. Used for education in Italian and Ticino (Lombard) speaking areas. See main entry under Italy.

Lombard [lmo] 303,000 in Switzerland (1995). Ticino Canton and Graubünden in the Mesolcina District and two districts south of St. Moritz, central southeast Switzerland. *Dialect:* Ticinese (Ticino, Tessinian, Ticines, Ticinees). *Lg Use:* Used more extensively in Switzerland than in Italy. 14.5% of the population of Switzerland speak 'Italian' every day (1990 census). Ticinese is the form of Lombard used in the home in Italy. Speakers are adequately bilingual in Standard Italian. See main entry under Italy.

Romani, Sinte [rmo] 21,000 in Switzerland (1993 Johnstone). *Other:* Christian. See main entry under Serbia and Montenegro.

Romansch (Rheto-Romance, Rhaeto-Romance, Romansh, Romanche) [roh] 40,000 (1990 census). Borders of Switzerland, Austria, Italy; Graubünden Canton, Grisons valley of Surselva, valley of Voderrhein; Engadin and Val Mustair, southeast Switzerland. *Class:* Indo-European, Italic, Romance, Italo-Western, Western, Gallo-Iberian, Gallo-Romance, Gallo-Rhaetian, Rhaetian. *Dialects:* Lower Engadine (Vallader-Lower Engadine, Grisons), Upper Engadine (Puter-Upper Engadine), Sursilvan (Surselva, Sutsilvan-Hinterrhein), Sursilvan-Oberland, Surmiran-Albula. Friulian, Ladin, and Romansch are separate languages (R. A. Hall, Jr., personal communication 1978). Lexical similarity 78% with Italian and French, 76% with Catalan, 74% with Spanish, Sardinian, and Portuguese, 72% with Romanian. *Lg Use:*

Official language. An official written language is in common use now, called Grischuna. All dialects taught in school. Speakers are bilingual. Standard German is the language of instruction in school. *Lg Dev:* Taught in primary schools. Newspapers. Bible: 1679–1953.

Schwyzerdütsch (Alemannisch) [gsw] 4,215,000 in Switzerland (1990 census). Population total all countries: 6,044,000. Central, south central, north central, northeast, and eastern cantons. Also spoken in Austria, France, Germany, Liechtenstein. *Class:* Indo-European, Germanic, West, High German, German, Upper German, Alemannic. *Dialects:* Bern (Bärndütsch), Zurich, Lucerne, Basel, Obwald, Appenzell, St. Gallen, Graubenden-Grisons (Valserisch), Wallis. Swiss varieties are High Alemannisch (most) and Highest Alemannisch (several in central Switzerland). Not functionally intelligible to speakers of Standard German. Each canton has a separate variety, many of which are unintelligible to each other's speakers. Only a few of the 20 to 70 varieties are listed as dialects (subdialects). Close to Schwäbisch in south central Germany. *Lg Use:* 93.3% of German speakers in Switzerland speak a Swiss German dialect, and 66.4% speak dialect only, and no high German (1990 census). 72% of the entire population of Switzerland speaks Schwyzerdütsch every day (1990 census). Used in some schools and churches. They have a strong social function, being used to maintain the borders of regions or cantons, or even to keep one village different from another. They also draw the line between Germans, Swiss, and Austrians. All speakers are actively or passively bilingual in Standard German. Standard German is the language of instruction in school. *Lg Dev:* Grammar. NT: 1984. *Other:* Called 'Schwyzerdütsch' in Switzerland, and 'Alsatian' in France. There is an important literature.

Swiss-French Sign Language (Langage Gestuelle) [ssr] 1,000 (1986 Gallaudet Univ.). *Class:* Deaf sign language. *Dialects:* Some regional lexical variations in the French area are tied to specific schools. There are local Swiss signs and imported French signs. *Lg Use:* Sign language is now taught in a bilingual program in Geneva. The status of signing has been low, but is now improving. *Lg Dev:* TV. *Other:* French Sign Language is used some in the French area.

Swiss-German Sign Language (Natürliche Gebärde) [sgg] 6,000 (1986 Gallaudet Univ.). *Class:* Deaf sign language. *Other:* Some regional lexical variations in German areas are tied to specific schools. The status of signing has been low, but is now improving. In schools in the German area there is a strong oralist tradition.

Swiss-Italian Sign Language [slf] 200 (1986 Gallaudet Univ.). *Class:* Deaf sign language. *Other:* The status of signing has been low, but is now improving.

Walser (Walscher) [wae] 10,000 in Switzerland (2004). Population total all countries: 22,780. Ethnic population: 21,900 (1980 C. Buchli). Bosco-Gurin, Canton Ticino; Wallis, Simplon; Graubunden, Obersaxen; Valsertal (Vals, St. Martin); Safiental (Valendas, Versam, Tenna, Safien); Rheinwald (Medels, Nufenen, Splngen, Sufers, Hinterrhein, Avers); Schanfigg (Arosa, Langwiesn); Albula (Mutten, Schmitte Wiesen); Landquart (Davos, Klosters, Furna, Says, St. Antonien, Valzeina). 26 communities in Switzerland, and 7 former ones. Also spoken in Austria, Italy, Liechtenstein. *Class:* Indo-European, Germanic, West, High German, German, Upper German, Alemannic. *Dialects:* Ancestors came from the Wallis Canton between the 12th and 13th centuries. Close but different from Schwyzerdütsch

spoken in Wallis Canton in Switzerland. Different from Cimbrian, Mocheno, or Bavarian.

Turkey (Europe)

Also see Turkey in Asia for a listing of languages in Asia. The number of languages listed for Turkey (Europe) is 12. Of those, 11 are living languages and 1 is extinct.

Albanian, Tosk [als] 15,000 in Turkey (1980). 1,075 monolinguals (1965 census). Ethnic population: 65,000 in Turkey. Scattered in western Turkey. *Lg Use:* 96% of speakers can use Turkish as second language. *Other:* Muslim (Sunni). See main entry under Albania.

Armenian (Haieren, Somkhuri, Ermenice, Armjanski) [hye] 40,000 in Turkey (1980). 1,022 monolinguals (1965 census). Ethnic population: 70,000 in Turkey (1980). Many in Istanbul, and a few scattered across eastern Turkey. The Hemshin (Hamshen) are Armenian Muslims, living near the Laz. *Dialect:* Eastern Armenian. *Lg Use:* 96% bilingual in Turkish. *Other:* Christian. See main entry under Armenia.

Balkan Gagauz Turkish (Balkan Turkic) [bgx] 327,000 in Turkey (1993 Johnstone). Population includes 7,000 Surguch (1965) and 320,000 Yuruk. Population total all countries: 331,000. Yuruk dialect on the west coast in Macedonia. Also spoken in Greece, Macedonia. *Class:* Altaic, Turkic, Southern, Turkish. *Dialect:* Gajol, Gerlovo Turks, Karamanli, Kyzylbash, Surguch, Tozluk Turks, Yuruk (Yoruk, Konyar). *Other:* Distinct from Gagauz of Moldova, Bulgaria, and Romania. Christian.

Bulgarian (Pomak) [bul] 300,000 in Turkey (2001 Johnstone and Mandryk). Population includes refugees from Bulgaria. Scattered in Edirne and other western provinces. *Dialect:* Pomak. *Lg Use:* Spoken by Muslim Pomaks in Turkey and Greece. 93% bilingual in Turkish. *Other:* Muslim (Sunni). See main entry under Bulgaria.

Domari (Middle Eastern Romani, Tsigene, Gypsy) [rmt] 28,461 in Turkey (2000 WCD). Mainly in western Turkey, some in eastern Turkey. *Dialects:* Karachi, Beludji, Marashi. *Other:* 500,000 Gypsies in Turkey speak Domari or varieties of Romani (Gunnemark and Kenrick 1985). Muslim. See main entry under Iran.

Greek [ell] 4,000 in Turkey (1993). Istanbul city. *Other:* Nearly all Greeks have now emigrated from Turkey. There were 1,500,000 in Turkey in 1900. See main entry under Greece.

Ladino (Dzhudezmo, Judeo Spanish, Sefardi, Judezmo, Hakitia, Haketia, Spanyol) [lad] 8,000 in Turkey (1976). Ethnic population: 15,000. Mainly in Istanbul; some in Izmirin. *Lg Use:* Chief language of Sefardic Jews. The Donme are a Ladino-speaking group in Turkey, adherents of Shabbetai Zevi (Zvi). Nearly all also use Turkish. *Other:* Jewish. See main entry under Israel.

Pontic [pnt] 4,535 in Turkey (1965 Mackridge). Northest Turkey, easternmost part of Pontic-speaking region. *Other:* Muslim. See main entry under Greece.

Romani, Balkan [rmn] 25,000 Arlija in Turkey. *Dialect:* Arlija (Erli). *Other:* Muslim. See main entry under Serbia and Montenegro.

Serbian (Bosnian) [srp] 20,000 in Turkey (1980). 2,345 monolinguals (1965 census). Ethnic population: 61,000. Scattered in western Turkey. *Lg Use:* 95% bilingual in Turkish. *Other:* Muslim. See main entry under Serbia and Montenegro.

Tatar [tat] Istanbul and perhaps other places. *Other:* Muslim. See main entry under Russia (Europe).

Ubykh (Ubyx, Pekhi, Oubykh) [uby] Extinct. Haci Osman village, near the Sea of Marmara, near Istanbul. *Class:* North Caucasian, West Caucasian, Ubyx. *Lg Use:* The last fully competent speaker, Tevfik Esen, of Haci Osman, died in Istanbul October 1992. A century ago there were 50,000 speakers in the Caucasus valleys east of the Black Sea. Most migrated to Turkey in 1894. The ethnic group now speaks a distinct dialect of Adyghe.

Ukraine

Ukraine. 47,732,079. National or official language: Ukrainian. 233,100 square miles. Literacy rate: 99%. Also includes Abkhaz (952), Armenian (54,000), Balkan Romani, Baltic Romani, Bashkir (3,672), Belarusan (440,000), Bulgarian (234,000), Crimean Turkish (200,000), Czech (21,000), Dargwa (634), Eastern Yiddish (634,000), Erzya (19,000), Gagauz, Georgian (24,000), Kazakh (7,555), Lak (574), Latvian (2,600), Lezgi (1,708), Northern Uzbek (10,563), Osetin (4,554), Polish (1,140,068), Russian (11,335,000), Serbian (5,000), Slovak, Standard German (38,000), Tajiki (2,215), Tatar (90,542), Tosk Albanian (5,000), Turkish. Information mainly from B. Podolsky 1985; B. Comrie 1987. The number of languages listed for Ukraine is 11. Of those, 10 are living languages and 1 is extinct. See map on page 850.

Gothic [got] Extinct. Bulgaria and central Europe. *Class:* Indo-European, Germanic, East. *Dialects:* Crimean Gothic, Ostrogoth, Visigoth. *Lg Dev:* Bible: 520. *Other:* Some settlements survived in Crimea until the 18th century (Bloomfield 1933).
Greek [ell] 7,205 in Ukraine (1970 census). Ethnic population: 106,909. Donetsk oblast, town of Mariupol, 18 villages. *Dialect:* Mariupol Greek (Tavro-Rumeic, Crimeo-Rumeic). *Lg Use:* Most ethnic Greeks speak Russian as first language. Some speak Urum (Podolsky). See main entry under Greece.
Hungarian (Magyar) [hun] 176,000 in Ukraine (2001 Johnstone and Mandryk). Transcarpathian Ukraine. *Lg Use:* 95% speak it as first language. *Other:* Christian. See main entry under Hungary.
Jakati (Jati, Jatu, Jat, Jataki, Kayani, Musali) [jat] 29,250 in Ukraine (2000 WCD). Population total all countries: 30,615. Kabul (25 families); Jalalabad (50 families); Charikar (15 families). Also spoken in Afghanistan. *Class:* Indo-European, Indo-Iranian, Indo-Aryan, Northwestern zone, Lahnda. *Dialects:* Related to Western Panjabi. *Other:* Different from Jadgali of Pakistan. Nomadic. Ironsmiths; fortune tellers. Muslim.
Romani, Carpathian [rmc] Ukraine, Transcarpathia. One dialect is in east Hungary, south Poland, and Galicia; another in Transylvania, Romania; others in Czech Republic and Slovakia, USA. *Other:* Ethnic group: Ungrike Romá (Ukraine). Christian. See main entry under Czech Republic.
Romani, Vlax [rmy] Eastern and western Ukraine, Odessa, Transcarpathia. *Dialects:* Ukrainian Vlax Romani, Central Vlax Romani, Kalderash. *Other:* Vlax from the former USSR are called 'Rusurja'. Ethnic groups: Sárvi (left-bank Ukraine), Volóxuja (right-bank Ukraine), Chache (Moldavia), Kalderari (Moldavia, Ukraine, Odessa, Transcarpathia), Lovári (Ukraine). Christian. See main entry under Romania.
Romanian (Rumanian, Moldavian, Daco-Romanian) [ron] 250,000 in Ukraine (2004). Historically the regions of Bucovina and southern Basarabia (Chernowitz or Cernauti regions) were incorporated into the USSR from Romania by the Ribentrop-Molotov treaty in 1939. *Other:* Mountain slope. See main entry under Romania.
Rusyn (Ruthenian, Carpathian, Carpatho-Rusyn) [rue] 560,120 in Ukraine (2000). Population total all countries: 610,120. Transcarpathian Oblast of Ukraine. Also possibly in Romania. Also spoken in Slovakia. *Class:* Indo-European, Slavic, East. *Dialects:* Rusyn is called a dialect

of Ukrainian, but speakers are reported to consider themselves distinct from Ukrainians. *Lg Use:* Standard Ukrainian used for literature, signs. *Lg Dev:* Radio programs. TV. Dictionary. *Other:* Christian.
Ukrainian [ukr] 31,058,000 in Ukraine (1993). Population total all countries: 39,441,842. Ethnic population: 37,419,000 (1993 Johnstone). Western Ukraine, adjacent republics. Also spoken in Argentina, Armenia, Azerbaijan, Belarus, Brazil, Canada, Estonia, Georgia, Hungary, Kazakhstan, Kyrgyzstan, Latvia, Lithuania, Moldova, Paraguay, Poland, Romania, Russia (Asia), Serbia and Montenegro, Slovakia, Tajikistan, Turkmenistan, USA, Uzbekistan. *Class:* Indo-European, Slavic, East. *Dialects:* Northwest Ukrainian, Southwest Ukrainian, East Ukrainian. Dialect differences are slight. *Lg Use:* Official language. 83% speak it as first language. *Lg Dev:* Cyrillic script. Grammar. Bible: 1903–1999. *Other:* Christian.
Ukrainian Sign Language [ukl] *Class:* Deaf sign language.
Urum [uum] 94,983 in Ukraine (2000 WCD). A few villages in the Donetsk Oblast of southeastern Ukraine. 10 villages total. *Other:* Spoken by ethnic 'Greeks'. See main entry under Georgia.

United Kingdom

United Kingdom of Great Britain and Northern Ireland. 60,270,708. National or official languages: English, Welsh, French (regional). Literacy rate: 97% to 99%. Also includes Assyrian Neo-Aramaic (5,000), Bengali (400,000), Eastern Panjabi (471,000), Estonian (14,000), Greek (200,000), Gujarati (140,000), Hakka Chinese (10,000), Hebrew (8,000), Hindi (243), Italian (200,000), Japanese (12,000), Judeo-Iraqi Arabic, Kashmiri (115,000), Kirmanjki, Latvian (12,000), Leeward Caribbean Creole English, Lithuanian, Malayalam (21,000), Maltese (40,900), Mandarin Chinese (12,000), Mirpur Panjabi (20,000), Moroccan Spoken Arabic (5,800), Northern Kurdish (23,766), Northern Pashto, Parsi (75,000), Portuguese (17,000), Seraiki, Shelta (30,000), Sindhi (25,000), Somali (1,600), Southern Pashto (87,000), Southwestern Caribbean Creole English (170,000), Sylheti (300,000), Tagalog (74,000), Ta'izzi-Adeni Spoken Arabic (29,000), Tamil (40,000), Turkish (60,000), Urdu (400,000), Vietnamese (22,000), Western Farsi (12,000), Western Panjabi (102,500), Yoruba (12,000), Yue Chinese (300,000), people from Ghana, Nigeria, Guyana, West Indies. Information mainly from I. Hancock 1974, 1984, 1986; M. Stephens 1976; R. McCrum, W. Cran, R. MacNeil 1986; B. Comrie 1987. Blind population: 116,414. Deaf population: 909,000 to 3,524,725 (1998). Deaf institutions: 468 in England, 2 in Northern Ireland, 14 in Scotland, 34 in Wales. The number of languages listed for United Kingdom is 18. Of those, 12 are living languages, 2 are second language without mother-tongue speakers, and 4 are extinct. See map on page 845.

Angloromani (English Romani, Romani English, Romanichal, Pogadi Chib, Posh 'N' Posh) [rme] 90,000 in Britain (1990 I. Hancock). Population total all countries: 195,000. England, Wales, Scotland. Also spoken in Australia, South Africa, USA. *Class:* Mixed Language, English-Romani. *Dialects:* Angloromani not inherently intelligible with Welsh Romani, Traveller Swedish, Traveller Norwegian, or Traveller Danish. The grammar is basically English with heavy Romani lexical borrowing. Many dialects. *Lg Use:* It has been spoken in the United Kingdom for 500 years. "The Romanichal population must be considered as being more actively determined to retain the ethnic language than some other British minorities" (I. Hancock).

British Sign Language (BSL) [bfi] 40,000 first-language users (1984 Deuchar), out of 909,000 deaf, of which the majority probably have some degree of sign language competence (1977 Deuchar). United Kingdom including Northern Ireland, Scotland. *Class:* Deaf sign language. *Dialects:* Not inherently intelligible to users of American Sign Language. The deaf community is cohesive, so communication is good despite regional differences. *Lg Use:* Good regional and national organizations for the deaf. Signed interpretation is required in court, and provided in some other situations. Sign language instruction for parents of deaf children. Many sign language classes for hearing people. There is an organization for sign language teachers. There is a committee on national sign language. Sign language was used before 1644. Deaf schools were established in the late 18th century. There is increasing desire to train deaf children in BSL. *Lg Dev:* Films. TV. Videos. Dictionary. Grammar. *Other:* British Signed English is different from American Signed English.

Cornish (Kernowek, Kernewek, Curnoack) [cor] A number of people under 20 years of age are first-language speakers. There are 500 speakers who use Cornish, and about 100 others who speak it fluently (2003). Ethnic population: 468,425 (1991 census). Duchy of Cornwall, southwest England. A few in Canada and Australia. *Class:* Indo-European, Celtic, Insular, Brythonic. *Dialects:* Related to Breton, Welsh, Gaulish (extinct), Irish Gaelic, Manx Gaelic, Scots Gaelic. *Lg Use:* Religious services are still held in Cornish. There are evening classes, correspondence courses, summer camps, children's play groups. There is a Cornish Language Board. It became extinct as a first language in 1777, but is being revived. Some children grow up bilingual in English. *Lg Dev:* Taught in some schools. NT: 2000. *Other:* There are a small number of second-language speakers in Canada and Australia. Christian, secular.

English [eng] 55,000,000 in United Kingdom (1984). 508,000,000 including second-language speakers (1999 WA). Population total all countries: 309,352,280. Also spoken in American Samoa, Andorra, Anguilla, Antigua and Barbuda, Aruba, Australia, Bahamas, Barbados, Belize, Bermuda, Botswana, British Indian Ocean Territory, British Virgin Islands, Brunei, Cambodia, Cameroon, Canada, Cayman Islands, China, Cook Islands, Denmark, Dominica, Dominican Republic, Ecuador, Eritrea, Ethiopia, Falkland Islands, Fiji, Finland, Gambia, Germany, Ghana, Gibraltar, Greece, Grenada, Guadeloupe, Guam, Guyana, Honduras, India, Ireland, Israel, Italy, Jamaica, Japan, Kenya, Kiribati, South Korea, Lebanon, Lesotho, Liberia, Malawi, Malaysia (Peninsular), Malta, Marshall Islands, Mauritius, Mexico, Micronesia, Montserrat, Namibia, Nauru, Netherlands Antilles, New Zealand, Nigeria, Niue, Norfolk Island, Northern Mariana Islands, Norway, Pakistan, Palau, Papua New Guinea, Philippines, Pitcairn, Puerto Rico, Rwanda, Saint Helena, Saint Kitts and Nevis, Saint Lucia, Saint Pierre and Miquelon, Saint Vincent and the Grenadines, Samoa, Saudi Arabia, Seychelles, Sierra Leone, Singapore, Solomon Islands, Somalia, South Africa, Sri Lanka, Suriname, Swaziland, Switzerland, Tanzania, Tokelau, Tonga, Trinidad and Tobago, Turks and Caicos Islands, U.S. Virgin Islands, Uganda, United Arab Emirates, USA, Vanuatu, Venezuela, Zambia, Zimbabwe. *Class:* Indo-European, Germanic, West, English. *Dialects:* Cockney, Scouse, Geordie, West Country, East Anglia, Birmingham (Brummy, Brummie), South Wales, Edinburgh, Belfast, Cornwall, Cumberland, Central Cumberland, Devonshire, East Devonshire, Dorset, Durham, Bolton Lancashire, North Lancashire, Radcliffe Lancashire, Northumberland, Norfolk, Newcastle Northumberland, Tyneside Northumberland, Lowland Scottish, Somerset, Sussex, Westmorland, North Wiltshire, Craven Yorkshire, North Yorkshire, Sheffield Yorkshire, West Yorkshire. Lexical similarity 60% with German, 27% with French, 24% with Russian. *Lg Use:* National language. *Lg Dev:* Dictionary. Grammar. Bible: 1382–2002. *Other:* SVO; prepositions; genitives after noun heads; articles, adjectives, numerals before noun heads; question word initial; word order distinguishes subject, object, indirect objects, given and new information, topic and comment; active and passive; causative; comparative; consonant and vowel clusters; nontonal. Island, plains, hills. Deciduous forest. Christian.

French [fra] 14,000 in England (1976 Stephens). Channel Islands. *Dialects:* Jerriais, Dgernesiais. *Lg Use:* Official language on Channel Islands. French is only spoken by about 11% of the population of Channel Islands, mainly older adults. See main entry under France.

Gaelic, Hiberno-Scottish (Gaoidhealg, Hiberno-Scottish Classical Common Gaelic) [ghc] Extinct. Ireland and Scotland. *Class:* Indo-European, Celtic, Insular, Goidelic. *Lg Dev:* Roman script. Bible: 1690. *Other:* Archaic literary language based on 12th century Irish, formerly used by professional classes in Ireland until the 17th century and Scotland until the 18th century. VSO.

Gaelic, Irish (Irish, Erse, Gaeilge) [gle] 95,000 in United Kingdom (2004). Belfast and counties of Fermanagh and Armagh, Northern Ireland. See main entry under Ireland.

Gaelic, Scottish (Gàidhlig, Gaelic, Scots Gaelic, Albannach Gaidhlig, Erse) [gla] 58,650 in United Kingdom (2003 census). Population total all countries: 62,175. North and central counties of Ross, islands of Hebrides and Skye, Glasgow. Also spoken in Australia, Canada, USA. *Class:* Indo-European, Celtic, Insular, Goidelic. *Dialect:* East Sutherlandshire. Church Gaelic is based on the Perthshire dialect of 200 years ago, and is at a distance from spoken dialects. East Sutherlandshire dialect is so different from other spoken dialects as to be a barrier to communication. *Lg Use:* Books and journals are produced on various topics. Resurgence of interest in Scottish Gaelic in the 1990s has been given a boost by the establishing of Scotland's own Parliament, for the first time in 300 years. In some communities it is primarily used in the home, in church, and for social purposes. In bilingual areas Gaelic usually is first language of instruction for most primary subjects. *Lg Dev:* Literacy rate in first language: 50% (1971 census). Taught in primary schools. Gaelic Medium Education schools have been set up. Newspapers. Radio programs. Bible: 1801–1992. *Other:* The status is rising since the establishment of the Scots Parliament. VSO.

Manx (Gaelg, Gailck, Manx Gaelic) [glv] Extinct. Ethnic population: On the Isle of Man: 77,000 residents (1998 UN). Isle of Man, part of the British Isles, a Crown Dependency, with its own Parliament, laws, currency, and taxation. The United Kingdom represents the Isle of Man at the United Nations. *Class:* Indo-European, Celtic, Insular, Goidelic. *Dialects:* Close to Scottish Gaelic. *Lg Use:* It became extinct in 1974 as a first language. There are efforts to revive it. Second language for several hundred who have mainly learned it as adults. Children are taught it in play-groups. Used for some public functions. *Lg Dev:* Different from Scottish Gaelic orthography. Grammar. Bible: 1773. *Other:* It was supplanted by Manx Vernacular English, which in turn is now being supplanted by other varieties of English. VSO.

Norn [nrn] Extinct. Shetland and Orkney Islands. *Class:* Indo-European, Germanic, North, West Scandinavian.

Lg Use: Became extinct after the islands were ceded to Scotland in the 15th century.

Old Kentish Sign Language [okl] Extinct. Kent. *Class:* Deaf sign language. *Other:* The apparent ancestor of Martha's Vineyard Sign Language.

Polari (Parlare, Parlary, Palarie, Palari, Parlyaree) [pld] *Class:* Unclassified. *Other:* An in-group language among theatrical and circus people. Speakers are gays. Some observers trace its roots to sailors and seafarers, alleging that it derived from a maritime lingua franca. Second language only.

Romani, Vlax (Romenes, Rom, Tsigane) [rmy] 4,100 in United Kingdom (2004). *Dialects:* Kalderash, Lovari. *Other:* Christian. See main entry under Romania.

Romani, Welsh [rmw] England and Wales. *Class:* Indo-European, Indo-Iranian, Indo-Aryan, Central zone, Romani, Northern. *Dialects:* Not inherently intelligible with Angloromani. *Other:* Ethnic groups: Volshanange, Kalá. Christian.

Scots [sco] 100,000 in United Kingdom (1999 Billy Kay). Some population estimates are much higher. Population total all countries: 200,000. All of Scotland except highlands: lowlands: Aberdeen to Ayrshire. Northern Ireland. Also spoken in Ireland. *Class:* Indo-European, Germanic, West, English. *Dialects:* Insular, Northern Scots, Southern Scots, Ulster. Difficult intelligibility among dialects. Northern Scots on the Scottish Islands is considered by some to be a different language (Shetlandic or Orcadian). Lallans is the main literary dialect. Ulster Scots has its own development group. Scots is closest to English and Frisian. *Lg Use:* 1,500,000 speak it as second language. Used with family and friends. All ages. English is considered to be the language of education and religion. *Lg Dev:* Literacy rate in second language: 97% English. Poetry. Magazines. Dictionary. NT: 1901–1984. *Other:* SVO; prepositions; genitives, articles, adjectives, numerals before noun heads; relatives without noun heads; question word initial; 2 prefixes, 1 suffix; word order distinguishes subjects, objects, indirect objects, given and new information, topic and comment; affixes indicate genitive case of noun phrase; passives; comparatives; CVC; nontonal. Christian.

Traveller Scottish (Scottish Cant, Scottish Traveller Cant) [trl] 4,000 in Scotland. Also spoken in Australia, USA. *Class:* Unclassified. *Other:* A blend language of High Romani and Elizabethan Cant. The earliest texts go back to the sixteenth century. Not Gypsies. Nomadic in Scotland. In USA they travel but have a fixed base.

Welsh (Cymraeg) [cym] 508,098 in United Kingdom (1991 census). Out of 575,102 speakers in 1971, it included 32,700 monolinguals, 542,402 bilinguals (1971 census). Population total all countries: 536,258. Northern, western, and southern Wales. Also spoken in Argentina, Canada. *Class:* Indo-European, Celtic, Insular, Brythonic. *Dialects:* Northern Welsh, Southern Welsh, Patagonian Welsh. *Lg Use:* Official language. 19% of the Welsh population speak the language, and 33% are able to understand it (1998). Literature being produced. The Royal National Eisteddfod meets annually. 44,600 between 5 and 9 years old speak Welsh, 47,100 between 10 and 14 years old (1991). 88% of those questioned believe they should be proud of Welsh, and that it should be treated equally with English. There is an increase in the number of parents choosing a Welsh-medium education for their children. *Lg Dev:* 525 Welsh primary and secondary schools provide Welsh-medium education to over 82,000 children (1999). Compulsory in most Welsh schools. Magazines. Radio programs. TV. Dictionary. Grammar. Bible: 1588–1988. *Other:* VSO.

Yinglish [yib] *Lg Use:* Speakers also use English. *Other:* Professor Joshua A. Fishman says, "'Yinglish' is a variety of English influenced by Yiddish (lexically, particularly, but also grammatically and phonetically). Any good English dictionary will now include 50–100 (or more) 'borrowings from Yiddish' (= Yinglish)....Since the variety is only used...(by speakers who can always speak 'proper English') Yinglish is never a first language acquired by the usual process of intergenerational transmission. French, Spanish, and Russian counterparts (also a Hebrew counterpart) also exist, but are more restricted in nature, both in size as well as in availability to non-Jews." Jewish. Second language only. See main entry under USA.

Vatican State

The Holy See. 480 (1998 UN). National or official language: Latin. Information mainly from B. Comrie 1987. The number of languages listed for Vatican State is 3. Of those, 1 is a living language and 2 are second language without mother-tongue speakers.

Italian [ita] 1,000 in Vatican State (2004). See main entry under Italy.

Latin (Latina) [lat] *Class:* Indo-European, Italic, Latino-Faliscan. *Lg Use:* National language. Used in Roman Catholic liturgy. There is an effort to revive it. The Vatican Latin Foundation was established in 1976. *Lg Dev:* Radio programs. Dictionary. Bible: 1385–1906. *Other:* Second language only.

Monastic Sign Language [mzg] Monastic communities, especially in Europe. *Class:* Sign language. *Dialects:* Anglo-Saxon Monastic Sign Language, Augustinian Sign Language, Benedictine Sign Language, Cistercian Sign Language, Trappist Sign Language. *Lg Use:* A second-language means of communicating while maintaining vows of silence. Not a deaf sign language. *Other:* Second language only.

Pacific

American Samoa

Territory of American Samoa. 57,902. National or official language: English. A USA territory. 7 islands: Tutuila, Aunuu, Manua Islands (Ta'u, Olosega, Ofu), Rose, Swains. Literacy rate: 98%. Also includes Japanese (1,500), Korean, Tokelauan (100), Tongan (800). Information mainly from S. Wurm and S. Hattori 1981; N. Besnier OIEL 1992. The number of languages listed for American Samoa is 2. Of those, both are living languages.

English [eng] 1,248 in American Samoa, foreign born (1970 census). *Lg Use:* Official language. 15,050 mainly second-language speakers. See main entry under United Kingdom.

Samoan [smo] 56,700 in American Samoa (1999). *Lg Use:* Speakers in American Samoa are highly bilingual in English. *Other:* Fishermen; canning. Christian. See main entry under Samoa.

Australia

Commonwealth of Australia. 19,913,144. 170,000 are of Aboriginal descent, of whom 47,000 have some knowledge of an Aboriginal language. National or official language: English. Includes Cocos Islands (569 in 1981), Christmas Island (3,000 in 1983), and Norfolk Island (1,800 in 1985). Literacy rate: 99%. Also includes Adyghe, Afrikaans (12,655), Assyrian Neo-Aramaic (30,000), Basque, Chaldean Neo-Aramaic, Eastern Yiddish, Estonian, Fijian Hindustani, Greek (106,677), Hebrew, Hungarian (5,764), Indo-Portuguese, Italian (500,000), Japanese (12,000), Korean (37,000), Lao, Latvian (25,000), Lithuanian (10,000), Maltese, Mambae, Northern Kurdish (11,000), Northern Uzbek, Nung, Piemontese, Polish (13,782), Pukapuka (140), Romanian, Scottish Gaelic, Senaya, Serbian (38,753), Slovenian, Spanish, Standard German (135,000), Sylheti, Tai Dam, Tongan, Traveller Scottish, Turkish (40,000), Turoyo (2,000), Unserdeutsch, Uyghur, Vietnamese (35,000), Western Cham, Western Farsi (11,000), Yue Chinese, Malay and Indonesian (35,000), Arabic (250,000), Chinese (190,000), many other languages of Europe. Information mainly from W. J. and L. F. Oates 1970; S.

Wurm and S. Hattori 1981; P. Black 1983; J. Hudson 1987; B. Waters 1989; A. Schmidt 1990. Blind population: 28,000. Deaf population: 90,000 to 196,008 (1998). Deaf institutions: 116. The number of languages listed for Australia is 273. Of those, 231 are living languages, 3 are second language without mother-tongue speakers, and 39 are extinct. See maps beginning on page 854.

Adynyamathanha (Wailpi, Wailbi, Waljbi, Wipie, Ad'n'amadana, Anjimatana, Anjiwatana, Archualda, Benbakanjamata, Binbarnja, Gadjnjamada, Jandali, Kanjimata, Keydnjmarda, Mardala, Nimalda, Nuralda, Unyamootha, Umbertana) [adt] 20 (1990 Schmidt). South Australia, Flinders Ranges area, Nepabunna. *Class:* Australian, Pama-Nyungan, South-West, Yura. *Dialects:* Related to Guyani, Banggarla, Nugunu, and Narungga, which may be extinct. *Lg Use:* Speakers also use English. *Lg Dev:* Grammar. *Other:* Nearly extinct.

Aghu Tharnggalu (Kuku-Mini, Ikarranggali) [ggr] Extinct. Queensland, Cape York Peninsula, Laura. *Class:* Australian, Pama-Nyungan, Paman, Rarmul Pama.

Alawa (Kallana, Leealowa) [alh] 17 to 20 (1991 M. Sharpe). There are 4 partial first-language speakers. Roper River, Arnhem Land, Northern Territory. *Class:* Australian, Gunwingguan, Maran, Alawic. *Lg Use:* Young people speak Kriol and understand only a little Alawa. All speakers use Kriol. *Lg Dev:* Dictionary. Grammar. *Other:* Nearly extinct.

Alngith [aid] 3 (1981 Wurm and Hattori). Queensland, northeast Cape York Peninsula just north of Weipa. *Class:* Australian, Pama-Nyungan, Paman, Northern Pama. *Other:* Nearly extinct.

Alyawarr (Alyawarra, Alyawarre, Aljawara, Iliaura, Yowera) [aly] 1,500 (1991 Hoogenrad). Sandover and Tennant Creek areas, Northern Territory and Queensland. *Class:* Australian, Pama-Nyungan, Arandic. *Dialects:* Related to Arrernte, Arrernte Akerre, Anmatyerre, Kaytetye. *Lg Use:* Speakers have low proficiency in English. *Lg Dev:* Literacy rate in second language: 40%. Roman script. Dictionary. Grammar. Bible portions: 1996–2002.

Amarag (Wureidbug, Amurag) [amg] 5. Goulburn Island, Oenpelli, Northern Territory. *Class:* Australian,

Yiwaidjan, Amaragic. *Lg Use:* May be extinct (Black 1983). *Other:* Nearly extinct.

Ami (Ame, Amijangal) [amy] 30 to 35 (1983 Black). Northern Territory, Coast along Anson Bay, southwest of Darwin. *Class:* Australian, Daly, Bringen-Wagaydy, Wagaydy. *Dialects:* May be intelligible with Wadjiginy. *Lg Use:* Speakers also use Kriol. *Other:* Nearly extinct.

Andegerebinha (Andigibinha, Antekerrepinhe) [adg] 10 (1981 Wurm and Hattori). Northern Territory, Hay River, Pituri Creek area, east of Alyawarra. *Class:* Australian, Pama-Nyungan, Arandic. *Other:* Nearly extinct.

Angloromani (Romanichal, English Romani, Pogadi Chib) [rme] 5,000 in Australia (1985). See main entry under United Kingdom.

Anindilyakwa (Aninhdhilyagwa, Andiljangwa, Andilyaugwa, Enindiljaugwa, Ingura, Wanindilyaugwa, Groote Eylandt, Enindhilyagwa) [aoi] 1,000 (1983 Black). Groote Eylandt, Northern Territory, Gulf of Carpenteria. *Class:* Australian, Gunwingguan, Enindhilyagwa. *Lg Use:* Most young people also use English. *Lg Dev:* Dictionary. Grammar. Bible portions: 1976–1993. *Other:* SOV. Coastal, island. Scrub forest. Sea level to 200 meters. Hunter-gatherers traditionally.

Anmatyerre (Anmatjirra) [amx] 800 (1983 Black). Northern Territory, Mt. Allen, Northwest Alice Springs Region. *Class:* Australian, Pama-Nyungan, Arandic. *Dialect:* Eastern Anmatyerre, Western Anmatyerre (Kalenthelkwe, Kelenthwelkere, Kelentheyewelrere). *Lg Dev:* Dictionary. *Other:* Traditional religion, Christian.

Antakarinya (Andagarinya) [ant] 50 (1981 Wurm and Hattori). Northeast area of South Australia. *Class:* Australian, Pama-Nyungan, South-West, Wati. *Dialects:* Closest to Warnman and Western Desert Language. *Lg Use:* People generally speak Kriol. *Other:* Nearly extinct.

Arabana [ard] 8 (1981 Wurm and Hattori). South Australia, west side of Lake Eyre to Stuart Range, Maree, Port Augusta. *Class:* Australian, Pama-Nyungan, Karnic, Palku. *Lg Dev:* Dictionary. Grammar. *Other:* Nearly extinct.

Areba [aea] 2 (1981 Wurm and Hattori). Queensland, southwestern Cape York Peninsula, Bilbert River, northeast of Normanton. *Class:* Australian, Pama-Nyungan, Paman, Norman Pama. *Other:* Nearly extinct.

Arrarnta, Western (Aranda, Arunta) [are] 1,000 (1981 Wurm and Hattori). Northern Territory, Alice Springs area, Hermannsburg. *Class:* Australian, Pama-Nyungan, Arandic. *Dialects:* Western Aranda, Akerre (Akara), Southern Aranda. Close to Alyawarr and Gaididj. Wurm and Hattori (1981) and Ruhlen (1987) treat Western Arrarnta and Eastern Arrernte as separate languages. *Lg Use:* Southern Aranda is nearly extinct. *Lg Dev:* Dictionary. Grammar. NT: 1956. *Other:* SOV. Plains. Savannah. Hunter-gatherers.

Arrernte, Eastern (Eastern Aranda, Arunta) [aer] 2,175 (2000 WCD). Northern Territory, Alice Springs area (Mparntwe), Santa Teresa (Ltyentye Apurte), Alcoota, Harts Range (Artetyerre), Bonya (Uthipe Atherre), Amoonguna (Amwengkwerne). *Class:* Australian, Pama-Nyungan, Arandic. *Dialects:* Mparntwe Arrernte, Ikngerripenhe, Akarre, Antekerrepenh. Related to Mparntwe Arrernte, Alyawarr, Arrernte Akarre, Anmatyerre, Kaytetye, Western Arrarnta. *Lg Use:* English bilingual program in operation at a school at Santa Teresa. *Lg Dev:* Literacy rate in first language: 10%. Literacy rate in second language: 50%. Radio programs. TV. Videos. Dictionary. Grammar. *Other:* SOV. Plains. Savannah. Hunter-gatherers.

Atampaya [amz] 4 (1981 Wurm and Hattori). Queensland, extreme northern Cape York Peninsula, Eliot Creek. *Class:* Australian, Pama-Nyungan, Paman, Northern Pama. *Other:* Nearly extinct.

Australian Aborigines Sign Language [asw] Southern, central, and western desert regions, coastal Arnhem Land, some islands of north coast, western side of Cape York Peninsula, islands of Torres Strait. *Class:* Sign language. *Dialects:* Not related to Australian Sign Language. *Lg Use:* Used by hearing Aborigines as an alternate form of communication with speakers of other languages. Other nondeaf sign languages are used by some groups, such as Aranda, Warlpiri, Warumungu, during periods of mourning or hunting. Several such sign languages are also used by deaf persons. *Other:* Second language only.

Australian Sign Language (Auslan) [asf] 14,000 (1991 Hyde and Power). *Class:* Deaf sign language. *Dialects:* Related to British Sign Language, with influences also from Irish and American sign languages. *Lg Use:* Some signed interpretation in court, for college students, at important public events. Australian Signed English is distinct from Australian Sign Language. It is a manual system for English spelling, used by hearing people for communication with the deaf. It is used in teaching the deaf, and officially so in New South Wales. *Lg Dev:* Taught in primary schools. Films. TV. Videos. Dictionary. Grammar. Bible portions: 1999–2002. *Other:* The earliest schools for the deaf were established by British deaf immigrants in 1860. Many agencies for the deaf. There is sign language instruction for parents of deaf children. There is a committee on national sign language.

Awabakal (Awabagal) [awk] Extinct. Lake Macquarie, south from Newcastle, New South Wales. *Class:* Australian, Pama-Nyungan, Worimi. *Dialects:* Awabagal, Cameeragal, Wonarua. *Lg Dev:* Bible portions: 1891.

Ayabadhu [ayd] 6 (1981 Wurm and Hattori). Queensland, Cape York Peninsula, north of the Coleman River, south of Coen. *Class:* Australian, Pama-Nyungan, Paman, Middle Pama. *Other:* Nearly extinct.

Badimaya (Widimaya, Parti-Maya) [bia] 20 (1966 Voegelin and Voegelin). Western Australia, northeast of Moora to south of Cue; east to Paynes Find; west to Mullewa. *Class:* Australian, Pama-Nyungan, South-West, Wadjari. *Dialects:* Related to Wajarri. *Lg Use:* Linguists at Yamaji Language Centre working on a draft dictionary and wordlist. *Other:* Nearly extinct.

Bandjalang (Bandjelang, Bogganger, Bundala, Gidabal, Yugumbe) [bdy] 10 (1983 R. M. W. Dixon). New South Wales, northeastern, Woodenbong. *Class:* Australian, Pama-Nyungan, Bandjalangic. *Dialects:* Gidabal (Gidhabal), Yugumbir. *Lg Use:* All speakers also use English. *Lg Dev:* Dictionary. Bible portions. *Other:* Nearly extinct.

Bandjigali (Baarrundji, Barindji, Marrawarra, Maruara) [bjd] 1 (1981 Wurm and Hattori). New South Wales, northwest, north, and west of White Cliffs. *Class:* Australian, Pama-Nyungan, Baagandji. *Other:* Nearly extinct.

Banggarla (Bangala, Banggala, Bahanga-La, Barngarla, Bungeha, Bungela, Pangkala, Pakarla, Pankalla, Parnkala, Parnkalla, Punkalla, Kortabina) [bjb] Extinct. South Australia, Port Lincoln to the head of Spencer Gulf. *Class:* Australian, Pama-Nyungan, South-West, Yura.

Bardi (Baadi, Bard, Baardi, Badi) [bcj] 20 (1999 Claire Bowern). Population includes 16 Bardi, 3 Jawi. One Arm Point Aboriginal Community, Lombadina Aboriginal Community, Broome, Derby, Western Kimberley Region Western Australia. *Class:* Australian, Nyulnyulan. *Dialects:* Bardi, Jawi. Intelligibility is adequate between Bardi and Jawi dialects. Related to Nyikina, Warwa, Djawi, Nimanbur, Nyulnyul, Dyaberdyaber, Dyugun, Yawuru. *Lg Use:* Children and adolescents can understand Bardi, but never seem to speak it. They use English as their language. Speakers are over 40 years old.

No monolinguals. English and Kriol are the second languages. English is generally spoken in the community, Kriol with Aboriginals from farther east. *Lg Dev:* Literacy rate in second language: 60% in English. There is a feeling that English or Bardi are the languages that should be written, not Kriol. There is a government program in the primary school. Dictionary. Grammar. *Other:* Christian. Nearly extinct.

Barrow Point [bpt] 1 (1981 Wurm and Hattori). Queensland, Cape York Peninsula, Barrow Point on Princess Charlotte Bay and inland. *Class:* Australian, Pama-Nyungan, Guugu Yimidhirr. *Other:* Nearly extinct.

Bayali (Biyali, Darambal, Orambul, Charumbul, Darawal, Darumbal, Kooinmarburra, Kuinmurbara, Ningebal, Tarumbal, Tharumbal, Urambal, Warabal, Yetimarala) [bjy] Extinct. Queensland, from the mouth of the Fitzroy River inland to Boomer Range at Marlborough, Yeppon, Yamba, and Rockhampton. *Class:* Australian, Pama-Nyungan, Waka-Kabic, Kingkel.

Bayungu (Baiong, Baiung, Biong, Bajungu, Pajungu, Payungu, Giong, Mulgarnoo) [bxj] 6 (1981 Wurm and Hattori). Western Australia, lower Lyndon and Minilya rivers, West Pilbara. *Class:* Australian, Pama-Nyungan, South-West, Kanyara. *Lg Dev:* Dictionary. *Other:* Nearly extinct.

Bidyara (Bidjara, Bitjara, Bithara) [bym] 20 (1981 Wurm and Hattori). Queensland, between Tambo and Augathella, Warrego River and Langlo River. *Class:* Australian, Pama-Nyungan, Maric. *Lg Use:* Speakers are shifting to English. *Other:* Ruhlen (1987) says it is extinct. Nearly extinct.

Biri (Wirri) [bzr] Extinct. Queensland southeast of Charters Towers. *Class:* Australian, Pama-Nyungan, Maric. *Lg Dev:* Grammar.

Broome Pearling Lugger Pidgin (Broom Creole, Koepang Talk, Malay Talk, Japanese Pidgin English) [bpl] 40 speakers. Broome, Lombardinie, Beagle Bay, La Grange, One Arm Point, Derby. *Class:* Pidgin, Malay based. *Lg Use:* Used as a lingua franca on pearling boats to communicate between Malays, Japanese, Chinese, and Aborigines. *Other:* Some Japanese and Aboriginal creole or pidgin English words. Second language only.

Bunaba (Punapa, Bunuba) [bck] 50 to 100 (1990 Schmidt). Fitzroy Crossing area, Western Australia. *Class:* Australian, Bunaban. *Lg Use:* Speakers are shifting to Kriol. Only older adults. Children only know a few words; their first language is Kriol (Hudson 1987:16). *Lg Dev:* Dictionary. Grammar.

Burarra (Anbarra, Burada, Bureda, Burera, Gidjingaliya Gujingalia, Gujalabiya, Gun-Guragone, Barera, Bawera, Jikai, Tchikai) [bvr] 400 to 600 (1990 Schmidt). Maningrida, Arnhem Land, Northern Territory. *Class:* Australian, Gunwingguan, Burarran. *Dialects:* Gunardba (Gun-nartpa) is a related language which may be extinct, or may be an alternate name. *Lg Dev:* Dictionary. Grammar. NT: 1991. *Other:* SOV. Coastal. Scrub forest. Hunter-gatherers.

Burduna (Buduna, Boordoona, Budina, Budoona, Purduna, Pinneegooroo, Poodena, Poordoona, Purduma) [bxn] 3 (1981 Wurm and Hattori). Henry and upper Lyndon rivers. *Class:* Australian, Pama-Nyungan, South-West, Kanyara. *Other:* Nearly extinct.

Dagoman [dgn] Extinct. Northern Territory. *Class:* Australian, Gunwingguan, Yangmanic. *Dialects:* Was very close to Wardaman.

Darling (Kula, Baagandji, Southern Baagandji) [drl] 5. Darling River Basin, New South Wales. *Class:* Australian, Pama-Nyungan, Baagandji. *Dialects:* Kula, Wiljakali (Wilyagali), Bagundji (Baagandji, Bagandji). Bagundji dialect is widely understood by others (1970 Oates). *Other:* Nearly extinct.

Dayi (Dhay'yi, Dha'i) [dax] 200 (1983 Black). Arnhem Land, Roper River, Yirrkala, Lake Evella, Galiwinku, Numbulwam, Northern Territory. *Class:* Australian, Pama-Nyungan, Yuulngu, Dhuwal. *Dialects:* Dhalwangu, Djarrwark. *Lg Use:* The clans are active, but the position of the language is weak because of scattering and children speaking other languages, such as Djambarrpuyngu. Speakers also use Djambarrpuyngu, Gumatj, Dhuwal, and English.

Dhalandji (Talandji, Dalandji, Dalendi, Djalendi, Tallainga, Talandi, Talaindji, Talangee, Taloinga, Thalanyji, Thalantji) [dhl] 20 (1981 Wurm and Hattori). Western Australia, head of Exmouth Gulf, inland to Ashburton River, West Pilbara. *Class:* Australian, Pama-Nyungan, South-West, Dhalandji. *Lg Use:* Speakers are reported to be highly bilingual in English. *Lg Dev:* Dictionary. *Other:* Nearly extinct.

Dhangu (Dangu, Dhangu'mi, Djangu) [dhg] 350 (1983 Black). Population includes 200 in Gaalpu, 150 in Wangurri. Elcho Island, Arnhem Land, Northern Territory. *Class:* Australian, Pama-Nyungan, Yuulngu, Dhangu. *Dialects:* Dhangu-Djangu, Gaalpu (Kalbu), Wangurri, Ngaymil, Rirratjingu, Golumala. *Lg Use:* Speakers also use Djambarrpuyngu. *Lg Dev:* Bible portions: 1977. *Other:* Yolngu-Matha means 'people language'. SVO, SOV if O is a pronoun or deictic. Coastal. Scrub forest. Hunter-gatherers; fishermen.

Dhargari (Targari, Dal'gari, Tarkarri, Thargari, Tharrgari, Tharrkari) [dhr] 6 (1981 Wurm and Hattori). Western Australia, Kennedy Range, upper Minilya and lower Lyons rivers, West Pilbara. *Class:* Australian, Pama-Nyungan, South-West, Inland Ngayarda. *Lg Dev:* Dictionary. *Other:* Ruhlen classifies it in a separate Mantharda group. Nearly extinct.

Dhurga (Dhu'rga, Durga, Thoorga, Tharumba) [dhu] Extinct. New South Wales, Bermagui to Jervis Bay. *Class:* Australian, Pama-Nyungan, Yuin.

Dhuwal (Duala, Dual, Wulamba) [duj] 500 (1983 Black). Population includes 200 Djapu, 160 Liyagalawumirr (clan names). Roper River, Arnhem Land, Northern Territory. *Class:* Australian, Pama-Nyungan, Yuulngu, Dhuwal. *Dialects:* Dhuwaya, Dhuwal, Liyagalawumirr, Marrangu, Marrakulu, Djapu, Liyagalawumirr, Datiwuy. *Lg Use:* Speakers also use Djambarrpuyngu. *Lg Dev:* Dictionary. Grammar.

Dieri (Diyari) [dif] Extinct. South Australia, Leigh Creek. *Class:* Australian, Pama-Nyungan, Karnic, Karna. *Dialects:* Related to Garuwali, Marrula, Midhaga, Yarluyandi, all of which may be extinct. *Lg Dev:* Grammar. NT: 1897.

Dirari (Dhirari) [dit] 1 (1981 Wurm and Hattori). South Australia, east of Lake Eyre North. *Class:* Australian, Pama-Nyungan, Karnic, Karna. *Other:* Nearly extinct.

Djambarrpuyngu (Djambarbwingu, Jambapuing, Jambapuingo) [djr] 450 (1983 Black). Elcho Island, Northern Territory. *Class:* Australian, Pama-Nyungan, Yuulngu, Dhuwal. *Lg Use:* Lingua franca for 2,000 (1990 UBS). *Lg Dev:* Dictionary. Grammar. Bible portions: 1977–1993.

Djamindjung (Jaminjung) [djd] 30 (1990 Schmidt). Victoria River, Northern Territory. *Class:* Australian, Djamindjungan. *Dialect:* Ngaliwuru (Ngaliwerra). Reports indicate that Djamindjung and Ngaliwuru are so close as to be one language; only some older adults can distinguish the difference. *Lg Use:* No monolinguals. Ngarinman or Kriol are the second languages. *Lg Dev:* Dictionary. Grammar. *Other:* Nearly extinct.

Djangun (Jangun Djanggun, Adho-Adhom, Butju, Chungki, Chunkumberries, Chunkunburra, Koko-Mudju, Mutyu, Ngaigungo, Koko-Tyankun) [djf] 1 (1981 Wurm and Hattori). Queensland, from Mt. Mulligan south to

Alma-den, east to Dimbula, west to Mungana. *Class:* Australian, Pama-Nyungan, Yalandyic. *Other:* Nearly extinct.

Djauan (Jawan, Adowen, Kumertuo, Jawony, Jawoyn) [djn] 100 (1983 Black). Bamyili settlement, Northern Territory, and Katherine. *Class:* Australian, Gunwingguan, Djauanic. *Lg Use:* Used only rarely by people over 50 years of age. Speakers have low proficiency in English, some also use Ngalkbun or Kriol. All education is in Kriol and English. *Lg Dev:* Dictionary. Grammar.

Djawi [djw] 1 (1981 Wurm and Hattori). Western Australia, islands from King Sound to Brunswick Bay. *Class:* Australian, Nyulnyulan. *Other:* Nearly extinct.

Djeebbana (Ndjébbana, Gunavidji) [djj] 100. West Arnhem Land, north coast around Maningrida. *Class:* Australian, Gunwinngguan, Burarran. *Dialects:* Not closely related to other languages. *Lg Use:* 100 partial second-language speakers (1991). Most speakers also speak Gunwinggu and another Burarran language. *Lg Dev:* Dictionary. Grammar. *Other:* Gunavidji is the name of the people, Ndjébbana of the language. Different from Gunawitji, an alternate name for Gunwinggu.

Djinang (Jandijinung) [dji] 250 (1982 SIL). Ramingining, Goyder, and Blyth rivers, Arnhem Land, Northern Territory. *Class:* Australian, Pama-Nyungan, Yuulngu, Djinang. *Dialects:* Djadiwitjibi, Mildjingi, Wulaki, Balurbi, Murrungun, Manyarring. *Lg Use:* There are varying degrees of bilingualism in Ganalbingu (Djinba dialect), Gupapuyngu, Djambarrpuyngu, Dhuwal, or Dhuwala. There is limited use of English. Wulaki speakers also use Burarra. *Lg Dev:* Dictionary. Grammar. Bible portions: 1985–1987. *Other:* Speakers intermarry with the Djinba. Coastal, riverine. Scrub forest. Hunter-gatherers (formerly).

Djinba [djb] 60 to 90 (1989 Waters). Population includes 70 Ganalbingu (1983 Black). Dabi is nearly extinct (1991 SIL). Ngangalala, Arnhem Land, Northern Territory, southeast adjoining Djinang area. *Class:* Australian, Pama-Nyungan, Yuulngu, Djinang. *Dialects:* Ganalbingu, Dabi, Mandjalpingu. Lexical similarity 60% with Djinang. *Lg Use:* Some Ritarungo use this as second language. Some use Djinang as second language, some Djambarrpuyngu. *Other:* Speakers intermarry with the Djinang. Riverine. Scrub forest.

Djingili (Djingulu, Jingali, Tjingilu, Chingalee, Djingila, Lee, Chunguloo, Tchingalee, Jingulu) [jig] 10 (1997). Newcastle Waters, Ash Burton Range area, Elliott, Northern Territory, Elsey Station. *Class:* Australian, West Barkly. *Lg Use:* Speakers are shifting to Kriol. *Lg Dev:* Dictionary. Grammar. *Other:* Nearly extinct.

Djiwarli (Djwarli, Tjiwarli, Thiin) [djl] 1 (1981 Wurm and Hattori). Western Australia, northwest, north of Mount Augustus. *Class:* Australian, Pama-Nyungan, South-West, Inland Ngayarda. *Other:* Ruhlen (1987) classifies it in a separate Mantharda group. Nearly extinct.

Dyaabugay (Dyabugay, Tjapukai, Bulum-Bulum, Check-Cull, Chewlie, Djabugai, Hileman, Kodgotto, Kikonjunkulu, Kokonyungalo, Koko-Tjumbundji, Ngarlkajie, Orlow, Tjabakai-Thandji, Tjabogaijanji, Tjankir, Tjankun, Tjapunkandji, Tjunbundji) [dyy] 3 (1981 Wurm and Hattori). Queensland, Barron River from south of Mareeba to Kuranda, north to Port Douglas on a plateau. *Class:* Australian, Pama-Nyungan, Yidinic. *Dialects:* Njakali (Nyakali, Nyagali), Dyaabugay, Gulay. *Lg Dev:* Dictionary. *Other:* Nearly extinct.

Dyaberdyaber (Jabirr-Jabirr) [dyb] 3 (1981 Wurm and Hattori). Western Australia, coast south of Beagle Bay and inland. *Class:* Australian, Nyulnyulan. *Other:* Nearly extinct.

Dyangadi (Djan-Gadi, Dainggati, Boorkutti, Burgadi, Dangadi, Dangati, Danggadi, Danggetti, Ghangatty,

Tangetti, Thangatti, Thangatty) [dyn] 5 (1981 Wurm and Hattori). New South Wales, Kempsey area, Armidale, Macleay River. *Class:* Australian, Pama-Nyungan, Dyangadi. *Other:* Ruhlen (1987) says it is extinct. Nearly extinct.

Dyirbal (Djirubal) [dbl] 40 to 50 (1983 R. M. W. Dixon). Northeast Queensland, Herberton south to headwaters of Herbert River, to Cashmere, at Ravenshoe, Millaa Millaa, and Woodleigh, east to Tully Falls. *Class:* Australian, Pama-Nyungan, Dyirbalic. *Dialects:* Dyiru, Girramay (Keramai), Gulnguy (Gulngay), Mamu, Ngadjan (Ngatjan). *Lg Dev:* Dictionary. Grammar. *Other:* Nearly extinct.

Dyugun (Jukun) [dyd] 2 (1981 Wurm and Hattori). Western Australia, coast around Broome and inland. *Class:* Australian, Nyulnyulan. *Other:* Nearly extinct.

English [eng] 15,682,000 in Australia (1987). *Dialect:* Australian Standard English, Aboriginal English, Neo-Nyungar (Noonga, Noongar, Noogar). *Lg Use:* National language. *Other:* Minor regional dialect differences. Neo-Nyungar is the community dialect of the Nyungar people. See main entry under United Kingdom.

Erre (Ere, Ari) [err] 1 (1981 Wurm and Hattori). Northern Territory, Red Lily area west of Oenpelli; around East Alligator River, Mt. Howship. *Class:* Australian, Giimbiyu. *Other:* Nearly extinct.

Flinders Island (Yalgawarra) [fln] 3 (1981 Wurm and Hattori). Queensland, Cape York Peninsula, Flinders Island, Princess Charlotte Bay. *Class:* Australian, Pama-Nyungan, Flinders Island. *Other:* Nearly extinct.

Gadjerawang (Gadjerong, Kajirrawung) [gdh] 3 (1981 Wurm and Hattori). Western Australia and Northern Territory, north coast from Wyndham to mouth of Victoria River and inland. *Class:* Australian, Djeragan. *Other:* Nearly extinct.

Gagadu (Gaagudju, Kakdjuan, Kakdju, Kakadu, Abdedal, Abiddul, Kakakta) [gbu] 6 (1981 Wurm and Hattori). Northern Territory, Oenpelli. *Class:* Australian, Gunwinngguan, Gagudjuan. *Lg Use:* All also use another Aboriginal language. *Lg Dev:* Dictionary. Grammar. *Other:* Nearly extinct.

Gambera (Gamberre, Gambre, Gamgre, Guwan, Kambera) [gma] 6 (1981 Wurm and Hattori). Western Australia, Admiralty Gulf, far northern Kimberleys area. *Class:* Australian, Wororan. *Other:* Nearly extinct.

Gamilaraay (Camileroi, Gamilaroi, Kamilaroi) [kld] 3 (1997 Coonabarabran Public School). Barwon, Bundarra, Balonne rivers, Liverpool Plains and upper Hunter River, central northern New South Wales. *Class:* Australian, Pama-Nyungan, Wiradhuric. *Lg Use:* Members of one family still speak the language and teach in schools as community visitors. *Lg Dev:* Dictionary. *Other:* Nearly extinct.

Ganggalida (Kangkalita, Ganggalita, Jugula, Jakula, Yukala, Yukulta, Yugulda, Yokula) [gcd] 5 (1981 Wurm and Hattori). Near Bourketown, Queensland. *Class:* Australian, Pama-Nyungan, Tangic. *Dialects:* Kangkalita, Nguburindi. *Lg Use:* All speakers are older adults. *Lg Dev:* Dictionary. Grammar. *Other:* Nearly extinct.

Gangulu [gnl] Extinct. Queensland around Isaac River, west of Marlborough. *Class:* Australian, Pama-Nyungan, Maric.

Garawa (Karawa, Leearrawa, Gaarwa, Garrwa) [gbc] 200 (1990 Schmidt). There may be 10 speakers of the Wanji dialect (2000 Nick Adams). Borroloola, Northern Territory and Doomadgee, Queensland. Waanyi were originally in North Australia. *Class:* Australian, Garawan. *Dialect:* Wanji (Wainyi, Waanyi). *Lg Use:* Speakers also use Kriol. *Lg Dev:* Dictionary. Grammar. Bible portions: 1983. *Other:* Speakers intermarry with the Yanyuwa.

Garig-Ilgar [ilg] 4 (2003 N. Evans). Population includes 3 Ilgar, 1 Garig. Mainland of Cobourg Peninsula, around

Port Essington, Northern Territory. *Class:* Australian, Yiwaidjan, Yiwaidjic. *Dialects:* Ilgar, Garig. *Other:* Nearly extinct.

Giyug [giy] 2 (1981 Wurm and Hattori). Peron Islands in Anson Bay, southwest of Darwin. *Class:* Australian, Daly, Bringen-Wagaydy, Wagaydy. *Other:* Nearly extinct.

Gooniyandi (Guniandi, Guniandi, Gunian, Kunian, Kuniyan, Guniyan, Guniyn, Kunan, Koneyandi, Konejandi) [gni] 100 (1990 Schmidt). Gogo, Fossil Downs, Louisa, and Margaret River stations, Western Australia. *Class:* Australian, Bunaban. *Lg Use:* Peile says it is nearly extinct. Speakers are shifting to Kriol. *Lg Dev:* Dictionary. Grammar. *Other:* Nearly extinct.

Gudanji (Kurdanji, Ngarnga) [nji] 3 (1981 Wurm and Hattori). Northern Territory, Barkly Tableland, northeast of Lake Woods, Tennant Creek, Elliott, and Borroloola. *Class:* Australian, West Barkly. *Dialects:* Binbinka, Ngarnga. *Other:* Binbinka possibly extinct. Nearly extinct.

Gugadj [ggd] 1 (1981 Wurm and Hattori). Queensland, north coast from west of Karumba inland on Norman River. *Class:* Australian, Pama-Nyungan, Paman, Flinders Pama. *Other:* Nearly extinct.

Gugu Badhun [gdc] 2 (1981 Wurm and Hattori). Queensland, west of Ingham and Abergowrie almost to Einasleigh. *Class:* Australian, Pama-Nyungan, Maric. *Other:* Nearly extinct.

Gugu Warra (Guguwarra, Kuku-Wara) [wrw] Extinct. Queensland, Cape York Peninsula, west bank of Normanby River. *Class:* Australian, Pama-Nyungan, Paman, Mbariman.

Gugubera (Kukubera, Koko Bera, Koko Pera, Berang, Paperyn, Kok Kaber) [kkp] 15 (1991 SIL). Ethnic population: 50 (1990 Schmidt). Around the mouth of Mission River, Mitchell River, Queensland. *Class:* Australian, Pama-Nyungan, Paman, Coastal Pama. *Lg Use:* Most use Kunjen as second language, some use Torres Strait Creole. The ethnic group has poor comprehension of English. *Other:* Nearly extinct.

Guguyimidjir (Kukuyimidir, Koko Imudji, Gugu Yimijir, Guugu Yimithirr, Gugu-Yimidhirr) [kky] 20 to 30 (1991 Wayne Rosendale). 200 to 300 know and understand the language but prefer English. Ethnic population: 400 (1990 Schmidt). Hopevale, Queensland. *Class:* Australian, Pama-Nyungan, Guugu-Yimidhirr. *Lg Use:* Children understand Guguyimidjir, but speak only a little, and mainly speak Aboriginal English. *Lg Dev:* Dictionary. Grammar. Bible portions: 1940. *Other:* Nearly extinct.

Gumatj (Gomadj, Gumait, Gumaj) [gnn] 300 (1983 Black). Yirrkala, Northern Territory. *Class:* Australian, Pama-Nyungan, Yuulngu, Dhuwal. *Dialect:* Mangalili. *Lg Use:* Many also use Gupapuyngu, some English. *Lg Dev:* NT: 1985. *Other:* SOV. Coastal. Scrub forest. Hunter-gatherers.

Gungabula [gyf] 2 (1981 Wurm and Hattori). Queensland, around Injune. *Class:* Australian, Pama-Nyungan, Maric. *Other:* Nearly extinct.

Gunwinggu (Gunawitji, Mayali, Kunwinjku, Gunwinjgu) [gup] 1,511 (2000 WCD). Oenpelli, Arnhem Land, Northern Territory, Maningrida, Croker Island. *Class:* Australian, Gunwingguan, Gunwinggic. *Dialects:* Gumadir, Muralidban, Gunei, Gundjeipme, Naiali. *Lg Use:* Some Ngalkbun use this as a second language. Many domains. Some children speakers. *Lg Dev:* Dictionary. Grammar. Bible portions: 1942–1993.

Gunya [gyy] 3 (1981 Wurm and Hattori). Queensland, around Wyandra. *Class:* Australian, Pama-Nyungan, Maric. *Other:* Nearly extinct.

Gupapuyngu (Gobabingo, Gubabwingu) [guf] 450 (1983 Black). 500 in other Dhuwal varieties besides those listed. Milingimbi, Arnhem Land, Northern Territory, and Elcho Islands. *Class:* Australian, Pama-Nyungan, Yuulngu,

Dhuwal. *Dialects:* Gupapuyngu, Madarrpa, Manggalili, Munyuku, Wubulkarra, Walangu. About 45 related dialects. Close to Gumatj. *Lg Use:* 950 second-language speakers. Children are learning Djambarrpuyngu. Others use that, Gumaj or other Aboriginal languages as second language. *Lg Dev:* Bible portions: 1967. *Other:* SOV, OVS. Coastal. Scrub forest. Sea level to 50 meters. Hunter-gatherers.

Guragone (Gurrogone, Gurrgoni, Gorogone, Gun-Guragone, Gungorogone, Gunagoragone, Gutjertabia) [gge] 20 (1990 Schmidt). Arnhem Land, south of Maningrida, along the Mann River, northwest of the Rembarrnga language, east of the Gunwinygu language. *Class:* Australian, Gunwinggguan, Burarran. *Lg Use:* All speakers also use Burarra or Gunwinggu. *Other:* Nearly extinct.

Gurdjar (Kurtjjar) [gdj] 30 (1981 Wurm and Hattori). Northeastern side of Norman River, Normanton, western Queensland. *Class:* Australian, Pama-Nyungan, Paman, Norman Pama. *Dialects:* Speakers say it is similar to Kunggar. *Lg Use:* Gurdjar is in daily use by older adults, but children prefer English. *Other:* Nearly extinct.

Gureng Gureng (Gurreng Gurreng, Gureng-Gureng) [gnr] Extinct. Queensland, southeast, around Abercorn, north Burnett River District. *Class:* Australian, Pama-Nyungan, Waka-Kabic, Than. *Dialects:* The Gurreng Gurreng dialect is a 'heavier' one that uses the trilled 'r'. *Lg Use:* Still spoken as a second or third language by fewer than 100 children and adults. Guweng may be a dialect. Related to Daribalang and Gabi, which may be extinct. *Lg Dev:* Dictionary.

Gurinji (Gurindji, Wurlayi) [gue] 250 (1983 Black). Population includes 400 partial speakers. Victoria River and Wave Hill, Kalkaringi, Northern Territory. *Class:* Australian, Pama-Nyungan, South-West, Ngumbin. *Dialect:* Malngin, Wanyjirra (Wandjirra). *Lg Use:* All also use Kriol. *Lg Dev:* Bible portions: 1981–1986. *Other:* There is a mixed 'Gurinji children's language' formed from Gurinji and Kriol.

Guwamu [gwu] 1 (1981 Wurm and Hattori). Queensland, between St. George, Moonie River, Surat, Maranoa River. *Class:* Australian, Pama-Nyungan, Maric. *Other:* Nearly extinct.

Guyani (Kuyani, Kijani, Kwiani) [gvy] Extinct. South Australia, south Yorke Peninsula. *Class:* Australian, Pama-Nyungan, South-West, Yura. *Dialects:* Close to Narungga.

Iwaidja (Iwaydja, Iwaidji, Ibadjo, Eiwaja, Jiwadja, Limba, Karadjee) [ibd] 150 (2000 N. Evans). Croker Island, Northern Territory. *Class:* Australian, Yiwaidjan, Yiwaidjic. *Dialect:* Iwaydja. *Lg Use:* Some domains. Some children speakers. Speakers also use English. *Lg Dev:* Dictionary. Grammar.

Jarnango (Yan-Nhangu, Nangu, Yanangu) [jay] 40 (1983 Black). Two of the most western Crocodile Islands, adjacent to Cape Stewart, Maningrida and Milingimbi, Northern Territory. *Class:* Australian, Pama-Nyungan, Yuulngu, Dhangu. *Dialects:* Garmalangga, Gurjindi. *Lg Use:* People generally speak Djambarrpuyngu, Gupapuyngu, or Burarra. *Other:* Nearly extinct.

Jaru (Djaru, Jaroo, Tjaru, Wawari) [ddj] 250 (1981 Wurm and Hattori). Halls Creek, Ringers Soak, southeastern Kimberley Region Western Australia. *Class:* Australian, Pama-Nyungan, South-West, Ngumbin. *Dialects:* Nyininy, Djaru. Nyininy is inherently intelligible with Jaru (Black 1983). *Lg Use:* Children speak Kriol or Aboriginal English. *Lg Dev:* Dictionary. Grammar.

Kala Lagaw Ya (Kala Yagaw Ya, Yagar Yagar, Mabuiag, Kala Lagau Langgus, Langus, Kala Lagaw) [mwp] 3,000 to 4,000 (1990 Schmidt). Western Torres Strait Islands, Queensland; including Mabuiag, Badu, Moa, Kubin, Saibai, Boigu, Dauan, Yam, Sue, Yorke,

Coconut, Thursday, Bamaga Islands; Townsville. *Class:* Australian, Pama-Nyungan, Kala Lagaw Ya. *Dialect:* Kalaw Kawaw. *Lg Use:* Outside the language area those younger than 30 are likely to speak Torres Strait Creole. *Lg Dev:* Dictionary. Grammar. NT: 1994. *Other:* SOV. Islands: volcanic, coral. Tropical island; trade wind dry season, monsoon wet; moderate rainfall. Sea level to 400 meters. Hunters; fishermen; agriculturalists.

Kalarko (Malpa, Malba, Galaagu, Kalako, Kalakul, Kalaaku) [kba] Extinct. Fraser and Bremer ranges area, Western Australia. *Class:* Australian, Pama-Nyungan, South-West, Mirning.

Kalkutung (Galgaduun, Galgadungu, Kalkatungu, Kalkadoon) [ktg] Extinct. Mt. Isa area, Queensland. *Class:* Australian, Pama-Nyungan, Galgadungic. *Lg Use:* Members of the ethnic group now speak English.

Kamu (Gamor) [xmu] 2 (1967). Northern Territory, south of Darwin, east of Daly River. *Class:* Australian, Daly, Malagmalag, Daly Proper. *Other:* Possibly extinct. Nearly extinct.

Kanju (Kandju, Kaantyu, Gandju, Gandanju, Kamdhue, Kandyu, Kanyu, Karnu, Jabuda, Neogulada, Yaldiye-Ho) [kbe] 50 (1981 Wurm and Hattori). Central Cape York, Queensland. *Class:* Australian, Pama-Nyungan, Paman, Northeastern Pama. *Other:* Nearly extinct.

Karadjeri (Karajarri, Karrajarri, Garadjiri, Garadyari, Guradjara, Gard'are) [gbd] 12 (1991 SIL). Roebuck Bay to seventy miles inland, Broome, Western Australia, La Grange mission. *Class:* Australian, Pama-Nyungan, South-West, Marngu. *Lg Use:* Speakers are shifting to Aboriginal English. *Other:* Nearly extinct.

Kariyarra (Kariera, Karriara, Kariyara, Gariera) [vka] Extinct. Western Australia, south of Port Hedland. *Class:* Australian, Pama-Nyungan, South-West, Coastal Ngayarda.

Kayardild (Gajadilt, Gajardild, Gayadilt, Gayardild, Gayardilt, Kaiadilt, Malununda) [gyd] 6 (2000 Evans). Ethnic population: 150. Queensland, Bentinck Island, Gulf of Carpentaria. *Class:* Australian, Pama-Nyungan, Tangic. *Lg Use:* Speakers are shifting to English. *Lg Dev:* Dictionary. Grammar. *Other:* Nearly extinct.

Kaytetye (Kaiditj, Kaititj, Gaididj) [gbb] 200 (1983 Black). North of Alice Springs, Northern Territory. *Class:* Australian, Pama-Nyungan, Arandic. *Dialects:* Related to Alyawarr. *Lg Use:* People generally speak Kriol.

Kitja (Kija, Gidja, Kidja) [gia] 100 (1983 Black). Near Hall's Creek and Turkey Creek, Western Australia. *Class:* Australian, Djeragan. *Dialects:* Closest to Miriwung. Related to Kuluwarrang (Guluwarin, Guluwarung). *Lg Use:* Speakers are shifting to Kriol. *Lg Dev:* Grammar. Bible portions: 1978. *Other:* Nomadic. SOV. Hills. Savannah. 100 to 400 meters. Hunter-gatherers.

Kokata (Gugada, Kokitta, Koocatho, Koogurda, Kokatha, Kugurda, Kukata, Madutara, Maduwonga, Wanggamadu, Wongamardu) [ktd] 3 (1981 Wurm and Hattori). South Australia, Pimba, Mt. Eba, Coober Peby. *Class:* Australian, Pama-Nyungan, South-West, Wati. *Dialects:* Different from Kukatja. *Other:* People may adequately understand Pintupi or Pitjantjatjara. Nearly extinct.

Kriol (Roper-Bamyili Creole) [rop] 10,000 (1991 B. Borneman SIL). Roper River, Katherine areas, Ngukurr, Northern Territory; Kimberley Region Western Australia; Gulf Country, Lower Cape York Peninsula, Queensland. *Class:* Creole, English based, Pacific. *Dialects:* Roper River Kriol (Roper River Pidgin), Bamyili Creole, Barkly Kriol, Fitzroy Valley Kriol, Daly River Kriol. Kimberley Kriol has many differences with Ngukkur Kriol. Both Kriol and Torres Strait Creole are spreading, and are nearly overlapping in Queensland. *Lg Use:* 10,000 second-language speakers (1991 SIL). Preschool children may not be bilingual in another language. There are many first-language Kriol speakers who are not fully bilingual in English or in Aboriginal languages. *Lg Dev:* NT: 1991. *Other:* SVO. Coastal plains. Savannah, scrub forest. Sea level to 1,000 meters. Pastoralists; hunter-gatherers.

Kukatja (Kukaja, Gugadja) [kux] 300 (1983 Black). Balgo, Lake Gregory and area to the east, south of Halls Creek, Western Australia. *Class:* Australian, Pama-Nyungan, South-West, Wati. *Dialects:* Different from Kokata. *Lg Use:* Bilingual in Pintupi-Luritja, Ngaanyatjarra, Martu Wangka, or Walmajarri.

Kuku-Mangk (Kugu-Mangk) [xmq] 1 (1981 Wurm and Hattori). Queensland, Cape York Peninsula, east coast south of Aurukun. *Class:* Australian, Pama-Nyungan, Paman, Middle Pama. *Other:* Nearly extinct.

Kuku-Mu'inh (Kugu-Mu'inh) [xmp] 7 (1981 Wurm and Hattori). Queensland, Cape York Peninsula, east coast south of Aurukun. *Class:* Australian, Pama-Nyungan, Paman, Middle Pama. *Other:* Nearly extinct.

Kuku-Muminh (Kugu-Muminh, Wik Muminh, Wik-Mumin, Kugu) [xmh] 31 (1981 Wurm and Hattori). Queensland, Cape York Peninsula, east coast south of Aurukun. *Class:* Australian, Pama-Nyungan, Paman, Middle Pama. *Other:* Nearly extinct.

Kuku-Ugbanh (Kugu-Ugbanh) [ugb] 6 (1981 Wurm and Hattori). Queensland, west coast Cape York Peninsula below Aurukun. *Class:* Australian, Pama-Nyungan, Paman, Middle Pama. *Other:* Nearly extinct.

Kuku-Uwanh (Kugu-Uwanh) [uwa] 40 (1981 Wurm and Hattori). Queensland, Cape York Peninsula, east coast south of Aurukun. *Class:* Australian, Pama-Nyungan, Paman, Middle Pama. *Other:* Nearly extinct.

Kuku-Yalanji (Guguyalanji, Koko-Yalanji, Kuku-Yalangi) [gvn] 700 (2000 SIL). Wujal-Wujal, Bloomfield River, Daintree and Mossman, Queensland, between Cooktown and Mossman. Centers are Wujal-Wujal, Bloomfield River (Ayton), Daintree, and Mossman. *Class:* Australian, Pama-Nyungan, Yalandyic. *Dialects:* Kuku-Nyungkul, Kuku-Biraji. *Lg Use:* Vigorous. Oral use in traditional religion, oral and some written use in religious services. Oral tradition. Positive language attitude. All also use English. Perhaps 25 can also speak Kuku-Yimidji. *Lg Dev:* Literacy rate in first language: 14%. 100 can read Kuku-Yalanji, 30 can write it. Limited oral use as a subject of study. Dictionary. NT: 1985. *Other:* SOV. Coastal, mountain slope. Scrub forest. Hunter-gatherers formerly, now laborers. Christian, traditional religion, syncretism.

Kumbainggar (Gumbaingari, Gumbaynggir, Kumbaingeri, Gambalamam, Baanbay) [kgs] 10 (2000). New South Wales, Grafton and north coast. *Class:* Australian, Pama-Nyungan, Gumbaynggiric. *Dialects:* Also related to Yaygirr. *Other:* Nearly extinct.

Kunbarlang (Gunbalang, Walang, Warlang, Gungalang, Gunbarlang) [wlg] 50 to 100 (1983 Black). Oenpelli, Maningrida, and Goulburn Island, Northern Territory. *Class:* Australian, Gunwingguan, Gunwinggic. *Lg Use:* Members of the ethnic group generally speak Gunwinggu. *Lg Dev:* Grammar. *Other:* Nearly extinct.

Kungarakany (Gungaragan, Gunerakan, Kangarraga, Kungarakan, Gungarakanj) [ggk] Extinct. Northern Territory, Finniss River. South of Darwin around Darwin River and Rum Jungle. *Class:* Australian, Gunwingguan, Gungaraganyan. *Lg Use:* The last speaker died in 1989. *Lg Dev:* Dictionary. Grammar.

Kunggara (Gunggara, Kunggera, Goom-Gharra) [kvs] 10 (1971 SIL). Normanton, Delta, Queensland. *Class:* Australian, Pama-Nyungan, Paman, Norman Pama. *Other:* Nearly extinct.

Kunggari (Coongurri, Ungorri, Gungari, Gunggari) [kgl] 10. Upper Nebine and Mungallala Creeks, Queensland. *Class:* Australian, Pama-Nyungan, Maric. *Dialects:*

Related to Birria, which may be extinct. *Other:* Possibly extinct. Nearly extinct.

Kunjen (Guguminjen, Kukumindjen) [kjn] 20 to 25 (1991 Bruce Sommer). 40 with some knowledge. Ethnic population: 300 (1991 Bruce Sommer). Wrotham Park, Kowanyama, Edward River, Queensland. *Class:* Australian, Pama-Nyungan, Paman, Central Pama. *Dialect:* Ulkulu, Oykangand (Olgol, Olgolo, Olgel, Ogondyan). *Lg Use:* Speakers are shifting to Torres Strait Creole. Most also use other Aboriginal languages, English, or Kriol. *Lg Dev:* Bible portions: 1967. *Other:* Nearly extinct.

Kurrama (Kurama, Gurama, Karama, Korama) [vku] 50 (1981 Wurm and Hattori). Western Australia, northwest, southeast of Pannawonica. *Class:* Australian, Pama-Nyungan, South-West, Coastal Ngayarda. *Lg Use:* Speakers also use English. *Other:* Nearly extinct.

Kuthant [xut] 3 (1981 Wurm and Hattori). Queensland, southwest Cape York Peninsula, north of Karumba and Normanton. *Class:* Australian, Pama-Nyungan, Paman, Norman Pama. *Other:* Ruhlen (1987) says it is extinct. Nearly extinct.

Kuuku-Ya'u (Ya'o, Koko-Ja'o, Kokoyao, Bagadji, Pakadji) [kuy] 100 (1981 Wurm and Hattori). Queensland, northeastern Cape York Peninsula south of Temple Bay. *Class:* Australian, Pama-Nyungan, Paman, Northeastern Pama. *Lg Use:* Speakers also use Torres Strait Creole.

Kwini (Gwini, Gwiini, Cuini, Gunin, Wunambal, Goonan, Kunan) [gww] 50 (1979 Black). Kalumburu, Western Australia. *Class:* Australian, Wororan. *Lg Use:* Children may know some of the language, but most speak Aboriginal English as first language. *Lg Dev:* Grammar. *Other:* Known in the area as 'Kwini', the name of the people. 'Goonan' (Kunan) is the name of the language. 'Gwini' is the Wunambal word for 'east' and was used by some people to refer to the Gunin and Yeidji.

Lamu-Lamu (Lamulamul, Lamalama, Lama-Lama, Mba Rumbathama) [lby] 1 (1981 Wurm and Hattori). Bamiga, Queensland, and Coen. *Class:* Australian, Pama-Nyungan, Paman, Lamalamic. *Other:* Ethnic groups include Baganambia, Gan-Ganda, Wurangung. Nearly extinct.

Laragia (Larakia, Larakiya, Laragiya, Gulumirrgin) [lrg] 6 (1983 Black). Darwin area, Northern Territory. *Class:* Australian, Laragiyan. *Lg Use:* All speak English. *Lg Dev:* Dictionary. Grammar. *Other:* May be extinct. Nearly extinct.

Lardil (Ladil, Lardill, Laierdila, Kunana) [lbz] 2 (2000 Evans). Mornington Island, Queensland. *Class:* Australian, Pama-Nyungan, Lardil. *Dialects:* Related to Kayardild, Nyangga, Yugulda. Initiated males learn Damin, which has a very different phonology from Lardil (1992 R. M. W. Dixon OIEL, Vol. 1, p. 137). *Lg Dev:* Dictionary. Grammar. *Other:* Nearly extinct.

Leningitij (Linngithig, Linngithigh) [lnj] Extinct. Winduwinda area, Queensland. *Class:* Australian, Pama-Nyungan, Paman, Northern Pama.

Limilngan (Manadja, Minitji) [lmc] 3 (1981 Wurm and Hattori). Northern Territory, Arnhem Land, between Mary River and W. Alligator River, from coast and inland. *Class:* Australian, Limilngan-Wulna. *Lg Dev:* Dictionary. Grammar. *Other:* It may be the same as Lemil (Norweilimil; Oates 1970:29) or Manaidja (Manatja, Mandatja; Oates 1970:220). Nearly extinct.

Madngele (Matngala, Matngele, Warat, Madngela, Maangella, Mandella, Muttangulla) [zml] 15 to 20 (1983 Black). Northern Territory, south of Darwin and Daly River, west bank of Muldiva River. *Class:* Australian, Daly, Malagmalag, Daly Proper. *Dialects:* Related to Kamu and Yunggor, which may be extinct. *Lg Dev:* Dictionary. Grammar. *Other:* Nearly extinct.

Malay, Cocos Islands (Cocos, Kokos, Kukus) [coa] 1,000 in Australia. Population includes 495 in Cocos Islands (1987), 558 on Christmas Island (1987). Cocos (Keeling) Islands, and Christmas Island. *Lg Use:* Vigorous. Young people also use English, but as the age increases the knowledge of English decreases. *Other:* Muslim. See main entry under Malaysia (Sabah).

Malgana (Maljanna, Maldjana, Malkana) [vml] Extinct. Western Australia, Shark Bay, south of Wooramel River to near Hamelin Pool. *Class:* Australian, Pama-Nyungan, South-West, Malgana.

Manangkari [znk] Extinct. Cobourg Peninsula, Northern Territory. *Class:* Australian, Yiwaidjan, Yiwaidjic. *Dialects:* Close to Iwaidja.

Manda [zma] 25 (1983 Black). Northern Territory, coast southwest of Anson Bay, southwest of Darwin. *Class:* Australian, Daly, Bringen-Wagaydy, Wagaydy. *Lg Use:* Speakers also use Kriol or English. *Other:* Nearly extinct.

Mandandanyi (Mandandanjnjdji) [zmk] 1 (1981 Wurm and Hattori). Queensland, around Roma from Maranoa River to near Miles and Wandoan. *Class:* Australian, Pama-Nyungan, Maric. *Other:* Nearly extinct.

Mangala (Mangalaa, Mangarla, Manala, Minala, Djawali, Djuwali, Jiwali, Jiwarli, Koalgurdi, Yalmbau) [mem] Extinct. Broome, Jurgurra Creek, Edgar Range, southwest Fitzroy, West Pilbara, Western Australia. *Class:* Australian, Pama-Nyungan, South-West, Mangala. *Lg Use:* Members of the ethnic group now speak Kriol or Aboriginal English. *Lg Dev:* Dictionary. Grammar. *Other:* Extinct in 1986.

Mangarayi (Mungerry, Mangarai, Manggarai, Mungarai, Mangarrayi, Ngarrabadji) [mpc] 50 (1983 Black). Mataranka and Elsey stations, Northern Territory. *Class:* Australian, Gunwingguan, Mangarayic. *Lg Use:* Speakers are shifting to Kriol. *Other:* Different from Mangerr (Mangerei). Nearly extinct.

Mangerr (Mengerrdji, Mangerei, Mennagi, Mangeri, Giimbiyu) [zme] 1 (1981 Wurm and Hattori). Arnhem Land around Oenpelli. *Class:* Australian, Giimbiyu. *Dialects:* Intelligible with Urningangg (Black). *Other:* Nearly extinct.

Mara (Leelalwarra, Leelawarra, Mala, Marra) [mec] 15 (1991 M. Sharpe). Roper River area, Arnhem Land, Northern Territory. *Class:* Australian, Gunwingguan, Maran, Mara. *Dialects:* Related to Warndarrang and Yugul, which may be extinct. *Lg Use:* Most speak Kriol or English as second language. *Lg Dev:* Dictionary. Grammar. *Other:* Speakers intermarry with the Yanyuwa. Nearly extinct.

Maranunggu (Merranunggu, Emmi, Warrgat) [zmr] 15 to 20 (1983 Black). Southwest of Darwin, inland from Anson Bay, east of Manda. *Class:* Australian, Daly, Bringen-Wagaydy, Wagaydy. *Lg Use:* Young people speak Kriol. *Lg Dev:* Dictionary. Grammar. *Other:* Nearly extinct.

Margany (Marrganj) [zmc] 1 (1981 Wurm and Hattori). Queensland, between Quilpie and Wyandra, Bulloo River and Paroo River. *Class:* Australian, Pama-Nyungan, Maric. *Other:* Nearly extinct.

Margu (Ajokoot, Jaako, Terutong, Terrutong, Marrgu, Raffles Bay, Croker Island, Yaako, Yako) [mhg] 1 (2000 Evans). Croker Island, Northern Territory. *Class:* Australian, Yiwaidjan, Margic. *Other:* May be extinct. Nearly extinct.

Maridan (Meradan) [zmd] 20 (1981 Wurm and Hattori). Southwest of Darwin, north of Moyle River, east of Magadige. *Class:* Australian, Daly, Bringen-Wagaydy, Bringen. *Other:* Nearly extinct.

Maridjabin (Maretyabin, Maridyerbin, Maredyerbin) [zmj] 20 (1970 Oates). Northern Territory, inland from Anson Bay, south of Mariyedi and Manda, southwest of Darwin. *Class:* Australian, Daly, Bringen-Wagaydy, Bringen. *Dialects:* May be intelligible with Marithiel or

Maringarr. *Lg Use:* Speakers also use Kriol. *Other:* Nearly extinct.

Marimanindji (Maramarandji, Maramanandji, Marimanindu, Murinmanindji, Marramaninjsji) [zmm] 15 (1983 Black). Northern Territory, south of Darwin and Daly River, west of Muldiva River, near headwaters. *Class:* Australian, Daly, Bringen-Wagaydy, Bringen. *Other:* Nearly extinct.

Maringarr (Marenggar, Maringa) [zmt] 30 to 40 (1983 Black). Northern Territory south of Moyle River, southwest of Darwin. *Class:* Australian, Daly, Bringen-Wagaydy, Bringen. *Dialect:* Maranunggu (Marranunga, Maramanunggu, Merranunggu, Warrgat). May be intelligible with other Bringen languages. Lexical similarity 40% with Mullukmulluk and Murrinh-Patha. *Lg Use:* Speakers also use Kriol. *Other:* Nearly extinct.

Marithiel (Maridhiyel, Marithiyel, Marrithiyel, Maridhiel, "Brinken," "Bringen," Berringen) [mfr] 25 (1983 Black). 30 to 50 miles south of Daly River and central Daly River; Daly River Mission, Bagot, Delissaville, Roper River Mission, Northern Territory. *Class:* Australian, Daly, Bringen-Wagaydy, Bringen. *Dialect:* Marithiel, Nganygit, Mare-Ammu (Mari-Ammu). *Lg Use:* Speakers are shifting to Kriol. 50 second-language speakers. *Lg Dev:* Dictionary. Grammar. *Other:* The people dislike the name "Brinken." Nearly extinct.

Mariyedi [zmy] 20 (1981 Wurm and Hattori). Inland from Anson Bay, south of Manda, southwest of Darwin. *Class:* Australian, Daly, Bringen-Wagaydy, Bringen. *Other:* Nearly extinct.

Marti Ke (Magati-Ge, Magadige, Mati Ke, Magati Gair) [zmg] 10 (2001 Alexander). Ethnic population: 100. Wadeye, Northern Territory, coast south from Moyle River estuary to Port Keat, southwest of Darwin. *Class:* Australian, Daly, Bringen-Wagaydy, Bringen. *Dialects:* Close to Marringarr, Marrathiel. *Lg Use:* Second-language speakers 50. Speakers are older adults. Some speakers also use Murrinh Patha, English, or Kriol. *Other:* Nearly extinct.

Martu Wangka (Mardo, Targudi) [mpj] 720 (1991 SIL). Population includes 100 in Wankajunga (1991). Western Australia, Jigalong area, western side of Lake Disappointment, Great Sandy Desert. *Class:* Australian, Pama-Nyungan, South-West, Wati. *Dialects:* Manyjilyjara (Mantjiltjara), Kartujarra (Kartutjara, Kardutjara, Kadaddjara, Kardutjarra, Kiadjara, Gardudjara, Gagudjara), Puditara (Budidjara, Putujara), Yulparitja (Yilparitja, Yulbaridja), Wangkajunga (Wangkajungka). Mantjiltjara and Kartutjara are two ethnic groups speaking almost identical dialects. High inherent intelligibility between Yulparitja and Wangkajunga. Speakers of the 4 dialects can use the same written language with possible minor adjustments, including vocabulary change, partly needed because of cultural identity factors. *Lg Use:* Puditara dialect is extinct. Speakers also use Walmajarri, Kukatja, or Kriol. *Lg Dev:* Dictionary. Grammar. Bible portions: 1981–1994.

Martuyhunira (Martuthunira) [vma] 5 (1981 Wurm and Hattori). Western Australia, northwest coast southwest of Dampier and inland. *Class:* Australian, Pama-Nyungan, South-West, Coastal Ngayarda. *Lg Dev:* Dictionary. Grammar. *Other:* Nearly extinct.

Maung (Gunmarung, Mawung, Gun-Marung) [mph] 200 (1983 Black). Goulburn Island, Arnhem Land, Northern Territory. *Class:* Australian, Yiwaidjan, Yiwaidjic. *Dialects:* Garig is reported to be related. *Lg Use:* Speakers also use English or Gunwinggu with some limitations. *Lg Dev:* Dictionary. Grammar. Bible portions: 1960.

Mayaguduna (Mayi-Kutuna) [xmy] 2. Queensland, near north coast, inland between Leichhardt River and Flinders River. *Class:* Australian, Pama-Nyungan, Paman,

Mayabic. *Other:* Ruhlen (1987) says it is extinct. Nearly extinct.

Maykulan (Mayi-Kulan, Wunamara, Mayi-Thakurti, Mayi-Yapi) [mnt] Extinct. Canobie, Queensland. *Class:* Australian, Pama-Nyungan, Paman, Mayabic.

Mbabaram (Mbara) [vmb] 2 (1981 Wurm and Hattori). *Class:* Australian, Pama-Nyungan, Paman, Southern Pama. *Other:* Nearly extinct.

Mbara [mvl] Extinct. *Class:* Australian, Pama-Nyungan, Mbara.

Mbariman-Gudhinma (Rimang-Gudinhma) [zmv] 3 (1981 Wurm and Hattori). Queensland, Cape York Peninsula, southwest coast of Princess Charlotte Bay. *Class:* Australian, Pama-Nyungan, Paman, Mbariman. *Other:* Nearly extinct.

Meriam (Miriam-Mir, Miriam, Mer, Mir, East Torres) [ulk] 300 to 400 (1991 Rod Kennedy). Murray Island, Eastern Torres Strait Islands, Queensland. Not in Papua New Guinea. *Class:* Trans-New Guinea, Trans-Fly-Bulaka River, Trans-Fly, Eastern Trans-Fly. *Dialects:* Boigu, Bulgai, Buglial, Tagota. *Lg Use:* Most also use Torres Strait Creole. *Lg Dev:* Dictionary. Grammar. Bible portions: 1879–1902.

Miriwung (Mirung, Merong, Miriwun, Miriwoong) [mep] 10 to 20 (1990 Schmidt). Kununurra, Western Australia, and Turkey Creek. *Class:* Australian, Djeragan. *Lg Use:* Some older adults speak Miriwung. The young people use only Kriol. Most older adults speak Kriol. *Lg Dev:* Dictionary. Grammar. *Other:* Nearly extinct.

Miwa (Bagu) [vmi] 4 (1981 Wurm and Hattori). Western Australia, Drysdale River, far northern Kimberleys area. *Class:* Australian, Wororan. *Other:* Nearly extinct.

Mudbura (Mudburra, Karranga, Pinkangama) [mwd] 50 (1983 Black). Victoria River to Barkly Tablelands, Northern Territory. *Class:* Australian, Pama-Nyungan, South-West, Ngumbin. *Lg Use:* Most also use English and other Aboriginal languages. Very few monolinguals. *Other:* Nearly extinct.

Mullukmulluk (Malak-Malak, Malagmalag, Ngolak-Wonga, Nguluwongga) [mpb] 9 to 11 (1988 SIL). Northern bank of Daly River, Northern Territory. *Class:* Australian, Daly, Malagmalag, Malagmalag Proper. *Lg Use:* Speakers are shifting to Kriol. *Lg Dev:* Dictionary. Grammar. *Other:* Nearly extinct.

Muluridyi (Binjara, Kokomoloroij, Kokomoloroitji, Kookanoona, Molloroidyi, Mooloroiji, Mularitchee, Mullridgey, Mulurutji, Waluridji) [vmu] 1 (1981 Wurm and Hattori). Queensland, headwaters of Mitchell River to Mt. Carbine, Rumula, Mareeba, Woodville. *Class:* Australian, Pama-Nyungan, Yalandyic. *Other:* Nearly extinct.

Murrinh-Patha (Murinbada, Murinbata, Garama) [mwf] 900 (1990 Schmidt). Port Keats area, Wadeye, Northern Territory. *Class:* Australian, Daly, Murrinh-Patha. *Dialects:* Murrinhpatha, Murrinhkura, Murrinhdiminin. *Lg Use:* Port Keats about 90% of speakers: English, other Aboriginal languages. *Lg Dev:* Dictionary. Grammar. Bible portions: 1982. *Other:* SOV. Coastal. Tropical savannah. 50 to 100 meters. Hunter-gatherers; fishermen (traditionally).

Muruwari (Murawari, Muruwarri) [zmu] 1 (1981 Wurm and Hattori). Queensland and New South Wales from Bollon, Dirranbandi, Weilmoringle, Bourke, almost to Cunnamulla. *Class:* Australian, Pama-Nyungan, Muruwaric. *Lg Dev:* Dictionary. *Other:* Nearly extinct.

Nakara (Kokori, Nagara, Nakkara) [nck] 75 to 100 (1983 Black). Maningrida, Arnhem Land, Northern Territory, Goulburn Island. *Class:* Australian, Gunwingguan, Burarran. *Lg Use:* Members of the ethnic group generally speak Burarra or Djeebbana. *Lg Dev:* Grammar.

Nangikurrunggurr (Ngenkikurrunggur, Ngangikarangurr, Ngankikurrunkurr, Nangikurunggurr)

[nam] 275 (1988 SIL). Population includes 40 Ngengiwumerri (1983 Black). Junction of Flora and Daly rivers, Daly River Mission, Tipperary Station, Northern Territory. *Class:* Australian, Daly, Murrinh-Patha. *Dialects:* Tyemeri (Moil, Ngankikurrunkurr), Ngenkiwumerri (Nangumiri, Nangiomeri, Angomerry, Marewumiri, Nangimera, Ngangomori), Ngangi-Tjemerri, Ngangi-Wumeri. Lexical similarity 84% with Ngengiwumerri dialect. *Lg Use:* Main language in Daly River group. Speakers also use Kriol or English. *Lg Dev:* Dictionary. Grammar.

Narrinyeri (Ngarinyeri, Ngarrindjeri, Yaralde) [nay] Extinct. South Australia. *Class:* Australian, Pama-Nyungan, Ngarinyeric-Yithayithic. *Dialects:* Related to Ngayawung and Yuyu (Ngarrket). *Lg Dev:* Bible portions: 1864.

Narungga (Narangga, Nanunga, Naranga, Narranga, Narranggu, Narrangu) [nnr] Extinct. South Australia, south Yorke Peninsula. *Class:* Australian, Pama-Nyungan, South-West, Yura. *Dialects:* Adjabdurah (Adjahdurah), Turra. *Other:* May have become extinct in 1936.

Ngaanyatjarra (Nyanganyatjara, Ngaanyatjara, Ngaanjatjarra) [ntj] 1,200 (1995 D. Hackett). Warburton Ranges, Western Australia. *Class:* Australian, Pama-Nyungan, South-West, Wati. *Lg Use:* Speakers also use English. *Lg Dev:* Literacy rate in first language: 11%. Grammar. NT: 1991.

Ngadjunmaya (Badonjunga, Bardojunga, Ngadju, Ngadjunmaia, Ngadjumaja, Ngatjumay, Ngatju, Tchaakalaaga) [nju] 10 (1981 Wurm and Hattori). Western Australia, Eyre's Sand Patch, Goddard Creek to Port Malcolm, to Fraser Range, to Naretha and Point Culver, at Mount Andres, Russell Range, Balladonia, and Norseman. *Class:* Australian, Pama-Nyungan, South-West, Mirning. *Dialects:* Related to Kalarko. *Other:* Nearly extinct.

Ngalakan (Hongalla, Ngalangan) [nig] 10 (1981 Wurm and Hattori). Roper River area, Northern Territory. *Class:* Australian, Gunwingguan, Rembargic. *Dialects:* Related to Ngalkbun and Rembarranga. *Lg Dev:* Grammar. *Other:* Nearly extinct.

Ngalkbun (Ngalkbon, Dalabon, Buin, Boun, Buan, Bouin, Buwan, Gundangbon, Ngalabon, Nalabon, Dangbon) [ngk] 20 (2000 N. Evans). Oenpelli, Arnhem Land, Northern Territory, Katherine area. *Class:* Australian, Gunwingguan, Ngalkbun. *Lg Use:* A few children. Some Rembarunga use this as a second language. Ngalkbun used for a few domains. Most speak Kriol, and some speak Rembarrnga or Gunwinggu as second language. *Lg Dev:* Dictionary. Grammar. *Other:* Nearly extinct.

Ngamini (Yarluyandji, Karangura) [nmv] 2 (1981 Wurm and Hattori). South Australia around Narburton Creek. *Class:* Australian, Pama-Nyungan, Karnic, Karna. *Other:* Nearly extinct.

Ngandi [nid] Extinct. Upper Wilton River, Northern Territory. *Class:* Australian, Gunwingguan, Enindhilyagwa.

Nganyaywana (Nganjaywana, Aniwan) [nyx] Extinct. New South Wales, northeastern, between Inverell, Ashford, and Glen Innes. *Class:* Australian, Pama-Nyungan, Dyangadi.

Ngarinman (Airiman, Hainman, Ngaiman, Ngrarmun) [nbj] 170 (1983 Black). Victoria River around Jasper Creek, Northern Territory. *Class:* Australian, Pama-Nyungan, South-West, Ngumbin. *Dialect:* Bilinara (Pilinara). *Lg Use:* Members of the ethnic group generally speak Kriol.

Ngarinyin (Ungarinyin, Ungarinjin) [ung] 82 (1981 Wurm and Hattori). Derby to King River, Kimberley, Western Australia. *Class:* Australian, Wororan. *Dialect:* Wilawila, Wolyamidi, Guwidj, Wurla (Worla, Worlaja, Wula, Ola, Walar, Wuladja, Wuladjangari). *Lg Use:* Children may know some of the language. Most children speak Kriol as

first language. *Lg Dev:* Dictionary. Grammar. *Other:* A different Wurla is described by Alan Rumsey 1990, reported to still be spoken. OSV, VOS. Interfluvial, coastal. Savannah. Formerly hunter-gatherers, now station hands and country town workers.

Ngarla [nlr] 8 (1991 SIL). 10 partial speakers. Western Australia, Port Hedland area. *Class:* Australian, Pama-Nyungan, South-West, Inland Ngayarda. *Other:* Nearly extinct.

Ngarluma (Ngaluma, Gnalouma, Gnalluma, Ngallooma) [nrl] 70 (1970 C.G. von Brandenstein). Western Australia, northwest coast around Roebourne and inland. *Class:* Australian, Pama-Nyungan, South-West, Coastal Ngayarda. *Lg Use:* Speakers are shifting to English. *Other:* Nearly extinct.

Ngawun [nxn] 1 (1981 Wurm and Hattori). Queensland, southwest of Croydon, between Flinders River and Norman River. *Class:* Australian, Pama-Nyungan, Paman, Mayabic. *Other:* Nearly extinct.

Ngura [nbx] 6 (1981 Wurm and Hattori). Population includes 1 Punthamara, 4 Wongkumara, 2 Badjiri, and 1 Kalali. Northwestern New South Wales and southwestern Queensland. *Class:* Australian, Pama-Nyungan, Karnic, Ngura. *Dialects:* Punthamara (Bundhamara), Kalali (Galali, Garlali), Wongkumara (Wangkumara, Wangumarra), Badjiri, Bidjara, Dhiraila, Garandala, Mambangura, Mingbari, Ngurawarla, Yarumarra. Wurm and Hattori list the dialects as separate languages. *Other:* Nearly extinct.

Ngurmbur (Ngormbur, Gnormbur, Gnumbu, Koarnbut, Ngumbur, Oormbur) [nrx] 1 (1981 Wurm and Hattori). Northern Territory, Arnhem Land, between West and South Alligator rivers, northeast of Umbugarla. *Class:* Australian, Umbugarla-Ngumbur. *Other:* Nearly extinct.

Nhuwala [nhf] 10 (1981 Wurm and Hattori). Western Australia, northwest, Barrow and Monte Bello Islands and nearby coast. *Class:* Australian, Pama-Nyungan, South-West, Coastal Ngayarda. *Other:* Wordick says it may be extinct. Nearly extinct.

Nijadali (Njijapali, Nyiypali, Nyiyabali, Bailko, Balygu, Palyku, Paljgu, Balgu, Jauna) [nad] 6 (1990 SIL). Western Australia, Marblebar, and possibly some at Nulagine. *Class:* Australian, Pama-Nyungan, South-West, Nijadali. *Lg Use:* Members of the ethnic group generally use Aboriginal English or Nyangumarta. *Other:* Two groups: Bailko and Jauna. Nearly extinct.

Nimanbur (Nimanburru) [nmp] 2 (1981 Wurm and Hattori). Western Australia, southwest of King Sound, and inland. *Class:* Australian, Nyulnyulan. *Other:* Nearly extinct.

Nugunu (Nukuna, Doora, Njuguna, Nokunna, Noocoona, Nookoona, Nuguna, Nukana, Nukunnu, Nukunu, Pukunna, Tjura, Tyura, Wallaroo, Warra, Wongaidya) [nnv] Extinct. South Australia, south of Gugada people to coast west to Fowler's Bay and east to Streaky Bay, eastern Spencer Gulf. *Class:* Australian, Pama-Nyungan, South-West, Yura. *Lg Dev:* Dictionary.

Nungali [nug] 2 (1981 Wurm and Hattori). Upper Daly River area, Northern Territory. *Class:* Australian, Djamindjungan. *Lg Dev:* Grammar. *Other:* Nearly extinct.

Nunggubuyu (Nunggubuju, Wubuy, Yingkwira) [nuy] 300 (1991 M. Hore ANG). 400 partial- or second-language speakers. Numbulwar, east Arnhem Land, Northern Territory. *Class:* Australian, Gunwingguan, Enindhilyagwa. *Dialects:* Not intelligible with other languages. *Lg Use:* Most Ritharrngu speakers around Numbulwar understand it fairly well. Children understand Nunggubuyu, but speak Kriol. *Lg Dev:* Dictionary. Grammar. Bible portions: 1946–1993. *Other:* Coastal. Sea level to 30 meters. Hunter-gatherers.

Nyamal (Gnamo, Namel, Njamal, Njamarl, Nyamel) [nly] 20 to 30 (1991 SIL). Western Australia, northwest, around Bamboo Creek, Marble Bar, Nullagine, to coast just east of Port Hedland. *Class:* Australian, Pama-Nyungan, South-West, Inland Ngayarda. *Lg Use:* Children speak Nyangumarta or English. *Other:* Nearly extinct.

Nyangga (Janga, Jangaa, Jangga, Njangga, Yanggal, Jang-Kala, Njanggala, Yangkaal, Yangarella, Yuckamurri) [nny] 1 (1981 Wurm and Hattori). Queensland, head of Gilbert River, south of Forsayth to Gledswood and Gregory Range to Oak Park and Glenora; Northern Territory, coast east of Robinson River. *Class:* Australian, Pama-Nyungan, Tangic. *Other:* Reported to be the same as Ganggalida (Yugulda, Jakula). Nearly extinct.

Nyangumarta (Nyangumarda, Nyangumata) [nna] 520 (1991 SIL). Marble Bar, Port Hedlund, Tjalku Wara, Western Australia. *Class:* Australian, Pama-Nyungan, South-West, Marngu. *Lg Dev:* Dictionary. Grammar.

Nyawaygi (Nawagi) [nyt] 3 (1981). Northeast Queensland, Herberton south to headwaters of Herbert River, to Cashmere, at Ravenshoe, Millaa Millaa and Woodleigh, east to Tully Falls. *Class:* Australian, Pama-Nyungan, Dyirbalic. *Dialects:* Related to Wulguru, Bindal, and Yuru, which may be extinct. *Other:* Nearly extinct.

Nyigina (Nyikina, Njigina) [nyh] 50 (1981 Wurm and Hattori). Lower Fitzroy River, Western Australia. *Class:* Australian, Nyulnyulan. *Lg Use:* Children speak Kriol or Aboriginal English as first language. Most speak Walmatjari, Kriol, or English as second language. *Lg Dev:* Dictionary. Grammar. *Other:* Nearly extinct.

Nyulnyul [nyv] 1 (2001 McGregor). Western Australia, West Kimberley, coast around Beagle Bay. *Class:* Australian, Nyulnyulan. *Lg Dev:* Grammar. *Other:* Nearly extinct.

Nyunga (Nyungar, Neo-Nyunga) [nys] Extinct. Southwest Australia. *Class:* Australian, Pama-Nyungan, South-West, Nyungar. *Lg Use:* Former Nyungar languages: Tjapanmay, Karlamay, Pipelman (Pipalman), Ngatjumay, Kwetjman, Mirnong, Kaniyang Pindjarup, Whadjuk. There are about 8,000 people who are descended from the Nyunga and speak a mixture of English and Nyunga. They are sometimes called 'Noonga', 'Noongar', or 'Noogar', and their speech 'Neo-Nyunga'.

Pakanha (Bakanha) [pkn] 10 (1981 Wurm and Hattori). Queensland, central Cape York Peninsula, south of Coleman River. *Class:* Australian, Pama-Nyungan, Paman, Middle Pama. *Other:* Nearly extinct.

Panytyima (Pandjima, Panjtjima, Bandjima, Panjima, Panyjima, Banjima) [pnw] 50 (1972 B. Geytenbeek). Western Australia, northwest, east southeast of Tom Price. *Class:* Australian, Pama-Nyungan, South-West, Inland Ngayarda. *Dialects:* Related to Yinawongga, Ngarlawangga, Ngarla, Tjurruru, which may be extinct, and Nyamal. *Lg Use:* Speakers also use Yindjibarndi or English. *Lg Dev:* Dictionary. Grammar. *Other:* Nearly extinct.

Pini (Piniritjara, Pirniritjara, Bini, Birni) [pii] 10. Three Rivers, Western Australia. *Class:* Australian, Pama-Nyungan, South-West, Wati. *Other:* Possibly extinct. Nearly extinct.

Pinigura (Binigura, Pinikura) [pnv] 5 (1981 Wurm and Hattori). Western Australia, northwest, inland on Duck Creek. *Class:* Australian, Pama-Nyungan, South-West, Dhalandji. *Other:* Nearly extinct.

Pintiini (Pindiini, Wangada, Wanggaji, Wangkatja, Wonga, Wongai-I, Wonggaii) [pti] 200 to 300 (1983 Black). Western Australia, northern margin of Nullabor Plain from north of Hughes. *Class:* Australian, Pama-Nyungan, South-West, Wati. *Lg Use:* Speakers also use Pitjantjatjara or Ngaanyatjarra.

Pintupi-Luritja (Pintubi, Binddibu, Loridja) [piu] 800 (1983 Black). 90% monolingual. Papunya settlement, Yuendumu and Kintore, Northern Territory, and Balgo Hills, Western Australia. *Class:* Australian, Pama-Nyungan, South-West, Wati. *Lg Use:* About 10% also use English. *Lg Dev:* Dictionary. Grammar. NT: 1981.

Pirlatapa (Biladaba) [bxi] Extinct. South Australia, around Lake Blanche and Lake Callabonn. *Class:* Australian, Pama-Nyungan, Karnic, Karna. *Dialects:* It was close to Diyari. *Lg Use:* The language became extinct in the 1960s.

Pitcairn-Norfolk (Pitcairn English) [pih] *Lg Use:* An in-group language used to assist in the preservation of identity. The people speak Standard Brirish English as first language. There may be no speakers on the Australian mainland. *Other:* Christian. Second language only. See main entry under Norfolk Island.

Pitjantjatjara (Pitjantjara) [pjt] 2,500 (1995 Paul Eckert). 80% monolingual. Pitjantjatjara Freehold lands, northwest South Australia, surrounding areas, and Yalata. *Class:* Australian, Pama-Nyungan, South-West, Wati. *Dialect:* Yankunytjatjara, Pitjantjatjara (Pithantjarra). *Lg Use:* 500 second-language speakers. About 20% also use English. *Lg Dev:* Literacy rate in first language: 50% to 70%. Literacy rate in second language: 10% to 15%. Roman script. Dictionary. Grammar. NT: 2002.

Pitta Pitta (Pita Pita, Pitha-Pitha, Bidhabidha, Bida-Bida) [pit] 2 (1981 Wurm and Hattori). Boulia, Queensland. *Class:* Australian, Pama-Nyungan, Karnic, Palku. *Dialects:* Related to Gangalanya, Garanya, Lhanima, Ngurlubulu, Ragaya, Rangwa, Yurlayurlanya, which may be extinct, and Wanggamala. *Other:* Distinct from Pita Pita. Nearly extinct.

Rembarunga (Rembarranga, Rembarrnga, Rainbargo, Kaltuy) [rmb] 150 (1983 Black). Roper River area, Maningrida and outstations, Katherine area, Northern Territory. *Class:* Australian, Gunwingguan, Rembargic. *Lg Use:* Few children seem to be learning the language. Speakers also use Kriol, Ngalkbun, or Gunwinggu. *Lg Dev:* Dictionary. Grammar.

Ritarungo (Ritarnugu, Ritharngu, Ridharrngu, Ritharrngu, Ridarngo, Wagelak, Wawilag) [rit] 300 (1983 Black). Eastern Arnhem Land (Rose River, Roper River), Northern Territory. *Class:* Australian, Pama-Nyungan, Yuulngu, Dhuwal. *Lg Use:* Some also use Kriol or Djinba. *Lg Dev:* Dictionary. Grammar.

Thayore (Kuuk Thaayoore, Kuuk Thaayorre, Thaayore, Thayorre, Taior, Gugudayor, Kuktayor, Kukudayore, Behran) [thd] 150 (1991 SIL). Ethnic population: 350 (1982 A. Hall). Between Edward and Coleman rivers, Western Cape York, Queensland. *Class:* Australian, Pama-Nyungan, Paman, Western Pama. *Lg Dev:* Dictionary. Bible portions: 1981. *Other:* SVO. Coastal. Desert, savannah, scrub forest. Sea level. Hunter-gatherers; fishermen.

Thaypan (Kuku-Thaypan) [typ] 2 (1981 Wurm and Hattori). Queensland, central Cape York Peninsula, Coleman River. *Class:* Australian, Pama-Nyungan, Paman, Rarmul Pama. *Dialects:* Related to Takalak. *Other:* Nearly extinct.

Thurawal (Dharawal, Dharawaal, Turrubul) [tbh] Extinct. Port Hacking to Shoalhaven River, New South Wales. *Class:* Australian, Pama-Nyungan, Yuin. *Dialect:* Wadiwadi (Wodiwodi). *Lg Use:* Members of the ethnic group now speak English or Aboriginal English.

Tiwi [tiw] 1,500 (1983 Black). Population includes nonfluent speakers. Bathurst and Melville Islands, Nguiu, Northern Territory. *Class:* Australian, Tiwian. *Lg Use:* Speakers also use English. *Lg Dev:* Dictionary. Grammar. Bible portions: 1979–1985. *Other:* SVO. Coastal, islands. Scrub forest. Sea level. Hunter-gatherers formerly; now laborers; craftsmen.

Tjurruru (Tjururu) [tju] Extinct. Western Australia, northwest, Hardey River, southwest of Tom Price. *Class:* Australian, Pama-Nyungan, South-West, Inland Ngayarda.

Torres Strait Creole (Torres Strait Pidgin, Torres Strait Broken, Cape York Creole, Lockhart Creole, West Torres) [tcs] 23,400 (1989 J. Holm). Torres Strait Islands, towns on upper Cape York and some towns on the east coast of north Queensland. *Class:* Creole, English based, Pacific. *Dialects:* Ap-Ne-Ap, Modern Langus. Lexical similarity 80% with English. *Lg Use:* Trade language between the western and central islanders and the eastern islanders. Second-language speakers. *Other:* A creolization of Tok Pisin or Bislama and Kala Lagau Langgus.

Tyaraity (Dyeraidy, Daktjerat, Tjerait, Djeradj, Djerag, Kuwema) [woa] 10 (1983 Black). Delissaville, Northern Territory. They were originally near the mouth of the Reynold River. *Class:* Australian, Daly, Malagmalag, Malagmalag Proper. *Lg Use:* All or most also use English. *Other:* Nearly extinct.

Umbindhamu [umd] 6 (1981 Wurm and Hattori). Queensland, Cape York Peninsula, north of Coen. *Class:* Australian, Pama-Nyungan, Paman, Umbindhamuic. *Other:* Nearly extinct.

Umbugarla (Mbakarla) [umr] 3 (1981 Wurm and Hattori). Northern Territory, Arnhem Land, southeast of Limilngan, between Mary River and South Alligator River. *Class:* Australian, Umbugarla-Ngumbur. *Lg Dev:* Dictionary. Grammar. *Other:* Nearly extinct.

Umbuygamu (Moroba-Lama) [umg] 7 (1981 Wurm and Hattori). Queensland, Cape York Peninsula, east coast of Princess Charlotte Bay. *Class:* Australian, Pama-Nyungan, Paman, Lamalamic. *Other:* Nearly extinct.

Umpila [ump] 100 (1981 Wurm and Hattori). Cape Sidmouth and north nearly to Night Island, Queensland. *Class:* Australian, Pama-Nyungan, Paman, Northeastern Pama. *Lg Use:* Speakers are shifting to Torres Strait Creole. Only a few older people know Umpila. The middle generation has varying proficiency.

Uradhi [urf] 2 (1981 Wurm and Hattori). Queensland, northeast Cape York Peninsula, North Alice Creek. *Class:* Australian, Pama-Nyungan, Paman, Northern Pama. *Dialects:* Related to Gudang, Wuthati, Luthigh (Mpalitjanh), Yinwum, Ngkoth, Aritinngithigh, Mbiywom, Andyingit. *Other:* Nearly extinct.

Urningangg (Uningangk, Wuningak) [urc] 10 (1983 Black). Arnhem Land, northwest; upper reaches of Alligator River. *Class:* Australian, Giimbiyu. *Dialects:* Intelligible with Mangerr. *Lg Dev:* Dictionary. Grammar. *Other:* Nearly extinct.

Wadjiginy (Wogaity, Wagaydy) [wdj] 12 (1988 SIL). Southwest of Darwin along coast and inland along Finniss River. *Class:* Australian, Daly, Bringen-Wagaydy, Wagaydy. *Dialect:* Pungupungu (Kuwama, Patjtjamalh, Kandjerramal). *Lg Use:* Members of the ethnic group speak Kriol, but many understand Wadjiginy when the older people speak it. *Other:* Nearly extinct.

Wadjigu [wdu] 1 (1981 Wurm and Hattori). Queensland, southwest of Fairbairn Reservoir. *Class:* Australian, Pama-Nyungan, Maric. *Other:* Nearly extinct.

Wagaya (Wakaya, Waagai, Waagi, Wagai, Wagaja, Waggaia, Wakaja, Wakkaja, Warkya, Worgai, Worgaia, Workia, Leewakya, Ukkia) [wga] 10 (1983 Black). Northern Territory, Avon Downs, Camooweal, Austral Downs, area north of Lake Nash. *Class:* Australian, Pama-Nyungan, Wagaya-Warluwaric, Warluwara-Thawa. *Other:* Nearly extinct.

Wageman (Wogeman, Wagiman) [waq] 10 (2000). South of Pine Creek, Tipperary Station, and Bagot, Northern Territory. *Class:* Australian, Gunwingguan, Wagiman. *Lg Use:* Members of the ethnic group now speak Kriol. *Lg Dev:* Dictionary. Grammar. *Other:* Nearly extinct.

Wajarri (Watjari, Watjarri, Wadjari, Wadjeri) [wbv] 50 (1981 W. Douglas). Ethnic population: 200 or fewer (1981 W. Douglas). Mt. Magnet to Geraldton, Western Australia. *Class:* Australian, Pama-Nyungan, South-West, Wadjari. *Dialects:* Related to Badimaya. *Lg Use:* Members of the ethnic group generally speak English. *Other:* Nearly extinct.

Wakawaka (Wakka, Waga, Wagawaga, Waga-Waga, Enibura, Nukunukubara) [wkw] 3 (1981 Wurm and Hattori). Nanango north to Mt. Perry, west to Boyne River, at Kingaroy, Murgon, and Gayndah, Queensland. *Class:* Australian, Pama-Nyungan, Waka-Kabic, Miyan. *Dialects:* Duungidjawu, Wagawaga. Related to Wuliwuli, Barunggam, Gayabara, Muringam, which may be extinct. *Lg Use:* Most speak English as second language. *Other:* Nearly extinct.

Walmajarri (Walmatjari, Walmatjiri, Walmajiri, Wolmeri, Pililuna) [wmt] 1,000 (1990 Schmidt). Western Australia, along the Fitzroy River valley, Lake Gregory and La Grange. *Class:* Australian, Pama-Nyungan, South-West, Ngumbin. *Dialect:* Djuwarliny (Juwaliny, Tjuwalinj). The western group speaks Juwaliny. *Lg Use:* Some children understand and respond to Walmajarri, but their first language is Kriol. *Lg Dev:* Dictionary. Grammar. Bible portions: 1978–1985. *Other:* SOV. Plains. Semidesert. Hunter-gatherers.

Wambaya (Wambaia, Wambaja, Wombya, Wom-By-A, Umbaia, Yumpia) [wmb] 12 (1981 Wurm and Hattori). Northern Territory, Barkly Tableland, headwaters of Limmen Bight and McArthur rivers, and east of Lake Woods. *Class:* Australian, West Barkly. *Dialects:* Wambaya, Binbinga (Binbinka), Gudandji. Black (1983) says the dialects are inherently intelligible. *Lg Use:* Speakers are shifting to Kriol. *Lg Dev:* Dictionary. Grammar. *Other:* Nearly extinct.

Wamin (Agwamin) [wmi] 1 (1981 Wurm and Hattori). Queensland, south central Cape York Peninsula, Einasleigh River, northwest of Einasleigh. *Class:* Australian, Pama-Nyungan, Paman, Southern Pama. *Lg Dev:* Dictionary. Grammar. *Other:* Nearly extinct.

Wandarang (Wandaran, Warndarang, Wuyarrawala) [wnd] Extinct. Arnhem Land, Roper River area, Northern Territory. *Class:* Australian, Gunwingguan, Maran, Mara. *Dialects:* Related to Mara. *Lg Use:* Members of the ethnic group now speak Kriol. *Lg Dev:* Dictionary. Grammar.

Wangaaybuwan-Ngiyambaa [wyb] 12 (1981 Wurm and Hattori). New South Wales, Darling River, Barwon River, Yanda Creek, Bogan River. *Class:* Australian, Pama-Nyungan, Wiradhuric. *Dialects:* Wangaaybuwan (Wongaibon, Wombungee, Wongagibun, Wonghibon, Wonghi, Wonjhibon), Ngiyambaa (Giamba, Narran, Noongaburrah, Ngeumba, Ngiamba, Ngiumba, Ngjamba, Ngumbarr), Wayilwan (Waljwan). *Other:* Nearly extinct.

Wanggamala [wnm] 1 (1981 Wurm and Hattori). Northern Territory, Hay River, south of Andegerebinha. *Class:* Australian, Pama-Nyungan, Karnic, Palku. *Other:* Nearly extinct.

Wangganguru [wgg] 8 (1981 Wurm and Hattori). Northern Territory, southeast corner. *Class:* Australian, Pama-Nyungan, Karnic, Palku. *Other:* Nearly extinct.

Wanman (Warnman, Nanidjara, Nyaani) [wbt] 20 (1973 SIL). Western Australia, Marble Bar area, Nullagine Station, Strelley. *Class:* Australian, Pama-Nyungan, South-West, Wati. *Lg Use:* Members of the ethnic group generally speak Kriol, English, Martu Wangka, or Nyangumarta. *Other:* Nearly extinct.

Waray (Warray, Warrai, Arwur, Awarai, Awarra) [wrz] 4 (1981 Wurm and Hattori). Adelaide River area, Northern Territory. *Class:* Australian, Gunwingguan, Warayan. *Lg Dev:* Grammar. *Other:* Nearly extinct.

Wardaman (Wadaman, Waderman, Waduman, Warda'man, Warduman, Wartaman, Wardman, Wordman) [wrr] 50 (1983 Black). Northern Territory, upper Daly River. *Class:* Australian, Gunwingguan, Yangmanic. *Dialects:* Close to Yangman and Dagoman, which are extinct. *Lg Use:* Members of the ethnic group generally speak Kriol. *Lg Dev:* Dictionary. Grammar. *Other:* Nearly extinct.

Wariyangga (Warriyangka) [wri] Extinct. Western Australia, southeast of Mount Augustus, West Pilbara. *Class:* Australian, Pama-Nyungan, South-West, Inland Ngayarda. *Lg Dev:* Dictionary. *Other:* Ruhlen (1987) classifies it in a separate Mantharda group.

Warlmanpa (Walmala) [wrl] 50 (1981 Wurm and Hattori). Northern Territory, Mount Leichhardt area. *Class:* Australian, Pama-Nyungan, South-West, Ngarga. *Lg Use:* Members of the ethnic group generally speak Kriol. *Other:* Nearly extinct.

Warlpiri (Walbiri, Elpira, Ilpara, Wailbri, Walpiri, Walmama, Ngaliya, Ngardilpa) [wbp] 3,000 (1990 Schmidt). Northern Territory, Yuendumu, Ali Curung Willowra, Alice Springs, Katherine, Darwin, and Lajamanu. *Class:* Australian, Pama-Nyungan, South-West, Ngarga. *Dialects:* Related to Warlmanpa. *Lg Dev:* Dictionary. Grammar. NT: 2001. *Other:* SOV. Plains. Desert. Hunter-gatherers; nomadic.

Warluwara (Maula, Mauula, Mawula, Walookera, Walugera, Waluwara, Wollegara, Yunnalinka, Kapula, Parnkarra) [wrb] 3 (1981 Wurm and Hattori). Queensland, Roxborough Downs. *Class:* Australian, Pama-Nyungan, Wagaya-Warluwaric, Warluwara-Thawa. *Other:* Nearly extinct.

Warrgamay (Biyay) [wgy] 3 (1981 Wurm and Hattori). Queensland, coast south of Hinchinbrook Island, and inland along Herbert River. *Class:* Australian, Pama-Nyungan, Dyirbalic. *Other:* Nearly extinct.

Warrwa (Warwa, Warrawai) [wwr] 2 (2001 McGregor). Western Australia, West Kimberley, Derby Region. *Class:* Australian, Nyulnyulan. *Lg Dev:* Grammar. *Other:* Nearly extinct.

Warumungu (Warramunga) [wrm] 200 (1983 Black). Tennant Creek area, Northern Territory. *Class:* Australian, Pama-Nyungan, Warumungic. *Lg Use:* Members of the ethnic group generally speak Kriol.

Warungu (Warrungu, Gugu-Badhun, Gudjala) [wrg] 2 (1981 Wurm and Hattori). Queensland, northeast of Einasleigh. *Class:* Australian, Pama-Nyungan, Maric. *Dialects:* Related to Ngaygungu and Yirandhali. *Lg Dev:* Grammar. *Other:* Nearly extinct.

Wik-Epa (Wik-Ep) [wie] 3 (1981 Wurm and Hattori). Queensland, Cape York Peninsula, southeast of Aurukun. *Class:* Australian, Pama-Nyungan, Paman, Middle Pama. *Other:* Nearly extinct.

Wik-liyanh [wij] 40 (1981 Wurm and Hattori). Queensland, central Cape York Peninsula, southwest of Coen. *Class:* Australian, Pama-Nyungan, Paman, Middle Pama. *Other:* Nearly extinct.

Wik-Keyangan [wif] 3 (1981 Wurm and Hattori). Queensland, Cape York Peninsula, southeast of Aurukun. *Class:* Australian, Pama-Nyungan, Paman, Middle Pama. *Other:* Nearly extinct.

Wik-Me'anha (Wik-Em'an) [wih] 12 (1981 Wurm and Hattori). Queensland, Cape York Peninsula, southeast of Aurukun. *Class:* Australian, Pama-Nyungan, Paman, Middle Pama. *Other:* Nearly extinct.

Wik-Mungkan (Wik-Munkan, Wik-Mungkhn, Munkan) [wim] 400 (1990 Schmidt). Edward River to Aurukun, Queensland. *Class:* Australian, Pama-Nyungan, Paman, Middle Pama. *Lg Use:* 600 second-language speakers. Some also use English. *Lg Dev:* Dictionary. Grammar. NT: 1985.

Wik-Ngathana [wig] 126 (1981 Wurm and Hattori). Queensland, Cape York Peninsula, west coast below Aurukun. *Class:* Australian, Pama-Nyungan, Paman, Middle Pama.

Wikalkan (Wikngatara, Wik-Ngathara, Wik-Ngathrr, Wik-Ngatharra) [wik] 86 (1981 Wurm and Hattori). Aurukun, Queensland. *Class:* Australian, Pama-Nyungan, Paman, Middle Pama. *Dialects:* Wik-Ngandjara (Ngandjara), Ngadanja. *Lg Use:* Young people speak Wik-Mungkan.

Wikngenchera (Ngandjara, Nantjara, Ngantjeri, Wik-Nantjara, Wik Njinturawik-Nganhcara) [wua] 50 (1970 Oates). Aurukun, Queensland. *Class:* Australian, Pama-Nyungan, Paman, Middle Pama. *Dialects:* Related to Wikngathara (Wikalkan). *Lg Use:* All young people speak Wik-Mungkan. *Other:* Nearly extinct.

Wilawila (Wila-Wila) [wil] 2 (1981 Wurm and Hattori). Western Australia, central Kimberleys. *Class:* Australian, Wororan. *Other:* Nearly extinct.

Wiradhuri (Wiradhurri, Wiradjuri, Berrembeel, Warandgeri, Werogery, Wiiratheri, Wira-Athoree, Wiraduri, Wirajeree, Wirashuri, Wiratheri, Wirracharee, Wiraidyuri, Wirrai'yarrai, Wooragurie, Wordjerg) [wrh] 3 (1981 Wurm and Hattori). New South Wales, from Murray River to Macquarie River, along Lachlan River from junction with Murrumbidgee River to Parkes. *Class:* Australian, Pama-Nyungan, Wiradhuric. *Other:* Nearly extinct.

Wirangu (Nhawu, Njangga, Nyangga, Warrangoo, Wirongu, Wironguwongga, Wirrung, Wirrunga) [wiw] 2 (1981 Wurm and Hattori). South Australia, coast between head of Bight and Streaky Bay and inland to Ooldea Region. *Class:* Australian, Pama-Nyungan, South-West, Wirangu. *Other:* Nearly extinct.

Worimi (Kattang, Gadhang, Gadang, Warimi, Gadjang, Birbay) [kda] Extinct. Between Hunter and Hastings rivers, from Port Macquarie to Hawkesbury River, New South Wales. *Class:* Australian, Pama-Nyungan, Worimi. *Lg Use:* Members of the ethnic group now speak English.

Worora (Worrorra) [unp] 20 (1990 Schmidt). Derby area, Collier Bay, Western Australia. *Class:* Australian, Wororan. *Dialects:* Worora, Unggumi. *Lg Use:* 150 second-language speakers (1983 R. M. W. Dixon). Children may know some of the language. Many also use English, Aboriginal English, or Kriol. *Lg Dev:* Grammar. Bible portions: 1930–1943. *Other:* Nearly extinct.

Wuliwuli [wlu] Extinct. Queensland, southwestern, Dawson River, Baralaba, Banana, Theodore. *Class:* Australian, Pama-Nyungan, Waka-Kabic, Miyan.

Wulna [wux] 1 (1981 Wurm and Hattori). Arnhem Land around Darwin, mouth of Adelaide River and inland. *Class:* Australian, Limilngan-Wulna. *Other:* Nearly extinct.

Wunambal (Unambal, Wumnabal, Wunambullu, Yeidji, Yeithi, Jeidji, Jeithi) [wub] 20 (1990 A. Schmidt). Kalumburu, Wyndham and Mowanjum, Western Australia. *Class:* Australian, Wororan. *Dialects:* Wunambal, Gambera, Miwa. *Lg Use:* People generally speak Kriol. Children may know some of the language, but most speak Kriol, Aboriginal English, or Standard Australian English as first language. *Lg Dev:* Grammar. *Other:* Different from Kwini. 'Yeidji' means 'talk, speech'. Nearly extinct.

Wurrugu [wur] Extinct. Cobourg Peninsula, Northern Territory. *Class:* Australian, Yiwaidjan, Yiwaidjic. *Dialects:* Close to Iwaidja.

Yalarnnga [ylr] Extinct. Queensland around Burke River and Dajarra. *Class:* Australian, Pama-Nyungan, Galgadungic.

Yandruwandha [ynd] 2 (1981 Wurm and Hattori). South Australia around Moomba, and east into Queensland. *Class:* Australian, Pama-Nyungan, Karnic, Karna. *Other:* Nearly extinct.

Yangman (Jungman, Dagoman) [jng] Extinct. Ethnic population: 50 (1983 Black). Elsey Creek, Northern Territory, and Katherine. *Class:* Australian, Gunwingguan, Yangmanic. *Dialects:* Very close to Wardaman. *Lg Use:* Members of the ethnic group now speak English or Kriol.

Yankunytjatjara (Yankunjtjatjarra, Yankuntatjara, Jangkundjara, Kulpantja) [kdd] 200 to 300 (1985 Cliff Goddard). Yalata, Musgrave, and Everard Ranges, and the eastern part of Pitjantjatjara freehold lands and surrounding areas, South Australia. *Class:* Australian, Pama-Nyungan, South-West, Wati. *Lg Use:* Speakers also use Pitjantjatjara. *Lg Dev:* Dictionary. Grammar.

Yanyuwa (Yanyula, Janjula, Anyula, Wadiri, Yanula, Aniula, Anula, Leeanuwa) [jao] 70 to 100 (1990 Schmidt). Ethnic population: 113 (2000 WCD). Borroloola, Northern Territory and Doomadgee, Queensland. *Class:* Australian, Pama-Nyungan, Yanyuwan. *Lg Use:* Speakers intermarry with the Garawa or Mara. Wives learn the husband's language but use their own with members of their own group. Children usually speak the mother's language, but boys at puberty learn and then speak the father's language. All speak Kriol or English, and some speak Garawa as second language. *Lg Dev:* Bible portions: 1980. *Other:* SVO. Coastal plains. Savannah, scrub forest. Hunter-gatherers traditionally.

Yawarawarga [yww] 1 (1981 Wurm and Hattori). South Australia and Queensland, north of Cooper Creek, southeast of Lake Yamma Yamma. *Class:* Australian, Pama-Nyungan, Karnic, Karna. *Dialects:* Related to Midhaga, Karuwardi, Marulta. *Other:* Nearly extinct.

Yawuru (Jaudjibara, Jawdjibara, Jawdjibara, Yaudjibara, Yaudijbaia, Yawjibara, Jawadjag, Winjawindjagu) [ywr] 30 (2001 K. Hosokawa). Western Australia, coast south of Broome and inland. *Class:* Australian, Nyulnyulan. *Dialects:* Northern Yawuru, Southern Coastal Yawuru, Eastern Inland Yawuru. Related to Nyikina, Warrwa, Ngumbarl, Nimanburru, Jabirrjabirr, Nyulnyul, Bardi, Jawi. *Lg Use:* None use it as primary language. *Lg Dev:* Dictionary. Grammar. *Other:* Coastal dunes, riverine. Savannah, acacia woods. Fishermen; hunters. Nearly extinct.

Yidiny (Yidini, Idinji, Boolboora, Deba, Eneby, Gerrah, Gijow, Gillah, Guwamal, Idin Idindji, Idin-Wudjar, Indindji, Jidindji, Kitba, Maimbie, Mungera Ohalo, Pegullo-Bura, Warra-Warra, Warryboora, Woggil, Yetinji, Yiddinji, Yidin, Yidindji, Yitintyi, Yukkaburra) [yii] 12 (1981 Wurm and Hattori). Queensland, formerly Atherton Region. A few now at Palm Island Babinda, north to Gordonvale. *Class:* Australian, Pama-Nyungan, Yidinic. *Dialects:* Gunggay, Yidiny, Madyay. *Lg Dev:* Dictionary. Grammar. *Other:* Nearly extinct.

Yindjibarndi (Jindjibandi, Yinjtjipartnti) [yij] 500 to 600 (1990 Schmidt). Roebourne, Western Australia, surrounding towns and stations. *Class:* Australian, Pama-Nyungan, South-West, Coastal Ngayarda. *Lg Use:* Speakers also use English or Aboriginal English. *Lg Dev:* Dictionary. Grammar. *Other:* SVO. Coastal, riverine. Desert. Sea level to 200 meters. Hunter-gatherers; fishermen.

Yindjilandji (Injdjiladji, Bularnu, Dhidhanu) [yil] 1 (1981 Wurm and Hattori). Northern Territory, northeast of Wonarah. *Class:* Australian, Pama-Nyungan, Wagaya-Warluwaric, Warluwara-Thawa. *Other:* Nearly extinct.

Yinggarda (Inggarda, Ingara, Ingarda, Ingarra, Ingarrah, Inparra, Jinggarda, Yingkarta, Kakarakala) [yia] 5 (1981 Wurm and Hattori). Western Australia, coast at Shark Bay between Gascoyne and Wooramel rivers, inland to Red Hill, West Pilbara. *Class:* Australian, Pama-Nyungan, South-West, Yinggarda. *Dialects:* Related to Malgana which is extinct, Nhanda which is nearly extinct (handful

of speakers, Blevins 1995), and Bulinya which may be extinct. *Lg Dev:* Dictionary. Grammar. *Other:* Ruhlen (1987) says it is extinct. Nearly extinct.

Yir Yoront (Yir Yiront, Jir Joront, Gwandera, Kokomindjen, Mandjoen, Millera, Mind'jana, Mundjun, Myunduno) [yiy] 15 (1991 Bruce Sommer). Queensland, west central Cape York Peninsula, just southeast of Edward River. *Class:* Australian, Pama-Nyungan, Paman, Yir Yoront. *Dialects:* Dangedl (Dhanu'un, Djudjan, Dudjym), Gorminang, Jir'jorond (Jirmel Mel-Jir, Ngamba'wandh, Yirmel, Yirtangettle, Yir Thangedl, Yirtutiym). *Lg Use:* Most members of the ethnic group speak Torres Strait Creole. Some second-language speakers. Understanding of English is poor. *Lg Dev:* Dictionary. Grammar. *Other:* Nearly extinct.

Yugambal (Yugumbal, Yugabeh, Yugambeh, Jugumbir, Jukamba, Manaldjali, Minjanbal, Ngarrubul, Ngarrbal) [yub] Extinct. Queensland, Logan and Albert river basins from Jimboomba to MacPherson Range. *Class:* Australian, Pama-Nyungan, Yugambal. *Lg Dev:* Grammar.

Cook Islands

Cook Islands. 21,200. National or official language: English. A New Zealand self-governing territory. 15 islands including Danger, Manahiki, Rakahanga, Penrhyn (Tongareva), Pukapuka islands. Literacy rate: 92% to 94%. Also includes Niue (196). Information mainly from S. Wurm and S. Hattori 1981; N. Besnier OIEL 1992. The number of languages listed for Cook Islands is 5. Of those, all are living languages. See map on page 853.

English [eng] 683 in Cook Islands (1966 UN report). *Lg Use:* Official language. See main entry under United Kingdom.

Penrhyn (Tongareva, Mangarongaro, Penrhynese) [pnh] 600 (1981 Wurm and Hattori). Northern Cook Islands, Penrhyn Island. *Class:* Austronesian, Malayo-Polynesian, Central-Eastern, Eastern Malayo-Polynesian, Oceanic, Central-Eastern Oceanic, Remote Oceanic, Central Pacific, East Fijian-Polynesian, Polynesian, Nuclear, East, Central, Tahitic. *Dialects:* Almost intelligible with Rarotongan. *Lg Use:* Speakers also use Rarotongan. *Other:* Disappearing rapidly. The language spoken on Palmerstone Island is reported to be a mixture of Penrhynese and Yorkshire English.

Pukapuka (Bukabukan, Pukapukan) [pkp] 840 in Cook Islands (1997). Population total all countries: 2,030. Ethnic population: 1,200 (1997). Pukapuka and Nasau islands, northern Cook Islands; some in Rarotonga. Also spoken in Australia, New Zealand. *Class:* Austronesian, Malayo-Polynesian, Central-Eastern, Eastern Malayo-Polynesian, Oceanic, Central-Eastern Oceanic, Remote Oceanic, Central Pacific, East Fijian-Polynesian, Polynesian, Nuclear, Samoic-Outlier, Pukapuka. *Dialects:* Not intelligible with Rarotongan or other Cook Islands languages. Related to Samoan. *Other:* Unwritten. VSO, VOS. Fishermen; agriculturalists; copra production.

Rakahanga-Manihiki (Manihiki-Rakahanga) [rkh] 2,500 in Cook Islands (1981 Wurm and Hattori). Population total all countries: 5,000. Northern Cook Islands, Rakahanga and Manihiki islands. Also spoken in New Zealand. *Class:* Austronesian, Malayo-Polynesian, Central-Eastern, Eastern Malayo-Polynesian, Oceanic, Central-Eastern Oceanic, Remote Oceanic, Central Pacific, East Fijian-Polynesian, Polynesian, Nuclear, East, Central, Tahitic. *Dialects:* Limited intelligibility of Rarotongan. *Other:* Unwritten. Fishermen; agriculturalists: taro, coconuts.

Rarotongan (Cook Island, Cook Islands Maori, Maori, Kuki Airani, Rarotongan-Mangaian) [rar] 16,800 in Cook Islands (1979 Government report). Population total all countries: 42,669. 13 inhabited Cook Islands. Also spoken in French Polynesia, New Zealand. _Class:_ Austronesian, Malayo-Polynesian, Central-Eastern, Eastern Malayo-Polynesian, Oceanic, Central-Eastern Oceanic, Remote Oceanic, Central Pacific, East Fijian-Polynesian, Polynesian, Nuclear, East, Central, Tahitic. _Dialects:_ Mitiaro, Mauke, Atiu, Mangaia, Rarotonga, Aitutaki. Lexical similarity 83% with Paumotu, 79% with Hawaiian, 75% with Mangareva, 73% with Marquesan. _Lg Use:_ Trade language. _Lg Dev:_ Bible: 1851–1888. _Other:_ Prepositions. Fishermen; agriculturalists: arrowroot, coconut, sweet potato, yams, taro, banana, citrus fruit, pineapple, papaya, mango, chestnut. Christian.

Fiji

Republic of Fiji. 880,874. Population includes ethnic Fijian 46.2%, Indian 48.6%, Chinese and European 5.2%. National or official languages: Fijian, Fijian Hindustani, English. 325 islands, 100 inhabited. Land area 7,000 square miles. Literacy rate: 80% to 90%. Also includes Eastern Panjabi, Gujarati, Malayalam, Pitcairn-Norfolk, Samoan (1,139), Tamil, Telugu, Tongan (1,220), Tuvaluan (488), Urdu, Wallisian, Chinese (5,500). Information mainly from A. J. Schütz 1972; S. Wurm and S. Hattori 1981; P. Geraghty 1983. Blind population: 392. Deaf population: 46,321. The number of languages listed for Fiji is 10. Of those, all are living languages. See map on page 856.

English [eng] 4,929 Europeans in Fiji (1976 census). An additional 10,276 or 1.8% of population (1976 census) are part-European, and speak English and Fijian. _Lg Use:_ Official language. Also used by many urban Chinese (4,652 in 1976), Rotuman, occasionally by Indians, rarely by Fijians (P. Geraghty 1981). There are also reports of a Fijian Pidgin English. Main language of commerce, education, government. See main entry under United Kingdom.

Fijian (Fiji, Standard Fijian, Eastern Fijian, Nadroga, Nadronga) [fij] 330,441 in Fiji (1996 census). Population includes 10,000 in Kadavu (1,500 Nabukelevu), 20,000 in Northeast Viti Levu. Population total all countries: 334,061. Eastern half of Viti Levu and its eastern offshore islands, Kadavu Island, Vanua Levu and its offshore islands, Nayau, Lakeba, Oneata, Moce, Komo, Namuka, Kabara, Vulaga, Ogea, Vatoa islands as first language; other areas of Fiji as second language. Also spoken in Nauru, New Zealand, Vanuatu. _Class:_ Austronesian, Malayo-Polynesian, Central-Eastern, Eastern Malayo-Polynesian, Oceanic, Central-Eastern Oceanic, Remote Oceanic, Central Pacific, East Fijian-Polynesian, East Fijian. _Dialects:_ Kadavu (Ono, Tavuki, Nabukelevu), Southeast Viti Levu (Waidina, Lutu, Nandrau, Naimasimasi), Bau (Bauan, Mbau), Northeast Viti Levu (Tokaimalo, Namena, Lovoni), Central Vanua Levu (Baaravi, Seaqaaqaa, Nabalebale, Savusavu), Northeast Vanua Levu (Labasa, Dogotuki Saqani, Korolau), Southeast Vanua Levu (Navatu-C, Tunuloa, Naweni, Baumaa), West Vanua Levu (Navatu-B, Soolevu, Bua, Navakasiga). The southern part of Vanua Levu has several dialects similar to Bau. On the northern part of Vanua Levu and adjacent islands people speak a variety somewhat related to Bau. Bau is very similar to Standard Fijian, used as traditional lingua franca among Fijians. _Lg Use:_ National language. 320,000 second-language users (1991 UBS). _Lg Dev:_ Newspapers. Radio programs. Dictionary. Grammar. Bible: 1864. _Other:_ VOS. Lumbermen; agriculturalists: taro, yams, breadfruit, bananas, sugarcane; molasses; copra production; coconut oil; miners: gold, copper; fishermen. Christian, traditional religion.

Fijian, Western (Fiji, Nadroga, Nadronga) [wyy] 57,000 (1977 Lincoln). Population includes 38,500 in Waya (Waya and Ba-Navosa), 18,500 in Nadroga. Fiji Islands, western half of Viti Levu, Waya Islands. _Class:_ Austronesian, Malayo-Polynesian, Central-Eastern, Eastern Malayo-Polynesian, Oceanic, Central-Eastern Oceanic, Remote Oceanic, Central Pacific, West Fijian-Rotuman, West Fijian. _Dialects:_ Nuclear Western Fijian (Nadrogaa, Tubaniwai, Baaravi), Waya (Nakoroboya, Noikoro, Magodro).

Gone Dau (Gonedau) [goo] 686 (2000). Eastern Fiji, Gone and Dau islands off western Vanua Levu. _Class:_ Austronesian, Malayo-Polynesian, Central-Eastern, Eastern Malayo-Polynesian, Oceanic, Central-Eastern Oceanic, Remote Oceanic, Central Pacific, East Fijian-Polynesian, East Fijian. _Dialects:_ Dialect chain to Bau (Standard) Fijian at the opposite end. Speakers learn Standard Fijian; it is not inherently intelligible to them.

Hindustani, Fijian (Fijian Hindi) [hif] 380,000 in Fiji (1991 UBS). Also spoken in Australia, USA. _Class:_ Indo-European, Indo-Iranian, Indo-Aryan, East Central zone. _Dialects:_ No significant regional variation. A type of Awadhi, also influenced by Bhojpuri. _Lg Use:_ Official language. Spoken by all of Indian ancestry in Fiji, including ethnic Tamil (6,663), Gujarati (6,203), Urdu, Telugu (2,008), Gurmukhi (Panjabi, 1,167), Bengali (17,875), Malayalam. A small Gujarati community speak Gujarati at home, and a few others, mainly older people, speak their traditional languages. _Lg Dev:_ Literacy rate in second language: 85%. Newspapers. Radio programs. Bible portions. _Other:_ Speakers were brought by the British to work as indentured laborers from 1879 until the 1920s. SOV; verb conjugations have been simplified from Standard Hindi. Agriculturalists: sugarcane, rice, vegetables; shopkeepers; small businessmen; professional people. Hindu, Muslim, Christian, Sikh.

Kiribati (Gilbertese, Ikiribati) [gil] 5,300 in Fiji (1988). Population includes 3,000 or more Banaban. _Dialect:_ Banaban. _Other:_ Christian. See main entry under Kiribati.

Lauan (Lau) [llx] 16,000 (1981 P. Geraghty). Eastern Fiji Islands, Lau, Nayau, Lakeba, Oneata, Moce, Komo, Namuka, Kabara, Vulaga, Ogea, Vatoa islands. _Class:_ Austronesian, Malayo-Polynesian, Central-Eastern, Eastern Malayo-Polynesian, Oceanic, Central-Eastern Oceanic, Remote Oceanic, Central Pacific, East Fijian-Polynesian, East Fijian. _Dialects:_ Lau, Vanua Balavu. In the middle of the East Fijian dialect chain; a cluster of dialects. Has some similarities to Bau Fijian; may be inherently intelligible with it. _Other:_ Agriculturalists: yams, taro, breadfruit, sugarcane, coconut; fishermen. Traditional religion.

Lomaiviti [lmv] 1,627 (2000 WCD). Islands east of Viti Levu: Koro, Makogai, Levuka, Ovalau, Batiki, Nairai, Gau. _Class:_ Austronesian, Malayo-Polynesian, Central-Eastern, Eastern Malayo-Polynesian, Oceanic, Central-Eastern Oceanic, Remote Oceanic, Central Pacific, East Fijian-Polynesian, East Fijian.

Namosi-Naitasiri-Serua (Namosi-Naitaasiri-Seerua) [bwb] 1,627 (2000 WCD). Namosi, Serua, Naitasiri provinces. _Class:_ Austronesian, Malayo-Polynesian, Central-Eastern, Eastern Malayo-Polynesian, Oceanic, Central-Eastern Oceanic, Remote Oceanic, Central Pacific, West Fijian-Rotuman, West Fijian. _Dialects:_ Batiwai, Tubai, Nalea. Namosi is a divergent variety of West Fijian. The dialects listed may be separate languages.

Rotuman (Rotuna, Rutuman) [rtm] 9,000 (1991 UBS). Population includes 2,500 on Rotuma, 300 overseas (1990 J. Vamarasi). Rotuma Island. _Class:_ Austronesian, Malayo-Polynesian, Central-Eastern, Eastern Malayo-Polynesian, Oceanic, Central-Eastern Oceanic, Remote Oceanic, Central Pacific, West Fijian-Rotuman, Rotuman.

Lg Dev: Dictionary. Grammar. Bible: 1999. *Other:* Agriculturalists; fishermen; copra production.

French Polynesia

French Overseas Territory of French Polynesia. 266,339. National or official languages: French, Tahitian. Includes Marquesas Islands, Gambier Islands, Austral Islands, Tuamotu Archipelago, Tahiti and the Society Islands. Literacy rate: 82% to 95%. Also includes Rapa Nui, Rarotongan (869). Information mainly from S. Wurm and S. Hattori 1981; N. Besnier 1992. The number of languages listed for French Polynesia is 9. Of those, all are living languages. See map on page 857.

Austral (Tubuai-Rurutu) [aut] 8,000 (1987). Austral (Tubuai) Islands. *Class:* Austronesian, Malayo-Polynesian, Central-Eastern, Eastern Malayo-Polynesian, Oceanic, Central-Eastern Oceanic, Remote Oceanic, Central Pacific, East Fijian-Polynesian, Polynesian, Nuclear, East, Central, Tahitic. *Dialects:* Raivavae, Rimatara, Rurutu, Tubuai. *Lg Use:* Speakers seem to be shifting to Tahitian. Speakers on Raivavae may be less bilingual.

Chinese, Hakka (Hakka) [hak] 19,200 in French Polynesia (1987). *Other:* Many are shifting to Tahitian. Buddhist, Christian, Chinese traditional religion. See main entry under China.

French [fra] 25,668 in French Polynesia (2000 WCD). *Lg Use:* Official language. 50,215 attending French schools, second-language users (1978). See main entry under France.

Mangareva (Mangarevan) [mrv] 1,600 (1987). Gambier Islands, Mangareva Island, Rikitea settlement. *Class:* Austronesian, Malayo-Polynesian, Central-Eastern, Eastern Malayo-Polynesian, Oceanic, Central-Eastern Oceanic, Remote Oceanic, Central Pacific, East Fijian-Polynesian, Polynesian, Nuclear, East, Central, Marquesic. *Dialects:* Lexical similarity 75% with Rarotongan, 73% with Marquesan, 72% with Paumotu, 50% to 68% with Tahitian. *Lg Use:* Some bilingualism in Tahitian; 65% average comprehension of those tested. *Lg Dev:* Bible portions: 1908. *Other:* Sea level to 440 meters. Agriculturalists: breadfruit, coconut, banana, plantain, sugarcane, taro, sweet potato, yams, arrowroot, turmeric, pandanus; fishermen. Traditional religion.

Marquesan, North [mrq] 3,400 (1981 Wurm and Hattori). Marquesas Islands: Hatutu, Nuku Hiva, Ua Huka, Ua Pou islands. *Class:* Austronesian, Malayo-Polynesian, Central-Eastern, Eastern Malayo-Polynesian, Oceanic, Central-Eastern Oceanic, Remote Oceanic, Central Pacific, East Fijian-Polynesian, Polynesian, Nuclear, East, Central, Marquesic. *Dialects:* Hatutu, Nuku Hiva, Ua Huka, Ua Pou. Wurm and Hattori (1981) list North Marquesan and South Marquesan as two languages. The dialects of North Marquesan are all inherently intelligible. 50% intelligibility of Tahitian. Lexical similarity 45% to 67% with Tahitian, 73% with Mangareva and Rarotonga, 70% with Hawaiian, 29% with Paumotu. *Lg Dev:* NT: 1995. *Other:* Fishermen; agriculturalists: breadfruit, coconut, banana, manioc, taro, melon, sweet potato, lettuce, tomato, orange, grapefruit, coffee; copra production.

Marquesan, South [mqm] 2,100 (1981 Wurm and Hattori). Marquesas Islands: Hiva Oa, Tahuta, Fatu Hiva islands. *Class:* Austronesian, Malayo-Polynesian, Central-Eastern, Eastern Malayo-Polynesian, Oceanic, Central-Eastern Oceanic, Remote Oceanic, Central Pacific, East Fijian-Polynesian, Polynesian, Nuclear, East, Central, Marquesic. *Dialects:* Hiva Oa, Tahuta, Fatu Hiva. The dialects listed are inherently intelligible. Wurm and Hattori (1981) list North Marquesan as a separate language.

Lg Dev: Bible portions: 1858–1905. *Other:* Fishermen; agriculturalists.

Rapa (Rapan) [ray] 521 (1998 Kenji Rutter, U. of Hawaii). Austral Islands, Rapa (Rapa Iti) Island, 2 villages, Ha'urei and 'Area. *Class:* Austronesian, Malayo-Polynesian, Central-Eastern, Eastern Malayo-Polynesian, Oceanic, Central-Eastern Oceanic, Remote Oceanic, Central Pacific, East Fijian-Polynesian, Polynesian, Nuclear, East, Central. *Dialects:* May be a dialect of Tubuai-Rurutu (Austral). *Lg Use:* School teachers desire to preserve Rapa. Children speak French among themselves. Some children are monolingual in French. Tahitian is used in church. School attendance is required to age 14; instruction is in French. French proficiency is limited. *Other:* Up to 600 meters. Agriculturalists: taro, coconut, orange, banana, coffee; fishermen; animal husbandry: goats, cattle. Christian.

Tahitian [tah] 117,000 in French Polynesia (1977 census). Population includes several thousand non-Tahitians. Population total all countries: 124,262. Society Islands and some islands in the Tuamotus including the Mihiroa group. Also spoken in New Caledonia, New Zealand, Vanuatu. *Class:* Austronesian, Malayo-Polynesian, Central-Eastern, Eastern Malayo-Polynesian, Oceanic, Central-Eastern Oceanic, Remote Oceanic, Central Pacific, East Fijian-Polynesian, Polynesian, Nuclear, East, Central, Tahitic. *Dialects:* Lexical similarity 85% with Rarotongan, 76% with Hawaiian. *Lg Use:* Official language. *Lg Dev:* Dictionary. Bible: 1838–1913. *Other:* Agriculturalists: taro, yams, sweet potato, corn, eggplant, tomato, melon, lettuce, coconut, breadfruit, Tahitian chestnut, mango, banana, coffee; fishermen; animal husbandry: pigs, cattle.

Tuamotuan (Pa'umotu) [pmt] 14,400 (1987). Population includes 6,700 on Tuamotu (1977 census), 2,000 in Tahiti (1977 Voegelin and Voegelin). Tuamotu, Tahiti. *Class:* Austronesian, Malayo-Polynesian, Central-Eastern, Eastern Malayo-Polynesian, Oceanic, Central-Eastern Oceanic, Remote Oceanic, Central Pacific, East Fijian-Polynesian, Polynesian, Nuclear, East, Central, Tahitic. *Dialects:* Vahitu, Tapuhoe, Napuka, Reao, Fangatau (Tupitimoake), Parata (Putahi), Marangai. Lexical similarity 83% with Rarotongan, 77% with Hawaiian. *Lg Use:* Dialect variations are being leveled out as people use more Tahitian. Speakers on Napuka and Reao may have less proficiency in Tahitian.

Guam

Guam. 166,090. National or official languages: Chamorro, English. USA territory. Geographically southernmost of the Mariana Islands. Literacy rate: 96%. Also includes Chuukese, Japanese (2,500), Korean (4,000), Palauan, Pingelapese, Tagalog (24,000), Chinese (2,000), people from the Philippines (30,000). Information mainly from Byron Bender 1971, 1996; K. Rehg 1991, 1996; J. Ellis 1996. The number of languages listed for Guam is 2. Of those, both are living languages. See map on page 858.

Chamorro (Tjamoro) [cha] 62,500 in Guam (1991 Bender and Rehg). Population total all countries: 76,705. Also spoken in Northern Mariana Islands. *Class:* Austronesian, Malayo-Polynesian, Chamorro. *Dialects:* Chamorro, Rotanese Chamorro. *Lg Use:* National language. Active language use. Language gaining in importance. Taught at the University of Guam. *Lg Dev:* Dictionary. Grammar. Bible portions: 1908–1992. *Other:* Influence from Spanish. SVO, VSO. Coral plateau, volcanic. Tropical. 200 to 400 meters. Christian.

English [eng] 28,800 in Guam (1987). *Lg Use:* National language. *Other:* USA military and dependents. See main entry under United Kingdom.

Kiribati

Repubic of Kiribati. Formerly Gilbert Islands, part of the British Gilbert and Ellice Islands Colony. 100,798. National or official languages: Kiribati, English. 38 islands and atolls; land area is 32.5 square miles, spread over nearly 2 million square miles of ocean at the equator. Literacy rate: 90%. Also includes Tuvaluan (500). Information mainly from B. Bender 1996; K. Rehg 1996. The number of languages listed for Kiribati is 2. Of those, both are living languages.

English [eng] 492 in Kiribati (2000). *Lg Use:* Official language. See main entry under United Kingdom.
Kiribati (I-Kiribati, Gilbertese, Ikiribati) [gil] 58,320 in Kiribati (1987). Population total all countries: 67,790. Also spoken in Fiji, Nauru, Solomon Islands, Tuvalu, Vanuatu. *Class:* Austronesian, Malayo-Polynesian, Central-Eastern, Eastern Malayo-Polynesian, Oceanic, Central-Eastern Oceanic, Remote Oceanic, Micronesian, Micronesian Proper, Ikiribati. *Dialect:* Banaban. North-south dialect division. In Tuvalu, the Nui dialect is inherently intelligible with Kiribati, but has vocabulary and pronunciation differences. Lexical similarity 26% with Ponapean. *Lg Use:* National language. Vigorous. Only 30% of the speakers are effectively bilingual in Kiribati and English. *Lg Dev:* Most are literate in Kiribati, but little material is available. Dictionary. Bible: 1893–1954. *Other:* The language and speakers are called 'I-Kiribati'. VOS. Fishermen; sailors; agriculturalists; copra production. Christian.

Marshall Islands

Formerly part of the U.S. Trust Territory of the Pacific Islands. 57,738. National or official languages: Marshallese, English. Double chain of 1,225 islands and reefs, 68 square miles of land. Literacy rate: 85%. Information mainly from B. W. Bender 1996; K. L. Rehg 1996; J. Ellis 1996. The number of languages listed for Marshall Islands is 2. Of those, both are living languages.

English [eng] 600 in Marshall Islands (2004). *Lg Use:* Official language. See main entry under United Kingdom.
Marshallese (Ebon) [mah] 43,900 in Marshall Islands (1979 Bender). Also spoken in Nauru. *Class:* Austronesian, Malayo-Polynesian, Central-Eastern, Eastern Malayo-Polynesian, Oceanic, Central-Eastern Oceanic, Remote Oceanic, Micronesian, Micronesian Proper, Marshallese. *Dialects:* Rälik, Ratak. Two inherently intelligible dialects. Speech on Ujelang, the westernmost island, is slightly less homogeneous. Lexical similarity 33% with Ponapean. *Lg Use:* Official language. Vigorous. *Lg Dev:* Dictionary. Grammar. Bible: 1982. *Other:* Copra production, coconut oil.

Micronesia

Federated States of Micronesia. Formerly part of the U.S. Trust Territory of the Pacific Islands. 108,155. National or official languages: Chuukese, Kosraean, Pohnpeian, Yapese, English. It includes the states of Yap, Chuuk (Truk), Pohnpei (Ponape), and Kosrae (Kusaie). 607 islands, 270.8 square miles of land, spread over more than 1 million square miles of ocean. Capital: Palikir. Literacy rate: 85%. Also includes Japanese, Chinese. Information mainly from B. W. Bender 1996; K. L. Rehg 1996; J. Ellis 1996. The number of languages listed for Micronesia is 18. Of those, all are living languages. See map on page 859.

Chuukese (Chuuk, Truk, Trukese, Ruk, Lagoon Chuukese) [chk] 38,341 in Micronesia (1989 census). Chuuk Lagoon, Caroline Islands, some on Ponape. Also spoken in Guam. *Class:* Austronesian, Malayo-Polynesian, Central-Eastern, Eastern Malayo-Polynesian, Oceanic, Central-Eastern Oceanic, Remote Oceanic, Micronesian, Micronesian Proper, Ponapeic-Trukic, Trukic. *Dialects:* East Lagoon, Fayichuck. *Lg Use:* National language. Vigorous. Total 45,000 including second-language users (1991 UBS). *Lg Dev:* Dictionary. Grammar. Bible: 1989–2001. *Other:* Island. Agriculturalists; copra production.
English [eng] 5,341 in Micronesia (2000). *Lg Use:* Official language. See main entry under United Kingdom.
Kapingamarangi (Kirinit) [kpg] 3,000 (1995 SIL). Population includes 1,500 on Kapingamarangi and 1,500 in Porakiet village on Ponape. Kapingamarangi and Ponape islands, Caroline Islands. *Class:* Austronesian, Malayo-Polynesian, Central-Eastern, Eastern Malayo-Polynesian, Oceanic, Central-Eastern Oceanic, Remote Oceanic, Central Pacific, East Fijian-Polynesian, Polynesian, Nuclear, Samoic-Outlier, Ellicean. *Dialects:* Lexical similarity 55% with Nukuoro, 54% with Rarotongan, 53% with Samoan, 51% with Paumotu, 50% with Tahitian. *Lg Use:* Vigorous. *Lg Dev:* Dictionary. NT: 2000. *Other:* There is intermarriage with Nukuoro people. SVO, VSO. Agriculturalists: taro, breadfruit, banana, coconut, pandanus; fishermen; livestock: pigs, poultry; woodcarvers.
Kosraean (Kusaie, Kosrae) [kos] 8,000 in Micronesia (2001 Johnstone and Mandryk). Kusaie Island, Caroline Islands. Also spoken in Nauru. *Class:* Austronesian, Malayo-Polynesian, Central-Eastern, Eastern Malayo-Polynesian, Oceanic, Central-Eastern Oceanic, Remote Oceanic, Micronesian, Micronesian Proper, Kusaiean. *Dialects:* Lelu-Tafunsak, Malen-Utwe. Lexical similarity 26% with Ponapean. *Lg Use:* National language. Vigorous. *Lg Dev:* Dictionary. Grammar. Bible: 1928.
Mokilese (Mokil, Mwoakilese, Mwoakiloa) [mkj] 1,050 (1979 Bender). Fewer than 500 on Mokil Atoll. Mokil (Mwoakiloa) Atoll, east of Carolines, and on Pohnpei Island. *Class:* Austronesian, Malayo-Polynesian, Central-Eastern, Eastern Malayo-Polynesian, Oceanic, Central-Eastern Oceanic, Remote Oceanic, Micronesian, Micronesian Proper, Ponapeic-Trukic, Ponapeic. *Dialects:* Lexical similarity 79% with Pingelapese, 75% with Ponapean. *Lg Use:* Vigorous. Speakers also use Ponapean. *Lg Dev:* Dictionary. Grammar.
Mortlockese (Mortlock, Nomoi) [mrl] 5,904 (1989 census). Population includes 1,692 in Upper Mortlock, 1,757 in Mid Mortlock, 2,455 in Lower Mortlock, about 1,000 elsewhere. Mortlock Islands, 70 miles southeast of Truk, Caroline Islands. A large group of Lower Mortlock speakers are on Ponape Island. *Class:* Austronesian, Malayo-Polynesian, Central-Eastern, Eastern Malayo-Polynesian, Oceanic, Central-Eastern Oceanic, Remote Oceanic, Micronesian, Micronesian Proper, Ponapeic-Trukic, Trukic. *Dialects:* Upper Mortlock, Mid Mortlock, Lower Mortlock. 75% intelligibility of Pulapese, 18% of Satawal, 8% of Woleaian. Lexical similarity 80% to 85% with Chuukese, 83% with Puluwat, 82% with Satawal, 81% with Carolinian, 78% with Woleaian, 72% with Ulithi. *Lg Use:* Vigorous. *Lg Dev:* NT: 1883.
Namonuito (Namon Weite) [nmt] 944 (1989 census). Magur, Ono, Onari, Piserarh, Ulul islands, Carolines. *Class:* Austronesian, Malayo-Polynesian, Central-Eastern, Eastern Malayo-Polynesian, Oceanic, Central-Eastern Oceanic, Remote Oceanic, Micronesian, Micronesian Proper, Ponapeic-Trukic, Trukic. *Lg Use:* Vigorous.
Ngatik Men's Creole (Ngatikese Men's Language, Ngatikese) [ngm] 700. Population includes 500 on atoll

(1983 Poyer), 200 on Ponape. Ngatik (Sapuahfik) Atoll, east of the Caroline Islands. *Class:* Creole, English based, Pacific. *Dialects:* A creolized language from the Sapuahfik dialect of Ponapean and English whose genesis is the direct result of a massacre in 1837 of adult males on Ngatik by British traders. *Lg Use:* Women and children understand it. Spoken by adult males who are also native bilinguals of the Sapuahfik dialect of Ponapean. *Other:* Agriculturalists: coconut; fishermen; animal husbandry: pigs.

Nguluwan [nuw] 50 (2000 Osamu Sakiyama). Ngulu atoll, between the Yap Islands and Belau Islands. *Class:* Mixed Language, Yapese-Ulithi. *Dialects:* Phonology from Ulithian and grammar and lexicon from Yapese. *Lg Use:* Speakers are shifting to Yapese. *Other:* Nearly extinct.

Nukuoro (Nukoro, Nuguor) [nkr] 860 (1993 Johnstone). Population includes 125 on Ponape. Nukuoro Island, Caroline Islands. *Class:* Austronesian, Malayo-Polynesian, Central-Eastern, Eastern Malayo-Polynesian, Oceanic, Central-Eastern Oceanic, Remote Oceanic, Central Pacific, East Fijian-Polynesian, Polynesian, Nuclear, Samoic-Outlier, Ellicean. *Dialects:* Lexical similarity 55% with Kapingamarangi. *Lg Use:* Vigorous. Many older speakers also use Ponapean. *Lg Dev:* Literacy rate in second language: 80%. NT: 1986. *Other:* SVO, VSO. Fishermen (net, spear, rod); agriculturalists: taro; copra production; animal husbandry.

Pááfang [pfa] 1,318 (1989 census). Hall Islands (Nomwin, Fananu, Marilo, Ruo), Carolines. *Class:* Austronesian, Malayo-Polynesian, Central-Eastern, Eastern Malayo-Polynesian, Oceanic, Central-Eastern Oceanic, Remote Oceanic, Micronesian, Micronesian Proper, Ponapeic-Trukic, Trukic. *Dialects:* Indications of convergence with Chuukese. *Lg Use:* Highly bilingual in Chuukese. *Other:* No published dictionary or grammar.

Pingelapese (Pingelap, Pingilapese) [pif] 2,500 in Micronesia. 500 on Pingelap, about 2,000 on Ponape. Population total all countries: 3,000. Pingelap and Ponape. Also spoken in Guam, USA. *Class:* Austronesian, Malayo-Polynesian, Central-Eastern, Eastern Malayo-Polynesian, Oceanic, Central-Eastern Oceanic, Remote Oceanic, Micronesian, Micronesian Proper, Ponapeic-Trukic, Ponapeic. *Dialects:* Lexical similarity 81% with Pohnpeian, 79% with Mokilese. *Lg Use:* Vigorous. Speakers also use Ponapean.

Pohnpeian (Ponapean) [pon] 29,000 (2001 Johnstone and Mandryk). Population includes 24,000 on Pohnpei, 3,425 on outer islands, 275 elsewhere. Pohnpei Island, Caroline Islands. *Class:* Austronesian, Malayo-Polynesian, Central-Eastern, Eastern Malayo-Polynesian, Oceanic, Central-Eastern Oceanic, Remote Oceanic, Micronesian, Micronesian Proper, Ponapeic-Trukic, Ponapeic. *Dialects:* Kiti, Ponapean, Sapwuahfik. Lexical similarity 81% with Pingelapese, 75% with Mokilese, 36% with Chuuk. *Lg Use:* National language. Vigorous. *Lg Dev:* Dictionary. Grammar. Bible: 1994.

Puluwatese (Puluwat) [puw] 1,364 (1989 census). Polowat, Pollap, Houk (Pulusuk), and Tamtam islands, Carolines. *Class:* Austronesian, Malayo-Polynesian, Central-Eastern, Eastern Malayo-Polynesian, Oceanic, Central-Eastern Oceanic, Remote Oceanic, Micronesian, Micronesian Proper, Ponapeic-Trukic, Trukic. *Dialects:* Puluwatese, Pulapese, Pulusukese. 64% intelligibility of Satawalese, 40% of Woleaian, 21% of Ulithian. Pulap speakers may need separate literature. Lexical similarity 88% with Satawalese and Carolinian, 83% with Mortlock, 82% with Woleaian, 81% with Chuukese, 72% with Ulithian. *Lg Use:* Vigorous. Speakers have low proficiency in English. *Lg Dev:* Dictionary.

Satawalese [stw] 458 (1987 Yap census). Satawal Island, Carolines. *Class:* Austronesian, Malayo-Polynesian, Central-Eastern, Eastern Malayo-Polynesian, Oceanic, Central-Eastern Oceanic, Remote Oceanic, Micronesian, Micronesian Proper, Ponapeic-Trukic, Trukic. *Dialects:* 60% intelligibility of Ulithian and Woleaian. Lexical similarity 95% with Carolinian, 88% with Woleaian and Puluwat, 82% with Mortlockese, 79% with Chuukese, 77% with Ulithian. *Lg Use:* Vigorous. *Other:* No published dictionary or grammar.

Ulithian [uli] 3,000 (1987 UBS). Ulithi, Ngulu, Sorol, Fais islands, eastern Caroline Islands. *Class:* Austronesian, Malayo-Polynesian, Central-Eastern, Eastern Malayo-Polynesian, Oceanic, Central-Eastern Oceanic, Remote Oceanic, Micronesian, Micronesian Proper, Ponapeic-Trukic, Trukic. *Dialects:* 85% intelligibility of Woleaian, 57% of Satawalese, very low intelligibility of Pulapese and Chuuk. Lexical similarity 74% to 80% with Woleaian, 77% with Satawalese, 74% with Carolinian, 72% with Puluwatese and Mortlockese, 68% with Chuuk. *Lg Use:* Semiofficial status. Vigorous. *Lg Dev:* Grammar. NT: 1995. *Other:* Christian, traditional religion.

Woleaian [woe] 1,631 (1987 Yap census). Woleai (Wottegai), Falalus, Seliap (Sulywap), Falalop (Falalap), Tegailap (Tagalap), Paliau, Mariang, Eauripik, Faraulep, Elato, Lamotrek, Ifaluk islands, eastern Caroline Islands. The first 5 listed are inhabited. 22 islands total, Yap State. *Class:* Austronesian, Malayo-Polynesian, Central-Eastern, Eastern Malayo-Polynesian, Oceanic, Central-Eastern Oceanic, Remote Oceanic, Micronesian, Micronesian Proper, Ponapeic-Trukic, Trukic. *Dialects:* Woleaian, Lamotrek. 84% intelligibility of Satawalese, 81% of Ulithian, 50% of Sonsorol, very low of Pulapese and Chuukese. Lexical similarity 88% with Satawalese and Carolinian, 82% with Puluwatese, 80% with Ulithian, 78% with Mortlockese, 75% with Chuukese. *Lg Use:* Vigorous. Positive language attitude. Speakers have low proficiency in English. *Lg Dev:* Dictionary. Grammar.

Yapese [yap] 6,592 (1987 Yap census). Yap Island, 10 islands, Caroline Islands. *Class:* Austronesian, Malayo-Polynesian, Central-Eastern, Eastern Malayo-Polynesian, Oceanic, Yapese. *Lg Use:* National language. Vigorous. *Lg Dev:* Dictionary. Grammar. NT: 1973. *Other:* VSO. Mountain, plateau, coral reef, volcanic. Mangrove swamps, coconut groves. 4 to 200 meters. Agriculturalists: yams, banana, betel nut, breadfruit, Tahitian chestnut, mango, papaya, cassava, sweet potato, sugarcane, turmeric; animal husbandry: pigs, poultry; fishermen. Traditional religion, Christian.

Nauru

Republic of Nauru. Naoero. 12,809. National or official languages: Nauruan, English. One coral island, 9 square miles. Literacy rate: 99%. Also includes Fijian (180), Kiribati (1,700), Kosraean, Marshallese, Tuvaluan (789), Yue Chinese (626). Information mainly from B. Bender and K. Rehg 1991. The number of languages listed for Nauru is 3. Of those, all are living languages.

Chinese Pidgin English [cpi] *Class:* Pidgin, English based, Pacific. *Other:* Currently spoken.

English [eng] 714 in Nauru (2000). *Lg Use:* National language. 7,254 including second-language users (1979 Government figures). See main entry under United Kingdom.

Nauruan [nau] 6,000 (1991 Bender and Rehg). Nauru Island, Pleasant Island, isolated atoll west of Kiribati. *Class:* Austronesian, Malayo-Polynesian, Central-Eastern, Eastern Malayo-Polynesian, Oceanic, Central-Eastern

Oceanic, Remote Oceanic, Micronesian, Nauruan. *Lg Use:* Official language. Used as a second language by 1,000 Kiribati, Tuvalu, Kosraean, or Marshallese. Children not learning Nauru. Almost all also use English. *Lg Dev:* Bible: 1918. *Other:* School attendance is required from age 6 to 17. Fishermen; phosphate miners. Christian.

New Caledonia

New Caledonia. 213,679. Melanesian 45%. National or official language: French. A French territory. Literacy rate: 85% among Melanesians. Also includes Tahitian (7,000), Vietnamese (5,000), Chinese (500). Information mainly from S. Wurm and S. Hattori 1981; S. Schooling 1990; P. A. Geraghty 1988; D. T. Tryon 1995. Blind population: 30. The number of languages listed for New Caledonia is 40. Of those, 39 are living languages and 1 is extinct. See map on page 860.

Ajië (Houailou, Wailu, Wai, Anjie, A'jie) [aji] 4,044 (1996 census). Houailou: east coast Monéo to Kouaoua and inland valleys. *Class:* Austronesian, Malayo-Polynesian, Central-Eastern, Eastern Malayo-Polynesian, Oceanic, Central-Eastern Oceanic, Remote Oceanic, New Caledonian, Southern, South, Wailic. *Lg Use:* Language of wider communication. Vigorous. *Lg Dev:* Taught at secondary and junior college levels, and various other schools. Grammar. NT: 1922. *Other:* Regional language and 'church language'.

Arhâ (Ara) [aqr] 35 (1996 census). Poya, upper valleys. *Class:* Austronesian, Malayo-Polynesian, Central-Eastern, Eastern Malayo-Polynesian, Oceanic, Central-Eastern Oceanic, Remote Oceanic, New Caledonian, Southern, South, Wailic. *Dialects:* Different from Arho. *Lg Use:* Reported to be bilingual in Ajië. *Other:* Nearly extinct.

Arhö (Aro) [aok] 62 (1996 census). Poya, Cradji, and Nékliai villages. *Class:* Austronesian, Malayo-Polynesian, Central-Eastern, Eastern Malayo-Polynesian, Oceanic, Central-Eastern Oceanic, Remote Oceanic, New Caledonian, Southern, South, Wailic. *Lg Use:* Reported to be nearing extinction. Speakers also use Ajië. *Other:* Different from Arhâ.

Bislama (Bichelamar) [bis] 1,200 in New Caledonia (1982 SIL). Mainly in Noumea. All from Vanuatu. See main entry under Vanuatu.

Bwatoo [bwa] 300 (1982 SIL). Voh-Kone: Baco, Gatope, Oundjo; Poya: Népou. *Class:* Austronesian, Malayo-Polynesian, Central-Eastern, Eastern Malayo-Polynesian, Oceanic, Central-Eastern Oceanic, Remote Oceanic, New Caledonian, Northern, North, Hmwaveke. *Dialects:* May be a dialect of Haveke. Wurm and Hattori (1981) treat it as a dialect of Voh-Kone.

Caac (Moenebeng) [msq] 890 (1996 census). Pouébo, northeast coast. *Class:* Austronesian, Malayo-Polynesian, Central-Eastern, Eastern Malayo-Polynesian, Oceanic, Central-Eastern Oceanic, Remote Oceanic, New Caledonian, Northern, Extreme Northern. *Dialects:* Pouébo (Pwebo), La Conception (St. Louis).

Cemuhî (Camuhi, Camuki, Tyamuhi, Wagap) [cam] 2,051 (1996 census). Touho: east coast from Congouma to Wagap and inland valleys. *Class:* Austronesian, Malayo-Polynesian, Central-Eastern, Eastern Malayo-Polynesian, Oceanic, Central-Eastern Oceanic, Remote Oceanic, New Caledonian, Northern, Central. *Lg Dev:* Dictionary. Grammar. *Other:* Tonal.

Dehu (De'u, Drehu, Lifou, Lifu) [dhv] 11,338 (1996 census). Lifou, Loyalty Islands. *Class:* Austronesian, Malayo-Polynesian, Central-Eastern, Eastern Malayo-Polynesian, Oceanic, Central-Eastern Oceanic, Remote Oceanic, Loyalty Islands. *Dialects:* Losi, Wete. *Lg Use:* Vigorous. *Lg Dev:* Taught at secondary and junior college

levels, and various other schools. Dictionary. Grammar. Bible: 1890. *Other:* Min is an old language of respect. Word order depends on tense.

Dumbea (Ndumbea, Naa Dubea, Dubea, Drubea) [duf] 946 (1996 census). Paita on the west coast, Ounia on the east coast. *Class:* Austronesian, Malayo-Polynesian, Central-Eastern, Eastern Malayo-Polynesian, Oceanic, Central-Eastern Oceanic, Remote Oceanic, New Caledonian, Southern, Extreme Southern. *Lg Dev:* Dictionary. Grammar. *Other:* Tonal.

French [fra] 53,400 in New Caledonia (1987). Mainly Noumea. *Lg Use:* Official language. See main entry under France.

Futuna, East (Futunian) [fud] 3,000 in New Caledonia (1986). *Lg Use:* Speakers also use French. *Other:* Different from Futuna-Aniwa (West Futuna) in Vanuatu. Migrant workers. See main entry under Wallis and Futuna.

Fwâi (Poai, Yengen, Yehen) [fwa] 1,131 (1996 census). Hiènghène on the east coast; Ouenguip to Pindache and lower valleys. *Class:* Austronesian, Malayo-Polynesian, Central-Eastern, Eastern Malayo-Polynesian, Oceanic, Central-Eastern Oceanic, Remote Oceanic, New Caledonian, Northern, North, Nemi. *Lg Dev:* Dictionary.

Haeke (Aeke, 'Aeke, Haeake) [aek] 100 (1982 SIL). Voh-Kone: Baco. *Class:* Austronesian, Malayo-Polynesian, Central-Eastern, Eastern Malayo-Polynesian, Oceanic, Central-Eastern Oceanic, Remote Oceanic, New Caledonian, Haekic. *Dialects:* Wurm and Hattori (1981) treat it as a dialect of Voh-Kone. *Lg Use:* Speakers are reported to be bilingual in a neighboring dialect. *Other:* Nearly extinct.

Haveke (Aveke, 'Aveke) [hvk] 300 (1982 SIL). Voh-Kone: Gatope, Oundjo, Tiéta. *Class:* Austronesian, Malayo-Polynesian, Central-Eastern, Eastern Malayo-Polynesian, Oceanic, Central-Eastern Oceanic, Remote Oceanic, New Caledonian, Northern. *Dialects:* Bwatoo may be a dialect. Wurm and Hattori (1981) treat it as a dialect of Voh-Kone.

Hmwaveke ('Moaveke, Ceta, Faa Ceta) [mrk] 300 (1982 SIL). Voh: Tiéta. *Class:* Austronesian, Malayo-Polynesian, Central-Eastern, Eastern Malayo-Polynesian, Oceanic, Central-Eastern Oceanic, Remote Oceanic, New Caledonian, Northern, North, Hmwaveke. *Dialects:* Wurm and Hattori (1981) treat it as a dialect of Voh-Kone.

Iaai (Iai, Yai) [iai] 1,562 (1996 census). Ouvéa Island, Loyalty Islands. *Class:* Austronesian, Malayo-Polynesian, Central-Eastern, Eastern Malayo-Polynesian, Oceanic, Central-Eastern Oceanic, Remote Oceanic, Loyalty Islands. *Lg Dev:* Taught in primary schools. Grammar. Bible: 1901. *Other:* VOS.

Javanese, New Caledonian [jas] 6,750 (1987). Noumea. *Class:* Austronesian, Malayo-Polynesian, Javanese. *Lg Use:* Young people understand Javanese, but speak French. *Other:* Migrant workers who came primarily between 1900 and 1938. Since World War II there has been continuing migration in both directions by individuals and families. The language is influenced by French, in contrast to the Javanese of Indonesia, which is influenced by Indonesian. Muslim (Sunni).

Jawe (Njawe, Diahoue, Oubatch, Ubach) [jaz] 729 (1996 census). Northeast coast from Tchamboenne to Tao and upper valleys. *Class:* Austronesian, Malayo-Polynesian, Central-Eastern, Eastern Malayo-Polynesian, Oceanic, Central-Eastern Oceanic, Remote Oceanic, New Caledonian, Northern, North, Nemi. *Lg Dev:* Dictionary.

Kumak (Koumac, Fwa-Goumak) [nee] 947 (1996 census). Northwest coast of Koumac (Kumak dialect) and Poum (Nenema dialect). *Class:* Austronesian, Malayo-Polynesian, Central-Eastern, Eastern Malayo-Polynesian, Oceanic, Central-Eastern Oceanic, Remote Oceanic, New

Caledonian, Northern, Extreme Northern. *Dialect:* Kumak, Nenema (Nelema). *Lg Dev:* Grammar.

Mea (Ha Mea, Hameha) [meg] 300 (1982 SIL). La Foa: upper valleys. *Class:* Austronesian, Malayo-Polynesian, Central-Eastern, Eastern Malayo-Polynesian, Oceanic, Central-Eastern Oceanic, Remote Oceanic, New Caledonian, Southern. *Dialects:* Some influences from Tiri. Wurm and Hattori (1981) treat it as a dialect of Tiri. *Lg Dev:* Dictionary.

Neku [nek] 221 (1996 census). Bourail, lower valley. *Class:* Austronesian, Malayo-Polynesian, Central-Eastern, Eastern Malayo-Polynesian, Oceanic, Central-Eastern Oceanic, Remote Oceanic, New Caledonian, Southern, South, Wailic.

Nemi [nem] 325 (2000 Tryon). East coast: upper valleys north of Hiènghène, and west coast at Voh: Ouélis and upper valley. *Class:* Austronesian, Malayo-Polynesian, Central-Eastern, Eastern Malayo-Polynesian, Oceanic, Central-Eastern Oceanic, Remote Oceanic, New Caledonian, Northern, North, Nemi. *Lg Dev:* Dictionary.

Nengone (Maré, Iwatenu) [nen] 6,500 (2000 Tryon). Mare, Loyalty Islands. *Class:* Austronesian, Malayo-Polynesian, Central-Eastern, Eastern Malayo-Polynesian, Oceanic, Central-Eastern Oceanic, Remote Oceanic, Loyalty Islands. *Dialects:* Iwatenu is a dialect of respect. *Lg Use:* Vigorous. *Lg Dev:* Taught at secondary and junior college levels, and various other schools. Dictionary. Grammar. Bible: 1903. *Other:* Word order depends on tense.

Numee (Naa Numee, Kapone, Touaouru, Ouen, Kwenyii, Kunie, Tuaaru, Duauru, Uen, Wen, Naa-Wee) [kdk] 1,814 (1996 census). Yate, Touaouru and Goro on main island south coast (Numee dialect), Isle Ouen (Ouen dialect), and Isle of Pines (Kwenyii). *Class:* Austronesian, Malayo-Polynesian, Central-Eastern, Eastern Malayo-Polynesian, Oceanic, Central-Eastern Oceanic, Remote Oceanic, New Caledonian, Southern, Extreme Southern. *Dialects:* Numee (Touaouru), Ouen, Kwenyii (Kunie). *Lg Dev:* Grammar. *Other:* Distinct from Nume of Vanuatu. Tonal.

Nyâlayu [yly] 1,522 (1996 census). North coast, Belep Island, Arama, and Balade. *Class:* Austronesian, Malayo-Polynesian, Central-Eastern, Eastern Malayo-Polynesian, Oceanic, Central-Eastern Oceanic, Remote Oceanic, New Caledonian, Northern, Extreme Northern. *Dialects:* Yalayu, Belep.

Orowe (Boewe) [bpk] 587 (1996 census). Bourail upper valleys: Ni, Pothé, Bouirou, Azareu. *Class:* Austronesian, Malayo-Polynesian, Central-Eastern, Eastern Malayo-Polynesian, Oceanic, Central-Eastern Oceanic, Remote Oceanic, New Caledonian, Southern, South, Wailic.

Paicî (Pati, Paaci, Ci, Ponerihouen) [pri] 5,498 (1996 census). East coast between Poindimié and Ponérihouen and inland valleys. *Class:* Austronesian, Malayo-Polynesian, Central-Eastern, Eastern Malayo-Polynesian, Oceanic, Central-Eastern Oceanic, Remote Oceanic, New Caledonian, Northern, Central. *Lg Use:* Vigorous. *Lg Dev:* Taught at secondary and junior college levels. Dictionary. Bible portions: 1998. *Other:* Tonal.

Pije (Pinje, Pindje) [piz] 161 (1996 census). Hiènghène: Tipindjé, Tiendanite, and Pouépaï. *Class:* Austronesian, Malayo-Polynesian, Central-Eastern, Eastern Malayo-Polynesian, Oceanic, Central-Eastern Oceanic, Remote Oceanic, New Caledonian, Northern, North, Nemi. *Lg Dev:* Dictionary.

Pwaamei (Poamei) [pme] 219 (1996 census). Voh: Ouélis, Témala, Tiéta. *Class:* Austronesian, Malayo-Polynesian, Central-Eastern, Eastern Malayo-Polynesian, Oceanic, Central-Eastern Oceanic, Remote Oceanic, New Caledonian, Northern, North.

Pwapwa (Poapoa) [pop] 16 (1996 census). Voh: Boyen. *Class:* Austronesian, Malayo-Polynesian, Central-Eastern,

Eastern Malayo-Polynesian, Oceanic, Central-Eastern Oceanic, Remote Oceanic, New Caledonian, Northern, North. *Other:* Nearly extinct.

Tayo ("Kaldosh," "Caldoche," Patois, Patois de St-Louis) [cks] 2,000 (1996 C. Corne). Southern, Ploum, Mont-Dore, and especially Saint Louis, near Noumea, and Paita. *Class:* Creole, French based. *Dialects:* Not intelligible with French. *Lg Use:* Used as first language by some who are also bilingual in French and as second language by others, mainly Wallis Islanders. *Lg Dev:* Grammar.

Tiri (Ciri, Ha-Tiri, Tinrin) [cir] 264 (1996 census). La Foa: lower valleys. *Class:* Austronesian, Malayo-Polynesian, Central-Eastern, Eastern Malayo-Polynesian, Oceanic, Central-Eastern Oceanic, Remote Oceanic, New Caledonian, Southern, South, Zire-Tiri. *Dialects:* Speakers have some comprehension of Mea. *Lg Dev:* Dictionary. Grammar. *Other:* SVO, VOS.

Uvean, West (Faga-Uvea, Fagauvea) [uve] 1,107 (1996 census). Northern and southern parts of Ouvea Atoll, Loyalty Islands. *Class:* Austronesian, Malayo-Polynesian, Central-Eastern, Eastern Malayo-Polynesian, Oceanic, Central-Eastern Oceanic, Remote Oceanic, Central Pacific, East Fijian-Polynesian, Polynesian, Nuclear, Samoic-Outlier, Futunic. *Lg Dev:* Dictionary. *Other:* Different from East Uvean on Uvea Island in the Wallis Islands. May be VSO. Atoll. Fishermen; agriculturalists: taro, sweet potato; hunters.

Vamale ('Moaeke, Hmwaeke, Pamale) [mkt] 150 (1982 SIL). East coast: (Vamale dialect) Téganpaïk, Tiouandé; west coast: (Hmwaeke dialect) Voh, Tiéta. *Class:* Austronesian, Malayo-Polynesian, Central-Eastern, Eastern Malayo-Polynesian, Oceanic, Central-Eastern Oceanic, Remote Oceanic, New Caledonian, Northern. *Dialects:* Vamale, Hmwaeke. *Lg Use:* Hmwaeke dialect nearly extinct.

Waamwang (Wamoang) [wmn] Extinct. Voh, north. *Class:* Austronesian, Malayo-Polynesian, Central-Eastern, Eastern Malayo-Polynesian, Oceanic, Central-Eastern Oceanic, Remote Oceanic, New Caledonian, Northern, North, Hmwaveke.

Wallisian (Uvean, East Uvean, Wallisien) [wls] 19,376 in New Caledonia (2000 WCD). Noumea. *Other:* Speakers are originally from Uvea Island in Wallis and Futuna. It has borrowed heavily from Tongan. Tongan is increasingly influenced by English and Wallisian by French. See main entry under Wallis and Futuna.

Xârâcùù (Xaracii, Anesu, Haraneu, Kanala, Canala) [ane] 3,784 (1996 census). Canala, east coast and inland valleys. *Class:* Austronesian, Malayo-Polynesian, Central-Eastern, Eastern Malayo-Polynesian, Oceanic, Central-Eastern Oceanic, Remote Oceanic, New Caledonian, Southern, South, Xaracuu-Xarague. *Lg Dev:* Taught in primary schools. Dictionary. *Other:* SVO, VOS.

Xaragure (Aragure, 'Aragure, Haragure, Thio) [axx] 566 (1996 census). Thio, east coast, and Ouinane on west coast. *Class:* Austronesian, Malayo-Polynesian, Central-Eastern, Eastern Malayo-Polynesian, Oceanic, Central-Eastern Oceanic, Remote Oceanic, New Caledonian, Southern, South, Xaracuu-Xarague. *Other:* SVO, VOS.

Yuaga (Yuanga, Thuanga, Juanga, Nua, Nyua) [nua] 1,992 (1996 census). Inland valleys between Gomen (Thuanga dialect) and Bondé (Juanga dialect). *Class:* Austronesian, Malayo-Polynesian, Central-Eastern, Eastern Malayo-Polynesian, Oceanic, Central-Eastern Oceanic, Remote Oceanic, New Caledonian, Northern, Extreme Northern. *Dialects:* Thuanga, Juanga. *Lg Dev:* Grammar.

Zire (Zira, Sirhe, Siche, Sîshëë, Nerë) [sih] 4 (1996 census). Bourail, coastal plain. *Class:* Austronesian, Malayo-Polynesian, Central-Eastern, Eastern Malayo-Polynesian, Oceanic, Central-Eastern Oceanic, Remote

Oceanic, New Caledonian, Southern, South, Zire-Tiri. *Lg Dev:* Grammar. *Other:* Nearly extinct.

New Zealand

New Zealand. 3,993,817. National or official languages: English, Maori. Two main islands, several smaller ones. Literacy rate: 99%. Also includes Afrikaans, Assyrian Neo-Aramaic, Fijian (3,090), Hakka Chinese, Hindi (11,200), Japanese (3,000), Korean, Latvian, Niue (5,688), Pukapuka (1,050), Rakahanga-Manihiki (2,500), Rarotongan (25,000), Samoan (50,000), Tahitian (262), Tokelauan (1,737), Tongan (3,965), Tuvaluan (604), Yue Chinese (20,000), Arabic (4,000), Chinese (600), from India (15,000). Information mainly from S. Wurm and S. Hattori 1981; N. Besnier 1992; D. T. Tryon 1995. Blind population: 3,687. Deaf institutions: 29. The number of languages listed for New Zealand is 4. Of those, 3 are living languages and 1 is a second language without mother-tongue speakers. See map on page 861.

English [eng] 3,213,000 in New Zealand (1987). *Lg Use:* Official language. See main entry under United Kingdom.
Maori (New Zealand Maori) [mri] 50,000 to 70,000 (1991 Fishman, p. 231). 100,000 who understand it, but do not speak it (1995 Maori Language Commission). Ethnic population: 530,000 (2002 Honolulu Advertiser). Far north, east coast, North Island. *Class:* Austronesian, Malayo-Polynesian, Central-Eastern, Eastern Malayo-Polynesian, Oceanic, Central-Eastern Oceanic, Remote Oceanic, Central Pacific, East Fijian-Polynesian, Polynesian, Nuclear, East, Central, Tahitic. *Dialects:* North Auckland, South Island, Taranaki, Wanganui, Bay of Plenty, Rotorua-Taupo, Moriori. Formerly fragmented into a number of regional dialects, some of which diverged quite radically from what has become the standard dialect. Lexical similarity 71% with Hawaiian, 57% with Samoan. *Lg Use:* Used officially for legal needs. Until the 20th century spoken throughout New Zealand. The Moriori dialect in the Chatham Islands is extinct. 30,000 to 50,000 adult speakers over 15 years old (1995 Maori Language Commission). 33% of fluent speakers are over 60 years old, 38% are between 45 and 59. All or most use English as second language. *Lg Dev:* 322 government-funded Maori language schools, including for preschoolers. Grammar. Bible: 1858–1952. *Other:* VSO. Volcanic plateau. Christian.
New Zealand Sign Language [nzs] *Class:* Deaf sign language. *Lg Use:* The first school for the deaf was established in 1878. Sign language used since the 1800s. It developed informally among deaf people because the oralist method only was used in schools. It has some features in common with British sign languages and some from other countries. Some signed interpretation used in court and at important public events. There is a committee on national sign language. *Lg Dev:* TV. Dictionary. Grammar. *Other:* There is a manual system for spelling.
Pitcairn-Norfolk (Pitcairn English) [pih] *Lg Use:* Developed from mutineers settling on Pitcairn in 1790. Some people were removed to Norfolk in 1859. An in-group language used to assist in the preservation of identity. People speak standard English as first language. *Other:* Christian. Second language only. See main entry under Norfolk Island.

Niue

Niue. 2,082 (1997 Honolulu Advertiser). National or official language: English. One coral island, 100 square miles. A New Zealand self-governing territory. Literacy rate: 99% to 100%. Also includes Tongan. Information mainly from N.

Besnier 1992. The number of languages listed for Niue is 2. Of those, both are living languages.

English [eng] 78 in Niue (2004). *Lg Use:* National language. Second-language speakers in Niue: 2,082. See main entry under United Kingdom.
Niue (Niuean, "Niuefekai") [niu] 2,027 in Niue (1998). Population total all countries: 7,941. Also spoken in Cook Islands, New Zealand, Tonga. *Class:* Austronesian, Malayo-Polynesian, Central-Eastern, Eastern Malayo-Polynesian, Oceanic, Central-Eastern Oceanic, Remote Oceanic, Central Pacific, East Fijian-Polynesian, Polynesian, Tongic. *Dialects:* Close to Tongan. *Lg Dev:* Bible: 1904. *Other:* Christian.

Norfolk Island

Norfolk Island. 1,700 (1994 Honolulu Advertiser). National or official language: English. An External Territory of Australian. Information mainly from M. Adler 1977. The number of languages listed for Norfolk Island is 2. Of those, 1 is a living language and 1 is a second language without mother-tongue speakers.

English [eng] 1,678 in Norfolk Island (1980 Government report). *Lg Use:* Official language. See main entry under United Kingdom.
Pitcairn-Norfolk (Pitcairn English) [pih] 580 on Norfolk Island (1989 Holm). Norfolk Island, Pitcairn. There are some second generation Pitcairn Islanders in Australia and New Zealand. Also spoken in Australia, Fiji, New Zealand, Pitcairn. *Class:* Cant, English-Tahitian. *Dialect:* Norfolk English. Slightly different variety than in Pitcairn. *Lg Use:* An in-group language used to assist in the preservation of identity. People speak Standard British English as first language. *Other:* Developed from mutineers settling on Pitcairn in 1790. Some were removed to Norfolk in 1859. Agriculturalists: breadfruit, banana, pineapple, passion fruit, watermelon, mango, custard apple, orange, lime, lemon, grapefruit. Second language only.

Northern Mariana Islands

Commonwealth of the Northern Mariana Islands (USA). 78,252. National or official languages: Carolinian, Chamorro, English. Includes Rota, Aguiguan, Tinian, Saipan, Farallon de Medinilla, Anatahan, Sariguan, Guguan, Alamagan, Pagan, Agrihan, Asuncion, Maug Islands, Farallon de Pajaros. Also includes Japanese, Korean (5,200), Sonsorol, Chinese (5,800), people from the Philippines (28,000). Information mainly from F. Jackson 1983; B. Bender 1971, 1996; K. Rehg 1991, 1996; J. Ellis 1996–1999. The number of languages listed for Northern Mariana Islands is 4. Of those, all are living languages. See map on page 858.

Carolinian (Saipan Carolinian, Southern Carolinian) [cal] 3,000 (1990 census). Saipan, Anatahan, and Agrihan islands, Carolines. *Class:* Austronesian, Malayo-Polynesian, Central-Eastern, Eastern Malayo-Polynesian, Oceanic, Central-Eastern Oceanic, Remote Oceanic, Micronesian, Micronesian Proper, Ponapeic-Trukic, Trukic. *Dialects:* Southern Carolinian has 95% lexical similarity with Satawalese, 88% with Woleaian and Puluwatese; 81% with Mortlockese; 78% with Chuukese, 74% with Ulithian. *Lg Use:* National language. Semiofficial status. All speakers on Saipan also use Chamorro or English. *Lg Dev:* Dictionary. *Other:* Fishermen mainly; agriculturalists: vegetables; livestock: cattle, pigs, goats.

Chamorro (Tjamoro) [cha] 14,205 in Northern Mariana Islands (1990). Population includes 11,466 on on Saipan (1990), 1,502 on Rota (1990), 1,231 on Tinian (1990); 62,500 on Guam (1991 Bender and Rehg). Alamagan Island. *Lg Use:* National language. A trade language on Saipan. 90,000 including second-language users. Some bilingualism in English. *Other:* Christian. See main entry under Guam.

English [eng] *Lg Use:* National language. See main entry under United Kingdom.

Tanapag (Northern Carolinian, Tallabwog) [tpv] 4,400 (2004). West central coast of Saipan, Tanapag community. *Class:* Austronesian, Malayo-Polynesian, Central-Eastern, Eastern Malayo-Polynesian, Oceanic, Central-Eastern Oceanic, Remote Oceanic, Micronesian, Micronesian Proper, Ponapeic-Trukic, Trukic. *Dialects:* Close to Namonuito of Micronesia. *Lg Use:* Members of the ethnic group under 30 do not speak Tanapag, but Chamorro. They are working to promote Tanapag. Speakers have low proficiency in English or Chamorro.

Palau

Republic of Palau. Republic of Belaw. Formerly part of the U.S. Trust Territory of the Pacific Islands. 20,016. National or official languages: Palauan (all states except Sonsorol, Tobi, Angaur), English, Sonsorol (in Sonsorol), Tobian (in Tobi), Japanese (in Angaur). 200 islands. Literacy rate: 85%. Also includes Japanese, Chinese, other people from Asia and the Pacific. Information mainly from B. W. Bender 1996; K. L. Rehg 1996; J. Ellis 1996. The number of languages listed for Palau is 4. Of those, all are living languages. See map on page 862.

English [eng] *Lg Use:* Official language. See main entry under United Kingdom.

Palauan (Belauan, Palau) [pau] 14,825 in Palau (2000 WCD). Palau Islands. Also spoken in Guam. *Class:* Austronesian, Malayo-Polynesian, Palauan. *Dialects:* Little dialect variation. *Lg Use:* Official language in all states except Sonsorol, Tobi, Angaur. Vigorous. *Lg Dev:* Dictionary. Grammar. NT: 1964. *Other:* SVO. Agriculturalists: taro, cassava; fishermen; government workers; merchants.

Sonsorol (Sonsorolese) [sov] 600 in Palau (1981 Wurm and Hattori). Approximately 60 on the outer islands: Sonsoral 29, Pulo Anna 25, Merir 5. The number of outer islanders resident on the main island of Palau is unclear from the 1990 census. Pulo Anna, Merir, Helen, and Sonsorol islands. Also spoken in Northern Mariana Islands. *Class:* Austronesian, Malayo-Polynesian, Central-Eastern, Eastern Malayo-Polynesian, Oceanic, Central-Eastern Oceanic, Remote Oceanic, Micronesian, Micronesian Proper, Ponapeic-Trukic, Trukic. *Dialects:* Sonsorolese, Pulo Anna. There are significant linguistic differences between the Tobian variety and Sonsorolese; similar to or greater than differences between, e.g., Puluwat and Namonuito. 50% intelligibility of Woleaian, less of the remainder of the Trukic continuum. Lexical similarity 69% with Ulithi. *Lg Use:* Official language in state of Sonsorol. Reported to be completely bilingual in Palauan. *Lg Dev:* Grammar.

Tobian (Tobi, Hatohobei) [tox] 22 (1995 SIL). Tobi (Hatohobei) Island and near the capitol. *Class:* Austronesian, Malayo-Polynesian, Central-Eastern, Eastern Malayo-Polynesian, Oceanic, Central-Eastern Oceanic, Remote Oceanic, Micronesian, Micronesian Proper, Ponapeic-Trukic, Trukic. *Dialects:* There are significant linguistic differences between Tobian and Sonsorolese, although they are often treated as one language. *Lg Use:* Official language in state of Tobi.

Reported to be highly bilingual in Palauan and bicultural. *Other:* Nearly extinct.

Papua New Guinea

Papua New Guinea. 5,420,280. Papuan 78%, Melanesian 20%. National or official languages: Hiri Motu, Tok Pisin, English. 600 islands. Literacy rate: 32% to 43%. Also includes Chinese, people from the Philippines, India. Information mainly from J. C. Anceaux 1961; A. Healey 1964; K. Franklin 1968; G. Sankoff 1968; J. A. Z'Graggen 1969, 1971, 1975; K. McElhanon 1970, 1978; B. Hooley 1971; B. Hooley and K. McElhanon 1970; R. D. Shaw 1973, 1981; S. Wurm and S. Hattori 1981; M. Ross 1988; L. Carrington 1996; SIL 1971–2003. Blind population: 12,500. The number of languages listed for Papua New Guinea is 830. Of those, 820 are living languages and 10 are extinct. See maps beginning on page 863.

Abadi (Gabadi, Kabadi) [kbt] 2,121 (2003 SIL). Central Province, north of Galley Reach. *Class:* Austronesian, Malayo-Polynesian, Central-Eastern, Eastern Malayo-Polynesian, Oceanic, Western Oceanic, Papuan Tip, Peripheral, Central Papuan, West Central Papuan, Gabadi. *Dialects:* Lexical similarity 53% with Toura (closest). *Lg Use:* All ages. Positive language attitude. Many in younger generation use Tok Pisin or English. *Lg Dev:* Abadi used in primary education for first 3 years. *Other:* Gabadi is the Motu name. Coastal. Savannah. Sea level. Swidden agriculturalists.

Abaga [abg] 5 (1994 SIL). Ethnic population: 1,200 (1975 SIL). Eastern Highlands Province, Goroka District. *Class:* Trans-New Guinea, Main Section, Central and Western, Huon-Finisterre, Finisterre, Abaga. *Lg Use:* Speakers also use Kamano or Benabena. *Other:* Nearly extinct.

Abau (Green River) [aau] 7,267 (2000 census). Sandaun Province, Green River District, Sepik and Green rivers. Not in Papua, Indonesia. *Class:* Sepik-Ramu, Sepik, Upper Sepik, Abau. *Lg Dev:* Grammar. Bible portions: 1990. *Other:* Some form of whistle speech reported.

Abom [aob] 15 (2002 SIL). Western Province, a few older adult speakers in Tewara, Lewada, and Mutam villages. *Class:* Trans-New Guinea, Trans-Fly-Bulaka River, Trans-Fly, Tirio. *Dialects:* Lexical similarity 14% with Bitur, 12% with Baramu, 11% with Makayam, 9% with Were, 4% with Idi and Agob. *Lg Use:* All speakers are older adults (2002). Middle-aged generation understand only rudiments. Children do not speak or understand Abom. *Other:* Nearly extinct.

Abu (Adjora, Adjoria, Azao) [ado] 3,221 (1990 census). East Sepik Province, Angoram District, 19 villages; Madang Province, Bogia District, 8 villages, western side of lower Ramu River. *Class:* Sepik-Ramu, Ramu, Ramu Proper, Grass, Grass Proper. *Dialects:* Abu, Auwa, Sabu. Auwa may be a different language. *Lg Dev:* Bible portions: 1969. *Other:* Riverine, interfluvial. Swamp, tropical forest. 15 to 30 meters.

Adzera (Azera, Atzera, Acira) [azr] 20,675 (1988 Holzknecht). Population includes 367 Ngariawan (1978 McElhanon), 497 Sarasira (1988 Holzknecht), 990 Sukurum (1990). Morobe Province, Markham Valley, Kaiapit District, Leron River. *Class:* Austronesian, Malayo-Polynesian, Central-Eastern, Eastern Malayo-Polynesian, Oceanic, Western Oceanic, North New Guinea, Huon Gulf, Markham, Upper, Adzera. *Dialects:* Yarus, Amari, Azera, Ngarowapum, Tsumanggorun, Guruf-Ngariawang (Ngariawan), Sarasira (Sirasira), Sukurum. The dialects form a cluster. *Lg Use:* Speakers also use Tok Pisin. *Lg Dev:* Grammar. NT: 1976.

Aekyom (Awin, Aiwin, Akium, West Awin) [awi] 8,000 (1987 UBS). Western Province, Kiunga area. *Class:*

Trans-New Guinea, Main Section, Central and Western, Central and South New Guinea-Kutubuan, Central and South New Guinea, Awin-Pare. *Dialects:* North Awin, South Awin, East Awin. *Lg Dev:* Literacy rate in first language: below 5%. Literacy rate in second language: 5% to 15%. NT: 1987.

Agarabi (Agarabe, Bare) [agd] 26,996 (2000 census). Eastern Highlands Province, Kainantu District. *Class:* Trans-New Guinea, Main Section, Central and Western, East New Guinea Highlands, Eastern, Gadsup-Auyana-Awa. *Dialects:* Close to Gadsup. *Lg Dev:* Literacy rate in first language: below 5%. Literacy rate in second language: 15% to 25%. Grammar. Bible portions: 1970. *Other:* SOV. Mountain slope. Savannah. 1,640 meters. Swidden agriculturalists.

Agi [aif] 955 (2003 SIL). Sandaun Province. *Class:* Torricelli, Wapei-Palei, Palei.

Agob (Dabu) [kit] 2,436 (2000 census). Population includes 1,437 Agob, 542 Ende, 457 Kawam. Western Province, along the Pahoturi River and southern coast. *Class:* Trans-New Guinea, Trans-Fly-Bulaka River, Trans-Fly, Pahoturi. *Dialects:* Agob, Ende, Kawam. One end of a dialect chain stretching to Idi. Ende and Kawam are closest to Agob. Distinct from, but related to Idi (Tame) and Waia. *Lg Dev:* Literacy rate in first language: below 5%. Literacy rate in second language: 5% to 15%. *Other:* 3 government schools. SOV. Riverine, Coastal. Savannah, lowland forest, palm swamp. Sea level to 5 meters. Swidden agriculturalists; hunters.

Aigon (Bao, Apsokok, Psohoh) [aix] 2,000 (2003 SIL). West New Britain Province, Gasmata and Mosa Rural LLGs, inland from Akolet and Avau, between Avio and Amgen rivers, extending to the northern side of the Whiteman Range. *Class:* Austronesian, Malayo-Polynesian, Central-Eastern, Eastern Malayo-Polynesian, Oceanic, Western Oceanic, North New Guinea, Ngero-Vitiaz, Vitiaz, Southwest New Britain, Arawe-Pasismanua, Pasismanua. *Dialects:* Bao (Do), Apsokok (Psohoh, Sokhok, Psokhok, Psokok), Aigon. In the Kaulong (Pasismanua) dialect cluster. Lexical similarity 83% between Aigon and Bao. *Lg Use:* All ages. *Other:* Different from Bau in Madang Province. Mountain slope. Tropical Forest. Sea level to 1,194 meters. Swidden agriculturalists. Christian, traditional religion.

Aiklep (Moewehafen, Eklep, Agerlep, Kaul) [mwg] 3,697 (1991 SIL). West New Britain Province, southwest coast and inland, Aviklo Island near Kandrian,Ais, Asailo, Yumielo, Analo villages. *Class:* Austronesian, Malayo-Polynesian, Central-Eastern, Eastern Malayo-Polynesian, Oceanic, Western Oceanic, North New Guinea, Ngero-Vitiaz, Vitiaz, Southwest New Britain, Arawe-Pasismanua, Arawe, West Arawe. *Dialects:* Dialect cluster with Gimi and Apalik.

Aiku (Minendon, Menandon, Malek) [mzf] 1,132 (2003 SIL). Sandaun Province, Maimai Namblo Division, Wemil village, and more in West Palei Division. *Class:* Torricelli, Wapei-Palei, Palei.

Aimele (Kware) [ail] 138 (2000). Southwest corner of Southern Highlands Province around Mt. Bosavi; Western Province around Lake Campbell. Most have moved to Wawoi Falls area of Western Province. *Class:* Trans-New Guinea, Main Section, Central and Western, Central and South New Guinea-Kutubuan, Central and South New Guinea, Bosavi.

Ainbai [aic] 100 (2003 SIL). Sandaun Province, Vanimo District, south of Bewani station. 2 villages. *Class:* Trans-New Guinea, Northern, Border, Bewani. *Dialects:* Lexical similarity 30% with Manem, 25% with Pagi.

Aiome (Ayom) [aki] 751 (1981 Wurm and Hattori). Madang Province, 70 miles west of Madang city, scattered houses. *Class:* Sepik-Ramu, Ramu, Ramu Proper,

Annaberg, Aian. *Other:* Mountain slope, valleys. 50 to 100 meters. Agriculturalists: sweet potato, sugarcane, bananas; animal husbandry: pigs. Traditional religion.

Ak [akq] 75 (2000 S. Wurm). Sandaun Province. *Class:* Sepik-Ramu, Sepik, Yellow River. *Dialects:* Closest to Namia and Awun.

Akolet [akt] 954 (1982 SIL). West New Britain Province, south coast and islands around Awio Bay. *Class:* Austronesian, Malayo-Polynesian, Central-Eastern, Eastern Malayo-Polynesian, Oceanic, Western Oceanic, North New Guinea, Ngero-Vitiaz, Vitiaz, Southwest New Britain, Arawe-Pasismanua, Arawe, East Arawe. *Dialects:* Dialect cluster. *Lg Use:* Speakers also use Tok Pisin or English. *Other:* 3 primary schools, provincial secondary school, vocational school. Raised coral coast. Tropical forest.

Akoye (Akoinkake, Lohiki, Obi, Mai-Hea-Ri, Maihiri, Angoya, Akoyi) [miw] 800 (1998 SIL). Gulf Province, Kaberofe District, valleys between the Nabo Range and the Albert Mountains, Lohiki River. The largest group is living in a settlement in Kerema. *Class:* Trans-New Guinea, Main Section, Central and Western, Angan, Angan Proper. *Dialects:* Close to Ivori. Similar to Tainae. *Lg Use:* Little pride in the language. *Lg Dev:* Literacy rate in first language: below 5%. Literacy rate in second language: below 5%. *Other:* SOV; postpositions. Mountain slope, coastal. Tropical forest. Sea level to 900 meters. Agriculturalists. Traditional religion.

Akrukay [afi] 246 (2003 SIL). Madang Province. *Class:* Sepik-Ramu, Ramu, Ramu Proper, Goam, Tamolan.

Alamblak [amp] 1,527 (2000 census). East Sepik Province, Angoram District. 9 villages (900 speakers) on Middle Karawari and Wagupmeri rivers. Another dialect has 4 villages (400 speakers) near Kuvanmas Lake. *Class:* Sepik-Ramu, Sepik, Sepik Hill, Alamblak. *Dialects:* Kuvenmas, Karawari. *Lg Dev:* Literacy rate in first language: 15% to 25%. Literacy rate in second language: 15% to 25%. Grammar. NT: 2003. *Other:* Karawari is distinct from Karawari in the Pondo branch. Traditional religion, Christian.

Alatil (Aru, Eru) [alx] 176 (2003 SIL). Sandaun Province. *Class:* Torricelli, Wapei-Palei, Palei.

Alekano (Gahuku, Gafuku, Gahuku-Gama) [gah] 25,000 (1999 SIL). Eastern Highlands Province, Goroka District, centered around the town of Goroka. *Class:* Trans-New Guinea, Main Section, Central and Western, East New Guinea Highlands, East-Central, Gahuku-Benabena. *Dialects:* Close to Tokano, Dano, Yaweyuha, Siane, Benabena. *Lg Use:* Many parents do not teach the language to their children. All speakers are probably fluent in Tok Pisin. They use it in the market or streets along with Alekano. Those under 35 who have had extensive schooling may know English, but do not use it on the streets. *Lg Dev:* Literacy rate in first language: 25% to 50%. Literacy rate in second language: 50% to 75%. Grammar. NT: 1973–1986. *Other:* Christian.

Ama (Sawiyanu) [amm] 475 (1990 census). East Sepik Province, Ambunti District, Waniap Creek, south of the Sepik River, south of Namia. Villages: Ama (Wopolu I), Wopolu II (Nokonufa), Kauvia (Kawiya), Yonuwai; all on hills rising from the swamp. *Class:* Left May. *Dialects:* Dialects have converged into one. *Lg Dev:* Literacy rate in first language: 25% to 50%. Literacy rate in second language: 15% to 25%. NT: 1990. *Other:* Seminomadic. SOV. 100 to 200 meters. Hunters; sago. Christian, traditional religion.

Amaimon [ali] 1,781 (2003 SIL). Madang Province. *Class:* Trans-New Guinea, Madang-Adelbert Range, Adelbert Range, Pihom-Isumrud-Mugil, Pihom, Amaimon.

Amal (Alai) [aad] 831 (2003 SIL). Sandaun Province, on Wagana River, near the confluence with Wanibe Creek. *Class:* Sepik-Ramu, Sepik, Upper Sepik, Iwam.

Amanab [amn] 4,419 (2003 SIL). Sandaun Province, Amanab District. Not in Papua, Indonesia. *Class:* Trans-New Guinea, Northern, Border, Waris. *Lg Dev:* Literacy rate in first language: 25% to 50%. Literacy rate in second language: 25% to 50%. Taught in primary schools. Grammar. NT: 2001. *Other:* SOV. Mountain slope. Tropical forest. 300 to 600 meters. Swidden agriculturalists. Traditional religion, Christian.

Amara (Longa, Bibling) [aie] 1,170 (2000 D. Tryon). West New Britain Province, northwest coast. *Class:* Austronesian, Malayo-Polynesian, Central-Eastern, Eastern Malayo-Polynesian, Oceanic, Western Oceanic, North New Guinea, Ngero-Vitiaz, Vitiaz, Southwest New Britain, Amara. *Dialects:* Related to Mouk-Aria and Lamogai. *Lg Use:* Close to 100% bilingualism with Bariai. Because of intermarriage, most children learn Bariai first, and many never become proficient in Amara. Also high bilingualism in Tok Pisin. *Lg Dev:* Dictionary.

Ambakich (Aion, Porapora) [aew] 770 (2003 SIL). Ethnic population: 1,964 (2003 SIL). East Sepik Province. *Class:* Sepik-Ramu, Ramu, Ramu Proper, Grass, Grass Proper. *Dialects:* Northern Ambakich (Antanau), Southern Ambakich. *Lg Use:* Very low vitality. All speakers older than 20 years. Interest in language retention. Many parents say they want their children to know Ambakich; however, they often speak Tok Pisin to their children. Nearly all speakers also speak Tok Pisin, those under 20 speak it primarily. Tok Pisin is used in many domains, including home, cultural, social, official (court), and with outsiders. *Lg Dev:* 41% of ethnic group (10 years and older) literate in at least one language (2000 census). *Other:* SOV. Riverine. Swampland. Swidden agriculturalists. Christian.

Ambulas (Abulas, Abelam) [abt] 44,000 (1991 SIL). Population includes 27,000 in Wosera (1991 SIL), 9,000 in Maprik (1991 SIL), 8,000 in Wingei (1991 SIL). East Sepik Province, Maprik District. *Class:* Sepik-Ramu, Sepik, Middle Sepik, Ndu. *Dialects:* Maprik, Wingei, Wosera-Kamu, Wosera-Mamu. *Lg Dev:* Literacy rate in first language: 25% to 50%. Literacy rate in second language: 50% to 75%. NT: 1983–1996. *Other:* OSV. Riverine, valleys. Tropical forest. 250 to 500 meters. Swidden agriculturalists. Traditional religion, Christian.

Amele (Amale) [aey] 5,300 (1987 SIL). Madang Province, Madang District, in the hills up from Astrolabe Bay, between the Gum and Gogol rivers. 40 hamlets. *Class:* Trans-New Guinea, Madang-Adelbert Range, Madang, Mabuso, Gum. *Dialects:* Huar, Jagahala, Haija. Related to Gumalu, Sihan, Isebe, Bau, Panim. *Lg Dev:* Literacy rate in first language: 75% to 100%. Literacy rate in second language: 75% to 100%. Grammar. NT: 1997. *Other:* SOV.

Amto (Ki, Siwai, Siawi, Siafli) [amt] 200 (2000 S. Wurm). Ethnic population: 200 to 300. Sandaun Province, Amanab District and Rocky Peak District, south of the Upper Sepik River, toward the headwaters of the Left May River on the Samaia River. Villages: Amto, Habiyon (Sernion). *Class:* Amto-Musan. *Dialects:* Amto, Siawi. *Lg Use:* All ages. Speakers also use Sinou, most speak Tok Pisin. *Lg Dev:* Literacy rate in first language: 20% to 25%. Literacy rate in second language: 20% to 25%. Bible portions: 1992– 1998. *Other:* Acculturating rapidly. SOV; postpositions; genitives before noun heads; adjectives after noun heads; relatives without noun heads; question word final; maximum prefixes: 1, maximum suffixes: 3, causatives, comparatives; CV, CVV, CVVV, CCV, CCCV, nontonal. Interfluvial, mountain slope. Tropical forest, swamp. 60 to 160 meters. Hunters. Traditional religion, Christian.

Anam (Pondoma) [pda] 1,069 (2003 SIL). Madang Province, villages around Josephstaal. *Class:* Trans-New Guinea, Madang-Adelbert Range, Adelbert Range, Josephstaal-Wanang, Josephstaal, Pomoikan. *Lg Use:* Speakers also use Anamgura, Mum, Tok Pisin. *Other:* Different villages are shifting to Anamgura, Mum, or Tok Pisin. Mountain slope, riverine. Swidden agriculturalists; sago gatherers.

Anamgura (Ikundun, Mindivi) [imi] 1,253 (1990 census). Madang Province, northwest of Josephstaal. *Class:* Trans-New Guinea, Madang-Adelbert Range, Adelbert Range, Josephstaal-Wanang, Josephstaal.

Andarum [aod] 1,084 (1981 Wurm and Hattori). Madang Province. *Class:* Sepik-Ramu, Ramu, Ramu Proper, Goam, Ataitan. *Dialects:* Related to Kanggape.

Andra-Hus (Ahus, Ha'us) [anx] 1,309 (2000). Manus Province, Andra and Hus islands. *Class:* Austronesian, Malayo-Polynesian, Central-Eastern, Eastern Malayo-Polynesian, Oceanic, Admiralty Islands, Eastern, Manus, East.

Anem (Karaiai) [anz] 550 (2003 SIL). West New Britain Province, northwest coast and inland. *Class:* East Papuan, Yele-Solomons-New Britain, New Britain, Anem. *Lg Use:* Speakers in one village among the Bariai use Bariai as second language.

Aneme Wake (Abie, Abia) [aby] 650 (1990 SIL). Oro Province, Afore District, both sides of Owen Stanley Range, Central Province; north from Ianu along Foasi and Domara creeks. *Class:* Trans-New Guinea, Main Section, Eastern, Central and Southeastern, Yareban. *Dialects:* Mori, Buniabura, Auwaka, Jari, Doma. Lexical similarity 65% to 73% with Moikodi (closest). *Lg Use:* Speakers also use Motu or Yareba. *Lg Dev:* NT: 1988. *Other:* Foothills.

Angaatiha (Langimar, Angataha, Angaatiya, Angaataha) [agm] 2,100 (2003 BTA). Morobe Province, Menyamya District. *Class:* Trans-New Guinea, Main Section, Central and Western, Angan. *Lg Dev:* Grammar. Bible portions: 1976–1980. *Other:* SOV. Mountain slope. Tropical forest. 1,400 to 1,600 meters. Swidden agriculturalists.

Angal (East Angal, Mendi) [age] 18,614 (WCD 2000). Southern Highlands Province, Mendi area, north into Mendi Valley, west into Lai Valley, east bank, west of Mt. Giluwe. *Class:* Trans-New Guinea, Main Section, Central and Western, East New Guinea Highlands, West-Central, Angal-Kewa. *Lg Dev:* Bible portions: 1990. *Other:* SOV, Time-Subject-Object-Location-Verb. Mountain slope. Highland forest. 1,300 to 2,500 meters. Swidden agriculturalists.

Angal Enen (South Angal Heneng, South Mendi, Nembi) [aoe] 22,000 (1995 UBS). Southern Highlands Province, 10 to 12 km south of Nipa, north of the Erave River, east of Lake Kutubu, west of Lai Valley. *Class:* Trans-New Guinea, Main Section, Central and Western, East New Guinea Highlands, West-Central, Angal-Kewa. *Dialect:* Megi. *Lg Dev:* Grammar. Bible portions: 1968–1996. *Other:* SOV, Time-Subject-Object-Location-Verb. Mountain slope. Highland forest. 1,300 to 2,500 meters. Swidden agriculturalists.

Angal Heneng (Augu, West Mendi, West Angal Heneng, Agarar, Wage, Katinja) [akh] 40,000 (1994 V. Schlatter). Southern Highlands Province, south of Margarima and Kandep, north of Lake Kutubu, west of the Lai Valley. *Class:* Trans-New Guinea, Main Section, Central and Western, East New Guinea Highlands, West-Central, Angal-Kewa. *Dialects:* Waola (Wala), Augu, Nipa. *Lg Dev:* NT: 1978. *Other:* SOV, Time-Subject-Object-Location-Verb. Mountain slope. Highland forest. 1,300 to 2,500 meters. Swidden agriculturalists.

Angor (Watapor, Senagi, Anggor) [agg] 1,266 (1990 census). Population includes 836 in Nai, 430 in Samanai.

Sandaun Province, Amanab District. 11 villages. *Class:* Trans-New Guinea, Senagi. *Dialects:* Nai (Central Angor), Samanai (Southern Angor). *Lg Dev:* Literacy rate in second language: 15% to 25%. Grammar. NT: 2001. *Other:* SOV. Lowland, foothills. Tropical forest. 150 to 500 meters. Swidden agriculturalists.

Angoram (Pondo, Tjimundo, Olem) [aog] 8,215 (2003 SIL). East Sepik Province, along lower Sepik River, Angoram District. *Class:* Sepik-Ramu, Nor-Pondo, Pondo. *Lg Use:* Speakers also use Tok Pisin.

Anjam (Bogati, Bom, Bogajim, Bogadjim, Lalok) [boj] 2,019 (2003 SIL). Madang Province, Astrolabe Bay District. *Class:* Trans-New Guinea, Madang-Adelbert Range, Madang, Rai Coast, Mindjim. *Lg Dev:* NT: 2000. *Other:* SOV. Coastal. Tropical forest. Sea level. Swidden agriculturalists. Christian, traditional religion, cargo cult.

Ankave (Angave) [aak] 1,600 (1987 SIL). Gulf Province, Kerema District, in the valleys of the Mbwei and Swanson rivers. *Class:* Trans-New Guinea, Main Section, Central and Western, Angan, Angan Proper. *Dialects:* Sawuve, Wiyagwa, Wunavai, Miyatnu, Ankai, Bu'u. *Lg Dev:* Literacy rate in first language: below 5%. Literacy rate in second language: below 5%. NT: 1991. *Other:* Traditional religion.

Anor [anj] 981 (2000). Madang Province. *Class:* Sepik-Ramu, Ramu, Ramu Proper, Annaberg, Aian.

Anuki (Gabobora) [aui] 500 (2000 Wurm). North coast, Cape Vogel, Milne Bay Province. *Class:* Austronesian, Malayo-Polynesian, Central-Eastern, Eastern Malayo-Polynesian, Oceanic, Western Oceanic, Papuan Tip, Nuclear, North Papuan Mainland-D'Entrecasteaux, Anuki. *Dialects:* Lexical similarity 49% to 57% with Gapapaiwa (closest).

Ap Ma (Kambot, Ap Ma Botin, Botin) [kbx] 7,000 (1990 UBS). Angoram District, East Sepik Province. *Class:* Sepik-Ramu, Ramu, Ramu Proper, Grass, Grass Proper. *Dialect:* Kambaramba. *Lg Dev:* NT: 1999.

Apali (Emerum, Apal) [ena] 985 (2003 SIL). Madang Province, upper Ramu River area, Aiome District. *Class:* Trans-New Guinea, Madang-Adelbert Range, Adelbert Range, Josephstaal-Wanang, Wanang, Emuan. *Dialects:* Aki, Aci. *Lg Dev:* Literacy rate in first language: 5% to 25%. Literacy rate in second language: 25% to 50%. Bible portions: 1993.

Apalik (Palik, Ambul) [apo] 374 (1979 census). West New Britain Province, islands off the south coast between the Andru and Johanna rivers. *Class:* Austronesian, Malayo-Polynesian, Central-Eastern, Eastern Malayo-Polynesian, Oceanic, Western Oceanic, North New Guinea, Ngero-Vitiaz, Vitiaz, Southwest New Britain, Arawe-Pasismanua, Arawe, West Arawe. *Dialects:* In a dialect chain with Gimi and Aiklep. *Lg Use:* Positive language attitude.

Arafundi (Alfendio) [arf] 733 (1981 Wurm and Hattori). East Sepik Province, on the Arafundi River. *Class:* Sepik-Ramu, Ramu, Ramu Proper, Arafundi. *Dialect:* Meakambut. *Other:* Meakambut may be a separate language.

Arammba (Aramba, Serkisetavi, Upper Morehead, Serki) [stk] 967 (2003 SIL). Western Province, Morehead Subprovince, southwest of Suki. *Class:* Trans-New Guinea, Trans-Fly-Bulaka River, Trans-Fly, Morehead and Upper Maro rivers, Tonda. *Lg Dev:* Literacy rate in first language: below 5%. Literacy rate in second language: below 5%. *Other:* 2 community schools. Swamp, savannah. Below 300 meters.

Arapesh, Bumbita (Weri) [aon] 4,335 (2003 SIL). East Sepik Province, Maprik District, Torricelli Mountains, south of Wom, 13 villages. *Class:* Torricelli, Kombio-Arapesh, Arapesh. *Dialects:* Bonahoi, Urita, Timingir, Weril, Werir. Weril and Werir are inherently intelligible to each other's speakers. Lexical similarity 21% with

Southern Arapesh, 30% with Bukiyip. *Lg Use:* 40% to 60% of the ethnic group speaks Bumbita. Middle-aged and older speakers use Bumbita, and in 2 villages younger members use it. Elsewhere younger members mainly use Tok Pisin. Speakers also use Tok Pisin. *Lg Dev:* Literacy rate in first language: 15% to 25%. Literacy rate in second language: 25% to 50%. For beginning literacy Weril and Werir use different materials. *Other:* Mountain slope. Agriculturalists: taro, tobacco; animal husbandry: pigs.

Arawum [awm] 60 (2000 Wurm). Madang Province. *Class:* Trans-New Guinea, Madang-Adelbert Range, Madang, Rai Coast, Kabenau. *Dialects:* Related to Siroi, Pulabu, Kolom, Lemio.

Are (Mukawa) [mwc] 1,231 (1973 SIL). Milne Bay Province, tip of Cape Vogel. *Class:* Austronesian, Malayo-Polynesian, Central-Eastern, Eastern Malayo-Polynesian, Oceanic, Western Oceanic, Papuan Tip, Nuclear, North Papuan Mainland-D'Entrecasteaux, Are-Taupota, Are. *Dialects:* Close to Gapapaiwa. Lexical similarity 47% to 55% with Doga (closest). *Lg Dev:* Grammar. Bible: 1925.

Ari [aac] 50 (2000 S. Wurm). Ari and Serea villages, Aramia River area, Western Province. *Class:* Trans-New Guinea, Main Section, Central and Western, Gogodala-Suki, Gogodala. *Lg Use:* Speakers also use Gogodala.

Aribwatsa (Lae, Lahe) [laz] Extinct. Morobe Province, lower Wamped River. *Class:* Austronesian, Malayo-Polynesian, Central-Eastern, Eastern Malayo-Polynesian, Oceanic, Western Oceanic, North New Guinea, Huon Gulf, Markham, Lower, Busu. *Lg Use:* Members of the ethnic group now speak Bukawa, living in Bukawa villages of Butibum and Kamkumun at Lae.

Aribwaung (Aribwaungg, Yalu, Jaloc) [ylu] 1,000 (1994). Morobe Province, lower Markham Valley, Yalu village. *Class:* Austronesian, Malayo-Polynesian, Central-Eastern, Eastern Malayo-Polynesian, Oceanic, Western Oceanic, North New Guinea, Huon Gulf, Markham, Lower, Busu. *Dialects:* Close to Musom, Guwot, Sirak, Wampar. *Other:* Jaloc is the Yabem spelling of the village name.

Arifama-Miniafia (Miniafia-Arifama) [aai] 3,469 (2000). Four locations along the coast of Cape Nelson and Collingwood Bay, Oro Province, Tufi District. 20 to 25 villages. *Class:* Austronesian, Malayo-Polynesian, Central-Eastern, Eastern Malayo-Polynesian, Oceanic, Western Oceanic, Papuan Tip, Nuclear, North Papuan Mainland-D'Entrecasteaux, Are-Taupota, Are. *Dialects:* Arifama, Miniafia. Lexical similarity 39% with Ubir. *Lg Use:* Speakers also use English, Motu, or other neighboring languages. *Lg Dev:* Literacy rate in second language: 10%. Bible portions: 1990. *Other:* SOV. Coastal. Tropical forest, mangrove swamp. Sea level to 200 meters. Fishermen; swidden agriculturalists.

Arop-Lukep (Siasi, Siassi, Tolokiwa, Moromiranga, Lukep, Arop-Lokep) [apr] 3,015 (2000 census). Three islands in the Siassi chain in the Vitiaz Strait. Arop dialect on Long Island, Madang Province, Saidor District. Lokep dialect on Tolokiwa Island and the north tip of Umboi Island, Morobe Province, Siassi District. Madang Province, Rai Coast District, east of Saidor. *Class:* Austronesian, Malayo-Polynesian, Central-Eastern, Eastern Malayo-Polynesian, Oceanic, Western Oceanic, North New Guinea, Ngero-Vitiaz, Vitiaz, Korap. *Dialects:* Arop (Poono), Lokep (Lukep, Lokewe). *Lg Dev:* Literacy rate in first language: 75% to 100%. Literacy rate in second language: 50% to 75%. Bible portions: 1990–1993. *Other:* Different from Arop-Sissano in Sandaun Province. SVO.

Arop-Sissano (Arop) [aps] 1,150 (1998). Sandaun Province, Aitape District, Arop village. *Class:* Austronesian, Malayo-Polynesian, Central-Eastern, Eastern Malayo-Polynesian, Oceanic, Western Oceanic, North

New Guinea, Schouten, Siau. *Dialects:* Related to Sissano, Malol, and Sera, but different enough to be a separate language. *Lg Dev:* Literacy rate in first language: 15% to 25%. Literacy rate in second language: 25% to 50%. Bible portions: 1988–1994. *Other:* 863 people killed in July 1998 tsunami.

Aruamu (Mikarew, Ariawiai, Makarup, Makarub, Mikarup, Mikarew-Ariaw) [msy] 8,000 (1990 UBS). Madang Province, west of Bogia. *Class:* Sepik-Ramu, Ramu, Ramu Proper, Ruboni, Misegian. *Lg Dev:* Literacy rate in first language: 5% to 25%. Literacy rate in second language: 50% to 75%. Bible portions: 1996.

Aruek (Djang) [aur] 740 (2003 SIL). Sandaun Province, north of Kombio. *Class:* Torricelli, Kombio-Arapesh, Kombio.

Aruop (Lauisaranga, Lau'u) [lsr] 700 (1991 SIL). Sandaun Province, 6 villages. *Class:* Torricelli, Wapei-Palei, Palei. *Other:* 1 community school. Mountain ridge. 800 meters.

Asaro'o (Morafa) [mtv] 1,245 (2003 SIL). Madang Province, southeast of Saidor. At least 4 villages. *Class:* Trans-New Guinea, Main Section, Central and Western, Huon-Finisterre, Finisterre, Warup. *Dialects:* Related to Muratayak, Bulgebi, Degenan, Forak, Guya, Gwahatike, Yagomi. *Other:* Morafa is a clan name. Coastal, mountain slope. Sea level to 400 meters.

Asas (Kow) [asd] 333 (1981 Wurm and Hattori). Madang Province. *Class:* Trans-New Guinea, Madang-Adelbert Range, Madang, Rai Coast, Evapia. *Dialects:* Related to Sinsauru, Sausi, Kesawai, Dumpu.

Askopan (Eivo) [eiv] 1,200 (1981 Wurm and Hattori). Mountains of south central Bougainville Province. *Class:* East Papuan, Bougainville, West, Rotokas. *Dialects:* Close to Kunua.

Atemble (Atemple-Apris, Atemple) [ate] 60 (2000 Wurm). Madang Province. *Class:* Trans-New Guinea, Madang-Adelbert Range, Adelbert Range, Josephstaal-Wanang, Wanang, Atan.

Au [avt] 8,000 (2000 census). 20% monolingual. Sandaun Province, Lumi District, 19 villages in the foothills of the Torricelli Mountains. *Class:* Torricelli, Wapei-Palei, Wapei. *Lg Use:* Some also use Tok Pisin. *Lg Dev:* Literacy rate in second language: 25% to 50%. Grammar. NT: 1982. *Other:* SVO; extensive agreement system. Mountain slope. Tropical forest. 200 to 600 meters. Hunter-gatherers.

'Auhelawa (Nuakata, Kurada, 'Urada) [kud] 1,200 (1998 SIL). 30% monolingual. Milne Bay Province, Normanby Island, Sehuleya District. *Class:* Austronesian, Malayo-Polynesian, Central-Eastern, Eastern Malayo-Polynesian, Oceanic, Western Oceanic, Papuan Tip, Nuclear, Suauic. *Dialects:* Lexical similarity 52% with Duau (closest). *Lg Use:* Some speakers also use Dobu. *Lg Dev:* Literacy rate in first language: 85%. Literacy rate in second language: 85%. Bible portions: 1986–1993. *Other:* Volcanic islands. Tropical forest. Sea level to 300 meters. Agriculturalists: yams; fishermen. Christian, traditional religion.

Auwe (Simog) [smf] 410 (2003 SIL). Sandaun Province, Amanab District, Simog and Watape villages. *Class:* Trans-New Guinea, Northern, Border, Waris. *Lg Dev:* Literacy rate in second language: 50% to 75%.

Avau (Awau) [avb] 621 (2002 SIL). West New Britain Province, south coast and islands around Gasmata. *Class:* Austronesian, Malayo-Polynesian, Central-Eastern, Eastern Malayo-Polynesian, Oceanic, Western Oceanic, North New Guinea, Ngero-Vitiaz, Vitiaz, Southwest New Britain, Arawe-Pasismanua, Arawe, East Arawe. *Dialect:* Gasmata. *Lg Use:* Speakers also use Tok Pisin or English. *Other:* Raised coral coast. Tropical forest.

Awa (Mobuta) [awb] 2,054 (2003 SIL). Okapa and Kainantu districts, Eastern Highlands Province. *Class:*

Trans-New Guinea, Main Section, Central and Western, East New Guinea Highlands, Eastern, Gadsup-Auyana-Awa. *Dialects:* Tauna, Ilakia, Northeast Awa, South Awa. *Lg Dev:* Literacy rate in first language: 25% to 50%. Literacy rate in second language: 25% to 50%. Dictionary. Grammar. NT: 1974–1997. *Other:* SOV. Mountain slope. Tropical forest. 1,700 to 1,800 meters. Peasant agriculturalists.

Awad Bing (Biliau, Sengam, Samang, Semang, Bing, Awad Gey) [bcu] 1,150 (2000 SIL). Madang Province, 7 villages west of Saidor, Astrolabe Bay area. *Class:* Austronesian, Malayo-Polynesian, Central-Eastern, Eastern Malayo-Polynesian, Oceanic, Western Oceanic, North New Guinea, Ngero-Vitiaz, Vitiaz, Bel, Astrolabe. *Dialects:* Biliau, Yamai, Suit, Galeg, Yori. Distinct from, but close to, Mindiri and Wab. Four dialects. *Lg Use:* Vigorous. A few Ngaing speakers speak it for trade. All domains. All ages. Positive language attitude. All or most speak Tok Pisin as second language. Some also speak some English. A few can speak the church language, Gedaged. *Lg Dev:* Literacy rate in first language: 61%. Literacy rate in second language: 61%. 700 can read and write it. Bible portions: 1992. *Other:* Vernacular elementary schools planned. Coastal, hills. Copra production; agriculturalists; fishermen; fish marketers. Traditional religion, Christian.

Awar [aya] 1,094 (2003 SIL). Madang Province. *Class:* Sepik-Ramu, Ramu, Ramu Proper, Ruboni, Ottilien. *Dialects:* Awar, Nubia.

Awara [awx] 1,627 (1994 govt. figure). 35% monolingual. Morobe Province, Lae District, near the Wantoat. *Class:* Trans-New Guinea, Main Section, Central and Western, Huon-Finisterre, Finisterre, Wantoat. *Dialects:* There is some dialect variation within Awara. Wantoat, Wapu, and Awara are part of a language chain, with Awara being the western end. Lexical similarity 60% to 70% with Wantoat and Wapu. *Lg Use:* Tok Pisin is used as second language. Use of Wantoat is passive. *Lg Dev:* Literacy rate in first language: below 1%. Literacy rate in second language: 3%. *Other:* SOV. Mountain ridge, plateau. Tropical forest, savannah. 1,000 to 1,800 meters. Swidden agriculturalists: coffee.

Awiyaana (Auyana) [auy] 11,110 (2000). Kainantu, Okapa districts, Eastern Highlands Province. 15 villages. *Class:* Trans-New Guinea, Main Section, Central and Western, East New Guinea Highlands, Eastern, Gadsup-Auyana-Awa. *Lg Dev:* NT: 1984. *Other:* SOV. Mountain ridge. Tropical forest. 1,208 to 1,988 meters. Agriculturalists.

Awtuw (Kamnum, Autu) [kmn] 506 (2003 SIL). Sandaun Province. *Class:* Sepik-Ramu, Sepik, Ramu. *Dialects:* Related to Karawa, Pouye. *Lg Dev:* Grammar. *Other:* Tropical forest. 300 to 400 meters. Sago gatherers.

Awun (Awon) [aww] 400 (2003 SIL). Sandaun Province, east of Namia. *Class:* Sepik-Ramu, Sepik, Yellow River. *Dialects:* Related to Namia and Ak.

Ayi [ayq] 433 (2000 census). Southeast corner of Sandaun Province, Wan Wan Division, 3 villages. *Class:* Sepik-Ramu, Sepik, Tama. *Dialects:* Close to Pasi. *Lg Use:* Men also use Tok Pisin. *Other:* Agriculturalists; fishermen. Traditional religion.

Bagupi [bpi] 50 (2000 Wurm). Madang Province. *Class:* Trans-New Guinea, Madang-Adelbert Range, Madang, Mabuso, Hanseman. *Dialects:* Related languages: Rapting, Wamas, Samosa, Murupi, Saruga, Nake, Mosimo, Garus, Yoidik, Rempi, Silopi, Utu, Mawan, Baimak, Matepi, Gal, Garuh, Kamba. *Lg Use:* 40% of the ethnic group speaks Bagupi.

Bahinemo (Bahenemo, Gahom, Wogu, Yigai, Inaru) [bjh] 550 (1998 NTM). East Sepik Province, Ambunti District, Hunstein Range, south of the Sepik River. 4 villages.

Class: Sepik-Ramu, Sepik, Sepik Hill, Bahinemo. *Lg Use:* Speakers also use Tok Pisin. *Lg Dev:* Literacy rate in first language: 5% to 15%. Literacy rate in second language: 15% to 25%. Bible portions: 1973–1983. *Other:* Mountain slope. Tropical forest. 60 to 1,000 meters. Hunter-gatherers; sago palm. Christian, traditional religion.

Baibai [bbf] 345 (2000 census). Sandaun Province, Amanab District. *Class:* Kwomtari-Baibai, Baibai. *Lg Use:* Vigorous. Few people have any comprehension of Tok Pisin. *Other:* The nearest school is a day's walk away. Virgin forest, sago swamp.

Baimak [bmx] 653 (2003 SIL). Madang Province, 20 miles west of Madang city. *Class:* Trans-New Guinea, Madang-Adelbert Range, Madang, Mabuso, Hanseman. *Dialects:* Related to Gal.

Baluan-Pam [blq] 1,000 (1982 SIL). Manus Province, Baluan and Pam islands. *Class:* Austronesian, Malayo-Polynesian, Central-Eastern, Eastern Malayo-Polynesian, Oceanic, Admiralty Islands, Eastern, Southeast Islands. *Dialects:* Baluan, Pam. Two close dialects; Baluan is the larger one. *Lg Use:* Speakers are moderately bilingual in Lou or Titan. *Other:* SVO. Win Nesien cult.

Bamu (Bamu Kiwai) [bcf] 6,313 (2000 census). Population includes 964 Gama. Western Province from the mouth of the Bamu River to 50 miles upriver. *Class:* Trans-New Guinea, Trans-Fly-Bulaka River, Trans-Fly, Kiwaian. *Dialects:* Gama, Lower Bamu, Sisiame, Upper Bamu (Middle Bamu), Nuhiro. Gama dialect may be a separate language. Closely related to Kiwai and less closely to Waboda. Lexical similarity below 80% between Gama dialect and Lower Bamu, the closest other Bamu dialect. *Lg Dev:* Literacy rate in first language: 5% to 10%. Literacy rate in second language: 5% to 15%. Bible portions: 1952–2001. *Other:* Riverine. Swamp. Sea level to 2 meters. Hunter-gatherers.

Banaro (Banar, Banara) [byz] 2,484 (1991 SIL). Madang and East Sepik provinces. 2 villages. *Class:* Sepik-Ramu, Ramu, Ramu Proper, Grass, Banaro. *Lg Dev:* Literacy rate in first language: 5% to 25%. Literacy rate in second language: 50% to 75%. *Other:* Traditional religion, Christian.

Bannoni (Banoni, Tsunari) [bcm] 1,000 (1977 Lincoln). Bougainville Province, southwestern Bougainville. *Class:* Austronesian, Malayo-Polynesian, Central-Eastern, Eastern Malayo-Polynesian, Oceanic, Western Oceanic, Meso Melanesian, New Ireland, South New Ireland-Northwest Solomonic, Piva-Banoni. *Lg Dev:* Grammar.

Barai [bbb] 800 (2003 SIL). Inland Oro Province, Afore District, on the Managalas Plateau. Birarie dialect is in Umuate, Naokanane, Itokama, Madokoro villages. *Class:* Trans-New Guinea, Main Section, Eastern, Central and Southeastern, Koiarian, Baraic. *Dialects:* Birarie, Muguani. Lexical similarity 50% with Managalsi. *Lg Dev:* Literacy rate in first language: 50%. Literacy rate in second language: 50% to 60%. NT: 1994. *Other:* SOV. Interfluvial. Tropical forest. 700 to 900 meters. Swidden agriculturalists. Christian, traditional religion.

Baramu [bmz] 853 (2000 census). Western Province, southern bank of lower Fly River; Baramura, Tirio (Madiri), Tirio 2, and Tapila villages. *Class:* Trans-New Guinea, Trans-Fly-Bulaka River, Trans-Fly, Tirio. *Dialects:* Lexical similarity 33% with Bitur, 32% with Makayam, 27% with Were. *Other:* Different from Bitur, Makayam and Were.

Bargam (Mugil, Saker) [mlp] 3,750 (2003 SIL). Madang Province, Madang District, North Coast Road just opposite Karkar Island. *Class:* Trans-New Guinea, Madang-Adelbert Range, Adelbert Range, Pihom-Isumrud-Mugil, Mugil. *Lg Use:* Vigorous. All domains. Oral and written use in some schools, some use in religious services. Used by most adults over 20 years of age. Speakers are

ambivalent toward Bargam. Speakers use Tok Pisin, and a few use Garus, Megiar, or Matukar as second languages. Many parents are choosing to teach Tok Pisin first. Occasionally children become bilingual in Bargam. *Lg Dev:* Literacy rate in first language: More than 50%. Dictionary. NT: 2001. *Other:* The name 'Mugil' refers to an RC station. 'Saker' is a rare word referring to strength or stability. Coastal, foothills. Tropical forest. Agriculturalists: coffee; cocoa and copra production; portable saw mills; fish ponds. Christian, syncretism.

Bariai ("Kabana") [bch] 1,380 (1998 SIL). West New Britain Province, east of Cape Gloucester, northwest coast. *Class:* Austronesian, Malayo-Polynesian, Central-Eastern, Eastern Malayo-Polynesian, Oceanic, Western Oceanic, North New Guinea, Ngero-Vitiaz, Ngero, Bariai. *Dialects:* Lexical similarity 72% with Kove, 76% with Lusi. *Lg Use:* Speakers also use Tok Pisin. *Lg Dev:* Literacy rate in first language: 40.5% (adults). Literacy rate in second language: 82.5% (adults). Bible portions: 1998. *Other:* "Kabana" is a name acceptable to the three eastern villages, but offensive to the majority of the population. SVO; prepositions, 14% of syllables are closed; morphologically less complex than most Austronesian languages. Coastal. Tropical forest. Swidden agriculturalists; fishermen.

Bariji (Aga Bereho) [bjc] 456 (2000). Oro Province, on the south bank of the Bariji River. *Class:* Trans-New Guinea, Main Section, Eastern, Central and Southeastern, Yareban. *Dialects:* Lexical similarity 49% with Moikodi. *Lg Use:* Speakers also use Hiri Motu and some know Moikodi or Yareba.

Barok (Komalu, Kanapit, Kulubi, Kolube, Kanalu) [bjk] 2,116 (1985). New Ireland, south central, east and west coasts. 15 villages. *Class:* Austronesian, Malayo-Polynesian, Central-Eastern, Eastern Malayo-Polynesian, Oceanic, Western Oceanic, Meso Melanesian, New Ireland, Madak. *Dialects:* Usen, Barok. *Lg Dev:* Bible portions: 1929.

Baruga [bjz] 2,227 (2003 SIL). Population includes 796 Tafota, 987 Bareji, and 444 Mado. Oro Province, Tufi District, in the Musa and Bariji (Bareji) River flood plains. The Gaina, Bariji, and Yareba border them to the south. The Okeina dialect of Ewage-Notu, Ambe Tofo, Korafe-Mokorua, Miniafia-Arifama, Ubir, and Maisin speakers border them to the east. Dyke Ackland Bay is to the north. *Class:* Trans-New Guinea, Main Section, Eastern, Binanderean, Binanderean Proper. *Dialects:* Bareji, Baruga, Mado, Tafota Baruga. Lexical similarity 56% to 61% with Korafe and Gaina (Dutton 1971), 43% with Ewage dialect of Ewage-Notu. *Lg Use:* Vigorous. Wives of Baruga men who are not Baruga learn it. All domains. Some use in religious services. Speakers are preparing books in Baruga. Oral literature. All ages. Positive language attitude. Some speakers also use Hiri Motu, Ewage, Korafe, Tok Pisin, or English. *Lg Dev:* Literacy rate in first language: 60%. Literacy rate in second language: 60%. Bible portions: 1995. *Other:* Speakers go to Port Moresby and other towns to work. They prefer to retire in Baruga territory. SOV. Riverine, coastal. Tropical forest. Sea level to 60 meters. Swidden agriculturalists; fishermen; hunters. Christian, traditional religion.

Baruya (Barua, Yipma) [byr] 6,600 (1990 census). Eastern Highlands Province, Marawaka District. *Class:* Trans-New Guinea, Main Section, Central and Western, Angan, Angan Proper. *Dialect:* Wantakia, Baruya, Gulicha, Usirampia (Wuzuraabya). *Lg Dev:* Literacy rate in first language: 10% to 20%. Literacy rate in second language: 15% to 25%. Dictionary. NT: 1992. *Other:* 'Yipma' is the name most acceptable to speakers of most dialects. SOV. Mountain slope. Tropical forest, savannah. 1,040 to 3,459 meters. Swidden agriculturalists.

Bau [bbd] 3,058 (2000). Madang Province. *Class:* Trans-New Guinea, Madang-Adelbert Range, Madang, Mabuso, Gum. *Dialects:* Related to Sihan, Gumalu, Isebe, Amele, Panim. *Other:* Different from Bao in New Britain, an Oceanic language.

Bauwaki (Bawaki) [bwk] 398 (1980 census). Most are at Amau (Mori River), Central Province, extending into Oro Province. *Class:* Trans-New Guinea, Main Section, Eastern, Central and Southeastern, Mailuan. *Dialects:* Dutton says this is a bridge language between the Mailuan and Yareban families. Lexical similarity 66% with Abia (closest), 39% with Domu. *Lg Use:* 85% to 100% of speakers also use Magi, Suau, Motu, or English.

Beami (Bedamini, Bedamuni, Mougulu) [beo] 4,200 (1981 Wurm and Hattori). Western Province, east of Nomad, extending into Southern Highlands Province. *Class:* Trans-New Guinea, Main Section, Central and Western, Central and South New Guinea-Kutubuan, Central and South New Guinea, Bosavi. *Dialects:* Komofio, North Beami. *Lg Dev:* Literacy rate in first language: 5% to 15%. Literacy rate in second language: 15% to 25%. NT: 1991.

Bebeli (Benaule, Banaule, Kapore, Beli) [bek] 1,050 (1982 SIL). West New Britain Province, Stettin Bay, Cape Hoskins area. *Class:* Austronesian, Malayo-Polynesian, Central-Eastern, Eastern Malayo-Polynesian, Oceanic, Western Oceanic, North New Guinea, Ngero-Vitiaz, Vitiaz, Southwest New Britain, Arawe-Pasismanua, Arawe, East Arawe. *Other:* Different from Beli in Sandaun Province.

Beli (Mukili, Akuwagel, Makarim) [bey] 2,202 (2000). Population includes 1,400 in area and 53 outside. Sandaun Province, west of Mehek. *Class:* Torricelli, Maimai, Beli. *Other:* Different from Bebeli (Beli) in West New Britain.

Benabena (Bena) [bef] 45,000 (1998 NTM). Eastern Highlands Province, Goroka District. *Class:* Trans-New Guinea, Main Section, Central and Western, East New Guinea Highlands, East-Central, Gahuku-Benabena. *Lg Dev:* Literacy rate in first language: 25% to 50%. Literacy rate in second language: 50% to 75%. Grammar. NT: 1983. *Other:* Mountain valley. Savannah, tropical forest. 1,500 to 2,000 meters. Swidden agriculturalists. Traditional religion, Christian.

Bepour [bie] 50 (2000 Wurm). Madang Province. *Class:* Trans-New Guinea, Madang-Adelbert Range, Adelbert Range, Pihom-Isumrud-Mugil, Pihom, Kumilan. *Dialects:* Related to Mauwake, Moere. *Lg Use:* 40% of the ethnic group speaks Bepour.

Berinomo (Bitara) [bit] 353 (2000 census). East Sepik Province, April River. Bitara and Kagiru villages. *Class:* Sepik-Ramu, Sepik, Sepik Hill, Bahinemo. *Dialect:* Bitara, Kagiru (Apowasi). *Lg Use:* Speakers are moderately bilingual in Tok Pisin.

Biangai [big] 1,400 (1991 SIL). 50% monolingual. Morobe Province, Wau District, headwaters of the Bulolo River. 7 villages. *Class:* Trans-New Guinea, Main Section, Eastern, Central and Southeastern, Goilalan, Kunimaipa. *Dialects:* Ngowiye, Yongolei. *Lg Use:* Some speakers use Tok Pisin as second language. *Lg Dev:* Literacy rate in first language: 50%. Literacy rate in second language: 75% to 100%. The literacy rate remains high because of the number of children attending school. The vernacular literacy rate has dropped because of the deaths of adult readers and the shift of children to Tok Pisin. NT: 1985. *Other:* SOV. Interfluvial, mountain slope. Mixed forests. 950 to 1,100 meters. Swidden agriculturalists.

Biem (Bam) [bmc] 1,455 (1981 Wurm and Hattori). East Sepik Province, Viai, Blupblup, Kadovar, and Bam islands east of Wewak. *Class:* Austronesian, Malayo-Polynesian, Central-Eastern, Eastern Malayo-Polynesian, Oceanic, Western Oceanic, North New Guinea, Schouten, Kairiru-Manam, Manam.

Bikaru (Pikaru, Bugalu) [bic] 100 (1981 Wurm and Hattori). East Sepik Province, headwaters of April River. *Class:* Sepik-Ramu, Sepik, Sepik Hill, Sanio. *Lg Dev:* Literacy rate in first language: below 5%. Literacy rate in second language: 5% to 15%. *Other:* Nomadic. Traditional religion.

Bilakura [bql] 30 (2000 Wurm). Madang Province. *Class:* Trans-New Guinea, Madang-Adelbert Range, Adelbert Range, Pihom-Isumrud-Mugil, Pihom, Numugenan. *Dialects:* Related languages: Usan, Yaben, Yarawata, Parawen, Ukuriguma. *Other:* Nearly extinct.

Bilbil (Bilibil) [brz] 1,246 (2003 SIL). Madang Province, coast just south of Madang town. *Class:* Austronesian, Malayo-Polynesian, Central-Eastern, Eastern Malayo-Polynesian, Oceanic, Western Oceanic, North New Guinea, Ngero-Vitiaz, Vitiaz, Bel, Nuclear Bel, Northern.

Bilur (Birar) [bxf] 2,304 (2000). East New Britain Province, Gazelle Peninsula, 9 villages southeast of Cape Gazelle. *Class:* Austronesian, Malayo-Polynesian, Central-Eastern, Eastern Malayo-Polynesian, Oceanic, Western Oceanic, Meso Melanesian, New Ireland, South New Ireland-Northwest Solomonic.

Bimin [bhl] 2,250 (2003 SIL). Sandaun Province, Bak-Bimin District, and Western Province. *Class:* Trans-New Guinea, Main Section, Central and Western, Central and South New Guinea-Kutubuan, Central and South New Guinea, Ok, Mountain. *Dialects:* Bim, Nimtep Weng. Close to Faiwol. *Lg Dev:* Literacy rate in first language: below 5%. Literacy rate in second language: 5% to 15%. Vernacular primary schools. Bible portions: 1995–2000. *Other:* Much intermarriage and cultural exchange with Oksapmin. Mountain slope, valley. Tropical forest. 600 to 2,000 meters. Swidden agriculturalists; hunters.

Bina [bmn] Extinct. Central Province, north of Baibara. *Class:* Austronesian, Malayo-Polynesian, Central-Eastern, Eastern Malayo-Polynesian, Oceanic, Western Oceanic, Papuan Tip, Peripheral, Central Papuan, Oumic, Magoric.

Binahari [bxz] 764 (1980 census). Central Province, both sides of a range of hills inland from Cloudy Bay. *Class:* Trans-New Guinea, Main Section, Eastern, Central and Southeastern, Mailuan. *Dialects:* Neme (Nemea), Ma. Lexical similarity 70% with Morawa (closest). *Lg Use:* Most speakers also use Magi, Suau, Hiri Motu, or English.

Binandere (Ioma Binandere) [bhg] 6,902 (2003 SIL). Oro Province, along the Eia, Gira, Ope, Mambere, and Kumusi rivers, between Zia and Ambasi; a few in Morobe Province. *Class:* Trans-New Guinea, Main Section, Eastern, Binanderean, Binanderean Proper. *Dialects:* Aeka (Aiga), Ambasi (Tain-Daware, Davari, Dawari), Binandere. Lexical similarity 50% to 54% with Suena and Zia, 67% with Ambasi. *Lg Use:* Speakers who live near the coast are more bilingual. *Lg Dev:* Literacy rate in first language: 25% to 50%. Literacy rate in second language: 25% to 50%. Grammar. Bible portions: 1912–1949. *Other:* SOV. Sago swamp, plains. Sea level to 100 meters. Fishermen; hunters; swidden agriculturalists: tobacco; wood carvers; potters. Christian, traditional religion.

Bine (Oriomo, Pine) [bon] 2,000 (1987 SIL). Western Province, Daru District, south of Fly River. *Class:* Trans-New Guinea, Trans-Fly-Bulaka River, Trans-Fly, Eastern Trans-Fly. *Dialects:* Kunini, Boze-Giringarede, Sogal, Masingle, Tate, Irupi-Drageli, Sebe. *Lg Dev:* Literacy rate in first language: 50% to 75%. Literacy rate in second language: 25% to 50%. NT: 1993. *Other:* SOV. Coastal, riverine. Tropical forest, mangrove swamp, savannah. Sea level. Fishermen; swidden agriculturalists.

Binumarien (Binumaria, Binamarir) [bjr] 360 (1990 census). Eastern Highlands Province, Kainantu District. *Class:* Trans-New Guinea, Main Section, Central and

Western, East New Guinea Highlands, Eastern, Tairora. *Lg Dev:* Literacy rate in first language: 75% to 100%. Literacy rate in second language: 75% to 100%. NT: 1983. *Other:* Some form of whistle speech reported. SOV. Mountain slope. Tropical forest. 1,350 meters. Swidden agriculturalists.

Bipi (Sisi-Bipi) [biq] 1,200 (1990 SIL). Manus Province, west coast, Maso, Matahei, and Salapai villages, Bipi and Sisi islands. *Class:* Austronesian, Malayo-Polynesian, Central-Eastern, Eastern Malayo-Polynesian, Oceanic, Admiralty Islands, Eastern, Manus, West. *Dialects:* Close to Loniu. *Other:* SVO.

Bisis (Yambiyambi) [bnw] 500 (1986 SIL). East Sepik Province, Hunstein Range, Ambunti District, next to the Bahinemo, between the Lower Salumei River and Chambri Lake. 3 villages. *Class:* Sepik-Ramu, Sepik, Sepik Hill, Bahinemo. *Lg Use:* Highly bilingual in Tok Pisin. *Other:* Mountain slope. Tropical forest. Hunter-gatherers, sago palm. Traditional religion, Christian.

Bisorio (Inyai-Gadio-Bisorio, Iniai) [bir] 255 (2003 SIL). Population includes 50 to 100 Pikaru. East Sepik Province, headwaters of the Karawari, Wagupmeri, and Korosameri rivers; villages of Bisorio, Iniai, Gadio. *Class:* Trans-New Guinea, Main Section, Central and Western, East New Guinea Highlands, West-Central, Enga. *Dialect:* Pikaru (Bikaru). Lexical similarity 70% with Nete. *Lg Dev:* NT: 1993.

Bitur (Mutum, Paswam, Dudi, Bituri) [mcc] 856 (2000 census). Western Province, southern bank and hinterland of Fly River; Upiara, Bisuaka, Petom, Tewara and Kasimap villages. *Class:* Trans-New Guinea, Trans-Fly-Bulaka River, Trans-Fly, Tirio. *Dialects:* Lexical similarity 52% with Makayam, 35% with Were, 33% with Baramu. *Other:* Distinct from Makayam, Were, and Baramu.

Biwat (Mundugumor, Munduguma) [bwm] 3,042 (2003 SIL). East Sepik Province, lower and middle Yuat River. *Class:* Sepik-Ramu, Ramu, Yuat-Langam, Yuat-Maramba, Yuat. *Dialects:* Related to Kyenele, Changriwa, Mekmek, Kyenele, Bun.

Biyom (Sasime) [bpm] 379 (1981 Wurm and Hattori). Madang Province, southeast of Gende. *Class:* Trans-New Guinea, Madang-Adelbert Range, Adelbert Range, Brahman. *Dialects:* Related to Isabi, Tauya, Faita.

Blafe (Tonda, Indorodoro) [bfh] 667 (2003 SIL). Western Province, west of Nambo language. Indorodoro town is center. *Class:* Trans-New Guinea, Trans-Fly-Bulaka River, Trans-Fly, Morehead and Upper Maro rivers, Tonda. *Dialects:* Mblafe, Ránmo. Different from Ara (Rouku), although related. *Lg Dev:* Literacy rate in first language: 5%. Literacy rate in second language: 5% to 15%.

Bo (Po, Sorimi) [bpw] 85 (1998 NTM). Sandaun Province, the heart of the western range; Bo, Kobaru, Kaumifi, Nigyama Umarita villages. Western range, close to the border of Sandaun Province, near Right May River, East Sepik Province. *Class:* Left May. *Dialects:* Kaboru, Nikiyama, Umuruta. *Lg Dev:* Literacy rate in second language: 50%. *Other:* The area is seldom entered by outsiders. Unconfirmed as a separate language. Mountain slope, valley. Tropical forest. 150 meters. Hunter-gatherers. Traditional religion.

Bogaya (Pogaya, Bogaia) [boq] 300 (1981 Wurm and Hattori). Western Province, some also in base of northern neck of Southern Highlands Province. *Class:* Trans-New Guinea, Main Section, Central and Western, Central and South New Guinea-Kutubuan, Central and South New Guinea, Duna-Bogaya. *Lg Dev:* Literacy rate in first language: below 5%. Literacy rate in second language: below 5%.

Boikin (Boiken, Nucum, Yangoru, Yengoru) [bzf] 31,328 (2003 SIL). East Sepik Province, Yangoru District. *Class:*

Sepik-Ramu, Sepik, Middle Sepik, Ndu. *Dialects:* West Boikin, Central Boikin, East Boikin, Munji, Haripmor, Kwusaun, Kunai, Island Boikin. *Lg Use:* 30% monolingual. Others use Tok Pisin as second language. *Lg Dev:* Literacy rate in first language: 5% to 15%. Literacy rate in second language: 50% to 75%. Bible portions: 1971–1979.

Bola (Bakovi, Bola-Bakovi) [bnp] 13,746 (2000 census). Population includes 2,253 Harua. West New Britain Province, northeast coast, most of Willaumez Peninsula. Harua is on the east side of Kimbe. *Class:* Austronesian, Malayo-Polynesian, Central-Eastern, Eastern Malayo-Polynesian, Oceanic, Western Oceanic, Meso Melanesian, Willaumez. *Dialects:* Harua (Karua, Xarua, Garua, Mai), Bola. Harua is a dialect that has developed as a result of a group of people being resettled on an oil palm plantation. *Lg Dev:* NT: 1934. *Other:* 11 vernacular preparatory schools.

Bongu [bpu] 854 (2000 census). Madang Province, Astrolabe Bay, Rai Coast. *Class:* Trans-New Guinea, Madang-Adelbert Range, Madang, Rai Coast, Mindjim.

Bonkiman [bop] 175 (1991 SIL). 40% monolingual. Madang and Morobe provinces. *Class:* Trans-New Guinea, Main Section, Central and Western, Huon-Finisterre, Finisterre, Yupna. *Lg Use:* Speakers also use Tok Pisin. Passive bilingualism with neighboring languages.

Borei (Gamei, Gamai, Mborei, Mbore) [gai] 2,090 (2003 SIL). Madang Province, Bogia District. *Class:* Sepik-Ramu, Ramu, Ramu Proper, Ruboni, Ottilien. *Dialects:* Boroi, Borewar, Botbot. *Lg Dev:* Literacy rate in first language: 5% to 25%. Literacy rate in second language: 50% to 75%.

Borong (Naama, Kosorong) [ksr] 2,069 (2000 census). Morobe Province, Finschhafen District, 5 villages and 5 hamlets in the central Huon Peninsula between the Kuat and Burum rivers, south of Mindik airstrip. Burum and Kuat are tributaries of the Mongi River. Many live in Lae and other towns. *Class:* Trans-New Guinea, Main Section, Central and Western, Huon-Finisterre, Huon, Eastern. *Dialects:* Kosorong, Yangeborong. *Lg Use:* Vigorous. Used in religious services. Use of Tok Pisin is increasing and Kâte decreasing as second language. *Lg Dev:* NT: 2002. *Other:* SOV; postpositions; long and short vowels. Mountain slope. Tropical forest. 500 to 1,500 to meters. Swidden agriculturalists.

Boselewa (Bosilewa, Bosalewa, Mwani'u) [bwf] 614 (1999 SIL). Milne Bay Province, north shore of Fergusson Island. *Class:* Austronesian, Malayo-Polynesian, Central-Eastern, Eastern Malayo-Polynesian, Oceanic, Western Oceanic, Papuan Tip, Nuclear, North Papuan Mainland-D'Entrecasteaux, Dobu-Duau. *Dialects:* Lexical similarity 61% with Galeya (closest). *Lg Use:* 40% of the ethnic group speak Boselewa. Multilingual in neighboring languages.

Bosngun (Bosman) [bqs] 1,225 (2000). 20% monolingual. Madang Province. *Class:* Sepik-Ramu, Ramu, Ramu Proper, Ruboni, Ottilien. *Lg Use:* Others use Tok Pisin as second language.

Bragat (Alauagat, Yauan) [aof] 460 (2003 SIL). Sandaun Province, 4 villages. *Class:* Torricelli, Wapei-Palei, Palei. *Dialects:* Most closely related to Aru. *Other:* 1 community school. Mountain ridge. 460 to 550 meters.

Brem (Barem, Bunabun, Bunubun, Bububun) [buq] 1,190 (2003 SIL). Madang Province, including Bunabun village. *Class:* Trans-New Guinea, Madang-Adelbert Range, Adelbert Range, Pihom-Isumrud-Mugil, Isumrud, Mabuan. *Other:* Speakers refer to themselves as 'Brem' or 'Barem'.

Breri (Kuanga) [brq] 1,100 (1986 PBT). Madang Province, lower Ramu Valley, 80 miles west of Madang City. *Class:* Sepik-Ramu, Ramu, Ramu Proper, Goam, Tamolan.

Dialects: Related to Kominimung, Igana, Itutang. *Other:* Swampy plain.

Buang, Mangga (Manga Buang, Kaidemui) [mmo] 3,000 (1986 SIL). Morobe Province, mid-upper Snake River area, Mumeng District. *Class:* Austronesian, Malayo-Polynesian, Central-Eastern, Eastern Malayo-Polynesian, Oceanic, Western Oceanic, North New Guinea, Huon Gulf, South, Hote-Buang, Buang. *Dialects:* Lagis, Kwasang. *Lg Use:* Speakers also use Tok Pisin. *Lg Dev:* Literacy rate in first language: 50% to 75%. Literacy rate in second language: 50% to 75%. NT: 1981. *Other:* SVO. Mountain slope. Savannah. 670 to 1,830 meters. Swidden agriculturalists. Christian, traditional religion.

Buang, Mapos (Mapos, Central Buang) [bzh] 10,484 (2000). 30% monolingual. Morobe Province, middle Snake River area, Mumeng District. 10 villages. *Class:* Austronesian, Malayo-Polynesian, Central-Eastern, Eastern Malayo-Polynesian, Oceanic, Western Oceanic, North New Guinea, Huon Gulf, South, Hote-Buang, Buang. *Dialects:* Wagau, Mambump, Buweyeu, Wins, Chimbuluk, Papakene, Mapos. Lexical similarity 61% between Mambump and Mangga. *Lg Use:* Vigorous. People in cities are more likely to speak Tok Pisin to children. All domains. Some oral and written use in village schools, community development, oral and written use in church. Personal letters. All ages. Children in towns understand Buang, but speak Tok Pisin. Positive language attitude. Speakers also use Tok Pisin. *Lg Dev:* Literacy rate in first language: 50% to 75%. Literacy rate in second language: 50% to 75%. Grammar. NT: 1978. *Other:* SVO. Mountain slope. Scrub forest, tropical forest. 1,500 to 2,000 meters. Swidden agriculturalists; vegetables, coffee; animal husbandry: cattle. Christian, traditional religion.

Budibud (Nada) [btp] 309 (2000). 15% monolingual. Milne Bay Province, Lachlan Islands, 50 miles east of Woodlark Island. *Class:* Austronesian, Malayo-Polynesian, Central-Eastern, Eastern Malayo-Polynesian, Oceanic, Western Oceanic, Papuan Tip, Peripheral, Kilivila-Louisiades, Kilivila. *Dialects:* Most closely related to Muyuw. Lexical similarity 65% with Muyuw. *Lg Use:* Speakers use Muyuw as second language. *Other:* The name 'Nada' is no longer used. Christian, traditional religion.

Bugawac (Bukawa, Bukaua, Bukawac, Kawa, Kawac, Yom Gawac) [buk] 9,694 (1978 McElhanon). 40% monolingual. Morobe Province, coast of Huon Gulf. *Class:* Austronesian, Malayo-Polynesian, Central-Eastern, Eastern Malayo-Polynesian, Oceanic, Western Oceanic, North New Guinea, Huon Gulf, North. *Dialects:* Close to Yabem. *Lg Use:* Yabem is decreasingly used in religious services. Yabem bilingual proficiency is decreasing with those educated in Yabem up to the 1960s. Tok Pisin is the second language. *Lg Dev:* Literacy rate in first language: 80%. Literacy rate in second language: 15% to 25%. Bugawac primary schools in about half the Bukawa villages. NT: 2001.

Buhutu (Bohutu, Buhulu, Yaleba, Siasiada) [bxh] 1,350 (2003 SIL). 20% monolingual. Eastern tip of Papua, Sagarai Valley, Milne Bay Province, Alotau (Rabaraba) District. *Class:* Austronesian, Malayo-Polynesian, Central-Eastern, Eastern Malayo-Polynesian, Oceanic, Western Oceanic, Papuan Tip, Nuclear, Suauic. *Dialects:* Lexical similarity 68% with Suau. *Lg Use:* Vigorous. Also spoken as second language by Kakabai, Sinaki, Haigwai (Naura), Wagawaga. All domains. Local administration, commerce, some religious services, personal letters, oral literature. All ages. Positive language attitude. About 75% have speaking and listening competence in 2 or 3 other languages. Many older adults also use Suau or Tawala, but this has declined since the mission schools were replaced by an English

medium government school. Fewer than 20% know some Motu, Tok Pisin has come in since the early 1990s, and is known to some extent by 50%. *Lg Dev:* Literacy rate in first language: 75%. Literacy rate in second language: 75%. Taught in primary schools. *Other:* Riverine, valleys, lowland, coastal, mountain slope. Mangrove swamp. Up to 1,500 meters. Gardeners; hunters; oil palm; coconut plantation; lumbermen. Christian.

Bukiyip (Bukiyúp, Mountain Arapesh) [ape] 16,233 (2003 SIL). East Sepik Province, west Yangoru District, Torricelli Mountains. *Class:* Torricelli, Kombio-Arapesh, Arapesh. *Dialect:* Coastal Arapesh, Bukiyip (Mountain Arapesh). Lexical similarity 60% with Mufian. *Lg Dev:* Literacy rate in first language: 15% to 25%. Literacy rate in second language: 25% to 50%. Grammar. NT: 1994. *Other:* SVO; 14 noun classes; noun phrase concordance. Mountain slope. Scrub forest, tropical forest. 300 to 500 meters. Swidden agriculturalists.

Bulgebi [bmp] 50 (2000 Wurm). Madang Province, 10 miles southeast of Saidor. *Class:* Trans-New Guinea, Main Section, Central and Western, Huon-Finisterre, Finisterre, Warup. *Dialects:* Related to Asaro'o, Muratayak, Degenan, Forak, Guya, Gwahatike, Yagomi. *Lg Use:* 40% of the ethnic group speaks Bulgebi.

Bulu [bjl] 906 (2000 census). West New Britain Province, Willaumez Peninsula. *Class:* Austronesian, Malayo-Polynesian, Central-Eastern, Eastern Malayo-Polynesian, Oceanic, Western Oceanic, Meso Melanesian, Willaumez. *Lg Use:* Speakers also use Bola.

Bun [buv] 481 (2003 SIL). East Sepik Province. *Class:* Sepik-Ramu, Ramu, Yuat-Langam, Yuat-Maramba, Yuat. *Dialects:* Related to Changriwa, Mekmek, Biwat, Kyenele. *Lg Dev:* Literacy rate in second language: 25% to 50%.

Buna [bvn] 750 (2003 SIL). East Sepik Province, Angoram District. *Class:* Torricelli, Marienberg. *Dialects:* Kasmin, Masan. Apparently 2 dialects: 1 in Kasmin, Boig, Waskurin, and Arapang villages, and 1 in Masan, Mangan, and Garien villages. *Lg Dev:* Literacy rate in first language: below 5%. Literacy rate in second language: 15% to 25%.

Bunama [bdd] 4,000 (1993 SIL). Milne Bay Province, southern Normanby Island, Esa'ala District. *Class:* Austronesian, Malayo-Polynesian, Central-Eastern, Eastern Malayo-Polynesian, Oceanic, Western Oceanic, Papuan Tip, Nuclear, North Papuan Mainland-D'Entrecasteaux, Dobu-Duau. *Dialects:* Bunama, Barabara, Sawatupwa, Lomitawa, Sipupu, Weyoko, Meudana, Kerorogea, Kumalahu, Kasikasi, Sawabwala. Lexical similarity 66% with Mwatebu, 75% with most Dobu dialects. *Lg Use:* Speakers have low proficiency in Dobu. *Lg Dev:* Literacy rate in first language: 85%. Literacy rate in second language: 85%. NT: 1991. *Other:* Volcanic islands. Tropical forest. Sea level to 300 meters. Agriculturalists: yams. Traditional religion, Christian.

Bungain [but] 3,597 (2003 SIL). East Sepik Province. Yaugiba is one village. *Class:* Torricelli, Marienberg. *Lg Dev:* Literacy rate in second language: 50% to 75%.

Burui [bry] 256 (2000). East Sepik Province, Ambunti District, Sepik Plains south of Maprik, Burui village, north of Pagwi. *Class:* Sepik-Ramu, Sepik, Middle Sepik, Ndu. *Lg Use:* Most adults are fluent in Gaikundi. *Lg Dev:* Literacy rate in first language: below 5%. Literacy rate in second language: 25% to 50%.

Burum-Mindik (Bulum, Burum, Mindik, Somba-Siawari) [bmu] 8,253 (2000 census). 1,000 monolingual. Population includes 5,500 in Somba, 4,500 in Siawari. Morobe Province, Finschhafen District, 30 villages in Central Huon Peninsula, south of Cromwell Range, Burum River valley and some western slopes of Kuat River. (Burum and Kuat are tributaries of the main Mongi River.) Many live in towns, 1,000 in Lae, scattered groups in Port Moresby and other towns. 3 airstrips: Ogeramnang, Mindik, Nomanene. *Class:* Trans-New Guinea, Main Section, Central and Western, Huon-Finisterre, Huon, Western. *Dialects:* Somba, Siawari. Lexical similarity 92% between the dialects. *Lg Use:* Vigorous. All domains. Local administration, commerce. All ages. Positive language attitude. Tok Pisin is the main second language, used by most. English use is increasing slowly. Kâte is the church language, but decreasing in use. 5,000 can speak all 4 languages. *Lg Dev:* Literacy rate in first language: 80%. Literacy rate in second language: 80% to 90%. 7,000 can read it, 6,000 can write it. Taught in primary and secondary schools. NT: 1996. *Other:* 'Bulum' is the Kâte name for them. Place of origin of cargo cults in Morobe Province. 7 community schools. There has been a self-help movement since 1975. SOV; postpositions. Mountain slope. Tropical forest. 500 to 1,700 meters. Swidden agriculturalists.

Bwaidoka (Bwaidoga) [bwd] 6,500 (2000 SIL). 50% monolingual. Milne Bay Province, southeast tip of Goodenough Island and west Fergusson Island, Bolubolu District. *Class:* Austronesian, Malayo-Polynesian, Central-Eastern, Eastern Malayo-Polynesian, Oceanic, Western Oceanic, Papuan Tip, Nuclear, North Papuan Mainland-D'Entrecasteaux, Bwaidoga. *Dialects:* Mataitai, Wagifa, Kilia, Lauwela, Bwaidoga, Faiyava, Belebele I, Bebebele Ii, Kalauna, Kiliva. Lexical similarity 72% with Iduna (closest). *Lg Use:* Vigorous. Speakers of Diodio, Iamalele, and Kaninuwa use Bwaidoka as second language. Bwaidoka was used as a lingua franca to communicate with other language speakers. All domains. It is the main language used in church, along with Dobu. Oral and written use in local commerce. All ages. Bwaidoka speakers have a positive attitude toward it. They consider Iduna to be a less important language. Speakers use Dobu as second language. English is used as the teaching medium in schools and for government. *Lg Dev:* Literacy rate in first language: 65%. Literacy rate in second language: 65% to 75%. Bible portions: 1934–1994. *Other:* Half of the children are in school. Island, mountain slope, plains. Agriculturalists.

Bwanabwana (Tubetube) [tte] 2,015 (1994 SIL). 30% monolingual. Milne Bay Province, Bwanabwana District, Engineer Islands, Laseinie Islands, Ware Island, Kitai Island and southeast peninsula of Basilaki Island. *Class:* Austronesian, Malayo-Polynesian, Central-Eastern, Eastern Malayo-Polynesian, Oceanic, Western Oceanic, Papuan Tip, Nuclear, Suauic. *Dialects:* Wale (Wari, Ware), Kwalaiwa. Lexical similarity 52% with Duau (closest). *Lg Use:* Important language at the center of the trade route. Older people know Dobu, the traditional church language, and language of kula trade. Some also use Dobu, Suau, Tawala, Duau, or Misima. *Lg Dev:* Literacy rate in first language: 25% to 50%. Literacy rate in second language: 25% to 50%. NT: 2004.

Chambri (Tshamberi, Tchambuli) [can] 1,700 (1991). East Sepik Province, marsh dwellers east and north of Sepik Hill area, southeastern shore and island in Chambri Lake. 4 villages. *Class:* Sepik-Ramu, Nor-Pondo, Pondo. *Lg Use:* Speakers are highly bilingual in Tok Pisin. *Lg Dev:* Literacy rate in first language: below 5%. Literacy rate in second language: 15% to 25%. *Other:* Wealth comes from fishing. Fishermen; poultry husbandry; turtle catching. Traditional religion.

Changriwa [cga] 688 (2003 SIL). East Sepik Province. *Class:* Sepik-Ramu, Ramu, Yuat-Langam, Yuat-Maramba, Yuat. *Dialects:* Related languages: Mekmek, Kyenele, Biwat, Bun.

Chenapian (Tsenap, Zenap, Chenap) [cjn] 178 (2003 SIL). East Sepik Province, on the Sepik River west of Wogamusin. 1 village. *Class:* Sepik-Ramu, Sepik, Upper Sepik, Wogamusin. *Lg Use:* Many Tok Pisin speakers. Some youth are learning English. *Lg Dev:* Literacy rate in first language: below 5%. Literacy rate in second language: below 5%.

Chuave (Tjuave) [cjv] 23,107 (1981 Wurm and Hattori). Population includes 4,290 Sua (1962 Wurm). Simbu Province, Chuave District. *Class:* Trans-New Guinea, Main Section, Central and Western, East New Guinea Highlands, Central, Chimbu. *Dialects:* Elimbari, Kebai, Gomia, Chuave, Sua. Kebai is distinct, but intelligible. *Lg Dev:* Literacy rate in first language: 50% to 75%. Literacy rate in second language: 25% to 50%. NT: 1992–1994. *Other:* SOV. Mountain mesa. Savannah. 1,500 to 2,200 meters. Swidden agriculturalists.

Dadibi (Daribi, Karimui) [mps] 10,000 (1988 SIL). 10% monolingual. Southern Simbu Province, Karimui District, eastern corner of Southern Highlands Province. 28 villages. *Class:* Trans-New Guinea, Teberan-Pawaian, Teberan. *Dialect:* Erave. Those villages have minor dialect differences from standard Dadibi in the Karimui and Negabo areas. *Lg Use:* Speakers in 2 or 3 villages on the Erave River have high proficiency in Folopa. They also use Tok Pisin. *Lg Dev:* Literacy rate in first language: 50% to 75%. Literacy rate in second language: 50% to 75%. Grammar. Bible: 2001. *Other:* SOV. Plateau. Tropical forest. 1,000 to 1,150 meters. Swidden agriculturalists. Christian, traditional religion.

Daga (Dimuga, Nawp) [dgz] 6,000 (1991 SIL). Milne Bay Province, Rabaraba District, and Central Province, Abau District. *Class:* Trans-New Guinea, Main Section, Eastern, Central and Southeastern, Dagan. *Lg Dev:* Literacy rate in first language: 25% to 50%. Literacy rate in second language: 25% to 50%. Grammar. NT: 1974.

Dambi [dac] 711 (2000). Morobe Province, Mumeng District. *Class:* Austronesian, Malayo-Polynesian, Central-Eastern, Eastern Malayo-Polynesian, Oceanic, Western Oceanic, North New Guinea, Huon Gulf, South, Hote-Buang, Buang, Mumeng. *Dialects:* In the Mumeng language cluster. Some intelligibility of Kumalu. *Lg Dev:* Literacy rate in first language: 15% to 25%. Literacy rate in second language: 25% to 50%. *Other:* SVO. Mountain slope. Tropical forest. 300 to 900 meters. Swidden agriculturalists.

Danaru [dnr] 257 (2003 SIL). Madang Province. *Class:* Trans-New Guinea, Madang-Adelbert Range, Madang, Rai Coast, Peka. *Dialects:* Related to Sop, Urigina, Sumau.

Dano (Upper Asaro, Asaro) [aso] 30,000 (1987 SIL). Eastern Highlands Province, Goroka District. *Class:* Trans-New Guinea, Main Section, Central and Western, East New Guinea Highlands, East-Central, Gahuku-Benabena. *Dialects:* Upper Asaro, Lunube Mado, Bohena, Amaizuho, Kongi. *Lg Dev:* Literacy rate in first language: 15% to 25%. Literacy rate in second language: 25% to 50%. NT: 1989. *Other:* SOV. Mountain slope. Savannah. 1,500 to 2,300 meters. Peasant agriculturalists.

Daonda [dnd] 169 (2003 SIL). Sandaun Province, Amanab District near Imonda. *Class:* Trans-New Guinea, Northern, Border, Waris. *Lg Use:* Adults can understand Waris.

Dawawa (Dawana) [dww] 2,500 (1994 SIL). 20% monolingual. West and inland from Wedau in Milne Bay Province, Rabaraba District. *Class:* Austronesian, Malayo-Polynesian, Central-Eastern, Eastern Malayo-Polynesian, Oceanic, Western Oceanic, Papuan Tip, Nuclear, North Papuan Mainland-D'Entrecasteaux, Kakabai. *Dialects:* Lexical similarity 58% with Kakabai. *Lg Use:* Used in the home and village. Older speakers know Wedau, Motu, and English. Wedau is used primarily in church. *Lg Dev:* NT: 2002. *Other:* Mountain slope.

Dedua [ded] 5,000 (1991 SIL). Morobe Province, Sialum District, headwaters of the Masaweng and Tewae rivers, south of Mt. Besenona. *Class:* Trans-New Guinea, Main Section, Central and Western, Huon-Finisterre, Huon, Eastern. *Dialects:* Dzeigoc, Fanic. *Lg Dev:* Literacy rate in first language: 80%. Literacy rate in second language: 80%. Bible portions: 1990–1999. *Other:* Mountain slope. Swidden agriculturalists.

Degenan [dge] 789 (2003 SIL). Madang Province. *Class:* Trans-New Guinea, Main Section, Central and Western, Huon-Finisterre, Finisterre, Warup. *Dialects:* Related to Asaro'o, Muratayak, Bulgebi, Forak, Guya, Gwahatike, Yagomi.

Dera (Dra, Mangguar, Komberatoro, Kamberataro, Kamberatoro) [kbv] 687 in Papua New Guinea. Sandaun Province, Amanab District, both sides of the Faringi River. *Dialects:* North Kamberataro, South Kamberataro, Mengau, Lihen, Duka-Ekor. See main entry under Indonesia (Papua).

Dia (Alu, Metru, Galu) [dia] 1,835 (2003 SIL). Sandaun Province. *Class:* Torricelli, Wapei-Palei, Wapei.

Dibiyaso (Bainapi, Pikiwa, Dibiasu) [dby] 1,953 (2000 Census). Western Province, villages of Makapa, Pikiwa, and Bamustu, via Balimo. *Class:* Trans-New Guinea, Main Section, Central and Western, Central and South New Guinea-Kutubuan, Central and South New Guinea, Bosavi. *Dialects:* Lexical similarity 19% with Turumsa, 15% with Doso. *Lg Use:* Vigorous. All domains, home, social events, cultural events. Vernacular instruction first two years. All ages. Strong sense of separate identity from the dominant Gogodala. All levels of bilingualism in Gogodala. Speakers also use Kamula, Doso, English, Hiri Motu, or Tok Pisin. *Lg Dev:* Literacy rate in second language: 5% to 50%. Taught in primary schools. *Other:* SOV. Riverine. Tropical forest. Below 100 meters. Hunter-gatherers. Christian, traditional religion.

Dima (Dimadima, Jimajima) [jma] 754 (2001 SIL). 15% monolinguals. Milne Bay Province, along the coast east of Moi Bay almost to Posaposa Harbor, and along the Ruaba River. *Class:* Trans-New Guinea, Main Section, Eastern, Central and Southeastern, Dagan. *Dialects:* Lexical similarity 41% with Daga (closest). *Lg Use:* All domains. Used in the home if both parents are Dima, cultural events if no nonspeakers present. All ages. All Dima speakers learn at least the nearest neighboring language which might be Anuki, Gapapaiwa, Maiwa, Are, or Doga. The older generation also uses Motu while the younger generation uses English and some Tok Pisin. *Other:* SOV. Coastal. Savannah. Sea level to 200 meters. Swidden agriculturalists. Christian, traditional religion.

Dimir (Boskien, Bosiken) [dmc] 3,820 (2003 SIL). Madang Province. *Class:* Trans-New Guinea, Madang-Adelbert Range, Adelbert Range, Pihom-Isumrud-Mugil, Isumrud, Dimir. *Lg Use:* Speakers also use Tok Pisin.

Diodio [ddi] 2,184 (2000). 20% monolingual. Milne Bay Province, west coast of Goodenough Island. *Class:* Austronesian, Malayo-Polynesian, Central-Eastern, Eastern Malayo-Polynesian, Oceanic, Western Oceanic, Papuan Tip, Nuclear, North Papuan Mainland-D'Entrecasteaux, Bwaidoga. *Dialects:* Iauiaula, Utalo, Awale, Central Diodio. Lexical similarity 66% with Bwaidoka (closest). *Lg Use:* All domains, home, religion. Speakers also use Bwaidoka. *Lg Dev:* Literacy rate in second language: Many speakers.

Dobu [dob] 10,000 (1998 SIL). 60% monolingual. Milne Bay Province, Esa'ala District, Sanaroa, Dobu, and parts of Fergusson and Normanby islands. 500 villages. *Class:* Austronesian, Malayo-Polynesian, Central-Eastern, Eastern Malayo-Polynesian, Oceanic, Western Oceanic, Papuan Tip, Nuclear, North Papuan Mainland-D'Entrecasteaux, Dobu-Duau. *Dialect:* Galubwa, Sanaroa, Ubuia, Central Dobu, Loboda (Roboda, Dawada-Siausi). Lexical similarity 56% with Morima (closest). *Lg Use:* Trade

language of most of D'entrecasteaux Islands. Lingua franca for 100,000 (1987 SIL). Speakers have some proficiency in Motu, English, adjacent languages. *Lg Dev:* Literacy rate in first language: 90%. Literacy rate in second language: 90%. Dictionary. Bible: 1928. *Other:* Many schools. SOV. Volcanic islands. Tropical forest. Sea level to 300 meters. Agriculturalists: yams.

Doga (Magabara) [dgg] 200 (2000 Wurm). Milne Bay Province, north coast of Cape Vogel. *Class:* Austronesian, Malayo-Polynesian, Central-Eastern, Eastern Malayo-Polynesian, Oceanic, Western Oceanic, Papuan Tip, Nuclear, North Papuan Mainland-D'Entrecasteaux, Are-Taupota, Are. *Dialects:* Lexical similarity 7% to 55% with Are (closest). *Lg Use:* 60% of the ethnic group speaks Doga. 60% of young people know English, others Anuki and Dima. *Lg Dev:* Literacy rate in second language: most young people.

Doghoro [dgx] 267 (2000 census). Oro Province, Tufi District, in the Musa and Bariji (Bareji) River flood plains, Bendorode and Sebagha villages. *Class:* Trans-New Guinea, Main Section, Eastern, Binanderean, Binanderean Proper. *Lg Use:* All domains. *Other:* SOV. Riverine, coastal. Tropical forest. Sea level to 60 meters. Swidden agriculturalists; fishermen; hunters. Christian, traditional religion.

Dom [doa] 12,000 (1994 NTM). Simbu Province, mainly south of the Wahgi River from Kundiawa west of the Sinasina area. *Class:* Trans-New Guinea, Main Section, Central and Western, East New Guinea Highlands, Central, Chimbu. *Dialect:* Era. *Lg Dev:* Bible portions.

Domu (Dom) [dof] 947 (2000). Central Province, coast east of Cape Rodney and inland. *Class:* Trans-New Guinea, Main Section, Eastern, Central and Southeastern, Mailuan. *Dialects:* Lexical similarity 66% with Bauwaki (closest). *Lg Use:* 85% to 100% of the speakers also use Mailu, Suau, Hiri Motu, English.

Domung [dev] 2,000 (1991 SIL). Tapen, Madang Province. *Class:* Trans-New Guinea, Main Section, Central and Western, Huon-Finisterre, Finisterre, Yupna.

Doromu (Doram) [kqc] 1,600 (2002 SIL). Central Province, south of Mt. Obree, west of Mt. Brown. *Class:* Trans-New Guinea, Main Section, Eastern, Central and Southeastern, Manubaran. *Dialect:* Kokila, Koriko, Koki (Doromu). Lexical similarity 63% with Maria (closest).

Doso [dol] 700 (1973 D. Shaw). Western Province, Aramia River and Wawoi Falls areas, near the Kamula. *Class:* Unclassified. *Other:* A separate language from Kamula.

Duau [dva] 3,550 (1991 SIL). 20% monolingual. Milne Bay Province, Sawabwala, Normanby islands. *Class:* Austronesian, Malayo-Polynesian, Central-Eastern, Eastern Malayo-Polynesian, Oceanic, Western Oceanic, Papuan Tip, Nuclear, North Papuan Mainland-D'Entrecasteaux, Dobu-Duau. *Dialects:* Mwalukwasia, Somwadina, Guleguleu (Guragureu), Dawada, Siausi. Dialects are diverse. No central or dominant dialect. Lexical similarity 75% with Bunama, 52% with Mwatebu, Auhelawa, and Tubetube. *Lg Use:* Trade language. Speakers also use Dobu. Dobu used some in schools. *Lg Dev:* There are many schools, but the literacy rate is low. *Other:* Christian, traditional religion.

Duduela [duk] 469 (1981 Wurm and Hattori). Madang Province. *Class:* Trans-New Guinea, Madang-Adelbert Range, Madang, Rai Coast, Nuru. *Dialects:* Related to Kwato, Ogea, Uya, Rerau, Jilim, Yangulam.

Dumpu (Watifa, Watiwa) [wtf] 510 (2003 SIL). Madang Province, two villages: Bebei and Dumpu. *Class:* Trans-New Guinea, Madang-Adelbert Range, Madang, Rai Coast, Evapia. *Dialects:* Related to Sinsauru, Asas, Sausi, Kesawai. *Lg Use:* All men use Tok Pisin as second language.

Dumun (Bai) [dui] 35 (2000 Wurm). Madang Province. *Class:* Trans-New Guinea, Madang-Adelbert Range, Madang, Rai Coast, Yaganon. *Dialects:* Related to Yabong, Ganglau, Saep. *Other:* Nearly extinct.

Duna (Yuna) [duc] 11,000 (1991 SIL). Southern Highlands Province, Lake Kopiago and Koroba districts, some in Western Highlands Province. *Class:* Trans-New Guinea, Main Section, Central and Western, Central and South New Guinea-Kutubuan, Central and South New Guinea, Duna-Bogaya. *Lg Dev:* NT: 1976.

Duwet (Guwet, Guwot, Waing) [gve] 398 (1988 Holzknecht). Morobe Province, Busu River area. *Class:* Austronesian, Malayo-Polynesian, Central-Eastern, Eastern Malayo-Polynesian, Oceanic, Western Oceanic, North New Guinea, Huon Gulf, Markham, Lower, Busu.

Edolo (Etoro, Edolo Ado, Etolo) [etr] 1,668 (2000 census). 60% monolingual. Southern Highlands Province, Tari District, and Western Province, Nomad District; southwest of Mt. Sisa, 16 villages. *Class:* Trans-New Guinea, Main Section, Central and Western, Central and South New Guinea-Kutubuan, Central and South New Guinea, Bosavi. *Dialects:* Eastern Edolo, Western Edolo. Lexical similarity 38% with Beami. *Lg Use:* Vigorous. All domains. Spoken and some written use in religious services, Local use in commerce. All ages. Positive language attitude. 30% can also use Huli, Onobasulu, or Beami. *Lg Dev:* Literacy rate in first language: 15% to 20%. Literacy rate in second language: 25% to 50%. Bible portions: 1997. *Other:* SOV; (C)V(V). Mountain slope. Tropical forest. 365 to 1,000 meters. Swidden agriculturalists. Christian.

Eitiep [eit] 501 (2003 SIL). East Sepik Province, southwest of Kombio, and partially in Sandaun Province, across Bongos River. *Class:* Torricelli, Kombio-Arapesh, Kombio. *Dialects:* Close to Kombio.

Elepi (Samap) [ele] 327 (2003 SIL). East Sepik Province, coast around Samap. *Class:* Torricelli, Marienberg. *Lg Dev:* Literacy rate in first language: below 5%. Literacy rate in second language: 25% to 50%.

Elkei (Olkoi) [elk] 1,642 (2000 census). Sandaun Province. *Class:* Torricelli, Wapei-Palei, Wapei. *Dialects:* At least 3 dialects.

Elu [elu] 216 (1983 SIL). Manus Province, north coast of Manus Island. *Class:* Austronesian, Malayo-Polynesian, Central-Eastern, Eastern Malayo-Polynesian, Oceanic, Admiralty Islands, Eastern, Manus, East. *Lg Use:* Most speakers also use Kurti. *Other:* SVO.

Enga (Caga, Tsaga, Tchaga) [enq] 164,750 (1981 Wurm and Hattori). Population includes 12,000 in Sau (1990 UBS). Enga Province. The Maramuni are nomadic, and are in the lower reaches of the central range. *Class:* Trans-New Guinea, Main Section, Central and Western, East New Guinea Highlands, West-Central, Enga. *Dialects:* Kandepe, Layapo, Tayato, Mae (Mai, Wabag), Maramuni (Malamuni), Kaina, Kapona, Sau (Sau Enga, Wapi), Yandapo, Lapalama 1, Lapalama 2, Laiagam, Sari. Mae is the standard dialect; all understand it. Layapo is between Mae and Kyaka. *Lg Use:* Trade language. *Lg Dev:* Dictionary. NT: 1979–1988. *Other:* SOV. Mountain slope. Scrub forest. 1,200 to 2,700 meters. Swidden agriculturalists.

English [eng] 50,000 in Papua New Guinea (1987). *Lg Use:* Official language. *Lg Dev:* Taught in primary schools. See main entry under United Kingdom.

Erave (Pole, South Kewa, Kewa South) [kjy] 10,000 (2000 census). Southern Highlands Province. *Class:* Trans-New Guinea, Main Section, Central and Western, East New Guinea Highlands, West-Central, Angal-Kewa. *Lg Dev:* NT: 1993.

Ere (Nane, E) [twp] 1,030 (1980 census). Manus Province, south coast, Drabitou, Lohe, Londru, Metawari, Pau, Piterait, Taui-Undrau, Hatwara, and Loi villages. *Class:*

Austronesian, Malayo-Polynesian, Central-Eastern, Eastern Malayo-Polynesian, Oceanic, Admiralty Islands, Eastern, Manus, East. *Lg Use:* Speakers have high proficiency in Kele. *Other:* SVO.

Ese ("Managulasi," "Managalasi") [mcq] 10,000 (2000 SIL). Oro Province, Popondetta District, southeast of the Omie. *Class:* Trans-New Guinea, Main Section, Eastern, Central and Southeastern, Koiarian, Baraic. *Dialects:* Muaturaina, Chimona, Dea, Akabafa, Nami, Mesari, Averi, Afore, Minjori, Oko, Wakue, Numba, Jimuni, Karira. *Lg Use:* Vigorous. All domains. Personal letters. All ages. Positive language attitude. 50% monolingual. Others use Tok Pisin, English, or Hiri Motu as second language. The use of Hiri Motu is diminishing. The younger generation does not know it. *Lg Dev:* Literacy rate in first language: 50%. Taught in primary schools. Newspapers. Radio programs. Dictionary. NT: 1975–1999. *Other:* "Managalasi" is a pejorative Hiri Motu term used by the coastal people to refer to the Ese people. Mountain slope. Agriculturalists: taro, bananas, pineapple, coffee, vegetables, fruit. Traditional religion.

Ewage-Notu (Notu, Ewage) [nou] 12,900 (1988 SIL). Oro Province, Popondetta District, on the coast between Bakumbari and Pongani. *Class:* Trans-New Guinea, Main Section, Eastern, Binanderean, Binanderean Proper. *Dialect:* Ewage-Notu, Yega (Gona, Okeina, Okena). *Lg Dev:* Literacy rate in first language: 75% to 100%. Literacy rate in second language: 75% to 100%. NT: 1987. *Other:* Also spoken by the Soverapa people. People do not like the name 'Ewage' in the Ovo Bay, Dongani, and Ako areas. The name 'Ewage' is preferred in the Buna and Gona areas where the name 'Notu' is not liked. SOV. Coastal. Tropical forest. Sea level to 60 meters. Fishermen; swidden agriculturalists.

Faita [faj] 50 (2000 Wurm). Madang Province. *Class:* Trans-New Guinea, Madang-Adelbert Range, Adelbert Range, Brahman. *Dialects:* Related to Biyom, Isabi, Tauya.

Faiwol (Faiwolmin, Fegolmin, Angkiyakmin, Wokeimin) [fai] 4,500 (1987 SIL). Western Province, Tabubil District, at the headwaters of the Fly and Palmer rivers. Not in Papua, Indonesia. *Class:* Trans-New Guinea, Main Section, Central and Western, Central and South New Guinea-Kutubuan, Central and South New Guinea, Ok, Mountain. *Dialects:* Angkiyakmin, Faiwolmin, Wopkeimin. Many dialects. *Lg Dev:* Literacy rate in first language: 25% to 40%. Literacy rate in second language: 30% to 40%. NT: 1995. *Other:* SOV. Mountain slope. Gallery forest. 70 to 1,600 meters. Swidden agriculturalists.

Fas (Bembi) [fqs] 1,600 (1988 SIL). Sandaun Province, Amanab and Aitape districts. *Class:* Kwomtari-Baibai, Kwomtari. *Dialects:* Eastern Fas, Western Fas. Dialect differences are small. *Other:* SOV. Mountain slope, riverine. Tropical forest. 200 to 600 meters. Hunter-gatherers; agriculturalists.

Fasu (Namome) [faa] 1,200 (1981 Wurm and Hattori). Population includes 750 Fasu, 300 Namuni, 150 Some. Southern Highlands Province, Nipa District, south into Gulf Province and west to the Kikori River in Western Province. *Class:* Trans-New Guinea, Main Section, Central and Western, Central and South New Guinea-Kutubuan, Kutubuan, West. *Dialects:* Some, Kaibu (Kaipu), Namome (Namumi, Namuni). *Lg Dev:* Literacy rate in first language: 75% to 100%. Literacy rate in second language: 75% to 100%. Dictionary. Grammar. NT: 1976–1995. *Other:* Wurm and Hattori treat Some and Namuni as separate languages.

Fembe (Sinale, Agala) [agl] 350 (1986 SIL). Western Province, Upper Strickland River. *Class:* Trans-New Guinea, Main Section, Central and Western, Central and South New Guinea-Kutubuan, Central and South New

Guinea, East Strickland. *Dialects:* Closest to Kalamo and Konai. *Lg Dev:* Literacy rate in first language: below 5%. Literacy rate in second language: below 5%. *Other:* Bogaia language speakers have moved into Fembe territory, dividing the Fembe into 2 geographical areas.

Finongan (Finungwa, Finungwan) [fag] 1,300 (2002 SIL). 3% monolinguals. Morobe Province. *Class:* Trans-New Guinea, Main Section, Central and Western, Huon-Finisterre, Finisterre, Erap. *Lg Use:* All ages. *Other:* 1,000 to 1,200 meters. Christian.

Fiwaga (Fimaga, Fiwage) [fiw] 300 (1981 Wurm and Hattori). Southern Highlands Province, northeast of Tama. *Class:* Trans-New Guinea, Main Section, Central and Western, Central and South New Guinea-Kutubuan, Kutubuan, East.

Foi (Foe, Mubi River) [foi] 2,800 (1980 UBS). Southern Highlands Province, east and south of Lake Kutubu and Mubi River. *Class:* Trans-New Guinea, Main Section, Central and Western, Central and South New Guinea-Kutubuan, Kutubuan, East. *Dialects:* Ifigi, Kafa, Kutubu, Mubi. *Lg Dev:* NT: 1978.

Folopa (Podopa, Polopa, Podoba, Foraba) [ppo] 3,000 (1985 SIL). Gulf Province, Baimuru District, Kerabi Valley; also in Southern Highlands Province. 20 villages. *Class:* Trans-New Guinea, Teberan-Pawaian, Teberan. *Dialects:* Ro (Keai, Worugl), Bara (Harahui, Harahu), Sesa (Mamisa, Songu, Ibukairu), Kewah, Tebera, Aurei, Waraga, Pupitau, Boro, Suri, Siligi, Sopese, Keba-Wopasali. Closest to Dadibi. *Lg Dev:* Bible portions: 1978–1989. *Other:* Some form of whistle speech reported. SOV. Mountain slope. Tropical forest. 600 to 1,000 meters. Hunters; gatherers; agriculturalists.

Forak [frq] 283 (2003 SIL). Madang Province, Saidor District, Mamgak village, 5 miles west and inland from Seure on the coast. *Class:* Trans-New Guinea, Main Section, Central and Western, Huon-Finisterre, Finisterre, Warup. *Dialects:* Related to Asaro'o, Muratayak, Bulgebi, Degenan, Guya, Gwahatike, Yagomi. *Lg Use:* Speakers also use Muratayak or Asaro'o. *Other:* Mountain slope.

Fore [for] 17,000 (1991 SIL). Eastern Highlands Province, Okapa District. *Class:* Trans-New Guinea, Main Section, Central and Western, East New Guinea Highlands, East-Central, Fore. *Dialects:* Pamusa (South Fore), North Central Fore. *Lg Dev:* Literacy rate in first language: 25% to 50%. Literacy rate in second language: 25% to 50%. Dictionary. Grammar. NT: 1970–1974. *Other:* SOV.

Fuyug (Fuyuge, Fuyughe, Mafufu) [fuy] 14,000 (2003 SIL). Central Province, Goilala District, Owen Stanley Range. *Class:* Trans-New Guinea, Main Section, Eastern, Central and Southeastern, Goilalan. *Dialects:* Central Udab, Northeast Fuyug, North-South Udab, West Fuyug. Lexical similarity 35% with Biangai, 33% with Kunimaipa, 29% with Weri, 27% with Tauade. *Lg Dev:* Literacy rate in first language: 5%. Literacy rate in second language: 10%. Grammar. Bible portions: 1973–1994. *Other:* SOV; (C)V(C)(C); postpositions. Mountain valleys. Pandanus forest. 335 to 2,600 meters.

Gabutamon [gav] 329 (2003 SIL). Madang Province, 10 miles west southwest of Gali. *Class:* Trans-New Guinea, Main Section, Central and Western, Huon-Finisterre, Finisterre, Yupna. *Dialects:* Related to Yupna, Ma.

Gadsup [gaj] 22,061 (2000 census). Eastern Highlands Province, Kainantu District. *Class:* Trans-New Guinea, Main Section, Central and Western, East New Guinea Highlands, Eastern, Gadsup-Auyana-Awa. *Dialects:* Oyana (Oiyana), Gadsup. Related to Ontenu. *Lg Dev:* Literacy rate in first language: 25% to 50%. Literacy rate in second language: 50% to 75%. NT: 1981. *Other:* Some form of whistle speech reported. SOV. Mountain slope. Tropical forest. 1,538 meters. Swidden agriculturalists.

Gaikundi (Gaikunti) [gbf] 1,196 (2000). East Sepik Province, Ambunti District, Sepik Plains south of Maprik, east of Pagwi. *Class:* Sepik-Ramu, Sepik, Middle Sepik, Ndu. *Lg Dev:* Literacy rate in first language: below 5%. Literacy rate in second language: 25% to 50%. Bible portions: 1978.

Gaina [gcn] 1,406 (1971 Dutton). Population includes 1,000 in Bareji, 130 in Gaina. Oro Province, next to the Baruga, the villages around Iwuji. *Class:* Trans-New Guinea, Main Section, Eastern, Binanderean, Binanderean Proper. *Dialects:* Bareji (Baredji), Gaina. Lexical similarity 61% with Dogoro (closest). *Other:* Sago swamp.

Gal (Baimak, Weim) [gap] 335 (2003 SIL). Madang Province, on the Gogol River. *Class:* Trans-New Guinea, Madang-Adelbert Range, Madang, Mabuso, Hanseman.

Galeya (Garea) [gar] 3,414 (2000). 30% monolingual. Milne Bay Province, northeast coast, Fergusson Island. *Class:* Austronesian, Malayo-Polynesian, Central-Eastern, Eastern Malayo-Polynesian, Oceanic, Western Oceanic, Papuan Tip, Nuclear, North Papuan Mainland-D'Entrecasteaux, Dobu-Duau. *Dialect:* Wadalei, Gameta, Urua, Basima, Sebutuia, Garea (Galeya). Lexical similarity 61% with Boselewa (closest). Galeya and Basima dialects have 80% lexical similarity. *Lg Use:* Speakers also use Dobu. *Other:* Less than half of children are in school. Coastal. Christian, traditional religion.

Ganglau [ggl] 468 (2003 SIL). Madang Province. *Class:* Trans-New Guinea, Madang-Adelbert Range, Madang, Rai Coast, Yaganon. *Dialects:* Related languages: Yabong, Dumun, Saep.

Gants (Gaj) [gao] 1,884 (1981 Wurm and Hattori). Madang Province. *Class:* Trans-New Guinea, Main Section, Central and Western, East New Guinea Highlands, Kalam, Gants.

Gapapaiwa (Manape, Gapa, Paiwa) [pwg] 2,383 (2003 SIL). Milne Bay Province, Makamaka District, south coast of Cape Vogel and inland along the Ruaba River. *Class:* Austronesian, Malayo-Polynesian, Central-Eastern, Eastern Malayo-Polynesian, Oceanic, Western Oceanic, Papuan Tip, Nuclear, North Papuan Mainland-D'Entrecasteaux, Are-Taupota, Are. *Dialects:* Lexical similarity 73% with Ghayavi (Boanaki, closest). *Lg Use:* English used in religious services. Only older adults can speak Wedau. Tok Pisin is seldom heard, and men are more fluent than women. *Lg Dev:* Literacy rate in first language: 80%. Literacy rate in second language: 80%. Vernacular primary schools. Dictionary. Grammar. Bible portions: 1997. *Other:* A number of well-educated people. SOV; CV; nontonal. Coastal. Tropical and gallery forest. Sea level to 50 meters. Swidden agriculturalists; coconut palm; fishermen.

Garus (Ate, Em, Kurupi) [gyb] 2,652 (2003 SIL). Madang Province, Astrolabe Bay. *Class:* Trans-New Guinea, Madang-Adelbert Range, Madang, Mabuso, Hanseman. *Dialects:* Related to Bagupi, Matepi, Mosimo, Murupi, Rapting, Samosa, Silopi. *Lg Use:* Speakers are becoming more bilingual. *Lg Dev:* Literacy rate in first language: below 5%. Literacy rate in second language: 25% to 50%.

Gedaged (Bel, Graged, Star, Star-Ragetta, Tiara, Mitebog, Ragetta, Rio, Sek, Szeak-Bagili) [gdd] 6,954 (2003 SIL). Madang Province; Sek, Yabob, Karkar, and Bagabag islands, Astrolabe Bay, and coastal villages around Madang. *Class:* Austronesian, Malayo-Polynesian, Central-Eastern, Eastern Malayo-Polynesian, Oceanic, Western Oceanic, North New Guinea, Ngero-Vitiaz, Vitiaz, Bel, Nuclear Bel, Northern. *Lg Dev:* Literacy rate in first language: 25% to 50%. Literacy rate in second language: 50% to 100%. NT: 1960.

Gende (Bundi, Gene, Gendeka) [gaf] 8,000 (1987 SIL). Madang Province, Bundi District near Bundi. *Class:*

Trans-New Guinea, Main Section, Central and Western, East New Guinea Highlands, East-Central, Gende. *Lg Use:* Vigorous. Speakers also use Tok Pisin. *Other:* Mountain slope. 1,200 to 2,000 meters. Traditional religion.

Ghayavi (Galavi, Boianaki, Boanaki, Boinaki, Boanai) [bmk] 2,807 (2000). Milne Bay Province, Alotau District, Weraura Local Government Area, north coast along Goodenough Bay from Uga in the west to Wadobuna in the east, including Rabaraba. *Class:* Austronesian, Malayo-Polynesian, Central-Eastern, Eastern Malayo-Polynesian, Oceanic, Western Oceanic, Papuan Tip, Nuclear, North Papuan Mainland-D'Entrecasteaux, Are-Taupota, Are. *Dialects:* Lexical similarity 76% with Gapapaiwa (closest), 46% with Wedau. *Lg Use:* Wedau, Gapapaiwa, and English are the second languages. Wedau people were traditional rivals, and there are reservations toward the use of Wedau. *Lg Dev:* Most speakers are literate. There are adequate schools in the area, but Ghayavi does not seem to be used for instruction. *Other:* The alternate names given are in reports written by outsiders.

Gimi [gim] 22,463 (1981 Wurm and Hattori). Eastern Highlands Province, Okapa District. *Class:* Trans-New Guinea, Main Section, Central and Western, East New Guinea Highlands, East-Central, Fore. *Dialect:* East Gimi, West Gimi (Gouno). *Lg Dev:* Literacy rate in first language: 5% to 15%. Literacy rate in second language: 5% to 15%. NT: 1994. *Other:* Traditional religion, Christian.

Gimi (Loko) [gip] 3,697 (1982 SIL). West New Britain Province, southwest coast and inland, Johanna River to Anu River. *Class:* Austronesian, Malayo-Polynesian, Central-Eastern, Eastern Malayo-Polynesian, Oceanic, Western Oceanic, North New Guinea, Ngero-Vitiaz, Vitiaz, Southwest New Britain, Arawe-Pasismanua, Arawe, West Arawe. *Dialects:* Dialect continuum with Aiklep and Apalik. *Lg Dev:* Literacy rate in first language: 25% to 50%. Literacy rate in second language: 25% to 50%. NT: 2000. *Other:* Different from Gimi in Eastern Highlands Province.

Ginuman (Dime) [gnm] 1,442 (2000). Milne Bay Province, Mt. Simpson to coast at Naraka. *Class:* Trans-New Guinea, Main Section, Eastern, Central and Southeastern, Dagan. *Dialects:* Lexical similarity 42% with Kanasi (Dombosaina village).

Girawa (Begasin, Begesin, Bagasin) [bbr] 4,000 (1981 Wurm and Hattori). Madang Province, Ramu District. *Class:* Trans-New Guinea, Madang-Adelbert Range, Madang, Mabuso, Kokon. *Dialects:* Related to Munit, Kein. *Lg Dev:* Literacy rate in first language: 25% to 50%. Literacy rate in second language: 25% to 50%. NT: 1994. *Other:* SOV. Mountain slope. Tropical forest. 300 to 1,000 meters. Swidden agriculturalists.

Gitua (Gitoa, Kelana) [ggt] 759 (2000). Morobe Province, north coast of Huon Peninsula. *Class:* Austronesian, Malayo-Polynesian, Central-Eastern, Eastern Malayo-Polynesian, Oceanic, Western Oceanic, North New Guinea, Ngero-Vitiaz, Ngero, Tuam. *Lg Use:* 70% of the ethnic group speaks Gitua. Most or some key domains. 30% of children. Positive language attitude.

Gizrra (Gizra) [tof] 1,050 (2002 SIL). Western Province, South Fly Area, north-northeast of the Torres Strait island of Saibai, villages of Kulalae, Ngomtono, Barnap, Kupere, and Waidoro. *Class:* Trans-New Guinea, Trans-Fly-Bulaka River, Trans-Fly, Eastern Trans-Fly. *Dialects:* Western Gizra, Waidoro. *Lg Dev:* Literacy rate in first language: 15% (including semiliterates). Literacy rate in second language: 80% (including semiliterates). *Other:* SOV. Coastal, interfluvial. Savannah, wooded freshwater

swamp, mangroves. 3 to 12 meters. Swidden agriculturalists. Christian, traditional religion.

Gnau [gnu] 1,325 (2000 census). Sandaun Province, Namblo Census Division, northwest of Maimai. *Class:* Torricelli, Wapei-Palei, Wapei.

Gobasi (Nomad) [goi] 1,100 (1993 ECP). Western Province. *Class:* Trans-New Guinea, Main Section, Central and Western, Central and South New Guinea-Kutubuan, Central and South New Guinea, East Strickland. *Dialects:* Gobasi (Bibo), Honibo, Oibae (Oiba). Related to Samo and Kubo. *Lg Dev:* Literacy rate in first language: 5% to 10%. Literacy rate in second language: 10% to 15%. Two vernacular primary schools.

Gogodala (Gogodara) [ggw] 10,000 (1991 UBS). Western Province, north bank of Fly River, Aramia River. 301 villages. *Class:* Trans-New Guinea, Main Section, Central and Western, Gogodala-Suki, Gogodala. *Dialects:* Closest to Ari. *Lg Dev:* Literacy rate in first language: 15% to 25%. Literacy rate in second language: 25% to 50%. NT: 1981.

Golin (Gollum, Gumine) [gvf] 51,105 (1981 Wurm and Hattori). Simbu Province, Gumine District. *Class:* Trans-New Guinea, Main Section, Central and Western, East New Guinea Highlands, Central, Chimbu. *Dialects:* Yuri, Kia (Kiari), Golin, Keri, Marigl. Close to Dom. *Lg Use:* Nondiri is not a language, but a village where the Mian bush people live. They speak Golin. *Lg Dev:* Literacy rate in first language: 25% to 50%. Literacy rate in second language: 25% to 50%. Grammar. NT: 1980.

Gorakor [goc] 2,741 (1979 census). Morobe Province, Mumeng District, including Yanta. *Class:* Austronesian, Malayo-Polynesian, Central-Eastern, Eastern Malayo-Polynesian, Oceanic, Western Oceanic, North New Guinea, Huon Gulf, South, Hote-Buang, Buang, Mumeng. *Dialect:* Yanta. In the Mumeng language chain. Some intelligibility of Patep. *Lg Dev:* Literacy rate in first language: 15% to 25%. Literacy rate in second language: 25% to 50%. *Other:* SVO. Mountain slope. Tropical forest. 300 to 900 meters. Swidden agriculturalists.

Gorovu (Gorova, Yerani) [grq] 15 (2000 Wurm). East Sepik Province, Bangapela village, Ramu River. *Class:* Sepik-Ramu, Ramu, Ramu Proper, Grass, Grass Proper. *Lg Use:* Used in the home. No children speak Gorovu. Banaro is replacing Gorovu. *Other:* Nearly extinct.

Guhu-Samane (Paiawa, Tahari, Muri, Bia, Mid-Waria) [ghs] 12,761 (2000 census). Morobe Province, Lae District, and a few in Oro Province, from Kanoma and Sidema villages northward. *Class:* Trans-New Guinea, Main Section, Eastern, Binanderean, Guhu-Samane. *Dialect:* Sekare. Lexical similarity 18% with Suena and Zia (closest). *Lg Dev:* Literacy rate in first language: 50% to 75%. Literacy rate in second language: 50% to 75%. NT: 1975–1983.

Gumalu [gmu] 580 (2003 SIL). Madang Province. *Class:* Trans-New Guinea, Madang-Adelbert Range, Madang, Mabuso, Gum. *Dialects:* Related to Sihan, Amele, Isebe, Bau, Panim.

Gumawana (Gumasi, Domdom) [gvs] 469 (2000 census). 50% monolingual. Milne Bay Province, Esa'ala District, Amphlett Islands; a group of about 25 islands north of Fergusson. 7 villages. *Class:* Austronesian, Malayo-Polynesian, Central-Eastern, Eastern Malayo-Polynesian, Oceanic, Western Oceanic, Papuan Tip, Nuclear, North Papuan Mainland-D'Entrecasteaux, Gumawana. *Dialects:* Lexical similarity 48% with Galeya, 47% with Dobu (closest). *Lg Use:* Vigorous. All domains. Used in local administration, commerce, education, spoken use in religious services, personal letters. It is the primary language of children. Positive language attitude. Speakers also use Dobu, Kilivila, Boselewa, Maiodom, or Galeya. *Lg Dev:* Literacy rate in first language: 95%. Literacy rate in second language: 75% to 100%. Grammar. Bible portions: 1992–1999. *Other:* People do not mix with others. Islands, mountain slope. Potters. Christian.

Guntai [gnt] 346 (2003 SIL). Western Province, Morehead District. *Class:* Trans-New Guinea, Trans-Fly-Bulaka River, Trans-Fly, Morehead and Upper Maro rivers, Tonda. *Dialect:* Kan.

Guramalum [grz] 3 or 4 (1987 SIL). New Ireland Province. *Class:* Austronesian, Malayo-Polynesian, Central-Eastern, Eastern Malayo-Polynesian, Oceanic, Western Oceanic, Meso Melanesian, New Ireland, South New Ireland-Northwest Solomonic, Patpatar-Tolai. *Other:* Nearly extinct.

Guriaso [grx] 162 (2003 SIL). Sandaun Province, Amanab District. *Class:* Kwomtari-Baibai, Kwomtari. *Other:* Distinct language from Kwomtari.

Gusan [gsn] 794 (1980 census). Morobe Province. *Class:* Trans-New Guinea, Main Section, Central and Western, Huon-Finisterre, Finisterre, Erap.

Guya (Guiarak, Guyarak) [gka] 131 (1981 Wurm and Hattori). Madang Province, 10 to 15 miles west of Seure. *Class:* Trans-New Guinea, Main Section, Central and Western, Huon-Finisterre, Finisterre, Warup. *Dialects:* Related to Asaro'o, Muratayak, Bulgebi, Degenan, Forak, Gwahatike, Yagomi. *Other:* Guiarak is a village name.

Gwahatike (Gwatike, Dahating) [dah] 1,571 (2003 SIL). Madang Province, Saidor District, several villages south of Saidor. *Class:* Trans-New Guinea, Main Section, Central and Western, Huon-Finisterre, Finisterre, Warup. *Dialects:* Gwahatike, Gwahamere, Gora, Gwapti. Related to Asaro'o, Muratayak, Bulgebi, Degenan, Forak, Guya, Yagomi. *Lg Use:* All speakers also use Tok Pisin. *Lg Dev:* Literacy rate in first language: 30%. Literacy rate in second language: 70%. NT: 1999. *Other:* SOV. Foothills. 550 meters. Swidden agriculturalists. Christian, traditional religion, cargo cult.

Gweda (Garuwahi) [grw] 26 (2001 SIL). Milne Bay Province, Alotau District, Maramatana Local Council Area, Garuwahi village. *Class:* Austronesian, Malayo-Polynesian, Central-Eastern, Eastern Malayo-Polynesian, Oceanic, Western Oceanic, Papuan Tip, Nuclear, North Papuan Mainland-D'Entrecasteaux, Are-Taupota, Taupota. *Dialects:* Closest to Haigwai. Lexical similarity 71% with Wa'ema, 69% with Taupota, 68% with Naura, 67% with Kapulika, 64% with Topura, 63% with Tawala, 53% with Wedau. *Lg Use:* Only 2 older adults, and their children and grandchildren who use Gweda with them. Speakers also use Wedau, Taupota, Motu, or English. *Other:* Nearly extinct.

Hahon (Hanon) [hah] 1,300 (1977 Lincoln). Northwest Bougainville Province. *Class:* Austronesian, Malayo-Polynesian, Central-Eastern, Eastern Malayo-Polynesian, Oceanic, Western Oceanic, Meso Melanesian, New Ireland, South New Ireland-Northwest Solomonic, Nehan-North Bougainville, Saposa-Tinputz. *Dialects:* Kurur, Ratsua, Aravia. *Other:* Moderate acculturation.

Haigwai (Naura, Kapulika, Garaghwaghi) [hgw] 1,060 (2000 census). 15% monolingual. Milne Bay Province, Alotau District, Huhu Local Government Area, inland from the head of Milne Bay between Hagita and Waigani estates and the mountains to the west. *Class:* Austronesian, Malayo-Polynesian, Central-Eastern, Eastern Malayo-Polynesian, Oceanic, Western Oceanic, Papuan Tip, Nuclear, North Papuan Mainland-D'Entrecasteaux, Are-Taupota, Taupota. *Dialects:* Naura, Kapulika. Naura and Gweda agree that Gweda is the closest to Haigwai. Naura has 68% lexical similarity with Gweda, Kapulika has 65% with Taupota, both dialects have 52% with Wedau, 48% with Maiwala. *Lg Use:* Positive language attitude. Some speakers know some Suau, Tawala, Wedau,

English, or Motu. *Lg Dev:* One vernacular elementary school.

Hakö (Haku) [hao] 5,000 (1982 SIL). Bougainville Province, North Bougainville District, northeastern Buka Island. *Class:* Austronesian, Malayo-Polynesian, Central-Eastern, Eastern Malayo-Polynesian, Oceanic, Western Oceanic, Meso Melanesian, New Ireland, South New Ireland-Northwest Solomonic, Nehan-North Bougainville, Buka, Halia. *Dialect:* Lontes. *Lg Dev:* Literacy rate in first language: 75% to 100%. Literacy rate in second language: 75% to 100%. *Other:* SVO. Coastal, coral escarpment. Tropical forest, deciduous forest. Sea level to 70 meters. Fishermen; intensive agriculturalists; cocoa and copra production.

Halia (Tasi) [hla] 20,000 (1994 SIL). Bougainville Province, North Bougainville District, northeastern Buka Island. *Class:* Austronesian, Malayo-Polynesian, Central-Eastern, Eastern Malayo-Polynesian, Oceanic, Western Oceanic, Meso Melanesian, New Ireland, South New Ireland-Northwest Solomonic, Nehan-North Bougainville, Buka, Halia. *Dialects:* Hanahan, Hangan, Touloun (Tulon, Tulun), Selau. *Lg Dev:* Literacy rate in first language: 75% to 100%. Literacy rate in second language: 75% to 100%. Dictionary. Grammar. NT: 1978. *Other:* Distinct from Tulun in Manus Province (see Tulu-Bohuai). SVO. Coastal, coral escarpment. Tropical forest, deciduous forest. Sea level to 70 meters. Fishermen; intensive agriculturalists; cocoa and copra production.

Hamtai (Hamday, Kapau, Kamea, Watut, "Kukukuku") [hmt] 45,000 (1998 Tom Palmer). Gulf Province, Kukipi District, along the Tauri River inland east to the Ladedamu River; Morobe Province, Lae District, Kodama Range into Bulolo-Watut divide, across to Mt. Grosse and north to Mt. Taylor. *Class:* Trans-New Guinea, Main Section, Central and Western, Angan, Angan Proper. *Dialects:* Wenta, Howi, Pmasa'a, Hamtai, Kaintiba. *Lg Dev:* Grammar. NT: 1974. *Other:* The people dislike the name "Kukukuku." The name 'Kamea' is used in Gulf Province. 500 to 2,000 meters.

Hanga Hundi (Kwasengen, West Wosera) [wos] 6,008 (1983 SIL). East Sepik Province, Pagwi District. 16 villages. *Class:* Sepik-Ramu, Sepik, Middle Sepik, Ndu. *Dialects:* Close to Ambulas. *Lg Dev:* Literacy rate in first language: 5% to 15%. Literacy rate in second language: 5% to 15%. *Other:* 3 community schools. Hills. Savannah, swamp. 50 to 100 meters.

Haruai (Harway, Waibuk, Wiyaw, Wiyau, Wovan, Taman) [tmd] 1,000 (1988 B. Comrie). Many are monolingual. Madang Province, southwest corner, southwest Mid-Ramu (Simbai) District, western Schrader Range, west of the Kobon. *Class:* Trans-New Guinea, Main Section, East New Guinea Highlands, Piawi. *Dialects:* North Waibuk (Hamil), Central Waibuk (Mambar), South Waibuk (Arama). Related to Pinai-Hagahai, though not inherently intelligible with Haruai. Word taboo is practiced, but does not seem to impede intelligibility among related language varieties. Lexical similarity 37% with Aramo, 35% with Kobon. *Lg Use:* Speeches and sermons by outsiders are always translated into Haruai. All ages. Young men are likely to know Tok Pisin or Kobon, many children speak good Tok Pisin, and many women are at least communicatively competent in Tok Pisin (Comrie). *Other:* 'Haruai' is self name. Some similarities to Kalam languages due to borrowing (Comrie). More loanwords from Kobon are used in the northern area. SOV; postpositions (few); genitives precede noun heads; possessives, adjectives, numerals, relative clauses follow noun heads; postclitic demonstratives; suffixes; V, CV, VC, CVC. Mountain slope. Tropical forest. 600 to 2,000 meters. Swidden agriculturalists.

Hermit (Agomes, Luf, Maron) [llf] Extinct. Western Manus Province, Luf and Maron islands in Hermit Islands. *Class:* Austronesian, Malayo-Polynesian, Central-Eastern, Eastern Malayo-Polynesian, Oceanic, Admiralty Islands, Eastern, Manus, West.

Hewa (Sisimin) [ham] 2,147 (1986 P. Vollrath SIL). Population includes 290 in Yoliapi (1982 SIL). Southern Highlands Province, Koroba District; Enga Province, Lagaip District; Sandaun Province, Telefomin District. Lagaip River area, in the mountains north of Duna and Ipili language area, from 8 miles south of the Lagaip River and northward up to the high peaks of the Central Range, which is the political and physical boundary between the Sepik region and the highlands, a land area basically 50 miles from east to west and 20 miles maximum north to south, or 1,000 sq. miles of area. *Class:* Sepik-Ramu, Sepik, Sepik Hill, Sanio. *Dialects:* Upper Lagaip, Central Lagaip, Lower Lagaip, North Hewa. *Lg Use:* Vigorous. All domains. Oral and written use in religion. All ages. Speakers view use of Hewa as normal. Bilingual level estimates for Tok Pisin: 0 85%, 1 8%, 2 5%, 3 2%, 4 0%, 5 0%; English: 0 99%, 1 1%, 2–5 0%; Ipili: 0 98%, 1–5 2%; Duna: 0 96%, 1 2%, 2 1%, 3 1%, 4 0%, 5 0%; Oksapmin: 0 99%, 1–5 1%. 1,600 or more are monolingual. 550 can use Tok Pisin, Ipili, Duna, Oksapmin, or English. *Lg Dev:* Literacy rate in first language: below 2%. Literacy rate in second language: 5% to 15%. 25 or fewer can read it, 10 or fewer can write it. Bible portions: 1985. *Other:* Seminomadic. SOV. Mountain slope. Tropical forest. 480 to 1,700 meters. Swidden agriculturalists; hunter-gatherers traditionally. Traditional religion, Christian.

Heyo (Arinua, Arinwa, Arima, Lolopani, Wan Wan, Wanib, Ruruhip) [auk] 2,708 (2000 census). 10% monolinguals. Sandaun Province, Nuku District. *Class:* Torricelli, Maimai, Maimai Proper. *Dialects:* Lexical similarity 60% with Yahang. *Lg Use:* Older men use Tok Pisin with difficulty; older women are monolingual. Two primary schools where English is used. Tok Pisin use more in the north than in the south. *Other:* The people call themselves 'Wanib'. Yahang is also called 'Ruruhip'. SVO. Hills, plains. Tropical forest, sago swamp. 50 to 150 meters. Swidden agriculturalists. Traditional religion, Christian.

Hote (Ho'tei, Hotec, Malei) [hot] 2,237 (2000 census). Population includes 1,909 Hote and 328 Misim. Morobe Province, Lae District, Francisco River area. *Class:* Austronesian, Malayo-Polynesian, Central-Eastern, Eastern Malayo-Polynesian, Oceanic, Western Oceanic, North New Guinea, Huon Gulf, South, Hote-Buang, Hote. *Dialect:* Hote, Misim (Musim, Ombalei). Lexical similarity 90% between Hote and Misim, 70% with Yamap. *Lg Use:* Speakers consider them all to be one language. *Lg Dev:* Literacy rate in first language: 30% to 50%. Literacy rate in second language: 40% to 65%. Bible portions: 1988.

Hula (Vulaa) [hul] 3,000 (1987 SIL). Central Province, Hood Peninsula. *Class:* Austronesian, Malayo-Polynesian, Central-Eastern, Eastern Malayo-Polynesian, Oceanic, Western Oceanic, Papuan Tip, Peripheral, Central Papuan, Sinagoro-Keapara. *Lg Dev:* NT: 1954.

Huli (Huli-Hulidana, Huri) [hui] 70,000 (1991 UBS). Southern Highlands Province around Tari, and southern fringe of Enga Province. *Class:* Trans-New Guinea, Main Section, Central and Western, East New Guinea Highlands, West-Central, Huli. *Lg Dev:* Literacy rate in first language: 50% to 75%. Literacy rate in second language: 50% to 75%. Grammar. Bible: 2003.

Humene [huf] 935 (2000). Central Province, lower edge of Sogeri Plateau and adjacent plain between Gaire and Kapakapa villages. Manugoro is principal village. *Class:* Trans-New Guinea, Main Section, Eastern, Central and Southeastern, Kwalean. *Dialects:* Lagume (Lakume, Manukolu), Humene. Lexical similarity 65% to 74% with Kwale (closest). *Lg Use:* Some speakers know Hiri Motu and Motu, some English.

Iamalele (Yamalele) [yml] 2,800 (1987 SIL). 40% monolingual. Milne Bay Province, Bwaidoka District, west Fergusson Island. *Class:* Austronesian, Malayo-Polynesian, Central-Eastern, Eastern Malayo-Polynesian, Oceanic, Western Oceanic, Papuan Tip, Nuclear, North Papuan Mainland-D'Entrecasteaux, Bwaidoga. *Dialects:* Didigavu, Gwabegwabe, Masimasi, Central Yamalele, Southern Yamalele. Lexical similarity 64% with Kalokalo (closest). *Lg Use:* Some speakers also use Bwaidoka and Dobu. *Lg Dev:* Literacy rate in first language: 50% to 75%. Literacy rate in second language: 50% to 75%. Dictionary. NT: 1984–1999. *Other:* SOV. Coastal, mountain slope. Tropical forest. Sea level to 1,500 meters. Swidden agriculturalists.

Iatmul (Big Sepik, Ngepma Kwundi, Gepma Kwudi, Gepma Kwundi) [ian] 8,442 (2003 SIL). East Sepik Province, Ambunti and Angoram districts, Sepik River villages from Tambunum to Japandai, Kundungay area. *Class:* Sepik-Ramu, Sepik, Middle Sepik, Ndu. *Dialects:* Nyaura, Palimbei. *Lg Dev:* Literacy rate in first language: 5% to 15%. Literacy rate in second language: 25% to 50%. NT: 1975. *Other:* Riverine. Fishermen; sago gatherers.

Idi (Tame, Dimsisi, Dimisi, Diblaeg) [idi] 1,608 (2000 census). Population includes 774 Idi, 834 Tame. Western Province, northwest of Agob, east of Nambo language. *Class:* Trans-New Guinea, Trans-Fly-Bulaka River, Trans-Fly, Pahoturi. *Dialects:* Tame, Idi. One end of a dialect cluster stretching to Agob. Distinct from but close to Agob. *Lg Dev:* Literacy rate in first language: below 5%. Literacy rate in second language: 50%. *Other:* Primary schools. Lowland. Savannah, tropical forest, palm swamp. Sea level to 5 meters. Hunters; swidden agriculturalists.

Iduna (Vivigana, Vivigani) [viv] 6,000 (1984 SIL). Milne Bay Province, north coast, Goodenough Island, Esa'ala District. *Class:* Austronesian, Malayo-Polynesian, Central-Eastern, Eastern Malayo-Polynesian, Oceanic, Western Oceanic, Papuan Tip, Nuclear, North Papuan Mainland-D'Entrecasteaux, Bwaidoga. *Dialects:* Waibula, Ufaufa, Idakamenai, Belebele, Kalauna, Goiala, Ufufu, Central Vivigani. Lexical similarity 72% with Bwaidoka (closest). *Lg Dev:* Literacy rate in first language: 75% to 100%. Literacy rate in second language: 75% to 100%. Grammar. NT: 1983–2003. *Other:* Three-quarters of the children are in school.

Igana [igg] 200 (2003 SIL). Madang Province, west of Josephstaal. *Class:* Sepik-Ramu, Ramu, Ramu Proper, Goam, Tamolan. *Dialects:* Related to Romkun, Breri, Kominimung, Akrukay, Itutang, Inapang.

Ikobi-Mena (Kopo-Monia, Kasere, Wailemi, Meni, Ikobi Kairi) [meb] 650 (1977 SIL). Population includes 350 Ikobi, 300 Mena (1981 Wurm and Hattori). Gulf Province, south of Kibirowi Island, around upper Omati River and around Middle Turama River. *Class:* Trans-New Guinea, Turama-Kikorian, Turama-Omatian. *Dialects:* Meni, Mena, Pimuru, Gorau, Utabi. Closest language is Omati (Mini). Wurm and Hattori treat Ikobi and Mena as separate languages. *Lg Dev:* Literacy rate in first language: below 5%. Literacy rate in second language: below 5%.

Imbongu (Imbo Ungu, Ibo Ugu, Imbonggo, Awa, Aua, Au, Imbo Ungo) [imo] 42,500 (2000 census). 15% monolingual. Southern Highlands Province, Ialibu District. *Class:* Trans-New Guinea, Main Section, Central and Western, East New Guinea Highlands, Central, Hagen, Kaugel. *Dialect:* Awa (Aua, Au). *Lg Use:* Vigorous.

Speakers of other languages also speak it. All domains. Used in local administration, commerce, oral and written use in religion, beginning in education, personal letters. All ages. Positive language attitude. Speakers also use Tok Pisin, Kewa, Wiru, or English. *Lg Dev:* Literacy rate in first language: 25% to 50%. Literacy rate in second language: 15% to 25%. NT: 1997. *Other:* Mountain slope. 1,700 to 2,200 meters. Agriculturalists. Christian.

Imonda [imn] 250 (1994 SIL). Sandaun Province, Amanab District, near Imonda airstrip. *Class:* Trans-New Guinea, Northern, Border, Waris. *Lg Dev:* Grammar. *Other:* A separate language from Waris.

Inapang (Midsivindi) [mzu] 1,611 (1990 census). Madang Province, Josephstaal Subdistrict. *Class:* Sepik-Ramu, Ramu, Ramu Proper, Goam, Tamolan.

Inoke-Yate (Inoke, Yate) [ino] 10,000 (1993 SIL). Eastern Highlands Province, Okapa District. *Class:* Trans-New Guinea, Main Section, Central and Western, East New Guinea Highlands, East-Central, Kamano-Yagaria. *Lg Dev:* Literacy rate in first language: 50% to 75%. Literacy rate in second language: 50% to 75%. NT: 1992.

Ipiko (Ipikoi, Higa, Epai) [ipo] 200 (1977 SIL). Gulf Province, 5 miles up Pie River beyond Baimuri, villages of Ipiko and Pahemuba. *Class:* Trans-New Guinea, Inland Gulf, Ipiko. *Dialects:* Slightly related to Minanibai and Mubami. *Lg Use:* Vigorous. *Lg Dev:* Literacy rate in first language: below 5%. Literacy rate in second language: below 5%. *Other:* Seminomadic. Lowland. Tropical forest, swamp. Below 300 meters.

Ipili (Ipili-Paiela, Ipili-Payala) [ipi] 26,000 (2002 SIL). 50% monolinguals. Enga Province around Porgera patrol post. *Class:* Trans-New Guinea, Main Section, Central and Western, East New Guinea Highlands, West-Central, Enga. *Dialects:* Porgera, Paiela, Tipinini. The Paiela and Pogera dialects have minor lexical differences. The Tipinini dialect is more like Enga. *Lg Use:* Vigorous. Used in the home. Positive language attitude. *Lg Dev:* Low motivation for literacy. Roman script. Bible portions: 1978. *Other:* SOV. Mountain slope. Tropical forest. 1,500 to 2,200 meters. Swidden agriculturalists. Christian, traditional religion.

Isabi (Maruhia) [isa] 280 (1981 Wurm and Hattori). Madang Province. *Class:* Trans-New Guinea, Madang-Adelbert Range, Adelbert Range, Brahman. *Dialects:* Related languages: Biyom, Tauya, Faita.

Isebe (Balahaim) [igo] 913 (1981 Wurm and Hattori). Madang Province, northern bank of Gum River, west of Madang Town. *Class:* Trans-New Guinea, Madang-Adelbert Range, Madang, Mabuso, Gum. *Dialects:* Isebe, Urukun, Mirkuk. Related to Sihan, Gumalu, Amele, Bau, Panim. *Other:* Mountain slope. 60 to 250 meters. Swidden agriculturalists. Christian, traditional religion, cargo cult.

Iteri (Alowiemino, Laro, Iyo, Yinibu, Rocky Peak) [itr] 475 (2003 SIL). Sandaun Province, Rocky Peak Mountains. *Class:* Left May. *Lg Use:* Some speakers also use Ama. *Lg Dev:* NT: 2000. *Other:* Area seldom entered by outsiders. The Iteri are called the 'Rocky Peak' people.

Itutang [itu] 220 (1981 Wurm and Hattori). East Sepik Province. *Class:* Sepik-Ramu, Ramu, Ramu Proper, Goam, Tamolan. *Dialects:* Related to Romkun, Breri, Kominimung, Akrukay, Igana, Inapang.

Iwal (Kaiwa) [kbm] 1,500 (1987 SIL). Morobe Province, Lae District, between Wau and Salamaua. *Class:* Austronesian, Malayo-Polynesian, Central-Eastern, Eastern Malayo-Polynesian, Oceanic, Western Oceanic, North New Guinea, Huon Gulf, South, Kaiwa. *Dialects:* Close to Yabem. *Lg Dev:* Literacy rate in first language: 15% to 25%. Literacy rate in second language: 25% to 50%. NT: 1984.

Iwam (May River) [iwm] 3,000 (1998 NTM). East Sepik Province, Ambunti District, Mowi and Iyomempwi

villages on the Sepik River and villages on the May River and surrounding lakes and tributaries as far as Premai village. *Class:* Sepik-Ramu, Sepik, Upper Sepik, Iwam. *Dialects:* Close to Amal and Sepik Iwam. *Lg Dev:* Literacy rate in first language: 5% to 15%. Literacy rate in second language: 5% to 15%. Bible portions: 1990–1998. *Other:* Traditional religion.

Iwam, Sepik (Yawenian) [iws] 2,500 (1987 SIL). East Sepik Province, Ambunti District. Villages along the Sepik River, and on lagoons north and south of the river, from Iniok village downstream to the Leonard Schultze River. *Class:* Sepik-Ramu, Sepik, Upper Sepik, Iwam. *Lg Dev:* Literacy rate in first language: 25% to 50%. Literacy rate in second language: 25% to 50%. NT: 1989. *Other:* Riverine. Sago gatherers; fishermen.

Iyo (Naho, Nabu, Nahu, Ndo, Bure) [nca] 6,900 (2003 SIL). Madang Province, on the southern slopes of the Finisterre Mountains along the Nahu (Gusap) and Bure rivers, on the northern slopes along the Kipuro (Yangdala) and Kasang (Mot) rivers. *Class:* Trans-New Guinea, Main Section, Central and Western, Huon-Finisterre, Finisterre, Gusap-Mot. *Dialects:* Lexical similarity 54% with Rawa. *Lg Use:* Used in the home, church, community. *Lg Dev:* Literacy rate in first language: below 5%. Literacy rate in second language: 25% to 50%. Vernacular preschools in operation. Grammar. Bible portions: 1998–2000.

Jilim [jil] 647 (2000 census). Madang Province. *Class:* Trans-New Guinea, Madang-Adelbert Range, Madang, Rai Coast, Nuru. *Dialects:* Related to Kwato, Ogea, Usu, Duduela, Rerau, Yangulam.

Juwal (Mambe, Muniwara, Tumara, Tumaru) [mwb] 1,444 (2000 census). East Sepik Province, about 20 miles south southeast of Wewak. *Class:* Torricelli, Marienberg.

Kaian (Kayan) [kct] 322 (1981 Wurm and Hattori). Madang Province. *Class:* Sepik-Ramu, Ramu, Ramu Proper, Ruboni, Ottilien.

Kaiep (Samap) [kbw] 300 (1993 SIL). East Sepik Province, coast around Taul at Kep. *Class:* Austronesian, Malayo-Polynesian, Central-Eastern, Eastern Malayo-Polynesian, Oceanic, Western Oceanic, North New Guinea, Schouten, Kairiru-Manam, Kairiru. *Lg Use:* 70% of the ethnic group speaks Kaiep. Speakers also use Manam. *Lg Dev:* Literacy rate in second language: 50% to 75%.

Kairak [ckr] 750 (1988 SIL). East New Britain Province, Gazelle Peninsula. *Class:* East Papuan, Yele-Solomons-New Britain, New Britain, Baining-Taulil. *Lg Use:* Speakers also use Uramat. *Other:* There is a primary school. Mountain slope, foothills.

Kairiru [kxa] 3,507 (1981 R. Wivell). East Sepik Province, Wewak District, Kairiru, Yuo, Karesau Islands, several coastal villages on the mainland between Cape Karawop and Cape Samein, and northern and western Mushu Island. *Class:* Austronesian, Malayo-Polynesian, Central-Eastern, Eastern Malayo-Polynesian, Oceanic, Western Oceanic, North New Guinea, Schouten, Kairiru-Manam, Kairiru. *Dialects:* Close to Kaiep. *Lg Use:* Speakers are highly bilingual in Tok Pisin. *Lg Dev:* Literacy rate in first language: below 5%. Literacy rate in second language: 25% to 50%. Dictionary. Grammar.

Kakabai (Igora) [kqf] 900 (2003 SIL). 15% monolingual. Milne Bay Province, Alotau District, Weraura and Suau Local Government Areas, inland villages, eastern tip of Papua. *Class:* Austronesian, Malayo-Polynesian, Central-Eastern, Eastern Malayo-Polynesian, Oceanic, Western Oceanic, Papuan Tip, Nuclear, North Papuan Mainland-D'Entrecasteaux, Kakabai. *Dialects:* North Kakabai, South Kakabai. *Lg Use:* Kakabai serves as group identity.

Speakers have some degree of bilingualism in Wedau, Dawawa, English, or Motu. *Other:* People move whole villages.

Kaki Ae (Tate, Raepa Tati, Tati, Lorabada, Lou) [tbd] 512 (2000 census). Gulf Province, southeast of Kerema. *Class:* Trans-New Guinea, Eleman, Tate. *Dialects:* Different from Torricelli (Lou) in East Sepik Province or Lou in Manus Province. *Lg Use:* 40% of the ethnic group speaks Kaki Ae. Speakers also use Toaripi. *Other:* Sea level to 15 meters.

Kalam (Aforo, Karam) [kmh] 15,000 (1991 SIL). Madang Province, Ramu District, and in Western Highlands Province, Hagen District, along the north side of the Jimi River into the Kaironk Valley. *Class:* Trans-New Guinea, Main Section, Central and Western, East New Guinea Highlands, Kalam, Kalam-Kobon. *Dialects:* Related to Gants, Kobon. *Lg Dev:* Literacy rate in first language: below 5%. Literacy rate in second language: 15% to 25%. Grammar. NT: 1992. *Other:* SOV. Mountain slope. Savannah. 1,500 to 2,000 meters. Swidden agriculturalists.

Kalou (Yawa) [ywa] 1,370 (2003 SIL). Sandaun Province, northwest of Hauna in the Sepik Iwam area. *Class:* Sepik-Ramu, Sepik, Tama. *Other:* Lowland. Tropical forest, swamp.

Kaluli (Bosavi) [bco] 2,500 (1994 SIL). Southern Highlands Province, extending into Western Province, on the northern and western slopes of Mt. Bosavi. *Class:* Trans-New Guinea, Main Section, Central and Western, Central and South New Guinea-Kutubuan, Central and South New Guinea, Bosavi. *Dialects:* Ologo, Kaluli, Walulu, Kugenesi. No significant dialect differences. Close to but different from Kasua. *Lg Use:* Bilingual level estimates for Tok Pisin: 0 60%, 1 20%, 2 15%, 3 5%, 4 0%, 5 0%; English: 0 89%, 1 8%, 2–5 3%. Some speakers between 15 and 25 years old speak a little Tok Pisin for common topics. *Lg Dev:* Literacy rate in first language: 5%. Literacy rate in second language: 10%. Bible portions: 1997–1998. *Other:* 'Bosavi' is a geographic name. SOV; prepositions; articles, adjectives, numerals after noun heads; question word initial; 1–4 prefixes; word order important; affixes indicate case; verb affixes mark person; ergativity; CV, CVC, CVV; tonal. Mountain slope. Tropical forest. 800 meters. Swidden agriculturalists. Traditional religion, Christian.

Kamano (Kamano-Kafe) [kbq] 63,170 (2000 census). Eastern Highlands Province, Kainantu and Henganofi districts. *Class:* Trans-New Guinea, Main Section, Central and Western, East New Guinea Highlands, East-Central, Kamano-Yagaria. *Lg Dev:* Literacy rate in first language: 25% to 50%. Literacy rate in second language: 25% to 50%. Dictionary. NT: 1977–1982. *Other:* SOV. Mountain slope. Savannah, scrub forest. 1,800 meters. Swidden agriculturalists: coffee cash crop.

Kamasa [klp] 7 (2003 SIL). Morobe Province, in part of the Katsiong census unit. *Class:* Trans-New Guinea, Main Section, Central and Western, Angan, Angan Proper. *Lg Use:* Used in the home. *Other:* Nearly extinct.

Kamasau (Wand Tuan) [kms] 964 (2003 SIL). East Sepik Province, Wewak District. Segi is in Kamasau, Tring, and Wau villages, Hagi in Kenyari, Ghini in Yibab, Wandomi, and Wobu. *Class:* Torricelli, Marienberg. *Dialects:* Hagi, Segi, Ghini. *Lg Dev:* Literacy rate in first language: 15% to 25%. Literacy rate in second language: 50% to 75%. Dictionary. NT: 1998.

Kambaira [kyy] 135 (1971 Wurm). Eastern Highlands Province, Kainantu District. *Class:* Trans-New Guinea, Main Section, Central and Western, East New Guinea Highlands, Eastern, Kambaira. *Lg Use:* Speakers also use Binumarien, Gadsup. *Other:* Trilingual in Binumarien, Gadsup.

Kamula (Wawoi) [xla] 800 (1998 SIL). Villages of Kamiyami (Wasapea), Aramia River area, and Keseki and Somokopa, Wawoi Falls area, Western Province. *Class:* Trans-New Guinea, Main Section, Central and Western, Central and South New Guinea-Kutubuan, Central and South New Guinea, Awin-Pare. *Dialects:* The closest language is Pare (G. Reesink SIL 1976). *Lg Use:* Some also use Gogodala or Doso. *Lg Dev:* Literacy rate in first language: 25% to 50%. Literacy rate in second language: 25% to 50%. Literacy is increasing as more children and adults are learning to read. Two vernacular primary schools. Bible portions: 1996–2000. *Other:* Riverine. Tropical forest. Below 100 meters. Hunter-gatherers.

Kanasi (Sona) [soq] 2,200 (1998 SIL). Milne Bay Province, Rabaraba District, on both sides of the main range river valleys from Mt. Thomson. *Class:* Trans-New Guinea, Main Section, Eastern, Central and Southeastern, Dagan. *Dialects:* Lexical similarity 51% with Ginuman (closest). *Lg Dev:* Literacy rate in first language: 15% to 25%. Literacy rate in second language: 15% to 25%. Grammar. NT: 1997.

Kandas (King) [kqw] 480 (1972 Beaumont). New Ireland Province, southwest coast, Watpi, King, and Kait villages. *Class:* Austronesian, Malayo-Polynesian, Central-Eastern, Eastern Malayo-Polynesian, Oceanic, Western Oceanic, Meso Melanesian, New Ireland, South New Ireland-Northwest Solomonic, Patpatar-Tolai. *Lg Use:* 70% of the ethnic group speaks Kandas. Most domains.

Kandawo (Narake) [gam] 4,000 (2003 SIL). Western Highlands Province, Hagen District in the upper Jimi headwaters, on the slopes of Mt. Wilhelm. *Class:* Trans-New Guinea, Main Section, Central and Western, East New Guinea Highlands, Central, Jimi. *Lg Dev:* Literacy rate in first language: below 5%. Literacy rate in second language: 5% to 15%. Bible portions: 1989–1998. *Other:* Mountain slope.

Kanggape (Igom) [igm] 1,082 (1981 Wurm and Hattori). Madang Province, west of Tanggu. *Class:* Sepik-Ramu, Ramu, Ramu Proper, Goam, Ataitan. *Dialects:* Related to Andarum, Tangu, Tanguat.

Kaniet [ktk] Extinct. Manus Province, Anchorite and Kaniet Islands, western. *Class:* Austronesian, Malayo-Polynesian, Central-Eastern, Eastern Malayo-Polynesian, Oceanic, Admiralty Islands, Western. *Lg Use:* Extinct since 1950.

Kaningra (Kaningara) [knr] 300 (2000 Wurm). East Sepik Province, Blackwater River just south of Kuvanmas Lake, 2 villages. *Class:* Sepik-Ramu, Sepik, Sepik Hill, Alamblak. *Lg Use:* 40% of the ethnic group speaks Kaningra. Highly bilingual in Tok Pisin. *Lg Dev:* Literacy rate in first language: below 5%. Literacy rate in second language: below 5%.

Kaninuwa (Kaokao, Wataluma) [wat] 360 (2001). 10% monolingual. Milne Bay Province, village of Sivesive and one other small village as well as two villages on the north of Goodenough Island. *Class:* Austronesian, Malayo-Polynesian, Central-Eastern, Eastern Malayo-Polynesian, Oceanic, Western Oceanic, Papuan Tip, Nuclear, North Papuan Mainland-D'Entrecasteaux, Are-Taupota, Are. *Dialects:* Lexical similarity 51% with Iduna (closest). *Lg Use:* 70% of the ethnic group speaks Kaninuwa. Most key domains. Older people use Dobu also. 60% of the children speak Kaninuwa. Speakers also use Bwaidoka, Motu, or Iduna. *Lg Dev:* Literacy rate in first language: high. Highly literate in English. *Other:* 'Wataluma' is name of adjacent mission station. 'Kaokao' is used by other people on Goodenough Island.

Kanite [kmu] 8,000 (1991 SIL). Eastern Highlands Province, Okapa District. *Class:* Trans-New Guinea, Main Section, Central and Western, East New Guinea Highlands, East-Central, Kamano-Yagaria. *Dialects:*

Close to Keyagana, Inoke-Yate. *Lg Dev:* Literacy rate in first language: 25% to 50%. Literacy rate in second language: 25% to 50%. NT: 1980–2002.

Kapin (Sambio, Taiak, Tayek, Katumene) [tbx] 2,351 (1979 census). Morobe Province, Mumeng District, Bulolo District, 5 villages in the hills southwest of Mumeng, and settlements in Wau and Lae. *Class:* Austronesian, Malayo-Polynesian, Central-Eastern, Eastern Malayo-Polynesian, Oceanic, Western Oceanic, North New Guinea, Huon Gulf, South, Hote-Buang, Buang. *Dialect:* Kapin, Garawa (Gawawa). May be a member of the Mumeng language chain. *Lg Use:* All domains. All ages. Tok Pisin is used with others by all under the age of 40, and by men and half the women over 40. Tok Pisin is used in church; Yabem was the former church language. Kumalu and English are used by some. *Lg Dev:* Literacy rate in second language: possibly 10% are fluent readers, 25% halting. *Other:* SVO; prepositions; genitives before nouns, adjectives, numerals, relatives after noun heads, V, CV, CVC, CVV, CVVC, CVCC, VC; nontonal. Mountain valley. Tropical forest, gallery forest. 450 to 1,000 meters. Swidden agriculturalists, coffee producers; gold traders. Traditional religion.

Kapriman (Wasare, Mugumute) [dju] 1,638 (2003 SIL). East Sepik Province, Blackwater River and Korosameri River, 6 villages. *Class:* Sepik-Ramu, Sepik, Sepik Hill, Bahinemo. *Dialects:* Kapriman, Karambit. *Lg Dev:* Literacy rate in first language: below 5%. Literacy rate in second language: 5% to 15%.

Kara (Lemusmus, Lemakot) [leu] 5,000 (1998 SIL). New Ireland Province, northern New Ireland District. *Class:* Austronesian, Malayo-Polynesian, Central-Eastern, Eastern Malayo-Polynesian, Oceanic, Western Oceanic, Meso Melanesian, New Ireland, Lavongai-Nalik. *Dialects:* East Kara, West Kara, Lauan-Nonopai, Ngavalus-Lossuk, Luburua. *Lg Dev:* NT: 1997. *Other:* SVO. Coastal. Tropical forest. Sea level to 300 meters. Swidden agriculturalists.

Karami [xar] Extinct. Gulf Province, on Western Province border, northeast of Tao-Suamoto. *Class:* Trans-New Guinea, Inland Gulf, Minanibai.

Karawa (Bulawa) [xrw] 63 (2003 SIL). Sandaun Province, Lumi District, Pulwa (Bulawa) village. *Class:* Sepik-Ramu, Sepik, Ram. *Dialects:* Related to Awtuw, Pouye. Lexical similarity 67% with Pouye. *Lg Use:* Speakers are shifting to Pouye. In 1995, the children were speaking Pouye as their first language. Pouye speakers consider Karawa to be part of their language. *Other:* Nearly extinct.

Kare [kmf] 384 (1981 Wurm and Hattori). Madang Province. *Class:* Trans-New Guinea, Madang-Adelbert Range, Madang, Mabuso, Kare. *Lg Dev:* Literacy rate in first language: 25% to 50%. Literacy rate in second language: 50% to 75%.

Karkar-Yuri (Yuri, Karkar) [yuj] 1,142 (1994 SIL). Sandaun Province, Amanab District, along the Papua, Indonesia border. *Class:* Language Isolate. *Dialects:* North Central Yuri, Auia-Tarauwi, Usari. *Lg Dev:* Literacy rate in first language: 25% to 50%. Literacy rate in second language: 25% to 50%. NT: 1994. *Other:* SOV. Mountain slope. Tropical forest. 100 to 700 meters. Swidden agriculturalists.

Karnai ("Barim") [bbv] 915 (2000 D. Tryon). Morobe Province, 4 villages on mainland near Wasu and 3 on southwestern Umboi Island; Madang Province, 2 or 3 villages east of Saidor. *Class:* Austronesian, Malayo-Polynesian, Central-Eastern, Eastern Malayo-Polynesian, Oceanic, Western Oceanic, North New Guinea, Ngero-Vitiaz, Vitiaz, Korap. *Other:* "Barim" used by outsiders and is not acceptable to native speakers. Coastal.

Karore [xkx] 550 (2003 SIL). West New Britain Province, Kandrian District, between the Andru and Johanna rivers.

Class: Austronesian, Malayo-Polynesian, Central-Eastern, Eastern Malayo-Polynesian, Oceanic, Western Oceanic, North New Guinea, Ngero-Vitiaz, Vitiaz, Southwest New Britain, Arawe-Pasismanua, Pasismanua. *Dialects:* Dialect chain with Kaulong and Getmata.

Kasua [khs] 600 (1990 SIL). Southern Highlands Province, east and south of Mt. Bosavi, northeastern corner of Western Province, and northwestern corner of Gulf Province, 6 villages. *Class:* Trans-New Guinea, Main Section, Central and Western, Central and South New Guinea-Kutubuan, Central and South New Guinea, Bosavi.

Kâte (Kai, Kâte Dong) [kmg] 6,125 (1978 McElhanon). Morobe Province, Finschhafen District. *Class:* Trans-New Guinea, Main Section, Central and Western, Huon-Finisterre, Huon, Eastern. *Dialects:* Magobineng (Bamota), Wamora (Wamola), Wemo, Parec, Wana. Those listed as dialects may be separate languages. *Lg Use:* Used by Lutherans as a religious language in the area for 80,000 (1980 UBS). *Lg Dev:* Literacy rate in first language: 25% to 50%. Literacy rate in second language: 50% to 75%. Dictionary. Bible: 1978. *Other:* Christian.

Kaulong (Pasismanua, Kowlong) [pss] 4,000 (2000 Tryon). West New Britain Province, Kandrian District, southwest hinterland. *Class:* Austronesian, Malayo-Polynesian, Central-Eastern, Eastern Malayo-Polynesian, Oceanic, Western Oceanic, North New Guinea, Ngero-Vitiaz, Vitiaz, Southwest New Britain, Arawe-Pasismanua, Pasismanua. *Dialects:* Kaulong, East Inland Kaulong. Dialect cluster. Miu, Bao, and Senseng are treated as dialects by Wurm and Hattori. *Lg Dev:* Bible portions: 1992. *Other:* SVO. Mountain slope. Tropical forest. 25 to 500 meters. Swidden agriculturalists.

Kawacha (Kawatsa) [kcb] 12 (2000 Wurm). Morobe Province, east of Ampale, in part of the Katsiong census unit. *Class:* Trans-New Guinea, Main Section, Central and Western, Angan, Angan Proper. *Lg Use:* 30% or less of the ethnic group speaks Kawacha. Used in the home. No children speak Kawacha. Speakers also use Yagwoia. *Other:* Nearly extinct.

Keapara (Keopara, Kerepunu) [khz] 19,400 (2000 D. Tryon). Central Province, coast from east of Hood Peninsula to Lalaura west of Cape Rodney. 3 villages. *Class:* Austronesian, Malayo-Polynesian, Central-Eastern, Eastern Malayo-Polynesian, Oceanic, Western Oceanic, Papuan Tip, Peripheral, Central Papuan, Sinagoro-Keapara. *Dialects:* Babaga, Kalo, Keapara (Keopara), Aroma (Arona, Aloma, Galoma), Maopa, Wanigela, Kapari, Lalaura. Dialect continuum to Hula. *Lg Dev:* Bible portions: 1892–1905. *Other:* High educational standard and income level. Coastal.

Kein (Bemal) [bmh] 1,750 (2000 census). Madang Province, Trans-Gogol District. *Class:* Trans-New Guinea, Madang-Adelbert Range, Madang, Mabuso, Kokon. *Dialects:* Related to Girawa, Munit. *Lg Use:* Some speakers are bilingual in Tok Pisin. *Other:* SOV. Interfluvial. Tropical forest. Above 40 meters. Agriculturalists. Traditional religion.

Kela (Gela, Kelana, Laukanu) [kcl] 2,145 (1980 census). Morobe Province, southern coast of Huon Gulf, between Salamaua and Kui, Paiawa River. 10 villages. *Class:* Austronesian, Malayo-Polynesian, Central-Eastern, Eastern Malayo-Polynesian, Oceanic, Western Oceanic, North New Guinea, Huon Gulf, North. *Lg Dev:* Literacy rate in first language: 15% to 25%. Literacy rate in second language: 15% to 25%. *Other:* Coastal.

Kele (Gele') [sbc] 600 (1982 SIL). Manus Province, south coast inland, Buyang, Droia, Kawaliap, Koruniat, Tingau. *Class:* Austronesian, Malayo-Polynesian, Central-Eastern, Eastern Malayo-Polynesian, Oceanic, Admiralty Islands, Eastern, Manus, East. *Lg Use:* Speakers also use Kurti or Ere. *Other:* SVO. Win Nesien cult.

Kenati (Kenathi, Ganati, Aziana) [gat] 950 (1990 census). Eastern Highlands Province, Wonenara District. All 3 villages are within ten miles of Wonenara. *Class:* Trans-New Guinea, Main Section, Central and Western, East New Guinea Highlands, Kenati. *Lg Dev:* Bible portions: 1989. *Other:* Mountain slope. Agriculturalists: sweet potatoes, yams, bananas, coffee. Traditional religion, Christian.

Kerewo (Kerewa, Kerewa-Goari) [kxz] 2,200 (1975 Wurm). Gulf Province, west bank of Omati River, east and inland to Samoa village. *Class:* Trans-New Guinea, Trans-Fly-Bulaka River, Trans-Fly, Kiwaian. *Dialect:* Gibario (Goaribari). *Lg Dev:* Literacy rate in first language: 15% to 25%. Literacy rate in second language: 5% to 15%. Bible portions: 1926–1941.

Kesawai (Namuya) [xes] 767 (2003 SIL). Madang Province. *Class:* Trans-New Guinea, Madang-Adelbert Range, Madang, Rai Coast, Evapia. *Dialects:* Related to Sinsauru, Asas, Sausi, Dumpu.

Keuru (Keuro, Belepa, Haura, Haura Haela) [xeu] 4,523 (1981 Wurm and Hattori). Gulf Province, from the mouth of the Purari River east to the Bairu River. *Class:* Trans-New Guinea, Eleman, Eleman Proper, Western. *Dialect:* Aheave.

Kewa, East [kjs] 45,000 (2000 census). Southern Highlands Province, Ialibu and Kagua districts. *Class:* Trans-New Guinea, Main Section, Central and Western, East New Guinea Highlands, West-Central, Angal-Kewa. *Lg Dev:* Literacy rate in first language: 15% to 25%. Literacy rate in second language: 25% to 50%. NT: 2004.

Kewa, West (Pasuma) [kew] 45,000 (2000 census). Southern Highlands Province, Kagua and Mendi districts. *Class:* Trans-New Guinea, Main Section, Central and Western, East New Guinea Highlands, West-Central, Angal-Kewa. *Lg Dev:* Dictionary. Grammar. NT: 1973–2004. *Other:* SOV. Mountain mesa. Tropical forest, some savannah, scrub forest. Below 2,000 meters. Swidden agriculturalists, some cash crops.

Keyagana (Keigana, Keiagana, Ke'yagana) [kyg] 12,284 (1981 Wurm and Hattori). Okapa and Henganofi districts, Eastern Highlands Province. *Class:* Trans-New Guinea, Main Section, Central and Western, East New Guinea Highlands, East-Central, Kamano-Yagaria. *Lg Dev:* Literacy rate in first language: 15% to 25%. Literacy rate in second language: 25% to 50%. NT: 2003.

Khehek (Levei-Drehet, Levei-Ndrehet) [tlx] 1,600 (1991 SIL). Manus Province, Soparibeu District. Ndrehet, Levei, and Bucho villages; Ndrehet is the center. *Class:* Austronesian, Malayo-Polynesian, Central-Eastern, Eastern Malayo-Polynesian, Oceanic, Admiralty Islands, Eastern, Manus, West. *Dialects:* Levei (Lebei, Lebej), Drehet (Khehek, Chehek, Chechek), Bucho. Those in the Levei area speak a dialect closely related to that of Bucho in the south. A distinct language from Tulu-Bohuai.

Kibiri (Porome, Polome) [prm] 1,100 (1977 SIL). Gulf Province, Kikori District, near Aird Hills, on several tributaries of Kikori River, villages of Tipeowo, Doibo, Paile, Babaguina, Ero, and Wowa. *Class:* Language Isolate. *Dialects:* Aird Hills (Kibiri), Porome. Unrelated to other languages in Gulf Province. *Lg Dev:* Literacy rate in first language: 15% to 25%. Literacy rate in second language: 5% to 15%. *Other:* Different from Kairi, which is also called Kibiri.

Kilivila (Kiriwina) [kij] 20,000 (2000 Tryon). 60% monolingual. Milne Bay Province, Trobriand Islands. *Class:* Austronesian, Malayo-Polynesian, Central-Eastern, Eastern Malayo-Polynesian, Oceanic, Western Oceanic, Papuan Tip, Peripheral, Kilivila-Louisiades, Kilivila. *Dialects:* Kitava, Vakuta, Sinaketa. Various dialects. Lexical similarity 68% with Muyuw. Kitava Island has 80% lexical similarity. *Lg Use:* Speakers also use Dobu.

Lg Dev: Dictionary. Grammar. NT: 1985. *Other:* Many schools. Agriculturalists: yams, sweet potato, taro, cassava, greens, coconuts. Christian, traditional religion.

Kilmeri (Kilmera) [kih] 2,823 (2003 SIL). Sandaun Province, Vanimo District near Ossima. 15 villages. *Class:* Trans-New Guinea, Northern, Border, Bewani. *Dialects:* Western Kilmeri (Isi), Eastern Kilmeri (Ossima). *Lg Use:* Speakers are using Tok Pisin primarily. *Lg Dev:* Bible portions: 1880.

Kinalakna [kco] 219 (1978 McElhanon). Morobe Province. *Class:* Trans-New Guinea, Main Section, Central and Western, Huon-Finisterre, Huon, Western.

Kire (Gire, Giri, Kire-Puire) [geb] 2,419 (2003 SIL). Madang Province, lower Ramu, around Garati village. *Class:* Sepik-Ramu, Ramu, Ramu Proper, Ruboni, Misegian. *Lg Dev:* Literacy rate in first language: 5% to 25%. Literacy rate in second language: 50% to 75%. NT: 2002.

Kis [kis] 220 (2000 D. Tryon). East Sepik Province, 10 to 20 miles south southeast of Samap, inland from the coast. *Class:* Austronesian, Malayo-Polynesian, Central-Eastern, Eastern Malayo-Polynesian, Oceanic, Western Oceanic, North New Guinea, Schouten, Kairiru-Manam, Manam.

Kiwai, Northeast (Gibaio) [kiw] 4,400 (1986 Foley). Population includes 1,300 in Kope, 700 in Gibaio, 1,700 in Urama, 700 in Arigibi. Gulf Province. *Class:* Trans-New Guinea, Trans-Fly-Bulaka River, Trans-Fly, Kiwaian. *Dialects:* Gibaio, Kope (Gope, Era River), Urama, Arigibi (Anigibi). *Lg Dev:* Literacy rate in first language: 15% to 25%. Literacy rate in second language: 25% to 50%. *Other:* Wurm and Hattori treat Arigibi as a separate language.

Kiwai, Southern [kjd] 9,700 (1975 Wurm). Population includes 3,800 in Coast, 1,000 in Daru, 4,500 in Island Kiwai, 400 in Doumori. Western Province, Fly River Delta. *Class:* Trans-New Guinea, Trans-Fly-Bulaka River, Trans-Fly, Kiwaian. *Dialects:* Doumori, Coast Kiwai, Southern Coast Kiwai, Daru Kiwai, Eastern Kiwai, Island Kiwai. *Lg Dev:* Literacy rate in first language: 15% to 25%. Literacy rate in second language: 15% to 25%. NT: 1960.

Kobol (Koguman) [kgu] 716 (2000 census). Madang Province. *Class:* Trans-New Guinea, Madang-Adelbert Range, Adelbert Range, Pihom-Isumrud-Mugil, Pihom, Omosan. *Dialects:* Related to Pal.

Kobon [kpw] 6,000 (1991 SIL). Madang Province, Middle Ramu District, and Western Highlands Province on Kaironk River in lower Jimi River area north of Mt. Hagen. *Class:* Trans-New Guinea, Main Section, Central and Western, East New Guinea Highlands, Kalam, Kalam-Kobon. *Lg Dev:* Literacy rate in first language: 5% to 15%. Literacy rate in second language: 5% to 15%. Grammar. Bible portions: 1988. *Other:* SOV. Mountain slope. Tropical forest. 1,000 to 2,000 meters. Swidden agriculturalists.

Koiali, Mountain (Mountain Koiari) [kpx] 1,700 (1975 SIL). 50% monolingual. Central Province, Port Moresby District, north of Koita, Koiari, and Barai. One village is Efogi. *Class:* Trans-New Guinea, Main Section, Eastern, Central and Southeastern, Koiarian, Koiaric. *Dialects:* Lexical similarity 50% to 57% with Grass Koiari (closest). *Lg Use:* Speakers also use Motu. *Lg Dev:* Literacy rate in second language: 25% to 50%. Grammar. NT: 1981. *Other:* SOV. Mountain slope. Tropical forest. 800 to 1,400 meters. Swidden agriculturalists.

Koiari, Grass (Koiari) [kbk] 1,700 (2000 Wurm). 10% monolingual. Central Province, east of Port Moresby and to coast. *Class:* Trans-New Guinea, Main Section, Eastern, Central and Southeastern, Koiarian, Koiaric. *Dialects:* Hogeri, Lahada, Omani. Lexical similarity 60% to 65% with Koitabu (closest). *Lg Use:* Speakers also use Hiri Motu or English. *Lg Dev:* Dictionary. Grammar.

Koitabu (Koita) [kqi] 2,700 (2000 Wurm). Central Province, around Port Moresby. *Class:* Trans-New Guinea, Main Section, Eastern, Central and Southeastern, Koiarian, Koiaric. *Dialects:* West Koita, East Koita. Lexical similarity 60% to 65% with Grass Koiari (closest). *Lg Use:* Bilingual level estimates for Hiri Motu: 0 33%, 1 10%, 2 20%, 3 20%, 4 13%, 5 4%; Motu: 0 80%, 1 5%, 2 5%, 3 5%, 4 5%, 5 0%. Some also use Hiri Motu, Motu, Tok Pisin, or English. *Other:* Traditionally hunters; agriculturalists.

Koiwat [kxt] 450 (1975 SIL). East Sepik Province, Ambunti District, Koiwat, Kamangaui, Seraba and Paiambit villages, between the Munguma and Nagam rivers. *Class:* Sepik-Ramu, Sepik, Middle Sepik, Ndu.

Kol (Kole, Kola) [kol] 4,000 (1991 SIL). Population includes 1,300 Sui, Kol (1987). East New Britain Province, Pomio District, inland from Open Bay to the coast at Waterfall Bay. Most are on the south side of the Island. *Class:* East Papuan, Yele-Solomons-New Britain, New Britain. *Dialect:* Sui, Kol (Nakgaktai). *Other:* SVO. Mountain mesa. Tropical forest. Sea level to 800 meters. Swidden agriculturalists.

Kolom [klm] 472 (2003 SIL). Madang Province. *Class:* Trans-New Guinea, Madang-Adelbert Range, Madang, Rai Coast, Kabenau.

Koluwawa (Kalokalo) [klx] 900 (1998 SIL). Milne Bay Province, northwest tip of Fergusson Island. *Class:* Austronesian, Malayo-Polynesian, Central-Eastern, Eastern Malayo-Polynesian, Oceanic, Western Oceanic, Papuan Tip, Nuclear, North Papuan Mainland-D'Entrecasteaux, Bwaidoga. *Dialects:* Lexical similarity 64% with Iamalele (closest), and then Bwaidoka. *Lg Use:* Speakers also use Minaveha. *Lg Dev:* Literacy rate in first language: 50% to 80%. Literacy rate in second language: 50% to 80%. *Other:* Sea level to 30 meters. Christian.

Komba (Neng Den) [kpf] 15,000 (2000 SIL). Morobe Province, Kabwum District. Selepet language to the northwest, Timbe language to the west, Saruwaget Mountains to the south, Cromwell Mountains to the east. *Class:* Trans-New Guinea, Main Section, Central and Western, Huon-Finisterre, Huon, Western. *Dialects:* East Komba, Central Komba, West Central Komba, Border Komba, West Komba. *Lg Use:* Vigorous. All domains. Komba and Tok Pisin used in church, songs. Positive language attitude. 60% know some Tok Pisin, 50% know some English. English used in school. *Lg Dev:* Literacy rate in first language: 40%. Literacy rate in second language: 50% to 75%. NT: 1980. *Other:* SVO. Mountain slope. Savannah. 1,330 to 2,000 meters. Swidden agriculturalists: coffee as cash crop. Christian.

Kombio (Endangen) [xbi] 2,970 (2003 SIL). East Sepik Province, Dreikikir District, Torricelli Mountains 31 villages. *Class:* Torricelli, Kombio-Arapesh, Kombio. *Dialects:* North Kombio (Mwi), West-Central Kombio (Wampukuamp), South Kombio (Yanimoi). The Mwi dialect is more distinct from the others and speakers have some difficulty in comprehension between dialects. *Lg Use:* Speakers are shifting to Tok Pisin. *Lg Dev:* Literacy rate in second language: 25% to 35%. Bible portions: 2001. *Other:* People refer to themselves as 'Akwun'. SVO. Foothills, mountain ridge. Tropical rainforest. No significant natural water source but high water table. 270 to 1,000 meters. Agriculturalists: yams, sweet potato, coffee, cacao; coconut, sago.

Kominimung [xoi] 320 (2003 SIL). Madang Province. *Class:* Sepik-Ramu, Ramu, Ramu Proper, Goam, Tamolan. *Dialects:* Related to Romkun, Breri, Igana, Akrukay, Itutang, Inapang.

Konai (Mirapmin) [kxw] 600 (1991 SIL). Western Province, west side of Upper Strickland River. *Class:* Trans-New Guinea, Main Section, Central and Western,

Central and South New Guinea-Kutubuan, Central and South New Guinea, East Strickland. *Dialects:* Closest to Kalamo and Agala. *Lg Dev:* Literacy rate in first language: below 5%. Literacy rate in second language: below 5%.

Konomala [koa] 800 (1985 SIL). New Ireland Province, southeastern coast. 8 villages. *Class:* Austronesian, Malayo-Polynesian, Central-Eastern, Eastern Malayo-Polynesian, Oceanic, Western Oceanic, Meso Melanesian, New Ireland, South New Ireland-Northwest Solomonic, Patpatar-Tolai. *Dialects:* Laket, Konomala. *Lg Use:* There has been major shift to Siar.

Kopar [xop] 229 (1981 Wurm and Hattori). East Sepik Province. *Class:* Sepik-Ramu, Nor-Pondo, Nor. *Dialects:* Related to Murik.

Korafe (Korape, Korafi, Kwarafe, Kailikaili) [kpr] 3,625 (2003 SIL). Population includes 2,755 in Korafe dialect and 850 in Yegha dialect living in the area. Oro Province, Tufi District, on the headlands (fiord system) of Cape Nelson. *Class:* Trans-New Guinea, Main Section, Eastern, Binanderean, Binanderean Proper. *Dialect:* Korafe, Yegha (Yega, Mokorua). Yega dialect is distinct from Gona, also called 'Yega'. Gaina may also be a dialect. Lexical similarity 56% to 61% with Baruga (closest), 50% with Ewage dialect of Ewage Notu (Dutton 1971). *Lg Use:* Some also use English, Tok Pisin, or Hiri Motu. *Lg Dev:* Literacy rate in first language: 75% to 100%. Literacy rate in second language: 75% to 100%. Grammar. NT: 1984. *Other:* SOV. Coastal. Tropical forest. Sea level to 300 meters. Fishermen; swidden agriculturalists.

Korak [koz] 512 (2003 SIL). Madang Province. *Class:* Trans-New Guinea, Madang-Adelbert Range, Adelbert Range, Pihom-Isumrud-Mugil, Isumrud, Kowan.

Koro [kxr] 400 (1983 SIL). Manus Province. *Class:* Austronesian, Malayo-Polynesian, Central-Eastern, Eastern Malayo-Polynesian, Oceanic, Admiralty Islands, Eastern, Manus, East. *Dialects:* Close to, and possibly intelligible with, Papitalai. *Lg Use:* All domains. All ages. *Other:* SVO.

Koromira [kqj] 1,562 (1990 SIL). Population includes 1,448 Koromira and 114 Koianu. Bougainville Province, Kieta District, central mountains and southeast coast. *Class:* East Papuan, Bougainville, East, Nasioi. *Dialects:* Koromira, Koianu. *Other:* Koianu may need separate literature. SOV. Mountain slope, coastal. Tropical forest. Swidden agriculturalists: cash crops.

Kosena [kze] 2,000 (1987 SIL). Eastern Highlands Province, Kainantu and Okapa districts. *Class:* Trans-New Guinea, Main Section, Central and Western, East New Guinea Highlands, Eastern, Gadsup-Auyana-Awa. *Lg Dev:* Literacy rate in first language: 5% to 15%. Literacy rate in second language: 5% to 15%. NT: 1980. *Other:* SOV. Mountain ridge. Tropical forest. 1,200 to 2,000 meters. Agriculturalists.

Kovai (Umboi, Kobai, Kowai) [kqb] 4,500 (1991 SIL). Morobe Province, Siassi District, Umboi or Rooke Island, 12 villages. *Class:* Trans-New Guinea, Main Section, Central and Western, Huon-Finisterre, Huon, Kovai. *Lg Dev:* Literacy rate in first language: 15% to 25%. Literacy rate in second language: 15% to 25%. Bible portions: 1993. *Other:* Plateau. Traditional religion.

Kove [kvc] 6,750 (1994 SIL). West New Britain Province, northwest coast. 24 villages, most on small islands off the coast. *Class:* Austronesian, Malayo-Polynesian, Central-Eastern, Eastern Malayo-Polynesian, Oceanic, Western Oceanic, North New Guinea, Ngero-Vitiaz, Ngero, Bariai. *Lg Dev:* Grammar. *Other:* A separate language from Kaliai. Many highly educated people. Coastal, coral islands. Sea level. Swidden agriculturalists; fishermen.

Kowaki [xow] 25 (2000 Wurm). Madang Province. *Class:* Trans-New Guinea, Madang-Adelbert Range,

Adelbert Range, Pihom-Isumrud-Mugil, Pihom, Tiboran. *Dialects:* Related to Mawak, Pamosu, Musar, Wanambre. *Other:* Nearly extinct.

Krisa [ksi] 421 (2003 SIL). Sandaun Province near coast. *Class:* Sko, Krisa. *Dialects:* Related to Rawo, Puari, Warapu.

Kuanua (Tolai, Gunantuna, Tinata Tuna, Tuna, Blanche Bay, New Britain Language) [ksd] 61,000 (1991 SIL). East New Britain Province, Rabaul District, Gazelle Peninsula. *Class:* Austronesian, Malayo-Polynesian, Central-Eastern, Eastern Malayo-Polynesian, Oceanic, Western Oceanic, Meso Melanesian, New Ireland, South New Ireland-Northwest Solomonic, Patpatar-Tolai. *Dialects:* Vunadidir, Rapitok, Raluana, Vanumami, Livuan, Matupit, Kokopo, Kabakada, Nodup, Kininanggunan, Rakunei, Rebar, Watom, Masawa. *Lg Use:* Trade language on New Britain and New Ireland. 20,000 second-language speakers (1985 UBS). *Lg Dev:* Bible: 1983. *Other:* 'Tolai' is the name of the people.

Kube (Mongi, Hube) [kgf] 6,000 (1987 SIL). Morobe Province, Dindiu District, at the eastern headwaters of the Mongi River, on the eastern slopes of the lower Kua River valley and Foris River Valley. *Class:* Trans-New Guinea, Main Section, Central and Western, Huon-Finisterre, Huon, Eastern. *Dialect:* Kurungtufu, Yoangen (Yoanggeng). *Other:* Mountain slope. Swidden agriculturalists.

Kubo [jko] 1,000. Western Province, Lake Murray District, northern half of Upper Strickland Census District, east of Strickland River, north of the Samo. *Class:* Trans-New Guinea, Main Section, Central and Western, Central and South New Guinea-Kutubuan, Central and South New Guinea, East Strickland. *Dialects:* Related to Samo and Gobasi. *Lg Dev:* Literacy rate in first language: 10% to 15%. Literacy rate in second language: 15% to 20%. One vernacular primary school. Bible portions: 1996–1999. *Other:* Interfluvial. Tropical forest, swamp. 120 to 200 meters. Swidden agriculturalists.

Kumalu (Kumara) [ksl] 2,583 (1979 census). Morobe Province, Mumeng District. *Class:* Austronesian, Malayo-Polynesian, Central-Eastern, Eastern Malayo-Polynesian, Oceanic, Western Oceanic, North New Guinea, Huon Gulf, South, Hote-Buang, Buang, Mumeng. *Dialects:* A member of the Mumeng language cluster. Some intelligibility of Dambi. *Lg Dev:* Literacy rate in first language: 15% to 25%. Literacy rate in second language: 25% to 50%. *Other:* SVO. Mountain slope. Tropical forest. 300 to 900 meters. Swidden agriculturalists.

Kuman (Chimbu, Simbu) [kue] 80,000 (1994 SIL). 10,000 monolinguals. Simbu Province, northern third, overlapping into Minj Subprovince of Western Highlands Province. *Class:* Trans-New Guinea, Main Section, Central and Western, East New Guinea Highlands, Central, Chimbu. *Dialects:* Kuman, Nagane (Genagane, Genogane), Yongomugi. *Lg Use:* Language of wider communication. Vigorous. Major language of the area. All domains. Oral use in local administration, in the first 3 grades in school, religion, local commerce. All ages. Positive language attitude. 70,000 use Tok Pisin as second language. 20,000 can also use English or various neighboring languages. *Lg Dev:* Literacy rate in first language: 12%. Literacy rate in second language: 25% to 40%. 10,000 can read and write it. Dictionary. Bible portions: 1968–1995. *Other:* SOV; clause chaining, auxiliary verbs with adjuncts. Mountain valley. Tropical forest, savannah. 1,200 to 4,500 meters. Swidden agriculturalists: coffee. Christian, traditional religion.

Kumukio (Kumokio) [kuo] 552 (1978 McElhanon). Morobe Province. *Class:* Trans-New Guinea, Main Section, Central and Western, Huon-Finisterre, Huon, Western.

Kuni [kse] 4,500 (1993 SIL). Central Province, Kairuku and southwest Goilala districts, towards Port Moresby, south of Mekeo. *Class:* Austronesian, Malayo-Polynesian, Central-Eastern, Eastern Malayo-Polynesian, Oceanic, Western Oceanic, Papuan Tip, Peripheral, Central Papuan, West Central Papuan, Nuclear. *Dialects:* Lexical similarity 52% with Lala, 47% with Mekeo, 40% with Waima, the closest varieties. *Lg Dev:* Literacy rate in first language: 25% to 50%. Literacy rate in second language: 25% to 50%.

Kuni-Boazi (Boazi, Boadji, Bwadji, Kuni, Kuini) [kvg] 2,500 (2001 SIL). Western Province, Lake Murray District. None now in Papua, Indonesia (1978 SIL). *Class:* Trans-New Guinea, Main Section, Central and Western, Marind, Boazi. *Dialects:* Kuni, Wamak, Khoamak, Sengeze, Ingias, Aewa. Related to Zimakani and Marind. *Lg Dev:* Literacy rate in first language: 40%. Literacy rate in second language: 40% to 50%. 14 vernacular primary schools. Bible portions: 1997–2003. *Other:* Some are educated. Speakers of different dialects do not share a common language name. Lake and lagoon shores, riverine. Fishermen; hunters; some swidden agriculturalists; sago gatherers.

Kunimaipa [kup] 11,000 (1991 SIL). Population includes 1,429 in Morobe Province (1978 McElhanon). Central Province, northern Goilala District; Morobe Province, Wau District. *Class:* Trans-New Guinea, Main Section, Eastern, Central and Southeastern, Goilalan, Kunimaipa. *Dialects:* Karuama, Kâte (Hate), Gajili (Gajila, Gazili, Hazili). *Lg Use:* Speakers also use Tok Pisin. *Lg Dev:* Literacy rate in first language: 15% to 25%. Literacy rate in second language: 25% to 50%. Grammar. NT: 1990. *Other:* SOV. Mountain slope. Tropical forest. 1,500 to 2,000 meters. Swidden agriculturalists. Traditional religion, Christian.

Kunja (Lower Morehead, Thundai-Kanza, Peremka) [pep] 294 (2003 SIL). Western Province, extreme southwest. *Class:* Trans-New Guinea, Trans-Fly-Bulaka River, Trans-Fly, Morehead and Upper Maro rivers, Tonda. *Dialects:* Gambadi, Semariji, Kánchá, Kámá. Related to Kanum, Aramba, Bothar, Rouku. *Other:* Swamp, savannah. Below 300 meters.

Kuot (Kuat, Panaras) [kto] 2,400 (2002 SIL). New Ireland Province, northwest coast. 9 villages. *Class:* East Papuan, Yele-Solomons-New Britain, New Britain, Kuot. *Lg Use:* Vigorous on the west coast. Speakers also use Tok Pisin. *Lg Dev:* Literacy rate in first language: 75% to 85%. Literacy rate in second language: 75% to 95%. NT: 2001. *Other:* Coastal.

Kurti (Kuruti, Kuruti-Pare, Ndrugul) [ktm] 3,000 (2002 SIL). Manus Province, north central coast. *Class:* Austronesian, Malayo-Polynesian, Central-Eastern, Eastern Malayo-Polynesian, Oceanic, Admiralty Islands, Eastern, Manus, East. *Lg Use:* Vigorous. All domains. Oral use in first 3 grades of school, religious services, personal letters. All ages. Positive language attitude. 95% use Tok Pisin, 30% use English as second languages, 30% can use Kele or Mondropolon. *Lg Dev:* Literacy rate in first language: 50%. Literacy rate in second language: 50% to 75%. Radio programs. Bible portions: 1999–2000. *Other:* SVO. Hills, coastal. Tropical forest. Christian.

Kwanga (Kawanga, Gawanga) [kwj] 10,000 (2001 SIL). East Sepik Province, extending beyond the western boundary of Maprik District; Makru-Klaplei Division, Nuku District; Saundaun Province, east of Mehek. 40 villages. *Class:* Sepik-Ramu, Sepik, Middle Sepik, Nukuma. *Dialects:* Apos, Bongos (Bongomamsi, Bongomaise, Nambi), Tau (Kubiwat), Wasambu, Yubanakor (Daina). A dialect cluster of 5 subdialects, 2 main dialects. *Lg Dev:* Literacy rate in first language: 5% to 15%. Literacy rate in second language: 15% to 25%.

NT: 1991. *Other:* OSV. Plains. Tropical forest. 50 to 60 meters. Swidden agriculturalists.

Kwato (Waupe) [kop] 778 (1981 Wurm and Hattori). Madang Province. *Class:* Trans-New Guinea, Madang-Adelbert Range, Madang, Rai Coast, Nuru. *Dialects:* Related to Uya, Ogea, Duduela, Rerau, Jilim, Yangulam.

Kwoma (Washkuk) [kmo] 3,000 (2003 SIL). East Sepik Province, Ambunti District, along the Sepik River, along the Sanchi River, 12 villages. *Class:* Sepik-Ramu, Sepik, Middle Sepik, Nukuma. *Dialects:* Kwoma (Washkuk), Nukuma. *Lg Dev:* Literacy rate in first language: 5% to 15%. Literacy rate in second language: 15% to 25%. Dictionary. Grammar. NT: 1975. *Other:* Mountain slope, riverine. 50 meters. Swidden agriculturalists; sago; fishermen.

Kwomtari [kwo] 600 (1998 SIL). Sandaun Province, Amanab District, north of Namia. 6 villages. *Class:* Kwomtari-Baibai, Kwomtari. *Dialects:* West Central Kwomtari, Ekos-Yenabi-Maragin. *Lg Use:* Used in the home and village life. Some men and boys and a few women can communicate in Tok Pisin. *Other:* One school. Tropical forest, swamp. 100 to 300 meters. Hunter-gatherers. Traditional religion, Christian.

Kyaka (Baiyer, Enga-Kyaka) [kyc] 15,368 (1981 Wurm and Hattori). Enga Province. *Class:* Trans-New Guinea, Main Section, Central and Western, East New Guinea Highlands, West-Central, Enga. *Lg Dev:* Dictionary. NT: 1973.

Kyenele (Keñele, Keyele, Kenen Birang, Kyenying-Barang, Kenying Bulang, Miyak) [kql] 1,253 (2003 SIL). East Sepik Province, Giling village, Yuat River. *Class:* Sepik-Ramu, Ramu, Yuat-Langam, Yuat-Maramba, Yuat. *Lg Dev:* Bible portions: 1994.

Label [lbb] 144 (1979 census). New Ireland Province, southwest coast, Nasko and Tampakar villages. *Class:* Austronesian, Malayo-Polynesian, Central-Eastern, Eastern Malayo-Polynesian, Oceanic, Western Oceanic, Meso Melanesian, New Ireland, South New Ireland-Northwest Solomonic, Patpatar-Tolai.

Labu (Labu', Labo, Hapa) [lbu] 1,600 (1989 SIL). Population includes 800 in Labu-Butu. Morobe Province, coast near the mouth of the Markham River. 3 communities: Labu-Butu, Labu-Miti, and Labu-Tali. *Class:* Austronesian, Malayo-Polynesian, Central-Eastern, Eastern Malayo-Polynesian, Oceanic, Western Oceanic, North New Guinea, Huon Gulf, Markham, Lower, Labu. *Lg Use:* Children are taught Tok Pisin first; use of Tok Pisin is active. The culture seems in decline. Used in the home, especially when older people are present. *Lg Dev:* Grammar. *Other:* Those who attend school learn English. Yabem was the church language, and there were schools in Yabem. The economy is strong.

Laeko-Libuat (Laeko, Laeko-Limbuat) [lkl] 719 (2003 SIL). Population includes 518 in area and 20 outside. Sandaun Province, Torricelli Mountains, west of Mehek. *Class:* Torricelli, Maimai, Laeko-Libuat.

Lala (Nala, Ala'ala, Pokau, Nara) [nrz] 989 (2003 SIL). Central Province, between Kuni and Waima, just inland from the coast and south of Yule Island. *Class:* Austronesian, Malayo-Polynesian, Central-Eastern, Eastern Malayo-Polynesian, Oceanic, Western Oceanic, Papuan Tip, Peripheral, Central Papuan, West Central Papuan, Nuclear. *Dialects:* Lexical similarity 57% with Toura (closest). *Lg Use:* All ages. Positive language attitude. Many of younger generation use Tok Pisin. Hiri Motu is used by some older generation. *Lg Dev:* Lala used in primary education for first 3 years. Grammar. *Other:* Riverine. Savannah. Sea level. Swidden agriculturalists.

Lamogai (Mulakaino, Akiuru) [lmg] 3,653 (1980 Johnston). West New Britain Province, northwest interior, and 2 regions on the south coast. *Class:* Austronesian,

Malayo-Polynesian, Central-Eastern, Eastern Malayo-Polynesian, Oceanic, Western Oceanic, North New Guinea, Ngero-Vitiaz, Vitiaz, Southwest New Britain, Bibling. *Dialects:* Ibanga (Ivanga), Pulie-Rauto (Rauto, Roto), Lomogai, Musen, Paret. *Lg Dev:* NT: 1996. *Other:* Mountain slope, valley, coastal. Tropical forest. Agriculturalists; fishermen; hunters, gatherers. Christian, traditional religion.

Langam [lnm] 424 (2003 SIL). East Sepik Province. *Class:* Sepik-Ramu, Ramu, Yuat-Langam, Mongol-Langam. *Dialects:* Related to Mongol, Yaul.

Lantanai [lni] 300 (1990 SIL). Bougainville Province, Kieta District, Piruneu' village. *Class:* East Papuan, Bougainville, East, Nasioi. *Other:* The language was quite different from others in the Nasioi group, but it may have converged to be more like Koromira or Nasioi.

Laua (Labu) [luf] 1 (1987 SIL). Central Province, north and west of Laua. *Class:* Trans-New Guinea, Main Section, Eastern, Central and Southeastern, Mailuan. *Other:* Different from Austronesian Labu in Morobe Province. May be extinct. Nearly extinct.

Lavatbura-Lamusong (Lamasong) [lbv] 1,308 (1972 Beaumont). New Ireland Province, central. *Class:* Austronesian, Malayo-Polynesian, Central-Eastern, Eastern Malayo-Polynesian, Oceanic, Western Oceanic, Meso Melanesian, New Ireland, Madak. *Dialect:* Ugana, Kontu, Lavatbura, Lamusong (Lamasong).

Lawunuia (Nagarige, Nagarege, Naghareghe, Piva) [tgi] 550 (1977 Lincoln). Bougainville Province, Piva River. *Class:* Austronesian, Malayo-Polynesian, Central-Eastern, Eastern Malayo-Polynesian, Oceanic, Western Oceanic, Meso Melanesian, New Ireland, South New Ireland-Northwest Solomonic, Piva-Banoni. *Dialect:* Amun.

Leipon (Pitilu, Pityilu) [lek] 650 (1977 Lincoln). Manus Province, Lolo village, Hauwai, Ndrilo, and Pityilu islands. *Class:* Austronesian, Malayo-Polynesian, Central-Eastern, Eastern Malayo-Polynesian, Oceanic, Admiralty Islands, Eastern, Manus, East. *Lg Use:* Speakers have high proficiency in Lele. *Other:* SVO.

Lele (Lele Hai, Hai, Usiai, Moanus, Manus, Elu-Kara) [lle] 1,300 (1982 SIL). Manus Province, Manus Island. *Class:* Austronesian, Malayo-Polynesian, Central-Eastern, Eastern Malayo-Polynesian, Oceanic, Admiralty Islands, Eastern, Manus, East. *Dialect:* Sabon. *Lg Dev:* NT: 1956. *Other:* SVO. Coastal, island. Tropical forest. Sea level. Swidden agriculturalists; cocoa and copra production; rubber; fishermen.

Lembena (Nanimba Pii, Uyalipa Pii, Lembena Pii, Wapi Pii) [leq] 1,756 (2000 census). 750 monolinguals. Enga Province, northeast corner, and into East Sepik Province. 8 villages: Eleme, Yambaitoko, Saut Isataele, Mosope, Itopeno, Pipitesa, Madawesa (Olimolo), and Mokosele. *Class:* Trans-New Guinea, Main Section, Central and Western, East New Guinea Highlands, West-Central, Enga. *Lg Use:* Vigorous. All domains. Some oral and written use in church, oral use in local commerce. All ages. Positive language attitude. 50% use Enga, Tok Pisin, or English as second language. Enga is the language of wider communication in the area. *Lg Dev:* Literacy rate in first language: 3%. Literacy rate in second language: below 5%. 2% can write it. No vernacular schools in Lembena area. *Other:* SOV. Mountain slope. Tropical forest. 80 to 1,520 meters. Swidden agriculturalists: coffee, peanuts. Christian.

Lemio [lei] 271 (2003 SIL). Madang Province, several villages on coast near Saidor. *Class:* Trans-New Guinea, Madang-Adelbert Range, Madang, Rai Coast, Kabenau.

Lenkau [ler] 250 (1982 SIL). Ethnic population: 250 (2000 Tryon). Manus Province, southwest Rambutyo Island. 1 village only. *Class:* Austronesian, Malayo-Polynesian, Central-Eastern, Eastern Malayo-Polynesian,

Oceanic, Admiralty Islands, Eastern, Southeast Islands. *Lg Use:* Vigorous. Most domains. All ages. Speakers also use Titan or Penchal. *Other:* SVO.

Lesing-Gelimi (Lesing-Atui, Atui) [let] 929 (1982 SIL). Eastern end of West New Britain Province, south coast, Kaskas Island and Amio village (Lesing dialect), Atui Island and Paronga village (Gelimi dialect). *Class:* Austronesian, Malayo-Polynesian, Central-Eastern, Eastern Malayo-Polynesian, Oceanic, Western Oceanic, North New Guinea, Ngero-Vitiaz, Vitiaz, Southwest New Britain, Arawe-Pasismanua, Arawe, East Arawe. *Dialect:* Lesing, Gelimi (Atui). *Lg Use:* Speakers have receptive bilingualism in Mangseng. Tok Pisin is also used. *Other:* 3 primary schools. Atui is an island name. Raised coral coast. Tropical forest.

Lihir (Lir) [lih] 12,571 (2000 census). New Ireland Province, Lihir Island, and 3 smaller islands. *Class:* Austronesian, Malayo-Polynesian, Central-Eastern, Eastern Malayo-Polynesian, Oceanic, Western Oceanic, Meso Melanesian, New Ireland, Tabar. *Lg Dev:* Vernacular primary schools. *Other:* Coastal, island. Tropical forest. Sea level. Fishermen; swidden agriculturalists; gold miners. Christian, traditional religion.

Likum [lib] 80 (2000 Wurm). Manus Province. *Class:* Austronesian, Malayo-Polynesian, Central-Eastern, Eastern Malayo-Polynesian, Oceanic, Admiralty Islands, Eastern, Manus, West. *Lg Use:* Speakers also use Lindrou. *Other:* SVO.

Lilau (Ngaimbom) [lll] 449 (1981 Wurm and Hattori). Madang Province, Bogia District. *Class:* Torricelli, Monumbo.

Loniu (Lonio, Ndroku) [los] 460 (1977 Lincoln). Manus Province, Lolak and Loniu villages, south coast of Los Negros Island. *Class:* Austronesian, Malayo-Polynesian, Central-Eastern, Eastern Malayo-Polynesian, Oceanic, Admiralty Islands, Eastern, Manus, Mokoreng-Loniu. *Dialects:* Close to Bipi. *Lg Use:* 70% of the ethnic group speaks Loniu. Most domains. All ages. Moderate bilingualism in Lele and Papitalai. *Lg Dev:* Dictionary. Grammar. *Other:* SVO.

Lote (Uvol) [uvl] 5,500 (2004 SIL). East New Britain Province, Pomio District, southeast coast and inland near Cape Dampier. *Class:* Austronesian, Malayo-Polynesian, Central-Eastern, Eastern Malayo-Polynesian, Oceanic, Western Oceanic, North New Guinea, Ngero-Vitiaz, Vitiaz, Mengen. *Lg Dev:* Literacy rate in first language: 30%. Literacy rate in second language: 60% to 85%. Several vernacular primary schools. Bible portions: 1993–1996. *Other:* Mountain slope. Tropical forest. Sea level to 300 meters. Swidden agriculturalists; fishermen.

Lou [loj] 1,000 (1994 SIL). Manus Province, Lou Island. *Class:* Austronesian, Malayo-Polynesian, Central-Eastern, Eastern Malayo-Polynesian, Oceanic, Admiralty Islands, Eastern, Southeast Islands. *Dialect:* Rei. Three very similar dialects. Rei is dominant. *Lg Use:* Speakers also use Baluan-Pam or Titan. *Other:* Different from Torricelli (Lou) in East Sepik Province or Tate (Lou) in Gulf Province. SVO.

Lusi (Kaliai) [khl] 2,000 (1994 SIL). West New Britain Province, northwest coast. *Class:* Austronesian, Malayo-Polynesian, Central-Eastern, Eastern Malayo-Polynesian, Oceanic, Western Oceanic, North New Guinea, Ngero-Vitiaz, Ngero, Bariai. *Dialect:* Kaliai. *Lg Dev:* Grammar. *Other:* A distinct language from Kove.

Ma (Mawam, Mebu) [mjn] 570 (2003 SIL). Ethnic population: 570. Madang Province, 10 to 20 miles southwest of Saidor, Mibu village and Tariknan village along with hamlets of each village. *Class:* Trans-New Guinea, Main Section, Central and Western, Huon-Finisterre, Finisterre, Yupna. *Dialect:* Mina. Related to Nankina (Jerung). *Lg Use:* Vigorous. Used in the home.

All ages. Interest in language retention and literacy. Tok Pisin is used only in the presence of outsiders and in their church services. Tok Pisin words are intermixed with the Ma language in cases where such a word is not indigenous to their culture. *Lg Dev:* Literacy rate in second language: 20%. Roman script. *Other:* 1,100 to 1,600 meters. Agriculturalists; hunters; animal husbandry: pigs, sheep. Traditional religion, Christian.

Madak (Mandak, Lelet) [mmx] 3,000 (1985 UBS). New Ireland Province, Central New Ireland District. *Class:* Austronesian, Malayo-Polynesian, Central-Eastern, Eastern Malayo-Polynesian, Oceanic, Western Oceanic, Meso Melanesian, New Ireland, Madak. *Dialects:* Danu, Katingan, Lelet, Mesi, Malom. *Lg Dev:* NT: 1995.

Madi (Gira) [grg] 383 (2003 SIL). Madang Province. *Class:* Trans-New Guinea, Main Section, Central and Western, Huon-Finisterre, Finisterre, Gusap-Mot.

Magori [zgr] 100 (2000 Wurm). Central Province, eastern end of Table Bay, lower reaches of Bailebo-Tavenei River. *Class:* Austronesian, Malayo-Polynesian, Central-Eastern, Eastern Malayo-Polynesian, Oceanic, Western Oceanic, Papuan Tip, Peripheral, Central Papuan, Oumic, Magoric. *Dialects:* Closest to Suau. Vocabulary is heavily influenced by Mailu. Ouma, Yoba, and Bina are separate languages. *Lg Use:* Speakers are bilingual or trilingual in Suau, the Gadaisu dialect of Suau, Mailu, or Hiri Motu. *Other:* Probably extinct. Nearly extinct.

Maia (Saki, Pila, Suaro, Turutap, Yakiba, Maya, Banar) [sks] 4,346 (2000 census). Population includes 3,712 in main dialect, 634 in southern dialect. Madang Province, Bogia District, on the mainland south of Manam Island. *Class:* Trans-New Guinea, Madang-Adelbert Range, Adelbert Range, Pihom-Isumrud-Mugil, Kaukombaran. *Lg Dev:* Literacy rate in first language: 25% to 50%. Literacy rate in second language: 50% to 75%. Bible portions: 1988.

Maiadomu (Maiadom) [mzz] 726 (2000 census). Milne Bay Province, Bwaidoka District, East Fergusson Island. *Class:* Austronesian, Malayo-Polynesian, Central-Eastern, Eastern Malayo-Polynesian, Oceanic, Western Oceanic, Papuan Tip, Nuclear, North Papuan Mainland-D'Entrecasteaux, Bwaidoga. *Dialects:* Lexical similarity 62% with Iamalele, 35% with Boselewa, 32% with Gameta, 20% with Dobu. *Lg Dev:* Literacy rate in first language: 5% to 10%. Literacy rate in second language: 20% to 30%. *Other:* Coastal, mountain slope. Tropical forest, savannah. Sea level to 400 meters. Agriculturalists; fishermen.

Maiani (Tani, Banara, Wagimuda, Miani South) [tnh] 3,036 (2003 SIL). Madang Province, Bogia District. *Class:* Trans-New Guinea, Madang-Adelbert Range, Adelbert Range, Pihom-Isumrud-Mugil, Pihom, Kaukombaran. *Dialects:* Different from Mala (Banara). *Lg Dev:* Literacy rate in first language: 25% to 50%. Literacy rate in second language: 50% to 75%. Bible portions: 1982–1988.

Mailu (Magi) [mgu] 6,000 (1980 UBS). Central Province, south coast, Gadaisu to Baramata, Table Bay and Toulon Island. *Class:* Trans-New Guinea, Main Section, Eastern, Central and Southeastern, Mailuan. *Dialects:* Domara, Darava, Asiaoro, Derebai, Island, Geagea, Borebo, Ilai, Baibara. Related to Laua. *Lg Dev:* NT: 1936–1979. *Other:* Education standard above average.

Maisin (Maisan) [mbq] 2,612 (2000 census). Population includes 600 in Kosirava dialect. Oro Province, villages along coast of Collingwood Bay and Kosirava swamp. *Class:* Austronesian, Malayo-Polynesian, Central-Eastern, Eastern Malayo-Polynesian, Oceanic, Western Oceanic, Papuan Tip, Nuclear, Maisin. *Dialects:* Kosirava, Maisin. No closely related languages. Dialects have 73% lexical similarity, but there is little interaction between the speakers. *Lg Use:* Many Maisin are fluent in Korafe, Ubir, and English. *Lg Dev:* Literacy varies from 20% to 80% in different areas. Taught in primary schools. Grammar. *Other:* SOV. Coastal. Swamp. Sea level. Swidden agriculturalists; fishermen.

Maiwa [mti] 1,400 (1998 SIL). Milne Bay Province, Rabaraba District, on the northern slopes and foothills of the Meneao Range eastward from the Mt. Tantam Valley of the Ruaba River; it reaches the coast of Moi Biri Bay, extending into Oro Province. *Class:* Trans-New Guinea, Main Section, Eastern, Central and Southeastern, Dagan. *Dialects:* Maiwa, Oren, Manigara, Gairen, Gwareta. Closest lexical similarity is with Mapena at 41%. *Lg Use:* English is used in religious services. Some speakers also use Motu. *Other:* Lowland. Swamp.

Maiwala [mum] 2,448 (2000 census). Milne Bay Province, Alotau District, Huhu Local Government Area, at the head of Milne Bay. *Class:* Austronesian, Malayo-Polynesian, Central-Eastern, Eastern Malayo-Polynesian, Oceanic, Western Oceanic, Papuan Tip, Nuclear, North Papuan Mainland-D'Entrecasteaux, Are-Taupota, Taupota. *Dialects:* Maiwala is the major dialect. Lexical similarity 67% with Tawala at Diwala village (closest). *Lg Use:* Speakers know English, Suau, Tawala, some Motu. *Lg Dev:* Taught in primary schools. *Other:* Two schools.

Makayam (Aturu, Atura, Adulu, Makaeyam, Tirio) [aup] 1,298 (2003 SIL). Western Province, Sumogi Island in Fly Estuary, Adulu, Lewada, and Suame villages. Giribam dialect spoken in Janor village. *Class:* Trans-New Guinea, Trans-Fly-Bulaka River, Trans-Fly, Tirio. *Dialect:* Giribam. Lexical similarity 79% with Giribam, 52% with Bitur, 47% with Were, 32% with Baramu. *Lg Use:* Lewada and Suame reported consistent use of the vernacular by children. The 82 residents of Janor village include native speakers of both Bitur and Makayam. The children use both Bitur and Makayam. Giribam is reportedly the sole language of the home in Janor village. Aduru village reported children starting to use English amongst themselves.

Makolkol [zmh] 7 (1988 SIL). East New Britain Province, Gazelle Peninsula. *Class:* East Papuan, Yele-Solomons-New Britain, New Britain, Baining-Taulil. *Other:* Nearly extinct.

Mala (Malala, Pay, Pai, Alam, Banara, Dagoi, Hatzfeldhafen, Dagui) [ped] 1,390 (2003 SIL). Madang Province, Bogia District. *Class:* Trans-New Guinea, Madang-Adelbert Range, Adelbert Range, Pihom-Isumrud-Mugil, Pihom, Kaukombaran. *Lg Use:* Increasing use of Tok Pisin. *Lg Dev:* Literacy rate in first language: 25% to 50%. Literacy rate in second language: 50% to 75%. Bible portions: 1982–1988. *Other:* Distinct from Maiani (Banara), and from Pei (Pai) in Walio group. SOV. Coastal. Savannah, scrub, tropical forest. Sea level. Swidden agriculturalists; fishermen.

Malalamai (Bonga) [mmt] 548 (2003 SIL). Madang Province, Rai coast east and west of Saidor; Malalamai and Bonga villages. *Class:* Austronesian, Malayo-Polynesian, Central-Eastern, Eastern Malayo-Polynesian, Oceanic, Western Oceanic, North New Guinea, Ngero-Vitiaz, Ngero, Bariai.

Malas [mkr] 650 (2003 SIL). Madang Province near Tokain. *Class:* Trans-New Guinea, Madang-Adelbert Range, Adelbert Range, Pihom-Isumrud-Mugil, Isumrud, Mabuan.

Malasanga [mqz] 900 (2000 census). Morobe Province, north coast, two villages: Malasanga and Singorokai. *Class:* Austronesian, Malayo-Polynesian, Central-Eastern, Eastern Malayo-Polynesian, Oceanic, Western Oceanic, North New Guinea, Ngero-Vitiaz, Vitiaz, Korap. *Dialects:* Malasanga, Singorokai. Separate from Karnai. *Lg Use:* All ages.

Male (Koliku) [mdc] 972 (2000 census). Madang Province, coast south of Bom. *Class:* Trans-New Guinea, Madang-Adelbert Range, Madang, Rai Coast, Mindjim. *Dialects:* Related to Bongu and Anjam.

Maleu-Kilenge (Idne) [mgl] 5,200 (1983 census). Population includes 1,561 Kilenge. West New Britain Province, Talasea District, western tip. *Class:* Austronesian, Malayo-Polynesian, Central-Eastern, Eastern Malayo-Polynesian, Oceanic, Western Oceanic, North New Guinea, Ngero-Vitiaz, Vitiaz, Kilenge-Maleu. *Dialect:* Maleu, Kilenge (Kaitarolea). Lexical similarity 93% between Maleu and Kilenge. *Lg Use:* All or nearly the whole Kilenge ethnic group speaks Kilenge. Kilenge dialect: all ages. *Lg Dev:* Literacy rate in first language: 25% to 50%. Literacy rate in second language: 50% to 75%. Bible portions: 1990. *Other:* Wurm and Hattori (1981), and M. Ross (1988) treat Maleu and Kilenge as separate languages. SVO. Coastal, mountain slope, volcanic. Savannah, tropical forest. Swidden agriculturalists.

Mali (Gaktai) [gcc] 2,200 (1988 SIL). East New Britain Province, eastern Gazelle Peninsula. *Class:* East Papuan, Yele-Solomons-New Britain, New Britain, Baining-Taulil. *Dialects:* A distinct language within the Baining ethnic group. Two dialects. *Other:* Several primary schools. Mountain slope, coastal.

Malinguat (Tshwosh, Tshuosh, Kwaruwikwundi, Sepik Plains) [sic] 9,000 (1986 PBT). East Sepik Province, Maprik District, Sepik Plains south of Maprik. *Class:* Sepik-Ramu, Sepik, Middle Sepik, Ndu. *Dialects:* Koiwat, Burui, Chimbian, Central Sawos, Eastern Sawos. Close to Gaikundi.

Malol (Malon, Malolo) [mbk] 3,330. Sandaun Province, around Malol village. *Class:* Austronesian, Malayo-Polynesian, Central-Eastern, Eastern Malayo-Polynesian, Oceanic, Western Oceanic, North New Guinea, Schouten, Siau. *Other:* Distinct enough from Sissano, Arop-Sissano, and Sera that it will probably need separate literature.

Mamaa (Mama) [mhf] 198 (1978 McElhanon). Morobe Province, 1 village. *Class:* Trans-New Guinea, Main Section, Central and Western, Huon-Finisterre, Finisterre, Erap.

Mamusi (Kakuna) [kdf] 6,000 (1985 SIL). East New Britain Province, southeast coast, inland on the Melkoi and Torlu rivers. Inland villages are up to 40 km from the coast. *Class:* Austronesian, Malayo-Polynesian, Central-Eastern, Eastern Malayo-Polynesian, Oceanic, Western Oceanic, North New Guinea, Ngero-Vitiaz, Vitiaz, Mengen. *Dialect:* Mamusi, Melkoi (Kakuna). *Lg Use:* Used in the home and village. Speakers also use Tok Pisin. *Lg Dev:* Literacy rate in second language: only young people. *Other:* Scattered village schools. 900 meters.

Manam (Manum) [mva] 7,949 (2003 SIL). Manam and Boesa islands, Madang Province, Bogia District, and in Sepa and Wanami on the adjacent mainland. *Class:* Austronesian, Malayo-Polynesian, Central-Eastern, Eastern Malayo-Polynesian, Oceanic, Western Oceanic, North New Guinea, Schouten, Kairiru-Manam, Manam. *Dialect:* Wanami. Related to Wogeo, Biem, Sepa, Medebur. *Lg Dev:* Grammar. NT: 1996. *Other:* Different from Manem. SOV. Coastal. Tropical forest. Sea level to 300 meters. Swidden agriculturalists.

Manambu [mle] 2,105 (2003 SIL). East Sepik Province, Ambunti Subprovince, 3 villages along the Sepik River. *Class:* Sepik-Ramu, Sepik, Middle Sepik, Ndu. *Lg Dev:* Literacy rate in first language: 5% to 15%. Literacy rate in second language: 15% to 25%. NT: 1979. *Other:* Different from Manumbo in Madang Province. Riverine. 50 meters. Fishermen; sago gatherers. Traditional religion, Christian.

Mandara (Madara, Tabar) [tbf] 2,500 (1985 SIL). New Ireland Province, Simberi, Tatau, Tabar and one other island. *Class:* Austronesian, Malayo-Polynesian, Central-Eastern, Eastern Malayo-Polynesian, Oceanic, Western Oceanic, Meso Melanesian, New Ireland, Lavongai-Nalik. *Dialects:* Simberi, Tatau, Tabar. *Lg Dev:* 6 Mandara prep schools and 7 primary schools.

Manem (Yeti, Jeti, Wembi, Skofro) [jet] 500 in Papua New Guinea (1993 SIL). Population total all countries: 900. Sandaun Province, 1 village; Skotiau. Also spoken in Indonesia (Papua). *Class:* Trans-New Guinea, Northern, Border, Waris. *Dialects:* Lexical similarity 50% with Waris. *Lg Dev:* Significant literacy in Tok Pisin and Bahasa Indonesia. *Other:* Different from Manam.

Mangseng (Mangsing, Masegi, Maseki) [mbh] 2,500 (1998 SIL). West New Britain and East New Britain provinces, area south of Commodore Bay (north coast, West New Britain), through to Montagu Harbor (south coast of East New Britain) on the east and through to Fulleborn Harbor (south coast of West New Britain) on the west. *Class:* Austronesian, Malayo-Polynesian, Central-Eastern, Eastern Malayo-Polynesian, Oceanic, Western Oceanic, North New Guinea, Ngero-Vitiaz, Vitiaz, Southwest New Britain, Arawe-Pasismanua, Arawe. *Dialects:* Umua, Marapu. Arawe chain isolate, most closely related to West Arawe. *Lg Dev:* Literacy rate in first language: 25% to 50%. Literacy rate in second language: 25% to 50%. NT: 1999.

Mape [mlh] 5,117 (1978 McElhanon). Morobe Province along the Mape River. *Class:* Trans-New Guinea, Main Section, Central and Western, Huon-Finisterre, Huon, Eastern. *Dialects:* Naga, Mape, Nigac, Fukac. Close to Kâte, which is the lingua franca. *Lg Use:* Naga and Nigac dialects may be extinct.

Mapena [mnm] 274 (1973 SIL). Milne Bay Province, around Mt. Gwoira. *Class:* Trans-New Guinea, Main Section, Eastern, Central and Southeastern, Dagan. *Dialects:* Lexical similarity 51% with Daga (closest).

Maramba [myd] 300 (1981 Wurm and Hattori). East Sepik Province. *Class:* Sepik-Ramu, Ramu, Yuat-Langam, Yuat-Maramba, Maramba.

Mari (Hop) [hob] 810 (2000 D. Tryon). Madang Province, upper Ramu River. 4 villages. *Class:* Austronesian, Malayo-Polynesian, Central-Eastern, Eastern Malayo-Polynesian, Oceanic, Western Oceanic, North New Guinea, Huon Gulf, Markham, Upper, Mountain. *Other:* Different from Mari of East Sepik Province and Mari of Western Province.

Mari [mbx] 80 (2000 Wurm). East Sepik Province, near Mari Lake and on Salumei River. *Class:* Sepik-Ramu, Sepik, Sepik Hill, Bahinemo. *Lg Use:* Used only in the home. A few children speak Mari. People neutral toward Mari. Speakers are highly bilingual in Tok Pisin. *Other:* Different from Mari of Madang Province and Mari of Western Province.

Maria (Manubara) [mds] 870 (1980 census). Central Province, Marshall Lagoon to Mt. Brown; a remote area. *Class:* Trans-New Guinea, Main Section, Eastern, Central and Southeastern, Manubaran. *Dialects:* Didigaru, Maria, Gebi, Oibu, Amota, Imila, Uderi. Lexical similarity 63% with Doromu (closest).

Marik (Dami, Ham) [dad] 3,500 (1998 SIL). Madang Province, Madang District, inland around Gogol River. 10 villages. *Class:* Austronesian, Malayo-Polynesian, Central-Eastern, Eastern Malayo-Polynesian, Oceanic, Western Oceanic, North New Guinea, Ngero-Vitiaz, Vitiaz, Bel, Nuclear Bel, Southern. *Dialects:* Northern Marik, Western Marik, Southern Marik. *Lg Dev:* Bible portions: 1989. *Other:* SOV. Interfluvial. Tropical forest. Above 40 meters. Agriculturalists.

Maring (Mareng, Yoadabe-Watoare) [mbw] 11,000 (1998 SIL). Western Highlands Province, Hagen District. A small number are over the Bismarck Range in Madang Province. 18 villages. *Class:* Trans-New Guinea, Main Section, Central and Western, East New Guinea Highlands, Central, Jimi. *Dialects:* Central Maring, Eastern Maring, Timbunki, Tsuwenki, Karamba, Kambegl. Speakers of all dialects understand the central one. *Lg Dev:* Literacy rate in first language: below 5%. Literacy rate in second language: below 5%. Grammar. Bible portions: 1974–1979. *Other:* SOV. Mountain slope. Tropical forest. 400 to 2,734 meters. Swidden agriculturalists.

Matepi [mqe] 284 (2003 SIL). Madang Province. *Class:* Trans-New Guinea, Madang-Adelbert Range, Madang, Mabuso, Hanseman. *Dialects:* Related to Rapting, Wamas, Samosa, Murupi, Saruga, Nake, Mosimo, Garus, Yoidik, Rempi, Silopi, Utu, Mawan, Baimak, Bagupi, Gal, Garuh, Bemal.

Mato (Nenaya, Nengaya, Nineia) [met] 580 (2002 SIL). Morobe Province, north coast of Huon Peninsula, near Morobe-Madang provincial border, Uruwa River plain 38 km west of Wasu, 20 km north of Sapmanga, approximately 55 km southeast of Saidor. *Class:* Austronesian, Malayo-Polynesian, Central-Eastern, Eastern Malayo-Polynesian, Oceanic, Western Oceanic, North New Guinea, Ngero-Vitiaz, Vitiaz, Roinji-Nenaya. *Dialects:* Bonea, Nanaya. Lexical similarity 67% with Ronji, 39% with Karnai and Arop-Lukep, 38% with Malasanga, 29% with Sio, 23% with Tuam-Mutu. *Lg Dev:* Literacy rate in first language: 4%. Literacy rate in second language: 41%. *Other:* SVO. Mountain slope, coastal. Savannah, tropical forest. Sea level to 550 meters. Swidden agriculturalists. Christian, traditional religion.

Matukar [mjk] 434 (2003 SIL). Ethnic population: 434. Madang Province, 40 miles north of Madang town around Matukar. *Class:* Austronesian, Malayo-Polynesian, Central-Eastern, Eastern Malayo-Polynesian, Oceanic, Western Oceanic, North New Guinea, Ngero-Vitiaz, Vitiaz, Bel, Nuclear Bel, Northern. *Dialects:* Related to Gedaged. *Lg Use:* All ages. *Other:* Coastal.

Mauwake (Ulingan, Mawake) [mhl] 2,392 (2003 SIL). Madang Province, Bogia District, east of Malala High School. *Class:* Trans-New Guinea, Madang-Adelbert Range, Adelbert Range, Pihom-Isumrud-Mugil, Pihom, Kumilan. *Dialects:* Related to Moere. *Lg Dev:* Literacy rate in first language: 25% to 50%. Literacy rate in second language: 50% to 75%. NT: 1998. *Other:* Christian, traditional religion.

Mawak [mjj] 25 (2000 Wurm). Madang Province, southwest of Mauwake. *Class:* Trans-New Guinea, Madang-Adelbert Range, Adelbert Range, Pihom-Isumrud-Mugil, Pihom, Tiboran. *Dialects:* Related to Hinahon. *Other:* Nearly extinct.

Mawan [mcz] 471 (2003 SIL). Madang Province, Gogol River area. *Class:* Trans-New Guinea, Madang-Adelbert Range, Madang, Mabuso, Hanseman. *Lg Use:* Speakers are older adults. Speakers also use Tok Pisin.

Mbo-Ung (Tembalo, Bo-Ung, Mboung) [mux] 40,948 (2000 census). Western Highlands Province, Hagen District. Some also in Tambul and Lower Kaugel districts. *Class:* Trans-New Guinea, Main Section, Central and Western, East New Guinea Highlands, Central, Hagen, Kaugel. *Dialects:* Miyemu (Miyem), Mara-Gomu, Tembalo (Tembaglo). *Lg Use:* Some also use Medlpa. *Lg Dev:* Bible portions: 1989–1990. *Other:* SOV. Mountain slope and valley. 1,000 to 2,400 meters.

Mbula (Mangap-Mbula, Mangaaba, Mangaawa, Mangaava, Mangap. Kaimanga) [mna] 2,500 (1991 SIL). Morobe Province, Siassi District, 6 villages on eastern Umboi Island, 1 village on Sakar Island. *Class:* Austronesian,

Malayo-Polynesian, Central-Eastern, Eastern Malayo-Polynesian, Oceanic, Western Oceanic, North New Guinea, Ngero-Vitiaz, Vitiaz, Mangap-Mbula. *Dialects:* Mbula (Central Mbula), Northern Mbula, Gauru, Sakar. *Lg Dev:* Literacy rate in first language: 15% to 25%. Literacy rate in second language: 25% to 50%. Grammar. NT: 1997. *Other:* SVO; prepositions. Coastal. Tropical forest. Sea level. Swidden agriculturalists. Christian, traditional religion.

Medebur [mjm] 514 (2003 SIL). Ethnic population: 514. Madang Province, coast just north of Sikor at Medebur. *Class:* Austronesian, Malayo-Polynesian, Central-Eastern, Eastern Malayo-Polynesian, Oceanic, Western Oceanic, North New Guinea, Schouten, Kairiru-Manam, Manam. *Dialects:* Related to Wogeo, Biem, Sepa, Manam. *Lg Use:* All ages.

Mehek (Nuku, Me'ek, Driafleisuma, Indinogosima) [nux] 6,300 (1994 SIL). Sandaun Province, Nuku District, Makru-Klaplei area, lower foothills of Torricelli Mountains, southeast of Siliput. 9 large villages. *Class:* Sepik-Ramu, Sepik, Tama. *Dialects:* Lexical similarity 51% with Pahi (closest). *Lg Use:* Vigorous. Used in the home and village life. Positive language attitude. Speakers also use Tok Pisin. *Lg Dev:* Literacy rate in second language: 50% to 75%. *Other:* 50% or more of the children are in primary school. Mountain slope.

Mekeo (Mekeo-Kovio) [mek] 19,000 (2003 SIL). Central Province, Kaiyuku District, inland, bounded on the west by the Waima, on the east by the Kuni and Kunimaipa. Extends into Gulf Province. *Class:* Austronesian, Malayo-Polynesian, Central-Eastern, Eastern Malayo-Polynesian, Oceanic, Western Oceanic, Papuan Tip, Peripheral, Central Papuan, West Central Papuan, Nuclear. *Dialect:* East Mekeo, West Mekeo, North Mekeo, Northwest Mekeo (Kovio). Kovio is a peripheral dialect. The four dialects are mutually unintelligible to each other's speakers, except for North and West Mekeo, but most Mekeo are reported to have familiarity with neighboring dialects. Kovio, however, is not contiguous to the other dialects. Kovio has 81% lexical similarity with West Mekeo and North Mekeo, and 79% with East Mekeo. West and East Mekeo have 87% lexical similarity. North Mekeo has 99% lexical similarity with West Mekeo and 87% with East Mekeo. Mekeo has 41% with Waima. *Lg Use:* Positive language attitude. *Lg Dev:* Grammar. NT: 1998. *Other:* "Kovio" is pejorative in some contexts. The educational standard is above average.

Mekmek [mvk] 1,036 (1981 Wurm and Hattori). East Sepik Province. *Class:* Sepik-Ramu, Ramu, Yuat-Langam, Yuat-Maramba, Yuat. *Dialects:* Related to Changriwa, Kyenele, Biwat, Bun.

Melpa (Medlpa, Hagen) [med] 130,000 (1991 SIL). Western Highlands Province, Hagen District. *Class:* Trans-New Guinea, Main Section, Central and Western, East New Guinea Highlands, Central, Hagen. *Dialect:* Tembagla. Only slight dialect differences. *Lg Dev:* Literacy rate in first language: 5% to 15%. Literacy rate in second language: 25% to 50%. NT: 1965–1995. *Other:* Swidden agriculturalists: sweet potatoes, yams, taro, maize, coffee. Traditional religion, Christian.

Mende (Seim) [sim] 5,697 (2003 SIL). Sandaun Province, Nuku District, fifteen villages east of Mehek. *Class:* Sepik-Ramu, Sepik, Middle Sepik, Nukuma. *Dialects:* Lexical similarity 49% to nearest Kwanga village. *Other:* 'Wamsak' is a village, not a language name.

Mengen (Poeng) [mee] 8,400 (1982 SIL). East New Britain Province, Pomio District, Jacquinot Bay and inland. 20 villages. *Class:* Austronesian, Malayo-Polynesian, Central-Eastern, Eastern Malayo-Polynesian, Oceanic, Western Oceanic, North New Guinea, Ngero-

Vitiaz, Vitiaz, Mengen. *Dialects:* North Coast Mengen (Maeng), South Coast Mengen (Poeng), Bush Mengen (Inland Mengen, Longueinga). Some linguists separate Poeng (Mengen 1, Bush Mengen) and Maeng (Mengen 2, Orford, Maenge) into two languages (see, for example, Ross and Tryon 2000). *Lg Dev:* Literacy rate in first language: 5% to 15%. Literacy rate in second language: 25% to 50%. NT: 2003. *Other:* SVO. Coastal. Tropical forest. Sea level to 70 meters. Fishermen; swidden agriculturalists.

Menya (Menye, Menyama) [mcr] 20,000 (1998 SIL). Morobe Province, Menyamya District, north along the Tauri River and its tributaries. *Class:* Trans-New Guinea, Main Section, Central and Western, Angan, Angan Proper. *Lg Dev:* Literacy rate in first language: 5% to 15%. Literacy rate in second language: 15% to 25%. Bible portions: 1995. *Other:* SOV. Mountain slope. Tropical forest, savannah. 1,100 to 2,300 meters. Swidden agriculturalists.

Meramera (Ubili, Melamela) [mxm] 2,000 (1995 SIL). 5% monolingual. West New Britain Province, Bialla District, northwest coast. *Class:* Austronesian, Malayo-Polynesian, Central-Eastern, Eastern Malayo-Polynesian, Oceanic, Western Oceanic, Meso Melanesian, Willaumez. *Dialect:* Lolobao. *Lg Use:* Moderately vigorous. Some neighboring-language speakers speak it. All domains to each other. Some use in church. Oral literature. All ages. They are not proud of their language, but they say it speaks to their hearts. More than 90% can use Mengen or Kol. English is the language used in school. *Lg Dev:* Literacy rate in first language: 0% to 5%. Literacy rate in second language: 50% to 75%. Vernacular school discontinued. *Other:* SVO. Coastal. Sea level. Swidden agriculturalists; cocoa; fishermen; copra production; oil palm. Christian.

Mese (Mesem, Momolili, Momalili) [mci] 4,000 (1997 census). Morobe Province, Lae District, Boana Subdistrict, interior north of Lae. 14 villages: Samanzing, Biliman, Tusulu, Hobu, Zezegi, Momolili, Zitare, Malapipi, Kwamu, Busu, Nomenga, Zitale-Ogaw, Tuzing, Kaisia. Sambuen is a border community with both Nabak and Mese speakers. *Class:* Trans-New Guinea, Main Section, Central and Western, Huon-Finisterre, Huon, Western. *Dialects:* West-Central Mese, East Mese, Momolili, Zezagi. *Lg Use:* Men 50 years old and older can speak either Yabem or Kâte. Most adults under 30 also use Tok Pisin. *Lg Dev:* Literacy rate in first language: below 5%. Literacy rate in second language: 5% to 15%. Bible portions: 1996–1997. *Other:* Community schools at Hobu and Samanzing. SOV; adjectives, numerals after noun heads; verb affixes mark number; CV, CVC, CVV, CCV, VC, V; nontonal. Mountain slope. Tropical forest. 600 to 1,700 meters. Swidden agriculturalists: coffee. Christian, traditional religion.

Mian (Mianmin) [mpt] 2,200 (1981 Wurm and Hattori). Sandaun Province, Telefomin District, north part of the Fak (Hak) and Aki River valleys, headwaters of the August River and upper May River. Villages: Nenebil, Suganga, Blimo, and Wagarabai. *Class:* Trans-New Guinea, Main Section, Central and Western, Central and South New Guinea-Kutubuan, Central and South New Guinea, Ok, Mountain. *Dialects:* Upper August River, Usage, Mianmin. Dialects have 75% to 83% lexical similarity. *Lg Dev:* Literacy rate in first language: 25% to 50%. Literacy rate in second language: 25% to 50%. NT: 1986. *Other:* 'Mianmin' is the name for the people.

Miani (Bonaputa-Mopu, Tani, Miani North) [pla] 1,500 (1987 SIL). Madang Province, Bogia District, inland. *Class:* Trans-New Guinea, Madang-Adelbert Range, Adelbert Range, Pihom-Isumrud-Mugil, Pihom, Kaukombaran. *Lg Dev:* Literacy rate in first language:

25% to 50%. Literacy rate in second language: 50% to
75%. Bible portions: 1982.

Migabac (Migaba') [mpp] 1,300 (1990 SIL). Morobe
Province, Masaweng River area. 5 villages divided among
3 dialects: Hudewa and Waringai; Ago; Butengka and
Kapawa. *Class:* Trans-New Guinea, Main Section, Central
and Western, Huon-Finisterre, Huon, Eastern. *Dialects:*
North Migabac, South Migabac, Central Migabac. *Lg Use:*
Speakers also use Kâte, the lingua franca.

Minanibai (Pepeha, Eme-Eme, Hei) [mcv] 300 (1981
Wurm and Hattori). Ikobi Kairi and Goaribari Census
districts, near the mouth of the Omati River, Gulf
Province. *Class:* Trans-New Guinea, Inland Gulf,
Minanibai. *Dialects:* Related to Mubami. *Lg Use:* Might
be extinct.

Minaveha (Minavega, Kukuya) [mvn] 2,000 (2002 SIL).
600 monolinguals. Milne Bay Province, Bolubolu District,
southwest tip of Fergusson Island near Mapamoiwa
station. *Class:* Austronesian, Malayo-Polynesian, Central-
Eastern, Eastern Malayo-Polynesian, Oceanic, Western
Oceanic, Papuan Tip, Nuclear, North Papuan Mainland-
D'Entrecasteaux, Are-Taupota, Taupota. *Dialects:* Lexical
similarity 60% with Iamalele (closest), Koluawawa, and
Bwaidoka. *Lg Use:* Vigorous. Koluwawa speakers use it
as second language. All domains. Used in preschool, oral
literature. All ages. Positive language attitude. Some
bilingualism in Dobu, which is the lingua franca. About
1,200 can also speak some English, Bwaidoka, Iamalele,
or Koluwawa. English use is increasing slowly. *Lg Dev:*
Literacy rate in first language: 35%. Literacy rate in
second language: 15% to 25%. 800 can read it, 200 can
write it. Dictionary. Bible portions: 1993–1995. *Other:*
'Kukuya' is the name of a prominent village. There is
little arable land, and population increase endangers the
future of agriculture. SOV. Coastal, mountain slope.
Agriculturalists. Traditional religion, Christian.

Mindiri [mpn] 80 (2000 Wurm). Madang Province, along
the Rai Coast west of Saidor, 1 village. *Class:*
Austronesian, Malayo-Polynesian, Central-Eastern, Eastern
Malayo-Polynesian, Oceanic, Western Oceanic, North
New Guinea, Ngero-Vitiaz, Vitiaz, Bel, Astrolabe.
Dialects: Close to Biliau and Wab.

Minigir (Lungalunga) [vmg] 598 (2000 WCD). East New
Britain Province, Gazelle Peninsula, Lungalunga village
on Ataliklikun Bay. *Class:* Austronesian, Malayo-
Polynesian, Central-Eastern, Eastern Malayo-Polynesian,
Oceanic, Western Oceanic, Meso Melanesian, New
Ireland, South New Ireland-Northwest Solomonic, Mono-
Uruava. *Lg Use:* 40% of the ethnic group speak Minigir.
Most key domains. All ages.

Misima-Paneati (Panaieti, Panaeati, Paneyate, Paneate,
Panayeti) [mpx] 18,000 (2002 SIL). 4,000 monolinguals.
Milne Bay Province, Misima District, Misima Island,
Panaieti, and all the islands of the Calvados Chain (not
including) Panawina, Alcester, Ole, and Tewatewan
Islands, and Bowagis on Woodlark Island. 32 villages.
Class: Austronesian, Malayo-Polynesian, Central-Eastern,
Eastern Malayo-Polynesian, Oceanic, Western Oceanic,
Papuan Tip, Peripheral, Kilivila-Louisiades, Misima.
Dialects: Nasikwabw (Tokunu), Tewatewa. Lexical
similarity 33% with Nimowa and Dobu (closest). *Lg Use:*
Some use it as a second language. *Lg Dev:* Literacy rate
in first language: 75% to 80%. Literacy rate in second
language: 75% to 80%. Many schools. Many go to
secondary school, one secondary school on Misima. NT:
1947–1998. *Other:* SOV. Coastal. Tropical forest. Sea
level to 1,000 meters. Swidden agriculturalists.

Miu (Myu) [mpo] 500 (1998 NTM). West New Britain
Province, Gimi Rauto District, southwest interior. *Class:*
Austronesian, Malayo-Polynesian, Central-Eastern, Eastern
Malayo-Polynesian, Oceanic, Western Oceanic, North

New Guinea, Ngero-Vitiaz, Vitiaz, Southwest New
Britain, Arawe-Pasismanua, Pasismanua. *Dialects:* A
separate language from Kaulong. *Lg Use:* 40% of the
ethnic group speak Miu. All ages. *Lg Dev:* Literacy rate
in first language: 20%. Literacy rate in second language:
20%. NT: 2003. *Other:* The people live in hamlets of 1 or
2 families. SVO; some minor affixation. Mountain slope,
foothills. Tropical forest. 100 to 600 meters. Agriculturalists: taro, sweet potato, cassava, cucumber, papaya,
banana, pineapple, coconut, maize; animal husbandry:
pigs. Traditional religion, Christian.

Moere [mvq] 50 (2000 Wurm). Madang Province. *Class:*
Trans-New Guinea, Madang-Adelbert Range, Adelbert
Range, Pihom-Isumrud-Mugil, Pihom, Kumilan. *Dialects:*
Related to Mauwake, Bepour.

Moikodi (Doriri) [mkp] 571 (1981 Wurm and Hattori).
50% are monolingual. Oro Province, north slopes of Owen
Stanley Range around Mt. Brown down to Komi west of
Foasi Creek. *Class:* Trans-New Guinea, Main Section,
Eastern, Central and Southeastern, Yareban. *Dialects:*
Several dialects. Lexical similarity 65% to 73% with
Aneme Wake (closest). *Lg Use:* Speakers also use Hiri
Motu.

Mokerang (Mokareng, Mokoreng) [mft] 200 (1981 Wurm
and Hattori). Manus Province, north Los Negros Island
and Ndrilo Island. *Class:* Austronesian, Malayo-
Polynesian, Central-Eastern, Eastern Malayo-Polynesian,
Oceanic, Admiralty Islands, Eastern, Manus, Mokoreng-
Loniu. *Lg Use:* All ages. *Other:* SVO.

Molima (Ebadidi, Salakahadi, Morima, Fagululu) [mox]
3,186 (1972 census). Population includes 416 in Fagululu,
600 in Salakahadi. Milne Bay Province, 'Esa'ala District,
West Fergusson Island, inland villages of the Salakahadi
and Ebadidi areas, central west coast (Fagululu) and
central south coast (Molima). *Class:* Austronesian,
Malayo-Polynesian, Central-Eastern, Eastern Malayo-
Polynesian, Oceanic, Western Oceanic, Papuan Tip,
Nuclear, North Papuan Mainland-D'Entrecasteaux,
Bwaidoga. *Dialects:* Tala'ai, Ai'alu, Tosila'ai. One dialect
is on the coast, two dialects are remote in the mountains.
Lexical similarity 56% with Dobu. *Lg Use:* Church
leaders, community leaders, traders, and travellers also use
Dobu. *Lg Dev:* Literacy rate in first language: 15% to
30%. Literacy rate in second language: 15% to 30%. Bible
portions: 1996–1997. *Other:* 'Molima' refers to the whole
area, as well as the south coast only; 'Ebadidi',
'Salakahadi', and 'Fagululu' to parts of it. Mountain slope,
coastal. Tropical forest. Sea level to 500 meters. Swidden
agriculturalists; hunters; gatherers; fishermen. Traditional
religion, Christian.

Momare (Momale, Momole) [msz] 650 (2003 SIL).
Morobe Province, north of Masaweng River. *Class:*
Trans-New Guinea, Main Section, Central and Western,
Huon-Finisterre, Huon, Eastern. *Lg Use:* Speakers are
older adults. Most also use Kâte.

Mondropolon [npn] 300 (1981 Wurm and Hattori).
Manus Province, north central coast, Manus Island. *Class:*
Austronesian, Malayo-Polynesian, Central-Eastern, Eastern
Malayo-Polynesian, Oceanic, Admiralty Islands, Eastern,
Manus, West. *Lg Use:* All ages. Positive language
attitude. Most also use Kurti. *Other:* SVO.

Mongol [mgt] 336 (2003 SIL). East Sepik Province.
Class: Sepik-Ramu, Ramu, Yuat-Langam, Mongol-
Langam. *Dialects:* Related to Langam, Yaul.

Monumbo [mxk] 412 (2003 SIL). Madang Province,
Bogia District. *Class:* Torricelli, Monumbo.

Morawa [mze] 755 (1973 SIL). Central Province, south
coast around Cloudy Bay. *Class:* Trans-New Guinea,
Main Section, Eastern, Central and Southeastern, Mailuan.
Dialects: Lexical similarity 70% with Binahari (closest).
Lg Use: Most speakers also use Magi, Suau, Hiri Motu, or

English. Suau used in religious services. Hiri Motu has been used as a trade language.

Moresada (Murisapa, Murusapa-Sarewa) [msx] 197 (1981 Wurm and Hattori). Madang Province. *Class:* Trans-New Guinea, Madang-Adelbert Range, Adelbert Range, Josephstaal-Wanang, Josephstaal, Pomoikan.

Morigi (Morigi Island, Wariadai, Turama River Kiwai, Dabura) [mdb] 700 (1975 Wurm). Gulf Province, Lower Turama Census Division. *Class:* Trans-New Guinea, Trans-Fly-Bulaka River, Trans-Fly, Kiwaian. *Lg Dev:* Literacy rate in first language: below 5%. Literacy rate in second language: below 5%.

Mosimo [mqv] 50 (2000 Wurm). Madang Province. *Class:* Trans-New Guinea, Madang-Adelbert Range, Madang, Mabuso, Hanseman. *Dialects:* Related to Rapting, Wamas, Samosa, Murupi, Saruga, Nake, Matepi, Garus, Yoidik, Rempi, Silopi, Utu, Mawan, Baimak, Bagupi, Gal, Garuh, Kamba.

Motu (True Motu, Pure Motu) [meu] 14,000 (1981 Wurm and Hattori). Central Province, in and around Port Moresby, villages along the coast from Manumanu, Galley Reach, to GabaGaba (Kapakapa). *Class:* Austronesian, Malayo-Polynesian, Central-Eastern, Eastern Malayo-Polynesian, Oceanic, Western Oceanic, Papuan Tip, Peripheral, Central Papuan, Sinagoro-Keapara. *Dialects:* Western Motu, Eastern Motu. *Lg Dev:* Dictionary. Bible: 1973. *Other:* Government schools in all villages.

Motu, Hiri (Police Motu, Pidgin Motu, Hiri) [hmo] Very few first-language speakers (1992 T. Dutton). Central Province, in and around Port Moresby area, also throughout Oro, Central, Gulf, and part of Milne Bay provinces, some in Western Province. *Class:* Pidgin, Motu based. *Dialects:* Austronesian Hiri Motu, Papuan Hiri Motu. Linguistically a pidginization of True Motu. Also influenced by English, Tok Pisin, and Polynesian languages. Speakers of Hiri Motu cannot understand Motu. There are phonological and grammatical differences. Lexical similarity 90% with Motu. *Lg Use:* Official language. 120,000 second-language speakers (1989 J. Holm). Papuan Hiri Motu is more widespread and considered as the standard. *Lg Dev:* Literacy rate in first language: below 5%. Dictionary. Bible: 1994.

Mouk-Aria (Aria-Mouk) [mwh] 626 (1982 SIL). West New Britain Province, southeast coast to northwest coast, Kandrian District. *Class:* Austronesian, Malayo-Polynesian, Central-Eastern, Eastern Malayo-Polynesian, Oceanic, Western Oceanic, North New Guinea, Ngero-Vitiaz, Vitiaz, Southwest New Britain, Bibling. *Dialects:* Mouk (Mok), Tourai. *Lg Dev:* NT: 1994.

Mubami (Tao-Suamato, Tao-Suame, Dausuami, Dausame, Ta) [tsx] 1,730 (2002 SIL). Western Province, northeastern corner, middle and lower Wawoi River and Guavi River, villages of Parieme, Sogae (Sipsi), Diwami, Kubeai, Waliho (Warehou), Paueme, Ugu (Kala) on Aramia River. *Class:* Trans-New Guinea, Inland Gulf, Minanibai. *Dialects:* Lexical similarity 42% with Minanibai (closest). *Lg Use:* Vigorous. Used in the home and cultural events, social events along with other languages. Vernacular instruction first two years. All ages. Positive language attitude. Some speakers also use English, Tok Pisin, Hiri Motu, Hoyahoya, Bamu, or Gogodala. Women tend to control fewer languages than men. Many women are monolingual. *Lg Dev:* Literacy rate in first language: below 5%. Literacy rate in second language: below 5%. Taught in primary schools. *Other:* SOV. Lowland. Forests, swamp. Below 100 meters. Traditional religion, Christian.

Muduapa (Vitu, Witu) [wiv] 8,800 (1991 SIL). West New Britain Province, Talasea District, Vitu and Mudua islands

off the northwest coast. *Class:* Austronesian, Malayo-Polynesian, Central-Eastern, Eastern Malayo-Polynesian, Oceanic, Western Oceanic, Meso Melanesian, Bali-Vitu. *Dialects:* 2 or 3 dialects. The variety spoken on Mudua Island may be a separate language. Related to Bali. *Lg Dev:* Literacy rate in first language: 15% to 25%. Literacy rate in second language: 75% to 100%. Two or more vernacular primary schools. Bible portions: 2001. *Other:* 'Vitu' is the name of the island. Islands, coastal. Sea level to 300 meters. Swidden agriculturalists; fishermen; copra production.

Mufian (Southern Arapesh, Muhiang, Muhian) [aoj] 11,000 (1998 SIL). Population includes 6,000 Filifita (1999 SIL). East Sepik Province, Maprik District, Torricelli Mountains, west of Maprik. 36 villages. *Class:* Torricelli, Kombio-Arapesh, Arapesh. *Dialects:* Supari, Balif, Filifita (Ilahita), Iwam-Nagalemb, Nagipaem. *Lg Dev:* Literacy rate in first language: Filifita 15% to 25%; Mufian: 15% to 25%. Literacy rate in second language: Filifita 50% to 75%; Mufian 50% to 75%. NT: 1988–1998. *Other:* SVO; 14 noun classes; noun phrase concordance. Plains. Tropical forest. 200 to 300 meters. Swidden agriculturalists.

Mulaha [mfw] Extinct. Central Province, just southeast of Gaile on the coast. *Class:* Trans-New Guinea, Main Section, Eastern, Central and Southeastern, Kwalean. *Dialects:* Mulaha, Iaibu. *Other:* Coastal.

Mum (Katiati) [kqa] 3,286 (1981 Wurm and Hattori). Madang Province. *Class:* Trans-New Guinea, Madang-Adelbert Range, Adelbert Range, Josephstaal-Wanang, Josephstaal, Sikan. *Dialects:* Related to Sileibi. *Lg Dev:* Literacy rate in first language: 5% to 25%. Literacy rate in second language: 25% to 50%.

Munit [mtc] 911 (2003 SIL). Madang Province, Trans-Gogol District. *Class:* Trans-New Guinea, Madang-Adelbert Range, Madang, Mabuso, Kokon. *Dialects:* Related to Girawa, Kein.

Munkip [mpv] 137 (1978 McElhanon). Morobe Province, two villages. *Class:* Trans-New Guinea, Main Section, Central and Western, Huon-Finisterre, Finisterre, Erap. *Dialects:* Closest to Uri.

Muratayak (Asat, Murataik) [asx] 811 (2003 SIL). Madang Province, Rai Coast District, east of Saidor. *Class:* Trans-New Guinea, Main Section, Central and Western, Huon-Finisterre, Finisterre, Warup. *Dialects:* Related to Asaro'o, Bulgebi, Degenan, Forak, Guya, Gwahatike, Yagomi. *Lg Use:* People in Yagomi villages are said to speak Muratayak. *Other:* Coastal, mountain slope. Sea level to 1,200 meters.

Murik (Nor, Nor-Murik Lakes) [mtf] 1,000 (2000 Wurm). East Sepik Province, Angoram District, on the coast west of the mouth of the Sepik River. *Class:* Sepik-Ramu, Nor-Pondo, Nor. *Dialects:* Related to Kopar. *Lg Use:* Speakers also use Tok Pisin or English. *Lg Dev:* Literacy rate in first language: below 5%. Literacy rate in second language: 25% to 50%.

Murupi [mqw] 301 (1981 Wurm and Hattori). Madang Province. *Class:* Trans-New Guinea, Madang-Adelbert Range, Madang, Mabuso, Hanseman. *Dialects:* Related to Rapting, Wamas, Samosa, Mosimo, Saruga, Nake, Matepi, Garus, Yoidik, Rempi, Silopi, Utu, Mawan, Baimak, Bagupi, Gal, Garuh, Kamba.

Musak [mmq] 355 (1981 Wurm and Hattori). Madang Province, west of Astrolabe Bay on the Ramu River. *Class:* Trans-New Guinea, Madang-Adelbert Range, Adelbert Range, Josephstaal-Wanang, Wanang, Emuan.

Musan (Musian, Musa) [mmp] 70 (2000 Wurm). Sandaun Province, village east of Amto. *Class:* Amto-Musan. *Dialects:* Lexical similarity 29% with Amto. Amto and Musan 3% lexical similarity with Odiai, 18 miles north.

Both average 7% lexical similarity with Left May languages. *Other:* Frequent interaction with Amto.

Musar (Aregerek) [mmi] 684 (1981 Wurm and Hattori). Madang Province, inland, west of Tokain. *Class:* Trans-New Guinea, Madang-Adelbert Range, Adelbert Range, Pihom-Isumrud-Mugil, Pihom, Tiboran. *Dialects:* Related languages: Kowaki, Mawak, Pamosu, Wanambre.

Musom (Misatik) [msu] 200 (2000 Wurm). Morobe Province, tributary of the Busu River. *Class:* Austronesian, Malayo-Polynesian, Central-Eastern, Eastern Malayo-Polynesian, Oceanic, Western Oceanic, North New Guinea, Huon Gulf, Markham, Lower, Busu. *Dialects:* A member of the Azera dialect cluster.

Mussau-Emira (Emira-Mussau, Musau-Emira, Mussau, Musao) [emi] 5,000 (2003 SIL). Ethnic population: 5,000, including 3,500 who are resident in the traditional area (2000 J. Brownie SIL). New Ireland Province, St. Matthias Islands (Mussau and Emira), 150 km northwest of Kavieng. About 30% of the people live outside the language area, the majority in Kavieng. Some in Port Moresby, Lae, Goroka, Madang. *Class:* Austronesian, Malayo-Polynesian, Central-Eastern, Eastern Malayo-Polynesian, Oceanic, St. Matthias. *Dialects:* Emira, Western Mussau, Southern Mussau, Eastern Mussau. *Lg Use:* Vigorous. Nearly all of the ethnic group speaks Mussau-Emira. Parents pass it on to children in the traditional area, and some elsewhere, except in mixed marriages. The Tenis ethnic group use this as second language. Most domains, local administration, commerce, teaching medium in early grades, oral and some written use in church, personal letters. Positive language attitude. All but the youngest children speak Tok Pisin. All have varying fluency in English. *Lg Dev:* Literacy rate in first language: 80% to 95%. Literacy rate in second language: 80% to 95%. Vernacular prep schools since 1994. Dictionary. Grammar. *Other:* SVO. Island, coastal. Tropical forest. Sea level to 200 meters. Swidden agriculturalists; fishermen. Christian.

Mutu (Tuam-Mutu, Tuam, Tuom) [tuc] 3,000 (1998 SIL). Morobe Province, 6 villages on the 6 Siassi Islands south of Umboi Island: Mandok, Malai, Aronai, Tuam, Mutu Malau, and Aramot, and Yam village on Umboi Island. *Class:* Austronesian, Malayo-Polynesian, Central-Eastern, Eastern Malayo-Polynesian, Oceanic, Western Oceanic, North New Guinea, Ngero-Vitiaz, Ngero, Tuam. *Dialects:* Mutu, Tuam, Malai. *Lg Dev:* Literacy rate in second language: 25%. *Other:* SVO; prepositions. Island, coastal. Fishermen; traders. Christian, traditional religion.

Muyuw (Muyu, Muyua, Murua, Muruwa, Muyuwa) [myw] 6,000 (1998). 3,000 monolinguals. Population includes 1,000 to 1,200 Iwa. Milne Bay Province, Losuia District, Woodlark Island. *Class:* Austronesian, Malayo-Polynesian, Central-Eastern, Eastern Malayo-Polynesian, Oceanic, Western Oceanic, Papuan Tip, Peripheral, Kilivila-Louisiades, Kilivila. *Dialects:* Yanaba, Lougaw (Gawa), Wamwan, Nawyem, Iwa. The Iwa dialect is halfway between Muyuw and Kilivila. Lexical similarity 68% with Kilivila. *Lg Use:* Speakers also use Dobu, Kilivila, or Misima. *Lg Dev:* Literacy rate in first language: 75%. Literacy rate in second language: 75%. 30% of the children are in government schools. Dictionary. NT: 1976–1996. *Other:* SVO. Islands, coral, volcanic. Tropical forest. Sea level to 100 meters. Swidden agriculturalists.

Mwatebu [mwa] 120 (2000 Wurm). 10% monolingual. Milne Bay Province, Normanby Island, north central coast, one village. *Class:* Austronesian, Malayo-Polynesian, Central-Eastern, Eastern Malayo-Polynesian, Oceanic, Western Oceanic, Papuan Tip, Nuclear, North Papuan Mainland-D'Entrecasteaux, Dobu-Duau. *Dialects:* Lexical similarity 49% with Dobu (closest). *Lg Use:* Speakers

also use Duau or Dobu. *Lg Dev:* Literacy rate in second language: low.

Naasioi (Nasioi, Kieta, Kieta Talk, Aunge) [nas] 10,000 (1990 SIL). Bougainville Province, Kieta District, central mountains and southeast coast. *Class:* East Papuan, Bougainville, East, Nasioi. *Dialects:* Naasioi, Kongara, Orami (Guava), Pakia-Sideronsi. *Lg Dev:* Literacy rate in first language: 50% to 75%. Literacy rate in second language: 50% to 75%. NT: 1994. *Other:* SOV. Mountain slope, coastal. Tropical forest. Sea level to 1,000 meters. Swidden agriculturalists: cash crops. Christian, traditional religion.

Nabak (Naba, Wain) [naf] 16,000 (1994 SIL). Morobe Province, Lae District, eastern headwaters of the Busu River. 52 villages and 30 settlements. *Class:* Trans-New Guinea, Main Section, Central and Western, Huon-Finisterre, Huon, Western. *Lg Dev:* Literacy rate in first language: 50% to 75%. Literacy rate in second language: 50% to 75%. NT: 1998. *Other:* SOV. Mountain slope, coastal, interfluvial. Tropical forest. Swidden agriculturalists. Christian, traditional religion.

Nabi (Mitang, Metan, Nambieb) [mty] 615 (2003 SIL). Sandaun Province. 3 villages. *Class:* Torricelli, Wapei-Palei, Palei. *Other:* Speakers in 2 villages prefer 'Nabi', in 1 they prefer 'Metan'.

Nafi (Sirak) [srf] 157 (1988 Holzknecht). Morobe Province, Busu River. *Class:* Austronesian, Malayo-Polynesian, Central-Eastern, Eastern Malayo-Polynesian, Oceanic, Western Oceanic, North New Guinea, Huon Gulf, Markham, Lower, Busu.

Nai (Biaka, Amini) [bio] 595 (2003 SIL). Sandaun Province, Amanab District, adjacent to and southeast of the Angor language. 3 large villages. *Class:* Kwomtari-Baibai, Baibai. *Lg Dev:* Literacy rate in first language: 5% to 15%. Literacy rate in second language: 5% to 15%. *Other:* No schools, but speakers desire education. Hills, plain.

Nakama [nib] 983 (1980 census). Morobe Province, 6 villages in rugged terrain west and northwest of Boana of the south side of Saruwaged Range. *Class:* Trans-New Guinea, Main Section, Central and Western, Huon-Finisterre, Finisterre, Erap. *Dialects:* North Nakama, South Nakama. *Other:* Mountain slope. 1,000 to 1,300 meters. Swidden agriculturalists.

Nakanai (Nakonai) [nak] 13,000 (1981 Wurm and Hattori). West New Britain Province, Hoskins District, northwest coast. 42 villages. *Class:* Austronesian, Malayo-Polynesian, Central-Eastern, Eastern Malayo-Polynesian, Oceanic, Western Oceanic, Meso Melanesian, Willaumez. *Dialects:* Losa (Loso, Auka), Bileki (Lakalai, Muku, Mamuga), Vere (Vele, Tarobi), Ubae (Babata), Maututu. *Lg Dev:* Grammar. NT: 1983. *Other:* Major language of the Nakanai family. Agriculturalists: bananas, sweet potatoes, palm oil; animal husbandry: pigs; cocoa and copra production. Christian, traditional religion.

Nake (Ale) [nbk] 173 (1981 Wurm and Hattori). Madang Province, northwest of Madang. *Class:* Trans-New Guinea, Madang-Adelbert Range, Madang, Mabuso, Hanseman.

Nakwi [nax] 275 (2003 SIL). East Sepik Province, south of Ama language. Villages; Nakwi-Amasu, Augot (Mumupra, Sari), Tiki, Uwau. *Class:* Left May. *Dialects:* Lexical similarity 71% between Nakwi and Nimo. *Lg Dev:* Literacy rate in second language: 1%. *Other:* Village locations change frequently. Acculturation is slight. Foothills. Tropical forest, swamp. 30 to 40 meters. Hunter-gatherers; some gardens. Traditional religion.

Nali (Yiru) [nss] 1,800 (1982 SIL). Population includes 200 Okro (2000 D. Tryon). Manus Province, southeast Manus Island, and southwest coast, northwest of Titan. *Class:* Austronesian, Malayo-Polynesian, Central-Eastern, Eastern Malayo-Polynesian, Oceanic, Admiralty Islands, Eastern, Manus, East. *Dialect:* Okro. Tryon 2000 makes Okro

(200) and Nali (1,800) separate languages. *Lg Use:* 40% of the ethnic group speaks Okro. Most key domains. 60% of children speak the Okro dialect. Positive language attitude. Speakers are moderately bilingual in Lele. *Lg Dev:* Literacy rate in first language: 75% to 100%. Literacy rate in second language: 50% to 75%. Bible portions: 1991. *Other:* SVO. Coastal, hills. Tropical forest. Sea level to 200 meters. Agriculturalists; hunters; fishermen.

Nalik (Lugagon, Fesoa, Fessoa) [nal] 5,138 (1990 census). New Ireland Province, north central, 14 villages from 70 to 115 km from Kavieng on the east coast, and 3 villages on the west coast. Some in urban areas. *Class:* Austronesian, Malayo-Polynesian, Central-Eastern, Eastern Malayo-Polynesian, Oceanic, Western Oceanic, Meso Melanesian, New Ireland, Lavongai-Nalik. *Other:* SVO. Coastal. Tropical forest. Sea level to 300 meters. Swidden agriculturalists; cacao plantations; fishermen; oil palm.

Nama [nmx] 1,196 (2003 SIL). Western Province, Morehead District, Ngaraita, Mata and Daraia villages immediately east of Morehead. *Class:* Trans-New Guinea, Trans-Fly-Bulaka River, Trans-Fly, Morehead and Upper Maro rivers, Nambu.

Namat [nkm] 175 (2000 census). Western Province, Morehead District, Mibini village south of Morehead. *Class:* Trans-New Guinea, Trans-Fly-Bulaka River, Trans-Fly, Morehead and Upper Maro rivers, Nambu.

Nambo (Arufe, Nambu, Namna) [ncm] 713 (2003 SIL). Western Province, Morehead District, five villages (Arufe, Gubam, Bebdeben, Pongariki and Derideri) bordering the Idi and Nen languages. *Class:* Trans-New Guinea, Trans-Fly-Bulaka River, Trans-Fly, Morehead and Upper Maro rivers, Nambu. *Dialects:* Nambo, Namna. The Namna dialect, spoken in Pongariki and Derideri, is being replaced by the Nambo dialect. Children in Derideri learn only the Nambo dialect. *Lg Dev:* Bible portions: 1974.

Namia (Namie, Yellow River, Nemia, Edawapi, Lujere) [nnm] 4,944 (2003 SIL). Sandaun Province (19 villages), Yellow River District, Panewai village, East Sepik Province (1 village). Areas are called Edwaki, Ameni, Wiyari, Lawo, Pabei, Iwane. *Class:* Sepik-Ramu, Sepik, Yellow River. *Dialects:* Closest to Ak and Awun. Lexical similarity 13% with Abau, 12% with May River Iwam. *Lg Dev:* Literacy rate in first language: 5% to 15%. Literacy rate in second language: 50% to 75%. Four vernacular primary schools, started in 2000. Grammar. Bible portions: 1996–2002. *Other:* SOV; postpositions; consonant clusters; vowel glides; 6 phonemic vowels. Swamp, savannah. Sea level to 50 meters. Hunter-gatherers: sago (primarily); agriculturalists (some).

Namiae [nvm] 1,200 (2003 SIL). Inland Oro Province, Afore District, on the Managalas Plateau, Kuae, Kokoro, Tahama, Sorefuna, Ubuvara villages. *Class:* Trans-New Guinea, Main Section, Eastern, Central and Southeastern, Koiarian, Baraic. *Lg Dev:* NT: 2003. *Other:* SOV. Interfluvial. Tropical forest. 700 to 900 meters. Swidden agriculturalists. Christian, traditional religion.

Namo (Mari, Dorro) [mxw] 385 (2003 SIL). Western Province, Morehead District, Mari and Tais villages on the south coast, extending inland. *Class:* Trans-New Guinea, Trans-Fly-Bulaka River, Trans-Fly, Morehead and Upper Maro rivers, Nambu. *Lg Dev:* Literacy rate in first language: below 5%. Literacy rate in second language: below 5%. *Other:* Different from Mari of East Sepik Province, and Mari of Madang Province.

Nankina [nnk] 2,500 (1991 SIL). Madang Province, Saidor District, in the upper Nankina River valley. *Class:* Trans-New Guinea, Main Section, Central and Western, Huon-Finisterre, Finisterre, Yupna. *Lg Dev:* Literacy rate in first language: 5% to 15%. Literacy rate in second language: 25% to 50%. Bible portions: 1990. *Other:* SOV.

Mountain slope. Tropical forest. 1,000 to 2,000 meters. Swidden agriculturalists. Traditional religion, Christian.

Narak (Ganja) [nac] 6,223 (2000 census). 70% monolingual. Western Highlands Province, Hagen District, middle Jimi near Tabibuga. *Class:* Trans-New Guinea, Main Section, Central and Western, East New Guinea Highlands, Central, Jimi. *Dialects:* Close to Maring, North Wahgi, Kandawo. No significant dialect differences. *Lg Use:* Vigorous. All domains. Religious services. All ages. Positive language attitude. 30% can use Tok Pisin. A few can use some English. *Lg Dev:* Literacy rate in first language: 15%. Literacy rate in second language: 5% to 15%. Transfer primer from Tok Pisin. 10% can write Narak. NT: 1981. *Other:* Some form of whistle speech reported. SOV. Mountain slope. Tropical forest. 550 to 2,750 meters. Swidden agriculturalists: coffee. Christian.

Nauna (Naune) [ncn] 100 (2000 Wurm). Manus Province, Nauna Island. 1 village. *Class:* Austronesian, Malayo-Polynesian, Central-Eastern, Eastern Malayo-Polynesian, Oceanic, Admiralty Islands, Eastern, Southeast Islands. *Lg Use:* Speakers also use Titan. *Other:* SVO.

Nawaru (Sirio) [nwr] 190 (1990 SIL). Oro Province, around upper Musa River valley. *Class:* Trans-New Guinea, Main Section, Eastern, Central and Southeastern, Yareban. *Dialects:* Very close to Yareba. *Lg Use:* Speakers also use Hiri Motu or Yareba.

Nehan (Nissan, Nihan) [nsn] 6,500 (2003 SIL). Bougainville Province, Nissan Island. *Class:* Austronesian, Malayo-Polynesian, Central-Eastern, Eastern Malayo-Polynesian, Oceanic, Western Oceanic, Meso Melanesian, New Ireland, South New Ireland-Northwest Solomonic, Nehan-North Bougainville, Nehan. *Dialect:* Nehan, Pinipel (Pinipin). Not closely related to other languages. *Lg Dev:* Literacy rate in first language: 25% to 50%. Literacy rate in second language: 50% to 75%. Grammar. *Other:* Little acculturation.

Nek [nif] 1,500 (2002 SIL). Morobe Province, Nawaeb District, 5 villages in rugged terrain north of Boana on the south side of the Saruwaged Range. *Class:* Trans-New Guinea, Main Section, Central and Western, Huon-Finisterre, Finisterre, Erap. *Dialects:* East Nek, West Nek. Lexical similarity 65% with Nuk, less than 60% with Nakama. *Lg Dev:* Literacy rate in first language: 5% to 15%. Literacy rate in second language: 50% to 75%. Bible portions: 1999. *Other:* SOV. Mountain slope. Tropical forest. 1,000 to 1,300 meters. Swidden agriculturalists. Christian.

Nekgini [nkg] 430 (1981 Wurm and Hattori). Madang Province, west of Mot River. *Class:* Trans-New Guinea, Main Section, Central and Western, Huon-Finisterre, Finisterre, Gusap-Mot. *Lg Use:* Used in the home and village life. Speakers also use Tok Pisin. *Other:* One community school. Coastal, foothills.

Neko [nej] 315 (1981 Wurm and Hattori). Madang Province, coast near Biliau. *Class:* Trans-New Guinea, Main Section, Central and Western, Huon-Finisterre, Finisterre, Gusap-Mot. *Lg Use:* Used in the home and village life. Speakers also use Tok Pisin. *Other:* One community school. Coastal, foothills.

Neme [nex] 305 (2002 SIL). Western Province, Morehead District, Keru and Mitere villages northeast of Morehead. *Class:* Trans-New Guinea, Trans-Fly-Bulaka River, Trans-Fly, Morehead and Upper Maro rivers, Nambu.

Nen [nqn] 250 (2002 SIL). Western Province, Morehead District, Bimadeben village, between Nambo and Idi languages. *Class:* Trans-New Guinea, Trans-Fly-Bulaka River, Trans-Fly, Morehead and Upper Maro rivers, Nambu.

Nend (Nent, Angaua) [anh] 2,000 (1991 UBS). Madang Province, between the Ramu and Sogeram rivers, around

Pasinkap village. *Class:* Trans-New Guinea, Madang-Adelbert Range, Adelbert Range, Josephstaal-Wanang, Wanang, Atan. *Lg Dev:* Literacy rate in first language: 5% to 25%. Literacy rate in second language: 25% to 50%. Grammar. *Other:* 'Angaua' is the people's name. Mountain ridge. Swamp. 50 to 300 meters. Swidden agriculturalists; sago gatherers; hunters. Traditional religion, Christian.

Nete (Iniai, Malamauda, Malaumanda) [net] 1,000 (1982 SIL). East Sepik Province, adjoining the Hewa area. 3 villages. *Class:* Trans-New Guinea, Main Section, Central and Western, East New Guinea Highlands, West-Central, Enga. *Dialects:* Lexical similarity 70% with Bisorio of East Sepik. *Lg Dev:* Literacy rate in first language: 0%. Literacy rate in second language: below 1%. *Other:* 800 to 900 meters.

Ngaing (Sor, Mailang) [nnf] 2,023 (2000 census). Madang Province, 15 villages, foothills from coast to Finisterre Range, southwest of Saidor. *Class:* Trans-New Guinea, Main Section, Central and Western, Huon-Finisterre, Finisterre, Gusap-Mot. *Lg Use:* Vigorous. *Other:* 3 community schools. Foothills. Tropical forest. Sea level to 1,000 meters. Swidden agriculturalists. Christian, traditional religion, cargo cult.

Ngala (Kara, Sogap, Swagup) [nud] 178 (2003 SIL). East Sepik Province, one village in Ambunti District. *Class:* Sepik-Ramu, Sepik, Middle Sepik, Ndu. *Lg Dev:* Literacy rate in first language: below 5%. Literacy rate in second language: 15% to 25%.

Ngalum [szb] 8,000 in Papua New Guinea (1981). Sandaun Province. *Dialects:* Ngalum, Apmisibil, Sibil. See main entry under Indonesia (Papua).

Nii (Ek Nii) [nii] 12,000 (1991 SIL). Western Highlands Province, Hagen District. *Class:* Trans-New Guinea, Main Section, Central and Western, East New Guinea Highlands, Central, Wahgi. *Lg Dev:* NT: 1980. *Other:* SOV. Mountain slope, valley. Pine forest, bamboo. 1,500 meters. Intensive agriculturalists.

Niksek (Meiyari, Sumwari) [gbe] 926 (2003 SIL). East Sepik Province, at the headwaters of the eastern branch of the Leonhard Schultze and upper Niksek (April) rivers. 200 are at a new settlement at Niksek airport. Also at Sumwari, and a few in 2 other villages. *Class:* Sepik-Ramu, Sepik, Sepik Hill, Sanio. *Dialects:* Gabiano (Kabiano), Meiyari ("Paka"), Setiali. *Lg Dev:* Literacy rate in first language: below 5%. Literacy rate in second language: 5% to 15%. *Other:* Patrolled from Oksapmin. Speakers have limited comprehension of oral or written Tok Pisin. SOV. Mountain slope. Tropical forest. 900 to 1,500 meters. Swidden agriculturalists.

Nimi [nis] 1,381 (1980 census). Morobe Province, upper Erap River, south of the Saruwaged Range. *Class:* Trans-New Guinea, Main Section, Central and Western, Huon-Finisterre, Finisterre, Erap. *Other:* Mountain slope. 1,330 to 1,830 meters. Swidden agriculturalists.

Nimo (Nimo-Wasawai) [niw] 350 (1998 NTM). East Sepik Province, southeast of Ama language. Villages; Nimo (Boyemo), Wasuai, Didipas (including Uburu site), Yuwaitri (moved from Aimi site to Wanawo site), Fowiom, Uwawi, Wamwiu, Binuto, Arakau. *Class:* Left May. *Dialects:* Lexical similarity 71% between Nakwi and Nimo. *Lg Dev:* Bible portions. *Other:* Village locations change frequently. Acculturation is slight.

Nimoa (Nimowa) [nmw] 1,100 (census). 40% monolingual. Milne Bay Province, Misima District, group of islands just west of Sud-Est. *Class:* Austronesian, Malayo-Polynesian, Central-Eastern, Eastern Malayo-Polynesian, Oceanic, Western Oceanic, Papuan Tip, Peripheral, Kilivila-Louisiades, Nimoa-Sudest. *Dialects:* Panawina, Sabari, Panatinani, Western Point. Lexical similarity 44% with Tagula (closest). *Lg Use:* Most

speakers have high proficiency in Misima. *Lg Dev:* Bible portions: 1979–1984. *Other:* Half of the children are in school.

Ningera (Nagira, Negira, Ninggera) [nby] 147 (2003 SIL). Sandaun Province, Vanimo District, east of Vanimo, north of Bewani and Ossima. *Class:* Trans-New Guinea, Northern, Border, Bewani. *Lg Dev:* Literacy rate in second language: 50% to 75%.

Ninggerum (Ninggrum, Ninggirum, Ningerum, Niyium, Kativa, Kasiwa, Obgwo, Tedi, Tidi) [nxr] 5,146 in Papua New Guinea (2000 census). 40% are monolingual. Population total all countries: 6,146. Western Province between the Ok Birim and Ok Tedi rivers, extending east of the Ok Tedi to the main road linking Kiunga and Tabubil, and north to the main mountain range. Also spoken in Indonesia (Papua). *Class:* Trans-New Guinea, Main Section, Central and Western, Central and South New Guinea-Kutubuan, Central and South New Guinea, Ok, Lowland. *Dialects:* Kasuwa, Daupka. *Lg Use:* Vigorous. All domains. Used in preschool and first 2 grades, oral use in religious services, songs, local commerce. All ages. Positive language attitude. 10% can speak Hiri Motu, 5% English, 50% Tok Pisin, 5% also speak neighboring languages (Yongkom, Faiwol, Telefol). *Lg Dev:* Literacy rate in first language: 5%. Literacy rate in second language: 5% to 15%. *Other:* About half the population died from 1950–1975 because of western diseases. Interfluvial. Tropical forest. Below 100 to 500 meters. Swidden agriculturalists; copper mine workers; lumbermen; animal husbandry: pigs, chickens, fish, rabbits; market gardening. Traditional religion, Christian.

Ningil [niz] 952 (2000 census). Sandaun Province. *Class:* Torricelli, Wapei-Palei, Wapei. *Dialects:* Related to Olo, Yau, Yis, Valman. *Lg Dev:* Literacy rate in second language: 25% to 50%. *Other:* 600 meters.

Nobonob (Butelkud-Guntabak, Garuh, Nobanob, Nobnob) [gaw] 2,500 (2002 SIL). Madang Province, Madang District. *Class:* Trans-New Guinea, Madang-Adelbert Range, Madang, Mabuso, Hanseman. *Dialect:* Ari (Ati, A'i). *Lg Use:* Moderately vigorous. Wagi speakers use Nobonob as second language. All domains, personal letters, oral literature. All ages. Positive language attitude. 1,800 can speak Tok Pisin. 300 to 400 can also speak Bel, Kamba, or Rempi. Tok Pisin is increasing in use. *Lg Dev:* Literacy rate in first language: 16%. Literacy rate in second language: 25% to 75%. 400 or fewer can read it, 200 to 400 can write it. NT: 1990. *Other:* SOV. Mountain slope. Tropical forest. Sea level to 300 meters. Swidden agriculturalists; fish cannery workers.

Nomane [nof] 4,645 (1981 Wurm and Hattori). Simbu Province. *Class:* Trans-New Guinea, Main Section, Central and Western, East New Guinea Highlands, Central, Chimbu. *Dialects:* Nomane, Kiari. *Other:* Mountain slope. Swidden agriculturalists.

Nomu [noh] 807 (1978 McElhanon). Morobe Province, northern coast, Huon Peninsula. *Class:* Trans-New Guinea, Main Section, Central and Western, Huon-Finisterre, Huon, Western. *Lg Use:* Speakers also use Ono.

Notsi (Nochi) [ncf] 1,836 (2000 census). New Ireland Province, Central New Ireland District, east coast. *Class:* Austronesian, Malayo-Polynesian, Central-Eastern, Eastern Malayo-Polynesian, Oceanic, Western Oceanic, Meso Melanesian, New Ireland, Tabar. *Lg Dev:* Literacy rate in second language: 80% to 100%. One primary school, two more planned to start in 2002. Bible portions: 1995. *Other:* SVO. Coastal. Tropical forest. Sea level. Swidden agriculturalists; fishermen; oil palm.

Nuk [noc] 1,009 (1980 census). Morobe Province, 8 villages in rugged terrain northeast of Boana on the south side of Saruwaged Range. *Class:* Trans-New Guinea,

Main Section, Central and Western, Huon-Finisterre, Finisterre, Erap. *Dialects:* North Nuk, South Nuk. *Other:* Mountain slope. 1,000 to 1,500 meters. Swidden agriculturalists.

Nukna (Komutu) [klt] 850 (2003 SIL). Morobe Province, lower Timbe River valley. *Class:* Trans-New Guinea, Main Section, Central and Western, Huon-Finisterre, Finisterre, Uruwa.

Nukumanu (Tasman) [nuq] 700 (2003 SIL). Bougainville Province, Atolls District, Nukumanu Atoll. *Class:* Austronesian, Malayo-Polynesian, Central-Eastern, Eastern Malayo-Polynesian, Oceanic, Central-Eastern Oceanic, Remote Oceanic, Central Pacific, East Fijian-Polynesian, Polynesian, Nuclear, Samoic-Outlier, Ellicean. *Dialects:* Tryon says it is distinct from Takuu (Nukuria) in Papua New Guinea and Luangiua (Ontong Java) in Solomon Islands. Speakers have contact with Luangiua.

Nukuria (Nuguria, Nahoa, Fead) [nur] 550 (2003 SIL). Bougainville Province, Atolls District, northeast of Bougainville Island, Nukuria Atoll. *Class:* Austronesian, Malayo-Polynesian, Central-Eastern, Eastern Malayo-Polynesian, Oceanic, Central-Eastern Oceanic, Remote Oceanic, Central Pacific, East Fijian-Polynesian, Polynesian, Nuclear, Samoic-Outlier, Ellicean. *Other:* Distinct from Takuu and Nukumanu in Papua New Guinea and Sikiana and Luanguia (Ontong Java) in Solomon Islands.

Numanggang (Manggang, Numangang, Numangan, Boana, Kai, Ngain, Sugu) [nop] 2,262 (2000 census). Few monolinguals. Morobe Province, Lae District, north Nadzab. 10 villages. A few also in Lae, Mt. Hagen, and Rabaul. *Class:* Trans-New Guinea, Main Section, Central and Western, Huon-Finisterre, Finisterre, Erap. *Dialects:* East Numanggang, West Numanggang. *Lg Use:* Vigorous. In towns more Tok Pisin is used. All domains, in town meetings, church, local commerce. All ages. Positive language attitude. The younger generation mainly speak Tok Pisin, and the older generation speak some Kâte as second language. Some also speak some English, Nakama, Nabak, or German. *Lg Dev:* Literacy rate in first language: 25%. Literacy rate in second language: 25%. Bible portions: 1984–1994. *Other:* SOV. Mountain slope. Tropical forest. Swidden agriculturalists: coffee, vegetables, cardamom. Christian.

Numbami (Siboma, Sipoma) [sij] 270 (1978 McElhanon). Morobe Province, Lae District, one village on the coast. *Class:* Austronesian, Malayo-Polynesian, Central-Eastern, Eastern Malayo-Polynesian, Oceanic, Western Oceanic, North New Guinea, Huon Gulf, Numbami. *Lg Use:* The use of Yabem in religious services is declining.

Nyindrou (Lindrou, Lindau, Salien, Nyada) [lid] 4,200 (1998 SIL). Few monolinguals. Manus Province, Manus Island. 10 villages around the west coast of Manus. *Class:* Austronesian, Malayo-Polynesian, Central-Eastern, Eastern Malayo-Polynesian, Oceanic, Admiralty Islands, Eastern, Manus, West. *Dialect:* Babon. The Babon dialect is in 3 southern villages. *Lg Use:* Vigorous. All domains. Used in first 3 grades in school. Oral and written use in church. Oral use in local commerce. All ages. Positive language attitude. Bilingual level estimates for Bipi: 0 73%, 1 8%, 2 19%, 3–5 0%; Harengam: 0 84%, 1 9%, 2 7%, 3–5 0%; Sori: 1 89%, 1 6%, 2 5%, 3–5 0%; Levei: 0 94%, 1 2%, 2 4%, 3–5 0%. *Lg Dev:* Literacy rate in first language: 50%. Literacy rate in second language: 50% to 75%. 30% can write it. Radio programs. NT: 2001. *Other:* SVO. Coastal. Tropical forest. Sea level to 30 meters. Fishermen; hunters; agriculturalists. Christian.

Odiai (Busa, Busan, Uriai) [bhf] 244 (2000 census). Sandaun Province, Amanab District, north of Upper Sepik River, west of Namia. 3 villages. Yare is north and east, Abau is south and west, Biaka is northwest. *Class:* Language Isolate. *Other:* No schools. Some intermarriage

with the Yale. Lowland swamps. 100 meters. Hunter-gatherers.

Odoodee (Kalamo, Nomad, Tomu, Tomu River, Ododei) [kkc] 486 (2002 SIL). Western Province from south bank of middle Rentoul River past the middle Tomu River to Wawoi Falls. Villages of Tulusi (Hesif), Hasalibi, Kalamo (Wawoi Falls). *Class:* Trans-New Guinea, Main Section, Central and Western, Central and South New Guinea-Kutubuan, Central and South New Guinea, East Strickland. *Dialects:* Closest to Samo-Kubo and Konai. *Lg Dev:* Literacy rate in first language: 15%. Literacy rate in second language: 15%. *Other:* 'Kalamo' is the name of one of the clans living at Wawoi Falls. The speakers call themselves 'Odoodee'. SOV. Interfluvial. Tropical forest. Swidden agriculturalists; hunters; gatherers.

Ogea (Erima, Nuru) [eri] 2,209 (2003 SIL). Madang Province, Astrolabe Bay. *Class:* Trans-New Guinea, Madang-Adelbert Range, Madang, Rai Coast, Nuru. *Dialects:* Related to Uya, Duduela, Kwato, Rerau, Jilim, Yangulam. *Lg Dev:* Literacy rate in second language: 65%. Bible portions: 1981. *Other:* SOV. Coastal. Tropical forest. Sea level. Swidden agriculturalists.

Oksapmin [opm] 8,000 (1991 SIL). Sandaun Province, Telefomin District, bordering on the southwest of the Sepik Hill languages. *Class:* Trans-New Guinea, Oksapmin. *Dialects:* Not closely related to any other language. Several dialects. *Lg Dev:* Literacy rate in first language: 25% to 50%. Literacy rate in second language: 25% to 50%. Dictionary. NT: 1992. *Other:* SOV. Mountain slope. Tropical forest. 1,300 to 2,300 meters. Swidden agriculturalists.

Olo (Orlei) [ong] 13,667 (2003 SIL). Sandaun Province, Lumi District. 55 villages. *Class:* Torricelli, Wapei-Palei, Wapei. *Dialects:* Payi (Pay, North Olo), Wapi (Wape, South Olo). Related to Yis, Yau, Ningil, Valman. *Lg Dev:* NT: 1997. *Other:* Different from Wapi in Enga Province. SVO. Mountain slope, coastal. Tropical forest. 20 to 1,600 meters. Swidden agriculturalists.

Omati (Mini) [mgx] 800 (1977 SIL). Gulf Province, villages on Omati River: Gihiteri, Iba, Gibidai, Kiberi, Kamairo. *Class:* Trans-New Guinea, Turama-Kikorian, Turama-Omatian. *Dialects:* Lexical similarity 53% with Ikobi-Mena. *Other:* Each village also has Joso and Juko language speakers. One school. Lowland limestone pinnacle region.

Omie (Aomie, Upper Managalasi) [aom] 800 (1993 SIL). 400 monolinguals. Oro Province, Kokoda, Upper Kumusi, and Afore districts, northwest of Managalasi, Mamama River, and Upper Kumusi Valley. *Class:* Trans-New Guinea, Main Section, Eastern, Central and Southeastern, Koiarian, Baraic. *Dialects:* Asapa, Zuwadza, Gora-Bomahouji. *Lg Use:* Some speakers use Hiri Motu or English as second language. *Lg Dev:* Literacy rate in first language: 25% to 50%. Literacy rate in second language: 25% to 50%. Grammar. NT: 1991. *Other:* SOV. Mountain slope, riverine, interfluvial. Tropical forest. 545 to 1,500 meters. Swidden agriculturalists; animal husbandry: pigs.

One, Inebu (Oni, Inebu, Onele, Aunalei) [oin] 1,300 (2000 Crowther). Ethnic population: 1,300. Sandaun Province, Lumi District, West Waipei Division, between East Bewani and West Torricelli ranges, Inebu, Kalema, Windiple, Alkula villages. *Class:* Torricelli, West Wapei, One. *Dialects:* Close to Kabore One, Northern One, Southern One, Kwamtim One, Molmo One. *Lg Use:* All domains except church. All ages. Speakers have routine bilingual proficiency in Tok Pisin, but inadequate for abstract and complex concepts. *Other:* Mountain slope. Christian.

One, Kabore (Oni, Kabore, Onele, Aunalei) [onk] 300 (2000 Crowther). Ethnic population: 300. Sandaun Province, Lumi District, West Waipei Division, between

East Bewani and West Torricelli ranges, Abore, Sapin, Kara, Wamtip villages, Kabore Station. *Class:* Torricelli, West Wapei, One. *Dialects:* Close to Inebu One, Northern One, Southern One, Kwamtim One, Molmo One. *Lg Use:* All domains except church. All ages. Speakers have routine bilingual proficiency in Tok Pisin, but inadequate for abstract and complex concepts. Tok Pisin heard more in this area because of a community school. *Other:* Mountain slope. Christian.

One, Kwamtim (Oni, Kuamtim, Kwamtim, Aunalei) [okk] 150 (2000 Crowther). Ethnic population: 150. Sandaun Province, Lumi District, West Waipei Division, between East Bewani and West Torricelli ranges, Kuamtim village. *Class:* Torricelli, West Wapei, One. *Dialects:* Close to Kabore One, Inebu One, Northern One, Kwamtim One, Molmo One. *Lg Use:* All domains except church. All ages. Speakers have routine bilingual proficiency in Tok Pisin, but inadequate for abstract and complex concepts. *Other:* Mountain slope. Christian.

One, Molmo (Aunalei, Onele, Oni, Molmo) [aun] 500 (2000 Crowther). Ethnic population: 500 (2000). Sandaun Province. Between East Bewani and West Torricelli ranges, West Waipei Division, Molmo, Wisoli, Anononti, Laurela, Pusa villages. *Class:* Torricelli, West Wapei, One. *Dialects:* North Aunalei, Central Aunalei, South Aunalei. Close to One Kabore, One Inebu, One Northern, One Southern, One Kwamtim. *Lg Use:* 200 speakers of other One languages use it as second language when in One Molmo villages. All domains except church. All ages. Speakers have routine bilingual proficiency in Tok Pisin, but inadequate for abstract and complex concepts. Tok Pisin used in church only. Other One languages used when visiting those villages. *Lg Dev:* Literacy rate in second language: 5% in Tok Pisin. *Other:* Mountain slope. Christian.

One, Northern (Onele, Oni, Aunalei) [onr] 2,000 (2000 Crowther). Ethnic population: 2,000. Sandaun Province. Between East Bewani and West Torricelli ranges, Lumi District, West Waipei Division, Romei, Parara, Wolwale, Koiniri, Karantu villages. *Class:* Torricelli, West Wapei, One. *Dialects:* Close to Kabore One, Inebu One, Southern One, Kwamtim One, Molmo One. *Lg Use:* All domains except church. All ages. Speakers have routine bilingual proficiency in Tok Pisin, but inadequate for abstract and complex concepts. *Other:* Mountain slope. Christian.

One, Southern (Onele, Oni, Aunalei) [osu] 200 (2000 Crowther). Ethnic population: 200. Sandaun Province, Lumi District, West Waipei Division, between East Bewani and West Torricelli ranges, Romei, Parara, Wolwale, Koiniri, Karantu villages. *Class:* Torricelli, West Wapei, One. *Dialects:* Close to Kabore One, Inebu One, Northern One, Kwamtim One, Molmo One. *Lg Use:* All domains except church. All ages. Speakers have routine bilingual proficiency in Tok Pisin, but inadequate for abstract and complex concepts. *Other:* Mountain slope. Christian.

Onjob (Onjab) [onj] 150 (2000 Wurm). Oro Province, Koreat and Naukwate villages. *Class:* Trans-New Guinea, Main Section, Eastern, Central and South-eastern, Dagan. *Dialects:* Lexical similarity 30% with Maiwa (closest). *Lg Use:* Speakers also use English or Ubir. *Lg Use:* Literacy rate in second language: English, Ubir.

Ono [ons] 5,500 (1993 SIL). Morobe Province, Finschhafen District. *Class:* Trans-New Guinea, Main Section, Central and Western, Huon-Finisterre, Huon, Western. *Dialects:* Ziwe, Amugen. *Lg Use:* Spoken as a second language by 1,000 Nomu and Sialum (Voegelin and Voegelin 1977). *Lg Dev:* Literacy rate in first language: 25% to 50%. Literacy rate in second language: 50% to 75%. NT: 1991. *Other:* SOV. Mountain slope.

Savannah, tropical forest, gallery forest. Sea level to 2,000 meters. Swidden agriculturalists.

Onobasulu (Onabasulu) [onn] 700 (2000 SIL). 50% are monolingual. Southern Highlands Province midway between Mt. Sisa and Mt. Bosavi. *Class:* Trans-New Guinea, Main Section, Central and Western, Central and South New Guinea-Kutubuan, Central and South New Guinea, Bosavi. *Lg Use:* Vigorous. All domains. Oral and written use in preschool and adult literacy. All ages. It is the first language children learn. Also used by Edolo speakers as a second language. Positive language attitude. Speakers also use Kaluli, Edolo, or Tok Pisin. *Lg Dev:* Literacy rate in first language: 43%. Literacy rate in second language: 15% to 25%. 300 can read it, 200 can write it. Bible portions: 1996. *Other:* SOV. Mountain slope. 700 to 1,000 meters. Swidden agriculturalists. Christian.

Ontenu (Ontena) [ont] 3,000 (1996 SIL). Eastern Highlands Province, Kainantu District. *Class:* Trans-New Guinea, Main Section, Central and Western, East New Guinea Highlands, Eastern, Gadsup-Auyana-Awa. *Dialects:* Related to Gadsup. *Other:* SOV. Mountain slope. Tropical forest. 1,538 meters. Swidden agriculturalists.

Opao [opo] 1,116 (1973 H. A. Brown). Gulf Province, near Orokolo and Keuru. *Class:* Trans-New Guinea, Eleman, Eleman Proper, Western.

Orokaiva (Orakaiva, Ke, Kaiva) [ork] 33,300 (1989 SIL). 20% monolingual. Population includes 4,300 Hunjara (1973 SIL), 2,000 Aeka (1981 Wurm and Hattori). Oro Province, Popondetta District between the Hunjara, Notu, Binandere and Managalasi. 200 villages. Some in Port Moresby, Wewak, Madang, and Lae. *Class:* Trans-New Guinea, Main Section, Eastern, Binanderean, Binanderean Proper. *Dialects:* Kokoda, Hunjara, Ajeka, Etija (Sose, Sohe), Ehija (Ihane, Ifane), Harava, Aeka. *Lg Use:* Vigorous. All domains. Local administration, commerce. Oral and written use in church. Personal letters. Oral literature. All ages. Speakers are positive about Orokaiva. Young men sometimes prefer Tok Pisin. Over 80% speak Tok Pisin, 20% also speak English, a few of older adults also speak Motu. *Lg Dev:* Literacy rate in first language: 15%. Literacy rate in second language: 15% to 25%. 5,000 can read and write it. Taught in primary schools. Radio programs. Grammar. NT: 1988. *Other:* SOV. Interfluvial. Tropical forest. 200 to 800 meters. Swidden agriculturalists: coffee; oil palm workers; cocoa and copra production; rubber. Christian, traditional religion.

Orokolo (West Elema, Kairu-Kaura, Haira, Kaipi, Vailala, Bailala, Muru, Muro) [oro] 13,000 (1977 SIL). Gulf Province, from mouth of Purari River east to Bairu River. Kerema is a main town. *Class:* Trans-New Guinea, Eleman, Eleman Proper, Western. *Lg Dev:* Literacy rate in first language: 25% to 50%. Literacy rate in second language: 25% to 50%. Dictionary. NT: 1963.

Ouma [oum] Extinct. Central Province, south coast around Labu. *Class:* Austronesian, Malayo-Polynesian, Central-Eastern, Eastern Malayo-Polynesian, Oceanic, Western Oceanic, Papuan Tip, Peripheral, Central Papuan, Oumic.

Oune (Ounge, Dapera) [oue] 1,900 (1990 SIL). Bougainville Province, Kieta District, central mountains and southeast coast. *Class:* East Papuan, Bougainville, East, Nasioi. *Dialects:* Most dialects are not functionally intelligible with Nasioi.

Owenia (Owena, Owenda, Waijara, Waisara) [wsr] 349 (1981 Wurm and Hattori). Eastern Highlands Province, Obura District. *Class:* Trans-New Guinea, Main Section, Central and Western, East New Guinea Highlands, Eastern, Owenia.

Owiniga (Samo, Bero, Taina) [owi] 330 (1998 NTM). East Sepik Province, southeast of Nimo language. Villages: Yei, Amu, Inagri, Samo. *Class:* Left May.

Lg Dev: Bible portions: 1991. *Other:* Traditional culture. Traditional religion, Christian.

Oya'oya (Kuiaro, Simagahi, Daiomuni, Loani) [oyy] 367 (1990 census). Milne Bay Province, Samarai-Murua District, Bwanabwana Local Government Area, southeast tip of the Papuan mainland facing China Strait. *Class:* Austronesian, Malayo-Polynesian, Central-Eastern, Eastern Malayo-Polynesian, Oceanic, Western Oceanic, Papuan Tip, Nuclear, Suauic. *Dialects:* Dialect cluster. Lexical similarity 61% with Wagawaga, 46% with Saliba, 31% with Tawala, 48% with Buhutu. *Other:* No schools. Children travel by boat to various offshore islands for school.

Pagi (Pagei, Bembi) [pgi] 2,136 (2003 SIL). Sandaun Province, Vanimo District, Bewani Subdistrict, 5 villages, east and southeast of the Kilmeri. *Class:* Trans-New Guinea, Northern, Border, Bewani. *Dialects:* Western Pagi (Bewani), Eastern Pagi (Imbinis). Related to Kilmeri and Ningera.

Pahi (Lugitama, Wansum, Riahoma) [lgt] 845 (2000 census). Sandaun Province, extending north in Maimai Namblo Division. *Class:* Sepik-Ramu, Sepik, Tama. *Dialects:* Related to Pasi, Kalou, Mehek, Yessan-Mayo.

Pak-Tong (Tong-Pak) [pkg] 970 (1977 Lincoln). Manus Province, Pak and Tong islands. *Class:* Austronesian, Malayo-Polynesian, Central-Eastern, Eastern Malayo-Polynesian, Oceanic, Admiralty Islands, Eastern, Pak-Tong. *Dialects:* Pak, Tong. 2 nearly identical dialects; Pak is larger. *Other:* SVO.

Pal (Abasakur) [abw] 1,159 (2000 census). Madang Province. *Class:* Trans-New Guinea, Madang-Adelbert Range, Adelbert Range, Pihom-Isumrud-Mugil, Pihom, Omosan. *Dialects:* Related to Kobol.

Pamosu (Hinihon) [hih] 1,503 (2000 SIL). Madang Province, north central, Adelbert Range. *Class:* Trans-New Guinea, Madang-Adelbert Range, Adelbert Range, Pihom-Isumrud-Mugil, Pihom, Tiboran. *Dialects:* Related to Kowaki (nearly extinct). *Lg Use:* Vigorous. All ages. Speakers also use Tok Pisin. Some of older generation can speak Pal. *Other:* Mountain slope. Tropical Forest. 1,000 to 1,300 meters. Swidden agriculturalists. Christian, traditional religion.

Panim [pnr] 420 (2003 SIL). Madang Province just west of Madang city. *Class:* Trans-New Guinea, Madang-Adelbert Range, Madang, Mabuso, Gum. *Dialects:* Related to Gumalu, Sihan, Isebe, Bau, Amele.

Papapana [ppn] 120 (2000 Wurm). Bougainville Province. *Class:* Austronesian, Malayo-Polynesian, Central-Eastern, Eastern Malayo-Polynesian, Oceanic, Western Oceanic, Meso Melanesian, New Ireland, South New Ireland-Northwest Solomonic, Nehan-North Bougainville, Papapana.

Papi (Paupe) [ppe] 70 (2000 Wurm). Sandaun Province, middle Sepik Region, one village on the Frieda River. *Class:* Sepik-Ramu, Leonhard Schultze, Papi. *Dialects:* Lexical similarity 29% with Suarmin, closest. *Lg Use:* Nearly all speakers have some knowledge of Tok Pisin. *Lg Dev:* Literacy rate in second language: 2% to 3%.

Papitalai [pat] 520 (1977 Lincoln). Manus Province, Naringel and Papitalai, Los Negros Island. *Class:* Austronesian, Malayo-Polynesian, Central-Eastern, Eastern Malayo-Polynesian, Oceanic, Admiralty Islands, Eastern, Manus, East. *Dialects:* 3 dialects. Close to Koro. *Lg Use:* Speakers are moderately bilingual in Loniu. *Other:* SVO. Shore dwellers. Fishermen; hunters; animal husbandry: pigs.

Parawen (Para) [prw] 429 (1981 Wurm and Hattori). Madang Province. *Class:* Trans-New Guinea, Madang-Adelbert Range, Adelbert Range, Pihom-Isumrud-Mugil, Pihom, Numugenan.

Pare (Pa, Akium-Pare) [ppt] 2,000 (1990 UBS). Western Province. *Class:* Trans-New Guinea, Main Section,

Central and Western, Central and South New Guinea-Kutubuan, Central and South New Guinea, Awin-Pare. *Lg Dev:* Literacy rate in first language: below 5%. Literacy rate in second language: 5% to 15%. Bible portions: 1978–1980.

Pasi (Besi) [psq] 356 (2000 census). Southeast corner of Sandaun Province, Wan Wan Division, 3 villages. *Class:* Sepik-Ramu, Sepik, Tama. *Dialects:* Close to Ayi.

Patep (Ptep) [ptp] 1,700 (2003 SIL). Morobe Province, Mumeng District. *Class:* Austronesian, Malayo-Polynesian, Central-Eastern, Eastern Malayo-Polynesian, Oceanic, Western Oceanic, North New Guinea, Huon Gulf, South, Hote-Buang, Buang, Mumeng. *Dialect:* Dengalu. In the Mumeng dialect chain. Some intelligibility of Gorakor and Zenag. *Lg Dev:* Grammar. NT: 1986. *Other:* SVO. Mountain slope. Tropical forest. 300 to 900 meters. Swidden agriculturalists.

Patpatar (Gelik, Patpari) [gfk] 7,000 (1998 SIL). New Ireland Province, Namatanai District, south central. *Class:* Austronesian, Malayo-Polynesian, Central-Eastern, Eastern Malayo-Polynesian, Oceanic, Western Oceanic, Meso Melanesian, New Ireland, South New Ireland-Northwest Solomonic, Patpatar-Tolai. *Dialects:* Pala, Sokirik, Patpatar. *Lg Dev:* Literacy rate in first language: 75% to 100%. Literacy rate in second language: 75% to 100%. NT: 1997.

Pawaia (Pavaia, Sira, Aurama, Tudahwe, Yasa) [pwa] 4,000 (1991 SIL). Simbu Province, Karimui District, and Gulf Province, Purari River near Oroi. Some also in Eastern Highlands Province. *Class:* Trans-New Guinea, Teberan-Pawaian, Pawaian. *Dialects:* Aurama (Turoha, Uri), Hauruha. *Lg Dev:* Literacy rate in first language: below 5%. Literacy rate in second language: below 5%. NT: 2000. *Other:* Traditional religion, Christian.

Paynamar [pmr] 150 (1975 Z'Graggen). Madang Province. *Class:* Trans-New Guinea, Madang-Adelbert Range, Adelbert Range, Josephstaal-Wanang, Wanang, Paynamar.

Pei (Pai) [ppq] 208 (1981 Wurm and Hattori). Sandaun Province, middle Sepik Region, Hauna and Walio (Leonhard Schultze) River. *Class:* Sepik-Ramu, Leonhard Schultze, Walio. *Dialects:* Close to Walio. *Lg Use:* Speakers are learning Walio. Very limited comprehension of Tok Pisin. *Other:* Different from Mala (Pai) in Madang Province. Christian.

Pele-Ata (Wasi, Uase, Uasi, Uasilau, Peleata) [ata] 1,900 (1991 SIL). West New Britain Province, Nakanai District, inland from Bongula Bay. *Class:* East Papuan, Yele-Solomons-New Britain, New Britain, Wasi. *Dialects:* Pele, Ata. *Lg Dev:* NT: 1996.

Penchal [pek] 550 (1982 SIL). Manus Province, Rambutyo Island. *Class:* Austronesian, Malayo-Polynesian, Central-Eastern, Eastern Malayo-Polynesian, Oceanic, Admiralty Islands, Eastern, Southeast Islands. *Dialects:* 3 nearly identical dialects. *Lg Use:* Speakers are moderately bilingual in Titan. *Other:* SVO.

Petats [pex] 2,000 (1975 SIL). Bougainville Province, Buka Passage District, Petats, Pororan, and Hitau islands off the west coast of Buka Island. *Class:* Austronesian, Malayo-Polynesian, Central-Eastern, Eastern Malayo-Polynesian, Oceanic, Western Oceanic, Meso Melanesian, New Ireland, South New Ireland-Northwest Solomonic, Nehan-North Bougainville, Buka. *Dialects:* Hitau-Pororan, Matsungan, Sumoun. Sumoun may be a dialect. *Lg Use:* Trade language. 8,000 second-language speakers (1977 Voegelin and Voegelin). *Lg Dev:* Literacy rate in first language: 75% to 100%. Literacy rate in second language: 75% to 100%. Bible portions: 1934–1978.

Piame (Biami) [pin] 100 (1981 Wurm and Hattori). Sandaun Province, middle Sepik Region, headwaters of the Niksek (April) and Walio (Leonhard Schultz) rivers.

Class: Sepik-Ramu, Sepik, Sepik Hill, Sanio. *Lg Use:* About 3 speakers of Tok Pisin. *Lg Dev:* Literacy rate in first language: below 5%. Literacy rate in second language: below 5%. *Other:* First contact with outsiders in 1982.

Pinai-Hagahai (Pinaye, Pinai, Hagahai, Wapi, Aramo, Miamia) [pnn] 600 (1997 SIL). Border area of Enga, Madang, Western Highlands, and East Sepik provinces. *Class:* Trans-New Guinea, Main Section, East New Guinea Highlands, Piawi. *Dialects:* Luya-Ginam-Mamusi, Pinai. The dialects have 78% lexical similarity with each other. They have 33% with Haruai, 19% with Kobon, 8% with Enga. *Lg Use:* Some speakers are partially bilingual in Enga, Tok Pisin, or Haruai. *Other:* Speakers in Enga Province use 'Pinai' to refer to the entire language group. Those in Madang Province use 'Hagahai' to refer to themselves, suggested to them by a medical anthropologist. 'Wapi' or 'Miamia' are sometimes used by the Enga, 'Aramo' by Haruai speakers. Medical workers report widespread health problems. Mountain slope. 100 to 1,300 meters. Hunter-gatherers; swidden agriculturalists.

Piu (Sanbiau, Lanzog, Kuruko) [pix] 100 (2000 Wurm). Morobe Province, upper Watut River, one village. *Class:* Austronesian, Malayo-Polynesian, Central-Eastern, Eastern Malayo-Polynesian, Oceanic, Western Oceanic, North New Guinea, Huon Gulf, South, Hote-Buang, Buang. *Other:* Distinct from Pyu in Sandaun Province.

Ponam [ncc] 420 (1977 Lincoln). Manus Province, Ponam Island. *Class:* Austronesian, Malayo-Polynesian, Central-Eastern, Eastern Malayo-Polynesian, Oceanic, Admiralty Islands, Eastern, Manus, East. *Dialects:* Close to Andra-Hus. *Lg Use:* Moderately bilingual in Kurti. *Other:* SVO.

Pouye (Bouye) [bye] 960 (2003 SIL). Sandaun Province. *Class:* Sepik-Ramu, Sepik, Ram. *Dialects:* Related to Awtuw, Karawa. Lexical similarity 67% with Karawa.

Puari [pux] 35 (2003 SIL). Sandaun Province, coast around Puari. *Class:* Sko, Krisa. *Dialects:* Related to Rawo, Krisa, Warapu. *Lg Dev:* Literacy rate in second language: 50% to 75%. *Other:* Nearly extinct.

Pulabu [pup] 116 (1981 Wurm and Hattori). Madang Province. *Class:* Trans-New Guinea, Madang-Adelbert Range, Madang, Rai Coast, Kabenau. *Dialects:* Related to Siroi, Arawum, Kolom, Lemio.

Purari (Koriki, Evorra, Namau, Iai, Maipua) [iar] 7,000 (1991 UBS). Gulf Province, between Kapaina Inlet and Orokolo language, Purari River. *Class:* Trans-New Guinea, Eleman, Purari. *Dialect:* Iai (Namau). Apparently unrelated to other languages of Gulf Province. *Lg Dev:* Literacy rate in first language: below 5%. Literacy rate in second language: 5% to 15%. NT: 1920.

Pyu [pby] 100 (1978 SIL). Village of Biake No. 2 on the October River just east of Papua, Indonesia border. Not in Papua, Indonesia. *Class:* Kwomtari-Baibai, Pyu. *Other:* Different from Austronesian Piu in Morobe Province.

Qaqet (Maqaqet, Kakat, Makakat, Baining) [byx] 6,350 (1988 SIL). East New Britain Province, Gazelle Peninsula. *Class:* East Papuan, Yele-Solomons-New Britain, New Britain, Baining-Taulil. *Dialects:* 2 dialects. *Lg Dev:* NT: 1996. *Other:* Several primary schools. Mountain slope, coastal.

Ramoaaina (Duke of York, Ramuaina) [rai] 10,266 (2000 census). East New Britain Province, Kokopo District, Duke of York Islands. *Class:* Austronesian, Malayo-Polynesian, Central-Eastern, Eastern Malayo-Polynesian, Oceanic, Western Oceanic, Meso Melanesian, New Ireland, South New Ireland-Northwest Solomonic, Patpatar-Tolai. *Dialects:* Makada, Molot (Main Island), Aalawa (Aalawaa, Alawa, Mioko, Ulu, South Islands). Makada dialect is very different. Possibly not intelligible to speakers of other dialects. *Lg Use:* Vigorous. All domains. Language of instruction in schools, local

administration, commerce. All ages. Younger children are monolingual. Positive language attitude. Most speakers also use Tok Pisin. Most older than 50 can also use Kuanua (Tolai). People 20 to 50 who have finished secondary school can speak some English. Language used in first three years of school (prep, grades 1 to 2). From grade 3 English is used. *Lg Dev:* Literacy rate in first language: 50%. Literacy rate in second language: 75% to 100%. Most adults can read it, 10% can write it. Videos. Bible portions: 1882–2002. *Other:* SVO. Coastal, coral islands. Tropical forest, highly cultivated. Sea level to 40 meters. Fishermen; swidden agriculturalists. Christian, traditional religion.

Ramopa (Keriaka, Kereaka) [kjx] 1,000 (1981 Wurm and Hattori). Bougainville Province, northwest Bougainville Island, south of Rapoisi. *Class:* East Papuan, Bougainville, West, Keriaka. *Dialects:* Lexical similarity 19% with Rapoisi. *Lg Use:* Few also use Tok Pisin. *Other:* Traditional religion, Christian.

Rao (Annaberg, Rao Breri) [rao] 6,000 (1992 UBS). Madang Province, Keram River area, lower Ramu Valley, 80 miles west of Madang city. *Class:* Sepik-Ramu, Ramu, Ramu Proper, Annaberg, Rao. *Dialects:* Li'o, Ndramini'o. *Lg Dev:* NT: 2000. *Other:* Plains. Swamp. Traditional religion.

Rapoisi (Kunua, Konua) [kyx] 3,500 (1998 SIL). Bougainville Province, northwest Bougainville Island, Kunua District. Most villages are inland. *Class:* East Papuan, Bougainville, West. *Dialects:* Related to Eivo, Kereaka, Rotokas. *Lg Use:* Vigorous. Tok Pisin used in schools. *Lg Dev:* Bible portions: 1994. *Other:* Christian, traditional religion.

Rapting [rpt] 332 (1981 Wurm and Hattori). Madang Province. *Class:* Trans-New Guinea, Madang-Adelbert Range, Madang, Mabuso, Hanseman. *Dialects:* Related to Murupi, Wamas, Samosa, Mosimo, Saruga, Nake, Matepi, Garus, Yoidik, Rempi, Silopi, Utu, Mawan, Baimak, Bagupi, Gal, Garuh, Kamba.

Rawa (Raua, Erawa, Erewa) [rwo] 11,500 (1998 SIL). Population includes 7,000 Rawa and 4,500 Karo. Madang Province, Upper Ramu District (Rawa dialect), Rai Coast District (Karo dialect). The two dialects are on opposite sides of the Finisterre Range. *Class:* Trans-New Guinea, Main Section, Central and Western, Huon-Finisterre, Finisterre, Gusap-Mot. *Dialects:* Rawa, Karo. *Lg Dev:* Literacy rate in first language: 20% Rawa, below 1% Karo. Literacy rate in second language: 25% Rawa, 50% Karo. Grammar. NT: 1992–2001. *Other:* SOV. Mountain slope. Tropical forest. Sea level to 2,200 meters. Swidden agriculturalists: sweet potatoes, cash crops (coffee and vegetables).

Rawo [rwa] 640 (2003 SIL). Sandaun Province coast around Rawo and Leitre. *Class:* Sko, Krisa. *Dialects:* Related to Krisa, Puari, Warapu. *Lg Dev:* Literacy rate in second language: 50% to 75%.

Rema (Bothar) [bow] Extinct. Western Province, Morehead District. Not in Papua, Indonesia. *Class:* Trans-New Guinea, Trans-Fly-Bulaka River, Trans-Fly, Morehead and Upper Maro rivers, Tonda. *Dialects:* Related to Aramba, Kanum. *Other:* Swamp, savannah. Below 300 meters.

Rempi (Rempin, A'e, Erempi) [rmp] 1,594 (2003 SIL). Madang Province. *Class:* Trans-New Guinea, Madang-Adelbert Range, Madang, Mabuso, Hanseman.

Rerau [rea] 588 (2000 census). Madang Province. *Class:* Trans-New Guinea, Madang-Adelbert Range, Madang, Rai Coast, Nuru. *Dialects:* Related to Kwato, Ogea, Uya, Duduela, Jilim, Yangulam.

Romkun (Romkuin) [rmk] 632 (2003 SIL). Madang Province. *Class:* Sepik-Ramu, Ramu, Ramu Proper, Goam, Tamolan.

Ronji (Roinji, Gali) [roe] 449 (2003 SIL). 2 villages, one each in Madang and Morobe provinces, north coast of Huon Peninsula, 50 km northwest of Wasu, 30 km north-northwest of Sapmanga, about 45 km southeast of Saidor. *Class:* Austronesian, Malayo-Polynesian, Central-Eastern, Eastern Malayo-Polynesian, Oceanic, Western Oceanic, North New Guinea, Ngero-Vitiaz, Vitiaz, Roinji-Nenaya. *Dialects:* Lexical similarity 67% with Mato, 46% with Karnai, 45% with Malasanga, 44% with Arop-Lukep, 33% with Sio, 28% with Tuam-Mutu. *Other:* Mato language schools are operating in both villages. SVO. Coastal. Savannah. Sea level. Swidden agriculturalists. Christian, traditional religion.

Rotokas [roo] 4,320 (1981 Wurm and Hattori). Bougainville Province, Central Bougainville District, central mountains. 28 villages. *Class:* East Papuan, Bougainville, West, Rotokas. *Dialects:* Pipipaia, Aita, Atsilima. *Lg Dev:* Literacy rate in first language: 50% to 75%. Literacy rate in second language: 50% to 75%. Dictionary. NT: 1982. *Other:* SOV. Mountain slope, coastal. Tropical forest. Sea level to 700 meters. Swidden agriculturalists; intensive agriculturalists: cocoa and other cash crops.

Rumu (Kairi, Rumuwa, Dumu, Tumu, Kibiri, Kai-Iri) [klq] 1,000 (1985 UBS). Gulf Province, Kikori District, north of Kikori on the Kikori, Sirebi, and Tiviri rivers. *Class:* Trans-New Guinea, Turama-Kikorian, Kairi. *Lg Dev:* Literacy rate in first language: below 5%. Literacy rate in second language: 5% to 15%. Bible portions: 1965–1993. *Other:* A distinct language from Kibiri (Porome).

Saep [spd] 550 (2003 SIL). Madang Province, Gowar River area, Rai coast, 75 miles east of Madang. *Class:* Trans-New Guinea, Madang-Adelbert Range, Madang, Rai Coast, Yaganon. *Dialects:* Related to Dumun. *Lg Dev:* Literacy rate in first language: below 5%. *Other:* Mountainous. Coconuts.

Safeyoka (Ampale, Ampele, Ambari, Ampeeli-Wojokeso) [apz] 2,388 (1980 census). Morobe Province, Kaiapit, Lae-Wamba, and Menyamya districts. *Class:* Trans-New Guinea, Main Section, Central and Western, Angan, Angan Proper. *Dialect:* Aiewomba, Wajakes (Wocokeso). *Lg Use:* Speakers also use Tok Pisin or Yabem. *Lg Dev:* Literacy rate in first language: 5% to 15%. Literacy rate in second language: 25% to 50%. Grammar. NT: 1989. *Other:* SOV. Mountain slope. Tropical forest. 1,000 to 1,500 meters. Swidden agriculturalists. Traditional religion, Christian.

Sakam [skm] 510 (1978 McElhanon). Morobe Province. *Class:* Trans-New Guinea, Main Section, Central and Western, Huon-Finisterre, Finisterre, Uruwa. *Other:* The most divergent Uruwa language.

Saliba [sbe] 2,300 (2000 Oetzel). Sariba and Rogeia islands, and parts of the mainland across from Rogeia Island, China Strait, Milne Bay Province. *Class:* Austronesian, Malayo-Polynesian, Central-Eastern, Eastern Malayo-Polynesian, Oceanic, Western Oceanic, Papuan Tip, Nuclear, Suauic. *Dialects:* Saliba, Logeya. Distinct from Suau. *Lg Use:* Vigorous. All domains. Used in some village preschools, some churches. All ages. All children under school age are monolingual. Positive language attitude. About 1,000 use basic English as second language. Very few also know Tok Pisin. English is the language used in school. Older people know Suau, because it was the school language until 1968. *Lg Dev:* Literacy rate in first language: 87%. Grammar. *Other:* Islands, coastal. Copra production; fishermen. Christian, Baha'i.

Salt-Yui (Salt, Salt-Iui, Yui, Iui) [sll] 6,500 (1981 Wurm and Hattori). Simbu Province, Gumine District. 10 villages. *Class:* Trans-New Guinea, Main Section, Central and Western, East New Guinea Highlands, Central, Chimbu. *Dialects:* Close to Nondiri. *Lg Dev:* NT: 1978.

Sam (Songum) [snx] 779 (2000 census). Madang Province, just inland and south of Bongu, Songum, Buan, and Wongbe villages. *Class:* Trans-New Guinea, Madang-Adelbert Range, Madang, Rai Coast, Mindjim. *Other:* 'Songum' is a village name, 'Sam' means language. Coastal. Sea level to 90 meters.

Samberigi (Sau, Sanaberigi) [ssx] 3,125 (1981 Wurm and Hattori). Southern Highlands Province, Lake Kutubu District, east of Erave. *Class:* Trans-New Guinea, Main Section, Central and Western, East New Guinea Highlands, West-Central, Angal-Kewa. *Lg Dev:* NT: 1993.

Samo (Daba, Nomad, Supei) [smq] 900 (2001 SIL). Western Province, Lake Murray District, southern Upper Strickland Census District, east of the Strickland River, north of Nomad. *Class:* Trans-New Guinea, Main Section, Central and Western, Central and South New Guinea-Kutubuan, Central and South New Guinea, East Strickland. *Lg Use:* Speakers also use Hiri Motu. *Lg Dev:* Literacy rate in first language: 5% to 15%. Literacy rate in second language: 20% to 25%. One primary school to start 2001. Bible portions: 1980. *Other:* Interfluvial. Swamp, tropical forest. 100 to 150 meters. Swidden agriculturalists; hunter-gatherers. Traditional religion, Christian.

Samosa [swm] 90 (2000 Wurm). Madang Province. *Class:* Trans-New Guinea, Madang-Adelbert Range, Madang, Mabuso, Hanseman. *Dialects:* Related to Murupi, Wamas, Rapting, Mosimo, Saruga, Nake, Matepi, Garus, Yoidik, Rempi, Silopi, Utu, Mawan, Baimak, Bagupi, Gal, Garuh, Kamba.

Saniyo-Hiyewe [sny] 644 (1981 Wurm and Hattori). East Sepik Province, Ambunti District, foothills of the Wogamus River basin. Saniyo dialect: Pukapuki, Sio, Hanasi, Salunapi, Malapute'e villages; Hiyewe dialect: Maposi village. *Class:* Sepik-Ramu, Sepik, Sepik Hill, Sanio. *Dialects:* Saniyo (Sanio), Hiyowe (Hiowe). Related to Niksek ("Paka"). *Lg Dev:* Literacy rate in first language: 5% to 15%. Literacy rate in second language: 15% to 25%. Bible portions: 1983–1984. *Other:* Seminomadic. SOV. Interfluvial. Tropical forest. 100 meters. Hunter-gatherers; agriculturalists.

Saposa [sps] 1,400 (1998 SIL). Bougainville Province, Buka District, chain of islands south of Buka Island off northwest coast of Bougainville. *Class:* Austronesian, Malayo-Polynesian, Central-Eastern, Eastern Malayo-Polynesian, Oceanic, Western Oceanic, Meso Melanesian, New Ireland, South New Ireland-Northwest Solomonic, Nehan-North Bougainville, Saposa-Tinputz. *Dialect:* Taiof, Saposa (Fa Saposa). *Lg Dev:* Literacy rate in first language: 75% to 100%. Literacy rate in second language: 75% to 100%. NT: 2001.

Saruga [sra] 129 (1981 Wurm and Hattori). Madang Province. *Class:* Trans-New Guinea, Madang-Adelbert Range, Madang, Mabuso, Hanseman.

Sauk [skc] 605 (1978 McElhanon). Morobe Province. *Class:* Trans-New Guinea, Main Section, Central and Western, Huon-Finisterre, Finisterre, Erap.

Sausi (Uya) [ssj] 1,452 (2003 SIL). Madang Province. *Class:* Trans-New Guinea, Madang-Adelbert Range, Madang, Rai Coast, Evapia. *Dialects:* Related to Sinsauru, Asas, Kesawai, Dumpu.

Seimat (Ninigo) [ssg] 1,000 (1992 SIL). Western Manus Province, on the Ninigo Islands and Anchorite Islands. *Class:* Austronesian, Malayo-Polynesian, Central-Eastern, Eastern Malayo-Polynesian, Oceanic, Admiralty Islands, Western. *Other:* SVO.

Selepet (Selepe) [spl] 7,000 (1988 SIL). Morobe Province, Kabwum District, valleys of the Pumune and Kiari rivers. *Class:* Trans-New Guinea, Main Section, Central and Western, Huon-Finisterre, Huon, Western.

Dialects: North Selepet, South Selepet. *Lg Dev:* Literacy rate in first language: 25% to 50%. Literacy rate in second language: 25% to 50%. Dictionary. Grammar. NT: 1986. *Other:* Christian, traditional religion.

Sene [sej] 10 (1978 McElhanon). Morobe Province. *Class:* Trans-New Guinea, Main Section, Central and Western, Huon-Finisterre, Huon, Eastern. *Other:* Nearly extinct.

Sengo [spk] 522 (2003 SIL). East Sepik Province, Ambunti District, Sengo village, west-northwest of Pagwi. *Class:* Sepik-Ramu, Sepik, Middle Sepik, Ndu. *Lg Use:* Most adults are fluent in Iatmul.

Sengseng (Asengseng) [ssz] 1,750 (2003 SIL). West New Britain Province, southwest interior. *Class:* Austronesian, Malayo-Polynesian, Central-Eastern, Eastern Malayo-Polynesian, Oceanic, Western Oceanic, North New Guinea, Ngero-Vitiaz, Vitiaz, Southwest New Britain, Arawe-Pasismanua, Pasismanua. *Dialects:* Wurm and Hattori treat it as a dialect of Kaulong. *Lg Dev:* Literacy rate in second language: 30%. Bible portions: 1992. *Other:* 300 to 450 meters.

Sepa [spe] 697 (2003 SIL). Madang Province, coast south of Manam Island around Bogia. *Class:* Austronesian, Malayo-Polynesian, Central-Eastern, Eastern Malayo-Polynesian, Oceanic, Western Oceanic, North New Guinea, Schouten, Kairiru-Manam, Manam. *Dialects:* Related to Wogeo, Biem, Manam, Medebur.

Sepen [spm] 650 (2003 SIL). Madang Province. *Class:* Sepik-Ramu, Ramu, Ramu Proper, Ruboni, Misegian.

Sera (Ssia, Serra) [sry] 432 (1981 Wurm and Hattori). Sandaun Province, around Serai, one village. *Class:* Austronesian, Malayo-Polynesian, Central-Eastern, Eastern Malayo-Polynesian, Oceanic, Western Oceanic, North New Guinea, Schouten, Siau. *Lg Dev:* Literacy rate in second language: 50% to 75%. *Other:* Coastal.

Seta [stf] 155 (1981 Wurm and Hattori). Sandaun Province. *Class:* Torricelli, West Wapei. *Lg Dev:* Literacy rate in second language: 50% to 75%.

Setaman [stm] 200 (1981 Wurm and Hattori). Sandaun Province. *Class:* Trans-New Guinea, Main Section, Central and Western, Central and South New Guinea-Kutubuan, Central and South New Guinea, Ok, Mountain.

Seti [sbi] 164 (2003 SIL). Sandaun Province. *Class:* Torricelli, West Wapei. *Lg Dev:* Literacy rate in second language: 50% to 75%.

Sewa Bay (Duau Pwata) [sew] 1,516 (1972 census). 20% monolingual. Milne Bay Province, center of Normanby Island around Sewa Bay. *Class:* Austronesian, Malayo-Polynesian, Central-Eastern, Eastern Malayo-Polynesian, Oceanic, Western Oceanic, Papuan Tip, Nuclear, North Papuan Mainland-D'Entrecasteaux, Dobu-Duau. *Dialects:* Miadeba, Bwakera, Maiabare, Darubia, Sewataitai, Sibonai, Central Sewa Bay. The dialects are very diverse. Lexical similarity 45% with Dobu (closest). *Lg Use:* Speakers also use Dobu. *Other:* Christian, traditional religion.

Sialum [slw] 642 (1978 McElhanon). Morobe Province. *Class:* Trans-New Guinea, Main Section, Central and Western, Huon-Finisterre, Huon, Western. *Lg Use:* Speakers also use Ono.

Siane (Siani) [snp] 28,978 (2000 census). Eastern Highlands Province, Watabung and Unggai census divisions (16,000), Goroka District. Simbu Province, Nambaiyufa Census Division (11,000). *Class:* Trans-New Guinea, Main Section, Central and Western, East New Guinea Highlands, East-Central, Siane. *Dialects:* Kolepa, Yamofowe, Komongu, Komoigaleka, Kemanimowe, Ona, Keto, Laiya, Fowe, Olumba, Lambau, Alango, Yandime, Wando. Separate literature in Komongu and Lambau dialects. *Lg Dev:* Literacy rate in first language: 25% to 50%. Literacy rate in second language: 25% to 50%. NT: 1991–1996. *Other:* SOV. Mountain slope. Forest. 1,700 to

2,500 meters. Agriculturalists; some cash crops: coffee, vegetables.

Siar-Lak (Siar, Lambom, Lamassa, Lak) [sjr] 2,076 (2000 census). Southern New Ireland Province, Namatanai District. *Class:* Austronesian, Malayo-Polynesian, Central-Eastern, Eastern Malayo-Polynesian, Oceanic, Western Oceanic, Meso Melanesian, New Ireland, South New Ireland-Northwest Solomonic, Patpatar-Tolai. *Lg Use:* Tok Pisin is second language. English used in schools. *Other:* SVO. Coastal.

Sibe (Sibbe, Sibe-Nagovisi, Nagovisi) [nco] 5,000 (1975 SIL). Bougainville Province, Buin District. *Class:* East Papuan, Bougainville, East, Nasioi. *Lg Dev:* Literacy rate in second language: 75% to 100%. Bible portions: 1984. *Other:* Moderate acculturation.

Sihan [snr] 568 (2003 SIL). Madang Province. *Class:* Trans-New Guinea, Madang-Adelbert Range, Madang, Mabuso, Gum. *Dialects:* Related to Gumalu, Amele, Isebe, Bau, Panim.

Sileibi [sbq] 259 (1981 Wurm and Hattori). Madang Province. *Class:* Trans-New Guinea, Madang-Adelbert Range, Adelbert Range, Josephstaal-Wanang, Josephstaal, Sikan. *Dialects:* Related to Katiati.

Siliput (Mai, Maimai, Sokorok) [mkc] 515 (2003 SIL). Population includes 242 in Makru-Klaplei plus 21 elsewhere. Sandaun Province, Seleput village, Makru-Klaplei Division, Nuku District, north of Mehek. *Class:* Torricelli, Maimai, Maimai Proper. *Dialects:* Lexical similarity 30% with Yahang. *Lg Dev:* Literacy rate in second language: 25% to 50%. *Other:* Different from Selepet.

Silopi [xsp] 185 (2003 SIL). Madang Province. *Class:* Trans-New Guinea, Madang-Adelbert Range, Madang, Mabuso, Hanseman. *Dialects:* Related to Murupi, Wamas, Rapting, Mosimo, Saruga, Nake, Matepi, Garus, Yoidik, Rempi, Samosa, Utu, Mawan, Baimak, Bagupi, Gal, Garuh, Kamba.

Simbali (Asimbali) [smg] 387 (2004 SIL). East New Britain Province, Gazelle Peninsula. *Class:* East Papuan, Yele-Solomons-New Britain, New Britain, Baining-Taulil. *Lg Use:* Many have comprehension in Mali. *Other:* Mountain slope, foothills.

Simbari (Chimbari) [smb] 3,036 (1990 census). Eastern Highlands Province, Marawaka District. *Class:* Trans-New Guinea, Main Section, Central and Western, Angan, Angan Proper. *Lg Use:* A government school teaches children in English and Tok Pisin. *Other:* Swidden agriculturalists: sweet potatoes, cassava, coffee; hunters; gatherers; animal husbandry: pigs, poultry. Traditional religion, Christian.

Simeku [smz] 1,898 (1980 SIL). Population includes 1,183 Koopei and 715 Mainoki. Bougainville Province, Kieta District, central mountains. Mainoki is on the west slope and Koopei on the east slope. *Class:* East Papuan, Bougainville, East, Nasioi. *Dialects:* Mainoki (Mainoke), Koopei (Kopei). Not functionally intelligible with Nasioi. *Other:* The people are culturally conservative.

Sinagen (Galu, Metru) [siu] 328 (2003 SIL). Sandaun Province. *Class:* Torricelli, Wapei-Palei, Wapei.

Sinasina [sst] 50,079 (1981 Wurm and Hattori). Simbu Province. *Class:* Trans-New Guinea, Main Section, Central and Western, East New Guinea Highlands, Central, Chimbu. *Dialects:* Tabare, Guna. Close to Dom and Golin. *Lg Dev:* NT: 1975.

Sinaugoro (Sinagoro) [snc] 15,000 (1991 SIL). Central Province, Rigo District, south of Kwikila. *Class:* Austronesian, Malayo-Polynesian, Central-Eastern, Eastern Malayo-Polynesian, Oceanic, Western Oceanic, Papuan Tip, Peripheral, Central Papuan, Sinagoro-Keapara. *Dialects:* Ikolu, Balawaia, Saroa, Babagarupu, Kwaibida, Taboro, Kwaibo, Alepa, Omene, Tubulamo, Ikega, Boku,

Buaga, Wiga, Vora, Kubuli, Oruone. Boku dialect may be most central. Lexical similarity 70% to 75% with Kalo (closest), 65% to 70% with Hula. *Lg Use:* Motu and Hiri Motu fairly well known. *Lg Dev:* Literacy rate in second language: 50% to 75%. Dictionary. Grammar. NT: 1995.

Sinsauru (Kow) [snz] 505 (2003 SIL). Madang Province, near Dumpu. *Class:* Trans-New Guinea, Madang-Adelbert Range, Madang, Rai Coast, Evapia. *Dialect:* Saipa. Related to Asas, Sausi, Kesawai, Dumpu.

Sio (Sigawa) [xsi] 3,500 (1987 SIL). Morobe Province, Wasu District, mainland near Sio Island. *Class:* Austronesian, Malayo-Polynesian, Central-Eastern, Eastern Malayo-Polynesian, Oceanic, Western Oceanic, North New Guinea, Ngero-Vitiaz, Vitiaz, Sio. *Lg Dev:* Literacy rate in first language: 50% to 75%. Literacy rate in second language: 50% to 75%. NT: 1995. *Other:* Swidden agriculturalists.

Siroi (Suroi) [ssd] 1,309 (2003 SIL). Madang Province, Saidor District. Kumisanger is one village; not a separate language. 5 villages. *Class:* Trans-New Guinea, Madang-Adelbert Range, Madang, Rai Coast, Kabenau. *Dialects:* Related to Arawum, Pulabu, Kolom, Lemio. *Lg Use:* Vigorous. All domains. Used in local commerce. All ages. Young children are monolingual. Positive language attitude. Speakers also use Tok Pisin, and other neighboring languages. Some know Bel, the former church language. Tok Pisin and English used in schools. *Lg Dev:* Literacy rate in first language: 50%. Grammar. NT: 1975–2000. *Other:* Coastal, mountain slope. Coastal plains. copra production; merchants. Christian.

Sissano (Sisano, Sinano, Sinama) [sso] 300 (2000 Wurm). Ethnic population: 4,776 (1990 census). Sandaun Province, Aitape District, around Sissano. *Class:* Austronesian, Malayo-Polynesian, Central-Eastern, Eastern Malayo-Polynesian, Oceanic, Western Oceanic, North New Guinea, Schouten, Siau. *Dialects:* Related to Arop-Sissano, Malol, Sera, Tumleo, Yakamul, Suain. *Lg Dev:* Literacy rate in first language: 15% to 25%. Literacy rate in second language: 50% to 75%. *Other:* SVO. Coastal. Tropical forest. Sea level. Fishermen.

Siwai (Motuna) [siw] 6,600. Population includes 600 in Baitsi. Bougainville Province, southeastern. *Class:* East Papuan, Bougainville, East, Buin. *Dialect:* Baitsi (Sigisigero). *Lg Dev:* NT: 1977.

Solong (Arove, Arawe, Pililo) [aaw] 2,200 (1981 Wurm and Hattori). West New Britain Province, southwestern coast. *Class:* Austronesian, Malayo-Polynesian, Central-Eastern, Eastern Malayo-Polynesian, Oceanic, Western Oceanic, North New Guinea, Ngero-Vitiaz, Vitiaz, Southwest New Britain, Arawe-Pasismanua, Arawe, West Arawe. *Dialect:* Arawe. Dialect cluster. Understood by all along the coast. *Lg Use:* Speakers also use Tok Pisin or English. *Other:* The language is called 'Solong', the people 'Arove'. 3 primary schools. Raised coral coast. Tropical forest. Christian, traditional religion.

Solos [sol] 3,200 (1977 Lincoln). Bougainville Province, central and southwest Buka Island. *Class:* Austronesian, Malayo-Polynesian, Central-Eastern, Eastern Malayo-Polynesian, Oceanic, Western Oceanic, Meso Melanesian, New Ireland, South New Ireland-Northwest Solomonic, Nehan-North Bougainville, Solos. *Lg Dev:* Literacy rate in first language: 50% to 75%. Literacy rate in second language: 50% to 75%.

Som [smc] 80 (2000 Wurm). Morobe Province. *Class:* Trans-New Guinea, Main Section, Central and Western, Huon-Finisterre, Finisterre, Uruwa.

Sonia [siq] 300 (1988 Shaw). Western Province and Southern Highlands Province, 10 to 20 miles west and southwest of Bosavi. *Class:* Trans-New Guinea, Main Section, Central and Western, Central and South New Guinea-Kutubuan, Central and South New Guinea, Bosavi.

Lg Dev: Literacy rate in first language: below 5%. Literacy rate in second language: below 5%.

Sop (Kari, Usino) [urw] 2,250 (2003 SIL). Madang Province, Usino-Bundi District, Usino Subdistrict, northeast of the Ramu Valley. *Class:* Trans-New Guinea, Madang-Adelbert Range, Madang, Rai Coast, Peka. *Dialects:* Related to Sumau, Urigina, Danaru. *Other:* Riverine.

Sori-Harengan [sbh] 570 (1977 Lincoln). Manus Province, Sori is on the northwest coast of Manus Island and on the Sori and Harengan islands off the coast. *Class:* Austronesian, Malayo-Polynesian, Central-Eastern, Eastern Malayo-Polynesian, Oceanic, Admiralty Islands, Eastern, Manus, West. *Dialects:* Sori, Harengan. 2 nearly identical dialects. *Lg Use:* Speakers are moderately bilingual in Nyindrou. *Other:* SVO.

Sowanda (Waina, Wina, Wanya, Wanja) [sow] 1,000 in Papua New Guinea (1982 SIL). Population total all countries: 1,212. Sandaun Province, Amanab District. Also spoken in Indonesia (Papua). *Class:* Trans-New Guinea, Northern, Border, Waris. *Dialects:* Punda-Umeda (Umada), Waina. May be 2 languages. *Lg Use:* Little use of Tok Pisin.

Suarmin (Duranmin, Akiapmin) [seo] 140 (2000 Wurm). Sandaun Province, Telefomin District, a few hamlets on the Kenu River, a tributary of the Om River. Near Duranmin airstrip. *Class:* Sepik-Ramu, Leonhard Schultze, Papi. *Dialects:* Lexical similarity 29% with Papi. *Lg Use:* Young people are bilingual in Telefol. Speakers middle aged and older are not bilingual.

Suau [swp] 6,795 (1981 Wurm and Hattori). 10% monolingual. Milne Bay Province, southeastern extremity of the Papua mainland. *Class:* Austronesian, Malayo-Polynesian, Central-Eastern, Eastern Malayo-Polynesian, Oceanic, Western Oceanic, Papuan Tip, Nuclear, Suauic. *Dialects:* Daui (Fife Bay), Sinaki (Gaidasu, Gadaisu), Leileiafa, Bona Bona, Dahuni, Suau, Bonarua. *Lg Use:* Lingua franca of 14,000 along part of the south coast. *Lg Dev:* Literacy rate in second language: high. NT: 1956–1962.

Sudest (Tagula, Sud-Est, Vanga, Vanatina) [tgo] 2,000 (1987 SIL). Milne Bay Province, Yama-Yele District, Tagula Island, west of Rossel Island, at the end of the Calvados chain. *Class:* Austronesian, Malayo-Polynesian, Central-Eastern, Eastern Malayo-Polynesian, Oceanic, Western Oceanic, Papuan Tip, Peripheral, Kilivila-Louisiades, Nimoa-Sudest. *Dialects:* Rambuso (Rewa), Eastern Point, Pamela, Griffin Point (Nine Hills, Nanhil), Jelewaga. Lexical similarity 44% with Nimowa (closest). *Lg Use:* 40% monolingual. Others use Misima or Nimowa as second language. *Lg Dev:* Literacy rate in first language: 50% to 70%. Literacy rate in second language: 75% to 90%. Dictionary. *Other:* Half of the children are in school. Island. Sea level to 250 meters. Swidden agriculturalists; fishermen; some hunting.

Suena (Yema, Yarawe, Yarawi) [sue] 3,000 (2000 SIL). Ethnic population: 3,000 (2000 SIL). Morobe Province, Lae District, north of Yekora. *Class:* Trans-New Guinea, Main Section, Eastern, Binanderean, Binanderean Proper. *Lg Use:* The Yarawi are apparently a people group who spoke Suena around 1910 to 1978, but today may speak a dialect of Binandere as their first language (2000). Speakers also use Tok Pisin or English. *Lg Dev:* Literacy rate in first language: 75% to 100%. Literacy rate in second language: 75% to 100%. Grammar. NT: 1978. *Other:* Christian, traditional religion.

Suganga (Wagarabai, North Mianmin) [sug] 700 (1981 Wurm and Hattori). Sandaun Province, Amanab District. *Class:* Trans-New Guinea, Main Section, Central and Western, Central and South New Guinea-Kutubuan, Central and South New Guinea, Ok, Mountain. *Dialects:* Close to Mianmin.

Suki (Wiram) [sui] 3,512 (2003 SIL). Western Province, Lake Suki. *Class:* Trans-New Guinea, Main Section, Central and Western, Gogodala-Suki, Suki. *Lg Use:* English used in schools, which go through 6th grade. Hiri Motu also used. *Lg Dev:* Literacy rate in first language: 5% to 15%. Literacy rate in second language: 15% to 25%. NT: 1982.

Sulka [sua] 2,500 (1991 SIL). East New Britain Province, East Pomio District, Wide Bay coast. *Class:* East Papuan, Yele-Solomons-New Britain, New Britain, Sulka. *Dialects:* A dialect chain. *Lg Dev:* Literacy rate in first language: 25% to 50%. Literacy rate in second language: 75% to 100%. NT: 1997. *Other:* Several primary schools. Riverine. Swamp.

Sumariup (Sogoba, Latoma) [siv] 80 (1993 SIL). East Sepik Province, Upper Wagupmeri River. 1 village. *Class:* Sepik-Ramu, Sepik, Sepik Hill, Bahinemo. *Lg Use:* Speakers also use Alamblak or Tok Pisin. *Lg Dev:* Literacy rate in second language: 5% to 15%.

Sumau (Kari, Garia, Sumau-Garia) [six] 2,575 (2003 SIL). Madang Province, low mountain ranges between the Ramu and Naru rivers. *Class:* Trans-New Guinea, Madang-Adelbert Range, Madang, Rai Coast, Peka. *Dialects:* Possibly 2 dialects. Related to Sop, Urigina, Danaru. *Other:* SOV. Mountain ridge, river valley. Lowlands forest. 120 to 1,000 meters. Agriculturalists: taro.

Sursurunga [sgz] 3,000 (1991 SIL). South central New Ireland Province, Namatanai District. *Class:* Austronesian, Malayo-Polynesian, Central-Eastern, Eastern Malayo-Polynesian, Oceanic, Western Oceanic, Meso Melanesian, New Ireland, South New Ireland-Northwest Solomonic, Patpatar-Tolai. *Lg Dev:* Literacy rate in first language: 75% to 100%. Literacy rate in second language: 50% to 75%. Bible portions: 1979–1987.

Susuami [ssu] 10 (2000 Wurm). Morobe Province, Upper Watut Valley outside Bulolo. *Class:* Trans-New Guinea, Main Section, Central and Western, Angan. *Dialects:* Most closely related to Kamasa. *Lg Use:* Used in the home. Speakers are older adults. Speakers also use Angaatiha. *Other:* Nearly extinct.

Tabo (Waya) [knv] 3,000 (2002 SIL). Western Province, lower Aramia River villages of Waya, Saiwase, Galu, Alagi; Bamu River village of Alikinapi; lower Fly River villages of Kenedibi, Urio, and Wagumi-Sarau; Segero Creek village of Segero. *Class:* Trans-New Guinea, Trans-Fly-Bulaka River, Waia. *Dialects:* Aramia River, Fly River. The dialects have 60% lexical similarity, but nearly identical syntax and grammar. *Lg Dev:* Literacy rate in first language: 28%. Literacy rate in second language: 33%. Bible portions: 1990–2002.

Tabriak (Karawari) [tzx] 2,082 (2003 SIL). East Sepik Province, near Chambri, lower Karawari River. 9 villages. *Class:* Sepik-Ramu, Nor-Pondo, Pondo. *Dialects:* Closest to Kopar (Watam). Distinct from the Karawari dialect of Alamblak. *Lg Use:* Speakers have high proficiency in Tok Pisin.

Tai (Tay) [taw] 900 (1990 UBS). Madang Province, southwest, Dundrom village. *Class:* Trans-New Guinea, Main Section, Central and Western, East New Guinea Highlands, Kalam, Unclassified. *Lg Dev:* Bible portions: 1995. *Other:* 1,200 meters.

Taiap (Gapun) [gpn] 80 (2000 S. Wurm). East Sepik Province, Gapun village. *Class:* Sepik-Ramu, Gapun. *Dialects:* Not closely related to any other language. *Lg Use:* All speakers older than 10 years. *Lg Dev:* Literacy rate in first language: below 5%. Literacy rate in second language: 15% to 25%. *Other:* 'Taiap' is the language, 'Gapun' the village.

Tainae (Ivori) [ago] 1,000 (1991 SIL). Gulf Province, Ivori-Swanson District. The main villages are Pio, Famba, and Paiguna. *Class:* Trans-New Guinea, Main

Section, Central and Western, Angan, Angan Proper. *Dialects:* Close to Angoya. *Lg Dev:* Literacy rate in first language: below 5%. Literacy rate in second language: below 5%.

Tairora, North (Tairora) [tbg] 6,000 (2003 SIL). Eastern Highlands Province, Kainantu and Obura districts, south of Kainantu. *Class:* Trans-New Guinea, Main Section, Central and Western, East New Guinea Highlands, Eastern, Tairora. *Dialects:* Aantantara (Andandara), Arau-Varosia (Arau-Barosia), Arokaara (Arokara), Saiqora (Sai'ora), Tairora. Most closely related to South Tairora and Binumarien. *Lg Dev:* Literacy rate in first language: 75%. Literacy rate in second language: 50%. NT: 1979. *Other:* SOV. Hills, mountain slope. Savannah, forest. 1,200 to 1,800 meters. Hunters; agriculturalists.

Tairora, South (Omwunra-Toqura) [omw] 7,000 (2003 SIL). Eastern Highlands Province, Kainantu and Obura districts, south of Kainantu. *Class:* Trans-New Guinea, Main Section, Central and Western, East New Guinea Highlands, Eastern, Tairora. *Dialects:* Aatasaara (Atakara), Haaviqinra-Oraura (Habina-Oraura), Omwunra-Toqura (Obura-To'okena), Vaira-Ntosara (Baira), Veqaura (Meauna), Vinaata-Konkompira (Pinata-Konkombira). Most closely related to North Tairora and Waffa. *Lg Dev:* Literacy rate in first language: 75%. Literacy rate in second language: 50%. NT: 1994–2000. *Other:* SOV. Mountain slope. Savannah, forest. 1,600 to 2,000 meters. Hunters; agriculturalists.

Tairuma (Uaripi) [uar] 4,000 (1993 SIL). Gulf Province, Uaripi and several other villages near Toaripi. *Class:* Trans-New Guinea, Eleman, Eleman Proper, Eastern. *Lg Dev:* Literacy rate in first language: below 5%. Literacy rate in second language: 5% to 15%.

Takia [tbc] 19,619 (2003 SIL). Southern half of Karkar Island, Bagabag Island, and coastal villages Megiar and Serang, Madang Province, Madang District. *Class:* Austronesian, Malayo-Polynesian, Central-Eastern, Eastern Malayo-Polynesian, Oceanic, Western Oceanic, North New Guinea, Ngero-Vitiaz, Vitiaz, Bel, Nuclear Bel, Northern. *Dialects:* Megiar, Serang. *Lg Use:* Domains of use are being gradually reduced. Children are increasingly inclined to not use or learn Takia. All also use Tok Pisin, and many use English. Tok Pisin used at the hospital and wharf. Many marry into other language groups, and their children speak Tok Pisin or English. *Lg Dev:* Literacy rate in first language: 50% to 75%. Literacy rate in second language: 50% to 75%. People usually write in Gedaged, Tok Pisin, or English. NT: 1999.

Takuu (Tauu, Taku, Tau, Mortlock) [nho] 1,750 (2003 SIL). Bougainville Province, Atolls District, northeast of Bougainville, Takuu Atoll, Mortlock village. *Class:* Austronesian, Malayo-Polynesian, Central-Eastern, Eastern Malayo-Polynesian, Oceanic, Central-Eastern Oceanic, Remote Oceanic, Central Pacific, East Fijian-Polynesian, Polynesian, Nuclear, Samoic-Outlier, Ellicean. *Dialects:* Distinct from Nukumanu and Nukuria in Papua New Guinea and Ontong Java and Sikaiana in Solomon Islands, although very closely related. *Lg Use:* Most of the key domains. Positive language attitude.

Tami [tmy] 1,500 (2003 SIL). Population includes 681 Wanam dialect, 567 Taemi dialect. Morobe Province, Tami Islands and mainland villages south of Finschhafen. *Class:* Austronesian, Malayo-Polynesian, Central-Eastern, Eastern Malayo-Polynesian, Oceanic, Western Oceanic, North New Guinea, Ngero-Vitiaz, Vitiaz, Tami. *Dialects:* Wanam, Taemi. *Lg Use:* Older speakers also use Yabem, the church language. *Lg Dev:* Literacy rate in first language: below 5%. Literacy rate in second language: 25% to 50%. Bible portions: 2000. *Other:* SVO. Coastal, island. Tropical forest. Sea level. Swidden agriculturalists; fishermen; wood carving.

Tangga (Tanga) [tgg] 5,800 (1990 SIL). New Ireland Province, Tanga Islands, Anir (Feni) Island, three villages on New Ireland. *Class:* Austronesian, Malayo-Polynesian, Central-Eastern, Eastern Malayo-Polynesian, Oceanic, Western Oceanic, Meso Melanesian, New Ireland, South New Ireland-Northwest Solomonic, Patpatar-Tolai. *Dialects:* Tanga, Anir (Feni), Maket. *Lg Dev:* Dictionary.

Tanggu (Tanggum, Tangu) [tgu] 3,000 (1991 SIL). Madang Province, Bogia District. *Class:* Sepik-Ramu, Ramu, Ramu Proper, Goam, Ataitan. *Lg Dev:* Bible portions: 1993. *Other:* Forests. Agriculturalists; hunters; gatherers.

Tanguat [tbs] 745 (2003 SIL). Madang Province. *Class:* Sepik-Ramu, Ramu, Ramu Proper, Goam, Ataitan.

Tauade (Tauata) [ttd] 11,000 (1991 SIL). Central Province, Goilala District toward the northeast. *Class:* Trans-New Guinea, Main Section, Eastern, Central and Southeastern, Goilalan. *Dialects:* Lexical similarity 44% with Kunimaipa (closest). *Lg Dev:* Literacy rate in first language: 15% to 25%. Literacy rate in second language: 5% to 15%. RC schools teach in Tauade. *Other:* 1,000 meters.

Taulil [tuh] 800 (2000 Wurm). East New Britain Province, Gazelle Peninsula. *Class:* East Papuan, Yele-Solomons-New Britain, New Britain, Baining-Taulil. *Dialects:* Taulil, Butam. *Lg Use:* The Butam dialect is extinct (1981). Speakers also use Kuanua.

Taupota [tpa] 1,276 (2001 SIL). Milne Bay Province, Alotau District, Maramatana Local Government Area, on East Cape facing Goodenough Bay from Wamawamana to Garuwahi including Taupota village. *Class:* Austronesian, Malayo-Polynesian, Central-Eastern, Eastern Malayo-Polynesian, Oceanic, Western Oceanic, Papuan Tip, Nuclear, North Papuan Mainland-D'Entrecasteaux, Are-Taupota, Taupota. *Dialects:* Probably a dialect chain with Wa'ema to the south and Wedau to the west. Lexical similarity 81% with Topura village of Wedau, 69% with central Wedau, 76% with Wa'ema, 56% with Tawala, 53% with Maiwala. *Lg Use:* Most speakers have low proficiency in Tawala or Wedau. *Other:* Two schools.

Tauya (Inafosa) [tya] 347 (1981 Wurm and Hattori). Madang Province. *Class:* Trans-New Guinea, Madang-Adelbert Range, Adelbert Range, Brahman. *Dialects:* Related to Biyom, Isabi, Faita. *Lg Dev:* Grammar.

Tawala (Tawara, Tavara) [tbo] 20,000 (2000 census). Milne Bay Province, Alotau District, from Awaiama to East Cape, north and south shores of Milne Bay, Sideia and Basilaki islands. *Class:* Austronesian, Malayo-Polynesian, Central-Eastern, Eastern Malayo-Polynesian, Oceanic, Western Oceanic, Papuan Tip, Nuclear, North Papuan Mainland-D'Entrecasteaux, Are-Taupota, Taupota. *Dialects:* Awayama (Awaiama, Awalama), Huhuna, Kehelala (Keherara, East Cape), Lelehudi, Diwinai (Divinai), Labe (Rabe), Yaleba (Wagawaga, Gwawili, Gwavili, Ealeba), Bohilai (Bohira'i, Basilaki), Sideya (Sideia). *Lg Use:* Trade language for Milne Bay area. 40% monolingual. Speakers have some proficiency in Dobu, Suau, Motu, Wedau. Most speakers know some English. *Lg Dev:* Literacy rate in first language: 50% to 75%. Literacy rate in second language: 50% to 75%. Grammar. NT: 1985. *Other:* SVO. Mountain slope, coastal. Tropical forest. Sea level. Fishermen; peasant agriculturalists; industrialists: copra production; palm oil.

Telefol (Telefomin, Telefolmin, Teleefool) [tlf] 5,400 (1994 SIL). Sandaun Province, Telefomin District. *Class:* Trans-New Guinea, Main Section, Central and Western, Central and South New Guinea-Kutubuan, Central and South New Guinea, Ok, Mountain. *Dialects:* Telefol, Feramin. *Lg Dev:* Literacy rate in first language: 5% to 15%. Literacy rate in second language: 25% to 50%. Dictionary. Grammar. NT: 1988. *Other:* Some form of

whistle speech reported. SOV. Mountain slope. Tropical forest. 800 to 2,600 meters. Swidden agriculturalists.

Tenis (Tench) [tns] 30 (2000 Wurm). New Ireland Province, Tench Island. *Class:* Austronesian, Malayo-Polynesian, Central-Eastern, Eastern Malayo-Polynesian, Oceanic, St. Matthias. *Lg Use:* Speakers have high proficiency in Mussau-Emira. *Other:* Nearly extinct.

Teop [tio] 5,000 (1991 SIL). Bougainville Province, Tinputz District, northeastern. *Class:* Austronesian, Malayo-Polynesian, Central-Eastern, Eastern Malayo-Polynesian, Oceanic, Western Oceanic, Meso Melanesian, New Ireland, South New Ireland-Northwest Solomonic, Nehan-North Bougainville, Saposa-Tinputz. *Dialects:* Wainanana, Losiara (Raosiara), Taunita, Melilup, Petspets. Raosiara may be a dialect. *Lg Dev:* Literacy rate in first language: 75% to 100%. Literacy rate in second language: 75% to 100%. Bible portions: 1958–1966.

Terebu (Terepu, Turupu, Turubu) [trb] 128 (1990). East Sepik Province, coast southeast of Taul, village of Turubu. *Class:* Austronesian, Malayo-Polynesian, Central-Eastern, Eastern Malayo-Polynesian, Oceanic, Western Oceanic, North New Guinea, Schouten, Kairiru-Manam, Kairiru. *Other:* Coastal.

Terei (Buin, Telei, Rugara) [buo] 26,500 (2003 SIL). Southern Bougainville Province, Buin District. *Class:* East Papuan, Bougainville, East, Buin. *Dialects:* Closest to Uisai. *Lg Dev:* Literacy rate in first language: 50% to 75%. Literacy rate in second language: 75% to 100%. Bible portions: 1973–1978.

Tiang (Djaul) [tbj] 791 (1972 Beaumont). New Ireland Province, eastern part of Djaul Island. *Class:* Austronesian, Malayo-Polynesian, Central-Eastern, Eastern Malayo-Polynesian, Oceanic, Western Oceanic, Meso Melanesian, New Ireland, Lavongai-Nalik. *Other:* SVO. Coastal. Tropical forest. Sea level to 300 meters. Swidden agriculturalists.

Tifal (Tifalmin) [tif] 3,600 (2003 SIL). Sandaun Province, Telefomin District. *Class:* Trans-New Guinea, Main Section, Central and Western, Central and South New Guinea-Kutubuan, Central and South New Guinea, Ok, Mountain. *Dialects:* Tifal, Asbalmin. *Lg Use:* Vigorous. All domains. Used in preschool. Oral and written use in churches. Oral use in local commerce. Personal letters. All ages. Positive language attitude. Most use Tok Pisin, Telefol, Faiwol, or Opti. *Lg Dev:* Literacy rate in first language: 6%. 300 can read and write it. NT: 1998. *Other:* SOV. Mountain slope. Scrub forest, tropical forest. 1,600 to 2,300 meters. Swidden agriculturalists. Christian.

Tigak (Omo) [tgc] 6,000 (1991 SIL). Northern New Ireland Province, Kavieng District, and western Djaul Island. *Class:* Austronesian, Malayo-Polynesian, Central-Eastern, Eastern Malayo-Polynesian, Oceanic, Western Oceanic, Meso Melanesian, New Ireland, Lavongai-Nalik. *Dialects:* Island Tigak, West Tigak, Central Tigak, South Tigak. *Lg Dev:* Grammar. Bible portions: 1912–1972. *Other:* SVO. Coastal. Tropical forest. Sea level to 300 meters. Swidden agriculturalists.

Timbe [tim] 11,000 (1991 SIL). 60% are monolingual (women and older men). Morobe Province, Kabwum District, Timbe River valley and tributaries. *Class:* Trans-New Guinea, Main Section, Central and Western, Huon-Finisterre, Huon, Western. *Dialects:* Central Timbe, North Timbe, South Timbe. *Lg Use:* Vigorous. Weliki speakers use Timbe as second language. All domains. Used in education, local commerce. Oral and written use in church. Letter writing. All ages. Positive language attitude. All working-age men use Tok Pisin for work. 20% also know Kâte, the language formerly used in the church. *Lg Dev:* Literacy rate in first language: 50%. Literacy rate in second language: 50% to 75%. NT: 1987. *Other:* SOV. Mountain slope. Tropical forest. 1,000 meters. Swidden agriculturalists: coffee. Christian, traditional religion.

Tinputz (Vasuii, Wasoi, Timputs, Vasui) [tpz] 3,900 (1991 SIL). Bougainville Province, Teop-Tinputz District. *Class:* Austronesian, Malayo-Polynesian, Central-Eastern, Eastern Malayo-Polynesian, Oceanic, Western Oceanic, Meso Melanesian, New Ireland, South New Ireland-Northwest Solomonic, Nehan-North Bougainville, Saposa-Tinputz. *Dialects:* Vasui, Vavoehpoa', Vaene', Vado-Vaene', Vapopeo', Vapopeo'-Rausaura, Vado. *Lg Dev:* Literacy rate in first language: 50% to 75%. Literacy rate in second language: 50% to 75%. At least ten vernacular primary schools. Bible portions: 1975–1983. *Other:* Moderate acculturation. Their name for themselves is 'Vasuii'. SVO. Mountain slope. Tropical forest. Sea level to 1,000 meters. Swidden agriculturalists.

Titan (Manus, Moanus, Tito, M'bunai) [ttv] 3,850 (1992 SIL). Manus Province on the following islands - Manus (southeast coast), Tawi, Wal, M'buke, Johnson, Baluan, Tilianu, Bundro, Rambutyo. *Class:* Austronesian, Malayo-Polynesian, Central-Eastern, Eastern Malayo-Polynesian, Oceanic, Admiralty Islands, Eastern, Manus, East. *Dialects:* 2 dialects, 'r' speakers on southeast Manus Island, 'l' speakers on outlying islands. Intelligibility between speakers of 'r' and 'l' dialects is 100%. *Lg Use:* Vigorous. All Titans use Tok Pisin as a second language. A small percent of Titan speakers also use English. *Lg Dev:* Literacy rate in first language: 75% to 100%. Literacy rate in second language: 50% to 75%. *Other:* The trading ring was described by Margaret Mead. SVO. Coastal. Coconut trees. Sea level. Copra production. Christian, traditional religion.

Toaripi (Motumotu, East Elema) [tqo] 23,000 (1977 SIL). Gulf Province, Cape Possession to Cape Cupola. Kerema is a main town. *Class:* Trans-New Guinea, Eleman, Eleman Proper, Eastern. *Dialects:* Kaipi (Melaripi), Toaripi (Moripi-Iokea, Moveave), Sepoe. *Lg Dev:* Literacy rate in first language: 15% to 25%. Literacy rate in second language: 15% to 25%. Bible: 1983.

Tobo [tbv] 2,230 (1980 census). Morobe Province, upper Kuat River valley, south of Cromwell Range. *Class:* Trans-New Guinea, Main Section, Central and Western, Huon-Finisterre, Huon, Western. *Other:* Two community schools. Mountain slope. 1,665 to 1,900 meters. Swidden agriculturalists.

Tok Pisin (Pisin, Pidgin, Neomelanesian, New Guinea Pidgin English, Melanesian English) [tpi] 121,000 (2003 SIL). 50,000 monolinguals. Mainly in the northern half of the country, and now well established in Port Moresby, and into other regions. *Class:* Creole, English based, Pacific. *Dialects:* There are dialect differences between lowlands, highlands, and the islands. The highlands lexicon has more English influence (J. Holm). *Lg Use:* Official language. The first language of some people in mixed urban areas. The main means of communication between speakers of different languages. The most frequently used language in Parliament and commerce. Some second-language users speak a 'broken' Pidgin. Where it is the first language, it is passed on to children by parents. 4,000,000 second-language speakers. All domains. Used in schools, churches, government, commerce. All ages. Positive language attitude. *Lg Dev:* Literacy rate in second language: 40% to 45%. Newspapers. Radio programs. TV. Dictionary. Grammar. Bible: 1989. *Other:* Agriculturalists; merchants. Christian, traditional religion.

Tokano (Tokama, Gamuso, Zuhuzoho, Zuhozoho, Yufiyufa, Zaka) [zuh] 6,000 (1982 SIL). Eastern Highlands Province, Goroka District. *Class:* Trans-New Guinea, Main Section, Central and Western, East New Guinea Highlands, East-Central, Gahuku-Benabena.

Dialects: Lower Asaro, Zuhuzoho. *Lg Use:* Speakers also use Dano, Alekano, or Tok Pisi. *Lg Dev:* Bible portions: 1979.

Tomoip (Tumuip, Tumie, Tomoyp, Tomoive) [tqp] 700 (1982 SIL). East New Britain Province, Wide Bay to Waterfall Bay and interior. *Class:* Austronesian, Malayo-Polynesian, Central-Eastern, Eastern Malayo-Polynesian, Oceanic, Western Oceanic, Meso Melanesian, New Ireland, Tomoip.

Torau (Rorovana) [ttu] 605 (1963 SIL). Bougainville Province, southeast coast, north of Kieta. *Class:* Austronesian, Malayo-Polynesian, Central-Eastern, Eastern Malayo-Polynesian, Oceanic, Western Oceanic, Meso Melanesian, New Ireland, South New Ireland-Northwest Solomonic, Mono-Uruava. *Lg Use:* Speakers have declined in number during the last 150 years. *Lg Dev:* Literacy rate in first language: 75% to 100%. Literacy rate in second language: 75% to 100%. *Other:* Fairly acculturated. Coastal. Swamp. Agriculturalists: sweet potatoes.

Torricelli (Lou, Anamagi) [tei] 517 (2003 SIL). East Sepik Province, Maprik District and partially in Sandaun Province, west of Kombio, 5 villages. *Class:* Torricelli, Kombio-Arapesh, Kombio. *Dialects:* West Torricelli, East Torricelli. 2 dialects. *Lg Dev:* Literacy rate in first language: below 5%. Literacy rate in second language: 15% to 25%. *Other:* Different from Lou in Manus Province or Tate (Lou) in Gulf Province.

Toura (Doura) [don] 335 (2003 SIL). Central Province, around Galley Reach. *Class:* Austronesian, Malayo-Polynesian, Central-Eastern, Eastern Malayo-Polynesian, Oceanic, Western Oceanic, Papuan Tip, Peripheral, Central Papuan, West Central Papuan, Nuclear. *Dialects:* Lexical similarity 57% with Lala, 54% with Motu. *Lg Use:* All ages. Positive language attitude. Many of the younger generation use Tok Pisin or English. Some speakers also use Abadi. *Lg Dev:* Toura used in primary education for first 3 years. *Other:* Riverine. Savannah; gallery forest. Sea level. Swidden agriculturalists.

Tulu-Bohuai (Pahavai, Pelipowai, Bohuai, Bowai, Pohuai, Bohuai-Tulu) [rak] 1,400 (1982 SIL). Manus Province, Bohuai, Peli Island, Pelipowai. *Class:* Austronesian, Malayo-Polynesian, Central-Eastern, Eastern Malayo-Polynesian, Oceanic, Admiralty Islands, Eastern, Manus, West. *Dialect:* Keli, Bohuai, Tulu (Tulun, Tjudun). Close to Levei-Ndrehet. *Lg Use:* Speakers also use Kurti, Titan, or Ere.

Tuma-Irumu (Upper Irumu, Tuma, Irumu) [iou] 1,500 (1998 SIL). Morobe Province, Kaiapit District, Wantoat Subdistrict. *Class:* Trans-New Guinea, Main Section, Central and Western, Huon-Finisterre, Finisterre, Wantoat. *Lg Dev:* Literacy rate in first language: 75%. Literacy rate in second language: 75%. NT: 1997. *Other:* Mountain slope. 1,000 to 1,350 meters. Swidden agriculturalists.

Tumleo [tmq] 793 (2003 SIL). Sandaun Province, Tumleo Island, and coast around Aitape. *Class:* Austronesian, Malayo-Polynesian, Central-Eastern, Eastern Malayo-Polynesian, Oceanic, Western Oceanic, North New Guinea, Schouten, Siau. *Lg Dev:* Literacy rate in second language: 50% to 75%.

Tungag (Tungak, Lavongai, Lavangai, Dang) [lcm] 12,000 (1990 SIL). New Ireland Province, Lamet District, New Hanover Island, Tingwon and Umbukul Islands. *Class:* Austronesian, Malayo-Polynesian, Central-Eastern, Eastern Malayo-Polynesian, Oceanic, Western Oceanic, Meso Melanesian, New Ireland, Lavongai-Nalik. *Lg Use:* Primary education in English. Tok Pisin and some Tungag used in church. *Lg Dev:* Grammar. NT: 1999. *Other:* Center of Johnson cargo cult. SVO. Coastal. Tropical forest. Sea level to 300 meters. Swidden agriculturalists. Christian, cargo cult.

Turaka [trh] 25 (2000 Wurm). Milne Bay Province, 5 miles southwest of Radarada and Ruaba. *Class:* Trans-New Guinea, Main Section, Eastern, Central and Southeastern, Dagan. *Lg Dev:* People want their own literacy program. *Other:* Nearly extinct.

Turumsa [tqm] 5 (2002 SIL). Western Province, Middle Fly District, Makapa village. *Class:* Unclassified. *Dialects:* Lexical similarity 19% with Turumsa, 15% with Doso. *Lg Use:* Speakers are older adults. Speakers also use Dibiyaso, Doso, Kamula, Gogodala, or Hiri Motu. *Other:* SOV. Riverine. Tropical forest. Below 100 meters. Hunter-gatherers. Nearly extinct.

Tuwari [tww] 122 (1981 Wurm and Hattori). Sandaun Province, middle Sepik Region, upper Walio (Leonhard Schultze) River. A few also near Akiapmin south of the Central Range. *Class:* Sepik-Ramu, Leonhard Schultze, Walio. *Lg Dev:* Literacy rate in second language: 0%.

Uare (Kwale, Kware) [ksj] 1,300 (1996 SIL). Central Province, Rigo Inland District, on the coast south of Port Moresby, Kemp Welsh and Hunter rivers. *Class:* Trans-New Guinea, Main Section, Eastern, Central and Southeastern, Kwalean. *Dialects:* Garihe (Garia), Uare (Kwale). Lexical similarity 65% to 74% with Humeme (closest). *Lg Dev:* Bible portions: 1994. *Other:* Different from Kware in the Bosavi family, Western Province.

Ubir (Ubiri, Kubiri) [ubr] 2,560 (2000 census). Oro Province, Tufi District, coast of Collingwood Bay on the Kwagila River. *Class:* Austronesian, Malayo-Polynesian, Central-Eastern, Eastern Malayo-Polynesian, Oceanic, Western Oceanic, Papuan Tip, Nuclear, North Papuan Mainland-D'Entrecasteaux, Are-Taupota, Are. *Dialects:* Lexical similarity 27% with Miniafia (closest). *Lg Use:* Also spoken by the Maisin and Miniafia speakers. *Lg Dev:* NT: 1997.

Ufim [ufi] 550 (1978 McElhanon). Morobe Province. *Class:* Trans-New Guinea, Main Section, Central and Western, Huon-Finisterre, Finisterre, Gusap-Mot.

Uisai [uis] 2,500 (1991 SIL). Bougainville Province, southern, Buin District. *Class:* East Papuan, Bougainville, East, Buin. *Lg Dev:* Literacy rate in first language: 50% to 75%. Literacy rate in second language: 50% to 75%. Bible portions: 1986. *Other:* High plateau. 600 to 900 meters.

Ukuriguma [ukg] 166 (2003 SIL). Madang Province. *Class:* Trans-New Guinea, Madang-Adelbert Range, Adelbert Range, Pihom-Isumrud-Mugil, Pihom, Numugenan. *Dialects:* Related to Wanuma, Yaben, Yarawata, Parawen, Bilakura.

Ulau-Suain (Suain) [svb] 2,797 (2003 SIL). Sandaun Province, coast around Ulau 1, Ulau 2, and Suain. *Class:* Austronesian, Malayo-Polynesian, Central-Eastern, Eastern Malayo-Polynesian, Oceanic, Western Oceanic, North New Guinea, Schouten, Siau. *Lg Dev:* Literacy rate in second language: 25% to 50%.

Umanakaina (Gwedena, Gweda, Gwede, Gvede, Umanikaina) [gdn] 2,400 (1987 SIL). Milne Bay Province, Rabaraba District, on the coast of Goodenough Bay, inland between Mt. Gwoira and Mt. Simpson. *Class:* Trans-New Guinea, Main Section, Eastern, Central and Southeastern, Dagan. *Dialects:* Upper Ugu River, East Umanakaina. At least two dialects. Lexical similarity 23% with Ginuman (closest). *Lg Use:* Some speak some English. *Lg Dev:* Literacy rate in first language: 25% to 50%. Literacy rate in second language: 15% to 25%. NT: 1999. *Other:* 'Umanakaina' is the name used by the people. SOV. Mountain slope. Tropical forest. 500 to 1,200 meters. Swidden agriculturalists.

Umbu-Ungu (Ubu Ugu, Kaugel, Kauil, Gawigl, Gawil, Kakoli) [ubu] 34,154 (2000 census). Western Highlands Province, Tambul (No-Penge dialect) and Lower Kaugel (Kala dialect) districts, extending into Southern Highlands Province (Andelale dialect). *Class:* Trans-New Guinea, Main Section, Central and Western, East New Guinea Highlands, Central, Hagen, Kaugel. *Dialects:* Kala (Mendo-Kala), No-Penge, Andelale. *Lg Use:* Some speakers understand Medlpa. *Lg Dev:* NT: 1995–1998. *Other:* SOV. Mountain slope and valley. Scrub forest. 2,000 to 3,000 meters. Swidden agriculturalists.

Umeda [upi] 289 (2003 SIL). Sandaun Province, Amanda District, south of Imonda. *Class:* Trans-New Guinea, Northern, Border, Bewani.

Uneapa (Bali) [bbn] 10,000 (1998 SIL). West New Britain Province, Talasea District, Unea (Bali) Island off the northwest coast. *Class:* Austronesian, Malayo-Polynesian, Central-Eastern, Eastern Malayo-Polynesian, Oceanic, Western Oceanic, Meso Melanesian, Bali-Vitu. *Other:* 'Bali' is the outsiders' name for the island, which the people call 'Unea'.

Unserdeutsch (Rabaul Creole German) [uln] 100 in Papua New Guinea. Population includes 15 in New Britain, a few in other parts of Papua New Guinea and the rest in southeastern Queensland, Australia (1981 C. Volker). East New Britain Province, Rabaul. Also spoken in Australia. *Class:* Creole, German based. *Lg Use:* The descendant of a pidginized form of Standard German which originated in the Gazelle Peninsula of New Britain during German colonial times among the Catholic mixed-race ('Vunapope') community. With increased mobility and intermarriage, it has been disappearing in the last few decades. Most speakers are older adults, although many younger members of the community can understand it. All speakers are fluent in at least two of the following: Standard German, English, or Tok Pisin. Some can also speak Kuanua. *Lg Dev:* Grammar. *Other:* Nearly extinct.

Ura (Uramät, Uramit, Uramet, Uramot, Auramot) [uro] 1,900 (1991 SIL). East New Britain Province, Gazelle Peninsula. *Class:* East Papuan, Yele-Solomons-New Britain, New Britain, Baining-Taulil. *Lg Dev:* Literacy rate in first language: 15% to 25%. Literacy rate in second language: 15% to 25%. *Other:* 'Uramät' refers to the people. There are several primary schools. Mountain slope.

Urapmin [urm] 366 (2003 SIL). Sandaun Province, Telefomin District. *Class:* Trans-New Guinea, Main Section, Central and Western, Central and South New Guinea-Kutubuan, Central and South New Guinea, Ok, Mountain. *Other:* Geographically and linguistically between Tifal and Telefol.

Urat [urt] 6,279 (2003 SIL). Population includes 2,476 in Wasep Ngau, 2,058 in Wusyep Yehre, 1,208 in Wasep Yam, and 547 in Wusyep Tep. East Sepik Province, Dreikikir District, southwest of Wom, south of Kombio. 20 major villages and several hamlets. *Class:* Torricelli, Wapei-Palei, Urat. *Dialects:* Wasep Nau (North Urat), Wusyep Yehre (Central Urat), Wasep Yam (South Urat), Wusyep Tep (East Urat). *Lg Use:* In the Wusyep Yehre dialect area most children understand, but do not speak the language. *Lg Dev:* Literacy rate in first language: 50%. Literacy rate in second language: 25% to 50%. Bible portions: 1993.

Uri (Urii, Uri Vehees, Erap) [uvh] 2,500 (1991 SIL). Morobe Province, Boana District. *Class:* Trans-New Guinea, Main Section, Central and Western, Huon-Finisterre, Finisterre, Erap. *Dialects:* East Urii, West Urii. *Lg Dev:* Literacy rate in first language: 25% to 50%. Literacy rate in second language: 25% to 50%. NT: 1984. *Other:* SOV. Mountain slope. Savannah, tropical forest. 200 to 1,000 meters. Swidden agriculturalists.

Urigina (Uriginau, Origanau) [urg] 1,404 (1981 Wurm and Hattori). Madang Province, 30 miles downstream. *Class:* Trans-New Guinea, Madang-Adelbert Range, Madang, Rai Coast, Peka. *Dialects:* Related to Sop, Danaru, Sumau. *Other:* Cargo cult.

Urim (Kalp) [uri] 3,742 (2003 SIL). East Sepik Province, Maprik Subdistrict, extending into Sandaun Province, Nuku Subdistrict, southwest of Kombio. 16 villages. *Class:* Torricelli, Urim. *Dialects:* Kukwo, Yangkolen. *Lg Dev:* Literacy rate in first language: 25% to 50%. Literacy rate in second language: 50% to 75%. Bible portions: 1981–1992. *Other:* SVO. Foothills. Tropical forest. 450 to 500 meters. Swidden agriculturalists. Christian, traditional religion.

Urimo (Yaugiba) [urx] 799 (2003 SIL). East Sepik Province. *Class:* Torricelli, Marienberg. *Dialects:* Related to Elepi. *Lg Dev:* Literacy rate in first language: below 5%. Literacy rate in second language: 25% to 50%.

Uruava [urv] Extinct. Bougainville Province, southeastern coast. *Class:* Austronesian, Malayo-Polynesian, Central-Eastern, Eastern Malayo-Polynesian, Oceanic, Western Oceanic, Meso Melanesian, New Ireland, South New Ireland-Northwest Solomonic, Mono-Uruava.

Usan (Wanuma) [wnu] 1,400 (1991 SIL). Madang Province, Madang District. *Class:* Trans-New Guinea, Madang-Adelbert Range, Adelbert Range, Pihom-Isumrud-Mugil, Pihom, Numugenan. *Dialects:* Related to Yarawata, Bilakura, Ukuriguma. *Lg Dev:* Literacy rate in second language: 50% to 75%. Grammar. NT: 2001. *Other:* SOV. Mountain slope. Tropical forest. 600 to 1,200 meters. Swidden agriculturalists.

Usarufa (Usurufa, Uturupa) [usa] 1,300 (1996 SIL). Eastern Highlands Province, Okapa District. *Class:* Trans-New Guinea, Main Section, Central and Western, East New Guinea Highlands, Eastern, Gadsup-Auyana-Awa. *Lg Dev:* Literacy rate in first language: 25% to 50%. Literacy rate in second language: 15% to 25%. Grammar. NT: 1980.

Utarmbung (Osum) [omo] 1,166 (2003 SIL). Madang Province. *Class:* Trans-New Guinea, Madang-Adelbert Range, Adelbert Range, Josephstaal-Wanang, Josephstaal, Osum.

Utu [utu] 583 (1981 Wurm and Hattori). Madang Province. *Class:* Trans-New Guinea, Madang-Adelbert Range, Madang, Mabuso, Hanseman.

Uya (Usu) [usu] 272 (2003 SIL). Madang Province, Trans-Gogol District. *Class:* Trans-New Guinea, Madang-Adelbert Range, Madang, Rai Coast, Nuru. *Dialects:* Related to Kwato, Ogea, Duduela, Rerau, Jilim, Yangulam.

Valman (Koroko) [van] 1,740 (2003 SIL). Sandaun Province. *Class:* Torricelli, Wapei-Palei, Wapei. *Dialects:* Related to Olo, Yau, Ningil, Yis.

Vanimo (Manimo, Wanimo, Duso) [vam] 2,667 (2000 census). Sandaun Province, Vanimo District. 3 villages. Not in Papua, Indonesia. *Class:* Sko, Vanimo. *Dialects:* 2 dialects. Related to Wutung. *Other:* Many highly educated speakers. Coastal. Sea level to 150 meters.

Vehes (Buasi, Vehees) [val] 70 (2000 Wurm). Morobe Province, one village near the coast between Salamaua and Lae. *Class:* Austronesian, Malayo-Polynesian, Central-Eastern, Eastern Malayo-Polynesian, Oceanic, Western Oceanic, North New Guinea, Huon Gulf, South, Hote-Buang, Buang. *Dialects:* Lexical similarity 60% with Buang (closest).

Wab (Som) [wab] 120 (2000 Wurm). Madang Province, north coast of Huon Peninsula. 2 villages next to Saidor: Wab and Saui. *Class:* Austronesian, Malayo-Polynesian, Central-Eastern, Eastern Malayo-Polynesian, Oceanic, Western Oceanic, North New Guinea, Ngero-Vitiaz, Vitiaz, Bel, Astrolabe. *Dialects:* Related to Mindiri and Biliau.

Waboda (Wabuda) [kmx] 2,750 (2003 SIL). Western Province, Wabuda Island, and the north bank of the Fly River mouth. Meipani, Tirere, Maduduo, Sagero, Wapi, Gesoa, Dameratamu, and Kabaturi villages. *Class:* Trans-New Guinea, Trans-Fly-Bulaka River, Trans-Fly, Kiwaian. *Lg Dev:* Literacy rate in first language: 5% to 15%. Literacy rate in second language: 15% to 25%.

Wadaginam (Wadaginamb) [wdg] 947 (2003 SIL). Madang Province. *Class:* Trans-New Guinea, Madang-Adelbert Range, Adelbert Range, Josephstaal-Wanang, Josephstaal, Wadaginam.

Wa'ema (Waiema) [wag] 1,023 (2000 census). Milne Bay Province, Alotau District, Huhu Local Government Area, the area from Giligili Estates to Turnbull War Memorial, near the head of Milne Bay north to, but not crossing, the East Cape coastal range. *Class:* Austronesian, Malayo-Polynesian, Central-Eastern, Eastern Malayo-Polynesian, Oceanic, Western Oceanic, Papuan Tip, Nuclear, North Papuan Mainland-D'Entrecasteaux, Are-Tapota, Taupota. *Dialects:* Wa'ema seems to be in a dialect chain with Taupota. Tawala is not intelligible to Wa'ema speakers. Lexical similarity 76% with Taupota, 69% with Maiwala, 54% with Tawala. *Lg Use:* Speakers know some Wedau, Tawala, English, and Motu. *Lg Dev:* One Wa'ema primary school.

Waffa [waj] 1,300 (1988 SIL). Morobe Province, Kaiapit District, headwaters of Waffa River, 3 major villages and 2 smaller ones. *Class:* Trans-New Guinea, Main Section, Central and Western, East New Guinea Highlands, Eastern, Tairora. *Lg Use:* Vigorous. Some North Tairora traders also use Waffa. All domains. Oral and written use in church. All ages. Positive language attitude. Tok Pisin is used by those who have access to a school, English to those with access to a secondary school. *Lg Dev:* Literacy rate in first language: 90%. Literacy rate in second language: 50% to 75%. Dictionary. NT: 1975–1988. *Other:* Mountain slope. 300 to 2,400 meters. Agriculturalists: coffee cash crop. Christian.

Wagawaga (Baeaula, Gamadoudou, Gibara, Kilakilana) [wgw] 1,294 (1990 census). 10% monolingual. Milne Bay Province, Alotau District, Huhu Local Government Area, south shore of Milne Bay. *Class:* Austronesian, Malayo-Polynesian, Central-Eastern, Eastern Malayo-Polynesian, Oceanic, Western Oceanic, Papuan Tip, Nuclear, Suauic. *Dialects:* Wagawaga (Baeaula), Gamadoudou. Lexical similarity 61% with Oya'oya, 31% with Tawala, 55% with Buhutu. *Lg Use:* Speakers also use Suau, Hiri Motu, and Tawala. *Other:* Two schools.

Wagi (Foran, Furan, Kamba, Mis-Kemba) [fad] 3,378 (2003 SIL). Madang Province, 7 miles northwest of Madang. 5 villages: Mis, Kamba, Foran, Kauris, and Silibob. *Class:* Trans-New Guinea, Madang-Adelbert Range, Madang, Mabuso, Hanseman. *Dialects:* May be closest to Nobonob. Lexical similarity 30% with Ari dialect of Nobonob. *Lg Use:* Speakers also use Ari, Nobonob, or Tok Pisin. *Lg Dev:* Literacy rate in first language: 5% to 25%. Literacy rate in second language: 50% to 75%. *Other:* SOV; adjectives, numerals follow noun head; verb affixes mark person, number; CV, CVC, VC, V; nontonal. Mountain slope, coastal. Tropical forest. Sea level to 300 meters. Swidden agriculturalists, marginally peasant: cacao, coconuts, coffee.

Wahgi (Mid Wahgi) [wgi] 39,000 (1999 SIL). Western Highlands Province, Minj District, overlapping into Simbu Province, South of the Wahgi River. *Class:* Trans-New Guinea, Main Section, Central and Western, East New Guinea Highlands, Central, Wahgi. *Dialects:* Kup-Minj (Kumai), Pukamigl-Andegabu, Kunjip, Kambia, Mid-Wahgi. *Lg Dev:* Dictionary. Grammar. NT: 1989.

Wahgi, North [whg] 47,000 (1999 SIL). Western Highlands Province, Minj District, overlapping into Simbu Province. North Wahgi is on the north side of the Wahgi River, and on both sides of the Sepik-Wahgi Divide. *Class:* Trans-New Guinea, Main Section, Central and Western, East New Guinea Highlands, Central, Wahgi.

Dialect: Banz-Nondugl. *Other:* Between 2 to 5 dialects of North Wahgi.

Waima (Roro) [rro] 15,000 (2000 census). Central Province, Bereina District, near Kairuku, shores of Hall Sound, between Yule Island and mainland, 65 miles northwest of Port Moresby. *Class:* Austronesian, Malayo-Polynesian, Central-Eastern, Eastern Malayo-Polynesian, Oceanic, Western Oceanic, Papuan Tip, Peripheral, Central Papuan, West Central Papuan, Nuclear. *Dialects:* Waima, Paitana, Roro. Roro and Paitana populations are smaller and scattered. Lexical similarity 45% with Kuni (closest), 99% among all three dialects. *Lg Use:* Used in the home, traditional ceremonies, play, public meetings, religious services. All speakers agree Waima is the main dialect. *Lg Dev:* Taught in primary schools. Radio programs. NT: 2003. *Other:* Many schools. SOV. Coastal.

Walio [wla] 227 (2003 SIL). East Sepik Province. *Class:* Sepik-Ramu, Leonhard Schultze, Walio. *Dialects:* Lexical similarity 12% with Yabio.

Wamas [wmc] 218 (2000 WCD). Madang Province, 10 villages. *Class:* Trans-New Guinea, Madang-Adelbert Range, Madang, Mabuso, Hanseman.

Wampar (Laewomba, Laewamba, Laiwomba) [lbq] 5,150 (1990). Morobe Province, lower Markham and Wamped rivers. *Class:* Austronesian, Malayo-Polynesian, Central-Eastern, Eastern Malayo-Polynesian, Oceanic, Western Oceanic, North New Guinea, Huon Gulf, Markham, Lower, Wampar. *Dialects:* Lexical similarity 50% with Adzera. *Lg Dev:* NT: 1984.

Wampur [waz] 360 (1990). Morobe Province, Wanton River. *Class:* Austronesian, Malayo-Polynesian, Central-Eastern, Eastern Malayo-Polynesian, Oceanic, Western Oceanic, North New Guinea, Huon Gulf, Markham, Upper, Mountain. *Dialects:* Closest to Mari. Lexical similarity 50% with Adzera. *Lg Use:* Most key domains. Positive language attitude.

Wanambre (Vanambere) [wnb] 589 (2003 SIL). Madang Province. *Class:* Trans-New Guinea, Madang-Adelbert Range, Adelbert Range, Pihom-Isumrud-Mugil, Pihom, Tiboran.

Wanap (Kayik) [wnp] 1,066 (2003 SIL). Sandaun Province, north of Mehek, northeast of Siliput. *Class:* Torricelli, Wapei-Palei, Palei. *Dialects:* Related to Agi, Aru, Aruop, Bragat, Nabi.

Wantoat [wnc] 8,201 (1978 McElhanon). Population includes 393 Bam (1978 McElhanon) and 492 Yagawak (1981 Wurm and Hattori). Morobe Province, Kaiapit District, Wantoat, Leron, and Bam rivers. *Class:* Trans-New Guinea, Main Section, Central and Western, Huon-Finisterre, Finisterre, Wantoat. *Dialects:* Wapu (Leron), Central Wantoat, Bam, Yagawak (Kandomin). *Lg Dev:* Literacy rate in second language: 25% to 50%. NT: 1975. *Other:* Saseng is a village; not a separate language.

Wára (Rouku, Wärä, Yumbar, Upper Morehead, Kamindjo, Tjokwai, Tokwasa, Vara, Ara) [tci] 696 (2002 SIL). Western Province, Morehead District, villages immediately west of Morehead. *Class:* Trans-New Guinea, Trans-Fly-Bulaka River, Trans-Fly, Morehead and Upper Maro rivers, Tonda. *Dialects:* Wára, Kómnjo, Anta, Wèré. *Lg Dev:* Literacy rate in first language: 5% to 15%. Literacy rate in second language: 5% to 15%. *Other:* 4 primary schools. Swamp, savannah. Below 300 meters. Traditional religion.

Warapu [wra] 300 (2000 Wurm). Ethnic population: 1,602 including 442 nonresidents (1983 census). Sandaun Province, coast near Sera and Sissano, northwest peninsula of the Sissano lagoon, around Sumo and Ramu towns. *Class:* Sko, Krisa. *Dialects:* Related to Krisa, Rawo, Puari. *Lg Dev:* Literacy rate in second language: 50% to 75%.

Waris (Walsa) [wrs] 2,500 in Papua New Guinea. Population total all countries: 4,000. Sandaun Province,

Amanab District, around Wasengla. Also spoken in Indonesia (Papua). *Class:* Trans-New Guinea, Northern, Border, Waris. *Lg Dev:* Literacy rate in first language: 5% to 15%. Literacy rate in second language: 5% to 15%. Dictionary. NT: 2003. *Other:* Different from Wari or Wares.

Waruna [wrv] 600 (1991 SIL). Western Province, Aramia River area, Waruna village. *Class:* Trans-New Guinea, Main Section, Central and Western, Gogodala-Suki, Gogodala. *Dialects:* Lexical similarity 50% with Ari. *Lg Use:* Speakers also use Gogodala.

Wasembo (Gusap, Yankowan, Biapim) [gsp] 586 (1980 census). Morobe Province, west of Ufim. *Class:* Trans-New Guinea, Madang-Adelbert Range, Adelbert Range, Pihom-Isumrud-Mugil, Pihom, Wasembo.

Waskia (Woskia, Vaskia) [wsk] 15,938 (2003 SIL). Madang Province, Madang District, Karkar Island. *Class:* Trans-New Guinea, Madang-Adelbert Range, Adelbert Range, Pihom-Isumrud-Mugil, Isumrud, Kowan. *Dialects:* Closest to Korak. *Lg Dev:* Dictionary. Grammar. NT: 1985. *Other:* Volcanic island, mountain slope.

Watakataui (Waxe) [wtk] 350 (1998). East Sepik Province, on a branch of the middle Korosameri River. 2 villages. *Class:* Sepik-Ramu, Sepik, Sepik Hill, Bahinemo. *Lg Use:* All also use Tok Pisin. *Lg Dev:* Literacy rate in first language: below 25%. Literacy rate in second language: 25% to 50%. Bible portions: 1991.

Watam (Marangis) [wax] 590 (2003 SIL). Madang and East Sepik provinces, near the mouth of the Ramu River. *Class:* Sepik-Ramu, Ramu, Ramu Proper, Ruboni, Ottilien.

Watut, Middle (Silisili, Maraliinan, Maralinan, Watut) [mpl] 1,350 (1990 SIL). Morobe Province, Mumeng District, lower Watut Valley, 7 villages. *Class:* Austronesian, Malayo-Polynesian, Central-Eastern, Eastern Malayo-Polynesian, Oceanic, Western Oceanic, North New Guinea, Huon Gulf, Markham, Watut. *Lg Use:* Used in the home and village life. Yabem used in religious services. *Other:* Lowlands to 330 meters. Swidden agriculturalists: betelnut cash crop; gold.

Watut, North (Unank, Onank, Unangg, Watut) [una] 465 (1988 Holzknecht). Morobe Province, Mumeng District, Kaiapit area, Waffa Valley. *Class:* Austronesian, Malayo-Polynesian, Central-Eastern, Eastern Malayo-Polynesian, Oceanic, Western Oceanic, North New Guinea, Huon Gulf, Markham, Watut. *Dialects:* Holzknecht says Unank combines with part of Silisili and part of Maraliinan to form one language, North Watut. *Lg Use:* 70% of the ethnic group speaks North Watut. Most key domains. 60% of the children speak North Watut.

Watut, South [mcy] 889 (1988 Holzknecht). Morobe Province, southern or lower Watut River. 5 villages. *Class:* Austronesian, Malayo-Polynesian, Central-Eastern, Eastern Malayo-Polynesian, Oceanic, Western Oceanic, North New Guinea, Huon Gulf, Markham, Watut. *Dialects:* Maralango (Maralangko), Dangal (Danggal). *Other:* Holzknecht says Maralango and Dangal are one language.

Wedau (Wedaun, Wedawan) [wed] 2,200 (2000 D. Tryon). 900 monolinguals. Milne Bay Province, Rabaraba District, Weraura Local Government Area, on the mainland from Kuvira Bay to Dogura along the north coast. *Class:* Austronesian, Malayo-Polynesian, Central-Eastern, Eastern Malayo-Polynesian, Oceanic, Western Oceanic, Papuan Tip, Nuclear, North Papuan Mainland-D'Entrecasteaux, Are-Taupota, Taupota. *Dialects:* Topura, Yapoa, Lavora, Kwamana. *Lg Use:* Trade language of northeast Papua. Lingua franca for 5,000 (1985 UBS). It is understood some in Oro Province. *Lg Dev:* NT: 1927–1980.

Weliki (Weleki, Karangi) [klh] 200 (1990 SIL). Morobe Province, lower Timbe River valley. 2 villages. *Class:* Trans-New Guinea, Main Section, Central and Western, Huon-Finisterre, Finisterre, Uruwa. *Lg Use:* Those in one village are highly proficient in Timbe.

Were [wei] 492 (2000 census). Western Province, Dewara (Weredai) village. *Class:* Trans-New Guinea, Trans-Fly-Bulaka River, Trans-Fly, Tirio. *Other:* Different from Makayam, Bitur, and Baramu.

Weri (Weli, Wele) [wer] 4,163 (1978 McElhanon). Morobe Province, Wau District, headwaters of Biaru, Waria, and Ono rivers. *Class:* Trans-New Guinea, Main Section, Eastern, Central and Southeastern, Goilalan, Kunimaipa. *Dialects:* Sim, Biaru-Waria, Ono. *Lg Dev:* Literacy rate in first language: 50% to 75%. Literacy rate in second language: 50% to 75%. Grammar. NT: 1984.

Wiaki (Wiakei) [wii] 766 (2003 SIL). Sandaun Province, north of Beli, Laeko-Libuat. *Class:* Torricelli, Maimai, Wiaki.

Wiarumus (Imandi, Mandi) [tua] 162 (1981 Wurm and Hattori). East Sepik Province, Mandi village, on coast about 12 km southeast of Wewak. *Class:* Torricelli, Marienberg. *Lg Use:* Only people over 60 are still speakers, middle-aged people can understand it, but only speak a few phrases, young people do not understand the language. Of 400 people in the village, there are very few speakers. Interest in revitalization. *Lg Dev:* Roman script. *Other:* Coastal. Sea level to 40 meters.

Wipi (Oriomo, Jibu, Gidra) [gdr] 3,500 (1999 Shim). Western Province, eastern third of area between Fly Delta, estuary, and south coast. *Class:* Trans-New Guinea, Trans-Fly-Bulaka River, Trans-Fly, Eastern Trans-Fly. *Dialects:* Dorogori, Abam, Peawa, Ume, Kuru, Woigo, Wonie, Iamega, Gamaewe, Podari, Wipim, Kapal, Rual, Guiam, Yuta. *Lg Dev:* Literacy rate in first language: 25% to 50%. Literacy rate in second language: 25% to 50%. NT: 2001. *Other:* 'Gidra' is a Bine term meaning 'bush'.

Wiru (Witu) [wiu] 15,292 (1981 Wurm and Hattori). Southern Highlands Province, Ialibu District. *Class:* Trans-New Guinea, Main Section, Central and Western, East New Guinea Highlands, Wiru. *Lg Dev:* Literacy rate in first language: 50% to 75%. Literacy rate in second language: 25% to 50%. Grammar. NT: 1990.

Wogamusin (Wongamusin) [wog] 700 (1998 SIL). East Sepik Province, Ambunti District. 4 villages. *Class:* Sepik-Ramu, Sepik, Upper Sepik, Wogamusin. *Lg Use:* Many Tok Pisin speakers. Some young people learning English. *Lg Dev:* Literacy rate in first language: below 5%. Literacy rate in second language: 15% to 25%.

Wogeo (Uageo) [woc] 1,624 (2003 SIL). Vokeo and Koil islands, East Sepik Province. *Class:* Austronesian, Malayo-Polynesian, Central-Eastern, Eastern Malayo-Polynesian, Oceanic, Western Oceanic, North New Guinea, Schouten, Kairiru-Manam, Manam. *Dialects:* Related to Manam, Biem, Sepa, Medebur. *Lg Use:* Speakers also use Tok Pisin. *Lg Dev:* Literacy rate in first language: below 5%. Literacy rate in second language: 5% to 15%. *Other:* SOV. Coastal. Tropical forest. Swidden agriculturalists.

Wom (Wam) [wmo] 4,264 (2003 SIL). East Sepik Province, east of Wara Sikau, Maprik District. 12 villages, foothills of Torricelli Mountains, 22 km west northwest of Maprik in Dreikikir District, Maprik Province. *Class:* Torricelli, Kombio-Arapesh, Kombio. *Dialects:* 2 slightly different dialects. *Lg Use:* Vigorous. Speakers also use Tok Pisin. *Lg Dev:* Literacy rate in first language: below 5%. Literacy rate in second language: 50% to 75%. *Other:* One school. Cargo cult.

Wutung (Udung) [wut] 903 (2003 SIL). Sandaun Province, Vanimo District, coast bordering Papua, Indonesia, including Sangke village. *Class:* Sko, Vanimo. *Lg Dev:* Literacy rate in second language: 50% to 75%. *Other:* Coastal.

Wuvulu-Aua (Aua-Viwulu, Viwulu-Aua) [wuv] 1,000 (1982 SIL). Western Manus Province, Aua, Durour, Maty, and Wuvulu islands. *Class:* Austronesian, Malayo-Polynesian, Central-Eastern, Eastern Malayo-Polynesian, Oceanic, Admiralty Islands, Western. *Dialect:* Aua, Wuvulu (Wuu). 2 nearly identical dialects. *Other:* SVO. Atolls. Sea level to 10 meters. Agriculturalists; fishermen.

Yabem (Laulabu, Jabem, Jabim, Yabim) [jae] 2,084 (1978 McElhanon). Morobe Province, Huon Peninsula, coast near Finschhafen. *Class:* Austronesian, Malayo-Polynesian, Central-Eastern, Eastern Malayo-Polynesian, Oceanic, Western Oceanic, North New Guinea, Huon Gulf, North. *Lg Use:* Used by Lutherans as a religious language throughout the area (1981 UBS). *Lg Dev:* NT: 1924–1974. *Other:* Christian.

Yaben [ybm] 702 (1981 Wurm and Hattori). Madang Province. *Class:* Trans-New Guinea, Madang-Adelbert Range, Adelbert Range, Pihom-Isumrud-Mugil, Pihom, Numugenan. *Dialects:* Related to Usan, Yarawata, Bilakura, Parawen, Ukuriguma.

Yabong [ybo] 370 (1970 SIL). Madang Province. *Class:* Trans-New Guinea, Madang-Adelbert Range, Madang, Rai Coast, Yaganon.

Yagaria [ygr] 21,116 (1982 SIL). Eastern Highlands Province, Goroka District. *Class:* Trans-New Guinea, Main Section, Central and Western, East New Guinea Highlands, East-Central, Kamano-Yagaria. *Dialects:* Kami-Kulaka, Move, Ologuti, Dagenava, Kamate, Hira, Hua (Huva), Kotom. *Lg Dev:* Dictionary. Grammar. NT: 1977.

Yagomi [ygm] 283 (2003 SIL). Madang Province, Saidor District, Yagomi village, on the coast southeast of Seure. *Class:* Trans-New Guinea, Main Section, Central and Western, Huon-Finisterre, Finisterre, Warup. *Other:* May be the same as Muratayak. Coastal.

Yagwoia (Kokwaiyakwa, Yeghuye) [ygw] 9,000 (1987 SIL). Morobe Province, Menyamya District, extending into Gulf Province; Eastern Highlands Province, one section west of the Tauri River, the other north of Menye. *Class:* Trans-New Guinea, Main Section, Central and Western, Angan, Angan Proper. *Dialects:* Close to Chimbari, Hamtai, Barua, Menya. Closest, Menya. *Lg Use:* All domains. They speak Tok Pisin with routine proficiency to outsiders. *Lg Dev:* Literacy rate in first language: 5% to 15%. Literacy rate in second language: 5% to 15% in Tok Pisin. *Other:* 5 ethnic groups: Iwalaqamalje, Hiqwaye, Hiqwase, Gwase, Heqwangilye. SOV. Mountain slope. Pine forest, deciduous forest. 1,200 to 2,000 meters. Swidden agriculturalists.

Yahang (Ya'unk, Ruruhip, Ruruhi'ip) [rhp] 1,429 (2003 SIL). Population includes 1,116 in area and 66 outside. Sandaun Province, west of Mehek. *Class:* Torricelli, Maimai, Maimai Proper. *Dialects:* Lexical similarity 60% with Heyo (Arinua). *Other:* Arinua also called 'Ruruhip'.

Yakaikeke [ykk] 100 (1998 SIL). Milne Bay Province, Alotau District, Weraura Local Government Area, on Goodenough Bay between Wedau and Radava, Near Manubada at Diruna only. *Class:* Austronesian, Malayo-Polynesian, Central-Eastern, Eastern Malayo-Polynesian, Oceanic, Western Oceanic, Papuan Tip, Nuclear, North Papuan Mainland-D'Entrecasteaux, Are-Taupota, Taupota. *Dialects:* Lexical similarity 65% with Wedau (closest), 58% with Kwamana, 48% with Ghayavi (at Radava).

Yakamul (Ali) [ykm] 3,463 (2003 SIL). Sandaun Province, coast between Paup and Yakamul, and Ali, Seleo, and Angel islands. *Class:* Austronesian, Malayo-Polynesian, Central-Eastern, Eastern Malayo-Polynesian, Oceanic, Western Oceanic, North New Guinea, Schouten,

Siau. *Dialects:* Ali, Yakamul. *Lg Dev:* Literacy rate in second language: 50% to 75%. *Other:* Coastal, islands.

Yale (Nagatman, Nagatiman, Yarë, Yade) [nce] 600 (1991 SIL). 5% monolingual. Sandaun Province, Amanab District, west of Namia. Kwomtari is north, Abau is south, Busa is southwest, Biaka is west, Anggor and Amanab are northwest. 6 villages. *Class:* Language Isolate. *Dialects:* 2 very similar dialects. *Lg Use:* Vigorous. All domains. Used in church, local commerce. All ages. Positive language attitude. Most men up to 35 years old have routine proficiency in Tok Pisin. There is some intermarriage with the Odiai, Abau, and Kwomtari. *Lg Dev:* Literacy rate in first language: 5% to 15%. Literacy rate in second language: 15% to 25%. *Other:* 'Nagatman' is a corrupted name of 1 village, not a language name. SOV. Tropical forest, sago swamps. 100 meters. Hunter-gatherers; some cultivation: sugarcane, tobacco, sweet potatoes, taro. No cash crops. Christian, syncretism.

Yamap [ymp] 1,581 (2000 census). Morobe Province, Francisco River area. *Class:* Austronesian, Malayo-Polynesian, Central-Eastern, Eastern Malayo-Polynesian, Oceanic, Western Oceanic, North New Guinea, Huon Gulf, South, Hote-Buang, Hote. *Dialects:* Close to Hote and Misim.

Yambes [ymb] 1,078 (2003 SIL). East Sepik Province, Maprik District, northwest of Wom, east and southeast of Kombio, 4 villages. *Class:* Torricelli, Kombio-Arapesh, Kombio. *Dialects:* West Yambes, East Yambes. *Lg Dev:* Literacy rate in first language: below 5%. Literacy rate in second language: 15% to 25%.

Yangulam [ynl] 405 (2000 census). Madang Province. *Class:* Trans-New Guinea, Madang-Adelbert Range, Madang, Rai Coast, Nuru. *Dialects:* Related to Kwato, Ogea, Uya, Duduela, Rerau, Jilim.

Yapunda (Reiwo) [yev] 60 (2000 Wurm). Sandaun Province. *Class:* Torricelli, Wapei-Palei, Wapei.

Yarawata [yrw] 127 (2003 SIL). Madang Province. *Class:* Trans-New Guinea, Madang-Adelbert Range, Adelbert Range, Pihom-Isumrud-Mugil, Pihom, Numugenan. *Dialects:* Related to Usan, Yaben, Bilakura, Parawen, Ukuriguma.

Yareba (Middle Musa) [yrb] 750 (1981 Wurm and Hattori). Oro Province, Popondetta District. *Class:* Trans-New Guinea, Main Section, Eastern, Central and Southeastern, Yareban. *Lg Use:* Speakers are highly bilingual in Hiri Motu. *Lg Dev:* Literacy rate in first language: 75% to 100%. Literacy rate in second language: 50% to 75%. Dictionary. Grammar. NT: 1973.

Yau (Uruwa) [yuw] 1,700 (1991 SIL). Morobe Province, Kabwum District. Villages include Worin, Yawan, Kotet, Mitmit, Mup, Sindamon. *Class:* Trans-New Guinea, Main Section, Central and Western, Huon-Finisterre, Finisterre, Uruwa. *Dialects:* Northern Yau, Headwaters Yau. The dialects listed are also names of villages. *Lg Dev:* Literacy rate in first language: 50% to 75%. Literacy rate in second language: 50% to 75%. NT: 1997. *Other:* It is different from Yau which is Torricelli. Mountain slope. 930 to 1,500 meters. Swidden agriculturalists.

Yau [yyu] 144 (2003 SIL). Sandaun Province. 1 village. *Class:* Torricelli, Wapei-Palei, Wapei. *Dialects:* Related to Olo, Yis, Ningil, Valman. Lexical similarity 63% with Olo and Yis. *Lg Dev:* Literacy rate in second language: 50% to 75%. *Other:* Different from Yau in Uruwa group and the Yau dialect of Yessan-Mayo. 1,200 to 1,600 meters.

Yaul [yla] 1,210 (2003 SIL). East Sepik Province. *Class:* Sepik-Ramu, Ramu, Yuat-Langam, Mongol-Langam. *Dialects:* Related to Langam, Mongol.

Yaweyuha (Yabiyufa, Yawiyuha) [yby] 2,000 (1991 SIL). Eastern Highlands Province, Goroka District. *Class:* Trans-New Guinea, Main Section, Central and Western,

East New Guinea Highlands, East-Central, Siane. *Lg Dev:* NT: 1982.

Yawiyo (Yabio) [ybx] 100 (1977 Voegelin and Voegelin). Sandaun Province, 10 miles east of Duranmin. 3 villages. *Class:* Sepik-Ramu, Leonhard Schultze, Walio. *Dialects:* Lexical similarity 7% with Papi. *Lg Use:* Most use Saniyo-Hiyewe as second language.

Yekora [ykr] 1,000 (1995 SIL). Morobe Province, 2 villages near Morobe government station. *Class:* Trans-New Guinea, Main Section, Eastern, Binanderean, Binanderean Proper. *Dialects:* Close to Mawae. *Lg Use:* Speakers also use Suena or Zia.

Yele (Yelejong, Rossel, Yela, Yeletnye, Yelidnye) [yle] 3,750 (1998 Rossel Health Centres). 400 monolinguals. Ethnic population: 3,750 (1998). Milne Bay Province, Misima District, Rossel Island at eastern end of Calvados chain, and 500 in Port Moresby and Alotau. *Class:* East Papuan, Yele-Solomons-New Britain, Yele-Solomons, Yele. *Dialects:* Daminyu, Bou, Wulanga, Jinjo, Abaletti, Jaru. Lexical similarity 8% with Daga (closest). *Lg Use:* Vigorous. All domains. Oral use in preschool and elementary school, local administration, commerce. Oral and written use in churches. All ages. Positive language attitude. Half the children have elementary education in English. 1,200 can also speak Misima or English. Misima introduced as church language in the 1930s, English for trade and administration in about 1900, for elementary education in about 1948. *Lg Dev:* Literacy rate in first language: 29%. Literacy rate in second language: 75% to 100%. 1,100 can read it, 450 can write it. Dictionary. Grammar. NT: 1987. *Other:* SOV; postpositions. Coastal, island. Tropical forest. Sea level to 830 meters. Swidden agriculturalists. Christian.

Yelogu (Kaunga, Buiamanambu) [ylg] 162 (2003 SIL). East Sepik Province, one village in Ambunti District. *Class:* Sepik-Ramu, Sepik, Middle Sepik, Ndu.

Yerakai (Yerekai) [yra] 390 (1981 Wurm and Hattori). East Sepik Province, Ambunti District, southeast near government station, 2 villages. *Class:* Sepik-Ramu, Sepik, Middle Sepik, Yerakai. *Dialects:* Lexical similarity 6% with Middle Sepik languages. *Lg Dev:* Literacy rate in second language: 25% to 50%. *Other:* Hills. Traditional religion, Christian.

Yessan-Mayo (Mayo-Yesan, Maio-Yesan, Yasyin, Yesan) [yss] 1,988 (2000 census). East Sepik Province, Ambunti District, Sandaun Province, Wan Wan Division, south of Mehek. 10 villages. *Class:* Sepik-Ramu, Sepik, Tama. *Dialects:* Yawu (Yau, Yaw, Warasai), Mayo-Yessan. *Lg Dev:* Literacy rate in first language: 15% to 25%. Literacy rate in second language: 50% to 75%. Grammar. NT: 1980–2004. *Other:* Yawu is distinct from Yau which is Torricelli or Yau which is Trans-New Guinea. Riverine. Tropical forest. 50 meters. Fishermen; swidden agriculturalists; hunter-gatherers. Christian, traditional religion.

Yetfa (Inisine, Biaksi, Biksi) [yet] 200 in Papua New Guinea (1992 SIL). South of the Green River, and into Papua, Indonesia. See main entry under Indonesia (Papua).

Yil [yll] 2,472 (2000 census). Sandaun Province, northwest of Au. 16 villages. *Class:* Torricelli, Wapei-Palei, Wapei. *Dialects:* Lexical similarity 23% with Au. *Lg Dev:* Literacy rate in second language: 15% to 25%. *Other:* Mountain slope. Tropical forest. 1,200 to 1,800 meters.

Yimas [yee] 300 (2000 Wurm). East Sepik Province, near Chambri, Arafundi River, middle Karawari River. *Class:* Sepik-Ramu, Nor-Pondo, Pondo. *Dialects:* Related to Karawari. *Lg Dev:* Literacy rate in first language: below 5%. Literacy rate in second language: 15% to 25%. Grammar.

Yis [yis] 325 (2003 SIL). Sandaun Province. 5 villages. *Class:* Torricelli, Wapei-Palei, Wapei. *Dialects:* Different dialects in each village. Related languages: Olo, Yau, Ningil, Valman. *Other:* Mountain slope.

Yoba [yob] Extinct. Central Province, north of Magori. *Class:* Austronesian, Malayo-Polynesian, Central-Eastern, Eastern Malayo-Polynesian, Oceanic, Western Oceanic, Papuan Tip, Peripheral, Central Papuan, Oumic, Magoric. *Dialects:* Related to Magori. *Lg Use:* 2 nonprimary speakers left (1981 Wurm and Hattori).

Yoidik [ydk] 766 (2003 SIL). Madang Province. *Class:* Trans-New Guinea, Madang-Adelbert Range, Madang, Mabuso, Hanseman.

Yonggom (Yongom, Yongkom) [yon] 4,000 (1997 SIL). Western Province along the Fly and Tedi (Alice) rivers and towards Lake Murray. *Class:* Trans-New Guinea, Main Section, Central and Western, Central and South New Guinea-Kutubuan, Central and South New Guinea, Ok, Lowland. *Dialects:* Lexical similarity 80% with North Muyu, 70% with South Muyu, 30% with Ninggerum. *Lg Dev:* Literacy rate in first language: 50% to 75%. Literacy rate in second language: 50% to 75%. NT: 2004.

Yopno (Yupna) [yut] 7,200 (2000 census). Madang Province and Morobe Province. *Class:* Trans-New Guinea, Main Section, Central and Western, Huon-Finisterre, Finisterre, Yupna. *Dialects:* Kewieng, Nokopo, Wandabong, Isan. Related to Ma, Gabutamon. *Lg Dev:* Literacy rate in first language: 25% to 35%. Literacy rate in second language: 50% to 75%. Bible portions: 1979–1993. *Other:* SOV. Mountain slope. Swidden agriculturalists. Christian, traditional religion.

Zenag (Zenang) [zeg] 1,818 (1979 census). Morobe Province, Mumeng District. *Class:* Austronesian, Malayo-Polynesian, Central-Eastern, Eastern Malayo-Polynesian, Oceanic, Western Oceanic, North New Guinea, Huon Gulf, South, Hote-Buang, Buang, Mumeng. *Dialect:* Latep. In Mumeng dialect chain. Some intelligibility of Patep. *Other:* SVO. Mountain slope. Tropical forest. 300 to 900 meters. Swidden agriculturalists.

Zia (Tsia, Lower Waria, Ziya) [zia] 3,943 (1978 McElhanon). Population includes 3,000 Zia (1991 SIL), 943 Mawae. Morobe Province, Lae District near the mouth of the Waria River. *Class:* Trans-New Guinea, Main Section, Eastern, Binanderean, Binanderean Proper. *Dialects:* Zia, Mawae. Lexical similarity 68% with Yekora (closest). *Lg Dev:* Literacy rate in first language: 75% to 100%. Literacy rate in second language: 75% to 100%. NT: 1982.

Zimakani (Baegwa, Dea, Bagwa Zimakani) [zik] 1,500 (1990 UBS). Western Province, south end of Lake Murray. *Class:* Trans-New Guinea, Main Section, Central and Western, Marind, Boazi. *Dialects:* Zimakani, Bagwa (Begua, Mbegu), Dea. Related to Kuni (Boazi). *Lg Dev:* Literacy rate in first language: 5% to 15%. Literacy rate in second language: 15% to 25%. NT: 1989.

Pitcairn

Pitcairn. 46 (1998 UN). National or official language: English. A British colony. Information mainly from M. Adler 1977. The number of languages listed for Pitcairn is 2. Of those, 1 is a living language and 1 is a second language without mother-tongue speakers.

English [eng] 46 (1998 UN). *Lg Use:* Official language. See main entry under United Kingdom.

Pitcairn-Norfolk [pih] 36 on Pitcairn (2002). Pitcairn Island, Norfolk Island, Fiji, and some second-generation Pitcairn Islanders in Australia and New Zealand. *Dialect:* Pitcairn English. *Lg Use:* Developed from mutineers settling on Pitcairn in 1790. Some were removed to Norfolk in 1859. Slightly different variety from that in Norfolk. An in-group language to assist in the preservation of identity. People speak Standard British English as first language. *Other:* Christian. Second language only. See main entry under Norfolk Island.

Samoa

Independent State of Samoa, Malotuto'atasi o Samoa i Sisifo. 200,000. Samoan 93%, mixed 7%. National or official languages: Samoan, English. 2 large islands, several smaller ones. Literacy rate: 97%. Information mainly from S. Wurm and S. Hattori 1981; N. Besnier 1992. The number of languages listed for Samoa is 2. Of those, both are living languages.

English [eng] 200 in Samoa (2004). *Lg Use:* Official language. See main entry under United Kingdom.

Samoan [smo] 199,377 in Samoa (1999). Population total all countries: 370,337. Also spoken in American Samoa, Fiji, New Zealand, Tonga, USA. *Class:* Austronesian, Malayo-Polynesian, Central-Eastern, Eastern Malayo-Polynesian, Oceanic, Central-Eastern Oceanic, Remote Oceanic, Central Pacific, East Fijian-Polynesian, Polynesian, Nuclear, Samoic-Outlier, Samoan. *Dialects:* No significant dialect variations, but significant phonological and lexical differences between formal and colloquial speech. Lexical similarity 70% with Wallisian, 67% with Rarotongan, 66% with Tongan, 62% with Paumotu. *Lg Use:* Official language. *Lg Dev:* Dictionary. Bible: 1855–1970. *Other:* VSO. Agriculturalists. Christian.

Solomon Islands

Solomon Islands. 523,617. Melanesian 94%, Polynesian 4%, Micronesian 1.5%. National or official language: English. Double chain of 6 large islands and many smaller ones. Literacy rate: 5% to 60%; average years of schooling 4.4. Also includes Chinese (1,000). Information mainly from E. M. Todd 1975; S. Wurm and S. Hattori 1981; D. T. Tryon and B. D. Hackman 1983; M. Ross 1988; D. T. Tryon 1995; SIL 1977–2003. The number of languages listed for Solomon Islands is 74. Of those, 70 are living languages and 4 are extinct. See map on page 884.

Amba (Aba, Nembao, Utupua) [utp] 593 (1999 SIL). Aveta, Matembo, and Nembao villages, Utupua Island, Temotu Province. *Class:* Austronesian, Malayo-Polynesian, Central-Eastern, Eastern Malayo-Polynesian, Oceanic, Central-Eastern Oceanic, Remote Oceanic, Eastern Outer Islands, Utupua. *Lg Use:* Speakers also use Pijin. *Lg Dev:* Literacy rate in first language: 10% to 30%. Literacy rate in second language: 25% to 50%. *Other:* SVO. Mountain slope, coastal. Tropical forest. Sea level to 350 meters. Agriculturalists; fishermen.

Anuta [aud] 267 (1999 SIL). Anuta Island. *Class:* Austronesian, Malayo-Polynesian, Central-Eastern, Eastern Malayo-Polynesian, Oceanic, Central-Eastern Oceanic, Remote Oceanic, Central Pacific, East Fijian-Polynesian, Polynesian, Nuclear, Samoic-Outlier, Futunic. *Lg Dev:* Literacy rate in first language: 10% to 30%. Literacy rate in second language: 25% to 50%.

'Are'are (Areare) [alu] 17,800 (1999 SIL). South Malaita Island. *Class:* Austronesian, Malayo-Polynesian, Central-Eastern, Eastern Malayo-Polynesian, Oceanic, Central-Eastern Oceanic, Southeast Solomonic, Malaita-San Cristobal, Malaita, Southern. *Dialect:* 'Are'are, Marau (Marau Sound). *Lg Dev:* Literacy rate in first language: 30% to 60%. Literacy rate in second language: 25% to 50%. Bible portions: 1957. *Other:* SVO. Mountain slope, coastal. Tropical forest. 100 to 1,000 meters. Hunters; agriculturalists.

Arosi [aia] 6,750 (1999 SIL). Northwest Makira (San Cristobal) Island. *Class:* Austronesian, Malayo-Polynesian, Central-Eastern, Eastern Malayo-Polynesian, Oceanic, Central-Eastern Oceanic, Southeast Solomonic, Malaita-San Cristobal, San Cristobal. *Dialects:* Wango, Arosi. Many dialects. *Lg Dev:* Literacy rate in first language: 30% to 60%. Literacy rate in second language: 25% to 50%. Active literacy program. Dictionary. Grammar. Bible portions: 1905–2002.

Asumboa (Asumbua, Asumuo) [aua] 10 (1999 SIL). Asumbuo village, Utupua Island, Temotu Province. *Class:* Austronesian, Malayo-Polynesian, Central-Eastern, Eastern Malayo-Polynesian, Oceanic, Central-Eastern Oceanic, Remote Oceanic, Eastern Outer Islands, Utupua. *Lg Use:* Bilingual level estimates for Pijin: 1 0%, 2 0%, 3+ 33%, 4 67%, 5 0%. Speakers also use Amba or Nyisunggu. *Lg Dev:* Literacy rate in first language: 10% to 30%. Literacy rate in second language: 25% to 50%. *Other:* SVO. Mountain slope, coastal. Tropical forest. Sea level to 350 meters. Agriculturalists; fishermen. Nearly extinct.

Ayiwo (Naaude, Aïwo, Gnivo, Nivo, Nifilole, Lomlom, Reef Islands, Reefs) [nfl] 8,400 (1999 SIL). Population includes 4,500 on Reef Islands, others on Santa Cruz, and 1,000 in Honiara (2000 John Rentz SIL). Santa Cruz Islands, eastern Solomons, Temotu Province. Lomlom is the main island, Fenualoa, Nibanga Nede, and Nibanga Temaa islands, many villages scattered along the north coast of Santa Cruz, and Honiara. Not on reef outlier islands. *Class:* East Papuan, Reef Islands-Santa Cruz. *Lg Use:* Vigorous. Used in religious services, commerce. Positive language attitude. Good speakers respected, Pijin borrowings disliked. Probably fewer than 10% of adults are unable to speak Pijin. Some speak nearby Pileni. Most do not understand English. Written English used in church. *Lg Dev:* Literacy rate in first language: Few. Literacy rate in second language: 25% to 50%. The orthography has not been standardized so there are few readers. Taught in primary and secondary schools. Radio programs. *Other:* Coral atolls. Sea level to 30 meters. Copra production; beche de mer (trepang) production; fishermen. Christian.

Babatana (Mbambatana, East Choiseul) [baa] 5,600 (1999 SIL). East Choiseul Island. *Class:* Austronesian, Malayo-Polynesian, Central-Eastern, Eastern Malayo-Polynesian, Oceanic, Western Oceanic, Meso Melanesian, New Ireland, South New Ireland-Northwest Solomonic, Choiseul. *Dialects:* Babatana, Sengan (Sengga, Sisingga, Senga), Kuboro (Kumboro), Katazi, Lömaumbi, Avasö. Related to Ririo. *Lg Use:* Trade language. There are second-language speakers. *Lg Dev:* NT: 1960–1998.

Baeggu (Baegu, Mbaenggu) [bvd] 5,900 (1999 SIL). North Malaita Island. *Class:* Austronesian, Malayo-Polynesian, Central-Eastern, Eastern Malayo-Polynesian, Oceanic, Central-Eastern Oceanic, Southeast Solomonic, Malaita-San Cristobal, Malaita, Northern. *Dialects:* Baelelea and Baegu are about equally intelligible with To'abaita and Lau. *Lg Dev:* Literacy rate in first language: 30% to 60%. Literacy rate in second language: 25% to 50%. *Other:* SVO. Mountain slope, coastal. Tropical forest. 100 to 1,000 meters. Hunters; agriculturalists.

Baelelea (Mbaelelea) [bvc] 8,800 (1999 SIL). North Malaita Island. *Class:* Austronesian, Malayo-Polynesian, Central-Eastern, Eastern Malayo-Polynesian, Oceanic, Central-Eastern Oceanic, Southeast Solomonic, Malaita-San Cristobal, Malaita, Northern. *Dialects:* Baelelea and Baegu are about equally intelligible with To'abaita and Lau. *Lg Dev:* Literacy rate in first language: 30% to 60%. Literacy rate in second language: 25% to 50%. *Other:* SVO. Mountain slope, coastal. Tropical forest. 100 to 1,000 meters. Hunters; agriculturalists.

Bauro (Marmaregho, Mamarego) [bxa] 3,420 (1999 SIL). Central Makira (San Cristobal) Island. *Class:*

Austronesian, Malayo-Polynesian, Central-Eastern, Eastern Malayo-Polynesian, Oceanic, Central-Eastern Oceanic, Southeast Solomonic, Malaita-San Cristobal, San Cristobal. *Dialects:* Haununu (Hauhunu), Bauro, Rawo (Ravo). There is a deep linguistic division between Bauro and Arosi. The Mamaregho variety is reported to be the 'bush' variety. Another variety is Ngaoni. *Lg Dev:* Literacy rate in first language: 10% to 30%. Literacy rate in second language: 25% to 50%. Bible portions: 1922. *Other:* The purported Mamaregho language has not been found (1986 G. Simons SIL).

Bilua (Mbilua, Vella Lavella) [blb] 8,740 (1999 SIL). Vella Lavella Island, Western Province. *Class:* East Papuan, Yele-Solomons-New Britain, Yele-Solomons, Central Solomons. *Lg Use:* There are second-language users. *Lg Dev:* Literacy rate in first language: 30% to 60%. Literacy rate in second language: 25% to 50%. Dictionary. Grammar. NT: 1995. *Other:* 'Vella Lavella' is a geographical name used in some lists as a language name.

Birao (Mbirao) [brr] 5,900 (1999 SIL). Eastern Guadalcanal Island. *Class:* Austronesian, Malayo-Polynesian, Central-Eastern, Eastern Malayo-Polynesian, Oceanic, Central-Eastern Oceanic, Southeast Solomonic, Gela-Guadalcanal, Guadalcanal.

Blablanga (Gema, Goi) [blp] 1,772 (1999 SIL). Santa Isabel Island, villages of Popoheo and Hovukoilo in Maringe District and from Ghove to Biluro on Hograno coast. *Class:* Austronesian, Malayo-Polynesian, Central-Eastern, Eastern Malayo-Polynesian, Oceanic, Western Oceanic, Meso Melanesian, New Ireland, South New Ireland-Northwest Solomonic, Santa Isabel, Central. *Dialects:* Slight dialect differences. *Lg Use:* Speakers converse in Cheke Holo (Maringe).

Bughotu (Bugoto, Bugota, Bugotu, Mbughotu, Mahaga) [bgt] 4,048 (1999 SIL). Santa Isabel Island, southeast end from Suma to Horara, and on Furona Island off the northwest coast of Kia District. *Class:* Austronesian, Malayo-Polynesian, Central-Eastern, Eastern Malayo-Polynesian, Oceanic, Central-Eastern Oceanic, Southeast Solomonic, Gela-Guadalcanal, Bughotu. *Dialects:* Hageulu, Vulava. Related to vernaculars on Guadalcanal. Close affinity to Gela. Literature in Bughotu will also reach Gao—a total of 2,191 speakers, or 2% of the Island. *Lg Use:* Trade language. Used in the church. Different from other languages of Santa Isabel. Except for Gao, speakers of other Santa Isabel languages cannot communicate with Bughotu speakers except through Pijin. *Lg Dev:* Literacy rate in first language: 30% to 60%. Literacy rate in second language: 50% to 75%. Dictionary. Grammar. NT: 1914–1934.

Cheke Holo (A'ara, Kubonitu, Holo) [mrn] 10,840 (1999 SIL). 1,500 monolinguals. Central Santa Isabel Island, on Maringe side from village of Gnulahaghe southeast to Kuma'ihaui; on Hograno coast in several villages in Kia District; and scattered villages in Gao-Bughotu Region. *Class:* Austronesian, Malayo-Polynesian, Central-Eastern, Eastern Malayo-Polynesian, Oceanic, Western Oceanic, Meso Melanesian, New Ireland, South New Ireland-Northwest Solomonic, Santa Isabel, East. *Dialects:* Maringe (Maringhe), Hograno (Hogirano). *Lg Use:* Trade language. Vigorous. Most important language of Santa Isabel apart from Bughotu. Second language of many speakers of other languages. Literature in this language could be used by the Blablanga and Gao, Kokota, and Zazao. Used in kindergartens, religious services, commerce. People are proud of Cheke Holo. Others recognize it as the major language of the island. At least 80% can speak another language. Some speak Bughotu. *Lg Dev:* Literacy rate in first language: 50%. Literacy rate in second language: 30% to 35%. 5,500 can read and write. Dictionary. Grammar. NT: 1993. *Other:* Coastal, riverine. Dense forest. Sea level to 1,200 meters. Subsistence agriculturalists; fishermen; government workers; church workers. Christian.

Dori'o (Kwarekwareo) [dor] 2,406 (1999 SIL). West central Malaita Island. *Class:* Austronesian, Malayo-Polynesian, Central-Eastern, Eastern Malayo-Polynesian, Oceanic, Central-Eastern Oceanic, Southeast Solomonic, Malaita-San Cristobal, Malaita, Southern. *Dialects:* Lexical similarity 71% with 'Are'are. *Other:* SVO. Mountain slope, coastal. Tropical forest. 100 to 1,000 meters. Hunters; agriculturalists.

Dororo (Doriri) [drr] Extinct. New Georgia. *Class:* East Papuan, Yele-Solomons-New Britain, Yele-Solomons, Kazukuru. *Dialects:* May have been a Kazukuru dialect.

Duke (Nduke, Ndughore, Kolombangara) [nke] 2,312 (1999 SIL). Kolombangara Island, Western Province. *Class:* Austronesian, Malayo-Polynesian, Central-Eastern, Eastern Malayo-Polynesian, Oceanic, Western Oceanic, Meso Melanesian, New Ireland, South New Ireland-Northwest Solomonic, New Georgia, West. *Dialects:* Close to Lungga and Roviana. *Lg Use:* All domains. All ages. They prefer to read English over Pijin. Bilingual level estimates for Roviana: 0 7%, 1 11%, 2 24%, 3 58%, 4 0%, 5 0%. They also speak Pijin, Marovo, or English for some purposes. For historical reasons they use Marovo for Scripture. Marovo is the Seventh Day Adventist lingua franca—Roviana used by Methodists. Most are SDA. SDA schools teach English. They use Roviana to the Roviana, Marovo to the Marovo, English to tourists, Pijin domestically and to all others. *Lg Dev:* Literacy rate in second language: 40% fluently, 60% haltingly. Motivation for literacy high. *Other:* Christian, Baha'i.

English [eng] *Lg Use:* National language. See main entry under United Kingdom.

Fagani (Faghani) [faf] 902 (1999 SIL). Northwest Makira Island. *Class:* Austronesian, Malayo-Polynesian, Central-Eastern, Eastern Malayo-Polynesian, Oceanic, Central-Eastern Oceanic, Southeast Solomonic, Malaita-San Cristobal, San Cristobal. *Dialects:* Fagani, Rihu'a, Agufi. *Lg Dev:* Literacy rate in second language: 25% to 50%. *Other:* Tryon says this is separate from Arosi.

Fataleka [far] 6,703 (1999 SIL). Malaita Island. *Class:* Austronesian, Malayo-Polynesian, Central-Eastern, Eastern Malayo-Polynesian, Oceanic, Central-Eastern Oceanic, Southeast Solomonic, Malaita-San Cristobal, Malaita, Northern. *Dialects:* Wurm and Hattori (1981) treat it as a dialect of To'abaita. Intelligibility of the Baegu variety of To'abaita is reported to be high, but of To'abaita is much less. Lexical similarity 82% with Kwara'ae, 76% with Lau. *Lg Use:* Used in the home. All ages. Bilingual level estimates for Pijin: 0 0%, 1 0%, 2 20%, 3 60%, 4 20%, 5 0%; Kwara'ae: 0 0%, 1 0%, 2 50%, 3 30%, 4 20%, 5 0%; Lau: 0 0%, 1 0%, 2 60%, 3 20%, 4 20%, 5 0%. *Lg Dev:* Literacy rate in first language: 30% to 60%. Literacy rate in second language: 25% to 50%. *Other:* SVO. Mountain slope, coastal. Tropical forest. 100 to 1,000 meters. Hunters; agriculturalists.

Gao (Nggao) [gga] 1,215 (1999 SIL). Central Isabel Island, from Tausese southeast to Floakora Point. The principal village is Poro. *Class:* Austronesian, Malayo-Polynesian, Central-Eastern, Eastern Malayo-Polynesian, Oceanic, Western Oceanic, Meso Melanesian, New Ireland, South New Ireland-Northwest Solomonic, Santa Isabel, East. *Lg Use:* All domains. All ages. Most also use Cheke Holo and Bughotu. *Other:* There are a number of mixed marriages.

Gela (Nggela, Florida Islands) [nlg] 11,876 (1999 SIL). Gela, Florida Islands, Guadalcanal (immigrants), and Savo Islands, central Solomons. *Class:* Austronesian, Malayo-Polynesian, Central-Eastern, Eastern Malayo-Polynesian,

Oceanic, Central-Eastern Oceanic, Southeast Solomonic, Gela-Guadalcanal, Gela. *Lg Dev:* Literacy rate in first language: 30% to 60%. Literacy rate in second language: 25% to 50%. NT: 1923. *Other:* Similar to Lengo in north Guadalcanal. Agriculturalists: root vegetables, coconut; fishermen; copra production. Christian.

Ghanongga (Ganongga, Kubokota, Kumbokota) [ghn] 2,508 (1999 SIL). North Ranonga Island, Western Province. *Class:* Austronesian, Malayo-Polynesian, Central-Eastern, Eastern Malayo-Polynesian, Oceanic, Western Oceanic, Meso Melanesian, New Ireland, South New Ireland-Northwest Solomonic, New Georgia, West. *Dialects:* Related to Lungga, Simbo.

Ghari (Gari, Tangarare, Sughu, West Guadalcanal) [gri] 12,119 (1999 SIL). Population includes 7,113 Ghari, 953 Gae, 3,019 Ndi, 487 Nginia, 547 Tandai-Nggaria. Guadalcanal Island, west, northwest and north central coast. *Class:* Austronesian, Malayo-Polynesian, Central-Eastern, Eastern Malayo-Polynesian, Oceanic, Central-Eastern Oceanic, Southeast Solomonic, Gela-Guadalcanal, Guadalcanal. *Dialects:* Gae (Qae, Nggae), Geri (Nggeri), Ndi (Vaturanga), Nginia, Tandai-Nggaria (Tanaghai), Ghari. *Lg Use:* Trade language. *Lg Dev:* Literacy rate in first language: 30% to 60%. Literacy rate in second language: 25% to 50%. Grammar. Bible: 1998.

Gula'alaa (Kwai, Ngongosila) [gmb] 1,568 (1999 SIL). Kwai and Ngongosila islands on the east side of Kwara'ae, Malaita. *Class:* Austronesian, Malayo-Polynesian, Central-Eastern, Eastern Malayo-Polynesian, Oceanic, Central-Eastern Oceanic, Southeast Solomonic, Malaita-San Cristobal, Malaita, Northern. *Dialects:* Might be intelligible with Lau or Kwara'ae. Lexical similarity 85% with Lau and Kwara'ae. *Other:* SVO. Coral reef. Salt water. Sea level to 1 meter. Fishermen; craftsmen.

Guliguli (Gulili) [gli] Extinct. New Georgia. *Class:* East Papuan, Yele-Solomons-New Britain, Yele-Solomons, Kazukuru. *Dialects:* Possibly was a Kazukuru dialect.

Hoava [hoa] 459 (1999 SIL). North Marovo Lagoon, New Georgia Island, Western Province. *Class:* Austronesian, Malayo-Polynesian, Central-Eastern, Eastern Malayo-Polynesian, Oceanic, Western Oceanic, Meso Melanesian, New Ireland, South New Ireland-Northwest Solomonic, New Georgia, West. *Dialects:* Close to Kusaghe. *Lg Use:* All ages. Speakers also use Roviana.

Kahua (Anganiwai, Anganiwei, Wanoni, Narihua) [agw] 3,000 (1998 SIL). South Makira (San Cristobal) Island. *Class:* Austronesian, Malayo-Polynesian, Central-Eastern, Eastern Malayo-Polynesian, Oceanic, Central-Eastern Oceanic, Southeast Solomonic, Malaita-San Cristobal, San Cristobal. *Lg Use:* Trade language. There are second-language users. *Lg Dev:* Literacy rate in first language: 30% to 60%. Literacy rate in second language: 25% to 50%. NT: 1986.

Kazukuru [kzk] Extinct. New Georgia. *Class:* East Papuan, Yele-Solomons-New Britain, Yele-Solomons, Kazukuru.

Kiribati (Gilbertese, Ikiribati) [gil] 1,230 in Solomon Islands (1998 SIL). One area on Gizo Island and one area on Choiseul Island. *Other:* The British relocated them here in the 1950s. Christian. See main entry under Kiribati.

Kokota [kkk] 530 (1999 SIL). Santa Isabel, villages of Sisiga and Ghoveo on the northeast coast and Hurepelo on southwest coast. *Class:* Austronesian, Malayo-Polynesian, Central-Eastern, Eastern Malayo-Polynesian, Oceanic, Western Oceanic, Meso Melanesian, New Ireland, South New Ireland-Northwest Solomonic, Santa Isabel, Central. *Lg Use:* Speakers can converse in Cheke Holo and Zabana.

Kusaghe (Kusage, Kushage) [ksg] 2,395 (1999 SIL). North New Georgia Island, Western Province. *Class:*

Austronesian, Malayo-Polynesian, Central-Eastern, Eastern Malayo-Polynesian, Oceanic, Western Oceanic, Meso Melanesian, New Ireland, South New Ireland-Northwest Solomonic, New Georgia, West. *Dialects:* Close to Roviana. *Lg Use:* Speakers also use Kusaghe.

Kwaio (Koio) [kwd] 13,249 (1999 SIL). Central Malaita Island. *Class:* Austronesian, Malayo-Polynesian, Central-Eastern, Eastern Malayo-Polynesian, Oceanic, Central-Eastern Oceanic, Southeast Solomonic, Malaita-San Cristobal, Malaita, Northern. *Dialects:* Closer to Kwara'ae than to 'Are'are. *Lg Dev:* Dictionary. Grammar. *Other:* SVO. Mountain slope, coastal. Tropical forest. 100 to 1,000 meters. Hunters; agriculturalists: sweet potato. Traditional religion.

Kwara'ae (Fiu) [kwf] 32,433 (1999 SIL). Central Malaita Island. *Class:* Austronesian, Malayo-Polynesian, Central-Eastern, Eastern Malayo-Polynesian, Oceanic, Central-Eastern Oceanic, Southeast Solomonic, Malaita-San Cristobal, Malaita, Northern. *Lg Use:* Largest indigenous vernacular in the Solomons. Many second-language users. *Lg Dev:* Literacy rate in first language: 30% to 60%. Literacy rate in second language: 25% to 50%. NT: 1961–2003. *Other:* SVO. Mountain slope, coastal. Tropical forest. 100 to 1,000 meters. Hunters; agriculturalists.

Laghu (Lagu, Katova) [lgb] 15 (1999 SIL). Santa Isabel, villages of Baolo and Samasodu in the Kia District. *Class:* Austronesian, Malayo-Polynesian, Central-Eastern, Eastern Malayo-Polynesian, Oceanic, Western Oceanic, Meso Melanesian, New Ireland, South New Ireland-Northwest Solomonic, Santa Isabel, West. *Lg Use:* Most key domains. *Other:* Nearly extinct.

Lau [llu] 16,937 (1999 SIL). Northeast Malaita Island. *Class:* Austronesian, Malayo-Polynesian, Central-Eastern, Eastern Malayo-Polynesian, Oceanic, Central-Eastern Oceanic, Southeast Solomonic, Malaita-San Cristobal, Malaita, Northern. *Dialect:* Suafa, Lau, Dai (Ndai). *Lg Dev:* Literacy rate in first language: 30% to 60%. Literacy rate in second language: 25% to 50%. Dictionary. NT: 1929–1992. *Other:* SVO. Coral reef. Sea level to 1 meter. Fishermen; craftsmen.

Lavukaleve (Laube, Laumbe, Russell Island) [lvk] 1,783 (1999 SIL). Russell Islands, northwest of Guadalcanal, central Solomons. *Class:* East Papuan, Yele-Solomons-New Britain, Yele-Solomons, Central Solomons.

Lengo (Ruavatu, Tasemboko) [lgr] 13,752 (1999 SIL). Population includes 13,594 Lengo and 158 Ghaimuta. North and east central Guadalcanal Island. *Class:* Austronesian, Malayo-Polynesian, Central-Eastern, Eastern Malayo-Polynesian, Oceanic, Central-Eastern Oceanic, Southeast Solomonic, Gela-Guadalcanal, Gela. *Dialects:* Aola, Paripao, Ghaimuta (Ghua), Lengo. *Lg Dev:* Literacy rate in first language: 30% to 60%. Literacy rate in second language: 25% to 50%.

Longgu (Logu) [lgu] 1,894 (1999 SIL). East coast of Guadalcanal Island. *Class:* Austronesian, Malayo-Polynesian, Central-Eastern, Eastern Malayo-Polynesian, Oceanic, Central-Eastern Oceanic, Southeast Solomonic, Malaita-San Cristobal, Malaita, Longgu. *Dialects:* Brought over long ago by settlers from Malaita; probably not intelligible with Malaitan languages. *Lg Dev:* Dictionary.

Lungga (Luga, Luqa) [lga] 2,767 (1999 SIL). South Ranonga Island, Western Province. *Class:* Austronesian, Malayo-Polynesian, Central-Eastern, Eastern Malayo-Polynesian, Oceanic, Western Oceanic, Meso Melanesian, New Ireland, South New Ireland-Northwest Solomonic, New Georgia, West. *Dialects:* Close to Duke (Nduke). Ghanongga, and Simbo are related but separate languages. *Lg Dev:* Literacy rate in first language: 30% to 60%. Literacy rate in second language: 25% to 50%. NT: 2004.

Malango [mln] 4,135 (1999 SIL). Central Guadalcanal Island. *Class:* Austronesian, Malayo-Polynesian, Central-Eastern, Eastern Malayo-Polynesian, Oceanic, Central-Eastern Oceanic, Southeast Solomonic, Gela-Guadalcanal, Guadalcanal.

Marovo [mvo] 8,094 (1999 SIL). South New Georgia Island, Marovo Lagoon, Vangunu Island, and Nggatokae Island; Western Province. *Class:* Austronesian, Malayo-Polynesian, Central-Eastern, Eastern Malayo-Polynesian, Oceanic, Western Oceanic, Meso Melanesian, New Ireland, South New Ireland-Northwest Solomonic, New Georgia, East. *Lg Use:* Trade language. *Lg Dev:* Literacy rate in first language: 30% to 60%. Literacy rate in second language: 25% to 50%. Bible: 1956. *Other:* Second most important language of the New Georgia group.

Mono (Alu, Mono-Alu) [mte] 3,337 (1999 SIL). Population includes 657 Mono, 2,266 Alu, 14 Fauro. Treasury Island (Mono), Shortland Island (Alu, Alo), Fauro Island (Fauro). *Class:* Austronesian, Malayo-Polynesian, Central-Eastern, Eastern Malayo-Polynesian, Oceanic, Western Oceanic, Meso Melanesian, New Ireland, South New Ireland-Northwest Solomonic, Mono-Uruava. *Dialects:* Mono, Alu (Alo), Fauro. *Lg Dev:* Literacy rate in first language: 30% to 60%. Literacy rate in second language: 25% to 50%.

Nanggu [ngr] 210 (1999 SIL). Santa Cruz Island. *Class:* East Papuan, Reef Islands-Santa Cruz. *Lg Use:* Most also use Santa Cruz.

Ontong Java (Luangiua, Leuangiua, Lord Howe) [ojv] 2,367 (1999 SIL). Luangiua Atoll (Lord Howe Island), 130 miles from Santa Isabel Island. *Class:* Austronesian, Malayo-Polynesian, Central-Eastern, Eastern Malayo-Polynesian, Oceanic, Central-Eastern Oceanic, Remote Oceanic, Central Pacific, East Fijian-Polynesian, Polynesian, Nuclear, Samoic-Outlier, Ellicean. *Dialects:* Luangiua, Pelau. Close to Sikaiana in the Solomon Islands, and to Takuu and Nukumanu in Papua New Guinea. *Lg Dev:* Literacy rate in first language: 30% to 60%. Literacy rate in second language: 25% to 50% literate. Grammar. NT: 1998. *Other:* VSO, SVO.

Oroha (Mara Ma-Siki, Oraha) [ora] 38 (1999 SIL). South Malaita Island. *Class:* Austronesian, Malayo-Polynesian, Central-Eastern, Eastern Malayo-Polynesian, Oceanic, Central-Eastern Oceanic, Southeast Solomonic, Malaita-San Cristobal, Malaita, Southern. *Lg Use:* Speakers appear to be bilingual in Sa'a. *Lg Dev:* Dictionary. *Other:* Nearly extinct.

Owa (Anganiwai, Anganiwei, Wanoni, Narihua) [stn] 3,069 (1999 SIL). South Makira (San Cristobal), Santa Ana and Santa Catalina islands. *Class:* Austronesian, Malayo-Polynesian, Central-Eastern, Eastern Malayo-Polynesian, Oceanic, Central-Eastern Oceanic, Southeast Solomonic, Malaita-San Cristobal, San Cristobal. *Dialects:* Tawarafa (Star Harbour), Santa Ana (Owa Raha), Santa Catalina (Owa Riki). Formerly thought to be a dialect of Kahua. *Lg Dev:* Bible portions: 1927.

Pijin (Solomons Pidgin, Neo-Solomonic) [pis] 24,390 (1999 SIL). *Class:* Creole, English based, Pacific. *Dialects:* Basic vocabulary is closer to standard English than is Tok Pisin of Papua New Guinea. Grammar shows Melanesian features. Pronunciation varies according to local languages. Historically related to Tok Pisin of Papua New Guinea and Bislama of Vanuatu. Intelligibility of Bislama is quite high. *Lg Use:* Language of wider communication. Creolization in progress. 306,984 second- or third-language speakers (1999 SIL). *Lg Dev:* Literacy rate in first language: 60%. Literacy rate in second language: 50%. Dictionary. NT: 1993.

Pileni (Pilheni) [piv] 1,142 (1999 SIL). Matema, Taumako, Nupani, Nukapu, Pileni, Nifiloli in the Duff and Reef islands. *Class:* Austronesian, Malayo-Polynesian, Central-Eastern, Eastern Malayo-Polynesian, Oceanic, Central-Eastern Oceanic, Remote Oceanic, Central Pacific, East Fijian-Polynesian, Polynesian, Nuclear, Samoic-Outlier, Futunic. *Dialects:* Matema, Taumako (Duff), Nupani, Nukapu, Pileni, Aua. The Pileni and Taumako dialects differ in significant ways. *Lg Dev:* Literacy rate in first language: 30% to 60%. Literacy rate in second language: 25% to 50%. Grammar. *Other:* SVO.

Rennell-Belona (Rennell, Rennellese-Bellonese, Rennellese) [mnv] 3,191 (1999 SIL). Rennell and Bellona Islands, Central Solomons. *Class:* Austronesian, Malayo-Polynesian, Central-Eastern, Eastern Malayo-Polynesian, Oceanic, Central-Eastern Oceanic, Remote Oceanic, Central Pacific, East Fijian-Polynesian, Polynesian, Nuclear, Samoic-Outlier, Futunic. *Dialects:* Munggava (Rennell, Mugaba), Mungiki (Mugiki, Bellonese, Bellona). *Lg Dev:* Literacy rate in first language: 30% to 60%. Literacy rate in second language: 25% to 50%. Dictionary. NT: 1994. *Other:* VSO.

Rennellese Sign Language [rsi] 1 (1986 Gallaudet University). Rennell Island. *Class:* Deaf sign language. *Lg Use:* Developed about 1915 by Kagobai, the first deaf person. Used also by hearing people. *Other:* Nearly extinct.

Ririo [rri] 79 (1999 SIL). Choiseul Island. *Class:* Austronesian, Malayo-Polynesian, Central-Eastern, Eastern Malayo-Polynesian, Oceanic, Western Oceanic, Meso Melanesian, New Ireland, South New Ireland-Northwest Solomonic, Choiseul. *Dialects:* Close to Babatana.

Roviana (Robiana, Ruviana, Rubiana) [rug] 9,871 (1999 SIL). North central New Georgia, Roviana Lagoon, Vonavona Lagoon; Western Province. *Class:* Austronesian, Malayo-Polynesian, Central-Eastern, Eastern Malayo-Polynesian, Oceanic, Western Oceanic, Meso Melanesian, New Ireland, South New Ireland-Northwest Solomonic, New Georgia, West. *Lg Use:* Trade language. Trade language previously in Western Province and as far north as Buka and Bougainville in Papua New Guinea. It is being replaced as a lingua franca by Pijin in Western Province, and is now used as a second language mainly by those over 30 years old. 16,000 second-language users (1987 UBS). *Lg Dev:* Literacy rate in first language: 30% to 60%. Literacy rate in second language: 25% to 50%. Dictionary. NT: 1953–1995. *Other:* VSO.

Sa'a (Saa, South Malaita, Apae'aa) [apb] 11,519 (1999 SIL). Population includes 7,298 Sa'a, 3,304 Ulawa, and 917 Uki Ni Masi. South Malaita Island, Ulawa Island, Three Sisters Islands. *Class:* Austronesian, Malayo-Polynesian, Central-Eastern, Eastern Malayo-Polynesian, Oceanic, Central-Eastern Oceanic, Southeast Solomonic, Malaita-San Cristobal, Malaita, Southern. *Dialect:* Ulawa, Uki Ni Masi (Ugi). *Lg Use:* Uki Ni Masi is nearly extinct. *Lg Dev:* Literacy rate in first language: 30% to 60%. Literacy rate in second language: 25% to 50%. Dictionary. Grammar. NT: 1911–1927. *Other:* SVO. Mountain slope, coastal. Tropical forest. 100 to 1,000 meters. Hunters; agriculturalists: yams, taro, banana, coconut, breadfruit; fishermen; animal husbandry: pigs. Traditional religion.

Santa Cruz (Natögu, Nendö, Nambakaengö, Mbanua) [stc] 5,899 (1999 SIL). Population includes 4,276 Londai and 1,623 Nea. Santa Cruz Islands, Eastern Solomons. *Class:* East Papuan, Reef Islands-Santa Cruz. *Dialects:* Ndeni (Deni), Te Motu, Londai, Nea, Nooli, Lvova (Lwowa), Mbanua. Speakers of most dialects understand Lwowa and Mbanua well. Nea and Nooli dialects may be sufficiently diverse to require adapted literature. *Lg Dev:* Literacy rate in first language: 25% to 50%. Literacy rate in second language: 15% to 25%. Bible portions: 1985–1991. *Other:* Fishermen.

Savosavo (Savo Island, Savo) [svs] 2,415 (1999 SIL). Savo Island, north of Guadalcanal, Central Solomons.

Class: East Papuan, Yele-Solomons-New Britain, Yele-Solomons, Central Solomons. *Lg Use:* Use of Savosavo is declining among the younger generation. Speakers also use Pijin.

Sikaiana (Sikayana) [sky] 731 (1999 SIL). Sikaiana Atoll, Central Solomons. *Class:* Austronesian, Malayo-Polynesian, Central-Eastern, Eastern Malayo-Polynesian, Oceanic, Central-Eastern Oceanic, Remote Oceanic, Central Pacific, East Fijian-Polynesian, Polynesian, Nuclear, Samoic-Outlier, Ellicean. *Dialects:* Close to Luangiua (Ontong Java). *Lg Dev:* Dictionary. *Other:* SVO.

Simbo (Sibo, Madeggusu, Mandeghughusu) [sbb] 2,701 (1999 SIL). Simbo (Eddystone) Island, Western Province. *Class:* Austronesian, Malayo-Polynesian, Central-Eastern, Eastern Malayo-Polynesian, Oceanic, Western Oceanic, Meso Melanesian, New Ireland, South New Ireland-Northwest Solomonic, New Georgia, West. *Dialects:* Distinct from Lungga and Ghanongga. *Lg Use:* Use of Roviana is decreasing.

Talise (Talisi, Tolo) [tlr] 12,525 (1999 SIL). Population includes 5,944 in Talise, 2,087 in Moli, 4,494 in Koo. Guadalcanal Island, southeast to southwest coast. *Class:* Austronesian, Malayo-Polynesian, Central-Eastern, Eastern Malayo-Polynesian, Oceanic, Central-Eastern Oceanic, Southeast Solomonic, Gela-Guadalcanal, Guadalcanal. *Dialects:* Talise, Tolo, Moli, Poleo, Koo (Inakona), Malagheti. *Lg Dev:* Dictionary. Grammar.

Tanema (Tanima) [tnx] 3 (1999 SIL). Ethnic population: 190 (1998 SIL). Emua village, Vanikolo Island, Temotu Province. *Class:* Austronesian, Malayo-Polynesian, Central-Eastern, Eastern Malayo-Polynesian, Oceanic, Central-Eastern Oceanic, Remote Oceanic, Eastern Outer Islands, Vanikoro. *Lg Use:* Members of the ethnic group now speak Pijin or Teanu. *Other:* SVO. Mountain slope, coastal. Tropical forest. Sea level to 1,000 meters. Agriculturalists; fishermen. Nearly extinct.

Tanimbili (Nyisunggu) [tbe] 15 (1999 SIL). Tanimbili village, Utupua Island, Temotu Province. *Class:* Austronesian, Malayo-Polynesian, Central-Eastern, Eastern Malayo-Polynesian, Oceanic, Central-Eastern Oceanic, Remote Oceanic, Eastern Outer Islands, Utupua. *Lg Use:* Bilingual level estimates for Amba: 0 27%, 1 0%, 2 0%, 3+ 40%, 4 33%, 5 0%; Pijin: 0 0%, 1 0%, 2 0%, 3 47%, 4 53%, 5 0%. Speakers also use Asumbuo. *Other:* SVO. Mountain slope, coastal. Tropical forest. Sea level to 350 meters. Agriculturalists; fishermen. Nearly extinct.

Teanu (Buma, Puma) [tkw] 24 (1999 SIL). Puma, Lavaka, Emua, and Lale villages, Vanikolo Island, Temotu Province. *Class:* Austronesian, Malayo-Polynesian, Central-Eastern, Eastern Malayo-Polynesian, Oceanic, Central-Eastern Oceanic, Remote Oceanic, Eastern Outer Islands, Vanikoro. *Lg Use:* Speakers also use Pijin. *Lg Dev:* Literacy rate in first language: 30% to 60%. Literacy rate in second language: 25% to 50%. *Other:* Speakers prefer the name 'Teanu'. SVO. Mountain slope, coastal. Tropical forest. Sea level to 1,000 meters. Agriculturalists; fishermen. Nearly extinct.

Tikopia [tkp] 3,324 (1999 SIL). Tikopia Island. *Class:* Austronesian, Malayo-Polynesian, Central-Eastern, Eastern Malayo-Polynesian, Oceanic, Central-Eastern Oceanic, Remote Oceanic, Central Pacific, East Fijian-Polynesian, Polynesian, Nuclear, Samoic-Outlier, Futunic. *Dialects:* Related to Anuta. *Lg Dev:* Literacy rate in first language: 30% to 60%. Literacy rate in second language: 25% to 50%. Bible portions: 1989. *Other:* SVO, VSO. Agriculturalists: sago.

To'abaita (To'ambaita, Malu, Malu'u) [mlu] 12,572 (1999 SIL). North Malaita Island. *Class:* Austronesian, Malayo-Polynesian, Central-Eastern, Eastern Malayo-Polynesian, Oceanic, Central-Eastern Oceanic, Southeast Solomonic, Malaita-San Cristobal, Malaita, Northern.

Dialects: Baelelea and Baegu are about equally intelligible
with To'abaita and Lau. *Lg Dev:* Literacy rate in first
language: 30% to 60%. Literacy rate in second language:
25% to 50%. Dictionary. NT: 1923. *Other:* SVO.
Mountain slope, coastal. Tropical forest. 100 to 1,000
meters. Hunters; agriculturalists.

Touo (Baniata, Lokuru, Mbaniata) [tqu] 1,874 (1999
census). South Rendova Island, Western Province. *Class:*
East Papuan, Yele-Solomons-New Britain, Yele-Solomons,
Central Solomons. *Lg Use:* All ages. High level of
bilingualism in Pijin and Marovo. Bilingualism of speakers
in Roviana is decreasing.

Ughele (Ugele) [uge] 1,202 (1999 SIL). North end of
Rendova Island, Western Province. *Class:* Austronesian,
Malayo-Polynesian, Central-Eastern, Eastern Malayo-
Polynesian, Oceanic, Western Oceanic, Meso Melanesian,
New Ireland, South New Ireland-Northwest Solomonic,
New Georgia, West. *Lg Use:* Bilingual level estimates for
Roviana: 0 0%, 1 0%, 2 30%, 3–5 70%.

Vaghua (Tavula, Tavola, Vagua) [tva] 1,960 (1999 SIL).
Tavula, Choiseul Island. *Class:* Austronesian, Malayo-
Polynesian, Central-Eastern, Eastern Malayo-Polynesian,
Oceanic, Western Oceanic, Meso Melanesian, New
Ireland, South New Ireland-Northwest Solomonic,
Choiseul. *Dialects:* Close to Varisi.

Vangunu [mpr] 907 (1999 SIL). Population includes 399
Bareke, 508 Vangunu. North Vangunu Island (Bareke),
southwest Vangunu Island (Vangunu), Western Province.
Class: Austronesian, Malayo-Polynesian, Central-Eastern,
Eastern Malayo-Polynesian, Oceanic, Western Oceanic,
Meso Melanesian, New Ireland, South New Ireland-
Northwest Solomonic, New Georgia, East. *Dialects:* Bareke
(Mbareke), Vangunu. *Lg Use:* Speakers also use Marovo.

Vano (Vanikoro, Vanikolo) [vnk] Extinct. Lale and Lavaka
villages, Vanikolo Island, Temotu Province. *Class:*
Austronesian, Malayo-Polynesian, Central-Eastern, Eastern
Malayo-Polynesian, Oceanic, Central-Eastern Oceanic,
Remote Oceanic, Eastern Outer Islands, Vanikoro. *Lg Use:*
Members of the ethnic group now speak Pijin or Teanu.
Other: SVO. Mountain slope, coastal. Tropical forest. Sea
level to 1,000 meters. Agriculturalists; fishermen.

Varisi (Varese) [vrs] 5,161 (1999 SIL). Northeast Choiseul
Island. *Class:* Austronesian, Malayo-Polynesian, Central-
Eastern, Eastern Malayo-Polynesian, Oceanic, Western
Oceanic, Meso Melanesian, New Ireland, South New
Ireland-Northwest Solomonic, Choiseul. *Dialects:* Ghone,
Varisi. Close to Vaghua. *Lg Dev:* Bible portions: 1995.

Wala (Langalanga) [lgl] 6,978 (1999 SIL). West central
Malaita Island. *Class:* Austronesian, Malayo-Polynesian,
Central-Eastern, Eastern Malayo-Polynesian, Oceanic,
Central-Eastern Oceanic, Southeast Solomonic, Malaita-San
Cristobal, Malaita, Northern. *Dialects:* Lexical similarity
56% with Kwaio; 66% with Kwara'ae. *Other:* SVO. Coral
reef. Sea level to 1 meter. Fishermen; craftsmen.

Zabana (Kia) [kji] 3,355 (2003 SIL). Santa Isabel Island
from Samasodu on the southwest side up to Kia village
and down the northeast side to Baolo village. *Class:*
Austronesian, Malayo-Polynesian, Central-Eastern, Eastern
Malayo-Polynesian, Oceanic, Western Oceanic, Meso
Melanesian, New Ireland, South New Ireland-Northwest
Solomonic, Santa Isabel, West. *Dialects:* Borrowings from
Roviana. Closest to Cheke Holo. *Lg Use:* Speakers also
use Cheke Holo. *Lg Dev:* Literacy rate in first language:
30% to 60%. Literacy rate in second language: 25% to
50%. Literature could also be used for Kokota and Zazao
speakers. Grammar.

Zazao (Jajao, Kilokaka) [jaj] 10 (1999 SIL). Central Isabel
Island, village of Kilokaka on Hograno coast. *Class:*
Austronesian, Malayo-Polynesian, Central-Eastern, Eastern
Malayo-Polynesian, Oceanic, Western Oceanic, Meso
Melanesian, New Ireland, South New Ireland-Northwest

Solomonic, Santa Isabel, Central. *Lg Use:* Some key
domains. People are mildly supportive. Speakers can
converse in Cheke Holo (Maringe) and Zabana. *Other:*
Nearly extinct.

Tokelau

Formerly called Union Islands. 1,458. National or official
language: English. A New Zealand self-governing territory.
Three atolls: Atafu, Nukunono, Fakaofo. Literacy rate: 94%.
Information mainly from N. Besnier 1992. The number of
languages listed for Tokelau is 2. Of those, both are living
languages.

English [eng] 40 in Tokelau (2004). *Lg Use:* National
language. Used in schools. See main entry under United
Kingdom.

Tokelauan (Tokelau) [tkl] 1,405 in Tokelau (2004).
Population total all countries: 3,242. Also spoken in
American Samoa, New Zealand, USA. *Class:*
Austronesian, Malayo-Polynesian, Central-Eastern,
Eastern Malayo-Polynesian, Oceanic, Central-Eastern
Oceanic, Remote Oceanic, Central Pacific, East Fijian-
Polynesian, Polynesian, Nuclear, Samoic-Outlier,
Tokelauan. *Dialects:* There are dialect differences among
the three atolls. Intelligible with Tuvaluan. Close to
Samoan. Tokelauans read the Samoan Bible and some
speak some Samoan. *Lg Use:* Most who live in Tokelau
have very rudimentary knowledge of English as a second
language. *Lg Dev:* Taught in primary schools. Grammar.
Bible portions: 2000. *Other:* Fishermen mainly;
agriculturalists: coconut, taro, breadfruit, banana,
arrowroot. Christian, traditional religion.

Tonga

Kingdom of Tonga. Pulèanga Tonga. 110,237. National
or official languages: Tongan, English. Constitutional
monarchy. 169 islands, 36 inhabited. 270 square miles.
Literacy rate: 93% to 100%. Also includes , Chinese (200).
Information mainly from S. Wurm and S. Hattori 1981; N.
Besnier 1992. The number of languages listed for Tonga is
4. Of those, 3 are living languages and 1 is extinct. See map
on page 885.

English [eng] *Lg Use:* Official language. See main entry
under United Kingdom.

Niuafo'ou [num] 690 (1981 SIL). Niuafo'ou and 'Eua
islands. *Class:* Austronesian, Malayo-Polynesian, Central-
Eastern, Eastern Malayo-Polynesian, Oceanic, Central-
Eastern Oceanic, Remote Oceanic, Central Pacific, East
Fijian-Polynesian, Polynesian, Nuclear, Samoic-Outlier,
East Uvean-Niuafo'ou. *Dialects:* Probably a dialect of
East Uvean (Wallisian).

Niuatoputapu [nkp] Extinct. Ethnic population: 1,630
(1981). Niuatoputapu Island. *Class:* Austronesian,
Malayo-Polynesian, Central-Eastern, Eastern Malayo-
Polynesian, Oceanic, Central-Eastern Oceanic, Remote
Oceanic, Central Pacific, East Fijian-Polynesian,
Polynesian, Nuclear, Samoic-Outlier. *Lg Use:* Known
from a few words collected by Westerners in the 17th
century. Became extinct before the 19th century. The
ethnic group now speaks Tongan.

Tongan (Tonga) [ton] 96,334 in Tonga (1998). Population
total all countries: 105,319. Also spoken in American
Samoa, Australia, Canada, Fiji, New Zealand, Niue, USA,
Vanuatu. *Class:* Austronesian, Malayo-Polynesian, Central-
Eastern, Eastern Malayo-Polynesian, Oceanic, Central-
Eastern Oceanic, Remote Oceanic, Central Pacific, East
Fijian-Polynesian, Polynesian, Tongic. *Dialects:* Close to
Niue. There are slight dialect differences from north to

south. Lexical similarity 86% with Wallisian, 66% with Samoan. *Lg Use:* National language. The ethnic group is predominantly monolingual in Tongan (1997 J. Siegel). *Lg Dev:* Newspapers. Radio programs. Dictionary. Bible: 1862–1966. *Other:* VSO. Agriculturalists.

Tuvalu

Formerly Ellice Islands. 11,468. National or official language: Tuvaluan. 9 islands. Literacy rate: 96%. Information mainly from B. Bender and K. Rehg 1991. The number of languages listed for Tuvalu is 2. Of those, both are living languages.

Kiribati (Gilbertese, Ikiribati) [gil] 870 in Tuvalu (1987). Nui, a northern island. *Dialect:* Nui (Nuian). *Lg Use:* Vigorous. A part of Tuvalu culture. *Other:* Christian. See main entry under Kiribati.

Tuvaluan (Ellice, Ellicean, Tuvalu) [tvl] 10,670 in Tuvalu (1998). Population total all countries: 13,051. Tuvalu, 7 of the 9 inhabited islands. Also spoken in Fiji, Kiribati, Nauru, New Zealand. *Class:* Austronesian, Malayo-Polynesian, Central-Eastern, Eastern Malayo-Polynesian, Oceanic, Central-Eastern Oceanic, Remote Oceanic, Central Pacific, East Fijian-Polynesian, Polynesian, Nuclear, Samoic-Outlier, Ellicean. *Dialects:* North Tuvaluan (Nanumanga, Nanumea, Niutao), South Tuvaluan (Nukufetau, Vaitupu, Funafuti, Nukulaelae). Not intelligible with Samoan, which was formerly used as a mission language. Tuvalu is intelligible with Tokelau. The southern dialect is official. *Lg Use:* Official language. Vigorous. *Lg Dev:* Literacy rate in first language: Most people. Bible: 1987. *Other:* Little Tuvalu literature is available. Christian.

Vanuatu

Republic of Vanuatu. Ripablik Blong Vanuatu. Formerly New Hebrides. 202,609. Population includes 175,700 Melanesian (92%). National or official languages: Bislama, English, French. Y-shaped chain of 80 islands. Land area 13,000 square kilometers. Literacy rate: 61% to 90%. 85% to 90% of school age children attend school (1977 WA). Also includes Fijian (350), Kiribati (370), Tahitian, Tongan, Vietnamese (770), Wallisian (775), Chinese (300). Information mainly from D. T. Tryon 1971, 1976, 1978, 1995; S. Wurm and S. Hattori 1981. The number of languages listed for Vanuatu is 110. Of those, 109 are living languages and 1 is extinct. See maps beginning on page 886.

Akei (Tasiriki) [tsr] 650 (1981 Wurm and Hattori). Southwestern Santo. *Class:* Austronesian, Malayo-Polynesian, Central-Eastern, Eastern Malayo-Polynesian, Oceanic, Central-Eastern Oceanic, Remote Oceanic, North and Central Vanuatu, Northeast Vanuatu-Banks Islands, West Santo. *Dialects:* Close to Fortsenal. Complex dialect chain. *Lg Dev:* Bible portions: 1909–1924.

Ambae, East (Omba, Oba, Aoba, Walurigi, Northeast Aoba, Northeast Ambae) [omb] 5,000 (1991 UBS). Ambae (Leper's) Island. *Class:* Austronesian, Malayo-Polynesian, Central-Eastern, Eastern Malayo-Polynesian, Oceanic, Central-Eastern Oceanic, Remote Oceanic, North and Central Vanuatu, Northeast Vanuatu-Banks Islands, East Vanuatu. *Dialects:* Lombaha (Lobaha), Longana, Lolokaro (Lolokara, Lolsiwoi). About 15 dialects. *Lg Dev:* Bible portions: 1971–1986. *Other:* SVO. Christian.

Ambae, West (Opa) [nnd] 4,500 (1983 SIL). West Ambae (Aoba, Leper's) Island. *Class:* Austronesian, Malayo-Polynesian, Central-Eastern, Eastern Malayo-Polynesian, Oceanic, Central-Eastern Oceanic, Remote

Oceanic, North and Central Vanuatu, Northeast Vanuatu-Banks Islands, East Vanuatu. *Dialect:* Walaha, Nduindui (Duindui). Many dialects. *Lg Dev:* NT: 1984.

Amblong [alm] 150 (1983 SIL). South Santo. *Class:* Austronesian, Malayo-Polynesian, Central-Eastern, Eastern Malayo-Polynesian, Oceanic, Central-Eastern Oceanic, Remote Oceanic, North and Central Vanuatu, Northeast Vanuatu-Banks Islands, West Santo. *Dialects:* Close to Narango and Morouas. *Lg Use:* 70% of the ethnic group speaks Amblong. Most domains. 30% to 50% of children speak Amblong. Positive language attitude.

Ambrym, North [mmg] 2,850 (1983 SIL). North Ambrym Island. *Class:* Austronesian, Malayo-Polynesian, Central-Eastern, Eastern Malayo-Polynesian, Oceanic, Central-Eastern Oceanic, Remote Oceanic, North and Central Vanuatu, Northeast Vanuatu-Banks Islands, East Vanuatu. *Dialects:* Magam, Olal. *Other:* Volcanic island. Traditional religion.

Ambrym, Southeast [tvk] 1,800 (1983 SIL). Southeast Ambrym Island. *Class:* Austronesian, Malayo-Polynesian, Central-Eastern, Eastern Malayo-Polynesian, Oceanic, Central-Eastern Oceanic, Remote Oceanic, North and Central Vanuatu, Northeast Vanuatu-Banks Islands, East Vanuatu. *Dialects:* Taveak (Taviak), Endu, Toak, Penapo. *Lg Dev:* Bible portions: 1949. *Other:* Links with Paama linguistically. Traditional religion.

Aneityum (Aniteum, Aneiteumese, Anejom) [aty] 600 (1983 SIL). Aneityum Island. *Class:* Austronesian, Malayo-Polynesian, Central-Eastern, Eastern Malayo-Polynesian, Oceanic, Central-Eastern Oceanic, South Vanuatu, Aneityum. *Lg Dev:* Literacy rate in first language: 30% to 60%. Literacy rate in second language: 50% to 75%. Bible: 1879. *Other:* Some simplification of the subject marking system has occurred.

Aore [aor] 1 (1982 SIL). Mafea Island, East Santo. *Class:* Austronesian, Malayo-Polynesian, Central-Eastern, Eastern Malayo-Polynesian, Oceanic, Central-Eastern Oceanic, Remote Oceanic, North and Central Vanuatu, Northeast Vanuatu-Banks Islands, West Santo. *Dialects:* Close to Malo and Tutuba. *Other:* Nearly extinct.

Apma (Central Raga) [app] 4,500 (1983 SIL). Central Pentecost (Raga). *Class:* Austronesian, Malayo-Polynesian, Central-Eastern, Eastern Malayo-Polynesian, Oceanic, Central-Eastern Oceanic, Remote Oceanic, North and Central Vanuatu, Northeast Vanuatu-Banks Islands, East Vanuatu. *Dialects:* Bwatnapni, Loltong, Melsisi, Suru-Bo, Suru-Marani. *Lg Dev:* Bible portions: 1977.

Araki [akr] 8. Araki Island, south Santo. *Class:* Austronesian, Malayo-Polynesian, Central-Eastern, Eastern Malayo-Polynesian, Oceanic, Central-Eastern Oceanic, Remote Oceanic, North and Central Vanuatu, Northeast Vanuatu-Banks Islands, West Santo. *Lg Use:* Only older adult speakers in 2 families. Tangoa is used as first or second language. *Other:* Nearly extinct.

Aulua (Aulua Bay) [aul] 300 (1983 SIL). East Malekula. *Class:* Austronesian, Malayo-Polynesian, Central-Eastern, Eastern Malayo-Polynesian, Oceanic, Central-Eastern Oceanic, Remote Oceanic, North and Central Vanuatu, Northeast Vanuatu-Banks Islands, Malekula Coastal. *Dialects:* Onesso, Boinelang. *Lg Use:* 70% of the ethnic group speaks Aulua. Most key domains. 60% of the children speak Aulua. Positive language attitude. *Lg Dev:* Bible portions: 1894–1925.

Axamb (Ahamb) [ahb] 525 (1983 SIL). South Malekula. *Class:* Austronesian, Malayo-Polynesian, Central-Eastern, Eastern Malayo-Polynesian, Oceanic, Central-Eastern Oceanic, Remote Oceanic, North and Central Vanuatu, Northeast Vanuatu-Banks Islands, Malekula Coastal. *Lg Dev:* Bible portions: 1935.

Baetora [btr] 540 (1983 SIL). Maewo Island. *Class:* Austronesian, Malayo-Polynesian, Central-Eastern, Eastern

Malayo-Polynesian, Oceanic, Central-Eastern Oceanic, Remote Oceanic, North and Central Vanuatu, Northeast Vanuatu-Banks Islands, East Vanuatu. *Dialects:* Nasawa, Talise, Narovorovo. Considerable dialect variation.

Baki (Burumba, Paki) [bki] 200 (1981 Wurm and Hattori). West Epi. *Class:* Austronesian, Malayo-Polynesian, Central-Eastern, Eastern Malayo-Polynesian, Oceanic, Central-Eastern Oceanic, Remote Oceanic, North and Central Vanuatu, Northeast Vanuatu-Banks Islands, Epi, Lamenu-Baki, Baki-Bierebo. *Dialects:* Slight dialect variation. *Lg Use:* 60% of the ethnic group speaks Baki. Some or most key domains. 30% of the children speak Baki. Positive language attitude. Many Bierebo use Baki as second language. *Lg Dev:* Literacy rate in first language: below 1%. Literacy rate in second language: 5% to 15%. Bible portions: 1886–1987.

Bierebo (Bonkovia-Yevali) [bnk] 450 (1983 SIL). West Epi, south of the Lamenu, north of the Baki. *Class:* Austronesian, Malayo-Polynesian, Central-Eastern, Eastern Malayo-Polynesian, Oceanic, Central-Eastern Oceanic, Remote Oceanic, North and Central Vanuatu, Northeast Vanuatu-Banks Islands, Epi, Lamenu-Baki, Baki-Bierebo. *Lg Use:* 70% of the ethnic group speaks Bierebo. Some or most key domains. 40% of the children speak Bierebo. Positive language attitude. Many speakers also use Baki.

Bieria (Bieri, Vovo, Wowo) [brj] 170 (1981 Wurm and Hattori). Population includes 100 in Vovo, 70 in Bieria. South Epi, between the Maii and the Lewo. *Class:* Austronesian, Malayo-Polynesian, Central-Eastern, Eastern Malayo-Polynesian, Oceanic, Central-Eastern Oceanic, Remote Oceanic, North and Central Vanuatu, Northeast Vanuatu-Banks Islands, Epi, Bieria-Maii. *Dialect:* Bieria, Vovo (Wowo). Wurm and Hattori treat Bieria and Vovo as separate languages. *Lg Use:* 70% of the ethnic group speaks Bieria. Some or most domains. 40% of children speak Bieria. Positive language attitude. Speakers may be bilingual in Baki. *Lg Dev:* Literacy rate in first language: below 1%. Literacy rate in second language: 5% to 15%. Bible portions: 1898.

Bislama (Bichelamar) [bis] 5,000 in Vanuatu (2001 Naito and Tryon). Population total all countries: 6,200. Also spoken in New Caledonia. *Class:* Creole, English based, Pacific. *Dialects:* Unlike Tok Pisin (Papua New Guinea) and Pijin (Solomon Islands) there are some French loanwords. Partially intelligible with Pijin and Tok Pisin. *Lg Use:* Official language. The majority of the population of 128,000 understand and use it as a lingua franca. Widely used in commerce, government, internal dealings. Language of parliament. Used orally in education. *Lg Dev:* Literacy rate in first language: 10% to 30%. Literacy rate in second language: 25% to 50%. Newspapers. Radio programs. TV. Dictionary. Grammar. Bible: 1998.

Burmbar (Vartavo, Banan Bay) [vrt] 525 (1983 SIL). Southeast Malekula. *Class:* Austronesian, Malayo-Polynesian, Central-Eastern, Eastern Malayo-Polynesian, Oceanic, Central-Eastern Oceanic, Remote Oceanic, North and Central Vanuatu, Northeast Vanuatu-Banks Islands, Malekula Coastal. *Dialects:* Some dialect differences.

Butmas-Tur (Ati) [bnr] 525 (1983 SIL). East central Santo. *Class:* Austronesian, Malayo-Polynesian, Central-Eastern, Eastern Malayo-Polynesian, Oceanic, Central-Eastern Oceanic, Remote Oceanic, North and Central Vanuatu, East Santo, South.

Dakaka (Baiap, South Ambrym) [bpa] 600 (1983 SIL). South Ambrym. *Class:* Austronesian, Malayo-Polynesian, Central-Eastern, Eastern Malayo-Polynesian, Oceanic, Central-Eastern Oceanic, Remote Oceanic, North and Central Vanuatu, Northeast Vanuatu-Banks Islands, East Vanuatu. *Dialect:* Sesivi. Several dialects.

Dixon Reef [dix] 50 (1982 SIL). Southwest Malekula. *Class:* Austronesian, Malayo-Polynesian, Central-Eastern,

Eastern Malayo-Polynesian, Oceanic, Central-Eastern Oceanic, Remote Oceanic, North and Central Vanuatu, Malekula Interior, Small Nambas. *Lg Use:* 80% of the ethnic group speaks Dixon Reef. Most key domains. 40% of children speak Dixon Reef. Positive language attitude.

Efate, North [llp] 3,000 (1983 SIL). Northern Efate Island, Nguna, Tongoa, and several smaller islands, southeast Epi. *Class:* Austronesian, Malayo-Polynesian, Central-Eastern, Eastern Malayo-Polynesian, Oceanic, Central-Eastern Oceanic, Remote Oceanic, North and Central Vanuatu, Northeast Vanuatu-Banks Islands, Central Vanuatu. *Dialects:* Nguna (Guna, Tongoa, Ngunese), Buninga, Sesake, Emau, Paunangis, Livara. *Lg Dev:* Literacy rate in first language: 30% to 60%. Literacy rate in second language: 50% to 75%. Bible: 1972. *Other:* SVO (for Nguna).

Efate, South (Fate, Erakor, Southern Efate) [erk] 3,750 (1983 SIL). Efate Island. *Class:* Austronesian, Malayo-Polynesian, Central-Eastern, Eastern Malayo-Polynesian, Oceanic, Central-Eastern Oceanic, Remote Oceanic, North and Central Vanuatu, Northeast Vanuatu-Banks Islands, Central Vanuatu. *Lg Dev:* Literacy rate in first language: 10% to 30%. Literacy rate in second language: 50% to 75%. NT: 1889–1930.

Emae (Emwae, Mae, Mwae, Emai, Mai) [mmw] 200 (1981 Wurm and Hattori). Emae; Three Hills Island, Sesake Island, two villages. *Class:* Austronesian, Malayo-Polynesian, Central-Eastern, Eastern Malayo-Polynesian, Oceanic, Central-Eastern Oceanic, Remote Oceanic, Central Pacific, East Fijian-Polynesian, Polynesian, Nuclear, Samoic-Outlier, Futunic. *Dialects:* No dialect variation. *Lg Use:* 70% of the ethnic group speaks Emae. 50% of the children speak Emae. Positive language attitude. Speakers use North Efate (Tongoan) as second language. *Lg Dev:* Literacy rate in first language: below 1%. Literacy rate in second language: 50% to 75%. *Other:* SVO.

English [eng] 1,900 in Vanuatu (1995). *Lg Use:* Official language. First-language speakers are from the United Kingdom. See main entry under United Kingdom.

Eton (Epwau, Eastern Efate) [etn] 500 (1989 census). Southeastern Efate Island at Eton, Pang Pang, and surrounding villages. *Class:* Austronesian, Malayo-Polynesian, Central-Eastern, Eastern Malayo-Polynesian, Oceanic, Central-Eastern Oceanic, Remote Oceanic, North and Central Vanuatu, Northeast Vanuatu-Banks Islands, Central Vanuatu. *Dialects:* Eton, Pang Pang. Formerly thought to be a dialect of South Efate. 88% inherent intelligibility of Lelepa, 64% of South Efate. *Lg Use:* Pang Pang dialect is nearly extinct. All ages. Speakers also use Bislama, English, French, South Efate, Lelepa, or North Efate.

Fortsenal [frt] 150 (1983 SIL). Central Santo. *Class:* Austronesian, Malayo-Polynesian, Central-Eastern, Eastern Malayo-Polynesian, Oceanic, Central-Eastern Oceanic, Remote Oceanic, North and Central Vanuatu, Northeast Vanuatu-Banks Islands, West Santo. *Dialects:* Close to Akei. *Lg Use:* 80% of the ethnic group speaks Fortsenal. Most key domains. 70% of children speak Fortsenal. Positive language attitude.

French [fra] 6,300 in Vanuatu (1995). *Lg Use:* Official language. See main entry under France.

Futuna-Aniwa (West Futuna-Aniwa, Erronan) [fut] 600 (1981 Wurm and Hattori). (West) Futuna and Aniwa Islands, east of Tanna. *Class:* Austronesian, Malayo-Polynesian, Central-Eastern, Eastern Malayo-Polynesian, Oceanic, Central-Eastern Oceanic, Remote Oceanic, Central Pacific, East Fijian-Polynesian, Polynesian, Nuclear, Samoic-Outlier, Futunic. *Dialects:* West Futuna (Fotuna), Aniwa (Anewa). There are significant differences between the West Futunan and Aniwan dialects. *Lg Dev:* Literacy rate in first language: 30% to 60%. Literacy rate in second language: 50% to 75%. NT: 1898. *Other:* Distinct from (East) Futuna on Futuna Island in French Territory of Wallis and Futuna. SVO, VS. Fishermen; agriculturalists: taro, yams, sweet potato, coconut, fig, breadfruit, banana, native cabbage, sugarcane, chestnut, arrowroot; animal husbandry: pigs, poultry.

Hano (Raga, Lamalanga, North Raga, Vunmarama, Qatvenua, Bwatvenua) [lml] 7,000 (1991 UBS). North Pentecost (Raga, Whitsuntide Island) and southern Maewo (Aurora) Island. *Class:* Austronesian, Malayo-Polynesian, Central-Eastern, Eastern Malayo-Polynesian, Oceanic, Central-Eastern Oceanic, Remote Oceanic, North and Central Vanuatu, Northeast Vanuatu-Banks Islands, East Vanuatu. *Dialects:* Slight dialect differences. *Lg Use:* Trade language. *Lg Dev:* Bible portions: 1908–1989. *Other:* 'Hano' is the name preferred locally.

Hiw (Torres, Torres Island) [hiw] 120 (1983 SIL). Torres Islands. *Class:* Austronesian, Malayo-Polynesian, Central-Eastern, Eastern Malayo-Polynesian, Oceanic, Central-Eastern Oceanic, Remote Oceanic, North and Central Vanuatu, Northeast Vanuatu-Banks Islands, East Vanuatu. *Lg Use:* 80% of the ethnic group speaks Hiw. Most key domains retained for Hiw. 70% of children speak Hiw. Positive language attitude. *Lg Dev:* Bible portions: 1894–1900.

Ifo (Utaha) [iff] Extinct. Erromanga Island, southern Vanuatu. *Class:* Austronesian, Malayo-Polynesian, Central-Eastern, Eastern Malayo-Polynesian, Oceanic, Central-Eastern Oceanic, South Vanuatu, Erromanga. *Other:* The last speaker died in 1954.

Katbol (Tembimbe-Katbol, Taremp, Tisvel) [tmb] 450 (1983 SIL). Central Malekula. *Class:* Austronesian, Malayo-Polynesian, Central-Eastern, Eastern Malayo-Polynesian, Oceanic, Central-Eastern Oceanic, Remote Oceanic, North and Central Vanuatu, Malekula Interior, Malekula Central. *Lg Use:* 70% of the ethnic group speaks Katbol. Most key domains. 60% of children speak Katbol. Positive language attitude.

Koro [krf] 105 (1983 SIL). Gaua Island of the Banks Islands, villages of Koro and Mekeon. *Class:* Austronesian, Malayo-Polynesian, Central-Eastern, Eastern Malayo-Polynesian, Oceanic, Central-Eastern Oceanic, Remote Oceanic, North and Central Vanuatu, Northeast Vanuatu-Banks Islands, East Vanuatu. *Lg Use:* 70% of the ethnic group speaks Koro. Most key domains. 60% of the children speak Koro. Positive language attitude.

Kwamera [tnk] 2,500 (1989 SIL). Southeast Tanna. *Class:* Austronesian, Malayo-Polynesian, Central-Eastern, Eastern Malayo-Polynesian, Oceanic, Central-Eastern Oceanic, South Vanuatu, Tanna. *Dialects:* 2 main dialects. *Lg Dev:* Grammar. NT: 1890.

Labo (Mewun, Meaun, Nide) [mwi] 350 (1981 Wurm and Hattori). Southwest Bay, Malekula. *Class:* Austronesian, Malayo-Polynesian, Central-Eastern, Eastern Malayo-Polynesian, Oceanic, Central-Eastern Oceanic, Remote Oceanic, North and Central Vanuatu, Malekula Interior, Labo. *Lg Use:* 70% of the ethnic group speaks Labo. Most key domains. 30% of the children speak Labo. Positive language attitude. *Lg Dev:* Bible portions: 1905. *Other:* Hunters; fishermen; agriculturalists: yams. Traditional religion.

Lakona (Lakon, Gaua, Gog) [lkn] 300 (1983 SIL). Gaua Island, Banks Group. *Class:* Austronesian, Malayo-Polynesian, Central-Eastern, Eastern Malayo-Polynesian, Oceanic, Central-Eastern Oceanic, Remote Oceanic, North and Central Vanuatu, Northeast Vanuatu-Banks Islands, East Vanuatu. *Lg Use:* 70% of the ethnic group speaks Lakona. Most key domains. 60% of children speak Lakona. Positive language attitude. English is used by the teachers and in classes only. Outside communications and commerce are in Bislama. Religious services are in Lakona or Bislama, not English. Some monolinguals. *Other:* Two primary schools.

Lamenu (Lewo, Varmali) [lmu] 750 (1986 SIL). Very few monolinguals. Shefa Province, Lamenu Island, and the northwest tip of Epi Island, Varmali Region. Some in Sara village. Some live in Port Vila and Luganville. *Class:* Austronesian, Malayo-Polynesian, Central-Eastern, Eastern Malayo-Polynesian, Oceanic, Central-Eastern Oceanic, Remote Oceanic, North and Central Vanuatu, Northeast Vanuatu-Banks Islands, Epi, Lamenu-Baki, Lamenu-Lewo. *Lg Use:* Vigorous. Used in kindergarten, oral and some written use in church, oral use in commerce. Positive language attitude. Most speak Bislama for wider communication. Half speak some English, which is used in schools. Some also speak Paama. *Lg Dev:* Literacy rate in first language: below 1%. Literacy rate in second language: 15% to 25%. Bible portions: 1987. *Other:* At one time the population of Lamenu and Epi was over 14,000, but it was reduced to 800 by the early 1900s because of disease and economic dependence. Volcanic island, hills. Copra production; tourism; fishermen; agriculturalists. Christian.

Larevat (Laravat) [lrv] 150 (1983 SIL). Central Malekula. *Class:* Austronesian, Malayo-Polynesian, Central-Eastern, Eastern Malayo-Polynesian, Oceanic, Central-Eastern Oceanic, Remote Oceanic, North and Central Vanuatu, Malekula Interior, Malekula Central. *Lg Use:* 70% of the ethnic group speaks Larevat. Most key domains. 60% of children speak Larevat. Positive language attitude.

Lehali (Teqel, Tekel) [tql] 150 (1983 SIL). Ureparapara Island, Banks Group. *Class:* Austronesian, Malayo-Polynesian, Central-Eastern, Eastern Malayo-Polynesian, Oceanic, Central-Eastern Oceanic, Remote Oceanic, North and Central Vanuatu, Northeast Vanuatu-Banks Islands, East Vanuatu. *Dialects:* Close to Lehalurup. *Lg Use:* 70% of the ethnic group speaks Lehali. Most key domains. 60% of children speak Lehali. Positive language attitude.

Lehalurup (Ureparapara, East Ureparapara) [urr] 90 (1983 SIL). Ureparapara Island, Banks Group. *Class:* Austronesian, Malayo-Polynesian, Central-Eastern, Eastern Malayo-Polynesian, Oceanic, Central-Eastern Oceanic, Remote Oceanic, North and Central Vanuatu, Northeast Vanuatu-Banks Islands, East Vanuatu. *Dialects:* Close to Lehali. *Lg Use:* 70% of the ethnic group speaks Lehalurup. Most key domains. 60% of children speak Lehalurup. Positive language attitude.

Lelepa (Havannah Harbour) [lpa] 400 (1989 census). Lelepa Island, and Mangaliliu and Napkoa on western Efate Island. *Class:* Austronesian, Malayo-Polynesian, Central-Eastern, Eastern Malayo-Polynesian, Oceanic, Central-Eastern Oceanic, Remote Oceanic, North and Central Vanuatu, Northeast Vanuatu-Banks Islands, Central Vanuatu. *Dialects:* Formerly thought to be a dialect of North Efate. Also related to South Efate. 84% inherent intelligibility of Eton, 88% of South Efate. *Lg Use:* All ages. Speakers also use Bislama, South Efate, North Efate, English, or French. *Lg Dev:* Bible portions: 1877–1883. *Other:* SVO.

Lenakel [tnl] 6,500 (1988 SIL). West central Tanna. *Class:* Austronesian, Malayo-Polynesian, Central-Eastern, Eastern Malayo-Polynesian, Oceanic, Central-Eastern Oceanic, South Vanuatu, Tanna. *Dialects:* Loanatit, Nerauya, Itonga, Ikyoo. Complex dialect chain; up to 10 dialects (Wurm and Hattori). *Lg Dev:* Bible portions: 1900–1902. *Other:* SVO.

Letemboi (Small Nambas) [nms] 305 (1983 SIL). South Malekula. *Class:* Austronesian, Malayo-Polynesian, Central-Eastern, Eastern Malayo-Polynesian, Oceanic, Central-Eastern Oceanic, Remote Oceanic, North and Central Vanuatu, Malekula Interior, Small Nambas.

Lg Use: 70% of the ethnic group speaks Letemboi. Most
key domains. 60% of children speak Letemboi. Positive
language attitude.

Lewo (Varsu) [lww] 750 (1986 SIL). East Epi Island,
Varsu and Varmali regions. *Class:* Austronesian, Malayo-
Polynesian, Central-Eastern, Eastern Malayo-Polynesian,
Oceanic, Central-Eastern Oceanic, Remote Oceanic, North
and Central Vanuatu, Northeast Vanuatu-Banks Islands,
Epi, Lamenu-Baki, Lamenu-Lewo. *Dialects:* Tasiko,
Mate-Nul-Filakara. *Lg Dev:* Literacy rate in first
language: below 1%. Literacy rate in second language:
5% to 15%. Bible portions: 1892–1990.

Lingarak (Bushman's Bay) [lgk] 210 (1983 SIL).
Malekula. *Class:* Austronesian, Malayo-Polynesian,
Central-Eastern, Eastern Malayo-Polynesian, Oceanic,
Central-Eastern Oceanic, Remote Oceanic, North and
Central Vanuatu, Malekula Interior, Malekula Central.
Lg Use: 70% of the ethnic group speaks Lingarak. Most
key domains. 60% of children speak Lingarak. Positive
language attitude.

Litzlitz (Litzlitz-Visele) [lzl] 330 (1983 SIL). Malekula.
Class: Austronesian, Malayo-Polynesian, Central-Eastern,
Eastern Malayo-Polynesian, Oceanic, Central-Eastern
Oceanic, Remote Oceanic, North and Central Vanuatu,
Malekula Interior, Malekula Central. *Lg Use:* 70% of the
ethnic group speak Litzlitz. Most key domains. 60% of
children speak Litzlitz. Positive language attitude.

Lonwolwol (Craig Cove, Fali, Fanting) [crc] 600 (1983
SIL). West Ambrym Island and several hundred in Maat
village on Efate Island. *Class:* Austronesian, Malayo-
Polynesian, Central-Eastern, Eastern Malayo-Polynesian,
Oceanic, Central-Eastern Oceanic, Remote Oceanic, North
and Central Vanuatu, Northeast Vanuatu-Banks Islands,
East Vanuatu. *Dialects:* 2 main dialects. *Lg Dev:* Bible
portions: 1899–1949.

Lorediakarkar [lnn] 335 (2000 WCD). Central east coast,
Santo Island. *Class:* Austronesian, Malayo-Polynesian,
Central-Eastern, Eastern Malayo-Polynesian, Oceanic,
Central-Eastern Oceanic, Remote Oceanic, North and
Central Vanuatu, East Santo, South. *Dialects:* Close to the
Shark Bay language. *Lg Use:* 40% of the ethnic group
speaks Lorediakarkar. Few key domains. A few children
speak Lorediakarkar. People are mildly supportive toward
Lorediakarkar.

Mae [mme] 750 (1983 SIL). Population includes North
Small Nambas. Malekula. *Class:* Austronesian, Malayo-
Polynesian, Central-Eastern, Eastern Malayo-Polynesian,
Oceanic, Central-Eastern Oceanic, Remote Oceanic, North
and Central Vanuatu, Northeast Vanuatu-Banks Islands,
Malekula Coastal. *Dialect:* North Small Nambas.

Maewo, Central (Maevo, Tanoriki) [mwo] 350 (1981
Wurm and Hattori). Maewo (Aurora) Island. *Class:*
Austronesian, Malayo-Polynesian, Central-Eastern, Eastern
Malayo-Polynesian, Oceanic, Central-Eastern Oceanic,
Remote Oceanic, North and Central Vanuatu, Northeast
Vanuatu-Banks Islands, East Vanuatu. *Dialects:* Lotora,
Tanoriki, Peterara. Dialects or closely related dying
languages: Arata, Bangoro. *Lg Use:* 70% of the ethnic
group speaks Maewo. Most key domains. 60% of children
speak Maewo. Positive language attitude. *Lg Dev:* Bible
portions: 1906.

Mafea (Mavea) [mkv] 50 (1981 Wurm and Hattori). East
Santo, Mafea Island. *Class:* Austronesian, Malayo-
Polynesian, Central-Eastern, Eastern Malayo-Polynesian,
Oceanic, Central-Eastern Oceanic, Remote Oceanic, North
and Central Vanuatu, Northeast Vanuatu-Banks Islands,
West Santo. *Lg Use:* 40% of the ethnic group speaks
Mafea. Most or some key domains. 30% of children speak
Mafea. People are mildly supportive toward Mafea.

Maii (Mae-Morae, Mafilau) [mmm] 100 (1981 Wurm and
Hattori). Mafilau village, southwest Epi, north of the

Bieria, south of the Baki. *Class:* Austronesian, Malayo-
Polynesian, Central-Eastern, Eastern Malayo-Polynesian,
Oceanic, Central-Eastern Oceanic, Remote Oceanic, North
and Central Vanuatu, Northeast Vanuatu-Banks Islands,
Epi, Bieria-Maii. *Dialects:* No dialect variation. *Lg Use:*
70% of the ethnic group speaks Maii. Most key domains.
60% of children speak Maii. Positive language attitude.
Lg Dev: Literacy rate in first language: below 1%.
Literacy rate in second language: 5% to 15%.

Malfaxal (Malvaxal-Toman Island, Taman, Tomman)
[mlx] 600 (1983 SIL). South Malekula. *Class:*
Austronesian, Malayo-Polynesian, Central-Eastern,
Eastern Malayo-Polynesian, Oceanic, Central-Eastern
Oceanic, Remote Oceanic, North and Central Vanuatu,
Northeast Vanuatu-Banks Islands, Malekula Coastal.
Dialect: Orierh (Na'ahai). *Lg Dev:* Bible portions: 1919.

Malo [mla] 1,500 (1981 Wurm and Hattori). Malo Island,
three adjacent small islands and south Tangoa. *Class:*
Austronesian, Malayo-Polynesian, Central-Eastern,
Eastern Malayo-Polynesian, Oceanic, Central-Eastern
Oceanic, Remote Oceanic, North and Central Vanuatu,
Northeast Vanuatu-Banks Islands, West Santo. *Dialects:*
Avunatari (North Malo), Ataripoe (South Malo). Close to
Aore and Tutuba. *Lg Use:* Southern dialect is extinct.
Lg Dev: Dictionary. NT: 1954.

Malua Bay (Espiegle Bay, Middle Nambas) [mll] 300
(1983 SIL). Northwest coast of Malekula. *Class:*
Austronesian, Malayo-Polynesian, Central-Eastern,
Eastern Malayo-Polynesian, Oceanic, Central-Eastern
Oceanic, Remote Oceanic, North and Central Vanuatu,
Northeast Vanuatu-Banks Islands, Malekula Coastal.
Dialects: Several dialects. *Lg Use:* 70% of the ethnic
group speaks Malua Bay. Most key domains. 60% of
children speak it. Positive language attitude.

Maragus (Maragaus) [mrs] 10 (1971 Tryon). Central
north Malekula. *Class:* Austronesian, Malayo-Polynesian,
Central-Eastern, Eastern Malayo-Polynesian, Oceanic,
Central-Eastern Oceanic, Remote Oceanic, North and
Central Vanuatu, Malekula Interior, Malekula Central.
Lg Use: People are mildly supportive toward Maragus.
Other: Nearly extinct.

Marino (Naone, North Maewo) [mrb] 180 (1983 SIL).
North Maewo. *Class:* Austronesian, Malayo-Polynesian,
Central-Eastern, Eastern Malayo-Polynesian, Oceanic,
Central-Eastern Oceanic, Remote Oceanic, North and
Central Vanuatu, Northeast Vanuatu-Banks Islands, East
Vanuatu.

Maskelynes (Kuliviu, Maskelyne Islands) [klv] 1,200
(1990 UBS). South Malekula, Maskelyne Islets. *Class:*
Austronesian, Malayo-Polynesian, Central-Eastern,
Eastern Malayo-Polynesian, Oceanic, Central-Eastern
Oceanic, Remote Oceanic, North and Central Vanuatu,
Northeast Vanuatu-Banks Islands, Malekula Coastal.
Dialects: Some dialect differences. *Lg Dev:* Bible
portions: 1906.

Mele-Fila (Fila-Mele) [mxe] 2,000 (1980 UBS). Over
1,000 in Mele village on Efate, 500 on Fila Island (1977
Voegelin and Voegelin). Fila Island in Vila Harbor, Mele
village on South Efate. *Class:* Austronesian, Malayo-
Polynesian, Central-Eastern, Eastern Malayo-Polynesian,
Oceanic, Central-Eastern Oceanic, Remote Oceanic,
Central Pacific, East Fijian-Polynesian, Polynesian,
Nuclear, Samoic-Outlier, Futunic. *Dialects:* Fila (Efira,
Fira, Ifira), Mele. There are significant differences
between the Mele and Fila dialects. *Lg Use:* Speakers
also use South Efate. *Lg Dev:* Literacy rate in first
language: 5% to 10%. Literacy rate in second language:
75% to 100%. NT: 1993. *Other:* SVO.

Merei (Lametin) [lmb] 400 (1997 J. Chung). Central
Santo, north of Morouas, between the Lape and Ora
rivers. *Class:* Austronesian, Malayo-Polynesian, Central-

Eastern, Eastern Malayo-Polynesian, Oceanic, Central-Eastern Oceanic, Remote Oceanic, North and Central Vanuatu, Northeast Vanuatu-Banks Islands, West Santo. *Dialect:* Winiv. *Lg Use:* 70% of the ethnic group speaks Merei. Most key domains. 60% of children speak Merei. Positive language attitude. Men and school children are able to speak Bislama. *Other:* 'Merei' is the name used by speakers. Valleys, highland. Christian.

Merlav (Merelava, Merlav-Merig) [mrm] 1,350. Population includes 1,200 Merlav, 150 Merig. Mere Lava Island and Merig Island, Banks Group. *Class:* Austronesian, Malayo-Polynesian, Central-Eastern, Eastern Malayo-Polynesian, Oceanic, Central-Eastern Oceanic, Remote Oceanic, North and Central Vanuatu, Northeast Vanuatu-Banks Islands, East Vanuatu. *Dialects:* Mwerig (Merig), West Mwerelawa, Matliwag.

Morouas (Moruas) [mrp] 150 (1983 SIL). Central Santo. *Class:* Austronesian, Malayo-Polynesian, Central-Eastern, Eastern Malayo-Polynesian, Oceanic, Central-Eastern Oceanic, Remote Oceanic, North and Central Vanuatu, Northeast Vanuatu-Banks Islands, West Santo. *Dialects:* Several dialects. Possibly a dialect cluster with Amblong and Narango. *Lg Use:* 70% of the ethnic group speaks Morouas. Most key domains. 60% of children speak Morouas. Positive language attitude.

Mosina (Mosin) [msn] 400 (1981 Wurm and Hattori). Vanua Lava, Banks Group. *Class:* Austronesian, Malayo-Polynesian, Central-Eastern, Eastern Malayo-Polynesian, Oceanic, Central-Eastern Oceanic, Remote Oceanic, North and Central Vanuatu, Northeast Vanuatu-Banks Islands, East Vanuatu. *Dialect:* Vetumboso, Vures (Vuras, Vureas, Avreas). Mosina and Vures have 88% lexical similarity. *Lg Use:* Most key domains. Positive language attitude.

Mota [mtt] 450 (1983 SIL). Mota (Sugarloaf) Island, Banks Group. *Class:* Austronesian, Malayo-Polynesian, Central-Eastern, Eastern Malayo-Polynesian, Oceanic, Central-Eastern Oceanic, Remote Oceanic, North and Central Vanuatu, Northeast Vanuatu-Banks Islands, East Vanuatu. *Lg Use:* Formerly a lingua franca. 70% of the ethnic group speaks Mota. Most key domains. 60% of children speak Mota. Positive language attitude. *Lg Dev:* Literacy rate in first language: 30% to 60%. Literacy rate in second language: 75% to 100%. Dictionary. Bible: 1912.

Motlav (Motalava) [mlv] 1,275 (1983 SIL). Mota Lava (Saddle) Island, Banks Group. *Class:* Austronesian, Malayo-Polynesian, Central-Eastern, Eastern Malayo-Polynesian, Oceanic, Central-Eastern Oceanic, Remote Oceanic, North and Central Vanuatu, Northeast Vanuatu-Banks Islands, East Vanuatu. *Dialect:* Volow (Valuva, Valuwa, Valuga).

Mpotovoro [mvt] 180 (1983 SIL). North tip of Malekula. *Class:* Austronesian, Malayo-Polynesian, Central-Eastern, Eastern Malayo-Polynesian, Oceanic, Central-Eastern Oceanic, Remote Oceanic, North and Central Vanuatu, Northeast Vanuatu-Banks Islands, Malekula Coastal. *Lg Use:* 70% of the ethnic group speaks Mpotovoro. Most key domains. 60% of the children speak Mpotovoro. Positive language attitude.

Namakura (Makura) [nmk] 2,850 (1983 SIL). North Efate, Tongoa, Tongariki. *Class:* Austronesian, Malayo-Polynesian, Central-Eastern, Eastern Malayo-Polynesian, Oceanic, Central-Eastern Oceanic, Remote Oceanic, North and Central Vanuatu, Northeast Vanuatu-Banks Islands, Central Vanuatu. *Dialects:* Tongoa Island, Tongariki Island, Buninga, Makura (Emwae Island), Mataso. *Lg Dev:* Literacy rate in first language: below 1%. Literacy rate in second language: 25% to 50%.

Nambas, Big [nmb] 1,800 (1983 SIL). Northwest Malekula. *Class:* Austronesian, Malayo-Polynesian, Central-Eastern, Eastern Malayo-Polynesian, Oceanic,

Central-Eastern Oceanic, Remote Oceanic, North and Central Vanuatu, Malekula Interior, Malekula Central. *Lg Dev:* Literacy rate in first language: below 1%. Literacy rate in second language: 5% to 15%. NT: 1986.

Narango [nrg] 160 (1981 Wurm and Hattori). South Santo Island. *Class:* Austronesian, Malayo-Polynesian, Central-Eastern, Eastern Malayo-Polynesian, Oceanic, Central-Eastern Oceanic, Remote Oceanic, North and Central Vanuatu, Northeast Vanuatu-Banks Islands, West Santo. *Dialects:* Several dialects. Close to Amblong and Morouas. *Lg Use:* 70% of the ethnic group speaks Narango. Most key domains. 60% of children speak Narango. Positive language attitude.

Nasarian [nvh] 20 (1983 SIL). Southwest coast of Malekula. *Class:* Austronesian, Malayo-Polynesian, Central-Eastern, Eastern Malayo-Polynesian, Oceanic, Central-Eastern Oceanic, Remote Oceanic, North and Central Vanuatu, Malekula Interior, Malekula Central. *Lg Use:* 20% to 60% of the ethnic group speaks Nasarian. Some key domains. A few children speak Nasarian. Positive language attitude. *Other:* Nearly extinct.

Navut [nsw] 525 (1983 SIL). West central Santo. *Class:* Austronesian, Malayo-Polynesian, Central-Eastern, Eastern Malayo-Polynesian, Oceanic, Central-Eastern Oceanic, Remote Oceanic, North and Central Vanuatu, Northeast Vanuatu-Banks Islands, West Santo. *Dialects:* Close to Malmariv.

Nokuku (Nogugu) [nkk] 160 (1981 Wurm and Hattori). Northwest Santo. *Class:* Austronesian, Malayo-Polynesian, Central-Eastern, Eastern Malayo-Polynesian, Oceanic, Central-Eastern Oceanic, Remote Oceanic, North and Central Vanuatu, Northeast Vanuatu-Banks Islands, West Santo. *Lg Use:* 40% of the ethnic group speaks Nokuku. Most key domains retained. 60% of children speak Nokuku. Positive language attitude. *Lg Dev:* Bible portions: 1901–1918.

Nume (Tarasag, Gaua) [tgs] 450 (1983 SIL). Gaua Island. *Class:* Austronesian, Malayo-Polynesian, Central-Eastern, Eastern Malayo-Polynesian, Oceanic, Central-Eastern Oceanic, Remote Oceanic, North and Central Vanuatu, Northeast Vanuatu-Banks Islands, East Vanuatu. *Lg Use:* 70% of the ethnic group speaks Nume. Most key domains. 60% of children speak Nume. Positive language attitude. *Lg Dev:* Literacy rate in first language: 1% to 5%. Literacy rate in second language: 50% to 75%. *Other:* Distinct from Numee of New Caledonia.

Paama (Paama-Lopevi, Pauma, Paamese) [pma] 6,000 (1996 SIL). Paama, one village on east Epi (Lopevi), a large group in Vila. *Class:* Austronesian, Malayo-Polynesian, Central-Eastern, Eastern Malayo-Polynesian, Oceanic, Central-Eastern Oceanic, Remote Oceanic, North and Central Vanuatu, Northeast Vanuatu-Banks Islands, East Vanuatu. *Dialects:* North Paama, South Paama. Close to Southeast Ambrym. *Lg Dev:* Literacy rate in first language: 5% to 10%. Literacy rate in second language: 75% to 100%. Dictionary. Grammar. NT: 1944.

Piamatsina [ptr] 150 (1981 Wurm and Hattori). Northwest Santo Island. *Class:* Austronesian, Malayo-Polynesian, Central-Eastern, Eastern Malayo-Polynesian, Oceanic, Central-Eastern Oceanic, Remote Oceanic, North and Central Vanuatu, Northeast Vanuatu-Banks Islands, West Santo. *Dialects:* Close to Vunapu. *Lg Use:* 70% of the ethnic group speaks Piamatsina. Most key domains. 60% of children speak Piamatsina. Positive language attitude.

Polonombauk [plb] 225 (1983 SIL). Southeast Santo Island. *Class:* Austronesian, Malayo-Polynesian, Central-Eastern, Eastern Malayo-Polynesian, Oceanic, Central-Eastern Oceanic, Remote Oceanic, North and Central Vanuatu, East Santo, South. *Lg Use:* 20% to 60% of the ethnic group speaks Polonombauk. Most key domains. A few to half the children speak Polonombauk. Positive language attitude.

Port Sandwich [psw] 750 (1983 SIL). Southeast Malekula Island. *Class:* Austronesian, Malayo-Polynesian, Central-Eastern, Eastern Malayo-Polynesian, Oceanic, Central-Eastern Oceanic, Remote Oceanic, North and Central Vanuatu, Northeast Vanuatu-Banks Islands, Malekula Coastal. *Dialects:* Several dialects.

Port Vato [ptv] 750 (1983 SIL). Southwest Ambrym Island. *Class:* Austronesian, Malayo-Polynesian, Central-Eastern, Eastern Malayo-Polynesian, Oceanic, Central-Eastern Oceanic, Remote Oceanic, North and Central Vanuatu, Northeast Vanuatu-Banks Islands, East Vanuatu. *Lg Dev:* Bible portions: 1899.

Repanbitip [rpn] 90 (1983 SIL). East Malekula Island. *Class:* Austronesian, Malayo-Polynesian, Central-Eastern, Eastern Malayo-Polynesian, Oceanic, Central-Eastern Oceanic, Remote Oceanic, North and Central Vanuatu, Malekula Interior, Small Nambas. *Lg Use:* 70% of the ethnic group speaks Repanbitip. Most key domains. 60% of children speak Repanbitip. Positive language attitude.

Rerep (Pangkumu, Pangkumu Bay) [pgk] 375 (1983 SIL). East Malekula Island. *Class:* Austronesian, Malayo-Polynesian, Central-Eastern, Eastern Malayo-Polynesian, Oceanic, Central-Eastern Oceanic, Remote Oceanic, North and Central Vanuatu, Northeast Vanuatu-Banks Islands, Malekula Coastal. *Dialect:* Tisman. *Lg Use:* 70% of the ethnic group speaks Rerep. Most key domains. 60% of children speak Rerep. Positive language attitude. *Lg Dev:* Bible portions: 1892–1913.

Roria [rga] 150 (1983 SIL). Central Santo Island. *Class:* Austronesian, Malayo-Polynesian, Central-Eastern, Eastern Malayo-Polynesian, Oceanic, Central-Eastern Oceanic, Remote Oceanic, North and Central Vanuatu, Northeast Vanuatu-Banks Islands, West Santo. *Dialects:* Some dialect differences. *Lg Use:* 70% of the ethnic group speaks Roria. Most key domains. 60% of children speak Roria. Positive language attitude.

Sa [sax] 1,800 (1983 SIL). South Raga Island. *Class:* Austronesian, Malayo-Polynesian, Central-Eastern, Eastern Malayo-Polynesian, Oceanic, Central-Eastern Oceanic, Remote Oceanic, North and Central Vanuatu, Northeast Vanuatu-Banks Islands, East Vanuatu. *Dialects:* Ponorwal (South Raga), Lolatavola, Ninebulo.

Sakao (Hog Harbour, Santo, Sakau) [sku] 1,500 (1983 SIL). Northeast Santo Island. *Class:* Austronesian, Malayo-Polynesian, Central-Eastern, Eastern Malayo-Polynesian, Oceanic, Central-Eastern Oceanic, Remote Oceanic, North and Central Vanuatu, East Santo, North. *Dialect:* Livara (Liara). *Lg Use:* The Livara dialect is extinct. *Lg Dev:* Bible portions: 1905–1949. *Other:* More divergent linguistically with some Polynesian characteristics. Agriculturalists: yams, sweet potato, sugarcane, banana, coconut, breadfruit; fishermen; animal husbandry: pigs.

Seke [ske] 300 (1983 SIL). Central Raga Island. *Class:* Austronesian, Malayo-Polynesian, Central-Eastern, Eastern Malayo-Polynesian, Oceanic, Central-Eastern Oceanic, Remote Oceanic, North and Central Vanuatu, Northeast Vanuatu-Banks Islands, East Vanuatu. *Lg Use:* 70% of the ethnic group speaks Seke. Most key domains. 30% of children speak Seke. Positive language attitude.

Shark Bay [ssv] 225 (1983 SIL). East Santo on Litaro (Pilot) Island and also on the coast at Shark Bay. *Class:* Austronesian, Malayo-Polynesian, Central-Eastern, Eastern Malayo-Polynesian, Oceanic, Central-Eastern Oceanic, Remote Oceanic, North and Central Vanuatu, East Santo, South. *Dialects:* Close to Lorediakarkar. *Lg Use:* 40% of the ethnic group speaks Shark Bay. Some key domains. 30% of children speak Shark Bay. Positive language attitude.

Sie (Eromanga, Erromanga, Erramanga) [erg] 1,352 (2000 WCD). Erromanga Island, southern Vanuatu. *Class:* Austronesian, Malayo-Polynesian, Central-Eastern, Eastern Malayo-Polynesian, Oceanic, Central-Eastern Oceanic, South Vanuatu, Erromanga. *Dialects:* Yoku (Enyau), Potnariven, Sie (Sorung). *Lg Dev:* NT: 1909.

South West Bay (Sinesip, Seniang, Na'ahai) [sns] 250 (1981 Wurm and Hattori). Southwest Malekula Island. *Class:* Austronesian, Malayo-Polynesian, Central-Eastern, Eastern Malayo-Polynesian, Oceanic, Central-Eastern Oceanic, Remote Oceanic, North and Central Vanuatu, Northeast Vanuatu-Banks Islands, Malekula Coastal. *Lg Use:* 70% of the ethnic group speaks South West Bay. Most key domains. 60% of children speak it. Positive language attitude. *Lg Dev:* Bible portions: 1905. *Other:* Hunters; fishermen; agriculturalists: yams.

Sowa [sww] 20 (1971 Tryon). Central Raga Island. *Class:* Austronesian, Malayo-Polynesian, Central-Eastern, Eastern Malayo-Polynesian, Oceanic, Central-Eastern Oceanic, Remote Oceanic, North and Central Vanuatu, Northeast Vanuatu-Banks Islands, East Vanuatu. *Lg Use:* 70% of the ethnic group speaks Sowa. Most key domains. 30% of children speak Sowa. Positive language attitude. *Other:* Nearly extinct.

Tambotalo [tls] 50 (1981 Wurm and Hattori). Southeast Santo, Tambotalo village. *Class:* Austronesian, Malayo-Polynesian, Central-Eastern, Eastern Malayo-Polynesian, Oceanic, Central-Eastern Oceanic, Remote Oceanic, North and Central Vanuatu, Northeast Vanuatu-Banks Islands, West Santo. *Lg Use:* 70% of the ethnic group speaks Tambotalo. Most key domains. 30% of children speak Tambotalo. Positive language attitude.

Tangoa (Santo) [tgp] 800 (2001 SIL). Tangoa Island, off south Santo, four villages. *Class:* Austronesian, Malayo-Polynesian, Central-Eastern, Eastern Malayo-Polynesian, Oceanic, Central-Eastern Oceanic, Remote Oceanic, North and Central Vanuatu, Northeast Vanuatu-Banks Islands, West Santo. *Lg Use:* Vigorous. Code switching with Bislams does occur. Used by Araki people as first or second language. All domains. All ages. Positive language attitude. *Lg Dev:* Literacy rate in first language: 30% to 60%. Literacy rate in second language: 50% to 75%. Bible portions: 1892–2001. *Other:* Distinct from Tongoa (Namakura and North Efate languages).

Tanna, North [tnn] 2,000 (1988 SIL). North Tanna. *Class:* Austronesian, Malayo-Polynesian, Central-Eastern, Eastern Malayo-Polynesian, Oceanic, Central-Eastern Oceanic, South Vanuatu, Tanna. *Dialects:* East Tanna, West Tanna, Imafin. Two major dialects. There is a dialect chain. Close to Whitesands. *Lg Use:* Bislama is used as second language, but many women and some men do not understand it. *Lg Dev:* Literacy rate in first language: below 1%. Literacy rate in second language: 5% to 15%. Bible portions: 1990–2000. *Other:* SVO. Agriculturalists: coconut; copra production.

Tanna, Southwest [nwi] 2,250 (1983 SIL). Southwest Tanna Island. *Class:* Austronesian, Malayo-Polynesian, Central-Eastern, Eastern Malayo-Polynesian, Oceanic, Central-Eastern Oceanic, South Vanuatu, Tanna. *Dialects:* Nowai, Nvhal. A complex dialect chain (Wurm and Hattori). *Other:* Agriculturalists: coconut; copra production.

Tasmate [tmt] 150 (1983 SIL). West Santo Island. *Class:* Austronesian, Malayo-Polynesian, Central-Eastern, Eastern Malayo-Polynesian, Oceanic, Central-Eastern Oceanic, Remote Oceanic, North and Central Vanuatu, Northeast Vanuatu-Banks Islands, West Santo. *Dialects:* Some dialect differences. *Lg Use:* 70% of the ethnic group speaks Tasmate. Most key domains. 60% of children speak Tasmate. Positive language attitude.

Tiale (Malmariv) [mnl] 150 (1983 SIL). North central Santo. *Class:* Austronesian, Malayo-Polynesian, Central-Eastern, Eastern Malayo-Polynesian, Oceanic, Central-Eastern Oceanic, Remote Oceanic, North and Central Vanuatu, Northeast Vanuatu-Banks Islands, West Santo. *Dialects:* Close to Navut. *Lg Use:* 70% of the ethnic group speaks Tiale. Most key domains. 60% of children speak Tiale. Positive language attitude.

Toga (Lo, Loh-Toga, Torres) [lht] 315 (1983 SIL). Torres Islands. *Class:* Austronesian, Malayo-Polynesian, Central-Eastern, Eastern Malayo-Polynesian, Oceanic, Central-Eastern Oceanic, Remote Oceanic, North and Central Vanuatu, Northeast Vanuatu-Banks Islands, East Vanuatu. *Lg Use:* 70% of the ethnic group speaks Toga. Most of the key domains. 60% of children speak Toga. Positive language attitude. *Lg Dev:* Bible portions: 1900.

Tolomako (Tolomako-Jereviu, Big Bay, Marina) [tlm] 450 (1983 SIL). Big Bay, Santo Island. *Class:* Austronesian, Malayo-Polynesian, Central-Eastern, Eastern Malayo-Polynesian, Oceanic, Central-Eastern Oceanic, Remote Oceanic, North and Central Vanuatu, Northeast Vanuatu-Banks Islands, West Santo. *Dialects:* Slight dialect differences. *Lg Use:* 70% of the ethnic group speaks Tolomako. Most key domains. 30% of children speak Tolomako. Positive language attitude. *Lg Dev:* Bible portions: 1904–1909.

Tutuba [tmi] 150 (1983 SIL). Tutuba Island, south Santo. *Class:* Austronesian, Malayo-Polynesian, Central-Eastern, Eastern Malayo-Polynesian, Oceanic, Central-Eastern Oceanic, Remote Oceanic, North and Central Vanuatu, Northeast Vanuatu-Banks Islands, West Santo. *Dialects:* Close to Aore and Malo. *Lg Use:* 40% of the ethnic group speaks Tutuba. Most key domains. 30% of children speak Tutuba. Positive language attitude.

Unua (Onua) [onu] 525. Population includes 50 in Bush Unua. East Malekula Island. *Class:* Austronesian, Malayo-Polynesian, Central-Eastern, Eastern Malayo-Polynesian, Oceanic, Central-Eastern Oceanic, Remote Oceanic, North and Central Vanuatu, Northeast Vanuatu-Banks Islands, Malekula Coastal. *Dialect:* Bush Unua. Several dialects. *Lg Dev:* Bible portions: 1892–1913.

Ura [uur] 6 (1998 T. Crowley). North Erromanga Island, southern Vanuatu. *Class:* Austronesian, Malayo-Polynesian, Central-Eastern, Eastern Malayo-Polynesian, Oceanic, Central-Eastern Oceanic, South Vanuatu, Erromanga. *Lg Use:* Speakers are older adults. *Lg Dev:* Dictionary. Grammar. *Other:* Nearly extinct.

Uripiv-Wala-Rano-Atchin [upv] 6,000 (1988 SIL). Population includes 1,375 Atchin, 3,450 Uripiv-Wala-Rano. Northeast Malekula and nearby islands. *Class:* Austronesian, Malayo-Polynesian, Central-Eastern, Eastern Malayo-Polynesian, Oceanic, Central-Eastern Oceanic, Remote Oceanic, North and Central Vanuatu, Northeast Vanuatu-Banks Islands, Malekula Coastal. *Dialect:* Uripiv, Wala-Rano, Atchin (Nale). Dialect chain from Uripiv in the south to Atchin in the north. Lexical similarity 85% at the extremes of the dialect chain. *Lg Dev:* Literacy rate in first language: 10% to 30%. Literacy rate in second language: 25% to 50%. Bible portions: 1893–1989.

Valpei (Valpei-Hukua, Valpay) [vlp] 300 (1983 SIL). Northwest Santo Island. *Class:* Austronesian, Malayo-Polynesian, Central-Eastern, Eastern Malayo-Polynesian, Oceanic, Central-Eastern Oceanic, Remote Oceanic, North and Central Vanuatu, Northeast Vanuatu-Banks Islands, West Santo. *Lg Use:* 70% of the ethnic group speaks Valpei. Most key domains. 60% of children speak Valpei. Positive language attitude.

Vao [vao] 1,350 (1983 SIL). Vao Island, north Malekula. *Class:* Austronesian, Malayo-Polynesian, Central-Eastern,

Eastern Malayo-Polynesian, Oceanic, Central-Eastern Oceanic, Remote Oceanic, North and Central Vanuatu, Northeast Vanuatu-Banks Islands, Malekula Coastal. *Other:* Agriculturalists: yams, banana, taro, pineapple, cabbage, coconut, breadfruit; fishermen; animal husbandry: pigs.

Vatrata (Vanua Lava) [vlr] 600 (1983 SIL). Vanua Lava Island. *Class:* Austronesian, Malayo-Polynesian, Central-Eastern, Eastern Malayo-Polynesian, Oceanic, Central-Eastern Oceanic, Remote Oceanic, North and Central Vanuatu, Northeast Vanuatu-Banks Islands, East Vanuatu. *Dialects:* Leon, Pak (Bek), Sasar (Lem). *Lg Use:* Leon, Sasar, and Pak dialects are extinct.

Vinmavis (Lambumbu) [vnm] 210 (1983 SIL). Central west Malekula Island. *Class:* Austronesian, Malayo-Polynesian, Central-Eastern, Eastern Malayo-Polynesian, Oceanic, Central-Eastern Oceanic, Remote Oceanic, North and Central Vanuatu, Malekula Interior, Malekula Central. *Dialect:* Winiv. *Lg Use:* 70% of the ethnic group speaks Vinmavis. Most key domains. 60% of children speak Vinmavis. Positive language attitude.

Vunapu [vnp] 375 (1983 SIL). Northwest Santo Island. *Class:* Austronesian, Malayo-Polynesian, Central-Eastern, Eastern Malayo-Polynesian, Oceanic, Central-Eastern Oceanic, Remote Oceanic, North and Central Vanuatu, Northeast Vanuatu-Banks Islands, West Santo. *Dialects:* Close to Piamatsina. *Lg Use:* 70% of the ethnic group speaks Vunapu. Most key domains. 60% of children speak Vunapu. Positive language attitude.

Wailapa [wlr] 100 (1981 Wurm and Hattori). Southwest Santo Island. *Class:* Austronesian, Malayo-Polynesian, Central-Eastern, Eastern Malayo-Polynesian, Oceanic, Central-Eastern Oceanic, Remote Oceanic, North and Central Vanuatu, Northeast Vanuatu-Banks Islands, West Santo. *Dialects:* A dialect chain with Akei and Penantsiro at the extremes; they are not inherently intelligible. *Lg Use:* 70% of the ethnic group speaks Wailapa. Most key domains. 60% of children speak Wailapa. Positive language attitude.

Wetamut [wwo] 157 (2000 WCD). Gaua Island of the Banks Group, villages of Dorig and Kweteon. *Class:* Austronesian, Malayo-Polynesian, Central-Eastern, Eastern Malayo-Polynesian, Oceanic, Central-Eastern Oceanic, Remote Oceanic, North and Central Vanuatu, Northeast Vanuatu-Banks Islands, East Vanuatu. *Dialects:* Slight dialect differences. *Lg Use:* 70% of the ethnic group speaks Wetamut. Most key domains. 60% of children speak Wetamut. Positive language attitude.

Whitesands (Napuanmen, Whitsands) [tnp] 3,500 (1988 SIL). Tanna Island, east coast. *Class:* Austronesian, Malayo-Polynesian, Central-Eastern, Eastern Malayo-Polynesian, Oceanic, Central-Eastern Oceanic, South Vanuatu, Tanna. *Dialects:* Weasisi (Wassisi), Lometimeti. *Lg Dev:* Literacy rate in first language: 1% to 5%. Literacy rate in second language: 5% to 15%. NT: 1924. *Other:* SVO.

Wusi (Wusi-Kerepua) [wsi] 170 (1977 Lincoln). West Santo Island. *Class:* Austronesian, Malayo-Polynesian, Central-Eastern, Eastern Malayo-Polynesian, Oceanic, Central-Eastern Oceanic, Remote Oceanic, North and Central Vanuatu, Northeast Vanuatu-Banks Islands, West Santo. *Dialects:* Some dialect differences. *Lg Use:* 70% of the ethnic group speaks Wusi. Most key domains. 60% of children speak Wusi. Positive language attitude.

Wallis and Futuna

French Overseas Territory of Wallis and Futuna. 15,880. National or official language: French. Literacy rate: 95%. Information mainly from B. Biggs 1980; S. Wurm and S. Hattori 1981; N. Besnier 1992. The number of languages listed for Wallis and Futuna is 3. Of those, all are living languages.

French [fra] 120 in Wallis and Futuna (1993 Johnstone). *Lg Use:* National language. See main entry under France.

Futuna, East (Futunian) [fud] 3,600 on Futuna (1987). Population total all countries: 6,600. Futuna Island. Different from Futuna Island (West Futuna) in Vanuatu. Also spoken in New Caledonia. *Class:* Austronesian, Malayo-Polynesian, Central-Eastern, Eastern Malayo-Polynesian, Oceanic, Central-Eastern Oceanic, Remote Oceanic, Central Pacific, East Fijian-Polynesian, Polynesian, Nuclear, Samoic-Outlier, Futunic. *Dialects:* Not intelligible with Wallisian (East Uvean). *Lg Use:* Speakers also use French. *Lg Dev:* Dictionary. Bible: 2000. *Other:* Different from Futuna-Aniwa (West Futuna)

in Vanuatu. Agriculturalists: coconut, taro, breadfruit, yams, sweet potato, sugarcane, banana, arrowroot; animal husbandry: pigs, chickens; fishermen. Christian, traditional religion.

Wallisian (Uvean, East Uvean, Wallisien) [wls] 9,617 in Wallis and Futuna (2000 WCD). Population total all countries: 29,768. Uvea Island is their original home. Also spoken in Fiji, New Caledonia, Vanuatu. *Class:* Austronesian, Malayo-Polynesian, Central-Eastern, Eastern Malayo-Polynesian, Oceanic, Central-Eastern Oceanic, Remote Oceanic, Central Pacific, East Fijian-Polynesian, Polynesian, Nuclear, Samoic-Outlier, East Uvean-Niuafo'ou. *Dialects:* Some dialect divergence between Wallis Islands and New Caledonia. Not functionally intelligibile with Tongan. *Lg Dev:* Bible portions: 1971.

Bibliography

Abas, Hussen, ed. 1985. *Lontara*. Majalah Universitas Hasanuddin No 28. Ujung Pandang: Percetakan Lembaga Penerbitan Universitas Hasanuddin.

Abrahams, R. G. 1967. *The peoples of Greater Unyamwezi, Tanzania*. London: International African Institute.

Acebes, Argentina. 1966. Indígenas en Argentina. In *XXXVI Congreso Internacional de Americanistas, España 1964: Actas y Memorias,* Tomo 3, pp. 543–546. Sevilla.

Acton, Thomas and Donald Kenrick, eds. 1984. *Romani Rokkeripen Todivvus*. London: Romanestan Publications.

Addleton, Jonathan S. 1986. The importance of regional languages in Pakistan. *Al-Mushir* 28(2):55–80.

Adelaar, Karl Alexander. 1985. *Proto-Malayic: The reconstruction of its phonology and part of its lexicon and morphology*. Alblasserdam: Offsetdrukkerij Kanters B. V.

Adelaar, Karl Alexander. 1995. Minangkabau. In Tyron, ed., pp. 433–441.

Adler, Max K. 1977a. *Pidgins, creoles, and lingua francas, a sociolinguistic study*. Hamburg: Helmut Buske Verlag.

Adler, Max K. 1977b. *Welsh and the other dying languages in Europe*. Hamburg: Helmut Buske Verlag.

Afido, Pedro, Gregório Firmino, John Heins, Samba Mbuub, and Manuel Trinta. 1989. *Seminario sobre a padronização da ortografia de línguas moçambícanas*. Maputo: Faculdade de Letras, Universidade Eduardo Mondlane.

Agard, Frederick B. 1975. Toward a taxonomy of language split, Part One: Phonology. *Leuvense Bijdragen* 64(3–4):293–312.

Agard, Frederick B. 1984. *A course in Romance linguistics*. Vol. 2, *A diachronic view*. Washington, D.C.: Georgetown University Press.

Agesthialingom, S. and S. Sakthivel. 1973. *A bibliography for the study of Nilgiri hill tribes*. Annamalainagar: Annamalai University.

Akiner, Shirin. 1983. *Islamic peoples of the Soviet Union*. London: Kegan Paul International.

Ali, Salah Mohamed. 1988. The unity of the Somali language despite the barrier of regional language variants. In Annarita Puglielli, ed., *Proceedings of the Third International Congress of Somali Studies,* pp. 90–98. Rome: Il Pensiero Scientifico.

Allen, Jerry and Conrad Hurd. 1963a. *Languages of the Bougainville District*. Port Moresby: Summer Institute of Linguistics.

Allen, Jerry and Conrad Hurd. 1963b. *Languages of the Cape Hoskins Patrol Post Division of the Talasea Sub-district New Britain*. Port Moresby: Summer Institute of Linguistics.

Alleyne, Mervyn C. 1980. *Comparative Afro-American*. Ann Arbor: Karoma.

Alleyne, Mervyn C. n.d. *A linguistic perspective on the Caribbean*. Washington, D.C.: The Woodrow Wilson International Center for Scholars.

Allin, Trevor. 1976. *A grammar of Resígaro*. Horsleys Green, United Kingdom: Summer Institute of Linguistics.

Al-Tajir, Mahdi Abdalla. 1982. *Language and linguistic origins in Bahrain: The Baharnah dialect of Arabic*. London: Kegan Paul International.

Anceaux, J. C. 1961. *The linguistic situation in the islands of Yapen, Kurudu, Nau, and Miosnum, New Guinea*. The Hague: Martinus Nijhoff.

Anceaux, J. C. 1978. The linguistic position of Southeast Sulawesi: A preliminary outline. In S. A. Wurm and Lois Carrington, eds., *Proceedings of the Second International Conference on Austronesian Linguistics,* Fascicle 1. Pacific Linguistics C-61, pp. 275–283. Canberra: Australian National University

Anderson, Franklin Scott. 1987. *The lexicon of Fanagolo*. Carbondale: Southern Illinois University.

Andersson, Lars-Gunnar and Tore Janson. 1997. *Languages in Botswana: Language ecology in southern Africa*. Gaborone: Longman Botswana.

Andrews, Peter Alford, ed. 1989. *Ethnic groups in the Republic of Turkey*. Wiesbaden: Dr. Ludwig Reichert Verlag.

Andrzejewski, B. W. 1975a. The role of indicator particles in Somali. *Afroasiatic Linguistics* 1(6): 1–69.

Andrzejewski, B. W. 1975b. Verbs with vocalic mutation in Somali and their significance for Hamitico-Semitic comparative studies. In James Bynon and Theodora Bynon, eds., *Hamitico-Semitica,* pp. 361–367. The Hague: Mouton.

Andrzejewski, B. W. 1978. The development of a national orthography in Somalia and the modernization of the Somali language. *Horn of Africa* 1(3):39–45.

Andvik, Eric. 1993. Tshangla verb inflections: A preliminary sketch. *Linguistics of the Tibeto-Burman Area* 16(1):75–136.

Andvik, Eric. 1999. Tshangla grammar. Ph.D. dissertation. University of Oregon, Eugene.

Antworth, Evan L. 1979. *A grammatical sketch of Botolan Sambal*. Philippine Journal of *Linguistics,* Special Monograph Issue No. 8. Manila: Linguistic Society of the Philippines.

Applegate, Joseph R. 1970. The Berber languages. In Sebeok, ed., pp. 586–661.

Arango, Raúl and Enrique Sánchez. 1998. *Los pueblos indígenas de Colombia, 1997*. Bogotá: Tercer Mundo Editores and Departamento Nacional de Planeación.

Arango Montoya, P. Francisco MXY. 1977. *Colombia atlas indigenista.* Bogotá: Ministerio de Educación Nacional.

Arbues, Lilia R. 1960. The Negritos as a minority group in the Philippines. *Philippine Sociological Review* 8(1/2).

Armstrong, Robert G. 1955a. The Igala. In *Peoples of the Niger-Benue Confluence, Ethnographic Survey of Africa, Western Africa,* Part X, pp. 77–90. London: International African Institute.

Armstrong, Robert G. 1955b. The Idoma-speaking peoples. In *Peoples of the Niger-Benue Confluence, Ethnographic Survey of Africa, Western Africa,* Part X, pp. 91–155. London: International African Institute.

Arnott, D. W. 1970. *The nominal and verbal systems of Fula.* Oxford: Clarendon Press.

Arveiller, R. 1967. *Études sur le parler de Monaco.* Monaco: Comité National des Traditions Monégasques.

Aschmann, Richard P. 1993. *Proto Witotoan.* Summer Institute of Linguistics and the University of Texas at Arlington Publications in Linguistics 114. Dallas.

Atlas Linguistique de l'Afrique Central. 1984, 1988. Bangui: Agence de Coopération Culturelle et Technique.

Atlas National du Senegal. 1977. Paris: l'Institut Géographique National.

Backstrom, Peter C. and Carla F. Radloff, eds. 1992. *Languages of northern areas.* Sociolinguistic Survey of Northern Pakistan, Vol. 2. Islamabad: National Institute of Pakistan Studies, Quaid-i-Azam University and Summer Institute of Linguistics.

Bahuchet, Serge. 1985. *Les pygmées aka et la forêt centrafricaine: Ethnologie écologique.* Paris: SELAF.

Bailey, T. Grahame. 1915. *Linguistic studies from the Himalayas.* London: The Royal Asiatic Society.

Baker, Philip. 1972. *Kreol: A description of Mauritian Creole.* London: C. Hurst & Co.

Baker, Philip and R. Ramnak. 1985. Mauritian Bhojpuri: An Indo-Aryan language spoken in a predominantly creolphone society. In Stephen A. Wurm, ed., *Papers in Pidgin and Creole Linguistics,* No. 4. Pacific Linguistics A-72, pp. 215–238. Canberra: Australian National University.

Barbour, Stephen and Patrick Stevenson. 1990. *Variation in German: A critical approach to German sociolinguistics.* Cambridge: Cambridge University Press.

Barker, Milton E. 1966. Proto-Vietnamuong initial labial consonants. *Van-hóa Nguyêt-san* 12:491–500.

Barr, Donald F., Sharon G. Barr, and C. Salombe. 1979. *Languages of Central Sulawesi: Checklist, preliminary classification, language maps, wordlists.* Ujung Pandang: Summer Institute of Linguistics and Hasanuddin University.

Barreteau, Daniel, ed. 1978. *Inventaire des études linguistiques sur les pays d'Afrique noire d'expression française et sur Madagascar.* Paris: Conseil International de la Langue Française.

Barreteau, Daniel and Paul Newman. 1978. Les langues tchadiques. In Barreteau, ed., pp. 291–330.

Barrett, David B., ed. 1982. *World Christian encyclopedia: A comparative study of churches and religions in the modern world A.D. 1900–2000.* Nairobi: Oxford University Press.

Barry, Abdoulaye. 1987. The Joola languages: Subgrouping and reconstruction. Ph.D. dissertation. University of London, School of African and Oriental Studies.

Bartholomew, Doris. 1965. The reconstruction of Otopamean (Mexico). Ph.D. dissertation. University of Chicago.

Barz, R. and J. Siegel, eds., 1988. *Language transplanted: The development of overseas Hindi.* Wiesbaden: Otto Harrasowitz.

Barz, R. and Y. K. Yadav. 1993. *An introduction to Hindi and Urdu,* fifth edition. New Delhi: Munshiram Manoharlal.

Bastin, Yvonne. 1978. Les langues Bantoues. In Barreteau, ed., pp. 123–185.

Bateson, Mary Catherine. 1967. *Arabic language handbook.* Washington D.C.: Center for Applied Linguistics.

Baxter, Alan N. 1988. *A grammar of Kristang (Malacca Creole Portuguese).* Pacific Linguistics B-95. Canberra: Australian National University.

Beaumont, C. L. 1972. New Ireland languages: A review. In *Papers in Linguistics of Melanesia,* No. 3. Pacific Linguistics A-35, pp. 1–41. Canberra: Australian National University.

Behnstedt, Peter. 1985. *Die nordjemenitischen Dialaekte.* Teil 1: *Atlas.* Wiesbaden: Dr. Ludwig Reichert Verlag.

Behnstedt, Peter and Manfred Woidich. 1988. *Die ägyptisch-arabischen Dialekte,* 3 vols. Wiesbaden: Dr. Ludwig Reichert Verlag.

Beidelman, T. O. 1967. *The matrilineal peoples of eastern Tanzania.* London: International African Institute.

Beltran, Joan S. 1986. *L'estandard occidental: Una proposta sobre l'estandard català a les terres del darrer tram de l'Ebre.* Barcelona: Generalitat de Catalunya.

Bender, Byron W. 1971. Micronesian languages. In Sebeok, ed., 1971b, pp. 426–465.

Bender, Byron and Kenneth L. Rehg. 1991. Micronesian languages in jeopardy? Presented at the Sixth International Conference of Austronesian Linguistics, Honolulu, Hawaii. May 1991.

Bender, Byron W. and Alfred Capelle. 1996. Dealing with the ABCs of Marshallese over twenty years. In France Mugler and John Lynch, eds., *Pacific languages in education,* pp. 36–75. Suva: University of the South Pacific, Institute of Pacific Studies.

Bender, M. Lionel. 1971. The languages of Ethiopia. *Anthropological Linguistics* 13(5):165–288.

Bender, M. Lionel. 1975. *The Ethiopian Nilo-Saharans.* Addis Ababa: s.n.

Bender, M. Lionel, ed. 1976. *The non-Semitic languages of Ethiopia.* Monograph No. 5, Occasional Papers Series, Committee on Ethiopian Studies. East Lansing: African Studies Center, Michigan State University.

Bender, M. Lionel, ed. 1983a. *Nilo-Saharan language studies.* East Lansing: African Studies Center, Michigan State University.

Bender, M. Lionel. 1983b. Majang phonology and morphology. In Bender, ed., pp. 114–147.

Bender, M. Lionel. 1983c. Remnant languages. In Bender, ed., pp. 336–354.

Bender, M. Lionel. 1989. Eastern Jebel languages. In M. Lionel Bender, ed., *Topics in Nilo-Saharan Linguistics.* Hamburg: Helmut Buske Verlag.

Bendor-Samuel, John. 1971. Niger-Congo, Gur. In Sebeok, ed., 1971a, pp. 141–178.

Bendor-Samuel, John, ed. 1989. *The Niger-Congo Languages.* Lanham, Maryland: University Press of America.

Benedict, Paul K. 1975. *Austro-Thai language and culture with a glossary of roots.* New Haven: Human Relations Area Files Press.

Besnier, Nico. 1992. Polynesian languages. In Bright, ed., Vol. 3, pp. 245–251.

Bhurhanuddin, B. H. 1979. Bahasa-bahasa daerah di Sulawesi Tenggara. Kendari. ms.

Biber, Douglas. 1984. Pragmatic roles in Central Somali narrative discourse. *Studies in African Linguistics* 15:1–26.

Bickerton, Derek. 1974. Priorities in creole studies. In De Camp and Hancock, eds., pp. 85–87.

Bickerton, Derek and Aquilas Escalante. 1970. Palenquero: A Spanish-based creole of northern Colombia. *Lingua* 24:254–267.

Biggs, Bruce. 1957. Testing intelligibility among Yuman languages. *International Journal of American Linguistics* 23:57–62.

Biggs, Bruce. 1980. The position of East Uvean and Anutan in the Polynesian language family. *Journal of the Linguistic Society of New Zealand* 23:115–134.

Bimson, Kent D. 1978. Comparative reconstruction of Proto-Northern-Western Mande. Ph.D. dissertation. University of California, Los Angeles.

Bista, Dor Bahadur. 1996. *People of Nepal,* sixth edition. Kathmandu: Ratna Pustak Bhandar.

Black, Paul. 1983. *Aboriginal languages of the Northern Ter ritory.* Darwin: School of Australian Linguistics, Darwin Community College.

Blair, Frank. 1990. *Survey on a shoestring: A manual for small-scale language surveys.* Summer Institute of Linguistics and the University of Texas at Arlington Publications in Linguistics 96. Dallas.

Blanchet, Phillippe. 1986. Idiome spécifique et culture populaire: Le français régional de Provence. Doctoral dissertation. Sorbonne University, Paris.

Blust, Robert A. 1974. The Proto-North Sarawak vowel deletion hypothesis. Ph.D. dissertation. University of Hawaii, Honolulu.

Blust, Robert A. 1977. The Proto-Austronesian pronouns and Austronesian subgrouping: A preliminary report. *Working Papers in Linguistics*

9(2):1–15. Honolulu: Department of Linguistics, University of Hawaii.

Blust, Robert A. 1981. The Soboyo reflexes of Proto-Austronesian *S. In Robert A. Blust, ed., *Historical Linguistics in Indonesia, Part 1.* NUSA, Linguistic Studies in Indonesian and Languages in Indonesia, Vol. 10, pp. 21–30. Jakarta: Badan Penyelenggara Seri Nusa, Universitas Atma Jaya.

Blust, Robert A. 1983–1984. More on the position of the languages of eastern Indonesia. *Oceanic Linguistics* 22/23:1–28.

Blust, Robert A. 1999. Subgrouping, circularity and extinction: Some issues in Austronesian comparative linguistics. In Elizabeth Zeitoun and Paul Jen-Kuei Li, eds., *Selected papers from the Eighth International Conference on Austronesian Linguistics,* pp. 31–94. Symposium Series of the Institute of Linguistics (Preparatory Office), Academia Sinica 1. Taipei: Institute of Linguistics (Preparatory Office), Academia Sinica.

Boeder, R. B. 1984. *Silent majority: A history of the Lomwe in Malawi.* Pretoria: Africa Institute of South Africa.

Borg, Alexander. 1985. *Cypriot Arabic.* Stuttgart: Deutsch Morgenlaendische Gesellschaft.

Bourgue, François. 1976. Los caminos de los hijos del cielo. Estudio socio-territorial de los Kawillary del Cananarí y del Apaporis. *Revista Colombiana de Antropología,* pp. 101–146. Bogotá: Instituto Colombiano de Cultura.

Boutin, Michael E., comp. 1986. *Indigenous groups of Sabah: An annotated bibliography of linguistic and anthropological sources: Supplement 1.* Sabah Museum Monograph 1, part 2. Kota Kinabalu: Sabah Museum.

Boutin, Michael E. and Alanna Y. Boutin. 1985. Report on the languages of Banggi and Balambangan. *Sabah Society Journal* 8(1):89–92.

Boyeldieu, Pascal. 1977. *Etudes phonologiques tchadiennes.* Paris: SELAF.

Boyeldieu, Pascal. 1985. *La langue lua ('niellim').* Paris: Maison des Sciences de l'Homme, SELAF.

Bradley, C. Henry. 1968. A method for determining dialectal boundaries and relationships. *América Indígena* 28:751–760.

Brenzinger, Matthias. 1997. *Moving to survive: Kxoe communities in arid lands. Hunter-gatherers in transition: Language, identity, and conceptualization among the Khoisan.* Khoisau–Forum 2. Köln.

Breton, Roland J. L. 1979. Ethnies et langues. In Georges Laclavère, ed., *Atlas de la République Unie du Cameroun,* pp. 31–35. Paris: Éditions Jeune Afrique.

Breton, Roland J. L. 1981a. Groupe A10: Lundu-Mbo, Oroko-Ngoe. *Map of Oroko-Ngoe language group of SW Cameroon.* Yaoundé: D.G.R.S.T., C.R.E.A.

Breton, Roland J. L. 1981b. *Les ethnies.* Paris: Presses Universitaires de France.

Breton, Roland J. L. 1986. Cartes linguistiques (Cameroun, Centrafrique, Congo, Gabon, Zaïre, Tchad) in *Conference des Ministres de l'Education Nationale des Etats de'expression française.*

Breton, Roland J. L. 1991a. The handicaps of language planning in Africa. In *Joshua A. Fishman, Festschrift.* No. 3, *Language planning.* Amsterdam: John Benjamins.

Breton, Roland J. L. 1991b. *Geolinguistics: Language dynamics and ethno-linguistic geography.* Ottawa: University of Ottawa Press.

Breton, Roland J. L. 1993. Is there a Furu language group? An investigation on the Cameroon-Nigeria border. *Journal of West African Languages* 23(2):97–118.

Breton, Roland J. L. 1996. The dynamics of ethno-linguistic communities as the central factor in language policy and planning. *International Journal of the Sociology of Language* 118:163–179.

Breton, Roland J. L. 1997. *Atlas of the languages and ethnic communities of South Asia.* New Delhi: Sage Publications India.

Breton, Roland J. L. and D. Louder. 1993. The linguistic geography of Acadiana. In Dean Louder and Eric Waddell, eds., *French America: Mobility, identity, and minority experience across the continent.* Baton Rouge: Louisiana State University Press.

Bright, William, ed. 1992. *International encyclopedia of linguistics,* 4 vols. New York: Oxford University Press.

Bromley, Myron. 1967. The linguistic relationships of Grand Valley Dani: A lexico-statistical classification. *Oceania* 37(4):286–308.

Brown, J. Marvin. 1965. *From ancient Thai to modern dialects.* Bangkok: Social Science Association Press of Thailand.

Browne, Wayles, Ewa Dornisch, Natash Kondrashova, and Draga Zec, eds. 1997. *Annual Workshop on Formal Approaches to Slavic Linguistics: the Cornell Meeting, 1995.* Michigan Slavic Materials No. 39. Ann Arbor: Michigan Slavic Publications.

Bruhn, Thea C. 1989. Passages: Life, the universe, and language proficiency assessment. In *Georgetown University Round Table on Languages and Linguistics 1989,* pp. 245–254. Washington, D.C.: Georgetown University Press.

Bryan, Margaret A. 1959. *The Bantu languages of Africa.* London: Oxford University Press.

Buddruss, Georg. 1960. *Die Sprach von Wotapur und Katarqala.* Bonn: Selbstverlag des Orientalischen Seminars der Universitat Bonn.

Bulakarima, Umara. 1986. Is Mobar a Kanuri dialect? *Annals of Borno* 3:81–90.

Bulletin of the Department of Anthropology. 1987. Calcutta: Anthropological Survey of India.

Bunn, Gordon and Graham Scott. 1963. *Languages of the Mount Hagen Sub-district.* Port Moresby: Summer Institute of Linguistics.

Burling, Robbins. 1998. The Tibeto-Burman languages of Northeast India. ms.

Burmeister, Jonathan L. 1976. A comparison of variable nouns in Anyi-Sanvi and Nzema. *Annales* 9:7–19.

Burnham, Eugene C. 1976. The place of Haroi in the Chamic languages. M.A. thesis. University of Texas at Arlington

Busenitz, Robert L. 1991. Lexicostatistic and sociolinguistic survey of Balantak and Andio. In Friberg, ed., pp. 7–22.

Butt, Audrey J. 1966. The present state of ethnology in Latin America: The Guianas. In *XXXVI Congreso Internacional de Americanistas, España 1964: Actas y Memorias,* Tomo 3, pp. 19–37. Sevilla.

Callaghan, Catherine A. 1998. More evidence for Yok-Utian: A re-analysis of the Dixon and Kroeber sets. Paper read at the Society for the Study of the Indigenous Languages of the Americas at the Linguistic Society of America meeting, New York. January 11, 1998.

Campbell, Lyle and David Oltrogge. 1980. Proto-Tol (Jicaque). *International Journal of American Linguistics* 46:205–223.

Campbell, Lyle and Marianne Mithun, eds. 1979. *The languages of native America: Historical and comparative assessment.* Austin: University of Texas Press.

Capell, Arthur. 1962a. *A linguistic survey of the southwestern Pacific.* South Pacific Commission, Technical Paper No. 136. Noumea: South Pacific Commission.

Capell, Arthur. 1962b. Oceanic linguistics today. *Current Anthropology* 3:371–428.

Capell, Arthur. 1968. Lexicostatistical study of the languages of Choiseul Island, British Solomon Islands. In *Papers in Linguistics of Melanesia,* No. 1. Pacific Linguistics A-15, pp. 1–25. Canberra: Australian National University.

Capo, Hounkpati B. C. 1986. *Renaissance du Gbe, une language de l'Afrique Occidentale. Etude critique sur les langues ajatado: l'Ewe, le Fon, le Gen, l'Aja, le Gun, etc.* Lomé: Université du Bénin, Institut National des Sciences de l'Education.

Caprile, Jean Pierre, ed. 1977. *Etudes phonologiques tchadiennes.* Paris: SELAF.

Capron, Jean. 1973. *Communautes villageoises Mali-Haute Volta Bwa,* Vol. 1. Paris: Institut d'Ethnologie.

Carr, Elizabeth Ball. 1972. *Da Kine Talk: From Pidgin to Standard English in Hawaii.* Honolulu: The University Press of Hawaii.

Carrington, Lawrence D. 1984. *St. Lucian Creole: A descriptive analysis.* Hamburg: Helmut Buske.

Carrington, Lois. 1996. *A linguistic bibliography of the New Guinea area.* Pacific Linguistics D-90. Canberra: Australian National University.

Casad, Eugene H. 1974. *Dialect intelligibility testing.* SIL Publications in Linguistics and Related Fields, No. 38. Norman, Oklahoma: Summer Institute of Linguistics.

Cassanelli, Lee V. 1982. *The shaping of Somali society: Reconstructing the history of a pastoral people, 1600–1900.* Philadelphia: University of Pennsylvania Press.

Cavalli-Sforza, Luigi Luca, ed. 1986. *African Pygmies.* Orlando, Florida: Academic Press.

Cense, A. A. and E. M. Uhlenbeck. 1958. *A critical survey of studies on the languages of Borneo.* Bibliographical Series No. 2. The Hague: Martinus Nijhoff.

Central Institute of Indian Languages. 1973. *Distribution of languages in India in states and union territories, inclusive of mother-tongues.* Mysore.

Cerrón-Palomino, Rodolfo. 1976. *Gramática quechua: Junín-Huanca.* Lima: Ministerio de Educación.

Chafe, Wallace L. 1962. Estimates regarding the present speakers of North American Indian languages. *International Journal of American Linguistics* 28:162–171.

Chafe, Wallace L. 1965. Corrected estimates regarding speakers of Indian languages. *International Journal of American Linguistics* 31:345–346.

Chagnoux, H. and A. Haribou. 1980. *Les Comores. Que sais-je?* Paris: Presses Universitaires de France.

Chamanga, M. A. and N. J. Gueunie. 1966–1967. *Recherches sur l'instrumentalisation du comorien.* Cahiers d'Etudes Africaines, Vol. 17. The Hague: Mouton.

Chamberlain, James R. 1984. The Tai dialects of Khammoun Province, Laos: Their diversity and origins. *The Science of Language* 4:62–95.

Chamberlain, James R. 1998. The origin of the Sek: Implications for Tai and Vietnamese history. Paper presented at the International Conference on Tai Studies, Institute of Language and Culture for Rural Development of Mahidol University, Bangkok. July 29–31, 1998.

Chamberlain, James R. Mene: A Tai dialect originally spoken in Nghe An (Nghe Tinh), Vietnam. Preliminary linguistic observations and historical implications. *Journal of the Siam Society* 79:103–123.

Chamberlain, James R., Charles Alton, Latsamay Silavong. 1996. *Socio-economic and cultural survey: Nam Theun 2 Project Area.* Part 2, Appendix 2, *Be-Tai ethnolinguistic family.* CARE International and Lao People's Democratic Republic.

Chase-Sardi, Miguel. 1987. *Derecho consuetudinario Chamacoco.* Asunción: Asociación Indigenista del Paraguay, RP Ediciones.

Chazee, Laurent. 1995. *Atlas des ethnies et des sous-ethnies du Laos.* Bangkok.

Chetrit, Joseph. 1985. Judeo-Arabic and Judeo-Spanish in Morocco and their sociolinguistic interaction. In Fishman, ed., pp. 261–279.

Claassen, Oren and Kenneth McElhanon. 1970. Languages of the Finisterre Range—New Guinea. *Pacific Linguistics A-23,* pp. 45–78. Canberra: Australian National University.

Clairis, Christos. 1982. Les Qawasqar. Thesis. Sorbonne, Paris.

Clammer, J. R. 1976. *Literacy and social change: A case study of Fiji.* Leiden: E. J. Brill.

Classe, A. 1957a. Phonetics of the Silbo Gomero. *Archivum Linguisticum* 9(1):44–61.

Classe, A. 1957b. The whistled language of La Gomero. *Scientific American* 196(4):111–120.

Cloarec-Heiss, France. 1978. Étude preliminaire à une dialectologie banda. In Raymond Boyd and France Cloarec-Heiss, *Études Comparatives.* Bibliothèque de la SELAF 65, pp. 11–42. Paris: SELAF.

Clouse, Duane. 1997. Towards a reconstruction and reclassification of the Lakes Plain languages of Irian Jaya. In Karl J. Franklin, ed., *Papers in Papuan Linguistics 2.* Pacific Linguistics A-85, pp. 133–236. Canberra: Australian National University.

Coelho, V. H. 1967. *Sikkim and Bhutan.* New Delhi: Indraprastha Press.

Cohen, David. 1963. *Le dialecte Arabe Hassaniya de Mauritanie.* Paris: Librairie C. Klincksieck.

Cohen, David. 1985. Judeo-Arabic of North Africa. In Fishman, ed., pp. 246–260.

Cohen, Pedro I. and others. 1976. El inglés criollo de Panamá. *Primeras Jornadas Lingüísticas.* Panamá: Editorial Universitaria.

Collins, James. 1983. *The historical relationships of the languages of central Maluku, Indonesia.* Pacific Linguistics D-47. Canberra: Australian National University.

Collins, James. 1995. *Bibliografi Dialek Melayu Di Pulau Sumatera.* Kuala Lumpur: Dewan Bahasa dan Pustaka Kementerian Pedidikan Malaysia

Comrie, Bernard, ed. 1987. *The world's major languages.* New York: Oxford University Press.

Connell, Bruce. 1994. The Lower Cross languages: A prolegomena to the classification of the Cross River languages. *Journal of West African Languages* 24(1):3–46.

Connell, Bruce and K. B. Maison. 1994. A Cameroun homeland for the Lower Cross languages? *Sprache und Geschichte in Afrika* 15:47–90.

Conrad, Robert and Wayne Dye. 1975. Some language relationships in the Upper Sepik Region of Papua New Guinea. In *Papers in New Guinea Linguistics,* No. 18. Pacific Linguistics A-40, pp.1–35. Canberra: Australian National University

Cook, Edwin A. 1966. Narak: Language or dialect? *Journal of the Polynesian Society* 75:437–444.

Coon, Carleton Stevens. 1931. *Tribes of the Rif.* Harvard African Studies, Vol. IX. Cambridge, Mass: Peabody Museum of Harvard University.

Corne, Chris. 1999. *The development of new vernaculars in the French colonial world.* Westminster Creolistics Series, Vol. 5. Battlebridge Publications.

Cortina-Borja, Mario and Leopoldo Valiñas C. 1989. Some remarks on Uto-Aztecan classification. *International Journal of American Linguistics* 55(2):214–239.

Creider, Chet A. 1981. The tonal system of proto-Kalenjin. In Schadeberg and Bender, eds., pp. 19–39.

Crozier, D. H. and R. M. Blench, eds. 1992. *An index of Nigerian languages,* second edition. Dallas: Summer Institute of Linguistics.

Curnow, Timothy Jowan. 1998. Why Paez is not a Barbacoan language: The nonexistence of "Moguex" and the use of early sources.

International Journal of American Linguistics 64(4):338–351.

Cusihuamán G., Antonio. 1976. *Gramática quechua: Cuzco-Collao.* Lima: Ministerio de Educación.

Dalby, T. D. P. 1962. Language distribution in Sierra Leone: 1961–1962. *Sierra Leone Language Review* 1:62–67.

Dan Nghiem Van, et al. 1993. *Ethnic minorities of Vietnam.* Hanoi: The Gioi Publishers.

Dawkins, R. M. 1916. *Modern Greek in Asia Minor.* Cambridge: Cambridge University Press.

Day, Richard R. 1974. Decreolization: Coexistent systems and the post-creole continuum. In De Camp and Hancock, eds., pp. 38–45.

De Camp, David. 1968. The field of creole language studies. Presented at the Conference on Pidginization and Creolization, University of the West Indies, Jamaica. April 9–12, 1968.

De Camp, David and Ian F. Hancock, eds. 1974. *Pidgins and creoles: Current trends and prospects.* Washington, D.C.: Georgetown University Press.

Decker, Kendall D., ed. 1992. *Languages of Chitral.* Sociolinguistic Survey of Northern Pakistan, Vol. 5. Islamabad: National Institute of Pakistan Studies, Quaid-i-Azam University and Summer Institute of Linguistics.

Delafosse, Maurice. 1904. *Vocabulaires comparatifs de plus de soixante langues ou dialectes parlés à la Côte d'Ivoire et dans les régions limitrophes.* Paris: Laroux.

Demesse, L. 1978. *Changements techno-économiques et sociaux chez les Pygmées Babinga (Nord-Congo et Sud-Centrafrique).* Paris: SELAF.

Dentan, R. K. 1968. *The Semai: A nonviolent people of Malaya.* New York: Holt, Rinehart and Winston.

Derbyshire, Desmond C. 1977. Word order universals and the existence of OVS languages. *Linguistic Inquiry* 8:590–599.

Derbyshire, Desmond C. 1979. Hixkaryana syntax. Ph.D. dissertation. University of London.

Derbyshire, Desmond C. and Geoffrey K. Pullum, eds. 1986. *Handbook of Amazonian Languages,* Vol. 1. Berlin: Mouton de Gruyter.

Derbyshire, Desmond C. and Geoffrey K. Pullum, eds. 1990. *Handbook of Amazonian Languages,* Vol. 2. Berlin: Mouton de Gruyter.

Derbyshire, Desmond C. and Geoffrey K. Pullum, eds. 1991. *Handbook of Amazonian Languages,* Vol. 3. Berlin: Mouton de Gruyter.

Dieu, Michel and Patrick Renaud, eds. 1983. *Atlas linguistique du Cameroun.* Yaoundé: Délégation Générale à la Recherche Scientifique et Technique.

Dimmendaal, Gerrit J. 1983. Topics in a grammar of Turkana. In Bender, ed., pp. 239–271.

Dimmendaal, Gerrit J. 1989. On language death of Eastern Africa. In Dorian, ed., pp. 13–32.

Doerfer, Gerhard, with Wolfram Hesche, Hartwig Scheinhardt, and Semih Tezcan. 1971. *Khalaj materials.* Uralic and Altaic Series, Vol. 115, Indiana University Publications. Bloomington.

Doornbos, Paul and M. Lionel Bender. 1983. Languages of Wadai-Darfur. In Bender, ed., pp. 42–79.

Dorian, Nancy C., ed. 1989. *Investigating obsolescence: Studies in language contraction and death.* Studies in the Social and Cultural Foundations of Language, 7. Cambridge: Cambridge University Press.

Dorji, C. T. 1997. *An introduction to Bhutanese languages.* Vikas Publishing House.

Douglas, Leonora Mosende, ed. 1986. *World Christianity: Oceania.* Monrovia: MARC.

Douglas, Wilfred. 1976. *The Aboriginal languages of the South-West of Australia.* Canberra: Australian Institute of Aboriginal Studies.

Dreyer, June Teufel. 1976. *China's forty millions: Minority nationalities and national integration in the People's Republic of China.* Harvard East Asia Series No. 87.

Drower, Ethel S. 1939. *The Mandaeans of Iraq and Iran.* Oxford University Press.

Du Nay, André. 1977. *The Early History of the Rumanian Language.* Edward Sapir Monograph Series in Language, Culture, and Cognition, No. 3. Lake Bluff, Illinois: Jupiter Press. [Foreword by Robert Hall]

Duboc, Général. 1935. *Mauritanie.* Paris: L. Fournier.

Dupree, Louis. 1980. *Afghanistan.* Princeton: Princeton University Press.

Durbin, Marshall and Haydee Seijas. 1973. Proto Hianacoto: Guaque-Carijona-Hianacoto Umaua. *International Journal of American Linguistics* 39(1):22–31.

Dutton, T. E. 1969. *The peopling of Central Papua: Some preliminary observations.* Pacific Linguistics B-9. Canberra: Australian National University.

Dutton, T. E. 1970. Notes on the languages of the Rigo area of the Central District of Papua. In S. A. Wurm and D. C. Laycock, eds., *Pacific Linguistic Studies in Honour of Arthur Capell.* Pacific Linguistics C-13, pp. 879–983. Canberra: Australian National University.

Dutton, T. E. 1971. Languages of southeast Papua; a preliminary report. In *Papers in New Guinea Linguistics,* No. 14. Pacific Linguistics A-28, pp. 1–46. Canberra: Australian National University.

Dwyer, David J. 1989. Mande. In Bendor-Samuel, pp. 47–66.

Dye, W., P. Townsend, and W. Townsend. 1968. The Sepik Hill languages: A preliminary report. *Oceania* 39:(2)146–156.

Dyen, Isidore. 1962. The lexicostatistical classification of the Malayopolynesian languages. *Language* 38:38–46.

Dyen, Isidore. 1963. *The lexicostatistical classification of the Austronesian languages.* New Haven: Yale University.

Dyen, Isidore. 1965. *A lexicostatistical classification of the Austronesian languages.* Indiana University Publications in Anthropology and Linguistics, Memoir 19. *International Journal of American Linguistics* 31:1, supplement.

Ebert, Karen 1994. *The structure of Kiranti languages, comparative grammar and texts, Kiranti subordination in the South Asian areal context.* Zürich: ASAS.

Edmondson, Jerold A., ed. 1990. *Kadai: Discussions in Kadai and S.E. Asian linguistics.* Fiftieth Anniversary Kadai. Kadai II. Arlington: University of Texas.

Edmondson, Jerold A. and David Solnit, eds. 1988. *Comparative Kadai: Linguistic studies beyond Tai.* Summer Institute of Linguistics and the University of Texas at Arlington Publications in Linguistics 86. Dallas.

Edmondson, Jerold A. and David Solnit, eds. 1997. *Comparative Kadai: The Tai branch.* Summer Institute of Linguistics and the University of Texas at Arlington Publications in Linguistics 124. Dallas.

Egerod, Søren C. 1974. Sino-Tibetan languages. In *Encyclopaedia Britannica* 16:796–806.

Egland, Steven, Doris Bartholomew, and Saul Cruz Ramos. 1983. *La inteligibilidad interdialectal en México: Resultados de algunos sondeos.* Mexico, D. F.: Instituto Lingüístico de Verano.

Elkins, Richard E. 1967. Major grammatical patterns of Western Bukidnon Manobo. Ph.D. dissertation. University of Hawaii, Honolulu.

Ellis, Jim. 1991. Language intelligibility testing across Micronesia. Presented at the Sixth International Conference of Austronesian Linguistics.

Encyclopedic dictionary of Chinese Linguistics. 1991. Jiangxi Educational Publishing House.

Eriksen, Thomas H. 1990. Linguistic diversity and the quest for national identity: The case of Mauritius. *Ethnic and Racial Studies* 13(1):1–24.

Everett, Daniel L. 1983. Á língua pirahã e a teoria da sintaxe: Descrição, perspectivas, e teoria. Ph.D. dissertation. Universidade Estadual de Campinas.

Fagerberg, Sonja. 1978–1979. A brief survey of Pulaar/Fulfulde dialects in West Africa. New York: United Bible Societies. ms.

Farhadi, A. G. Raven. 1967. *Languages.* Kabul: Kabul Times Publishing Agency.

Fasold, Ralph. 1984. *The sociolinguistics of society,* Vol. I. Oxford: Basil Blackwell.

Ferlus, Michel. 1996. Langues et peuples viet-muong. *Mon-Khmer Studies* 16:7–28. Mahidol University, Salaya, Thailand and The Summer Institute of Linguistics. Dallas.

Fischer, Wolfdietrich and Otto Jastrow. 1980. *Handbuch der arabischen Dialekte.* Wiesbaden: Harrassowitz.

Fishman, Joshua A., ed. 1985. *Readings in the sociology of Jewish languages.* Leiden: E. J. Brill.

Fishman, Joshua A. 1988. Language spread and language policy for endangered languages. In Peter H. Lowenberg, ed., *Language spread and language policy: Issues, implications, and case studies,* pp. 1–15. Washington, D.C.: Georgetown University Press.

Fishman, Joshua A. 1991. *Reversing language shift.* Clevedon: Multilingual Matters, Ltd.

Fishman, Joshua A., C. A. Ferguson, and J. Das Gupta, eds. 1968. *Language problems of developing nations.* New York: Wiley.

Fleisch, H. 1974. *Études d'Arabe dialectal.* Beyrouth.

Foley, William A. 1986. *The Papuan languages of New Guinea.* Cambridge: Cambridge University Press.

Forte, Janette. 1990. *The populations of Guyanese Amerindian settlements.* University of Guyana, Amerindian Research Unit.

Frank, David B. 1993. Political, religious, and economic factors affecting language choice in St. Lucia. *International Journal of the Sociology of Language* 102:39–56.

Franklin, Karl. 1968. Languages of the Gulf District: A preview. In *Papers in New Guinea Linguistics,* No. 8. Pacific Linguistics A-16, pp. 19–44. Canberra: Australian National University.

Friberg, Timothy, ed. 1987. *South Sulawesi Sociolinguistic Surveys.* Workpapers in Indonesian Languages and Cultures, Vol. 5. Ujung Pandang: Summer Institute of Linguistics.

Friberg, Timothy, ed. 1991. *More Sulawesi sociolinguistic surveys,* 1987–1991. Workpapers in Indonesian Linguistics (and Cultures) 11. Ujung Pandang: Summer Institute of Linguistics.

Friberg, Timothy and Thomas V. Laskowske. 1988. South Sulawesi languages, 1988. Presented at the Fifth International Conference on Austronesian Linguistics.

Frick, E. and M. Bolli. 1971. Inventaire préliminaire des langues et dialectes en Côte-d'Ivoire. In *Actes du Huitième Congrès International de Linguistique Africaine* 1:395–416.

Fu Maoji, ed. 1991. *Tibeto-Burman sounds and vocabulary.* Beijing: Zhongguo Shihui Kexue Chubanshe.

Fussman, Gerard. 1972. *Atlas linguistique des perlers dardes et kafirs,* 2 vols. Paris: Ecole Française d'Extreme Orient.

Fussman, Gerard. 1989. Languages as a source for history. In A. H. Dani, ed., *History of northern areas of Pakistan,* pp. 43–58. Islamabad: National Institute of Historical and Cultural Research.

Gallman, Andrew F. 1983. Proto East Mindanao and its internal relationships. Ph.D. dissertation. University of Texas at Arlington.

Galtier, Gerard. 1980. Problèmes dialectologiques et phonographématiques del parlers mandingues. Thèse de 3ème Cycle. University of Paris.

Garbell, Irene. 1965. *The Jewish Neo-Aramaic dialect of Persian Azerbaijan: Linguistic analysis and folkloristic texts.* Janua Linguarum, Series Practica, III. The Hague: Mouton.

Geraghty, Paul A. 1983. *The history of the Fijian languages. Oceanic Linguistics,* Special Publication 19. Honolulu: University of Hawaii Press.

Geraghty, Paul A. 1988. Proto New Caledonian and its relationships. Presented at the Fifth International Conference on Austronesian Linguistics.

Gerteiny, Alfred G. 1967. *Mauritania.* New York: Frederick A. Praeger.

Gibson, Michael. 1988. The Munichi language: With particular reference to verb morphology. Thesis. Reading University.

Gloria, Heidi K. 1987. *The Bagobos: Their ethnohistory and acculturation.* Quezon City, Philippines: New Day Publishers.

Godfrey, Thomas James and Wesley M. Collins. 1987. *Una encuesta dialectal en el area mam de Guatemala.* Guatemala: Summer Institute of Linguistics.

Gohain, B. C., compiler. 1971. *Annexure to the tribal map of India.* Calcutta: Anthropological Survey of India.

Gold, David L. 1974. Jewish intralinguistics. *Sociological Abstracts,* Supplement 47(1), p. 344.

Goldbert de Goodbar, Perla. 1975. *Cuento tradicional araucano; transcripción fonológica, traducción, y análisis.* Buenos Aires: Centro de Investigaciones en Ciencias de la Educación.

Goodman, Morris. 1964. *A comparative study of Creole French dialects.* The Hague: Mouton.

Goyvaerts, D. L. 1983. Some aspects of Logo phonology and morphology. In Bender, ed., pp. 272–279.

Gran Enciclopèdia Catalana. 1978–1988. Barcelona: Enciclopèdia Catalana.

Greenberg, Joseph H. 1963. *The languages of Africa.* Indiana University Research Center in Anthropology, Folklore, and Linguistics, Publication 25. The Hague: Mouton.

Greenberg, Joseph H. 1987. *Language in the Americas.* Stanford: Stanford University Press.

Gregerson, Kenneth J. 1976. Tongue-root and register in Mon-Khmer. In Philip N. Jenner, Laurence C. Thompson, and Stanley Starosta, eds., *Austroasiatic studies, part I. Oceanic Linguistics,* Special Publication 13, pp. 323–369.

Grierson, G. A., ed. 1903–1928. *Linguistic survey of India,* 3 vols. Calcutta: Government of India, Central Publication Branch.

Grimes, Barbara D. 1988. Exploring the socio-linguistics of Ambonese Malay. Presented at the Fifth International Conference on Austronesian Languages.

Grimes, Barbara D. 1994. Cloves and nutmeg, traders and wars: Language contact in the Spice Islands. In T. Dutton and D. T. Tryon, eds., *Language contact and change in the Austronesian world.* Trends in Linguistics: Studies and Monographs 77, pp. 251–274. Berlin: Mouton de Gruyter.

Grimes, Barbara F. 1985. Comprehension and language attitudes in relation to language choice for literature and education in pre-literate societies. *Journal of Multilingual and Multicultural Development* 6(2):165–181.

Grimes, Barbara F. 1985. Language attitudes: Identity, distinctiveness, survival in the Vaupes. *Journal of Multilingual and Multicultural Development* 6(5):389–401.

Grimes, Barbara F. 1986. Regional and other nonstandard dialects of major languages. *Notes on Linguistics* 35:19–39.

Grimes, Barbara F. 1987a. How bilingual is bilingual? *Notes on Linguistics* 40:3–23.

Grimes, Barbara F. 1987b. The Summer Institute of Linguistics second language oral proficiency evaluation. *Notes on Linguistics* 40:24–54.

Grimes, Barbara F. 1988. Why test intelligibility? *Notes on Linguistics* 42:39–64.

Grimes, Barbara F. 1989. Special considerations for creole surveys. *Notes on Linguistics* 47:41–63.

Grimes, Barbara F. 1994. Evaluating the Hawaii Creole English situation. *Notes on Literature in Use and Language Programs* 39:39–60.

Grimes, Charles E. 1992. The Buru Language of eastern Indonesia. Ph.D. dissertation. Australian National University, Canberra.

Grimes, Charles E. 1995. *Digging for the roots of language death in eastern Indonesia: The cases of Kayeli and Hukumina.* Published as ERIC Clearinghouse on Languages and Linguistics Document No. ED 384 231, Washington, D.C.: U.S. Department of Education. Paper presented at LSA meetings in New Orleans, 1995.

Grimes, Charles E., ed. 2000. *Spices from the East: Papers in languages of eastern Indonesia.* Pacific Linguistics 503. Canberra: Australian National University.

Grimes, Charles E. and Barbara D. Grimes. 1983. *Languages of the North Moluccas: A preliminary lexicostatistic classification.* Ambon: Pattimura University and the Summer Institute of Linguistics.

Grimes, Charles E. and Barbara D. Grimes. 1987. *Languages of South Sulawesi.* Pacific Linguistics, Series D-78. Canberra: Australian National University.

Grimes, Charles E., Tom Therik, Barbara Dix Grimes, and Max Jacob. 1997. *A guide to the people and languages of Nusa Tenggara.* Center for Regional Studies, Paradigma, Series B, No. 1 Kupang: Artha Wacana Press.

Grimes, Joseph E. 1964. Measures of linguistic divergence. In H. G. Lunt, ed., *Proceedings of the Ninth International Congress of Linguists,* pp. 44–50. The Hague: Mouton.

Grimes, Joseph E. 1974a. Dialects as optimal communication networks. *Language* 50:260–269.

Grimes, Joseph E. 1974b. *Word lists and languages.* Technical Report No. 2. Ithaca, New York: Cornell University, Department of Modern Languages and Linguistics.

Grimes, Joseph E. 1986. Area norms of language size. In B. F. Elson, ed., *Language in global perspective: Papers in honor of the fiftieth anniversary of the Summer Institute of Linguistics,* pp. 5–19. Dallas: Summer Institute of Linguistics.

Grimes, Joseph E. 1988. Correlations between vocabulary similarity and intelligibility. *Notes on Linguistics* 41:19–33.

Grimes, Joseph E. 1989. Interpreting sample variation in intelligibility tests. In Thomas J. Walsh, ed., *Synchronic and diachronic approaches to linguistic variation and change.* Georgetown University Round Table on Languages and Linguistics 1988, pp. 138–146. Washington, D.C.: Georgetown University Press.

Grimes, Joseph E. 1995. Language endangerment in the Pacific. *Oceanic Linguistics* 34(1):1–12.

Grimes, Joseph E. 1995. *Language survey reference guide.* Dallas: Summer Institute of Linguistics.

Grimes, Joseph E. and Frederick B. Agard. 1959. Measures of phonological divergence in Romance. *Language* 35:598–604.

Grjunberg, A. L. 1963. *The language of the northern Azerbaijan Tats.* Leningrad. [in Russian]

Grjunberg, A. L. 1968. *Languages of the Eastern Hindu Kush.* Moscow.

Grjunberg, A. L. 1971. *A dialektologii Dardskix jazykov (Glangali i Zemiaki).* Moscow.

Grünberg, Georg and Friedl Grünberg. 1978. Los Guaraní occidentales. In Augusto Roa Bisto, ed., *Las culturas condenadas,* pp. 178–193. Mexico: Siglo XXI Editorial.

Güldemann, Tom. 1998. *San languages for education: A linguistic short survey and proposal, on behalf of the Molteno Early Literacy and Language Development Project in Namibia.* Okahandja: National Institute of Educational Development, Ministry of Basic Education and Culture.

Gudschinsky, Sarah C. 1953. Proto-Mazateco. *Ciencias Sociales: MCCM* 12, pp. 171–174. Mexico: Universidad Nacional Autónoma de México.

Gudschinsky, Sarah C. 1959. *Proto-Popotecan: A comparative study of Popolocan and Mixtecan.* Indiana University Research Center, Memoir 15, Supplement to *International Journal of American Linguistics* 25:2.

Gudschinsky, Sarah C. 1964. The ABCs of lexicostatistics (glottochronology). In Dell Hymes, ed., *Language in culture and society,* pp. 612–622. New York: Harper and Row.

Gunn, H. D. 1953. *Peoples of the plateau region of northern Nigeria.* London: International African Institute.

Gunn, H. D. 1956. *Peoples of the central area of northern Nigeria.* London: International African Institute.

Gunn, H. D. and F. P. Conant. 1960. *Peoples of the middle Niger region of northern Nigeria.* London: International African Institute.

Gunnemark, Erik and Donald Kenrick. 1985. *A geolinguistic handbook.* Sweden: Gunnemark.

Gurung, G. M. 1989. *The Chepangs: A study in continuity and change.* Kathmandu: Centre for Nepal and Asian Studies.

Guthrie, Malcolm. 1948. *The classification of the Bantu languages.* Oxford: Oxford University Press.

Guthrie, Malcolm. 1967–1971. *Comparative Bantu,* 4 vols. Farnborough: Gregg International Publishers.

Haacke, Wilfrid H. G. and Edward E. Elderkin, eds. 1997. *Namibian languages: Reports and papers.* Namibian African Studies, Vol. 4. Cologne: Rudiger Koppe Verlag.

Haby, Eden. 1975. *Les Assyriens d'Union Sovietique.* Cahiers du Mohde Russe et Sovietique 176.

Hagège, C. 1973. *Profil d'un parler arabe du Tchad.* Paris: P. Geuthner.

Hahn, Reinhold F. 1990. *An annotated sample of Ili Turki.* Acta Orientalia Hungaricae 43

Hale, Austin. 1982. *Research on Tibeto-Burman Languages.* Trends in Linguistics: State-of-the-Art Report 14. Berlin: Mouton.

Hale, K., M. Krauss, L. Watahomigie, A. Yamamoto, C. Craig, L. Masayevsa Jeane, and N. England. 1992. Endangered languages. *Language* 68:1–42.

Hall, Edward. 1983. *Ghanaian languages.* Accra: Asempa.

Hall, Robert A., Jr. 1966. *Pidgin and creole languages.* Ithaca: Cornell University Press.

Hall, Robert A., Jr. 1974. *External history of the Romance languages.* New York: American Elsevier Publishing Co.

Hallberg, Daniel G., ed. 1992. *Pashto, Waneci, Ormuri.* Sociolinguistic Survey of Northern Pakistan, Vol. 4. Islamabad: National Institute of Pakistan Studies, Quaid-i-Azam University and Summer Institute of Linguistics.

Hancock, Ian F. 1969. The Malacca Creoles and their language. *Afrasia* 3:38–45.

Hancock, Ian F. 1974. Shelta: A problem of classification. In De Camp and Hancock, eds., pp. 130–137.

Hancock, Ian F. ed., 1979. *Romani sociolinguistics. International Journal of the Sociology of Language* 19. The Hague: Mouton.

Hancock, Ian F. 1984a. Romani and Angloromani. In P. Trudgill, ed., *Language in the British Isles,* pp. 367–383. Cambridge: Cambridge University Press.

Hancock, Ian F. 1984b. Shelta and Polari. In P. Trudgill, ed., *Language in the British Isles,* pp. 384–403. Cambridge: Cambridge University Press.

Hancock, Ian F. 1984c. The social and linguistic development of Angloromani. In Acton and Kenrick, eds., pp. 89–122.

Hancock, Ian F. 1985. A preliminary structural sketch of Trinidad Creole French. *Amsterdam Creole Studies* 8:27–40.

Hancock, Ian F. 1986a. On the classification of Afro-Seminole Creole. In Michael Montgomery and Guy Bailey, eds., *Language variety in the South: Perspectives in black and white,* pp. 85–101. University: University of Alabama Press.

Hancock, Ian F. 1986b. The cryptolectal speech of the American roads: Traveler Cant and American Angloromani. *American Speech* 61:206–220.

Hancock, Ian F. 1987a. A preliminary classification of the Anglophone Atlantic Creoles, with syntactic data from thirty-three representative dialects. In Glenn Gilbert, ed., *Pidgin and Creole languages: Essays in memory of John E. Reinecke,* pp. 264–334. Honolulu: The University Press of Hawaii.

Hancock, Ian F. 1987b. Componentiality and the origins of Gullah. In Mary W. Helms, ed., *Sea and land. Proceedings of the Southern Anthropological Society,* Vol. 21. Athens: University of Georgia Press.

Hancock, Ian F. 1987c. *Romani: The language of the Gypsies.* Gamut 23.

Hancock, Ian F. 1987d. The function of the Gypsy myth. *Roma* 27:35–44.

Hancock, Ian F. 1988a. The development of Romani linguistics. In A. Jazery and W. Winter, eds., *Languages and cultures: Studies in honor of*

Edgar C. Polomé, pp. 183–223. The Hague: Mouton.

Hancock, Ian F. 1988b. Creole language provenance and the African component. Presented at the International Round-Table on Africanisms in Afro-American Language Varieties. The University of Georgia, Athens, Georgia. February 25–27, 1988.

Hancock, Ian F. 1990. *A grammar of the Hungarian-Slovak (Carpathian, Bashaldo, Romungro) Romani language.* Manchaca, Texas: International Romani Union.

Hancock, Ian F. 1991. The social and linguistic development of Scandoromani. In Ernst H. Jahr, ed., *Language contact in Scandinavia. Proceedings of the Fifth International Tromso Symposium.* Berlin: Mouton de Gruyter.

Hansford, Keir, John Bendor-Samuel, and Ron Stanford. 1976. *An index of Nigerian languages.* Studies in Nigerian Languages, No. 5. Accra, Ghana: Summer Institute of Linguistics.

Hanson, F. A. 1970. *The society and history on a Polynesian island.* Boston: Little, Brown and Co.

Hansson, G. 1991. *The Rai of eastern Nepal: Ethnic and linguistic grouping. Findings of the Linguistic Survey of Nepal.* Kathmandu: CNAS.

Harmon, David. 1995. The status of the world's languages as reported in Ethnologue. *Southwest Journal of Linguistics* 14(1–2):1–28.

Harmon, David. 1996. Losing species, losing languages: Connections between biological and linguistic diversity. *Southwest Journal of Linguistics* 15(1–2):89–108.

Harris, Tracy K. 1994. *Death of a language.* Newark: University of Delaware Press.

Haugen, Einar. 1992. Scandinavian languages. In Bright, ed., Vol. 3, pp. 375–379.

Hayes, Curtis W., Jacob Ornstein, and William W. Gage 1977. Appendix: Languages of the world. In *ABC's of languages and linguistics.* Silver Spring, Maryland: Institute of Modern Languages, Inc.

Headland, Thomas N. 1985. Imposed values and aid rejection among Casiguran Agta. In P. Bion Griffin and Agnes Estioko-Griffin, eds., *The Agta of northeastern Luzon: Recent studies,* pp. 102–118. Cebu City, Philippines: University of San Carlos.

Headland, Thomas N. 1987. Negrito religions: Negritos of the Philippine Islands. In Mircea Eliade, ed., *The encyclopedia of religion,* Vol. 10, pp. 348–349. New York: MacMillan.

Healey, Alan. 1964. The Ok language family in New Guinea. Ph.D. dissertation. Australian National University, Canberra.

Hedinger, Robert. 1984. A comparative-historical study of the Manenguba languages (Bantu A.15 MBO cluster) of Cameroon. Ph.D. dissertation. University of London.

Heijdra, Martin. 1998. Who were the Laka? A survey of Scriptures in the minority languages of southwest China. *The East Asian Library Journal* 8.1, Spring.

Heine, Bernd. 1968. *Die Verbreitung und Gliederung der Togorestsprachen.* Kölner Beiträge zur Afrikanistik, Band). Berlin: Dietrich Reimer.

Heine, Bernd and Wilhelm J. G. Möhlig. 1980. *Language and dialect atlas of Kenya,* Vol. 1. Berlin: Deitrich Reimer Verlag.

Hetzron, Robert, ed., 1997. *The Semitic languages.* New York: Routledge.

Hickerson, Harold, Glen D. Turner, and Nancy P. Hickerson. 1952. Testing procedures for estimating transfer of information among Iroquois dialects and languages. *International Journal of American Linguistics* 18:1–8.

Himmelmann, Nikolaus P. 2001. *Sourcebook on Tomini-Tolitoli languages. General information and word lists.* Pacific Linguistics 511. Canberra: Australian National University.

Hoberman, Robert D. 1988a. Emphasis harmony in a modern Aramaic dialect. *Language* 64:1–26.

Hoberman, Robert D. 1988b. *The syntax and semantics of verb morphology in modern Aramaic: A Jewish dialect of Iraqi Kurdistan.* New Haven: American Oriental Society.

Hodgson, Brian Houghton. 1874. Sifán and Hórsók vocabularies. *Journal of the Royal Asiatic Society of Bengal* 22:117–151.

Holes, Clive. 1988. The typology of Omani Arabic dialects. In *Proceedings of the BRIMES International Conference on Middle Eastern Studies.* Leeds: University of Leeds.

Holes, Clive. 1990. *Gulf Arabic.* New York: Routledge.

Holm, John. 1989. *Pidgins and Creoles,* Vols. 1, 2. Cambridge: Cambridge University Press.

Hombert, Jean-Marie. 1980. Le groupe noun. In Hyman and Voorhoeve, eds., *Les classes nominales dans le bantou des Grassfields. L'expansion bantoue,* Vol. 1, pp. 143–163.

Hombert, Jean-Marie and L. Hyman, eds. 1999. *Recent advances in Bantu historical linguistics.* Stanford. Center for the Study of Language and Information.

Hooley, Bruce A. 1971. Austronesian languages of the Morobe District, Papua New Guinea. *Oceanic Linguistics* 10:79–151.

Hooley, Bruce A. and Kenneth McElhanon. 1970. Languages of the Morobe District—New Guinea. In Wurm, S. A. and D. C. Laycock, eds., *Pacific Linguistic Studies in Honour of Arthur Capell.* Pacific Linguistics C-13, pp. 1065–1094. Canberra: Australian National University.

Hopkins, Bradley Lynn. 1995. Contribution à une étude de la syntaxe Diola-Fogny. Ph.D. dissertation. Université Cheikh Anta Diop de Dakar.

Hopper, Janice H., ed. 1967. *Indians of Brazil in the Twentieth Century,* ICR Studies 2. Washington D.C.: Institute for Cross-Cultural Research.

Hu, C. T. 1970. *The education of national minorities in Communist China.* Washington, D.C.: U.S. Government Printing Office, Catalog HE 5.214:141–146.

Hudson, Joyce. 1987. *Languages of the Kimberley region.* Broome, WA: Catholic Education Kimberly Regional Office.

Hugoniot, Richard D., ed. 1970. *A bibliographical index of the lesser known languages and dialects of India and Nepal.* Kathmandu: Summer Institute of Linguistics.

Hunter, Brian. 1995. *The statesman's yearbook: Statistical and historical annual of the states of the world for the year 1995–1996.* London: MacMillan.

Huntingford, G. W. B. 1953. *The northern Nilo-Hamites.* London: International African Institute.

Huntingford, G. W. B. 1953. *The south Nilo-Hamites.* London: International African Institute.

Hussainmiya, B. A. 1986. *Melayu Bahasa: Some preliminary observations on the Malay Creole of Sri Lanka.* Sari 4. Kuala Lampur: Universiti Kebangsaan Malaysia.

Huttar, George L. 1981. Some Kwa-like features of Djuka syntax. *Studies in African Linguistics* 12:291–323.

Huttar, George L. 1983. On the study of Creole lexicons. In Lawrence D. Carrington, Dennis Craig, and Ramon T. Dandare, eds., *Studies in Caribbean languages,* pp. 82–29. St. Augustine, Trinidad: Society for Caribbean Linguistics.

Hyman, Larry M. 1980. Babanki and the Ring Group. In Hyman and Voorhoeve, eds., pp. 225–258.

Hyman, Larry M. and Jan Voorhoeve, eds. 1980. *Les classes nominales dans le bantou des Grassfields. L'expansion bantoue,* Vol. 1. Paris: SELAF.

Ingemann, Frances and John Duitsman. 1976. A survey of Grebo dialects in Liberia. *Liberian Studies Journal* VII(2):121–131.

Ingemann, Frances, John Duitsman, and William Doe. 1972. A survey of Krahn dialects in Liberia. *University of Liberia Journal.*

Ingham, Bruce. 1982. *Northeast Arabian dialects.* London: Kegan Paul International.

Ingham, Bruce. 1994. *Najdi Arabic: Central Arabian.* Amsterdam: John Benjamins.

International encyclopedia of linguistics, 4 vols. Bright, William, ed. 1992. New York: Oxford University Press.

Iyanga Pendi, Agusto. 1991. *Préstamos en la lengua nDowe de Guinea Ecuatorial.* Valencia: NAU Libres, Periodista Badia 10.

Izadi, Mehrdad. 1993. *The Kurds: A concise handbook.* Cambridge: Harvard University Press.

Jackson, Frederick. 1983. The internal and external relationships of the Trukic languages of Micronesia. Ph.D. dissertation. University of Hawaii, Honolulu.

Jacquot, André. 1971. *Les langues du Congo-Brazzaville: Inventaire et classification.* In Cahiers ORSTROM, Série Sciences Humaines, Vol. VIII, No. 4.

Jacquot, André. 1978. Le Gabon. In Barreteau, ed., pp. 493–503.

Janhunen, Juha. 1989. A Sino-Finnish joint expedition to the minority nationalities of northern China. *Suomalais-Ugrilaisen Seuran Aikakauskiria* 82:277–279.

Jastrow, Otto. 1971. Ein neuaramaischen Dielekt aus dem Vilayet Siirt (Ustanatolien). *ZDub* 121:215–222.

Jastrow, Otto. 1978. *Die Mesopotamisch-Arabishen qeltu-Dialekte,* 2 vols. Wiesbaden: Franz Steiner GMBH.

Jastrow, Otto. 1988. *Der Neuaramaische Dialect von Hertevin (Provinz Siirt).* Wiesbaden: Karassowitz.

Jensen, Allen A. 1985. Sistemas indígenas de classificação de aves: Aspectos comparativos, ecológicos e evolutivos. Ph.D. dissertation. Universidade Estadual de Campinas.

Jernudd, Bjorn H. 1968. Linguistic integration and national development: A case study of the Jebel Mara area, Sudan. In Fishman, Ferguson, and Das Gupta, eds., pp. 167–181.

Jernudd, Bjorn H. and Muhammad H. Ibrahim. 1986. Aspects of Arabic sociolinguistics. *International Journal of the Sociology of Language* 61. Berlin: Mouton de Gruyter.

Jha, Sudhakar. 1958. *The formation of the Maithili language.* London: Luzac.

Johnstone, Patrick. 1993. *Operation World.* Grand Rapids: Zondervan Publishing House.

Johnstone, Patrick and Jason Mandryk. 2001. *Operation World.* Waynesboro: Paternoster Lifestyle

Johnstone, T. M. 1967. *Eastern Arabian dialect studies.* London: Oxford University Press.

Johnstone, T. M. 1987. *Mehri lexicon and English-Mehri word-list.* London: SOAS.

Jones, Robert B. 1988. Proto-Burmese as a test of reconstruction. In Caroline Duncan-Rose and Theo Vennemann, eds., *On Language: Rhetorica, phonologica, syntactica. A festschrift for Robert P. Stockwell,* pp. 203–211. London: Routledge.

Jones, Schuyler. 1974. *Men of influence in Nuristan.* London: Seminar Press.

Jungraithmayr, H. 1971. How many Mimi languages are there? *Africana Marburgensia* 4(2):62–69.

Jungraithmayr, H. 1978. A lexical comparison of Darfur and Wadai Daju. In Thelwall, ed., pp. 145–154.

Kakumasu, James Y. 1976. Urubú sign language. *International Journal of American Linguistics* 34:275–281.

Kanyoro, Rachel Angogo. 1983. *Unity in diversity: A linguistic survey of the Abaluhyia of western Kenya.* Wien: Beitrage zur Afrikanistik.

Kaseng, Syahruddin. 1978. *Kedudukan dan fungsi bahasa Makassar di Sulawesi Selatan.* Jakarta: Pusat Pembinaan dan Pengembangan Bahasa.

Kaseng, Syahruddin, et al. 1983. Pemetaan Bahasa di Sulawesi Tenggara. Ujung Pandang. ms.

Kastenholz, Raimund. 1996. *Sprachgeschichte im West-Mande: Methoden und Rekonstruktionen. Mande Languages and Linguistics,* Vol. 2. Cologne: Rudiger, Koppe Verlag.

Katzner, Kenneth. 1975. *The languages of the world.* New York: Funk and Wagnalls.

Kaye, Alan S. 1988. Review of Bjorn H. Jernudd and Muhammad H. Ibrahim, *Aspects of Arabic sociolinguistics, International Journal of the Sociology of Language 1986. Language* 64:210.

Kazakevitch, Olga and Kazuto Matsumura, eds. 2002. *Indigenous minority languages of Russia:*

Bibliographical guide. Moscow: Institute of Linguistics, Russian Academy of Sciences

Kedrebeogo, G., Z. Yago, and T. Hien. 1988. *Burkina Faso: Carte linguistique.* Institut Géographique du Burkina and Institut de Recherche des Sciences Sociales et Humaines.

Key, Mary Ritchie. 1979. *The grouping of South American Indian languages.* Tübingen: Gunter Narr Verlag.

Kibrik, Aleksandr E. 1991. The problem of endangered languages in the USSR. In Robins and Uhlenbeck, eds., pp. 257–273.

King, Julie K. and John Wayne King, eds. 1984. *Languages of Sabah: A survey report.* Pacific Linguistics C-78. Canberra: Australian National University.

Kirk, Paul L. 1970. Dialect intelligibility testing: The Mazatec study. *International Journal of American Linguistics* 36:205–211.

Klein, Harriet E. Manelis and Louisa R. Stark. 1977. Indian languages of the Paraguayan Chaco. *Anthropological Linguistics* 19.8.

Klein, Harriet E. Manelis and Louisa R. Stark, eds. 1985. *South American Indian languages: Retrospect and prospect.* Austin: University of Texas Press.

Kloss, Heinz and Grant D. McConnell. 1974. *Linguistic composition of the nations of the world,* Vol. 1, *Central and Western South Asia.* Quebec: International Center for Research on Bilingualism.

Kloss, Heinz and Grant D. McConnell. 1978. *Linguistic composition of the nations of the world,* Vol. 2, *North America.* Quebec: International Center for Research on Bilingualsm.

Koentjaraningrat, ed. 1971. *Manusia dan kebudayaan di Indonesia.* Jakarta: Djambatan.

Krauss, Michael. 1992. The world's languages in crisis. *Language* 68:4-10.

Krauss, Michael E. 1979. Na-Dene and Eskimo-Aleut. In Campbell and Mithun, eds., pp. 803–901.

Krauss, Michael E. 1995. *The indigenous languages of the North: A report on their present state.* Fairbanks, Alaska: Alaska Native Language Center, University of Alaska Fairbanks.

Kroeger, Paul R. 1985. Linguistic relations among the Dusunic groups in the Kota Marudu District. *Borneo Research Bulletin* 17(1):31–46.

Kroeger, Paul R. 1986. Intelligibility patterns in Sabah and the problem of prediction. In Paul Geraghty, Lois Carrington, and S. A. Wurm, eds., *Focal 1: Papers from the Fourth International Congress on Austronesian Linguistics.* Pacific Linguistics C-93, pp. 309–339. Canberra: Australian National University.

Krupa, Viktor. 1973. *Polynesian languages, a survey of research.* The Hague: Mouton.

Kullavanajaya, Pranee and Theraphan L-Thongkum. 1998. Linguistic criteria for determining Tai ethnic groups: Case studies on Central and Southwestern Tais. Paper presented at The International Conference on Tai Studies, Institute of Language and Culture for Rural Development of Mahidol University, Bangkok. July 29–31, 1998.

Kuter, Lois. 1989. Breton vs. French: Language and the opposition of political, economic, social, and cultural values. In Nancy C. Dorian, ed., *Investigating obsolescence: Studies in language contraction and death,* pp. 75–90. Cambridge: Cambridge University Press.

Ladefoged, Peter, Ruth Glick, and Clive Criper. 1972. *Language in Uganda.* London: Oxford University Press.

Lafarge, Francine. 1978. Etudes phonologiques des parlers kosop (Kim) et gerep (Djouman), groupe kim (Adamawa). Mayo Kebbi, Tchad. Thèse 3e cycle, Université de Paris III.

Lajard, M. 1891. Le langage siffle des Canaries. *Bulletin de la Societe d'Anthropologie de Paris* 2:469–483.

Lamberti, Marcello. 1986. *Map of Somali dialects in the Somali Democratic Republic.* Hamburg: Helmut Buske Verlag.

Lamberti, Marcello. 1988. The origin of the Jiiddu of Somalia. In Annarita Puglielli, ed., *Proceedings of the Third International Congress of Somali Studies,* pp. 3–10. Rome: Il Pensiero Scientifico.

Landaburu, Jon. 1978. El tratamiento gramatical de la verdad en la lengua andoque. *Revista Colombiana de Antropología,* 20:81–100. Bogotá: Instituto Colombiano de Antropología.

Langdon, Margaret. 1968. The Proto-Yuman demonstrative system. *Folia Linguistica* 2(1):61–81.

Langdon, Margaret. 1974. *Comparative Hokan-Coahuiltecan studies.* The Hague: Mouton.

Larsen, Thomas W. 1984. Case markings and subjecthood in Kipeá Kirirí. In *Proceedings of the Tenth Annual Meeting of the Berkeley Linguistic Society,* pp. 189–205.

Law, Gail. 1982. *Chinese churches handbook.* Hong Kong: Chinese Coordination Centre of World Evangelism.

Laycock, D. C. 1965. *The Ndu language family (Sepik District), New Guinea.* Linguistic Circle of Canberra Publications C-1. Canberra: Australian National University.

Laycock, D. C. 1968. Languages of the Lumi Sub-district (West Sepik District), New Guinea. *Oceanic Linguistics* 7(1):36–66.

Laycock, D. C. 1973. *Sepik languages checklist and preliminary classification.* Pacific Linguistics Series B-25. Canberra: Australian National University.

Le Page, R. B. 1960. *Jamaican Creole: A historical introduction to Jamaican Creole,* Creole Language Studies, No. 1. London: MacMillan.

Lebar, Frank M., ed. 1972. *Ethnic groups of insular Southeast Asia,* Vol. 1. New Haven: Human Relations Area Files Press.

Lebar, Frank M., Gerald C. Hickey, and John K. Musgrave. 1964. *Ethnic groups of mainland Southeast Asia.* New Haven: Human Relations Area Files Press.

Lehmann, Winfred P. 1975. *Language and linguistics in the People's Republic of China.* Austin: University of Texas Press.

Leroy, Jacqueline. 1980. The Ngemba group: Mankon, Bangangu, Mundum I, Bafut, Nkwen,

Bambui, Pinyin, Awing. In Hyman and Voorhoeve, eds., pp. 111–141.

Li Fang-gui. 1973. Languages and dialects of China. *Journal of Chinese Linguistics* 1:1–13.

Li Fang-gui. 1977. *A handbook of comparative Tai.* Honolulu: University of Hawaii Press.

Li, Paul Jen-kuei. 1987. The preglottalised stops in Bunun. In D. C. Laycock and Werner Winter, eds., *Papers presented to Professor S. A. Wurm on his 65th birthday.* Pacific Linguistics C-100, pp. 381–387. Canberra: Australian National University.

Liang Min. 1987. The origins of the Kam-Sui peoples. *Zhongguo Minzushi Yanjiu* 1.2.

Liang Min. 1990. The Buyang language. In Edmondson, ed., pp. 13–21.

Lieberson, Stanley. 1981. *Language diversity and language contact.* Stanford: Stanford University Press.

Lim, S. 1977. *Listing Austronesian languages,* Parts 1, 2.

Lim, S. 1981. Baba Malay, the language of the "Straits-born" Chinese. M.A. thesis. Monash University, Australia.

Liu Guangkun. 1998. *Research on Mawo Qiang.* Chengdu: Sichuan Minorities Press.

Loewen, Jacob A. 1963. Choco I: Introduction and bibliography. *International Journal of American Linguistics* 29(3):239–263.

Loewen, Jacob A. 1963. Choco II: Phonological problems. *International Journal of American Linguistics* 29(4):357–371.

Lokpari, Basa Vyalisha. 1981. *Introduction aux langues de l'Ituri, Colloque sur l'Enseignement des langues caïroises.* Bunia: CANDIP et Institut Supérieure Pédagogique.

Longacre, Robert. 1957. *Proto-Mixtecan.* Indiana University Research Center Publication 5, Supplement to *International Journal of American Linguistics* 23.4.

Longacre, Robert. 1967. Systemic comparison and reconstruction. In Norman McQuown, ed., *Handbook of Middle American Indians,* Vol. 5, pp. 117–159. Austin: University of Texas Press.

Loos, Eugene E. 1973. Algunas implicaciones de la reconstrucción de un fragmento de la gramática del proto-pano. *Estudios Panos 2,* Serie Lingüística Peruana 11, pp. 263–282. Yarinacocha, Peru: Instituto Lingüístico de Verano.

Lopis, J. 1980. Phonologie et morphologie du noon, parler de Ngente. Thèse de 3e cycle, Paris III.

Lorenzino, Gerardo A. 1999. *The Angolar Creole Portuguese of São Tomé: Its grammar and sociolinguistic history.* Muenchen: Lincom.

Lorimer, D. L. R. 1922. *The phonology of the Baktiari, Badakhshani, and Madaglashti dialects of Modern Persian.* London: Royal Asiatic Society.

Loukotka, Čestmír. 1968. *Classification of South American Indian Languages.* Reference series, Vol. 7. Johannes Wilbert, ed. Los Angeles, California: University of California, Latin American Center.

Lukas, Johannes. 1937. *A study of the Kanuri language: Grammar and vocabulary.* London: Oxford University Press.

Lyon, Patricia J. 1975. Dislocación tribal y clasificación lingüística en la zona del río Madre de Dios. In *XXXIX Congreso Internacional de Americanistas: Actas y Memorias,* Vol. 5, pp. 185–207.

MacKinnon, C. 2002. The dialect of Xorramâbâd and comparative notes on other Lor dialects. *Studia Iranica* 31:103–138.

Maclean, Arthur J. 1893. *Grammar of the dialects of vernacular Syriac.* Cambridge: Cambridge University Press, reprinted 1979 Amsterdam: Philo Press.

Macuch, Rudolf. 1965. *Handbook of classical and modern Mandaic.* Berlin: deGruyter.

Mahapatra, B. P. Malto. 1979. *An ethnosemantic study.* Mysore: Central Institute of Indian Languages.

Maho, J.F. 1998. *Few people, many tongues: The languages of Namibia.* Windhoek: Gamsberg Macmillan.

Manessy, Gabriel. 1961. *Le bwamu et ses dialectes.* Publication de la Section de Langues et Litteraires, No. 9. Dakar: Universite de Dakar, Fac. des Lettres et Sciences Humaines.

Manessy, Gabriel. 1975. *Les langues Oti-Volta: Classification généalogique d'un groupe de langues voltaïques.* Paris: SELAF.

Manessy, Gabriel. 1981. Langues voltaïques. In Perrot, ed., *Les langues de l'Afrique subsahariene,* Part 1, pp. 103–110.

Mansur, Abdalla Omar. 1988. A lexical aspect of Somali and East Cushitic languages. In Annarita Puglielli, ed., *Proceedings of the Third International Congress of Somali Studies,* pp. 11–18. Rome: Il Pensiero Scientifico.

Mapes, Glynn. 1990. Linguistic Lazarus: Cornish language is back from the dead. *The Wall Street Journal,* May 16, 1990, p. A1.

Marcais, Ph. 1977. *Esquisse grammaticale de L'Arabe Maghrebin.* Paris: Librairie d'Amerique et d'Orient.

Marchese, Lynell. 1979. *Atlas linguistique des langues Kru.* Abidjan: Université d'Abidjan.

Marrison, Geoffrey Edward. 1967. The classification of the Naga languages of north east India. Vol. I, II. Ph.D. dissertation. University of London.

Martens, Michael. 1989. The Badaic languages of Central Sulawesi. In Sneddon, ed., pp. 19–53.

Martin, Peter W. 1991. Whither the indigenous languages of Brunei Darussalem? *Oceanic Linguistics* 34(1):29–39.

Martin, Peter W., Conrad Oxog, and Gloria Poedjosoedarmo, eds. 1996. *Language use and language change in Brunei Darussalam.* Athens: Ohio University Center for International Studies.

Marty, Paul. 1930. Les Nimadi, Maures sauvages et chasseurs. *Herperis* 11:119–124.

Masica, Colin P. 1991. *The Indo-Aryan languages.* Cambridge: Cambridge University Press.

Masyhuda, M. 1971. *Bahasa Kaili Pamona.* Palu: Yayasan Kebudayaan.

Mathis, Steve L., III, ed. 1980. *International directory of services for the deaf.* Washington, D.C.: Gallaudet University.

Matisoff, James A. 1991. Endangered languages of Mainland Southeast Asia. In Robins and Uhlenbeck, eds., pp. 189–228.

Matisoff, James A., Stephen P. Baron, and John B. Lowe. 1996. *Languages and dialects of Tibeto-Burman.* STEDT Monograph Series, No. 2, James A. Matisoff, General Editor, Center for Southeast Asia Studies. Berkeley: University of California Press.

Matteson, Esther, Alva Wheeler, Frances L. Jackson, Nathan E. Waltz, and Diana R. Christian. 1972. *Comparative studies in Amerindian languages.* The Hague: Mouton.

Maurer, Phillippe. 1995. *L'Angolar. Un créole afro-portugais parlé à São Tomé; Notes de grammaire, textes, vocabulaires.* Hamburg: Helmut Buske Verlag.

Maybury-Lewis, David, and James Howe. 1979. *The Indian peoples of Paraguay, problems and prospects.* USAID Paraguay.

Mayers, Marvin K. 1960. The linguistic unity of Pocoman-Pocomchi. *International Journal of American Linguistics* 26:290–300.

Mayers, Marvin K., ed. 1966a. *Languages of Guatemala.* Janua Linguarum, Series Practica 23. The Hague: Mouton.

Mayers, Marvin K. 1966b. Linguistic comparisons [between Mayan languages]. In Mayers, ed., 1966a, pp. 272–302.

McAlpin, David W. 1981. *Proto-Elamo-Dravidian: The evidence and its implications.* Philadelphia: The American Philosophical Society.

McConnell, Grant D., ed., 1995. *The written languages of the world: A survey of the degree and modes of use.* Vol. 4: *China.* Quebec: Laval University Press.

McCrum, Robert, William Cran, and Robert MacNeil. 1986. *The story of English.* New York: Elisabeth Sifton Books, Viking.

McElhanon, Kenneth A. 1967. Preliminary observations on Huon Peninsula languages. *Oceanic Linguistics* 6:1–45.

McElhanon, Kenneth A. 1970. The Selepet language within the Finisterre-Huon phylum (New Guinea). Ph.D. dissertation. Australian National University.

McElhanon, Kenneth A. 1971. Classifying New Guinea languages. *Anthropos* 66:120–144.

McElhanon, Kenneth A. 1978. *A classification of the languages of the Morobe Province, Papua New Guinea with the linguistic situation of individual villages.* Canberra: Department of Linguistics, Australian National University.

McFarland, Curtis D. 1980. *A linguistic atlas of the Philippines.* Tokyo: University of Foreign Studies, Institute for the Study of Languages and Cultures of Asia and Africa.

McGregor, William. 1988. *Handbook of Kimberley Languages.* Vol. 1, *General Information.* Pacific Linguistics C-105. Canberra: Australian National University.

McKaughan, Howard P. and Michael L. Forman. 1981. Pidgin in Hawaii: 'Da Kine' talk serves useful purposes. *Ampersand* 14(4):11–15.

McKinney, Carol V. 1985. The Bajju of central Nigeria: A case study of religious and social change. M.A. thesis. University of Michigan, Ann Arbor.

McQuown, Norman. 1955. The indigenous languages of Latin America. *American Anthropologist* 57:501–570.

McVey, Ruth T., ed. 1963. *Indonesia.* New Haven: Human Relations Area Files.

Mead, David E. 1998. Proto-Bungku-Tolaki: Reconstruction of its phonology and aspects of its morphosyntax. Ph.D. dissertation. Rice University.

Mead, David E. 1999. *The Bungku-Tolaki languages of South-Eastern Sulawesi, Indonesia.* Pacific Linguistics D-91. Canberra: Australian National University.

Meillet, Antoine and Marcel Cohen, eds. 1952. *Les langues du monde.* Paris: Campion.

Menges, K. H. 1968. *The Turkic language and peoples.* Wiesbaden: Otto Harrassowitz.

Menkhaus, K. J. 1989. Rural transformation and the roots of underdevelopment in Somalia's lower Jubba valley. Ph.D. dissertation. University of South Carolina, Columbia.

Messing, Gordon M. 1980. Politics and national language in Albania. In Frans Van Coetsem and Linda R. Waugh, eds., *Contributions to historical linguistics,* pp. 270–280. Leiden: E. J. Brill.

Middleton, J. 1955. Notes on the political organization of the Madi of Uganda. *African Studies* 14.1.

Middleton, J. 1960. *Lugbara religion: Ritual and authority among an East African people.* London: Oxford University Press.

Middleton, John. 1965. *The Lugbara of Uganda.* New York: Holt, Rinehart and Winston.

Migliazza, Ernest A. 1977. Languages of the Rio Branco-Rio Orinoco region: Current status. ms.

Miller, Philip E. 1993. *Karaite separatism in nineteenth-century Russia.* Cincinnati: Hebrew Union College Press.

Miller, Wick R. 1984. The classification of the Uto-Aztecan languages based on lexical evidence. *International Journal of American Linguistics* 50(1):1–24.

Mills, R. F. 1975. Proto South Sulawesi and Proto Austronesian phonology. Ph.D. dissertation. University of Michigan, Ann Arbor.

Mills, R. F. 1981. Additional addenda. In Robert A. Blust, ed., *Historical linguistics in Indonesia,* Part 1. NUSA, Linguistic Studies in Indonesian and Languages in Indonesia, Vol. 10, pp. 59–82. Jakarta: Badan Penyelenggara Seri Nusa, Universitas Atma Jaya.

Ministry of Development, Sultanate of Oman. 1996. *General census of population, housing and establishments 1993—Detailed publication of the results of the census.*

Minnich, R. Herbert. 1974. Mennonites in Latin America: Number and distribution. *The Mennonite Quarterly Review,* Vol. 48.

Mohan, Peggy and Paul Zador. 1986. Discontinuity in a Life Cycle: The death of Trinidad Bhojpuri. *Language* 62:291–319.

Monan, James and Daisy Y. Noval-Morales. 1979. *A primer on the Negritos of the Philippines.* Manila: Philippine Business for Social Progress.

Moñino, Yves, ed. 1988. *Lexique comparatif des langues Oubanguiennes.* Paris: Librairie Orientaliste Paul Geuthner S.A.

Morgenstierne, Georg. 1974. Languages of Nuristan and surrounding regions. In Karl Jettmas, ed., *Cultures of the Hindu Kush: Selected papers from the Hindu-Kush Cultural Conference held in Moesgard 1970,* pp. 1–10. Wiesbaden: Franz Steiner Verlag.

Moulton, William G. 1985. *Mutual intelligibility among speakers of early German dialects.* Presented at Germania Conference. Washington, D.C.: Georgetown University.

Mühlhäusler, Peter. 1987. *Identifying and mapping the pidgins and creoles of the Pacific.* Duisburg: Linguistic Agency, University of Duisburg.

Muller, Siegfried H. 1964. *The world's living languages.* New York: Frederick Ungar.

Murane, Elizabeth, ed. 1975. *Bibliography of the Summer Institute of Linguistics Papua New Guinea Branch 1956 to 1975.* Ukarumpa: Summer Institute of Linguistics.

Murdock, George Peter. 1959. *Africa: Its peoples and their culture history.* New York: McGraw-Hill.

Naden, Tony. 1989. Gur. In Bendor-Samuel, ed., pp. 141–168.

Nagore, Francho. 1989. *Gramática de la lengua aragonesa,* fifth edition. Zaragoza: Mira Editores, S.A.

Naito, Maho and Darrell Tryon. 2001. The sociolinguistic situation in Vanuatu. In Shibata and Shhionoya, eds., *Languages of the South Pacific Rim,* Vol. 1, pp.114–120. Osaka, Japan: Endangered Languages of the Pacific Rim.

Nakano, A. 1986. The Turoyo language today. *Journal of Assyrian Academic Studies.*

Needham, R. 1954. Penan and Punan. *Journal of the Malayan Branch of the Royal Asiatic Society* 27(1):73–83.

Newman, Paul. 1977. Chadic classification and reconstructions. *Afroasiatic Linguistics* 5:1–42. Malibu, California: Undena Publications.

Newmark, Leonard, Philip Hubbard, and Peter Prifti. 1982. *Standard Arabic: A reference grammar for students.* Stanford: Stanford University Press.

Nicolai, Robert. 1979. Le Songhay Central: Niamey. *Études Linguistiques* 1(2):33–69.

Nicolai, Robert. 1981. Les dialectes du Songhay: Contributions a l'etude des changements linguistiques. Ph.D. dissertation. Société d'Études Linguistiques et Anthropologiques de France, Paris.

Nicolai, Robert. 1983. Position, structure, and classification of Songay. In Bender, ed., pp. 11–41.

Nida, Eugene A. and Harold Fehderau. 1970. Indigenous pidgins and koines. *International Journal of American Linguistics* 36:146–155.

Nida, Eugene A., ed. 1972. *The book of a thousand tongues,* second edition. New York: United Bible Societies.

Nigam, R. C. 1972. *Language handbook on mother tongue in census.* Census of India 1971, Census Centenary Monograph 10. New Delhi: Office of the Registrar General, Government of India, Ministry of Home Affairs.

Noble, G. Kingsley. 1965. *Proto-Arawakan and its descendants.* Indiana University Publications in Anthropology and Linguistics No. 38. Bloomington: Indiana University.

Noorduyn, J. 1991a. *A critical survey of studies on the languages of Sulawesi.* Leiden: KITLV Press.

Noorduyn, J. 1991b. The languages of Sulawesi. In H. Steinhaver, ed., *Papers in Austronesian Linguistics,* No. 1. Pacific Linguistics A-81, pp. 137–150. Canberra: Australian National University.

Nurse, Derek. 1982. Segeju and Daisu: A case study of evidence from oral tradition and comparative linguistics. *History in Africa* 9:175–208.

Nurse, Derek. 1999. Towards a historical classification of East African Bantu languages. In Hombert and Hyman, eds., pp. 1–43.

Nyrop, Richard F., et al. 1974. *Area handbook for India.* Washington, D.C.: American University.

Nyrop, Richard F., ed, 1986. *The Yemens: Country studies.* Washington, D. C.: American University.

Oates, W. J. and Lynette F. Oates. 1970. *A revised linguistic survey of Australia.* Canberra: Australian Institute of Aboriginal Studies.

Oberling, Pierre. 1974. *The Qashqa'i nomads of Fars.* The Hague: Mouton.

Odden, David. 1983. Aspects of Didinga phonology and morphology. In Bender, ed., pp. 148–176.

Ohannessian, Sirarpi and Mubanga E. Kashoki, eds. 1978. *Language in Zambia.* London: International African Institute.

O'Leary, Clare F., ed. 1992. Sociolinguistic Survey of Northern Pakistan, 5 vols. Islamabad: National Institute of Pakistan Studies, Quaid-i-Azam University and Summer Institute of Linguistics.

Olson, Kenneth S. 1996. On the comparison and classification of Banda dialects. In Lisa M. Dobrin, Kora Singer, and Lisa McNair, eds., *CLS 32, Papers from the Main Session,* pp. 267–283. Chicago: Chicago Linguistic Society.

Oltrogge, David. 1977 Proto-Jicaque Subtiaba-Tequistlateco: A comparative reconstruction. M.A. thesis. University of Texas at Arlington.

Omar, Asmah Haji. 1983. *The Malay peoples of Malaysia and their languages.* Kuala Lumpur: Dewan Bahasa Dan Pustaka, Kementerian Pelajaran Malaysia.

Ostapirat, Weera. 2000. Proto-Kra. *Linguistics of the Tibeto-Burman Area* 23(1):1–251.

Osumi, Midori. 2001. The sociolinguistic situation in New Caledonia. In Shibata and Shhionoya, eds., *Languages of the South Pacific Rim,* Vol. 1, pp. 106–112. Osaka, Japan: Endangered Languages of the Pacific Rim. [in Japanese]

Ottenheimer, H. J. and M. Ottenheimer. 1976. The classification of the languages of the Comoro Islands. *Africana Linguistica* 18(9):408–415.

Otterloo, Roger Van. 1979. *A Kalenjin dialect study.* Nairobi: Summer Institute of Linguistics.

Ouane, Adama. 1986. Aperçu sociolinguistique du Mali In *Promotion et Intégration des Langues Nationales dans les Systèmes Educatifs.* CONFEMEN. Paris: Editions Champion.

Owens, Jonathan. 1985. Arabic dialects of Chad and Nigeria. *Journal of Arabic Linguistics* 14:45–61. Wiesbaden: Harrassowitz.

Painter, Colin. 1966. *Linguistic field notes from Banda and language maps of the Guang speaking areas of Ghana, Togo, and Dahomey.* Institute of African Studies, No. 7. University of Ghana.

Painter, Colin. 1967. The distribution of Guang in Ghana and a statistical pre-testing on twenty-five idiolects. *Journal of West African Languages* 4(1):25–78.

Pallesen, A. Kemp. 1984. Culture contact and language convergence. Ph.D. dissertation. University of California, Berkeley.

Paper, Herbert H., ed. 1978. *Jewish languages: Theme and variation.* Cambridge, Massachusetts: Association for Jewish Studies.

Parker, Gary J. 1976. *Gramática quechua: Ancash-Huaylas.* Lima: Ministerio de Educación.

Parker, Stephen. 1988. Some universal aspects of coalescence processes confirmed by Chamicuro phonology and morphology. M.A. thesis. University of Texas at Arlington.

Parkin, Robert. 1991. *A guide to AA speakers and their languages. Oceanic Linguistics,* Special Publication No. 23. Honolulu: University of Hawaii Press.

Patai, Bridglal, ed. 1972. *The early history of Malawi.* London: Longman.

Pawley, Andrew and Lawrence A. Reid. 1980. The evolution of transitive constructions in Austronesian. In Paz Buenaventura Naylor, ed., *Austronesian studies,* Michigan Papers on South and Southeast Asia 15, pp. 103–130. Ann Arbor: University of Michigan.

Payne, David L. 1978. Phonology and morphology of Axininca (Apurucayali Campa). Ph.D. dissertation. University of Texas at Austin.

Payne, David L. 1985. The genetic classification of Resigaro. *International Journal of American Linguistics* 51:222–231.

Payne, David L. 1987. Some morphological elements of Maipuran Arawakan: Agreement affixes and the genitive construction. *Language Sciences* 9:57–75.

Payne, David L. 1988a. On proposing deep genetic relationships in Amazonian languages: The case of Candoshi and Maipuran Arawakan languages. Presented at the Society for the Study of Indigenous Languages of the Americas.

Payne, David L. 1988b. Una visión panorámica de la familia lingüística arawak. Presented at the Tercer Seminario-Taller para el Estudio Preliminar del Atlas Etnolingüístico Colombiano.

Payne, David L. 1991. A classification of Maipuran (Arawakan) languages based on shared lexical retentions. In Derbyshire and Pullum, eds., pp. 355–499.

Payne, Doris L. 1985a. Aspects of the grammar of Yagua: A typological perspective. Ph.D. dissertation. University of California, Los Angeles.

Payne, Doris L. 1985b. *-ta* in Zaparoan and Peba-Yaguan. *International Journal of American Linguistics* 51:529–531.

Payne, J. R. 1987. Iranian Languages. In Comrie, ed., pp. 514–522.

Payne, Ronald and Kalpana Vora. 1991. Radio brings Latin back from the dead. *The European,* September 27, 1991.

Payne, Thomas E. 1985. Participant coding in Yagua discourse. Ph.D. dissertation. University of California, Los Angeles.

Perrot, Jean, ed. 1981. *Les langues dans le monde ancien et moderne.* Paris: Centre National de la Recherche Scientifique.

Persson, Andrew. 1984. The relationships of the languages of the Sudan. In *Occasional Papers in the Study of Sudanese Languages* 3, pp. 1–5. Juba: University of Juba, SIL, and IRL.

Phillips, Kathleen. 1979. The initial standardization of the Yambeta language. D.E.S. dissertation. University of Yaoundé, Cameroon.

Pinnow, Heinz-Jurgen. 1963. The position of the Munda languages within the Austroasiatic language family. In H. L. Shorto, ed., *Linguistic comparison in South East Asia and the Pacific.* London: School of Oriental and African Studies.

Platiel, S. 1978. Les langues Mandé. In D. Barreteau, ed., *Inventaire des études linguistiques sur les pays d'Afrique noire d'expression française et sur Madagascar.* Paris: Conseil International de la Langue Française.

Podolsky, Baruch. 1985. Notes on the Urum language. *Rovanik Orientalistyczny,* T 44, z.2, pp. 59–66.

Pollet, E. 1971. *La société Soninké (Dyahunn, Mali).* Brussels: Editions de l'Université de Bruxelles.

Polman, Katrien. 1981. *The Central Moluccas: An annotated bibliography.* KITLV Bibliographical Series 12. Dordrecht: Foris Publications.

Polomé, E. C. and C. P. Hill, eds. 1980. *Language in Tanzania.* London: Oxford University Press for the IAI.

Poppe, Nicholas. 1970. *Mongolian language handbook.* Washington: Center for Applied Linguistics.

Prachakij-karacak, Phraya. 1995. *Some languages of Siam,* translated and annotated by David Thomas and Sophana Srichampa. Institute of Language and Culture for Rural Development, Mahidol University.

Prochazka, Theodore Jr. 1988. *Saudi Arabian dialects.* London: Kegan Paul International.

Purnama, Karyono. 1991. *The sociolinguistic pattern of use of Standard Malay in Brunei Darussalam.* Brunei Darussalam: Department of Malay Language and Linguistics, Universiti

Brunei Darussalam (presented at ICAL 6, Honolulu).

Purnell, Herbert C. 1970. Toward a reconstruction of Proto-Miao-Yao. Ph.D. dissertation. Cornell University, Ithaca, New York.

Quackenbush, Edward M. 1988. From Sonsoral to Truk: A dialect chain. Ph.D. dissertation. University of Michigan, Ann Arbor.

Quakenbush, John Stephen. 1989. *Language use and proficiency in a multilingual setting: A sociolinguistic survey of Agutaynen speakers in Palawan, Philippines.* Manila: Linguistic Society of the Philippines.

Ramer, Alexis Manaster. 1995. On the subject of Malagasy imperatives. *Oceanic Linguistics* 34(1):203–210.

Ramponi, E. 1937. Religion and divination of the Logbara tribe of North-Uganda. *Anthropos* 32.

Ramsey, Robert. 1987. *The languages of China.* Princeton: Princeton University Press.

Ravines, Rogger and Rosalía Ávalos de Matos. 1988. *Atlas etnolingüístico del Perú.* Lima: Instituto Andino de Artes Populares del Convenio Andrés Bello, Comisión Nacional del Perú.

Redinha, Jose. 1970. *Distribuição étnica da Província de Angol,* sixth edition. Centro de Informação e Turismo de Angola.

Reesink, G. 1976. Languages of the Aramia River Area. In *Papers in New Guinea Linguistics,* No. 19. Pacific Linguistics A-45, pp. 1–37. Canberra: Australian National University.

Rehg, Kenneth L. and Byron W. Bender. 1988. Lexical transfer from Marshallese to Mokilese: A study in intra-Micronesian borrowing. Presented at the Fifth International Conference on Austronesian Linguistics.

Reid, Lawrence A. n.d. The Alta languages of the Philippines. Honolulu: Social Science Research Institute, University of Hawaii. ms.

Reid, Lawrence A. 1971. *Philippine minor languages: Word lists and phonologies. Oceanic Linguistics,* Special Publication 8.

Reid, Lawrence A. 1982. The demise of Proto-Philippines. In Amran Halim et al., eds., *Papers from the Third International Conference on Austronesian Linguistics,* Vol. 2, *Tracking the travellers.* Pacific Linguistics, C–75, pp. 201–216. Canberra: Australian National University.

Remijsen, Albert C. L. 2001. *Word-prosodic systems of Raja Ampat languages.* The Netherlands: Landelijke Onderzoekschool Taalwetenschap [Netherlands Graduate School of Linguistics].

Rennie, John Keith. 1973. Christianity, colonialism and the origins of nationalism among the Ndau of Mozambique. Ph.D. dissertation. Northwestern University, Chicago

Rensch, Calvin R. 1966. Comparative Otomanguean phonology. Ph.D. dissertation. University of Pennsylvania, Philadelphia.

Rensch, Calvin R. 1968. *Proto Chinantec phonology.* Papeles de la Chinantla 6, Serie Científica 10. México: Museo Nacional de Antropología.

Rensch, Calvin R., Calinda E. Hallberg, and Clare F. O'Leary, eds. 1992. *Hindko and Gujari.*

Sociolinguistic Survey of Northern Pakistan, Vol. 3. Islamabad: National Institute of Pakistan Studies, Quaid-i-Azam University and Summer Institute of Linguistics.

Rensch, Calvin R., Sandra J. Decker, and Daniel G. Hallberg, eds. 1992. *Languages of Kohistan.* Sociolinguistic Survey of Northern Pakistan, Vol. 1. Islamabad: National Institute of Pakistan Studies, Quaid-i-Azam University and Summer Institute of Linguistics.

Report of the Commission of Enquiry into South West African Affairs. 1962–1963. Pretoria.

Ribeiro, Darcy. 1957. Culturas e linguas indígenas do Brasil. *Educação e Ciencias Sociais* 2.6.

Ribeiro, Darcy and Mary Ruth Wise. 1979. *Grupos étnicos de la Amazonía Peruana.* Comunidades y Culturas Peruanas No. 13. Lima: Instituto Lingüístico de Verano.

Rickford, John R. 1974. The insights of the mesolect. In De Camp and Hancock, eds., pp. 92–117.

Ring, Andy. 1997. *Revisiting the Central Volta region. Research Review,* Supplement 12. Legon: Institute of African Studies, University of Ghana.

Riviere, Jean-Claude. 1982. *Situation des langues d'Oc. L'information grammaticale.* Paris 12:13.

Robins, R. H. and E. M. Uhlenbeck, eds. 1991. *Endangered languages.* Oxford: Berg Publishers.

Robles, Carlos. 1964. Investigaciones lingüísticas sobre los grupos indígenas del estado de Baja California. *Anales del Instituto Nacional de Antropología e Historia* 17:275–301.

Rodrigues, Aryon D. 1958. Classification of Tupi-Guarani. *International Journal of American Linguistics* 24:231–234.

Roesler, Calvin. 1972. The phonology of the Ajam dialect of Asmat. M.A. thesis. Hartford Seminary Foundation.

Romaine, Suzanne. 1988. *Pidgin and creole languages.* London: Longman.

Ross, Malcolm D. 1988. *Proto Oceanic and the Austronesian languages of western Melanesia.* Pacific Linguistics C-98. Canberra: Australian National University.

Rottland, Franz. 1981. The segmental morphology of proto-Southern Nilotic. In Schadeberg and Bender, eds., pp. 5–17.

Rottland, Franz. 1983. Southern Nilotic. In Bender, ed., pp. 208–238.

Ruhlen, Merritt. 1975. *A guide to the languages of the world.* Stanford University Language Universals Project.

Ruhlen, Merritt. 1987. *A guide to the world's languages.* Vol. 1, *Classification.* Stanford: Stanford University Press.

Rutkis, J., ed. 1967. *Latvia: Country and people.* Stockholm: Latvian National Foundation.

Sacks, Oliver. 1989. *Seeing voices.* Berkeley: University of California Press.

Saeed, John I. 1982. Central Somali—A grammatical outline. *Afroasiatic Linguistics* 8(2):2–43.

Saenz-Badillos, Angel. 1993. *A history of the Hebrew language.* Cambridge: Cambridge University Press.

Salzner, Richard. 1960. *Sprachenatlas des Indopazifischen Raumes.* Wiesbaden: Otto Harrassowitz.

Samarin, William J. 1971. Adamawa-Eastern. In Sebeok, ed., 1971a, pp. 213–244.

Sandager, Oliver K. 1986. *Sign languages around the world.* North Hollywood: OK Publishing.

Sandefur, John R. 1984. A language coming of age: Kriol of North Australia. M.A. thesis. University of Western Australia, Perth.

Sandefur, John R. 1990. *Kriol and Torres Strait Creole: Where do they meet?* Occasional Bulletin 44. Darwin: Nungalinya College.

Sankoff, Gillian. 1968. Social aspects of multilingualism in New Guinea. Ph.D. dissertation. McGill University.

Sapir, J. David. 1971. West Atlantic: An inventory of the languages, their noun class systems and consonant alternation. In Sebeok, ed., 1971a, pp. 45–58.

Sara, Solomon I. 1974. *A description of modern Chaldean.* The Hague: Mouton.

Sasse, Hans-Jürgen. 1987. Kuschitische Sprachen. *Studium Linguistik* 21:78–99.

Sather, Clifford. 1997. *The Bajau Laut.* Oxford: Oxford University Press.

Schadeberg, Thilo C. 1981a. *A survey of Kordofanian I: Heiban Group.* SUGIA Beiheft I. Hamburg: Buske Verlag.

Schadeberg, Thilo C. 1981b. The classification of the Kadugli language group. In Schadeberg and Bender, eds., pp. 291–305.

Schadeberg, Thilo C. and M. Lionel Bender, eds. 1981. *Nilo-Saharan.* Dordrecht: Foris Publications.

Schenker, A. M. and E. Stankiewicz, eds. 1980. *The Slavic literary languages: Formation and development.* New Haven: Yale Concilium on International and Area Studies.

Schmidt, Annette. 1990. *The loss of Australia's Aboriginal language heritage.* The Institute Report Series. Canberra: Aboriginal Studies Press.

Schooling, Stephen. 1990. *Language maintenance in Melanesia: Sociolinguistics and social networks in New Caledonia.* Summer Institute of Linguistics and the University of Texas at Arlington Publications in Linguistics 91. Dallas.

Schreck, Harley and David Barrett, eds. 1987. *Unreached peoples: Clarifying the task.* Monrovia, California: MARC.

Schütz, Albert J. 1972. *The languages of Fiji.* Oxford: Clarendon.

Scriptures of the world. 1996. New York: United Bible Societies.

Scruggs, Terri R. 1982. Rapport linguistique de l'enquête menée à Bokito. Yaoundé: Société Internationale de Linguistique. ms.

Sebeok, Thomas A., ed. 1963. *Soviet and East European linguistics.* Current Trends in Linguistics, Vol. 1. The Hague: Mouton.

Sebeok, Thomas A., ed. 1967. *Linguistics in East Asia and Southeast Asia.* Current Trends in Linguistics, Vol. 2. The Hague: Mouton.

Sebeok, Thomas A., ed. 1968. *Ibero-American and Caribbean linguistics.* Current Trends in Linguistics, Vol. 4. The Hague: Mouton.

Sebeok, Thomas A., ed. 1969. *Linguistics in South Asia.* Current Trends in Linguistics, Vol. 5. The Hague: Mouton.

Sebeok, Thomas A., ed. 1970. *Southwest Asia and North Africa.* Current Trends in Linguistics, Vol. 6. The Hague: Mouton.

Sebeok, Thomas A., ed. 1971a. *Linguistics in Sub-Saharan Africa.* Current Trends in Linguistics, Vol. 7. The Hague: Mouton.

Sebeok, Thomas A., ed. 1971b. *Linguistics in Oceania.* Current Trends in Linguistics, Vol. 8. The Hague: Mouton.

Sebeok, Thomas A., ed. 1977. *Native languages of the Americas,* Vols. 1, 2. New York: Plenum.

Seidensticker, Wilhelm and Gizachew Adamu. 1986. *A bibliographical guide to Borno studies 1821–1983.* Maiduguri: University of Maiduguri.

Shackle, C. 1979. Problems of classification in Pakistan Punjab. *Transaction of the Philological Society,* pp. 191–210.

Shackle, C. 1980. Hindko in Kohat and Peshawar. *Bulletin of the School of Oriental and African Studies* 43(3):482–510.

Shafer, Robert. 1955. Classification of the Sino-Tibetan languages. *Word* 11:94–111.

Shapiro, Michael C. and Harold F. Schiffman. 1981. *Language and society in South Asia.* Delhi: Motilal Banarsidass.

Sharma, Jagdish Chander. 1971. Pronouns in Gade Lohar dialect. In H. S. Biligiri, ed., *Papers and talks.* Mysore: Central Institute of Indian Languages.

Sharma, Jagdish Chander. 1982. *Gojri grammar.* Mysore: Central Institute of Indian Linguistics.

Shashi, Padma Shri S. S., ed. 1994. *Encyclopedia of Indian tribes.* New Delhi: Anmol Publications.

Shaw, R. D. 1973. A tentative classification of the languages of the Mt. Bosavi Region. *Pacific Linguistics Series C,* 26:187–215.

Shaw, R. D. 1981. The Bosavi language family: An interim report. Presented at the 1981 Congress of the Linguistic Society of Papua New Guinea.

Shellabear, W. G. 1913. Baba Malay, an introduction to the language of the Straits-born Chinese. *Journal of the Royal Asiatic Society (Straits Branch)* 65:49–63.

Shibatani, Masayoshi. 1990. *The languages of Japan.* Cambridge: Cambridge University Press.

Shnukal, Annette. 1982. Why Torres Strait "Broken English" is not English. In Jeanie Bell, ed., *Aboriginal languages and the question of a national language policy,* pp. 25–35. Alice Springs, Northwest Territories: Aboriginal Language Association.

Showalter, Stuart D. 1991. Surveying sociolinguistic aspects of interethnic contact in rural Burkina Faso: An adaptive methodological approach. Ph.D. dissertation. Georgetown University, Washington, D.C.

Siegel, Jeff. 1991. Language maintenance of Overseas Hindi. *Anuario del seminario de filologica vasca "Julio de Urquijo"* 25(2):91–114.

Silzer, Peter J., Heljä Heikkinen, and Duane Clouse. 1986. *Peta lokasi bahasa-bahasa daerah di propinsi Irian Jaya,* Seri D, No. 1. Jayapura: Program Kerjasama Universitas Cenderawasih and Summer Institute of Linguistics.

Simmons-McDonald, Hazel. 1994. Comparative patterns in the acquisition of English negation by native speakers of (St. Lucian) French Creole and English. *Language Learning* 44(1):29–74.

Simons, Gary F. 1979. *Language variation and limits to communication,* Technical Report No. 3., NSF Grant No. BNS 76–06031. DMLL, Cornell University.

Simons, Gary F. 1982. Word taboo and comparative Austronesian linguistics. *Pacific Linguistics* C-76, pp. 157–226. Canberra: Australian National University.

Simons, Linda. 1983. A comparison of the pidgins of Solomon Islands and Papua New Guinea. In *Papers in Pidgin and Creole Linguistics,* No. 3. Pacific Linguistics A-65, pp. 121–137. Canberra: Australian National University.

Singh, K. S. 1994. *The scheduled tribes.* Anthropological Survey of India. Calcutta: Oxford University Press.

Singh, K. S. 1995. *The scheduled castes.* Anthropological Survey of India. Calcutta: Oxford University Press.

Singh, K. S. 2003. *People of India: Assam,* Vol. XV. Calcutta: Seagull Books.

Singh, Nagendra. 1972. *Bhutan: A kingdom in the Himalayas.* New Delhi: Thomson.

Sirk, Ü. 1981. The South Sulawesi group and neighbouring languages. *Indonesia Circle* 25:29–36.

Sirk, Ü. 1983. *The Buginese language.* Moscow: Nauka Publishing House.

Smalley, W. A. ed. 1976. *Phonemes and orthography: Language planning in ten minority languages of Thailand.* Canberra: Department of Linguistics, Research School of Pacific Linguistics, Australian National University.

Smedal, Olaf H. 1987. *Lom – Indonesia – English and English – Lom Wordlists accompanied by four Lom Texts.* NUSA: Linguistic Studies of Indonesian and Other Languages in Indonesia, Vol. 28/29. Jakarta: Badan Penyelenggaraan Seri Nusa, Universitas Katolik Indonesia Atma Jaya.

Smieja, Birgit. 2002. *Language pluralism in Botswana—hope or hurdle: A sociolinguistic survey on language use and language attitudes in Botswana with special reference to the status and use of English.* Frankfurt: Peter Lang.

Smith, Kenneth D. 1968. Sedang dialects. M.A. thesis. University of North Dakota, Grand Forks.

Smith, Kenneth D. 1972. *A phonological reconstruction of Proto-North-Bahnaric.* Language Data-Asia Pacific Studies 3. Santa Ana: Summer Institute of Linguistics.

Smith, Kenneth D. 1973. Eastern north Bahnaric: Cua and Kotua. *Mon-Khmer Studies* 4:113–118.

Sneddon, J. N., comp. 1981. Southern Part of Celebres (Sulawesi). In Wurm and Hattori, eds., No. 44.

Sneddon, J. N. 1988. The position of Lolak. Presented at the Fifth International Congress of Austronesian Linguistics.

Sneddon, J. N. 1989. The north Sulawesi microgroups: In search of higher level connections. In James N. Sneddon, ed., *Studies in Sulawesi Linguistics: Part I.* NUSA, Linguistic Studies in Indonesian and Languages in Indonesia, Vol. 31, pp. 83–107. Jakarta: Badan Penyelenggara Seri Nusa, Universitas Katolik Indonesia Atma Jaya.

Sneddon, J. N. 1993. The drift towards final open syllables in Sulawesi languages. *Oceanic Linguistics* 32: 1–44.

Sobelman, Harvey, ed. 1962. *Arabic dialect studies: A selected bibliography.* Washington, D.C.: Center for Applied Linguistics and Middle East Institute.

Soto Ruiz, Clodoaldo. 1976. *Gramática quechua: Ayacucho-Chanca.* Lima: Ministerio de Educación.

Southall, A. W. 1956. *Alur society.* Cambridge: W. Seffer & Sons.

Sperl, Savitri Rambissoon.1980. From Indians to Trinidadians: A study of the relationship between language, behaviour, socio-economic and cultural factors in a Trinidad village. Ph. D. dissertation. University of York.

Sreedhar, M. V. 1974. *Naga Pidgin: A sociolinguistic study of inter-lingual communication pattern in Nagaland.* Mysore: Central Institute of Indian Languages.

Staalsen, P. 1975. The languages of the Sawos Region. *Anthropos* 70:6–16.

Stahl, Wilmar. 1982, 1986. *Escenario indígena chaqueño pasado y presente.* Filadelfia, Paraguay: Asociación de Servicios de Cooperación Indígena-Menonita.

Stallcup, Kenneth l. 1980a. La géographie linguistique des Grassfields. In Hyman and Voorhoeve, eds., pp. 43–57.

Stallcup, Kenneth I. 1980b. The Momo languages. In Hyman and Voorhoeve, eds., pp. 194–223.

Stallcup, Kenneth I. 1980c. Noun classes in Esimbi. In Larry M. Hyman, ed., *Noun classes in the Grassfields Bantu borderland.* Southern California Occasional Papers in Linguistics No. 8. Los Angeles: University of Southern California.

Stampe, David L., ed. 1965. Recent work in Munda linguistics, Part I. Abstracts and Translations. *International Journal of American Linguistics* 31(1):332–341.

Stampe, David L., ed. 1966a. Recent work in Munda linguistics, Part II. Abstracts and Translations. *International Journal of American Linguistics* 32(1):74–80.

Stampe, David L., ed. 1966b. Recent work in Munda linguistics, Part III. Abstracts and Translations.

International Journal of American Linguistics 32(2):164–168.

Stampe, David L., ed. 1966c. Recent work in Munda linguistics, Part IV. Abstracts and Translations. *International Journal of American Linguistics* 32(4):390–397.

Stanley, George Edward. 1968. The indigenous languages of South West Africa. *Anthropological Linguistics* 10:5–18.

Stephens, Meic. 1976. *Linguistic minorities in western Europe.* Llandysul, Wales: Gomer.

Stevenson, Roland C. 1956. A survey of the phonetics and grammatical structure of the Nuba Mountain languages, with particular reference to Otoro, Katcha and Nyimang. *Afrika und Ubersee* 40:110–112.

Stevenson, Roland C. 1981. Adjectives in Nyimang, with special reference to *k*- and *t*- prefixes. In Schadeberg and Bender, eds., pp. 151–165.

Stevenson, Roland C. 1984. *The Nuba people of Kordofan Province An ethnographic survey.* Khartoum: Graduate College, University of Khartoum.

Steward, Julian Haynes, ed. 1946–1959. *Handbook of South American Indians,* 7 vols. Washington, D.C.: U.S. Government Printing Office.

Stewart, John Massie. 1971. Niger-Congo, Kwa. In Sebeok, ed., 1971a, pp. 179–212.

Stewart, William A. 1962. Creole languages of the Caribbean. In Frank A. Rice, ed., *Study of the role of second languages in Asia, Africa, and Latin America,* pp. 34–53. Washington, D.C.: Center for Applied Linguistics of the Modern Language Association of America.

Stigand, C. H. 1925. *Equatoria: The Lado Enclave,* pp. 19, 89. London: Constable & Co.

Stilo, D. L. 1981. The Tati languages group in the sociolinguistic context of Northwestern Iran and Transcaucasia. *Iranian Studies* 14(3–4):137–187.

Stokes, J. F. G. 1965. Language in Rapa. *Journal of the Polynesian Society* 64:315–340.

Stokoe, William and Rolf Kuschel. 1979. *A field guide for sign language research.* Silver Spring: Linstok Press.

Stoltzfus, Ronald Dean. 1974. Toward defining centers for indigenous literature programs: A problem of language communication. M.A. thesis. Cornell University, Ithaca, New York.

Strand, Richard F. 1973. Notes on the Nuristani and Dardic languages. *Journal of the American Oriental Society* 93(3):297–305.

Strecker, David. 1987. The Hmong-Mien languages. *Linguistics of the Tibeto-Burman Area* 10(2):1–11.

Strecker, David. 1989. Hmongic noun prefixes. Presented at the Linguistic Society of America Annual Meeting, December 1989.

Sun Hongkai, Lu Shaozun, Zhang Jichuan, and Ouyang Jueya. 1980. *The languages of the Menba, Luoba, and Deng peoples.* Beijing: Chinese Social Science Publishing House.

Sun, Tianshin Jackson. 1993. A historical-comparative study of the Tan (Mirish) branch in Tibeto-Burman. Ph.D. dissertation. University of California, Berkeley.

Susnik, Branislava. 1986–1987. *Los aborígenes del Paraguay, VII/1, Lenguas chaqueñas.* Asunción: Museo Etnográfico "Andres Barbero."

Swift, Jeremy. 1975. *The Sahara.* Amsterdam: Time-Life International.

Taber, Mark. 1993. Towards a better understanding of the languages of Maluku. *Oceanic Linguistics* 32.2.

Tarpent, Marie-Lucie and Daythal Kendall. 1998. On the relationship between Takelma and Kalapuyan: Another look at 'Takelman'. Paper presented at the Society for the Study of the Indigenous Languages of the American, January 1998, New York.

Tax, Sol. 1960. Aboriginal languages of Latin America. *Current Anthropology* 1:430–436.

Taylor, Brian K. 1962. *The Western Lacustrine Bantu.* London: International African Institute.

Taylor, Carrie. 1982. Les langues de l'arrondissement de Bokito: Esquisse d'une enquête sociolinguistique. Yaoundé: Société Internationale de Linguistique. ms.

Taylor, Douglas. 1977. *Languages of the West Indies.* Baltimore: Johns Hopkins University Press.

Taylor, Paul. 1991. *The folk biology of the Tobelo people: A study in folk classification.* Washington, D.C.: Smithsonian Institution Press.

Teeuw, A. 1961. *A critical survey of studies on Malay and Bahasa Indonesia.* Bibliographical Series No. 5. The Hague: Martinus Nijhoff.

Thelwall, Robin, ed. 1978. *Aspects of language in the Sudan.* Occasional Papers in Linguistics and Language Learning, No. 5. Coleraine: New University of Ulster.

Thelwall, Robin. 1981. Lexicostatistical subgrouping and lexical reconstruction of the Daju group. In Schadeberg and Bender, eds., pp. 167–185.

Thelwall, Robin. 1983. Meidob Nubian: Phonology, grammatical notes and basic vocabulary. In Bender, pp. 97–113.

Thelwall, Robin. 1983. Twampa phonology. In Bender, ed., pp. 323–335.

Thieberger, N., comp. 1990. *Handbook of South Western Australian languages south of the Kimberley regions.* Port Hedland, WA: Pilbara Aboriginal Language Centre.

Thiessen, Jack. 1963. *Studien zum deutschsprachigen Wortschatz der kanadischen Mennoniten.* Marburg: Elwert Verlag.

Thomas, Bertram. n.d. Four strange tongues from south Arabia: The Hadara group. *Proceedings of the British Academy,* Vol. XXIII. London: Humphrey Milford Amen House EC.

Thomas, David D. 1966. Mon-Khmer subgroupings in Vietnam. In N. Zide, ed., *Studies in comparative Austroasiatic linguistics,* pp. 194–202. The Hague: Mouton.

Thomas, David D. 1969. Mon-Khmer in North Vietnam. *Mon-Khmer Studies* 3:74–75.

Thomas, David D. 1976. South Bahnaric and other Mon-Khmer numeral systems. *Linguistics* 174:65–80.

Thomas, David D. 1980. The place of Alak, Tampuan, and West Bahnaric. *Mon-Khmer Studies* 8:171–186.

Thomas, David D. and Robert K. Headley, Jr. 1970. More on Mon-Khmer subgroupings. *Lingua* 25:398–418.

Thomas, Jacqueline M. C. and Serge Bahuchet, eds. 1983. *Encyclopedia des Pygmées Aka.* Paris: SELAF.

Thompson, E. David. 1983. Kunama: Phonology and noun phrase. In Bender, ed., pp. 281–322.

Tiendrebeogo, Gerard. 1983. *Langues et groupes ethniques de Haute Volta.* Abidjan: Institut de Linguistique Appliquee et l'Agence de Cooperation Culturelle et Technique.

Tiendrebeogo, Gerard and Zakaria Yago. 1983. *Situation des langues parlees en Haute Volta.* Abidjan: Institut de Linguistique Appliquee et l'Agence de Cooperaqtion Culturelle et Technique.

Tippett, A. R. 1970. *Peoples of Southwest Ethiopia.* Pasadena: William Carey Library.

Titiev, Mischa. 1951. *Araucanian culture in transition.* Occasional Contributions from the Museum of Anthropology of the University of Michigan, No. 15. Ann Arbor: University of Michigan Press.

Toba, Sueyoshi. 1976. National language and ethnic minority languages in Nepal. In *Symposium Nepal,* 1975, Vol. 4, pp. 30–36. Japan-Nepal Society. [in Japanese]

Toba, Sueyoshi. 1983. A phonological reconstruction of Proto-Northern Rai. M.A. thesis. University of Texas at Arlington.

Toba, Sueyoshi. 1991. *A bibliography of Nepalese languages and linguistics.* Kathmandu: Linguistic Society of Nepal.

Todd, Evelyn. M. 1975. The Solomon language family. In Wurm, ed., pp. 805–846.

Todd, Loreto and Ian Hancock. 1986. *International English Usage.* London: Croom Helm.

Torero, Alfredo F. 1970. Lingüística e historia de la sociedad andina. *Anales Científicos* 8(3–4):231–264.

Tovar, Antonio. 1961. *Catálogo de las lenguas de América del Sur.* Buenos Aires: Editorial Sudamérica.

Tovar, Antonio. 1966. Notas de campo sobre el idioma Chorote. In *XXXVI Congreso Internacional de Americanistas, España 1964: Actas y Memorias,* Tomo 2. Sevilla.

Tran Tri Doi. 1996. The languages that constitute the Viet-Muong group. *Ngon-Ngu* 3:28–34. Hanoi: The Linguistics Institute of Vietnam.

Travis, Edgar W. 1986. *A lexicostatistic survey of the languages indigenous to Ambon Island.* Ambon: Pattimura University and the Summer Institute of Linguistics.

Troike, Rudolph C. 1969. The glottochronology of six Turkic languages. *International Journal of American Linguistics* 35:183–191.

Troike, Rudolph C. 1970. The linguistic classi-fication of Cochimí. Paper presented at the Hokan Conference, University of California, San Diego.

Trudgill, Peter and G. A. Tzavaras. 1977. Why Albanian-Greeks are not Albanians. In Howard Giles, ed., *Language, ethnicity and intergroup relations.* London: Academic Press, chapter 7.

Tryon, Darrell T. 1971. The contemporary language situation in the New Hebrides. Presented at the 28th International Congress of Orientalists.

Tryon, Darrell T. 1976. *New Hebrides languages: An internal classification.* Pacific Linguistics C-50. Canberra: Australian National University.

Tryon, Darrell T. 1978. The languages of the New Hebrides: Internal and external relationships. In S. A. Wurm and Lois Carrington, eds., *Second International Conference on Austronesian Languages: Proceedings,* Fascicle 1. Pacific Linguistics C-61, pp. 877–902. Canberra: Australian National University.

Tryon, Darrell T. 1981. Towards a classification of Solomon Islands languages. Presented at Third International Conference of Austronesian Linguistics.

Tryon, Darrell T, ed. 1995. *Comparative Austronesian dictionary: An introduction to Austronesian studies,* Parts 1–4. Berlin: Mouton de Gruyter.

Tryon, D. T. and B. D. Hackman. 1983. *Solomon Islands languages: An internal classification.* Pacific Linguistics C-72. Canberra: Australian National University.

Tsuchida, Shigeru. 1976. *Reconstruction of Proto-Tsouic phonology.* Tokyo: Institute of Asian and African Languages and Cultures, University of Foreign Language.

Tucker, Archibald N. 1967 (1940). *The Eastern Sudanic languages.* Vol. 1. London: Dawsons for IAI.

Tucker, Archibald N. and M. A. Bryan. 1957. *Linguistic survey of the northern Bantu borderland.* London: Oxford University Press.

Tucker, Archibald N. and M. A. Bryan. 1966. *The non-Bantu languages of North-Eastern Africa.* Handbook of African Languages, Part III. Oxford: Oxford University Press.

T'ung-ho, Tung et al. 1964. *A descriptive study of the Tsou language, Formosa.* Taipei: Institute of History and Philology, Academia Sinica.

Turnbull, Colin M. 1972. *The mountain people.* New York: Simon & Schuster.

Tuttle, Edward F. 1988. Review of Glauco Sanga, *Dialettologia Lombarda, Lingue e culture popolari.* Pavia: Universita di Pavia, Dipartimento di Scienza della Letterature (Aurora Edizione) 1984. *Language* 64:208–209.

Ubels, Edward H. 1975. An historical-comparative study of some West Bamileke dialects. M.A. thesis. University of Toronto.

Uhlenbeck, E. M. 1964. *A critical survey of studies on the languages of Java and Madura.* Bibliographical Series No. 7. The Hague: Martinus Nijhoff.

United Bible Societies. 1978–1997. *World translations progress reports and supplements.* London: United Bible Societies.

Unseth, Peter. 1988. The validity and unity of the 'Southeast Surma' language grouping. *Northeast African Studies* 10(2–3):151–163.

Unseth, Peter. 1990. *Linguistic bibliography of the non-Semitic languages of Ethiopia.* Ethiopian Series Monograph 20. East Lansing and Addis Ababa: African Studies Center, Michigan State University and Institute of Ethiopian Studies, Addis Ababa University.

Urvoy, Y. 1942. *Petit atlas ethno-demographique du Soudan entre Sénégal et Tchad.* Mémoire de L'IFAN No. 5. Paris V: Librairie Larose.

Valenzuela, Pilar. 1988. Clasificación de iñapari. Presented at the Symposium on Arawakan Linguistics, Forty-sixth International Congress of Americanists.

Van Cleve, John. 1986. *Encyclopedia of deaf people and deafness.* Washington, D.C.: Gallaudet University.

Van den Berg, Rene. 1991. Muna dialects and Munic languages: Towards a recontruction. In Ray Harlow, ed., *VICAL 2: Western Austronesian and contact languages: Papers from the Fifth International Conference on Austronesian Linguistics,* pp. 21–51. Auckland: Linguistic Society of New Zealand.

Van der Merwe, I. J. and L. O. van Niekerk. 1994. *Language in South Africa: Distribution and change.* Stellenbosch: Dept. of Geography, University of Stellenbosch.

Van Driem, George. 1993. *The grammar of Dzongkha.* Dzongkha Development Commission, Royal Government of Bhutan.

VanBulck, Gaston and Peter Hackett. 1956. Report of the eastern team (Oubangui to Great Lakes). In *Linguistic Survey of the Northern Bantu Borderland 1,* pp. 63–122. London: Oxford University Press for International Africa Institute.

Vanderaa, Larry. 1991. *A survey for Christian Reformed World Missions of missions and churches in West Africa.* Grand Rapids: Christian Reformed World Missions.

Vansina, J. 1966. *Regions culturelles du Congo. Introduction à l'ethnolographic du Congo.* Brussels: Centre de Recherche et d'Information Sociopolitiques.

Vérin, Pierre, Conrad P. Kottak and Peter Gorlin. 1969. The glottochronology of Malagasy speech communities. *Oceanic Linguistics* 8(1): 26–83.

Visser, Hessel. 2000. Language and cultural empowerment of the Khoesan people: The Naro experience. In Herman M. Batibo and Birgit Smieja, eds., *Botswana: The future of the minority languages,* pp. 193–215. Frankfurt: Peter Lang.

Vitale, A. J. 1980. Kisetla: linguistic and sociolinguistic aspects of a Pidgin Swahili of Kenya. *Anthropological Linguistics* 22(2):47–65.

Voegelin, C. F. and F. M. Voegelin. 1965a. *Languages of the world: Sino-Tibetan,* Fascicle 4. *Anthropological Linguistics* 7.5 (May 1965).

Voegelin, C. F. and F. M. Voegelin. 1965b. *Languages of the world: Sino-Tibetan,* Fascicle 5. *Anthropological Linguistics* 7.6 (June 1965).

Voegelin, C. F. and F. M. Voegelin. 1965c. *Languages of the world: Indo-European,* Fascicle 1. *Anthropological Linguistics* 7.8 (November 1965).

Voegelin, C. F. and F. M. Voegelin. 1977. *Classification and index of the world's languages.* New York: Elsevier North Holland.

Voeltz, Erhardt. 1979. The languages and dialects of the Southwest Province of Cameroon. Presented at the Tenth Annual Conference on African Linguistics, University of Illinois, Urbana.

Von Fuerer-Haimendorf, Christoph. 1985. *Tribes of India: The struggle for survival.* Delhi: Oxford University Press.

Voorhoeve, C. L. 1968. The Central and South New Guinea Phylum. In *Papers in New Guinea Linguistics,* No. 8. Pacific Linguistics A-16, pp. 1–17. Canberra: Australian National University.

Voorhoeve, C. L. 1975. *Languages of Irian Jaya: Checklist, preliminary classification, language maps, word lists.* Pacific Linguistics B-31. Canberra: Australian National University.

Voorhoeve, P. 1955. *A critical survey of studies on the languages of Sumatra.* Bibliographical Series No. 1. The Hague: Martinus Nijhoff.

Voroshil, Q. 1972. On the trilingualism of the Udi. In *Problems of Bilingualism and Multilingualism.* Moscow.

Vossen, Rainier. 1981. *The Eastern Nilotes: Linguistic and historical reconstructions.* Köln: University of Köln.

Vossen, Rainier. 1983. Comparative Eastern Nilotic. In Bender, pp. 177–207.

Vydrine, Valentin. 2000. Review of Raimund Kastenholz, Sprachgeschichte im West-Mande: Methoden und Rekonstruktionen. *Journal of African Languages and Linguistics* 21(1):106–118.

Wagner, C. Peter and Edward R. Dayton, eds. 1979–1984. *Unreached peoples.* Elgin, Illinois: David C. Cook.

Walker, Dale F. 1976. *A grammar of the Lampung language: The Pesisir dialect of Way Lima.* NUSA, Linguistic Studies in Indonesian and Languages in Indonesia, Vol 2. Jakarta: Badan Penyelenggara Seri Nusa.

Walton, Janice R. and David C. Moody. 1984. The east coast Bajau languages. In King and King, eds., pp. 113–123.

Wang Fushi. 1985. *Sketch of the Miao language.* Beijing: Nationalities Publishing House.

Ward, Jack. 1969. *Working Papers No. 4.* Honolulu: Department of Linguistics, University of Hawaii.

Wares, Alan C. 1965. A comparative study of Yuman consonantism. Ph.D. dissertation. University of Texas, Austin and 1968 The Hague: Mouton.

Wares, Alan C. 1979, 1985, 1986. *Bibliography of the Summer Institute of Linguistics 1935–1985,* Vols. 1–3. Dallas: Summer Institute of Linguistics.

Waters, Bruce. 1989. Djinang and Djinba: *A grammatical and historical perspective.* Pacific Linguistics C-114. Canberra: Australian National University.

Watters, John R. 1981. A phonology and morphology of Ejagham—with notes on dialect variation. Ph.D. dissertation. University of California, Los Angeles.

Welmers, William E. 1971a. Checklist of language and dialect names. In Sebeok, ed., 1971a, pp. 759–900.

Welmers, William E. 1971b. Christian missions and language policies. In Sebeok, ed., 1971a, pp. 559–569.

Welmers, William E. 1971c. Niger-Congo, Mande. In Sebeok, ed., 1971a, pp. 113–140.

Welmers, William E. 1973. *African language structures.* Berkeley: University of California Press.

Westermann, Diedrich and M. A. Bryan. 1970. *Handbook of African languages,* Part II. Folkestone: Dawsons.

Whinnom, Keith. 1956. *Spanish contact vernaculars in the Philippine Islands.* Hong Kong: Hong Kong University Press.

White, John Claude. 1971. *Sikhim and Bhutan: Twenty-one years on the North-East Frontier (1887–1908).* Delhi: Vivek.

Whiteford, Scott. 1981. *Workers from the north.* Austin: University of Texas Press.

Whiteley, Wilfred H. 1969. *Swahili: The rise of a national language.* London: Methuen & Co.

Whiteley, Wilfred H., ed. 1974. *Language in Kenya.* Nairobi: Oxford University Press, Dar es Salaam.

Widlok, Thomas. 1997. Akhoe pragmatics, Haiom identity and the Khoekhoe language. In Haacke and Elderkin, eds., pp. 117–153.

Williams, Gordon, ed. 1993. *Enquête sociolinguistique sur les langues Cangin de la région de Thiès au Sénégal.* Cahiers de Recherche Linguistique No. 3. Dakar: Société Internationale de Linguistique.

Williamson, Kay. 1971. The Benue-Congo languages and Ijo. In Sebeok, ed., 1971a, pp. 245–306.

Willamson, Kay and Roger Blench. 2000. Niger Congo. In Bernd Heine and Derek Nurse, eds., *African languages: An introduction,* pp. 10–42. Cambridge: Cambridge University Press.

Willis, Roy G. 1966. *The Fipa and related peoples of southwest Tanzania and northeast Zambia.* London: International African Institute.

Wilson, Darryl. 1969. The Binandere language family. *Papers in New Guinea Linguistics,* No. 9. Pacific Linguistics A-18, pp. 65–85. Canberra: Australian National University.

Wimbish, John. 1989. *WORDSURV: A program for analyzing language survey word lists.* Occasional Publications in Academic Computing 13. Dallas: Summer Institute of Linguistics.

Winer, Lise. 1993. *Varieties of English around the world: Trinidad and Tobago.* Amsterdam: John Benjamins.

Winsa, Birger. 1998. *Language attitudes and social identity—Oppression and revival of a minority language in Sweden.* Canberra: Applied Linguistics Association of Australia.

Wise, Mary Ruth. 1976. Apuntes sobre la influencia Inca entre los amuesha: Factor que oscurece la clasificación de su idioma. *Revista del Museo Nacional* XLII:355–366.

Wise, Mary Ruth. 1983. Lenguas indígenas de la Amazonía Peruana: Historia y estado presente. *América Indígena* 43(4):823–848.

Wise, Mary Ruth. 1988. Comparative morphosyntax and subgrouping of Maipuran Arawakan languages. Presented at the Symposium on Arawakan Linguistics, 46th International Congress of Americanists.

Wise, Mary Ruth. 1990. Valence-changing affixes in Maipuran Arawakan languages. In Doris Payne, ed., *Amazonian linguistics: Studies in lowland South American languages,* pp. 86–116. Austin: University of Texas Press.

Wismann, Lynn and Margaret Walsh. 1987. *Signs of Morocco.* U.S. Peace Corps.

Wittmann, Henri, ed. 1991. *Les langues Signées. Revue québécoise de linguistique théorique et appliquée* 10.1.

Wonderly, William L. and Eugene A. Nida. 1963. Linguistics and Christian missions. *Anthropological Linguistics* 5:104–144.

World Almanac and Book of Facts. 1999. Mahwah, N.J.: World Almanac Books.

World Christian encyclopedia: A comparative study of churches and religions in the modern world A.D. 1900–2000. Barrett, David B., ed. 1982. Nairobi: Oxford University Press.

Wurm, Stephen A. 1961. The linguistic situation in the Highlands Districts of Papua and New Guinea. *Australian Territories* 1(2):14–23.

Wurm, Stephen A. 1971. The Papuan linguistic situation. In Sebeok, ed., 1971b, pp. 541–657.

Wurm, Stephen A. 1972. *Languages of Australia and Tasmania.* Janua Linguarum, Series Critica, 1. The Hague: Mouton.

Wurm, Stephen A., ed. 1975. *Papuan languages and the New Guinea linguistic scene. New Guinea area languages and language study,* Vol. 1. Pacific Linguistics Series C-38. Canberra: Australian National University.

Wurm, Stephen A. and Shirô Hattori, eds. 1981. *Language atlas of the Pacific area.* Canberra: The Australian Academy of the Humanities in collaboration with the Japan Academy.

Wurm, Stephen A., B. T'sou, D. Bradley, Li Rong, Xiong Zhenghui, Zhang Zehnxing, Fu Maoji, Wang Jun, Dob, eds. 1987. *Language atlas of China,* Parts 1, 2. Pacific Linguistics C-102. Hong Kong: Longman Group Ltd.

Young, Colville N. 1973. Belize Creole: A study of the creolized English spoken in the city of Belize, in its social and cultural setting. Ph.D. dissertation. University of York.

Young, Oliver Gordon. 1962. *The hilltribes of northern Thailand,* second edition. Siam Society Monograph 1. Bangkok

Zavadovskii, Yurii Nikolaevich. 1962. *The Arabic dialects of the Maghrib.* Moscow: The Publishing House of Eastern Literature. [in Russian]

Zeshan, Ulrike. 2000. *Sign language in Indo-Pakistan: A description of a signed language.* Amsterdam: John Benjamins.

Z'Graggen, J. A. 1969. *Classificatory and typological studies in languages of the western Madang District New Guinea.* Canberra: Australian National University.

Z'Graggen, J. A. 1971. *Classificatory and typological studies in languages of the Madang District.* Pacific Linguistics C-19. Canberra: Australian National University.

Z'Graggen, J. A. 1975. *The languages of the Madang District, Papua New Guinea.* Pacific Linguistics B-41. Canberra: Australian National University.

Zhao Xiangru and Reinhard F. Hahn. 1989. The Ili Turk people and their language. *Central Asiatic Journal* 33:3–4.

Zorc, R. David. 1986. The genetic relationships of Philippine languages. In Paul Geraghty, Lois Carrington, and S. A. Wurm, eds., *FOCAL II: Papers from the Fourth International Conference on Austronesian Linguistics.* Pacific Linguistics C-94, pp. 147–173. Canberra: Australian National University.

Part II
Language Maps

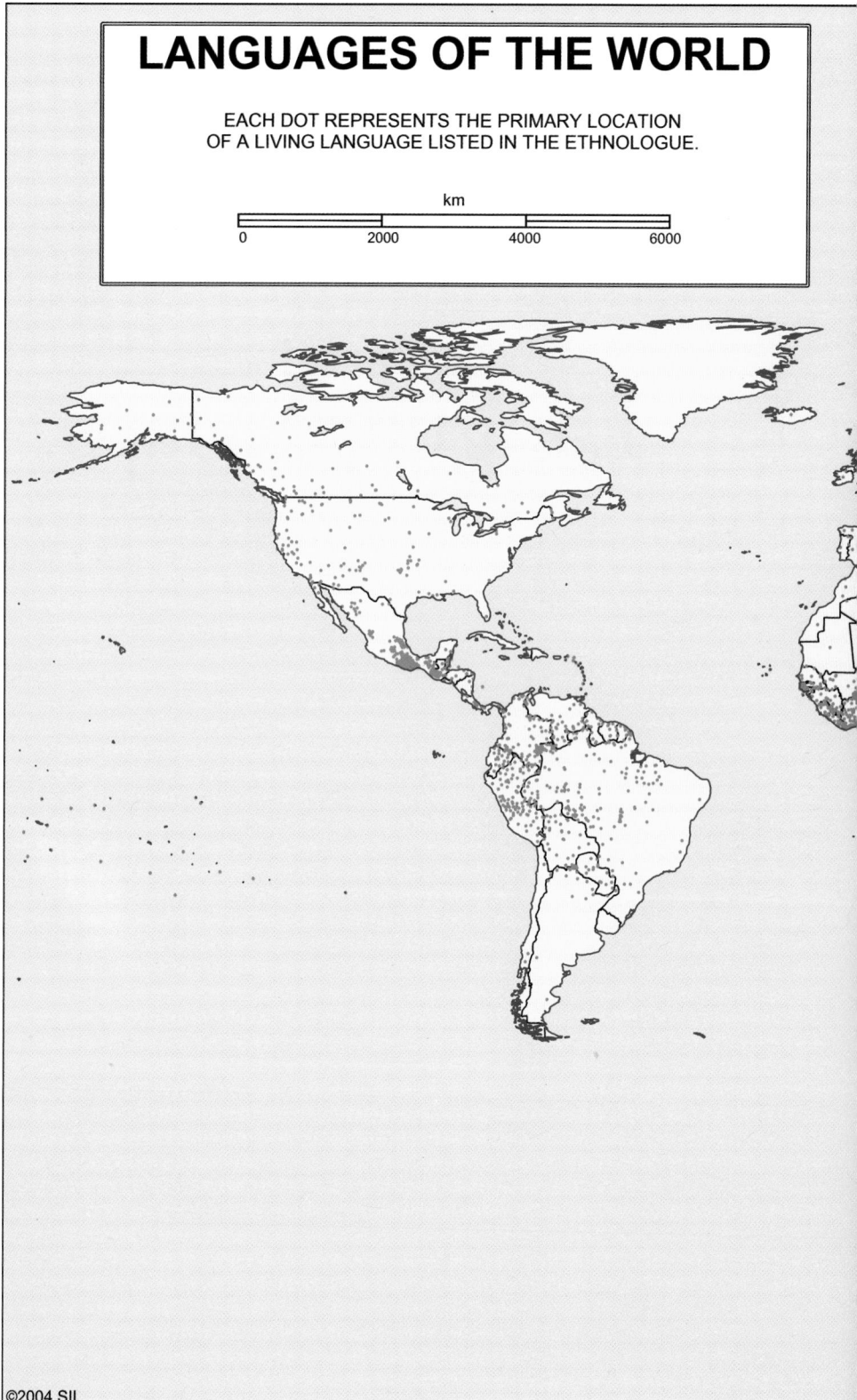

LANGUAGES OF THE WORLD

EACH DOT REPRESENTS THE PRIMARY LOCATION
OF A LIVING LANGUAGE LISTED IN THE ETHNOLOGUE.

km

| 0 | 2000 | 4000 | 6000 |

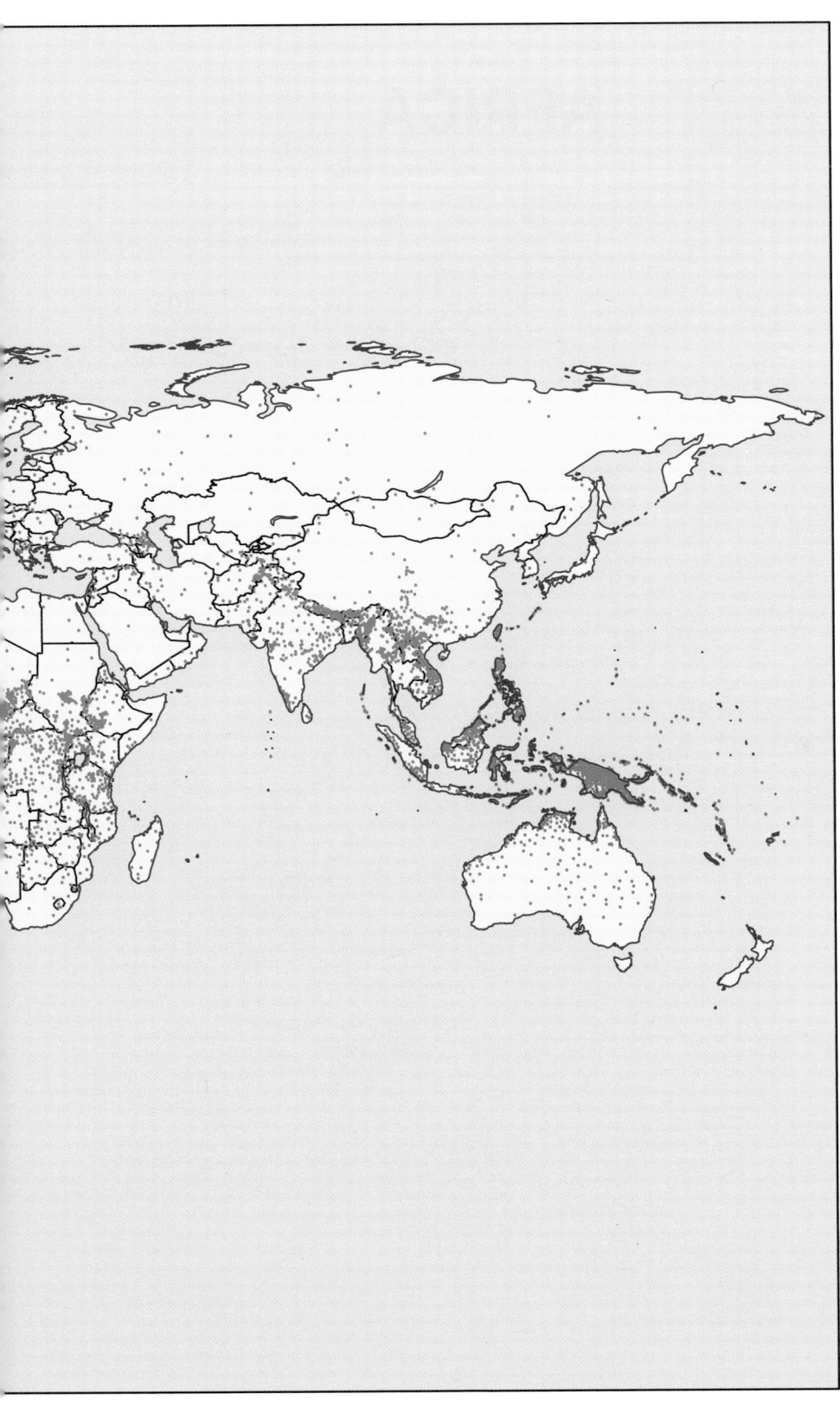

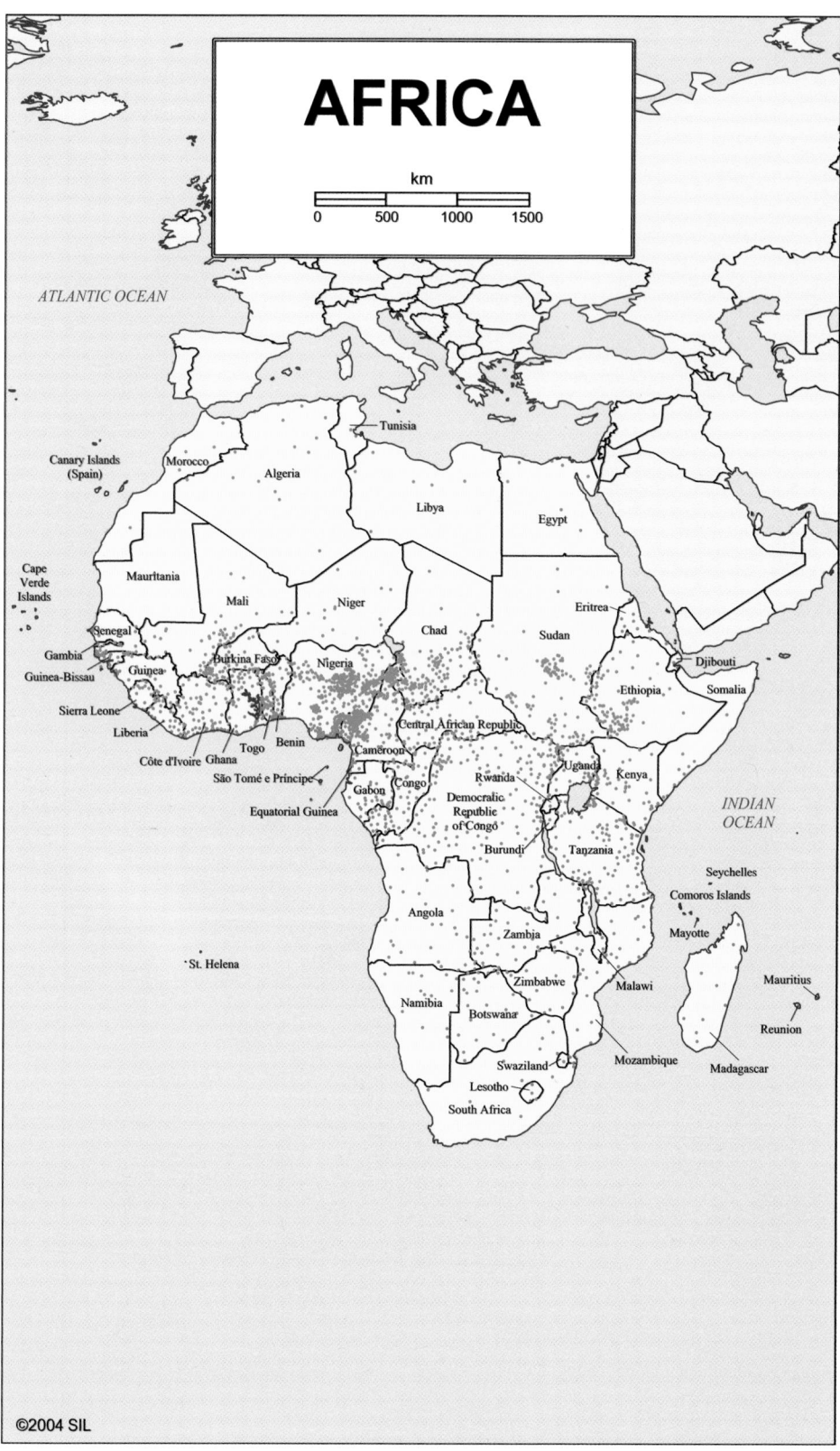

AFRICA

km

| 0 | 500 | 1000 | 1500 |

ATLANTIC OCEAN

Tunisia

Canary Islands
(Spain)

Morocco

Algeria

Libya

Egypt

Cape
Verde
Islands

Mauritania

Mali

Niger

Chad

Sudan

Eritrea

Senegal

Gambia

Guinea-Bissau

Guinea

Burkina Faso

Nigeria

Djibouti

Ethiopia

Somalia

Sierra Leone

Liberia

Côte d'Ivoire

Ghana

Togo

Benin

Cameroon

Central African Republic

São Tomé e Príncipe

Gabon

Congo

Rwanda

Uganda

Kenya

Equatorial Guinea

Democratic
Republic
of Congo

INDIAN
OCEAN

Burundi

Tanzania

Seychelles

Comoros Islands

Angola

Zambia

Mayotte

St. Helena

Zimbabwe

Malawi

Mauritius

Namibia

Botswana

Reunion

Swaziland

Mozambique

Madagascar

Lesotho

South Africa

©2004 SIL

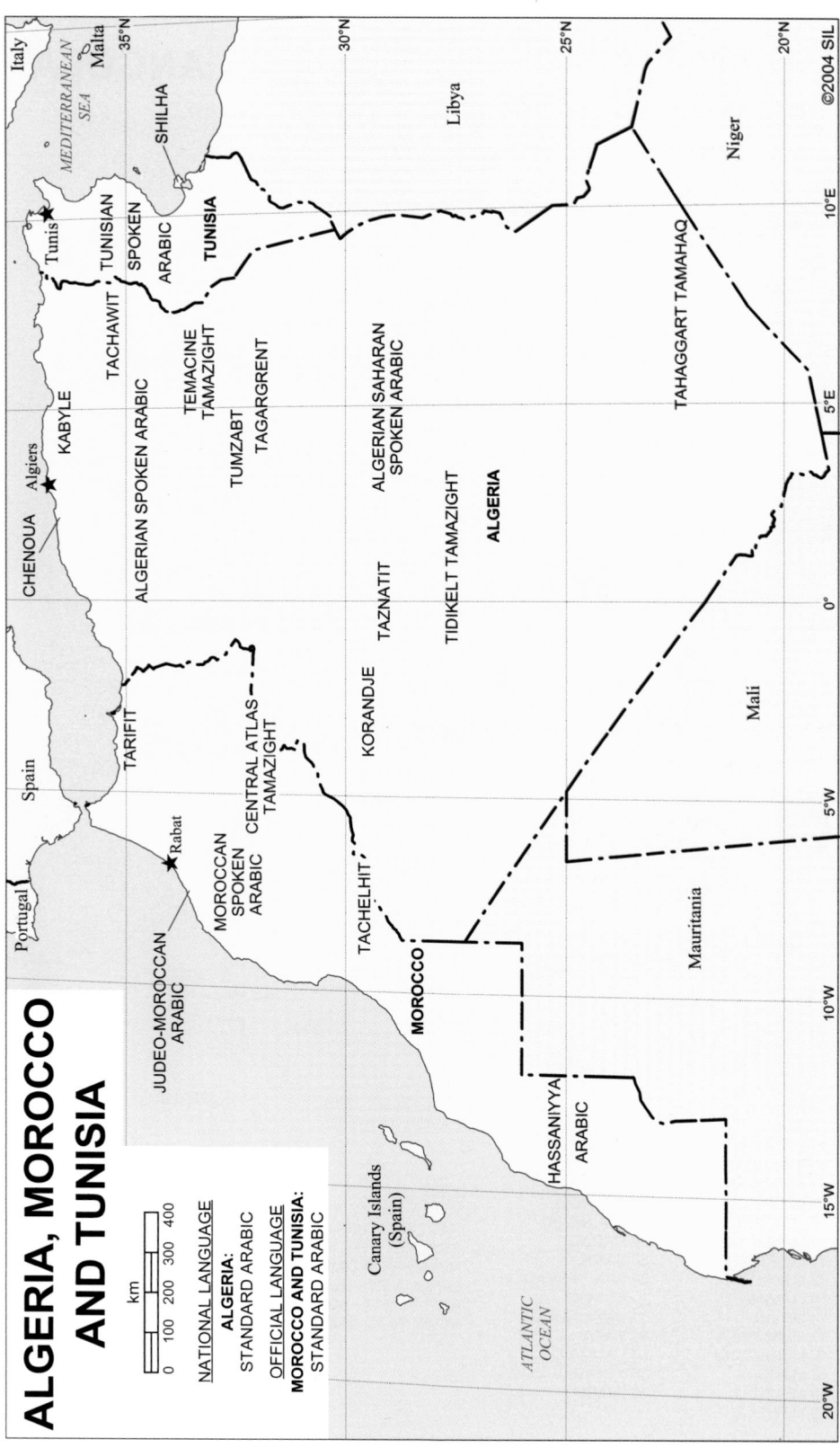

ALGERIA, MOROCCO AND TUNISIA

km

0 100 200 300 400

NATIONAL LANGUAGE
ALGERIA:
STANDARD ARABIC

OFFICIAL LANGUAGE
MOROCCO AND TUNISIA:
STANDARD ARABIC

©2004 SIL

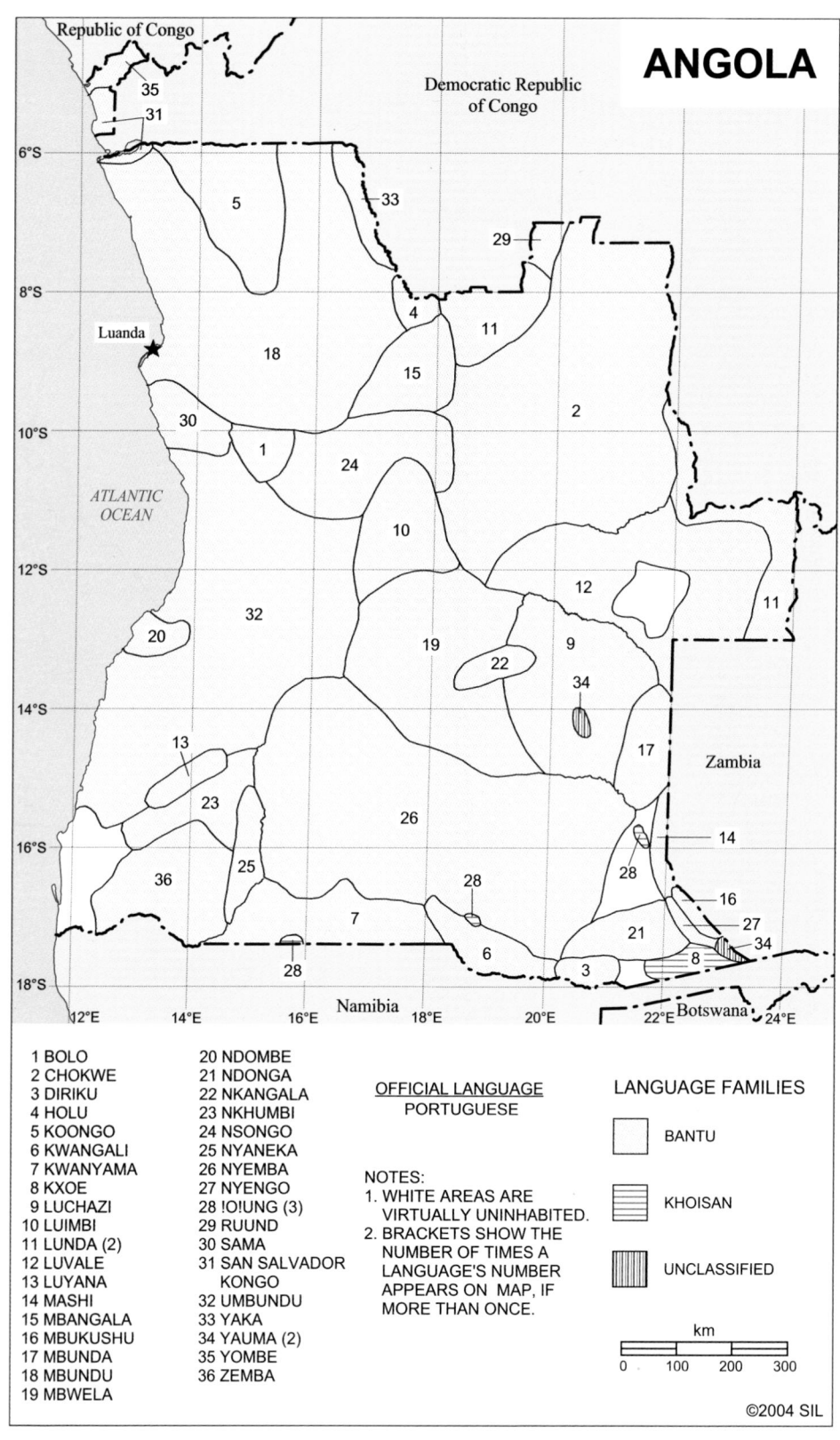

ANGOLA

Republic of Congo

Democratic Republic
of Congo

Luanda

ATLANTIC
OCEAN

Zambia

Namibia

Botswana

1 BOLO	20 NDOMBE
2 CHOKWE	21 NDONGA
3 DIRIKU	22 NKANGALA
4 HOLU	23 NKHUMBI
5 KOONGO	24 NSONGO
6 KWANGALI	25 NYANEKA
7 KWANYAMA	26 NYEMBA
8 KXOE	27 NYENGO
9 LUCHAZI	28 !O!UNG (3)
10 LUIMBI	29 RUUND
11 LUNDA (2)	30 SAMA
12 LUVALE	31 SAN SALVADOR
13 LUYANA	KONGO
14 MASHI	32 UMBUNDU
15 MBANGALA	33 YAKA
16 MBUKUSHU	34 YAUMA (2)
17 MBUNDA	35 YOMBE
18 MBUNDU	36 ZEMBA
19 MBWELA	

OFFICIAL LANGUAGE
PORTUGUESE

NOTES:
1. WHITE AREAS ARE
   VIRTUALLY UNINHABITED.
2. BRACKETS SHOW THE
   NUMBER OF TIMES A
   LANGUAGE'S NUMBER
   APPEARS ON MAP, IF
   MORE THAN ONCE.

LANGUAGE FAMILIES

BANTU

KHOISAN

UNCLASSIFIED

km
0   100   200   300

©2004 SIL

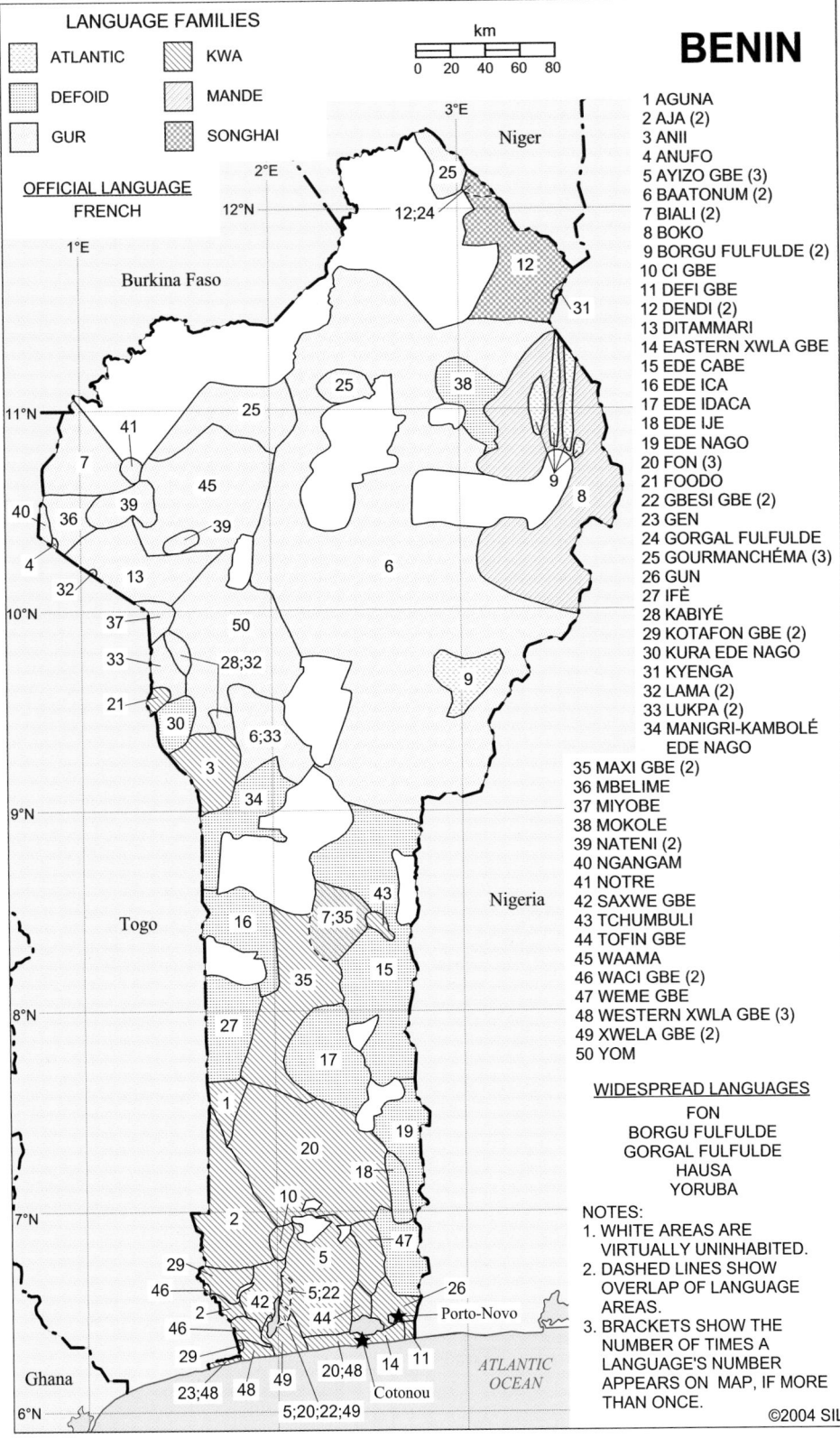

LANGUAGE FAMILIES

- ATLANTIC
- DEFOID
- GUR
- KWA
- MANDE
- SONGHAI

km
0 20 40 60 80

BENIN

OFFICIAL LANGUAGE
FRENCH

1 AGUNA
2 AJA (2)
3 ANII
4 ANUFO
5 AYIZO GBE (3)
6 BAATONUM (2)
7 BIALI (2)
8 BOKO
9 BORGU FULFULDE (2)
10 CI GBE
11 DEFI GBE
12 DENDI (2)
13 DITAMMARI
14 EASTERN XWLA GBE
15 EDE CABE
16 EDE ICA
17 EDE IDACA
18 EDE IJE
19 EDE NAGO
20 FON (3)
21 FOODO
22 GBESI GBE (2)
23 GEN
24 GORGAL FULFULDE
25 GOURMANCHÉMA (3)
26 GUN
27 IFÈ
28 KABIYÉ
29 KOTAFON GBE (2)
30 KURA EDE NAGO
31 KYENGA
32 LAMA (2)
33 LUKPA (2)
34 MANIGRI-KAMBOLÉ
   EDE NAGO
35 MAXI GBE (2)
36 MBELIME
37 MIYOBE
38 MOKOLE
39 NATENI (2)
40 NGANGAM
41 NOTRE
42 SAXWE GBE
43 TCHUMBULI
44 TOFIN GBE
45 WAAMA
46 WACI GBE (2)
47 WEME GBE
48 WESTERN XWLA GBE (3)
49 XWELA GBE (2)
50 YOM

WIDESPREAD LANGUAGES
FON
BORGU FULFULDE
GORGAL FULFULDE
HAUSA
YORUBA

NOTES:
1. WHITE AREAS ARE
   VIRTUALLY UNINHABITED.
2. DASHED LINES SHOW
   OVERLAP OF LANGUAGE
   AREAS.
3. BRACKETS SHOW THE
   NUMBER OF TIMES A
   LANGUAGE'S NUMBER
   APPEARS ON MAP, IF MORE
   THAN ONCE.

©2004 SIL

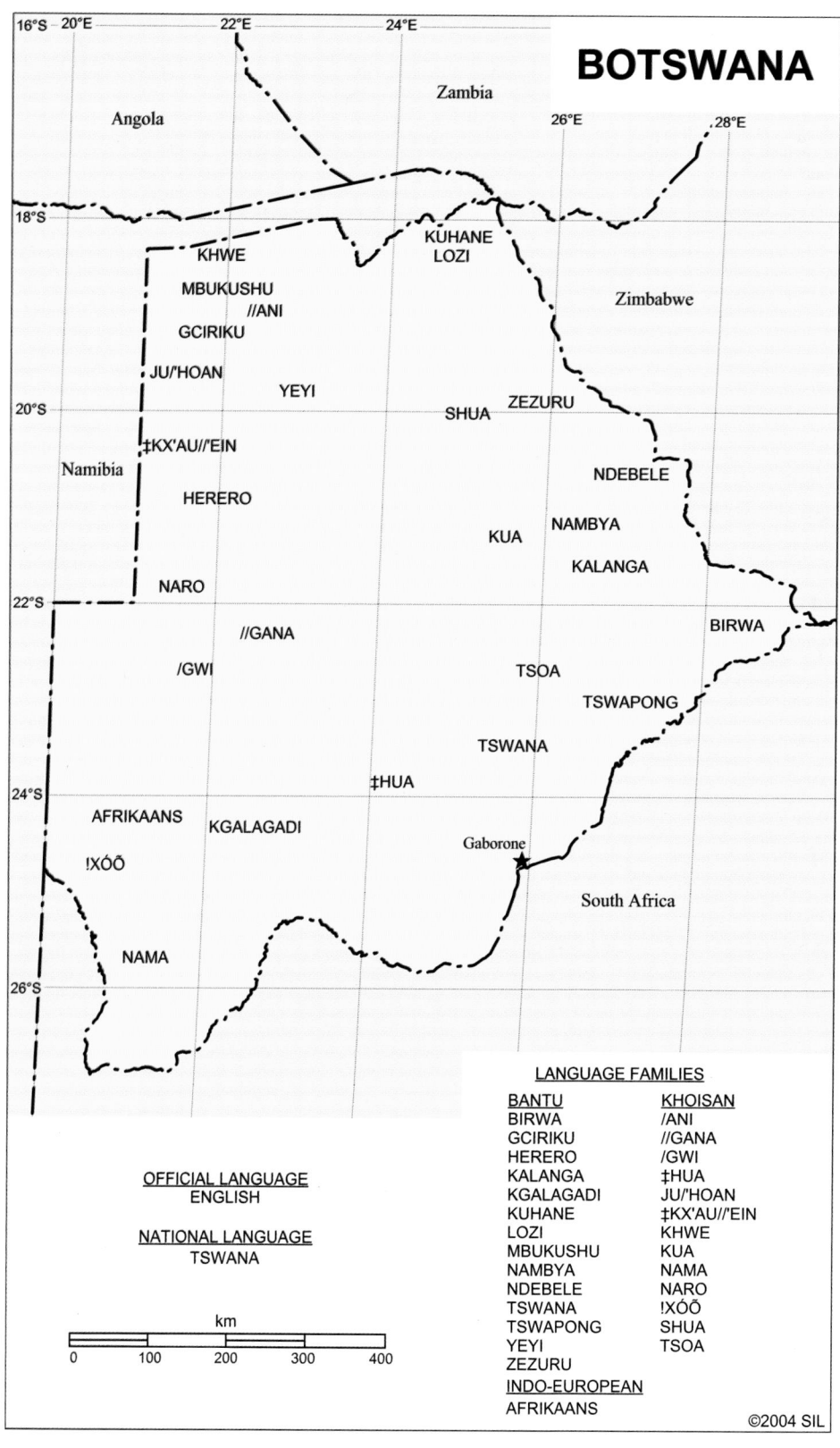

BOTSWANA

LANGUAGE FAMILIES

BANTU	KHOISAN
BIRWA	/ANI
GCIRIKU	//GANA
HERERO	/GWI
KALANGA	‡HUA
KGALAGADI	JU/'HOAN
KUHANE	‡KX'AU//'EIN
LOZI	KHWE
MBUKUSHU	KUA
NAMBYA	NAMA
NDEBELE	NARO
TSWANA	!XÓÕ
TSWAPONG	SHUA
YEYI	TSOA
ZEZURU	

INDO-EUROPEAN

AFRIKAANS

OFFICIAL LANGUAGE
ENGLISH

NATIONAL LANGUAGE
TSWANA

km

0   100   200   300   400

©2004 SIL

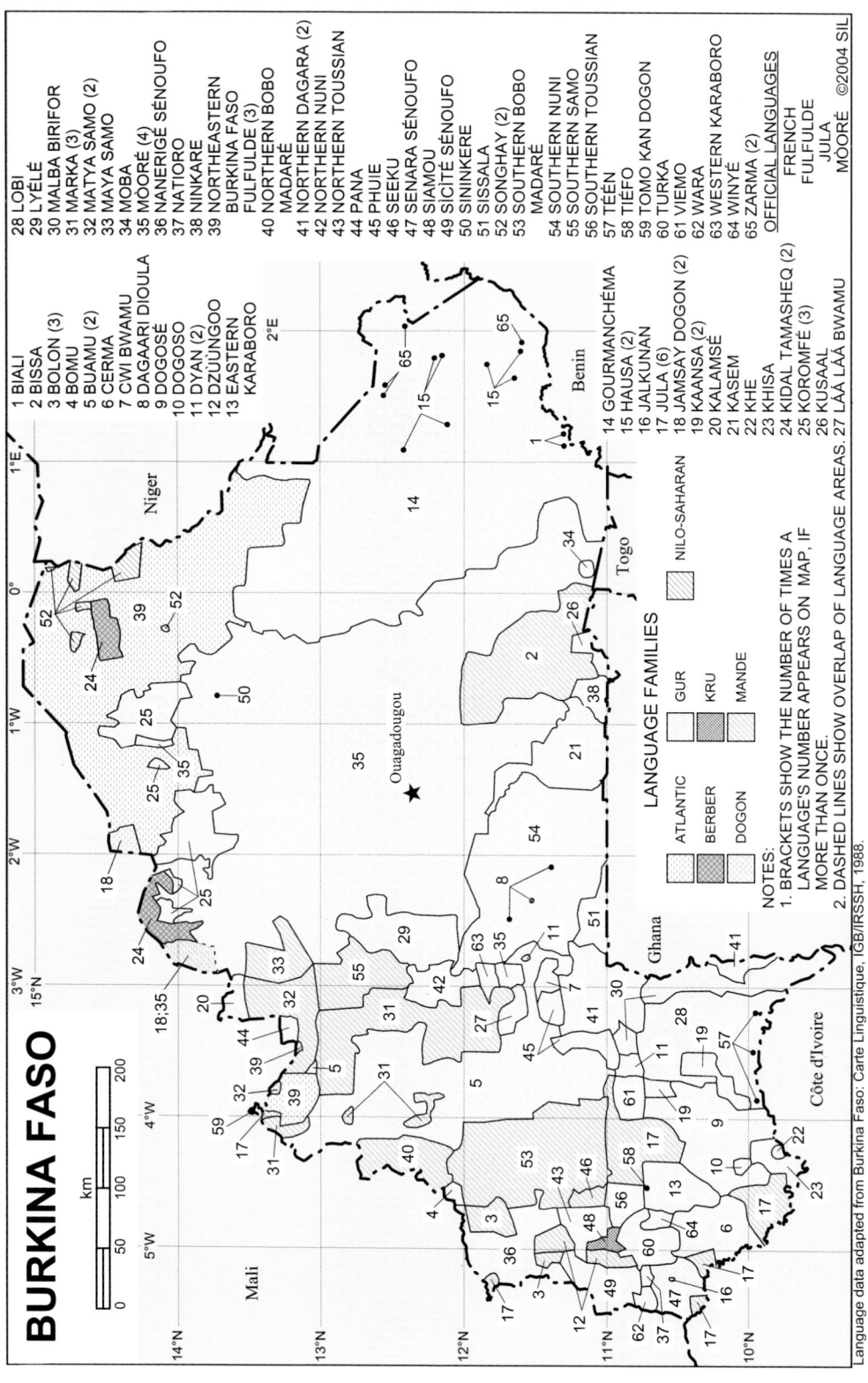

BURKINA FASO

Language data adapted from Burkina Faso: Carte Linguistique, IGB/IRSSH, 1988.

MÖORÉ ©2004 SIL

1 BIALI	28 LOBI
2 BISSA	29 LYÉLÉ
3 BOLON (3)	30 MALBA BIRIFOR
4 BOMU	31 MARKA (3)
5 BUAMU (2)	32 MATYA SAMO (2)
6 CERMA	33 MAYA SAMO
7 CWI BWAMU	34 MOBA
8 DAGAARI DIOULA	35 MÖORÉ (4)
9 DOGOSÉ	36 NANERIGÉ SÉNOUFO
10 DOGOSO	37 NATIORO
11 DYAN (2)	38 NINKARE
12 DZÚÚNGOO	39 NORTHEASTERN
13 EASTERN	BURKINA FASO
KARABORO	FULFULDE (3)
	40 NORTHERN BOBO
14 GOURMANCHÉMA	MADARÉ
15 HAUSA (2)	41 NORTHERN DAGARA (2)
16 JALKUNAN	42 NORTHERN NUNI
17 JULA (6)	43 NORTHERN TOUSSIAN
18 JAMSAY DOGON (2)	44 PANA
19 KAANSA (2)	45 PHUIE
20 KALAMSÉ	46 SEEKU
21 KASEM	47 SENARA SÉNOUFO
22 KHE	48 SIAMOU
23 KHISA	49 SICÍTÉ SÉNOUFO
24 KIDAL TAMASHEQ (2)	50 SININKERE
25 KOROMFÉ (3)	51 SISSALA
26 KUSAAL	52 SONGHAY (2)
27 LÁÁ LÁÁ BWAMU	53 SOUTHERN BOBO
	MADARÉ
	54 SOUTHERN NUNI
	55 SOUTHERN SAMO
	56 SOUTHERN TOUSSIAN
	57 TÉÉN
	58 TIÉFO
	59 TOMO KAN DOGON
	60 TURKA
	61 VIEMO
	62 WARA
	63 WESTERN KARABORO
	64 WINYÉ
	65 ZARMA (2)

OFFICIAL LANGUAGES
FRENCH
FULFULDE
JULA
MÖORÉ

LANGUAGE FAMILIES

ATLANTIC
BERBER
DOGON
GUR
KRU
MANDE
NILO-SAHARAN

NOTES:
1. BRACKETS SHOW THE NUMBER OF TIMES A LANGUAGE'S NUMBER APPEARS ON MAP, IF MORE THAN ONCE.
2. DASHED LINES SHOW OVERLAP OF LANGUAGE AREAS.

Mali

Niger

Benin

Togo

Ghana

Côte d'Ivoire

Ouagadougou

Cameroon: Index Of Languages

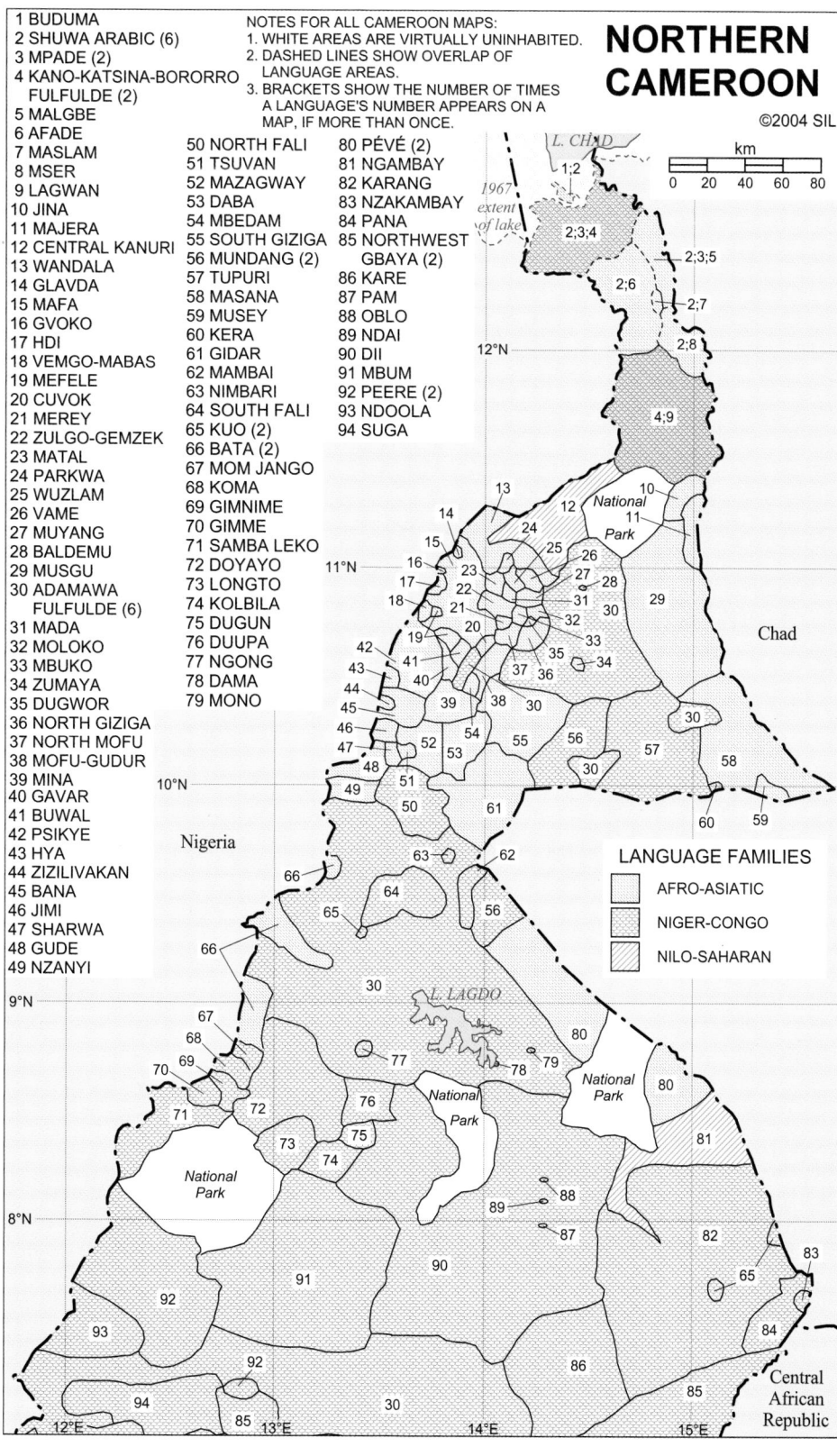

1 BUDUMA
2 SHUWA ARABIC (6)
3 MPADE (2)
4 KANO-KATSINA-BORORRO
   FULFULDE (2)
5 MALGBE
6 AFADE
7 MASLAM
8 MSER
9 LAGWAN
10 JINA
11 MAJERA
12 CENTRAL KANURI
13 WANDALA
14 GLAVDA
15 MAFA
16 GVOKO
17 HDI
18 VEMGO-MABAS
19 MEFELE
20 CUVOK
21 MEREY
22 ZULGO-GEMZEK
23 MATAL
24 PARKWA
25 WUZLAM
26 VAME
27 MUYANG
28 BALDEMU
29 MUSGU
30 ADAMAWA
   FULFULDE (6)
31 MADA
32 MOLOKO
33 MBUKO
34 ZUMAYA
35 DUGWOR
36 NORTH GIZIGA
37 NORTH MOFU
38 MOFU-GUDUR
39 MINA
40 GAVAR
41 BUWAL
42 PSIKYE
43 HYA
44 ZIZILIVAKAN
45 BANA
46 JIMI
47 SHARWA
48 GUDE
49 NZANYI

50 NORTH FALI
51 TSUVAN
52 MAZAGWAY
53 DABA
54 MBEDAM
55 SOUTH GIZIGA
56 MUNDANG (2)
57 TUPURI
58 MASANA
59 MUSEY
60 KERA
61 GIDAR
62 MAMBAI
63 NIMBARI
64 SOUTH FALI
65 KUO (2)
66 BATA (2)
67 MOM JANGO
68 KOMA
69 GIMNIME
70 GIMME
71 SAMBA LEKO
72 DOYAYO
73 LONGTO
74 KOLBILA
75 DUGUN
76 DUUPA
77 NGONG
78 DAMA
79 MONO

80 PÉVÉ (2)
81 NGAMBAY
82 KARANG
83 NZAKAMBAY
84 PANA
85 NORTHWEST
   GBAYA (2)
86 KARE
87 PAM
88 OBLO
89 NDAI
90 DII
91 MBUM
92 PEERE (2)
93 NDOOLA
94 SUGA

NOTES FOR ALL CAMEROON MAPS:
1. WHITE AREAS ARE VIRTUALLY UNINHABITED.
2. DASHED LINES SHOW OVERLAP OF
   LANGUAGE AREAS.
3. BRACKETS SHOW THE NUMBER OF TIMES
   A LANGUAGE'S NUMBER APPEARS ON A
   MAP, IF MORE THAN ONCE.

NORTHERN CAMEROON

©2004 SIL

LANGUAGE FAMILIES

AFRO-ASIATIC
NIGER-CONGO
NILO-SAHARAN

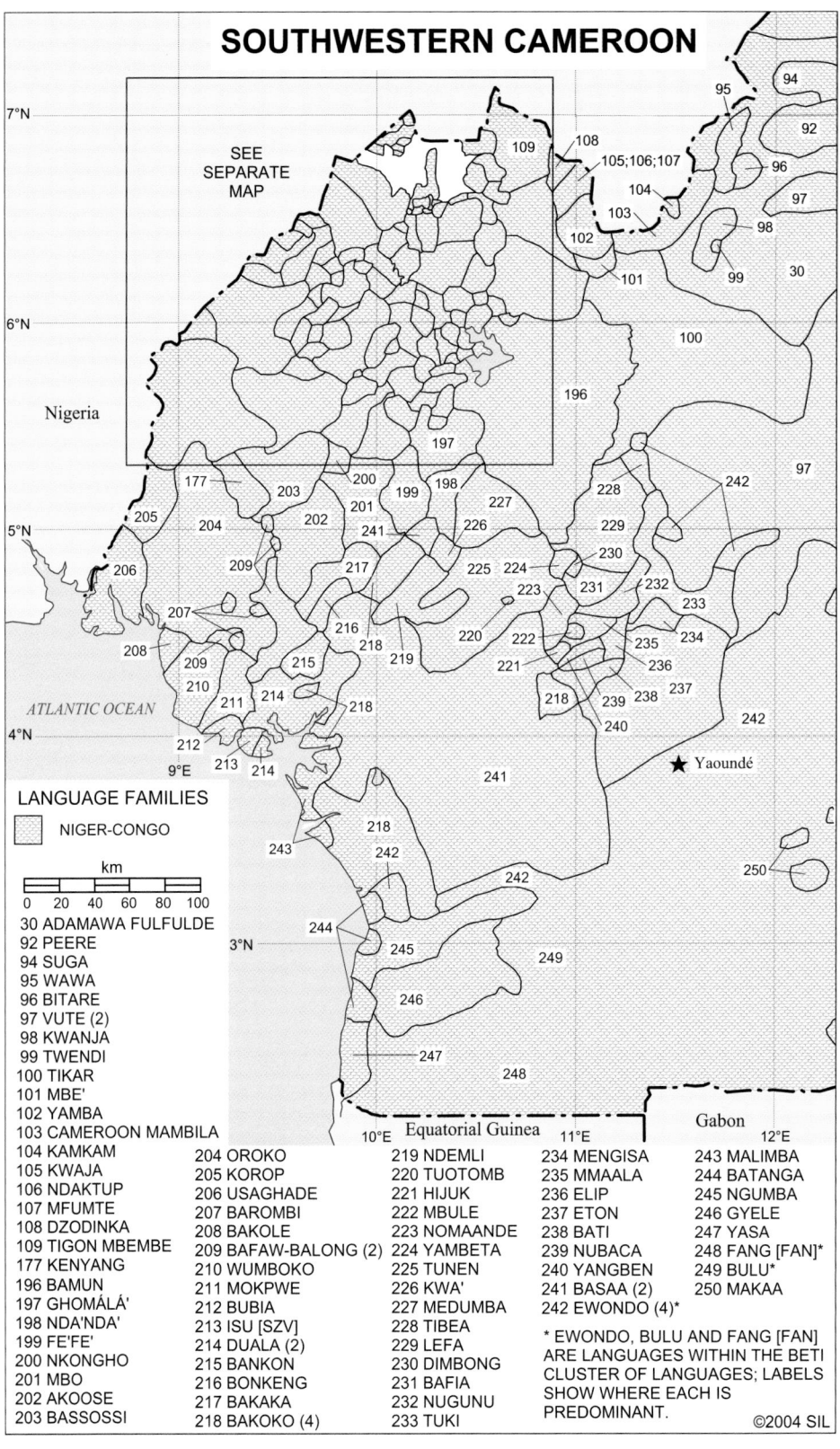

SOUTHWESTERN CAMEROON

7°N

SEE
SEPARATE
MAP

6°N

Nigeria

5°N

ATLANTIC OCEAN

4°N

9°E

★ Yaoundé

109
108
105;106;107
104
103
102
101
100
99
30
97
95
94
92
96
97
98

196
197
177
203
200
199 198
201
202
241
204
205
206
207
208
209
210
211
212
213 214
214
215
216
217
218
219
220
221
222
223
224
225
226
227
228
229
230
231
232
233
234
235
236
237
238 239
240
242
243
244
245
246
247
248
249
250

Equatorial Guinea

Gabon

10°E   11°E   12°E

3°N

LANGUAGE FAMILIES

NIGER-CONGO

km
0 20 40 60 80 100

30 ADAMAWA FULFULDE
92 PEERE
94 SUGA
95 WAWA
96 BITARE
97 VUTE (2)
98 KWANJA
99 TWENDI
100 TIKAR
101 MBE'
102 YAMBA
103 CAMEROON MAMBILA
104 KAMKAM
105 KWAJA
106 NDAKTUP
107 MFUMTE
108 DZODINKA
109 TIGON MBEMBE
177 KENYANG
196 BAMUN
197 GHOMÁLÁ'
198 NDA'NDA'
199 FE'FE'
200 NKONGHO
201 MBO
202 AKOOSE
203 BASSOSSI

204 OROKO
205 KOROP
206 USAGHADE
207 BAROMBI
208 BAKOLE
209 BAFAW-BALONG (2)
210 WUMBOKO
211 MOKPWE
212 BUBIA
213 ISU [SZV]
214 DUALA (2)
215 BANKON
216 BONKENG
217 BAKAKA
218 BAKOKO (4)

219 NDEMLI
220 TUOTOMB
221 HIJUK
222 MBULE
223 NOMAANDE
224 YAMBETA
225 TUNEN
226 KWA'
227 MEDUMBA
228 TIBEA
229 LEFA
230 DIMBONG
231 BAFIA
232 NUGUNU
233 TUKI

234 MENGISA
235 MMAALA
236 ELIP
237 ETON
238 BATI
239 NUBACA
240 YANGBEN
241 BASAA (2)
242 EWONDO (4)*

243 MALIMBA
244 NGUMBA
245 NGUMBA
246 GYELE
247 YASA
248 FANG [FAN]*
249 BULU*
250 MAKAA

* EWONDO, BULU AND FANG [FAN]
ARE LANGUAGES WITHIN THE BETI
CLUSTER OF LANGUAGES; LABELS
SHOW WHERE EACH IS
PREDOMINANT.

©2004 SIL

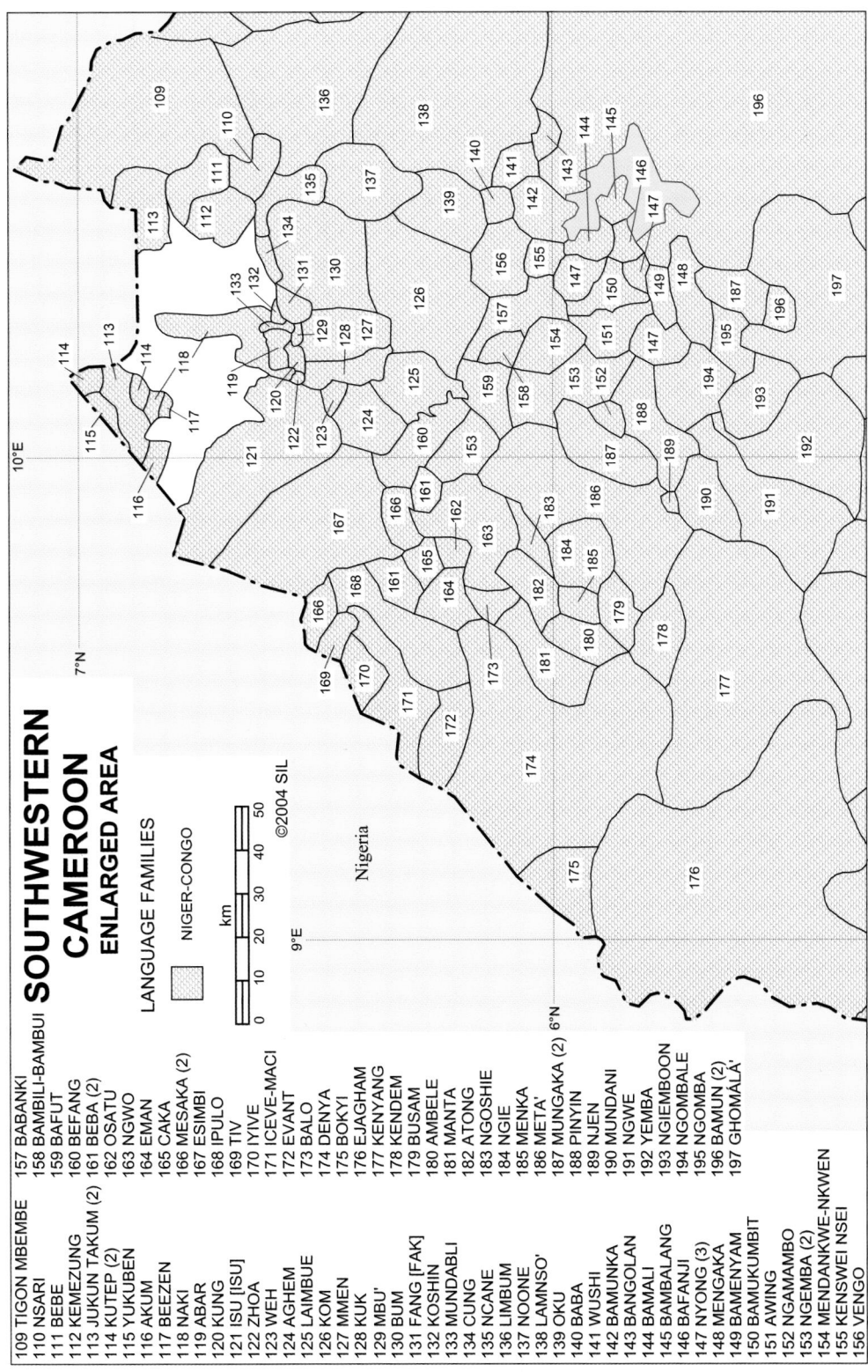

SOUTHWESTERN CAMEROON ENLARGED AREA

LANGUAGE FAMILIES

NIGER-CONGO

km

0 10 20 30 40 50

©2004 SIL

Nigeria

109 TIGON MBEMBE	157 BABANKI
110 NSARI	158 BAMBILI-BAMBUI
111 BEBE	159 BAFUT
112 KEMEZUNG	160 BEFANG
113 JUKUN TAKUM (2)	161 BEBA (2)
114 KUTEP (2)	162 OSATU
115 YUKUBEN	163 NGWO
116 AKUM	164 EMAN
117 BEEZEN	165 CAKA
118 NAKI	166 MESAKA (2)
119 ABAR	167 ESIMBI
120 KUNG	168 IPULO
121 ISU [ISU]	169 TIV
122 ZHOA	170 IYIVE
123 WEH	171 ICEVE-MACI
124 AGHEM	172 EVANT
125 LAIMBUE	173 BALO
126 KOM	174 DENYA
127 MMEN	175 BOKYI
128 KUK	176 EJAGHAM
129 MBU'	177 KENYANG
130 BUM	178 KENDEM
131 FANG [FAK]	179 BUSAM
132 KOSHIN	180 AMBELE
133 MUNDABLI	181 MANTA
134 CUNG	182 ATONG
135 NCANE	183 NGOSHIE
136 LIMBUM	184 NGIE
137 NOONE	185 MENKA
138 LAMNSO'	186 META'
139 OKU	187 MUNGAKA (2)
140 BABA	188 PINYIN
141 WUSHI	189 NJEN
142 BAMUNKA	190 MUNDANI
143 BANGOLAN	191 NGWE
144 BAMALI	192 YEMBA
145 BAMBALANG	193 NGIEMBOON
146 BAFANJI	194 NGOMBALE
147 NYONG (3)	195 NGOMBA
148 MENGAKA	196 BAMUN (2)
149 BAMENYAM	197 GHOMALA'
150 BAMUKUMBIT	
151 AWING	
152 NGAMAMBO	
153 NGEMBA (2)	
154 MENDANKWE-NKWEN	
155 KENSWEI NSEI	
156 VENGO	

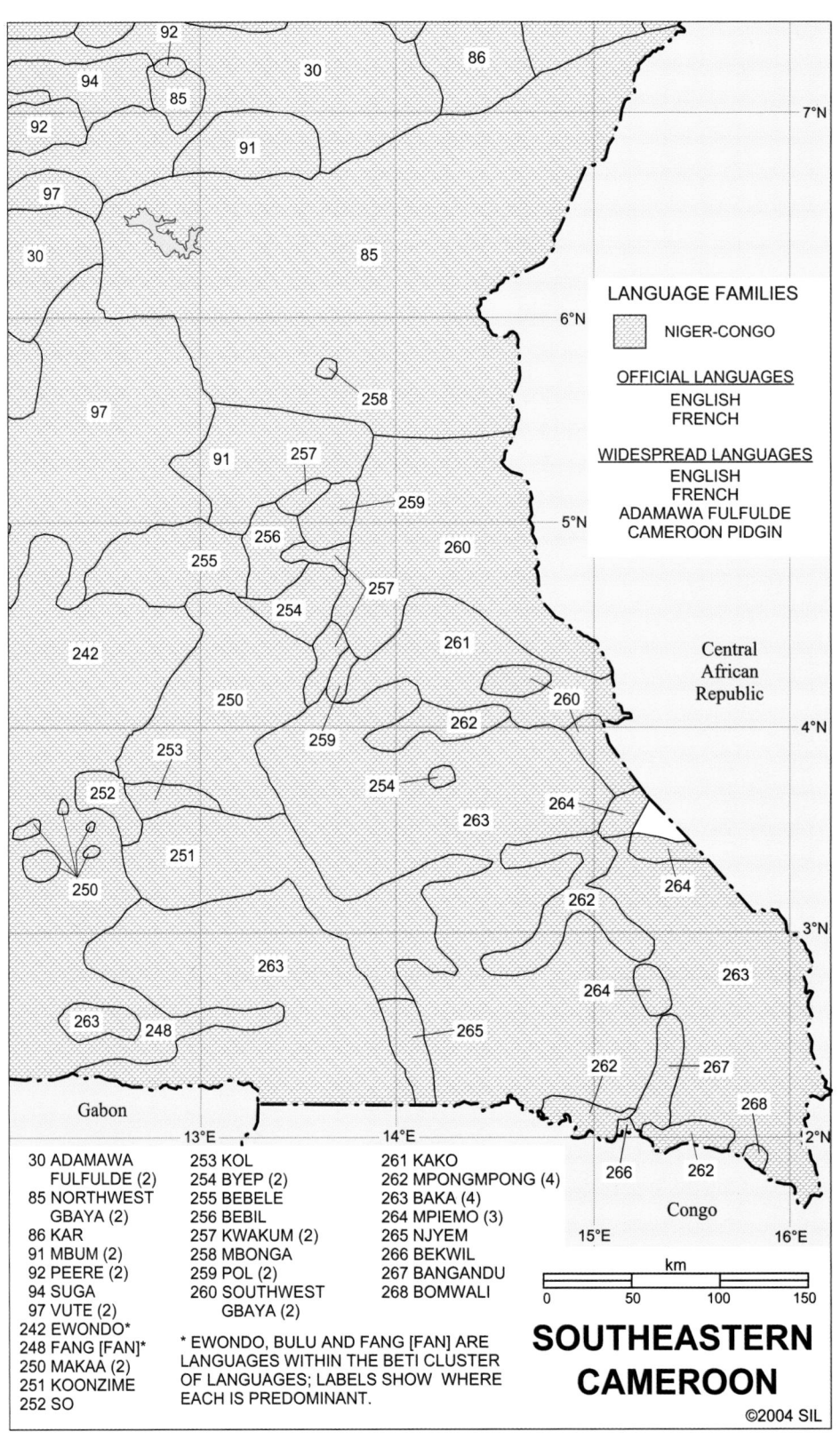

LANGUAGE FAMILIES

NIGER-CONGO

OFFICIAL LANGUAGES
ENGLISH
FRENCH

WIDESPREAD LANGUAGES
ENGLISH
FRENCH
ADAMAWA FULFULDE
CAMEROON PIDGIN

Central
African
Republic

Gabon

Congo

km

SOUTHEASTERN
CAMEROON

©2004 SIL

30 ADAMAWA
FULFULDE (2)
85 NORTHWEST
GBAYA (2)
86 KAR
91 MBUM (2)
92 PEERE (2)
94 SUGA
97 VUTE (2)
242 EWONDO*
248 FANG [FAN]*
250 MAKAA (2)
251 KOONZIME
252 SO

253 KOL
254 BYEP (2)
255 BEBELE
256 BEBIL
257 KWAKUM (2)
258 MBONGA
259 POL (2)
260 SOUTHWEST
GBAYA (2)

261 KAKO
262 MPONGMPONG (4)
263 BAKA (4)
264 MPIEMO (3)
265 NJYEM
266 BEKWIL
267 BANGANDU
268 BOMWALI

* EWONDO, BULU AND FANG [FAN] ARE
LANGUAGES WITHIN THE BETI CLUSTER
OF LANGUAGES; LABELS SHOW WHERE
EACH IS PREDOMINANT.

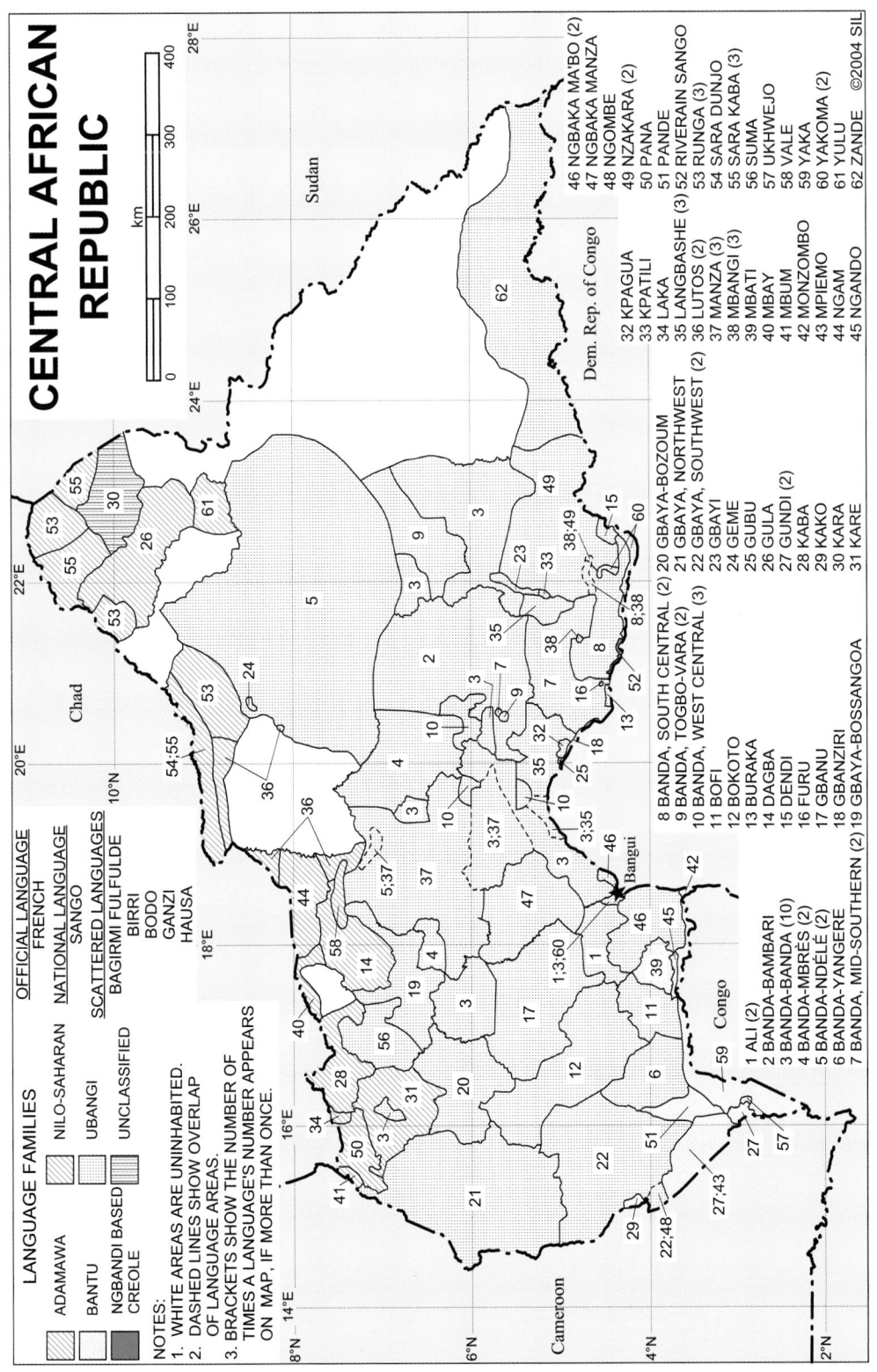

CENTRAL AFRICAN REPUBLIC

©2004 SIL

LANGUAGE FAMILIES

ADAMAWA

NILO-SAHARAN

BANTU

UBANGI

NGBANDI BASED CREOLE

UNCLASSIFIED

OFFICIAL LANGUAGE
FRENCH

NATIONAL LANGUAGE
SANGO

SCATTERED LANGUAGES
BAGIRMI FULFULDE
BIRRI
BODO
GANZI
HAUSA

NOTES:
1. WHITE AREAS ARE UNINHABITED.
2. DASHED LINES SHOW OVERLAP OF LANGUAGE AREAS.
3. BRACKETS SHOW THE NUMBER OF TIMES A LANGUAGE'S NUMBER APPEARS ON MAP, IF MORE THAN ONCE.

1 ALI (2)
2 BANDA-BAMBARI
3 BANDA-BANDA (10)
4 BANDA-MBRÈS (2)
5 BANDA-NDÉLÉ (2)
6 BANDA-YANGERE
7 BANDA, MID-SOUTHERN (2)
8 BANDA, SOUTH CENTRAL (2)
9 BANDA, TOGBO-VARA (2)
10 BANDA, WEST CENTRAL (3)
11 BOFI
12 BOKOTO
13 BURAKA
14 DAGBA
15 DENDI
16 FURU
17 GBANU
18 GBANZIRI
19 GBAYA-BOSSANGOA
20 GBAYA-BOZOUM
21 GBAYA, NORTHWEST
22 GBAYA, SOUTHWEST (2)
23 GBAYI
24 GEME
25 GUBU
26 GULA
27 GUNDI (2)
28 KABA
29 KAKO
30 KARA
31 KARE
32 KPAGUA
33 KPATILI
34 LAKA
35 LANGBASHE (3)
36 LUTOS (2)
37 MANZA (3)
38 MBANGI (3)
39 MBATI
40 MBAY
41 MBUM
42 MONZOMBO
43 MPIEMO
44 NGAM
45 NGANDO
46 NGBAKA MA'BO (2)
47 NGBAKA MANZA
48 NGOMBE
49 NZAKARA (2)
50 PANA
51 PANDE
52 RIVERAIN SANGO
53 RUNGA (3)
54 SARA DUNJO
55 SARA KABA (3)
56 SUMA
57 UKHWEJO
58 VALE
59 YAKA
60 YAKOMA (2)
61 YULU
62 ZANDE

Sudan

Dem. Rep. of Congo

Chad

Cameroon

Congo

Bangui

km
0 100 200 300 400

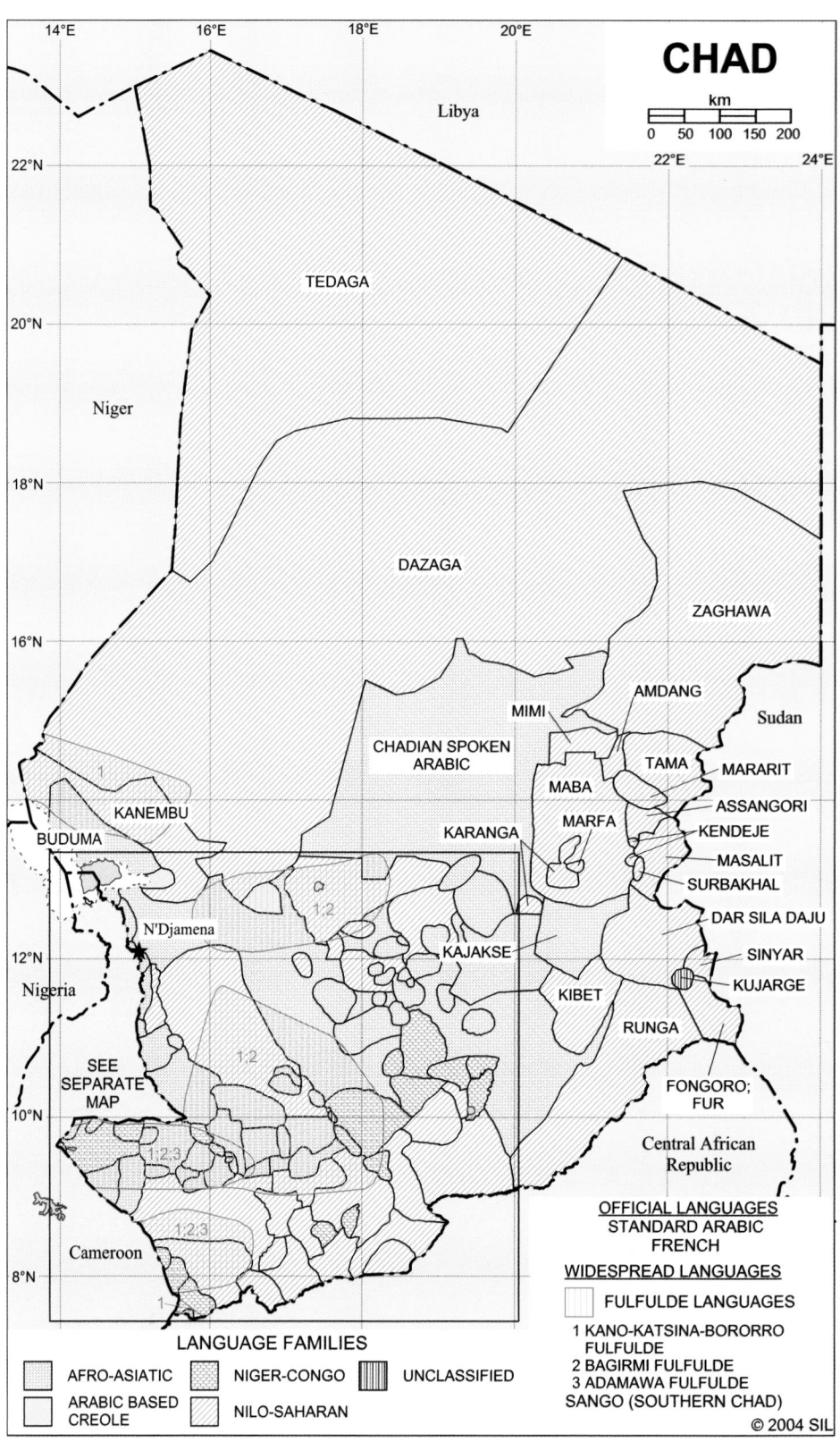

LANGUAGE FAMILIES

AFRO-ASIATIC

ARABIC BASED CREOLE

NIGER-CONGO

NILO-SAHARAN

UNCLASSIFIED

OFFICIAL LANGUAGES
STANDARD ARABIC
FRENCH

WIDESPREAD LANGUAGES

FULFULDE LANGUAGES

1 KANO-KATSINA-BORORRO FULFULDE
2 BAGIRMI FULFULDE
3 ADAMAWA FULFULDE
SANGO (SOUTHERN CHAD)

CHAD

km
0 50 100 150 200

Libya

TEDAGA

Niger

DAZAGA

ZAGHAWA

Sudan

AMDANG

MIMI

CHADIAN SPOKEN ARABIC

TAMA

MARARIT

MABA

ASSANGORI

MARFA

KENDEJE

KARANGA

MASALIT

SURBAKHAL

DAR SILA DAJU

KANEMBU

BUDUMA

N'Djamena

KAJAKSE

SINYAR

KUJARGE

KIBET

Nigeria

RUNGA

SEE SEPARATE MAP

FONGORO; FUR

Central African Republic

Cameroon

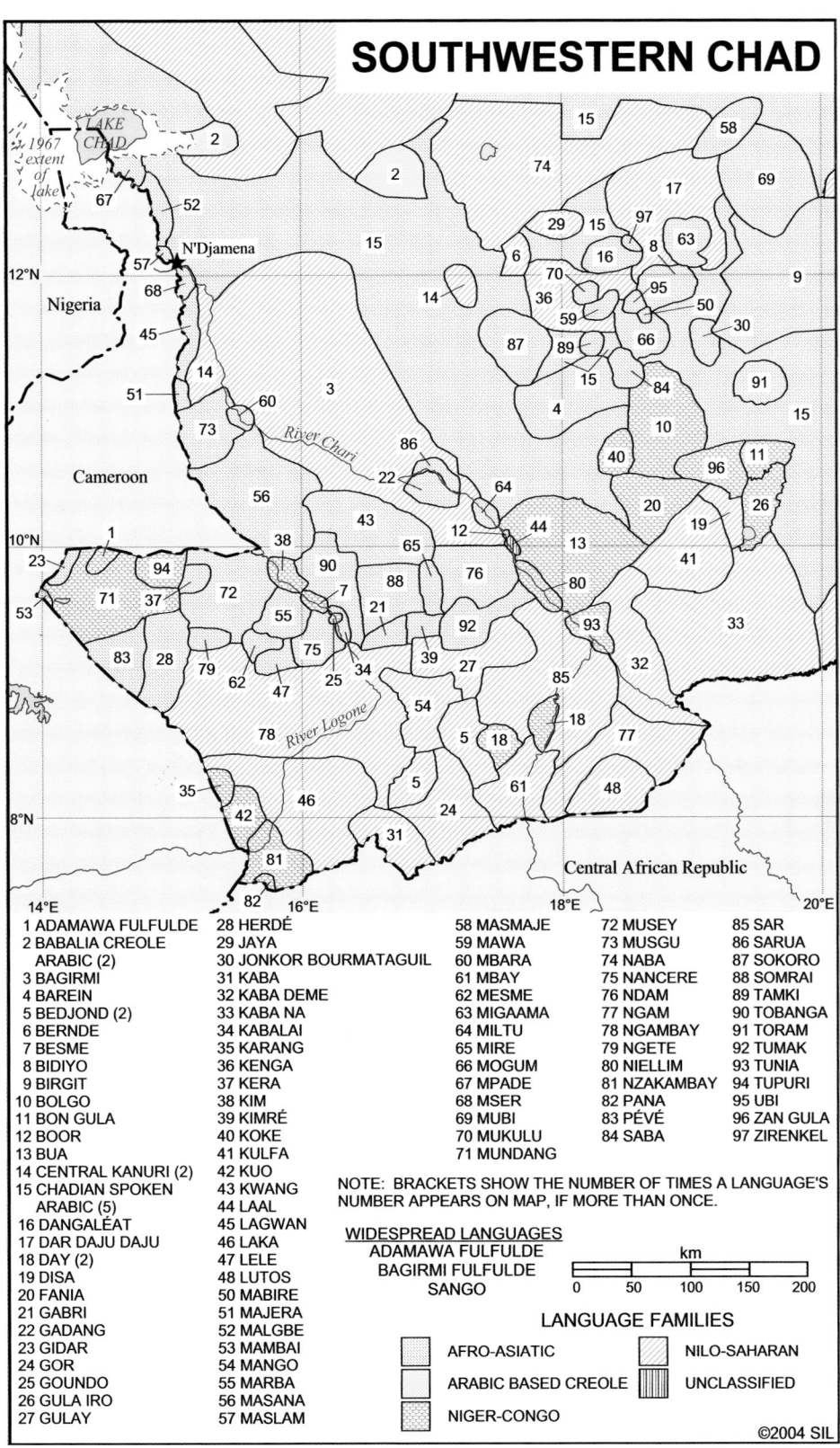

SOUTHWESTERN CHAD

1967 extent of lake

LAKE CHAD

N'Djamena

Nigeria

Cameroon

Central African Republic

River Chari

River Logone

1 ADAMAWA FULFULDE	28 HERDÉ	58 MASMAJE	72 MUSEY	85 SAR
2 BABALIA CREOLE ARABIC (2)	29 JAYA	59 MAWA	73 MUSGU	86 SARUA
	30 JONKOR BOURMATAGUIL	60 MBARA	74 NABA	87 SOKORO
3 BAGIRMI	31 KABA	61 MBAY	75 NANCERE	88 SOMRAI
4 BAREIN	32 KABA DEME	62 MESME	76 NDAM	89 TAMKI
5 BEDJOND (2)	33 KABA NA	63 MIGAAMA	77 NGAM	90 TOBANGA
6 BERNDE	34 KABALAI	64 MILTU	78 NGAMBAY	91 TORAM
7 BESME	35 KARANG	65 MIRE	79 NGETE	92 TUMAK
8 BIDIYO	36 KENGA	66 MOGUM	80 NIELLIM	93 TUNIA
9 BIRGIT	37 KERA	67 MPADE	81 NZAKAMBAY	94 TUPURI
10 BOLGO	38 KIM	68 MSER	82 PANA	95 UBI
11 BON GULA	39 KIMRÉ	69 MUBI	83 PÉVÉ	96 ZAN GULA
12 BOOR	40 KOKE	70 MUKULU	84 SABA	97 ZIRENKEL
13 BUA	41 KULFA	71 MUNDANG		
14 CENTRAL KANURI (2)	42 KUO			
15 CHADIAN SPOKEN ARABIC (5)	43 KWANG			
16 DANGALÉAT	44 LAAL			
17 DAR DAJU DAJU	45 LAGWAN			
18 DAY (2)	46 LAKA			
19 DISA	47 LELE			
20 FANIA	48 LUTOS			
21 GABRI	50 MABIRE			
22 GADANG	51 MAJERA			
23 GIDAR	52 MALGBE			
24 GOR	53 MAMBAI			
25 GOUNDO	54 MANGO			
26 GULA IRO	55 MARBA			
27 GULAY	56 MASANA			
	57 MASLAM			

NOTE: BRACKETS SHOW THE NUMBER OF TIMES A LANGUAGE'S NUMBER APPEARS ON MAP, IF MORE THAN ONCE.

WIDESPREAD LANGUAGES
ADAMAWA FULFULDE
BAGIRMI FULFULDE
SANGO

km
0　50　100　150　200

LANGUAGE FAMILIES

AFRO-ASIATIC

ARABIC BASED CREOLE

NIGER-CONGO

NILO-SAHARAN

UNCLASSIFIED

©2004 SIL

COMOROS, MADAGASCAR AND MAYOTTE

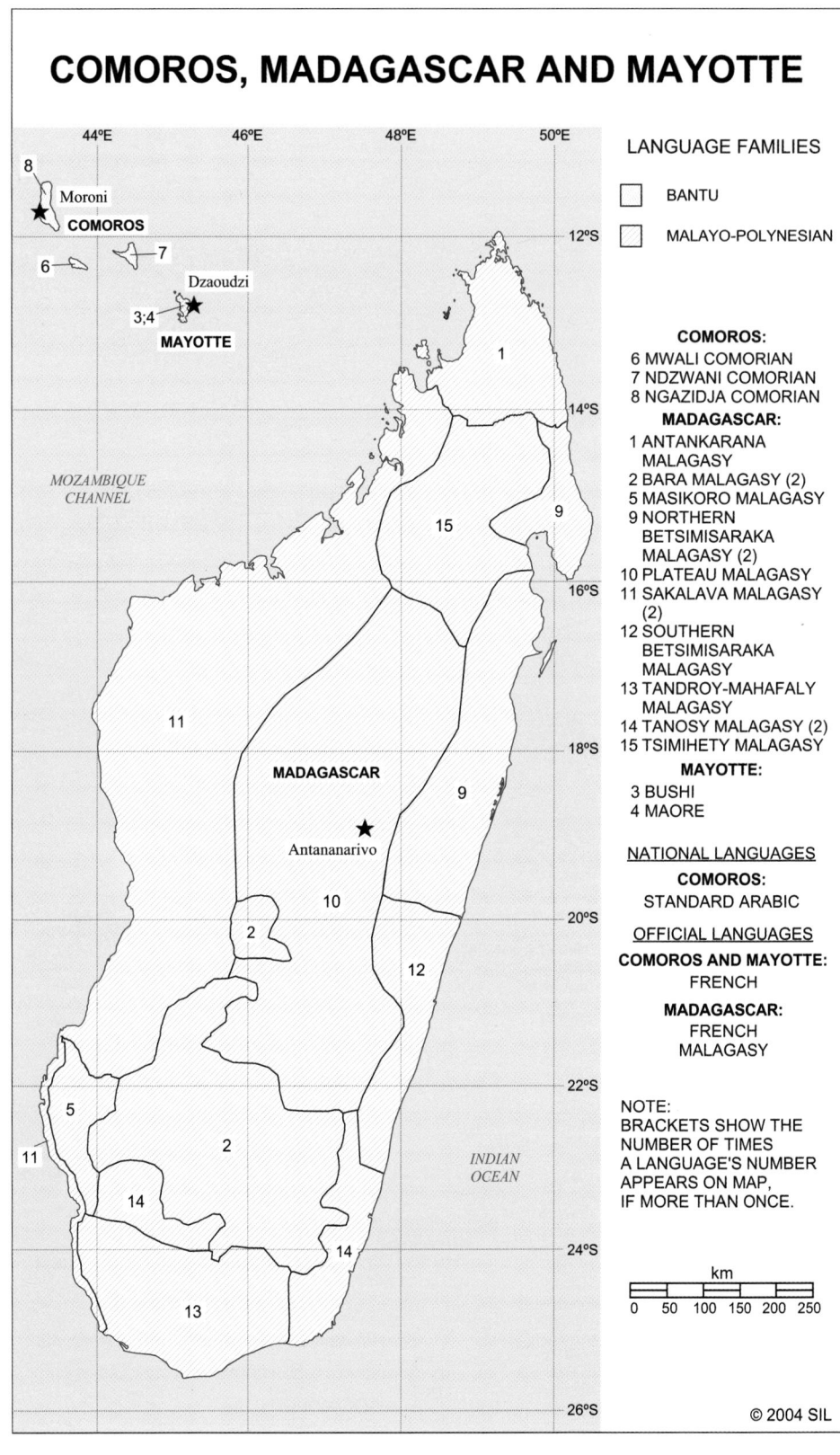

LANGUAGE FAMILIES

☐ BANTU

☐ MALAYO-POLYNESIAN

COMOROS:
6 MWALI COMORIAN
7 NDZWANI COMORIAN
8 NGAZIDJA COMORIAN
MADAGASCAR:
1 ANTANKARANA
  MALAGASY
2 BARA MALAGASY (2)
5 MASIKORO MALAGASY
9 NORTHERN
  BETSIMISARAKA
  MALAGASY (2)
10 PLATEAU MALAGASY
11 SAKALAVA MALAGASY
  (2)
12 SOUTHERN
  BETSIMISARAKA
  MALAGASY
13 TANDROY-MAHAFALY
  MALAGASY
14 TANOSY MALAGASY (2)
15 TSIMIHETY MALAGASY
MAYOTTE:
3 BUSHI
4 MAORE

NATIONAL LANGUAGES
COMOROS:
STANDARD ARABIC

OFFICIAL LANGUAGES
COMOROS AND MAYOTTE:
FRENCH

MADAGASCAR:
FRENCH
MALAGASY

NOTE:
BRACKETS SHOW THE
NUMBER OF TIMES
A LANGUAGE'S NUMBER
APPEARS ON MAP,
IF MORE THAN ONCE.

km
0 50 100 150 200 250

© 2004 SIL

1 AKWA	44 TEKE-EBOO
2 BANGANDU	45 TEKE-FUUMU
3 BEEMBE	46 TEKE-IBALI
4 BEKWIL	47 TEKE-KUKUYA
5 BOBANGI	48 TEKE-LAALI
6 BOMITABA	49 TEKE-NZIKOU
7 BOMWALI	50 TEKE-TEGE
8 BONGILI (3)	51 TEKE-TSAAYI
9 BONJO (2)	52 TEKE-TYEE
10 BWISI	53 TSAANGI
11 DIBOLE	54 VILI
12 DOONDO	55 WUMBVU
13 FANG	56 YAKA
14 GBAYA	57 YOMBE
15 KAAMBA	
16 KAKO	
17 KOONGO	
18 KOTA (2)	
19 KOYO	
20 KUNYI	
21 LAARI	
22 LIKUBA	
23 LIKWALA (2)	
24 LUMBU	
25 MBANDJA	
26 MBANGWE	
27 MBERE	
28 MBOKO	
29 MBOSI	
30 MOI	
31 MONZOMBO	
32 MPYEMO	
33 NDASA	
34 NGBAKA	
35 NGOM	
36 NGUNDI	
37 NGUNGWEL	
38 NJEBI	
39 NJYEM	
40 OMBAMBA	
41 POMO	
42 PUNU	
43 SUUNDI	

OFFICIAL LANGUAGE
FRENCH

NATIONAL LANGUAGES
KITUBA
LINGALA

CONGO

LANGUAGE FAMILIES

ADAMAWA-UBANGI

BANTU

km
0   50   100   150   200

©2004 SIL

NOTES:
1. WHITE AREAS ARE SPARSELY INHABITED.
2. AKA IS MAINLY SPOKEN NORTH OF THE DASHED LINE.
3. BRACKETS SHOW THE NUMBER OF TIMES A LANGUAGE'S NUMBER APPEARS ON MAP, IF MORE THAN ONCE.

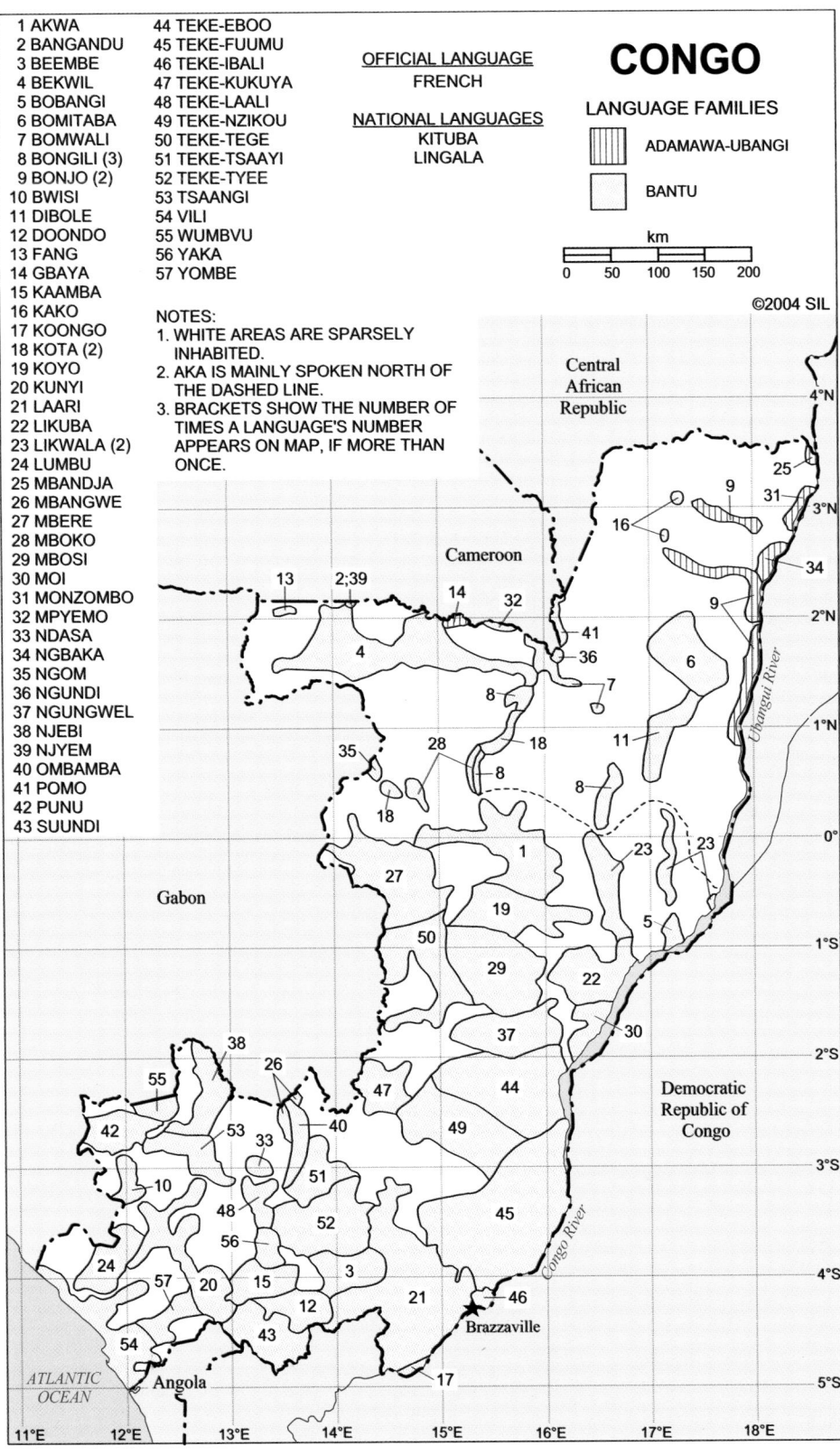

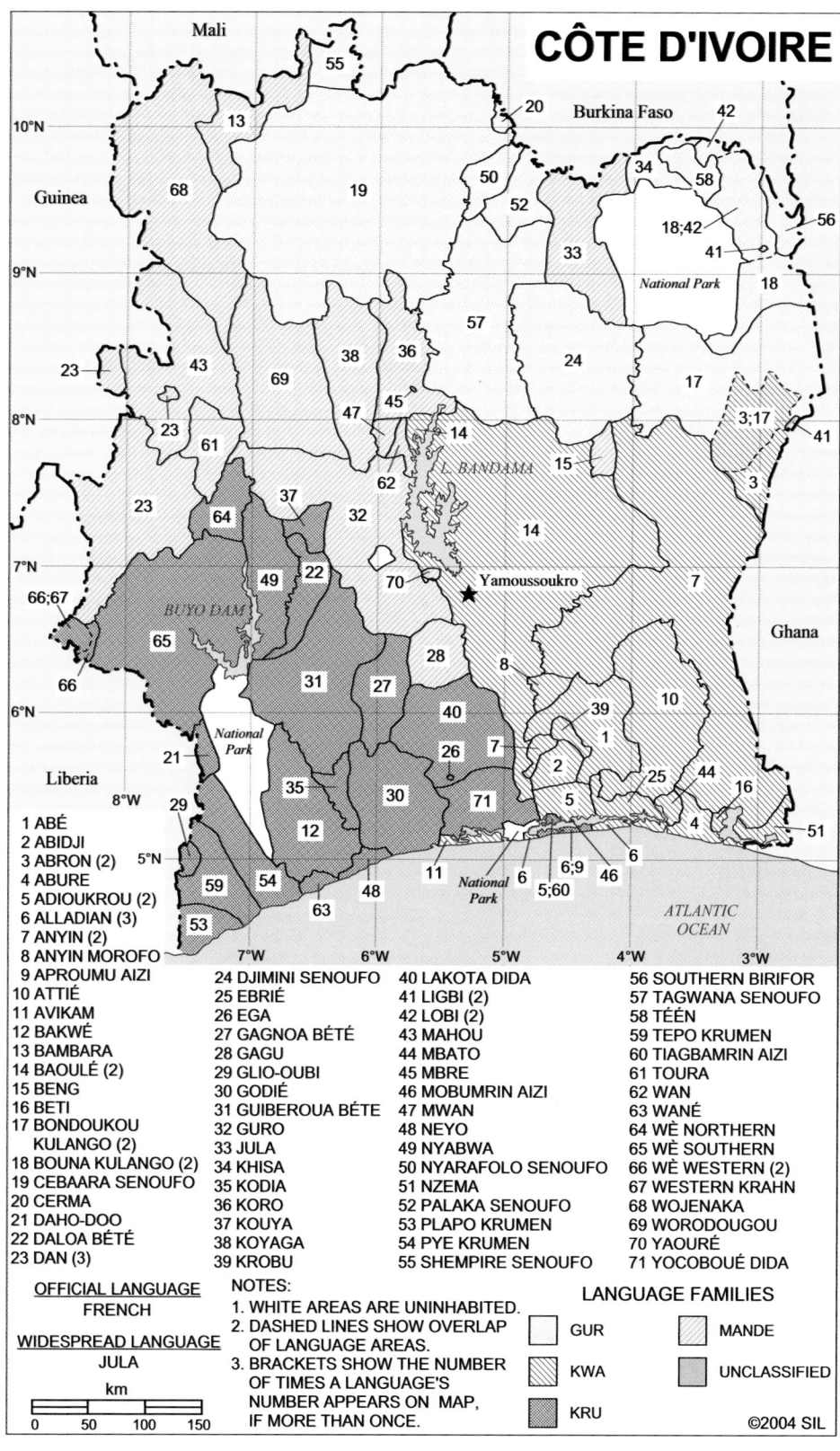

CÔTE D'IVOIRE

1 ABÉ
2 ABIDJI
3 ABRON (2)
4 ABURE
5 ADIOUKROU (2)
6 ALLADIAN (3)
7 ANYIN (2)
8 ANYIN MOROFO
9 APROUMU AIZI
10 ATTIÉ
11 AVIKAM
12 BAKWÉ
13 BAMBARA
14 BAOULÉ (2)
15 BENG
16 BETI
17 BONDOUKOU
    KULANGO (2)
18 BOUNA KULANGO (2)
19 CEBAARA SENOUFO
20 CERMA
21 DAHO-DOO
22 DALOA BÉTÉ
23 DAN (3)

24 DJIMINI SENOUFO
25 EBRIÉ
26 EGA
27 GAGNOA BÉTÉ
28 GAGU
29 GLIO-OUBI
30 GODIÉ
31 GUIBEROUA BÉTE
32 GURO
33 JULA
34 KHISA
35 KODIA
36 KORO
37 KOUYA
38 KOYAGA
39 KROBU

40 LAKOTA DIDA
41 LIGBI (2)
42 LOBI (2)
43 MAHOU
44 MBATO
45 MBRE
46 MOBUMRIN AIZI
47 MWAN
48 NEYO
49 NYABWA
50 NYARAFOLO SENOUFO
51 NZEMA
52 PALAKA SENOUFO
53 PLAPO KRUMEN
54 PYE KRUMEN
55 SHEMPIRE SENOUFO

56 SOUTHERN BIRIFOR
57 TAGWANA SENOUFO
58 TÉÉN
59 TEPO KRUMEN
60 TIAGBAMRIN AIZI
61 TOURA
62 WAN
63 WANÉ
64 WÈ NORTHERN
65 WÈ SOUTHERN
66 WÈ WESTERN (2)
67 WESTERN KRAHN
68 WOJENAKA
69 WORODOUGOU
70 YAOURÉ
71 YOCOBOUÉ DIDA

OFFICIAL LANGUAGE
FRENCH

WIDESPREAD LANGUAGE
JULA

km
0   50   100   150

NOTES:
1. WHITE AREAS ARE UNINHABITED.
2. DASHED LINES SHOW OVERLAP
   OF LANGUAGE AREAS.
3. BRACKETS SHOW THE NUMBER
   OF TIMES A LANGUAGE'S
   NUMBER APPEARS ON MAP,
   IF MORE THAN ONCE.

LANGUAGE FAMILIES

GUR

KWA

KRU

MANDE

UNCLASSIFIED

©2004 SIL

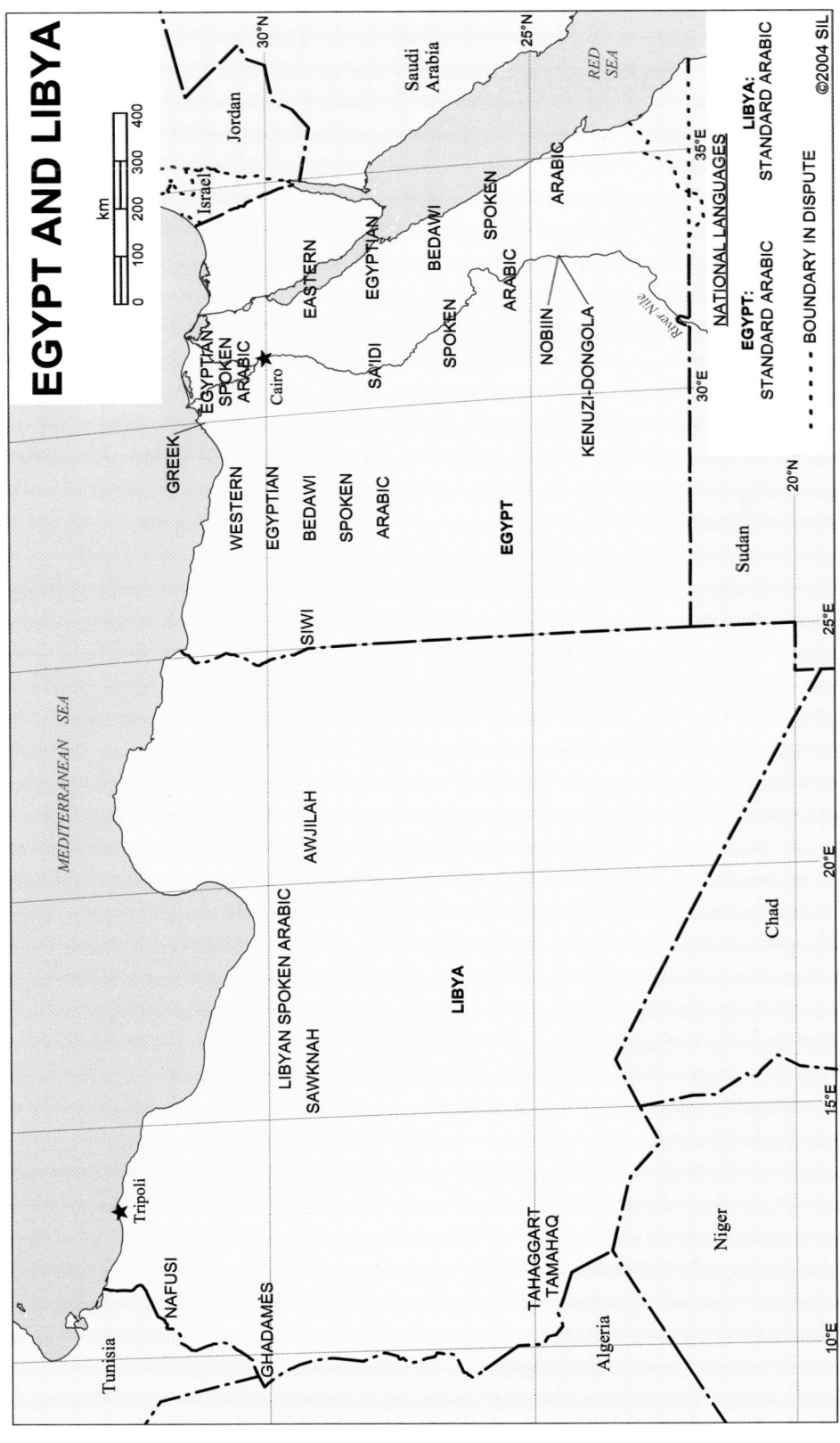

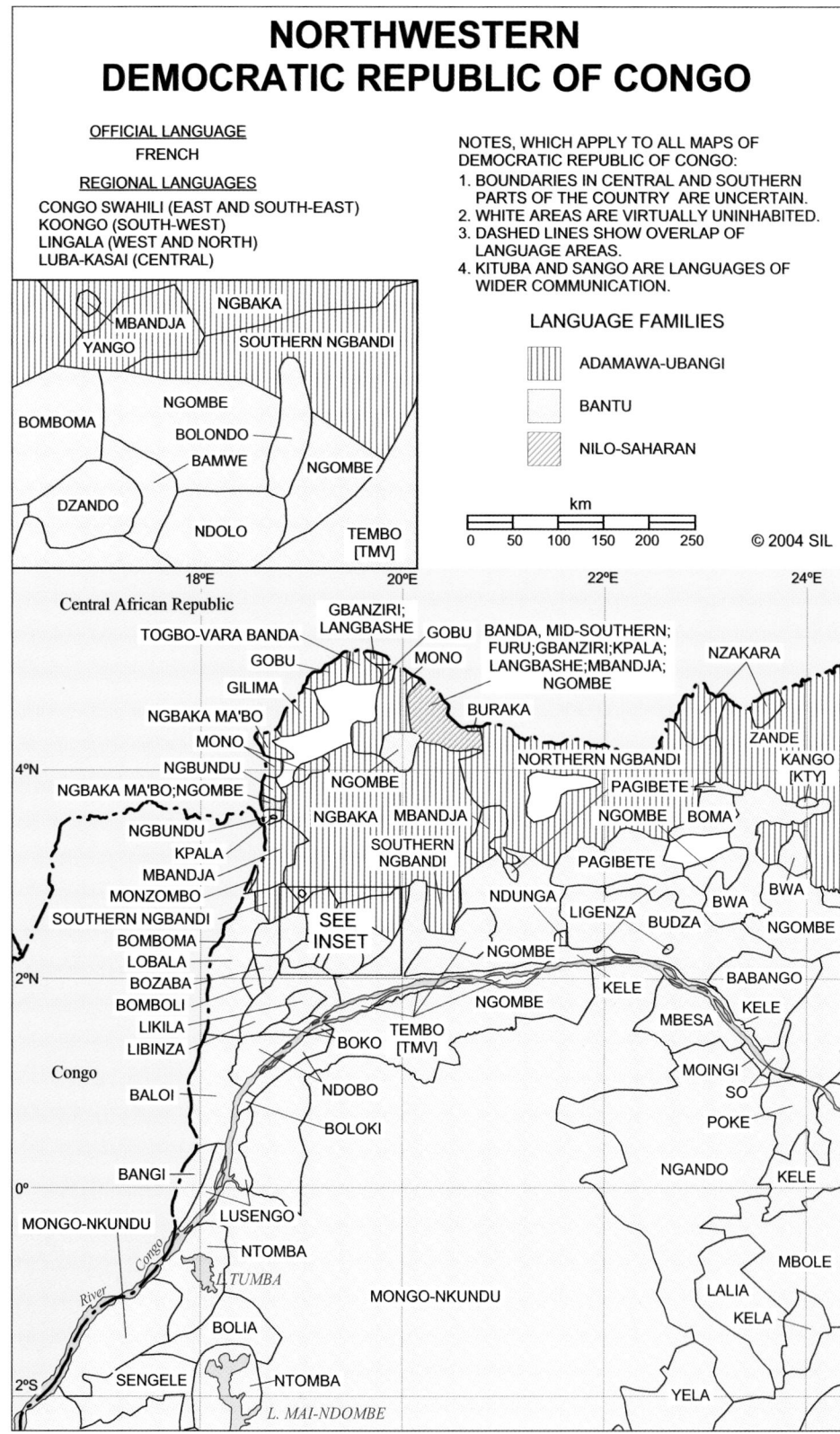

NORTHWESTERN
DEMOCRATIC REPUBLIC OF CONGO

OFFICIAL LANGUAGE
FRENCH

REGIONAL LANGUAGES
CONGO SWAHILI (EAST AND SOUTH-EAST)
KOONGO (SOUTH-WEST)
LINGALA (WEST AND NORTH)
LUBA-KASAI (CENTRAL)

NOTES, WHICH APPLY TO ALL MAPS OF
DEMOCRATIC REPUBLIC OF CONGO:
1. BOUNDARIES IN CENTRAL AND SOUTHERN
   PARTS OF THE COUNTRY ARE UNCERTAIN.
2. WHITE AREAS ARE VIRTUALLY UNINHABITED.
3. DASHED LINES SHOW OVERLAP OF
   LANGUAGE AREAS.
4. KITUBA AND SANGO ARE LANGUAGES OF
   WIDER COMMUNICATION.

LANGUAGE FAMILIES

ADAMAWA-UBANGI

BANTU

NILO-SAHARAN

km
0   50   100   150   200   250

© 2004 SIL

NORTHEASTERN
DEMOCRATIC REPUBLIC OF CONGO

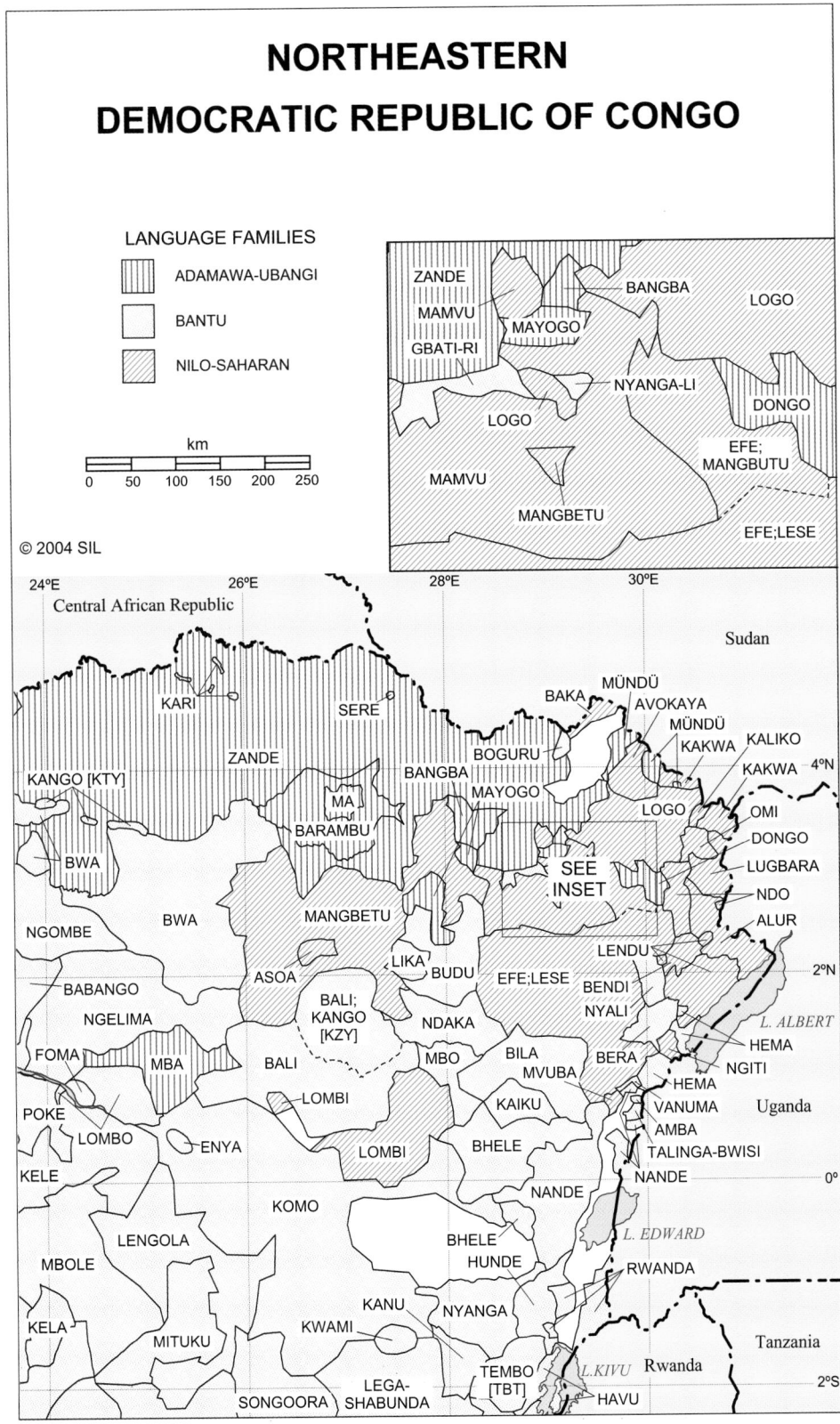

LANGUAGE FAMILIES

ADAMAWA-UBANGI

BANTU

NILO-SAHARAN

km

0 50 100 150 200 250

© 2004 SIL

SOUTHWESTERN
DEMOCRATIC REPUBLIC OF CONGO

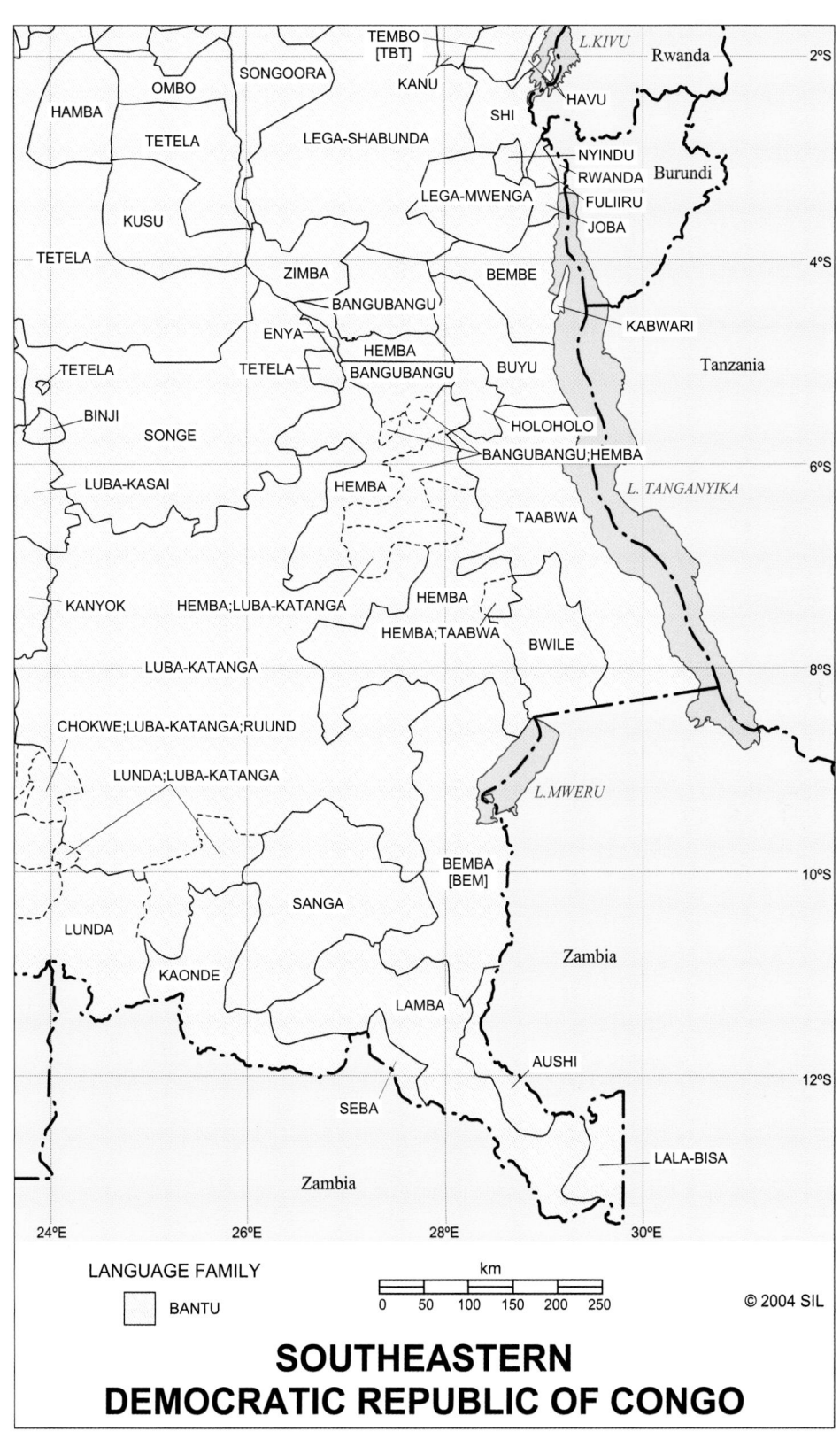

LANGUAGE FAMILY

BANTU

km

0 50 100 150 200 250

© 2004 SIL

SOUTHEASTERN
DEMOCRATIC REPUBLIC OF CONGO

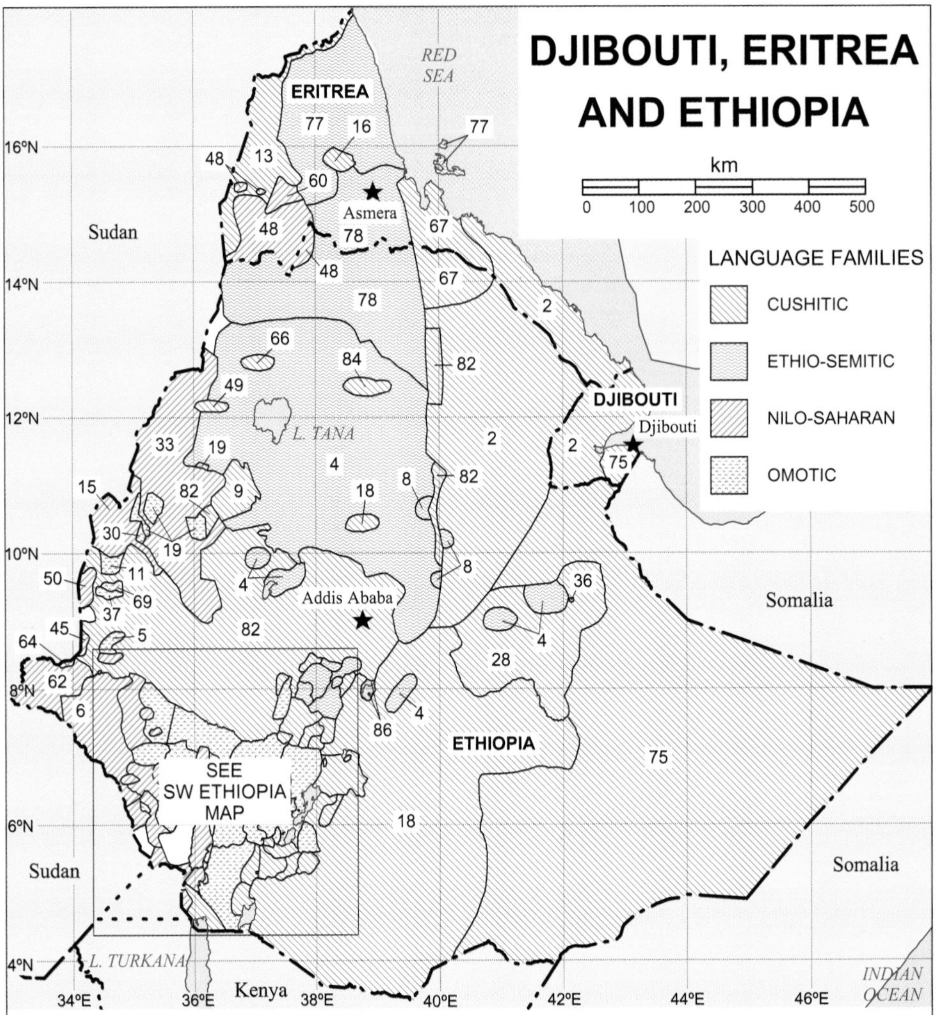

DJIBOUTI, ERITREA AND ETHIOPIA

km

0 100 200 300 400 500

LANGUAGE FAMILIES

- CUSHITIC
- ETHIO-SEMITIC
- NILO-SAHARAN
- OMOTIC

RED SEA

ERITREA

Asmera

DJIBOUTI

Djibouti

Sudan

L. TANA

Addis Ababa

ETHIOPIA

Somalia

SEE SW ETHIOPIA MAP

Somalia

Sudan

L. TURKANA

Kenya

INDIAN OCEAN

DJIBOUTI:

2 AFAR
75 SOMALI

ERITREA:

2 AFAR
13 BEDAWI
16 BILEN
48 KUNAMA (2)
60 NARA
67 SAHO
77 TIGRE (2)
78 TIGRIGNA

ETHIOPIA:

2 AFAR
4 AMHARIC (4)
5 ANFILLO
6 ANUAK
8 ARGOBBA (2)
9 AWNGI
11 BAMBASSI
15 BERTA
18 BORANA-ARSI-GUJI OROMO (2)
19 BORO (2)
28 EASTERN OROMO
30 GANZA
33 GUMUZ
36 HARARI
37 HOZO

45 KOMO
48 KUNAMA
49 KUNFAL
50 KWAMA
62 NUER
64 OPUUO
66 QIMANT
67 SAHO
69 SEZE
75 SOMALI
78 TIGRIGNA
82 WEST CENTRAL OROMO (4)
84 XAMTANGA
86 ZAY

- - - - - - - - - -
BOUNDARY IN DISPUTE

NATIONAL LANGUAGES
DJIBOUTI:
FRENCH
ERITREA:
STANDARD ARABIC
ENGLISH
ETHIOPIA:
AMHARIC
ENGLISH
TIGRIGNA

OFFICIAL LANGUAGE
ERITREA:
TIGRIGNA

SCATTERED LANGUAGES
ERITREA:
STANDARD ARABIC
SUDANESE ARABIC
TA'IZZI-ADENI ARABIC

NOTES:
1. WHITE AREAS ARE VIRTUALLY UNINHABITED.
2. BRACKETS SHOW THE NUMBER OF TIMES A LANGUAGE'S NUMBER APPEARS ON THE MAP OF ITS COUNTRY, IF MORE THAN ONCE.

© 2004 SIL

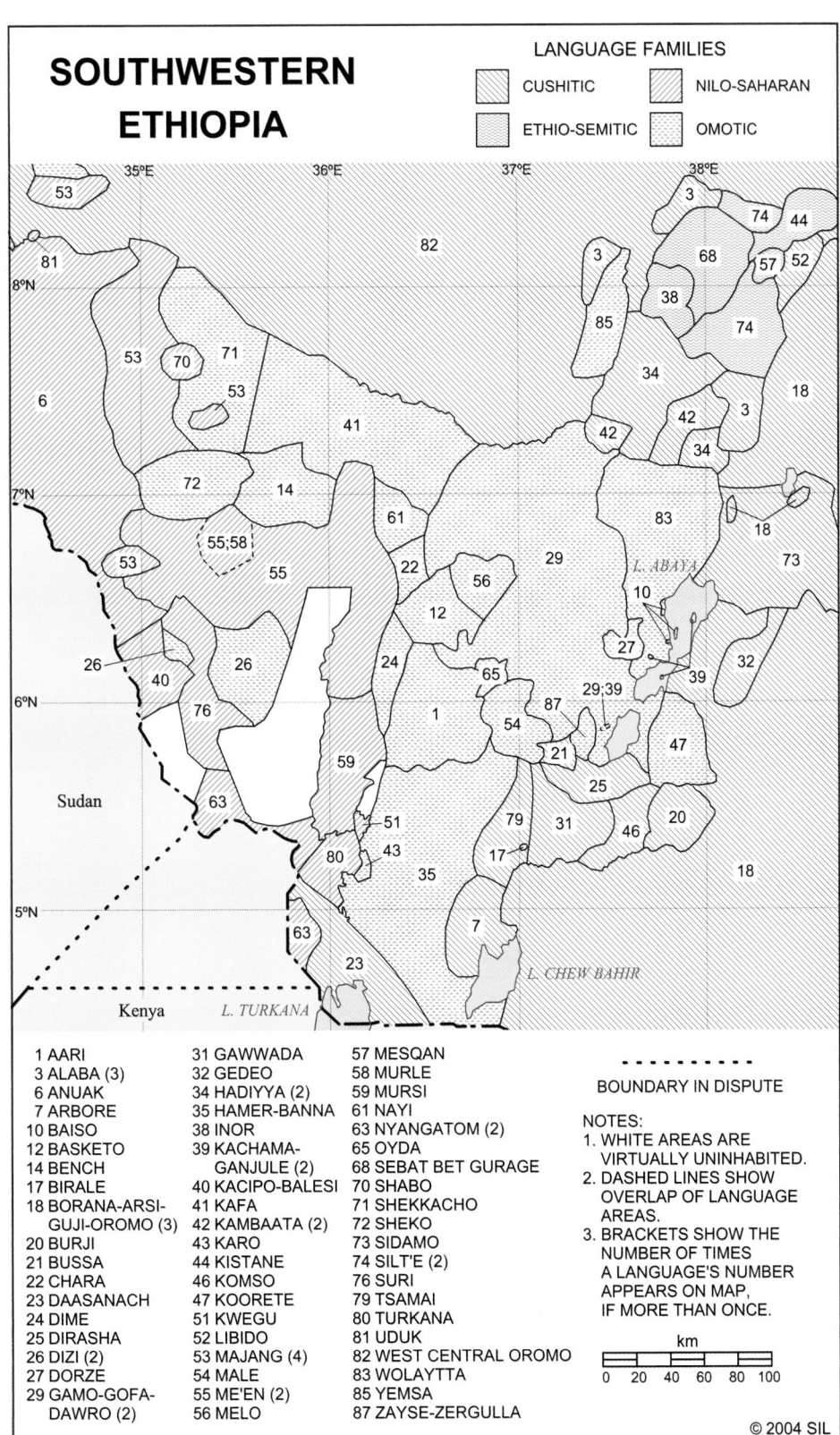

SOUTHWESTERN ETHIOPIA

LANGUAGE FAMILIES

CUSHITIC   NILO-SAHARAN

ETHIO-SEMITIC   OMOTIC

1 AARI	31 GAWWADA	57 MESQAN
3 ALABA (3)	32 GEDEO	58 MURLE
6 ANUAK	34 HADIYYA (2)	59 MURSI
7 ARBORE	35 HAMER-BANNA	61 NAYI
10 BAISO	38 INOR	63 NYANGATOM (2)
12 BASKETO	39 KACHAMA-	65 OYDA
14 BENCH	GANJULE (2)	68 SEBAT BET GURAGE
17 BIRALE	40 KACIPO-BALESI	70 SHABO
18 BORANA-ARSI-	41 KAFA	71 SHEKKACHO
GUJI-OROMO (3)	42 KAMBAATA (2)	72 SHEKO
20 BURJI	43 KARO	73 SIDAMO
21 BUSSA	44 KISTANE	74 SILT'E (2)
22 CHARA	46 KOMSO	76 SURI
23 DAASANACH	47 KOORETE	79 TSAMAI
24 DIME	51 KWEGU	80 TURKANA
25 DIRASHA	52 LIBIDO	81 UDUK
26 DIZI (2)	53 MAJANG (4)	82 WEST CENTRAL OROMO
27 DORZE	54 MALE	83 WOLAYTTA
29 GAMO-GOFA-	55 ME'EN (2)	85 YEMSA
DAWRO (2)	56 MELO	87 ZAYSE-ZERGULLA

- - - - - - - - - -

BOUNDARY IN DISPUTE

NOTES:
1. WHITE AREAS ARE VIRTUALLY UNINHABITED.
2. DASHED LINES SHOW OVERLAP OF LANGUAGE AREAS.
3. BRACKETS SHOW THE NUMBER OF TIMES A LANGUAGE'S NUMBER APPEARS ON MAP, IF MORE THAN ONCE.

km

0 20 40 60 80 100

© 2004 SIL

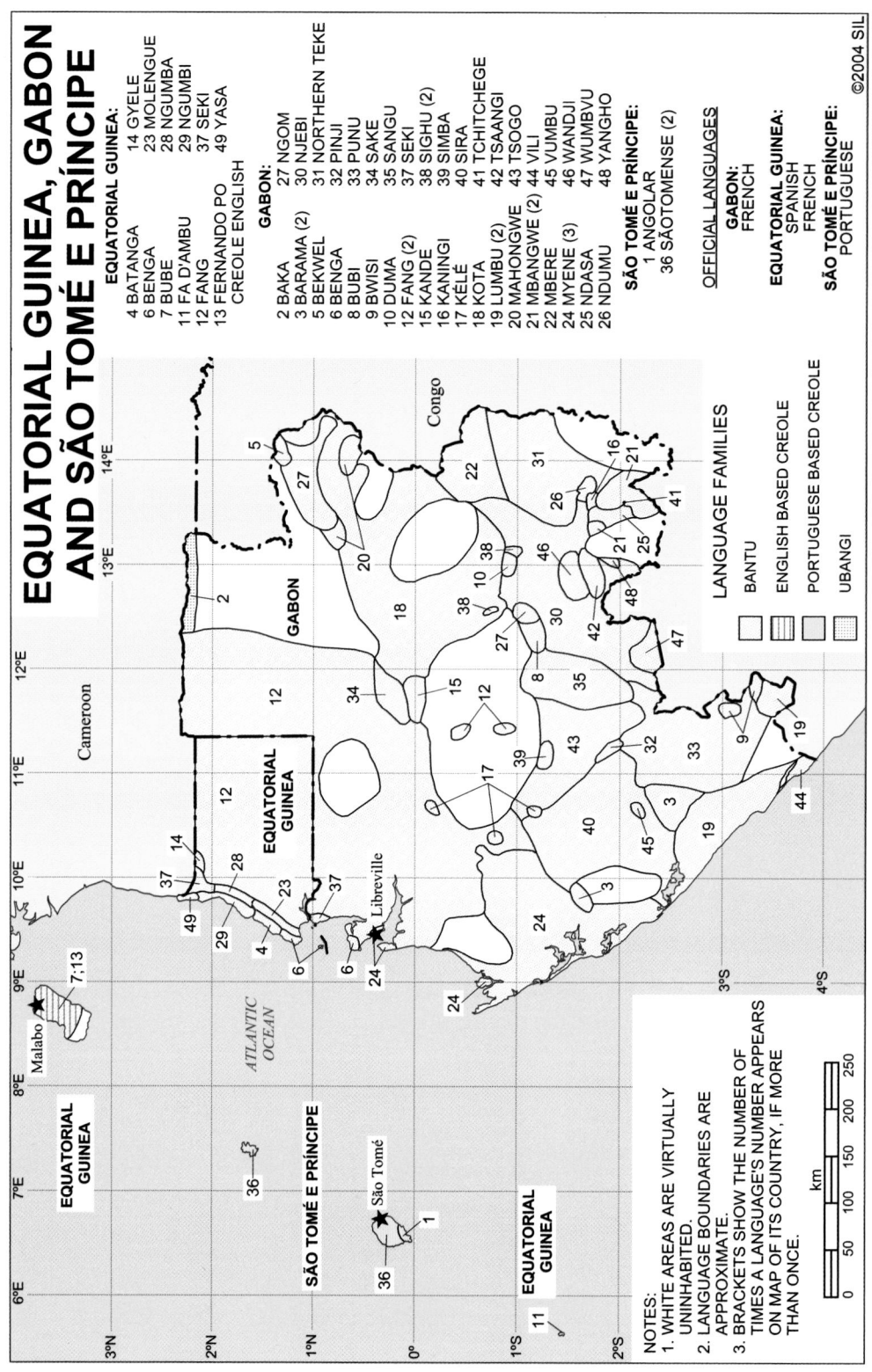

EQUATORIAL GUINEA, GABON AND SÃO TOMÉ E PRÍNCIPE

©2004 SIL

EQUATORIAL GUINEA:

4 BATANGA	14 GYELE
6 BENGA	23 MOLENGUE
7 BUBE	28 NGUMBA
11 FA D'AMBU	29 NGUMBI
12 FANG	37 SEKI
13 FERNANDO PO	49 YASA
CREOLE ENGLISH	

GABON:

2 BAKA	27 NGOM
3 BARAMA (2)	30 NJEBI
5 BEKWEL	31 NORTHERN TEKE
6 BENGA	32 PINJI
8 BUBI	33 PUNU
9 BWISI	34 SAKE
10 DUMA	35 SANGU
12 FANG (2)	37 SEKI
15 KANDE	38 SIGHU (2)
16 KANINGI	39 SIMBA
17 KÉLÉ	40 SIRA
18 KOTA	41 TCHITCHEGE
19 LUMBU (2)	42 TSAANGI
20 MAHONGWE	43 TSOGO
21 MBANGWE (2)	44 VILI
22 MBERE	45 VUMBU
24 MYENE (3)	46 WANDJI
25 NDASA	47 WUMBVU
26 NDUMU	48 YANGHO

SÃO TOMÉ E PRÍNCIPE:

1 ANGOLAR
36 SÃOTOMENSE (2)

OFFICIAL LANGUAGES

GABON:
FRENCH

EQUATORIAL GUINEA:
SPANISH
FRENCH

SÃO TOMÉ E PRÍNCIPE:
PORTUGUESE

LANGUAGE FAMILIES

☐	BANTU
☐	ENGLISH BASED CREOLE
☐	PORTUGUESE BASED CREOLE
☐	UBANGI

NOTES:
1. WHITE AREAS ARE VIRTUALLY UNINHABITED.
2. LANGUAGE BOUNDARIES ARE APPROXIMATE.
3. BRACKETS SHOW THE NUMBER OF TIMES A LANGUAGE'S NUMBER APPEARS ON MAP OF ITS COUNTRY, IF MORE THAN ONCE.

km

0   50   100   150   200   250

EQUATORIAL GUINEA

SÃO TOMÉ E PRÍNCIPE

EQUATORIAL GUINEA

Cameroon

Congo

GABON

EQUATORIAL GUINEA

Libreville

São Tomé

Malabo

ATLANTIC OCEAN

3°N   2°N   1°N   0°   1°S   2°S

6°E   7°E   8°E   9°E   10°E   11°E   12°E   13°E   14°E

3°S   4°S

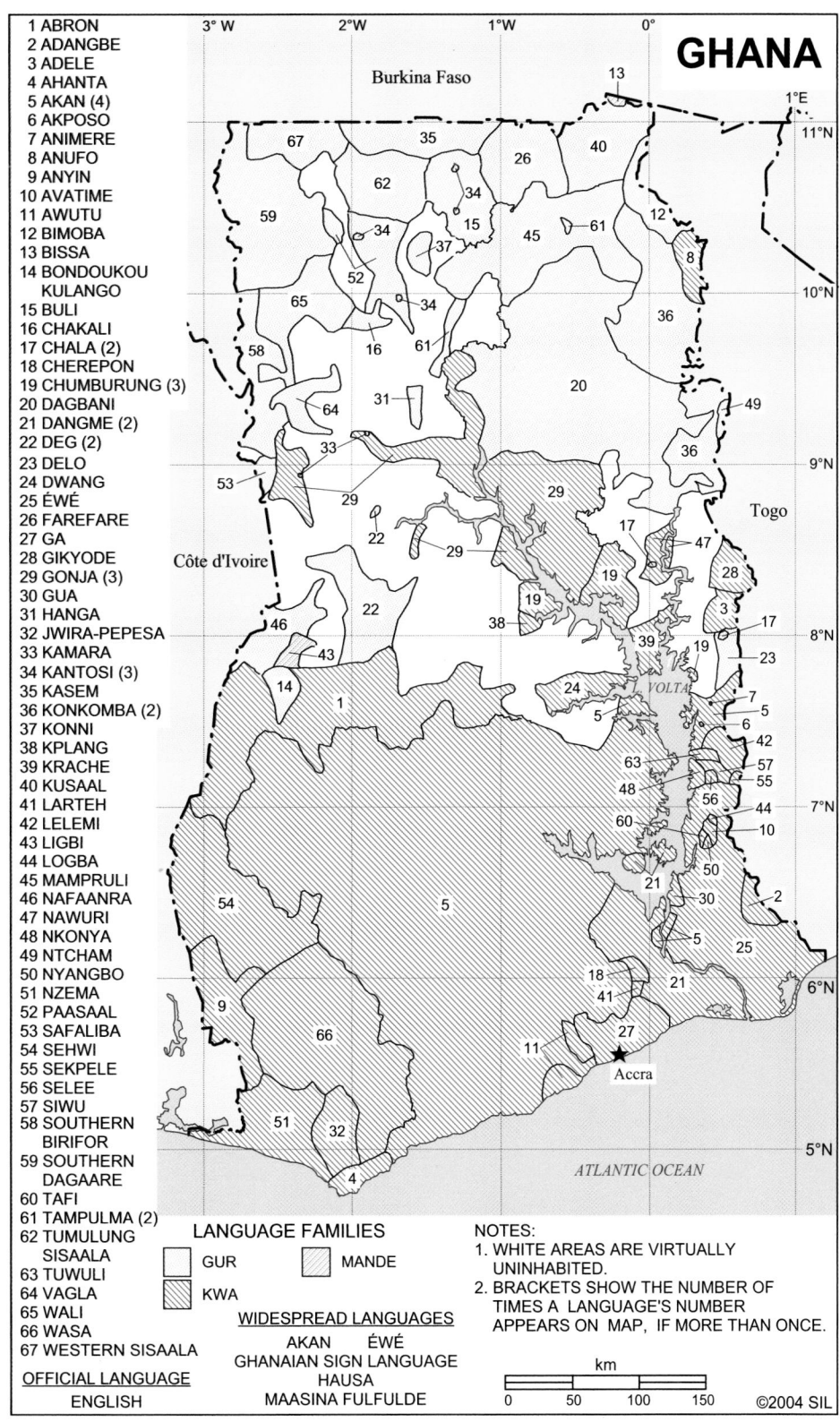

1 ABRON
2 ADANGBE
3 ADELE
4 AHANTA
5 AKAN (4)
6 AKPOSO
7 ANIMERE
8 ANUFO
9 ANYIN
10 AVATIME
11 AWUTU
12 BIMOBA
13 BISSA
14 BONDOUKOU
   KULANGO
15 BULI
16 CHAKALI
17 CHALA (2)
18 CHEREPON
19 CHUMBURUNG (3)
20 DAGBANI
21 DANGME (2)
22 DEG (2)
23 DELO
24 DWANG
25 ÉWÉ
26 FAREFARE
27 GA
28 GIKYODE
29 GONJA (3)
30 GUA
31 HANGA
32 JWIRA-PEPESA
33 KAMARA
34 KANTOSI (3)
35 KASEM
36 KONKOMBA (2)
37 KONNI
38 KPLANG
39 KRACHE
40 KUSAAL
41 LARTEH
42 LELEMI
43 LIGBI
44 LOGBA
45 MAMPRULI
46 NAFAANRA
47 NAWURI
48 NKONYA
49 NTCHAM
50 NYANGBO
51 NZEMA
52 PAASAAL
53 SAFALIBA
54 SEHWI
55 SEKPELE
56 SELEE
57 SIWU
58 SOUTHERN
   BIRIFOR
59 SOUTHERN
   DAGAARE
60 TAFI
61 TAMPULMA (2)
62 TUMULUNG
   SISAALA
63 TUWULI
64 VAGLA
65 WALI
66 WASA
67 WESTERN SISAALA

OFFICIAL LANGUAGE
   ENGLISH

GHANA

Burkina Faso

Côte d'Ivoire

Togo

VOLTA

Accra

ATLANTIC OCEAN

LANGUAGE FAMILIES

GUR   MANDE

KWA

WIDESPREAD LANGUAGES
   AKAN   ÉWÉ
GHANAIAN SIGN LANGUAGE
        HAUSA
MAASINA FULFULDE

NOTES:
1. WHITE AREAS ARE VIRTUALLY
   UNINHABITED.
2. BRACKETS SHOW THE NUMBER OF
   TIMES A LANGUAGE'S NUMBER
   APPEARS ON MAP, IF MORE THAN ONCE.

km

0   50   100   150

©2004 SIL

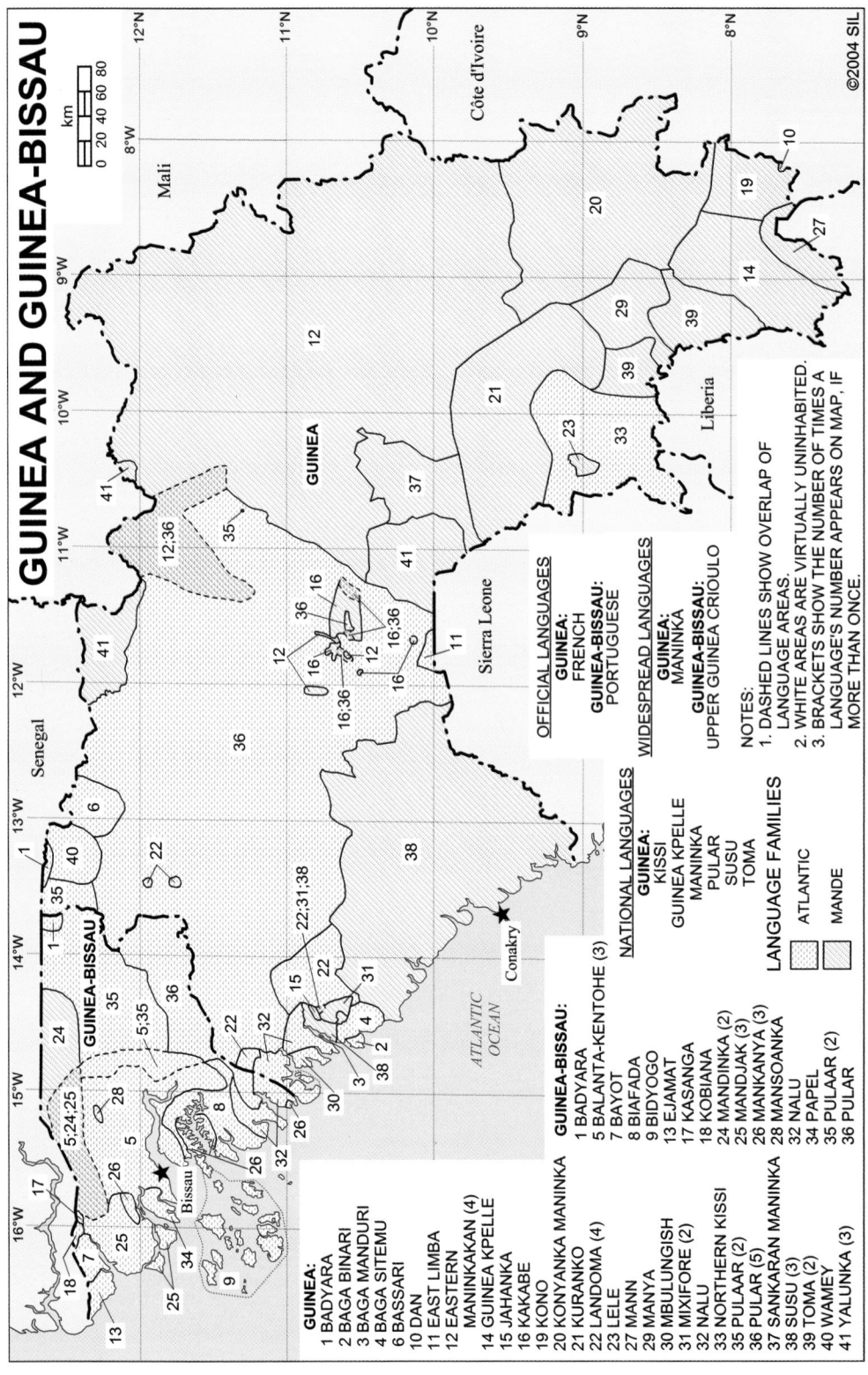

GUINEA AND GUINEA-BISSAU

©2004 SIL

km
0 20 40 60 80

GUINEA:
1 BADYARA
2 BAGA BINARI
3 BAGA MANDURI
4 BAGA SITEMU
6 BASSARI
10 DAN
11 EAST LIMBA
12 EASTERN
  MANINKAKAN (4)
14 GUINEA KPELLE
15 JAHANKA
16 KAKABE
19 KONO
20 KONYANKA MANINKA
21 KURANKO
22 LANDOMA (4)
23 LELE
27 MANN
29 MANYA
30 MBULUNGISH
31 MIXIFORE (2)
32 NALU
33 NORTHERN KISSI
35 PULAAR (2)
36 PULAR (5)
37 SANKARAN MANINKA
38 SUSU (3)
39 TOMA (2)
40 WAMEY
41 YALUNKA (3)

GUINEA-BISSAU:
1 BADYARA
5 BALANTA-KENTOHE (3)
7 BAYOT
8 BIAFADA
9 BIDYOGO
13 EJAMAT
17 KASANGA
18 KOBIANA
24 MANDINKA (2)
25 MANDJAK (3)
26 MANSOANKA
28 MANSOANKA
32 NALU
34 PAPEL
35 PULAAR (2)
36 PULAR

LANGUAGE FAMILIES

▨ ATLANTIC

▨ MANDE

NATIONAL LANGUAGES

GUINEA:
KISSI
GUINEA KPELLE
MANINKA
PULAR
SUSU
TOMA

OFFICIAL LANGUAGES

GUINEA:
FRENCH
GUINEA-BISSAU:
PORTUGUESE

WIDESPREAD LANGUAGES

GUINEA:
MANINKA
GUINEA-BISSAU:
UPPER GUINEA CRIOULO

NOTES:
1. DASHED LINES SHOW OVERLAP OF
   LANGUAGE AREAS.
2. WHITE AREAS ARE VIRTUALLY UNINHABITED.
3. BRACKETS SHOW THE NUMBER OF TIMES A
   LANGUAGE'S NUMBER APPEARS ON MAP, IF
   MORE THAN ONCE.

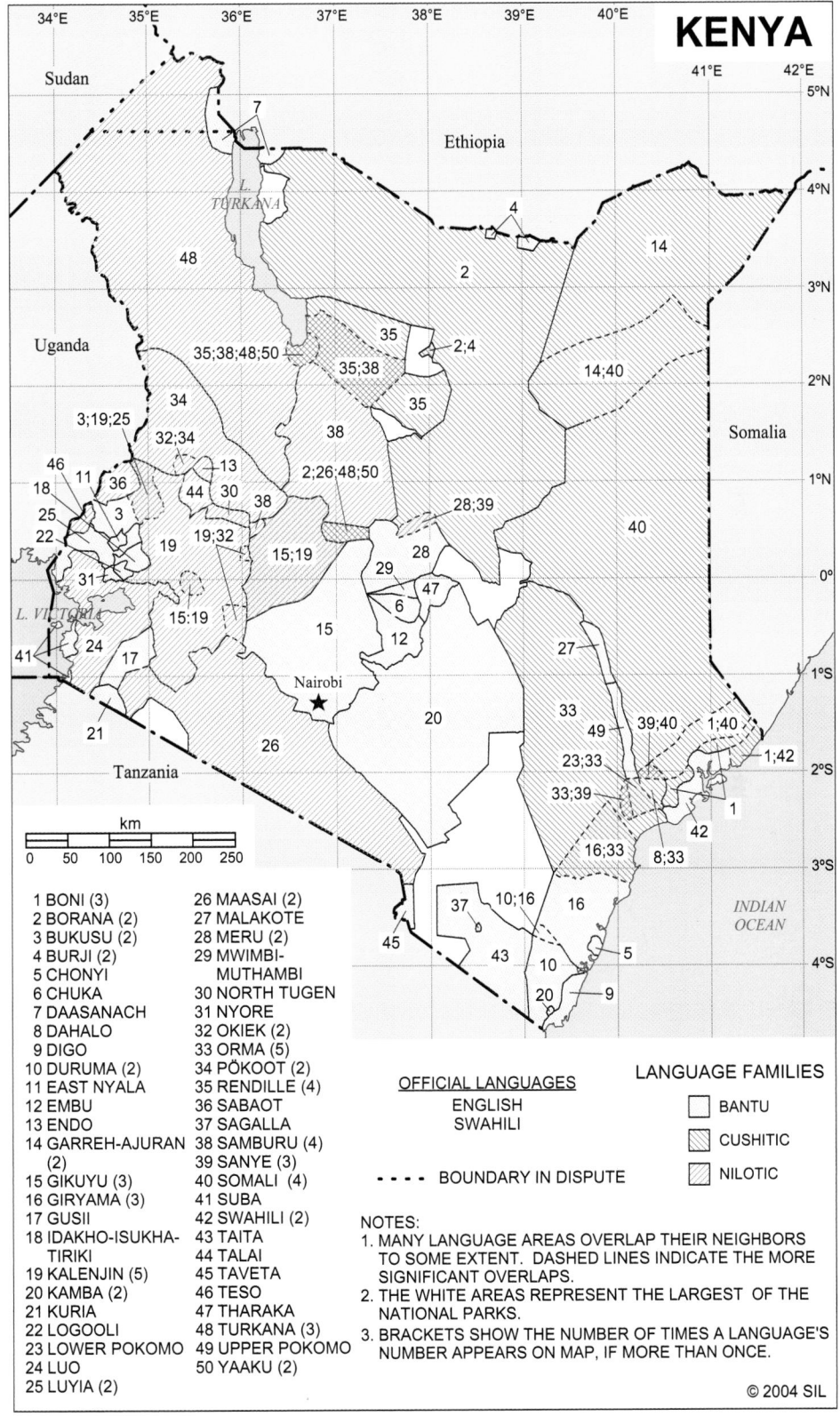

KENYA

1 BONI (3)	26 MAASAI (2)
2 BORANA (2)	27 MALAKOTE
3 BUKUSU (2)	28 MERU (2)
4 BURJI (2)	29 MWIMBI-
5 CHONYI	MUTHAMBI
6 CHUKA	30 NORTH TUGEN
7 DAASANACH	31 NYORE
8 DAHALO	32 OKIEK (2)
9 DIGO	33 ORMA (5)
10 DURUMA (2)	34 PÖKOOT (2)
11 EAST NYALA	35 RENDILLE (4)
12 EMBU	36 SABAOT
13 ENDO	37 SAGALLA
14 GARREH-AJURAN	38 SAMBURU (4)
(2)	39 SANYE (3)
15 GIKUYU (3)	40 SOMALI (4)
16 GIRYAMA (3)	41 SUBA
17 GUSII	42 SWAHILI (2)
18 IDAKHO-ISUKHA-	43 TAITA
TIRIKI	44 TALAI
19 KALENJIN (5)	45 TAVETA
20 KAMBA (2)	46 TESO
21 KURIA	47 THARAKA
22 LOGOOLI	48 TURKANA (3)
23 LOWER POKOMO	49 UPPER POKOMO
24 LUO	50 YAAKU (2)
25 LUYIA (2)	

OFFICIAL LANGUAGES
ENGLISH
SWAHILI

- - - - BOUNDARY IN DISPUTE

LANGUAGE FAMILIES

☐ BANTU

▨ CUSHITIC

▨ NILOTIC

NOTES:
1. MANY LANGUAGE AREAS OVERLAP THEIR NEIGHBORS TO SOME EXTENT. DASHED LINES INDICATE THE MORE SIGNIFICANT OVERLAPS.
2. THE WHITE AREAS REPRESENT THE LARGEST OF THE NATIONAL PARKS.
3. BRACKETS SHOW THE NUMBER OF TIMES A LANGUAGE'S NUMBER APPEARS ON MAP, IF MORE THAN ONCE.

© 2004 SIL

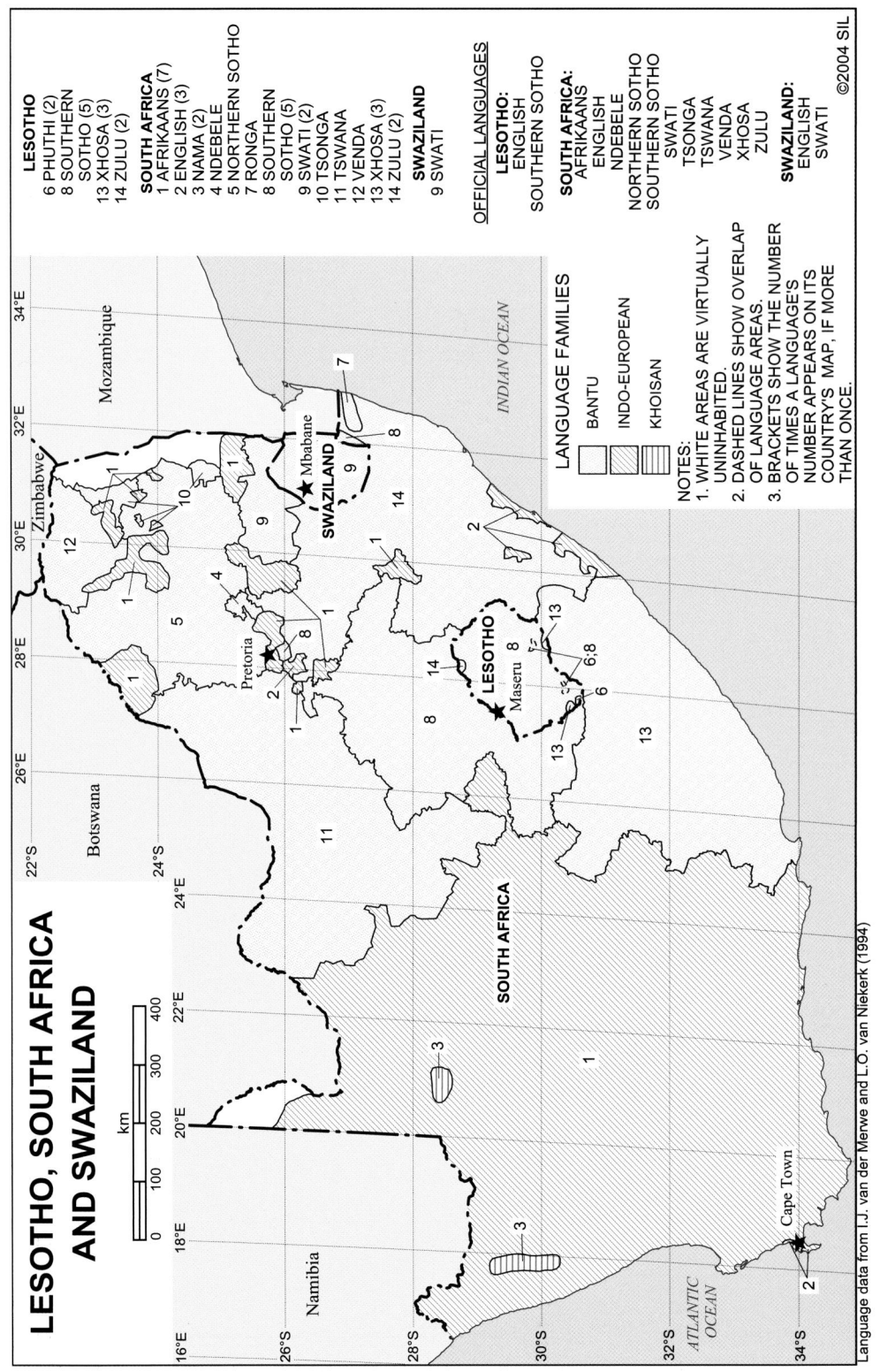

LESOTHO, SOUTH AFRICA AND SWAZILAND

LESOTHO
6 PHUTHI (2)
8 SOUTHERN SOTHO (5)
13 XHOSA (3)
14 ZULU (2)

SOUTH AFRICA
1 AFRIKAANS (7)
2 ENGLISH (3)
3 NAMA (2)
4 NDEBELE
5 NORTHERN SOTHO
7 RONGA
8 SOUTHERN SOTHO (5)
9 SWATI (2)
10 TSONGA
11 TSWANA
12 VENDA
13 XHOSA (3)
14 ZULU (2)

SWAZILAND
9 SWATI

OFFICIAL LANGUAGES

LESOTHO:
ENGLISH
SOUTHERN SOTHO

SOUTH AFRICA:
AFRIKAANS
ENGLISH
NDEBELE
NORTHERN SOTHO
SOUTHERN SOTHO
SWATI
TSONGA
TSWANA
VENDA
XHOSA
ZULU

SWAZILAND:
ENGLISH
SWATI

©2004 SIL

LANGUAGE FAMILIES
BANTU
INDO-EUROPEAN
KHOISAN

NOTES:
1. WHITE AREAS ARE VIRTUALLY UNINHABITED.
2. DASHED LINES SHOW OVERLAP OF LANGUAGE AREAS.
3. BRACKETS SHOW THE NUMBER OF TIMES A LANGUAGE'S NUMBER APPEARS ON ITS COUNTRY'S MAP, IF MORE THAN ONCE.

Language data from I.J. van der Merwe and L.O. van Niekerk (1994)

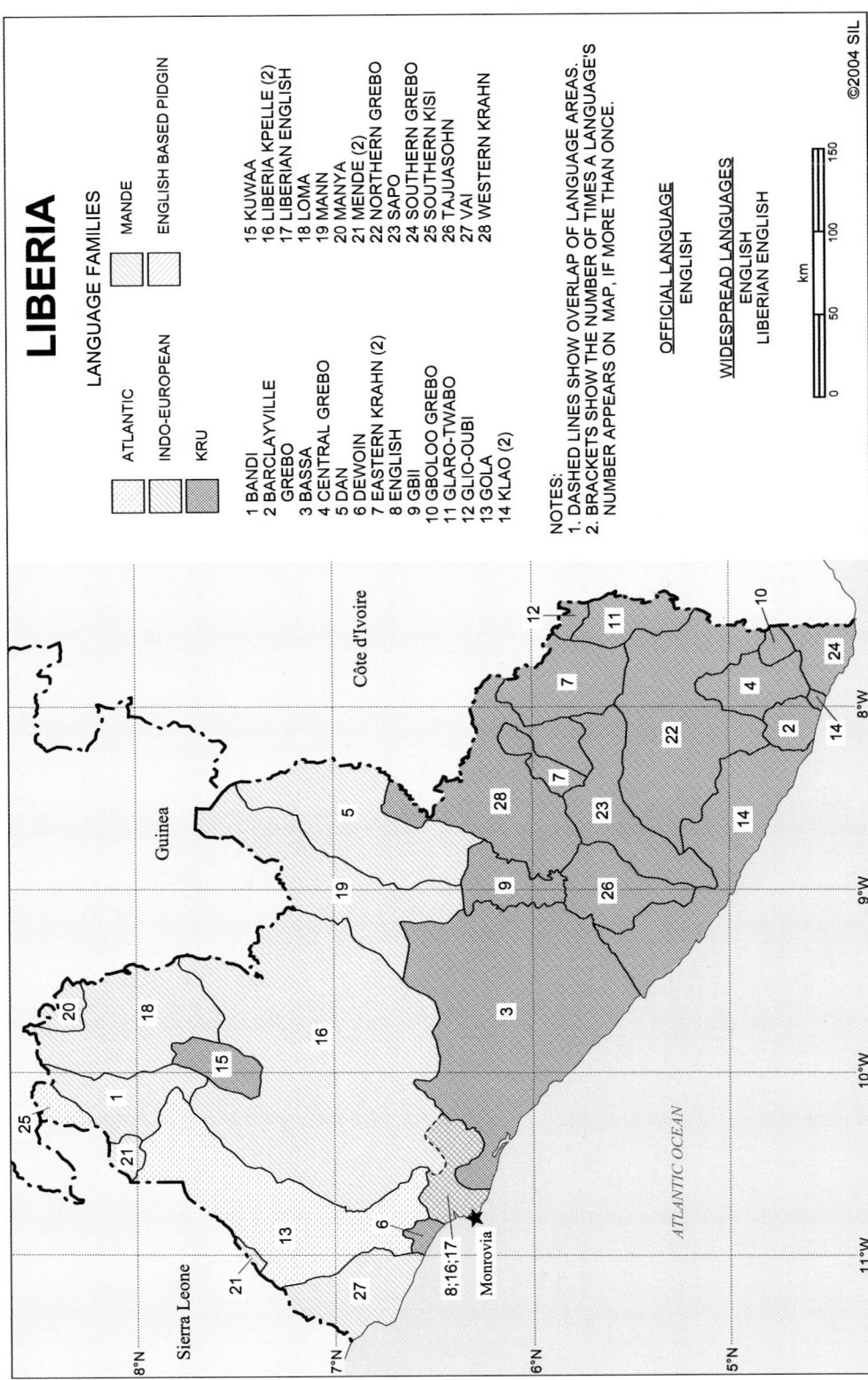

LIBERIA

LANGUAGE FAMILIES

ATLANTIC

INDO-EUROPEAN

KRU

MANDE

ENGLISH BASED PIDGIN

1 BANDI
2 BARCLAYVILLE GREBO
3 BASSA
4 CENTRAL GREBO
5 DAN
6 DEWOIN
7 EASTERN KRAHN (2)
8 ENGLISH
9 GBII
10 GBOLOO GREBO
11 GLARO-TWABO
12 GLIO-OUBI
13 GOLA
14 KLAO (2)

15 KUWAA
16 LIBERIA KPELLE (2)
17 LIBERIAN ENGLISH
18 LOMA
19 MANN
20 MANYA
21 MENDE (2)
22 NORTHERN GREBO
23 SAPO
24 SOUTHERN GREBO
25 SOUTHERN KISI
26 TAJUASOHN
27 VAI
28 WESTERN KRAHN

NOTES:
1. DASHED LINES SHOW OVERLAP OF LANGUAGE AREAS.
2. BRACKETS SHOW THE NUMBER OF TIMES A LANGUAGE'S NUMBER APPEARS ON MAP, IF MORE THAN ONCE.

OFFICIAL LANGUAGE
ENGLISH

WIDESPREAD LANGUAGES
ENGLISH
LIBERIAN ENGLISH

©2004 SIL

km
0   50   100   150

Sierra Leone

Guinea

Côte d'Ivoire

ATLANTIC OCEAN

Monrovia

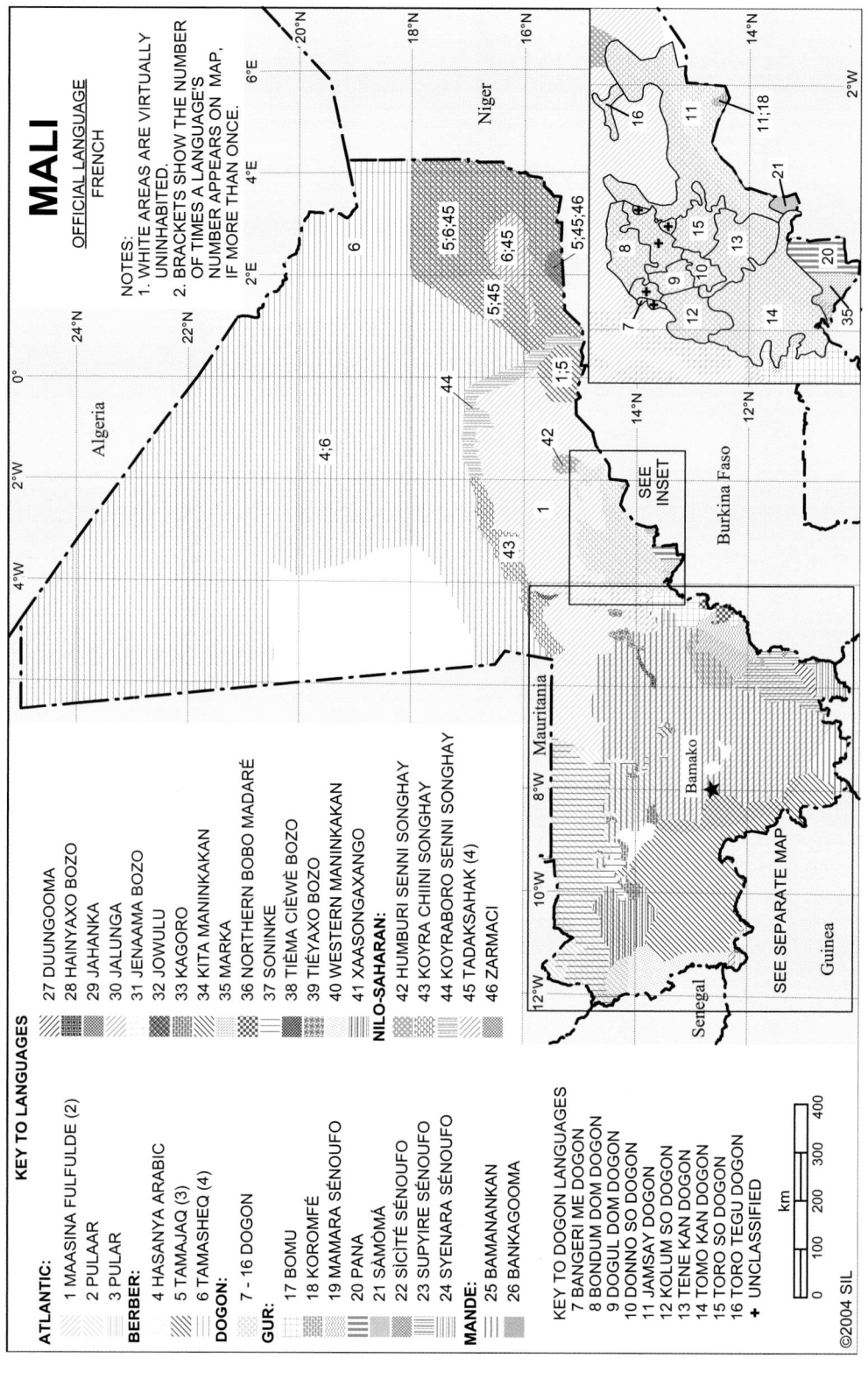

MALI

<u>OFFICIAL LANGUAGE</u>
FRENCH

NOTES:
1. WHITE AREAS ARE VIRTUALLY UNINHABITED.
2. BRACKETS SHOW THE NUMBER OF TIMES A LANGUAGE'S NUMBER APPEARS ON MAP, IF MORE THAN ONCE.

KEY TO LANGUAGES

ATLANTIC:
1 MAASINA FULFULDE (2)
2 PULAAR
3 PULAR

BERBER:
4 HASANYA ARABIC
5 TAMAJAQ (3)
6 TAMASHEQ (4)

DOGON:
7 - 16 DOGON

GUR:
17 BOMU
18 KOROMFÉ
19 MAMARA SÉNOUFO
20 PANA
21 SÀMÒMÁ
22 SICÌTÉ SÉNOUFO
23 SUPYIRE SÉNOUFO
24 SYENARA SÉNOUFO

MANDE:
25 BAMANANKAN
26 BANKAGOOMA

27 DUUNGOOMA
28 HAINYAXO BOZO
29 JAHANKA
30 JALUNGA
31 JENAAMA BOZO
32 JOWULU
33 KAGORO
34 KITA MANINKAKAN
35 MARKA
36 NORTHERN BOBO MADARÉ
37 SONINKE
38 TIÉMA CIÉWÉ BOZO
39 TIÉYAXO BOZO
40 WESTERN MANINKAKAN
41 XAASONGAXANGO

NILO-SAHARAN:
42 HUMBURI SENNI SONGHAY
43 KOYRA CHIINI SONGHAY
44 KOYRABORO SENNI SONGHAY
45 TADAKSAHAK (4)
46 ZARMACI

KEY TO DOGON LANGUAGES
7 BANGERI ME DOGON
8 BONDUM DOM DOGON
9 DOGUL DOM DOGON
10 DONNO SO DOGON
11 JAMSAY DOGON
12 KOLUM SO DOGON
13 TENE KAN DOGON
14 TOMO KAN DOGON
15 TORO SO DOGON
16 TORO TEGU DOGON
+ UNCLASSIFIED

km
0   100   200   300   400

©2004 SIL

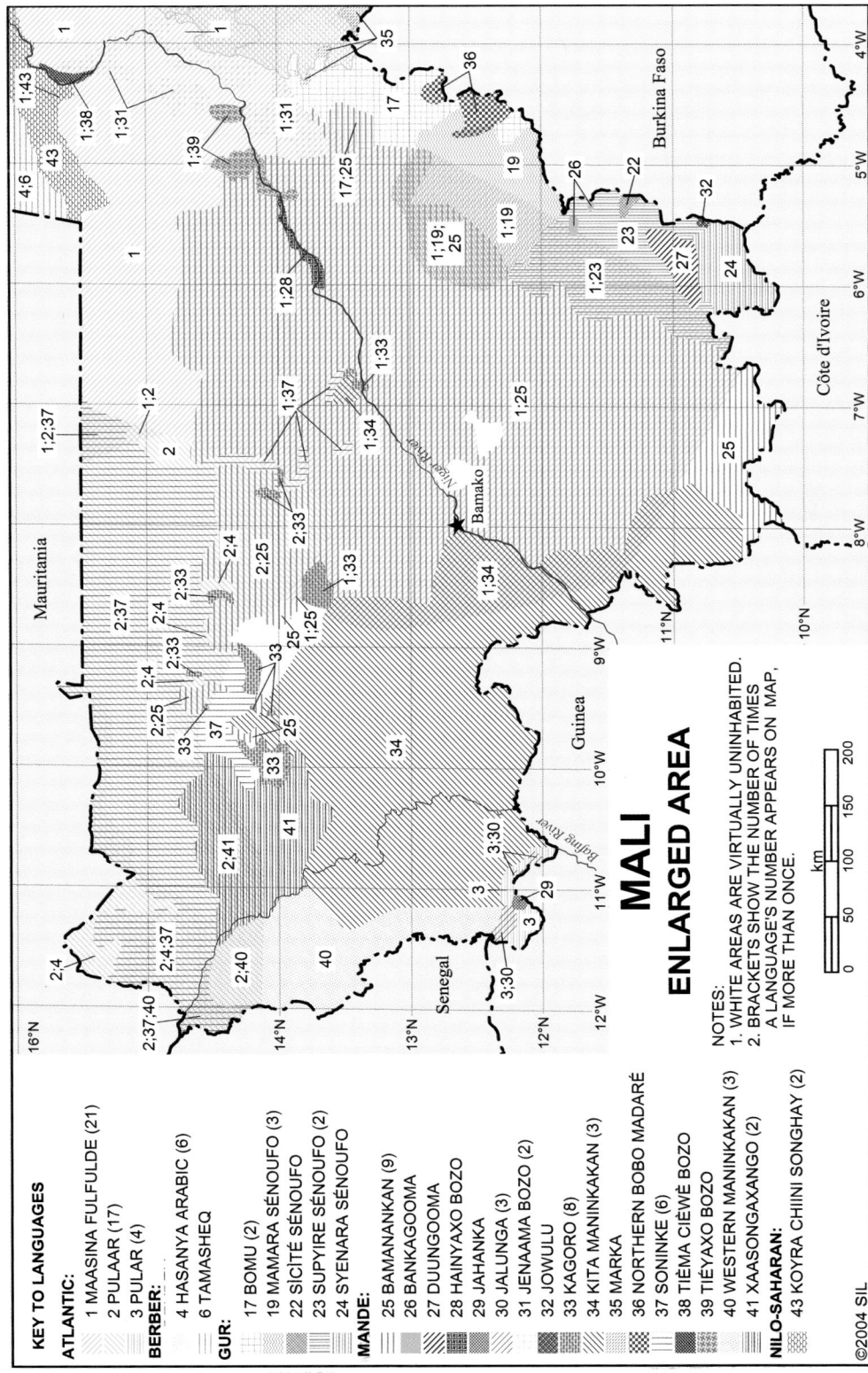

MALI
ENLARGED AREA

NOTES:
1. WHITE AREAS ARE VIRTUALLY UNINHABITED.
2. BRACKETS SHOW THE NUMBER OF TIMES A LANGUAGE'S NUMBER APPEARS ON MAP, IF MORE THAN ONCE.

km

0   50   100   150   200

KEY TO LANGUAGES

ATLANTIC:
1 MAASINA FULFULDE (21)
2 PULAAR (17)
3 PULAR (4)

BERBER:
4 HASANYA ARABIC (6)
6 TAMASHEQ

GUR:
17 BOMU (2)
19 MAMARA SÉNOUFO (3)
22 SICITÉ SÉNOUFO
23 SUPYIRE SÉNOUFO (2)
24 SYENARA SÉNOUFO

MANDE:
25 BAMANANKAN (9)
26 BANKAGOOMA
27 DUUNGOOMA
28 HAINYAXO BOZO
29 JAHANKA
30 JALUNGA (3)
31 JENAAMA BOZO (2)
32 JOWULU
33 KAGORO (8)
34 KITA MANINKAKAN (3)
35 MARKA
36 NORTHERN BOBO MADARÉ
37 SONINKE (6)
38 TIÉMA CIÉWÉ BOZO
39 TIÉYAXO BOZO
40 WESTERN MANINKAKAN (3)
41 XAASONGAXANGO (2)

NILO-SAHARAN:
43 KOYRA CHIINI SONGHAY (2)

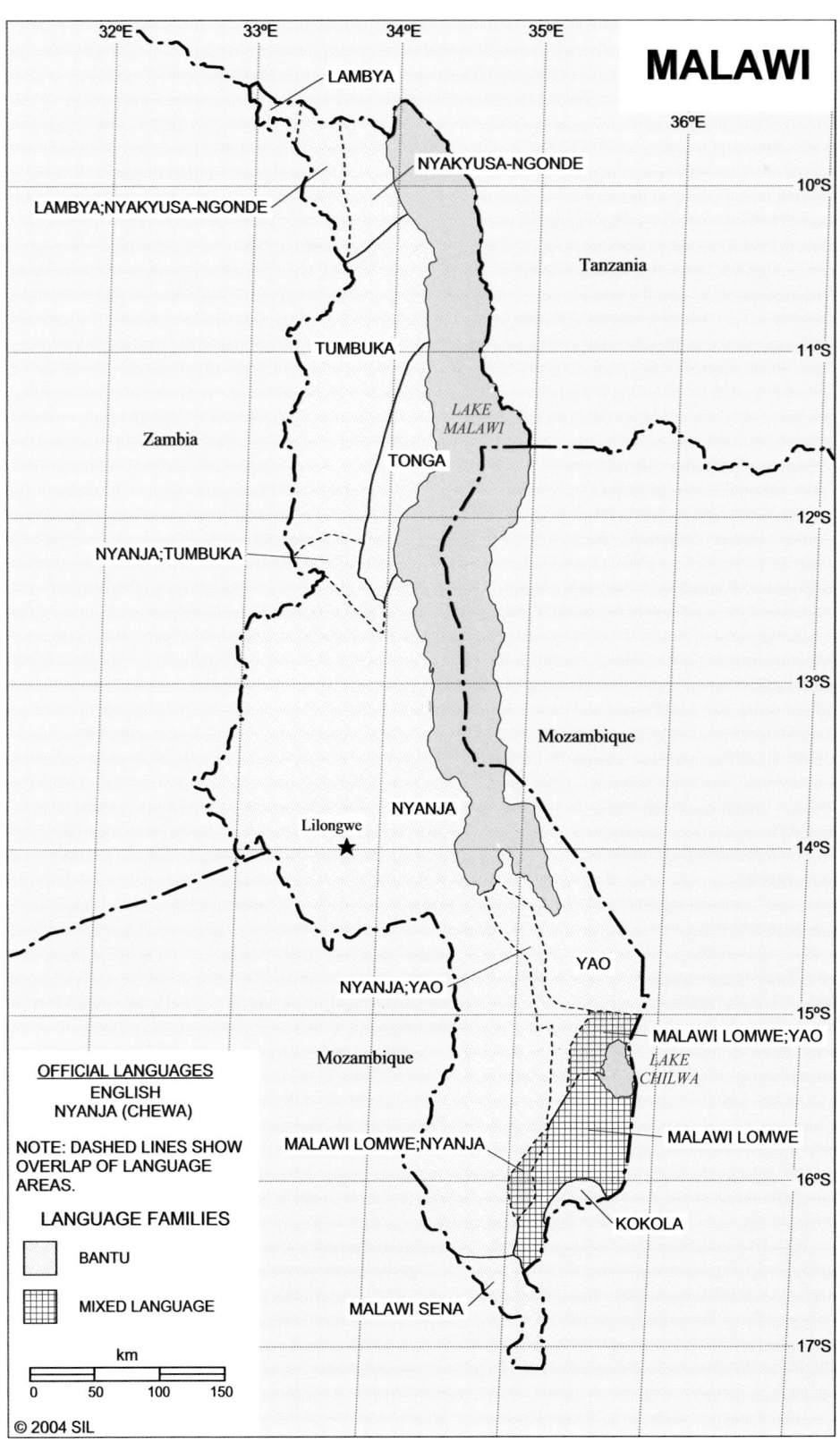

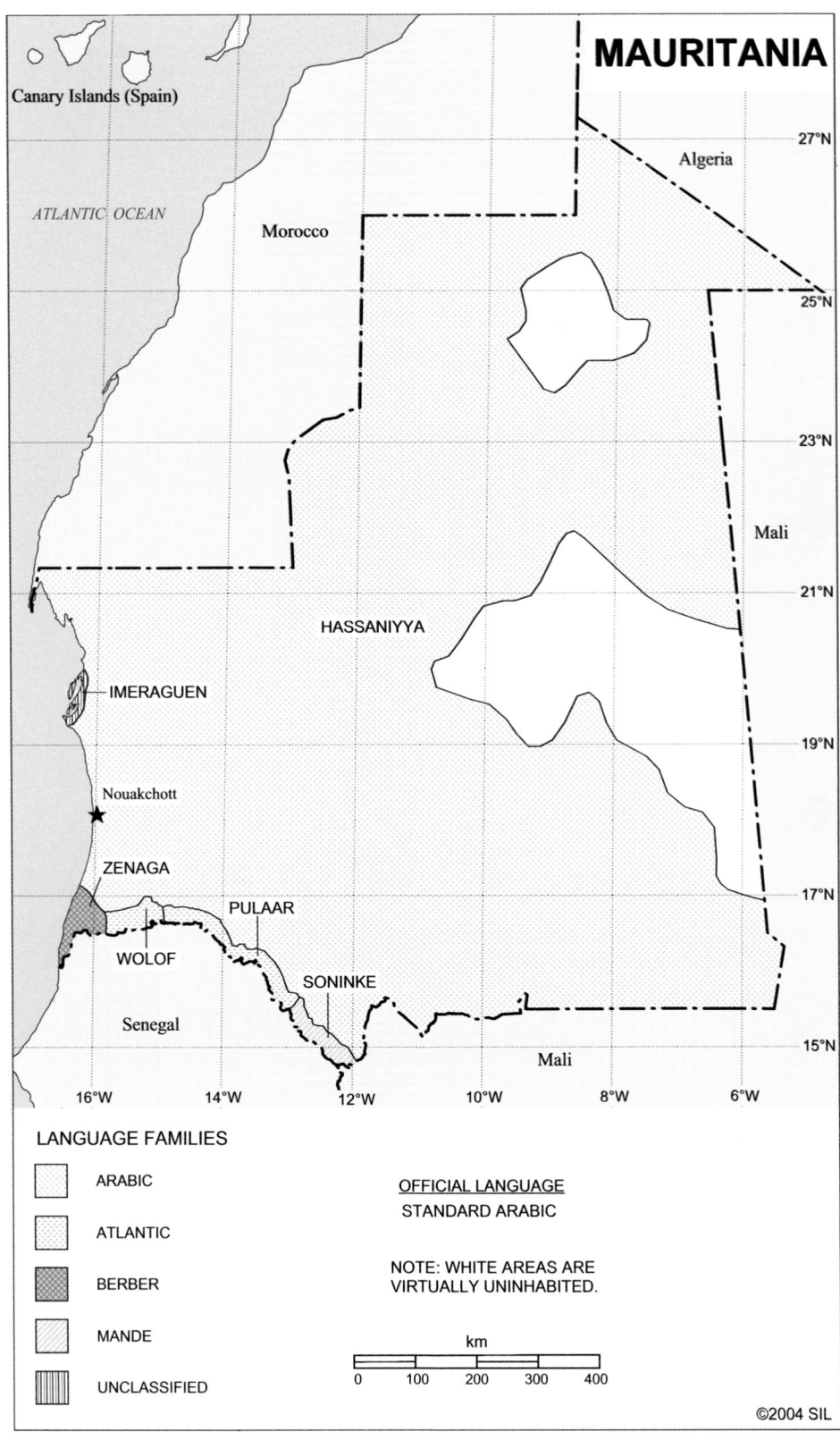

MAURITANIA

Canary Islands (Spain)

ATLANTIC OCEAN

27°N

Algeria

Morocco

25°N

23°N

Mali

21°N

HASSANIYYA

IMERAGUEN

19°N

Nouakchott

ZENAGA

17°N

PULAAR

WOLOF

SONINKE

Senegal

Mali

15°N

16°W   14°W   12°W   10°W   8°W   6°W

LANGUAGE FAMILIES

- ARABIC
- ATLANTIC
- BERBER
- MANDE
- UNCLASSIFIED

OFFICIAL LANGUAGE
STANDARD ARABIC

NOTE: WHITE AREAS ARE
VIRTUALLY UNINHABITED.

km

0   100   200   300   400

©2004 SIL

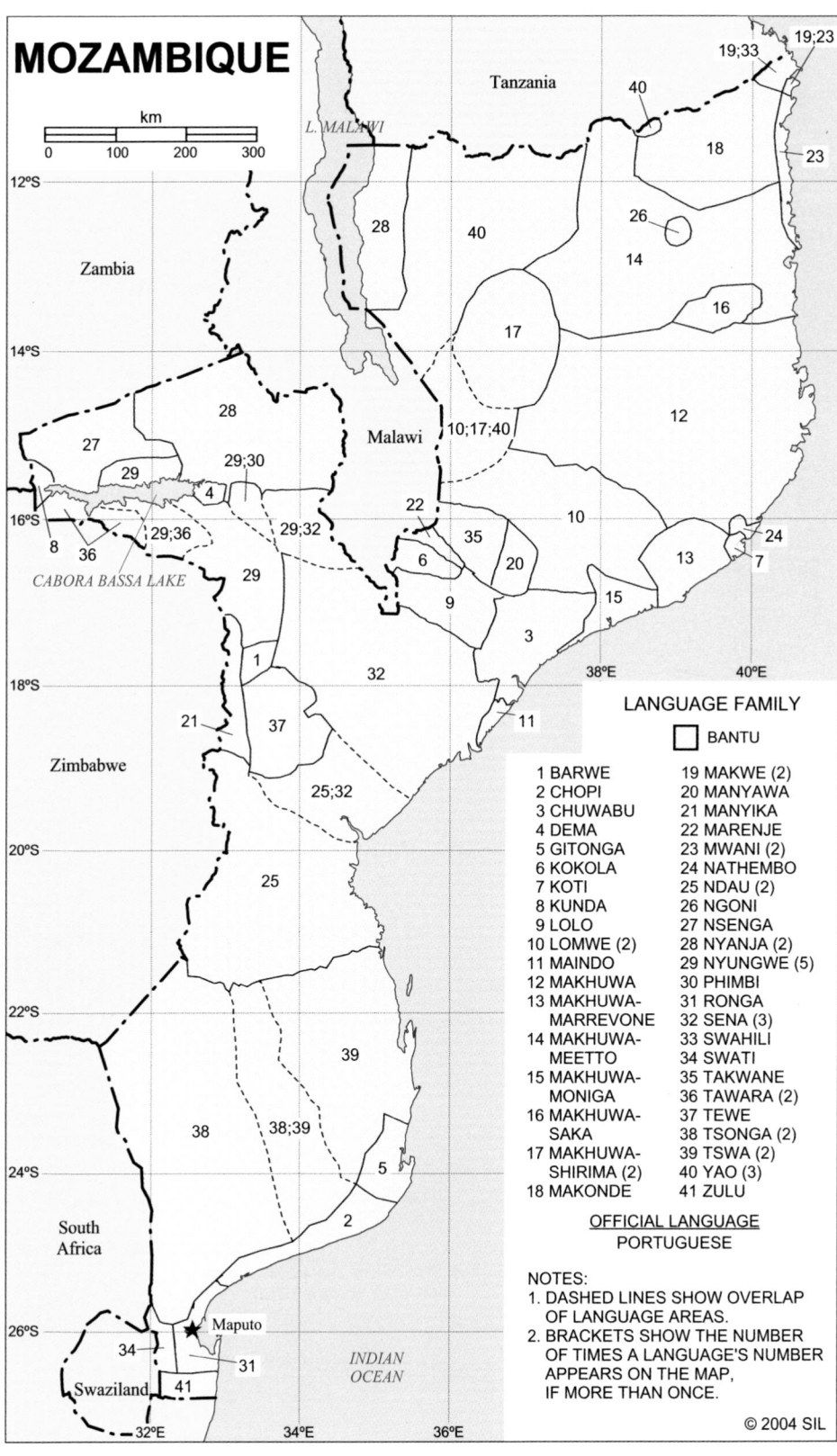

MOZAMBIQUE

LANGUAGE FAMILY

☐ BANTU

1 BARWE	19 MAKWE (2)
2 CHOPI	20 MANYAWA
3 CHUWABU	21 MANYIKA
4 DEMA	22 MARENJE
5 GITONGA	23 MWANI (2)
6 KOKOLA	24 NATHEMBO
7 KOTI	25 NDAU (2)
8 KUNDA	26 NGONI
9 LOLO	27 NSENGA
10 LOMWE (2)	28 NYANJA (2)
11 MAINDO	29 NYUNGWE (5)
12 MAKHUWA	30 PHIMBI
13 MAKHUWA-	31 RONGA
MARREVONE	32 SENA (3)
14 MAKHUWA-	33 SWAHILI
MEETTO	34 SWATI
15 MAKHUWA-	35 TAKWANE
MONIGA	36 TAWARA (2)
16 MAKHUWA-	37 TEWE
SAKA	38 TSONGA (2)
17 MAKHUWA-	39 TSWA (2)
SHIRIMA (2)	40 YAO (3)
18 MAKONDE	41 ZULU

OFFICIAL LANGUAGE
PORTUGUESE

NOTES:
1. DASHED LINES SHOW OVERLAP OF LANGUAGE AREAS.
2. BRACKETS SHOW THE NUMBER OF TIMES A LANGUAGE'S NUMBER APPEARS ON THE MAP, IF MORE THAN ONCE.

© 2004 SIL

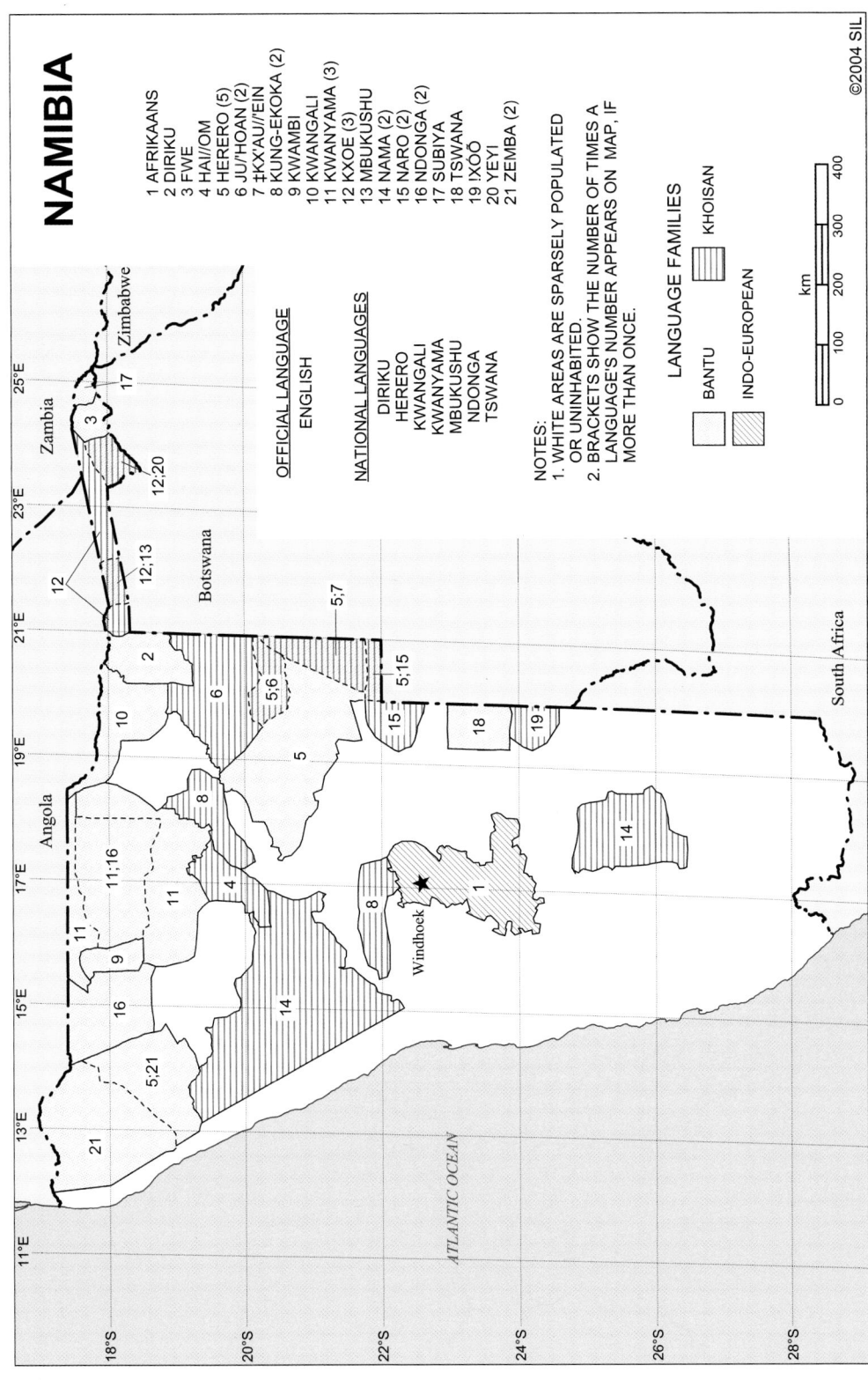

NAMIBIA

1 AFRIKAANS
2 DIRIKU
3 FWE
4 HAI//OM
5 HERERO (5)
6 JU/'HOAN (2)
7 ‡KX'AU//'EIN
8 KUNG-EKOKA (2)
9 KWAMBI
10 KWANGALI
11 KWANYAMA (3)
12 KXOE (3)
13 MBUKUSHU
14 NAMA (2)
15 NARO (2)
16 NDONGA (2)
17 SUBIYA
18 TSWANA
19 !XOŌ
20 YEYI
21 ZEMBA (2)

OFFICIAL LANGUAGE
ENGLISH

NATIONAL LANGUAGES
DIRIKU
HERERO
KWANGALI
KWANYAMA
MBUKUSHU
NDONGA
TSWANA

NOTES:
1. WHITE AREAS ARE SPARSELY POPULATED
   OR UNINHABITED.
2. BRACKETS SHOW THE NUMBER OF TIMES A
   LANGUAGE'S NUMBER APPEARS ON MAP, IF
   MORE THAN ONCE.

LANGUAGE FAMILIES

BANTU   KHOISAN

INDO-EUROPEAN

km
0   100   200   300   400

©2004 SIL

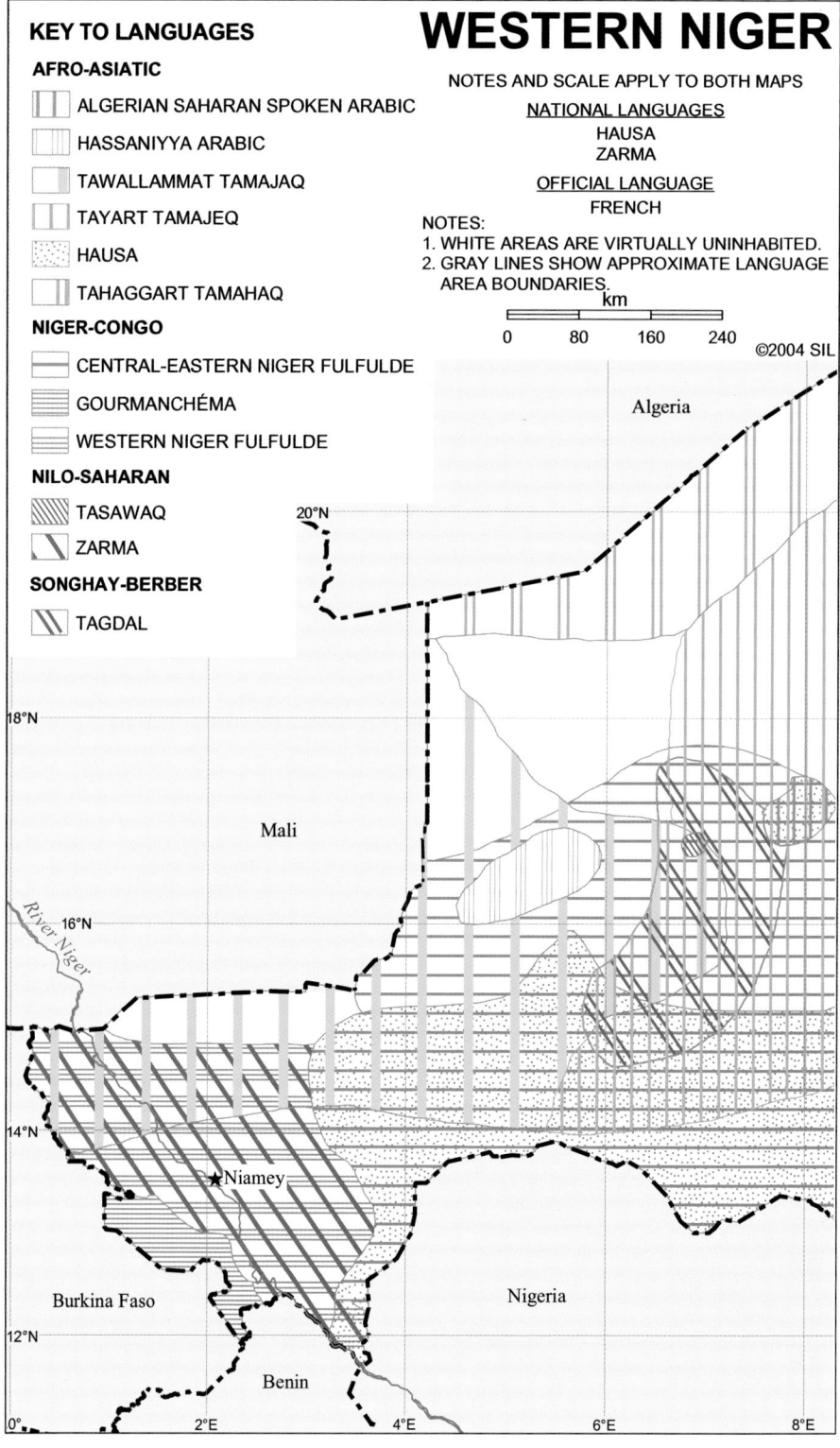

WESTERN NIGER

KEY TO LANGUAGES

AFRO-ASIATIC

- ALGERIAN SAHARAN SPOKEN ARABIC
- HASSANIYYA ARABIC
- TAWALLAMMAT TAMAJAQ
- TAYART TAMAJEQ
- HAUSA
- TAHAGGART TAMAHAQ

NIGER-CONGO

- CENTRAL-EASTERN NIGER FULFULDE
- GOURMANCHÉMA
- WESTERN NIGER FULFULDE

NILO-SAHARAN

- TASAWAQ
- ZARMA

SONGHAY-BERBER

- TAGDAL

NOTES AND SCALE APPLY TO BOTH MAPS

NATIONAL LANGUAGES
HAUSA
ZARMA

OFFICIAL LANGUAGE
FRENCH

NOTES:
1. WHITE AREAS ARE VIRTUALLY UNINHABITED.
2. GRAY LINES SHOW APPROXIMATE LANGUAGE AREA BOUNDARIES.

km

0   80   160   240

©2004 SIL

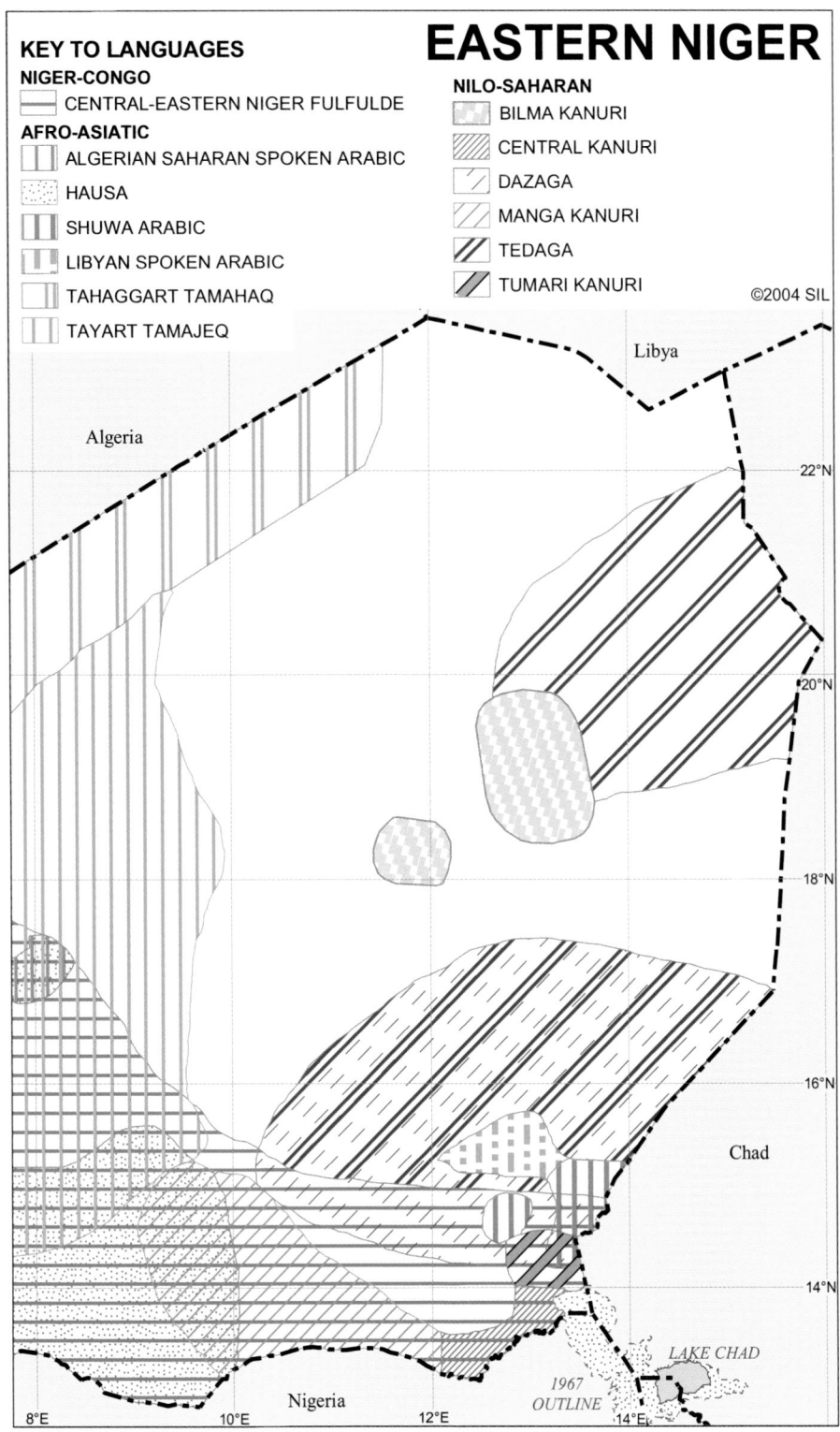

KEY TO LANGUAGES

NIGER-CONGO
- CENTRAL-EASTERN NIGER FULFULDE

AFRO-ASIATIC
- ALGERIAN SAHARAN SPOKEN ARABIC
- HAUSA
- SHUWA ARABIC
- LIBYAN SPOKEN ARABIC
- TAHAGGART TAMAHAQ
- TAYART TAMAJEQ

EASTERN NIGER

NILO-SAHARAN
- BILMA KANURI
- CENTRAL KANURI
- DAZAGA
- MANGA KANURI
- TEDAGA
- TUMARI KANURI

©2004 SIL

Libya

Algeria

22°N

20°N

18°N

16°N

Chad

14°N

LAKE CHAD

Nigeria

1967 OUTLINE

8°E   10°E   12°E   14°E

Nigeria: Index Of Languages

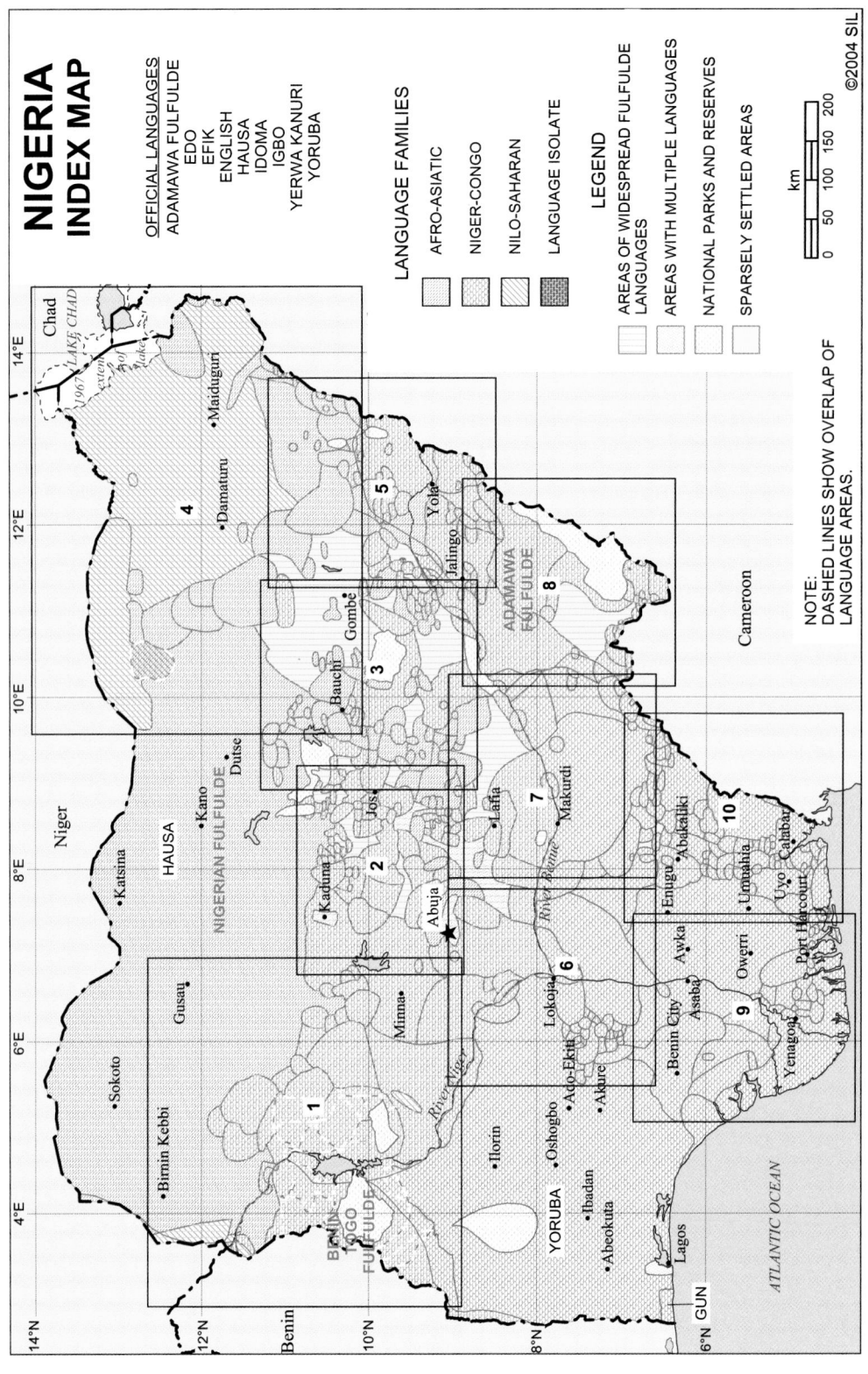

NIGERIA INDEX MAP

OFFICIAL LANGUAGES
ADAMAWA FULFULDE
EDO
EFIK
ENGLISH
HAUSA
IDOMA
IGBO
YERWA KANURI
YORUBA

LANGUAGE FAMILIES

AFRO-ASIATIC

NIGER-CONGO

NILO-SAHARAN

LANGUAGE ISOLATE

LEGEND

AREAS OF WIDESPREAD FULFULDE LANGUAGES

AREAS WITH MULTIPLE LANGUAGES

NATIONAL PARKS AND RESERVES

SPARSELY SETTLED AREAS

NOTE:
DASHED LINES SHOW OVERLAP OF LANGUAGE AREAS.

©2004 SIL

km
0 50 100 150 200

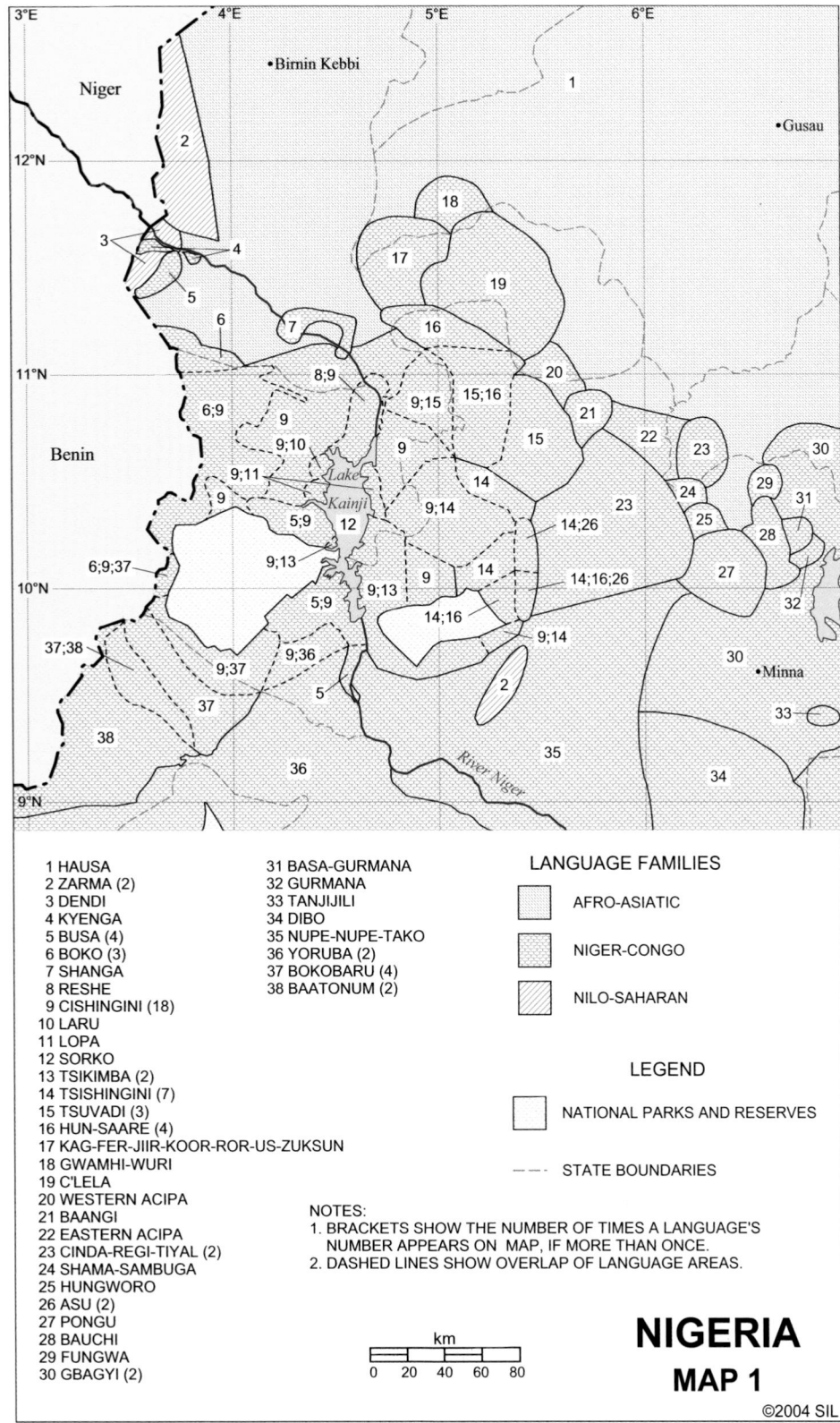

1 HAUSA
2 ZARMA (2)
3 DENDI
4 KYENGA
5 BUSA (4)
6 BOKO (3)
7 SHANGA
8 RESHE
9 CISHINGINI (18)
10 LARU
11 LOPA
12 SORKO
13 TSIKIMBA (2)
14 TSISHINGINI (7)
15 TSUVADI (3)
16 HUN-SAARE (4)
17 KAG-FER-JIIR-KOOR-ROR-US-ZUKSUN
18 GWAMHI-WURI
19 C'LELA
20 WESTERN ACIPA
21 BAANGI
22 EASTERN ACIPA
23 CINDA-REGI-TIYAL (2)
24 SHAMA-SAMBUGA
25 HUNGWORO
26 ASU (2)
27 PONGU
28 BAUCHI
29 FUNGWA
30 GBAGYI (2)

31 BASA-GURMANA
32 GURMANA
33 TANJIJILI
34 DIBO
35 NUPE-NUPE-TAKO
36 YORUBA (2)
37 BOKOBARU (4)
38 BAATONUM (2)

LANGUAGE FAMILIES

AFRO-ASIATIC

NIGER-CONGO

NILO-SAHARAN

LEGEND

NATIONAL PARKS AND RESERVES

–––– STATE BOUNDARIES

NOTES:
1. BRACKETS SHOW THE NUMBER OF TIMES A LANGUAGE'S
   NUMBER APPEARS ON MAP, IF MORE THAN ONCE.
2. DASHED LINES SHOW OVERLAP OF LANGUAGE AREAS.

km
0   20   40   60   80

NIGERIA
MAP 1

©2004 SIL

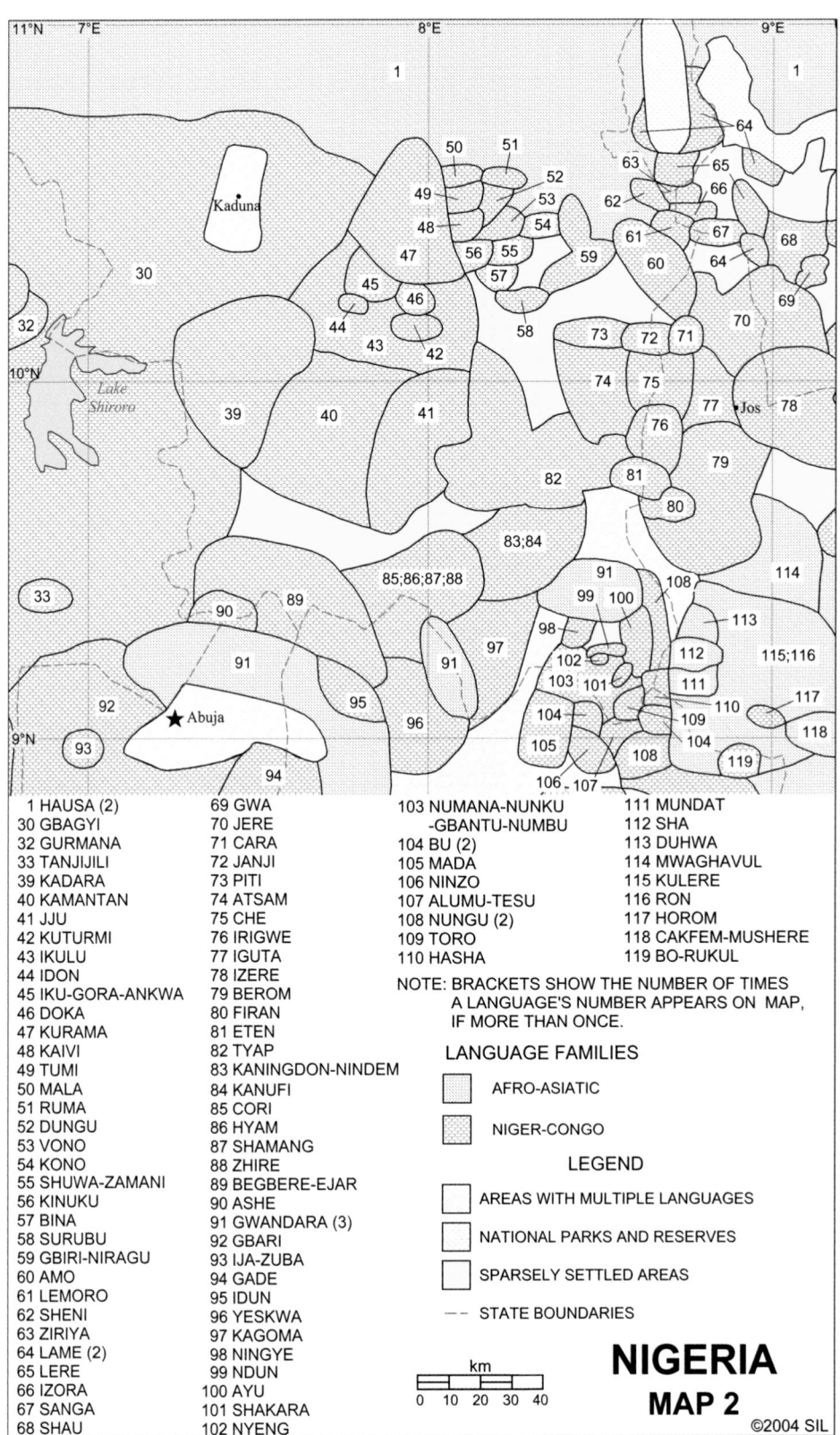

1 HAUSA (2)
30 GBAGYI
32 GURMANA
33 TANJIJILI
39 KADARA
40 KAMANTAN
41 JJU
42 KUTURMI
43 IKULU
44 IDON
45 IKU-GORA-ANKWA
46 DOKA
47 KURAMA
48 KAIVI
49 TUMI
50 MALA
51 RUMA
52 DUNGU
53 VONO
54 KONO
55 SHUWA-ZAMANI
56 KINUKU
57 BINA
58 SURUBU
59 GBIRI-NIRAGU
60 AMO
61 LEMORO
62 SHENI
63 ZIRIYA
64 LAME (2)
65 LERE
66 IZORA
67 SANGA
68 SHAU

69 GWA
70 JERE
71 CARA
72 JANJI
73 PITI
74 ATSAM
75 CHE
76 IRIGWE
77 IGUTA
78 IZERE
79 BEROM
80 FIRAN
81 ETEN
82 TYAP
83 KANINGDON-NINDEM
84 KANUFI
85 CORI
86 HYAM
87 SHAMANG
88 ZHIRE
89 BEGBERE-EJAR
90 ASHE
91 GWANDARA (3)
92 GBARI
93 IJA-ZUBA
94 GADE
95 IDUN
96 YESKWA
97 KAGOMA
98 NINGYE
99 NDUN
100 AYU
101 SHAKARA
102 NYENG

103 NUMANA-NUNKU
   -GBANTU-NUMBU
104 BU (2)
105 MADA
106 NINZO
107 ALUMU-TESU
108 NUNGU (2)
109 TORO
110 HASHA

111 MUNDAT
112 SHA
113 DUHWA
114 MWAGHAVUL
115 KULERE
116 RON
117 HOROM
118 CAKFEM-MUSHERE
119 BO-RUKUL

NOTE: BRACKETS SHOW THE NUMBER OF TIMES
    A LANGUAGE'S NUMBER APPEARS ON MAP,
    IF MORE THAN ONCE.

LANGUAGE FAMILIES

AFRO-ASIATIC

NIGER-CONGO

LEGEND

AREAS WITH MULTIPLE LANGUAGES

NATIONAL PARKS AND RESERVES

SPARSELY SETTLED AREAS

– – STATE BOUNDARIES

km
0   10   20   30   40

NIGERIA
MAP 2
©2004 SIL

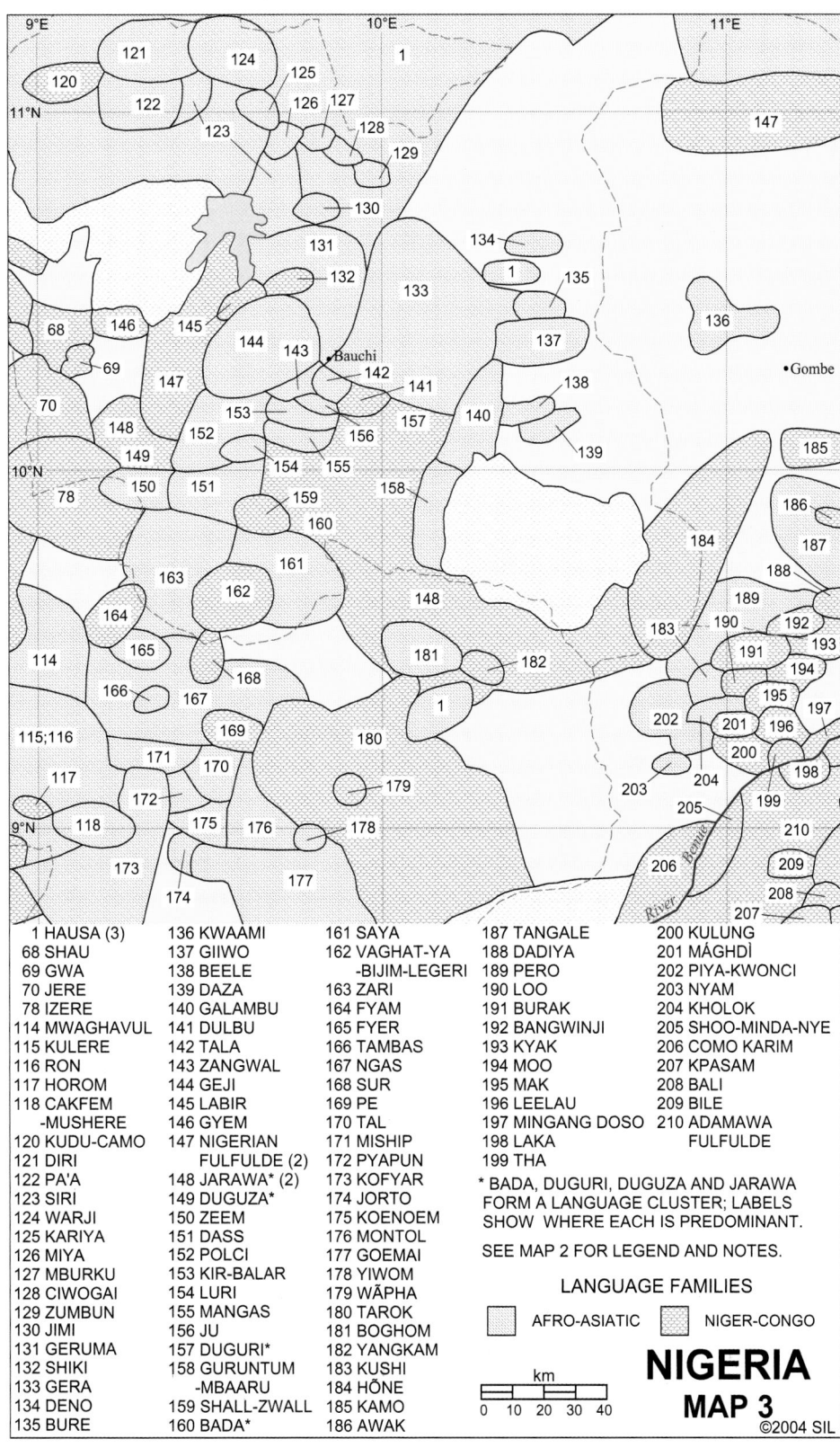

1 HAUSA (3)	136 KWAAMI	161 SAYA	187 TANGALE	200 KULUNG
68 SHAU	137 GIIWO	162 VAGHAT-YA	188 DADIYA	201 MÁGHDÌ
69 GWA	138 BEELE	-BIJIM-LEGERI	189 PERO	202 PIYA-KWONCI
70 JERE	139 DAZA	163 ZARI	190 LOO	203 NYAM
78 IZERE	140 GALAMBU	164 FYAM	191 BURAK	204 KHOLOK
114 MWAGHAVUL	141 DULBU	165 FYER	192 BANGWINJI	205 SHOO-MINDA-NYE
115 KULERE	142 TALA	166 TAMBAS	193 KYAK	206 COMO KARIM
116 RON	143 ZANGWAL	167 NGAS	194 MOO	207 KPASAM
117 HOROM	144 GEJI	168 SUR	195 MAK	208 BALI
118 CAKFEM	145 LABIR	169 PE	196 LEELAU	209 BILE
-MUSHERE	146 GYEM	170 TAL	197 MINGANG DOSO	210 ADAMAWA
120 KUDU-CAMO	147 NIGERIAN	171 MISHIP	198 LAKA	FULFULDE
121 DIRI	FULFULDE (2)	172 PYAPUN	199 THA	
122 PA'A	148 JARAWA* (2)	173 KOFYAR		
123 SIRI	149 DUGUZA*	174 JORTO	* BADA, DUGURI, DUGUZA AND JARAWA	
124 WARJI	150 ZEEM	175 KOENOEM	FORM A LANGUAGE CLUSTER; LABELS	
125 KARIYA	151 DASS	176 MONTOL	SHOW WHERE EACH IS PREDOMINANT.	
126 MIYA	152 POLCI	177 GOEMAI		
127 MBURKU	153 KIR-BALAR	178 YIWOM	SEE MAP 2 FOR LEGEND AND NOTES.	
128 CIWOGAI	154 LURI	179 WÃPHA		
129 ZUMBUN	155 MANGAS	180 TAROK	LANGUAGE FAMILIES	
130 JIMI	156 JU	181 BOGHOM		
131 GERUMA	157 DUGURI*	182 YANGKAM	AFRO-ASIATIC NIGER-CONGO	
132 SHIKI	158 GURUNTUM	183 KUSHI		
133 GERA	-MBAARU	184 HŌNE		
134 DENO	159 SHALL-ZWALL	185 KAMO	km	**NIGERIA**
135 BURE	160 BADA*	186 AWAK	0 10 20 30 40	**MAP 3**

©2004 SIL

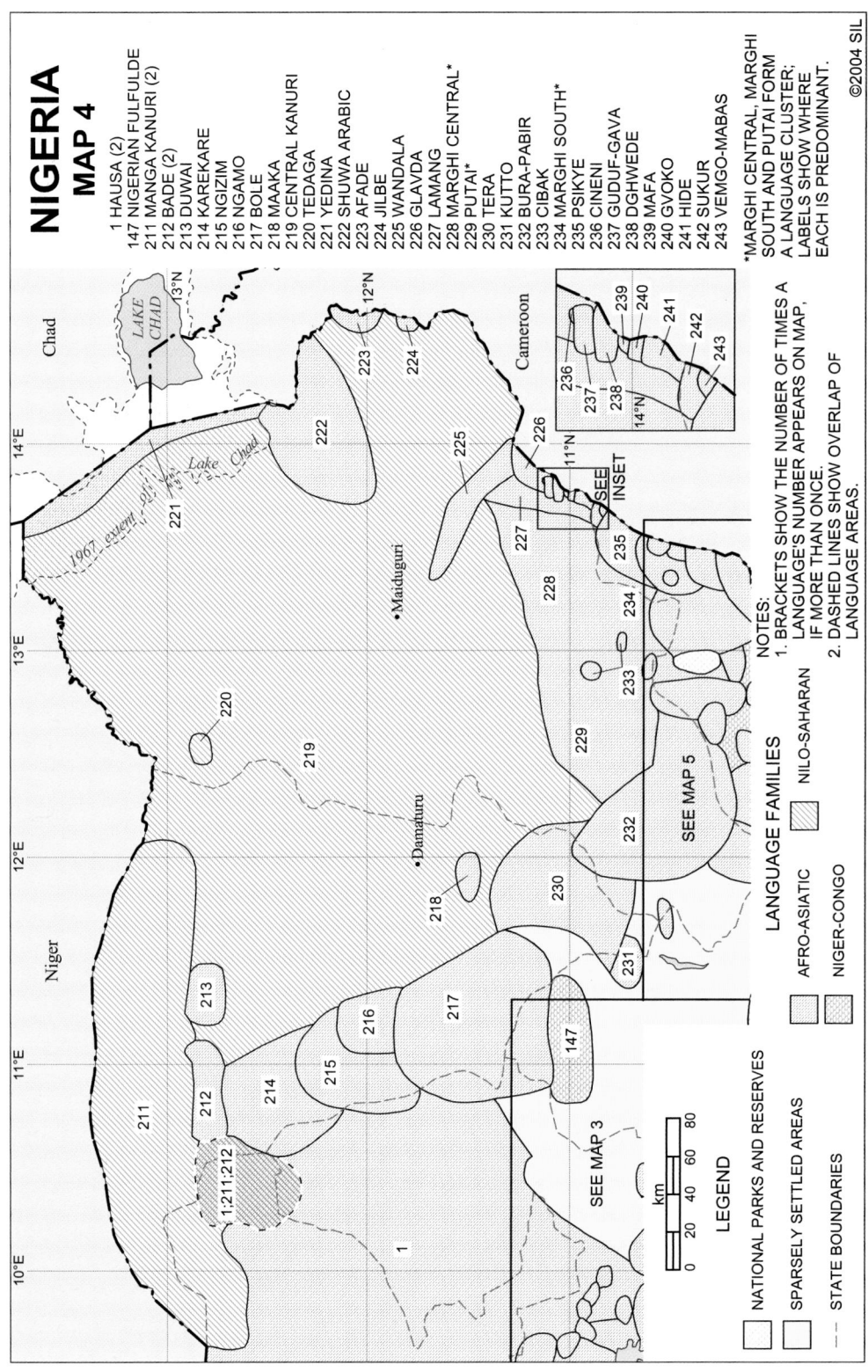

NIGERIA
MAP 4

1 HAUSA (2)
147 NIGERIAN FULFULDE
211 MANGA KANURI (2)
212 BADE (2)
213 DUWAI
214 KAREKARE
215 NGIZIM
216 NGAMO
217 BOLE
218 MAAKA
219 CENTRAL KANURI
220 TEDAGA
221 YEDINA
222 SHUWA ARABIC
223 AFADE
224 JILBE
225 WANDALA
226 GLAVDA
227 LAMANG
228 MARGHI CENTRAL*
229 PUTAI*
230 TERA
231 KUTTO
232 BURA-PABIR
233 CIBAK
234 MARGHI SOUTH*
235 PSIKYE
236 CINENI
237 GUDUF-GAVA
238 DGHWEDE
239 MAFA
240 GVOKO
241 HIDE
242 SUKUR
243 VEMGO-MABAS

*MARGHI CENTRAL, MARGHI SOUTH AND PUTAI FORM A LANGUAGE CLUSTER; LABELS SHOW WHERE EACH IS PREDOMINANT.

©2004 SIL

Chad

LAKE CHAD

13°N

12°N

11°N

14°N

Lake Chad

1967 extent of Lake Chad

•Maiduguri

•Damaturu

Niger

Cameroon

SEE INSET

SEE MAP 5

SEE MAP 3

1:211:212

10°E 11°E 12°E 13°E 14°E

NOTES:
1. BRACKETS SHOW THE NUMBER OF TIMES A LANGUAGE'S NUMBER APPEARS ON MAP, IF MORE THAN ONCE.
2. DASHED LINES SHOW OVERLAP OF LANGUAGE AREAS.

LANGUAGE FAMILIES

AFRO-ASIATIC

NIGER-CONGO

NILO-SAHARAN

LEGEND

NATIONAL PARKS AND RESERVES

SPARSELY SETTLED AREAS

STATE BOUNDARIES

km
0 20 40 60 80

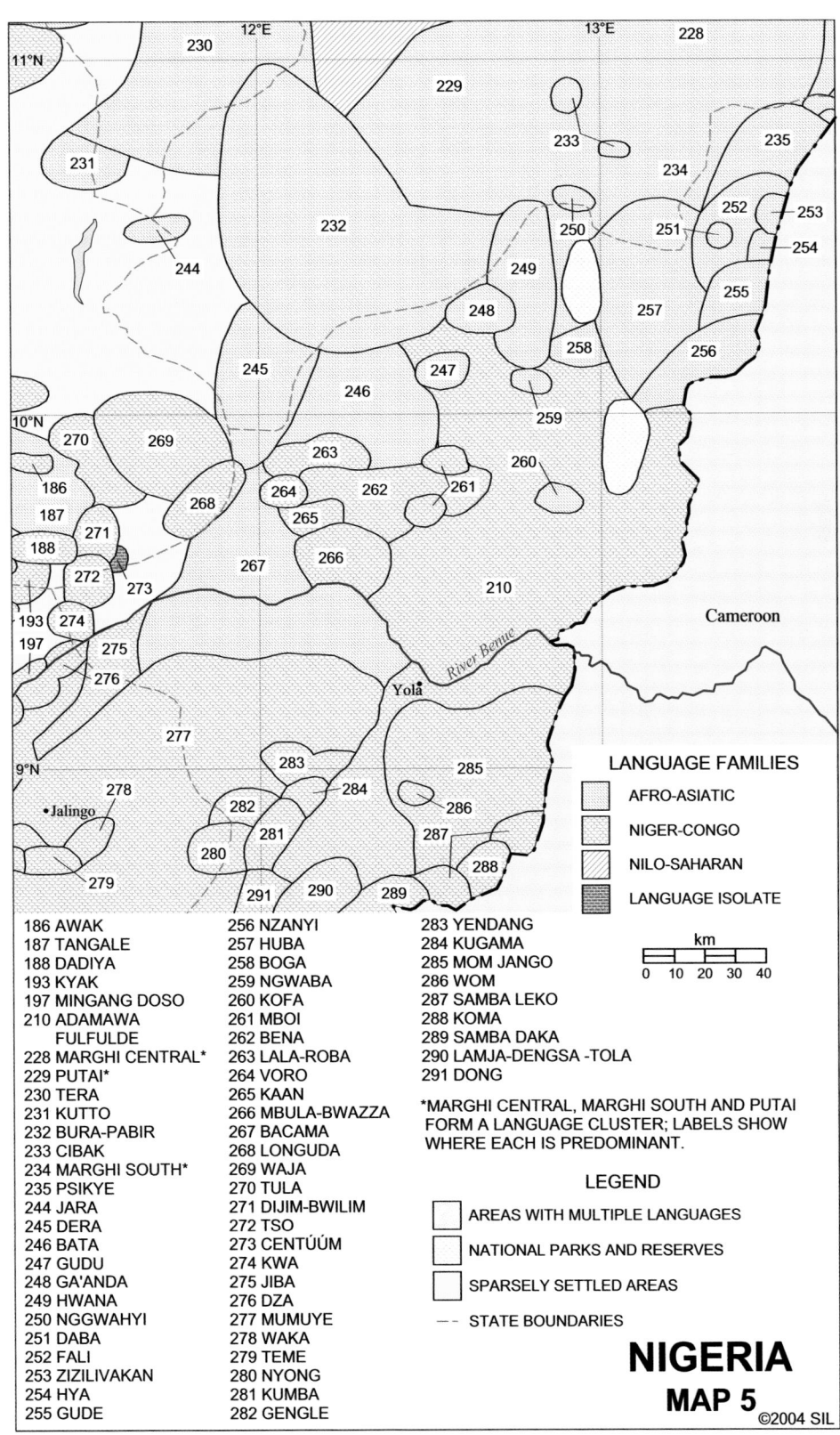

LANGUAGE FAMILIES

AFRO-ASIATIC

NIGER-CONGO

NILO-SAHARAN

LANGUAGE ISOLATE

186 AWAK	256 NZANYI	283 YENDANG
187 TANGALE	257 HUBA	284 KUGAMA
188 DADIYA	258 BOGA	285 MOM JANGO
193 KYAK	259 NGWABA	286 WOM
197 MINGANG DOSO	260 KOFA	287 SAMBA LEKO
210 ADAMAWA	261 MBOI	288 KOMA
FULFULDE	262 BENA	289 SAMBA DAKA
228 MARGHI CENTRAL*	263 LALA-ROBA	290 LAMJA-DENGSA -TOLA
229 PUTAI*	264 VORO	291 DONG
230 TERA	265 KAAN	
231 KUTTO	266 MBULA-BWAZZA	
232 BURA-PABIR	267 BACAMA	*MARGHI CENTRAL, MARGHI SOUTH AND PUTAI
233 CIBAK	268 LONGUDA	FORM A LANGUAGE CLUSTER; LABELS SHOW
234 MARGHI SOUTH*	269 WAJA	WHERE EACH IS PREDOMINANT.
235 PSIKYE	270 TULA	
244 JARA	271 DIJIM-BWILIM	LEGEND
245 DERA	272 TSO	
246 BATA	273 CENTÚÚM	AREAS WITH MULTIPLE LANGUAGES
247 GUDU	274 KWA	
248 GA'ANDA	275 JIBA	NATIONAL PARKS AND RESERVES
249 HWANA	276 DZA	
250 NGGWAHYI	277 MUMUYE	SPARSELY SETTLED AREAS
251 DABA	278 WAKA	
252 FALI	279 TEME	-- STATE BOUNDARIES
253 ZIZILIVAKAN	280 NYONG	
254 HYA	281 KUMBA	**NIGERIA**
255 GUDE	282 GENGLE	**MAP 5**

km
0 10 20 30 40

©2004 SIL

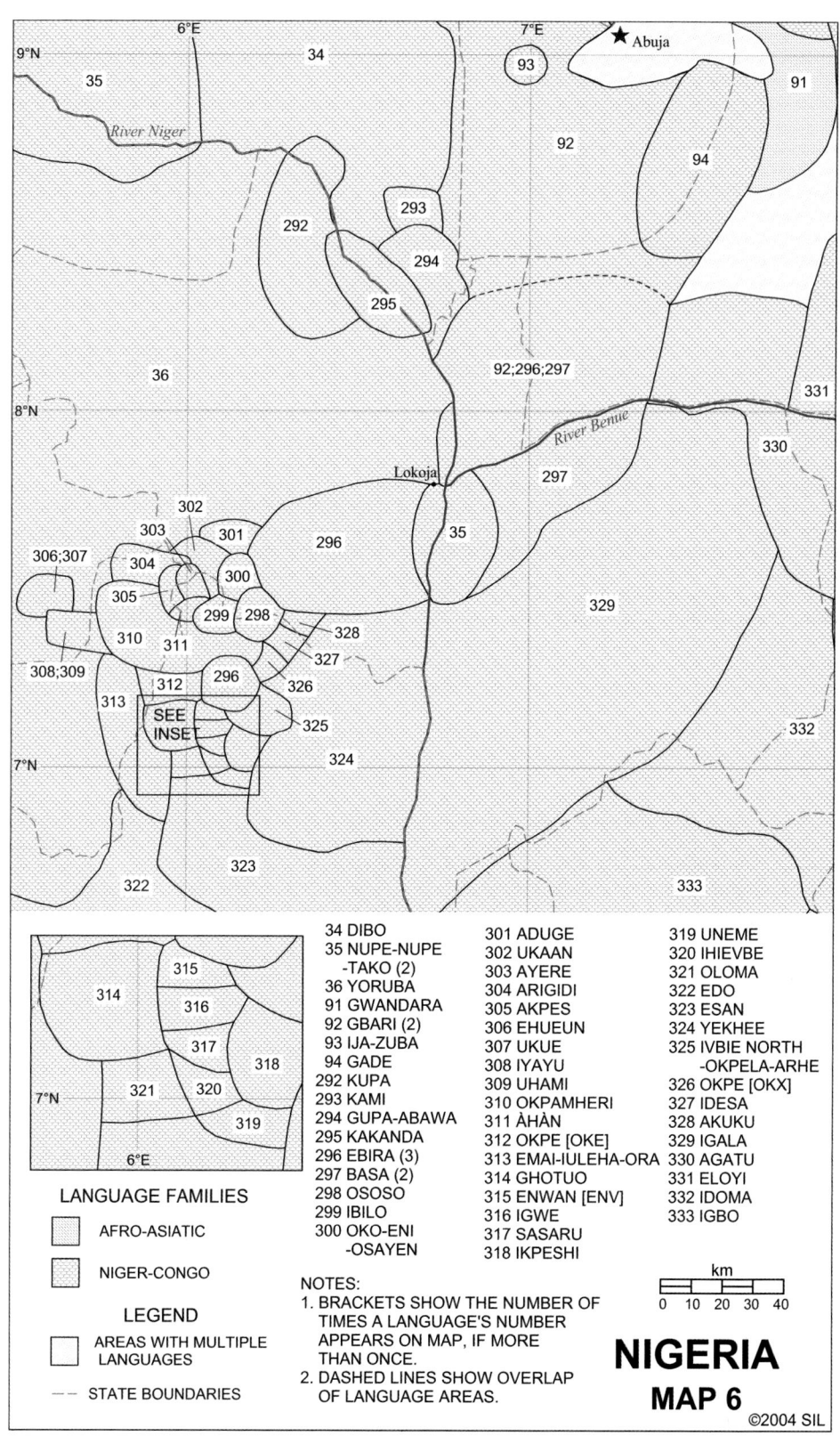

LANGUAGE FAMILIES

☐ AFRO-ASIATIC

☐ NIGER-CONGO

LEGEND

☐ AREAS WITH MULTIPLE
   LANGUAGES

-- STATE BOUNDARIES

34 DIBO
35 NUPE-NUPE
   -TAKO (2)
36 YORUBA
91 GWANDARA
92 GBARI (2)
93 IJA-ZUBA
94 GADE
292 KUPA
293 KAMI
294 GUPA-ABAWA
295 KAKANDA
296 EBIRA (3)
297 BASA (2)
298 OSOSO
299 IBILO
300 OKO-ENI
   -OSAYEN

301 ADUGE
302 UKAAN
303 AYERE
304 ARIGIDI
305 AKPES
306 EHUEUN
307 UKUE
308 IYAYU
309 UHAMI
310 OKPAMHERI
311 ÀHÀN
312 OKPE [OKE]
313 EMAI-IULEHA-ORA
314 GHOTUO
315 ENWAN [ENV]
316 IGWE
317 SASARU
318 IKPESHI

319 UNEME
320 IHIEVBE
321 OLOMA
322 EDO
323 ESAN
324 YEKHEE
325 IVBIE NORTH
   -OKPELA-ARHE
326 OKPE [OKX]
327 IDESA
328 AKUKU
329 IGALA
330 AGATU
331 ELOYI
332 IDOMA
333 IGBO

NOTES:
1. BRACKETS SHOW THE NUMBER OF
   TIMES A LANGUAGE'S NUMBER
   APPEARS ON MAP, IF MORE
   THAN ONCE.
2. DASHED LINES SHOW OVERLAP
   OF LANGUAGE AREAS.

km
0 10 20 30 40

NIGERIA
MAP 6
©2004 SIL

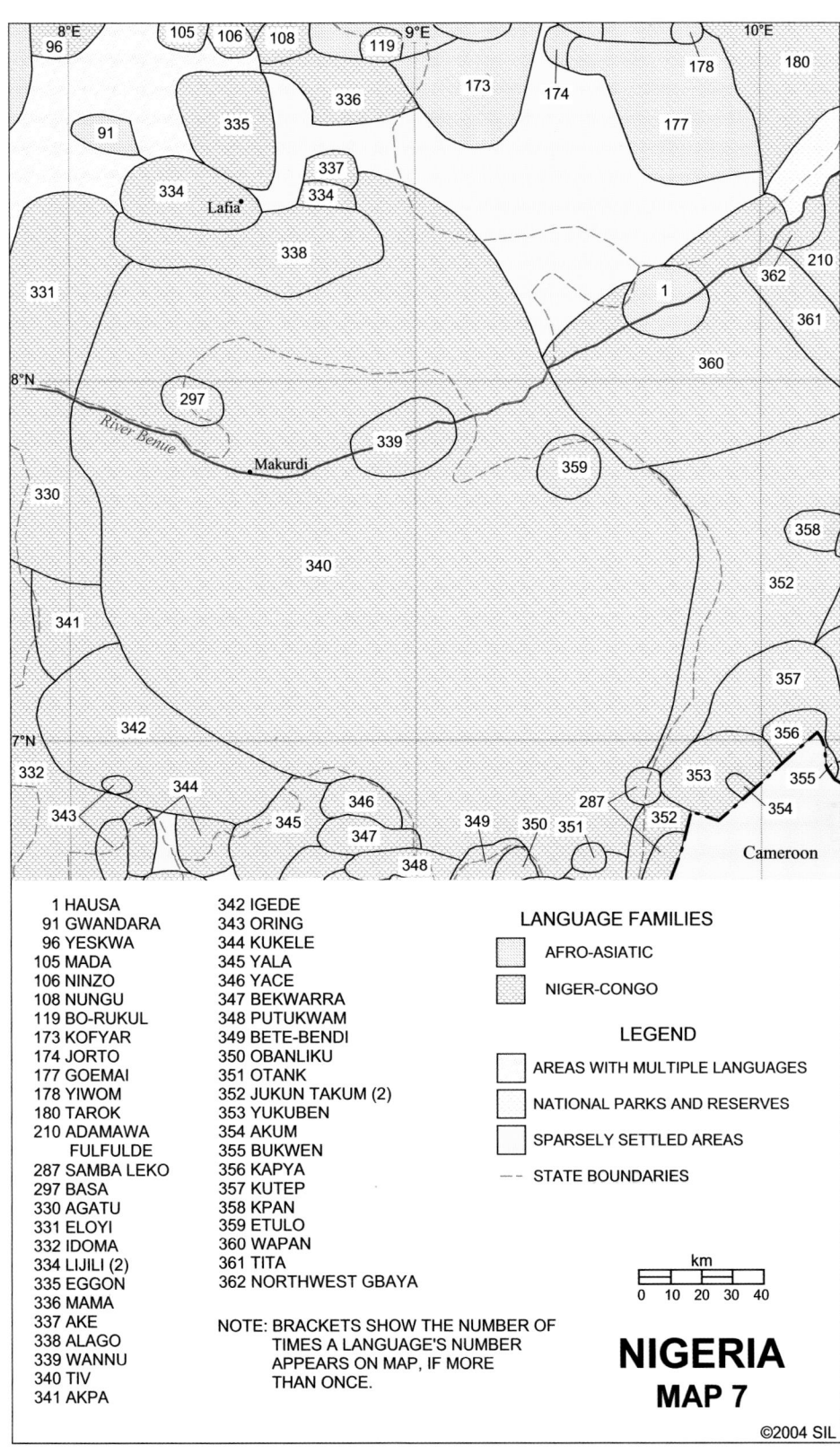

1 HAUSA
91 GWANDARA
96 YESKWA
105 MADA
106 NINZO
108 NUNGU
119 BO-RUKUL
173 KOFYAR
174 JORTO
177 GOEMAI
178 YIWOM
180 TAROK
210 ADAMAWA
    FULFULDE
287 SAMBA LEKO
297 BASA
330 AGATU
331 ELOYI
332 IDOMA
334 LIJILI (2)
335 EGGON
336 MAMA
337 AKE
338 ALAGO
339 WANNU
340 TIV
341 AKPA

342 IGEDE
343 ORING
344 KUKELE
345 YALA
346 YACE
347 BEKWARRA
348 PUTUKWAM
349 BETE-BENDI
350 OBANLIKU
351 OTANK
352 JUKUN TAKUM (2)
353 YUKUBEN
354 AKUM
355 BUKWEN
356 KAPYA
357 KUTEP
358 KPAN
359 ETULO
360 WAPAN
361 TITA
362 NORTHWEST GBAYA

NOTE: BRACKETS SHOW THE NUMBER OF
        TIMES A LANGUAGE'S NUMBER
        APPEARS ON MAP, IF MORE
        THAN ONCE.

LANGUAGE FAMILIES

AFRO-ASIATIC

NIGER-CONGO

LEGEND

AREAS WITH MULTIPLE LANGUAGES

NATIONAL PARKS AND RESERVES

SPARSELY SETTLED AREAS

-- STATE BOUNDARIES

km
0 10 20 30 40

NIGERIA
MAP 7

©2004 SIL

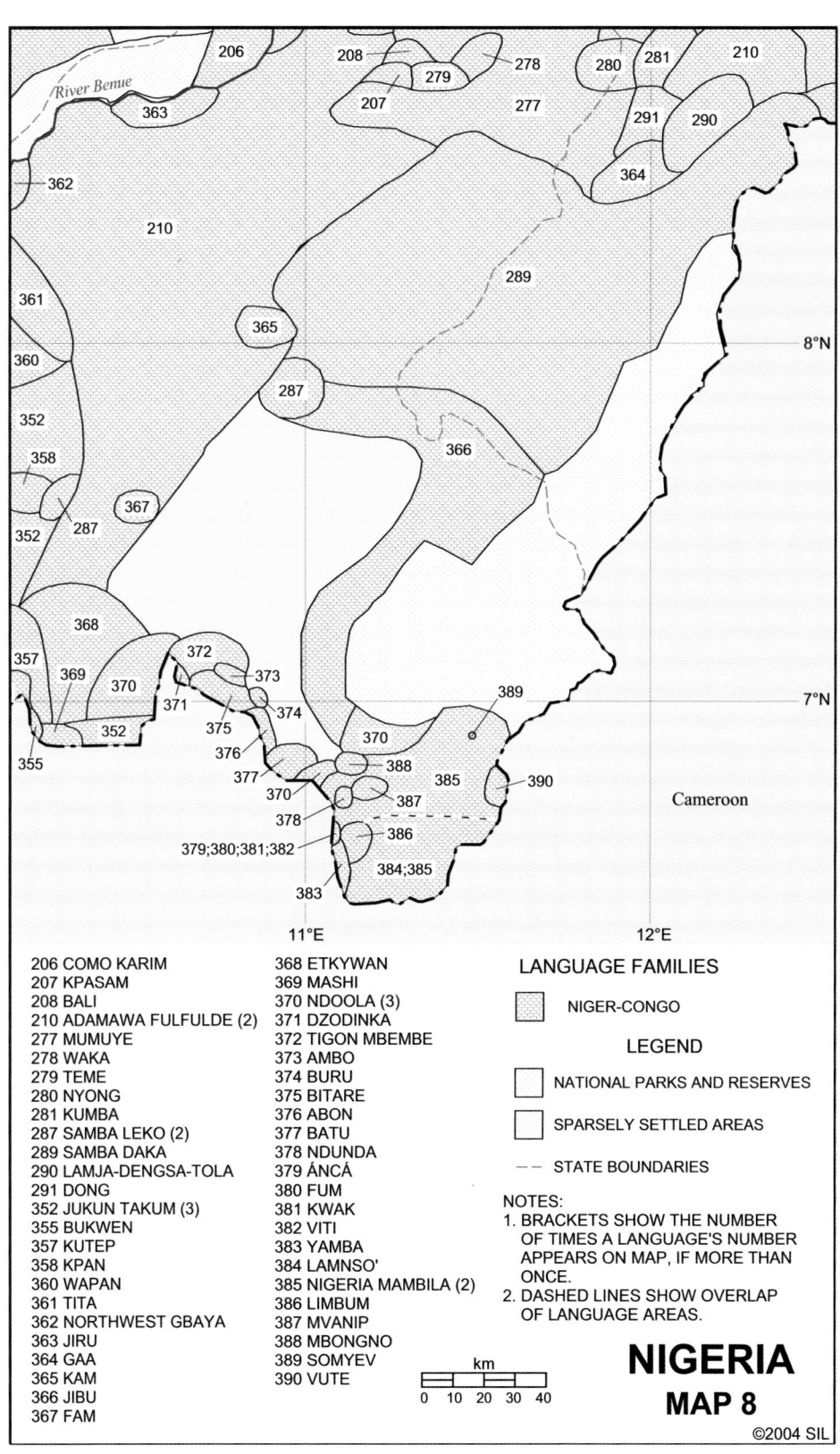

206 COMO KARIM
207 KPASAM
208 BALI
210 ADAMAWA FULFULDE (2)
277 MUMUYE
278 WAKA
279 TEME
280 NYONG
281 KUMBA
287 SAMBA LEKO (2)
289 SAMBA DAKA
290 LAMJA-DENGSA-TOLA
291 DONG
352 JUKUN TAKUM (3)
355 BUKWEN
357 KUTEP
358 KPAN
360 WAPAN
361 TITA
362 NORTHWEST GBAYA
363 JIRU
364 GAA
365 KAM
366 JIBU
367 FAM

368 ETKYWAN
369 MASHI
370 NDOOLA (3)
371 DZODINKA
372 TIGON MBEMBE
373 AMBO
374 BURU
375 BITARE
376 ABON
377 BATU
378 NDUNDA
379 ÁNCÁ
380 FUM
381 KWAK
382 VITI
383 YAMBA
384 LAMNSO'
385 NIGERIA MAMBILA (2)
386 LIMBUM
387 MVANIP
388 MBONGNO
389 SOMYEV
390 VUTE

LANGUAGE FAMILIES

NIGER-CONGO

LEGEND

NATIONAL PARKS AND RESERVES

SPARSELY SETTLED AREAS

— — STATE BOUNDARIES

NOTES:
1. BRACKETS SHOW THE NUMBER
   OF TIMES A LANGUAGE'S NUMBER
   APPEARS ON MAP, IF MORE THAN
   ONCE.
2. DASHED LINES SHOW OVERLAP
   OF LANGUAGE AREAS.

km
0 10 20 30 40

NIGERIA
MAP 8

©2004 SIL

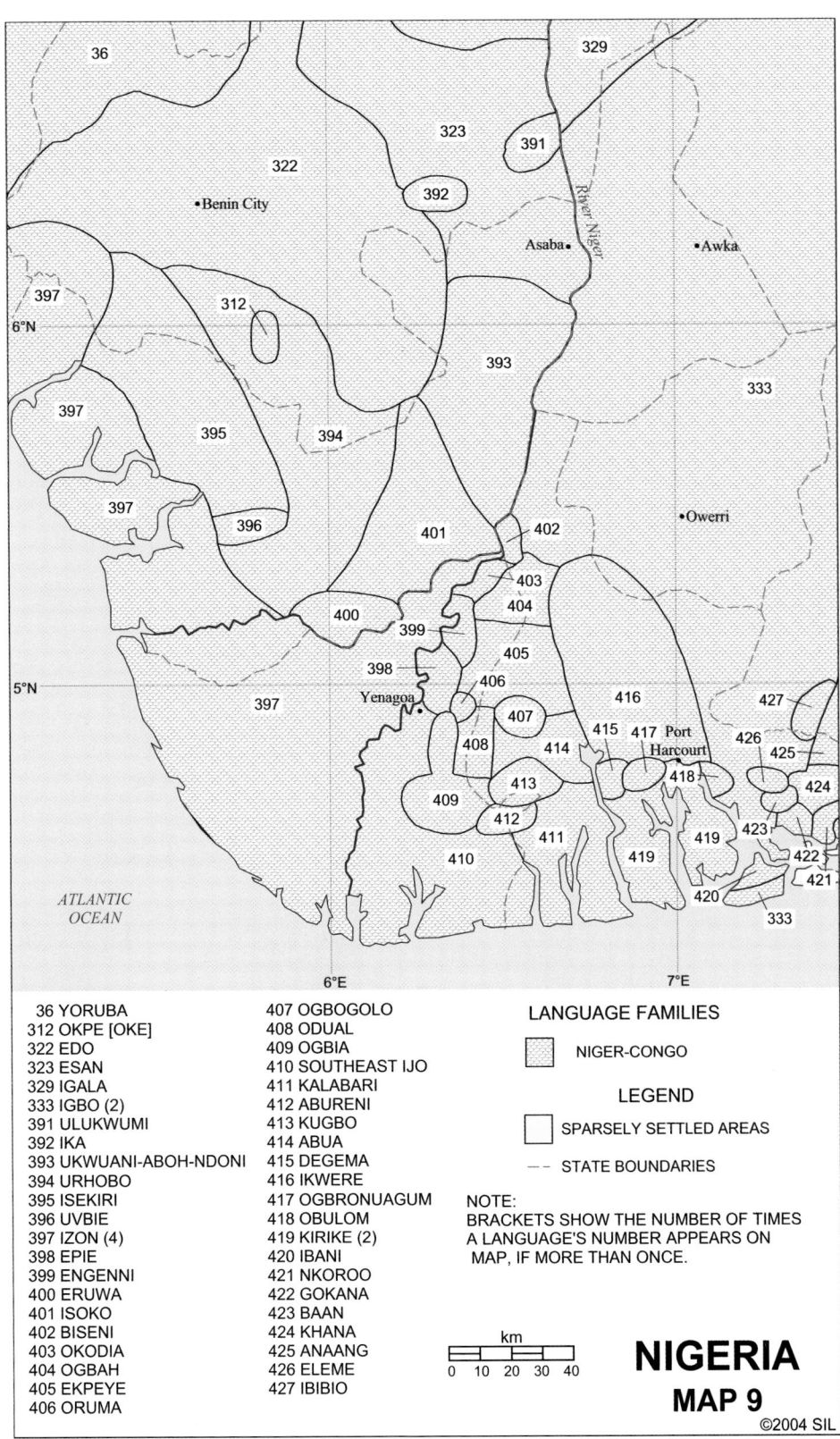

36 YORUBA
312 OKPE [OKE]
322 EDO
323 ESAN
329 IGALA
333 IGBO (2)
391 ULUKWUMI
392 IKA
393 UKWUANI-ABOH-NDONI
394 URHOBO
395 ISEKIRI
396 UVBIE
397 IZON (4)
398 EPIE
399 ENGENNI
400 ERUWA
401 ISOKO
402 BISENI
403 OKODIA
404 OGBAH
405 EKPEYE
406 ORUMA

407 OGBOGOLO
408 ODUAL
409 OGBIA
410 SOUTHEAST IJO
411 KALABARI
412 ABURENI
413 KUGBO
414 ABUA
415 DEGEMA
416 IKWERE
417 OGBRONUAGUM
418 OBULOM
419 KIRIKE (2)
420 IBANI
421 NKOROO
422 GOKANA
423 BAAN
424 KHANA
425 ANAANG
426 ELEME
427 IBIBIO

LANGUAGE FAMILIES

NIGER-CONGO

LEGEND

SPARSELY SETTLED AREAS

-- STATE BOUNDARIES

NOTE:
BRACKETS SHOW THE NUMBER OF TIMES
A LANGUAGE'S NUMBER APPEARS ON
MAP, IF MORE THAN ONCE.

km
0 10 20 30 40

NIGERIA
MAP 9

©2004 SIL

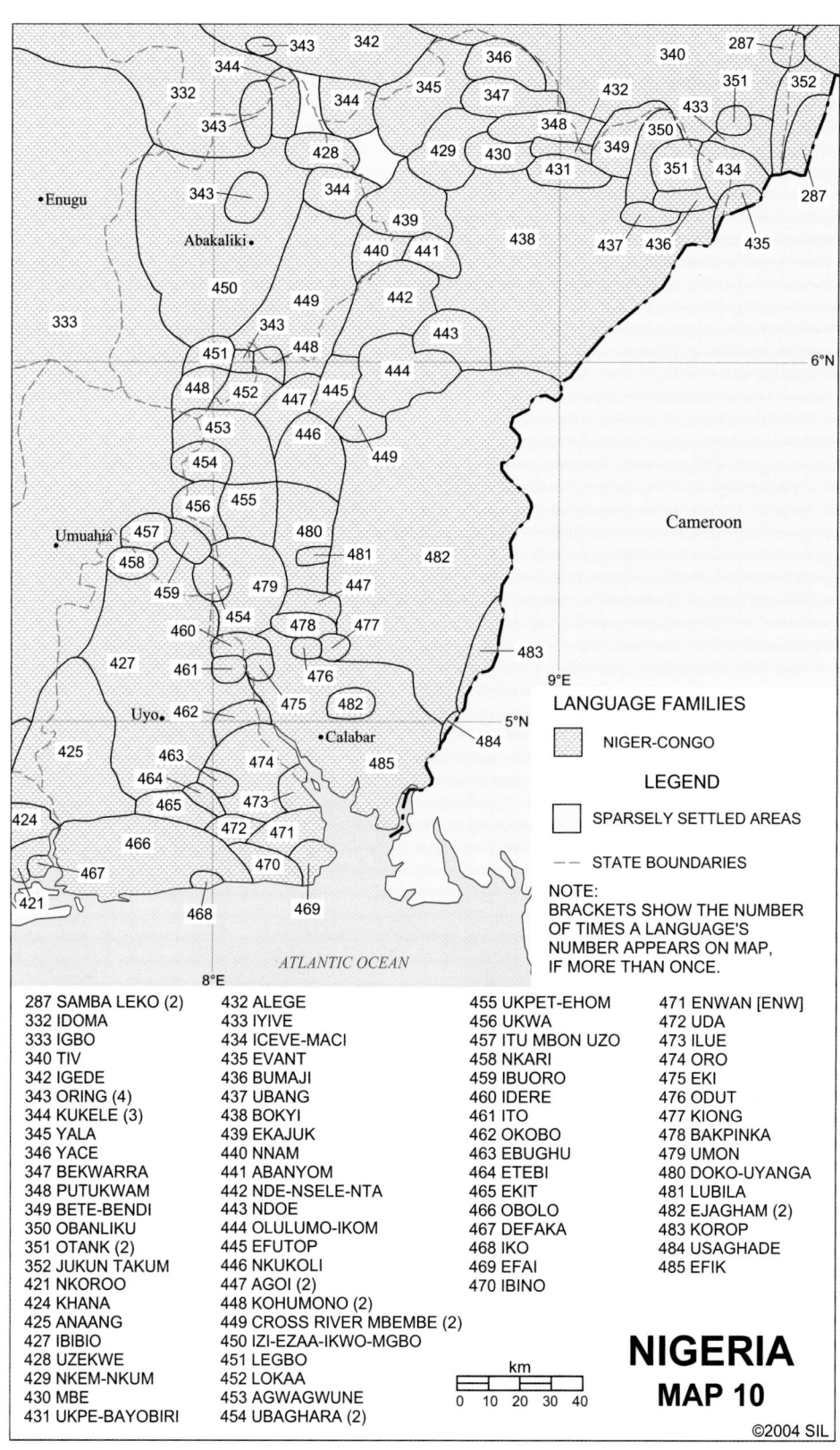

LANGUAGE FAMILIES

NIGER-CONGO

LEGEND

SPARSELY SETTLED AREAS

– – STATE BOUNDARIES

NOTE:
BRACKETS SHOW THE NUMBER
OF TIMES A LANGUAGE'S
NUMBER APPEARS ON MAP,
IF MORE THAN ONCE.

287 SAMBA LEKO (2)
332 IDOMA
333 IGBO
340 TIV
342 IGEDE
343 ORING (4)
344 KUKELE (3)
345 YALA
346 YACE
347 BEKWARRA
348 PUTUKWAM
349 BETE-BENDI
350 OBANLIKU
351 OTANK (2)
352 JUKUN TAKUM
421 NKOROO
424 KHANA
425 ANAANG
427 IBIBIO
428 UZEKWE
429 NKEM-NKUM
430 MBE
431 UKPE-BAYOBIRI

432 ALEGE
433 IYIVE
434 ICEVE-MACI
435 EVANT
436 BUMAJI
437 UBANG
438 BOKYI
439 EKAJUK
440 NNAM
441 ABANYOM
442 NDE-NSELE-NTA
443 NDOE
444 OLULUMO-IKOM
445 EFUTOP
446 NKUKOLI
447 AGOI (2)
448 KOHUMONO (2)
449 CROSS RIVER MBEMBE (2)
450 IZI-EZAA-IKWO-MGBO
451 LEGBO
452 LOKAA
453 AGWAGWUNE
454 UBAGHARA (2)

455 UKPET-EHOM
456 UKWA
457 ITU MBON UZO
458 NKARI
459 IBUORO
460 IDERE
461 ITO
462 OKOBO
463 EBUGHU
464 ETEBI
465 EKIT
466 OBOLO
467 DEFAKA
468 IKO
469 EFAI
470 IBINO

471 ENWAN [ENW]
472 UDA
473 ILUE
474 ORO
475 EKI
476 ODUT
477 KIONG
478 BAKPINKA
479 UMON
480 DOKO-UYANGA
481 LUBILA
482 EJAGHAM (2)
483 KOROP
484 USAGHADE
485 EFIK

km
0 10 20 30 40

NIGERIA
MAP 10

©2004 SIL

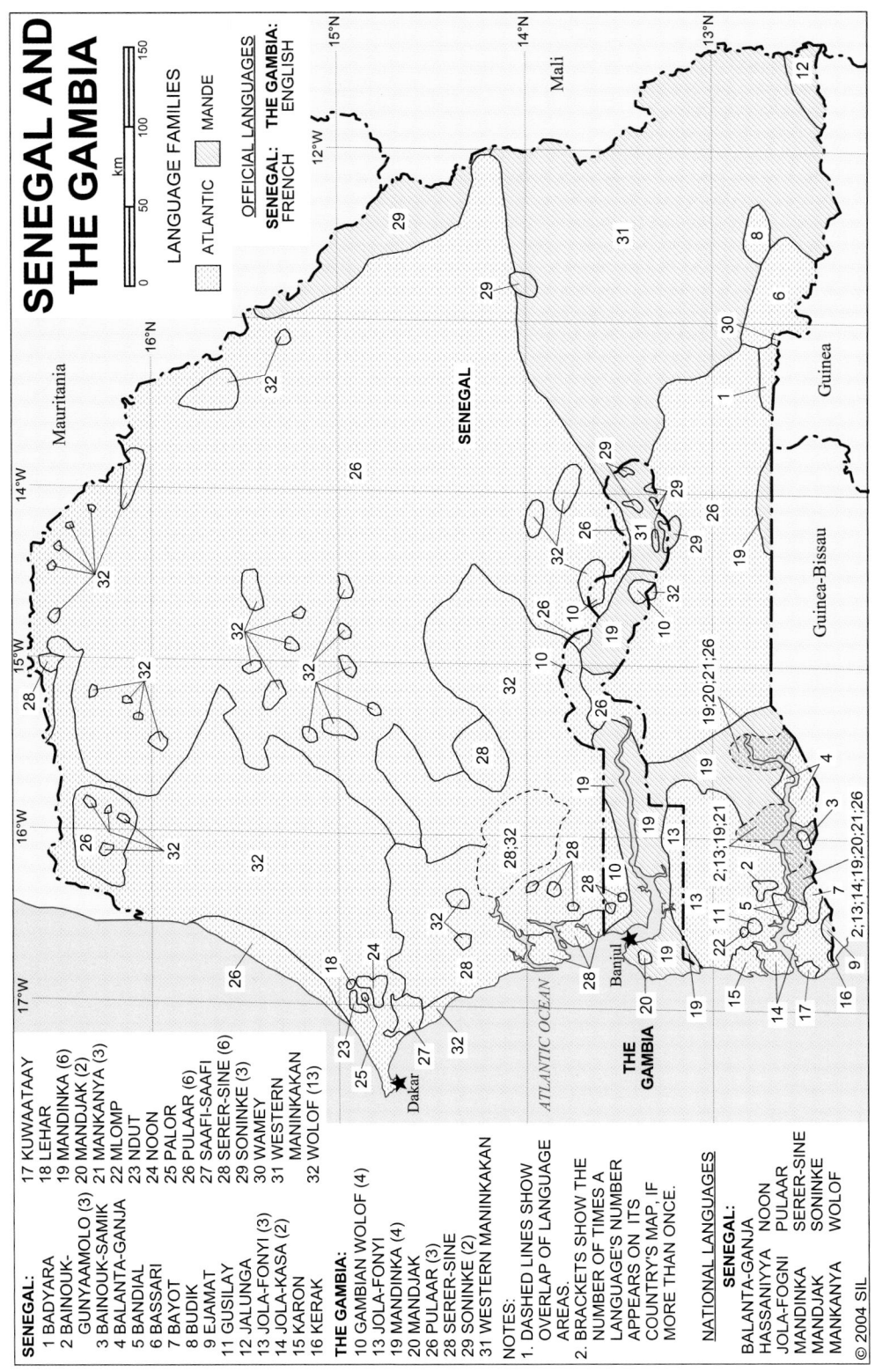

SENEGAL AND THE GAMBIA

LANGUAGE FAMILIES
- ATLANTIC
- MANDE

OFFICIAL LANGUAGES
SENEGAL: FRENCH
THE GAMBIA: ENGLISH

km
0   50   100   150

SENEGAL:
1 BADYARA
2 BAINOUK-GUNYAAMOLO (3)
3 BAINOUK-SAMIK
4 BALANTA-GANJA
5 BANDIAL
6 BASSARI
7 BAYOT
8 BUDIK
9 EJAMAT
11 GUSILAY
12 JALUNGA
13 JOLA-FONYI (3)
14 JOLA-KASA (2)
15 KARON
16 KERAK
17 KUWAATAAY
18 LEHAR
19 MANDINKA (6)
20 MANDJAK (2)
21 MANKANYA (3)
22 MLOMP
23 NDUT
24 NOON
25 PALOR
26 PULAAR (6)
27 SAAFI-SAAFI
28 SERER-SINE (6)
29 SONINKE (3)
30 WAMEY
31 WESTERN MANINKAKAN
32 WOLOF (13)

THE GAMBIA:
10 GAMBIAN WOLOF (4)
13 JOLA-FONYI
19 MANDINKA (4)
20 MANDJAK
26 PULAAR (3)
28 SERER-SINE
29 SONINKE (2)
31 WESTERN MANINKAKAN

NOTES:
1. DASHED LINES SHOW OVERLAP OF LANGUAGE AREAS.
2. BRACKETS SHOW THE NUMBER OF TIMES A LANGUAGE'S NUMBER APPEARS ON ITS COUNTRY'S MAP, IF MORE THAN ONCE.

NATIONAL LANGUAGES
SENEGAL:
BALANTA-GANJA
HASSANIYYA
JOLA-FOGNI
MANDINKA
MANDJAK
MANKANYA
NOON
PULAAR
SERER-SINE
SONINKE
WOLOF

© 2004 SIL

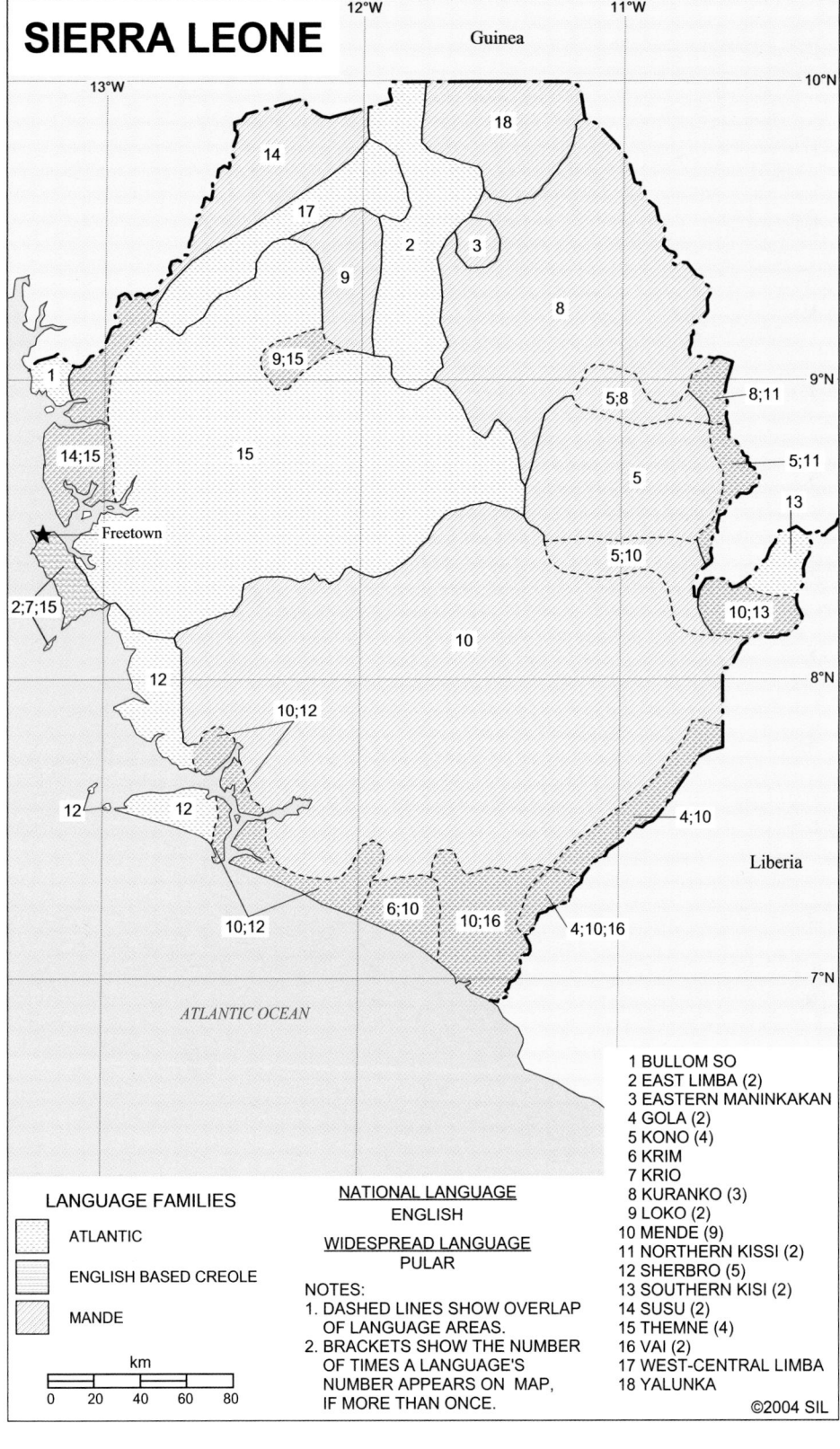

SIERRA LEONE

Guinea

Freetown

ATLANTIC OCEAN

Liberia

LANGUAGE FAMILIES

- ATLANTIC
- ENGLISH BASED CREOLE
- MANDE

km
0 20 40 60 80

NATIONAL LANGUAGE
ENGLISH

WIDESPREAD LANGUAGE
PULAR

NOTES:
1. DASHED LINES SHOW OVERLAP
   OF LANGUAGE AREAS.
2. BRACKETS SHOW THE NUMBER
   OF TIMES A LANGUAGE'S
   NUMBER APPEARS ON MAP,
   IF MORE THAN ONCE.

1 BULLOM SO
2 EAST LIMBA (2)
3 EASTERN MANINKAKAN
4 GOLA (2)
5 KONO (4)
6 KRIM
7 KRIO
8 KURANKO (3)
9 LOKO (2)
10 MENDE (9)
11 NORTHERN KISSI (2)
12 SHERBRO (5)
13 SOUTHERN KISI (2)
14 SUSU (2)
15 THEMNE (4)
16 VAI (2)
17 WEST-CENTRAL LIMBA
18 YALUNKA

©2004 SIL

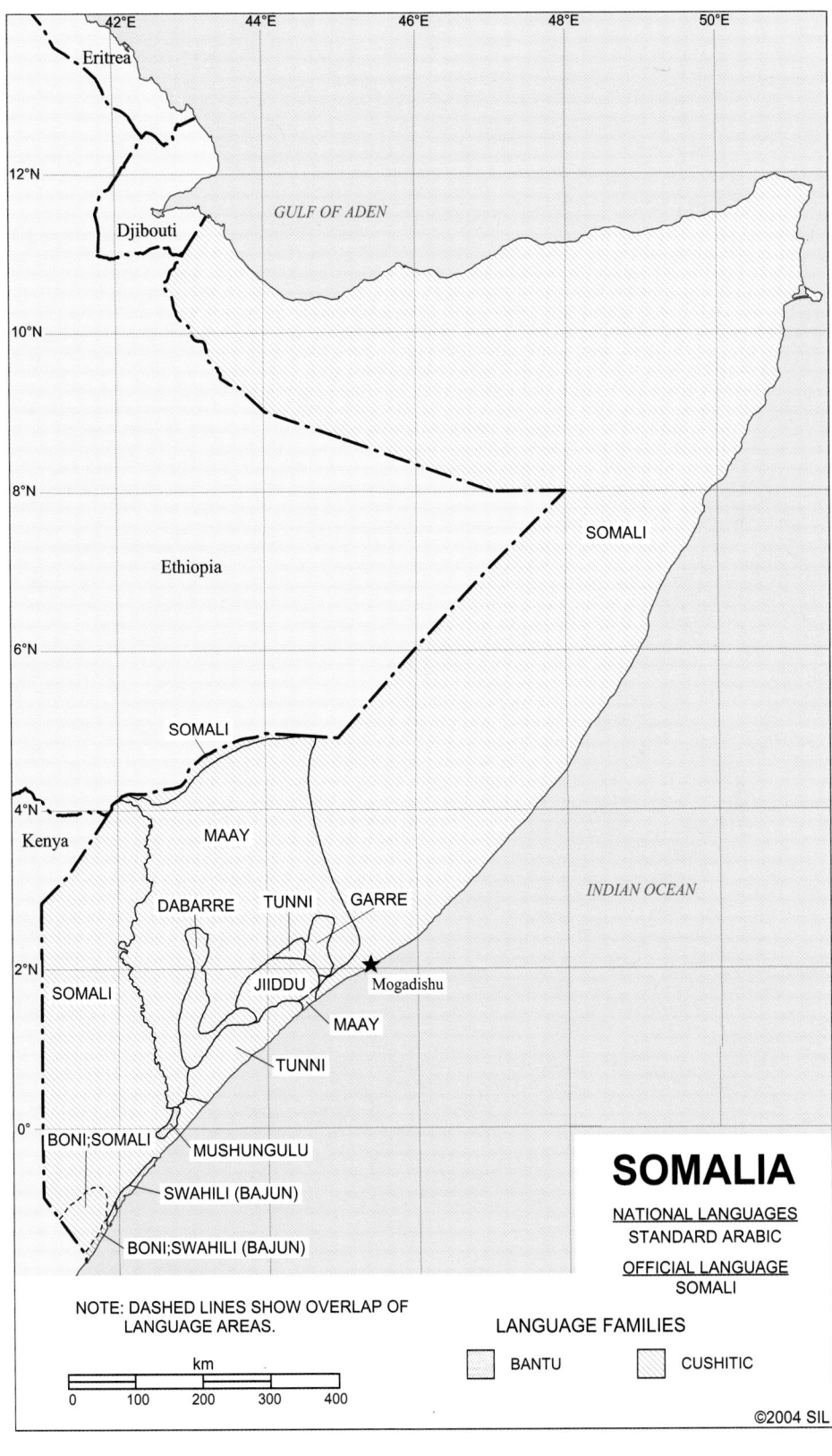

SOMALIA

NATIONAL LANGUAGES
STANDARD ARABIC

OFFICIAL LANGUAGE
SOMALI

NOTE: DASHED LINES SHOW OVERLAP OF
LANGUAGE AREAS.

LANGUAGE FAMILIES

BANTU   CUSHITIC

km

0   100   200   300   400

©2004 SIL

SUDAN - ENLARGED AREA

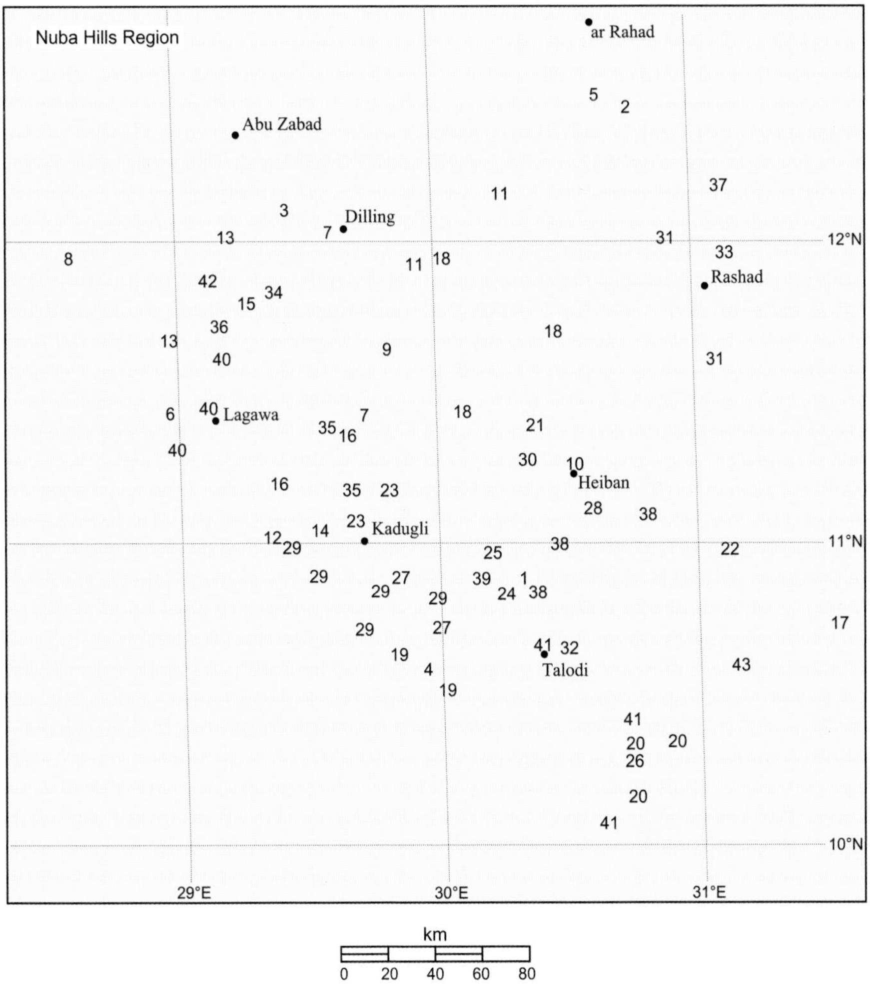

Nuba Hills Region

NOTE: BRACKETS SHOW THE NUMBER OF TIMES A LANGUAGE'S
NUMBER APPEARS ON MAP, IF MORE THAN ONCE.

1 ACHERON	23 LOGORIK (2)
2 AFITTI	24 LUMUN
3 AMA	25 MORO
4 DAGIK	26 NDING
5 DAIR	27 NGILE (2)
6 DAR FUR DAJU	28 OTORO
7 DILLING (2)	29 SHATT (5)
8 EL HUGEIRAT	30 SHWAI
9 GHULFAN	31 TAGOI (2)
10 HEIBAN	32 TALODI
11 KADARU (2)	33 TEGALI
12 KANGA	34 TEMEIN
13 KARKO (2)	35 TESE (2)
14 KATCHA-KADUGLI-MIRI	36 TIMA
15 KATLA	37 TINGAL
16 KEIGA (2)	38 TIRA (3)
17 KO	39 TOCHO
18 KOALIB (3)	40 TULISHI (3)
19 KRONGO (2)	41 TUMTUM (3)
20 LAFOFA (3)	42 WALI
21 LARO	43 WARNANG
22 LOGOL	

WESTERN TANZANIA

NATIONAL
LANGUAGE
SWAHILI

4 BEMBE
5 BENA
6 BENDE (2)
8 BUNGU
10 DATOOGA (5)
14 FIPA (2)
15 GOGO
18 HA (2)
19 HADZA
20 HANGAZA
21 HAYA (2)
22 HEHE
23 IKIZU
24 IKOMA
25 IRAQW
26 ISANZU
27 JITA
28 KABWA
32 KARA
33 KEREWE (2)
34 KIMBU (3)
35 KINGA
36 KISI
37 KONONGO
38 KURIA
40 KWAYA
42 LAMBYA
45 LUO
51 MALILA
52 MAMBWE-
   LUNGU
53 MANDA
55 MATENGO
61 MPOTO
62 MWERA [MJH]
64 NDALI
71 NGONI
73 NGURIMI
74 NILAMBA
76 NYAKYUSA-
   NGONDE (2)
77 NYAMBO
78 NYAMWANGA
79 NYAMWEZI (2)
80 NYATURU
81 NYIHA
83 PANGWA
84 PIMBWE (2)
88 RUNGWA
90 SAFWA (2)
93 SANGU (2)
96 SHUBI (2)
97 SIZAKI
98 SUBA
99 SUBI (3)
100 SUKUMA (5)
101 SUMBWA
104 TONGWE
106 VINZA
108 WANDA
109 WANJI
111 ZANAKI
114 ZINZA (3)

© 2004 SIL

NOTES:
1. DASHED LINES SHOW OVERLAP OF
   LANGUAGE AREAS.
2. WHITE AREAS ARE MOSTLY UNINHABITED.
3. BRACKETS SHOW THE NUMBER OF TIMES
   A LANGUAGE'S NUMBER APPEARS ON MAP,
   IF MORE THAN ONCE.

LANGUAGE FAMILIES

BANTU   KHOISAN

CUSHITIC   NILOTIC

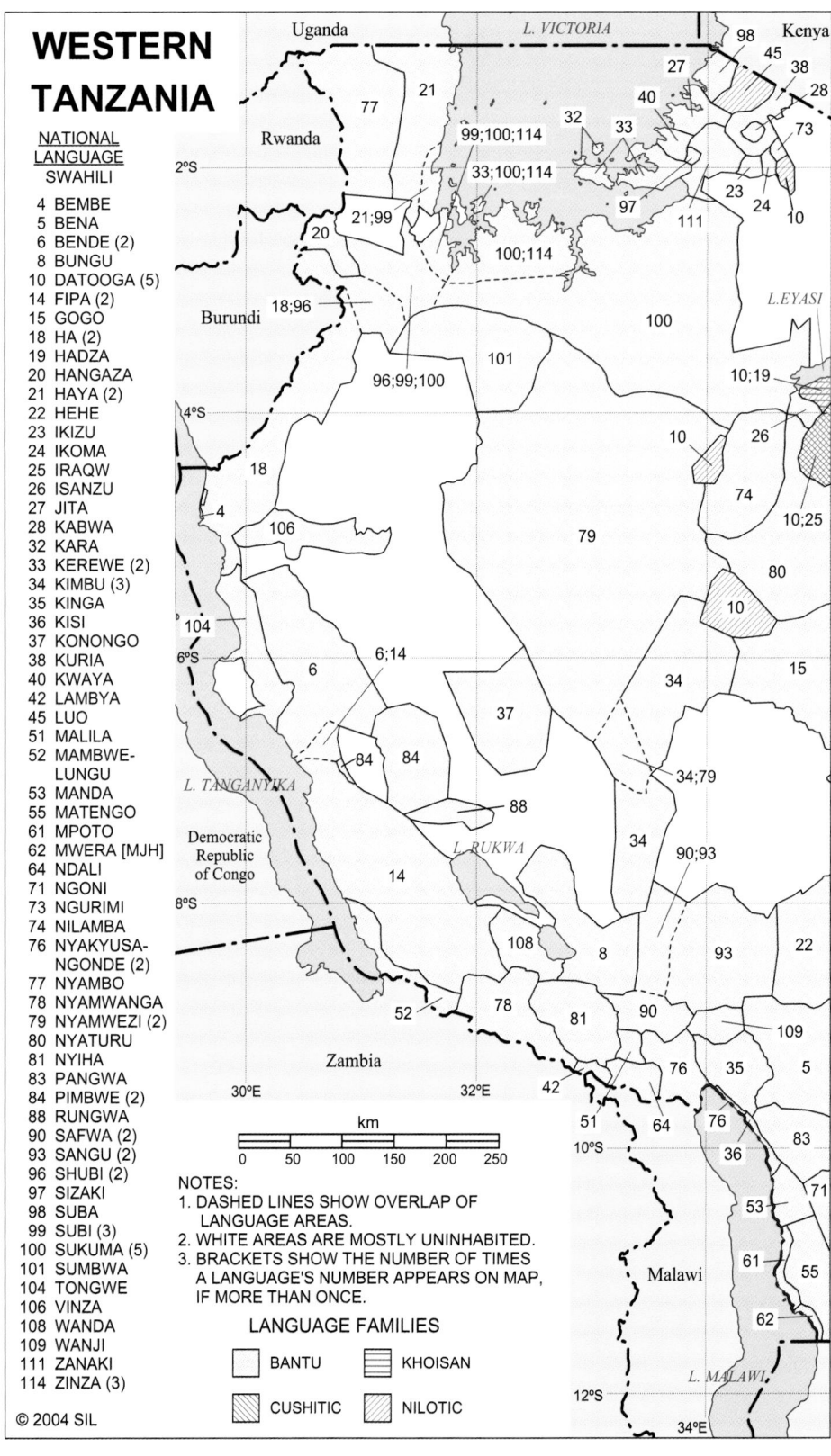

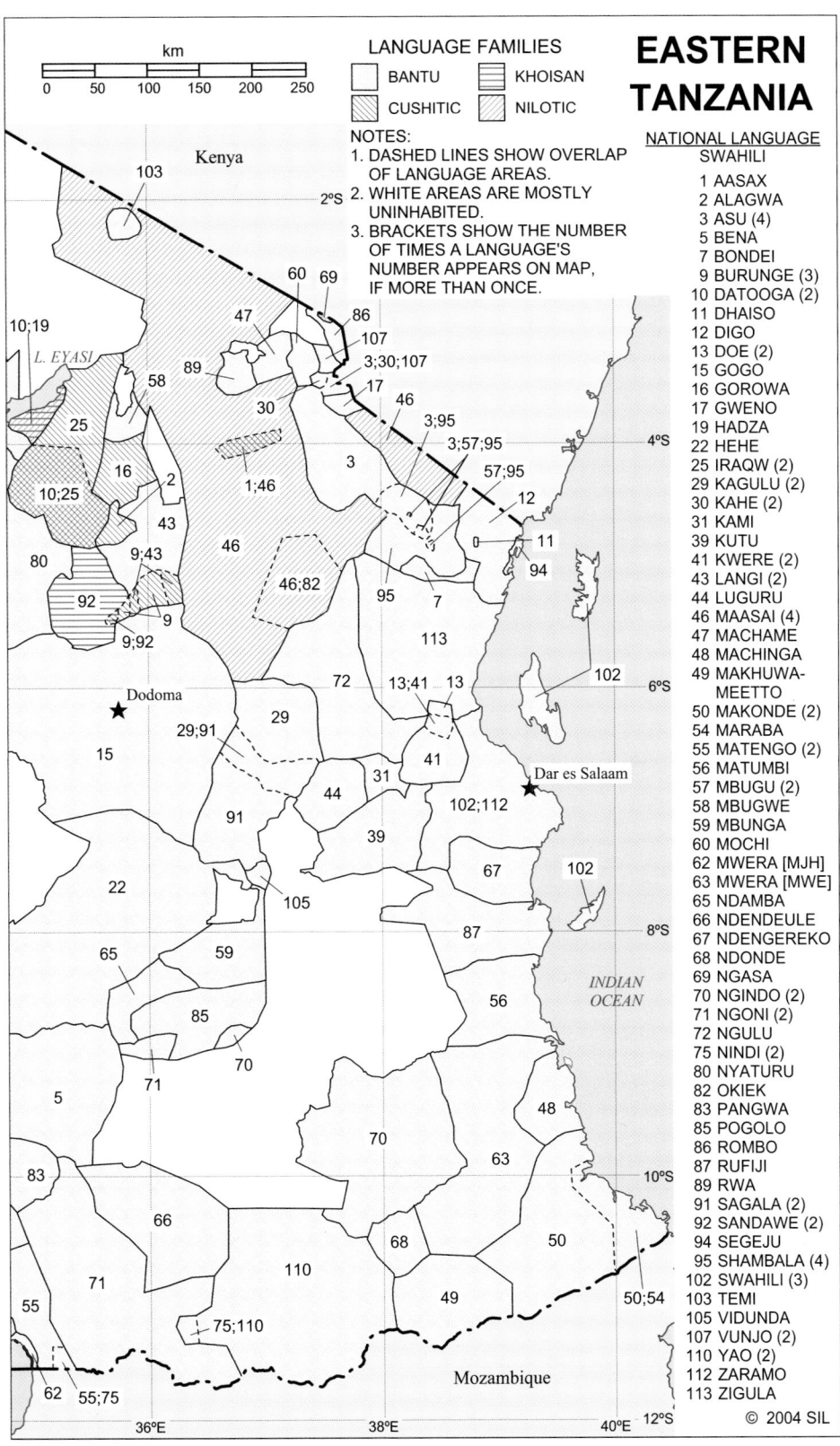

km

0 50 100 150 200 250

LANGUAGE FAMILIES

BANTU KHOISAN

CUSHITIC NILOTIC

NOTES:
1. DASHED LINES SHOW OVERLAP OF LANGUAGE AREAS.
2. WHITE AREAS ARE MOSTLY UNINHABITED.
3. BRACKETS SHOW THE NUMBER OF TIMES A LANGUAGE'S NUMBER APPEARS ON MAP, IF MORE THAN ONCE.

EASTERN TANZANIA

NATIONAL LANGUAGE
SWAHILI

1 AASAX
2 ALAGWA
3 ASU (4)
5 BENA
7 BONDEI
9 BURUNGE (3)
10 DATOOGA (2)
11 DHAISO
12 DIGO
13 DOE (2)
15 GOGO
16 GOROWA
17 GWENO
19 HADZA
22 HEHE
25 IRAQW (2)
29 KAGULU (2)
30 KAHE (2)
31 KAMI
39 KUTU
41 KWERE (2)
43 LANGI (2)
44 LUGURU
46 MAASAI (4)
47 MACHAME
48 MACHINGA
49 MAKHUWA-
    MEETTO
50 MAKONDE (2)
54 MARABA
55 MATENGO (2)
56 MATUMBI
57 MBUGU (2)
58 MBUGWE
59 MBUNGA
60 MOCHI
62 MWERA [MJH]
63 MWERA [MWE]
65 NDAMBA
66 NDENDEULE
67 NDENGEREKO
68 NDONDE
69 NGASA
70 NGINDO (2)
71 NGONI (2)
72 NGULU
75 NINDI (2)
80 NYATURU
82 OKIEK
83 PANGWA
85 POGOLO
86 ROMBO
87 RUFIJI
89 RWA
91 SAGALA (2)
92 SANDAWE (2)
94 SEGEJU
95 SHAMBALA (4)
102 SWAHILI (3)
103 TEMI
105 VIDUNDA
107 VUNJO (2)
110 YAO (2)
112 ZARAMO
113 ZIGULA

Kenya

Dodoma

Dar es Salaam

INDIAN OCEAN

Mozambique

© 2004 SIL

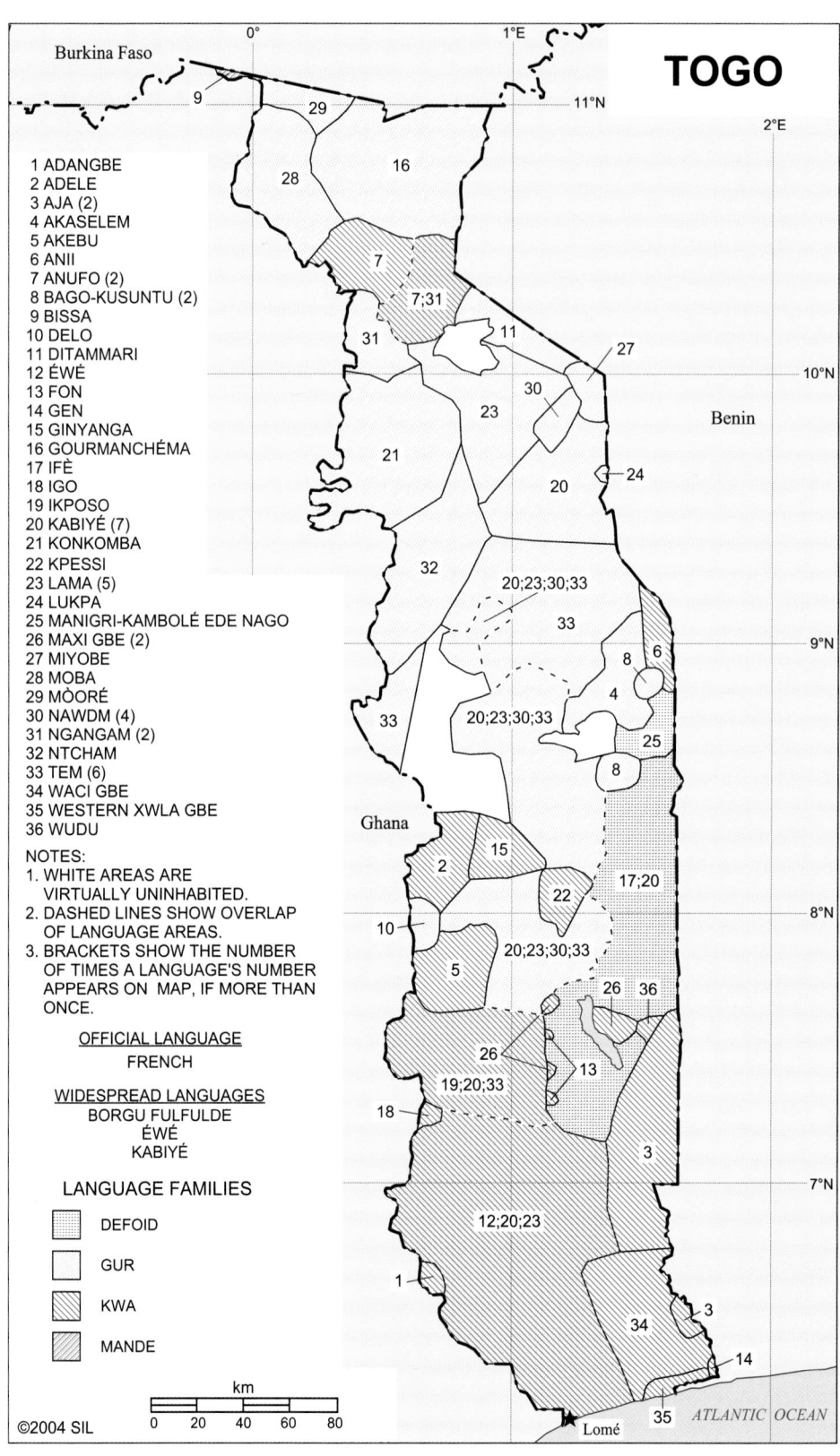

TOGO

Burkina Faso

Benin

Ghana

1 ADANGBE
2 ADELE
3 AJA (2)
4 AKASELEM
5 AKEBU
6 ANII
7 ANUFO (2)
8 BAGO-KUSUNTU (2)
9 BISSA
10 DELO
11 DITAMMARI
12 ÉWÉ
13 FON
14 GEN
15 GINYANGA
16 GOURMANCHÉMA
17 IFÈ
18 IGO
19 IKPOSO
20 KABIYÉ (7)
21 KONKOMBA
22 KPESSI
23 LAMA (5)
24 LUKPA
25 MANIGRI-KAMBOLÉ EDE NAGO
26 MAXI GBE (2)
27 MIYOBE
28 MOBA
29 MÒORÉ
30 NAWDM (4)
31 NGANGAM (2)
32 NTCHAM
33 TEM (6)
34 WACI GBE
35 WESTERN XWLA GBE
36 WUDU

NOTES:
1. WHITE AREAS ARE
   VIRTUALLY UNINHABITED.
2. DASHED LINES SHOW OVERLAP
   OF LANGUAGE AREAS.
3. BRACKETS SHOW THE NUMBER
   OF TIMES A LANGUAGE'S NUMBER
   APPEARS ON MAP, IF MORE THAN
   ONCE.

OFFICIAL LANGUAGE
FRENCH

WIDESPREAD LANGUAGES
BORGU FULFULDE
ÉWÉ
KABIYÉ

LANGUAGE FAMILIES

DEFOID

GUR

KWA

MANDE

km
0   20   40   60   80

©2004 SIL

ATLANTIC OCEAN

Lomé

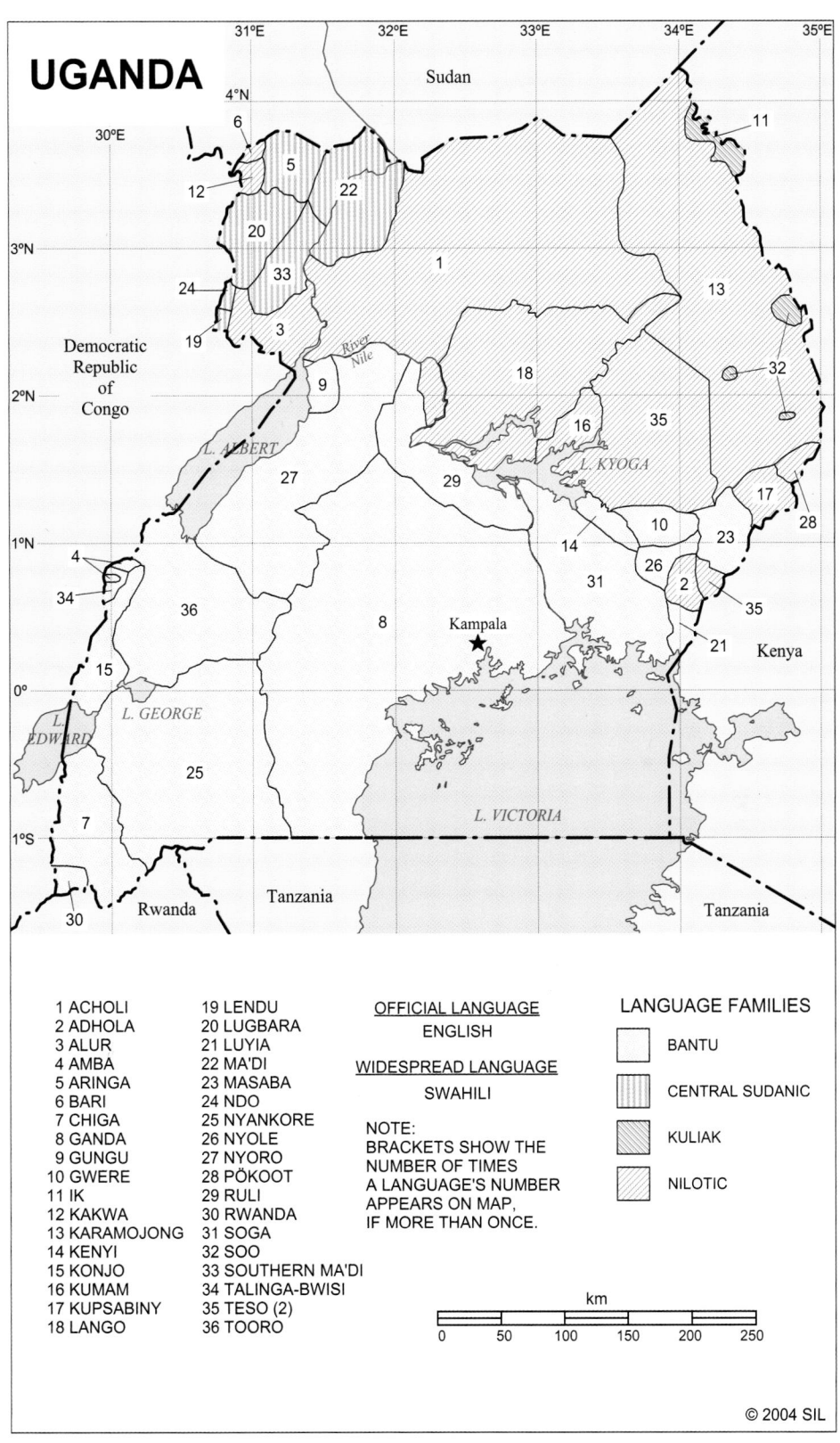

UGANDA

Sudan

Democratic Republic of Congo

Kampala

Kenya

Rwanda

Tanzania

Tanzania

River Nile

L. ALBERT

L. KYOGA

L. GEORGE

L. EDWARD

L. VICTORIA

1 ACHOLI	19 LENDU
2 ADHOLA	20 LUGBARA
3 ALUR	21 LUYIA
4 AMBA	22 MA'DI
5 ARINGA	23 MASABA
6 BARI	24 NDO
7 CHIGA	25 NYANKORE
8 GANDA	26 NYOLE
9 GUNGU	27 NYORO
10 GWERE	28 PÖKOOT
11 IK	29 RULI
12 KAKWA	30 RWANDA
13 KARAMOJONG	31 SOGA
14 KENYI	32 SOO
15 KONJO	33 SOUTHERN MA'DI
16 KUMAM	34 TALINGA-BWISI
17 KUPSABINY	35 TESO (2)
18 LANGO	36 TOORO

OFFICIAL LANGUAGE
ENGLISH

WIDESPREAD LANGUAGE
SWAHILI

NOTE:
BRACKETS SHOW THE
NUMBER OF TIMES
A LANGUAGE'S NUMBER
APPEARS ON MAP,
IF MORE THAN ONCE.

LANGUAGE FAMILIES

BANTU

CENTRAL SUDANIC

KULIAK

NILOTIC

km
0   50   100   150   200   250

© 2004 SIL

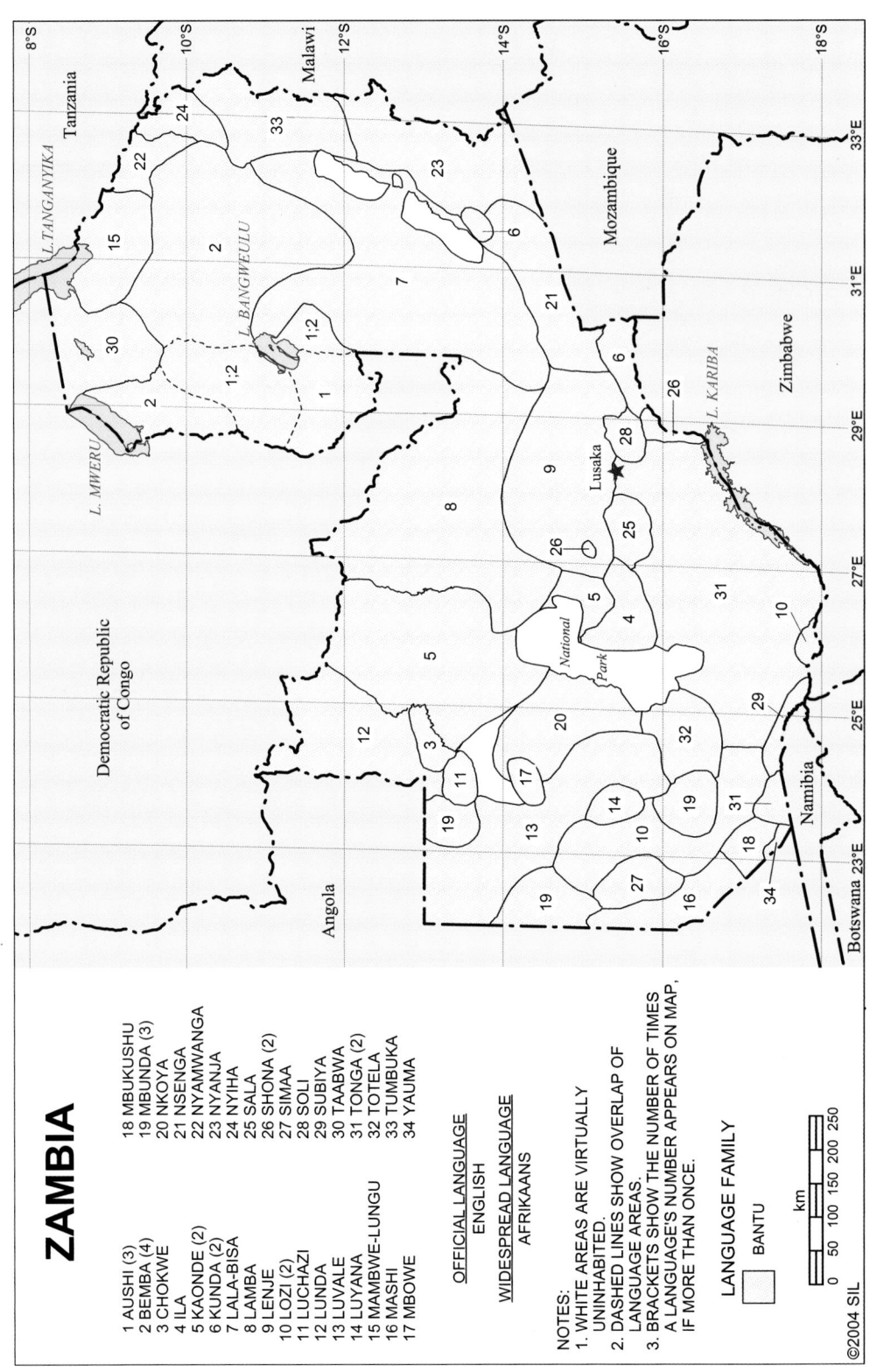

ZAMBIA

1 AUSHI (3)
2 BEMBA (4)
3 CHOKWE
4 ILA
5 KAONDE (2)
6 KUNDA (2)
7 LALA-BISA
8 LAMBA
9 LENJE
10 LOZI (2)
11 LUCHAZI
12 LUNDA
13 LUVALE
14 LUYANA
15 MAMBWE-LUNGU
16 MASHI
17 MBOWE

18 MBUKUSHU
19 MBUNDA (3)
20 NKOYA
21 NSENGA
22 NYAMWANGA
23 NYANJA
24 NYIHA
25 SALA
26 SHONA (2)
27 SIMAA
28 SOLI
29 SUBIYA
30 TAABWA
31 TONGA (2)
32 TOTELA
33 TUMBUKA
34 YAUMA

OFFICIAL LANGUAGE
ENGLISH

WIDESPREAD LANGUAGE
AFRIKAANS

NOTES:
1. WHITE AREAS ARE VIRTUALLY
UNINHABITED.
2. DASHED LINES SHOW OVERLAP OF
LANGUAGE AREAS.
3. BRACKETS SHOW THE NUMBER OF TIMES
A LANGUAGE'S NUMBER APPEARS ON MAP,
IF MORE THAN ONCE.

LANGUAGE FAMILY

BANTU

km
0 50 100 150 200 250

©2004 SIL

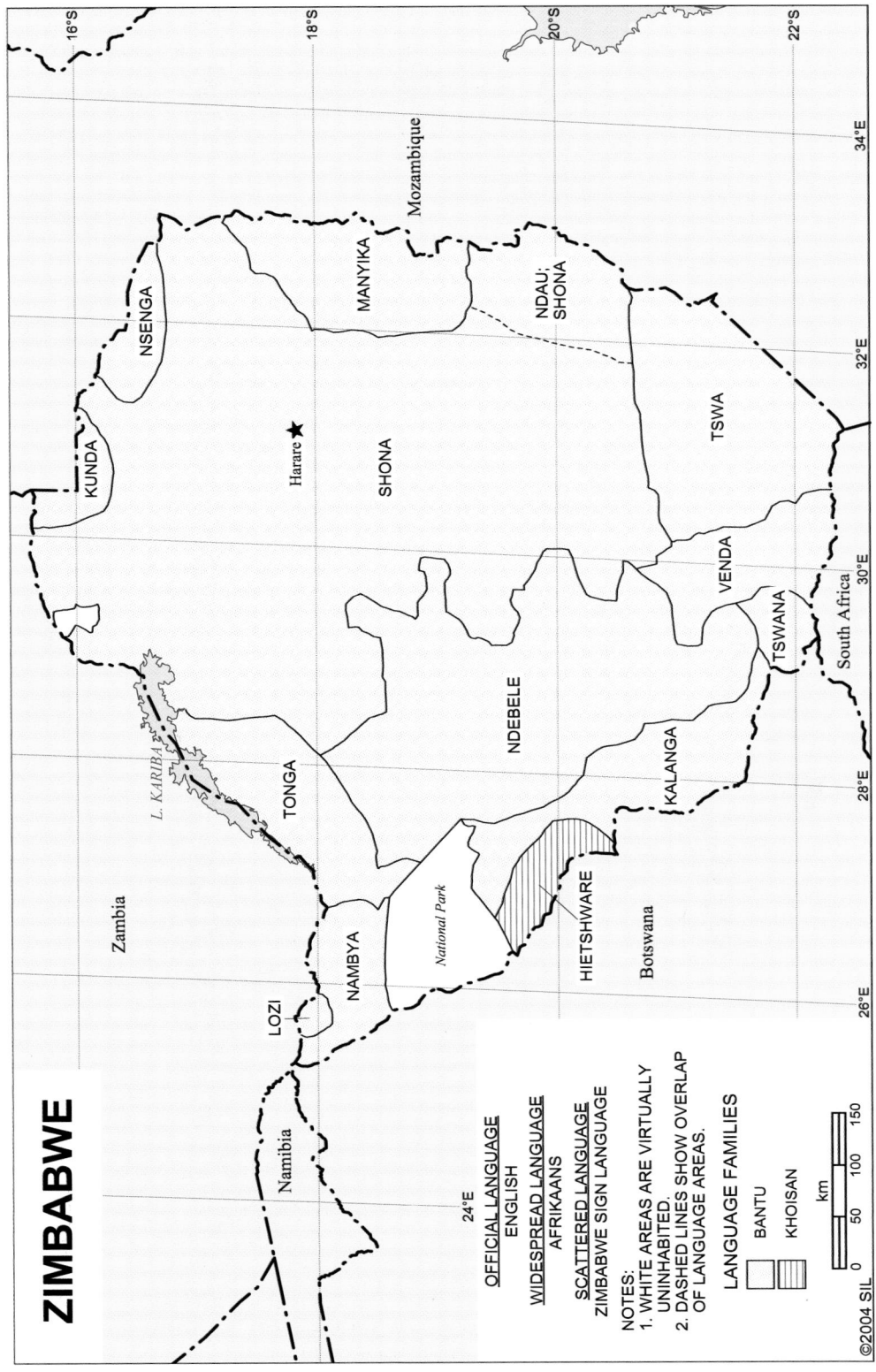

ZIMBABWE

OFFICIAL LANGUAGE
ENGLISH
WIDESPREAD LANGUAGE
AFRIKAANS
SCATTERED LANGUAGE
ZIMBABWE SIGN LANGUAGE

NOTES:
1. WHITE AREAS ARE VIRTUALLY
   UNINHABITED.
2. DASHED LINES SHOW OVERLAP
   OF LANGUAGE AREAS.

LANGUAGE FAMILIES

BANTU
KHOISAN

km
0   50   100   150

©2004 SIL

THE AMERICAS

km

0	1000	2000	3000

Greenland

Alaska (USA)

Canada

St. Pierre and Miquelon

USA

Bermuda

Hawaii (USA)

Mexico

PACIFIC OCEAN

ATLANTIC OCEAN

Belize

Nicaragua

Guatemala
El Salvador
Honduras
Costa Rica
Panama

Guyana
Venezuela
Suriname
French Guiana

Colombia

Ecuador

Peru

Brazil

Bolivia

Paraguay

Chile

Argentina
Uruguay

Falkland Islands

©2004 SIL

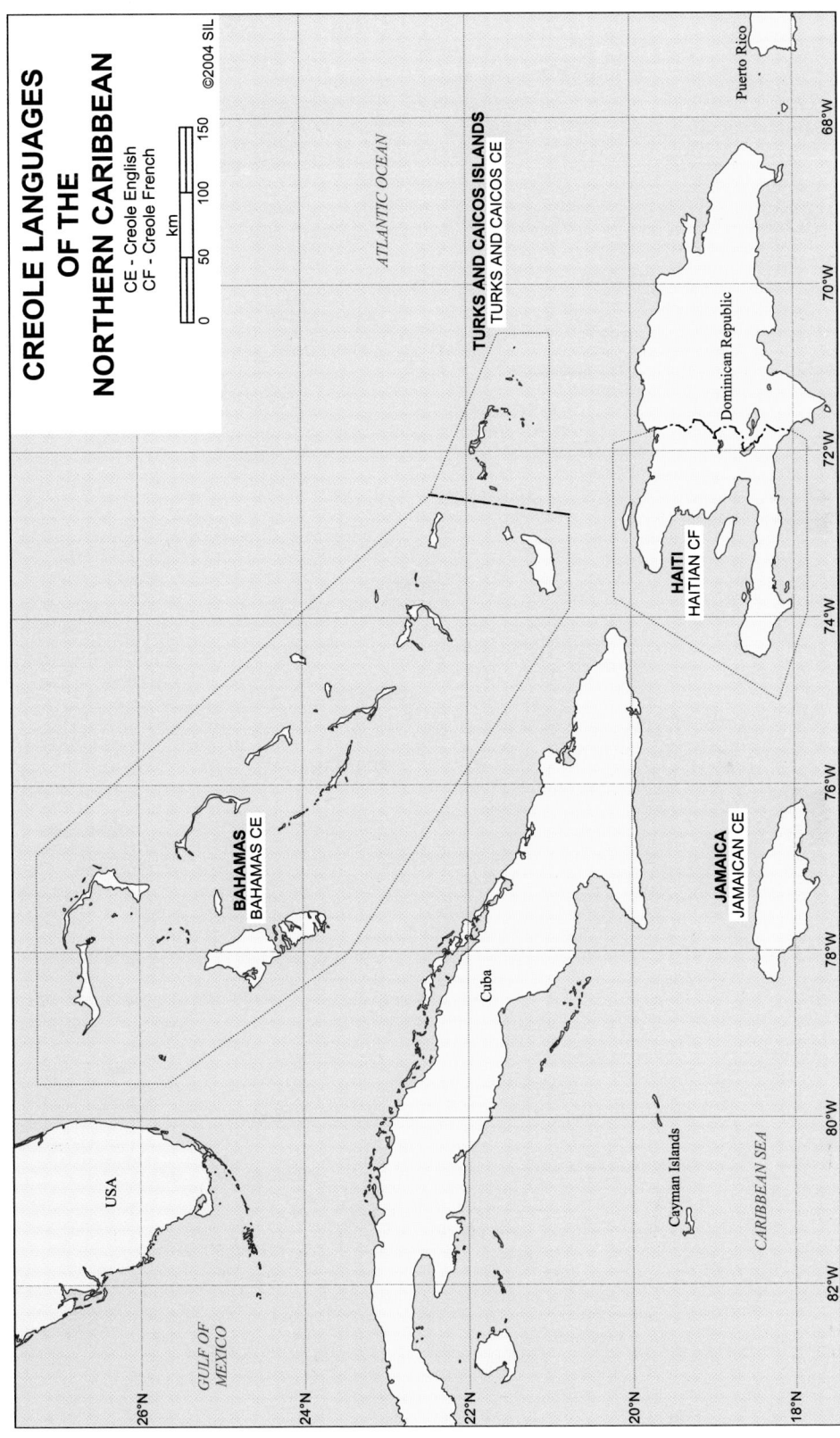

CREOLE LANGUAGES
OF THE
NORTHERN CARIBBEAN

CE - Creole English
CF - Creole French

km

0   50   100   150

©2004 SIL

ATLANTIC OCEAN

TURKS AND CAICOS ISLANDS
TURKS AND CAICOS CE

Puerto Rico

Dominican Republic

HAITI
HAITIAN CF

BAHAMAS
BAHAMAS CE

Cuba

JAMAICA
JAMAICAN CE

USA

Cayman Islands

CARIBBEAN SEA

GULF OF
MEXICO

26°N
24°N
22°N
20°N
18°N

82°W   80°W   78°W   76°W   74°W   72°W   70°W   68°W

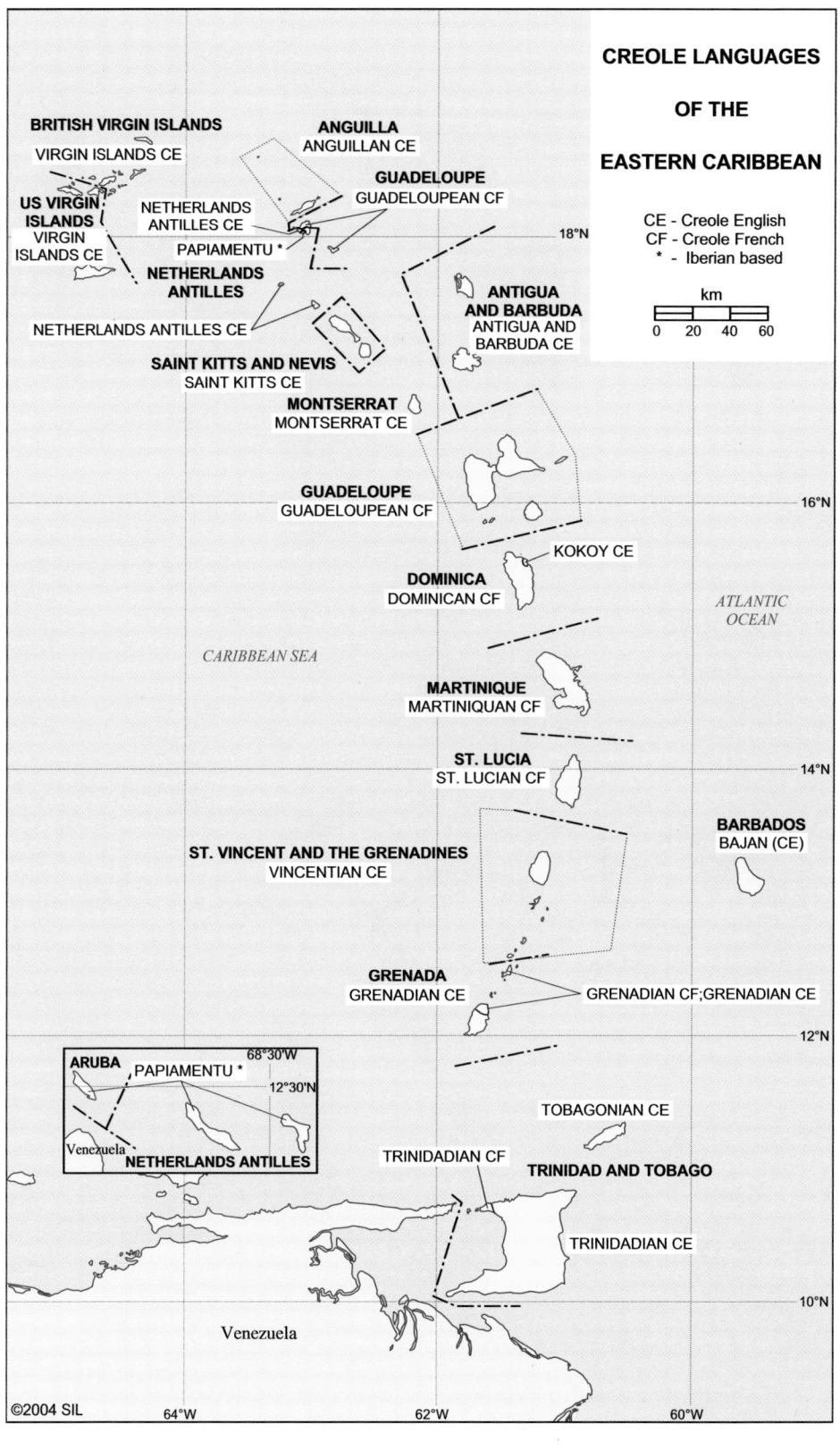

CREOLE LANGUAGES

OF THE

EASTERN CARIBBEAN

CE - Creole English
CF - Creole French
* - Iberian based

km

0   20   40   60

BRITISH VIRGIN ISLANDS
VIRGIN ISLANDS CE

ANGUILLA
ANGUILLAN CE

GUADELOUPE
GUADELOUPEAN CF

US VIRGIN
ISLANDS
VIRGIN
ISLANDS CE

NETHERLANDS
ANTILLES CE

PAPIAMENTU *

NETHERLANDS
ANTILLES

18°N

NETHERLANDS ANTILLES CE

ANTIGUA
AND BARBUDA
ANTIGUA AND
BARBUDA CE

SAINT KITTS AND NEVIS
SAINT KITTS CE

MONTSERRAT
MONTSERRAT CE

GUADELOUPE
GUADELOUPEAN CF

16°N

KOKOY CE

DOMINICA
DOMINICAN CF

ATLANTIC
OCEAN

CARIBBEAN SEA

MARTINIQUE
MARTINIQUAN CF

ST. LUCIA
ST. LUCIAN CF

14°N

BARBADOS
BAJAN (CE)

ST. VINCENT AND THE GRENADINES
VINCENTIAN CE

GRENADA
GRENADIAN CE

GRENADIAN CF;GRENADIAN CE

12°N

ARUBA
PAPIAMENTU *

68°30'W

12°30'N

Venezuela

NETHERLANDS ANTILLES

TOBAGONIAN CE

TRINIDADIAN CF

TRINIDAD AND TOBAGO

TRINIDADIAN CE

10°N

Venezuela

©2004 SIL

64°W

62°W

60°W

ARGENTINA
AND CHILE

NATIONAL LANGUAGE
(BOTH COUNTRIES)
SPANISH

LANGUAGE FAMILIES

	ALACALUFAN
	ARAUCANIAN
	AUSTRONESIAN
	AYMARAN
	CHON
	TUPI
	LULE-VILELA
	MATACO-GUAICURU
	QUECHUAN

NOTE: DASHED LINES SHOW
OVERLAP OF LANGUAGE AREAS.
©2004 SIL

1 SOUTH BOLIVIAN QUECHUA
2 WICHÍ LHAMTÉS NOCTEN
3 NIVACLE
4 IYOJWA'JA CHOROTE
5 IYO'WUJWA CHOROTE
6 TAPIETÉ
7 WICHÍ LHAMTÉS GÜISNAY
8 WESTERN ARGENTINE
  GUARANÍ
9 WICHÍ LHAMTÉS VEJOZ

Chile - Easter Island

RAPA NUI

CHILEAN QUECHUA

CENTRAL AYMARA

PILAGÁ

TOBA

MBYÁ
GUARANÍ

KAIWÁ

VILELA

SANTIAGO
DEL
ESTERO
QUICHUA

MOCOVÍ

MAPUDUNGUN

HUILLICHE

MAPUDUNGUN

TEHUELCHE

QAWASQAR

Peru

Bolivia

Paraguay

Brazil

See Inset

CHILE

Argentina

Santiago

ARGENTINA

Buenos Aires

Paraná River

Uruguay

ATLANTIC OCEAN

PACIFIC OCEAN

km
0 100 200 300

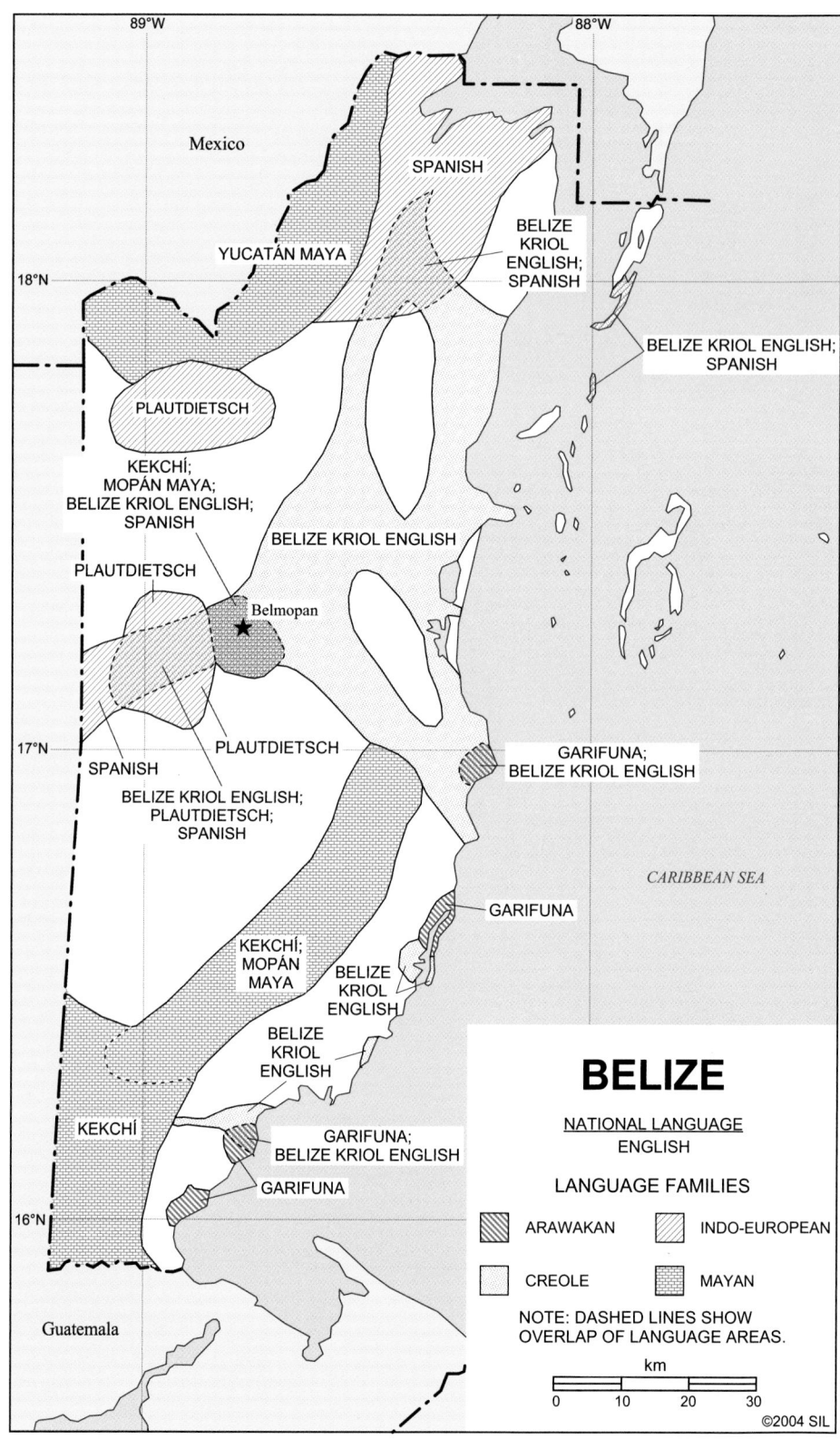

89°W

Mexico

SPANISH

BELIZE
KRIOL
ENGLISH;
SPANISH

YUCATÁN MAYA

88°W

BELIZE KRIOL ENGLISH;
SPANISH

18°N

PLAUTDIETSCH

KEKCHÍ;
MOPÁN MAYA;
BELIZE KRIOL ENGLISH;
SPANISH

PLAUTDIETSCH

BELIZE KRIOL ENGLISH

Belmopan

PLAUTDIETSCH

17°N

SPANISH

BELIZE KRIOL ENGLISH;
PLAUTDIETSCH;
SPANISH

GARIFUNA;
BELIZE KRIOL ENGLISH

GARIFUNA

CARIBBEAN SEA

KEKCHÍ;
MOPÁN
MAYA

BELIZE
KRIOL
ENGLISH

BELIZE
KRIOL
ENGLISH

KEKCHÍ

GARIFUNA;
BELIZE KRIOL ENGLISH

GARIFUNA

16°N

Guatemala

BELIZE

<u>NATIONAL LANGUAGE</u>
ENGLISH

LANGUAGE FAMILIES

ARAWAKAN   INDO-EUROPEAN

CREOLE   MAYAN

NOTE: DASHED LINES SHOW
OVERLAP OF LANGUAGE AREAS.

km

0   10   20   30

©2004 SIL

BOLIVIA

NATIONAL LANGUAGE
SPANISH

LANGUAGE FAMILIES

ARAWAKAN	QUECHUAN
AYMARAN	TACANAN
URU-CHIPAYA	TUPI
MACRO-GE	ZAMUCOAN
MATACO-GUAICURU	LANGUAGE ISOLATE
MOSETENAN	UNCLASSIFIED
PANOAN	

NOTES:
1. DASHED LINES SHOW OVERLAP OF LANGUAGE AREAS.
2. BRACKETS SHOW THE NUMBER OF TIMES A LANGUAGE'S
   NUMBER APPEARS ON MAP IF MORE THAN ONCE.

1 ARAONA
2 AYOREO (3)
3 BAURE
4 CAVINEÑA
5 CENTRAL AYMARA
6 CHÁCOBO
7 CHIPAYA
8 CHIQUITANO (2)
9 EASTERN BOLIVIAN GUARANÍ (2)
10 ESE EJJA (3)
11 GUARAYU
12 IGNACIANO
13 ITONAMA
14 IYO'WUJWA CHOROTE
15 LECO
16 MOVIMA
17 NORTH BOLIVIAN QUECHUA
18 PACAHUARA
19 SIRIONÓ
20 SOUTH BOLIVIAN QUECHUA
21 TACANA
22 TAPIETÉ
23 TOBA
24 TRINITARIO
25 TSIMANÉ
26 URU
27 WESTERN BOLIVIAN GUARANÍ (2)
28 WICHÍ LHAMTÉS NOCTEN
29 YAMINAHUA
30 YUQUI
31 YURACARE

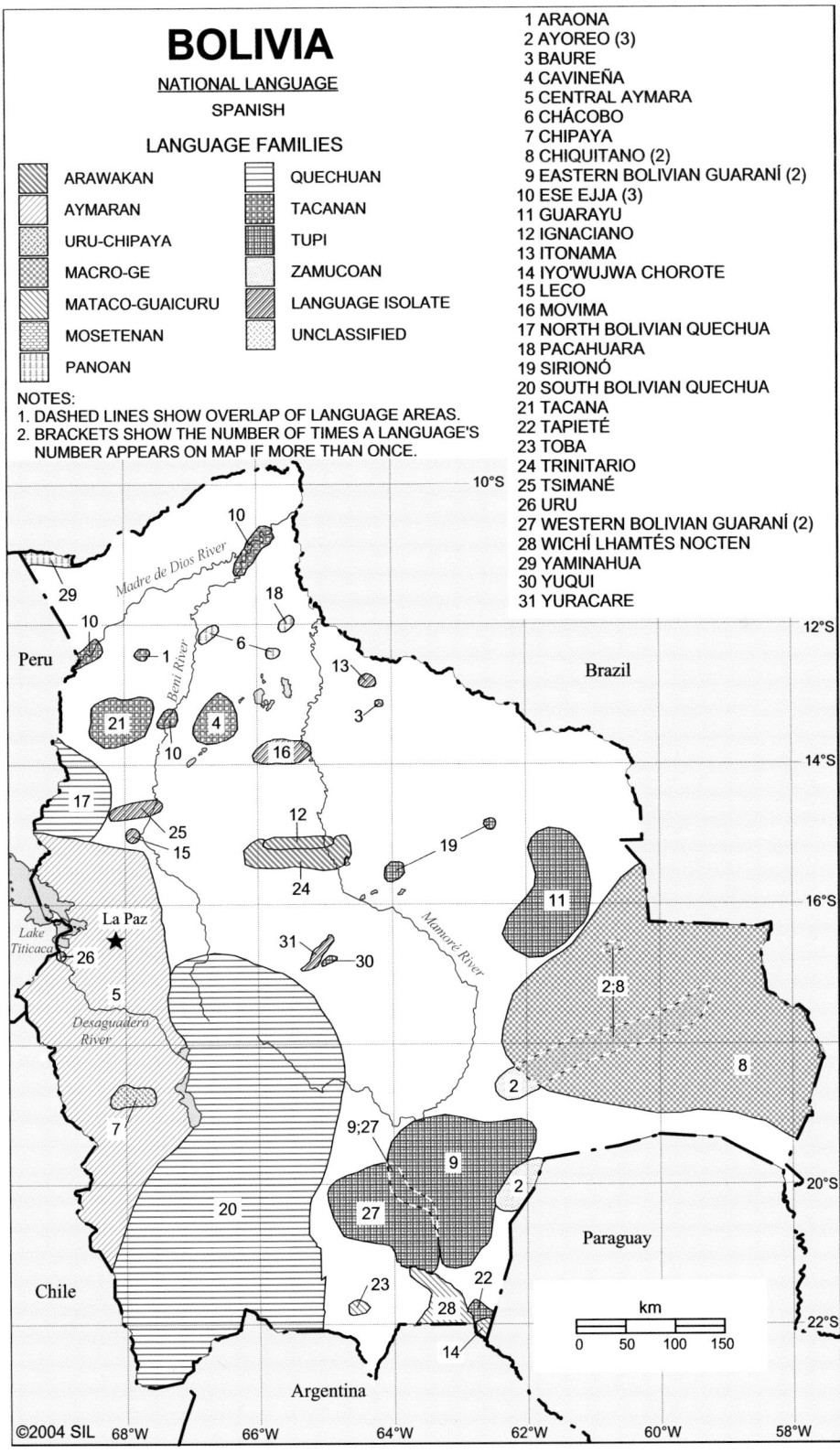

©2004 SIL

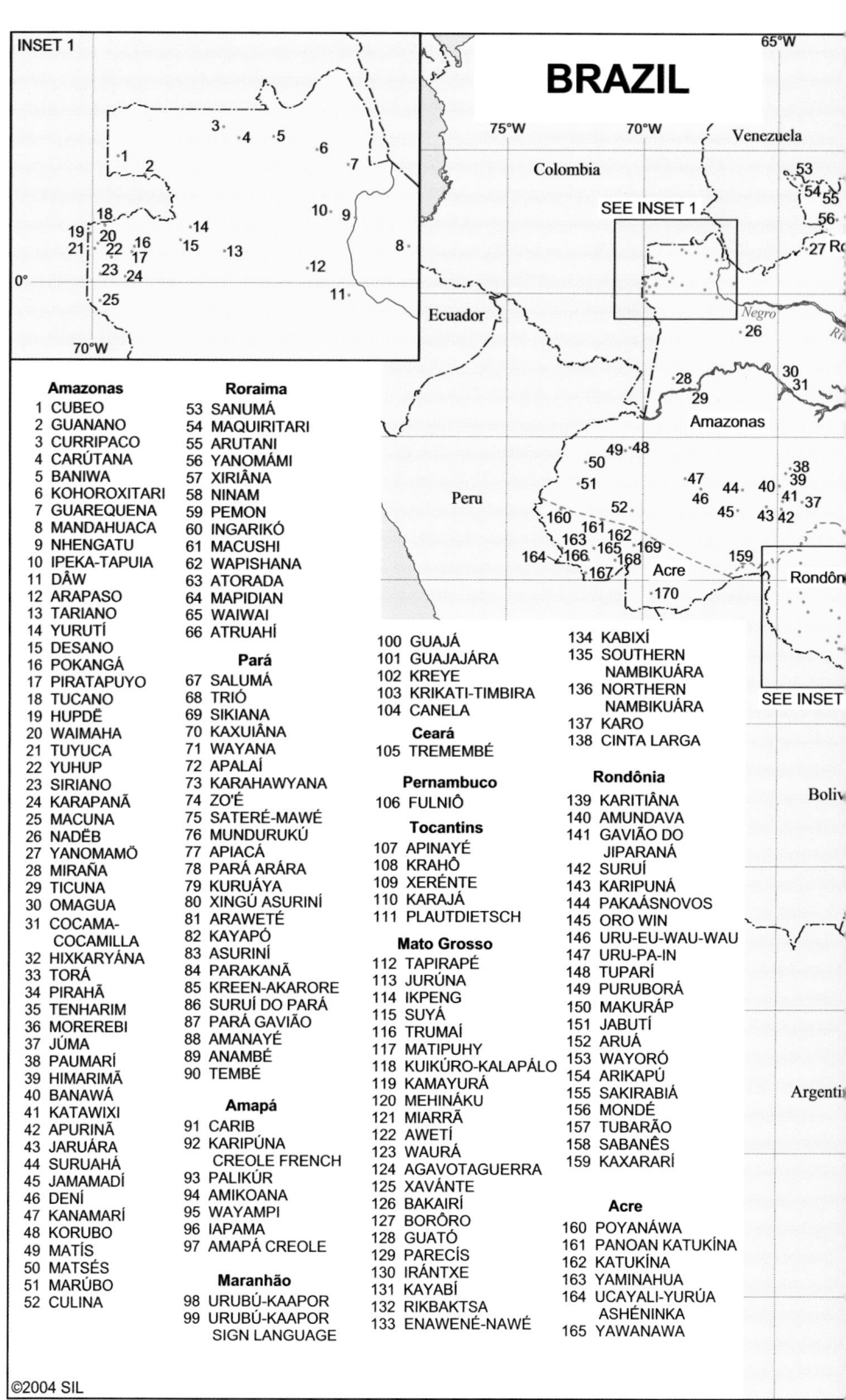

Amazonas
1 CUBEO
2 GUANANO
3 CURRIPACO
4 CARÚTANA
5 BANIWA
6 KOHOROXITARI
7 GUAREQUENA
8 MANDAHUACA
9 NHENGATU
10 IPEKA-TAPUIA
11 DÂW
12 ARAPASO
13 TARIANO
14 YURUTÍ
15 DESANO
16 POKANGÁ
17 PIRATAPUYO
18 TUCANO
19 HUPDË
20 WAIMAHA
21 TUYUCA
22 YUHUP
23 SIRIANO
24 KARAPANÃ
25 MACUNA
26 NADËB
27 YANOMAMÖ
28 MIRAÑA
29 TICUNA
30 OMAGUA
31 COCAMA-
   COCAMILLA
32 HIXKARYÁNA
33 TORÁ
34 PIRAHÃ
35 TENHARIM
36 MOREREBI
37 JÚMA
38 PAUMARÍ
39 HIMARIMÃ
40 BANAWÁ
41 KATAWIXI
42 APURINÃ
43 JARUÁRA
44 SURUAHÁ
45 JAMAMADÍ
46 DENÍ
47 KANAMARÍ
48 KORUBO
49 MATÍS
50 MATSÉS
51 MARÚBO
52 CULINA

Roraima
53 SANUMÁ
54 MAQUIRITARI
55 ARUTANI
56 YANOMÁMI
57 XIRIÃNA
58 NINAM
59 PEMON
60 INGARIKÓ
61 MACUSHI
62 WAPISHANA
63 ATORADA
64 MAPIDIAN
65 WAIWAI
66 ATRUAHÍ

Pará
67 SALUMÁ
68 TRIÓ
69 SIKIANA
70 KAXUIÃNA
71 WAYANA
72 APALAÍ
73 KARAHAWYANA
74 ZO'É
75 SATERÉ-MAWÉ
76 MUNDURUKÚ
77 APIACÁ
78 PARÁ ARÁRA
79 KURUÁYA
80 XINGÚ ASURINÍ
81 ARAWETÉ
82 KAYAPÓ
83 ASURINÍ
84 PARAKANÃ
85 KREEN-AKARORE
86 SURUÍ DO PARÁ
87 PARÁ GAVIÃO
88 AMANAYÉ
89 ANAMBÉ
90 TEMBÉ

Amapá
91 CARIB
92 KARIPÚNA
   CREOLE FRENCH
93 PALIKÚR
94 AMIKOANA
95 WAYAMPI
96 IAPAMA
97 AMAPÁ CREOLE

Maranhão
98 URUBÚ-KAAPOR
99 URUBÚ-KAAPOR
   SIGN LANGUAGE

100 GUAJÁ
101 GUAJAJÁRA
102 KREYE
103 KRIKATI-TIMBIRA
104 CANELA

Ceará
105 TREMEMBÉ

Pernambuco
106 FULNIÔ

Tocantins
107 APINAYÉ
108 KRAHÔ
109 XERÉNTE
110 KARAJÁ
111 PLAUTDIETSCH

Mato Grosso
112 TAPIRAPÉ
113 JURÚNA
114 IKPENG
115 SUYÁ
116 TRUMAÍ
117 MATIPUHY
118 KUIKÚRO-KALAPÁLO
119 KAMAYURÁ
120 MEHINÁKU
121 MIARRÃ
122 AWETÍ
123 WAURÁ
124 AGAVOTAGUERRA
125 XAVÁNTE
126 BAKAIRÍ
127 BORÔRO
128 GUATÓ
129 PARECÍS
130 IRÁNTXE
131 KAYABÍ
132 RIKBAKTSA
133 ENAWENÉ-NAWÉ

134 KABIXÍ
135 SOUTHERN
   NAMBIKUÁRA
136 NORTHERN
   NAMBIKUÁRA
137 KARO
138 CINTA LARGA

Rondônia
139 KARITIÂNA
140 AMUNDAVA
141 GAVIÃO DO
   JIPARANÁ
142 SURUÍ
143 KARIPUNÁ
144 PAKAÁSNOVOS
145 ORO WIN
146 URU-EU-WAU-WAU
147 URU-PA-IN
148 TUPARÍ
149 PURUBORÁ
150 MAKURÁP
151 JABUTÍ
152 ARUÁ
153 WAYORÓ
154 ARIKAPÚ
155 SAKIRABIÁ
156 MONDÉ
157 TUBARÃO
158 SABANÊS
159 KAXARARÍ

Acre
160 POYANÁWA
161 PANOAN KATUKÍNA
162 KATUKÍNA
163 YAMINAHUA
164 UCAYALI-YURÚA
   ASHÉNINKA
165 YAWANAWA

©2004 SIL

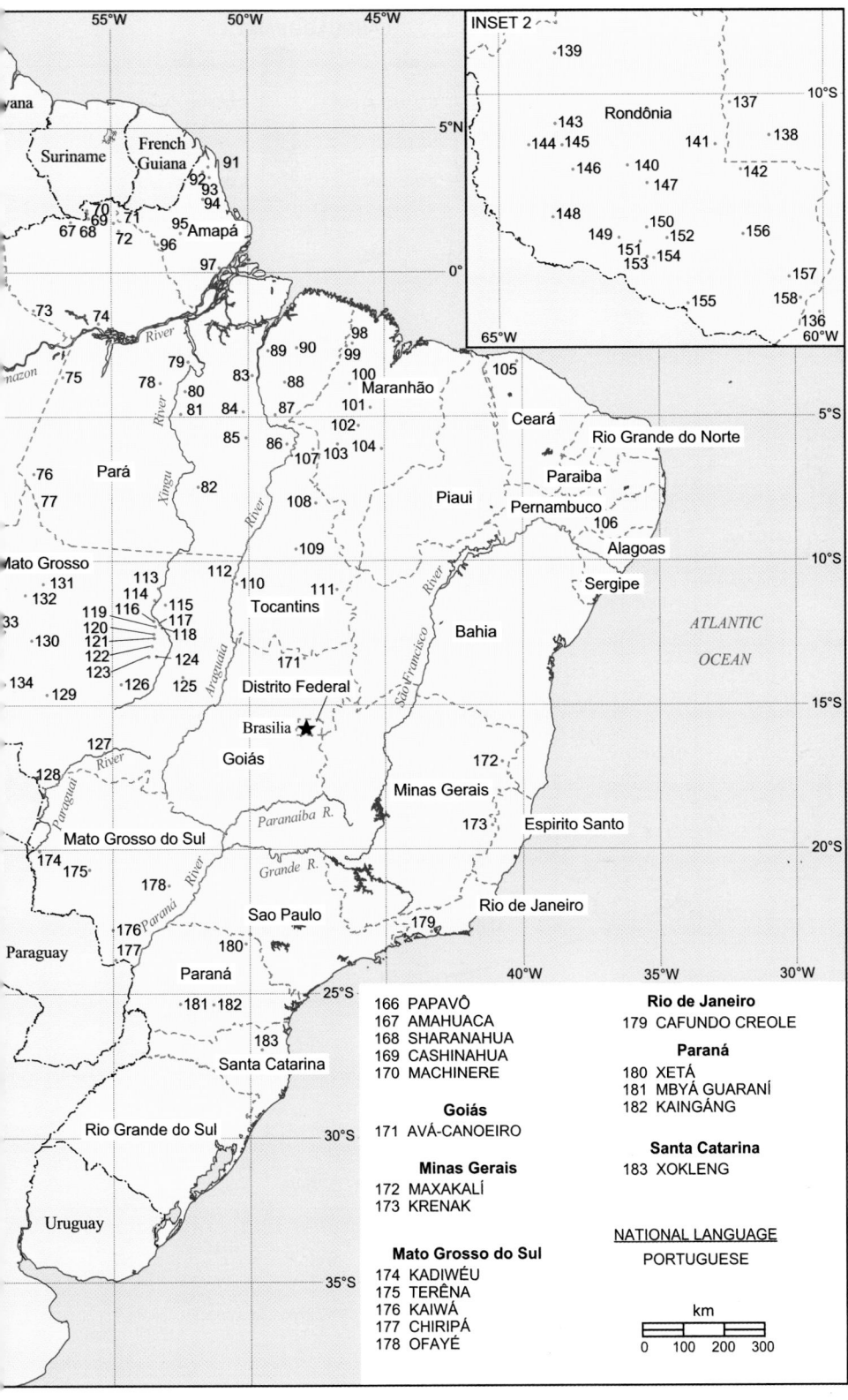

INSET 2

139

Rondônia

137   10°S

5°N   143   141   138
        144 145
           146   140   142
                       147

                148   150
                     149   152   156
                          151
                          153 154

                             155   158   157

65°W   136
                                                         60°W

Suriname

French
Guiana   91

92
93
94
70   95 Amapá
69 71
67 68   72   96

97   0°

73   74

River

79   98
89 90   99
75   78   83   88   100   105
80   Maranhão
81 84   87   101
85   86   102   Ceará   5°S
107 103 104
107   Rio Grande do Norte

76   Pará   Paraiba
82   Piaui   Pernambuco
77   108   106

109   Alagoas   10°S

Mato Grosso   Sergipe
131   112 110 111
132   113   Tocantins
114
119 116 115 117   Bahia   ATLANTIC
33   120   118
130 121   OCEAN
122   124
123   171
134   129 126 125

Distrito Federal   15°S

127   Brasilia ★

128   Goiás

Minas Gerais
172
Paranaiba R.   Espirito Santo
173
Mato Grosso do Sul   20°S

174
175   178   Grande R.

Sao Paulo   Rio de Janeiro
176 Paraná
Paraguay 177   180
179
Paraná

181 182   25°S

183
Santa Catarina

Rio Grande do Sul   30°S

Uruguay

35°S

166 PAPAVÔ
167 AMAHUACA
168 SHARANAHUA
169 CASHINAHUA
170 MACHINERE

Goiás
171 AVÁ-CANOEIRO

Minas Gerais
172 MAXAKALÍ
173 KRENAK

Mato Grosso do Sul
174 KADIWÉU
175 TERÊNA
176 KAIWÁ
177 CHIRIPÁ
178 OFAYÉ

Rio de Janeiro
179 CAFUNDO CREOLE

Paraná
180 XETÁ
181 MBYÁ GUARANÍ
182 KAINGÁNG

Santa Catarina
183 XOKLENG

NATIONAL LANGUAGE
PORTUGUESE

km

0   100   200   300

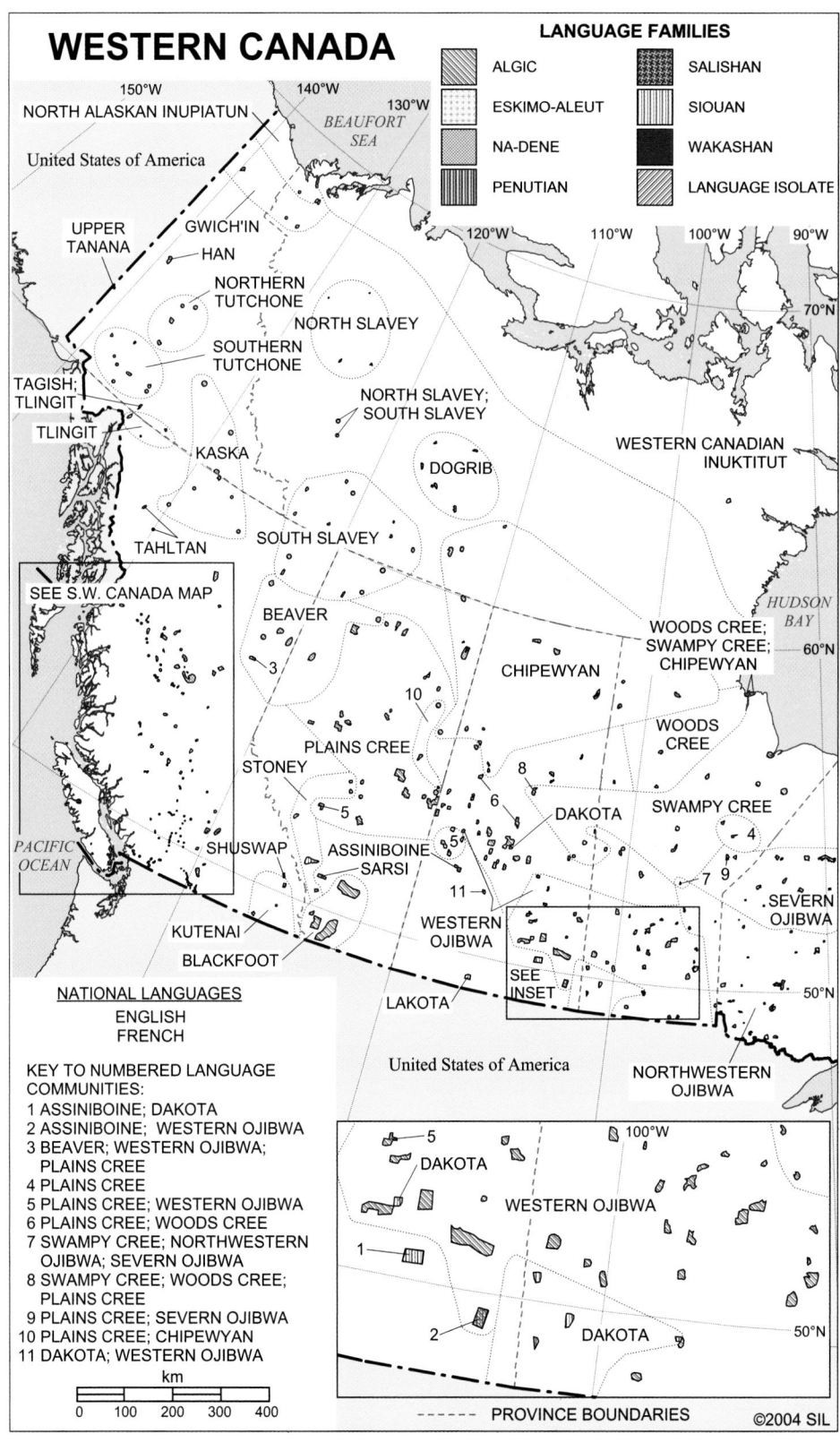

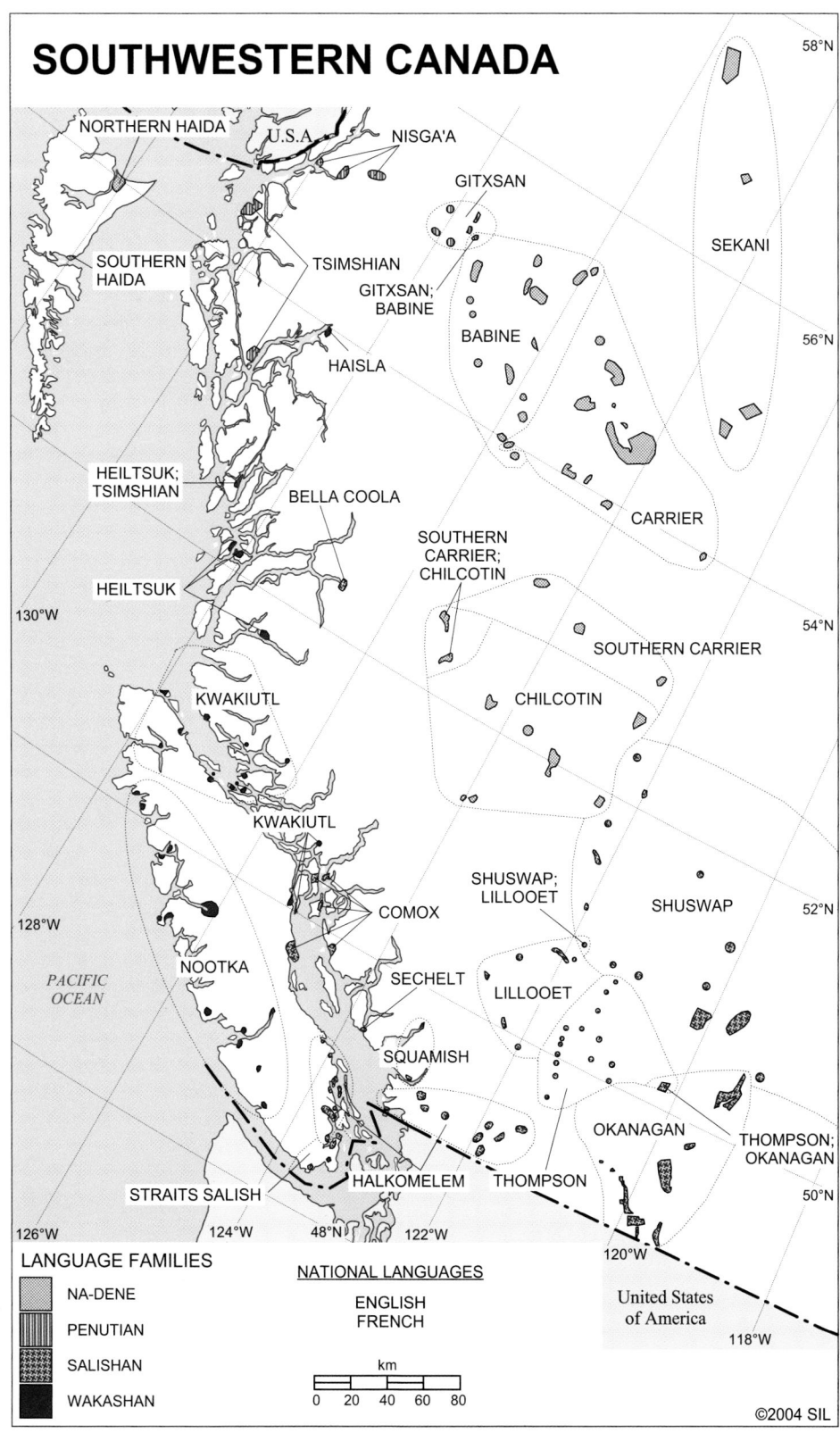

SOUTHWESTERN CANADA

58°N

NORTHERN HAIDA

U.S.A.

NISGA'A

GITXSAN

SEKANI

SOUTHERN
HAIDA

TSIMSHIAN

GITXSAN;
BABINE

56°N

BABINE

HAISLA

HEILTSUK;
TSIMSHIAN

BELLA COOLA

CARRIER

SOUTHERN
CARRIER;
CHILCOTIN

HEILTSUK

130°W

54°N

SOUTHERN CARRIER

KWAKIUTL

CHILCOTIN

KWAKIUTL

SHUSWAP;
LILLOOET

COMOX

SHUSWAP

52°N

128°W

LILLOOET

PACIFIC
OCEAN

NOOTKA

SECHELT

OKANAGAN

SQUAMISH

THOMPSON;
OKANAGAN

STRAITS SALISH

HALKOMELEM

THOMPSON

50°N

126°W

124°W

48°N

122°W

120°W

United States
of America

118°W

LANGUAGE FAMILIES

NATIONAL LANGUAGES

NA-DENE

ENGLISH
FRENCH

PENUTIAN

SALISHAN

km

WAKASHAN

0   20   40   60   80

©2004 SIL

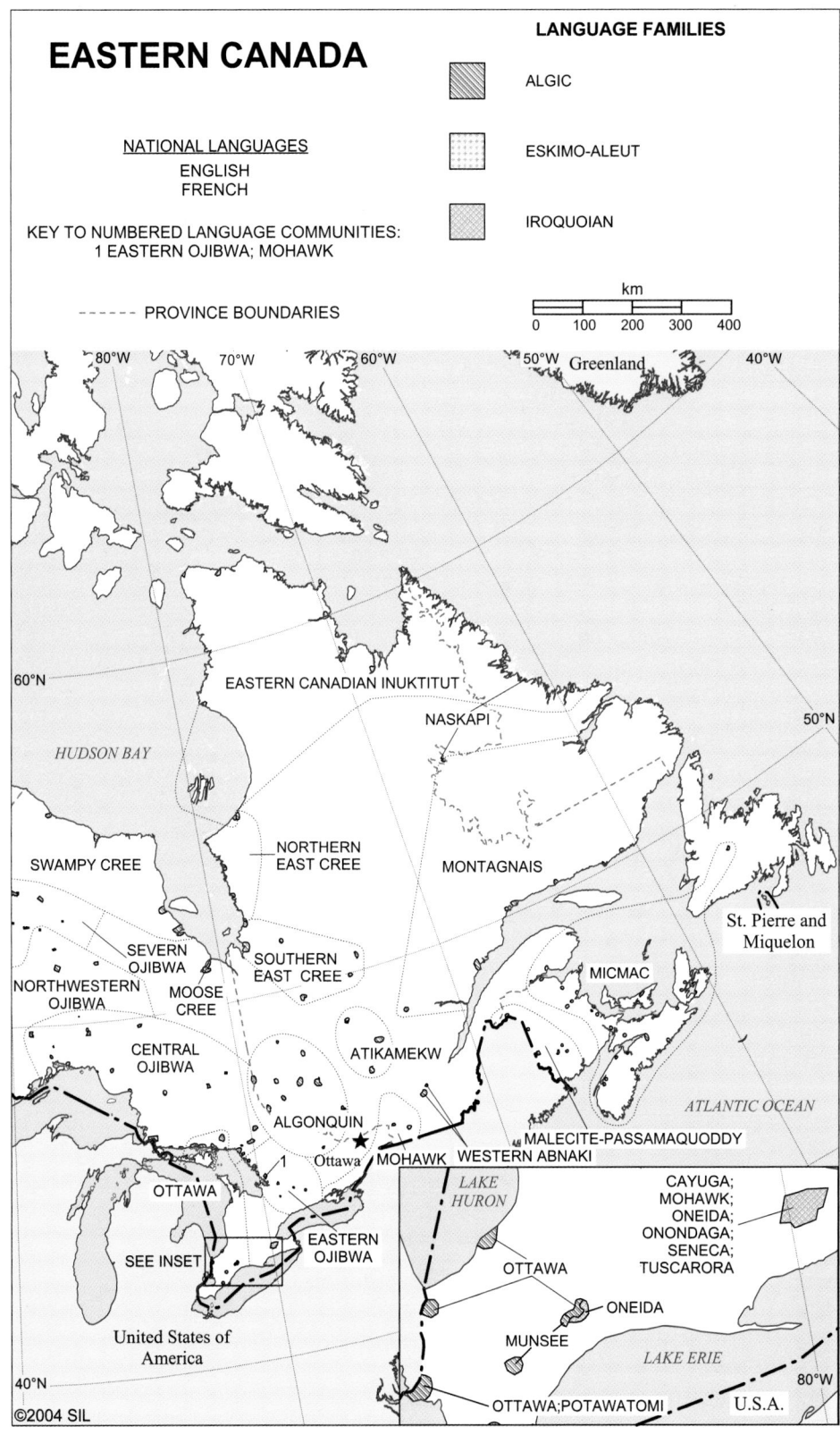

EASTERN CANADA

LANGUAGE FAMILIES

ALGIC

ESKIMO-ALEUT

IROQUOIAN

NATIONAL LANGUAGES
ENGLISH
FRENCH

KEY TO NUMBERED LANGUAGE COMMUNITIES:
1 EASTERN OJIBWA; MOHAWK

----- PROVINCE BOUNDARIES

km
0 100 200 300 400

80°W   70°W   60°W   50°W Greenland   40°W

60°N

50°N

EASTERN CANADIAN INUKTITUT

NASKAPI

HUDSON BAY

NORTHERN
EAST CREE   MONTAGNAIS

SWAMPY CREE

St. Pierre and
Miquelon

SEVERN
OJIBWA   SOUTHERN
EAST CREE
NORTHWESTERN   MOOSE
OJIBWA   CREE

MICMAC

CENTRAL
OJIBWA   ATIKAMEKW

ATLANTIC OCEAN

ALGONQUIN

1   Ottawa   MOHAWK   WESTERN ABNAKI
OTTAWA   MALECITE-PASSAMAQUODDY

EASTERN
OJIBWA
SEE INSET

United States of
America

40°N

©2004 SIL

LAKE
HURON

CAYUGA;
MOHAWK;
ONEIDA;
ONONDAGA;
SENECA;
TUSCARORA

OTTAWA
ONEIDA

MUNSEE

LAKE ERIE

OTTAWA;POTAWATOMI   U.S.A.

80°W

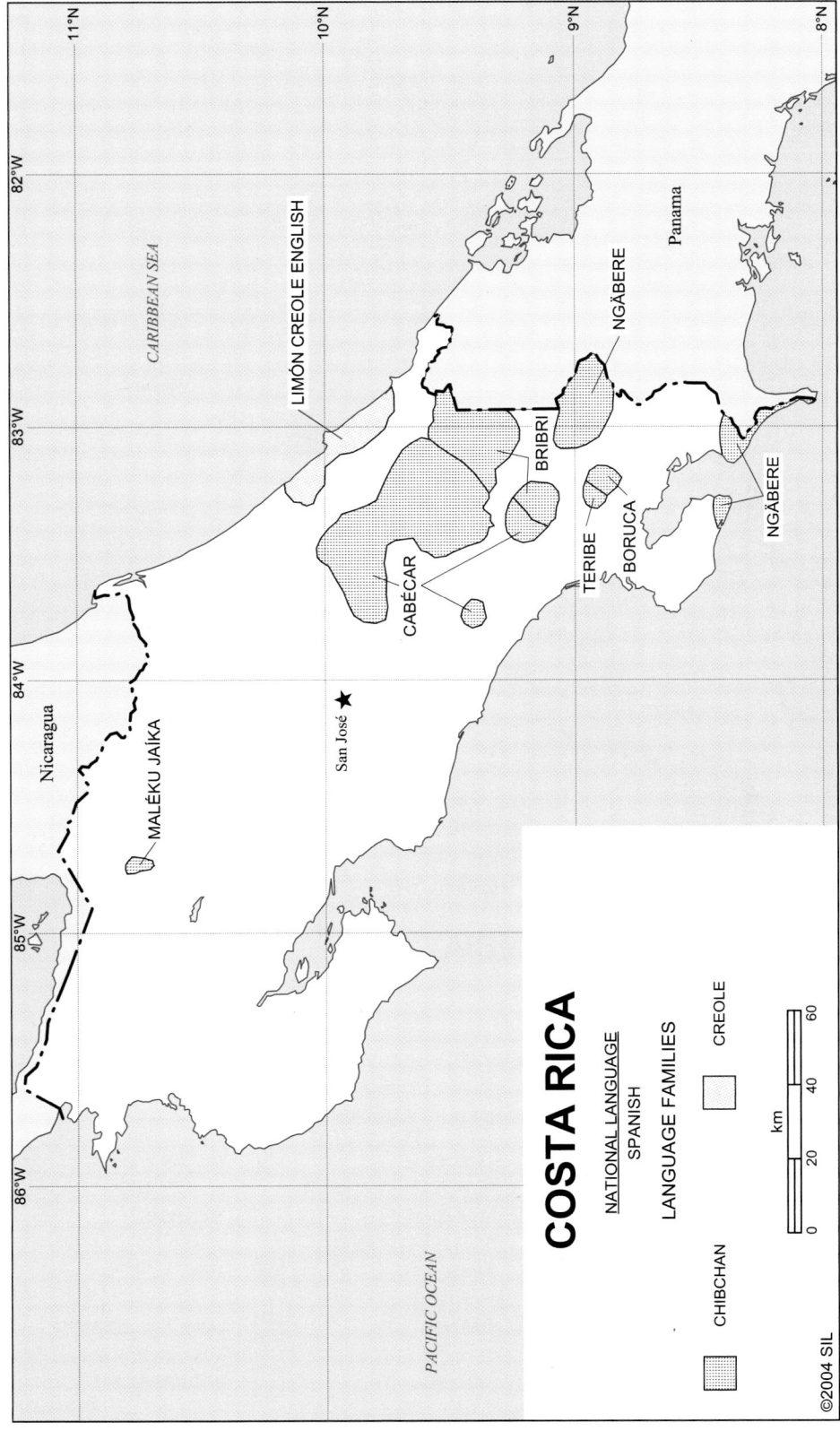

CARIBBEAN SEA

LIMÓN CREOLE ENGLISH

NGÄBERE

BRIBRI

Panama

CABÉCAR

TERIBE

BORUCA

NGÄBERE

Nicaragua

MALÉKU JAÍKA

San José

85°W

86°W

PACIFIC OCEAN

COSTA RICA

NATIONAL LANGUAGE
SPANISH

LANGUAGE FAMILIES

CHIBCHAN

CREOLE

km

0   20   40   60

©2004 SIL

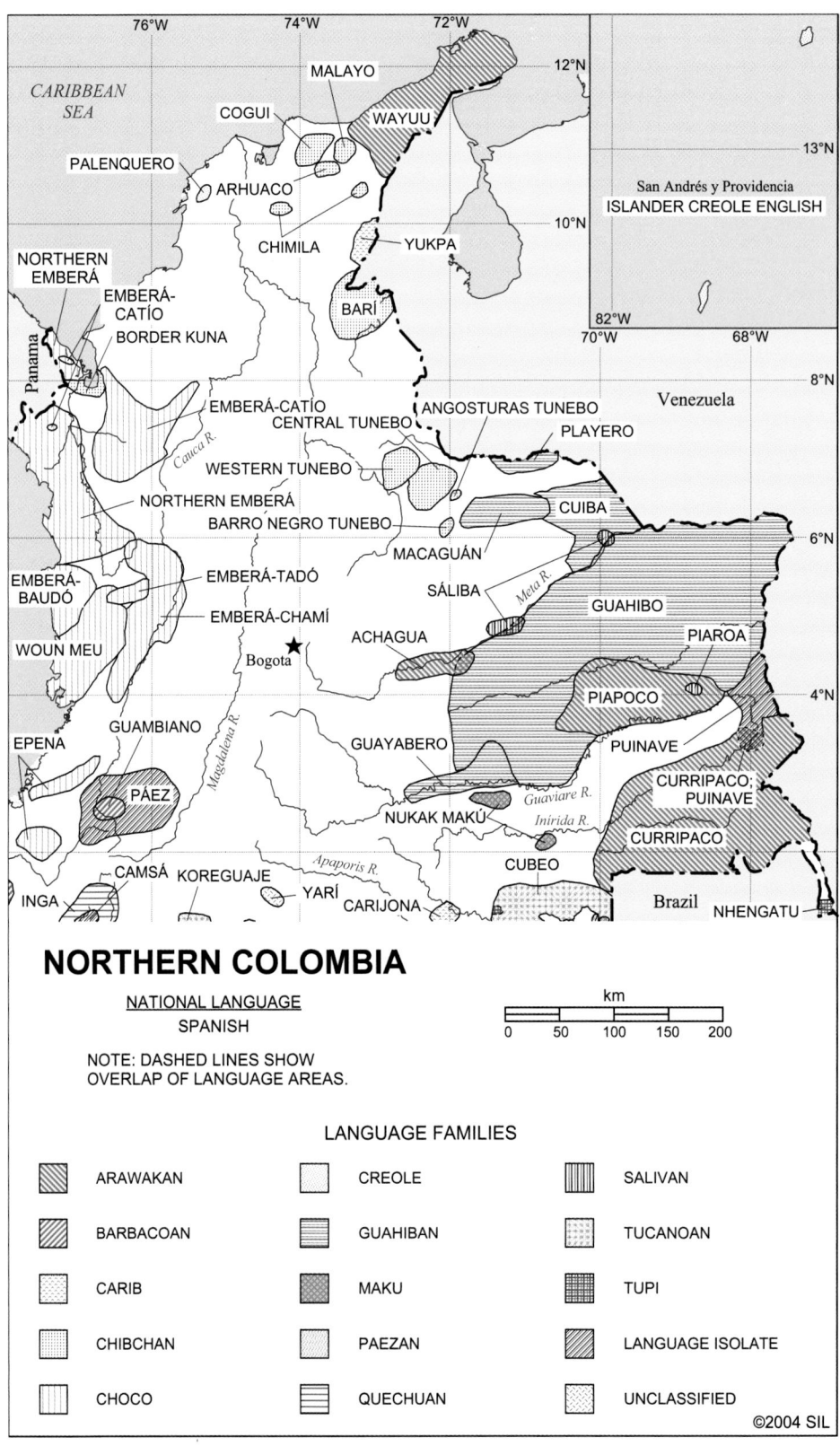

NORTHERN COLOMBIA

NATIONAL LANGUAGE
SPANISH

km
0   50   100   150   200

NOTE: DASHED LINES SHOW
OVERLAP OF LANGUAGE AREAS.

LANGUAGE FAMILIES

ARAWAKAN	CREOLE	SALIVAN
BARBACOAN	GUAHIBAN	TUCANOAN
CARIB	MAKU	TUPI
CHIBCHAN	PAEZAN	LANGUAGE ISOLATE
CHOCO	QUECHUAN	UNCLASSIFIED

©2004 SIL

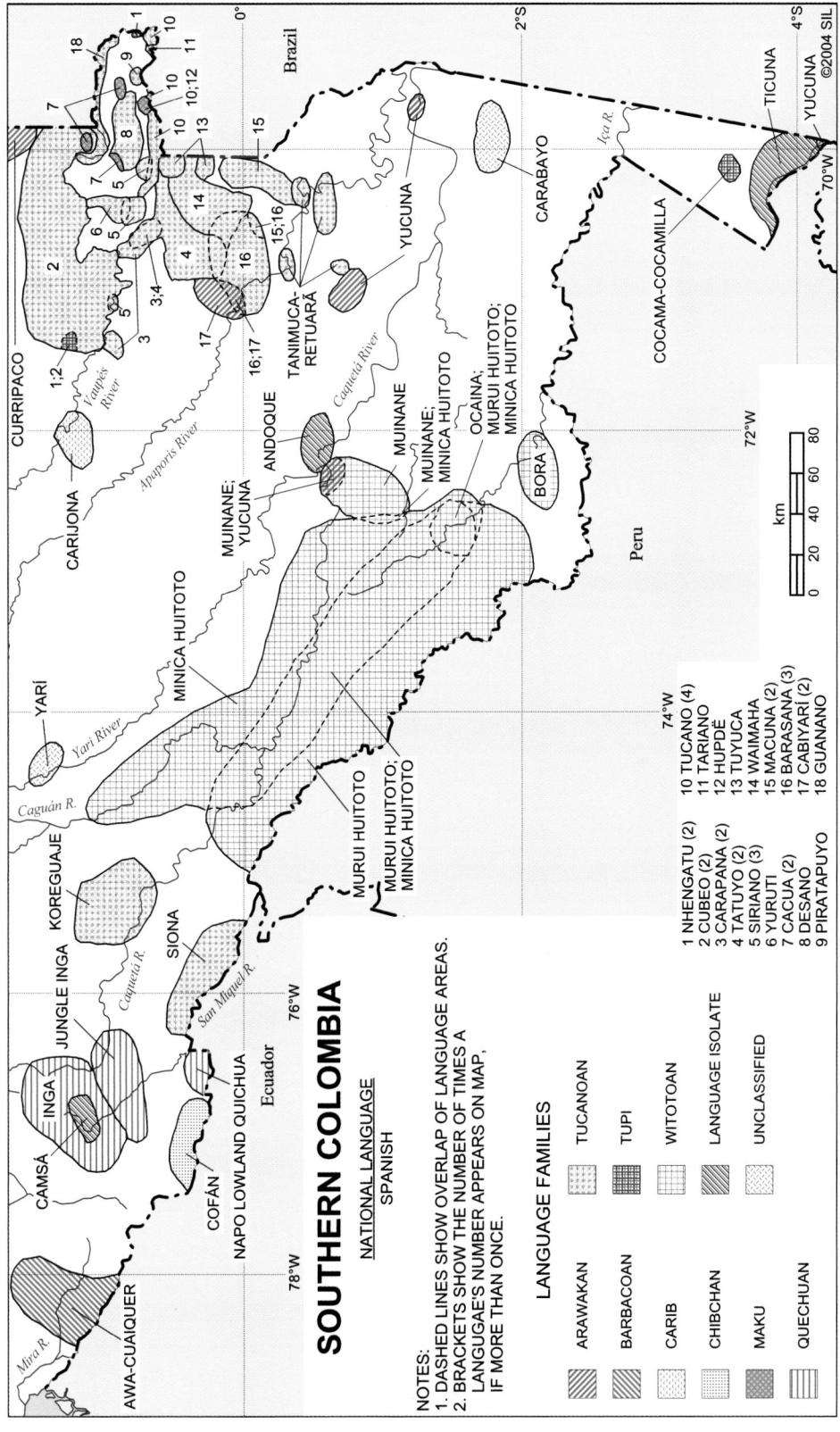

SOUTHERN COLOMBIA

NATIONAL LANGUAGE
SPANISH

NOTES:
1. DASHED LINES SHOW OVERLAP OF LANGUAGE AREAS.
2. BRACKETS SHOW THE NUMBER OF TIMES A
LANGUGAE'S NUMBER APPEARS ON MAP,
IF MORE THAN ONCE.

LANGUAGE FAMILIES

ARAWAKAN
BARBACOAN
CARIB
CHIBCHAN
MAKU
QUECHUAN

TUCANOAN
TUPI
WITOTOAN
LANGUAGE ISOLATE
UNCLASSIFIED

1 NHENGATU (2)
2 CUBEO (2)
3 CARAPANA (2)
4 TATUYO (2)
5 SIRIANO (3)
6 YURUTI
7 CACUA (2)
8 DESANO
9 PIRATAPUYO

10 TUCANO (4)
11 TARIANO
12 HUPDË
13 TUYUCA
14 WAIMAHA
15 MACUNA (2)
16 BARASANA (3)
17 CABIYARI (2)
18 GUANANO

©2004 SIL

km
0 20 40 60 80

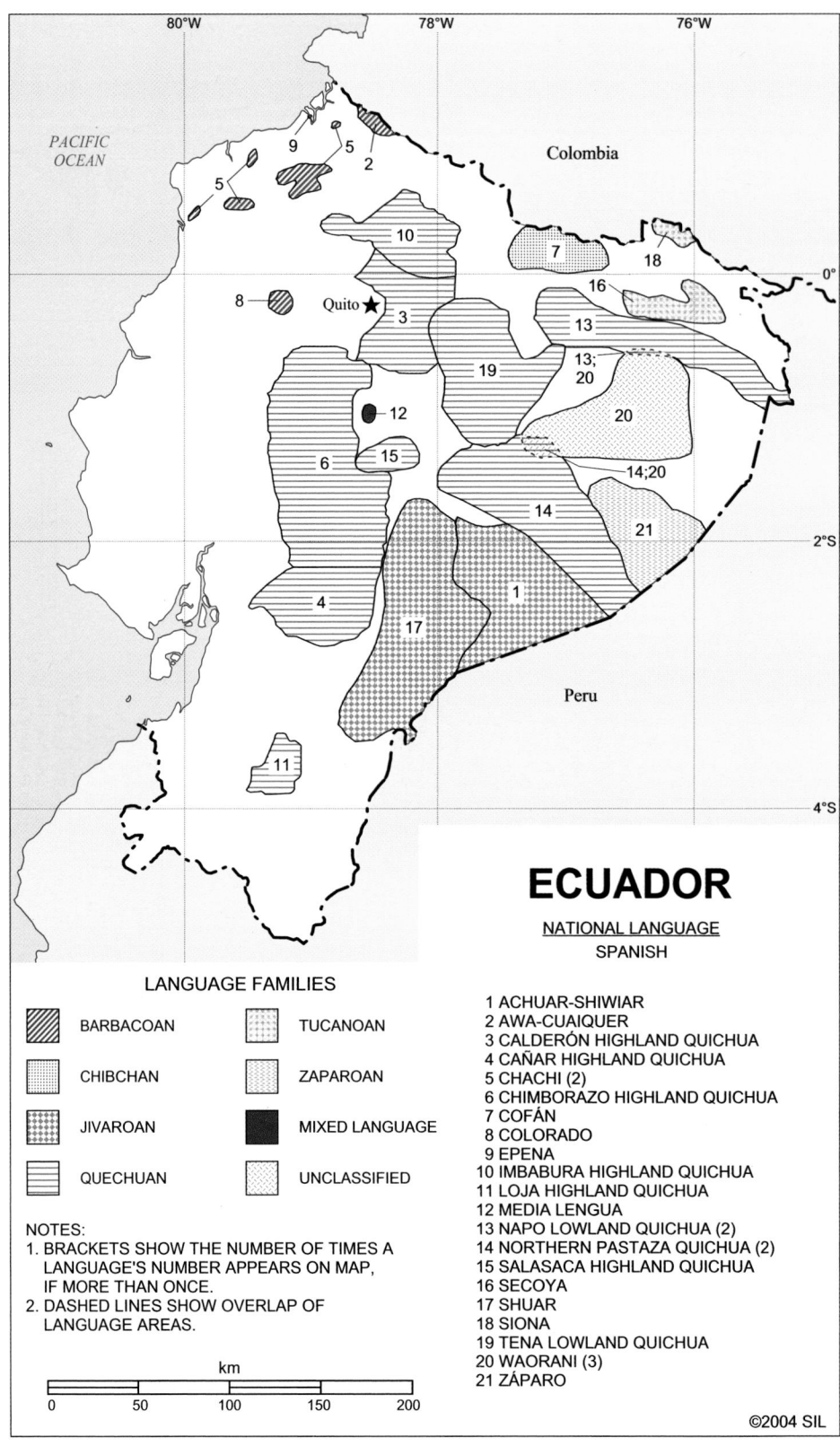

ECUADOR

<u>NATIONAL LANGUAGE</u>
SPANISH

LANGUAGE FAMILIES

BARBACOAN

CHIBCHAN

JIVAROAN

QUECHUAN

TUCANOAN

ZAPAROAN

MIXED LANGUAGE

UNCLASSIFIED

NOTES:
1. BRACKETS SHOW THE NUMBER OF TIMES A LANGUAGE'S NUMBER APPEARS ON MAP, IF MORE THAN ONCE.
2. DASHED LINES SHOW OVERLAP OF LANGUAGE AREAS.

km
0   50   100   150   200

1 ACHUAR-SHIWIAR
2 AWA-CUAIQUER
3 CALDERÓN HIGHLAND QUICHUA
4 CAÑAR HIGHLAND QUICHUA
5 CHACHI (2)
6 CHIMBORAZO HIGHLAND QUICHUA
7 COFÁN
8 COLORADO
9 EPENA
10 IMBABURA HIGHLAND QUICHUA
11 LOJA HIGHLAND QUICHUA
12 MEDIA LENGUA
13 NAPO LOWLAND QUICHUA (2)
14 NORTHERN PASTAZA QUICHUA (2)
15 SALASACA HIGHLAND QUICHUA
16 SECOYA
17 SHUAR
18 SIONA
19 TENA LOWLAND QUICHUA
20 WAORANI (3)
21 ZÁPARO

©2004 SIL

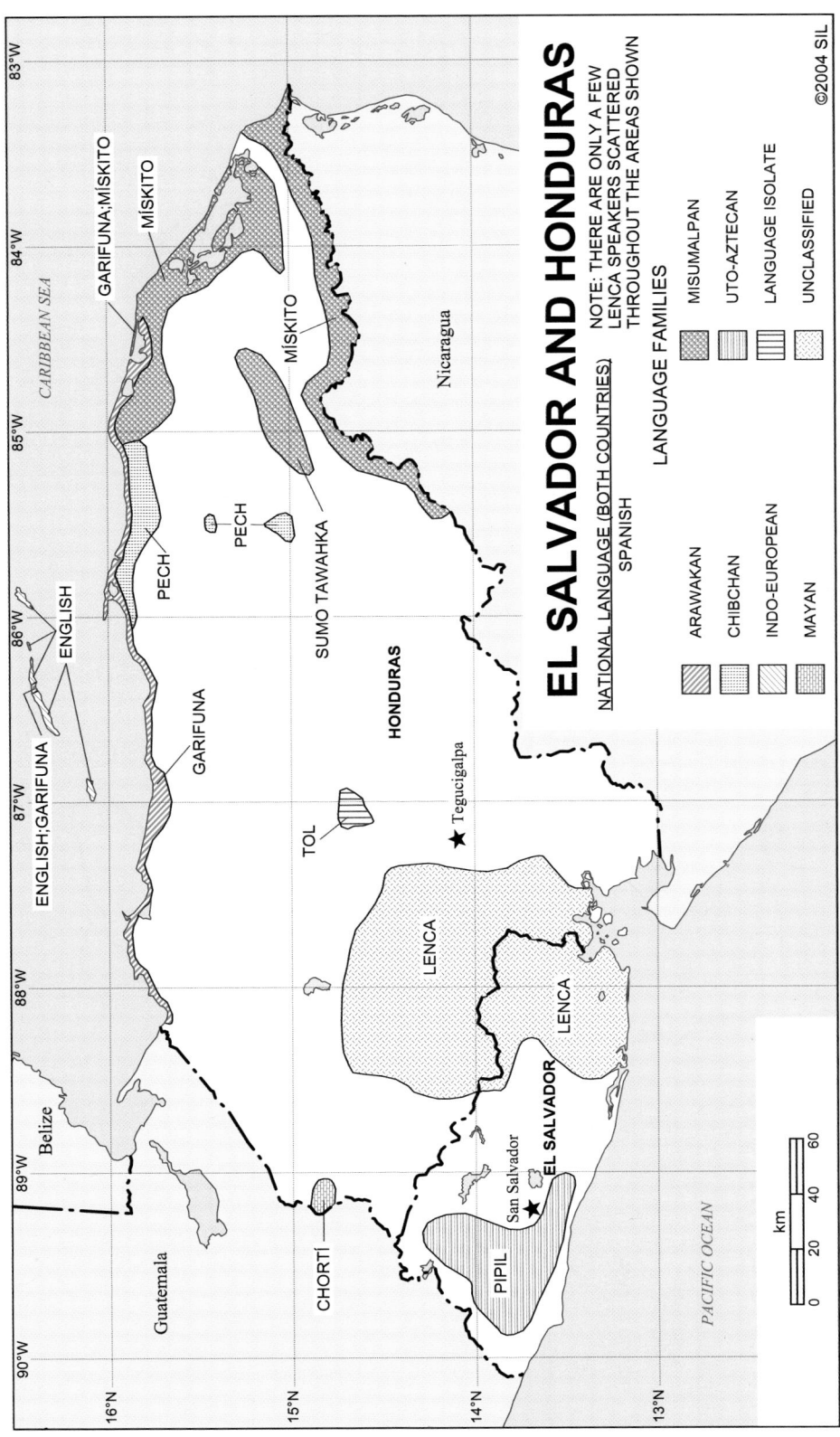

EL SALVADOR AND HONDURAS

NOTE: THERE ARE ONLY A FEW
LENCA SPEAKERS SCATTERED
THROUGHOUT THE AREAS SHOWN

NATIONAL LANGUAGE (BOTH COUNTRIES)
SPANISH

LANGUAGE FAMILIES

ARAWAKAN
CHIBCHAN
INDO-EUROPEAN
MAYAN

MISUMALPAN
UTO-AZTECAN
LANGUAGE ISOLATE
UNCLASSIFIED

CARIBBEAN SEA

PACIFIC OCEAN

Belize

Guatemala

HONDURAS

Nicaragua

EL SALVADOR

★ Tegucigalpa

★ San Salvador

GARIFUNA;MISKITO
MISKITO
MISKITO
SUMO TAWAHKA
PECH
PECH
ENGLISH
ENGLISH;GARIFUNA
GARIFUNA
TOL
LENCA
LENCA
CHORTÍ
PIPIL

km
0   20   40   60

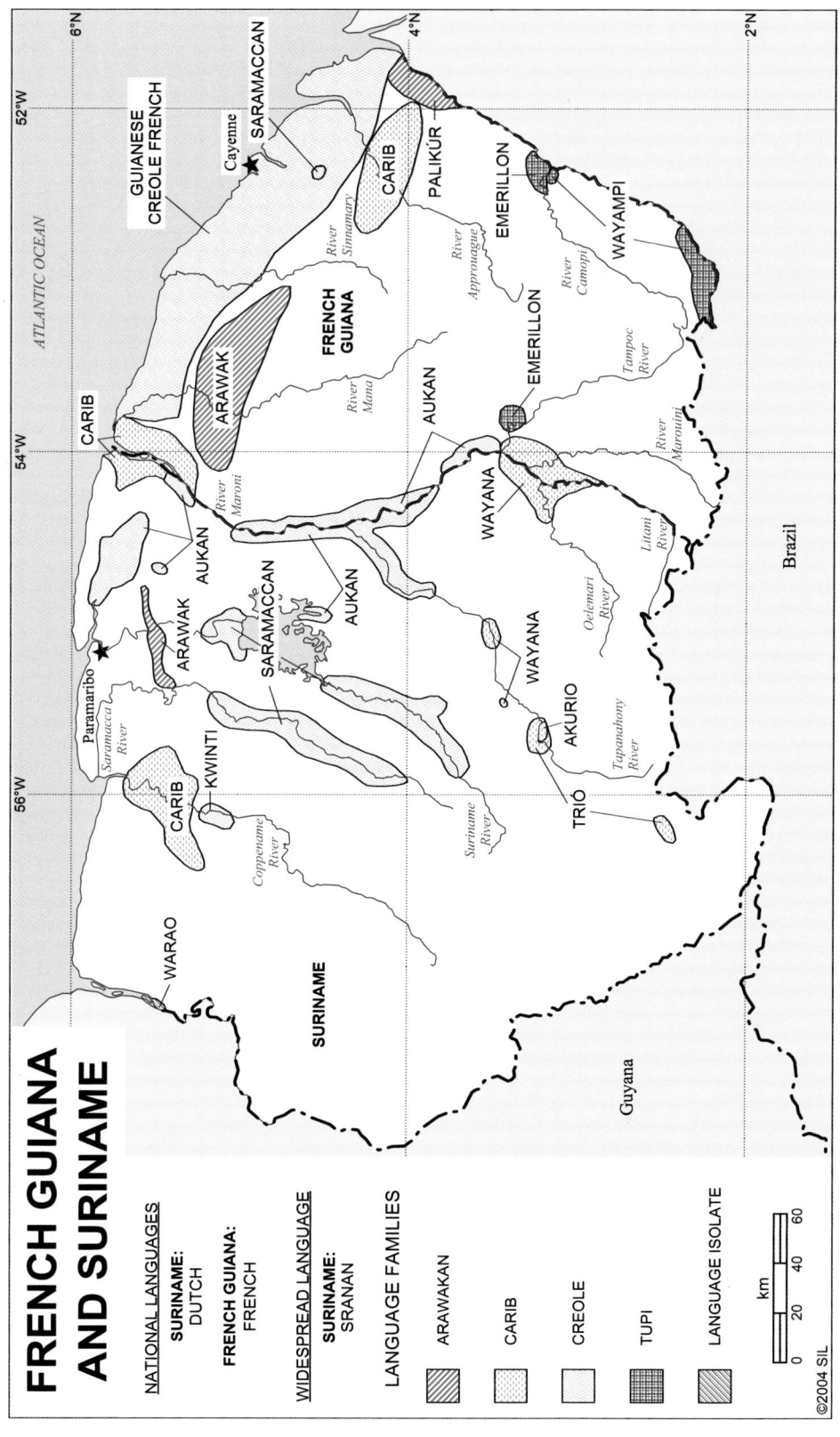

FRENCH GUIANA
AND SURINAME

NATIONAL LANGUAGES
  SURINAME:
  DUTCH

  FRENCH GUIANA:
  FRENCH

WIDESPREAD LANGUAGE
  SURINAME:
  SRANAN

LANGUAGE FAMILIES

ARAWAKAN

CARIB

CREOLE

TUPI

LANGUAGE ISOLATE

km
0   20   40   60

©2004 SIL

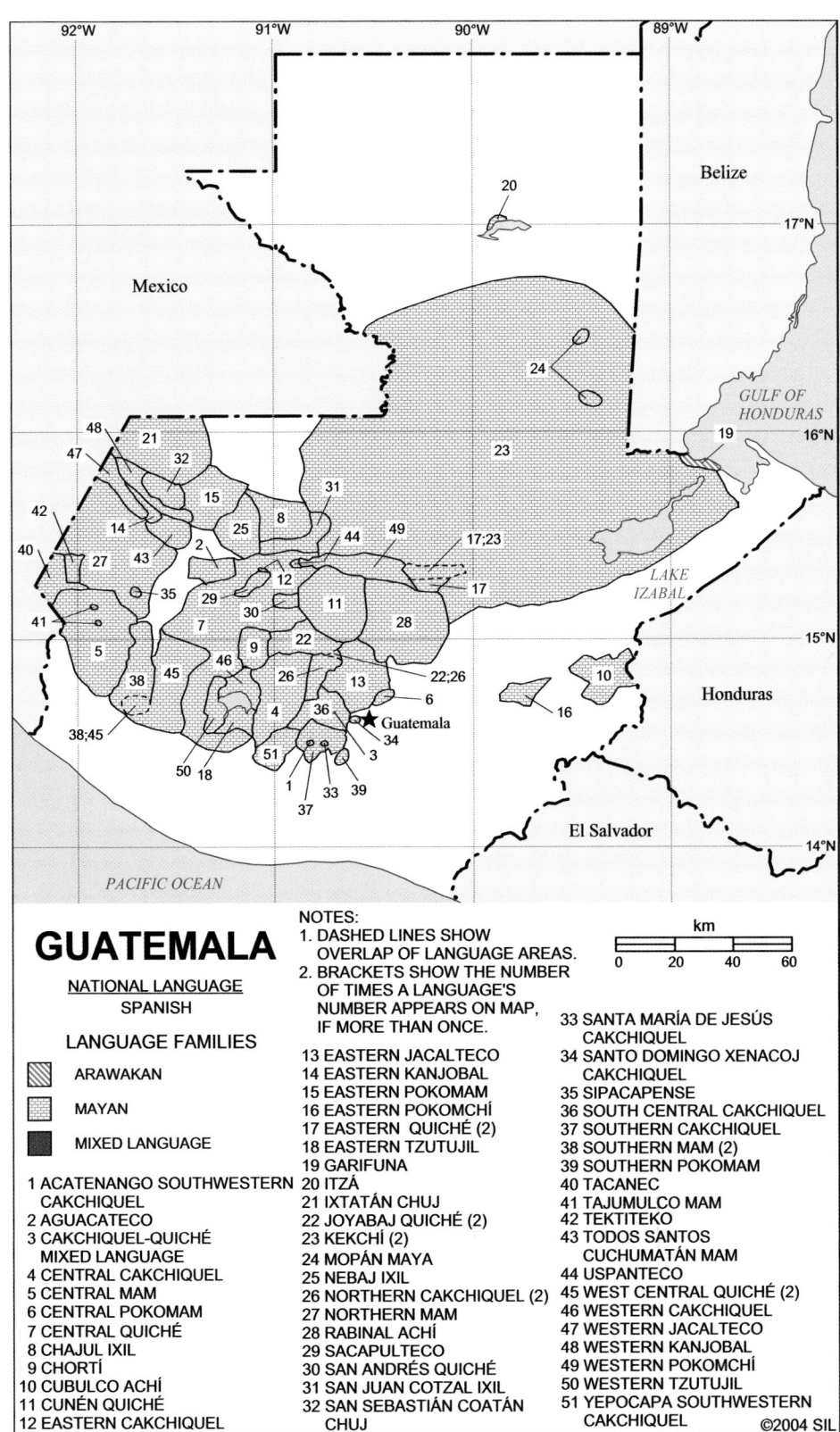

GUATEMALA

©2004 SIL

NATIONAL LANGUAGE
SPANISH

LANGUAGE FAMILIES

ARAWAKAN

MAYAN

MIXED LANGUAGE

1 ACATENANGO SOUTHWESTERN
  CAKCHIQUEL
2 AGUACATECO
3 CAKCHIQUEL-QUICHÉ
  MIXED LANGUAGE
4 CENTRAL CAKCHIQUEL
5 CENTRAL MAM
6 CENTRAL POKOMAM
7 CENTRAL QUICHÉ
8 CHAJUL IXIL
9 CHORTÍ
10 CUBULCO ACHÍ
11 CUNÉN QUICHÉ
12 EASTERN CAKCHIQUEL

NOTES:
1. DASHED LINES SHOW
  OVERLAP OF LANGUAGE AREAS.
2. BRACKETS SHOW THE NUMBER
  OF TIMES A LANGUAGE'S
  NUMBER APPEARS ON MAP,
  IF MORE THAN ONCE.

13 EASTERN JACALTECO
14 EASTERN KANJOBAL
15 EASTERN POKOMAM
16 EASTERN POKOMCHÍ
17 EASTERN QUICHÉ (2)
18 EASTERN TZUTUJIL
19 GARIFUNA
20 ITZÁ
21 IXTATÁN CHUJ
22 JOYABAJ QUICHÉ (2)
23 KEKCHÍ (2)
24 MOPÁN MAYA
25 NEBAJ IXIL
26 NORTHERN CAKCHIQUEL (2)
27 NORTHERN MAM
28 RABINAL ACHÍ
29 SACAPULTECO
30 SAN ANDRÉS QUICHÉ
31 SAN JUAN COTZAL IXIL
32 SAN SEBASTIÁN COATÁN
  CHUJ

33 SANTA MARÍA DE JESÚS
  CAKCHIQUEL
34 SANTO DOMINGO XENACOJ
  CAKCHIQUEL
35 SIPACAPENSE
36 SOUTH CENTRAL CAKCHIQUEL
37 SOUTHERN CAKCHIQUEL
38 SOUTHERN MAM (2)
39 SOUTHERN POKOMAM
40 TACANEC
41 TAJUMULCO MAM
42 TEKTITEKO
43 TODOS SANTOS
  CUCHUMATÁN MAM
44 USPANTECO
45 WEST CENTRAL QUICHÉ (2)
46 WESTERN CAKCHIQUEL
47 WESTERN JACALTECO
48 WESTERN KANJOBAL
49 WESTERN POKOMCHÍ
50 WESTERN TZUTUJIL
51 YEPOCAPA SOUTHWESTERN
  CAKCHIQUEL

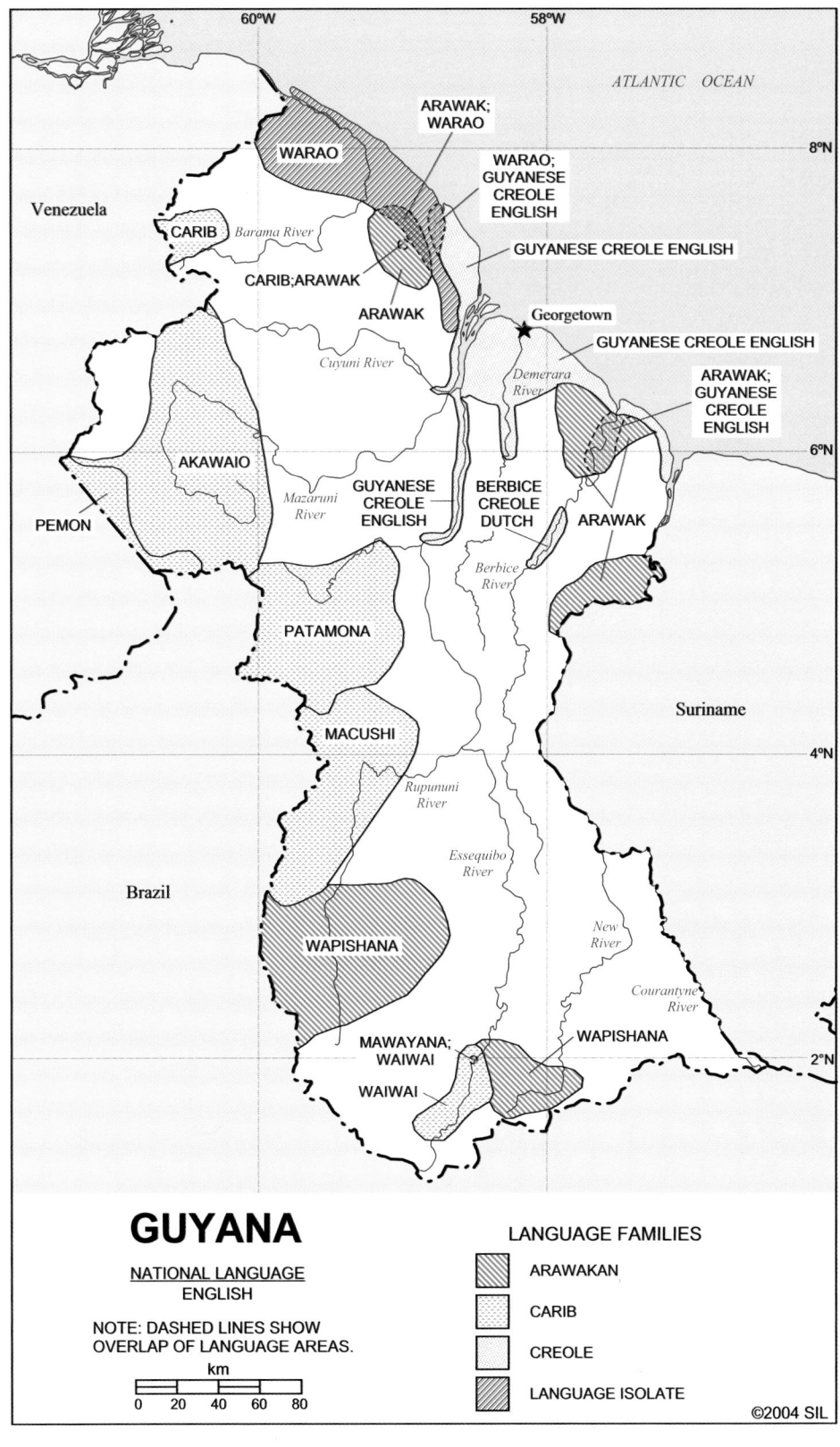

GUYANA

NATIONAL LANGUAGE
ENGLISH

NOTE: DASHED LINES SHOW
OVERLAP OF LANGUAGE AREAS.

km
0 20 40 60 80

LANGUAGE FAMILIES

ARAWAKAN

CARIB

CREOLE

LANGUAGE ISOLATE

©2004 SIL

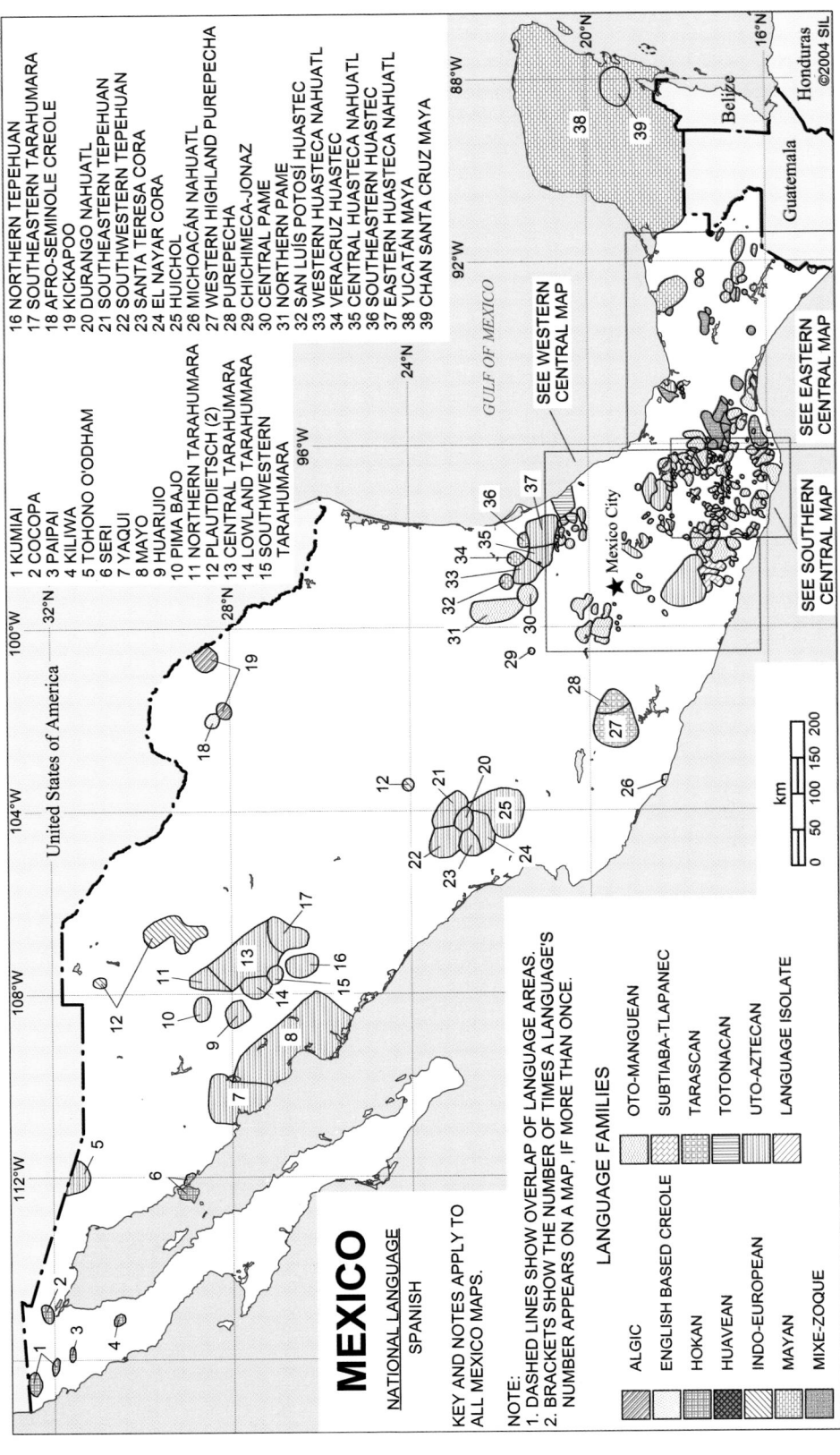

MEXICO

NATIONAL LANGUAGE
SPANISH

KEY AND NOTES APPLY TO
ALL MEXICO MAPS.

NOTE:
1. DASHED LINES SHOW OVERLAP OF LANGUAGE AREAS.
2. BRACKETS SHOW THE NUMBER OF TIMES A LANGUAGE'S
NUMBER APPEARS ON A MAP, IF MORE THAN ONCE.

LANGUAGE FAMILIES

ALGIC
ENGLISH BASED CREOLE
HOKAN
HUAVEAN
INDO-EUROPEAN
MAYAN
MIXE-ZOQUE

OTO-MANGUEAN
SUBTIABA-TLAPANEC
TARASCAN
TOTONACAN
UTO-AZTECAN
LANGUAGE ISOLATE

1 KUMIAI
2 COCOPA
3 PAIPAI
4 KILIWA
5 TOHONO O'ODHAM
6 SERI
7 YAQUI
8 MAYO
9 HUARIJIO
10 PIMA BAJO
11 NORTHERN TARAHUMARA
12 PLAUTDIETSCH (2)
13 CENTRAL TARAHUMARA
14 LOWLAND TARAHUMARA
15 SOUTHWESTERN
   TARAHUMARA

16 NORTHERN TEPEHUAN
17 SOUTHEASTERN TARAHUMARA
18 AFRO-SEMINOLE CREOLE
19 KICKAPOO
20 DURANGO NAHUATL
21 SOUTHEASTERN TEPEHUAN
22 SOUTHWESTERN TEPEHUAN
23 SANTA TERESA CORA
24 EL NAYAR CORA
25 HUICHOL
26 MICHOACÁN NAHUATL
27 WESTERN HIGHLAND PUREPECHA
28 PUREPECHA
29 CHICHIMECA-JONAZ
30 CENTRAL PAME
31 NORTHERN PAME
32 SAN LUIS POTOSÍ HUASTEC
33 WESTERN HUASTECA NAHUATL
34 VERACRUZ HUASTEC
35 CENTRAL HUASTECA NAHUATL
36 SOUTHEASTERN HUASTEC
37 EASTERN HUASTECA NAHUATL
38 YUCATÁN MAYA
39 CHAN SANTA CRUZ MAYA

United States of America

GULF OF MEXICO

Mexico City

SEE WESTERN
CENTRAL MAP

SEE EASTERN
CENTRAL MAP

SEE SOUTHERN
CENTRAL MAP

Belize

Guatemala

Honduras

©2004 SIL

km
0 50 100 150 200

Mexico: Index Of Languages

WESTERN CENTRAL MEXICO

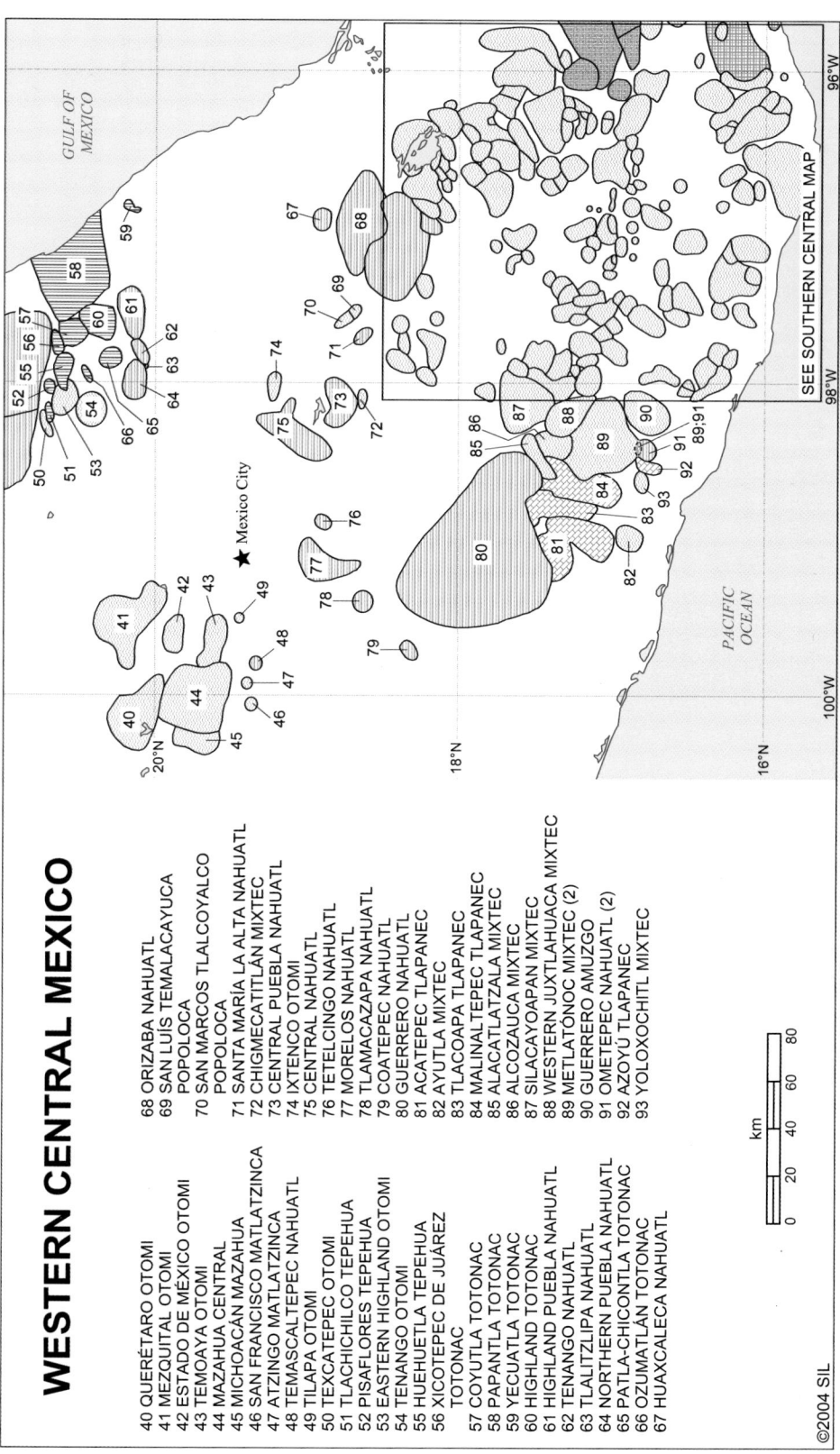

40 QUERÉTARO OTOMI
41 MEZQUITAL OTOMI
42 ESTADO DE MÉXICO OTOMI
43 TEMOAYA OTOMI
44 MAZAHUA CENTRAL
45 MICHOACÁN MAZAHUA
46 SAN FRANCISCO MATLATZINCA
47 ATZINGO MATLATZINCA
48 TEMASCALTEPEC NAHUATL
49 TILAPA OTOMI
50 TEXCATEPEC OTOMI
51 TLACHICHILCO TEPEHUA
52 PISAFLORES TEPEHUA
53 EASTERN HIGHLAND OTOMI
54 TENANGO OTOMI
55 HUEHUETLA TEPEHUA
56 XICOTEPEC DE JUÁREZ
   TOTONAC
57 COYUTLA TOTONAC
58 PAPANTLA TOTONAC
59 YECUATLA TOTONAC
60 HIGHLAND TOTONAC
61 HIGHLAND PUEBLA NAHUATL
62 TENANGO NAHUATL
63 TLALITZLIPA NAHUATL
64 NORTHERN PUEBLA NAHUATL
65 PATLA-CHICONTLA TOTONAC
66 OZUMATLÁN TOTONAC
67 HUAXCALECA NAHUATL

68 ORIZABA NAHUATL
69 SAN LUIS TEMALACAYUCA
   POPOLOCA
70 SAN MARCOS TLALCOYALCO
   POPOLOCA
71 SANTA MARÍA LA ALTA NAHUATL
72 CHIGMECATITLÁN MIXTEC
73 CENTRAL PUEBLA NAHUATL
74 IXTENCO OTOMI
75 CENTRAL NAHUATL
76 TETELCINGO NAHUATL
77 MORELOS NAHUATL
78 TLAMACAZAPA NAHUATL
79 COATEPEC NAHUATL
80 GUERRERO NAHUATL
81 ACATEPEC TLAPANEC
82 AYUTLA MIXTEC
83 TLACOAPA TLAPANEC
84 MALINALTEPEC TLAPANEC
85 ALACATLATZALA MIXTEC
86 ALCOZAUCA MIXTEC
87 SILACAYOAPAN MIXTEC
88 WESTERN JUXTLAHUACA MIXTEC
89 METLATÓNOC MIXTEC (2)
90 GUERRERO AMUZGO
91 OMETEPEC NAHUATL (2)
92 AZOYÚ TLAPANEC
93 YOLOXOCHITL MIXTEC

km

0   20   40   60   80

EASTERN CENTRAL MEXICO

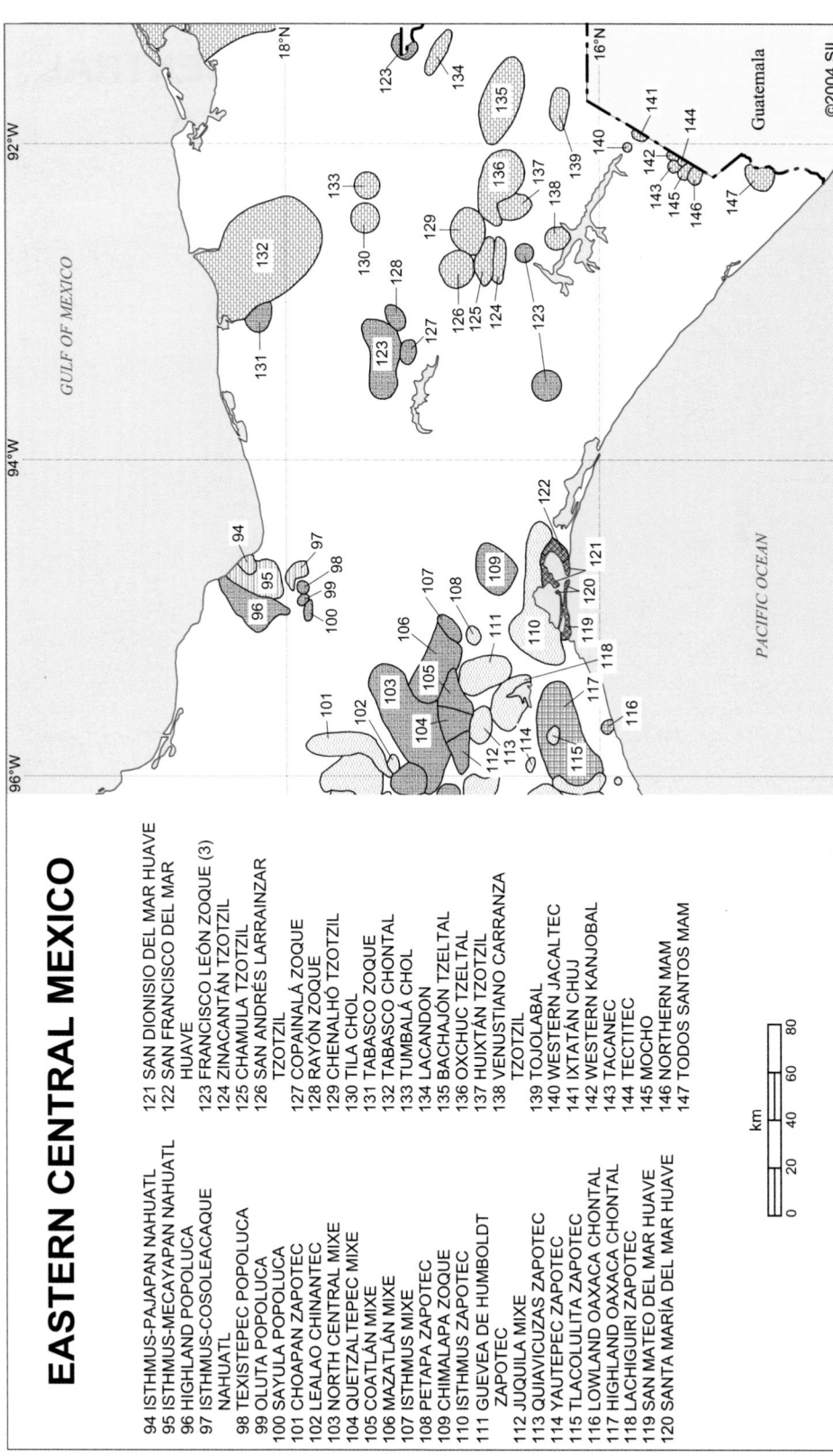

94 ISTHMUS-PAJAPAN NAHUATL
95 ISTHMUS-MECAYAPAN NAHUATL
96 HIGHLAND POPOLUCA
97 ISTHMUS-COSOLEACAQUE
    NAHUATL
98 TEXISTEPEC POPOLUCA
99 OLUTA POPOLUCA
100 SAYULA POPOLUCA
101 CHOAPAN ZAPOTEC
102 LEALAO CHINANTEC
103 NORTH CENTRAL MIXE
104 QUETZALTEPEC MIXE
105 COATLÁN MIXE
106 MAZATLÁN MIXE
107 ISTHMUS MIXE
108 PETAPA ZAPOTEC
109 CHIMALAPA ZOQUE
110 ISTHMUS ZAPOTEC
111 GUEVEA DE HUMBOLDT
     ZAPOTEC
112 JUQUILA MIXE
113 QUIAVICUZAS ZAPOTEC
114 YAUTEPEC ZAPOTEC
115 TLACOLULITA ZAPOTEC
116 LOWLAND OAXACA CHONTAL
117 HIGHLAND OAXACA CHONTAL
118 LACHIGUIRI ZAPOTEC
119 SAN MATEO DEL MAR HUAVE
120 SANTA MARÍA DEL MAR HUAVE

121 SAN DIONISIO DEL MAR HUAVE
122 SAN FRANCISCO DEL MAR
     HUAVE
123 FRANCISCO LEÓN ZOQUE (3)
124 ZINACANTÁN TZOTZIL
125 CHAMULA TZOTZIL
126 SAN ANDRÉS LARRAINZAR
     TZOTZIL
127 COPAINALÁ ZOQUE
128 RAYÓN ZOQUE
129 CHENALHÓ TZOTZIL
130 TILA CHOL
131 TABASCO ZOQUE
132 TABASCO CHONTAL
133 TUMBALÁ CHOL
134 LACANDON
135 BACHAJÓN TZELTAL
136 OXCHUC TZELTAL
137 HUIXTÁN TZOTZIL
138 VENUSTIANO CARRANZA
     TZOTZIL
139 TOJOLABAL
140 WESTERN JACALTEC
141 IXTATÁN CHUJ
142 WESTERN KANJOBAL
143 TACANEC
144 TECTITEC
145 MOCHO
146 NORTHERN MAM
147 TODOS SANTOS MAM

km

0   20   40   60   80

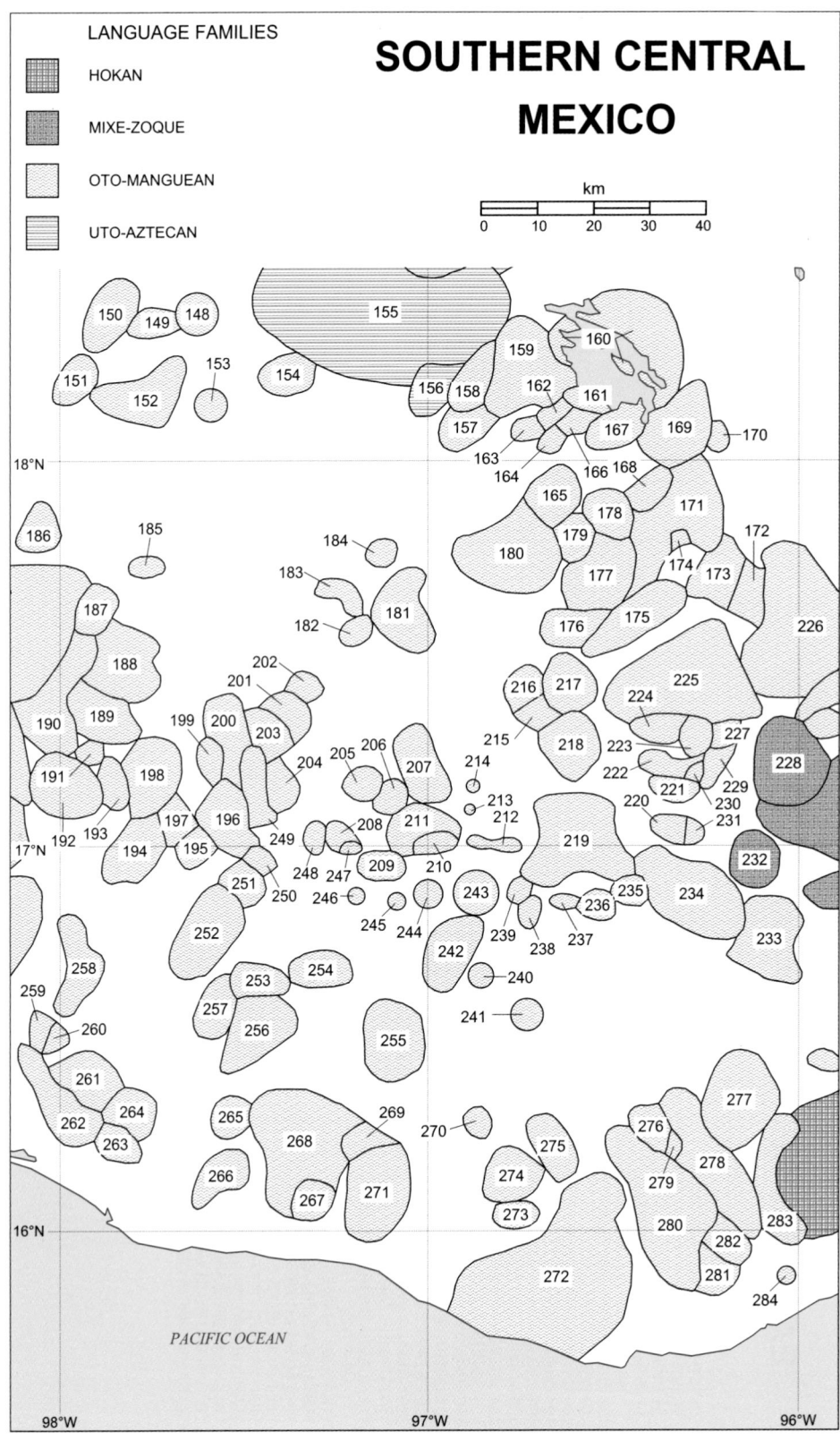

LANGUAGE FAMILIES

HOKAN

MIXE-ZOQUE

OTO-MANGUEAN

UTO-AZTECAN

SOUTHERN CENTRAL MEXICO

km

0   10   20   30   40

18°N

17°N

16°N

PACIFIC OCEAN

98°W

97°W

96°W

Mexico, Southern Central: Key To Languages

148 Coyotepec Popoloca
149 San Felipe Otlaltepec Popoloca
150 Santa Inés Ahuatempan Popoloca
151 Southern Puebla Mixtec
152 Chazumba Mixtec
153 Mezontla Popoloca
154 San Juan Atzingo Popoloca
155 Southeastern Puebla Nahuatl
156 Northern Oaxaca Nahuatl
157 Mazatlán Mazatec
158 San Jerónimo Tecóatl Mazatec
159 Huautla Mazatec
160 Soyaltepec Mazatec
161 Ixcatlán Mazatec
162 Coatzospan Mixtec
163 Cuyamecalco Mixtec
164 Chiquihuitlán Mazatec
165 Teutila Cuicatec
166 Ayautla Mazatec
167 Jalapa De Díaz Mazatec
168 Usila Chinantec
169 Ojitlán Chinantec
170 Chiltepec Chinantec
171 Palantla Chinantec
172 Tepinapa Chinantec
173 Ozumacín Chinantec
174 Valle Nacional Chinantec
175 Comaltepec Chinantec
176 Quiotepec Chinantec
177 Tepetotutla Chinantec
178 Tlacoatzintepec Chinantec
179 Sochiapan Chinantec
180 Tepeuxila Cuicatec
181 Apasco-Apoala Mixtec
182 Soyaltepec Mixtec
183 Chochotec
184 Ixcatec
185 Cacaloxtepec Mixtec
186 Northwest Oaxaca Mixtec
187 Tezoatlán Mixtec
188 Northern Tlaxiaco Mixtec
189 Mixtepec Mixtec
190 Juxtlahuaca Mixtec
191 San Martín Itunyoso Triqui
192 Copala Triqui
193 Chicahuaxtla Triqui

194 Southwestern Tlaxiaco Mixtec
195 Santa Lucía Monteverde Mixtec
196 San Miguel El Grande Mixtec
197 Atatláhuca Mixtec
198 Ocotepec Mixtec
199 Sinicahua Mixtec
200 Magdalena Peñasco Mixtec
201 Diuxi-Tilantongo Mixtec
202 Tidaá Mixtec
203 Yucuañe Mixtec
204 San Juan Teita Mixtec
205 Mitlatongo Mixtec
206 Tamazola Mixtec
207 Southeastern Nochixtlán Mixtec
208 Yutanduchi Mixtec
209 Huitepec Mixtec
210 Tlazoyaltepec Mixtec
211 Peñoles Mixtec
212 Zaachila Zapotec
213 Tejalapan Zapotec
214 Mazaltepec Zapotec
215 Yareni Zapotec
216 Aloápam Zapotec
217 Sierra De Juárez Zapotec
218 Southeastern Ixtlán Zapotec
219 San Juan Guelavía Zapotec
220 Santa Catarina Albarradas Zapotec
221 Cajonos Zapotec
222 Zoogocho Zapotec
223 Tabaa Zapotec
224 Southern Rincon Zapotec
225 Rincón Zapotec
226 Lalana Chinantec
227 Yatee Zapotec
228 Totontepec Mixe
229 Yalálag Zapotec
230 Yatzachi Zapotec
231 Santo Domingo Albarradas Zapotec
232 Tlahuitoltepec Mixe
233 San Pedro Quiatoni Zapotec
234 Mitla Zapotec
235 Güilá Zapotec
236 Chichicapan Zapotec
237 Tilquiapan Zapotec
238 Ocotlán Zapotec

239 Santa Inés Yatzechi Zapotec
240 Ayoquesco Zapotec
241 Coatecas Altas Zapotec
242 Lachixío Zapotec
243 Asunción Mixtepec Zapotec
244 El Alto Zapotec
245 Totomachapan Zapotec
246 Elotepec Zapotec
247 San Miguel Piedras Mixtec
248 Sindihui Mixtec
249 Tijaltepec Mixtec
250 Tacahua Mixtec
251 Yosondúa Mixtec
252 Itundujia Mixtec
253 Amoltepec Mixtec
254 Zaniza Zapotec
255 Texmelucan Zapotec
256 Zenzontepec Chatino
257 Ixtayutla Mixtec
258 Santa María Zacatepec Mixtec
259 San Pedro Amuzgos Amuzgo
260 Ipalapa Amuzgo
261 San Juan Colorado Mixtec
262 Pinotepa Nacional Mixtec
263 Jamiltepec Mixtec
264 Chayuco Mixtec
265 Tataltepec Chatino
266 Tututepec Mixtec
267 Zacatepec Chatino
268 Western Highland Chatino
269 Eastern Highland Chatino
270 San Vicente Coatlán Zapotec
271 Nopala Chatino
272 Loxicha Zapotec
273 San Baltazar Loxicha Zapotec
274 Coatlán Zapotec
275 Miahuatlán Zapotec
276 Amatlán Zapotec
277 Quioquitani-Quierí Zapotec
278 Mixtepec Zapotec
279 San Agustín Mixtepec Zapotec
280 Ozolotepec Zapotec
281 Santiago Xanica Zapotec
282 Xanaguía Zapotec
283 Santa María Quiegolani Zapotec
284 Xadani Zapotec

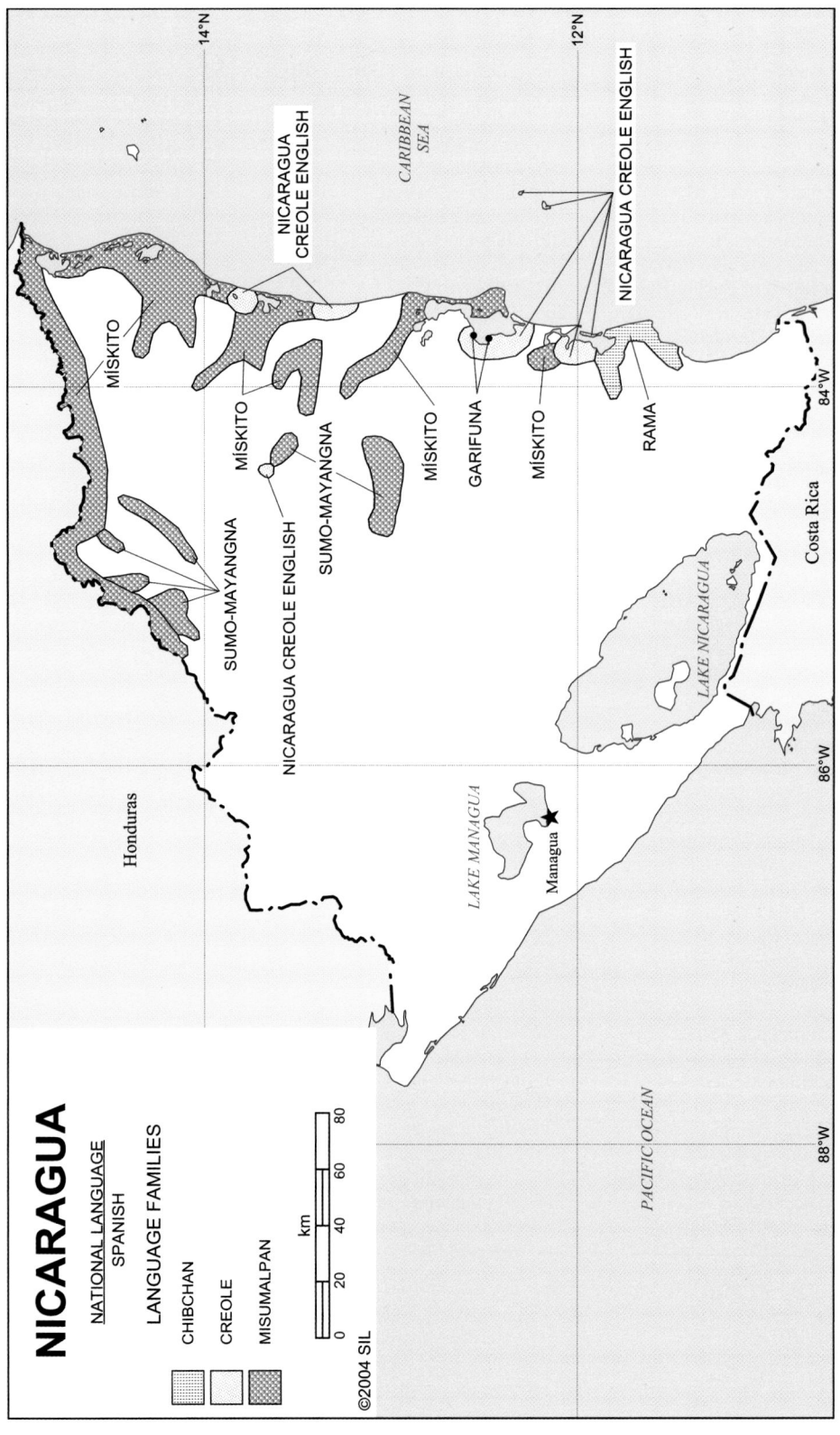

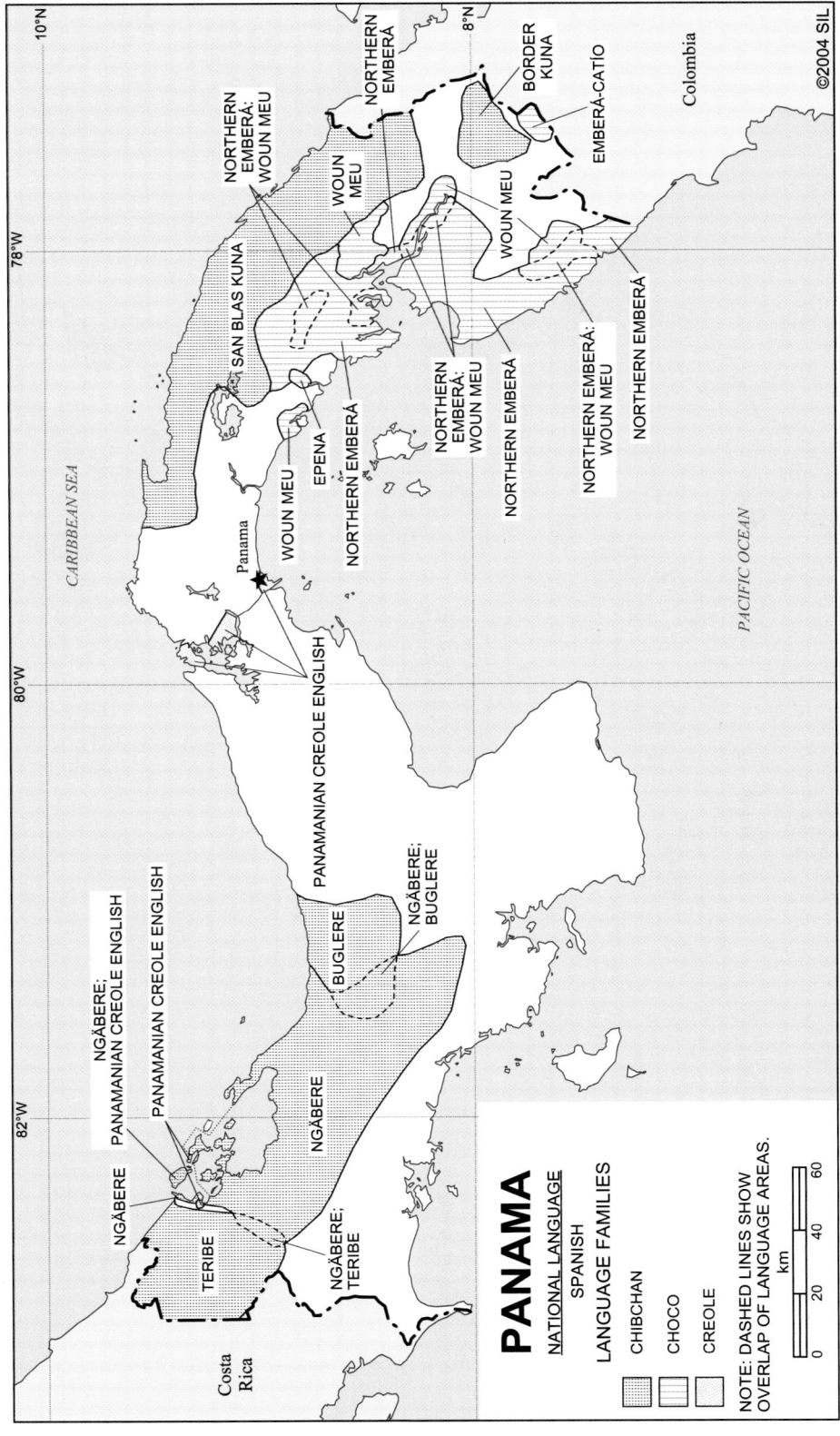

PANAMA

NATIONAL LANGUAGE
SPANISH

LANGUAGE FAMILIES

CHIBCHAN
CHOCO
CREOLE

NOTE: DASHED LINES SHOW
OVERLAP OF LANGUAGE AREAS.

km

0   20   40   60

Costa
Rica

NGÄBERE

NGÄBERE;
PANAMANIAN CREOLE ENGLISH

TERIBE

NGÄBERE;
TERIBE

NGÄBERE

BUGLERE

NGÄBERE;
BUGLERE

PANAMANIAN CREOLE ENGLISH

PANAMANIAN CREOLE ENGLISH

Panama

WOUN MEU

EPENA

NORTHERN EMBERÁ

SAN BLAS KUNA

NORTHERN
EMBERÁ:
WOUN MEU

WOUN
MEU

NORTHERN
EMBERÁ

NORTHERN
EMBERÁ:
WOUN MEU

NORTHERN EMBERÁ

WOUN MEU

NORTHERN EMBERÁ

NORTHERN EMBERÁ:
WOUN MEU

NORTHERN EMBERÁ

BORDER
KUNA

EMBERÁ-CATÍO

Colombia

CARIBBEAN SEA

PACIFIC OCEAN

10°N

8°N

78°W

80°W

82°W

©2004 SIL

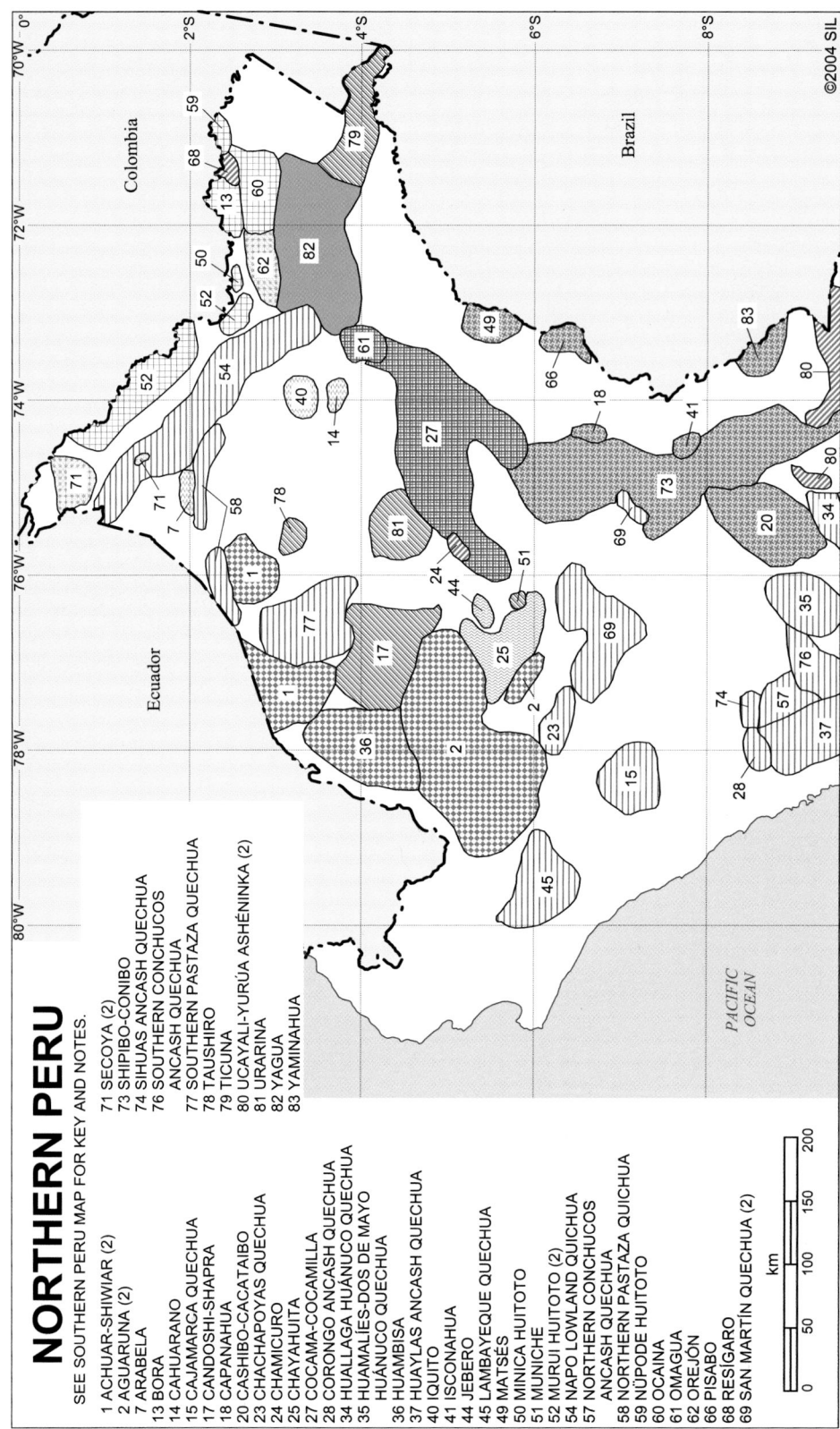

NORTHERN PERU

SEE SOUTHERN PERU MAP FOR KEY AND NOTES.

1 ACHUAR-SHIWIAR (2)
2 AGUARUNA (2)
7 ARABELA
13 BORA
14 CAHUARANO
15 CAJAMARCA QUECHUA
17 CANDOSHI-SHAPRA
18 CAPANAHUA
20 CASHIBO-CACATAIBO
23 CHACHAPOYAS QUECHUA
24 CHAMICURO
25 CHAYAHUITA
27 COCAMA-COCAMILLA
28 CORONGO ANCASH QUECHUA
34 HUALLAGA HUÁNUCO QUECHUA
35 HUAMALÍES-DOS DE MAYO
   HUÁNUCO QUECHUA
36 HUAMBISA
37 HUAYLAS ANCASH QUECHUA
40 IQUITO
41 ISCONAHUA
44 JEBERO
45 LAMBAYEQUE QUECHUA
49 MATSÉS
50 MINICA HUITOTO
51 MUNICHE
52 MURUI HUITOTO (2)
54 NAPO LOWLAND QUICHUA
57 NORTHERN CONCHUCOS
   ANCASH QUECHUA
58 NORTHERN PASTAZA QUICHUA
59 NÜPODE HUITOTO
60 OCAINA
61 OMAGUA
62 OREJÓN
66 PISABO
68 RESÍGARO
69 SAN MARTÍN QUECHUA (2)

71 SECOYA (2)
73 SHIPIBO-CONIBO
74 SIHUAS ANCASH QUECHUA
76 SOUTHERN CONCHUCOS
   ANCASH QUECHUA
77 SOUTHERN PASTAZA QUECHUA
78 TAUSHIRO
79 TICUNA
80 UCAYALI-YURÚA ASHÉNINKA (2)
81 URARINA
82 YAGUA
83 YAMINAHUA

km
0   50   100   150   200

©2004 SIL

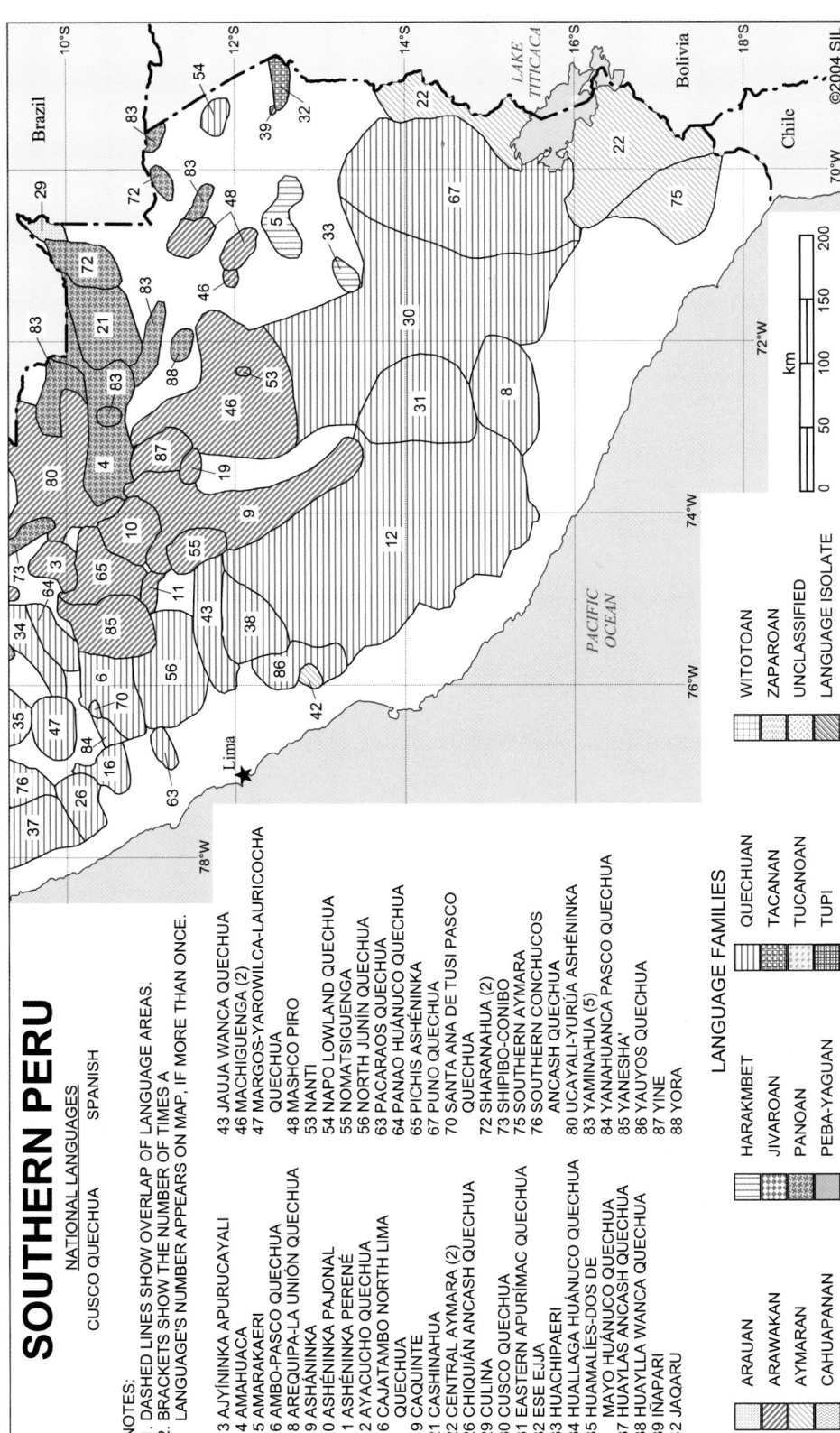

SOUTHERN PERU

NATIONAL LANGUAGES

CUSCO QUECHUA   SPANISH

NOTES:
1. DASHED LINES SHOW OVERLAP OF LANGUAGE AREAS.
2. BRACKETS SHOW THE NUMBER OF TIMES A LANGUAGE'S NUMBER APPEARS ON MAP, IF MORE THAN ONCE.

3 AJYÍNINKA APURUCAYALI
4 AMAHUACA
5 AMARAKAERI
6 AMBO-PASCO QUECHUA
8 AREQUIPA-LA UNIÓN QUECHUA
9 ASHÁNINKA
10 ASHÉNINKA PAJONAL
11 ASHÉNINKA PERENÉ
16 CAJATAMBO NORTH LIMA QUECHUA
19 CAQUINTE
21 CASHINAHUA
22 CENTRAL AYMARA (2)
26 CHIQUIÁN ANCASH QUECHUA
29 CULINA
30 CUSCO QUECHUA
31 EASTERN APURÍMAC QUECHUA
32 ESE EJJA
33 HUACHIPAERI
34 HUALLAGA HUÁNUCO QUECHUA
35 HUAMALÍES-DOS DE MAYO HUÁNUCO QUECHUA
37 HUAYLAS ANCASH QUECHUA
38 HUAYLLA WANCA QUECHUA
39 IÑAPARI
42 JAQARU
43 JAUJA WANCA QUECHUA
46 MACHIGUENGA (2)
47 MARGOS-YAROWILCA-LAURICOCHA QUECHUA
48 MASHCO PIRO
53 NANTI
54 NAPO LOWLAND QUECHUA
55 NOMATSIGUENGA
56 NORTH JUNÍN QUECHUA
63 PACARAOS QUECHUA
64 PANAO HUÁNUCO QUECHUA
65 PICHIS ASHÉNINKA
67 PUNO QUECHUA
70 SANTA ANA DE TUSI PASCO QUECHUA
72 SHARANAHUA (2)
73 SHIPIBO-CONIBO
75 SOUTHERN AYMARA
76 SOUTHERN CONCHUCOS ANCASH QUECHUA
80 UCAYALI-YURÚA ASHÉNINKA
83 YAMINAHUA (5)
84 YANAHUANCA PASCO QUECHUA
85 YANESHA'
86 YAUYOS QUECHUA
87 YINE
88 YORA

LANGUAGE FAMILIES

ARAUAN	HARAKMBET
ARAWAKAN	JIVAROAN
AYMARAN	PANOAN
CAHUAPANAN	PEBA-YAGUAN

WITOTOAN	QUECHUAN
ZAPAROAN	TACANAN
UNCLASSIFIED	TUCANOAN
LANGUAGE ISOLATE	TUPI

©2004 SIL

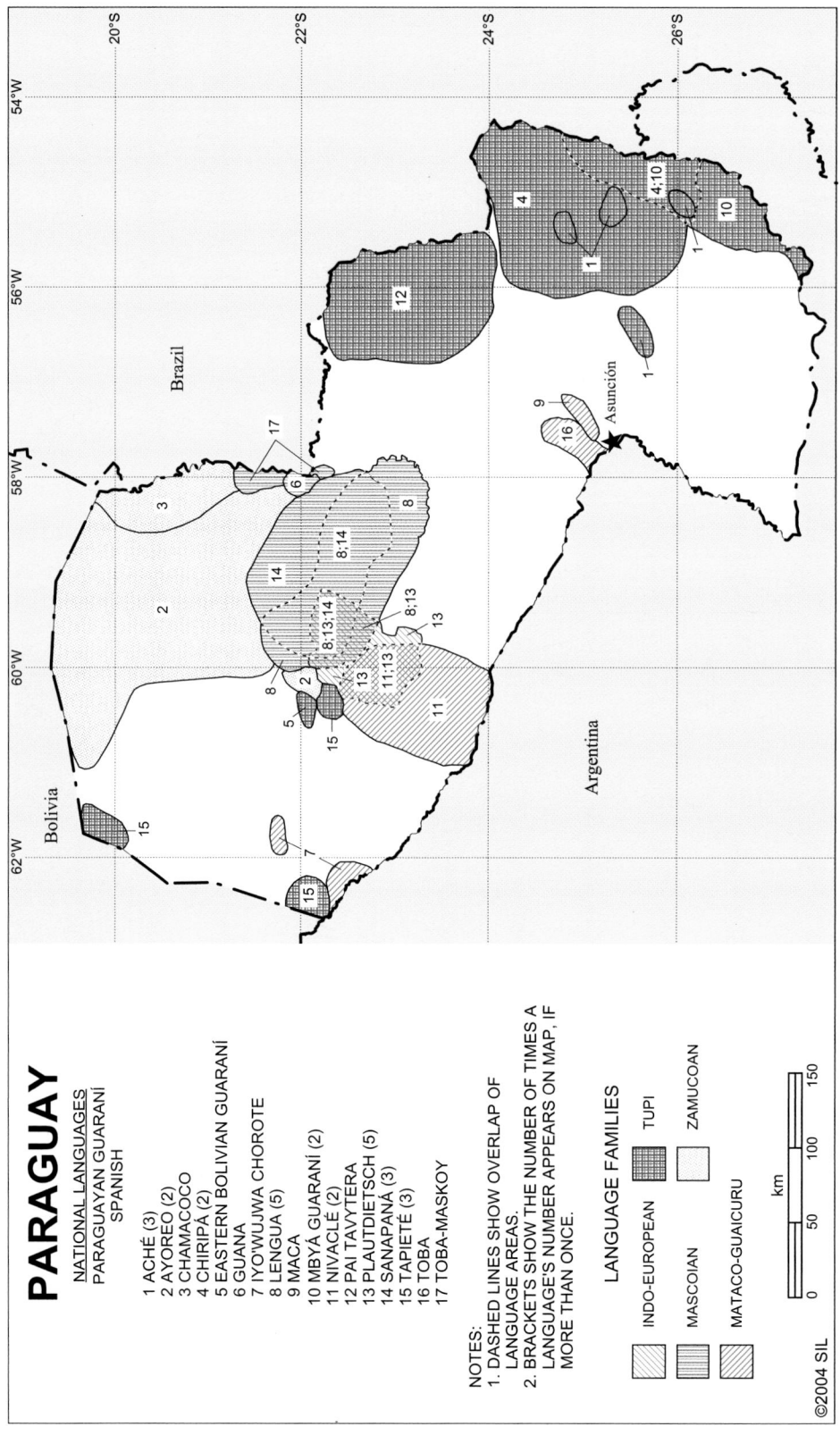

PARAGUAY

NATIONAL LANGUAGES
PARAGUAYAN GUARANÍ
SPANISH

1 ACHÉ (3)
2 AYOREO (2)
3 CHAMACOCO
4 CHIRIPÁ (2)
5 EASTERN BOLIVIAN GUARANÍ
6 GUANA
7 IYO'WUJWA CHOROTE
8 LENGUA (5)
9 MACA
10 MBYÁ GUARANÍ (2)
11 NIVACLÉ (2)
12 PAI TAVYTERA
13 PLAUTDIETSCH (5)
14 SANAPANÁ (3)
15 TAPIETÉ (3)
16 TOBA
17 TOBA-MASKOY

NOTES:
1. DASHED LINES SHOW OVERLAP OF
   LANGUAGE AREAS.
2. BRACKETS SHOW THE NUMBER OF TIMES A
   LANGUAGE'S NUMBER APPEARS ON MAP, IF
   MORE THAN ONCE.

LANGUAGE FAMILIES

INDO-EUROPEAN	TUPI
MASCOIAN	ZAMUCOAN
MATACO-GUAICURU	

km
0   50   100   150

©2004 SIL

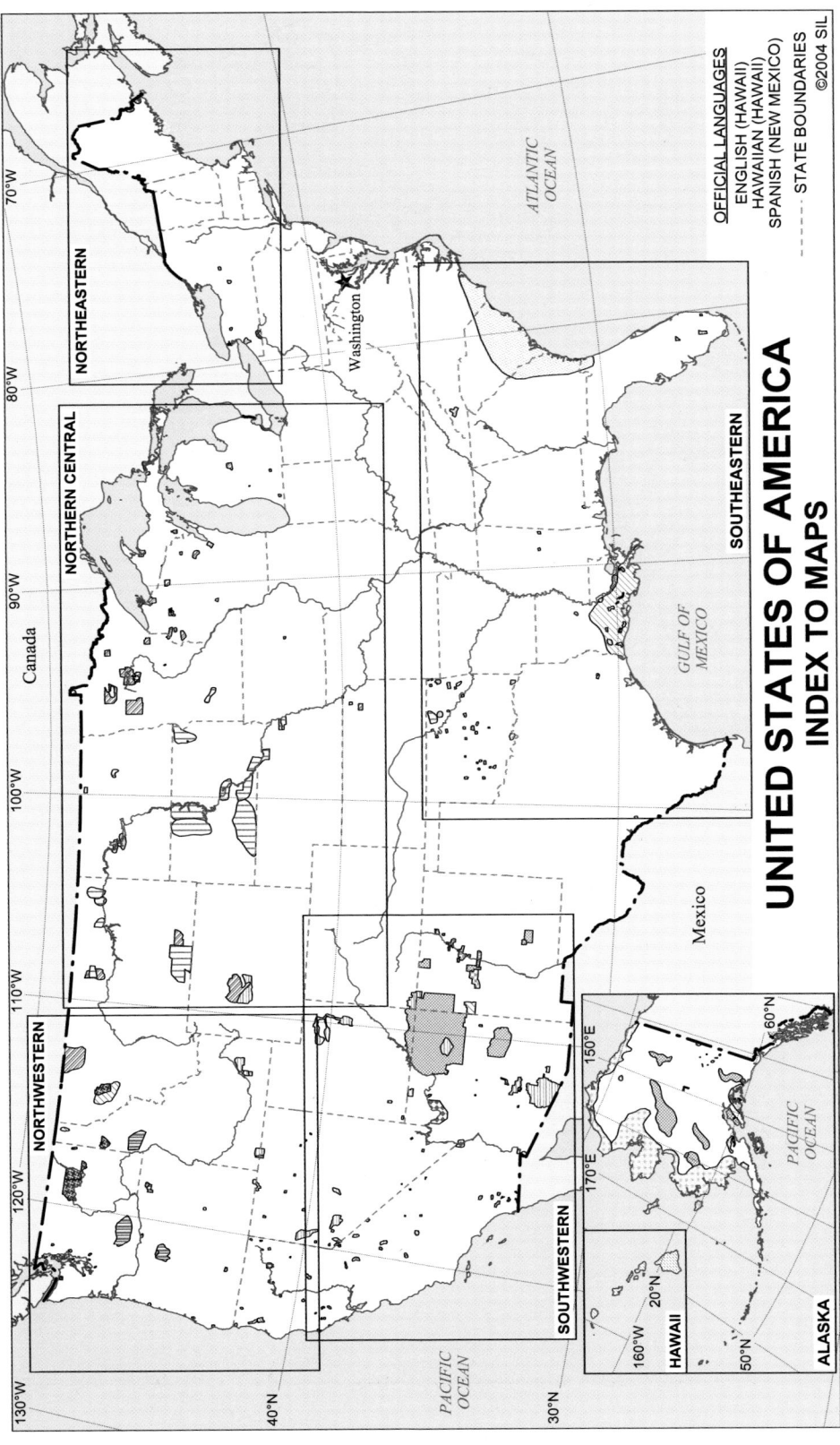

UNITED STATES OF AMERICA

INDEX TO MAPS

OFFICIAL LANGUAGES
ENGLISH (HAWAII)
HAWAIIAN (HAWAII)
SPANISH (NEW MEXICO)
------ STATE BOUNDARIES
©2004 SIL

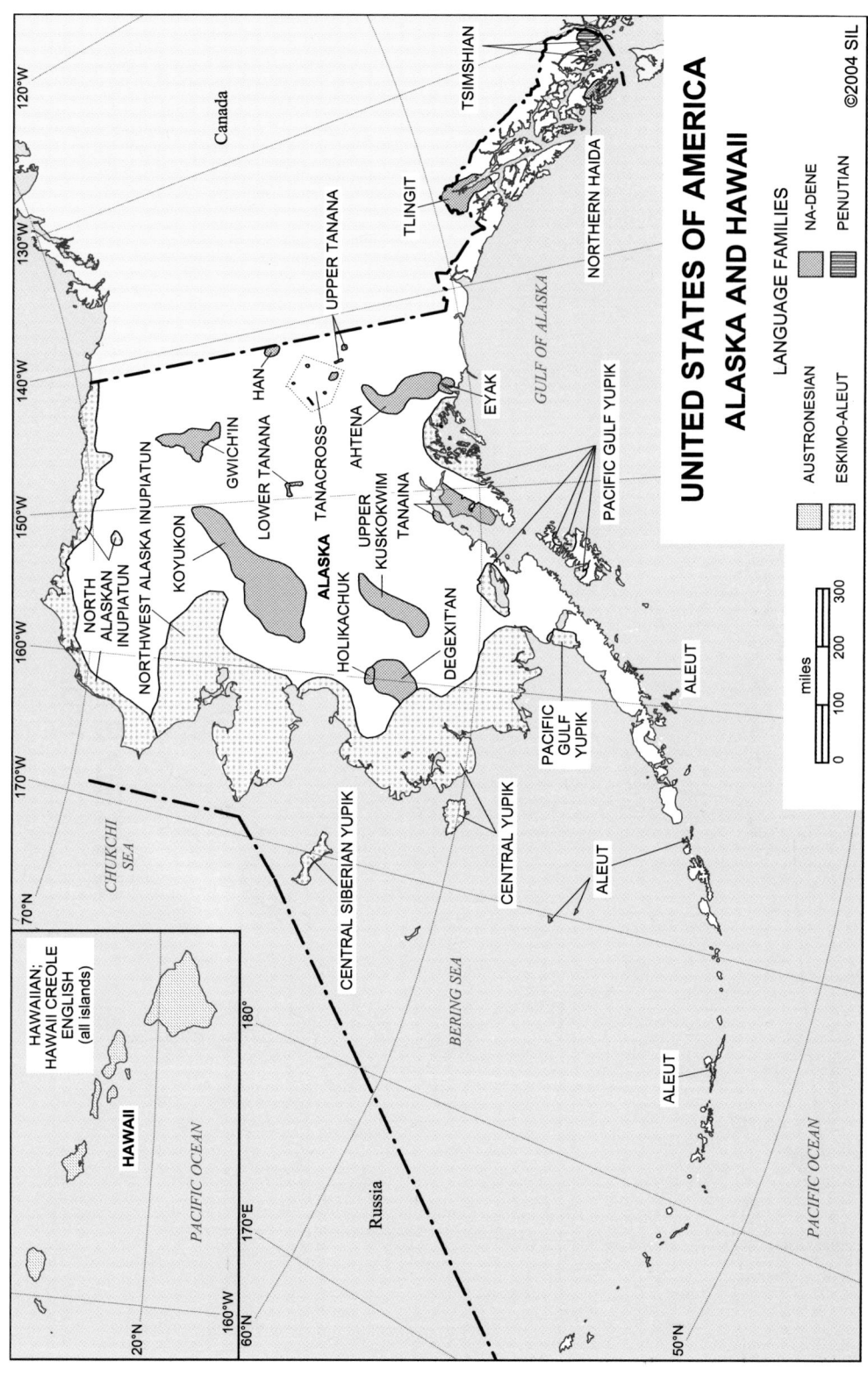

UNITED STATES OF AMERICA
ALASKA AND HAWAII

LANGUAGE FAMILIES

NA-DENE

PENUTIAN

AUSTRONESIAN

ESKIMO-ALEUT

©2004 SIL

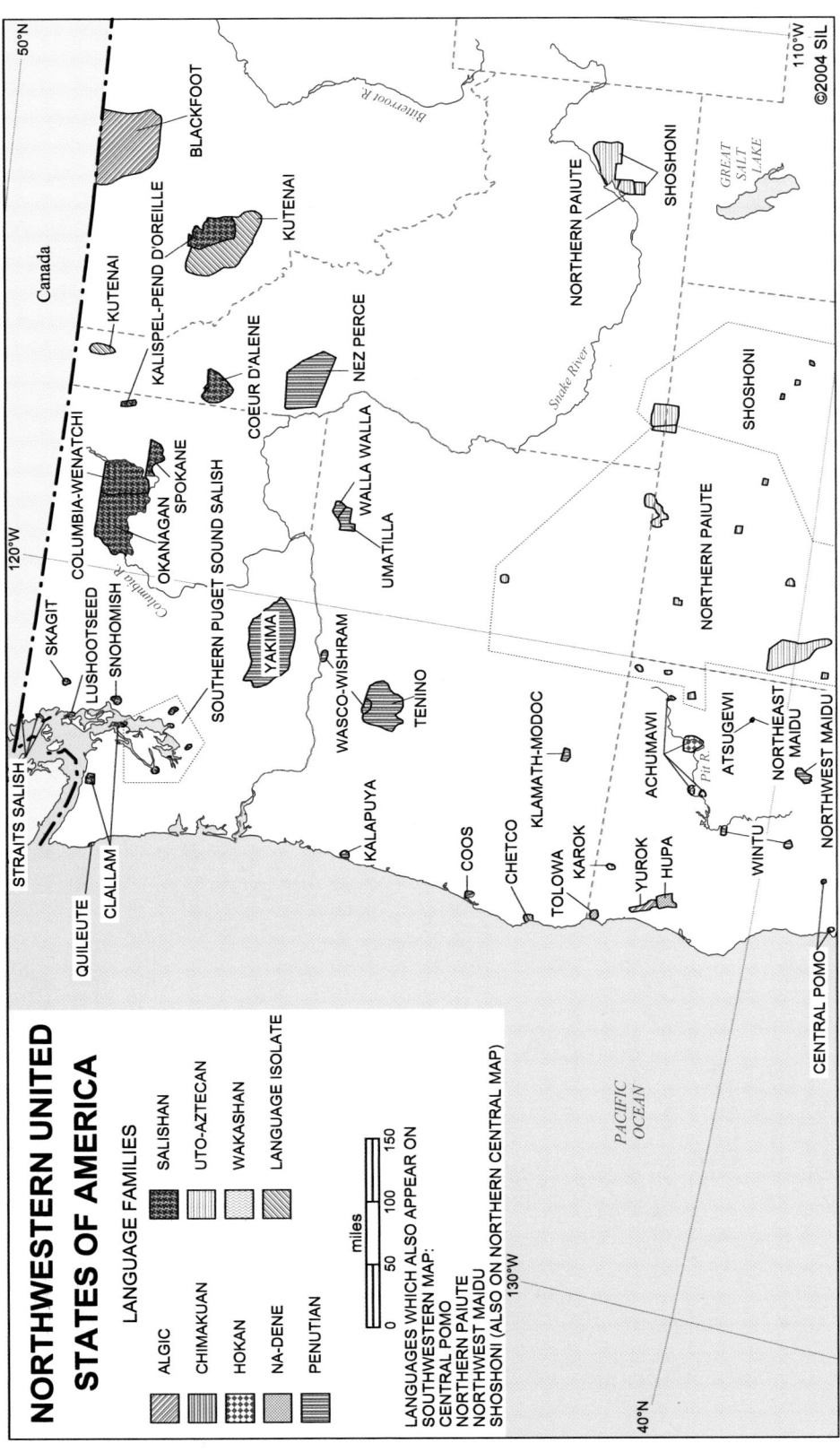

NORTHWESTERN UNITED STATES OF AMERICA

LANGUAGE FAMILIES

- ALGIC
- CHIMAKUAN
- HOKAN
- NA-DENE
- PENUTIAN

- SALISHAN
- UTO-AZTECAN
- WAKASHAN
- LANGUAGE ISOLATE

miles

0   50   100   150

LANGUAGES WHICH ALSO APPEAR ON
SOUTHWESTERN MAP:
CENTRAL POMO
NORTHERN PAIUTE
NORTHWEST MAIDU
SHOSHONI (ALSO ON NORTHERN CENTRAL MAP)

©2004 SIL

50°N

110°W

120°W

130°W

40°N

Canada

Bitterroot R.

Snake River

Columbia R.

Pit R.

GREAT SALT LAKE

PACIFIC OCEAN

BLACKFOOT

KALISPEL-PEND D'OREILLE

KUTENAI

KUTENAI

KUTENAI

COEUR D'ALENE

NEZ PERCE

COLUMBIA-WENATCHI

OKANAGAN

SPOKANE

SOUTHERN PUGET SOUND SALISH

SKAGIT

LUSHOOTSEED

SNOHOMISH

STRAITS SALISH

QUILEUTE

CLALLAM

YAKIMA

WALLA WALLA

UMATILLA

WASCO-WISHRAM

TENINO

KALAPUYA

COOS

CHETCO

TOLOWA

KAROK

YUROK

HUPA

KLAMATH-MODOC

ACHUMAWI

ATSUGEWI

WINTU

NORTHEAST MAIDU

NORTHWEST MAIDU

CENTRAL POMO

NORTHERN PAIUTE

NORTHERN PAIUTE

SHOSHONI

SHOSHONI

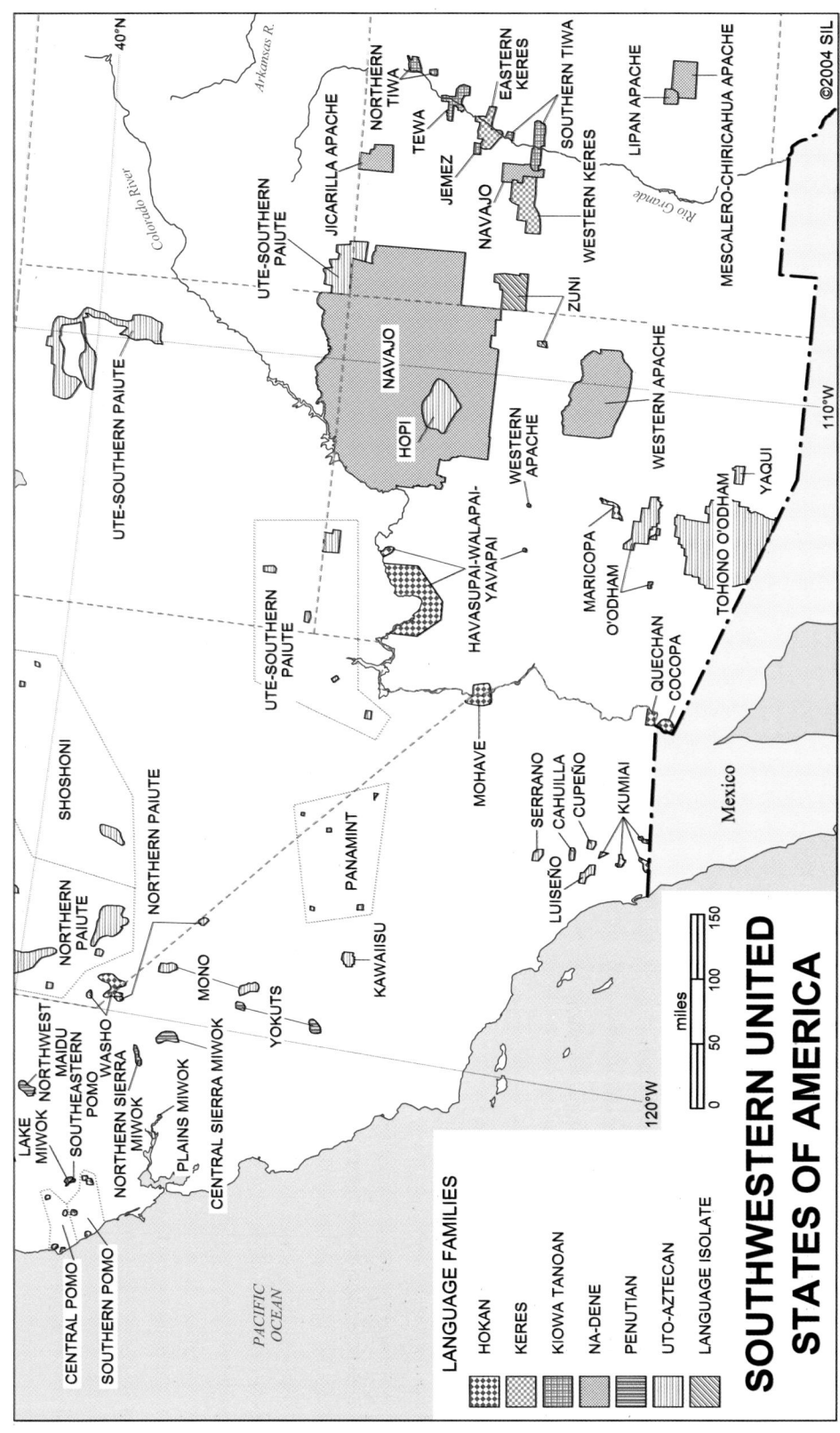

SOUTHWESTERN UNITED STATES OF AMERICA

©2004 SIL

LANGUAGE FAMILIES

- HOKAN
- KERES
- KIOWA TANOAN
- NA-DENE
- PENUTIAN
- UTO-AZTECAN
- LANGUAGE ISOLATE

miles

0   50   100   150

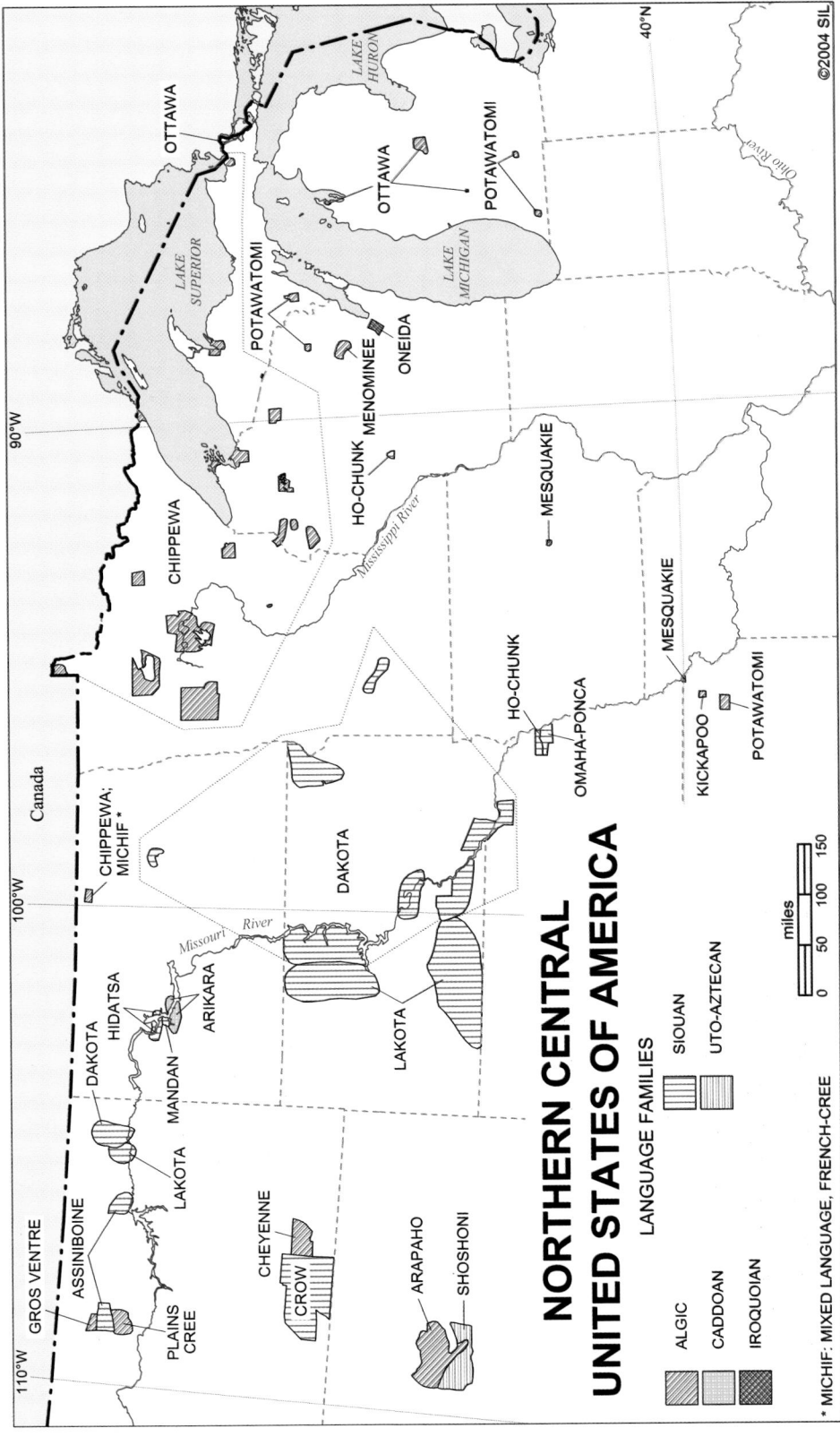

NORTHERN CENTRAL UNITED STATES OF AMERICA

LANGUAGE FAMILIES

ALGIC

CADDOAN

IROQUOIAN

SIOUAN

UTO-AZTECAN

miles

0   50   100   150

* MICHIF: MIXED LANGUAGE, FRENCH-CREE

©2004 SIL

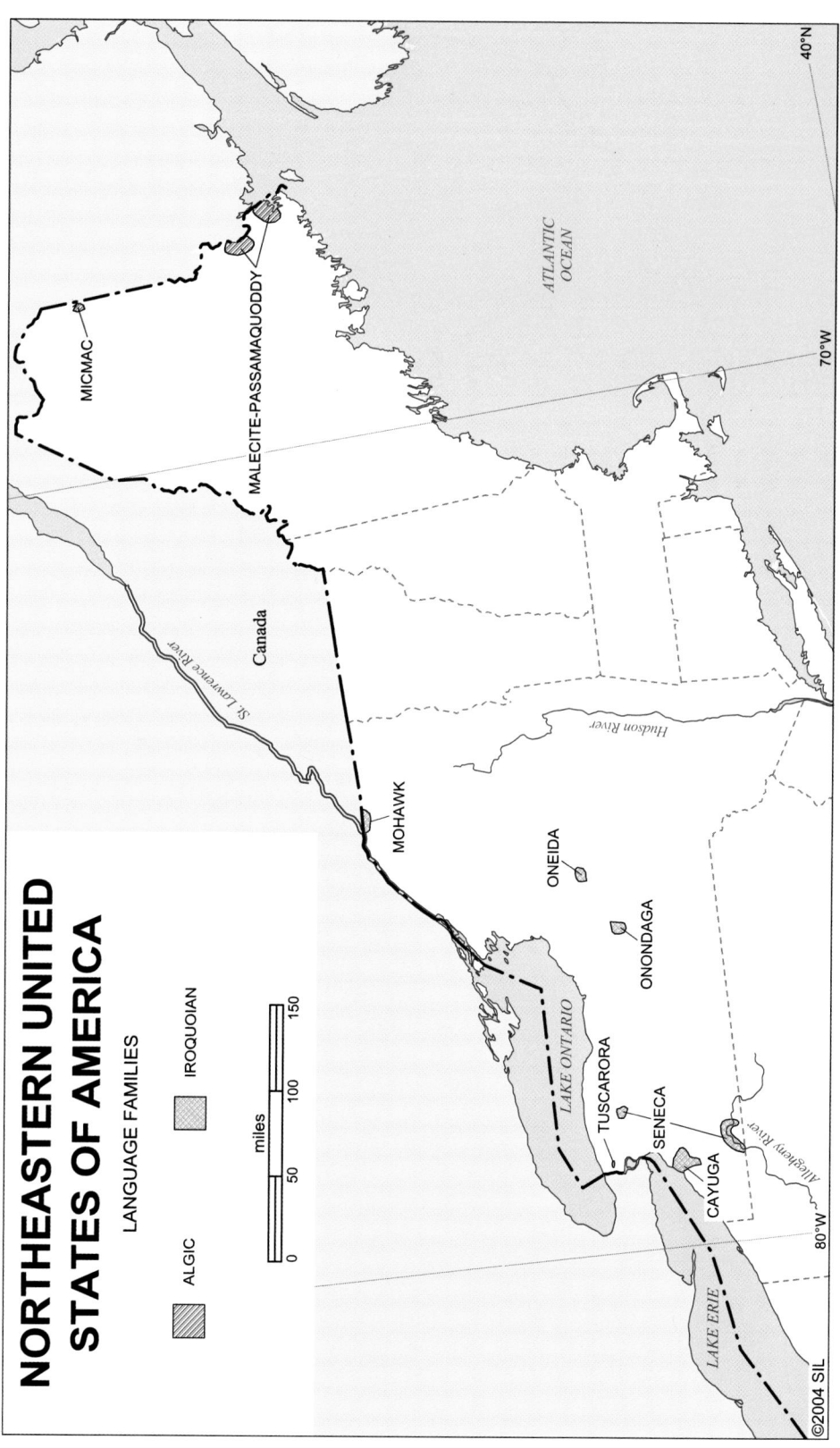

NORTHEASTERN UNITED STATES OF AMERICA

LANGUAGE FAMILIES

ALGIC

IROQUOIAN

©2004 SIL

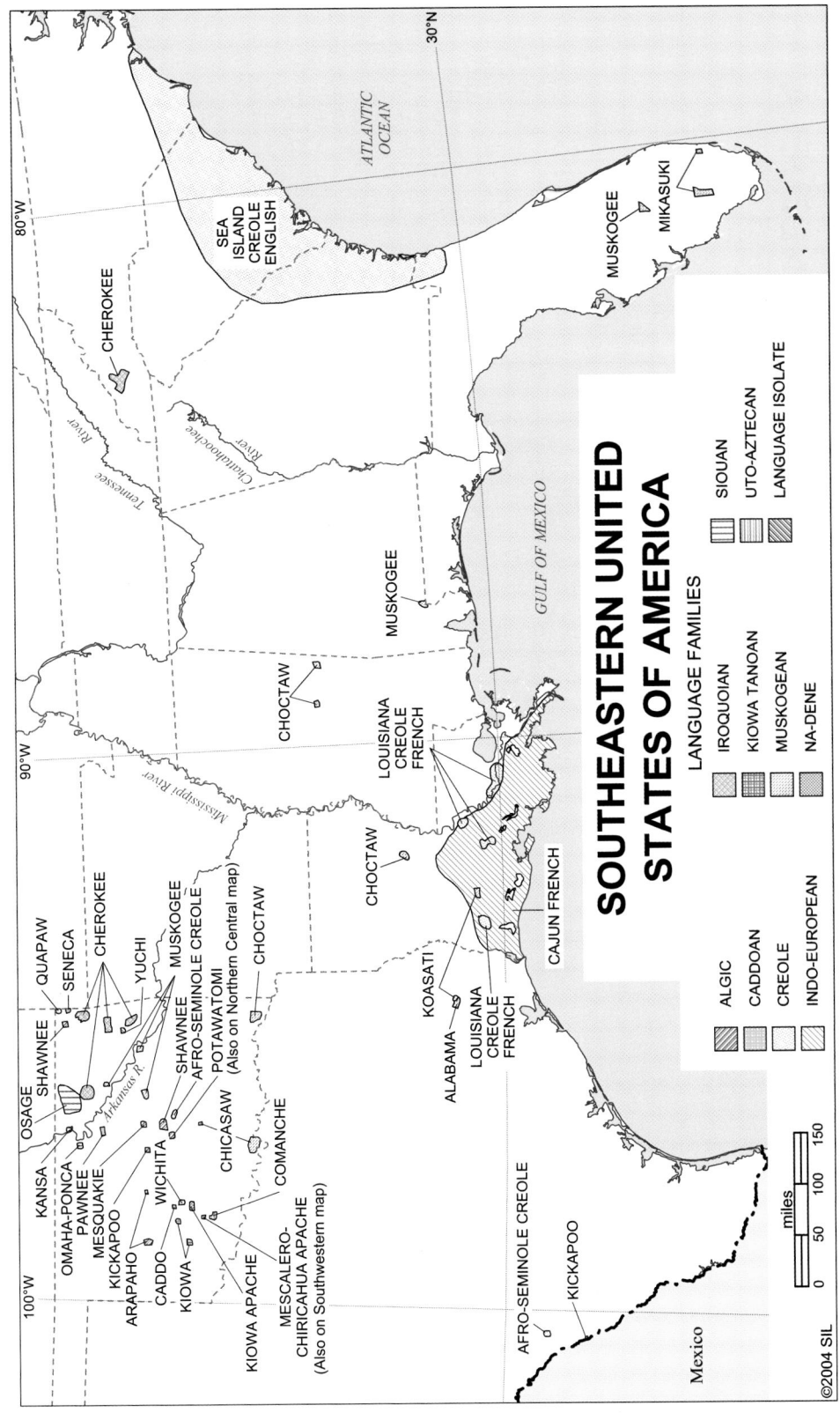

SOUTHEASTERN UNITED STATES OF AMERICA

LANGUAGE FAMILIES

ALGIC

CADDOAN

CREOLE

INDO-EUROPEAN

IROQUOIAN

KIOWA TANOAN

MUSKOGEAN

NA-DENE

SIOUAN

UTO-AZTECAN

LANGUAGE ISOLATE

©2004 SIL

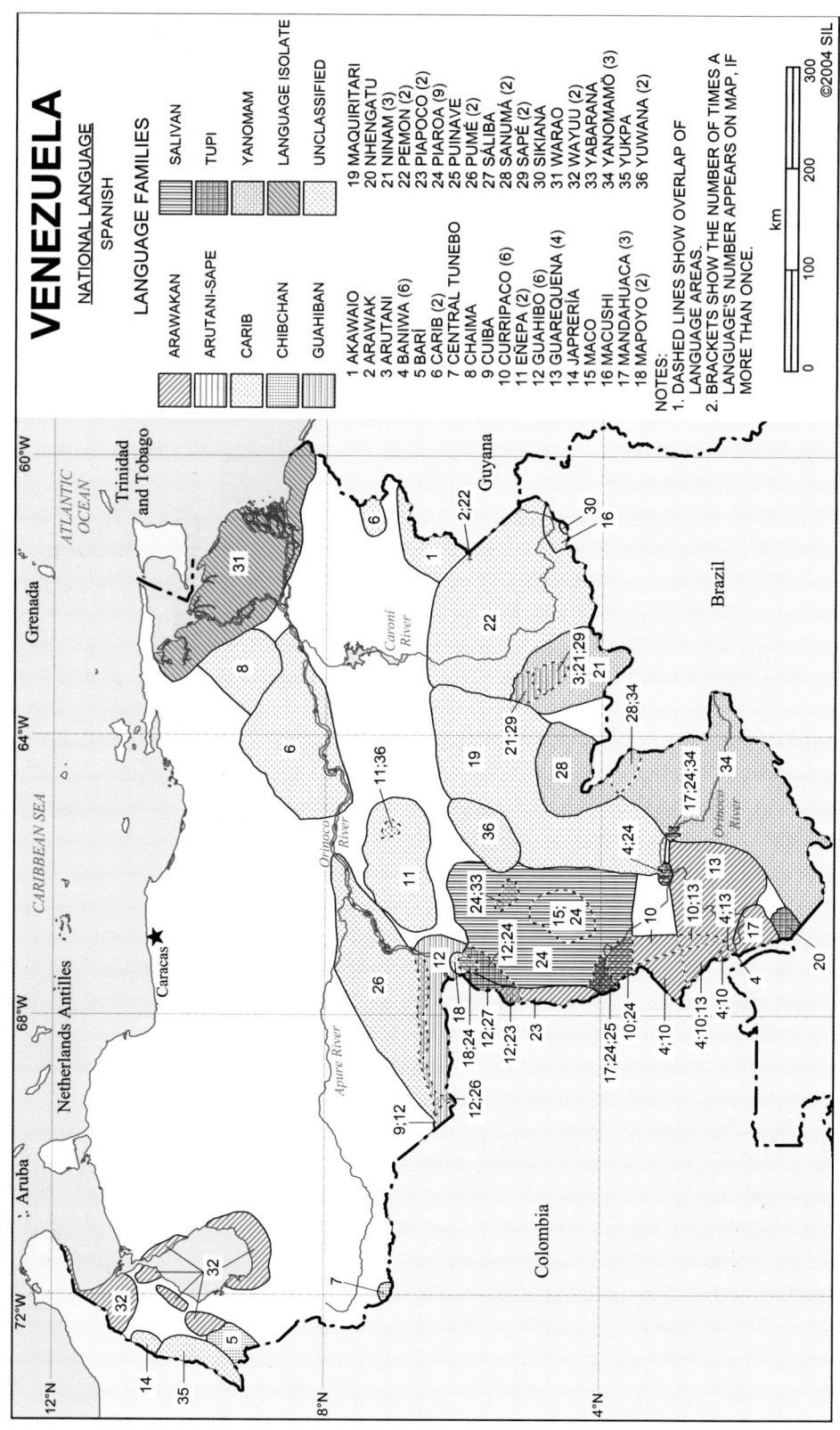

VENEZUELA

NATIONAL LANGUAGE
SPANISH

LANGUAGE FAMILIES

ARAWAKAN

ARUTANI-SAPE

CARIB

CHIBCHAN

GUAHIBAN

SALIVAN

TUPI

YANOMAM

LANGUAGE ISOLATE

UNCLASSIFIED

1 AKAWAIO
2 ARAWAK
3 ARUTANI
4 BANIWA (6)
5 BARÍ
6 CARIB (2)
7 CENTRAL TUNEBO
8 CHAIMA
9 CUIBA
10 CURRIPACO (6)
11 EÑEPA (2)
12 GUAHIBO (6)
13 GUAREQUENA (4)
14 JAPRERÍA
15 MACO
16 MACUSHI
17 MANDAHUACA (3)
18 MAPOYO (2)

19 MAQUIRITARI
20 NHENGATU
21 NINAM (3)
22 PEMON (2)
23 PIAPOCO (2)
24 PIAROA (9)
25 PUINAVE
26 PUMÉ (2)
27 SÁLIBA
28 SANUMÁ (2)
29 SAPÉ (2)
30 SIKIANA
31 WARAO
32 WAYUU (2)
33 YABARANA
34 YANOMAMÖ (3)
35 YUKPA
36 YUWANA (2)

NOTES:
1. DASHED LINES SHOW OVERLAP OF LANGUAGE AREAS.
2. BRACKETS SHOW THE NUMBER OF TIMES A LANGUAGE'S NUMBER APPEARS ON MAP, IF MORE THAN ONCE.

©2004 SIL

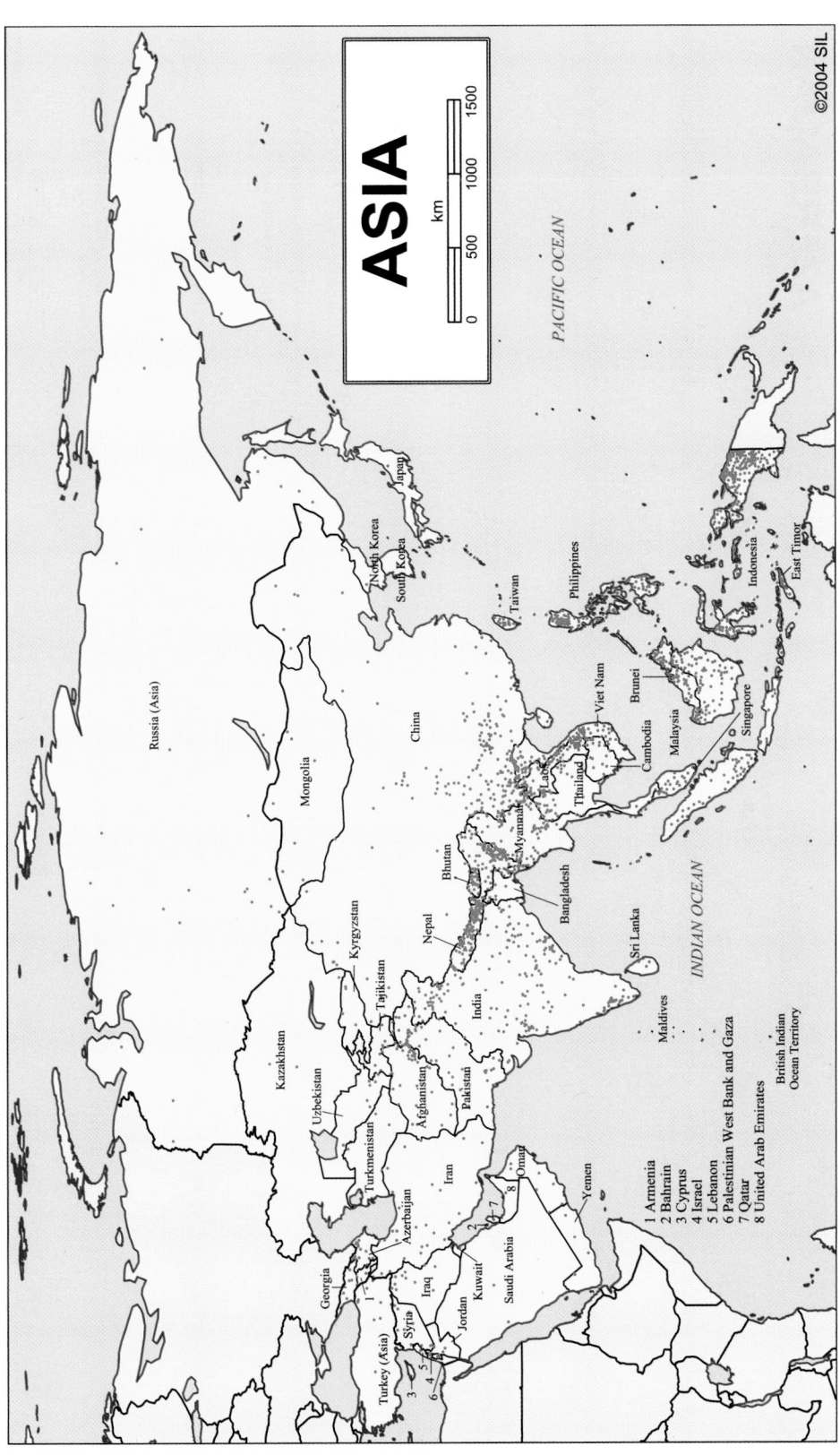

©2004 SIL

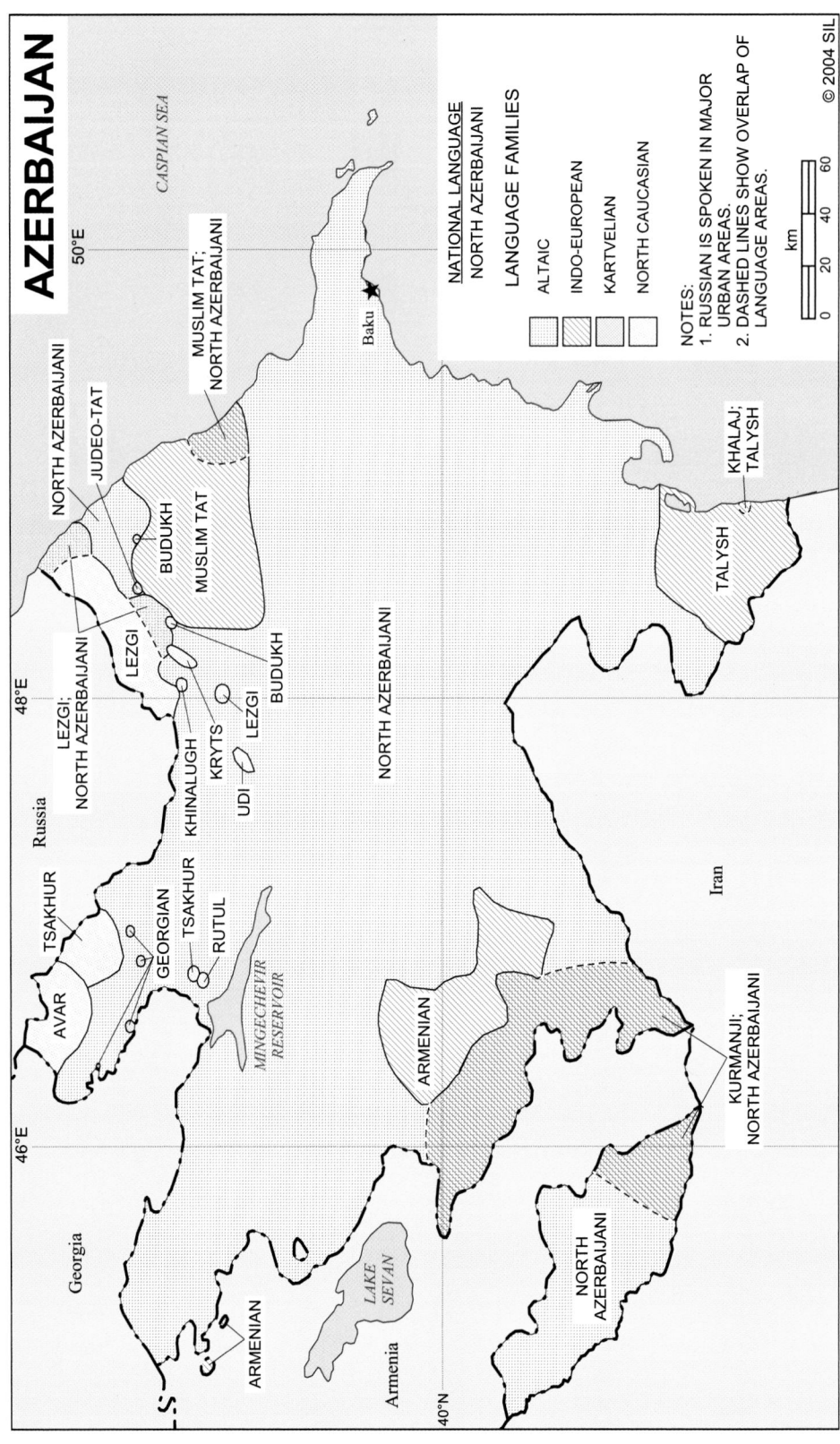

AZERBAIJAN

CASPIAN SEA

Baku

NORTH AZERBAIJANI

NORTH AZERBAIJANI

JUDEO-TAT

MUSLIM TAT;
NORTH AZERBAIJANI

BUDUKH

MUSLIM TAT

LEZGI;
NORTH AZERBAIJANI

LEZGI

BUDUKH

KHINALUGH

KRYTS

UDI

LEZGI

Russia

TSAKHUR

GEORGIAN

TSAKHUR

RUTUL

AVAR

MINGECHEVIR
RESERVOIR

Georgia

LAKE
SEVAN

ARMENIAN

Armenia

ARMENIAN

ARMENIAN

NORTH
AZERBAIJANI

KURMANJI;
NORTH AZERBAIJANI

Iran

TALYSH

KHALAJ;
TALYSH

NATIONAL LANGUAGE
NORTH AZERBAIJANI

LANGUAGE FAMILIES

ALTAIC

INDO-EUROPEAN

KARTVELIAN

NORTH CAUCASIAN

NOTES:
1. RUSSIAN IS SPOKEN IN MAJOR
   URBAN AREAS.
2. DASHED LINES SHOW OVERLAP OF
   LANGUAGE AREAS.

km

0   20   40   60

© 2004 SIL

50°E

48°E

46°E

40°N

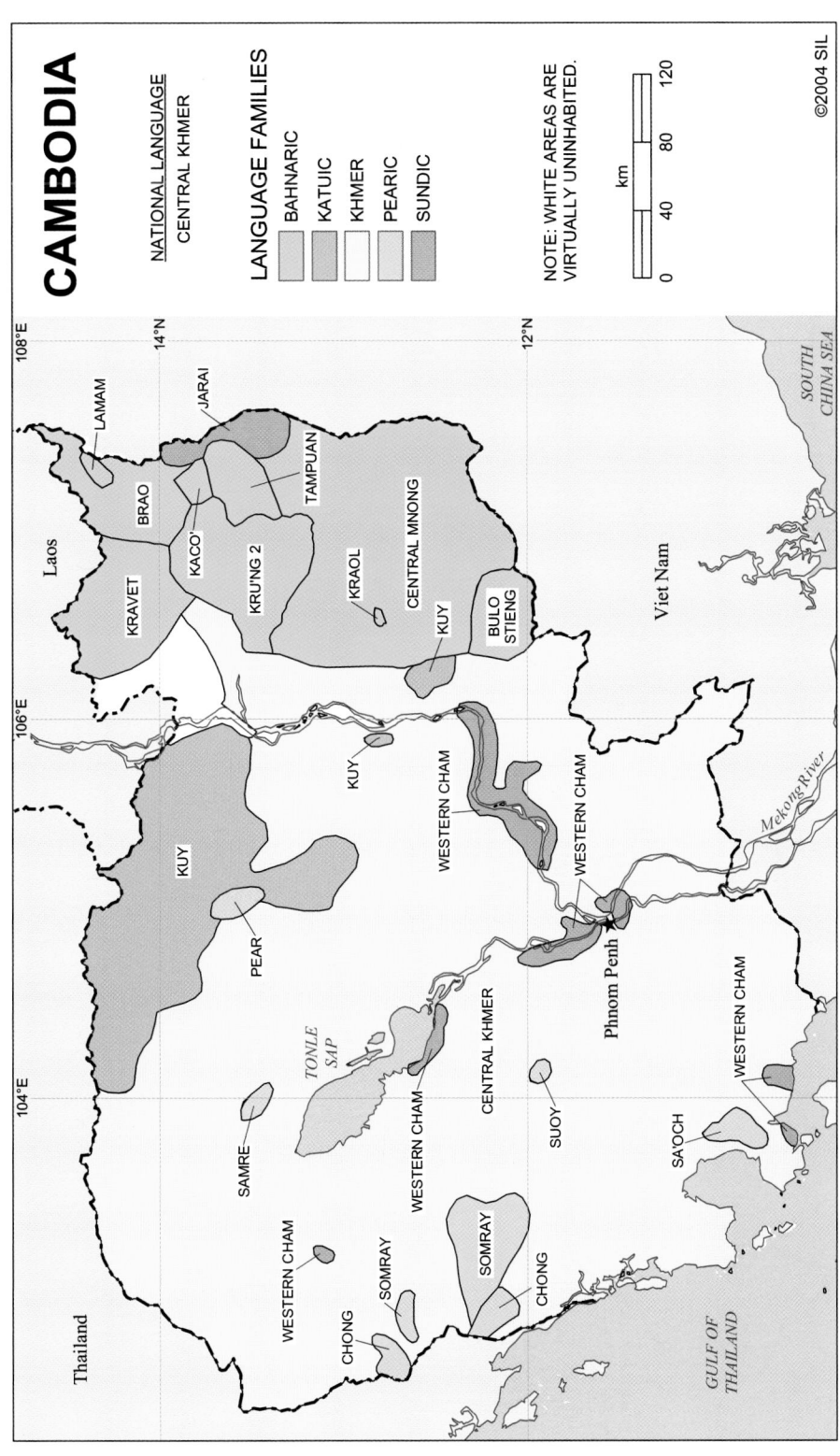

CAMBODIA

NATIONAL LANGUAGE
CENTRAL KHMER

LANGUAGE FAMILIES

BAHNARIC
KATUIC
KHMER
PEARIC
SUNDIC

NOTE: WHITE AREAS ARE
VIRTUALLY UNINHABITED.

km

0   40   80   120

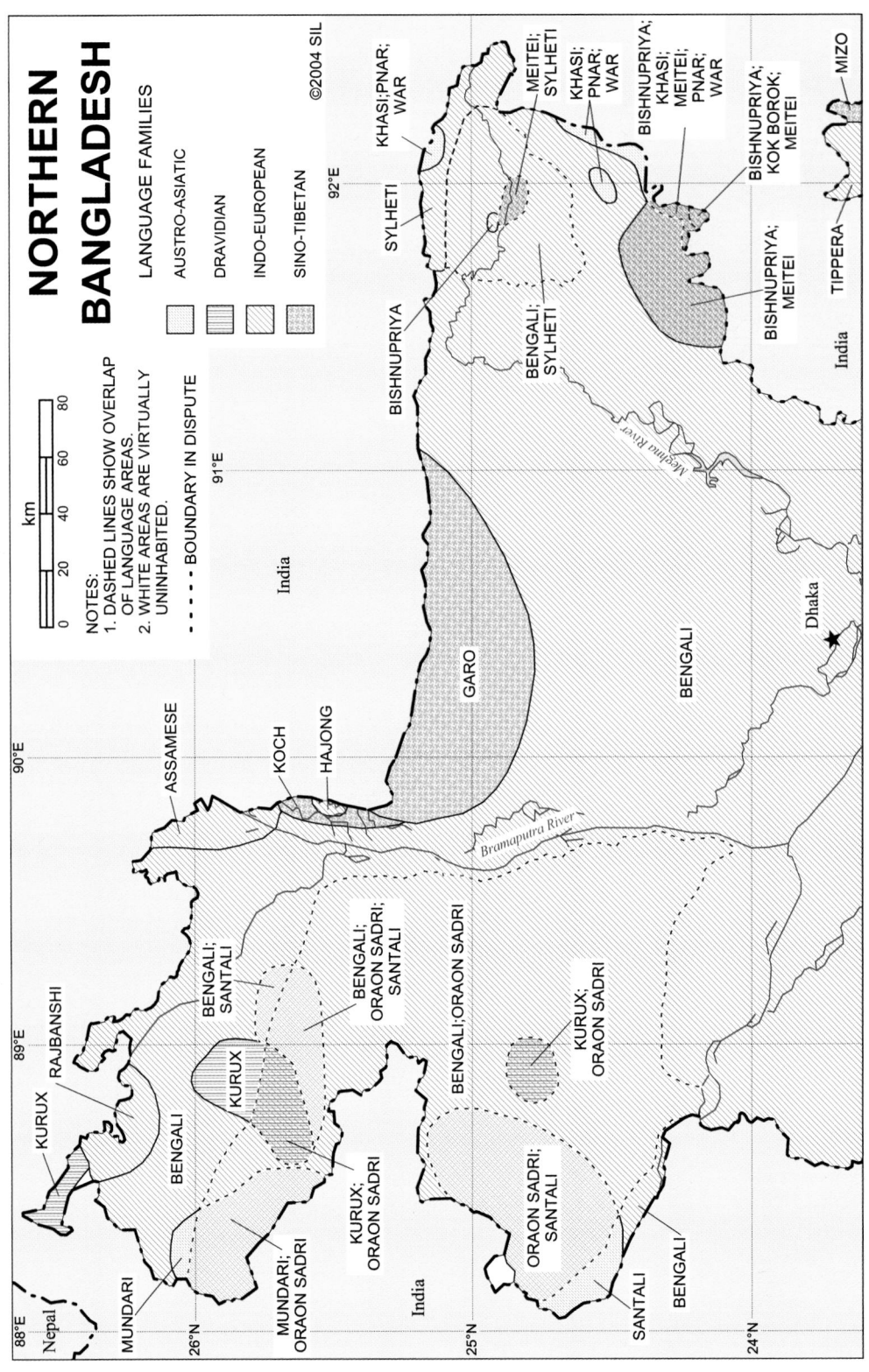

SOUTHERN BANGLADESH

LANGUAGE FAMILIES

INDO-EUROPEAN

SINO-TIBETAN

- - - BOUNDARY IN DISPUTE

NOTES:
1. DASHED LINES SHOW OVERLAP OF LANGUAGE AREAS.
2. WHITE AREAS ARE VIRTUALLY UNINHABITED.

ISLANDS ARE BENGALI UNLESS SHOWN OTHERWISE

km

0 20 40 60 80

©2004 SIL

BAY OF BENGAL

India

Myanmar

Dhaka

Padma River

Bhairab River

BENGALI

BENGALI

BENGALI

ARAKANESE; BENGALI

ARAKANESE; BENGALI

ARAKANESE; BENGALI

ARAKANESE; BURMESE

ARAKANESE

ARAKANESE; MRU

ARAKANESE;CHAKMA

MIZO

MIZO

MIZO

MIZO

PANKHU

TANGCHANGYA

SHENDU

ASHO CHIN

CHAK

KHUMI CHIN

TIPPERA

RIANG

KOK BOROK

USUI

China: Index Of Languages

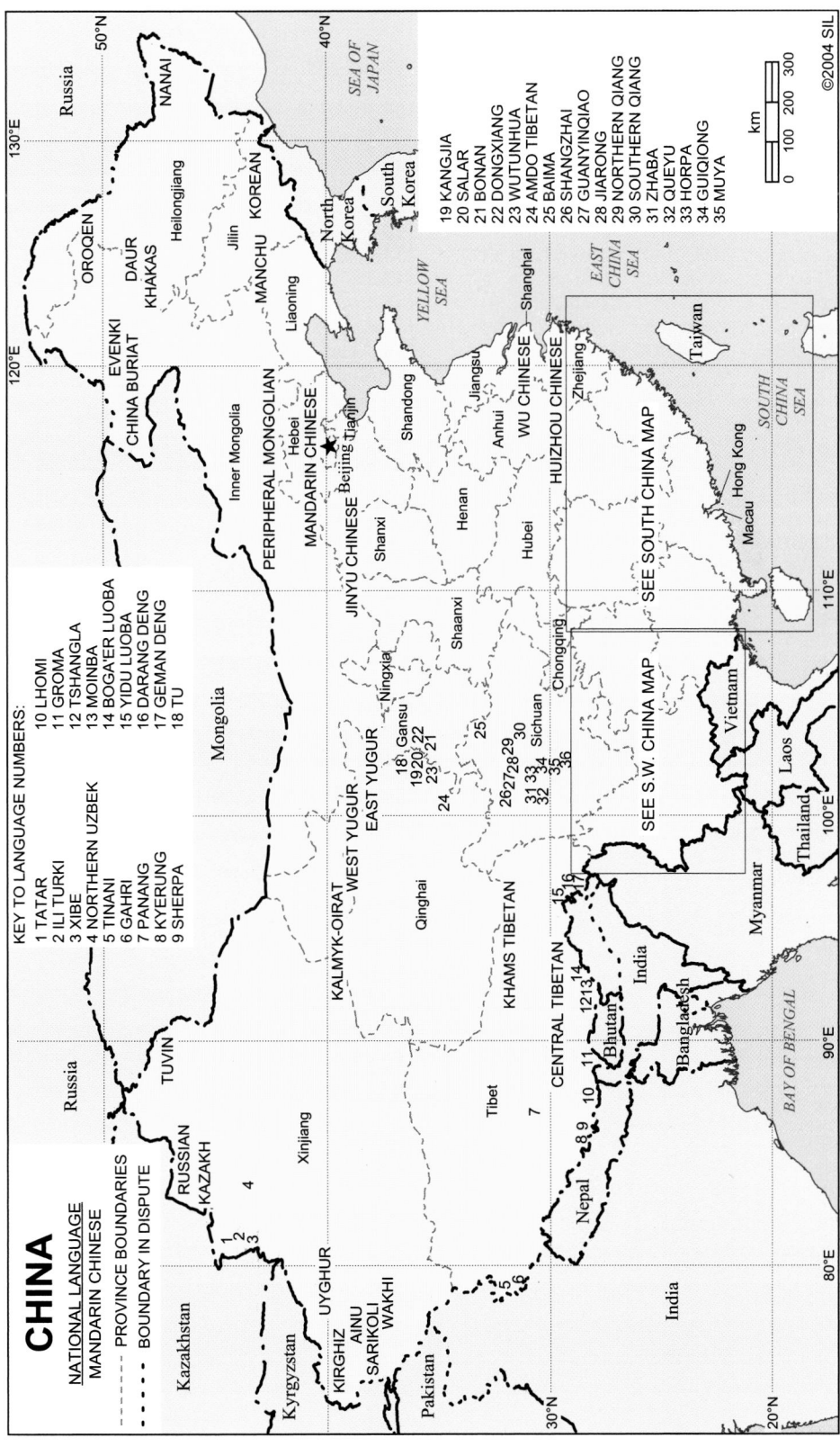

CHINA

NATIONAL LANGUAGE
MANDARIN CHINESE

--- --- PROVINCE BOUNDARIES

–·–·– BOUNDARY IN DISPUTE

KEY TO LANGUAGE NUMBERS:

1 TATAR	10 LHOMI
2 ILI TURKI	11 GROMA
3 XIBE	12 TSHANGLA
4 NORTHERN UZBEK	13 MOINBA
5 TINANI	14 BOGA'ER LUOBA
6 GAHRI	15 YIDU LUOBA
7 PANANG	16 DARANG DENG
8 KYERUNG	17 GEMAN DENG
9 SHERPA	18 TU

19 KANGJIA	28 JIARONG
20 SALAR	29 NORTHERN QIANG
21 BONAN	30 SOUTHERN QIANG
22 DONGXIANG	31 ZHABA
23 WUTUNHUA	32 QUEYU
24 AMDO TIBETAN	33 HORPA
25 BAIMA	34 GUIQIONG
26 SHANGZHAI	35 MUYA
27 GUANYINQIAO	

©2004 SIL

km
0 100 200 300

SEE SOUTH CHINA MAP

SEE S.W. CHINA MAP

China, Southwestern: Key To Languages

37 Atuence	73 Pale Palaung	106 Tai Dón	139 Western Mashan
38 Shixing	74 Shwe Palaung	107 U	Hmong
39 Namuyi	75 Riang	108 Kaduo	140 Central Mashan
40 Northern Pumi	76 Limi Yi	109 Biyo	Hmong
41 Sichuan Yi	77 Tai Nüa	110 Hani	141 Northern Mashan
42 Drung	78 Mili Yi	111 Blang	Hmong
43 Choni	79 Southern Lolopho	112 Kang	142 Eastern Huishui
44 Nung	Yi	113 Parauk	Hmong
45 Ayi	80 Eastern Lalu Yi	114 Wa	143 Central Huishui
46 Lisu	81 Maru	115 Lahu	Hmong
47 Nusu	82 Eshan-Xinping Yi	116 Bisu	144 Southwestern
48 Zauzou	83 Ache Yi	117 Lahu Shi	Huishui Hmong
49 Lashi	84 Sani Yi	118 Akha	145 Southern Guiyang
50 Northern Bai	85 Axi Yi	119 Kon Keu	Hmong
51 Central Bai	86 Awu Yi	120 Western Lawa	146 Northern Guiyang
52 Southern Pumi	87 Azhe Yi	121 Kuanhua	Hmong
53 Naxi	88 Puwa Yi	122 Kemiehua	147 Northern Huishui
54 Lipo	89 Poluo Yi	123 Man Met	Hmong
55 Wumeng Yi	90 Bugan	124 Hu	148 Luopohe Hmong
56 Naluo Yi	91 Buyang	125 Buyuan Jinuo	149 Chonganjiang
57 Wuding-Luquan Yi	92 Kim Mun	126 Youle Jinuo	Hmong
58 Miqie Yi	93 Laqua	127 Lü	150 Northern Qiandong
59 Hmong Njua	94 Lachi	128 Khmu	Hmong
60 Dayao Yi	95 Southeastern Lolo	129 Buxinhua	151 T'en
61 Central Yi	Yi	130 Bit	152 Mak
62 Southern Bai	96 Pa Di	131 Northeastern Dian	153 Sui
63 Western Yi	97 Muji Yi	Hmong	154 Ai-Cham
64 Xishan Lalu Yi	98 Mang	132 Wusa Yi	155 Bolyu
65 Western Lalu Yi	99 Tai Dam	133 Guizhou Yi	156 Yerong
66 Achang	100 Pula Yi	134 Hmong Daw	157 Western Xiangxi
67 Pela	101 Southern Yi	135 Gelao	Hmong
68 Jingpho	102 Tai Hongjin	136 Southwestern	158 Southern Zhuang
69 Xiandao	103 Tai Ya	Guiyang Hmong	159 Maonan
70 Kado	104 Honi	137 Bouyei	160 Bu-Nao Bunu
71 Rumai Palaung	105 Yuanjiang-Mojiang	138 Southern Mashan	161 Northern Zhuang
72 Zaiwa	Yi	Hmong	162 Vietnamese

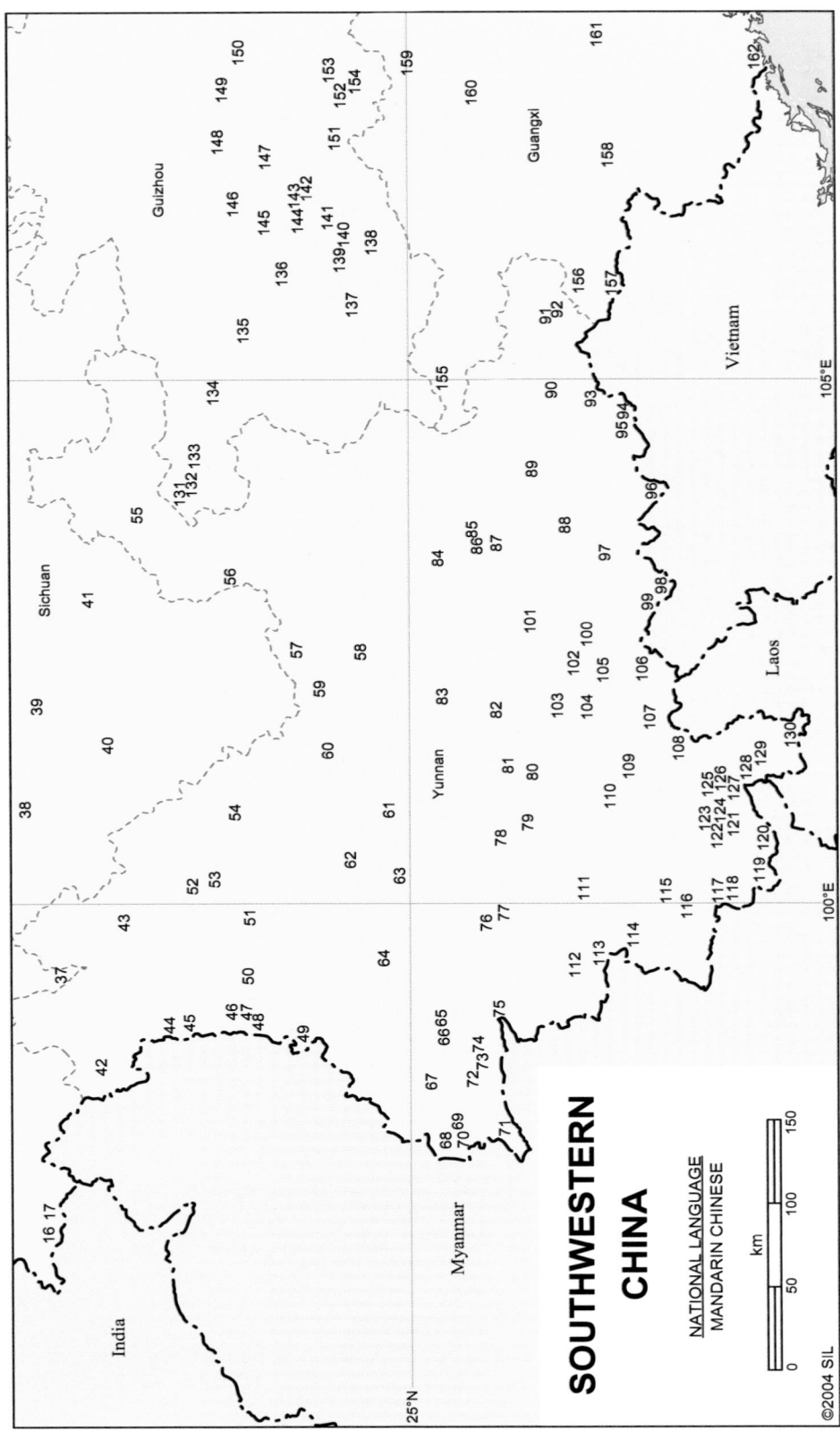

SOUTHWESTERN
CHINA

NATIONAL LANGUAGE
MANDARIN CHINESE

km

0   50   100   150

©2004 SIL

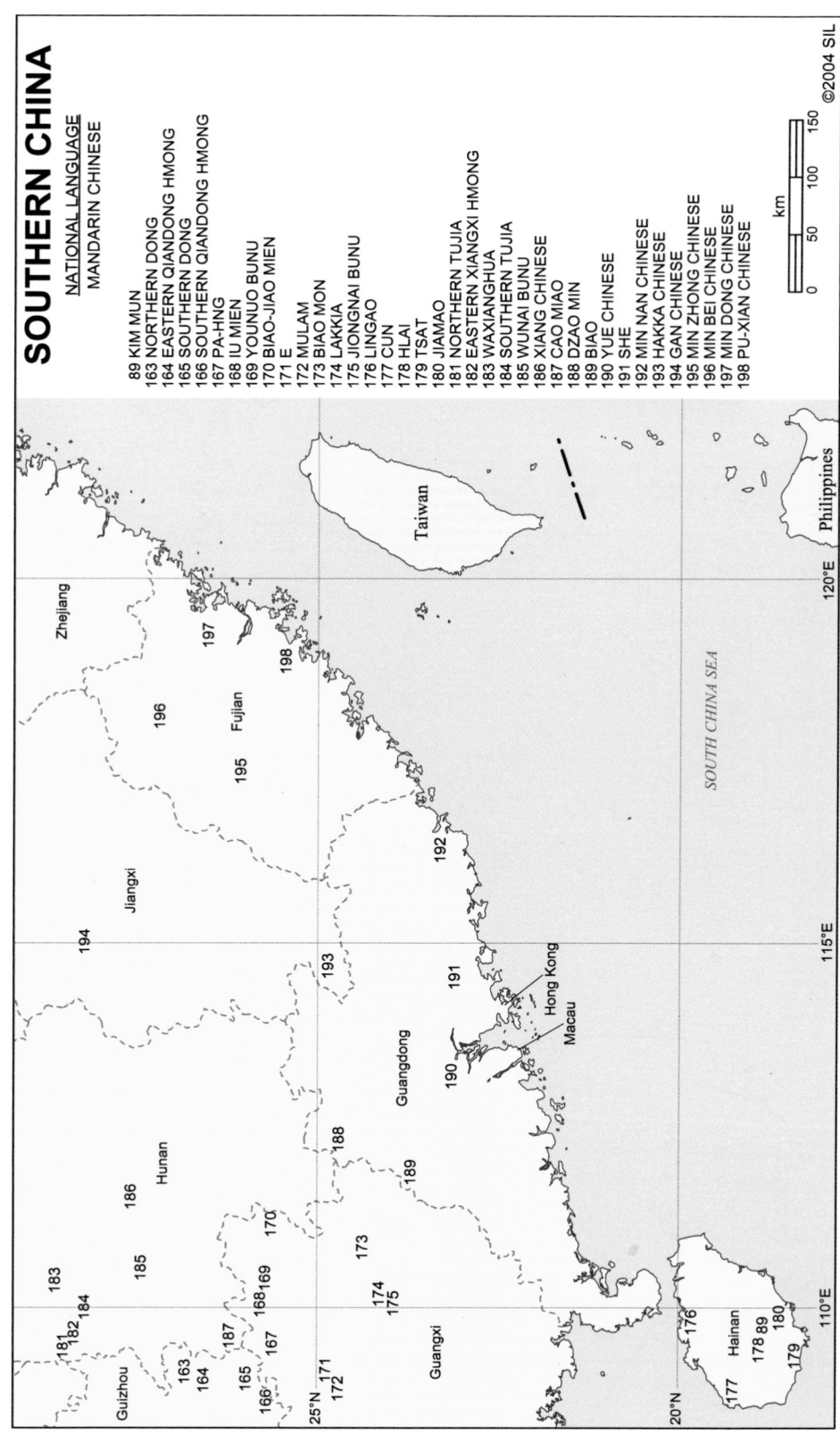

SOUTHERN CHINA

NATIONAL LANGUAGE
MANDARIN CHINESE

89 KIM MUN
163 NORTHERN DONG
164 EASTERN QIANDONG HMONG
165 SOUTHERN DONG
166 SOUTHERN QIANDONG HMONG
167 PA-HNG
168 IU MIEN
169 YOUNUO BUNU
170 BIAO-JIAO MIEN
171 E
172 MULAM
173 BIAO MON
174 LAKKIA
175 JIONGNAI BUNU
176 LINGAO
177 CUN
178 HLAI
179 TSAT
180 JIAMAO
181 NORTHERN TUJIA
182 EASTERN XIANGXI HMONG
183 WAXIANGHUA
184 SOUTHERN TUJIA
185 WUNAI BUNU
186 XIANG CHINESE
187 CAO MIAO
188 DZAO MIN
189 BIAO
190 YUE CHINESE
191 SHE
192 MIN NAN CHINESE
193 HAKKA CHINESE
194 GAN CHINESE
195 MIN ZHONG CHINESE
196 MIN BEI CHINESE
197 MIN DONG CHINESE
198 PU-XIAN CHINESE

©2004 SIL

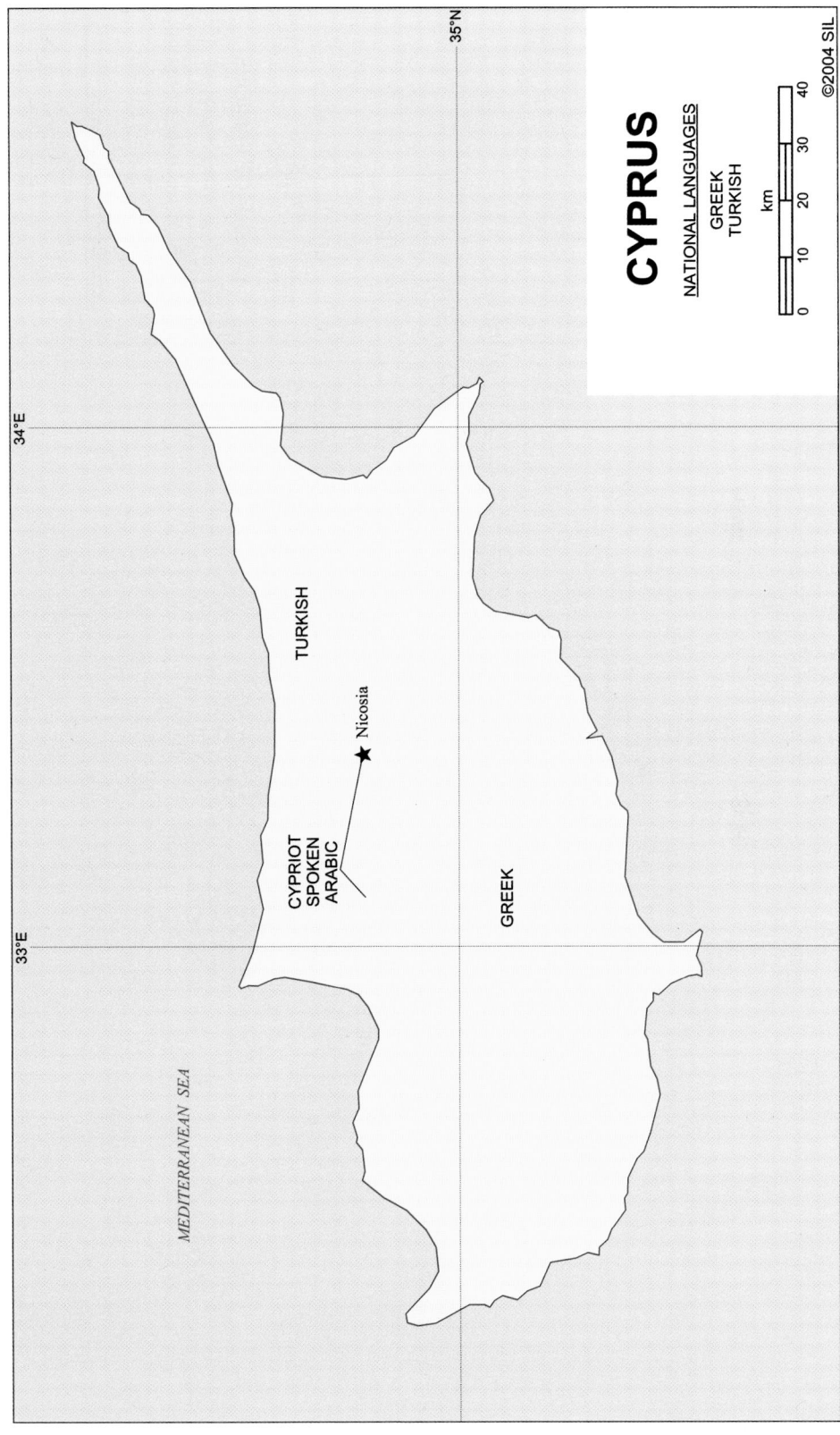

MEDITERRANEAN SEA

TURKISH

CYPRIOT
SPOKEN
ARABIC

★ Nicosia

GREEK

34°E

33°E

35°N

CYPRUS

<u>NATIONAL LANGUAGES</u>

GREEK
TURKISH

km

0   10   20   30   40

©2004 SIL

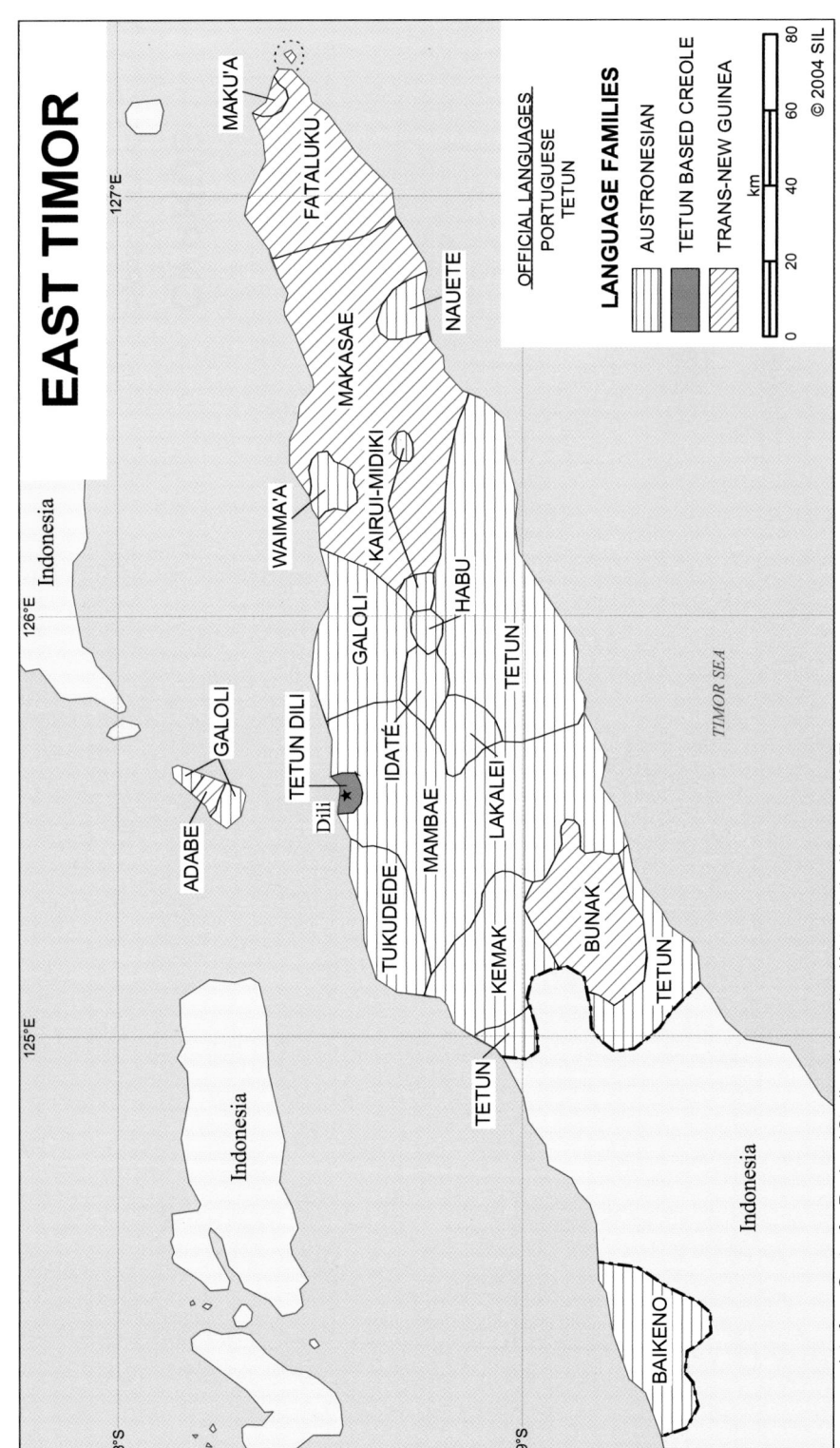

EAST TIMOR

127°E

126°E

125°E

8°S

9°S

Indonesia

Indonesia

Indonesia

TIMOR SEA

MAKU'A

FATALUKU

MAKASAE

NAUETE

KAIRUI-MIDIKI

WAIMA'A

GALOLI

HABU

TETUN

TETUN DILI

IDATÉ

MAMBAE

LAKALEI

BUNAK

TETUN

Dili

ADABE

GALOLI

TUKUDEDE

KEMAK

TETUN

BAIKENO

OFFICIAL LANGUAGES
PORTUGUESE
TETUN

LANGUAGE FAMILIES

AUSTRONESIAN

TETUN BASED CREOLE

TRANS-NEW GUINEA

km

0   20   40   60   80

© 2004 SIL

Language data from Centre for Regional Studies, Universitas Kristen Artha Wacana (1997)

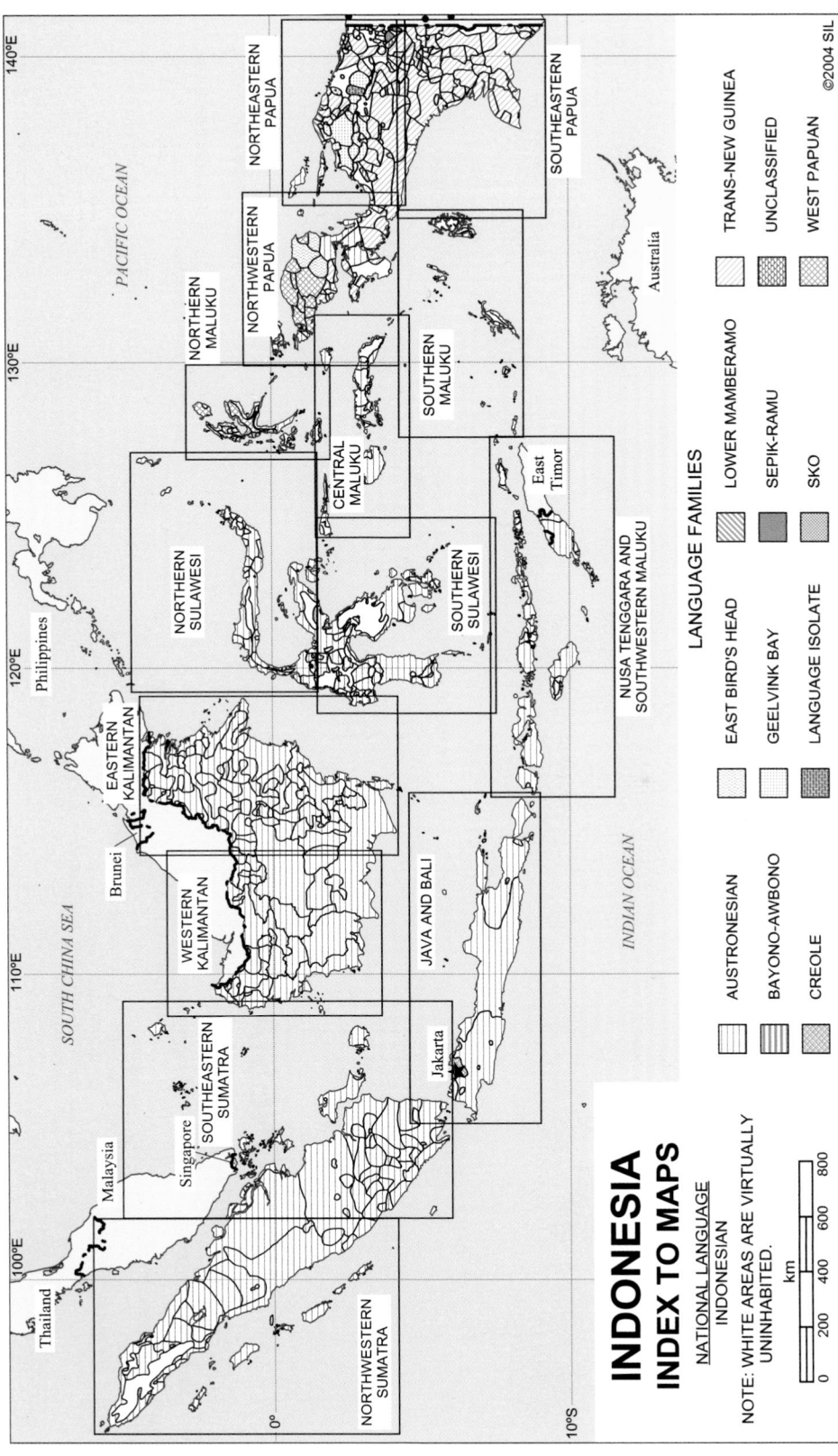

INDONESIA
INDEX TO MAPS

NATIONAL LANGUAGE
INDONESIAN

NOTE: WHITE AREAS ARE VIRTUALLY
UNINHABITED.

km

| 0 | 200 | 400 | 600 | 800 |

LANGUAGE FAMILIES

AUSTRONESIAN

BAYONO-AWBONO

CREOLE

EAST BIRD'S HEAD

GEELVINK BAY

LANGUAGE ISOLATE

LOWER MAMBERAMO

SEPIK-RAMU

SKO

TRANS-NEW GUINEA

UNCLASSIFIED

WEST PAPUAN

©2004 SIL

NORTHEASTERN PAPUA

SOUTHEASTERN PAPUA

NORTHWESTERN PAPUA

NORTHERN MALUKU

SOUTHERN MALUKU

CENTRAL MALUKU

NORTHERN SULAWESI

SOUTHERN SULAWESI

NUSA TENGGARA AND SOUTHWESTERN MALUKU

EASTERN KALIMANTAN

WESTERN KALIMANTAN

JAVA AND BALI

SOUTHEASTERN SUMATRA

NORTHWESTERN SUMATRA

PACIFIC OCEAN

SOUTH CHINA SEA

INDIAN OCEAN

Australia

East Timor

Philippines

Brunei

Jakarta

Singapore

Malaysia

Thailand

140°E

130°E

120°E

110°E

100°E

0°

10°S

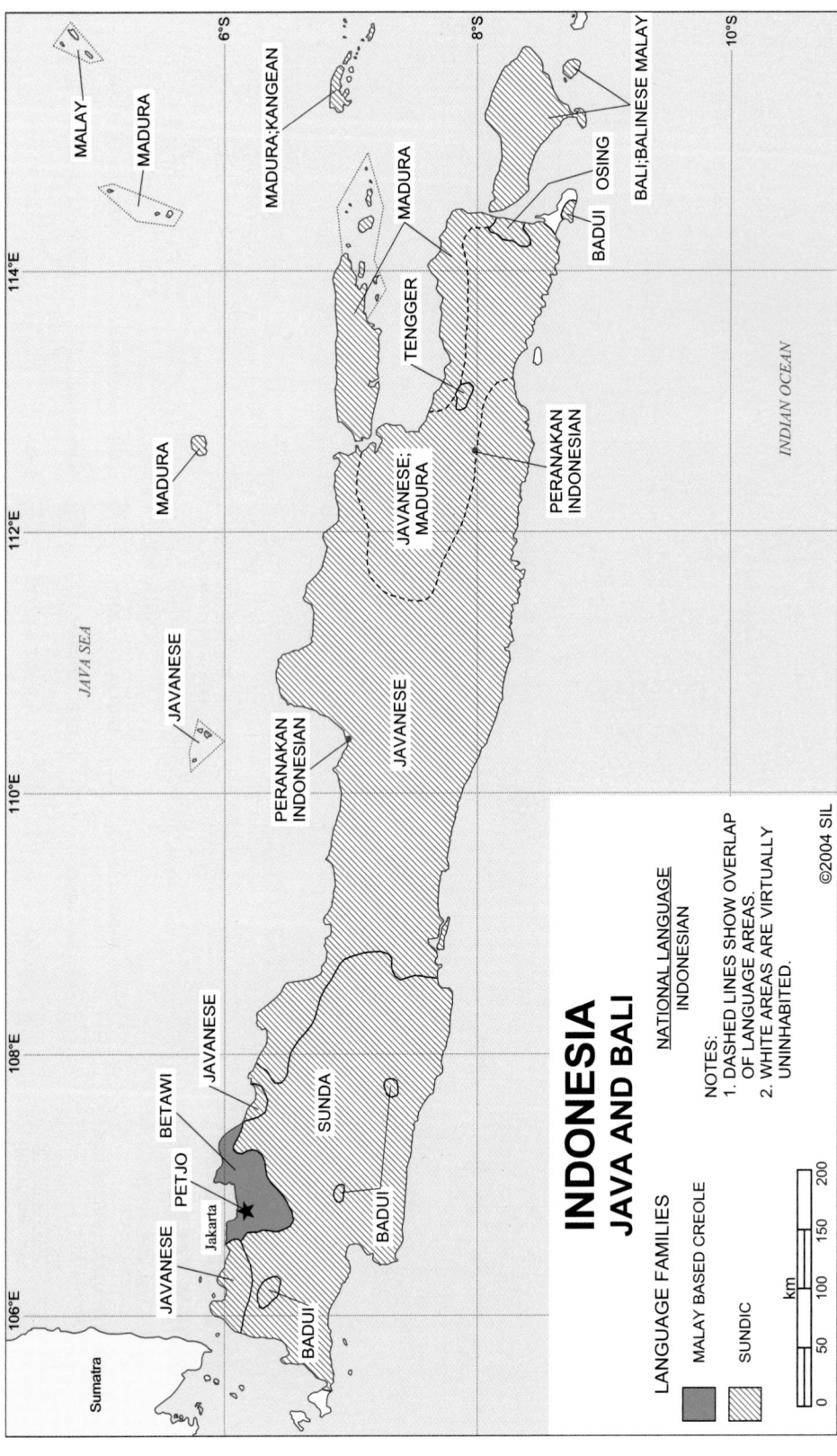

LANGUAGE FAMILIES

NATIONAL LANGUAGE
INDONESIAN

MALAY BASED CREOLE

SUNDIC

NOTES:
1. DASHED LINES SHOW OVERLAP
   OF LANGUAGE AREAS.
2. WHITE AREAS ARE VIRTUALLY
   UNINHABITED.

INDONESIA
JAVA AND BALI

©2004 SIL

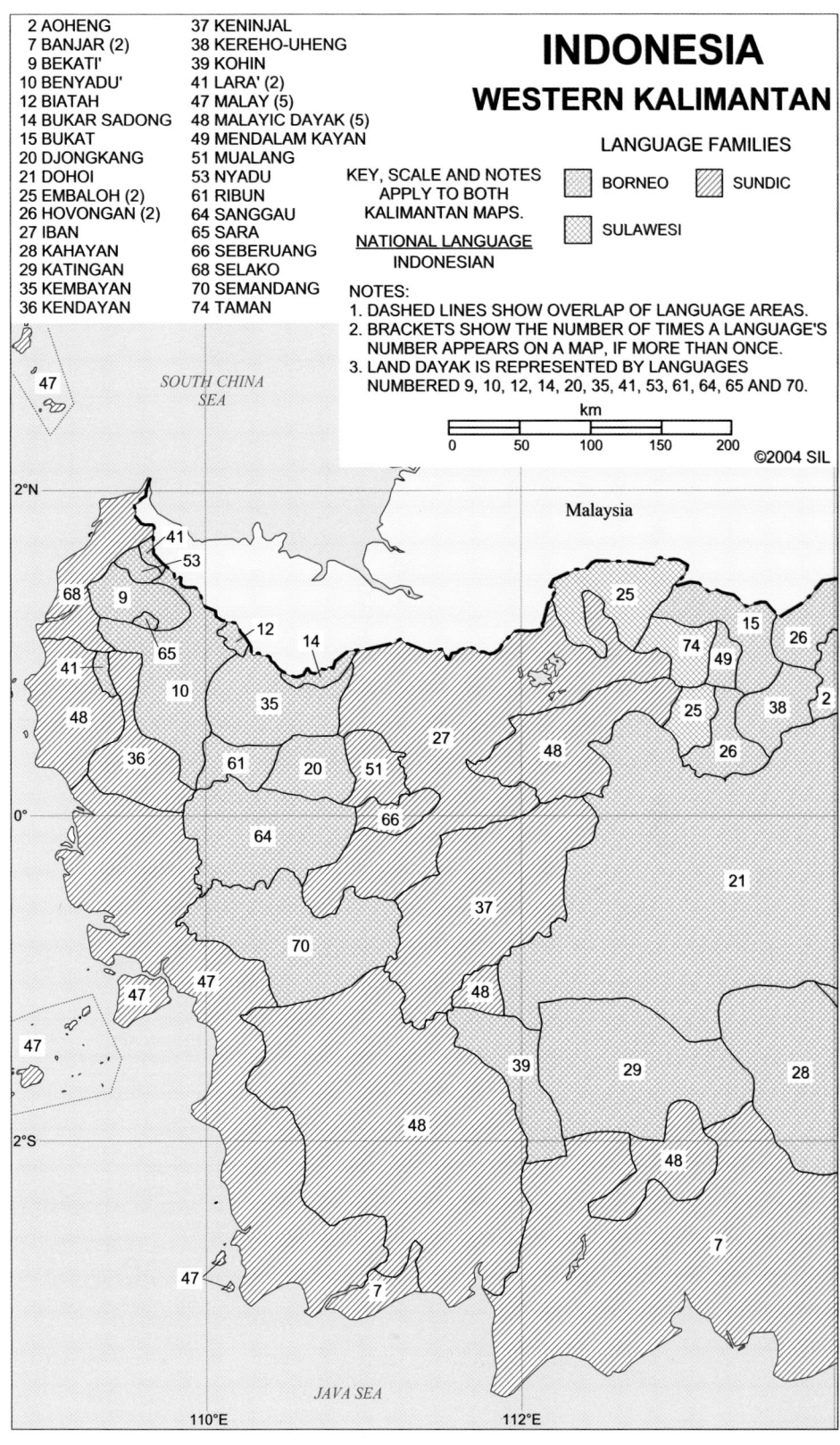

2 AOHENG
7 BANJAR (2)
9 BEKATI'
10 BENYADU'
12 BIATAH
14 BUKAR SADONG
15 BUKAT
20 DJONGKANG
21 DOHOI
25 EMBALOH (2)
26 HOVONGAN (2)
27 IBAN
28 KAHAYAN
29 KATINGAN
35 KEMBAYAN
36 KENDAYAN

37 KENINJAL
38 KEREHO-UHENG
39 KOHIN
41 LARA' (2)
47 MALAY (5)
48 MALAYIC DAYAK (5)
49 MENDALAM KAYAN
51 MUALANG
53 NYADU
61 RIBUN
64 SANGGAU
65 SARA
66 SEBERUANG
68 SELAKO
70 SEMANDANG
74 TAMAN

INDONESIA
WESTERN KALIMANTAN

LANGUAGE FAMILIES

BORNEO   SUNDIC

SULAWESI

KEY, SCALE AND NOTES
 APPLY TO BOTH
 KALIMANTAN MAPS.

NATIONAL LANGUAGE
 INDONESIAN

NOTES:
1. DASHED LINES SHOW OVERLAP OF LANGUAGE AREAS.
2. BRACKETS SHOW THE NUMBER OF TIMES A LANGUAGE'S
   NUMBER APPEARS ON A MAP, IF MORE THAN ONCE.
3. LAND DAYAK IS REPRESENTED BY LANGUAGES
   NUMBERED 9, 10, 12, 14, 20, 35, 41, 53, 61, 64, 65 AND 70.

km
0   50   100   150   200

©2004 SIL

SOUTH CHINA SEA

Malaysia

JAVA SEA

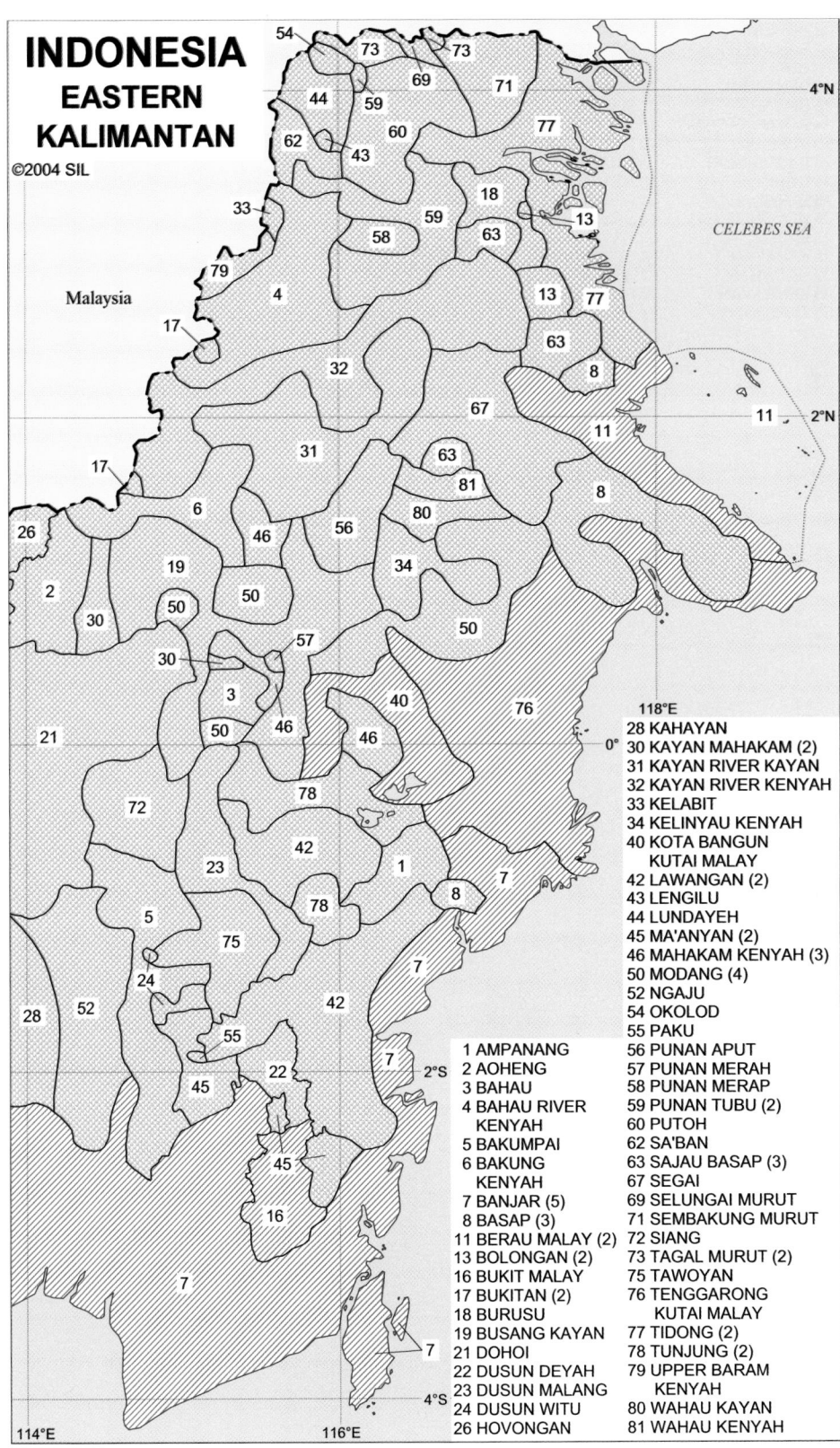

INDONESIA
EASTERN
KALIMANTAN
©2004 SIL

Malaysia

CELEBES SEA

28 KAHAYAN
30 KAYAN MAHAKAM (2)
31 KAYAN RIVER KAYAN
32 KAYAN RIVER KENYAH
33 KELABIT
34 KELINYAU KENYAH
40 KOTA BANGUN
   KUTAI MALAY
42 LAWANGAN (2)
43 LENGILU
44 LUNDAYEH
45 MA'ANYAN (2)
46 MAHAKAM KENYAH (3)
50 MODANG (4)
52 NGAJU
54 OKOLOD
55 PAKU
56 PUNAN APUT
57 PUNAN MERAH
58 PUNAN MERAP
59 PUNAN TUBU (2)
60 PUTOH
62 SA'BAN
63 SAJAU BASAP (3)
67 SEGAI
69 SELUNGAI MURUT
71 SEMBAKUNG MURUT
72 SIANG
73 TAGAL MURUT (2)
75 TAWOYAN
76 TENGGARONG
   KUTAI MALAY
77 TIDONG (2)
78 TUNJUNG (2)
79 UPPER BARAM
   KENYAH
80 WAHAU KAYAN
81 WAHAU KENYAH

1 AMPANANG
2 AOHENG
3 BAHAU
4 BAHAU RIVER
   KENYAH
5 BAKUMPAI
6 BAKUNG
   KENYAH
7 BANJAR (5)
8 BASAP (3)
11 BERAU MALAY (2)
13 BOLONGAN (2)
16 BUKIT MALAY
17 BUKITAN (2)
18 BURUSU
19 BUSANG KAYAN
21 DOHOI
22 DUSUN DEYAH
23 DUSUN MALANG
24 DUSUN WITU
26 HOVONGAN

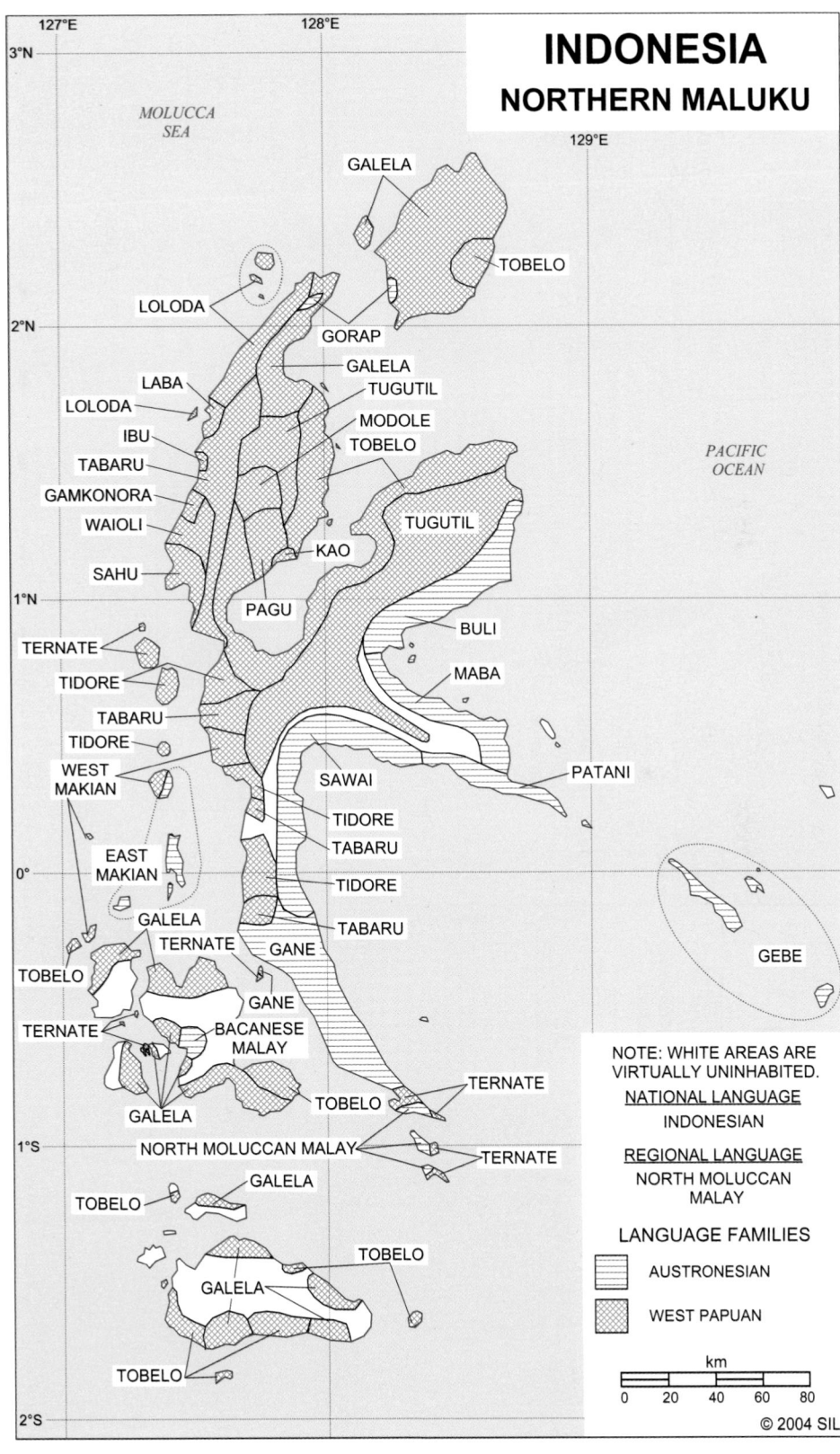

INDONESIA
NORTHERN MALUKU

MOLUCCA SEA

GALELA

TOBELO

LOLODA

GORAP

GALELA

LABA

TUGUTIL

LOLODA

MODOLE

IBU

TOBELO

TABARU

GAMKONORA

WAIOLI

TUGUTIL

SAHU

KAO

PAGU

PACIFIC OCEAN

TERNATE

BULI

TIDORE

MABA

TABARU

TIDORE

WEST MAKIAN

SAWAI

PATANI

TIDORE

TABARU

EAST MAKIAN

TIDORE

GALELA

TABARU

TERNATE

GANE

GEBE

TOBELO

GANE

TERNATE

BACANESE MALAY

GALELA

TERNATE

TOBELO

TERNATE

NORTH MOLUCCAN MALAY

GALELA

TOBELO

TOBELO

GALELA

TOBELO

NOTE: WHITE AREAS ARE VIRTUALLY UNINHABITED.

NATIONAL LANGUAGE
INDONESIAN

REGIONAL LANGUAGE
NORTH MOLUCCAN MALAY

LANGUAGE FAMILIES

AUSTRONESIAN

WEST PAPUAN

km
0   20   40   60   80

© 2004 SIL

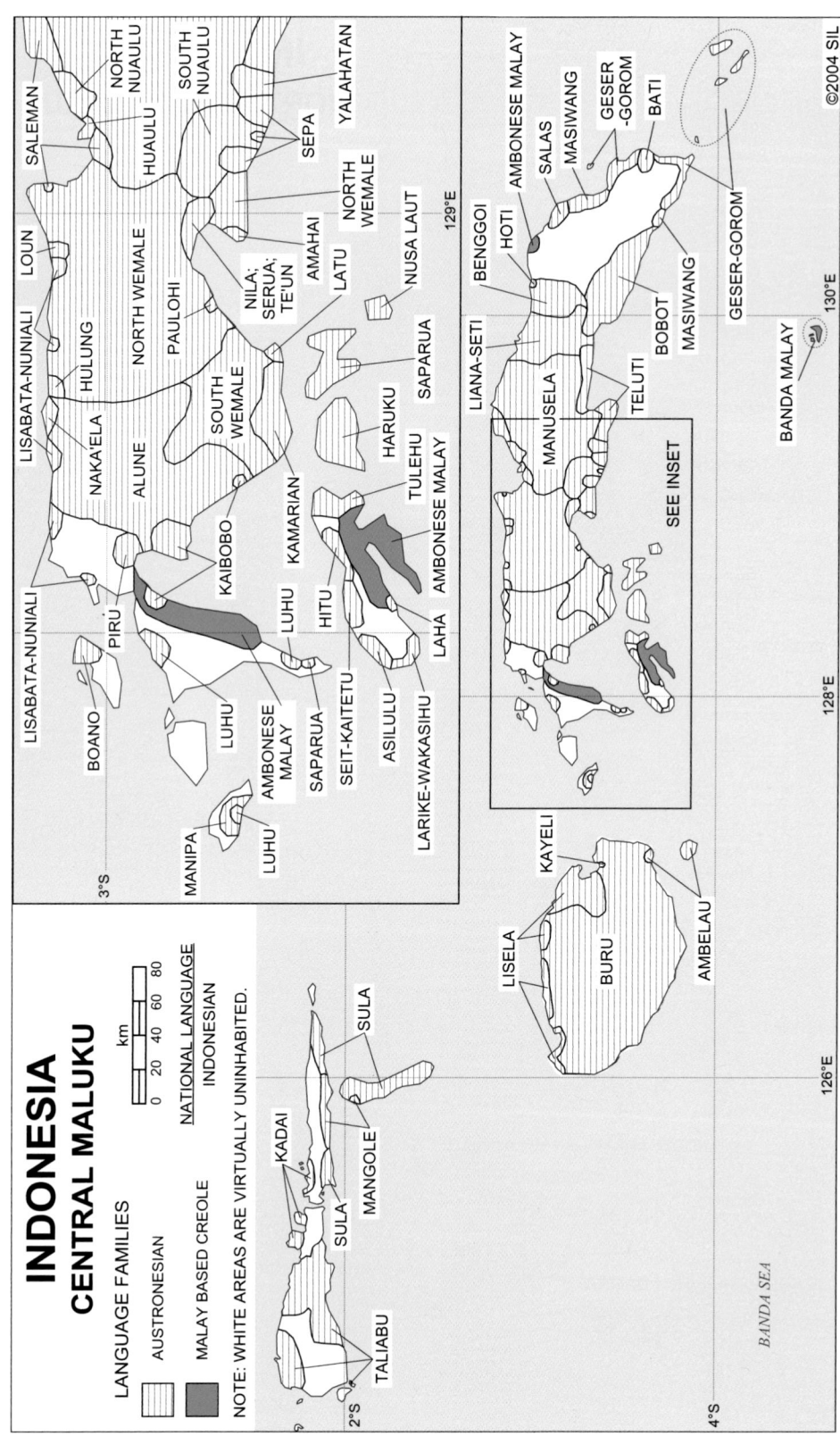

INDONESIA
CENTRAL MALUKU

LANGUAGE FAMILIES

AUSTRONESIAN

MALAY BASED CREOLE

NOTE: WHITE AREAS ARE VIRTUALLY UNINHABITED.

NATIONAL LANGUAGE
INDONESIAN

km
0 20 40 60 80

©2004 SIL

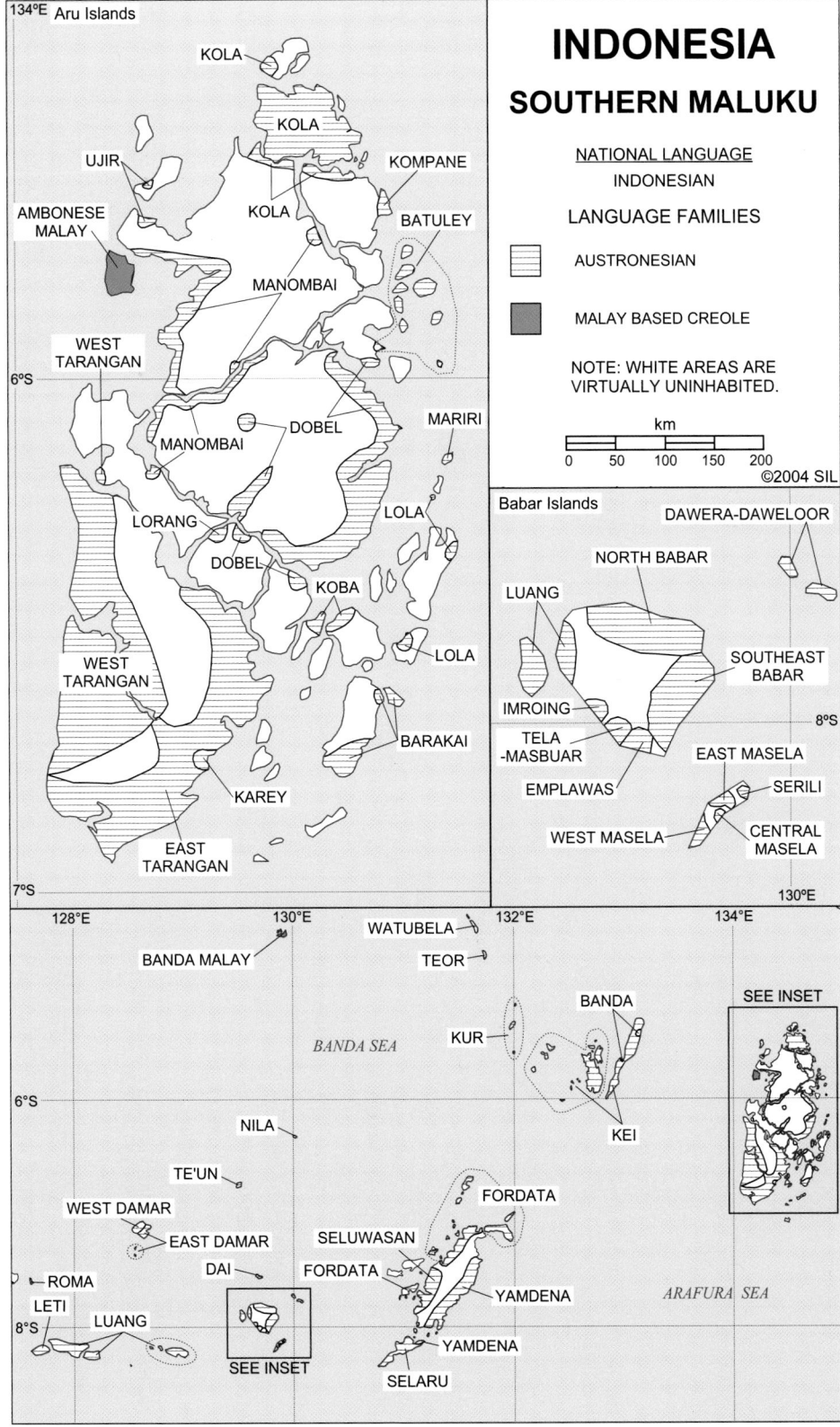

INDONESIA
SOUTHERN MALUKU

<u>NATIONAL LANGUAGE</u>
INDONESIAN

LANGUAGE FAMILIES

AUSTRONESIAN

MALAY BASED CREOLE

NOTE: WHITE AREAS ARE
VIRTUALLY UNINHABITED.

km

0   50   100   150   200

©2004 SIL

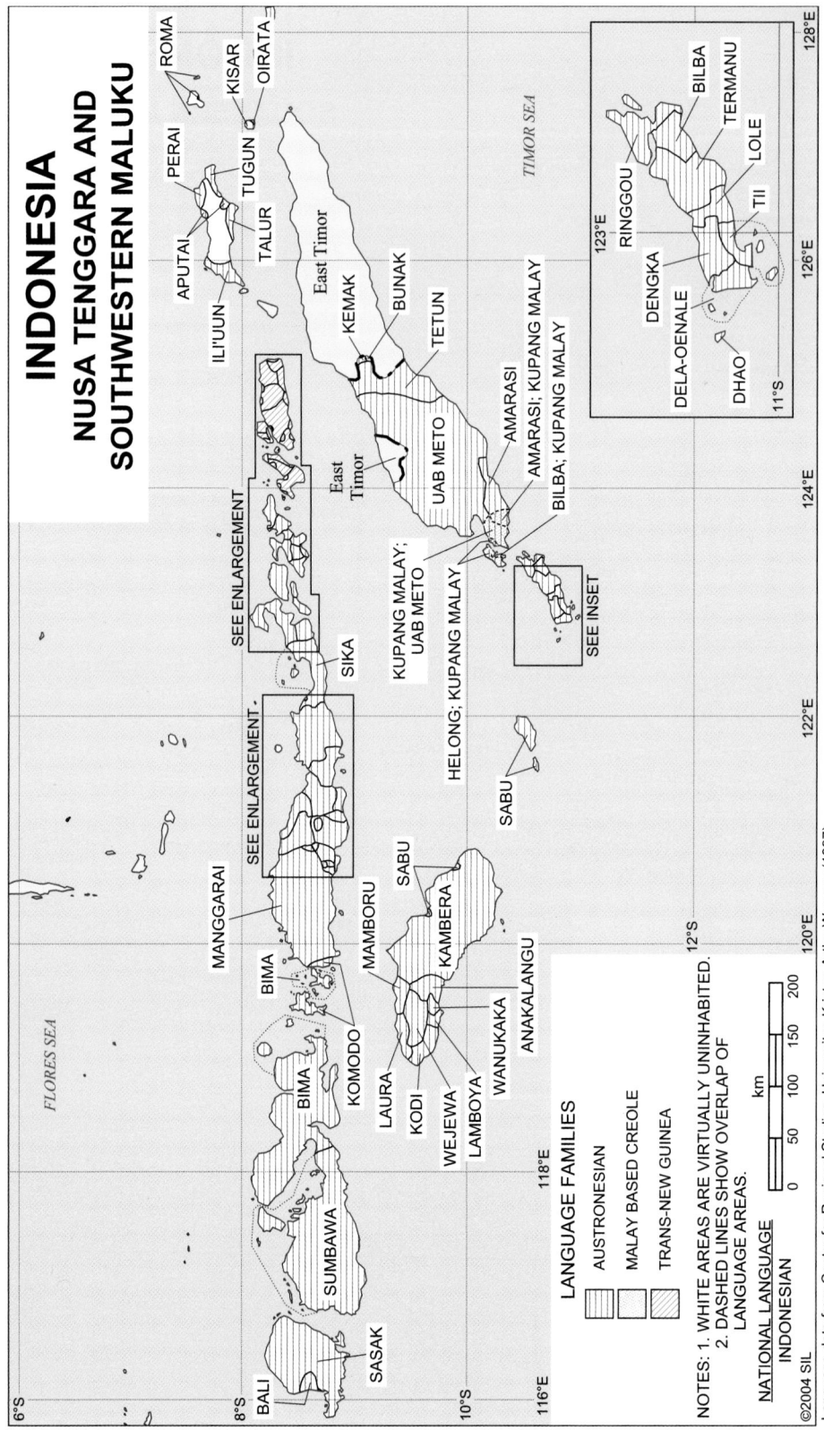

INDONESIA
NUSA TENGGARA AND
SOUTHWESTERN MALUKU

LANGUAGE FAMILIES

AUSTRONESIAN
MALAY BASED CREOLE
TRANS-NEW GUINEA

NOTES: 1. WHITE AREAS ARE VIRTUALLY UNINHABITED.
2. DASHED LINES SHOW OVERLAP OF
LANGUAGE AREAS.

NATIONAL LANGUAGE
INDONESIAN

km
0   50   100   150   200

©2004 SIL

Language data from Centre for Regional Studies, Universitas Kristen Artha Wacana (1997)

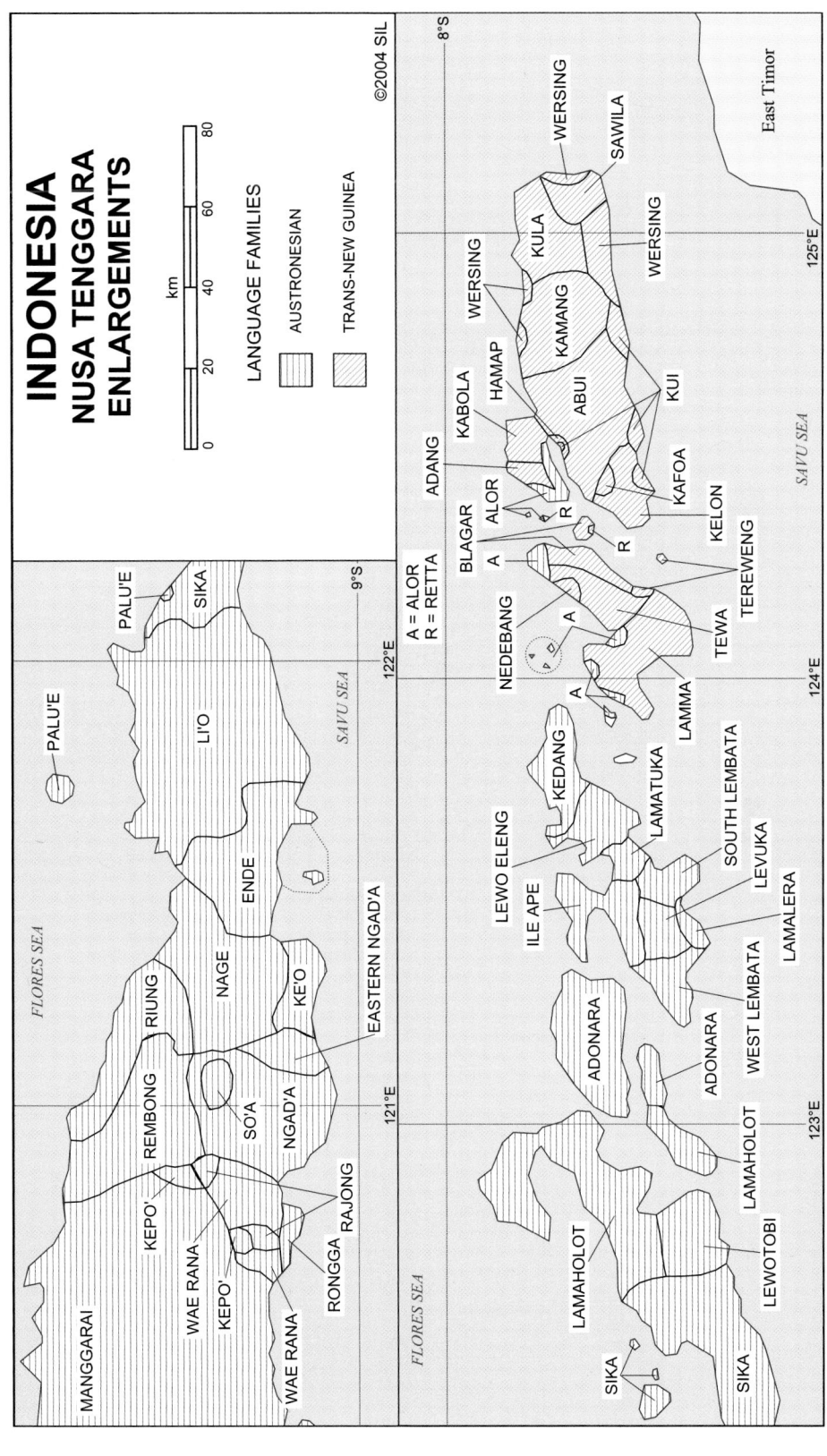

INDONESIA
NUSA TENGGARA
ENLARGEMENTS

©2004 SIL

LANGUAGE FAMILIES

AUSTRONESIAN

TRANS-NEW GUINEA

A = ALOR
R = RETTA

Language data from Center for Regional Studies, Universitas Kristen Artha Wacana (1997)

Indonesia, Papua: Index Of Languages

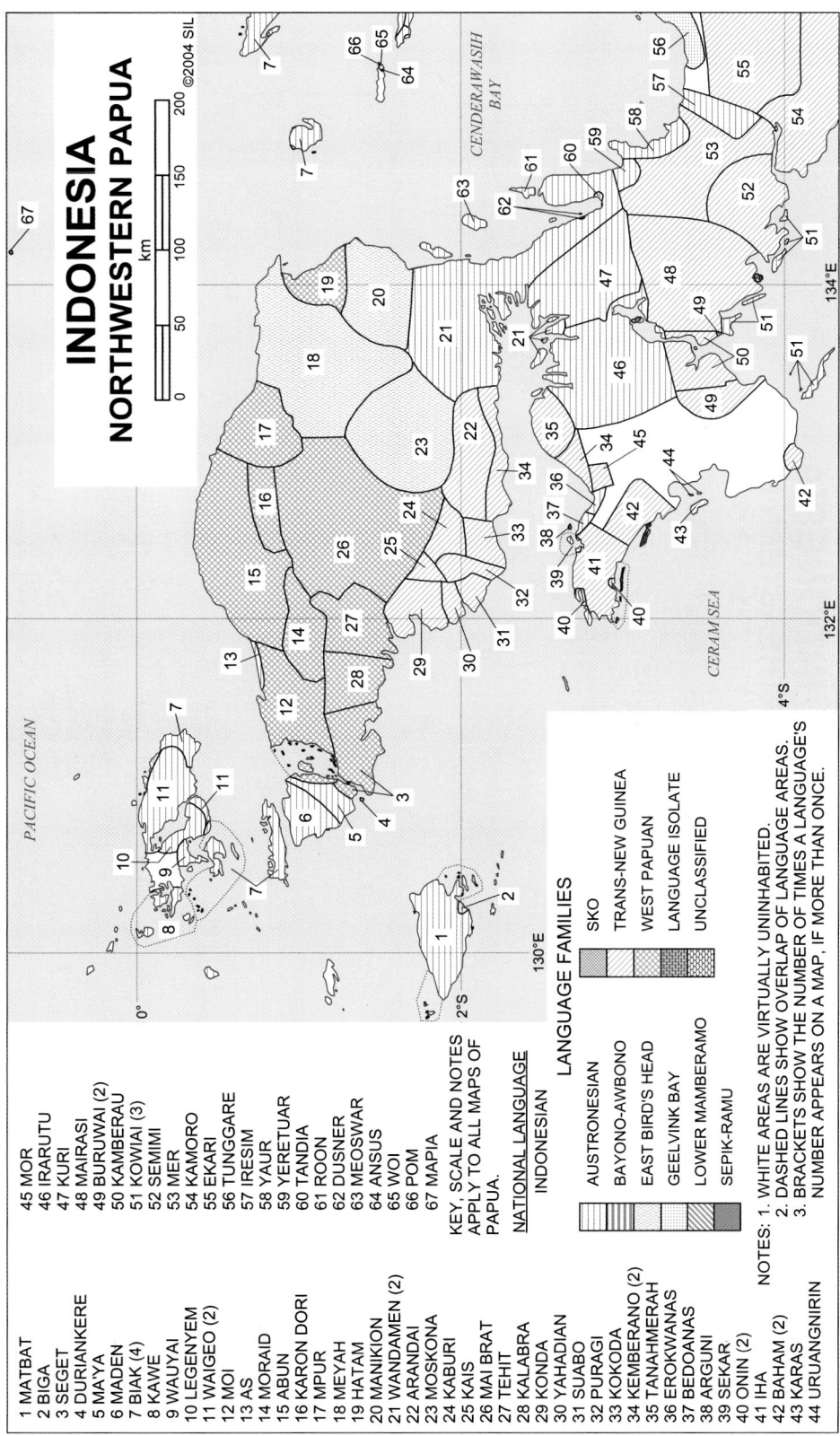

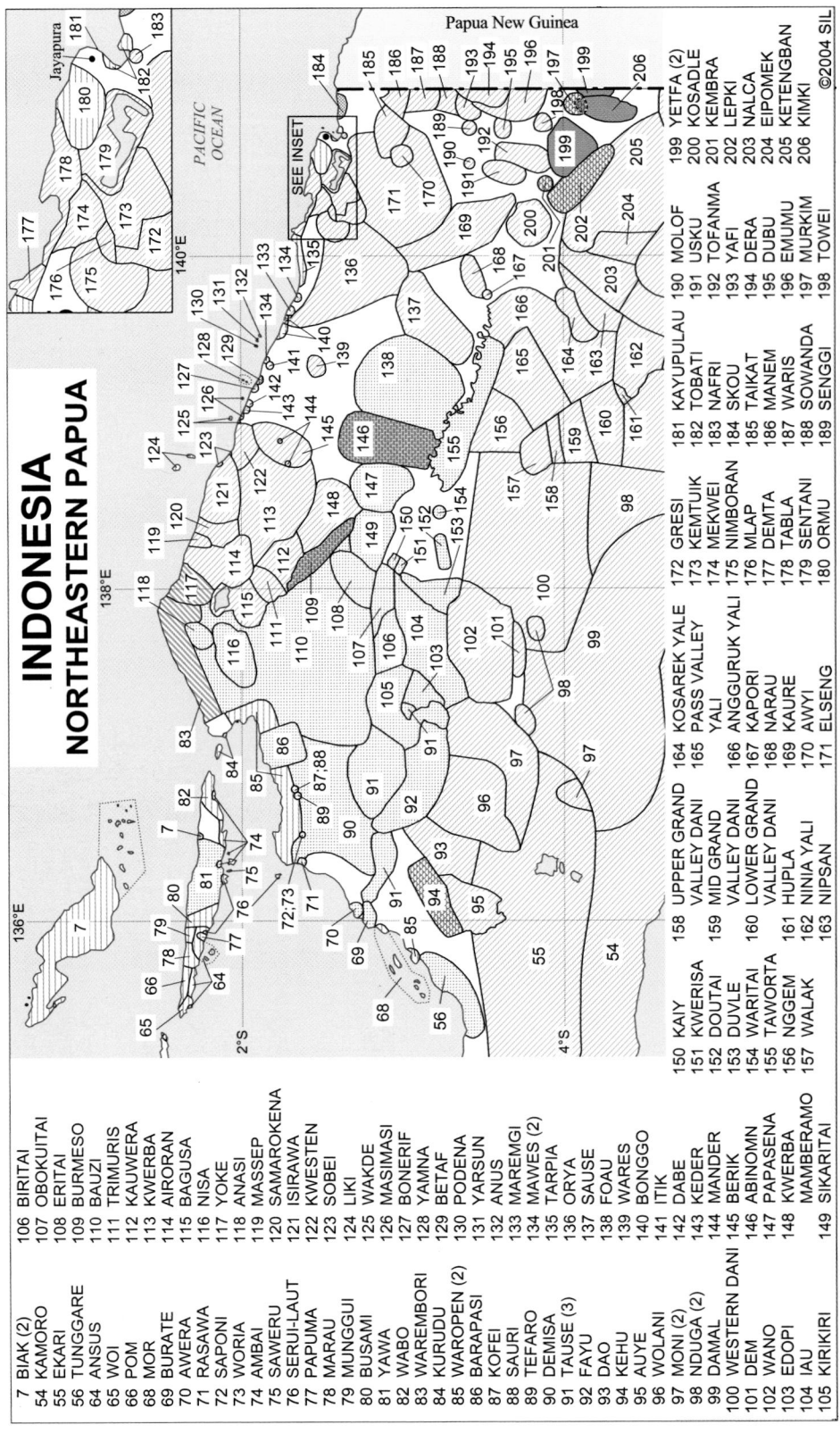

INDONESIA NORTHEASTERN PAPUA

©2004 SIL

#	Name	#	Name
7	BIAK (2)	106	BIRITAI
54	KAMORO	107	OBOKUITAI
55	EKARI	108	ERITAI
56	TUNGGARE	109	BURMESO
64	ANSUS	110	BAUZI
65	WOI	111	TRIMURIS
66	POM	112	KAUWERA
68	MOR	113	KWERBA
69	BURATE	114	AIRORAN
70	AWERA	115	BAGUSA
71	RASAWA	116	NISA
72	SAPONI	117	YOKE
73	WORIA	118	ANASI
74	AMBAI	119	MASSEP
75	SAWERU	120	SAMAROKENA
76	SERUI-LAUT	121	ISIRAWA
77	PAPUMA	122	KWESTEN
78	MARAU	123	SOBEI
79	MUNGGUI	124	LIKI
80	BUSAMI	125	WAKDE
81	YAWA	126	MASIMASI
82	WABO	127	BONERIF
83	WAREMBORI	128	YAMNA
84	KURUDU	129	BETAF
85	WAROPEN (2)	130	PODENA
86	BARAPASI	131	YARSUN
87	KOFEI	132	ANUS
88	SAURI	133	MAREMGI
89	TEFARO	134	MAWES (2)
90	DEMISA	135	TARPIA
91	TAUSE (3)	136	ORYA
92	FAYU	137	SAUSE
93	DAO	138	FOAU
94	KEHU	139	WARES
95	AUYE	140	BONGGO
96	WOLANI	141	ITIK
97	MONI (2)	142	DABE
98	NDUGA (2)	143	KEDER
99	DAMAL	144	MANDER
100	WESTERN DANI	145	BERIK
101	DEM	146	ABINOMN
102	WANO	147	PAPASENA
103	EDOPI	148	KWERBA MAMBERAMO
104	IAU	149	SIKARITAI
105	KIRIKIRI		

#	Name	#	Name
150	KAIY	172	GRESI
151	KWERISA	173	KEMTUIK
152	DOUTAI	174	MEKWEI
153	DUVLE	175	NIMBORAN
154	WARITAI	176	MLAP
155	TAWORTA	177	DEMTA
156	NGGEM	178	TABLA
157	WALAK	179	SENTANI
158	UPPER GRAND VALLEY DANI	180	ORMU
159	MID GRAND VALLEY DANI	181	KAYUPULAU
160	LOWER GRAND VALLEY DANI	182	TOBATI
161	HUPLA	183	NAFRI
162	NINIA YALI	184	SKOU
163	NIPSAN	185	TAIKAT
164	KOSAREK YALE	186	MANEM
165	PASS VALLEY YALI	187	WARIS
166	ANGGURUK YALI	188	SOWANDA
167	KAPORI	189	SENGGI
168	NARAU	190	MOLOF
169	KAURE	191	USKU
170	AWYI	192	TOFANMA
171	ELSENG	193	YAFI
		194	DERA
		195	DUBU
		196	EMUMU
		197	MURKIM
		198	TOWEI
		199	YETFA (2)
		200	KOSADLE
		201	KEMBRA
		202	LEPKI
		203	NALCA
		204	EIPOMEK
		205	KETENGBAN
		206	KIMKI

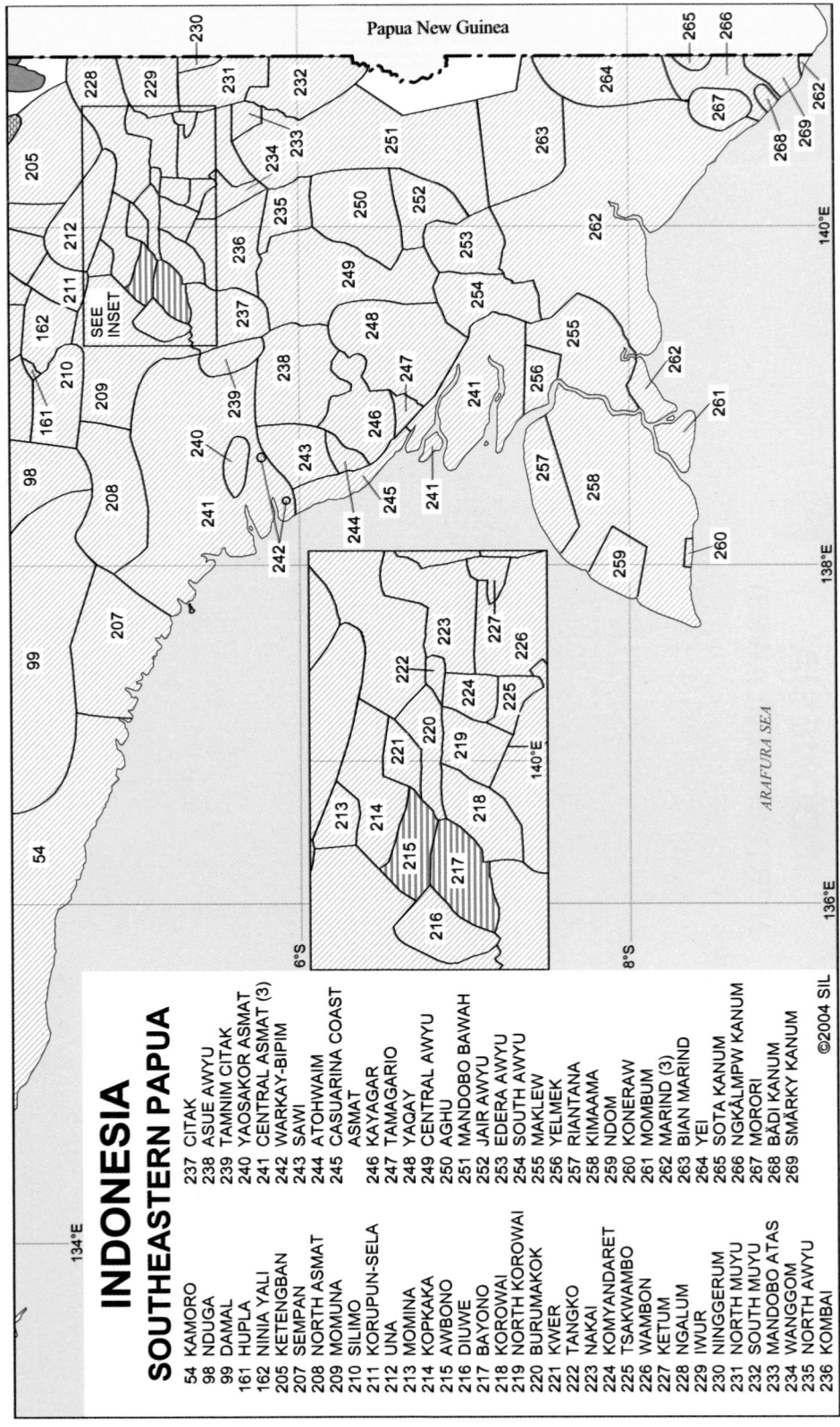

Papua New Guinea

ARAFURA SEA

©2004 SIL

INDONESIA
SOUTHEASTERN PAPUA

54 KAMORO	237 CITAK
98 NDUGA	238 ASUE AWYU
99 DAMAL	239 TAMNIM CITAK
161 HUPLA	240 YAOSAKOR ASMAT
162 NINIA YALI	241 CENTRAL ASMAT (3)
205 KETENGBAN	242 WARKAY-BIPIM
207 SEMPAN	243 SAWI
208 NORTH ASMAT	244 ATOHWAIM
209 MOMUNA	245 CASUARINA COAST
210 SILIMO	ASMAT
211 KORUPUN-SELA	246 KAYAGAR
212 UNA	247 TAMAGARIO
213 MOMINA	248 YAQAY
214 KOPKAKA	249 CENTRAL AWYU
215 AWBONO	250 AGHU
216 DIUWE	251 MANDOBO BAWAH
217 BAYONO	252 JAIR AWYU
218 KOROWAI	253 EDERA AWYU
219 NORTH KOROWAI	254 SOUTH AWYU
220 BURUMAKOK	255 MAKLEW
221 KWER	256 YELMEK
222 TANGKO	257 RIANTANA
223 NAKAI	258 KIMAAMA
224 KOMYANDARET	259 NDOM
225 TSAKWAMBO	260 KONERAW
226 WAMBON	261 MOMBUM
227 KETUM	262 MARIND (3)
228 NGALUM	263 BIAN MARIND
229 IWUR	264 YEI
230 NINGGERUM	265 SOTA KANUM
231 NORTH MUYU	266 NGKÂLMPW KANUM
232 SOUTH MUYU	267 MORORI
233 MANDOBO ATAS	268 BÂDI KANUM
234 WANGGOM	269 SMÄRKY KANUM
235 NORTH AWYU	
236 KOMBAI	

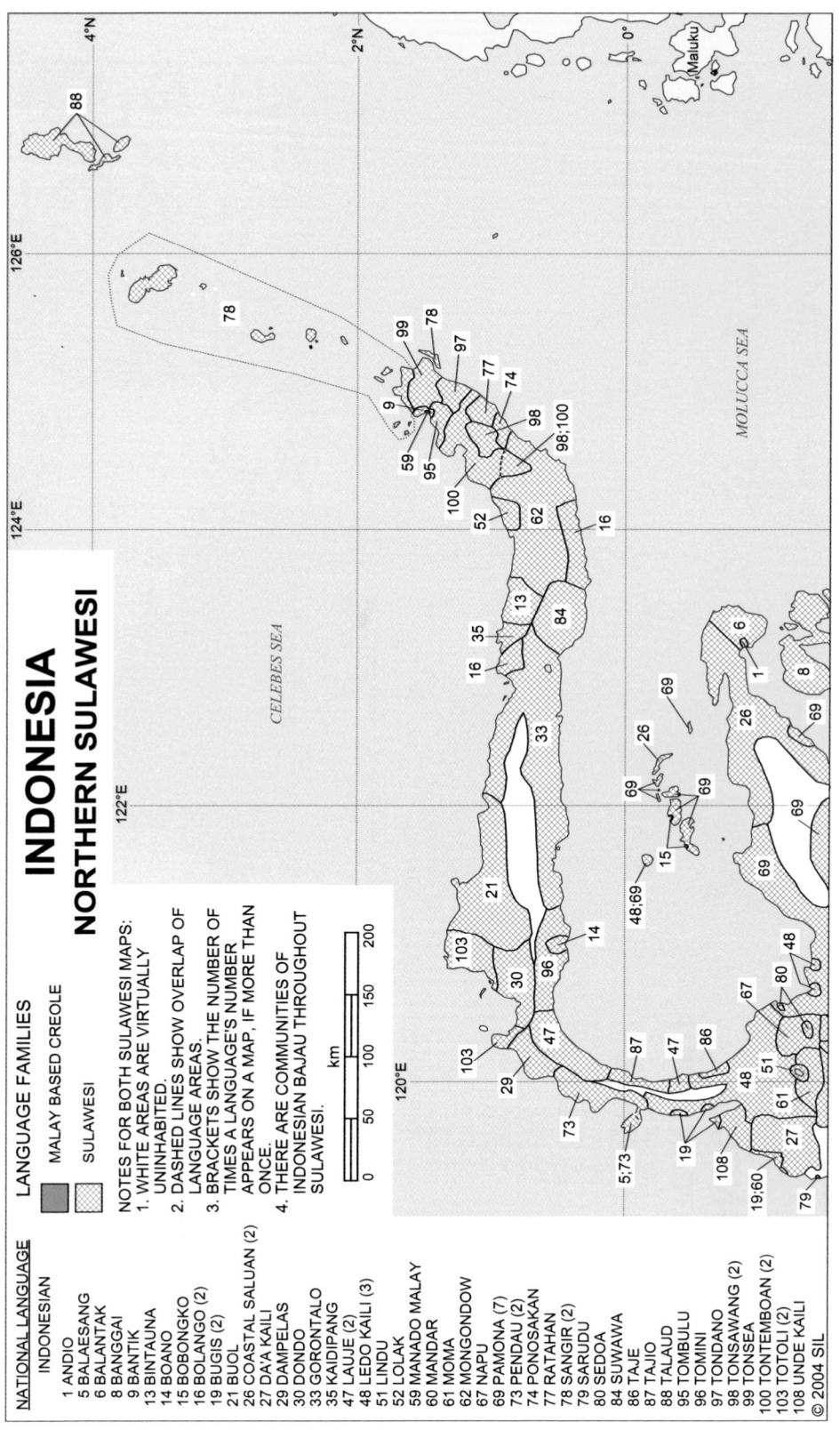

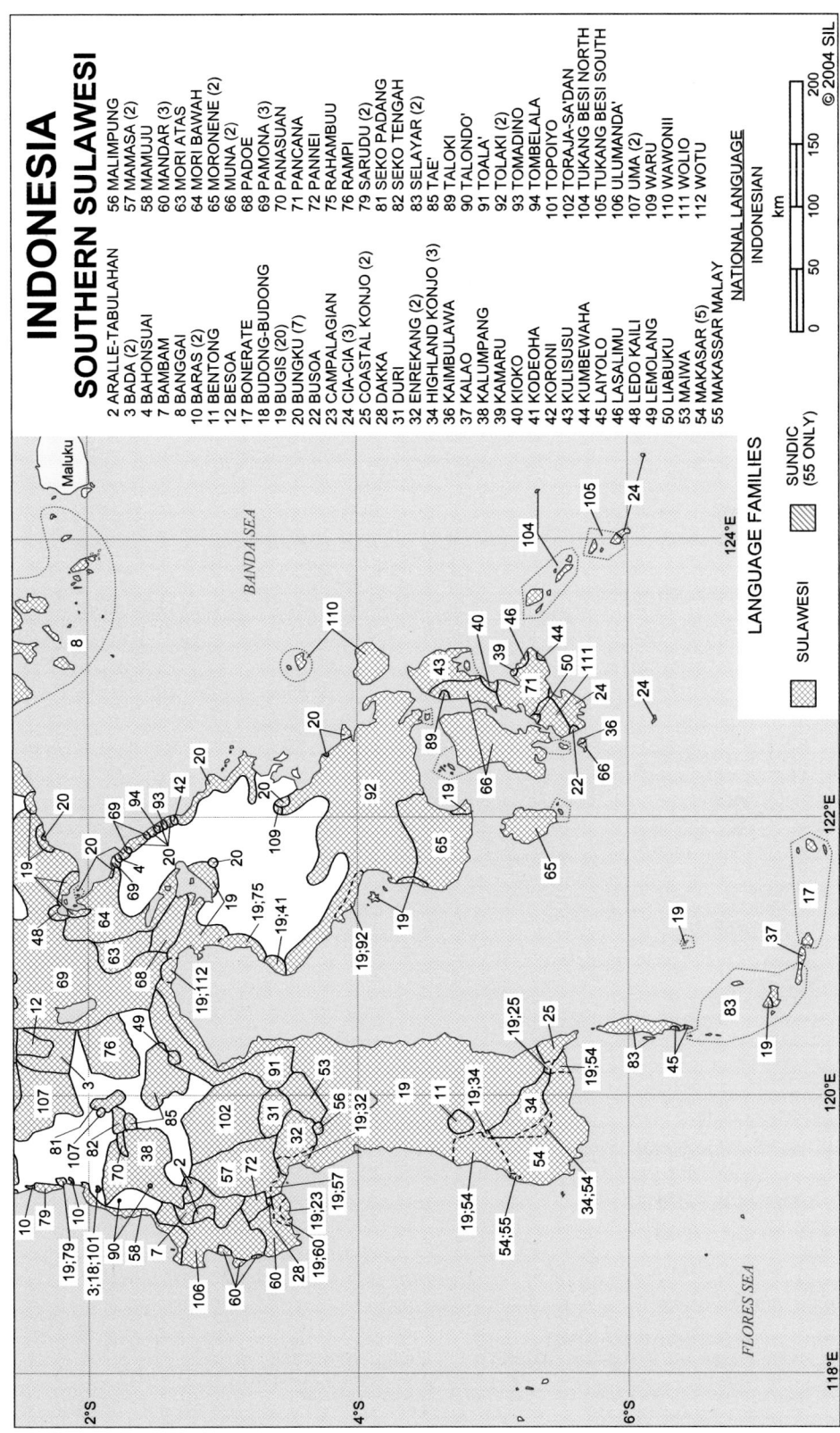

INDONESIA
SOUTHERN SULAWESI

2 ARALLE-TABULAHAN
3 BADA (2)
4 BAHONSUAI
7 BAMBAM
8 BANGGAI
10 BARAS (2)
11 BENTONG
12 BESOA
17 BONERATE
18 BUDONG-BUDONG
19 BUGIS (20)
20 BUNGKU (7)
22 BUSOA
23 CAMPALAGIAN
24 CIA-CIA (3)
25 COASTAL KONJO (2)
28 DAKKA
31 DURI
32 ENREKANG (2)
34 HIGHLAND KONJO (3)
36 KAIMBULAWA
37 KALAO
38 KALUMPANG
39 KAMARU
40 KIOKO
41 KODEOHA
42 KORONI
43 KULISUSU
44 KUMBEWAHA
45 LAIYOLO
46 LASALIMU
48 LEDO KAILI
49 LEMOLANG
50 LIABUKU
53 MAIWA
54 MAKASAR (5)
55 MAKASSAR MALAY

56 MALIMPUNG
57 MAMASA (2)
58 MAMUJU
60 MANDAR (3)
63 MORI ATAS
64 MORI BAWAH
65 MORONENE (2)
66 MUNA (2)
68 PADOE
69 PAMONA (3)
70 PANASUAN
71 PANCANA
72 PANNEI
75 RAHAMBUU
76 RAMPI
79 SARUDU (2)
81 SEKO PADANG
82 SEKO TENGAH
83 SELAYAR (2)
85 TAE'
89 TALOKI
90 TALONDO'
91 TOALA'
92 TOLAKI (2)
93 TOMADINO
94 TOMBELALA
101 TOPOIYO
102 TORAJA-SA'DAN
104 TUKANG BESI NORTH
105 TUKANG BESI SOUTH
106 ULUMANDA'
107 UMA (2)
109 WARU
110 WAWONII
111 WOLIO
112 WOTU

NATIONAL LANGUAGE
INDONESIAN

km
0   50   100 150 200
© 2004 SIL

LANGUAGE FAMILIES

SULAWESI

SUNDIC
(55 ONLY)

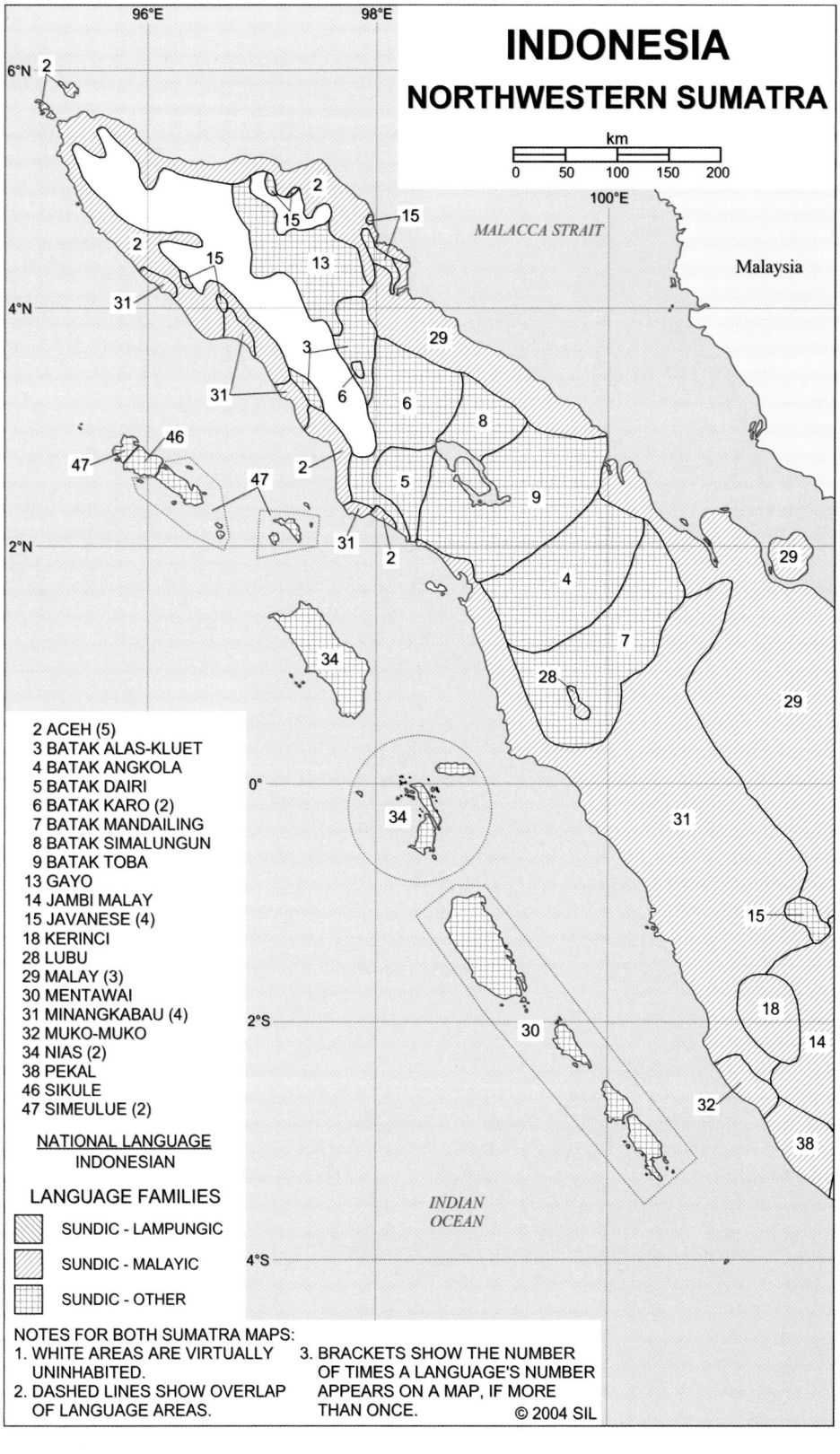

INDONESIA
NORTHWESTERN SUMATRA

km
0   50   100   150   200

MALACCA STRAIT

Malaysia

MALAYSIA

INDIAN OCEAN

2 ACEH (5)
3 BATAK ALAS-KLUET
4 BATAK ANGKOLA
5 BATAK DAIRI
6 BATAK KARO (2)
7 BATAK MANDAILING
8 BATAK SIMALUNGUN
9 BATAK TOBA
13 GAYO
14 JAMBI MALAY
15 JAVANESE (4)
18 KERINCI
28 LUBU
29 MALAY (3)
30 MENTAWAI
31 MINANGKABAU (4)
32 MUKO-MUKO
34 NIAS (2)
38 PEKAL
46 SIKULE
47 SIMEULUE (2)

NATIONAL LANGUAGE
INDONESIAN

LANGUAGE FAMILIES

SUNDIC - LAMPUNGIC

SUNDIC - MALAYIC

SUNDIC - OTHER

NOTES FOR BOTH SUMATRA MAPS:
1. WHITE AREAS ARE VIRTUALLY UNINHABITED.
2. DASHED LINES SHOW OVERLAP OF LANGUAGE AREAS.
3. BRACKETS SHOW THE NUMBER OF TIMES A LANGUAGE'S NUMBER APPEARS ON A MAP, IF MORE THAN ONCE.

© 2004 SIL

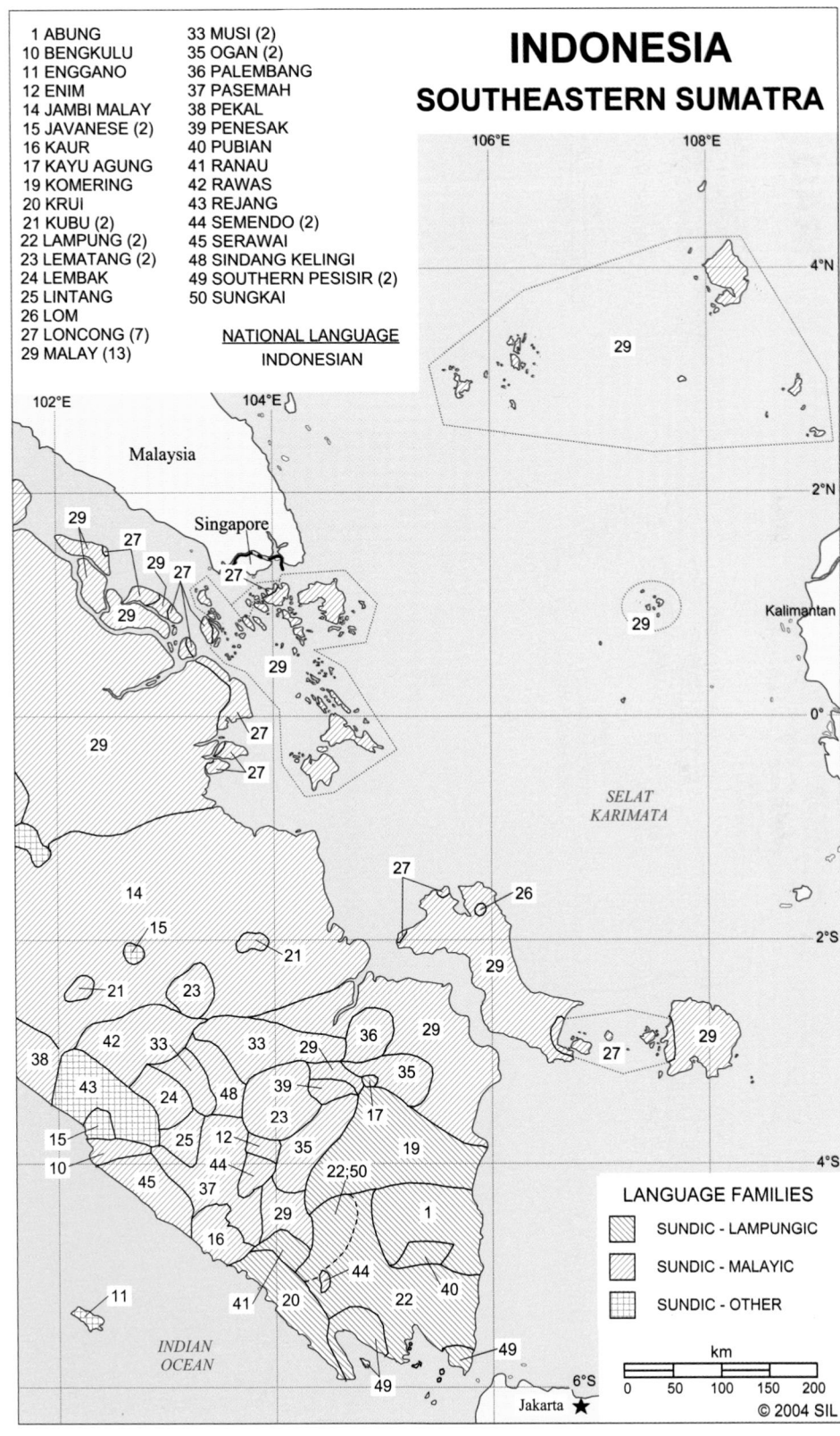

1 ABUNG
10 BENGKULU
11 ENGGANO
12 ENIM
14 JAMBI MALAY
15 JAVANESE (2)
16 KAUR
17 KAYU AGUNG
19 KOMERING
20 KRUI
21 KUBU (2)
22 LAMPUNG (2)
23 LEMATANG (2)
24 LEMBAK
25 LINTANG
26 LOM
27 LONCONG (7)
29 MALAY (13)

33 MUSI (2)
35 OGAN (2)
36 PALEMBANG
37 PASEMAH
38 PEKAL
39 PENESAK
40 PUBIAN
41 RANAU
42 RAWAS
43 REJANG
44 SEMENDO (2)
45 SERAWAI
48 SINDANG KELINGI
49 SOUTHERN PESISIR (2)
50 SUNGKAI

NATIONAL LANGUAGE
INDONESIAN

INDONESIA
SOUTHEASTERN SUMATRA

LANGUAGE FAMILIES

SUNDIC - LAMPUNGIC

SUNDIC - MALAYIC

SUNDIC - OTHER

© 2004 SIL

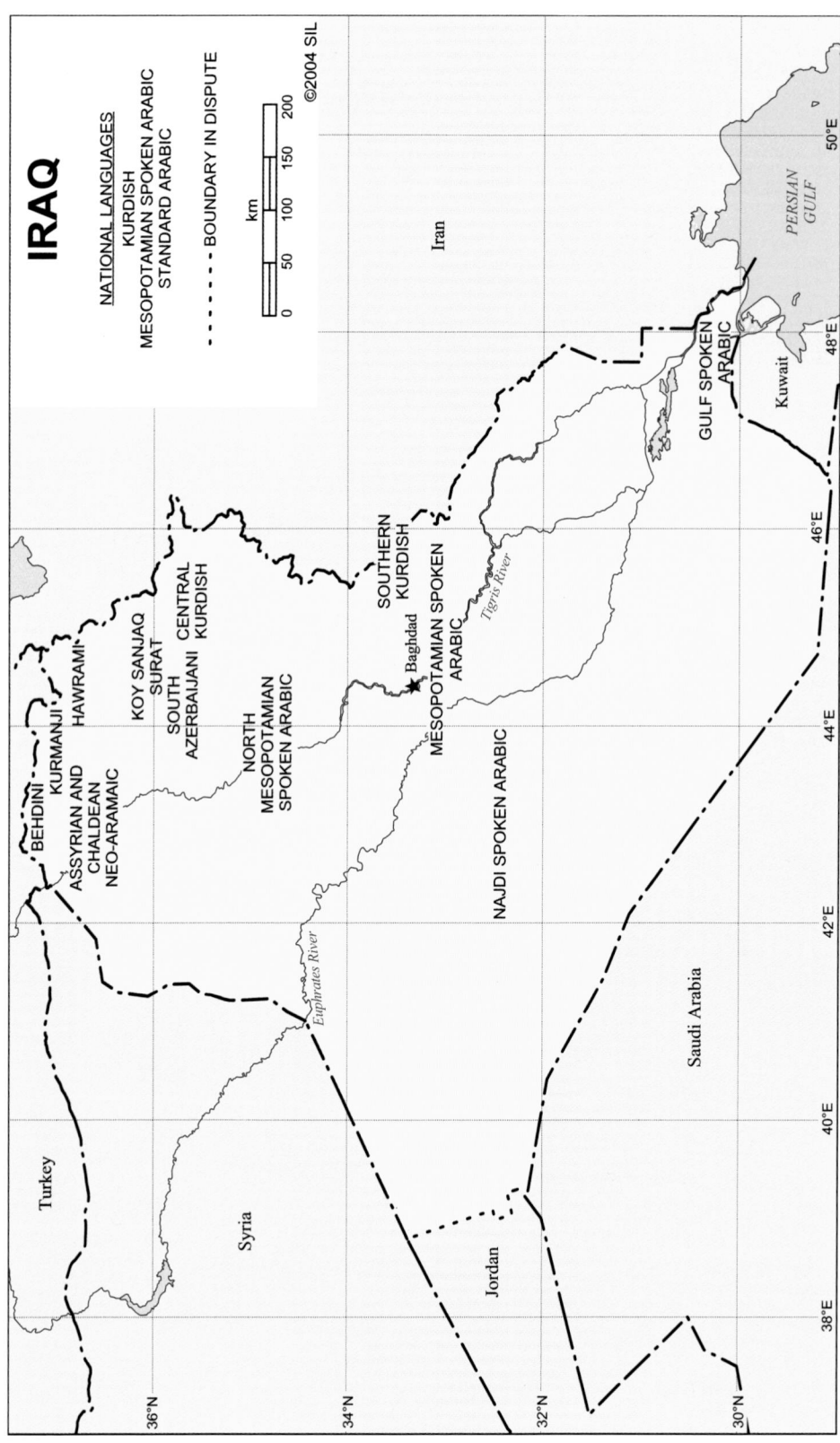

IRAQ

<u>NATIONAL LANGUAGES</u>
KURDISH
MESOPOTAMIAN SPOKEN ARABIC
STANDARD ARABIC

- - - - - BOUNDARY IN DISPUTE

km
0   50   100   150   200

©2004 SIL

Turkey

Syria

Jordan

Saudi Arabia

Iran

Kuwait

PERSIAN GULF

Baghdad

Euphrates River

Tigris River

BEHDINI
KURMANJI
HAWRAMI
ASSYRIAN AND CHALDEAN NEO-ARAMAIC
KOY SANJAQ SURAT
SOUTH AZERBAIJANI
CENTRAL KURDISH
NORTH MESOPOTAMIAN SPOKEN ARABIC
SOUTHERN KURDISH
MESOPOTAMIAN SPOKEN ARABIC
NAJDI SPOKEN ARABIC
GULF SPOKEN ARABIC

36°N
34°N
32°N
30°N

38°E   40°E   42°E   44°E   46°E   48°E   50°E

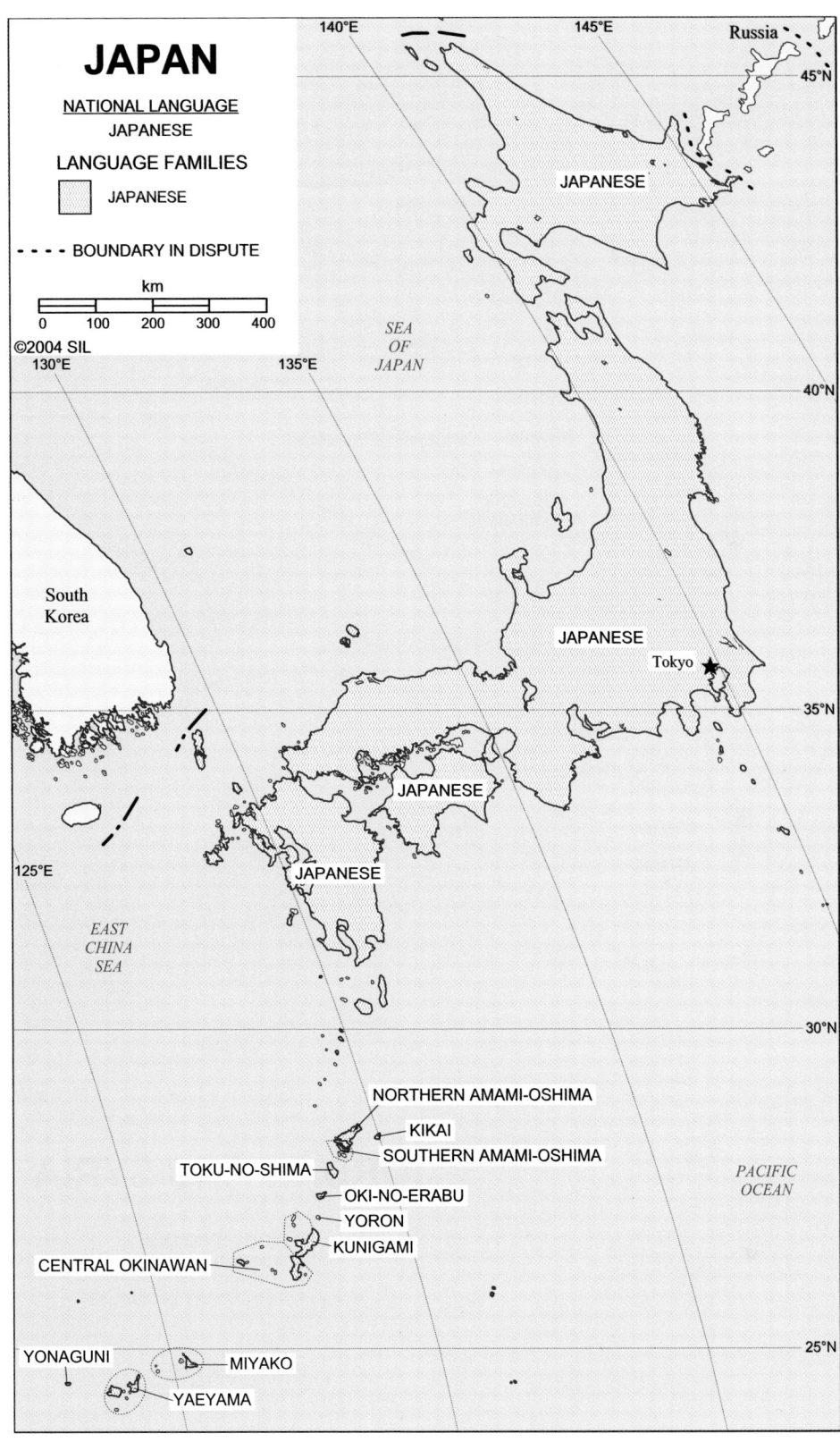

JAPAN

NATIONAL LANGUAGE
JAPANESE

LANGUAGE FAMILIES

JAPANESE

- - - - BOUNDARY IN DISPUTE

km

0   100   200   300   400

©2004 SIL

130°E   135°E

140°E   145°E   Russia

45°N

JAPANESE

SEA OF JAPAN

40°N

South Korea

JAPANESE   Tokyo ★

35°N

JAPANESE

JAPANESE

125°E

EAST CHINA SEA

30°N

NORTHERN AMAMI-OSHIMA

KIKAI

SOUTHERN AMAMI-OSHIMA

TOKU-NO-SHIMA

PACIFIC OCEAN

OKI-NO-ERABU

YORON

KUNIGAMI

CENTRAL OKINAWAN

25°N

YONAGUNI   MIYAKO

YAEYAMA

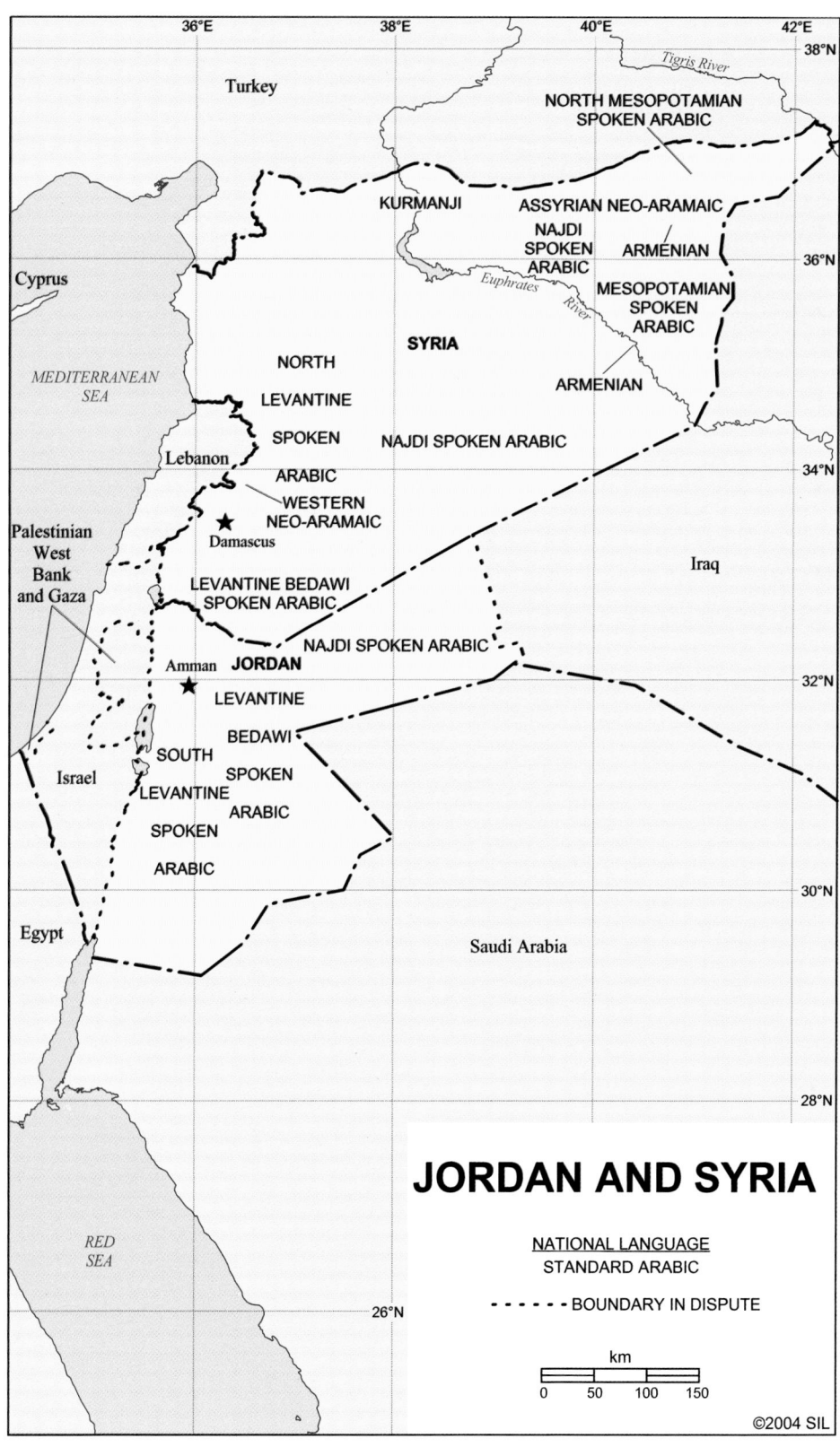

JORDAN AND SYRIA

<u>NATIONAL LANGUAGE</u>
STANDARD ARABIC

- - - - - BOUNDARY IN DISPUTE

km
0   50   100   150

©2004 SIL

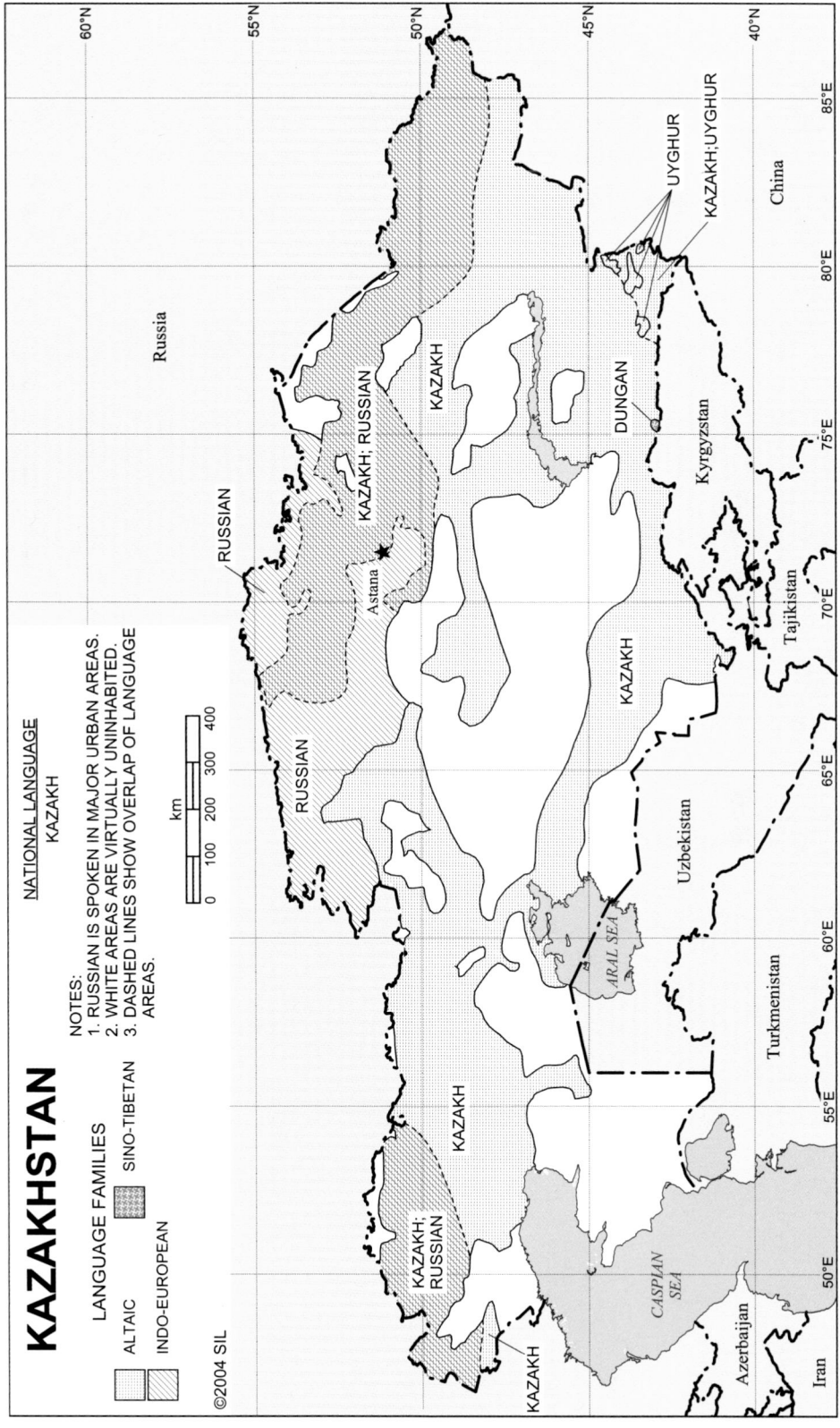

KAZAKHSTAN

LANGUAGE FAMILIES

ALTAIC

INDO-EUROPEAN

SINO-TIBETAN

NATIONAL LANGUAGE
KAZAKH

NOTES:
1. RUSSIAN IS SPOKEN IN MAJOR URBAN AREAS.
2. WHITE AREAS ARE VIRTUALLY UNINHABITED.
3. DASHED LINES SHOW OVERLAP OF LANGUAGE
   AREAS.

km

0   100   200   300   400

©2004 SIL

Russia

RUSSIAN

KAZAKH; RUSSIAN

KAZAKH

UYGHUR

KAZAKH;UYGHUR

China

DUNGAN

Astana

RUSSIAN

KAZAKH

Kyrgyzstan

Tajikistan

KAZAKH; RUSSIAN

KAZAKH

Uzbekistan

ARAL SEA

Turkmenistan

KAZAKH

CASPIAN SEA

Azerbaijan

Iran

60°N

55°N

50°N

45°N

40°N

50°E   55°E   60°E   65°E   70°E   75°E   80°E   85°E

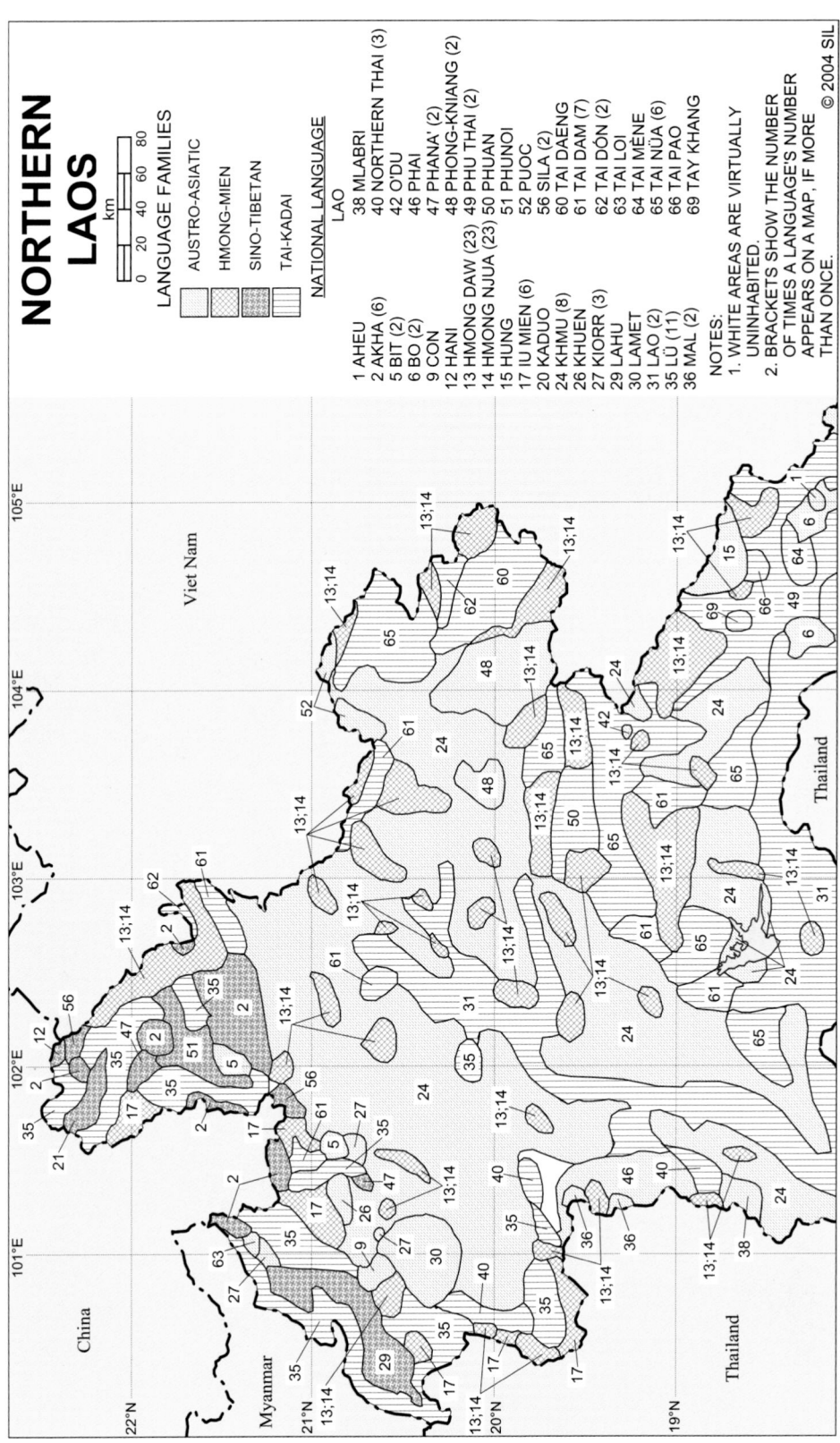

NORTHERN LAOS

km
0 20 40 60 80

LANGUAGE FAMILIES
AUSTRO-ASIATIC
HMONG-MIEN
SINO-TIBETAN
TAI-KADAI

NATIONAL LANGUAGE
LAO

© 2004 SIL

1 AHEU
2 AKHA (6)
5 BIT (2)
6 BO (2)
9 CON
12 HANI
13 HMONG DAW (23)
14 HMONG NJUA (23)
15 HUNG
17 IU MIEN (6)
20 KADUO
24 KHMU (8)
26 KHUEN
27 KIORR (3)
29 LAHU
30 LAMET
31 LAO (2)
35 LÜ (11)
36 MAL (2)
38 MLABRI
40 NORTHERN THAI (3)
42 O'DU
46 PHAI
47 PHANA' (2)
48 PHONG-KNIANG (2)
49 PHU THAI (2)
50 PHUAN
51 PHUNOI
52 PUOC
56 SILA (2)
60 TAI DAENG
61 TAI DAM (7)
62 TAI DÒN (2)
63 TAI LOI
64 TAI MÈNE
65 TAI NÜA (6)
66 TAI PAO
69 TAY KHANG

NOTES:
1. WHITE AREAS ARE VIRTUALLY UNINHABITED.
2. BRACKETS SHOW THE NUMBER OF TIMES A LANGUAGE'S NUMBER APPEARS ON A MAP, IF MORE THAN ONCE.

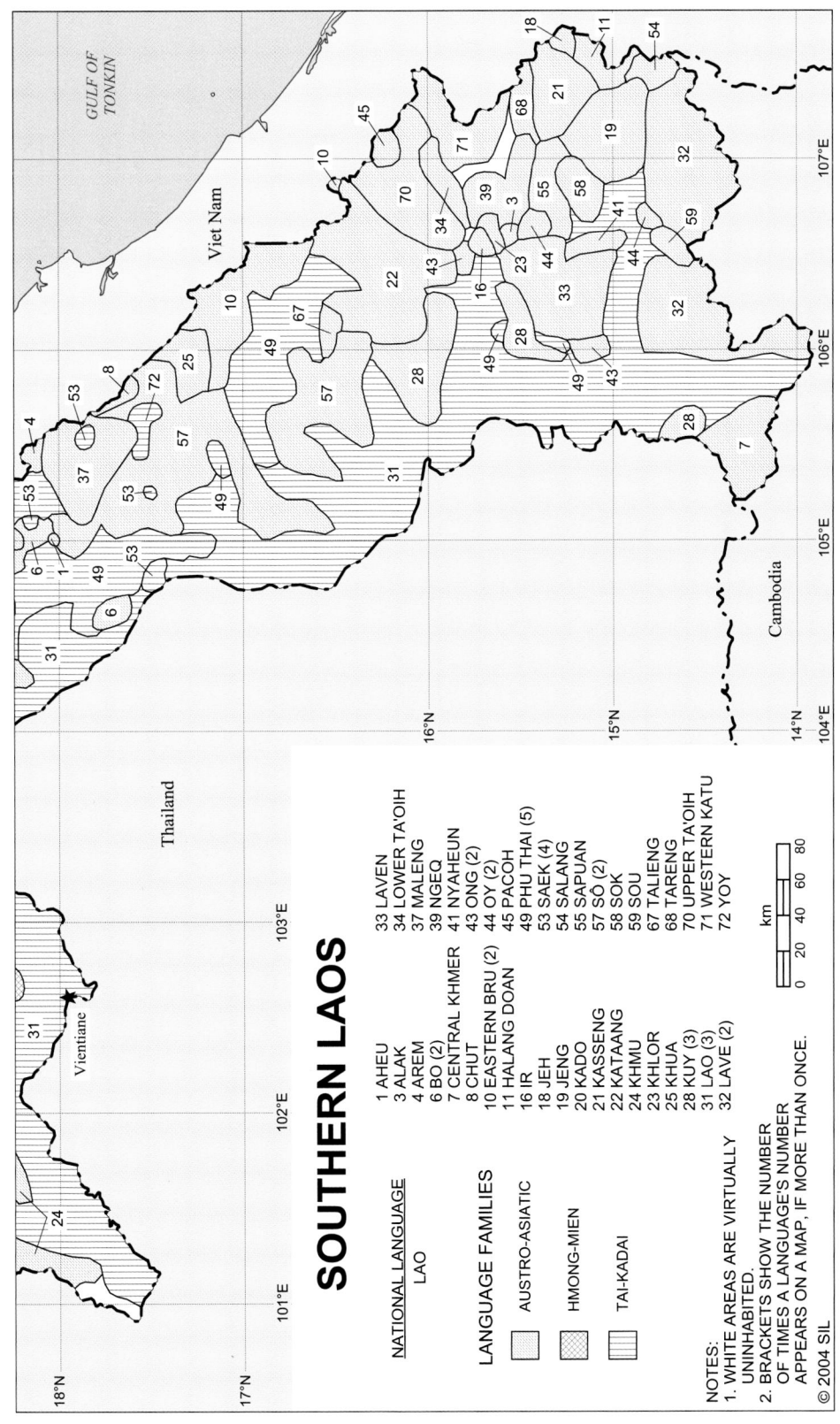

SOUTHERN LAOS

NATIONAL LANGUAGE
LAO

LANGUAGE FAMILIES

AUSTRO-ASIATIC

HMONG-MIEN

TAI-KADAI

1 AHEU	33 LAVEN
3 ALAK	34 LOWER TA'OIH
4 AREM	37 MALENG
6 BO (2)	39 NGEQ
7 CENTRAL KHMER	41 NYAHEUN
8 CHUT	43 ONG (2)
10 EASTERN BRU (2)	44 OY (2)
11 HALANG DOAN	45 PACOH
16 IR	49 PHU THAI (5)
18 JEH	53 SAEK (4)
19 JENG	54 SALANG
20 KADO	55 SAPUAN
21 KASSENG	57 SÔ (2)
22 KATAANG	58 SOK
24 KHMU	59 SOU
23 KHLOR	67 TALIENG
25 KHUA	68 TARENG
28 KUY (3)	70 UPPER TA'OIH
31 LAO (3)	71 WESTERN KATU
32 LAVE (2)	72 YOY

km

0 20 40 60 80

NOTES:
1. WHITE AREAS ARE VIRTUALLY UNINHABITED.
2. BRACKETS SHOW THE NUMBER OF TIMES A LANGUAGE'S NUMBER APPEARS ON A MAP, IF MORE THAN ONCE.

© 2004 SIL

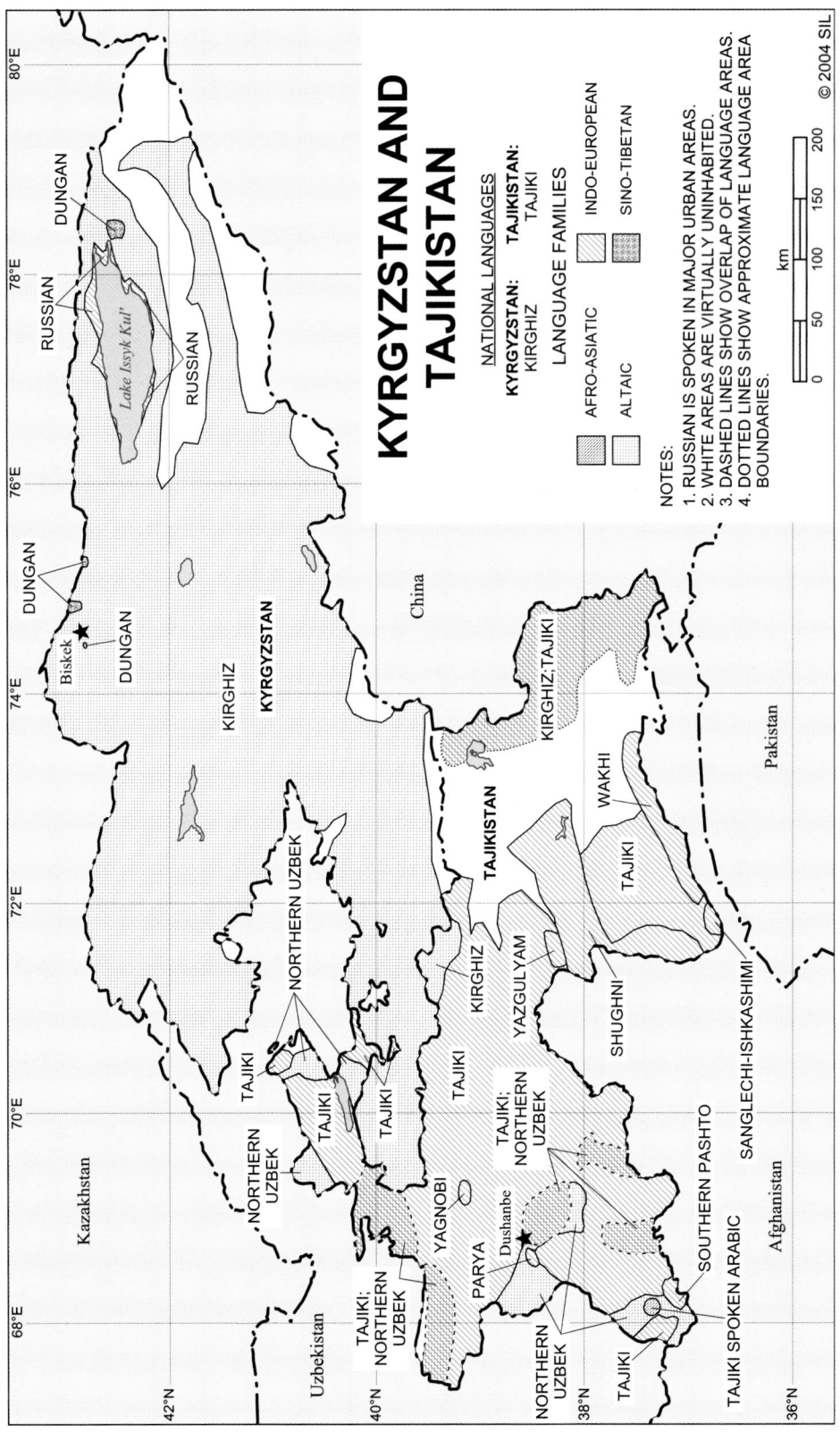

KYRGYZSTAN AND TAJIKISTAN

NATIONAL LANGUAGES
KYRGYZSTAN: TAJIKISTAN:
KIRGHIZ   TAJIKI

LANGUAGE FAMILIES
AFRO-ASIATIC   INDO-EUROPEAN
ALTAIC   SINO-TIBETAN

NOTES:
1. RUSSIAN IS SPOKEN IN MAJOR URBAN AREAS.
2. WHITE AREAS ARE VIRTUALLY UNINHABITED.
3. DASHED LINES SHOW OVERLAP OF LANGUAGE AREAS.
4. DOTTED LINES SHOW APPROXIMATE LANGUAGE AREA BOUNDARIES.

© 2004 SIL

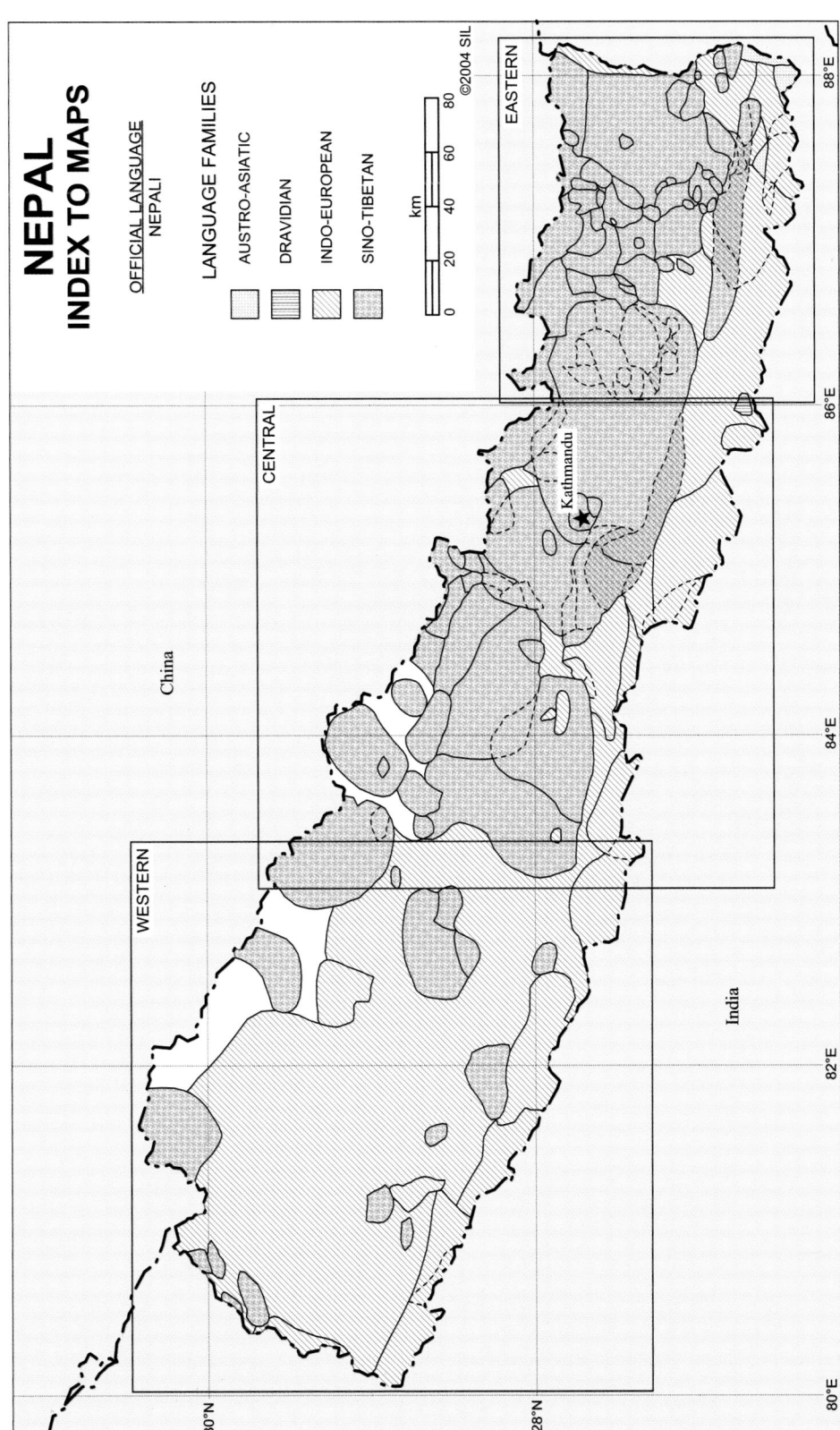

NEPAL
INDEX TO MAPS

OFFICIAL LANGUAGE
NEPALI

LANGUAGE FAMILIES

AUSTRO-ASIATIC

DRAVIDIAN

INDO-EUROPEAN

SINO-TIBETAN

km

0   20   40   60   80

©2004 SIL

EASTERN

CENTRAL

WESTERN

China

Kathmandu

India

88°E

86°E

84°E

82°E

80°E

30°N

28°N

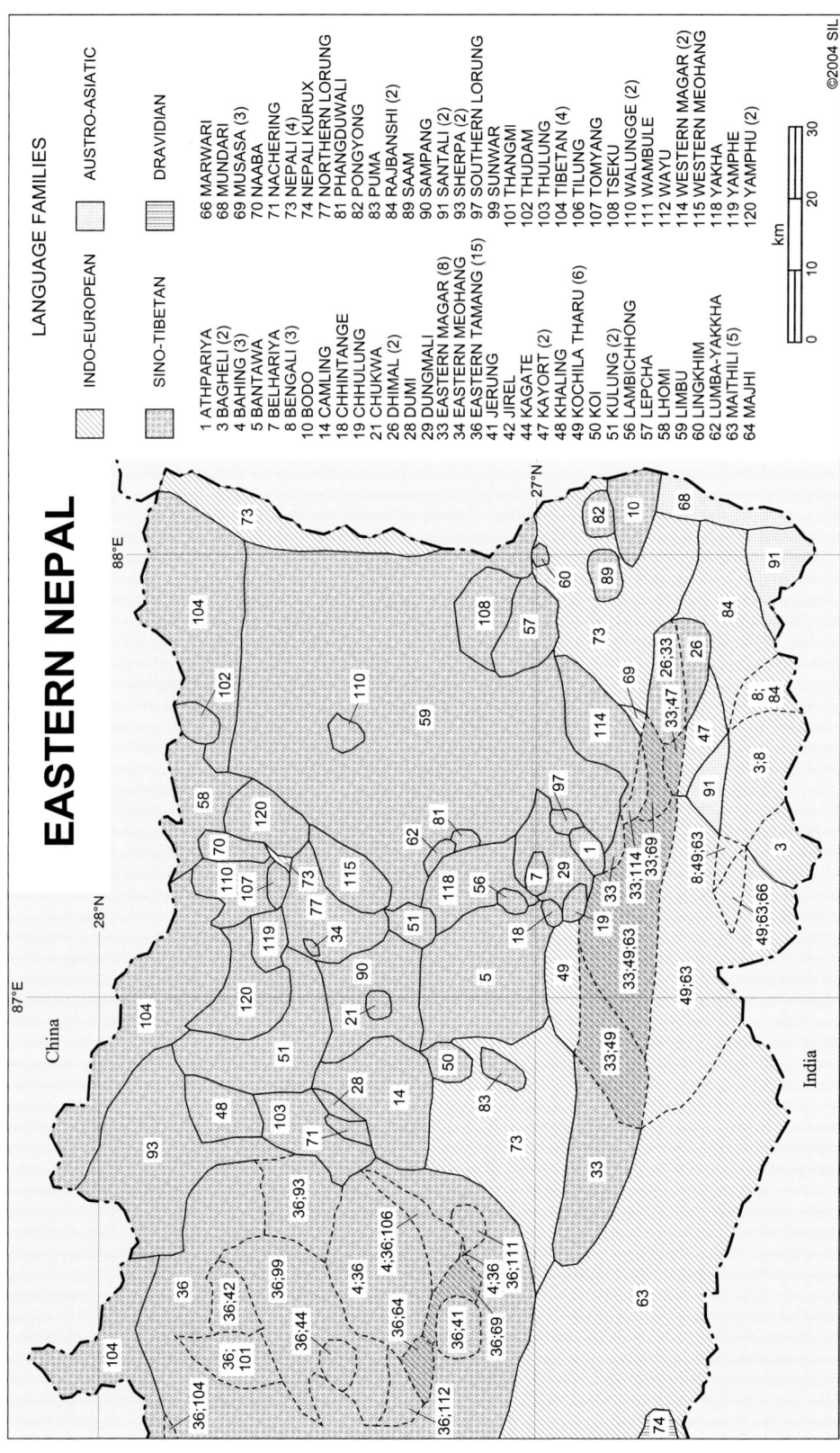

CENTRAL NEPAL

©2004 SIL

LANGUAGE FAMILIES

▨ INDO-EUROPEAN	▦ DRAVIDIAN
▨ SINO-TIBETAN	

2 AWADHI (2)
6 BARAAMU
9 BHOJPURI (4)
11 BOTE-MAJHI (2)
12 BUHYAL
15 CHANTYAL
17 CHEPANG (4)
20 CHITWANIA THARU (2)
23 DARAI (2)
25 DHANWAR (2)
27 DOLPO (2)
30 DZONGKHA
31 EASTERN GORKHA TAMANG (4)
32 EASTERN GURUNG
33 EASTERN MAGAR (2)
36 EASTERN TAMANG (6)
38 HELAMBU SHERPA (2)
39 HINDI
45 KAIKE
49 KOCHILA THARU
53 KUMHALI
54 KUTANG GHALE
55 KYERUNG (2)

61 LOWA
63 MAITHILI (5)
65 MANANGBA
66 MARWARI (3)
72 NAR PHU
73 NEPALI (4)
74 NEPALI KURUX
75 NEWAR
76 NORTHERN GHALE
78 NORTHWESTERN TAMANG
79 NUBRI
80 PALPA
92 SEKE
96 SOUTHERN GHALE (2)
98 SOUTHWESTERN TAMANG (3)
100 THAKALI
104 TIBETAN (4)
105 TICHURONG
109 TSUM
113 WESTERN GURUNG (2)
114 WESTERN MAGAR
117 WESTERN TAMANG (4)

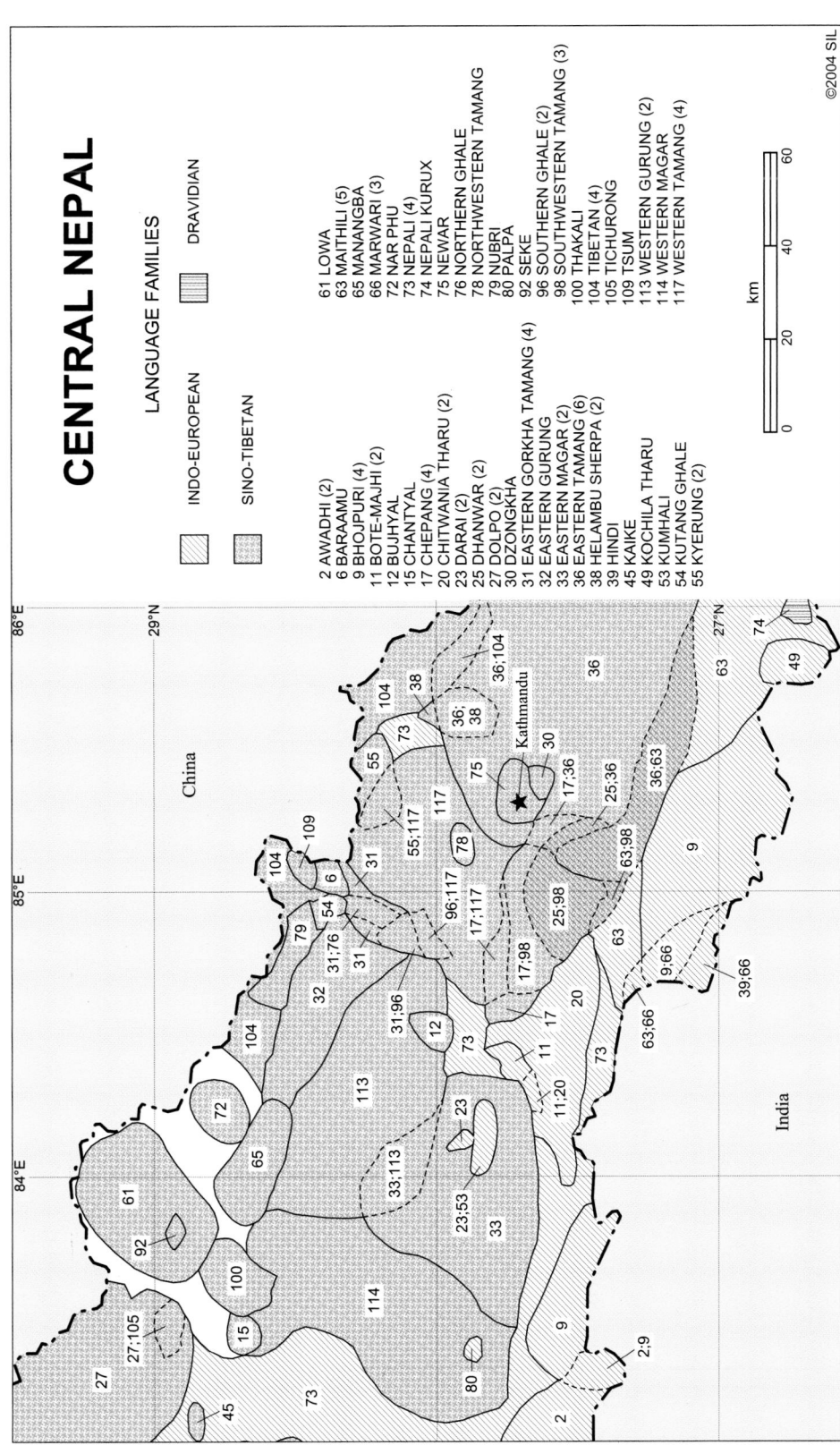

km
0   20   40   60

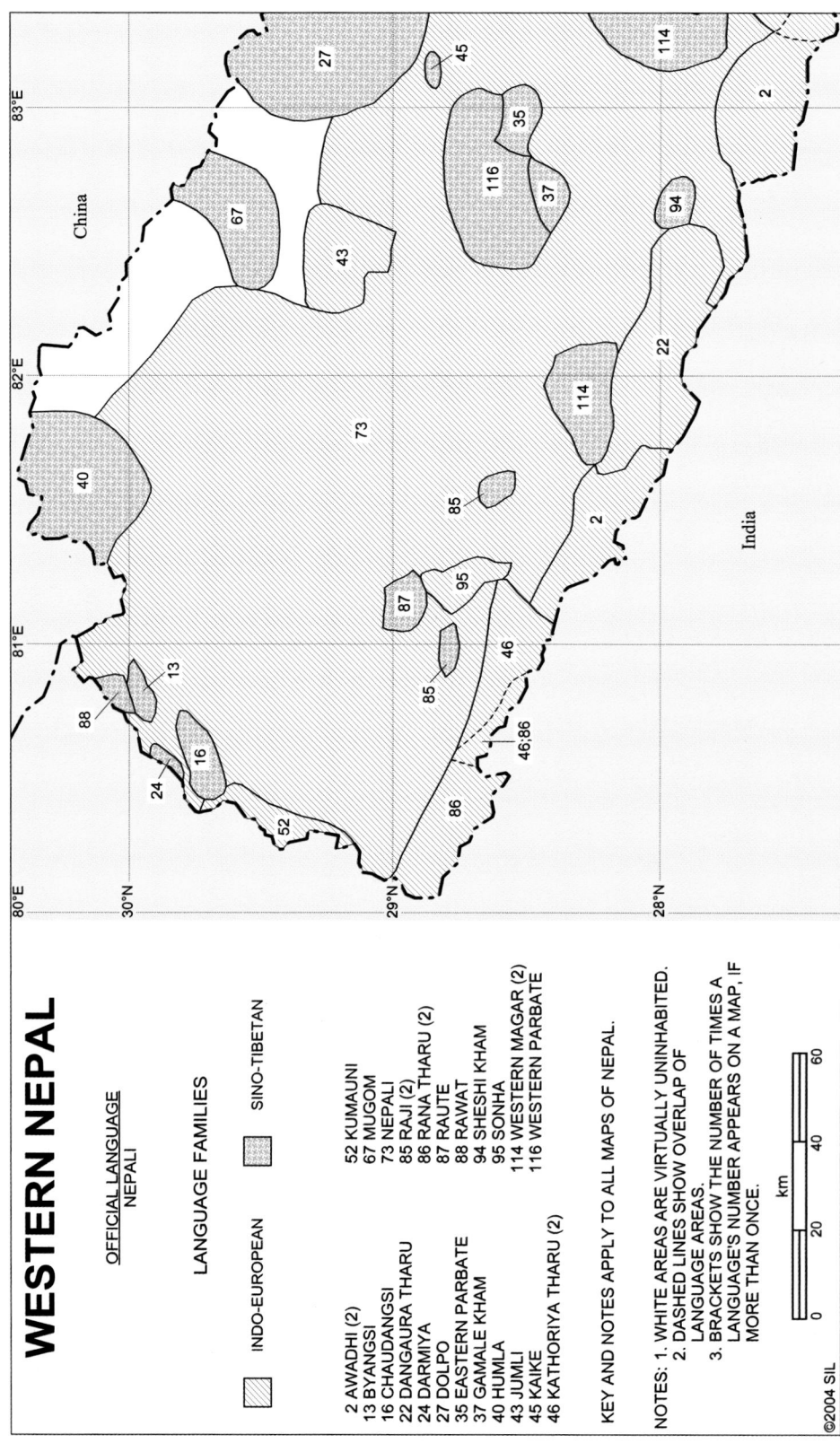

WESTERN NEPAL

OFFICIAL LANGUAGE
NEPALI

LANGUAGE FAMILIES

INDO-EUROPEAN

SINO-TIBETAN

2 AWADHI (2)
13 BYANGSI
16 CHAUDANGSI
22 DANGAURA THARU
24 DARMIYA
27 DOLPO
35 EASTERN PARBATE
37 GAMALE KHAM
40 HUMLA
43 JUMLI
45 KAIKE
46 KATHORIYA THARU (2)

52 KUMAUNI
67 MUGOM
73 NEPALI
85 RAJI (2)
86 RANA THARU (2)
87 RAUTE
88 RAWAT
94 SHESHI KHAM
95 SONHA
114 WESTERN MAGAR (2)
116 WESTERN PARBATE

KEY AND NOTES APPLY TO ALL MAPS OF NEPAL.

NOTES: 1. WHITE AREAS ARE VIRTUALLY UNINHABITED.
2. DASHED LINES SHOW OVERLAP OF
LANGUAGE AREAS.
3. BRACKETS SHOW THE NUMBER OF TIMES A
LANGUAGE'S NUMBER APPEARS ON A MAP, IF
MORE THAN ONCE.

km

0   20   40   60

©2004 SIL

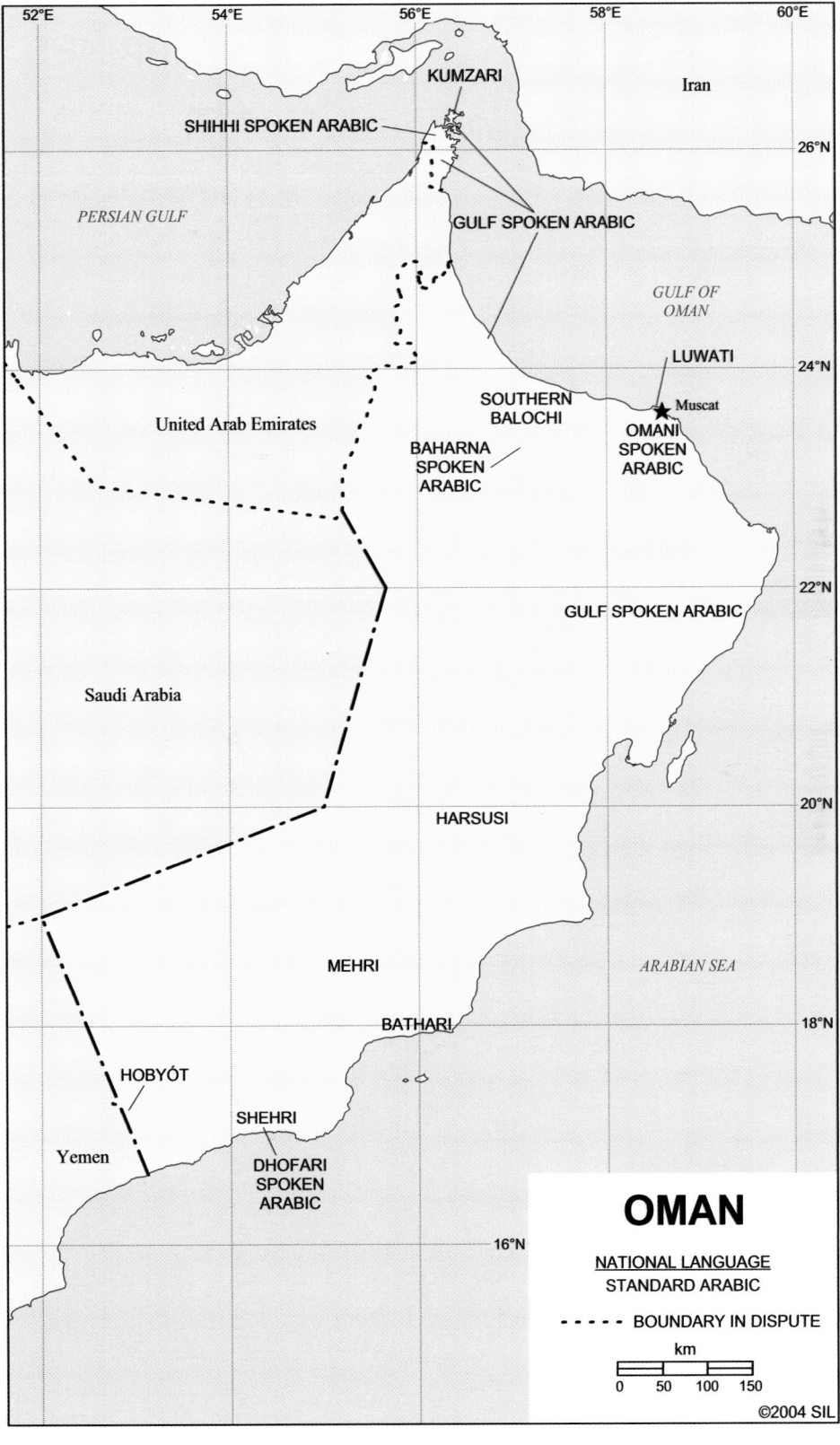

52°E   54°E   56°E   58°E   60°E

KUMZARI   Iran

SHIHHI SPOKEN ARABIC

26°N

PERSIAN GULF

GULF SPOKEN ARABIC

GULF OF OMAN

LUWATI   24°N

Muscat

SOUTHERN
BALOCHI

OMANI
SPOKEN
ARABIC

United Arab Emirates

BAHARNA
SPOKEN
ARABIC

GULF SPOKEN ARABIC   22°N

Saudi Arabia

20°N

HARSUSI

MEHRI   *ARABIAN SEA*

BATHARI   18°N

HOBYÓT

SHEHRI

Yemen

DHOFARI
SPOKEN
ARABIC

16°N

OMAN

NATIONAL LANGUAGE
STANDARD ARABIC

- - - - BOUNDARY IN DISPUTE

km

0   50   100   150

©2004 SIL

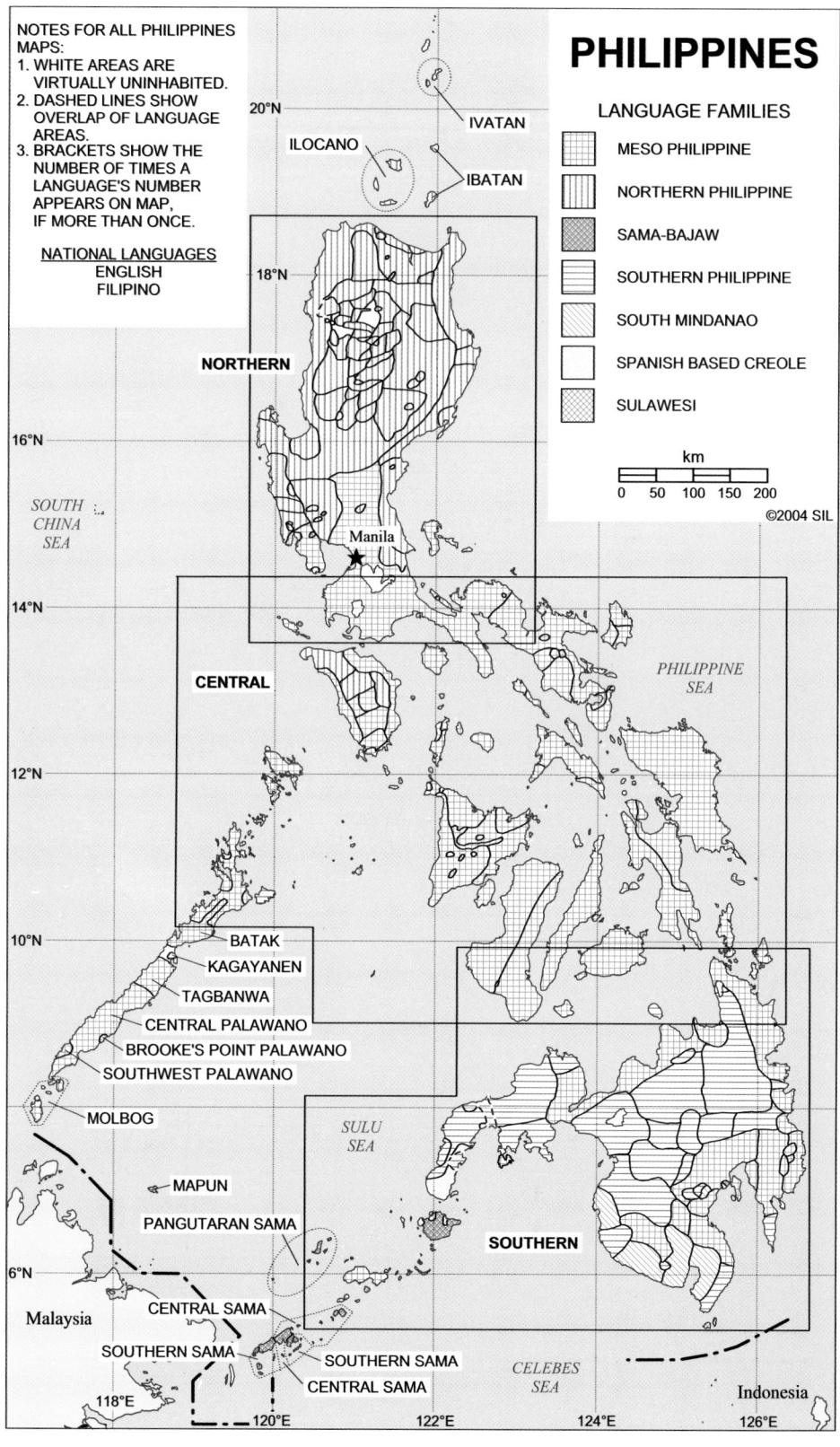

NOTES FOR ALL PHILIPPINES MAPS:
1. WHITE AREAS ARE VIRTUALLY UNINHABITED.
2. DASHED LINES SHOW OVERLAP OF LANGUAGE AREAS.
3. BRACKETS SHOW THE NUMBER OF TIMES A LANGUAGE'S NUMBER APPEARS ON MAP, IF MORE THAN ONCE.

NATIONAL LANGUAGES
ENGLISH
FILIPINO

PHILIPPINES

LANGUAGE FAMILIES

MESO PHILIPPINE

NORTHERN PHILIPPINE

SAMA-BAJAW

SOUTHERN PHILIPPINE

SOUTH MINDANAO

SPANISH BASED CREOLE

SULAWESI

km
0   50   100   150   200

©2004 SIL

IVATAN
ILOCANO
IBATAN

NORTHERN

SOUTH CHINA SEA

Manila

CENTRAL

PHILIPPINE SEA

BATAK
KAGAYANEN
TAGBANWA
CENTRAL PALAWANO
BROOKE'S POINT PALAWANO
SOUTHWEST PALAWANO
MOLBOG

SULU SEA

MAPUN
PANGUTARAN SAMA

SOUTHERN

Malaysia

CENTRAL SAMA
SOUTHERN SAMA
SOUTHERN SAMA
CENTRAL SAMA

CELEBES SEA

Indonesia

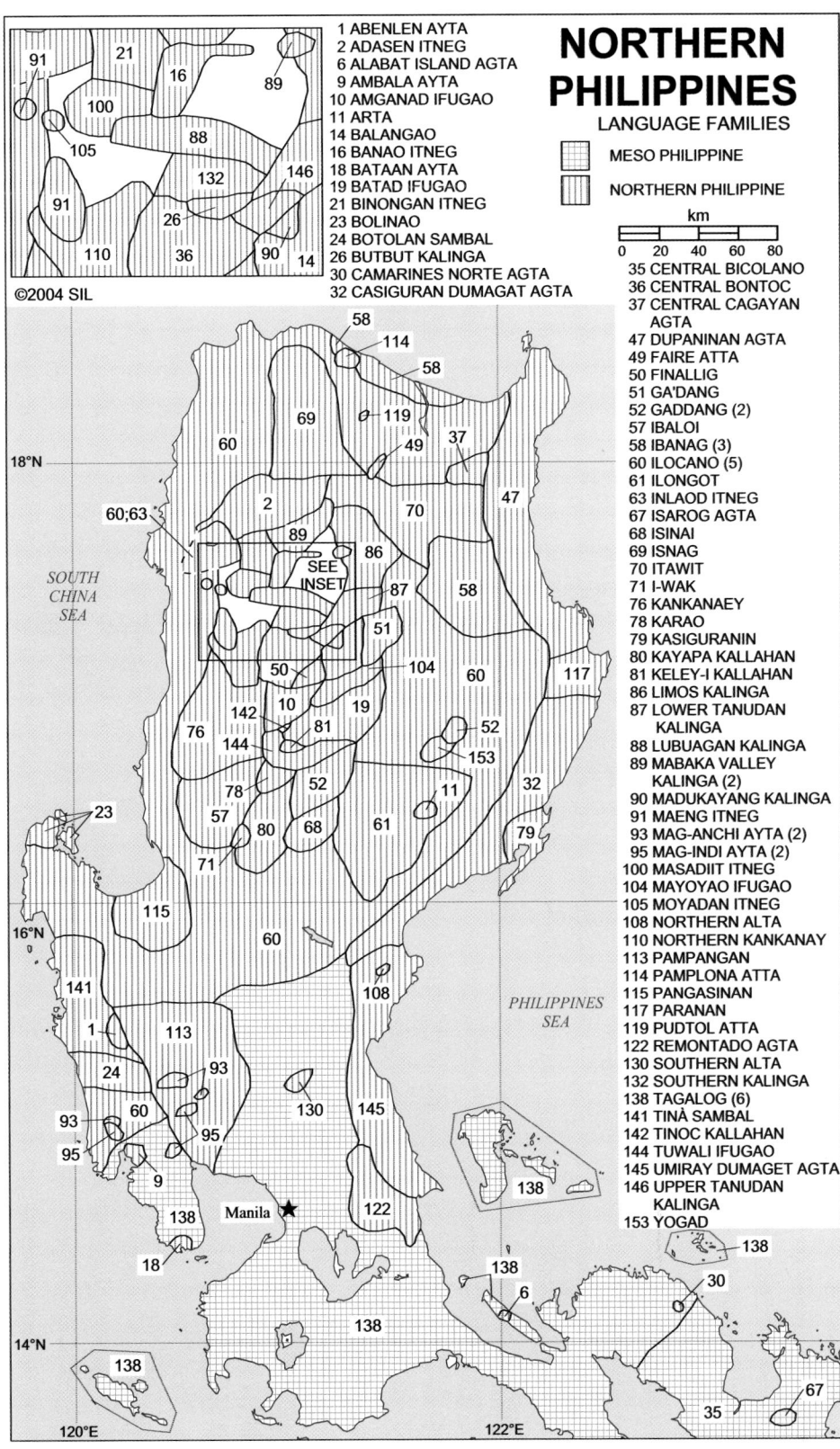

NORTHERN PHILIPPINES
LANGUAGE FAMILIES

1 ABENLEN AYTA
2 ADASEN ITNEG
6 ALABAT ISLAND AGTA
9 AMBALA AYTA
10 AMGANAD IFUGAO
11 ARTA
14 BALANGAO
16 BANAO ITNEG
18 BATAAN AYTA
19 BATAD IFUGAO
21 BINONGAN ITNEG
23 BOLINAO
24 BOTOLAN SAMBAL
26 BUTBUT KALINGA
30 CAMARINES NORTE AGTA
32 CASIGURAN DUMAGAT AGTA
35 CENTRAL BICOLANO
36 CENTRAL BONTOC
37 CENTRAL CAGAYAN AGTA
47 DUPANINAN AGTA
49 FAIRE ATTA
50 FINALLIG
51 GA'DANG
52 GADDANG (2)
57 IBALOI
58 IBANAG (3)
60 ILOCANO (5)
61 ILONGOT
63 INLAOD ITNEG
67 ISAROG AGTA
68 ISINAI
69 ISNAG
70 ITAWIT
71 I-WAK
76 KANKANAEY
78 KARAO
79 KASIGURANIN
80 KAYAPA KALLAHAN
81 KELEY-I KALLAHAN
86 LIMOS KALINGA
87 LOWER TANUDAN KALINGA
88 LUBUAGAN KALINGA
89 MABAKA VALLEY KALINGA (2)
90 MADUKAYANG KALINGA
91 MAENG ITNEG
93 MAG-ANCHI AYTA (2)
95 MAG-INDI AYTA (2)
100 MASADIIT ITNEG
104 MAYOYAO IFUGAO
105 MOYADAN ITNEG
108 NORTHERN ALTA
110 NORTHERN KANKANAY
113 PAMPANGAN
114 PAMPLONA ATTA
115 PANGASINAN
117 PARANAN
119 PUDTOL ATTA
122 REMONTADO AGTA
130 SOUTHERN ALTA
132 SOUTHERN KALINGA
138 TAGALOG (6)
141 TINÀ SAMBAL
142 TINOC KALLAHAN
144 TUWALI IFUGAO
145 UMIRAY DUMAGET AGTA
146 UPPER TANUDAN KALINGA
153 YOGAD

MESO PHILIPPINE

NORTHERN PHILIPPINE

km
0   20   40   60   80

©2004 SIL

SOUTH CHINA SEA

PHILIPPINES SEA

Manila

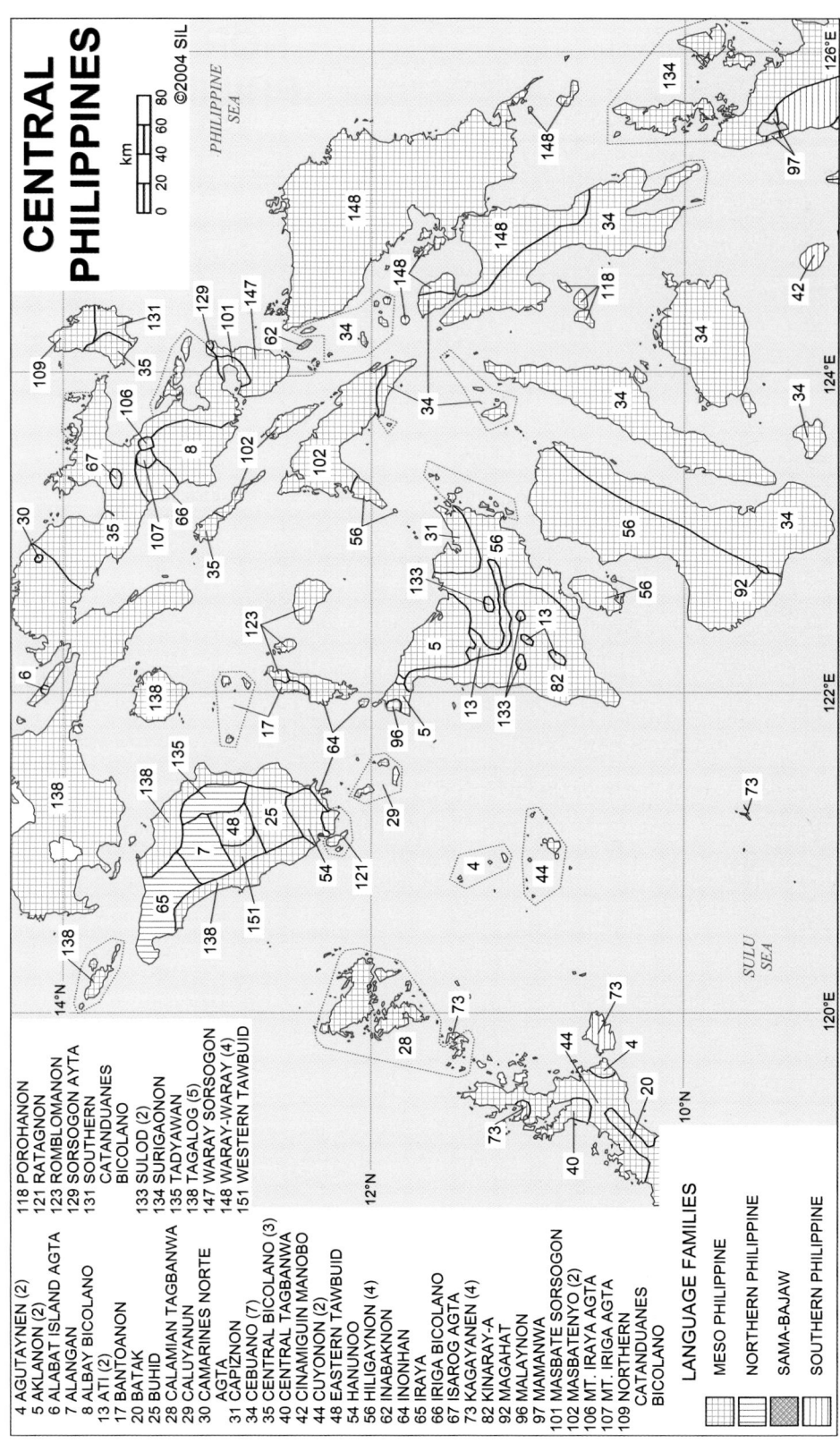

CENTRAL PHILIPPINES

©2004 SIL

km
0 20 40 60 80

PHILIPPINE SEA

SULU SEA

4 AGUTAYNEN (2)
5 AKLANON (2)
6 ALABAT ISLAND AGTA
7 ALANGAN
8 ALBAY BICOLANO
13 ATI (2)
17 BANTOANON
20 BATAK
25 BUHID
28 CALAMIAN TAGBANWA
29 CALUYANUN
30 CAMARINES NORTE AGTA
31 CAPIZNON
34 CEBUANO (7)
35 CENTRAL BICOLANO (3)
40 CENTRAL TAGBANWA
42 CINAMIGUIN MANOBO
44 CUYONON (2)
48 EASTERN TAWBUID
54 HANUNOO
56 HILIGAYNON (4)
62 INABAKNON
64 INONHAN
65 IRAYA
66 IRIGA BICOLANO
67 ISAROG AGTA
73 KAGAYANEN (4)
82 KINARAY-A
92 MAGAHAT
96 MALAYNON
97 MAMANWA
101 MASBATE SORSOGON
102 MASBATENYO (2)
106 MT. IRAYA AGTA
107 MT. IRIGA AGTA
109 NORTHERN CATANDUANES BICOLANO

118 POROHANON
121 RATAGNON
123 ROMBLOMANON
129 SORSOGON AYTA
131 SOUTHERN CATANDUANES BICOLANO
133 SULOD (2)
134 SURIGAONON
135 TADYAWAN
138 TAGALOG (5)
147 WARAY SORSOGON
148 WARAY-WARAY (4)
151 WESTERN TAWBUID

LANGUAGE FAMILIES

MESO PHILIPPINE

NORTHERN PHILIPPINE

SAMA-BAJAW

SOUTHERN PHILIPPINE

SOUTHERN PHILIPPINES

LANGUAGE FAMILIES

MESO PHILIPPINE

SAMA-BAJAW

SOUTHERN PHILIPPINE

SOUTH MINDANAO

SPANISH BASED CREOLE

SULAWESI

km

0 20 40 60 80

©2004 SIL

3 AGUSAN MANOBO
12 ATA MANOBO
15 BALANGINGI (3)
22 BINUKID
27 BUTUANON
33 CATAELANO MANDAYA
34 CEBUANO (7)
38 CENTRAL SAMA
39 CENTRAL SUBANEN (2)
41 CHAVACANO (4)
42 CINAMIGUIN MANOBO
43 COTABATO MANOBO (2)
45 DAVAWENYO (2)
46 DIBABAWON MANOBO
53 GIANGAN
55 HIGAONON
56 HILIGAYNON (2)
59 ILIANEN MANOBO
72 KAGAN KALAGAN
74 KALAGAN (2)
75 KAMAYO
77 KARAGA MANDAYA
83 KOLIBUGAN
     SUBANON (5)
84 KORONADAL BLAAN
85 LAPUYAN SUBANUN
92 MAGAHAT
94 MAGUINDANAO
97 MAMANWA
98 MANSAKA
99 MARANAO
103 MATIGSALUG MANOBO
111 NORTHERN SUBANEN
112 OBO MANOBO

116 PANGUTARAN SAMA
120 RAJAH KABUNSUWAN
     MANOBO
124 SANGAB MANDAYA
125 SANGIL
126 SANGIR
127 SARANGANI BLAAN
128 SARANGANI MANOBO (2)
134 SURIGAONON
136 TAGABAWA
137 TAGAKAULU KALAGAN
139 TAUSUG (2)
140 TBOLI
143 TIRURAY
149 WESTERN BUKIDNON
     MANOBO
150 WESTERN SUBANON (2)
152 YAKAN

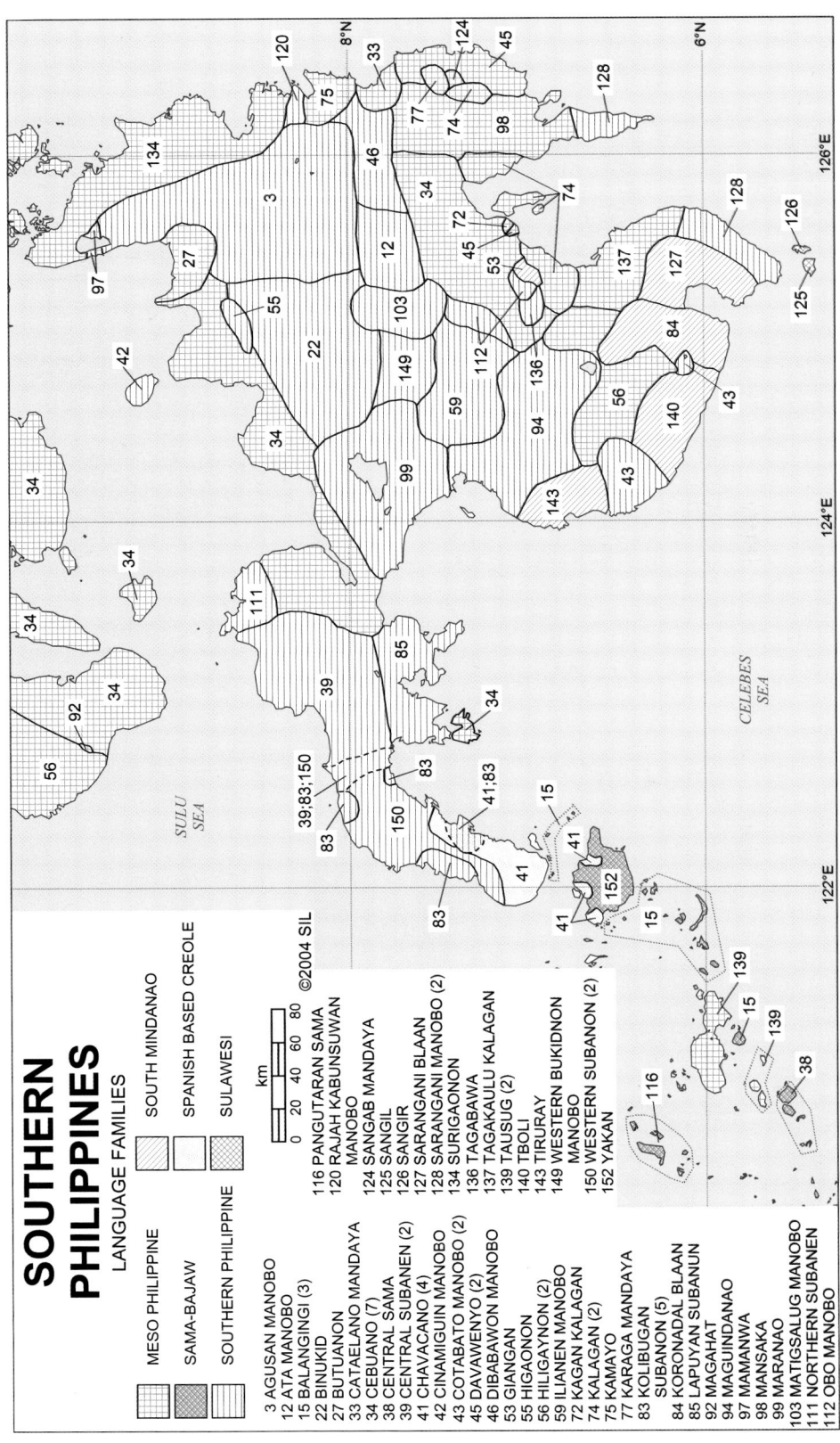

SULU SEA

CELEBES SEA

8°N

6°N

122°E

124°E

126°E

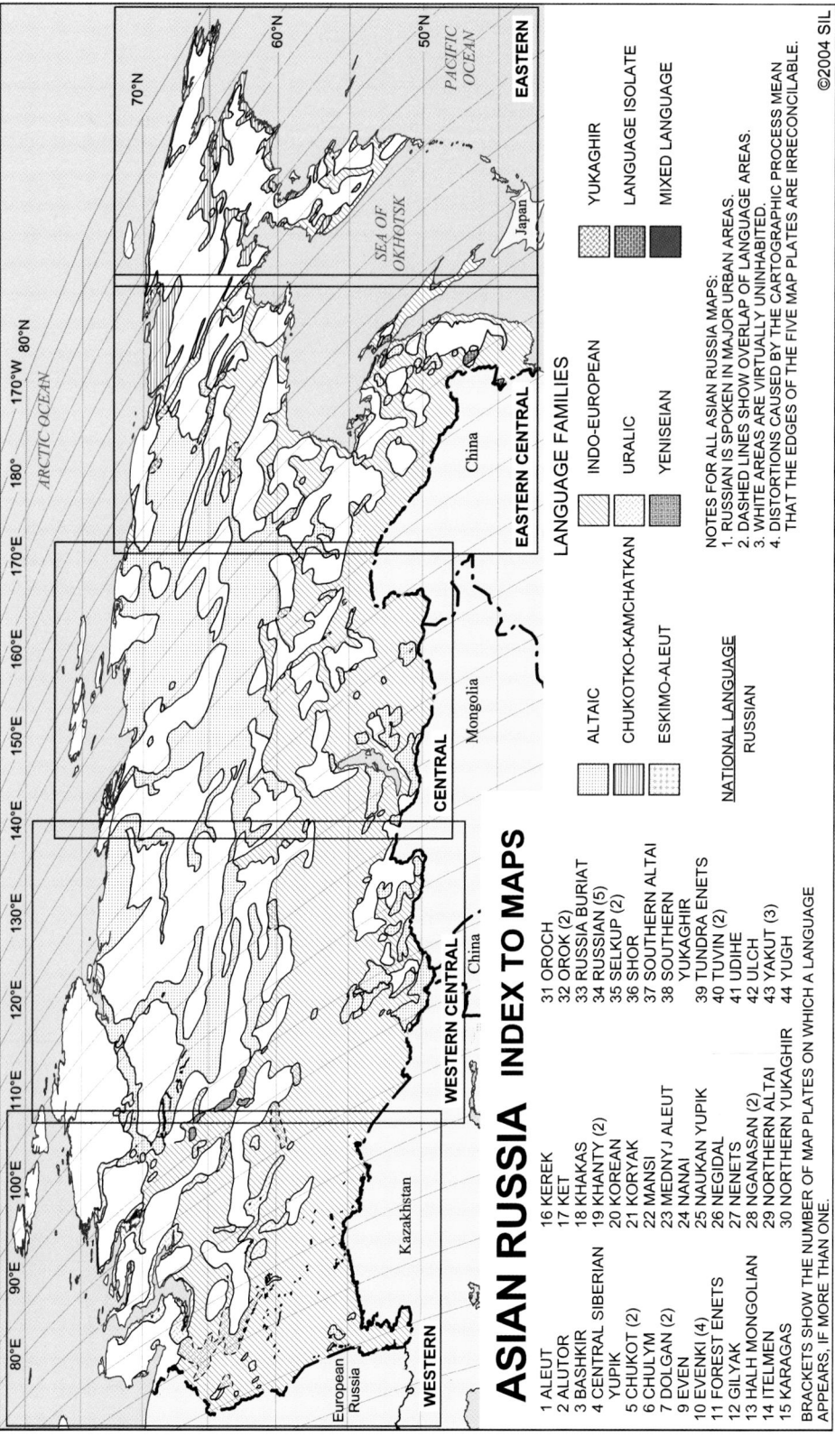

ASIAN RUSSIA   INDEX TO MAPS

1 ALEUT
2 ALUTOR
3 BASHKIR
4 CENTRAL SIBERIAN
   YUPIK
5 CHUKOT (2)
6 CHULYM
7 DOLGAN (2)
8 EVEN
9 EVEN
10 EVENKI (4)
11 FOREST ENETS
12 GILYAK
13 HALH MONGOLIAN
14 ITELMEN
15 KARAGAS

16 KEREK
17 KET
18 KHAKAS
19 KHANTY (2)
20 KOREAN
21 KORYAK
22 MANSI
23 MEDNYJ ALEUT
24 NANAI
25 NAUKAN YUPIK
26 NEGIDAL
27 NENETS
28 NGANASAN (2)
29 NORTHERN ALTAI
30 NORTHERN YUKAGHIR

31 OROCH
32 OROK (2)
33 RUSSIA BURIAT
34 RUSSIAN (5)
35 SELKUP (2)
36 SHOR
37 SOUTHERN ALTAI
38 SOUTHERN
   YUKAGHIR
39 TUNDRA ENETS
40 TUVIN (2)
41 UDIHE
42 ULCH
43 YAKUT (3)
44 YUGH

BRACKETS SHOW THE NUMBER OF MAP PLATES ON WHICH A LANGUAGE
APPEARS, IF MORE THAN ONE.

LANGUAGE FAMILIES

ALTAIC
CHUKOTKO-KAMCHATKAN
ESKIMO-ALEUT

INDO-EUROPEAN
URALIC
YENISEIAN

YUKAGHIR
LANGUAGE ISOLATE
MIXED LANGUAGE

NATIONAL LANGUAGE
RUSSIAN

NOTES FOR ALL ASIAN RUSSIA MAPS:
1. RUSSIAN IS SPOKEN IN MAJOR URBAN AREAS.
2. DASHED LINES SHOW OVERLAP OF LANGUAGE AREAS.
3. WHITE AREAS ARE VIRTUALLY UNINHABITED.
4. DISTORTIONS CAUSED BY THE CARTOGRAPHIC PROCESS MEAN
   THAT THE EDGES OF THE FIVE MAP PLATES ARE IRRECONCILABLE.

©2004 SIL

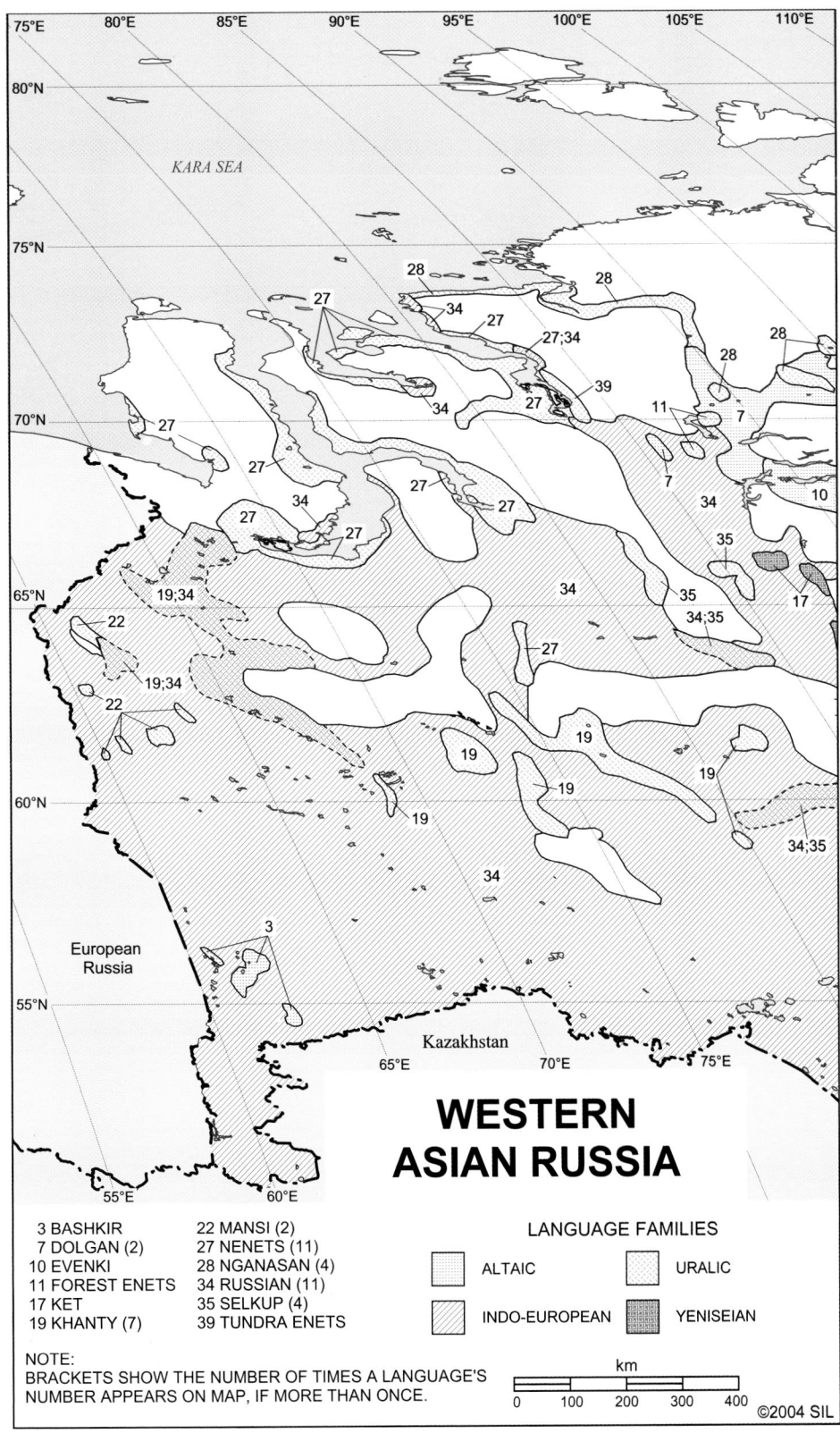

WESTERN ASIAN RUSSIA

3 BASHKIR
7 DOLGAN (2)
10 EVENKI
11 FOREST ENETS
17 KET
19 KHANTY (7)

22 MANSI (2)
27 NENETS (11)
28 NGANASAN (4)
34 RUSSIAN (11)
35 SELKUP (4)
39 TUNDRA ENETS

LANGUAGE FAMILIES

ALTAIC

URALIC

INDO-EUROPEAN

YENISEIAN

NOTE:
BRACKETS SHOW THE NUMBER OF TIMES A LANGUAGE'S
NUMBER APPEARS ON MAP, IF MORE THAN ONCE.

km
0   100   200   300   400

©2004 SIL

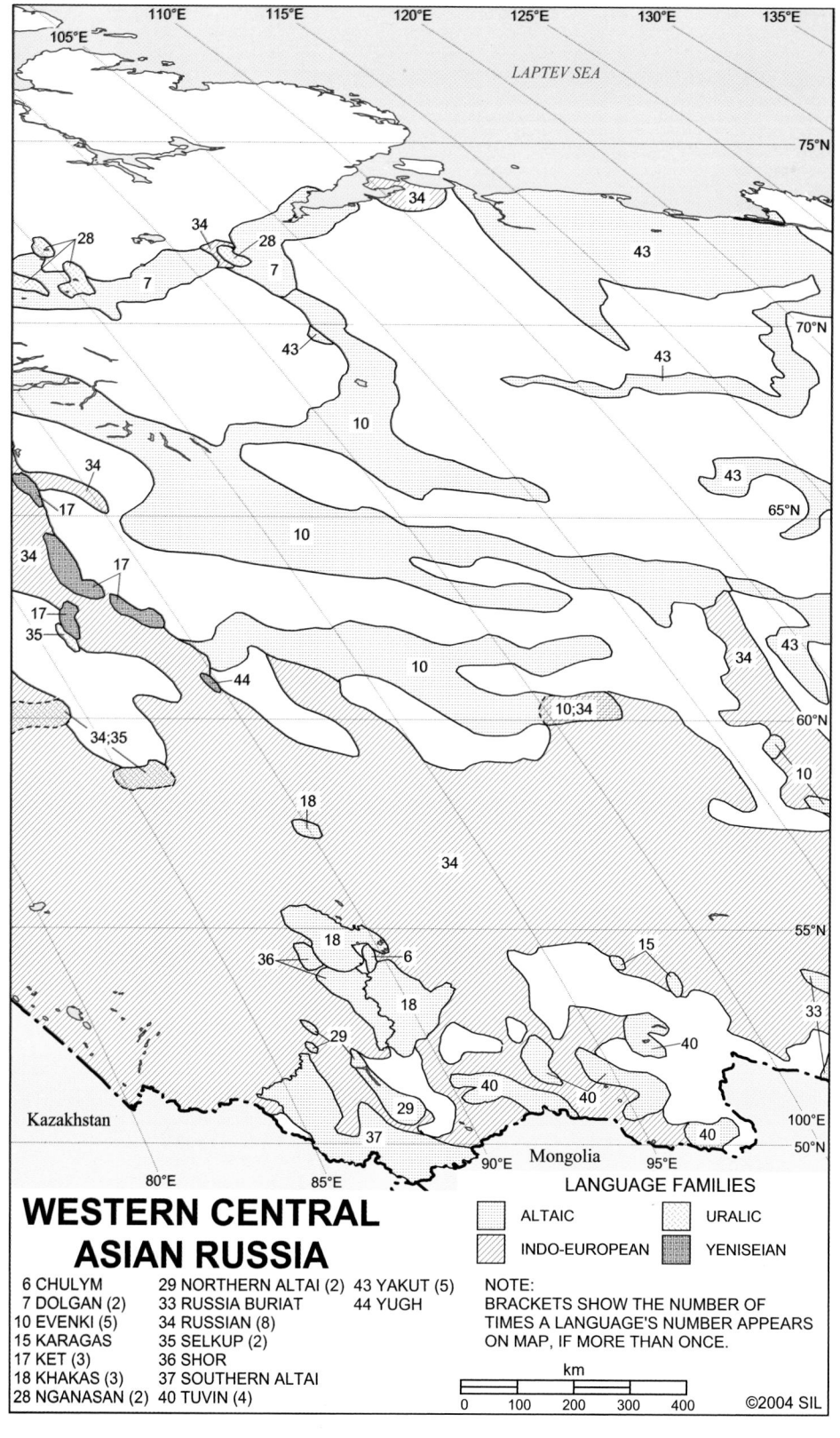

WESTERN CENTRAL ASIAN RUSSIA

LANGUAGE FAMILIES

ALTAIC	URALIC
INDO-EUROPEAN	YENISEIAN

6 CHULYM
7 DOLGAN (2)
10 EVENKI (5)
15 KARAGAS
17 KET (3)
18 KHAKAS (3)
28 NGANASAN (2)

29 NORTHERN ALTAI (2)
33 RUSSIA BURIAT
34 RUSSIAN (8)
35 SELKUP (2)
36 SHOR
37 SOUTHERN ALTAI
40 TUVIN (4)

43 YAKUT (5)
44 YUGH

NOTE:
BRACKETS SHOW THE NUMBER OF
TIMES A LANGUAGE'S NUMBER APPEARS
ON MAP, IF MORE THAN ONCE.

km

0   100   200   300   400

©2004 SIL

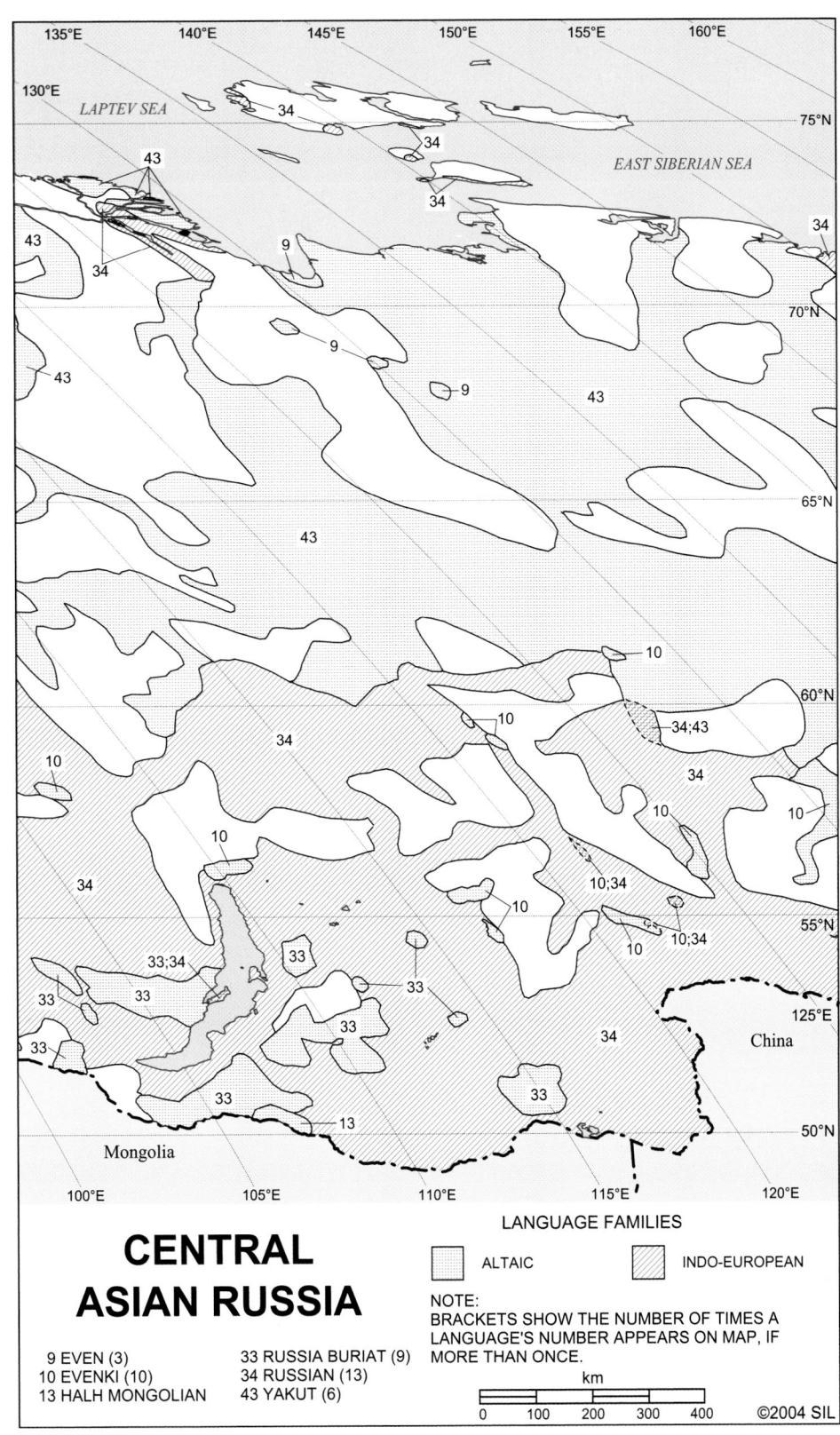

135°E 140°E 145°E 150°E 155°E 160°E
130°E
LAPTEV SEA 75°N
34
43 34
EAST SIBERIAN SEA
34
43
34 34
9
43
43 70°N
9
43
9 43 65°N
43
43
10
10 60°N
34 10 34;43
34
10 10
10
34 10;34
10 34
10 55°N
10;34
10
33;34 33
33 33 125°E
33 33 China
33 33
33 34
34
33
33
13 50°N
Mongolia
100°E 105°E 110°E 115°E 120°E

LANGUAGE FAMILIES

CENTRAL
ASIAN RUSSIA

ALTAIC   INDO-EUROPEAN

NOTE:
BRACKETS SHOW THE NUMBER OF TIMES A
LANGUAGE'S NUMBER APPEARS ON MAP, IF
MORE THAN ONCE.

9 EVEN (3)   33 RUSSIA BURIAT (9)
10 EVENKI (10)   34 RUSSIAN (13)
13 HALH MONGOLIAN   43 YAKUT (6)

km
0   100   200   300   400

©2004 SIL

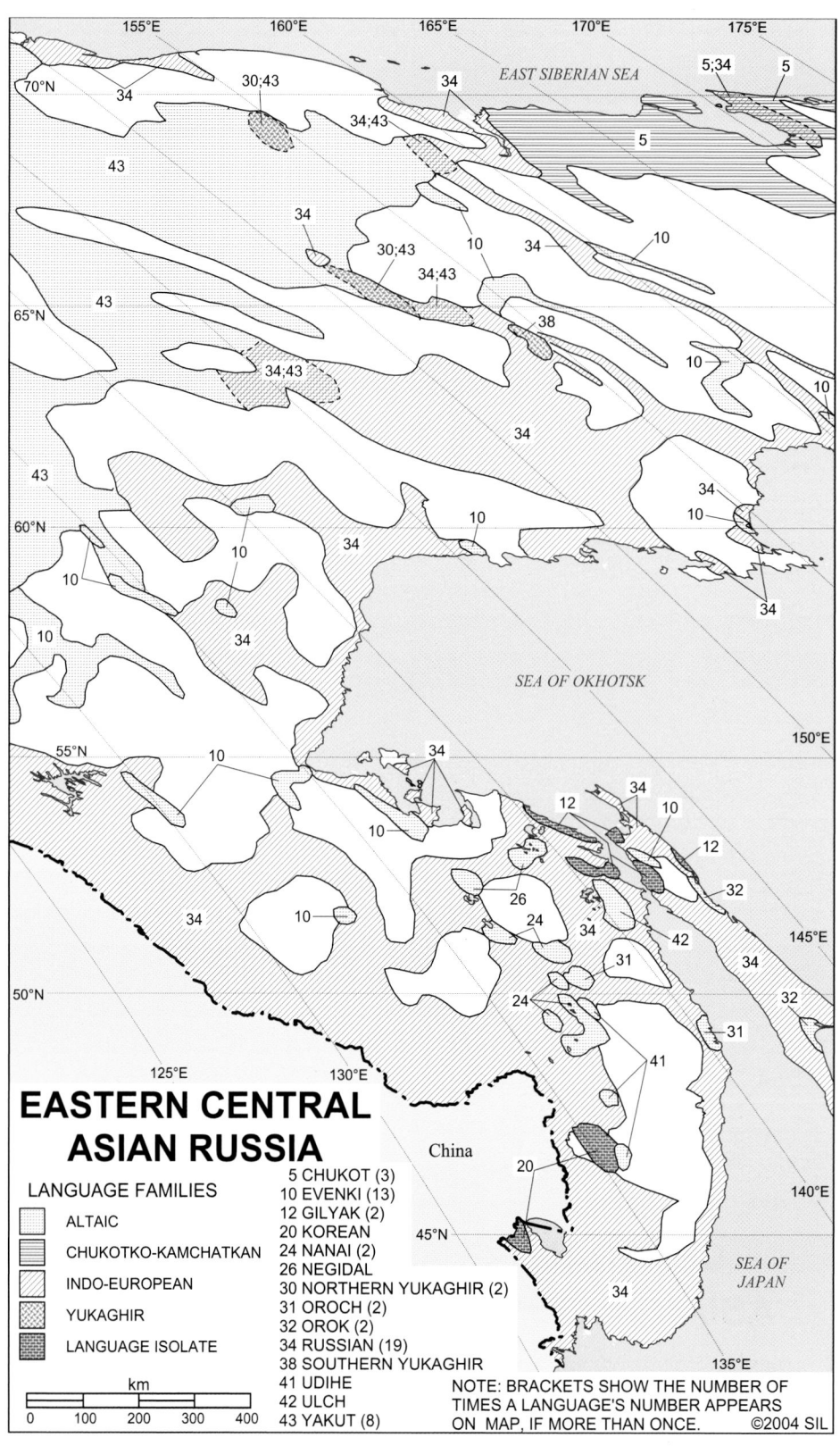

EASTERN CENTRAL
ASIA RUSSIA

LANGUAGE FAMILIES

- ALTAIC
- CHUKOTKO-KAMCHATKAN
- INDO-EUROPEAN
- YUKAGHIR
- LANGUAGE ISOLATE

km
0   100   200   300   400

5 CHUKOT (3)
10 EVENKI (13)
12 GILYAK (2)
20 KOREAN
24 NANAI (2)
26 NEGIDAL
30 NORTHERN YUKAGHIR (2)
31 OROCH (2)
32 OROK (2)
34 RUSSIAN (19)
38 SOUTHERN YUKAGHIR
41 UDIHE
42 ULCH
43 YAKUT (8)

NOTE: BRACKETS SHOW THE NUMBER OF
TIMES A LANGUAGE'S NUMBER APPEARS
ON MAP, IF MORE THAN ONCE.   ©2004 SIL

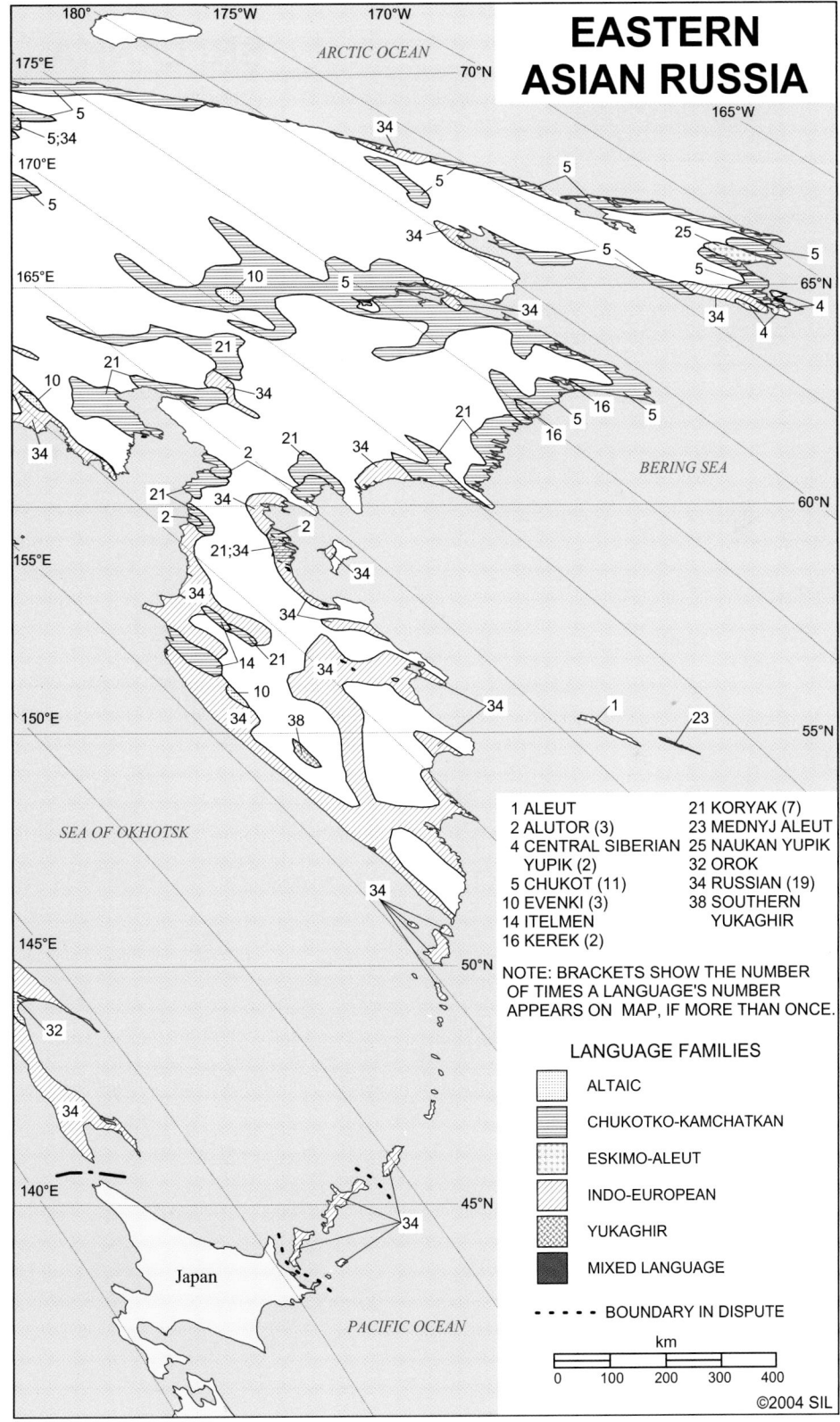

EASTERN ASIAN RUSSIA

1 ALEUT
2 ALUTOR (3)
4 CENTRAL SIBERIAN
   YUPIK (2)
5 CHUKOT (11)
10 EVENKI (3)
14 ITELMEN
16 KEREK (2)

21 KORYAK (7)
23 MEDNYJ ALEUT
25 NAUKAN YUPIK
32 OROK
34 RUSSIAN (19)
38 SOUTHERN
   YUKAGHIR

NOTE: BRACKETS SHOW THE NUMBER
OF TIMES A LANGUAGE'S NUMBER
APPEARS ON MAP, IF MORE THAN ONCE.

LANGUAGE FAMILIES

ALTAIC

CHUKOTKO-KAMCHATKAN

ESKIMO-ALEUT

INDO-EUROPEAN

YUKAGHIR

MIXED LANGUAGE

- - - - BOUNDARY IN DISPUTE

km
0   100   200   300   400

©2004 SIL

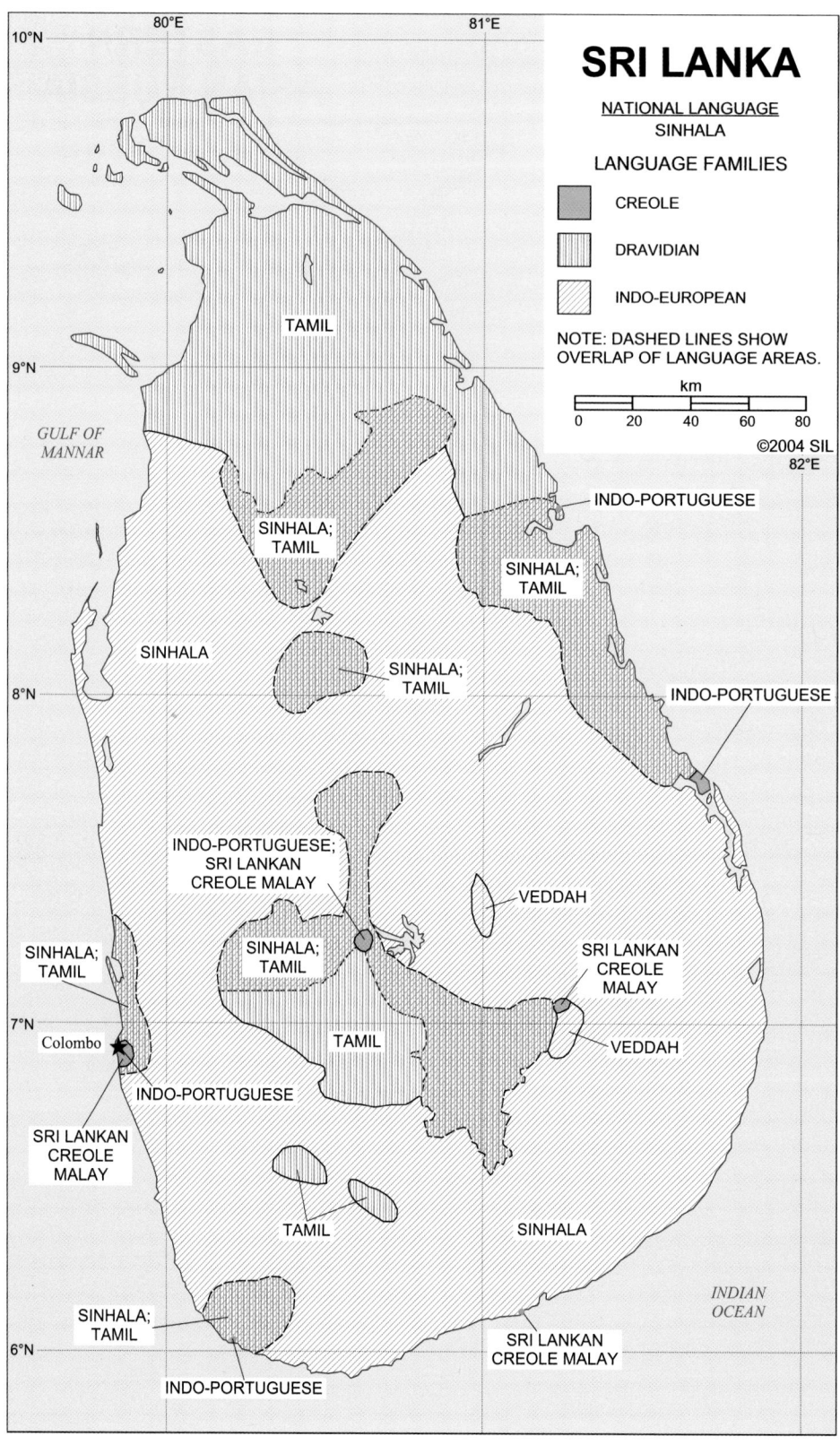

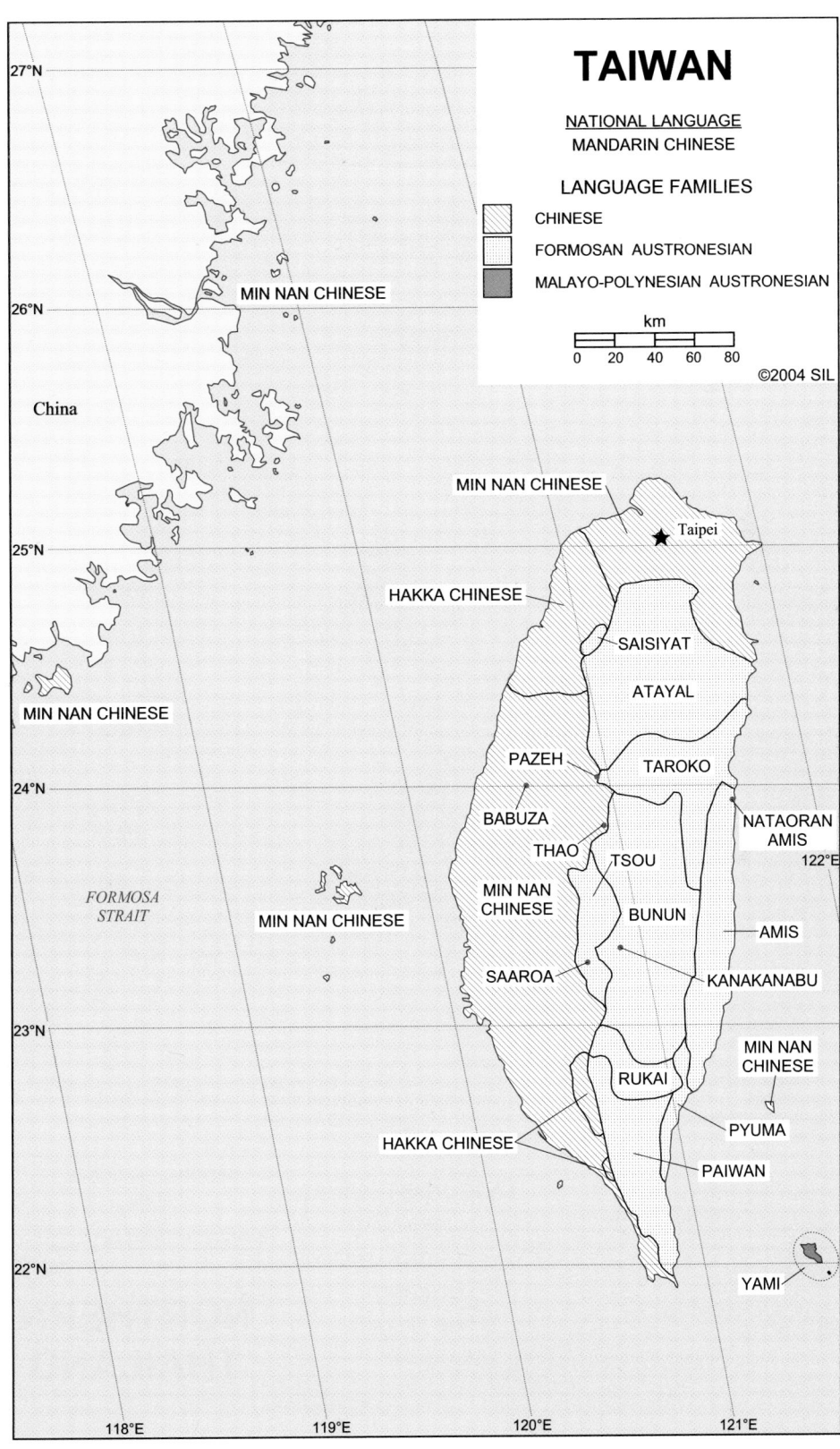

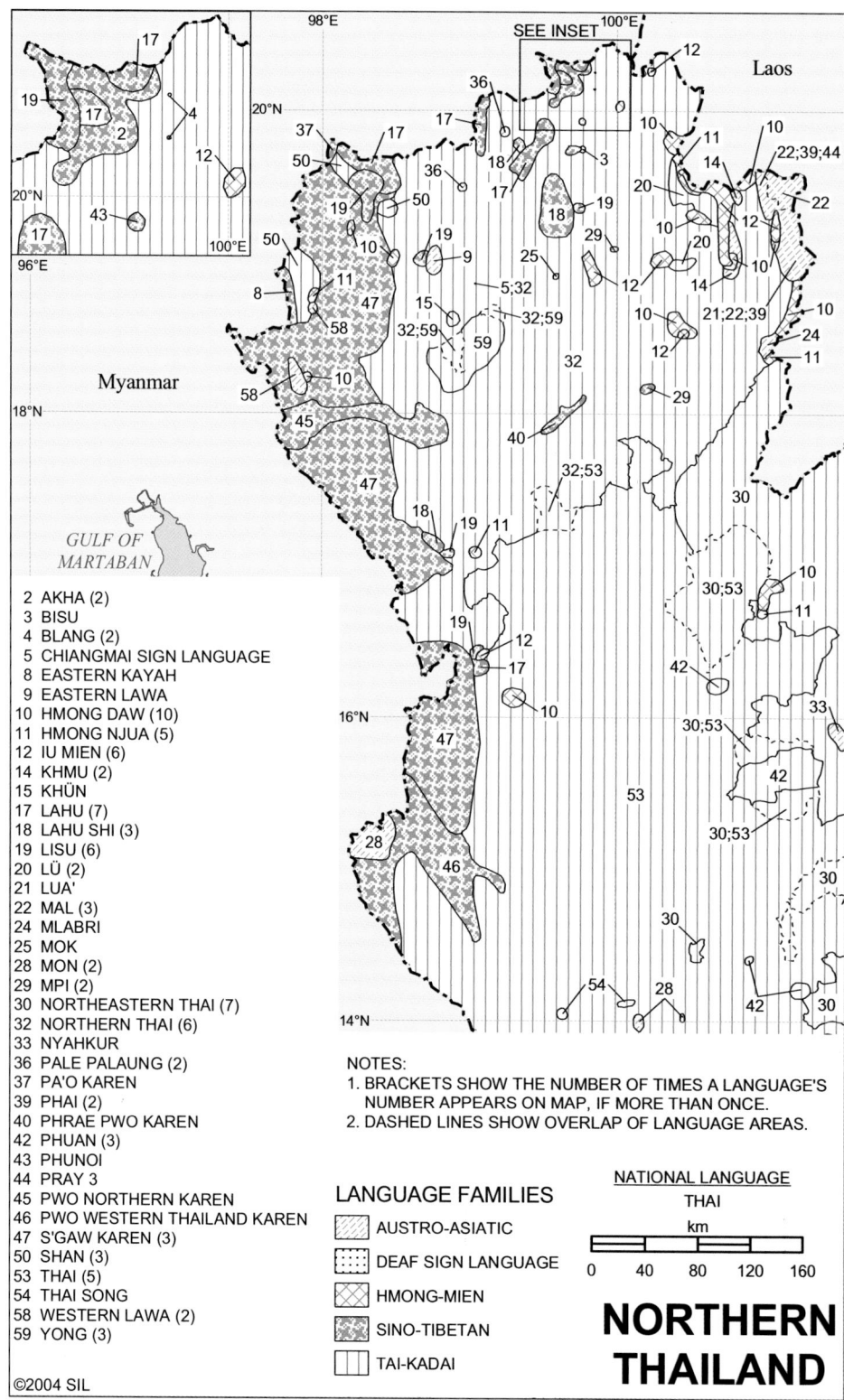

2 AKHA (2)
3 BISU
4 BLANG (2)
5 CHIANGMAI SIGN LANGUAGE
8 EASTERN KAYAH
9 EASTERN LAWA
10 HMONG DAW (10)
11 HMONG NJUA (5)
12 IU MIEN (6)
14 KHMU (2)
15 KHÜN
17 LAHU (7)
18 LAHU SHI (3)
19 LISU (6)
20 LÜ (2)
21 LUA'
22 MAL (3)
24 MLABRI
25 MOK
28 MON (2)
29 MPI (2)
30 NORTHEASTERN THAI (7)
32 NORTHERN THAI (6)
33 NYAHKUR
36 PALE PALAUNG (2)
37 PA'O KAREN
39 PHAI (2)
40 PHRAE PWO KAREN
42 PHUAN (3)
43 PHUNOI
44 PRAY 3
45 PWO NORTHERN KAREN
46 PWO WESTERN THAILAND KAREN
47 S'GAW KAREN (3)
50 SHAN (3)
53 THAI (5)
54 THAI SONG
58 WESTERN LAWA (2)
59 YONG (3)

©2004 SIL

NOTES:
1. BRACKETS SHOW THE NUMBER OF TIMES A LANGUAGE'S
   NUMBER APPEARS ON MAP, IF MORE THAN ONCE.
2. DASHED LINES SHOW OVERLAP OF LANGUAGE AREAS.

LANGUAGE FAMILIES

AUSTRO-ASIATIC

DEAF SIGN LANGUAGE

HMONG-MIEN

SINO-TIBETAN

TAI-KADAI

NATIONAL LANGUAGE
THAI

km

0   40   80   120   160

NORTHERN
THAILAND

Language data based on data from the Institute of Language and Culture for Rural Development, Mahidol University, Bangkok

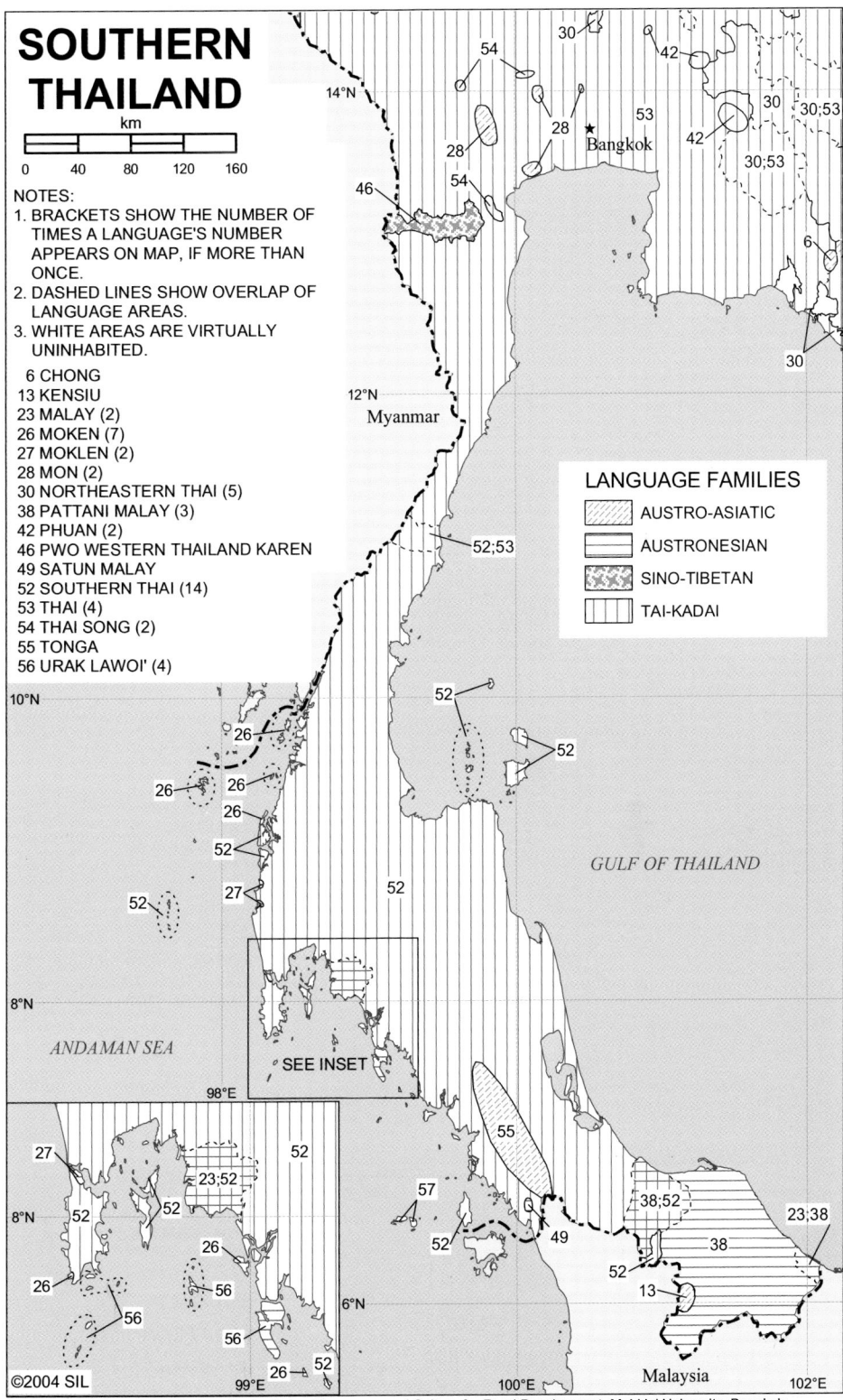

SOUTHERN THAILAND

km

0   40   80   120   160

NOTES:
1. BRACKETS SHOW THE NUMBER OF TIMES A LANGUAGE'S NUMBER APPEARS ON MAP, IF MORE THAN ONCE.
2. DASHED LINES SHOW OVERLAP OF LANGUAGE AREAS.
3. WHITE AREAS ARE VIRTUALLY UNINHABITED.

 6 CHONG
13 KENSIU
23 MALAY (2)
26 MOKEN (7)
27 MOKLEN (2)
28 MON (2)
30 NORTHEASTERN THAI (5)
38 PATTANI MALAY (3)
42 PHUAN (2)
46 PWO WESTERN THAILAND KAREN
49 SATUN MALAY
52 SOUTHERN THAI (14)
53 THAI (4)
54 THAI SONG (2)
55 TONGA
56 URAK LAWOI' (4)

LANGUAGE FAMILIES

AUSTRO-ASIATIC

AUSTRONESIAN

SINO-TIBETAN

TAI-KADAI

14°N

12°N
Myanmar

10°N

8°N

ANDAMAN SEA

SEE INSET

98°E

8°N

99°E

6°N

100°E

Bangkok

GULF OF THAILAND

Malaysia

102°E

©2004 SIL

Language data based on data from the Institute of Language and Culture for Rural Development, Mahidol University, Bangkok

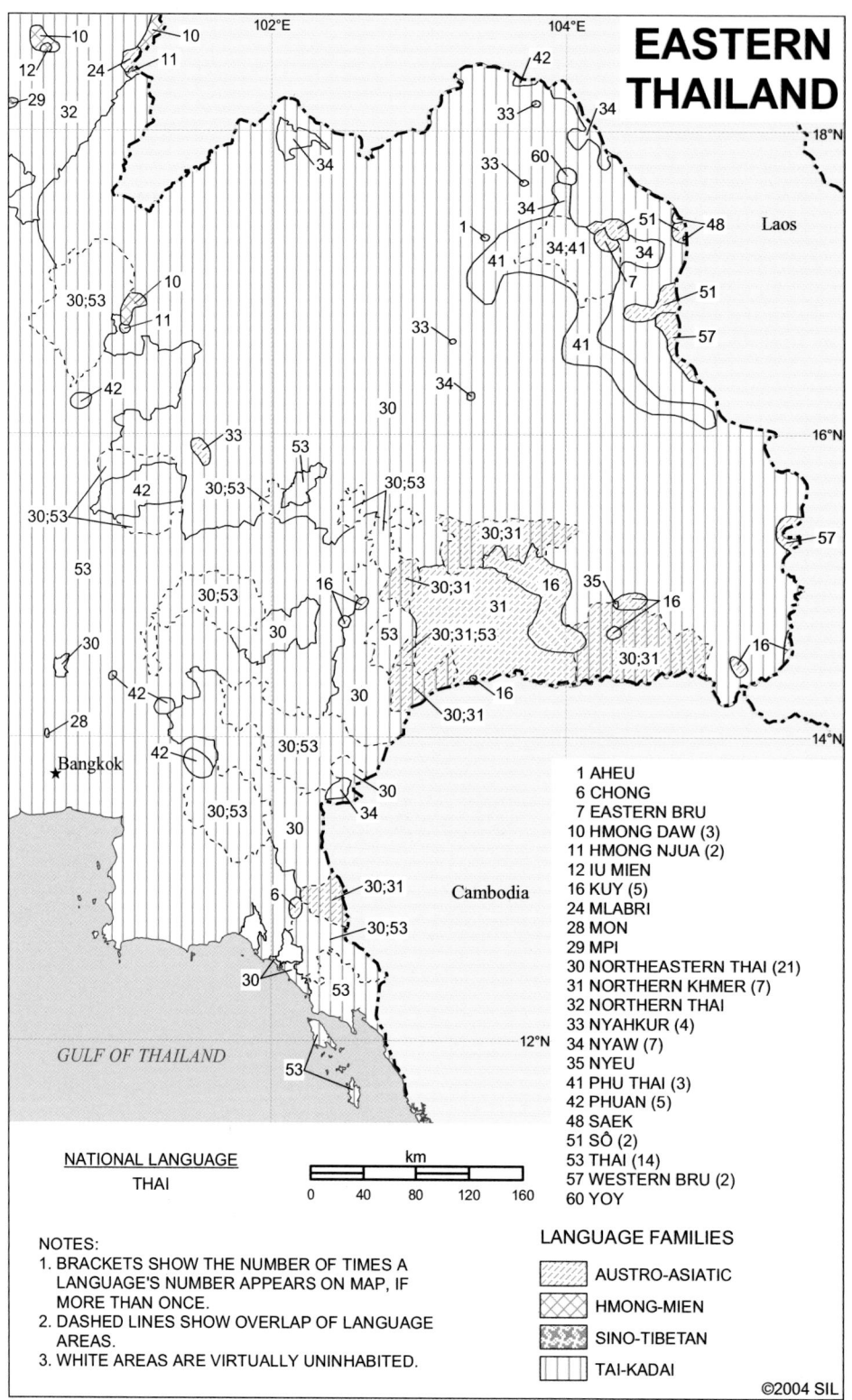

EASTERN THAILAND

102°E   104°E

18°N

Laos

16°N

14°N

Cambodia

12°N

Bangkok

GULF OF THAILAND

NATIONAL LANGUAGE
THAI

km
0 40 80 120 160

1 AHEU
6 CHONG
7 EASTERN BRU
10 HMONG DAW (3)
11 HMONG NJUA (2)
12 IU MIEN
16 KUY (5)
24 MLABRI
28 MON
29 MPI
30 NORTHEASTERN THAI (21)
31 NORTHERN KHMER (7)
32 NORTHERN THAI
33 NYAHKUR (4)
34 NYAW (7)
35 NYEU
41 PHU THAI (3)
42 PHUAN (5)
48 SAEK
51 SÔ (2)
53 THAI (14)
57 WESTERN BRU (2)
60 YOY

NOTES:
1. BRACKETS SHOW THE NUMBER OF TIMES A
   LANGUAGE'S NUMBER APPEARS ON MAP, IF
   MORE THAN ONCE.
2. DASHED LINES SHOW OVERLAP OF LANGUAGE
   AREAS.
3. WHITE AREAS ARE VIRTUALLY UNINHABITED.

LANGUAGE FAMILIES

AUSTRO-ASIATIC
HMONG-MIEN
SINO-TIBETAN
TAI-KADAI

©2004 SIL

Language data based on data from the Institute of Language and Culture for Rural Development, Mahidol University, Bangkok

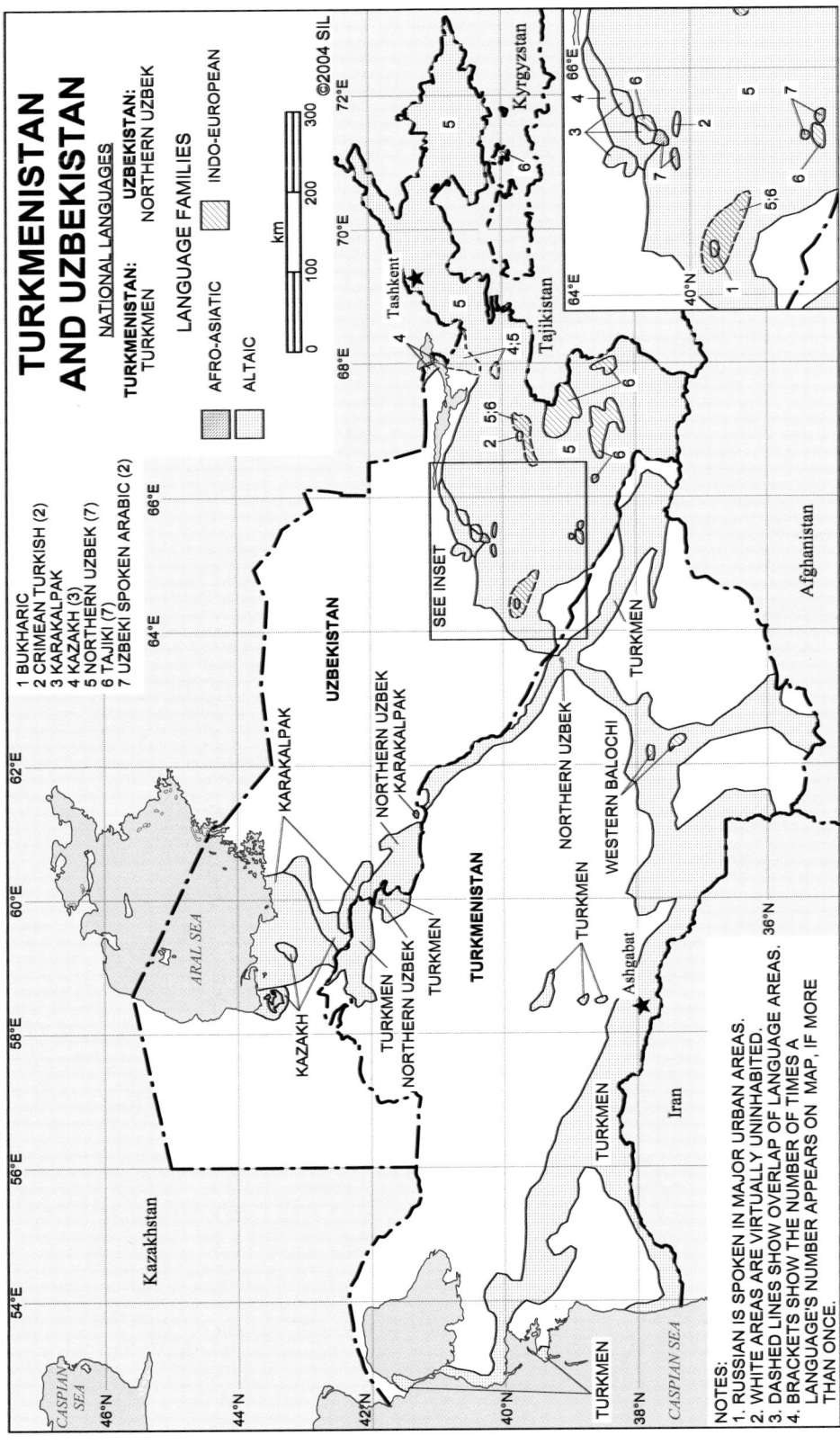

TURKMENISTAN AND UZBEKISTAN

NATIONAL LANGUAGES

TURKMENISTAN:
TURKMEN

UZBEKISTAN:
NORTHERN UZBEK

LANGUAGE FAMILIES

AFRO-ASIATIC

ALTAIC

INDO-EUROPEAN

1 BUKHARIC
2 CRIMEAN TURKISH (2)
3 KARAKALPAK
4 KAZAKH (3)
5 NORTHERN UZBEK (7)
6 TAJIKI (7)
7 UZBEKI SPOKEN ARABIC (2)

©2004 SIL

km

0   100   200   300

NOTES:
1. RUSSIAN IS SPOKEN IN MAJOR URBAN AREAS.
2. WHITE AREAS ARE VIRTUALLY UNINHABITED.
3. DASHED LINES SHOW OVERLAP OF LANGUAGE AREAS.
4. BRACKETS SHOW THE NUMBER OF TIMES A
   LANGUAGE'S NUMBER APPEARS ON MAP, IF MORE
   THAN ONCE.

Kazakhstan

ARAL SEA

CASPIAN SEA

UZBEKISTAN

TURKMENISTAN

KARAKALPAK

NORTHERN UZBEK
KARAKALPAK

KAZAKH

TURKMEN
NORTHERN UZBEK

TURKMEN

TURKMEN

NORTHERN UZBEK

WESTERN BALOCHI

TURKMEN

Ashgabat

Iran

TURKMEN

CASPIAN SEA

SEE INSET

Tashkent

Tajikistan

Kyrgyzstan

Afghanistan

TURKMEN

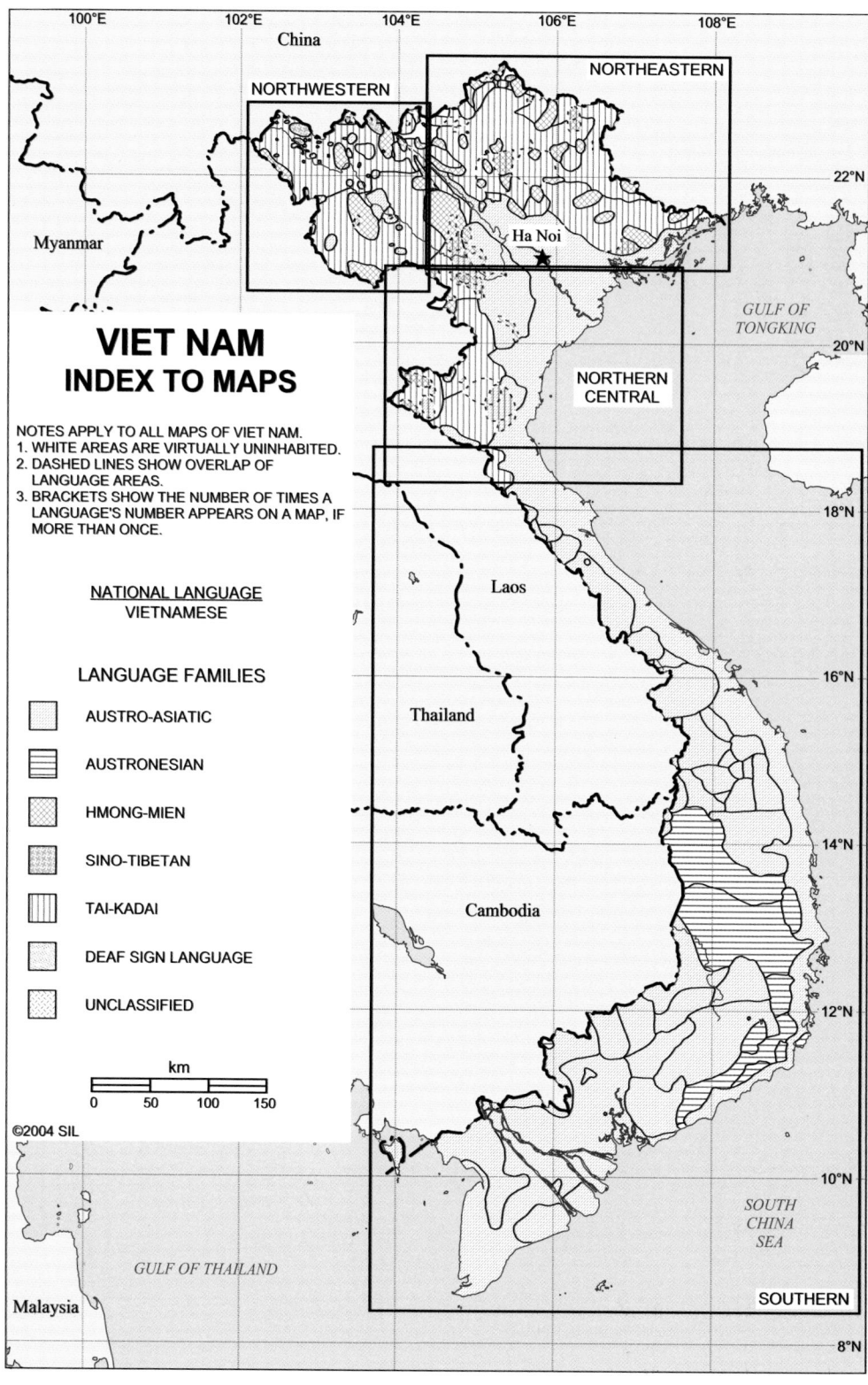

VIET NAM
INDEX TO MAPS

NOTES APPLY TO ALL MAPS OF VIET NAM.
1. WHITE AREAS ARE VIRTUALLY UNINHABITED.
2. DASHED LINES SHOW OVERLAP OF
   LANGUAGE AREAS.
3. BRACKETS SHOW THE NUMBER OF TIMES A
   LANGUAGE'S NUMBER APPEARS ON A MAP, IF
   MORE THAN ONCE.

NATIONAL LANGUAGE
VIETNAMESE

LANGUAGE FAMILIES

AUSTRO-ASIATIC

AUSTRONESIAN

HMONG-MIEN

SINO-TIBETAN

TAI-KADAI

DEAF SIGN LANGUAGE

UNCLASSIFIED

km
0   50   100   150

©2004 SIL

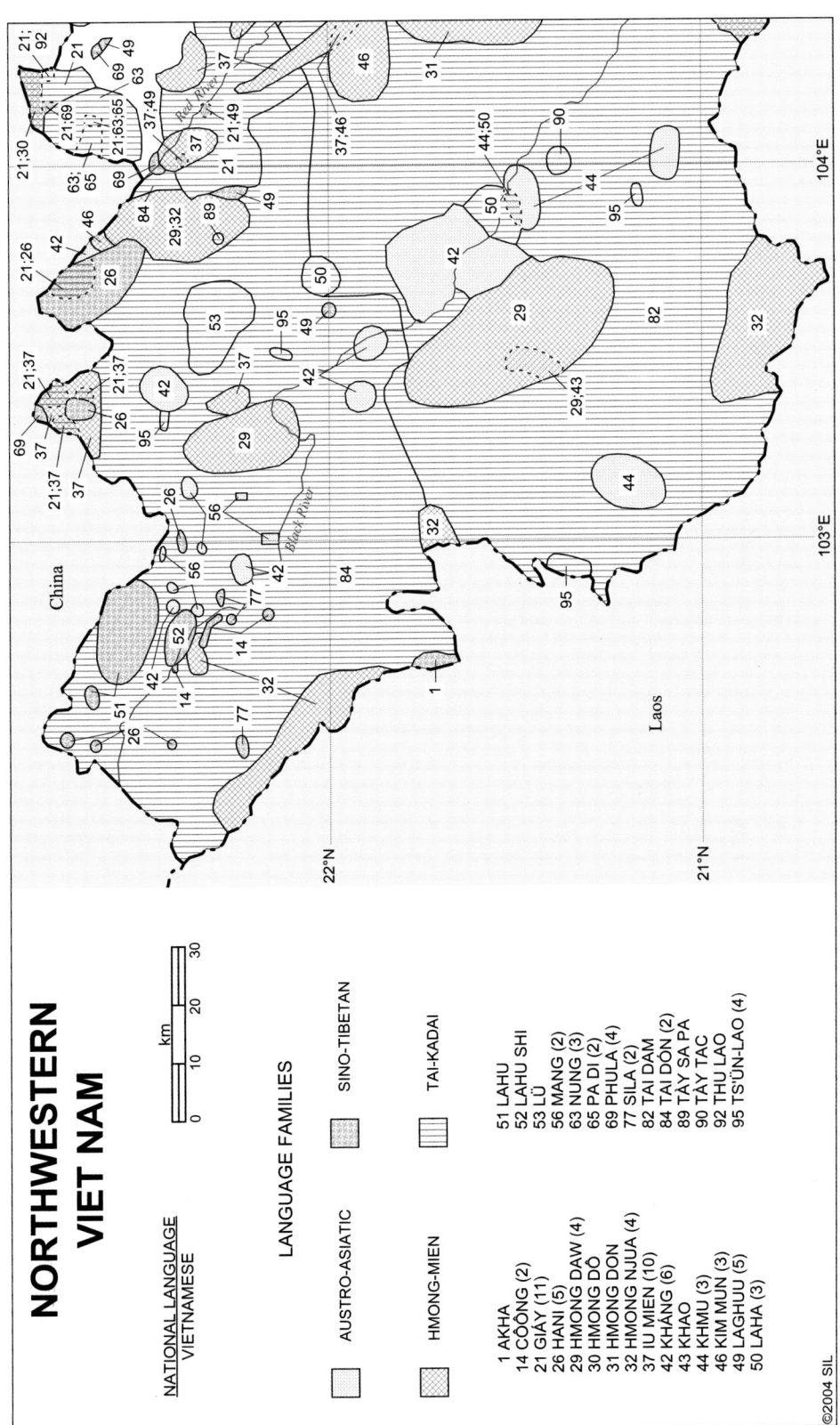

NORTHWESTERN VIET NAM

NATIONAL LANGUAGE
VIETNAMESE

LANGUAGE FAMILIES

AUSTRO-ASIATIC

HMONG-MIEN

SINO-TIBETAN

TAI-KADAI

1 AKHA
14 CÔÔNG (2)
21 GIÁY (11)
26 HANI (5)
29 HMONG DAW (4)
30 HMONG DÔ
31 HMONG DON
32 HMONG NJUA (4)
37 IU MIEN (10)
42 KHÁNG (6)
43 KHAO
44 KHMU (3)
46 KIM MUN (3)
49 LAGHUU (5)
50 LAHA (3)
51 LAHU
52 LAHU SHI
53 LÜ
56 MANG (2)
63 NUNG (3)
65 PA DI (2)
69 PHULA (4)
77 SILA (2)
82 TAI DAM
84 TAI DÓN (2)
89 TÁY SA PA
90 TÁY TAC
92 THU LAO
95 TS'ÜN-LAO (4)

©2004 SIL

China

Laos

22°N

21°N

104°E

103°E

Red River

Black River

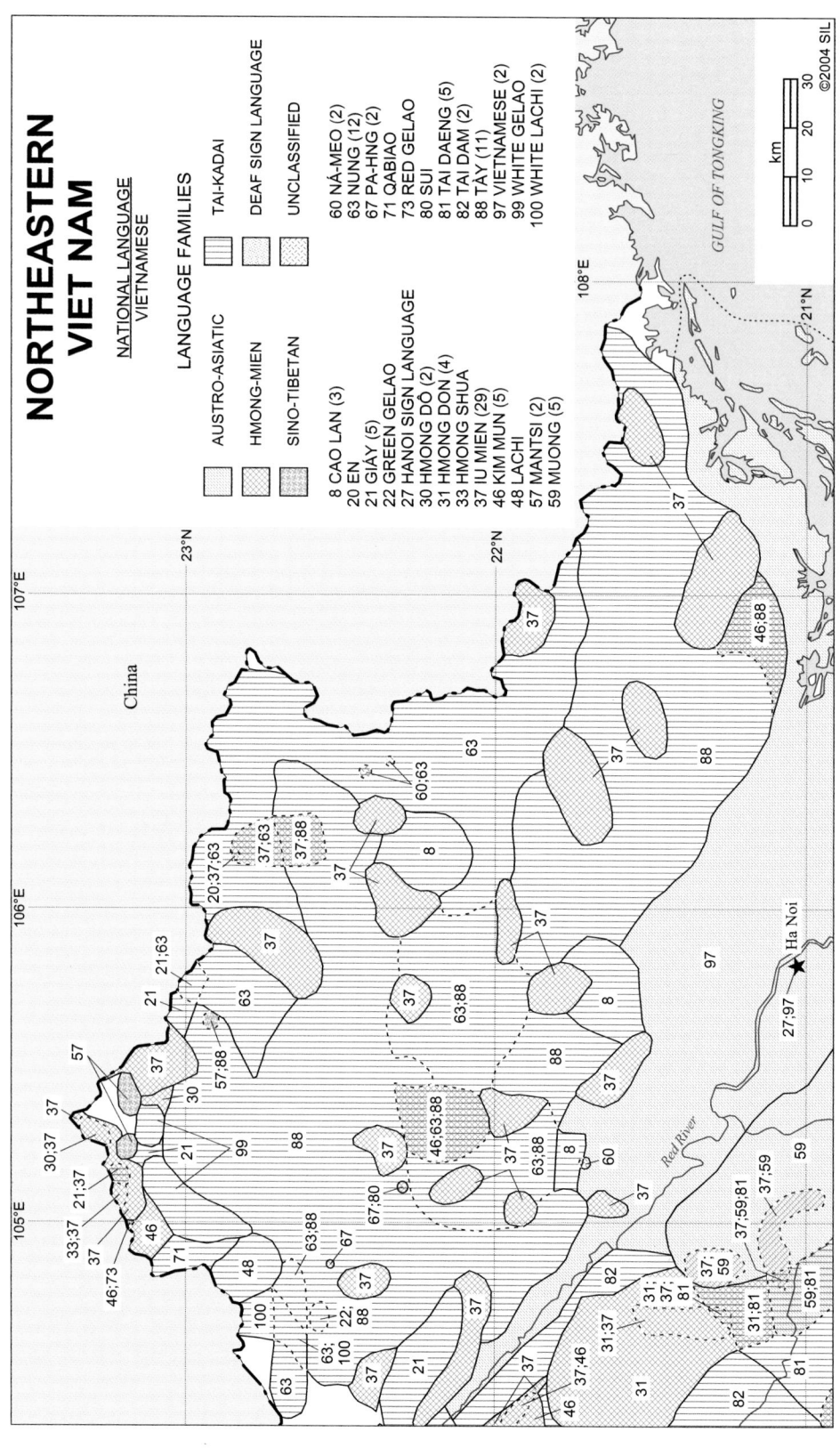

NORTHEASTERN VIET NAM

NATIONAL LANGUAGE
VIETNAMESE

LANGUAGE FAMILIES

AUSTRO-ASIATIC

HMONG-MIEN

SINO-TIBETAN

TAI-KADAI

DEAF SIGN LANGUAGE

UNCLASSIFIED

8 CAO LAN (3)
20 EN
21 GIÁY (5)
22 GREEN GELAO
27 HANOI SIGN LANGUAGE
30 HMONG ĐỎ (2)
31 HMONG ĐON (4)
33 HMONG SHUA
37 IU MIEN (29)
46 KIM MUN (5)
48 LACHI
57 MANTSI (2)
59 MUONG (5)

60 NÁ-MEO (2)
63 NUNG (12)
67 PA-HNG (2)
71 QABIAO
73 RED GELAO
80 SUI
81 TAI DAENG (5)
82 TAI DAM (2)
88 TÀY (11)
97 VIETNAMESE (2)
99 WHITE GELAO
100 WHITE LACHI (2)

©2004 SIL

GULF OF TONGKING

km

China

Red River

Ha Noi

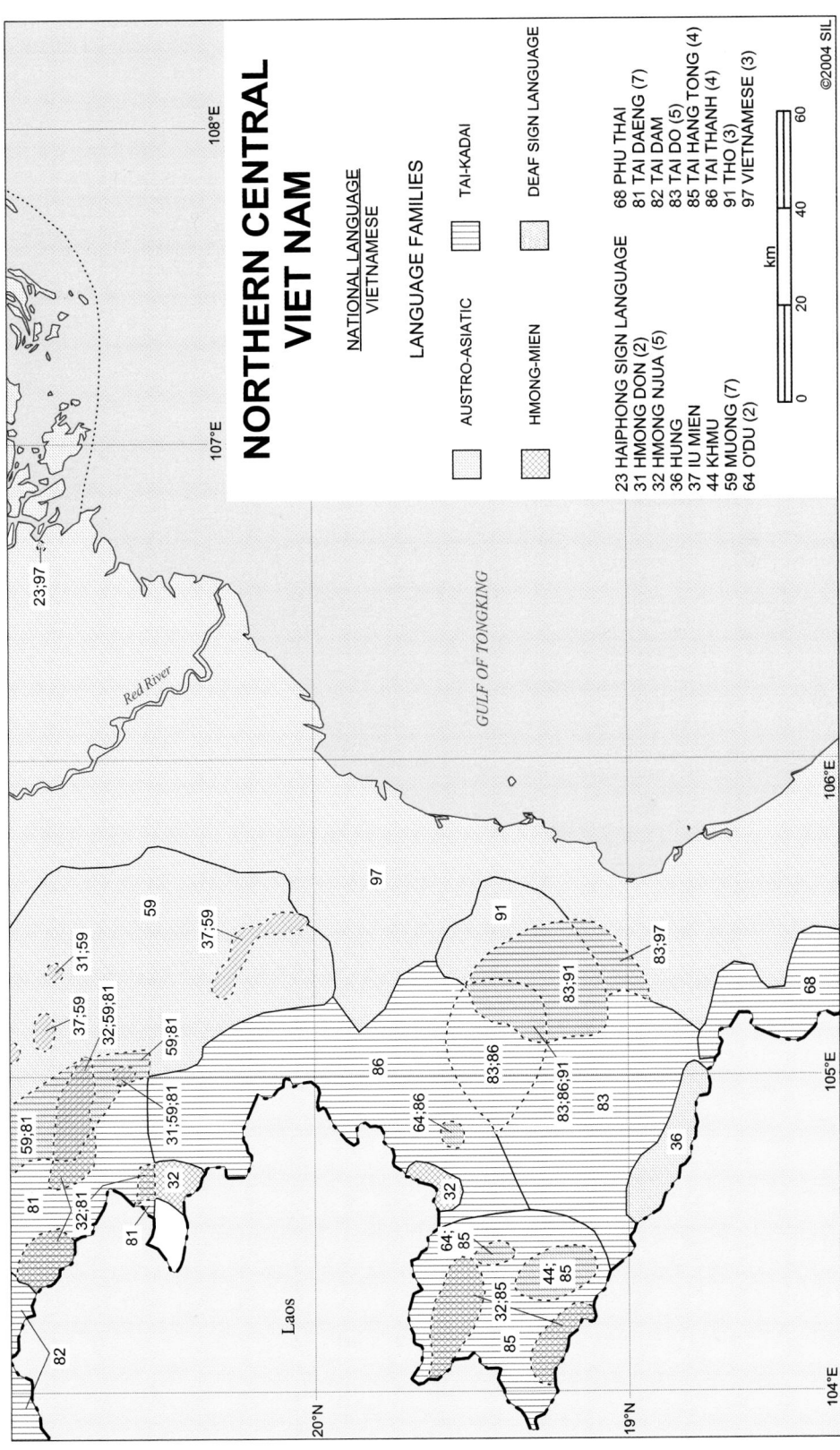

NORTHERN CENTRAL VIET NAM

<u>NATIONAL LANGUAGE</u>
VIETNAMESE

LANGUAGE FAMILIES

AUSTRO-ASIATIC

HMONG-MIEN

TAI-KADAI

DEAF SIGN LANGUAGE

23 HAIPHONG SIGN LANGUAGE
31 HMONG DON (2)
32 HMONG NJUA (5)
36 HUNG
37 IU MIEN
44 KHMU
59 MUONG (7)
64 O'DU (2)

68 PHU THAI
81 TAI DAENG (7)
82 TAI DAM
83 TAI DO (5)
85 TAI HANG TONG (4)
86 TAI THANH (4)
91 THO (3)
97 VIETNAMESE (3)

©2004 SIL

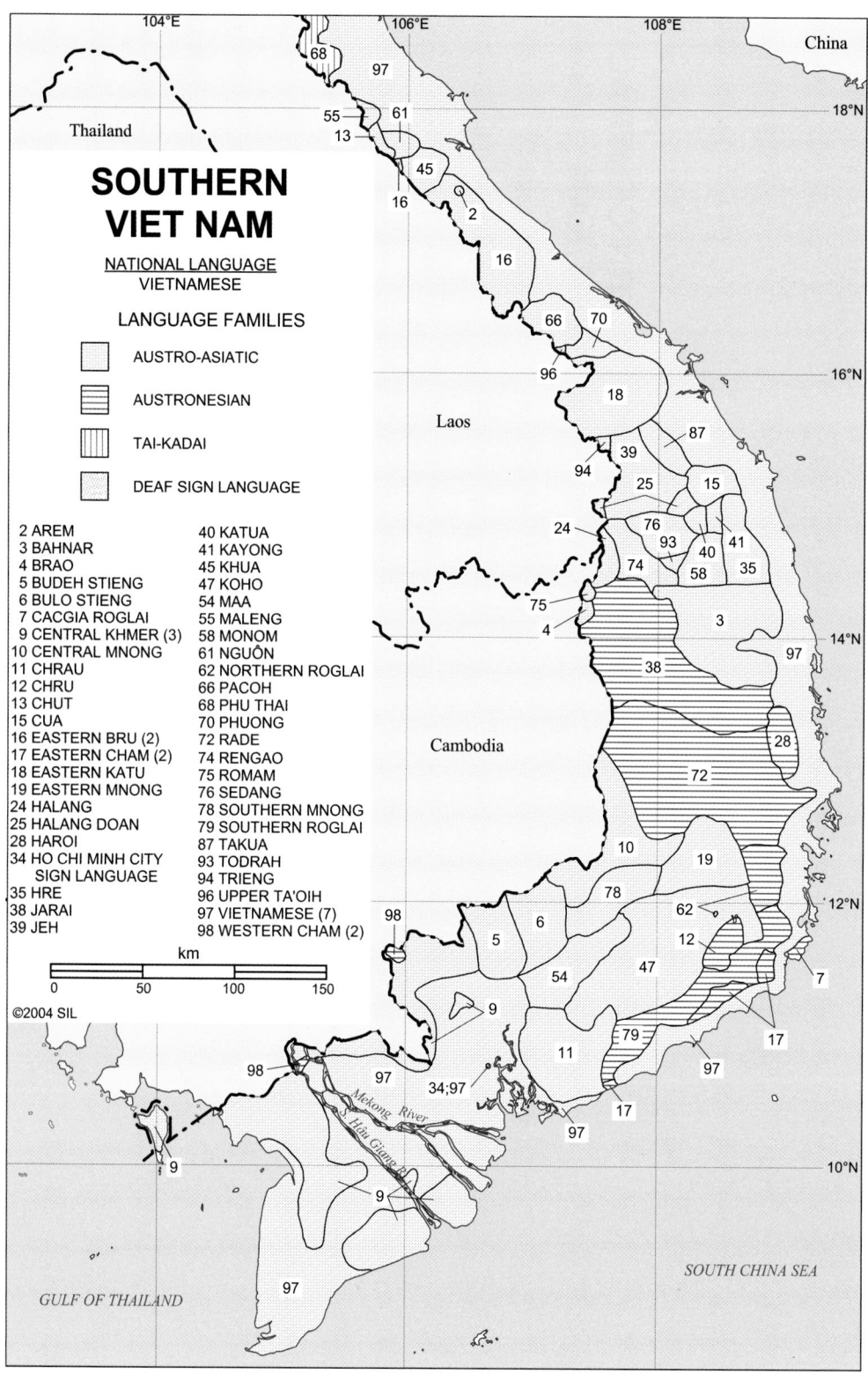

SOUTHERN VIET NAM

NATIONAL LANGUAGE
VIETNAMESE

LANGUAGE FAMILIES

AUSTRO-ASIATIC

AUSTRONESIAN

TAI-KADAI

DEAF SIGN LANGUAGE

2 AREM
3 BAHNAR
4 BRAO
5 BUDEH STIENG
6 BULO STIENG
7 CACGIA ROGLAI
9 CENTRAL KHMER (3)
10 CENTRAL MNONG
11 CHRAU
12 CHRU
13 CHUT
15 CUA
16 EASTERN BRU (2)
17 EASTERN CHAM (2)
18 EASTERN KATU
19 EASTERN MNONG
24 HALANG
25 HALANG DOAN
28 HAROI
34 HO CHI MINH CITY
    SIGN LANGUAGE
35 HRE
38 JARAI
39 JEH

40 KATUA
41 KAYONG
45 KHUA
47 KOHO
54 MAA
55 MALENG
58 MONOM
61 NGUÔN
62 NORTHERN ROGLAI
66 PACOH
68 PHU THAI
70 PHUONG
72 RADE
74 RENGAO
75 ROMAM
76 SEDANG
78 SOUTHERN MNONG
79 SOUTHERN ROGLAI
87 TAKUA
93 TODRAH
94 TRIENG
96 UPPER TA'OIH
97 VIETNAMESE (7)
98 WESTERN CHAM (2)

km

0   50   100   150

©2004 SIL

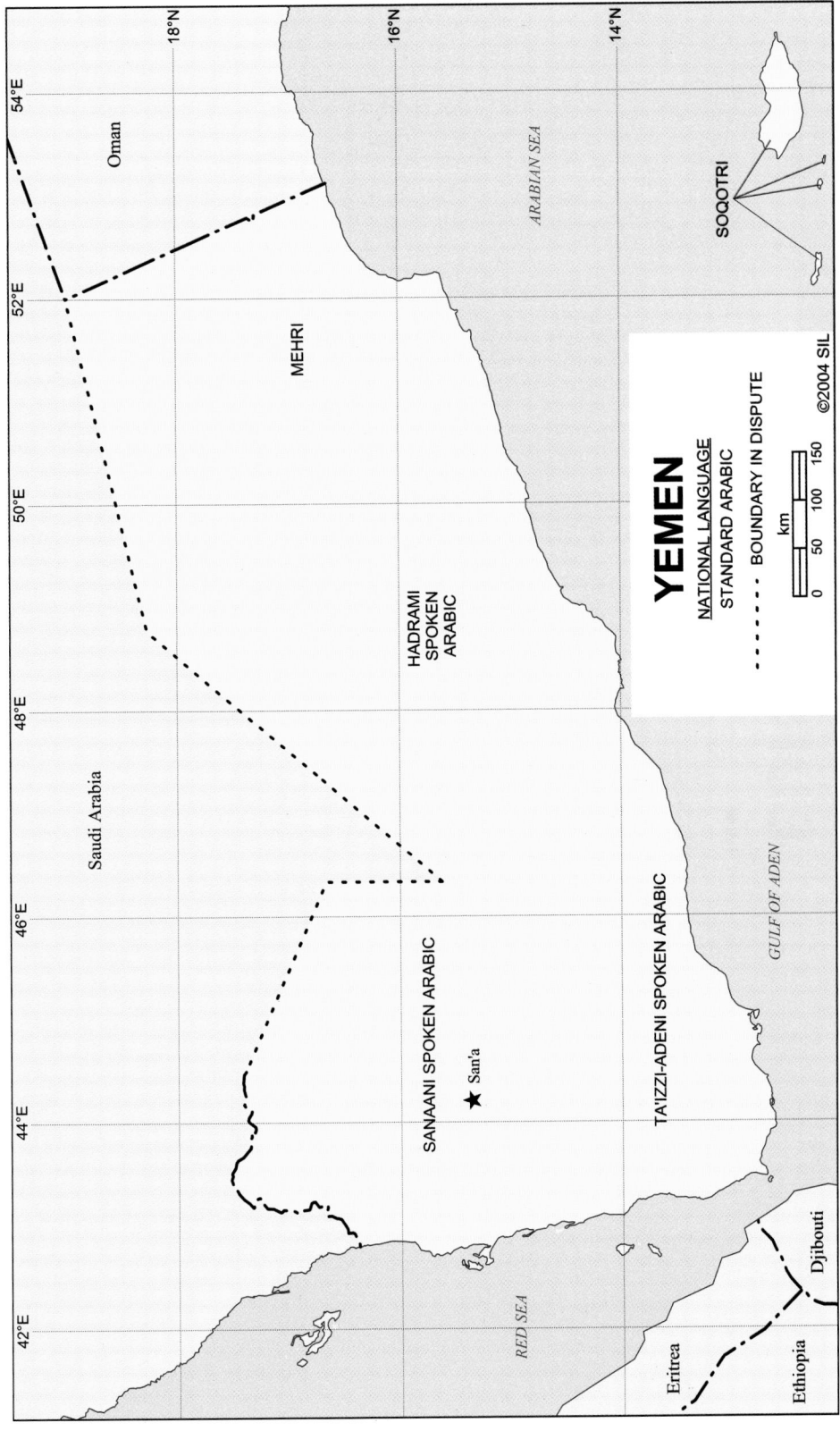

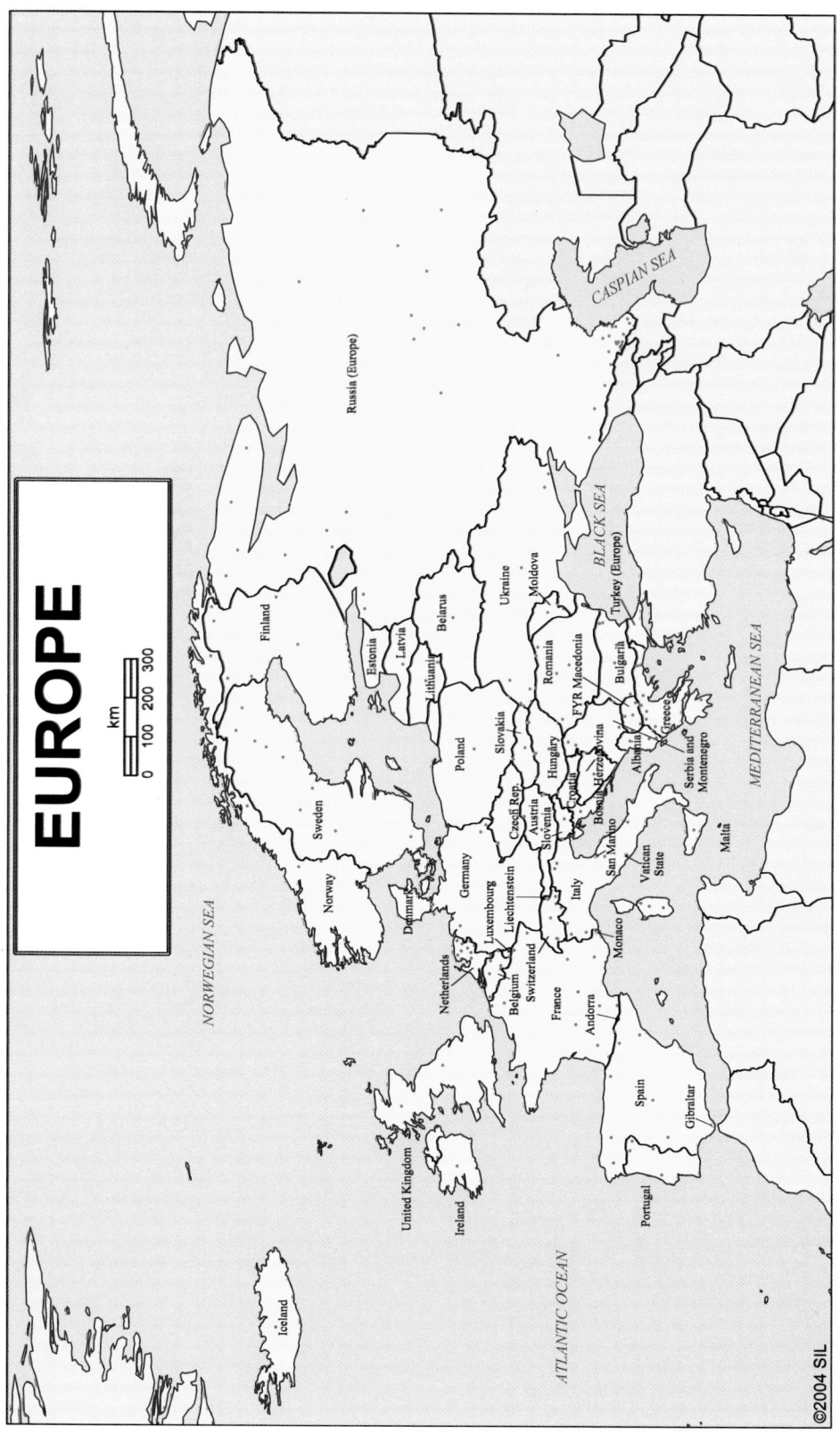

EUROPE

km

0 100 200 300

NORWEGIAN SEA

ATLANTIC OCEAN

MEDITERRANEAN SEA

BLACK SEA

CASPIAN SEA

Iceland

United Kingdom

Ireland

Portugal

Spain

Gibraltar

Andorra

France

Monaco

Belgium

Netherlands

Switzerland

Luxembourg

Liechtenstein

Germany

Denmark

Norway

Sweden

Finland

Estonia

Latvia

Lithuania

Belarus

Poland

Ukraine

Moldova

Czech Rep.

Slovakia

Austria

Slovenia

Hungary

Croatia

Italy

San Marino

Vatican State

Bosnia Herzegovina

Serbia and Montenegro

Romania

Malta

Albania

FYR Macedonia

Bulgaria

Greece

Turkey (Europe)

Russia (Europe)

©2004 SIL

WESTERN FRISIAN

NORTH SEA

GRONINGS*

DUTCH

WESTERN FRISIAN

DRENTS*

STELLINGWERFS*

SALLANDS*

Amsterdam

TWENTS*

The Hague

VELUWS*

DUTCH

52°N

NETHERLANDS

ACHTERHOEKS*

ZEEUWS

VLAAMS

DUTCH

VLAAMS

DUTCH;FRENCH

LIMBURGISCH

Germany

Brussels

STANDARD GERMAN

FRENCH;
PICARD

FRENCH;
PICARD

DUTCH;
LIMBURGISCH

BELGIUM

FRENCH;
WALLOON

FRENCH;
PICARD

**OFFICIAL REGIONAL
LANGUAGES**

BELGIUM:
PICARD
STANDARD GERMAN

NETHERLANDS:
ACHTERHOEKS*
DRENTS*
GRONINGS*
LIMBURGISCH
SALLANDS*
STELLINGWERFS*
TWENTS*
VELUWS*
WESTERN FRISIAN

France

FRENCH

Luxembourg

FRENCH;
LUXEMBOURGEOIS

* THESE LANGUAGES FORM A CLUSTER
REFERRED TO AS NEDERSAKSISCH
(LOW SAXON), WHICH HAS THE
STATUS OF A REGIONAL LANGUAGE
IN THE NETHERLANDS.

NOTES:
1. DASHED LINES SHOW OVERLAP OF
LANGUAGE AREAS.
2. IN THE NETHERLANDS PRACTICALLY ALL DIALECT
AND OTHER INDIGENOUS LANGUAGE SPEAKERS
ARE ALSO FLUENT IN DUTCH.
3. IN BELGIUM DUTCH IS COMMONLY CALLED FLEMISH.

NATIONAL LANGUAGES

BELGIUM:
DUTCH
FRENCH

NETHERLANDS:
DUTCH

LANGUAGE FAMILIES

GERMANIC

ROMANCE

km

0   20   40   60   80

BELGIUM AND
NETHERLANDS

©2004 SIL

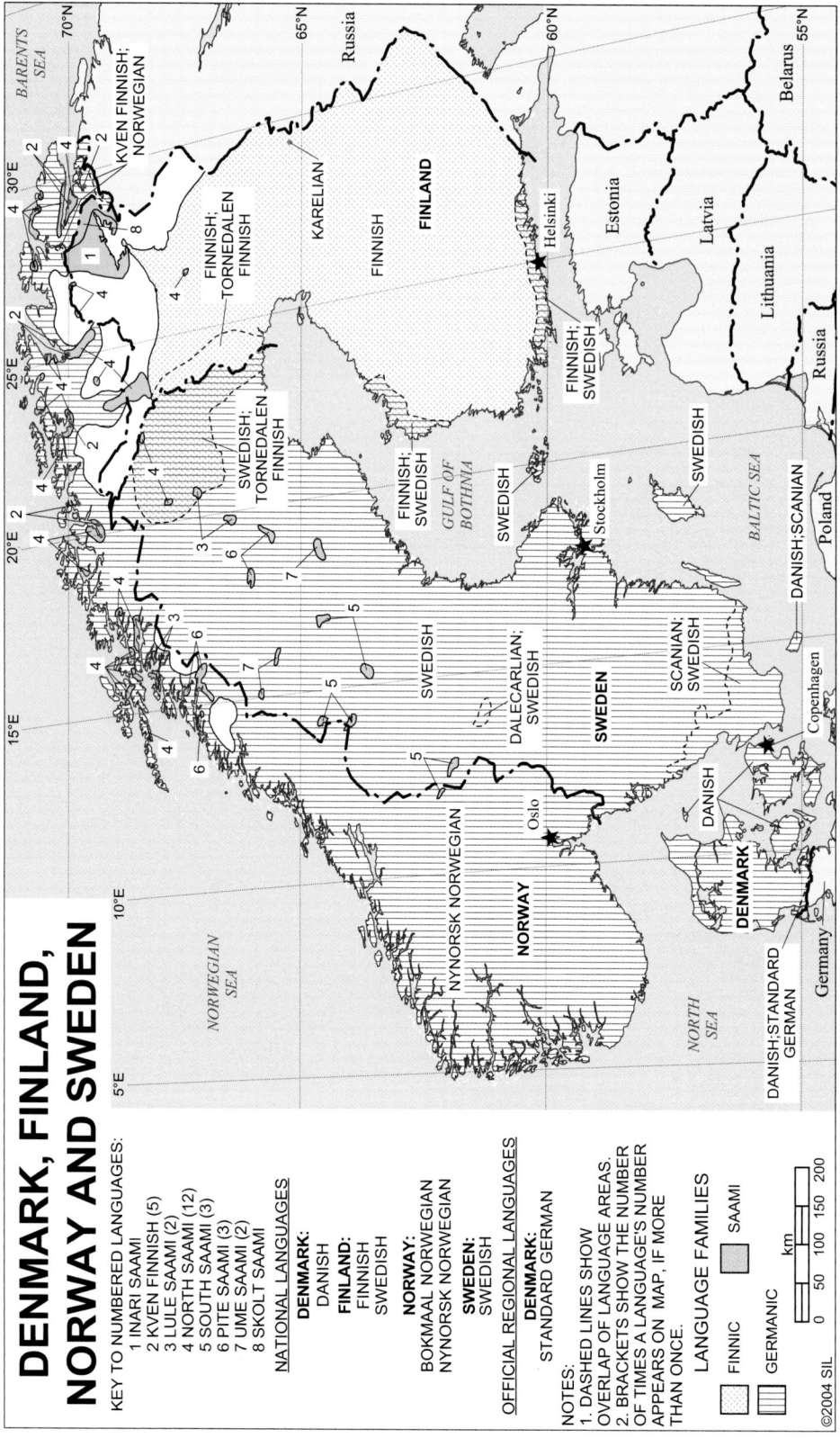

DENMARK, FINLAND, NORWAY AND SWEDEN

KEY TO NUMBERED LANGUAGES:
1 INARI SAAMI
2 KVEN FINNISH (5)
3 LULE SAAMI (2)
4 NORTH SAAMI (12)
5 SOUTH SAAMI (3)
6 PITE SAAMI (3)
7 UME SAAMI (2)
8 SKOLT SAAMI

NATIONAL LANGUAGES

DENMARK:
DANISH

FINLAND:
FINNISH
SWEDISH

NORWAY:
BOKMAAL NORWEGIAN
NYNORSK NORWEGIAN

SWEDEN:
SWEDISH

OFFICIAL REGIONAL LANGUAGES

DENMARK:
STANDARD GERMAN

NOTES:
1. DASHED LINES SHOW
OVERLAP OF LANGUAGE AREAS.
2. BRACKETS SHOW THE NUMBER
OF TIMES A LANGUAGE'S NUMBER
APPEARS ON MAP, IF MORE
THAN ONCE.

LANGUAGE FAMILIES

FINNIC　　　SAAMI

GERMANIC

km
0 50 100 150 200

©2004 SIL

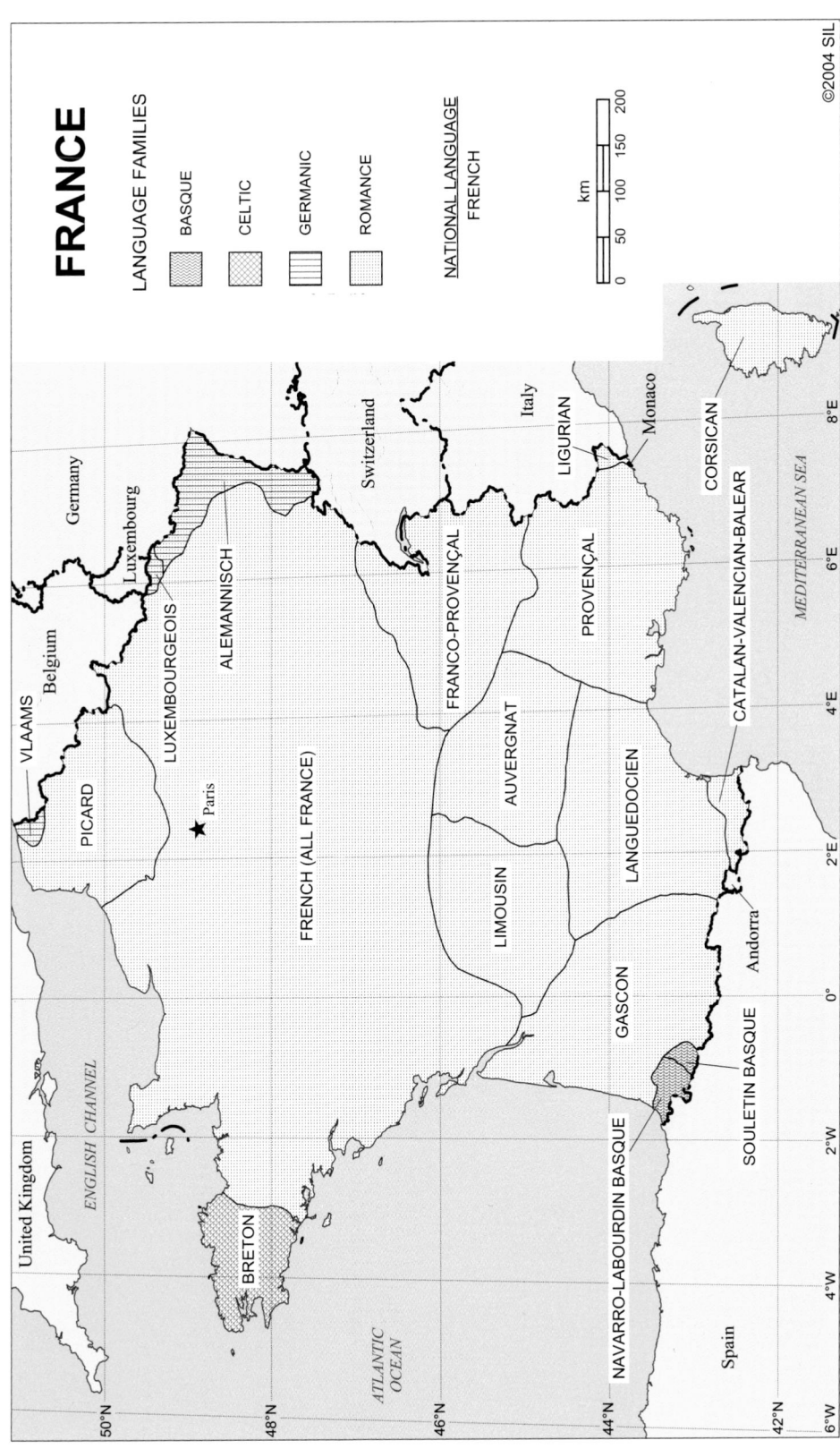

FRANCE

LANGUAGE FAMILIES

- BASQUE
- CELTIC
- GERMANIC
- ROMANCE

NATIONAL LANGUAGE
FRENCH

km

0   50   100   150   200

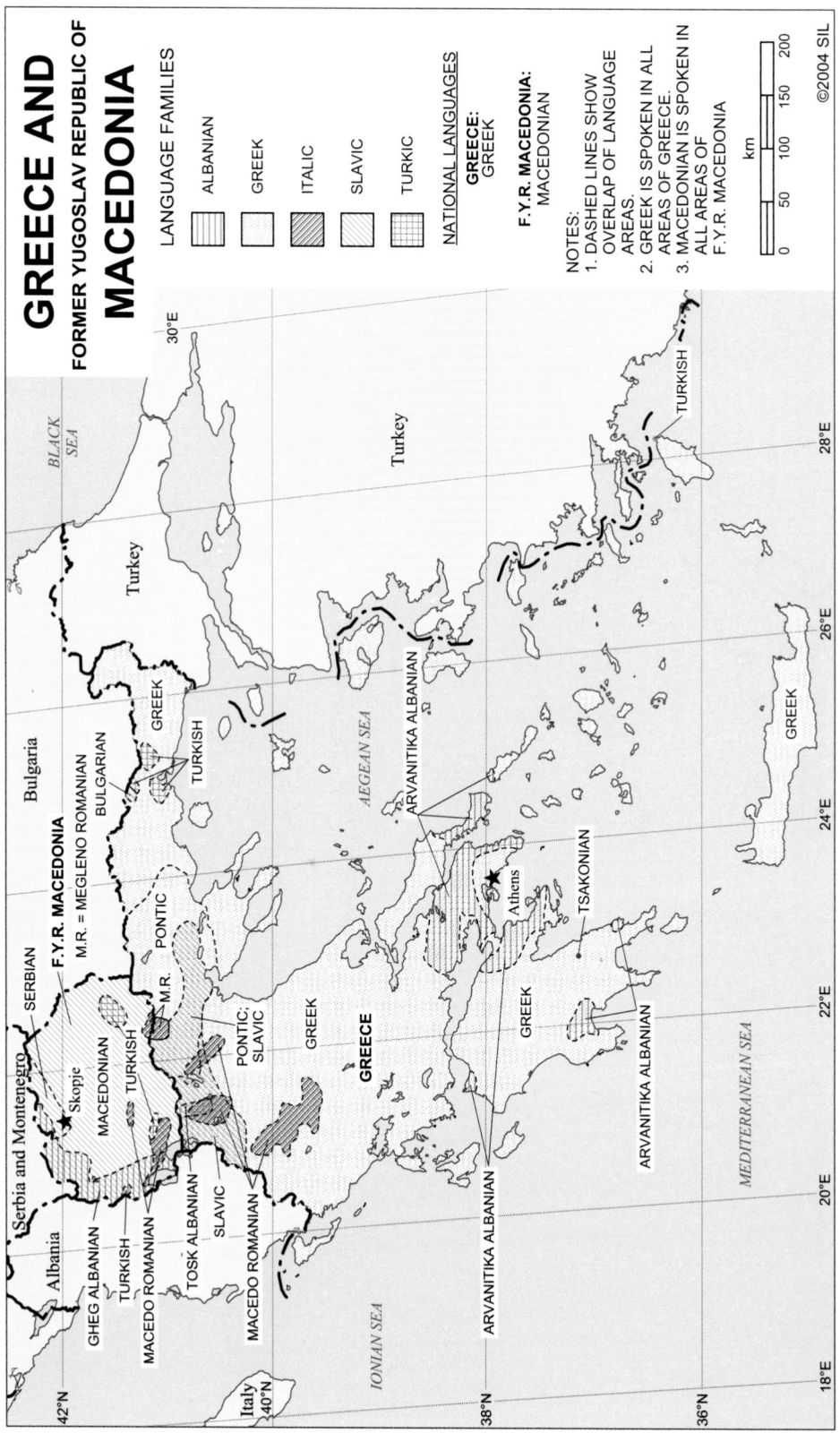

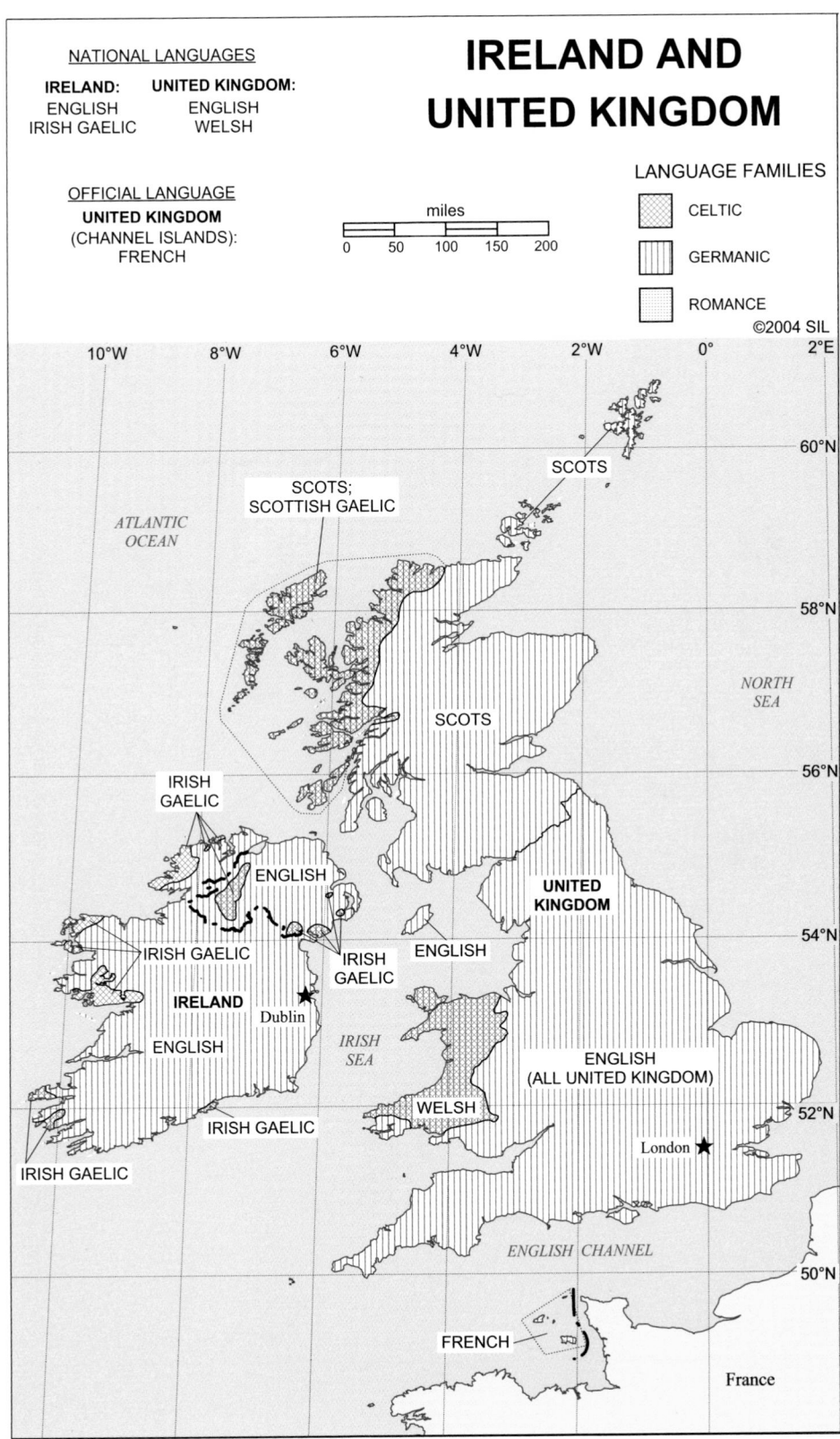

NATIONAL LANGUAGES

IRELAND: **UNITED KINGDOM:**
ENGLISH   ENGLISH
IRISH GAELIC   WELSH

OFFICIAL LANGUAGE

UNITED KINGDOM
(CHANNEL ISLANDS):
FRENCH

IRELAND AND
UNITED KINGDOM

LANGUAGE FAMILIES

CELTIC

GERMANIC

ROMANCE

©2004 SIL

miles

0   50   100   150   200

10°W   8°W   6°W   4°W   2°W   0°   2°E

60°N

SCOTS

SCOTS;
SCOTTISH GAELIC

ATLANTIC
OCEAN

58°N

NORTH
SEA

SCOTS

56°N

IRISH
GAELIC

ENGLISH

**UNITED
KINGDOM**

54°N

IRISH GAELIC

IRISH
GAELIC

ENGLISH

IRELAND   Dublin ★

IRISH
SEA

ENGLISH

ENGLISH
(ALL UNITED KINGDOM)

52°N

IRISH GAELIC

WELSH

London ★

IRISH GAELIC

ENGLISH CHANNEL

50°N

FRENCH

France

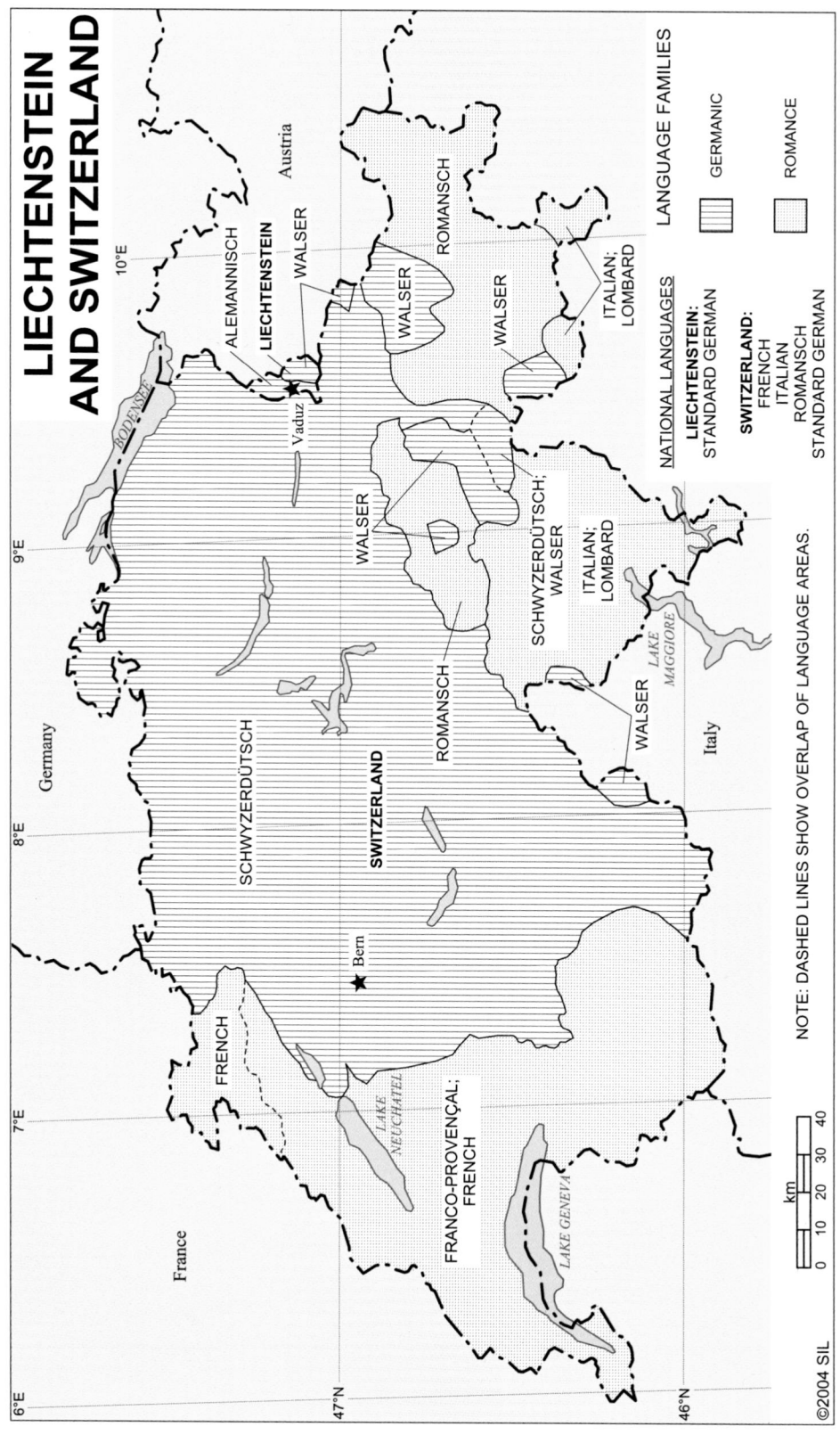

LIECHTENSTEIN AND SWITZERLAND

Germany

France

Austria

Italy

BODENSEE

LAKE NEUCHATEL

LAKE GENEVA

LAKE MAGGIORE

★ Vaduz

★ Bern

ALEMANNISCH

LIECHTENSTEIN

WALSER

ROMANSCH

WALSER

WALSER

ITALIAN; LOMBARD

WALSER

SCHWYZERDÜTSCH

SWITZERLAND

ROMANSCH

SCHWYZERDÜTSCH; WALSER

ITALIAN; LOMBARD

WALSER

FRENCH

FRANCO-PROVENÇAL; FRENCH

LANGUAGE FAMILIES

GERMANIC

ROMANCE

NATIONAL LANGUAGES

LIECHTENSTEIN:
STANDARD GERMAN

SWITZERLAND:
FRENCH
ITALIAN
ROMANSCH
STANDARD GERMAN

NOTE: DASHED LINES SHOW OVERLAP OF LANGUAGE AREAS.

km

0   10   20   30   40

©2004 SIL

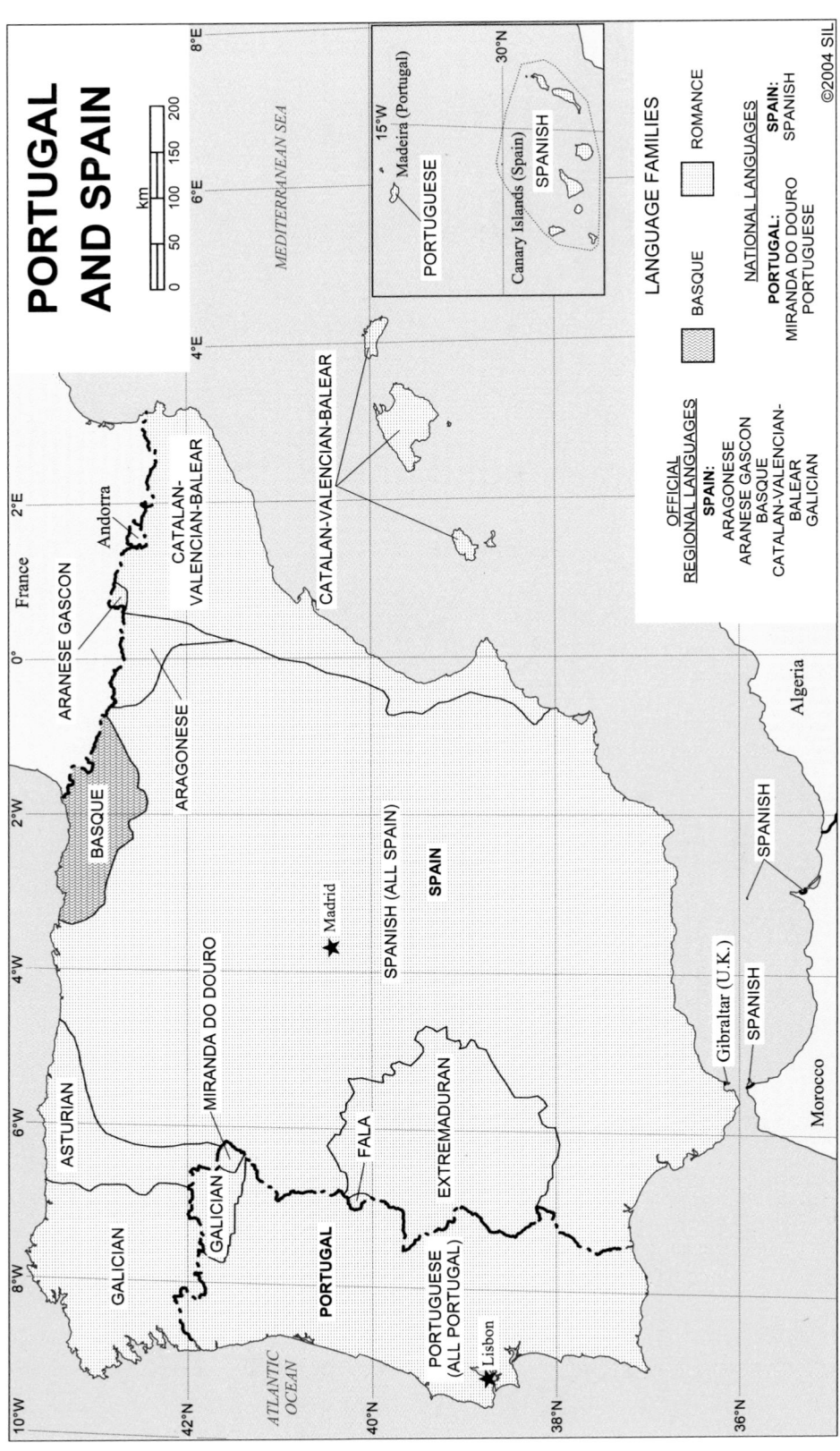

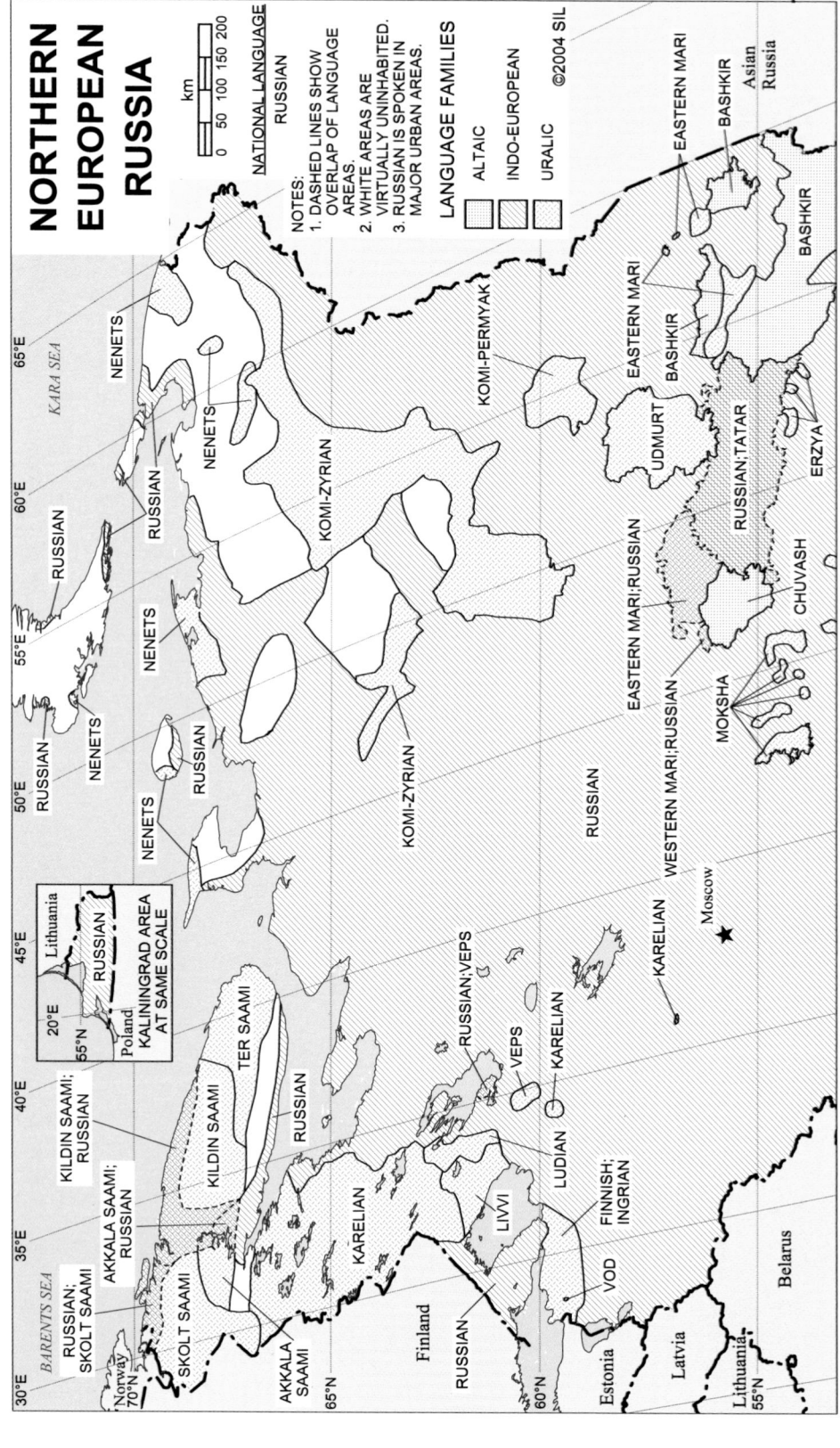

NORTHERN EUROPEAN RUSSIA

km

0 50 100 150 200

NATIONAL LANGUAGE
RUSSIAN

NOTES:
1. DASHED LINES SHOW OVERLAP OF LANGUAGE AREAS.
2. WHITE AREAS ARE VIRTUALLY UNINHABITED.
3. RUSSIAN IS SPOKEN IN MAJOR URBAN AREAS.

LANGUAGE FAMILIES

ALTAIC

INDO-EUROPEAN

URALIC

©2004 SIL

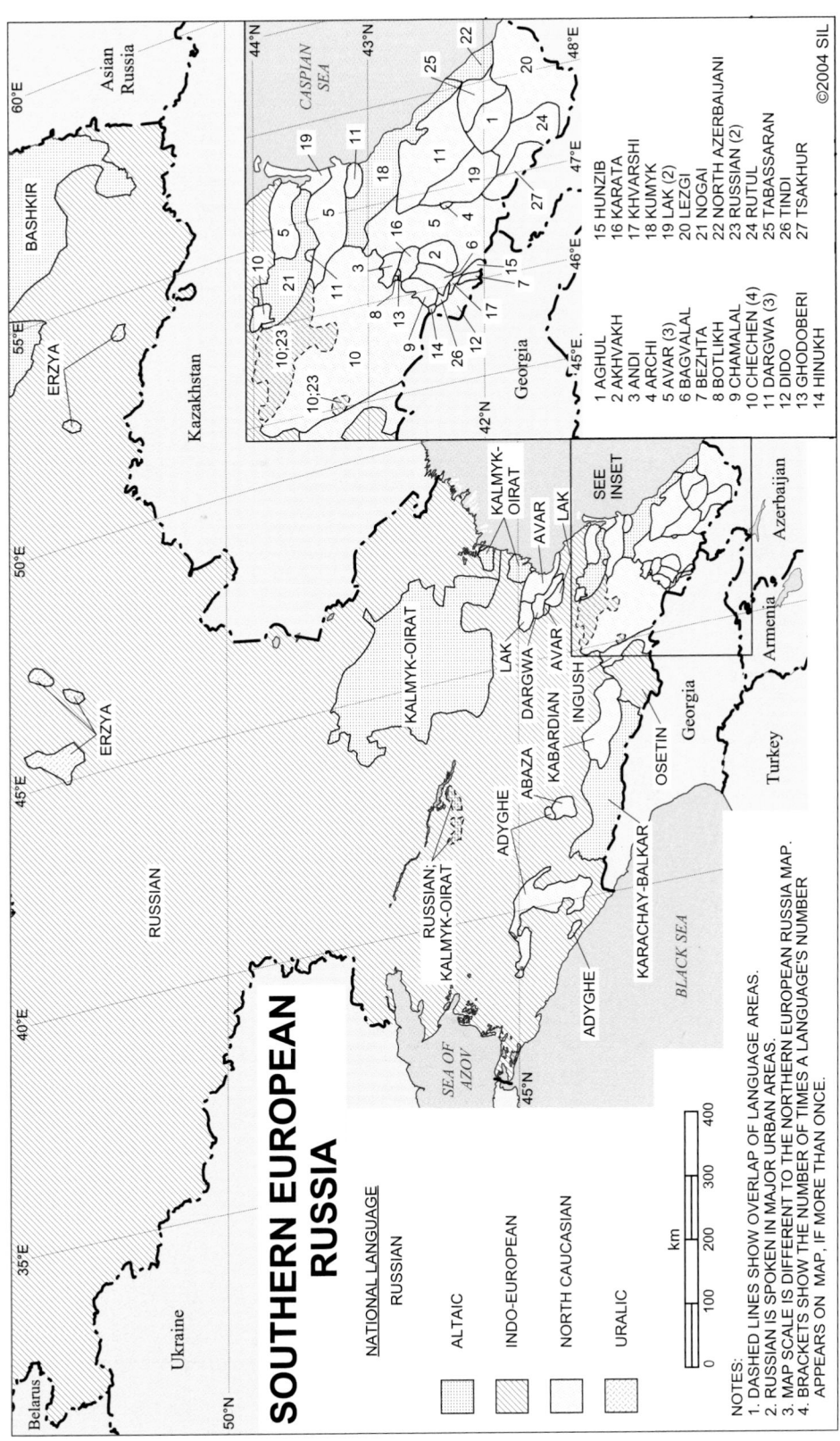

SOUTHERN EUROPEAN RUSSIA

NATIONAL LANGUAGE
RUSSIAN

ALTAIC

INDO-EUROPEAN

NORTH CAUCASIAN

URALIC

km
0   100   200   300   400

NOTES:
1. DASHED LINES SHOW OVERLAP OF LANGUAGE AREAS.
2. RUSSIAN IS SPOKEN IN MAJOR URBAN AREAS.
3. MAP SCALE IS DIFFERENT TO THE NORTHERN EUROPEAN RUSSIA MAP.
4. BRACKETS SHOW THE NUMBER OF TIMES A LANGUAGE'S NUMBER
   APPEARS ON MAP, IF MORE THAN ONCE.

1 AGHUL
2 AKHVAKH
3 ANDI
4 ARCHI
5 AVAR (3)
6 BAGVALAL
7 BEZHTA
8 BOTLIKH
9 CHAMALAL
10 CHECHEN (4)
11 DARGWA (3)
12 DIDO
13 GHODOBERI
14 HINUKH
15 HUNZIB
16 KARATA
17 KHVARSHI
18 KUMYK
19 LAK (2)
20 LEZGI
21 NOGAI
22 NORTH AZERBAIJANI
23 RUSSIAN (2)
24 RUTUL
25 TABASSARAN
26 TINDI
27 TSAKHUR

©2004 SIL

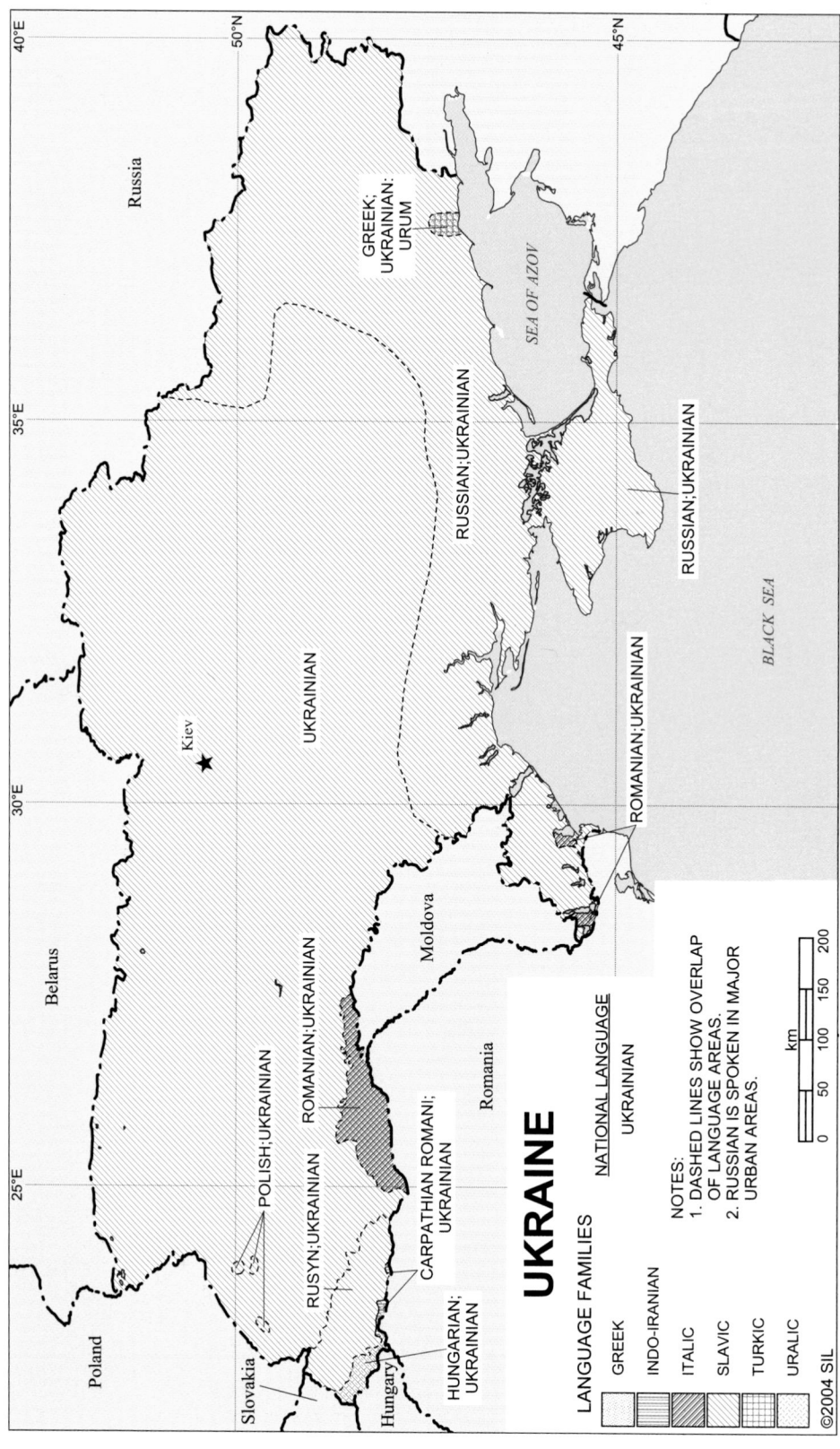

40°E · 50°N · 45°N

Russia

GREEK;
UKRAINIAN;
URUM

SEA OF AZOV

35°E

RUSSIAN;UKRAINIAN

RUSSIAN;UKRAINIAN

Kiev

UKRAINIAN

BLACK SEA

30°E

ROMANIAN;UKRAINIAN

Belarus

Moldova

POLISH;UKRAINIAN

ROMANIAN;UKRAINIAN

25°E

RUSYN;UKRAINIAN

Romania

CARPATHIAN ROMANI;
UKRAINIAN

Poland

Slovakia

HUNGARIAN;
UKRAINIAN

Hungary

UKRAINE

LANGUAGE FAMILIES   NATIONAL LANGUAGE

GREEK   UKRAINIAN

INDO-IRANIAN

ITALIC   NOTES:
                           1. DASHED LINES SHOW OVERLAP
SLAVIC   OF LANGUAGE AREAS.
                           2. RUSSIAN IS SPOKEN IN MAJOR
TURKIC   URBAN AREAS.

URALIC

km
0   50 100 150 200

©2004 SIL

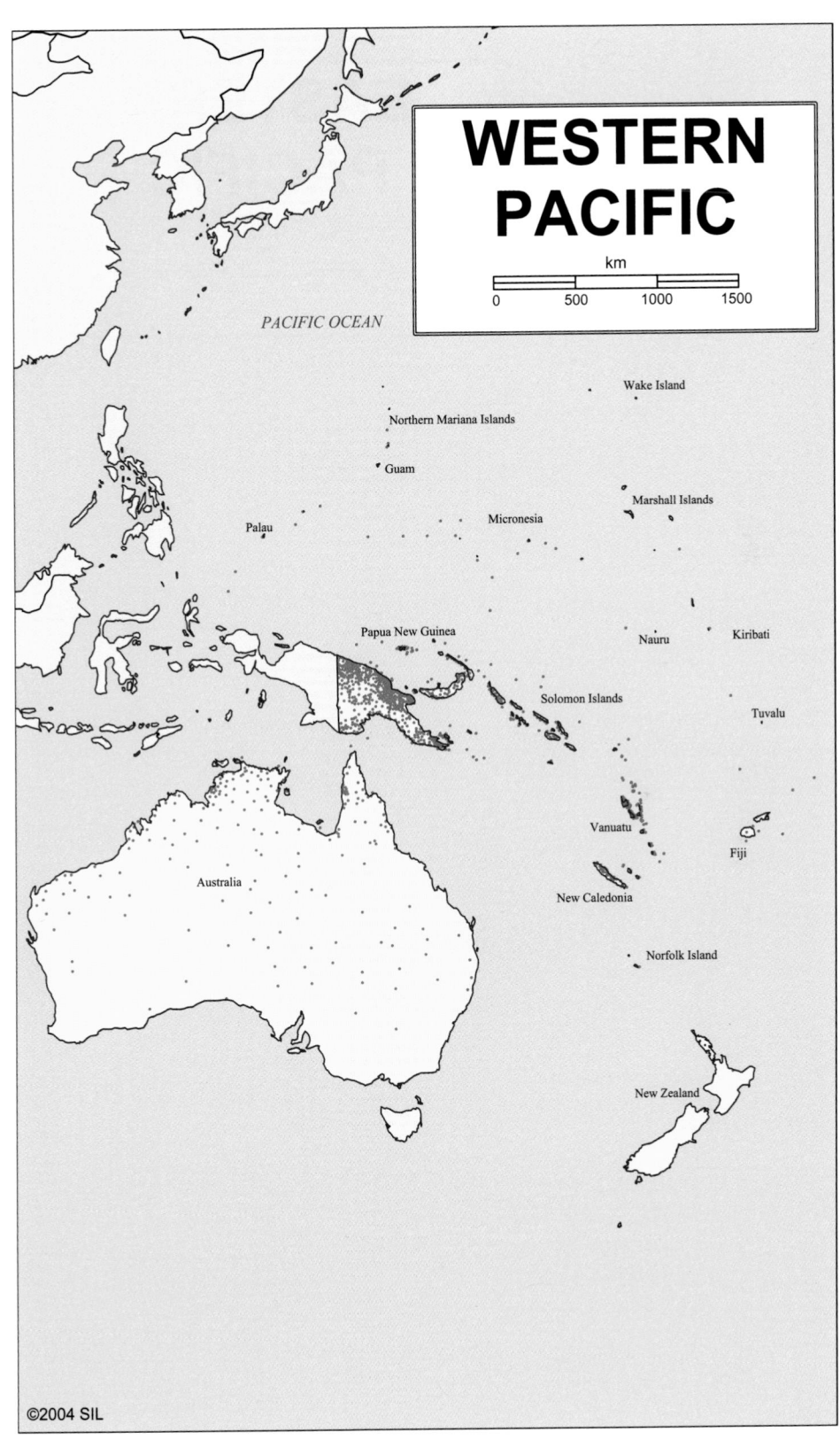

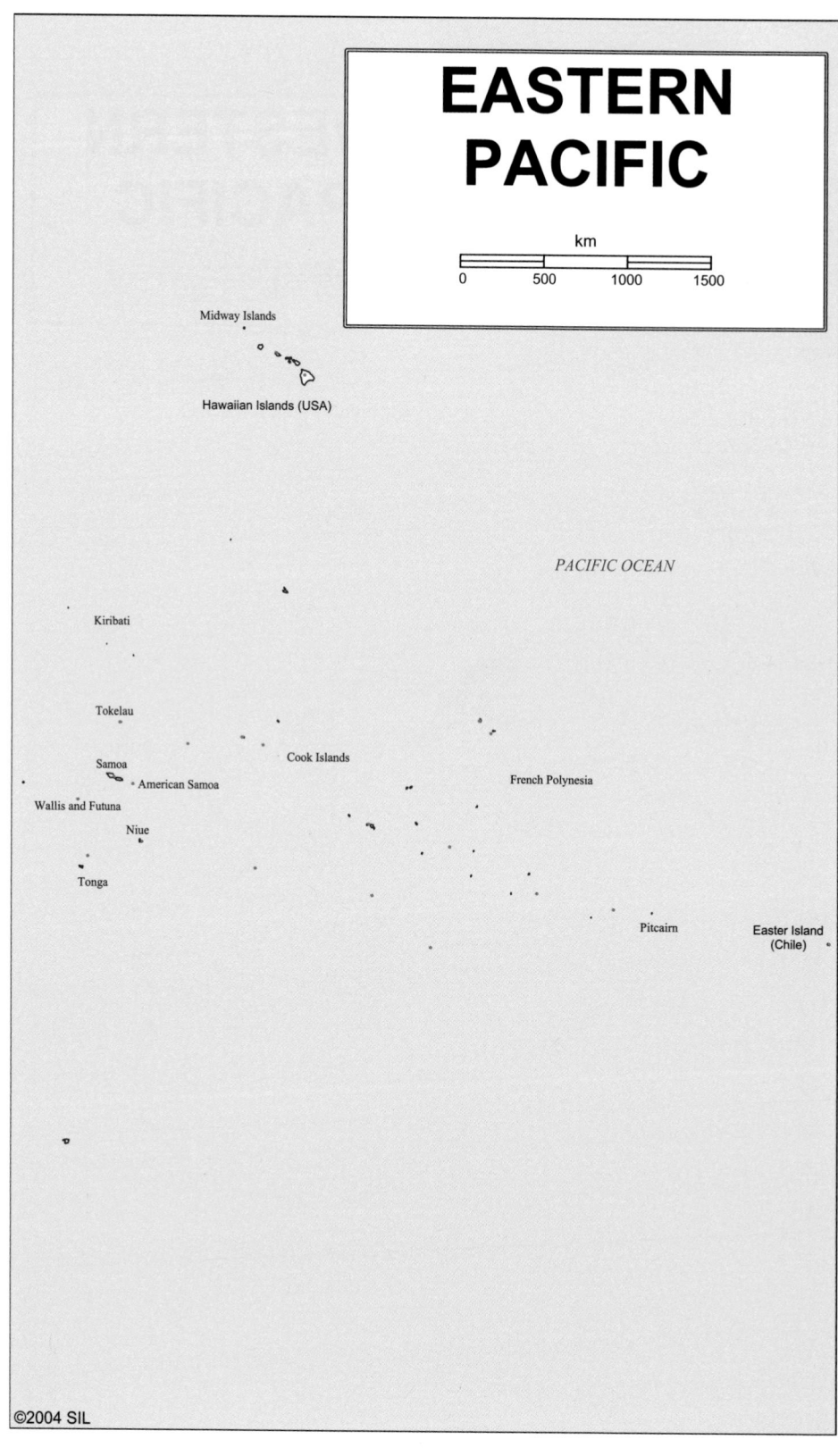

EASTERN PACIFIC

km

0   500   1000   1500

Midway Islands

Hawaiian Islands (USA)

PACIFIC OCEAN

Kiribati

Tokelau

Samoa

American Samoa

Cook Islands

French Polynesia

Wallis and Futuna

Niue

Tonga

Pitcairn

Easter Island (Chile)

©2004 SIL

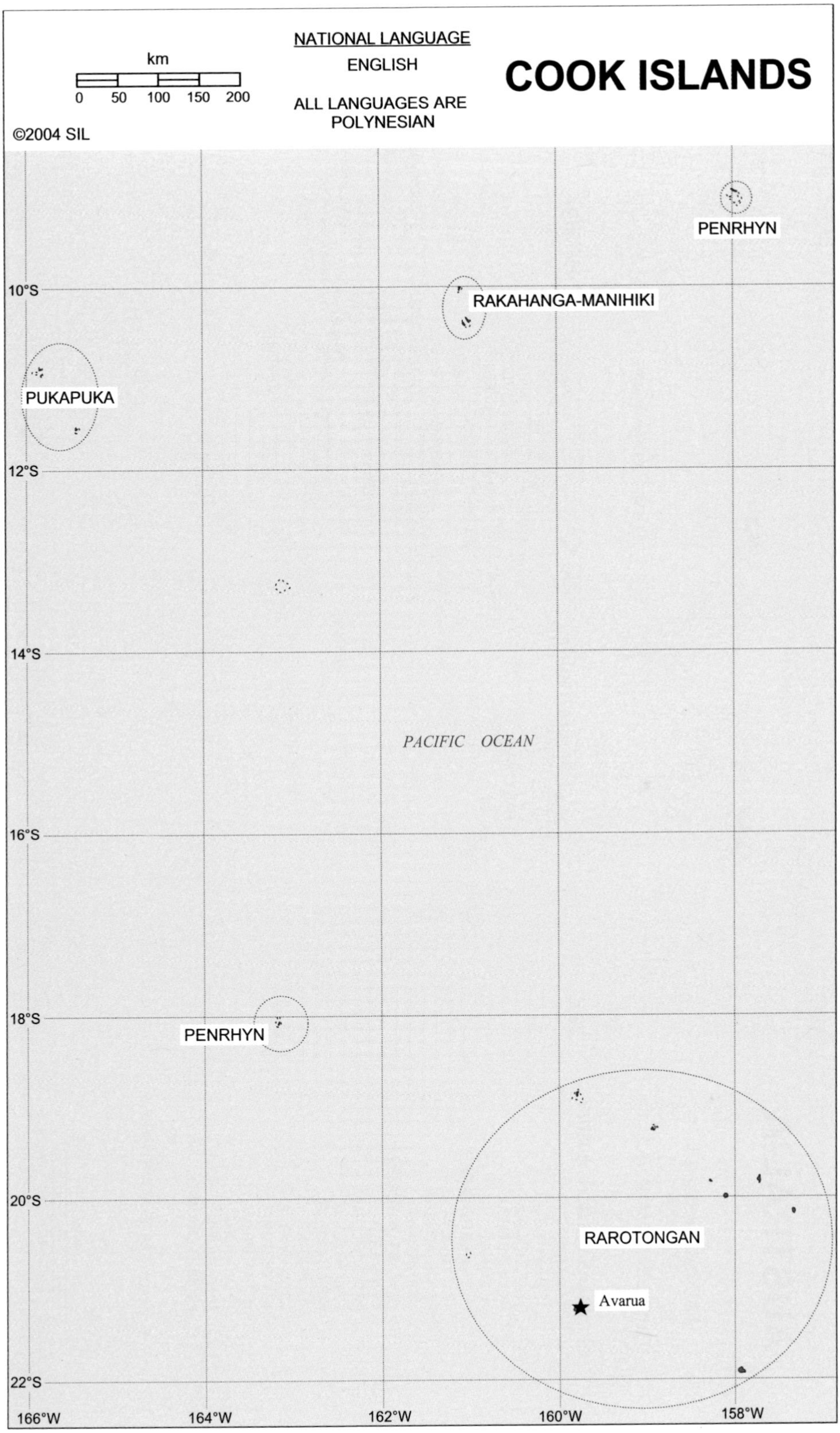

NATIONAL LANGUAGE

ENGLISH

ALL LANGUAGES ARE
POLYNESIAN

COOK ISLANDS

km

0   50   100   150   200

©2004 SIL

PENRHYN

10°S

RAKAHANGA-MANIHIKI

PUKAPUKA

12°S

14°S

PACIFIC   OCEAN

16°S

18°S

PENRHYN

20°S

RAROTONGAN

★ Avarua

22°S

166°W   164°W   162°W   160°W   158°W

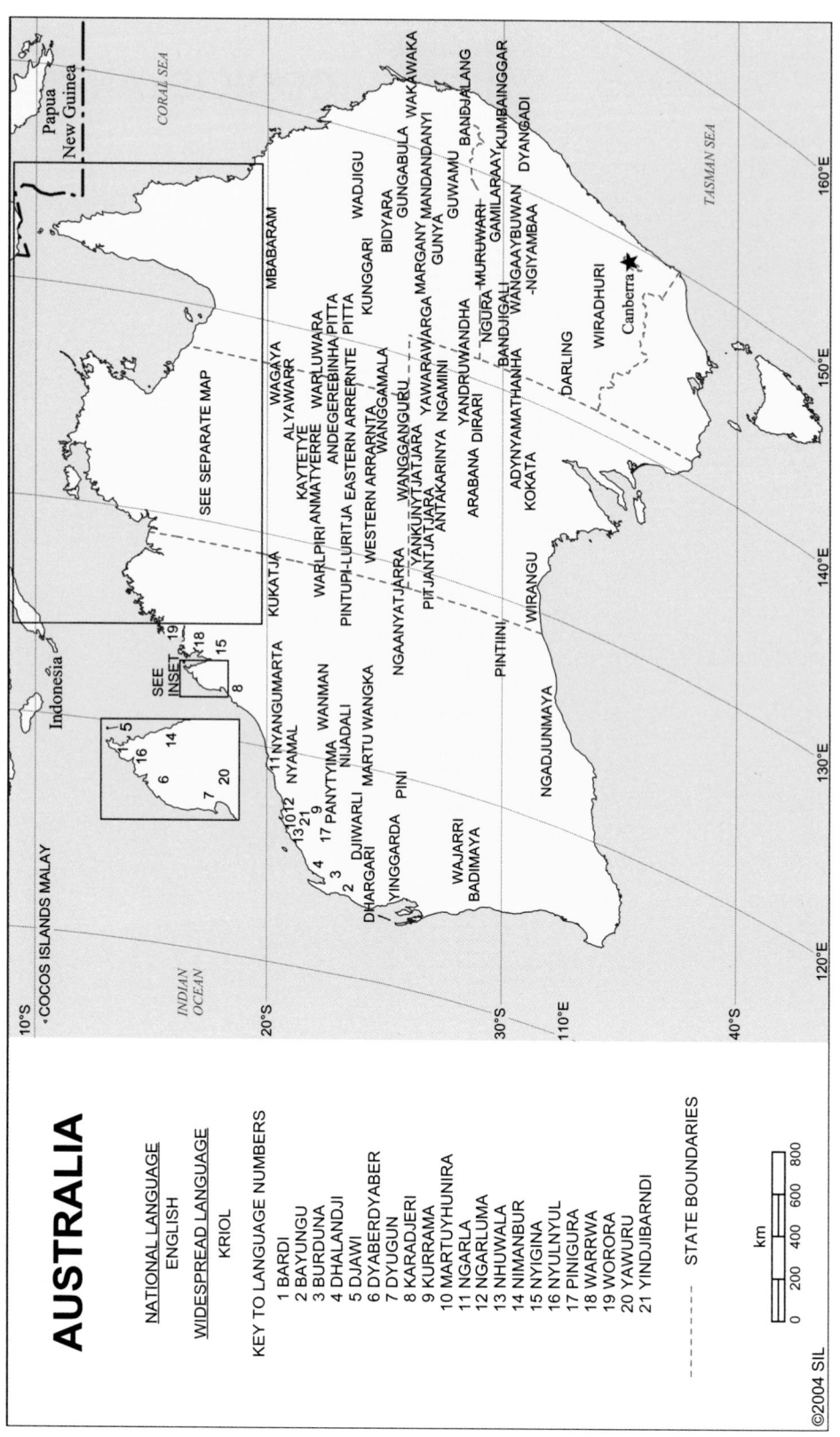

AUSTRALIA

NATIONAL LANGUAGE
ENGLISH

WIDESPREAD LANGUAGE
KRIOL

KEY TO LANGUAGE NUMBERS

1 BARDI
2 BAYUNGU
3 BURDUNA
4 DHALANDJI
5 DJAWI
6 DYABERDYABER
7 DYUGUN
8 KARADJERI
9 KURRAMA
10 MARTUYHUNIRA
11 NGARLA
12 NGARLUMA
13 NHUWALA
14 NIMANBUR
15 NYIGINA
16 NYULNYUL
17 PINIGURA
18 WARRWA
19 WORORA
20 YAWURU
21 YINDJIBARNDI

- - - - - STATE BOUNDARIES

km

0   200   400   600   800

©2004 SIL

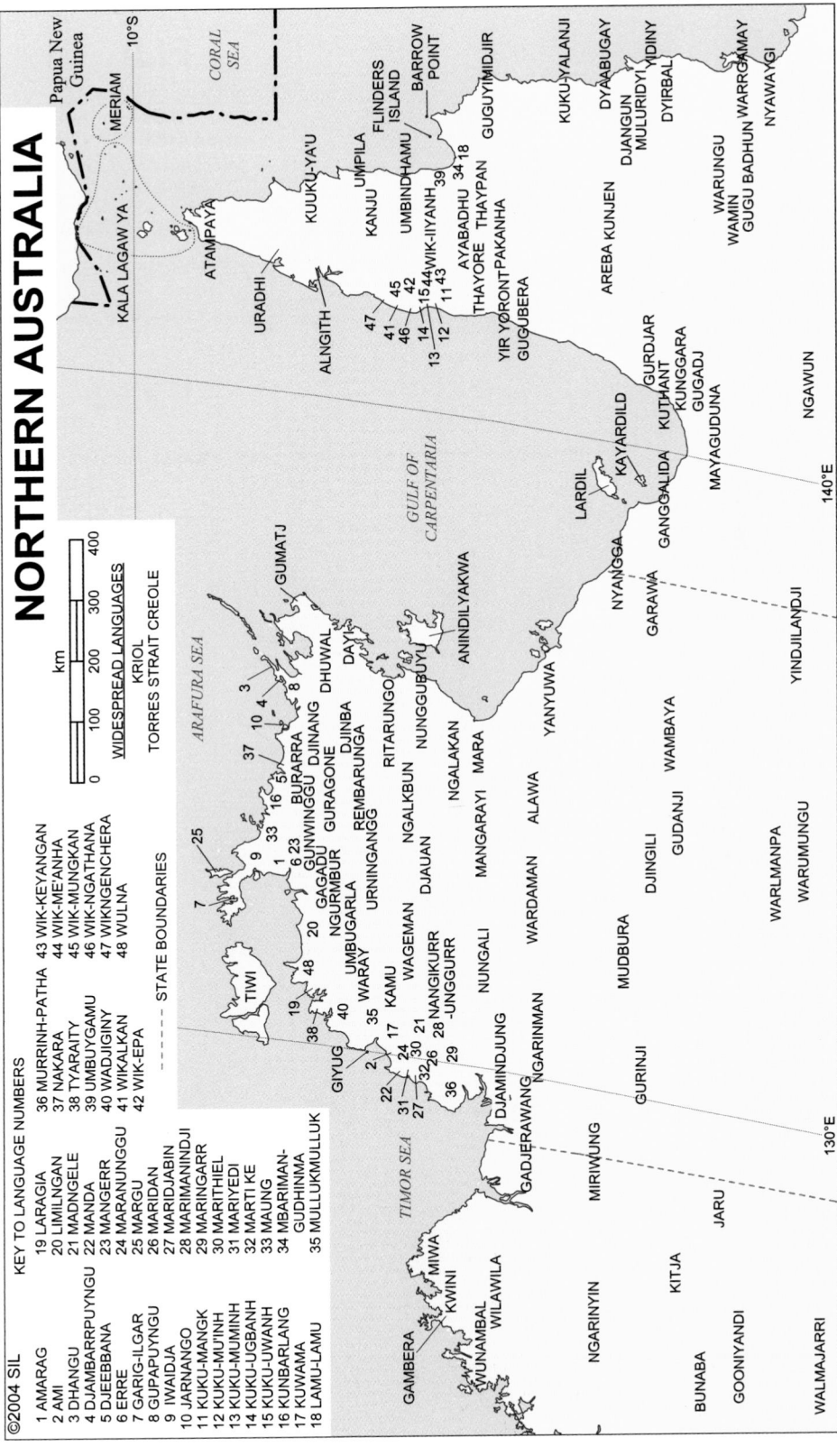

NORTHERN AUSTRALIA

KEY TO LANGUAGE NUMBERS

1 AMARAG	19 LARAGIA	36 MURRINH-PATHA
2 AMI	20 LIMILNGAN	37 NAKARA
3 DHANGU	21 MADNGELE	38 TYARAITY
4 DJAMBARRPUYNGU	22 MANDA	39 UMBUYGAMU
5 DJEEBBANA	23 MANGERR	40 WADJIGINY
6 ERRE	24 MARANUNGGU	41 WIKALKAN
7 GARIG-ILGAR	25 MARGU	42 WIK-EPA
8 GUPAPUYNGU	26 MARIDAN	43 WIK-KEYANGAN
9 IWAIDJA	27 MARIDJABIN	44 WIK-ME'ANHA
10 JARNANGO	28 MARIMANINDJI	45 WIK-MUNGKAN
11 KUKU-MANGK	29 MARINGARR	46 WIK-NGATHANA
12 KUKU-MUINH	30 MARITHIEL	47 WADJIGINY
13 KUKU-MUMINH	31 MARIYEDI	48 WULNA
14 KUKU-UGBANH	32 MARTI KE	
15 KUKU-UWANH	33 MAUNG	
16 KUNBARLANG	34 MBARIMAN-GUDHINMA	
17 KUWAMA	35 MULLUKMULLUK	
18 LAMU-LAMU		

WIDESPREAD LANGUAGES
KRIOL
TORRES STRAIT CREOLE

------ STATE BOUNDARIES

km
0   100   200   300   400

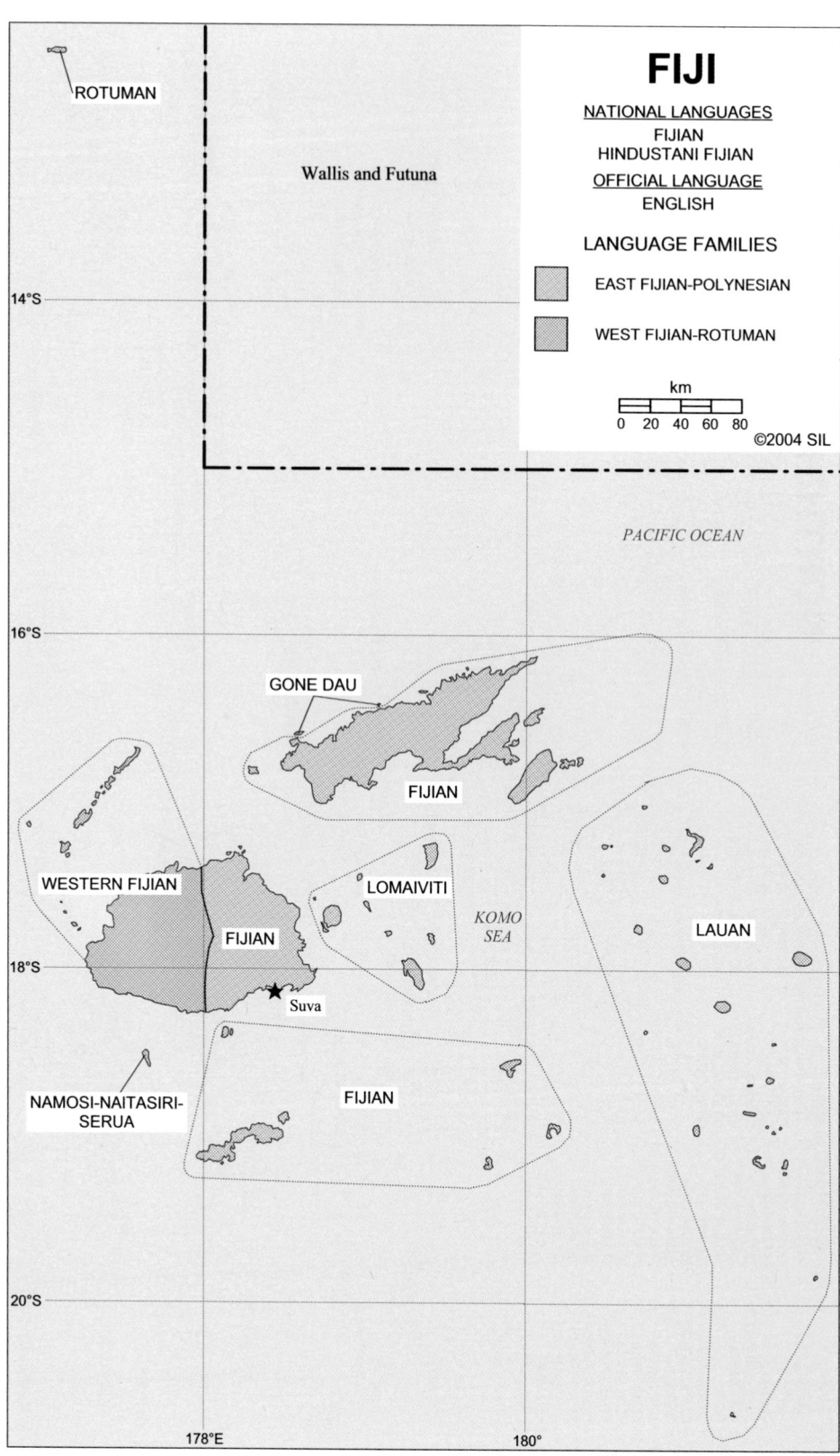

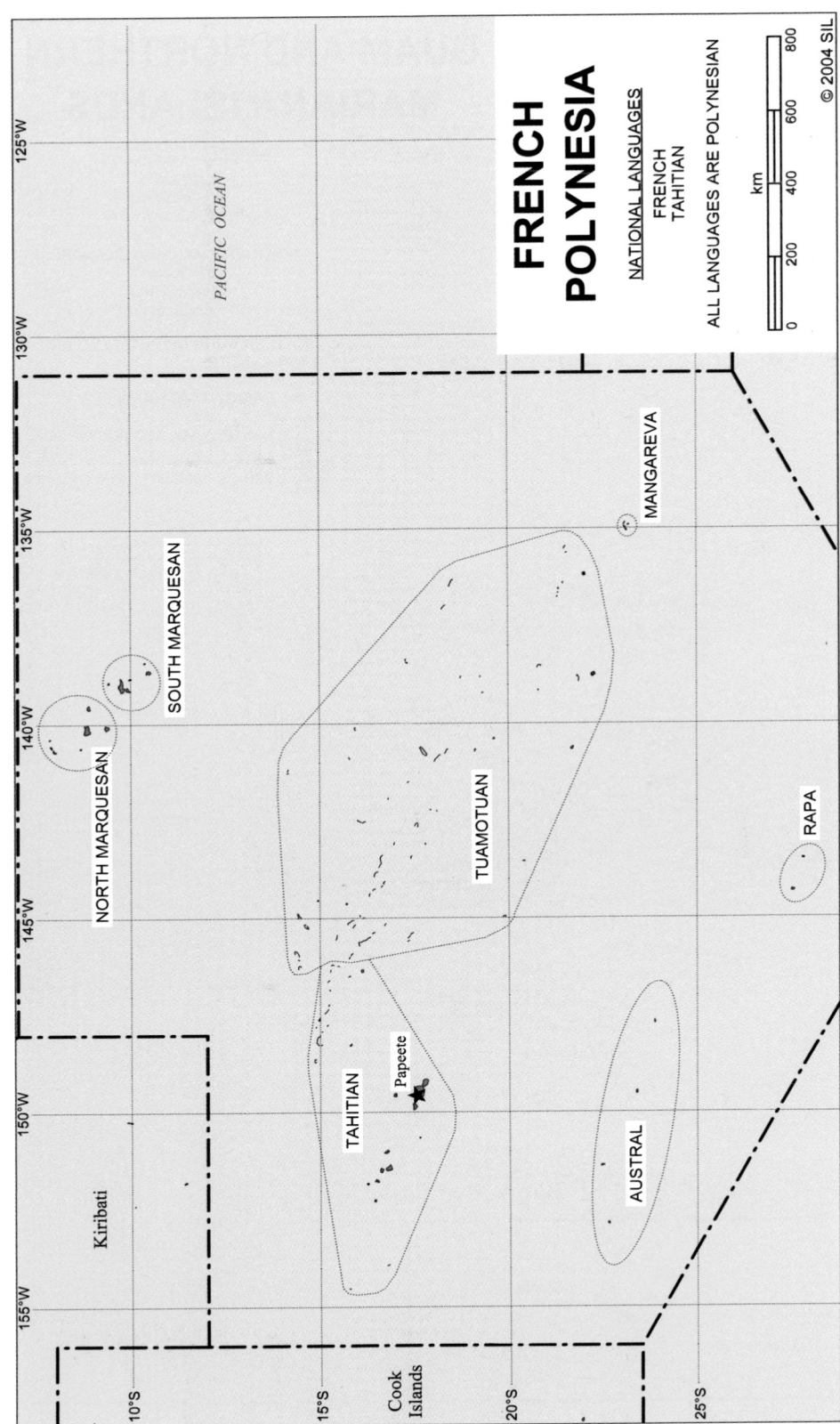

FRENCH POLYNESIA

NATIONAL LANGUAGES
FRENCH
TAHITIAN

ALL LANGUAGES ARE POLYNESIAN

km

0   200   400   600   800

© 2004 SIL

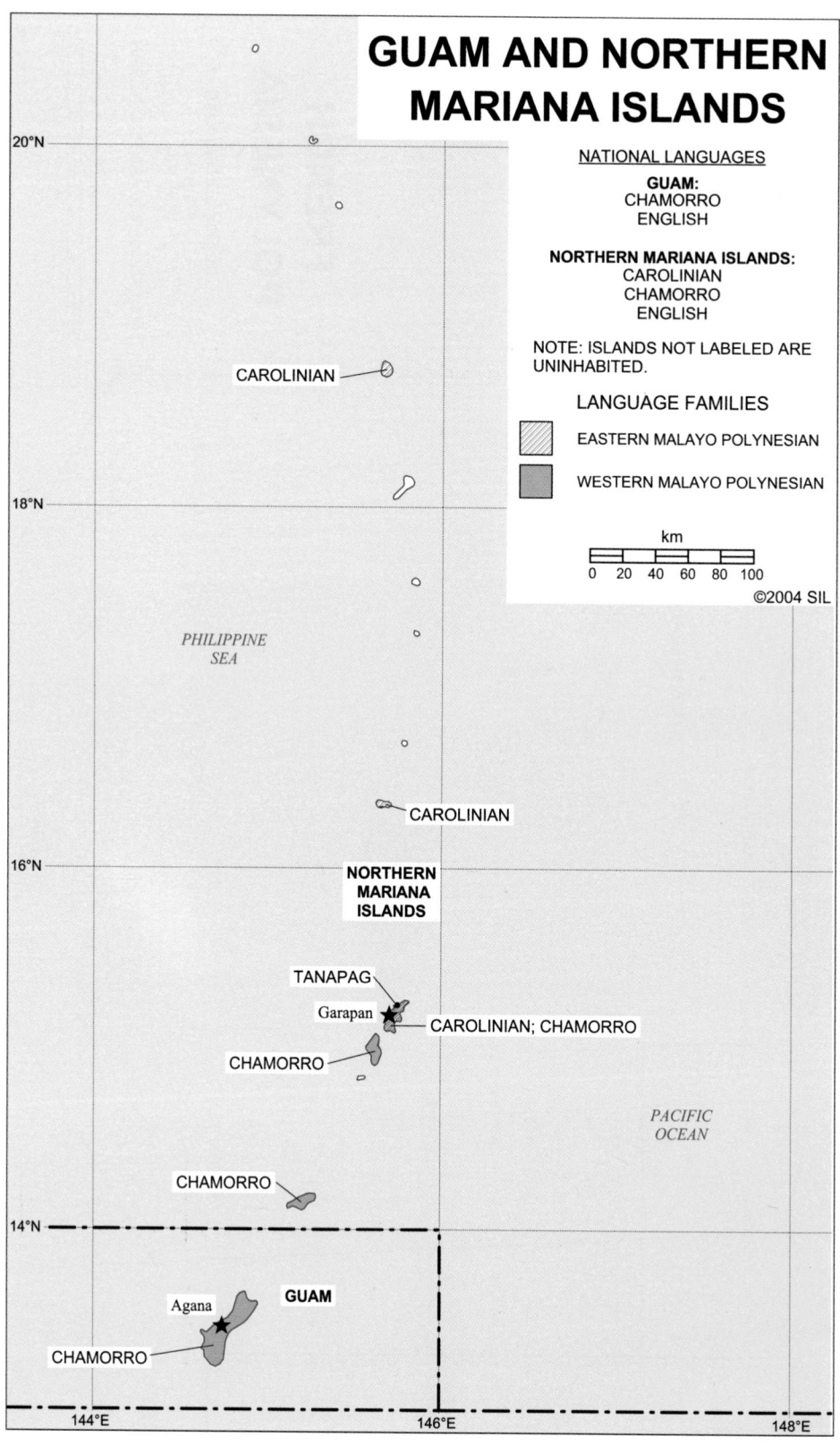

GUAM AND NORTHERN MARIANA ISLANDS

NATIONAL LANGUAGES

GUAM:
CHAMORRO
ENGLISH

NORTHERN MARIANA ISLANDS:
CAROLINIAN
CHAMORRO
ENGLISH

NOTE: ISLANDS NOT LABELED ARE UNINHABITED.

LANGUAGE FAMILIES

EASTERN MALAYO POLYNESIAN

WESTERN MALAYO POLYNESIAN

km
0 20 40 60 80 100

©2004 SIL

20°N

CAROLINIAN

18°N

PHILIPPINE SEA

CAROLINIAN

16°N

NORTHERN MARIANA ISLANDS

TANAPAG
Garapan
CHAMORRO
CAROLINIAN; CHAMORRO

PACIFIC OCEAN

CHAMORRO

14°N

Agana **GUAM**

CHAMORRO

144°E 146°E 148°E

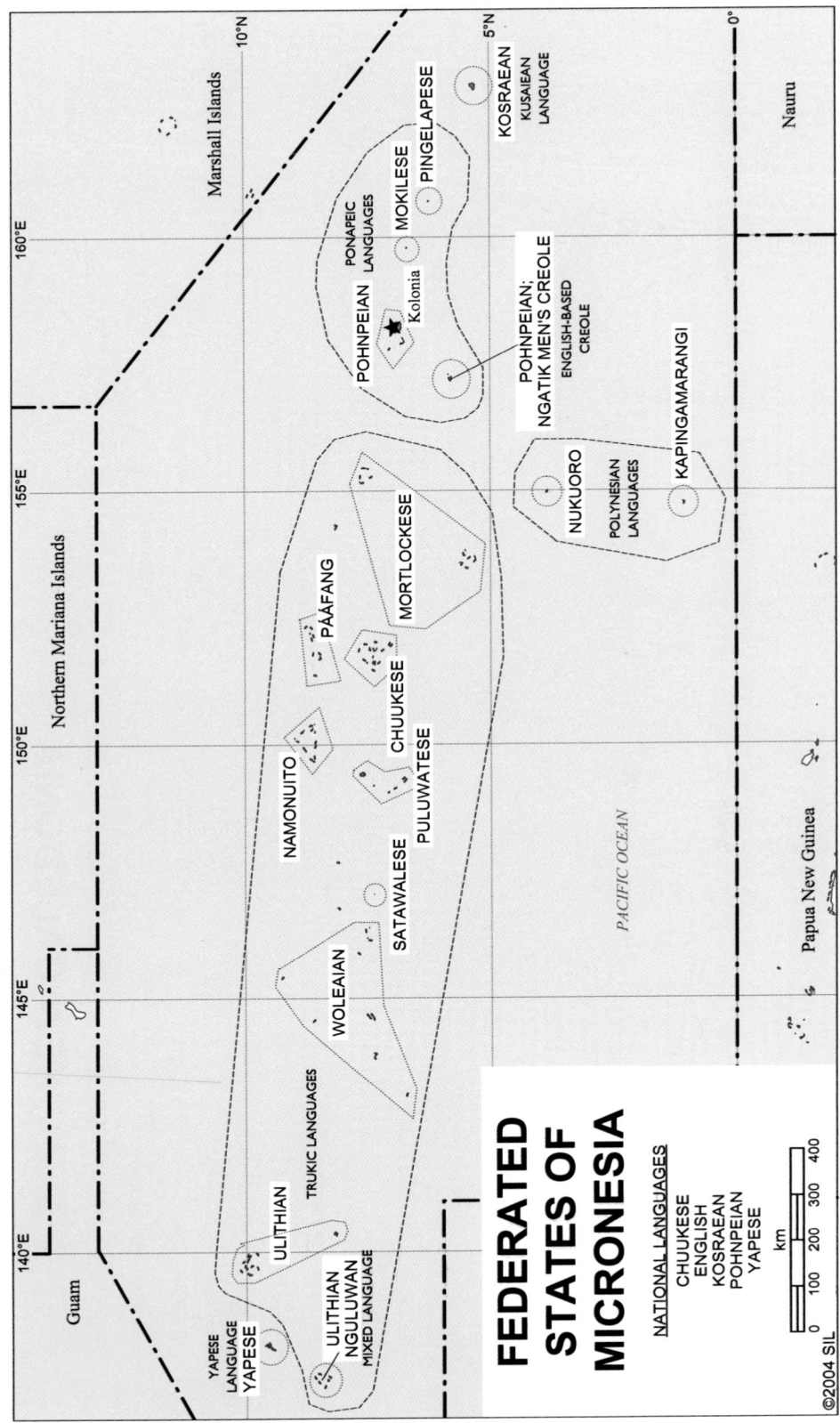

FEDERATED
STATES OF
MICRONESIA

NATIONAL LANGUAGES
CHUUKESE
ENGLISH
KOSRAEAN
POHNPEIAN
YAPESE

©2004 SIL

km
0 100 200 300 400

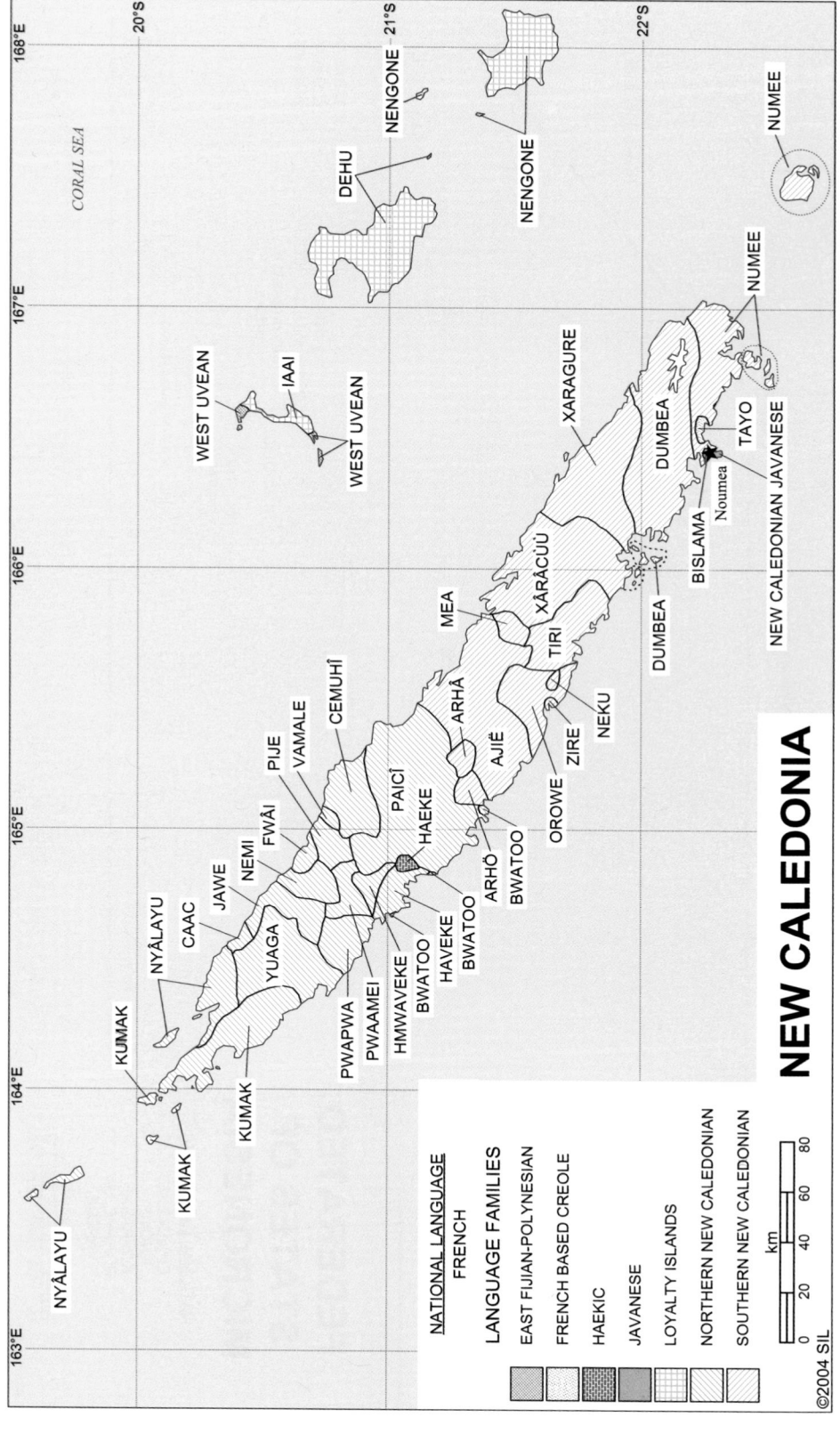

NEW CALEDONIA

NATIONAL LANGUAGE
FRENCH

LANGUAGE FAMILIES

EAST FIJIAN-POLYNESIAN

FRENCH BASED CREOLE

HAEKIC

JAVANESE

LOYALTY ISLANDS

NORTHERN NEW CALEDONIAN

SOUTHERN NEW CALEDONIAN

km

0   20   40   60   80

©2004 SIL

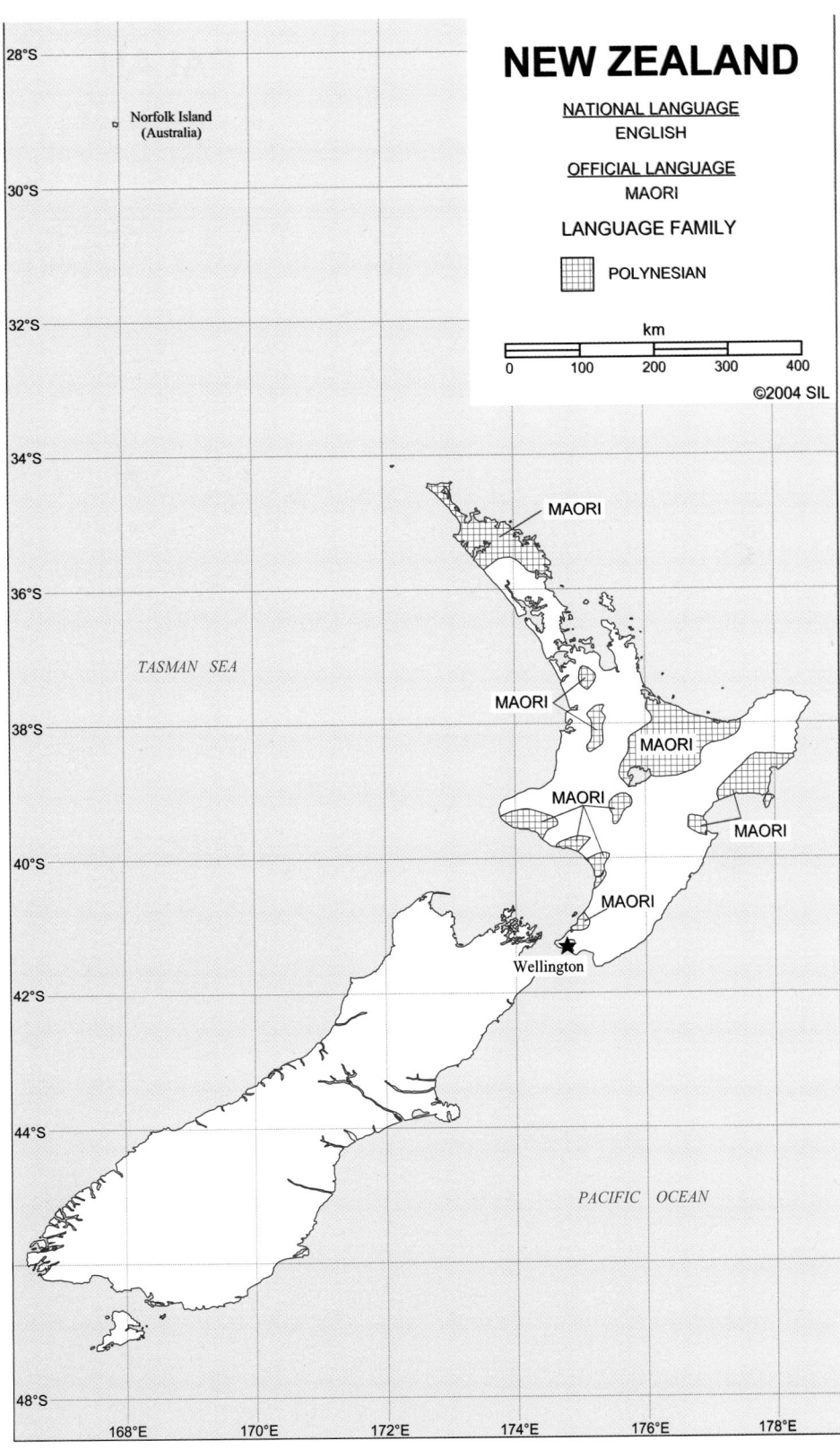

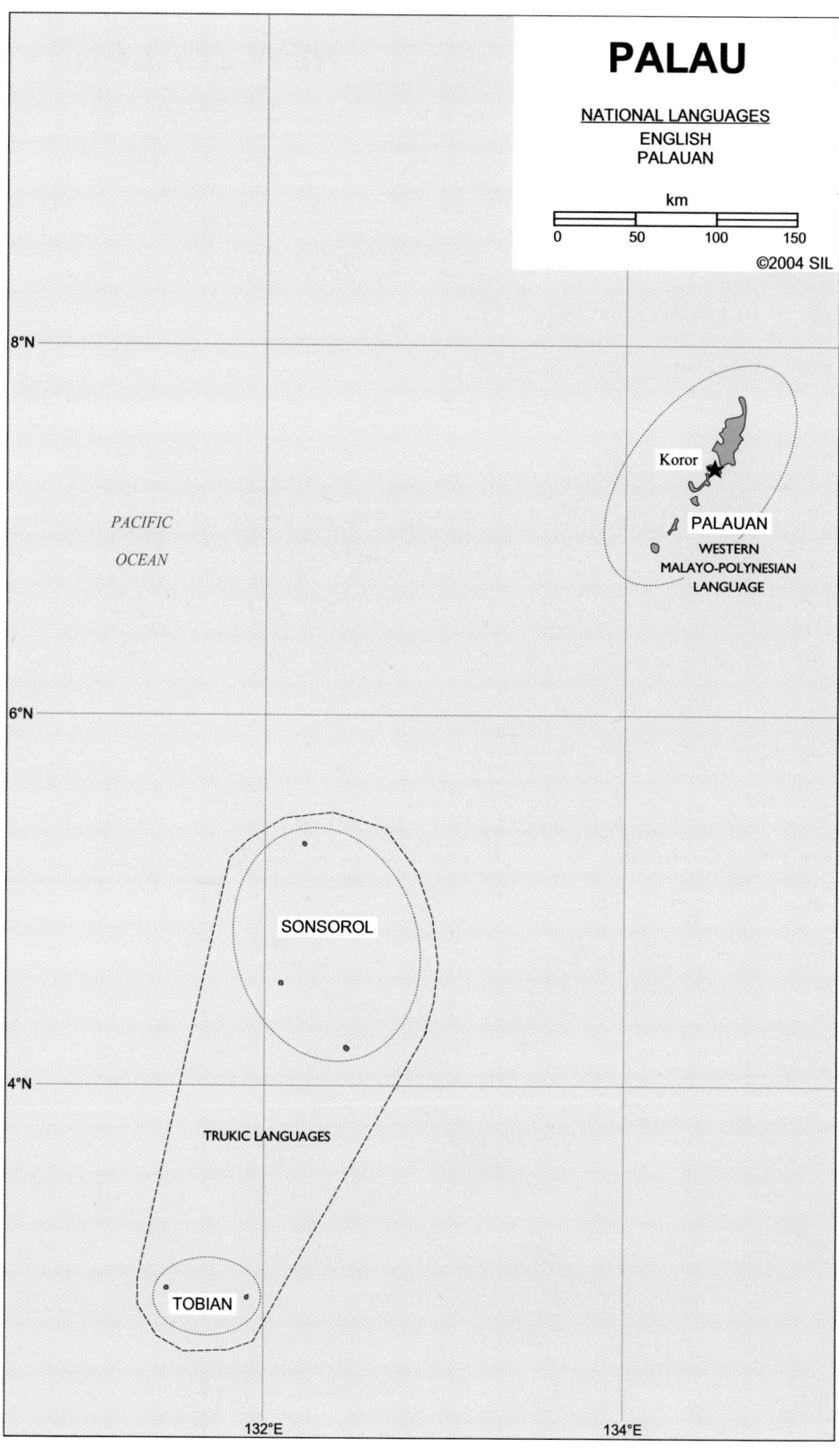

PALAU

NATIONAL LANGUAGES
ENGLISH
PALAUAN

km

| 0 | 50 | 100 | 150 |

©2004 SIL

8°N

Koror

PALAUAN
WESTERN
MALAYO-POLYNESIAN
LANGUAGE

PACIFIC

OCEAN

6°N

SONSOROL

4°N

TRUKIC LANGUAGES

TOBIAN

132°E   134°E

Papua New Guinea: Index Of Languages

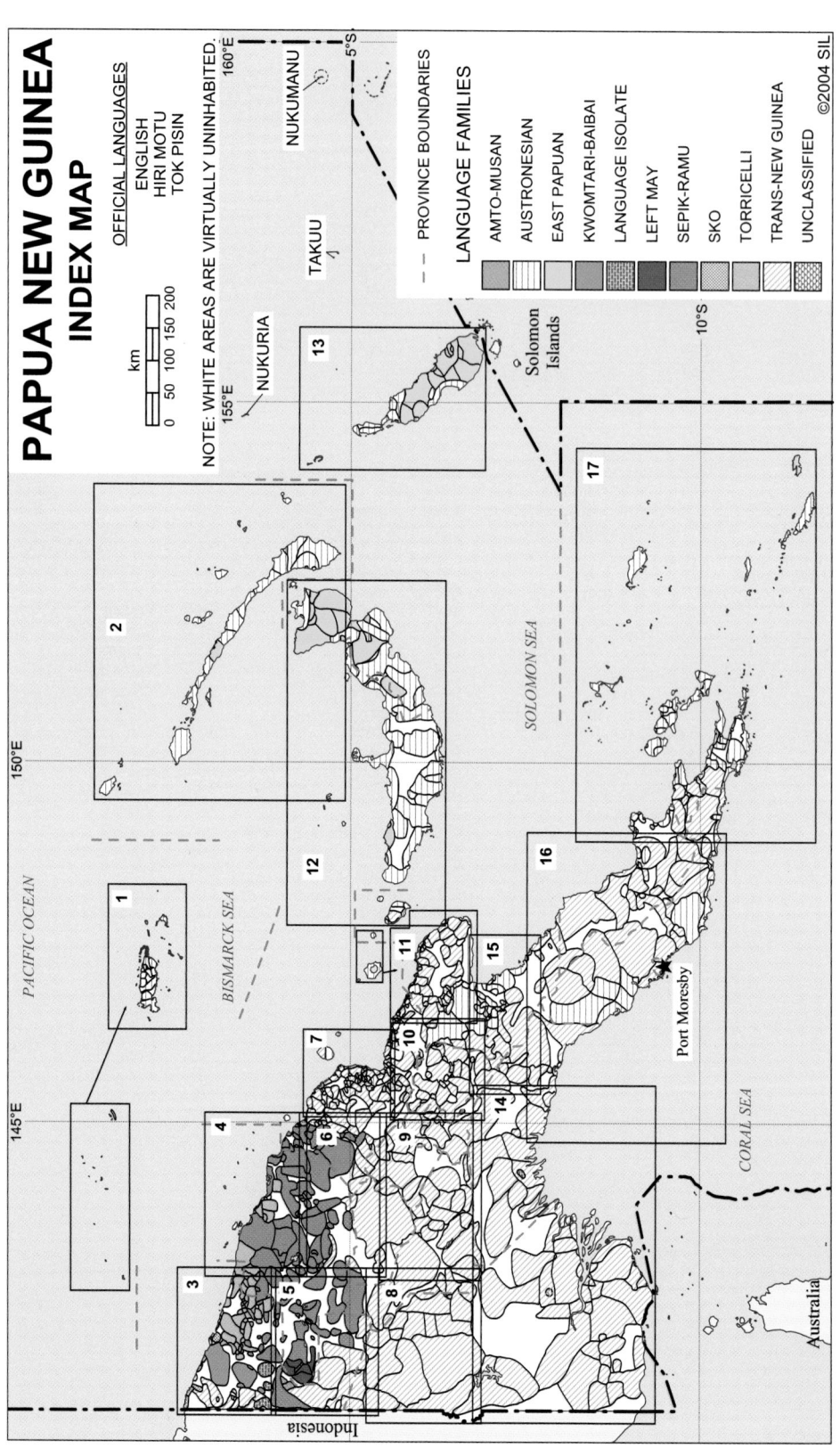

PAPUA NEW GUINEA
INDEX MAP

OFFICIAL LANGUAGES
ENGLISH
HIRI MOTU
TOK PISIN

km
0 50 100 150 200

NOTE: WHITE AREAS ARE VIRTUALLY UNINHABITED.

- - - PROVINCE BOUNDARIES

LANGUAGE FAMILIES

AMTO-MUSAN
AUSTRONESIAN
EAST PAPUAN
KWOMTARI-BAIBAI
LANGUAGE ISOLATE
LEFT MAY
SEPIK-RAMU
SKO
TORRICELLI
TRANS-NEW GUINEA
UNCLASSIFIED

©2004 SIL

NUKUMANU

TAKUU

NUKURIA

Solomon
Islands

5°S

10°S

160°E

155°E

150°E

145°E

PACIFIC OCEAN

BISMARCK SEA

SOLOMON SEA

CORAL SEA

Port Moresby

Indonesia

Australia

1 2 3 4 5 6 7 8 9 10 11 12 13 14 15 16 17

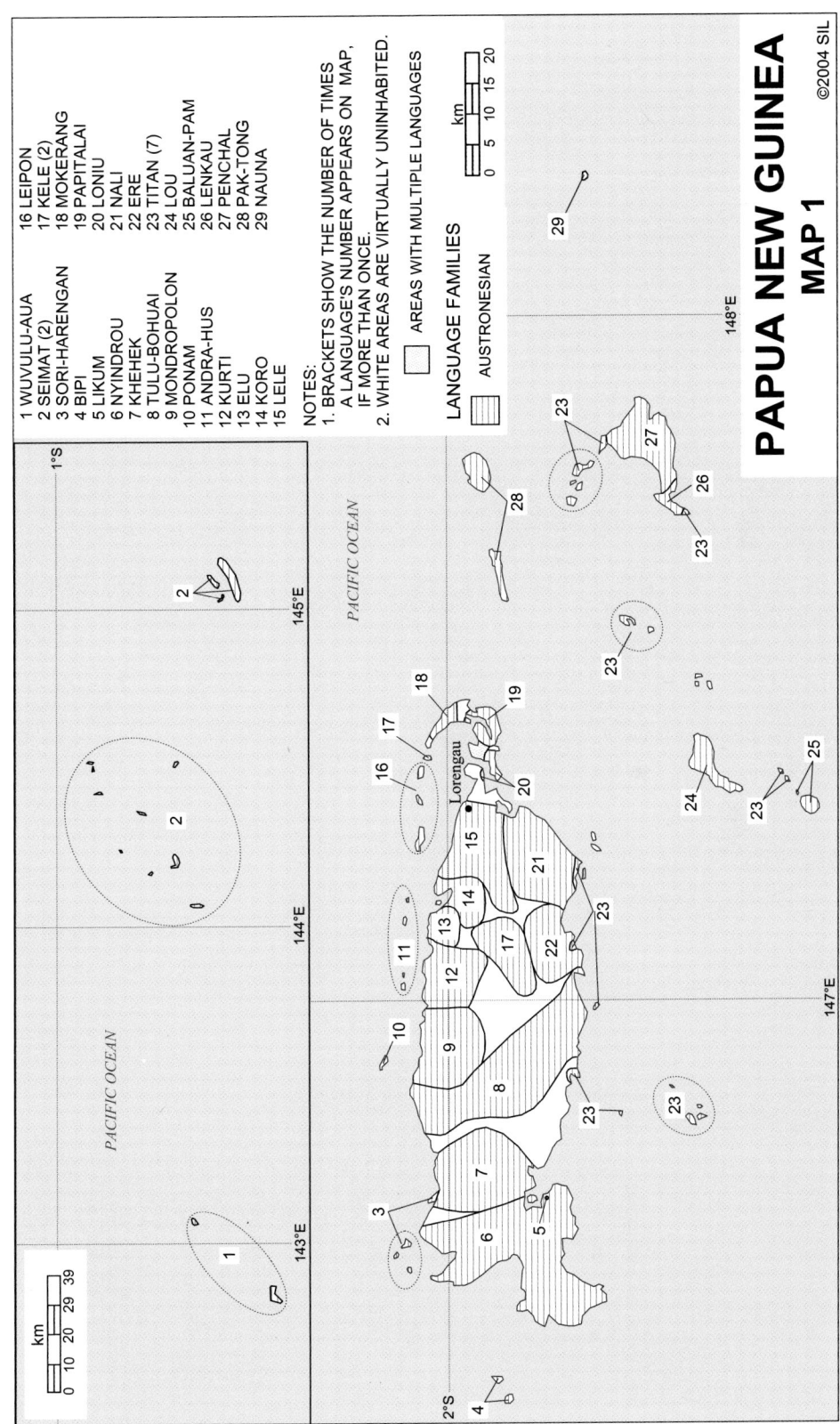

PAPUA NEW GUINEA
MAP 1

©2004 SIL

NOTES:
1. BRACKETS SHOW THE NUMBER OF TIMES A LANGUAGE'S NUMBER APPEARS ON MAP, IF MORE THAN ONCE.
2. WHITE AREAS ARE VIRTUALLY UNINHABITED.

LANGUAGE FAMILIES

AREAS WITH MULTIPLE LANGUAGES

AUSTRONESIAN

1 WUVULU-AUA
2 SEIMAT (2)
3 SORI-HARENGAN
4 BIPI
5 LIKUM
6 NYINDROU
7 KHEHEK
8 TULU-BOHUAI
9 MONDROPOLON
10 PONAM
11 ANDRA-HUS
12 KURTI
13 ELU
14 KORO
15 LELE
16 LEIPON
17 KELE (2)
18 MOKERANG
19 PAPITALAI
20 LONIU
21 NALI
22 ERE
23 TITAN (7)
24 LOU
25 BALUAN-PAM
26 LENKAU
27 PENCHAL
28 PAK-TONG
29 NAUNA

PACIFIC OCEAN

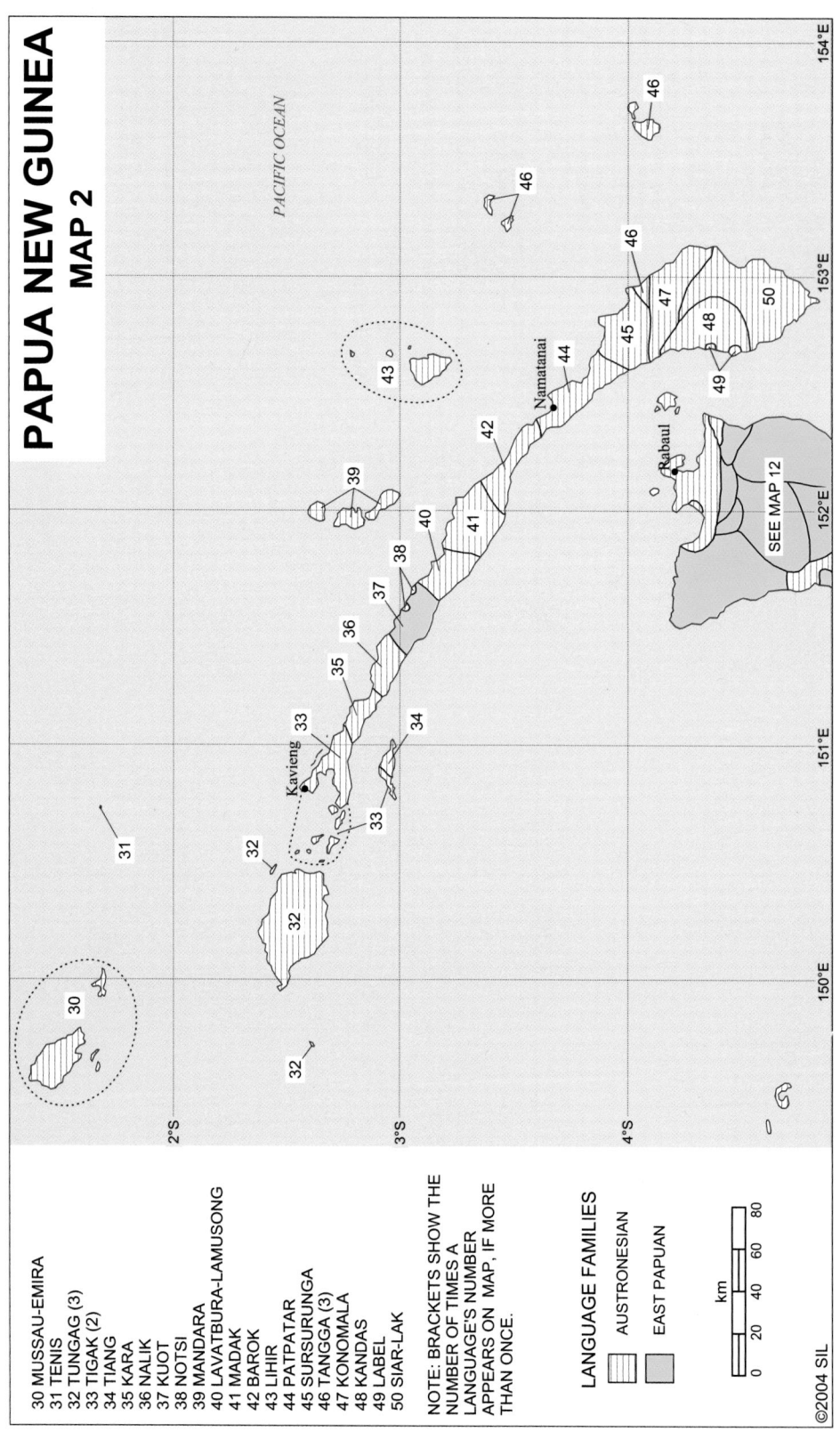

PAPUA NEW GUINEA
MAP 2

PACIFIC OCEAN

30 MUSSAU-EMIRA
31 TENIS
32 TUNGAG (3)
33 TIGAK (2)
34 TIANG
35 KARA
36 NALIK
37 KUOT
38 NOTSI
39 MANDARA
40 LAVATBURA-LAMUSONG
41 MADAK
42 BAROK
43 LIHIR
44 PATPATAR
45 SURSURUNGA
46 TANGGA (3)
47 KONOMALA
48 KANDAS
49 LABEL
50 SIAR-LAK

NOTE: BRACKETS SHOW THE
NUMBER OF TIMES A
LANGUAGE'S NUMBER
APPEARS ON MAP, IF MORE
THAN ONCE.

LANGUAGE FAMILIES

AUSTRONESIAN

EAST PAPUAN

km
0   20   40   60   80

©2004 SIL

Kavieng
Namatanai
Rabaul
SEE MAP 12

2°S
3°S
4°S

150°E   151°E   152°E   153°E   154°E

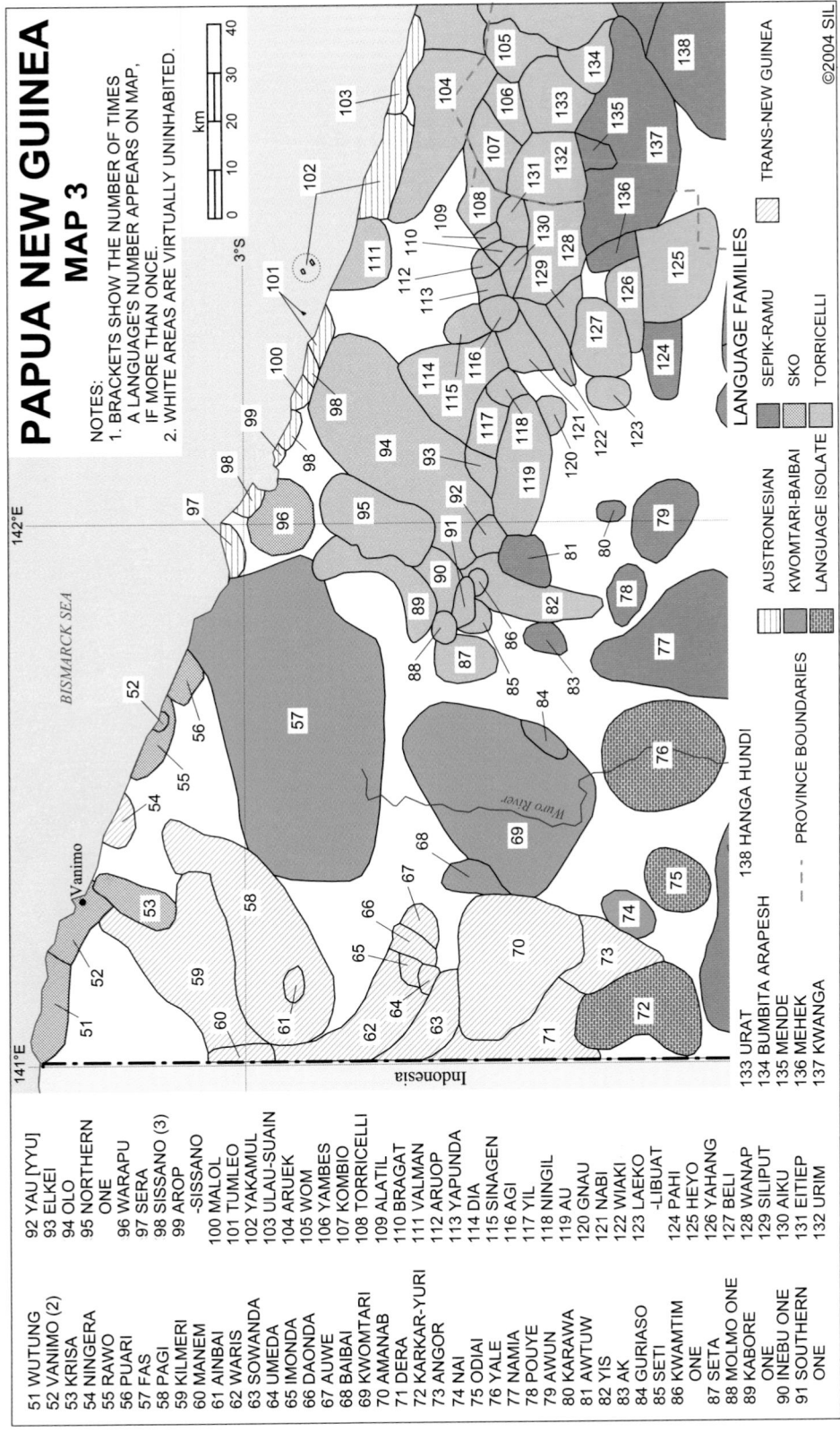

PAPUA NEW GUINEA
MAP 3

NOTES:
1. BRACKETS SHOW THE NUMBER OF TIMES A LANGUAGE'S NUMBER APPEARS ON MAP, IF MORE THAN ONCE.
2. WHITE AREAS ARE VIRTUALLY UNINHABITED.

©2004 SIL

LANGUAGE FAMILIES

AUSTRONESIAN
KWOMTARI-BAIBAI
LANGUAGE ISOLATE
SEPIK-RAMU
SKO
TORRICELLI
TRANS-NEW GUINEA

--- PROVINCE BOUNDARIES

51 WUTUNG
52 VANIMO (2)
53 KRISA
54 NINGERA
55 RAWO
56 PUARI
57 FAS
58 PAGI
59 KILMERI
60 MANEM
61 AINBAI
62 WARIS
63 SOWANDA
64 UMEDA
65 IMONDA
66 DAONDA
67 AUWE
68 BAIBAI
69 KWOMTARI
70 AMANAB
71 DERA
72 KARKAR-YURI
73 ANGOR
74 NAI
75 ODIAI
76 YALE
77 NAMIA
78 POUYE
79 AWUN
80 KARAWA
81 AWTUW
82 YIS
83 AK
84 GURIASO
85 SETI
86 KWAMTIM ONE
87 SETA
88 MOLMO ONE
89 KABORE ONE
90 INEBU ONE
91 SOUTHERN ONE
92 YAU [YYU]
93 ELKEI
94 OLO
95 NORTHERN ONE
96 WARAPU
97 SERA
98 SISSANO (3) -SISSANO
99 AROP -SISSANO
100 MALOL
101 TUMLEO
102 YAKAMUL
103 ULAU-SUAIN
104 ARUEK
105 WOM
106 YAMBES
107 KOMBIO
108 TORRICELLI
109 ALATIL
110 BRAGAT
111 VALMAN
112 ARUOP
113 YAPUNDA
114 DIA
115 SINAGEN
116 AGI
117 YIL
118 NINGIL
119 AU
120 GNAU
121 NABI
122 WIAKI
123 LAEKO -LIBUAT
124 PAHI
125 HEYO
126 YAHANG
127 BELI
128 WANAP
129 SILIPUT
130 AIKU
131 EITIEP
132 URIM
133 URAT
134 BUMBITA ARAPESH
135 MENDE
136 MEHEK
137 KWANGA
138 HANGA HUNDI

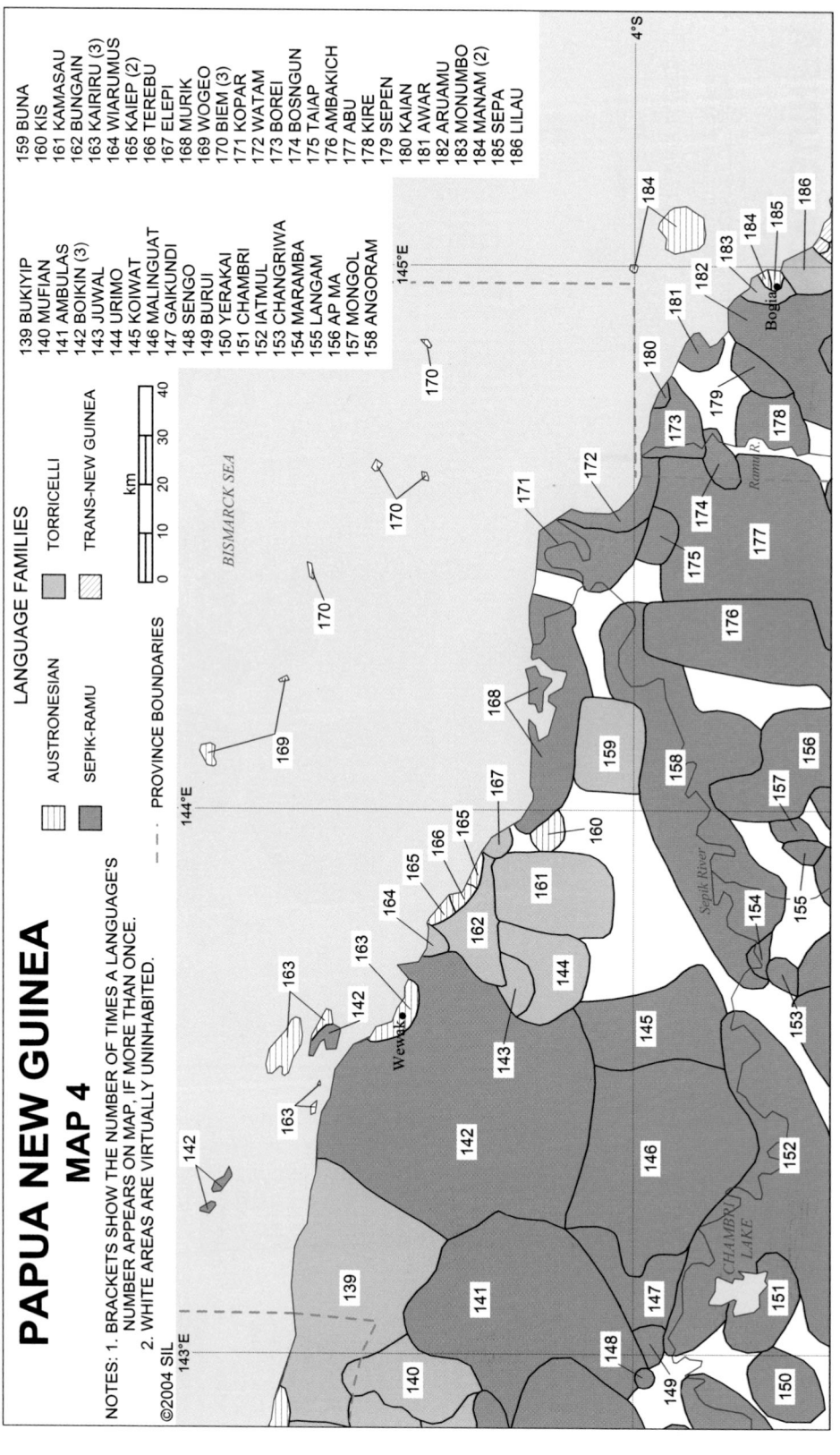

PAPUA NEW GUINEA
MAP 4

NOTES: 1. BRACKETS SHOW THE NUMBER OF TIMES A LANGUAGE'S
NUMBER APPEARS ON MAP, IF MORE THAN ONCE.
2. WHITE AREAS ARE VIRTUALLY UNINHABITED.

©2004 SIL

LANGUAGE FAMILIES

AUSTRONESIAN
SEPIK-RAMU
TORRICELLI
TRANS-NEW GUINEA

– – – · PROVINCE BOUNDARIES

km
0   10   20   30   40

139 BUKIYIP
140 MUFIAN
141 AMBULAS
142 BOIKIN (3)
143 JUWAL
144 URIMO
145 KOIWAT
146 MALINGUAT
147 GAIKUNDI
148 SENGO
149 BURUI
150 YERAKAI
151 CHAMBRI
152 IATMUL
153 CHANGRIWA
154 MARAMBA
155 LANGAM
156 AP MA
157 MONGOL
158 ANGORAM

159 BUNA
160 KIS
161 KAMASAU
162 BUNGAIN
163 KAIRIRU (3)
164 WIARUMUS
165 KAIEP (2)
166 TEREBU
167 ELEPI
168 MURIK
169 WOGEO
170 BIEM (3)
171 KOPAR
172 WATAM
173 BOREI
174 BOSNGUN
175 TAIAP
176 AMBAKICH
177 ABU
178 KIRE
179 SEPEN
180 KAIAN
181 AWAR
182 ARUAMU
183 MONUMBO
184 MANAM (2)
185 SEPA
186 LILAU

BISMARCK SEA

Sepik River

Ramu R.

CHAMBRI LAKE

Wewak

Bogia

143°E   144°E   145°E   4°S

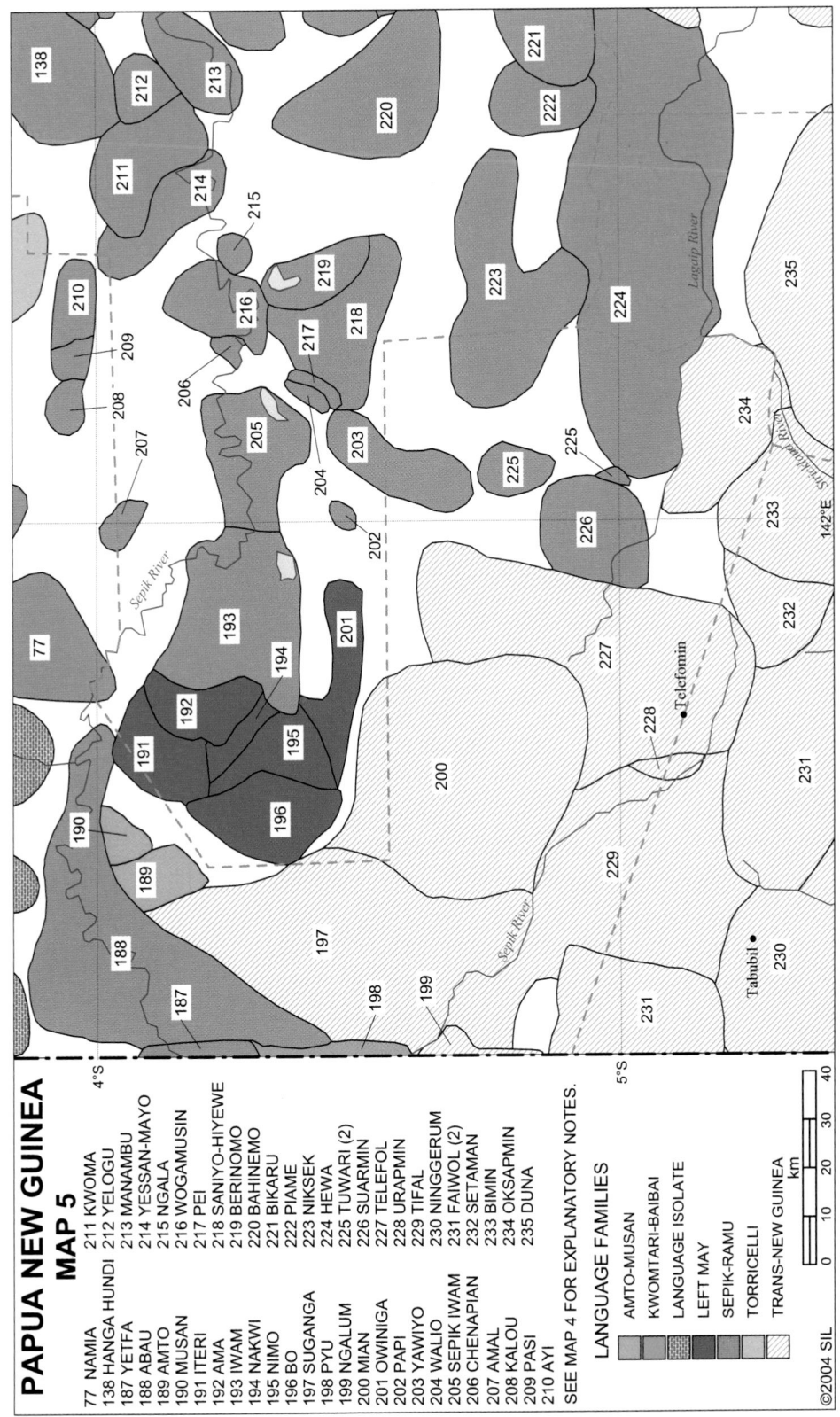

PAPUA NEW GUINEA
MAP 5

77 NAMIA	211 KWOMA	
138 HANGA HUNDI	212 YELOGU	
187 YETFA	213 MANAMBU	
188 ABAU	214 YESSAN-MAYO	
189 AMTO	215 NGALA	
190 MUSAN	216 WOGAMUSIN	
191 ITERI	217 PEI	
192 AMA	218 SANIYO-HIYEWE	
193 IWAM	219 BERINOMO	
194 NAKWI	220 BAHINEMO	
195 NIMO	221 BIKARU	
196 BO	222 PIAME	
197 SUGANGA	223 NIKSEK	
198 PYU	224 HEWA	
199 NGALUM	225 TUWARI (2)	
200 MIAN	226 SUARMIN	
201 OWININGA	227 TELEFOL	
202 PAPI	228 URAPMIN	
203 YAWIYO	229 TIFAL	
204 WALIO	230 NINGGERUM	
205 SEPIK IWAM	231 FAIWOL (2)	
206 CHENAPIAN	232 SETAMAN	
207 AMAL	233 BIMIN	
208 KALOU	234 OKSAPMIN	
209 PASI	235 DUNA	
210 AYI		

SEE MAP 4 FOR EXPLANATORY NOTES.

LANGUAGE FAMILIES

- AMTO-MUSAN
- KWOMTARI-BAIBAI
- LANGUAGE ISOLATE
- LEFT MAY
- SEPIK-RAMU
- TORRICELLI
- TRANS-NEW GUINEA

km

0   10   20   30   40

©2004 SIL

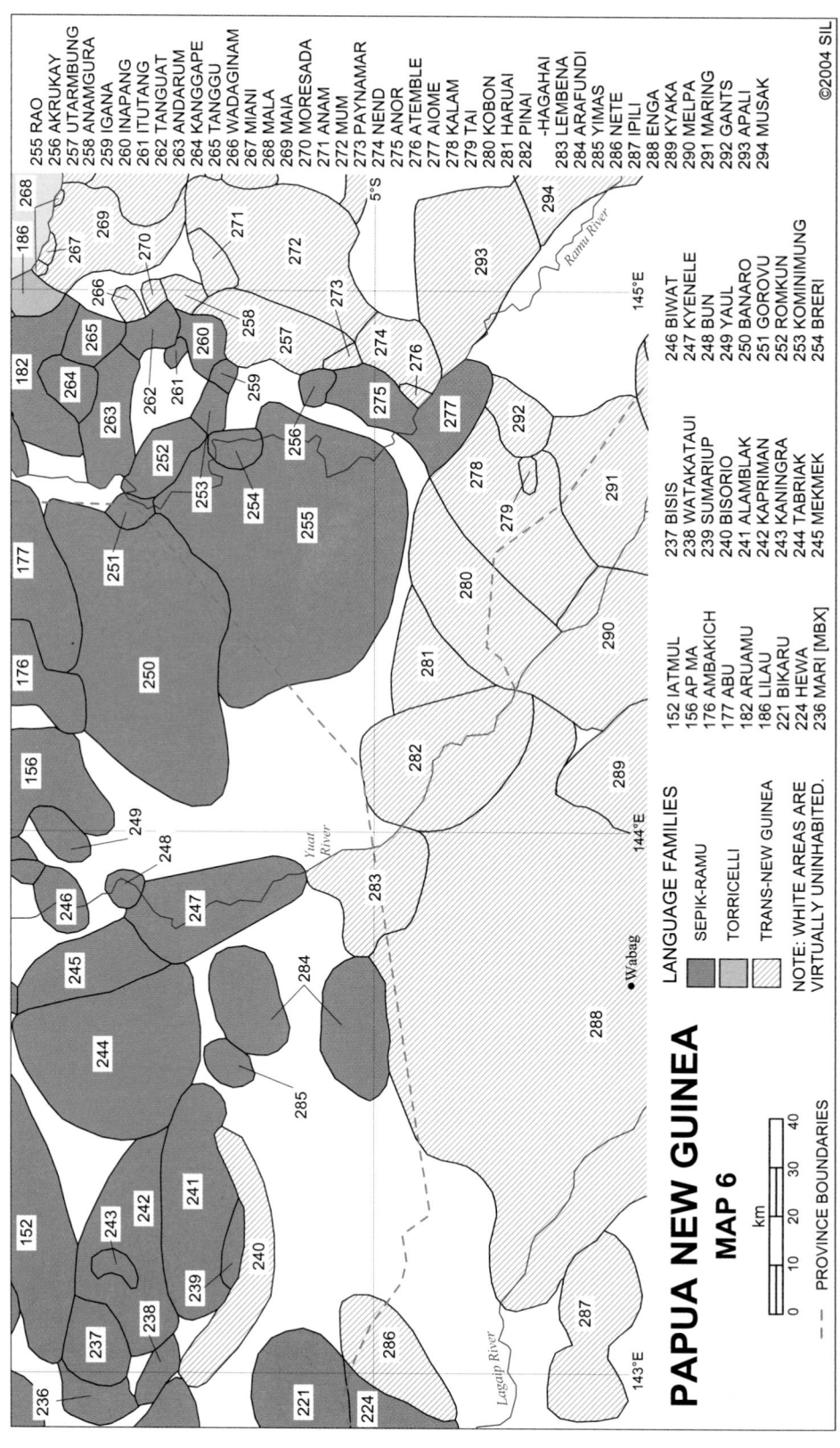

PAPUA NEW GUINEA
MAP 6

©2004 SIL

255 RAO
256 AKRUKAY
257 UTARMBUNG
258 ANAMGURA
259 IGANA
260 INAPANG
261 ITUTANG
262 TANGUAT
263 ANDARUM
264 KANGGAPE
265 TANGGU
266 WADAGINAM
267 MIANI
268 MALA
269 MAIA
270 MORESADA
271 ANAM
272 MUM
273 PAYNAMAR
274 NEND
275 ANOR
276 ATEMBLE
277 AIOME
278 KALAM
279 TAI
280 KOBON
281 HARUAI
282 PINAI
 -HAGAHAI
283 LEMBENA
284 ARAFUNDI
285 YIMAS
286 NETE
287 IPILI
288 ENGA
289 KYAKA
290 MELPA
291 MARING
292 GANTS
293 APALI
294 MUSAK

246 BIWAT
247 KYENELE
248 BUN
249 YAUL
250 BANARO
251 GOROVU
252 ROMKUN
253 KOMINIMUNG
254 BRERI

237 BISIS
238 WATAKATAUI
239 SUMARIUP
240 BISORIO
241 ALAMBLAK
242 KAPRIMAN
243 KANINGRA
244 TABRIAK
245 MEKMEK

152 IATMUL
156 AP MA
176 AMBAKICH
177 ABU
182 ARUAMU
186 LILAU
221 BIKARU
224 HEWA
236 MARI [MBX]

LANGUAGE FAMILIES

SEPIK-RAMU

TORRICELLI

TRANS-NEW GUINEA

NOTE: WHITE AREAS ARE
VIRTUALLY UNINHABITED.

km
0   10   20   30   40

- - -   PROVINCE BOUNDARIES

Ramu River

Yuat River

Lagaip River

Wabag

5°S

145°E

144°E

143°E

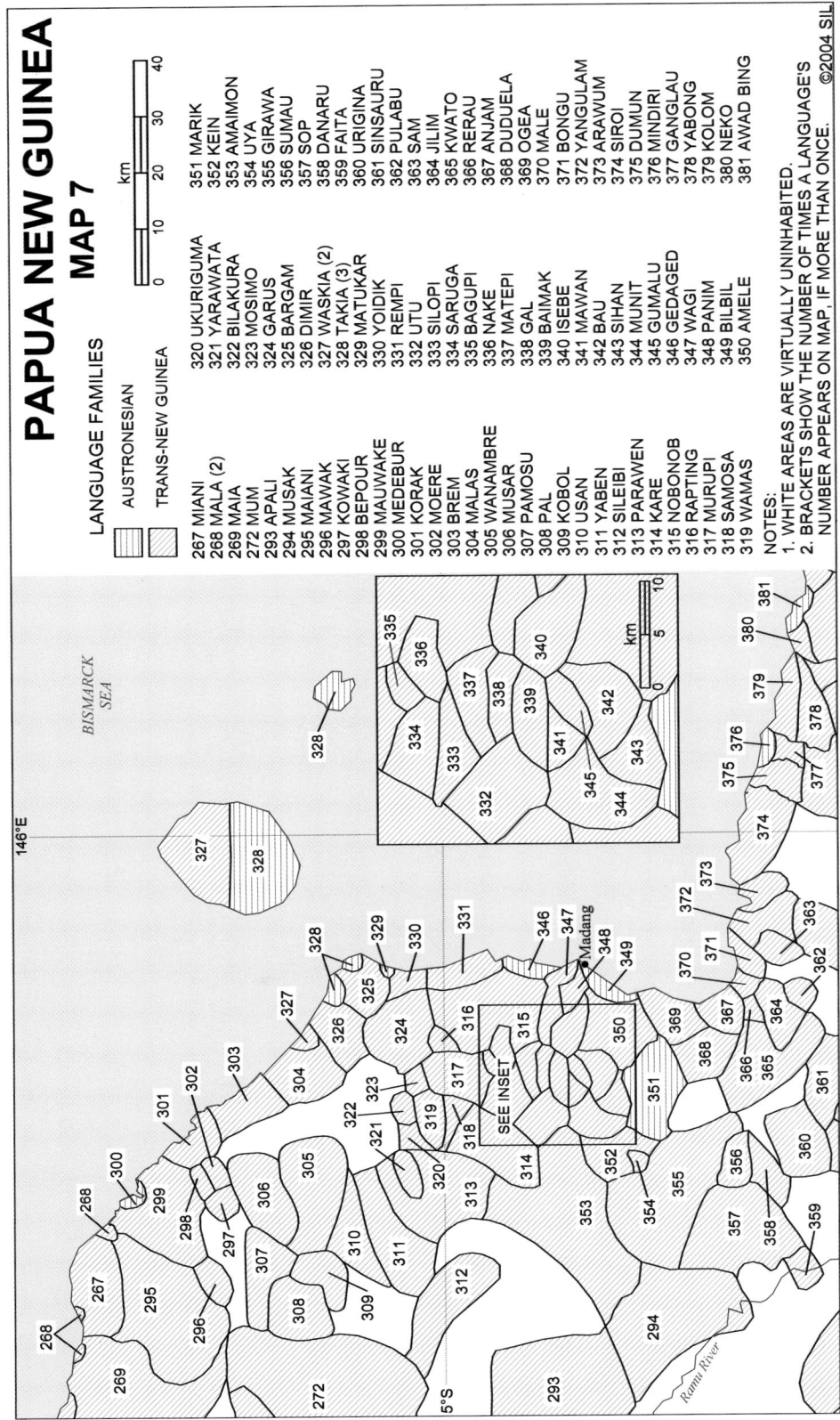

PAPUA NEW GUINEA
MAP 7

LANGUAGE FAMILIES

AUSTRONESIAN

TRANS-NEW GUINEA

267 MIANI	320 UKURIGUMA
268 MALA (2)	321 YARAWATA
269 MAIA	322 BILAKURA
272 MUM	323 MOSIMO
293 APALI	324 GARUS
294 MUSAK	325 BARGAM
295 MAIANI	326 DIMIR
296 MAWAK	327 WASKIA (2)
297 KOWAKI	328 TAKIA (3)
298 BEPOUR	329 MATUKAR
299 MAUWAKE	330 YOIDIK
300 MEDEBUR	331 REMPI
301 KORAK	332 UTU
302 MOERE	333 SILOPI
303 BREM	334 SARUGA
304 MALAS	335 BAGUPI
305 WANAMBRE	336 NAKE
306 MUSAR	337 MATEPI
307 PAMOSU	338 GAL
308 PAL	339 BAIMAK
309 KOBOL	340 ISEBE
310 USAN	341 MAWAN
311 YABEN	342 BAU
312 SILEIBI	343 SIHAN
313 PARAWEN	344 MUNIT
314 KARE	345 GUMALU
315 NOBONOB	346 GEDAGED
316 RAPTING	347 WAGI
317 MURUPI	348 PANIM
318 SAMOSA	349 BILBIL
319 WAMAS	350 AMELE

351 MARIK	
352 KEIN	
353 AMAIMON	
354 UYA	
355 GIRAWA	
356 SUMAU	
357 SOP	
358 DANARU	
359 FAITA	
360 URIGINA	
361 SINSAURU	
362 PULABU	
363 SAM	
364 JILIM	
365 KWATO	
366 RERAU	
367 ANJAM	
368 DUDUELA	
369 OGEA	
370 MALE	
371 BONGU	
372 YANGULAM	
373 ARAWUM	
374 SIROI	
375 DUMUN	
376 MINDIRI	
377 GANGLAU	
378 YABONG	
379 KOLOM	
380 NEKO	
381 AWAD BING	

NOTES:
1. WHITE AREAS ARE VIRTUALLY UNINHABITED.
2. BRACKETS SHOW THE NUMBER OF TIMES A LANGUAGE'S NUMBER APPEARS ON MAP, IF MORE THAN ONCE.

©2004 SIL

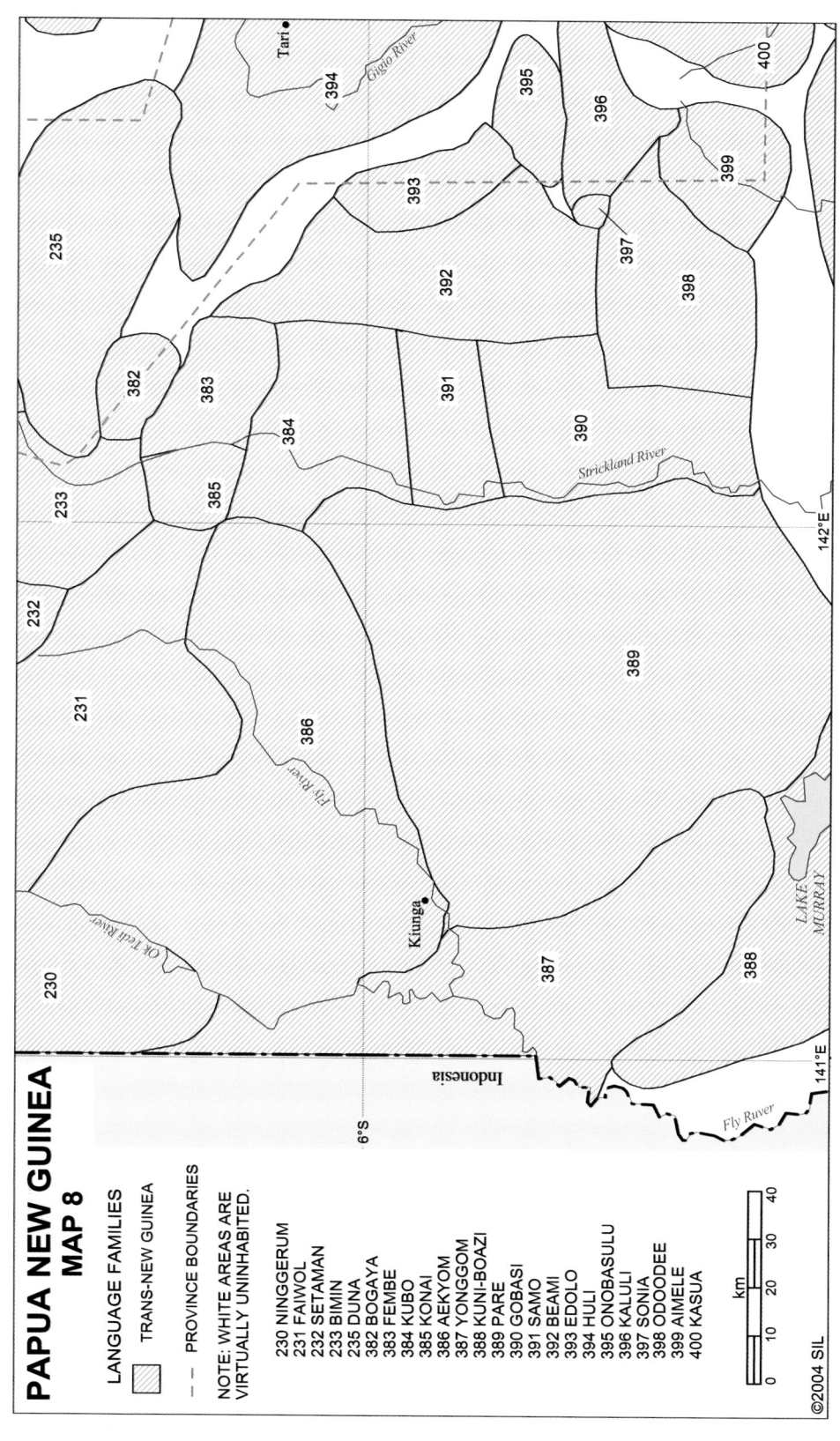

PAPUA NEW GUINEA
MAP 8

LANGUAGE FAMILIES

TRANS-NEW GUINEA

PROVINCE BOUNDARIES

NOTE: WHITE AREAS ARE
VIRTUALLY UNINHABITED.

230 NINGGERUM
231 FAIWOL
232 SETAMAN
233 BIMIN
235 DUNA
382 BOGAYA
383 FEMBE
384 KUBO
385 KONAI
386 AEKYOM
387 YONGGOM
388 KUNI-BOAZI
389 PARE
390 GOBASI
391 SAMO
392 BEAMI
393 EDOLO
394 HULI
395 ONOBASULU
396 KALULI
397 SONIA
398 ODOODEE
399 AIMELE
400 KASUA

km
0 10 20 30 40

©2004 SIL

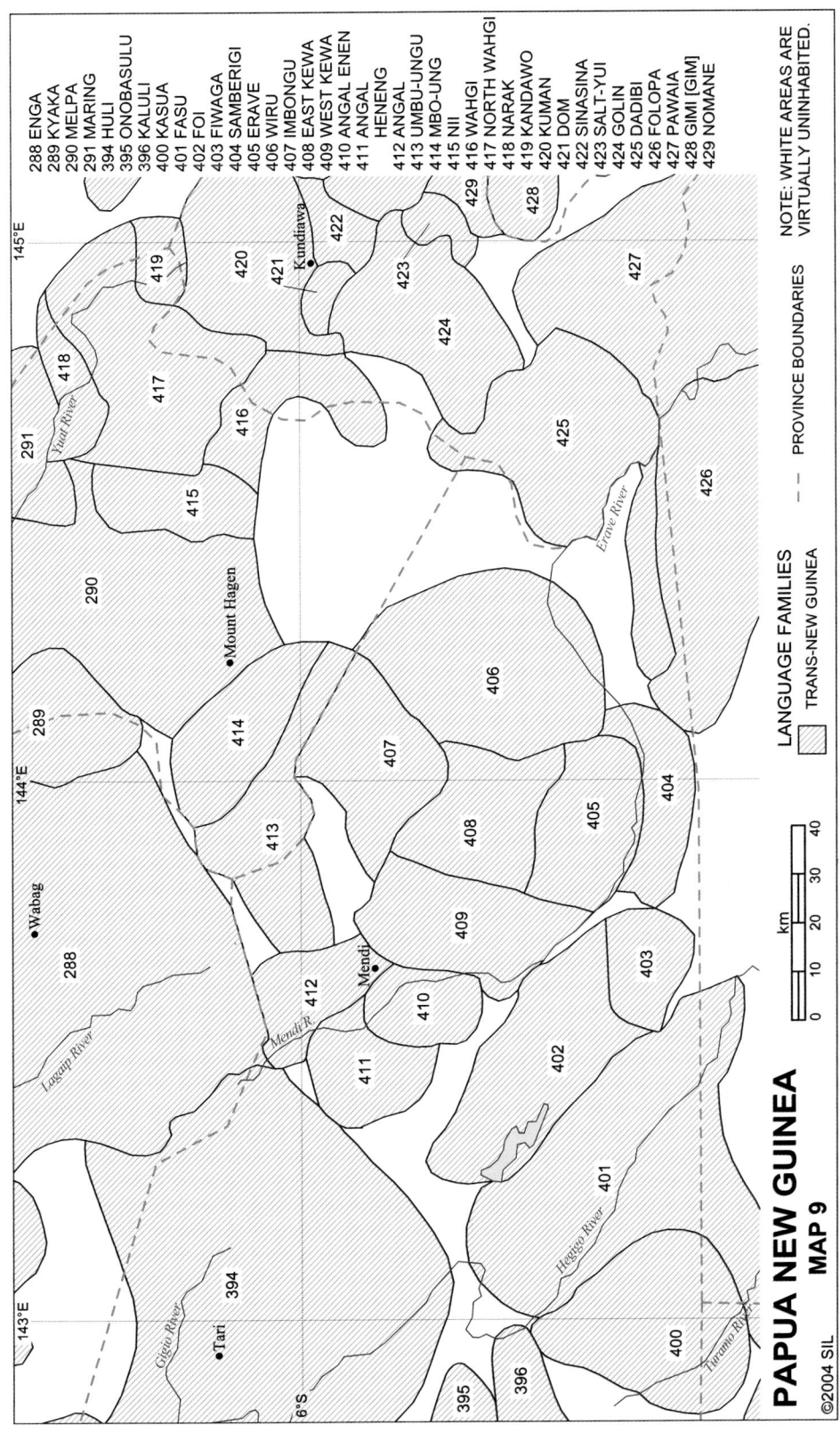

PAPUA NEW GUINEA
MAP 9

©2004 SIL

LANGUAGE FAMILIES

TRANS-NEW GUINEA

– – – PROVINCE BOUNDARIES

NOTE: WHITE AREAS ARE
VIRTUALLY UNINHABITED.

288 ENGA
289 KYAKA
290 MELPA
291 MARING
394 HULI
395 ONOBASULU
396 KALULI
400 KASUA
401 FASU
402 FOI
403 FIWAGA
404 SAMBERIGI
405 ERAVE
406 WIRU
407 IMBONGU
408 EAST KEWA
409 WEST KEWA
410 ANGAL ENEN
411 ANGAL
     HENENG
412 ANGAL
413 UMBU-UNGU
414 MBO-UNG
415 NII
416 WAHGI
417 NORTH WAHGI
418 NARAK
419 KANDAWO
420 KUMAN
421 DOM
422 SINASINA
423 SALT-YUI
424 GOLIN
425 DADIBI
426 FOLOPA
427 PAWAIA
428 GIMI [GIM]
429 NOMANE

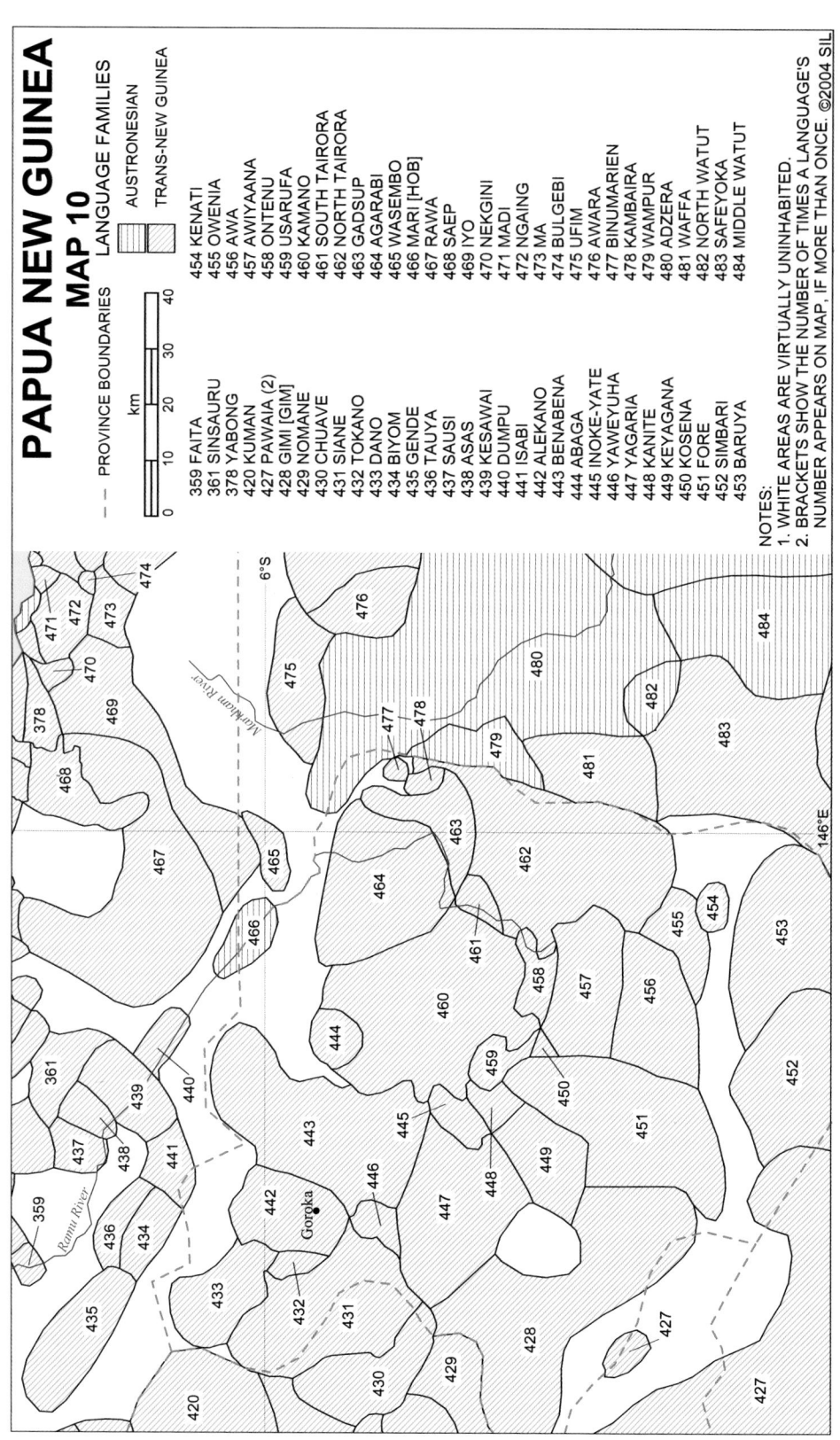

PAPUA NEW GUINEA
MAP 10

-- - PROVINCE BOUNDARIES

LANGUAGE FAMILIES

AUSTRONESIAN

TRANS-NEW GUINEA

km
0   10   20   30   40

359 FAITA
361 SINSAURU
378 YABONG
420 KUMAN
427 PAWAIA (2)
428 GIMI [GIM]
429 NOMANE
430 CHUAVE
431 SIANE
432 TOKANO
433 DANO
434 BIYOM
435 GENDE
436 TAUYA
437 SAUSI
438 ASAS
439 KESAWAI
440 DUMPU
441 ISABI
442 ALEKANO
443 BENABENA
444 ABAGA
445 INOKE-YATE
446 YAWEYUHA
447 YAGARIA
448 KANITE
449 KEYAGANA
450 KOSENA
451 FORE
452 SIMBARI
453 BARUYA

454 KENATI
455 OWENIA
456 AWA
457 AWIYAANA
458 ONTENU
459 USARUFA
460 KAMANO
461 SOUTH TAIRORA
462 NORTH TAIRORA
463 GADSUP
464 AGARABI
465 WASEMBO
466 MARI [HOB]
467 RAWA
468 SAEP
469 IYO
470 NEKGINI
471 MADI
472 NGAING
473 MA
474 BULGEBI
475 UFIM
476 AWARA
477 BINUMARIEN
478 KAMBAIRA
479 WAMPUR
480 ADZERA
481 WAFFA
482 NORTH WATUT
483 SAFEYOKA
484 MIDDLE WATUT

NOTES:
1. WHITE AREAS ARE VIRTUALLY UNINHABITED.
2. BRACKETS SHOW THE NUMBER OF TIMES A LANGUAGE'S NUMBER APPEARS ON MAP, IF MORE THAN ONCE. ©2004 SIL

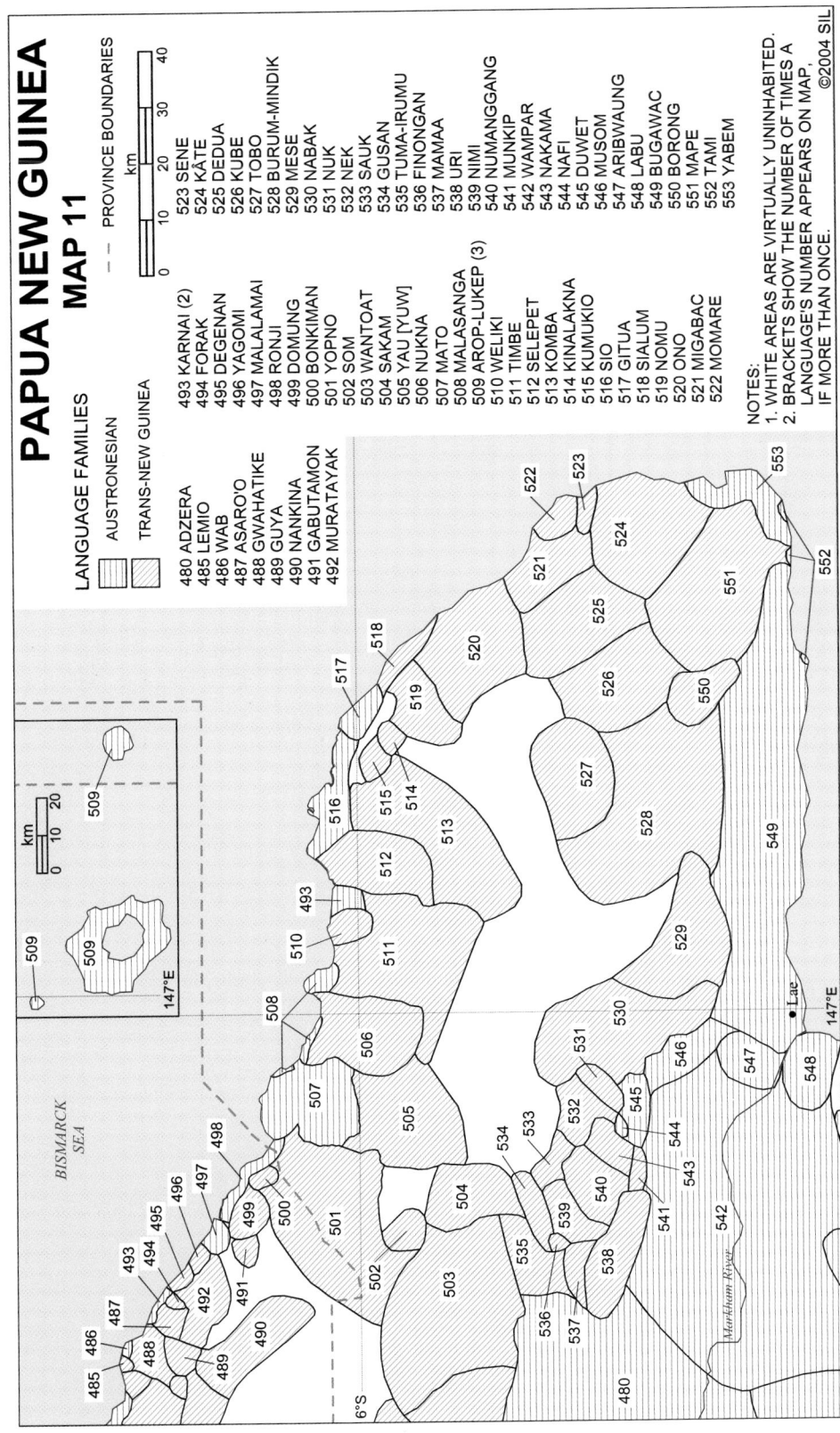

PAPUA NEW GUINEA
MAP 11

LANGUAGE FAMILIES

- AUSTRONESIAN
- TRANS-NEW GUINEA

--- PROVINCE BOUNDARIES

km
0 10 20 30 40

480 ADZERA
485 LEMIO
486 WAB
487 ASARO'O
488 GWAHATIKE
489 GUYA
490 NANKINA
491 GABUTAMON
492 MURATAYAK
493 KARNAI (2)
494 FORAK
495 DEGENAN
496 YAGOMI
497 MALALAMAI
498 RONJI
499 DOMUNG
500 BONKIMAN
501 YOPNO
502 SOM
503 WANTOAT
504 SAKAM
505 YAU [YUW]
506 NUKNA
507 MATO
508 MALASANGA
509 AROP-LUKEP (3)
510 WELIKI
511 TIMBE
512 SELEPET
513 KOMBA
514 KINALAKNA
515 KUMUKIO
516 SIO
517 GITUA
518 SIALUM
519 NOMU
520 ONO
521 MIGABAC
522 MOMARE
523 SENE
524 KÂTE
525 DEDUA
526 KUBE
527 TOBO
528 BURUM-MINDIK
529 MESE
530 NABAK
531 NUK
532 NEK
533 SAUK
534 GUSAN
535 TUMA-IRUMU
536 FINONGAN
537 MAMAA
538 URI
539 NIMI
540 NUMANGGANG
541 MUNKIP
542 WAMPAR
543 NAKAMA
544 NAFI
545 DUWET
546 MUSOM
547 ARIBWAUNG
548 LABU
549 BUGAWAC
550 BORONG
551 MAPE
552 TAMI
553 YABEM

NOTES:
1. WHITE AREAS ARE VIRTUALLY UNINHABITED.
2. BRACKETS SHOW THE NUMBER OF TIMES A LANGUAGE'S NUMBER APPEARS ON MAP, IF MORE THAN ONCE.

©2004 SIL

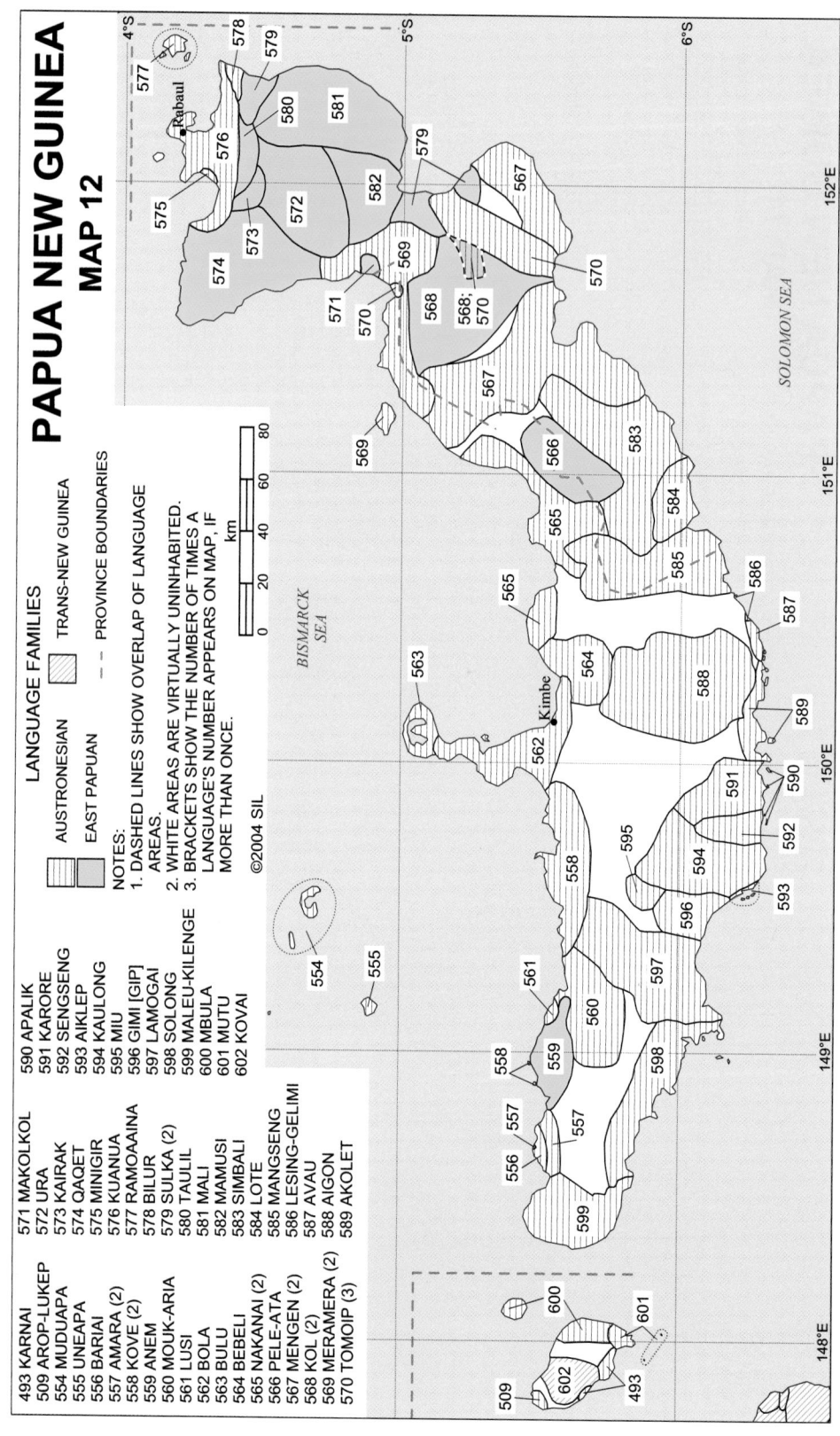

PAPUA NEW GUINEA
MAP 12

LANGUAGE FAMILIES

AUSTRONESIAN
EAST PAPUAN
TRANS-NEW GUINEA
– – – PROVINCE BOUNDARIES

NOTES:
1. DASHED LINES SHOW OVERLAP OF LANGUAGE AREAS.
2. WHITE AREAS ARE VIRTUALLY UNINHABITED.
3. BRACKETS SHOW THE NUMBER OF TIMES A LANGUAGE'S NUMBER APPEARS ON MAP, IF MORE THAN ONCE.

©2004 SIL

km
0 20 40 60 80

493 KARNAI
509 AROP-LUKEP
554 MUDUAPA
555 UNEAPA
556 BARIAI
557 AMARA (2)
558 KOVE (2)
559 ANEM
560 MOUK-ARIA
561 LUSI
562 BOLA
563 BULU
564 BEBELI
565 NAKANAI (2)
566 PELE-ATA
567 MENGEN (2)
568 KOL (2)
569 MERAMERA (2)
570 TOMOIP (3)
571 MAKOLKOL
572 URA
573 KAIRAK
574 QAQET
575 MINIGIR
576 KUANUA
577 RAMOAAINA
578 BILUR
579 SULKA (2)
580 TAULIL
581 BOLA
582 MAMUSI
583 SIMBALI
584 LOTE
585 MANGSENG
586 LESING-GELIMI
587 AVAU
588 AIGON
589 AKOLET
590 APALIK
591 KARORE
592 SENGSENG
593 AIKLEP
594 KAULONG
595 MIU
596 GIMI [GIP]
597 LAMOGAI
598 SOLONG
599 MALEU-KILENGE
600 MBULA
601 MUTU
602 KOVAI

BISMARCK SEA

SOLOMON SEA

Rabaul

Kimbe

4°S
5°S
6°S

148°E 149°E 150°E 151°E 152°E

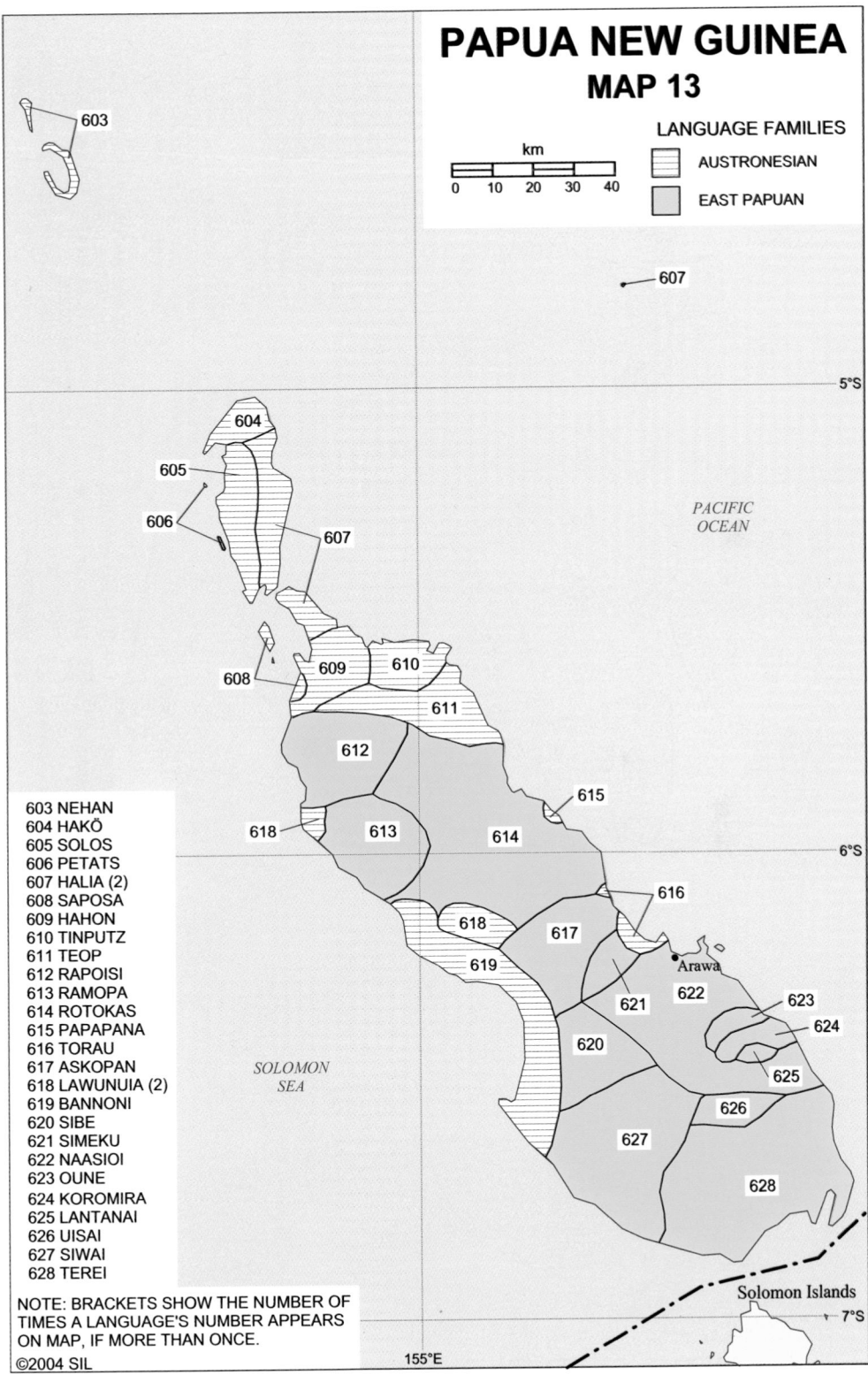

PAPUA NEW GUINEA
MAP 13

km

0   10   20   30   40

LANGUAGE FAMILIES

AUSTRONESIAN

EAST PAPUAN

603 NEHAN
604 HAKÖ
605 SOLOS
606 PETATS
607 HALIA (2)
608 SAPOSA
609 HAHON
610 TINPUTZ
611 TEOP
612 RAPOISI
613 RAMOPA
614 ROTOKAS
615 PAPAPANA
616 TORAU
617 ASKOPAN
618 LAWUNUIA (2)
619 BANNONI
620 SIBE
621 SIMEKU
622 NAASIOI
623 OUNE
624 KOROMIRA
625 LANTANAI
626 UISAI
627 SIWAI
628 TEREI

NOTE: BRACKETS SHOW THE NUMBER OF
TIMES A LANGUAGE'S NUMBER APPEARS
ON MAP, IF MORE THAN ONCE.

©2004 SIL

PACIFIC
OCEAN

SOLOMON
SEA

Arawa

Solomon Islands

155°E

5°S

6°S

7°S

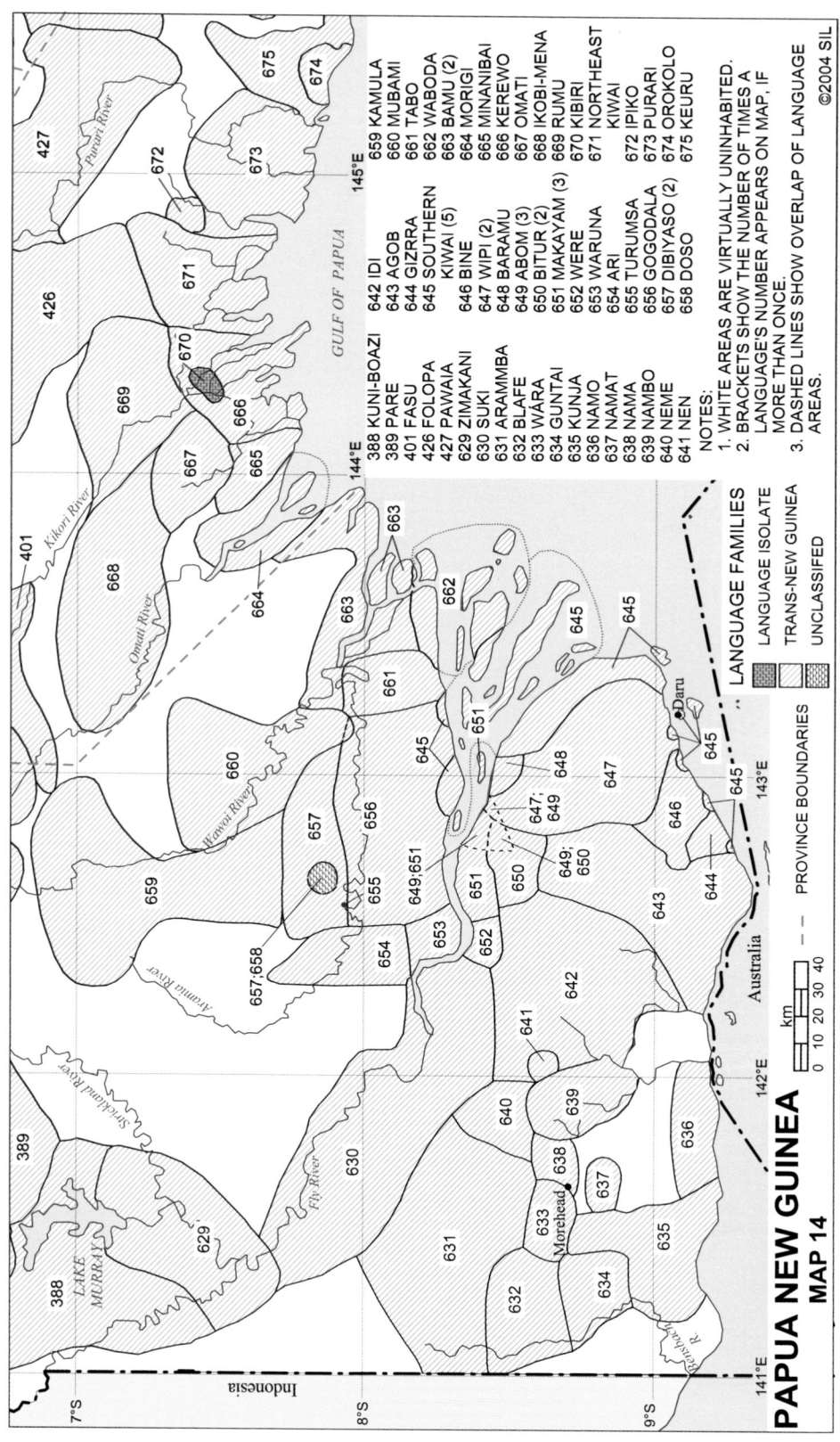

PAPUA NEW GUINEA
MAP 14

©2004 SIL

388 KUNI-BOAZI	642 IDI	659 KAMULA
389 PARE	643 AGOB	660 MUBAMI
401 FASU	644 GIZRRA	661 TABO
426 FOLOPA	645 SOUTHERN	662 WABODA
427 PAWAIA	KIWAI (5)	663 BAMU (2)
629 ZIMAKANI	646 BINE	664 MORIGI
630 SUKI	647 WIPI (2)	665 MINANIBAI
631 ARAMMBA	648 BARAMU	666 KEREWO
632 BLAFE	649 ABOM (3)	667 OMATI
633 WARA	650 BITUR (2)	668 IKOBI-MENA
634 GUNTAI	651 MAKAYAM (3)	669 RUMU
635 KUNJA	652 WERE	670 KIBIRI
636 NAMO	653 WARUNA	671 NORTHEAST
637 NAMAT	654 ARI	KIWAI
638 NAMA	655 TURUMSA	672 IPIKO
639 NAMBO	656 GOGODALA	673 PURARI
640 NEME	657 DIBIYASO (2)	674 OROKOLO
641 NEN	658 DOSO	675 KEURU

NOTES:
1. WHITE AREAS ARE VIRTUALLY UNINHABITED.
2. BRACKETS SHOW THE NUMBER OF TIMES A LANGUAGE'S NUMBER APPEARS ON MAP, IF MORE THAN ONCE.
3. DASHED LINES SHOW OVERLAP OF LANGUAGE AREAS.

LANGUAGE FAMILIES

LANGUAGE ISOLATE

TRANS-NEW GUINEA

UNCLASSIFIED

--- PROVINCE BOUNDARIES

km
0 10 20 30 40

GULF OF PAPUA

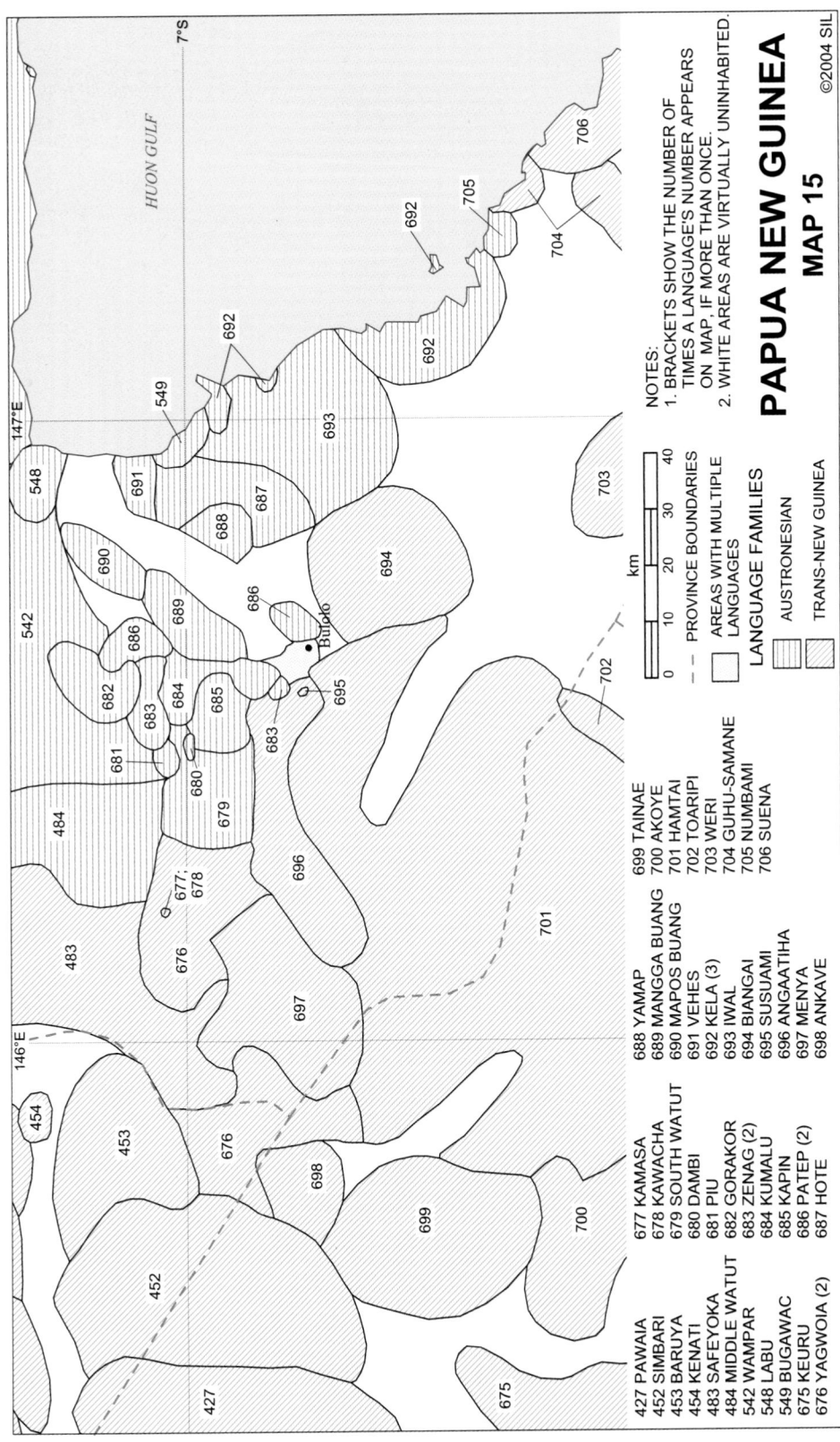

PAPUA NEW GUINEA

MAP 15

©2004 SIL

NOTES:
1. BRACKETS SHOW THE NUMBER OF TIMES A LANGUAGE'S NUMBER APPEARS ON MAP, IF MORE THAN ONCE.
2. WHITE AREAS ARE VIRTUALLY UNINHABITED.

km
0 10 20 30 40

PROVINCE BOUNDARIES

AREAS WITH MULTIPLE LANGUAGES

LANGUAGE FAMILIES

AUSTRONESIAN

TRANS-NEW GUINEA

427 PAWAIA
452 SIMBARI
453 BARUYA
454 KENATI
483 SAFEYOKA
484 MIDDLE WATUT
542 WAMPAR
548 LABU
549 BUGAWAC
675 KEURU
676 YAGWOIA (2)

677 KAMASA
678 KAWACHA
679 SOUTH WATUT
680 DAMBI
681 PIU
682 GORAKOR
683 ZENAG (2)
684 KUMALU
685 KAPIN
686 PATEP (2)
687 HOTE

688 YAMAP
689 MANGGA BUANG
690 MAPOS BUANG
691 VEHES
692 KELA (3)
693 IWAL
694 BIANGAI
695 SUSUAMI
696 ANGAATIHA
697 MENYA
698 ANKAVE

699 TAINAE
700 AKOYE
701 HAMTAI
702 TOARIPI
703 WERI
704 GUHU-SAMANE
705 NUMBAMI
706 SUENA

HUON GULF

Bulolo

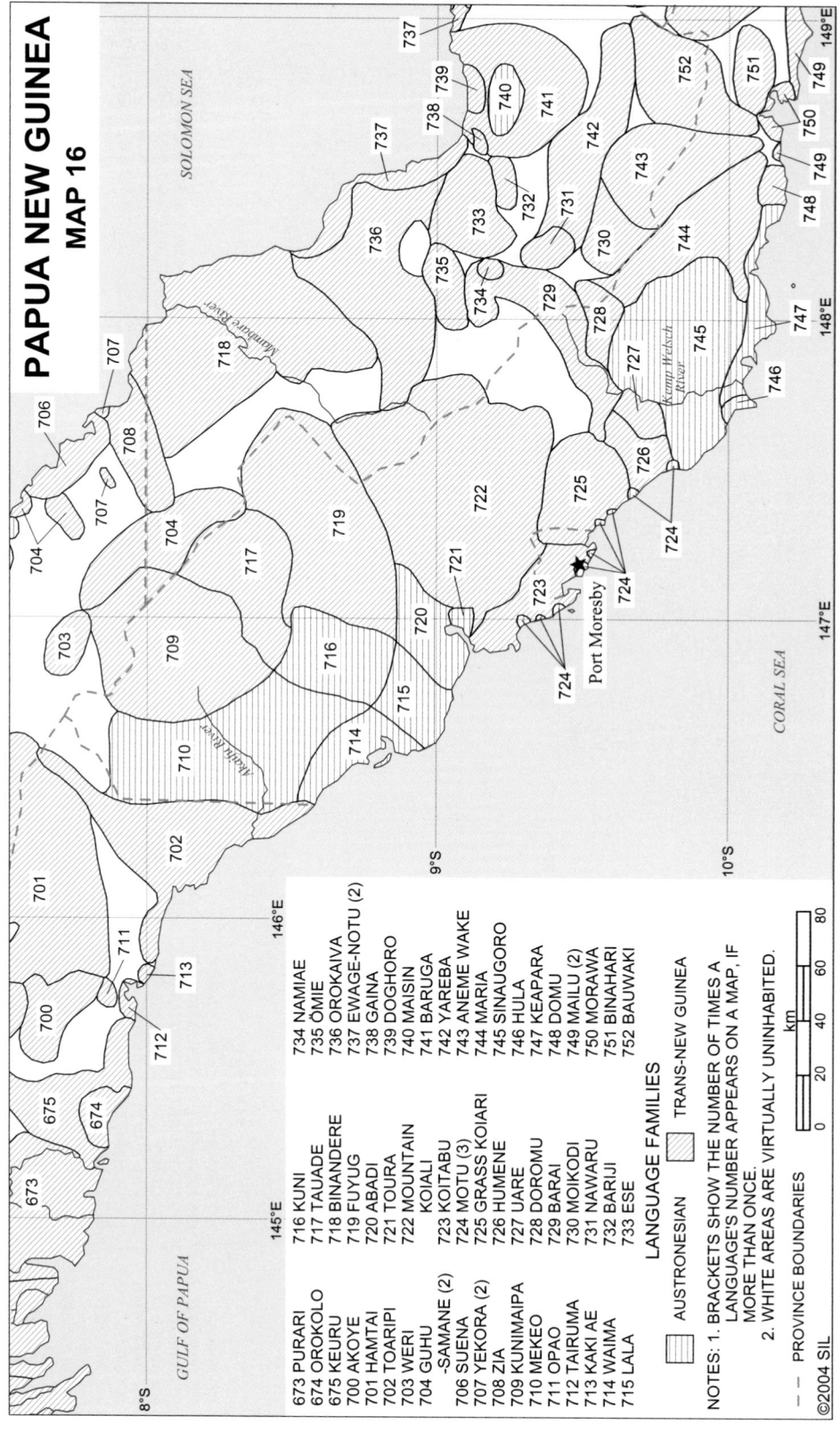

PAPUA NEW GUINEA
MAP 16

673 PURARI
674 OROKOLO
675 KEURU
700 AKOYE
701 HAMTAI
702 TOARIPI
703 WERI
704 GUHU
   -SAMANE (2)
706 SUENA
707 YEKORA (2)
708 ZIA
709 KUNIMAIPA
710 MEKEO
711 OPAO
712 TAIRUMA
713 KAKI AE
714 WAIMA
715 LALA

716 KUNI
717 TAUADE
718 BINANDERE
719 FUYUG
720 ABADI
721 TOURA
722 MOUNTAIN
   KOIALI
723 KOITABU
724 MOTU (3)
725 GRASS KOIARI
726 HUMENE
727 UARE
728 DOROMU
729 BARAI
730 MOIKODI
731 NAWARU
732 BARIJI
733 ESE

734 NAMIAE
735 ŌMIE
736 OROKAIVA
737 EWAGE-NOTU (2)
738 GAINA
739 DOGHORO
740 MAISIN
741 BARUGA
742 YAREBA
743 ANEME WAKE
744 MARIA
745 SINAUGORO
746 HULA
747 KEAPARA
748 DOMU
749 MAILU (2)
750 MORAWA
751 BINAHARI
752 BAUWAKI

LANGUAGE FAMILIES

AUSTRONESIAN   TRANS-NEW GUINEA

NOTES: 1. BRACKETS SHOW THE NUMBER OF TIMES A
            LANGUAGE'S NUMBER APPEARS ON A MAP, IF
            MORE THAN ONCE.
        2. WHITE AREAS ARE VIRTUALLY UNINHABITED.

-- -- PROVINCE BOUNDARIES

km
0   20   40   60   80

©2004 SIL

GULF OF PAPUA

SOLOMON SEA

CORAL SEA

Port Moresby

Mambare River

Kumusi River

Kemp Welch River

8°S
9°S
10°S

145°E   146°E   147°E   148°E   149°E

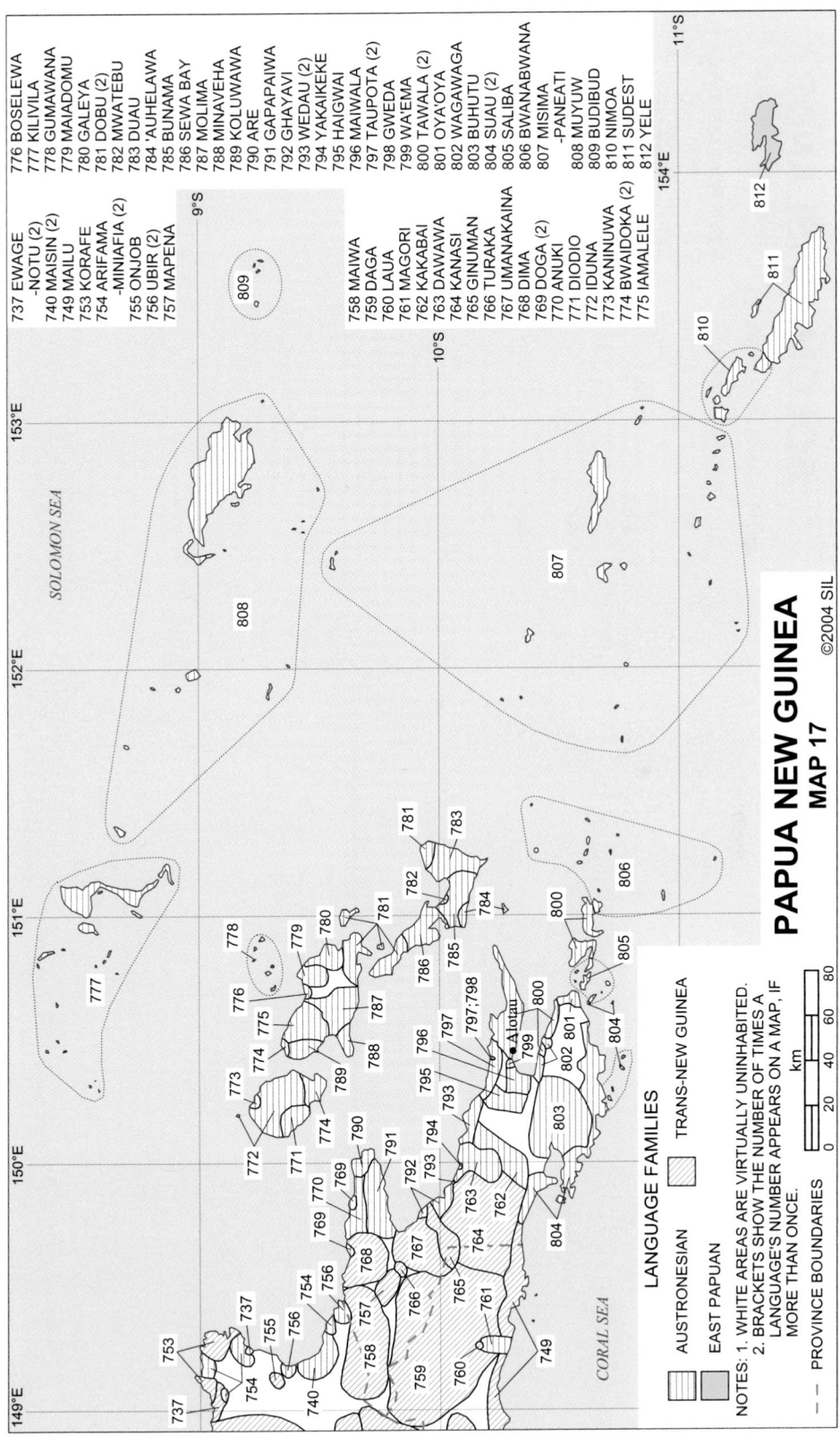

PAPUA NEW GUINEA
MAP 17
©2004 SIL

LANGUAGE FAMILIES

AUSTRONESIAN

EAST PAPUAN

TRANS-NEW GUINEA

NOTES: 1. WHITE AREAS ARE VIRTUALLY UNINHABITED.
2. BRACKETS SHOW THE NUMBER OF TIMES A
LANGUAGE'S NUMBER APPEARS ON A MAP, IF
MORE THAN ONCE.

-- - PROVINCE BOUNDARIES

km
0 20 40 60 80

737 EWAGE
   -NOTU (2)
740 MAISIN (2)
749 MAILU
753 KORAFE
754 ARIFAMA
   -MINIAFIA (2)
755 ONJOB
756 UBIR (2)
757 MAPENA

758 MAIWA
759 DAGA
760 LAUA
761 MAGORI
762 KAKABAI
763 DAWAWA
764 KANASI
765 GINUMAN
766 TURAKA
767 UMANAKAINA
768 DIMA
769 DOGA (2)
770 ANUKI
771 DIODIO
772 IDUNA
773 KANINUWA
774 BWAIDOKA (2)
775 IAMALELE

776 BOSELEWA
777 KILIVILA
778 GUMAWANA
779 MAIADOMU
780 GALEYA
781 DOBU (2)
782 MWATEBU
783 DUAU
784 'AUHELAWA
785 BUNAMA
786 SEWA BAY
787 MOLIMA
788 MINAVEHA
789 KOLUWAWA
790 ARE
791 GAPAPAIWA
792 GHAYAVI
793 WEDAU (2)
794 YAKAIKEKE
795 HAIGWAI
796 MAIWALA
797 TAUPOTA (2)
798 GWEDA
799 WA'EMA
800 TAWALA (2)
801 OYA'OYA
802 WAGAWAGA
803 BUHUTU
804 SUAU (2)
805 SALIBA
806 BWANABWANA
807 MISIMA
   -PANEATI
808 MUYUW
809 BUDIBUD
810 NIMOA
811 SUDEST
812 YELE

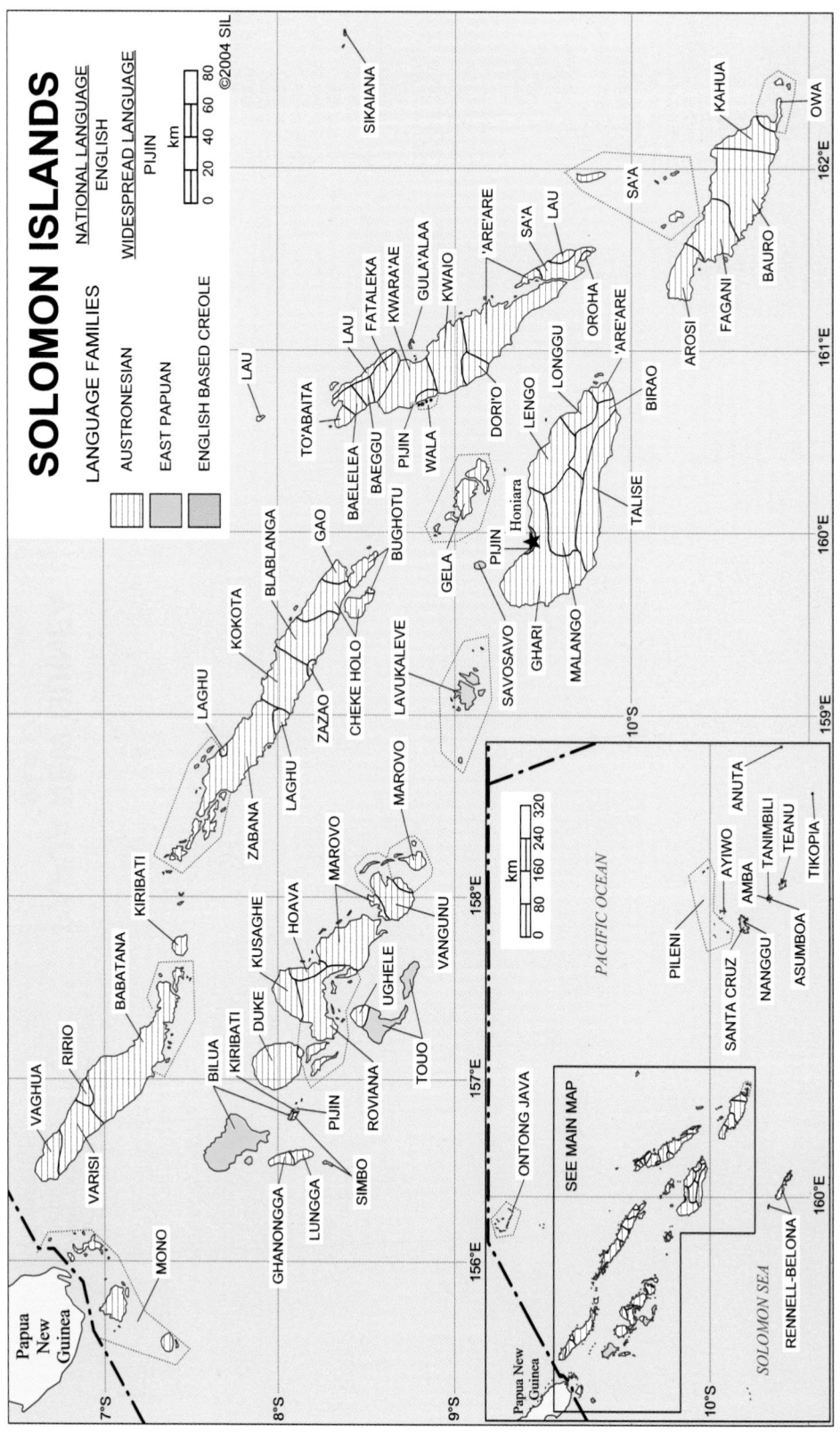

SOLOMON ISLANDS

NATIONAL LANGUAGE
ENGLISH

WIDESPREAD LANGUAGE
PIJIN

LANGUAGE FAMILIES

AUSTRONESIAN

EAST PAPUAN

ENGLISH BASED CREOLE

©2004 SIL

km
0 20 40 60 80

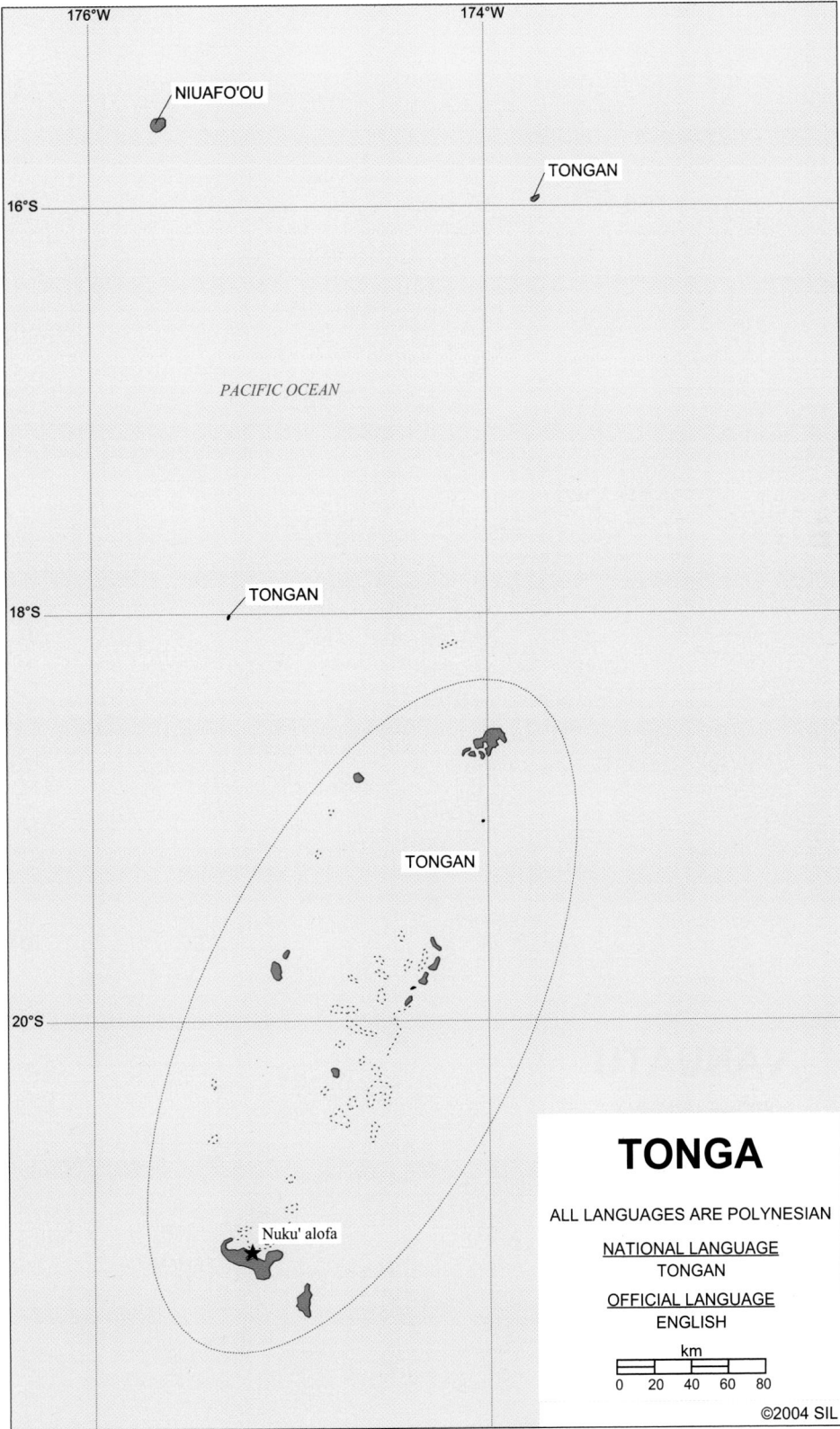

176°W   174°W

NIUAFO'OU

TONGAN

16°S

PACIFIC OCEAN

TONGAN

18°S

TONGAN

20°S

Nuku' alofa

TONGA

ALL LANGUAGES ARE POLYNESIAN

NATIONAL LANGUAGE
TONGAN

OFFICIAL LANGUAGE
ENGLISH

km

0   20   40   60   80

©2004 SIL

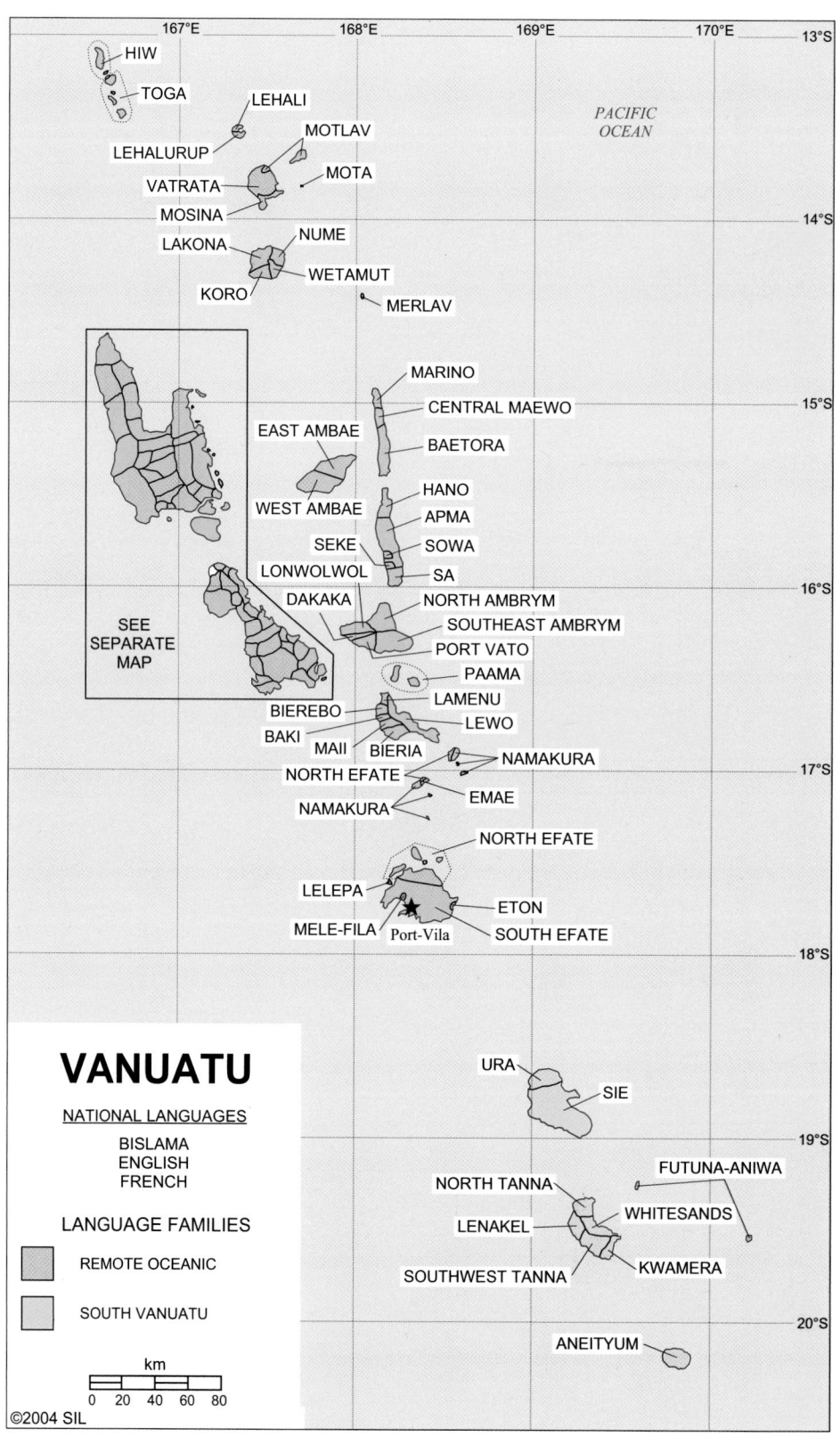

PACIFIC OCEAN

HIW
TOGA
LEHALI
LEHALURUP
MOTLAV
VATRATA
MOTA
MOSINA
LAKONA
NUME
KORO
WETAMUT
MERLAV

MARINO
CENTRAL MAEWO
EAST AMBAE
BAETORA
WEST AMBAE
HANO
APMA
SEKE
SOWA
LONWOLWOL
SA
DAKAKA
NORTH AMBRYM
SOUTHEAST AMBRYM
PORT VATO
PAAMA
LAMENU
BIEREBO
LEWO
BAKI
MAII
BIERIA
NORTH EFATE
NAMAKURA
EMAE
NAMAKURA
NORTH EFATE
LELEPA
ETON
MELE-FILA
Port-Vila
SOUTH EFATE

SEE SEPARATE MAP

URA
SIE

FUTUNA-ANIWA
NORTH TANNA
WHITESANDS
LENAKEL
SOUTHWEST TANNA
KWAMERA

ANEITYUM

VANUATU

NATIONAL LANGUAGES

BISLAMA
ENGLISH
FRENCH

LANGUAGE FAMILIES

REMOTE OCEANIC

SOUTH VANUATU

km

0 20 40 60 80

©2004 SIL

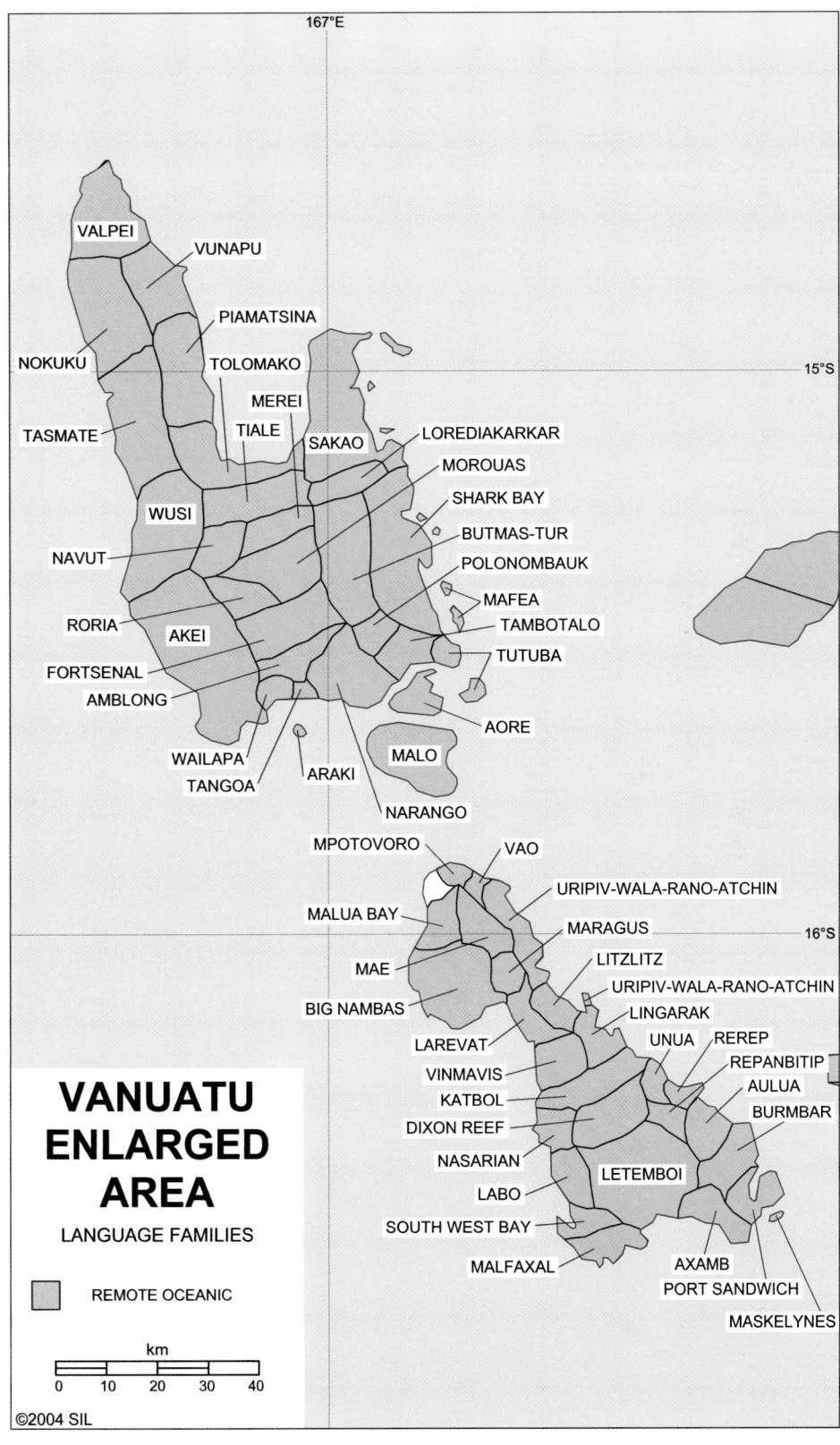

167°E

VALPEI

VUNAPU

PIAMATSINA

NOKUKU   TOLOMAKO   15°S

MEREI

TASMATE   TIALE   SAKAO   LOREDIAKARKAR

MOROUAS

SHARK BAY

WUSI   BUTMAS-TUR

POLONOMBAUK

NAVUT

MAFEA

TAMBOTALO

RORIA   AKEI   TUTUBA

FORTSENAL

AMBLONG

AORE

WAILAPA   MALO

TANGOA   ARAKI

NARANGO

MPOTOVORO   VAO

URIPIV-WALA-RANO-ATCHIN

MALUA BAY

MARAGUS   16°S

MAE   LITZLITZ

BIG NAMBAS   URIPIV-WALA-RANO-ATCHIN

LINGARAK

LAREVAT   UNUA   REREP

VINMAVIS   REPANBITIP

KATBOL   AULUA

DIXON REEF   BURMBAR

NASARIAN   LETEMBOI

LABO

SOUTH WEST BAY

AXAMB

MALFAXAL   PORT SANDWICH

MASKELYNES

**VANUATU
ENLARGED
AREA**

LANGUAGE FAMILIES

REMOTE OCEANIC

km

0   10   20   30   40

©2004 SIL

Part III
Indexes

Language Name Index

This index lists every name that appears in Part I as a primary or alternate name of a language or dialect. The following abbreviations are used in the index entries: *alt.* 'alternate name for', *alt. dial.* 'alternate dialect name for', *dial.* 'primary dialect name for', *pej. alt.* 'pejorative alternate name for', and *pej. alt. dial.* 'pejorative alternate dialect name for'. The index entry gives the primary name for the language with which the given name is associated, followed by the unique three-letter language code in square brackets. The numbers identify the pages on which the language entries using the indexed name may be found. If the list of page references includes the entry in the primary country, it is listed first.

A Fala de Xálima, *alt.* Fala [fax], 560
A Fala do Xálima, *alt.* Faa [fax], 560
A Nden, *alt.* Abun [kgr], 410
A-Dham, *alt. dial.* Rade [rad], 526
A-Hmao, *alt.* Hmong, Northeastern Dian [hmd], 334
A-La Cong, *alt. dial.* Bahnar [bdq], 521
A-Pucikwar [apq], 353
A-Rem, *alt.* Arem [aem], 521
A'a Sama, *alt. dial.* Sama, Southern [ssb], 458
Aachterhoeks, *alt.* Achterhoeks [act], 548
Aage, *alt.* Esimbi [ags], 61
Aaimasa, *alt. dial.* Kunama [kun], 112
Aal Murrah, *alt. dial.* Arabic, Najdi Spoken [ars], 508
Aalawa, *dial.* Ramoaaina [rai], 622
Aalawaa, *alt. dial.* Ramoaaina [rai], 622
Aaleira, *alt.* Laro [lro], 192
Aantantara, *dial.* Tairora, North [tbg], 626
A'ara, *alt.* Cheke Holo [mrn], 635
Aarai, *alt.* Aari [aiz], 112
Aari [aiz], 112
Aariya [aay], 353
Aasá, *alt.* Aasáx [aas], 197
Aasáx [aas], 197
Aatasaara, *dial.* Tairora, South [omw], 626
|Aaye, *alt. dial.* Shua [shg], 48
Aba, *alt.* Amba [utp], 634
alt. Shor [cjs], 506
dial. Tibetan [bod], 388
Abá, *alt.* Avá-Canoeiro [avv], 225
Abaali, *alt.* Bali [bcn], 154
Abaangi, *alt. dial.* Gwamhi-Wuri [bga], 161
Ababda, *dial.* Bedawi [bej], 112
Abaca, *alt. dial.* Ilongot [ilk], 495
Abacama, *alt.* Bacama [bcy], 154
Abacha, *alt.* Basa [bzw], 154

Abadekh, *alt. dial.* Adyghe [ady], 552
Abadhi, *alt.* Awadhi [awa], 468
Abadi [kbt], 587
alt. Awadhi [awa], 354, 468
alt. Tsuvadi [tvd], 176
Abadzeg, *alt. dial.* Adyghe [ady], 552
Abadzex, *dial.* Adyghe [ady], 552
Abaga [abg], 587
Abai, *dial.* Putoh [put], 395
Abai Sungai [abf], 456
Abak, *dial.* Anaang [anw], 153
Abaka, *dial.* Ilongot [ilk], 495
Abakan, *alt.* Kpan [kpk], 167
Abakan Tatar, *alt.* Khakas [kjh], 505, 337
Abakay Spanish, *alt. dial.* Chavacano [cbk], 493
Abaknon, *alt.* Inabaknon [abx], 495
Abaknon Sama, *alt.* Inabaknon [abx], 495
Abakoum, *alt.* Kwakum [kwu], 65
Abakpa, *alt. dial.* Ejagham [etu], 159, 60
Abakum, *alt.* Kwakum [kwu], 65
Abakwariga, *alt.* Hausa [hau], 162
Abaletti, *dial.* Yele [yle], 633
Abam, *dial.* Wipi [gdr], 632
Abancay, *dial.* Quechua, Eastern Apurímac [qve], 291
Abane, *alt.* Baniva [bvv], 311
Abangba, *alt.* Bangba [bbe], 97
Abanliku, *alt.* Obanliku [bzy], 172
Abanyai, *alt. dial.* Kalanga [kck], 216
Abanyom [abm], 152
Abanyum, *alt.* Abanyom [abm], 152
Abar [mij], 56
Abarambo, *alt.* Barambu [brm], 97
Abasakur, *alt.* Pal [abw], 621
Abathwa, *alt.* ‖Xegwi [xeg], 187
Abatonga, *alt. dial.* Ndau [ndc], 216
Abatsa, *alt.* Basa [bzw], 154
Abau [aau], 587
Abaw, *alt.* Bankon [abb], 58
Abawa, *dial.* Gupa-Abawa [gpa], 161

Abayongo, *dial.* Agwagwune [yay], 153
Abaza [abq], 552, 518
Abazin, *alt.* Abaza [abq], 552, 518
Abazintsy, *alt.* Abaza [abq], 552, 518
Abbé, *alt.* Abé [aba], 90
Abbey, *alt.* Abé [aba], 90
Abbey-Ve, *alt. dial.* Abé [aba], 90
Abbruzzesi, *dial.* Romani, Sinte [rmo], 557
'Abd Al-Kuri, *dial.* Soqotri [sqt], 528
Abdal, *alt.* Ainu [aib], 326
Abdedal, *alt.* Gagadu [gbu], 570
Abe, *dial.* Anyin [any], 91
Abé [aba], 90
Abedju-Azaki, *dial.* Lugbara [lgg], 103
Àbéélé, *alt.* Beele [bxq], 155
Abefang, *alt. dial.* Befang [bby], 58
Abelam, *alt.* Ambulas [abt], 589
Abenaki, *alt.* Abnaki, Eastern [aaq], 297
alt. Abnaki, Western [abe], 235
Abenaqui, *alt.* Abnaki, Western [abe], 235
Abendago, *alt.* Yali, Pass Valley [yac], 426
A'beng, *dial.* Garo [grt], 362
Abeng, *dial.* Garo [grt], 321
A'bengya, *alt. dial.* Garo [grt], 362
Abenlen, *alt.* Ayta, Abenlen [abp], 492
Abenlen Ayta, *see* Ayta, Abenlen [abp], 492
Abewa, *alt.* Asu [aum], 154
Abgue, *dial.* Birgit [btf], 79
Abhor, *alt.* Adi [adi], 353
Abi, *alt.* Abé [aba], 90
Abia, *alt.* Aneme Wake [aby], 589
Abiddul, *alt.* Gagadu [gbu], 570
Abidji [abi], 88
Abie, *alt.* Aneme Wake [aby], 589
Abiem, *dial.* Dinka, Southwestern [dik], 190
Abigar, *alt. dial.* Nuer [nus], 117
dial. Nuer [nus], 194

Abigira, *alt.* Abishira [ash], 285
Abiji, *alt.* Abidji [abi], 88
Abiliang, *dial.* Dinka, Northeastern [dip], 189
Abini, *dial.* Agwagwune [yay], 153
Abinomn [bsa], 410
Abinsi, *alt.* Wannu [jub], 177
Abipon [axb], 219
Abiquira, *alt.* Abishira [ash], 285
Abira, *alt.* Eñepa [pbh], 311
Abiri, *alt.* Mararit [mgb], 83
   alt. dial. Agwagwune [yay], 153
Abishira [ash], 285
Abisi, *alt.* Piti [pcn], 173
Abiyi, *alt.* Mararit [mgb], 83
Abkar, *dial.* Maba [mde], 83
Abkhaz [abk], 352, 518
Ableg-Salegseg, *alt. dial.* Kalinga, Lubuagan [knb], 497
Abnaki, Eastern [aaq], 297
Abnaki, Western [abe], 235
Abo, *alt.* Bankon [abb], 58
   alt. Mulam [mlm], 340
   dial. Bokyi [bky], 156
   dial. Ukwuani-Aboh-Ndoni [ukw], 176
Abō, *alt.* Abon [abo], 153
Aboh, *alt. dial.* Ukwuani-Aboh-Ndoni [ukw], 176
Abohi, *alt.* Awadhi [awa], 354, 468
Abom [aob], 587
Abon [abo], 153
Abong, *alt.* Abon [abo], 153
Abonwa, *alt.* Abure [abu], 91
Abor, *alt.* Adi [adi], 353
   alt. Luoba, Boga'er [adi], 339
Aboriginal English, *alt. dial.* English [eng], 570
Aborlan Tagbanwa, *alt.* Tagbanwa [tbw], 502
Aboro, *alt.* Berom [bom], 155
'Abotee, *alt.* Vute [vut], 73
Abou Charib, *alt. dial.* Mararit [mgb], 83
Abouré, *alt.* Abure [abu], 91
Abra-De-Ilog, *dial.* Iraya [iry], 495
Abri, *alt.* Koalib [kib], 192
Abron [abr], 122, 91
Abruzzese, *dial.* Italian [ita], 544
Absheron, *dial.* Tat, Muslim [ttt], 320
Abu [ado], 586
   alt. dial. Bokyi [bky], 156
   alt. dial. Bu [jid], 156
   dial. Abu [ado], 586
Abu Sharib, *alt. dial.* Mararit [mgb], 83
Abu Sharin, *alt. dial.* Mararit [mgb], 83
Abu Sinun, *dial.* Kanga [kcp], 191

Abua [abn], 153
Abuan, *alt.* Abua [abn], 153
Abui [abz], 406
Abujhmadia, *alt. dial.* Maria [mrr], 375
Abujhmaria, *alt. dial.* Maria [mrr], 375
Abujmar Maria, *alt. dial.* Maria [mrr], 375
Abujmaria, *dial.* Maria [mrr], 375
Abujmariya, *alt. dial.* Maria [mrr], 375
Abukeia, *alt.* Avokaya [avu], 188, 96
Abul, *alt.* Heiban [hbn], 191
Abulas, *alt.* Ambulas [abt], 589
Abuldugu, *dial.* Burun [bdi], 189
Abule, *alt.* Abure [abu], 91
Abuloma, *alt.* Obulom [obu], 172
Abun [kgr], 410
Abun Je, *dial.* Abun [kgr], 410
Abun Ji, *dial.* Abun [kgr], 410
Abun Tat, *dial.* Abun [kgr], 410
Abung [abl], 435
Abure [abu], 91
Abureni [mgj], 153
Aburlin Negrito, *alt.* Ayta, Abenlen [abp], 492
Abuya, *alt. dial.* Dinka, Northeastern [dip], 189
'Abwetee, *alt.* Vute [vut], 73
Abxazo, *alt.* Abkhaz [abk], 352, 518
Abyssinian, *alt.* Amharic [amh], 113
Abzhui, *dial.* Abkhaz [abk], 352, 518
Acadian, *alt.* French, Cajun [frc], 300
   alt. dial. French [fra], 237
Acadien, *alt. dial.* French [fra], 237
Acahuayo, *alt.* Akawaio [ake], 256, 311
   alt. Ingarikó [ake], 227
Acang, *alt.* Achang [acn], 326, 456
Acatec, *alt.* Akateko [knj], 253
   alt. Kanjobal, Western [knj], 263
Acateco, *alt.* Akateko [knj], 253
   alt. Kanjobal, Western [knj], 263
Acatenango Southwestern Cakchiquel, *alt.* Kaqchikel, Akatenango Southwestern [ckk], 254
Acatepec, *dial.* Tlapanec, Acatepec [tpx], 275
Acatepec Tlapanec, *see* Tlapanec, Acatepec [tpx], 275
Acatlán Mixtec, *alt.* Mixtec, Southern Puebla [mit], 269
Acawayo, *alt.* Akawaio [ake], 311
Acchami, *dial.* Nepali [nep], 476
Accra, *alt.* Ga [gaa], 125
Aceh [ace], 435
Acewaio, *alt.* Akawaio [ake], 256, 311

   alt. Ingarikó [ake], 227
Acgachemem, *alt. dial.* Luiseño [lui], 304
Achagua [aca], 243
Ach'ang, *alt.* Achang [acn], 326
Achang [acn], 326, 456
Achanti, *alt. dial.* Akan [aka], 123
Acharian, *alt. dial.* Georgian [kat], 352
Achawa, *alt.* Yao [yao], 141, 149, 206, 215
Ache, *alt.* Ashe [ahs], 154
Aché [guq], 284
Ache Yi, *see* Yi, Ache [yif], 347
Achehnese, *alt.* Aceh [ace], 435
Achero, *alt. dial.* Nachering [ncd], 476
Acheron [acz], 187
Achi', Cubulco [acc], 253
Achi', Rabinal [acr], 253
A'chick, *dial.* Garo [grt], 362
A'chik, *alt. dial.* Garo [grt], 362
Achik, *dial.* Garo [grt], 321
Achinese, *alt.* Aceh [ace], 435
Achipa, *alt.* Acipa, Eastern [acp], 153
   alt. Acipa, Western [awc], 153
Achlo, *alt.* Igo [ahl], 208
Acholi [ach], 210, 187
Achomawi, *alt.* Achumawi [acv], 297
Achomi, *alt.* Lari [lrl], 440
Achpar, *alt. dial.* Qimant [ahg], 118
Achterhoek, *alt.* Achterhoeks [act], 548
Achterhoeks [act], 548
Achual, *alt.* Achuar-Shiwiar [acu], 285, 250
Achuale, *alt.* Achuar-Shiwiar [acu], 285, 250
Achuar, *alt.* Achuar-Shiwiar [acu], 285, 250
Achuar-Shiwiar [acu], 285, 250
Achuara, *alt.* Achuar-Shiwiar [acu], 285, 250
Achumawi [acv], 297
Achung, *alt.* Achang [acn], 326
Aci, *alt.* Zaiwa [atb], 349, 467
   dial. Apali [ena], 590
Acilowe, *alt.* Lomwe [ngl], 147
Acipa, Eastern [acp], 153
Acipa, Western [awc], 153
Acipanci, *alt.* Acipa, Eastern [acp], 153
   alt. Acipa, Western [awc], 153
Acira, *alt.* Adzera [azr], 587
Acoli, *alt.* Acholi [ach], 210, 187
Acoma, *dial.* Keres, Western [kjq], 303
Acooli, *alt.* Acholi [ach], 210, 187
Acra, *alt.* Ga [gaa], 125

Acre Arara, *alt.* Sharanahua
  [mcd], 232
Acroá [acs], 224
Aculo, *alt.* Deg [mzw], 124, 92
Ac'ye, *alt.* Lashi [lsi], 465
Acye, *alt.* Lashi [lsi], 338
Ada, *alt.* Kuturmi [khj], 167
  dial. Dangme [ada], 124
Adabe [adb], 350
Adal, *alt.* Afar [aar], 112
Adamawa Fulani, *alt.* Fulfulde,
  Adamawa [fub], 61, 80
Adamawa Fulfulde, *see* Fulfulde,
  Adamawa [fub], 61, 80, 160, 190
Adamorobe Sign Language
  [ads], 122
Adan, *alt.* Adangbe [adq], 122, 206
  dial. Éwé [ewe], 207
Adang [adn], 406
  dial. Lundayeh [lnd], 460
Adangbe [adq], 122, 206
Adangme, *alt.* Dangme [ada], 124
Adantonwi, *alt.* Adangbe
  [adq], 122, 206
Adap [adp], 322
Adara, *alt.* Kadara [kad], 165
Adarawa, *dial.* Hausa [hau], 162
Adare, *alt.* Harari [har], 115
Adarinnya, *alt.* Harari [har], 115
Adaru, *dial.* Carútana [cru], 226
Adasen, *alt.* Itneg, Adasen [tiu], 496
Adasen Itneg, *see* Itneg, Adasen
  [tiu], 496
Addasen, *alt.* Itneg, Adasen
  [tiu], 496
Addasen Tinguian, *alt.* Itneg,
  Adasen [tiu], 496
Addo, *alt.* Edo [bin], 158
Adea, *alt.* Hadiyya [hdy], 115
Adeeyah, *alt.* Bube [bvb], 110
Adeka, *alt. dial.* Bauchi [bsf], 155
Adele [ade], 206, 122
'Aden, *dial.* Arabic, Judeo-Yemeni
  [jye], 444, 528
Adeni, *dial.* Arabic, Ta'izzi-Adeni
  Spoken [acq], 528
Aderawa, *dial.* Hausa [hau], 152
Adere, *alt.* Dzodinka [add], 60, 158
  alt. Harari [har], 115
Aderinya, *alt.* Harari [har], 115
Adewada, *dial.* Maria [mrr], 375
Adgawan, *dial.* Manobo, Agusan
  [msm], 499
Adham, *dial.* Rade [rad], 526
Adhiang, *alt. dial.* Dinka,
  Southwestern [dik], 190
Adho-Adhom, *alt.* Djangun
  [djf], 569
Adhola [adh], 210
Adi [adi], 353

alt. Adi, Galo [adl], 353
alt. Kowiai [kwh], 418
alt. Luoba, Boga'er [adi], 339
Adi Dravida, *dial.* Tamil [tam], 388
Adi, Galo [adl], 353
Adi-Bokar, *alt.* Luoba, Boga'er
  [adi], 339
Adi-Gallong, *alt.* Adi, Galo
  [adl], 353
Adi-Galo, *alt.* Adi, Galo [adl], 353
Adiangok, *alt. dial.* Bakoko
  [bkh], 57
Adibom, *dial.* Odual [odu], 172
Adie, *dial.* Bakoko [bkh], 57
Adihup, *alt.* Hatam [had], 415
  dial. Hatam [had], 415
Adija, *alt.* Bube [bvb], 110
Adijaya, *dial.* Kowiai [kwh], 418
Adikimmu Sukur, *alt.* Sukur
  [syk], 175
Adilabad, *alt. dial.* Gondi, Southern
  [ggo], 363
Adim, *dial.* Agwagwune [yay], 153
Adioukrou [adj], 91
Adiri, *alt.* Dzodinka [add], 60, 158
Adivasi Oriya, *see* Oriya, Adivasi
  [ort], 382
Adivasi Wagdi, *dial.* Wagdi
  [wbr], 390
Adiwasi Garasia, *see* Garasia,
  Adiwasi [gas], 362
Adiwasi Girasia, *alt.* Garasia,
  Adiwasi [gas], 362
Adiwasi Gujarati, *alt.* Garasia,
  Adiwasi [gas], 362
Adiwasi Oriya, *alt.* Oriya, Adivasi
  [ort], 382
Adiya, *alt.* Hadiyya [hdy], 115
  alt. Ravula [yea], 384
  dial. Ravula [yea], 384
Adiyan, *alt.* Ravula [yea], 384
Adiye, *alt.* Hadiyya [hdy], 115
Adja, *alt.* Aja [aja], 187
  alt. Aja [ajg], 42, 206
Adjabdurah, *dial.* Narungga
  [nnr], 575
Adjahdurah, *alt. dial.* Narungga
  [nnr], 575
Adjer, *alt. dial.* Soninke [snk], 144,
  95, 122, 131, 145, 182
Adjiga, *alt. dial.* Avokaya [avu], 188
Adjio, *alt.* Tajio [tdj], 433
Adjora, *alt.* Abu [ado], 586
Adjoria, *alt.* Abu [ado], 586
Adjukru, *alt.* Adioukrou [adj], 91
Adjumani, *alt. dial.* Ma'di
  [mhi], 211
Adjumba, *alt. dial.* Myene
  [mye], 121
Adkibba, *alt.* Murle [mur], 193

Adkuri, *dial.* Halbi [hlb], 363
Adlai, *alt.* Roglai, Northern [rog], 526
Ad'n'amadana, *alt.*
  Adynyamathanha [adt], 567
Ado, *dial.* Kaili, Ledo [lew], 429
Adoma, *alt. dial.* C'lela [dri], 157
Adona, *alt.* Rer Bare [rer], 118
Adonara [adr], 406
Adong, *alt.* Idun [ldb], 163
  alt. dial. Mambwe-Lungu [mgr], 214
Ador, *alt. dial.* Dinka, South Central
  [dib], 190
Adora, *alt.* Airoran [air], 410
Adouma, *alt.* Duma [dma], 120
Adowen, *alt.* Djauan [djn], 570
Adoyo, *dial.* Anuak [anu], 113
Adsawa, *alt.* Yao [yao], 141, 149,
  206, 215
Adsoa, *alt.* Yao [yao], 141, 149, 215
Adu, *dial.* Tabaru [tby], 404
Aduge [adu], 153
Adulu, *alt.* Makayam [aup], 611
Aduma, *alt.* Duma [dma], 120
Adun, *dial.* Mbembe, Cross River
  [mfn], 163
Adyaktye, *alt.* Kakanda [kka], 165
Adygei, *alt.* Adyghe [ady], 552
Adygey, *alt.* Adyghe [ady], 552, 442,
  444, 447, 510, 518, 547
Adyghe [ady], 552, 442, 444, 447,
  510, 518, 547
Adynyamathanha [adt], 567
Adyoukrou, *alt.* Adioukrou
  [adj], 91
Adyukru, *alt.* Adioukrou [adj], 91
Adyumba, *alt. dial.* Myene
  [mye], 121
Adzera [azr], 587
Adzerma, *alt.* Zarma [dje], 152, 55,
  178
  alt. Zarmaci [dje], 145
Adzhar, *dial.* Georgian [kat], 352
Adzu Balaka, *alt. dial.* Caka
  [ckx], 59
Adzu Batanga, *alt. dial.* Caka
  [ckx], 59
A'e, *alt.* Rempi [rmp], 622
Aejauroh, *alt.* Sawi [saw], 422
Aeka, *dial.* Binandere [bhg], 593
  dial. Orokaiva [ork], 620
'Aeke, *alt.* Haeke [aek], 584
Aeke, *alt.* Haeke [aek], 584
Aekyom [awi], 587
Aer [aeq], 483
Aeroran, *alt.* Airoran [air], 410
Aeta Negrito, *alt.* Sambal, Botolan
  [sbl], 501
Aewa, *dial.* Kuni-Boazi [kvg], 608
Af-Ashraaf, *alt. dial.* Somali
  [som], 185

Af-Bajuun, *alt. dial.* Swahili [swh], 185
Af-Boon, *alt.* Boon [bnl], 184
Af-Chimwiini, *alt. dial.* Swahili [swh], 185
Af-Dabarre, *alt.* Dabarre [dbr], 184
Af-Garre, *alt.* Garre [gex], 184
Af-Helledi, *dial.* Maay [ymm], 184
Af-Iroole, *alt. dial.* Dabarre [dbr], 184
Af-Jiiddu, *alt.* Jiiddu [jii], 184
Af-Kareti, *alt.* Komso [kxc], 116
Af-Maay, *alt.* Maay [ymm], 184
Af-Maay Tiri, *alt.* Maay [ymm], 184
Af-Maxaad Tiri, *alt.* Somali [som], 185
Af-May, *alt.* Maay [ymm], 184
Af-Maymay, *alt.* Maay [ymm], 184
Af-Soomaali, *alt.* Somali [som], 185
Af-Tunni, *alt.* Tunni [tqq], 185
Afa, *alt.* Pa'a [pqa], 173
   dial. Arigidi [aqg], 154
Afada, *alt.* Afade [aal], 153
Afade [aal], 153, 56
Afadeh, *alt.* Afade [aal], 153, 56
Afakani, *alt.* Defaka [afn], 157
Afan Mao, *alt.* Kwama [kmq], 116
Afan Oromo, *alt.* Oromo, Borana-Arsi-Guji [gax], 117
   alt. Oromo, West Central [gaz], 118
Afanci, *alt.* Pa'a [pqa], 173
Afango, *alt.* Berom [bom], 155
Afao, *alt.* Eloyi [afo], 159
Afar [aar], 112, 109, 111
'Afar Af, *alt.* Afar [aar], 112
Afaraf, *alt.* Afar [aar], 112, 109, 111
Afatime, *alt.* Avatime [avn], 123
Afawa, *alt.* Pa'a [pqa], 173
Afenmai, *alt.* Yekhee [ets], 177
Aferike, *alt. dial.* Putukwam [afe], 173
Affa, *alt. dial.* Arigidi [aqg], 154
Affade, *alt.* Afade [aal], 153, 56
Affiniam, *dial.* Bandial [bqj], 180
Affitti, *alt.* Afitti [aft], 187
Afghan, *alt.* Pashto, Northern [pbu], 317
   alt. Pashto, Southern [pbt], 520
Afghan Farsi, *alt. dial.* Farsi, Eastern [prs], 315
Afghana-Yi Nasfurush, *alt.* Parya [paq], 513, 317
Afghana-Yi Siyarui, *alt.* Parya [paq], 513, 317
Afghani, *pej. alt.* Pashto, Southern [pbt], 441
Afikpo, *dial.* Igbo [ibo], 163
Afitti [aft], 187
Afizare, *alt.* Izere [fiz], 164
Afizarek, *alt.* Izere [fiz], 164

Afkabiye, *alt.* Guduf-Gava [gdf], 161
Afo, *alt.* Eloyi [afo], 159
   alt. dial. Bafaw-Balong [bwt], 56
Afore, *dial.* Ese [mcq], 598
Aforo, *alt.* Kalam [kmh], 604
Afrikaans [afr], 185, 46, 140, 149, 213
Afrike, *dial.* Putukwam [afe], 173
Afro-Guyanese Creole, *dial.* Guyanese Creole English [gyn], 257
Afro-Seminol Criollo, *alt.* Afro-Seminole Creole [afs], 259
Afro-Seminole, *alt.* Afro-Seminole Creole [afs], 297, 259
Afro-Seminole Creole [afs], 297, 259
Afsar, *alt. dial.* Azerbaijani, South [azb], 438, 315
Afshar, *alt. dial.* Azerbaijani, South [azb], 438, 315
Afshari, *dial.* Azerbaijani, South [azb], 438, 315
Afu, *alt.* Eloyi [afo], 159
Afughe, *alt. dial.* Bafut [bfd], 56
Afunatam, *alt. dial.* Nde-Nsele-Nta [ndd], 170
Afungwa, *alt.* Fungwa [ula], 160
Afusare, *alt.* Izere [fiz], 164
Aga, *alt.* Kanuri, Central [knc], 81
   dial. Buriat, China [bxu], 329
   dial. Buriat, Mongolia [bxm], 461
Aga Bereho, *alt.* Bariji [bjc], 592
Agachemem, *alt. dial.* Luiseño [lui], 304
Agadez, *alt. dial.* Tamajeq, Tayart [thz], 152
Agala, *alt.* Fembe [agl], 598
Agalo, *dial.* Gumuz [guk], 115
Agam, *dial.* Minangkabau [min], 436
Agamoru, *alt. dial.* Avokaya [avu], 188
Agar, *alt.* Dinka, South Central [dib], 190
   dial. Dinka, South Central [dib], 190
Agarabe, *alt.* Agarabi [agd], 588
Agarabi [agd], 588
Agarar, *alt.* Angal Heneng [akh], 589
Agari, *alt. dial.* Gbiri-Niragu [grh], 160
   alt. dial. Lame [bma], 168
Agari of Kolaba, *dial.* Konkani [knn], 369
Agaria, *alt.* Agariya [agi], 353
Agariya [agi], 353
Agatu [agc], 153
Agau, *alt.* Awngi [awn], 113
   alt. dial. Ju|'hoan [ktz], 47, 150
Agaunshe, *dial.* Tsikimba [kdl], 175
Agaushi, *alt.* Tsikimba [kdl], 175

Agavotaguerra [avo], 224
Agavotokueng, *alt.* Agavotaguerra [avo], 224
Agavotoqueng, *alt.* Agavotaguerra [avo], 224
Agaw, *alt.* Awngi [awn], 113
Agawinya, *alt.* Xamtanga [xan], 119
Agbaragba, *alt.* Efutop [ofu], 158
Agbarho, *dial.* Urhobo [urh], 176
Agbawi, *alt. dial.* Gbari [gby], 160
Agbiri, *alt. dial.* Gbiri-Niragu [grh], 160
   alt. dial. Lame [bma], 168
Agbo, *alt.* Legbo [agb], 168
Agbome, *dial.* Fon [fon], 43
Agbon, *dial.* Urhobo [urh], 176
Age, *alt.* Esimbi [ags], 61
Ageer, *dial.* Dinka, Northeastern [dip], 189
Ageir, *alt. dial.* Dinka, Northeastern [dip], 189
Ager, *alt. dial.* Dinka, Northeastern [dip], 189
Agere, *alt.* Begbere-Ejar [bqv], 155
Agerlep, *alt.* Aiklep [mwg], 588
Agew, *alt.* Awngi [awn], 113
Agharia, *alt.* Agariya [agi], 353
Aghem [agq], 56
Agholo, *dial.* Ogbia [ogb], 172
Aghu [ahh], 410
Aghu Tharnggalu [ggr], 567
Aghul [agx], 552
Aghulshuy, *alt.* Aghul [agx], 552
Agi [aif], 588
   dial. Moru [mgd], 193
Agiba, *alt.* Murle [mur], 193
Agiryama, *alt.* Giryama [nyf], 133
Agiyan, *alt.* Agta, Camarines Norte [abd], 490
Agnagan, *alt.* Ginyanga [ayg], 207
Agnang, *alt.* Denya [anv], 60
Agni, *alt.* Anyin [any], 91, 123
Ago, *alt.* Igo [ahl], 208
Agob [kit], 588
   dial. Agob [kit], 588
Agoi [ibm], 153
   dial. Gen [gej], 207, 45
Agolok, *alt. dial.* Tyap [kcg], 176
Agoma, *alt.* Kagoma [kdm], 165
Agomes, *alt.* Hermit [llf], 602
Agona, *dial.* Akan [aka], 123
Agoria, *alt.* Agariya [agi], 353
Agotime, *alt.* Adangbe [adq], 122, 206
Agouisiri, *alt.* Abishira [ash], 285
Agow, *alt.* Awngi [awn], 113
Agrab, *dial.* Birgit [btf], 79
Agta, Alabat Island [dul], 490
Agta, Camarines Norte [abd], 490

||**Aisan**, *alt.* Naro [nhr], 48
Aiso, *alt.* Kais [kzm], 415
Aisorski, *alt.* Assyrian Neo-Aramaic [aii], 442, 319, 352, 510
Aissuari, *alt. dial.* Omagua [omg], 231
Aita, *dial.* Rotokas [roo], 623
Aiton [aio], 353
Aitonia, *alt.* Aiton [aio], 353
Aitutaki, *dial.* Rarotongan [rar], 579
Aiwanat, *dial.* Yupik, Central Siberian [ess], 507
Aiwin, *alt.* Aekyom [awi], 587
Aïwo, *alt.* Ayiwo [nfl], 635
Aiyangar, *dial.* Tamil [tam], 388
Aiyar, *dial.* Tamil [tam], 388
||**'Aiye**, *dial.* Shua [shg], 48
Aiysyen, *alt.* Haitian Creole French [hat], 258, 250, 253
Aizi, Aproumu [ahp], 91
Aizi, Mobumrin [ahm], 91
Aizi, Tiagbamrin [ahi], 91
Aizuare, *dial.* Omagua [omg], 231
Aja (Benin) [ajg], 42, 206
  Aja (Sudan) [aja], 187
  alt. Ajawa [ajw], 153
Ajachema, *alt. dial.* Luiseño [lui], 304
Ajachemem, *alt. dial.* Luiseño [lui], 304
Ajagbe, *alt.* Aja [ajg], 42, 206
Ajagua, *alt.* Achagua [aca], 243
Ajak, *alt. dial.* Dinka, South Central [dib], 190
  alt. dial. Dinka, Southwestern [dik], 190
Ajam, *alt. dial.* Asmat, Central [cns], 411
Ajamaru, *alt.* Mai Brat [ayz], 419
Ajanci, *alt.* Ajawa [ajw], 153
Ajanji, *alt.* Janji [jni], 164
Ajau, *alt.* Awyu, Central [awu], 412
Ajawa [ajw], 153
  alt. Yao [yao], 141, 149, 206, 215
Aje, *dial.* Arigidi [aqg], 154
Ajeka, *dial.* Orokaiva [ork], 620
Ajer, *alt. dial.* Soninke [snk], 131
Aji, *alt.* Zaiwa [atb], 349
  dial. Malay [mly], 436
Ajibba, *alt.* Murle [mur], 193, 117
A'jie, *alt.* Ajië [aji], 584
Ajië [aji], 584
Ajigu, *dial.* Avokaya [avu], 96
Ajiri of Hazara, *dial.* Gujari [gju], 363
Ajiw, *dial.* Mpur [akc], 420
Ajja, *alt.* Aja [aja], 187
Ajjer, *alt. dial.* Tamahaq, Tahaggart [thv], 37, 139, 152

'Ajmaan, *alt. dial.* Arabic, Najdi Spoken [ars], 508
Ajmeri, *alt.* Merwari [wry], 375
'Ajnabi, *alt.* Lingua Franca [pml], 209
Ajo, *alt.* Majang [mpe], 116
Ajokoot, *alt.* Margu [mhg], 573
Ajomang, *alt.* Talodi [tlo], 195
Ajong Dit, *alt. dial.* Dinka, Southwestern [dik], 190
Ajong Thi, *alt. dial.* Dinka, Southwestern [dik], 190
Ajra, *dial.* Gun [guw], 45
Ajugu, *alt. dial.* Avokaya [avu], 96
  dial. Avokaya [avu], 188
Ajuh, *dial.* Lawangan [lbx], 394
Ajujure, *alt.* Arára, Pará [aap], 225
Ajukru, *alt.* Adioukrou [adj], 91
Ajumba, *dial.* Myene [mye], 121
Ajuran, *dial.* Garreh-Ajuran [ggh], 133
Ajure, *alt. dial.* Kadara [kad], 165
Ajurú, *alt.* Wayoró [wyr], 234
Ajuuraan, *alt. dial.* Garreh-Ajuran [ggh], 133
Ajyéninka, *alt.* Ajyíninka Apurucayali [cpc], 286
Ajyíninka Apurucayali [cpc], 286
Ak [akq], 588
  alt. dial. Nogai [nog], 556
Ak'a, *alt.* Akha [ahk], 462, 326, 449, 513, 521
Aka ([soh], 187
  Yaka (Central African Republic) [axk], 87
  alt. Akha [ahk], 462, 326, 449, 513, 521
  alt. Asoa [asv], 96
  alt. Hruso [hru], 364
  alt. Yaka [axk], 78
Aka Lel, *dial.* Nisi [dap], 381
Aka-Bea [abj], 353
Aka-Beada, *alt.* Aka-Bea [abj], 353
Aka-Bo [akm], 353
Aka-Cari [aci], 353
Aka-Jeru [akj], 353
Aka-Kede [akx], 353
Aka-Kol [aky], 353
Aka-Kora [ack], 353
Akab, *alt.* Kallahan, Kayapa [kak], 497
Akabafa, *dial.* Ese [mcq], 598
Akaha, *alt. dial.* Ijo, Southeast [ijs], 163
Akajo, *alt.* Ekajuk [eka], 159
Akajuk, *alt.* Ekajuk [eka], 159
Akalak, *alt.* Katla [kcr], 192
Akan [aka], 123
Akanda, *alt.* Kakanda [kka], 165
Akande, *alt.* Kulere [kul], 167

Akandi, *alt.* Kulere [kul], 167
Akani, *dial.* Nanai [gld], 506
Akany Kok, *alt. dial.* Dinka, Southwestern [dik], 190
Akaplass, *alt.* Abure [abu], 91
Akar-Bale [acl], 353
Akara, *alt.* Toposa [toq], 196
  alt. dial. Arrarnta, Western [are], 568
Akarre, *dial.* Arrernte, Eastern [aer], 568
Akasele, *alt.* Akaselem [aks], 206
Akaselem [aks], 206
Akassa, *dial.* Ijo, Southeast [ijs], 163
Akateko [knj], 253
Akatenango Southwestern Kaqkchikel, *see* Kaqkchikel, Akatenango Southwestern [ckk], 254
Akawai, *alt.* Akawaio [ake], 256, 311
  alt. Ingarikó [ake], 227
Akawaio [ake], 256, 311
  alt. Ingarikó [ake], 227
Akayon, *alt.* Kiong [kkm], 166
Ake [aik], 153
Akebou, *alt.* Akebu [keu], 206
Akebu [keu], 206
Akei [tsr], 640
Akele, *alt.* Kélé [keb], 120
Aker, *alt. dial.* Dinka, South Central [dib], 190
Akern Jok, *alt. dial.* Dinka, Southwestern [dik], 190
Akerre, *dial.* Arrarnta, Western [are], 568
Akewara, *alt.* Suruí do Pará [mdz], 232
Akewere, *alt.* Suruí do Pará [mdz], 232
Akha [ahk], 462, 326, 449, 513, 521
Akhoe, *dial.* Kung-Ekoka [knw], 150
Akhty, *dial.* Lezgi [lez], 555
Akhvakh [akv], 552
Aki, *alt.* Banggai [bgz], 427
  alt. dial. Tuki [bag], 72
  dial. Apali [ena], 590
Akiapmin, *alt.* Suarmin [seo], 625
Akido, *pej. alt.* Tolaki [lbw], 433
Akie, *alt.* Attié [ati], 91
  alt. Okiek [oki], 135, 203
Akiek, *alt.* Okiek [oki], 135, 203
Akimba, *alt.* Tsikimba [kdl], 175
Akimel O'odham, *dial.* Tohono O'odham [ood], 309
Akit, *dial.* Kerinci [kvr], 436
Akita, *alt.* Okodia [okd], 172
Akium, *alt.* Aekyom [awi], 587
Akium-Pare, *alt.* Pare [ppt], 621
Akiuru, *alt.* Lamogai [lmg], 609
Akiza, *alt.* Ninzo [nin], 171

Akjuet, *alt. dial.* Dinka,
Southwestern [dik], 190
Akkala Saami, *see* Saami, Akkala
[sia], 556
Akkhusha, *alt. dial.* Dargwa
[dar], 553
Akkin, *alt. dial.* Chechen [che], 553
Aklan, *alt.* Aklanon [akl], 491
Aklano, *alt.* Aklanon [akl], 491
Aklanon [akl], 491
Aklanon-Bisayan, *alt.* Aklanon
[akl], 491
Akn, *dial.* Armenian [hye], 318
Ako, *alt. dial.* Fulfulde, Kano-
Katsina-Bororro [fuv], 61, 80
alt. dial. Fulfulde, Nigerian
[fuv], 160
dial. Akha [ahk], 462
dial. Bada [bhz], 427
dial. Ekpeye [ekp], 159
Akoerio, *alt.* Akurio [ako], 295
Akoinkake, *alt.* Akoye [miw], 588
Akoiyang, *alt.* Kiong [kkm], 166
Akokolemu, *alt.* Kumam [kdi], 211
Akolet [akt], 588
Akoli, *alt.* Acholi [ach], 210, 187
Akono, *dial.* Yoruba [yor], 178
Akonto, *alt.* Mbembe, Tigon
[nza], 66, 170
Akoon, *alt. dial.* Dinka, Northeastern
[dip], 189
Akoose [bss], 56
Akosi, *alt.* Akoose [bss], 56
Akoye [miw], 588
Akoyi, *alt.* Akoye [miw], 588
Akpa [akf], 153
Akpafu, *dial.* Siwu [akp], 128
Akpafu-Lolobi, *alt.* Siwu [akp], 128
Akpanzhi, *alt. dial.* Jukun Takum
[jbu], 63, 165
alt. dial. Kpan [kpk], 167
Akparabong, *alt. dial.* Ndoe
[nbb], 170
Akpe, *alt.* Anii [blo], 207
dial. Anii [blo], 42, 207
Akpes [ibe], 153
alt. dial. Akpes [ibe], 153
Akpese, *alt.* Kpelle, Guinea
[gkp], 129
Akpet, *alt. dial.* Ukpet-Ehom
[akd], 176
Akpet-Ehom, *alt.* Ukpet-Ehom
[akd], 176
Akpo-Mgbu-Tolu, *dial.* Ikwere
[ikw], 164
Akposo [kpo], 123
alt. Ikposo [kpo], 208
Akposso, *alt.* Akposo [kpo], 123
alt. Ikposo [kpo], 208
Akpoto, *alt. dial.* Idoma [idu], 163

Akpwakum, *alt.* Kwakum [kwu], 65
Akre, *dial.* Kurdish, Northern
[kmr], 443
Akrukay [afi], 588
Aksana, *alt. dial.* Qawasqar
[alc], 243
Aksanás, *dial.* Qawasqar [alc], 243
Aku, *alt.* Li'o [ljl], 408
alt. dial. Befang [bby], 58
dial. Krio [kri], 183
Akuapem, *dial.* Akan [aka], 123
Akuapim, *alt. dial.* Akan [aka], 123
Akuên, *alt.* Xavánte [xav], 234
Akuku [ayk], 153
Akule, *alt. dial.* Yendang [yen], 178
Akuliyo, *alt.* Akurio [ako], 295
Akum [aku], 56, 153
alt. Kumam [kdi], 211
alt. dial. Ngemba [nge], 69
Akunakuna, *pej. alt.* Agwagwune
[yay], 153
Akunnu, *dial.* Akpes [ibe], 153
Akurakura, *alt.* Agwagwune
[yay], 153
Akuri, *alt.* Akurio [ako], 295
Akurijo, *alt.* Akurio [ako], 295
Akurio [ako], 295
Akuriyo, *alt.* Akurio [ako], 295
Akurmi, *alt.* Kurama [krh], 167
Akurumi, *alt.* Kurama [krh], 167
Akusha, *dial.* Dargwa [dar], 553
Akuwagel, *alt.* Beli [bey], 593
Akwa [akw], 88
dial. Pongu [png], 173
Akwa'ala, *alt.* Paipai [ppi], 273
Akwang, *alt. dial.* Dinka,
Southwestern [dik], 190
Akwanto, *alt.* Mbembe, Tigon
[nza], 170
Akwapem Twi, *alt. dial.* Akan
[aka], 123
Akwapi, *alt. dial.* Akan [aka], 123
Akwaya, *alt.* Asuriní [asu], 225
Akwaya Motom, *alt. dial.* Iceve-
Maci [bec], 63
Akwen, *alt.* Xavánte [xav], 234
Akweto, *alt.* Nsari [asj], 70
Akweya, *alt.* Akpa [akf], 153
Akyab, *alt. dial.* Chittagonian
[cit], 321, 463
Akye, *alt.* Ake [aik], 153
alt. Attié [ati], 91
Akyem Bosome, *dial.* Akan
[aka], 123
Al Arabiya, *alt.* Arabic, Standard
[arb], 508
Al Fus-Ha, *alt.* Arabic, Standard
[arb], 508
Al-Hasâ, *dial.* Arabic, Gulf Spoken
[afb], 437

Al-Hasaa, *dial.* Arabic, Gulf Spoken
[afb], 508
Al-Qasiim, *alt. dial.* Arabic, Najdi
Spoken [ars], 508
Al-Shihuh, *alt.* Arabic, Shihhi
Spoken [ssh], 520
Ala, *alt.* Ashe [ahs], 154
alt. Wali [wlx], 128
Ala'ala, *alt.* Lala [nrz], 609
Alaba [alw], 112
Alabama [akz], 297
Alabat Island Agta, *see* Agta,
Alabat Island [dul], 490
Alabat Island Dumagat, *alt.* Agta,
Alabat Island [dul], 490
Alacaluf, *alt.* Qawasqar [alc], 243
Alacalufe, *alt.* Qawasqar [alc], 243
Alacatlatzala Mixtec, *see* Mixtec,
Alacatlatzala [mim], 265
Alada, *alt.* Gun [guw], 45
dial. Gun [guw], 45, 161
Alada-Gbe, *alt.* Gun [guw], 45
alt. dial. Gun [guw], 161
Alag-Bako, *dial.* Iraya [iry], 495
Alago [ala], 153
Alagwa [wbj], 197
Alagwaisi, *alt.* Alagwa [wbj], 197
Alagwase, *alt.* Alagwa [wbj], 197
Alai, *alt.* Amal [aad], 589
Alak [alk], 449
Alakaman, *dial.* Abui [abz], 406
Alakamat, *alt.* Huaulu [hud], 399
Alaki, *alt.* Laki [lki], 440
Alakong, *dial.* Bahnar [bdq], 521
Alalao, *alt.* Padoe [pdo], 432
Alam, *alt.* Mala [ped], 611
Alama, *alt.* Quichua, Northern
Pastaza [qvz], 251, 293
Alamatu, *alt. dial.* Ngemba [nge], 69
Alamblak [amp], 588
Alan, *alt.* Allar [all], 353
Åland Islands Swedish, *dial.*
Swedish [swe], 535
Alangan [alj], 491
Alango, *dial.* Siane [snp], 624
Alangua, *dial.* Anyin [any], 91
Alanmar, *alt.* Allar [all], 353
Alante, *alt.* Balanta-Ganja [bjt], 179
alt. Balanta-Kentohe [ble], 130
Alar, *alt.* Allar [all], 353
dial. Buriat, Russia [bxr], 504
Alas, *dial.* Batak Alas-Kluet [btz], 435
Alas-Kluet Batak, *alt.* Batak Alas-
Kluet [btz], 435
Alasai, *dial.* Pashayi, Northwest
[glh], 317
Alatening, *dial.* Ngemba [nge], 69
Alatesu, *dial.* Nambikuára, Southern
[nab], 230
Alatil [alx], 588

Alatining, *alt. dial.* Ngemba [nge], 69

Alauagat, *alt.* Bragat [aof], 594

Alawa [alh], 567
alt. Alagwa [wbj], 197
alt. dial. Ramoaaina [rai], 622

Albanian, Arbëreshë [aae], 543

Albanian, Arvanitika [aat], 540

Albanian, Gheg [aln], 557, 529, 532, 547

Albanian, Tosk [als], 529, 540, 563

Albannach Gaidhlig, *alt.* Gaelic, Scottish [gla], 565

Albany River Ojibwa, *dial.* Ojibwa, Northwestern [ojb], 240

Albarradas Zapotec, *alt.* Zapotec, Santo Domingo Albarradas [zas], 280

Albay Bicolano, *see* Bicolano, Albay [bhk], 493

Alcantaranon, *dial.* Inonhan [loc], 495

Alcozauca Mixtec, *see* Mixtec, Alcozauca [xta], 266

Aldan Timpton, *dial.* Evenki [evn], 504

Ale, *alt.* Nake [nbk], 616

Alealum, *alt.* Malayalam [mal], 374, 509

Alechuxa, *dial.* Manchu [mnc], 339

Alege [alf], 153

Alegi, *alt.* Alege [alf], 153

Alekano [gah], 588

Alemán Coloneiro, *alt.* German, Colonia Tovar [gct], 311

Alemannic, *alt.* Alemannisch [gsw], 530, 535, 538, 546

Alemannisch [gsw], 530, 535, 538, 546
alt. Schwyzerdütsch [gsw], 563

Aleng, *alt.* Mon [mnw], 516

Alepa, *dial.* Sinaugoro [snc], 624

Aleut [ale], 297, 495
alt. Yupik, Pacific Gulf [ems], 310

Aleut, Mednyj [mud], 503

Alevica, *alt.* Kirmanjki [kiu], 518

Alfendio, *alt.* Arafundi [arf], 590

Alfold, *dial.* Hungarian [hun], 542

Algerian, *alt.* Arabic, Algerian Spoken [arq], 39

Algerian Saharan Spoken Arabic, *see* Arabic, Algerian Saharan Spoken [aao], 39, 151

Algerian Sign Language [asp], 39

Algerian Spoken Arabic, *see* Arabic, Algerian Spoken [arq], 39

Algherese, *alt. dial.* Catalan-Valencian-Balear [cat], 559

dial. Catalan-Valencian-Balear [cat], 543

Algiers, *dial.* Arabic, Algerian Spoken [arq], 39

Algonkin, *alt.* Algonquin [alq], 235

Algonquin [alq], 235

Ali [aiy], 74
alt. Yakamul [ykm], 632
dial. Yakamul [ykm], 632

Aliab, *alt. dial.* Dinka, South Central [dib], 190

Aliap, *dial.* Dinka, South Central [dib], 190

Alibamu, *alt.* Alabama [akz], 297

Alifokpa, *dial.* Yace [ekr], 177

Aliki, *alt.* Biritai [bqq], 413
alt. Eritai [ert], 415
alt. Obokuitai [afz], 421

Alile, *dial.* Paraujano [pbg], 312

Alinga, *alt. dial.* Tunen [baz], 72

Alingar, *dial.* Pashayi, Southeast [psi], 317

Alis, *alt. dial.* Quechua, Yauyos [qux], 292

Alis I Run, *alt. dial.* Ron [cla], 174

Alitta, *alt. dial.* Bugis [bug], 428

Aliutor, *alt.* Alutor [alr], 503

Aljamia, *alt.* Lingua Franca [pml], 209

Aljawara, *alt.* Alyawarr [aly], 567

Alkali, *alt.* Baiso [bsw], 113

Alkansea, *alt.* Quapaw [qua], 307

Allaaba, *alt.* Alaba [alw], 112

Alladian [ald], 91

Alladyan, *alt.* Alladian [ald], 91

Allagia, *alt.* Alladian [ald], 91

Allagian, *alt.* Alladian [ald], 91

Allagir, *dial.* Osetin [oss], 352, 519

Allan, *alt.* Allar [all], 353

Allang, *dial.* Larike-Wakasihu [alo], 396

Allar [all], 353
alt. Gadaba, Pottangi Ollar [gdb], 361

Almatson, *alt. dial.* Ngemba [nge], 69

Almomoloya Náhuatl, *alt.* Nahuatl, Temascaltepec [nhv], 272

Alngith [aid], 567

Alo, *alt. dial.* Mono [mte], 637

Aloa, *dial.* Kwang [kvi], 82

Aloápam Zapotec, *see* Zapotec, Aloápam [zaq], 277

Aloekoe, *alt. dial.* Aukan [djk], 295

Aloma, *alt. dial.* Keapara [khz], 605

Alomwe, *alt.* Lomwe [ngl], 147

Along, *alt. dial.* Akoose [bss], 56

Alor [aol], 406
alt. Adang [adn], 406
dial. Dinka, Northwestern [diw], 190

Alorese, *alt.* Alor [aol], 406

Aloro, *alt.* Alur [alz], 96, 210

Alowiemino, *alt.* Iteri [itr], 603

Alpin, *alt. dial.* Provençal [prv], 537

Alpine Lombard, *dial.* Lombard [lmo], 544

Alqosh, *dial.* Chaldean Neo-Aramaic [cld], 443

Alsacien, *alt. dial.* Alemannisch [gsw], 535

Alsatian, *dial.* Alemannisch [gsw], 535

Alsea [aes], 298

Alséya, *alt.* Alsea [aes], 298

Alta, Northern [aqn], 491

Alta, Southern [agy], 491

Altai, *alt.* Altai, Southern [alt], 503

Altai Proper, *dial.* Altai, Southern [alt], 503

Altai, Northern [atv], 503

Altai, Southern [alt], 503

Altai-Kizhi, *alt. dial.* Altai, Southern [alt], 503

Altaj Kizi, *alt. dial.* Altai, Southern [alt], 503

Alto Bayano, *alt. dial.* Kuna, San Blas [cuk], 283

Alto Navarro Meridional, *dial.* Basque [eus], 559

Alto Navarro Septentrional, *dial.* Basque [eus], 559

Alto Piemontese, *alt. dial.* Piemontese [pms], 545

Alto Ucayali, *alt. dial.* Shipibo-Conibo [shp], 293

Altoaragonés, *alt.* Aragonese [arg], 558

Alu, *alt.* Dia [dia], 597
alt. Mono [mte], 637
dial. Mono [mte], 637

Alu Kurumba, *see* Kurumba, Alu [xua], 371

Alu Kurumba Nonstandard Kannada, *alt.* Kurumba, Alu [xua], 371

Alua, *alt.* Alur [alz], 96, 210

Aluku, *dial.* Aukan [djk], 295

Alukuyana, *alt.* Wayana [way], 296, 234, 252

Alulu, *alt.* Alur [alz], 96, 210

Alumbis, *dial.* Tagal Murut [mvv], 458, 395

Alumu, *alt.* Alumu-Tesu [aab], 153
dial. Alumu-Tesu [aab], 153

Alumu-Tesu [aab], 153

Alune [alp], 396

Alur [alz], 96, 210

Aluru, *dial.* Lugbara [lgg], 103

Alutiiq, *alt.* Yupik, Pacific Gulf [ems], 310

Alutor [alr], 503

Alutor Proper, *alt. dial.* Alutor [alr], 503
Alutorskij, *dial.* Alutor [alr], 503
Aluu, *dial.* Ikwere [ikw], 164
Alvir, *dial.* Alviri-Vidari [avd], 437
Alviri, *alt. dial.* Alviri-Vidari [avd], 437
Alviri-Vidari [avd], 437
Alyawarr [aly], 567
Alyawarra, *alt.* Alyawarr [aly], 567
Alyawarre, *alt.* Alyawarr [aly], 567
Alyk, *dial.* Kryts [kry], 319
Alyutor, *alt.* Alutor [alr], 503
Ama (Papua New Guinea) [amm], 588
   Ama (Sudan) [nyi], 187
Amaarro, *alt.* Kooreete [kqy], 116
Amabi, *alt. dial.* Uab Meto [aoz], 410
Amabusmana, *alt.* ‖Xegwi [xeg], 187
Amacacore, *alt.* Iquito [iqu], 288
Amadi, *alt.* Ma [msj], 103
Amadiya, *dial.* Lishana Deni [lsd], 445
Amadiye, *dial.* Kurdish, Northern [kmr], 443
Amage, *alt.* Yanesha' [ame], 293
Amaguaco, *alt.* Amahuaca [amc], 286
Amagues, *alt.* Yanesha' [ame], 293
Amahai [amq], 396
Amahei, *alt.* Amahai [amq], 396
Amahuaca [amc], 286, 224
Amaimon [ali], 588
Amaizuho, *dial.* Dano [aso], 596
Amaje, *alt.* Yanesha' [ame], 293
Amajo, *alt.* Yanesha' [ame], 293
Amal [aad], 589
Amala, *alt.* Mala [ruy], 169
Amale, *alt.* Amele [aey], 589
Amam, *alt.* Bambassi [myf], 113
   alt. Kwama [kmq], 116
Amami-Oshima, Northern [ryn], 446
Amami-Oshima, Southern [ams], 446
Amampa, *alt.* Sherbro [bun], 177
Aman, *alt. dial.* Eman [emn], 60
Amana, *alt. dial.* Eman [emn], 60
   dial. Maninkakan, Eastern [emk], 129
Amanab [amn], 589
Amanage, *alt.* Amanayé [ama], 224
Amanajé, *alt.* Amanayé [ama], 224
Amanatun, *alt. dial.* Uab Meto [aoz], 410
Amanavil, *alt. dial.* Eman [emn], 60
Amanayé [ama], 224
Amanda-Afi, *dial.* Batu [btu], 150

Amangbetu, *alt.* Mangbetu [mdj], 104
Amani, *alt. dial.* Eman [emn], 60
Amankgqwigqwi, *alt.* ‖Xegwi [xeg], 187
Amanuban, *alt. dial.* Uab Meto [aoz], 410
Amanuban-Amanatun, *dial.* Uab Meto [aoz], 410
Amanubang, *alt. dial.* Uab Meto [aoz], 410
Amanyé, *alt.* Amanayé [ama], 224
Amapá Creole [amd], 224
Amapari Wayampi, *dial.* Wayampi [oym], 233
Amar, *alt.* Hamer-Banna [amf], 115
Amar Tita, *alt.* Ninzo [nin], 171
Amara [aie], 589
   dial. Bedawi [bej], 112
Amaracaire, *alt.* Amarakaeri [amr], 286
Amarag [amg], 567
Amarakaeri [amr], 286
Amarakaire, *alt.* Amarakaeri [amr], 286
Amarasi [aaz], 406
Amarcocche, *alt.* Hamer-Banna [amf], 115
Amari, *dial.* Adzera [azr], 587
Amariba, *dial.* Wapishana [wap], 257, 233
Amarigna, *alt.* Amharic [amh], 113
Amarinya, *alt.* Amharic [amh], 113
Amarro, *alt.* Kooreete [kqy], 116
Amaruwa, *dial.* Cuiba [cui], 244, 311
Amatenango del Valle, *dial.* Tzeltal, Bachajón [tzb], 276
Amatlán Zapotec, *see* Zapotec, Amatlán [zpo], 277
Amawaca, *alt.* Amahuaca [amc], 224
Amawaka, *alt.* Amahuaca [amc], 286
Amawáka, *alt.* Amahuaca [amc], 224
Amayo, *dial.* Eman [emn], 60
Amazigh, *alt.* Tamajaq, Tawallammat [ttq], 152
   alt. Tamajeq, Tayart [thz], 152
Amazonas, *alt.* Quechua, Chachapoyas [quk], 290
Amazonas Macusa, *pej. alt.* Carabayo [cby], 244
Amba (Solomon Islands) [utp], 634
   Amba (Uganda) [rwm], 210, 96
Ambabiko, *alt. dial.* Befang [bby], 58
Ambae, East [omb], 640
Ambae, West [nnd], 640
Ambai [amk], 410
   dial. Ambai [amk], 410

Ambai-Menawi, *alt.* Ambai [amk], 410
Ambakich [aew], 589
Ambala Agta, *alt.* Ayta, Ambala [abc], 492
Ambala Ayta, *see* Ayta, Ambala [abc], 492
Ambala Sambal, *alt.* Ayta, Ambala [abc], 492
Ambali, *alt. dial.* Teke, Ibali [tek], 108
Ambandi, *alt.* Piya-Kwonci [piy], 173
Ambange, *dial.* Dogon, Kolum So [dkl], 142
Ambaquista, *alt. dial.* Mbundu [kmb], 41
Ambari, *alt.* Safeyoka [apz], 623
Ambasi, *dial.* Binandere [bhg], 593
Ambawang, *dial.* Kendayan [knx], 393
Ambede, *alt.* Mbere [mdt], 121
Ambel, *alt.* Waigeo [wgo], 424
Ambelau [amv], 396
Ambele [ael], 56
Am'beng, *alt. dial.* Garo [grt], 362
Ambeno, *alt.* Baikeno [bkx], 350
Ambenu, *alt.* Baikeno [bkx], 350
Amber, *alt.* Waigeo [wgo], 424
Amberbaken, *alt.* Mpur [akc], 420
Amberi, *alt.* Waigeo [wgo], 424
Amblau, *alt.* Ambelau [amv], 396
Amblong [alm], 640
Ambo [amb], 153
   alt. Ndonga [ndo], 150, 41
   dial. Lala-Bisa [leb], 214, 102
Ambo-Pasco Quechua, *see* Quechua, Ambo-Pasco [qva], 289
Ambodhi, *alt.* Awadhi [awa], 354, 468
Ambodi, *dial.* Vasavi [vas], 390
Ambodia, *alt. dial.* Vasavi [vas], 390
Ambonese, *alt.* Malay, Ambonese [abs], 401
Ambonese Malay, *see* Malay, Ambonese [abs], 401
Ambong, *alt.* Malay, Ambonese [abs], 401
Ambrym, North [mmg], 640
Ambrym, Southeast [tvk], 640
Ambual, *dial.* Keningau Murut [kxi], 457
Ambuela, *alt.* Mbwela [mfu], 41
Ambuella, *alt.* Mbwela [mfu], 41
Ambul, *alt.* Apalik [apo], 590
Ambulas [abt], 589
Ambule, *alt.* Wambule [wme], 482
Ambumi, *dial.* Wandamen [wad], 425

Amchauke, *alt. dial.* Bantawa [bap], 468
Amchoke, *alt. dial.* Bantawa [bap], 468
Amdang [amj], 78
Amdo, *alt.* Tibetan, Amdo [adx], 344
Amdo Tibetan, *see* Tibetan, Amdo [adx], 344
Ame, *alt.* Ami [amy], 568
Amegi, *alt.* Biseni [ije], 155
Amele [aey], 589
Amenfi, *dial.* Wasa [wss], 128
Amengi, *dial.* Mamvu [mdi], 103
Amenguaca, *alt.* Amahuaca [amc], 224
Amer, *alt.* Hamer-Banna [amf], 115
Amerax [aex], 298
American Sign Language [ase], 298, 235, 253
American Spanish, *dial.* Spanish [spa], 560
Ameridish, *alt.* Yinglish [yib], 310
Ameslan, *alt.* American Sign Language [ase], 298, 235, 253
Ameuhaque, *alt.* Amahuaca [amc], 286
Amfoan, *alt. dial.* Uab Meto [aoz], 410
Amfoan-Fatule'u-Amabi, *dial.* Uab Meto [aoz], 410
Amfuang, *alt. dial.* Uab Meto [aoz], 410
Amganad, *alt.* Ifugao, Amganad [ifa], 495
Amganad Ifugao, *see* Ifugao, Amganad [ifa], 495
Amharic [amh], 113, 444
Ami [amy], 568
alt. Amis [ami], 511
Amia, *alt.* Amis [ami], 511
Amiangba, *alt.* Barambu [brm], 97
Amiangbwa, *alt.* Barambu [brm], 97
Amienois, *alt. dial.* Picard [pcd], 537
Amies, *alt. dial.* Picard [pcd], 537
Amijangal, *alt.* Ami [amy], 568
Amikoana [akn], 224
Amikuân, *alt.* Amikoana [akn], 224
Amina, *alt.* Ga [gaa], 125
Amini, *alt.* Nai [bio], 616
Amiol, *alt. dial.* Dinka, Southwestern [dik], 190
Amis [ami], 511
Amis, Nataoran [ais], 511
Amish Pennsylvania German, *dial.* German, Pennsylvania [pdc], 301, 237
|**Amkwe**, *dial.* Naro [nhr], 48
Ammar, *alt.* Hamer-Banna [amf], 115
Amniapé, *alt.* Kanoé [kxo], 228
Amo [amo], 153

Amoishe, *alt.* Yanesha' [ame], 293
Amok, *alt.* Mok [mqt], 516
Amoltepec Mixtec, *see* Mixtec, Amoltepec [mbz], 266
Amon, *alt.* Amo [amo], 153
alt. Umon [umm], 176
Amondawa, *alt.* Amundava [adw], 224
Among, *alt.* Amo [amo], 153
Amongme, *dial.* Damal [uhn], 413
Amono, *alt.* Mono [mnh], 104
Amorua, *alt. dial.* Cuiba [cui], 244, 311
dial. Guahibo [guh], 245
Amota, *dial.* Maria [mds], 612
Amou Oblou, *dial.* Akposo [kpo], 123
dial. Ikposo [kpo], 208
Amoy, *alt. dial.* Chinese, Min Nan [nan], 330, 454, 508
dial. Chinese, Min Nan [nan], 511
Ampale, *alt.* Safeyoka [apz], 623
Ampanang [apg], 392
Ampari, *alt. dial.* Dogon, Kolum So [dkl], 142
Ampas, *alt.* Molof [msl], 420
Ampeeli-Wojokeso, *alt.* Safeyoka [apz], 623
Ampele, *alt.* Safeyoka [apz], 623
Ampeyi, *alt. dial.* Nupe-Nupe-Tako [nup], 171
Ampezzano, *dial.* Ladin [lld], 544
Ampibabo, *dial.* Lauje [law], 430
Ampibabo-Lauje, *alt.* Lauje [law], 430
Ampika, *alt.* Bole [bol], 156
Amravati, *dial.* Gondi, Northern [gno], 362
Amri [ajz], 353
Amri Karbi, *alt.* Amri [ajz], 353
Amto [amt], 589
dial. Amto [amt], 589
Amtul, *alt.* Tal [tal], 175
Amu, *dial.* Swahili [swh], 136
Amubre-Katsi, *dial.* Bribri [bzd], 249
Amueixa, *alt.* Yanesha' [ame], 293
Amuese, *alt.* Yanesha' [ame], 293
Amuesha, *alt.* Yanesha' [ame], 293
Amuetamo, *alt.* Yanesha' [ame], 293
Amugen, *dial.* Ono [ons], 620
Amun, *dial.* Lawunuia [tgi], 609
Amundava [adw], 224
Amundawa, *alt.* Amundava [adw], 224
Amung, *alt.* Damal [uhn], 413
dial. Damal [uhn], 413
Amung Kal, *alt.* Damal [uhn], 413
Amungme, *alt.* Damal [uhn], 413

Amur, *dial.* Gilyak [niv], 504
Amurag, *alt.* Amarag [amg], 567
Amuru, *dial.* Boro [bwo], 114
Amutoura, *alt.* Saisiyat [xsy], 512
Amuy, *alt.* Damal [uhn], 413
Amuzgo de San Pedro Amuzgos, *alt.* Amuzgo, San Pedro Amuzgos [azg], 259
Amuzgo de Santa María Ipalapa, *alt.* Amuzgo, Ipalapa [azm], 259
Amuzgo, Guerrero [amu], 259
Amuzgo, Ipalapa [azm], 259
Amuzgo, San Pedro Amuzgos [azg], 259
Amwi, *alt.* War [aml], 322, 390
alt. dial. War [aml], 390
Àmzírív, *alt.* Zizilivakan [ziz], 74, 178
Ana, *alt.* Ede Nago, Manigri-Kambolé [xkb], 43
alt. Ifè [ife], 208, 45
Ana-Ife, *alt.* Ifè [ife], 45
Ana-Ifé, *alt.* Ifè [ife], 208
Anaang [anw], 153
Anabeze, *alt. dial.* Jere [jer], 165
Anafejanzi, *alt.* Janji [jni], 164
Anago, *alt.* Ifè [ife], 45
Anaguta, *alt.* Iguta [nar], 163
Anakalang, *alt.* Anakalangu [akg], 406
Anakalangu [akg], 406
Anakola, *alt.* Batak Angkola [akb], 435
Anaktuvik Pass Inupiatun, *dial.* Inupiatun, North Alaskan [esi], 302
Anal [anm], 354, 462
Anam [pda], 589
Anamagi, *alt.* Torricelli [tei], 628
Anambé [aan], 224
Anamgura [imi], 589
Anana, *alt.* Guanano [gvc], 227, 245
Anandjoobi, *alt. dial.* Anii [blo], 207
Anang, *alt.* Anaang [anw], 153
Ananin, *alt.* Gros Ventre [ats], 301
Ananjubi, *alt. dial.* Anii [blo], 207
Anapia, *alt.* Omagua [omg], 289, 231
Anar, *alt.* Saami, Inari [smn], 535
Anarak, *dial.* Nayini [nyq], 441
Anarya, *dial.* Bhili [bhb], 356
Anasi [bpo], 411
Anatolian, *alt.* Turkish [tur], 519
Anatolian Cluster, *dial.* Arabic, Mesopotamian Spoken [acm], 442
Anatri, *dial.* Chuvash [chv], 553
Anauli, *dial.* Turkmen [tuk], 520, 442
Anawla, *alt. dial.* Gujarati [guj], 363
Anbarra, *alt.* Burarra [bvr], 569
Áncá [acb], 154

dial. Kxoe [xuu], 186

‖**Ani-Khoe**, *alt. dial.* Khwe [xuu], 47

Anibau, *alt. dial.* Jere [jer], 165

Anigibi, *alt. dial.* Kiwai, Northeast [kiw], 606

Anii [blo], 42, 207

‖**Anikxoe**, *alt. dial.* Khwe [xuu], 47

Animere [anf], 123

Anindilyakwa [aoi], 568

Aninhdhilyagwa, *alt.* Anindilyakwa [aoi], 568

Anini-Y, *alt. dial.* Kinaray-A [krj], 498

Aniocha, *dial.* Igbo [ibo], 163

Anir, *dial.* Tangga [tgg], 627

Anirago, *alt. dial.* Gbiri-Niragu [grh], 160

Aniula, *alt.* Yanyuwa [jao], 579

Aniwa, *dial.* Futuna-Aniwa [fut], 641

Aniwan, *alt.* Nganyaywana [nyx], 575

Anjam [boj], 590

Anjie, *alt.* Ajië [aji], 584

Anjimatana, *alt.* Adynyamathanha [adt], 567

Anjiwatana, *alt.* Adynyamathanha [adt], 567

Anjouan, *alt. dial.* Comorian [swb], 87, 140

alt. dial. Maore [swb], 146

Anjuski, *dial.* Udihe [ude], 507

Ankai, *dial.* Ankave [aak], 590

Ankave [aak], 590

Ankober, *dial.* Argobba [agj], 113

Ankpa, *dial.* Igala [igl], 163

Ankulu, *alt.* Ikulu [ikl], 164

Ankwai, *alt.* Goemai [ank], 161

Ankwe, *alt.* Goemai [ank], 161

Ankwei, *alt.* Goemai [ank], 161

Anlo, *alt.* Igo [ahl], 208

alt. dial. Éwé [ewe], 124, 207

Anmatjirra, *alt.* Anmatyerre [amx], 568

Anmatyerre [amx], 568

Anna, *alt. dial.* Zaghawa [zag], 87

Annaberg, *alt.* Rao [rao], 622

Annamese, *alt.* Vietnamese [vie], 527, 346

Annamite French, *alt.* Tay Boi [tas], 527

Annang, *alt.* Anaang [anw], 153

Annobonense, *alt.* Fa D'ambu [fab], 111

Annobonés, *alt.* Fa D'ambu [fab], 111

Annobonese, *alt.* Fa D'ambu [fab], 111

Ano, *dial.* Anyin [any], 91

Anodöub, *alt.* Nadëb [mbj], 230

Anong, *alt.* Nung [nun], 466, 341

Anoong, *alt.* Nung [nun], 466, 341

Anor [anj], 590

Anorubuna, *alt. dial.* Jere [jer], 165

Anosangobari, *alt. dial.* Jere [jer], 165

Anowuru, *alt.* Lemoro [ldj], 168

Anpika, *alt. dial.* Bole [bol], 156

Ansakara, *alt.* Nzakara [nzk], 77, 106

Anserma [ans], 243

Anserna, *alt.* Anserma [ans], 243

Anshuenkuan Nyarong, *alt.* Atuence [atf], 326

alt. dial. Tibetan [bod], 388

Ansita, *alt.* Opuuo [lgn], 117, 194

Ansotano, *alt. dial.* Aragonese [arg], 558

Ansus [and], 411

Anta, *alt.* Manta [myg], 66

dial. Wára [tci], 631

Antabamba, *alt. dial.* Quechua, Arequipa-La Unión [qxu], 289

dial. Quechua, Eastern Apurímac [qve], 291

Antakarinya [ant], 568

Antalaotra, *alt.* Bushi [buc], 145

Antanau, *alt. dial.* Ambakich [aew], 589

Antankarana Malagasy, *see* Malagasy, Antankarana [xmv], 140

Antarbedi, *alt.* Braj Bhasha [bra], 357

dial. Braj Bhasha [bra], 357

Antarvedi, *alt.* Braj Bhasha [bra], 357

Antekerrepenh, *dial.* Arrernte, Eastern [aer], 568

Antekerrepinhe, *alt.* Andegerebinha [adg], 568

Antesaka, *alt.* Malagasy, Southern Betsimisaraka [bjq], 140

Antigua and Barbuda Creole English [aig], 219

Antiguan Creole English, *dial.* Antigua and Barbuda Creole English [aig], 219

Antipolo Ifugao, *alt.* Kallahan, Keley-I [ify], 497

Antiqueño, *alt.* Kinaray-A [krj], 498

Antra, *dial.* Kuy [kdt], 451

Antsukh, *alt. dial.* Avar [ava], 553

Antwerps, *dial.* Vlaams [vls], 531

Anu [anl], 462

alt. Nung [nun], 466, 341

dial. Gua [gwx], 125

Añú, *alt.* Paraujano [pbg], 312

Anuak [anu], 187, 113

Anufo [cko], 123, 42, 207

Anuki [aui], 590

Anula, *alt.* Yanyuwa [jao], 579

Anum, *alt. dial.* Gua [gwx], 125

Anum-Boso, *alt.* Gua [gwx], 125

Anung, *alt.* Nung [nun], 466, 341

Anupe, *alt. dial.* Nupe-Nupe-Tako [nup], 171

Anupecwayi, *alt. dial.* Nupe-Nupe-Tako [nup], 171

Anuperi, *alt. dial.* Nupe-Nupe-Tako [nup], 171

Anus [auq], 411

Anuta [aud], 634

Anwain, *alt.* Esan [ish], 159

Anyah, *alt.* Denya [anv], 60

Anyama, *dial.* Ogbia [ogb], 172

Anyan, *alt.* Denya [anv], 60

Anyang, *alt.* Denya [anv], 60

dial. Ngemba [nge], 69

dial. Sui [swi], 344

Anyanga, *alt.* Ginyanga [ayg], 207

Anyar, *alt.* Akum [aku], 56, 153

Anyaran, *alt.* Ukaan [kcf], 176

Anyep, *alt. dial.* Ndoe [nbb], 170

Anyi, *alt.* Anyin [any], 91, 123

Anyima, *alt.* Lenyima [ldg], 168

Anyimere, *alt.* Animere [anf], 123

Anyin [any], 91, 123

Anyin Morofo [mtb], 91

Anyuak, *alt.* Anuak [anu], 187, 113

Anyugba, *dial.* Igala [igl], 163

Anyula, *alt.* Yanyuwa [jao], 579

Anywa, *alt.* Anuak [anu], 187, 113

Anywak, *alt.* Anuak [anu], 187, 113

Anyx, *dial.* Lezgi [lez], 555

Ao, *alt.* Naga, Ao [njo], 377

Ao Naga, *see* Naga, Ao [njo], 377

Ao Tá, *dial.* Muong [mtq], 525

Aoaqui, *alt.* Arutani [atx], 225, 311

Aoba, *alt.* Ambae, East [omb], 640

Aoheng [pni], 392

Aola, *dial.* Lengo [lgr], 637

Aoluguya, *dial.* Evenki [evn], 332

Aomie, *alt.* Ömie [aom], 619

Aona, *alt.* Ona [ona], 220

Aoniken, *alt.* Tehuelche [teh], 220

Aore [aor], 640

Aorr, *alt.* Naga, Ao [njo], 377

Aoshedd, *alt.* Naga, Khiamniungan [nky], 378

A'ou, *dial.* Gelao [gio], 333

Aoudjila, *alt.* Awjilah [auj], 139

Aouei, *alt.* Kuy [kdt], 451

Aowin, *dial.* Anyin [any], 123

Ap Ma [kbx], 590

Ap Ma Botin, *alt.* Ap Ma [kbx], 590

Ap-Ne-Ap, *dial.* Torres Strait Creole [tcs], 577

Apa, *alt.* Apatani [apt], 354

dial. Kpan [kpk], 167

Apabhramsa, *alt.* Maithili [mai], 373, 475

187, 197, 209, 320, 442, 444, 448, 449, 453, 482, 490, 503, 510, 520, 528

Arabic, Sudanese Creole [pga], 187

Arabic, Sudanese Spoken [apd], 188

Arabic, Ta'izzi-Adeni Spoken [acq], 528, 109

Arabic, Tajiki Spoken [abh], 315, 513

Arabic, Tunisian Spoken [aeb], 209

Arabic, Uzbeki Spoken [auz], 521

Arabic, Western Egyptian Bedawi Spoken [ayl], 110

Arabized Hebrew, *alt. dial.* Hebrew [heb], 444

Arabkir, *dial.* Armenian [hye], 318

Aradigi, *alt.* Ratagnon [btn], 500

Arafundi [arf], 590

Arago, *alt.* Alago [ala], 153

Aragoieraz, *alt.* Aragonese [arg], 558

Aragonés, *alt.* Aragonese [arg], 558

Aragonese [arg], 558
dial. Spanish [spa], 560

Aragu, *alt.* Alago [ala], 153

'Aragure, *alt.* Xaragure [axx], 585

Aragure, *alt.* Xaragure [axx], 585

Araikurioko, *alt.* Sikaritai [tty], 423

Arakan Manobo, *dial.* Manobo, Obo [obo], 499

Arakanese [mhv], 462, 320, 354

Araki [akr], 640
dial. Farsi, Western [pes], 439

Aralle, *dial.* Aralle-Tabulahan [atq], 427

Aralle-Tabulahan [atq], 427

Arama, *alt. dial.* Haruai [tmd], 601

Aramanik [aam], 197

Aramba, *alt.* Arammba [stk], 590

Aramia River, *dial.* Tabo [knv], 626

'Aramit, *alt.* Hulaulá [huy], 445

Arammba [stk], 590

Aramo, *alt.* Pinai-Hagahai [pnn], 622

Aranadan [aaf], 354

Aranatan, *alt.* Aranadan [aaf], 354

Aranda, *alt.* Arrarnta, Western [are], 568

Arandai [jbj], 411
alt. Kemberano [bzp], 412
alt. dial. Arandai [jbj], 411

Arandui, *alt.* Gawar-Bati [gwt], 316, 484

Aranés, *alt.* Gascon, Aranese [gsc], 560

Aranese, *alt.* Gascon, Aranese [gsc], 560
dial. Gascon [gsc], 537

Aranese Gascon, *see* Gascon [gsc], 560

Aranese Occitan, *alt.* Gascon, Aranese [gsc], 560

Arangka'a, *dial.* Talaud [tld], 433

Araona [aro], 222

Aráp, *dial.* Jarai [jra], 523, 325

Arapaço, *alt.* Arapaso [arj], 225

Arapaho [arp], 298

Arapaso [arj], 225

Arapesh, Bumbita [aon], 590

Arapium, *alt.* Sateré-Mawé [mav], 231

Arara, *alt.* Júma [jua], 227
dial. Carútana [cru], 226

Arára, *alt.* Karo [arr], 228

Arara do Amazonas, *alt.* Carútana [cru], 226

Arara do Beiradão, *alt.* Arára, Mato Grosso [axg], 225

Arára do Jiparaná, *alt.* Karo [arr], 228

Arara do Rio Branco, *alt.* Arára, Mato Grosso [axg], 225

Arára, Mato Grosso [axg], 225

Arára, Pará [aap], 225

Arara-Karo, *alt.* Karo [arr], 228

Arara-Shawanawa, *dial.* Katukína, Panoan [knt], 229

Ararapina, *dial.* Katukína, Panoan [knt], 229

Ararawa, *alt. dial.* Katukína, Panoan [knt], 229

Arasairi, *dial.* Huachipaeri [hug], 288

Araspaso, *alt.* Arapaso [arj], 225

Arau-Barosia, *alt. dial.* Tairora, North [tbg], 626

Arau-Varosia, *dial.* Tairora, North [tbg], 626

Araucano, *alt.* Mapudungun [arn], 220
pej. alt. Mapudungun [arn], 242

Arauine, *alt.* Awetí [awe], 225

Arauite, *alt.* Awetí [awe], 225

Arava, *dial.* Tamil [tam], 388

Aravia, *dial.* Hahon [hah], 601

Arawá, *alt.* Arua [aru], 225

Arawak [arw], 295, 252, 257, 311

Arawe, *alt.* Solong [aaw], 625
dial. Solong [aaw], 625

Araweté [awt], 225

Arawum [awm], 590

Arayans, *alt.* Malaryan [mjq], 374

Arbanasi, *dial.* Albanian, Tosk [als], 529

Arbel, *dial.* Lishanid Noshan [aij], 445

Arbëreshë, *alt.* Albanian, Arbëreshë [aae], 543

Arbëreshë Albanian, *see* Albanian, Arbëreshë [aae], 543

Arberichte, *alt.* Albanian, Arvanitika [aat], 540

Arbil, *alt. dial.* Lishanid Noshan [aij], 445

Arbili, *alt. dial.* Kurdish, Central [ckb], 443

Arbora, *alt.* Arbore [arv], 113

Arbore [arv], 113

Arborense, *dial.* Sardinian, Campidanese [sro], 545

Archi [aqc], 553

Archin, *alt.* Archi [aqc], 553

Archintsy, *alt.* Archi [aqc], 553

Archualda, *alt.* Adynyamathanha [adt], 567

Arctic Red River, *dial.* Gwich'in [gwi], 237, 301

Arctic Village Gwich'in, *dial.* Gwich'in [gwi], 237, 301

Arderi, *alt.* Dzodinka [add], 60

Ardido, *alt. dial.* Dza [jen], 158

Are [mwc], 590
alt. dial. Muyu, North [kti], 421

Aré, *alt.* Xetá [xet], 234

'Are'are [alu], 634
dial. 'Are'are [alu], 634

Areare, *alt.* 'Are'are [alu], 634

Areba [aea], 568

Arecuna, *dial.* Pemon [aoc], 312, 231, 257

Aregerek, *alt.* Musar [mmi], 616

Aregwe, *alt.* Irigwe [iri], 164

Arekuna, *alt. dial.* Pemon [aoc], 312, 231, 257

Arem [aem], 521, 450

Arequena, *alt.* Guarequena [gae], 311, 227

Arequipa Quechua, *alt.* Quechua, Arequipa-La Unión [qxu], 289

Arequipa-La Unión Quechua, *see* Quechua, Arequipa-La Unión [qxu], 289

Aret, *dial.* Pashayi, Northeast [aee], 317

Arewa, *dial.* Hausa [hau], 162, 152

Arfak, *alt.* Meyah [mej], 420

Argentine Sign Language [aed], 219

Argo, *alt.* Alago [ala], 153

Argobba [agj], 113

Argoeni, *alt.* Arguni [agf], 411

Arguni [agf], 411

Arguni Bay, *alt.* Irarutu [irh], 415

Arhâ [aqr], 584

Arhe, *dial.* Ivbie North-Okpela-Arhe [atg], 164

Arhö [aok], 584

Arhuaco [arh], 243

Ari [aac], 590
  alt. Aari [aiz], 112
  alt. Erre [err], 570
  dial. Nobonob [gaw], 618
Aria, *alt. dial.* Pamona [bcx], 432
  alt. dial. Uma [ppk], 434
Aria-Mouk, *alt.* Mouk-Aria
  [mwh], 615
Ariana, *alt.* Omagua [omg], 289, 231
Ariangulu, *alt.* Sanye [ssn], 136
Ariawiai, *alt.* Aruamu [msy], 591
Aribwatsa [laz], 590
Aribwaung [ylu], 590
Aribwaungg, *alt.* Aribwaung
  [ylu], 590
Aricapú, *alt.* Arikapú [ark], 225
Aricuna, *alt. dial.* Pemon [aoc], 312,
  231, 257
Ariégeois, *dial.* Gascon [gsc], 537
Arifama, *dial.* Arifama-Miniafia
  [aai], 590
Arifama-Miniafia [aai], 590
Arigibi, *alt. dial.* Kiwai, Northeast
  [kiw], 606
Arigidi [aqg], 154
Arigidí, *dial.* Arigidi [aqg], 154
Arihini, *alt.* Baré [bae], 311
  alt. Mandahuaca [mht], 312
Arikapú [ark], 225
Arikara [ari], 298
Arikaree, *alt.* Arikara [ari], 298
Arikari, *alt.* Arikara [ari], 298
Arikaris, *alt.* Arikara [ari], 298
Arikem [ait], 225
Ariken, *alt.* Arikem [ait], 225
Arima, *alt.* Heyo [auk], 602
Aringa [luc], 210
Arinua, *alt.* Heyo [auk], 602
Arinwa, *alt.* Heyo [auk], 602
Ariom, *dial.* Biak [bhw], 412
Aripaktsa, *alt.* Rikbaktsa [rkb], 232
Ariseachi Tarahumara, *alt.*
  Tarahumara, Northern [thh], 274
Arkan Valley, *dial.* Manobo, Ilianen
  [mbi], 499
Arkansas, *alt.* Quapaw [qua], 307
Arleng Alam, *alt.* Karbi [mjw], 366
Arlija, *alt. dial.* Romani, Balkan
  [rmn], 541
  dial. Romani, Balkan [rmn], 557,
  532, 537, 539, 545, 547, 563
Arma [aoh], 243
Arman, *dial.* Even [eve], 504
Armani, *alt.* Armenian [hye], 437
Armanski, *alt.* Armenian [hye], 453
Armati, *alt.* Kwerba [kwe], 418
Armenian [hye], 318, 319, 350, 437,
  442, 444, 448, 453, 510, 563
Armenian Bosa, *alt.* Lomavren
  [rmi], 319

Armenian Bosha, *alt.* Lomavren
  [rmi], 319, 510
Armenian Sign Language
  [aen], 319
Armina, *alt.* Romanian, Macedo
  [rup], 541, 529, 532, 547
Armjanski, *alt.* Armenian [hye], 319,
  350, 437, 444, 510, 563
Armjanski Yazyk, *alt.* Armenian
  [hye], 318
Armopa, *alt.* Bonggo [bpg], 413
Arnais, *alt.* Gascon, Aranese
  [gsc], 560
Arnaut, *alt.* Albanian, Tosk [als], 529
Arnebuab Bisa, *alt.* Lomavren
  [rmi], 510
Arniya, *alt.* Khowar [khw], 486
Aro, *alt.* Aari [aiz], 112
  alt. Arhö [aok], 584
Arogbo, *dial.* Izon [ijc], 164
Arohun, *dial.* Fon [fon], 43
Aroi, *alt.* Haroi [hro], 523
Arokaara, *dial.* Tairora, North
  [tbg], 626
Arokara, *alt. dial.* Tairora, North
  [tbg], 626
Arokwa, *alt.* Eruwa [erh], 159
Aroma, *alt. dial.* C'lela [dri], 157
  dial. Keapara [khz], 605
Aromanian, *alt.* Romanian, Macedo
  [rup], 541, 532, 552
Aromunian, *alt.* Romanian, Macedo
  [rup], 529, 547
Arona, *alt. dial.* Keapara [khz], 605
Arop, *alt.* Arop-Sissano [aps], 590
  dial. Arop-Lukep [apr], 590
Arop-Lokep, *alt.* Arop-Lukep
  [apr], 590
Arop-Lukep [apr], 590
Arop-Sissano [aps], 590
Aropen, *alt.* Waropen [wrp], 425
Arosario, *alt.* Malayo [mbp], 246
Arosi [aia], 635
  dial. Arosi [aia], 635
Arove, *alt.* Solong [aaw], 625
Arowak, *alt.* Arawak [arw], 295, 257,
  311
Arpitan, *alt.* Franco-Provençal
  [frp], 536
Arrapahoe, *alt.* Arapaho [arp], 298
Arrarnta, Western [are], 568
Arrernte, Eastern [aer], 568
Arringeu, *alt.* Pongu [png], 173
Arsario, *alt.* Malayo [mbp], 246
Arsi, *dial.* Oromo, Borana-Arsi-Guji
  [gax], 117
Arso, *alt.* Taikat [aos], 423
Arta [atz], 491
Arthare, *alt.* Athpariya [aph], 468
  alt. Dungmali [raa], 471

Arthare-Khesang, *alt.* Athpariya
  [aph], 468
  alt. Dungmali [raa], 471
Artois, *alt. dial.* Picard [pcd], 537
Arton, *alt. dial.* Hértevin [hrt], 518
Artu Ehtremeñu, *alt. dial.*
  Extremaduran [ext], 560
Artvin, *dial.* Armenian [hye], 318
Artwin, *alt. dial.* Armenian [hye], 318
Aru, *alt.* Alatil [alx], 588
  alt. Jaqaru [jqr], 288
Arua [aru], 225
  dial. Lugbara [lgg], 211
Aruá [arx], 225
Aruachi, *alt. dial.* Aruá [arx], 225
Aruaco, *alt.* Arhuaco [arh], 243
Aruamu [msy], 591
Aruáshi, *dial.* Aruá [arx], 225
Aruba English, *dial.* English
  [eng], 221
Aruek [aur], 591
Arufe, *alt.* Nambo [ncm], 617
Arughunya, *dial.* Odual [odu], 172
Arui, *alt.* Serui-Laut [seu], 423
Arum, *alt. dial.* Alumu-Tesu
  [aab], 153
Arum-Cesu, *alt.* Alumu-Tesu [aab],
  153
Arum-Chessu, *alt.* Alumu-Tesu
  [aab], 153
Arum-Tesu, *alt.* Alumu-Tesu
  [aab], 153
Arumaka, *dial.* Kula [tpg], 408
Arumanian, *alt.* Romanian, Macedo
  [rup], 541, 529, 532, 547
Arumbi, *dial.* Lese [les], 102
Arumun, *alt.* Romanian, Macedo
  [rup], 529
Arunamese, *alt.* Nefamese
  [nef], 381
Arundum, *alt. dial.* Tagal Murut
  [mvv], 458, 395
Arung, *alt.* Naga, Zeme [nzm], 381
Arunta, *alt.* Arrarnta, Western
  [are], 568
  alt. Arrernte, Eastern [aer], 568
Aruop [lsr], 591
Arupai, *dial.* Maritsauá [msp], 230
Arusa, *dial.* Maasai [mas], 134
Arusha, *alt. dial.* Maasai [mas], 134
  dial. Maasai [mas], 201
Arusi, *alt. dial.* Oromo, Borana-Arsi-
  Guji [gax], 117
Aruskush-Daqqushchu, *dial.* Tat,
  Muslim [ttt], 320
Arussi, *alt. dial.* Oromo, Borana-Arsi-
  Guji [gax], 117
Arut, *dial.* Malayic Dayak
  [xdy], 394
Arutani [atx], 225, 311

Arvanitic, *alt.* Albanian, Arvanitika [aat], 540
Arvanitika, *alt.* Albanian, Arvanitika [aat], 540
alt. Albanian, Tosk [als], 540
Arvanitika Albanian, *see* Albanian, Arvanitika [aat], 540
Arwala, *dial.* Tugun [tzn], 405
Arwur, *alt.* Waray [wrz], 577
Arzeu, *dial.* Tarifit [rif], 40
As [asz], 411
Asa, *dial.* Iraqw [irk], 199
Asá, *alt.* Aasáx [aas], 197
Asahyue, *alt.* Sehwi [sfw], 127
Asak, *alt.* Aasáx [aas], 197
alt. Kado [kdv], 464, 337, 450
Asake, *alt.* Sake [sak], 121
Asambe, *alt.* Assamese [asm], 354, 320
Asami, *alt.* Assamese [asm], 354, 320
Asamiya, *alt.* Assamese [asm], 354
Asande, *alt.* Zande [zne], 109
Asanga, *alt.* Sanga [xsn], 174
alt. dial. Jere [jer], 165
Asante, *dial.* Akan [aka], 123
Asanti, *alt. dial.* Akan [aka], 123
Asapa, *dial.* Ömie [aom], 619
Asaro, *alt.* Dano [aso], 596
Asaro'o [mtv], 591
Asas [asd], 591
Asat, *alt.* Muratayak [asx], 615
Asax, *alt.* Aasáx [aas], 197
Asbalmin, *dial.* Tifal [tif], 627
Aschingini, *alt.* Cishingini [asg], 151
Ase, *dial.* Akpes [ibe], 153
Asebi, *dial.* Pongu [png], 173
Asen, *dial.* Akan [aka], 123
Asengseng, *alt.* Sengseng [ssz], 624
Asento, *dial.* Gun [guw], 161
Aser, *alt. dial.* Soninke [snk], 144, 95, 122, 131, 145, 182
Asera, *dial.* Tolaki [lbw], 433
Ashaganna, *alt.* Cishingini [asg], 151
Ashaninca, *alt.* Ajyíninka Apurucayali [cpc], 286
Asháninca, *alt.* Asháninka [cni], 286
Asháninka [cni], 286
Ashante Twi, *alt. dial.* Akan [aka], 123
Ashe [ahs], 154
Ashen, *dial.* Tsikimba [kdl], 175
Ashéninca, *alt.* Ashéninca Pajonal [cjo], 286
Ashéninca Apurucayali, *alt.* Ajyíninka Apurucayali [cpc], 286
Ashéninca Perené, *alt.* Ashéninca Perené [prq], 286
Ashéninka Pajonal [cjo], 286
Ashéninka Perené [prq], 286

Ashéninka, Pichis [cpu], 286
Ashéninka, South Ucayali [cpy], 286
Ashéninka, Ucayali-Yurúa [cpb], 286, 225
Ashing, *dial.* Adi [adi], 353
Ashingini, *alt.* Cishingini [asg], 151
alt. Tsishingini [tsw], 176
Ashiti, *dial.* Kurdish, Northern [kmr], 519
Ashkar, *alt. dial.* Abaza [abq], 552, 518
Ashkaraua, *dial.* Abaza [abq], 552, 518
Ashkharik, *dial.* Armenian [hye], 318
Ashkun [ask], 315
Ashkund, *alt.* Ashkun [ask], 315
Ashkuni, *alt.* Ashkun [ask], 315
Ashlushlay, *alt.* Nivaclé [cag], 285, 220
Asho, *alt.* Chin, Asho [csh], 462
Asho Chin, *see* Chin, Asho [csh], 462, 321
Asholio, *alt. dial.* Tyap [kcg], 176
Ashraaf, *alt. dial.* Somali [som], 185
Ashree, *alt.* Asuri [asr], 354
Ashreti, *dial.* Phalura [phl], 488
Ashtiani [atn], 438
dial. Ashtiani [atn], 438
Ashtikulin, *dial.* Lak [lbe], 555
Ashtiyani, *alt.* Ashtiani [atn], 438
Ashu, *alt.* Chin, Asho [csh], 462
Ashuku, *dial.* Mbembe, Tigon [nza], 66, 170
Ashuruveri, *dial.* Ashkun [ask], 315
Ashuwa, *alt.* Abaza [abq], 552
Asi, *alt.* Alagwa [wbj], 197
Asian Swahili, *alt.* Cutchi-Swahili [ccl], 132, 198
Asianara, *alt.* Buruwai [asi], 413
Asiaoro, *dial.* Mailu [mgu], 610
Asiatic Yupik, *alt.* Yupik, Central Siberian [ess], 507
Asienara, *alt.* Buruwai [asi], 413
Asifabad, *dial.* Kolami, Southeastern [nit], 369
Asiga, *alt.* Leyigha [ayi], 168
dial. Asilulu [asl], 396
Asilulu [asl], 396
Asimbali, *alt.* Simbali [smg], 624
Asiq, *alt.* Bantoanon [bno], 492
Askopan [eiv], 591
ASL, *alt.* American Sign Language [ase], 298, 235, 253
Asmat Darat, *alt.* Citak [txt], 413
alt. Citak, Tamnim [tml], 413
Asmat, Casuarina Coast [asc], 411
Asmat, Central [cns], 411

Asmat, North [nks], 411
Asmat, Yaosakor [asy], 411
Asoa [asv], 96
Asobse, *alt.* Bassossi [bsi], 58
Asolio, *alt. dial.* Tyap [kcg], 176
Asom, *alt.* Como Karim [cfg], 157
alt. dial. Pol [pmm], 71
Asong, *alt.* Assangori [sjg], 78
dial. Akha [ahk], 462
Asonga, *dial.* Ngumbi [nui], 111
dial. Yasa [yko], 111, 122
Asongori, *alt.* Sungor [sjg], 195
Aspromonte, *dial.* Greek [ell], 544
Assa, *alt.* Aasáx [aas], 197
Assagori, *alt.* Sungor [sjg], 195
Assaikio, *dial.* Alago [ala], 153
Assaka, *dial.* Caka [ckx], 59
Assam Khamti, *dial.* Khamti [kht], 465, 367
Assamese [asm], 354, 320
Assangori [sjg], 78
Assem, *dial.* Jagoi [sne], 459
Assi, *dial.* Jumli [jml], 472
Assiga, *alt.* Leyigha [ayi], 168
Assiniboin, *alt.* Assiniboine [asb], 235, 298
Assiniboine [asb], 235, 298
Assoungor, *alt.* Assangori [sjg], 78
Assumbo, *alt.* Ipulo [ass], 63
Assur, *alt.* Asuri [asr], 354
Assuriní, *alt.* Asuriní [asu], 225
Assuriní do Tocantins, *alt.* Asuriní [asu], 225
Assyrian, *alt.* Assyrian Neo-Aramaic [aii], 442, 510
Assyrian Neo-Aramaic [aii], 442, 319, 352, 438, 510
Assyrianci, *alt.* Assyrian Neo-Aramaic [aii], 442
Assyriski, *alt.* Assyrian Neo-Aramaic [aii], 442, 510
Astara, *dial.* Talysh [tly], 320
Astiani, *alt.* Ashtiani [atn], 438
Astor, *alt. dial.* Shina [scl], 488
Astori, *dial.* Shina [scl], 488
Astrachan, *alt. dial.* Armenian [hye], 318
Astrakhan, *dial.* Armenian [hye], 318
Astrakhân, *dial.* Armenian [hye], 437
Astur-Leonese, *alt.* Asturian [ast], 559
Asturian [ast], 559, 551
Asturian-Leonese, *alt.* Asturian [ast], 559, 551
Asturianu, *alt.* Asturian [ast], 559
Asu (Nigeria) [aum], 154
Asu (Tanzania) [asa], 197
Asua, *alt.* Asoa [asv], 96

Asuae, *alt.* Asoa [asv], 96
Asuati, *alt.* Asoa [asv], 96
Asue Awyu, *see* Awyu, Asue [psa], 412
Asumbo, *alt.* Ipulo [ass], 63
  alt. Iyive [uiv], 164
Asumboa [aua], 635
Asumbua, *alt.* Asumboa [aua], 635
Asumuo, *alt.* Asumboa [aua], 635
Asunción Mixtepec Zapotec, *see* Zapotec, Asunción Mixtepec [zoo], 277
Asungore, *alt.* Assangori [sjg], 78
  alt. Sungor [sjg], 195
Asura, *alt.* Asuri [asr], 354
Asuri [asr], 354
Asuriní [asu], 225
Asuriní de Koatinema, *alt.* Asuriní, Xingú [asn], 225
Asuriní do Trocará, *alt.* Asuriní [asu], 225
Asurini do Xingu, *alt.* Asuriní, Xingú [asn], 225
Asuriní, Xingú [asn], 225
Aswanik, *alt.* Soninke [snk], 144, 95, 122, 145
Ata [atm], 491
  dial. Pele-Ata [ata], 621
Ata Manobo, *see* Manobo, Ata [atd], 499
Ata of Davao, *alt.* Manobo, Ata [atd], 499
Ata-Man, *alt.* Magahat [mtw], 498
Ataba, *dial.* Obolo [ann], 172
Atacameño, *alt.* Kunza [kuz], 242
Ataiyal, *alt.* Atayal [tay], 511
Atak, *alt.* Jiru [jrr], 165
Atakapa [aqp], 298
Atakar, *alt. dial.* Tyap [kcg], 176
Atakara, *alt. dial.* Tairora, South [omw], 626
Atakat, *dial.* Tyap [kcg], 176
Atakora Fulfulde, *dial.* Fulfulde, Borgu [fue], 207
Atala, *dial.* Degema [deg], 157
Atam, *alt.* Hatam [had], 415
  alt. dial. Nde-Nsele-Nta [ndd], 170
Atamanu, *alt.* Yalahatan [jal], 405
Atampaya [amz], 568
Atao Manobo, *alt.* Manobo, Ata [atd], 499
Ataripoe, *dial.* Malo [mla], 643
Atatláhuca Mixtec, *see* Mixtec, Atatláhuca [mib], 266
Ataura, *alt.* Adabe [adb], 350
Atauro, *alt.* Adabe [adb], 350
Atauru, *alt.* Adabe [adb], 350
Atayal [tay], 511
Atche, *alt.* Attié [ati], 91

Atchin, *alt. dial.* Uripiv-Wala-Rano-Atchin [upv], 646
Ate, *alt.* Garus [gyb], 599
  alt. dial. Ivbie North-Okpela-Arhe [atg], 164
Atemble [ate], 591
Atemple, *alt.* Atemble [ate], 591
Atemple-Apris, *alt.* Atemble [ate], 591
Aten, *alt.* Eten [etx], 159
Atesino, *dial.* Ladin [lld], 544
Ateso, *alt.* Teso [teo], 213, 136
Ath Paharia Rai, *alt.* Athpariya [aph], 468
Athapre, *alt.* Athpariya [aph], 468
Athoc, *dial.* Dinka, Southeastern [dks], 190
Athoic, *alt. dial.* Dinka, Southeastern [dks], 190
Athpagari, *alt.* Belhariya [byw], 469
Athpahariya, *alt.* Belhariya [byw], 469
Athpare, *alt.* Athpariya [aph], 468
  alt. Belhariya [byw], 469
Athpariya [aph], 468
  alt. Belhariya [byw], 469
Athpre, *alt.* Athpariya [aph], 468
Athu, *alt.* Asu [asa], 197
Ati [atk], 491
  alt. Biritai [bqq], 413
  alt. Butmas-Tur [bnr], 641
  alt. Kinaray-A [krj], 498
  alt. Kutep [kub], 167, 64
  alt. Obokuitai [afz], 421
  alt. Sikaritai [tty], 423
  alt. dial. Nobonob [gaw], 618
Atiahu, *alt.* Bobot [bty], 397
Aticherak, *alt. dial.* Tyap [kcg], 176
Aticum, *alt.* Uamué [uam], 233
Atie, *alt.* Attié [ati], 91
Atihkamekw, *alt.* Atikamekw [atj], 235
Atikamek, *alt.* Atikamekw [atj], 235
Atikamekw [atj], 235
Atikum, *alt.* Uamué [uam], 233
Atimelang, *dial.* Abui [abz], 406
Atina, *dial.* Laz [lzz], 352
Atinggola, *dial.* Bolango [bld], 428
Atinjo, *alt.* Mai Brat [ayz], 419
Atiri, *alt.* Nomatsiguenga [not], 289
Atisa, *dial.* Epie [epi], 159
Atissa, *alt. dial.* Epie [epi], 159
Atitlán Mixe, *alt.* Mixe, North Central [neq], 265
  dial. Mixe, North Central [neq], 265
Atiu, *dial.* Rarotongan [rar], 579
Atjeh, *alt.* Aceh [ace], 435
Atjehnese, *alt.* Aceh [ace], 435
Atka, *alt. dial.* Aleut [ale], 297
Atkan, *alt. dial.* Aleut [ale], 297, 495

Atlacomulco-Temascalcingo, *dial.* Mazahua Central [maz], 264
Atlamajalcingo del Monte, *dial.* Mixtec, Alacatlatzala [mim], 265
Atna, *alt.* Ahtena [aht], 297
Atnebar, *alt. dial.* Kei [kei], 399
Ato Majang, *alt.* Majang [mpe], 116
Ato Majanger-Onk, *alt.* Majang [mpe], 116
Atoc, *alt. dial.* Dinka, Southeastern [dks], 190
Atohwaim [aqm], 411
Atoktou, *alt. dial.* Dinka, Southwestern [dik], 190
A'tong [aot], 354
Atong [ato], 56
Atonga, *alt. dial.* Ndau [ndc], 216
Atoni, *alt.* Uab Meto [aoz], 410
Atorad, *alt.* Atorada [aox], 225
Atorada [aox], 257, 225
Atorai, *alt.* Atorada [aox], 257, 225
  dial. Wapishana [wap], 233
Atori, *alt.* Kais [kzm], 415
Ator'ti, *alt.* Atorada [aox], 257, 225
Atrato, *alt.* Emberá, Northern [emp], 283, 245
Atroahy, *alt.* Atruahí [atr], 225
Atroaí, *alt.* Atruahí [atr], 225
Atroarí, *alt.* Atruahí [atr], 225
Atrowari, *alt.* Atruahí [atr], 225
Atruahi, *dial.* Atruahí [atr], 225
Atruahí [atr], 225
Atrush, *dial.* Lishana Deni [lsd], 445
Atsahuaca [atc], 286
Atsam [cch], 154
  alt. Ai-Cham [aih], 326
Atsang, *alt.* Achang [acn], 326, 456
Atsang-Bangwa, *alt.* Yemba [ybb], 74
Atscholi, *alt.* Acholi [ach], 210, 187
Atse, *alt. dial.* Hmong Njua [blu], 334
Atshe, *alt.* Attié [ati], 91
Atshi, *alt.* Zaiwa [atb], 349, 467
Atsi, *alt.* Zaiwa [atb], 349, 467
Atsi-Maru, *alt.* Zaiwa [atb], 349
Atsilima, *dial.* Rotokas [roo], 623
Atsina, *alt.* Gros Ventre [ats], 301
Atsiri, *alt.* Ashéninka Pajonal [cjo], 286
Atsugewi [atw], 298
Atta, Faire [azt], 491
Atta, Pamplona [att], 491
Atta, Pudtol [atp], 491
Attaka, *alt. dial.* Tyap [kcg], 176
Attakar, *alt. dial.* Tyap [kcg], 176
Attayal, *alt.* Atayal [tay], 511
Atte, *alt. dial.* Ivbie North-Okpela-Arhe [atg], 164
Attié [ati], 91
Attikamek, *alt.* Atikamekw [atj], 235

Avio, *alt.* Awyu, Central [awu], 412
Aviritu, *alt. dial.* Ndo [ndp], 212, 105
Avirxiri, *alt.* Abishira [ash], 285
Avokaya [avu], 188, 96
Avokaya Pur, *dial.* Avokaya [avu], 96
Avreas, *alt. dial.* Mosina [msn], 644
Avukaya, *alt.* Avokaya [avu], 188, 96
Avunatari, *dial.* Malo [mla], 643
Awa [awb], 591
  alt. Awa-Cuaiquer [kwi], 243, 250
  alt. Busuu [bju], 59
  alt. Imbongu [imo], 602
  alt. Wa [wbm], 346
  dial. Imbongu [imo], 602
Awá, *alt.* Guajá [gvj], 227
Awá Guajá, *alt.* Guajá [gvj], 227
Awa Pit, *alt.* Awa-Cuaiquer [kwi], 243
Awa-Cuaiquer [kwi], 243, 250
'Awaazim, *alt. dial.* Arabic, Najdi Spoken [ars], 508
Awabagal, *alt.* Awabakal [awk], 568
dial. Awabakal [awk], 568
Awabakal [awk], 568
Awad Bing [bcu], 591
Awad Gey, *alt.* Awad Bing [bcu], 591
Awadhi [awa], 354, 468
Awaeté, *alt.* Asuriní, Xingú [asn], 225
  alt. Parakanã [pak], 231
Awaiama, *alt. dial.* Tawala [tbo], 627
Awaiya, *alt.* Yalahatan [jal], 405
Awak [awo], 154
Awakateko [agu], 253
Awake, *alt.* Arutani [atx], 225
Awaké, *alt.* Arutani [atx], 311
Awalama, *alt. dial.* Tawala [tbo], 627
Awale, *dial.* Diodio [ddi], 597
Awan, *dial.* Dinka, Southwestern [dik], 190
Awana, *alt.* Avá-Canoeiro [avv], 225
Awannu, *alt.* Wannu [jub], 177
Awano, *alt.* Aguano [aga], 285
Awapit, *alt.* Awa-Cuaiquer [kwi], 250
Awar [aya], 591
  dial. Awar [aya], 591
Awara [awx], 591
Awarai, *alt.* Waray [wrz], 577
Awarra, *alt.* Waray [wrz], 577
Awaté, *alt.* Asuriní, Xingú [asn], 225
Awau, *alt.* Avau [avb], 591
Awawar, *alt.* Awngi [awn], 113
Awayama, *dial.* Tawala [tbo], 627
Awbono [awh], 411

A'we, *alt.* Xavánte [xav], 234
  dial. Garo [grt], 362
Awe, *alt. dial.* Zaghawa [zag], 87
  dial. Pengo [peg], 383
Aweer, *alt.* Boni [bob], 132
Aweera, *alt.* Boni [bob], 132
Awege, *dial.* Pongu [png], 173
Aweikoma, *alt.* Xokleng [xok], 234
Awembak, *dial.* Moni [mnz], 420
Awembiak, *alt. dial.* Moni [mnz], 420
Awera [awr], 411
Awetí [awe], 225
Awetö, *alt.* Awetí [awe], 225
Awi, *alt.* Awing [azo], 56
  alt. Awngi [awn], 113
Awiaka, *alt.* Auyokawa [auo], 154
Awin, *alt.* Aekyom [awi], 587
Awing [azo], 56
Awit, *dial.* Talaud [tld], 433
Awiya, *alt.* Awngi [awn], 113
Awiyaana [auy], 591
Awje, *alt.* Awyi [auw], 412
Awji, *alt.* Awyi [auw], 412
Awjilah [auj], 139
Awju, *alt.* Awyu, Central [awu], 412
Awka, *alt. dial.* Igbo [ibo], 163
Awlan, *alt. dial.* Éwé [ewe], 207
Awngi [awn], 113
Awo-Sumakuyu, *alt.* Ulumanda' [ulm], 434
Awok, *alt.* Awak [awo], 154
Awon, *alt.* Awun [aww], 591
Awori, *dial.* Yoruba [yor], 178
Aworo, *dial.* Yoruba [yor], 178
Awromani, *alt.* Hawrami [hac], 439
Awtuw [kmn], 591
Awu Yi, *see* Yi, Awu [yiu], 347
Awun [aww], 591
Awuna, *alt.* Aguna [aug], 42
  dial. Éwé [ewe], 124
Awutu [afu], 123
  dial. Awutu [afu], 123
Awya, *alt.* Awyu, Central [awu], 412
Awye, *alt.* Awyi [auw], 412
Awyi [auw], 412
Awyu, *alt.* Awyu, North [yir], 412
Awyu, Asue [psa], 412
Awyu, Central [awu], 412
Awyu, Edera [awy], 412
Awyu, Jair [awv], 412
Awyu, North [yir], 412
Awyu, South [aws], 412
Axamb [ahb], 640
Axe, *alt.* Aché [guq], 284
Axels, *dial.* Zeeuws [zea], 549
Axi Yi, *see* Yi, Axi [yix], 347
Axibo, *alt.* Yi, Axi [yix], 347
Axininka Campa, *pej. alt.*
  Ajyíninka Apurucayali [cpc], 286

Axipo, *alt.* Yi, Axi [yix], 347
Axluslay, *alt.* Nivaclé [cag], 285
Axvax, *alt.* Akhvakh [akv], 552
Aya, *alt.* Ayu [ayu], 154
Ayabadhu [ayd], 568
Ayacucho Quechua, *see* Quechua, Ayacucho [quy], 289
Ayam, *alt. dial.* Asmat, Central [cns], 411
Ayamaru, *alt.* Mai Brat [ayz], 419
Ayan, *alt.* Bassari [bsc], 180, 129, 131
Ayan-Maya, *dial.* Evenki [evn], 504
Ayane, *alt.* Baniva [bvv], 311
Ayangan Ifugao, *dial.* Ifugao, Batad [ifb], 495
Ayao, *alt.* Yao [yao], 141
Ayat, *alt. dial.* Dinka, Southwestern [dik], 190
Ayautla Mazatec, *see* Mazatec, Ayautla [vmy], 264
Ayawa, *alt.* Yao [yao], 141, 149, 206, 215
Ayaya, *alt.* Guajá [gvj], 227
Ayerbense, *alt. dial.* Aragonese [arg], 558
Ayere [aye], 154
Ayi (China) [ayx], 326
  Ayi (Papua New Guinea) [ayq], 591
Ayiga, *alt.* Leyigha [ayi], 168
Ayigha, *alt.* Leyigha [ayi], 168
Ayikiben, *alt.* Yukuben [ybl], 178, 74
Ayiwo [nfl], 635
Ayizo, *alt.* Gbe, Ayizo [ayb], 44
Ayizo Gbe, *see* Gbe, Ayizo [ayb], 44
Ayizo-Ci, *alt.* Gbe, Ci [cib], 44
Ayizo-Gbe, *alt.* Gbe, Ayizo [ayb], 44
Ayizo-Kobe, *dial.* Gbe, Ayizo [ayb], 44
Ayizo-Seto, *dial.* Gbe, Ayizo [ayb], 44
Ayizo-Tori, *dial.* Gbe, Ayizo [ayb], 44
Ayki, *alt.* Runga [rou], 86, 77
Aykindang, *alt.* Runga [rou], 86, 77
Aymallal, *alt. dial.* Kistane [gru], 116
Aymara, Central [ayr], 222, 219, 242, 287
Aymara, Southern [ayc], 287
Aymasa, *alt. dial.* Kunama [kun], 112
Aymellel, *alt. dial.* Kistane [gru], 116
Aynallu, *dial.* Azerbaijani, South [azb], 438
Aynu, *alt.* Ainu [aib], 326
Ayo, *alt.* Mulam [mlm], 340
  alt. Yao [yao], 141, 149, 206, 215
Ayom, *alt.* Aiome [aki], 588
Ayoquesco Zapotec, *see* Zapotec, Ayoquesco [zaf], 277
Ayoré, *alt.* Ayoreo [ayo], 284, 222

Ayoreo [ayo], 284, 222
Ayotzintepec, *dial.* Chinantec, Ozumacín [chz], 261
Ayt Waziten, *dial.* Ghadamès [gha], 139
Ayta Abenlen Sambal, *alt.* Ayta, Abenlen [abp], 492
Ayta Hambali, *alt.* Sambal, Botolan [sbl], 501
   dial. Sambal, Botolan [sbl], 501
Ayta, Abenlen [abp], 492
Ayta, Ambala [abc], 492
Ayta, Bataan [ayt], 492
Ayta, Mag-Anchi [sgb], 492
Ayta, Mag-Indi [blx], 492
Ayta, Sorsogon [ays], 492
Ayta, Tayabas [ayy], 492
Ayu [ayu], 154
Ayuk, *alt.* Mixe, Totontepec [mto], 265
Ayun, *dial.* Jola-Kasa [csk], 180
Ayurú, *alt.* Wayoró [wyr], 234
Ayutla Mixtec, *see* Mixtec, Ayutla [miy], 266
Ayzo, *alt.* Gbe, Ayizo [ayb], 44
Aza, *alt. dial.* Dazaga [dzg], 151
Azaghvana, *alt.* Dghwede [dgh], 157
Azande, *alt.* Zande [zne], 109, 78, 196
Azángaro-Huangáscar-Chocos, *dial.* Quechua, Yauyos [qux], 292
Azangori, *alt.* Sungor [sjg], 195
Azanguri, *alt.* Assangori [sjg], 78
Azao, *alt.* Abu [ado], 586
Azargi, *alt.* Hazaragi [haz], 316, 485
Azawagh, *dial.* Tagdal [tda], 152
Azbinawa, *alt.* Tamajaq, Tawallammat [ttq], 175
Azelle, *alt. dial.* Jere [jer], 165
Azer, *dial.* Soninke [snk], 144, 95, 122, 131, 145, 182
Azera, *alt.* Adzera [azr], 587
   dial. Adzera [azr], 587
Azerbaijan, *alt.* Azerbaijani, North [azj], 319
Azerbaijani, North [azj], 319, 319
Azerbaijani, South [azb], 438, 315, 443, 510, 518
Azerbaydzhani, *alt.* Azerbaijani, North [azj], 319, 319
Azeri, *alt.* Azerbaijani, South [azb], 438, 315, 518
Azeri Turk, *alt.* Azerbaijani, North [azj], 319, 319
Azhe Yi, *see* Yi, Azhe [yiz], 347
Azhiga, *dial.* Pongu [png], 173
Azi, *alt.* Zaiwa [atb], 349, 467
Aziana, *alt.* Kenati [gat], 606
Azom, *dial.* Pol [pmm], 71

Azonyu, *alt. dial.* Naga, Southern Rengma [nre], 379
Azora, *alt.* Izora [cbo], 164
Azoyú Tlapanec, *see* Tlapanec, Azoyú [tpc], 275
'Azumeina, *alt.* Marba [mpg], 83
Azumeina, *alt.* Marba [mpg], 83
Azumu, *alt.* Kurama [krh], 167
Azza, *alt. dial.* Dazaga [dzg], 151
Azzaga, *alt. dial.* Dazaga [dzg], 151
'Ba, *alt.* Bua [bub], 79
Ba, *alt.* Aka-Bo [akm], 353
   alt. Amo [amo], 153
Ba Mali, *alt. dial.* Kenyah, Sebob [sib], 459
Ba Pai Yao, *alt.* Dzao Min [bpn], 332
Ba-Buche, *alt. dial.* Gamo-Ningi [bte], 160
Ba-Hi, *alt. dial.* Pacoh [pac], 525
Ba-Mbutu, *alt. dial.* Gamo-Ningi [bte], 160
Ba'a, *alt.* Lole [llg], 408
   dial. Lole [llg], 408
Baa, *alt.* Kwa [kwb], 167
Baä, *alt.* Lole [llg], 408
Baada, *alt.* Kunama [kun], 112
Baaden, *alt.* Kunama [kun], 112
Baadi, *alt.* Bardi [bcj], 568
Ba'adu, *dial.* Afar [aar], 111
Ba'adu, *alt. dial.* Afar [aar], 112
Baadu, *alt. dial.* Afar [aar], 112
Baagandji, *alt.* Darling [drl], 569
   alt. dial. Darling [drl], 569
Baagato, *alt. dial.* Mpongmpong [mgg], 68
   dial. Bangandu [bgf], 88
Baale, *alt. dial.* Kacipo-Balesi [koe], 115
Baali, *alt.* Bali [bcp], 96
Ba'amang, *dial.* Ngaju [nij], 394
Baan [bvj], 154
Baan-Ogoi, *alt.* Baan [bvj], 154
Baanbay, *alt.* Kumbainggar [kgs], 572
Baangi [bqx], 154
Baangingi', *alt.* Balangingi [sse], 492, 456
Baaravi, *alt. dial.* Fijian [fij], 580
   alt. dial. Fijian, Western [wyy], 580
Baardi, *alt.* Bardi [bcj], 568
Baarrundji, *alt.* Bandjigali [bjd], 568
Baate, *alt.* Ifè [ife], 208, 45
Baati, *alt. dial.* Bwa [bww], 99
Baato Baloi, *alt.* Baloi [biz], 96
Baatombu, *alt.* Baatonum [bba], 42
Baatonu, *alt.* Baatonum [bba], 42
Baatonum [bba], 42, 154
Baatonun, *alt.* Baatonum [bba], 154

Baatonun-Kwara, *alt.* Baatonum [bba], 154
Baaza, *alt.* Kunama [kun], 112
Baazayn, *alt.* Kunama [kun], 112
Baazen, *alt.* Kunama [kun], 112
Baba [bbw], 56
   alt. Malay, Baba [mbf], 509
   dial. Galoli [gal], 350
Baba Indonesian, *alt.* Indonesian, Peranakan [pea], 391
Baba Malay, *see* Malay, Baba [mbf], 509, 455
Babadji, *alt.* Beba [bfp], 58
Babadjou, *dial.* Ngombale [nla], 70
Babaga, *dial.* Keapara [khz], 605
Babagarupu, *dial.* Sinaugoro [snc], 624
Babal, *alt. dial.* Marghi Central [mrt], 169
Babalia, *alt.* Arabic, Babalia Creole [bbz], 78
   alt. Berakou [bxv], 79
Babalia Creole Arabic, *see* Arabic, Babalia Creole [bbz], 78
Babaliya, *alt.* Arabic, Babalia Creole [bbz], 78
Ba'ban, *alt.* Abon [abo], 153
Babango [bbm], 96
Babanki [bbk], 56
Babar, North [bcd], 396
Babar, Southeast [vbb], 396
Babasi, *alt. dial.* Mesaka [iyo], 67
Babata, *alt. dial.* Nakanai [nak], 616
Babatana [baa], 635
   dial. Babatana [baa], 635
Baba'zhi, *alt.* Beba [bfp], 58
Babbe, *dial.* Khana [ogo], 166
Babessi, *alt.* Wushi [bse], 73
Babete, *dial.* Ngomba [jgo], 69
Babine [bcr], 235
Babine Carrier, *alt.* Babine [bcr], 235
Babinga, *alt.* Aka [axk], 87
   alt. Baka [bkc], 56, 120
   alt. Gyele [gyi], 62, 111
   pej. alt. Yaka [axk], 78
Babino, *alt.* Saami, Akkala [sia], 556
Babinsk, *alt.* Saami, Akkala [sia], 556
Babir, *alt.* Bura-Pabir [bwr], 156
Babiruwa, *alt.* Eritai [ert], 415
Bable, *alt. dial.* Asturian [ast], 559, 551
Babok, *alt. dial.* Mandjak [mfv], 131, 122
Babole, *alt.* Dibole [bvx], 88
Babon, *dial.* Nyindrou [lid], 619
Babong, *dial.* Bakaka [bqz], 57
Baboute, *alt.* Vute [vut], 73
Babri, *alt.* Bauria [bge], 355

Babrua, *alt.* Eritai [ert], 415
Babruwa, *alt.* Eritai [ert], 415
Babue, *alt. dial.* Oroko [bdu], 71
Babungo, *alt.* Vengo [bav], 73
Babur, *alt.* Bura-Pabir [bwr], 156
Baburiwa, *alt.* Eritai [ert], 415
Babusa, *alt.* Babuza [bzg], 511
Babute, *alt.* Vute [vut], 177
Babuyan, *alt.* Batak [bya], 492
  alt. Ibatan [ivb], 494
Babuza [bzg], 511
Babwa, *alt. dial.* Kwa' [bko], 65
Babylonian Talmudic Aramaic,
  alt. Jewish Babylonian Aramaic
  [tmr], 443
Bac, *alt.* Bats [bbl], 352
Baca, *alt.* Nubaca [baf], 70
  dial. Swati [ssw], 197, 186
Bacadin, *dial.* Avar [ava], 553
Bacairí, *alt.* Bakairí [bkq], 225
Bacama [bcy], 154
Bacan, *alt.* Malay, Bacanese
  [btj], 401
Bacanese Malay, *see* Malay,
  Bacanese [btj], 401
Bacavès, *alt.* Catalan-Valencian-
  Balear [cat], 559, 529
Bacenga, *alt.* Tuki [bag], 72
  alt. dial. Tuki [bag], 72
Baceve, *alt. dial.* Iceve-Maci
  [bec], 163
Bacha, *alt.* Kwegu [xwg], 116
Bachadi, *dial.* Malvi [mup], 374
Bachajón Tzeltal, *see* Tzeltal,
  Bachajón [tzb], 276
Bachama, *alt.* Bacama [bcy], 154
Bache, *alt.* Che [ruk], 156
Bacheve, *alt.* Iceve-Maci [bec], 63
  alt. dial. Iceve-Maci [bec], 63
  dial. Iceve-Maci [bec], 163
Bachit-Gashish, *dial.* Berom
  [bom], 155
Baco, *alt. dial.* Aari [aiz], 112
Bada (Indonesia) [bhz], 427
  Bada (Nigeria) [bau], 154
  alt. Kunama [kun], 112
  dial. Bada [bhz], 427
Bada', *alt.* Bada [bhz], 427
Báda, *alt.* Cacua [cbv], 244
Badag, *alt.* Badaga [bfq], 354
Badaga [bfq], 354
Badagu, *alt.* Badaga [bfq], 354
Badak, *alt.* Bauria [bge], 355
Badakhshi, *alt.* Farsi, Eastern
  [prs], 484
Badanchi, *alt.* Bada [bau], 154
Badang, *alt.* Madang [mqd], 460
Badara, *alt.* Badyara [pbp], 128
Badara Duguri, *dial.* Duguri
  [dbm], 158

Badawa, *alt.* Bada [bau], 154
Bade [bde], 154
Bade-Kado, *alt. dial.* Bade
  [bde], 154
Baden, *alt.* Kunama [kun], 112
Baderwali, *alt.* Bhadrawahi
  [bhd], 355
Badeshi [bdz], 483
Badhani, *dial.* Garhwali [gbm], 360
Badi, *alt.* Bardi [bcj], 568
Bädi Kanum, *see* Kanum, Bädi
  [khd], 416
Badian, *alt.* Badyara [pbp], 128, 130,
  179
Badie, *alt. dial.* Bété, Gagnoa
  [btg], 92
Badimaya [bia], 568
Badin, *dial.* Sindhi Bhil [sbn], 489
Badinani, *alt.* Kurdish, Northern
  [kmr], 443
Badiotto, *dial.* Ladin [lld], 544
Badittu, *alt.* Koorete [kqy], 116
Badjande, *alt.* Zande [zne], 109, 78,
  196
Badjara, *alt.* Badyara [pbp], 128,
  130, 179
Badjaranke, *alt.* Badyara [pbp], 179
Badjava, *alt.* Ngad'a [nxg], 409
Badjaw, *alt.* Bajau, Indonesian
  [bdl], 427
Badjia, *dial.* Ewondo [ewo], 61
Badjiri, *dial.* Ngura [nbx], 575
Badjo, *alt.* Bajau, Indonesian
  [bdl], 427
Badjoue, *alt. dial.* Koonzime
  [ozm], 64
Badoni, *dial.* Maindo [cwb], 147
Badonjunga, *alt.* Ngadjunmaya
  [nju], 575
Badou, *alt. dial.* Akposo [kpo], 123
  alt. dial. Ikposo [kpo], 208
Badouma, *alt.* Duma [dma], 120
Badrohi, *alt.* Bhadrawahi [bhd], 355
Baduga, *alt.* Badaga [bfq], 354
Badugu, *alt.* Badaga [bfq], 354
Badui [bac], 391
Badung, *alt. dial.* Bali [ban], 391
Badwe'e, *dial.* Koonzime [ozm], 64
Badyara [pbp], 128, 130, 179
Badyaranke, *alt.* Badyara
  [pbp], 128, 130
Badzumbo, *alt.* Ipulo [ass], 63
Ba'e, *alt.* Mang [zng], 525, 339
Baeaula, *alt.* Wagawaga [wgw], 630
  alt. dial. Wagawaga [wgw], 630
Baebunta, *alt.* Lemolang [ley], 430
Baeggu [bvd], 635
Baegu, *alt.* Baeggu [bvd], 635
Baegwa, *alt.* Zimakani [zik], 634
Baele, *alt. dial.* Zaghawa [zag], 87

Baelelea [bvc], 635
Baetora [btr], 640
Bafang, *alt.* Fe'fe' [fmp], 61
  alt. dial. Fe'fe' [fmp], 61
Bafangi, *alt.* Bafanji [bfj], 56
Bafanio, *alt. dial.* Budu [buu], 98
Bafanji [bfj], 56
Bafanyi, *alt.* Bafanji [bfj], 56
Bafatá Creole, *dial.* Crioulo, Upper
  Guinea [pov], 131
Bafaw, *dial.* Bafaw-Balong [bwt], 56
Bafaw-Balong [bwt], 56
Bafeuk, *dial.* Ewondo [ewo], 61
Baffinland Eskimo, *dial.* Inuktitut,
  Eastern Canadian [ike], 238
Bafia [ksf], 56
Bafmen, *alt.* Mmen [bfm], 67
Bafmeng, *alt.* Mmen [bfm], 67
Bafo, *alt. dial.* Bafaw-Balong
  [bwt], 56
Bafou, *alt.* Yemba [ybb], 74
Bafoumeng, *alt.* Mmen [bfm], 67
Bafowu, *alt. dial.* Bafaw-Balong
  [bwt], 56
Bafreng, *alt. dial.* Mendankwe-
  Nkwen [mfd], 67
Bafuchu, *alt.* Ngamambo [nbv], 69
Bafumen, *alt.* Mmen [bfm], 67
Bafun, *dial.* Bakaka [bqz], 57
Bafut [bfd], 56
  dial. Bafut [bfd], 56
Bafwakoyi, *dial.* Budu [buu], 98
Bafwandaka, *dial.* Bali [bcp], 96
Bag Lachi, *alt. dial.* Lachi [lbt], 338
Baga Binari [bcg], 128
Baga Foré, *alt.* Mbulungish
  [mbv], 130
Baga Kakissa, *alt.* Baga Sobané
  [bsv], 128
Baga Kaloum [bqf], 128
Baga Koga [bgo], 128
Baga Manduri [bmd], 128
Baga Mboteni [bgm], 128
Baga Monson, *alt.* Mbulungish
  [mbv], 130
Baga Sitemu [bsp], 128
Baga Sobané [bsv], 128
Bagadji, *alt.* Kuuku-Ya'u [kuy], 573
Bagahak, *alt. dial.* Ida'an [dbj], 456
Bagam, *dial.* Mengaka [xmg], 67
Bagandji, *alt. dial.* Darling [drl], 569
Bagando, *alt.* Bangandu [bgf], 57,
  88
Bagando-Ngombe, *alt.* Ngombe
  [nmj], 77
Bagandou, *alt.* Ngando [ngd], 77
Bagangte, *alt.* Medumba [byv], 67
Bagangu, *dial.* Ngemba [nge], 69
Bagari, *alt.* Bagri [bgq], 354, 483
Bagasin, *alt.* Girawa [bbr], 600

Balaaben, *alt.* Yukuben [ybl], 178, 74

Balaban, *alt.* Tadyawan [tdy], 502

Balaesan, *alt.* Balaesang [bls], 427

Balaesang [bls], 427

Balafi, *alt. dial.* Fe'fe' [fmp], 61

Balagnini, *alt.* Balangingi [sse], 456

Balahaim, *alt.* Isebe [igo], 603

Balaisang, *alt.* Balaesang [bls], 427

Balait, *dial.* Lundayeh [lnd], 460

Balait Jati, *alt.* Belait [beg], 324

Balakeo, *dial.* Benggoi [bgy], 397

Balakhani, *dial.* Tat, Muslim [ttt], 320

Balali, *alt. dial.* Meohang, Western [raf], 476

Balamata, *alt.* Palumata [pmc], 403

Balambu, *alt.* Barambu [brm], 97

Balanda, *alt.* Balanta-Ganja [bjt], 179 *alt.* Balanta-Kentohe [ble], 130

Balangao [blw], 492

Balangao Bontoc, *alt.* Balangao [blw], 492

Balangaw, *alt.* Balangao [blw], 492

Balangingi [sse], 492, 456 *dial.* Balangingi [sse], 492

Balangingi Bajau, *alt.* Balangingi [sse], 456

Balanguingui, *alt.* Balangingi [sse], 492

Balanian, *alt.* Balangingi [sse], 456

Balanini, *alt.* Balangingi [sse], 456

Balanipa, *dial.* Mandar [mdr], 431

Balanka, *alt. dial.* Anii [blo], 207 *dial.* Anii [blo], 42

Balant, *alt.* Balanta-Ganja [bjt], 179 *alt.* Balanta-Kentohe [ble], 130

Balanta, *alt.* Balanta-Kentohe [ble], 130

Balanta-Ganja [bjt], 179

Balanta-Kentohe [ble], 130

Balantak [blz], 427

Balante, *alt.* Balanta-Ganja [bjt], 179 *alt.* Balanta-Kentohe [ble], 130

Balantian, *alt.* Nyadu [nxj], 395

Balantiang, *alt.* Nyadu [nxj], 395

Balaongwe, *dial.* Kgalagadi [xkv], 47

Balar, *alt. dial.* Kir-Balar [kkr], 166

Balatchi, *dial.* Ngiemboon [nnh], 69

Balatok-Itneg, *alt. dial.* Kalinga, Lubuagan [knb], 497

Balatok-Kalinga, *alt. dial.* Kalinga, Lubuagan [knb], 497

Bala'u, *alt.* Balau [blg], 458

Balau [blg], 458

Balawaia, *dial.* Sinaugoro [snc], 624

Balbalasang, *alt. dial.* Kalinga, Lubuagan [knb], 497

Balda, *alt.* Matal [mfh], 66

Baldam, *alt. dial.* Mískito [miq], 282

Baldamu, *alt.* Baldemu [bdn], 57

Baldare, *alt.* Baldemu [bdn], 57

Baldemu [bdn], 57

Bale, *alt.* Akar-Bale [acl], 353 *alt.* Lendu [led], 102 *alt.* Selee [snw], 127 *alt. dial.* Kacipo-Balesi [koe], 115

Balear, *alt. dial.* Catalan-Valencian-Balear [cat], 559

Balearic, *dial.* Catalan-Valencian-Balear [cat], 559

Balegete, *alt.* Evant [bzz], 159, 61

Balen, *alt.* Bilen [byn], 112

Balendru, *alt.* Lendu [led], 102

Balengue, *alt.* Molengue [bxc], 111

Balep, *dial.* Ndoe [nbb], 170

Baler Negrito, *alt.* Alta, Northern [aqn], 491

Balese, *alt.* Lese [les], 102

Balesi, *dial.* Kacipo-Balesi [koe], 115

Baletha, *alt.* Lendu [led], 102

Balgarski, *alt.* Bulgarian [bul], 532

Balgu, *alt.* Nijadali [nad], 575

Bali (Democratic Republic of Congo) [bcp], 96

Bali (Nigeria) [bcn], 154

Balinese [ban], 391

alt. Mungaka [mhk], 68

alt. Uneapa [bbn], 629

alt. dial. Mungaka [mhk], 68

dial. Teke, Ibali [tek], 108

Bali Aga, *pej. alt. dial.* Bali [ban], 391

Bali Holma, *alt.* Holma [hod], 162

Bali Nyonga, *dial.* Mungaka [mhk], 68

Bali Sign Language [bqy], 391

'Bali'ba, *dial.* Moru [mgd], 193

Baliem Valley Dani, *alt.* Dani, Mid Grand Valley [dnt], 413

Baliet, *alt. dial.* Dinka, Southwestern [dik], 190

Balif, *dial.* Mufian [aoj], 615

Balignini, *alt.* Balangingi [sse], 456

Balikpapan, *dial.* Malay [mly], 436

Balimbing, *dial.* Sama, Southern [ssb], 500

Balin, *alt. dial.* Mongolian, Peripheral [mvf], 339

Balinese, *alt.* Bali [ban], 391

Balinese Malay, *see* Malay, Balinese [mhp], 392

Balingian, *dial.* Melanau [mel], 460

Baliwon, *alt.* Ga'dang [gdg], 494

Balkan Gagauz Turkish [bgx], 563, 547

Balkan Romani, *see* Romani, Balkan [rmn], 557, 441, 532, 537,

539, 541, 542, 545, 547, 548, 551, 563

Balkan Turkic, *alt.* Balkan Gagauz Turkish [bgx], 563, 547

Balkar, *dial.* Karachay-Balkar [krc], 554

Balkar-Tsalakan, *alt. dial.* Lak [lbe], 555

Balke, *alt.* Barwe [bwg], 147

Balkh Arabic, *dial.* Arabic, Tajiki Spoken [abh], 315

Balkhu-Sisneri, *alt. dial.* Jerung [jee], 472

Ballante, *alt.* Balanta-Ganja [bjt], 179 *alt.* Balanta-Kentohe [ble], 130

Ballo-Kai-Pomo, *alt.* Pomo, Central [poo], 307

'Balo, *alt.* Kpasam [pbn], 167

Balo [bqo], 57

Balobo, *alt.* Likila [lie], 103 *alt. dial.* Mabaale [mmz], 103

Balochi, *alt.* Balochi, Eastern [bgp], 355

Balochi, Eastern [bgp], 483, 355

Balochi, Southern [bcc], 483, 438, 482, 520

Balochi, Western [bgn], 476, 315, 438, 520

Baloci, *alt.* Balochi, Eastern [bgp], 483, 355 *alt.* Balochi, Southern [bcc], 483, 438, 482, 520 *alt.* Balochi, Western [bgn], 476, 315, 438, 520

Baloga, *alt.* Ayta, Mag-Indi [blx], 492

Baloi [biz], 96

Baloki, *alt.* Boloki [bkt], 98

Balom, *alt.* Lefa [lfa], 65

Balombi, *alt.* Barombi [bbi], 58

Balon, *alt. dial.* Bafaw-Balong [bwt], 56

Balondo, *dial.* Bakaka [bqz], 57

Balondo Ba Diko, *alt. dial.* Oroko [bdu], 71

Balondo Ba Nanga, *alt. dial.* Oroko [bdu], 71

Balong, *dial.* Bafaw-Balong [bwt], 56

Baloum, *alt.* Ghomálá' [bbj], 62

Baloumbou, *alt.* Lumbu [lup], 120

Balsapuertino, *alt.* Chayahuita [cbt], 287

Baltap, *alt.* Montol [mtl], 170

Baltap-Lalin, *dial.* Montol [mtl], 170

Balti [bft], 483, 355

Baltic Romani, *see* Romani, Baltic [rml], 550, 546, 546

Baltistani, *alt.* Balti [bft], 483, 355

Baluan, *dial.* Baluan-Pam [blq], 592

Baluan-Pam [blq], 592
Baluchi, *alt.* Balochi, Eastern
  [bgp], 483
  alt. Balochi, Southern [bcc], 483,
  438, 482, 520
  alt. Balochi, Western [bgn], 476,
  315, 438, 520
Baluci, *alt.* Balochi, Eastern
  [bgp], 483, 355
  alt. Balochi, Southern [bcc], 483,
  438, 482, 520
  alt. Balochi, Western [bgn], 476,
  315, 438, 520
Balud, *alt.* Blaan, Sarangani
  [bps], 493
Balue, *alt. dial.* Oroko [bdu], 71
Baluga, *alt.* Alta, Southern [agy], 491
Balung, *alt. dial.* Bafaw-Balong
  [bwt], 56
Balungada, *alt.* Nedebang
  [nec], 409
Baluombila, *dial.* Poke [pof], 107
Balurbi, *dial.* Djinang [dji], 570
Balvi, *dial.* Godwari [gdx], 362
Balwa, *alt.* Akar-Bale [acl], 353
Balxar-Calakan, *alt. dial.* Lak
  [lbe], 555
Balygu, *alt.* Nijadali [nad], 575
Bam, *alt.* Biem [bmc], 593
  alt. dial. Wantoat [wnc], 631
Bama, *alt.* Burmese [mya], 462, 321
  alt. Nagumi [ngv], 69
  dial. Dogon, Jamsay [djm], 142, 50
Bamachaka, *alt.* Burmese
  [mya], 462, 321
Bamako Sign Language
  [bog], 141
Bamali [bbq], 57
Bamana, *alt.* Bambara [bam], 49, 91
Bamanakan, *alt.* Bamanankan
  [bam], 141
  alt. Bambara [bam], 49, 91
Bamanankan [bam], 141
Bamanyeka, *alt.* Manyika
  [mxc], 216
Bamassa, *alt.* Limassa [bme], 76
Bambaa, *alt.* Hukumina [huw], 399
Bambaama, *alt.* Mbama
  [mbm], 120
Bambadion-Dogoso, *alt.* Dogoso
  [dgs], 50
Bambadion-Dokhosié, *alt.*
  Dogoso [dgs], 50
Bambadion-Kheso, *alt.* Khe
  [kqg], 52
Bambala, *alt.* Burji [bji], 114, 132
Bambalang [bmo], 56
Bambam [ptu], 427
Bambam Hulu, *dial.* Bambam
  [ptu], 427

Bambara [bam], 49, 91
  alt. Bamanankan [bam], 141
  alt. dial. Lame [bma], 168
Bambaro, *alt. dial.* Lame [bma], 168
Bambassi [myf], 113
  dial. Bambassi [myf], 113
Bambeiro, *alt. dial.* Mbundu
  [kmb], 41
Bambele, *alt. dial.* Tuki [bag], 72
Bambenga, *pej. alt.* Yaka [axk], 78
Bambenzele, *dial.* Aka [axk], 87
Bambeshi, *alt.* Bambassi [myf], 113
Bambili, *alt.* Bambili-Bambui
  [baw], 57
  dial. Bambili-Bambui [baw], 57
Bambili-Bambui [baw], 57
Bambo, *alt. dial.* Lala-Bisa [leb], 102
Bamboko, *alt.* Wumboko [bqm], 73
Bambolang, *alt.* Bambalang
  [bmo], 56
Bamboma, *alt.* Teke-Eboo [ebo], 90
Bamboute, *alt.* Vute [vut], 73
Bambuba, *alt.* Mvuba [mxh], 105
Bambui, *dial.* Bambili-Bambui
  [baw], 57
Bambuka, *alt.* Kyak [bka], 168
Bambuku, *alt.* Wumboko [bqm], 73
Bambuluwe, *alt.* Awing [azo], 56
Bambur, *alt.* Kulung [bbu], 167
Bamburo, *alt. dial.* Lame [bma], 168
Bambutu, *alt. dial.* Ngemba
  [nge], 69
Bambutuku, *alt.* Vanuma [vau], 109
Bamechom, *alt. dial.* Ngemba [nge],
  69
Bamekon, *alt.* Kom [bkm], 64
Bamenda, *alt. dial.* Mendankwe-
  Nkwen [mfd], 67
Bamendjin, *alt. dial.* Mengaka
  [xmg], 67
Bamendjinda, *dial.* Ngomba
  [jgo], 69
Bamendjing, *alt. dial.* Mengaka
  [xmg], 67
Bamendjo, *dial.* Ngomba [jgo], 69
Bamenjou, *alt. dial.* Ghomálá'
  [bbj], 62
Bamenkombit, *alt.* Bamukumbit
  [bqt], 57
Bamenkoumbit, *alt.* Bamukumbit
  [bqt], 57
Bamenkumbo, *dial.* Ngomba
  [jgo], 69
Bamenyam [bce], 57
Bamenyan, *alt.* Bamenyam [bce], 57
Bamessing, *alt.* Kenswei Nsei
  [ndb], 64
Bamessingue, *dial.* Ngombale
  [nla], 70
Bamesso, *dial.* Ngomba [jgo], 69

Bameta, *alt.* Meta' [mgo], 67
  alt. dial. Meta' [mgo], 67
Bamete, *alt. dial.* Ngomba [jgo], 69
Bamileke-Bandjoun, *alt.* Ghomálá'
  [bbj], 62
Bamileke-Fe'fe', *alt.* Fe'fe'
  [fmp], 61
Bamileke-Kwa, *alt.* Kwa' [bko], 65
Bamileke-Medumba, *alt.*
  Medumba [byv], 67
Bamileke-Mengaka, *alt.* Mengaka
  [xmg], 67
Bamileke-Nda'nda', *alt.* Nda'nda'
  [nnz], 69
Bamileke-Ngiemboon, *alt.*
  Ngiemboon [nnh], 69
Bamileke-Ngomba, *alt.* Ngomba
  [jgo], 69
Bamileke-Ngombale, *alt.*
  Ngombale [nla], 70
Bamileke-Ngwe, *alt.* Ngwe
  [nwe], 70
Bamileke-Ngyemboon, *alt.*
  Ngiemboon [nnh], 69
Bamileke-Yemba, *alt.* Yemba
  [ybb], 74
Baminge, *alt.* Ngie [ngj], 69
Bamitaba, *alt.* Bomitaba [zmx], 88
Bamongo, *alt.* Bushoong [buf], 98
Bamota, *alt. dial.* Kâte [kmg], 605
Bamoukoumbit, *alt.* Bamukumbit
  [bqt], 57
Bamoum, *alt.* Bamun [bax], 57
Bamoun, *alt.* Bamun [bax], 57
Bamoungong, *dial.* Ngiemboon
  [nnh], 69
Bamu [bcf], 592
Bamu Kiwai, *alt.* Bamu [bcf], 592
Bamukumbit [bqt], 57
Bamum, *alt.* Bamun [bax], 57
Bamumbo, *dial.* Mundani [mnf], 68
Bamumbu, *alt. dial.* Mundani
  [mnf], 68
Bamun [bax], 57
Bamundum 1, *alt. dial.* Ngemba
  [nge], 69
Bamundum 2, *alt. dial.* Ngemba
  [nge], 69
Bamunka [bvm], 57
Bamunkum, *alt.* Bamukumbit
  [bqt], 57
Bamunkun, *alt.* Bamunka [bvm], 57
Bamusso, *alt.* Bakole [kme], 57
Bamvele, *alt.* Bebele [beb], 58
  alt. dial. Tuki [bag], 72
  dial. Ewondo [ewo], 61
Bamvuba, *alt.* Mvuba [mxh], 105
Bamwe [bmg], 96
Bamyili Creole, *dial.* Kriol
  [rop], 572

Ban Khor Sign Language
  [bfk], 514
Ban Manus, *alt.* Rawat [jnl], 385
Ban Rauts, *alt.* Rawat [jnl], 385
Ban Yao, *alt.* Iu Mien [ium], 336
Bana [bcw], 57
  alt. Bahnar [bdq], 521
  alt. Hamer-Banna [amf], 115
  alt. dial. Fe'fe' [fmp], 61
  alt. dial. Mundang [mua], 68
  dial. Uma [ppk], 434
Bana', *alt.* Phana' [phq], 452
Banaban, *dial.* Kiribati [gil], 582,
  580
Banadan, *alt.* Balangingi [sse], 456
Banag, *alt.* Panang [pcr], 342
Banagere, *alt.* Mesaka [iyo], 67
Banai, *dial.* Koch [kdq], 368, 321
Banaka, *alt. dial.* Batanga [bnm], 58
Banala, *dial.* Kenga [kyq], 82
Banama, *dial.* Kenga [kyq], 82
Banan Bay, *alt.* Burmbar [vrt], 641
Banana, *pej. alt.* Masana [mcn], 83,
  66
Banana', *dial.* Malayic Dayak
  [xdy], 394
Banang, *alt.* Panang [pcr], 342
Banamma, *alt.* Musey [mse], 85, 68
Banamma Ho, *alt.* Musey [mse], 68
Banamma Ho Ho, *alt.* Musey
  [mse], 85
Banao, *alt.* Itneg, Banao [bjx], 496
Banao Itneg, *see* Itneg, Banao
  [bjx], 496
Banao Pikekj, *dial.* Itneg, Banao
  [bjx], 496
Banapari, *dial.* Bagheli [bfy], 354,
  468
Banaphari, *dial.* Bundeli [bns], 357
Banar, *alt.* Banaro [byz], 592
  alt. Maia [sks], 610
Banara, *alt.* Banaro [byz], 592
  alt. Maiani [tnh], 610
  alt. Mala [ped], 611
Banaro [byz], 592
Banat, *dial.* Romanian [ron], 552, 548
Banauá, *alt.* Banawá [bnh], 225
Banaue Ifugao, *dial.* Ifugao,
  Amganad [ifa], 495
Banaule, *alt.* Bebeli [bek], 593
Banava, *alt.* Kaili, Unde [unz], 429
Banavá, *alt.* Banawá [bnh], 225
Banawa, *alt.* Kaili, Unde [unz], 429
Banawá [bnh], 225
Banchapai, *dial.* Muria, Western
  [mut], 377
Banda [bnd], 396
  alt. Ligbi [lig], 126, 94
  alt. Nafaanra [nfr], 126
  alt. dial. Chumburung [ncu], 124

  alt. dial. Shoo-Minda-Nye [bcv], 174
Banda Aceh, *dial.* Aceh [ace], 435
Banda Central Sud, *alt.* Banda,
  Mid-Southern [bjo], 74
Banda de Bria, *alt. dial.* Banda-
  Banda [bpd], 75
Banda Malay, *see* Malay, Banda
  [bpq], 401
Banda of Bambari, *alt.* Banda-
  Bambari [liy], 75
Banda of Bria, *alt. dial.* Banda-
  Banda [bpd], 75
Banda of Mbrès, *alt.* Banda-Mbrès
  [bqk], 75
Banda of Mbrés, *alt.* Banda-Mbrès
  [bqk], 188
Banda of Ndélé, *alt.* Banda-Ndélé
  [bfl], 75, 188
Banda, Mid-Southern [bjo], 74,
  97, 188
Banda, South Central [lnl], 74,
  97
Banda, Togbo-Vara [tor], 97, 74,
  188
Banda, West Central [bbp], 74,
  188
Banda-Bambari [liy], 75
Banda-Banda [bpd], 75, 188
  dial. Banda-Banda [bpd], 75
Banda-Kpaya, *dial.* Banda-Ndélé
  [bfl], 188
Banda-Mbre, *alt.* Banda-Mbrès
  [bqk], 75, 188
Banda-Mbrès [bqk], 75, 188
Banda-Ndélé [bfl], 75, 188
  dial. Banda-Ndélé [bfl], 75
Banda-Yangere [yaj], 75
Bandangao, *alt. dial.* Banda-Ndélé
  [bfl], 75
Bandari, *dial.* Farsi, Western
  [pes], 439
Bandas, *alt. dial.* Dass [dot], 157
Bandawa, *alt. dial.* Shoo-Minda-Nye
  [bcv], 174
Bande, *alt.* Bandi [bza], 137
  alt. Budik [tnr], 180
  alt. dial. Ngemba [nge], 69
Bande', *alt. dial.* Ngemba [nge], 69
Bandem, *alt.* Ndemli [nml], 69
Bandeng, *alt. dial.* Mungaka
  [mhk], 68
  alt. dial. Ngemba [nge], 69
Bandi [bza], 137
Bandial [bqj], 180
  alt. dial. Bandial [bqj], 180
Bandja-Baboontou, *alt. dial.*
  Fe'fe' [fmp], 61
Bandjalang [bdy], 568
Bandjarese, *alt.* Banjar [bjn], 392,
  456

Bandjelang, *alt.* Bandjalang
  [bdy], 568
Bandjigali [bjd], 568
Bandjima, *alt.* Panytyima [pnw], 576
Bandjoun, *alt.* Ghomálá' [bbj], 62
  alt. dial. Ghomálá' [bbj], 62
Bandobo, *dial.* Tikar [tik], 72
Bandougou, *dial.* Siamou [sif], 54
Bandoumou, *alt.* Ndumu
  [nmd], 121
Bandu, *dial.* Thai, Northern
  [nod], 517
Bandzabi, *alt.* Njebi [nzb], 121
Bandzhogi, *alt.* Chin, Zotung
  [czt], 463
Bane, *dial.* Ewondo [ewo], 61
Baneka, *dial.* Bakaka [bqz], 57
Banen, *alt.* Tunen [baz], 72
Banend, *alt.* Tunen [baz], 72
Banenge, *dial.* Bahing [bhj], 468
Banfora-Sienena, *dial.* Cerma
  [cme], 50
Bang, *alt.* Mambila, Cameroon
  [mcu], 66
  alt. Mambila, Nigeria [mzk], 169
  dial. Mfumte [nfu], 67
Bang-Ling, *dial.* Tupuri [tui], 87
Bang-Were, *dial.* Tupuri [tui], 87
Banga, *alt.* Rukai [dru], 512
  alt. dial. Gwamhi-Wuri [bga], 161
  dial. Kaba Na [kwv], 81
  dial. Mboi [moi], 170
Banga-Bhasa, *alt.* Bengali
  [ben], 320
Bangad, *dial.* Kalinga, Southern
  [ksc], 497
Bangala [bxg], 97
  alt. Banggarla [bjb], 568
  alt. Bengali [ben], 320, 355, 469
  alt. Lambadi [lmn], 372
  alt. Mbangala [mxg], 41
Bangalam, *alt. dial.* Murle
  [mur], 117
Bangalema, *alt.* Ngelima [agh], 106
**Bangalore-Chennai-Hyderabad
  Sign Language**, *dial.* Indian
  Sign Language [ins], 365
**Bangalore-Madras Sign
  Language**, *dial.* Indian Sign
  Language [ins], 365
Bangan, *alt. dial.* Fe'fe' [fmp], 61
Banganci, *alt. dial.* Gwamhi-Wuri
  [bga], 161
Bangando, *alt.* Bangandu [bgf], 57,
  88
Bangando-Ngombe, *alt.* Ngombe
  [nmj], 77
Bangandou, *alt.* Ngando [ngd], 77
Bangandu [bgf], 57, 88
Bangang, *dial.* Mundani [mnf], 68

Bangangte, *alt.* Medumba [byv], 67
Bangani, *dial.* Garhwali [gbm], 360
Bangantu, *alt.* Bangandu [bgf], 57
alt. dial. Mpongmpong [mgg], 68
Bangaru, *alt.* Haryanvi [bgc], 364
Bangaru Proper, *dial.* Haryanvi [bgc], 364
Bangassogo, *dial.* Samo, Maya [sym], 53
Bangawa, *alt. dial.* Gwamhi-Wuri [bga], 161
Bangay, *alt.* Bonggi [bdg], 456
Bangba [bbe], 97
Bangba Lo, *alt.* Chaudangsi [cdn], 358
Bangba Lwo, *alt.* Chaudangsi [cdn], 469
Bangbani, *alt.* Chaudangsi [cdn], 358
Bangbinda, *alt.* Ngbinda [nbd], 106
Bangdale, *alt.* Nachering [ncd], 476
dial. Nachering [ncd], 476
Bangdel Tûm, *alt.* Nachering [ncd], 476
Bangdile, *alt.* Nachering [ncd], 476
Bangela, *alt.* Likila [lie], 103
Bangelima, *alt.* Ngelima [agh], 106
Banger, *alt.* Haryanvi [bgc], 364
Bangeri Me, *alt.* Dogon, Bangeri Me [dba], 142
Bangeri Me Dogon, *see* Dogon, Bangeri Me [dba], 142
Banggai [bgz], 427
Banggala, *alt.* Banggarla [bjb], 568
Banggarla [bjb], 568
Banggi, *alt.* Bonggi [bdg], 456
dial. Bajau, West Coast [bdr], 456
Banggi Dusun, *alt.* Bonggi [bdg], 456
Bangi [bni], 97
alt. Bobangi [bni], 88
Banginda, *dial.* Gbaya, Northwest [gya], 61
Bangingi Sama, *alt.* Balangingi [sse], 492
Bangjinge, *alt.* Bangwinji [bsj], 154
Bangka, *dial.* Malay [mly], 436
Bangkalan, *dial.* Madura [mad], 392
Bangkalon, *alt. dial.* Madura [mad], 392
Bangla, *alt.* Bengali [ben], 320, 355, 469
dial. Samba Leko [ndi], 72
Bangla-Bhasa, *alt.* Bengali [ben], 355, 469
Banglori, *alt.* Kannada [kan], 366
Bangni, *alt.* Nisi [dap], 381
dial. Nisi [dap], 381
Bango, *alt.* Nubaca [baf], 70

Bangobango, *alt.* Bangubangu [bnx], 97
Bangolan [bgj], 58
Bangom, *alt.* Ngom [nra], 121, 89
Bangomo, *alt.* Ngom [nra], 121, 89
Bangon, *alt.* Buhid [bku], 493
alt. Tawbuid, Eastern [bnj], 502
Bangoul, *dial.* Day [dai], 80
Bangri, *alt.* Haryanvi [bgc], 364
dial. Bagirmi [bmi], 78
Bangru, *alt.* Haryanvi [bgc], 364
alt. dial. Hruso [hru], 364
dial. Koma [kmy], 64
Bangubangu [bnx], 97
dial. Bangubangu [bnx], 97
Bangui, *dial.* Befang [bby], 58
Bangunji, *alt.* Bangwinji [bsj], 154
Bangwa, *alt.* Yemba [ybb], 74
alt. dial. Ngemba [nge], 69
Bangwe, *alt. dial.* Befang [bby], 58
dial. Sena [seh], 149
Bangwi, *alt. dial.* Befang [bby], 58
Bangwinji [bsj], 154
Banhum, *alt.* Bainouk-Gunyaamolo [bcz], 179
alt. Bainouk-Gunyuño [bab], 130
Bani Khaalid, *alt. dial.* Arabic, Najdi Spoken [ars], 508
Baniata, *alt.* Touo [tqu], 639
Baniba, *alt.* Baniwa [bwi], 225, 311
Baninge, *alt.* Ngie [ngj], 69
Baniua do Içana, *alt.* Baniwa [bwi], 225, 311
Baniva [bvv], 311
alt. Baniwa [bwi], 225, 311
dial. Baniva [bvv], 311
Baniwa [bwi], 225, 311
Banja, *alt.* Mbandja [zmz], 89
alt. Ngamambo [nbv], 69
Banjaal, *alt.* Bandial [bqj], 180
Banjangi, *alt.* Kenyang [ken], 64
Banjar [bjn], 392, 456
Banjar Malay, *alt.* Banjar [bjn], 392, 456
Banjara, *alt.* Lambadi [lmn], 372
Banjarese, *alt.* Banjar [bjn], 392, 456
Banjari, *alt.* Lambadi [lmn], 372
Banjima, *alt.* Panytyima [pnw], 576
Banjiram, *alt. dial.* Longuda [lnu], 169
Banjogi, *alt.* Chin, Zotung [czt], 463
Banjong, *alt. dial.* Ngemba [nge], 69
Banjori, *alt.* Lambadi [lmn], 372
Banjoun-Baham, *alt.* Ghomálá' [bbj], 62
Banjun, *alt.* Ghomálá' [bbj], 62
Banjur, *alt. dial.* Iban [iba], 393
Banjuri, *alt.* Lambadi [lmn], 372
Banka, *alt.* Bankagooma [bxw], 141

alt. dial. Fe'fe' [fmp], 61
Bankagoma, *alt.* Bankagooma [bxw], 141
Bankagooma [bxw], 141
Bankagoroma, *alt.* Bankagooma [bxw], 141
Bankaje, *alt.* Bankagooma [bxw], 141
Bankal, *dial.* Jarawa [jar], 165
Bankala, *alt. dial.* Jarawa [jar], 165
Banke, *dial.* Tharu, Dangaura [thl], 480
Bankon [abb], 58
Bankoti, *alt.* Konkani [knn], 369
alt. dial. Konkani [knn], 369
Bankutu, *alt.* Nkutu [nkw], 106
Banlol, *dial.* Ma'ya [slz], 420
Banna, *alt.* Hamer-Banna [amf], 115
Bannochi, *alt. dial.* Pashto, Central [pst], 488
Bannock, *dial.* Paiute, Northern [pao], 306
Bannoni [bcm], 592
Bannu, *alt. dial.* Pashto, Central [pst], 488
Bannuchi, *dial.* Pashto, Central [pst], 488
Banoho, *alt.* Batanga [bnm], 110, 58
Banoko, *alt. dial.* Batanga [bnm], 58
Banoni, *alt.* Bannoni [bcm], 592
Bano'o, *alt.* Batanga [bnm], 110, 58
dial. Batanga [bnm], 58
Banoo, *alt.* Batanga [bnm], 110, 58
alt. dial. Batanga [bnm], 58
Banpara Naga, *alt.* Naga, Wancho [nnp], 380
Bansaw, *alt.* Lamnso' [lns], 65, 168
Bansbali, *dial.* Chambeali [cdh], 358
Banso, *alt.* Lamnso' [lns], 65, 168
Banso', *alt.* Lamnso' [lns], 65, 168
Bansyari, *dial.* Chambeali [cdh], 358
Banta, *alt.* Manta [myg], 66
dial. Themne [tem], 184
Bantaba, *alt.* Bantawa [bap], 468
Bantaeng, *dial.* Konjo, Coastal [kjc], 430
Bantakpa, *alt.* Manta [myg], 66
Bantalang, *alt.* Rukai [dru], 512
Bantar, *dial.* Maithili [mai], 475
dial. Musasa [smm], 476
Bantaurang, *alt.* Rukai [dru], 512
Bantawa [bap], 468
Bantawa Dum, *alt.* Bantawa [bap], 468
Bantawa Rai, *alt.* Bantawa [bap], 468
Bantawa Yong, *alt.* Bantawa [bap], 468
Bantawa Yüng, *alt.* Bantawa [bap], 468

Bantayan, *dial.* Hiligaynon [hil], 494
Banten, *dial.* Javanese [jav], 391
  dial. Sunda [sun], 392
Banti, *dial.* Mundani [mnf], 68
Bantian, *dial.* Lawangan [lbx], 394
Bantik [bnq], 428
Bantoanon [bno], 492
Banton, *dial.* Bantoanon [bno], 492
Banu, *alt.* Gbanu [gbv], 75
Banuwang, *dial.* Lawangan [lbx], 394
Banya, *dial.* Ngwo [ngn], 70
Banyai, *alt. dial.* Kalanga [kck], 216
Banyang, *alt.* Kenyang [ken], 64
Banyangi, *alt.* Kenyang [ken], 64
Banyok, *dial.* Sibu [sdx], 461
Banyuk, *alt.* Bainouk-Gunyaamolo [bcz], 179
  alt. Bainouk-Gunyuño [bab], 130
Banyum, *alt.* Bainouk-Gunyaamolo [bcz], 179
  alt. Bainouk-Gunyuño [bab], 130
Banyun, *alt.* Bainouk-Gunyaamolo [bcz], 179
  alt. Bainouk-Gunyuño [bab], 130
Banyung, *alt.* Bainouk-Gunyaamolo [bcz], 179
  alt. Bainouk-Gunyuño [bab], 130
Banyuq, *alt. dial.* Kayan, Murik [mxr], 459
Banyuwangi, *alt.* Osing [osi], 392
Banz-Nondugl, *dial.* Wahgi, North [whg], 630
Banza, *alt. dial.* Mabaale [mmz], 103
Banziri, *alt.* Gbanziri [gbg], 73, 99
Bao, *alt.* Aigon [aix], 588
  dial. Aigon [aix], 588
Bao'an, *alt.* Bonan [peh], 328
Baojing, *dial.* Tujia, Northern [tji], 345
Baokan, *alt. dial.* Bookan [bnb], 456
Baol, *dial.* Wolof [wol], 182, 145
Baonan, *alt.* Bonan [peh], 328
Baori, *alt.* Bauria [bge], 355
Baorias, *alt.* Bagri [bgq], 354, 483
Baoulé [bci], 92
Bapa, *alt.* Baba [bbw], 56
Bapai, *dial.* Yaqay [jaq], 426
Bapakum, *alt.* Baba [bbw], 56
Bape, *alt.* Dimbong [dii], 60
  dial. Bafia [ksf], 56
Bapinyi, *alt.* Pinyin [pny], 71
Bapo, *dial.* Krumen, Tepo [ted], 93, 138
Bapu, *alt.* Anasi [bpo], 411
Bapuku, *dial.* Batanga [bnm], 110, 58
Bapuu, *alt. dial.* Batanga [bnm], 110, 58
Bar, *alt.* Anuak [anu], 113
Bara, *alt.* Bodo [brx], 357, 469

alt. Ghera [ghr], 484
dial. Bole [bol], 156
dial. Folopa [ppo], 599
Bará, *alt.* Pokangá [pok], 231
pej. alt. Waimaha [bao], 248, 233
Bara Malagasy, *see* Malagasy, Bara [bhr], 140
Bara Sona, *alt.* Pokangá [pok], 231
Bara-Bare, *alt. dial.* Ngaju [nij], 394
Bara-Jida, *alt.* Bakumpai [bkr], 392
Baraa, *alt. dial.* Mandjak [mfv], 131, 122, 181
Baraamu [brd], 468
Baraan, *alt.* Blaan, Koronadal [bpr], 493
Barabaig, *alt. dial.* Datooga [tcc], 198
Barabaik, *alt. dial.* Datooga [tcc], 198
Barabara, *dial.* Bunama [bdd], 595
Barabayga, *alt. dial.* Datooga [tcc], 198
Barabayiiga, *dial.* Datooga [tcc], 198
Barabo, *dial.* Anyin [any], 91
Baragaon, *alt. dial.* Lowa [loy], 474
Baragaun, *alt. dial.* Lowa [loy], 474
Baragaunle, *dial.* Lowa [loy], 474
Barage, *dial.* Dhatki [mki], 484
Baraguyu, *alt. dial.* Maasai [mas], 134, 201
Barahuwi, *dial.* Balochi, Southern [bcc], 482
Barai [bbb], 592
Barain, *alt. dial.* Fulfulde, Northeastern Burkina Faso [fuh], 51
Baraïn, *alt.* Barein [bva], 78
Baraka, *dial.* Bissa [bib], 123
Barakai [baj], 396
  dial. Barakai [baj], 396
Barake, *alt.* Domari [rmt], 448, 510
  dial. Domari [rmt], 448, 510
Baraki, *alt.* Ormuri [oru], 487
Baraks, *alt.* Ormuri [oru], 487, 317
Barakwena Barakwengo, *pej. alt.* Kxoe [xuu], 150
Barala, *alt. dial.* Mahou [mxx], 94
Baralaka, *alt. dial.* Mahou [mxx], 94
Baram, *alt.* Baraamu [brd], 468
  dial. Polci [plj], 173
Baram Dutse, *alt. dial.* Polci [plj], 173
Baram Kajan, *alt.* Kayan, Baram [kys], 459
Baram Kayan, *see* Kayan, Baram [kys], 459
Barama [bbg], 120
Barambo, *alt.* Barambu [brm], 97
Barambu [brm], 97

Baramu [bmz], 592
Baranci, *alt. dial.* Jarawa [jar], 165
Barang, *alt. dial.* Polci [plj], 173
Barang-Barang, *alt.* Laiyolo [lji], 430
  dial. Laiyolo [lji], 430
Barangan, *alt.* Tawbuid, Eastern [bnj], 502
Barani, *dial.* Fulfulde, Northeastern Burkina Faso [fuh], 51
Baraniire, *alt. dial.* Fulfulde, Northeastern Burkina Faso [fuh], 51
Baraog, *alt.* Parauk [prk], 466, 342
Baraoke, *dial.* Wa [wbm], 346
Barapasi [brp], 412
Baras [brs], 428
  dial. Tagbanwa, Calamian [tbk], 502
Barasana [bsn], 243
Barasano, *alt.* Pokangá [pok], 231
  alt. Waimaha [bao], 248
Barashe, *dial.* Lishana Deni [lsd], 445
Barat, *dial.* Orya [ury], 422
Barau, *alt.* Kemberano [bzp], 412
  dial. Kemberano [bzp], 412
Barauana, *alt.* Baré [bae], 311
Barauna, *alt.* Baré [bae], 311
Barawa, *alt.* Dass [dot], 157
Barawahing, *pej. alt.* Abui [abz], 406
Barawana, *alt.* Baré [bae], 311
Barazana, *alt.* Waimaha [bao], 233
Barba, *alt.* Baatonum [bba], 42, 154
Barbacoas [bpb], 243
Barbadian Creole English, *alt.* Bajan [bjs], 221
Barbados, *alt.* Umotína [umo], 233
Barbaig, *alt. dial.* Datooga [tcc], 198
Barbalin, *alt.* Bagvalal [kva], 553
Barbareño [boi], 298
Barbari, *alt.* Aimaq [aiq], 315
Barbaricino, *dial.* Sardinian, Logudorese [src], 545
Barbuda Creole English, *dial.* Antigua and Barbuda Creole English [aig], 219
Barburr, *alt.* Bura-Pabir [bwr], 156
Barclayville Grebo, *see* Grebo, Barclayville [gry], 138
Bard, *alt.* Bardi [bcj], 568
Bardangal, *dial.* Daju, Dar Daju [djc], 79
Bardeskari, *dial.* Konkani, Goanese [gom], 369
Bardi [bcj], 568
  dial. Bardi [bcj], 568
Bardiya, *dial.* Tharu, Dangaura [thl], 480

Basese, *dial.* Aka [axk], 87
Bashaka, *alt.* Bashkardi [bsg], 438
Bashaldo, *alt.* Romani, Carpathian [rmc], 533, 558
Bashamma, *alt.* Bacama [bcy], 154
Bashar, *alt.* Yangkam [bsx], 177
Basharawa, *alt.* Yangkam [bsx], 177
Bashgaadi, *dial.* Balochi, Southern [bcc], 482
Bashgali, *alt.* Kati [bsh], 316, 486
Bashgharik, *alt.* Kalami [gwc], 485
Bashilele, *alt.* Lele [lel], 102
Bashiri, *alt.* Yangkam [bsx], 177
Bashkardi [bsg], 438
Bashkarik, *alt.* Kalami [gwc], 485
Bashkir [bak], 553
Bashkort, *alt.* Bashkir [bak], 553
Basho, *dial.* Denya [anv], 60
Bashua, *alt. dial.* Bokyi [bky], 156
Basic Zulu, *alt.* Fanagalo [fng], 185, 213
Basila, *alt.* Anii [blo], 42, 207
Basilaki, *alt. dial.* Tawala [tbo], 627
Basili, *alt.* Sere [swf], 107
Basilicatan, *alt. dial.* Napoletano-Calabrese [nap], 545
Basima, *alt. dial.* Galeya [gar], 599
Basing, *alt.* Moken [mwt], 466, 516
Basinyari, *dial.* Nuni, Southern [nnw], 53
Basiq, *dial.* Romblomanon [rol], 500
Basiri, *alt.* Sere [swf], 107
Baskatta, *alt.* Basketo [bst], 113
Basketo [bst], 113
Basketto, *alt.* Basketo [bst], 113
Baso, *pej. alt.* Abinomn [bsa], 410
Basoo, *alt.* Bakoko [bkh], 57
Basoo Ba Die, *alt. dial.* Bakoko [bkh], 57
Basoo Ba Likol, *alt. dial.* Bakoko [bkh], 57
Basoo D'edea, *alt. dial.* Bakoko [bkh], 57
Basosi, *alt.* Bassossi [bsi], 58
Basossi, *alt.* Bassossi [bsi], 58
Basque [eus], 559
Basque Calo, *dial.* Caló [rmr], 559, 536, 551
Basque, Navarro-Labourdin [bqe], 535
Basque, Souletin [bsz], 536
Basquort, *alt.* Bashkir [bak], 553
Basria, *alt.* Bauria [bge], 355
Bassa [bsq], 137, 183
  alt. Basaa [bas], 58
  alt. dial. Ngwo [ngn], 70
Bassa Nge, *alt. dial.* Nupe-Nupe-Tako [nup], 171
Bassa-Kaduna, *alt.* Basa-Gumna [bsl], 155

Bassa-Komo, *pej. alt.* Basa [bzw], 154
Bassa-Kontagora [bsr], 155
Bassa-Kwomu, *pej. alt.* Basa [bzw], 154
Bassan, *alt. dial.* Izon [ijc], 164
Bassar, *alt.* Ntcham [bud], 209, 127
Bassari [bsc], 180, 129, 131
  alt. Ntcham [bud], 209, 127
Bassein, *dial.* Karen, Pwo Western [pwo], 464
Bassein Pwo Karen, *alt.* Karen, Pwo Western [pwo], 464
Basseri, *dial.* Farsi, Western [pes], 439
Bassila, *alt.* Anii [blo], 42, 207
Bassing, *alt. dial.* Ngombale [nla], 70
Basso, *alt. dial.* Bakoko [bkh], 57
  alt. dial. Ngombale [nla], 70
  dial. Basaa [bas], 58
Basso Piemontese, *alt. dial.* Piemontese [pms], 545
Bassossi [bsi], 58
Bastari, *alt.* Halbi [hlb], 363
  dial. Halbi [hlb], 363
Basti, *alt. dial.* Bhojpuri [bho], 356
Bastia, *alt. dial.* Corsican [cos], 536
Basturia, *alt.* Bhatri [bgw], 356
Basua, *dial.* Bokyi [bky], 156, 59
Basurudo, *dial.* Epena [sja], 251, 283
Basurudó, *dial.* Epena [sja], 245
Baswo, *alt. dial.* Bokyi [bky], 156
Bat, *alt.* Bada [bau], 154
Bata [bta], 155, 58
Bata-Ndeewe, *alt. dial.* Bata [bta], 58
Bataan, *dial.* Tagalog [tgl], 502
Bataan Ayta, *see* Ayta, Bataan [ayt], 492
Bataan Ayta, *alt.* Ayta, Bataan [ayt], 492
Bataan Sambal, *alt.* Ayta, Bataan [ayt], 492
Batad, *alt.* Ifugao, Batad [ifb], 495
Batad Ifugao, *see* Ifugao, Batad [ifb], 495
Batad Ifugao, *dial.* Ifugao, Batad [ifb], 495
Batadji, *alt.* Beba [bfp], 58
Batahari, *alt.* Bathari [bhm], 482
Batak [bya], 492
Batak Alas-Kluet [btz], 435
Batak Angkola [akb], 435
Batak Dairi [btd], 435
Batak Karo [btx], 435
Batak Mandailing [btm], 435
Batak Simalungun [bts], 435
Batak Toba [bbc], 435

Batang, *alt. dial.* Tibetan [bod], 388
Batang Lupar, *dial.* Iban [iba], 459, 324, 393
Batanga [bnm], 110, 58
  alt. dial. Oroko [bdu], 71
  dial. Batanga [bnm], 58
  dial. Caka [ckx], 59
Batangan, *alt.* Buhid [bku], 493
  alt. Tawbuid, Eastern [bnj], 502
Batangan Taubuid, *alt.* Tawbuid, Western [twb], 502
Batangas, *dial.* Tagalog [tgl], 502
Batanta Island, *dial.* Ma'ya [slz], 420
Batavi, *alt.* Betawi [bew], 391
Batawi, *alt.* Betawi [bew], 391
Bataxan, *alt. dial.* Daur [dta], 331, 461
Batcham, *dial.* Ngiemboon [nnh], 69
Batchenga, *alt.* Tuki [bag], 72
Bateg, *alt.* Batek [btq], 454
Batek [btq], 454
Batek De', *dial.* Batek [btq], 454
Batek Iga, *dial.* Batek [btq], 454
Batek Nong, *alt. dial.* Batek [btq], 454
Batek Teh, *dial.* Jehai [jhi], 454
Batek Teq, *dial.* Batek [btq], 454
Batem-Da-Kai-Ee, *alt.* Kato [ktw], 303
Bateq, *alt.* Batek [btq], 454
Batera Kohistani, *alt.* Bateri [btv], 483
Baterawal, *alt.* Bateri [btv], 483
Baterawal Kohistani, *alt.* Bateri [btv], 483
Bateri [btv], 483, 355
Bateri Kohistani, *alt.* Bateri [btv], 483
Batha, *alt.* Lendu [led], 102
  dial. Arabic, Chadian Spoken [shu], 78
Bathara, *alt.* Bathari [bhm], 528, 482
Bathari [bhm], 528, 482
Bathi, *dial.* Panjabi, Eastern [pan], 383
Bati (Cameroon) [btc], 58
  Bati (Indonesia) [bvt], 396
  alt. dial. Bwa [bww], 99
  alt. dial. Mungaka [mhk], 68
Bati Ba Ngong, *alt.* Bati [btc], 58
Bati de Brousse, *alt.* Bati [btc], 58
Batibo, *alt.* Meta' [mgo], 67
  alt. dial. Meta' [mgo], 67
Baticola, *dial.* Guaraní, Mbyá [gun], 227
Batie, *alt.* Ghomálá' [bbj], 62
Batin, *alt. dial.* Malay, Jambi [jax], 436

alt. Ngbandi, Northern [ngb], 105
Bazaar Malay, *alt.* Malay, Sabah [msi], 457
alt. dial. Malay [mly], 455, 436
Bazen, *alt.* Kunama [kun], 112
Bazenda, *alt.* Zande [zne], 109
Bazezuru, *alt. dial.* Shona [sna], 216
Bazhi, *alt.* Beba [bfp], 58
Bazigar [bfr], 355
Bazuzura, *alt. dial.* Shona [sna], 216
Bazza, *alt. dial.* Kamwe [hig], 166
Bbadha, *alt.* Lendu [led], 102
Bbaledha, *alt.* Lendu [led], 102
Bbate, *dial.* Mbay [myb], 84
Be, *alt.* Deno [dbb], 157
dial. Éwé [ewe], 207
Bê, *alt.* Lingao [onb], 338
Be:da, *dial.* Arabic, Judeo-Yemeni [jye], 444, 528
Bea, *alt.* Aka-Bea [abj], 353
alt. Mambila, Cameroon [mcu], 66
Beada, *alt.* Aka-Bea [abj], 353
Beafada, *alt.* Biafada [bif], 131
Beami [beo], 593
Bearlake, *dial.* Slavey, North [scs], 241
Béarnais, *dial.* Gascon [gsc], 537
Beaufort, *dial.* Dusun, Central [dtp], 456
Beaufort Murut, *dial.* Timugon Murut [tih], 458
Beaver [bea], 235
Beba [bfp], 58
Beba', *alt.* Beba [bfp], 58
Beba-Befang, *alt.* Befang [bby], 58
alt. dial. Befang [bby], 58
Bebadji, *alt.* Beba [bfp], 58
Bebaroe, *alt.* Yamba [yam], 73
Bebayaga, *alt.* Baka [bkc], 56
Bebayaka, *alt.* Baka [bkc], 56
Bebe [bzv], 58
Bebebele li, *dial.* Bwaidoka [bwd], 596
Bebele [beb], 58
Bebeli [bek], 593
Bebende, *alt. dial.* Makaa [mcp], 65
Bebent, *dial.* Makaa [mcp], 65
Bebi, *dial.* Obanliku [bzy], 172
Bebil [bxp], 58
Bébote, *dial.* Bedjond [bjv], 79
Bechati, *dial.* Mundani [mnf], 68
Bechere, *alt.* Iceve-Maci [bec], 63
alt. dial. Iceve-Maci [bec], 163
Becheve, *alt.* Iceve-Maci [bec], 63
alt. dial. Iceve-Maci [bec], 163
Bechitin, *alt.* Bezhta [kap], 553
Beda, *alt.* Veddah [ved], 510
Bedamini, *alt.* Beami [beo], 593
Bedamuni, *alt.* Beami [beo], 593
Bedanga, *dial.* Sokoro [sok], 86

Bedauye, *alt.* Bedawi [bej], 188, 112
Bedawi [bej], 188, 112
alt. Arabic, Eastern Egyptian Bedawi Spoken [avl], 110
alt. Arabic, Gulf Spoken [afb], 482
alt. Arabic, Levantine Bedawi Spoken [avl], 448, 489, 510
alt. Arabic, Najdi Spoken [ars], 510
alt. Arabic, South Levantine Spoken [ajp], 490
alt. Arabic, Western Egyptian Bedawi Spoken [ayl], 110
Bedàwie, *alt.* Bedawi [bej], 112
Bedawiye, *alt.* Bedawi [bej], 188, 112
Bedawye, *alt.* Bedawi [bej], 112
Bedda, *alt.* Veddah [ved], 510
Bedde, *alt.* Bade [bde], 154
Bede, *alt.* Bade [bde], 154
dial. Yeskwa [yes], 178
Bédégué, *dial.* Mbay [myb], 84
Bedere, *alt.* Adele [ade], 206
Bedfola, *alt.* Biafada [bif], 131
Bedia, *alt.* Kudmali [kyw], 370
alt. Panchpargania [tdb], 382
Bedik, *alt.* Budik [tnr], 180
Bediondo, *alt.* Bedjond [bjv], 79
Bediondo Mbai, *alt.* Bedjond [bjv], 79
Bedja, *alt.* Bedawi [bej], 188, 112
Bedjond [bjv], 79
dial. Bedjond [bjv], 79
Bédjonde, *alt.* Bedjond [bjv], 79
Bedjondo, *alt.* Bedjond [bjv], 79
Bédjou, *dial.* Mbay [myb], 84
Bedoanas [bed], 412
Beduanda, *dial.* Temuan [tmw], 455
Beduba, *alt.* Iresim [ire], 415
Bedwi, *alt.* Bedawi [bej], 112
Bedya, *alt.* Bedawi [bej], 112
Beege, *dial.* Musgu [mug], 68, 85
Beeke [bkf], 97
Beekuru, *alt. dial.* Befang [bby], 58
Beele [bxq], 155
Beembe [beq], 88
alt. Bembe [bmb], 97, 197
Beer, *alt. dial.* Dinka, Northeastern [dip], 189
Beetjuans, *alt.* Tswana [tsn], 48, 186, 217
Beezen [bnz], 58
Befang [bby], 58
dial. Befang [bby], 58
Befe, *alt.* Bafut [bfd], 56
Befi, *alt.* Kenswei Nsei [ndb], 64
Befon, *alt. dial.* Nde-Nsele-Nta [ndd], 170
Befun, *alt.* Abanyom [abm], 152
Bega, *alt.* Gumuz [guk], 115
alt. dial. Chhattisgarhi [hne], 358
Bega-Tse, *alt.* Gumuz [guk], 115

Begahak, *alt. dial.* Ida'an [dbj], 456
Begak, *dial.* Ida'an [dbj], 456
Begasin, *alt.* Girawa [bbr], 600
Begbere-Ejar [bqv], 155
Begbungba, *alt.* Bakpinka [bbs], 154
Bege, *alt.* Njalgulgule [njl], 194
Begesin, *alt.* Girawa [bbr], 600
Begi, *alt.* Njalgulgule [njl], 194
Begi-Mao, *alt.* Hozo [hoz], 115
Begi-Nibum, *alt. dial.* Yambeta [yat], 73
Beginci, *dial.* Semandang [sdm], 395
Bego, *alt.* Baygo [byg], 188
Begua, *alt. dial.* Zimakani [zik], 634
Behdini, *alt.* Kurdish, Northern [kmr], 443
Behe, *dial.* Dayak, Land [dyk], 393
Behere, *dial.* Koi [kkt], 473
Beheve, *alt. dial.* Iceve-Maci [bec], 163
Behie, *alt.* Nugunu [yas], 70
Behli, *alt.* Beli [blm], 189
Behoa, *alt.* Besoa [bep], 428
Behran, *alt.* Thayore [thd], 576
Beiço de Pau, *dial.* Suyá [suy], 232
Beifang Fangyan, *alt.* Chinese, Mandarin [cmn], 329
Beigo, *alt.* Baygo [byg], 188
Beik, *alt. dial.* Burmese [mya], 462
Beili, *alt.* Beli [blm], 189
Beilla, *dial.* Komo [xom], 192
Beir, *alt.* Murle [mur], 193, 117
Beira, *dial.* Portuguese [por], 551
Beirut, *dial.* Domari [rmt], 510
Beja, *alt.* Bedawi [bej], 188, 112
Bejamse, *alt. dial.* Chumburung [ncu], 124
Bejwan, *alt.* Bajelani [bjm], 443
Bek, *alt. dial.* Vatrata [vlr], 646
Beka, *alt.* Aka [axk], 87
dial. Yaka [axk], 78
Beká, *alt.* Yaka [axk], 78
Bekati' [bei], 392
Beke, *alt.* Beeke [bkf], 97
alt. Daju, Dar Fur [daj], 189
alt. Nugunu [yas], 70
Bekeni, *dial.* Bali [bcp], 96
Beketan, *alt.* Bukitan [bkn], 392, 459
Bekiau, *alt.* Bisaya, Brunei [bsb], 324
alt. Bisaya, Sarawak [bsd], 459
Beko, *alt.* Baygo [byg], 188
alt. Njalgulgule [njl], 194
Bekoe, *alt.* Gyele [gyi], 62, 111
Bekol, *alt.* Kol [biw], 64
Bekombo, *alt. dial.* Oroko [bdu], 71
Bekoose, *alt.* Akoose [bss], 56
Bekpak, *alt.* Bafia [ksf], 56
Bekunde, *alt. dial.* Oroko [bdu], 71

Bekwa', *alt. dial.* Kwa' [bko], 65
Bekwarra [bkv], 155
Bekwel, *alt.* Bekwil [bkw], 88, 58, 120
Bekwie, *alt.* Bekwil [bkw], 120
Bekwil [bkw], 88, 58, 120
Bekwiri, *alt.* Mokpwe [bri], 68
Bekworra, *alt.* Bekwarra [bkv], 155
Bekye, *dial.* Dwang [nnu], 120
Bel, *alt.* Gedaged [gdd], 599
Bela, *alt.* Pela [bxd], 342
    alt. dial. Pamona [bcx], 432
Belagar, *alt.* Blagar [beu], 406
Belait [beg], 324
Belala, *alt. dial.* Pamona [bcx], 432
Belana, *alt. dial.* Temuan [tmw], 455
Belanas, *alt. dial.* Temuan [tmw], 455
Belana'u, *alt.* Melanau [mel], 460, 325
Belanda, *alt.* Belanda Viri [bvi], 189
    dial. Temuan [tmw], 455
Belanda Bor [bxb], 188
Belanda Viri [bvi], 189
Belandas, *alt. dial.* Temuan [tmw], 455
Belani, *alt.* Lohar, Gade [gda], 372
Belante, *alt.* Balanta-Ganja [bjt], 179
    alt. Balanta-Kentohe [ble], 130
Belantikan, *dial.* Malayic Dayak [xdy], 394
Belarusan [bel], 530, 550
Belarusian, *alt.* Belarusan [bel], 530
Belauan, *alt.* Palauan [pau], 587
Belayan, *dial.* Kayan, Busang [bfg], 393
Bele, *alt.* Beele [bxq], 155
    dial. Fali, South [fal], 61
Belebele, *dial.* Iduna [viv], 602
Belebele I, *dial.* Bwaidoka [bwd], 596
Beledugu, *dial.* Bamanankan [bam], 141
Belegete, *alt.* Evant [bzz], 159, 61
Belen, *alt.* Bilen [byn], 112
Beleni, *alt.* Bilen [byn], 112
Belep, *dial.* Nyâlayu [yly], 585
Belepa, *alt.* Keuru [xeu], 606
Belfast, *dial.* English [eng], 565
Belgian Picard, *dial.* Picard [pcd], 531
Belgian Sign Language [bvs], 530
Belhare, *alt.* Belhariya [byw], 469
Belhariya [byw], 469
'Beli, *alt.* Beli [blm], 189
Beli (Papua New Guinea) [bey], 593
    Beli (Sudan) [blm], 189
    alt. Bebeli [bek], 593
Belibi, *alt.* Elip [ekm], 60

Belide, *dial.* Malay [mly], 436
Belip, *alt.* Elip [ekm], 60
Belitung, *dial.* Malay [mly], 436
Belize Kriol English [bzj], 221
Bella Bella, *dial.* Heiltsuk [hei], 238
Bella Coola [blc], 235
Bellari [brw], 355
Bellawa, *alt.* Beele [bxq], 155
Belle, *alt.* Kuwaa [blh], 138
Belleh, *alt.* Kuwaa [blh], 138
Bellona, *alt. dial.* Rennell-Belona [mnv], 638
Bellonese, *alt. dial.* Rennell-Belona [mnv], 638
Belo, *alt.* Tetun [tet], 410, 351
Beloh, *alt. dial.* Lawangan [lbx], 394
Belom, *alt.* Lom [mfb], 436
Belorussian, *alt.* Belarusan [bel], 530
Belsetán, *alt. dial.* Aragonese [arg], 558
Beltir, *dial.* Khakas [kjh], 505, 337
Belu, *alt.* Tetun [tet], 410, 351
Belu Selatan, *alt. dial.* Tetun [tet], 410, 351
Belu Utara, *alt. dial.* Tetun [tet], 410, 351
Belubaa, *alt.* Bilba [bpz], 406
Belubn, *alt.* Kensiu [kns], 515
Beludji, *dial.* Domari [rmt], 563
Bemal, *alt.* Kein [bmh], 605
Bemar, *alt. dial.* Ngambay [sba], 85
Bemba (Democratic Republic of Congo) [bmy], 97
    Bemba (Zambia) [bem], 213, 97
Bembala, *alt.* Burji [bji], 114
Bembe [bmb], 97, 197
    alt. Beembe [beq], 88
    dial. Mabaale [mmz], 103
Bembi, *alt.* Fas [fqs], 598
    alt. Pagi [pgi], 621
Bemili, *dial.* Bali [bcp], 96
Bemina, *alt. dial.* Makaa [mcp], 65
Bémour, *dial.* Laka [lap], 83
Ben, *alt.* Beng [nhb], 92
    alt. Moba [mfq], 208, 52
Bena (Nigeria) [yun], 155
    Bena (Tanzania) [bez], 197
    alt. Benabena [bef], 593
    alt. Voro [vor], 177
Benaadir, *alt. dial.* Somali [som], 185
Benabena [bef], 593
Benaffarera, *alt. dial.* Basque, Navarro-Labourdin [bqe], 535
Benarsi, *alt. dial.* Bhojpuri [bho], 356
Benasqués, *alt. dial.* Aragonese [arg], 558
Benaule, *alt.* Bebeli [bek], 593

Benbakanjamata, *alt.* Adynyamathanha [adt], 567
Bench [bcq], 113
    dial. Bench [bcq], 113
Bencho, *alt. dial.* Bench [bcq], 113
Bencoolen, *alt.* Bengkulu [bke], 435
Bende [bdp], 197
    alt. Islander Creole English [icr], 246
Bendi [bct], 97
    dial. Bete-Bendi [btt], 155
    dial. Hlai [lic], 333
Bendi Lolo, *alt.* Qabiao [laq], 526
Bene, *dial.* Bulu [bum], 59
Benedictine Sign Language, *dial.* Monastic Sign Language [mzg], 566
Benehes, *dial.* Modang [mxd], 394
Beneraf, *alt.* Bonerif [bnv], 413
Benesho, *alt. dial.* Bench [bcq], 113
Beng [nhb], 92
Benga [bng], 110, 120
Bengali [ben], 320, 355, 469, 508
Bengali of Cachar, *alt.* Sylheti [syl], 388
Bengan, *alt.* Bogan [bgh], 328
Benge, *alt. dial.* Bwa [bww], 99
    dial. Bobo Madaré, Northern [bbo], 141
    dial. Bobo Madaré, Southern [bwq], 49
Benggaulu, *dial.* Uma [ppk], 434
Benggoi [bgy], 397
    dial. Benggoi [bgy], 397
Bengkulu [bke], 435
Bengni-Boga'er, *alt.* Luoba, Boga'er [adi], 339
Bengoi, *alt.* Benggoi [bgy], 397
Benguet-Igorot, *alt.* Ibaloi [ibl], 494
Beni Iznassen, *alt. dial.* Tarifit [rif], 146, 40
Beni Shangul, *alt.* Berta [wti], 113
    pej. alt. Berta [wti], 189
Beni Sheko, *dial.* Kelo [xel], 192
Beni Snassen, *alt. dial.* Tarifit [rif], 146
Beni-Amir, *dial.* Bedawi [bej], 188, 112
Benin, *alt.* Edo [bin], 158
Benin Pidgin, *dial.* Pidgin, Nigerian [pcm], 173
Benin-Togo Fulfulde, *see* Fulfulde, Borgu [fue], 160
Benin-Togo Fulfulde, *alt.* Fulfulde, Borgu [fue], 44, 207
Benkonjo, *alt.* Ukhwejo [ukh], 78
Benkulan, *alt.* Bengkulu [bke], 435
Benoye, *dial.* Ngambay [sba], 85
Bentenan, *alt.* Ratahan [rth], 432

Bentian, *alt. dial.* Lawangan [lbx], 394
Bentoeni, *alt.* Wandamen [wad], 425
Bentong [bnu], 428
Bentuni, *alt.* Wandamen [wad], 425
Benua, *alt.* Temuan [tmw], 455
  dial. Lawangan [lbx], 394
Benyadu' [byd], 392
Benyi, *alt.* Mmaala [mmu], 67
Benza, *dial.* Ligenza [lgz], 102
Benzing, *alt.* Mengaka [xmg], 67
Beo, *alt. dial.* Talaud [tld], 433
  dial. Ngelima [agh], 106
Béogé, *alt.* Baygo [byg], 188
Beothuc, *alt.* Beothuk [bue], 235
Beothuk [bue], 235
Bepour [bie], 593
Beqaa Arabic, *dial.* Arabic, North Levantine Spoken [apc], 453
Bera [brf], 97
  dial. Kako [kkj], 63
Berad, *dial.* Telugu [tel], 388
Berakou [bxv], 79
Berang, *alt.* Gugubera [kkp], 571
  dial. Dayak, Land [dyk], 393
Berar Marathi, *alt.* Varhadi-Nagpuri [vah], 389
Berari, *alt.* Varhadi-Nagpuri [vah], 389
Berau, *alt.* Malay, Berau [bve], 394
  dial. Basap [bdb], 392
Berau Malay, *see* Malay, Berau [bve], 394
Beraur, *alt.* Kalabra [kzz], 416
Berawan [lod], 459
Berba, *alt.* Baatonum [bba], 42, 154
  alt. Biali [beh], 42, 49
Berberi, *alt.* Aimaq [aiq], 315
Berbice Creole Dutch [brc], 257
Berbou, *dial.* Tso [ldp], 176
Berdama, *alt.* Nama [naq], 150, 48, 186
Bere, *alt.* Mbre [mka], 94
  alt. dial. Mbula-Bwazza [mbu], 170
Beregadougou-Toumousseni, *dial.* Turka [tuz], 55
Berembun, *dial.* Temuan [tmw], 455
Berens River Ojibwa, *dial.* Ojibwa, Northwestern [ojb], 240
Bereya, *dial.* Banda-Banda [bpd], 75
Bergamasco, *alt. dial.* Lombard [lmo], 544
Bergdamara, *alt.* Nama [naq], 150, 48, 186
Bergit, *alt.* Birgit [btf], 79
Bergotés, *alt. dial.* Aragonese [arg], 558
Berguid, *alt.* Birgit [btf], 79
Beri, *alt.* Bari [bfa], 188, 210
  alt. Chewong [cwg], 454
  alt. Zaghawa [zag], 196, 87

Beri-Aa, *alt.* Zaghawa [zag], 196, 87
Beria, *alt.* Zaghawa [zag], 87
  alt. dial. Zaghawa [zag], 87
Beriberi, *alt.* Kanuri, Central [knc], 166
  pej. alt. Kanuri, Central [knc], 63, 81, 152, 191
Berick, *alt.* Berik [bkl], 412
Berik [bkl], 412
Berin, *alt.* Jumjum [jum], 191
Bering, *alt. dial.* Aleut [ale], 495
Bering Strait Inupiatun, *alt. dial.* Inupiatun, Northwest Alaska [esk], 302
Bering Strait Yupik, *alt.* Yupik, Central Siberian [ess], 310, 507
Beringov, *dial.* Aleut [ale], 495
Berinomo [bit], 593
Berka, *alt. dial.* Kunama [kun], 112
Bermejo Vejoz, *dial.* Wichí Lhamtés Vejoz [wlv], 220
Bermudan English, *dial.* English [eng], 222
Bern, *dial.* Schwyzerdütsch [gsw], 563
Bernde [bdo], 79
Bero, *alt.* Owiniga [owi], 620
  dial. Mesme [zim], 84
Berom [bom], 155
Berrembeel, *alt.* Wiradhuri [wrh], 578
Berri, *alt.* Zaghawa [zag], 196, 87
Berrichon, *dial.* French [fra], 536
Berrik, *alt.* Berik [bkl], 412
Berringen, *alt.* Marithiel [mfr], 574
Berta [wti], 113, 189
Bertha, *alt.* Berta [wti], 113
Berti [byt], 189
Berum, *alt.* Berom [bom], 155
Besali, *dial.* Mundani [mnf], 68
Besaya, *alt.* Bisaya, Brunei [bsb], 324
  alt. Bisaya, Sabah [bsy], 456
Beseki, *alt.* Seki [syi], 111
Besema, *alt.* Bacama [bcy], 154
Besemah, *alt.* Pasemah [pse], 437
Besembo, *dial.* Kako [kkj], 63
Beseme, *alt.* Besme [bes], 79
Besemme, *alt.* Besme [bes], 79
Besep, *alt. dial.* Byep [mkk], 59
Besermyan, *alt. dial.* Udmurt [udm], 557
Besha, *alt. dial.* Byep [mkk], 59
Beshada, *alt.* Hamer-Banna [amf], 115
Besi, *alt.* Pasi [psq], 621
  alt. dial. Meta' [mgo], 67
Besisi [mhe], 454
Beslenei, *alt.* Kabardian [kbd], 554
  alt. dial. Kabardian [kbd], 554

Beslenej, *alt. dial.* Kabardian [kbd], 554
Besleri, *alt.* Mina [hna], 67
  dial. Mina [hna], 67
Besme [bes], 79
Besoa [bep], 428
Beta, *dial.* Dayak, Land [dyk], 393
Betaf [bfe], 412
Bétanure, *dial.* Lishana Deni [lsd], 445
Betau, *alt. dial.* Semai [sea], 455
Betawi [bew], 391
Betawi Malay, *alt.* Betawi [bew], 391
Betaya, *alt.* Tucano [tuo], 248
Bete [byf], 155
  alt. Bata [bta], 155
  alt. Biete [biu], 356
  dial. Bete-Bendi [btt], 155
Bété, Daloa [bev], 92
Bété, Gagnoa [btg], 92
Béte, Guiberoua [bet], 92
Bete-Bendi [btt], 155
Betef, *alt.* Itik [itx], 415
Beten, *dial.* Kwakum [kwu], 65
Bethel Yupik, *alt. dial.* Yupik, Central [esu], 310
Bethen, *alt. dial.* Kwakum [kwu], 65
Bethuck, *alt.* Beothuk [bue], 235
Bethuk, *alt.* Beothuk [bue], 235
Beti (Cameroon) [btb], 58
  Beti (Côte d'Ivoire) [eot], 92
  dial. Ewondo [ewo], 61
Betise', *dial.* Besisi [mhe], 454
Betisek, *alt. dial.* Besisi [mhe], 454
Betoya, *alt.* Tucano [tuo], 248
Betsileo, *dial.* Malagasy, Plateau [plt], 140
Betsinga, *alt.* Tuki [bag], 72
Betta Kurumba, *see* Kurumba, Betta [xub], 371
Betta Kurumba Nonstandard Tamil, *alt.* Kurumba, Betta [xub], 371
Bette, *alt. dial.* Bete-Bendi [btt], 155
Bette-Bendi, *alt.* Bete-Bendi [btt], 155
Betul, *dial.* Gondi, Northern [gno], 362
Betzinga, *alt.* Tuki [bag], 72
Beu, *dial.* Wè Southern [gxx], 95
Bevelands, *dial.* Zeeuws [zea], 549
Bewani, *alt. dial.* Pagi [pgi], 621
Bewil, *alt. dial.* Makaa [mcp], 65
Bexita, *alt.* Bezhta [kap], 553
Beygo, *alt.* Baygo [byg], 188
Beyidzolo, *dial.* Eton [eto], 61
Bezanozano, *dial.* Malagasy, Plateau [plt], 140

Bezhedukh, *dial.* Adyghe [ady], 552
Bezhehux-Temirgoi, *alt. dial.*
  Adyghe [ady], 552
Bezheta, *alt.* Bezhta [kap], 553
Bezhita, *alt.* Bezhta [kap], 553
Bezhta [kap], 553
  dial. Bezhta [kap], 553
Bezhti, *alt.* Bezhta [kap], 553
Bezshagh, *dial.* Abaza [abq], 552,
  518
Bghai Karen, *alt.* Karen, Bwe
  [bwe], 464
Bgu, *alt.* Bonggo [bpg], 413
Bhaca, *dial.* Xhosa [xho], 187
Bhadauri, *dial.* Bundeli [bns], 357
Bhaderbhai Jamu, *alt.*
  Bhadrawahi [bhd], 355
Bhaderwali Pahari, *alt.*
  Bhadrawahi [bhd], 355
Bhadrava, *alt.* Bhadrawahi [bhd], 355
Bhadrawahi [bhd], 355
Bhadri, *alt.* Bhadrawahi [bhd], 355
Bhagira, *dial.* Logo [log], 103
Bhagoria, *alt.* Bhili [bhb], 356
Bhaipei, *alt.* Vaiphei [vap], 389
Bhakha, *alt.* Kanauji [bjj], 366
Bhalay [bhx], 355
Bhalesi, *dial.* Bhadrawahi [bhd], 355
Bhalu, *dial.* Sampang [rav], 478
Bhamam, *alt.* Cham, Eastern
  [cjm], 522
Bhamani, *alt. dial.* Maria [mrr], 375
Bhamani Maria, *dial.* Maria
  [mrr], 375
Bhamragarh, *dial.* Gondi, Southern
  [ggo], 363
Bhandara, *dial.* Gondi, Northern
  [gno], 362
Bhandari, *dial.* Konkani [knn], 369
Bhar, *alt.* Bharia [bha], 355
Bharat, *alt.* Bharia [bha], 355
Bharia [bha], 355
Bharmauri, *dial.* Gaddi [gbk], 361
Bharmauri Bhadi, *alt.* Gaddi
  [gbk], 361
Bhatbali, *dial.* Dogri [dgo], 360
Bhateali, *alt.* Bhattiyali [bht], 356
Bhatia, *dial.* Sindhi [snd], 387
Bhatiali Pahari, *alt.* Bhattiyali
  [bht], 356
Bhatiari, *alt. dial.* Bengali [ben], 355
  dial. Bengali [ben], 469
Bhatiyali, *alt.* Bhattiyali [bht], 356
Bhatneri, *alt. dial.* Panjabi, Eastern
  [pan], 383
Bhatola [btl], 355
Bhatra, *alt.* Bhatri [bgw], 356
Bhatri [bgw], 356
Bhatti, *alt. dial.* Panjabi, Eastern
  [pan], 383

Bhattiani, *dial.* Garhwali
  [gbm], 360
Bhattiyali [bht], 356
Bhattra, *alt.* Bhatri [bgw], 356
Bhattri, *alt.* Bhatri [bgw], 356
Bhatyiana, *dial.* Panjabi, Eastern
  [pan], 383
Bhawalpuri, *alt. dial.* Seraiki
  [skr], 386
Bhawnagari, *alt. dial.* Gujarati
  [guj], 363
Bhaya [bhe], 484
Bhele [bhy], 98
Bhiét, *alt. dial.* Mnong, Central
  [cmo], 525
Bhil, *alt.* Bhili [bhb], 356
Bhilala, *alt.* Bhilali [bhi], 356
Bhilali [bhi], 356
Bhilbari, *alt.* Bhili [bhb], 356
Bhilboli, *alt.* Bhili [bhb], 356
Bhili [bhb], 356
  alt. Wagdi [wbr], 390
Bhilki, *alt.* Sansi [ssi], 386, 488
Bhilla, *alt.* Bhili [bhb], 356
Bhilodi, *alt.* Bhili [bhb], 356
  alt. Wagdi [wbr], 390
  dial. Bhili [bhb], 356
Bhilori, *alt.* Noiri [noi], 381
Bhim, *dial.* Bhili [bhb], 356
Bhoi-Khasi, *dial.* Khasi [kha], 367
Bhojapuri, *alt.* Bhojpuri [bho], 356,
  469
Bhojpuri [bho], 356, 145, 469
Bhojpuri Tharu, *dial.* Bhojpuri
  [bho], 469
Bhokha, *alt.* Tibetan [bod], 324
Bhomiyari, *alt. dial.* Powari
  [pwr], 384
Bhonda Bhasha, *alt.* Bondo
  [bfw], 357
Bhoo, *dial.* Yaouré [yre], 96
Bhoria, *alt.* Bauria [bge], 355
Bhotea of Upper Kinnauri, *alt.*
  Kinnauri, Bhoti [nes], 368
Bhoti Gurung, *alt. dial.* Lowa
  [loy], 474
Bhoti Kinnauri, *see* Kinnauri, Bhoti
  [nes], 368
Bhoti of Baltistan, *alt.* Balti
  [bft], 355
Bhotia, *alt.* Byangsi [bee], 358
  alt. Jad [jda], 365
  alt. Tibetan [bod], 388, 481
  alt. Tibetan, Central [bod], 344
Bhotia of Baltistan, *alt.* Balti
  [bft], 483
Bhotia of Bhutan, *alt.* Dzongkha
  [dzo], 323, 471
Bhotia of Dukpa, *alt.* Dzongkha
  [dzo], 323

Bhotia of Lahul, *alt.* Tinani
  [lbf], 345
Bhottada, *alt.* Bhatri [bgw], 356
Bhottara, *alt.* Bhatri [bgw], 356
Bhotte, *alt.* Ghale, Kutang [ght], 471
Bhoyar Powari, *dial.* Powari
  [pwr], 384
Bhoyari, *alt. dial.* Malvi [mup], 374
  alt. dial. Powari [pwr], 384
Bhoyaroo, *alt. dial.* Powari
  [pwr], 384
Bhozpuri, *alt.* Bhojpuri [bho], 356,
  469
Bhramu, *alt.* Baraamu [brd], 468
Bhuani, *dial.* Nimadi [noe], 381
Bhubaliya Lohar, *alt.* Lohar, Gade
  [gda], 372
Bhubhi, *alt.* Bubi [buw], 120
Bhugelkhud, *alt.* Bagheli [bfy], 354,
  468
Bhuiyar, *alt. dial.* Powari [pwr], 384
Bhujel Kham, *dial.* Parbate, Eastern
  [kif], 477
Bhuksa, *dial.* Braj Bhasha [bra], 357
Bhulia, *dial.* Chhattisgarhi [hne], 358
Bhulla, *alt.* Rawat [jnl], 385
Bhumia, *alt.* Bharia [bha], 355
  alt. dial. Chhattisgarhi [hne], 358
Bhumij, *alt. dial.* Mundari [muw],
  376
Bhumij Munda, *alt. dial.* Mundari
  [muw], 376
Bhumij Thar, *alt. dial.* Mundari
  [muw], 376
Bhumiya, *alt.* Bharia [bha], 355
Bhumjiya, *alt.* Bhunjia [bhu], 356
Bhumtam, *alt.* Bumthangkha [kjz],
  323
Bhunjia [bhu], 356
  dial. Halbi [hlb], 363
Bhunjiya, *alt.* Bhunjia [bhu], 356
Bhuria, *alt. dial.* Powari [pwr], 384
Bhutanese, *alt.* Dzongkha
  [dzo], 323, 471
Bi-Gimu, *alt.* Jimi [jmi], 165
Bia, *alt.* Guhu-Samane [ghs], 599
  alt. Yuqui [yuq], 224
Biabo, *dial.* Grebo, Gbaloo [gec], 138
Biada, *alt.* Aka-Bea [abj], 353
Biadju, *alt.* Ngaju [nij], 394
Biafada [bif], 131
Biafar, *alt.* Biafada [bif], 131
Biai, *dial.* Krahn, Western [krw], 138,
  93
Biak [bhw], 412
Biak-Numfor, *alt.* Biak [bhw], 412
Biaka, *alt.* Nai [bio], 616
Biakpan, *dial.* Ubaghara [byc], 176
Biaksi, *alt.* Yetfa [yet], 426, 633
Biali [beh], 42, 49

Biami, *alt.* Piame [pin], 621
Bian, *alt.* Marind, Bian [bpv], 419
Bian Marind, *see* Marind, Bian [bpv], 419
Bianda, *alt. dial.* Gbaya, Southwest [mdo], 76
Biangai [big], 593
Biangwala, *dial.* Lamma [lev], 408
Bianjiida, *dial.* Datooga [tcc], 198
Biao [byk], 327
Biao Chao, *alt.* Biao-Jiao Mien [bje], 327
Biao Mien, *alt.* Biao Mon [bmt], 327
  alt. dial. Biao-Jiao Mien [bje], 327
Biao Min, *dial.* Biao-Jiao Mien [bje], 327
Biao Mon [bmt], 327
  dial. Biao Mon [bmt], 327
Biao-Jiao Mien [bje], 327
Biaoman, *alt.* Biao Mon [bmt], 327
Biaomin, *alt. dial.* Biao-Jiao Mien [bje], 327
Biapim, *alt.* Wasembo [gsp], 631
Biarnese, *alt. dial.* Gascon [gsc], 537
Biaru-Waria, *dial.* Weri [wer], 632
Biat, *dial.* Mnong, Central [cmo], 525, 326
Biatah [bth], 459, 392
Biate, *alt.* Biete [biu], 356
Biba, *alt.* Beba [bfp], 58
Biba-Bifang, *alt.* Befang [bby], 58
Bibaali, *alt.* Bali [bcn], 154
Bibaya, *alt.* Baka [bkc], 56
Bibeng, *dial.* Basaa [bas], 58
Bibling, *alt.* Amara [aie], 589
Bibo, *alt. dial.* Gobasi [goi], 600
Biboki, *alt. dial.* Uab Meto [aoz], 410
Biboki-Insana, *dial.* Uab Meto [aoz], 410
Bibot, *alt. dial.* Zari [zaz], 178
Bicek, *alt.* Basaa [bas], 58
Bichelamar, *alt.* Bislama [bis], 641, 584
Bicolano, Albay [bhk], 493
Bicolano, Central [bcl], 493
Bicolano, Iriga [bto], 493
Bicolano, Northern Catanduanes [cts], 493
Bicolano, Southern Catanduanes [bln], 493
Bicoli, *alt.* Maba [mqa], 401
Bida, *alt. dial.* Ngemba [nge], 69
Bida-Bida, *alt.* Pitta Pitta [pit], 576
Bidayah, *alt. dial.* Bukar Sadong [sdo], 459, 392
Bidayuh, *alt. dial.* Bukar Sadong [sdo], 459, 392
Bïde, *alt.* Araweté [awt], 225
Bideyat, *alt. dial.* Zaghawa [zag], 196, 87

Bideyu, *alt.* Biatah [bth], 392
  alt. dial. Bukar Sadong [sdo], 459
Bidhabidha, *alt.* Pitta Pitta [pit], 576
Bidikili, *alt. dial.* Gbanu [gbv], 75
'Bidio, *alt.* Bidiyo [bid], 79
Bidio, *alt.* Bidiyo [bid], 79
Bidire, *alt.* Adele [ade], 206, 122
Bidiya, *alt.* Bidiyo [bid], 79
'Bidiyo, *alt.* Bidiyo [bid], 79
Bidiyo [bid], 79
Bidiyo-Waana, *alt.* Bidiyo [bid], 79
Bidjara, *alt.* Bidyara [bym], 569
  dial. Ngura [nbx], 575
Bidjir, *dial.* Kenga [kyq], 82
Bidjouki, *alt. dial.* Mpiemo [mcx], 77, 68
  alt. dial. Mpyemo [mcx], 89
Bidjuki, *dial.* Mpiemo [mcx], 77, 68
  dial. Mpyemo [mcx], 89
Bidor, *alt. dial.* Semai [sea], 455
Biduanda, *alt. dial.* Temuan [tmw], 455
Bidyara [bym], 569
Bidyo, *alt.* Bidiyo [bid], 79
Bidyogo [bjg], 131
Bidyola, *alt.* Biafada [bif], 131
Bielorussian, *alt.* Belarusan [bel], 530
Biem [bmc], 593
Bierebo [bnk], 641
Bieri, *alt.* Biali [beh], 42, 49
  alt. Bieria [brj], 641
Bieria [brj], 641
  dial. Bieria [brj], 641
Biete [biu], 356
Bifang, *alt.* Befang [bby], 58
  alt. dial. Befang [bby], 58
Big Bay, *alt.* Tolomako [tlm], 646
Big Bolgo, *alt. dial.* Bolgo [bvo], 79
Big Flowery Miao, *alt.* Hmong, Northeastern Dian [hmd], 334
Big Nambas, *see* Nambas, Big [nmb], 644
Big Sepik, *alt.* Iatmul [ian], 602
Big Woods French, *dial.* French, Cajun [frc], 300
Biga [bhc], 413
  alt. Sobei [sob], 423
Bigawguno, *dial.* Bidiyo [bid], 79
Bigola, *alt.* Badyara [pbp], 128, 130, 179
Bih, *dial.* Rade [rad], 526
Bihak, *dial.* Semandang [sdm], 395
Bihar Ho, *alt.* Ho [hoc], 364
Bihari, *alt.* Bhojpuri [bho], 356
  alt. Magahi [mag], 373
  alt. Maithili [mai], 373, 475
Bihi, *dial.* Ghale, Kutang [ght], 471
Bihor, *alt.* Birhor [biy], 356

Biira, *alt.* Fulfulde, Adamawa [fub], 61, 80
Biisa, *alt. dial.* Lala-Bisa [leb], 214
Biishah, *alt. dial.* Arabic, Najdi Spoken [ars], 508
Bijago, *alt.* Bidyogo [bjg], 131
Bijang Bai, *alt.* Bai, Northern [bfc], 327
Bijapur, *dial.* Kannada [kan], 366
Bijapuri, *dial.* Deccan [dcc], 360
Bijari, *alt. dial.* Kurdish, Southern [sdh], 440
Bijbhasha, *alt.* Braj Bhasha [bra], 357
Bijie, *dial.* Yi, Guizhou [yig], 347
Bijil, *dial.* Barzani Jewish Neo-Aramaic [bjf], 444
Bijil Neo-Aramaic, *alt.* Barzani Jewish Neo-Aramaic [bjf], 444
Bijilan, *dial.* Zauzou [zal], 349
Bijim, *dial.* Vaghat-Ya-Bijim-Legeri [bij], 177
Bijobe, *alt.* Miyobe [soy], 45, 208
Bijogo, *alt.* Bidyogo [bjg], 131
Bijori [bix], 356
Bijougot, *alt.* Bidyogo [bjg], 131
Bijuga, *alt.* Bidyogo [bjg], 131
Bik, *alt.* Judeo-Tat [jdt], 445, 319, 554
Bika, *dial.* Hani [hni], 333
Bikaka, *alt. dial.* Ukhwejo [ukh], 78
Bikaneri, *alt. dial.* Marwari [rwr], 375
Bikaru [bic], 593
  alt. dial. Bisorio [bir], 594
Bikele, *dial.* Kol [biw], 64
Bikele-Bikay, *alt.* Kol [biw], 64
Bikele-Bikeng, *alt.* Kol [biw], 64
Biken, *alt. dial.* Makaa [mcp], 65
Bikeng, *dial.* Kol [biw], 64
Bikin, *dial.* Udihe [ude], 507
Bikol, *alt.* Bicolano, Central [bcl], 493
Bikol Sorsogon, *alt.* Sorsogon, Waray [srv], 501
Bikom, *alt.* Kom [bkm], 64
Bikshi, *alt. dial.* Lorung, Northern [lbr], 474
Biksi, *alt.* Yetfa [yet], 426, 633
Biksit, *dial.* Lorung, Northern [lbr], 474
Bikuab, *alt.* Biatah [bth], 459
Bikya [byb], 58
Bikyek, *alt.* Basaa [bas], 58
Bil, *alt. dial.* Semai [sea], 455
Bila [bip], 98
  dial. Tsonga [tso], 149, 217
Bilaala, *alt. dial.* Naba [mne], 85
Bilaan, *alt.* Blaan, Sarangani [bps], 493
Biladaba, *alt.* Pirlatapa [bxi], 576

Bilakura [bql], 593
Bilala, *dial.* Naba [mne], 85
Bilanes, *alt.* Blaan, Koronadal
  [bpr], 493
Bilaspuri [kfs], 356
Bilaspuri Pahari, *alt.* Bilaspuri
  [kfs], 356
Bilayn, *alt.* Bilen [byn], 112
Bilba [bpz], 406
  dial. Bilba [bpz], 406
Bilbaa, *alt.* Bilba [bpz], 406
Bilbil [brz], 593
Bile [bil], 155
Bilein, *alt.* Bilen [byn], 112
Bileki, *dial.* Nakanai [nak], 616
Bilembo-Mango, *dial.* Lega-
  Mwenga [lgm], 102
Bilen [byn], 112
Bileno, *alt.* Bilen [byn], 112
Bili, *alt.* Bhele [bhy], 98
  alt. Bile [bil], 155
  dial. Mono [mnh], 104
Biliau, *alt.* Awad Bing [bcu], 591
  dial. Awad Bing [bcu], 591
Bilibil, *alt.* Bilbil [brz], 593
Bilichi, *dial.* Karen, Paku [kpp], 464
Bilin, *alt.* Bilen [byn], 112
Bilinara, *dial.* Ngarinman [nbj], 575
Biliri, *dial.* Tangale [tan], 175
Bilkire Fulani, *alt. dial.* Fulfulde,
  Adamawa [fub], 61, 80
Bilkiri, *alt. dial.* Fulfulde, Adamawa
  [fub], 61, 80
Billanchi, *alt.* Bile [bil], 155
Bille, *alt.* Bile [bil], 155
Bilma, *dial.* Kanuri, Bilma
  [bms], 152
Bilma Kanuri, *see* Kanuri, Bilma
  [bms], 152
Biloxi [bll], 298
Biltine, *alt.* Amdang [amj], 78
  alt. dial. Arabic, Chadian Spoken
  [shu], 78
Biltum, *alt.* Burushaski [bsk], 484
Bilua [blb], 635
Bilur [bxf], 593
Bim, *dial.* Bimin [bhl], 593
Bima [bhp], 406
  dial. Bima [bhp], 406
  dial. Oroko [bdu], 71
Bimanese, *alt.* Bima [bhp], 406
Bimbaan, *alt. dial.* Tringgus [trx],
  461
Bimbia, *alt.* Isu [szv], 63
Bime, *dial.* Ketengban [xte], 417
Bimin [bhl], 593
Bimoba [bim], 123
Bimu, *alt.* Mpiemo [mcx], 77, 68
  alt. Mpyemo [mcx], 89
Bina (Nigeria) [byj], 155

Bina (Papua New Guinea) [bmn], 593
Binadan, *alt.* Balangingi [sse], 456
Binahari [bxz], 593
Binamarir, *alt.* Binumarien [bjr], 593
Binandere [bhg], 593
  dial. Binandere [bhg], 593
Binari, *alt.* Baga Binari [bcg], 128
Binatang, *dial.* Basap [bdb], 392
Binatangan, *alt.* Tawbuid, Eastern
  [bnj], 502
Binawa, *alt.* Bina [byj], 155
Binbarnja, *alt.* Adynyamathanha
  [adt], 567
Binbinga, *dial.* Wambaya
  [wmb], 577
Binbinka, *alt. dial.* Wambaya
  [wmb], 577
  dial. Gudanji [nji], 571
Bindafum, *alt. dial.* Byep [mkk], 59
Binddibu, *alt.* Pintupi-Luritja
  [piu], 576
Bindi, *alt.* Ngiti [niy], 106
Bindji, *alt.* Binji [bpj], 98
Bine [bon], 593
Bing, *alt.* Awad Bing [bcu], 591
Binga, *alt.* Aka [axk], 87
  dial. Yulu [yul], 78, 109, 196
Bingird, *dial.* Kurdish, Central
  [ckb], 443
Bingkokak, *alt. dial.* Tolaki
  [lbw], 433
Bingkolu, *alt. dial.* Uma [ppk], 434
Bini, *alt.* Edo [bin], 158
  alt. Pini [pii], 576
  alt. dial. Yoruba [yor], 178
  dial. Anyin [any], 91
Binigura, *alt.* Pinigura [pnv], 576
Binisaya, *alt.* Cebuano [ceb], 493
  alt. Waray-Waray [war], 502
Binja, *alt.* Songoora [sod], 108
  dial. Ngombe [ngc], 106
  dial. Zimba [zmb], 109
Binjara, *alt.* Muluridyi [vmu], 574
Binjhia, *alt.* Bijori [bix], 356
Binjhwari, *dial.* Chhattisgarhi
  [hne], 358
Binji [bpj], 98
Binli, *dial.* Hanunoo [hnn], 494
Binna, *alt.* Bena [yun], 155
Binobolinao, *alt.* Bolinao [smk], 493
Binokid, *alt.* Binukid [bkd], 493
Binongan Itneg, *see* Itneg,
  Binongan [itb], 496
Binongko, *dial.* Tukang Besi South
  [bhq], 434
Binta', *alt. dial.* Timugon Murut
  [tih], 458
Bintauna [bne], 428
Bintucua, *alt.* Arhuaco [arh], 243
Bintuhan, *alt.* Kaur [vkk], 436

Bintuk, *alt.* Arhuaco [arh], 243
Bíntukua, *alt.* Arhuaco [arh], 243
Bintulu [bny], 459
Bintuni, *alt.* Wandamen [wad], 425
  dial. Wandamen [wad], 425
Binuang, *alt. dial.* Mamasa
  [mqj], 431
**Binuang-Paki-Batetanga-
  Anteapi**, *alt. dial.* Mamasa
  [mqj], 431
Binukid [bkd], 493
Binukid Manobo, *alt.* Binukid
  [bkd], 493
Binumaria, *alt.* Binumarien [bjr], 593
Binumarien [bjr], 593
Binza, *alt. dial.* Ngombe [ngc], 106
Binzabi, *alt.* Njebi [nzb], 89
Bio, *alt.* Biyo [byo], 327
  alt. dial. Aari [aiz], 112
Bionah, *alt. dial.* Dayak, Land
  [dyk], 393
Biong, *alt.* Bayungu [bxj], 569
Biotu, *pej. alt.* Isoko [iso], 164
Bipi [biq], 594
Bipim, *alt.* Warkay-Bipim [bgv], 425
Bipim As-So, *alt.* Warkay-Bipim
  [bgv], 425
Biqueno, *alt.* Baikeno [bkx], 350
Bira, *alt. dial.* Ebira [igb], 158
  alt. dial. Konjo, Coastal [kjc], 430
Biraan, *alt.* Blaan, Koronadal
  [bpr], 493
Birahui, *alt.* Brahui [brh], 484, 315,
  438
Birale [bxe], 114
Birao [brr], 635
Birar, *alt.* Bilur [bxf], 593
  dial. Nanai [gld], 506
Birarie, *dial.* Barai [bbb], 592
Biratak, *alt. dial.* Dayak, Land
  [dyk], 393
Birbay, *alt.* Worimi [kda], 578
Birelle, *alt.* Birale [bxe], 114
Birgid, *alt.* Birgit [btf], 79
  alt. Birked [brk], 189
Birgit [btf], 79
Birguid, *alt.* Birked [brk], 189
Birhar, *alt.* Birhor [biy], 356
Birhor [biy], 356
  alt. Kurux [kru], 371
Birhore, *alt.* Birhor [biy], 356
Biri [bzr], 569
  alt. Belanda Viri [bvi], 189
  alt. Biritai [bqq], 413
  alt. Birri [bvq], 75
  alt. dial. Ebira [igb], 158
  alt. dial. Teso [teo], 213
Birifo, *alt.* Birifor, Malba [bfo], 49
  alt. Birifor, Southern [biv], 123, 92
Birifor, *dial.* Birifor, Malba [bfo], 49

Bogos, *alt.* Bilen [byn], 112
Bogota, *alt.* Buglere [sab], 283
Bogoto, *alt.* Bokoto [bdt], 75
Bogu, *alt.* Bonggo [bpg], 413
Bogue, *alt.* Esimbi [ags], 61
Bogung, *alt.* Baatonum [bba], 42, 154
Boguru [bqu], 189
  dial. Boguru [bqu], 189
Bogyel, *alt.* Gyele [gyi], 62, 111
Bogyeli, *alt.* Gyele [gyi], 62, 111
Boh, *dial.* Kenyah, Mahakam [xkm], 394
Boh Bakung, *dial.* Kenyah, Bakung [boc], 393
Bohaan, *dial.* Buriat, Russia [bxr], 504
Bohairic, *dial.* Coptic [cop], 110
Bohena, *dial.* Dano [aso], 596
Bohilai, *dial.* Tawala [tbo], 627
Bohira'i, *alt. dial.* Tawala [tbo], 627
Boholano, *dial.* Cebuano [ceb], 493
Bohom, *alt.* Boghom [bux], 155
Bohoyeri, *alt. dial.* Powari [pwr], 384
Bohtan, *alt. dial.* Chaldean Neo-Aramaic [cld], 443
Bohtan Neo-Aramaic [bhn], 352, 503
Bohuai, *alt.* Tulu-Bohuai [rak], 628
  alt. dial. Tulu-Bohuai [rak], 628
Bohuai-Tulu, *alt.* Tulu-Bohuai [rak], 628
Bohutu, *alt.* Buhutu [bxh], 595
Boi, *alt. dial.* Vaghat-Ya-Bijim-Legeri [bij], 177
Boi Bi, *dial.* Muong [mtq], 525
Boi Gadaba, *alt.* Gadaba, Bodo [gbj], 361
Boianaki, *alt.* Ghayavi [bmk], 600
Boigu, *dial.* Meriam [ulk], 574
Boiken, *alt.* Boikin [bzf], 594
Boikin [bzf], 594
Boinaki, *alt.* Ghayavi [bmk], 600
Boinelang, *dial.* Aulua [aul], 640
Boje, *dial.* Bokyi [bky], 156
Bojie, *alt. dial.* Bokyi [bky], 156
Bojigniji, *alt.* Aka-Bea [abj], 353
Bojigyab, *alt.* Aka-Bea [abj], 353
Bojiin, *alt.* Limbum [lmp], 65
Bojpury, *dial.* Bhojpuri [bho], 145
Bok, *alt.* Taworta [tbp], 424
  alt. dial. Penan, Western [pne], 460, 325
  alt. dial. Sabaot [spy], 135
  dial. Mandjak [mfv], 131, 122, 181
Bok Penan, *dial.* Penan, Western [pne], 460, 325
Boka, *alt.* Boga [bvw], 155
  alt. Bolon [bof], 49

alt. dial. Manyika [mxc], 216, 148
Bokabo, *dial.* Gagu [ggu], 93
Bokai, *dial.* Termanu [twu], 410
Bokan, *alt. dial.* Bookan [bnb], 456
Bokar, *alt.* Luoba, Boga'er [adi], 339
  dial. Adi [adi], 353
Bokare, *dial.* Gbaya, Southwest [mdo], 76
Bokari, *alt. dial.* Gbaya, Southwest [mdo], 76
Boken, *alt. dial.* Bookan [bnb], 456
Bokhan, *alt. dial.* Buriat, Russia [bxr], 504
Bokharan, *alt.* Bukharic [bhh], 444
Bokharian, *alt.* Bukharic [bhh], 521
Bokharic, *alt.* Bukharic [bhh], 444, 521
Boki, *alt.* Bokyi [bky], 156, 59
  dial. Bokyi [bky], 59
Bokiba, *alt.* Bongili [bui], 88
Bokiyim, *alt.* Boghom [bux], 155
Bokko, *alt.* Boko [bqc], 42, 155
Bokkos, *dial.* Ron [cla], 174
Bokmaal, *alt.* Norwegian, Bokmål [nob], 549
Bokmål, *alt.* Norwegian, Bokmål [nob], 549
Bokmål Norwegian, *see* Norwegian, Bokmål [nob], 549
Boko (Benin) [bqc], 42, 155
  Boko (Democratic Republic of Congo) [bkp], 98
  alt. Longto [wok], 65
Bokobaru [bus], 156
Bokod, *dial.* Ibaloi [ibl], 494
Bokodo, *alt.* Bokoto [bdt], 75
Bokoki, *alt.* Bolia [bli], 98
Bokon, *alt. dial.* Bookan [bnb], 456
Bokonya, *alt.* Boko [bqc], 42, 155
Bokonzi, *dial.* Bomboma [bws], 98
Bokor, *alt.* Daju, Dar Sila [dau], 189
Bokorike, *alt.* Daju, Dar Sila [dau], 80, 189
Bokoruge, *alt.* Daju, Dar Sila [dau], 80, 189
Bokota, *alt.* Buglere [sab], 283
Bokotá, *dial.* Buglere [sab], 283
Bokoto [bdt], 75
  dial. Bokoto [bdt], 75
Bokoy, *dial.* Ligenza [lgz], 102
Bokpan, *dial.* Bokoto [bdt], 75
Bokpoto, *alt.* Bokoto [bdt], 75
Boku, *dial.* Sinaugoro [snc], 624
Bokun, *alt. dial.* Bookan [bnb], 456
Bokwa, *dial.* Gagu [ggu], 93
  dial. Glavda [glw], 161
Bokwa-Kendem, *alt.* Kendem [kvm], 63
Bokyi [bky], 156, 59

Bol Murut, *alt. dial.* Tagal Murut [mvv], 458, 395
Bola [bnp], 594
  alt. Mankanya [knf], 131, 181
  alt. Pela [bxd], 342
  dial. Bola [bnp], 594
Bola-Bakovi, *alt.* Bola [bnp], 594
Bolaang Itang, *alt. dial.* Kaidipang [kzp], 429
Bolaang Mongondow, *alt.* Mongondow [mog], 431
Bolaghain, *dial.* Pashayi, Northwest [glh], 317
Bolaka, *alt.* Buraka [bkg], 75
Bolanchi, *alt.* Bole [bol], 156
Bolang Itang, *alt. dial.* Kaidipang [kzp], 429
Bolango [bld], 428
  dial. Bolango [bld], 428
Bolano, *alt.* Boano [bzl], 428
Bolawa, *alt.* Bole [bol], 156
Bole [bol], 156
  dial. Vagla [vag], 128
Bole Murut, *alt. dial.* Tagal Murut [mvv], 458, 395
Boleka, *alt.* Desano [des], 226, 245
Boleki, *alt.* Boloki [bkt], 98
Bolemba, *dial.* Mbati [mdn], 77
Boleri, *alt. dial.* Dadiya [dbd], 157
Bolewa, *alt.* Bole [bol], 156
Bolgo [bvo], 79
Bolgo Dugag, *dial.* Bolgo [bvo], 79
Bolgo Kubar, *dial.* Bolgo [bvo], 79
Boli, *alt. dial.* Gbaya, Southwest [mdo], 76
Bolia [bli], 98
Bolinao [smk], 493
Bolinao Sambal, *alt.* Bolinao [smk], 493
Bolinao Zambal, *alt.* Bolinao [smk], 493
Bolivian Mataco, *pej. alt.* Wichí Lhamtés Nocten [mtp], 224
Bolivian Sign Language [bvl], 222
Bolo [blv], 40
Bolo Djarma, *dial.* Berakou [bxv], 79
Boloi, *alt.* Baloi [biz], 96
Bolok, *alt. dial.* Helong [heg], 407
Boloki [bkt], 98
Bolom, *alt.* Bullom So [buy], 183, 129
Bolon [bof], 49
Bolondo [bzm], 98
Bolong, *dial.* Kenga [kyq], 82
Bolongan [blj], 392
Bolongo, *alt. dial.* Mongo-Nkundu [lol], 104

Bolos Point, *dial.* Agta, Dupaninan [duo], 490

Boloven, *alt.* Laven [lbo], 451

Bolton Lancashire, *dial.* English [eng], 565

Bolu, *dial.* Geji [gji], 160

Bolupi, *dial.* Ligenza [lgz], 102

Bolyu [ply], 328

Bom [bmf], 183
  alt. Anjam [boj], 590
  alt. Bum [bmv], 59
  alt. Chin, Bawm [bgr], 358, 321, 463

Bom Futuro, *dial.* Jamamadí [jaa], 227

Boma [boh], 98
  alt. Teke-Eboo [ebo], 90
  alt. dial. Izon [ijc], 164

Boma Kasai, *alt.* Boma [boh], 98

Bomali, *alt.* Bomwali [bmw], 88, 59

Bomam, *alt. dial.* Bahnar [bdq], 521

Boman, *alt. dial.* Mpongmpong [mgg], 68

Bomang, *dial.* Burmese [mya], 321

Bomasa, *alt.* Limassa [bme], 76

Bomassa, *alt.* Limassa [bme], 76

Bombali, *dial.* Themne [tem], 184

Bombaro, *alt. dial.* Lame [bma], 168

Bombay Gujarati, *alt. dial.* Gujarati [guj], 363

Bombay Sign Language, *dial.* Indian Sign Language [ins], 365

Bombe, *alt.* Beba [bfp], 58

Bomberawa, *alt. dial.* Lame [bma], 168

Bombi-Ngbanja, *dial.* Bila [bip], 98

Bombo, *alt.* Mpongmpong [mgg], 68

Bomboko, *alt.* Wumboko [bqm], 73

Bomboli [bml], 98

Bomboma [bws], 98

Bombongo, *alt.* Bomboli [bml], 98

Bombori, *dial.* Katla [kcr], 192

Bome, *alt.* Bom [bmf], 183

Bomitaba [zmx], 88

Bomo, *alt.* Bom [bmf], 183

Bomokandi, *dial.* Kango [kty], 100

Bompaka, *alt. dial.* Teressa [tef], 388

Bompoka, *dial.* Teressa [tef], 388

Bomu [bmq], 137, 49
  dial. Gokana [gkn], 161

Bomu Tegu, *alt.* Dogon, Toro So [dts], 142

Bomudi, *dial.* Ngumbi [nui], 111

Bomui, *dial.* Yasa [yko], 111, 122

Bomvana, *dial.* Xhosa [xho], 187

Bomwali [bmw], 88, 59

Bon, *alt.* Bankon [abb], 58
  alt. Bon Gula [glc], 79
  alt. Boni [bob], 132

dial. Basaa [bas], 58

Bon Goula, *alt.* Bon Gula [glc], 79

Bon Gula [glc], 79

Bon Shwai, *alt. dial.* Dinka, Southwestern [dik], 190

Bona, *dial.* Anyin [any], 91

Bona Bona, *dial.* Suau [swp], 625

Bonahoi, *dial.* Arapesh, Bumbita [aon], 590

Bonan [peh], 328

Bonaputa-Mopu, *alt.* Miani [pla], 613

Bonarua, *dial.* Suau [swp], 625

Bonda, *alt.* Bondo [bfw], 357
  alt. Suwawa [swu], 433

Bonde, *alt.* Bondei [bou], 197

Bondei [bou], 197

Bondeya, *alt.* Korku [kfq], 369

Bondili, *alt.* Bundeli [bns], 357

Bondjiel, *alt.* Gyele [gyi], 62, 111

Bondo [bfw], 357

Bondo-Poraja, *alt.* Bondo [bfw], 357

Bondonga, *alt.* Ndunga [ndt], 105

Bondoukou Kulango, *see* Kulango, Bondoukou [kzc], 94, 126

Bondoy, *alt. dial.* Korku [kfq], 369

Bonduku Kulango, *alt.* Kulango, Bondoukou [kzc], 126

Bondum Dom Dogon, *see* Dogon, Bondum Dom [dbu], 142

Bondum-Dom, *alt.* Dogon, Bondum Dom [dbu], 142

Bone, *dial.* Bugis [bug], 428

Bone Hau, *dial.* Kalumpang [kli], 429

Bonea, *dial.* Mato [met], 612

Bonefa, *alt.* Nisa [njs], 421

Bonek, *alt.* Tuotomb [ttf], 72

Bonerate [bna], 428
  dial. Bonerate [bna], 428

Bonerif [bnv], 413

Bonfia, *alt.* Masiwang [bnf], 402

Bong, *alt.* Kintaq [knq], 454

Bòng Mieu, *alt.* Cua [cua], 522

Bong Miew, *alt.* Cua [cua], 522

Bonga, *alt.* Malalamai [mmt], 611

Bongao, *dial.* Sama, Southern [ssb], 500

Bonggi [bdg], 456

Bonggo [bpg], 413

Bongili [bui], 88

Bongiri, *alt.* Bongili [bui], 88

Bongken, *alt.* Bonkeng [bvg], 59

Bongo [bot], 189
  alt. Bonggo [bpg], 413
  alt. Nubaca [baf], 70
  dial. Banda, Mid-Southern [bjo], 74

Bongo Talk, *alt.* Jamaican Creole English [jam], 259

Bong'om, *alt. dial.* Sabaot [spy], 135

Bongomaise, *alt. dial.* Kwanga [kwj], 608

Bongomamsi, *alt. dial.* Kwanga [kwj], 608

Bong'omeek, *dial.* Sabaot [spy], 135

Bongor, *dial.* Masana [mcn], 83, 66

Bongor-Jodo-Tagal-Berem-Gunu, *dial.* Musey [mse], 85

Bongos, *dial.* Kwanga [kwj], 608

Bongu [bpu], 594

Bongwe, *alt.* Yasa [yko], 73, 111, 122

Boni [bob], 132, 184
  alt. dial. Aukan [djk], 295

Boniange, *dial.* Libinza [liz], 102

Bonjo [bok], 88

Bonkeng [bvg], 59

Bonkeng-Pendia, *alt.* Bonkeng [bvg], 59

Bonkenge, *alt.* Bonkeng [bvg], 59

Bonkiman [bop], 594

Bonkovia-Yevali, *alt.* Bierebo [bnk], 641

Bonny, *alt.* Ibani [iby], 162

Bonny-Opobo, *dial.* Igbo [ibo], 163

Bonom, *alt.* Monom [moo], 525

Bonotsek, *alt.* Atayal [tay], 511

Bontawa, *alt.* Bantawa [bap], 468

Bonthain, *alt. dial.* Konjo, Coastal [kjc], 430

Bontoc, Central [bnc], 493

Bontok, *alt.* Bontoc, Central [bnc], 493

Bonu, *dial.* Wambule [wme], 482

Bonum, *alt. dial.* Fali, North [fll], 61

Bonzio, *dial.* Mbati [mdn], 77

Bo'o, *dial.* Biak [bhw], 412

Boo, *alt.* Boko [bqc], 42, 155
  alt. Teke-Eboo [ebo], 90
  dial. Toura [neb], 95

Boõ, *alt.* Teke-Eboo [ebo], 90

Boobe, *alt.* Bube [bvb], 110

Boodla, *alt. dial.* Dass [dot], 157

Book, *dial.* Sabaot [spy], 135

Bookan [bnb], 456
  alt. dial. Bookan [bnb], 456

Boolboora, *alt.* Yidiny [yii], 579

Boombe, *alt.* Bube [bvb], 110

Boomu, *alt.* Bomu [bmq], 137, 49

Boon [bnl], 184

Boonan, *alt.* Gahri [bfu], 361

Booni, *dial.* Farefare [gur], 124
  dial. Ninkare [gur], 53

Boor [bvf], 79

Booran, *alt.* Borana [gax], 132
  alt. dial. Oromo, Borana-Arsi-Guji [gax], 185

Boordoona, *alt.* Burduna [bxn], 569

Boorim, *dial.* Bokyi [bky], 156

Boorkutti, *alt.* Dyangadi [dyn], 570
Boot, *alt. dial.* Zari [zaz], 178
Boow, *dial.* Dii [dur], 60
Bopchi, *alt.* Korku [kfq], 369
Bor, *alt.* Dinka, Southeastern [dks], 190
  dial. Dinka, Southeastern [dks], 190
Bor Athoic, *alt. dial.* Dinka, Southeastern [dks], 190
Bor Gok, *alt. dial.* Dinka, Southeastern [dks], 190
Bor Muthun, *dial.* Naga, Wancho [nnp], 380
Bor Mutonia, *alt. dial.* Naga, Wancho [nnp], 380
Bora [boa], 287, 243
  alt. Miraña [boa], 230
  dial. Bora [boa], 243
Boraan, *alt.* Borana [gax], 132
Borae, *alt. dial.* Chumburung [ncu], 124
Borai, *alt.* Hatam [had], 415
Borail Sadri, *dial.* Sadri, Oraon [sdr], 322
Boraka, *alt.* Buraka [bkg], 75, 98
Boran, *alt.* Borana [gax], 132
  alt. dial. Oromo, Borana-Arsi-Guji [gax], 117, 185
  dial. Borana [gax], 132
Borana [gax], 132
  dial. Oromo, Borana-Arsi-Guji [gax], 117, 185
Borana-Arsi-Guji Oromo, *see* Oromo, Borana-Arsi-Guji [gax], 117, 185
Borathoi, *alt. dial.* Dinka, Southeastern [dks], 190
Borcala, *dial.* Azerbaijani, North [azj], 319, 319
Borch, *dial.* Rutul [rut], 556
Border Komba, *dial.* Komba [kpf], 607
Border Kuna, *see* Kuna, Border [kvn], 246, 283
Bordo, *alt. dial.* Kimré [kqp], 82
Borduria, *alt.* Naga, Nocte [njb], 379
Bore, *alt.* Bomu [bmq], 137, 49
Borebo, *dial.* Mailu [mgu], 610
Borei [gai], 594
Borena, *alt. dial.* Oromo, Borana-Arsi-Guji [gax], 117
Borewar, *dial.* Borei [gai], 594
Borgawa, *alt.* Baatonum [bba], 154
Borgu, *alt.* Baatonum [bba], 154
  alt. Maba [mde], 83
Borgu Fulfulde, *see* Fulfulde, Borgu [fue], 44, 207
Bori, *alt. dial.* Fali, North [fll], 61
  dial. Adi [adi], 353
Boritsu, *alt.* Yukuben [ybl], 178, 74

Boriwen, *alt.* Laven [lbo], 451
Borna [bxx], 98
Borneo, *dial.* Malay [mly], 436
Bornholm, *dial.* Scanian [scy], 533
Bornholmsk, *dial.* Scanian [scy], 562
Bornouan, *alt.* Kanuri, Central [knc], 63, 81
Bornouans, *alt.* Kanuri, Central [knc], 63, 81, 152, 191
Bornu, *alt.* Kanuri, Central [knc], 166, 63, 81, 152, 191
Boro [bwo], 114
  alt. Bodo [brx], 357, 469
  alt. Bora [boa], 243
  alt. Miraña [boa], 230
  alt. dial. Ngelima [agh], 106
  dial. Folopa [ppo], 599
Boro-Aboro, *alt.* Berom [bom], 155
Boroa, *alt.* ‖Xegwi [xeg], 187
Borobo, *dial.* Grebo, Central [grv], 138
Borodda, *alt.* Wolaytta [wal], 119
Boroi, *dial.* Borei [gai], 594
Boroma, *dial.* Acipa, Eastern [acp], 153
Boromeso, *alt.* Burmeso [bzu], 413
Borong [ksr], 594
Boroni, *alt.* Bodo [brx], 357, 469
Bororo, *alt. dial.* Fulfulde, Kano-Katsina-Bororro [fuv], 61, 80
  dial. Fulfulde, Nigerian [fuv], 160
Borôro [bor], 226
Bororro, *alt. dial.* Fulfulde, Kano-Katsina-Bororro [fuv], 61, 80
Borpika, *alt.* Bole [bol], 156
Borrom, *alt.* Boghom [bux], 155
Borto, *alt.* Itik [itx], 415
Boruca [brn], 249
Borujerdi, *dial.* Luri, Northern [lrc], 440
Borumesso, *alt.* Burmeso [bzu], 413
Borun, *alt.* Burun [bdi], 189
Borunca, *alt.* Boruca [brn], 249
Bosa, *alt.* Lomavren [rmi], 319, 510
Bosalewa, *alt.* Boselewa [bwf], 594
Bosambi, *dial.* Budza [bja], 98
Bosavi, *alt.* Kaluli [bco], 604
Bosele, *alt.* Sekpele [lip], 127
Boselewa [bwf], 594
Bosha, *alt.* Lomavren [rmi], 319, 510
  alt. dial. Kafa [kbr], 116
Bosho, *dial.* Machame [jmc], 193
Bosiken, *alt.* Dimir [dmc], 597
Bosilewa, *alt.* Boselewa [bwf], 594
Boskien, *alt.* Dimir [dmc], 597
Bosman, *alt.* Bosngun [bqs], 594
Bosngun [bqs], 594
Bosnian [bos], 531
  alt. Serbian [srp], 563

Bosnik, *dial.* Biak [bhw], 412
Boso, *alt.* Bozo, Hainyaxo [bzx], 142
  alt. Bozo, Jenaama [bze], 142
  alt. Bozo, Tièma Cièwè [boo], 142
  alt. Bozo, Tiéyaxo [boz], 142
  dial. Gua [gwx], 125
Boso Bozo, *alt.* Sorko [bze], 175
Bosoa, *alt.* Busoa [bup], 428
Bosoko, *dial.* Gbaya, Southwest [mdo], 76
Bossangoa, *dial.* Gbaya-Bossangoa [gbp], 76
Bossouka, *alt. dial.* Gbaya, Southwest [mdo], 76
Bossoum, *dial.* Fali, North [fll], 61
Bota, *alt.* Bubia [bbx], 59
Botahari, *alt.* Bathari [bhm], 528
Botai, *dial.* Gbari [gby], 160
Botani, *alt. dial.* Kurdish, Northern [kmr], 519
Botbot, *dial.* Borei [gai], 594
Bote-Majhi [bmj], 469
Botel Tabago, *alt.* Yami [tao], 512
Botel Tobago, *alt.* Yami [tao], 512
Bothar, *alt.* Rema [bow], 622
Boti, *dial.* Kurdish, Northern [kmr], 519
Botin, *alt.* Ap Ma [kbx], 590
Botlikh [bph], 553
  dial. Botlikh [bph], 553
Botlix, *alt.* Botlikh [bph], 553
Boto, *dial.* Zari [zaz], 178
Bötö, *alt.* Nde-Gbite [ned], 170
Botocudos, *alt.* Xokleng [xok], 234
Botolan Sambal, *see* Sambal, Botolan [sbl], 501
Botolan Zambal, *alt.* Sambal, Botolan [sbl], 501
Botteng, *dial.* Ulumanda' [ulm], 434
Botteng-Tappalang, *alt.* Ulumanda' [ulm], 434
Botunga, *dial.* Mbole [mdq], 104
Bou, *dial.* Yele [yle], 633
Boua, *alt.* Bua [bub], 79
  alt. Bwa [bww], 99
Bouaka, *alt.* Ngbaka Ma'bo [nbm], 77, 89, 105
Bouamou, *alt.* Buamu [box], 50
Bouanila, *alt. dial.* Dibole [bvx], 88
Boudjou, *alt. dial.* Tuki [bag], 72
Boudouma, *alt.* Buduma [bdm], 79, 59
  alt. Yedina [bdm], 177
Boúe, *dial.* Khana [ogo], 166
Boufale, *dial.* Kabiyé [kbp], 208
Bouin, *alt.* Ngalkbun [ngk], 575
Bouiok, *alt.* Saisiyat [xsy], 512
Bouka, *alt. dial.* Banda-Mbrès [bqk], 75, 188

Boukhou, *dial.* Saafi-Saafi [sav], 182
Boulahay, *alt.* Mefele [mfj], 67
Boulala, *alt. dial.* Naba [mne], 85
Boulba, *alt.* Notre [bly], 46
Boulbe, *alt.* Fulfulde, Adamawa [fub], 61, 80
Boulonnais, *alt. dial.* Picard [pcd], 537
Boulou, *alt.* Bulu [bum], 59
Boumoali, *alt.* Bomwali [bmw], 88, 59
Boumpe, *alt.* Mende [men], 183, 139
Boun, *alt.* Ngalkbun [ngk], 575
Bouna, *dial.* Day [dai], 80
Bouna Koulango, *alt.* Kulango, Bouna [nku], 126
Bouna Kulango, *see* Kulango, Bouna [nku], 94, 126
Bounou, *dial.* Samo, Maya [sym], 53
Bouraka, *alt.* Buraka [bkg], 75, 98
Bourbonnais, *dial.* French [fra], 536
Bourguignon, *dial.* French [fra], 536
Bouriya, *dial.* Korku [kfq], 369
Bourrah, *alt.* Bura-Pabir [bwr], 156
Bousso, *alt.* Buso [bso], 79
Boute, *alt.* Vute [vut], 73
Bouye, *alt.* Pouye [bye], 622
Bouyei [pcc], 328
   alt. Giáy [pcc], 523
Bouyei 1, *alt. dial.* Bouyei [pcc], 328
Bouyei 2, *alt. dial.* Bouyei [pcc], 328
Bouyei 3, *alt. dial.* Bouyei [pcc], 328
Bouze, *pej. alt.* Loma [lom], 138
Boven-Mbian, *alt.* Marind, Bian [bpv], 419
Bowai, *alt.* Tulu-Bohuai [rak], 628
Bowili, *alt.* Tuwuli [bov], 128
Bowiri, *alt.* Tuwuli [bov], 128
Bowom, *alt. dial.* Dinka, Northeastern [dip], 189
Boyali, *dial.* Gbaya-Bozoum [gbq], 76
Boyanese, *alt. dial.* Madura [mad], 392, 509
Boyao, *dial.* Ai-Cham [aih], 326
Boyela, *alt.* Yela [yel], 109
Boyerahmadi, *dial.* Luri, Southern [luz], 440
Bozaba [bzo], 98
Boze-Giringarede, *dial.* Bine [bon], 593
Bozo, Hainyaxo [bzx], 142
Bozo, Jenaama [bze], 142
Bozo, Tièma Cièwè [boo], 142
Bozo, Tiéyaxo [boz], 142
Bozom, *alt.* Gbaya-Bozoum [gbq], 76
   dial. Gbaya-Bozoum [gbq], 76

Brabants, *dial.* Dutch [nld], 531
   dial. Vlaams [vls], 531
Brabori, *alt.* Dida, Lakota [dic], 92
Bragat [aof], 594
Brahmani, *dial.* Varhadi-Nagpuri [vah], 389
Brahmu, *alt.* Baraamu [brd], 468
Brahudi, *alt.* Brahui [brh], 438
Brahui [brh], 484, 315, 438
Brahuidi, *alt.* Brahui [brh], 484
Brahuigi, *alt.* Brahui [brh], 484
Brahuiki, *alt.* Brahui [brh], 315
Braj, *alt.* Braj Bhasha [bra], 357
   alt. Kanauji [bjj], 366
Braj Bhakha, *alt.* Braj Bhasha [bra], 357
Braj Bhasha [bra], 357
   dial. Braj Bhasha [bra], 357
Braj Kanauji, *alt.* Kanauji [bjj], 366
Brame, *alt. dial.* Mankanya [knf], 131, 181
Bramu, *alt.* Baraamu [brd], 468
Brao [brb], 325, 522
   alt. Lave [brb], 451
Braou, *alt.* Brao [brb], 325, 522
   alt. Lave [brb], 451
Brasiliano, *alt.* Tupinambá [tpn], 233
Brasilica, *alt.* Tupinambá [tpn], 233
Brasmi, *dial.* Dumi [dus], 471
Brass Ijo, *alt.* Ijo, Southeast [ijs], 163
Brassa, *alt.* Balanta-Ganja [bjt], 179
   alt. Balanta-Kentohe [ble], 130
Brat, *alt.* Mai Brat [ayz], 419
Brathela, *alt. dial.* Gujarati [guj], 363
Brau, *alt.* Brao [brb], 522
   alt. Lave [brb], 451
Bravanese, *alt. dial.* Swahili [swh], 185
Brawbaw, *dial.* Thao [ssf], 512
Brazilian Calão, *dial.* Caló [rmr], 559, 226, 551
Brazilian Portuguese, *dial.* Portuguese [por], 551
Brazilian Sign Language [bzs], 226
Bre, *alt.* Karen, Brek [kvl], 464
   alt. Mbre [mka], 94
Brec, *alt.* Karen, Brek [kvl], 464
Brek, *alt.* Karen, Brek [kvl], 464
Brek Karen, *see* Karen, Brek [kvl], 464
Brem [buq], 594
Bren, *alt.* Kháng [kjm], 524
Breri [brq], 594
Breton [bre], 536
Brezhoneg, *alt.* Breton [bre], 536
Bri, *alt.* Braj Bhasha [bra], 357
Bri-La, *alt. dial.* Jeh [jeh], 523
Bria, *alt. dial.* Banda-Banda [bpd], 75
Bribri [bzd], 249

Brignan, *alt.* Avikam [avi], 91
Brij Bhasha, *alt.* Braj Bhasha [bra], 357
Brijia, *alt.* Bijori [bix], 356
   dial. Asuri [asr], 354
Briju, *alt.* Braj Bhasha [bra], 357
Bringen, *pej. alt.* Marithiel [mfr], 574
Brinjari, *alt.* Lambadi [lmn], 372
Brinken, *pej. alt.* Marithiel [mfr], 574
Brinya, *alt.* Avikam [avi], 91
Brissa, *alt. dial.* Anyin [any], 123
British Sign Language [bfi], 565
Brokkat [bro], 322
Brokpa, *alt.* Brokpake [sgt], 322
   alt. Brokskat [bkk], 357
   alt. Shina [scl], 488
Brokpa of Dah-Hanu, *alt.* Brokskat [bkk], 357
Brokpake [sgt], 322
Brokskad, *alt.* Brokkat [bro], 322
Brokskat [bkk], 357
Bron, *alt.* Abron [abr], 122, 91
Brong, *alt.* Abron [abr], 122, 91
Brooke's Point Palawan, *alt.* Palawano, Brooke's Point [plw], 500
Brooke's Point Palawano, *see* Palawano, Brooke's Point [plw], 500
Broom Creole, *alt.* Broome Pearling Lugger Pidgin [bpl], 569
Broome Pearling Lugger Pidgin [bpl], 569
Brosa, *alt. dial.* Anyin [any], 123
Brou, *alt.* Brao [brb], 325, 522
   alt. Bru, Eastern [bru], 522
   alt. Lave [brb], 451
B'ru, *alt.* Bru, Western [brv], 514
Bru, *alt.* Bru, Eastern [bru], 522
   alt. Sô [sss], 452
Bru Dong Sen Keo, *dial.* Bru, Eastern [bru], 514
Bru Kok Sa-At, *dial.* Bru, Eastern [bru], 514
Bru, Eastern [bru], 450, 514, 522
Bru, Western [brv], 514
Bruit, *dial.* Melanau [mel], 460
Bruj, *alt.* Braj Bhasha [bra], 357
Brulé, *dial.* Lakota [lkt], 303
Brummie, *alt. dial.* English [eng], 565
Brummy, *alt. dial.* English [eng], 565
Brunca, *alt.* Boruca [brn], 249
Brunei [kxd], 324, 456
   dial. Brunei [kxd], 456
Brunei Bisaya, *see* Bisaya, Brunei [bsb], 324
Brunei Malay, *dial.* Brunei [kxd], 324

Brunei Murut, *alt.* Lundayeh [lnd], 324

Brunei-Kadaian, *alt.* Brunei [kxd], 324, 456

Brung, *dial.* Kelabit [kzi], 459

Brunka, *alt.* Boruca [brn], 249

Brushaski, *alt.* Burushaski [bsk], 484

Bruu, *alt.* Bru, Western [brv], 514

BSL, *alt.* British Sign Language [bfi], 565

Bu [jid], 156
  alt. Mundabli [boe], 68
  dial. Bu [jid], 156

Bu Dang, *dial.* Mnong, Central [cmo], 525, 326

Bu Giiwo, *alt.* Giiwo [kks], 161

Bu Nar, *dial.* Mnong, Central [cmo], 525, 326

Bu Rung, *dial.* Mnong, Central [cmo], 525, 326

Bu-Hwan, *alt.* Taroko [trv], 512

Bu-Nao Bunu, *see* Bunu, Bu-Nao [bwx], 328

Bu-Nong, *alt.* Nung [nut], 525

Bua [bub], 79
  alt. Bwa [bww], 99
  alt. dial. Fijian [fij], 580
  dial. Tae' [rob], 428

Bua Ponrang, *alt. dial.* Bugis [bug], 428

Buaga, *dial.* Sinaugoro [snc], 624

Bual, *alt.* Buol [blf], 428
  alt. Buwal [bhs], 59

Bualkhaw Chin, *see* Chin, Bualkhaw [cbl], 463

Buamu [box], 50

Buan, *alt.* Ngalkbun [ngk], 575

Buang, Mangga [mmo], 595

Buang, Mapos [bzh], 595

Buano, *alt.* Boano [bzn], 397

Buasi, *alt.* Vehes [val], 630

Bubalia, *alt.* Arabic, Babalia Creole [bbz], 78
  alt. Berakou [bxv], 79

Bubanda, *dial.* Mono [mnh], 104

Bubangi, *alt.* Bangi [bni], 97
  alt. Bobangi [bni], 88

Bube [bvb], 110

Bubi [buw], 120
  alt. Bube [bvb], 110
  dial. Kélé [keb], 120

Bubia [bbx], 59

Bubis, *dial.* Citak [txt], 413

Bubu, *alt. dial.* Gula [kcm], 191

Bububun, *alt.* Brem [buq], 594

Bubukun, *alt.* Bunun [bnn], 511

Bubure, *alt.* Bure [bvh], 156
  alt. Vute [vut], 73

Bucho, *dial.* Khehek [tlx], 606

Bud-Kat, *alt.* Kinnauri, Bhoti [nes], 368

Budai, *dial.* Rukai [dru], 512

Budamono, *dial.* Gbaya, Southwest [mdo], 76

Budang, *alt.* Mnong, Central [cmo], 525

Budanoh, *dial.* Dayak, Land [dyk], 393

Budapest, *dial.* Hungarian Sign Language [hsh], 542

Budeh Stieng, *see* Stieng, Budeh [stt], 526

Budibud [btp], 595

Budidjara, *alt. dial.* Martu Wangka [mpj], 574

Budigri, *dial.* Gbanu [gbv], 75

Budik [tnr], 180

Budina, *alt.* Burduna [bxn], 569

Budip, *dial.* Stieng, Bulo [sti], 326

Budíp, *alt.* Stieng, Bulo [sti], 526

Budja, *alt.* Budza [bja], 98

Budjago, *alt.* Bidyogo [bjg], 131

Budon Kakanda, *dial.* Kakanda [kka], 165

Budong, *alt.* Mnong, Central [cmo], 525, 326

Budong-Budong [bdx], 428

Budoona, *alt.* Burduna [bxn], 569

Budu [buu], 98

Budug, *alt.* Budukh [bdk], 319

Budugi, *alt.* Budukh [bdk], 319

Budugum, *alt. dial.* Masana [mcn], 83
  dial. Masana [mcn], 66

Budukh [bdk], 319
  dial. Budukh [bdk], 319

Buduma [bdm], 79, 59
  alt. Yedina [bdm], 177
  dial. Yedina [bdm], 177

Buduna, *alt.* Burduna [bxn], 569

Budux, *alt.* Budukh [bdk], 319

Budza [bja], 98

Budzaba, *alt.* Bozaba [bzo], 98

Bue, *alt.* Huitoto, Murui [huu], 288, 245

Buek, *alt. dial.* Gaam [tbi], 190

Buela, *alt.* Bwela [bwl], 99

Buem, *alt.* Lelemi [lef], 126

Buena Vista Chontal, *dial.* Chontal, Tabasco [chf], 262

Buende, *alt. dial.* Koongo [kng], 101

Bueng, *dial.* Aceh [ace], 435

Bufe, *alt.* Bafut [bfd], 56
  alt. dial. Bafut [bfd], 56

Bufumbwa, *dial.* Rwanda [kin], 178

Bug, *alt.* Mangayat [myj], 193

Buga, *alt.* Mangayat [myj], 193

Buga-Khwe, *alt. dial.* Khwe [xuu], 47

Buga-Kxoe, *dial.* Khwe [xuu], 47
  dial. Kxoe [xuu], 150

Bugago, *alt.* Bidyogo [bjg], 131

Bugalu, *alt.* Bikaru [bic], 593

Bugan [bbh], 328

Bugau, *alt. dial.* Iban [iba], 393
  dial. Iban [iba], 459, 324

Bugawac [buk], 595

Buge, *dial.* Vagla [vag], 128

Bughotu [bgt], 635

Bugi, *alt.* Bugis [bug], 428

Buginese, *alt.* Bugis [bug], 428, 456

Bugis [bug], 428, 456

Bugkalut, *alt.* Ilongot [ilk], 495

Buglere [sab], 283

Buglial, *dial.* Meriam [ulk], 574

Bugombe, *dial.* Bhele [bhy], 98

Bugongo, *alt. dial.* Pande [bkj], 77

Bugota, *alt.* Bughotu [bgt], 635

Bugoto, *alt.* Bughotu [bgt], 635

Bugotu, *alt.* Bughotu [bgt], 635

Bugre, *alt.* Guaraní, Mbyá [gun], 227
  alt. Kaingáng [kgp], 228
  alt. Xokleng [xok], 234

Bugsuk Palawano, *alt. dial.* Palawano, Brooke's Point [plw], 500

Bugudum, *dial.* Masana [mcn], 83

Buguli, *alt.* Phuie [pug], 53

Bugumbe, *dial.* Kuria [kuj], 134

Bugun [bgg], 357
  dial. Sulung [suv], 388

Buguri, *alt.* Phuie [pug], 53

Buguru, *alt.* Boguru [bqu], 189

Buhagana, *alt.* Macuna [myy], 246, 229

Buhi, *dial.* Bicolano, Albay [bhk], 493

Buhid [bku], 493

Buhi'non, *alt. dial.* Bicolano, Albay [bhk], 493

Buhulu, *alt.* Buhutu [bxh], 595

Buhutu [bxh], 595

Bui, *alt.* Bouyei [pcc], 328

Buiamanambu, *alt.* Yelogu [ylg], 633

Builsa, *alt.* Buli [bwu], 123

Buin, *alt.* Ngalkbun [ngk], 575
  alt. Terei [buo], 627

Buinak, *dial.* Kumyk [kum], 519

Buinaksk, *dial.* Kumyk [kum], 555

Buja, *alt.* Budza [bja], 98

Bujal, *alt.* Bujhyal [byh], 469

Bujeba, *alt.* Ngumba [nmg], 111

Bujhel, *alt.* Bujhyal [byh], 469

Bujhyal [byh], 469

Buji, *dial.* Jere [jer], 165

Bujiyel, *dial.* Sanga [xsn], 174

Bujwe, *alt.* Buyu [byi], 99

Buka, *alt.* Bukar Sadong [sdo], 459, 392

dial. Banda-Mbrès [bqk], 75, 188

Bukabukan, *alt.* Pukapuka
[pkp], 579

Bukakhwe, *alt. dial.* Khwe [xuu], 47

Bukala, *dial.* Mongo-Nkundu
[lol], 104

Bukalot, *alt.* Ilongot [ilk], 495

Bukambero, *alt. dial.* Laura
[lur], 408

Bukar, *alt.* Bukar Sadong [sdo], 459,
392

Bukar Bidayuh, *alt. dial.* Bukar
Sadong [sdo], 392

dial. Bukar Sadong [sdo], 459

Bukar Sadong [sdo], 459, 392

dial. Bukar Sadong [sdo], 459, 392

Bukat [bvk], 392

Bukau, *alt. dial.* Timugon Murut
[tih], 458

Bukaua, *alt.* Bugawac [buk], 595

Bukawa, *alt.* Bugawac [buk], 595

Bukawac, *alt.* Bugawac [buk], 595

Bukhara Arabic, *alt.* Arabic, Tajiki
Spoken [abh], 513

Bukharan, *alt.* Bukharic [bhh], 444,
521

Bukharian, *alt.* Bukharic [bhh], 444

Bukharic [bhh], 444, 521

Bukharin, *alt.* Bukharic [bhh], 521

Bukidnon, *alt.* Binukid [bkd], 493

alt. Magahat [mtw], 498

alt. Sulod [srg], 501

Bukil, *alt.* Buhid [bku], 493

Bukira, *dial.* Kuria [kuj], 134

Bukit, *alt.* Malay, Bukit [bvu], 394

Bukit Malay, *see* Malay, Bukit
[bvu], 394

Bukitan [bkn], 392, 459

Bukiyip [ape], 595

alt. dial. Bukiyip [ape], 595

Bukiyúp, *alt.* Bukiyip [ape], 595

Bukongo, *alt. dial.* Pande [bkj], 77

Bukow, *alt. dial.* Timugon Murut
[tih], 458

Bukpi, *dial.* Chin, Paite [pck], 359

Bukpui, *alt. dial.* Chin, Paite
[pck], 359

Buksa [tkb], 357

Buku, *dial.* Campalagian [cml], 428

Bukueta, *alt.* Buglere [sab], 283

Bukukhi, *alt.* Budukh [bdk], 319

Bukum, *alt. dial.* Boguru [bqu], 189

Bukuma, *alt.* Ogbronuagum
[ogu], 172

Bukun, *alt. dial.* Bookan [bnb], 456

Bukur, *alt. dial.* Boguru [bqu], 189

dial. Boguru [bqu]

Bukuru, *alt. dial.* Boguru [bqu], 189

Bukurumi, *alt.* Kurama [krh], 167

Bukusu [bxk], 132

dial. Bukusu [bxk], 132

Bùkwák, *alt.* Kwak [kwq], 168

Bukwen [buz], 156

Bul, *alt. dial.* Nuer [nus], 194

Bula, *alt.* Mafa [maf], 169

alt. Mefele [mfj], 67

Bulacan, *dial.* Tagalog [tgl], 502

Bulagat, *dial.* Buriat, Russia
[bxr], 504

Bulahai, *alt.* Mafa [maf], 169

alt. Mefele [mfj], 67

Bulai, *alt.* Palaung, Pale [pce], 342

Bulala, *alt. dial.* Naba [mne], 85

Bulalakaw, *dial.* Inonhan [loc], 495

Bulalakawnon, *dial.* Hanunoo
[hnn], 494

Bulama, *alt. dial.* Mankanya
[knf], 131, 181

Bulanda, *alt.* Balanta-Ganja [bjt], 179

alt. Balanta-Kentohe [ble], 130

Bulang, *alt.* Blang [blr], 327, 462,
514

Bulanga, *alt.* Bolango [bld], 428

Bulanga-Uki, *alt.* Bolango [bld], 428

Bularnu, *alt.* Yindjilandji [yil], 579

Bulawa, *alt.* Karawa [xrw], 605

Bulba, *alt.* Notre [bly], 46

Buldit, *dial.* Opuuo [lgn], 194

Bule, *alt.* Vute [vut], 73

Bulei, *alt.* Palaung, Pale [pce], 342

dial. Palaung, Pale [pce], 342

Buleleng, *alt. dial.* Bali [ban], 391

Bulem, *alt.* Bullom So [buy], 183,
129

'Bulengee, *dial.* Wali [wlx], 128

Bulgai, *dial.* Meriam [ulk], 574

Bulgar, *alt.* Chuvash [chv], 553

Bulgar Gagauz, *dial.* Gagauz
[gag], 532, 551

Bulgar Gagauzi, *dial.* Gagauz
[gag], 547

Bulgarian [bul], 532, 540, 547, 551,
557, 563

Bulgarian Sign Language [bqn],
532

Bulgebi [bmp], 595

Buli (Ghana) [bwu], 123

Buli (Indonesia) [bzq], 397

alt. dial. Mongo-Nkundu [lol], 104

dial. Buli [bzq], 397

dial. Gbaya, Southwest [mdo], 76

dial. Polci [plj], 173

Bulia, *alt.* Bolia [bli], 98

Bulisa, *alt.* Buli [bwu], 123

Bulla, *alt. dial.* Sheko [she], 118

Bullin, *alt.* Bullom So [buy], 183, 129

Bullom So [buy], 183, 129

Bullun, *alt.* Bullom So [buy], 183,
129

Bulo, *dial.* Pannei [pnc], 432

dial. Stieng, Bulo [sti], 326

Bulo Stieng, *see* Stieng, Bulo
[sti], 526, 326

Bulu (Cameroon) [bum], 59

Bulu (Papua New Guinea) [bjl], 595

alt. Seki [syi], 111

Bulud Upi, *alt.* Ida'an [dbj], 456

Buluf, *dial.* Jola-Fonyi [dyo], 180

Buluh Kuning, *alt. dial.* Ma'anyan
[mhy], 394

Buluki, *alt.* Boloki [bkt], 98

Bulukumba, *alt. dial.* Bugis
[bug], 428

Bulum, *alt.* Burum-Mindik
[bmu], 595

Bulum-Bulum, *alt.* Dyaabugay
[dyy], 570

Bulungan, *alt.* Bolongan [blj], 392

dial. Basap [bdb], 392

Bulunge, *alt.* Burunge [bds], 197

Bulunits, *alt.* Mbulungish [mbv], 130

Buluyiema, *dial.* Loma [lom], 138

Bum [bmv], 59

alt. Bom [bmf], 183

alt. dial. Mbum [mdd], 66

Buma, *alt.* Boma [boh], 98

alt. Teanu [tkw], 638

alt. Turkana [tuv], 137

Buma-Kxoe, *dial.* Kxoe [xuu], 150,
40

Bumaji [byp], 156

Bumal, *dial.* Bambam [ptu], 427

Bumali, *alt.* Bomwali [bmw], 88, 59

Bumbira, *dial.* Haya [hay], 199

Bumbita Arapesh, *see* Arapesh,
Bumbita [aon], 590

Bumboko, *alt.* Wumboko [bqm], 73

Bumbong, *alt.* Dimbong [dii], 60

Bumboret, *alt. dial.* Kalasha
[kls], 486

Bumdemba, *dial.* Meohang, Western
[raf], 476

Bume, *alt.* Turkana [tuv], 137

Bumo, *dial.* Izon [ijc], 164

Bumtang, *alt.* Bumthangkha
[kjz], 323

Bumtangkha, *alt.* Bumthangkha
[kjz], 323

Bumtanp, *alt.* Bumthangkha
[kjz], 323

Bumthang, *alt.* Bumthangkha
[kjz], 323

Bumthangkha [kjz], 323

Bumthapkha, *alt.* Bumthangkha
[kjz], 323

Bumwangi, *dial.* Lusengo [lse], 103

Bun [buv], 595

alt. Bon Gula [glc], 79

Buna [bvn], 595

alt. Bena [yun], 155

alt. Mbum [mdd], 66
alt. Voro [vor], 177
Buna', *alt.* Bunak [bfn], 350, 406
Buna Kulango, *alt.* Kulango, Bouna [nku], 126
Bunaba [bck], 569
Bunabun, *alt.* Brem [buq], 594
Bunak [bfn], 350, 406
Bunake, *alt.* Bunak [bfn], 350, 406
Bunaki, *alt.* Naki [mff], 69
Bunama [bdd], 595
  dial. Bunama [bdd], 595
Bunan, *alt.* Bunun [bnn], 511
  alt. Gahri [bfu], 361, 332
  alt. dial. Dayak, Land [dyk], 393
Bunao, *alt.* Bunu, Bu-Nao [bwx], 328
Bunaq, *alt.* Bunak [bfn], 350, 406
Bunberawa, *alt. dial.* Lame [bma], 168
Bunda, *alt.* Suwawa [swu], 433
  dial. Suwawa [swu], 433
Bundala, *alt.* Bandjalang [bdy], 568
Bunde, *dial.* Loma [lom], 138
Bundeli [bns], 357
Bundelkhandi, *alt.* Bundeli [bns], 357
Bundhamara, *alt. dial.* Ngura [nbx], 575
Bundi, *alt.* Gende [gaf], 599
Bundu, *dial.* Dusun, Central [dtp], 456
Bundum, *dial.* Tuki [bag], 72
Bune, *alt.* Suwawa [swu], 433
Bung [bqd], 59
Bungain [but], 595
Bungase, *dial.* Ligbi [lig], 126
Bungbinda, *alt.* Ngbinda [nbd], 106
Bungeha, *alt.* Banggarla [bjb], 568
Bungela, *alt.* Banggarla [bjb], 568
Bunggu, *alt.* Kaili, Da'a [kzf], 429
Bungi, *alt.* Bobangi [bni], 88
Bungili, *alt.* Bongili [bui], 88
Bungiri, *alt.* Bongili [bui], 88
Bungku [bkz], 428
  dial. Bungku [bkz], 428
Bungla, *dial.* Saam [raq], 478
Bungnu, *alt.* Kamkam [bgu], 63
  alt. Mbongno [bgu], 170
Bungo, *dial.* Bongo [bot], 189
Bungu [wun], 197
  alt. Bongo [bot], 189
Bungun, *alt.* Kamkam [bgu], 63
  alt. Mbongno [bgu], 170
Buniabura, *dial.* Aneme Wake [aby], 589
Buninga, *dial.* Efate, North [llp], 641
  dial. Namakura [nmk], 644
Bunji, *alt. dial.* Shina [scl], 488
  dial. Manyika [mxc], 216, 148
Bunjia, *alt.* Bhunjia [bhu], 356

Bunju, *alt. dial.* Tuki [bag], 72
Bunjwali, *dial.* Kashmiri [kas], 367
Bunong, *alt.* Mnong, Central [cmo], 326
  dial. Mnong, Southern [mnn], 525
Bunta, *alt.* Áncá [acb], 154
Bunti, *alt.* Bunun [bnn], 511
Bunu, *alt.* Kamkam [bgu], 63
  alt. Mbongno [bgu], 170
  alt. dial. Jere [jer], 165
  dial. Yoruba [yor], 178
Bunu, Bu-Nao [bwx], 328
Bunu, Jiongnai [pnu], 328
Bunu, Wunai [bwn], 328
Bunu, Younuo [buh], 329
Bunuba, *alt.* Bunaba [bck], 569
Bunubun, *alt.* Brem [buq], 594
Bunum, *alt.* Bunun [bnn], 511
Bunun [bnn], 511
Bunuo, *dial.* Bunu, Bu-Nao [bwx], 328
Buol [blf], 428
Buoncwai, *alt. dial.* Dinka, Southwestern [dik], 190
Bupuran, *alt.* Papora-Hoanya [ppu], 512
Bur:aad, *alt.* Buriat, Mongolia [bxm], 461
Bura, *alt.* Bura-Pabir [bwr], 156
  dial. Taita [dav], 136
Bura Hyilhawul, *alt. dial.* Bura-Pabir [bwr], 156
Bura Kokura, *dial.* Tera [ttr], 175
Bura Mabang, *alt.* Maba [mde], 83
Bura Pela, *alt. dial.* Bura-Pabir [bwr], 156
Bura-Pabir [bwr], 156
Buraadiiga, *dial.* Datooga [tcc], 198
Burada, *alt.* Burarra [bvr], 569
Buradiga, *alt. dial.* Datooga [tcc], 198
Buraga, *alt. dial.* Kui [kvd], 408
Burak [bys], 156
Buraka [bkg], 75, 98
Buram, *alt.* Dagik [dec], 189
  alt. dial. Mankanya [knf], 131, 181
Burama, *dial.* Mankanya [knf], 131, 181
Burarra [bvr], 569
Burate [bti], 413
Burba, *alt.* Biali [beh], 49
Burduna [bxn], 569
Bure [bvh], 156
  alt. Iyo [nca], 603
Buré, *alt.* Zo'é [pto], 234
Bureadiga, *alt. dial.* Datooga [tcc], 198
Bureda, *alt.* Burarra [bvr], 569
Burera, *alt.* Burarra [bvr], 569
Burgadi, *alt.* Dyangadi [dyn], 570

Burgandi, *dial.* Tamil [tam], 388
Burgenland Croatian, *dial.* Croatian [hrv], 530
Burgu, *alt.* Baatonum [bba], 42, 154
Buriah-Weth-Laturake, *alt. dial.* Alune [alp], 396
Buriat, China [bxu], 329
Buriat, Mongolia [bxm], 461
Buriat, Russia [bxr], 504
Buriat-Mongolian, *alt.* Buriat, China [bxu], 329
  alt. Buriat, Mongolia [bxm], 461
  alt. Buriat, Russia [bxr], 504
Burig, *alt.* Purik [prx], 384
Burigskat, *alt.* Purik [prx], 384
Buriram, *dial.* Khmer, Northern [kxm], 515
Burja, *alt.* Bijori [bix], 356
Burji [bji], 114, 132
Burjin, *alt.* Anuak [anu], 113
Burkanawa, *alt.* Mburku [bbt], 170
Burkeneji, *alt.* Samburu [saq], 136
Burma, *alt.* Boghom [bux], 155
Burma Tamil, *dial.* Tamil [tam], 388
Burmbar [vrt], 641
Burmese [mya], 462, 321
  dial. Burmese [mya], 462
Burmese Karen, *alt.* Karen, S'gaw [ksw], 464, 514
Burmeso [bzu], 413
Burnay Ifugao, *dial.* Ifugao, Amganad [ifa], 495
Buro, *alt.* Deg [mzw], 92
Burogo, *alt.* Rogo [rod], 174
Burom, *alt.* Boghom [bux], 155
Burra, *alt.* Bura-Pabir [bwr], 156
Burrum, *alt.* Boghom [bux], 155
Burta, *alt.* Berta [wti], 113, 189
Buru (Indonesia) [mhs], 397
  Buru (Nigeria) [bqw], 156
  alt. Deg [mzw], 124
  alt. Lisela [lcl], 400
  alt. Tamagario [tcg], 423
  dial. Banda-Banda [bpd], 75
  dial. Ngelima [agh], 106
Burubora, *alt.* Puruborá [pur], 232
Burucaki, *alt.* Burushaski [bsk], 484
Burucaski, *alt.* Burushaski [bsk], 484
Buruese, *alt.* Buru [mhs], 397
Burui [bry], 595
  dial. Malinguat [sic], 611
Burulo, *dial.* Ma'di [mhi], 193
Burum, *alt.* Boghom [bux], 155
  alt. Burum-Mindik [bmu], 595
Burum-Mindik [bmu], 595
Burumakok [aip], 413
Burumba, *alt.* Baki [bki], 641
Burumeso, *alt.* Burmeso [bzu], 413
Burun [bdi], 189

alt. Uduk [udu], 119, 196
Burunca, *alt.* Boruca [brn], 249
Burunge [bds], 197
Burungi, *alt.* Burunge [bds], 197
Burusa, *alt.* Notre [bly], 46
Burushaki, *alt.* Burushaski [bsk], 484
Burushaski [bsk], 484
Burushki, *alt.* Burushaski [bsk], 484
Burusu [bqr], 392
Buruwa, *dial.* Kimré [kqp], 82
Buruwai [asi], 413
Buryat, *alt.* Buriat, China [bxu], 329
alt. Buriat, Mongolia [bxm], 461
alt. Buriat, Russia [bxr], 504
Burzhan, *dial.* Bashkir [bak], 553
Busa [bqp], 156
alt. Odiai [bhf], 619
Busa-Bisã, *alt.* Busa [bqp], 156
Busa-Boko, *alt.* Boko [bqc], 42
Busa-Bokobaru, *alt.* Bokobaru [bus], 156
Busam [bxs], 56
Busami [bsm], 413
Busan, *alt.* Odiai [bhf], 619
Busang, *alt.* Kayan, Busang [bfg], 393
alt. dial. Dayak, Land [dyk], 393
Busang Kayan, *see* Kayan, Busang [bfg], 393
Busano, *alt.* Busa [bqp], 156
Buseni, *alt.* Biseni [ije], 155
Busere Bongo, *dial.* Bongo [bot], 189
Bush Mengen, *dial.* Mengen [mee], 613
Bush Unua, *dial.* Unua [onu], 646
Bush-C, *alt.* ‖Xegwi [xeg], 187
Bushama, *alt.* Shama-Sambuga [sqa], 174
Bushi [buc], 145
Bushman's Bay, *alt.* Lingarak [lgk], 643
Bushong, *alt.* Bushoong [buf], 98
Bushongo, *alt.* Bushoong [buf], 98
Bushoong [buf], 98
Busi, *dial.* Obanliku [bzy], 172
Busillu Sisala, *alt.* Sisaala, Western [ssl], 128
Buso [bso], 79
Busoa [bup], 428
Busoong, *alt.* Bushoong [buf], 98
Bussa [dox], 114
Bussanchi, *alt.* Busa [bqp], 156
Busso, *alt.* Buso [bso], 79
Busu Djanga, *dial.* Lusengo [lse], 103
Busuu [bju], 59
Busy, *pej. alt.* Loma [lom], 138
But, *alt. dial.* Moinba [mob], 376

Buta, *alt. dial.* Gamo-Ningi [bte], 160
Butam, *dial.* Taulil [tuh], 627
Butanglu, *alt.* Paiwan [pwn], 511
Butbut, *alt.* Kalinga, Butbut [kyb], 497
Butbut Kalinga, *see* Kalinga, Butbut [kyb], 497
Bute, *alt.* Vute [vut], 73, 177
Bute Bamnyo, *dial.* Vute [vut], 73
Buteha, *dial.* Daur [dta], 331, 461
Butelkud-Guntabak, *alt.* Nobonob [gaw], 618
Buti, *alt.* Vute [vut], 177
Butju, *alt.* Djangun [djf], 569
Butmas-Tur [bnr], 641
Buton, *alt.* Cia-Cia [cia], 429
alt. Tukang Besi North [khc], 434
alt. Tukang Besi South [bhq], 434
alt. Wolio [wlo], 458
Butonese, *alt.* Cia-Cia [cia], 429
alt. Wolio [wlo], 458
Butuanon [btw], 493
Butung, *alt.* Cia-Cia [cia], 429
alt. Wolio [wlo], 458
Butuo Yi, *dial.* Yi, Sichuan [iii], 348
Bu'u, *dial.* Ankave [aak], 590
Buu, *alt. dial.* Geji [gji], 160
Buu I, *dial.* Pokomo, Lower [poj], 135
Buu II, *dial.* Pokomo, Lower [poj], 135
Buu III, *dial.* Pokomo, Lower [poj], 135
Buurak, *alt.* Burak [bys], 156
Buwahg, *dial.* Gaam [tbi], 190
Buwal [bhs], 59
Buwan, *alt.* Ngalkbun [ngk], 575
Buweyeu, *dial.* Buang, Mapos [bzh], 595
Buxara Arabic, *alt.* Arabic, Tajiki Spoken [abh], 513
Buxinhua [bxt], 329
Buy, *alt.* Kobiana [kcj], 131, 181
Buya [byy], 99
dial. Loko [lok], 183
Buyaka, *alt.* Sentani [set], 423
Buyang [byu], 329
Buyei, *alt.* Bouyei [pcc], 328
Buyi, *alt.* Bouyei [pcc], 328
alt. Buyu [byi], 99
alt. Giáy [pcc], 523
Buyu [byi], 99
Buyuan, *alt.* Jinuo, Buyuan [jiy], 336
Buyuan Jinuo, *see* Jinuo, Buyuan [jiy], 336
Buyui, *alt.* Bouyei [pcc], 328
Buzaba, *alt.* Bozaba [bzo], 98
Buzawa, *dial.* Kalmyk-Oirat [xal], 554
Buzi, *dial.* Yeskwa [yes], 178
pej. alt. Loma [lom], 138

Buzu, *alt.* Tamajaq, Tawallammat [ttq], 175
Bvanuma, *alt.* Vanuma [vau], 109
Bveri, *dial.* Fali, North [fll], 61
Bviri, *alt.* Belanda Viri [bvi], 189
alt. Birri [bvq], 75
Bvukoo, *alt.* Oku [oku], 71
Bvumba, *dial.* Manyika [mxc], 216, 148
Bwa [bww], 99
alt. Bua [bub], 79
Bwadji, *alt.* Kuni-Boazi [kvg], 608
Bwaidoga, *alt.* Bwaidoka [bwd], 596
dial. Bwaidoka [bwd], 596
Bwaidoka [bwd], 596
Bwaka, *alt.* Ngbaka Ma'bo [nbm], 77, 89, 105
dial. Mbati [mdn], 77
Bwakera, *dial.* Sewa Bay [sew], 624
Bwal, *alt. dial.* Kofyar [kwl], 166
Bwamu, *alt.* Buamu [box], 50
Bwamu, Cwi [bwy], 50
Bwamu, Láá Láá [bwj], 50
Bwana, *dial.* Nuni, Southern [nnw], 53
Bwanabwana [tte], 596
Bwara, *alt.* Boor [bvf], 79
Bwareba, *alt.* Bacama [bcy], 154
Bwatnapni, *dial.* Apma [app], 640
Bwatoo [bwa], 584
Bwatvenua, *alt.* Hano [lml], 642
Bwa'za, *alt. dial.* Mbula-Bwazza [mbu], 170
Bwaza, *alt. dial.* Mbula-Bwazza [mbu], 170
Bwazza, *dial.* Mbula-Bwazza [mbu], 170
Bwe, *alt.* Karen, Bwe [bwe], 464
Bwe Karen, *see* Karen, Bwe [bwe], 464
Bween, *dial.* Fali [fli], 159
Bweko, *dial.* Yasa [yko], 111, 122
Bwela [bwl], 99
Bwende, *dial.* Koongo [kng], 101
Bwile [bwc], 213, 99
Bwilim, *dial.* Dijim-Bwilim [cfa], 158
Bwirege, *dial.* Kuria [kuj], 134
Bwisha, *dial.* Rwanda [kin], 107
Bwisi [bwz], 88, 120
Bwissi, *alt.* Talinga-Bwisi [tlj], 212, 108
Bwol, *dial.* Kofyar [kwl], 166
Bwoncwai, *alt. dial.* Dinka, Southwestern [dik], 190
Bwo'ol, *alt.* Buol [blf], 428
Bworo, *alt.* Boro [bwo], 114
Byabe, *dial.* Norra [nrr], 466
Byangkho Lwo, *alt.* Byangsi [bee], 358, 469

Byangkhopa, *alt.* Byangsi [bee], 358
Byangsi [bee], 358, 469
Byangskat, *alt.* Changthang [cna], 358
Byanshi, *alt.* Byangsi [bee], 358, 469
Byansi, *alt.* Byangsi [bee], 358, 469
Byanskat, *alt.* Changthang [cna], 358
Byasi, *alt.* Byangsi [bee], 469
Byau Min, *alt.* Biao-Jiao Mien [bje], 327
Byelorussian, *alt.* Belarusan [bel], 530, 550
Byep [mkk], 59
   dial. Byep [mkk], 59
Byoki, *alt.* Bokyi [bky], 59
Byrre, *alt. dial.* Mbum [mdd], 66
Bzedux, *alt. dial.* Adyghe [ady], 552
Bzhedug, *alt. dial.* Adyghe [ady], 552
Bzyb, *dial.* Abkhaz [abk], 352, 518
Ca', *dial.* Fe'fe' [fmp], 61
Ca Giong, *alt.* Kayong [kxy], 515
Ca Tua, *alt.* Katua [kta], 523
Caabankeere, *alt. dial.* Fulfulde, Borgu [fue], 44
Caabe, *alt.* Ede Cabe [cbj], 43
Caac [msq], 584
Caapor, *alt.* Urubú-Kaapor [urb], 233
Cabanapo, *alt.* Pomo, Central [poo], 307
Cabanatit, *alt.* Toba-Maskoy [tmf], 285
Cabaran, *alt.* Kavalan [ckv], 511
Cabe, *alt.* Ede Cabe [cbj], 43
Cabeça Seca, *alt. dial.* Gavião do Jiparaná [gvo], 226
Cabécar [cjp], 249
Cabichí, *alt.* Kabixí [xbx], 228
Cabinda, *alt.* Koongo [kng], 40
Cabishi, *alt.* Kabixí [xbx], 228
Cabiuarí, *alt.* Cabiyarí [cbb], 243
Cabiyarí [cbb], 243
Cabo, *dial.* Mískito [miq], 282
Caboverdiano, *alt.* Kabuverdianu [kea], 74
Cabrai, *alt.* Kabiyé [kbp], 208, 45, 125
Cabrais, *alt.* Kabiyé [kbp], 208, 45, 125
Caca Weranos, *alt.* Chimila [cbg], 244
Cacahue, *alt.* Kakauhua [kbf], 242
Cacaloxtepec Mixtec, *see* Mixtec, Cacaloxtepec [miu], 266
Cacaopera [ccr], 252
Cacataibo de Mariscal, *dial.* Cashibo-Cacataibo [cbr], 287
Cacataibo de Sinchi Roca, *dial.* Cashibo-Cacataibo [cbr], 287

Cacche', *alt.* Q'eqchi' [kek], 256
Cacché, *alt.* Kekchí [kek], 221, 252
Cac'chiquel Mam, *alt.* Chicomuceltec [cob], 260
Caceteiros, *alt.* Korubo [xor], 229
Cacgia Roglai, *see* Roglai, Cacgia [roc], 526
Cachabel, *alt.* K'iche', Central [quc], 255
Cachari, *alt.* Kachari [xac], 366
Cacheu-Ziguinchor Creole, *dial.* Crioulo, Upper Guinea [pov], 131, 180
Cachibo, *alt.* Cashibo-Cacataibo [cbr], 287
Cachomashiri, *pej. alt.* Caquinte [cot], 287
Cachuena, *alt. dial.* Waiwai [waw], 233
Cachuy, *alt. dial.* Jaqaru [jqr], 288
Caci, *alt. dial.* Suri [suq], 119, 195
Cacibo, *alt.* Cashibo-Cacataibo [cbr], 287
Cacra-Hongos, *dial.* Quechua, Yauyos [qux], 292
Cacua [cbv], 244
Cadauapuritana, *alt. dial.* Curripaco [kpc], 226
Caddo [cad], 298
Caddoe, *alt.* Caddo [cad], 298
Cadegomeño, *alt.* Cochimi [coj], 262
Cadegomo, *alt.* Cochimi [coj], 262
Cadien, *alt.* French, Cajun [frc], 300
Cadoe Loang, *alt.* Chru [cje], 522
Cadong, *alt.* Sedang [sed], 526
Cadorino, *dial.* Ladin [lld], 544
Caduvéo, *alt.* Kadiwéu [kbc], 228
Caeli, *alt.* Kayeli [kzl], 399
Caffino, *alt.* Kafa [kbr], 116
Caffre, *pej. alt.* Xhosa [xho], 187
Cafre, *pej. alt.* Xhosa [xho], 187
Cafundo Creole [ccd], 226
Caga, *alt.* Enga [enq], 598
Cagani, *dial.* Luri, Northern [lrc], 440
Cagayan, *alt.* Gaddang [gad], 494
Cagayan de Sulu, *alt.* Mapun [sjm], 499, 457
Cagayancillo, *alt.* Kagayanen [cgc], 496
Cagayano, *alt.* Mapun [sjm], 499
Cagayano Cillo, *alt.* Kagayanen [cgc], 496
Cagayanon, *alt.* Mapun [sjm], 499, 457
Cagere, *dial.* Pongu [png], 173
Cagliare, *dial.* Sardinian, Campidanese [sro], 545

Cagliari, *alt. dial.* Sardinian, Campidanese [sro], 545
Cagliaritan, *alt. dial.* Sardinian, Campidanese [sro], 545
Cagua [cbh], 244
Cahivo, *alt.* Cashibo-Cacataibo [cbr], 287
Caho, *alt.* Koho [kpm], 524
Cahto, *alt.* Kato [ktw], 303
Cahtúo, *alt.* Extremaduran [ext], 560
Cahtúö, *alt.* Extremaduran [ext], 560
Cahuapa, *alt.* Chayahuita [cbt], 287
Cahuapana, *dial.* Chayahuita [cbt], 287
Cahuarano [cah], 287
Cahuilla [chl], 299
Cai, *alt.* Burun [bdi], 189
   alt. dial. Suri [suq], 119, 195
Caia, *dial.* Sena [seh], 149
Caiabi, *alt.* Kayabí [kyz], 229
Cailloma Quechua, *dial.* Quechua, Puno [qxp], 292
Caiman Nuevo, *alt.* Kuna, Border [kvn], 246, 283
Caingang, *alt.* Kaingáng [kgp], 228
Caingua, *alt.* Kaiwá [kgk], 228, 220
Cairene Arabic, *dial.* Arabic, Egyptian Spoken [arz], 110
Cairui, *alt.* Kairui-Midiki [krd], 351
Caiua, *alt.* Kaiwá [kgk], 228
Caiwa, *alt.* Kaiwá [kgk], 228
Caiwá, *alt.* Kaiwá [kgk], 220
Cajamarca Quechua, *see* Quechua, Cajamarca [qvc], 290
Cajan, *alt.* French, Cajun [frc], 300
Cajatambo North Lima Quechua, *see* Quechua, Cajatambo North Lima [qvl], 290
Cajeli, *alt.* Kayeli [kzl], 399
Cajonos Zapotec, *see* Zapotec, Cajonos [zad], 277
Cajonos Zapotec, *dial.* Zapotec, Cajonos [zad], 277
Cajun, *alt.* French, Cajun [frc], 300
Cajun French, *see* French, Cajun [frc], 300
Caka [ckx], 59
Cakchiquel, *alt.* Kaqkchikel, Central [cak], 254
Cakchiquel Mam, *alt.* Chicomuceltec [cob], 260, 253
Cakfem-Mushere [cky], 156
Cakke, *dial.* Duri [mvp], 429
Cala, *alt.* Chala [cll], 123
Cala-Cala, *alt.* C'lela [dri], 157
Calabar, *alt.* Efik [efi], 158
Calabrian Albanian, *dial.* Albanian, Arbëreshë [aae], 543
Calabro-Sicilian, *alt.* Sicilian [scn], 545

Calaisis, *alt. dial.* Picard [pcd], 537
Calamian Tagbanwa, *see* Tagbanwa, Calamian [tbk], 502
Calamiano, *alt.* Tagbanwa, Calamian [tbk], 502
Calanasan, *dial.* Isnag [isd], 496
Calão, *alt.* Caló [rmr], 551
　alt. dial. Caló [rmr], 559, 551
Calatravanhon, *dial.* Bantoanon [bno], 492
Calcutta Sign Language, *dial.* Indian Sign Language [ins], 365
Calderón Highland Quichua, *see* Quichua, Calderón Highland [qud], 251
Calderón Quichua, *alt.* Quichua, Calderón Highland [qud], 251
Caldoche, *pej. alt.* Tayo [cks], 585
Calebasses, *alt.* Kenswei Nsei [ndb], 64
Caliana, *alt.* Sapé [spc], 312
Calibugan, *alt.* Subanon, Kolibugan [skn], 501
Callahuaya, *alt.* Callawalla [caw], 222
Callawalla [caw], 222
Calo, *alt.* Caló [rmr], 226
Caló [rmr], 559, 226, 536, 551
Caluyanen, *alt.* Caluyanun [clu], 493
Caluyanhon, *alt.* Caluyanun [clu], 493
Caluyanun [clu], 493
Cam, *alt. dial.* Dijim-Bwilim [cfa], 158
Cam Mu, *alt.* Khmu [kjg], 524
Cama, *alt.* Ebrié [ebr], 92
　dial. Lefa [lfa], 65
Camaiura, *alt.* Kamayurá [kay], 228
Camajere, *dial.* Pongu [png], 173
Camalal, *alt.* Chamalal [cji], 553
Caman, *alt.* Ebrié [ebr], 92
Camaracota, *dial.* Pemon [aoc], 231
Camaracoto, *dial.* Pemon [aoc], 312, 257
Camarines Norte Agta, *see* Agta, Camarines Norte [abd], 490
Camba, *alt.* Kamba [xba], 228
　dial. Bugis [bug], 428
Cambap, *alt.* Twendi [twn], 72
Cambeba, *alt.* Omagua [omg], 289, 231
Cambeeba, *alt.* Omagua [omg], 289
Cambela, *alt.* Omagua [omg], 289, 231
Cambodian, *alt.* Khmer, Central [khm], 325, 524
Cambodian Cham, *alt.* Cham, Western [cja], 325, 514, 522

Cambresis, *alt. dial.* Picard [pcd], 537
Cameali, *alt.* Chambeali [cdh], 358
Cameeragal, *dial.* Awabakal [awk], 568
Camëntsëä, *alt.* Camsá [kbh], 244
Camerija, *alt.* Albanian, Tosk [als], 540
　dial. Albanian, Tosk [als], 529
Cameron, *alt. dial.* Semai [sea], 455
Cameroon Creole English, *alt.* Pidgin, Cameroon [wes], 71
Cameroon Mambila, *see* Mambila, Cameroon [mcu], 66
Cameroon Pidgin, *see* Pidgin, Cameroon [wes], 71
Camileroi, *alt.* Gamilaraay [kld], 570
Camling [rab], 469
Camo, *dial.* Kudu-Camo [kov], 167
Camonayan, *dial.* Agta, Dupaninan [duo], 490
Camorta, *dial.* Nicobarese, Central [ncb], 381
Camotes, *alt.* Porohanon [prh], 500
Camotlán Mixe, *dial.* Mixe, Coatlán [mco], 265
Campa, *pej. alt.* Ajyíninka Apurucayali [cpc], 286
　pej. alt. Ashéninka [cni], 286
　pej. alt. Ashéninka Pajonal [cjo], 286
Campalagian [cml], 428
　dial. Campalagian [cml], 428
Campeba, *alt.* Omagua [omg], 289, 231
Campidanese, *alt.* Sardinian, Campidanese [sro], 545
Campidanese Sardinian, *see* Sardinian, Campidanese [sro], 545
Campidese, *alt.* Sardinian, Campidanese [sro], 545
Campo, *alt.* Kumiai [dih], 263, 303
Campo Marino Albanian, *dial.* Albanian, Arbëreshë [aae], 543
Campuon, *alt.* Tampuan [tpu], 326
Camsá [kbh], 244
Camtho [cmt], 185
Camucones, *alt.* Tidong [tid], 395, 458
Camuhi, *alt.* Cemuhî [cam], 584
Camuki, *alt.* Cemuhî [cam], 584
Camuru, *alt. dial.* Kariri-Xocó [kzw], 228
Canaanic, *alt.* Knaanic [czk], 533
Canala, *alt.* Xârâcùù [ane], 585
Canamanti, *alt.* Jamamadí [jaa], 227
Canamarí, *alt.* Kanamarí [knm], 228
Cañar Highland Quichua, *see* Quichua, Cañar Highland [qxr], 251
Canarese, *alt.* Kannada [kan], 366
　alt. Kurumba [kfi], 371

Cañaris, *dial.* Quechua, Lambayeque [quf], 291
Canary Islands Spanish, *dial.* Spanish [spa], 560
Cancuc, *alt.* Tzeltal, Oxchuc [tzh], 276
Candelaria Loxicha Zapotec, *dial.* Zapotec, Loxicha [ztp], 278
Candoshi, *alt.* Candoshi-Shapra [cbu], 287
Candoshi-Shapra [cbu], 287
Candoxi, *alt.* Candoshi-Shapra [cbu], 287
Cane, *alt.* Ncane [ncr], 69
Canela [ram], 226
Canelos Quichua, *alt.* Quichua, Northern Pastaza [qvz], 251
Canga-Peba, *alt.* Omagua [omg], 289, 231
Cangala, *alt.* Nkangala [nkn], 41
Cangin, *dial.* Noon [snf], 181
Canglo Monba, *alt.* Tshangla [tsj], 345
Cangluo Menba, *alt.* Tshangla [tsj], 345, 389
Cangva, *alt.* Zhuang, Northern [ccx], 349
Canichana [caz], 222
Caning, *alt.* Shatt [shj], 195
Caño Padilla-La Laguna, *dial.* Yukpa [yup], 248
Canoa, *alt.* Avá-Canoeiro [avv], 225
Canoe, *alt.* Avá-Canoeiro [avv], 225
Canoé, *alt.* Kanoé [kxo], 228
Canoeiro, *alt.* Rikbaktsa [rkb], 232
Canoeiros, *alt.* Avá-Canoeiro [avv], 225
Canpa, *alt.* Rangkas [rgk], 384
Cansu, *dial.* Pongu [png], 173
Cant, *alt.* Shelta [sth], 543
Cantel Quiché, *alt.* K'iche', West Central [qut], 255
Cantilan, *dial.* Surigaonon [sul], 502
Cantonese, *alt.* Chinese, Yue [yue], 331, 283, 324, 391, 454, 508, 514
　dial. Chinese, Yue [yue], 454
Cao Lan [mlc], 522, 329
Cao Lan-Sán Chi, *alt.* Cao Lan [mlc], 522, 329
Cao Miao [cov], 329
Caodeng, *alt. dial.* Jiarong [jya], 336
Caolan, *alt.* Cao Lan [mlc], 522, 329
Capa, *alt.* Quapaw [qua], 307
Capanahua [kaq], 287
Cape Afrikaans, *dial.* Afrikaans [afr], 185
Cape Cors, *alt. dial.* Corsican [cos], 536

Cape Draping Gelao, *alt.* Gelao, Green [giq], 522
Cape Hottentot, *alt.* Xiri [xii], 187
Cape York Creole, *alt.* Torres Strait Creole [tcs], 577
Capisano, *alt.* Capiznon [cps], 493
Capiseño, *alt.* Capiznon [cps], 493
Capiznon [cps], 493
Caposho, *alt.* Maxakalí [mbl], 230
Cappadocian Greek [cpg], 540
Capul, *alt.* Inabaknon [abx], 495
Capuleño, *alt.* Inabaknon [abx], 495
Caquetá, *alt.* Koreguaje [coe], 246
Caquinte [cot], 287
Caquinte Campa, *alt.* Caquinte [cot], 287
Car, *alt.* Nicobarese, Car [caq], 381
Car Nicobarese, *see* Nicobarese, Car [caq], 381
Cara [cfd], 156
  dial. Shua [shg], 48
Carabayo [cby], 244
Caramanta [crf], 244
Carapana [cbc], 244
  alt. Karapanã [cbc], 228
Carapanã, *alt.* Karapanã [cbc], 228
Carapana-Tapuya, *alt.* Carapana [cbc], 244
Carapató, *alt.* Tingui-Boto [tgv], 233
Caras-Pretas, *alt.* Mundurukú [myu], 230
Caravare, *alt.* Kuruáya [kyr], 229
Care, *alt. dial.* Sena [seh], 149
Cargese, *dial.* Greek [ell], 537
Cari, *alt.* Aka-Cari [aci], 353
Carib [car], 311, 226, 252, 257, 295
Carib Motilón, *alt.* Yukpa [yup], 248
Carib, Island [crb], 250, 295
Caribbean Hindustani, *see* Hindustani, Caribbean [hns], 295, 257, 296
Caribbean Javanese, *see* Javanese, Caribbean [jvn], 295, 252
Caribe, *alt.* Carib [car], 311, 226, 252, 257, 295
  alt. Garifuna [cab], 258, 221, 253, 282
Caribou Eskimo, *dial.* Inuktitut, Western Canadian [ikt], 238
Carihona, *alt.* Carijona [cbd], 244
Carijona [cbd], 244
Cariña, *alt.* Carib [car], 311, 226, 252, 257, 295
Caripuna, *alt.* Karipuná [kuq], 228
Caritiana, *alt.* Karitiâna [ktn], 228
Carmel, *alt. dial.* Ohlone, Southern [css], 306
Carnico, *dial.* Friulian [fur], 544
Carnijó, *alt.* Fulniô [fun], 226

Carolina Algonquian [crr], 299
Carolinian [cal], 586
Carpathian, *alt.* Rusyn [rue], 564, 558
Carpathian Romani, *see* Romani, Carpathian [rmc], 533, 542, 550, 551, 558, 564
Carpatho-Rusyn, *alt.* Rusyn [rue], 564, 558
Carraga Mandaya, *alt.* Mandaya, Karaga [mry], 498
Carriacou Creole English, *dial.* Grenadian Creole English [gcl], 253
Carrier [crx], 236
Carrier, Southern [caf], 236
Carútana [cru], 226
Casa, *alt.* Jola-Kasa [csk], 180
Cashibo, *dial.* Cashibo-Cacataibo [cbr], 287
Cashibo-Cacataibo [cbr], 287
Cashinahua [cbs], 287, 226
Cashinahuá, *alt.* Cashinahua [cbs], 226
Cashmeeree, *alt.* Kashmiri [kas], 367, 486
Cashmiri, *alt.* Kashmiri [kas], 367, 486
Cashquiha, *alt.* Guana [gva], 284
Cashubian, *alt.* Kashubian [csb], 550
Casiguran Dumagat, *alt.* Agta, Casiguran Dumagat [dgc], 490
Casiguran Dumagat Agta, *see* Agta, Casiguran Dumagat [dgc], 490
Casiguranin, *alt.* Kasiguranin [ksn], 498
Caska, *alt.* Kaska [kkz], 238
Cassanga, *alt.* Kasanga [ccj], 131
Cassubian, *alt.* Kashubian [csb], 550
Castellano, *alt.* Spanish [spa], 560, 222, 243, 249, 251, 252, 256, 258, 274, 283, 284, 293, 308
Castilian, *alt.* Spanish [spa], 560, 529
  dial. Spanish [spa], 560
Castillan, *alt.* Spanish [spa], 538
Casu, *alt.* Asu [asa], 197
Casuarina Coast Asmat, *see* Asmat, Casuarina Coast [asc], 411
Cataelano Mandaya, *see* Mandaya, Cataelano [mst], 498
Català, *alt.* Catalan-Valencian-Balear [cat], 559, 529
Catalán, *alt.* Catalan-Valencian-Balear [cat], 559, 529
Catalan-Rousillonese, *dial.* Catalan-Valencian-Balear [cat], 559

Catalan-Valencian-Balear [cat], 559, 529, 536, 543
Catalonian, *alt.* Catalan-Valencian-Balear [cat], 559
Catalonian Calo, *dial.* Caló [rmr], 559, 536, 551
Catalonian Sign Language [csc], 560
Catauian, *alt. dial.* Waiwai [waw], 233
Catauichi, *alt.* Katawixi [xat], 228
Catauixi, *alt.* Katawixi [xat], 228
Catawba [chc], 299
Catawian, *alt. dial.* Waiwai [waw], 233
Catawishi, *alt.* Katawixi [xat], 228
Catawixi, *alt.* Katawixi [xat], 228
Cateelenyo, *alt.* Mandaya, Cataelano [mst], 498
Catio, *alt.* Emberá-Catío [cto], 245
Catío, *alt.* Emberá-Catío [cto], 283
Catrú, *alt.* Emberá-Baudó [bdc], 245
Catuquina, *alt.* Katukína [kav], 228
  alt. Katukína, Panoan [knt], 229
Cauca [cca], 244
Caundu, *dial.* Pongu [png], 173
Cauque Mixed Language, *alt.* Kaqkchikel-K'iche' Mixed Language [ckz], 255
Cauqui, *dial.* Jaqaru [jqr], 288
Caura, *dial.* Sanumá [xsu], 232
Cauyarí, *alt.* Cabiyarí [cbb], 243
Cauzuh, *pej. alt.* Xhosa [xho], 187
Cavcuvenskij, *dial.* Koryak [kpy], 505
Cavina, *alt.* Araona [aro], 222
Cavineña [cav], 222
Caviteño, *dial.* Chavacano [cbk], 493
Cawai, *alt.* Atsam [cch], 154
Cawdur, *dial.* Turkmen [tuk], 520
Cawe, *alt.* Atsam [cch], 154
Cawi, *alt.* Atsam [cch], 154
Caxibo, *alt.* Cashibo-Cacataibo [cbr], 287
Caxinawa, *alt.* Cashinahua [cbs], 287
Caxinawá, *alt.* Cashinahua [cbs], 287, 226
Caxur, *alt.* Tsakhur [tkr], 320, 557
Cayambe Quichua, *alt.* Quichua, Calderón Highland [qud], 251
Cayapa, *alt.* Chachi [cbi], 250
Caylloma Quechua, *dial.* Quechua, Cusco [quz], 290
Cayman Islands English, *dial.* English [eng], 242
Cayor, *dial.* Wolof [wol], 182, 145
Cayua, *alt.* Kaiwá [kgk], 228
Cayubaba [cyb], 222

Cayuga [cay], 236, 299
Cayuvava, *alt.* Cayubaba [cyb], 222
Cayuwaba, *alt.* Cayubaba [cyb], 222
Cazama, *alt.* Khwe [xuu], 214
	alt. Kxoe [xuu], 40
Cebaara Senoufo, *see* Senoufo,
	Cebaara [sef], 94
Cebu, *dial.* Cebuano [ceb], 493
Cebuano [ceb], 493
Ceemba, *dial.* Ntcham [bud], 209
Cele, *dial.* Xhosa [xho], 187
Cellate, *alt.* Besisi [mhe], 454
Celle, *alt.* Jeri Kuo [jek], 93
Celle San Vito, *dial.* Franco-
	Provençal [frp], 543
Cemba, *alt.* Akaselem [aks], 206
Cemdalsk, *dial.* Evenki [evn], 504
Cemual, *alt. dial.* Kalenjin [kln], 133
Cemuhî [cam], 584
Cen, *dial.* Berom [bom], 155
Cen Berom, *alt.* Berom [bom], 155
Cen Tuum, *alt.* Centúúm [cet], 156
Cenge, *alt.* Kenga [kyq], 82
	dial. Kenga [kyq], 82
Cenka, *alt.* Kyenga [tye], 45
Cenrana, *alt. dial.* Mandar
	[mdr], 431
Central, *dial.* Limba, West-Central
	[lia], 183
Central Abuan, *dial.* Abua [abn],
	153
Central Afar, *alt. dial.* Afar
	[aar], 112
	dial. Afar [aar], 111
Central Alaskan Yupik, *alt.*
	Yupik, Central [esu], 310
Central Ambon, *alt.* Laha
	[lhh], 400
Central American Carib, *alt.*
	Garifuna [cab], 258, 221, 253,
	282
Central Amis, *dial.* Amis
	[ami], 511
Central and North Pohjanmaa,
	dial. Finnish [fin], 534
Central Angor, *alt. dial.* Angor
	[agg], 589
Central Aragonese, *dial.*
	Aragonese [arg], 558
Central Asian Arabic, *alt.* Arabic,
	Tajiki Spoken [abh], 513
	alt. Arabic, Uzbeki Spoken
	[auz], 521
Central Asmat, *see* Asmat, Central
	[cns], 411
Central Asturian, *alt. dial.*
	Asturian [ast], 551
	dial. Asturian [ast], 559
Central Atlas, *dial.* Tamazight,
	Central Atlas [tzm], 146

Central Atlas Tamazight, *see*
	Tamazight, Central Atlas
	[tzm], 146, 40
Central Aunalei, *dial.* One, Molmo
	[aun], 620
Central Awyu, *see* Awyu, Central
	[awu], 412
Central Aymara, *see* Aymara,
	Central [ayr], 222, 219, 242, 287
Central Aztec, *alt.* Nahuatl, Central
	[nhn], 270
Central Bai, *see* Bai, Central
	[bca], 326
Central Bassa, *dial.* Bassa
	[bsq], 137
Central Bavarian, *dial.* Bavarian
	[bar], 530, 533, 538, 543
Central Belarusan, *dial.* Belarusan
	[bel], 530
Central Bété, *alt.* Béte, Guiberoua
	[bet], 92
Central Bicolano, *see* Bicolano,
	Central [bcl], 493
Central Bohemian, *dial.* Czech
	[ces], 533
Central Boikin, *dial.* Boikin
	[bzf], 594
Central Bolivian Quechua, *alt.*
	Quechua, South Bolivian
	[quh], 223, 220
Central Bomitaba, *dial.* Bomitaba
	[zmx], 88
Central Bontoc, *see* Bontoc,
	Central [bnc], 493
Central Buang, *alt.* Buang, Mapos
	[bzh], 595
Central Bunun, *dial.* Bunun
	[bnn], 511
Central Buru, *dial.* Buru
	[mhs], 397
Central Cagayan Agta, *see* Agta,
	Central Cagayan [agt], 490
Central Campidanese, *dial.*
	Sardinian, Campidanese [sro], 545
Central Carrier, *alt.* Carrier
	[crx], 236
Central Catalan, *dial.* Catalan-
	Valencian-Balear [cat], 559
Central Chuwabo, *dial.* Chuwabu
	[chw], 147
Central Colloquial Maithili, *dial.*
	Maithili [mai], 373
Central Crimean, *dial.* Crimean
	Turkish [crh], 521, 518, 532, 551
Central Cumberland, *dial.* English
	[eng], 565
Central Damara, *dial.* Nama
	[naq], 150
Central Dangaleat, *dial.* Dangaléat
	[daa], 80

Central Danish, *alt.* Danish
	[dan], 533
Central Dhatki, *dial.* Dhatki
	[mki], 484
Central Dibole, *dial.* Dibole
	[bvx], 88
Central Dinka, *alt.* Dinka, South
	Central [dib], 190
Central Diodio, *dial.* Diodio
	[ddi], 597
Central Dobu, *alt. dial.* Dobu
	[dob], 597
Central Dusun, *see* Dusun, Central
	[dtp], 456
Central East Alune, *dial.* Alune
	[alp], 396
Central East Sasak, *alt. dial.*
	Sasak [sas], 409
Central Emiliano, *dial.* Emiliano-
	Romagnolo [eml], 543
Central Ersu, *alt. dial.* Ersu
	[ers], 332
Central Extremaduran, *dial.*
	Extremaduran [ext], 560
Central Gogo, *alt. dial.* Gogo
	[gog], 198
Central Gourmanchema, *dial.*
	Gourmanchéma [gux], 51
Central Grand Valley Dani, *alt.*
	Dani, Mid Grand Valley [dnt], 413
Central Grebo, *see* Grebo, Central
	[grv], 138
Central Guangdong, *alt. dial.*
	Chinese, Hakka [hak], 329
Central Guéré, *alt.* Wè Southern
	[gxx], 95
Central Guizhou, *alt. dial.* Bouyei
	[pcc], 328
Central Huancayo, *alt. dial.*
	Quechua, Huaylla Wanca
	[qvw], 291
Central Huasteca Nahuatl, *see*
	Nahuatl, Central Huasteca [nch],
	270
Central Huishui Hmong, *see*
	Hmong, Central Huishui [hmc], 334
Central Huishui Miao, *alt.*
	Hmong, Central Huishui [hmc], 334
Central Ibibio, *dial.* Ibibio
	[ibb], 162
Central Igede, *alt. dial.* Igede
	[ige], 163
Central Isan, *dial.* Thai,
	Northeastern [tts], 517
Central Jibbali, *dial.* Shehri
	[shv], 483
Central Juxtlahuaca Mixtec, *alt.*
	Mixtec, Juxtlahuaca [vmc], 267
Central Kadazan, *alt.* Dusun,
	Central [dtp], 456

Central Sedang, *dial.* Sedang [sed], 526

Central Sel'kup, *alt. dial.* Selkup [sel], 506

Central Selk'up, *alt. dial.* Selkup [sel], 506

Central Sentani, *dial.* Sentani [set], 423

Central Sewa Bay, *dial.* Sewa Bay [sew], 624

Central Shilha, *alt.* Tamazight, Central Atlas [tzm], 146, 40

Central Siberian Yupik, *see* Yupik, Central Siberian [ess], 310, 507

Central Sierra Miwok, *see* Miwok, Central Sierra [csm], 305

Central Sikka, *alt. dial.* Sika [ski], 409

Central Sinama, *alt.* Sama, Central [sml], 500, 458

Central Sindhi, *alt. dial.* Sindhi [snd], 488

Central Sola de Vega Zapotec, *alt.* Zapotec, Texmelucan [zpz], 280

Central Songai, *alt.* Songhay [hmb], 54 *alt.* Songhay, Humburi Senni [hmb], 144

Central Soqotri, *dial.* Soqotri [sqt], 528

Central South Sasak, *alt. dial.* Sasak [sas], 409

Central Subanen, *see* Subanen, Central [syb], 501

Central Tabukang, *alt. dial.* Sangir [sxn], 432

Central Tagbanwa, *see* Tagbanwa, Central [tgt], 502

Central Tai, *alt.* Thai [tha], 517

Central Talyshi, *dial.* Talysh [tly], 442

Central Tarahumara, *see* Tarahumara, Central [tar], 274

Central Tày, *dial.* Tày [tyz], 527

Central Tboli, *dial.* Tboli [tbl], 502

Central Teke, *alt.* Teke-Eboo [ebo], 90

Central Tharaka, *alt. dial.* Tharaka [thk], 136

Central Thulung, *dial.* Thulung [tdh], 481

Central Tibetan, *see* Tibetan, Central [bod], 344

Central Tibetan, *alt.* Tibetan [bod], 388, 481

Central Tigak, *dial.* Tigak [tgc], 627

Central Timbe, *dial.* Timbe [tim], 627

Central Tunebo, *see* Tunebo, Central [tuf], 248, 312

Central Tuvin, *dial.* Tuvin [tyv], 507

Central Udab, *dial.* Fuyug [fuy], 599

Central Uma, *alt. dial.* Uma [ppk], 434

Central Urat, *alt. dial.* Urat [urt], 629

Central Uyghur, *dial.* Uyghur [uig], 346

Central Vanua Levu, *dial.* Fijian [fij], 580

Central Veps, *alt. dial.* Veps [vep], 557

Central Vietnamese, *dial.* Vietnamese [vie], 527

Central Villa Alta Zapotec, *alt.* Zapotec, Tabaa [zat], 280

Central Vivigani, *dial.* Iduna [viv], 602

Central Vlax Romani, *dial.* Romani, Vlax [rmy], 556, 564

Central Waibuk, *dial.* Haruai [tmd], 601

Central Wakhi, *dial.* Wakhi [wbl], 513

Central Walloon, *dial.* Walloon [wln], 531

Central Wantoat, *dial.* Wantoat [wnc], 631

Central West Alune, *dial.* Alune [alp], 396

Central West Gurage, *alt.* Sebat Bet Gurage [sgw], 118

Central West Sasak, *alt. dial.* Sasak [sas], 409

Central Yamalele, *dial.* Iamalele [yml], 602

Central Yana, *dial.* Yana [ynn], 310

Central Yawa, *dial.* Yawa [yva], 426

Central Yi, *see* Yi, Central [ycl], 347

Central Yupik, *see* Yupik, Central [esu], 310

Central-Eastern Niger Fulfulde, *see* Fulfulde, Central-Eastern Niger [fuq], 151

Central-Eastern Tamang, *dial.* Tamang, Eastern [taj], 479

Central-Western Agrigentino, *alt. dial.* Sicilian [scn], 545

Central-Western Ijo, *alt.* Izon [ijc], 164

Centúúm [cet], 156

Cep, *dial.* Acipa, Western [awc], 153

Cerma [cme], 50, 92

Cerro Grande Totonac, *dial.* Totonac, Coyutla [toc], 276

Cerumba, *dial.* Shwai [shw], 195

Cestina, *alt.* Czech [ces], 533

Ceta, *alt.* Hmwaveke [mrk], 584

Cevenda, *alt.* Venda [ven], 217

Cewa, *alt. dial.* Nyanja [nya], 148, 215

Cez, *alt.* Dido [ddo], 554

Cha', *dial.* Mmen [bfm], 67

Cha kawaida, *dial.* Mbugu [mhd], 202

Cha ndani, *dial.* Mbugu [mhd], 202

Cha' Palaachi, *alt.* Chachi [cbi], 250

Chaari, *alt. dial.* Zeem [zua], 178

Chabakano, *alt.* Chavacano [cbk], 493

Chabao, *dial.* Jiarong [jya], 336

Chachapoyas Quechua, *see* Quechua, Chachapoyas [quk], 290

Chachi [cbi], 250

Chaco Pilagá, *dial.* Pilagá [plg], 220

Chaco Sur, *alt.* Toba [tob], 220

Chácobo [cao], 222

Chad Arabic, *alt.* Arabic, Chadian Spoken [shu], 78

Chadian Arabic, *alt.* Arabic, Chadian Spoken [shu], 78 *alt.* Arabic, Shuwa [shu], 154

Chadian Sign Language [cds], 79

Chadian Spoken Arabic, *see* Arabic, Chadian Spoken [shu], 78

Chadian Spoken Arabic, *alt.* Arabic, Shuwa [shu], 56

Chadic Arabic, *alt.* Arabic, Shuwa [shu], 151

Chagatai [chg], 520 *alt. dial.* Turkmen [tuk], 318

Chaghatay, *alt.* Chagatai [chg], 520

Chaha, *dial.* Sebat Bet Gurage [sgw], 118

Chaha'er, *alt. dial.* Mongolian, Peripheral [mvf], 339

Chahar, *dial.* Mongolian, Peripheral [mvf], 339

Chahar-Aimaq, *alt.* Aimaq [aiq], 315

Chahi, *dial.* Nyaturu [rim], 203

Chai, *dial.* Suri [suq], 119, 195

Chaibasa-Thakurmunda, *dial.* Ho [hoc], 364

Chail, *dial.* Torwali [trw], 489

Chaima [ciy], 311

Chajul Ixil, *see* Ixil, Chajul [ixj], 254

Chak [ckh], 462, 321 *dial.* Ghale, Kutang [ght], 471

Chakali [cli], 123

Chakama, *alt.* Chakma [ccp], 358

Chakavski, *alt. dial.* Croatian [hrv], 532

Chakfem, *alt.* Cakfem-Mushere [cky], 156

Chakhar, *alt. dial.* Mongolian, Peripheral [mvf], 339

Chakhesang, *alt.* Naga, Chokri [nri], 377

Chakma [ccp], 321, 358

Chakosi, *alt.* Anufo [cko], 123, 42, 207

Chakpa, *alt. dial.* Meitei [mni], 375 *dial.* Kado [kdv], 464, 337, 450

Chakriaba, *alt.* Xakriabá [xkr], 234

Chakrima Naga, *alt.* Naga, Chokri [nri], 377

Chakroma, *dial.* Naga, Angami [njm], 377

Chakru, *alt.* Naga, Chokri [nri], 377

Chal, *alt.* Rutul [rut], 556

Chala [cll], 123 *pej. alt.* Ron [cla], 174

Chalah, *dial.* Chrau [crw], 522

Chalas, *dial.* Pashayi, Northeast [aee], 317

Chaldean, *alt.* Chaldean Neo-Aramaic [cld], 443

Chaldean Neo-Aramaic [cld], 443

Chalgari, *alt.* Waneci [wne], 489

Chali, *alt.* Chalikha [tgf], 323 *alt. dial.* Bru, Eastern [bru], 450 *dial.* Komo [xom], 192

Chalikha [tgf], 323

Chalipkha, *alt.* Chalikha [tgf], 323

Challa, *pej. alt.* Ron [cla], 174

Chalun, *dial.* Chrau [crw], 522

Cham, *alt.* Cham, Western [cja], 325, 514, 522 *alt. dial.* Dijim-Bwilim [cfa], 158 *alt. dial.* Mak [mkg], 339 *dial.* Iu Mien [ium], 523

Cham Chang, *alt.* Naga, Tase [nst], 466, 380

Cham, Eastern [cjm], 522

Cham, Western [cja], 325, 514, 522

Cham-Re, *alt.* Hre [hre], 523

Chama, *pej. alt.* Ese Ejja [ese], 222, 288

Chamacoco [ceg], 284

Chamacoco Bravo, *dial.* Chamacoco [ceg], 284

Chamalal [cji], 553

Chamalin, *alt.* Chamalal [cji], 553

Chaman, *alt.* Mang [zng], 525, 339

Chamar, *alt.* Chamari [cdg], 358

Chamari [cdg], 358

Chamarwa, *alt.* Haryanvi [bgc], 364

Chamaya, *alt.* Chambeali [cdh], 358

Chamba, *alt.* Akaselem [aks], 206 *alt.* Pattani [lae], 383

Chamba Daka, *alt.* Samba Daka [ccg], 174

Chamba Lahuli, *alt.* Pattani [lae], 383

Chamba Leeko, *alt.* Samba Leko [ndi], 72

Chamba Leko, *alt.* Samba Leko [ndi], 174

Chamba-Lahuli, *dial.* Pattani [lae], 383

Chambeali [cdh], 358

Chambhar Boli, *alt.* Chamari [cdg], 358

Chambhari, *alt.* Chamari [cdg], 358

Chambiali, *alt.* Chambeali [cdh], 358

Chambiyali, *alt.* Chambeali [cdh], 358

Chamboa, *alt.* Karajá [kpj], 228

Chambri [can], 596

Chamchang, *alt. dial.* Naga, Tase [nst], 380

Chami, *alt.* Emberá-Chamí [cmi], 245

Chamicolo, *alt.* Chamicuro [ccc], 287

Chamicura, *alt.* Chamicuro [ccc], 287

Chamicuro [ccc], 287

Chamiyali Pahari, *alt.* Chambeali [cdh], 358

Chamling, *alt.* Camling [rab], 469

Chamlinge Rai, *alt.* Camling [rab], 469

Chamo, *alt. dial.* Kudu-Camo [kov], 167

Chamorro [cha], 581, 587 *dial.* Chamorro [cha], 581

Champhung, *alt.* Naga, Tangkhul [nmf], 380

Chamula, *alt.* Tzotzil, Chamula [tzc], 277

Chamula Tzotzil, *see* Tzotzil, Chamula [tzc], 277

Chamus, *dial.* Samburu [saq], 136

Chamya, *alt.* Chambeali [cdh], 358

Chan, *alt.* Laz [lzz], 519, 352

Chan Santa Cruz Maya, *see* Maya, Chan Santa Cruz [yus], 264

Chana, *alt.* Chinali [cih], 359 *alt.* Guana [gqn], 227

Chañabal, *alt.* Tojolabal [toj], 275

Chanal, *alt.* Tzeltal, Oxchuc [tzh], 276

Chanal Cancuc, *dial.* Tzeltal, Oxchuc [tzh], 276

Chanco, *alt.* Woun Meu [noa], 284

Chandari, *dial.* Halbi [hlb], 363

Chandinahua, *dial.* Sharanahua [mcd], 293, 232

Chandpuri, *dial.* Garhwali [gbm], 360

Chané [caj], 219

dial. Guaraní, Western Argentine [gui], 220

Chang, *alt.* Naga, Chang [nbc], 377 *dial.* Kuy [kdt], 515

Chang Chá, *alt.* Giáy [pcc], 523

Chang Naga, *see* Naga, Chang [nbc], 377

Chang-Jing, *dial.* Chinese, Gan [gan], 329

Changa, *alt. dial.* Ndau [ndc], 148 *alt. dial.* Tsonga [tso], 149, 217 *dial.* Ndau [ndc], 216

Changana, *alt.* Tsonga [tso], 197 *dial.* Tsonga [tso], 186, 149, 217

Changki, *dial.* Naga, Ao [njo], 377

Changnoi, *dial.* Naga, Wancho [nnp], 380

Changnyu, *dial.* Naga, Konyak [nbe], 378

Chango, *alt.* Sangu [snq], 121

Changping, *alt.* Biao Mon [bmt], 327

Changriwa [cga], 596

Changs-Skat, *alt.* Changthang [cna], 358

Changsapa Boli, *alt.* Pattani [lae], 383

Changsen, *alt. dial.* Chin, Thado [tcz], 359 *dial.* Chin, Thado [tcz], 463

Changtang, *alt.* Changthang [cna], 358

Changtang Ladakhi, *alt.* Changthang [cna], 358

Changthang [cna], 358

Changyanguh, *alt.* Naga, Chang [nbc], 377

Changyi, *dial.* Chinese, Xiang [hsn], 331

Chanka, *alt.* Quechua, Ayacucho [quy], 289

Channali, *alt.* Chinali [cih], 359

Chanpa Lo, *alt.* Chaudangsi [cdn], 358

Chantel, *alt.* Chantyal [chx], 469

Chantyal [chx], 469

Chanuri, *alt.* Laz [lzz], 519, 352

Chanzan, *alt.* Laz [lzz], 519, 352

Chao Kong Meng, *alt. dial.* Biao-Jiao Mien [bje], 327

Chao-Shan, *dial.* Chinese, Min Nan [nan], 330

Chaobon, *pej. alt.* Nyahkur [cbn], 516

Chaocha Pai, *alt.* Koreguaje [coe], 246

Chaochow, *alt. dial.* Chinese, Min Nan [nan], 454, 508, 514 *dial.* Chinese, Min Nan [nan], 324, 391

Chaodon, *pej. alt.* Nyahkur [cbn], 516

Chaoue, *alt. dial.* Mpade [mpi], 68, 84

Chaouia, *alt.* Tachawit [shy], 39

Chaoxian, *alt.* Korean [kor], 337

Chaozhou, *alt. dial.* Chinese, Min Nan [nan], 330, 508
dial. Chinese, Min Nan [nan], 514

Chapai, *alt.* Chuj, Ixtatán [cnm], 262

Chapara, *dial.* Candoshi-Shapra [cbu], 287

Chaplino, *dial.* Yupik, Central Siberian [ess], 310, 507

Chapogir, *alt.* Evenki [evn], 504

Chapultenango, *dial.* Zoque, Francisco León [zos], 282

Chapurreáu, *pej. alt.* Fala [fax], 560

Char, *alt. dial.* Avar [ava], 553, 319

Char Aimaq, *alt.* Aimaq [aiq], 315

Chara [cra], 114
alt. Cara [cfd], 156

Charani, *dial.* Bhili [bhb], 356

Chararana, *alt. dial.* Guana [gva], 284

Charazani, *dial.* Quechua, North Bolivian [qul], 223

Charberd, *alt. dial.* Armenian [hye], 318

Chari Chong, *dial.* Chin, Falam [flm], 358

Chari-Baguirmi, *dial.* Arabic, Chadian Spoken [shu], 78

Chariar, *alt.* Aka-Cari [aci], 353

Charlang, *alt. dial.* Bakhtiari [bqi], 438

Charotari, *alt. dial.* Gujarati [guj], 363

Charumba, *alt.* Zakhring [zkr], 390

Charumbul, *alt.* Bayali [bjy], 569

Chasan Yao, *alt.* Kim Mun [mji], 337

Chashan, *alt.* Lashi [lsi], 465

Chashan Yao, *alt.* Lakkia [lbc], 338

Chashanhua, *alt.* Lashi [lsi], 338

Chasi, *alt.* Alagwa [wbj], 197

Chasu, *alt.* Asu [asa], 197

Cha't-An, *alt.* Chatino, Western Highland [ctp], 260

Chatans, *alt.* Allar [all], 353

Chatgam, *alt. dial.* Sauria Paharia [mjt], 386

Chatino de la Zona Alta Occidental, *alt.* Chatino, Western Highland [ctp], 260

Chatino de la Zona Alta Oriental, *alt.* Chatino, Eastern Highland [cly], 259

Chatino de San Marcos Zacatepec, *alt.* Chatino, Zacatepec [ctz], 260

Chatino, Eastern Highland [cly], 259

Chatino, Nopala [cya], 259

Chatino, Tataltepec [cta], 260

Chatino, Western Highland [ctp], 260

Chatino, Zacatepec [ctz], 260

Chatino, Zenzontepec [czn], 260

Chattare, *alt. dial.* Limbu [lif], 474

Chatthare, *alt. dial.* Limbu [lif], 474

Chatthare Yakthungba Pan, *alt. dial.* Limbu [lif], 474

Chau Ko', *alt.* Moken [mwt], 466, 516

Chau Pok, *alt.* Moklen [mkm], 516

Chaudangsi [cdn], 358, 469

Chaudans Lo, *alt.* Chaudangsi [cdn], 358

Chaudary, *alt.* Tharu, Dangaura [thl], 388

Chaudary Tharu, *alt.* Tharu, Dangaura [thl], 480

Chaudhabis, *dial.* Jumli [jml], 472

Chaudhari, *alt.* Chodri [cdi], 359
alt. Tharu, Dangaura [thl], 388

Chaudhari Tharu, *alt.* Tharu, Dangaura [thl], 480

Chaudhuri, *alt.* Tharu, Dangaura [thl], 388

Chaudri, *alt.* Chodri [cdi], 359

Chauma, *alt.* Maa [cma], 524

Chaun, *dial.* Chukot [ckt], 504

Chaungtha [ccq], 462

Chaupal, *alt.* Surajpuri [sjp], 388

Chaura [crv], 358

Chaurahi, *alt.* Churahi [cdj], 359

Chaurasia, *alt.* Wambule [wme], 482

Chaurasya, *alt.* Wambule [wme], 482

Chauro, *alt.* Chrau [crw], 522

Chavacano [cbk], 493, 456
alt. dial. Chavacano [cbk], 493

Chavante, *alt.* Oti [oti], 231
alt. Xávante [xav], 234

Chavchuven, *alt. dial.* Koryak [kpy], 505

Chavdur, *dial.* Turkmen [tuk], 442

Chaw Talay, *alt.* Urak Lawoi' [urk], 518

Chawai, *alt.* Atsam [cch], 154

Chawe, *alt.* Atsam [cch], 154

Chawi, *alt.* Atsam [cch], 154
alt. Chayahuita [cbt], 287
alt. Tachawit [shy], 39

Chawia, *dial.* Taita [dav], 136

Chawiyana, *alt.* Hixkaryána [hix], 227

Chawnam, *alt.* Urak Lawoi' [urk], 518

Chawng, *alt.* Chong [cog], 325, 514

Chawte, *alt.* Naga, Chothe [nct], 377

Chawuncu, *pej. alt.* Guaraní, Eastern Bolivian [gui], 284
pej. alt. Guaraní, Western Argentine [gui], 220

Chayabita, *alt.* Chayahuita [cbt], 287

Chayahuita [cbt], 287
dial. Chayahuita [cbt], 287

Chayawita, *alt.* Chayahuita [cbt], 287

Chayhuita, *alt.* Chayahuita [cbt], 287

Chayma, *alt.* Chaima [ciy], 311

Chayuco Mixtec, *see* Mixtec, Chayuco [mih], 266

Chazumba Mixtec, *see* Mixtec, Chazumba [xtb], 266

Che [ruk], 156

Che Ma, *alt.* Maa [cma], 524

Che-Hwan, *alt.* Taroko [trv], 512

Cheberloi, *alt. dial.* Chechen [che], 553

Chebero, *alt.* Jebero [jeb], 288

Chechek, *alt. dial.* Khehek [tlx], 606

Chechen [che], 553, 448

Check-Cull, *alt.* Dyaabugay [dyy], 570

Chedepo, *dial.* Grebo, Northern [gbo], 138

Chedi, *alt.* Lisu [lis], 339

Cheha, *alt. dial.* Sebat Bet Gurage [sgw], 118

Chehalis, *alt.* Chehalis, Upper [cjh], 299

Chehalis, Lower [cea], 299

Chehalis, Upper [cjh], 299

Chehek, *alt. dial.* Khehek [tlx], 606

Cheju Island, *dial.* Korean [kor], 448

Cheke, *alt.* Gude [gde], 161, 62

Cheke Holo [mrn], 635

Chekiri, *alt.* Isekiri [its], 164

Chelan, *alt. dial.* Columbia-Wenatchi [col], 300

Chelgerd, *alt. dial.* Bakhtiari [bqi], 438

Cheli, *alt.* Lisu [lis], 339

Chemakum, *alt.* Chimakum [cmk], 299

Chemant, *alt. dial.* Qimant [ahg], 118

Chemehuevi, *dial.* Ute-Southern Paiute [ute], 309

Chemgui, *alt. dial.* Adyghe [ady], 552

Chen, *dial.* Naga, Konyak [nbe], 378

Chena, *dial.* Tanana, Lower [taa], 308

Chenalhó Tzotzil, *see* Tzotzil, Chenalhó [tze], 277

Chenaló, *alt.* Tzotzil, Chenalhó [tze], 277

Chenap, *alt.* Chenapian [cjn], 596

Chenapian [cjn], 596

Chenba'erhu, *dial.* Evenki [evn], 332

Chenberom, *alt.* Berom [bom], 155

Chenchu [cde], 358

Chenchucoolam, *alt.* Chenchu [cde], 358

Chenchwar, *alt.* Chenchu [cde], 358

Cheng, *alt.* Jeng [jeg], 450

Chengkung-Kwangshan, *dial.* Amis [ami], 511

Chenoua [cnu], 39

Chenswar, *alt.* Chenchu [cde], 358

Chentel, *alt.* Chantyal [chx], 469

Chepang [cdm], 469

Cheq Wong, *alt.* Chewong [cwg], 454

Cherangany, *dial.* Kalenjin [kln], 133

Chere, *alt.* Sere [swf], 107

Cheremis, *alt.* Mari, Eastern [mhr], 555

alt. Mari, Western [mrj], 555

Cherepon [cpn], 123

Cheres, *alt. dial.* Jah Hut [jah], 454

Cheribon, *alt. dial.* Javanese [jav], 391

Cherii, *dial.* Wali [wlx], 128

Cherkes, *alt.* Adyghe [ady], 518

alt. dial. Kabardian [kbd], 554

Cherokee [chr], 299

Cherrapunji, *alt. dial.* Khasi [kha], 321

dial. Khasi [kha], 367

Cherre, *alt.* Karo [kxh], 116

Cheslatta, *dial.* Carrier, Southern [caf], 236

Cheso, *alt. dial.* Aragonese [arg], 558

Cheta, *alt.* Xetá [xet], 234

Chetco [ctc], 299

Cheva, *alt. dial.* Nyanja [nya], 140

Chewa, *alt.* Nyanja [nya], 140

dial. Nyanja [nya], 140, 148, 215

Chewlie, *alt.* Dyaabugay [dyy], 570

Che'wong, *alt.* Chewong [cwg], 454

Chewong [cwg], 454

Cheyenne [chy], 299

Chhantel, *alt.* Chantyal [chx], 469

Chhapkoa, *dial.* Kulung [kle], 473

Chhathar, *alt. dial.* Limbu [lif], 474

Chhattare, *alt. dial.* Limbu [lif], 474

Chhattisgarhi [hne], 358

Chhattisgarhi Proper, *dial.* Chhattisgarhi [hne], 358

Chhika-Chhiki, *alt.* Angika [anp], 354, 468

Chhilling, *alt.* Chhulung [cur], 470

Chhindwara, *dial.* Gondi, Northern [gno], 362

Chhindwara Bundeli, *dial.* Bundeli [bns], 357

Chhintang, *alt.* Chhintange [ctn], 470

Chhintange [ctn], 470

Chholung, *alt.* Chhulung [cur], 470

Chhori, *alt.* Chiru [cdf], 359

Chhulung [cur], 470

Chhûlûng Rûng, *alt.* Chhulung [cur], 470

Chi, *dial.* Mak [mkg], 339

Ch'iang, *alt.* Qiang, Northern [cng], 342

alt. Qiang, Southern [qxs], 342

Chiangmai Sign Language [csd], 514

Chiangrai, *dial.* Iu Mien [ium], 514

Chiapanec [cip], 260

Chiapaneco, *alt.* Chiapanec [cip], 260

Chiarong, *alt.* Jiarong [jya], 336

Chiasu, *alt.* Asu [asa], 197

Chibabava, *alt. dial.* Ndau [ndc], 148

Chibbak, *alt.* Cibak [ckl], 157

Chibbuk, *alt.* Cibak [ckl], 157

Chibcha [chb], 244

Chibemba, *alt.* Bemba [bem], 213

Chibhali, *alt.* Pahari-Potwari [phr], 487

dial. Pahari-Potwari [phr], 487

Chibito, *alt.* Hibito [hib], 288

Chibok, *alt.* Cibak [ckl], 157

Chibuk, *alt.* Cibak [ckl], 157

Chicahuaxtla Trique, *alt.* Triqui, Chicahuaxtla [trs], 276

Chicahuaxtla Triqui, *see* Triqui, Chicahuaxtla [trs], 276

Chicano, *alt.* Yuwana [yau], 313

Chicao, *alt.* Ikpeng [txi], 227

Chichamachu, *alt.* Bajelani [bjm], 443

Chichanga, *alt. dial.* Ndau [ndc], 148, 216

Chichawa, *alt.* Yao [yao], 215

Chichewa, *alt. dial.* Nyanja [nya], 140, 148

Chichicapan Zapotec, *see* Zapotec, Chichicapan [zpv], 278

Chichicastenango Eastern Quiché, *alt.* K'iche', Eastern [quu], 255

Chichimeca, *alt.* Pame, Central [pbs], 273

Chichimeca-Jonaz [pei], 260

Chichonyi, *alt.* Chonyi [coh], 132

Chichwabo, *alt.* Chuwabu [chw], 147

Chickasaw [cic], 299

Chicomuceltec [cob], 260, 253

Chicomulcelteco, *alt.* Chicomuceltec [cob], 260

Chicunda, *alt.* Kunda [kdn], 147

Chidigo, *alt.* Digo [dig], 132, 198

Chiech, *alt. dial.* Dinka, South Central [dib], 190

Chiehn, *alt. dial.* Krahn, Eastern [kqo], 138

Chiem, *alt.* Cham, Eastern [cjm], 522

alt. Cham, Western [cja], 522

Chiem Thành, *alt.* Cham, Eastern [cjm], 522

Chiengceng, *alt.* Jeng [jeg], 450

Chiengmai Sign Language, *alt.* Chiangmai Sign Language [csd], 514

Chientung Miao, *alt.* Hmong, Northern Qiandong [hea], 335

Chiga [cgg], 210

Chigmecatitlán Mixtec, *see* Mixtec, Chigmecatitlán [mii], 266

Chigogo, *alt.* Gogo [gog], 198

Chihuahua Pima Bajo, *dial.* Pima Bajo [pia], 273

Chiila, *alt.* Ila [ilb], 213

Chik Barik, *alt.* Panchpargania [tdb], 382

Chikagulu, *alt.* Kagulu [kki], 199

Chikahonde, *alt.* Kaonde [kqn], 213, 101

Chikalanga, *alt.* Kalanga [kck], 216, 47

Chikamanga, *dial.* Tumbuka [tum], 141, 215

Chikano, *alt.* Yuwana [yau], 313

Chikaonde, *alt.* Kaonde [kqn], 213, 101

Chikaranga, *alt. dial.* Shona [sna], 216

Chikena, *alt.* Sikiana [sik], 232, 296, 312

Chikide, *alt. dial.* Guduf-Gava [gdf], 161

Chikobo, *alt.* Izora [cbo], 164

Chikonono, *alt. dial.* Yao [yao], 149

Chikriaba, *alt.* Xakriabá [xkr], 234

Chikuahane, *alt.* Subiya [sbs], 151, 215

Chikuhane, *alt.* Kuhane [sbs], 47

Chikunda, *alt.* Kunda [kdn], 216, 147, 214

Chikuya, *alt.* Teke-Kukuya [kkw], 90

Chikwahane, *alt.* Subiya [sbs], 151, 215

Chil, *dial.* Koho [kpm], 524

dial. Mnong, Eastern [mng], 525

Chilala, *alt.* C'lela [dri], 157

Chilamba, *alt.* Lamba [lam], 214, 102

Chilao, *alt.* Gelao [gio], 333

Chilapalapa, *dial.* Fanagalo [fng], 216

Chilas, *alt. dial.* Pashayi, Northeast [aee], 317
alt. dial. Shina [scl], 488

Chilasi Kohistani, *dial.* Shina [scl], 488

Chilcotin [clc], 236

Chilean Quechua, *see* Quechua, Chilean [cqu], 243

Chilean Sign Language [csg], 242

Chilela, *alt.* C'lela [dri], 157

Chilenje, *alt.* Lenje [leh], 214

Chiliss, *alt.* Chilisso [clh], 484

Chilisso [clh], 484

Chiliwack, *dial.* Halkomelem [hur], 238, 301

Chilowe, *alt.* Lomwe [ngl], 147

Chiltepec Chinantec, *see* Chinantec, Chiltepec [csa], 260

Chilu Wunda, *alt.* Ruund [rnd], 41

Chiluchazi, *alt.* Luchazi [lch], 41, 214

Chiluimbi, *alt.* Luimbi [lum], 41

Chilunda, *alt.* Lunda [lun], 214, 41, 103

Chiluvale, *alt.* Luvale [lue], 214, 41

Chiluwunda, *alt.* Ruund [rnd], 107

Chima-Nishey, *dial.* Waigali [wbk], 318

Chimakonde, *alt.* Makonde [kde], 201, 148

Chimakum [cmk], 299

Chimalapa Zoque, *see* Zoque, Chimalapa [zoh], 281

Chimané, *alt.* Tsimané [cas], 224

Chimanyika, *alt.* Manyika [mxc], 216, 148

Chimariko [cid], 299

Chimatengo, *alt.* Matengo [mgv], 201

Chimaviha, *alt. dial.* Makonde [kde], 148

Chimba, *alt.* Zemba [dhm], 42

Chimbalazi, *alt. dial.* Swahili [swh], 136, 185

Chimbari, *alt.* Simbari [smb], 624

Chimbian, *dial.* Malinguat [sic], 611

Chimborazo Highland Quichua, *see* Quichua, Chimborazo Highland [qug], 251

Chimbu, *alt.* Kuman [kue], 608

Chimbuluk, *dial.* Buang, Mapos [bzh], 595

Chimbunda, *alt.* Mbunda [mck], 214, 41

Chimila [cbg], 244

Chimmezyan, *alt.* Tsimshian [tsi], 242, 309

Chimona, *dial.* Ese [mcq], 598

Chimpoto, *alt.* Mpoto [mpa], 202

Chimwera, *alt.* Mwera [mwe], 202

Chimwiini, *alt. dial.* Swahili [swh], 185

Chin, Asho [csh], 462, 321

Chin, Bawm [bgr], 358, 321, 463

Chin, Bualkhaw [cbl], 463

Chin, Chinbon [cnb], 463

Chin, Daai [dao], 463

Chin, Falam [flm], 463, 321, 358

Chin, Haka [cnh], 463, 321, 357

Chin, Khumi [cnk], 463, 321, 359

Chin, Khumi Awa [cka], 463

Chin, Mara [mrh], 359, 463

Chin, Matu [hlt], 359

Chin, Mro [cmr], 463

Chin, Mün [mwq], 463

Chin, Ngawn [cnw], 463

Chin, Paite [pck], 359, 463

Chin, Senthang [sez], 463

Chin, Siyin [csy], 463

Chin, Tawr [tcp], 463

Chin, Tedim [ctd], 463, 359

Chin, Thado [tcz], 359, 463

Chin, Zotung [czt], 463

China Buriat, *see* Buriat, China [bxu], 329

Chinal, *alt.* Chinali [cih], 359

Chinali [cih], 359

Chinambya, *alt.* Nambya [nmq], 209, 48

Chinamukuni, *alt.* Lenje [leh], 214

Chinamwanga, *alt.* Nyamwanga [mwn], 203

Chinantec, Chiltepec [csa], 260

Chinantec, Comaltepec [cco], 260

Chinantec, Lalana [cnl], 260

Chinantec, Lealao [cle], 260

Chinantec, Ojitlán [chj], 260

Chinantec, Ozumacín [chz], 261

Chinantec, Palantla [cpa], 261

Chinantec, Quiotepec [chq], 261

Chinantec, Sochiapan [cso], 261

Chinantec, Tepetotutla [cnt], 261

Chinantec, Tepinapa [cte], 261

Chinantec, Tlacoatzintepec [ctl], 261

Chinantec, Usila [cuc], 261

Chinantec, Valle Nacional [cvn], 261

Chinanteco de Ayotzintepec, *alt.* Chinantec, Ozumacín [chz], 261

Chinanteco de San Juan Lalana, *alt.* Chinantec, Lalana [cnl], 260

Chinanteco de San Juan Lealao, *alt.* Chinantec, Lealao [cle], 260

Chinanteco de Santiago Tlatepusco, *alt.* Chinantec, Palantla [cpa], 261

Chinatú Tarahumara, *dial.* Tarahumara, Southeastern [tcu], 275

Chinbok, *pej. alt.* Chin, Mün [mwq], 463

Chinbon, *alt.* Chin, Chinbon [cnb], 463

Chinbon Chin, *see* Chin, Chinbon [cnb], 463

Chincha Quechua, *see* Quechua, Chincha [qxc], 290

Chindali, *alt.* Ndali [ndh], 202

Chindau, *alt.* Ndau [ndc], 148, 216

Chinderi, *alt. dial.* Chumburung [ncu], 124

Chindonde, *alt.* Ndonde Hamba [njd], 202

Chindonde Hamba, *alt.* Ndonde Hamba [njd], 202

Chindwin Chin, *alt.* Chin, Chinbon [cnb], 463

Chinese Indonesian, *alt.* Indonesian, Peranakan [pea], 391

Chinese Malay, *alt.* Malay, Baba [mbf], 509, 455

Chinese Nung, *alt.* Chinese, Yue [yue], 522

Chinese Pidgin English [cpi], 583

Chinese Shan, *alt.* Tai Nüa [tdd], 344, 453, 467, 517

Chinese Sign Language [csl], 329

Chinese Tai, *alt.* Tai Nüa [tdd], 344

Chinese, Gan [gan], 329

Chinese, Hakka [hak], 329, 252, 283, 295, 324, 391, 454, 508, 511, 514, 581

Chinese, Huizhou [czh], 329

Chinese, Jinyu [cjy], 329

Chinese, Mandarin [cmn], 329, 324, 391, 454, 461, 494, 508, 511, 514

Chinese, Min Bei [mnp], 330, 508

Chinese, Min Dong [cdo], 330, 324, 391, 454, 508, 514

Chinese, Min Nan [nan], 330, 324, 391, 454, 494, 508, 511, 514

Chinese, Min Zhong [czo], 330

Chinese, Pu-Xian [cpx], 330, 454, 508

Chinese, Wu [wuu], 330

Chinese, Xiang [hsn], 331
Chinese, Yue [yue], 331, 283, 324, 391, 454, 494, 508, 514, 522
Ching, *alt.* Mak [mkg], 339
　alt. Vietnamese [vie], 527, 346
　dial. Mak [mkg], 339
Ching Miao, *alt. dial.* Hmong Njua [blu], 334
Chinga, *alt. dial.* Tuki [bag], 72
Chingalee, *alt.* Djingili [jig], 570
Chingalese, *alt.* Sinhala [sin], 509
Chinghizi, *dial.* Aimaq [aiq], 315
Chingkao, *dial.* Naga, Konyak [nbe], 378
Chinglang, *dial.* Naga, Konyak [nbe], 378
Chingmengu, *alt.* Naga, Phom [nph], 379
Chingoni, *alt.* Ngoni [ngo], 202, 148
　dial. Nyanja [nya], 215
Chingpaw, *alt.* Jingpho [kac], 464, 336
Chingp'o, *alt.* Jingpho [kac], 464, 336
Chingthang, *dial.* Karbi [mjw], 366
Chinguil, *dial.* Zan Gula [zna], 87
Chinimakonde, *alt.* Makonde [kde], 201, 148
Chinook [chh], 299
Chinook Jargon, *alt.* Chinook Wawa [chn], 236, 299
Chinook Pidgin, *alt.* Chinook Wawa [chn], 236, 299
Chinook Wawa [chn], 236, 299
Chinsenga, *alt.* Nsenga [nse], 215, 148, 216
Chintang, *alt.* Chhintange [ctn], 470
Chintang Rûng, *alt.* Chhintange [ctn], 470
Chintoor Koya, *alt. dial.* Koya [kff], 370
Chinyanja, *alt.* Nyanja [nya], 140, 148, 215, 216
Chinyungwi, *alt.* Nyungwe [nyu], 148
Chip, *alt.* Miship [mjs], 170
Chipaya [cap], 222
Chipeta, *alt. dial.* Nyanja [nya], 215
Chipewyan [chp], 236
Chipiajes [cbe], 244
Chipodzo, *alt. dial.* Sena [seh], 149
Chipogolo, *alt.* Pogolo [poy], 204
Chipogoro, *alt.* Pogolo [poy], 204
Chipoka, *alt. dial.* Tumbuka [tum], 141
　dial. Tumbuka [tum], 215
Chippewa [ciw], 299
　alt. Ottawa [otw], 306
Chiquel, *alt.* K'iche', Central [quc], 255

Chiquena, *alt.* Sikiana [sik], 232, 312
Chiquián Ancash Quechua, *see* Quechua, Chiquián Ancash [qxa], 290
Chiquiana, *alt.* Sikiana [sik], 232, 312
Chiquihuitlán Mazatec, *see* Mazatec, Chiquihuitlán [maq], 264
Chiquitano [cax], 222
Chiquito, *alt.* Chiquitano [cax], 222
Chir, *alt.* Mandari [mqu], 193
Chirag, *dial.* Dargwa [dar], 553
Chiricahua, *dial.* Apache, Mescalero-Chiricahua [apm], 298
Chirichano, *alt.* Sanumá [xsu], 312
　alt. Sapé [spc], 312
Chiricoa, *dial.* Cuiba [cui], 244, 311
Chiriguano, *pej. alt.* Guaraní, Eastern Bolivian [gui], 223, 284
　pej. alt. Guaraní, Western Argentine [gui], 220
Chirima, *alt.* Makhuwa-Shirima [vmk], 147
Chiripá [nhd], 284, 220, 226
Chiripo, *dial.* Cuiba [cui], 244
Chiripon, *alt.* Cherepon [cpn], 123
Chiripong, *alt.* Cherepon [cpn], 123
Chiripuno, *alt.* Arabela [arl], 286
Chiripunu, *alt.* Arabela [arl], 286
Chiriqui, *alt.* Ngäbere [gym], 283
Chiriquí, *alt. dial.* Ngäbere [gym], 283
Chirmar, *alt. dial.* Bengali [ben], 355
　dial. Bengali [ben], 469
Chiroro-Kursi, *dial.* Kanga [kcp], 191
Chirr, *dial.* Naga, Yimchungru [yim], 380
Chirripó, *alt.* Cabécar [cjp], 249
　dial. Cabécar [cjp], 249
Chiru [cdf], 359
Chirue, *alt. dial.* Sena [seh], 149
Chisak, *dial.* Garo [grt], 362
Chisalampasu, *alt.* Salampasu [slx], 107
Chisena, *alt.* Sena [seh], 149
　alt. Sena, Malawi [swk], 140
Chisenji, *alt. dial.* Ndau [ndc], 148
Chishinga, *dial.* Bemba [bem], 213
Chishona, *alt.* Shona [sna], 216, 215
Chisingini, *alt.* Cishingini [asg], 151
Chisoli, *alt.* Soli [sby], 215
Chistabino, *alt. dial.* Aragonese [arg], 558
Chita Pardhi, *alt.* Pardhi [pcl], 383
Chitawan Tharu, *alt.* Tharu, Chitwania [the], 480
Chitembo, *alt.* Tembo [tbt], 108
Chitimacha [ctm], 299

Chitkhuli, *alt.* Kinnauri, Chitkuli [cik], 368
Chitkuli, *alt.* Kinnauri, Chitkuli [cik], 368
Chitkuli Kinnauri, *see* Kinnauri, Chitkuli [cik], 368
Chitodi Lohar, *alt.* Lohar, Gade [gda], 372
Chitonahua, *alt. dial.* Yaminahua [yaa], 293
Chitonga, *alt.* Tonga [tog], 141
　alt. Tonga [toi], 215, 217
　dial. Tonga [toi], 215, 217
Chitpavani, *dial.* Konkani, Goanese [gom], 369
Chitrali, *alt.* Khowar [khw], 486
Chitrari, *alt.* Khowar [khw], 486
Chittagong, *dial.* Chin, Asho [csh], 321
Chittagonian [cit], 321, 463
Chittagonian Bengali, *alt.* Chittagonian [cit], 321
Chitties Creole Malay, *alt.* Malaccan Creole Malay [ccm], 454
Chittoriya Lohar, *alt.* Lohar, Gade [gda], 372
Chituan Tharu, *alt.* Tharu, Chitwania [the], 480
Chitumbuka, *alt.* Tumbuka [tum], 141, 215
　dial. Tumbuka [tum], 141, 215
Chitwania Tharu, *see* Tharu, Chitwania [the], 480
Chiupei, *alt. dial.* Zhuang, Northern [ccx], 349
Chiute, *alt.* Tewe [twx], 149
Chiutse, *alt.* Rawang [raw], 466, 385
Chivenda, *alt.* Venda [ven], 187, 217
Chividunda, *alt.* Vidunda [vid], 205
Chiwaro, *alt.* Shuar [jiv], 251
Chiwemba, *alt.* Bemba [bem], 213, 97
Chiwere, *alt. dial.* Iowa-Oto [iow], 302
Chixanga, *alt. dial.* Ndau [ndc], 148, 216
Chiyao, *alt.* Yao [yao], 141, 149, 206, 215
Chizezuru, *alt. dial.* Shona [sna], 216
Chizima, *alt.* Naga, Lotha [njh], 378
Cho, *alt.* Chin, Mün [mwq], 463
Cho-Rai, *alt.* Jarai [jra], 523, 325
Choa, *alt.* Arabic, Shuwa [shu], 56
Choapan Zapotec, *see* Zapotec, Choapan [zpc], 278
Chobba, *alt.* Huba [hbb], 162
Chocama, *alt.* Woun Meu [noa], 284
Chocangacakha [cgk], 323
Chocho, *alt.* Chochotec [coz], 261

Chochotec [coz], 261
Choctaw [cho], 299
Chode, *alt.* Gikyode [acd], 125
Chodhari, *alt.* Chodri [cdi], 359
Chodri [cdi], 359
Chogor, *dial.* Bumthangkha
  [kjz], 323
Choha, *dial.* Naga, Konyak
  [nbe], 378
Choi-Salmst, *alt. dial.* Armenian
  [hye], 318
Choimi, *alt.* Naga, Lotha [njh], 378
Chokfem, *alt.* Cakfem-Mushere
  [cky], 156
Chokobo, *alt.* Izora [cbo], 164
Chokosi, *alt.* Anufo [cko], 123, 42,
  207
Chokossi, *alt.* Anufo [cko], 42, 207
Chokri, *alt.* Naga, Chokri [nri], 377
Chokri Naga, *see* Naga, Chokri
  [nri], 377
Chokwe [cjk], 99, 40, 213
Ch'ol de Sabanilla, *alt.* Chol,
  Tumbalá [ctu], 261
Chol, Tila [cti], 261
Chol, Tumbalá [ctu], 261
Cholimi, *alt.* Naga, Ao [njo], 377
Chollado, *dial.* Korean [kor], 448
Cholo, *alt.* Emberá, Northern
  [emp], 283, 245
  alt. Epena [sja], 245, 251, 283
  dial. Nung [nun], 466, 341
Cholón [cht], 287
Choluteca, *alt.* Chorotega [cjr], 249
Chom, *alt.* Hre [hre], 523
Chombrau, *alt.* Arem [aem], 521,
  450
Chombulon, *alt.* Tchumbuli [bqa],
  46
Chomo, *alt.* Como Karim [cfg], 157
Chomrau, *alt.* Arem [aem], 521,
  450
Chona, *alt.* Choni [cda], 331
Choncharu, *alt.* Chenchu [cde], 358
Chone, *alt.* Choni [cda], 331
Chong [cog], 325, 514
Chonganjiang Hmong, *see*
  Hmong, Chonganjiang [hmj], 334
Chong'anjiang Miao, *alt.* Hmong,
  Chonganjiang [hmj], 334
Chong'e, *alt.* Kushi [kuh], 167
Chongka, *alt.* Tomyang [tmx], 481
Chongli, *dial.* Naga, Ao [njo], 377
Choni [cda], 331
Chontal de la Costa de
  Oaxaca, *alt.* Chontal, Lowland
  Oaxaca [clo], 262
Chontal de la Sierra de
  Oaxaca, *alt.* Chontal, Highland
  Oaxaca [chd], 261

Chontal, Highland Oaxaca
  [chd], 261
Chontal, Lowland Oaxaca
  [clo], 262
Chontal, Tabasco [chf], 262
Chonyi [coh], 132
Ch'opa, *alt.* Rawang [raw], 466, 385
Chope, *alt. dial.* Acholi [ach], 210
Chopechop, *alt.* Bamali [bbq], 57
Chopi [cce], 147
  alt. dial. Acholi [ach], 210
Chor, *alt.* Jarai [jra], 523, 325
Chorei, *dial.* Chin, Falam [flm], 463,
  321, 358
Chori, *alt.* Cori [cry], 157
Choro, *alt.* Chrau [crw], 522
Choroba, *alt. dial.* Gonja [gjn], 125
Chorote, Iyojwa'ja [crt], 220
Chorote, Iyo'wujwa [crq], 220,
  222, 284
Chorotega [cjr], 249
  dial. Chorotega [cjr], 249
Choroti, *alt.* Chorote, Iyojwa'ja
  [crt], 220
  alt. Chorote, Iyo'wujwa [crq], 220,
  222, 284
Ch'orti' [caa], 253, 258
Choru, *alt.* Chru [cje], 522
Choruba, *alt. dial.* Gonja [gjn], 125
Choskule, *dial.* Tilung [tij], 481
Chota Nagpuri, *alt.* Sadri [sck], 385
Chote, *dial.* Bodo [brx], 357
Chothe, *alt.* Naga, Chothe [nct], 377
Chothe Naga, *see* Naga, Chothe
  [nct], 377
Choudhara, *alt.* Chodri [cdi], 359
Choudhary, *alt.* Chodri [cdi], 359
Chougoule, *alt. dial.* Mefele
  [mfj], 67
Choupal, *alt.* Surajpuri [sjp], 388
Chourase, *alt.* Wambule [wme], 482
Chourasia, *alt.* Wambule [wme], 482
Choushan, *alt. dial.* Chinese, Min
  Nan [nan], 330
Chowa, *alt.* Arabic, Chadian Spoken
  [shu], 78
  alt. Arabic, Shuwa [shu], 56
Chowdhary, *alt.* Chodri [cdi], 359
Chowra, *alt.* Chaura [crv], 358
Chowte, *alt.* Naga, Chothe [nct], 377
Chrai, *alt.* Jarai [jra], 523, 325
Ch'rame, *alt.* Pumi, Northern
  [pmi], 342
Chrau [crw], 522
Chrau Hma, *alt.* Chru [cje], 522
Chrishana, *alt. dial.* Romanian
  [ron], 548
Christian Neo-Aramaic, *alt.*
  Senaya [syn], 441
Chru [cje], 522

Chtimi, *alt.* Picard [pcd], 537, 531
Chu, *alt.* Chru [cje], 522
Chu Ru, *alt.* Chru [cje], 522
Chuabo, *alt.* Chuwabu [chw], 147
Chuala, *alt.* Guana [gqn], 227
Chuan Miao, *alt.* Hmong Daw
  [mww], 334, 514
Chuana, *alt.* Tswana [tsn], 48, 186,
  217
  dial. Kuna, San Blas [cuk], 283
Chuanchientien Miao, *alt.* Hmong
  Njua [blu], 334, 514
Chuang, *alt.* Zhuang, Northern
  [ccx], 349
Chuanqiandian Miao, *alt.* Hmong
  Njua [blu], 334, 514
Chuave [cjv], 596
  dial. Chuave [cjv], 596
Chuba, *alt.* Chewong [cwg], 454
Chubo, *alt.* Meta' [mgo], 67
Chuchee, *alt.* Chukot [ckt], 504
Chudy, *pej. alt.* Veps [vep], 557
Chuf, *alt. dial.* Shughni [sgh], 513
Chug, *dial.* Moinba [mob], 376
Chugach, *dial.* Yupik, Pacific Gulf
  [ems], 310
Chugach Eskimo, *pej. alt.* Yupik,
  Pacific Gulf [ems], 310
Chuh, *alt.* Chuj, Ixtatán [cnm], 253
Chuhari, *pej. alt.* Veps [vep], 557
Chuhe, *alt.* Chuj, Ixtatán [cnm], 253
Chui-Huan, *alt.* Thao [ssf], 512
Chuihwan, *alt.* Thao [ssf], 512
Chuil Quiché, *alt.* K'iche', Cunén
  [cun], 255
Chuj de San Mateo Ixtatán, *alt.*
  Chuj, Ixtatán [cnm], 253, 262
Chuj, Ixtatán [cnm], 253, 262
Chuj, San Sebastián Coatán
  [cac], 253
Chuje, *alt.* Chuj, Ixtatán [cnm], 253
Chuka [cuh], 132
Chukcha, *alt.* Chukot [ckt], 504
Chukchee, *alt.* Chukot [ckt], 504
Chukchi, *alt.* Chukot [ckt], 504
Chukhari, *pej. alt.* Veps [vep], 557
Chukkol, *alt.* Nyong [muo], 171
Chukot [ckt], 504
Chuksang, *dial.* Seke [skj], 478
Chuku, *alt.* Chuka [cuh], 132
Chukwa [cuw], 470
Chulikata, *alt.* Luoba, Yidu
  [clk], 339
  pej. alt. Idu-Mishmi [clk], 364
Chulikotta, *pej. alt.* Idu-Mishmi
  [clk], 364
Chulim, *alt.* Chulym [clw], 504
Chulla, *alt.* Shilluk [shk], 195
Chulung, *alt.* Chhulung [cur], 470
Chülüng, *alt.* Chhulung [cur], 470

Chulupe, *pej. alt.* Nivaclé [cag], 285, 220

Chulupi, *pej. alt.* Nivaclé [cag], 220

Chulupí, *pej. alt.* Nivaclé [cag], 285

Chulupie, *pej. alt.* Nivaclé [cag], 285, 220

Chulym [clw], 504

Chulym Tatar, *alt.* Chulym [clw], 504

Chulym-Turkish, *alt.* Chulym [clw], 504

Chuma, *dial.* Quechua, North Bolivian [qul], 223

Chumash [chs], 299

Chumburung [ncu], 124

Chung, *alt.* Achang [acn], 456 *alt.* Lisu [lis], 339

Chung Cha, *alt.* Giáy [pcc], 523

Chung-Chia, *alt.* Bouyei [pcc], 328

Ch'ungch'ongdo, *dial.* Korean [kor], 448

Chungki, *alt.* Djangun [djf], 569

Chungli, *alt. dial.* Naga, Ao [njo], 377

Chunguloo, *alt.* Djingili [jig], 570

Chunkumberries, *alt.* Djangun [djf], 569

Chunkunburra, *alt.* Djangun [djf], 569

Chunmat, *dial.* Bumthangkha [kjz], 323

Chuqu, *dial.* Chinese, Wu [wuu], 330

Chuquisaca, *dial.* Quechua, South Bolivian [quh], 223

Churahi [cdj], 359

Churahi Pahari, *alt.* Churahi [cdj], 359

Churai Pahari, *alt.* Churahi [cdj], 359

Churari, *dial.* Romani, Vlax [rmy], 551, 542

Churarícko, *alt. dial.* Romani, Vlax [rmy], 551

Churi, *alt.* Suri [suq], 119

Churi-Wali, *dial.* Domari [rmt], 315

Churo, *alt. dial.* Mandjak [mfv], 131, 122, 181

Churu, *alt.* Chru [cje], 522

Churupi, *pej. alt.* Nivaclé [cag], 220

Churupí, *pej. alt.* Nivaclé [cag], 285

Chut [scb], 522, 450

Chutiya, *alt.* Deori [der], 360

Chutobikha, *dial.* Nyenkha [neh], 324

Chuty, *dial.* Jarai [jra], 523, 325

Chuufi, *alt.* Bafanji [bfj], 56

Chuuk, *alt.* Chuukese [chk], 582

Chuukese [chk], 582

Chuvash [chv], 553

Chuwabo, *alt.* Chuwabu [chw], 147

Chuwabu [chw], 147

Chuwau, *alt.* Tsoa [hio], 48

Chuy, *alt. dial.* Altai, Southern [alt], 503

Chwabo, *alt.* Chuwabu [chw], 147

Chwagga, *dial.* Hai‖om [hgm], 149

Chwaka, *dial.* Giryama [nyf], 133

Chwambo, *alt.* Maindo [cwb], 147

Chwana, *alt.* Tswana [tsn], 217

Chware, *alt.* Hietshware [hio], 216 *alt.* Tsoa [hio], 48

Chxala, *dial.* Laz [lzz], 352

Chyanam, *alt.* Rangkas [rgk], 384

Ci, *alt.* Gbe, Ci [cib], 44 *alt.* Paicî [pri], 585

Ci Gbe, *see* Gbe, Ci [cib], 44

Cia-Cia [cia], 429

Ciara, *alt.* Chara [cra], 114

Cibaangi, *alt.* Baangi [bqx], 154

Cibak [ckl], 157

Cibalke, *alt.* Barwe [bwg], 147

Cibbo, *alt.* Tso [ldp], 176

Cibecue, *dial.* Apache, Western [apw], 298

Cic, *alt. dial.* Dinka, South Central [dib], 190

Cicak, *alt.* Citak [txt], 413

Cicewa, *alt. dial.* Nyanja [nya], 148

Cicolano-Reatino-Aquilano, *dial.* Italian [ita], 544

Cicopi, *alt.* Chopi [cce], 147

Cicuabo, *alt.* Chuwabu [chw], 147

Cidanda, *alt. dial.* Ndau [ndc], 148

Cidondo, *alt. dial.* Ndau [ndc], 148

Ciec, *dial.* Dinka, South Central [dib], 190

Ciem, *alt. dial.* Dinka, South Central [dib], 190

Cien, *dial.* Nuer [nus], 194

Cifipa, *alt.* Fipa [fip], 198

Ciga, *alt.* Chiga [cgg], 210

Cigány, *alt.* Romani, Balkan [rmn], 542 *alt.* Romani, Carpathian [rmc], 542 *alt.* Romani, Vlax [rmy], 542

Cigbe, *alt.* Gbe, Ci [cib], 44

Cigova, *alt. dial.* Ndau [ndc], 148

Ciikuhane, *alt.* Subiya [sbs], 151

Ciina, *alt.* Lenje [leh], 214

Ciita, *alt.* Opuuo [lgn], 117, 194

Cikabanga, *dial.* Fanagalo [fng], 213

Cikide, *dial.* Guduf-Gava [gdf], 161

Cikobu, *alt.* Izora [cbo], 164

Cikonono, *alt. dial.* Yao [yao], 149

Cikosowan, *dial.* Amis, Nataoran [ais], 511

Cikunda, *alt.* Kunda [kdn], 216, 147

Cilowe, *alt.* Lomwe [ngl], 147

Cilungu, *alt. dial.* Mambwe-Lungu [mgr], 201

Cimakale, *alt. dial.* Yao [yao], 149, 215

Cimakonde, *alt.* Makonde [kde], 148

Cimanganja, *alt. dial.* Nyanja [nya], 140

Cimashanga, *alt. dial.* Ndau [ndc], 148

Cimassaninga, *alt. dial.* Yao [yao], 149, 215

Cimbangala, *alt.* Mbangala [mxg], 41

Cimbrian [cim], 543

Cimel, *alt. dial.* Dinka, Southwestern [dik], 190

Cimulin, *dial.* Qiang, Northern [cng], 342

Cimwera, *alt.* Mwera [mwe], 202

Cin Haw, *alt. dial.* Chinese, Mandarin [cmn], 514

Cinamiguin, *alt.* Manobo, Cinamiguin [mkx], 499

Cinamiguin Manobo, *see* Manobo, Cinamiguin [mkx], 499

Cinda, *dial.* Cinda-Regi-Tiyal [cdr], 157

Cinda-Regi-Tiyal [cdr], 157

Cindanda, *alt. dial.* Ndau [ndc], 148

Cindau, *alt. dial.* Ndau [ndc], 148

Cineni [cie], 157

Cingalese, *alt.* Sinhala [sin], 509

Cingoni, *alt. dial.* Nyanja [nya], 148

Cini, *alt. dial.* Niellim [nie], 85

Cinta Larga [cin], 226

Cinyambe, *alt. dial.* Tonga [toh], 149

Cinyanja, *alt. dial.* Nyanja [nya], 148

Cinyungwe, *alt.* Nyungwe [nyu], 148

Ciokwe, *alt.* Chokwe [cjk], 99, 40, 213

Cip, *alt.* Miship [mjs], 170

Cipeta, *alt. dial.* Nyanja [nya], 140, 215

Cipimbwe, *alt.* Pimbwe [piw], 204

Cipodzo, *alt. dial.* Sena [seh], 149

Circassian, *alt.* Adyghe [ady], 552, 518

Cirebon, *dial.* Javanese [jav], 391 *dial.* Sunda [sun], 392

Ciri, *alt.* Tiri [cir], 585

Cirimba, *alt. dial.* Longuda [lnu], 169

Cirma, *alt. dial.* Suri [suq], 119, 195

Cis-Baikalia, *dial.* Evenki [evn], 504

Cisafwa, *alt.* Safwa [sbk], 204

Cisena, *alt.* Sena [seh], 149 *alt.* Sena, Malawi [swk], 140

Cishingini [asg], 151

Ethnologue

Cistercian Sign Language, *dial.*
Monastic Sign Language
[mzg], 566
Cita, *alt.* Opuuo [lgn], 117, 194
Citak [txt], 413
Citak, Tamnim [tml], 413
Citlang, *dial.* Newar [new], 476
Citrali, *alt.* Khowar [khw], 486
Ci'uli', *alt. dial.* Atayal [tay], 511
Ciute, *alt.* Tewe [twx], 149
Cividale, *dial.* Slovenian [slv], 545
Civili, *alt.* Vili [vif], 90, 121
Ciwogai [tgd], 157
Ciyao, *alt.* Yao [yao], 149, 215
Ciyei, *alt.* Yeyi [yey], 48, 151
Ciyoombe, *alt. dial.* Vili [vif], 90, 121
Ckhala, *alt. dial.* Laz [lzz], 352
Clackama, *dial.* Chinook [chh], 299
Clallam [clm], 300
Classical Arabic, *dial.* Arabic, Standard [arb], 508
Classical Aztec, *alt.* Nahuatl, Classical [nci], 270
Classical Greek, *dial.* Greek, Ancient [grc], 541
Classical Mandaean, *alt.* Mandaic, Classical [myz], 441
Classical Mandaic, *see* Mandaic, Classical [myz], 441
Classical Nahuatl, *see* Nahuatl, Classical [nci], 270
Classical Quechua, *see* Quechua, Classical [qwc], 290
Classical Syriac, *alt.* Syriac [syc], 519
Clata, *alt.* Giangan [bgi], 494
Clear Lake Pomo, *alt.* Pomo, Eastern [peb], 307
C'lela [dri], 157
Co, *alt. dial.* Cua [cua], 522
Co-Don, *alt. dial.* Koho [kpm], 524
Coaiquer, *alt.* Awa-Cuaiquer [kwi], 243
Coana, *alt.* Tswana [tsn], 48, 186, 217
Coast Kiwai, *dial.* Kiwai, Southern [kjd], 606
Coast Miwok, *see* Miwok, Coast [csi], 305
Coast Tsimshian, *alt.* Tsimshian [tsi], 309
dial. Tsimshian [tsi], 242
Coastal Arapesh, *dial.* Bukiyip [ape], 595
Coastal Balochi, *dial.* Balochi, Southern [bcc], 483
Coastal Guerrero Mixtec, *alt.* Mixtec, Ayutla [miy], 266

Coastal Inupiatun, *alt. dial.* Inupiatun, Northwest Alaska [esk], 302
Coastal Kadazan, *see* Kadazan, Coastal [kzj], 457
Coastal K'iche', *dial.* K'iche', West Central [qut], 255
Coastal Konjo, *see* Konjo, Coastal [kjc], 430
Coastal Makhuwa, *alt.* Makhuwa-Marrevone [xmc], 147
Coastal Makwe, *dial.* Makwe [ymk], 148
Coastal Mixtec, *alt.* Mixtec, Pinotepa Nacional [mio], 268
Coastal Saluan, *see* Saluan, Coastal [loe], 432
Coastal Tihaamah, *dial.* Arabic, Hijazi Spoken [acw], 508
Coastal Tupian, *alt.* Nhengatu [yrl], 230
Coastal-Inland, *dial.* Tanaina [tfn], 308
Coatecas Altas Zapotec, *see* Zapotec, Coatecas Altas [zca], 278
Coatepec Aztec, *alt.* Nahuatl, Coatepec [naz], 270
Coatepec Nahuatl, *see* Nahuatl, Coatepec [naz], 270
Coatlán Mixe, *see* Mixe, Coatlán [mco], 265
Coatlán Mixe, *dial.* Mixe, Coatlán [mco], 265
Coatlán Zapotec, *see* Zapotec, Coatlán [zps], 278
Coatlán Zapotec, *alt.* Zapotec, San Vicente Coatlán [zpt], 279
Coatzospan Mixtec, *see* Mixtec, Coatzospan [miz], 266
Cobari, *alt. dial.* Sanumá [xsu], 312
Cobari Kobali, *alt.* Yanomamö [guu], 313
Cobaría Tunebo, *alt.* Tunebo, Central [tuf], 248
Cobariwa, *alt.* Yanomamö [guu], 313
alt. dial. Sanumá [xsu], 312
Cobecha, *dial.* Tchumbuli [bqa], 46
Cobiana, *alt.* Kobiana [kcj], 131, 181
Coc Mun, *alt.* Kim Mun [mji], 524
Cocama, *alt.* Cocama-Cocamilla [cod], 287, 226, 244
dial. Cocama-Cocamilla [cod], 287, 226
Cocama-Cocamilla [cod], 287, 226, 244
Cocamilla, *alt. dial.* Cocama-Cocamilla [cod], 226
dial. Cocama-Cocamilla [cod], 287
Cocche, *alt.* Hamer-Banna [amf], 115

Cochabamba, *dial.* Quechua, South Bolivian [quh], 223
Coche, *alt.* Camsá [kbh], 244
Cochetimi, *alt.* Cochimi [coj], 262
Cochima, *alt.* Cochimi [coj], 262
Cochimi [coj], 262
Cochimí, *alt.* Kumiai [dih], 263
Cochimtee, *alt.* Cochimi [coj], 262
Cochin, *dial.* Marathi [mar], 374
Cochiti, *dial.* Keres, Eastern [kee], 303
Cockney, *dial.* English [eng], 565
Cocoli, *alt.* Landoma [ldm], 129
Cocomaricopa, *alt.* Maricopa [mrc], 304
Cocopa [coc], 262, 300
Cocopá, *alt.* Cocopa [coc], 262
Cocopah, *alt.* Cocopa [coc], 262, 300
Cocos, *alt.* Malay, Cocos Islands [coa], 457, 573
Cocos Islands Malay, *see* Malay, Cocos Islands [coa], 457, 573
Coeur d'Alene [crd], 300
Cofán [con], 250, 244
Cogapacori, *pej. alt.* Nanti [cox], 289
Coghui, *alt.* Cogui [kog], 244
Cogniagui, *alt.* Wamey [cou], 130
Cogui [kog], 244
Coho, *alt.* Koho [kpm], 524
Coicoyán, *dial.* Mixtec, Western Juxtlahuaca [jmx], 270
Coicoyán Mixtec, *alt.* Mixtec, Western Juxtlahuaca [jmx], 270
Cok, *alt. dial.* Dinka, South Central [dib], 190
Cokobanci, *alt.* Izora [cbo], 164
Cokobo, *alt.* Izora [cbo], 164
Cokwe, *alt.* Chokwe [cjk], 99, 40, 213
Col, *alt.* Kiorr [xko], 451, 465
alt. dial. Cua [cua], 522
Colh, *alt.* Mundari [muw], 376, 321
Colla, *alt. dial.* Quechua, South Bolivian [quh], 220
Colo, *alt.* Shilluk [shk], 195
dial. Thuri [thu], 195
Colombia Cuna, *alt.* Kuna, Border [kvn], 246, 283
Colombian Sign Language [csn], 244
Colonia Tovar German, *see* German, Colonia Tovar [gct], 311
Colorado [cof], 250
Columbia, *dial.* Columbia-Wenatchi [col], 300
Columbia River Sahaptin, *alt.* Umatilla [uma], 309
Columbia-Wenatchi [col], 300

Columbian, *alt. dial.* Columbia-Wenatchi [col], 300
Colville, *dial.* Okanagan [oka], 306
Comaltepec Chinantec, *see* Chinantec, Comaltepec [cco], 260
Comanche [com], 300
Combe, *alt.* Ngumbi [nui], 111
Comematsa, *dial.* Barasana [bsn], 243
Comeya, *alt.* Kumiai [dih], 263
Comitancillo Mam, *alt.* Mam, Central [mvc], 255
Comiteco, *alt.* Tojolabal [toj], 275
Common Kartvelian, *alt.* Georgian [kat], 352
Common Somali, *alt.* Somali [som], 185, 119
Como, *alt.* Komo [xom], 192
Como Karim [cfg], 157
Comores Swahili, *alt.* Comorian [swb], 87, 140
alt. Maore [swb], 146
Comorian [swb], 87, 140
alt. Maore [swb], 146
Comorian, Mwali [wlc], 87
Comorian, Ndzwani [wni], 87
Comorian, Ngazidja [zdj], 87
Comoro, *alt.* Comorian [swb], 87, 140
alt. Maore [swb], 146
Comox [coo], 236
Comox-Sliammon, *alt.* Comox [coo], 236
Compeva, *alt.* Omagua [omg], 289, 231
Con [cno], 450
alt. Kiorr [xko], 451, 465
Cona Monba, *alt.* Moinba [mob], 340
Concepción, *dial.* Chiquitano [cax], 222
Conchucos Quechua, *alt.* Quechua, Northern Conchucos Ancash [qxn], 291
alt. Quechua, Southern Conchucos Ancash [qxo], 292
Concorinum, *alt.* Konkani [knn], 369
Concow, *alt.* Maidu, Northwest [mjd], 304
Condul, *dial.* Nicobarese, Southern [nik], 381
Cone, *alt.* Choni [cda], 331
Conestoga, *alt.* Susquehannock [sqn], 308
Congo, *alt.* Kongo, San Salvador [kwy], 101, 40
alt. Koongo [kng], 101, 40, 88
Congo Nyoro, *alt.* Hema [nix], 100
Congo Pol, *alt.* Pol [pmm], 71

alt. Pomo [pmm], 89
Congo Swahili, *see* Swahili, Congo [swc], 108
Conhague, *alt.* Wamey [cou], 182, 130
Coniagui, *alt.* Wamey [cou], 182, 130
Coniba, *alt. dial.* Shipibo-Conibo [shp], 293
Conibo, *dial.* Shipibo-Conibo [shp], 293
Connacht, *dial.* Gaelic, Irish [gle], 542
Conob, *alt.* Akateko [knj], 253
alt. Kanjobal, Western [knj], 263
alt. Q'anjob'al, Eastern [kjb], 256
Conoy, *alt.* Piscataway [psy], 307
Conso, *alt.* Komso [kxc], 116
Constantine, *dial.* Arabic, Algerian Spoken [arq], 39
Constantinople, *dial.* Armenian [hye], 318
Conta-Reddi, *alt.* Mukha-Dora [mmk], 376
Contaquiro, *alt.* Yine [pib], 294
Coo, *alt.* Bwamu, Cwi [bwy], 50
Cook Island, *alt.* Rarotongan [rar], 579
Cook Islands Maori, *alt.* Rarotongan [rar], 579
Côông [cnc], 522
Coongurri, *alt.* Kunggari [kgl], 572
Coorge, *alt.* Kodagu [kfa], 368
Coos [csz], 300
Copainalá Zoque, *see* Zoque, Copainalá [zoc], 281
Copala Trique, *alt.* Triqui, Copala [trc], 276
Copala Triqui, *see* Triqui, Copala [trc], 276
Copalita Zapotec, *alt.* Zapotec, Loxicha [ztp], 278
Copi, *alt.* Chopi [cce], 147
dial. Chopi [cce], 147
Copper, *alt.* Aleut, Mednyj [mud], 503
Copper Eskimo, *pej. alt. dial.* Inuktitut, Western Canadian [ikt], 238
Copper Inuit, *alt. dial.* Inuktitut, Western Canadian [ikt], 238
Copper Inuktitut, *dial.* Inuktitut, Western Canadian [ikt], 238
Copper Island Aleut, *alt.* Aleut, Mednyj [mud], 503
Copper Island Attuan, *alt.* Aleut, Mednyj [mud], 503
Copper River, *alt.* Ahtena [aht], 297
Coppersmith, *alt. dial.* Romani, Vlax [rmy], 551

Coptic [cop], 110
Coquille [coq], 300
Cor, *alt. dial.* Cua [cua], 522
Cora de el Nayar, *alt.* Cora, El Nayar [crn], 262
Cora, El Nayar [crn], 262
Cora, Santa Teresa [cok], 262
Coreguaje, *alt.* Koreguaje [coe], 246
Cori [cry], 157
Corina, *alt.* Culina [cul], 226
Cornish [cor], 565
Cornouaillais, *dial.* Breton [bre], 536
Cornwall, *dial.* English [eng], 565
Coro, *dial.* Anuak [anu], 113
Coroá, *alt.* Acroá [acs], 224
Coroado, *alt.* Kaingáng [kgp], 228
alt. Puri [prr], 231
Coroados, *alt.* Kaingáng [kgp], 228
Corogaama, *alt.* Bozo, Jenaama [bze], 142
Corogama, *alt.* Sorko [bze], 175
Coroma, *dial.* Bribri [bzd], 249
Corongo Ancash Quechua, *see* Quechua, Corongo Ancash [qwa], 290
Correguaje, *alt.* Koreguaje [coe], 246
Corse, *alt.* Corsican [cos], 536, 543
Corsi, *alt.* Corsican [cos], 536, 543
Corsican [cos], 536, 543
Corso, *alt.* Corsican [cos], 536, 543
Corsu, *alt.* Corsican [cos], 536, 543
Corumbiara, *alt.* Tubarão [tba], 233
Coso, *alt.* Panamint [par], 306
Cosoleacaque Aztec, *alt.* Nahuatl, Isthmus-Cosoleacaque [nhk], 271
Cossyah, *alt.* Khasi [kha], 321
Costa Rican Sign Language [csr], 249
Costanoan, *pej. alt.* Ohlone, Northern [cst], 306
pej. alt. Ohlone, Southern [css], 306
Cotabambas, *dial.* Quechua, Eastern Apurímac [qve], 291
Cotabateño, *alt. dial.* Chavacano [cbk], 493
Cotabato Manobo, *see* Manobo, Cotabato [mta], 499
Cotahuasi, *dial.* Quechua, Arequipa-La Unión [qxu], 289
Cotahuasi Quechua, *alt.* Quechua, Arequipa-La Unión [qxu], 289
Coti, *alt.* Koti [eko], 147
Coto, *alt.* Orejón [ore], 289
Cotobato Chavacano, *dial.* Chavacano [cbk], 493
Cotocoli, *alt.* Tem [kdh], 209, 46, 128

Cotzocón Mixe, *dial.* Mixe, North
Central [neq], 265
Country Sign, *alt.* Jamaican
Country Sign Language [jcs], 258
Coushatta, *alt.* Koasati [cku], 303
Covahloc, *alt. dial.* Sanapaná
[sap], 285
Covavitis, *alt. dial.* Sanapaná
[sap], 285
Cowichan, *dial.* Halkomelem
[hur], 238, 301
Cowlitz [cow], 300
Coxima [kox], 244
Coyaima [coy], 244
dial. Yukpa [yup], 248
Coyotepec Popoloca, *see*
Popoloca, Coyotepec [pbf], 273
Coyotero, *alt.* Apache, Western
[apw], 298
Coyultita, *dial.* Huichol [hch], 263
Coyutla Totonac, *see* Totonac,
Coyutla [toc], 276
Craig Cove, *alt.* Lonwolwol
[crc], 643
Crange, *alt.* Kreye [xre], 229
Craô, *alt.* Krahô [xra], 229
Craven Yorkshire, *dial.* English
[eng], 565
Cree, *alt.* Ojibwa, Severn [ojs], 240
Cree, Moose [crm], 236
Cree, Plains [crk], 236, 300
Cree, Swampy [csw], 236
Cree, Woods [cwd], 236
Creek, *alt.* Muskogee [mus], 305
dial. Muskogee [mus], 305
Crenge, *alt.* Kreye [xre], 229
Crenye, *alt.* Kreye [xre], 229
Creola, *alt.* Belize Kriol English
[bzj], 221
Creole, *alt.* Krio [kri], 183
alt. Seselwa Creole French
[crs], 182
Creolese, *alt.* Guyanese Creole
English [gyn], 257, 295
Creolized Attuan, *alt.* Aleut,
Mednyj [mud], 503
Creq, *dial.* Hre [hre], 523
Creye, *alt.* Kreye [xre], 229
Crichana, *alt.* Ninam [shb], 230
Crimea, *dial.* Armenian [hye], 318
Crimean Gothic, *dial.* Gothic
[got], 564
Crimean Nogai, *alt. dial.* Crimean
Turkish [crh], 521, 518, 532, 551
Crimean Tatar, *alt.* Crimean
Turkish [crh], 521, 518, 532, 551
Crimean Turkish [crh], 521, 518,
532, 551
Crimeo-Rumeic, *alt. dial.* Greek
[ell], 564

Criollo, *alt.* Fernando Po Creole
English [fpe], 111
Crioulo, *alt.* Karipúna Creole French
[kmv], 228
Crioulo, Upper Guinea
[pov], 131, 180
Crisca, *alt.* Xavánte [xav], 234
Croatan, *alt.* Lumbee [lmz], 304
Croatia Sign Language [csq], 532
Croatian [hrv], 532, 530, 531, 542,
543, 558
dial. Croatian [hrv], 531, 542, 543,
558
Croker Island, *alt.* Margu
[mhg], 573
Cross River Mbembe, *see*
Mbembe, Cross River [mfn], 163
Cross River Pidgin, *dial.* Pidgin,
Nigerian [pcm], 173
Crow [cro], 300
Cru, *alt.* Chru [cje], 522
Cruzan, *dial.* Virgin Islands Creole
English [vic], 297
Cruzeño [crz], 300
Cù Te, *alt.* Lachi [lbt], 524
Cu Tho, *alt.* Khmer, Central
[khm], 524
Cu-Tê, *alt.* Lachi [lbt], 524
Cua [cua], 522
alt. Kua [tyu], 47
Cuabo, *alt.* Chuwabu [chw], 147
Cuaiquer, *alt.* Awa-Cuaiquer
[kwi], 243, 250
Cuana, *alt.* Tswana [tsn], 48, 186,
217
Cuangar, *alt.* Kwangali [kwn], 40
Cuanhama, *alt.* Kwanyama [kua], 40
Cuanhoca, *alt.* Kwadi [kwz], 40
Cuatzoquitengo, *dial.* Mixtec,
Alacatlatzala [mim], 265
Cuba Sign Language [csf], 249
Cubeo [cub], 244, 226
Cubeu, *alt.* Cubeo [cub], 226
Cubulco Achi', *see* Achi', Cubulco
[acc], 253
Cucapá, *alt.* Cocopa [coc], 262, 300
Cuchi, *alt.* Kachchi [kfr], 366, 140,
485
Cuchimí, *alt.* Kumiai [dih], 263
Cuchudua, *dial.* Jamamadí [jaa], 227
Cucupá, *alt.* Cocopa [coc], 262
Cudaxar, *dial.* Dargwa [dar], 553
Cuepe, *alt.* Kwadi [kwz], 40
Cueva, *alt. dial.* Kuna, San Blas
[cuk], 283
Cugani, *alt.* Konkani [knn], 369
Cùi Chu, *alt.* Giáy [pcc], 523
Cuiba [cui], 244, 311
Cuiba-Wámonae, *alt.* Cuiba
[cui], 244

Cuicatec, Tepeuxila [cux], 262
Cuicatec, Teutila [cut], 262
Cuicatlán Mixtec, *alt.* Mixtec,
Cuyamecalco [xtu], 267
Cuicutl, *alt.* Kuikúro-Kalapálo
[kui], 229
Cuini, *alt.* Kwini [gww], 573
Cuiva, *alt.* Cuiba [cui], 244, 311
Cujareno, *alt.* Mashco Piro
[cuj], 288
Cujareño, *alt.* Mashco Piro
[cuj], 288
Cujazi, *alt.* Luchazi [lch], 214
Cujubi, *alt.* Puruborá [pur], 232
Cukwa Ring, *alt.* Chukwa
[cuw], 470
Cule, *alt.* Tsamai [tsb], 119
Culina [cul], 226, 287
Cullo, *alt. dial.* Gamo-Gofa-Dawro
[gmo], 114
Cumanagoto [cuo], 311
Cumanasho, *alt.* Maxakalí
[mbl], 230
Cumata, *alt.* Ipeka-Tapuia [paj], 227
Cumberland, *dial.* English
[eng], 565
Cumeral [cum], 245
Cun [cuq], 331
Cun-Hua, *alt.* Cun [cuq], 331
Cuna, *alt.* Kuna, Border [kvn], 246,
283
Cunama, *alt.* Kunama [kun], 112
Cunén K'iche', *see* K'iche', Cunén
[cun], 255
Cunén Quiché, *alt.* K'iche', Cunén
[cun], 255
Cunenteco K'iche', *alt.* K'iche',
Cunén [cun], 255
Cunenteco Quiché, *alt.* K'iche',
Cunén [cun], 255
Cung [cug], 59
alt. Tai Ya [cuu], 344
Cunhua, *alt.* Cun [cuq], 331
Cuni, *alt. dial.* Niellim [nie], 85
Cunimía, *alt.* Guayabero [guo], 245
Cunipusana, *alt.* Baré [bae], 311
alt. Mandahuaca [mht], 312
Cunuana, *alt.* Maquiritari
[mch], 312
dial. Maquiritari [mch], 229
Cuoi, *alt.* Kuy [kdt], 515, 451
alt. Tho [tou], 527
Cuói, *alt.* Hung [hnu], 523
Cuoi Cham, *alt.* Tho [tou], 527
dial. Tho [tou], 527
Cuona Menba, *alt.* Moinba
[mob], 340
Cuona Monpa, *alt.* Moinba
[mob], 340
Cupeño [cup], 300

alt. Yangman [jng], 579
Dagomba, *alt.* Dagbani [dag], 124
Dagu, *alt.* Daju, Dar Fur [daj], 189
Dagui, *alt.* Mala [ped], 611
Daguor, *alt.* Daur [dta], 331, 461
Dagur, *alt.* Daur [dta], 331, 461
Dahalo [dal], 132
Dahanmu, *dial.* Bomu [bmq], 137
Dahating, *alt.* Gwahatike [dah], 601
Dahejia, *alt. dial.* Bonan [peh], 328
Daho-Doo [das], 92
Dahomeen, *alt.* Fon [fon], 43, 207
Dahuni, *dial.* Suau [swp], 625
Dai [dij], 397
　alt. Chin, Daai [dao], 463
　alt. Day [dai], 80
　alt. Hlai [lic], 333
　alt. Lü [khb], 339
　alt. dial. Lau [llu], 637
Dai Kong, *alt.* Tai Nüa [tdd], 344
Dai Le, *alt.* Lü [khb], 339
Dai Na, *alt.* Tai Nüa [tdd], 344
Dai Nuea, *alt.* Tai Nüa [tdd], 344
Daido, *alt. dial.* Pamona [bcx], 432
Daier, *alt.* Dair [drb], 189
Daigok, *alt. dial.* Pemon [aoc], 312
Daina, *alt. dial.* Kwanga [kwj], 608
Dainggati, *alt.* Dyangadi [dyn], 570
Daiomuni, *alt.* Oya'oya [oyy], 621
Dair [drb], 189
Dairi, *alt.* Batak Dairi [btd], 435
Daiso, *alt.* Dhaiso [dhs], 198
Daisu, *alt.* Dhaiso [dhs], 198
Daiya, *alt.* Tai Ya [cuu], 344
Daiya-Ataiyal, *alt.* Taroko [trv], 512
Daja, *dial.* Aceh [ace], 435
　dial. Akpes [ibe], 153
Dajiahe, *alt. dial.* Bonan [peh], 328
Dajishan, *dial.* Qiang, Southern
　[qxs], 342
Dajo, *alt.* Daju, Dar Daju [djc], 79
Dajou, *alt.* Daju, Dar Daju [djc], 79
　alt. Daju, Dar Sila [dau], 80
Daju, *alt.* Daju, Dar Daju [djc], 79
　alt. Daju, Dar Sila [dau], 80
Daju Ferne, *alt.* Daju, Dar Fur
　[daj], 189
Daju Mongo, *alt.* Daju, Dar Daju
　[djc], 79
Daju Oum Hadjer, *alt.* Daju, Dar
　Daju [djc], 79
Daju, Dar Daju [djc], 79
Daju, Dar Fur [daj], 189
Daju, Dar Sila [dau], 80, 189
Dak Sut Sedang, *dial.* Sedang
　[sed], 526
Daka, *alt.* Dirim [dir], 158
　alt. Samba Daka [ccg], 174
Dakaka [bpa], 641
Dakakari, *alt.* C'lela [dri], 157

Dakalla, *alt. dial.* Katcha-Kadugli-
　Miri [xtc], 191
Dakani, *alt. dial.* Urdu [urd], 389
Dakao, *dial.* Bisu [bii], 327
Dakarkari, *alt.* C'lela [dri], 157
Dakenei, *alt.* Baniwa [bwi], 225
Dakheczjha, *alt. dial.* Bonan [peh],
　328
Dakhini, *dial.* Urdu [urd], 389
Dakhota, *alt. dial.* Dakota [dak], 297
Dakka [dkk], 429
　alt. Dirim [dir], 158
　alt. Samba Daka [ccg], 174
Dakkarkari, *alt.* C'lela [dri], 157
Daklan, *dial.* Ibaloi [ibl], 494
Dakota [dak], 297, 237
　dial. Dakota [dak], 297, 237
Dakpa, *alt.* Brokpake [sgt], 322
　alt. Takpa [tkk], 344
　dial. Banda, West Central [bbp], 74
Dakpakha [dka], 323
Daktjerat, *alt.* Tyaraity [woa], 577
Dakunza, *dial.* Gumuz [guk], 191
Dakwa, *dial.* Kamwe [hig], 166
Dala, *alt.* Fur [fvr], 190
Dalabon, *alt.* Ngalkbun [ngk], 575
Dalad, *alt. dial.* Melanau [mel], 460
Dalandji, *alt.* Dhalandji [dhl], 569
Dalat, *dial.* Melanau [mel], 460
Daldi, *dial.* Konkani, Goanese
　[gom], 369
Dalecarlian [dlc], 561
Dalendi, *alt.* Dhalandji [dhl], 569
Dal'gari, *alt.* Dhargari [dhr], 569
Dali, *dial.* Bai, Southern [bfs], 327
　dial. Lelak [llk], 460
Dalit Murut, *dial.* Paluan [plz], 458
Dallol, *dial.* Fulfulde, Western Niger
　[fuh], 151
Dalmaal, *alt.* Dalecarlian [dlc], 561
Dalmatian [dlm], 532
Daloa Bété, *see* Bété, Daloa
　[bev], 92
Daloka, *alt.* Ngile [jle], 194
　dial. Ngile [jle], 194
Dalong, *alt.* Darlong [dln], 321, 359
　alt. Pe [pai], 173
Daloua Bété, *alt.* Bété, Daloa
　[bev], 92
Dalska, *alt.* Dalecarlian [dlc], 561
Daly River Kriol, *dial.* Kriol
　[rop], 572
Dam, *alt.* Ndam [ndm], 85
　dial. Bagirmi [bmi], 78
Dam de Bousso, *alt.* Buso [bso], 79
Dam Fer, *alt.* Kara [kah], 76
Dama [dmm], 59
　alt. Bete-Bendi [btt], 155
　alt. Daasanach [dsh], 114, 132
　alt. Mursi [muz], 117

alt. Nama [naq], 48, 186
　alt. dial. Mbembe, Tigon [nza], 66,
　170
Damagaram, *dial.* Hausa [hau], 152
Damal [uhn], 413
　dial. Damal [uhn], 413
Damani, *alt. dial.* Konkani [knn], 369
Damaqua, *alt.* Nama [naq], 48, 186
Damar, East [dmr], 397
Damar, West [drn], 397
Damara, *alt.* Nama [naq], 48, 186
　dial. Nama [naq], 150
Damat, *dial.* Maasai [mas], 134
Damata, *dial.* Mambae [mgm], 351
Damba, *dial.* Katcha-Kadugli-Miri
　[xtc], 191
Dambi [dac], 596
　dial. Sagalla [tga], 136
Dambiya, *alt. dial.* Migaama
　[mmy], 84
Dambro, *alt.* Thai, Southern
　[sou], 517
Dambya, *alt. dial.* Qimant
　[ahg], 118
Damedi, *alt.* Dameli [dml], 484
Damel, *alt.* Dameli [dml], 484
Dameli [dml], 484
Dami, *alt.* Marik [dad], 612
Damia, *alt.* Dameli [dml], 484
Damilo, *alt.* Brokpake [sgt], 322
Daminyu, *dial.* Yele [yle], 633
Damlale, *alt. dial.* Vame [mlr], 73
Dammai, *alt.* Sajalong [sjl], 385
Damot, *alt.* Awngi [awn], 113
Dampal, *alt.* Dampelas [dms], 429
Dampelas [dms], 429
Dampelasa, *alt.* Dampelas
　[dms], 429
Damraw, *alt.* Boor [bvf], 79
Damti, *alt. dial.* Koma [kmy], 167
Damulian, *alt.* Tamil [tam], 388
Dan [daf], 92, 129, 137
　alt. Dyan [dya], 51
　alt. dial. Sheko [she], 118
Dan Lai, *dial.* Hung [hnu], 523
Dan Muure, *dial.* Peere [pfe], 71
Dana, *alt.* Kaba Na [kwv], 81
Danakil, *pej. alt.* Afar [aar], 112, 109,
　111
Danal, *alt.* Dangaléat [daa], 80
Danaru [dnr], 596
Danau [dnu], 463
Danaw, *alt.* Danau [dnu], 463
Danba, *alt.* Horpa [ero], 335
Danda, *dial.* Ndau [ndc], 148
Dandami Madiya, *alt.* Maria,
　Dandami [daq], 375
Dandami Maria, *see* Maria,
　Dandami [daq], 375
Dandawa, *alt.* Dendi [ddn], 43, 157

Dandzongka, *alt.* Sikkimese [sip], 387

Dang, *alt.* Giáy [pcc], 523
alt. Kedang [ksx], 407
alt. Tharu, Dangaura [thl], 388
alt. Tungag [lcm], 628
dial. Tharu, Dangaura [thl], 480

Dangadi, *alt.* Dyangadi [dyn], 570

Dangal, *alt.* Dangaléat [daa], 80
dial. Watut, South [mcy], 631

Dangaléat [daa], 80

Dangali, *alt.* Humla [hut], 472
alt. Tharu, Dangaura [thl], 388

Dangarik, *alt.* Phalura [phl], 488

Dangati, *alt.* Dyangadi [dyn], 570

Dangauli, *alt.* Tharu, Dangaura [thl], 480

Dangaura Tharu, *see* Tharu, Dangaura [thl], 480, 388

Dangbe, *alt.* Adangbe [adq], 122, 206

Dangbon, *alt.* Ngalkbun [ngk], 575

Dangedl, *dial.* Yir Yoront [yiy], 579

Danggadi, *alt.* Dyangadi [dyn], 570

Danggal, *alt. dial.* Watut, South [mcy], 631

Danggetti, *alt.* Dyangadi [dyn], 570

Dangha, *alt.* Tharu, Dangaura [thl], 480, 388

Dangi, *alt.* Dhanki [dhn], 360
dial. Braj Bhasha [bra], 357

Dangla, *alt.* Dangaléat [daa], 80

Dangme [ada], 124

Dangora, *alt.* Tharu, Dangaura [thl], 480, 388

Dangri, *alt.* Dhanki [dhn], 360
dial. Khandesi [khn], 367

Dangs Bhil, *alt.* Dhanki [dhn], 360

Dangu, *alt.* Dhangu [dhg], 569

Dangura, *alt.* Tharu, Dangaura [thl], 480, 388

Dani, *alt.* Dení [dny], 226

Dani Barat, *alt.* Dani, Western [dnw], 414

Dani, Lower Grand Valley [dni], 413

Dani, Mid Grand Valley [dnt], 413

Dani, Upper Grand Valley [dna], 414

Dani, Western [dnw], 414

Dani-Kurima, *alt. dial.* Dani, Lower Grand Valley [dni], 413

Daniel Carrion, *alt.* Quechua, Yanahuanca Pasco [qur], 292

Danisa, *alt. dial.* Shua [shg], 48

Dänisch, *alt.* Danish [dan], 538

Danish [dan], 533, 252, 538, 542

Danish Sign Language [dsl], 533

Danisi, *dial.* Shua [shg], 48

Danisis, *alt. dial.* Shua [shg], 48

Danjongka, *alt.* Sikkimese [sip], 387

Dankyira, *dial.* Akan [aka], 123

Dano [aso], 596

Danshe, *dial.* Zeem [zua], 178

Dansk, *alt.* Danish [dan], 533, 538

Danu, *dial.* Burmese [mya], 462
dial. Madak [mmx], 610

Danube-Tisza, *dial.* Hungarian [hun], 542

Danubian, *alt.* Romani, Vlax [rmy], 551, 531
dial. Turkish [tur], 519, 521, 532, 552

Danuwar, *alt.* Dhanwar [dha], 360
alt. Dhanwar [dhw], 470

Danuwar Rai, *alt.* Dhanwar [dhw], 470

Danyouka, *alt.* Sikkimese [sip], 387

Dao [daz], 414
alt. Dhao [nfa], 406

Dao Ao Dai, *alt.* Kim Mun [mji], 524

Dao Do, *alt.* Iu Mien [ium], 523
dial. Iu Mien [ium], 523

Dao Ho, *dial.* Kim Mun [mji], 337

Dao Lam Dinh, *alt.* Kim Mun [mji], 524

Dao Lan Tien, *dial.* Iu Mien [ium], 523

Dao Lo Gang, *dial.* Iu Mien [ium], 523

Dao Quan Trang, *alt.* Kim Mun [mji], 524
dial. Kim Mun [mji], 337

Dao Thanh Phan, *alt.* Iu Mien [ium], 523

Dao Thanh Y, *alt.* Kim Mun [mji], 524

Daofu, *dial.* Horpa [ero], 335

Daofuhua, *alt. dial.* Horpa [ero], 335

Daonda [dnd], 596

Daongdung, *dial.* Balangingi [sse], 492

Daosahaq, *alt.* Tadaksahak [dsq], 144

Daoussahaq, *alt.* Tadaksahak [dsq], 144

Daoussak, *alt.* Tadaksahak [dsq], 144

Dap, *alt.* Brokpake [sgt], 322

Dapalan, *dial.* Talaud [tld], 433

Dapera, *alt.* Oune [oue], 620

Daphla, *pej. alt.* Nisi [dap], 381

Dapitan, *dial.* Subanen, Northern [stb], 501

Dapo, *dial.* Krumen, Tepo [ted], 93, 138

Dapzal, *dial.* Chin, Paite [pck], 359

Dapzar, *alt. dial.* Chin, Paite [pck], 359

Daqishan, *alt. dial.* Qiang, Southern [qxs], 342

Dar Daju Daju, *see* Daju, Dar Daju [djc], 79

Dar El Kabira, *dial.* Tulishi [tey], 196

Dar Fur Daju, *see* Daju, Dar Fur [daj], 189

Dar Sila Daju, *see* Daju, Dar Sila [dau], 80, 189

Daraga, *dial.* Bicolano, Albay [bhk], 493

Daragawan, *alt. dial.* Isnag [isd], 496

Darai [dry], 470

Darambal, *alt.* Bayali [bjy], 569

Darang, *alt.* Darang Deng [dat], 331

Darang Deng [dat], 331

Darang Dengyu, *alt.* Darang Deng [dat], 331

Darasa, *alt.* Gedeo [drs], 115

Darassa, *alt.* Gedeo [drs], 115

Darava, *dial.* Mailu [mgu], 610

Darawal, *alt.* Bayali [bjy], 569

Darbé, *dial.* Gabri [gab], 80

Darel, *alt. dial.* Shina [scl], 488

Dargi, *alt.* Dargwa [dar], 553

Dargin, *alt.* Dargwa [dar], 553

Dargintsy, *alt.* Dargwa [dar], 553

Dargwa [dar], 553

Darha, *alt.* Tause [tad], 424

Dari, *alt.* Dari, Zoroastrian [gbz], 438
alt. Deori [der], 360
alt. Farsi, Eastern [prs], 315, 484
dial. Farsi, Eastern [prs], 315
dial. Pévé [lme], 86

Dari, Zoroastrian [gbz], 438

Daribi, *alt.* Dadibi [mps], 596

Darien, *alt.* Emberá, Northern [emp], 283

Darién, *alt.* Emberá, Northern [emp], 245

Dariena, *alt.* Emberá, Northern [emp], 283, 245

Dariganga, *dial.* Mongolian, Halh [khk], 461, 505

Darimiya, *alt.* Darmiya [drd], 359, 470

Darjula, *dial.* Nepali [nep], 476

Darkhat [drh], 461

Darling [drl], 569

Darlong [dln], 321, 359

Darmani, *alt.* Darmiya [drd], 359

Darmiya [drd], 359, 470

Daro, *dial.* Daro-Matu [dro], 459

Daro-Matu [dro], 459

Daroro, *alt. dial.* Tyap [kcg], 176

Darra, *alt.* Ngile [jle], 194

Darrai Nur, *dial.* Pashayi, Southeast [psi], 317

Deibula, _dial._ Korupun-Sela [kpq], 418

Deing, _dial._ Tewa [twe], 410

Deirate, _dial._ Tause [tad], 424

Dejah, _alt._ Dusun Deyah [dun], 393

Dejbuk, _dial._ Dargwa [dar], 553

Dek [dek], 60

Dekini, _alt._ Deccan [dcc], 360

Dekka, _alt._ Samba Daka [ccg], 174

Dekoka, _dial._ Gumuz [guk], 191

Dekshi, _alt. dial._ Dass [dot], 157

Dekwambre, _alt._ Mpur [akc], 420

Dela, _dial._ Dela-Oenale [row], 406

Dela-Oenale [row], 406

Delang, _dial._ Malayic Dayak [xdy], 394

Delaware, _alt._ Munsee [umu], 239
alt. Unami [unm], 309

Delaware, Pidgin [dep], 300

Delen, _alt._ Dilling [dil], 189

Delha, _alt._ Dela-Oenale [row], 406
alt. dial. Dela-Oenale [row], 406

Delhi Sign Language, _dial._ Indian Sign Language [ins], 365

Deli, _dial._ Malay [mly], 436

Delnoserbski, _alt._ Sorbian, Lower [dsb], 539

Delo [ntr], 124, 207

Delta Pidgin, _dial._ Pidgin, Nigerian [pcm], 173

Delta Pwo Karen, _alt._ Karen, Pwo Western [pwo], 464

Delta River Yuman, _alt._ Cocopa [coc], 300

Dem [dem], 414

Dema [dmx], 147
alt. Tupuri [tui], 72

Demam, _alt. dial._ Iban [iba], 393

Demba, _alt._ Tefaro [tfo], 424

Dembiya, _dial._ Qimant [ahg], 118

Dembo, _alt. dial._ Thuri [thu], 195

Dembya, _alt. dial._ Qimant [ahg], 118

Demen, _alt. dial._ Thuri [thu], 195

Demenggong-Waibron-Bano, _alt._ Mekwei [msf], 420

Demik, _alt._ Keiga [kec], 192
dial. Keiga [kec], 192

Demisa [dei], 414
alt. dial. Shua [shg], 48

Demsa, _dial._ Bata [bta], 155

Demsa Bata, _alt._ Bata [bta], 155

Demshin, _dial._ Miya [mkf], 170

Demta [dmy], 414

Demwa, _dial._ Vame [mlr], 73

Dena'ina, _alt._ Tanaina [tfn], 308

Denawa, _alt._ Deno [dbb], 157

Dendi (Benin) [ddn], 43, 157
Dendi (Central African Republic) [deq], 75

Dendje, _alt. dial._ Kaba Na [kwv], 81

Dene, _alt._ Chipewyan [chp], 236

Dené, _alt._ Slavey, North [scs], 241
alt. Slavey, South [xsl], 241

Deng, _alt._ Samba Daka [ccg], 174
alt. dial. Gola [gol], 183
dial. Gola [gol], 138

Dengalu, _dial._ Patep [ptp], 621

Dengebu, _alt._ Dagik [dec], 189

Dengese [dez], 99

Dengka [dnk], 406

Dengkwop, _alt. dial._ Ghomálá' [bbj], 62

Dengsa, _dial._ Lamja-Dengsa-Tola [ldh], 168

Dengurume, _alt._ Ngurimi [ngq], 203

Deni, _alt. dial._ Santa Cruz [stc], 638

Dení [dny], 226

Denje, _alt. dial._ Kaba Na [kwv], 81

Denjong, _alt._ Sikkimese [sip], 387

Denjongkha, _alt._ Sikkimese [sip], 387

Denjongpa, _alt._ Sikkimese [sip], 387

Denjonka, _alt._ Sikkimese [sip], 387

Denjonke, _alt._ Sikkimese [sip], 387

Denkel, _pej. alt._ Afar [aar], 112, 111

Deno [dbb], 157

Dentong, _alt._ Bentong [bnu], 428

Denwa, _alt._ Deno [dbb], 157

Denwar, _alt._ Dhanwar [dhw], 470

Denya [anv], 60

Deo Tien, _dial._ Iu Mien [ium], 523

Deokhar, _alt. dial._ Tharu, Dangaura [thl], 480

Deokhuri, _dial._ Tharu, Dangaura [thl], 480

Deokri, _alt. dial._ Tharu, Dangaura [thl], 480

Deori [der], 360

Deple, _dial._ Bakwé [bjw], 91

Deq, _alt. dial._ Batek [btq], 454

Dera (Indonesia) [kbv], 414, 597
Dera (Nigeria) [kna], 157

Derasa, _alt._ Gedeo [drs], 115

Derasanya, _alt._ Gedeo [drs], 115

Derawali, _dial._ Seraiki [skr], 488

Derbend, _dial._ Azerbaijani, North [azj], 319
dial. Judeo-Tat [jdt], 445, 554

Derbent, _dial._ Azerbaijani, North [azj], 319

Derbet, _alt. dial._ Kalmyk-Oirat [xal], 554

Dere, _dial._ Gokana [gkn], 161

Derebai, _dial._ Mailu [mgu], 610

Deresa, _alt._ Gedeo [drs], 115

Deressia, _alt. dial._ Tobanga [tng], 87

Dermuha, _dial._ Karen, Paku [kpp], 464

Dersimki, _alt._ Kirmanjki [kiu], 518

Derung River, _alt. dial._ Drung [duu], 332

Deruwo, _dial._ Waja [wja], 177

Desa, _alt. dial._ Iban [iba], 393

Desána, _alt._ Desano [des], 245

Desâna, _alt._ Desano [des], 226

Desano [des], 226, 245

Desari, _alt._ Haryanvi [bgc], 364

Deshia, _alt._ Oriya, Desiya [dso], 382

Desi, _alt._ Deccan [dcc], 360

Desia, _alt._ Oriya, Desiya [dso], 382
alt. dial. Urdu [urd], 389

Desin Dola', _alt._ Duano' [dup], 454

Desiya, _alt._ Oriya, Desiya [dso], 382

Desiya Oriya, _see_ Oriya, Desiya [dso], 382

Dessana, _alt._ Desano [des], 245

Dessano, _alt._ Desano [des], 226

Dessaulya, _dial._ Garhwali [gbm], 360

Desua, _alt. dial._ Gumuz [guk], 191

Deswali, _alt._ Bhojpuri [bho], 356
dial. Haryanvi [bgc], 364

Detah-Ndilo, _dial._ Dogrib [dgr], 237

Deti, _dial._ Shua [shg], 48

De'u, _alt._ Dehu [dhv], 584

Deuri, _alt._ Deori [der], 360

Deutsch, _alt._ German, Standard [deu], 538

Deutsche Gebärdensprache, _alt._ German Sign Language [gsg], 538

Devechi, _dial._ Tat, Muslim [ttt], 320

Devehi, _alt._ Maldivian [div], 374

Devonshire, _dial._ English [eng], 565

Dewansala, _alt._ Yakha [ybh], 482

Dewiya, _dial._ Gumuz [guk], 191

Dewoi, _alt._ Dewoin [dee], 137

Dewoin [dee], 137

Dewri, _alt._ Deori [der], 360

Dey, _alt._ Dewoin [dee], 137

Dezfuli [def], 438

Dezhfili, _alt._ Dezfuli [def], 438

Dfola, _alt._ Biafada [bif], 131

Dgernesiais, _dial._ French [fra], 565

Dghwede [dgh], 157

Dgiéh, _alt._ Trieng [stg], 527

Dgs, _alt._ German Sign Language [gsg], 538

Dhading, _alt. dial._ Tamang, Western [tdg], 480
dial. Tamang, Northwestern [tmk], 479

Dha'i, _alt._ Dayi [dax], 569

Dhaiso [dhs], 198

Dhalandji [dhl], 569

Dhalla, _alt. dial._ Katcha-Kadugli-Miri [xtc], 191

Dhalwangu, _dial._ Dayi [dax], 569

Dhanagari, _alt._ Varhadi-Nagpuri [vah], 389

dial. Konkani [knn], 369
Dhangar, *alt.* Kurux, Nepali [kxl], 473
Dhangu [dhg], 569
Dhangu-Djangu, *dial.* Dhangu [dhg], 569
Dhangu'mi, *alt.* Dhangu [dhg], 569
Dhanka, *alt.* Dhanki [dhn], 360
Dhanki [dhn], 360
Dhankuta, *alt. dial.* Bantawa [bap], 468
Dhanora, *dial.* Muria, Western [mut], 377
Dhanusa, *dial.* Tharu, Kochila [thq], 481
Dhanu'un, *alt. dial.* Yir Yoront [yiy], 579
Dhanvar, *alt.* Dhanwar [dha], 360
   alt. Dhanwar [dhw], 470
Dhanwar (India) [dha], 360
   Dhanwar (Nepal) [dhw], 470
Dhao [nfa], 406
Dharawaal, *alt.* Thurawal [tbh], 576
Dharawal, *alt.* Thurawal [tbh], 576
Dharba, *dial.* Duruwa [pci], 361
Dhargari [dhr], 569
Dharthi, *dial.* Sirmauri [srx], 387
Dharua, *alt.* Kudmali [kyw], 370
Dharwar, *alt. dial.* Deccan [dcc], 360
Dhati, *alt.* Dhatki [mki], 484
Dhatki [mki], 484, 360
Dhay'yi, *alt.* Dayi [dax], 569
Dhe Boodho, *alt. dial.* Thuri [thu], 195
Dhe Colo, *alt. dial.* Thuri [thu], 195
Dhe Luwo, *alt.* Luwo [lwo], 193
Dhe Lwo, *alt.* Luwo [lwo], 193
Dhe Thuri, *alt.* Thuri [thu], 195
Dhed, *alt. dial.* Konkani [knn], 369
Dhed Gujari, *alt.* Khandesi [khn], 367
Dhedi, *alt. dial.* Varhadi-Nagpuri [vah], 389
Dhekaru, *alt.* Degaru [dgu], 360
Dhelki Kharia, *dial.* Kharia [khr], 367
Dhibali, *alt.* Bali [bcp], 96
Dhidhanu, *alt.* Yindjilandji [yil], 579
Dhimal [dhi], 470, 360
Dhimba, *alt.* Zemba [dhm], 42, 151
Dhimorong, *alt.* Moro [mor], 193
Dhiraila, *dial.* Ngura [nbx], 575
Dhirari, *alt.* Dirari [dit], 569
Dhirasha, *alt.* Dirasha [gdl], 114
Dhitoro, *alt.* Otoro [otr], 194
Dho Alur, *alt.* Alur [alz], 96, 210
Dho Anywaa, *alt.* Anuak [anu], 187
Dhobi, *alt.* Dhodia [dho], 360
Dhocolo, *alt.* Shilluk [shk], 195

Dhodia [dho], 360
Dhofari, *alt.* Arabic, Dhofari Spoken [adf], 482
Dhofari Spoken Arabic, *see* Arabic, Dhofari Spoken [adf], 482
Dhogaryali, *alt.* Dogri [dgo], 360
Dhogri, *alt. dial.* Vasavi [vas], 390
Dholewari, *alt. dial.* Malvi [mup], 374
Dholubi, *alt. dial.* Katcha-Kadugli-Miri [xtc], 191
Dholuo, *alt.* Luo [luo], 134, 201
Dhopadhola, *alt.* Adhola [adh], 210
Dhopaluo, *alt. dial.* Acholi [ach], 210
Dhore, *alt.* Dhodia [dho], 360
Dhori, *alt.* Dhodia [dho], 360
Dhowari, *alt.* Dhodia [dho], 360
Dhruva, *alt.* Duruwa [pci], 361
Dhundari [dhd], 360
Dhundari-Marwari, *alt.* Dhundari [dhd], 360
Dhundi-Kairali, *alt.* Pahari-Potwari [phr], 487
   alt. dial. Pahari-Potwari [phr], 487
Dhungri Garasia, *alt.* Garasia, Rajput [gra], 362
Dhunkuria, *alt.* Lohar, Gade [gda], 372
Dhu'rga, *alt.* Dhurga [dhu], 569
Dhurga [dhu], 569
Dhuri, *alt.* Suri [suq], 119
Dhuru, *alt.* Maria, Dandami [daq], 375
Dhurwa, *alt.* Duruwa [pci], 361
Dhuwal [duj], 569
   dial. Dhuwal [duj], 569
Dhuwaya, *dial.* Dhuwal [duj], 569
Di, *alt.* Ding [diz], 99
Di-Ang, *alt.* Palaung, Pale [pce], 466, 516
Di-Pri, *alt. dial.* Mnong, Central [cmo], 525
Dia [dia], 597
   alt. Buol [blf], 428
   alt. dial. Sakata [skt], 104
Diabe, *dial.* Gbaya-Bozoum [gbq], 76
Diahói, *alt. dial.* Tenharim [pah], 232
Diahoue, *alt.* Jawe [jaz], 584
Diakhanke, *alt.* Jahanka [jad], 129, 143
   alt. dial. Maninkakan, Western [mlq], 181
Diakkanke, *alt.* Jahanka [jad], 129, 143
   alt. dial. Maninkakan, Western [mlq], 181
Dialonke, *alt.* Jalunga [yal], 143
   alt. Yalunka [yal], 130, 184
Dialonké, *alt.* Jalunga [yal], 180

Dialu, *alt.* Zapotec, Lachixío [zpl], 278
Diamala, *dial.* Senoufo, Djimini [dyi], 95
Dian, *alt.* Dampelas [dms], 429
   alt. Dyan [dya], 51
Dian Dongbei Yi, *alt.* Yi, Wuding-Luquan [ywq], 348
Diandongbei, *alt.* Hmong, Northeastern Dian [hmd], 334
Diarbekir, *alt. dial.* Armenian [hye], 318
Diawara, *alt.* Soninke [snk], 144
Diba, *alt.* Tuvin [tyv], 507, 345, 462
Dibabaon, *alt.* Manobo, Dibabawon [mbd], 499
Dibabawon Manobo, *see* Manobo, Dibabawon [mbd], 499
Dibagat-Kabugao, *dial.* Isnag [isd], 496
Dibagat-Kabugao-Isneg, *alt.* Isnag [isd], 496
Dibatchua, *pej. alt.* Kango [kzy], 100
Dibate, *dial.* Gumuz [guk], 115
Dibiasu, *alt.* Dibiyaso [dby], 597
Dibiyaso [dby], 597
Diblaeg, *alt.* Idi [idi], 602
Dibo [dio], 157
Dibole [bvx], 88
Diboum, *dial.* Basaa [bas], 58
Dibum, *dial.* Meohang, Eastern [emg], 475
Dicamay Agta, *see* Agta, Dicamay [duy], 490
Dicamay Dumagat, *alt.* Agta, Dicamay [duy], 490
Dida, Lakota [dic], 92
Dida, Yocoboué [gud], 92
Didayi, *alt.* Gata' [gaq], 362
Didei, *alt.* Gata' [gaq], 362
Didessa, *alt.* Bambassi [myf], 113
Didi, *dial.* Kaliko [kbo], 100
Didigaru, *dial.* Maria [mds], 612
Didigavu, *dial.* Iamalele [yml], 602
Didinaht, *alt. dial.* Nootka [noo], 240
'Di'dinga, *alt.* Didinga [did], 189
Didinga [did], 189
Didiu, *alt.* Cochimi [coj], 262
Dido [ddo], 554
Didoi, *alt.* Dido [ddo], 554
Didra, *alt.* Todrah [tdr], 527
Didrah, *alt.* Todrah [tdr], 527
Didxsaj, *alt.* Zapotec, Mitla [zaw], 279
Di'e, *dial.* Ai-Cham [aih], 326
Die, *alt.* Jeh [jeh], 523, 450
Dieguéño, *alt.* Kumiai [dih], 263, 303
Dieko, *alt.* Dida, Lakota [dic], 92

Dieri [dif], 569
Diés, *alt.* Ega [ega], 92
Digam, *dial.* Mpade [mpi], 68, 84
Digaro, *alt.* Darang Deng [dat], 331
  alt. Digaro-Mishmi [mhu], 360
Digaro-Mishmi [mhu], 360
Digaru, *alt.* Digaro-Mishmi
  [mhu], 360
Digenja, *alt.* Ligenza [lgz], 102
Digger, *pej. alt.* Maidu, Northwest
  [mjd], 304
Digo [dig], 132, 198
Digoel, *alt.* Muyu, South [kts], 421
Digor, *dial.* Osetin [oss], 352, 519
Digueño, *alt.* Kumiai [dih], 303
Digul, *alt.* Muyu, South [kts], 421
Digüt, *alt.* Gavião do Jiparaná
  [gvo], 226
Dih Bri, *dial.* Mnong, Central
  [cmo], 525, 326
Dihina, *dial.* Gawwada [gwd], 115
Dihok, *dial.* Chaldean Neo-Aramaic
  [cld], 443
Dii [dur], 60
  alt. Bata [bta], 58
Diidz Zë, *alt.* Zapotec, Xanaguía
  [ztg], 281
Diila, *alt.* Kunama [kun], 112
Diir, *alt. dial.* Polci [plj], 173
Dije, *alt.* Tumak [tmc], 87
Dijim, *dial.* Dijim-Bwilim [cfa], 158
Dijim-Bwilim [cfa], 158
Dikaka, *alt.* Kako [kkj], 63
Dikango, *alt.* Kango [kzy], 100
Dikayu, *dial.* Subanen, Northern
  [stb], 501
Dikele, *alt.* Kélé [keb], 120
Dikini, *dial.* Maraghei [vmh], 441
Dikku Kaji, *alt.* Sadri [sck], 385
Diko, *alt. dial.* Gbagyi [gbr], 160
Dikota, *alt. dial.* Ngando [ngd], 77
Dikuta, *dial.* Ngando [ngd], 77
Dilaut-Badjao, *dial.* Sama, Central
  [sml], 500
Dili Tetum, *alt.* Tetun Dili [tdt], 351
Dilling [dil], 189
  dial. Dilling [dil], 189
Dilpali, *alt. dial.* Bantawa [bap], 468
Dim, *alt. dial.* Agwagwune
  [yay], 153
  dial. Chin, Paite [pck], 359
Dima [jma], 597
  alt. Dime [dim], 114
Dimadima, *alt.* Dima [jma], 597
Dimali, *dial.* Nachering [ncd], 476
Dimasa [dis], 360
  dial. Dimasa [dis], 360
Dimasa Kachari, *alt.* Dimasa [dis],
  360
Dimba, *alt.* Zemba [dhm], 42

Dimbambang, *alt. dial.* Bakoko
  [bkh], 57
Dimbong [dii], 60
Dime [dim], 114
  alt. Ginuman [gnm], 600
Dimeo, *dial.* Mofu-Gudur [mif], 68
Dimili, *alt.* Dimli [diq], 518
Dimilki, *alt.* Kirmanjki [kiu], 518
Dimir [dmc], 597
Dimisi, *alt.* Idi [idi], 602
Dimli [diq], 518
Dimmuk, *dial.* Kofyar [kwl], 166
Dimodongo, *alt.* Krongo [kgo], 192
Dimotiki, *dial.* Greek [ell], 540
Dimpi, *dial.* Chin, Paite [pck], 359
Dimsisi, *alt.* Idi [idi], 602
Dimu, *alt. dial.* Sabu [hvn], 409
Dimuga, *alt.* Daga [dgz], 596
Dimuk, *alt. dial.* Kofyar [kwl], 166
Din, *alt.* Ding [diz], 99
Dindje, *alt. dial.* Kaba Na [kwv], 81
Diné, *alt.* Navajo [nav], 305
Ding [diz], 99
Dingando, *alt.* Ngando [ngd], 77
Dingi, *alt.* Dungu [dbv], 158
Dinik, *alt.* Afitti [aft], 187
Dinje, *alt. dial.* Kaba Na [kwv], 81
Dinka Ibrahim, *alt. dial.* Dinka,
  Northeastern [dip], 189
Dinka, Northeastern [dip], 189
Dinka, Northwestern [diw], 190
Dinka, South Central [dib], 190
Dinka, Southeastern [dks], 190
Dinka, Southwestern [dik], 190
Dinler, *dial.* Turkish [tur], 519, 521,
  532, 547
Dio, *alt.* Kaidipang [kzp], 429
  dial. Zande [zne], 196
Diobass, *dial.* Saafi-Saafi [sav], 182
Diodio [ddi], 597
Dioi, *alt.* Bouyei [pcc], 328
  alt. Giáy [pcc], 523
  alt. Yoy [yoy], 518, 453
Diola-Fogny, *alt.* Jola-Fonyi
  [dyo], 180, 118, 131
Diola-Kasa, *alt.* Jola-Kasa [csk], 180
Diongor Guera, *alt.* Mukulu
  [moz], 85
Dionkor, *alt.* Migaama [mmy], 84
Diore, *alt. dial.* Kayapó [txu], 229
Dioula, *alt.* Jula [dyu], 51, 93, 143
Dioula Véhiculaire, *alt. dial.* Jula
  [dyu], 93
Dir, *dial.* Polci [plj], 173
Dir Kohistani, *alt.* Kalami
  [gwc], 485
Diraasha, *alt.* Dirasha [gdl], 114
Dirang, *alt. dial.* Moinba [mob], 376
Dirari [dit], 569
Dirasha [gdl], 114

Dirayta, *alt.* Dirasha [gdl], 114
Dire, *alt.* Gata' [gaq], 362
Diri [dwa], 158
  alt. Kalami [gwc], 485
Diria, *alt.* Chorotega [cjr], 249
  alt. dial. Chorotega [cjr], 249
Diriko, *alt.* Diriku [diu], 149, 40
  alt. Gciriku [diu], 47
Diriku [diu], 149, 40
  alt. Gciriku [diu], 47
Dirim [dir], 158
  dial. Samba Daka [ccg], 174
Dirin, *alt.* Dirim [dir], 158
Diriya, *alt.* Diri [dwa], 158
Dirma, *alt. dial.* Suri [suq], 119, 195
Dirong-Guruf, *dial.* Zaghawa
  [zag], 87
Dirrim, *alt.* Dirim [dir], 158
Dirwali, *alt.* Kalami [gwc], 485
Dirya, *alt.* Diri [dwa], 158
Diryawa, *alt.* Diri [dwa], 158
Disa [dsi], 80
Dishili, *alt.* Sur [tdl], 175
Diso, *alt.* Maru [mhx], 465, 340
Disoha, *dial.* Gumuz [guk], 191
Dispoholnon, *dial.* Inonhan
  [loc], 495
Ditamari, *alt.* Ditammari [tbz], 43
Ditammari [tbz], 43, 207
Ditaylin Alta, *alt.* Alta, Northern
  [aqn], 491
Ditaylin Dumagat, *alt.* Alta,
  Northern [aqn], 491
Ditinat, *alt. dial.* Nootka [noo], 240
Ditti, *alt.* Afitti [aft], 187
Diu, *alt.* Bolango [bld], 428
  dial. Bilba [bpz], 406
Dìu, *alt.* Iu Mien [ium], 523
Diula, *alt.* Jula [dyu], 51, 93, 143
Diuwe [diy], 414
Diuxi-Tilantongo Mixtec, *see*
  Mixtec, Diuxi-Tilantongo [xtd], 267
Divehi, *alt.* Maldivian [div], 461
Divehi Bas, *alt.* Maldivian
  [div], 461, 374
Divehli, *alt.* Maldivian [div], 461, 374
Divinai, *alt. dial.* Tawala [tbo], 627
Divo, *dial.* Dida, Yocoboué [gud], 92
Diwala, *alt.* Duala [dua], 60
Diwinai, *dial.* Tawala [tbo], 627
Dixon Reef [dix], 641
Diyarbakir, *alt. dial.* Armenian
  [hye], 318
Diyari, *alt.* Dieri [dif], 569
Diyi, *alt.* Jukun Takum [jbu], 165
Diyu, *alt.* Jukun Takum [jbu], 63
Dizfuli, *alt.* Dezfuli [def], 438
Dizhe, *alt.* Zapotec, Amatlán
  [zpo], 277
Dizi [mdx], 114

Dogon, Bangeri Me [dba], 142
Dogon, Bondum Dom [dbu], 142
Dogon, Dogul Dom [dbg], 142
Dogon, Donno So [dds], 142
Dogon, Jamsay [djm], 142, 50
Dogon, Kolum So [dkl], 142
Dogon, Tene Kan [dtk], 142
Dogon, Tomo Kan [dtm], 142, 50
Dogon, Toro So [dts], 142
Dogon, Toro Tegu [dtt], 142
Dogoridi, *dial.* Otoro [otr], 194
Dogosé [dos], 50
Dogoso [dgs], 50
　alt. Dogon, Toro So [dts], 142
Dogotuki Saqani, *alt. dial.* Fijian
　[fij], 580
Dogri [dgo], 360
　dial. Dogri [dgo], 360
　dial. Vasavi [vas], 390
Dogri Jammu, *alt.* Dogri [dgo], 360
Dogri Pahari, *alt.* Dogri [dgo], 360
Dogri-Kangri, *alt.* Dogri [dgo], 360
Dogrib [dgr], 237
Dogul Dom Dogon, *see* Dogon,
　Dogul Dom [dbg], 142
Dogul-Dom, *alt.* Dogon, Dogul Dom
　[dbg], 142
Dogwa, *alt. dial.* Sotho, Northern
　[nso], 186
Dohe, *alt.* Doe [doe], 198
Dohoi [otd], 393
　dial. Dohoi [otd], 393
Dohuk, *dial.* Lishana Deni [lsd], 445
Doi, *dial.* Kaili, Ledo [lew], 429
　dial. Tai Loi [tlq], 467, 453
Doibel, *alt.* Dobel [kvo], 397
Dok Acoli, *alt.* Acholi [ach], 210, 187
Doka [dbi], 158
　dial. Logo [log], 103
　dial. Miship [mjs], 170
Doka-Poara, *alt.* Tuyuca [tue], 233
Dokhobe, *alt.* Dogosé [dos], 50
Dokhosié, *alt.* Dogosé [dos], 50
Doko, *dial.* Ngombe [ngc], 106
Doko-Uyanga [uya], 158
Dokshi, *alt. dial.* Zeem [zua], 178
Dokskat, *alt.* Brokskat [bkk], 357
Dolakha, *alt.* Thangmi [thf], 480, 344
　alt. dial. Newar [new], 476
Dolgan [dlg], 504
Doliki, *dial.* Mukulu [moz], 85
'Dolimi, *dial.* Wali [wlx], 128
Dolkhali, *dial.* Newar [new], 476
Dolnoserbski, *alt.* Sorbian, Lower
　[dsb], 539
Dolomite, *alt.* Ladin [lld], 544
Dolores Cora, *dial.* Cora, Santa
　Teresa [cok], 262
Dolpa Tibetan, *alt.* Dolpo
　[dre], 470

Dolpike, *alt.* Dolpo [dre], 470
Dolpo [dre], 470
Dom [doa], 597
　alt. Domari [rmt], 360, 444, 490
　alt. Domu [dof], 597
Doma, *alt.* Abron [abr], 122, 91
　alt. Domaaki [dmk], 484
　dial. Alago [ala], 153
　dial. Aneme Wake [aby], 589
Domaaki [dmk], 484
Domaki, *dial.* Domari [rmt], 360
Domara, *dial.* Mailu [mgu], 610
Domari [rmt], 438, 110, 139, 190,
　315, 360, 443, 444, 448, 490, 510,
　554, 563
Domba, *alt.* Lohar, Gade [gda], 372
　dial. Manyika [mxc], 216, 148
Dombano, *alt.* Arandai [jbj], 411
　dial. Arandai [jbj], 411
Dombe [dov], 215
　alt. Ndombe [ndq], 41
Dombiali, *alt.* Lohar, Gade
　[gda], 372
Dombo, *alt. dial.* Thuri [thu], 195
Domdom, *alt.* Gumawana [gvs], 600
Dominican Creole French
　[acf], 250
Dominican English, *dial.* English
　[eng], 250
Dominican Sign Language
　[doq], 250
Domkhoe, *dial.* ‖Gana [gnk], 46
Dommara, *alt. dial.* Telugu [tel], 388
Domno, *dial.* Dogon, Jamsay
　[djm], 142, 50
Domo, *dial.* Masana [mcn], 83, 66
Domona, *alt.* Fulfulde, Adamawa
　[fub], 61, 80
Dompa, *alt. dial.* Uma [ppk], 434
Dompago, *alt.* Lukpa [dop], 45, 208
Dompo [doy], 124
Domra, *dial.* Bhojpuri [bho], 356
Domra Magu Hiya, *alt.* Domari
　[rmt], 360
Domu [dof], 597
Domung [dev], 597
Donde, *alt. dial.* Makonde [kde], 148
Dondi, *alt. dial.* Pol [pmm], 71
Dondo [dok], 429
　alt. Doondo [dde], 88
　dial. Ndau [ndc], 148
Dondongo, *dial.* Maba [mde], 83
Donegal, *dial.* Gaelic, Irish [gle], 542
Dong [doh], 158
　alt. dial. Cua [cua], 522
　dial. Mumuye [mzm], 170
　pej. alt. Iu Mien [ium], 523
Dong, Northern [doc], 331
Dong, Southern [kmc], 331
Donga, *alt.* Dong [doh], 158

　alt. Dongo [doo], 99
　alt. Kambaata [ktb], 116
　alt. dial. Jukun Takum [jbu], 63, 165
　dial. Kpan [kpk], 167
Dongari, *alt.* Dogri [dgo], 360
Dongay, *alt. dial.* Jagoi [sne], 459
Dongiro, *alt.* Nyangatom [nnj], 117
Dongjol, *dial.* Dinka, Northeastern
　[dip], 189
Dongnu, *dial.* Bunu, Bu-Nao
　[bwx], 328
Dongo [doo], 99
　alt. Mbundu [kmb], 41
　dial. Gbaya [krs], 190
Dongo Ko, *alt.* Dongo [doo], 99
Dongola, *dial.* Kenuzi-Dongola
　[kzh], 192, 110
Dongola-Kenuz, *alt.* Kenuzi-
　Dongola [kzh], 192, 110
Dongolawi, *alt.* Kenuzi-Dongola
　[kzh], 192, 110
Dongotono [ddd], 190
Dongshan Lalu Yi, *alt.* Yi, Western
　[ywt], 348
Dongshan Yao, *alt. dial.* Biao-Jiao
　Mien [bje], 327
Dongxiang [sce], 332
Donno So, *dial.* Dogon, Donno So
　[dds], 142
Donno So Dogon, *see* Dogon,
　Donno So [dds], 142
Donyanyo, *alt.* Doyayo [dow], 60
Donyayo, *alt.* Doyayo [dow], 60
Donyiro, *alt.* Nyangatom [nnj], 117
Doobe, *alt. dial.* Koma [kmy], 167
Doohyaayo, *alt.* Doyayo [dow], 60
Dooka, *dial.* Gbaya, Southwest
　[mdo], 62
　dial. Guruntum-Mbaaru [grd], 161
Doome, *alt. dial.* Koma [kmy], 167
Doompas, *alt.* Dumpas [dmv], 456
Doondo [dde], 88
D'oopace, *alt.* Bussa [dox], 114
Door, *alt. dial.* Nuer [nus], 194, 117
Doora, *alt.* Nugunu [nnv], 575
Doowaayo, *alt.* Doyayo [dow], 60
Dooyaayo, *alt.* Doyayo [dow], 60
Dooyayo, *alt.* Doyayo [dow], 60
D'opaasunte, *alt.* Bussa [dox], 114
Dor, *alt.* Bongo [bot], 189
　dial. Chrau [crw], 522
　dial. Nuer [nus], 194
Dor Koi, *alt. dial.* Koya [kff], 370
Dora, *alt. dial.* Koya [kff], 370
Dora Koi, *alt. dial.* Koya [kff], 370
Doram, *alt.* Doromu [kqc], 597
Dörböd, *alt. dial.* Kalmyk-Oirat
　[xal], 554
Dorbor, *dial.* Gbii [ggb], 137
Dorbot, *dial.* Kalmyk-Oirat [xal], 337

Dörböt, *dial.* Kalmyk-Oirat [xal], 554
Dordar, *dial.* Naga, Ao [njo], 377
Dorhosié-Finng, *alt.* Dogoso [dgs], 50
Dorhosié-Noirs, *alt.* Dogoso [dgs], 50
Dorhossié, *alt.* Dogosé [dos], 50
Dorhosye, *alt.* Dogosé [dos], 50
Doria, *alt.* Dhodia [dho], 360
Dori'o [dor], 636
Doriri, *alt.* Dororo [drr], 636
  alt. Moikodi [mkp], 614
Dorla Koitur, *alt. dial.* Koya [kff], 370
Dorla Koya, *alt. dial.* Koya [kff], 370
Dorli, *dial.* Koya [kff], 370
Dormon, *dial.* Gabri [gab], 80
Doro, *alt. dial.* Chrau [crw], 522
Doro Doghosié, *alt.* Dogosé [dos], 50
Dorobe, *dial.* Otoro [otr], 194
Dorobé, *alt.* Dogosé [dos], 50
Dorobo, *alt.* Mediak [mwx], 202
  alt. Mosiro [mwy], 202
  dial. Grebo, Central [grv], 138
  pej. alt. Aasáx [aas], 197
  pej. alt. Aramanik [aam], 197
  pej. alt. Kisankasa [kqh], 200
Dorogori, *dial.* Wipi [gdr], 632
Doromu [kqc], 597
  alt. dial. Doromu [kqc], 597
Dororo [drr], 636
Dorosie, *alt.* Dogosé [dos], 50
Dorossé, *alt.* Dogosé [dos], 50
Dorossié-Fing, *alt.* Dogoso [dgs], 50
Dorot, *dial.* Gayo [gay], 430
Dorpat, *alt. dial.* Estonian [est], 534, 534
Dorro, *alt.* Namo [mxw], 617
Dorset, *dial.* English [eng], 565
Dorsha, *dial.* Sheko [she], 118
Dorunkecha, *dial.* Tilung [tij], 481
Dorze [doz], 114
Dosanga, *alt.* Doko-Uyanga [uya], 158
Doso [dol], 597
  alt. Mingang Doso [mko], 170
Dosobou, *alt.* Edopi [dbf], 414
Dot, *alt. dial.* Cua [cua], 522
  dial. Dass [dot], 157
Dotali, *alt. dial.* Nepali [nep], 476
Doteli, *dial.* Nepali [nep], 476
Dott, *alt. dial.* Dass [dot], 157
Dou, *alt.* Edopi [dbf], 414
Douala, *alt.* Duala [dua], 60
Doué, *alt. dial.* Pévé [lme], 86
Doufou, *alt.* Edopi [dbf], 414

Dougne, *alt.* Jonkor Bourmataguil [jeu], 81
  dial. Jonkor Bourmataguil [jeu], 81
Dougour, *alt.* Dugwor [dme], 60
Douguia, *alt. dial.* Malgbe [mxf], 65
  dial. Malgbe [mxf], 83
Doukhobour Russian, *dial.* Russian [rus]
Douma, *alt.* Duma [dma], 120
Doumbou, *alt.* Ndumu [nmd], 121
Doume, *alt. dial.* Vame [mlr], 73
Doumori, *dial.* Kiwai, Southern [kjd], 606
Douna, *dial.* Turka [tuz], 55
Dounje, *alt. dial.* Kaba Na [kwv], 81
Doupa, *alt.* Duupa [dae], 60
Doura, *alt.* Toura [don], 628
Dourbeye, *dial.* Fali, North [fll], 61
Dourou, *alt.* Dii [dur], 60
Douroun, *dial.* Mofu, North [mfk], 67
Doutai [tds], 414
Douvangar, *alt.* Mofu, North [mfk], 67
Dowayayo, *alt.* Doyayo [dow], 60
Dowayo, *alt.* Doyayo [dow], 60
Dowyan, *alt.* Tiwa [lax], 389
Doxká-Poárá, *alt.* Tuyuca [tue], 233
Doyaayo, *alt.* Doyayo [dow], 60
Doyau, *alt.* Doyayo [dow], 60
Doyayo [dow], 60
Dra, *alt.* Dera [kbv], 414, 597
  alt. dial. Polci [plj], 173
Dramandougou-Nyarafo, *dial.* Tiéfo [tiq], 55
Dras, *alt. dial.* Shina [scl], 488
Drasi, *dial.* Shina [scl], 387
Drehet, *dial.* Khehek [tlx], 606
Drehu, *alt.* Dehu [dhv], 584
Drente, *alt.* Drents [drt], 548
Drents [drt], 548
Driafleisuma, *alt.* Mehek [nux], 613
Dro, *alt. dial.* Malgbe [mxf], 65
Drokpakay, *alt.* Brokpake [sgt], 322
Dromois, *alt. dial.* Provençal [prv], 537
Drori, *alt.* Deori [der], 360
Dru, *dial.* Tibetan [bod], 388
Drubea, *alt.* Dumbea [duf], 584
Drukai, *alt.* Rukai [dru], 512
Drukay, *alt.* Rukai [dru], 512
Drukha, *alt.* Dzongkha [dzo], 323, 471
Drukke, *alt.* Dzongkha [dzo], 323, 471
Druna, *alt.* Ngiti [niy], 106
Drung [duu], 332
Druze Arabic, *alt. dial.* Arabic, North Levantine Spoken [apc], 453
Dschang, *alt.* Yemba [ybb], 74

  alt. dial. Yemba [ybb], 74
Dschugha, *alt. dial.* Armenian [hye], 318
Dschulfa, *alt. dial.* Armenian [hye], 318
Du, *alt.* Duungooma [dux], 142
Du-Ropp-Rim, *dial.* Berom [bom], 155
Dua Boccoe, *alt. dial.* Bugis [bug], 428
Dual, *alt.* Dhuwal [duj], 569
Duala [dua], 60
  alt. Dhuwal [duj], 569
Dualla, *alt.* Duala [dua], 60
Duan, *alt.* Halang Doan [hld], 523, 450
Duano' [dup], 454
Duau [dva], 597
Duau Pwata, *alt.* Sewa Bay [sew], 624
Duauru, *alt.* Numee [kdk], 585
Dubala, *alt.* Dubli [dub], 360
Dubea, *alt.* Dumbea [duf], 584
Duber-Kandia, *dial.* Kohistani, Indus [mvy], 486
Dubla, *alt.* Dubli [dub], 360
Dubli [dub], 360
Dubu [dmu], 414
Ducligan Ifugao, *dial.* Ifugao, Batad [ifb], 495
Dudh Kharia, *dial.* Kharia [khr], 367
Dudi, *alt.* Bitur [mcc], 594
Dudjym, *alt. dial.* Yir Yoront [yiy], 579
Duduela [duk], 597
Duff, *alt. dial.* Pileni [piv], 637
Duga, *alt.* Barambu [brm], 97
Dugarwa, *alt.* Duguri [dbm], 158
Dugbo, *dial.* Krumen, Pye [pye], 93
Dugiya, *alt. dial.* Malgbe [mxf], 65
Dugujur, *dial.* Otoro [otr], 194
Dugun [ndu], 60
Dugunza, *alt. dial.* Gumuz [guk], 191
Dugur, *dial.* Merey [meq], 67
Duguranchi, *alt.* Duguri [dbm], 158
Dugurawa, *alt.* Duguri [dbm], 158
Duguri [dbm], 158
  dial. Birgit [btf], 79
Dugusa, *alt.* Duguza [dza], 158
Duguza [dza], 158
Dugwor [dme], 60
Duhlian Twang, *alt.* Mizo [lus], 376
Duhtu, *dial.* Tsou [tsu], 512
Duhwa [kbz], 158
Dui, *alt.* Duli [duz], 60
  alt. Kuy [kdt], 451
Duindui, *alt. dial.* Ambae, West [nnd], 640

Duisalongmei, *alt.* Naga, Kharam [kfw], 378
Duka, *alt.* Hun-Saare [dud], 162
Duka-Ekor, *dial.* Dera [kbv], 597
Dukai, *alt.* Rukai [dru], 512
Dukaiya, *dial.* Ocaina [oca], 289, 246
Dukanchi, *alt.* Hun-Saare [dud], 162
Dukanci, *alt.* Hun-Saare [dud], 162
Dukawa, *alt.* Hun-Saare [dud], 162
Duke [nke], 636
Duke of York, *alt.* Ramoaaina [rai], 622
Dukpa, *alt.* Dzongkha [dzo], 323
Dukpu, *dial.* Banda, Mid-Southern [bjo], 74, 188
Dukslinu, *dial.* Sindhi [snd], 488
Dukuna, *alt. dial.* Gumuz [guk], 191
Dukunza, *alt. dial.* Gumuz [guk], 191
Dukuri, *alt.* Duguri [dbm], 158
Dukwa, *alt.* Hun-Saare [dud], 162
Dukwara, *dial.* Otoro [otr], 194
Dulangan Manobo, *alt.* Manobo, Cotabato [mta], 499
Dulbu [dbo], 158
Duli [duz], 60
Dulien, *alt.* Mizo [lus], 376
dial. Mizo [lus], 321, 466
Duliit, *alt. dial.* Dinka, Southwestern [dik], 190
Dulong, *alt.* Drung [duu], 332
dial. Jingpho [kac], 464, 336
Dulong River, *dial.* Drung [duu], 332
Duma [dma], 120
Dumaki, *alt.* Domaaki [dmk], 484
Dumaring, *dial.* Basap [bdb], 392
Dumbea [duf], 584
Dumbeli, *alt. dial.* Dimli [diq], 518
Dumbo, *alt.* Kemezung [dmo], 63
Dumbu, *alt.* Ndumu [nmd], 121
Dumbule, *alt.* Mbule [mlb], 66
Dumbuli, *dial.* Dimli [diq], 518
Dumi [dus], 471
Dumi Bo'o, *alt.* Dumi [dus], 471
Dumi Bro, *alt.* Dumi [dus], 471
Dumoga, *dial.* Mongondow [mog], 431
Dumpas [dmv], 456
Dumpo, *alt.* Dompo [doy], 124
Dumpu [wtf], 597
Dumu, *alt.* Rumu [klq], 623
Dumun [dui], 598
Dumut, *alt.* Mandobo Atas [aax], 419
alt. Mandobo Bawah [bwp], 419
Duna [duc], 598
Dung, *dial.* Moken [mwt], 466, 516
Dungan [dng], 449, 448
Dungari Garasia, *alt.* Garasia, Rajput [gra], 362

Dungi, *alt.* Dungu [dbv], 158
Dungmali [raa], 471
Dungmali Pûk, *alt.* Dungmali [raa], 471
Dungmali-Bantawa, *alt.* Dungmali [raa], 471
Dungra Bhil [duh], 361
Dungri, *alt. dial.* Vasavi [vas], 390
Dungri Grasia, *alt.* Garasia, Rajput [gra], 362
Dungu [dbv], 158
Dunjawa, *alt.* Dungu [dbv], 158
Dunje, *dial.* Kaba Na [kwv], 81
Dunu, *alt.* Bata [bta], 155
Duoluo, *dial.* Gelao [gio], 333
Duon, *alt.* Lü [khb], 524
Duoxu, *alt.* Ersu [ers], 332
dial. Ersu [ers], 332
Dupa, *alt.* Duupa [dae], 60
Dupaninan Agta, *see* Agta, Dupaninan [duo], 490
Dura [drq], 471
Duram, *alt. dial.* Korupun-Sela [kpq], 418
Durango Aztec, *alt.* Nahuatl, Durango [nln], 270
Durango Nahuatl, *see* Nahuatl, Durango [nln], 270
Durani, *dial.* Pashto, Northern [pbu], 317
Duranmin, *alt.* Suarmin [seo], 625
Durga, *alt.* Dhurga [dhu], 569
Durham, *dial.* English [eng], 565
Duri [mvp], 429
Duriankari, *alt.* Duriankere [dbn], 414
Duriankere [dbn], 414
Durop, *alt.* Korop [krp], 167, 64
Durr-Baraza, *dial.* Dass [dot], 157
Durru, *alt.* Dii [dur], 60
Duru, *alt.* Dii [dur], 60
Durum, *alt. dial.* Mofu, North [mfk], 67
Duruma [dug], 132
Duruwa [pci], 361
Durva, *alt.* Duruwa [pci], 361
Dusan, *alt.* Dusun, Central [dtp], 456
Dusner [dsn], 414
Dusnir, *alt.* Dusner [dsn], 414
Duso, *alt.* Vanimo [vam], 630
Dusum, *alt.* Dusun, Central [dtp], 456
Dusun, *alt.* Dusun, Central [dtp], 456
alt. Dusun, Sugut [kzs], 456
alt. Tutong 1 [ttx], 325
Dusun Balangan, *dial.* Ma'anyan [mhy], 394
Dusun Dayak, *alt.* Rungus [drg], 458
Dusun Deyah [dun], 393

Dusun Malang [duq], 393
dial. Dusun Malang [duq], 393
Dusun Murut, *dial.* Keningau Murut [kxi], 457
Dusun Pepas, *dial.* Dusun Witu [duw], 393
Dusun Segama, *dial.* Kinabatangan, Upper [dmg], 457
Dusun Sinulihan, *dial.* Dusun, Central [dtp], 456
Dusun Witu [duw], 393
dial. Dusun Witu [duw], 393
Dusun, Central [dtp], 456
Dusun, Sugut [kzs], 456
Dusun, Tambunan [kzt], 456
Dusun, Tempasuk [tdu], 456
Dusur, *alt.* Dusun, Central [dtp], 456
Dutch [nld], 548, 221, 282, 295, 531, 536
Dutch Creole, *alt.* Negerhollands [dcr], 297
Dutch Sign Language [dse], 548
Duungidjawu, *dial.* Wakawaka [wkw], 577
Duungo, *alt.* Duungooma [dux], 142
Duungooma [dux], 142
Duupa [dae], 60
Duurum, *dial.* Geruma [gea], 161
Duvde, *alt.* Duvle [duv], 414
Duve, *alt.* Duvle [duv], 414
Duvelands, *dial.* Zeeuws [zea], 549
Duvele, *alt.* Duvle [duv], 414
Duvle [duv], 414
Duvre, *alt.* Duvle [duv], 414
Duwai [dbp], 158
Duwamish, *dial.* Salish, Southern Puget Sound [slh], 307
Duwe, *alt. dial.* Wandala [mfi], 73
Duwet [gve], 598
Duwinna, *alt. dial.* Nafusi [jbn], 139
alt. dial. Shilha [jbn], 209
Dwags, *alt.* Takpa [tkk], 344
alt. dial. Tibetan [bod], 388
Dwala, *alt.* Duala [dua], 60
Dwan, *alt.* Dwang [nnu], 120
Dwang [nnu], 120
Dwar, *dial.* Biak [bhw], 412
Dwat, *alt. dial.* Dass [dot], 157
Dwela, *alt.* Duala [dua], 60
Dwemu, *dial.* Bomu [bmq], 137
Dwera, *dial.* Ligbi [lig], 126
Dwingi, *alt.* Dungu [dbv], 158
Dxana, *alt.* ‖Gana [gnk], 46
Dya, *alt.* Dyan [dya], 51
Dyaabugay [dyy], 570
dial. Dyaabugay [dyy], 570
Dyabarma, *alt.* Zarma [dje], 152, 55, 178
alt. Zarmaci [dje], 145
Dyaberdyaber [dyb], 570

Dyabugay, *alt.* Dyaabugay [dyy], 570
Dyair, *alt.* Aghu [ahh], 410
alt. Awyu, North [yir], 412
Dyakanke, *alt.* Jahanka [jad], 129, 143
Dyala, *alt.* Jalkunan [bxl], 51
Dyalanu, *alt.* Jalkunan [bxl], 51
Dyalonke, *alt.* Jalunga [yal], 143, 180
alt. Yalunka [yal], 130
Dyamala, *alt. dial.* Senoufo, Djimini [dyi], 95
Dyamsay Tegu, *alt.* Dogon, Jamsay [djm], 142, 50
Dyan [dya], 51
Dyane, *alt.* Dyan [dya], 51
Dyangadi [dyn], 570
Dyanu, *alt.* Dyan [dya], 51
Dyarma, *alt.* Zarma [dje], 152, 55, 178
alt. Zarmaci [dje], 145
Dye, *alt.* Ngangam [gng], 209, 46
Dyegueme, *alt. dial.* Serer-Sine [srr], 122
dial. Serer-Sine [srr], 182
Dyeraidy, *alt.* Tyaraity [woa], 577
Dyerma, *alt.* Zarma [dje], 152, 55, 178
alt. Zarmaci [dje], 145
Dyimini, *alt.* Senoufo, Djimini [dyi], 95
Dyirbal [dbl], 570
Dyiru, *dial.* Dyirbal [dbl], 570
Dyokay, *alt.* Rukai [dru], 512
Dyola, *alt.* Jola-Fonyi [dyo], 180
Dyolof, *dial.* Wolof [wol], 182, 145
Dyongor, *alt.* Migaama [mmy], 84
Dyongor Guera, *alt.* Mukulu [moz], 85
Dyoula, *alt.* Jula [dyu], 51, 93, 143
Dyugun [dyd], 570
Dyula, *alt.* Jula [dyu], 51, 93, 143
Dyumba, *alt. dial.* Myene [mye], 121
Dyurop, *alt.* Korop [krp], 64
Dza [jen], 158
Dzad, *alt.* Jad [jda], 365
alt. dial. Tibetan [bod], 388
Dzalakha [dzl], 323
Dzalamat, *alt.* Dzalakha [dzl], 323
Dzalamo, *alt.* Zaramo [zaj], 206
Dzama, *alt.* Nafaanra [nfr], 126
Dzamba, *alt.* Bangi [bni], 97
alt. Bobangi [bni], 88
alt. dial. Koongo [kng], 101
dial. Baloi [biz], 96
Dzambazi, *dial.* Romani, Balkan [rmn], 557, 532, 537, 539, 547
Dzando [dzn], 99

Dzanggali, *alt.* Rawat [jnl], 478, 385
Dzao Min [bpn], 332
Dzaui, *dial.* Carútana [cru], 226
Dzawi, *alt. dial.* Carútana [cru], 226
Dzaze, *alt.* Piapoco [pio], 312
Dzeigoc, *dial.* Dedua [ded], 596
Dzek, *alt.* Kryts [kry], 319
Dzeke, *alt. dial.* Dibole [bvx], 88
Dzem, *alt.* Njyem [njy], 70, 89
Dzemay, *alt.* Fulfulde, Adamawa [fub], 61, 80
Dzerngu, *alt. dial.* Marghi Central [mrt], 169
Dzhek, *alt.* Kryts [kry], 319
dial. Kryts [kry], 319
Dzheki, *alt.* Kryts [kry], 319
Dzhemshid, *alt. dial.* Aimaq [aiq], 315
Dzhidi [jpr], 444, 438
Dzhudezmo, *alt.* Ladino [lad], 445, 563
Dzhuhuric, *alt.* Judeo-Tat [jdt], 445, 319, 554
Dzhulfa, *alt. dial.* Armenian [hye], 437
dial. Armenian [hye], 318
Dzhunyan, *alt.* Dungan [dng], 449
Dzibi-Dzonga, *alt. dial.* Tswa [tsc], 149, 186, 217
Dzihana, *alt. dial.* Giryama [nyf], 133
Dzili, *dial.* Jingpho [kac], 464, 336
Dzimou, *alt.* Koonzime [ozm], 64
Dzinda, *alt.* Zinza [zin], 206
Dzindza, *alt.* Zinza [zin], 206
Dzing, *alt.* Ding [diz], 99
Dzivi, *alt. dial.* Tswa [tsc], 149
Dzodinka [add], 60, 158
Dzodzinka, *alt.* Dzodinka [add], 60
Dzonga, *alt. dial.* Tsonga [tso], 186, 149, 217
Dzonga-Dzibi, *alt. dial.* Tswa [tsc], 149
Dzongkha [dzo], 323, 361, 471
Dzowo, *alt.* Ligbi [lig], 126
Dzubucua, *alt. dial.* Kariri-Xocó [kzw], 228
Dzubukuá, *dial.* Kariri-Xocó [kzw], 228
Dzukish, *dial.* Lithuanian [lit], 546
Dzukiskai, *alt. dial.* Lithuanian [lit], 546
Dzumbo, *alt.* Kemezung [dmo], 63
Dzumdzum, *alt. dial.* Mina [hna], 67
Dzuna, *dial.* Naga, Angami [njm], 377
Dzunza, *dial.* Pokomo, Lower [poj], 135
Dzu'oasi, *alt.* Juǀ'hoan [ktz], 47, 150
dial. Juǀ'hoan [ktz], 47, 150
Dzùùngoo [dnn], 51
dial. Dzùùngoo [dnn], 51

Dzwabo, *dial.* Sotho, Northern [nso], 186
E [eee], 332
alt. Ere [twp], 598
E Je, *dial.* Grebo, Northern [gbo], 138
E Lokop, *alt.* Samburu [saq], 136
E-De, *alt.* Rade [rad], 526
E-Xin Yi, *alt.* Yi, Eshan-Xinping [yiv], 347
Ealeba, *alt. dial.* Tawala [tbo], 627
East Adonara, *dial.* Adonara [adr], 406
East Ambae, *see* Ambae, East [omb], 640
East Angal, *alt.* Angal [age], 589
East Anglia, *dial.* English [eng], 565
East Awin, *dial.* Aekyom [awi], 587
East Bafwangada, *dial.* Budu [buu], 98
East Baikeno, *alt. dial.* Baikeno [bkx], 350
East Banggai, *dial.* Banggai [bgz], 427
East Bay, *dial.* Ohlone, Northern [cst], 306
East Boikin, *dial.* Boikin [bzf], 594
East Boki, *alt. dial.* Bokyi [bky], 156
East Bulgarian Romani, *dial.* Romani, Balkan [rmn], 532
East Cape, *alt. dial.* Tawala [tbo], 627
East Cape Afrikaans, *dial.* Afrikaans [afr], 185
East Central Friulian, *dial.* Friulian [fur], 544
East Central Mixe, *alt.* Mixe, Mazatlán [mzl], 265
East Central Quiché, *alt.* K'iche', Eastern [quu], 255
East Central Tlacolula Zapotec, *alt.* Zapotec, Mitla [zaw], 279
East Chachapoyas, *alt. dial.* Quechua, Chachapoyas [quk], 290
East Choiseul, *alt.* Babatana [baa], 635
East Circassian, *alt.* Kabardian [kbd], 554
East Cree, Northern [crl], 237
East Cree, Southern [crj], 237
East Damar, *see* Damar, East [dmr], 397
East Dangaleat, *dial.* Dangaléat [daa], 80
East Devonshire, *dial.* English [eng], 565
East Dogri, *dial.* Dogri [dgo], 360
East Elema, *alt.* Toaripi [tqo], 628
East Futuna, *see* Futuna, East [fud], 647, 584
East Gimi, *dial.* Gimi [gim], 600

East Godaveri, *alt. dial.* Telugu [tel], 388

East Gogo, *alt. dial.* Gogo [gog], 198

East Gorontalo, *dial.* Gorontalo [gor], 429

East Greenlandic, *alt. dial.* Inuktitut, Greenlandic [kal], 252

East Guizhou Miao, *alt.* Hmong, Northern Qiandong [hea], 335

East Gurage, *alt.* Silt'e [xst], 119

East Gwari, *alt.* Gbagyi [gbr], 160

East Inland Kaulong, *dial.* Kaulong [pss], 605

East Kalamsé, *alt. dial.* Kalamsé [knz], 51

East Kara, *dial.* Kara [leu], 605

East Kasem, *dial.* Kasem [xsm], 52

East Kewa, *see* Kewa, East [kjs], 606

East Khowar, *dial.* Khowar [khw], 486

East Koita, *dial.* Koitabu [kqi], 607

East Komba, *dial.* Komba [kpf], 607

East Kongo, *dial.* Koongo [kng], 101

East Lagoon, *dial.* Chuukese [chk], 582

East Latvian, *dial.* Latvian [lav], 546

East Lele, *alt. dial.* Lele [llc], 129

East Limba, *see* Limba, East [lma], 129, 183

East Mafa, *dial.* Mafa [maf], 65

East Makian, *see* Makian, East [mky], 401

East Makian, *dial.* Makian, East [mky], 401

East Marsela, *alt.* Masela, East [vme], 402

East Masela, *see* Masela, East [vme], 402

East Mekeo, *dial.* Mekeo [mek], 613

East Mese, *dial.* Mese [mci], 613

East Mori, *alt.* Mori Bawah [xmz], 431

East Nda'nda', *alt. dial.* Nda'nda' [nnz], 69

East Nek, *dial.* Nek [nif], 617

East Numanggang, *dial.* Numanggang [nop], 619

East Nyala, *see* Nyala, East [nle], 135

East Oki-No-Erabu, *dial.* Oki-No-Erabu [okn], 447

East Olodiama, *dial.* Izon [ijc], 164

East Orya, *alt. dial.* Orya [ury], 422

East Paraná, *alt.* Guana [gqn], 227

East Pokot, *dial.* Pökoot [pko], 135

East Prussian, *alt. dial.* Saxon, Low [nds], 539

East Pua Pray, *alt.* Lua' [prb], 516

East Sakhalin Gilyak, *dial.* Gilyak [niv], 504

East Sentani, *dial.* Sentani [set], 423

East Slovakian Romani, *dial.* Romani, Carpathian [rmc], 533, 558

East Solor, *dial.* Adonara [adr], 406

East Songhay, *alt.* Songhay, Koyraboro Senni [ses], 144

East Sumba, *alt.* Kambera [xbr], 407

East Sumbanese, *alt.* Kambera [xbr], 407

East Sutherlandshire, *dial.* Gaelic, Scottish [gla], 565

East Tanna, *dial.* Tanna, North [tnn], 645

East Tarakiri, *dial.* Izon [ijc], 164

East Tarangan, *see* Tarangan, East [tre], 404

East Toraja, *alt.* Tae' [rob], 428 *alt.* Toala' [tlz], 433

East Torres, *alt.* Meriam [ulk], 574

East Torricelli, *dial.* Torricelli [tei], 628

East Trangan, *alt.* Tarangan, East [tre], 404

East Ukrainian, *dial.* Ukrainian [ukr], 564

East Umanakaina, *dial.* Umanakaina [gdn], 629

East Urat, *alt. dial.* Urat [urt], 629

East Ureparapara, *alt.* Lehalurup [urr], 642

East Urii, *dial.* Uri [uvh], 629

East Uvean, *alt.* Wallisian [wls], 647, 585

East Valley Zapotec, *alt.* Zapotec, Mitla [zaw], 279

East Veluws, *dial.* Veluws [vel], 549

East Vod, *dial.* Vod [vot], 557

East Waylla, *dial.* Quechua, Huaylla Wanca [qvw], 291

East Yambes, *dial.* Yambes [ymb], 633

East Yawa, *dial.* Yawa [yva], 426

East Yugur, *see* Yugur, East [yuy], 348

Easter Island, *alt.* Rapa Nui [rap], 243

Eastern, *alt.* Jakalteko, Eastern [jac], 254
dial. Muthuvan [muv], 377
dial. Romani, Vlax [rmy], 551

Eastern Abnaki, *see* Abnaki, Eastern [aaq], 297

Eastern Acheron, *dial.* Acheron [acz], 187

Eastern Acipa, *see* Acipa, Eastern [acp], 153

Eastern Addasen, *dial.* Itneg, Adasen [tiu], 496

Eastern Aka, *alt. dial.* Aka [axk], 87

Eastern Aleut, *dial.* Aleut [ale], 297

Eastern Angami, *alt.* Naga, Chokri [nri], 377

Eastern Anmatyerre, *dial.* Anmatyerre [amx], 568

Eastern Apurímac Quechua, *see* Quechua, Eastern Apurímac [qve], 291

Eastern Apurímac Quechua, *dial.* Quechua, Cusco [quz], 290

Eastern Aragonese, *dial.* Aragonese [arg], 558

Eastern Aranda, *alt.* Arrernte, Eastern [aer], 568

Eastern Arctic Eskimo, *pej. alt.* Inuktitut, Eastern Canadian [ike], 238

Eastern Argentina Guaraní, *alt.* Guaraní, Mbyá [gun], 220

Eastern Armenian, *dial.* Armenian [hye], 318, 437, 563

Eastern Arrernte, *see* Arrernte, Eastern [aer], 568

Eastern Asturian, *dial.* Asturian [ast], 559

Eastern Bade, *alt.* Duwai [dbp], 158

Eastern Balochi, *see* Balochi, Eastern [bgp], 483, 355

Eastern Bantawa, *dial.* Bantawa [bap], 468

Eastern Bété, *alt.* Bété, Gagnoa [btg], 92

Eastern Birgit, *dial.* Birgit [btf], 79

Eastern Bisa, *alt. dial.* Bissa [bib], 123

Eastern Bobo Oule, *alt.* Buamu [box], 50

Eastern Bobo Wule, *alt.* Buamu [box], 50

Eastern Bokyi, *dial.* Bokyi [bky], 156

Eastern Bolivian Guaraní, *see* Guaraní, Eastern Bolivian [gui], 223, 284

Eastern Bolivian Guaraní, *alt.* Guaraní, Western Argentine [gui], 220

Eastern Bontoc, *alt.* Finallig [bkb], 494

Eastern Border Pwo Karen, *alt. dial.* Karen, Pwo Eastern [kjp], 464

Eastern Broach Gujarati, *alt. dial.* Gujarati [guj], 363

Eastern Bru, *see* Bru, Eastern [bru], 450, 514, 522

Eastern Bwe, *alt.* Karen, Geba [kvq], 458

Eastern Cagayan Agta, *alt.* Agta, Dupaninan [duo], 490

Eastern Cajamarca, *dial.* Quechua, Cajamarca [qvc], 290

Eastern Cakchiquel, *alt.* Kaqchikel, Eastern [cke], 254

Eastern Canadian Eskimo, *pej. alt.* Inuktitut, Eastern Canadian [ike], 238

Eastern Canadian Inuktitut, *see* Inuktitut, Eastern Canadian [ike], 238

Eastern Carib, *alt. dial.* Carib [car], 226, 252, 295

Eastern Central Sierra Miwok, *dial.* Miwok, Central Sierra [csm], 305

Eastern Cham, *see* Cham, Eastern [cjm], 522

Eastern Chepang, *dial.* Chepang [cdm], 469

Eastern Cherokee, *alt. dial.* Cherokee [chr], 299

Eastern Dan, *alt. dial.* Dan [daf], 92

Eastern Danish, *alt.* Scanian [scy], 562, 533

Eastern Dengka, *dial.* Dengka [dnk], 406

Eastern Dhatki, *dial.* Dhatki [mki], 484

Eastern Dhimal, *dial.* Dhimal [dhi], 470, 360

Eastern Dinka, *alt.* Dinka, Southeastern [dks], 190

Eastern Ditammari, *dial.* Ditammari [tbz], 43, 207

Eastern Duka, *dial.* Hun-Saare [dud], 162

Eastern Duun, *alt.* Dzùùngoo [dnn], 51

Eastern Duvle, *dial.* Duvle [duv], 414

Eastern East-Guizhou Miao, *alt.* Hmong, Eastern Qiandong [hmq], 334

Eastern Edolo, *dial.* Edolo [etr], 598

Eastern Efate, *alt.* Eton [etn], 641

Eastern Egyptian Bedawi Arabic, *dial.* Arabic, Levantine Bedawi Spoken [avl], 448, 489

Eastern Egyptian Bedawi Spoken Arabic, *see* Arabic, Eastern Egyptian Bedawi Spoken [avl], 110

Eastern Ejagham, *alt. dial.* Ejagham [etu], 60

dial. Ejagham [etu], 159

Eastern Emiliano, *dial.* Emiliano-Romagnolo [eml], 543

Eastern Ersu, *alt. dial.* Ersu [ers], 332

Eastern Farsi, *see* Farsi, Eastern [prs], 315, 484

Eastern Fas, *dial.* Fas [fqs], 598

Eastern Fijian, *alt.* Fijian [fij], 580

Eastern Frisian, *see* Frisian, Eastern [frs], 538

Eastern Fulani, *alt.* Fulfulde, Adamawa [fub], 61, 80

Eastern Fulfulde, *alt.* Fulfulde, Adamawa [fub], 160

Eastern Garifuna, *dial.* Garifuna [cab], 258

Eastern Gitxsan, *alt. dial.* Gitxsan [git], 237

Eastern Gorkha Tamang, *see* Tamang, Eastern Gorkha [tge], 479

Eastern Guaymí, *alt. dial.* Ngäbere [gym], 283

Eastern Gujari, *dial.* Gujari [gju], 485

Eastern Gurung, *see* Gurung, Eastern [ggn], 471

Eastern Helambu Sherpa, *dial.* Helambu Sherpa [scp], 472

Eastern Highland Chatino, *see* Chatino, Eastern Highland [cly], 259

Eastern Highland Otomi, *see* Otomi, Eastern Highland [otm], 272

Eastern Huasteca Aztec, *alt.* Nahuatl, Eastern Huasteca [nhe], 271

Eastern Huasteca Nahuatl, *see* Nahuatl, Eastern Huasteca [nhe], 271

Eastern Huichol, *alt. dial.* Huichol [hch], 263

Eastern Huishui Hmong, *see* Hmong, Eastern Huishui [hme], 334

Eastern Huishui Miao, *alt.* Hmong, Eastern Huishui [hme], 334

Eastern Inland Yawuru, *dial.* Yawuru [ywr], 579

Eastern Isirawa, *dial.* Isirawa [srl], 415

Eastern Jakalteko, *see* Jakalteko, Eastern [jac], 254

Eastern James Bay Cree Southern Dialect, *alt.* East Cree, Southern [crj], 237

Eastern Jamiltepec-Chayuco Mixtec, *alt.* Mixtec, Chayuco [mih], 266

Eastern Jamiltepec-San Cristobal Mixtec, *alt.* Mixtec, Jamiltepec [mxt], 267

Eastern Japanese, *dial.* Japanese [jpn], 446

Eastern Jiarong, *alt. dial.* Jiarong [jya], 336

Eastern Jibbali, *dial.* Shehri [shv], 483

Eastern Jikany, *dial.* Nuer [nus], 194

Eastern Juxtlahuaca Mixtec, *alt.* Mixtec, Mixtepec [mix], 267

Eastern Kadazan, *alt.* Kadazan, Labuk-Kinabatangan [dtb], 457

Eastern Kalebwe, *dial.* Songe [sop], 108

Eastern Kalibugan, *alt. dial.* Subanen, Central [syb], 501

Eastern Kanjobal, *alt.* Q'anjob'al, Eastern [kjb], 256

Eastern Kaqchikel, *see* Kaqchikel, Eastern [cke], 254

Eastern Karaboro, *see* Karaboro, Eastern [xrb], 51

Eastern Karaim, *dial.* Karaim [kdr], 546

Eastern Kativiri, *dial.* Kati [bsh], 316, 486

Eastern Katu, *see* Katu, Eastern [ktv], 523

Eastern Kayah, *see* Kayah, Eastern [eky], 465, 515

Eastern Keliko, *dial.* Keliko [kbo], 192

Eastern Keres, *see* Keres, Eastern [kee], 303

Eastern Keres Pueblo, *alt.* Keres, Eastern [kee], 303

Eastern Khams, *dial.* Tibetan, Khams [khg], 345

Eastern Khanti, *alt. dial.* Khanty [kca], 505

Eastern K'iche', *see* K'iche', Eastern [quu], 255

Eastern Kilmeri, *dial.* Kilmeri [kih], 606

Eastern Kituba, *dial.* Kituba [ktu], 101

Eastern Kiwai, *dial.* Kiwai, Southern [kjd], 606

Eastern Klaoh, *dial.* Klao [klu], 138

Eastern Kolibugan, *dial.* Subanen, Central [syb], 501

Eastern Koromfe, *dial.* Koromfé [kfz], 143

Eastern Krahn, *see* Krahn, Eastern [kqo], 138

Eastern Kran, *alt.* Krahn, Eastern [kqo], 138

Eastern Kurmanji, *alt.* Kurdish, Northern [kmr], 440

Eastern Kusaal, *alt. dial.* Kusaal [kus], 126

Eastern Lalu Yi, *see* Yi, Eastern Lalu [yit], 347

Eastern Lawa, *see* Lawa, Eastern [lwl], 515

Eastern Libyan Arabic, *dial.* Arabic, Libyan Spoken [ayl], 139 *dial.* Arabic, Western Egyptian Bedawi Spoken [ayl], 110

Eastern Lisu, *alt.* Lipo [lpo], 339

Eastern Livonian, *dial.* Liv [liv], 546

Eastern Lombard, *dial.* Lombard [lmo], 544

Eastern Low Navarrese, *dial.* Basque, Navarro-Labourdin [bqe], 535

Eastern Luba, *alt.* Hemba [hem], 100

Eastern Macina, *dial.* Fulfulde, Maasina [ffm], 143

Eastern Magar, *see* Magar, Eastern [mgp], 475, 373

Eastern Maithili, *dial.* Maithili [mai], 373

Eastern Malinke, *alt.* Maninkakan, Eastern [emk], 129, 183

Eastern Mampruli, *dial.* Mampruli [maw], 126

Eastern Manggarai, *dial.* Manggarai [mqy], 409

Eastern Maninkakan, *see* Maninkakan, Eastern [emk], 129, 183

Eastern Mari, *see* Mari, Eastern [mhr], 555

Eastern Maring, *dial.* Maring [mbw], 612

Eastern Mbum, *alt.* Karang [kzr], 81

Eastern Mehri, *dial.* Mehri [gdq], 528

Eastern Meohang, *see* Meohang, Eastern [emg], 475

Eastern Miahuatlán Zapotec, *alt.* Zapotec, Mixtepec [zpm], 279

Eastern Min, *alt.* Chinese, Min Dong [cdo], 330, 514

Eastern Mixe, *alt.* Mixe, Isthmus [mir], 265

Eastern Mixtec, *alt.* Mixtec, Peñoles [mil], 268

Eastern Mnong, *see* Mnong, Eastern [mng], 525

Eastern Montagnais, *dial.* Montagnais [moe], 239

Eastern Motu, *dial.* Motu [meu], 615

Eastern Muna, *alt. dial.* Muna [mnb], 431

Eastern Muria, *see* Muria, Eastern [emu], 376

Eastern Mussau, *dial.* Mussau-Emira [emi], 616

Eastern Muya, *dial.* Muya [mvm], 340

Eastern Nahane, *alt.* Kaska [kkz], 238

Eastern Namuyi, *dial.* Namuyi [nmy], 341

Eastern Naskapi, *alt. dial.* Naskapi [nsk], 239

Eastern Ngad'a, *see* Ngad'a, Eastern [nea], 409

Eastern Nihiri, *dial.* Varli [vav], 390

Eastern Nonmetafonetica, *dial.* Sicilian [scn], 545

Eastern Nuer, *dial.* Nuer [nus], 117

Eastern Ocotlán Zapotec, *alt.* Zapotec, Chichicapan [zpv], 278

Eastern Ojibwa, *see* Ojibwa, Eastern [ojg], 240

Eastern Ojibwa, *alt.* Ottawa [otw], 306

Eastern Oromo, *see* Oromo, Eastern [hae], 118

Eastern Otomi, *alt.* Otomi, Eastern Highland [otm], 272

Eastern Pagi, *dial.* Pagi [pgi], 621

Eastern Pahari, *alt.* Nepali [nep], 476, 323, 381

Eastern Panjabi, *see* Panjabi, Eastern [pan], 383, 135, 509

Eastern Parbate, *see* Parbate, Eastern [kif], 477

Eastern Pattani, *dial.* Pattani [lae], 383

Eastern Penan, *see* Penan, Eastern [pez], 460, 325

Eastern Pochutla Zapotec, *alt.* Zapotec, Xadani [zax], 281

Eastern Point, *dial.* Sudest [tgo], 625

Eastern Pokomam, *alt.* Poqomam, Eastern [poa], 255

Eastern Pokomchí, *alt.* Poqomchi', Eastern [poh], 256

Eastern Pomo, *see* Pomo, Eastern [peb], 307

Eastern Popoloca, *alt.* Popoloca, San Juan Atzingo [poe], 273

Eastern Poqomam, *see* Poqomam, Eastern [poa], 255

Eastern Poqomchi', *see* Poqomchi', Eastern [poh], 256

Eastern Putla Mixtec, *alt.* Mixtec, Itundujia [mce], 265

Eastern Q'anjob'al, *see* Q'anjob'al, Eastern [kjb], 256

Eastern Qiandong Hmong, *see* Hmong, Eastern Qiandong [hmq], 334

Eastern Qiandong Miao, *alt.* Hmong, Eastern Qiandong [hmq], 334

Eastern Quiché, *alt.* K'iche', Eastern [quu], 255

Eastern Rajbanshi, *dial.* Rajbanshi [rjb], 384, 477

Eastern Rote, *alt.* Bilba [bpz], 406 *alt.* Ringgou [rgu], 409

Eastern Ruli, *dial.* Ruli [ruc], 212

Eastern Sawos, *dial.* Malinguat [sic], 611

Eastern She, *alt. dial.* She [shx], 343

Eastern Shuswap, *dial.* Shuswap [shs], 241

Eastern Sola de Vega Zapotec, *alt.* Zapotec, Lachixío [zpl], 278

Eastern Suri, *alt.* Suri [suq], 119

Eastern Swampy Cree, *dial.* Cree, Swampy [csw], 236

Eastern Swedish, *dial.* Swedish [swe], 562

Eastern Syriac, *dial.* Syriac [syc], 519

Eastern Tamang, *see* Tamang, Eastern [taj], 479, 388

Eastern Tatar, *dial.* Tatar [tat], 556

Eastern Tawbuid, *see* Tawbuid, Eastern [bnj], 502

Eastern Tày, *dial.* Tày [tyz], 527

Eastern Teke, *alt.* Teke, Ibali [tek], 108 *alt.* Teke-Ibali [tek], 90

Eastern Tetun, *dial.* Tetun [tet], 410, 351

Eastern Thai, *alt.* Lao [lao], 445

Eastern Thami, *dial.* Thangmi [thf], 480

Eastern Thulung, *dial.* Thulung [tdh], 481

Eastern Tlacolula Zapotec, *alt.* Zapotec, San Pedro Quiatoni [zpf], 279

Eastern Tlapanec, *alt.* Tlapanec, Malinaltepec [tcf], 275

Eastern Toposa, *dial.* Toposa
[toq], 196
Eastern Tumut, *alt. dial.*
Mongolian, Peripheral [mvf], 339
Eastern Tunebo, *alt.* Tunebo,
Barro Negro [tbn], 248
Eastern Tz'utujil, *see* Tz'utujil,
Eastern [tzj], 256
Eastern Uma, *alt. dial.* Uma
[ppk], 434
Eastern Vogul, *dial.* Mansi
[mns], 505
Eastern Waimaha, *dial.* Waimaha
[bao], 248
Eastern Wakhi, *dial.* Wakhi
[wbl], 346, 513
Eastern Walloon, *dial.* Walloon
[wln], 531
Eastern West-Hunan Miao, *alt.*
Hmong, Eastern Xiangxi
[muq], 334
Eastern Xiangxi Hmong, *see*
Hmong, Eastern Xiangxi
[muq], 334
Eastern Xiangxi Miao, *alt.*
Hmong, Eastern Xiangxi
[muq], 334
Eastern Xwla Gbe, *see* Gbe,
Eastern Xwla [gbx], 44
Eastern Yagnobi, *dial.* Yagnobi
[yai], 513
Eastern Yakha, *dial.* Yakha
[ybh], 482
Eastern Yanomami, *dial.*
Yanomamö [guu], 313, 234
Eastern Yi, *alt.* Yi, Guizhou
[yig], 347
Eastern Yiddish, *see* Yiddish,
Eastern [ydd], 446, 546
Eastern Yogor, *alt.* Yugur, East
[yuy], 348
Eastphalian, *dial.* Saxon, Low
[nds], 539
Ebadidi, *alt.* Molima [mox], 614
Ebang, *alt.* Heiban [hbn], 191
Ebe, *alt.* Asu [aum], 154
Ebekwara, *alt.* Bekwarra [bkv], 155
Ebembe, *alt.* Bembe [bmb], 97, 197
Eben, *alt.* Even [eve], 504
Eberã, *alt.* Emberá, Northern
[emp], 245
Ebera Bedea, *alt.* Emberá, Northern
[emp], 283
Eberã Bed'ea, *alt.* Emberá,
Northern [emp], 245
Ebeteng, *alt. dial.* Ukpet-Ehom
[akd], 176
Ebhele, *alt.* Bhele [bhy], 98
Ebila, *alt.* Bila [bip], 98
Ebina, *alt.* Bena [yun], 155

alt. Voro [vor], 177
Ebira [igb], 158
Ebiri, *alt.* Mararit [mgb], 83
Ebitoso, *dial.* Chamacoco [ceg], 284
Ebkuo, *alt.* Oku [oku], 71
Ebode, *dial.* Lala-Roba [lla], 163
Eboh, *alt. dial.* Ukwuani-Aboh-Ndoni
[ukw], 176
Ebon, *alt.* Marshallese [mah], 582
Eboo Teke, *see* Teke-Eboo
[ebo], 108
Eboo Teke, *alt.* Teke-Eboo [ebo], 90
Eboom, *alt.* Teke-Eboo [ebo], 90
Eborna, *alt.* Borna [bxx], 98
Eboze, *alt. dial.* Jere [jer], 165
Ebrié [ebr], 92
Ebu, *dial.* Igala [igl], 163
Ebudu, *alt.* Budu [buu], 98
Ebughu [ebg], 158
Ebugombe, *alt. dial.* Bhele [bhy], 98
Ebuja, *alt.* Budza [bja], 98
Ebuku, *dial.* Bomboma [bws], 98
Ebuna, *alt.* Bena [yun], 155
alt. Voro [vor], 177
Ebwe, *alt.* Éwé [ewe], 124
Eche, *dial.* Igbo [ibo], 163
Echidzindza, *alt.* Zinza [zin], 206
Echijinja, *alt.* Zinza [zin], 206
Echijita, *alt.* Jita [jit], 199
Echisubia, *alt.* Kuhane [sbs], 47
alt. Subiya [sbs], 151, 215
Echitotela, *alt.* Totela [ttl], 215, 151
Echiungu, *alt.* Bungu [wun], 197
Echoaldi, *dial.* Guana [gva], 284
Echonoana, *alt. dial.* Guana
[gva], 284
Echuabo, *alt.* Chuwabu [chw], 147
Echuku, *alt. dial.* Akpes [ibe], 153
Echuwabo, *alt.* Chuwabu [chw], 147
Ecijita, *alt.* Jita [jit], 199
Ecizinza, *alt.* Zinza [zin], 206
Ecuadorian Sign Language
[ecs], 251
Ecuadorian Siona, *dial.* Secoya
[sey], 251
Ecun, *dial.* Buyang [byu], 329
E'da, *alt. dial.* Kalumpang [kli], 429
Edangabo, *dial.* Haya [hay], 199
Edawapi, *alt.* Namia [nnm], 617
Ede Cabe [cbj], 43
Ede Ica [ica], 43
Ede Idaca [idd], 43
Ede Ife, *alt.* Ifè [ife], 45
Ede Ije [ijj], 43
Ede Nago [nqg], 43
Ede Nago, Kura [nqk], 43
Ede Nago, Manigri-Kambolé
[xkb], 43, 207
Ede-Yoruba, *alt.* Yoruba [yor], 46
Edeh, *alt.* Rade [rad], 526

Edera Awyu, *see* Awyu, Edera
[awy], 412
Edheidhei, *pej. alt. dial.* Koti
[eko], 147
Edi, *dial.* Galoli [gal], 350
Ediamat, *alt.* Ejamat [eja], 131, 180
Ediba, *alt.* Kohumono [bcs], 166
Edimala, *alt.* Alta, Northern [aqn],
491
Edinburgh, *dial.* English [eng], 565
Edirne, *dial.* Turkish [tur], 519, 521
Ediro, *dial.* Engenni [enn], 159
Editode Edai, *alt.* Eritai [ert], 415
Ediu-Adig, *alt.* Kadiwéu [kbc], 228
Ediya, *alt.* Bube [bvb], 110
Edjagam, *alt.* Ejagham [etu], 60
Edo [bin], 158
dial. Kaili, Ledo [lew], 429
Edolo [etr], 598
Edolo Ado, *alt.* Edolo [etr], 598
Edopi [dbf], 414
Edulia, *alt.* Barasana [bsn], 243
Eduria, *alt.* Barasana [bsn], 243
Edyenge Dom, *alt.* Dogon, Kolum
So [dkl], 142
Eenthlit, *alt. dial.* Lengua [leg], 284
Eerã, *alt.* Emberá, Northern
[emp], 283
E'erduosite, *alt. dial.* Mongolian,
Peripheral [mvf], 339
Eerwee, *alt. dial.* Bokyi [bky], 156
Eesti, *alt.* Estonian [est], 534, 534
Efai [efa], 158
Efate, North [llp], 641
Efate, South [erk], 641
Efe [efe], 99
alt. Éwé [ewe], 124
Effiat, *alt.* Efai [efa], 158
Effium, *alt. dial.* Oring [org], 172
Effurun, *alt.* Uvbie [evh], 176
Efifa, *dial.* Akpes [ibe], 153
Efik [efi], 158
Efira, *alt. dial.* Mele-Fila [mxe], 643
Eftawagaria, *dial.* Romani, Sinte
[rmo], 539
Efutop [ofu], 158
Efutu, *dial.* Awutu [afu], 123
Ega [ega], 92
Egba, *dial.* Yoruba [yor], 178, 46
Egbedna, *dial.* Ikwere [ikw], 164
Egbema, *dial.* Igbo [ibo], 163
dial. Izon [ijc], 164
Egbira, *alt.* Ebira [igb], 158
Egbura, *alt.* Ebira [igb], 158
Egede, *alt.* Igede [ige], 163
Egejo, *alt. dial.* Pagibete [pae], 107
Egene, *alt.* Engenni [enn], 159
Eger, *dial.* Hungarian Sign Language
[hsh], 542
Egezo, *alt. dial.* Pagibete [pae], 107

Egezon, *alt. dial.* Pagibete [pae], 107
Eggon [ego], 158
Eghom, *alt. dial.* Mbembe, Cross River [mfn], 163
Egnih, *dial.* Ogbah [ogc], 172
Egon, *alt.* Eggon [ego], 158
Egongot, *dial.* Ilongot [ilk], 495
Egu, *alt. dial.* Ebira [igb], 158
Egun, *alt.* Gun [guw], 45
  alt. dial. Gun [guw], 161
Egwa, *alt.* Ega [ega], 92
Egypt Sign Language [esl], 110
Egyptian Spoken Arabic, *see* Arabic, Egyptian Spoken [arz], 110
Eh Je, *alt. dial.* Grebo, Northern [gbo], 138
Ehija, *dial.* Orokaiva [ork], 620
Ehkili, *alt.* Shehri [shv], 483
Eho Mbo, *alt. dial.* Mbo [mbo], 66
Ehob Mkaa, *alt. dial.* Bakaka [bqz], 57
Ehobe Belon, *alt. dial.* Bakaka [bqz], 57
Ehom, *dial.* Ukpet-Ehom [akd], 176
Ehoue, *alt. dial.* Aja [ajg], 42, 206
Ehow Mba, *alt. dial.* Mbo [mbo], 66
Ehtremeñu, *alt.* Extremaduran [ext], 560
Ehueun [ehu], 159
Ehwe, *alt.* Éwé [ewe], 207
Eibe, *alt.* Éwé [ewe], 124, 207
|**Eikusi**, *alt. dial.* !Xóõ [nmn], 48, 151
Eipo, *alt.* Eipomek [eip], 414
Eipomek [eip], 414
Eitiep [eit], 598
Eivissenc, *alt. dial.* Catalan-Valencian-Balear [cat], 559
Eivo, *alt.* Askopan [eiv], 591
Eiwaja, *alt.* Iwaidja [ibd], 571
Ejagam, *alt.* Ejagham [etu], 60
Ejagham [etu], 159, 60
Ejaham, *alt.* Ejagham [etu], 60
Ejamat [eja], 131, 180
Ejar, *dial.* Begbere-Ejar [bqv], 155
Ejine, *dial.* Mongolian, Peripheral [mvf], 339
Ejwe, *alt.* Ejagham [etu], 60
Ek Nii, *alt.* Nii [nii], 618
Ekagi, *alt.* Ekari [ekg], 414
Ekajuk [eka], 159
Ekama, *dial.* Mbembe, Cross River [mfn], 163
Ekamtulufu, *alt. dial.* Nde-Nsele-Nta [ndd], 170
Ekamu, *alt. dial.* Mbembe, Cross River [mfn], 163
Ekari [ekg], 414
Ekaw, *alt.* Akha [ahk], 462, 326, 449, 513, 521
Ekegusii, *alt.* Gusii [guz], 133

Ekele, *alt.* Kele [khy], 101
Eket, *alt.* Ekit [eke], 159
Ekhirit, *dial.* Buriat, Russia [bxr], 504
Eki [eki], 159
  dial. Bebele [beb], 58
Ekibena, *alt.* Bena [bez], 197
Ekiguria, *alt.* Kuria [kuj], 134
Ekihaya, *alt.* Haya [hay], 199
Ekikerebe, *alt.* Kerewe [ked], 199
Ekikinga, *alt.* Kinga [zga], 200
Ekikira, *alt. dial.* Nande [nnb], 105
Ekikumbule, *alt. dial.* Nande [nnb], 105
Ekimate, *alt. dial.* Nande [nnb], 105
Ekin, *alt. dial.* Ejagham [etu], 159, 60
Ekinyambo, *alt.* Nyambo [now], 203
Ekipangwa, *alt.* Pangwa [pbr], 203
Ekisanza, *alt. dial.* Konjo [koo], 211, 101
  alt. dial. Nande [nnb], 105
Ekishu, *alt. dial.* Nande [nnb], 105
Ekisongoora, *dial.* Nande [nnb], 105
Ekiswaga, *alt. dial.* Nande [nnb], 105
Ekit [eke], 159
Ekitangi, *alt. dial.* Nande [nnb], 105
Ekiti, *dial.* Yoruba [yor], 178
Ekiyira, *alt. dial.* Nande [nnb], 105
Ekiziba, *dial.* Haya [hay], 199
Ekkpahia, *alt.* Ekpeye [ekp], 159
Eklenjuy, *alt.* Chorote, Iyojwa'ja [crt], 220
Eklep, *alt.* Aiklep [mwg], 588
Ekoi, *alt.* Ejagham [etu], 159, 60
Ekoka-!Xû, *alt.* Kung-Ekoka [knw], 150
Ekoko-!Xû, *alt.* Kung-Ekoka [knw], 40
Ekokoma, *alt.* Mbembe, Cross River [mfn], 163
Ekombe, *dial.* Oroko [bdu], 71
Ekonda, *alt. dial.* Mongo-Nkundu [lol], 104
Ekonda Mongo, *dial.* Mongo-Nkundu [lol], 104
Ekos-Yenabi-Maragin, *dial.* Kwomtari [kwo], 609
Ekoti, *alt.* Koti [eko], 147
  dial. Koti [eko], 147
Ekoyo, *alt.* Koyo [koh], 88
Ekpabya, *alt.* Ekpeye [ekp], 159
Ekpaffia, *alt.* Ekpeye [ekp], 159
Ekparabong, *dial.* Ndoe [nbb], 170
Ekpari, *alt.* Yace [ekr], 177
Ekpeebhe, *alt.* Akebu [keu], 206
Ekpenmen, *alt.* Ehueun [ehu], 159
  alt. Ukue [uku], 176
Ekpenmi, *alt.* Ukue [uku], 176
Ekperi, *alt. dial.* Ngwo [ngn], 70

  dial. Yekhee [ets], 177
Ekpeshe, *alt.* Ikpeshi [ikp], 164
Ekpetiama, *dial.* Izon [ijc], 164
Ekpeye [ekp], 159
Ekpimi, *alt.* Ehueun [ehu], 159
Ekpon, *dial.* Esan [ish], 159
Ekpwo, *alt.* Oku [oku], 71
Ekumbe, *alt. dial.* Oroko [bdu], 71
Ekumuru, *alt.* Kohumono [bcs], 166
Ekuri, *alt.* Nkukoli [nbo], 171
Ekwala, *alt.* Likwala [kwc], 89
Ekware, *alt.* Mpur [akc], 420
El Akheimar, *alt. dial.* Ngile [jle], 194
El Alto Zapotec, *see* Zapotec, El Alto [zpp], 278
El Amira, *alt. dial.* Lafofa [laf], 192
El Hagarat, *alt.* El Hugeirat [elh], 190
El Hugeirat [elh], 190
El Molo [elo], 132
El Nayar, *alt. dial.* Cora, El Nayar [crn], 262
El Nayar Cora, *see* Cora, El Nayar [crn], 262
El Salvadoran Sign Language, *alt.* Salvadoran Sign Language [esn], 252
Elaka, *alt. dial.* Eman [emn], 60
Elat, *dial.* Banda [bnd], 396
Elati, *dial.* Cherokee [chr], 299
Elbasan-Tirana, *dial.* Albanian, Gheg [aln], 529
Eleko, *alt. dial.* Lusengo [lse], 103
Eleku, *alt. dial.* Lusengo [lse], 103
Elele, *dial.* Ikwere [ikw], 164
Elembe, *dial.* Nkutu [nkw], 106
Eleme [elm], 159
Elepi [ele], 598
Eleuth, *alt. dial.* Kalmyk-Oirat [xal], 337, 461
Elgeyo, *alt. dial.* Kalenjin [kln], 133
Elgumi, *alt.* Teso [teo], 213
Eli, *dial.* Banda [bnd], 396
Elimbari, *dial.* Chuave [cjv], 596
Eling, *dial.* Tunen [baz], 72
Elip [ekm], 60
Eliri, *alt.* Nding [eli], 194
Elkei [elk], 598
Ellice, *alt.* Tuvaluan [tvl], 640
Ellicean, *alt.* Tuvaluan [tvl], 640
Ellinika, *alt.* Greek [ell], 540
Ellyria, *alt.* Lokoya [lky], 192
Elmolo, *alt.* El Molo [elo], 132
Elog Mpoo, *alt. dial.* Bakoko [bkh], 57
Elomay, *alt.* Bainouk-Gunyaamolo [bcz], 179
  alt. Bainouk-Gunyuño [bab], 130
Elomwe, *alt.* Lomwe [ngl], 147

Elong, *alt. dial.* Akoose [bss], 56
Elopi, *alt.* Edopi [dbf], 414
Elotepec Zapotec, *see* Zapotec,
   Elotepec [zte], 278
Elowa, *dial.* Ligenza [lgz], 102
Eloyi [afo], 159
Elpaputi, *alt.* Elpaputih [elp], 398
Elpaputih [elp], 398
Elpira, *alt.* Warlpiri [wbp], 578
Elsaessisch, *alt. dial.* Alemannisch
   [gsw], 535
Elseng [mrf], 414
Elt Ulid, *dial.* Ghadamès [gha], 139
Elu [elu], 598
   dial. Isoko [iso], 164
Elu-Kara, *alt.* Lele [lle], 609
Elun, *alt. dial.* Bandial [bqj], 180
Elunay, *alt.* Bainouk-Gunyaamolo
   [bcz], 179
   alt. Bainouk-Gunyuño [bab], 130
Elunchun, *alt.* Oroqen [orh], 341
Elung, *dial.* Akoose [bss], 56
Eluosi, *alt.* Russian [rus], 343
Elyut, *alt. dial.* Kalmyk-Oirat [xal],
   337, 461
Em, *alt.* Garus [gyb], 599
Ema, *alt.* Kemak [kem], 351, 407
Emae [mmw], 641
Emai, *alt.* Emae [mmw], 641
   dial. Emai-Iuleha-Ora [ema], 159
Emai-Iuleha-Ora [ema], 159
Emaka, *alt.* Makhuwa-Marrevone
   [xmc], 147
Emakhuwa, *alt.* Makhuwa
   [vmw], 147
Emakhuwa-Emoniga, *alt.*
   Makhuwa-Moniga [mhm], 147
Emakhuwana, *alt. dial.* Makhuwa
   [vmw], 147
   alt. dial. Makhuwa-Marrevone
   [xmc], 147
Emakua, *alt.* Makhuwa [vmw], 147
Eman [emn], 60
Emane, *alt.* Eman [emn], 60
Emarendje, *alt.* Marenje [vmr], 148
Emarle, *alt. dial.* Okpamheri
   [opa], 172
Emathipane, *alt. dial.* Makhuwa
   [vmw], 147
Emau, *dial.* Efate, North [llp], 641
Emba, *alt.* Hemba [hem], 100
Embaloh [emb], 393
Embena, *alt.* Emberá-Catío
   [cto], 245, 283
Embená Tadó, *alt.* Emberá-Tadó
   [tdc], 245
Emberá, Northern [emp], 283,
   245
Emberá-Baudó [bdc], 245
Emberá-Catío [cto], 245, 283

Emberá-Chamí [cmi], 245
Emberá-Saija, *alt.* Epena [sja], 245,
   251, 283
Emberá-Tadó [tdc], 245
Embosi, *alt.* Mbosi [mdw], 89
Embu [ebu], 132
   dial. Embu [ebu], 132
Embudja, *alt.* Budza [bja], 98
Eme-Eme, *alt.* Minanibai [mcv], 614
Emede, *dial.* Isoko [iso], 164
Emela, *alt.* Naga, Mao [nbi], 378
Emereñon, *alt.* Emerillon [eme], 252
Emerillon [eme], 252
Emerilon, *alt.* Emerillon [eme], 252
Emerum, *alt.* Apali [ena], 590
Emeto, *alt.* Makhuwa-Meetto
   [mgh], 147
   alt. dial. Makhuwa-Meetto
   [mgh], 201
Emfinu, *alt.* Mfinu [zmf], 104
Emhalhe, *alt. dial.* Okpamheri
   [opa], 172
Emilian, *alt.* Emiliano-Romagnolo
   [eml], 543
Emiliano, *alt.* Emiliano-Romagnolo
   [eml], 543
Emiliano-Romagnolo [eml], 543,
   557
Emira, *dial.* Mussau-Emira [emi], 616
Emira-Mussau, *alt.* Mussau-Emira
   [emi], 616
Emmi, *alt.* Maranunggu [zmr], 573
Emoa, *alt.* Macuna [myy], 246
Emok [emo], 284
Emoniga, *alt.* Makhuwa-Moniga
   [mhm], 147
Emoro, *alt.* Lemoro [ldj], 168
Emowhua, *dial.* Ikwere [ikw], 164
Empamela, *alt. dial.* Makhuwa-
   Marrevone [xmc], 147
   dial. Makhuwa [vmw], 147
Empawa, *dial.* Jagoi [sne], 459
Empera, *alt.* Emberá, Northern
   [emp], 283
Emperã, *alt.* Emberá, Northern
   [emp], 245
Empesa Poko, *dial.* Lusengo
   [lse], 103
Emplawas [emw], 398
Empui, *alt.* Naga, Zeme [nzm], 381
Emughan, *dial.* Abua [abn], 153
Emumu [enr], 414
Emvane So, *dial.* So [sox], 72
Emwae, *alt.* Emae [mmw], 641
Emwae Island, *alt. dial.* Namakura
   [nmk], 644
Emwaja, *dial.* Makhuwa [vmw], 147
En [enc], 522
   dial. Wa [wbm], 467
Ena, *alt.* Enya [gey], 99

Enaharra, *alt. dial.* Makhuwa-
   Marrevone [xmc], 147
   dial. Makhuwa [vmw], 147
Enatthembo, *alt. dial.* Koti
   [eko], 147
Enawené-Nawé [unk], 226
Encabellao, *alt.* Secoya [sey], 293
Endangen, *alt.* Kombio [xbi], 607
Ende [end], 406
   alt. Baras [brs], 428
   dial. Agob [kit], 588
   dial. Ende [end], 406
Ende Malay, *alt. dial.* Malay
   [mly], 436
Endeh, *alt.* Ende [end], 406
   alt. dial. Ende [end], 406
Endekan, *alt.* Enrekang [ptt], 429
Endekan Timur, *alt.* Enrekang
   [ptt], 429
Endeve, *alt.* Opata [opt], 272
Endo [enb], 133
   dial. Endo [enb], 133
Endo-Marakwet, *alt.* Endo
   [enb], 133
Endu, *dial.* Ambrym, Southeast
   [tvk], 640
Eneby, *alt.* Yidiny [yii], 579
Eneeme, *alt. dial.* Mbembe, Tigon
   [nza], 170
   dial. Mbembe, Tigon [nza], 66
Enegegny, *dial.* Inor [ior], 115
Enenga, *dial.* Myene [mye], 121
Enenlhit, *alt.* Toba-Maskoy
   [tmf], 285
Eñepa [pbh], 311
Enets, Forest [enf], 504
Enets, Tundra [enh], 504
Eneuene-Mare, *alt.* Enawené-Nawé
   [unk], 226
Enga [enq], 598
Enga-Kyaka, *alt.* Kyaka [kyc], 609
Engenni [enn], 159
Enger, *alt.* Yugur, East [yuy], 348
Engganese, *alt.* Enggano
   [eno], 435
Enggano [eno], 435
Enggipiloe, *alt.* Damal [uhn], 413
Enggipilu, *dial.* Damal [uhn], 413
Enggros, *alt.* Tobati [tti], 424
English [eng], 565, 46, 49, 60, 112,
   114, 122, 124, 133, 137, 140, 145,
   149, 159, 178, 179, 182, 183, 184,
   185, 197, 198, 210, 213, 215, 219,
   221, 222, 234, 237, 242, 250, 252,
   253, 257, 258, 282, 294, 295, 296,
   297, 300, 324, 325, 332, 361, 444,
   453, 454, 484, 494, 509, 540, 542,
   547, 567, 570, 579, 580, 581, 582,
   583, 585, 586, 587, 598, 634, 636,
   639, 641

English Romani, *alt.* Angloromani [rme], 564, 298, 568
Engungwel, *alt.* Ngungwel [ngz], 89
Enhen, *alt. dial.* Curripaco [kpc], 226
Enhwe, *dial.* Isoko [iso], 164
Eni, *dial.* Oko-Eni-Osayen [oks], 172
Enibura, *alt.* Wakawaka [wkw], 577
Enim [eni], 435
Enimaca, *alt.* Maca [mca], 285
Enimaga, *alt.* Maca [mca], 285
Enindhilyagwa, *alt.* Anindilyakwa [aoi], 568
Enindiljaugwa, *alt.* Anindilyakwa [aoi], 568
Enkelembu, *alt.* Kanum, Bädi [khd], 416
　alt. Kanum, Ngkâlmpw [kcd], 416
　alt. Kanum, Smärky [kxq], 416
　alt. Kanum, Sota [krz], 416
Enkun, *dial.* Jingpho [kac], 336
Enlai, *dial.* Makhuwa [vmw], 147
　dial. Makhuwa-Marrevone [xmc], 147
Enlit, *alt. dial.* Sanapaná [sap], 285
Enmylinskij, *dial.* Chukot [ckt], 504
Enna, *alt. dial.* Agwagwune [yay], 153
　alt. dial. Bugis [bug], 428
Ennebergisch, *alt. dial.* Ladin [lld], 544
Ennemor, *alt.* Inor [ior], 115
Enneqor, *dial.* Silt'e [xst], 119
Enner, *alt. dial.* Inor [ior], 115
Enoah, *dial.* Ewondo [ewo], 61
Enrekang [ptt], 429
　dial. Enrekang [ptt], 429
Entiat, *alt. dial.* Columbia-Wenatchi [col], 300
Enurmin, *dial.* Chukot [ckt], 504
Enwan (Akwa Ibom State) [enw], 159
　Enwan (Edu State) [env], 159
Enxet, *alt.* Lengua [leg], 284
Enya [gey], 99
Enyara, *dial.* Makhuwa [vmw], 147
Enyau, *alt. dial.* Sie [erg], 645
Enyembe, *dial.* Abidji [abi], 88
Enyong, *dial.* Ibibio [ibb], 162
Enzeb, *alt.* Hunzib [huz], 554
Eotile, *alt.* Beti [eot], 92
Epai, *alt.* Ipiko [ipo], 603
Epe, *alt.* Eloyi [afo], 159
Epena [sja], 245, 251, 283
　alt. dial. Bomitaba [zmx], 88
Epená, *alt.* Epena [sja], 251
Epéna Pedée, *alt.* Epena [sja], 245, 251, 283
Epena Saija, *alt.* Epena [sja], 283
Epená Saija, *alt.* Epena [sja], 245, 251

Epera, *alt.* Emberá-Catío [cto], 283
Eperã Pedea, *alt.* Emberá, Northern [emp], 245
Epie [epi], 159
Epie-Atissa, *alt.* Epie [epi], 159
Epigi, *dial.* Ndumu [nmd], 121
Epimi, *alt.* Ehueun [ehu], 159
Epinmi, *alt.* Ukue [uku], 176
Epwau, *alt.* Eton [etn], 641
Equinao, *alt.* Guana [gqn], 227
Er-Gwar, *alt. dial.* Kag-Fer-Jiir-Koor-Ror-Us-Zuksun [gel], 165
Era, *dial.* Dom [doa], 597
Era River, *alt. dial.* Kiwai, Northeast [kiw], 606
Eraans, *alt.* Ida'an [dbj], 456
Erai, *alt.* Eritai [ert], 415
　alt. Ili'uun [ilu], 399
Erakor, *alt.* Efate, South [erk], 641
Erakwa, *alt.* Eruwa [erh], 159
Erâmani, *alt.* Armenian [hye], 437
Eranadans, *alt.* Aranadan [aaf], 354
Erankad, *alt.* Gahri [bfu], 361
Erap, *alt.* Uri [uvh], 629
Erati, *alt. dial.* Makhuwa-Saka [xsq], 147
Eravallan, *alt.* Irula [iru], 365
Erave [kjy], 598
　dial. Dadibi [mps], 596
Erawa, *alt.* Rawa [rwo], 622
Eray, *dial.* Ili'uun [ilu], 399
Erbore, *alt.* Arbore [arv], 113
Ere [twp], 598
　alt. Erre [err], 570
　dial. Guanyinqiao [jiq], 333
Éré, *alt. dial.* Kim [kia], 82
Eref, *dial.* Daju, Dar Daju [djc], 79
Eregba, *dial.* Kpan [kpk], 167
Erei, *dial.* Agwagwune [yay], 153
Eremagok, *alt.* Patamona [pbc], 257
Erempi, *alt.* Rempi [rmp], 622
Erenga, *alt.* Sungor [sjg], 195
　dial. Sungor [sjg], 195
Erevan, *dial.* Armenian [hye], 318
　dial. Azerbaijani, North [azj], 319
Erewa, *alt.* Rawa [rwo], 622
Ergali, *dial.* Guanyinqiao [jiq], 333
Ergong, *alt.* Horpa [ero], 335
Erhsu, *alt.* Ersu [ers], 332
Eri, *alt.* Eritai [ert], 415
Erikbatsa, *alt.* Rikbaktsa [rkb], 232
Erikpatsa, *alt.* Rikbaktsa [rkb], 232
Erima, *alt.* Ogea [eri], 619
Eritai [ert], 415
Eriwan, *alt. dial.* Armenian [hye], 318
Erli, *alt. dial.* Romani, Balkan [rmn], 539, 541, 545, 563
Ermeni Dili, *alt.* Armenian [hye], 318

Ermenice, *alt.* Armenian [hye], 318, 319, 350, 437, 444, 453, 510, 563
Ermitaño, *dial.* Chavacano [cbk], 493
Ermiteño, *alt. dial.* Chavacano [cbk], 493
Ernga, *alt.* Korwa [kfp], 370
Erohwa, *alt.* Eruwa [erh], 159
Erokh, *alt.* Iraqw [irk], 199
Erokwanas [erw], 415
Eromanga, *alt.* Sie [erg], 645
Erorup, *alt.* Korop [krp], 64
Erramanga, *alt.* Sie [erg], 645
Erre [err], 570
Erromanga, *alt.* Sie [erg], 645
Erronan, *alt.* Futuna-Aniwa [fut], 641
Ersari, *dial.* Turkmen [tuk], 318
Erse, *alt.* Gaelic, Irish [gle], 542, 565
　alt. Gaelic, Scottish [gla], 565
Ersu [ers], 332
　dial. Ersu [ers], 332
Eru, *alt.* Alatil [alx], 588
Eru-Eu-Wau-Wau, *alt.* Uru-Eu-Wau-Wau [urz], 233
Erukala, *alt.* Irula [iru], 365
　alt. Yerukula [yeu], 390
Eruku Bhasha, *alt.* Yerukula [yeu], 390
Erushu, *alt. dial.* Arigidi [aqg], 154
Erúsú, *dial.* Arigidi [aqg], 154
Eruwa [erh], 159
Ervato-Ventuari, *dial.* Sanumá [xsu], 232
Erwan, *alt. dial.* Bokyi [bky], 156
Eryuan, *dial.* Bai, Central [bca], 326
Erzenka, *alt. dial.* Armenian [hye], 318
Erzerum, *alt. dial.* Armenian [hye], 318
Erzgebirgisch, *dial.* German, Standard [deu], 533
　dial. Saxon, Upper [sxu], 539
Erzia, *alt.* Erzya [myv], 554
Erzincan, *alt. dial.* Armenian [hye], 318
Erzurum, *alt. dial.* Armenian [hye], 318
Erzya [myv], 554
Es-Saare, *alt. dial.* Hun-Saare [dud], 162
Esa, *alt.* Esan [ish], 159
Esaaka, *alt.* Makhuwa-Saka [xsq], 147
　alt. dial. Makhuwa-Saka [xsq], 147
　alt. dial. Koti [eko], 147
Esakaji, *alt.* Nathembo [nte], 148
　alt. dial. Koti [eko], 147
Esambi Kipya, *alt. dial.* Songe [sop], 108
Esan [ish], 159
Esangaje, *alt. dial.* Koti [eko], 147

Esangaji, *alt. dial.* Koti [eko], 147
Esari, *dial.* Turkmen [tuk], 520, 442
Esaro, *alt.* Duriankere [dbn], 414
Esary, *alt. dial.* Turkmen [tuk], 442
Esaun, *dial.* Citak [txt], 413
Ese [mcq], 598
  dial. Arigidi [aqg], 154
Ese Eja, *alt.* Ese Ejja [ese], 222, 288
Ese Ejja [ese], 222, 288
Ese Exa, *alt.* Ese Ejja [ese], 222, 288
Ese'ejja, *alt.* Ese Ejja [ese], 288
Esel, *dial.* Bekwil [bkw], 58
Esfahani, *dial.* Farsi, Western [pes], 439
Eshan Nasu, *dial.* Yi, Eshan-Xinping [yiv], 347
Eshan-Xinping Yi, *see* Yi, Eshan-Xinping [yiv], 347
Eshira, *alt.* Sira [swj], 121
Eshirima, *alt.* Makhuwa-Shirima [vmk], 147
Eshisango, *alt.* Sangu [sbp], 204
Eshkashimi, *alt. dial.* Sanglechi-Ishkashimi [sgl], 317
Eshkashmi, *alt. dial.* Sanglechi-Ishkashimi [sgl], 513
Eshtehardi [esh], 438
Esiluyana, *alt.* Luyana [lyn], 214
Esimbi [ags], 61
Esimbowe, *alt.* Mbowe [mxo], 214
  alt. dial. Luyana [lyn], 214, 41
Esingee, *alt. dial.* Teke, Ibali [tek], 108
Esiriun, *alt.* Watubela [wah], 405
Eskimo, *pej. alt.* Inupiatun, North Alaskan [esi], 302, 238
  pej. alt. Inupiatun, Northwest Alaska [esk], 302
  pej. alt. Yupik, Central Siberian [ess], 507
Eskisehir, *dial.* Turkish [tur], 519, 521
Eso, *alt.* So [soc], 108
Español, *alt.* Spanish [spa], 560, 222, 243, 249, 251, 252, 256, 258, 274, 283, 284, 293, 308
Esperanto [epo], 536
Espiegle Bay, *alt.* Malua Bay [mll], 643
Essang, *dial.* Talaud [tld], 433
Essel, *alt. dial.* Bekwil [bkw], 58
Essele, *dial.* Eton [eto], 61
Esselen [esq], 300
Essequibo, *dial.* Skepi Creole Dutch [skw], 257
Essimbi, *alt.* Esimbi [ags], 61
Essin, *dial.* Bayot [bda], 180
Essouma, *alt.* Esuma [esm], 92

Estado de México Otomi, *see* Otomi, Estado de México [ots], 272
Estonian [est], 534, 534
Estonian Romani, *dial.* Romani, Baltic [rml], 550, 546
Estonian Sign Language [eso], 534
Estonian Swedish, *alt. dial.* Swedish [swe], 562
Estracharia, *dial.* Romani, Sinte [rmo], 539
Estrella, *dial.* Cabécar [cjp], 249
Estremenho, *dial.* Portuguese [por], 551
Esuku, *dial.* Akpes [ibe], 153
Esulalu, *dial.* Jola-Kasa [csk], 180
Esulit, *dial.* Ili'uun [ilu], 399
Esuma [esm], 92
Esumbu, *dial.* Lusengo [lse], 103
Esuulaalur, *alt. dial.* Jola-Kasa [csk], 180
Et-Hun, *alt. dial.* Hun-Saare [dud], 162
Et-Jiir, *alt. dial.* Kag-Fer-Jiir-Koor-Ror-Us-Zuksun [gel], 165
Et-Kag, *alt. dial.* Kag-Fer-Jiir-Koor-Ror-Us-Zuksun [gel], 165
Et-Maror, *alt. dial.* Kag-Fer-Jiir-Koor-Ror-Us-Zuksun [gel], 165
Et-Us, *alt. dial.* Kag-Fer-Jiir-Koor-Ror-Us-Zuksun [gel], 165
Et-Zuksun, *alt. dial.* Kag-Fer-Jiir-Koor-Ror-Us-Zuksun [gel], 165
Etapally Gondi, *dial.* Gondi, Southern [ggo], 363
Etapally Maria, *dial.* Maria [mrr], 375
Etebi [etb], 159
Etekwe, *alt.* Etkywan [ich], 159
Etelena, *alt.* Terêna [ter], 232
Eten [etx], 159
Ethiopian, *alt.* Amharic [amh], 113
Ethiopian Sign Language [eth], 114
Ethiopic, *alt.* Geez [gez], 115, 112
Etien, *alt.* Eten [etx], 159
Etija, *dial.* Orokaiva [ork], 620
Etkye, *alt. dial.* Kpan [kpk], 167
Etkywan [ich], 159
Etla Zapotec, *alt.* Zapotec, Mazaltepec [zpy], 278
  alt. Zapotec, Yareni [zae], 281
Etna Bay, *alt.* Semimi [etz], 422
Eto, *alt.* Giangan [bgi], 494
Etoh, *alt.* Atong [ato], 56
Etolo, *alt.* Edolo [etr], 598
Eton (Cameroon) [eto], 61
  Eton (Vanuatu) [etn], 641
  dial. Eton [etn], 641
Etongo, *dial.* Ipulo [ass], 63

Etono, *alt. dial.* Agwagwune [yay], 153
  alt. dial. Ubaghara [byc], 176
Etoro, *alt.* Edolo [etr], 598
Etossio, *alt.* Teso [teo], 213
Etsako, *alt.* Yekhee [ets], 177
Etsakor, *alt.* Yekhee [ets], 177
Etteittei, *pej. alt. dial.* Koti [eko], 147
Etulo [utr], 159
Etung, *alt.* Ejagham [etu], 60
Etuno, *alt. dial.* Agwagwune [yay], 153
  alt. dial. Ebira [igb], 158
Eturo, *alt.* Etulo [utr], 159
Euchavante, *alt.* Oti [oti], 231
Eue, *alt.* Éwé [ewe], 124
Eunda Kolonkadhi, *dial.* Ndonga [ndo], 150
Euphrates Cluster, *dial.* Arabic, Mesopotamian Spoken [acm], 442, 510
Europanto [eur], 531
European Oirat, *alt.* Kalmyk-Oirat [xal], 554
Europeanized Hebrew, *alt. dial.* Hebrew [heb], 444
Euskera, *alt.* Basque [eus], 559
Evadi, *alt.* Tsuvadi [tvd], 176
Evalue, *dial.* Nzema [nzi], 127
Evand, *alt.* Evant [bzz], 159, 61
Evant [bzz], 159, 61
Eve, *alt.* Éwé [ewe], 124, 207
Even [eve], 504
Evenki [evn], 332, 461, 504
Evhro, *pej. alt.* Uvbie [evh], 176
Eviia, *alt.* Bubi [buw], 120
Evji, *alt.* Duwai [dbp], 158
Evorra, *alt.* Purari [iar], 622
Evouzok, *dial.* Ewondo [ewo], 61
Evrie, *alt.* Uvbie [evh], 176
Ewage, *alt.* Ewage-Notu [nou], 598
Ewage-Notu [nou], 598
  dial. Ewage-Notu [nou], 598
Ewdokia, *dial.* Armenian [hye], 318
Éwé [ewe], 124, 207
Ewen, *alt.* Even [eve], 504
Ewenke, *alt.* Evenki [evn], 332
Ewenki, *alt.* Evenki [evn], 332, 504
Ewodi, *alt. dial.* Duala [dua], 60
Ewondo [ewo], 61
Ewota, *alt.* Bubia [bbx], 59
Ewumbonga, *alt. dial.* Mbembe, Cross River [mfn], 163
Ewundu, *alt.* Ewondo [ewo], 61
Extremaduran [ext], 560
Extremeño, *alt.* Extremaduran [ext], 560
Eyabida, *alt.* Emberá-Catío [cto], 245
Eyak [eya], 300

Eyan, *alt.* Denya [anv], 60
Eyansi, *alt.* Yansi [yns], 109
Eyanzi, *alt.* Yansi [yns], 109
Eye, *alt.* Eñepa [pbh], 311
Eza, *alt. dial.* Izi-Ezaa-Ikwo-Mgbo
[izi], 164
alt. dial. Sebat Bet Gurage [sgw],
118
Ezaa, *dial.* Izi-Ezaa-Ikwo-Mgbo
[izi], 164
Êzdîkî, *alt.* Kurdish, Northern
[kmr], 319
Ezei, *alt. dial.* Agwagwune [yay], 153
Ezekwe, *alt.* Uzekwe [eze], 176
Ezelle, *alt. dial.* Jere [jer], 165
Ezeshio, *alt.* Kamakan [vkm], 228
Ezha, *dial.* Sebat Bet Gurage
[sgw], 118
Ezo, *alt. dial.* Ainu [ain], 446, 503
Ezopong, *alt. dial.* Mbembe, Cross
River [mfn], 163
Fa', *dial.* Fe'fe' [fmp], 61
Fa D'ambu [fab], 111
Fa Saposa, *alt. dial.* Saposa [sps],
623
Fa-C-Aka, *alt.* Aka [soh], 187
Faa Ceta, *alt.* Hmwaveke [mrk], 584
Faake, *alt.* Phake [phk], 384
Faala, *alt. dial.* Karanga [kth], 82
Faale-Piyew, *dial.* Tupuri [tui], 87
Fa'awa, *alt.* Pa'a [pqa], 173
Fabla Aragonesa, *alt.* Aragonese
[arg], 558
Fablas, *dial.* Haitian Creole French
[hat], 258
Facé, *alt. dial.* Sula [szn], 404
Facei, *alt. dial.* Sula [szn], 404
Fachara, *alt.* Cara [cfd], 156
Fachi, *dial.* Kanuri, Bilma [bms], 152
Fada, *alt.* Biafada [bif], 131
Fada Ngurma, *dial.* Fulfulde,
Northeastern Burkina Faso
[fuh], 51
Fadan Wate, *alt.* Ninzo [nin], 171
Fadashi, *dial.* Berta [wti], 113, 189
Fadawa, *dial.* Kanuri, Central
[knc], 166, 63, 81, 191
Fadicca, *alt.* Nobiin [fia], 110
alt. dial. Nobiin [fia], 194
Fadicha, *alt.* Nobiin [fia], 110
alt. dial. Nobiin [fia], 194
Fadija, *alt.* Nobiin [fia], 110
alt. dial. Nobiin [fia], 194
Fadiro, *alt.* Bambassi [myf], 113
Fadjulu, *alt. dial.* Bari [bfa], 188, 210
Fadyut-Palmerin, *alt. dial.* Serer-
Sine [srr], 122
dial. Serer-Sine [srr], 182
Faetar, *alt. dial.* Franco-Provençal
[frp], 543

Faeto, *dial.* Franco-Provençal
[frp], 543
Faga-Uvea, *alt.* Uvean, West
[uve], 585
Fagani [faf], 636
dial. Fagani [faf], 636
Fagauvea, *alt.* Uvean, West
[uve], 585
Faghani, *alt.* Fagani [faf], 636
Fagnia, *alt.* Fania [fni], 80
Fagudu, *dial.* Sula [szn], 404
Fagululu, *alt.* Molima [mox], 614
Faia, *dial.* Kirikiri [kiy], 417
Faire Atta, *see* Atta, Faire [azt], 491
Fairi, *dial.* Biak [bhw], 412
Faishang, *dial.* Miya [mkf], 170
Faita [faj], 598
Faiwol [fai], 598
Faiwolmin, *alt.* Faiwol [fai], 598
dial. Faiwol [fai], 598
Faiyava, *dial.* Bwaidoka [bwd], 596
Fajelu, *alt. dial.* Bari [bfa], 188, 210
Fajulu, *alt. dial.* Bari [bfa], 210
Fak, *alt.* Lefa [lfa], 65
Fakanchi, *alt. dial.* Kag-Fer-Jiir-
Koor-Ror-Us-Zuksun [gel], 165
Fakanci, *alt.* Kag-Fer-Jiir-Koor-Ror-
Us-Zuksun [gel], 165
Fakara, *alt.* Cara [cfd], 156
Fakkanci, *alt.* Kag-Fer-Jiir-Koor-
Ror-Us-Zuksun [gel], 165
Fala [fax], 560
alt. dial. Karanga [kth], 82
Falahu, *alt. dial.* Sula [szn], 404
Falam, *alt.* Chin, Falam [flm], 463,
321
Falam Chin, *see* Chin, Falam
[flm], 463, 321, 358
Fali [fli], 159
alt. Lonwolwol [crc], 643
Fali du Bele-Fere, *alt. dial.* Fali,
South [fal], 61
Fali du Peske-Bori, *alt. dial.* Fali,
North [fll], 61
Fali Kangou, *alt. dial.* Fali, South
[fal], 61
Fali of Baissa [fah], 160
Fali of Jilbu, *alt.* Zizilivakan
[ziz], 74, 178
Fali of Kiriya, *dial.* Kamwe
[hig], 166
Fali of Mijilu, *dial.* Kamwe
[hig], 166
Fali of Mubi, *alt.* Fali [fli], 159
Fali of Muchella, *alt.* Fali
[fli], 159
Fali, North [fll], 61
Fali, South [fal], 61
Fali-Bele, *alt. dial.* Fali, South
[fal], 61

Fali-Bossoum, *alt. dial.* Fali, North
[fll], 61
Fali-Dourbeye, *alt. dial.* Fali, North
[fll], 61
Fali-Tinguelin, *dial.* Fali, South
[fal], 61
Fall Indians, *alt.* Gros Ventre
[ats], 301
Fallam, *alt.* Chin, Falam [flm], 463,
321, 358
Fallani, *alt.* Chaldean Neo-Aramaic
[cld], 443
Falor, *alt.* Palor [fap], 181
Fam [fam], 160
Fama-Teis-Kua, *dial.* Krongo
[kgo], 192
Fan-Foron-Heikpang, *dial.* Berom
[bom], 155
Fana, *alt.* Fania [fni], 80
Fanagalo [fng], 185, 213, 216
Fanakalo, *pej. alt.* Fanagalo
[fng], 185, 213, 216
Fanating, *alt.* Kafoa [kpu], 407
Fanawbuid, *alt.* Tawbuid, Eastern
[bnj], 502
alt. Tawbuid, Western [twb], 502
Fanekolo, *pej. alt.* Fanagalo [fng],
185, 213, 216
Fang (Cameroon) [fak], 61
Fang (Equatorial Guinea) [fan], 111,
61, 88, 120
dial. Fang [fan], 61
Fangatau, *dial.* Tuamotuan
[pmt], 581
Fania [fni], 80
Faniagara, *dial.* Wara [wbf], 55
Fanian, *alt.* Fania [fni], 80
Fanic, *dial.* Dedua [ded], 596
Fannai, *dial.* Mizo [lus], 376
Fante, *dial.* Akan [aka], 123
Fantera, *dial.* Nafaanra [nfr], 126
Fanti, *alt. dial.* Akan [aka], 123
Fanting, *alt.* Lonwolwol [crc], 643
Fantuan, *alt. dial.* Tyap [kcg], 176
Fanya, *alt.* Fania [fni], 80
Fanyan, *alt.* Fania [fni], 80
Far Eastern Manggarai, *alt.*
Riung [riu], 409
Far Western Muria, *see* Muria, Far
Western [fmu], 376
Faran, *alt.* Firan [fir], 160
Faranah, *alt.* Maninka, Sankaran
[msc], 129
Faranga, *dial.* Kendeje [klf], 82
Farangao, *alt.* Balangao [blw], 492
Faranyao, *alt.* Mairasi [zrs], 419
Fare, *dial.* Lese [les], 102
Farefare [gur], 124
Faroese [fao], 533
Fars, Northwestern [faz], 439

Fjaalib, *dial.* Balanta-Ganja [bjt], 179
Fkar, *dial.* Tehit [kps], 424
Flaai Taal, *alt.* Tsotsitaal [fly], 186
Flakkees, *dial.* Zeeuws [zea], 549
Flamand, *alt.* Vlaams [vls], 531, 538, 549
Flathead-Kalispel, *alt.* Kalispel-Pend D'oreille [fla], 302
Flemish, *alt.* Vlaams [vls], 538, 549
Fleo, *dial.* Wè Southern [gxx], 95
Flinders Island [fln], 570
Florida Islands, *alt.* Gela [nlg], 636
Florutz, *alt. dial.* Mócheno [mhn], 545
Floup, *alt.* Ejamat [eja], 131, 180
Flowery Lachi, *alt. dial.* Lachi [lbt], 338
Flowery Lisu, *alt. dial.* Lisu [lis], 339, 465
Flowery Lolo, *alt.* Mantsi [nty], 525
Flowery Miao, *alt.* Hmong, Northeastern Dian [hmd], 334
Flup, *alt.* Ejamat [eja], 131, 180
Fluplands, *dial.* Zeeuws [zea], 549
Fluvial, *dial.* Jola-Kasa [csk], 180
Fly River, *dial.* Tabo [knv], 626
Fly Taal, *alt.* Tsotsitaal [fly], 186
Fo, *alt.* Fon [fon], 43, 207
  alt. So [sox], 72
Foau [flh], 415
Fobano, *alt. dial.* Aragonese [arg], 558
Fodara, *dial.* Senoufo, Cebaara [sef], 94
Foe, *alt.* Foi [foi], 599
Fogbe, *alt.* Fon [fon], 43, 207
Fogi, *dial.* Buru [mhs], 397
Fohr-Amrum, *alt. dial.* Frisian, Northern [frr], 538
Foi [foi], 599
  alt. Edopi [dbf], 414
  alt. Iau [tmu], 415
  dial. Iau [tmu], 415
Foja, *alt.* Abinomn [bsa], 410
Folepi, *dial.* Mundani [mnf], 68
Folopa [ppo], 599
Foma [fom], 99
Fomopea, *alt.* Ngwe [nwe], 70
Fon [fon], 43, 207
Fon-Gbe, *alt.* Fon [fon], 207
Fondanti, *alt. dial.* Fe'fe' [fmp], 61
Fondebougou, *dial.* Senoufo, Tagwana [tgw], 95
Fondjomekwet, *alt. dial.* Fe'fe' [fmp], 61
Fong, *dial.* Ewondo [ewo], 61
Fongbe, *alt.* Fon [fon], 43
Fongoro [fgr], 80
Foni, *alt.* Pa'a [pqa], 173
Fonnu, *alt.* Fon [fon], 43, 207

Fontem, *alt.* Ngwe [nwe], 70
Fonyi, *dial.* Jola-Fonyi [dyo], 180
Foochow, *alt. dial.* Chinese, Min Dong [cdo], 330, 508, 514
  dial. Chinese, Min Dong [cdo], 324, 454
Foodo [fod], 44
Foolo, *dial.* Senoufo, Djimini [dyi], 95
Fopo-Bua, *dial.* Grebo, Northern [gbo], 138
For, *alt.* Fur [fvr], 190, 80
Fora, *alt.* Fur [fvr], 190
  dial. Balanta-Kentohe [ble], 130
Foraba, *alt.* Folopa [ppo], 599
Forak [frq], 599
Foran, *alt.* Wagi [fad], 630
Forcalquieren, *alt. dial.* Provençal [prv], 537
Fordata [frd], 398
Fordata-Larat I, *dial.* Fordata [frd], 398
Fordata-Larat II, *dial.* Fordata [frd], 398
Fordunga, *alt.* Fur [fvr], 190
Fore [for], 599
Foredafa, *alt. dial.* Yaminahua [yaa], 293
Foreke Dschang, *alt. dial.* Yemba [ybb], 74
Forest Bira, *alt.* Bila [bip], 98
Forest Enets, *see* Enets, Forest [enf], 504
Forest Maninka, *see* Maninka, Forest [myq], 94
Forest Maninka, *alt. dial.* Wojenaka [jod], 95
Forest Nivaclé, *dial.* Nivaclé [cag], 285, 220
Forest Yurak, *dial.* Nenets [yrk], 506
Formosan, *alt.* Siraya [fos], 512
  alt. dial. Chinese, Min Nan [nan], 511
Fornió, *alt.* Fulniô [fun], 226
Forok, *alt.* Fur [fvr], 190
Foron, *alt.* Firan [fir], 160
Fort Yukon Gwich'in, *dial.* Gwich'in [gwi], 237, 301
Forta, *alt.* Fur [fvr], 190
Fortsenal [frt], 641
Fotouni, *alt.* Fe'fe' [fmp], 61
  alt. dial. Fe'fe' [fmp], 61
Fotuna, *alt. dial.* Futuna-Aniwa [fut], 641
Foula Fouta, *alt.* Pular [fuf], 130, 143
Foulfoulde, *alt.* Fulfulde, Adamawa [fub], 61, 80
Four, *alt.* Fur [fvr], 80

Fourgoula, *dial.* Senoufo, Tagwana [tgw], 95
Fouta Dyalon, *alt.* Pular [fuf], 130, 143, 182, 184
Foute, *alt.* Vute [vut], 73
Fowe, *dial.* Siane [snp], 624
Fox, *dial.* Mesquakie [sac], 304
Foya, *alt.* Abinomn [bsa], 410
Fraase, *alt.* Balanta-Ganja [bjt], 179
Frafra, *alt.* Farefare [gur], 124
  alt. Ninkare [gur], 53
  dial. Ninkare [gur], 53
Franc-Comtois, *dial.* French [fra], 536
Français, *alt.* French [fra], 536, 237, 531, 544, 548, 562
Français Acadien, *alt.* French, Cajun [frc], 300
Franche-Comtois, *dial.* French [fra], 562
Francisco León Zoque, *see* Zoque, Francisco León [zos], 282
Franco-Ontarien, *alt. dial.* French [fra], 237
Franco-Provençal [frp], 536, 543, 562
Franconian, *alt.* Mainfränkisch [vmf], 539
Fränkisch, *alt.* Frankish [frk], 538
Frankish [frk], 538
  alt. Luxembourgeois [ltz], 546, 537
Frans Vlaams, *alt. dial.* Vlaams [vls], 549
  dial. Vlaams [vls], 538
Frase, *alt.* Balanta-Kentohe [ble], 130
Frassilongo, *dial.* Mócheno [mhn], 545
French [fra], 536, 39, 44, 51, 55, 61, 75, 80, 87, 88, 93, 99, 109, 111, 120, 129, 140, 143, 145, 146, 151, 178, 180, 182, 207, 209, 237, 252, 253, 258, 259, 295, 325, 453, 529, 531, 544, 546, 548, 562, 565, 581, 584, 641, 647
French Cree, *alt.* Michif [crg], 305, 239
French Guianese Creole French, *alt.* Guianese Creole French [gcr], 252
French Sign Language [fsl], 536, 207
French, Cajun [frc], 300
Fribourgois, *alt. dial.* French [fra], 562
Fries, *alt.* Frisian, Western [fri], 548
Frioulan, *alt.* Friulian [fur], 544
Frioulian, *alt.* Friulian [fur], 544
Frisian, Eastern [frs], 538
Frisian, Northern [frr], 538
Frisian, Western [fri], 548

Friulano, *alt.* Friulian [fur], 544
Friulian [fur], 544
Frysk, *alt.* Frisian, Western [fri], 548
FSL, *alt.* French Sign Language
   [fsl], 536
   alt. Philippine Sign Language
   [psp], 500
Ftour, *alt.* Hide [xed], 162
   alt. dial. Hdi [xed], 62
Fu, *alt.* Bafut [bfd], 56
Fu Khla, *alt.* Phula [phh], 525, 342
Fu-Guang, *dial.* Chinese, Gan
   [gan], 329
Fucaka, *alt.* Pa'a [pqa], 173
Fuchow, *alt. dial.* Chinese, Min
   Dong [cdo], 330, 508, 514
Fuch'ye, *alt.* Nung [nun], 466, 341
Fu'da, *alt. dial.* Ghomálá' [bbj], 62
Fufula, *dial.* Wali [wlx], 128
Fuga of Jimma, *dial.* Yemsa
   [jnj], 119
Fugar, *alt. dial.* Yekhee [ets], 177
Fujian, *alt. dial.* Chinese, Min Nan
   [nan], 324, 508, 514
   dial. Chinese, Min Nan [nan], 391
Fujianese, *alt. dial.* Chinese, Min
   Nan [nan], 454
Fukac, *dial.* Mape [mlh], 612
Fukien, *alt. dial.* Chinese, Min Nan
   [nan], 514
Fukienese, *alt. dial.* Chinese, Min
   Nan [nan], 508
   dial. Chinese, Min Nan [nan], 454
Ful, *alt.* Fulfulde, Adamawa [fub], 61,
   80
Fula, *alt.* Fulfulde, Adamawa
   [fub], 61, 160
   alt. Fulfulde, Central-Eastern Niger
   [fuq], 151
   alt. Fulfulde, Western Niger
   [fuh], 151
   alt. Koromfé [kfz], 52
Fula Forro, *alt. dial.* Pulaar
   [fuc], 131
Fula Fulbe, *alt.* Fulfulde, Adamawa
   [fub], 80
Fula Peta, *dial.* Pular [fuf], 130
Fula Preto, *alt. dial.* Pulaar
   [fuc], 130, 131
Fulacunda, *dial.* Pulaar [fuc], 181,
   122, 130, 131
Fulajon Kan, *alt.* Kakabe
   [kke], 129
Fulakunda, *alt. dial.* Pulaar [fuc],
   181, 122, 130, 131
Fulani, *alt.* Fulfulde, Adamawa [fub],
   160
   alt. Fulfulde, Borgu [fue], 207
   alt. Fulfulde, Central-Eastern Niger
   [fuq], 151

alt. Fulfulde, Western Niger
   [fuh], 151
alt. Pulaar [fuc], 122
Fulanke, *dial.* Maninkakan, Kita
   [mwk], 143
Fulatanchi, *alt.* Fulfulde, Adamawa
   [fub], 160
Fulbe, *alt.* Fulfulde, Adamawa
   [fub], 61
   alt. Fulfulde, Central-Eastern Niger
   [fuq], 151
   alt. Fulfulde, Kano-Katsina-Bororro
   [fuv], 61, 80
   alt. Fulfulde, Maasina [ffm], 125
   alt. Fulfulde, Western Niger
   [fuh], 151
   alt. Pular [fuf], 130, 184
Fulbe Jeeri, *alt.* Pulaar [fuc], 122
   alt. dial. Pulaar [fuc], 181, 143
Fulbe-Borgu, *alt.* Fulfulde, Borgu
   [fue], 44
Fulero, *alt.* Fuliiru [flr], 99
Fulfulde, *alt.* Fulfulde, Adamawa
   [fub], 61
   alt. Fulfulde, Gorgal [fuh], 44
Fulfulde Jalon, *alt.* Pular [fuf], 130,
   143
Fulfulde Pulaar, *alt.* Pulaar [fuc],
   130
Fulfulde Western Niger, *alt.*
   Fulfulde, Gorgal [fuh], 44
Fulfulde, Adamawa [fub], 61, 80,
   160, 190
Fulfulde, Bagirmi [fui], 80, 75
Fulfulde, Benin-Togo [fue], 160
Fulfulde, Borgu [fue], 44, 207
Fulfulde, Central-Eastern Niger
   [fuq], 151
Fulfulde, Gorgal [fuh], 44
Fulfulde, Kano-Katsina-Bororro
   [fuv], 61, 80
Fulfulde, Maasina [ffm], 143, 125
Fulfulde, Nigerian [fuv], 160
**Fulfulde, Northeastern Burkina
   Faso** [fuh], 51
Fulfulde, Western Niger
   [fuh], 151
Fulfulde-Pulaar, *alt.* Pulaar
   [fuc], 122, 131
Fuliiru [flr], 99
Fuliru, *alt.* Fuliiru [flr], 99
Fulkunda, *alt. dial.* Pulaar [fuc], 181,
   122, 130, 131
Fullo Fuuta, *alt.* Pular [fuf], 130,
   143, 182, 184
Fulniô [fun], 226
   dial. Fulniô [fun], 226
Fulse, *alt.* Koromfé [kfz], 52
   dial. Koromfé [kfz], 52
Fuluka, *alt.* Kusu [ksv], 101

Fulup, *alt.* Ejamat [eja], 131, 180
Fum [fum], 160
Fuma, *alt.* Foma [fom], 99
Funafuti, *alt. dial.* Tuvaluan
   [tvl], 640
Funai, *dial.* Helong [heg], 407
Fundi, *dial.* Swahili [swh], 136
Fung, *alt. dial.* Tunen [baz], 72
Fungom, *dial.* Mmen [bfm], 67
Fungor, *alt.* Ko [fuj], 192
Fungur, *alt.* Ko [fuj], 192
Fungwa [ula], 160
Fungwe, *alt. dial.* Tumbuka
   [tum], 141
   dial. Tumbuka [tum], 215
Funika, *alt.* Mfinu [zmf], 104
Funsile, *alt.* Paasaal [sig], 127
Fur [fvr], 190, 80
Fura-Pawa, *alt.* El Molo [elo], 132
Furakang, *alt.* Fur [fvr], 190
Furan, *alt.* Wagi [fad], 630
Furati, *alt.* Arabic, Mesopotamian
   Spoken [acm], 442, 510
Furawi, *alt.* Fur [fvr], 190
Furlan, *alt.* Friulian [fur], 544
Furniô, *alt.* Fulniô [fun], 226
Fursum, *dial.* Miya [mkf], 170
Furu [fuu], 99, 75
   alt. Bikya [byb], 58
   alt. Bishuo [bwh], 59
   alt. Busuu [bju], 59
Furupagha, *dial.* Izon [ijc], 164
Fusap, *alt. dial.* Ghomálá' [bbj], 62
Fut, *alt.* Bafut [bfd], 56
Futa Fula, *alt.* Pular [fuf], 130, 143,
   182, 184
Futa Jallon, *alt.* Pular [fuf], 130,
   143, 182, 184
Futa Toro, *alt. dial.* Pulaar [fuc], 130
Fute, *alt.* Vute [vut], 177
Futu, *dial.* Kamwe [hig], 166
Futuna, East [fud], 647, 584
Futuna-Aniwa [fut], 641
Futunian, *alt.* Futuna, East
   [fud], 647, 584
Fuumu, *dial.* Teke-Fuumu [ifm], 90
Fuuta Jalon, *alt.* Pular [fuf], 130,
   143, 182, 184
Fuyug [fuy], 599
Fuyuge, *alt.* Fuyug [fuy], 599
Fuyughe, *alt.* Fuyug [fuy], 599
Fuzhou, *alt. dial.* Chinese, Min Dong
   [cdo], 454
   dial. Chinese, Min Dong [cdo], 330,
   508, 514
Fwa-Goumak, *alt.* Kumak
   [nee], 584
Fwâi [fwa], 584
Fwe [fwe], 149
Fyam [pym], 160

Galambe, *alt.* Galambu [glo], 160
Galambi, *alt.* Galambu [glo], 160
Galambu [glo], 160
Galamjina, *dial.* Jibu [jib], 165
Galancho, *alt.* Chechen [che], 553
Galavda, *alt.* Glavda [glw], 161, 62
Galavi, *alt.* Ghayavi [bmk], 600
Galcha, *alt.* Tajiki [tgk], 513
Galebagla, *alt. dial.* Sisaala,
   Tumulung [sil], 127
Galeg, *dial.* Awad Bing [bcu], 591
Galego, *alt.* Galician [glg], 560, 551
Galela [gbi], 398
Galembi, *alt.* Galambu [glo], 160
Galera, *dial.* Nambikuára, Southern
   [nab], 230
Galeshi, *dial.* Gilaki [glk], 439
Galeya [gar], 599
   alt. dial. Galeya [gar], 599
Galgadungu, *alt.* Kalkutung
   [ktg], 572
Galgaduun, *alt.* Kalkutung
   [ktg], 572
Gali, *alt.* Ronji [roe], 623
Galibi, *alt.* Carib [car], 311, 252, 257
Galibí, *alt.* Carib [car], 226, 295
Galice [gce], 300
Galician [glg], 560, 551
   dial. Portuguese [por], 551
   dial. Romani, Carpathian [rmc], 542,
   550, 551
Galigalu, *alt.* Lishanid Noshan
   [aij], 445
Galiglu, *alt.* Hulaulá [huy], 445
Galihalu, *alt.* Lishán Didán [trg], 445
Galila, *dial.* Aari [aiz], 112
Galim, *alt.* Suga [sgi], 72
Galits, *dial.* Karaim [kdr], 546
Galke, *alt.* Ndai [gke], 69
Galla, *pej. alt.* Borana [gax], 132
   pej. alt. Oromo, Borana-Arsi-Guji
   [gax], 117
   pej. alt. Oromo, West Central
   [gaz], 118
Gallab, *alt.* Daasanach [dsh], 114
Galle Gurung, *alt.* Ghale, Southern
   [ghe], 471
Gallego, *alt.* Galician [glg], 560, 551
Galligna, *pej. alt.* Oromo, Borana-
   Arsi-Guji [gax], 117
Gallinas, *alt.* Vai [vai], 139, 184
Gallines, *alt.* Vai [vai], 139, 184
Gallinoméro, *alt.* Pomo, Southern
   [peq], 307
Gallinya, *pej. alt.* Oromo, Borana-
   Arsi-Guji [gax], 117
Gällivare Finnish, *dial.* Finnish,
   Tornedalen [fit], 561
Gallo, *dial.* French [fra], 536
Galloa, *alt. dial.* Myene [mye], 121

Gallong, *alt.* Adi, Galo [adl], 353
Gallurese, *alt.* Sardinian, Gallurese
   [sdn], 545
Gallurese Sardinian, *see*
   Sardinian, Gallurese [sdn], 545
Galo Adi, *see* Adi, Galo [adl], 353
Galoa, *alt. dial.* Myene [mye], 121
Galole, *alt.* Galoli [gal], 350
Galoleng, *alt.* Talur [ilw], 404
Galoli [gal], 350
   dial. Galoli [gal], 350
Galoma, *alt. dial.* Keapara [khz], 605
Galong, *alt.* Adi, Galo [adl], 353
Galos, *alt.* Chilisso [clh], 484
Galu, *alt.* Dia [dia], 597
   alt. Sinagen [siu], 624
Galua, *alt. dial.* Myene [mye], 121
Galuba, *alt.* Daasanach [dsh], 114
Galubwa, *dial.* Dobu [dob], 597
Galumpang, *alt.* Kalumpang
   [kli], 429
Galvaxdaxa, *alt.* Glavda [glw], 161,
   62
Galwa, *dial.* Myene [mye], 121
Gam, *alt.* Dong, Northern [doc], 331
   alt. Dong, Southern [kmc], 331
   alt. dial. Kwang [kvi], 82
Gama, *dial.* Bamu [bcf], 592
Gamadia, *dial.* Gujarati [guj], 363
Gamadoudou, *alt.* Wagawaga
   [wgw], 630
   dial. Wagawaga [wgw], 630
Gamaewe, *dial.* Wipi [gdr], 632
Gamai, *alt.* Borei [gai], 594
Gamale, *alt.* Kham, Gamale
   [kgj], 473
Gamale Kham, *see* Kham, Gamale
   [kgj], 473
Gamargu, *dial.* Wandala [mfi], 73,
   177
Gamati, *alt.* Gamit [gbl], 361
Gamawa, *alt.* Ngamo [nbh], 171
Gamb-Lai, *alt.* Ngambay [sba], 69
Gamba, *alt.* Belanda Viri [bvi], 189
   alt. Ngambay [sba], 85, 69
Gambadi, *dial.* Kunja [pep], 608
Gambai, *alt.* Ngambay [sba], 69
   dial. Tikar [tik], 72
Gambalamam, *alt.* Kumbainggar
   [kgs], 572
Gambar Leere, *alt. dial.* Saya
   [say], 174
Gambaye, *alt.* Ngambay [sba], 85,
   69
Gambera [gma], 570
   dial. Wunambal [wub], 578
Gamberre, *alt.* Gambera [gma], 570
Gambian Wolof, *see* Wolof,
   Gambian [wof], 122
Gamblai, *alt.* Ngambay [sba], 85

Gambo, *alt.* Nafaanra [nfr], 126
Gamboura, *dial.* Bana [bcw], 57
Gambre, *alt.* Gambera [gma], 570
Gamdugun, *dial.* Mina [hna], 67
Gamei, *alt.* Borei [gai], 594
Gamergou, *alt. dial.* Wandala
   [mfi], 73
Gamergu, *alt. dial.* Wandala
   [mfi], 73, 177
Gameta, *alt. dial.* Galeya [gar], 599
Gameti, *alt.* Gamit [gbl], 361
Gamgan, *alt.* Ngangam [gng], 46
Gamgre, *alt.* Gambera [gma], 570
Gamila, *dial.* Boro [bwo], 114
Gamilaraay [kld], 570
Gamilaroi, *alt.* Gamilaraay [kld], 570
Gamit [gbl], 361
Gamith, *alt.* Gamit [gbl], 361
Gamiya, *alt. dial.* Migaama [mmy],
   84
Gamkonora [gak], 398
Gammon, *alt.* Shelta [sth], 543
Gamo, *alt.* Ngamo [nbh], 171
   dial. Gamo-Gofa-Dawro [gmo], 114
   dial. Gamo-Ningi [bte], 160
Gamo-Gofa-Dawro [gmo], 114
Gamo-Ningi [bte], 160
Gamor, *alt.* Kamu [xmu], 572
Gamta, *alt.* Gamit [gbl], 361
Gamti, *alt.* Gamit [gbl], 361
   dial. Mawchi [mke], 375
Gamuso, *alt.* Tokano [zuh], 628
Gan, *alt.* Beng [nhb], 92
   alt. Chinese, Gan [gan], 329
   alt. Kaansa [gna], 51
Gan Chinese, *see* Chinese, Gan
   [gan], 329
‖Gana [gnk], 46
G‖ana, *alt.* ‖Gana [gnk], 46
Gana [gnq], 456
   dial. Lere [gnh], 168
Gana', *alt.* Gana [gnq], 456
G‖ana-Khwe, *alt.* ‖Gana [gnk], 46
Ganaan, *dial.* Kado [kdv], 464, 337,
   450
Ganádi, *dial.* Shua [shg], 48
Ganadugu, *dial.* Bamanankan
   [bam], 141
Ganagawa, *alt.* Dibo [dio], 157
G‖anakhwe, *dial.* ‖Gana [gnk], 46
Ganalbingu, *dial.* Djinba [djb], 570
Ganan, *alt. dial.* Kado [kdv], 464,
   337, 450
Ganang-Faishang, *dial.* Izere
   [fiz], 164
Gananwa, *dial.* Sotho, Northern
   [nso], 186
Ganaq, *alt.* Gana [gnq], 456
Ganati, *alt.* Kenati [gat], 606
Ganawuri, *alt.* Eten [etx], 159

Ganching, *dial.* Garo [grt], 362
Ganda [lug], 210
  alt. Ga'anda [gqa], 160
Ganda-Kiaka, *dial.* Haya [hay], 199
Gandanju, *alt.* Kanju [kbe], 572
Gandju, *alt.* Kanju [kbe], 572
Gandua, *dial.* Wawa [www], 73
!Gã!ne, *alt. dial.* Seroa [kqu], 186
Gane [gzn], 398
  alt. Kaansa [gna], 51
Ganet, *alt. dial.* Tamahaq, Tahaggart [thv], 37, 139, 152
Gang, *alt.* Acholi [ach], 210, 187
  alt. dial. Penan, Western [pne], 460, 325
Ganga, *alt.* Bushoong [buf], 98
Gangadi, *dial.* Garhwali [gbm], 360
Gangai, *alt.* Bagheli [bfy], 354, 468
Gangam, *alt.* Ngangam [gng], 209
Gangapari, *dial.* Awadhi [awa], 354, 468
Gangapariya, *alt. dial.* Garhwali [gbm], 360
!Gã!nge, *dial.* Seroa [kqu], 186
Gangela, *alt.* Nyemba [nba], 41
Ganggalida [gcd], 570
Ganggalita, *alt.* Ganggalida [gcd], 570
Ganglau [ggl], 599
Gangte [gnb], 361, 463
Ganguela, *alt.* Nyemba [nba], 41
Ganguella, *alt.* Nyemba [nba], 41
Gangulu [gnl], 570
Gangum, *alt.* Ngangam [gng], 209
Gani, *alt.* Gane [gzn], 398
Gani-Khwe, *alt. dial.* Khwe [xuu], 47
Ganja, *alt.* Narak [nac], 617
  alt. dial. Balanta-Ganja [bjt], 179
  dial. Azerbaijani, North [azj], 319
Ganjawle, *alt. dial.* Kachama-Ganjule [kcx], 115
Ganjule, *dial.* Kachama-Ganjule [kcx], 115
Gankui, *dial.* Oroqen [orh], 341
Ganongga, *alt.* Ghanongga [ghn], 636
Gansu, *alt. dial.* Dungan [dng], 449
Ganta, *dial.* Kachama-Ganjule [kcx], 115
Gante, *alt.* Gangte [gnb], 361, 463
Gants [gao], 599
Ganung-Rawang, *alt.* Rawang [raw], 466, 385
Ganwari, *alt.* Sadri [sck], 385
Ganza [gza], 115
  alt. dial. Gumuz [guk], 191
Ganzi [gnz], 75
  dial. Ganzi [gnz], 75
Ganzo, *alt.* Ganza [gza], 115

Ganzu, *dial.* Dungan [dng], 449
Gao [gga], 636
  alt. dial. Gelao [gio], 333
Gao Songhay, *alt.* Songhay, Koyraboro Senni [ses], 144
Gaoidhealg, *alt.* Gaelic, Hiberno-Scottish [ghc], 565
Gaolei, *dial.* Chinese, Yue [yue], 331
Gaoli, *dial.* Bundeli [bns], 357
Gaoyang, *alt. dial.* Chinese, Yue [yue], 331
Gapa, *alt.* Gapapaiwa [pwg], 599
Gapapaiwa [pwg], 599
Gapelta, *alt.* Fulfulde, Adamawa [fub], 61
Gapian, *alt. dial.* Provençal [prv], 537
Gapinji, *alt.* Pinji [pic], 121
Gapun, *alt.* Taiap [gpn], 626
Gar, *alt. dial.* Mnong, Eastern [mng], 525
  dial. Bada [bau], 154
  dial. Guruntum-Mbaaru [grd], 161
Gar Duguri, *dial.* Duguri [dbm], 158
Gara, *alt.* Lohar, Gade [gda], 372
Garadjiri, *alt.* Karadjeri [gbd], 572
Garadyari, *alt.* Karadjeri [gbd], 572
Garaganza, *alt. dial.* Nyamwezi [nym], 203
Garaghwaghi, *alt.* Haigwai [hgw], 601
Garaka, *alt.* Bada [bau], 154
Garama, *alt.* Murrinh-Patha [mwf], 574
Garandala, *dial.* Ngura [nbx], 575
Garap, *dial.* Kim [kia], 82
Garas, *alt.* Lohar, Lahul [lhl], 372
Garasia, Adiwasi [gas], 362
Garasia, Rajput [gra], 362
Garawa [gbc], 570
  alt. dial. Kapin [tbx], 605
Garawgino, *dial.* Bidiyo [bid], 79
Garbabi, *dial.* Jibu [jib], 165
Gard'are, *alt.* Karadjeri [gbd], 572
Gardenese, *dial.* Ladin [lld], 544
Gardudjara, *alt. dial.* Martu Wangka [mpj], 574
Gardulla, *alt.* Dirasha [gdl], 114
Garea, *alt.* Galeya [gar], 599
  alt. dial. Galeya [gar], 599
Garhwali [gbm], 360
Gari, *alt.* Ghari [gri], 636
  alt. dial. Garreh-Ajuran [ggh], 133
Garia, *alt.* Sumau [six], 626
  alt. dial. Uare [ksj], 629
Gariera, *alt.* Kariyarra [vka], 572
Garifuna [cab], 258, 221, 253, 282
Garífuna, *alt.* Garifuna [cab], 258, 253, 282
Garig, *dial.* Garig-Ilgar [ilg], 570

Garig-Ilgar [ilg], 570
Garihe, *dial.* Uare [ksj], 629
Garkin, *dial.* Lezgi [lez], 555
Garko, *alt.* Karko [kko], 191
Garlali, *alt. dial.* Ngura [nbx], 575
Garmalangga, *dial.* Jarnango [jay], 571
Garme, *alt.* Acheron [acz], 187
Garmiyani, *dial.* Kurdish, Central [ckb], 443
Garo [grt], 362, 321
  alt. dial. Kafa [kbr], 116
  alt. dial. Kimaragang [kqr], 457
Garoua, *alt. dial.* Fulfulde, Adamawa [fub], 61, 80
  dial. Bata [bta], 155
Garre [gex], 184
  alt. dial. Garreh-Ajuran [ggh], 133
Garreh, *dial.* Garreh-Ajuran [ggh], 133
Garreh-Ajuran [ggh], 133
Garrow, *alt.* Garo [grt], 362, 321
Garrusi, *dial.* Kurdish, Southern [sdh], 440
Garrwa, *alt.* Garawa [gbc], 570
Garua, *alt. dial.* Bata [bta], 155
  alt. dial. Bola [bnp], 594
Garuh, *alt.* Nobonob [gaw], 618
Garus [gyb], 599
Garuwahi, *alt.* Gweda [grw], 601
Garwa, *alt.* Kalami [gwc], 485
Garwe, *dial.* Ndau [ndc], 216
Garwi, *alt.* Kalami [gwc], 485
Gascon [gsc], 537
  alt. Gascon, Aranese [gsc], 560
Gascon, Aranese [gsc], 560
Gashan, *dial.* Naga, Tase [nst], 466
Gashua Bade, *dial.* Bade [bde], 154
Gashwali, *alt.* Garhwali [gbm], 360
Gasi, *dial.* Dera [kna], 157
Gasmata, *dial.* Avau [avb], 591
Gassan, *dial.* Marka [rkm], 52
Gata' [gaq], 362
Gatame, *alt.* Kachama-Ganjule [kcx], 115
Gataq, *alt.* Gata' [gaq], 362
Gato, *alt.* Komso [kxc], 116
Gats'ame, *alt.* Kachama-Ganjule [kcx], 115
Gatue, *dial.* Tharaka [thk], 136
Gaua, *alt.* Lakona [lkn], 642
  alt. Nume [tgs], 644
Gauar, *alt.* Gavar [gou], 61
Gaudi, *alt.* Gondi, Northern [gno], 362
Gauk, *alt. dial.* Dinka, South Central [dib], 190
Gaungtou, *alt.* Karen, Zayein [kxk], 465
Gaunle, *alt. dial.* Nepali [nep], 476

Gaur Kristen, *dial.* Teor [tev], 404
Gauri, *alt. dial.* Jingpho [kac], 464, 336
Gauru, *dial.* Mbula [mna], 612
Gauuari, *alt.* Sadri [sck], 385
Gauwada, *alt.* Gawwada [gwd], 115
Gava, *alt. dial.* Guduf-Gava [gdf], 161
Gavar [gou], 61
Gavião, *dial.* Gavião do Jiparaná [gvo], 226
Gavião do Jiparaná [gvo], 226
Gavião do Rondônia, *alt.* Gavião do Jiparaná [gvo], 226
Gavião, Pará [gvp], 226
Gavit, *alt.* Gamit [gbl], 361
Gavoko, *alt.* Gvoko [ngs], 161, 62
Gavot, *dial.* Provençal [prv], 537
Gawa, *alt. dial.* Muyuw [myw], 616
Gawaar, *alt. dial.* Nuer [nus], 194
Gawan Naw', *dial.* Maru [mhx], 465
Gawanga, *alt.* Kwanga [kwj], 608
Gawar, *alt.* Gavar [gou], 61
Gawar-Bati [gwt], 316, 484
Gawari, *alt.* Sadri [sck], 385
Gawata, *alt.* Gawwada [gwd], 115
Gawawa, *alt. dial.* Kapin [tbx], 605
Gawdi of Goa, *dial.* Marathi [mar], 374
Gawhara, *alt. dial.* Hawrami [hac], 439
Gawi, *dial.* Mser [kqx], 68, 84
Gawigl, *alt.* Umbu-Ungu [ubu], 629
Gawil, *alt.* Umbu-Ungu [ubu], 629
Gawir, *alt.* Marind [mrz], 419
  dial. Marind [mrz], 419
Gawri, *alt.* Kalami [gwc], 485
Gawwada [gwd], 115
Gaya, *dial.* Hausa [hau], 152
  dial. Kwang [kvi], 82
Gayadilt, *alt.* Kayardild [gyd], 572
Gayam, *dial.* Jibu [jib], 165
Gayar, *dial.* Guruntum-Mbaaru [grd], 161
Gayardild, *alt.* Kayardild [gyd], 572
Gayardilt, *alt.* Kayardild [gyd], 572
Gaye, *alt.* Andoa [anb], 286
Gayegi, *dial.* Gbari [gby], 160
Gayi, *alt. dial.* Obanliku [bzy], 172
Gaymona, *dial.* Gbaya, Northwest [gya], 61
Gayo [gay], 430
Gazaqi, *alt.* Kazakh [kaz], 439
Gazhuo, *alt.* Kaduo [ktp], 450, 337
Gazi [gzi], 439
Gaziantep, *dial.* Turkish [tur], 519, 521
Gazili, *alt. dial.* Kunimaipa [kup], 608

Gba Sor, *dial.* Bassa [bsq], 137
Gbabana, *dial.* Gbaya-Bossangoa [gbp], 76
Gbadi, *alt. dial.* Bété, Gagnoa [btg], 92
Gbadie, *alt. dial.* Bété, Gagnoa [btg], 92
Gbado, *dial.* Mbandja [zmz], 104
Gbadogo, *alt. dial.* Kaansa [gna], 51
Gbaeson, *dial.* Krahn, Western [krw], 138
Gbaga 1, *alt. dial.* Banda-Banda [bpd], 75
Gbaga-2, *alt. dial.* Banda, West Central [bbp], 74
Gbaga-Nord, *dial.* Banda, West Central [bbp], 74
Gbaga-South, *dial.* Banda-Banda [bpd], 75
Gbagili, *alt. dial.* Gbanu [gbv], 75
Gbagiri, *dial.* Gbanu [gbv], 75
Gbagye, *alt.* Gbagyi [gbr], 160
Gbagyi [gbr], 160
Gbagyi Nkwa, *dial.* Gbari [gby], 160
Gbaison, *alt. dial.* Krahn, Western [krw], 138
Gbaka, *alt.* Ngbaka Ma'bo [nbm], 77, 105
Gbakpwa, *alt.* Kpala [kpl], 101
Gbala, *alt.* Ngbaka Ma'bo [nbm], 89
Gbambiya, *dial.* Banda-Banda [bpd], 75
Gban, *alt.* Gagu [ggu], 93
Gbanda, *alt.* Avikam [avi], 91
Gbande, *alt.* Bandi [bza], 137
Gbandere, *alt.* Gbanziri [gbg], 73, 99
Gbandi, *alt.* Bandi [bza], 137
Gbane, *alt. dial.* Kono [kno], 183
Gbane Kando, *alt. dial.* Kono [kno], 183
Gbang, *alt.* Berom [bom], 155
Gbanmi-Sokun Kakanda, *dial.* Kakanda [kka], 165
Gbanou, *alt.* Gbanu [gbv], 75
Gbantu, *dial.* Numana-Nunku-Gbantu-Numbu [nbr], 171
Gbanu [gbv], 75
  dial. Gbanu [gbv], 75
Gbanzili, *alt.* Gbanziri [gbg], 73, 99
Gbanziri [gbg], 73, 99
Gbara, *alt.* Mo'da [gbn], 193
Gbarain, *dial.* Izon [ijc], 164
Gbaranmatu, *alt. dial.* Izon [ijc], 164
Gbarbo, *dial.* Krahn, Western [krw], 138
Gbari [gby], 160
Gbari Yamma, *alt.* Gbari [gby], 160

Gbarzon, *alt. dial.* Krahn, Western [krw], 138
Gbati-ri [gti], 99
Gbaya (Sudan) [krs], 190
  Northwest Gbaya [gya], 88
  alt. Gbaya, Northwest [gya], 75
Gbaya de Boda, *alt. dial.* Bokoto [bdt], 75
Gbaya de Bosangoa, *alt.* Gbaya-Bossangoa [gbp], 76
Gbaya de Bouar, *alt. dial.* Gbaya, Northwest [gya], 75
Gbaya de Bozoum, *alt.* Gbaya-Bozoum [gbq], 76
Gbaya Kara, *dial.* Gbaya, Northwest [gya], 75
Gbaya Nord-Ouest, *alt.* Gbaya, Northwest [gya], 75
Gbaya of Boda, *dial.* Bokoto [bdt], 75
Gbaya of Borro, *alt.* Gbaya-Bossangoa [gbp], 76
Gbaya of Bossangoa, *alt.* Gbaya-Bossangoa [gbp], 76
Gbaya Sud-Ouest, *alt.* Gbaya, Southwest [mdo], 76
Gbaya, Northwest [gya], 75, 61, 160
Gbaya, Southwest [mdo], 76, 62
Gbaya-Borro, *alt.* Gbaya-Bossangoa [gbp], 76
Gbaya-Bossangoa [gbp], 76
Gbaya-Bozoum [gbq], 76
Gbaya-Dara, *dial.* Gbaya [krs], 190
Gbaya-Gboko, *dial.* Gbaya [krs], 190
Gbaya-Mbodomo, *alt. dial.* Gbaya, Southwest [mdo], 62
Gbaya-Ndogo, *dial.* Gbaya [krs], 190
Gbaya-Ngbongbo, *dial.* Gbaya [krs], 190
Gbayaka, *alt. dial.* Yaka [axk], 78
Gbayi [gyg], 76
Gbe, *alt.* Éwé [ewe], 124
Gbe, Ayizo [ayb], 44
Gbe, Ci [cib], 44
Gbe, Defi [gbh], 44
Gbe, Eastern Xwla [gbx], 44
Gbe, Gbesi [gbs], 44
Gbe, Kotafon [kqk], 44
Gbe, Maxi [mxl], 44, 207
Gbe, Saxwe [sxw], 44
Gbe, Tofin [tfi], 44
Gbe, Waci [wci], 207, 45
Gbe, Weme [wem], 45
Gbe, Western Xwla [xwl], 45, 207
Gbe, Xwela [xwe], 45
Gbea, *alt.* Gbaya-Bossangoa [gbp], 76
  alt. dial. Gbaya, Northwest [gya], 160

Gbéan, *alt. dial.* Wè Northern [wob], 95

Gbeapo, *alt. dial.* Grebo, Northern [gbo], 138

Gbedde, *dial.* Yoruba [yor], 178

Gbee, *alt.* Gbii [ggb], 137

Gbekon, *dial.* Fon [fon], 43 *dial.* Gun [guw], 161

Gbende, *dial.* Banda-Bambari [liy], 75

Gbendembu, *dial.* Loko [lok], 183

Gbendere, *alt.* Yango [yng], 109

Gbeneku, *alt. dial.* Seeku [sos], 54

Gbense, *alt. dial.* Kono [kno], 183

Gbepo, *dial.* Grebo, Northern [gbo], 138

Gberi, *alt.* Mo'da [gbn], 193

Gbese, *alt.* Kpelle, Guinea [gkp], 129 *alt.* Kpelle, Liberia [xpe], 138

Gbesi Gbe, *see* Gbe, Gbesi [gbs], 44

Gbete, *dial.* Mbum [mdd], 66

Gbeya, *alt.* Gbaya-Bossangoa [gbp], 76 *dial.* Gbaya, Northwest [gya], 160

Gbeyãse, *dial.* Dogosé [dos], 50

Gbhu D Amar Randfa, *alt.* Ninzo [nin], 171

Gbi, *dial.* Banda, West Central [bbp], 74

Gbi-Dowlu, *alt.* Gbii [ggb], 137

Gbigbil, *alt.* Bebil [bxp], 58

Gbii [ggb], 137

Gbin, *dial.* Éwé [ewe], 207

Gbinna, *alt.* Bena [yun], 155

Gbiri, *dial.* Gbiri-Niragu [grh], 160

Gbiri-Niragu [grh], 160

Gblou Grebo, *alt.* Grebo, Gboloo [gec], 138

Gbo, *alt.* Legbo [agb], 168 *dial.* Krahn, Western [krw], 138 *dial.* Senoufo, Tagwana [tgw], 95

Gboare, *alt.* Bacama [bcy], 154

Gboati, *alt.* Bata [bta], 155

Gbobo, *alt. dial.* Krahn, Western [krw], 138 *alt. dial.* Wè Southern [gxx], 95

Gbogorose, *dial.* Dogosé [dos], 50

Gbokpa, *dial.* Gbe, Gbesi [gbs], 44

Gboloo, *alt.* Grebo, Gboloo [gec], 138

Gboloo Grebo, *see* Grebo, Gboloo [gec], 138

Gbongogbo, *alt. dial.* Limba, West-Central [lia], 183

Gboo, *dial.* Wè Southern [gxx], 95

Gbor, *dial.* Bassa [bsq], 137

Gborbo, *dial.* Krahn, Western [krw], 138

Gbote, *alt.* Gbati-ri [gti], 99

Gbowe-Hran, *dial.* Krumen, Pye [pye], 93

Gbugbla, *dial.* Dangme [ada], 124

Gbuhwe, *alt.* Lamang [hia], 168

Gbunde, *alt.* Bandi [bza], 137

Gbunhu, *alt.* Kamkam [bgu], 63 *alt.* Mbongno [bgu], 170

Gbwata, *alt.* Bata [bta], 155, 58

Gbwate, *alt.* Bata [bta], 155

Gciriku [diu], 47 *alt.* Diriku [diu], 149, 40

Gcwi, *alt.* |Gwi [gwj], 47

Ge, *alt.* Gen [gej], 207, 45 *alt. dial.* Befang [bby], 58 *alt. dial.* Hmong, Chonganjiang [hmj], 334

Geagea, *dial.* Mailu [mgu], 610

Gealeka, *dial.* Xhosa [xho], 187

Geba, *alt.* Karen, Geba [kvq], 458

Geba Karen, *see* Karen, Geba [kvq], 458

Gebe [gei], 398 *alt.* Gen [gej], 207

Gebi, *alt.* Gebe [gei], 398 *dial.* Maria [mds], 612

Geblet, *alt.* Shehri [shv], 483

Gebra, *alt. dial.* Borana [gax], 132 *alt. dial.* Oromo, Borana-Arsi-Guji [gax], 117

Gedaged [gdd], 599

Gedang, *alt. dial.* Hmong, Chonganjiang [hmj], 334

Geddeo, *alt.* Gedeo [drs], 115

Gede, *alt.* Gade [ged], 160

Gedegede, *dial.* Akpes [ibe], 153

Gedeo [drs], 115

Gederobo, *dial.* Grebo, Gboloo [gec], 138

Gedou Miao, *alt. dial.* Hmong, Chonganjiang [hmj], 334

Geechee, *alt.* Sea Island Creole English [gul], 307

Geedam, *dial.* Maria, Dandami [daq], 375

Ge'ez, *alt.* Geez [gez], 115, 112

Geez [gez], 115, 112

Geg, *alt.* Albanian, Gheg [aln], 557, 529, 547

Gegbe, *alt.* Gen [gej], 45

Gei, *alt. dial.* Hlai [lic], 333

Geja, *alt.* Ngulu [ngp], 203

Gejawa, *alt.* Geji [gji], 160

Geji [gji], 160 *dial.* Geji [gji], 160

Gejiahua, *dial.* Hmong, Chonganjiang [hmj], 334

Gekho, *alt.* Karen, Geko [ghk], 464

Gek'o, *alt.* Karen, Geko [ghk], 464

Geko Karen, *see* Karen, Geko [ghk], 464

Gekoyo, *alt.* Gikuyu [kik], 133

Gekxun, *dial.* Aghul [agx], 552

Gela [nlg], 636 *alt.* Kela [kcl], 605

Gelab, *alt.* Daasanach [dsh], 114

Gelaki, *alt.* Gilaki [glk], 439

Gelama, *dial.* Mundang [mua], 68

Gelanchi, *alt. dial.* Kag-Fer-Jiir-Koor-Ror-Us-Zuksun [gel], 165

Gelangali, *alt.* Grangali [nli], 316

Gelao [gio], 333

Gelao, Green [giq], 522

Gelao, Red [gir], 522

Gelao, White [giw], 522

Gele, *alt.* Fongoro [fgr], 80

Gele', *alt.* Kele [sbc], 605

Geleb, *alt.* Daasanach [dsh], 114, 132

Geleba, *alt.* Daasanach [dsh], 114, 132

Gelebda, *alt.* Glavda [glw], 161

Gelebinya, *alt.* Daasanach [dsh], 114

Gelekidoria, *dial.* Naga, Konyak [nbe], 378

Gelik, *alt.* Patpatar [gfk], 621

Gelilla, *alt.* Zay [zwa], 120

Gelimi, *alt. dial.* Lesing-Gelimi [let], 610

Gelo, *alt.* Gelao [gio], 333

Gelubba, *alt.* Daasanach [dsh], 114

Gelvaxdaxa, *alt.* Glavda [glw], 62

Gem Mun, *alt.* Kim Mun [mji], 337

Gema, *alt.* Blablanga [blp], 635 *alt.* Gyem [gye], 162

Geman Deng [gen], 333

Gemasakun, *alt.* Sukur [syk], 175

Gemawa, *alt.* Gyem [gye], 162

Gembanawa, *alt.* Gibanawa [gib], 161

Geme [geq], 76

Geme Kulagbolu, *dial.* Geme [geq], 76

Geme Tulu, *dial.* Geme [geq], 76

Gemjek, *alt.* Zulgo-Gemzek [gnd], 74

Gemu, *alt. dial.* Gamo-Gofa-Dawro [gmo], 114

Gemzek, *dial.* Zulgo-Gemzek [gnd], 74

Gen [gej], 207, 45 *dial.* Gen [gej], 207, 45

Gen-Gbe, *alt.* Gen [gej], 207, 45

Gena, *alt.* Mboi [moi], 170

Genagane, *alt. dial.* Kuman [kue], 608

Genawa, *alt.* Fyam [pym], 160

Gende [gaf], 599

Gendeka, *alt.* Gende [gaf], 599

Gendja, *alt.* Ligenza [lgz], 102

Gendok, *dial.* Kelon [kyo], 407

Gendza-Bali, *alt.* Ligenza [lgz], 102

Gene, *alt.* Gende [gaf], 599

General Israeli, *alt. dial.* Hebrew [heb], 444

General Urmi, *alt. dial.* Assyrian Neo-Aramaic [aii], 438

Genge, *alt. dial.* Gbagyi [gbr], 160

Gengele, *dial.* Songoora [sod], 108

Gengle [geg], 161

Gennaken, *alt.* Puelche [pue], 220

Genoan, *alt. dial.* Ligurian [lij], 544, 537, 548

Genoese, *dial.* Ligurian [lij], 544, 537, 548

Genogane, *alt. dial.* Kuman [kue], 608

Genovese, *alt. dial.* Ligurian [lij], 544, 537, 548

Gentoo, *alt.* Telugu [tel], 388

Genya, *alt.* Enya [gey], 99

Genyanga, *alt.* Ginyanga [ayg], 207

Geordie, *dial.* English [eng], 565

Georgia, *dial.* Sea Island Creole English [gul], 307

Georgian [kat], 352, 439, 518

Gepma Kwudi, *alt.* Iatmul [ian], 602

Gepma Kwundi, *alt.* Iatmul [ian], 602

Gera [gew], 161

Gerai, *dial.* Semandang [sdm], 395

Geral, *alt.* Nhengatu [yrl], 230, 246, 312

Gerawa, *alt.* Gera [gew], 161

Gere, *alt.* Wè Southern [gxx], 95
alt. Wè Western [wec], 95

Gerema, *alt.* Geruma [gea], 161

Gerep, *dial.* Kim [kia], 82

Gereut, *alt. dial.* Mócheno [mhn], 545

Gergere, *dial.* Gawwada [gwd], 115

Geri, *dial.* Ghari [gri], 636

Gerka, *alt.* Yiwom [gek], 178

Gerkanchi, *alt.* Yiwom [gek], 178

Gerkawa, *alt.* Yiwom [gek], 178

Gerlovo Turks, *alt. dial.* Balkan Gagauz Turkish [bgx], 563

Germa, *alt.* Geruma [gea], 161

German, *alt.* Plautdietsch [pdt], 222, 223

German Sign Language [gsg], 538

German Travellers, *alt.* Yeniche [yec], 540

German, Colonia Tovar [gct], 311

German, Hutterite [geh], 237, 300

German, Pennsylvania [pdc], 301, 237

German, Standard [deu], 538, 284, 448, 530, 531, 533, 542, 544, 546, 550, 551, 558, 562

Gerrah, *alt.* Yidiny [yii], 579

Gerse, *alt.* Kpelle, Guinea [gkp], 129

Geruma [gea], 161

Gerze, *alt.* Kpelle, Guinea [gkp], 129

Gesa, *alt.* Geser-Gorom [ges], 398

Gesawa, *alt. dial.* Jere [jer], 165

Gesda Dae, *dial.* Bauzi [bvz], 412

Geser, *alt.* Geser-Gorom [ges], 398

Geser-Gorom [ges], 398

Geshitsa, *alt. dial.* Horpa [ero], 335

Geshiza, *dial.* Horpa [ero], 335

Gesogo, *alt.* So [soc], 108

Gess, *dial.* Lorung, Southern [lrr], 474

Geta', *alt.* Gata' [gaq], 362

Getaq, *alt.* Gata' [gaq], 362

Get'eme, *alt.* Kachama-Ganjule [kcx], 115

Getou, *alt. dial.* Hmong, Chonganjiang [hmj], 334

Getsaayi, *alt.* Teke-Tsaayi [tyi], 90

Getsogo, *alt.* Tsogo [tsv], 121

Gevoko, *alt.* Gvoko [ngs], 161, 62

Gewe, *alt.* Gey [guv], 62

Gey [guv], 62

Gey Sinan, *alt.* Harari [har], 115

Gezawa, *alt.* Geji [gji], 160
alt. dial. Geji [gji], 160

Gezon, *alt. dial.* Pagibete [pae], 107

Ghaangala, *dial.* Laari [ldi], 88

Ghadamès [gha], 139

Ghagar, *alt. dial.* Domari [rmt], 110
alt. dial. Romani, Vlax [rmy], 551

Ghaimuta, *dial.* Lengo [lgr], 637

Ghale, Kutang [ght], 471

Ghale, Northern [ghh], 471

Ghale, Southern [ghe], 471

Ghalghay, *alt.* Ingush [inh], 554

Ghana Birifor, *alt.* Birifor, Southern [biv], 123

Ghanaian Sign Language [gse], 125

Ghangatty, *alt.* Dyangadi [dyn], 570

Ghanongga [ghn], 636

Ghao-Xong, *alt.* Hmong, Eastern Xiangxi [muq], 334
alt. Hmong, Western Xiangxi [mmr], 335

Ghap, *alt.* Mengaka [xmg], 67

Ghara, *alt.* Gahri [bfu], 361

Ghardaia, *alt.* Tumzabt [mzb], 40

Ghari [gri], 636
dial. Ghari [gri], 636

Gharti, *alt.* Bujhyal [byh], 469

Ghat, *dial.* Tamahaq, Tahaggart [thv], 37, 139, 152

Ghati, *dial.* Konkani [knn], 369

Ghayavi [bmk], 600

Ghboko, *alt.* Gvoko [ngs], 161, 62

Gheg, *alt.* Albanian, Gheg [aln], 529

Gheg Albanian, *see* Albanian, Gheg [aln], 557, 529, 532, 547

Ghekhol, *alt.* Karen, Geko [ghk], 464

Ghekhu, *alt.* Karen, Geko [ghk], 464

Gheko, *alt.* Karen, Geko [ghk], 464

Gheleba, *alt.* Daasanach [dsh], 114, 132

Ghena, *alt. dial.* Tera [ttr], 175

Ghera [ghr], 484

Ghetsogo, *alt.* Tsogo [tsv], 121

Ghibarama, *alt.* Barama [bbg], 120

Ghidole, *alt.* Dirasha [gdl], 114

Ghilzai, *dial.* Pashto, Northern [pbu], 317

Ghimarra, *alt.* Bench [bcq], 113

Ghini, *dial.* Kamasau [kms], 604

Ghisadi, *alt. dial.* Gujarati [guj], 363

Ghodoberi [gdo], 554

Ghol, *dial.* Dinka, Southeastern [dks], 190

Ghomálá' [bbj], 62

Ghomálá' Central, *dial.* Ghomálá' [bbj], 62

Ghomálá' North, *dial.* Ghomálá' [bbj], 62

Ghomálá' South, *dial.* Ghomálá' [bbj], 62

Ghomara [gho], 146

Ghond, *alt.* Gondi, Northern [gno], 362

Ghone, *dial.* Varisi [vrs], 639

Ghorani, *alt. dial.* Shughni [sgh], 318

Ghorbati, *alt. dial.* Domari [rmt], 438

Ghotuo [aaa], 161

Ghua, *alt. dial.* Lengo [lgr], 637

Ghujulan, *dial.* Parachi [prc], 317

Ghulfan [ghl], 191

Ghumghum, *alt.* Tabassaran [tab], 555

Ghuna, *alt. dial.* Tera [ttr], 175

Ghusbanggi, *dial.* Kham, Gamale [kgj], 473

Ghye, *alt.* Hya [hya], 62, 162

Gia-Rai, *alt.* Jarai [jra], 523, 325

Giahoi, *alt. dial.* Tenharim [pah], 232

Giai, *alt.* Giáy [pcc], 523

Giamba, *alt. dial.* Wangaaybuwan-Ngiyambaa [wyb], 577

Giang, *alt.* Giáy [pcc], 523
dial. Nung [nut], 525

Giang Ray, *alt.* Trieng [stg], 527

Giangan [bgi], 494

Gianyar, *alt. dial.* Bali [ban], 391

Giáy [pcc], 523

Gibaio, *alt.* Kiwai, Northeast [kiw], 606
dial. Kiwai, Northeast [kiw], 606

Gibanawa [gib], 161

Gibara, *alt.* Wagawaga [wgw], 630

Gibarama, *alt.* Barama [bbg], 120
Gibario, *dial.* Kerewo [kxz], 606
Gichugu, *dial.* Gikuyu [kik], 133
Gidabal, *alt.* Bandjalang [bdy], 568
dial. Bandjalang [bdy], 568
Gidar [gid], 62, 80
Gidder, *alt.* Gidar [gid], 62, 80
Gidgid, *alt.* Bade [bde], 154
Gidhabal, *alt. dial.* Bandjalang [bdy], 568
Gidire, *alt.* Adele [ade], 206, 122
Gidja, *alt.* Kitja [gia], 572
Gidjingaliya Gujingalia, *alt.* Burarra [bvr], 569
Gidole, *alt.* Dirasha [gdl], 114
Gidra, *alt.* Wipi [gdr], 632
Gie, *alt.* Jeh [jeh], 523, 450
Gie-Trieng, *alt.* Trieng [stg], 527
Giele, *alt.* Gyele [gyi], 62, 111
Gieli, *alt.* Gyele [gyi], 62, 111
Gigatl, *dial.* Chamalal [cji], 553
Gigikuyu, *alt.* Gikuyu [kik], 133
Giha, *alt.* Ha [haq], 199
Giimbiyu, *alt.* Mangerr [zme], 573
Giiwo [kks], 161
Giiz, *alt.* Geez [gez], 115, 112
Gijow, *alt.* Yidiny [yii], 579
Giklsan, *alt.* Gitxsan [git], 237
Gikolodjya, *alt. dial.* Anii [blo], 207
dial. Anii [blo], 42
Gikuyu [kik], 133
Gi∥kxigwi, *alt.* ∥Xegwi [xeg], 187
Gikyode [acd], 125
Gil Bagale, *dial.* Sisaala, Tumulung [sil], 127
Gilaki [glk], 439
Gilani, *alt.* Gilaki [glk], 439
Gilbagala, *dial.* Paasaal [sig], 127
Gilbertese, *alt.* Kiribati [gil], 582, 580, 636, 640
Gilempla, *alt. dial.* Anii [blo], 207
dial. Anii [blo], 42
Gilgit, *alt. dial.* Shina [scl], 488
Gilgiti, *dial.* Shina [scl], 488
Gili, *alt. dial.* Bana [bcw], 57
Gilika, *dial.* Yale, Kosarek [kkl], 426
Gilima [gix], 99
Gilipanes, *alt.* Ifugao, Tuwali [ifk], 495
Gillah, *alt.* Yidiny [yii], 579
Gilyak [niv], 504
Giman, *alt.* Gane [gzn], 398
Gimaras, *alt. dial.* Kinaray-A [krj], 498
Gimarra, *alt.* Bench [bcq], 113
Gimba, *dial.* Sagalla [tga], 136
Gimbaama, *alt.* Mbama [mbm], 120
Gimbala, *alt.* Mbala [mdp], 104
Gimbanawa, *alt.* Gibanawa [gib], 161

Gimbe, *alt.* Gimnime [gmn], 62
alt. dial. Koma [kmy], 167
Gimbunda, *alt.* Mbunda [mck], 214
alt. dial. Mpuono [zmp], 105
Gimi (Eastern Highlands) [gim], 600
Gimi (West New Britain) [gip], 600
Gimira, *alt.* Bench [bcq], 113
Gimma, *alt.* Gimme [kmp], 62
Gimme [kmp], 62
Gimnime [gmn], 62
Gimsbok Nama, *dial.* Nama [naq], 186
Gin, *alt.* Vietnamese [vie], 527, 346
dial. Koryak [kpy], 505
Ginabwal, *alt.* Ga'dang [gdg], 494
Ginaourou, *dial.* Natioro [nti], 53
Ginga, *alt. dial.* Mbundu [kmb], 41
!Gingkwe, *dial.* Naro [nhr], 48
Gingwak, *alt. dial.* Jarawa [jar], 165
G!inkwe, *dial.* Naro [nhr], 48
Ginukh, *alt.* Hinukh [gin], 554
Ginukhtsy, *alt.* Hinukh [gin], 554
Ginuman [gnm], 600
Ginux, *alt.* Hinukh [gin], 554
Ginyamunyinganyi, *dial.* Nyaturu [rim], 203
Ginyanga [ayg], 207
Gio, *alt.* Dan [daf], 92, 129, 137
Gio-Dan, *alt.* Dan [daf], 92, 129, 137
Gio-Lang, *alt. dial.* Bahnar [bdq], 521
Gio-Rai, *alt.* Jarai [jra], 523, 325
Giong, *alt.* Bayungu [bxj], 569
Gipende, *alt.* Phende [pem], 107
Giphende, *alt.* Phende [pem], 107
Gipuzkoan, *alt. dial.* Basque [eus], 559
Gira, *alt.* Madi [grg], 610
Girango, *dial.* Zanaki [zak], 206
Girasia, *alt.* Garasia, Adiwasi [gas], 362
alt. Garasia, Rajput [gra], 362
Girawa [bbr], 600
Gire, *alt.* Kire [geb], 606
Girga, *dial.* Sungor [sjg], 195
dial. Tama [tma], 86
Giri, *alt.* Kire [geb], 606
Giriama, *alt.* Giryama [nyf], 133
Giribam, *dial.* Makayam [aup], 611
Giripari, *dial.* Sirmauri [srx], 387
Giriwe, *alt. dial.* Krumen, Pye [pye], 93
Gironga, *alt.* Ronga [rng], 149
Girramay, *dial.* Dyirbal [dbl], 570
Girwali, *alt.* Garhwali [gbm], 360
Girwana, *dial.* Nyaturu [rim], 203
Giryama [nyf], 133
dial. Giryama [nyf], 133
Gisamjang, *alt. dial.* Datooga [tcc], 198

Gisamjanga, *dial.* Datooga [tcc], 198
Giseda, *alt. dial.* Anii [blo], 207
dial. Anii [blo], 42
Gisème, *alt. dial.* Anii [blo], 207
Gisewi, *alt. dial.* Tonga [toh], 149
Gisey, *alt. dial.* Masana [mcn], 83
Gishu, *alt. dial.* Masaba [myx], 211
Gisi, *alt.* Kisi, Southern [kss], 138
Gisida, *alt.* Anii [blo], 42, 207
Gisiga, *alt.* Giziga, North [gis], 62
alt. Giziga, South [giz], 62
Gisika, *alt.* Giziga, North [gis], 62
alt. Giziga, South [giz], 62
Gisira, *alt.* Sira [swj], 121
Gissi, *alt.* Kisi, Southern [kss], 183
Gisu, *alt.* Masaba [myx], 211
Gitano, *alt.* Caló [rmr], 559, 226, 536, 551
Gitksan, *alt.* Gitxsan [git], 237
Gitoa, *alt.* Gitua [ggt], 600
Gitonga Gy Khogani, *dial.* Tonga [toh], 149
Gitsken, *dial.* Gitxsan [git], 237
Gitua [ggt], 600
Gitxsan [git], 237
dial. Gitxsan [git], 237
Gityskyan, *alt.* Gitxsan [git], 237
Giur, *alt.* Luwo [lwo], 193
Giverom, *alt. dial.* Kofyar [kwl], 166
Giyug [giy], 571
Gizay, *dial.* Masana [mcn], 83, 66
Gizi, *alt.* Kisi, Southern [kss], 138
alt. Kissi, Northern [kqs], 129, 183
Giziga de Maroua, *alt.* Giziga, North [gis], 62
Giziga de Midjivin, *alt. dial.* Giziga, South [giz], 62
Giziga de Moutouroua, *alt. dial.* Giziga, South [giz], 62
Giziga, North [gis], 62
Giziga, South [giz], 62
Gizima, *dial.* Loma [lom], 138
Gizra, *alt.* Gizrra [tof], 600
Gizrra [tof], 600
Gjunej, *dial.* Lezgi [lez], 555
G'kelendeg, *alt.* Mbara [mpk], 84
G'kelendeng, *alt.* Mbara [mpk], 84
Glanda, *alt.* Glavda [glw], 161
Glanda-Khwe, *alt.* Khwe [xuu], 214
alt. Kxoe [xuu], 40
Glaro, *dial.* Glaro-Twabo [glr], 137
Glaro-Twabo [glr], 137
Glavda [glw], 161, 62
dial. Glavda [glw], 161
Glawlo, *dial.* Krumen, Tepo [ted], 93, 138
Glebo, *dial.* Grebo, Southern [grj], 138
Glesi, *alt.* Gresi [grs], 415

Glibe, *dial.* Godié [god], 93
Gliji, *dial.* Gen [gej], 207, 45
Glio, *alt.* Glio-Oubi [oub], 138, 93
Glio-Oubi [oub], 138, 93
Globo, *dial.* Grebo, Central [grv], 138
Gnalluma, *alt.* Ngarluma [nrl], 575
Gnalouma, *alt.* Ngarluma [nrl], 575
Gnamei, *alt.* Naga, Angami [njm], 377
Gnamo, *alt.* Nyamal [nly], 576
Gnau [gnu], 600
Gnivo, *alt.* Ayiwo [nfl], 635
Gnoore, *dial.* Mumuye [mzm], 170
Gnormbur, *alt.* Ngurmbur [nrx], 575
Gnumbu, *alt.* Ngurmbur [nrx], 575
Goa, *alt.* Makasar [mak], 430
alt. dial. Makasar [mak], 430
Goaa, *alt.* Mbato [gwa], 94
Goahibo, *alt.* Guahibo [guh], 245
Goahiva, *alt.* Guahibo [guh], 245
Goajiro, *alt.* Wayuu [guc], 248, 313
Goan, *alt.* Konkani, Goanese [gom], 369, 134
Goanese, *alt.* Konkani, Goanese [gom], 134
alt. dial. Konkani, Goanese [gom], 369
Goanese Konkani, *see* Konkani, Goanese [gom], 369, 134
Goari, *alt.* Sadri [sck], 385
Goaria [gig], 485
Goaribari, *alt. dial.* Kerewo [kxz], 606
Goba, *alt.* Ngwaba [ngw], 171
alt. dial. Shona [sna], 216, 215
Gobabingo, *alt.* Gupapuyngu [guf], 571
Gobasi [goi], 600
dial. Gobasi [goi], 600
Gobato, *dial.* Berta [wti], 113
Gobeyo, *alt.* Longto [wok], 65
Gobeze, *alt.* Bussa [dox], 114
dial. Gawwada [gwd], 115
Gobirawa, *dial.* Hausa [hau], 162, 152
Gobla, *alt. dial.* Gola [gol], 183
Gobu [gox], 100
alt. Gubu [gox], 76
Gobugdua, *alt. dial.* Korupun-Sela [kpq], 418
Godauli, *alt.* Garhwali [gbm], 360
Godavari Koya, *alt. dial.* Koya [kff], 370
Godda, *alt. dial.* Sauria Paharia [mjt], 386
Godi, *alt.* Gondi, Northern [gno], 362
Godié [god], 93
Godoberi, *alt.* Ghodoberi [gdo], 554

Godoberin, *alt.* Ghodoberi [gdo], 554
Godogodo, *alt.* Laka [lak], 168
Godwa, *alt.* Gadaba, Bodo [gbj], 361
Godwani, *dial.* Bagheli [bfy], 354, 468
Godwari [gdx], 362
Godye, *alt.* Godié [god], 93
Goemai [ank], 161
Goerees, *dial.* Zeeuws [zea], 549
Gofa, *dial.* Gamo-Gofa-Dawro [gmo], 114
Goffa, *alt. dial.* Gamo-Gofa-Dawro [gmo], 114
Gog, *alt.* Lakona [lkn], 642
Goggot, *alt. dial.* Kistane [gru], 116
Gogo [gog], 198
Gogodala [ggw], 600
Gogodara, *alt.* Gogodala [ggw], 600
Gogot, *alt. dial.* Kistane [gru], 116
Gogri, *alt.* Gujari [gju], 363, 485
Gogwama, *alt.* Kwama [kmq], 116
Gohar-Herkeri, *alt.* Lambadi [lmn], 372
Gohilwadi, *alt. dial.* Gujarati [guj], 363
Gohllaru, *alt.* Holiya [hoy], 364
Gohum, *alt.* Yukuben [ybl], 74
Goi, *alt.* Baan [bvj], 154
alt. Blablanga [blp], 635
Goiala, *dial.* Iduna [viv], 602
Gojal, *dial.* Wakhi [wbl], 489
Gojari, *alt.* Gujari [gju], 363, 316, 485
Goji, *alt.* Kushi [kuh], 167
Gojri, *alt.* Gujari [gju], 363, 316, 485
Gok, *dial.* Dinka, South Central [dib], 190
Gokana [gkn], 161
Goklan, *alt. dial.* Turkmen [tuk], 442
Goklen, *dial.* Turkmen [tuk], 520, 442
G!okwe, *dial.* Naro [nhr], 48
Gokwom, *alt.* Komo [xom], 192
Gol, *dial.* Bagirmi [bmi], 78
Gol Gadaba, *alt.* Gadaba, Mudhili [gau], 361
Gola [gol], 138, 183
alt. Badyara [pbp], 128, 130, 179
dial. Mumuye [mzm], 170
Golar, *dial.* Bahnar [bdq], 521
dial. Jarai [jra], 523, 325
Golari, *alt. dial.* Telugu [tel], 388
Golari-Kannada, *alt.* Holiya [hoy], 364
Gold, *alt.* Nanai [gld], 506, 341
Golden Palaung, *alt.* Palaung, Shwe [pll], 466, 342
Goldi, *alt.* Nanai [gld], 506, 341
Goliath, *alt.* Una [mtg], 424

Golin [gvf], 600
dial. Golin [gvf], 600
Gollango, *dial.* Gawwada [gwd], 115
Gollum, *alt.* Golin [gvf], 600
Golo, *alt.* Banda, West Central [bbp], 188
Golumala, *dial.* Dhangu [dhg], 569
Goma, *alt.* Kwama [kmq], 116
Gomadj, *alt.* Gumatj [gnn], 571
Gomantaki, *alt. dial.* Konkani, Goanese [gom], 369
Gomataki, *alt.* Konkani, Goanese [gom], 369, 134
Gombe, *dial.* Fulfulde, Adamawa [fub], 190
dial. Sena [seh], 149
Gombi, *alt.* Ngwaba [ngw], 171
Gombo, *alt.* Gumuz [guk], 115, 191
dial. Gumuz [guk], 191
Gomboro, *dial.* Samo, Maya [sym], 53
Gomia, *dial.* Chuave [cjv], 596
Gomjuer, *alt. dial.* Dinka, Southwestern [dik], 190
Gomme, *dial.* Koma [kmy], 167
Gommu Koya, *alt. dial.* Koya [kff], 370
Gomnome, *dial.* Koma [kmy], 167
Gomu, *alt.* Moo [gwg], 170
Gon Shan, *alt.* Khün [kkh], 465, 515
Gona, *alt. dial.* Ewage-Notu [nou], 598
Gondhla, *alt.* Tinani [lbf], 388
Gondi, *alt.* Gondi, Northern [gno], 362
Gondi, Northern [gno], 362
Gondi, Southern [ggo], 363
Gondiva, *alt.* Gondi, Northern [gno], 362
Gondla, *alt.* Tinani [lbf], 388, 345
Gondu, *alt.* Gondi, Northern [gno], 362
Gondwadi, *alt.* Gondi, Northern [gno], 362
Gone Dau [goo], 580
Gonedau, *alt.* Gone Dau [goo], 580
Gong, *alt.* Ngong [nnx], 70
alt. Ugong [ugo], 518
Gongdubikha, *alt.* Gongduk [goe], 323
Gongduk [goe], 323
Gonge, *dial.* Nzakambay [nzy], 71
dial. Pana [pnz], 77, 86
Gongla, *dial.* Mumuye [mzm], 170
Gongo, *alt.* Wongo [won], 109
Gongon Lobi, *dial.* Lobi [lob], 52
Goni, *alt.* Yeretuar [gop], 426
Gonja [gjn], 125
dial. Gonja [gjn], 125

Gono, *dial.* Dogon, Jamsay
[djm], 142, 50
Gonsomon, *dial.* Rungus [drg], 458
Goola, *alt.* Lambadi [lmn], 372
Goom, *dial.* Dii [dur], 60
Goom-Gharra, *alt.* Kunggara
[kvs], 572
Goonan, *alt.* Kwini [gww], 573
Goondile, *alt.* Gondi, Northern
[gno], 362
Gooniyandi [gni], 571
Gope, *alt. dial.* Kiwai, Northeast
[kiw], 606
Gor [gqr], 80
alt. dial. Gaam [tbi], 190
Gora, *dial.* Gwahatike [dah], 601
Gora-Bomahouji, *dial.* Ömie
[aom], 619
Gorachouqua, *alt.* Korana
[kqz], 186
Gorakhpuri, *alt. dial.* Bhojpuri
[bho], 356
Gorakor [goc], 600
Goram, *alt.* Geser-Gorom [ges], 398
alt. dial. Kofyar [kwl], 166
Goram Laut, *dial.* Geser-Gorom
[ges], 398
Gorama Kono, *alt. dial.* Kono
[kno], 183
Goran, *alt.* Geser-Gorom [ges], 398
Gorani, *alt.* Gurani [hac], 443
alt. Hawrami [hac], 439
alt. dial. Hawrami [hac], 439
Gorap [goq], 398
Gorau, *dial.* Ikobi-Mena [meb], 602
Gorawati, *dial.* Mewari [mtr], 375
Goraze, *alt.* Bussa [dox], 114
Gorbo, *dial.* Krahn, Eastern [kqo],
138
Gorgal Fulfulde, *see* Fulfulde,
Western Niger [fuh], 44
Gorgani, *dial.* Mazanderani
[mzn], 441
Gori, *alt.* Laal [gdm], 82
dial. Nuni, Southern [nnw], 53
Gorkha Gurung, *dial.* Gurung,
Eastern [ggn], 471
Gorkhali, *alt.* Nepali [nep], 476, 323,
381
dial. Nepali [nep], 381
Gorlos, *alt. dial.* Mongolian,
Peripheral [mvf], 339
Gormati, *alt.* Lambadi [lmn], 372
Gorminang, *dial.* Yir Yoront
[yiy], 579
Gorno-Mariy, *alt.* Mari, Western
[mrj], 555
Goroa, *alt.* Gorowa [gow], 192
Gorogone, *alt.* Guragone [gge], 571
Gorom, *alt.* Geser-Gorom [ges], 398

Gorong, *alt.* Geser-Gorom [ges], 398
Gorongosa, *dial.* Sena [seh], 149
Gorontalo [gor], 429
Gorontalo Kota, *dial.* Gorontalo
[gor], 429
Gorose, *dial.* Gawwada [gwd], 115
Gorova, *alt.* Gorovu [grq], 600
Gorovu [grq], 600
Gorowa [gow], 192
Gorrose, *alt. dial.* Gawwada
[gwd], 115
Gorum, *alt.* Parenga [pcj], 383
Gorum Sama, *alt.* Parenga
[pcj], 383
Gorwaa, *alt.* Gorowa [gow], 192
Gorwali, *alt.* Garhwali [gbm], 360
Goshute, *alt. dial.* Shoshoni
[shh], 308
Gosiute, *dial.* Shoshoni [shh], 308
Gothic [got], 564
Gotlandic, *alt. dial.* Swedish
[swe], 562
Gotte Koya, *alt. dial.* Koya
[kff], 370
Gouande, *dial.* Biali [beh], 42
Goude, *alt.* Gude [gde], 161, 62
Goudi, *alt.* Gondi, Northern
[gno], 362
Goudou, *alt. dial.* Dida, Yocoboué
[gud], 92
Goudwal, *alt.* Gondi, Northern
[gno], 362
Gouin, *alt.* Cerma [cme], 50, 92
Gouindougouba, *dial.* Cerma
[cme], 50
Goula, *alt.* Gula [glu], 81
alt. Gula [kcm], 76
alt. Zan Gula [zna], 87
alt. dial. Gula [kcm], 191
dial. Laka [lap], 83
Goula d'Iro, *alt.* Gula Iro [glj], 81
Goula Iro, *alt.* Gula Iro [glj], 81
Goulai, *alt.* Gulay [gvl], 81
Goulaye, *alt.* Gulay [gvl], 81
Goulei, *alt.* Gulay [gvl], 81
Goulfei, *alt.* Malgbe [mxf], 65, 83
alt. dial. Malgbe [mxf], 65
Goulfey, *alt.* Malgbe [mxf], 83
dial. Malgbe [mxf], 83
Goulimancema, *alt.*
Gourmanchéma [gux], 152
Goulmacema, *alt.* Gourmanchéma
[gux], 51
Goulmancema, *alt.* Gourmanchéma
[gux], 45
Goumaye, *alt. dial.* Masana
[mcn], 83
Goun, *alt.* Gun [guw], 45
alt. dial. Gun [guw], 161
Goundo [goy], 81

Gouno, *alt. dial.* Gimi [gim], 600
Gounou, *alt.* Nugunu [yas], 70
Gouraghie, *alt.* Sebat Bet Gurage
[sgw], 118
Gourara, *dial.* Taznatit [grr], 40
Gourma, *alt.* Gourmanchéma
[gux], 51, 152, 208
Gourmanchéma [gux], 51, 45, 152,
208
Gourmantche, *alt.* Gourmanchéma
[gux], 51, 45, 152, 208
dial. Fulfulde, Northeastern Burkina
Faso [fuh], 51
Gouro, *alt.* Guro [goa], 93
Gouwar, *alt.* Gavar [gou], 61
Gova, *alt.* Mbukushu [mhw], 150, 41,
47, 214
alt. dial. Shona [sna], 216, 215
dial. Ndau [ndc], 148
Govari, *dial.* Varhadi-Nagpuri
[vah], 389
Govari of Seoni, *dial.* Powari
[pwr], 384
Governor Generoso Manobo,
dial. Manobo, Sarangani [mbs], 499
Govhoroh, *alt. dial.* Banda-Banda
[bpd], 188
Govoro, *dial.* Banda-Banda
[bpd], 188
Gowa, *alt. dial.* Shona [sna], 215
dial. Makasar [mak], 430
Gowar-Bati, *alt.* Gawar-Bati
[gwt], 484
Gowari, *alt.* Gawar-Bati [gwt], 316,
484
Gowase, *alt.* Bussa [dox], 114
Gowlan [goj], 363
Gowli [gok], 363
Gowri, *alt.* Kalami [gwc], 485
Gowro [gwf], 485
alt. dial. Chhattisgarhi [hne], 358
Gozarkhani [goz], 439
Gozo, *dial.* Maltese [mlt], 547
Gozza, *dial.* Aari [aiz], 112
Graecae, *alt.* Greek [ell], 540
Graged, *alt.* Gedaged [gdd], 599
Gramsukraviri, *dial.* Ashkun
[ask], 315
Gramya, *alt. dial.* Gujarati [guj], 363
Grand Rapids, *dial.* Carrier
[crx], 236
Grangali [nli], 316
dial. Grangali [nli], 316
Grasia, *alt.* Garasia, Rajput [gra], 362
Grass Koiari, *see* Koiari, Grass
[kbk], 606
Grass Miao, *alt.* Cao Miao
[cov], 329
Grassland Mari, *dial.* Mari, Eastern
[mhr], 555

Guayakí, *pej. alt.* Aché [guq], 284
Guayaki-Ache, *alt.* Aché [guq], 284
Guayana, *alt.* Wayana [way], 252
Guayapi, *alt.* Wayampi [oym], 233
Guayba, *alt.* Guahibo [guh], 245
Guaymí, *alt.* Ngäbere [gym], 283
Guayqueri, *alt. dial.* Yabarana [yar], 313
Guayuyaco, *dial.* Inga, Jungle [inj], 246
Guazazzara, *alt.* Guajajára [gub], 227
Guba, *alt.* Shiki [gua], 174
  dial. Boro [bwo], 114
  dial. Gumuz [guk], 115
Gubabwingu, *alt.* Gupapuyngu [guf], 571
Gubang Itneg, *dial.* Itneg, Banao [bjx], 496
Gubat, *alt.* Sorsogon, Waray [srv], 501
  alt. dial. Hanunoo [hnn], 494
Gubatnon, *dial.* Hanunoo [hnn], 494
Gubawa, *alt.* Shiki [gua], 174
Gubi, *alt.* Shiki [gua], 174
  dial. Shiki [gua], 174
Gubu [gox], 76
  alt. Gobu [gox], 100
Gudandji, *dial.* Wambaya [wmb], 577
Gudanji [nji], 571
Gude [gde], 161, 62
Gudeni, *alt. dial.* Farefare [gur], 124
  dial. Ninkare [gur], 53
Gudenne, *alt. dial.* Farefare [gur], 124
Gudi, *dial.* Nungu [rin], 171
Gudjala, *alt.* Warungu [wrg], 578
Gudo, *alt.* Gudu [gdu], 161
Gudoji, *alt.* Dameli [dml], 484
Gudu [gdu], 161
Guduf, *dial.* Guduf-Gava [gdf], 161
Guduf-Gava [gdf], 161
Gudupe, *alt.* Guduf-Gava [gdf], 161
Gudur, *dial.* Mofu-Gudur [mif], 68
Gudwa, *alt.* Gadaba, Bodo [gbj], 361
Guebie, *alt. dial.* Bété, Gagnoa [btg], 92
Guébie, *alt.* Dida, Lakota [dic], 92
Guegue, *alt.* Albanian, Gheg [aln], 529
Guelebda, *alt.* Glavda [glw], 161, 62
Guelengdeng, *alt.* Mbara [mpk], 84
Guelili, *alt. dial.* Shilha [jbn], 209
Gueme, *alt.* Geme [geq], 76
Guemshek, *alt.* Zulgo-Gemzek [gnd], 74
Guéré, *alt.* Wè Southern [gxx], 95
  alt. Wè Western [wec], 95

Guerrero Amuzgo, *see* Amuzgo, Guerrero [amu], 259
Guerrero Aztec, *alt.* Nahuatl, Guerrero [ngu], 271
Guerrero Nahuatl, *see* Nahuatl, Guerrero [ngu], 271
Guerze, *alt.* Kpelle, Guinea [gkp], 129
Gueve, *alt.* Gey [guv], 62
Guevea de Humboldt Zapotec, *see* Zapotec, Guevea de Humboldt [zpg], 278
Gugada, *alt.* Kokata [ktd], 572
Gugadj [ggd], 571
Gugadja, *alt.* Kukatja [kux], 572
Gugbe, *alt.* Gun [guw], 45, 161
Gugiko, *dial.* Mukulu [moz], 85
Gugu, *dial.* Dayak, Land [dyk], 393
Gugu Badhun [gdc], 571
Gugu Warra [wrw], 571
Gugu Yimijir, *alt.* Guguyimidjir [kky], 571
Gugu-Badhun, *alt.* Warungu [wrg], 578
Gugu-Yimidhirr, *alt.* Guguyimidjir [kky], 571
Gugubera [kkp], 571
Gugudayor, *alt.* Thayore [thd], 576
Guguminjen, *alt.* Kunjen [kjn], 573
Guguwarra, *alt.* Gugu Warra [wrw], 571
Guguyalanji, *alt.* Kuku-Yalanji [gvn], 572
Guguyimidjir [kky], 571
Guha, *alt.* Holoholo [hoo], 100
Guhjali, *alt.* Wakhi [wbl], 318, 513
Guhu-Samane [ghs], 599
Guiam, *dial.* Wipi [gdr], 632
Guianese Creole French [gcr], 252
Guiarak, *alt.* Guya [gka], 601
Guibei, *dial.* Zhuang, Northern [ccx], 349
Guiberoua, *dial.* Béte, Guiberoua [bet], 92
Guiberoua Béte, *see* Béte, Guiberoua [bet], 92
Guibian, *dial.* Zhuang, Northern [ccx], 349
Guichicovi Mixe, *alt.* Mixe, Isthmus [mir], 265
Guichong, *alt.* Guiqiong [gqi], 333
Guicurú, *alt.* Kuikúro-Kalapálo [kui], 229
Guidar, *alt.* Gidar [gid], 62, 80
Guider, *alt.* Gidar [gid], 62
Guidiville, *dial.* Pomo, Northern [pej], 307
Güilá Zapotec, *see* Zapotec, Güilá [ztu], 278

Guilaki, *alt.* Gilaki [glk], 439
Guilani, *alt.* Gilaki [glk], 439
Guili, *alt. dial.* Bana [bcw], 57
Guilia, *alt.* Barein [bva], 78
  dial. Barein [bva], 78
Guimaras Island, *alt. dial.* Kinaray-A [krj], 498
Guimini Kan, *dial.* Dogon, Tene Kan [dtk], 142
Guin, *alt.* Cerma [cme], 92
  alt. Gen [gej], 207, 45
Guinaang, *dial.* Kalinga, Lubuagan [knb], 497
Guinaang Bontoc, *dial.* Bontoc, Central [bnc], 493
Guinan, *dial.* Chinese, Yue [yue], 331
Guinea Kpelle, *see* Kpelle, Guinea [gkp], 129
Guinea-Bissau Creole, *alt.* Crioulo, Upper Guinea [pov], 131
Guinean Sign Language [gus], 129
Guinzadan, *dial.* Kankanaey [kne], 498
Guipuzcoan, *dial.* Basque [eus], 559
Guipuzcoano, *alt. dial.* Basque [eus], 559
Guiqiong [gqi], 333
Guiren, *alt. dial.* Nung [nut], 525
Guirvidig, *alt. dial.* Musgu [mug], 85
Güisnay, *alt.* Wichí Lhamtés Güisnay [mzh], 220
Guissey, *alt. dial.* Masana [mcn], 83, 66
Guitry, *alt. dial.* Dida, Yocoboué [gud], 92
Guizhou Yi, *see* Yi, Guizhou [yig], 347
Guiziga, *alt.* Giziga, North [gis], 62
  alt. Giziga, South [giz], 62
Gujaaxet, *dial.* Bainouk-Gunyaamolo [bcz], 179
Gujalabiya, *alt.* Burarra [bvr], 569
Gujar, *alt.* Gujari [gju], 363
Gujarati [guj], 363, 133, 198, 210, 213, 485, 509
Gujari [gju], 363, 316, 485
Gujer, *alt.* Gujari [gju], 363, 485
Gujerathi, *alt.* Gujarati [guj], 363, 509
Gujerati, *alt.* Gujarati [guj], 363, 509
Guji, *dial.* Oromo, Borana-Arsi-Guji [gax], 117
Gujjari, *alt.* Gujari [gju], 363, 485
Gujji, *alt. dial.* Oromo, Borana-Arsi-Guji [gax], 117
Gujrathi, *alt.* Gujarati [guj], 363

Gujuri, *alt.* Gujari [gju], 363, 485
Gujuri Rajasthani, *alt.* Gujari
[gju], 316, 485
Gula (Central African Republic)
[kcm], 76, 191
  Gula (Chad) [glu], 81
  alt. Gola [gol], 183
  dial. Gula [kcm], 191
Gula du Mamoun, *alt.* Gula
[kcm], 76
Gula Guera, *alt.* Bon Gula [glc], 79
  alt. Zan Gula [zna], 87
Gula Iro [glj], 81
Gula'alaa [gmb], 636
Gulai, *alt.* Gulay [gvl], 81
Gulak, *dial.* Marghi Central
[mrt], 169
Gulamas, *dial.* Muna [mnb], 431
Gulanga, *alt.* Giangan [bgi], 494
Gulay [gvl], 81
  dial. Dyaabugay [dyy], 570
  dial. Gulay [gvl], 81
Gulbahar, *dial.* Pashayi, Northwest
[glh], 317
Gule [gly], 191
Guleguleu, *dial.* Duau [dva], 597
Gulei, *alt.* Gulay [gvl], 81
Gulf Arabic, *alt.* Arabic, Gulf
Spoken [afb], 442, 320, 437, 482,
503, 520
Gulf Spoken, *alt.* Arabic, Gulf
Spoken [afb], 508
Gulf Spoken Arabic, *see* Arabic,
Gulf Spoken [afb], 442, 320, 437,
449, 482, 503, 508, 520
Gulfan, *alt.* Ghulfan [ghl], 191
Gulfe, *alt.* Malgbe [mxf], 65
Gulfei, *alt.* Malgbe [mxf], 65, 83
Gulicha, *alt. dial.* Baruya [byr], 592
Guliguli [gli], 636
Gulili, *alt.* Guliguli [gli], 636
Gulimancema, *alt.* Gourmanchéma
[gux], 51, 45, 208
Gullah, *alt.* Sea Island Creole English
[gul], 307
Gulli, *dial.* Kurdish, Northern
[kmr], 443
Gulmancema, *alt.* Gourmanchéma
[gux], 51
Gulngay, *alt. dial.* Dyirbal [dbl], 570
Gulnguy, *dial.* Dyirbal [dbl], 570
Gulompaay, *alt.* Mlomp [mlo], 175
Gulud, *alt. dial.* Katla [kcr], 192
Gulumirrgin, *alt.* Laragia [lrg], 573
Gumadir, *dial.* Gunwinggu
[gup], 571
Gumait, *alt.* Gumatj [gnn], 571
Gumaj, *alt.* Gumatj [gnn], 571
Gumalu [gmu], 600
Gumasi, *alt.* Gumawana [gvs], 600

Gumatj [gnn], 571
Gumawana [gvs], 600
Gumay, *dial.* Masana [mcn], 83
Gumba, *alt.* Belanda Viri [bvi], 189
Gumbaingari, *alt.* Kumbainggar
[kgs], 572
Gumbang, *dial.* Jagoi [sne], 459
Gumbaynggir, *alt.* Kumbainggar
[kgs], 572
Gumer, *dial.* Sebat Bet Gurage
[sgw], 118
Gumine, *alt.* Golin [gvf], 600
Gumis, *alt.* Gumuz [guk], 115, 191
Gumsai, *dial.* Kui [kxu], 370
Gumuz [guk], 115, 191
Gumuzinya, *alt.* Gumuz [guk], 115
Gun [guw], 45, 161
  dial. Gun [guw], 161
Gun-Alada, *alt.* Gun [guw], 45, 161
Gun-Gbe, *alt.* Gun [guw], 45, 161
Gun-Guragone, *alt.* Burarra
[bvr], 569
  alt. Guragone [gge], 571
Gun-Marung, *alt.* Maung [mph], 574
Guna, *alt. dial.* Efate, North [llp], 641
  dial. Sinasina [sst], 624
Gunagoragone, *alt.* Guragone
[gge], 571
Gunantuna, *alt.* Kuanua [ksd], 608
Gunavidji, *alt.* Djeebbana [djj], 570
Gunawitji, *alt.* Gunwinggu
[gup], 571
Gunbalang, *alt.* Kunbarlang
[wlg], 572
Gunbarlang, *alt.* Kunbarlang
[wlg], 572
Gundangbon, *alt.* Ngalkbun
[ngk], 575
Gundi [gdi], 76
Gundjeipme, *dial.* Gunwinggu
[gup], 571
Gunei, *dial.* Gunwinggu [gup], 571
Gunerakan, *alt.* Kungarakany
[ggk], 572
Gunga, *alt.* Reshe [res], 173
Gungabula [gyf], 571
Gungalang, *alt.* Kunbarlang
[wlg], 572
Gunganchi, *alt.* Reshe [res], 173
Gungaragan, *alt.* Kungarakany
[ggk], 572
Gungarakanj, *alt.* Kungarakany
[ggk], 572
Gungari, *alt.* Kunggari [kgl], 572
Gungawa, *alt.* Reshe [res], 173
Gunggara, *alt.* Kunggara [kvs], 572
Gunggari, *alt.* Kunggari [kgl], 572
Gunggay, *dial.* Yidiny [yii], 579
Gungorogone, *alt.* Guragone [gge],
571

Gungu [rub], 210
Gunian, *alt.* Gooniyandi [gni], 571
Guniandi, *alt.* Gooniyandi [gni], 571
Gunin, *alt.* Kwini [gww], 573
Guniyan, *alt.* Gooniyandi [gni], 571
Guniyandi, *alt.* Gooniyandi
[gni], 571
Guniyn, *alt.* Gooniyandi [gni], 571
Gunmarung, *alt.* Maung [mph], 574
Guntai [gnt], 601
Guntur, *alt. dial.* Telugu [tel], 388
Gunu, *alt.* Nugunu [yas], 70
Gunua-Kena, *alt.* Tehuelche
[teh], 220
Gununa-Kena, *alt.* Tehuelche [teh],
220
Gunwinggu [gup], 571
Gunwinjgu, *alt.* Gunwinggu
[gup], 571
Gunya [gyy], 571
  alt. dial. Swahili [swh], 136
Gunyamoolo, *dial.* Bainouk-
Gunyaamolo [bcz], 179
Gunza, *alt. dial.* Gumuz [guk], 191
Gunzib, *alt.* Hunzib [huz], 554
Guo Garimani, *alt.* Dahalo
[dal], 132
Guoke-Puluo, *alt. dial.* Nusu
[nuf], 341
Guoyagui, *pej. alt.* Aché [guq], 284
Guoyu, *alt.* Chinese, Mandarin
[cmn], 329, 508, 511
Gupa, *dial.* Gupa-Abawa [gpa], 161
Gupa-Abawa [gpa], 161
Gupapuyngu [guf], 571
  dial. Gupapuyngu [guf], 571
Gura, *alt.* Mabaan [mfz], 193
  alt. dial. Gbiri-Niragu [grh], 160
  dial. Lame [bma], 168
  dial. Sebat Bet Gurage [sgw], 118
Guradjara, *alt.* Karadjeri [gbd], 572
Guragie, *alt.* Sebat Bet Gurage
[sgw], 118
Guragone [gge], 571
Gurague, *alt.* Sebat Bet Gurage
[sgw], 118
Guragureu, *alt. dial.* Duau
[dva], 597
Gurama, *alt.* Kurrama [vku], 572
Guramalum [grz], 601
Gurani [hac], 443
  alt. Bajelani [bjm], 443
  alt. Hawrami [hac], 439
  alt. dial. Hawrami [hac], 439
Gurara, *alt. dial.* Taznatit [grr], 40
Gurdjar [gdj], 571
Gurdung, *alt.* Guruntum-Mbaaru
[grd], 161
Gure, *alt. dial.* Gbiri-Niragu
[grh], 160

Gure-Kahugu, *alt.* Gbiri-Niragu [grh], 160
Gureng Gureng [gnr], 571
Gureng-Gureng, *alt.* Gureng Gureng [gnr], 571
Gurenne, *alt.* Farefare [gur], 124
  alt. Ninkare [gur], 53
  alt. dial. Farefare [gur], 124
Guresha, *alt.* Buli [bwu], 123
Gurezi, *alt. dial.* Shina [scl], 488
  dial. Shina [scl], 387
Gurgo, *dial.* Dayak, Land [dyk], 393
Gurgula [ggg], 485
Gurian, *dial.* Georgian [kat], 352
Guriaso [grx], 601
Gurindji, *alt.* Gurinji [gue], 571
Gurinji [gue], 571
Gurjar, *alt.* Gujari [gju], 363
Gurjindi, *dial.* Jarnango [jay], 571
Gurka, *alt.* Yiwom [gek], 178
Gurkhali, *alt.* Nepali [nep], 476, 323, 381
Gurma, *alt.* Gourmanchéma [gux], 51, 45, 152, 208
Gurmana [gvm], 161
Gurmarti, *alt.* Lambadi [lmn], 372
Gurmukhi, *alt.* Panjabi, Eastern [pan], 383, 135
Gurne, *alt.* Ninkare [gur], 53
Guro [goa], 93
Gurreh, *alt. dial.* Garreh-Ajuran [ggh], 133
Gurreng Gurreng, *alt.* Gureng Gureng [gnr], 571
Gurrgoni, *alt.* Guragone [gge], 571
Gurrogone, *alt.* Guragone [gge], 571
Gurrum, *alt. dial.* Jere [jer], 165
Gurtü, *alt.* Kurtokha [xkz], 323
Guru, *alt.* Luguru [ruf], 200
  dial. Dogon, Jamsay [djm], 142, 50
  dial. Shiki [gua], 174
Gurubi, *alt. dial.* Chumburung [ncu], 124
Guruf-Ngariawang, *dial.* Adzera [azr], 587
Guruka, *dial.* Safwa [sbk], 204
Gurumukhi, *alt.* Panjabi, Eastern [pan], 383, 135
Gurune, *alt.* Farefare [gur], 124
  dial. Farefare [gur], 124
Gurung, *alt.* Gurung, Western [gvr], 471
Gurung Kura, *alt.* Gurung, Western [gvr], 363
Gurung, Eastern [ggn], 471
Gurung, Western [gvr], 471, 363
Guruntum, *alt.* Guruntum-Mbaaru [grd], 161
Guruntum-Mbaaru [grd], 161
Gurvali, *alt.* Garhwali [gbm], 360

Gusan [gsn], 601
Gusap, *alt.* Wasembo [gsp], 631
Gusawa, *alt. dial.* Jere [jer], 165
Guse, *dial.* Toura [neb], 95
Gusii [guz], 133
Gusiilay, *alt.* Gusilay [gsl], 180
Gusilaay, *alt.* Gusilay [gsl], 180
Gusilay [gsl], 180
Gussum, *alt. dial.* Jere [jer], 165
Gustavia English, *dial.* English [eng], 253
Gusu, *dial.* Jere [jer], 165
Gusubou, *dial.* Tso [ldp], 176
Guta, *dial.* Manyika [mxc], 216, 148
Gutamal, *alt. dial.* Swedish [swe], 562
Gutjertabia, *alt.* Guragone [gge], 571
Gutnic, *alt. dial.* Swedish [swe], 562
Gutniska, *alt. dial.* Swedish [swe], 562
Gutob, *alt.* Gadaba, Bodo [gbj], 361
Gutop, *alt.* Gadaba, Bodo [gbj], 361
Gutu, *alt.* Gudu [gdu], 161
Guugu Yimithirr, *alt.* Guguyimidjir [kky], 571
Guvhu, *dial.* Venda [ven], 187
Guvja, *dial.* Kanuri, Central [knc], 166, 63, 81, 191
Guvvalollu, *alt.* Vaagri Booli [vaa], 389
Guwamal, *alt.* Yidiny [yii], 579
Guwamu [gwu], 571
Guwan, *alt.* Gambera [gma], 570
Guwet, *alt.* Duwet [gve], 598
Guwidj, *alt. dial.* Ngarinyin [ung], 575
Guwot, *alt.* Duwet [gve], 598
Guxhou, *alt. dial.* Chinese, Min Dong [cdo], 330, 508
Guya [gka], 601
Guyanais, *alt.* Guianese Creole French [gcr], 252
Guyane, *alt.* Guianese Creole French [gcr], 252
Guyane Creole, *alt.* Guianese Creole French [gcr], 252
Guyanese Creole, *alt.* Guyanese Creole English [gyn], 257, 295
Guyanese Creole English [gyn], 257, 295
Guyanese English, *dial.* English [eng], 257
Guyani [gvy], 571
Guyarak, *alt.* Guya [gka], 601
Guyennais, *dial.* Languedocien [lnc], 537
Guyuk, *alt. dial.* Longuda [lnu], 169
Guzawa, *alt. dial.* Jere [jer], 165
Guzii, *alt.* Gusii [guz], 133
Gvede, *alt.* Umanakaina [gdn], 629

Gvoko [ngs], 161, 62
Gwa [gwb], 161
  alt. Gua [gwx], 125
  alt. Mbato [gwa], 94
Gwabegwabe, *dial.* Iamalele [yml], 602
Gwadara Basa, *alt.* Basa-Gumna [bsl], 155
Gwadi Parekwa, *alt.* Parkwa [pbi], 71
Gwahamere, *dial.* Gwahatike [dah], 601
Gwahatike [dah], 601
  dial. Gwahatike [dah], 601
Gwak, *alt. dial.* Jarawa [jar], 165
Gwaka, *alt.* Ngbaka Ma'bo [nbm], 105
Gwama, *alt.* Kwama [kmq], 116
Gwamba, *alt.* Tsonga [tso], 149, 217
  dial. Tsonga [tso], 186
Gwamfanci, *alt. dial.* Gwamhi-Wuri [bga], 161
Gwamfi Gwamfawa, *alt. dial.* Gwamhi-Wuri [bga], 161
Gwamhi, *dial.* Gwamhi-Wuri [bga], 161
Gwamhi-Wuri [bga], 161
Gwana, *dial.* Hōne [juh], 162
Gwandaba, *alt. dial.* Longuda [lnu], 169
Gwandara [gwn], 161
Gwandara Eastern, *dial.* Gwandara [gwn], 161
Gwandara Gitata, *dial.* Gwandara [gwn], 161
Gwandara Karashi, *dial.* Gwandara [gwn], 161
Gwandara Koro, *dial.* Gwandara [gwn], 161
Gwandara Southern, *dial.* Gwandara [gwn], 161
Gwandera, *alt.* Yir Yoront [yiy], 579
Gwanje, *dial.* Wandala [mfi], 73, 177
Gwano, *dial.* Pokomo, Upper [pkb], 135
Gwanto, *alt. dial.* Numana-Nunku-Gbantu-Numbu [nbr], 171
Gwantu, *alt. dial.* Numana-Nunku-Gbantu-Numbu [nbr], 171
Gwapa, *alt. dial.* Tsonga [tso], 186
Gwapti, *dial.* Gwahatike [dah], 601
Gwara, *alt. dial.* Marghi Central [mrt], 169
Gwareta, *dial.* Maiwa [mti], 611
Gwari, *alt.* Gbagyi [gbr], 160
Gwari Matai, *alt.* Gbagyi [gbr], 160
Gwari Yamma, *alt.* Gbari [gby], 160

Gwasi, *dial.* Suba [suh], 136
Gwataley, *alt.* Batuley [bay], 396
Gwate, *alt.* Bata [bta], 58
Gwatike, *alt.* Gwahatike [dah], 601
Gwavili, *alt. dial.* Tawala [tbo], 627
Gwawili, *alt. dial.* Tawala [tbo], 627
Gwaza, *dial.* Nung [nun], 466, 341
Gwe, *alt.* Cerma [cme], 50, 92
  alt. dial. Sukuma [suk], 205
Gweda [grw], 601
  alt. Umanakaina [gdn], 629
Gwede, *alt.* Umanakaina [gdn], 629
Gwedena, *alt.* Umanakaina
  [gdn], 629
Gweetaawu, *dial.* Dan [daf], 92
Gwemarra, *alt. dial.* Sebat Bet
  Gurage [sgw], 118
Gwen, *alt.* Cerma [cme], 50, 92
Gwendele, *alt. dial.* Vame [mlr], 73
Gweno [gwe], 198
Gwéò, *dial.* Toura [neb], 95
Gwere [gwr], 210
Gweri, *alt.* Mo'da [gbn], 193
|Gwi [gwj], 47
G‖wi, *alt.* |Gwi [gwj], 47
G|wi, *alt.* |Gwi [gwj], 47
Gwibwen, *alt.* Neyo [ney], 94
Gwich'in [gwi], 237, 301
Gwiini, *alt.* Kwini [gww], 573
G‖wikhwe, *alt.* |Gwi [gwj], 47
G|wikhwe, *alt.* |Gwi [gwj], 47
G!wikwe, *alt.* |Gwi [gwj], 47
Gwini, *alt.* Kwini [gww], 573
Gwom, *alt.* Moo [gwg], 170
Gwomo, *alt.* Moo [gwg], 170
Gwomu, *alt.* Moo [gwg], 170
Gwong, *alt.* Kagoma [kdm], 165
Gwong Dung Waa, *alt.* Chinese,
  Yue [yue], 331
Gworam, *alt.* Lala-Roba [lla], 163
  dial. Kofyar [kwl], 166
Gwune, *alt.* Agwagwune [yay], 153
Gxana, *alt.* ‖Gana [gnk], 46
Gxanna, *alt.* ‖Gana [gnk], 46
Gyaazi, *alt. dial.* Geji [gji], 160
Gyakan, *dial.* Kwa [kwb], 167
Gyam, *alt.* Gyem [gye], 162
Gyaman, *alt.* Abron [abr], 122, 91
Gyange, *alt. dial.* Gbagyi [gbr], 160
Gyangiya, *alt.* Nyang'i [nyp], 212
Gyarong, *alt.* Jiarong [jya], 336
Gyarung, *alt.* Jiarong [jya], 336
Gyegem, *alt. dial.* Serer-Sine
  [srr], 182, 122
Gyele [gyi], 62, 111
Gyeli, *alt.* Gyele [gyi], 62, 111
Gyell-Kuru-Vwang, *dial.* Berom
  [bom], 155
Gyem [gye], 162
  alt. Fyam [pym], 160

Gyema, *alt.* Fyam [pym], 160
Gyemawa, *alt.* Gyem [gye], 162
Gyengyen, *alt. dial.* Gbagyi
  [gbr], 160
Gyeto, *dial.* Sebat Bet Gurage
  [sgw], 118
Gyirong, *alt.* Kyerung [kgy], 474
Gyo, *alt.* Dan [daf], 129, 137
Gyogo, *dial.* Ligbi [lig], 126
Gyong, *alt.* Kagoma [kdm], 165
Gypsy, *alt.* Domari [rmt], 438, 448,
  510, 563
  alt. Romani, Balkan [rmn], 532, 548
  alt. Romani, Kalo Finnish [rmf], 535
  alt. Romani, Vlax [rmy], 551, 531,
  542
Ha [haq], 199
  dial. Dzongkha [dzo], 323
  dial. Hlai [lic], 333
Ha Mea, *alt.* Mea [meg], 585
Ha Xa Phang, *alt.* Chinese, Yue
  [yue], 522
Ha-Tiri, *alt.* Tiri [cir], 585
Ha'aang, *alt. dial.* Ta'oih, Upper
  [tth], 453, 527
Haal, *alt.* Kasanga [ccj], 131
Haalpulaar, *alt.* Pulaar [fuc], 130
  alt. dial. Pulaar [fuc], 181, 122, 143,
  145
Haat, *alt.* O'du [tyh], 525
  pej. alt. O'du [tyh], 452
Haaviqinra-Oraura, *dial.* Tairora,
  South [omw], 626
Haavu, *alt.* Havu [hav], 100
Haayil, *alt. dial.* Arabic, Najdi Spoken
  [ars], 508
Habau, *dial.* Jarai [jra], 523, 325
Habban, *dial.* Arabic, Judeo-Yemeni
  [jye], 444, 528
Habe, *alt.* Hausa [hau], 162
Habenapo, *alt.* Pomo, Central [poo],
  307
Habina-Oraura, *alt. dial.* Tairora,
  South [omw], 626
Habu [hbu], 350
Habura, *dial.* Bhili [bhb], 356
Hachero, *alt. dial.* Nachering
  [ncd], 476
Hadaareb, *alt. dial.* Bedawi
  [bej], 188, 112
Hadang, *alt.* Sedang [sed], 526
Hadareb, *dial.* Bedawi [bej], 188,
  112
Hadauti, *alt.* Harauti [hoj], 364
Hadejiya, *dial.* Hausa [hau], 162
Hadem, *dial.* Hrangkhol [hra], 364
Hadendiwa, *alt. dial.* Bedawi
  [bej], 188
Hadendoa, *dial.* Bedawi [bej], 188,
  112

Hadendowa, *alt. dial.* Bedawi [bej],
  188, 112
Hadia, *alt.* Hadiyya [hdy], 115
Hadimu, *alt. dial.* Swahili [swh], 136
Hadiya, *alt.* Hadiyya [hdy], 115
Hadiyya [hdy], 115
Hadothi, *alt.* Harauti [hoj], 364
Hadoti, *alt.* Harauti [hoj], 364
Hadrami, *alt.* Arabic, Hadrami
  Spoken [ayh], 527
Hadrami Spoken Arabic, *see*
  Arabic, Hadrami Spoken [ayh], 527
Hadromi, *alt.* Arabic, Hadrami
  Spoken [ayh], 527
Hadya, *alt.* Hadiyya [hdy], 115
Hadyo, *dial.* Nyole [nuj], 212
Hadza [hts], 199
Hadzabi, *alt.* Hadza [hts], 199
Hadzapi, *alt.* Hadza [hts], 199
Haeake, *alt.* Haeke [aek], 584
Haeke [aek], 584
Haft-Lang, *dial.* Bakhtiari [bqi], 438
Hagahai, *alt.* Pinai-Hagahai
  [pnn], 622
Hagei, *dial.* Gelao [gio], 333
Hagen, *alt.* Melpa [med], 613
Hageulu, *dial.* Bughotu [bgt], 635
Hagi, *dial.* Kamasau [kms], 604
Hagueti, *alt.* Cashibo-Cacataibo
  [cbr], 287
Hahaintesu, *dial.* Nambikuára,
  Southern [nab], 230
Hahak, *dial.* Galoli [gal], 350
Hahon [hah], 601
Hahutan, *alt.* Ili'uun [ilu], 399
Hahutau, *alt.* Ili'uun [ilu], 399
Hai, *alt.* Lele [lle], 609
  dial. Banda-Banda [bpd], 75
  dial. Machame [jmc], 193
Hai Nam, *alt.* Chinese, Yue [yue],
  522
Haian Ami, *alt. dial.* Amis [ami], 511
Haiao, *alt.* Yao [yao], 141, 149, 215
Haida, Northern [hdn], 238, 301
Haida, Southern [hax], 238
Haieren, *alt.* Armenian [hye], 318,
  319, 350, 437, 444, 453, 510, 563
Haigwai [hgw], 601
Haija, *dial.* Amele [aey], 589
Haijong, *alt.* Hajong [haj], 363, 321
Haila'er, *dial.* Daur [dta], 331, 461
  dial. Evenki [evn], 332
Hailar, *alt. dial.* Daur [dta], 331, 461
Hailu, *dial.* Chinese, Hakka [hak], 511
Hain, *alt.* Bozo, Hainyaxo [bzx], 142
Hainan, *dial.* Chinese, Min Nan
  [nan], 330, 324, 514
Hainan Cham, *alt.* Tsat [huq], 345
Hainan Miao, *alt.* Kim Mun
  [mji], 337

Hainanese, *alt. dial.* Chinese, Min Nan [nan], 330
dial. Chinese, Min Nan [nan], 454, 508
Hainaut, *alt. dial.* Picard [pcd], 537
Hainman, *alt.* Ngarinman [nbj], 575
Hainte, *alt.* Chin, Paite [pck], 463
Hain‖um, *alt. dial.* Hai‖om [hgm], 149
Hainyaxo, *alt.* Bozo, Hainyaxo [bzx], 142
Hainyaxo Bozo, *see* Bozo, Hainyaxo [bzx], 142
Hai‖om [hgm], 149
Haiphong Sign Language [haf], 523
Haira, *alt.* Orokolo [oro], 620
|Hais, *alt. dial.* Shua [shg], 48
|Haise, *alt. dial.* Shua [shg], 48
Haisla [has], 238
Haithe, *alt.* Chin, Paite [pck], 359
Haitian Creole French [hat], 258, 250, 253
Haitian Vodoun Culture Language [hvc], 258
Haitshuari, *alt.* Tsoa [hio], 48
Haitshuwau, *alt.* Hietshware [hio], 216
Hajao, *alt.* Yao [yao], 206
Hajong [haj], 363, 321
Haka, *alt.* Bolo [blv], 40
alt. Chin, Haka [cnh], 463, 321, 357
Haka Chin, *see* Chin, Haka [cnh], 463, 321, 357
Hakei, *alt. dial.* Gelao [gio], 333
Haketia, *alt.* Ladino [lad], 563
alt. dial. Ladino [lad], 445
Haketiya, *alt. dial.* Ladino [lad], 445
Hakha, *alt.* Chin, Haka [cnh], 463
Hakhi, *alt. dial.* Gelao [gio], 333
Haki Piki, *alt.* Vaagri Booli [vaa], 389
Hakitia, *alt.* Ladino [lad], 563
alt. dial. Ladino [lad], 445
Hakka, *alt.* Chinese, Hakka [hak], 329, 324, 514, 581
Hakka Chinese, *see* Chinese, Hakka [hak], 329, 252, 283, 295, 324, 391, 454, 508, 511, 514, 581
Hakkipikkaru, *alt.* Vaagri Booli [vaa], 389
Hakö [hao], 601
Haku, *alt.* Hakö [hao], 601
Hal Kurumba, *alt.* Kurumba, Alu [xua], 371
Halaba, *alt.* Alaba [alw], 112
Halabi, *alt.* Halbi [hlb], 363
Halakwulup, *alt.* Qawasqar [alc], 243

Halam, *alt.* Chin, Falam [flm], 463, 321
dial. Chin, Falam [flm], 358
dial. Kok Borok [trp], 368, 321
Halam Chin, *alt.* Chin, Falam [flm], 358
Halang [hal], 523
alt. Salang [hal], 452
Halang Doan [hld], 523, 450
Halang Duan, *alt.* Halang Doan [hld], 523, 450
Halba, *alt.* Halbi [hlb], 363
Halbi [hlb], 363
dial. Oriya [ori], 382
Halchighol, *alt. dial.* Tu [mjg], 345
Halerman, *dial.* Kelon [kyo], 407
Halh, *alt.* Mongolian, Halh [khk], 461, 505
alt. dial. Mongolian, Halh [khk], 505
dial. Mongolian, Halh [khk], 461
Halh Mongolian, *see* Mongolian, Halh [khk], 461, 505
Halia [hla], 601
Halifoersch, *dial.* Marind [mrz], 419
Haliti, *alt.* Parecís [pab], 231
Halkomelem [hur], 238, 301
Hallaendska, *dial.* Scanian [scy], 533
Hallam, *alt.* Chin, Falam [flm], 358
Hallam Chin, *alt.* Chin, Falam [flm], 463, 321
Halländska, *dial.* Scanian [scy], 562
Hallari, *alt.* Gadaba, Pottangi Ollar [gdb], 361
Halotesu, *dial.* Nambikuára, Southern [nab], 230
Halpulaar, *alt. dial.* Pulaar [fuc], 122, 143
Haltu, *dial.* Chin, Matu [hlt], 359
Halumbung, *dial.* Sampang [rav], 478
Halvas, *alt.* Halbi [hlb], 363
Halvi, *alt.* Halbi [hlb], 363
Ham, *alt.* Hyam [jab], 162
alt. Marik [dad], 612
dial. Masana [mcn], 83
Hamacore, *alt.* Iquito [iqu], 288
Hamap [hmu], 407
Hamar, *alt.* Hamer-Banna [amf], 115
alt. Hmar [hmr], 364
Hamar-Koke, *alt.* Hamer-Banna [amf], 115
Hamba [hba], 100
alt. Amba [rwm], 210
alt. dial. Amba [rwm], 96
dial. Haya [hay], 199
dial. Nkutu [nkw], 106
Hambali Botolan, *alt. dial.* Sambal, Botolan [sbl], 501
Hambo, *alt.* Amba [rwm], 96

Hamday, *alt.* Hamtai [hmt], 601
Häme, *dial.* Finnish [fin], 534
Hameha, *alt.* Mea [meg], 585
Hamej, *alt.* Gule [gly], 191
Hamer, *alt.* Hamer-Banna [amf], 115
Hamer-Banna [amf], 115
Hamgyongdo, *dial.* Korean [kor], 448
Hamil, *alt. dial.* Haruai [tmd], 601
Hamirpuri, *dial.* Kangri [xnr], 366
Hammer, *alt.* Hamer-Banna [amf], 115
Hammercoche, *alt.* Hamer-Banna [amf], 115
Hamschen, *alt. dial.* Armenian [hye], 318
Hamshen, *dial.* Armenian [hye], 318
Hamtai [hmt], 601
dial. Hamtai [hmt], 601
Hamtik, *alt. dial.* Kinaray-A [krj], 498
Hamtiknon, *alt.* Kinaray-A [krj], 498
Hamung, *alt.* Damal [uhn], 413
Han [haa], 301, 238
alt. Chinese, Yue [yue], 522
Han Lachi, *alt. dial.* Lachi [lbt], 338
Han-Kutchin, *alt.* Han [haa], 301, 238
Hanahan, *dial.* Halia [hla], 601
Hanak, *dial.* Czech [ces], 533
Hanalulo, *alt.* Kallahan, Keley-I [ify], 497
Hananwa, *alt. dial.* Sotho, Northern [nso], 186
Handa, *dial.* Mboi [moi], 170
Handá, *alt.* ‖Ani [hnh], 46
Handa-Khwe, *alt.* ‖Ani [hnh], 46
Handádam, *alt.* ‖Ani [hnh], 46
Handakwe-Dam, *alt.* ‖Ani [hnh], 46
Handuri, *alt.* Hinduri [hii], 364
Hang, *alt.* Kháng [kjm], 524
Hàng Tong, *alt.* Tai Hang Tong [thc], 527
Hanga [hag], 125
alt. dial. Luyia [luy], 134
dial. Ngelima [agh], 106
Hanga Hundi [wos], 601
Hangala, *alt. dial.* Laari [ldi], 88
Hangan, *dial.* Halia [hla], 601
Hanganu, *alt. dial.* Tsonga [tso], 149, 217
Hangaza [han], 199
Hangiro, *dial.* Haya [hay], 199
Hangkhim, *alt. dial.* Bantawa [bap], 468
Hangkula, *alt. dial.* Nachering [ncd], 476

Hanguk Mal, *alt.* Korean [kor], 448
Hanguohua, *alt.* Korean [kor], 448
Hanhi, *alt.* Hani [hni], 333, 450
Hànhì, *alt.* Hani [hni], 523
Hani [hni], 333, 450, 523
Hani Proper, *alt.* Hani [hni], 333
Hanis, *alt.* Coos [csz], 300
Hanniu, *dial.* Tibetan [bod], 388
Hano [lml], 642
  dial. Tewa [tew], 308
Hanoi, *alt. dial.* Vietnamese [vie], 527
Hanoi Sign Language [hab], 523
Hanon, *alt.* Hahon [hah], 601
Hanonoo, *alt.* Hanunoo [hnn], 494
Hantong, *alt.* Ong [oog], 452
Hantong', *dial.* Ta'oih, Lower [tto], 453
Hanty, *alt.* Khanty [kca], 505
Hanunoo [hnn], 494
Hanyaxo, *alt.* Bozo, Hainyaxo [bzx], 142
Hanyeng, *alt.* Nyeng [nfg], 171
Hanyu, *alt.* Chinese, Mandarin [cmn], 329
Haohai, *dial.* Hani [hni], 333
Haoni, *alt.* Honi [how], 335
Haoulo, *alt. dial.* Krumen, Pye [pye], 93
Haoussa, *alt.* Hausa [hau], 162, 51, 62, 152
Hapa, *alt.* Labu [lbu], 609
Hapao Ifugao, *dial.* Ifugao, Tuwali [ifk], 495
Haq'aru, *alt.* Jaqaru [jqr], 288
Haqaru, *alt.* Jaqaru [jqr], 288
Haqearu, *alt.* Jaqaru [jqr], 288
Haquetiya, *alt.* Ladino [lad], 445
  alt. dial. Ladino [lad], 445
Har, *alt.* Santali [sat], 386, 322, 478
Haragure, *alt.* Xaragure [axx], 585
Harahu, *alt. dial.* Folopa [ppo], 599
Harahui, *alt. dial.* Folopa [ppo], 599
Haramosh, *alt. dial.* Shina [scl], 488
Haraneu, *alt.* Xârâcùù [ane], 585
Harar, *alt.* Oromo, Eastern [hae], 118
Harari [har], 115
Hararri, *alt.* Harari [har], 115
Harauti [hoj], 364
  dial. Harauti [hoj], 364
Harava, *dial.* Orokaiva [ork], 620
Harban, *alt. dial.* Shina [scl], 488
Hare, *dial.* Slavey, North [scs], 241
Hareme, *dial.* Maleng [pkt], 451
Harengan, *dial.* Sori-Harengan [sbh], 625
Harer, *alt.* Oromo, Eastern [hae], 118
Haria, *alt.* Kharia [khr], 367
Hariamba, *dial.* Dimasa [dis], 360
Hariani, *alt.* Haryanvi [bgc], 364

Harigaya, *dial.* Koch [kdq], 368, 321
Harijan, *alt.* Chinali [cih], 359
  dial. Tamil [tam], 388
Harijan Boli, *alt.* Kinnauri, Harijan [kjo], 368
Harijan Kinnauri, *see* Kinnauri, Harijan [kjo], 368
Haripmor, *dial.* Boikin [bzf], 594
Hariyani, *alt.* Haryanvi [bgc], 364
Harja, *alt.* Bodo Parja [bdv], 357
Harka Gurung, *alt.* Raute [rau], 478
Haroi [hro], 523
Harsi 'Aforit, *alt.* Harsusi [hss], 482
Harso, *dial.* Gawwada [gwd], 115
Harsusi [hss], 482
Harua, *dial.* Bola [bnp], 594
Haruai [tmd], 601
Haruku [hrk], 398
Harway, *alt.* Haruai [tmd], 601
Haryani, *alt.* Haryanvi [bgc], 364
Haryanvi [bgc], 364
Harzani [hrz], 439
Hasab, *dial.* Saafi-Saafi [sav], 182
Hasada, *dial.* Mundari [muw], 476
Hasada', *dial.* Mundari [muw], 376, 321
Hasala, *dial.* Bandi [bza], 137
Hasanya, *alt.* Arabic, Hassaniyya [mey], 146, 151
  alt. Hassaniyya [mey], 145
Hasanya Arabic, *see* Hassaniyya [mey], 141
Hasha [ybj], 162
Hasoria Bhil, *dial.* Koli, Wadiyara [kxp], 487
Hasoria Koli, *dial.* Koli, Wadiyara [kxp], 487
Hassani, *alt.* Arabic, Hasanya [mey], 141
  alt. Arabic, Hassaniyya [mey], 146, 151
  alt. Hassaniyya [mey], 145
Hassaniya, *alt.* Hassaniyya [mey], 145
Hassaniyya [mey], 145
  alt. Arabic, Hasanya [mey], 141
Hassaniyya Arabic, *see* Hassaniyya [mey], 146, 151
Hat, *alt.* O'du [tyh], 525
  dial. Khmu [kjg], 451
  pej. alt. O'du [tyh], 452
Hatam [had], 415
Hatang-Kayey, *alt.* Agta, Remontado [agv], 491
Hate, *alt.* Ninzo [nin], 171
  alt. dial. Kunimaipa [kup], 608
Hateruma, *dial.* Yaeyama [rys], 447
Hatigoria, *alt.* Naga, Ao [njo], 377
Hatohobei, *alt.* Tobian [tox], 587
Hatoma, *dial.* Yaeyama [rys], 447

Hatsa, *alt.* Hadza [hts], 199
Hattam, *alt.* Hatam [had], 415
Hatue, *alt.* Saleman [sau], 403
Hatumeten, *alt.* Bobot [bty], 397
Hatuolu, *dial.* Manusela [wha], 402
Hatusua, *dial.* Kaibobo [kzb], 399
Hatutu, *dial.* Marquesan, North [mrq], 581
Hatuwali, *alt. dial.* Bantawa [bap], 468
Hatzfeldhafen, *alt.* Mala [ped], 611
Haubi, *dial.* Langi [lag], 200
Hauhunu, *alt. dial.* Bauro [bxa], 635
Haununu, *dial.* Bauro [bxa], 635
Haura, *alt.* Keuru [xeu], 606
  dial. Tama [tma], 86
Haura Haela, *alt.* Keuru [xeu], 606
Hauruha, *dial.* Pawaia [pwa], 621
Ha'us, *alt.* Andra-Hus [anx], 589
Hausa [hau], 162, 45, 51, 62, 125, 152, 191
Hausa Sign Language [hsl], 162
Hausawa, *alt.* Hausa [hau], 162, 152
Háusi Kúta, *alt.* Yámana [yag], 243
Haussa, *alt.* Hausa [hau], 152
Haut Sorabe, *alt.* Sorbian, Upper [hsb], 539
Haut-Auvergnat, *dial.* Auvergnat [auv], 535
Haut-Kenyang, *alt. dial.* Kenyang [ken], 64
Haut-Languedocien, *dial.* Languedocien [lnc], 537
Haut-Limousin, *dial.* Limousin [lms], 537
Ha'uwa, *alt.* Rampi [lje], 432
Havannah Harbour, *alt.* Lelepa [lpa], 642
Havasupai, *dial.* Havasupai-Walapai-Yavapai [yuf], 301
Havasupai-Walapai-Yavapai [yuf], 301
Have, *dial.* Naga, Tase [nst], 380
Haveke [hvk], 584
Havoy, *alt. dial.* Naga, Tase [nst], 380
Havu [hav], 100
Havunese, *alt.* Sabu [hvn], 409
Haw, *alt.* Hani [hni], 333, 450, 523
  alt. dial. Chinese, Mandarin [cmn], 514
Hawai'i Creole English [hwc], 301
Hawai'i Pidgin, *alt.* Hawai'i Creole English [hwc], 301
Hawai'i Pidgin Sign Language [hps], 301
Hawaiian [haw], 302
Hawkip, *alt. dial.* Chin, Thado [tcz], 359
  dial. Chin, Thado [tcz], 463

High Latvian, *alt. dial.* Latvian [lav], 546

High Lugbara, *alt.* Lugbara [lgg], 211, 103

High Mari, *alt.* Mari, Western [mrj], 555

High Navarrese, *alt. dial.* Basque [eus], 559

High Piemontese, *dial.* Piemontese [pms], 545

Highland Arequipa, *alt. dial.* Quechua, Arequipa-La Unión [qxu], 289

Highland Bali, *dial.* Bali [ban], 391

Highland Chinantec, *alt.* Chinantec, Quiotepec [chq], 261

Highland Guerrero Mixtec, *alt.* Mixtec, Alacatlatzala [mim], 265

Highland Huarijío, *dial.* Huarijio [var], 262

Highland Inga, *alt.* Inga [inb], 246

Highland Konjo, *see* Konjo, Highland [kjk], 430

Highland Lithuanian, *alt. dial.* Lithuanian [lit], 546

Highland Mazatec, *alt.* Mazatec, Huautla [mau], 264

Highland Nung, *alt.* Nung [nut], 525

Highland Oaxaca Chontal, *see* Chontal, Highland Oaxaca [chd], 261

Highland Popoluca, *see* Popoluca, Highland [poi], 274

Highland Popoluca, *alt.* Popoluca, Highland [poi], 274

Highland Puebla Nahuatl, *see* Nahuatl, Highland Puebla [azz], 271

Highland Totonac, *see* Totonac, Highland [tos], 276

Highland Tzeltal, *alt.* Tzeltal, Oxchuc [tzh], 276

Highland Yao, *alt.* Iu Mien [ium], 336, 450, 514, 523

Higi, *alt.* Kamwe [hig], 166

Higir, *alt.* Nara [nrb], 112

Higsho, *dial.* Naga, Tase [nst], 380

Higtsii, *dial.* Naga, Tase [nst], 380

Hijazi, *alt.* Arabic, Hijazi Spoken [acw], 508, 111

Hijazi Spoken Arabic, *see* Arabic, Hijazi Spoken [acw], 508, 111

Hiji, *alt.* Kamwe [hig], 166

Hijuk [hij], 62

Hila, *dial.* Hitu [htu], 398

Hila-Kaitetu, *alt.* Seit-Kaitetu [hik], 403

Hildi, *dial.* Marghi South [mfm], 169

Hileman, *alt.* Dyaabugay [dyy], 570

Hiligainon, *alt.* Hiligaynon [hil], 494

Hiligaynon [hil], 494

    dial. Hiligaynon [hil], 494

Hill Angas, *dial.* Ngas [anc], 171

Hill Bura, *alt. dial.* Bura-Pabir [bwr], 156

Hill Dusun, *alt.* Kuijau [dkr], 457

Hill Geta', *dial.* Gata' [gaq], 362

Hill Jarawa, *alt.* Izere [fiz], 164

Hill Mada, *alt.* Eggon [ego], 158

Hill Mari, *alt.* Mari, Western [mrj], 555

Hill Maria, *alt.* Maria [mrr], 375

    alt. dial. Maria [mrr], 375

Hill Pantaram, *alt.* Malapandaram [mjp], 373

Hill Pulaya, *alt. dial.* Paliyan [pcf], 382

Hill Tarok, *alt. dial.* Tarok [yer], 175

Hill Tetun, *alt. dial.* Tetun [tet], 410, 351

Hilu Humba, *alt.* Kambera [xbr], 407

Hima, *alt. dial.* Ebira [igb], 158

    dial. Nyankore [nyn], 212

Himachali, *alt.* Mandeali [mjl], 374

Himarimã [hir], 227

Himba, *alt.* Zemba [dhm], 42, 151

Hin, *alt.* Nyaheun [nev], 452

Hina, *alt.* Mina [hna], 67

    alt. dial. Tera [ttr], 175

Hinapavosa, *alt.* Papora-Hoanya [ppu], 512

Hinaray-A, *alt.* Kinaray-A [krj], 498

Hinatsa, *alt.* Hidatsa [hid], 302

Hindi [hin], 364, 186, 211, 472

Hindi Dogri, *alt.* Dogri [dgo], 360

Hindki, *alt.* Hindko, Northern [hno], 485

    alt. Panjabi, Western [pnb], 383

Hindko, Northern [hno], 485

Hindko, Southern [hnd], 485

Hindu Sindhi, *alt. dial.* Sindhi [snd], 488

Hinduri [hii], 364

Hindustani, Caribbean [hns], 295, 257, 296

Hindustani, Fijian [hif], 580

Hinghua, *alt. dial.* Chinese, Pu-Xian [cpx], 330, 454, 508

Hinihon, *alt.* Pamosu [hih], 621

Hinna, *alt. dial.* Tera [ttr], 175

Hinukh [gin], 554

Hinux, *alt.* Hinukh [gin], 554

Hiochuwau, *alt.* Tsoa [hio], 48

Hiotshuwau, *alt.* Tsoa [hio], 48

Hiowe, *alt. dial.* Saniyo-Hiyewe [sny], 623

Hira, *dial.* Yagaria [ygr], 632

Hiraca, *alt.* Hidatsa [hid], 302

Hiranpur, *alt. dial.* Sauria Paharia [mjt], 386

Hirara, *alt. dial.* Miyako [mvi], 447

Hiri, *alt.* Motu, Hiri [hmo], 615

Hiri Motu, *see* Motu, Hiri [hmo], 615

Hiroi-Lamgang, *pej. alt.* Lamkang [lmk], 372, 465

Hishkaryana, *alt.* Hixkaryána [hix], 227

Hispanoromani, *alt.* Caló [rmr], 559

Hissala, *alt.* Sisaala, Tumulung [sil], 127

    alt. Sisaala, Western [ssl], 128

Hitadipa Nduga, *dial.* Nduga [ndx], 421

Hitau-Pororan, *dial.* Petats [pex], 621

Hitchiti, *alt.* Mikasuki [mik], 305

    dial. Mikasuki [mik], 305

Hitnü, *alt.* Macaguán [mbn], 246

Hitu [htu], 398

    dial. Hitu [htu], 398

Hiva Oa, *dial.* Marquesan, South [mqm], 581

Hiw [hiw], 642

Hixkariana, *alt.* Hixkaryána [hix], 227

Hixkaryána [hix], 227

Hiyowe, *dial.* Saniyo-Hiyewe [sny], 623

Hka Ko, *alt.* Akha [ahk], 449

Hka-Hku, *alt. dial.* Jingpho [kac], 464, 336

Hkaku, *dial.* Jingpho [kac], 464, 336

Hkaluk, *dial.* Naga, Tase [nst], 466

Hkamti, *alt.* Khamti [kht], 465, 367

Hkanung, *alt.* Rawang [raw], 466, 385

Hkauri, *alt. dial.* Jingpho [kac], 464, 336

Hkawa, *alt.* Blang [blr], 514

Hkun, *alt.* Khün [kkh], 465, 515

Hlai [lic], 333

Hlanganu, *alt. dial.* Tsonga [tso], 149, 217

Hlave, *dial.* Tsonga [tso], 186

Hlawthai, *dial.* Chin, Mara [mrh], 359, 463

Hlengwe, *dial.* Tswa [tsc], 149, 186, 217

Hloka, *alt.* Dzongkha [dzo], 361

Hlo'lan, *dial.* Maru [mhx], 465

Hlota, *alt.* Naga, Lotha [njh], 378

Hlubi, *dial.* Swati [ssw], 197, 186

    dial. Xhosa [xho], 187

Hm Nai, *alt.* Bunu, Wunai [bwn], 328

Hmanggona, *alt.* Nalca [nlc], 421

Hmar [hmr], 364

Hmari, *alt.* Hmar [hmr], 364
Hmong Daw [mww], 334, 450, 514, 523
Hmong Dô [hmv], 523
Hmong Don [hmf], 523
Hmong Gu Mba, *dial.* Hmong Daw [mww], 334, 450, 514
Hmong Hoa, *dial.* Hmong Njua [blu], 523
Hmong Leng, *alt.* Hmong Njua [blu], 450, 463, 523
Hmong Njua [blu], 334, 450, 463, 514, 523
Hmong Njwa, *alt.* Hmong Njua [blu], 450, 463, 523
Hmong Qua Mba, *alt. dial.* Hmong Daw [mww], 334, 450, 514
Hmong Shua [hmz], 523
Hmong Xi, *dial.* Hmong Daw [mww], 523
Hmong, Central Huishui [hmc], 334
Hmong, Central Mashan [hmm], 334
Hmong, Chonganjiang [hmj], 334
Hmong, Eastern Huishui [hme], 334
Hmong, Eastern Qiandong [hmq], 334
Hmong, Eastern Xiangxi [muq], 334
Hmong, Luopohe [hml], 334
Hmong, Northeastern Dian [hmd], 334
Hmong, Northern Guiyang [huj], 334
Hmong, Northern Huishui [hmi], 334
Hmong, Northern Mashan [hmp], 335
Hmong, Northern Qiandong [hea], 335
Hmong, Southern Guiyang [hmy], 335
Hmong, Southern Mashan [hma], 335
Hmong, Southern Qiandong [hms], 335
Hmong, Southwestern Guiyang [hmg], 335
Hmong, Southwestern Huishui [hmh], 335
Hmong, Western Mashan [hmw], 335
Hmong, Western Xiangxi [mmr], 335
Hmonono, *alt.* Nalca [nlc], 421
Hmu, *alt.* Hmong, Eastern Qiandong [hmq], 334

alt. Hmong, Northern Qiandong [hea], 335
alt. Hmong, Southern Qiandong [hms], 335
Hmwaeke, *alt.* Vamale [mkt], 585
dial. Vamale [mkt], 585
Hmwaveke [mrk], 584
Hñahñu, *alt.* Otomi, Mezquital [ote], 272
Hñatho, *alt.* Otomi, Estado de México [ots], 272
Hñohño, *alt.* Otomi, Querétaro [otq], 272
Ho [hoc], 364, 321
alt. Honi [how], 335
alt. Musey [mse], 68
dial. Chinese, Mandarin [cmn], 514
dial. Éwé [ewe], 207
Ho Chi Minh City Sign Language [hos], 523
Ho Muong Meridional, *alt.* Tho [tou], 527
Ho Nte, *alt.* She [shx], 343
Ho-Bau, *alt. dial.* Jarai [jra], 523, 325
Ho-Chunk [win], 302
‡Hoa, *alt.* ‡Hua [huc], 47
Hoa, *alt.* Chinese, Yue [yue], 522
Hoai Petel, *alt.* Tita [tdq], 175
‡Hoan, *alt.* ‡Hua [huc], 47
Hoanya, *dial.* Papora-Hoanya [ppu], 512
Hoava [hoa], 636
Hobi, *alt.* Hobyót [hoh], 483
Hobyót [hoh], 483
Hocák, *alt.* Ho-Chunk [win], 302
Hocak Wazijaci, *alt.* Ho-Chunk [win], 302
Hocank, *alt.* Ho-Chunk [win], 302
Hochalemannisch, *alt. dial.* Alemannisch [gsw], 530
Hochank, *alt.* Ho-Chunk [win], 302
Hoche, *alt.* Ulch [ulc], 507
Hockchew, *alt. dial.* Chinese, Min Bei [mnp], 508
Hod, *alt. dial.* Karen, Pwo Northern [pww], 514
Hodjo, *alt. dial.* Banda, West Central [bbp], 74
Hodrung, *dial.* Jarai [jra], 523, 325
Hoen, *alt.* Nyaheun [nev], 452
Hofuf, *alt. dial.* Arabic, Najdi Spoken [ars], 508
Hog Harbour, *alt.* Sakao [sku], 645
Hogeri, *dial.* Koiari, Grass [kbk], 606
Hoggar, *dial.* Tamahaq, Tahaggart [thv], 37, 139, 152
Hogirano, *alt. dial.* Cheke Holo [mrn], 635
Hogo, *alt.* Taroko [trv], 512

Hograno, *dial.* Cheke Holo [mrn], 635
Hoh, *dial.* Quileute [qui], 307
Hohe, *alt.* Assiniboine [asb], 298
Hohodena, *alt. dial.* Baniwa [bwi], 225
Hohodené, *dial.* Baniwa [bwi], 225
Hoi, *alt.* Haroi [hro], 523
Hoilluk, *alt. dial.* Chinese, Hakka [hak], 511
Hoiluk, *alt. dial.* Chinese, Hakka [hak], 511
Hoisan, *alt. dial.* Chinese, Yue [yue], 331
Hokchia, *dial.* Chinese, Min Bei [mnp], 508
Hoki Gelao, *alt.* Gelao, Green [giq], 522
Hokka, *alt.* Chinese, Hakka [hak], 329, 508
Hokkaido, *dial.* Ainu [ain], 446, 503
Hokkien, *alt. dial.* Chinese, Min Nan [nan], 324, 391, 454, 514
dial. Chinese, Min Nan [nan], 508
Hol-Chih, *alt.* Ulch [ulc], 507
Holadi, *alt. dial.* Gujarati [guj], 363
Holar, *alt.* Holiya [hoy], 364
Holari, *alt.* Holiya [hoy], 364
Hole, *alt.* Holiya [hoy], 364
Holi, *alt.* Ede Ije [ijj], 43
Holia, *alt. dial.* Konkani [knn], 369
Holian, *alt.* Holiya [hoy], 364
Holifoersch, *alt.* Marind [mrz], 419
Holikachuk [hoi], 302
Holiya [hoy], 364
Holkomelem, *alt.* Halkomelem [hur], 238, 301
Hollands, *alt.* Dutch [nld], 548
Hollar Gadbas, *alt.* Gadaba, Pottangi Ollar [gdb], 361
Holma [hod], 162
dial. Nzanyi [nja], 71
Holmestrand, *dial.* Norwegian Sign Language [nsl], 549
Holo, *alt.* Cheke Holo [mrn], 635
alt. Holu [hol], 40, 100
Holoholo [hoo], 100
Hololupai, *alt.* Maidu, Northwest [mjd], 304
Holom, *alt. dial.* Majera [xmj], 65, 83
Holu [hol], 40, 100
alt. Holiya [hoy], 364
dial. Holu [hol], 40
Hom, *alt. dial.* Ghomálá' [bbj], 62
Homa [hom], 191
Hombo, *alt.* Ombo [oml], 106
dial. Bangubangu [bnx], 97
Hombori Songhay, *alt.* Songhay, Humburi Senni [hmb], 144
Home, *dial.* Dii [dur], 60

Hona, *alt.* Hwana [hwo], 162
Honduran Mískito, *dial.* Mískito [miq], 282
Honduras Sign Language [hds], 258
Hőne [juh], 162
Hong Kong Cantonese, *alt. dial.* Chinese, Yue [yue], 331
Hong Yao, *alt. dial.* Bunu, Bu-Nao [bwx], 328
Hongalla, *alt.* Ngalakan [nig], 575
Hongshuihe, *dial.* Zhuang, Northern [ccx], 349
Honi [how], 335
Honibo, *dial.* Gobasi [goi], 600
Honitetu, *alt.* Wemale, South [tlw], 405
Hono', *alt. dial.* Seko Padang [skx], 433
Honpo, *dial.* Krumen, Tepo [ted], 93, 138
Honya, *alt.* Tupuri [tui], 72
Hoode, *dial.* Nzanyi [nja], 171
Hoopa, *alt.* Hupa [hup], 302
Hop, *alt.* Mari [hob], 612
Hopa, *alt. dial.* Laz [lzz], 352
Hopao, *dial.* Naga, Konyak [nbe], 378
Hopi [hop], 302
Hopland, *dial.* Pomo, Central [poo], 307
Hor, *alt.* Horo [hor], 81
   alt. Horpa [ero], 335
   alt. Santali [sat], 386, 322, 478
Hora, *alt.* Jorá [jor], 223
Horale, *dial.* Wemale, North [weo], 405
Hornjoserbski, *alt.* Sorbian, Upper [hsb], 539
Hornoserbski, *alt.* Sorbian, Upper [hsb], 539
Horo [hor], 81
   alt. Mundari [muw], 376, 321, 476
Horohoro, *alt.* Holoholo [hoo], 100
Horom [hoe], 162
Hororo, *dial.* Nyankore [nyn], 212
Horpa [ero], 335
Hórsók, *alt.* Horpa [ero], 335
Horu Muthun, *dial.* Naga, Wancho [nnp], 380
Horudahua, *alt. dial.* Yaminahua [yaa], 293
Horunahua, *alt. dial.* Yaminahua [yaa], 293
Horuru [hrr], 398
Hoshangabad, *alt. dial.* Malvi [mup], 374
Hoss, *dial.* Berom [bom], 155
Hotan, *dial.* Uyghur [uig], 346
Hote [hot], 602

dial. Hote [hot], 602
Hotea, *alt.* Sedang [sed], 526
Hoteang, *alt.* Sedang [sed], 526
Hotec, *alt.* Hote [hot], 602
Ho'tei, *alt.* Hote [hot], 602
Hoti [hti], 398
   alt. Yuwana [yau], 313
Hoton, *alt.* Chinese, Mandarin [cmn], 461
   alt. dial. Kalmyk-Oirat [xal], 461
Hottentot, *pej. alt.* Nama [naq], 150, 48, 186
Houailou, *alt.* Ajië [aji], 584
Houeda, *alt.* Gbe, Xwela [xwe], 45
Houla, *alt.* Gbe, Eastern Xwla [gbx], 44
Houlouf, *dial.* Mser [kqx], 68, 84
Hounar, *alt.* Besme [bes], 79
Hovongan [hov], 393
   dial. Hovongan [hov], 393
Howi, *dial.* Hamtai [hmt], 601
Howrami, *alt.* Hawrami [hac], 439
Hoy, *alt. dial.* Evenki [evn], 332
Hozo [hoz], 115
Hpon [hpo], 464
Hpön, *alt.* Hpon [hpo], 464
Hpungsi, *dial.* Rawang [raw], 466
Hpyin, *alt.* Pyen [pyy], 466
Hrangkhol [hra], 464, 364
Hre [hre], 523
   dial. Hre [hre], 523
Hrlak, *alt.* Alak [alk], 449
Hroi, *alt.* Haroi [hro], 523
Hroy, *alt.* Haroi [hro], 523
Hruso [hru], 364
   dial. Hruso [hru], 364
Hrusso, *alt.* Hruso [hru], 364
Hrvatski, *alt.* Croatian [hrv], 532
Hrway, *alt.* Haroi [hro], 523
Hsemtang, *alt.* Chin, Senthang [sez], 463
Hsen-Hsum, *alt.* Mok [mqt], 516
Hsiang, *alt.* Chinese, Xiang [hsn], 331
Hsianghsi Miao, *alt.* Hmong, Eastern Xiangxi [muq], 334
   alt. Hmong, Western Xiangxi [mmr], 335
Hsienyu, *alt. dial.* Chinese, Pu-Xian [cpx], 330
Hsinghua, *alt. dial.* Chinese, Min Dong [cdo], 391
   alt. dial. Chinese, Pu-Xian [cpx], 330, 454
Hsiukulan Ami, *alt. dial.* Amis [ami], 511
Ht'in, *alt.* Mal [mlf], 516
Htin, *alt.* Mal [mlf], 451
Htiselwang, *dial.* Rawang [raw], 466

!Hu, *alt.* Kung-Ekoka [knw], 150, 40
|Hû, *alt.* ‡Hua [huc], 47
Hu [huo], 335
|Hua, *alt.* ‡Hua [huc], 47
‡Hua [huc], 47
   dial. ‡Hua [huc], 47
Hua, *dial.* Yagaria [ygr], 632
Hua Lisu, *dial.* Lisu [lis], 339
Hua Miao, *alt.* Hmong, Northeastern Dian [hmd], 334
‡Hua-Owani, *alt.* ‡Hua [huc], 47
Huabei Guanhua, *dial.* Chinese, Mandarin [cmn], 329
Huachipaeri [hug], 288
Huachipaire, *alt.* Huachipaeri [hug], 288
   dial. Huachipaeri [hug], 288
Huadou Miao, *alt. dial.* Hmong, Chonganjiang [hmj], 334
Huailas, *alt. dial.* Quechua, Huaylas Ancash [qwh], 291
Huaipa, *dial.* Bisu [bii], 327
Huajuapan Mixtec, *alt.* Mixtec, Cacaloxtepec [miu], 266
Hualan Yao, *alt.* Bunu, Jiongnai [pnu], 328
Huallaga, *alt.* Cocama-Cocamilla [cod], 287
Huallaga Huánuco Quechua, *see* Quechua, Huallaga Huánuco [qub], 291
Hualngo, *alt.* Mizo [lus], 376, 321, 466
Hualo, *alt.* Bugan [bbh], 328
Hualpai, *alt. dial.* Havasupai-Walapai-Yavapai [yuf], 301
Huamalíes, *dial.* Quechua, Huamalíes-Dos de Mayo Huánuco [qvh], 291
Huamalíes-Dos de Mayo Huánuco Quechua, *see* Quechua, Huamalíes-Dos de Mayo Huánuco [qvh], 291
Huambisa [hub], 288
Huambiza, *alt.* Huambisa [hub], 288
Huamelula Chontal, *alt.* Chontal, Lowland Oaxaca [clo], 262
Huamelulteco, *alt.* Chontal, Lowland Oaxaca [clo], 262
Huamuê, *alt.* Uamué [uam], 233
Huana, *alt.* Hungana [hum], 100
Huanca Huaylla Quechua, *alt.* Quechua, Huaylla Wanca [qvw], 291
Huanca Jauja Quechua, *alt.* Quechua, Jauja Wanca [qxw], 291
Huancavelica, *dial.* Quechua, Ayacucho [quy], 289

Ichirungu, *alt. dial.* Mambwe-Lungu [mgr], 214
Ichirungwa, *alt.* Rungwa [rnw], 204
Ichitaabwa, *alt.* Taabwa [tap], 108, 215
Ichiwanda, *alt.* Wanda [wbh], 205
Ici-Ndali, *alt.* Ndali [ndh], 202
Ici-Rambia, *alt.* Lambya [lai], 200
Icietot, *alt.* Ik [ikx], 211
Icifipa, *alt.* Fipa [fip], 198
Icilambya, *alt.* Lambya [lai], 200
Icilungu, *alt. dial.* Mambwe-Lungu [mgr], 201
Icilungwa, *alt.* Rungwa [rnw], 204
Icimambwe, *alt. dial.* Mambwe-Lungu [mgr], 201
Iciwanda, *alt.* Wanda [wbh], 205
Ida, *alt.* Idu-Mishmi [clk], 364
Idaaca, *alt.* Ede Idaca [idd], 43
Ida'an [dbj], 456
   dial. Ida'an [dbj], 456
Idaan, *alt.* Ida'an [dbj], 456
Idaasa, *alt.* Ede Idaca [idd], 43
Idaca, *alt.* Ede Idaca [idd], 43
Idafan, *alt.* Irigwe [iri], 164
Idah, *dial.* Igala [igl], 163
Idahan, *alt.* Ida'an [dbj], 456
Idáìtsà, *alt.* Ede Idaca [idd], 43
Idakamenai, *dial.* Iduna [viv], 602
Idakho, *dial.* Idakho-Isukha-Tiriki [ida], 133
Idakho-Isukha-Tiriki [ida], 133
Idan, *alt.* Ida'an [dbj], 456
Idaté [idt], 350
Idaxo, *alt. dial.* Idakho-Isukha-Tiriki [ida], 133
Idayan, *alt.* Ida'an [dbj], 456
Ide, *alt.* Macuna [myy], 246
Idele, *alt. dial.* Befang [bby], 58
Idere [ide], 163
Idesa [ids], 163
Idi [idi], 602
   dial. Idi [idi], 602
Idin Idindji, *alt.* Yidiny [yii], 579
Idin-Wudjar, *alt.* Yidiny [yii], 579
Idinji, *alt.* Yidiny [yii], 579
Idioma de Senas de Nicaragua, *alt.* Nicaraguan Sign Language [ncs], 280
Idne, *alt.* Maleu-Kilenge [mgl], 611
Ido, *alt. dial.* Arigidi [aqg], 154
   alt. dial. Pamona [bcx], 432
Idoani, *alt.* Iyayu [iya], 164
Idoma [idu], 163
Idoma Central, *dial.* Idoma [idu], 163
Idoma Nokwu, *alt.* Alago [ala], 153
Idoma South, *dial.* Idoma [idu], 163
Idoma West, *dial.* Idoma [idu], 163

Idon [idc], 163
Idong, *alt.* Idon [idc], 163
Idongiro, *alt.* Nyangatom [nnj], 117
Idore'e, *alt. dial.* Pamona [bcx], 432
Idu, *alt.* Idu-Mishmi [clk], 364
Idu Lhoba, *alt.* Luoba, Yidu [clk], 339
Idu Mishmi, *alt.* Luoba, Yidu [clk], 339
Idu-Mishmi [clk], 364
Idua, *alt.* Ilue [ilv], 164
'Iduh, *alt.* O'du [tyh], 525, 452
Iduh, *alt.* O'du [tyh], 525, 452
Idum, *dial.* Mbe [mfo], 169
Idun [ldb], 163
Iduna [viv], 602
Iduwini, *dial.* Izon [ijc], 164
Idyoli Donge, *alt.* Dogon, Kolum So [dkl], 142
Ifane, *alt. dial.* Orokaiva [ork], 620
Ifa'ongota, *alt.* Birale [bxe], 114
Ife, *alt. dial.* Ede Ica [ica], 43
   dial. Igala [igl], 163
Ifè [ife], 208, 45
Ifigi, *dial.* Foi [foi], 599
Ifira, *alt. dial.* Mele-Fila [mxe], 643
Ifo [iff], 642
Ifugao, Amganad [ifa], 495
Ifugao, Batad [ifb], 495
Ifugao, Mayoyao [ifu], 495
Ifugao, Tuwali [ifk], 495
Ifuna, *dial.* Nyanga [nyj], 106
Ifunubwa, *alt.* Mbembe, Cross River [mfn], 163
Ifuumu, *alt. dial.* Teke-Fuumu [ifm], 90
Igabo, *pej. alt.* Isoko [iso], 164
Igala [igl], 163
Igan, *dial.* Melanau [mel], 460
Igana [igg], 602
Igara, *alt.* Igala [igl], 163
   dial. Ebira [igb], 158
Ìgàshí, *alt. dial.* Arigidi [aqg], 154
Igasi, *dial.* Arigidi [aqg], 154
Igbarra, *alt.* Ebira [igb], 158
Igbide, *alt. dial.* Isoko [iso], 164
Igbira, *alt.* Ebira [igb], 158
Igbiri, *alt. dial.* Gbiri-Niragu [grh], 160
Igbirra, *alt.* Ebira [igb], 158
Igbo [ibo], 163
   alt. Legbo [agb], 168
Igbonna, *dial.* Yoruba [yor], 178
Igbuduya, *dial.* Ekpeye [ekp], 159
Igburu-Usomini, *dial.* Ogbah [ogc], 172
Igedde, *alt.* Igede [ige], 163
Igede [ige], 163
Igembe, *dial.* Meru [mer], 134
Igikiga, *dial.* Rwanda [kin], 178

Igikuria, *alt.* Kuria [kuj], 200, 134
Ignaciano [ign], 223
Igo [ahl], 208
Igodor, *alt.* Ibaloi [ibl], 494
Igoji, *dial.* Meru [mer], 134
Igom, *alt.* Kanggape [igm], 604
Igonzabale, *alt.* Lega-Shabunda [lea], 102
Igora, *alt.* Kakabai [kqf], 603
Igorot, *alt.* Bontoc, Central [bnc], 493
Igu, *alt. dial.* Ebira [igb], 158
Iguambo, *dial.* Mundani [mnf], 68
Igueben, *dial.* Esan [ish], 159
Igumale, *alt. dial.* Idoma [idu], 163
Igumbo, *alt. dial.* Mundani [mnf], 68
Iguta [nar], 163
Igwaale, *alt. dial.* Idoma [idu], 163
Igwe [igw], 163
Igwuruta, *dial.* Ikwere [ikw], 164
Igyang, *dial.* Tarok [yer], 175
Igzennaian, *alt. dial.* Tarifit [rif], 40
Iha [ihp], 415
Iha Based Pidgin [ihb], 415
Iha-Saparua, *dial.* Saparua [spr], 403
Iha-Seram, *dial.* Saparua [spr], 403
Ihane, *alt. dial.* Orokaiva [ork], 620
Ihatum, *alt.* Osatu [ost], 71
Ihekwot, *alt. dial.* Iceve-Maci [bec], 63
Ihievbe [ihi], 163
Ihima, *alt. dial.* Ebira [igb], 158
Ihini, *alt.* Baré [bae], 311
   alt. Mandahuaca [mht], 312, 229
Ihobe Mbog, *alt. dial.* Bakaka [bqz], 57
Ihobe Mboong, *alt. dial.* Bakaka [bqz], 57
Ihuruana, *dial.* Maquiritari [mch], 229
Iiliit, *alt. dial.* Kunama [kun], 112
Iilit, *alt. dial.* Kunama [kun], 112
Iimutsu, *dial.* Tsou [tsu], 512
Ija, *dial.* Kaili, Ledo [lew], 429
Ija-Zuba [vki], 163
Ijaw, *alt.* Ijo, Southeast [ijs], 163
   alt. Izon [ijc], 164
Ijca, *alt.* Arhuaco [arh], 243
Ije, *alt.* Ede Ije [ijj], 43
Ijebu, *dial.* Yoruba [yor], 178
Ijekavski, *alt. dial.* Croatian [hrv], 532
Ijesha, *dial.* Yoruba [yor], 178
Ijiegu, *dial.* Yace [ekr], 177
Ijigbam, *alt. dial.* Idoma [idu], 163
Ijka, *alt.* Arhuaco [arh], 243
Ijo, *alt.* Izon [ijc], 164
Ijo, Southeast [ijs], 163
Ijoh, *dial.* Kensiu [kns], 454
Ijok, *alt. dial.* Kensiu [kns], 454

Ik [ikx], 211
Ika [ikk], 163
　alt. Arhuaco [arh], 243
　alt. dial. Ebira [igb], 158
Ikaiku, *alt.* Kaiku [kkq], 100
Ikalahan, *alt.* Kallahan, Kayapa [kak], 497
Ikalanga, *alt.* Kalanga [kck], 216, 47
　dial. Kalanga [kck], 47
Ikale, *dial.* Yoruba [yor], 178
Ikalebwe, *alt. dial.* Songe [sop], 108
Ikan, *alt.* Ukaan [kcf], 176
Ikarranggali, *alt.* Aghu Tharnggalu [ggr], 567
Ikaw, *alt.* Akha [ahk], 462, 326, 449, 513, 521
Ike, *alt.* Arhuaco [arh], 243
Ikega, *dial.* Sinaugoro [snc], 624
Ikela, *alt.* Kela [kel], 101
Ikeleve, *dial.* Kituba [ktu], 101
Ikibiri, *dial.* Izon [ijc], 164
Ikibungu, *alt.* Kimbu [kiv], 200
Ikiha, *alt.* Ha [haq], 199
Ikikuria, *alt.* Kuria [kuj], 200
Ikinata, *alt.* Ikoma [ntk], 199
Ikingonde, *alt.* Nyakyusa-Ngonde [nyy], 203, 140
Ikingurimi, *alt.* Ngurimi [ngq], 203
Ikinilamba, *alt.* Nilamba [nim], 203
Ikiniramba, *alt.* Nilamba [nim], 203
Ikinyakyusa, *alt.* Nyakyusa-Ngonde [nyy], 203
Ikinyarwanda, *alt.* Rwanda [kin], 178
Ikinyikyusa, *alt.* Nyakyusa-Ngonde [nyy], 140
Ikiribati, *alt.* Kiribati [gil], 582, 580, 636, 640
Ikiruguru, *alt.* Luguru [ruf], 200
Ikisenyi, *alt. dial.* Ikoma [ntk], 199
Ikito, *alt.* Iquito [iqu], 288
Ikizanaki, *alt.* Zanaki [zak], 206
Ikizu [ikz], 199
Ikngerripenhe, *dial.* Arrernte, Eastern [aer], 568
Iko [iki], 163
　alt. Doko-Uyanga [uya], 158
　dial. Agoi [ibm], 153
Ikó, *alt. dial.* Lika [lik], 102
Ikobi Kairi, *alt.* Ikobi-Mena [meb], 602
Ikobi-Mena [meb], 602
Ikokolemu, *alt.* Kumam [kdi], 211
Ikolu, *alt.* Ikulu [ikl], 164
　dial. Sinaugoro [snc], 624
Ikom, *dial.* Olulumo-Ikom [iko], 172
Ikoma [ntk], 199
Ikor, *alt.* Akha [ahk], 462, 326, 449, 513

Ikõro, *alt.* Gavião do Jiparaná [gvo], 226
Ikorom, *dial.* Akpes [ibe], 153
Ikot Ekpene, *dial.* Anaang [anw], 153
Ikota, *alt.* Kota [koq], 120, 88
Ikpan, *alt.* Kpan [kpk], 167
Ikpeng [txi], 227
Ikpeshe, *alt.* Ikpeshi [ikp], 164
Ikpeshi [ikp], 164
Ikponu, *dial.* Akposo [kpo], 123
　dial. Ikposo [kpo], 208
Ikposo [kpo], 208
　alt. Akposo [kpo], 123
Iku, *alt.* Iku-Gora-Ankwa [ikv], 164
　alt. dial. Befang [bby], 58
Iku-Gora-Ankwa [ikv], 164
Ikulu [ikl], 164
Ikumama, *alt.* Kumam [kdi], 211
　alt. Teso [teo], 213
Ikumbure, *dial.* Nyanga [nyj], 106
Ikumtale, *dial.* Mbe [mfo], 169
Ikun, *alt. dial.* Ubaghara [byc], 176
Ikundun, *alt.* Anamgura [imi], 589
Ikuta, *alt.* Kota [koq], 120, 88
Ikwere [ikw], 164
Ikweri, *dial.* Ngwo [ngn], 70
Ikwerre, *alt.* Ikwere [ikw], 164
Ikwerri, *alt.* Ikwere [ikw], 164
Ikwo, *dial.* Izi-Ezaa-Ikwo-Mgbo [izi], 164
Ikyoo, *dial.* Lenakel [tnl], 642
Il Konono, *alt.* Aasáx [aas], 197
Il-Arusha, *alt. dial.* Maasai [mas], 201
Ila [ilb], 213
　dial. Ila [ilb], 213
　dial. Yoruba [yor], 178
Ilaali, *alt.* Teke-Laali [lli], 90
Ilafuri, *dial.* Venda [ven], 187
Ilaga Western Dani, *alt.* Dani, Western [dnw], 414
Ilahita, *alt. dial.* Mufian [aoj], 615
Ilai, *dial.* Mailu [mgu], 610
Ilaje, *dial.* Yoruba [yor], 178
Ilakia, *dial.* Awa [awb], 591
Ilamba, *alt.* Nilamba [nim], 203
Ilammu, *dial.* Lepcha [lep], 372, 323, 474
Ilanon, *alt. dial.* Maguindanao [mdh], 498
Ilanum, *alt. dial.* Maguindanao [mdh], 498
Ilanun, *pej. alt.* Iranun [ill], 457
Ilao, *alt.* Gelao [gio], 333
Ilcamus, *alt. dial.* Samburu [saq], 136
Ile Ape [ila], 407
Ile Mandiri, *alt. dial.* Lamaholot [slp], 408

Ileka Ishile, *alt.* Lega-Mwenga [lgm], 102
Ileka-Igonzabale, *alt.* Lega-Shabunda [lea], 102
Ileme, *alt.* Uneme [une], 176
Ilentungen, *dial.* Manobo, Western Bukidnon [mbb], 499
Ileo, *alt.* Dengese [dez], 99
Ilgar, *dial.* Garig-Ilgar [ilg], 570
Ili Turki [ili], 336, 448
Ilianen, *alt.* Manobo, Ilianen [mbi], 499
Ilianen Manobo, *see* Manobo, Ilianen [mbi], 499
Iliaura, *alt.* Alyawarr [aly], 567
Iliit, *alt. dial.* Kunama [kun], 112
Iliku, *dial.* Lusengo [lse], 103
Ilimpeya, *dial.* Evenki [evn], 504
Ilir, *dial.* Malay, Jambi [jax], 436
Ilit, *dial.* Kunama [kun], 112
Iliun, *alt.* Ili'uun [ilu], 399
Ili'uun [ilu], 399
Iliwaki, *alt.* Talur [ilw], 404
　alt. dial. Talur [ilw], 404
Illanoan, *alt.* Iranun [ill], 457
Illanon, *alt. dial.* Maguindanao [mdh], 498
Illanoon, *alt.* Iranun [ill], 457
Illanos, *alt.* Iranun [ill], 457
Illanun, *alt.* Iranun [ill], 457
Illinois, *alt.* Miami [mia], 304
Illo, *dial.* Busa [bqp], 156
Illogo, *alt.* Hiligaynon [hil], 494
Ilmaumau, *alt.* Ili'uun [ilu], 399
　dial. Ili'uun [ilu], 399
Ilmedu, *alt.* Talur [ilw], 404
Ilocano [ilo], 495
Ilodji, *alt. dial.* Ede Ica [ica], 43
Ilois, *alt.* Seselwa Creole French [crs], 182
Ilokano, *alt.* Ilocano [ilo], 495
Iloko, *alt.* Ilocano [ilo], 495
Ilolo, *alt.* Lolo [llb], 147
Ilom, *dial.* Ixil, Chajul [ixj], 254
Ilomwe, *alt.* Lomwe [ngl], 147
Ilonggo, *alt.* Hiligaynon [hil], 494
Ilongot [ilk], 495
Iloodokilani, *dial.* Maasai [mas], 134
Ilpara, *alt.* Warlpiri [wbp], 578
Ilpokil, *dial.* Tugun [tzn], 405
Ilputih, *alt.* Aputai [apx], 396
　dial. Aputai [apx], 396
　dial. Talur [ilw], 404
Ilqan, *alt.* Even [eve], 504
Ilud, *dial.* Maguindanao [mdh], 498
Ilue [ilv], 164
Ilumbu, *alt.* Lumbu [lup], 120, 89
Ilwaki, *alt.* Talur [ilw], 404
　dial. Talur [ilw], 404
Ilwana, *alt.* Malakote [mlk], 134

Imaban, *alt.* Legbo [agb], 168
Imafin, *dial.* Tanna, North [tnn], 645
Imakua, *alt.* Makhuwa-Meetto [mgh], 201
Iman, *dial.* Udihe [ude], 507
Imandi, *alt.* Wiarumus [tua], 632
Imasi, *alt.* Sobei [sob], 423
Imbabura Highland Quichua, *see* Quichua, Imbabura Highland [qvi], 251
Imbana, *dial.* Mundang [mua], 68
Imbao'o, *alt.* Andio [bzb], 427
Imbara, *alt. dial.* Mundang [mua], 68
Imbatski-Ket, *alt.* Ket [ket], 505
Imbinis, *alt. dial.* Pagi [pgi], 621
Imbo, *alt.* Mbo [zmw], 104
Imbo Ungo, *alt.* Imbongu [imo], 602
Imbo Ungu, *alt.* Imbongu [imo], 602
Imbonggo, *alt.* Imbongu [imo], 602
Imbongu [imo], 602
Imeetto, *alt.* Makhuwa-Meetto [mgh], 147
Imenti, *dial.* Meru [mer], 134
Imeraguen [ime], 145
Imeretian, *dial.* Georgian [kat], 352
Imerxev, *dial.* Georgian [kat], 518
Imerxev Kartlian, *dial.* Georgian [kat], 352
Imila, *dial.* Maria [mds], 612
Imilangu, *alt. dial.* Luyana [lyn], 41 *dial.* Simaa [sie], 215
Imimkal, *alt.* Emumu [enr], 414
Imiv, *dial.* Isoko [iso], 164
Imo, *alt.* Chokwe [cjk], 99
Imona, *dial.* Ntomba [nto], 106
Imonda [imn], 603
Imraguen, *alt.* Imeraguen [ime], 145
Imroin, *alt.* Imroing [imr], 399
Imroing [imr], 399
Imyan, *dial.* Tehit [kps], 424
In, *alt.* Ir [irr], 450
In-lom, *alt.* Yale, Kosarek [kkl], 426
Inabaknon [abx], 495
Inafosa, *alt.* Tauya [tya], 627
Inagta of Mt. Iraya, *alt.* Agta, Mt. Iraya [atl], 490
Inakona, *alt. dial.* Talise [tlr], 638
Inallu, *alt. dial.* Azerbaijani, South [azb], 438
Inamari, *alt.* Iñapari [inp], 288
Inamwanga, *alt.* Nyamwanga [mwn], 215
Inanlu, *alt. dial.* Azerbaijani, South [azb], 438
Inanwatan, *alt.* Suabo [szp], 423
Inapang [mzu], 603
Iñapari [inp], 288
Inaquen, *alt.* Tehuelche [teh], 220
Inari Lappish, *pej. alt.* Saami, Inari [smn], 535

Inari Saami, *see* Saami, Inari [smn], 535
Inaru, *alt.* Bahinemo [bjh], 591
Inati, *alt.* Ati [atk], 491
Inauini, *dial.* Dení [dny], 226
Incahuasi, *dial.* Quechua, Lambayeque [quf], 291
Incha, *alt.* Ninzo [nin], 171
Inchazi, *alt.* Che [ruk], 156
Indaaka, *alt.* Ndaka [ndk], 102
Inde, *dial.* Kaili, Da'a [kzf], 429
Indenie, *dial.* Anyin [any], 91
Indi, *dial.* Pengo [peg], 383
Indi Ayta, *alt.* Ayta, Mag-Indi [blx], 492
Indian Sign Language [ins], 365, 321
Indigirka, *dial.* Even [eve], 504
Indindji, *alt.* Yidiny [yii], 579
Indinogosima, *alt.* Mehek [nux], 613
Indo-Guyanese Creole, *dial.* Guyanese Creole English [gyn], 257
Indo-Pakistani Sign Language, *alt.* Indian Sign Language [ins], 365
Indo-Portuguese [idb], 509, 365
Indonesian [ind], 391
Indonesian Bajau, *see* Bajau, Indonesian [bdl], 427
Indonesian Sign Language [inl], 391
Indonesian, Peranakan [pea], 391
Indorodoro, *alt.* Blafe [bfh], 594
Indramayu, *dial.* Javanese [jav], 391
Indri [idr], 191
Indun, *alt.* Ndun [nfd], 171
Indus, *dial.* Kohistani, Indus [mvy], 486
Indus Kohistani, *see* Kohistani, Indus [mvy], 486
Inebu, *alt.* One, Inebu [oin], 619
Inebu One, *see* One, Inebu [oin], 619
Inedua, *dial.* Engenni [enn], 159
Ineme, *alt.* Uneme [une], 176
Ineseño [inz], 302
Ineta, *dial.* Budu [buu], 98
Inga [inb], 246 *alt.* Quechua, Southern Pastaza [qup], 292
Inga, Jungle [inj], 246
Ingalik, *pej. alt.* Degexit'an [ing], 300
Ingalit, *pej. alt.* Degexit'an [ing], 300
Ingano, *alt.* Inga, Jungle [inj], 246 *alt.* Quichua, Napo Lowland [qvo], 251
Ingara, *alt.* Yinggarda [yia], 579
Ingarda, *alt.* Yinggarda [yia], 579
Ingaricó, *alt. dial.* Pemon [aoc], 231

Ingariko, *alt.* Patamona [pbc], 257
Ingarikó [ake], 227 *dial.* Pemon [aoc], 231
Ingarra, *alt.* Yinggarda [yia], 579
Ingarrah, *alt.* Yinggarda [yia], 579
Ingassana, *alt.* Gaam [tbi], 190
Ingelshi, *alt.* Tasawaq [twq], 152
Ingessana, *alt.* Gaam [tbi], 190
Inggarda, *alt.* Yinggarda [yia], 579
Ingias, *dial.* Kuni-Boazi [kvg], 608
Ingilo, *dial.* Georgian [kat], 352
‖Ing‖ke, *alt. dial.* N‖u [ngh], 186
Ingli, *alt.* Maba [mqa], 401
Ingrian [izh], 554
Ingul, *alt.* Ngul [nlo], 106
Ingulu, *alt.* Lomwe [ngl], 147
Ingundi, *alt.* Ngundi [ndn], 89
Ingundji, *alt. dial.* Lusengo [lse], 103
Ingura, *alt.* Anindilyakwa [aoi], 568
Ingus, *alt.* Ingush [inh], 554
Ingush [inh], 554
Ingwe, *alt.* Hungworo [nat], 162
Ingwo, *alt.* Hungworo [nat], 162
Inhambane, *alt.* Tonga [toh], 149
Iniai, *alt.* Bisorio [bir], 594 *alt.* Nete [net], 618
Inibaloi, *alt.* Ibaloi [ibl], 494
Inidem, *alt. dial.* Kaningdon-Nindem [kdp], 166
Inisine, *alt.* Yetfa [yet], 426, 633
Inja, *dial.* Mbole [mdq], 104
Injang, *alt.* Naga, Southern Rengma [nre], 379
Injdjiladji, *alt.* Yindjilandji [yil], 579
Injebi, *alt.* Njebi [nzb], 121, 89
Inkongo, *alt.* Luna [luj], 103
Inland Mengen, *alt. dial.* Mengen [mee], 613
Inland Pwo Eastern Karen, *alt. dial.* Karen, Pwo Eastern [kjp], 464
Inlaod, *alt.* Itneg, Inlaod [iti], 496
Inlaod Itneg, *see* Itneg, Inlaod [iti], 496
Inmeas, *alt.* Isinai [inn], 495
Inn Tea, *dial.* Oy [oyb], 452
Inneqor, *alt. dial.* Silt'e [xst], 119
Inner Mongolian, *alt.* Mongolian, Peripheral [mvf], 339
Inner Seraji, *alt. dial.* Pahari, Kullu [kfx], 382
Inner Siragi, *dial.* Pahari, Kullu [kfx], 382
Inntha, *alt.* Intha [int], 464
Innu, *alt.* Montagnais [moe], 239
Innu Aimun, *alt.* Montagnais [moe], 239
Innu Aimuun, *alt.* Naskapi [nsk], 239
Inoke, *alt.* Inoke-Yate [ino], 603
Inoke-Yate [ino], 603

Inonhan [loc], 495
Inor [ior], 115
Inparra, *alt.* Yinggarda [yia], 579
Inpui, *alt.* Naga, Inpui [nkf], 377
Inpui Naga, *see* Naga, Inpui [nkf], 377
Insanao, *alt. dial.* Uab Meto [aoz], 410
Insinai, *alt.* Isinai [inn], 495
Insular, *dial.* Scots [sco], 566
Insular Catalan, *alt. dial.* Catalan-Valencian-Balear [cat], 559
Interior Makwe, *dial.* Makwe [ymk], 148
Interior Saluan, *alt.* Saluan, Kahumamahon [slb], 432
Interlingua [ina], 537
Interlingua de Iala, *alt.* Interlingua [ina], 537
Intha [int], 464
Inuit, *alt.* Inuktitut, Eastern Canadian [ike], 238
Inuktitut, Eastern Canadian [ike], 238
Inuktitut, Greenlandic [kal], 252, 533
Inuktitut, Western Canadian [ikt], 238
Inupiaq, *alt.* Inupiatun, North Alaskan [esi], 238
Inupiat, *alt.* Inupiatun, North Alaskan [esi], 302, 238
Inupiatun, *alt.* Inupiatun, Northwest Alaska [esk], 302
Inupiatun, North Alaskan [esi], 302, 238
Inupiatun, Northwest Alaska [esk], 302
Inuvaken, *dial.* Amahuaca [amc], 224
Inuvialuktun, *alt.* Inuktitut, Western Canadian [ikt], 238
Inxokvari, *dial.* Khvarshi [khv], 555
Inyai-Gadio-Bisorio, *alt.* Bisorio [bir], 594
Inyanga, *alt.* Nyanga [nyj], 106
dial. Nyanga [nyj], 106
Inyangatom, *alt.* Nyangatom [nnj], 117
Inyima, *alt.* Lenyima [ldg], 168
Inyimang, *alt.* Ama [nyi], 187
Inyven, *alt. dial.* Komi-Permyak [koi], 555
Ioma Binandere, *alt.* Binandere [bhg], 593
Iombe, *alt.* Yombe [yom], 42
Ioullemmeden, *alt. dial.* Tamajaq [ttq], 144
alt. dial. Tamajaq, Tawallammet [ttq], 152

dial. Tamajaq, Tawallammat [ttq], 175
Iowa, *dial.* Iowa-Oto [iow], 302
Iowa-Oto [iow], 302
Ioway, *alt. dial.* Iowa-Oto [iow], 302
Ipai, *dial.* Kumiai [dih], 303
Ipalapa Amuzgo, *see* Amuzgo, Ipalapa [azm], 259
Ipande, *alt.* Pande [bkj], 77
Ipanga, *alt. dial.* Mongo-Nkundu [lol], 104
Ipeca, *alt.* Ipeka-Tapuia [paj], 227
Ipeka-Tapuia [paj], 227
Ipere, *alt.* Bhele [bhy], 98
Ipiko [ipo], 603
Ipikoi, *alt.* Ipiko [ipo], 603
Ipili [ipi], 603
Ipili-Paiela, *alt.* Ipili [ipi], 603
Ipili-Payala, *alt.* Ipili [ipi], 603
Ipitineri, *alt.* Amahuaca [amc], 286
Ipo, *dial.* Ikwere [ikw], 164
Ipoh, *dial.* Dayak, Land [dyk], 393
Ipounou, *alt.* Punu [puu], 89
Ipulo [ass], 63
Ipunu, *alt.* Punu [puu], 121, 89
Ipuricoto, *alt. dial.* Pemon [aoc], 231
Ipurinán, *alt.* Apurinã [apu], 225
Iqlim-Al-Kharrub Sunni Arabic, *dial.* Arabic, North Levantine Spoken [apc], 453
Iquita, *alt.* Iquito [iqu], 288
Iquito [iqu], 288
Ir [irr], 450
Irabu-Jima, *dial.* Miyako [mvi], 447
Irahutu, *alt.* Irarutu [irh], 415
Iraku, *alt.* Iraqw [irk], 199
Iramang, *dial.* Kula [tpg], 408
Iramba, *alt.* Lambya [lai], 200
alt. Nilamba [nim], 203
Iranche, *alt.* Irántxe [irn], 227
Irangi, *alt.* Langi [lag], 200
Irani, *alt.* Farsi, Western [pes], 439
Iranian Koine, *dial.* Assyrian Neo-Aramaic [aii], 438
Iranon, *alt. dial.* Maguindanao [mdh], 498
Iranon Maranao, *alt.* Iranun [ill], 457
Irántxe [irn], 227
dial. Irántxe [irn], 227
Iranum, *alt.* Iranun [ill], 457
Iranun [ill], 457
dial. Maguindanao [mdh], 498
Iranxe, *alt.* Irántxe [irn], 227
Iraqi Arabic, *alt.* Arabic, Mesopotamian Spoken [acm], 442
Iraqi Judeo-Arabic, *alt.* Arabic, Judeo-Iraqi [yhd], 444, 442
Iraqi Neo-Mandaic, *dial.* Mandaic [mid], 441

Iraqw [irk], 199
Irarutu [irh], 415
Irava, *alt.* Irula [iru], 365
Iraya [iry], 495
Irbore, *alt.* Arbore [arv], 113
Iregwe, *alt.* Irigwe [iri], 164
Iresim [ire], 415
Irhobo, *alt.* Isekiri [its], 164
Iri, *alt. dial.* Isoko [iso], 164
dial. Kadara [kad], 165
Iria, *alt.* Kamberau [irx], 416
Irianese, *alt. dial.* Malay [mly], 436
Iriemkena, *alt.* Airoran [air], 410
Iriga Bicolano, *see* Bicolano, Iriga [bto], 493
Irigwe [iri], 164
Irish, *alt.* Gaelic, Irish [gle], 542, 565
Irish Gaelic, *see* Gaelic, Irish [gle], 542, 565
Irish Sign Language [isg], 542
Irish Traveler Cant, *alt.* Shelta [sth], 543
Irob, *dial.* Saho [ssy], 118
Iroka, *alt. dial.* Yukpa [yup], 248
Iron, *dial.* Osetin [oss], 352, 519
Ironworker Romani, *dial.* Romani, Balkan [rmn], 532
Iroole, *alt. dial.* Dabarre [dbr], 184
Irri, *dial.* Isoko [iso], 164
Irruan, *dial.* Bokyi [bky], 156
Iru-Itu, *alt.* Uru [ure], 224
Iruan, *dial.* Bokyi [bky], 59
Irula [iru], 365
Irula Pallar, *dial.* Irula [iru], 365
Irulan, *alt.* Irula [iru], 365
Irular, *alt.* Irula [iru], 365
Irular Mozhi, *alt.* Irula [iru], 365
Irulavan, *alt.* Irula [iru], 365
Iruliga, *alt.* Irula [iru], 365
Iruligar, *alt.* Irula [iru], 365
Irumu, *alt.* Tuma-Irumu [iou], 628
Irupi-Drageli, *dial.* Bine [bon], 593
Irutu, *alt.* Irarutu [irh], 415
Iryavula, *alt.* Ravula [yea], 384
Isa, *alt.* Esan [ish], 159
Isaalung, *alt.* Sisaala, Tumulung [sil], 127
Isaan, *alt.* Thai, Northeastern [tts], 517
Isaanga, *alt.* Makhuwa-Saka [xsq], 147
Isabi [isa], 603
Isachanure, *alt.* Naga, Sangtam [nsa], 379
Isakara, *alt.* Shakara [nfk], 174
Isal, *alt.* Benggoi [bgy], 397
Isala, *dial.* Sisaala, Tumulung [sil], 127
Isam, *dial.* Pagu [pgu], 403
Isamal, *dial.* Kalagan [kqe], 497

Isan, *alt.* Thai, Northeastern [tts], 517
dial. Yopno [yut], 634
Isanga, *alt.* Sanga [xsn], 174
alt. dial. Jere [jer], 165
Isangele, *alt.* Usaghade [usk], 72, 176
Isangu, *alt.* Sangu [snq], 121
Isanzu [isn], 199
Isaro, *alt.* Kumba [ksm], 167
Isarog Agta, *see* Agta, Isarog [agk], 490
Iscamtho, *alt.* Camtho [cmt], 185
Iscobaquebu, *alt.* Isconahua [isc], 288
Isconahua [isc], 288
Isebe [igo], 603
dial. Isebe [igo], 603
Isekiri [its], 164
Iselema-Otu, *alt.* Isekiri [its], 164
Isenyi, *alt. dial.* Ikoma [ntk], 199
Ishan, *alt.* Esan [ish], 159
Ishanga, *alt.* Makhuwa-Saka [xsq], 147
Isharon Ki Zubann, *alt.* Pakistan Sign Language [pks], 487
Ishbukun, *alt. dial.* Bunun [bnn], 511
Ishe, *dial.* Ukaan [kcf], 176
Ishekiri, *alt.* Isekiri [its], 164
Ishibori, *alt. dial.* Nkem-Nkum [isi], 171
Ishigaki, *dial.* Yaeyama [rys], 447
Ishile, *alt.* Lega-Mwenga [lgm], 102
Ishimalilia, *alt.* Malila [mgq], 201
Ishinyiha, *alt.* Nyiha [nih], 203, 215
Ishira, *alt.* Sira [swj], 121
Ishiro, *alt.* Chamacoco [ceg], 284
alt. dial. Chamacoco [ceg], 284
Ishisafwa, *alt.* Safwa [sbk], 204
Ishkashim, *alt. dial.* Sanglechi-Ishkashimi [sgl], 317, 513
Ishkashimi, *alt. dial.* Sanglechi-Ishkashimi [sgl], 317
dial. Sanglechi-Ishkashimi [sgl], 513
Ishkashmi, *alt. dial.* Sanglechi-Ishkashimi [sgl], 317
Ishkoman, *dial.* Wakhi [wbl], 489
Ishpi, *dial.* Pashayi, Southwest [psh], 317
Ishua, *alt.* Uhami [uha], 176
Isi, *alt. dial.* Kilmeri [kih], 606
Isibiri, *alt. dial.* Nkem-Nkum [isi], 171
Isicamtho, *alt.* Camtho [cmt], 185
Isikula, *pej. alt.* Fanagalo [fng], 185, 213, 216
Isilololo, *alt.* Fanagalo [fng], 185, 213, 216
Isimbi, *alt.* Esimbi [ags], 61
Isimijeega, *alt. dial.* Datooga [tcc], 198

Isinai [inn], 495
Isinay, *alt.* Isinai [inn], 495
Isinde'bele, *alt.* Ndebele [nde], 216, 48
Isiokpo, *dial.* Ikwere [ikw], 164
Isipiki, *alt.* Fanagalo [fng], 185, 213, 216
Isira, *alt.* Sira [swj], 121
Isirawa [srl], 415
Isiswazi, *alt.* Swati [ssw], 197
Isixhosa, *alt.* Xhosa [xho], 187
Isizulu, *alt.* Zulu [zul], 187, 141, 149, 197
Isken, *dial.* Pashayi, Southwest [psh], 317
ISL, *alt.* Israeli Sign Language [isr], 445
Islami, *alt.* Urdu [urd], 389
Island, *dial.* Mailu [mgu], 610
Island Boikin, *dial.* Boikin [bzf], 594
Island Carib, *see* Carib, Island [crb], 250, 295
Island Chumash, *alt.* Cruzeño [crz], 300
Island Comox, *dial.* Comox [coo], 236
Island Helong, *alt. dial.* Helong [heg], 407
Island Kiwai, *dial.* Kiwai, Southern [kjd], 606
Island Tigak, *dial.* Tigak [tgc], 627
Islander Creole English [icr], 246
Isleño, *alt.* Cruzeño [crz], 300
Íslenska, *alt.* Icelandic [isl], 542
Isleta, *alt. dial.* Tiwa, Southern [tix], 309
Isleta Pueblo, *alt. dial.* Tiwa, Southern [tix], 309
Isnag [isd], 496
Isnay, *alt.* Isinai [inn], 495
Isneg, *alt.* Isnag [isd], 496
Isocenio, *alt. dial.* Guaraní, Western Argentine [gui], 220
Isoko [iso], 164
Isole Eolie, *dial.* Sicilian [scn], 545
Isombi, *alt. dial.* Budu [buu], 98
Isongo, *alt.* Mbati [mdn], 77
Isopo, *dial.* Lega-Mwenga [lgm], 102
Israeli Sign Language [isr], 445
Issala, *alt.* Sisaala, Tumulung [sil], 127
alt. Sisaala, Western [ssl], 128
Issan, *alt.* Thai, Northeastern [tts], 517
Issana, *alt.* Baniwa [bwi], 225
Issenyi, *dial.* Ikoma [ntk], 199
Issilita', *dial.* Bambam [ptu], 427
Issongo, *alt.* Mbati [mdn], 77

Istanbul, *alt. dial.* Armenian [hye], 318
Isthmus Aztec-Mecayapan, *alt.* Nahuatl, Isthmus-Mecayapan [nhx], 271
Isthmus Mixe, *see* Mixe, Isthmus [mir], 265
Isthmus Zapotec, *see* Zapotec, Isthmus [zai], 278
Isthmus-Cosoleacaque Nahuatl, *see* Nahuatl, Isthmus-Cosoleacaque [nhk], 271
Isthmus-Mecayapan Nahuatl, *see* Nahuatl, Isthmus-Mecayapan [nhx], 271
Isthmus-Pajapan Nahuatl, *see* Nahuatl, Isthmus-Pajapan [nhp], 271
Istrian, *dial.* Venetian [vec], 545, 532
Istriot [ist], 532
Istro Romanian, *see* Romanian, Istro [ruo], 532
Istro-Romanian, *alt.* Romanian, Istro [ruo], 532
Isu (Fako Division) [szv], 63
Isu (Menchum Division) [isu], 63
Isuama, *alt. dial.* Igbo [ibo], 163
Isubu, *alt.* Isu [szv], 63
Isukha, *dial.* Idakho-Isukha-Tiriki [ida], 133
Isuwu, *alt.* Isu [szv], 63
Isuxa, *alt. dial.* Idakho-Isukha-Tiriki [ida], 133
Ita, *alt.* Alta, Southern [agy], 491
Itak, *dial.* Ibibio [ibb], 162
Itakho, *alt. dial.* Idakho-Isukha-Tiriki [ida], 133
Italian [ita], 544, 112, 532, 537, 557, 558, 562, 566
Italian Sign Language [ise], 544
Italiano, *alt.* Italian [ita], 544
Italkian, *alt.* Judeo-Italian [itk], 544
Italon, *dial.* Ilongot [ilk], 495
Itanga, *alt.* Karo [arr], 228
Itangikom, *alt.* Kom [bkm], 64
Itangimbesa, *alt. dial.* Kom [bkm], 64
Itarok, *dial.* Tarok [yer], 175
Itarok Oga Asa, *dial.* Tarok [yer], 175
Itawes, *alt.* Itawit [itv], 496
Itawis, *alt.* Itawit [itv], 496
dial. Itawit [itv], 496
Itawit [itv], 496
Itbayaten, *dial.* Ivatan [ivv], 496
Itbeg Rugnot, *alt.* Agta, Mt. Iraya [atl], 490
Itchen, *alt.* Etkywan [ich], 159
Itebiege, *dial.* Isoko [iso], 164
Iteeji, *dial.* Kukele [kez], 167

alt. Shilha [jbn], 209
Jabali, *alt.* Hulaulá [huy], 445
Jaban, *alt.* Arandai [jbj], 411
Jabba, *alt.* Hyam [jab], 162
Jabem, *alt.* Yabem [jae], 632
Jabi, *alt. dial.* Ekari [ekg], 414
Jabim, *alt.* Yabem [jae], 632
Jabirr-Jabirr, *alt.* Dyaberdyaber [dyb], 570
Jabo, *dial.* Grebo, Southern [grj], 138
Jaborlang, *alt.* Babuza [bzg], 511
Jabotí, *alt.* Jabutí [jbt], 227
Jabsch, *alt.* Yelmek [jel], 426
Jabuda, *alt.* Kanju [kbe], 572
Jabung, *dial.* Abung [abl], 435
Jabutí [jbt], 227
Jacaltec, Western [jai], 263
Jacalteco, *alt.* Jakalteko, Eastern [jac], 254
Jacalteco del Oeste, *alt.* Jacaltec, Western [jai], 263
Jacaria, *dial.* Karipuná [kuq], 228
Jad [jda], 365
    dial. Tibetan [bod], 388
Jadeji, *dial.* Kachchi [kfr], 366, 485
    dial. Sindhi [snd], 387
Jadgali [jdg], 485, 439
Jadobafi, *dial.* Braj Bhasha [bra], 357
Jafga, *alt. dial.* Musgu [mug], 68, 85
Jafi, *alt.* Yafi [wfg], 426
Jafí, *alt.* Banawá [bnh], 225
Jafi Wagarindem, *alt.* Yafi [wfg], 426
Jafoo, *alt.* Kafoa [kpu], 407
Jafri, *dial.* Seraiki [skr], 386
Jagahala, *dial.* Amele [aey], 589
Jagai, *alt. dial.* Nuer [nus], 194
Jaganathapuram Koya, *dial.* Koya [kff], 370
Jagat, *dial.* Ghale, Northern [ghh], 471
Jagatai, *alt.* Chagatai [chg], 520
    alt. dial. Turkmen [tuk], 318
Jaggoi, *alt.* Jagoi [sne], 459
Jagoi [sne], 459
Jah Het, *alt.* Jah Hut [jah], 454
Jah Hut [jah], 454
Jahadian, *alt.* Yahadian [ner], 426
Jahai, *alt.* Jehai [jhi], 454
Jahalatan, *alt.* Yalahatan [jal], 405
Jahalatane, *alt.* Yalahatan [jal], 405
Jahanka [jad], 129, 143
    dial. Maninkakan, Western [mlq], 181, 122
Jahanque, *alt.* Jahanka [jad], 129, 143
    alt. dial. Maninkakan, Western [mlq], 181

Jahonque, *alt.* Jahanka [jad], 129, 143
    alt. dial. Maninkakan, Western [mlq], 181
Jahui, *alt. dial.* Tenharim [pah], 232
Jaintia, *dial.* Pnar [pbv], 384
Jaipuri, *alt.* Dhundari [dhd], 360
Jaipuria, *alt.* Naga, Nocte [njb], 379
Jair, *alt.* Awyu, North [yir], 412
Jair Awyu, *see* Awyu, Jair [awv], 412
Jaisalmeri, *alt. dial.* Marwari [rwr], 375
Jaiselmer, *alt.* Marwari [mve], 487
Jajao, *alt.* Zazao [jaj], 639
Jajura, *dial.* Cakfem-Mushere [cky], 156
Jakai, *alt.* Yaqay [jaq], 426
Jakalteko, Eastern [jac], 254
Jakalteko, Western [jai], 254
Jakanci, *alt.* Labir [jku], 168
Jakari, *alt.* Tabla [tnm], 423
Jakarta, *dial.* Malay [mly], 436
Jakarta Malay, *alt.* Betawi [bew], 391
Jakati [jat], 564, 316
Jakhachin, *dial.* Kalmyk-Oirat [xal], 337, 461
Jakoon, *alt.* Jakun [jak], 454
Jakphang, *dial.* Naga, Konyak [nbe], 378
Jaku, *alt.* Labir [jku], 168
Jaku'd, *alt.* Jakun [jak], 454
Jakud'n, *alt.* Jakun [jak], 454
Jakula, *alt.* Ganggalida [gcd], 570
Jakun [jak], 454
    alt. Labir [jku], 168
Jal, *alt.* Eten [etx], 159
Jalait, *alt. dial.* Mongolian, Peripheral [mvf], 339
Jalalam, *dial.* Karekare [kai], 166
Jalapa de Díaz Mazatec, *see* Mazatec, Jalapa de Díaz [maj], 264
Jalè, *alt.* Yali, Ninia [nlk], 426
Jalieza Zapotec, *dial.* Zapotec, San Juan Guelavía [zab], 279
Jalingo, *dial.* Mumuye [mzm], 170
Jalkia, *alt.* Barein [bva], 78
    dial. Barein [bva], 78
Jalkoti, *dial.* Shina, Kohistani [plk], 488
Jalkuna, *alt.* Jalkunan [bxl], 51
Jalkunan [bxl], 51
Jaloc, *alt.* Aribwaung [ylu], 590
Jalon, *alt.* Pular [fuf], 130
Jalonke, *alt.* Jalunga [yal], 143
    alt. Yalunka [yal], 130, 184
Jalonké, *alt.* Jalunga [yal], 180
Jalunga [yal], 143, 180
Jaly, *alt.* Yali, Ninia [nlk], 426

Jama, *alt.* Samba Daka [ccg], 174
Jama Mapun, *alt.* Mapun [sjm], 499, 457
Jamaican Country Sign Language [jcs], 258
Jamaican Creole English [jam], 259
Jamamadí [jaa], 227
Jamatia, *dial.* Kok Borok [trp], 368, 321
Jamba, *alt. dial.* Baloi [biz], 96
Jambapuing, *alt.* Djambarrpuyngu [djr], 569
Jambapuingo, *alt.* Djambarrpuyngu [djr], 569
Jambi Malay, *see* Malay, Jambi [jax], 436
Jambo, *alt.* Anuak [anu], 187, 113
Jamden, *alt.* Yamdena [jmd], 405
Jamdena, *alt.* Yamdena [jmd], 405
Jamee, *alt. dial.* Minangkabau [min], 436
James Bay Cree Southern Dialect, *alt.* East Cree, Southern [crj], 237
Jamesabad Aer, *dial.* Aer [aeq], 483
Jamiltepec Mixtec, *see* Mixtec, Jamiltepec [mxt], 267
Jaminawa, *alt.* Yaminahua [yaa], 224
Jaminawá, *alt.* Yaminahua [yaa], 293, 234
Jamindar Rai, *alt.* Athpariya [aph], 468
Jaminjung, *alt.* Djamindjung [djd], 569
Jampalam, *dial.* Wandala [mfi], 73, 177
Jampea, *dial.* Bajau, Indonesian [bdl], 427
Jamral, *alt. dial.* Malvi [mup], 374
Jamsay Dogon, *see* Dogon, Jamsay [djm], 142, 50
Jamshedi, *alt. dial.* Aimaq [aiq], 315
Jamshidi, *dial.* Aimaq [aiq], 315
Jamska, *alt.* Jamtska [jmk], 561
Jamtska [jmk], 561
Janbeba, *alt.* Omagua [omg], 231
Jandali, *alt.* Adynyamathanha [adt], 567
Jandavra [jnd], 485
Jander, *dial.* Wolof [wol], 182
Jandijinung, *alt.* Djinang [dji], 570
Janela, *alt.* Deg [mzw], 124, 92
Janera, *dial.* Barasana [bsn], 243
Jang, *alt.* Rejang [rej], 437
Jang-Kala, *alt.* Nyangga [nny], 576
Janga, *alt.* Nyangga [nny], 576

Jegu, *dial.* Mogum [mou], 84
Jeh [jeh], 523, 450
Jeh Bri La, *dial.* Jeh [jeh], 523, 450
Jeh Mang Ram, *dial.* Jeh [jeh], 523, 450
Jehai [jhi], 454
  dial. Jehai [jhi], 454
Jeher, *dial.* Kensiu [kns], 454
Jei, *alt.* Yei [jei], 426
Jeidji, *alt.* Wunambal [wub], 578
Jeinu Kuruba, *dial.* Kannada [kan], 366
Jeithi, *alt.* Wunambal [wub], 578
Jekaing, *alt. dial.* Nuer [nus], 194
Jekkino, *dial.* Bidiyo [bid], 79
Jekri, *alt.* Isekiri [its], 164
Jelai, *dial.* Semai [sea], 455
Jelalong Penan, *dial.* Penan, Western [pne], 460, 325
Jelewaga, *dial.* Sudest [tgo], 625
Jelgoore, *dial.* Fulfulde, Northeastern Burkina Faso [fuh], 51
Jeli Kuo, *alt.* Jeri Kuo [jek], 93
Jelkin, *alt. dial.* Barein [bva], 78
Jelkung, *alt.* Saba [saa], 86
Jelmek, *alt.* Yelmek [jel], 426
Jelmik, *alt.* Yelmek [jel], 426
Jeltulak, *dial.* Evenki [evn], 504
Jembayan, *dial.* Basap [bdb], 392
Jembrana, *alt. dial.* Bali [ban], 391
Jeme, *alt.* Geme [geq], 76
  alt. Naga, Zeme [nzm], 381
Jemez [tow], 302
Jemhwa, *dial.* Gumuz [guk], 191
Jemjem, *alt. dial.* Oromo, Borana-Arsi-Guji [gax], 117
  pej. alt. Suga [sgi], 72
Jen, *alt.* Dza [jen], 158
Jen Kurumba, *alt.* Kurumba, Jennu [xuj], 371
Jenaama Bozo, *see* Bozo, Jenaama [bze], 142
Jenaama Bozo, *alt.* Sorko [bze], 175
Jenama, *alt.* Sorko [bze], 175
Jeneponto, *alt. dial.* Makasar [mak], 430
Jeng [jeg], 450
  alt. Nzanyi [nja], 171, 71
  dial. Mumuye [mzm], 170
Jenge, *alt.* Nzanyi [nja], 171
Jengjeng, *alt.* Lanoh [lnh], 454
Jengre, *alt. dial.* Jere [jer], 165
Jenimu, *alt.* Awyu, Edera [awy], 412
  alt. Awyu, South [aws], 412
Jenisch, *alt.* Yeniche [yec], 540
Jenji, *alt.* Janji [jni], 164
Jenjo, *alt.* Dza [jen], 158

Jennu Kurumba, *see* Kurumba, Jennu [xuj], 371
Jennu Kurumba Nonstandard Kannada, *alt.* Kurumba, Jennu [xuj], 371
Jennu Nudi, *alt.* Kurumba, Jennu [xuj], 371
Jenures, *dial.* Biak [bhw], 412
Jenuwa, *dial.* Kutep [kub], 167, 64
Jepa-Matsi, *alt.* Macuna [myy], 246, 229
Jepal, *alt. dial.* Kofyar [kwl], 166
Jepel, *alt. dial.* Kofyar [kwl], 166
Jera, *alt.* Jara [jaf], 164
  alt. Jere [jer], 165
Jerba, *alt. dial.* Nafusi [jbn], 139
  dial. Shilha [jbn], 209
Jerbi, *dial.* Nafusi [jbn], 139
Jere [jer], 165
  dial. Jere [jer], 165
Jèrè, *dial.* Bobo Madaré, Northern [bbo], 49
Jeri Kuo [jek], 93
Jeriyawa, *alt. dial.* Jere [jer], 165
Jero, *alt.* Jerung [jee], 472
Jero Mala, *alt.* Jerung [jee], 472
Jerriais, *dial.* French [fra], 565
Jeru, *alt.* Aka-Jeru [akj], 353
Jerum, *alt.* Jerung [jee], 472
Jerung [jee], 472
Jerunge, *alt.* Jerung [jee], 472
Jessu, *alt. dial.* Longuda [lnu], 169
Jesús María Cora, *dial.* Cora, El Nayar [crn], 262
Jeti, *alt.* Manem [jet], 612, 419
Jeto, *alt. dial.* Banda-Bambari [liy], 75
Jewish Babylonian Aramaic [tmr], 443
Jewish Iraqi-Baghdadi Arabic, *alt.* Arabic, Judeo-Iraqi [yhd], 444, 442
Jewish Tat, *alt.* Judeo-Tat [jdt], 445, 319, 554
Jewish Tripolitanian-Libyan Arabic, *alt.* Arabic, Judeo-Tripolitanian [yud], 444
Jeywo, *alt.* Chamacoco [ceg], 284
Jezhu, *dial.* Gbari [gby], 160
Jhadpi, *dial.* Varhadi-Nagpuri [vah], 389
Jhalawadi, *alt. dial.* Gujarati [guj], 363
Jhaliya, *alt.* Bodo Parja [bdv], 357
Jhandoria, *alt.* Jandavra [jnd], 485
Jhangar, *alt.* Rawat [jnl], 478, 385
Jhanger, *alt.* Kurux, Nepali [kxl], 473
Jharawan, *dial.* Brahui [brh], 484, 438

Jharia, *alt.* Bodo Parja [bdv], 357
Jharkhandhi, *alt.* Sadri [sck], 385
Jharwa, *dial.* Assamese [asm], 354
Jherung, *alt.* Jerung [jee], 472
Jhodia Parja, *alt.* Bodo Parja [bdv], 357
Jhoria, *alt.* Muria, Western [mut], 377
Jhue, *dial.* Jarai [jra], 523, 325
Jhunjhunu-Churu, *dial.* Shekhawati [swv], 386
Ji, *alt. dial.* Nuer [nus], 117
Ji-Cha, *dial.* Chinese, Gan [gan], 329
Jiamao [jio], 336
Jiamuhua, *alt.* Ai-Cham [aih], 326
Jianchuan, *dial.* Bai, Central [bca], 326
Jiangxia Guanhua, *alt. dial.* Chinese, Mandarin [cmn], 329
Jiaochang, *dial.* Qiang, Southern [qxs], 342
Jiaogong Mian, *dial.* Biao-Jiao Mien [bje], 327
Jiarong [jya], 336
Jiba [juo], 165
Jibali, *alt.* Shehri [shv], 483
Jibana, *dial.* Giryama [nyf], 133
Jibanci, *alt.* Jibu [jib], 165
Jibaro, *alt.* Shuar [jiv], 251
Jibawa, *alt.* Jibu [jib], 165
Jibbali, *alt.* Shehri [shv], 483
Jibe, *alt.* Jiba [juo], 165
Jibi, *alt.* Jiba [juo], 165
Jibito, *alt.* Hibito [hib], 288
Jibu [jib], 165
  alt. Wipi [gdr], 632
Jibyal, *alt. dial.* Kofyar [kwl], 166
Jicaque, *alt.* Tol [jic], 258
Jicarilla Apache, *see* Apache, Jicarilla [apj], 298
Jida, *alt.* Bu [jid], 156
  alt. dial. Bu [jid], 156
Jida-Abu, *alt.* Bu [jid], 156
Jidda-Abu, *alt.* Bu [jid], 156
Jiddu, *alt.* Jiiddu [jii], 184
Jidha, *alt. dial.* Lendu [led], 102
Jidindji, *alt.* Yidiny [yii], 579
Jidyo, *alt. dial.* Ladino [lad], 445
Jie, *dial.* Karamojong [kdj], 211
Jiezi, *dial.* Salar [slr], 343
Jiiddu [jii], 184
Jiir, *dial.* Kag-Fer-Jiir-Koor-Ror-Us-Zuksun [gel], 165
Jijal, *alt. dial.* Kohistani, Indus [mvy], 486
Jijili, *alt.* Tanjijili [uji], 175
Jikai, *alt.* Burarra [bvr], 569
Jikain, *alt. dial.* Nuer [nus], 194
Jikany, *alt. dial.* Nuer [nus], 117

Jikrio Goth Aer, *dial.* Aer [aeq], 483
Jilama Bawang, *alt.* Bisaya, Brunei [bsb], 324
alt. Bisaya, Sabah [bsy], 456
Jilama Sungai, *alt.* Bisaya, Brunei [bsb], 324
alt. Bisaya, Sabah [bsy], 456
Jilbe [jie], 165
Jili, *alt. dial.* Jingpho [kac], 464, 336
Jilim [jil], 603
Jim Mun, *alt.* Kim Mun [mji], 337, 451
Jimajima, *alt.* Dima [jma], 597
Jimbin, *alt.* Zumbun [jmb], 178
Jimbinawa, *alt.* Zumbun [jmb], 178
Jimi (Cameroon) [jim], 63
Jimi (Nigeria) [jmi], 165
Jimjimen, *alt.* Jimi [jim], 63
Jimo, *alt. dial.* Bata [bta], 155
dial. Jimi [jim], 63
Jimuni, *dial.* Ese [mcq], 598
Jina [jia], 63
dial. Jina [jia], 63
Jinda, *alt. dial.* Cinda-Regi-Tiyal [cdr], 157
Jindjibandi, *alt.* Yindjibarndi [yij], 579
Jindwi, *dial.* Manyika [mxc], 216, 148
Jinet, *dial.* Hértevin [hrt], 518
Jing, *alt.* Vietnamese [vie], 527, 346
dial. Manchu [mnc], 339
Jinga, *alt. dial.* Mbundu [kmb], 41
Jingali, *alt.* Djingili [jig], 570
Jinggarda, *alt.* Yinggarda [yia], 579
Jinghpaw, *alt.* Jingpho [kac], 464, 336
Jinghuai Guanhua, *dial.* Chinese, Mandarin [cmn], 329
Jingjing, *dial.* Mina [hna], 67
Jingphaw, *alt.* Singpho [sgp], 387
Jingpho [kac], 464, 336
Jingpo, *alt.* Jingpho [kac], 336
Jingulu, *alt.* Djingili [jig], 570
Jingzhan, *dial.* Chinese, Huizhou [czh], 329
Jinhua, *alt.* Ai-Cham [aih], 326
dial. Chinese, Wu [wuu], 330
Jinja, *alt.* Zinza [zin], 206
Jinjo, *dial.* Yele [yle], 633
Jinkum, *alt.* Wapan [juk], 177
Jinleri, *alt. dial.* Shoo-Minda-Nye [bcv], 174
Jinmen, *alt.* Kim Mun [mji], 337, 524
Jinmini, *alt.* Senoufo, Djimini [dyi], 95
Jino, *alt.* Jinuo, Buyuan [jiy], 336
alt. Jinuo, Youle [jiu], 336

Jinping Dai, *alt.* Tai Dam [blt], 517
Jinuo, Buyuan [jiy], 336
Jinuo, Youle [jiu], 336
Jinyu, *alt.* Chinese, Jinyu [cjy], 329
Jinyu Chinese, *see* Chinese, Jinyu [cjy], 329
Jiongnai, *alt.* Bunu, Jiongnai [pnu], 328
Jiongnai Bunu, *see* Bunu, Jiongnai [pnu], 328
Jiongnaihua, *alt.* Bunu, Jiongnai [pnu], 328
Jipal, *dial.* Kofyar [kwl], 166
Jir Joront, *alt.* Yir Yoront [yiy], 579
Jirai, *dial.* Bata [bta], 155
Jirel [jul], 472
Jiri, *alt.* Jirel [jul], 472
Jirial, *alt.* Jirel [jul], 472
Jirim, *dial.* Mongolian, Peripheral [mvf], 339, 462
Jiriya, *alt.* Ziriya [zir], 178
Jir'jorond, *alt. dial.* Yir Yoront [yiy], 579
Jirmel Mel-Jir, *alt. dial.* Yir Yoront [yiy], 579
Jiru [jrr], 165
Jishishan, *dial.* Bonan [peh], 328
Jishu, *dial.* Chinese, Xiang [hsn], 331
Jita [jit], 199
Jivaro, *alt.* Achuar-Shiwiar [acu], 285, 250
alt. Shuar [jiv], 251
Jiw, *alt.* Guayabero [guo], 245
Jiwadja, *alt.* Iwaidja [ibd], 571
Jiwali, *alt.* Mangala [mem], 573
Jiwarli, *alt.* Mangala [mem], 573
Jiwele, *alt. dial.* Iowa-Oto [iow], 302
Jiwere, *alt. dial.* Iowa-Oto [iow], 302
Jixi, *dial.* Chinese, Huizhou [czh], 329
Jiye, *alt. dial.* Karamojong [kdj], 211
dial. Toposa [toq], 196
Jju [kaj], 165
Jluko, *dial.* Godié [god], 93
Jmii', *alt.* Chinantec, Comaltepec [cco], 260
Jo, *alt.* Jowulu [jow], 143
alt. Nyaw [nyw], 516
alt. dial. Ghomálá' [bbj], 62
Jo Alur, *alt.* Alur [alz], 96, 210
Jo Colo, *alt. dial.* Thuri [thu], 195
Jo Lwo, *alt.* Luwo [lwo], 193
Jo Thuri, *alt.* Thuri [thu], 195
Jo-Uda, *dial.* Mongolian, Peripheral [mvf], 339
Joari, *alt. dial.* Yanomámi [wca], 234
Joba [job], 100
Jobi, *dial.* Pom [pmo], 422
Jobikha, *alt.* Brokpake [sgt], 322
Joboka, *alt.* Naga, Wancho [nnp], 380

Jodhpuri, *alt. dial.* Marwari [rwr], 375
Jodi, *alt.* Yuwana [yau], 313
Jogo, *alt.* Ligbi [lig], 126, 94
Johari, *alt.* Rangkas [rgk], 384
Johode, *alt.* Dghwede [dgh], 157
Johor, *alt. dial.* Malay [mly], 436
Jojod, *alt.* Maco [wpc], 312
Jok, *alt. dial.* Dinka, Northeastern [dip], 189
Jokay, *alt.* Brokkat [bro], 322
Jokot, *dial.* Alur [alz], 210
Jola, *alt.* Jola-Fonyi [dyo], 180, 118, 131
Jola-Fogny, *alt.* Jola-Fonyi [dyo], 180, 118, 131
Jola-Fonyi [dyo], 180, 118, 131
Jola-Kasa [csk], 180
Jolaha, *dial.* Maithili [mai], 373
Jolfâ, *dial.* Armenian [hye], 437
Joloano, *alt.* Tausug [tsg], 458
Joloano Sulu, *alt.* Tausug [tsg], 395, 458
Jolof, *alt. dial.* Wolof [wol], 182, 145
Jolohano, *alt.* Tausug [tsg], 502
Jolong, *dial.* Bahnar [bdq], 521
Jomang, *alt.* Talodi [tlo], 195
Jompre, *pej. alt.* Kutep [kub], 167, 64
Jon Kule, *alt.* Kakabe [kke], 129
Jonam, *dial.* Alur [alz], 210
Jone, *alt.* Choni [cda], 331
dial. Tibetan, Khams [khg], 345
Jonga, *dial.* Tsonga [tso], 186, 149, 217
Jonggunu, *alt.* Moni [mnz], 420
Jongor, *alt.* Migaama [mmy], 84
Jonkha, *alt.* Dzongkha [dzo], 323, 471
Jonkor Bourmataguil [jeu], 81
Jonkor-Gera, *alt.* Mukulu [moz], 85
Jóola, *alt.* Jola-Fonyi [dyo], 180
Jóola-Kasa, *alt.* Jola-Kasa [csk], 180
Joole, *alt. dial.* Dza [jen], 158
Joole Manga, *alt.* Tha [thy], 175
Joore, *alt. dial.* Mòoré [mos], 52
Jopadhola, *alt.* Adhola [adh], 210
Jopará, *dial.* Guaraní, Paraguayan [gug], 284
Jorá [jor], 223
Jorai, *alt.* Jarai [jra], 523, 325
Jorajane, *dial.* Romani, Vlax [rmy]
Jordanian Sign Language [jos], 448
Jorto [jrt], 165
Jos-Zarazon, *alt.* Izere [fiz], 164
Jostu, *dial.* Mongolian, Peripheral [mvf], 339, 462
Jotafa, *alt.* Tobati [tti], 424

Joti, *alt.* Yuwana [yau], 313
Joto, *dial.* Banda-Bambari [liy], 75
Jowulu [jow], 143
Joyabaj K'iche', *see* K'iche',
   Joyabaj [quj], 255
Joyabaj Quiché, *alt.* K'iche',
   Joyabaj [quj], 255
Jro, *dial.* Chrau [crw], 522
Jru', *alt.* Laven [lbo], 451
Jruq, *alt.* Laven [lbo], 451
Ju [juu], 165
Ju Ba, *dial.* Mambila, Cameroon
   [mcu], 66
Ju Naare, *dial.* Mambila, Cameroon
   [mcu], 66
Juanauo, *alt.* Karipuná [kuq], 228
Juaneño, *dial.* Luiseño [lui], 304
Juang [jun], 365
Juanga, *alt.* Yuaga [nua], 585
   dial. Yuaga [nua], 585
Juango, *alt.* Juang [jun], 365
Juarzon, *dial.* Sapo [krn], 139
Jub-'adin, *dial.* Western Neo-
   Aramaic [amw], 510
Juba Arabic, *alt.* Arabic, Sudanese
   Creole [pga], 187
Jubb 'Adi:n, *alt. dial.* Western Neo-
   Aramaic [amw], 510
Juchen, *alt.* Nanai [gld], 341
Judeo Spanish, *alt.* Ladino
   [lad], 445, 563
Judeo-Aramaic, *alt.* Hulaulá
   [huy], 445
   alt. Lishana Deni [lsd], 445
Judeo-Berber [jbe], 445
Judeo-Comtadine, *alt.* Shuadit
   [sdt], 538
Judeo-Crimean Tatar [jct], 521
Judeo-Crimean Turkish, *alt.*
   Judeo-Crimean Tatar [jct], 521
Judeo-Czech, *dial.* Knaanic
   [czk], 533
Judeo-French, *alt.* Zarphatic
   [zrp], 538
Judeo-Georgian [jge], 445, 352
Judeo-German, *alt.* Yiddish,
   Eastern [ydd], 446, 546
   alt. Yiddish, Western [yih], 540
Judeo-Greek, *alt.* Yevanic
   [yej], 446
Judeo-Iraqi Arabic, *see* Arabic,
   Judeo-Iraqi [yhd], 444, 442
Judeo-Italian [itk], 544
Judeo-Moroccan Arabic, *see*
   Arabic, Judeo-Moroccan [aju], 444,
   146
Judeo-Persian, *alt.* Dzhidi
   [jpr], 444, 438
Judeo-Provençal, *alt.* Shuadit
   [sdt], 538

Judeo-Slavic, *alt.* Knaanic
   [czk], 533
Judeo-Tajik, *alt.* Bukharic
   [bhh], 444, 521
Judeo-Tat [jdt], 445, 319, 554
Judeo-Tatic, *alt.* Judeo-Tat
   [jdt], 445, 319, 554
Judeo-Tripolitanian Arabic, *see*
   Arabic, Judeo-Tripolitanian
   [yud], 444
Judeo-Tunisian Arabic, *see*
   Arabic, Judeo-Tunisian [ajt], 444,
   209
Judeo-Yemeni, *alt.* Arabic, Judeo-
   Yemeni [jye], 444, 528
Judeo-Yemeni Arabic, *see*
   Arabic, Judeo-Yemeni [jye], 444,
   528
Judezmo, *alt.* Ladino [lad], 445, 563
   dial. Ladino [lad], 445
Judi, *alt.* Dzhidi [jpr], 438
Judyo, *alt. dial.* Ladino [lad], 445
Jugari, *alt.* Arabic, Tajiki Spoken
   [abh], 513
   alt. Arabic, Uzbeki Spoken
   [auz], 521
Jugli, *alt. dial.* Naga, Tase [nst], 380
Jugula, *alt.* Ganggalida [gcd], 570
Jugumbir, *alt.* Yugambal [yub], 579
Juguure, *alt. dial.* Fulfulde, Borgu
   [fue], 44
Ju|'hoan [ktz], 47, 150
Juhuri, *alt.* Judeo-Tat [jdt], 445, 319,
   554
Jui, *alt.* Yoy [yoy], 518, 453
   dial. Mfumte [nfu], 67
Jukagir, *alt.* Yukaghir, Northern
   [ykg], 507
   alt. Yukaghir, Southern [yux], 499
Jukamba, *alt.* Yugambal [yub], 579
Jukon, *alt.* Wapan [juk], 177
Juku, *alt.* Wapan [juk], 177
Juku Junkun, *alt.* Wapan [juk], 177
Jukum, *alt.* Wapan [juk], 177
Jukun, *alt.* Dyugun [dyd], 570
   alt. Jukun Takum [jbu], 63, 165
Jukun Abinsi, *alt.* Wannu [jub], 177
Jukun Kona, *alt.* Jiba [juo], 165
Jukun Takum [jbu], 63, 165
Jukun Wapan, *alt.* Wapan
   [juk], 177
Jukun Wukari, *alt.* Wapan
   [juk], 177
Jula [dyu], 51, 93, 143
Juli, *alt.* Mambila, Cameroon
   [mcu], 66
Julud, *alt. dial.* Katla [kcr], 192
Júma [jua], 227
Jumam, *alt. dial.* Kim [kia], 82
Jumeli, *alt.* Jumli [jml], 472

Jumiaki, *alt.* Grangali [nli], 316
Jumjum [jum], 191
Jumla, *alt.* Jumli [jml], 472
Jumleli, *alt.* Jumli [jml], 472
Jumli [jml], 472
Jumu, *dial.* Yoruba [yor], 178
Juna, *alt.* Tatuyo [tav], 247
Jungle Inga, *see* Inga, Jungle
   [inj], 246
Jungle Spanish, *alt.* Spanish,
   Loreto-Ucayali [spq], 293
Jungman, *alt.* Yangman [jng], 579
Junguru, *dial.* Banda-Ndélé [bfl], 75,
   188
Junín Quechua, *alt.* Quechua,
   North Junín [qvn], 291
Junoi, *alt.* Oko-Juwoi [okj], 381
Ju'oasi, *alt.* Ju|'hoan [ktz], 47, 150
Jupdá Macú, *pej. alt.* Hupdë
   [jup], 227, 246
Juquila Mixe, *see* Mixe, Juquila
   [mxq], 265
Juquila Mixe, *dial.* Mixe, Juquila
   [mxq], 265
Jur, *alt.* Jur Modo [bex], 191
Jur Beli, *alt.* Beli [blm], 189
Jur Luo, *alt.* Luwo [lwo], 193
Jur Lwo, *alt.* Luwo [lwo], 193
Jur Manangeer, *alt. dial.* Thuri
   [thu], 195
Jur Modo [bex], 191
   alt. dial. Jur Modo [bex], 191
Jur Shol, *alt. dial.* Thuri [thu], 195
Jurassien, *alt. dial.* French [fra],
   562
Juray [juy], 365
Jurchen [juc], 335
Juriti, *alt.* Yurutí [yui], 249, 234
Juriti-Tapuia, *alt.* Yurutí [yui], 249
Jurua, *dial.* Jamamadí [jaa], 227
Jurúna [jur], 228
Jurupari, *dial.* Carútana [cru], 226
Juruti, *alt.* Yurutí [yui], 249, 234
Juruti-Tapuia, *alt.* Yurutí
   [yui], 234
Jutish [jut], 533
Jutlandish, *alt.* Jutish [jut], 533
Juujmii, *alt.* Chinantec, Ozumacín
   [chz], 261
Juwal [mwb], 603
Juwaliny, *alt. dial.* Walmajarri
   [wmt], 577
Juwoi, *alt.* Oko-Juwoi [okj], 381
Juwri, *alt.* Judeo-Tat [jdt], 445, 319,
   554
Juxtlahuaca Mixtec, *see* Mixtec,
   Juxtlahuaca [vmc], 267
Jwira, *dial.* Jwira-Pepesa [jwi], 125
Jwira-Pepesa [jwi], 125
Jwisince, *alt.* Masalit [mls], 193

Kachi, *alt.* Kachchi [kfr], 366, 140, 199, 485
  alt. Koli, Kachi [gjk], 486, 369
  dial. Koli, Kachi [gjk], 486, 369
Kachi Bhil, *dial.* Koli, Kachi [gjk], 486, 369
Kachi Gujarati, *alt.* Koli, Kachi [gjk], 486, 369
Kachi Koli, *see* Koli, Kachi [gjk], 486, 369
Kachi Meghwar, *alt. dial.* Koli, Kachi [gjk], 486, 369
Kachia, *dial.* Kadara [kad], 165
Kachichere, *dial.* Tyap [kcg], 176
Kachin, *alt.* Jingpho [kac], 464, 336
  alt. Singpho [sgp], 387
Kachmere, *alt. dial.* Karanga [kth], 82
Kachuana, *alt.* Kaxuiâna [kbb], 229
Kacipo, *dial.* Kacipo-Balesi [koe], 115
Kacipo-Balesi [koe], 191, 115
Kacmiri, *alt.* Kashmiri [kas], 367, 486
Kaco′ [xkk], 325
Kad Chensu, *alt.* Irula [iru], 365
Kada, *alt.* Gidar [gid], 62, 80
  alt. Kadar [kej], 366
Kada-Gbe, *alt. dial.* Gbe, Ayizo [ayb], 44
Kadaddjara, *alt. dial.* Martu Wangka [mpj], 574
Kadagbe, *dial.* Gbe, Ayizo [ayb], 44
Kadagi, *alt.* Kodagu [kfa], 368
Kadai [kzd], 399
  dial. Galela [gbi], 398
Kadaian, *alt. dial.* Brunei [kxd], 324, 456
Kadaklan, *dial.* Finallig [bkb], 494
Kadaklan-Barlig Bontoc, *alt.* Finallig [bkb], 494
Kadam, *alt.* Gimnime [gmn], 62
Kadar [kej], 366
Kadara [kad], 165
Kadaro, *alt.* Kadaru [kdu], 191
Kadaru [kdu], 191
  dial. Kadaru [kdu], 191
Kadas, *alt.* Paiwan [pwn], 511
  alt. Puyuma [pyu], 512
  alt. Rukai [dru], 512
Kadasan, *alt.* Dusun, Central [dtp], 456
Kadaupuritana, *alt. dial.* Baniwa [bwi], 225
Kadavu, *dial.* Fijian [fij], 580
Kadayan, *alt.* Dusun, Central [dtp], 456
  alt. Dusun, Sugut [kzs], 456
  alt. dial. Brunei [kxd], 324, 456

Kadazan Tangaa′, *alt.* Kadazan, Coastal [kzj], 457
Kadazan, Coastal [kzj], 457
Kadazan, Klias River [kqt], 457
Kadazan, Labuk-Kinabatangan [dtb], 457
Kadazan-Tagaro, *dial.* Dusun, Central [dtp], 456
Kàdenbà, *alt.* Bwamu, Láá Láá [bwj], 50
Kadero, *alt.* Kadaru [kdu], 191
Kaderu, *alt.* Kadaru [kdu], 191
Kadian, *alt. dial.* Brunei [kxd], 324, 456
Kadien, *alt. dial.* Brunei [kxd], 324, 456
Kadim-Kaban, *dial.* Cakfem-Mushere [cky], 156
Kadina, *dial.* Galela [gbi], 398
Kadir, *alt.* Kadar [kej], 366
Kadirgi, *alt.* Fur [fvr], 190
Kadiro, *dial.* Moru [mgd], 193
Kadiwéu [kbc], 228
Kadjakse, *alt.* Kajakse [ckq], 81
Kadjala, *dial.* Lama [las], 208, 45, 126
Kadjalla, *alt. dial.* Lama [las], 208, 45, 126
Kadjang, *alt. dial.* Konjo, Coastal [kjc], 430
Ka′do, *alt.* Pévé [lme], 71
Kado [kdv], 464, 337, 450
  alt. Caddo [cad], 298
  alt. Hausa [hau], 162
  alt. Kaduo [ktp], 337
  alt. Ulumanda′ [ulm], 434
  pej. alt. Herdé [hed], 81
  pej. alt. Pévé [lme], 86
Ka′do Herdé, *alt.* Herdé [hed], 81
Ka′do Ngueté, *alt.* Ngete [nnn], 85
Ka′do Pevé, *alt.* Pévé [lme], 86
Kadohadacho, *alt.* Caddo [cad], 298
Kadorih, *dial.* Dohoi [otd], 393
Kadu, *alt.* Kado [kdv], 464, 337, 450
  alt. Kaduo [ktp], 337
  dial. Kado [kdv], 464, 337, 450
Kadu Kurumba, *alt.* Kurumba, Betta [xub], 371
Kadu Sholigar, *alt.* Sholaga [sle], 387
Kadu-Ganaan, *alt.* Kado [kdv], 464
Kadugli, *dial.* Katcha-Kadugli-Miri [xtc], 191
Kadukali, *alt.* Kurux [kru], 371
Kadumodi, *alt.* Krongo [kgo], 192
Kadun, *alt. dial.* Vaghat-Ya-Bijim-Legeri [bij], 177
Kaduna, *alt. dial.* Gbagyi [gbr], 160
Kaduo [ktp], 450, 337

Kadyan, *alt. dial.* Brunei [kxd], 324, 456
Ka′e, *alt. dial.* Kadaru [kdu], 191
Kaele, *alt.* Mundang [mua], 85, 68
Kaesabu, *dial.* Cia-Cia [cia], 429
Kaeti, *pej. alt.* Mandobo Atas [aax], 419
  pej. alt. Mandobo Bawah [bwp], 419
Kafa [kbr], 116
  dial. Foi [foi], 599
  dial. Kafa [kbr], 116
Kafanchan, *dial.* Tyap [kcg], 176
Kaffa, *alt.* Kafa [kbr], 116
Kaffer, *pej. alt.* Xhosa [xho], 187
Kaffir, *pej. alt.* Xhosa [xho], 187
Kaficho, *alt.* Kafa [kbr], 116
Kafila, *alt. dial.* Bidiyo [bid], 79
Kafir, *dial.* Kadaru [kdu], 191
Kafire, *dial.* Senoufo, Cebaara [sef], 94
Kafoa [kpu], 407
Kafu, *dial.* Bullom So [buy], 183
Kafugu, *alt. dial.* Gbiri-Niragu [grh], 160
Kag, *dial.* Kag-Fer-Jiir-Koor-Ror-Us-Zuksun [gel], 165
Kag-Fer-Jiir-Koor-Ror-Us-Zuksun [gel], 165
Kaga, *dial.* Kanuri, Central [knc], 166, 63, 81, 191
  dial. Mono [mnh], 104
Kagaba, *alt.* Cogui [kog], 244
Kagama, *alt. dial.* Kanuri, Central [knc], 166, 63, 81, 191
Kagan Kalagan, *see* Kalagan, Kagan [kll], 497
Kagan Kalagan, *alt.* Kalagan, Kagan [kll], 497
Kagani, *alt.* Hindko, Northern [hno], 485
Kagankan, *dial.* Hanunoo [hnn], 494
Kagari, *alt.* Kanjari [kft], 366
Kagate [syw], 472
Kagate Bhote, *alt.* Kagate [syw], 472
Kagayan, *alt.* Mapun [sjm], 499, 457
Kagayanen [cgc], 496
Kagbaaga, *dial.* Bidyogo [bjg], 131
Kagbo, *dial.* Godié [god], 93
Kaggaba, *alt.* Cogui [kog], 244
Kaghani, *alt.* Hindko, Northern [hno], 485
Kagiru, *alt. dial.* Berinomo [bit], 593
Kagiuong, *alt.* Kayong [kxy], 515
Kagoma [kdm], 165
Kagoro [xkg], 143
  dial. Tyap [kcg], 176
Kagoué, *alt. dial.* Dida, Yocoboué [gud], 92

Kagu, *alt. dial.* Gbiri-Niragu [grh], 160
Kagulu [kki], 199
Kaguru, *alt.* Kagulu [kki], 199
Kagwahibm, *alt.* Júma [jua], 227
Kagwahiph, *alt.* Júma [jua], 227
Kagwahiv, *alt.* Júma [jua], 227
  alt. Tenharim [pah], 232
  dial. Tenharim [pah], 232
Kagwahiva, *alt.* Júma [jua], 227
  alt. Karipuná [kuq], 228
  alt. Tenharim [pah], 232
  alt. Uru-Eu-Wau-Wau [urz], 233
Kah So, *alt.* Sô [sss], 452
Kahaian, *alt.* Kahayan [xah], 393
Kahailin Ilway, *dial.* Tugun [tzn], 405
Kahajan, *alt.* Kahayan [xah], 393
Kahasi, *alt.* Khasi [kha], 367, 321
Kahayan [xah], 393
Kahe [hka], 199
Kahedupa, *alt. dial.* Tukang Besi North [khc], 434
Kahluri, *alt.* Bilaspuri [kfs], 356
Kahua [agw], 636
Kahugu, *alt. dial.* Gbiri-Niragu [grh], 160
Kahumamahon, *alt.* Saluan, Kahumamahon [slb], 432
Kahumamahon Saluan, *see* Saluan, Kahumamahon [slb], 432
Kai, *alt.* Kaiy [tcq], 416
  alt. Kâte [kmg], 605
  alt. Kei [kei], 399
  alt. Numanggang [nop], 619
Kai Po-Mo, *alt.* Kato [ktw], 303
Kai-Iri, *alt.* Rumu [klq], 623
Kaiadilt, *alt.* Kayardild [gyd], 572
Kaiama, *dial.* Bokobaru [bus], 156
Kaian [kct], 603
Kaibi, *alt.* Kaivi [kce], 165
Kaibobo [kzb], 399
  dial. Kaibobo [kzb], 399
Kaibu, *dial.* Fasu [faa], 598
Kaibubu, *alt.* Kaibobo [kzb], 399
Kaibus, *alt.* Tehit [kps], 424
Kaidemui, *alt.* Buang, Mangga [mmo], 595
Kaidipan, *alt.* Kaidipang [kzp], 429
  dial. Kaidipang [kzp], 429
Kaidipang [kzp], 429
Kaiditj, *alt.* Kaytetye [gbb], 572
Kaiep [kbw], 603
Kaigama, *dial.* Dza [jen], 158
Kaikadi [kep], 366
Kaikadia, *alt.* Kaikadi [kep], 366
Kaikai, *alt.* Kaikadi [kep], 366
Kaike [kzq], 473
Kaiko, *alt.* Kaiku [kkq], 100
Kaiku [kkq], 100

Kailali, *dial.* Tharu, Dangaura [thl], 480
Kaili, Da'a [kzf], 429
Kaili, Ledo [lew], 429
Kaili, Unde [unz], 429
Kailikaili, *alt.* Korafe [kpr], 607
Kailolo, *dial.* Haruku [hrk], 398
Kaimbé [xai], 228
Kaimbulawa [zka], 429
Kaina, *dial.* Enga [enq], 598
Kaingáng [kgp], 228
Kaingáng, São Paulo [zkp], 228
Kaintiba, *dial.* Hamtai [hmt], 601
Kaiova, *alt.* Kaiwá [kgk], 228
Kaipang, *dial.* Chin, Falam [flm], 358
Kaipi, *alt.* Orokolo [oro], 620
  dial. Toaripi [tqo], 628
Kaipu, *alt. dial.* Fasu [faa], 598
Kairak [ckr], 603
Kairatu, *dial.* Alune [alp], 396
Kairi, *alt.* Rumu [klq], 623
Kairiru [kxa], 603
Kairu-Kaura, *alt.* Orokolo [oro], 620
Kairui, *dial.* Kairui-Midiki [krd], 351
Kairui-Midiki [krd], 351
Kais [kzm], 415
Kais Metan, *dial.* Baikeno [bkx], 350
Kaisak, *alt.* Kazakh [kaz], 448, 461, 518
Kaitak, *alt. dial.* Dargwa [dar], 553
Kaitarolea, *alt. dial.* Maleu-Kilenge [mgl], 611
Kaitero, *alt.* Irarutu [irh], 415
Kaitetu, *dial.* Seit-Kaitetu [hik], 403
Kaititj, *alt.* Kaytetye [gbb], 572
Kaiva, *alt.* Orokaiva [ork], 620
Kaivi [kce], 165
Kaiwa, *alt.* Iwal [kbm], 603
Kaiwá [kgk], 228, 220
  dial. Kaiwá [kgk], 228
Kaiwai, *alt.* Kowiai [kwh], 418
Kaixien, *alt.* Lahu [lhu], 338, 524
Kaiy [tcq], 416
Kajabí, *alt.* Kayabí [kyz], 229
Kajagar, *alt.* Kayagar [kyt], 417
Kajaja, *alt.* Tingal [tie], 196
Kajakja, *alt.* Tingal [tie], 196
Kajakse [ckq], 81
Kajali [xkj], 439
Kajaman [kag], 459
Kajan, *alt.* Kayan, Busang [bfg], 393
Kajang, *alt.* Kayan, Busang [bfg], 393
  alt. Kayan, Kayan River [xkn], 393
  alt. dial. Konjo, Coastal [kjc], 430
Kajanga, *dial.* Maba [mde], 83
Kajangan, *alt. dial.* Maba [mde], 83
Kaje, *alt.* Jju [kaj], 165

Kajeli, *alt.* Kayeli [kzl], 399
Kajeske, *alt.* Kajakse [ckq], 81
Kajiang, *alt.* Stieng, Bulo [sti], 326
Kajire-'dulo, *dial.* Majera [xmj], 65, 83
Kajirrawung, *alt.* Gadjerawang [gdh], 570
Kajjara, *alt.* Birked [brk], 189
Kajji, *alt.* Jju [kaj], 165
Kajoa, *alt. dial.* Makian, East [mky], 401
  dial. Bajau, Indonesian [bdl], 427
Kajoko, *alt. dial.* Bidyogo [bjg], 131
Kajtak, *dial.* Dargwa [dar], 553
Kajumerah, *alt.* Kowiai [kwh], 418
Kajupulau, *alt.* Kayupulau [kzu], 417
Kajuru, *dial.* Kadara [kad], 165
Kaka, *alt.* Kako [kkj], 63, 76, 88
  alt. dial. Bakaka [bqz], 57
  pej. alt. Yamba [yam], 73, 177
Kakaa, *alt. dial.* Yedina [bdm], 177
Kakaba, *alt.* Kamkam [bgu], 63
  alt. Mbongno [bgu], 170
Kakabai [kqf], 603
Kakabe [kke], 129
Kakachhu-Ki Boli, *alt.* Dhanki [dhn], 360
Kakadu, *alt.* Gagadu [gbu], 570
Kakai, *dial.* Hawrami [hac], 439
Kakakta, *alt.* Gagadu [gbu], 570
Kakamega, *alt. dial.* Idakho-Isukha-Tiriki [ida], 133
Kakanda [kka], 165
Kakarakala, *alt.* Yinggarda [yia], 579
Kakari, *alt. dial.* Gujarati [guj], 363
Ka'kas, *alt. dial.* Tondano [tdn], 434
Kakas, *dial.* Tondano [tdn], 434
Kakat, *alt.* Qaqet [byx], 622
Kakauhua [kbf], 242
Kakayamba, *alt.* Yamba [yam], 73
Kakbarak, *alt.* Kok Borok [trp], 368
Kakdju, *alt.* Gagadu [gbu], 570
Kakdjuan, *alt.* Gagadu [gbu], 570
Kakhetian, *alt. dial.* Georgian [kat], 352
Kaki Ae [tbd], 604
Kakia, *dial.* !Xóõ [nmn], 48, 151
Kakihum [kxe], 166
Kako [kkj], 63, 76, 88
Kakoli, *alt.* Umbu-Ungu [ubu], 629
Kakolo, *alt.* Kagoro [xkg], 143
Kaksingri, *dial.* Suba [suh], 136
Kakua, *alt.* Kakwa [keo], 211, 191
Kakumega, *alt. dial.* Idakho-Isukha-Tiriki [ida], 133
Kakumo, *alt.* Ukaan [kcf], 176
  dial. Ukaan [kcf], 176
Kakuna, *alt.* Mamusi [kdf], 611
  alt. dial. Mamusi [kdf], 611

Kaliyuawan, *alt. dial.* Amis,
　Nataoran [ais], 511
Kalkadoon, *alt.* Kalkutung
　[ktg], 572
Kalkali, *alt.* Kallahan, Kayapa
　[kak], 497
Kalkatungu, *alt.* Kalkutung
　[ktg], 572
Kalkoti [xka], 486
Kalkus, *alt. dial.* Mandjak
　[mfv], 131, 122, 181
Kalkutung [ktg], 572
Kalla, *alt. dial.* Gbaya, Northwest
　[gya], 75, 61
Kallahan, Kayapa [kak], 497
Kallahan, Keley-I [ify], 497
Kallahan, Tinoc [tne], 498
Kallana, *alt.* Alawa [alh], 567
Kalmack, *alt.* Kalmyk-Oirat
　[xal], 554
Kalmuck, *alt.* Kalmyk-Oirat
　[xal], 554
Kalmuk, *alt.* Kalmyk-Oirat [xal], 554
Kalmyk-Oirat [xal], 554, 337, 461
Kalmytskii Jazyk, *alt.* Kalmyk-
　Oirat [xal], 554
Kalo, *alt. dial.* Nkutu [nkw], 106
　dial. Keapara [khz], 605
　dial. Mser [kqx], 68, 84
Kalo Finnish Romani, *see*
　Romani, Kalo Finnish [rmf], 535,
　561
Kaloeng, *alt. dial.* Thai, Northeastern
　[tts], 517
Kalokalo, *alt.* Koluwawa [klx], 607
Kalondama, *dial.* Lamma [lev], 408
Kalong, *alt.* Dimbong [dii], 60
　alt. Kelon [kyo], 407
Kalop, *dial.* Koho [kpm], 524
Kalosi, *dial.* Duri [mvp], 429
Kalou [ywa], 604
Kalounaye, *dial.* Jola-Fonyi
　[dyo], 180
Kalp, *alt.* Urim [uri], 630
Kalto, *alt.* Nahali [nlx], 381
Kaltungo, *dial.* Tangale [tan], 175
Kaltuy, *alt.* Rembarunga [rmb], 576
Kaluli [bco], 604
　dial. Kaluli [bco], 604
Kalum, *alt.* Baga Binari [bcg], 128
Kalumpang [kli], 429
Kalvadi, *dial.* Deccan [dcc], 360
Kalyokengnyu, *alt.* Naga,
　Khiamniungan [nky], 378, 466
Kam [kdx], 166
　alt. Dong, Northern [doc], 331
　alt. Dong, Southern [kmc], 331
　alt. Tibetan, Khams [khg], 345
Kam Mu'ang, *alt.* Thai, Northern
　[nod], 517

Kam Ti, *alt.* Khamti [kht], 465
Kama, *dial.* Kissi, Northern
　[kqs], 129, 183
Kamã, *pej. alt.* Dâw [kwa], 226
Kámá, *dial.* Kunja [pep], 608
Kamã Makú, *alt.* Dâw [kwa], 226
Kama Permyak, *alt.* Komi-Permyak
　[koi], 555
Kamaiurá, *alt.* Kamayurá [kay], 228
Kamakan [vkm], 228
Kamalan, *alt.* Kavalan [ckv], 511
Kaman, *alt.* Miju-Mishmi [mxj], 375
Kamana-Kamang, *dial.* Kamang
　[woi], 407
Kamanawa, *alt.* Katukína, Panoan
　[knt], 229
Kamang [woi], 407
　dial. Kamang [woi], 407
Kamanga, *alt. dial.* Tumbuka
　[tum], 141, 215
Kamanidi, *alt.* Gaam [tbi], 190
Kamannaua, *alt.* Katukína, Panoan
　[knt], 229
Kamano [kbq], 604
Kamano-Kafe, *alt.* Kamano
　[kbq], 604
Kamant, *alt. dial.* Qimant [ahg], 118
Kamantan [kci], 166
Kamanton, *alt.* Kamantan [kci], 166
Kamaoni, *alt.* Kumauni [kfy], 370
Kamar [keq], 366
　alt. Kurmukar [kfv], 371
Kamara [jmr], 125
　alt. dial. Kono [kno], 183
Kamaragakok, *alt. dial.* Pemon
　[aoc], 312
Kamari-Santali, *dial.* Santali
　[sat], 386, 322
Kamarian [kzz], 399
Kamariang, *alt.* Kamarian [kzz], 399
Kamaru [kgx], 429
Kamas [xas], 505
　alt. Karagas [kim], 505
Kamasa [klp], 604
Kamasau [kms], 604
Kamassian, *alt.* Kamas [xas], 505
　dial. Kamas [xas], 505
　dial. Khakas [kjh], 505, 337
Kamate, *dial.* Yagaria [ygr], 632
Kamathi, *alt. dial.* Telugu [tel], 388
Kamau, *alt.* Jiamao [jio], 336
Kamayirá, *alt.* Kamayurá [kay], 228
Kamayo [kyk], 498
Kamayurá [kay], 228
Kamba (Brazil) [xba], 228
　Kamba (Kenya) [kam], 133
　alt. Akaselem [aks], 206
　alt. Wagi [fad], 630
Kamba So, *alt.* Dogon, Donno So
　[dds], 142

Kambaata [ktb], 116
Kambaira [kyy], 604
Kambara, *alt.* Kambaata [ktb], 116
Kambaramba, *dial.* Ap Ma
　[kbx], 590
Kambari, *alt.* Cishingini [asg], 151
　alt. Tsikimba [kdl], 175
　alt. Tsishingini [tsw], 176
Kambariire, *alt. dial.* Fulfulde,
　Adamawa [fub], 61, 80
Kambata, *alt.* Kambaata [ktb], 116
Kambatta, *alt.* Kambaata [ktb], 116
Kambe, *dial.* Giryama [nyf], 133
Kambe-Kambero, *dial.*
　Kaimbulawa [zka], 429
Kambeba, *alt.* Omagua [omg], 289
Kambegl, *dial.* Maring [mbw], 612
Kambera [xbr], 407
　alt. Gambera [gma], 570
　dial. Kambera [xbr], 407
Kamberataro, *alt.* Dera [kbv], 414,
　597
Kamberatoro, *alt.* Dera [kbv], 597
Kamberau [irx], 416
Kamberchi, *alt.* Cishingini [asg], 151
　alt. Tsikimba [kdl], 175
　alt. Tsishingini [tsw], 176
Kamberi, *alt.* Tsuvadi [tvd], 176
Kamberri, *alt.* Cishingini [asg], 151
　alt. Tsikimba [kdl], 175
　alt. Tsishingini [tsw], 176
Kambia, *dial.* Wahgi [wgi], 630
Kambiwá [xbw], 228
Kambolé, *alt.* Ede Nago, Manigri-
　Kambolé [xkb], 207
Kambon, *alt.* Mandobo Atas
　[aax], 419
　alt. Mandobo Bawah [bwp], 419
Kambonsenga, *alt. dial.* Lala-Bisa
　[leb], 102
Kambot, *alt.* Ap Ma [kbx], 590
Kambowa, *dial.* Kioko [ues], 429
Kambu, *alt.* Limbum [lmp], 169
Kamburwama, *dial.* Wandala
　[mfi], 73, 177
Kamchadal, *alt.* Itelmen [itl], 505
Kamchatka, *alt.* Itelmen [itl], 505
　dial. Even [eve], 504
Kamda, *dial.* Tulishi [tey], 196
Kamdang, *alt. dial.* Tulishi
　[tey], 196
Kamdeshi, *alt.* Kamviri [xvi], 316,
　486
Kamdhue, *alt.* Kanju [kbe], 572
Kamea, *alt.* Hamtai [hmt], 601
Kamemtxa, *alt.* Camsá [kbh], 244
Kamen, *alt. dial.* Koryak [kpy], 505
Kamenskij, *dial.* Koryak [kpy], 505
Kamenz, *dial.* Sorbian, Upper
　[hsb], 539

Kamer, *dial.* Biak [bhw], 412
Kamesh, *alt. dial.* Azerbaijani, South [azb], 438
Kamet, *alt.* Lamet [lbn], 515
Kametsu, *dial.* Toku-No-Shima [tkn], 447
Kamhao, *alt. dial.* Chin, Tedim [ctd], 463, 359
Kamhau, *alt. dial.* Chin, Tedim [ctd], 463, 359
Kamhmu, *alt.* Khmu [kjg], 451, 337, 465, 515
Kamhow, *alt. dial.* Chin, Tedim [ctd], 463, 359
Kami (Nigeria) [kmi], 166
　Kami (Tanzania) [kcu], 199
　alt. Chin, Khumi [cnk], 321, 359
Kami-Kulaka, *dial.* Yagaria [ygr], 632
Kamia, *alt.* Kumiai [dih], 263, 303
Kamiai, *alt.* Kumiai [dih], 263
Kamigin, *alt.* Manobo, Cinamiguin [mkx], 499
Kamik, *alt.* Kamviri [xvi], 316, 486
Kamilaroi, *alt.* Gamilaraay [kld], 570
Kamindjo, *alt.* Wára [tci], 631
Kamino, *dial.* Batu [btu], 150
Kamiyahi, *alt.* Kumiai [dih], 263
Kamiyai, *alt.* Kumiai [dih], 263
|Kamka!e, *alt.* |Xam [xam], 187
Kamkam [bgu], 63
　alt. Mbongno [bgu], 170
Kamma So, *dial.* Dogon, Donno So [dds], 142
Kammu, *alt.* Khmu [kjg], 451, 337, 465, 515
Kammüang, *alt.* Thai, Northern [nod], 517
Kammyang, *alt.* Thai, Northern [nod], 517
Kamnum, *alt.* Awtuw [kmn], 591
Kamo [kcq], 166
Kamona, *alt. dial.* Bidyogo [bjg], 131
Kamora, *alt.* Kamoro [kgq], 416
Kamoro [kgq], 416
Kamorta, *alt. dial.* Nicobarese, Central [ncb], 381
Kampar, *alt. dial.* Semai [sea], 455
Kampong Ayer, *dial.* Brunei [kxd], 324
Kampung Baru, *alt.* Kais [kzm], 415
Kamrau, *alt.* Kamberau [irx], 416
Kamrup, *dial.* Garo [grt], 362
Kamsa, *alt.* Camsá [kbh], 244
Kamse, *alt.* Camsá [kbh], 244
Kamsiki, *alt.* Psikye [kvj], 71, 173
Kamsili, *alt. dial.* Ukhwejo [ukh], 78
Kamtapuri, *alt.* Rajbanshi [rjb], 384

Kamtuk, *alt.* Kemtuik [kmt], 417
Kamu [xmu], 572
　alt. Kamo [kcq], 166
　alt. Khmu [kjg], 451, 337, 465, 515
　alt. dial. Psikye [kvj], 71, 173
Kamuan', *alt. dial.* Ta'oih, Upper [tth], 453, 527
Kamuku, *alt.* Cinda-Regi-Tiyal [cdr], 157
Kamula [xla], 604
Kamurú, *dial.* Kariri-Xocó [kzw], 228
Kamviri [xvi], 316, 486
　dial. Kamviri [xvi], 316, 486
Kamwai-Marhai, *dial.* Kulere [kul], 167
Kamwe [hig], 166
Kan, *alt.* Chinese, Gan [gan], 329
　alt. Kaan [ldl], 165
　alt. Kaansa [gna], 51
　dial. Guntai [gnt], 601
　dial. Mbay [myb], 84
Kana, *alt.* Khana [ogo], 166
Kana Mabang, *alt.* Maba [mde], 83
Kanabu, *alt.* Kanakanabu [xnb], 511
Kanakanabu [xnb], 511
Kanakanavu, *alt.* Kanakanabu [xnb], 511
Kanakhoe, *alt.* ‖Gana [gnk], 46
　alt. dial. ‖Gana [gnk], 46
Kanakuru, *alt.* Dera [kna], 157
Kanala, *alt.* Xârâcùù [ane], 585
Kanalu, *alt.* Barok [bjk], 592
Kanam, *alt.* Koenoem [kcs], 166
　alt. dial. Jarawa [jar], 165
Kanamanti, *alt.* Jamamadí [jaa], 227
Kanamaré, *alt.* Kanamarí [knm], 228
Kanamarí [knm], 228
Kanambu, *alt.* Kanembu [kbl], 81
　alt. Kanuri, Tumari [krt], 152
Kanana, *alt.* Kalanga [kck], 216
Kanandjoho, *dial.* Ndumu [nmd], 121
Kanapit, *alt.* Barok [bjk], 592
Kanara, *alt.* Kukna [kex], 370
Kanara Konkani, *alt.* Kukna [kex], 370
Kanarese, *alt.* Kannada [kan], 366
Kanashi [xns], 366
Kanasi [soq], 604
　alt. Kanashi [xns], 366
Kanatang, *dial.* Kambera [xbr], 407
Kanauji [bjj], 366
Kanauji Proper, *dial.* Kanauji [bjj], 366
Kanauri, *alt.* Kinnauri [kfk], 368
　alt. Kinnauri, Chitkuli [cik], 368
Kanaury Anuskad, *alt.* Kinnauri [kfk], 368
Kanawari, *alt.* Kinnauri [kfk], 368

Kanawi, *alt.* Kinnauri [kfk], 368
Kánchá, *dial.* Kunja [pep], 608
Kanchanaburi Pwo Karen, *dial.* Karen, Pwo Western Thailand [kjp], 514
Kanchanpur, *dial.* Tharu, Dangaura [thl], 480
Kanda, *alt.* Kande [kbs], 120
　alt. Kui [kxu], 370
Kandaasi, *dial.* Fipa [fip], 198
Kandahar Pashto, *alt. dial.* Pashto, Southern [pbt], 317
Kandak, *dial.* Pashayi, Northeast [aee], 317
Kandar, *alt. dial.* Sangir [sxn], 432
　dial. Selaru [slu], 403
Kandas [kqw], 604
Kandawire, *dial.* Tumbuka [tum], 215
Kandawo [gam], 604
Kande [kbs], 120
　alt. Kulere [kul], 167
　dial. Lama [las], 208, 45
　dial. Tsonga [tso], 186
Kandepe, *dial.* Enga [enq], 598
Kandere, *dial.* Senoufo, Cebaara [sef], 94
Kandéré, *dial.* Lyélé [lee], 52
Kanderma, *alt. dial.* Tira [tic], 196
Kandh, *alt.* Kui [kxu], 370
Kandiali, *dial.* Dogri [dgo], 360
Kandjerramal, *alt. dial.* Wadjiginy [wdj], 577
Kandju, *alt.* Kanju [kbe], 572
Kandoashi, *dial.* Candoshi-Shapra [cbu], 287
Kandomin, *alt. dial.* Wantoat [wnc], 631
Kandoshi, *alt.* Candoshi-Shapra [cbu], 287
Kandula, *alt. dial.* Hawrami [hac], 439
Kandyu, *alt.* Kanju [kbe], 572
Kanela, *alt.* Canela [ram], 226
Kanembou, *alt.* Kanembu [kbl], 81
Kanembu [kbl], 81
　alt. Kanuri, Tumari [krt], 152
Kang [kyp], 450, 337
　alt. Tibetan, Khams [khg], 345
Kanga [kcp], 191
　dial. Kanga [kcp], 191
Kangaé, *alt. dial.* Sika [ski], 409
Kangana, *dial.* Lusengo [lse], 103
Kangar Bhat, *alt.* Kanjari [kft], 366
Kangarraga, *alt.* Kungarakany [ggk], 572
Kangean [kkv], 392
Kangeju, *alt.* Hadza [hts], 199
Kanggape [igm], 604

Kanggewot, *dial.* Muyu, North [kti], 421

Kangite, *alt.* Apurinã [apu], 225

Kangjia [kxs], 337

Kangkalita, *alt.* Ganggalida [gcd], 570
dial. Ganggalida [gcd], 570

Kango (Bas-Uélé District) [kty], 100
Kango (Tshopo District) [kzy], 100

Kango Pygmy, *alt.* Kango [kzy], 100

Kangou, *dial.* Fali, South [fal], 61

Kangra-Dogri, *alt.* Kangri [xnr], 366

Kangri [xnr], 366
alt. Kanjari [kft], 366

Kangu, *alt. dial.* Fali, South [fal], 61

Kangwondo, *alt. dial.* Korean [kor], 448

Kangyang Hui, *alt.* Kangjia [kxs], 337

Kangye, *alt. dial.* Gbari [gby], 160

Kanhobal, *alt.* Q'anjob'al, Eastern [kjb], 256

Kanichana, *alt.* Canichana [caz], 222

Kanien'kehaka, *alt.* Mohawk [moh], 305

Kaniet [ktk], 604

Kanigurami, *dial.* Ormuri [oru], 487, 317

Kanika, *dial.* Worodougou [jud], 96

Kanikeh, *dial.* Manusela [wha], 402

Kanikkar, *alt.* Kanikkaran [kev], 366

Kanikkaran [kev], 366

Kaningara, *alt.* Kaningra [knr], 604

Kaningdom, *dial.* Kaningdon-Nindem [kdp], 166

Kaningdon-Nindem [kdp], 166

Kaningi [kzo], 120

Kaningkon, *alt. dial.* Kaningdon-Nindem [kdp], 166

Kaningkwom, *alt. dial.* Kaningdon-Nindem [kdp], 166

Kaningra [knr], 604

Kaninjal, *alt.* Keninjal [knl], 393

Kaninjal Dayak, *alt.* Keninjal [knl], 393

Kaninkon, *alt. dial.* Kaningdon-Nindem [kdp], 166

Kaninuwa [wat], 604

Kanioka, *alt.* Kanyok [kny], 101

Kaniran, *alt.* Mairasi [zrs], 419

Kanite [kmu], 604

Kaniuá, *alt.* Marúbo [mzr], 230

Kanjaga, *alt.* Buli [bwu], 123

Kanjari [kft], 366

Kanjimata, *alt.* Adynyamathanha [adt], 567

Kanjiningi, *alt. dial.* Teke, Northern [teg], 121

Kanjobal de San Miguel Acatán, *alt.* Kanjobal, Western [knj], 263

Kanjobal, Western [knj], 263

Kanjri, *alt.* Kanjari [kft], 366

Kanju [kbe], 572

Kankan Maninka, *alt.* Maninkakan, Eastern [emk], 129, 183

Kankanaey [kne], 498

Kankanai, *alt.* Kankanaey [kne], 498

Kankanay, *alt.* Kankanaey [kne], 498

Kankanay, Northern [xnn], 498

Kanna, *alt.* Bada [bau], 154

Kannada [kan], 366

Kannauji, *alt.* Kanauji [bjj], 366

Kanneh, *alt. dial.* Krahn, Eastern [kqo], 138

Kannikan, *alt.* Kanikkaran [kev], 366

Kannikaran, *alt.* Kanikkaran [kev], 366

Kannikharan, *alt.* Kanikkaran [kev], 366

Kano, *alt.* Kanu [khx], 100
dial. Hausa [hau], 162

Kano-Katsina, *dial.* Fulfulde, Kano-Katsina-Bororro [fuv], 61, 80
dial. Fulfulde, Nigerian [fuv], 160

Kano-Katsina-Bororo Fulfulde, *alt.* Fulfulde, Nigerian [fuv], 160

Kano-Katsina-Bororo Fulfulde, *see* Fulfulde, Nigerian [fuv], 61, 80

Kanoé [kxo], 228

Kanoreunu Skad, *alt.* Kinnauri [kfk], 368

Kanorin Skad, *alt.* Kinnauri [kfk], 368

Kanorug Skadd, *alt.* Kinnauri [kfk], 368

Kanouri, *alt.* Kanuri, Bilma [bms], 152
alt. Kanuri, Central [knc], 166, 63, 81, 152, 191
alt. Kanuri, Manga [kby], 152, 166

Kanoury, *alt.* Kanuri, Bilma [bms], 152
alt. Kanuri, Central [knc], 166, 63, 81, 152, 191
alt. Kanuri, Manga [kby], 152, 166

Kanowit [kxn], 459

Kanpetiet Daai, *dial.* Chin, Daai [dao], 463

Kansa [ksk], 303

Kantana, *alt.* Mama [mma], 169

Kante, *alt. dial.* Lama [las], 208, 45

Kantewu, *dial.* Uma [ppk], 434

Kantilan, *alt. dial.* Surigaonon [sul], 502

Kantohe, *dial.* Balanta-Kentohe [ble], 130

Kantonsi, *alt.* Kantosi [xkt], 125, 51

Kantosi [xkt], 125, 51

Kantu', *alt. dial.* Iban [iba], 393

Kantua, *alt.* Ta'oih, Upper [tth], 453, 527

Kanu [khx], 100

Kanufi [kni], 166

Kanum, Bädi [khd], 416

Kanum, Ngkâlmpw [kcd], 416

Kanum, Smärky [kxq], 416

Kanum, Sota [krz], 416

Kanuri, Bilma [bms], 152

Kanuri, Central [knc], 166, 63, 81, 152, 191

Kanuri, Manga [kby], 152, 166

Kanuri, Tumari [krt], 152

Kanwar Khati, *alt.* Lohar, Gade [gda], 372

Kany, *alt. dial.* Nuer [nus], 117

Kanyak, *alt.* Naga, Konyak [nbe], 378

Kanyaw, *alt.* Karen, S'gaw [ksw], 464, 514

Kanyay, *alt.* Kenyah, Upper Baram [ubm], 460, 394
alt. Kenyah, Western [xky], 460

Kanyok [kny], 101

Kanyoka, *alt.* Kanyok [kny], 101

Kanyop, *alt.* Mandjak [mfv], 131, 122, 181

Kanyu, *alt.* Kanju [kbe], 572

Kanze, *alt.* Kansa [ksk], 303

Kao [kax], 399

Kaohsiung, *dial.* Taiwan Sign Language [tss], 512

Kaokao, *alt.* Kaninuwa [wat], 604

Kaokeep, *alt. dial.* Chin, Thado [tcz], 359
dial. Chin, Thado [tcz], 463

Kaokonau, *alt.* Kamoro [kgq], 416

Kaonde [kqn], 213, 101

Kaora, *alt.* Koda [cdz], 368

Kaoro, *dial.* Wè Western [wec], 95

Kaouara-Timba-Sindou-Koroni, *dial.* Natioro [nti], 53

Kaowerawedj, *alt.* Kauwera [xau], 416

Kaowlu, *alt. dial.* Wè Western [wec], 95

Kapagalan, *dial.* Timugon Murut [tih], 458

Kapal, *dial.* Wipi [gdr], 632

Kapampangan, *alt.* Pampangan [pam], 500

Kapanawa, *alt.* Capanahua [kaq], 287

Kapangan, *dial.* Kankanaey [kne], 498

Kapari, *dial.* Keapara [khz], 605

Kapau, *alt.* Hamtai [hmt], 601
Kapauku, *alt.* Ekari [ekg], 414
Kapaur, *alt.* Iha [ihp], 415
Kapauri, *alt.* Kapori [khp], 416
Kapawa, *alt.* Tha [thy], 175
Kapeso, *alt.* Bagusa [bqb], 412
Kapiangan, *alt.* Paiwan [pwn], 511
Kapin [tbx], 605
  dial. Kapin [tbx], 605
Kapinawá [xpn], 228
Kapingamarangi [kpg], 582
Kapitiauw, *alt.* Tarpia [suf], 423
Kapo, *alt. dial.* Krumen, Tepo [ted],
  93, 138
Kapon, *alt.* Akawaio [ake], 256
  alt. Patamona [pbc], 257
Kapona, *dial.* Enga [enq], 598
Kapone, *alt.* Numee [kdk], 585
Kapontori, *dial.* Pancana [pnp], 432
Kapore, *alt.* Bebeli [bek], 593
Kapori [khp], 416
Kapriman [dju], 605
  dial. Kapriman [dju], 605
Kapsiki, *alt.* Psikye [kvj], 71, 173
  alt. dial. Psikye [kvj], 71, 173
Kaptiauw, *alt.* Tarpia [suf], 423
Kapuas, *dial.* Kahayan [xah], 393
Kapucha, *alt.* Bezhta [kap], 553
Kapuchin, *alt.* Bezhta [kap], 553
Kapugu, *alt. dial.* Gbiri-Niragu
  [grh], 160
Kapul, *alt.* Inabaknon [abx], 495
Kapula, *alt.* Warluwara [wrb], 578
Kapulika, *alt.* Haigwai [hgw], 601
  dial. Haigwai [hgw], 601
Kaputiei, *dial.* Maasai [mas], 134
Kapwi, *alt.* Naga, Inpui [nkf], 377
Kapya [klo], 166
Kaqchiquel, *alt.* Kaqchikel, Central
  [cak], 254
**Kaqkchikel, Akatenango
  Southwestern** [ckk], 254
Kaqkchikel, Central [cak], 254
Kaqkchikel, Eastern [cke], 254
Kaqkchikel, Northern [ckc], 254
**Kaqkchikel, Santa María de
  Jesús** [cki], 254
**Kaqkchikel, Santo Domingo
  Xenacoj** [ckj], 254
Kaqkchikel, South Central
  [ckd], 254
Kaqkchikel, Southern [ckf], 254
Kaqkchikel, Western [ckw], 254
**Kaqkchikel, Yepocapa
  Southwestern** [cbm], 255
**Kaqkchikel-K'iche' Mixed
  Language** [ckz], 255
Kar, *alt.* Karaboro, Eastern [xrb], 51
  alt. dial. Kag-Fer-Jiir-Koor-Ror-Us-
  Zuksun [gel], 165

Kar Bhote, *alt.* Lhomi [lhm], 474
Kara (Central African Republic)
  [kah], 76
Kara (Papua New Guinea) [leu], 605
Kara (Tanzania) [reg], 199
alt. Gula [kcm], 76, 191
alt. Kirghiz [kir], 337
alt. Ngala [nud], 618
alt. dial. Nogai [nog], 556
pej. alt. dial. Qimant [ahg], 118
Kara de Soudan, *alt.* Gula
  [kcm], 76
Kara Kerre, *alt.* Hamer-Banna
  [amf], 115
Kara of Sudan, *alt.* Gula [kcm], 76,
  191
Kara-Kirgiz, *alt.* Kirghiz [kir], 449
Karabagh, *dial.* Armenian [hye], 318
Karabagh Shamakhi, *dial.*
  Armenian [hye], 437
Karabakh, *alt. dial.* Azerbaijani,
  North [azj], 319, 319
Karaboro, Eastern [xrb], 51
Karaboro, Western [kza], 52
Karacaylar, *alt.* Karachay-Balkar
  [krc], 554
Karachai, *alt.* Karachay-Balkar [krc],
  554
Karachaitsy, *alt.* Karachay-Balkar
  [krc], 554
Karachay, *alt.* Karachay-Balkar
  [krc], 554
  dial. Karachay-Balkar [krc], 554
Karachay-Balkar [krc], 554
Karachayla, *alt.* Karachay-Balkar
  [krc], 554
Karachi, *dial.* Domari [rmt], 438,
  554, 563
Karadjee, *alt.* Iwaidja [ibd], 571
Karadjeri [gbd], 572
Karaga, *alt. dial.* Alutor [alr], 503
Karaga Mandaya, *see* Mandaya,
  Karaga [mry], 498
Karagan, *dial.* Dayak, Land
  [dyk], 393
Karagas [kim], 505
  dial. Mator [mtm], 505
Karagass, *alt.* Karagas [kim], 505
Karagawan, *dial.* Isnag [isd], 496
Karaginskij, *dial.* Alutor [alr], 503
Karagwe, *alt.* Nyambo [now], 203
Karahawyana [xkh], 228
Karai Karai, *alt.* Karekare [kai], 166
Karaiai, *alt.* Anem [anz], 589
Karaikarai, *alt.* Karekare [kai], 166
Karaim [kdr], 546
Karaite, *alt.* Karaim [kdr], 546
Karajá [kpj], 228
Karajarri, *alt.* Karadjeri [gbd], 572
Karakalpak [kaa], 521, 316

Karakara, *dial.* Guruntum-Mbaaru
  [grd], 161
Karakati, *alt. dial.* Krikati-Timbira
  [xri], 229
Karakelang, *alt. dial.* Talaud
  [tld], 433
Karakelong, *alt. dial.* Talaud
  [tld], 433
Karakh, *alt. dial.* Avar [ava], 553
Karakir, *alt.* Jonkor Bourmataguil
  [jeu], 81
Karaklobuk, *alt.* Karakalpak
  [kaa], 521
Karam, *alt.* Kalam [kmh], 604
Karama, *alt.* Kurrama [vku], 572
Karamanli, *alt. dial.* Balkan Gagauz
  Turkish [bgx], 563
  dial. Turkish [tur], 519, 521
Karamba, *dial.* Maring [mbw], 612
Karambit, *dial.* Kapriman [dju], 605
Karami [xar], 605
Karamiananen, *alt.* Tagbanwa,
  Calamian [tbk], 502
Karamojong [kdj], 211
  dial. Karamojong [kdj], 211
Karang [kzr], 63, 81
  alt. Ngas [anc], 171
  dial. Karang [kzr], 63, 81
Karanga [kth], 82
  dial. Karanga [kth], 82
  dial. Shona [sna], 216
  dial. Zezuru [sna], 49
Karangan, *alt. dial.* Dayak, Land
  [dyk], 393
  dial. Basap [bdb], 392
Karangasem, *alt. dial.* Bali
  [ban], 391
Karangi, *alt.* Weliki [klh], 632
Karangura, *alt.* Ngamini [nmv], 575
Karani, *dial.* Mugom [muk], 476
Karanjan, *dial.* Worodougou
  [jud], 96
Karao [kyj], 498
Karapaná, *alt.* Carapana [cbc], 244
Karapanã [cbc], 228
Karapano, *alt.* Carapana [cbc], 244
Karapapak, *dial.* Azerbaijani, North
  [azj], 319, 319
Karapapakh, *dial.* Azerbaijani,
  South [azb], 438
Karapató, *alt.* Tingui-Boto
  [tgv], 233
Kararaó, *dial.* Kayapó [txu], 229
Karas [kgv], 416
Karata [kpt], 555
Karatai, *alt.* Karata [kpt], 555
Karataun, *dial.* Kalumpang
  [kli], 429
Karate, *alt.* Komso [kxc], 116
Karatin, *alt.* Karata [kpt], 555

Karutana, *alt.* Carútana [cru], 226
Kasaa, *dial.* Mumuye [mzm], 170
Kasaba, *alt. dial.* Irula [iru], 365
Kasanga [ccj], 131
Kasara, *dial.* Senoufo, Cebaara [sef], 94
Kasargod, *dial.* Marathi [mar], 374
Kasava, *alt. dial.* Irula [iru], 365
Kaschemiri, *alt.* Kashmiri [kas], 367, 486
Kasele, *alt.* Akaselem [aks], 206
Kasem [xsm], 52, 125
  dial. Kasem [xsm], 125
Kasena, *alt.* Kasem [xsm], 52, 125
Kaseng, *alt.* Kasseng [kgc], 450
Kasenga, *dial.* Bangubangu [bnx], 97
Kasere, *alt.* Ikobi-Mena [meb], 602
Kashani, *dial.* Farsi, Western [pes], 439
Kashaya [kju], 303
Kashgar-Yarkand, *dial.* Uyghur [uig], 318, 448
Kashkadarya Arabic, *alt.* Arabic, Uzbeki Spoken [auz], 521
Kashkai, *alt.* Qashqa'i [qxq], 441
Kashkari, *alt.* Khowar [khw], 486
Kashmere, *dial.* Karanga [kth], 82
Kashmir Gujuri, *alt.* Gujari [gju], 363, 485
Kashmiri [kas], 367, 486
Kashtawari, *alt. dial.* Kashmiri [kas], 367
Kashtwari, *alt. dial.* Kashmiri [kas], 367
Kashubian [csb], 550
Kashubian Proper, *dial.* Kashubian [csb], 550
Kashujana, *alt.* Kaxuiâna [kbb], 229
Kashuyana, *alt.* Kaxuiâna [kbb], 229
Kasieh, *dial.* Wemale, North [weo], 405
Kasigaon, *dial.* Tamang, Eastern Gorkha [tge], 479
Kasigau, *dial.* Sagalla [tga], 136
Kasiguranin [ksn], 498
Kasikasi, *dial.* Bunama [bdd], 595
Kasim, *alt.* Kasem [xsm], 52
Kasimbar, *alt.* Tajio [tdj], 433
Kasira, *alt.* Irarutu [irh], 415
Kasiui, *alt.* Watubela [wah], 405
Kasiwa, *alt.* Ninggerum [nxr], 618, 421
Kaska [kkz], 238
Kaski Gurung, *alt. dial.* Gurung, Western [gvr], 471
Kaskihá, *alt.* Guana [gva], 284
Kasmin, *dial.* Buna [bvn], 595
Kasoma, *dial.* Kalamsé [knz], 51
Kasonke, *alt.* Xaasongaxango [kao], 145

alt. Xasonga [kao], 182
Kasrapai, *alt.* Ninam [shb], 230
Kassadou Lele, *dial.* Lele [llc], 129
Kassanga, *alt.* Kasanga [ccj], 131
Kassem, *alt.* Kasem [xsm], 52
Kassena, *alt.* Kasem [xsm], 52, 125
Kassene, *alt.* Kasem [xsm], 125
Kasseng [kgc], 450
Kassi, *alt.* Khasi [kha], 367
Kasso, *alt.* Xaasongaxango [kao], 145
  alt. Xasonga [kao], 182
Kasson, *alt.* Xaasongaxango [kao], 145
  alt. Xasonga [kao], 182
Kassonke, *alt.* Xaasongaxango [kao], 145
  alt. Xasonga [kao], 182
Kastanista-Sitena, *alt. dial.* Tsakonian [tsd], 541
Kasua [khs], 605
Kasuba, *alt. dial.* Irula [iru], 365
Kasui, *alt.* Watubela [wah], 405
Kasuwa, *dial.* Ninggerum [nxr], 618
Kasuweri, *alt.* Kokoda [xod], 417
  dial. Kokoda [xod], 417
Kaszubski, *alt.* Kashubian [csb], 550
Kataang [kgd], 450
Katab, *alt.* Tyap [kcg], 176
  dial. Tyap [kcg], 176
Katabaga [ktq], 498
Kataf, *alt.* Tyap [kcg], 176
Katagum, *dial.* Hausa [hau], 162
Katai Meghwar, *dial.* Koli, Kachi [gjk], 486, 369
Katakari, *alt.* Katkari [kfu], 367
Katan, *alt.* Ullatan [ull], 389
Katang, *alt.* Kataang [kgd], 450
  alt. Kayong [kxy], 515
Katanga Swahili, *dial.* Swahili, Congo [swc], 108
Katari, *alt.* Katkari [kfu], 367
Katauixi, *alt.* Júma [jua], 227
Katausan, *alt.* Paiwan [pwn], 511
Kataut, *alt.* Muyu, North [kti], 421
Katawa, *alt.* Ebira [igb], 158
Katawian, *dial.* Waiwai [waw], 233, 257
Katawina, *alt. dial.* Waiwai [waw], 233, 257
Katawixi [xat], 228
Katazi, *dial.* Babatana [baa], 635
Katbol [tmb], 642
Katch, *alt.* Kachchi [kfr], 366, 485
Katcha, *dial.* Katcha-Kadugli-Miri [xtc], 191
Katcha-Kadugli-Miri [xtc], 191
Katchal, *dial.* Nicobarese, Central [ncb], 381
Katchi, *alt.* Kachchi [kfr], 366, 133, 140, 199, 485

alt. Koli, Kachi [gjk], 486, 369
Kâte [kmg], 605
  dial. Kunimaipa [kup], 608
Kâte Dong, *alt.* Kâte [kmg], 605
Katege, *alt.* Teke, Northern [teg], 121
  alt. dial. Teke, Northern [teg], 121
Kateghe, *dial.* Teke-Tege [teg], 90
Kateik, *alt. dial.* Katla [kcr], 192
Kath Bhote, *alt.* Lhomi [lhm], 474
Katharevousa, *dial.* Greek [ell], 540
Kathariya, *alt.* Tharu, Kathoriya [tkt], 480
Kathe, *alt.* Meitei [mni], 375, 321, 465
Kathi, *alt.* Meitei [mni], 375, 321, 465
Kathiawari, *alt. dial.* Kashmiri [kas], 367
Kathiyawadi, *dial.* Gujarati [guj], 363
Kathmandu-Pathan-Kirtipur, *dial.* Newar [new], 476
Kathodi, *alt.* Katkari [kfu], 367
Kathoriya Tharu, *see* Tharu, Kathoriya [tkt], 480
Kati [bsh], 316, 486
  dial. Dayak, Land [dyk], 393
Kati Metomka, *alt.* Muyu, South [kts], 421
Kati-Ninanti, *alt.* Muyu, North [kti], 421
Katia, *alt. dial.* !Xóõ [nmn], 48, 151
Katiara, *dial.* Senoufo, Tagwana [tgw], 95
Katiati, *alt.* Mum [kqa], 615
Katingan [kxg], 393
  dial. Madak [mmx], 610
Katingan Ngaju, *dial.* Katingan [kxg], 393
Katingan Ngawa, *dial.* Katingan [kxg], 393
Katinja, *alt.* Angal Heneng [akh], 589
Katio, *alt.* Emberá-Catío [cto], 245, 283
Katiola, *dial.* Senoufo, Tagwana [tgw], 95
Kativa, *alt.* Ninggerum [nxr], 618, 421
Kativiri, *alt.* Kati [bsh], 316, 486
Katiyai, *alt. dial.* Malvi [mup], 374
Katkari [kfu], 367
Katla [kcr], 192
Kato [ktw], 303
  alt. Kado [kdv], 464, 337
Katova, *alt.* Laghu [lgb], 637
Katsina, *dial.* Hausa [hau], 162, 152
Katsy, *alt.* Kryts [kry], 319
Kattalan, *alt.* Ullatan [ull], 389

Kattang, *alt.* Worimi [kda], 578
Kattea, *alt. dial.* !Xóõ [nmn], 48, 151
Kattu Nayaka, *alt.* Kurumba, Jennu [xuj], 371
Katu, *alt.* Kado [kdv], 464, 337, 450
Katu, Eastern [ktv], 523
Katu, Western [kuf], 450
Katua [kta], 523
Katuena, *alt. dial.* Waiwai [waw], 233
Katukína [kav], 228
Katukina do Juruá, *alt.* Katukína, Panoan [knt], 229
Katukina do Jutaí, *alt.* Katukína [kav], 228
Katukína, Panoan [knt], 229
Katumene, *alt.* Kapin [tbx], 605
Katvadi, *alt.* Katkari [kfu], 367
Katwena, *alt. dial.* Waiwai [waw], 233, 257
Ka'u, *alt.* Kao [kax], 399
Kau, *alt.* Kao [kax], 399
  alt. Ko [fuj], 192
  dial. Ko [fuj], 192
Kau Bru, *alt.* Riang [ria], 385, 322
Kauditan, *dial.* Tonsea [txs], 434
Kaugat, *alt.* Atohwaim [aqm], 411
Kaugel, *alt.* Umbu-Ungu [ubu], 629
Kauil, *alt.* Umbu-Ungu [ubu], 629
Kaukau, *alt.* ‡Kx'au‖'ein [aue], 150, 47
Kaukaue, *alt.* Kakauhua [kbf], 242
Kaul, *alt.* Aiklep [mwg], 588
Kauli, *alt.* Pahari, Kullu [kfx], 382
Kaulong [pss], 605
  dial. Kaulong [pss], 605
Kauma, *dial.* Giryama [nyf], 133
Kaunak, *alt.* Citak [txt], 413
Kaunga, *alt.* Yelogu [ylg], 633
Ka'ur, *alt.* Kaur [vkk], 436
Kaur [vkk], 436
Kaure [bpp], 416
Kaureh, *alt.* Kaure [bpp], 416
Kauri, *dial.* Jingpho [kac], 464, 336
Kauru, *alt.* Shuwa-Zamani [ksa], 174
  alt. dial. Lere [gnh], 168
Kautchy, *alt.* Kachchi [kfr], 366, 485
Kauwera [xau], 416
Kauwerawec, *alt.* Kauwera [xau], 416
Kauwerawetj, *alt.* Kauwera [xau], 416
Kauyarí, *alt.* Cabiyarí [cbb], 243
Kauyawa, *alt.* Kariya [kil], 166
Kavahiva, *alt.* Júma [jua], 227
Kavalan [ckv], 511
Kavanan, *alt.* Kavalan [ckv], 511
Kavarauan, *alt.* Kavalan [ckv], 511

Kavardi, *dial.* Chhattisgarhi [hne], 358
Kavet, *alt.* Kravet [krv], 325
Kavirondo, *alt.* Luo [luo], 201
Kavirondo Luo, *alt.* Luo [luo], 134
Kavor, *alt.* Koya [kff], 370
Kaw, *alt.* Akha [ahk], 462, 326, 449, 513, 521
  alt. Kansa [ksk], 303
  alt. Koshin [kid], 64
K'awa, *alt.* Wa [wbm], 467, 346
Kawa, *alt.* Blang [blr], 327, 462, 514
  alt. Bugawac [buk], 595
  alt. Wa [wbm], 467, 346
  dial. Lisabata-Nuniali [lcs], 400
Kawa Tadimini, *alt.* Kajakse [ckq], 81
Kawac, *alt.* Bugawac [buk], 595
Kawacha [kcb], 605
Kawahip, *alt.* Júma [jua], 227
Kawaib, *alt.* Júma [jua], 227
  alt. Tenharim [pah], 232
  alt. dial. Tenharim [pah], 232
Kawaiisu [xaw], 303
Kawait, *dial.* Maden [xmx], 419
Kawalib, *alt.* Koalib [kib], 192
Kawalké, *dial.* Kwang [kvi], 82
Kawam, *dial.* Agob [kit], 588
Kawama, *alt.* Otoro [otr], 194
Kawang, *dial.* Bajau, West Coast [bdr], 456
Kawanga, *alt.* Kwanga [kwj], 608
  alt. dial. Luyia [luy], 134
Kawanuwan, *alt.* Basay [byq], 511
Kawar, *dial.* Maithili [mai], 475
Kawari, *dial.* Halbi [hlb], 363
Kawarma, *alt.* Otoro [otr], 194
Kawathi, *alt.* Bagheli [bfy], 354, 468
Kawatsa, *alt.* Kawacha [kcb], 605
Kawayan, *dial.* Hiligaynon [hil], 494
Kawe [kgb], 416
Kaweinag, *alt.* Asmat, Casuarina Coast [asc], 411
Kawel, *alt. dial.* Kamang [woi], 407
Kawela, *alt.* Lamalera [lmr], 408
Kawera, *alt.* Kauwera [xau], 416
Kaweskar, *alt.* Qawasqar [alc], 243
Kawesqar, *alt.* Qawasqar [alc], 243
Kawiku, *dial.* Lunda [lun], 214
Kawillary, *alt.* Cabiyarí [cbb], 243
Kawkareik, *dial.* Karen, Pwo Eastern [kjp], 464
Kawki, *alt. dial.* Jaqaru [jqr], 288
Kawonde, *alt.* Kaonde [kqn], 213, 101
Kawwad'a, *alt.* Gawwada [gwd], 115
Kawwada, *alt.* Gawwada [gwd], 115
Kaxararí [ktx], 229
Kaxariri, *alt.* Kaxararí [ktx], 229

Kaxetian, *dial.* Georgian [kat], 352
Kaxib, *dial.* Akhvakh [akv], 552
  dial. Avar [ava], 553
Kaxinauá, *alt.* Cashinahua [cbs], 226
Kaxinawá, *alt.* Cashinahua [cbs], 287, 226
Kaxuiâna [kbb], 229
Kaxúyana, *alt.* Kaxuiâna [kbb], 229
Kaxynawa, *alt.* Cashinahua [cbs], 287, 226
Kaya, *alt.* Koya [kff], 370
Kayabí [kyz], 229
Kayagar [kyt], 417
Kayah, *alt.* Kayah, Eastern [eky], 465, 515
Kayah Li, *alt.* Kayah, Western [kyu], 465
Kayah, Eastern [eky], 465, 515
Kayah, Western [kyu], 465
Kayaman, *alt.* Kajaman [kag], 459
Kayan [pdu], 465
  alt. Kaian [kct], 603
Kayan Mahakam [xay], 393
Kayan River Bakung, *dial.* Kenyah, Bakung [boc], 393
Kayan River Kajan, *alt.* Kayan, Kayan River [xkn], 393
Kayan River Kayan, *see* Kayan, Kayan River [xkn], 393
Kayan River Kenya, *alt.* Kenyah, Kayan River [knh], 393
Kayan River Kenyah, *see* Kenyah, Kayan River [knh], 393
Kayan, Baram [kys], 459
Kayan, Busang [bfg], 393
Kayan, Kayan River [xkn], 393
Kayan, Mendalam [xkd], 393
Kayan, Murik [mxr], 459
Kayan, Rejang [ree], 459
Kayan, Wahau [whu], 393
Kayang, *alt.* Kayan [pdu], 465
Kayani, *alt.* Jakati [jat], 564, 316
Kayaniyut Kayan, *dial.* Kayan, Kayan River [xkn], 393
Kayaniyut Kenyah, *dial.* Kenyah, Kayan River [knh], 393
Kayapa, *alt.* Kallahan, Kayapa [kak], 497
Kayapa Kallahan, *see* Kallahan, Kayapa [kak], 497
Kayapó [txu], 229
Kayapó-Kradaú, *dial.* Kayapó [txu], 229
Kayapwe, *alt.* Záparo [zro], 252
Kayardild [gyd], 572
Kayasthi, *alt. dial.* Konkani [knn], 369
  dial. Sindhi [snd], 387
Kayauri, *alt.* Geji [gji], 160
Kayavar, *dial.* Malayalam [mal], 374

Kayay, *alt.* Kayah, Eastern [eky], 465, 515

Kayeli [kzl], 399
dial. Kayeli [kzl], 399

Kaygi, *alt.* Kayagar [kyt], 417

Kaygir, *alt.* Kayagar [kyt], 417

Kayik, *alt.* Wanap [wnp], 631

Kayinbyu, *alt.* Karen, Geba [kvq], 458

Kaykavski, *dial.* Croatian [hrv], 532

Kayla, *dial.* Qimant [ahg], 118

Kayoa, *alt. dial.* Makian, East [mky], 401

Kayobe, *alt.* Miyobe [soy], 45

Kayong [kxy], 515
alt. dial. Malayic Dayak [xdy], 394

Kayort [kyv], 473

Kayova, *alt.* Kaiwá [kgk], 228, 220

Kaytak, *alt. dial.* Dargwa [dar], 553

Kaytetye [gbb], 572

Kayu Agung [vky], 436

Kayumerah, *alt.* Kowiai [kwh], 418

Kayung, *dial.* Malayic Dayak [xdy], 394

Kayupulau [kzu], 417

Kazak, *alt.* Kazakh [kaz], 448, 337, 439

Kazakh [kaz], 448, 316, 337, 439, 461, 518
dial. Azerbaijani, North [azj], 319

Kazakhi, *alt.* Kazakh [kaz], 316, 439, 461, 518

Kazan, *alt. dial.* Tatar [tat], 556

Kazax, *alt.* Kazakh [kaz], 337, 461, 518

Kazikumukhtsy, *alt.* Lak [lbe], 555

Kazukuru [kzk], 636

Kbalan, *alt.* Kavalan [ckv], 511

Kdang, *alt.* Kedang [ksx], 407

Kdrao, *alt. dial.* Rade [rad], 526

Ke, *alt.* Chinese, Hakka [hak], 329, 508
alt. Orokaiva [ork], 620

Ke-Woya-Yaka, *alt. dial.* Limba, East [lma], 129, 183

Keai, *alt. dial.* Folopa [ppo], 599

Keaka, *alt.* Ejagham [etu], 60

Keana, *dial.* Alago [ala], 153

Keapara [khz], 605
dial. Keapara [khz], 605

Keb-Kaye, *alt.* Kabalai [kvf], 81

Keba-Wopasali, *dial.* Folopa [ppo], 599

Kebadi, *alt.* Zaghawa [zag], 196, 87

Kebai, *dial.* Chuave [cjv], 596

Kebanagung, *dial.* Rejang [rej], 437

Kebar, *alt.* Mpur [akc], 420

Kebbawa, *dial.* Hausa [hau], 162

Kebeenton, *dial.* Toussian, Northern [tsp], 55

Kebeirka, *alt.* Uduk [udu], 119, 196

Kebena, *alt. dial.* Kambaata [ktb], 116

Ke'bu, *alt.* Ndo [ndp], 105

Kebu, *alt.* Akebu [keu], 206
alt. Ndo [ndp], 212
alt. dial. Ndo [ndp], 212

Kebu Fula, *dial.* Pular [fuf], 130, 184

Kebumtamp, *alt.* Bumthangkha [kjz], 323

Kebun Kopi, *dial.* Kabola [klz], 407

Kebutu, *alt.* Ndo [ndp], 105
alt. dial. Ndo [ndp], 212

Kechan, *alt.* Quechan [yum], 307

Kecherda, *dial.* Tedaga [tuq], 175

Kechi, *alt. dial.* Balochi, Southern [bcc], 483

Kechia, *alt.* Chinese, Hakka [hak], 329, 508

Kecwan, *alt. dial.* Bokyi [bky], 156

Kedah, *dial.* Kensiu [kns], 454
dial. Malay [mly], 455

Kedah Malay, *see* Malay, Kedah [meo], 455

Kedah Malay, *alt.* Malay, Satun [meo], 516

Kedamaian Dusun, *alt.* Dusun, Tempasuk [tdu], 456

Kedang [ksx], 407

Kédang, *alt.* Kedang [ksx], 407

Kedangese, *alt.* Kedang [ksx], 407

Kedayan, *alt.* Dusun, Central [dtp], 456
alt. dial. Brunei [kxd], 456
dial. Brunei [kxd], 324

Kedde, *alt. dial.* Hai‖om [hgm], 149

Keddi, *alt. dial.* Hai‖om [hgm], 149

Kede, *alt.* Aka-Kede [akx], 353

Keder [kdy], 417

Kedi, *alt.* Laba [lau], 400
dial. Hai‖om [hgm], 149

Kedien, *alt. dial.* Brunei [kxd], 456

Kedien. Kerayan, *alt. dial.* Brunei [kxd], 324

Kedjom, *alt.* Babanki [bbk], 56

Kedyan, *alt. dial.* Brunei [kxd], 324, 456

Keekonyokie, *dial.* Maasai [mas], 134

Keembo, *dial.* Mbole [mdq], 104

Keenge, *dial.* Beembe [beq], 88

Keenok, *alt.* Asmat, North [nks], 411

Keerak, *alt.* Kerak [hhr], 181

Keeraku, *alt.* Kerak [hhr], 181

Ke'erkez, *alt.* Kirghiz [kir], 337

Ke'erqin, *alt. dial.* Mongolian, Peripheral [mvf], 339

Keewatin, *alt. dial.* Inuktitut, Western Canadian [ikt], 238

Kefa, *alt.* Kafa [kbr], 116

Keffa, *alt.* Kafa [kbr], 116

Keffi, *alt.* Eloyi [afo], 159

Kegberike, *alt.* Akebu [keu], 206

Kegengele, *alt. dial.* Songoora [sod], 108

Keh-Deo, *alt. dial.* Hmong, Chonganjiang [hmj], 334

Keha, *dial.* Tukudede [tkd], 351

Kehelala, *dial.* Tawala [tbo], 627

Kehena, *dial.* Naga, Angami [njm], 377

Keherara, *alt. dial.* Tawala [tbo], 627

Kehia, *alt.* Chinese, Hakka [hak], 508

Kehja, *alt.* Kenyah, Kayan River [knh], 393
alt. Kenyah, Kelinyau [xkl], 394
alt. Kenyah, Mahakam [xkm], 394

Kehlao, *alt.* Gelao [gio], 333

Kehloori Pahari, *alt.* Bilaspuri [kfs], 356

Kehluri, *alt.* Bilaspuri [kfs], 356

Kehu [khh], 417

Kei [kei], 399

Kei Besar, *dial.* Kei [kei], 399

Kei Kecil, *dial.* Kei [kei], 399

Keia, *alt. dial.* Tukudede [tkd], 351

Keiagana, *alt.* Keyagana [kyg], 606

Keiga [kec], 192
dial. Keiga [kec], 192

Keiga Girru, *alt.* Tese [keg], 195

Keiga Jirru, *alt.* Tese [keg], 195

Keiga-Al-Kheil, *alt.* Keiga [kec], 192

Keiga-Timero, *alt.* Keiga [kec], 192

Keigana, *alt.* Keyagana [kyg], 606

Kein [bmh], 605

Keiyo, *dial.* Kalenjin [kln], 133

Kejaman, *alt.* Kajaman [kag], 459

Kejeng, *alt.* Babanki [bbk], 56

Kejia, *alt.* Chinese, Hakka [hak], 329

Kejom, *alt.* Babanki [bbk], 56

Kek, *alt.* Chinese, Hakka [hak], 508

Keka-Talae, *alt. dial.* Termanu [twu], 410

Kekamba, *alt.* Kamba [kam], 133

Kekar, *alt. dial.* Oroch [oac], 506

Kekaungdu, *alt.* Karen, Geko [ghk], 464

Kekchi', *alt.* Q'eqchi' [kek], 256

Kekchí [kek], 221, 252

Kekem, *dial.* Mbo [mbo], 66

Kekhong, *alt.* Karen, Geko [ghk], 464

Keku, *alt.* Karen, Geko [ghk], 464

Kela (Democratic Republic of Congo) [kel], 101
Kela (Papua New Guinea) [kcl], 605

Kelabit [kzi], 459, 393

Kelai, *dial.* Segai [sge], 395

Kelana, *alt.* Gitua [ggt], 600

alt. Kela [kcl], 605

Kelanchi, *alt. dial.* Kag-Fer-Jiir-Koor-Ror-Us-Zuksun [gel], 165

Kelang, *dial.* Luhu [lcq], 401

Kelantan, *dial.* Malay [mly], 455

Kelao, *alt.* Gelao [gio], 333

Kelderashícko, *alt. dial.* Romani, Vlax [rmy], 551

Kele (Democratic Republic of Congo) [khy], 101

Kele (Papua New Guinea) [sbc], 605

alt. dial. Lusengo [lse], 103

Kélé [keb], 120

Keleb, *dial.* Avar [ava], 553

Kelenga, *alt.* Bozo, Hainyaxo [bzx], 142

Kelentheyewelrere, *alt. dial.* Anmatyerre [amx], 568

Kelenthwelkere, *alt. dial.* Anmatyerre [amx], 568

Keleo, *alt.* Gelao [gio], 333

Keley-I, *alt.* Kallahan, Keley-I [ify], 497

Keley-I Kalanguya, *alt.* Kallahan, Keley-I [ify], 497

Keley-I Kallahan, *see* Kallahan, Keley-I [ify], 497

Keleyqiq Ifugao, *alt.* Kallahan, Keley-I [ify], 497

Keli, *dial.* Tulu-Bohuai [rak], 628

Keliko [kbo], 192

alt. Kaliko [kbo], 100

Kelimuri, *dial.* Geser-Gorom [ges], 398

Kelinci, *alt. dial.* Kag-Fer-Jiir-Koor-Ror-Us-Zuksun [gel], 165

Kélinga, *alt.* Bozo, Hainyaxo [bzx], 142

Kelingan, *dial.* Maba [mde], 83

dial. Modang [mxd], 394

Kelingi, *alt.* Sindang Kelingi [sdi], 437

Kelinjau, *alt.* Kenyah, Kelinyau [xkl], 394

Kelinyau, *alt.* Kenyah, Kelinyau [xkl], 394

Kelinyau Kenyah, *see* Kenyah, Kelinyau [xkl], 394

Kelli-Ni, *alt. dial.* Kag-Fer-Jiir-Koor-Ror-Us-Zuksun [gel], 165

Kéllingua, *alt.* Bozo, Hainyaxo [bzx], 142

Kelo [xel], 192

dial. Kelo [xel], 192

Kelo-Beni Sheko, *alt.* Kelo [xel], 192

Kelon [kyo], 407

Kelong, *alt.* Kelon [kyo], 407

Kem Degne, *dial.* Blang [blr], 327

Kem Mun, *alt.* Kim Mun [mji], 337

Kemai, *alt.* Goemai [ank], 161

Kemak [kem], 351, 407

dial. Kemak [kem], 351, 407

Kemanat, *alt. dial.* Qimant [ahg], 118

Kemanimowe, *dial.* Siane [snp], 624

Kemant, *alt. dial.* Qimant [ahg], 118

Kemata, *alt.* Kambaata [ktb], 116

Kembata, *alt.* Kambaata [ktb], 116

Kembayan [xem], 393

Kemberano [bzp], 412

dial. Arandai [jbj], 411

Kembra [xkw], 417

Kemelom, *alt.* Mombum [mso], 420

Kemelomsch, *alt.* Mombum [mso], 420

Kemena Penan, *dial.* Kenyah, Western [xky], 460

Kemezung [dmo], 63

Kemi Saami, *see* Saami, Kemi [sjk], 535

Kemiehua [kfj], 337

Kemmungam, *alt.* Naga, Khiamniungan [nky], 378

Kemtuik [kmt], 417

Kemtuk, *alt.* Kemtuik [kmt], 417

Kemu, *alt.* Khmu [kjg], 337

dial. Wan [wan], 95

Ken, *alt.* Khengkha [xkf], 323

Ken-Khana, *dial.* Khana [ogo], 166

Kenai Peninsula, *dial.* Tanaina [tfn], 308

Kenat, *alt.* Bagheli [bfy], 354, 468

Kenathi, *alt.* Kenati [gat], 606

Kenati [gat], 606

Kendal, *alt. dial.* Kadaru [kdu], 191

Kendari, *alt. dial.* Tolaki [lbw], 433

Kendayan [knx], 393

dial. Kendayan [knx], 393

Kendayan Dayak, *alt.* Kendayan [knx], 393

Kendayan-Ambawang, *alt.* Kendayan [knx], 393

Kendeje [klf], 82

Kendem [kvm], 63

Kenderong, *dial.* Temiar [tea], 455

Keñele, *alt.* Kyenele [kql], 609

Kenen Birang, *alt.* Kyenele [kql], 609

Keneng, *alt.* Phong-Kniang [pnx], 452

Kenering, *dial.* Temiar [tea], 455

Keng, *alt.* Khengkha [xkf], 323

Kenga [kyq], 82

alt. Kyenga [tye], 168

Kenge, *alt.* Kenga [kyq], 82

Keni, *dial.* Rombo [rof], 204

Kenieba Maninka, *dial.* Maninkakan, Western [mlq], 143

Kenieng, *alt.* Phong-Kniang [pnx], 452

Keningau Dusun, *alt.* Gana [gnq], 456

Keningau Murut [kxi], 457

Keninjal [knl], 393

Kenja, *alt.* Kenyah, Kayan River [knh], 393

alt. Kenyah, Kelinyau [xkl], 394

alt. Kenyah, Mahakam [xkm], 394

alt. Kenyah, Upper Baram [ubm], 460, 394

alt. Kenyah, Western [xky], 460

Kenkha, *alt.* Khengkha [xkf], 323

Kenkü, *alt. dial.* Irántxe [irn], 227

Kense, *alt.* Kensiu [kns], 515

Kensense, *alt.* Kenswei Nsei [ndb], 64

Kenseu, *alt.* Kensiu [kns], 454, 515

Kensieu, *alt.* Kensiu [kns], 454, 515

Kensiu [kns], 454, 515

Kensiu Batu, *dial.* Kensiu [kns], 454

Kensiu Siong, *dial.* Kensiu [kns], 454

Kensiw, *alt.* Kensiu [kns], 454, 515

Kenswei Nsei [ndb], 64

Kenta, *alt.* Kintaq [knq], 454, 515

Kentaq Nakil, *dial.* Kensiu [kns], 454

Kente, *dial.* Kpan [kpk], 167

Kentin, *dial.* Kutep [kub], 167, 64

Kentohe, *alt. dial.* Balanta-Kentohe [ble], 130

Kentu, *alt.* Etkywan [ich], 159

alt. dial. Kpan [kpk], 167

Kentung Wa, *dial.* Wa [wbm], 467

Kenume, *alt.* Kanum, Bädi [khd], 416

alt. Kanum, Ngkâlmpw [kcd], 416

alt. Kanum, Smärky [kxq], 416

alt. Kanum, Sota [krz], 416

Kenuz, *alt. dial.* Kenuzi-Dongola [kzh], 192, 110

Kenuzi, *alt. dial.* Kenuzi-Dongola [kzh], 192, 110

Kenuzi-Dongola [kzh], 192, 110

Kenya, *alt.* Kenyah, Kayan River [knh], 393

alt. Kenyah, Kelinyau [xkl], 394

alt. Kenyah, Mahakam [xkm], 394

Kenyah, *alt.* Kenyah, Kayan River [knh], 393

alt. Kenyah, Kelinyau [xkl], 394

alt. Kenyah, Mahakam [xkm], 394

alt. Kenyah, Upper Baram [ubm], 460, 394

Kenyah, Bahau River [bwv], 393

Kenyah, Bakung [boc], 393, 459

Kenyah, Kayan River [knh], 393

Kenyah, Kelinyau [xkl], 394

Kenyah, Mahakam [xkm], 394
Kenyah, Sebob [sib], 459
Kenyah, Tutoh [ttw], 460
Kenyah, Upper Baram
   [ubm], 460, 394
Kenyah, Wahau [whk], 394
Kenyah, Western [xky], 460
Kenyan Sign Language [xki], 134
Kenyang [ken], 64
Kenyen, *dial.* Dwang [nnu], 120
Kenyi [lke], 211
   alt. Zhire [zhi], 178
   dial. Kgalagadi [xkv], 47
Kenying Bulang, *alt.* Kyenele
   [kql], 609
Kenzi, *alt. dial.* Kenuzi-Dongola
   [kzh], 110
Ke'o [xxk], 407
Keo, *alt.* Tho [tou], 527
Keopara, *alt.* Keapara [khz], 605
   alt. dial. Keapara [khz], 605
Kepere, *alt. dial.* Mbum [mdd], 66
Kepkiriwát [kpn], 229
Kepo' [kuk], 407
Kepoq, *alt.* Kepo' [kuk], 407
Ker, *alt.* Karaboro, Eastern [xrb], 51
Kera [ker], 82, 64
   dial. Mundari [muw], 476
Kera', *alt. dial.* Mundari [muw], 376
   dial. Mundari [muw], 321
Kerabit, *alt.* Kelabit [kzi], 459, 393
Kerak [hhr], 181
Keramai, *alt. dial.* Dyirbal
   [dbl], 570
Kerang, *alt.* Ngas [anc], 171
Kerayan, *alt. dial.* Brunei [kxd], 456
Kerdau, *dial.* Jah Hut [jah], 454
Kere, *alt.* Karo [kxh], 116
   alt. dial. Kag-Fer-Jiir-Koor-Ror-Us-
   Zuksun [gel], 165
   dial. Bambassi [myf], 113
   dial. Ngambay [sba], 85
Kereaka, *alt.* Ramopa [kjx], 622
Kerebe, *alt.* Kerewe [ked], 199
Kereho-Uheng [xke], 394
Kerei, *alt.* Karey [kyd], 399
Kerek [krk], 505
Kerekere, *alt.* Karekare [kai], 166
Kerema, *alt.* Nisa [njs], 421
Keremi, *alt.* Nyaturu [rim], 203
Keren, *dial.* Aghul [agx], 552
Kerend, *dial.* Hulaulá [huy], 445
Kerepunu, *alt.* Keapara [khz], 605
Keres, Eastern [kee], 303
Keres, Western [kjq], 303
Kerewa, *alt.* Kerewo [kxz], 606
Kerewa-Goari, *alt.* Kerewo
   [kxz], 606
Kerewe [ked], 199
Kerewo [kxz], 606

Kereyu, *dial.* Oromo, Borana-Arsi-
   Guji [gax], 117
Keri, *dial.* Golin [gvf], 600
Keri-Ni, *alt. dial.* Kag-Fer-Jiir-Koor-
   Ror-Us-Zuksun [gel], 165
Keriaka, *alt.* Ramopa [kjx], 622
Keriau Punan, *alt.* Kereho-Uheng
   [xke], 394
Kerifa, *alt.* Duhwa [kbz], 158
Kerinchi, *alt.* Kerinci [kvr], 436
Kerinci [kvr], 436
Kerinci-Minangkabau, *dial.*
   Minangkabau [min], 436
Keringani, *alt.* Karingani [kgn], 439
Kerintji, *alt.* Kerinci [kvr], 436
Kerkuki, *dial.* Kurdish, Central
   [ckb], 443
Kermancî, *alt.* Kurdish, Northern
   [kmr], 519
Kermani, *dial.* Farsi, Western
   [pes], 439
Kermanshahi, *dial.* Kurdish,
   Southern [sdh], 440, 443
Kermanshani, *alt. dial.* Kurdish,
   Southern [sdh], 440, 443
Kernewek, *alt.* Cornish [cor], 565
Kernowek, *alt.* Cornish [cor], 565
Keroi, *dial.* Kowiai [kwh], 418
Kerorogea, *dial.* Bunama [bdd], 595
Kerounja, *dial.* Tamang, Eastern
   Gorkha [tge], 479
Kerre, *alt.* Karo [kxh], 116
Kerrikerri, *alt.* Karekare [kai], 166
Kerta Mulya, *alt. dial.* Malayic
   Dayak [xdy], 394
Kesari, *dial.* Baan [bvj], 154
Kesawai [xes], 606
Kesengele, *alt.* Sengele [szg], 107
Keshikten, *alt. dial.* Mongolian,
   Peripheral [mvf], 339
Keshur, *alt.* Kashmiri [kas], 367
Keshuri, *alt.* Kashmiri [kas], 486
Kesongola, *alt.* Songoora [sod], 108
Kessi, *alt. dial.* Bugis [bug], 428
Kestane, *alt. dial.* Kistane [gru], 116
Kesu', *alt. dial.* Toraja-Sa'dan [sda],
   434
Kesui, *alt.* Watubela [wah], 405
Ket [ket], 505
Ketabi, *dial.* Farsi, Western
   [pes], 439
Ketagalan, *alt.* Ketangalan [kae], 511
Ketangalan [kae], 511
Ketchi', *alt.* Q'eqchi' [kek], 256
Ketchí, *alt.* Kekchí [kek], 221
Kete [kcv], 101
Ketebo, *alt. dial.* Teso [teo], 213
Keteghe, *dial.* Teke-Tege [teg], 90
Ketego, *alt.* Teke, Northern
   [teg], 121

Keteneneyu, *dial.* Naga, Southern
   Rengma [nre], 379
Ketengban [xte], 417
Ketiar Krau, *dial.* Jah Hut [jah], 454
Ketin, *dial.* Attié [ati], 91
Keto, *dial.* Siane [snp], 624
Ketuen, *alt.* Mbe [mfo], 169
Ketum [ktt], 417
Ketungau, *alt. dial.* Iban [iba], 393
Kety, *alt. dial.* Selkup [sel], 506
Keuro, *alt.* Keuru [xeu], 606
Keuru [xeu], 606
Kevat Boli, *alt.* Bagheli [bfy], 354,
   468
Kevati, *alt.* Bagheli [bfy], 354, 468
Kewa South, *alt.* Erave [kjy], 598
Kewa, East [kjs], 606
Kewa, West [kew], 606
Kewah, *dial.* Folopa [ppo], 599
Kewani, *alt.* Bagheli [bfy], 354, 468
Kewat, *alt.* Bagheli [bfy], 354, 468
Kewati, *alt.* Bagheli [bfy], 354, 468
Kewe, *dial.* Kabiyé [kbp], 208
Kewieng, *dial.* Yopno [yut], 634
Kewot, *alt.* Bagheli [bfy], 354, 468
Ke'yagana, *alt.* Keyagana [kyg], 606
Keyagana [kyg], 606
Keydnjmarda, *alt.* Adynyamathanha
   [adt], 567
Keyele, *alt.* Kyenele [kql], 609
Keylong Boli, *alt.* Gahri [bfu], 361
Keyo, *alt. dial.* Kalenjin [kln], 133
Kezami, *alt.* Naga, Khezha
   [nkh], 378
Kezands, *dial.* Zeeuws [zea], 549
Kfarze, *dial.* Turoyo [tru], 520
Kgaga, *dial.* Sotho, Northern
   [nso], 186
Kgalagadi [xkv], 47
   dial. Kgalagadi [xkv], 47
Kgatla, *dial.* Tswana [tsn], 48, 186
Kha Cau, *alt.* Khmu [kjg], 524
Kha Khmu, *alt.* Khmu [kjg], 515
Kha Ko, *alt.* Akha [ahk], 462, 326,
   513, 521
Kha Lamet, *alt.* Lamet [lbn], 451,
   515
Kha Mu Gia, *alt. dial.* Chut
   [scb], 522
Kha Nam Om, *alt. dial.* Maleng
   [pkt], 524
Kha Niang, *alt.* Puoc [puo], 452
Kha Pakatan, *alt. dial.* Maleng
   [pkt], 451
Kha Phay, *alt.* Phai [prt], 516
Kha Phong, *dial.* Maleng [pkt], 524
Kha Pray, *alt.* Phai [prt], 452
Kha Puhoc, *alt.* Puoc [puo], 525,
   452
Kha So, *alt.* Sô [sss], 517

Kha Tampuon, *alt.* Tampuan [tpu], 326

Kha Tong Luang, *alt.* Aheu [thm], 449

Khaang, *alt.* Kháng [kjm], 524

Khabenapo, *alt.* Pomo, Central [poo], 307

Khabit, *alt.* Bit [bgk], 450, 327

Khadar, *dial.* Haryanvi [bgc], 364

Khadi Boli, *alt.* Hindi [hin], 364

Khadia, *alt.* Kharia [khr], 367

Khae, *alt.* Lisu [lis], 339

Khael Baat, *alt.* Khaling [klr], 473, 367

Khael Bra, *alt.* Khaling [klr], 473, 367

Khaga, *alt. dial.* Sotho, Northern [nso], 186

Khahta, *alt.* Karen, Lahta [kvt], 464

Khaidak, *dial.* Kumyk [kum], 519

Khaikent, *dial.* Kumyk [kum], 555

Khairagarhi, *dial.* Chhattisgarhi [hne], 358

Khairari, *dial.* Mewari [mtr], 375

Khajuna, *alt.* Burushaski [bsk], 484

Khakas [kjh], 505, 337

Khakhae, *dial.* Kgalagadi [xkv], 47

Khakhas, *alt.* Khakas [kjh], 505, 337

Khakhass, *alt.* Khakas [kjh], 505, 337

Khako, *alt.* Akha [ahk], 462, 326, 449, 513, 521

Khal:mag, *alt.* Kalmyk-Oirat [xal], 554

Khalagari, *alt.* Kgalagadi [xkv], 47

Khalaj [kjf], 439, 319
alt. Khalaj, Turkic [klj], 439

Khalaj, Turkic [klj], 439

Khalakadi, *alt.* Kgalagadi [xkv], 47

Khalari, *dial.* Powari [pwr], 384

Khaliji, *alt.* Arabic, Gulf Spoken [afb], 442, 320, 437, 449, 482, 503, 520

Khaling [klr], 473, 367
dial. Bahing [bhj], 468

Khalinge Rai, *alt.* Khaling [klr], 473, 367

Khalkha, *alt. dial.* Mongolian, Halh [khk], 461
dial. Mongolian, Halh [khk], 505

Khalkha Mongolian, *alt.* Mongolian, Halh [khk], 461, 505

Khalkhal, *dial.* Takestani [tks], 441

Khaltahi, *alt.* Chhattisgarhi [hne], 358

Kham, Gamale [kgj], 473

Kham, Sheshi [kip], 473

|Kham-Ka-!k'e, *alt.* |Xam [xam], 187

Kham-Magar, *alt.* Parbate, Western [kjl], 477

Kham-Tai, *alt.* Khamti [kht], 367

Khamba [kbg], 367
alt. Tibetan, Khams [khg], 345

Khamba Khaadi, *alt.* Khamba [kbg], 367

Khambana-Makwakwe, *alt. dial.* Tswa [tsc], 149

Khambani, *alt. dial.* Tswa [tsc], 149
dial. Chopi [cce], 147

Khambu, *dial.* Kulung [kle], 473

Khamchi, *alt.* Raute [rau], 478

Khamed, *alt.* Lamet [lbn], 451

Khamen-Boran, *alt.* Kuy [kdt], 515, 451

Khamet, *alt.* Lamet [lbn], 451, 515

Khami, *alt.* Chin, Khumi [cnk], 463, 321, 359
dial. Chin, Khumi [cnk], 463, 321, 359

Khamiyang, *alt.* Khamyang [ksu], 367

Khamjang, *alt.* Khamyang [ksu], 367

Khamla, *dial.* Gowli [gok], 363

Khammouan, *dial.* Saek [skb], 452

Khamnigan, *alt.* Evenki [evn], 332, 461, 504

Khampa, *alt.* Tibetan, Khams [khg], 345

Khampti, *alt.* Khamti [kht], 465, 367

Khampti Shan, *alt.* Khamti [kht], 465

Khams, *alt.* Tibetan, Khams [khg], 345

Khams Bhotia, *alt.* Tibetan, Khams [khg], 345

Khams Tibetan, *see* Tibetan, Khams [khg], 345

Khams-Yal, *alt.* Tibetan, Khams [khg], 345

Khamseh, *dial.* Arabic, Gulf Spoken [afb], 437

Khamtanga, *alt.* Xamtanga [xan], 119

Khamti [kht], 465, 367

Khamti Shan, *alt.* Khamti [kht], 465, 367

Khamu, *alt.* Khmu [kjg], 451, 337, 515, 524

Khamuk, *alt.* Khmu [kjg], 451, 337, 465, 515

Khamyang [ksu], 367

Khana [ogo], 166
alt. Pomo, Central [poo], 307

Khanag, *alt. dial.* Tabassaran [tab], 555

Khandeshi, *alt.* Khandesi [khn], 367

Khandesi [khn], 367

dial. Khandesi [khn], 367

Khandi Shan, *alt.* Khamti [kht], 465

Khandish, *alt.* Khandesi [khn], 367

Kháng [kjm], 524

Kháng Ai, *alt. dial.* Kháng [kjm], 524

Kháng Clau, *dial.* Kháng [kjm], 524

Khangoi, *dial.* Naga, Tangkhul [nmf], 380

Khaniang, *alt.* Phong-Kniang [pnx], 452

Khanti, *alt.* Khanty [kca], 505

Khantis, *alt.* Khamti [kht], 367

Khanty [kca], 505

Khanung, *alt.* Nung [nun], 466, 341

Khao [xao], 524

Khao Ikor, *alt.* Akha [ahk], 521

Khao Kha Ko, *alt.* Akha [ahk], 462, 326, 449, 513

Khapa, *dial.* Naga, Nocte [njb], 379

Khaput, *alt. dial.* Kryts [kry], 319

Kharachin, *alt. dial.* Mongolian, Peripheral [mvf], 339, 462

Kharam Naga, *see* Naga, Kharam [kfw], 378

Kharaqan, *alt. dial.* Takestani [tks], 441

Kharbari, *dial.* Dumi [dus], 471

Kharberd, *dial.* Armenian [hye], 318

Kharchin, *alt. dial.* Mongolian, Peripheral [mvf], 339, 462

Kharchin-Tumut, *alt. dial.* Mongolian, Peripheral [mvf], 339

Khari Boli, *alt.* Hindi [hin], 364

Kharia [khr], 367

Kharia Thar [ksy], 367

Khariya, *alt.* Kharia [khr], 367

Kharlali, *dial.* Nachering [ncd], 476

Kharmangi, *alt. dial.* Shina [scl], 488

Khartamche, *dial.* Sampang [rav], 478

Khartoum, *dial.* Arabic, Sudanese Spoken [apd], 188

Khartoum Arabic, *alt.* Arabic, Sudanese Spoken [apd], 188

Kharvi, *alt.* Kharia [khr], 367

Kharwa, *dial.* Gujarati [guj], 363

Kharwari, *alt. dial.* Bhojpuri [bho], 356

Kharyuz, *dial.* Itelmen [itl], 505

Khas Nepali, *alt.* Jumli [jml], 472

Khasa, *alt.* Khasi [kha], 367
alt. Tigré [tig], 112, 195

Khasarli, *dial.* Turkmen [tuk], 520, 442

Khasav-Yurt, *dial.* Kumyk [kum], 519

Khasavyurt, *dial.* Kumyk [kum], 555

Khashi, *alt.* Khasi [kha], 367

Khasi [kha], 367, 321
  dial. Khasi [kha], 367, 321
Khasie, *alt.* Khasi [kha], 321
Khasiyas, *alt.* Khasi [kha], 367, 321
Khaskhong, *dial.* Phunoi [pho], 452, 517
Khaskura, *alt.* Nepali [nep], 476, 323, 381
Khasonke, *alt.* Xaasongaxango [kao], 145
  alt. Xasonga [kao], 182
Khassee, *alt.* Khasi [kha], 321
Khassonka, *alt.* Xaasongaxango [kao], 145
Khassonké, *alt.* Xaasongaxango [kao], 145
Khatalia, *dial.* Vasavi [vas], 390
Khatang, *dial.* Nganasan [nio], 506
Khatia, *alt. dial.* !Xóõ [nmn], 48, 151
Khatin, *alt.* Mal [mlf], 451, 516
Khatki, *alt. dial.* Seraiki [skr], 488
Khatola, *dial.* Bundeli [bns], 357
Khatria, *alt.* Kharia [khr], 367
Khatyrka, *dial.* Kerek [krk], 505
Khaungtou, *alt.* Karen, Zayein [kxk], 465
Khava, *alt. dial.* Ingrian [izh], 554
Khawar, *alt.* Khowar [khw], 486
Khayo, *dial.* Luyia [luy], 134
Khbit, *alt.* Bit [bgk], 450
Khe [kqg], 52
Khehek [tlx], 606
  alt. dial. Khehek [tlx], 606
Khek, *alt.* Chinese, Hakka [hak], 508
Khelma, *dial.* Sakechep [sch], 385
Khelobedu, *alt. dial.* Sotho, Northern [nso], 186
Khemsing, *alt. dial.* Naga, Tase [nst], 380
Khemungan, *alt.* Naga, Khiamniungan [nky], 378
Khen, *alt.* Khengkha [xkf], 323
Khen Lài, *dial.* Nung [nut], 525
Khengkha [xkf], 323
Khenkha, *alt.* Khengkha [xkf], 323
Kheria, *alt.* Kharia [khr], 367
Kherwara, *dial.* Wagdi [wbr], 390
Kherwari, *alt.* Khirwar [kwx], 368
Khesang, *dial.* Dungmali [raa], 471
Khesange, *alt. dial.* Dungmali [raa], 471
Kheso, *alt.* Khe [kqg], 52
|**Khessákhoe**, *dial.* ‖Gana [gnk], 46
Khetrani [xhe], 486
Kheysur, *alt. dial.* Georgian [kat], 352
Khezha, *alt.* Naga, Khezha [nkh], 378
Khezha Naga, *see* Naga, Khezha [nkh], 378

Khezhama, *alt.* Naga, Khezha [nkh], 378
Khi, *alt.* Gelao [gio], 333
  alt. Khisa [kqm], 52
Khi Khipa, *alt.* Khisa [kqm], 93, 52
Khiamngan, *alt.* Naga, Khiamniungan [nky], 378, 466
Khiamniungan, *alt.* Naga, Khiamniungan [nky], 378, 466
Khiamniungan Naga, *see* Naga, Khiamniungan [nky], 378, 466
Khieng, *alt.* Shendu [shl], 322, 383
Khienmungan, *alt.* Naga, Khiamniungan [nky], 378
Khik, *alt.* Wakhi [wbl], 489, 318, 346, 513
Khili, *alt.* Kohistani, Indus [mvy], 486
  alt. dial. Kohistani, Indus [mvy], 486
Khimi, *alt.* Chin, Khumi [cnk], 463
  dial. Chin, Khumi [cnk], 463, 321, 359
Khinalug, *alt.* Khinalugh [kjj], 319
Khinalugh [kjj], 319
Khinalugi, *alt.* Khinalugh [kjj], 319
Khiri, *alt.* Xiri [xii], 187
Khirwar [kwx], 368
Khirwara, *alt.* Khirwar [kwx], 368
Khisa [kqm], 93, 52
Khithaulhu, *dial.* Nambikuára, Southern [nab], 230
Khiurkilinskii, *alt.* Dargwa [dar], 553
Khlá Don, *alt.* Laha [lha], 524
Khlá Dung, *alt.* Laha [lha], 524
Khlá Liik, *alt.* Laha [lha], 524
Khlá Phlao, *alt.* Laha [lha], 524
Khlor [llo], 450
Khmer, *alt.* Khmer, Central [khm], 325
Khmer Lue, *alt.* Khmer, Northern [kxm], 515
Khmer, Central [khm], 325, 524
Khmer, Northern [kxm], 515
Khmu [kjg], 451, 337, 465, 515, 524
Khmu', *alt.* Khmu [kjg], 451, 337, 465, 515
Kho, *alt.* Bugun [bgg], 357
Kho Me, *alt.* Khmer, Central [khm], 524
Khoa, *alt.* Bugun [bgg], 357
Khoamak, *dial.* Kuni-Boazi [kvg], 608
Khocharkhotin, *dial.* Bezhta [kap], 553
Khoe, *alt.* Khwe [xuu], 47
  alt. Kxoe [xuu], 150, 186
Khoekhoe, *alt.* Nama [naq], 186
Khoekhoegowab, *pej. alt.* Nama [naq], 150

Khoekhoegowap, *pej. alt.* Nama [naq], 150
Khoeknoegowap, *alt.* Nama [naq], 186
Khoi, *alt.* Nama [naq], 186
Khoi-Salmst, *dial.* Armenian [hye], 437
Khoibu, *alt.* Naga, Khoibu [nkb], 378
Khoibu Maring, *alt.* Naga, Khoibu [nkb], 378
Khoibu Maring Naga, *alt.* Naga, Khoibu [nkb], 378
Khoibu Naga, *see* Naga, Khoibu [nkb], 378
Kho'ini [xkc], 439
Khoirao, *alt.* Naga, Thangal [nki], 380
Khoirao Naga, *alt.* Naga, Thangal [nki], 380
Khoke, *alt.* Koke [kou], 82
Khoksar, *dial.* Stod Bhoti [sbu], 387
Khoksar Bhoti, *alt. dial.* Stod Bhoti [sbu], 387
Khole, *alt. dial.* Santali [sat], 386, 322
Kholifa, *dial.* Themne [tem], 184
Kholok [ktc], 166
Kholung, *alt.* Kulung [kle], 473, 370
Khomakha, *dial.* Dzalakha [dzl], 323
‡**Khomani**, *alt.* N|u [ngh], 186
Khome, *alt.* Khmer, Central [khm], 524
Khomu, *alt.* Khmu [kjg], 451, 337, 465, 524
Khon Doi, *alt.* Blang [blr], 514
Khon Mung, *alt.* Thai, Northern [nod], 517
Khon Myang, *alt.* Thai, Northern [nod], 517
Khond, *alt.* Kui [kxu], 370
Khondh, *alt.* Kuvi [kxv], 371
Khondi, *alt.* Kui [kxu], 370
  alt. Kuvi [kxv], 371
  dial. Kui [kxu], 370
Khondo, *alt.* Kui [kxu], 370
Khong Kheng, *alt. dial.* Hung [hnu], 523
Khongzai, *alt. dial.* Chin, Thado [tcz], 359
  dial. Chin, Thado [tcz], 463
Khonoma, *dial.* Naga, Angami [njm], 377
Khoong, *alt.* Côông [cnc], 522
Khor, *dial.* Udihe [ude], 507
Khorasani, *alt.* Kurmanji [kmr], 520
  alt. dial. Farsi, Eastern [prs], 315
Khorasani Kurmanji, *alt.* Kurmanji [kmr], 520
  dial. Kurdish, Northern [kmr], 440
Khorasani Turkish [kmz], 439
Khorat Thai, *dial.* Thai [tha], 517

Kidal Tamasheq, *alt.* Tamasheq [taq], 144
Kidapawan Manobo, *alt.* Manobo, Obo [obo], 499
dial. Manobo, Obo [obo], 499
Kiddu, *alt. dial.* Katla [kcr], 192
Kidhaiso, *alt.* Dhaiso [dhs], 198
Kidigo, *alt.* Digo [dig], 132, 198
Kidja, *alt.* Kitja [gia], 572
Kidjia, *alt. dial.* Sakata [skt], 104
Kidoe, *alt.* Doe [doe], 198
Kidoondo, *alt.* Doondo [dde], 88
Kidzem, *alt.* Babanki [bbk], 56
Kidzom, *alt.* Babanki [bbk], 56
Kiefo, *alt.* Tiéfo [tiq], 55
Kiemba, *alt.* Hemba [hem], 100
Kiembara, *dial.* Samo, Maya [sym], 53
Kiembu, *alt.* Embu [ebu], 132
Kieta, *alt.* Naasioi [nas], 616
Kieta Talk, *alt.* Naasioi [nas], 616
Kifipa, *alt.* Fipa [fip], 198
Kifulero, *alt.* Fuliiru [flr], 99
Kifuliiru, *alt.* Fuliiru [flr], 99
Kiga, *alt.* Chiga [cgg], 210
alt. dial. Rwanda [kin], 178
Kigaguru, *alt.* Kagulu [kki], 199
Kigala, *dial.* Lega-Shabunda [lea], 102
Kigalulu, *alt.* Kagulu [kki], 199
Kighaangala, *alt. dial.* Laari [ldi], 88
Kigiriama, *alt.* Giryama [nyf], 133
Kigogo, *alt.* Gogo [gog], 198
Kigumu, *dial.* Amba [rwm], 96
Kigwe, *alt. dial.* Sukuma [suk], 205
Kigweno, *alt.* Gweno [gwe], 198
Kigyoma, *alt. dial.* Lega-Shabunda [lea], 102
Kiha, *alt.* Ha [haq], 199
Kihai, *dial.* Rwa [rwk], 204
Kihangaza, *alt.* Hangaza [han], 199
Kihavu, *alt.* Havu [hav], 100
Kihaya, *alt.* Haya [hay], 199
Ki|hazi, *dial.* !Xóõ [nmn], 48, 151
Kihehe, *alt.* Hehe [heh], 199
Kihema, *alt.* Hema [nix], 100
Kihema-Nord, *alt.* Lendu [led], 102
Kihemba, *alt.* Hemba [hem], 100
Kiholo, *alt.* Holu [hol], 40, 100
Kiholoholo, *alt.* Holoholo [hoo], 100
Kiholu, *alt.* Holu [hol], 40, 100
Kihumu, *alt.* Amba [rwm], 210
Kihunde, *alt.* Hunde [hke], 100
Kihungana, *alt.* Hungana [hum], 100
Kihyanzi, *alt. dial.* Amba [rwm], 210
dial. Amba [rwm], 96
Kiiraqw, *alt.* Iraqw [irk], 199
Kija, *alt.* Kitja [gia], 572
Kijang, *dial.* Kabiyé [kbp], 208

Kijani, *alt.* Guyani [gvy], 571
Kijau, *alt.* Kuijau [dkr], 457
Kijoba, *alt.* Joba [job], 100
Kikaamba, *alt.* Kaamba [xku], 88
Kikabeeux, *alt.* Kickapoo [kic], 263
Kikai [kzg], 446
Kikalanga, *alt.* Holoholo [hoo], 100
Kikamba, *alt.* Kamba [kam], 133
Kikami, *alt.* Kami [kcu], 199
Kikango, *alt.* Kango [kzy], 100
Kikapaux, *alt.* Kickapoo [kic], 263
Kikapoo, *alt.* Kickapoo [kic], 303
Kikapú, *alt.* Kickapoo [kic], 303, 263
Kikeenge, *alt. dial.* Beembe [beq], 88
Kikete, *alt.* Kete [kcv], 101
Kikima, *alt.* Cocopa [coc], 300
Kikimá, *alt.* Cocopa [coc], 262
Kikimbu, *alt.* Kimbu [kiv], 200
Kikinga, *alt.* Kinga [zga], 200
Kikisanga, *alt. dial.* Mwani [wmw], 148
Kikisi, *alt.* Kisi [kiz], 200
Kikomo, *alt.* Komo [kmw], 101
Kikongo, *alt.* Kongo, San Salvador [kwy], 101, 40
alt. Koongo [kng], 101, 40, 88
Kikongo Commercial, *alt.* Kituba [ktu], 101
Kikongo Simplifié, *alt.* Kituba [ktu], 101
Kikongo Ya Leta, *alt.* Kituba [ktu], 101
Kikongo-Kutuba, *alt.* Kituba [ktu], 101
Kikonjunkulu, *alt.* Dyaabugay [dyy], 570
Kikonongo, *alt.* Kononongo [kcz], 200
Kikoongo, *alt.* Kituba [mkw], 88
alt. Kongo, San Salvador [kwy], 101, 40
alt. Koongo [kng], 101, 40, 88
Kiksht, *dial.* Chinook [chh], 299
Kikuk, *alt.* Cibak [ckl], 157
Kikumo, *alt.* Komo [kmw], 101
Kikumu, *alt.* Komo [kmw], 101
Kikunyi, *alt.* Kunyi [njx], 88
Kikuria, *alt.* Kuria [kuj], 134
Kikusu, *alt.* Kusu [ksv], 101
Kikutu, *alt.* Kutu [kdc], 200
Kikuumu, *alt.* Komo [kmw], 101
Kikuwa, *alt.* Teke-Kukuya [kkw], 90
Kikuyu, *alt.* Gikuyu [kik], 133
Kikwame, *alt.* Kwami [ktf], 101
Kikwami, *alt.* Kwami [ktf], 101
Kikwere, *alt.* Kwere [cwe], 200
Kikwese, *alt.* Kwese [kws], 102
Ki‖kxigwi, *alt.* ‖Xegwi [xeg], 187
Kil, *alt. dial.* Koho [kpm], 524
Kila, *alt.* Somyev [kgt], 175

dial. Nanai [gld], 506
Kilakilana, *alt.* Wagawaga [wgw], 630
Kilangi, *alt.* Langi [lag], 200
Kilari, *alt.* Laadi [ldi], 41
alt. Laari [ldi], 88
Kilba, *alt.* Huba [hbb], 162
Kildani, *alt.* Chaldean Neo-Aramaic [cld], 443
Kildin Lappish, *pej. alt.* Saami, Kildin [sjd], 556
Kildin Saami, *see* Saami, Kildin [sjd], 556
Kilega, *alt.* Lega-Mwenga [lgm], 102
alt. Lega-Shabunda [lea], 102
Kilema, *alt. dial.* Vunjo [vun], 205
Kilen, *alt. dial.* Nanai [gld], 341
Kilendu, *alt.* Lendu [led], 102
Kilenge, *alt. dial.* Chopi [cce], 147
alt. dial. Maleu-Kilenge [mgl], 611
Kilengola, *alt.* Lengola [lej], 102
Kileta, *alt.* Kituba [ktu], 101
Kili, *alt.* Kele [khy], 101
alt. dial. Nanai [gld], 341
Kilia, *dial.* Bwaidoka [bwd], 596
Kilika, *alt.* Lika [lik], 102
alt. dial. Yale, Kosarek [kkl], 426
Kilikien, *dial.* Armenian [hye], 318
Kiliva, *dial.* Bwaidoka [bwd], 596
Kilivila [kij], 606
Kiliwa [klb], 263
Kiliwi, *alt.* Kiliwa [klb], 263
Killi, *alt.* Mundari [muw], 376
Kilmera, *alt.* Kilmeri [kih], 606
Kilmeri [kih], 606
Kilokaka, *alt.* Zazao [jaj], 639
Kilombeno Kibya, *alt. dial.* Songe [sop], 108
Kilop, *alt. dial.* Kim [kia], 82
Kiluba, *alt.* Luba-Katanga [lub], 103
Kiluguru, *alt.* Luguru [ruf], 200
Kilungu, *alt. dial.* Mambwe-Lungu [mgr], 201
Kim [kia], 82
alt. Krim [krm], 183
alt. dial. Kim [kia], 82
Kim Mien, *alt.* Iu Mien [ium], 523
Kim Mun [mji], 337, 451, 524
Kim-Ruwa, *alt. dial.* Kimré [kqp], 82
Kimaam, *alt.* Riantana [ran], 422
Kimaama [kig], 417
Kimaasai, *alt.* Maasai [mas], 201
Kimaghama, *alt.* Kimaama [kig], 417
Kimagoma, *alt.* Magoma [gmx], 201
Kimakua, *alt.* Makhuwa-Meetto [mgh], 201
Kimakwe, *alt.* Makwe [ymk], 148
alt. Maraba [ymk], 201

Kinyanga, *alt.* Nyanga [nyj], 106
Kinyarwanda, *alt.* Rwanda
  [kin], 178, 107
Kinyasa, *alt.* Manda [mgs], 201
  alt. Mpoto [mpa], 202
  alt. Mwera [mjh], 202
Kinyaturu, *alt.* Nyaturu [rim], 203
Kinyiha, *alt.* Nyiha [nih], 203
Kinyihanzu, *alt.* Isanzu [isn], 199
Kinyika, *alt.* Giryama [nyf], 133
Kinyisanzu, *alt.* Isanzu [isn], 199
Kinzimba, *alt.* Como Karim
  [cfg], 157
Kioki, *alt. dial.* Tolaki [lbw], 433
Kioko [ues], 429
  alt. Chokwe [cjk], 40
  dial. Kioko [ues], 429
Kiombi, *alt.* Yombe [yom], 109, 42,
  90
Kiong [kkm], 166
Kiong Nai, *alt.* Bunu, Jiongnai
  [pnu], 328
Kiorr [xko], 451, 465
Kiowa [kio], 300
Kiowa Apache, *see* Apache, Kiowa
  [apk], 298
Kipangwa, *alt.* Pangwa [pbr], 203
Kipchak, *dial.* Uzbek, Northern
  [uzn], 512
Kipeá, *alt.* Karirí-Xocó [kzw], 228
  dial. Karirí-Xocó [kzw], 228
Kipende, *alt.* Phende [pem], 107
Kipere, *alt.* Bhele [bhy], 98
Kipgen, *alt. dial.* Chin, Thado
  [tcz], 359
  dial. Chin, Thado [tcz], 463
Kipili, *alt.* Bhele [bhy], 98
Kipimbwe, *alt.* Pimbwe [piw], 204
Kipokomo, *alt.* Pokomo, Lower
  [poj], 135
Kipsigis, *dial.* Kalenjin [kln], 133
Kipsiikis, *alt. dial.* Kalenjin
  [kln], 133
Kipsikiis, *alt. dial.* Kalenjin
  [kln], 133
Kipsikis, *alt. dial.* Kalenjin
  [kln], 133
Kiput [kyi], 460
Kir, *alt.* Jiru [jrr], 165
  alt. Kir-Balar [kkr], 166
  alt. Mandari [mqu], 193
  dial. Kir-Balar [kkr], 166
Kir-Balar [kkr], 166
Kira, *alt.* Vagla [vag], 128
Kiramang, *dial.* Kui [kvd], 408
Kirangi, *alt.* Langi [lag], 200
Kiranti, *alt.* Bantawa [bap], 468
Kirari, *dial.* Bundeli [bns], 357
Kirawa, *dial.* Wandala [mfi], 177
Kirdi, *alt.* Karata [kpt], 555

Kirdi-Mora, *alt. dial.* Wandala
  [mfi], 73
Kire [geb], 606
Kire-Puire, *alt.* Kire [geb], 606
Kirega, *alt.* Lega-Mwenga [lgm], 102
  alt. Lega-Shabunda [lea], 102
Kiremi, *alt.* Nyaturu [rim], 203
Kirfi, *alt.* Giiwo [kks], 161
Kirghiz [kir], 449, 316, 337, 518
Kirghizi, *alt.* Kirghiz [kir], 316
Kirgiz, *alt.* Kirghiz [kir], 449, 316,
  337
Kiribati [gil], 582, 580, 636, 640
Kirifawa, *alt.* Giiwo [kks], 161
Kirifi, *alt.* Giiwo [kks], 161
Kirike [okr], 166
Kirikiri [kiy], 417
  dial. Kirikiri [kiy], 417
Kirikjir, *alt.* Lopa [lop], 169
Kirim, *alt.* Como Karim [cfg], 157
  alt. Krim [krm], 183
Kirimi, *alt.* Nyaturu [rim], 203
Kirin, *alt. dial.* Nanai [gld], 341
Kirinit, *alt.* Kapingamarangi
  [kpg], 582
Kirira, *alt.* Kirikiri [kiy], 417
Kiriri, *alt.* Xukurú [xoo], 234
Kiriri-Xokó, *alt.* Xukurú [xoo], 234
Kiristav, *dial.* Konkani [knn], 369
Kiriwina, *alt.* Kilivila [kij], 606
Kiriyenteken, *dial.* Manobo,
  Western Bukidnon [mbb], 499
Kirkpong, *alt. dial.* Katla [kcr], 192
Kirkuk, *dial.* Azerbaijani, South [azb],
  443
Kirma, *alt.* Cerma [cme], 50, 92
Kirmancî, *alt.* Kurdish, Northern
  [kmr], 519
Kirmanciya Jori, *alt.* Kurdish,
  Northern [kmr], 443
Kirmanjki [kiu], 518
Kirmico-Lek, *dial.* Tsakhur
  [tkr], 557
Kiroba, *dial.* Kuria [kuj], 200, 134
Kirombo, *alt.* Rombo [rof], 204
Kirovabad, *dial.* Azerbaijani, North
  [azj], 319
Kirr, *alt.* Kir-Balar [kkr], 166
Kiruguru, *alt.* Luguru [ruf], 200
Kiruihi, *alt.* Rufiji [rui], 204
Kirundi, *alt.* Rundi [run], 55
Kirungu, *alt. dial.* Mambwe-Lungu
  [mgr], 201
Kirwo, *alt.* Rwa [rwk], 204
Kiryol, *alt.* Crioulo, Upper Guinea
  [pov], 131
Kis [kis], 606
Kisa, *dial.* Luyia [luy], 134
Kisafwa, *alt.* Safwa [sbk], 204
Kisagala, *alt.* Sagala [sbm], 204

  alt. Sagalla [tga], 136
Kisagalla, *alt.* Sagalla [tga], 136
Kisagara, *alt.* Sagala [sbm], 204
Kisakata, *alt.* Sakata [skt], 104
Kisam, *alt.* Manta [myg], 66
Kisamajeng, *alt. dial.* Datooga [tcc],
  198
Kisambaa, *alt.* Shambala [ksb], 204
Kisambaeri, *dial.* Amarakaeri
  [amr], 286
Kisan, *alt.* Kurux [kru], 371
  dial. Kurux [kru], 371
  dial. Maithili [mai], 373, 475
Kisandawe, *alt.* Sandawe [sad], 204
Kisanga, *alt.* Sanga [sng], 107
  dial. Mwani [wmw], 148
Kisangu, *alt.* Sangu [sbp], 204
Kisankasa [kqh], 200
Kisar [kje], 400
Kisede, *alt. dial.* Lega-Shabunda
  [lea], 102
Kisegeju, *alt.* Segeju [seg], 204
Kiseguju, *alt.* Dhaiso [dhs], 198
Kisembombo, *alt. dial.* Zimba
  [zmb], 109
Kisetla, *alt.* Settla [sta], 215
Kisettla, *alt.* Settla [sta], 215
Kishamba, *alt. dial.* Swahili
  [swh], 136, 212
  dial. Sagalla [tga], 136
Kishambaa, *alt.* Shambala [ksb],
  204
Kishambala, *alt.* Shambala
  [ksb], 204
Kishanganjia, *alt. dial.* Bengali
  [ben], 355
Kishpignag, *dial.* Moinba
  [mob], 376
Kishtwari, *dial.* Kashmiri [kas], 367
Kisi [kiz], 200
  alt. Kisi, Southern [kss], 183
  alt. Kissi, Northern [kqs], 129, 183
Kisi, Southern [kss], 138, 183
Kisie, *alt.* Kissi, Northern [kqs], 129,
  183
Kisii, *alt.* Gusii [guz], 133
Kisikongo, *alt.* Kongo, San Salvador
  [kwy], 101, 40
Kisizaki, *alt.* Sizaki [szk], 204
Kisonde, *alt.* Sonde [shc], 108
Kisonga, *alt.* Songa [sgo], 108
Kisonge, *alt.* Songe [sop], 108
Kisongi, *alt.* Songe [sop], 108
Kisongo, *alt.* Songo [soo], 108
Kisongye, *alt.* Songe [sop], 108
Kisonjo, *alt.* Temi [soz], 205
Kisonko, *dial.* Maasai [mas], 134,
  201
Kisoonde, *alt.* Sonde [shc], 108
Kissama, *alt.* Sama [smd], 42

alt. Gbe, Kotafon [kqk], 44
alt. Kuo [xuo], 82, 64
alt. dial. Ko [fuj], 192
dial. Mende [men], 183
Kō, *alt.* Winyé [kst], 55
Ko Bashai, *dial.* Kota [kfe], 370
Koa, *alt.* Koya [kff], 370
Ko'al, *alt.* Kumiai [dih], 263
Koalgurdi, *alt.* Mangala [mem], 573
Koalib [kib], 192
Koaratira, *alt.* Kanoé [kxo], 228
Koarnbut, *alt.* Ngurmbur [nrx], 575
Koasati [cku], 303
Koassa, *alt.* Kauwera [xau], 416
alt. Kwerba [kwe], 418
Koba [kpd], 400
alt. Baga Koga [bgo], 128
alt. Yeyi [yey], 48, 151
Kobai, *alt.* Kovai [kqb], 607
Kobali, *alt. dial.* Sanumá [xsu], 312
Kobe, *alt.* Fania [fni], 80
dial. Sawai [szw], 403
Kobe-Kapka, *dial.* Zaghawa
[zag], 87
Kobeua, *alt.* Cubeo [cub], 244, 226
Kobewa, *alt.* Cubeo [cub], 244, 226
Kobéwa, *alt.* Cubeo [cub], 226
Kobi, *alt.* Hunde [hke], 100
dial. Liana-Seti [ste], 400
Kobi-Benggoi, *alt.* Benggoi
[bgy], 397
Kobiana [kcj], 131, 181
Kobo, *alt.* Mom Jango [ver], 170, 68
Kobochi, *alt.* Nzanyi [nja], 71
Koboi, *alt.* Naga, Inpui [nkf], 377
Kobol [kgu], 606
Kobola, *dial.* Abui [abz], 406
Kobon [kpw], 606
Kobotachi, *dial.* Bata [bta], 155
Kobotshi, *alt.* Nzanyi [nja], 171, 71
Kobro'or, *alt.* Dobel [kvo], 397
Kobroor, *alt.* Dobel [kvo], 397
Kobuk River Inupiatun, *alt. dial.*
Inupiatun, Northwest Alaska
[esk], 302
Koc, *alt.* Koch [kdq], 368, 321
Kocch, *alt.* Koch [kdq], 368, 321
Koce, *alt.* Koch [kdq], 368, 321
Koch [kdq], 368, 321
alt. Rajbanshi [rjb], 477
Kochboli, *alt.* Koch [kdq], 368, 321
Koche, *alt.* Rajbanshi [rjb], 477
Kochila Tharu, *see* Tharu, Kochila
[thq], 481, 388
Kochin-Kam, *alt. dial.* Komi-
Permyak [koi], 555
Kochuvelan, *alt.* Ullatan [ull], 389
Koda [cdz], 368
alt. Kurux [kru], 371
Kodagu [kfa], 368

Kodaku, *alt.* Koraku [ksz], 369
Kodava Thak, *alt.* Kodagu [kfa],
368
Kode, *alt.* Kholok [ktc], 166
Kodeoha [vko], 430
Kodgotto, *alt.* Dyaabugay
[dyy], 570
Kodhin, *alt.* Kadaru [kdu], 191
Kodhinniai, *alt.* Kadaru [kdu], 191
Kodi [kod], 407
Kodi Bangedo, *alt. dial.* Kodi
[kod], 407
Kodi Bokol, *dial.* Kodi [kod], 407
Kodia [kwp], 93
Kodoo, *dial.* Maba [mde], 83
Kodoro, *alt.* Kadaru [kdu], 191
Kodra, *alt.* Todrah [tdr], 527
Kodrao, *dial.* Rade [rad], 526
Kodu, *alt.* Kui [kxu], 370
dial. Koho [kpm], 524
Kodulu, *alt.* Kui [kxu], 370
Kodur, *alt. dial.* Kadaru [kdu], 191
Koegu, *alt.* Kwegu [xwg], 116
Koekhoegowap, *alt.* Nama
[naq], 48
Koenoem [kcs], 166
Koepang Talk, *alt.* Broome Pearling
Lugger Pidgin [bpl], 569
Kofa [kso], 166
alt. dial. Mfumte [nfu], 67
alt. dial. Mogum [mou], 84
Kofan, *alt.* Cofán [con], 244
Kofán, *alt.* Cofán [con], 250
Kofane, *alt.* Cofán [con], 250, 244
Kofei [kpi], 417
Koffa, *dial.* Mfumte [nfu], 67
dial. Mogum [mou], 84
Kofilo, *alt. dial.* Bidiyo [bid], 79
Kofyar [kwl], 166
dial. Kofyar [kwl], 166
Koga, *alt.* Baga Koga [bgo], 128
Kogapakori, *pej. alt.* Nanti
[cox], 289
Kogbe, *alt.* Gbe, Kotafon [kqk], 44
Kogi, *alt.* Cogui [kog], 244
Kognere, *alt. dial.* Karanga [kth], 82
Kogoro, *alt.* Boguru [bqu], 189
Kogui, *alt.* Cogui [kog], 244
Koguman, *alt.* Kobol [kgu], 606
Koguru, *alt.* Boguru [bqu], 189
dial. Boguru [bqu]
Koh, *alt.* Kuo [xuo], 82, 64
Kohama, *dial.* Yaeyama [rys], 447
Kohat Hindko, *dial.* Hindko,
Southern [hnd], 485
Kohati, *alt. dial.* Hindko, Southern
[hnd], 485
Kohelia, *alt.* Rathawi [rtw], 384
Kohgiluyeh, *dial.* Luri, Southern
[luz], 440

Kohi, *alt.* Koi [kkt], 473
Kohima, *dial.* Naga, Angami
[njm], 377
Kohin [kkx], 394
Kohistana, *alt.* Kalami [gwc], 485
Kohistani, *alt.* Kalami [gwc], 485
alt. Kohistani, Indus [mvy], 486
alt. Shina, Kohistani [plk], 488
Kohistani Shina, *see* Shina,
Kohistani [plk], 488
Kohistani, Indus [mvy], 486
Kohiste, *alt.* Kohistani, Indus
[mvy], 486
Kohistyo, *alt.* Shina, Kohistani
[plk], 488
Kohli, *alt.* Koli, Kachi [gjk], 486, 369
alt. dial. Varhadi-Nagpuri [vah], 389
Kohnadeh, *dial.* Pashayi, Northwest
[glh], 317
Koho [kpm], 524
Kohor, *alt.* Koho [kpm], 524
Kohoroxitari [kob], 229
Kohrang, *alt. dial.* Bakhtiari
[bqi], 438
Kohumono [bcs], 166
Koi [kkt], 473
alt. Koya [kff], 370
Koi Bo'o, *alt.* Koi [kkt], 473
Koi Gondi, *alt.* Gondi, Southern
[ggo], 363
alt. Koya [kff], 370
Koi Sanjaq Soorit, *alt.* Koy Sanjaq
Surat [kqd], 443
Koi-Sanjaq Sooret, *alt.* Koy
Sanjaq Surat [kqd], 443
Koiali, Mountain [kpx], 606
Koianu, *dial.* Koromira [kqj], 607
Koiari, *alt.* Koiari, Grass [kbk], 606
Koiari, Grass [kbk], 606
Koibal, *dial.* Kamas [xas], 505
Koijoe, *alt.* Kuijau [dkr], 457
Koine Greek, *dial.* Greek, Ancient
[grc], 541
Koio, *alt.* Kwaio [kwd], 637
Koirao, *alt.* Naga, Thangal [nki], 380
Koireng [nkd], 368
Koirng, *alt.* Koireng [nkd], 368
Koita, *alt.* Koitabu [kqi], 607
Koitabu [kqi], 607
Koitar, *alt.* Koya [kff], 370
Koiwai, *alt.* Kowiai [kwh], 418
Koiwat [kxt], 607
dial. Malinguat [sic], 611
Kojali, *alt.* Awadhi [awa], 354, 468
Kök, *alt.* Tuvin [tyv], 345, 462
Kok Borok [trp], 368, 321
Kok Chiang, *dial.* Ugong [ugo], 518
Kok Kaber, *alt.* Gugubera
[kkp], 571
Kök Mungak, *alt.* Tuvin [tyv], 507

Kokadi, *alt.* Kaikadi [kep], 366
Kokama, *alt.* Cocama-Cocamilla [cod], 287, 226, 244
Kokamilla, *alt. dial.* Cocama-Cocamilla [cod], 226
Kokant Shan, *dial.* Shan [shn], 467
Kokata [ktd], 572
Kokatha, *alt.* Kokata [ktd], 572
Kokbarak, *alt.* Kok Borok [trp], 368
Kokchulutan, *dial.* Tuvin [tyv], 462
Koke [kou], 82
Kokhola, *alt.* Kokola [kzn], 140
Koki, *alt. dial.* Doromu [kqc], 597
Kokila, *dial.* Doromu [kqc], 597
Kokitta, *alt.* Kokata [ktd], 572
Kokna, *alt.* Kukna [kex], 370
Kokni, *alt.* Kukna [kex], 370
Koko, *alt.* ‡Kx'au‖'ein [aue], 150, 47
Koko Bera, *alt.* Gugubera [kkp], 571
Koko Imudji, *alt.* Guguyimidjir [kky], 571
Koko Pera, *alt.* Gugubera [kkp], 571
Koko-Ja'o, *alt.* Kuuku-Ya'u [kuy], 573
Koko-Mudju, *alt.* Djangun [djf], 569
Koko-Tjumbundji, *alt.* Dyaabugay [dyy], 570
Koko-Tyankun, *alt.* Djangun [djf], 569
Koko-Yalanji, *alt.* Kuku-Yalanji [gvn], 572
Kokoda [xod], 417
dial. Orokaiva [ork], 620
Kokola [kzn], 140, 147
Kokomindjen, *alt.* Yir Yoront [yiy], 579
Kokomoloroij, *alt.* Muluridyi [vmu], 574
Kokomoloroitji, *alt.* Muluridyi [vmu], 574
Kokonyungalo, *alt.* Dyaabugay [dyy], 570
Kokopo, *dial.* Kuanua [ksd], 608
Kokori, *alt.* Nakara [nck], 574
Kokoroton Murut, *dial.* Bookan [bnb], 456
Kokos, *alt.* Malay, Cocos Islands [coa], 457, 573
Kokota [kkk], 636
Kokoy Creole English [aig], 250
Kokoyao, *alt.* Kuuku-Ya'u [kuy], 573
Kokraimoro, *alt.* Kayapó [txu], 229
Kokwaiyakwa, *alt.* Yagwoia [ygw], 632
Kol (Cameroon) [biw], 64
Kol (Papua New Guinea) [kol], 607
alt. Aka-Kol [aky], 353
alt. dial. Kol [kol], 607

dial. Cua [cua], 522
Kol North, *dial.* Kol [biw], 64
Kol South, *dial.* Kol [biw], 64
Kola [kvv], 400
alt. Kol [kol], 607
alt. Kula [tpg], 408
alt. Kurux [kru], 371
dial. Mazagway [dkx], 66
Kolai, *dial.* Shina, Kohistani [plk], 488
Kolaka, *alt.* Tolaki [lbw], 433
Kolam, *alt.* Kolami, Northwestern [kfb], 369
Kolamboli, *alt.* Kolami, Northwestern [kfb], 369
Kolami, Northwestern [kfb], 369
Kolami, Southeastern [nit], 369
Kolamy, *alt.* Kolami, Northwestern [kfb], 369
Kolana, *alt.* Wersing [kvw], 410
dial. Wersing [kvw], 410
Kolana-Wersin, *alt.* Wersing [kvw], 410
Kolango, *alt.* Kulango, Bondoukou [kzc], 126
Kolata, *alt. dial.* Ashkun [ask], 315
Kolbila [klc], 64
Kolbilari, *alt.* Kolbila [klc], 64
Kolbili, *alt.* Kolbila [klc], 64
Kolbilla, *alt.* Kolbila [klc], 64
Kolchan, *alt.* Kuskokwim, Upper [kuu], 303
Koldrong, *alt. dial.* Katla [kcr], 192
Kole, *alt.* Bakole [kme], 57
alt. Fongoro [fgr], 80
alt. Kanuri, Central [knc], 63, 81, 152, 191
alt. Kol [kol], 607
Kolela, *alt.* C'lela [dri], 157
Kolena, *alt.* Kolbila [klc], 64
Kolensusu, *alt.* Kulisusu [vkl], 430
Kolepa, *dial.* Siane [snp], 624
Kolere, *alt.* Kanuri, Central [knc], 63, 81
Kolhi, *alt.* Koli, Kachi [gjk], 486, 369
Kolhreng, *dial.* Kom [kmm], 369
Koli, *alt.* Koli, Kachi [gjk], 486, 369
alt. dial. Duala [dua], 60
dial. Domari [rmt], 438
dial. Konkani [knn], 369
Koli, Kachi [gjk], 486, 369
Koli, Parkari [kvx], 487
Koli, Wadiyara [kxp], 369, 487
Kolibugan, *alt.* Subanon, Kolibugan [skn], 501
Kolibugan Subanon, *see* Subanon, Kolibugan [skn], 501
Koliku, *alt.* Male [mdc], 611
Kolinsusu, *alt.* Kulisusu [vkl], 430

Kollanko, *alt. dial.* Gawwada [gwd], 115
Kollina, *alt.* Culina [cul], 287
Kolmi, *alt.* Kolami, Northwestern [kfb], 369
Kolo, *alt. dial.* Ogbia [ogb], 172
dial. Bima [bhp], 406
dial. Langi [lag], 200
Kolobo, *alt. dial.* Kim [kia], 82
Kolobuan, *alt. dial.* Kinabatangan, Upper [dmg], 457
Kolod, *alt.* Okolod [kqv], 395, 460
Koloi, *alt. dial.* Chin, Falam [flm], 358
Kolokuma-Opokuma, *dial.* Izon [ijc], 164
Kololo, *alt.* Lozi [loz], 214, 150, 216
Kolom [klm], 607
Kolombangara, *alt.* Duke [nke], 636
Kolong, *alt.* Marba [mpg], 83
alt. dial. Stod Bhoti [sbu], 387
Koloo, *dial.* Senoufo, Mamara [myk], 144
Kolop, *dial.* Kim [kia], 82
Kolour, *alt.* Okolod [kqv], 395, 460
Kolren, *alt.* Koireng [nkd], 368
Kols, *alt.* Winyé [kst], 55
Kölsch [ksh], 539
Kolsi, *alt.* Winyé [kst], 55
Kolta, *alt.* Saami, Skolt [sms], 535, 556
Koltta, *alt.* Saami, Skolt [sms], 535
Koluama, *dial.* Izon [ijc], 164
Kolube, *alt.* Barok [bjk], 592
Kolufaup, *alt.* Korowai [khe], 418
Kolum So Dogon, *see* Dogon, Kolum So [dkl], 142
Kolumbiara, *alt.* Tubarão [tba], 233
Kolur, *alt.* Okolod [kqv], 395, 460
dial. Lundayeh [lnd], 460
Koluwawa [klx], 607
Kolya, *alt.* Naga, Thangal [nki], 380
Kolyai, *dial.* Kurdish, Southern [sdh], 440, 443
Kolym, *alt.* Yukaghir, Southern [yux], 499
Kolyma, *alt.* Yukaghir, Southern [yux], 499
Kolyma-Omolon, *dial.* Even [eve], 504
Kom (Cameroon) [bkm], 64
Kom (India) [kmm], 369
alt. dial. Tegali [ras], 195
dial. Mfumte [nfu], 67
Kom Komba, *alt.* Konkomba [xon], 126
Kom Rem, *alt.* Kom [kmm], 369
Koma [kmy], 167, 64
alt. Bana [bcw], 57
alt. Ganza [gza], 115

alt. Komo [xom], 116

alt. Konni [kma], 126

dial. Kgalagadi [xkv], 47

Koma Damti, *dial.* Koma [kmy], 64

Koma Kadam, *alt.* Gimnime [gmn], 62

alt. dial. Koma [kmy], 167

Koma Kampana, *alt. dial.* Koma [kmy], 167

Koma Kompana, *alt.* Gimme [kmp], 62

Koma Ndera, *dial.* Koma [kmy], 64

Koma of Asosa, *alt.* Kwama [kmq], 116

Koma of Begi, *dial.* Komo [xom], 116

Koma of Daga, *alt.* Komo [xom], 192

dial. Komo [xom], 116

Komalu, *alt.* Barok [bjk], 592

Komasma, *dial.* Citak [txt], 413

Komawa, *alt.* Kwaami [ksq], 168

Komba [kpf], 607

Kombai [tyn], 417

Kombe, *alt.* Ngumbi [nui], 111

dial. Tuki [bag], 72

Komberatoro, *alt.* Dera [kbv], 597

Kombio [xbi], 607

Kombo, *dial.* Jola-Fonyi [dyo], 180

Komboy, *alt.* Kombai [tyn], 417

Kome, *alt. dial.* Tegali [ras], 195

Komerin, *alt.* Komering [kge], 436

Komering [kge], 436

Komfana, *alt.* Kompane [kvp], 400

Komi, *alt.* Komi-Zyrian [kpv], 555

dial. Barein [bva], 78

Komi-Perm, *alt.* Komi-Permyak [koi], 555

Komi-Permyak [koi], 555

Komi-Permyat, *alt.* Komi-Permyak [koi], 555

Komi-Zyrian [kpv], 555

Kominimung [xoi], 607

Komkar, *dial.* Adi [adi], 353

Komlama, *alt.* Gimnime [gmn], 62

Kómnjo, *dial.* Wára [tci], 631

Komo (Democratic Republic of Congo) [kmw], 101

Komo (Sudan) [xom], 192, 116

dial. Pangseng [pgs], 173

Komodo [kvh], 408

Komofio, *dial.* Beami [beo], 593

Komoigaleka, *dial.* Siane [snp], 624

Komolom, *alt.* Mombum [mso], 420

Komongu, *dial.* Siane [snp], 624

Komono, *alt.* Khisa [kqm], 93, 52

Komoro, *alt.* Comorian [swb], 87, 140

alt. Maore [swb], 146

Kompana, *alt.* Gimme [kmp], 62

Kompane [kvp], 400

Kompara, *alt.* Gimme [kmp], 62

Kompong Thom, *alt.* Pear [pcb], 326

Komso [kxc], 116

Komtao, *alt. dial.* Telugu [tel], 388

Komudago, *alt.* Kokoda [xod], 417

alt. dial. Kokoda [xod], 417

Komung, *alt.* Konni [kma], 126

Komutu, *alt.* Nukna [klt], 619

Komyandaret [kzv], 417

Kon Hring Sedang, *dial.* Sedang [sed], 526

Kon Keu [kkn], 337

Kon Ngam, *dial.* Ngam [nmc], 85

Kona, *alt.* Jiba [juo], 165

Konabem, *alt. dial.* Mpongmpong [mgg], 68

Konabembe, *alt. dial.* Mpongmpong [mgg], 68

Konai [kxw], 607

Konawe, *dial.* Tolaki [lbw], 433

Konch, *alt.* Koch [kdq], 368, 321

Kond, *alt.* Kuvi [kxv], 371

Konda [knd], 417

alt. dial. Konda-Dora [kfc], 369

dial. Mongo-Nkundu [lol], 104

dial. Ngwo [ngn], 70

Konda-Dora [kfc], 369

dial. Konda-Dora [kfc], 369

Konda-Reddi, *alt. dial.* Telugu [tel], 388

Kondair, *alt. dial.* Dinka, Southwestern [dik], 190

Konde, *alt.* Makonde [kde], 201, 148

alt. Nyakyusa-Ngonde [nyy], 203, 140

dial. Ronga [rng], 149, 186

Kondeha, *alt.* Kodeoha [vko], 430

Kondekar, *alt.* Gadaba, Mudhili [gau], 361

alt. Gadaba, Pottangi Ollar [gdb], 361

Kondin, *alt. dial.* Mansi [mns], 505

Kondja, *alt.* Kwanja [knp], 65

Kondjara, *alt.* Fur [fvr], 80

Kondjo, *alt.* Konjo, Coastal [kjc], 430

Kondkor, *alt.* Gadaba, Mudhili [gau], 361

alt. Gadaba, Pottangi Ollar [gdb], 361

Kondoa, *dial.* Langi [lag], 200

dial. Sagala [sbm], 204

Kondoma, *dial.* Shor [cjs], 506

Kondoma Tatar, *alt.* Shor [cjs], 506

Kondul, *alt. dial.* Nicobarese, Southern [nik], 381

Kone, *alt. dial.* Sotho, Northern [nso], 186

Koneá, *alt.* Arapaso [arj], 225

Konejandi, *alt.* Gooniyandi [gni], 571

Koneraw [kdw], 417

Koneyandi, *alt.* Gooniyandi [gni], 571

Kong, *alt.* Kom [bkm], 64

dial. Gbari [gby], 160

dial. Tikar [tik], 72

Kong Jula, *dial.* Jula [dyu], 93

Konga, *dial.* Lutos [ndy], 76

Kongampani, *alt.* Kompane [kvp], 400

Kongar, *dial.* Tamil [tam], 388

Kongara, *dial.* Naasioi [nas], 616

Kongba, *dial.* Gola [gol], 138

Kongbaa, *dial.* Gola [gol], 183

Kongbo, *dial.* Tibetan [bod], 388

Kongder, *alt. dial.* Dinka, Southwestern [dik], 190

Kongi, *dial.* Dano [aso], 596

Kongo, *alt.* Koongo [kng], 101, 40

Kongo, San Salvador [kwy], 101, 40

Kongola, *alt.* Kusu [ksv], 101

Kongola-Meno, *dial.* Nkutu [nkw], 106

Kongon, *dial.* Naga, Konyak [nbe], 378

Koni, *alt.* Konni [kma], 126

dial. Sotho, Northern [nso], 186

Koniag, *dial.* Yupik, Pacific Gulf [ems], 310

Koniag-Chugach, *alt.* Yupik, Pacific Gulf [ems], 310

Koniagi, *alt.* Wamey [cou], 130

Koniagui, *alt.* Wamey [cou], 182

Koniéré, *dial.* Karanga [kth], 82

Konike, *dial.* Themne [tem], 184

Konio, *dial.* Tolaki [lbw], 433

Konja, *alt.* Kwanja [knp], 65

Konjara, *alt.* Fur [fvr], 190, 80

Konjo [koo], 211, 101

Konjo Pegunungan, *alt.* Konjo, Highland [kjk], 430

Konjo Pesisir, *dial.* Konjo, Coastal [kjc], 430

Konjo, Coastal [kjc], 430

Konjo, Highland [kjk], 430

Konkan Standard, *alt.* Konkani [knn], 369

Konkanasths, *alt. dial.* Konkani, Goanese [gom], 369

Konkanese, *alt.* Konkani [knn], 369

Konkani [knn], 369

dial. Bhili [bhb], 356

Konkani, Goanese [gom], 369, 134

Konkau, *alt.* Maidu, Northwest [mjd], 304

Konkomba [xon], 126, 208
Konkow, *alt.* Maidu, Northwest
[mjd], 304
Konni [kma], 126
Konnoh, *alt.* Kono [kno], 183
Kono (Guinea) [knu], 129
Kono (Nigeria) [klk], 167
Kono (Sierra Leone) [kno], 183
Konobo, *alt. dial.* Krahn, Eastern
[kqo], 138
Konomala [koa], 607
dial. Konomala [koa], 607
Konongo [kcz], 200
alt. dial. Nyamwezi [nym], 203
Konorau, *alt.* Koneraw [kdw], 417
Konosarola, *alt.* Vagla [vag], 128
Konso, *alt.* Komso [kxc], 116
Konstantinopel, *alt. dial.*
Armenian [hye], 318
Kontoi, *alt.* Blang [blr], 327, 462,
514
Kontu, *alt. dial.* Lavatbura-Lamusong
[lbv], 609
Kontum, *dial.* Bahnar [bdq], 521
Konu, *alt.* Kono [klk], 167
Konua, *alt.* Rapoisi [kyx], 622
Kony, *alt. dial.* Sabaot [spy], 135
Konya, *alt.* Maninka, Konyanka
[mku], 129, 139
Konyagi, *alt.* Wamey [cou], 182, 130
Konyak, *alt.* Naga, Konyak
[nbe], 378
Konyak Naga, *see* Naga, Konyak
[nbe], 378
Konyakakan, *alt.* Maninka,
Konyanka [mku], 129, 139
Konyanka Maninka, *see* Maninka,
Konyanka [mku], 129, 139
Konyar, *alt. dial.* Balkan Gagauz
Turkish [bgx], 563, 547
Konyare, *alt. dial.* Karanga [kth], 82
Konyo, *alt.* Konjo, Highland
[kjk], 430
Konze, *alt.* Kansa [ksk], 303
Konzo, *alt.* Konjo [koo], 211, 101
Koo, *dial.* Talise [tlr], 638
Koocatho, *alt.* Kokata [ktd], 572
Koode, *alt.* Kholok [ktc], 166
Koogurda, *alt.* Kokata [ktd], 572
Kooinmarburra, *alt.* Bayali
[bjy], 569
Kookanoona, *alt.* Muluridyi
[vmu], 574
Kooki, *dial.* Ganda [lug], 210
Kookwila, *dial.* Dadiya [dbd], 157
Koola, *alt. dial.* Samba Leko
[ndi], 72
Koonawure, *alt.* Kinnauri [kfk], 368
Kooncimo, *alt.* Koonzime [ozm], 64
Koongo [kng], 101, 40, 88

Koony, *dial.* Sabaot [spy], 135
Koonzime [ozm], 64
alt. dial. Koonzime [ozm], 64
Koopei, *dial.* Simeku [smz], 624
Koor, *dial.* Kag-Fer-Jiir-Koor-Ror-Us-
Zuksun [gel], 165
Koo'ra, *alt.* Natioro [nti], 53
Koore, *alt.* Koorete [kqy], 116
Koorete [kqy], 116
Koosa, *alt.* Xhosa [xho], 187
alt. dial. Lunda [lun], 214
Koose, *alt.* Akoose [bss], 56
Kootenai, *alt.* Kutenai [kut], 238,
303
Kootenay, *alt.* Kutenai [kut], 238
Koozhime, *alt.* Koonzime [ozm], 64
Koozime, *alt.* Koonzime [ozm], 64
alt. dial. Koonzime [ozm], 64
Kopa, *alt. dial.* Amarasi [aaz], 406
dial. Bangba [bbe], 97
dial. Sotho, Northern [nso], 186
Kopar [xop], 607
Kope, *dial.* Kiwai, Northeast
[kiw], 606
Kopei, *alt. dial.* Simeku [smz], 624
Kopka, *alt.* Kopkaka [opk], 418
Kopkaka [opk], 418
Kopo-Monia, *alt.* Ikobi-Mena
[meb], 602
Kopti, *alt. dial.* Zari [zaz], 178
Kor, *alt. dial.* Cua [cua], 522
!Kora, *alt.* Korana [kqz], 186
Kora, *alt.* Aka-Kora [ack], 353
alt. Koda [cdz], 368
alt. Kurux [kru], 371
alt. Lambadi [lmn], 372
Korafe [kpr], 607
dial. Korafe [kpr], 607
Korafi, *alt.* Korafe [kpr], 607
Koraga, Korra [kfd], 369
Koraga, Mudu [vmd], 369
Koragar, *alt.* Koraga, Korra [kfd],
369
Koragara, *alt.* Koraga, Korra
[kfd], 369
Korak [koz], 607
Koraku [ksz], 369
Korakuure, *dial.* Fulfulde, Borgu
[fue], 44
Korali, *alt.* Koda [cdz], 368
Korama, *alt.* Kurrama [vku], 572
Korambar, *alt.* Kurumba [kfi], 371
Korana [kqz], 186
Korandje [kcy], 39
Korangi, *alt.* Koraga, Korra
[kfd], 369
Koranic Arabic, *alt. dial.* Arabic,
Standard [arb], 508
Koranko, *alt.* Kuranko [knk], 183,
129

Koranna, *alt.* Korana [kqz], 186
Koranti, *alt. dial.* Asuri [asr], 354
Korape, *alt.* Korafe [kpr], 607
Korapun, *alt.* Korupun-Sela
[kpq], 418
Koraput Oriya, *alt.* Oriya, Desiya
[dso], 382
Koraqua, *alt.* Korana [kqz], 186
Korara, *alt.* Uduk [udu], 119, 196
Korat, *alt. dial.* Thai [tha], 517
Korati, *alt.* Koda [cdz], 368
Korava, *alt.* Irula [iru], 365
alt. Yerukula [yeu], 390
Korbaffo, *alt. dial.* Termanu
[twu], 410
Korbafo, *dial.* Termanu [twu], 410
Korbo, *alt. dial.* Dangaléat [daa], 80
Korca, *dial.* Albanian, Tosk [als], 529
Korchi, *alt.* Yerukula [yeu], 390
Kordali, *dial.* Kurdish, Southern
[sdh], 440, 443
Kordi, *alt.* Kurdish, Central [ckb], 440
alt. Kurdish, Northern [kmr], 440
Kore, *alt.* Koda [cdz], 368
dial. Maasai [mas], 134
Korean [kor], 448, 337, 447, 448, 515
Korean Sign Language
[kvk], 449
|Koree-Khoe, *alt. dial.* Shua
[shg], 48
Koreguaje [coe], 246
Korekore, *dial.* Shona [sna], 216,
215
Koren, *alt.* Koireng [nkd], 368
Koresh-e Rostam [okh], 440
Ko'reuaju, *alt.* Koreguaje [coe], 246
Kori, *alt.* Koli, Kachi [gjk], 486, 369
alt. dial. Kaili, Ledo [lew], 429
dial. Dimli [diq], 518
Korido, *dial.* Biak [bhw], 412
Koriki, *alt.* Purari [iar], 622
Koriko, *alt. dial.* Doromu [kqc], 597
Korikori, *alt. dial.* Shona [sna], 215
Korim, *dial.* Biak [bhw], 412
Korindi, *alt. dial.* Tumtum [tbr], 196
Koring, *alt.* Oring [org], 172
Korintal, *dial.* Gula Iro [glj], 81
Koriok, *dial.* Otuho [lot], 194
Koripako, *alt.* Curripaco [kpc], 245,
226
Korispaso, *alt.* Curripaco
[kpc], 226
Korki, *alt.* Korku [kfq], 369
Korkora, *alt.* Kurdish, Central
[ckb], 440
Korku [kfq], 369
alt. Koraku [ksz], 369
Korla, *alt. dial.* Koya [kff], 370
Korlai Creole Portuguese
[vkp], 370

Koro (Côte d'Ivoire) [kfo], 93
Koro (Papua New Guinea) [kxr], 607
Koro (Vanuatu) [krf], 642
Koro Afiki, *alt.* Ija-Zuba [vki], 163
Koro Agwe, *alt.* Begbere-Ejar
[bqv], 155
Koro Funtu of Kafin Koro, *alt.*
Tanjijili [uji], 175
Koro Funtu of Minna, *alt.* Tanjijili
[uji], 175
Koro Ija, *alt.* Ija-Zuba [vki], 163
Koro Jula, *alt.* Koro [kfo], 93
Koro Lafia, *alt.* Lijili [mgi], 168
Koro Makama, *alt.* Ashe [ahs], 154
alt. Begbere-Ejar [bqv], 155
Koro Myamya, *alt.* Begbere-Ejar
[bqv], 155
Koro of Lafia, *alt.* Lijili [mgi], 168
Koro of Shakoyi, *alt.* Tanjijili
[uji], 175
Koro Zuba, *alt.* Ija-Zuba [vki], 163
Koroboré, *alt. dial.* Songhay
[hmb], 54
Koroboro Senni, *alt.* Songhay,
Koyraboro Senni [ses], 144
Korok, *alt. dial.* Dinka, Southwestern
[dik], 190
Koroka, *alt.* Kwadi [kwz], 40
alt. dial. Mahou [mxx], 94
Koroko, *alt.* Valman [van], 630
Korokoro, *alt. dial.* Orma [orc], 135
Korolau, *alt. dial.* Fijian [fij], 580
Korom Boye, *alt.* Kulere [kul], 167
Koromba, *alt.* Basa-Gurmana
[buj], 155
dial. Koromfé [kfz], 52
Koromfé [kfz], 52, 143
Koromira [kqj], 607
dial. Koromira [kqj], 607
Koron Ache, *alt.* Ashe [ahs], 154
dial. Begbere-Ejar [bqv], 155
Koron Ala, *alt.* Ashe [ahs], 154
Koron Panda, *dial.* Begbere-Ejar
[bqv], 155
Koronadal Bilaan, *alt.* Blaan,
Koronadal [bpr], 493
Koronadal Blaan, *see* Blaan,
Koronadal [bpr], 493
Korondougou, *dial.* Bozo, Jenaama
[bze], 142
Korongo, *alt.* Krongo [kgo], 192
Koroni [xkq], 430
Korop [krp], 167, 64
Koroshi [ktl], 440
Korowai [khe], 418
Korowai, North [krg], 418
Korra, *alt.* Fur [fvr], 190
alt. Koraga, Korra [kfd], 369
Korra Koraga, *see* Koraga, Korra
[kfd], 369

Korripako, *dial.* Curripaco
[kpc], 226
Korrose, *alt. dial.* Gawwada
[gwd], 115
Kortabina, *alt.* Banggarla [bjb], 568
Kortchi, *alt.* Gavar [gou], 61
Kortha, *alt. dial.* Maithili [mai], 373
Kortha Bihari, *alt. dial.* Maithili
[mai], 373
Korubo [xor], 229
Korupun, *dial.* Korupun-Sela
[kpq], 418
Korupun-Sela [kpq], 418
Korwa [kfp], 370
Koryak [kpy], 505
Kos, *alt. dial.* Abé [aba], 90
Kosa, *dial.* Lunda [lun], 214
Kosach, *alt.* Kazakh [kaz], 448, 461,
518
Kosadle [kiq], 418
Kosali, *alt.* Awadhi [awa], 354, 468
Kosare, *alt.* Kosadle [kiq], 418
Kosarek, *alt.* Yale, Kosarek
[kkl], 426
dial. Yale, Kosarek [kkl], 426
Kosarek Yale, *see* Yale, Kosarek
[kkl], 426
Kosena [kze], 607
Koseng, *alt.* Kasseng [kgc], 450
Koshan, *dial.* Aghul [agx], 552
Koshin [kid], 64
Koshti, *dial.* Powari [pwr], 384
Kosi, *alt.* Akoose [bss], 56
Kosian, *alt.* Balantak [blz], 427
Kosin, *alt.* Koshin [kid], 64
Kosirava, *dial.* Maisin [mbq], 610
Koso, *alt.* Panamint [par], 306
Koso Shoshone, *alt.* Panamint
[par], 306
Kosop, *dial.* Kim [kia], 82
Kosorong, *alt.* Borong [ksr], 594
dial. Borong [ksr], 594
Kosova, *alt.* Gusii [guz], 133
Kosove, *alt. dial.* Albanian, Gheg
[aln], 529
Kosrae, *alt.* Kosraean [kos], 582
Kosraean [kos], 582
Kossa, *alt.* Mende [men], 183, 139
Kosso, *alt.* Mende [men], 183, 139
Kosti, *dial.* Marathi [mar], 374
dial. Varhadi-Nagpuri [vah], 389
Kota (Gabon) [koq], 120, 88
Kota (India) [kfe], 370
alt. Kofa [kso], 166
alt. dial. Ngando [ngd], 77
Kota Agung, *dial.* Pesisir, Southern
[pec], 437
Kota Bangun Kutai Malay, *see*
Malay, Kota Bangun Kutai
[mqg], 394

Kota Belud, *dial.* Bajau, West Coast
[bdr], 456
Kota Bumi, *dial.* Abung [abl], 435
Kota Marudu Talantang [grm],
457
Kota Marudu Tinagas [ktr], 457
Kota-Waringin, *dial.* Malay
[mly], 436
Kotafoa, *dial.* Éwé [ewe], 124
Kotafon Gbe, *see* Gbe, Kotafon
[kqk], 44
Kotagu, *alt.* Kodagu [kfa], 368
Kotali, *dial.* Bhili [bhb], 356
Kotali Bhil, *dial.* Khandesi
[khn], 367
Kótedia, *alt.* Guanano [gvc], 227,
245
Kother-Tamil, *alt.* Kota [kfe], 370
Koti [eko], 147
Kotia Oriya, *alt.* Oriya, Adivasi
[ort], 382
Kotiria, *alt.* Guanano [gvc], 245
Kótirya, *alt.* Guanano [gvc], 227
Kotiya, *alt.* Oriya, Adivasi [ort], 382
Kotni, *dial.* Vasavi [vas], 390
Koto, *alt.* Orejón [ore], 289
alt. dial. Gula [kcm], 76
dial. Ebira [igb], 158
Kotofo, *alt.* Peere [pfe], 71, 173
alt. dial. Peere [pfe], 71
Kotogüt, *alt.* Tsakwambo
[kvz], 424
Kotoko, *alt.* Afade [aal], 153
Kotoko-Gana, *alt. dial.* Lagwan
[kot], 65, 83
Kotoko-Gulfei, *alt.* Malgbe
[mxf], 83
Kotoko-Kuseri, *alt.* Mser [kqx], 68,
84
Kotoko-Logone, *alt.* Lagwan [kot],
65, 83
Kotoko-Makari, *alt.* Mpade
[mpi], 84
Kotoko-Maltam, *alt.* Maslam
[msv], 84
Kotokoli, *alt.* Tem [kdh], 209, 46,
128
Kotokori, *alt.* Ebira [igb], 158
Kotom, *dial.* Yagaria [ygr], 632
Kotopo, *alt.* Peere [pfe], 71, 173
alt. dial. Peere [pfe], 71
Kotos, *dial.* Amarasi [aaz], 406
Kotpojo, *alt.* Peere [pfe], 71, 173
Kotta, *alt.* Kota [kfe], 370
Kotu, *alt.* Kota [koq], 120
Kotua Sedang, *dial.* Sedang [sed],
526
Kotule, *alt.* Tula [tul], 176
Kotvali, *alt. dial.* Bhili [bhb], 356
Kotwalia, *alt. dial.* Bhili [bhb], 356

Kotya, *dial.* Bozo, Jenaama
  [bze], 142
Kotyaxo, *alt. dial.* Bozo, Jenaama
  [bze], 142
Kotzebue Sound Inupiatun, *alt.*
  dial. Inupiatun, Northwest Alaska
  [esk], 302
Kouang, *alt.* Kwang [kvi], 82
Kouka, *alt. dial.* Naba [mne], 85
Koukouya, *alt.* Teke-Kukuya
  [kkw], 90
Koulango, *alt.* Kulango, Bondoukou
  [kzc], 126
  alt. Kulango, Bouna [nku], 94
Koulounkalan, *dial.* Maninkakan,
  Eastern [emk], 129
Koumac, *alt.* Kumak [nee], 584
Koumongou, *dial.* Ngangam
  [gng], 209
Kounte Lele, *dial.* Lele [llc], 129
Kouri, *alt. dial.* Yedina [bdm], 177
Kourousa, *alt. dial.* Maninkakan,
  Eastern [emk], 129
Kouseri, *alt.* Mser [kqx], 68
Koussassé, *alt.* Kusaal [kus], 52
Kousseri, *alt.* Mser [kqx], 68, 84
  alt. dial. Mser [kqx], 68, 84
Koussountou, *alt.* Bago-Kusuntu
  [bqg], 207
Koutin, *alt.* Peere [pfe], 71, 173
Koutine, *alt.* Peere [pfe], 71
Kouya [kyf], 93
Kouyou, *alt.* Koyo [koh], 88
Kovai [kqb], 607
Kove [kvc], 607
Kovio, *alt. dial.* Mekeo [mek], 613
Kow, *alt.* Asas [asd], 591
  alt. Sinsauru [snz], 625
Kowaao, *alt.* Kuwaa [blh], 138
Kowai, *alt.* Kovai [kqb], 607
Kowaki [xow], 607
Kowalib, *alt.* Koalib [kib], 192
Kowe-Adiwasi, *alt.* Kota [kfe], 370
Kowet, *alt.* Kravet [krv], 325
Kowiai [kwh], 418
Kowlong, *alt.* Kaulong [pss], 605
Kowohans, *alt.* Kurichiya [kfh], 371
Kowya, *alt.* Kouya [kyf], 93
Koxima, *alt.* Coxima [kox], 244
Koy Sanjaq, *dial.* Lishanid Noshan
  [aij], 445
Koy Sanjaq Sooret, *alt.* Koy
  Sanjaq Surat [kqd], 443
Koy Sanjaq Soorit, *alt.* Koy
  Sanjaq Surat [kqd], 443
Koy Sanjaq Surat [kqd], 443
Koya [kff], 370
  alt. Koyaga [kga], 93
  dial. Loko [lok], 183
  dial. Themne [tem], 184

Koyaa, *alt.* Koyaga [kga], 93
Koyaga [kga], 93
  dial. Koyaga [kga], 93
Koyaga Jula, *alt.* Koyaga [kga], 93
Koyagakan, *alt.* Koyaga [kga], 93
Koyaka, *alt.* Koyaga [kga], 93
Koyara, *alt.* Koyaga [kga], 93
Koyato, *alt.* Koya [kff], 370
Koyi, *alt.* Koi [kkt], 473
  alt. Koya [kff], 370
Koyo [koh], 88
  alt. Lokoya [lky], 192
  alt. dial. Gula [kcm], 191
  dial. Godié [god], 93
Koyong, *alt.* Halang [hal], 523
Koyra, *alt.* Koorete [kqy], 116
Koyra Chiini, *dial.* Songhay, Koyra
  Chiini [khq], 144
Koyra Chiini Songhay, *see*
  Songhay, Koyra Chiini [khq], 144
Koyra Senni, *alt.* Songhay,
  Koyraboro Senni [ses], 144
Koyra Senni Songhay, *alt.*
  Songhay, Koyraboro Senni
  [ses], 144
Koyraboro Senni Songhay, *see*
  Songhay, Koyraboro Senni
  [ses], 144
Koyta, *alt.* Nara [nrb], 112
Koyu, *alt.* Koi [kkt], 473
Koyu Bo', *alt.* Koi [kkt], 473
Koyukon [koy], 303
Kozymodemyan, *dial.* Mari,
  Western [mrj], 555
Kpa, *alt. dial.* Rade [rad], 526
  dial. Bafia [ksf], 56
  dial. Mende [men], 183
Kpagua [kuw], 76
Kpagwa, *alt.* Kpagua [kuw], 76
Kpakolo, *alt. dial.* Bété, Gagnoa
  [btg], 92
Kpakum, *alt.* Kwakum [kwu], 65
Kpala [kpl], 101
  alt. Gbaya [krs], 190
  alt. dial. Mazagway [dkx], 66
Kpalagha, *alt.* Senoufo, Palaka
  [plr], 95
Kpan [kpk], 167
Kpango, *alt.* Dzùùngoo [dnn], 51
  dial. Dzùùngoo [dnn], 51
Kpankpam, *alt.* Konkomba
  [xon], 126
Kpanten, *alt.* Kpan [kpk], 167
Kpanzon, *alt. dial.* Kpan [kpk], 167
Kpara, *alt.* Gbaya [krs], 190
Kparla, *alt.* Gbaya [krs], 190
Kpasam [pbn], 167
Kpase, *dial.* Fon [fon], 43
Kpasham, *alt.* Kpasam [pbn], 167
Kpashan, *alt. dial.* Tyap [kcg], 176

Kpasiya, *alt.* Gbayi [gyg], 76
Kpatere, *alt.* Kpatili [kym], 76
Kpati [koc], 167
Kpatili [kym], 76
Kpatiri, *alt.* Kpatili [kym], 76
Kpatogo, *alt. dial.* Kaansa [gna], 51
Kpatogoso, *alt. dial.* Kaansa
  [gna], 51
Kpeaply, *dial.* Krahn, Western
  [krw], 138
Kpele, *alt.* Kpelle, Guinea [gkp], 129
  alt. Kpelle, Liberia [xpe], 138
Kpelen, *dial.* Éwé [ewe], 207
Kpelese, *alt.* Kpelle, Guinea
  [gkp], 129
Kpelesetina, *alt.* Kpelle, Guinea
  [gkp], 129
Kpelle, Guinea [gkp], 129
Kpelle, Liberia [xpe], 138
Kpere, *alt. dial.* Mbum [mdd], 66
Kperese, *alt.* Kpelle, Guinea
  [gkp], 129
Kpese, *alt.* Kpelle, Guinea [gkp], 129
Kpesi, *alt.* Kpessi [kef], 208
Kpessi [kef], 208
Kpétsi, *alt.* Kpessi [kef], 208
Kpilakpila, *alt.* Yom [pil], 46
Kpla, *alt.* Gbe, Eastern Xwla [gbx], 44
Kplang [kph], 126
Kplebo, *dial.* Grebo, Barclayville
  [gry], 138
Kplor, *dial.* Gbii [ggb], 137
Kpo, *dial.* Gola [gol], 183
Kpongo, *alt.* Lika [lik], 102
Kporo, *alt. dial.* Mbembe, Tigon
  [nza], 170
  dial. Mbembe, Tigon [nza], 66
Kposo, *alt.* Akposo [kpo], 123
  alt. Ikposo [kpo], 208
Kpotopo, *alt. dial.* Peere [pfe], 71
Kpwaala, *alt.* Kpala [kpl], 101
Kpwate, *alt.* Kpan [kpk], 167
Kpwessi, *alt.* Kpelle, Guinea
  [gkp], 129
  alt. Kpelle, Liberia [xpe], 138
Krache [kye], 126
Krachi, *alt.* Krache [kye], 126
Krahn, *alt.* Krahn, Western
  [krw], 138, 93
Krahn, Eastern [kqo], 138
Krahn, Western [krw], 138, 93
Krahô [xra], 229
Krakye, *alt.* Krache [kye], 126
Kramang, *alt. dial.* Kui [kvd], 408
Kran, *alt.* Krahn, Eastern [kqo], 138
  alt. Krahn, Western [krw], 138
Kranaria, *dial.* Romani, Sinte
  [rmo], 539
Krangku, *alt.* Rawang [raw], 466,
  385

Krantiki, *dial.* Romani, Sinte [rmo], 539

Kranyeu, *dial.* Oy [oyb], 452

Kraô, *alt.* Krahô [xra], 229

Kraol [rka], 325

Kraseng, *alt.* Kasseng [kgc], 450

Krau, *dial.* Jah Hut [jah], 454

Kravet [krv], 325

Krawang, *alt. dial.* Sunda [sun], 392

Kre, *alt. dial.* Hre [hre], 523

Kredj, *alt.* Gbaya [krs], 190

Kreen-Akarore [kre], 229

Krei, *alt.* Karey [kyd], 399

Kreich, *alt.* Gbaya [krs], 190

Kreish, *alt.* Gbaya [krs], 190

Krem, *dial.* Bahnar [bdq], 521

Krem-Ye, *alt.* Kreye [xre], 229

Kren Akarore, *alt.* Kreen-Akarore [kre], 229

Krenak [kqq], 229

Kreol, *alt.* Morisyen [mfe], 145
 alt. Seselwa Creole French [crs], 182

Kreole, *alt.* Morisyen [mfe], 145

Krepe, *alt.* Éwé [ewe], 124, 207

Krepi, *alt.* Éwé [ewe], 124, 207

Kresh, *alt.* Gbaya [krs], 190

Kresh-Boro, *alt. dial.* Gbaya [krs], 190

Kresh-Hofra, *alt. dial.* Gbaya [krs], 190

Kresh-Ndogo, *alt. dial.* Gbaya [krs], 190

Kreye [xre], 229

Kreyol, *alt.* Guadeloupean Creole French [gcf], 253
 alt. Haitian Creole French [hat], 258, 250, 253

Kriang, *alt.* Ngeq [ngt], 451

Krikati-Timbira [xri], 229

Krim [krm], 183
 alt. dial. Armenian [hye], 318

Krimchak, *alt.* Judeo-Crimean Tatar [jct], 521

Krinkati, *dial.* Krikati-Timbira [xri], 229

Krio [kri], 183

Krio Fula, *dial.* Pular [fuf], 184

Kriol [rop], 572
 alt. Belize Kriol English [bzj], 221

Krisa [ksi], 608

Kristang, *alt.* Malaccan Creole Portuguese [mcm], 454

Kriulo, *alt.* Crioulo, Upper Guinea [pov], 131, 180

Krobo, *dial.* Dangme [ada], 124

Krobou, *alt.* Krobu [kxb], 93

Krobu [kxb], 93

Kroe, *alt.* Krui [krq], 436

Krokong, *dial.* Jagoi [sne], 459

Krom, *alt.* Khmer, Central [khm], 524

Krong, *alt. dial.* Khmu [kjg], 451

Krongo [kgo], 192

Krongo Abdalla, *dial.* Kanga [kcp], 191

Kroo, *alt.* Klao [klu], 138, 183

Kroumen, *alt.* Krumen, Pye [pye], 93
 alt. Krumen, Tepo [ted], 93, 138

Krowe, *alt.* Sika [ski], 409

Kru, *alt.* Chru [cje], 522
 alt. Klao [klu], 138, 183
 alt. Krumen, Tepo [ted], 93, 138

Kru Pidgin English, *dial.* Liberian English [lir], 138

Krueng, *alt.* Kru'ng 2 [krr], 325

Kru'i, *alt.* Krui [krq], 436

Krui [krq], 436

Krumen, *alt.* Krumen, Tepo [ted], 93, 138

Krumen, Plapo [ktj], 93

Krumen, Pye [pye], 93

Krumen, Tepo [ted], 93, 138

Krung 1, *dial.* Rade [rad], 526

Kru'ng 2 [krr], 325

Kryc, *alt.* Kryts [kry], 319

Kryts [kry], 319
 dial. Kryts [kry], 319

Kryz, *alt.* Kryts [kry], 319

Kryzy, *alt.* Kryts [kry], 319

Ksakautenh, *alt.* Kháng [kjm], 524

Ksing Mul, *alt.* Puoc [puo], 525, 452

KSL, *alt.* Kenyan Sign Language [xki], 134

Ktunaxa, *alt.* Kutenai [kut], 238, 303

!Ku, *alt.* Kung-Ekoka [knw], 150, 40

Ku Te, *alt.* Lachi [lbt], 338

Ku-Amba, *alt.* Amba [rwm], 210

Kua [tyu], 47

Kuahane, *alt.* Kuhane [sbs], 47

Ku'ahl, *alt.* Kumiai [dih], 263

Kuakua, *alt.* Piaroa [pid], 312, 247

Kuala, *dial.* Banjar [bjn], 392

Kuala Langot Besisi, *dial.* Besisi [mhe], 454

Kuala Lumpur Sign Language, *alt.* Selangor Sign Language [kgi], 455

Kuala Monsok Dusun, *dial.* Dusun, Central [dtp], 456

Kuala Tembeling, *dial.* Jah Hut [jah], 454

Kuala Tutoh, *alt. dial.* Kiput [kyi], 460

Kuamba, *alt.* Amba [rwm], 210, 96
 alt. dial. Amba [rwm], 96

Kuamtim, *alt.* One, Kwamtim [okk], 620

Kuan [uan], 451

Kuang, *alt.* Kwang [kvi], 82

Kuanga, *alt.* Breri [brq], 594

Kuangfu, *alt. dial.* Amis [ami], 511

Kuangsu-Bonggrang, *alt.* Mlap [kja], 420

Kuanhua [xnh], 337

Kuanua [ksd], 608

Kuanyama, *alt.* Kwanyama [kua], 40, 150

Kuap, *alt.* Biatah [bth], 459

Kuat, *alt.* Kuot [kto], 608

Kuay, *alt.* Kuy [kdt], 325
 dial. Kuy [kdt], 515

Kuba, *alt.* Bushoong [buf], 98
 alt. Kubi [kof], 167
 alt. Likuba [kxx], 89
 alt. Luna [luj], 103
 alt. Yeyi [yey], 48, 151
 dial. Azerbaijani, North [azj], 319
 dial. Lezgi [lez], 555

Kubachi, *dial.* Dargwa [dar], 553

Kubachin, *alt. dial.* Dargwa [dar], 553

Kubachintsy, *alt. dial.* Dargwa [dar], 553

Kubai, *alt.* Naga, Inpui [nkf], 377

Kuban, *alt. dial.* Kabardian [kbd], 554

Kubang, *alt. dial.* Sama, Southern [ssb], 458

Kubari, *dial.* Kanuri, Tumari [krt], 152

Kubawa, *alt.* Kubi [kof], 167

Kube [kgf], 608
 dial. Zaghawa [zag], 196

Kubi [kof], 167
 dial. Konda-Dora [kfc], 369

Kubiri, *alt.* Ubir [ubr], 629

Kubiwat, *alt. dial.* Kwanga [kwj], 608

Kubo [jko], 608

Kubokota, *alt.* Ghanongga [ghn], 636

Kubonitu, *alt.* Cheke Holo [mrn], 635

Kuboro, *dial.* Babatana [baa], 635

Kubu [kvb], 436

Kubuli, *dial.* Sinaugoro [snc], 624

Kubung, *alt. dial.* Sama, Southern [ssb], 458

Kubwa, *alt.* Cubeo [cub], 244, 226

Kuchbandhi, *dial.* Kanjari [kft], 366

Kuche, *alt.* Che [ruk], 156

Kuchi, *alt.* Koli, Kachi [gjk], 486, 369
 dial. Matumbi [mgw], 202

Kuchikoli, *alt.* Koli, Kachi [gjk], 369

Kucong, *alt.* Lahu Shi [kds], 451, 338, 465, 515, 524

Kuda, *alt.* Kurux [kru], 371
 alt. dial. Kudu-Camo [kov], 167

Kuda-Chamo, *alt.* Kudu-Camo [kov], 167

Kulpantja, *alt.* Yankunytjatjara [kdd], 579
Kulu, *alt.* Kulung [bbu], 167
  alt. dial. Kag-Fer-Jiir-Koor-Ror-Us-Zuksun [gel], 165
  alt. dial. Sarudu [sdu], 433
Kulu Boli, *alt.* Pahari, Kullu [kfx], 382
Kulu Pahari, *alt.* Pahari, Kullu [kfx], 382
Kulu Ring, *alt.* Kulung [kle], 473, 370
Kulubi, *alt.* Barok [bjk], 592
Kului, *alt.* Pahari, Kullu [kfx], 382
Kulun, *alt.* Kulon-Pazeh [uun], 511
Kulung (Nepal) [kle], 473, 370
  Kulung (Nigeria) [bbu], 167
  alt. Marba [mpg], 83
Kulung Muthun, *alt. dial.* Naga, Wancho [nnp], 380
Kulung Pun, *alt.* Pongyong [pgy], 477
Kuluno, *alt.* Kulung [bbu], 167
Kulur, *dial.* Saparua [spr], 403
Kuluunaay, *alt. dial.* Bandial [bqj], 180
Kulvi, *alt.* Pahari, Kullu [kfx], 382
Kulwali, *alt.* Pahari, Kullu [kfx], 382
Kulyna, *alt.* Culina [cul], 226, 287
Kuma, *alt.* Koma [kmy], 167, 64
Kumai, *alt. dial.* Wahgi [wgi], 630
Kumaju, *alt.* Kemezung [dmo], 63
Kumak [nee], 584
  dial. Kumak [nee], 584
Kumalahu, *dial.* Bunama [bdd], 595
Kumali, *alt.* Kumhali [kra], 473
Kumalu [ksl], 608
Kumam [kdi], 211
Kuman [kue], 608
  alt. Kumam [kdi], 211
  dial. Kuman [kue], 608
Kumaon, *alt.* Kumauni [kfy], 473
Kumaoni, *alt.* Kumauni [kfy], 370
Kumar, *alt.* Kumarbhag Paharia [kmj], 370
  alt. Kurmukar [kfv], 371
Kumara, *alt.* Kumalu [ksl], 608
Kumarbhag Paharia [kmj], 370
Kumau, *alt.* Kumauni [kfy], 370
Kumauni [kfy], 370, 473
Kumawani, *alt.* Kumauni [kfy], 370
Kumba [ksm], 167
  dial. Lusengo [lse], 103
Kumbaingeri, *alt.* Kumbainggar [kgs], 572
Kumbainggar [kgs], 572
Kumbale, *alt.* Kumhali [kra], 473
Kumbere, *dial.* Vute [vut], 73
Kumbewaha [xks], 430

Kumbhakar, *alt.* Kurmukar [kfv], 371
Kumbhari, *alt.* Varhadi-Nagpuri [vah], 389
  dial. Powari [pwr], 384
Kumbi, *dial.* Gudu [gdu], 161
Kumbo, *dial.* Izon [ijc], 164
  dial. Kpan [kpk], 167
Kumbokota, *alt.* Ghanongga [ghn], 636
Kumboro, *alt. dial.* Babatana [baa], 635
Kumbowei, *alt. dial.* Izon [ijc], 164
Kumbule, *dial.* Nande [nnb], 105
Kumertuo, *alt.* Djauan [djn], 570
Kumeyaai, *alt.* Kumiai [dih], 263
Kumeyaay, *alt.* Kumiai [dih], 263, 303
Kumfel, *alt.* Kunfal [xuf], 116
Kumgoni, *alt.* Kumauni [kfy], 370
Kumhale, *alt.* Kumhali [kra], 473
Kumhali [kra], 473
Kumhar, *alt.* Kurmukar [kfv], 371
Kumi, *alt.* Chin, Khumi [cnk], 321, 359
  alt. Toposa [toq], 196
Kumia, *alt.* Kumiai [dih], 263
Kumiai [dih], 263, 303
Kumiyana, *alt.* Hixkaryána [hix], 227
Kumkale, *alt.* Kumhali [kra], 473
Kumkh, *alt. dial.* Lak [lbe], 555
Kumman, *alt.* Kumauni [kfy], 370
Kumo, *alt.* Komo [kmw], 101
Kumokio, *alt.* Kumukio [kuo], 608
Kumu, *alt.* Komo [kmw], 101
Kumuk, *alt.* Kumyk [kum], 555, 519
Kumukio [kuo], 608
Kumuklar, *alt.* Kumyk [kum], 555, 519
Kumum, *alt.* Kumam [kdi], 211
Kumus, *alt.* Uduk [udu], 119, 196
Kumux, *dial.* Lak [lbe], 555
Kumwenu, *alt.* Khisa [kqm], 93, 52
Kumyk [kum], 555, 519
Kumyki, *alt.* Kumyk [kum], 555, 519
Kumzai, *alt.* Kumzari [zum], 483
Kumzari [zum], 483
Kuna de la Frontera, *alt.* Kuna, Border [kvn], 283
Kuna, Border [kvn], 246, 283
Kuna, San Blas [cuk], 283
Kunabe, *dial.* Kutep [kub], 167, 64
Kunabeeb, *alt. dial.* Mpongmpong [mgg], 68
Kunabembe, *dial.* Mpongmpong [mgg], 68
Kunabi, *alt.* Konkani [knn], 369
Kunai, *dial.* Boikin [bzf], 594
Kunama [kun], 112

Kunan, *alt.* Gooniyandi [gni], 571
  alt. Kwini [gww], 573
Kunana, *alt.* Lardil [lbz], 573
Kunant, *alt.* Mansoanka [msw], 131
Kunante, *alt.* Mansoanka [msw], 131
Kunar, *dial.* Pashayi, Southeast [psi], 317
Kunawari, *alt.* Kinnauri [kfk], 368
Kunawur, *alt.* Kinnauri [kfk], 368
Kunayaoni, *alt.* Kumauni [kfy], 370
Kunban, *dial.* Varhadi-Nagpuri [vah], 389
Kunbarlang [wlg], 572
Kunbau, *alt. dial.* Khandesi [khn], 367
Kunbi, *dial.* Khandesi [khn], 367
  dial. Varhadi-Nagpuri [vah], 389
Kunbille, *alt.* Bile [bil], 155
Kunda [kdn], 216, 147, 214
  alt. Animere [anf], 123
  alt. Seba [kdg], 107
  dial. Lusengo [lse], 103
  dial. Nyanja [nya], 215
Kundri, *dial.* Bundeli [bns], 357
Kundu, *alt. dial.* Oroko [bdu], 71
Kundur, *dial.* Mogholi [mhj], 316
Kunfal [xuf], 116
Kunfäl, *alt.* Kunfal [xuf], 116
Kunfel, *alt.* Kunfal [xuf], 116
!Kung, *alt.* Kung-Ekoka [knw], 150, 40
Kung [kfl], 64
  alt. Juǀ'hoan [ktz], 47, 150
  alt. Kung-Ekoka [knw], 150
Kung-Ekoka [knw], 150, 40
Kung-Gobabis, *alt.* ǂKx'auǁ'ein [aue], 150, 47
Kung-Tsumkwe, *alt.* Juǀ'hoan [ktz], 47, 150
Kungara, *alt.* Fur [fvr], 190
Kungarakan, *alt.* Kungarakany [ggk], 572
Kungarakany [ggk], 572
Kunggara [kvs], 572
Kunggari [kgl], 572
Kunggera, *alt.* Kunggara [kvs], 572
Kunha, *alt.* Kurux [kru], 371
Kunhar, *alt.* Kurux [kru], 371
Kuni [kse], 608
  alt. Kuni-Boazi [kvg], 608
  dial. Kuni-Boazi [kvg], 608
Kuni-Boazi [kvg], 608
Kunian, *alt.* Gooniyandi [gni], 571
Kunibum, *alt.* Emai-Iuleha-Ora [ema], 159
Kunie, *alt.* Numee [kdk], 585
  alt. dial. Numee [kdk], 585
Kunigami [xug], 447
Kunimaipa [kup], 608

Kunini, *alt. dial.* Shoo-Minda-Nye [bcv], 174
dial. Bine [bon], 593
Kuniyan, *alt.* Gooniyandi [gni], 571
Kunja [pep], 608
Kunjen [kjn], 573
Kunjip, *dial.* Wahgi [wgi], 630
Kunjut, *alt.* Burushaski [bsk], 484
Kunlang, *dial.* Rawang [raw], 466, 385
Kunna, *alt.* Kurux [kru], 371
Kunrukh, *alt.* Kurux [kru], 371
Kuntemba, *alt. dial.* Nateni [ntm], 46
Kunteni, *dial.* Nateni [ntm], 46
Kuntulishi, *alt.* Tulishi [tey], 196
Kunua, *alt.* Rapoisi [kyx], 622
Kunuk, *alt.* Kurux [kru], 371
Kunuzi, *alt. dial.* Kenuzi-Dongola [kzh], 192, 110
Kunwinjku, *alt.* Gunwinggu [gup], 571
Kunyi [njx], 88
Kunza [kuz], 242
Kunzakh, *dial.* Avar [ava], 553
Kuo [xuo], 82, 64
alt. Oku [oku], 71
Kuot [kto], 608
Kuoy, *alt.* Kuy [kdt], 515, 451
Kuoyu, *alt.* Chinese, Mandarin [cmn], 511
Kup-Minj, *dial.* Wahgi [wgi], 630
Kupa [kug], 167
Kupang, *alt.* Helong [heg], 407
alt. Malay, Kupang [mkn], 408
alt. dial. Malay [mly], 436
Kupang Malay, *see* Malay, Kupang [mkn], 408
Kupel, *alt.* Ketengban [xte], 417
Kupia [key], 371
Kupkaferrn, *pej. alt.* Nama [naq], 48
Kupkaffer, *pej. alt.* Nama [naq], 48
Kupome, *dial.* Naga, Tangkhul [nmf], 380
Kupsabiny [kpz], 211
alt. dial. Kupsabiny [kpz], 211
Kupsapiny, *alt. dial.* Kupsabiny [kpz], 211
Kupto, *alt.* Kutto [kpa], 167
Kupuca, *alt.* Bezhta [kap], 553
Kur [kuv], 400
alt. Lahu Shi [kds], 338
dial. Kag-Fer-Jiir-Koor-Ror-Us-Zuksun [gel], 165
Kur Galli, *alt.* Brahui [brh], 484, 315, 438
Kur-Urmi, *dial.* Evenki [evn], 504
Kurâ, *alt.* Bakairí [bkq], 225
Kura Ede Nago, *see* Ede Nago, Kura [nqk], 43

Kurada, *alt.* 'Auhelawa [kud], 591
Kurama [krh], 167
alt. Kurrama [vku], 572
Kuramwari, *alt.* Kurumba [kfi], 371
Kurangal, *dial.* Pashayi, Northeast [aee], 317
Kuranko [knk], 183, 129
Kurateg, *alt.* Makuráp [mpu], 229
Kurbat, *alt.* Domari [rmt], 448, 510
dial. Domari [rmt], 448
Kurbati, *dial.* Domari [rmt], 438, 510
Kurdanji, *alt.* Gudanji [nji], 571
Kurdar, *dial.* Pashayi, Northeast [aee], 317
Kurdi, *alt.* Kurdish, Central [ckb], 443, 440
alt. Kurdish, Northern [kmr], 519, 440, 510
Kurdî, *alt.* Kurdish, Northern [kmr], 519, 319, 352
Kurdish, Central [ckb], 443, 440
Kurdish, Northern [kmr], 519, 319, 319, 352, 440, 443, 453, 510
Kurdish, Southern [sdh], 440, 443
Kurdit, *alt.* Hulaulá [huy], 445
alt. Lishana Deni [lsd], 445
alt. Lishanid Noshan [aij], 445
Kurdy, *alt.* Kurdish, Central [ckb], 440
Kure, *dial.* Bobo Madaré, Northern [bbo], 49
Kuremban, *alt.* Kurumba [kfi], 371
Kurfey, *dial.* Hausa [hau], 152
Kuri [nbn], 418
alt. Korku [kfq], 369
alt. dial. Yedina [bdm], 177
Kuria [kuj], 200, 134
Kurichchia, *alt.* Kurichiya [kfh], 371
Kurichia, *alt.* Kurichiya [kfh], 371
Kurichiya [kfh], 371
Kurichiyars, *alt.* Kurichiya [kfh], 371
Kuril, *dial.* Ainu [ain], 446, 503
Kurima, *alt. dial.* Dani, Lower Grand Valley [dni], 413
Kurina, *alt.* Culina [cul], 287
Kuripaco, *alt.* Curripaco [kpc], 245
Kuripako, *alt.* Curripaco [kpc], 226, 311
Kuriyo, *alt.* Kuijau [dkr], 457
Kurja, *alt.* Kodagu [kfa], 368
Kurka, *alt.* Fur [fvr], 190
alt. Kurux [kru], 371
Kurku, *alt.* Korku [kfq], 369
Kurku-Ruma, *alt.* Korku [kfq], 369
Kurkuro, *alt.* Kuikúro-Kalapálo [kui], 229
Kurmali, *alt.* Kudmali [kyw], 370
Kurmali Thar, *alt.* Kudmali [kyw], 370

Kurmancî, *alt.* Kurdish, Northern [kmr], 519, 319, 319, 352, 440, 510
alt. Kurmanji [kmr], 520
Kurmanji [kmr], 520
alt. Kurdish, Northern [kmr], 519, 319, 319, 352, 440, 443, 510
Kurmi, *alt.* Kulfa [kxj], 82
dial. Kulfa [kxj], 82
Kurmukar [kfv], 371, 473
Kuro-Urmi, *dial.* Nanai [gld], 506
Kurondi, *alt. dial.* Tumtum [tbr], 196
Kurop, *alt.* Korop [krp], 167
Kuroshima, *dial.* Yaeyama [rys], 447
Kurrama [vku], 572
Kurripaco, *alt.* Curripaco [kpc], 245
Kurripako, *alt.* Curripaco [kpc], 311
Kurru Bhasha, *alt.* Yerukula [yeu], 390
Kursmadkha, *alt.* Chocangacakha [cgk], 323
Kurtala, *dial.* Kadaru [kdu], 191
Kurtat, *dial.* Osetin [oss], 352, 519
Kurteopkha, *alt.* Kurtokha [xkz], 323
Kürthöpka, *alt.* Kurtokha [xkz], 323
Kurthopkha, *alt.* Kurtokha [xkz], 323
Kurti [ktm], 608
Kurtjjar, *alt.* Gurdjar [gdj], 571
Kurtobikha, *alt.* Kurtokha [xkz], 323
Kurtokha [xkz], 323
Kurtopakha, *alt.* Kurtokha [xkz], 323
Kuru, *dial.* Wipi [gdr], 632
Kuruaia, *alt.* Kuruáya [kyr], 229
Kuruáya [kyr], 229
Kuruba, *alt.* Kurumba [kfi], 371
Kurubar, *alt.* Kurumba [kfi], 371
Kurubas Kuruban, *alt.* Kurumba [kfi], 371
Kuruchans, *alt.* Kurichiya [kfh], 371
Kurudu [kjr], 418
Kurug, *alt.* Kodagu [kfa], 368
Kurukh, *alt.* Kurux [kru], 371, 321
Kuruko, *alt.* Piu [pix], 622
Kurukuru, *dial.* Paumarí [pad], 231
Kuruma, *alt.* Koromfé [kfz], 52
alt. Kurumba [kfi], 371
Kurumali, *alt.* Kudmali [kyw], 370
Kuruman, *alt.* Kurumba [kfi], 371
Kurumans, *alt.* Kurumba [kfi], 371
Kurumar, *alt.* Kurumba [kfi], 371
Kurumba [kfi], 371
Kurumba Kannada, *alt.* Kurumba [kfi], 371
Kurumba, Alu [xua], 371
Kurumba, Betta [xub], 371

Kurumba, Jennu [xuj], 371
Kurumba, Mullu [kpb], 371
Kurumban, *alt.* Kurumba [kfi], 371
Kurumbar, *alt.* Kurumba [kfi], 371
Kurumbas, *alt.* Kurumba [kfi], 371
Kurumfe, *alt.* Koromfé [kfz], 52
Kurumi, *alt.* Kulfa [kxj], 82
Kurumvari, *alt.* Kurumba [kfi], 371
Kurunga, *alt.* Karanga [kth], 82
   alt. dial. Karanga [kth], 82
Kurungtufu, *dial.* Kube [kgf], 608
Kurungu, *alt.* Krongo [kgo], 192
Kurupi, *alt.* Garus [gyb], 599
Kurur, *dial.* Hahon [hah], 601
Kururu, *dial.* Kadaru [kdu], 191
Kurutha, *alt.* Yerukula [yeu], 390
Kuruti, *alt.* Kurti [ktm], 608
Kuruti-Pare, *alt.* Kurti [ktm], 608
Kuruvikkaran, *alt.* Vaagri Booli
   [vaa], 389
Kuruwer, *dial.* Kaba Deme [kwg], 81
Kurux [kru], 371, 321
Kurux, Nepali [kxl], 473
Kurya, *alt.* Kuria [kuj], 200, 134
Kurye, *alt.* Kuria [kuj], 200
Kurzeme, *alt. dial.* Liv [liv], 546
Kusa, *alt. dial.* Uab Meto [aoz], 410
Kusa-Manlea, *dial.* Uab Meto
   [aoz], 410
Kusaal [kus], 126, 52
Kusage, *alt.* Kusaghe [ksg], 636
Kusaghe [ksg], 636
Kusaie, *alt.* Kosraean [kos], 582
Kusale, *alt.* Kusaal [kus], 126, 52
Kusanda, *alt.* Kusunda [kgg], 473
Kusasi, *alt.* Kusaal [kus], 126, 52
Kuseki, *dial.* Yendang [yen], 178
Kuseri, *alt.* Mser [kqx], 68, 84
Kusgilo, *dial.* Opuuo [lgn], 194
Kushage, *alt.* Kusaghe [ksg], 636
Kushani, *alt. dial.* Shughni [sgh], 318
Kushar, *alt.* Bote-Majhi [bmj], 469
Kushe, *alt.* Kushi [kuh], 167
Kushi [kuh], 167
   alt. Bauchi [bsf], 155
|**Kusi**, *alt. dial.* !Xóõ [nmn], 48, 151
Kusibi, *alt.* Desano [des], 226, 245
Kusiilaay, *alt.* Gusilay [gsl], 180
Kusilay, *alt.* Gusilay [gsl], 180
Kuskokwim Yupik, *dial.* Yupik,
   Central [esu], 310
Kuskokwim, Upper [kuu], 303
Kuso, *alt.* Mbukushu [mhw], 41
Kusso, *alt.* Mbukushu [mhw], 150,
   47, 214
Kusu [ksv], 101
Kusunda [kgg], 473
Kusuntu, *dial.* Bago-Kusuntu
   [bqg], 207
Kusuri, *dial.* Tugutil [tuj], 405

Kusuwa, *alt. dial.* Amba [rwm], 210
   dial. Amba [rwm], 96
Kuta, *alt. dial.* Gbagyi [gbr], 160
Kutai, *alt.* Malay, Tenggarong Kutai
   [vkt], 394
Kutang Bhotia, *alt.* Nubri
   [kte], 477
Kutang Ghale, *see* Ghale, Kutang
   [ght], 471
Kutcha, *alt.* Naga, Zeme [nzm], 381
Kutchchi, *alt.* Kachchi [kfr], 366,
   485
Kutchie, *alt.* Kachchi [kfr], 366, 485
Kutchin, *alt.* Gwich'in [gwi], 237,
   301
Kuteb, *alt.* Kutep [kub], 167, 64
Kutenai [kut], 238, 303
Kutep [kub], 167, 64
Kutev, *alt.* Kutep [kub], 167, 64
Kuthant [xut], 573
Kuti, *dial.* Byangsi [bee], 358
Kutia-Dyapa, *alt. dial.* Katukína
   [kav], 228
Kutin, *alt.* Peere [pfe], 71, 173
Kutine, *alt.* Peere [pfe], 71, 173
Kutinn, *alt.* Peere [pfe], 71, 173
Kutkasen, *dial.* Azerbaijani, North
   [azj], 319
Kuto-Kute, *dial.* Sasak [sas], 409
Kutsu, *alt.* Kusu [ksv], 101
Kutsung, *alt.* Lahu Shi [kds], 451,
   338, 465, 515, 524
Kutswe, *alt. dial.* Sotho, Northern
   [nso], 186
Kutto [kpa], 167
Kúttò, *alt.* Kutto [kpa], 167
Kutu [kdc], 200
   alt. Yela [yel], 109
   dial. Libinza [liz], 102
   dial. Mongo-Nkundu [lol], 104
Kutubu, *dial.* Foi [foi], 599
Kutule, *alt.* Tula [tul], 176
   dial. Tula [tul], 176
Kuturmi [khj], 167
Kuuk Thaayoore, *alt.* Thayore
   [thd], 576
Kuuk Thaayorre, *alt.* Thayore
   [thd], 576
Kuuku, *dial.* Guruntum-Mbaaru
   [grd], 161
Kuuku-Ya'u [kuy], 573
Kuumu, *alt.* Komo [kmw], 101
Kuuy, *alt.* Kuy [kdt], 515
Kuvakan, *dial.* Bashkir [bak], 553
Kuvalan, *alt.* Kavalan [ckv], 511
Kuvale, *dial.* Herero [her], 150
Kuvarawan, *alt.* Kavalan [ckv], 511
Kuvenmas, *dial.* Alamblak
   [amp], 588
Kuvi [kxv], 371

Kuvi Kond, *alt.* Kuvi [kxv], 371
Kuvinga, *alt.* Kuvi [kxv], 371
Kuvoko, *alt.* Gvoko [ngs], 161, 62
Kuvuri, *alt. dial.* Kanuri, Central
   [knc], 166, 63, 81, 191
Kuwaa [blh], 138
Kuwaataay [cwt], 181
Kuwaiti Hadari Arabic, *dial.*
   Arabic, Gulf Spoken [afb], 449
Kuwama, *alt. dial.* Wadjiginy [wdj],
   577
Kuwarawan, *alt.* Kavalan [ckv], 511
Kuwema, *alt.* Tyaraity [woa], 577
Kuwi, *alt.* Kuvi [kxv], 371
Kuwuri, *alt. dial.* Kanuri, Tumari
   [krt], 152
Kuy [kdt], 515, 325, 451
   alt. Kui [kxu], 370
Kuy Anthua, *dial.* Kuy [kdt], 325
Kuy Antra, *dial.* Kuy [kdt], 325
Kuy Ma'ay, *alt. dial.* Kuy [kdt], 325
Kuy May, *dial.* Kuy [kdt], 325
Kuy Mlor, *dial.* Kuy [kdt], 325
Kuya, *alt.* Kouya [kyf], 93
   dial. Ndumu [nmd], 121
Kuyani, *alt.* Guyani [gvy], 571
Kuyobe, *alt.* Miyobe [soy], 45, 208
Kuyonon, *alt.* Cuyonon [cyo], 494
Kuyubi, *alt.* Puruborá [pur], 232
Kuyuk, *alt.* Zaghawa [zag], 196, 87
Kuyunon, *alt.* Cuyonon [cyo], 494
Kuzamani, *alt.* Shuwa-Zamani
   [ksa], 174
   alt. dial. Lere [gnh], 168
Kuznets Tatar, *alt.* Shor [cjs], 506
Kvalan, *alt.* Kavalan [ckv], 511
Kvanada, *alt.* Bagvalal [kva], 553
Kvanadin, *alt.* Bagvalal [kva], 553
Kvanxidatl, *dial.* Andi [ani], 553
Kven, *alt.* Finnish, Kven [fkv], 549
Kven Finnish, *see* Finnish, Kven
   [fkv], 549
Kvolyab, *alt.* Awbono [awh], 411
K'wa, *alt.* Blang [blr], 514
Kwa [kwb], 167
   alt. Ejagham [etu], 60
   alt. dial. Ejagham [etu], 159, 60
   dial. Fipa [fip], 198
   dial. Kwa [kwb], 167
Kwa' [bko], 65
   dial. Kwa' [bko], 65
Kwaa, *alt.* Kuwaa [blh], 138
Kwaafi, *dial.* Fipa [fip], 198
Kw'aal, *alt.* Kumiai [dih], 263
Kwa'alang, *alt. dial.* Kofyar
   [kwl], 166
Kwaami [ksq], 168
Kwabzak, *alt.* Tal [tal], 175
Kwac, *alt. dial.* Dinka, South Central
   [dib], 190

Kwadi [kwz], 40
Kwadia, *alt.* Kodia [kwp], 93
Kwadya, *alt.* Kodia [kwp], 93
Kw'adza [wka], 200
Kwagallak, *dial.* Kofyar [kwl], 166
Kwagiutl, *alt.* Kwakiutl [kwk], 238
Kwah, *alt.* Kwa [kwb], 167
Kwahane, *alt.* Kuhane [sbs], 47
Kwahu, *alt. dial.* Akan [aka], 123
Kwai, *alt.* Gula'alaa [gmb], 636
Kwaiailk, *alt.* Chehalis, Upper
    [cjh], 299
Kwaibida, *dial.* Sinaugoro [snc], 624
Kwaibo, *dial.* Sinaugoro [snc], 624
Kwaiker, *alt.* Awa-Cuaiquer
    [kwi], 243
Kwaio [kwd], 637
Kwaja [kdz], 65
Kwaji, *dial.* Mumuye [mzm], 170
Kwak [kwq], 168
    dial. Yamba [yam], 73
Kwakiutl [kwk], 238
Kwakum [kwu], 65
    dial. Kwakum [kwu], 65
Kwakwa, *alt.* Avikam [avi], 91
Kwakwagom, *dial.* Bokyi [bky],
    156
Kwakwak, *alt.* Kakwa [keo], 211,
    191
Kwak'wala, *alt.* Kwakiutl
    [kwk], 238
Kwakwi, *alt.* Firan [fir], 160
Kwal, *alt.* Irigwe [iri], 164
Kwala, *alt.* Kpala [kpl], 101
    alt. Likwala [kwc], 89
Kwalaiwa, *dial.* Bwanabwana
    [tte], 596
Kwale, *alt.* Uare [ksj], 629
    alt. dial. Uare [ksj], 629
    alt. dial. Ukwuani-Aboh-Ndoni
    [ukw], 176
Kwali, *dial.* Gbari [gby], 160
Kwalla, *alt. dial.* Kofyar [kwl], 166
Kwaludhi, *dial.* Ndonga [ndo], 150
Kwam, *alt.* Kwaami [ksq], 168
Kwama [kmq], 116
Kwamana, *dial.* Wedau [wed], 631
Kwamanchi, *alt.* Kwaami
    [ksq], 168
Kwamba, *alt.* Amba [rwm], 210, 96
Kwambi [kwm], 150
Kwame, *alt.* Kwami [ktf], 101
Kwamera [tnk], 642
Kwami [ktf], 101
    alt. Kwaami [ksq], 168
Kwamtim, *alt.* One, Kwamtim
    [okk], 620
Kwamtim One, *see* One, Kwamtim
    [okk], 620
Kwan, *alt.* Irigwe [iri], 164

Kwancama, *alt.* Kwanyama
    [kua], 40, 150
Kwandang, *alt. dial.* Gorontalo
    [gor], 429
Kwandara, *alt.* Gwandara [gwn], 161
Kwandi, *dial.* Luyana [lyn], 214, 41
Kwang [kvi], 82
    dial. Kwang [kvi], 82
Kwanga [kwj], 608
    dial. Luyana [lyn], 214
Kwangali [kwn], 150, 40
Kwangare, *alt.* Kwangali
    [kwn], 150, 40
Kwangari, *alt.* Kwangali [kwn], 150,
    40
Kwange, *alt. dial.* Zimba [zmb], 109
    dial. Gbari [gby], 160
Kwangfu, *alt. dial.* Amis [ami], 511
Kwangsu-Bonggrang, *alt.* Mlap
    [kja], 420
Kwanim Pa, *alt.* Uduk [udu], 119,
    196
Kwanja [knp], 65
Kwanjama, *alt.* Kwanyama
    [kua], 40, 150
Kwanka, *alt.* Vaghat-Ya-Bijim-Legeri
    [bij], 177
    alt. dial. Vaghat-Ya-Bijim-Legeri
    [bij], 177
Kwansu, *alt.* Mlap [kja], 420
Kwansu-Bonggrang, *alt.* Mlap
    [kja], 420
Kwanyama [kua], 40, 150
Kwapm, *alt. dial.* Zari [zaz], 178
Kwara'ae [kwf], 637
Kwarafe, *alt.* Korafe [kpr], 607
Kware, *alt.* Aimele [ail], 588
    alt. Uare [ksj], 629
Kwarekwareo, *alt.* Dori'o
    [dor], 636
Kwarra, *alt.* Mama [mma], 169
Kwarta Mataci, *dial.* Karekare
    [kai], 166
Kwaruwikwundi, *alt.* Malinguat
    [sic], 611
Kwasang, *dial.* Buang, Mangga
    [mmo], 595
Kwasap, *alt. dial.* Kim [kia], 82
Kwasengen, *alt.* Hanga Hundi
    [wos], 601
Kwasio, *dial.* Ngumba [nmg], 70,
    111
Kwassio, *alt. dial.* Ngumba
    [nmg], 70
Kwasu, *alt.* Ninzo [nin], 171
Kwatay, *alt.* Kuwaataay [cwt], 181
Kwato [kop], 609
Kwavi, *alt. dial.* Maasai [mas], 134,
    201
Kwawu, *dial.* Akan [aka], 123

Kwaya [kya], 200
    alt. dial. Iceve-Maci [bec], 63, 163
Kwayam, *dial.* Kanuri, Central
    [knc], 166, 63, 81, 191
Kwe, *alt.* Tsoa [hio], 48
Kwe-Etshori Kwee, *alt.* Tsoa
    [hio], 48
Kwe-Nee-Chee-Aht, *alt.* Makah
    [myh], 304
Kwe-Tshori, *alt.* Tsoa [hio], 48
Kwedi, *alt.* Mokpwe [bri], 68
Kweedishchaaht, *alt.* Makah
    [myh], 304
Kween, *alt.* Khuen [khf], 451, 337
Kwegi, *alt.* Kwegu [xwg], 116
Kwegu [xwg], 116
Kwele, *alt.* Kwere [cwe], 200
Kweli, *alt.* Mokpwe [bri], 68
Kwelshin, *alt. dial.* Chin, Falam
    [flm], 463
Kwem, *alt.* Mandobo Atas
    [aax], 419
Kwena, *dial.* Tswana [tsn], 48, 186
Kwéndré, *alt.* Guro [goa], 93
Kweni, *alt.* Guro [goa], 93
Kweny, *dial.* Sagala [sbm], 204
Kwenyii, *alt.* Numee [kdk], 585
    alt. dial. Numee [kdk], 585
Kwer [kwr], 418
Kwera, *alt.* Koorete [kqy], 116
Kwerba [kwe], 418
Kwerba Mamberamo [xwr], 418
Kwere [cwe], 200
Kwerisa [kkb], 418
Kwese [kws], 102
Kwesten [kwt], 418
Kwèyòl, *alt.* Dominican Creole
    French [acf], 250
Kwéyòl, *alt.* Saint Lucian Creole
    French [acf], 294
!Kwi, *dial.* !Xóõ [nmn], 48, 151
Kwi, *alt.* Lahu Shi [kds], 451, 338,
    465, 515, 524
Kwiani, *alt.* Guyani [gvy], 571
Kwifa, *alt. dial.* Sagala [sbm], 204
Kwijau, *alt.* Kuijau [dkr], 457
Kwikapa, *alt.* Cocopa [coc], 300
Kwikapá, *alt.* Cocopa [coc], 262
Kwili, *alt.* Mokpwe [bri], 68
Kwina, *alt.* Opuuo [lgn], 117, 194
Kwingsang, *alt.* Nung [nun], 466,
    341
Kwini [gww], 573
Kwinp'ang, *alt.* Nung [nun], 466,
    341
Kwinti [kww], 296
Kwiri, *alt.* Mokpwe [bri], 68
Kwiva, *alt. dial.* Sagala [sbm], 204
Kwoico Lo, *alt.* Sunwar [suz], 479
Kwoireng, *alt.* Koireng [nkd], 368

Kwojeffa, *alt.* Bura-Pabir [bwr], 156
Kwolacha, *alt. dial.* Qimant [ahg], 118
Kwolasa, *alt. dial.* Qimant [ahg], 118
Kwoll, *alt.* Irigwe [iri], 164
Kwollanyoch, *alt.* Awngi [awn], 113
Kwom, *alt.* Kwaami [ksq], 168
Kwoma [kmo], 609
  dial. Kwoma [kmo], 609
Kwomtari [kwo], 609
Kwonci, *dial.* Piya-Kwonci [piy], 173
Kwong, *alt.* Kagoma [kdm], 165
  alt. Kwang [kvi], 82
  alt. dial. Kofyar [kwl], 166
Kwono, *alt.* Kono [klk], 167
Kwoode, *alt.* Kholok [ktc], 166
Kwotto, *alt.* Ebira [igb], 158
Kwottu, *pej. alt.* Oromo, Eastern [hae], 118
Kwuizwu, *alt.* Dungan [dng], 449
Kwusaun, *dial.* Boikin [bzf], 594
‖Kxau, *alt. dial.* Nǀu [ngh], 186
ǂKx'au‖'ei, *alt.* ǂKx'au‖'ein [aue], 150, 47
ǂKx'au‖'ein [aue], 150, 47
Kxaxa, *alt. dial.* Sotho, Northern [nso], 186
Kxhalaxadi, *alt.* Kgalagadi [xkv], 47
Kxoe [xuu], 150, 40, 186
  alt. Khwe [xuu], 47, 214
Kxoedam, *alt.* Kxoe [xuu], 150, 40
  dial. Kxoe [xuu], 186
Kyabrat, *dial.* Maithili [mai], 475
Kyak [bka], 168
Kyaka [kyc], 609
Kyakanke, *alt. dial.* Maninkakan, Western [mlq], 181
Kyama, *alt.* Ebrié [ebr], 92
Kyan Kyar, *alt. dial.* Gwandara [gwn], 161
Kyang, *alt.* Chin, Asho [csh], 462
Kyango, *alt.* Brokskat [bkk], 357
Kyanton, *alt.* Etkywan [ich], 159
Kyanzi, *dial.* Amba [rwm], 210
Kyato, *alt.* Etkywan [ich], 159
Kyaura, *dial.* Ghale, Southern [ghe], 471
Kyenele [kql], 609
Kyenga [tye], 168, 45
Kyengkha, *alt.* Khengkha [xkf], 323
Kyentu, *alt. dial.* Kpan [kpk], 167
Kyenyemamba, *alt. dial.* Zimba [zmb], 109
Kyenying-Barang, *alt.* Kyenele [kql], 609
Kyerepong, *alt.* Cherepon [cpn], 123
Kyerung [kgy], 474, 338
Kyetho, *alt.* Karen, S'gaw [ksw], 464
Kyi, *alt.* Khasi [kha], 321

Kyibaku, *alt.* Cibak [ckl], 157
Kyirong, *alt.* Kyerung [kgy], 474
Kyo, *dial.* Naga, Lotha [njh], 378
Kyobe, *alt.* Miyobe [soy], 208
Kyode, *alt.* Gikyode [acd], 125
Kyokosi, *alt.* Anufo [cko], 123
Kyon, *dial.* Naga, Lotha [njh], 378
Kyonam, *alt.* Rangkas [rgk], 384
Kyong, *alt.* Naga, Lotha [njh], 378
  dial. Naga, Lotha [njh], 378
Kyongborong, *alt.* Chumburung [ncu], 124
Kyonggido, *alt. dial.* Korean [kor], 448
Kyongsangdo, *dial.* Korean [kor], 448
Kyou, *dial.* Naga, Lotha [njh], 378
Kypchak, *alt. dial.* Uzbek, Northern [uzn], 512
Kyzyl, *dial.* Khakas [kjh], 505, 337
Kyzylbash, *alt. dial.* Balkan Gagauz Turkish [bgx], 563
  dial. Azerbaijani, North [azj], 319
L-Arusha, *alt. dial.* Maasai [mas], 201
La, *alt.* Hlai [lic], 333
  alt. dial. Tai Nüa [tdd], 344
  dial. Wa [wbm], 467
La Chi, *alt.* Lachi [lbt], 524, 338
La Conception, *dial.* Caac [msq], 584
La Concordia, *dial.* Tzotzil, Huixtán [tzu], 277
La Ha, *alt.* Laha [lha], 524
La Ha Ung, *alt.* Laha [lha], 524
La Hu Si, *alt.* Lahu Shi [kds], 524
La Jalca, *dial.* Quechua, Chachapoyas [quk], 290
La Lingvo Internacia, *alt.* Esperanto [epo], 536
La Mesa del Nayar Cora, *dial.* Cora, El Nayar [crn], 262
La Nya, *alt.* Thai, Northern [nod], 517
La-Dang, *alt. dial.* Chru [cje], 522
La-Oang, *alt.* Roglai, Northern [rog], 526
La-Oor, *dial.* Lawa, Western [lcp], 515
Láá Láá Bwamu, *see* Bwamu, Láá Láá [bwj], 50
Laabe, *dial.* Laal [gdm], 82
Laadi [ldi], 41
  alt. Laari [ldi], 88
Laak, *alt. dial.* Nuer [nus], 194
Laal [gdm], 82
  dial. Laal [gdm], 82
La'alua, *alt.* Saaroa [sxr], 512
Laamang, *alt.* Lamang [hia], 168
Laame, *alt.* Gimnime [gmn], 62

  alt. dial. Koma [kmy], 167
Laamoot, *alt.* Omotik [omt], 135
Laany, *alt.* Dani, Western [dnw], 414
Laari [ldi], 88
La'arua, *alt.* Saaroa [sxr], 512
Laba [lau], 400
Labalekan, *alt.* Lembata, West [lmj], 408
Labasa, *alt. dial.* Fijian [fij], 580
Labbu, *alt.* Bai, Central [bca], 326
Labe, *dial.* Tawala [tbo], 627
Label [lbb], 609
Labhani, *alt.* Lambadi [lmn], 372
Labhani Muka, *alt.* Lambadi [lmn], 372
La'bi [lbi], 65
Labir [jku], 168
Labo [mwi], 642
  alt. Labu [lbu], 609
Labourdin, *dial.* Basque, Navarro-Labourdin [bqe], 535
Labrador Eskimo, *dial.* Inuktitut, Eastern Canadian [ike], 238
Labu [lbu], 609
  alt. Laua [luf], 609
  dial. Malay [mly], 436
Labu', *alt.* Labu [lbu], 609
Labu Basap, *alt. dial.* Malay [mly], 436
Labuan, *dial.* Rukai [dru], 512
Labuandiri, *dial.* Pancana [pnp], 432
Labuk, *alt. dial.* Kadazan, Labuk-Kinabatangan [dtb], 457
Labuk Kadazan, *alt.* Kadazan, Labuk-Kinabatangan [dtb], 457
Labuk-Kinabatangan Kadazan, *see* Kadazan, Labuk-Kinabatangan [dtb], 457
Labwor, *dial.* Acholi [ach], 210
Lac, *alt. dial.* Koho [kpm], 524
Lac Seul Ojibwa, *dial.* Ojibwa, Northwestern [ojb], 240
Lacandon [lac], 263
Lacanjá, *dial.* Lacandon [lac], 263
Lach, *alt. dial.* Koho [kpm], 524
  dial. Czech [ces], 533
Lachao-Yolotepec Chatino, *alt.* Chatino, Eastern Highland [cly], 259
Lachengpa, *alt.* Sikkimese [sip], 387
Lachi [lbt], 524, 338
Lachí, *alt.* Lachi [lbt], 524
Lachi, White [lwh], 524
Lachiguiri Zapotec, *see* Zapotec, Lachiguiri [zpa], 278
Lachik, *alt.* Lashi [lsi], 465
Lachikwaw, *alt.* Lashi [lsi], 465, 338
Lachirioag Zapotec, *see* Zapotec, Lachirioag [ztc], 278

Lachiruaj Zapotec, *alt.* Zapotec, Lachirioag [ztc], 278
Lachixío Zapotec, *see* Zapotec, Lachixío [zpl], 278
Lachungpa, *alt.* Sikkimese [sip], 387
Lacid, *alt.* Lashi [lsi], 465
Lacik, *alt.* Lashi [lsi], 465
Lacondê, *alt. dial.* Nambikuára, Northern [mbg], 230
Lactan, *alt.* Ratagnon [btn], 500
 dial. Kalagan [kqe], 497
Ladak, *alt.* Ladakhi [lbj], 372, 338
Ladakhi [lbj], 372, 338
Ladaphi, *alt.* Ladakhi [lbj], 372, 338
Ladhakhi, *alt.* Ladakhi [lbj], 372, 338
Ladi, *alt.* Laadi [ldi], 41
 alt. Laari [ldi], 88
Ladil, *alt.* Lardil [lbz], 573
Ladin [lld], 544
Ladino [lad], 445, 563
 dial. Ladino [lad], 445
Ladwags, *alt.* Ladakhi [lbj], 372, 338
Lae, *alt.* Aribwatsa [laz], 590
Laeko, *alt.* Laeko-Libuat [lkl], 609
 alt. dial. Samba Leko [ndi], 72
Laeko-Libuat [lkl], 609
Laeko-Limbuat, *alt.* Laeko-Libuat [lkl], 609
Laewamba, *alt.* Wampar [lbq], 631
Laewomba, *alt.* Wampar [lbq], 631
Lafana, *alt.* Lelemi [lef], 126
La'fi, *dial.* Fe'fe' [fmp], 61
Lafiit, *alt.* Lopit [lpx], 193
Lafit, *alt.* Lopit [lpx], 193
Lafite, *alt.* Lopit [lpx], 193
Lafofa [laf], 192
 dial. Lafofa [laf], 192
Laganyan, *alt.* Legenyem [lcc], 418
Lagarteiru, *dial.* Fala [fax], 560
Lagawe Ifugao, *dial.* Ifugao, Tuwali [ifk], 495
Lagba, *alt. dial.* Banda, South Central [lnl], 74
Laghman, *dial.* Pashayi, Southeast [psi], 317
Laghmani, *alt.* Parya [paq], 513, 317
Laghu [lgb], 637
Laghuu [lgh], 524
Lagis, *dial.* Buang, Mangga [mmo], 595
Lagoon Chuukese, *alt.* Chuukese [chk], 582
Lagos Pidgin, *dial.* Pidgin, Nigerian [pcm], 173
Lagouane, *alt.* Lagwan [kot], 65, 83
Lagowa, *dial.* Daju, Dar Fur [daj], 189

Lagu, *alt.* Laghu [lgb], 637
Lagubi, *alt.* Mambila, Cameroon [mcu], 66
 alt. Mambila, Nigeria [mzk], 169
Lagume, *dial.* Humene [huf], 602
Laguna, *alt. dial.* Keres, Western [kjq], 303
 dial. Triqui, Chicahuaxtla [trs], 276
Lagunan Murut, *alt. dial.* Tagal Murut [mvv], 458, 395
Lagwan [kot], 65, 83
Lagwane, *alt.* Lagwan [kot], 65, 83
Laha (Indonesia) [lhh], 400
 Laha (Viet Nam) [lha], 524
Laha Serani, *dial.* Teluti [tlt], 404
Lahada, *dial.* Koiari, Grass [kbk], 606
Lahanan [lhn], 460
Lahanda, *alt.* Panjabi, Western [pnb], 487, 383
Lahauli, *alt.* Tinani [lbf], 388, 345
Lahe, *alt.* Aribwatsa [laz], 590
Lahnda, *alt.* Panjabi, Western [pnb], 487, 383
Lahndi, *alt.* Panjabi, Western [pnb], 487, 383
Lahouli, *alt.* Tinani [lbf], 388, 345
Lahta, *alt.* Karen, Lahta [kvt], 464
Lahta Karen, *see* Karen, Lahta [kvt], 464
Lahu [lhu], 338, 451, 465, 515, 524
 alt. Avikam [avi], 91
Lahu Phung, *alt. dial.* Lahu [lhu], 524
Lahu Shi [kds], 451, 338, 465, 515, 524
Lahu Xi, *alt.* Lahu Shi [kds], 338
Lahul Bhoti, *alt.* Stod Bhoti [sbu], 387
Lahul Lohar, *see* Lohar, Lahul [lhl], 372
Lahuli, *alt.* Pattani [lae], 383
 alt. Tinani [lbf], 388
Lahuli of Bunan, *alt.* Gahri [bfu], 361, 332
Lahuli Tinan, *alt.* Tinani [lbf], 345
Lahuna, *alt.* Lahu [lhu], 338, 465, 524
Lahyj, *dial.* Tat, Muslim [ttt], 320
Lai, *alt.* Bolyu [ply], 328
 alt. Chin, Haka [cnh], 463, 321, 357
 alt. Hlai [lic], 333
 alt. Kabalai [kvf], 81
 dial. Gbaya, Northwest [gya], 75, 61
Lai Hawlh, *alt.* Chin, Haka [cnh], 357
Lai Pawi, *alt.* Chin, Haka [cnh], 357
Laia, *dial.* Loko [lok], 183
Laiagam, *dial.* Enga [enq], 598
Laierdila, *alt.* Lardil [lbz], 573

Laimbue [lmx], 65
Laimon, *alt.* Cochimi [coj], 262
Laiso, *alt. dial.* Chin, Falam [flm], 463
Laitokitok, *dial.* Maasai [mas], 134
Laiwomba, *alt.* Wampar [lbq], 631
Laiwonu, *dial.* Pamona [bcx], 432
Laiwui, *dial.* Tolaki [lbw], 433
Laiya, *dial.* Siane [snp], 624
Laiyen, *dial.* Moro [mor], 193
Laiyolo [lji], 430
 dial. Laiyolo [lji], 430
Laizao, *alt. dial.* Chin, Falam [flm], 463
Laizo, *dial.* Anal [anm], 354
 dial. Chin, Falam [flm], 463
Laizo-Shimhrin, *alt. dial.* Chin, Falam [flm], 463
Laji, *alt.* Lachi [lbt], 524, 338
Lajia, *alt.* Lakkia [lbc], 338
Lajolo, *alt. dial.* Laiyolo [lji], 430
Laju, *alt. dial.* Naga, Nocte [njb], 379
Lak [lbe], 555
 alt. Siar-Lak [sjr], 624
Laka (Chad) [lap], 83, 76
 Laka (Nigeria) [lak], 168
 alt. Karang [kzr], 63, 81
 alt. Lakkia [lbc], 338
Lakaalong, *alt.* Dimbong [dii], 60
Lakahia, *alt.* Kamoro [kgq], 416
Lakalai, *alt. dial.* Nakanai [nak], 616
Lakalei [lka], 351
Lakama'di, *dial.* Moru [mgd], 193
Lakatakura-Tika, *alt. dial.* Kunama [kun], 112
Lake, *dial.* Okanagan [oka], 306
Lake Buhi East, *alt.* Agta, Mt. Iraya [atl], 490
Lake Buhi West, *alt.* Agta, Mt. Iriga [agz], 491
Lake Miwok, *see* Miwok, Lake [lmw], 305
Lake of the Woods Ojibwa, *dial.* Ojibwa, Northwestern [ojb], 240
Laket, *dial.* Konomala [koa], 607
Lakha [lkh], 323
Lakher, *alt.* Chin, Mara [mrh], 359, 463
Lakhlokhi, *alt.* Lishán Didán [trg], 445
Lakhota, *alt.* Lakota [lkt], 303, 238
Lak'i, *alt.* Zay [zwa], 120
Laki [lki], 440
 alt. Lak [lbe], 555
 alt. Tolaki [lbw], 433
Lakia, *alt.* Lakkia [lbc], 338
Laking, *dial.* Maru [mhx], 465
Lakiung, *alt. dial.* Makasar [mak], 430
Lakja, *alt.* Lakkia [lbc], 338

Laqi, *alt.* Zay [zwa], 120
Laqua [laq], 338
  alt. Qabiao [laq], 526
Lara, *dial.* Ngambay [sba], 85
Lara' [lra], 460, 394
L'arabe du Tchad, *alt.* Arabic, Chadian Spoken [shu], 78
Laragia [lrg], 573
Laragiya, *alt.* Laragia [lrg], 573
Larakia, *alt.* Laragia [lrg], 573
Larakiya, *alt.* Laragia [lrg], 573
Laramanik, *alt.* Aramanik [aam], 197
Laranchi, *alt.* Laru [lan], 168
Larantuka, *alt. dial.* Lamaholot [slp], 408
  dial. Malay [mly], 436
Laraos, *dial.* Quechua, Yauyos [qux], 292
Larat, *alt.* Fordata [frd], 398
Laravat, *alt.* Larevat [lrv], 642
Larawa, *alt.* Laru [lan], 168
Larbawa, *alt. dial.* Kir-Balar [kkr], 166
Lardil [lbz], 573
Lardill, *alt.* Lardil [lbz], 573
Lare, *dial.* Kanuri, Central [knc], 166, 63, 81, 191
Laredo, *dial.* Dza [jen], 158
Larena, *dial.* Kula [tpg], 408
Larestani, *alt.* Lari [lrl], 440
Larevat [lrv], 642
Lari [lrl], 440
  alt. Laadi [ldi], 41
  alt. Laari [ldi], 88
  dial. Lari [lrl], 440
  dial. Sindhi [snd], 488, 387
Laria, *alt.* Chhattisgarhi [hne], 358
Lariang, *alt. dial.* Sarudu [sdu], 433
Lariim, *alt.* Narim [loh], 194
Larike, *dial.* Larike-Wakasihu [alo], 396
Larike-Wakasihu [alo], 396
Larim, *alt.* Narim [loh], 194
Lariminit, *alt.* Narim [loh], 194
Larimo, *alt.* Narim [loh], 194
Larkye, *alt.* Nubri [kte], 477
Laro [lro], 192
  alt. Iteri [itr], 603
  alt. Laru [lan], 168
  dial. Laro [lro], 192
Larteh [lar], 126
Laru [lan], 168
  alt. Laro [lro], 192
Lasalimu [llm], 430
Lasgerdi [lsa], 440
Lashi [lsi], 465, 338
Lashi-Maru, *alt.* Lashi [lsi], 465
Lashx, *dial.* Svan [sva], 352
Lasi [lss], 487

alt. Lashi [lsi], 465, 338
  dial. Sindhi [snd], 488, 387
Lassa, *dial.* Marghi Central [mrt], 169
Lassi, *alt.* Lasi [lss], 487
Lat, *alt. dial.* Koho [kpm], 524
Latagnun, *alt.* Ratagnon [btn], 500
Latan, *alt.* Ratagnon [btn], 500
Latar, *alt. dial.* Mundari [muw], 376
  dial. Mundari [muw], 321, 476
Late, *alt.* Larteh [lar], 126
Latep, *dial.* Zenag [zeg], 634
Latgalian, *alt. dial.* Latvian [lav], 546
Lati, *alt.* Lachi [lbt], 524, 338
Latin [lat], 566
Latin Anaunico, *alt. dial.* Lombard [lmo], 544
Latin Fiamazzo, *alt. dial.* Lombard [lmo], 544
Latina, *alt.* Latin [lat], 566
Latod, *alt.* Lotud [dtr], 457
Latoma, *alt.* Sumariup [siv], 626
Latooka, *alt.* Otuho [lot], 194
Lattuka, *alt.* Otuho [lot], 194
Latu [ltu], 400
Latud, *alt.* Lotud [dtr], 457
Latuka, *alt.* Otuho [lot], 194
Latuko, *alt.* Otuho [lot], 194
Latundê, *alt. dial.* Nambikuára, Northern [mbg], 230
Latuvi Zapotec, *alt.* Zapotec, Southeastern Ixtlán [zpd], 280
Latvian [lav], 546
Latvian Romani, *dial.* Romani, Baltic [rml], 550, 546
Latvian Sign Language [lsl], 546
Lau [llu], 637
  alt. Laka [lak], 168
  alt. Lauan [llx], 580
  alt. dial. Lau [llu], 637
  alt. dial. Nuer [nus], 194
  dial. Dinka, Southwestern [dik], 190
  dial. Lauan [llx], 580
Laua [luf], 609
Lauan [llx], 580
Lauan-Nonopai, *dial.* Kara [leu], 605
Laube, *alt.* Lavukaleve [lvk], 637
Lauda, *alt. dial.* Otuho [lot], 194
Laudje, *alt.* Lauje [law], 430
Lauisaranga, *alt.* Aruop [lsr], 591
Lauje [law], 430
Laukanu, *alt.* Kela [kcl], 605
Laulabu, *alt.* Yabem [jae], 632
Lauli, *dial.* Wejewa [wew], 410
Laumbe, *alt.* Lavukaleve [lvk], 637
Launa, *alt.* Lahu [lhu], 465, 524
Laungaw, *alt.* Maru [mhx], 465, 340

Laungwaw, *alt.* Maru [mhx], 465, 340
Laura [lur], 408
  dial. Laura [lur], 408
Laurentian [lre], 238
Laurowan, *dial.* Pashayi, Northwest [glh], 317
Lau'u, *alt.* Aruop [lsr], 591
Lauwela, *dial.* Bwaidoka [bwd], 596
Lava, *alt.* Lawa, Western [lcp], 338, 515
Lavangai, *alt.* Tungag [lcm], 628
Lavani, *alt.* Lambadi [lmn], 372
Lavatbura, *alt. dial.* Lavatbura-Lamusong [lbv], 609
Lavatbura-Lamusong [lbv], 609
Lave [brb], 451
  alt. Brao [brb], 325, 522
Laveh, *alt.* Brao [brb], 325, 522
  alt. Lave [brb], 451
Laven [lbo], 451
Lavongai, *alt.* Tungag [lcm], 628
Lavora, *dial.* Wedau [wed], 631
Lavua, *alt.* Lawa, Western [lcp], 338, 515
Lavüa, *alt.* Lawa, Western [lcp], 338, 515
Lavukaleve [lvk], 637
Lawa, *alt.* Bisu [bii], 327
  alt. Nyahkur [cbn], 516
  alt. Ugong [ugo], 518
  dial. Lawangan [lbx], 394
Lawa, Eastern [lwl], 515
Lawa, Western [lcp], 338, 515
Lawangan [lbx], 394
Lawas, *alt. dial.* Lundayeh [lnd], 460
Laweenjru, *alt.* Laven [lbo], 451
Lawele, *alt. dial.* Pancana [pnp], 432
Lawng, *alt.* Maru [mhx], 465, 340
Lawng Hsu, *dial.* Maru [mhx], 465
Lawoi, *alt.* Urak Lawoi' [urk], 518
Lawra Lobi, *alt. dial.* Dagara, Northern [dgi], 50
Lawta, *alt.* Urak Lawoi' [urk], 518
Lawunuia [tgi], 609
Lay, *alt.* Kabalai [kvf], 81
  alt. dial. Gbaya, Northwest [gya], 75, 61
Laya, *dial.* Koho [kpm], 524
  dial. Maguindanao [mdh], 498
Layakha [lya], 323
Layana, *dial.* Guana [gva], 284
Layapo, *dial.* Enga [enq], 598
Laydo, *dial.* Aari [aiz], 112
Laymon-Cochimi, *alt.* Cochimi [coj], 262
Laymonem, *alt.* Cochimi [coj], 262
Layolo, *alt. dial.* Laiyolo [lji], 430
Laz [lzz], 519, 352

Lemusmus, *alt.* Kara [leu], 605
Lemyo, *dial.* Chin, Asho [csh], 462, 321
Lenakel [tnl], 642
Lenape, *alt.* Unami [unm], 309
Lenca [len], 258, 252
Lendu [led], 102, 211
Lendu-Sud, *alt.* Ngiti [niy], 106
Lendumu, *alt.* Ndumu [nmd], 121
Lengadoucian, *alt.* Languedocien [lnc], 537
Lenge, *alt. dial.* Chopi [cce], 147
Lengese, *alt.* Dengese [dez], 99
Lengi, *alt.* Lenje [leh], 214
Lengilu [lgi], 394
Lengkayap, *dial.* Malay [mly], 436
Lengo [lgr], 637
   dial. Lengo [lgr], 637
Lengola [lej], 102
Lengora, *alt.* Lengola [lej], 102
Lengotia, *alt.* Bhili [bhb], 356
Lengua [leg], 284
   alt. Palenquero [pln], 246
Lengua Norte, *alt. dial.* Lengua [leg], 284
Lengua Sur, *alt. dial.* Lengua [leg], 284
Lenguaje de las Manos, *alt.* Mexican Sign Language [mfs], 265
Lenguaje de Signos Mexicano, *alt.* Mexican Sign Language [mfs], 265
Lenguaje Manual Mexicana, *alt.* Mexican Sign Language [mfs], 265
Lengue, *dial.* Chopi [cce], 147
Lengwe, *alt. dial.* Tswa [tsc], 149
Leningitij [lnj], 573
Lenje [leh], 214
   dial. Lenje [leh], 214
Lenji, *alt.* Lenje [leh], 214
Lenkaitahe, *alt.* Salas [sgu], 403
Lenkaran, *dial.* Azerbaijani, North [azj], 319
Lenkau [ler], 609
Lenkoran, *dial.* Azerbaijani, North [azj], 319
   dial. Talysh [tly], 320
Lenni-Lenape, *alt.* Unami [unm], 309
Lente, *dial.* Chin, Falam [flm], 463
Lentex, *dial.* Svan [sva], 352
Lenyima [ldg], 168
Leon, *dial.* Vatrata [vlr], 646
Leonais, *dial.* Breton [bre], 536
Leonese, *dial.* Asturian [ast], 559
Leonidio-Prastos, *alt. dial.* Tsakonian [tsd], 541
Lepcha [lep], 372, 323, 474
Lepki [lpe], 418

Lepo' Kulit, *dial.* Kenyah, Kelinyau [xkl], 394
Lepo Tau Kenya, *alt.* Madang [mqd], 460
Lepo Tau Kenyah, *alt.* Madang [mqd], 460
Lepu Potong, *dial.* Kelabit [kzi], 459
   dial. Lundayeh [lnd], 460
Lepu Tau, *alt.* Madang [mqd], 460
Leqi, *alt.* Lashi [lsi], 465, 338
Lera, *alt. dial.* Rwanda [kin], 178
Lerabain, *alt.* Kui [kvd], 408
Lerabaing, *alt. dial.* Kui [kvd], 408
Lere [gnh], 168
   alt. dial. Kanuri, Central [knc], 166
   dial. Bissa [bib], 49
Lerik, *dial.* Talysh [tly], 320
Leron, *alt. dial.* Wantoat [wnc], 631
Lesa, *alt.* Lese [les], 102
   alt. Sakata [skt], 104
   dial. Benggoi [bgy], 397
Lese [les], 102
Lese Dese, *alt. dial.* Lese [les], 102
Lese Karo, *dial.* Lese [les], 102
Leshon Knaan, *alt.* Knaanic [czk], 533
Leshuooopa, *alt.* Lisu [lis], 339
Lesighu, *alt.* Sighu [sxe], 121
Lesing, *dial.* Lesing-Gelimi [let], 610
Lesing-Atui, *alt.* Lesing-Gelimi [let], 610
Lesing-Gelimi [let], 610
Lesse, *alt.* Lese [les], 102
Lesser Antillean Creole French,
   alt. Dominican Creole French [acf], 250
   alt. Grenadian Creole French [acf], 253
   alt. Saint Lucian Creole French [acf], 294
   alt. Trinidadian Creole French [acf], 296
Lesser Kabardian, *alt. dial.* Kabardian [kbd], 554
Lesser Kabyle, *dial.* Kabyle [kab], 39
Lesuo, *alt.* Lisu [lis], 339
Lete, *alt.* Larteh [lar], 126
   dial. Tswana [tsn], 48
Letemboi [nms], 642
Leti (Cameroon) [leo], 65
   Leti (Indonesia) [lti], 400
Letia, *dial.* Lefa [lfa], 65
Letri Lgona, *alt.* Luang [lex], 401
Letsi, *alt.* Lashi [lsi], 465, 338
Letta-Batulappa-Kassa, *alt. dial.* Enrekang [ptt], 429
Lettisch, *pej. alt.* Latvian [lav], 546
Lettish, *pej. alt.* Latvian [lav], 546

Lettish Romani, *alt. dial.* Romani, Baltic [rml], 550, 546
Letuama, *alt.* Tanimuca-Retuarã [tnc], 247
Letuhama, *alt.* Tanimuca-Retuarã [tnc], 247
Letzburgisch, *alt.* Luxembourgeois [ltz], 546, 531, 539
Lëtzebuergesch, *alt.* Luxembourgeois [ltz], 546, 539
Leuangiua, *alt.* Ontong Java [ojv], 637
Levai, *alt. dial.* Hruso [hru], 364
Levantine, *alt.* Arabic, South Levantine Spoken [ajp], 444
Levantine Arabic, *alt.* Arabic, North Levantine Spoken [apc], 510, 453
   alt. Arabic, South Levantine Spoken [ajp], 448
Levantine Bedawi Arabic, *alt.* Arabic, Eastern Egyptian Bedawi Spoken [avl], 110
Levantine Bedawi Spoken Arabic, *see* Arabic, Eastern Egyptian Bedawi Spoken [avl], 448, 489, 510
Levei, *dial.* Khehek [tlx], 606
Levei-Drehet, *alt.* Khehek [tlx], 606
Levei-Ndrehet, *alt.* Khehek [tlx], 606
Levuka [lvu], 408
   dial. Levuka [lvu], 408
Lew, *dial.* Musey [mse], 85
Lewa, *dial.* Kambera [xbr], 407
Lewo [lww], 643
   alt. Lamenu [lmu], 642
Lewo Eleng [lwe], 408
Lewokukun, *alt.* Levuka [lvu], 408
Lewolaga, *alt. dial.* Lamaholot [slp], 408
Lewotobi [lwt], 408
Lewuka, *alt.* Levuka [lvu], 408
Leya, *dial.* Tonga [toi], 215, 217
Leyigha [ayi], 168
Leyte, *dial.* Cebuano [ceb], 493
Lezghi, *alt.* Lezgi [lez], 555, 320
Lezgi [lez], 555, 320
Lezgian, *alt.* Lezgi [lez], 555, 320
Lezgin, *alt.* Lezgi [lez], 555, 320
Lgalige, *alt.* Koalib [kib], 192
Lgona, *alt.* Luang [lex], 401
Lhao Vo, *alt.* Maru [mhx], 465, 340
Lhasa, *alt. dial.* Tibetan, Central [bod], 344
Lhengwe, *alt. dial.* Tswa [tsc], 149
Lho, *dial.* Nubri [kte], 477
Lho-Pa, *alt.* Luoba, Boga'er [adi], 339
   alt. Luoba, Yidu [clk], 339
Lhoba, *alt.* Adi [adi], 353

alt. Luoba, Boga'er [adi], 339

alt. Luoba, Yidu [clk], 339

Lhobikha, *alt.* Lhokpu [lhp], 323

Lhoket, *alt.* Lhomi [lhm], 474, 338, 372

Lhokpu [lhp], 323

Lhomi [lhm], 474, 338, 372

Lhoskad, *alt.* Dzongkha [dzo], 361

Lhota, *alt.* Naga, Lotha [njh], 378

Lhotshammikha, *alt.* Nepali [nep], 323

Lhukonzo, *alt.* Konjo [koo], 211

Li, *alt.* Hlai [lic], 333

alt. Lisu [lis], 339

alt. Mungaka [mhk], 68

Li Emteban, *alt. dial.* Buru [mhs], 397

Li Enyorot, *alt.* Lisela [lcl], 400

Li Hua, *alt. dial.* Chinese, Min Nan [nan], 330

Li-Hsaw, *alt.* Lisu [lis], 339, 465, 515

Li-Kari-Li, *alt.* Kari [kbj], 101

Li-Li-Sha, *alt.* Paiwan [pwn], 511

Li-Shaw, *alt.* Lisu [lis], 339, 465, 515

Lia Fehan, *alt. dial.* Tetun [tet], 410, 351

Lia Foho, *alt. dial.* Tetun [tet], 410, 351

Liabuka, *alt.* Liabuku [lix], 430

Liabuku [lix], 430

Liae, *dial.* Sabu [hvn], 409

Liah Bing, *dial.* Modang [mxd], 394

Liambata, *alt.* Salas [sgu], 403

Liambata-Kobi, *alt.* Liana-Seti [ste], 400

Liana, *alt.* Liana-Seti [ste], 400

Liana-Seti [ste], 400

Lianan, *alt.* Liana-Seti [ste], 400

Liang, *alt.* Riang [ril], 343

dial. Tulehu [tlu], 405

Liang Sek, *alt.* Riang [ril], 467

Lianghe, *dial.* Achang [acn], 326

Liangmai, *alt.* Koireng [nkd], 368

alt. Naga, Liangmai [njn], 378

Liangmai Naga, *see* Naga, Liangmai [njn], 378

Liangmei, *alt.* Koireng [nkd], 368

alt. Naga, Liangmai [njn], 378

Liangshan Nosu, *alt.* Yi, Sichuan [iii], 348

Liangshan Yi, *alt.* Yi, Sichuan [iii], 348

Lianhua, *dial.* She [shx], 343

Lianshan, *dial.* Zhuang, Northern [ccx], 349

Liara, *alt. dial.* Sakao [sku], 645

Liaro, *dial.* Kissi, Northern [kqs], 129, 183

Lias, *dial.* Finallig [bkb], 494

Libaali, *alt.* Bali [bcp], 96

Libbo, *alt.* Kaan [ldl], 165

Libbung, *dial.* Kelabit [kzi], 459

Libenge, *alt.* Bwa [bww], 99

Liberia Kpelle, *see* Kpelle, Liberia [xpe], 138

Liberian English [lir], 138

Liberian Pidgin English, *alt.* Liberian English [lir], 138

Liberian Standard English, *dial.* English [eng], 137

Libido [liq], 116

Libie, *alt.* Elip [ekm], 60

Libindja, *alt. dial.* Ngombe [ngc], 106

Libinja, *alt.* Libinza [liz], 102

alt. dial. Ngombe [ngc], 106

Libinza [liz], 102

Libisegahun, *dial.* Loko [lok], 183

Libo, *alt.* Kaan [ldl], 165

Libolo, *alt.* Bolo [blv], 40

Libon, *dial.* Bicolano, Albay [bhk], 493

Libua, *alt.* Bwa [bww], 99

Libwali, *alt.* Bwa [bww], 99

Libyan Sign Language [lbs], 139

Libyan Spoken Arabic, *see* Arabic, Libyan Spoken [ayl], 139, 151

Libyan Spoken Arabic, *alt.* Arabic, Western Egyptian Bedawi Spoken [ayl], 110

Libyan Vernacular Arabic, *alt.* Arabic, Libyan Spoken [ayl], 139, 151

Licela, *alt. dial.* Lisela [lcl], 400

Licella, *alt. dial.* Lisela [lcl], 400

Lichabool-Nalong, *dial.* Konkomba [xon], 126

Lichiang, *dial.* Naxi [nbf], 341

Liduma, *alt.* Duma [dma], 120

Liem Chau, *alt.* Chinese, Yue [yue], 522

Liet Enjorot, *alt.* Lisela [lcl], 400

Lietuvi, *alt.* Lithuanian [lit], 546

Lietuviskai, *alt.* Lithuanian [lit], 546

Lifoma, *alt.* Foma [fom], 99

Lifou, *alt.* Dehu [dhv], 584

Lifu, *alt.* Dehu [dhv], 584

Ligao, *dial.* Bicolano, Albay [bhk], 493

Ligbeln, *dial.* Konkomba [xon], 126

Ligbi [lig], 126, 94

Ligenza [lgz], 102

Liggo, *alt. dial.* Bari [bfa], 188

Ligili, *alt.* Lijili [mgi], 168

Ligo, *dial.* Bari [bfa], 188

Ligri, *dial.* Jarawa [jar], 165

Ligure, *alt.* Ligurian [lij], 544, 537, 548

Liguri, *alt.* Logorik [liu], 192

dial. Logorik [liu], 192

Ligurian [lij], 544, 537, 548

Líguru, *alt.* Ligurian [lij], 544

Ligwi, *alt.* Ligbi [lig], 126, 94

Lihen, *dial.* Dera [kbv], 597

Lihir [lih], 610

Lijiang, *alt. dial.* Naxi [nbf], 341

Lijili [mgi], 168

Lika [lik], 102

Liká, *alt. dial.* Lika [lik], 102

Likanantaí, *alt.* Kunza [kuz], 242

Likango, *alt.* Kango [kty], 100

alt. Kango [kzy], 100

Likanu, *alt.* Kanu [khx], 100

Likaw, *dial.* Bomboma [bws], 98

Likelo, *alt.* Kele [khy], 101

Likes-Utsia, *dial.* Mandjak [mfv], 131, 122, 181

Liki [lio], 418

alt. Sobei [sob], 423

Likila [lie], 103

Likó, *dial.* Lika [lik], 102

Likoka, *dial.* Lobala [loq], 103

Likolo, *dial.* Poke [pof], 107

Likoonli, *dial.* Konkomba [xon], 126

Likouala, *alt.* Likwala [kwc], 89

Likoya, *alt.* Gyele [gyi], 62, 111

Likpakpaln, *alt.* Konkomba [xon], 126

Likpe, *alt.* Sekpele [lip], 127

Likuba [kxx], 89

Likum [lib], 610

Likupang, *dial.* Tonsea [txs], 434

Likwala [kwc], 89

Lila, *dial.* C'lela [dri], 157

Lilau [lll], 610

Liliali, *alt. dial.* Kayeli [kzl], 399

Liliga, *alt. dial.* Lega-Shabunda [lea], 102

Liliká, *alt. dial.* Lika [lik], 102

Lilikó, *dial.* Lika [lik], 102

Lilima, *dial.* Kalanga [kck], 216, 47

Lillois, *alt. dial.* Picard [pcd], 537

Lillooet [lil], 238

Lima, *alt. dial.* Asilulu [asl], 396

dial. Lamba [lam], 214

Limarahing, *dial.* Blagar [beu], 406

Limassa [bme], 76

Limba, *alt.* Iwaidja [ibd], 571

alt. Malimba [mzd], 66

Limba, East [lma], 129, 183

Limba, West-Central [lia], 183

Limbang, *alt. dial.* Lundayeh [lnd], 460

Limbede, *alt.* Mbere [mdt], 89, 121

Limbo, *alt.* Limbu [lif], 372

Limbom, *alt.* Limbum [lmp], 65

Limboto, *alt. dial.* Gorontalo [gor], 429
Limbotto, *alt. dial.* Gorontalo [gor], 429
Limbu [lif], 474, 372
Limbudza, *alt.* Budza [bja], 98
Limbum [lmp], 65, 169
Limbur, *alt. dial.* Kamang [woi], 407
Limburgisch [lim], 548, 531, 539
Limburgs, *dial.* Vlaams [vls], 531
Limburgs Plat, *alt.* Limburgisch [lim], 548, 531, 539
Limera, *alt.* Ili'uun [ilu], 399
Limi, *alt.* Nyaturu [rim], 203
Limi Yi, *see* Yi, Limi [ylm], 347
Limilngan [lmc], 573
Limima, *alt. dial.* Kalanga [kck], 216
Limkhim, *alt.* Lingkhim [lii], 474
Limkow, *alt.* Lingao [onb], 338
Limón Creole English [jam], 249
Limonkpel, *dial.* Konkomba [xon], 126
Limoro, *alt.* Lemoro [ldj], 168
Limorro, *alt.* Lemoro [ldj], 168
Limos Kalinga, *see* Kalinga, Limos [kmk], 497
Limos-Liwan Kalinga, *alt.* Kalinga, Limos [kmk], 497
Limousin [lms], 537
Limpesa, *dial.* Lusengo [lse], 103
Linafiel, *dial.* Konkomba [xon], 126
Linangmanli, *dial.* Ntcham [bud], 209
Linaw-Qauqaul, *dial.* Basay [byq], 511
Lincha, *alt. dial.* Quechua, Yauyos [qux], 292
Lincheng, *dial.* Lingao [onb], 338
Linda, *dial.* Banda-Bambari [liy], 75
Lindau, *alt.* Nyindrou [lid], 619
Lindiri, *alt.* Nungu [rin], 171
Lindja, *dial.* Shi [shr], 107
Lindrou, *alt.* Nyindrou [lid], 619
Lindu [klw], 430
Linduan, *alt.* Lindu [klw], 430
Lingaayat, *dial.* Gowli [gok], 363
Lingala [lin], 103, 89
Lingao [onb], 338
Lingao Proper-Dengmai, *alt. dial.* Lingao [onb], 338
Lingarak [lgk], 643
Lingbe, *alt.* Ngbee [jgb], 106
Lingbee, *alt.* Ngbee [jgb], 106
Linggau, *alt.* Lembak [liw], 436
Lingi, *alt.* Bwela [bwl], 99
Lingkabau Sugut, *dial.* Tombonuwo [txa], 458
Lingkhim [lii], 474
Lingkhim Rai, *alt.* Lingkhim [lii], 474

Lingombe, *alt.* Ngombe [ngc], 106
Lingonda, *dial.* Bomboma [bws], 98
Lingotes, *alt.* Ilongot [ilk], 495
Lingua Franca [pml], 209
Língua Geral, *alt.* Nhengatu [yrl], 230
Lingua Gestual Portuguesa, *alt.* Portuguese Sign Language [psr], 551
Lingua Italiana Dei Segni, *alt.* Italian Sign Language [ise], 544
Linkabau, *alt. dial.* Tombonuwo [txa], 458
Linkhim, *alt.* Lingkhim [lii], 474
Linkow, *alt.* Lingao [onb], 338
Linngithig, *alt.* Leningitij [lnj], 573
Linngithigh, *alt.* Leningitij [lnj], 573
Lino, *alt.* Bomwali [bmw], 88, 59
Lintang [lnt], 436
Linyali, *alt.* Nyali [nlj], 106
Linyanga-le, *alt.* Nyanga-li [nyc], 106
Linyeli, *alt. dial.* Pande [bkj], 77
Linzeli, *alt. dial.* Pande [bkj], 77
Li'o [ljl], 408
  dial. Rao [rao], 622
Lio, *alt.* Li'o [ljl], 408
Lionese, *alt.* Li'o [ljl], 408
Lip'a, *alt.* Lisu [lis], 339
Lipan Apache, *see* Apache, Lipan [apl], 298
Lipanja, *alt. dial.* Mabaale [mmz], 103
Lipe, *alt.* Kunza [kuz], 242
Lipis, *alt. dial.* Semai [sea], 455
Lipkawa, *alt.* Kariya [kil], 166
  alt. Mburku [bbt], 170
Lipo [lpo], 339
Lipoto, *dial.* Lusengo [lse], 103
Liptaakoore, *dial.* Fulfulde, Northeastern Burkina Faso [fuh], 51
Lipuke, *dial.* Lachi [lbt], 338
Lipulio, *alt.* Lachi [lbt], 524, 338
Lipuliongtco, *dial.* Lachi [lbt], 338
Lipupi, *dial.* Lachi [lbt], 524, 338
Lipupõ, *alt.* Lachi, White [lwh], 524
Liputcio, *dial.* Lachi [lbt], 338
Lipute, *dial.* Lachi [lbt], 338
Liputiõ, *dial.* Lachi [lbt], 524, 338
Lir, *alt.* Lihir [lih], 610
Lir Talo, *alt.* Talur [ilw], 404
Lirang, *alt. dial.* Talaud [tld], 433
Lirong, *dial.* Kenyah, Sebob [sib], 459
Liru, *alt. dial.* Ersu [ers], 332
Lis, *alt.* Bagirmi [bmi], 78
  alt. Italian Sign Language [ise], 544
Lis Ma Run, *alt. dial.* Ron [cla], 174
Lisabata, *alt.* Lisabata-Nuniali [lcs], 400

Lisabata-Nuniali [lcs], 400
Lisabata-Timur, *dial.* Lisabata-Nuniali [lcs], 400
Lisaw, *alt.* Lisu [lis], 339, 465, 515
Lisbon, *dial.* Portuguese Sign Language [psr], 551
Lisela [lcl], 400
  dial. Lisela [lcl], 400
Lish, *alt. dial.* Moinba [mob], 376
Lishan Didan, *alt.* Barzani Jewish Neo-Aramaic [bjf], 444
Lishán Didán [trg], 445
Lishan Dideni, *alt.* Barzani Jewish Neo-Aramaic [bjf], 444
Lishan Hozaye, *alt.* Lishana Deni [lsd], 445
Lishan Hudaye, *alt.* Lishana Deni [lsd], 445
Lishana Atiga, *alt.* Syriac [syc], 519
Lishana Aturaya, *alt.* Assyrian Neo-Aramaic [aii], 442, 510
Lishana Axni, *alt.* Hulaulá [huy], 445
Lishana Deni [lsd], 445
Lishana Didán, *alt.* Lishanid Noshan [aij], 445
Lishana Kaldaya, *alt.* Chaldean Neo-Aramaic [cld], 443
Lishana Noshan, *alt.* Hulaulá [huy], 445
Lishanán, *alt.* Lishán Didán [trg], 445
Lishanid Nash Didán, *alt.* Lishán Didán [trg], 445
Lishanid Noshan [aij], 445
Lìsháù, *alt.* Shau [sqh], 174
Lishu, *alt.* Lisu [lis], 339
Lisi, *alt.* Bagirmi [bmi], 78
  alt. dial. Naba [mne], 85
Liso, *alt.* Lisu [lis], 339, 515
Lisongo, *alt.* Mbati [mdn], 77
Lissam, *dial.* Kutep [kub], 167, 64
Lissi, *alt.* Lese [les], 102
Lissongo, *alt.* Mbati [mdn], 77
Lissu, *alt.* Lisu [lis], 339
Lisu [lis], 339, 372, 465, 515
  dial. Ersu [ers], 332
Lisum, *dial.* Kayan, Rejang [ree], 459
Litauische, *alt.* Lithuanian [lit], 546
Litembo, *alt.* Tembo [tmv], 108
Literi Lagona, *alt.* Luang [lex], 401
Litewski, *alt.* Lithuanian [lit], 546
Lithiro, *alt.* Tira [tic], 196
Lithuanian [lit], 546
Lithuanian Romani, *dial.* Romani, Baltic [rml], 546
Lithuanian Sign Language [lls], 546
Litime, *dial.* Akposo [kpo], 123

Long Nawan, *dial.* Kenyah, Kayan River [knh], 393
Long Pata, *dial.* Berawan [lod], 459
Long Pokun, *dial.* Kenyah, Sebob [sib], 459
Long Puyungan, *dial.* Kenyah, Bahau River [bwv], 393
Long Semiang, *dial.* Kayan, Murik [mxr], 459
Long Terawan, *dial.* Berawan [lod], 459
Long Tutoh, *dial.* Kiput [kyi], 460
Long Wai, *alt. dial.* Modang [mxd], 394
Long Wat, *dial.* Kenyah, Tutoh [ttw], 460
Long We, *alt. dial.* Modang [mxd], 394
Long-Haired Lachi, *alt. dial.* Lachi [lbt], 524, 338
Longa, *alt.* Amara [aie], 589
alt. Longto [wok], 65
Longana, *dial.* Ambae, East [omb], 640
Longandu, *alt.* Ngando [nxd], 105
Longarim, *alt.* Narim [loh], 194
Longbia, *dial.* Kenyah, Kayan River [knh], 393
Longbo, *alt.* Longto [wok], 65
Longching, *dial.* Naga, Konyak [nbe], 378
Longchuan, *dial.* Achang [acn], 326
Longdu, *dial.* Chinese, Min Nan [nan], 330
Longe-Longe, *dial.* Shi [shr], 107
Longgu [lgu], 637
Longich, *alt.* Mbulungish [mbv], 130
Longkhai, *dial.* Naga, Konyak [nbe], 378
Longkhi, *alt. dial.* Naga, Tase [nst], 380
Longla, *dial.* Naga, Ao [njo], 377
Longmein, *dial.* Naga, Konyak [nbe], 378
Longmi, *dial.* Rawang [raw], 466
Longnan, *alt. dial.* Chinese, Hakka [hak], 329
Longo, *dial.* Mongo-Nkundu [lol], 104
dial. Zinza [zin], 206
Longolo, *dial.* Oroko [bdu], 71
Longombe, *dial.* Mongo-Nkundu [lol], 104
Longorban, *alt. dial.* Moro [mor], 193
Longoro, *dial.* Deg [mzw], 124
Longphi, *dial.* Naga, Tase [nst], 380
Longri, *dial.* Naga, Tase [nst], 466

Longshan, *dial.* Tujia, Northern [tji], 345
Longto [wok], 65
Longuda [lnu], 169
Longueinga, *alt. dial.* Mengen [mee], 613
Longura, *alt.* Longuda [lnu], 169
Longwa, *dial.* Naga, Konyak [nbe], 378
Longxi, *dial.* Qiang, Southern [qxs], 342
Lonio, *alt.* Loniu [los], 610
Loniu [los], 610
Lonkundo, *alt. dial.* Mongo-Nkundu [lol], 104
Lonkundu, *alt. dial.* Mongo-Nkundu [lol], 104
Lontes, *dial.* Hakö [hao], 601
Lontjong, *alt.* Loncong [lce], 436
Lonto, *alt.* Longto [wok], 65
alt. dial. Chumburung [ncu], 124
Lontomba, *alt.* Ntomba [nto], 106
Lonwolwol [crc], 643
Lonzo [lnz], 103
Loo [ldo], 169
alt. Noy [noy], 86
Loocnon, *alt.* Inonhan [loc], 495
Loodiya, *alt.* Dadiya [dbd], 157
Loofaa, *dial.* Dadiya [dbd], 157
Loofiyo, *dial.* Dadiya [dbd], 157
Looknon, *alt.* Inonhan [loc], 495
dial. Inonhan [loc], 495
Looma, *alt.* Loma [lom], 138
Loombo, *alt.* Ombo [oml], 106
Lop, *dial.* Uyghur [uig], 346
Lopa [lop], 169
alt. Lowa [loy], 474
Lopar, *alt.* Saami, Skolt [sms], 535, 556
Lopawa, *alt.* Lopa [lop], 169
Lophomi, *alt.* Naga, Sangtam [nsa], 379
Lopi [lov], 465
Lopid, *alt.* Lopit [lpx], 193
Lopit [lpx], 193
Loppit, *alt.* Lopit [lpx], 193
Loquia, *alt.* Lokoya [lky], 192
Lor, *alt.* Khlor [llo], 450
alt. Luri, Southern [luz], 440
Lorabada, *alt.* Kaki Ae [tbd], 604
Lorang [lrn], 401
Lorang Bukit, *alt.* Bisaya, Brunei [bsb], 324
alt. Bisaya, Sarawak [bsd], 459
Lord Howe, *alt.* Ontong Java [ojv], 637
Lorediakarkar [lnn], 643
Lorenzo, *alt.* Yanesha' [ame], 293
Loretano, *alt. dial.* Trinitario [trn], 224

Loreto, *dial.* Trinitario [trn], 224
Loreto-Ucayali Spanish, *see* Spanish, Loreto-Ucayali [spq], 293
Lorhon, *alt.* Téén [lor], 95, 55
Lori, *alt.* Bakhtiari [bqi], 438
alt. Luri, Northern [lrc], 440
alt. Luri, Southern [luz], 440
dial. Jur Modo [bex], 191
Lori-ye Jonubi, *alt.* Luri, Southern [luz], 440
Lori-ye Khaveri, *alt.* Bakhtiari [bqi], 438
Loridja, *alt.* Pintupi-Luritja [piu], 576
Lorma, *alt.* Loma [lom], 138
Loron, *alt.* Téén [lor], 95, 55
Lorraine, *dial.* French [fra], 536, 531
Lorung, Northern [lbr], 474
Lorung, Southern [lrr], 474
Lorwama, *dial.* Otuho [lot], 194
Los Reyes Metzontla Popoloca, *alt.* Popoloca, Mezontla [pbe], 273
Losa, *dial.* Nakanai [nak], 616
Losaka, *alt. dial.* Nkutu [nkw], 106
Losengo, *alt.* Lusengo [lse], 103
Losi, *dial.* Dehu [dhv], 584
Losiara, *dial.* Teop [tio], 627
Loso, *alt. dial.* Nakanai [nak], 616
Losso, *alt.* Lama [las], 208, 45, 126
alt. Nawdm [nmz], 209
Losu, *alt.* Nawdm [nmz], 209
Lotanga, *dial.* Oroko [bdu], 71
Lote [uvl], 610
Lotha, *alt.* Naga, Lotha [njh], 378
Lotha Naga, *see* Naga, Lotha [njh], 378
Lotora, *dial.* Maewo, Central [mwo], 643
Lotsu-Piri, *alt.* Tso [ldp], 176
Lotud [dtr], 457
Lotuho, *alt.* Otuho [lot], 194
Lotuka, *alt.* Otuho [lot], 194
Lotuko, *alt.* Otuho [lot], 194
Lotuni, *alt. dial.* Balochi, Southern [bcc], 483, 438, 482, 520
Lotuxo, *alt.* Otuho [lot], 194
Lou [loj], 610
alt. Kaki Ae [tbd], 604
alt. Torricelli [tei], 628
dial. Nuer [nus], 194
Loucheux, *alt.* Gwich'in [gwi], 237
alt. dial. Gwich'in [gwi], 237, 301
Loudo, *alt. dial.* Otuho [lot], 194
Lougaw, *dial.* Muyuw [myw], 616
Louisiana Creole French [lou], 304
Loulou, *alt. dial.* Giziga, South [giz], 62

Lukep, *alt.* Arop-Lukep [apr], 590
  alt. dial. Arop-Lukep [apr], 590
Lukete, *alt.* Kete [kcv], 101
Lukha, *alt.* Logol [lof], 192
Lukhai, *alt.* Mizo [lus], 376
Luko, *alt.* Lokaa [yaz], 169
Lukolwe, *dial.* Nkoya [nka], 214
Lukpa [dop], 45, 208
Lukshi, *alt. dial.* Zeem [zua], 178
  dial. Dass [dot], 157
Lukumel, *dial.* Parbate, Western
  [kjl], 477
Lul, *dial.* Anuak [anu], 113
Lulamogi, *alt. dial.* Soga [xog], 212
Lule, *alt.* Saami, Lule [smj], 561, 550
Lule Saami, *see* Saami, Lule
  [smj], 561, 550
Luleke, *dial.* Tsonga [tso], 186
Luli, *dial.* Domari [rmt], 438, 554
Luluba, *alt.* Olu'bo [lul], 194
Lulubo, *alt.* Olu'bo [lul], 194
Lulumo, *alt.* Olulumo-Ikom
  [iko], 172
Luluyia, *alt.* Luyia [luy], 134, 211
Lum Lao, *alt.* Lao [lao], 445
Lumadale, *alt.* Lambadi [lmn], 372
Lumaete, *dial.* Kayeli [kzl], 399
Lumaiti, *alt. dial.* Kayeli [kzl], 399
Luman, *alt. dial.* Tira [tic], 196
Lumara, *alt. dial.* Kayeli [kzl], 399
Lumasaba, *alt.* Masaba [myx], 211
Lumba-Yakkha [luu], 475
Lumbee [lmz], 304
Lumbi, *alt.* Lombi [lmi], 103
Lumbis, *alt. dial.* Tagal Murut [mvv],
  458, 395
Lumbu [lup], 120, 89
  alt. Limbu [lif], 372
  dial. Ila [ilb], 213
Lumbwa, *alt.* Maasai [mas], 201
Lumenya, *alt. dial.* Nyole [nuj], 212
Lummi, *dial.* Salish, Straits [str], 241,
  307
Lumun [lmd], 193
Lun Bawang, *alt.* Lundayeh
  [lnd], 324
  alt. dial. Lundayeh [lnd], 394
  dial. Lundayeh [lnd], 460
Lun Daya, *alt.* Lundayeh [lnd], 394,
  460
Lun Dayah, *alt.* Lundayeh [lnd], 394,
  460
  dial. Lundayeh [lnd], 460
Lun Daye, *alt.* Lundayeh [lnd], 394,
  324, 460
  dial. Lundayeh [lnd], 394
Lun Dayeh, *alt.* Lundayeh [lnd], 460
Lun Dayoh, *alt.* Lundayeh
  [lnd], 394, 460
Lun Lod, *alt.* Lundayeh [lnd], 460

Luna [luj], 103
Lunan, *dial.* Kenyah, Western
  [xky], 460
Lunanakha [luk], 323
Lund, *dial.* Mandjak [mfv], 131, 122,
  181
Lunda [lun], 214, 41, 103
  alt. Mbundu [kmb], 41
Lunda Kalunda, *dial.* Lunda
  [lun], 103
Lunda Kambove, *alt.* Ruund
  [rnd], 107
  dial. Lunda [lun], 103
Lunda Ndembu, *dial.* Lunda
  [lun], 103
Lunda-Kamboro, *alt.* Ruund [rnd],
  107
Lundaya, *alt.* Lundayeh [lnd], 394,
  460
Lundayeh [lnd], 394, 324, 460
Lundu, *alt.* Biatah [bth], 392
Lundur, *alt. dial.* Polci [plj], 173
Lundwe, *dial.* Ila [ilb], 213
Lungalunga, *alt.* Minigir
  [vmg], 614
Lungchang, *dial.* Naga, Tase
  [nst], 380
Lungga [lga], 637
Lungmi, *alt. dial.* Rawang [raw], 466
Lungri, *dial.* Naga, Tase [nst], 380
Lungu, *alt.* Idun [ldb], 163
  alt. dial. Mambwe-Lungu [mgr], 214,
  201
Lungulu, *alt. dial.* Nyakyusa-Ngonde
  [nyy], 203
Lungwa, *alt.* Rungwa [rnw], 204
Lun'gwiye, *alt.* Principense
  [pre], 179
Lunigiano, *dial.* Emiliano-
  Romagnolo [eml], 543
Luntu, *dial.* Salampasu [slx], 107
Luntumba, *alt.* Ntomba [nto], 106
Lunube Mado, *dial.* Dano
  [aso], 596
Lunyaneka, *alt.* Nyaneka [nyk], 41
Lunyole, *alt.* Nyole [nuj], 212
  alt. Nyore [nyd], 135
Lunyore, *alt.* Nyore [nyd], 135
Luo ([luw], 65
  Luo (Kenya and Tanzania) [luo], 134,
  201
Luoba, *alt.* Adi [adi], 353
Luoba, Boga'er [adi], 339
Luoba, Yidu [clk], 339
Luobohe Miao, *alt.* Hmong,
  Luopohe [hml], 334
Luobu, *alt. dial.* Uyghur [uig], 346
Luofu, *dial.* She [shx], 343
Luohua-Hayan-Baoxian, *alt. dial.*
  Hlai [lic], 333

Luopohe Hmong, *see* Hmong,
  Luopohe [hml], 334
Luoravetlan, *alt.* Chukot [ckt], 504
Luoshao, *dial.* Chinese, Xiang
  [hsn], 331
Luowu, *alt.* Yi, Awu [yiu], 347
Lupa, *alt.* Lopa [lop], 169
Luppa, *alt.* Naga, Tangkhul
  [nmf], 380
Luqa, *alt.* Lungga [lga], 637
Luquan Naso, *dial.* Yi, Wuding-
  Luquan [ywq], 348
Lur, *alt.* Alur [alz], 96, 210
  alt. Luri, Southern [luz], 440
Luragoli, *alt.* Logooli [rag], 134
Lurang, *dial.* Aputai [apx], 396
Luri [ldd], 169
  alt. Alur [alz], 96, 210
  alt. Bakhtiari [bqi], 438
  alt. Luri, Northern [lrc], 440
  alt. Luri, Southern [luz], 440
  dial. Kurdish, Southern [sdh], 440,
  443
Luri, Northern [lrc], 440
Luri, Southern [luz], 440
Luru, *alt.* Lara' [lra], 460, 394
Luruty-Tapuya, *alt.* Yurutí
  [yui], 249, 234
Lus, *dial.* Mfumte [nfu], 67
Lusa, *alt. dial.* Saya [say], 174
Lusaamia, *alt. dial.* Luyia [luy], 134
Lusabi, *alt. dial.* Nyole [nuj], 212
Lusago, *alt.* Mizo [lus], 376
Lusai, *alt.* Mizo [lus], 376, 321, 466
Lusamia, *alt. dial.* Luyia [luy], 134
Lusatian, *alt.* Sorbian, Lower
  [dsb], 539
Lusei, *alt.* Mizo [lus], 376
Lusenge, *dial.* Lega-Mwenga
  [lgm], 102
Lusengo [lse], 103
Lusengo Poto, *dial.* Lusengo
  [lse], 103
Lusernese Cimbrian, *dial.*
  Cimbrian [cim], 543
Lushai, *alt.* Mizo [lus], 376, 321, 466
Lushangi, *dial.* Nkoya [nka], 214
Lushei, *alt.* Mizo [lus], 376, 321,
  466
Lushi, *dial.* Zeem [zua], 178
Lushisa, *alt. dial.* Luyia [luy], 134
Lushnu, *alt.* Svan [sva], 352
Lushootseed [lut], 304
Lusi [khl], 610
Lusinga, *alt.* Singa [sgm], 212
Lusitano-Romani, *alt. dial.* Caló
  [rmr], 559, 551
Lusoga, *alt.* Soga [xog], 212
Lusong, *alt. dial.* Penan, Western
  [pne], 460, 325

Lusonge, *alt.* Songe [sop], 108
Lusu, *alt.* Lisu [lis], 339
Lutangan, *dial.* Balangingi
  [sse], 492
Lutango, *alt. dial.* Balangingi
  [sse], 492
Lutaos, *alt.* Bajau, Indonesian
  [bdl], 427
Lutayaos, *alt.* Bajau, Indonesian
  [bdl], 427
Lutchaz, *alt.* Luchazi [lch], 41
Lutenga, *alt. dial.* Soga [xog], 212
Lutha, *alt.* Naga, Lotha [njh], 378
Luti, *alt.* Domari [rmt], 438
Lutien, *dial.* Naxi [nbf], 341
Lutise, *dial.* Dogosé [dos], 50
Lutkuhwar, *alt.* Yidgha [ydg], 489
Luto, *alt. dial.* Lutos [ndy], 76, 83
Lutos [ndy], 76, 83
  dial. Lutos [ndy], 76
Lutshase, *alt.* Luchazi [lch], 41, 214
Lutu, *alt. dial.* Fijian [fij], 580
Lutze, *alt.* Nung [nun], 466, 341
Lutzu, *alt.* Nung [nun], 466, 341
Luu, *alt.* Khmu [kjg], 515
Luunda, *alt.* Ruund [rnd], 107, 41
  dial. Bemba [bem], 213
Luva, *alt.* Luba-Kasai [lua], 103
Luvale [lue], 214, 41
Luvuma, *dial.* Ganda [lug], 210
Luvure, *alt.* Vute [vut], 73
Luwa, *alt.* Lawa, Western [lcp], 338,
  515
  dial. Huba [hbb], 162
Luwangan, *alt.* Lawangan [lbx], 394
Luwati [luv], 483
Luwesa, *alt. dial.* Nyole [nuj], 212
Luwo [lwo], 193
Luwu, *alt.* Tae' [rob], 428
  alt. Yi, Awu [yiu], 347
  dial. Bugis [bug], 428
Luwu', *alt.* Toala' [tlz], 433
  alt. dial. Bugis [bug], 428
Luwunda, *alt.* Ruund [rnd], 107
Luxage, *alt.* Luchazi [lch], 41, 214
Luxembourgeois [ltz], 546, 531,
  537, 539
Luxembourgish, *alt.*
  Luxembourgeois [ltz], 546
Luxemburgian, *alt.*
  Luxembourgeois [ltz], 546, 539
Luxemburgish, *alt.*
  Luxembourgeois [ltz], 546
Luxi, *dial.* Achang [acn], 326
Luya-Ginam-Mamusi, *dial.* Pinai-
  Hagahai [pnn], 622
Luyana [lyn], 214, 41
Luyi, *alt.* Luyana [lyn], 214, 41
Luyia [luy], 134, 211
Luzimba, *alt.* Zemba [dhm], 151

Lüzü, *alt. dial.* Ersu [ers], 332
Lvova, *dial.* Santa Cruz [stc], 638
L'wa, *alt.* Lawa, Western [lcp], 338,
  515
Lwalu [lwa], 103
Lwamba, *alt.* Amba [rwm], 210
Lwena, *alt.* Luvale [lue], 214, 41
Lwimbe, *alt.* Luimbi [lum], 41
Lwimbi, *alt.* Luimbi [lum], 41
Lwindja, *alt. dial.* Shi [shr], 107
Lwisukha, *alt. dial.* Idakho-Isukha-
  Tiriki [ida], 133
Lwo, *alt.* Acholi [ach], 210, 187
  alt. Lango [laj], 211
  alt. Luwo [lwo], 193
Lwoo, *alt.* Acholi [ach], 210
  alt. Lango [laj], 211
Lwowa, *alt. dial.* Santa Cruz
  [stc], 638
Lxloukxle, *alt.* ‖Xegwi [xeg], 187
Ly, *alt.* Lü [khb], 339
Ly Ha, *dial.* Hung [hnu], 523
Lyaasa, *alt.* Yasa [yko], 73
Lyangmay, *alt.* Naga, Liangmai
  [njn], 378
Lyase, *alt.* Gwamhi-Wuri [bga], 161
Lyase-Ne, *alt.* Gwamhi-Wuri
  [bga], 161
Lyassa, *alt.* Yasa [yko], 111, 122
Lyélé [lee], 52
Lyen-Lyem, *alt. dial.* Chin, Falam
  [flm], 463
Lyengmai, *alt.* Koireng [nkd], 368
  alt. Naga, Liangmai [njn], 378
Lyente, *alt. dial.* Chin, Falam
  [flm], 463
Lying, *alt. dial.* Psikye [kvj], 173
Lyngngam, *dial.* Khasi [kha], 367,
  321
Lyo, *dial.* Mak [mkg], 339
Lyonnais, *dial.* Franco-Provençal
  [frp], 536
Lyons Sign Language [lsg], 537
Lyudic, *alt.* Ludian [lud], 555
Lyudikovian, *alt.* Ludian [lud], 555
Lyy, *dial.* Khmu [kjg], 451
Ma (Democratic Republic of Congo)
  [msj], 103
  Ma (Papua New Guinea) [mjn], 610
  alt. Kamo [kcq], 166
  alt. Maa [cma], 524
  alt. dial. Naba [mne], 85
  dial. Binahari [bxz], 593
Ma Buwal, *alt.* Buwal [bhs], 59
Ma Dala, *alt. dial.* Maba [mde], 83
Ma Krung, *alt.* Maa [cma], 524
Ma Ku, *alt.* Mlabri [mra], 516, 451
Ma Ndaba, *alt. dial.* Maba [mde], 83
Ma Ngan, *alt.* Maa [cma], 524
Ma To, *alt.* Maa [cma], 524

Ma Xop, *alt.* Maa [cma], 524
Ma-Gavar, *alt.* Gavar [gou], 61
Ma'a, *alt.* Mbugu [mhd], 202
Maa [cma], 524
  alt. Maasai [mas], 201
  alt. Mann [mev], 139, 130
Maa', *alt.* Maa [cma], 524
Maaban, *alt.* Mabaan [mfz], 193
Maacina, *alt.* Fulfulde, Maasina
  [ffm], 125
Ma'adi, *alt.* Ma'di [mhi], 211, 193
Ma'aging, *dial.* Kayan, Rejang
  [ree], 459
Maaka [mew], 169
Maaloula, *alt. dial.* Western Neo-
  Aramaic [amw], 510
Maalula, *alt.* Western Neo-Aramaic
  [amw], 510
  alt. dial. Western Neo-Aramaic
  [amw], 510
Maangella, *alt.* Madngele [zml], 573
Ma'anjan, *alt.* Ma'anyan [mhy], 394
Maanyak Dayak, *alt.* Ma'anyan
  [mhy], 394
Ma'anyan [mhy], 394
Maaq, *alt.* Maa [cma], 524
Maaro, *alt.* Oirata [oia], 402
Maasa, *alt.* Yasa [yko], 73, 111, 122
Ma'asae, *alt.* Makasae [mkz], 351
Maasai [mas], 134, 201
Maasina Fulfulde, *see* Fulfulde,
  Maasina [ffm], 143, 125
Maay [ymm], 184
Maba (Chad) [mde], 83
  Maba (Indonesia) [mqa], 401
Mabaa, *alt.* Maba [mde], 83
Mabaale [mmz], 103
Mabaan [mfz], 193
Mabahn, *dial.* Bassa [bsq], 137
Mabak, *alt.* Maba [mde], 83
Mabaka, *alt.* Kalinga, Mabaka Valley
  [kkg], 497
Mabaka Itneg, *alt.* Kalinga, Mabaka
  Valley [kkg], 497
Mabaka Valley Kalinga, *see*
  Kalinga, Mabaka Valley [kkg], 497
Mabale, *alt.* Mabaale [mmz], 103
Mabang, *alt.* Maba [mde], 83
Mabas, *alt. dial.* Vemgo-Mabas
  [vem], 177
  dial. Vemgo-Mabas [vem], 73
Mabe, *alt.* Mahei [mja], 465
Mabea, *alt.* Ngumba [nmg], 111
  alt. dial. Ngumba [nmg], 70
Mabendi, *alt.* Bendi [bct], 97
Mabeni, *alt.* Bendi [bct], 97
Mabi, *alt.* Ngumba [nmg], 111
  dial. Ngumba [nmg], 70
Mabiha, *alt. dial.* Makonde
  [kde], 148

Mabila, *alt.* Mambila, Nigeria [mzk], 169
Mabire [muj], 83
Mabiti, *alt.* Lika [lik], 102
Mablei, *dial.* Kalumpang [kli], 429
Ma'bo, *alt.* Ngbaka Ma'bo [nbm], 77, 89, 105
Mabo-Barkul, *alt.* Bo-Rukul [mae], 155
Mabo-Barukul, *alt.* Bo-Rukul [mae], 155
Mabodese, *alt. dial.* Mayogo [mdm], 104
Maboko, *dial.* Dzando [dzn], 99
Mabozo, *alt. dial.* Mayogo [mdm], 104
Mabri, *alt.* Mlabri [mra], 516, 451
Mabue, *alt.* Sateré-Mawé [mav], 231
Mabuiag, *alt.* Kala Lagaw Ya [mwp], 571
Maca [mca], 285
  alt. Makhuwa-Marrevone [xmc], 147
Macá, *alt.* Maca [mca], 285
Macaense, *alt.* Macanese [mzs], 339
Macaguaje [mcl], 246
Macaguán [mbn], 246
Macaguane, *alt.* Macaguán [mbn], 246
Macaísta, *dial.* Pidgin, Timor [tvy], 351
Macanese [mzs], 339
Macanipa, *alt.* Omagua [omg], 289, 231
Macao Creole Portuguese, *alt.* Macanese [mzs], 339
Macassai, *alt.* Makasae [mkz], 351
Macassar, *alt.* Makasar [mak], 430
Macassarese, *alt.* Makasar [mak], 430
Macau Cantonese, *alt. dial.* Chinese, Yue [yue], 331
Macedo Romanian, *see* Romanian, Macedo [rup], 541, 529, 532, 547, 552, 557
Macedo-Rumanian, *alt.* Romanian, Macedo [rup], 541, 529, 532, 547
Macedonian [mkd], 547, 529, 532
  alt. Slavic [mkd], 541
  dial. Turkish [tur], 547
Macedonian Gagauz, *dial.* Balkan Gagauz Turkish [bgx], 547
Macedonian Slavic, *alt.* Macedonian [mkd], 547, 529
  alt. Slavic [mkd], 541
Macedonian Turkish, *dial.* Turkish [tur], 532
Machambe, *alt.* Machame [jmc], 193
Machame [jmc], 193
Macharia, *dial.* Sindhi [snd], 488

Mache, *alt.* Bodo [brx], 469
Machicui, *alt.* Toba-Maskoy [tmf], 285
Machiguenga [mcb], 288
Machinere [mpd], 229
Machinga [mvw], 201
  dial. Yao [yao], 149
Macho, *alt.* Gurani [hac], 443
  alt. dial. Hawrami [hac], 439
Machongrr, *alt.* Naga, Chang [nbc], 377
Machoto, *alt.* Itonama [ito], 223
Machvanmcko, *alt. dial.* Romani, Vlax [rmy], 551
Machvano, *alt. dial.* Romani, Vlax [rmy], 531
  dial. Romani, Vlax [rmy], 551
Machwaya, *alt. dial.* Romani, Vlax [rmy], 531
Maci, *alt. dial.* Iceve-Maci [bec], 63
  dial. Iceve-Maci [bec], 163
Macina, *alt.* Fulfulde, Maasina [ffm], 143
Mackenzian, *alt.* Slavey, North [scs], 241
  alt. Slavey, South [xsl], 241
Mackenzie Delta Inupiatun, *alt. dial.* Inupiatun, North Alaskan [esi], 238
Mackenzie Inupiatun, *alt. dial.* Inupiatun, North Alaskan [esi], 238
Macleod Ganj, *dial.* Gaddi [gbk], 361
Maco [wpc], 312
Maconde, *alt.* Makonde [kde], 148
Macu de Cubeo, *alt.* Cacua [cbv], 244
Macu de Desano, *alt.* Cacua [cbv], 244
Macu de Guanano, *alt.* Cacua [cbv], 244
Macú de Tucano, *pej. alt.* Hupdë [jup], 227, 246
Macú-Paraná Cacua, *dial.* Cacua [cbv], 244
Macua, *alt.* Makhuwa [vmw], 147
Macue, *alt.* Makwe [ymk], 148
Macuna [myy], 246, 229
Macuni, *alt.* Maxakalí [mbl], 230
Macuráp, *alt.* Makuráp [mpu], 229
Macurapi, *alt.* Makuráp [mpu], 229
Macushi [mbc], 229, 257, 312
Macusi, *alt.* Macushi [mbc], 229, 257
Macussi, *alt.* Macushi [mbc], 257
Maczsa, *alt.* Nukak Makú [mbr], 246
Mad, *alt.* Kumarbhag Paharia [kmj], 370
  alt. Mal Paharia [mkb], 373
Mada (Cameroon) [mxu], 65
  Mada (Nigeria) [mda], 169

Mada Dutse, *alt.* Eggon [ego], 158
Mada Eggon, *alt.* Eggon [ego], 158
Madagascar Sign Language [mzc], 140
Madaglashti, *alt.* Farsi, Eastern [prs], 484
Madahaddi, *dial.* Godwari [gdx], 362
Madai Gang, *dial.* Bishnupriya [bpy], 357
Madak [mmx], 610
Madaka, *dial.* Bauchi [bsf], 155
Madang [mqd], 460
Madani, *dial.* Arabic, South Levantine Spoken [ajp], 448, 444, 490
Madar, *dial.* Tewa [twe], 410
Madara, *alt.* Mandara [tbf], 612
Madarrpa, *dial.* Gupapuyngu [guf], 571
Madda, *alt.* Mada [mda], 169
Madeán, *alt. dial.* Quechua, Yauyos [qux], 292
Madean-Viñac, *dial.* Quechua, Yauyos [qux], 292
Madeggusu, *alt.* Simbo [sbb], 638
Madeira-Azores, *dial.* Portuguese [por], 551
Mademang, *alt. dial.* Wersing [kvw], 410
Maden [xmx], 419
Madenassa, *alt. dial.* Shua [shg], 48
Madenasse, *alt. dial.* Shua [shg], 48
Mader, *alt.* Mal Paharia [mkb], 373
Madhavpur, *dial.* Jerung [jee], 472
Madhesi, *dial.* Bhojpuri [bho], 356
Madhura, *alt.* Madura [mad], 392, 509
Madhya Pradesh Marathi, *alt.* Varhadi-Nagpuri [vah], 389
Ma'di [mhi], 211, 193
  alt. Kaliko [kbo], 100
  alt. Morokodo [mgc], 193
Madi [grg], 610
  alt. Ma [msj], 103
  alt. Maria [mrr], 375
  alt. Saluan, Coastal [loe], 432
  alt. dial. Bari [bfa], 188
Ma'di, Southern [snm], 211
Madia, *alt.* Maria [mrr], 375
Madidwana, *alt.* Buruwai [asi], 413
Madihá, *alt.* Culina [cul], 226, 287
Madiin, *alt.* Komo [xom], 192, 116
Madija, *alt.* Culina [cul], 226, 287
Madik, *alt. dial.* Abun [kgr], 410
Madimadoko, *dial.* Mayogo [mdm], 104
Madingo, *alt.* Maninkakan, Eastern [emk], 183

Madinnisane, *alt. dial.* Shua [shg], 48

Madipia, *alt. dial.* Mayogo [mdm], 104

Ma'diti, *alt.* Ma'di [mhi], 211, 193

Maditi, *alt.* Kaliko [kbo], 100

Madiya, *alt.* Maria [mrr], 375
alt. Maria, Dandami [daq], 375

Madja Ngai, *alt. dial.* Sar [mwm], 86

Madjedje, *alt. dial.* Mayogo [mdm], 104

Madjingay, *alt. dial.* Sar [mwm], 86

Madjingaye, *alt. dial.* Sar [mwm], 86

Madka-Kinwat, *dial.* Kolami, Northwestern [kfb], 369

Madngela, *alt.* Madngele [zml], 573

Madngele [zml], 573

Mado, *dial.* Baruga [bjz], 592

Madoi Gang, *dial.* Bishnupriya [bpy], 321

Madole, *alt.* Modole [mqo], 402

Madrasi, *dial.* Tamil [tam], 388

Madrassi, *alt.* Kannada [kan], 366

Ma'du, *dial.* Morokodo [mgc], 193

Madu, *alt.* Enets, Tundra [enh], 504

Madube, *dial.* Marghi Central [mrt], 169

Madukayang Kalinga, *see* Kalinga, Madukayang [kmd], 497

Madungore, *alt.* Assangori [sjg], 78
alt. Sungor [sjg], 195

Madura [mad], 392, 509

Madurese, *alt.* Madura [mad], 392, 509

Maduri, *alt.* Baga Manduri [bmd], 128

Madutara, *alt.* Kokata [ktd], 572

Maduwonga, *alt.* Kokata [ktd], 572

Madyay, *dial.* Yidiny [yii], 579

Madyo, *alt.* Ma [msj], 103

Madzarin, *dial.* Fali [fli], 159

Mae [mme], 643
alt. Emae [mmw], 641
dial. Enga [enq], 598
dial. Jina [jia], 63

Mae Ping, *dial.* Karen, Pwo Northern [pww], 514

Mae Sarieng, *dial.* Karen, Pwo Northern [pww], 514

Mae-Morae, *alt.* Maii [mmm], 643

Maeng, *alt. dial.* Mengen [mee], 613

Maeng Itneg, *see* Itneg, Maeng [itt], 496

Maerkisch-Brandenburgisch, *alt. dial.* Saxon, Low [nds], 539

Maevo, *alt.* Maewo, Central [mwo], 643

Maewo, Central [mwo], 643

Mafa [maf], 65, 169
dial. Mafa [maf], 169

Mafea [mkv], 643

Mafilau, *alt.* Maii [mmm], 643

Mafindo, *alt. dial.* Kono [kno], 183

Mafoor, *alt.* Biak [bhw], 412

Mafoorsch, *alt.* Biak [bhw], 412

Mafufu, *alt.* Fuyug [fuy], 599

Mag-Anchi Ayta, *see* Ayta, Mag-Anchi [sgb], 492

Mag-Anchi Sambal, *alt.* Ayta, Mag-Anchi [sgb], 492

Mag-Indi Ayta, *see* Ayta, Mag-Indi [blx], 492

Mag-Indi Sambal, *alt.* Ayta, Mag-Indi [blx], 492

Maga, *alt.* Maaka [mew], 169
dial. Rukai [dru], 512

Magabara, *alt.* Doga [dgg], 597

Magadhi, *alt.* Magahi [mag], 373

Magadige, *alt.* Marti Ke [zmg], 574

Magahat [mtw], 498

Magahi [mag], 373

Magam, *dial.* Ambrym, North [mmg], 640

Magang, *alt. dial.* Geji [gji], 160

Magar, *alt.* Magar, Western [mrd], 475

Magar Nuwakot, *alt.* Magar, Western [mrd], 475

Magar, Eastern [mgp], 475, 373

Magar, Western [mrd], 475

Magara, *dial.* Nzanyi [nja], 171

Magari, *alt.* Magar, Eastern [mgp], 475, 373
alt. Magar, Western [mrd], 475

Magarkura, *alt.* Magar, Eastern [mgp], 373

Magati Gair, *alt.* Marti Ke [zmg], 574

Magati-Ge, *alt.* Marti Ke [zmg], 574

Magaya, *alt.* Magahi [mag], 373

Magbai, *alt. dial.* Mayogo [mdm], 104

Magbiambo, *dial.* Loko [lok], 183

Magdalena Peñasco Mixtec, *see* Mixtec, Magdalena Peñasco [xtm], 267

Mage, *alt. dial.* Naba [mne], 85

Magh, *alt.* Arakanese [mhv], 462
pej. alt. Arakanese [mhv], 320, 354

Magha, *alt.* Maaka [mew], 169

Maghai, *alt.* Magahi [mag], 373

Maghaya, *alt.* Magahi [mag], 373

Mághdì [gmd], 169

Maghi, *alt.* Arakanese [mhv], 462
pej. alt. Arakanese [mhv], 320, 354

Maghori, *alt.* Magahi [mag], 373

Maghrebi Arabic, *alt.* Arabic, Moroccan Spoken [ary], 146

alt. Arabic, Western Egyptian Bedawi Spoken [ayl], 110

Maghribi Colloquial Arabic, *alt.* Arabic, Moroccan Spoken [ary], 146

Magi, *alt.* Magahi [mag], 373
alt. Mailu [mgu], 610

Magindanaon, *alt.* Maguindanao [mdh], 498

Magindanaw, *alt.* Maguindanao [mdh], 498

Magingo, *alt.* Ngindo [nnq], 202

Magirona, *alt.* Matsés [mcf], 288

Magobineng, *dial.* Kâte [kmg], 605

Magodhi, *alt.* Magahi [mag], 373

Magodi, *alt. dial.* Tumbuka [tum], 215

Magodro, *alt. dial.* Fijian, Western [wyy], 580

Magoma [gmx], 201

Magongo, *alt. dial.* Oko-Eni-Osayen [oks], 172

Magori [zgr], 610

Magpet Manobo, *dial.* Manobo, Obo [obo], 499

Magra Ki Boli, *dial.* Bhili [bhb], 356

Magu, *alt.* Mvanip [mcj], 170

Maguindanao [mdh], 498

Magüta, *alt.* Ticuna [tca], 233

Magwaram. Maagwaram, *alt. dial.* Bade [bde], 154

Magyar, *alt.* Hungarian [hun], 542, 530, 551, 557, 558, 558, 564

Magyar Jelnyelv, *alt.* Hungarian Sign Language [hsh], 542

Mah, *alt.* Mann [mev], 139, 130

Mah Meri, *alt.* Besisi [mhe], 454

Maha, *alt.* Maaka [mew], 169

Mahaa, *dial.* Budu [buu], 98

Mahaga, *alt.* Bughotu [bgt], 635

Mahairi, *alt.* Omaha-Ponca [oma], 306

Mahakam Busang, *dial.* Kayan, Busang [bfg], 393

Mahakam Kenya, *alt.* Kenyah, Mahakam [xkm], 394

Mahakam Kenyah, *see* Kenyah, Mahakam [xkm], 394

Mahakam Kenyah, *dial.* Kenyah, Mahakam [xkm], 394

Mahakulung, *dial.* Kulung [kle], 473

Mahalhamadani, *dial.* Farsi, Western [pes], 439

Mahali [mjx], 373
alt. dial. Santali [sat], 386
dial. Luri, Northern [lrc], 440
dial. Santali [sat], 322

Mahanji, *dial.* Kinga [zga], 200

Maharashtra, *alt.* Marathi [mar], 374

Maharashtra Lamani, *dial.*
  Lambadi [lmn], 372
Maharathi, *alt.* Marathi [mar], 374
Mahari, *alt.* Halbi [hlb], 363
  dial. Konkani [knn], 369
  dial. Varhadi-Nagpuri [vah], 389
Maharra, *alt. dial.* Makhuwa
  [vmw], 147
Mahas, *alt.* Nobiin [fia], 110
  dial. Nobiin [fia], 194
Mahas-Fiadidja, *alt.* Nobiin
  [fia], 194, 110
Mahas-Fiyadikkya, *alt.* Nobiin
  [fia], 194
Mahasi, *alt. dial.* Nobiin [fia], 194
Mahass, *alt. dial.* Nobiin [fia], 194
Mahasu Pahari, *see* Pahari, Mahasu
  [bfz], 382
Mahasui, *alt.* Pahari, Mahasu
  [bfz], 382
Mahe, *alt.* Mahei [mja], 465
Mahei [mja], 465
Mahi, *alt.* Gbe, Maxi [mxl], 44, 207
Mahican [mjy], 304
Mahili, *alt.* Mahali [mjx], 373
  alt. dial. Santali [sat], 386
Mahinaku, *alt.* Mehináku
  [mmh], 230
Mahl, *alt.* Maldivian [div], 461, 374
Mahle, *alt.* Mahali [mjx], 373
  alt. dial. Santali [sat], 322
Mahli, *alt.* Mahali [mjx], 373
  alt. dial. Santali [sat], 386
Mahongwe [mhb], 120
Mahottari, *dial.* Tharu, Kochila
  [thq], 481
Mahou [mxx], 94
Mahoua, *alt.* Mawa [mcw], 84
Mahouka, *dial.* Mahou [mxx], 94
Mahri, *alt.* Mehri [gdq], 528, 449,
  483
Mahsudi, *alt.* Pashto, Central
  [pst], 488
Mahu, *alt.* Mahou [mxx], 94
Mahuan, *alt.* Tugun [tzn], 405
  dial. Tugun [tzn], 405
Mahuayana, *alt.* Mapidian
  [mpw], 229
  alt. Mawayana [mzx], 257
Mahum, *alt.* Ghomálá' [bbj], 62
Mahwa, *alt.* Mawa [mcw], 84
Mai, *alt.* Emae [mmw], 641
  alt. Siliput [mkc], 624
  alt. dial. Bola [bnp], 594
  alt. dial. Enga [enq], 598
Mai Brat [ayz], 419
Mai Ja, *alt.* Orejón [ore], 289
Mai-Hea-Ri, *alt.* Akoye [miw], 588
Maia [sks], 610
Maiabare, *dial.* Sewa Bay [sew], 624

Maiadom, *alt.* Maiadomu [mzz], 610
Maiadomu [mzz], 610
Maiak, *dial.* Burun [bdi], 189
Maiani [tnh], 610
Maibrat, *alt.* Mai Brat [ayz], 419
Maidu, Northeast [nmu], 304
Maidu, Northwest [mjd], 304
Maidu, Valley [vmv], 304
Maiduan, *alt.* Maidu, Northwest
  [mjd], 304
Maiduguri, *dial.* Kanuri, Central
  [knc], 63, 191
Maigo, *alt.* Mayogo [mdm], 104
Maiha, *dial.* Nzanyi [nja], 171
Maihiri, *alt.* Akoye [miw], 588
Maii [mmm], 643
Maikel, *alt.* Naga, Mao [nbi], 378
Maiko, *alt.* Mayogo [mdm], 104
Maikoti Kham, *alt.* Parbate,
  Western [kjl], 477
Mailang, *alt.* Ngaing [nnf], 618
Mailu [mgu], 610
Maima, *alt. dial.* Jamamadí [jaa], 227
Maimai, *alt.* Siliput [mkc], 624
Maimaka, *dial.* Mai Brat [ayz], 419
Maimbie, *alt.* Yidiny [yii], 579
Main Island, *alt. dial.* Ramoaaina
  [rai], 622
Maina, *alt.* Achuar-Shiwiar
  [acu], 285, 250
Maina-Kizhi, *alt. dial.* Altai,
  Southern [alt], 503
Maindo [cwb], 147
  dial. Chuwabu [chw], 147
Mainfränkisch [vmf], 539
Maïngao, *dial.* Laka [lap], 83
Maingtha, *alt.* Achang [acn], 326
  dial. Achang [acn], 456
Mainland Frisian, *alt. dial.* Frisian,
  Northern [frr], 538
Mainoke, *alt. dial.* Simeku
  [smz], 624
Mainoki, *dial.* Simeku [smz], 624
Mainypilgino, *dial.* Kerek [krk], 505
Maio-Yesan, *alt.* Yessan-Mayo
  [yss], 633
Maiongong, *alt.* Maquiritari
  [mch], 312
Maiopitian, *alt.* Mapidian
  [mpw], 229, 257
Maipua, *alt.* Purari [iar], 622
Mair, *alt.* Kohistani, Indus [mvy], 486
Mairasi [zrs], 419
Mairiri, *alt.* Mariri [mqi], 402
Maisan, *alt.* Maisin [mbq], 610
Maisawiet, *dial.* Mai Brat [ayz], 419
Maisefa, *dial.* Mai Brat [ayz], 419
Maisin [mbq], 610
  dial. Maisin [mbq], 610
Maitaria, *dial.* Rabha [rah], 384

Maite, *alt.* Mai Brat [ayz], 419
  dial. Mai Brat [ayz], 419
Maithili [mai], 373, 475
Maitili, *alt.* Maithili [mai], 373, 475
Maitli, *alt.* Maithili [mai], 373, 475
Maitoria, *alt. dial.* Rabha [rah], 384
Maitsi, *alt. dial.* Maquiritari
  [mch], 229
Maituri, *alt. dial.* Rabha [rah], 384
Maiwa (Indonesia) [wmm], 430
  Maiwa (Papua New Guinea)
  [mti], 611
  dial. Maiwa [mti], 611
Maiwala [mum], 611
Maiyã, *alt.* Kohistani, Indus
  [mvy], 486
Maiyach, *alt.* Karon Dori [kgw], 416
Maiyah, *dial.* Mai Brat [ayz], 419
Maiyon, *alt.* Kohistani, Indus
  [mvy], 486
Majak, *alt.* Mandjak [mfv], 181
Majang [mpe], 116
Majanjiro, *alt.* Majang [mpe], 116
Majbrat, *alt.* Mai Brat [ayz], 419
Maje, *alt. dial.* Kuna, San Blas
  [cuk], 283
Majene, *dial.* Mandar [mdr], 431
Majera [xmj], 65, 83
  dial. Majera [xmj], 65, 83
Majh-Kumaiya, *dial.* Garhwali
  [gbm], 360
Majhi [mjz], 475, 373
  dial. Panjabi, Eastern [pan], 383
Majhi-Korwa, *dial.* Korwa [kfp],
  370
Majhvar, *alt.* Majhwar [mmj], 373
Majhwar [mmj], 373
Maji, *alt.* Dizi [mdx], 114
Majiahua, *alt.* Chinese, Hakka
  [hak], 329
Majinda, *alt. dial.* Cinda-Regi-Tiyal
  [cdr], 157
Majingai, *dial.* Sar [mwm], 86
Majinngay, *alt. dial.* Sar
  [mwm], 86
Majna-Pil'ginskij, *alt. dial.* Kerek
  [krk], 505
Majubim, *alt.* Paranawát [paf], 231
Majugu, *alt.* Mayogo [mdm], 104
Majukayong, *alt.* Kalinga,
  Madukayang [kmd], 497
Majuruna, *alt.* Matsés [mcf], 288
Majuu, *alt.* Ngbee [jgb], 106
Mak (China) [mkg], 339
  Mak (Nigeria) [pbl], 169
  dial. Mak [mkg], 339
Mak'á, *alt.* Maca [mca], 285
Maka, *alt.* Byep [mkk], 59
  alt. Maaka [mew], 169
  alt. Maca [mca], 285

Malaccan, *alt.* Malaccan Creole Portuguese [mcm], 454, 509

Malaccan Creole Malay [ccm], 454

Malaccan Creole Portuguese [mcm], 454, 509

Malachini, *alt.* Pokomo, Lower [poj], 135

Malagasy [plt], 87

Malagasy, Antankarana [xmv], 140

Malagasy, Bara [bhr], 140

Malagasy, Masikoro [msh], 140

Malagasy, Northern Betsimisaraka [bmm], 140

Malagasy, Plateau [plt], 140

Malagasy, Sakalava [skg], 140

Malagasy, Southern Betsimisaraka [bjq], 140

Malagasy, Tandroy-Mahafaly [tdx], 140

Malagasy, Tanosy [txy], 140

Malagasy, Tsimihety [xmw], 140

Malagheti, *dial.* Talise [tlr], 638

Malagmalag, *alt.* Mullukmulluk [mpb], 574

Malahoi, *alt.* Dohoi [otd], 393

Malai, *dial.* Mutu [tuc], 616

Malai Arayan, *alt.* Malaryan [mjq], 374

Malai Paliyar, *alt.* Paliyan [pcf], 382

Malai Vedan, *alt.* Malavedan [mjr], 374

Malaikuravan, *alt.* Malankuravan [mjo], 373

Malak-Malak, *alt.* Mullukmulluk [mpb], 574

Malakanagiri Koya, *dial.* Koya [kff], 370

Malakhel [mld], 316

Malakka Besisi, *dial.* Besisi [mhe], 454

Malakkuravan, *alt.* Malankuravan [mjo], 373

Malakote [mlk], 134

Malal, *dial.* Themne [tem], 184

Malala, *alt.* Mala [ped], 611

Malalamai [mmt], 611

Malalulu, *dial.* Pokomo, Upper [pkb], 135

Malamauda, *alt.* Nete [net], 618

Malamba, *dial.* Budu [buu], 98

Malampashi, *alt.* Kanikkaran [kev], 366

Malamuni, *alt. dial.* Enga [enq], 598

Malang, *alt.* Madang [mqd], 460
alt. Maleng [pkt], 451, 524
dial. Maleng [pkt], 451

Malang-Pasuruan, *dial.* Javanese [jav], 391

Malanga, *dial.* Maba [mde], 83

Malangke-Ussu, *alt. dial.* Bugis [bug], 428

Malango [mln], 637

Malankudi, *alt.* Vishavan [vis], 390

Malankuravan [mjo], 373

Malapandaram [mjp], 373

Malapantaram, *alt.* Malapandaram [mjp], 373

Malaqueiro, *alt.* Malaccan Creole Portuguese [mcm], 454

Malaquenho, *alt.* Malaccan Creole Portuguese [mcm], 454

Malaquense, *alt.* Malaccan Creole Portuguese [mcm], 454

Malaquês, *alt.* Malaccan Creole Portuguese [mcm], 454

Malarkuti, *alt.* Vishavan [vis], 390

Malaryan [mjq], 374

Malas [mkr], 611

Malasanga [mqz], 611
dial. Malasanga [mqz], 611

Malatia, *alt. dial.* Armenian [hye], 318

Malatri, *alt.* Sauria Paharia [mjt], 386

Malatya, *dial.* Armenian [hye], 318

Malaueg, *alt. dial.* Itawit [itv], 496

Malaumanda, *alt.* Nete [net], 618

Malavedan [mjr], 374

Malavetan, *alt.* Malavedan [mjr], 374

Malavi, *alt.* Malvi [mup], 374

Malaweg, *dial.* Itawit [itv], 496

Malawi, *alt. dial.* Nyanja [nya], 140, 215

Malawi Lomwe, *see* Lomwe, Malawi [lon], 140

Malawi Sena, *see* Sena, Malawi [swk], 140

Malay [mly], 455, 324, 436, 509, 516
dial. Ati [atk], 491

Malay Talk, *alt.* Broome Pearling Lugger Pidgin [bpl], 569

Malay, Ambonese [abs], 401

Malay, Baba [mbf], 509, 455

Malay, Bacanese [btj], 401

Malay, Balinese [mhp], 392

Malay, Banda [bpq], 401

Malay, Berau [bve], 394

Malay, Bukit [bvu], 394

Malay, Cocos Islands [coa], 457, 573

Malay, Jambi [jax], 436

Malay, Kedah [meo], 455

Malay, Kota Bangun Kutai [mqg], 394

Malay, Kupang [mkn], 408

Malay, Makassar [mfp], 431

Malay, Manado [xmm], 431

Malay, North Moluccan [max], 401

Malay, Pattani [mfa], 516

Malay, Sabah [msi], 457

Malay, Satun [meo], 516

Malay, Tenggarong Kutai [vkt], 394

Malaya Tamil, *dial.* Tamil [tam], 388

Malayadiars, *dial.* Malankuravan [mjo], 373

Malayal, *alt.* Malayalam [mal], 509

Malayalam [mal], 374, 509
dial. Malayalam [mal], 374

Malayalam Muthuvan, *alt. dial.* Muthuvan [muv], 377

Malayalani, *alt.* Malayalam [mal], 374, 509

Malayali, *alt.* Malayalam [mal], 374

Malayarayan, *alt.* Malaryan [mjq], 374

Malayarayar, *alt.* Malaryan [mjq], 374

Malayic Dayak [xdy], 394

Malaynon [mlz], 498

Malayo [mbp], 246

Malayo-Portuguese, *alt.* Malaccan Creole Portuguese [mcm], 454

Malaysian Creole Portuguese, *alt.* Malaccan Creole Portuguese [mcm], 454, 509

Malaysian Minangkabau, *alt.* Negeri Sembilan Malay [zmi], 455

Malaysian Sign Language [xml], 455

Malayu, *alt.* Malay [mly], 455, 436

Malayu Ambon, *alt.* Malay, Ambonese [abs], 401

Malba, *alt.* Kalarko [kba], 572

Malba Birifor, *see* Birifor, Malba [bfo], 49

Malba-Birifor, *alt.* Birifor, Malba [bfo], 49

Malbe, *alt.* Malgbe [mxf], 65, 83

Maldavaca, *alt.* Baré [bae], 311
alt. Mandahuaca [mht], 312, 229

Maldivian [div], 461, 374

Maldjana, *alt.* Malgana [vml], 573

Male (Ethiopia) [mdy], 117
Male (Papua New Guinea) [mdc], 611

Male Arayans, *alt.* Malaryan [mjq], 374

Male Kudiya, *alt.* Kudiya [kfg], 370

Male Kuravan, *alt.* Malankuravan [mjo], 373

Malean, *alt.* Malayalam [mal], 374, 509

Malecite, *dial.* Malecite-Passamaquoddy [pqm], 238, 304

Mamalgha Munji, *dial.* Munji [mnj], 316

Mamanwa [mmn], 498

Mamanwa Negrito, *alt.* Mamanwa [mmn], 498

Mamaq, *dial.* Kerinci [kvr], 436

Mamara, *alt.* Senoufo, Mamara [myk], 144

Mamara Senoufo, *see* Senoufo, Mamara [myk], 144

Mamarego, *alt.* Bauro [bxa], 635

Mamasa [mqj], 431

Mamasani, *dial.* Luri, Southern [luz], 440

Mamba, *alt. dial.* Zimba [zmb], 109 *dial.* Vunjo [vun], 205

Mambae [mgm], 351

Mambai [mcs], 66, 83 *alt.* Mambae [mgm], 351 *dial.* Mambae [mgm], 351

Mambangura, *dial.* Ngura [nbx], 575

Mambar, *alt. dial.* Haruai [tmd], 601

Mambay, *alt.* Mambai [mcs], 66, 83

Mambaya, *alt. dial.* Pol [pmm], 71

Mambe, *alt.* Juwal [mwb], 603

Mambe', *dial.* Dii [dur], 60

Mambere, *alt.* Mambila, Cameroon [mcu], 66 *alt.* Mambila, Nigeria [mzk], 169

Mambetto, *alt.* Mangbetu [mdj], 104

Mambi, *dial.* Aralle-Tabulahan [atq], 427

Mambila de Gembu, *alt. dial.* Mambila, Cameroon [mcu], 66

Mambila, Cameroon [mcu], 66

Mambila, Nigeria [mzk], 169

Mambilla, *alt.* Mambila, Cameroon [mcu], 66 *alt.* Mambila, Nigeria [mzk], 169

Mambisa, *dial.* Alur [alz], 210

Mamboru [mvd], 408

Mambukush, *alt.* Mbukushu [mhw], 150, 41, 47, 214

Mambulu-Laporo, *alt. dial.* Cia-Cia [cia], 429

Mambump, *dial.* Buang, Mapos [bzh], 595

Mambwe, *dial.* Mambwe-Lungu [mgr], 214, 201

Mambwe-Lungu [mgr], 214, 201

Mame, *alt.* Tacanec [mtz], 274

Mamé, *alt.* Tacanec [mtz], 256

Mamedja, *alt.* Gaam [tbi], 190

Mamenyan, *alt.* Bamenyam [bce], 57

Mamgbay, *alt.* Mambai [mcs], 66, 83

Mamgbei, *alt.* Mambai [mcs], 66, 83

Mamidza, *alt.* Gaam [tbi], 190

Mamisa, *alt. dial.* Folopa [ppo], 599

Mamna'a, *dial.* Dii [dur], 60

Mamoedjoe, *alt.* Mamuju [mqx], 431

Mamoedjoesch, *alt.* Mamuju [mqx], 431

Mamori, *alt. dial.* Jamamadí [jaa], 227

Mamoria, *dial.* Jamamadí [jaa], 227

Mampa, *alt.* Sherbro [bun], 177

Mampoko, *dial.* Baloi [biz], 96

Mamprule, *alt.* Mampruli [maw], 126

Mampruli [maw], 126

Mampukush, *alt.* Mbukushu [mhw], 150, 41, 47, 214

Mampwa, *alt.* Sherbro [bun], 177

Mamu, *dial.* Dyirbal [dbl], 570

Mamudju, *alt.* Mamuju [mqx], 431

Mamuga, *alt. dial.* Nakanai [nak], 616

Mamuju [mqx], 431 *dial.* Mamuju [mqx], 431

Mamusi [kdf], 611 *dial.* Mamusi [kdf], 611

Mamvu [mdi], 103 *alt. dial.* Mamvu [mdi], 103

Mamwoh, *alt.* Menka [mea], 67

Man, *alt.* Iu Mien [ium], 450 *alt.* Manchu [mnc], 339 *dial.* Pana [pnz], 71

Mán, *pej. alt.* Cao Lan [mlc], 522, 329 *pej. alt.* Iu Mien [ium], 523

Man Cao-Lan, *pej. alt.* Cao Lan [mlc], 522, 329

Man Lan-Tien, *alt.* Kim Mun [mji], 451 *pej. alt.* Kim Mun [mji], 524

Man Lantien, *alt.* Kim Mun [mji], 337

Man Met [mml], 339

Man Pa Seng, *alt.* Pa-Hng [pha], 342

Mán Tráng, *alt.* Hmong Daw [mww], 523

Mana, *alt.* Fania [fni], 80

Manadja, *alt.* Limilngan [lmc], 573

Manado Malay, *see* Malay, Manado [xmm], 431

Manadonese, *dial.* Malay [mly], 436

Manadonese Malay, *alt.* Malay, Manado [xmm], 431

Managalasi, *pej. alt.* Ese [mcq], 598

Managobla, *dial.* Gola [gol], 183

Managua, *alt.* Cashibo-Cacataibo [cbr], 287

Managulasi, *pej. alt.* Ese [mcq], 598

Manajo, *alt.* Amanayé [ama], 224

Manala, *alt.* Mangala [mem], 573

Manaldjali, *alt.* Yugambal [yub], 579

Manam [mva], 611

Manambu [mle], 611

Mananahua, *alt.* Sensi [sni], 293

Manang, *alt.* Manangba [nmm], 475 *dial.* Mfumte [nfu], 67

Mananga, *dial.* Taliabu [tlv], 404

Manangba [nmm], 475

Manangbhot, *alt.* Manangba [nmm], 475

Manangbolt, *alt.* Manangba [nmm], 475

Manangeer, *dial.* Thuri [thu], 195

Manangi, *alt.* Manangba [nmm], 475

Manangkari [znk], 573

Manape, *alt.* Gapapaiwa [pwg], 599

Mañaries, *alt.* Machiguenga [mcb], 288

Manau, *alt.* Burmeso [bzu], 413

Manawadji, *dial.* Berakou [bxv], 79

Manawi, *dial.* Ambai [amk], 410

Manaxo, *alt.* Amanayé [ama], 224

Manay Mandayan, *alt.* Mandaya, Karaga [mry], 498

Manaze, *alt.* Amanayé [ama], 224

Manazo, *alt.* Amanayé [ama], 224

Manbae, *alt.* Mambae [mgm], 351

Manbai, *alt.* Mambai [mcs], 66, 83

Manbu, *alt.* Mang [zng], 525, 339

Mancagne, *alt.* Mankanya [knf], 131, 181

Mancang, *alt.* Mankanya [knf], 131, 181

Mancanha, *alt.* Mankanya [knf], 131, 181

Manchad, *alt.* Pattani [lae], 383

Manchati, *alt.* Karbi [mjw], 366 *alt.* Pattani [lae], 383

Manchhi Bhassa, *pej. alt.* Rongpo [rnp], 385

Manchinere, *alt.* Machinere [mpd], 229

Manchineri, *alt.* Machinere [mpd], 229

Manchu [mnc], 339

Manda (Australia) [zma], 573 Manda (India) [mha], 374 Manda (Tanzania) [mgs], 201 *dial.* Venda [ven], 187

Manda:yi, *alt.* Mandaic [mid], 441

Mandaba, *dial.* Maba [mde], 83

Mandaean, *alt.* Mandaic [mid], 441

Mandage, *alt.* Afade [aal], 56 *alt.* Malgbe [mxf], 83 *alt.* Maslam [msv], 84 *alt.* Mpade [mpi], 68, 84 *alt.* Mser [kqx], 68, 84

Mandague, *alt.* Mpade [mpi], 84
  alt. Mser [kqx], 84
Mandagué, *alt.* Maslam [msv], 84
  alt. Mpade [mpi], 68
Mandahuaca [mht], 312, 229
Mandaic [mid], 441
Mandaic, Classical [myz], 441
Mandailing Batak, *alt.* Batak
  Mandailing [btm], 435
Mandak, *alt.* Madak [mmx], 610
Mandal, *alt.* Bagheli [bfy], 354, 468
Mandala, *dial.* Maba [mde], 83
Mandan [mhq], 304
Mandandanjnjdji, *alt.*
  Mandandanyi [zmk], 573
Mandandanyi [zmk], 573
Mandankwe, *alt.* Mendankwe-
  Nkwen [mfd], 67
Mandar [mdr], 431
Mandara [tbf], 612
  alt. Wandala [mfi], 73, 177
  alt. dial. Wandala [mfi], 73
Mandara Montagnard, *alt.*
  Wandala [mfi], 73
Mandari [mqu], 193
  alt. Baga Manduri [bmd], 128
  alt. Mundari [muw], 376, 321, 476
  alt. dial. Bari [bfa], 210
Mandarin, *alt.* Chinese, Mandarin
  [cmn], 329, 461, 511
Mandarin Chinese, *see* Chinese,
  Mandarin [cmn], 329, 324, 391,
  454, 461, 494, 508, 511, 514
Mandauaca, *alt.* Mandahuaca
  [mht], 312, 229
Mandawaka, *alt.* Mandahuaca
  [mht], 312
Mandawáka, *alt.* Mandahuaca
  [mht], 229
Mandaya, *alt.* Manobo, Dibabawon
  [mbd], 499
Mandaya Mansaka, *alt.* Mansaka
  [msk], 499
Mandaya, Cataelano [mst], 498
Mandaya, Karaga [mry], 498
Mandaya, Sangab [myt], 498
Mande, *alt.* Garo [grt], 362, 321
  alt. Mandinka [mnk], 181
  alt. Maninkakan, Eastern [emk], 129,
  183
  alt. Nomaande [lem], 70
Mandé, *alt.* Mandinka [mnk], 122
Mandeali [mjl], 374
Mandeghughusu, *alt.* Simbo
  [sbb], 638
Mandelaut, *alt. dial.* Sama,
  Southern [ssb], 458
Mandella, *alt.* Madngele [zml], 573
Mandenyi, *alt.* Bullom So
  [buy], 183, 129

Mander [mqr], 419
Mandharsche, *alt.* Mandar
  [mdr], 431
Mandi, *alt.* Mandaic [mid], 441
  alt. Mandeali [mjl], 374
  alt. Nomaande [lem], 70
  alt. Wiarumus [tua], 632
Mandiali, *alt.* Mandeali [mjl], 374
Manding, *alt.* Mandinka [mnk], 181,
  122, 131
Mandinga, *alt.* Mandinka [mnk], 131
Mandingi, *alt.* Bullom So [buy], 183,
  129
Mandingo, *alt.* Mandinka
  [mnk], 181, 122, 131
  alt. Maninkakan, Eastern [emk], 183
  alt. Manya [mzj], 139, 130
Mandingue, *alt.* Mandinka
  [mnk], 181, 131
Mandinka [mnk], 181, 122, 131
Mandinque, *alt.* Mandinka
  [mnk], 181, 122, 131
Mandja, *alt.* Manza [mzv], 76
Mandjak [mfv], 131, 122, 181
Mandjalpingu, *dial.* Djinba
  [djb], 570
Mandjaque, *alt.* Mandjak
  [mfv], 131, 122, 181
Mandjoen, *alt.* Yir Yoront [yiy], 579
Mandju, *alt.* Ghomálá' [bbj], 62
Mandla, *dial.* Gondi, Northern
  [gno], 362
  dial. Tswa [tsc], 149
Mandlaha, *alt. dial.* Bagheli
  [bfy], 354, 468
Mando, *dial.* Kanembu [kbl], 81
Mandobbo, *alt.* Mandobo Atas
  [aax], 419
  alt. Mandobo Bawah [bwp], 419
Mandobo Atas [aax], 419
Mandobo Bawah [bwp], 419
Mandrica, *dial.* Albanian, Gheg
  [aln], 529
Manduka, *dial.* Nambikuára,
  Southern [nab], 230
Mandura, *dial.* Gumuz [guk], 115
Manduri, *alt.* Baga Manduri
  [bmd], 128
Mandusir, *dial.* Biak [bhw], 412
Mandyak, *alt.* Mandjak [mfv], 131,
  122, 181
Mandyam Brahmin, *dial.* Tamil
  [tam], 388
Mane, *dial.* Balanta-Kentohe
  [ble], 130
Manegir, *dial.* Evenki [evn], 504
Mañegu, *dial.* Fala [fax], 560
Manehas, *dial.* Bakaka [bqz], 57
Manem [jet], 612, 419
Maneo, *dial.* Manusela [wha], 402

Maneta, *alt. dial.* Wersing
  [kvw], 410
Mang [zng], 525, 339
  alt. dial. Taliabu [tlv], 404
  dial. Laka [lap], 83
  dial. Mumuye [mzm], 170
Mang Cong, *alt.* Sô [sss], 452
Mang U, *alt.* Mang [zng], 525, 339
Mang-Koong, *alt.* Sô [sss], 452
Manga, *alt.* Kanuri, Manga
  [kby], 152, 166
  alt. Mba [mfc], 104
  dial. Kanuri, Manga [kby], 152, 166
Manga Buang, *alt.* Buang, Mangga
  [mmo], 595
Manga Kanuri, *see* Kanuri, Manga
  [kby], 152, 166
Mangaaba, *alt.* Mbula [mna], 612
Mangaava, *alt.* Mbula [mna], 612
Mangaawa, *alt.* Mbula [mna], 612
Mangaia, *dial.* Rarotongan [rar], 579
Mangala [mem], 573
Mangalaa, *alt.* Mangala [mem], 573
Mangalili, *dial.* Gumatj [gnn], 571
Mangalore, *dial.* Konkani, Goanese
  [gom], 369
Mangambilis, *alt.* Dabe [dbe], 413
Manganitu, *dial.* Sangir [sxn], 432
Manganja, *dial.* Nyanja [nya], 140,
  215
Mangap-Mbula, *alt.* Mbula
  [mna], 612
Mangap. Kaimanga, *alt.* Mbula
  [mna], 612
Mangaragan Mandaya, *alt.*
  Mandaya, Karaga [mry], 498
Mangarai, *alt.* Mangarayi [mpc], 573
Mangarayi [mpc], 573
Mangareva [mrv], 581
Mangarevan, *alt.* Mangareva
  [mrv], 581
Mangari, *alt.* Magar, Eastern
  [mgp], 373
Mangarla, *alt.* Mangala [mem], 573
Mangarongaro, *alt.* Penrhyn
  [pnh], 579
Mangarrayi, *alt.* Mangarayi
  [mpc], 573
Mangas [zns], 169
Mangasara, *alt.* Makasar [mak], 430
Mangati, *pej. alt.* Datooga [tcc], 198
Mangaya, *alt.* Mangayat [myj], 193
Mangayat [myj], 193
Mangbai, *alt.* Mambai [mcs], 66, 83
Mangbaï de Biparé, *alt.* Mambai
  [mcs], 83
Mangbei, *alt.* Mambai [mcs], 66, 83
Mangbele, *alt.* Ngbee [jgb], 106
Mangbettu, *alt.* Mangbetu
  [mdj], 104

Mangbetu [mdj], 104
  dial. Mangbetu [mdj], 104
Mangbutu [mdk], 104
Mange, *alt. dial.* Taliabu [tlv], 404
Mange'e, *alt. dial.* Taliabu [tlv], 404
Mangehele, *dial.* Kagulu [kki], 199
Mangei, *alt. dial.* Taliabu [tlv], 404
Mangerei, *alt.* Mangerr [zme], 573
Mangeri, *alt.* Mangerr [zme], 573
Mangerr [zme], 573
Mangesh, *dial.* Chaldean Neo-
  Aramaic [cld], 443
Mangga Buang, *see* Buang,
  Mangga [mmo], 595
Manggalili, *dial.* Gupapuyngu
  [guf], 571
Manggang, *alt.* Numanggang
  [nop], 619
Manggar, *alt.* Magar, Eastern
  [mgp], 475, 373
  alt. Magar, Western [mrd], 475
Manggarai [mqy], 409
  alt. Mangarayi [mpc], 573
Mangghuer, *alt. dial.* Tu [mjg], 345
Mangguar, *alt.* Dera [kbv], 414, 597
Mangili-Waijelo, *dial.* Kambera
  [xbr], 407
Mangisa, *alt.* Mengisa [mct], 67
Mangkaak, *dial.* Kadazan, Labuk-
  Kinabatangan [dtb], 457
Mangkahak, *alt. dial.* Kadazan,
  Labuk-Kinabatangan [dtb], 457
Mangkak, *alt. dial.* Kadazan, Labuk-
  Kinabatangan [dtb], 457
Mangkatip, *alt. dial.* Bakumpai
  [bkr], 392
Mangkettan, *alt.* Bukitan
  [bkn], 392, 459
Mangki, *alt.* Kalumpang [kli], 429
  dial. Kalumpang [kli], 429
Mangkir, *alt.* Kalumpang [kli], 429
Mangkok, *alt. dial.* Kadazan, Labuk-
  Kinabatangan [dtb], 457
Mangkong, *alt.* Bamukumbit
  [bqt], 57
  alt. Sô [sss], 452
  dial. Bru, Eastern [bru], 522
Mangkunge, *dial.* Ngemba
  [nge], 69
Mango [mge], 83
  alt. dial. Fali, South [fal], 61
Mangoche, *dial.* Yao [yao], 141
Mangochi, *alt. dial.* Yao [yao], 149
Mangole [mqc], 402
Mangoli, *alt.* Mangole [mqc], 402
Mangsdekha, *alt.* Nyenkha
  [neh], 324
Mangseng [mbh], 612
Mangsing, *alt.* Mangseng
  [mbh], 612

Mangu-Ngutu, *alt.* Mangbutu
  [mdk], 104
Mangue, *alt.* Chorotega [cjr], 249
Mangum, *dial.* Deg [mzw], 124
Mangwato, *alt. dial.* Tswana
  [tsn], 217
Mani, *alt. dial.* Kohistani, Indus
  [mvy], 486
  alt. dial. Mpade [mpi], 68, 84
Mani-Iling, *alt. dial.* Musgu
  [mug], 68
Maniba, *alt.* Baniwa [bwi], 225, 311
Manide, *alt.* Agta, Camarines Norte
  [abd], 490
Manif, *alt.* Abun [kgr], 410
Manigara, *dial.* Maiwa [mti], 611
Manigri, *alt.* Ede Nago, Manigri-
  Kambolé [xkb], 43
Manigri-Kambolé Ede Nago, *see*
  Ede Nago, Manigri-Kambolé
  [xkb], 43, 207
Manihiki-Rakahanga, *alt.*
  Rakahanga-Manihiki [rkh], 579
Manika, *alt.* Manyika [mxc], 216,
  148
Manikion [mnx], 419
Manila, *dial.* Tagalog [tgl], 502
Maniling, *dial.* Musgu [mug], 68
Manimo, *alt.* Vanimo [vam], 630
Maninga, *alt.* Maninkakan, Western
  [mlq], 181
Maninka, *alt.* Maninkakan, Eastern
  [emk], 129
Maninka, Forest [myq], 94
Maninka, Konyanka [mku], 129,
  139
Maninka, Sankaran [msc], 129
Maninka-Mori, *alt.* Maninkakan,
  Eastern [emk], 183
  dial. Maninkakan, Eastern [emk], 129
Maninka-Western, *alt.*
  Maninkakan, Western [mlq], 181
Maninkakan, Eastern [emk], 129,
  183
Maninkakan, Kita [mwk], 143
Maninkakan, Western [mlq], 181,
  122, 143
Manipa [mqp], 402
Manipuri, *alt.* Meitei [mni], 375,
  321, 465
Manipuri Muslim, *alt. dial.* Meitei
  [mni], 375
Maniq, *alt.* Kensiu [kns], 515
Manitenére, *alt.* Machinere
  [mpd], 229
Maniterení, *alt.* Machinere
  [mpd], 229
Manitsawá, *alt.* Maritsauá
  [msp], 230
Maniwo, *alt.* Dao [daz], 414

Maniya, *alt.* Manya [mzj], 130
Manja, *alt.* Manza [mzv], 76
Manjaca, *alt.* Mandjak [mfv], 131,
  122, 181
Manjack, *alt.* Mandjak [mfv], 131,
  122, 181
Manjaco, *alt.* Mandjak [mfv], 131,
  122, 181
Manjacu, *alt.* Mandjak [mfv], 122
Manjak, *alt.* Mandjak [mfv], 181
Manjaku, *alt.* Mandjak [mfv], 131,
  181
Manjar, *alt.* Mandar [mdr], 431
Manjhi, *alt.* Majhi [mjz], 475, 373
  alt. Majhwar [mmj], 373
  alt. dial. Santali [sat], 386
  dial. Asuri [asr], 354
  dial. Santali [sat], 322
Manjhia, *alt.* Majhwar [mmj], 373
Manji-Kasa, *alt. dial.* Ligbi
  [lig], 126
Manjiak, *alt.* Mandjak [mfv], 131,
  122
Manjo, *alt.* Kafa [kbr], 116
Manjui, *alt.* Chorote, Iyo'wujwa
  [crq], 220, 222, 284
Manjuy, *alt.* Chorote, Iyo'wujwa
  [crq], 220, 222, 284
Mankaliya, *dial.* Kuranko [knk], 183
Mankanha, *alt.* Mankanya
  [knf], 131, 181
Mankanya [knf], 131, 181
Mankayan-Buguias, *dial.*
  Kankanaey [kne], 498
Manketa, *alt.* Bukitan [bkn], 392,
  459
Mankidi, *alt.* Birhor [biy], 356
Mankidia, *alt.* Birhor [biy], 356
Mankim, *dial.* Tikar [tik], 72
Mankon, *dial.* Ngemba [nge], 69
Mankoong, *alt.* Sô [sss], 452
Manlati, *alt.* Mal Paharia
  [mkb], 373
Manlea, *alt. dial.* Uab Meto
  [aoz], 410
Manmi, *alt.* Man Met [mml], 339
Manmit, *alt.* Man Met [mml], 339
Mann [mev], 139, 130
Manna-Dora [mju], 374
Mannadi, *alt.* Bagheli [bfy], 354,
  468
Mannan [mjv], 374
Manne, *alt.* Mannan [mjv], 374
Mannyod, *alt.* Mannan [mjv], 374
Mano, *alt.* Mann [mev], 139, 130
Manö, *alt.* Karen, Manumanaw
  [kxf], 464
Manoa, *alt.* Panobo [pno], 289
Manobai, *alt.* Manombai [woo], 402
Manobo, Agusan [msm], 499

Manobo, Ata [atd], 499
Manobo, Cinamiguin [mkx], 499
Manobo, Cotabato [mta], 499
Manobo, Dibabawon [mbd], 499
Manobo, Ilianen [mbi], 499
Manobo, Matigsalug [mbt], 499
Manobo, Obo [obo], 499
Manobo, Rajah Kabunsuwan
  [mqk], 499
Manobo, Sarangani [mbs], 499
Manobo, Western Bukidnon
  [mbb], 499
Manoita, *alt. dial.* Shipibo-Conibo
  [shp], 293
Manombai [woo], 402
Manouche, *alt.* Romani, Sinte
  [rmo], 448
  alt. dial. Romani, Sinte [rmo], 550
  dial. Romani, Sinte [rmo], 537, 545,
  549
Manowee, *alt.* Asmat, Central
  [cns], 411
Manpelle, *alt.* Mampruli [maw], 126
Mansa', *dial.* Tigré [tig], 112, 195
Mansaka [msk], 499
Mansfield-Ketchumstuck, *dial.*
  Tanacross [tcb], 308
Mansi [mns], 505
Mansibaber, *alt.* Meyah [mej], 420
Mansim, *alt.* Hatam [had], 415
Mansinyo, *dial.* Yuracare [yuz], 224
Mansiy, *alt.* Mansi [mns], 505
Mansoanca, *alt.* Mansoanka
  [msw], 131
Mansoanka [msw], 131
Manta [myg], 66
Mantangai, *dial.* Ngaju [nij], 394
Mantararen, *dial.* Lawangan
  [lbx], 394
Mantauran, *dial.* Rukai [dru], 512
Mantembu, *alt.* Yawa [yva], 426
Mantion, *alt.* Manikion [mnx], 419
Mantizula, *alt.* Maritsauá [msp], 230
Mantjiltjara, *alt. dial.* Martu
  Wangka [mpj], 574
Mantovano, *dial.* Emiliano-
  Romagnolo [eml], 543
Mantra, *dial.* Temuan [tmw], 455
Mantsi [nty], 525
Manu, *alt.* Karen, Manumanaw
  [kxf], 464
Manu Park Panoan, *alt.* Yora
  [mts], 294
Manua, *dial.* Mambae [mgm], 351
Manubara, *alt.* Maria [mds], 612
Manuche, *alt.* Romani, Sinte
  [rmo], 448
  alt. dial. Romani, Sinte [rmo], 537
  dial. Romani, Sinte [rmo], 550
Manuk, *dial.* Javanese [jav], 391

Manukai, *alt. dial.* Dayak, Land
  [dyk], 393
Manukolu, *alt. dial.* Humene
  [huf], 602
Manum, *alt.* Manam [mva], 611
Manumanaw, *alt.* Karen,
  Manumanaw [kxf], 464
Manumanaw Karen, *see* Karen,
  Manumanaw [kxf], 464
Manus, *alt.* Lele [lle], 609
  alt. Titan [ttv], 628
Manusela [wha], 402
Manush, *alt. dial.* Romani, Sinte
  [rmo], 537
Mañuwíin, *alt.* Tlapanec,
  Malinaltepec [tcf], 275
Manx [glv], 565
Manx Gaelic, *alt.* Manx [glv], 565
Manya [mzj], 139, 130
Manya Kan, *alt.* Manya [mzj], 139,
  130
Manyak, *alt.* Muya [mvm], 340
Manyang, *alt.* Kenyang [ken], 64
Manyarring, *dial.* Djinang [dji], 570
Manyawa [mny], 148
Manyeman, *alt. dial.* Kenyang
  [ken], 64
Manyemen, *alt. dial.* Kenyang
  [ken], 64
Manyika [mxc], 216, 148
Manyjilyjara, *dial.* Martu Wangka
  [mpj], 574
Manyok, *dial.* Bebele [beb], 58
Manyukai, *dial.* Dayak, Land
  [dyk], 393
Manyuke, *alt. dial.* Dayak, Land
  [dyk], 393
Manza [mzv], 76
Manzanero, *alt. dial.* Mapudungun
  [arn], 242
Manzari, *alt. dial.* Kohistani, Indus
  [mvy], 486
Mao, *alt.* Naga, Mao [nbi], 378
  alt. dial. Shan [shn], 467
  dial. Kanuri, Central [knc], 166, 63,
  81, 191
Mao Naga, *see* Naga, Mao [nbi], 378
Maoli, *alt. dial.* Konkani [knn], 369
Maonan [mmd], 340
Maopa, *dial.* Keapara [khz], 605
Maopityan, *alt.* Mapidian
  [mpw], 229, 257
Maore [swb], 146
  dial. Comorian [swb], 87
Maori [mri], 586
  alt. Rarotongan [rar], 579
Maou, *alt.* Mahou [mxx], 94
Mapache, *dial.* Carútana [cru], 226
Mapan, *alt. dial.* Mwaghavul
  [sur], 170

Mapanga, *dial.* Yasa [yko], 111, 122
Mapayo, *alt.* Mapoyo [mcg], 312
Mape [mlh], 612
  dial. Mape [mlh], 612
Mapena [mnm], 612
Maphekha, *alt.* Chocangacakha
  [cgk], 323
Mapi, *alt.* Yaqay [jaq], 426
Mapia [mpy], 419
  dial. Biak [bhw], 412
Mapian, *alt.* Mapia [mpy], 419
Mapidian [mpw], 229, 257
Mapiya-Kegata, *dial.* Ekari
  [ekg], 414
Mapodi, *alt.* Gude [gde], 161, 62
Mapor, *alt.* Lom [mfb], 436
Maporese, *alt.* Lom [mfb], 436
Mapos, *alt.* Buang, Mapos [bzh], 595
  dial. Buang, Mapos [bzh], 595
Mapos Buang, *see* Buang, Mapos
  [bzh], 595
Mapoye, *alt.* Mapoyo [mcg], 312
Mapoyo [mcg], 312
Mappa-Pana, *alt. dial.* Toraja-
  Sa'dan [sda], 434
Maprik, *dial.* Ambulas [abt], 589
Mapuche, *alt.* Mapudungun
  [arn], 242, 220
Mapuda, *alt.* Gude [gde], 161
Mapudungu, *alt.* Mapudungun
  [arn], 242, 220
Mapudungun [arn], 242, 220
Mapun [sjm], 499, 457
  alt. dial. Mwaghavul [sur], 170
Mapute, *alt.* Waru [wru], 435
Maputongo, *alt.* Mapudungun
  [arn], 220
Maqaqet, *alt.* Qaqet [byx], 622
Maqua, *alt.* Nama [naq], 150
Maquiri, *alt.* Kayabí [kyz], 229
Maquiritai, *alt.* Maquiritari
  [mch], 312, 229
Maquiritare, *alt.* Maquiritari
  [mch], 312, 229
Maquiritari [mch], 312, 229
Maquoua, *alt.* Makhuwa
  [vmw], 147
  alt. Makhuwa-Meetto [mgh], 201
Mar, *alt.* Mal Paharia [mkb], 373
Mara [mec], 573
  alt. Chin, Mara [mrh], 359, 463
  dial. Kaba Deme [kwg], 81
  dial. Malgbe [mxf], 65, 83
Mara Chin, *see* Chin, Mara
  [mrh], 359, 463
Mara Ma-Siki, *alt.* Oroha [ora], 637
Mara-Gomu, *dial.* Mbo-Ung
  [mux], 612
Maraba [ymk], 201
  alt. Marba [mpg], 83

alt. dial. Banda-Mbrès [bqk], 75, 188
dial. Makonde [kde], 201
Maracasero, *alt.* Malayo [mbp], 246
Maracha, *dial.* Lugbara [lgg], 211
Marachi, *dial.* Luyia [luy], 134
Maragang, *alt.* Kimaragang
[kqr], 457
Maragat, *alt.* Isnag [isd], 496
Maragaus, *alt.* Maragus [mrs], 643
Maraghei [vmh], 441
Maragoli, *alt.* Logooli [rag], 134
Maragooli, *alt.* Logooli [rag], 134
Maragua, *alt.* Sateré-Mawé
[mav], 231
Maragus [mrs], 643
Maraka, *alt.* Soninke [snk], 144, 122,
182
Marako, *alt.* Libido [liq], 116
Marakuet, *alt.* Endo [enb], 133
Marakwet, *alt.* Talai [tle], 136
Maralangko, *alt. dial.* Watut, South
[mcy], 631
Maralango, *dial.* Watut, South
[mcy], 631
Marale, *dial.* Chuwabu [chw], 147
Maraliinan, *alt.* Watut, Middle
[mpl], 631
Maralinan, *alt.* Watut, Middle
[mpl], 631
Maram, *alt.* Chin, Mara [mrh], 359,
463
alt. Naga, Maram [nma], 378
Maram Khullen Circle, *dial.* Naga,
Maram [nma], 378
Maram Naga, *see* Naga, Maram
[nma], 378
Marama, *alt.* Arakanese [mhv], 320
dial. Luyia [luy], 134
Maramanandji, *alt.* Marimanindji
[zmm], 574
Maramanunggu, *alt. dial.*
Maringarr [zmt], 573
Maramarandji, *alt.* Marimanindji
[zmm], 574
Maramba [myd], 612
Maramuni, *dial.* Enga [enq], 598
Maramuresh, *alt. dial.* Romanian
[ron], 548
Maran, *alt.* Amis [ami], 511
Maranao [mrw], 499
Maranaw, *alt.* Maranao [mrw], 499
Marangai, *dial.* Tuamotuan [pmt],
581
Marangis, *alt.* Watam [wax], 631
Marangu, *dial.* Vunjo [vun], 205
Maransé, *alt. dial.* Songhay
[hmb], 54
Maranunggu [zmr], 573
dial. Maringarr [zmt], 573
Marapu, *dial.* Mangseng [mbh], 612

Maraqo, *alt.* Libido [liq], 116
Marara, *dial.* Baga Sitemu [bsp], 128
Mararet, *alt.* Mararit [mgb], 83
Marari, *dial.* Powari [pwr], 384
Mararit [mgb], 83
dial. Mararit [mgb], 83
Marashi, *dial.* Domari [rmt], 563
dial. Kurdish, Northern [kmr], 519
Marathi [mar], 374
Marattiyan, *alt.* Vaagri Booli
[vaa], 389
Marau [mvr], 415
alt. dial. 'Are'are [alu], 634
Marau Sound, *alt. dial.* 'Are'are
[alu], 634
Marave, *alt. dial.* Nyanja [nya], 140,
215
Maravi, *alt. dial.* Nyanja [nya], 140,
215
Marawar, *alt.* Marwari [mve], 487
Maraworno, *alt.* Carib [car], 226,
295
Marba [mpg], 83
alt. Marfa [mvu], 83
Marchha, *dial.* Rongpo [rnp], 385
dial. Tibetan [bod], 388
pej. alt. Rongpo [rnp], 385
Marchha Pahari, *pej. alt.* Rongpo
[rnp], 385
Marda, *dial.* Kunama [kun], 112
Mardala, *alt.* Adynyamathanha
[adt], 567
Mardinli, *alt. dial.* Kurdish, Northern
[kmr], 453
Mardo, *alt.* Martu Wangka [mpj], 574
Mare, *alt. dial.* Bugis [bug], 428
Maré, *alt.* Nengone [nen], 585
Mare-Ammu, *alt. dial.* Marithiel
[mfr], 574
Marebbano, *dial.* Ladin [lld], 544
Maredyerbin, *alt.* Maridjabin
[zmj], 573
Maregaon, *dial.* Kolami,
Northwestern [kfb], 369
Maremgi [mrx], 419
Marendje, *alt.* Marenje [vmr], 148
Mareng, *alt.* Maring [mbw], 612
Marenggar, *alt.* Maringarr
[zmt], 573
Marengge, *alt.* Maremgi [mrx], 419
Marenje [vmr], 148
Marensé, *dial.* Songhay [hmb], 54
Maretyabin, *alt.* Maridjabin
[zmj], 573
Marevone, *alt.* Makhuwa-Marrevone
[xmc], 147
Marewumiri, *alt. dial.*
Nangikurrunggurr [nam], 574
Marfa [mvu], 83
Margaluri, *alt.* Mingrelian [xmf], 352

Margany [zmc], 573
Marghi, *alt.* Marghi Central
[mrt], 169
Marghi Central [mrt], 169
Marghi South [mfm], 169
Marghi West, *alt.* Putai [mfl], 173
Margi, *alt.* Marghi Central [mrt], 169
Margos-Yarowilca-Lauricocha
Quechua, *see* Quechua, Margos-
Yarowilca-Lauricocha [qvm], 291
Margosatubig, *alt.* Subanun,
Lapuyan [laa], 501
Margu [mhg], 573
Marhay, *alt.* Mundang [mua], 68
Mari (East Sepik Province)
[mbx], 612
Mari (Madang Province) [hob], 612
alt. Karon Dori [kgw], 416
alt. Mari, Eastern [mhr], 555
alt. Namo [mxw], 617
Mari, Eastern [mhr], 555
Mari, Western [mrj], 555
Mari-Ammu, *alt. dial.* Marithiel
[mfr], 574
Mari-Hills, *alt.* Mari, Western
[mrj], 555
Mari-Woods, *alt.* Mari, Eastern
[mhr], 555
Maria (India) [mrr], 375
Maria (Papua New Guinea)
[mds], 612
dial. Maria [mds], 612
Maria Gond, *alt.* Maria, Dandami
[daq], 375
Maria, Dandami [daq], 375
Mariape-Nahuqua, *alt.* Matipuhy
[mzo], 230
Maricopa [mrc], 304
Maridan [zmd], 573
Maridhiel, *alt.* Marithiel [mfr], 574
Maridhiyel, *alt.* Marithiel
[mfr], 574
Maridjabin [zmj], 573
Maridyerbin, *alt.* Maridjabin
[zmj], 573
Marie Galante Creole French,
dial. Guadeloupean Creole French
[gcf], 253
Marigang, *alt.* Kimaragang
[kqr], 457
Marigl, *dial.* Golin [gvf], 600
Marik [dad], 612
Marikai, *dial.* Barapasi [brp], 412
Marille, *alt.* Daasanach [dsh], 114,
132
Marimanindji [zmm], 574
Marimanindu, *alt.* Marimanindji
[zmm], 574
Marin Miwok, *dial.* Miwok, Coast
[csi], 305

Marina, *alt.* Tolomako [tlm], 646
Marinahua, *dial.* Sharanahua [mcd], 293, 232
Marinawa, *alt. dial.* Sharanahua [mcd], 293
Marináwa, *alt. dial.* Sharanahua [mcd], 232
Marind [mrz], 419
Marind, Bian [bpv], 419
Marinduque, *dial.* Tagalog [tgl], 502
Maring [mbw], 612
    alt. Naga, Maring [nng], 378
Maring Naga, *see* Naga, Maring [nng], 378
Maringa, *alt.* Maringarr [zmt], 573
Maringarr [zmt], 573
Maringe, *dial.* Cheke Holo [mrn], 635
Maringhe, *alt. dial.* Cheke Holo [mrn], 635
Marino [mrb], 643
Marip, *alt.* Jingpho [kac], 464, 336
Mariposas, *alt. dial.* Cuiba [cui], 244
Mariri [mqi], 402
Marithiel [mfr], 574
    dial. Marithiel [mfr], 574
Marithiyel, *alt.* Marithiel [mfr], 574
Maritime Gagauz, *dial.* Gagauz [gag], 532, 551
Maritime Gagauzi, *dial.* Gagauz [gag], 547
Maritime Provençal, *dial.* Provençal [prv], 537
Maritime Sign Language [nsr], 239
Maritsauá [msp], 230
Mariupol Greek, *dial.* Greek [ell], 564
Mariveles Ayta, *alt.* Ayta, Bataan [ayt], 492
Mariyedi [zmy], 574
Mark-Brandenburg, *dial.* Saxon, Low [nds], 539
Marka [rkm], 52, 143
    alt. Soninke [snk], 144, 95, 122, 131, 145, 182
Marka Dafing, *alt.* Marka [rkm], 52
Marka-Dafin, *alt.* Marka [rkm], 143
Marke, *dial.* Doyayo [dow], 60
Märkisch-Brandenburgisch, *alt. dial.* Saxon, Low [nds], 539
Markweta, *alt.* Endo [enb], 133
Marlasi, *alt.* Kola [kvv], 400
Marma, *alt.* Arakanese [mhv], 462, 320, 354
    dial. Arakanese [mhv], 320
Marmaregho, *alt.* Bauro [bxa], 635
Maroa, *alt. dial.* Tyap [kcg], 176

Marocasero, *alt.* Malayo [mbp], 246
Maron, *alt.* Hermit [llf], 602
Maronene, *alt.* Moronene [mqn], 431
Maronite, *alt.* Arabic, Cypriot Spoken [acy], 350
Marori, *alt.* Morori [mok], 420
Maros-Pangkep, *dial.* Makasar [mak], 430
Maroua, *dial.* Fulfulde, Adamawa [fub], 61, 80
Marova, *alt.* Marúbo [mzr], 230
Marovo [mvo], 637
Marpaharia, *alt.* Mal Paharia [mkb], 373
Marpha, *dial.* Thakali [ths], 480
Marquesan, North [mrq], 581
Marquesan, South [mqm], 581
Marquito, *alt.* Mískito [miq], 282, 258
Marra, *alt.* Mara [mec], 573
Marrakech, *dial.* Arabic, Moroccan Spoken [ary], 146
Marrakulu, *dial.* Dhuwal [duj], 569
Marramaninjsji, *alt.* Marimanindji [zmm], 574
Marrangu, *dial.* Dhuwal [duj], 569
Marranunga, *alt. dial.* Maringarr [zmt], 573
Marrawarra, *alt.* Bandjigali [bjd], 568
Marrevone, *alt.* Makhuwa-Marrevone [xmc], 147
Marrganj, *alt.* Margany [zmc], 573
Marrgu, *alt.* Margu [mhg], 573
Marrithiyel, *alt.* Marithiel [mfr], 574
Marry, *dial.* Yasa [yko], 111, 122
Marseillais, *alt. dial.* Provençal [prv], 537
Marseille Sign Language, *dial.* French Sign Language [fsl], 536
Marsela-South Babar, *alt.* Masela, Central [mxz], 402
Marsh French, *dial.* French, Cajun [frc], 300
Marshallese [mah], 582
Martha's Vineyard Sign Language [mre], 304
Marthi, *alt.* Marathi [mar], 374
Marti Ke [zmg], 574
Martiniquan Creole French [gcf], 259
Martu Wangka [mpj], 574
Martuthunira, *alt.* Martuyhunira [vma], 574
Martuyhunira [vma], 574
Maru [mhx], 465, 340
    alt. Mru [mro], 321
Maruara, *alt.* Bandjigali [bjd], 568
Marub, *dial.* Kopkaka [opk], 418

Maruba, *alt.* Marúbo [mzr], 230
Marúbo [mzr], 230
Maruhia, *alt.* Isabi [isa], 603
Maruongmai, *alt.* Naga, Rongmei [nbu], 379
Maruwa, *alt. dial.* Tyap [kcg], 176
Marva, *alt.* Giziga, North [gis], 62
Marvari, *alt.* Marwari [rwr], 375
Marwa, *alt. dial.* Tyap [kcg], 176
Marwadi, *alt.* Marwari [rwr], 475
Marwari (India) [rwr], 375, 475, 487
    Marwari (Pakistan) [mve], 487
Marwari Bhat, *dial.* Marwari [mve], 487
Marwari Bhil, *alt.* Marwari [mve], 487
    dial. Marwari [mve], 487
Marwari Ghera, *alt.* Gurgula [ggg], 485
Marwari Meghwar, *alt.* Marwari [mve], 487
    dial. Marwari [mve], 487
Marworno, *alt.* Carib [car], 226
Masa, *alt.* Masana [mcn], 83, 66
Masaaba, *alt.* Masaba [myx], 211
Masaba [myx], 211
Masadiit Boliney, *dial.* Itneg, Masadiit [tis], 496
Masadiit Itneg, *see* Itneg, Masadiit [tis], 496
Masadiit Sallapadan, *dial.* Itneg, Masadiit [tis], 496
Masai, *alt.* Maasai [mas], 134, 201
Masaká, *dial.* Tubarão [tba], 233
Masakin, *alt.* Dagik [dec], 189
    alt. Ngile [jle], 194
Masakin Buram, *alt. dial.* Ngile [jle], 194
Masakin Dagig, *alt.* Dagik [dec], 189
Masakin Gusar, *alt.* Dagik [dec], 189
    dial. Ngile [jle], 194
Masakin Tuwal, *dial.* Ngile [jle], 194
Masaku, *dial.* Kamba [kam], 133
Masale, *alt.* Masalit [mls], 83
Masalit [mls], 193, 83
Masama, *alt.* Andio [bzb], 427
    dial. Machame [jmc], 193
Masan, *dial.* Buna [bvn], 595
Masana [mcn], 83, 66
Masango, *alt.* Majang [mpe], 116
Masapua, *dial.* Tugun [tzn], 405
Masara, *alt.* Masalit [mls], 83
Masarete, *dial.* Buru [mhs], 397
Masarwa, *alt.* Tsoa [hio], 48
    alt. dial. !Xóõ [nmn], 48, 151
Masawa, *dial.* Kuanua [ksd], 608

Masbate Sorsogon, *see* Sorsogon, Masbate [bks], 501

Masbateño, *alt.* Masbatenyo [msb], 499

Masbatenyo [msb], 499

Masbuar-Tela, *alt.* Tela-Masbuar [tvm], 404

Masegi, *alt.* Mangseng [mbh], 612

Maseki, *alt.* Mangseng [mbh], 612

Masela, Central [mxz], 402

Masela, East [vme], 402

Masela, West [mss], 402

Masemola, *dial.* Sotho, Northern [nso], 186

Masemula, *alt. dial.* Sotho, Northern [nso], 186

Masenrempulu, *alt.* Duri [mvp], 429
  alt. Maiwa [wmm], 430

Masep, *alt.* Massep [mvs], 419

Masfeima, *dial.* Wandala [mfi], 73, 177

Mash, *alt.* Arakanese [mhv], 462, 320

Mashadi, *dial.* Farsi, Western [pes], 439

Mashanga, *alt. dial.* Ndau [ndc], 148

Mashasha, *dial.* Nkoya [nka], 214

Mashati, *dial.* Rombo [rof], 204

Mashco, *pej. alt.* Amarakaeri [amr], 286
  pej. alt. Huachipaeri [hug], 288
  pej. alt. Mashco Piro [cuj], 288

Mashco Piro [cuj], 288

Mashelle, *alt.* Bussa [dox], 114

Mashi (Nigeria) [jms], 169
  Mashi (Zambia) [mho], 214, 41, 150
  alt. Shi [shr], 107
  dial. Mashi [mho], 214, 41, 150

Mashiki, *alt.* Shiki [gua], 174

Mashile, *alt.* Bussa [dox], 114

Masholle, *alt.* Bussa [dox], 114

Mashuakwe, *alt.* Shua [shg], 48
  alt. dial. Shua [shg], 48

Masi, *alt.* Mashi [mho], 214, 41, 150

Masiguare, *alt. dial.* Cuiba [cui], 244
  dial. Cuiba [cui], 311

Masiin, *alt. dial.* Soninke [snk], 131

Masikoro Malagasy, *see* Malagasy, Masikoro [msh], 140

Masimasi [ism], 419
  dial. Iamalele [yml], 602

Masin-Lak, *alt.* Kui [kvd], 408

Masingbi, *dial.* Themne [tem], 184

Masingle, *dial.* Bine [bon], 593

Masinloc, *dial.* Sambal, Tinà [xsb], 501

Masiri, *dial.* Cia-Cia [cia], 429

Masiwang [bnf], 402

Masiware, *dial.* Cuiba [cui], 244

Maskelyne Islands, *alt.* Maskelynes [klv], 643

Maskelynes [klv], 643

Maskoy Pidgin [mhh], 285

Maslam [msv], 66, 84
  dial. Maslam [msv], 66, 84

Maslava, *alt.* Vame [mlr], 73
  alt. dial. Vame [mlr], 73

Masmadje, *alt.* Masmaje [mes], 84

Masmaje [mes], 84

Masongo, *alt.* Majang [mpe], 116

Masqan, *alt.* Mesqan [mvz], 117

Massa, *alt.* Masana [mcn], 83, 66

Massa de Guelengdeng, *alt.* Mbara [mpk], 84

Massaca, *alt. dial.* Tubarão [tba], 233

Massachusett, *alt.* Wampanoag [wam], 309

Massachusetts, *alt.* Wampanoag [wam], 309

Massagal, *dial.* Mofu-Gudur [mif], 68

Massaka, *alt.* Makuráp [mpu], 229

Massakal, *alt. dial.* Mofu-Gudur [mif], 68

Massalat [mdg], 84

Massali, *dial.* Talysh [tly], 320

Massalit, *alt.* Masalit [mls], 193, 83

Massaninga, *dial.* Yao [yao], 149, 215

Massenrempulu, *alt.* Duri [mvp], 429

Massep [mvs], 419

Masset, *alt.* Haida, Northern [hdn], 238, 301

Massolit, *alt.* Masalit [mls], 83

Massry, *alt.* Arabic, Egyptian Spoken [arz], 110

Mastanahua, *dial.* Sharanahua [mcd], 293

Masvingo School Sign, *dial.* Zimbabwe Sign Language [zib], 217

Maswanka, *alt.* Mansoanka [msw], 131

Mata, *alt.* Tupuri [tui], 72

Mataban-Moulmein, *dial.* Mon [mnw], 466

Matabello, *alt.* Watubela [wah], 405

Mataco, *pej. alt.* Wichí Lhamtés Güisnay [mzh], 220

Mataco Güisnay, *alt.* Wichí Lhamtés Güisnay [mzh], 220

Mataco Nocten, *alt.* Wichí Lhamtés Nocten [mtp], 224, 220

Mataco Pilcomayo, *alt.* Wichí Lhamtés Güisnay [mzh], 220

Mataco Vejoz, *alt.* Wichí Lhamtés Vejoz [wlv], 220

Matagalpa [mtn], 282

Mataitai, *dial.* Bwaidoka [bwd], 596

Matakam, *pej. alt.* Mafa [maf], 65, 169

Matal [mfh], 66

Matalaang, *dial.* Bajau, Indonesian [bdl], 427

Matambwe, *alt.* Makonde [kde], 201, 148

Matan, *dial.* Dayak, Land [dyk], 393

Matanai, *alt. dial.* Tontemboan [tnt], 434

Matana'i-Maore', *alt. dial.* Tontemboan [tnt], 434

Matangnga, *dial.* Bambam [ptu], 427

Matapi, *alt.* Yucuna [ycn], 248

Matapo, *dial.* Maasai [mas], 134

Mataso, *dial.* Namakura [nmk], 644

Matatlán Zapotec, *alt. dial.* Zapotec, Mitla [zaw], 279

Matawai, *alt. dial.* Saramaccan [srm], 296

Matawari, *dial.* Saramaccan [srm], 296

Mataweja, *alt.* Kwerba [kwe], 418

Matbat [xmt], 420

Matchi, *alt. dial.* Iceve-Maci [bec], 63, 163
  dial. Garo [grt], 362

Matchopa Nagnoo, *dial.* Moinba [mob], 376

Mate, *dial.* Nande [nnb], 105

Mate-Nul-Filakara, *dial.* Lewo [lww], 643

Matema, *dial.* Pileni [piv], 637

Matengo [mgv], 201

Matepi [mqe], 612

Materi, *dial.* Biali [beh], 42

Mathira, *dial.* Gikuyu [kik], 133

Mathsereng, *alt.* Nachering [ncd], 476

Mathwadi, *alt.* Noiri [noi], 381

Mati Ke, *alt.* Marti Ke [zmg], 574

Matia, *dial.* Asmat, Casuarina Coast [asc], 411

Matig-Salud, *dial.* Manobo, Matigsalug [mbt], 499

Matig-Salug Manobo, *alt.* Manobo, Matigsalug [mbt], 499

Matigsalug Manobo, *see* Manobo, Matigsalug [mbt], 499

Matino, *alt.* Davawenyo [daw], 494

Matipu, *alt.* Matipuhy [mzo], 230

Matipuhy [mzo], 230
  dial. Matipuhy [mzo], 230

Matís [mpq], 230

Matlala-Moletshi, *dial.* Sotho, Northern [nso], 186
Matlatzinca, *alt.* Matlatzinca, San Francisco [mat], 264
Matlatzinca de San Francisco de los Ranchos, *alt.* Matlatzinca, San Francisco [mat], 264
Matlatzinca, Atzingo [ocu], 263
Matlatzinca, San Francisco [mat], 264
Matliwag, *dial.* Merlav [mrm], 644
Matngala, *alt.* Madngele [zml], 573
Matngele, *alt.* Madngele [zml], 573
Mato [met], 612
   alt. Makhuwa-Meetto [mgh], 201
Mato Grosso Arára, *see* Arára, Mato Grosso [axg], 225
Matoewari, *alt. dial.* Saramaccan [srm], 296
Matoh, *alt.* Embaloh [emb], 393
Matoki, *alt. dial.* Bomitaba [zmx], 88
Matondoni, *dial.* Swahili [swh], 136
Mator [mtm], 505
   dial. Mator [mtm], 505
Matse, *alt.* Matsés [mcf], 230
Matsés [mcf], 288, 230
Matsiganga, *alt.* Machiguenga [mcb], 288
Matsigenka, *alt.* Machiguenga [mcb], 288
Matsungan, *dial.* Petats [pex], 621
Matsuvan, *alt.* Tsuvan [tsh], 72
Mattole [mvb], 304
Matu, *alt.* Maru [mhx], 465, 340
   dial. Daro-Matu [dro], 459
Matu Chin, *see* Nga La [hlt], 359
Matu Chin, *alt.* Nga La [hlt], 466
Matuari, *alt. dial.* Saramaccan [srm], 296
Matukar [mjk], 612
Matumba, *dial.* Manda [mgs], 201
Matumbi [mgw], 202
Matupi, *alt.* Chin, Matu [hlt], 359
Matupi Daai, *dial.* Chin, Daai [dao], 463
Matupit, *dial.* Kuanua [ksd], 608
Matwanly, *dial.* Rawang [raw], 466
Matya Samo, *see* Samo, Matya [stj], 53
Mau, *alt.* Mahou [mxx], 94
   alt. Shan [shn], 467
   alt. dial. Shan [shn], 467
Maubin, *dial.* Karen, Pwo Western [pwo], 464
Mauchi, *alt.* Mawchi [mke], 375
Maué, *alt.* Sateré-Mawé [mav], 231
Mauka, *alt.* Mahou [mxx], 94
Mauke, *alt.* Mahou [mxx], 94
   dial. Rarotongan [rar], 579

Maula, *alt.* Warluwara [wrb], 578
Mauligan, *alt. dial.* Tagal Murut [mvv], 458, 395
Maumbi, *dial.* Tonsea [txs], 434
Maumere, *alt.* Sika [ski], 409
Maunchi, *pej. alt.* Cishingini [asg], 151
Maung [mph], 574
   alt. dial. Iban [iba], 393
Maure, *alt.* Arabic, Hasanya [mey], 141
   alt. Arabic, Hassaniyya [mey], 146, 151
Mauri, *alt.* Arabic, Hasanya [mey], 141
   alt. Arabic, Hassaniyya [mey], 146, 151
Mauritian, *alt.* Morisyen [mfe], 145
Mauritian Bhojpuri, *dial.* Bhojpuri [bho], 145
Mauritius Creole French, *alt.* Morisyen [mfe], 145
Maurysen, *alt.* Morisyen [mfe], 145
Mauta, *alt.* Lamma [lev], 408
   alt. dial. Lamma [lev], 408
Maututu, *dial.* Nakanai [nak], 616
Mauula, *alt.* Warluwara [wrb], 578
Mauwake [mhl], 612
Mavar, *alt. dial.* Kanuri, Central [knc], 152
Mavchi, *alt.* Mawchi [mke], 375
Mavea, *alt.* Mafea [mkv], 643
Mavia, *alt. dial.* Makonde [kde], 148
Maviha, *dial.* Makonde [kde], 201, 148
Maw, *alt.* Mal Paharia [mkb], 373
   alt. dial. Shan [shn], 467
Mawa (Chad) [mcw], 84
   Mawa (Nigeria) [wma], 169
Mawachi, *alt.* Mawchi [mke], 375
Mawae, *dial.* Zia [zia], 634
Mawak [mjj], 612
Mawake, *alt.* Mauwake [mhl], 612
Mawam, *alt.* Ma [mjn], 610
Mawan [mcz], 612
Mawanchi, *pej. alt.* Cishingini [asg], 151
Mawanda, *alt.* Ndonde Hamba [njd], 202
Mawas, *alt.* Kensiu [kns], 515
Mawasi, *alt. dial.* Korku [kfq], 369
Mawayana [mzx], 257
   alt. Mapidian [mpw], 229
Mawchi [mke], 375
   dial. Mawchi [mke], 375
Mawchi Bhil, *alt.* Mawchi [mke], 375
Mawdo, *alt.* Mal Paharia [mkb], 373
Mawe, *alt.* Mann [mev], 139, 130
Mawé, *alt.* Sateré-Mawé [mav], 231

Mawer, *alt.* Mal Paharia [mkb], 373
   alt. dial. Tumak [tmc], 87
Mawer Nondi, *alt.* Mal Paharia [mkb], 373
Mawes [mgk], 420
Mawia, *alt. dial.* Makonde [kde], 148
Mawissi, *alt.* Talinga-Bwisi [tlj], 212, 108
Mawken, *alt.* Moken [mwt], 466, 516
Mawrang, *dial.* Naga, Tase [nst], 466
Mawshang, *alt.* Naga, Monsang [nmh], 378
Mawteik, *alt.* Kado [kdv], 464, 337
Mawula, *alt.* Warluwara [wrb], 578
Mawung, *alt.* Maung [mph], 574
Maxakalí [mbl], 230
Maxi, *alt.* Gbe, Maxi [mxl], 44
Maxi Gbe, *see* Gbe, Maxi [mxl], 44, 207
Maxi-Gbe, *alt.* Gbe, Maxi [mxl], 44, 207
Maxinéri, *alt.* Machinere [mpd], 229
Maxirona, *alt.* Matsés [mcf], 288
Maxubí, *alt.* Arikapú [ark], 225
Maxuruna, *alt.* Matsés [mcf], 288
May, *alt.* Chut [scb], 522, 450
   alt. dial. Chut [scb], 522
   dial. Chut [scb], 450
May River, *alt.* Iwam [iwm], 603
Ma'ya [slz], 420
   dial. Ma'ya [slz], 420
Maya, *alt.* Bali [bcn], 154
   alt. Itza' [itz], 254
   alt. Maia [sks], 610
Maya Mopán, *alt.* Maya, Mopán [mop], 221, 255
Maya Samo, *see* Samo, Maya [sym], 53
Maya, Chan Santa Cruz [yus], 264
Maya, Mopán [mop], 221, 255
Maya, Yucatán [yua], 264, 221
Maya-Tekiteko, *alt.* Tektiteko [ttc], 256
Mayaguduna [xmy], 574
Mayali, *alt.* Gunwinggu [gup], 571
Mayang, *dial.* Assamese [asm], 354
Mayangkhang, *alt.* Naga, Thangal [nki], 380
Mayaoyaw, *alt.* Ifugao, Mayoyao [ifu], 495
Mayar, *dial.* Stod Bhoti [sbu], 387
Mayar Bhoti, *alt. dial.* Stod Bhoti [sbu], 387
Mayari, *alt. dial.* Stod Bhoti [sbu], 387
Mayayero, *dial.* Cuiba [cui], 244
Mayeka [myc], 104

Mayi-Kulan, *alt.* Maykulan [mnt], 574

Mayi-Kutuna, *alt.* Mayaguduna [xmy], 574

Mayi-Thakurti, *alt.* Maykulan [mnt], 574

Mayi-Yapi, *alt.* Maykulan [mnt], 574

Mayiruna, *alt.* Matsés [mcf], 288

Mayko, *alt.* Mayogo [mdm], 104

Maykulan [mnt], 574

Mayna, *alt.* Omurano [omu], 289

Mayo [mfy], 264

Mayo-Plata, *dial.* Vame [mlr], 73

Mayo-Yesan, *alt.* Yessan-Mayo [yss], 633

Mayo-Yessan, *dial.* Yessan-Mayo [yss], 633

Mayogo [mdm], 104

Mayol, *alt.* Naga, Moyon [nmo], 379

Mayon Naga, *alt.* Naga, Moyon [nmo], 379

Mayongong, *alt.* Maquiritari [mch], 229

alt. dial. Maquiritari [mch], 229

Mayoruna, *alt.* Matsés [mcf], 288, 230

Mayotte, *alt. dial.* Comorian [swb], 87, 140

Mayoyao, *alt.* Ifugao, Mayoyao [ifu], 495

Mayoyao Ifugao, *see* Ifugao, Mayoyao [ifu], 495

Mayu, *dial.* Berta [wti], 113, 189

Mayugo, *alt.* Mayogo [mdm], 104

Mayuzuna, *alt.* Matsés [mcf], 288

Mayvasi Koli, *alt. dial.* Koli, Wadiyara [kxp], 487

Mazagwa, *dial.* Wandala [mfi], 73, 177

Mazagway [dkx], 66

Mazagway-Hidi, *alt.* Mazagway [dkx], 66

Mazahua Central [maz], 264

Mazahua, Michoacán [mmc], 264

Mazaltepec Zapotec, *see* Zapotec, Mazaltepec [zpy], 278

Mazandarani, *alt.* Mazanderani [mzn], 441

Mazanderani [mzn], 441

dial. Mazanderani [mzn], 441

Mazatec, Ayautla [vmy], 264

Mazatec, Chiquihuitlán [maq], 264

Mazatec, Huautla [mau], 264

Mazatec, Ixcatlán [mzi], 264

Mazatec, Jalapa de Díaz [maj], 264

Mazatec, Mazatlán [vmz], 264

Mazatec, San Jerónimo Tecóatl [maa], 265

Mazatec, Soyaltepec [vmp], 265

Mazateco de Huautla de Jimenez, *alt.* Mazatec, Huautla [mau], 264

Mazateco de la Sierra, *alt.* Mazatec, Huautla [mau], 264

Mazateco de Mazatlán Villa de Flores, *alt.* Mazatec, Mazatlán [vmz], 264

Mazateco de San Antonio Eloxochitlán, *alt.* Mazatec, San Jerónimo Tecóatl [maa], 265

Mazateco de San Felipe Jalapa de Díaz, *alt.* Mazatec, Jalapa de Díaz [maj], 264

Mazateco de San Jerónimo Tecóatl, *alt.* Mazatec, San Jerónimo Tecóatl [maa], 265

Mazateco de San Juan Chiquihuitlán, *alt.* Mazatec, Chiquihuitlán [maq], 264

Mazateco de San Miguel Soyaltepec, *alt.* Mazatec, Soyaltepec [vmp], 265

Mazateco de San Pedro Ixcatlán, *alt.* Mazatec, Ixcatlán [mzi], 264

Mazateco de Temascal, *alt.* Mazatec, Soyaltepec [vmp], 265

Mazatlán Mazatec, *see* Mazatec, Mazatlán [vmz], 264

Mazatlán Mixe, *see* Mixe, Mazatlán [mzl], 265

Mazera, *alt.* Majera [xmj], 83

Mazgarwa, *alt. dial.* Bade [bde], 154

Mazizuru, *alt. dial.* Shona [sna], 216

Maznoug, *dial.* Domari [rmt], 438, 554

Mazra, *alt. dial.* Majera [xmj], 65, 83

Mba [mfc], 104

Mba Rumbathama, *alt.* Lamu-Lamu [lby], 573

Mbaama, *alt.* Mbama [mbm], 120

alt. Ombamba [mbm], 89

Mbaan, *alt. dial.* Tringgus [trx], 461

Mbaanhu, *alt.* Mbalanhu [lnb], 150

Mbaaru, *dial.* Guruntum-Mbaaru [grd], 161

Mbabaram [vmb], 574

Mbacca, *alt.* Ngbaka Ma'bo [nbm], 77, 89, 105

Mbada, *alt.* Bada [bau], 154

Mbadawa, *alt.* Bada [bau], 154

Mbaelelea, *alt.* Baelelea [bvc], 635

Mbaenggu, *alt.* Baeggu [bvd], 635

Mbagani, *dial.* Songe [sop], 108

Mbah, *dial.* Mfumte [nfu], 67

M'bahouin, *alt.* Mbangwe [zmn], 120, 86

Mbahouin, *alt.* Mbangwe [zmn], 120, 86

Mbai, *alt.* Mbay [myb], 84, 77

dial. Gbaya, Northwest [gya], 61

dial. Kupsabiny [kpz], 211

Mbaise, *dial.* Igbo [ibo], 163

Mbaka, *alt.* Ngbaka Ma'bo [nbm], 77, 89, 105

dial. Mbundu [kmb], 41

Mbakarla, *alt.* Umbugarla [umr], 577

Mbaki, *alt. dial.* Kwakum [kwu], 65

Mbakolo, *dial.* Gbaya, Southwest [mdo], 76

Mbala [mdp], 104

dial. Yombe [yom], 109, 42, 90

Mbalangwe, *alt.* Subiya [sbs], 151

Mbalanhu [lnb], 150

Mbalantu, *alt.* Mbalanhu [lnb], 150

Mbalazi, *alt. dial.* Swahili [swh], 136, 185

Mbale, *alt.* Bushoong [buf], 98

dial. Taita [dav], 136

Mbali, *alt.* Mabaale [mmz], 103

alt. Umbundu [umb], 42

Mballa, *dial.* Mfumte [nfu], 67

Mbaloh, *alt.* Embaloh [emb], 393

Mbaluntu, *alt.* Mbalanhu [lnb], 150

Mbama [mbm], 120

alt. Nagumi [ngv], 69

alt. Ombamba [mbm], 89

Mbamba, *alt.* Mbama [mbm], 120

alt. Ombamba [mbm], 89

dial. Mbundu [kmb], 41

Mbambatana, *alt.* Babatana [baa], 635

Mbamu, *dial.* Eloyi [afo], 159

Mbana, *alt. dial.* Mundang [mua], 68

Mbandieru, *dial.* Herero [her], 150

Mbandja [zmz], 104, 89

Mbandza, *alt.* Mbandja [zmz], 104

Mbang, *alt. dial.* Mbay [myb], 84

dial. Bakoko [bkh], 57

dial. Basaa [bas], 58

Mbanga, *alt. dial.* Kaba Na [kwv], 81

Mbangala [mxg], 41

dial. Mbangala [mxg], 41

Mbangi [mgn], 77

Mbangui, *alt.* Mbangi [mgn], 77

Mbangwe [zmn], 120, 86

Mbaniata, *alt.* Touo [tqu], 639

Mbanja, *alt.* Mbandja [zmz], 104, 89

Mbanua, *alt.* Santa Cruz [stc], 638

dial. Santa Cruz [stc], 638

Mbanza, *alt.* Mbandja [zmz], 104, 89

Mbara (Australia) [mvl], 574

Mbara (Chad) [mpk], 84

alt. Mbabaram [vmb], 574

Mbara Kwengo, *alt.* Khwe [xuu], 214

Mbowe [mxo], 214
 dial. Luyana [lyn], 214, 41
Mbowela, *dial.* Nkoya [nka], 214
Mboxo, *alt.* Mboko [mdu], 89
Mboyakum, *alt.* Bambalang
 [bmo], 56
Mboyi, *alt.* Mboi [moi], 170
Mbre [mka], 94
 dial. Banda-Mbrès [bqk], 75, 188
Mbreme, *alt. dial.* Vame [mlr], 73
Mbrerewi, *dial.* Ngemba [nge], 69
Mbu, *alt.* Ngamambo [nbv], 69
Mbu' [muc], 66
Mbua, *alt.* Guaraní, Mbyá [gun], 227, 220, 284
Mbuba, *alt.* Mvuba [mxh], 105
Mbube Eastern, *alt.* Putukwam [afe], 173
Mbubem, *alt.* Yamba [yam], 73
Mbudja, *alt.* Budza [bja], 98
Mbuela, *alt.* Mbwela [mfu], 41
Mbughotu, *alt.* Bughotu [bgt], 635
Mbugu [mhd], 202
Mbugwe [mgz], 202
Mbui, *alt. dial.* Bambili-Bambui [baw], 57
Mbukambero, *alt. dial.* Laura [lur], 408
Mbuko [mqb], 66
Mbuku, *alt.* Mboko [mdu], 89
 alt. Mbuko [mqb], 66
Mbukuhu, *alt.* Mbukushu [mhw], 150, 41, 47, 214
Mbukushi, *alt.* Mbukushu [mhw], 150, 41, 47, 214
Mbukushu [mhw], 150, 41, 47, 214
Mbula [mna], 612
 dial. Mbula [mna], 612
 dial. Mbula-Bwazza [mbu], 170
Mbula-Bwazza [mbu], 170
Mbule [mlb], 66
Mbuli, *dial.* Ombo [oml], 106
Mbulu, *alt.* Iraqw [irk], 199
Mbulugwe, *alt.* Burunge [bds], 197
Mbulunge, *alt.* Iraqw [irk], 199
Mbulungish [mbv], 130
Mbum [mdd], 66, 77
 alt. Karang [kzr], 63
 alt. Nzakambay [nzy], 86
Mbum Bakal, *alt.* Karang [kzr], 81
Mbum Nzakambay, *alt.* Nzakambay [nzy], 86
Mbum-East, *alt.* Karang [kzr], 63
Mbumi, *dial.* Luyana [lyn], 214
M'bunai, *alt.* Titan [ttv], 628
Mbunda [mck], 214, 41
 alt. dial. Mpuono [zmp], 105
M'bundo, *alt.* Umbundu [umb], 42
Mbundu [kmb], 41

Mbundu Benguella, *alt.* Umbundu [umb], 42
Mbunga [mgy], 202
Mbunza, *alt. dial.* Gbaya, Southwest [mdo], 76
Mburkanci, *alt.* Mburku [bbt], 170
Mburku [bbt], 170
Mburugam, *alt.* Esimbi [ags], 61
Mbusuku, *alt. dial.* Gbaya, Southwest [mdo], 76
Mbuta, *alt. dial.* Gamo-Ningi [bte], 160
Mbute, *alt.* Vute [vut], 177
Mbutere, *alt.* Vute [vut], 177
Mbuti, *alt.* Lese [les], 102
Mbutu, *dial.* Ngemba [nge], 69
Mbuun, *alt. dial.* Mpuono [zmp], 105
Mbuunda, *alt.* Mbunda [mck], 214, 41
Mbuwe, *alt.* Mbugwe [mgz], 202
Mbwaanz, *dial.* Makaa [mcp], 65
Mbwaka, *alt.* Ngbaka Ma'bo [nbm], 105
Mbwase Nghuy, *alt. dial.* Bakaka [bqz], 57
Mbwela [mfu], 41
 alt. dial. Nkoya [nka], 214
Mbwera, *alt.* Mbwela [mfu], 41
 alt. dial. Nkoya [nka], 214
Mbwe'wi, *alt.* Awing [azo], 56
Mbwila, *dial.* Safwa [sbk], 204
Mbwisi, *alt.* Bwisi [bwz], 88, 120
Mbya, *alt.* Sirionó [srq], 223
Mbyá, *alt.* Guaraní, Mbyá [gun], 227, 220, 284
Mbyá Guaraní, *see* Guaraní, Mbyá [gun], 227, 220, 284
Mbyam, *dial.* Kwa' [bko], 65
Mbyemo, *alt.* Mpiemo [mcx], 77
 alt. Mpyemo [mcx], 89
Mcdermitt, *alt. dial.* Paiute, Northern [pao], 306
Mcgrath Ingalik, *alt.* Kuskokwim, Upper [kuu], 303
Mdhur, *alt. dial.* Rade [rad], 526
Mdundulu, *dial.* Luyana [lyn], 41
Me, *alt.* Matbat [xmt], 420
Me Mana, *alt.* Ekari [ekg], 414
Me-Wuk, *alt.* Miwok, Southern Sierra [skd], 305
Mea [meg], 585
Meadow Mari, *alt.* Mari, Eastern [mhr], 555
 alt. dial. Mari, Eastern [mhr], 555
Meah, *alt.* Meyah [mej], 420
Meakambut, *dial.* Arafundi [arf], 590
Meänkieli, *alt.* Finnish, Tornedalen [fit], 561
Mearim, *dial.* Guajajára [gub], 227

Meaun, *alt.* Labo [mwi], 642
Meauna, *alt. dial.* Tairora, South [omw], 626
Meax, *alt.* Meyah [mej], 420
Meban, *alt.* Mabaan [mfz], 193
Mebu, *alt.* Ma [mjn], 610
Mech, *alt.* Bodo [brx], 357, 469
 dial. Bodo [brx], 357
Meche, *alt.* Bodo [brx], 357, 469
Mechi, *alt.* Bodo [brx], 357, 469
Meci, *alt.* Bodo [brx], 357, 469
Mecklenburg-Anterior Pomerania, *dial.* Saxon, Low [nds], 539
Mecklenburgisch-Vorpommersch, *alt. dial.* Saxon, Low [nds], 539
Meco, *alt.* Chichimeca-Jonaz [pei], 260
Medang, *alt.* Madang [mqd], 460
Medebur [mjm], 613
Media Lengua [mue], 251
Mediak [mwx], 202
Medje, *alt. dial.* Mangbetu [mdj], 104
Medlpa, *alt.* Melpa [med], 613
Mednovskiy, *alt.* Ahtena [aht], 297
Medny, *alt.* Aleut, Mednyj [mud], 503
Mednyj Aleut, *see* Aleut, Mednyj [mud], 503
Medo, *alt.* Makhuwa-Meetto [mgh], 147
 dial. Makhuwa-Meetto [mgh], 201
Medogo, *dial.* Naba [mne], 85
Medumba [byv], 67
Medzime, *alt. dial.* Mpongmpong [mgg], 68
Mee, *alt.* Basaa [bas], 58
 dial. Ekari [ekg], 414
Mee Mana, *alt.* Ekari [ekg], 414
Me'ek, *alt.* Mehek [nux], 613
Meeka, *dial.* Mumuye [mzm], 170
Meembi, *alt.* Ndo [ndp], 105
Me'en [mym], 117
Meetto, *alt.* Makhuwa-Meetto [mgh], 147
Meewoc, *alt.* Miwok, Southern Sierra [skd], 305
Mefele [mfj], 67
 dial. Mefele [mfj], 67
Mefoor, *alt.* Biak [bhw], 412
Megahi, *alt.* Magahi [mag], 373
Megaka, *alt.* Mengaka [xmg], 67
Megam [mef], 321
 alt. dial. Khasi [kha], 367
Megi, *dial.* Angal Enen [aoe], 589
 dial. Kagulu [kki], 199
Megiar, *dial.* Takia [tbc], 626
Megili, *alt.* Lijili [mgi], 168
Megimba, *alt.* Ngemba [nge], 69

Meglenite, *alt.* Romanian, Megleno [ruq], 541
Meglenitic, *alt.* Romanian, Megleno [ruq], 541
Megleno Romanian, *see* Romanian, Megleno [ruq], 541, 547
Megrel, *alt.* Mingrelian [xmf], 352
Megruli, *alt.* Mingrelian [xmf], 352
Megyaw, *alt.* Hpon [hpo], 464
Mehalaan, *dial.* Bambam [ptu], 427
Mehara, *alt. dial.* Sabu [hvn], 409
Mehari, *alt.* Halbi [hlb], 363
  dial. Halbi [hlb], 363
Mehek [nux], 613
Meher, *alt.* Kisar [kje], 400
Mehinaco, *alt.* Mehináku [mmh], 230
Mehináku [mmh], 230
Mehri [gdq], 528, 449, 483
Mehriyet, *alt. dial.* Mehri [gdq], 528
Mehriyot, *alt. dial.* Mehri [gdq], 528
Mehtar, *alt.* Domari [rmt], 438
Meibuil, *dial.* Kabola [klz], 407
Meidob, *alt.* Midob [mei], 193
Meidoo, *alt.* Maidu, Northwest [mjd], 304
Meifu, *dial.* Hlai [lic], 333
Mein, *dial.* Izon [ijc], 164
Meitei [mni], 375, 321, 465
  dial. Meitei [mni], 375
Meiteilon, *alt.* Meitei [mni], 375
Meiteiron, *alt.* Meitei [mni], 375, 321, 465
Meithe, *alt.* Meitei [mni], 375, 321, 465
Meithei, *alt.* Meitei [mni], 375, 321, 465
Meixian, *alt. dial.* Chinese, Hakka [hak], 329
Meiyari, *alt.* Niksek [gbe], 618
  dial. Niksek [gbe], 618
Mejach, *alt.* Meyah [mej], 420
Mejah, *alt.* Meyah [mej], 420
Meje, *dial.* Mangbetu [mdj], 104
Mejicano de Zacapoaxtla, *alt.* Nahuatl, Highland Puebla [azz], 271
Meka, *alt.* Byep [mkk], 59
  alt. Marka [rkm], 52, 143
  alt. dial. Ghomálá' [bbj], 62
Mekaa, *alt.* Makaa [mcp], 65
Mekae, *alt.* Byep [mkk], 59
Mekaf, *alt.* Naki [mff], 69
Mekan, *alt.* Me'en [mym], 117
Mekay, *alt.* Byep [mkk], 59
Mekem, *alt.* Kanoé [kxo], 228
Mekéns, *alt.* Kanoé [kxo], 228
Mekeo [mek], 613

Mekeo-Kovio, *alt.* Mekeo [mek], 613
Mekey, *alt.* Byep [mkk], 59
Mekeyer, *pej. alt.* Shabo [sbf], 118
Mekmek [mvk], 613
Mekongga, *dial.* Tolaki [lbw], 433
Mekuk, *alt. dial.* Ngumba [nmg], 70
Mekwei [msf], 420
  alt. Moi [mxn], 420
Mekye, *alt.* Byep [mkk], 59
Melaju, *alt.* Malay [mly], 455, 436
Melamba, *alt.* Kenswei Nsei [ndb], 64
Melamela, *alt.* Meramera [mxm], 613
Melan So, *dial.* So [sox], 72
Melanau [mel], 460, 325
Melanesian English, *alt.* Tok Pisin [tpi], 628
Melaripi, *alt. dial.* Toaripi [tqo], 628
Melawi, *alt. dial.* Dohoi [otd], 393
Melayu, *alt.* Malay [mly], 455, 436, 509, 516
Melayu Bahasa, *alt.* Sri Lankan Creole Malay [sci], 509
Melayu Jakarte, *alt.* Betawi [bew], 391
Melayu Pasar, *dial.* Malay [mly], 436
Mele, *dial.* Gula [kcm], 76
  dial. Mele-Fila [mxe], 643
Mele Nadu Irula, *dial.* Irula [iru], 365
Mele-Fila [mxe], 643
Melejo, *alt.* Emerillon [eme], 252
Melete, *dial.* Tswana [tsn], 186
Melets Tatar, *alt.* Chulym [clw], 504
Meligan, *alt. dial.* Tagal Murut [mvv], 458, 395
Melilup, *dial.* Teop [tio], 627
Melkhin, *dial.* Chechen [che], 553
Melkoi, *alt. dial.* Mamusi [kdf], 611
Mella, *alt. dial.* Cuiba [cui], 311
Melo [mfx], 117
Melobong Rungus, *alt.* Rungus [drg], 458
Melokwo, *alt.* Moloko [mlw], 68
Melolo, *dial.* Kambera [xbr], 407
Melong, *dial.* Mbo [mbo], 66
Melpa [med], 613
Melsisi, *dial.* Apma [app], 640
Memagun, *alt.* Rungus [drg], 458
Memaloh, *alt.* Embaloh [emb], 393
Memba, *alt.* Tshangla [tsj], 389
Membakut Kadazan, *alt.* Kadazan, Coastal [kzj], 457
Membi, *alt. dial.* Ndo [ndp], 105
  dial. Ndo [ndp], 212
Membitu, *alt. dial.* Ndo [ndp], 105

Memboro, *alt.* Mamboru [mvd], 408
Memekere, *alt.* Dugwor [dme], 60
Memi, *alt.* Naga, Mao [nbi], 378
Memogun, *alt.* Rungus [drg], 458
Memoni [mby], 487
Men, *alt.* Kim Mun [mji], 337
  alt. Me'en [mym], 117
Men-Pa, *alt.* Moinba [mob], 376
Mena, *dial.* Ikobi-Mena [meb], 602
Menadonese, *alt. dial.* Malay [mly], 436
Menam, *alt.* Monom [moo], 525
Menandon, *alt.* Aiku [mzf], 588
Menba, *alt.* Moinba [mob], 376, 340
  alt. Tshangla [tsj], 324, 345, 389
Menchum, *alt.* Befang [bby], 58
Mendage, *alt.* Maslam [msv], 84
  alt. Mpade [mpi], 68, 84
  alt. Mser [kqx], 84
Mendalam Kajan, *alt.* Kayan, Mendalam [xkd], 393
Mendalam Kayan, *see* Kayan, Mendalam [xkd], 393
Mendankwe, *alt.* Mendankwe-Nkwen [mfd], 67
  dial. Mendankwe-Nkwen [mfd], 67
Mendankwe-Nkwen [mfd], 67
Mende (Papua New Guinea) [sim], 613
  Mende (Sierra Leone) [men], 183, 139
Mendeya, *alt.* Gumuz [guk], 115, 191
Mendi, *alt.* Angal [age], 589
  alt. Kensiu [kns], 454
Mendo-Kala, *alt. dial.* Umbu-Ungu [ubu], 629
Mendriq, *alt.* Minriq [mnq], 455
Mendyako, *alt.* Mandjak [mfv], 131
Mendzime, *alt. dial.* Mpongmpong [mgg], 68
Meneca, *alt.* Huitoto, Minica [hto], 245
Menemo, *dial.* Meta' [mgo], 67
Menemo-Mogamo, *alt.* Meta' [mgo], 67
Mengaka [xmg], 67
Mengambo, *alt.* Bamenyam [bce], 57
Mengau, *dial.* Dera [kbv], 597
Mengda, *dial.* Salar [slr], 343
Mengen [mee], 613
Mengerrdji, *alt.* Mangerr [zme], 573
Menggala, *dial.* Abung [abl], 435
Menggatal, *dial.* Dusun, Central [dtp], 456
Menggei, *alt.* Mekwei [msf], 420
Menggu, *alt.* Mongolian, Peripheral [mvf], 339

Menggwei, *alt.* Mekwei [msf], 420
Mengisa [mct], 67
Mengisa-Njowe, *alt.* Mengisa [mct], 67
Mengkasara, *alt.* Makasar [mak], 430
Mengkatip, *alt. dial.* Bakumpai [bkr], 392
Mengo, *alt.* Kensiu [kns], 515
Mengum, *dial.* Ngie [ngj], 69
Meni, *alt.* Ikobi-Mena [meb], 602
　alt. Kensiu [kns], 515
　dial. Ikobi-Mena [meb], 602
Menik, *alt.* Kensiu [kns], 515
Menindal, *alt.* Kuijau [dkr], 457
Menindaq, *alt.* Kuijau [dkr], 457
Meninggo, *alt.* Moskona [mtj], 420
Meningo, *alt.* Moskona [mtj], 420
Menipuri, *alt.* Meitei [mni], 375, 465
Menja, *alt.* Kwegu [xwg], 116
Menjuke, *alt. dial.* Dayak, Land [dyk], 393
Menka [mea], 67
Menku, *alt. dial.* Irántxe [irn], 227
Mennagi, *alt.* Mangerr [zme], 573
Mennonite German, *alt.* Plautdietsch [pdt], 241, 222, 223, 231, 249, 273, 307
Mennoniten Platt, *alt.* Plautdietsch [pdt], 241
Meno-Mene, *dial.* Sasak [sas], 409
Menominee [mez], 304
Menomini, *alt.* Menominee [mez], 304
Menorqui, *alt. dial.* Catalan-Valencian-Balear [cat], 559
Menpa, *alt.* Moinba [mob], 340
Menraq, *alt.* Minriq [mnq], 455
Menrik, *alt.* Minriq [mnq], 455
Menriq, *alt.* Minriq [mnq], 455
Mensa, *alt. dial.* Tigré [tig], 112, 195
Menta, *alt.* Manta [myg], 66
Mentawai [mwv], 436
Mentawei, *alt.* Mentawai [mwv], 436
Mentawi, *alt.* Mentawai [mwv], 436
Mentebah-Suruk, *dial.* Malayic Dayak [xdy], 394
Mentera, *alt. dial.* Temuan [tmw], 455
Mentuh Tapuh, *dial.* Bukar Sadong [sdo], 459
Menui, *dial.* Wawonii [wow], 435
Menya [mcr], 613
　dial. Nyole [nuj], 212
Menyama, *alt.* Menya [mcr], 613
Menye, *alt.* Menya [mcr], 613
Menyukai, *alt. dial.* Dayak, Land [dyk], 393

Menzime, *dial.* Mpongmpong [mgg], 68
Meo, *alt.* Hmong Njua [blu], 334, 450, 514
Meo Do, *alt.* Hmong, Eastern Xiangxi [muq], 334
　alt. Hmong, Western Xiangxi [mmr], 335
　alt. dial. Hmong Daw [mww], 523
Meo Kao, *alt.* Hmong Daw [mww], 334, 450, 514, 523
Meo Lai, *alt.* Pa-Hng [pha], 342
Meohang, Eastern [emg], 475
Meohang, Western [raf], 476
Meon, *alt.* Karon Dori [kgw], 416
Meoswar [mvx], 420
Me'pa, *alt.* Tlapanec, Acatepec [tpx], 275
Me'pa Wíʾìn, *alt.* Tlapanec, Acatepec [tpx], 275
Me'phaa, *alt.* Tlapanec, Acatepec [tpx], 275
　alt. Tlapanec, Azoyú [tpc], 275
　alt. Tlapanec, Malinaltepec [tcf], 275
Meqan, *alt.* Me'en [mym], 117
Mequem, *alt.* Kanoé [kxo], 228
Mequen, *alt.* Kanoé [kxo], 228
Mequens, *alt.* Kanoé [kxo], 228
Mer [mnu], 420
　alt. Meriam [ulk], 574
　dial. Bench [bcq], 113
Mera Sagtengpa, *alt.* Brokpake [sgt], 322
Meradan, *alt.* Maridan [zmd], 573
Meragsagstengkha, *alt.* Brokpake [sgt], 322
Meramera [mxm], 613
Merarit, *alt.* Mararit [mgb], 83
Meratei, *dial.* Dayak, Land [dyk], 393
Meratus, *alt.* Malay, Bukit [bvu], 394
Merau Malay, *alt.* Malay, Berau [bve], 394
Merdu, *alt.* Mursi [muz], 117
Mere, *alt.* Merey [meq], 67
　dial. Gula [kcm], 76
Merei [lmb], 643
Merelava, *alt.* Merlav [mrm], 644
Mereo, *alt.* Emerillon [eme], 252
Meretei, *alt. dial.* Dayak, Land [dyk], 393
Merey [meq], 67
Mereyo, *alt.* Emerillon [eme], 252
Mergel, *alt. dial.* Evenki [evn], 332
Merguese, *dial.* Burmese [mya], 462
Mergui, *alt. dial.* Burmese [mya], 462
Meri, *alt.* Merey [meq], 67

Meriam [ulk], 574
Merida, *alt.* Zaghawa [zag], 196, 87
Meridionale, *dial.* Sardinian, Campidanese [sro], 545
Merig, *alt. dial.* Merlav [mrm], 644
Merile, *alt.* Daasanach [dsh], 114
Merille, *alt.* Daasanach [dsh], 114
Merina, *dial.* Malagasy, Plateau [plt], 140
Meritu, *alt.* Mursi [muz], 117
Merlav [mrm], 644
Merlav-Merig, *alt.* Merlav [mrm], 644
Mernyang, *alt. dial.* Kofyar [kwl], 166
Merong, *alt.* Miriwung [mep], 574
Merranunggu, *alt.* Maranunggu [zmr], 573
　alt. dial. Maringarr [zmt], 573
Meru [mer], 134
　alt. dial. Rwa [rwk], 204
　dial. Meru [mer], 134
Merule, *alt.* Murle [mur], 193, 117
Merwari [wry], 375
　alt. Marwari [mve], 487
Mesa del Nayar, *alt. dial.* Cora, El Nayar [crn], 262
Mesaka [iyo], 67
Mesakin, *alt.* Ngile [jle], 194
Mesakin Qusar, *alt. dial.* Ngile [jle], 194
Mesara, *dial.* Sabu [hvn], 409
Mesari, *dial.* Ese [mcq], 598
Mescalero, *dial.* Apache, Mescalero-Chiricahua [apm], 298
Mescalero-Chiricahua Apache, *see* Apache, Mescalero-Chiricahua [apm], 298
Mese [mci], 613
　dial. Tunen [baz], 72
Mesem, *alt.* Mese [mci], 613
Mesengo, *alt.* Majang [mpe], 116
Meshed, *alt. dial.* Farsi, Western [pes], 439
Mesi, *dial.* Madak [mmx], 610
Mesiang, *dial.* Barakai [baj], 396
Mesing, *alt.* Kenswei Nsei [ndb], 64
Mesise, *dial.* Dogosé [dos], 50
Meskan, *alt.* Mesqan [mvz], 117
Mesketo, *alt.* Basketo [bst], 113
Meskhur-Javakhuri, *dial.* Georgian [kat], 352
Meskwakie, *alt.* Mesquakie [sac], 304
Mesme [zim], 84
Mesmedje, *alt.* Masmaje [mes], 84
Mesmes [mys], 117
Mesopotamian Gelet Arabic, *alt.* Arabic, Mesopotamian Spoken [acm], 442, 437, 510

Mesopotamian Qeltu Arabic,
  alt. Arabic, Mesopotamian Spoken
  [acm], 442
  alt. Arabic, North Mesopotamian
  Spoken [ayp], 442, 510
Mesopotamian Spoken Arabic,
  see Arabic, Mesopotamian Spoken
  [acm], 442, 437, 510
Mesqan [mvz], 117
Mesquakie [sac], 304
  dial. Mesquakie [sac], 304
Messa-Dote, *dial.* Sawai [szw], 403
Messaga, *alt.* Mesaka [iyo], 67
Messaga-Ekol, *alt.* Mesaka
  [iyo], 67
Messaka, *alt.* Mesaka [iyo], 67
Messeni, *alt. dial.* Senoufo, Cebaara
  [sef], 94
Messinese, *dial.* Sicilian [scn], 545
Meta' [mgo], 67
  alt. dial. Meta' [mgo], 67
Metabi, *alt.* Gaam [tbi], 190
Metan, *alt.* Nabi [mty], 616
Metemma, *dial.* Gumuz [guk], 115
Methli, *alt.* Maithili [mai], 373, 475
Meting, *alt.* Belait [beg], 324
Metis, *alt.* Michif [crg], 239
Metla-Kinwat, *dial.* Kolami,
  Southeastern [nit], 369
Metlatónoc Mixtec, *see* Mixtec,
  Metlatónoc [mxv], 267
Metnyo, *dial.* Waigeo [wgo], 424
Meto, *alt.* Makhuwa-Meetto
  [mgh], 147
  alt. Uab Meto [aoz], 410
  alt. dial. Makhuwa-Meetto [mgh],
  201
Mêto, *alt.* Makhuwa-Meetto [mgh],
  147
Metoki, *alt.* Kenuzi-Dongola
  [kzh], 110
Metoko, *alt.* Mituku [zmq], 104
Metomka, *alt.* Muyu, South
  [kts], 421
  dial. Muyu, South [kts], 421
Metru, *alt.* Dia [dia], 597
  alt. Sinagen [siu], 624
Metsam, *dial.* Waigeo [wgo], 424
Metta, *alt.* Meta' [mgo], 67
  alt. dial. Meta' [mgo], 67
Metto, *alt.* Makhuwa-Meetto [mgh],
  147
Metuali, *alt. dial.* Arabic, North
  Levantine Spoken [apc], 453
Meuay, *alt. dial.* Tai Dam [blt], 526,
  453
Meudana, *dial.* Bunama [bdd], 595
Mewadi, *alt.* Mewari [mtr], 375
Mewahang, *alt.* Meohang, Eastern
  [emg], 475

  alt. Meohang, Western [raf], 476
Mewari [mtr], 375
Mewasi, *dial.* Koli, Wadiyara
  [kxp], 487
Mewathi, *alt.* Mewati [wtm], 375
Mewati [wtm], 375
  dial. Haryanvi [bgc], 364
Mewoc, *alt.* Miwok, Southern Sierra
  [skd], 305
Mewun, *alt.* Labo [mwi], 642
Mexican Sign Language
  [mfs], 265
Mexicanero, *alt.* Nahuatl, Durango
  [nln], 270
Mexico, *dial.* Afro-Seminole Creole
  [afs], 297
Mexico Afro-Seminole, *dial.*
  Afro-Seminole Creole [afs], 259
Mextã, *alt.* Carapana [cbc], 244
  alt. Karapanã [cbc], 228
Mey Brat, *alt.* Mai Brat [ayz], 419
Meyach, *alt.* Meyah [mej], 420
Meyah [mej], 420
  alt. Moskona [mtj], 420
Meyobe, *alt.* Miyobe [soy], 45
Meyor, *alt.* Zakhring [zkr], 390
Meyu Ehtremeñu, *alt. dial.*
  Extremaduran [ext], 560
Mezama, *alt.* Naga, Zeme [nzm], 381
Mezime, *alt. dial.* Mpongmpong
  [mgg], 68
Mezimko, *dial.* Mukulu [moz], 85
Mezontla Popoloca, *see* Popoloca,
  Mezontla [pbe], 273
Mezquital Otomi, *see* Otomi,
  Mezquital [ote], 272
Mfangano, *dial.* Suba [suh], 136
Mfantse, *alt. dial.* Akan [aka], 123
Mfe, *dial.* Yamba [yam], 73
Mfengu, *dial.* Xhosa [xho], 187
Mfinu [zmf], 104
Mfumte [nfu], 67
Mfumu, *alt. dial.* Teke-Fuumu [ifm],
  90
Mfununga, *alt.* Mfinu [zmf], 104
Mfuti, *alt.* Vute [vut], 177
Mgao, *dial.* Swahili [swh], 205
Mgbakpa, *alt.* Hausa [hau], 162
Mgbato, *alt.* Mbato [gwa], 94
Mgbo, *alt. dial.* Izi-Ezaa-Ikwo-Mgbo
  [izi], 164
Mgoumba, *alt.* Ngumba [nmg], 111
  alt. dial. Ngumba [nmg], 70
Mhallami, *dial.* Kurdish, Northern
  [kmr], 453
Mhar, *alt.* Hmar [hmr], 364
Mi Marva, *alt.* Giziga, North [gis], 62
Mi Mijivin, *dial.* Giziga, South
  [giz], 62
Miadeba, *dial.* Sewa Bay [sew], 624

Miag-Ao, *alt. dial.* Kinaray-A
  [krj], 498
Miahuatlán Zapotec, *see* Zapotec,
  Miahuatlán [zam], 279
Mialát, *alt. dial.* Tenharim [pah], 232
Miambo, *alt. dial.* Dogon, Kolum So
  [dkl], 142
Miami [mia], 304
  dial. Miami [mia], 304
Miami-Illinois, *alt.* Miami [mia], 304
Miami-Myaamia, *alt.* Miami
  [mia], 304
Miamia, *alt.* Begbere-Ejar [bqv], 155
  alt. Pinai-Hagahai [pnn], 622
Miamilo, *alt. dial.* Bakaka [bqz], 57
Miamiya, *alt.* Begbere-Ejar
  [bqv], 155
Miamu, *dial.* Wan [wan], 95
Mian [mpt], 613
  alt. Iu Mien [ium], 336, 514
Mianchi, *dial.* Qiang, Southern
  [qxs], 342
Miango, *alt.* Irigwe [iri], 164
Miani [pla], 613
Miani North, *alt.* Miani [pla], 613
Miani South, *alt.* Maiani [tnh], 610
Mianka, *alt.* Senoufo, Mamara
  [myk], 144
Mianmin, *alt.* Mian [mpt], 613
  dial. Mian [mpt], 613
Miao, *alt.* Hmong Njua [blu], 334,
  450, 514
  alt. Hmong, Central Huishui [hmc],
  334
  alt. Hmong, Central Mashan
  [hmm], 334
  alt. Hmong, Eastern Huishui
  [hme], 334
  alt. Hmong, Eastern Qiandong
  [hmq], 334
  alt. Hmong, Northern Guiyang
  [huj], 334
  alt. Hmong, Northern Huishui
  [hmi], 334
  alt. Hmong, Northern Qiandong
  [hea], 335
  alt. Hmong, Southern Guiyang
  [hmy], 335
  alt. Hmong, Southern Mashan
  [hma], 335
  alt. Hmong, Southern Qiandong
  [hms], 335
  alt. Hmong, Southwestern Guiyang
  [hmg], 335
  alt. Hmong, Southwestern Huishui
  [hmh], 335
  alt. Hmong, Western Mashan
  [hmw], 335
Miao Lai, *alt. dial.* Hmong Daw
  [mww], 514

Miaro, *alt.* Awyu, Asue [psa], 412
Miaro Awyu, *alt.* Awyu, Asue [psa], 412
Miarrã [xmi], 230
Mibisu, *alt.* Bisu [bii], 327, 514
Mica, *dial.* Huitoto, Murui [huu], 288
Micari, *dial.* Nuni, Southern [nnw], 53
Miccosukee, *alt.* Mikasuki [mik], 305
Micha, *alt.* Yi, Miqie [yiq], 347
Michif [crg], 305, 239
Michoacan Aztec, *alt.* Nahuatl, Michoacán [ncl], 271
Michoacán Mazahua, *see* Mazahua, Michoacán [mmc], 264
Michoacán Nahuatl, *see* Nahuatl, Michoacán [ncl], 271
Michopdo, *alt.* Maidu, Northwest [mjd], 304
Micmac [mic], 239, 305
Mid Bisaya, *dial.* Bisaya, Sarawak [bsd], 459
Mid Grand Valley Dani, *see* Dani, Mid Grand Valley [dnt], 413
Mid Mortlock, *dial.* Mortlockese [mrl], 582
Mid Wahgi, *alt.* Wahgi [wgi], 630
Mid-Southern Banda, *see* Banda, Mid-Southern [bjo], 74, 97, 188
Mid-Wahgi, *dial.* Wahgi [wgi], 630
Mid-Waria, *alt.* Guhu-Samane [ghs], 599
Mida'a, *alt.* Majera [xmj], 65, 83
Midah, *alt.* Majera [xmj], 65, 83
Middle Atlas Berber, *alt.* Tamazight, Central Atlas [tzm], 146, 40
Middle Bamu, *alt. dial.* Bamu [bcf], 592
Middle Cherokee, *alt. dial.* Cherokee [chr], 299
Middle Chulym, *dial.* Chulym [clw], 504
Middle Eastern Romani, *alt.* Domari [rmt], 438, 443, 448, 510, 563
Middle Egypt Arabic, *dial.* Arabic, Sa'idi Spoken [aec], 110
Middle Kheng, *dial.* Khengkha [xkf], 323
Middle Lozyvin, *alt. dial.* Mansi [mns], 505
Middle Musa, *alt.* Yareba [yrb], 633
Middle Nambas, *alt.* Malua Bay [mll], 643
Middle River, *dial.* Carrier [crx], 236
Middle Tatar, *dial.* Tatar [tat], 556

Middle Watut, *see* Watut, Middle [mpl], 631
Mideastern Yiddish, *dial.* Yiddish, Eastern [ydd], 446
Midhi, *alt.* Idu-Mishmi [clk], 364
Midik, *alt. dial.* Kairui-Midiki [krd], 351
Midiki, *alt.* Kairui-Midiki [krd], 351
  alt. dial. Kairui-Midiki [krd], 351
Midin, *dial.* Turoyo [tru], 520
Midnapore Oriya, *dial.* Oriya [ori], 382
Midob [mei], 193
Midobi, *alt.* Midob [mei], 193
Midsivindi, *alt.* Inapang [mzu], 603
Midu, *alt.* Idu-Mishmi [clk], 364
Midwestern Yiddish, *dial.* Yiddish, Western [yih], 540
Midyat, *dial.* Turoyo [tru], 520
Mie'en, *alt.* Me'en [mym], 117
Mieken, *alt.* Me'en [mym], 117
Mien, *alt.* Iu Mien [ium], 336, 450, 514, 523
Mienge, *dial.* Bassossi [bsi], 58
Miere, *alt.* Mer [mnu], 420
Mieru, *alt. dial.* Bench [bcq], 113
Migaama [mmy], 84
  dial. Migaama [mmy], 84
Migaba', *alt.* Migabac [mpp], 614
Migabac [mpp], 614
Migam, *alt.* Megam [mef], 321
Migama, *alt.* Migaama [mmy], 84
Migangam, *alt.* Ngangam [gng], 209
Migani, *alt.* Moni [mnz], 420
Migili, *alt.* Lijili [mgi], 168
Mi'gmaq, *alt.* Micmac [mic], 239
Mi'gmaw, *alt.* Micmac [mic], 305
Miguelenho, *alt.* Puruborá [pur], 232
Miguelenno, *alt.* Puruborá [pur], 232
Miguhni, *alt. dial.* Ngwo [ngn], 70
Migulimancema, *alt.* Gourmanchéma [gux], 51, 45, 208
Mihavane, *alt.* Lomwe [ngl], 147
Mihavani, *alt.* Lomwe [ngl], 147
Mihawani, *alt.* Lomwe [ngl], 147
Miigmao, *alt.* Micmac [mic], 239, 305
Mijaranés Aranés, *dial.* Gascon, Aranese [gsc], 560
Miji, *alt.* Miju-Mishmi [mxj], 375
  alt. Sajalong [sjl], 385
Mijiem, *alt.* Ngangam [gng], 209
Mijili, *alt.* Lijili [mgi], 168
Mijong, *alt.* Abar [mij], 56
Miju, *alt.* Miju-Mishmi [mxj], 375
Miju-Mishmi [mxj], 375
Mìjuu, *dial.* Senoufo, Mamara [myk], 144
Mika, *alt.* Byep [mkk], 59

Mikair, *pej. alt.* Shabo [sbf], 118
Mikarew, *alt.* Aruamu [msy], 591
Mikarew-Ariaw, *alt.* Aruamu [msy], 591
Mikarup, *alt.* Aruamu [msy], 591
Mikasuki [mik], 305
  dial. Mikasuki [mik], 305
Mikasuki Seminole, *alt.* Mikasuki [mik], 305
Mikebwe, *dial.* Bangubangu [bnx], 97
Mikere, *dial.* Dugwor [dme], 60
Mikeyir, *pej. alt.* Shabo [sbf], 118
Mikifore, *alt.* Mixifore [mfg], 130
Mikik, *dial.* Tsakhur [tkr], 557
Mikir, *pej. alt.* Karbi [mjw], 366
Mikiri, *pej. alt.* Karbi [mjw], 366
Miklai, *alt.* Naga, Lotha [njh], 378
Mi'kmaq, *alt.* Micmac [mic], 239
Mi'kmaw, *alt.* Micmac [mic], 305
Miko, *dial.* Nung [nun], 466, 341
Milanau, *alt.* Melanau [mel], 460, 325
Milanese, *dial.* Lombard [lmo], 544
Milang, *dial.* Adi [adi], 353
Milano, *alt.* Melanau [mel], 460, 325
Milchan, *alt.* Kinnauri [kfk], 368
Milchanang, *alt.* Kinnauri [kfk], 368
Milchang, *alt.* Kinnauri [kfk], 368
Mildjingi, *dial.* Djinang [dji], 570
Mili Yi, *see* Yi, Mili [ymh], 347
Milikin, *alt.* Remun [lkj], 460
Millera, *alt.* Yir Yoront [yiy], 579
Millikin, *alt.* Remun [lkj], 460
Milo, *dial.* Nicobarese, Southern [nik], 381
Miltou, *alt.* Miltu [mlj], 84
Miltu [mlj], 84
Mima, *alt.* Amdang [amj], 78
  dial. Naga, Angami [njm], 377
Mime, *alt.* Mimi [miv], 84
Mimi [miv], 84
  alt. Amdang [amj], 78
Mímica, *alt.* Spanish Sign Language [ssp], 561
Mimika, *alt.* Kamoro [kgq], 416
Min Bei Chinese, *see* Chinese, Min Bei [mnp], 330, 508
Min Dong, *alt.* Chinese, Min Dong [cdo], 391
Min Dong Chinese, *see* Chinese, Min Dong [cdo], 330, 324, 391, 454, 508, 514
Min Nam, *alt.* Chinese, Min Nan [nan], 508
Min Nan, *alt.* Chinese, Min Nan [nan], 324, 391, 454, 494, 511, 514
Min Nan Chinese, *see* Chinese, Min Nan [nan], 330, 324, 391, 454, 494, 508, 511, 514

Min Pei, *alt.* Chinese, Min Bei [mnp], 330, 508

Min Yao, *alt.* Biao Mon [bmt], 327
alt. dial. Biao Mon [bmt], 327

Min Zhong Chinese, *see* Chinese, Min Zhong [czo], 330

Min-Ke, *alt. dial.* Chinese, Hakka [hak], 329

Mina (Cameroon) [hna], 67
Mina (India) [myi], 376
alt. Gen [gej], 207, 45
dial. Ma [mjn], 610

Mina Bhil, *alt.* Wagdi [wbr], 390

Mina Mina Gorong, *dial.* Geser-Gorom [ges], 398

Mina-Gen, *alt.* Gen [gej], 207, 45

Minaco, *alt.* Mehináku [mmh], 230

Minahasa, *alt.* Tombulu [tom], 434

Minahasan Malay, *alt.* Malay, Manado [xmm], 431

Minahassa, *alt.* Mongondow [mog], 431

Minahe, *alt. dial.* Mbo [mbo], 66

Minala, *alt.* Mangala [mem], 573

Minamanwa, *alt.* Mamanwa [mmn], 498

Minang, *alt.* Minangkabau [min], 436

Minangali, *dial.* Kalinga, Lower Tanudan [kml], 497

Minangkabau [min], 436

Minanibai [mcv], 614

Minansut, *alt.* Gana [gnq], 456
alt. Kuijau [dkr], 457

Minasbate, *alt.* Masbatenyo [msb], 499

Minavega, *alt.* Minaveha [mvn], 614

Minaveha [mvn], 614

Minbu, *dial.* Chin, Asho [csh], 462, 321

Minchia, *alt.* Bai, Central [bca], 326

Minda, *dial.* Shoo-Minda-Nye [bcv], 174

Mindanao, *dial.* Sangil [snl], 501

Mindanao Visayan, *dial.* Cebuano [ceb], 493

Mindat, *alt.* Chin, Mün [mwq], 463

Mindéra, *dial.* Kwang [kvi], 82

Mindik, *alt.* Burum-Mindik [bmu], 595

Mindiri [mpn], 614

Mindivi, *alt.* Anamgura [imi], 589

Mind'jana, *alt.* Yir Yoront [yiy], 579

Mindoumou, *alt.* Ndumu [nmd], 121

Mindumbu, *alt.* Ndumu [nmd], 121

Minduumo, *alt.* Ndumu [nmd], 121

Mine Kaffir, *pej. alt.* Fanagalo [fng], 185, 213, 216

Minendon, *alt.* Aiku [mzf], 588

Mineo, *dial.* Zulgo-Gemzek [gnd], 74

Minew, *alt. dial.* Zulgo-Gemzek [gnd], 74

Mingan, *alt. dial.* Mongolian, Peripheral [mvf], 339

Mingang Doso [mko], 170

Mingar, *alt.* Lembata, West [lmj], 408

Mingat, *dial.* Kalmyk-Oirat [xal], 337, 461

Mingbari, *dial.* Ngura [nbx], 575

Mingi, *alt.* Ngie [ngj], 69

Mingrelian [xmf], 352

Mínguíín, *alt.* Tlapanec, Tlacoapa [tpl], 275

Minh Huong, *alt.* Chinese, Yue [yue], 522

Minhasa, *alt.* Tombulu [tom], 434

Minhe, *dial.* Tu [mjg], 345

Mini, *alt.* Abureni [mgj], 153
alt. Kajakse [ckq], 81
alt. Omati [mgx], 619

Miniafia, *dial.* Arifama-Miniafia [aai], 590

Miniafia-Arifama, *alt.* Arifama-Miniafia [aai], 590

Minianka, *alt.* Senoufo, Mamara [myk], 144

Minica, *alt.* Huitoto, Minica [hto], 245

Minica Huitoto, *see* Huitoto, Minica [hto], 245, 288

Minica Huitoto, *alt.* Huitoto, Minica [hto], 288

Minigir [vmg], 614

Minir, *dial.* Naga, Yimchungru [yim], 380

Minitari, *alt.* Hidatsa [hid], 302

Minitji, *alt.* Limilngan [lmc], 573

Miniyanka, *alt.* Senoufo, Mamara [myk], 144

Minjanbal, *alt.* Yugambal [yub], 579

Minjanti, *alt.* Tibea [ngy], 72

Minjia, *alt.* Bai, Central [bca], 326

Minjimmina, *alt. dial.* Tulishi [tey], 196

Minjori, *dial.* Ese [mcq], 598

Minkia, *alt.* Bai, Central [bca], 326

Minna, *dial.* Kadara [kad], 165

Minnan, *alt.* Chinese, Min Nan [nan], 330, 324, 391, 454, 511, 514

Minnesota Border Chippewa, *dial.* Chippewa [ciw], 299

Minokok [mqq], 458

Minqi, *alt.* Yi, Miqie [yiq], 347

Minqua, *alt.* Susquehannock [sqn], 308

Minriq [mnq], 455

Mintamani, *alt.* Kais [kzm], 415

Mintil [mzt], 455

Mintra, *alt. dial.* Temuan [tmw], 455

Minungo, *dial.* Chokwe [cjk], 40, 213

Minya, *alt.* Senoufo, Mamara [myk], 144

Minyak, *alt.* Muya [mvm], 340

Minyong, *dial.* Adi [adi], 353

Mioko, *alt. dial.* Ramoaaina [rai], 622

Miomafo, *alt. dial.* Uab Meto [aoz], 410

Mios Num, *dial.* Biak [bhw], 412

Mipa, *alt. dial.* Kwa' [bko], 65

Mi'pha, *alt.* Tlapanec, Malinaltepec [tcf], 275

Miqie Yi, *see* Yi, Miqie [yiq], 347

Mir, *alt.* Meriam [ulk], 574

Mira, *alt.* Chin, Mara [mrh], 359, 463

Mira Sagtengpa, *alt.* Brokpake [sgt], 322

Mirabo, *alt.* Suabo [szp], 423

Miramar Chontal, *dial.* Chontal, Tabasco [chf], 262

Miraña [boa], 230
alt. dial. Miraña [boa], 230
dial. Bora [boa], 287, 243

Miranda do Douro [mwl], 551

Mirandesa, *alt.* Miranda do Douro [mwl], 551

Mirandese, *alt.* Miranda do Douro [mwl], 551

Miranha, *alt. dial.* Bora [boa], 243
dial. Miraña [boa], 230

Mirãnia, *alt. dial.* Miraña [boa], 230

Mirapmin, *alt.* Konai [kxw], 607

Miraski, *dial.* Kashmiri [kas], 367

Mirdha-Kharia, *dial.* Kharia [khr], 367

Mire [mvh], 84

Mirgami, *alt.* Mirgan [zrg], 376

Mirgan [zrg], 376
alt. dial. Urdu [urd], 389

Miri [mrg], 376
dial. Katcha-Kadugli-Miri [xtc], 191
dial. Narom [nrm], 460

Miriam, *alt.* Meriam [ulk], 574

Miriam-Mir, *alt.* Meriam [ulk], 574

Miriei, *alt.* Hatam [had], 415
dial. Hatam [had], 415

Miriti [mmv], 230

Miriti Tapuyo, *alt.* Miriti [mmv], 230

Miriti-Tapuia, *alt.* Miriti [mmv], 230

Miriwoong, *alt.* Miriwung [mep], 574

Miriwun, *alt.* Miriwung [mep], 574

Miriwung [mep], 574

Mirkan, *alt.* Mirgan [zrg], 376

Mirkuk, *dial.* Isebe [igo], 603

Mirlong, *dial.* Karbi [mjw], 366

Miroy, *alt.* Anuak [anu], 113
Mirpur Panjabi, *see* Panjabi, Mirpur [pmu], 380
Mirpuri, *alt.* Panjabi, Mirpur [pmu], 380
　dial. Pahari-Potwari [phr], 487
Mirriam, *dial.* Kofyar [kwl], 166
Mirung, *alt.* Miriwung [mep], 574
Mirzapuri, *dial.* Awadhi [awa], 354, 468
Mis-Kemba, *alt.* Wagi [fad], 630
Misaba, *alt.* Yi, Western [ywt], 348
Misamis Higaonon Manobo, *alt.* Higaonon [mba], 494
Misatik, *alt.* Musom [msu], 616
Misher, *alt. dial.* Tatar [tat], 556
Mishikhwutmetunee, *alt.* Coquille [coq], 300
Mishing, *alt.* Miri [mrg], 376
Miship [mjs], 170
Mishmi, *alt.* Digaro-Mishmi [mhu], 360
　alt. Miju-Mishmi [mxj], 375
Mishulundu, *dial.* Luyana [lyn], 41
Misim, *alt. dial.* Hote [hot], 602
Misima-Paneati [mpx], 614
Mising, *alt.* Miri [mrg], 376
Mískito [miq], 282, 258
Mískito Coast Creole English, *alt.* Nicaragua Creole English [bzk], 283
Mískitu, *alt.* Mískito [miq], 282, 258
Miskolc, *dial.* Hungarian Sign Language [hsh], 542
Misles, *dial.* Tsakhur [tkr], 557
Misman, *dial.* Asmat, Central [cns], 411
Mísquito, *alt.* Mískito [miq], 282, 258
Mississiou, *alt.* Sighu [sxe], 121
Missong, *alt.* Abar [mij], 56
Missouri, *alt. dial.* Iowa-Oto [iow], 302
Missouria, *alt. dial.* Iowa-Oto [iow], 302
Mistralien, *alt.* Provençal [prv], 537
Misu, *alt.* Bisu [bii], 327
Mitaa, *alt.* Meta' [mgo], 67
Mitang, *alt.* Nabi [mty], 616
Mitange, *dial.* Maindo [cwb], 147
Mitchif, *alt.* Michif [crg], 305
Mitebog, *alt.* Gedaged [gdd], 599
Mitei, *alt.* Meitei [mni], 375, 321, 465
Mithan, *alt. dial.* Naga, Wancho [nnp], 380
Mithe, *alt.* Meitei [mni], 375, 321, 465
Miti, *dial.* Naga, Tase [nst], 380
Mitiaro, *dial.* Rarotongan [rar], 579
Mitil, *alt.* Mintil [mzt], 455

Mitla Zapotec, *see* Zapotec, Mitla [zaw], 279
Mitlatongo Mixtec, *see* Mixtec, Mitlatongo [vmm], 267
Mitsogo, *alt.* Tsogo [tsv], 121
Mittu [mwu], 193
Mitua, *alt.* Baré [bae], 311
　alt. Mandahuaca [mht], 312
Mítua, *alt.* Guayabero [guo], 245
Mituku [zmq], 104
Mítus, *alt.* Guayabero [guo], 245
Miu [mpo], 614
Miutini, *dial.* Meru [mer], 134
Miwa [vmi], 574
　alt. Lobi [lob], 52, 94
　dial. Wunambal [wub], 578
Miwoc, *alt.* Miwok, Southern Sierra [skd], 305
Miwok, Bay [mkq], 305
Miwok, Central Sierra [csm], 305
Miwok, Coast [csi], 305
Miwok, Lake [lmw], 305
Miwok, Northern Sierra [nsq], 305
Miwok, Plains [pmw], 305
Miwok, Southern Sierra [skd], 305
Miwokan, *alt.* Miwok, Southern Sierra [skd], 305
Mixe de Atitlán, *alt.* Mixe, North Central [neq], 265
Mixe de San Juan Cotzocón, *dial.* Mixe, North Central [neq], 265
Mixe del Istmo, *alt.* Mixe, Isthmus [mir], 265
Mixe, Coatlán [mco], 265
Mixe, Isthmus [mir], 265
Mixe, Juquila [mxq], 265
Mixe, Mazatlán [mzl], 265
Mixe, North Central [neq], 265
Mixe, Quetzaltepec [pxm], 265
Mixe, Tlahuitoltepec [mxp], 265
Mixe, Totontepec [mto], 265
Mixifore [mfg], 130
Mixistlan, *dial.* Mixe, North Central [neq], 265
Mixtec, Alacatlatzala [mim], 265
Mixtec, Alcozauca [xta], 266
Mixtec, Amoltepec [mbz], 266
Mixtec, Apasco-Apoala [mip], 266
Mixtec, Atatláhuca [mib], 266
Mixtec, Ayutla [miy], 266
Mixtec, Cacaloxtepec [miu], 266
Mixtec, Chayuco [mih], 266
Mixtec, Chazumba [xtb], 266
Mixtec, Chigmecatitlán [mii], 266
Mixtec, Coatzospan [miz], 266

Mixtec, Cuyamecalco [xtu], 267
Mixtec, Diuxi-Tilantongo [xtd], 267
Mixtec, Huitepec [mxs], 267
Mixtec, Itundujia [mce], 265
Mixtec, Ixtayutla [vmj], 267
Mixtec, Jamiltepec [mxt], 267
Mixtec, Juxtlahuaca [vmc], 267
Mixtec, Magdalena Peñasco [xtm], 267
Mixtec, Metlatónoc [mxv], 267
Mixtec, Mitlatongo [vmm], 267
Mixtec, Mixtepec [mix], 267
Mixtec, Northern Tlaxiaco [xtn], 267
Mixtec, Northwest Oaxaca [mxa], 268
Mixtec, Ocotepec [mie], 268
Mixtec, Peñoles [mil], 268
Mixtec, Pinotepa Nacional [mio], 268
Mixtec, San Juan Colorado [mjc], 268
Mixtec, San Juan Teita [xtj], 268
Mixtec, San Miguel el Grande [mig], 268
Mixtec, San Miguel Piedras [xtp], 268
Mixtec, Santa Lucía Monteverde [mdv], 268
Mixtec, Santa María Zacatepec [mza], 268
Mixtec, Silacayoapan [mks], 268
Mixtec, Sindihui [xts], 269
Mixtec, Sinicahua [xti], 269
Mixtec, Southeastern Nochixtlán [mxy], 269
Mixtec, Southern Puebla [mit], 269
Mixtec, Southwestern Tlaxiaco [meh], 269
Mixtec, Soyaltepec [vmq], 269
Mixtec, Tacahua [xtt], 269
Mixtec, Tamazola [vmx], 269
Mixtec, Tezoatlán [mxb], 269
Mixtec, Tidaá [mtx], 269
Mixtec, Tijaltepec [xtl], 269
Mixtec, Tlazoyaltepec [mqh], 269
Mixtec, Tututepec [mtu], 269
Mixtec, Western Juxtlahuaca [jmx], 270
Mixtec, Yoloxochitl [xty], 270
Mixtec, Yosondúa [mpm], 270
Mixtec, Yucuañe [mvg], 270
Mixtec, Yutanduchi [mab], 270
Mixteco de Alacatlatzala, *alt.* Mixtec, Alacatlatzala [mim], 265
Mixteco de Alocozauca, *alt.* Mixtec, Alcozauca [xta], 266

Mixteco de Amoltepec, *alt.*
  Mixtec, Amoltepec [mbz], 266
Mixteco de Ayutla, *alt.* Mixtec,
  Ayutla [miy], 266
Mixteco de Cacaloxtepec, *alt.*
  Mixtec, Cacaloxtepec [miu], 266
Mixteco de Chayucu, *alt.* Mixtec,
  Chayuco [mih], 266
Mixteco de Chazumba, *alt.*
  Mixtec, Chazumba [xtb], 266
Mixteco de Chocho, *alt.* Mixtec,
  Apasco-Apoala [mip], 266
Mixteco de Cuyamecalco, *alt.*
  Mixtec, Cuyamecalco [xtu], 267
Mixteco de Diuxi-Tilantongo,
  alt. Mixtec, Diuxi-Tilantongo
  [xtd], 267
Mixteco de Huitepec, *alt.* Mixtec,
  Huitepec [mxs], 267
Mixteco de Jamiltepec, *alt.*
  Mixtec, Jamiltepec [mxt], 267
Mixteco de Juxtlahuaca, *alt.*
  Mixtec, Juxtlahuaca [vmc], 267
Mixteco de Mitlatongo, *alt.*
  Mixtec, Mitlatongo [vmm], 267
Mixteco de Nuxaá, *alt.* Mixtec,
  Southeastern Nochixtlán
  [mxy], 269
Mixteco de Pinotepa Nacional,
  alt. Mixtec, Pinotepa Nacional
  [mio], 268
**Mixteco de San Antonio
  Huitepec**, *alt.* Mixtec, Huitepec
  [mxs], 267
**Mixteco de San Antonio
  Sinicahua**, *alt.* Mixtec, Sinicahua
  [xti], 269
**Mixteco de San Bartolo
  Soyaltepec**, *alt.* Mixtec,
  Soyaltepec [vmq], 269
**Mixteco de San Bartolomé
  Yucuañe**, *alt.* Mixtec, Yucuañe
  [mvg], 270
**Mixteco de San Esteban
  Atatláhuca**, *alt.* Mixtec,
  Atatláhuca [mib], 266
**Mixteco de San Juan
  Coatzospan**, *alt.* Mixtec,
  Coatzospan [miz], 266
**Mixteco de San Juan
  Colorado**, *alt.* Mixtec, San Juan
  Colorado [mjc], 268
**Mixteco de San Juan
  Mixtepec**, *alt.* Mixtec, Mixtepec
  [mix], 267
Mixteco de San Juan Ñumí, *alt.*
  Mixtec, Northern Tlaxiaco
  [xtn], 267
Mixteco de San Juan Tamazola,
  alt. Mixtec, Tamazola [vmx], 269

**Mixteco de San Mateo
  Tepantepec**, *alt.* Mixtec, Peñoles
  [mil], 268
**Mixteco de San Pablo
  Tijaltepec**, *alt.* Mixtec, Tijaltepec
  [xtl], 269
**Mixteco de San Pedro
  Tututepec**, *alt.* Mixtec,
  Tututepec [mtu], 269
Mixteco de San Rafael, *alt.*
  Mixtec, Metlatónoc [mxv], 267
**Mixteco de Santa Cruz
  Itundujia**, *alt.* Mixtec, Itundujia
  [mce], 265
**Mixteco de Santa Cruz
  Tacahua**, *alt.* Mixtec, Tacahua
  [xtt], 269
**Mixteco de Santa María
  Chigmecatitlán**, *alt.* Mixtec,
  Chigmecatitlán [mii], 266
**Mixteco de Santa María
  Zacatepec**, *alt.* Mixtec, Santa
  María Zacatepec [mza], 268
Mixteco de Santiago Apoala,
  alt. Mixtec, Apasco-Apoala [mip],
  266
Mixteco de Santiago Ixtayutla,
  alt. Mixtec, Ixtayutla [vmj], 267
Mixteco de Santiago Nuyoo,
  alt. Mixtec, Southwestern Tlaxiaco
  [meh], 269
**Mixteco de Santiago
  Tlazoyaltepec**, *alt.* Mixtec,
  Tlazoyaltepec [mqh], 269
**Mixteco de Santiago
  Yosondúa**, *alt.* Mixtec, Yosondúa
  [mpm], 270
**Mixteco de Santo Domingo
  Nuxaá**, *alt.* Mixtec, Southeastern
  Nochixtlán [mxy], 269
**Mixteco de Santo Tomás
  Ocotepec**, *alt.* Mixtec, Ocotepec
  [mie], 268
**Mixteco de Tezoatlán de
  Segura y Luna**, *alt.* Mixtec,
  Tezoatlán [mxb], 269
Mixteco de Tidaá, *alt.* Mixtec,
  Tidaá [mtx], 269
Mixteco de Xochapa, *alt.* Mixtec,
  Alcozauca [xta], 266
Mixteco de Yucuná, *alt.*
  Mixtec, Northwest Oaxaca
  [mxa], 268
Mixteco de Yutanduchi, *alt.*
  Mixtec, Yutanduchi [mab], 270
Mixteco de Zaachila, *alt.* Mixtec,
  Huitepec [mxs], 267
**Mixteco del Noroeste de
  Oaxaca**, *alt.* Mixtec, Northwest
  Oaxaca [mxa], 268

**Mixteco del Oeste de
  Juxtlahuaca**, *alt.* Mixtec,
  Western Juxtlahuaca [jmx], 270
Mixteco del Sur de Puebla, *alt.*
  Mixtec, Southern Puebla [mit], 269
**Mixteco del Sureste de
  Nochixtlán**, *alt.* Mixtec,
  Southeastern Nochixtlán [mxy], 269
Mixtepec Mixtec, *see* Mixtec,
  Mixtepec [mix], 267
Mixtepec Zapotec, *see* Zapotec,
  Mixtepec [zpm], 279
Miya [mkf], 170
Miyak, *alt.* Kyenele [kql], 609
Miyako [mvi], 447
Miyako-Jima, *dial.* Miyako
  [mvi], 447
Miyang-Khang, *alt.* Naga, Thangal
  [nki], 380
Miyangho, *alt.* Yangho [ynh], 122
Miyao, *alt.* Muya [mvm], 340
Miyatnu, *dial.* Ankave [aak], 590
Miyawa, *alt.* Miya [mkf], 170
Miyem, *alt. dial.* Mbo-Ung
  [mux], 612
Miyemu, *dial.* Mbo-Ung [mux], 612
Miyobe [soy], 45, 208
Miza, *dial.* Moru [mgd], 193
Mizeran, *alt.* Bana [bcw], 57
Mizlime, *alt.* Wuzlam [udl], 73
Mizmast, *dial.* Aimaq [aiq], 315
Mizo [lus], 376, 321, 466
  dial. Mizo [lus], 376, 321, 466
Mizulo, *dial.* Lega-Mwenga
  [lgm], 102
Mjillem, *alt.* Niellim [nie], 85
Mjiuniang, *alt.* Cao Miao
  [cov], 329
M'kaang, *alt.* Chin, Daai [dao], 463
Mkako, *alt.* Kako [kkj], 63
Mkuu, *dial.* Rombo [rof], 204
Mkwet, *dial.* Fe'fe' [fmp], 61
Mla, *alt.* Mlabri [mra], 516, 451
Mla Bri, *alt.* Mlabri [mra], 516
Mla-Bri, *alt.* Mlabri [mra], 451
Mlabri [mra], 516, 451
Mlahsö [lhs], 510
Mlap [kja], 420
Mlomp [mlo], 175
Mlomp North, *alt.* Mlomp [mlo],
  175
Mlomp South, *alt. dial.* Jola-Kasa
  [csk], 180
Mmaala [mmu], 67
Mmala, *alt.* Mmaala [mmu], 67
Mmani, *alt.* Bullom So [buy], 183,
  129
  dial. Bullom So [buy], 183
Mme, *alt.* Mmen [bfm], 67
Mmen [bfm], 67

Mmfo, *alt.* Deg [mzw], 124, 92
Mndios do Coxodoá, *alt.* Suruahá [swx], 232
Mngahris, *alt. dial.* Tibetan, Central [bod], 344
Mnong Gar, *dial.* Mnong, Eastern [mng], 525
Mnong Kwanh, *dial.* Mnong, Eastern [mng], 525
Mnong Rolom, *dial.* Mnong, Eastern [mng], 525
Mnong, Central [cmo], 525, 326
Mnong, Eastern [mng], 525
Mnong, Southern [mnn], 525
Mnyam, *alt.* Kinnauri, Bhoti [nes], 368
Mo, *alt.* Deg [mzw], 124, 92
alt. Mak [mkg], 339
Mo Egon, *alt.* Eggon [ego], 158
Mo-Hua, *alt.* Mak [mkg], 339
Mo-Su, *pej. alt.* Naxi [nbf], 341
Moa, *alt.* Moba [mfq], 208, 52
dial. Luang [lex], 401
Moab, *alt.* Moba [mfq], 208, 52
'Moaeke, *alt.* Vamale [mkt], 585
Mòáka, *alt.* Aka [axk], 87
Moanus, *alt.* Lele [lle], 609
alt. Titan [ttv], 628
Moar, *alt.* Bimoba [bim], 123
alt. Liki [lio], 418
Moaraeri, *alt.* Morori [mok], 420
Moare, *alt.* Moba [mfq], 208, 52
'Moaveke, *alt.* Hmwaveke [mrk], 584
Moba [mfq], 208, 52
Mobango, *alt.* Babango [bbm], 96
Mobber, *alt. dial.* Kanuri, Central [knc], 152
Mober, *alt. dial.* Kanuri, Central [knc], 152
Mobesa, *alt.* Mbesa [zms], 104
Mobilian [mod], 305
Mobilian Jargon, *alt.* Mobilian [mod], 305
Mobou, *dial.* Kwang [kvi], 82
Mobu, *alt. dial.* Kwang [kvi], 82
Mobumrin Aizi, *see* Aizi, Mobumrin [ahm], 91
Mobuta, *alt.* Awa [awb], 591
Môc-Châu, *alt.* Tai Daeng [tyr], 526
Mocha, *alt.* Shekkacho [moy], 118
Mochda, *alt.* Carapana [cbc], 244
Mócheno [mhn], 545
Mochi [old], 202
Mochiahua, *alt.* Mak [mkg], 339
Mocho [mhc], 270
Mochuelo-Casanare-Cuiba, *dial.* Cuiba [cui], 244
Mochumi, *alt.* Naga, Chang [nbc], 377

Mochungrr, *alt.* Naga, Chang [nbc], 377
Mocigin, *alt.* Gude [gde], 161, 62
Mocoa, *alt.* Inga, Jungle [inj], 246
Mocobí, *alt.* Mocoví [moc], 220
Mocoví [moc], 220
Mod, *alt. dial.* Tumak [tmc], 87
Mo'da [gbn], 193
Modan, *alt.* Kuri [nbn], 418
Modang [mxd], 394
Modea, *dial.* Gumuz [guk], 191
Modele, *dial.* Befang [bby], 58
Modeli, *alt. dial.* Befang [bby], 58
Modelle, *alt. dial.* Befang [bby], 58
Moden, *alt. dial.* Tumak [tmc], 87
Modern Chaldean, *alt.* Chaldean Neo-Aramaic [cld], 443
Modern Langus, *dial.* Torres Strait Creole [tcs], 577
Modern Literary Arabic, *alt.* Arabic, Standard [arb], 320
alt. dial. Arabic, Standard [arb], 508
Modern Mandaic, *alt.* Mandaic [mid], 441
Modern Standard Arabic, *dial.* Arabic, Standard [arb], 508
Modern Tupi, *alt.* Nhengatu [yrl], 246, 312
Modern Tupí, *alt.* Nhengatu [yrl], 230
Modgel, *alt. dial.* Kwang [kvi], 82
Modh, *alt.* Maria [mrr], 375
Modi, *alt.* Maria [mrr], 375
dial. Kamwe [hig], 166
Modin, *alt. dial.* Tumak [tmc], 87
Modo, *alt.* Jur Modo [bex], 191
dial. Jur Modo [bex], 191
Modo Lali, *alt. dial.* Jur Modo [bex], 191
Modogo, *alt. dial.* Naba [mne], 85
Modole [mqo], 402
Modra, *alt.* Todrah [tdr], 527
Modunga, *alt.* Ndunga [ndt], 105
Moenebeng, *alt.* Caac [msq], 584
Moere [mvq], 614
Moewehafen, *alt.* Aiklep [mwg], 588
Mofa, *alt.* Mafa [maf], 65
Mofou, *alt.* Mofu-Gudur [mif], 68
Mofou de Goudour, *alt.* Mofu-Gudur [mif], 68
Mofu, *dial.* Biak [bhw], 412
Mofu de Douroum, *alt. dial.* Mofu, North [mfk], 67
Mofu de Meri, *alt.* Merey [meq], 67
Mofu South, *alt.* Mofu-Gudur [mif], 68
Mofu, North [mfk], 67
Mofu-Douvangar, *alt.* Mofu, North [mfk], 67

Mofu-Dugwor, *alt.* Dugwor [dme], 60
Mofu-Gudur [mif], 68
Mofu-Nord, *alt.* Mofu, North [mfk], 67
Mofu-Sud, *alt.* Mofu-Gudur [mif], 68
Mog, *alt.* Arakanese [mhv], 354
Mogana, *dial.* Yasa [yko], 111, 122
Moganda, *dial.* Ngumbi [nui], 111
Mogao, *alt.* Puragi [pru], 422
Mogareb, *alt.* Nara [nrb], 112
Mogari, *alt.* Afade [aal], 153
Mogh, *alt.* Arakanese [mhv], 462, 354
pej. alt. Arakanese [mhv], 320
Moghamo, *dial.* Meta' [mgo], 67
Moghamo-Menemo, *alt.* Meta' [mgo], 67
Moghol, *alt.* Mogholi [mhj], 316
Mogholi [mhj], 316
Mogimba, *alt.* Ngemba [nge], 69
Mogofin, *alt.* Mixifore [mfg], 130
Mogogodo, *alt.* Yaaku [muu], 137
Mogol, *alt.* Mogholi [mhj], 316
Mogou, *alt. dial.* Ngangam [gng], 209
Mogoum, *alt.* Mogum [mou], 84
Mogpha, *alt.* Karen, Paku [kpp], 464
Moguex, *alt.* Guambiano [gum], 245
Mogul, *alt.* Mogholi [mhj], 316
Mogum [mou], 84
Mogum Déle, *dial.* Mogum [mou], 84
Mogum Diguimi, *dial.* Mogum [mou], 84
Mogum Urmi, *dial.* Mogum [mou], 84
Mogwa, *alt.* Karen, Paku [kpp], 464
Mohave [mov], 305
Mohawk [moh], 239, 305
Mohegan-Montauk-Narragansett [mof], 305
Mohongia, *alt.* Naga, Nocte [njb], 379
Mohrano, *dial.* Sindhi Bhil [sbn], 489
Mohua, *alt.* Mak [mkg], 339
Mohung, *dial.* Naga, Konyak [nbe], 378
Moi (Congo) [mow], 89
Moi (Indonesia) [mxn], 420
alt. Hatam [had], 415
alt. Hre [hre], 523
alt. Mekwei [msf], 420
dial. Hatam [had], 415
Moi 1, *dial.* Muong [mtq], 525
Moi Bi, *alt. dial.* Muong [mtq], 525
Moi Da Vach, *alt.* Hre [hre], 523
Moi Luy, *alt.* Hre [hre], 523

Moifau, *alt. dial.* Hlai [lic], 333
Moikodi [mkp], 614
Moil, *alt. dial.* Nangikurrunggurr [nam], 574
Moinba [mob], 376, 340
Moingi [mwz], 104
Moire, *alt. dial.* Hatam [had], 415
Moissala Mbai, *alt.* Mbay [myb], 84
Moitanik, *dial.* Maasai [mas], 134
Moium, *alt.* Papel [pbo], 131
Moiyui, *alt.* Naga, Southern Rengma [nre], 379
Mojave, *alt.* Mohave [mov], 305
Mojiahua, *alt.* Mak [mkg], 339
Mojiang Nisu, *dial.* Yi, Yuanjiang-Mojiang [yym], 348
Mojo, *alt.* Ignaciano [ign], 223
Mojos, *alt.* Ignaciano [ign], 223
　alt. Trinitario [trn], 224
Mojung, *alt.* Naga, Chang [nbc], 377
Mok [mqt], 516
　alt. dial. Mouk-Aria [mwh], 615
Moka, *alt.* Byep [mkk], 59
Mokar, *alt.* Ga'anda [gqa], 160
Mokareng, *alt.* Mokerang [mft], 614
Mokélumne, *alt.* Miwok, Southern Sierra [skd], 305
Moken [mwt], 466, 516
Mokerang [mft], 614
Mokhev, *alt. dial.* Georgian [kat], 352
Mokil, *alt.* Mokilese [mkj], 582
Mokilese [mkj], 582
Mokilko, *alt.* Mukulu [moz], 85
　dial. Mukulu [moz], 85
Mokkan Tila Sadri, *dial.* Sadri, Oraon [sdr], 322
Moklen [mkm], 516
Moklum, *dial.* Naga, Tase [nst], 380
Mokmer, *alt. dial.* Biak [bhw], 412
Mokole [mkl], 45
Mokollé, *alt.* Mokole [mkl], 45
Mokomoko, *alt.* Muko-Muko [vmo], 436
Mokong, *dial.* Mofu-Gudur [mif], 68
Mokoreng, *alt.* Mokerang [mft], 614
Mokorua, *alt. dial.* Korafe [kpr], 607
Mokoulou, *alt.* Mukulu [moz], 85
Mokpe, *alt.* Mokpwe [bri], 68
Mokpwe [bri], 68
Mokri, *alt.* Kurdish, Central [ckb], 440
Moksela [vms], 402
Moksha [mdf], 556
Mokshan, *alt.* Moksha [mdf], 556
Mokulu, *alt.* Mukulu [moz], 85
Mokuru, *alt. dial.* Befang [bby], 58
Mokwale, *alt.* Mokole [mkl], 45
Mokyo, *alt.* Moloko [mlw], 68

Mol, *dial.* Muong [mtq], 525
Molala, *alt.* Molale [mbe], 305
Molale [mbe], 305
Molalla, *alt.* Molale [mbe], 305
Molao, *alt.* Mulam [mlm], 340
Molbog [pwm], 500, 458
Molbog Palawan, *alt.* Molbog [pwm], 500
Moldavan, *alt.* Romanian [ron], 548
　dial. Romanian [ron], 548
Moldavian, *alt.* Romanian [ron], 552, 542, 557, 564
　dial. Romanian [ron], 552
Moldova Sign Language [vsi], 548
Moldovean, *alt. dial.* Romanian [ron], 548
Moldovian, *alt. dial.* Romanian [ron], 548
Mole, *alt.* Mòoré [mos], 52, 143, 209
Molele, *alt.* Molale [mbe], 305
Molendji, *alt.* Molengue [bxc], 111
Molengue [bxc], 111
Moli, *dial.* Talise [tlr], 638
Moliba, *dial.* Dzando [dzn], 99
Molima [mox], 614
Molisano, *dial.* Italian [ita], 544
Molko, *alt.* Moloko [mlw], 68
Molkoa, *alt.* Moloko [mlw], 68
Molkwo, *alt.* Moloko [mlw], 68
Mollo, *alt. dial.* Uab Meto [aoz], 410
Mollo-Miomafo, *dial.* Uab Meto [aoz], 410
Molloroidyi, *alt.* Muluridyi [vmu], 574
Molmo, *alt.* One, Molmo [aun], 620
Molmo One, *see* One, Molmo [aun], 620
Molo [zmo], 193
　dial. Fordata [frd], 398
　dial. Gula [kcm], 76
　dial. Nyamusa-Molo [nwm], 194
Molo-Maru, *alt. dial.* Fordata [frd], 398
Molof [msl], 420
Moloko [mlw], 68
Molokwo, *alt.* Moloko [mlw], 68
Molot, *dial.* Ramoaaina [rai], 622
Molsom, *alt. dial.* Chin, Falam [flm], 358
Moluche, *dial.* Mapudungun [arn], 242
Molunga, *dial.* Dzando [dzn], 99
Mom Jango [ver], 170, 68
　dial. Mom Jango [ver], 170
Moma [myl], 431
Momale, *alt.* Momare [msz], 614
Momalili, *alt.* Mese [mci], 613
Momare [msz], 614
Momba, *alt.* Moinba [mob], 376, 340

Mombasa, *alt. dial.* Swahili [swh], 136
Mombe, *alt.* Nyakyusa-Ngonde [nyy], 203, 140
　alt. dial. Gbaya, Northwest [gya], 61
Mombesa, *alt.* Mbesa [zms], 104
Mombi, *alt. dial.* Ndo [ndp], 105
Mombo, *dial.* Dogon, Kolum So [dkl], 142
Momboi, *alt.* Mambai [mcs], 83
Mombum [mso], 420
Mombuttu, *alt.* Mangbutu [mdk], 104
Momfu, *alt. dial.* Mamvu [mdi], 103
Momi, *alt. dial.* Mom Jango [ver], 170
Momina [mmb], 420
Momogun, *alt.* Rungus [drg], 458
Momole, *alt.* Momare [msz], 614
Momolili, *alt.* Mese [mci], 613
　dial. Mese [mci], 613
Mompa, *alt.* Moinba [mob], 376, 340
Momu, *alt.* Gengle [geg], 161
Momuna [mqf], 420
Momveda, *dial.* Pagibete [pae], 107
Momvu, *alt. dial.* Mamvu [mdi], 103
Mon [mnw], 466, 516
　alt. Naga, Southern Rengma [nre], 379
　dial. Naga, Konyak [nbe], 378
　dial. Tho [tou], 527
Mon Nya, *alt. dial.* Mon [mnw], 466
Mon Tang, *alt. dial.* Mon [mnw], 466
Mon Te, *alt. dial.* Mon [mnw], 466
Mon-Non, *alt.* Mono [mru], 68
Mona, *alt.* Mwan [moa], 94
　alt. dial. Dijim-Bwilim [cfa], 158
Monachi, *alt.* Mono [mnr], 305
Monam, *alt.* Monom [moo], 525
Monao, *alt.* Burmeso [bzu], 413
Monastic Sign Language [mzg], 566
Monau, *alt.* Burmeso [bzu], 413
Monaxo, *alt.* Maxakalí [mbl], 230
Monba, *alt.* Moinba [mob], 376, 340
　alt. Tshangla [tsj], 345, 389
Monchon, *alt.* Mbulungish [mbv], 130
Moncó, *pej. alt.* Principense [pre], 179
Mondari, *alt.* Mandari [mqu], 193
　alt. Mundari [muw], 376, 321, 476
　dial. Bari [bfa], 210
Mondé [mnd], 230
Mondjembo, *alt.* Monzombo [moj], 89, 77
Mondo, *alt.* Mündü [muh], 193, 105
　alt. Sulod [srg], 501
　dial. Langi [lag], 200

Mondogossou, *dial.* Berakou [bxv], 79

Mondropolon [npn], 614

Mondu, *alt.* Mündü [muh], 193

Mondugu, *alt.* Ndunga [ndt], 105

Mondunga, *alt.* Ndunga [ndt], 105

Monebwa, *alt.* Karen, Paku [kpp], 464

Monégasque, *dial.* Ligurian [lij], 548

Mong Leng, *dial.* Hmong Daw [mww], 334, 450, 514

Mongaiyat, *alt.* Mangayat [myj], 193

Mongala Poto, *dial.* Lusengo [lse], 103

Mongbandi, *alt.* Ngbandi, Southern [nbw], 105

Mongbapele, *alt. dial.* Pagibete [pae], 107

Mongbay, *alt.* Mambai [mcs], 66, 83

Mongghul, *alt. dial.* Tu [mjg], 345

Monggol, *alt.* Mongolian, Peripheral [mvf], 339

Mönghsa, *alt.* Achang [acn], 326, 456

Mongi, *alt.* Kube [kgf], 608

Monglwe, *alt.* Tai Loi [tlq], 467, 453

Mongo, *alt.* Bushoong [buf], 98
alt. Mango [mge], 83
alt. Mongo-Nkundu [lol], 104
dial. Daju, Dar Sila [dau], 189
dial. Kuranko [knk], 183
dial. Lusengo [lse], 103

Mongo-Nkundu [lol], 104

Mongo-Sila, *alt.* Daju, Dar Sila [dau], 189

Mongol [mgt], 614
alt. Mongolian, Halh [khk], 461, 505
alt. Mongolian, Peripheral [mvf], 339

Mongolia Buriat, *see* Buriat, Mongolia [bxm], 461

Mongolian Buriat, *alt.* Buriat, Mongolia [bxm], 461

Mongolian Sign Language [msr], 461

Mongolian, Halh [khk], 461, 505

Mongolian, Peripheral [mvf], 339, 462

Mongondou, *alt.* Mongondow [mog], 431

Mongondow [mog], 431

Mongor, *alt.* Tu [mjg], 345

Mongour, *alt.* Tu [mjg], 345

Mongsen Khari, *dial.* Naga, Ao [njo], 377

Mongul, *alt.* Mogholi [mhj], 316

Monguna, *dial.* Ron [cla], 174

Monguor, *alt.* Tu [mjg], 345

Mongwandi, *alt.* Ngbandi, Northern [ngb], 105

alt. Ngbandi, Southern [nbw], 105

Moni [mnz], 420
alt. Kensiu [kns], 515

Monia, *dial.* Libinza [liz], 102

Moniga, *alt.* Makhuwa-Moniga [mhm], 147

Monik, *alt.* Kensiu [kns], 454, 515

Monimbo [mom], 283

Moning, *dial.* Perai [wet], 399

Moniq, *alt.* Kensiu [kns], 454, 515

Monjo, *alt. dial.* Ghomálá' [bbj], 62

Monjombo, *alt.* Monzombo [moj], 89, 77, 105

Monjoroku, *alt.* Mundurukú [myu], 230

Monkit, *dial.* Moinba [mob], 376

Monkole, *alt.* Mokole [mkl], 45

Monnepwa, *alt.* Karen, Paku [kpp], 464

Mono (Cameroon) [mru], 68
Mono (Democratic Republic of Congo) [mnh], 104
Mono (Solomon Islands) [mte], 637
Mono (USA) [mnr], 305
dial. Mono [mte], 637

Mono-Alu, *alt.* Mono [mte], 637

Mono-Jembo, *alt.* Monzombo [moj], 105

Monoarfu, *dial.* Biak [bhw], 412

Monocho, *alt.* Maxakalí [mbl], 230

Monogoy, *dial.* Marba [mpg], 83

Monom [moo], 525

Monpa, *alt.* Moinba [mob], 376, 340
alt. Olekha [ole], 324
alt. Tshangla [tsj], 324, 345, 389

Monr, *alt.* Naga, Angami [njm], 377

Monsang Naga, *see* Naga, Monsang [nmh], 378

Monshang, *alt.* Naga, Monsang [nmh], 378

Monshon, *alt.* Mbulungish [mbv], 130

Montagnais [moe], 239

Montal, *alt.* Montol [mtl], 170

Montauk, *dial.* Mohegan-Montauk-Narragansett [mof], 305

Monte Verde Mixtec, *dial.* Mixtec, Northern Tlaxiaco [xtn], 267

Montenegrin, *alt.* Serbian [srp], 557, 529, 531

Monterey, *dial.* Ohlone, Southern [css], 306

Montol [mtl], 170
dial. Montol [mtl], 170

Montserrat Creole English [aig], 282

Monu, *alt.* Karen, Manumanaw [kxf], 464

Monumbo [mxk], 614

Monzamboli, *dial.* Budza [bja], 98

Monzombo [moj], 89, 77, 105

Monzón, *dial.* Quechua, Huamalíes-Dos de Mayo Huánuco [qvh], 291

Monzumbo, *alt.* Monzombo [moj], 77, 105

Moo [gwg], 170

Mooi, *alt.* Mekwei [msf], 420
alt. Moi [mxn], 420

Moojanga, *alt.* Anuak [anu], 113

Mooloroiji, *alt.* Muluridyi [vmu], 574

Mooma, *dial.* Yasa [yko], 111, 122

Moonde, *dial.* Tobanga [tng], 87

Mo'or, *dial.* Waropen [wrp], 425

Moor, *alt.* Arabic, Hasanya [mey], 141
alt. Arabic, Hassaniyya [mey], 146, 151
alt. Bimoba [bim], 123

Mòoré [mos], 52, 143, 209

Mooringa, *alt. dial.* Frisian, Northern [frr], 538

Mooringer, *dial.* Frisian, Northern [frr], 538

Moose, *alt.* Mòoré [mos], 52, 209

Moose Cree, *see* Cree, Moose [crm], 236

Moosehide, *alt.* Han [haa], 301, 238

Mooso, *alt.* Lahu [lhu], 524

Mooyo, *alt. dial.* Karanga [kth], 82

Mopaga, *alt.* Karen, Paku [kpp], 464

Mopán Maya, *see* Maya, Mopán [mop], 221, 255

Mopane, *alt.* Maya, Mopán [mop], 221, 255

Mopha, *alt.* Karen, Paku [kpp], 464

Mopla, *alt.* Malayalam [mal], 374, 509

Moplah, *dial.* Malayalam [mal], 374

Mopo, *alt. dial.* Burun [bdi], 189

Mopoi, *alt.* Mapoyo [mcg], 312

Mopute, *alt.* Waru [wru], 435

Mopwa, *alt.* Karen, Paku [kpp], 464

Moqaddam, *dial.* Azerbaijani, South [azb], 438

Moquelumnan, *alt.* Miwok, Southern Sierra [skd], 305

Mor (Bomberai Peninsula) [moq], 420
Mor (Mor Islands) [mhz], 420

Mor2, *alt.* Mor [moq], 420

Mora, *alt.* Yawa [yva], 426
alt. dial. Yawa [yva], 426

Mora Brousse, *alt. dial.* Wandala [mfi], 73

Mora Massif, *alt. dial.* Wandala [mfi], 73

Morafa, *alt.* Asaro'o [mtv], 591

Moraid [msg], 420
Morang, *alt. dial.* Naga, Tase [nst], 380
Morangia, *dial.* Tharu, Kochila [thq], 388
Morangiya, *dial.* Tharu, Kochila [thq], 481
Moraori, *alt.* Morori [mok], 420
Morari, *alt.* Morori [mok], 420
Morato, *alt.* Uru [ure], 224
Moravian Romani, *dial.* Romani, Carpathian [rmc], 533, 558
Morawa [mze], 614
Morbo, *dial.* Bernde [bdo], 79
Mordoff, *alt.* Moksha [mdf], 556
Mordov, *alt.* Moksha [mdf], 556
Mordvin, *alt.* Erzya [myv], 554
Mordvin-Erzya, *alt.* Erzya [myv], 554
Mordvin-Moksha, *alt.* Moksha [mdf], 556
More, *alt.* Itene [ite], 223
  alt. Mòoré [mos], 52, 143, 209
Moreb, *dial.* Tagoi [tag], 195
Morela, *dial.* Hitu [htu], 398
Morelos Nahuatl, *see* Nahuatl, Morelos [nhm], 271
Moreno, *pej. alt.* Garifuna [cab], 221, 282
Morerebi [xmo], 230
Moresada [msx], 615
Mori, *alt. dial.* Maninkakan, Eastern [emk], 129
  dial. Aneme Wake [aby], 589
Mori Atas [mzq], 431
Mori Bawah [xmz], 431
Morie, *alt. dial.* Abé [aba], 90
Morigele, *dial.* Evenki [evn], 332
Morigi [mdb], 615
Morigi Island, *alt.* Morigi [mdb], 615
Moriil, *alt.* Zan Gula [zna], 87
Moriko, *dial.* Mukulu [moz], 85
Morille, *alt.* Daasanach [dsh], 114
Morima, *alt.* Molima [mox], 614
Moriori, *dial.* Maori [mri], 586
Moripi-Iokea, *alt. dial.* Toaripi [tqo], 628
Morisyen [mfe], 145
Morma, *alt.* Arakanese [mhv], 462, 354
  alt. dial. Arakanese [mhv], 320
Moro [mor], 193
  alt. Ayoreo [ayo], 284, 222
  alt. Tausug [tsg], 458
Moro Joloano, *alt.* Tausug [tsg], 502, 395
Moroa, *alt. dial.* Tyap [kcg], 176
Moroba-Lama, *alt.* Umbuygamu [umg], 577

Moroccan Arabic, *alt.* Arabic, Moroccan Spoken [ary], 146
Moroccan Colloquial Arabic, *alt.* Arabic, Moroccan Spoken [ary], 146
Moroccan Darija, *alt.* Arabic, Moroccan Spoken [ary], 146
Moroccan Sign Language [xms], 146
Moroccan Spoken Arabic, *see* Arabic, Moroccan Spoken [ary], 146
Morofo, *alt.* Anyin Morofo [mtb], 91
Morokodo [mgc], 193
  dial. Morokodo [mgc], 193
Morom, *alt.* Bernde [bdo], 79
  dial. Bernde [bdo], 79
Moromiranga, *alt.* Arop-Lukep [apr], 590
Moronahua, *alt. dial.* Yaminahua [yaa], 293
Moronene [mqn], 431
  alt. dial. Moronene [mqn], 431
Moronou, *dial.* Anyin [any], 91
Morori [mok], 420
Morotai, *dial.* Galela [gbi], 398
Morotoco, *alt.* Ayoreo [ayo], 284, 222
Morouas [mrp], 644
Morouba, *alt. dial.* Banda-Mbrès [bqk], 75, 188
Morre, *alt.* Zan Gula [zna], 87
Morta, *alt. dial.* Katcha-Kadugli-Miri [xtc], 191
Mortlock, *alt.* Mortlockese [mrl], 582
  alt. Takuu [nho], 626
Mortlockese [mrl], 582
Moru [mgd], 193
Moruas, *alt.* Morouas [mrp], 644
Moruba, *dial.* Banda-Mbrès [bqk], 75, 188
Morunahua, *alt. dial.* Yaminahua [yaa], 293
Moruwa'di, *dial.* Moru [mgd], 193
Morva, *alt.* Kurux [kru], 371
Morwa, *alt. dial.* Tyap [kcg], 176
Morwap, *pej. alt.* Elseng [mrf], 414
Mos, *alt.* Kensiu [kns], 515
  alt. Tonga [tnz], 518, 456
Mosana, *alt.* Moi [mxn], 420
Mosang, *dial.* Naga, Tase [nst], 380
Mosange, *alt.* Ndolo [ndl], 105
Mosca, *alt.* Chibcha [chb], 244
Moselle Franconian, *alt.* Luxembourgeois [ltz], 546, 539
Mosetén, *alt.* Tsimané [cas], 224
Moshang, *alt.* Naga, Monsang [nmh], 378
Moshi, *alt.* Mochi [old], 202
  alt. Mòoré [mos], 52, 143, 209

Mosi, *alt.* Mochi [old], 202
  alt. Musey [mse], 85, 68
Mosieno, *dial.* Teke, Ibali [tek], 108
Mosimo [mqv], 615
Mosin, *alt.* Mosina [msn], 644
Mosina [msn], 644
Mosiro [mwy], 202
Mosiye, *alt.* Bussa [dox], 114
Moskona [mtj], 420
Moslawi, *alt.* Arabic, North Mesopotamian Spoken [ayp], 442, 510
Moso, *alt.* Lahu [lhu], 338
  pej. alt. Naxi [nbf], 341
Mosquito, *alt.* Mískito [miq], 282, 258
Mossi, *alt.* Mòoré [mos], 52, 143, 209
Mosso, *pej. alt.* Naxi [nbf], 341
Mot, *alt. dial.* Tumak [tmc], 87
Mot-Mar, *dial.* Gula [kcm], 76
Mota [mtt], 644
Motalava, *alt.* Motlav [mlv], 644
Motchekin, *alt.* Gude [gde], 161, 62
Motembo, *alt.* Tembo [tmv], 108
Moti, *alt. dial.* Dimli [diq], 518
Motiem, *dial.* Ngangam [gng], 209
Motilón, *alt.* Barí [mot], 243, 311
  alt. Quechua, San Martín [qvs], 292
Motilone, *alt.* Barí [mot], 243, 311
Motin, *alt. dial.* Tumak [tmc], 87
Motki, *dial.* Dimli [diq], 518
Motlav [mlv], 644
Moto-Mara, *alt. dial.* Gula [kcm], 76
Motom, *alt. dial.* Iceve-Maci [bec], 163
Motomo, *alt. dial.* Iceve-Maci [bec], 63, 163
Motozintleco, *alt.* Mocho [mhc], 270
  dial. Mocho [mhc], 270
Motsuvan, *alt.* Tsuvan [tsh], 72
Motu [meu], 615
Motu, Hiri [hmo], 615
Motumotu, *alt.* Toaripi [tqo], 628
Motun, *alt. dial.* Tumak [tmc], 87
Motuna, *alt.* Siwai [siw], 625
Motuo, *alt.* Tshangla [tsj], 389
Motuo Menba, *alt.* Tshangla [tsj], 345
Mou, *alt.* Khmu [kjg], 451, 337, 465, 515
Mouamenam, *alt. dial.* Akoose [bss], 56
Mouan, *alt.* Mwan [moa], 94
Moubi, *alt.* Mubi [mub], 84
Mougo, *dial.* Mbay [myb], 84
Mougulu, *alt.* Beami [beo], 593
Mouhour, *alt. dial.* Mefele [mfj], 67
Mouk, *dial.* Mouk-Aria [mwh], 615
Mouk-Aria [mwh], 615

Mouktele, *alt.* Matal [mfh], 66

Moulmein, *alt. dial.* Karen, Pwo Eastern [kjp], 464

Moulmein Pwo Karen, *alt.* Karen, Pwo Eastern [kjp], 464

Mouloui, *alt.* Musgu [mug], 85

Mounan, *alt.* Muna [mnb], 431

Moundan, *alt.* Mundang [mua], 85, 68

Moundang, *alt.* Mundang [mua], 85, 68

Mount Lebanon Arabic, *alt. dial.* Arabic, North Levantine Spoken [apc], 453

Mountain, *dial.* Slavey, North [scs], 241

Mountain Arapesh, *alt.* Bukiyip [ape], 595

alt. dial. Bukiyip [ape], 595

Mountain Bashkir, *alt. dial.* Bashkir [bak], 553

Mountain Koiali, *see* Koiali, Mountain [kpx], 606

Mountain Koiari, *alt.* Koiali, Mountain [kpx], 606

Mountain Lawa, *alt.* Lawa, Western [lcp], 338, 515

Mountain Maidu, *alt.* Maidu, Northeast [nmu], 304

Mountain Pima, *alt.* Pima Bajo [pia], 273

Mountou, *alt.* Mündü [muh], 193, 105

Mourle, *alt.* Murle [mur], 193, 117

Mouroum, *alt. dial.* Ngambay [sba], 85

Mourro, *alt. dial.* Kibet [kie], 82

Mousgou, *alt.* Musgu [mug], 68, 85

Mousgoum, *alt.* Musgu [mug], 68, 85

Mousgoum de Guirvidig, *alt. dial.* Musgu [mug], 68, 85

Mousgoum de Guirvidik, *alt. dial.* Musgu [mug], 85

Mousgoum de Pouss, *alt. dial.* Musgu [mug], 68, 85

Mousgoun, *alt.* Musgu [mug], 68, 85

Moussei, *alt.* Musey [mse], 85, 68

Moussey, *alt.* Musey [mse], 85, 68

Mouton, *alt.* Tomini [txm], 434

Mouyenge, *alt.* Muyang [muy], 69

Mouyengue, *alt.* Muyang [muy], 69

Movar, *alt. dial.* Kanuri, Central [knc], 63

dial. Kanuri, Central [knc], 152

Move, *dial.* Yagaria [ygr], 632

Moveave, *alt. dial.* Toaripi [tqo], 628

Movima [mzp], 223

Mowchi, *alt.* Mawchi [mke], 375

Mowor, *alt. dial.* Kanuri, Central [knc], 152

dial. Kanuri, Central [knc], 63

Moxdoa, *alt.* Carapana [cbc], 244

Moxev, *dial.* Georgian [kat], 352

Moxo, *alt.* Ignaciano [ign], 223

Moxos, *alt.* Ignaciano [ign], 223

alt. Trinitario [trn], 224

Moyadan Itneg, *see* Itneg, Moyadan [ity], 496

Moyaka, *alt. dial.* Yaka [axk], 78

Moyo, *alt. dial.* Karanga [kth], 82

dial. Ma'di [mhi], 211

Moyon, *alt.* Naga, Moyon [nmo], 379

Moyon Naga, *see* Naga, Moyon [nmo], 379

Mozambican Sign Language [mzy], 148

Mozarabic [mxi], 560

Mozdok, *alt. dial.* Kabardian [kbd], 554

Mozhumi, *alt.* Naga, Southern Rengma [nre], 379

Mozome, *alt. dial.* Naga, Angami [njm], 377

Mpade [mpi], 68, 84

dial. Mpade [mpi], 68

Mpaka, *dial.* Mono [mnh], 104

Mpama, *dial.* Mongo-Nkundu [lol], 104

Mparntwe Arrernte, *dial.* Arrernte, Eastern [aer], 568

Mpezeni, *alt. dial.* Nsenga [nse], 215

Mpi [mpz], 516

Mpi-Mi, *alt.* Mpi [mpz], 516

Mpiemo [mcx], 77, 68

Mpo, *alt.* Mpiemo [mcx], 77, 68

alt. Mpyemo [mcx], 89

dial. Basaa [bas], 58

Mpomam, *dial.* Mpongmpong [mgg], 68

Mpompo, *alt.* Mpongmpong [mgg], 68

Mpondo, *dial.* Xhosa [xho], 187

Mpondomisi, *alt. dial.* Xhosa [xho], 187

Mpondomse, *dial.* Xhosa [xho], 187

Mpongmpong [mgg], 68

Mpongo, *dial.* Ntomba [nto], 106

Mpongoué, *alt. dial.* Myene [mye], 121

Mpongwe, *dial.* Myene [mye], 121

Mpopo, *alt.* Mpongmpong [mgg], 68

Mpoto [mpa], 202

Mpotovoro [mvt], 644

Mpu, *dial.* Ngungwel [ngz], 89

Mpumpum, *alt. dial.* Ngungwel [ngz], 89

Mpungwe, *alt. dial.* Myene [mye], 121

Mpuono [zmp], 105

dial. Mpuono [zmp], 105

Mpur [akc], 420

Mpus, *dial.* Musgu [mug], 68, 85

Mpuun, *alt. dial.* Mpuono [zmp], 105

Mpyemo [mcx], 89

alt. Mpiemo [mcx], 77, 68

dial. Mpiemo [mcx], 77

dial. Mpyemo [mcx], 89

Mrabri, *alt.* Mlabri [mra], 516, 451

Mras Tatar, *alt.* Shor [cjs], 506

Mrassa, *dial.* Shor [cjs], 506

Mrasu, *alt. dial.* Shor [cjs], 506

Mriak-Mriku, *dial.* Sasak [sas], 409

Mrima, *dial.* Swahili [swh], 205, 136

Mro, *alt.* Mru [mro], 376

dial. Chrau [crw], 522

Mro Chin, *see* Chin, Mro [cmr], 463

Mru [mro], 321, 376

Mrung, *alt.* Kok Borok [trp], 321

alt. Mru [mro], 321, 376

Mser [kqx], 68, 84

dial. Mser [kqx], 68, 84

Msir, *alt. dial.* Mser [kqx], 84

Mt. Elgon Maasai, *alt.* Sabaot [spy], 135

Mt. Goliath, *alt.* Una [mtg], 424

Mt. Iraya Agta, *see* Agta, Mt. Iraya [atl], 490

Mt. Iriga Agta, *see* Agta, Mt. Iriga [agz], 491

Mt. Iriga Negrito, *alt.* Agta, Mt. Iriga [agz], 491

Mtezi, *dial.* Kukele [kez], 167

Mthur, *alt.* Jarai [jra], 523, 325

Mtiul, *dial.* Georgian [kat], 352

Mu, *alt.* Naxi [nbf], 341

alt. Sekpele [lip], 127

Mu:du, *alt.* Koraga, Mudu [vmd], 369

Mual, *dial.* Muong [mtq], 525

Mualang [mtd], 394

Muan, *alt.* Mwan [moa], 94

Muana, *alt.* Mwan [moa], 94

Muane, *alt.* Mwani [wmw], 148

Mu'ang, *alt.* Thai, Northern [nod], 517

Muang, *alt.* Thai, Northern [nod], 453

Muasi, *alt. dial.* Korku [kfq], 369

Muatiamvua, *alt.* Ruund [rnd], 107, 41

Muaturaina, *dial.* Ese [mcq], 598

Mubadji, *alt.* Beba [bfp], 58

Mubako, *alt.* Nyong [muo], 71, 171

Mubami [tsx], 615

Mubi [mub], 84

alt. Gude [gde], 62

dial. Foi [foi], 599
Mubi River, *alt.* Foi [foi], 599
Muchella, *alt. dial.* Fali [fli], 159
Muckleshoot, *dial.* Salish, Southern Puget Sound [slh], 307
Mucoroca, *alt.* Kwadi [kwz], 40
Mud, *alt. dial.* Naba [mne], 85
Muda, *alt.* Mo'da [gbn], 193
Mudavan, *alt.* Muthuvan [muv], 377
Mudaye, *alt.* Gude [gde], 161, 62
Mudbura [mwd], 574
Mudburra, *alt.* Mudbura [mwd], 574
Muddali, *alt.* Pengo [peg], 383
Mudhili Gadaba, *see* Gadaba, Mudhili [gau], 361
Mudi, *alt.* Koda [cdz], 368
Mudia, *alt.* Muria, Western [mut], 377
Mudikora, *alt.* Koda [cdz], 368
Mudima, *alt.* Malimba [mzd], 66
Mudjétira, *pej. alt.* Suruí do Pará [mdz], 232
Mudjetíre, *pej. alt.* Suruí do Pará [mdz], 232
Mudjetíre-Suruí, *pej. alt.* Suruí do Pará [mdz], 232
Mudu, *dial.* Koraga, Korra [kfd], 369
Mudu Koraga, *see* Koraga, Mudu [vmd], 369
Muduapa [wiv], 615
Mudugar, *alt.* Muthuvan [muv], 377
Muduvan, *alt.* Muthuvan [muv], 377
Muduvar, *alt.* Muthuvan [muv], 377
Muename, *alt.* Muinane [bmr], 246
Muerzong, *dial.* Guanyinqiao [jiq], 333
Mufian [aoj], 615
Mufwa, *dial.* Burun [bdi], 189
Mugaba, *alt. dial.* Rennell-Belona [mnv], 638
Mugaja, *alt. dial.* Burun [bdi], 189
Mugali, *alt.* Mugom [muk], 476
dial. Mugom [muk], 476
Mugaly, *alt. dial.* Azerbaijani, North [azj], 319, 319
Mugange, *dial.* Sagalla [tga], 136
Mughaja, *dial.* Burun [bdi], 189
Mughalbandi, *dial.* Oriya [ori], 382
Mugiki, *alt. dial.* Rennell-Belona [mnv], 638
Mugil, *alt.* Bargam [mlp], 592
Mugo-Mborkoina, *alt. dial.* Burun [bdi], 189
Mugom [muk], 476, 376
Mugu, *alt.* Mugom [muk], 476
Muguani, *dial.* Barai [bbb], 592
Muguji, *dial.* Kwegu [xwg], 116
Mugum, *alt.* Mugom [muk], 476
alt. dial. Ghomálá' [bbj], 62

Mugumute, *alt.* Kapriman [dju], 605
Muhang, *alt. dial.* Lamaholot [slp], 408
Muher, *dial.* Sebat Bet Gurage [sgw], 118
Muhian, *alt.* Mufian [aoj], 615
Muhiang, *alt.* Mufian [aoj], 615
Muhso, *alt.* Lahu [lhu], 338, 451, 465, 515, 524
Muhsur, *alt.* Lahu [lhu], 515
Muhura, *dial.* Mefele [mfj], 67
Muhuru, *dial.* Suba [suh], 136
Muila, *alt. dial.* Nyaneka [nyk], 41
Muinana, *alt.* Muinane [bmr], 246
Muinane [bmr], 246
Muinane Huitoto, *alt.* Huitoto, Nüpode [hux], 288
Muinani, *alt.* Muinane [bmr], 246
Muirin, *dial.* Dargwa [dar], 553
Muisca, *alt.* Chibcha [chb], 244
Muji Yi, *see* Yi, Muji [ymj], 347
Muka, *alt.* Bamunka [bvm], 57
alt. dial. Melanau [mel], 460, 325
Mukah, *alt. dial.* Melanau [mel], 460, 325
Mukah-Oya, *dial.* Melanau [mel], 460, 325
Mukajai, *alt. dial.* Ninam [shb], 230
Mukamuga, *alt.* Kamoro [kgq], 416
Mukawa, *alt.* Are [mwc], 590
Mukha Dhora, *alt.* Mukha-Dora [mmk], 376
Mukha-Dora [mmk], 376
Mukhad, *alt.* Rutul [rut], 556
Mukhiya, *alt.* Sunwar [suz], 479
Muki, *alt.* Kanoé [kxo], 228
Mukili, *alt.* Beli [bey], 593
Muko-Muko [vmo], 436
Mukogodo, *alt.* Yaaku [muu], 137
Mukohn, *alt. dial.* Ngemba [nge], 69
Mukoquodo, *alt.* Yaaku [muu], 137
Mukri, *alt.* Kurdish, Central [ckb], 440
dial. Kurdish, Central [ckb], 443, 440
Muktele, *alt.* Matal [mfh], 66
Muktile, *alt.* Matal [mfh], 66
Muku, *alt. dial.* Nakanai [nak], 616
Mukulu [moz], 85
dial. Bemba [bem], 213
Mukuni, *alt.* Lenje [leh], 214
Mukuru, *alt. dial.* Befang [bby], 58
Mulaha [mfw], 615
dial. Mulaha [mfw], 615
Mulai, *alt. dial.* Makhuwa [vmw], 147
Mulak, *dial.* Malay [mly], 436
Mulakaino, *alt.* Lamogai [lmg], 609
Mulam [mlm], 340
Mulan, *alt.* Lamalera [lmr], 408
Mulao, *alt.* Mulam [mlm], 340
Mulao Miao, *alt.* Mulam [mlm], 340

Mularitchee, *alt.* Muluridyi [vmu], 574
Mulenge, *dial.* Rwanda [kin], 107
Mulgaon-Wangtang, *dial.* Meohang, Eastern [emg], 475
Mulgarnoo, *alt.* Bayungu [bxj], 569
Mulgi, *alt. dial.* Estonian [est], 534
dial. Estonian [est], 534
Mulgwe, *dial.* Marghi Central [mrt], 169
Muliao, *alt.* Mulam [mlm], 340
Mulimba, *alt.* Malimba [mzd], 66
Mullridgey, *alt.* Muluridyi [vmu], 574
Mullu Kurumba, *see* Kurumba, Mullu [kpb], 371
Mullukmulluk [mpb], 574
Mulonga, *dial.* Simaa [sie], 215
Mulou, *alt.* Mulam [mlm], 340
Mulsom, *dial.* Anal [anm], 354
Multani, *alt.* Seraiki [skr], 488, 386
dial. Seraiki [skr], 488
Mulu, *alt.* Maru [mhx], 465
Mulung, *dial.* Naga, Konyak [nbe], 378
Muluridyi [vmu], 574
Mulurutji, *alt.* Muluridyi [vmu], 574
Mulwi, *alt.* Musgu [mug], 68, 85
alt. dial. Musgu [mug], 68
Mulwi-Mogroum, *alt. dial.* Musgu [mug], 85
Mulwyin, *alt. dial.* Bacama [bcy], 154
Muly, *dial.* Estonian [est], 534
Mulyen, *dial.* Bacama [bcy], 154
Mum [kqa], 615
Mumaite, *alt. dial.* Kayeli [kzl], 399
Mumbai-Delhi Sign Language, *dial.* Indian Sign Language [ins], 365
Mumbake, *alt.* Nyong [muo], 71, 171
Mumbala, *alt. dial.* Yombe [yom], 109, 42, 90
Mumoni, *dial.* Kamba [kam], 133
Mumughadja, *alt. dial.* Burun [bdi], 189
Mumuye [mzm], 170
Mumviri, *dial.* Kati [bsh], 316, 486
Mun, *alt.* Kim Mun [mji], 337, 451, 524
alt. Mon [mnw], 466, 516
Mün, *alt.* Chin, Mün [mwq], 463
Mün Chin, *see* Chin, Mün [mwq], 463
Mun Xen, *alt.* Khmu [kjg], 524
Muna [mnb], 431
Munari, *alt.* Mundari [muw], 376, 321, 476

Munaseli Pandai, *dial.* Adabe [adb], 350

Munda, *alt.* Mundari [muw], 376, 321, 476
alt. dial. Mendankwe-Nkwen [mfd], 67

Munda Andhra Pradesh Gadaba, *dial.* Gadaba, Bodo [gbj], 361

Munda Orissa Gadaba, *dial.* Gadaba, Bodo [gbj], 361

Mundabli [boe], 68

Mundang [mua], 85, 68

Mundani [mnf], 68

Mundari [muw], 376, 321, 476
alt. Mandari [mqu], 193
alt. dial. Bari [bfa], 210

Mundat [mmf], 170

Mundjun, *alt.* Yir Yoront [yiy], 579

Mundo, *alt.* Mündü [muh], 193, 105

Mündü [muh], 193, 105

Munduguma, *alt.* Biwat [bwm], 594

Mundugumor, *alt.* Biwat [bwm], 594

Mundum 1, *alt. dial.* Ngemba [nge], 69

Mundum 2, *alt. dial.* Ngemba [nge], 69

Mundurucu, *alt.* Mundurukú [myu], 230

Mundurukú [myu], 230

Munegasc, *alt. dial.* Ligurian [lij], 548

Mung, *dial.* Phunoi [pho], 452, 517

Munga, *alt.* Leelau [ldk], 168
dial. Birri [bvq], 75

Munga Doso, *alt.* Mingang Doso [mko], 170

Munga Lelau, *alt.* Leelau [ldk], 168

Mungak, *alt.* Tuvin [tyv], 345, 462

Munga'ka, *alt.* Mungaka [mhk], 68

Mungaka [mhk], 68

Mungarai, *alt.* Mangarayi [mpc], 573

Mungera Ohalo, *alt.* Yidiny [yii], 579

Mungerry, *alt.* Mangarayi [mpc], 573

Munggai, *alt.* Mekwei [msf], 420

Munggava, *dial.* Rennell-Belona [mnv], 638

Mungge, *alt.* Mekwei [msf], 420

Munggui [mth], 421

Mungiki, *dial.* Rennell-Belona [mnv], 638

Mungo, *dial.* Duala [dua], 60

Mungom, *alt. dial.* Ncane [ncr], 69

Mungong, *alt. dial.* Ncane [ncr], 69

Mungray, *dial.* Naga, Tase [nst], 380

Mungu, *alt. dial.* Duala [dua], 60

Mungyen, *alt.* Ngamambo [nbv], 69

Muniche [myr], 289

Munichi, *alt.* Muniche [myr], 289

Munichino, *alt.* Muniche [myr], 289

Munin, *dial.* Andi [ani], 553

Munit [mtc], 615

Muniwara, *alt.* Juwal [mwb], 603

Munjani, *alt.* Munji [mnj], 316

Munjhan, *alt.* Munji [mnj], 316

Munji [mnj], 316
dial. Boikin [bzf], 594

Munjiwar, *alt.* Munji [mnj], 316

Munjuk, *alt.* Musgu [mug], 68, 85

Munkaf, *alt.* Naki [mff], 69

Munkan, *alt.* Wik-Mungkan [wim], 578

Munkei, *alt.* Mekwei [msf], 420

Munkip [mpv], 615

Münkü, *alt.* Irántxe [irn], 227
dial. Irántxe [irn], 227

Munsee [umu], 239

Munshi, *pej. alt.* Tiv [tiv], 175

Munster-Leinster, *dial.* Gaelic, Irish [gle], 542

Muntabi, *alt.* Gaam [tbi], 190

Muntean, *alt. dial.* Romanian [ron], 548

Muntenian, *dial.* Romanian [ron], 552, 548

Munukutuba, *alt.* Kituba [mkw], 88

Munyo, *dial.* Orma [orc], 135

Munyo Yaya, *alt. dial.* Orma [orc], 135

Munyuku, *dial.* Gupapuyngu [guf], 571

Munzombo, *alt.* Monzombo [moj], 89

Muong [mtq], 525

Mupun, *dial.* Mwaghavul [sur], 170

Mura, *dial.* Wandala [mfi], 73

Múra, *dial.* Pirahã [myp], 231

Múra-Pirahã, *alt.* Pirahã [myp], 231

Muralidban, *dial.* Gunwinggu [gup], 571

Murang Punan, *alt. dial.* Dayak, Land [dyk], 393

Murasi, *dial.* Sungor [sjg], 195

Murataik, *alt.* Muratayak [asx], 615

Muratayak [asx], 615

Murato, *alt.* Candoshi-Shapra [cbu], 287
dial. Carib [car], 257, 295

Muratu, *alt.* Uru [ure], 224

Murawari, *alt.* Muruwari [zmu], 574

Murcian, *dial.* Spanish [spa], 560

Murele, *alt.* Murle [mur], 117

Murelei, *alt.* Murle [mur], 193

Murgi, *alt.* Birked [brk], 189

Muri, *alt.* Guhu-Samane [ghs], 599
alt. Mer [mnu], 420
alt. Semimi [etz], 422

dial. Halbi [hlb], 363

Muria, *alt. dial.* Halbi [hlb], 363

Muria Gondi, *alt.* Muria, Western [mut], 377

Muria, Eastern [emu], 376

Muria, Far Western [fmu], 376

Muria, Western [mut], 377

Murik [mtf], 615

Murik Kayan, *see* Kayan, Murik [mxr], 459

Murinbada, *alt.* Murrinh-Patha [mwf], 574

Murinbata, *alt.* Murrinh-Patha [mwf], 574

Murinmanindji, *alt.* Marimanindji [zmm], 574

Murire, *alt.* Buglere [sab], 283

Muris, *alt.* Demta [dmy], 414

Murisapa, *alt.* Moresada [msx], 615

Murkim [rmh], 421

Murle [mur], 193, 117

Murmi, *alt.* Tamang, Western [tdg], 480

Muro, *alt.* Orokolo [oro], 620
alt. dial. Kibet [kie], 82

Murrinh-Patha [mwf], 574

Murrinhdiminin, *dial.* Murrinh-Patha [mwf], 574

Murrinhkura, *dial.* Murrinh-Patha [mwf], 574

Murrinhpatha, *dial.* Murrinh-Patha [mwf], 574

Murru, *dial.* Kibet [kie], 82

Murrungun, *dial.* Djinang [dji], 570

Mursi [muz], 117

Mursum, *dial.* Chin, Falam [flm], 358

Muru, *alt.* Orokolo [oro], 620

Murua, *alt.* Muyuw [myw], 616

Murui Huitoto, *see* Huitoto, Murui [huu], 288, 245

Murule, *alt.* Murle [mur], 193, 117

Murum, *dial.* Ngambay [sba], 85

Murung, *alt.* Mru [mro], 321, 376

Murung 1, *alt. dial.* Dohoi [otd], 393

Murung 2, *dial.* Siang [sya], 395

Murupi [mqw], 615

Murusapa-Sarewa, *alt.* Moresada [msx], 615

Murut, *alt.* Lundayeh [lnd], 324

Murut Padas, *alt. dial.* Timugon Murut [tih], 458

Muruthu, *alt.* Marathi [mar], 374

Muruwa, *alt.* Muyuw [myw], 616

Muruwari [zmu], 574

Muruwarri, *alt.* Muruwari [zmu], 574

Murzi, *alt.* Mursi [muz], 117

Murzu, *alt.* Mursi [muz], 117
Mus, *dial.* Armenian [hye], 318
Musa, *alt.* Musan [mmp], 613
Musahar, *alt.* Musasa [smm], 476
Musahari, *dial.* Bhojpuri [bho], 356
Musaia, *dial.* Yalunka [yal], 184
Musak [mmq], 615
Musali, *alt.* Jakati [jat], 564, 316
Musan [mmp], 613
Musao, *alt.* Mussau-Emira
    [emi], 616
Musar [mmi], 616
    dial. Maithili [mai], 475
Musasa [smm], 476
Musau-Emira, *alt.* Mussau-Emira
    [emi], 616
Musaya, *alt.* Musey [mse], 68
Musch, *alt. dial.* Armenian
    [hye], 318
Musei, *alt.* Musey [mse], 85, 68
Musemban, *alt.* Mundang [mua], 68
Musen, *dial.* Lamogai [lmg], 609
Museu, *alt.* Lahu [lhu], 451, 465
Musey [mse], 85, 68
Museyna, *alt.* Musey [mse], 85, 68
Musgoi, *dial.* Mazagway [dkx], 66
Musgoy, *alt. dial.* Mazagway
    [dkx], 66
Musgu [mug], 68, 85
Musgum, *alt.* Musgu [mug], 68, 85
Musgum-Pouss, *alt. dial.* Musgu
    [mug], 85
Mushang, *alt.* Naga, Monsang
    [nmh], 378
Mushuau Innu, *alt. dial.* Naskapi
    [nsk], 239
Mushunguli, *alt.* Mushungulu
    [xma], 185
Mushungulu [xma], 185
Musi [mui], 437
    dial. Rejang [rej], 437
Musian, *alt.* Musan [mmp], 613
Musiina, *alt.* Musey [mse], 68
Musim, *alt. dial.* Hote [hot], 602
Musiye, *alt.* Bussa [dox], 114
Muskogee [mus], 305
Muskum [mje], 85
Muslim Sindhi, *alt. dial.* Sindhi
    [snd], 488
Muslim Tat, *see* Tat, Muslim
    [ttt], 320, 442, 556
Muslim Tat, *alt.* Tat, Muslim
    [ttt], 320
Musoi, *alt.* Musey [mse], 68
Musom [msu], 616
Musqueam, *dial.* Halkomelem
    [hur], 238, 301
Mussar, *alt.* Lahu [lhu], 338, 524
Mussau, *alt.* Mussau-Emira
    [emi], 616

Mussau-Emira [emi], 616
Musseh Daeng, *alt. dial.* Lahu
    [lhu], 338, 451, 465, 515, 524
Musseh Kwi, *alt.* Lahu Shi
    [kds], 515
Musseh Lyang, *alt.* Lahu Shi
    [kds], 515
Musselmani, *alt. dial.* Bengali [ben],
    355
    dial. Bengali [ben], 469
Musser, *alt.* Lahu [lhu], 515
Musser Dam, *alt. dial.* Lahu
    [lhu], 338, 451, 465, 515, 524
Musso, *alt.* Lahu [lhu], 338, 451,
    465, 515, 524
Mussoi, *alt.* Musey [mse], 85, 68
Mussoy, *alt.* Musey [mse], 85, 68
Mussuh, *alt.* Lahu [lhu], 338, 451,
    465, 515, 524
Mussulman Tati, *alt.* Tat, Muslim
    [ttt], 320, 442, 556
Mustangi, *alt.* Lowa [loy], 474
Musuk, *alt.* Musgu [mug], 68, 85
Musunye, *dial.* Jonkor Bourmataguil
    [jeu], 81
Muta, *alt.* Meta' [mgo], 67
Mutair, *alt. dial.* Arabic, Najdi
    Spoken [ars], 508
Mutani, *alt.* Seraiki [skr], 386
Muthambi, *dial.* Mwimbi-Muthambi
    [mws], 135
Mutheit, *alt.* Karen, Pwo Western
    [pwo], 464
Muthuvan [muv], 377
Mutidi, *dial.* Nzanyi [nja], 171
Mutsun, *dial.* Ohlone, Southern
    [css], 306
Muttangulla, *alt.* Madngele [zml],
    573
Mutu [tuc], 616
    dial. Mutu [tuc], 616
Mutum, *alt.* Bitur [mcc], 594
Muturami, *dial.* Giziga, South
    [giz], 62
Muturua, *alt. dial.* Giziga, South
    [giz], 62
Muturwa, *alt. dial.* Giziga, South
    [giz], 62
Mututu, *alt.* Amdang [amj], 78
Mutuvar, *alt.* Muthuvan [muv], 377
Mutwang, *dial.* Rawang [raw], 466
Mutyu, *alt.* Djangun [djf], 569
Muungo, *alt. dial.* Duala [dua], 60
Muwasi, *alt. dial.* Korku [kfq], 369
Muxule, *dial.* Jina [jia], 63
Muxuli, *alt.* Jina [jia], 63
Muya [mvm], 340
    alt. Miya [mkf], 170
Muyang [muy], 69
Muyenge, *alt.* Muyang [muy], 69

Muyu, *alt.* Muyuw [myw], 616
    alt. Ninggerum [nxr], 421
Muyu, North [kti], 421
Muyu, South [kts], 421
Muyua, *alt.* Muyuw [myw], 616
Muyuw [myw], 616
Muyuwa, *alt.* Muyuw [myw], 616
Muywi, *alt. dial.* Meta' [mgo], 67
Muzgum, *alt.* Muskum [mje], 85
Muzuk, *alt.* Musgu [mug], 68
    dial. Musgu [mug], 68, 85
Mvae, *alt. dial.* Bakaka [bqz], 57
    dial. Fang [fan], 61
Mvan, *alt. dial.* Fang [fan], 61
Mvanip [mcj], 170
Mvanlip, *alt.* Mvanip [mcj], 170
Mvano, *alt.* Mvanip [mcj], 170
Mvanon, *alt.* Mvanip [mcj], 170
Mvanöp, *alt.* Mvanip [mcj], 170
Mvay, *alt. dial.* Fang [fan], 61
Mvedere, *alt. dial.* Banda-Banda
    [bpd], 75, 188
Mvegumba, *alt.* Belanda Viri
    [bvi], 189
Mvele, *alt.* Basaa [bas], 58
    alt. dial. Ewondo [ewo], 61
    alt. dial. Tuki [bag], 72
Mvete, *dial.* Ewondo [ewo], 61
Mvita, *dial.* Swahili [swh], 136
Mvo-Nangkok, *dial.* Eton [eto], 61
Mvog-Namve, *dial.* Eton [eto], 61
Mvog-Niengue, *dial.* Ewondo
    [ewo], 61
MVSL, *alt.* Martha's Vineyard Sign
    Language [mre], 304
Mvuba [mxh], 105
Mvuba-A, *alt.* Mvuba [mxh], 105
Mvumbo, *alt.* Ngumba [nmg], 111
    dial. Ngumba [nmg], 70
Mwa, *alt.* Mwan [moa], 94
Mwae, *alt.* Emae [mmw], 641
Mwaghavul [sur], 170
Mwahed, *alt. dial.* Bakaka [bqz], 57
Mwahet, *alt. dial.* Bakaka [bqz], 57
Mwali Comorian, *see* Comorian,
    Mwali [wlc], 87
Mwalu, *alt. dial.* Makonde
    [kde], 148
Mwalukwasia, *dial.* Duau
    [dva], 597
Mwamba, *dial.* Nyakyusa-Ngonde
    [nyy], 203
Mwambe, *alt. dial.* Makonde
    [kde], 148
Mwambong, *dial.* Akoose [bss], 56
Mwamenam, *dial.* Akoose [bss], 56
Mwan [moa], 94
Mwana, *alt. dial.* Dijim-Bwilim
    [cfa], 158
Mwanda, *dial.* Taita [dav], 136

Mwane, *alt.* Mwani [wmw], 148
Mwaneka, *alt. dial.* Bakaka [bqz], 57
Mwanga, *alt.* Nyamwanga
[mwn], 215, 203
Mwani [wmw], 148
dial. Haya [hay], 199
Mwani'u, *alt.* Boselewa [bwf], 594
Mwano, *alt. dial.* Dijim-Bwilim
[cfa], 158
Mwatebu [mwa], 616
Mwela, *alt.* Mwera [mwe], 202
Mwenyi, *dial.* Simaa [sie], 215
Mwera (Chimwera) [mwe], 202
Mwera (Nyasa) [mjh], 202
Mweri, *dial.* Nyamwezi [nym], 203
Mwerig, *dial.* Merlav [mrm], 644
Mwi, *alt. dial.* Kombio [xbi], 607
Mwiini, *alt. dial.* Swahili [swh], 185
Mwika, *dial.* Vunjo [vun], 205
Mwila, *alt. dial.* Nyaneka [nyk], 41
Mwimbi, *dial.* Mwimbi-Muthambi
[mws], 135
Mwimbi-Muthambi [mws], 135
Mwina, *dial.* Pokomo, Lower
[poj], 135
Mwini, *dial.* Swahili [swh], 185
Mwoakilese, *alt.* Mokilese
[mkj], 582
Mwoakiloa, *alt.* Mokilese [mkj], 582
Mwomo, *alt. dial.* Dijim-Bwilim
[cfa], 158
Mwona, *alt. dial.* Dijim-Bwilim
[cfa], 158
Mwulyin, *alt. dial.* Bacama
[bcy], 154
Mya Bura, *alt.* Bura-Pabir [bwr], 156
Myagatwa, *alt.* Zaramo [zaj], 206
Myamkat, *alt.* Kinnauri, Bhoti
[nes], 368
Myamskad, *alt.* Kinnauri, Bhoti
[nes], 368
Myang, *alt.* Thai, Northern
[nod], 517, 453
Myanmar, *alt.* Burmese [mya], 462
Myau, *alt.* Muyang [muy], 69
Myen, *alt.* Burmese [mya], 462, 321
alt. Iu Mien [ium], 336, 450, 514,
523
Myene [mye], 121
Myenge, *alt.* Muyang [muy], 69
Myet, *alt.* Sur [tdl], 175
Myfoorsch, *alt.* Biak [bhw], 412
Myimu, *dial.* Naga, Tase [nst], 466
Mykhanidy, *alt.* Rutul [rut], 556
Mynky, *alt. dial.* Irántxe [irn], 227
Myrato, *alt. dial.* Carib [car], 257,
295
Mysore Lamani, *alt. dial.* Lambadi
[lmn], 372
Myu, *alt.* Miu [mpo], 614

Myunduno, *alt.* Yir Yoront
[yiy], 579
Myy, *alt. dial.* Irántxe [irn], 227
Mzab, *alt.* Tumzabt [mzb], 40
Mzabi, *alt.* Tumzabt [mzb], 40
Mzangyim, *alt.* Nzanyi [nja], 71
Mzieme, *alt.* Naga, Mzieme
[nme], 379
Mzieme Naga, *see* Naga, Mzieme
[nme], 379
N-Batto, *alt.* Mbato [gwa], 94
Na [nbt], 377
alt. Kaba Na [kwv], 81
dial. Kaba Na [kwv], 81
dial. Lahu [lhu], 338, 451, 465, 515,
524
Na Kadok, *dial.* Saek [skb], 452
Na Nahek, *dial.* Galoli [gal], 350
Na Nhyang, *dial.* Kuy [kdt], 451
Ná-Meo [neo], 525
Naa Dubea, *alt.* Dumbea [duf], 584
Naa Numee, *alt.* Numee [kdk], 585
Naa-Wee, *alt.* Numee [kdk], 585
Naaba [nao], 476
Naaban, *dial.* Bangwinji [bsj], 154
Naadh, *alt.* Nuer [nus], 194
Na'ahai, *alt.* South West Bay
[sns], 645
alt. dial. Malfaxal [mlx], 643
Na'ai, *alt.* Nakai [nkj], 421
Naama, *alt.* Borong [ksr], 594
Naami, *alt.* Bebe [bzv], 58
Naan, *dial.* Dugun [ndu], 60
Naandi, *alt. dial.* Kalenjin [kln], 133
Naani, *alt.* Sénoufo, Nanerigé
[sen], 54
alt. dial. Farefare [gur], 124
Naapa, *alt.* Naaba [nao], 476
Naapaa, *alt.* Naaba [nao], 476
Naasioi [nas], 616
dial. Naasioi [nas], 616
Naath, *alt.* Nuer [nus], 194, 117
Naaude, *alt.* Ayiwo [nfl], 635
Naba [mne], 85
alt. Naaba [nao], 476
alt. Nabak [naf], 616
Nabai, *alt. dial.* Keningau Murut
[kxi], 457
Nabak [naf], 616
Nabalebale, *alt. dial.* Fijian [fij],
580
Nabaloi, *alt.* Ibaloi [ibl], 494
Nabanj, *dial.* Kulango, Bouna
[nku], 94, 126
Nabar, *dial.* Ili'uun [ilu], 399
Nabay, *dial.* Keningau Murut [kxi],
457
Nabdam, *alt. dial.* Farefare
[gur], 124
Nabde, *alt. dial.* Farefare [gur], 124

Nabdug, *alt. dial.* Farefare [gur], 124
Nabe, *alt.* Téén [lor], 95, 55
Nabesna, *alt.* Tanana, Upper
[tau], 308, 242
Nabi [mty], 616
alt. Kuri [nbn], 418
Nabit, *alt. dial.* Farefare [gur], 124
Nablos, *dial.* Domari [rmt], 510
Nabnam, *alt. dial.* Farefare
[gur], 124
Nabrug, *alt. dial.* Farefare [gur], 124
Nabt, *dial.* Farefare [gur], 124
Nabte, *alt. dial.* Farefare [gur], 124
Nabu, *alt.* Iyo [nca], 603
Nabukelevu, *alt. dial.* Fijian
[fij], 580
Nacchhering, *alt.* Nachering
[ncd], 476
Nacering Ra, *alt.* Nachering
[ncd], 476
Nachering [ncd], 476
Nachering Tûm, *alt.* Nachering
[ncd], 476
Nad'a, *alt.* Ngad'a [nxg], 409
Nada, *alt.* Budibud [btp], 595
Nadëb [mbj], 230
Nadeb Macu, *alt.* Nadëb [mbj], 230
Nadjamba, *dial.* Dogon, Bondum
Dom [dbu], 142
Nadöbö, *alt.* Nadëb [mbj], 230
Nadroga, *alt.* Fijian [fij], 580
alt. Fijian, Western [wyy], 580
Nadrogaa, *alt. dial.* Fijian, Western
[wyy], 580
Nadronga, *alt.* Fijian [fij], 580
alt. Fijian, Western [wyy], 580
Nafãã, *dial.* Senoufo, Mamara
[myk], 144
Nafaanra [nfr], 126
Nafaara, *alt.* Nafaanra [nfr], 126
Nafana, *alt.* Nafaanra [nfr], 126
alt. dial. Wojenaka [jod], 95
Nafar, *dial.* Azerbaijani, South
[azb], 438
Nafara, *dial.* Senoufo, Cebaara
[sef], 94
Nafarpi, *alt.* Kamoro [kgq], 416
Nafi [srf], 616
Nafri [nxx], 421
Nafukwá, *alt. dial.* Matipuhy
[mzo], 230
Nafunfia, *alt. dial.* Ron [cla], 174
Nafusi [jbn], 139
alt. Shilha [jbn], 209
Naga, *dial.* Balanta-Kentohe [ble],
130
dial. Bicolano, Central [bcl], 493
dial. Mape [mlh], 612
Naga Creole Assamese, *alt.*
Naga Pidgin [nag], 377

Nahuatl, Central Puebla [ncx], 270

Nahuatl, Classical [nci], 270

Nahuatl, Coatepec [naz], 270

Nahuatl, Durango [nln], 270

Nahuatl, Eastern Huasteca [nhe], 271

Nahuatl, Guerrero [ngu], 271

Nahuatl, Highland Puebla [azz], 271

Nahuatl, Huaxcaleca [nhq], 271

Nahuatl, Isthmus-Cosoleacaque [nhk], 271

Nahuatl, Isthmus-Mecayapan [nhx], 271

Nahuatl, Isthmus-Pajapan [nhp], 271

Nahuatl, Michoacán [ncl], 271

Nahuatl, Morelos [nhm], 271

Nahuatl, Northern Oaxaca [nhy], 271

Nahuatl, Northern Puebla [ncj], 271

Nahuatl, Ometepec [nht], 271

Nahuatl, Orizaba [nlv], 271

Nahuatl, Santa María la Alta [nhz], 272

Nahuatl, Southeastern Puebla [nhs], 272

Nahuatl, Tabasco [nhc], 272

Nahuatl, Temascaltepec [nhv], 272

Nahuatl, Tenango [nhi], 272

Nahuatl, Tetelcingo [nhg], 272

Nahuatl, Tlalitzlipa [nhj], 272

Nahuatl, Tlamacazapa [nuz], 272

Nahuatl, Western Huasteca [nhw], 272

Nahukuá, *alt. dial.* Matipuhy [mzo], 230

Nahuqua, *alt. dial.* Matipuhy [mzo], 230

Na'i, *alt.* Nakai [nkj], 421

Nai [bio], 616
dial. Angor [agg], 589

Naiali, *dial.* Gunwinggu [gup], 571

Naibedj, *alt.* Kwerba [kwe], 418

Naik Kurumba, *alt.* Kurumba, Jennu [xuj], 371

Naikan, *alt.* Kurumba, Jennu [xuj], 371

Naikdi, *dial.* Bhili [bhb], 356

Naiki, *dial.* Kolami, Southeastern [nit], 369

Naiman, *alt. dial.* Mongolian, Peripheral [mvf], 339

Naimasimasi, *alt. dial.* Fijian [fij], 580

Naindin, *dial.* Attié [ati], 91

Nairya Koli, *dial.* Koli, Wadiyara [kxp], 487

Najá, *dial.* Lacandon [lac], 263

Najdi Spoken Arabic, *see* Arabic, Najdi Spoken [ars], 508, 442, 448, 510

Najil, *dial.* Pashayi, Northwest [glh], 317

Najraan, *alt. dial.* Arabic, Najdi Spoken [ars], 508

Najran, *alt. dial.* Arabic, Najdi Spoken [ars], 508

Naka, *alt. dial.* Batanga [bnm], 110, 58
dial. Gbaya [krs], 190

Naka'ela [nae], 402

Nakai [nkj], 421

Nakama [nib], 616

Nakanai [nak], 616

Nakanna, *dial.* Evenki [evn], 504

Nakanyare, *alt.* Samba Daka [ccg], 174

Nakara [nck], 574

Nakare, *alt.* Bu [jid], 156

Nake [nbk], 616

Nakgaktai, *alt. dial.* Kol [kol], 607

Nakhchivan, *dial.* Azerbaijani, North [azj], 319

Nakhi, *alt.* Naxi [nbf], 341

Nakhichevan, *dial.* Azerbaijani, North [azj], 319

Naki [mff], 69

Nakkara, *alt.* Nakara [nck], 574

Na'klallam, *alt.* Clallam [clm], 300

Nakoda, *alt.* Stoney [sto], 241
alt. dial. Dakota [dak], 297

Nakonai, *alt.* Nakanai [nak], 616

Nakoroboya, *alt. dial.* Fijian, Western [wyy], 580

Nakota, *dial.* Dakota [dak], 297, 237

Nakukwa, *alt. dial.* Matipuhy [mzo], 230

Nákum, *alt.* Maidu, Northwest [mjd], 304

Nakwi [nax], 616

Nala, *alt.* Lala [nrz], 609

Nalabon, *alt.* Ngalkbun [ngk], 575

Nalca [nlc], 421

Nale, *alt. dial.* Uripiv-Wala-Rano-Atchin [upv], 646

Nalea, *dial.* Namosi-Naitasiri-Serua [bwb], 580

Nalguno, *dial.* Bidiyo [bid], 79

Nali [nss], 616
alt. dial. Naga, Angami [njm], 377

Nalik [nal], 617

Nalou, *alt.* Nalu [naj], 130, 131

Naltje, *alt.* Nalca [nlc], 421

Naltya, *alt.* Nalca [nlc], 421

Nalu [naj], 130, 131

Naluo Yi, *see* Yi, Naluo [ylo], 347

Nama (Namibia) [naq], 150, 48, 186

Nama (Papua New Guinea) [nmx], 617
alt. Bai, Central [bca], 326
dial. Mbembe, Tigon [nza], 66, 170
dial. Nama [naq], 150

Namakaban, *alt.* Tsou [tsu], 512

Namakura [nmk], 644

Namakwa, *alt.* Nama [naq], 150, 48, 186

Naman, *alt.* Nama [naq], 150, 48, 186

Namaqua, *alt.* Nama [naq], 150, 48, 186

Namasa, *alt.* Ligbi [lig], 126

Namat [nkm], 617

Namatalaki, *alt.* Abui [abz], 406

Namatota, *alt.* Kowiai [kwh], 418
dial. Kowiai [kwh], 418

Namatote, *alt.* Kowiai [kwh], 418

Namau, *alt.* Purari [iar], 622
alt. dial. Purari [iar], 622

Nambakaengö, *alt.* Santa Cruz [stc], 638

Nambas, Big [nmb], 644

Nambe, *dial.* Tewa [tew], 308

Namber Sacha, *dial.* Bahing [bhj], 468

Nambi, *alt. dial.* Kwanga [kwj], 608

Nambieb, *alt.* Nabi [mty], 616

Nambikuára, Northern [mbg], 230

Nambikuára, Southern [nab], 230

Nambikwara, *alt.* Nambikuára, Southern [nab], 230

Nambiomon-Mabur, *dial.* Yaqay [jaq], 426

Nambiquara, *alt.* Nambikuára, Southern [nab], 230

Nambo [ncm], 617
dial. Nambo [ncm], 617

Namboodiri, *dial.* Malayalam [mal], 374

Nambrong, *alt.* Nimboran [nir], 421

Nambu, *alt.* Nambo [ncm], 617

Nambya [nmq], 209, 48

Nambzya, *alt.* Nambya [nmq], 209, 48

Namchi, *pej. alt.* Doyayo [dow], 60

Namci, *pej. alt.* Doyayo [dow], 60

Namdrik, *alt.* Guambiano [gum], 245

Namel, *alt.* Nyamal [nly], 576

Namen, *alt.* Lahu [lhu], 338, 524

Namena, *alt. dial.* Fijian [fij], 580

Namfau, *alt.* Anal [anm], 354, 462

Nami, *dial.* Ese [mcq], 598

Namia [nnm], 617

Namiae [nvm], 617
Namibian Sign Language
  [nbs], 150
Namidama, *dial.* Nama [naq], 150
Namie, *alt.* Namia [nnm], 617
Namlung, *dial.* Kulung [kle], 473
Namna, *alt.* Nambo [ncm], 617
  dial. Nambo [ncm], 617
Namnam, *alt. dial.* Farefare
  [gur], 124
Namo [mxw], 617
Namome, *alt.* Fasu [faa], 598
  dial. Fasu [faa], 598
Namon Weite, *alt.* Namonuito
  [nmt], 582
Namonuito [nmt], 582
Namosi-Naitaasiri-Seerua, *alt.*
  Namosi-Naitasiri-Serua [bwb], 580
Namosi-Naitasiri-Serua
  [bwb], 580
Nampamela, *alt. dial.* Makhuwa
  [vmw], 147
  alt. dial. Makhuwa-Marrevone
  [xmc], 147
Namrung, *dial.* Nubri [kte], 477
Namsangia, *alt.* Naga, Nocte
  [njb], 379
Namshi, *pej. alt.* Doyayo [dow], 60
Namu, *alt. dial.* Mbembe, Tigon
  [nza], 66, 170
  dial. Rembong [reb], 409
Namumi, *alt. dial.* Fasu [faa], 598
Namuni, *alt. dial.* Fasu [faa], 598
Namunka, *dial.* Oroch [oac], 506
Namuya, *alt.* Kesawai [xes], 606
Namuyi [nmy], 341
Namuzi, *alt.* Namuyi [nmy], 341
Namwanga, *alt.* Nyamwanga
  [mwn], 215, 203
Namwezi, *alt.* Nyamwezi
  [nym], 203
Nan, *dial.* Thai, Northern [nod], 517,
  453
Ñanagua, *alt.* Tapieté [tpj], 282,
  220, 224
Nanai [gld], 506, 341
Nanaimo, *dial.* Halkomelem
  [hur], 238, 301
Nanaj, *alt.* Nanai [gld], 506
Nanaya, *dial.* Mato [met], 612
Nancere [nnc], 85
Nanchere, *alt.* Nancere [nnc], 85
Nancoury, *alt. dial.* Nicobarese,
  Central [ncb], 381
Nancowry, *dial.* Nicobarese, Central
  [ncb], 381
Nand, *alt.* Gowli [gok], 363
  dial. Gowli [gok], 363
Nande [nnb], 105
  dial. Nande [nnb], 105

Nandereke, *alt.* Sénoufo, Nanerigé
  [sen], 54
Nandergé, *alt.* Sénoufo, Nanerigé
  [sen], 54
Nandeva, *alt.* Tapieté [tpj], 282
Ñandeva, *alt.* Chiripá [nhd], 284,
  220, 226
Nandi, *alt.* Nande [nnb], 105
  dial. Kalenjin [kln], 133
Nandrau, *alt. dial.* Fijian [fij], 580
Nandu, *alt.* Ndun [nfd], 171
Nane, *alt.* Ere [twp], 598
Nanergé, *alt.* Sénoufo, Nanerigé
  [sen], 54
Nanergué, *alt.* Sénoufo, Nanerigé
  [sen], 54
Nanerigé Sénoufo, *see* Sénoufo,
  Nanerigé [sen], 54
Nanesa, *dial.* Kamoro [kgq], 416
Nangalami, *dial.* Grangali [nli], 316
Nangarach, *dial.* Pashayi, Northwest
  [glh], 317
Nangcere, *alt.* Nancere [nnc], 85
Nanggu [ngr], 637
Nangikurrunggurr [nam], 574
Nangikurunggurr, *alt.*
  Nangikurrunggurr [nam], 574
Nangimera, *alt. dial.*
  Nangikurrunggurr [nam], 574
Nangiomeri, *alt. dial.*
  Nangikurrunggurr [nam], 574
Nangjere, *alt.* Nancere [nnc], 85
Nangnda, *alt.* Bedjond [bjv], 79
Nangu, *alt.* Jarnango [jay], 571
Nangumiri, *alt. dial.*
  Nangikurrunggurr [nam], 574
Nanhil, *alt. dial.* Sudest [tgo], 625
Nanhua Lolopho, *dial.* Yi, Central
  [ycl], 347
Nanidjara, *alt.* Wanman [wbt], 577
Nanimba Pii, *alt.* Lembena
  [leq], 609
Nanjeri, *alt.* Nancere [nnc], 85
Nankana, *dial.* Ninkare [gur], 53
Nankani, *alt.* Farefare [gur], 124
  alt. Ninkare [gur], 53
  dial. Farefare [gur], 124
  dial. Ninkare [gur], 53
Nankanse, *alt. dial.* Farefare
  [gur], 124
Nankina [nnk], 617
Nano, *alt.* Umbundu [umb], 42
Nanomam, *dial.* Yanomámi
  [wca], 234
Nanping Baima, *alt. dial.* Baima
  [bqh], 327
Nanqa Poroja, *alt.* Bondo
  [bfw], 357
Nanshi Amis, *alt. dial.* Amis
  [ami], 511

Nantcere, *alt.* Nancere [nnc], 85
Nanti [cox], 289
Nanticoke [nnt], 305
Nantjara, *alt.* Wikngenchera
  [wua], 578
Nanumanga, *alt. dial.* Tuvaluan
  [tvl], 640
Nanumba, *alt. dial.* Dagbani
  [dag], 124
Nanumea, *alt. dial.* Tuvaluan [tvl],
  640
Nanunga, *alt.* Narungga [nnr], 575
Nanuni, *dial.* Dagbani [dag], 124
Nanwang, *dial.* Puyuma [pyu], 512
Nanzva, *alt.* Nambya [nmq], 209, 48
Na'o, *alt.* Nayi [noz], 117
Nao, *alt.* Nayi [noz], 117
Naò, *dial.* Toura [neb], 95
Nao Klao, *alt. dial.* Bunu, Bu-Nao
  [bwx], 328
Naogelao, *dial.* Bunu, Bu-Nao
  [bwx], 328
Naomam, *alt. dial.* Yanomámi
  [wca], 234
Naone, *alt.* Marino [mrb], 643
Naóti, *alt.* Nauete [nxa], 351
Naoudem, *alt.* Nawdm [nmz], 209,
  127
Napan, *dial.* Waropen [wrp], 425
Napanskij, *dial.* Itelmen [itl], 505
Napo, *alt.* Quechua, Napo Lowland
  [qvo], 291
Napo Kichua, *alt.* Quechua, Napo
  Lowland [qvo], 291
Napo Lowland Quechua, *see*
  Quechua, Napo Lowland
  [qvo], 291
Napo Lowland Quichua, *see*
  Quechua, Napo Lowland
  [qvo], 247, 251
Napo Quichua, *alt.* Quichua, Napo
  Lowland [qvo], 251
Napo-Tinambung, *alt. dial.*
  Mandar [mdr], 431
Napok, *alt.* Kwerba Mamberamo
  [xwr], 418
Napoletano, *dial.* Napoletano-
  Calabrese [nap], 545
Napoletano-Calabrese [nap], 545
Napu [npy], 432
Napuanmen, *alt.* Whitesands
  [tnp], 646
Napuka, *dial.* Tuamotuan [pmt], 581
Nar, *dial.* Nar Phu [npa], 476
  dial. Sar [mwm], 86
Nar Phu [npa], 476
Nar-Mä, *alt. dial.* Nar Phu [npa], 476
Nar-Phu, *alt.* Nar Phu [npa], 476
Nar-Tö, *alt. dial.* Nar Phu [npa], 476
Nara [nrb], 112

alt. Lala [nrz], 609
Narabunu, *alt. dial.* Jere [jer], 165
Naraguta, *alt.* Iguta [nar], 163
Narak [nac], 617
Narake, *alt.* Kandawo [gam], 604
Narakureavar, *alt.* Vaagri Booli
[vaa], 389
Narang, *dial.* Jola-Fonyi [dyo], 180
Naranga, *alt.* Narungga [nnr], 575
Narangga, *alt.* Narungga [nnr], 575
Narango [nrg], 644
Nararapi, *alt.* Sempan [xse], 423
Narau [nxu], 421
Narihua, *alt.* Kahua [agw], 636
alt. Owa [stn], 637
Nariim, *alt.* Narim [loh], 194
Narikkorava, *alt.* Vaagri Booli
[vaa], 389
Narim [loh], 194
Naringhol, *alt. dial.* Tu [mjg], 345
Narisati, *alt.* Gawar-Bati [gwt], 316,
484
Naro [nhr], 48, 150
Narom [nrm], 460
dial. Narom [nrm], 460
Narovorovo, *dial.* Baetora [btr], 640
Narran, *alt. dial.* Wangaaybuwan-
Ngiyambaa [wyb], 577
Narranga, *alt.* Narungga [nnr], 575
Narrangansett, *dial.* Mohegan-
Montauk-Narragansett [mof], 305
Narranggu, *alt.* Narungga [nnr], 575
Narrangu, *alt.* Narungga [nnr], 575
Narreweng, *alt. dial.* Dinka,
Southeastern [dks], 190
Narrinyeri [nay], 575
Narsati, *alt.* Gawar-Bati [gwt], 316,
484
Narum, *alt.* Narom [nrm], 460
Narungga [nnr], 575
Narym, *dial.* Selkup [sel], 506
Nasa Yuwe, *alt.* Páez [pbb], 246
Nasarian [nvh], 644
Nasawa, *dial.* Baetora [btr], 640
Nasi, *alt.* Naxi [nbf], 341
Nasikwabw, *dial.* Misima-Paneati
[mpx], 614
Nasioi, *alt.* Naasioi [nas], 616
Naskapi [nsk], 239
Naso, *alt.* Teribe [tfr], 284
Nasrani, *dial.* Malayalam [mal], 374
Nasring, *alt.* Nachering [ncd], 476
Nass, *alt.* Nisga'a [ncg], 240
Nat, *alt.* Kabutra [kbu], 485
Nata, *alt.* Ikoma [ntk], 199
Natabui, *alt.* Munggui [mth], 421
alt. dial. Marau [mvr], 415
Natagaimas [nts], 246
Natakan, *alt.* Mafa [maf], 65, 169
Natanzi [ntz], 441

Nataoran, *alt.* Amis, Nataoran
[ais], 511
dial. Amis, Nataoran [ais], 511
Nataoran Amis, *see* Amis,
Nataoran [ais], 511
Natarbora, *alt. dial.* Tetun [tet], 410,
351
Natawran, *alt.* Amis, Nataoran
[ais], 511
dial. Amis, Nataoran [ais], 511
Natchaba, *dial.* Moba [mfq], 208
Natchamba, *alt.* Ntcham [bud], 209
Natchez [ncz], 305
Natemba, *alt. dial.* Nateni [ntm], 46
Nateni [ntm], 46
dial. Nateni [ntm], 46
Nathembo [nte], 148
Natick, *alt.* Wampanoag [wam], 309
Natimba, *alt. dial.* Nateni [ntm], 46
Natioro [nti], 53
Natjoro, *alt.* Natioro [nti], 53
Natögu, *alt.* Santa Cruz [stc], 638
Natra, *alt.* Kabutra [kbu], 485
Nattu Muthuvan, *alt. dial.*
Muthuvan [muv], 377
Natukhai, *alt. dial.* Adyghe
[ady], 552
Naturalis, *dial.* Surigaonon
[sul], 502
Natürliche Gebärde, *alt.* Swiss-
German Sign Language [sgg], 563
Natuzaj, *dial.* Adyghe [ady], 552
Natyoro, *alt.* Natioro [nti], 53
Naudm, *alt.* Nawdm [nmz], 209, 127
Nauete [nxa], 351
Naueti, *alt.* Nauete [nxa], 351
Nauhete, *alt.* Nauete [nxa], 351
Naukan, *alt.* Yupik, Naukan
[ynk], 508
Naukan Yupik, *see* Yupik, Naukan
[ynk], 508
Naukanski, *alt.* Yupik, Naukan
[ynk], 508
Naumik, *dial.* Nauete [nxa], 351
Nauna [ncn], 617
Naune, *alt.* Nauna [ncn], 617
Nauote, *alt.* Nauete [nxa], 351
Nauoti, *alt.* Nauete [nxa], 351
Naura, *alt.* Haigwai [hgw], 601
dial. Haigwai [hgw], 601
Nauruan [nau], 583
Naut Aranés, *dial.* Gascon, Aranese
[gsc], 560
Nautley, *dial.* Carrier, Southern
[caf], 236
Navaho, *alt.* Navajo [nav], 305
Navajo [nav], 305
Navakasiga, *alt. dial.* Fijian
[fij], 580
Navarrese, *dial.* Spanish [spa], 560

Navarro-Labourdin, *alt.* Basque,
Navarro-Labourdin [bqe], 535
Navarro-Labourdin Basque, *see*
Basque, Navarro-Labourdin
[bqe], 535
Navatu-B, *alt. dial.* Fijian [fij], 580
Navatu-C, *alt. dial.* Fijian [fij], 580
Navut [nsw], 644
Nawa Sherpa, *alt.* Naaba [nao], 476
Nawagi, *alt.* Nyawaygi [nyt], 576
Nawaits, *alt. dial.* Konkani, Goanese
[gom], 369
Nawar, *alt.* Domari [rmt], 448, 510
dial. Domari [rmt], 438, 110, 448,
510
Nawari, *alt.* Domari [rmt], 444, 490
dial. Domari [rmt], 444, 490
Nawaru [nwr], 617
Nawat, *alt.* Pipil [ppl], 252
Nawathinehena [nwa], 306
Nawdam, *alt.* Nawdm [nmz], 209,
127
Nawdm [nmz], 209, 127
Naweni, *alt. dial.* Fijian [fij], 580
Nawp, *alt.* Daga [dgz], 596
Nawuri [naw], 127
Nawyem, *dial.* Muyuw [myw], 616
Naxi [nbf], 341
Nayar, *dial.* Malayalam [mal], 374
Nayi [noz], 117
Nayini [nyq], 441
dial. Nayini [nyq], 441
Naze, *dial.* Amami-Oshima, Northern
[ryn], 446
Nbangam, *alt.* Ngangam [gng], 209
Nbule, *alt.* Vute [vut], 73
N'bundo, *alt.* Mbundu [kmb], 41
Nbundu, *alt.* Mbundu [kmb], 41
Nbwaka, *alt.* Ngbaka Ma'bo
[nbm], 77, 89, 105
Ncane [ncr], 69
dial. Ncane [ncr], 69
Ncanm, *dial.* Ntcham [bud], 209
Ncha, *dial.* Ndaktup [ncp], 69
Ncham, *alt.* Ntcham [bud], 209, 127
Nchanti, *alt.* Ncane [ncr], 69
Nchimburu, *alt.* Chumburung
[ncu], 124
Nchobela, *alt. dial.* Ngombale
[nla], 70
Nchufie, *alt.* Bafanji [bfj], 56
Nchumbulu [nlu], 127
Nchumburung, *alt.* Chumburung
[ncu], 124
Nchummuru, *alt.* Chumburung
[ncu], 124
Nchumunu, *alt.* Dwang [nnu], 120
Ncqika, *alt. dial.* Xhosa [xho], 187
N'da, *dial.* Gagu [ggu], 93
Nda, *alt.* Mundang [mua], 85, 68

Nda'a, *alt.* Ngomba [jgo], 69
Ndaa, *alt.* Ngomba [jgo], 69
Ndaaka, *alt.* Ndaka [ndk], 102
Ndagam, *alt.* Nyong [muo], 71
Ndai [gke], 69
   alt. dial. Lau [llu], 637
Ndaka [ndk], 102
Ndaktup [ncp], 69
Ndali [ndh], 202, 140
   dial. Zanaki [zak], 206
Ndam [ndm], 85
Ndam Dik, *dial.* Ndam [ndm], 85
Ndam-Ndam, *dial.* Ndam [ndm], 85
Ndamba [ndj], 202
Ndambiya, *alt. dial.* Migaama
   [mmy], 84
Ndamm, *alt.* Ndam [ndm], 85
Nda'nda' [nnz], 69
Ndanda, *alt. dial.* Ndau [ndc], 148
Ndande, *alt.* Nande [nnb], 105
Ndano, *dial.* Shwai [shw], 195
Ndao, *alt.* Dhao [nfa], 406
Ndaoe, *alt.* Pendau [ums], 432
Ndaonese, *alt.* Dhao [nfa], 406
Ndara, *alt.* Wandala [mfi], 73, 177
   alt. dial. Rwanda [kin], 178
Ndasa [nda], 89, 121
Ndash, *alt.* Ndasa [nda], 121
Ndassa, *alt.* Ndasa [nda], 121
Ndau [ndc], 148, 216
   alt. Pendau [ums], 432
   dial. Ndau [ndc], 148
Ndaundau, *alt.* Dhao [nfa], 406
Ndauwa, *alt.* Nduga [ndx], 421
Nde, *dial.* Mungaka [mhk], 68
   dial. Nde-Nsele-Nta [ndd], 170
Nde-Gbite [ned], 170
Nde-Nsele-Nta [ndd], 170
Ndebele ([nde], 216, 48
   Ndebele, South [nbl], 186
Ndeewe, *dial.* Bata [bta], 58
Ndele, *dial.* Ikwere [ikw], 164
Ndem, *alt.* Dem [dem], 414
   alt. Nnam [nbp], 171
Ndema Sherbro, *dial.* Sherbro
   [bun], 177
Ndemba, *alt.* Ndemli [nml], 69
Ndembu, *dial.* Lunda [lun], 214
Ndemli [nml], 69
Ndendeule [dne], 202
Ndendeuli, *alt.* Ndendeule
   [dne], 202
Ndengeleko, *alt.* Ndengereko
   [ndg], 202
Ndengereko [ndg], 202
Ndengese, *alt.* Dengese [dez], 99
Ndeni, *dial.* Santa Cruz [stc], 638
Ndera, *dial.* Koma [kmy], 167
   dial. Pokomo, Upper [pkb], 135
Nderre, *dial.* Moro [mor], 193

Ndese, *dial.* Lese [les], 102
Ndhur, *dial.* Rade [rad], 526
Ndi, *alt.* Samba Leko [ndi], 174
   dial. Banda-Banda [bpd], 75
   dial. Ghari [gri], 636
Ndia, *dial.* Gikuyu [kik], 133
Ndii, *alt. dial.* Samba Leko [ndi], 72
Nding [eli], 194
Ndingi, *dial.* Koongo [kng], 40
Ndir, *alt.* Iyive [uiv], 164
Nditam, *dial.* Tikar [tik], 72
Ndjabi, *alt.* Njebi [nzb], 121, 89
Ndjak, *alt.* Mandjak [mfv], 181
Ndjébbana, *alt.* Djeebbana [djj], 570
Ndjeli, *alt. dial.* Pande [bkj], 77
Ndjem, *alt.* Njyem [njy], 70, 89
Ndjembe, *alt.* Wongo [won], 109
Ndjeme, *alt.* Njyem [njy], 70, 89
Ndjevi, *alt.* Njebi [nzb], 121
Ndjinini, *alt. dial.* Teke, Northern
   [teg], 121
Ndjuká, *alt.* Aukan [djk], 295
Ndlambe, *dial.* Xhosa [xho], 187
Ndmpo, *alt.* Dompo [doy], 124
Ndo [ndp], 212, 105
   alt. Iyo [nca], 603
   alt. dial. Ndo [ndp], 105
Ndo Oke'bu, *alt. dial.* Ndo
   [ndp], 212
Ndob, *alt.* Tikar [tik], 72
Ndobo [ndw], 105
Ndoe [nbb], 170
Ndogbang, *dial.* Tunen [baz], 72
Ndogo [ndz], 194
   alt. dial. Rwanda [kin], 178
Ndokama, *dial.* Basaa [bas], 58
Ndokbele, *dial.* Basaa [bas], 58
Ndokbiakat, *dial.* Tunen [baz], 72
Ndokpa, *dial.* Banda-Bambari
   [liy], 75
Ndokpenda, *dial.* Basaa [bas], 58
Ndoktuna, *dial.* Tunen [baz], 72
Ndola, *alt.* Ndoola [ndr], 171
Ndolo [ndl], 105
Ndom [nqm], 421
Ndombe [ndq], 41
Ndomde, *alt.* Ndonde Hamba
   [njd], 202
Ndome, *alt.* Tikar [tik], 72
Ndonde, *alt.* Ndonde Hamba
   [njd], 202
   alt. dial. Makonde [kde], 148
Ndonde Hamba [njd], 202
Ndonga [ndo], 150, 41
Ndonge, *dial.* Chopi [cce], 147
Ndongo, *alt.* Mbundu [kmb], 41
Ndoni, *dial.* Ukwuani-Aboh-Ndoni
   [ukw], 176
Ndoobo, *alt.* Ndobo [ndw], 105
Ndoola [ndr], 171, 69

Ndoolo, *alt.* Ndolo [ndl], 105
Ndoore, *alt.* Tupuri [tui], 72
Ndop-Bamessing, *alt.* Kenswei
   Nsei [ndb], 64
Ndop-Bamunka, *alt.* Bamunka
   [bvm], 57
Ndore, *alt.* Tupuri [tui], 72, 87
Ndoro, *alt.* Ndoola [ndr], 171, 69
Ndorobo, *alt.* Mediak [mwx], 202
   alt. Mosiro [mwy], 202
   pej. alt. Aasáx [aas], 197
   pej. alt. Aramanik [aam], 197
   pej. alt. El Molo [elo], 132
   pej. alt. Kisankasa [kqh], 200
   pej. alt. Okiek [oki], 135
   pej. alt. Omotik [omt], 135
   pej. alt. Yaaku [muu], 137
Ndoudja, *alt. dial.* Fali, South
   [fal], 61
Ndouka, *alt. dial.* Lutos [ndy], 76
Ndoukwa, *alt. dial.* Lutos [ndy], 76
Ndoute, *alt.* Ndut [ndv], 181
Ndramini'o, *dial.* Rao [rao], 622
Ndreme, *dial.* Vame [mlr], 73
Ndreng, *dial.* Naga, Lotha [njh], 378
Ndri, *alt. dial.* Banda-Banda [bpd], 75
Ndroku, *alt.* Loniu [los], 610
Ndrugul, *alt.* Kurti [ktm], 608
Ndruna, *alt.* Ngiti [niy], 106
Ndu, *alt.* Ndo [ndp], 212, 105
Ndu-Faa-Keelo, *alt.* Kelo [xel], 192
Nduga [ndx], 421
   dial. Lutos [ndy], 76
Ndughore, *alt.* Duke [nke], 636
Ndugwa, *alt.* Nduga [ndx], 421
Nduindui, *alt. dial.* Ambae, West
   [nnd], 640
Nduka, *dial.* Lutos [ndy], 76
Nduke, *alt.* Duke [nke], 636
Ndumbea, *alt.* Dumbea [duf], 584
Ndumbo, *alt.* Ndumu [nmd], 121
Ndumbu, *alt.* Ndumu [nmd], 121
Ndumu [nmd], 121
Ndun [nfd], 171
Ndunda [nuh], 171
   alt. Vidunda [vid], 205
Ndundulu, *alt. dial.* Luyana
   [lyn], 41
Ndundusana, *alt. dial.* Pagibete
   [pae], 107
Ndunga [ndt], 105
Ndura, *dial.* Pokomo, Upper
   [pkb], 135
Ndut [ndv], 181
Nduumo, *alt.* Ndumu [nmd], 121
Nduupa, *alt.* Duupa [dae], 60
Nduvum, *dial.* Vute [vut], 73
Ndxhonge, *dial.* Tswa [tsc], 149
Ndyak, *alt.* Mandjak [mfv], 131, 122
Ndyanger, *dial.* Wolof [wol], 145

Ndyuka, *alt.* Aukan [djk], 295
Ndyuka-Trio Pidgin [njt], 296
Ndzale, *alt. dial.* Mbembe, Tigon [nza], 66
Ndzawu, *alt.* Ndau [ndc], 148, 216
Ndzem, *alt.* Njyem [njy], 70, 89
Ndzundza, *alt.* Ndebele [nbl], 186
Ndzungle, *alt.* Limbum [lmp], 65
Ndzungli, *alt.* Limbum [lmp], 65
Ndzwani Comorian, *see* Comorian, Ndzwani [wni], 87
Ne Thu, *alt.* Lahu Shi [kds], 524
Nea, *dial.* Santa Cruz [stc], 638
Neabo, *alt. dial.* Wè Southern [gxx], 95
Neao, *dial.* Bauzi [bvz], 412
  dial. Wè Southern [gxx], 95
Neapolitan, *alt. dial.* Napoletano-Calabrese [nap], 545
Neapolitan-Calabrese, *alt.* Napoletano-Calabrese [nap], 545
Near-Eastern Gypsy, *alt.* Domari [rmt], 444, 490
Nebaj Ixil, *see* Ixil, Nebaj [ixi], 254
Nebaji, *dial.* Orejón [ore], 289
Nebee, *alt. dial.* Keningau Murut [kxi], 457
Nebes, *alt.* Kokoda [xod], 417
Nebome, *alt.* Pima Bajo [pia], 273
  alt. Tohono O'odham [ood], 309
Nebraska, *dial.* Ho-Chunk [win], 302
Necoslie, *dial.* Carrier [crx], 236
Nedderdütsch, *alt.* Saxon, Low [nds], 539
Neddersassisch, *alt.* Saxon, Low [nds], 539
Nedebang [nec], 409
Nédebang, *alt.* Nedebang [nec], 409
Nedek, *dial.* Yambeta [yat], 73
Nederlands, *alt.* Dutch [nld], 548, 531
Nedersaksisch, *alt.* Saxon, Low [nds], 539
Nee, *dial.* Fe'fe' [fmp], 61
Ñeegatú, *alt.* Nhengatu [yrl], 230
Neelishikari, *dial.* Pardhi [pcl], 383
Neenoá, *alt.* Miriti [mmv], 230
Neeshenam, *alt.* Nisenan [nsz], 306
Nefamese [nef], 381
Nefarpi, *alt.* Kamoro [kgq], 416
Neferipi, *alt.* Kamoro [kgq], 416
Nefusi, *alt.* Nafusi [jbn], 139
Negarotê, *alt. dial.* Nambikuára, Northern [mbg], 230
Negerhollands [dcr], 297
Negeri Besar, *alt. dial.* Kokoda [xod], 417
Negeri Lima, *alt. dial.* Asilulu [asl], 396

Negeri Sembilan Malay [zmi], 455
Neghidal, *alt.* Negidal [neg], 506
Negidal [neg], 506
Negidaly, *alt.* Negidal [neg], 506
Negira, *alt.* Ningera [nby], 618
Negri Besar, *dial.* Kokoda [xod], 417
Negueni-Klani, *dial.* Wara [wbf], 55
Nehan [nsn], 617
  dial. Nehan [nsn], 617
Nehina, *pej. alt.* Tolaki [lbw], 433
Nëhup, *dial.* Hupdë [jup], 227
Nejuu, *dial.* Senoufo, Mamara [myk], 144
Nek [nif], 617
Nekedi, *dial.* Bété, Gagnoa [btg], 92
Nekgini [nkg], 617
Neko [nej], 617
Neku [nek], 585
Nelema, *alt. dial.* Kumak [nee], 584
Nellore, *alt. dial.* Telugu [tel], 388
Nemadi, *alt.* Nimadi [noe], 381
Nemangbetu, *alt.* Mangbetu [mdj], 104
Nembao, *alt.* Amba [utp], 634
Nembe, *dial.* Ijo, Southeast [ijs], 163
Nembi, *alt.* Angal Enen [aoe], 589
Neme [nex], 617
  dial. Binahari [bxz], 593
Nemea, *alt. dial.* Binahari [bxz], 593
Nemi [nem], 585
Nemia, *alt.* Namia [nnm], 617
Nen [nqn], 617
Nenaya, *alt.* Mato [met], 612
Nend [anh], 617
Nendö, *alt.* Santa Cruz [stc], 638
Nenec, *alt.* Nenets [yrk], 506
Nenema, *alt. dial.* Kumak [nee], 584
Nenets [yrk], 506
Nenetsy, *alt.* Nenets [yrk], 506
Neng Den, *alt.* Komba [kpf], 607
Nengaya, *alt.* Mato [met], 612
Nengone [nen], 585
Nenni Nyo'o, *alt.* Tunen [baz], 72
Nent, *alt.* Nend [anh], 617
Nentse, *alt.* Nenets [yrk], 506
Nenusa-Maingas, *dial.* Talaud [tld], 433
Nenya, *dial.* Tumbuka [tum], 141, 215
Neo-Chaldean, *alt.* Chaldean Neo-Aramaic [cld], 443
Neo-Egyptian, *alt.* Coptic [cop], 110
Neo-Hellenic, *alt.* Greek [ell], 540
Neo-Mandaic, *alt.* Mandaic [mid], 441
Neo-Nyunga, *alt.* Nyunga [nys], 576

Neo-Nyungar, *alt. dial.* English [eng], 570
Neo-Solomonic, *alt.* Pijin [pis], 637
Neo-Syriac, *alt.* Assyrian Neo-Aramaic [aii], 442, 510
Neo-Western Aramaic, *alt.* Western Neo-Aramaic [amw], 510
Neogulada, *alt.* Kanju [kbe], 572
Neomelanesian, *alt.* Tok Pisin [tpi], 628
Nepa, *dial.* Evenki [evn], 504
Nepal Bhasa, *alt.* Newar [new], 476
Nepalese, *alt.* Nepali [nep], 476, 323, 381
Nepalese Sign Language [nsp], 476
Nepali [nep], 476, 323, 381
  dial. Nepali [nep], 381
Nepali Kurux, *see* Kurux, Nepali [kxl], 473
Nepo, *alt. dial.* Bugis [bug], 428
Nepoye, *alt.* Mapoyo [mcg], 312
Nera, *alt.* Nara [nrb], 112
Nerauya, *dial.* Lenakel [tnl], 642
Nerë, *alt.* Zire [sih], 585
Nerezim, *dial.* Turkmen [tuk], 520, 442
Nerigo, *alt.* Yahadian [ner], 426
Nerwa, *dial.* Lishana Deni [lsd], 445
Nesang, *alt.* Tukpa [tpq], 389
Nete [net], 618
Nethanar, *dial.* Duruwa [pci], 361
Netherlands Antilles Creole English [vic], 282
Netsilik, *dial.* Inuktitut, Western Canadian [ikt], 238
Neuch-Telois, *dial.* Franco-Provençal [frp], 562
Neuchatelais, *dial.* Franco-Provençal [frp], 536
Nevis Creole English, *dial.* Saint Kitts Creole English [aig], 294
Nevome, *alt.* Tohono O'odham [ood], 309
New Bargu, *alt. dial.* Buriat, China [bxu], 329
New Britain Language, *alt.* Kuanua [ksd], 608
New Busa, *dial.* Busa [bqp], 156
New Caledonian Javanese, *see* Javanese, New Caledonian [jas], 584
New Cham, *alt.* Cham, Western [cja], 325, 514, 522
New Guinea Pidgin English, *alt.* Tok Pisin [tpi], 628
New Norse, *alt.* Norwegian, Nynorsk [nno], 549

New Persian, *alt.* Farsi, Western [pes], 439
New Zealand Maori, *alt.* Maori [mri], 586
New Zealand Sign Language [nzs], 586
Newahang, *alt.* Meohang, Eastern [emg], 475
alt. Meohang, Western [raf], 476
Newahang Jimi, *alt.* Meohang, Eastern [emg], 475
alt. Meohang, Western [raf], 476
Newahang Yamphe, *alt.* Yamphe [yma], 482
Newang, *alt.* Meohang, Eastern [emg], 475
alt. Meohang, Western [raf], 476
Newange Rai, *alt.* Meohang, Eastern [emg], 475
alt. Meohang, Western [raf], 476
Newar [new], 476, 381
Newari, *pej. alt.* Newar [new], 476, 381
Newcastle Northumberland, *dial.* English [eng], 565
Newfoundland, *alt.* Beothuk [bue], 235
Newfoundland English, *dial.* English [eng], 237
Ney, *dial.* Kuranko [knk], 183
Neyo [ney], 94
alt. Wè Western [wec], 95
Nez Perce [nez], 306
Nfachara, *alt.* Cara [cfd], 156
Nfua, *alt.* Bokyi [bky], 156, 59
Nfumte, *alt.* Mfumte [nfu], 67
‖Ng, *alt. dial.* N∣u [ngh], 186
Ng‖-∣e, *alt. dial.* N∣u [ngh], 186
Nga, *alt.* Ngamambo [nbv], 69
Nga La [hlt], 466
Ngaaka, *alt.* Mungaka [mhk], 68
Ngaanjatjarra, *alt.* Ngaanyatjarra [ntj], 575
Ngaanyatjara, *alt.* Ngaanyatjarra [ntj], 575
Ngaanyatjarra [ntj], 575
Ngäbere [gym], 283
Ngabre, *alt.* Gabri [gab], 80
Ngac'ang, *alt.* Achang [acn], 326, 456
Ngacang, *alt.* Achang [acn], 326
Ngachang, *alt.* Achang [acn], 326, 456
Nga'da, *alt.* Ngad'a [nxg], 409
Ngad'a [nxg], 409
Ngada, *alt.* Ngad'a [nxg], 409
Ngad'a, Eastern [nea], 409
Ngadanja, *dial.* Wikalkan [wik], 578
Ngadha, *alt.* Ngad'a [nxg], 409

Ngadjan, *alt. dial.* Dyirbal [dbl], 570
Ngadju, *alt.* Ngadjunmaya [nju], 575
alt. Ngaju [nij], 394
Ngadjumaja, *alt.* Ngadjunmaya [nju], 575
Ngadjunmaia, *alt.* Ngadjunmaya [nju], 575
Ngadjunmaya [nju], 575
Ngae, *alt.* Ngeq [ngt], 451
Ngahm, *alt.* Ngam [nmc], 85
Ngaigungo, *alt.* Djangun [djf], 569
Ngaiman, *alt.* Ngarinman [nbj], 575
Ngaimbom, *alt.* Lilau [lll], 610
Ngain, *alt.* Beng [nhb], 92
alt. Numanggang [nop], 619
Ngaing [nnf], 618
Ngaju [nij], 394
Ngaju Dayak, *alt.* Ngaju [nij], 394
Nga'ka, *alt.* Mungaka [mhk], 68
Ngakom, *alt. dial.* Tegali [ras], 195
Ngala [nud], 618
alt. Bangala [bxg], 97
alt. Chin, Matu [hlt], 359
alt. Lingala [lin], 103, 89
dial. Chin, Khumi [cnk], 463, 321
Ngalabo, *dial.* Banda-Banda [bpd], 75
Ngalabon, *alt.* Ngalkbun [ngk], 575
Ngalakan [nig], 575
Ngalam, *alt. dial.* Murle [mur], 117
Ngalangan, *alt.* Ngalakan [nig], 575
Ngaliwerra, *alt. dial.* Djamindjung [djd], 569
Ngaliwuru, *dial.* Djamindjung [djd], 569
Ngaliya, *alt.* Warlpiri [wbp], 578
Ngalkbon, *alt.* Ngalkbun [ngk], 575
Ngalkbun [ngk], 575
Ngallooma, *alt.* Ngarluma [nrl], 575
Ngalo, *dial.* Day [dai], 80
Ngalum [szb], 421, 618
dial. Ngalum [szb], 421, 618
Ngaluma, *alt.* Ngarluma [nrl], 575
Ngam [nmc], 85, 77
dial. Fe'fe' [fmp], 61
dial. Kwang [kvi], 82
Ngam Gir Bor, *dial.* Ngam [nmc], 85
Ngam Tel, *dial.* Ngam [nmc], 85
Ngam Tira, *dial.* Ngam [nmc], 85
Ngama, *alt.* Ngam [nmc], 85, 77
Ngamambo [nbv], 69
Ng∣amani, *alt.* ǃXóõ [nmn], 48
Ngamawa, *alt.* Ngamo [nbh], 171
Ngambai, *alt.* Ngambay [sba], 85, 69
Ngamba'wandh, *alt. dial.* Yir Yoront [yiy], 579
Ngambay [sba], 85, 69
Ngambo, *alt.* Tibetan, Amdo [adx], 344

Ngamh, *alt.* Ngam [nmc], 85
Ngami, *alt.* Naga, Angami [njm], 377
Ngamini [nmv], 575
Ngamo [nbh], 171
Ngamsile, *alt. dial.* Ukhwejo [ukh], 78
Ngan, *alt.* Beng [nhb], 92
alt. Tày [tyz], 527
Nganasan [nio], 506
Ngandi [nid], 575
Ngandjara, *alt.* Wikngenchera [wua], 578
alt. dial. Wikalkan [wik], 578
Ngando (Central African Republic) [ngd], 77
Ngando (Democratic Republic of Congo) [nxd], 105
Ngando-Kota, *alt.* Ngando [ngd], 77
Ngandu, *alt.* Ngando [nxd], 105
Ngandyera [nne], 41
dial. Ndonga [ndo], 150
Ngangala, *alt.* Nkangala [nkn], 41
Ngangam [gng], 209, 46
Ngangan, *alt.* Ngangam [gng], 209
Ngangching, *dial.* Naga, Konyak [nbe], 378
Ngangea, *alt.* Nyang'i [nyp], 212
Ngangela, *alt.* Nyemba [nba], 41
Ngangi-Tjemerri, *dial.* Nangikurrunggurr [nam], 574
Ngangi-Wumeri, *dial.* Nangikurrunggurr [nam], 574
Ngangikarangurr, *alt.* Nangikurrunggurr [nam], 574
Ngangomori, *alt. dial.* Nangikurrunggurr [nam], 574
Ngangoulou, *alt.* Ngungwel [ngz], 89
Nganjaywana, *alt.* Nganyaywana [nyx], 575
Ngankikurrunkurr, *alt.* Nangikurrunggurr [nam], 574
alt. dial. Nangikurrunggurr [nam], 574
Nganshuenkuan, *alt.* Atuence [atf], 326
dial. Tibetan [bod], 388
Ngantjeri, *alt.* Wikngenchera [wua], 578
Nganyaywana [nyx], 575
Nganygit, *alt. dial.* Marithiel [mfr], 574
Nga'o, *dial.* Ende [end], 406
Ngao, *alt. dial.* Ende [end], 406
dial. Banda-Ndélé [bfl], 75
Ngao Fon, *alt.* Cun [cuq], 331
Ngaondéré, *alt. dial.* Fulfulde, Adamawa [fub], 61

Ngaoundéré, *alt. dial.* Fulfulde, Adamawa [fub], 80
Ngapo, *dial.* Banda-Bambari [liy], 75
Ngapore, *alt.* Nyang'i [nyp], 212
Ngapu, *alt. dial.* Banda-Bambari [liy], 75
Ngardilpa, *alt.* Warlpiri [wbp], 578
Ngare, *dial.* Mboko [mdu], 89
Ngari, *alt.* Naga, Thangal [nki], 380
   alt. dial. Tibetan, Central [bod], 344
Ngariawan, *alt. dial.* Adzera [azr], 587
Ngarinman [nbj], 575
Ngarinyeri, *alt.* Narrinyeri [nay], 575
Ngarinyin [ung], 575
Ngarla [nlr], 575
Ngarlkajie, *alt.* Dyaabugay [dyy], 570
Ngarluma [nrl], 575
Ngarnga, *alt.* Gudanji [nji], 571
   dial. Gudanji [nji], 571
Ngarowapum, *dial.* Adzera [azr], 587
Ngarrabadji, *alt.* Mangarayi [mpc], 573
Ngarrbal, *alt.* Yugambal [yub], 579
Ngarrindjeri, *alt.* Narrinyeri [nay], 575
Ngarrubul, *alt.* Yugambal [yub], 579
Ngas [anc], 171
Ngasa [nsg], 202
Ngatan, *dial.* Naga, Maram [nma], 378
Ngatana, *dial.* Pokomo, Lower [poj], 135
Ngatik Men's Creole [ngm], 582
Ngatikese, *alt.* Ngatik Men's Creole [ngm], 582
Ngatikese Men's Language, *alt.* Ngatik Men's Creole [ngm], 582
Ngatjan, *alt. dial.* Dyirbal [dbl], 570
Ngatju, *alt.* Ngadjunmaya [nju], 575
Ngatjumay, *alt.* Ngadjunmaya [nju], 575
Ngatsang, *alt.* Achang [acn], 326
Ngau, *alt. dial.* Banda-Ndélé [bfl], 75
Ngavalus-Lossuk, *dial.* Kara [leu], 605
Ngawn, *alt.* Chin, Ngawn [cnw], 463
Ngawn Chin, *see* Chin, Ngawn [cnw], 463
Ngawun [nxn], 575
Ngayaba, *alt.* Tibea [ngy], 72
Ngaymil, *dial.* Dhangu [dhg], 569
Ngazar, *dial.* Kanuri, Central [knc], 166, 63, 81, 191
Ngazidja, *alt.* Comorian, Ngazidja [zdj], 87
Ngazidja Comorian, *see* Comorian, Ngazidja [zdj], 87

Ngba Geme, *alt.* Geme [geq], 76
Ngbaka [nga], 105, 89
Ngbaka Gbaya, *alt.* Ngbaka [nga], 105
Ngbaka Limba, *alt.* Ngbaka Ma'bo [nbm], 77, 89, 105
Ngbaka Ma'bo [nbm], 77, 89, 105
Ngbaka Manza [ngg], 77
Ngbaka Minangende, *alt.* Ngbaka [nga], 105
Ngbako, *dial.* Kako [kkj], 63
Ngbala, *dial.* Banda-Ndélé [bfl], 75
Ngbandi, Northern [ngb], 105
Ngbandi, Southern [nbw], 105
Ngbandi-Ngiri, *alt.* Ngbandi, Southern [nbw], 105
Ngbandi-Sud, *alt.* Ngbandi, Southern [nbw], 105
Ngbang, *dial.* Dii [dur], 60
Ngbanyito, *alt.* Gonja [gjn], 125
Ngbee [jgb], 106
Ngbinda [nbd], 106
Ngbo, *alt. dial.* Izi-Ezaa-Ikwo-Mgbo [izi], 164
Ngbougou, *alt. dial.* Banda, South Central [lnl], 74, 97
Ngbugu, *dial.* Banda, South Central [lnl], 74, 97
Ngbundu [nuu], 106
Nge, *alt.* Vengo [bav], 73
Nge', *alt.* Ngeq [ngt], 451
Nge'dé, *alt.* Ngete [nnn], 85
Ngee, *dial.* Teke, Ibali [tek], 108
   dial. Teke-Ibali [tek], 90
Ngeh, *alt.* Ngeq [ngt], 451
Ngelima [agh], 106
Ngell-Kuru-Vwang, *alt. dial.* Berom [bom], 155
Ngemba [nge], 69
   alt. dial. Ngemba [nge], 69
   dial. Ghomálá' [bbj], 62
Ngembo, *alt.* Ngamambo [nbv], 69
Ngemere, *dial.* Koalib [kib], 192
Ngemu, *dial.* Naga, Tase [nst], 380
Ngen, *alt.* Bassossi [bsi], 58
   alt. Beng [nhb], 92
Ngende, *dial.* Bushoong [buf], 98
Ngene, *alt.* Engenni [enn], 159
Ngenge, *alt. dial.* Gbagyi [gbr], 160
Ngenkikurrunggur, *alt.* Nangikurrunggurr [nam], 574
Ngenkiwumerri, *dial.* Nangikurrunggurr [nam], 574
Ngeno-Ngene, *dial.* Sasak [sas], 409
Ngente, *dial.* Mizo [lus], 376, 321, 466
Ngeo, *pej. alt.* Shan [shn], 467, 517
Ngepma Kwundi, *alt.* Iatmul [ian], 602

Ngeq [ngt], 451
Ngete [nnn], 85
Ngeti, *alt.* Ngiti [niy], 106
Ngeto-Ngete, *dial.* Sasak [sas], 409
Ngeumba, *alt. dial.* Wangaaybuwan-Ngiyambaa [wyb], 577
Ngezzim, *alt.* Ngizim [ngi], 171
Nggae, *alt. dial.* Ghari [gri], 636
Nggao, *alt.* Gao [gga], 636
Nggaro, *alt. dial.* Kodi [kod], 407
Nggaura, *alt. dial.* Kodi [kod], 407
   dial. Lamboya [lmy], 408
Nggela, *alt.* Gela [nlg], 636
Nggem [nbq], 421
Nggeri, *alt. dial.* Ghari [gri], 636
Nggwahyi [ngx], 171
Nggweshe, *alt.* Gvoko [ngs], 161
Nggwoli, *dial.* Nzanyi [nja], 171
Nghuki, *alt.* N|u [ngh], 186
Nghwele, *alt.* Kwere [cwe], 200
Ngi, *alt.* Ngie [ngj], 69
Ngiamba, *alt. dial.* Wangaaybuwan-Ngiyambaa [wyb], 577
Ngiangeya, *alt.* Nyang'i [nyp], 212
Ngiao, *pej. alt.* Shan [shn], 467, 517
Ngiaw, *pej. alt.* Shan [shn], 467, 517
Ngie [ngj], 69
Ngiemboon [nnh], 69
Ngigua, *alt.* Popoloca, San Juan Atzingo [poe], 273
   alt. Popoloca, Santa Inés Ahuatempan [pca], 274
Ngile [jle], 194
Ngilemong, *dial.* Musgu [mug], 68
Ngili, *alt. dial.* Pande [bkj], 77
Ngin, *alt.* Beng [nhb], 92
Ngindere, *alt.* Kpatili [kym], 76
Ngindo [nnq], 202
Nginia, *dial.* Ghari [gri], 636
Nginyukwur, *dial.* Koalib [kib], 192
Ngio, *pej. alt.* Shan [shn], 467, 517
Ngiow, *pej. alt.* Shan [shn], 467, 517
Ngirere, *alt.* Koalib [kib], 192
   dial. Koalib [kib], 192
Ngishe, *alt.* Ngoshie [nsh], 70
Ngiti [niy], 106
Ngiumba, *alt. dial.* Wangaaybuwan-Ngiyambaa [wyb], 577
Ngiyambaa, *dial.* Wangaaybuwan-Ngiyambaa [wyb], 577
Ngizim [ngi], 171
Ngizmawa, *alt.* Ngizim [ngi], 171
Ngjamba, *alt. dial.* Wangaaybuwan-Ngiyambaa [wyb], 577
Ngkâlmpw Kanum, *see* Kanum, Ngkâlmpw [kcd], 416
‖Ng!ke, *alt. dial.* N|u [ngh], 186
Ngmamperli, *alt.* Mampruli [maw], 126

Ng'men, *alt.* Chin, Mün [mwq], 463
Ngnai, *alt.* Bunu, Wunai [bwn], 328
Ngnok, *alt.* Sherdukpen [sdp], 387
Ngo, *alt.* Vengo [bav], 73
  dial. Obolo [ann], 172
Ngo Chang, *alt.* Achang [acn], 326
Ngoahu, *dial.* Loko [lok], 183
Ngobere, *alt.* Ngäbere [gym], 283
Ngobo, *alt.* Gobu [gox], 100
  alt. Gubu [gox], 76
Ngobu, *alt.* Gobu [gox], 100
  alt. Gubu [gox], 76
Ngochang, *alt.* Achang [acn], 326,
  456
Ngodeni, *alt. dial.* Jina [jia], 63
Ngoe, *alt.* Bafaw-Balong [bwt], 56
Ngok Pa, *alt.* Kensiu [kns], 454, 515
Ngok-Kordofan, *dial.* Dinka,
  Northwestern [diw], 190
Ngok-Sobat, *dial.* Dinka,
  Northeastern [dip], 189
Ngoka, *dial.* Mbay [myb], 84
Ngokra, *alt. dial.* Kadaru [kdu], 191
Ngola, *alt.* Angolar [aoa], 179
  alt. dial. Banda-Banda [bpd], 75
  dial. Mbundu [kmb], 41
Ngolak-Wonga, *alt.* Mullukmulluk
  [mpb], 574
Ngoli, *alt.* Ngul [nlo], 106
Ngolo, *alt. dial.* Oroko [bdu], 71
Ngologa, *dial.* Kgalagadi [xkv], 47
Ngoluche, *alt. dial.* Mapudungun
  [arn], 242
Ngom [nra], 121, 89
Ngoma, *dial.* Bemba [bem], 213, 97
Ngomba [jgo], 69
  alt. Ngemba [nge], 69
Ngombale [nla], 70
Ngombe (Central African Republic)
  [nmj], 77
  Ngombe (Democratic Republic of
  Congo) [ngc], 106
  dial. Bushoong [buf], 98
Ngombe-Kaka, *alt.* Ngombe
  [nmj], 77
Ngombia, *alt. dial.* Bushoong
  [buf], 98
Ngomi, *dial.* Karang [kzr], 63, 81
Ngomo, *alt.* Ngom [nra], 121
Ngon, *alt.* Chin, Ngawn [cnw], 463
Ngonde, *alt.* Nyakyusa-Ngonde
  [nyy], 203, 140
  dial. Nyakyusa-Ngonde [nyy], 203
Ngondi, *dial.* Gundi [gdi], 76
  alt. Ngundi [ndn], 89
Ngong [nnx], 70
Ngonge, *alt. dial.* Nzakambay
  [nzy], 71
Ngongo [noq], 106
  alt. dial. Nkutu [nkw], 106

dial. Bushoong [buf], 98
Ngongosila, *alt.* Gula'alaa
  [gmb], 636
Ngoni [ngo], 202, 148
  alt. Zulu [zul], 141
  alt. dial. Nsenga [nse], 215
  alt. dial. Nyanja [nya], 215
  dial. Nyanja [nya], 140, 148
  dial. Tumbuka [tum], 215
Ngoobechop, *alt.* Bamali [bbq], 57
Ngoongo, *dial.* Yaka [yaf], 109, 42
Ngoreme, *alt.* Ngurimi [ngq], 203
Ngork, *alt. dial.* Dinka, Northeastern
  [dip], 189
Ngormbur, *alt.* Ngurmbur [nrx], 575
Ngorn, *alt.* Chin, Ngawn [cnw], 463
Ngoro, *dial.* Tuki [bag], 72
  dial. Vute [vut], 73
Ngoshe Sama, *alt.* Gvoko
  [ngs], 161
Ngoshe-Ndhang, *alt.* Gvoko
  [ngs], 161, 62
Ngoshi, *alt.* Gvoko [ngs], 161, 62
Ngoshie [nsh], 70
  dial. Glavda [glw], 161
Ngossi, *alt.* Gvoko [ngs], 161, 62
Ngouan, *alt.* Nguôn [nuo], 525
Ngougua, *alt. dial.* Lutos [ndy], 76
Ngoumba, *alt.* Ngumba [nmg], 111
  alt. dial. Ngumba [nmg], 70
Ngoutchoumi, *alt. dial.* Fali, South
  [fal], 61
Ngowiye, *dial.* Biangai [big], 593
Ngrarmun, *alt.* Ngarinman
  [nbj], 575
Ngruimi, *alt.* Ngurimi [ngq], 203
Ngubu, *alt. dial.* Banda, South
  Central [lnl], 97
Nguburindi, *dial.* Ganggalida
  [gcd], 570
Ng|u|ei, *alt. dial.* !Xóõ [nmn], 48,
  151
Nguemba, *alt.* Ngemba [nge], 69
  alt. Ngiemboon [nnh], 69
Ng|u|len, *dial.* !Xóõ [nmn], 48
Ng|u|en, *dial.* !Xóõ [nmn], 151
Ngueté, *alt.* Ngete [nnn], 85
Nguetté, *alt.* Ngete [nnn], 85
Nguin, *alt.* Beng [nhb], 92
Ng'uki, *alt.* N|u [ngh], 186
Ngul [nlo], 106
Ngulak, *alt.* Ik [ikx], 211
Ngulgule, *alt.* Njalgulgule [njl], 194
Nguli, *alt.* Ngul [nlo], 106
Ngulu [ngp], 203
  alt. Lomwe [ngl], 147
  alt. Ngul [nlo], 106
Nguluwan [nuw], 583
Nguluwongga, *alt.* Mullukmulluk
  [mpb], 574

Ngumba [nmg], 70, 111
  alt. dial. Ngumba [nmg], 70
Ngumbarr, *alt. dial.*
  Wangaaybuwan-Ngiyambaa
  [wyb], 577
Ngumbi [nui], 111
  alt. Nkhumbi [khu], 41
Ng'umbo, *dial.* Bemba [bem], 213
Ngumbur, *alt.* Ngurmbur [nrx], 575
Nguna, *dial.* Efate, North [llp], 641
Ngundi [ndn], 89
  alt. Gundi [gdi], 76
  dial. Lusengo [lse], 103
Ngundu [nue], 106
Ngunduna, *dial.* Koalib [kib], 192
Ngunese, *alt. dial.* Efate, North
  [llp], 641
Ngungulu, *alt.* Ngungwel [ngz], 89
Ngungwel [ngz], 89
Ng'uni, *dial.* Machame [jmc], 193
Nguni, *alt. dial.* Ngwo [ngn], 70
Ngunu, *alt. dial.* Ngwo [ngn], 70
Nguôn [nuo], 525
Nguqwurang, *dial.* Koalib
  [kib], 192
Ngura [nbx], 575
Ngurawarla, *dial.* Ngura [nbx], 575
Nguri, *dial.* Kanembu [kbl], 81
Ngurimi [ngq], 203
Ngurmbur [nrx], 575
Nguru, *alt.* Lomwe [ngl], 147
  alt. Lomwe, Malawi [lon], 140
  alt. Ngulu [ngp], 203
  alt. dial. Banda-Ndélé [bfl], 75, 188
  dial. Gula [kcm], 191
Nguruimi, *alt.* Ngurimi [ngq], 203
Ng|usan, *alt. dial.* !Xóõ [nmn], 48,
  151
Nguu, *alt.* Ngulu [ngp], 203
  alt. Vengo [bav], 73
Ngwa, *alt.* Vengo [bav], 73
  alt. dial. Ngemba [nge], 69
  dial. Igbo [ibo], 163
Ngwaa Móò, *alt.* Moo [gwg], 170
Ngwaba [ngw], 171
Ngwai Mungàn, *alt.* Mingang Doso
  [mko], 170
Ngwaketse, *dial.* Tswana [tsn], 48,
  186
Ngwalkwe, *alt.* Malgbe [mxf], 65,
  83
Ngwalungu, *dial.* Tsonga [tso], 149,
  217
Ngwandi, *alt.* Ngbandi, Northern
  [ngb], 105
  alt. Ngbandi, Southern [nbw], 105
Ngwané, *alt.* Wané [hwa], 95
Ngwato, *alt. dial.* Tswana [tsn], 48
  dial. Tswana [tsn], 186
Ngwatu, *dial.* Tswana [tsn], 48, 217

Ngwaw, *alt.* Ngwo [ngn], 70
alt. dial. Ngwo [ngn], 70
Ngwaxi, *alt.* Nggwahyi [ngx], 171
Ngwe [nwe], 70
alt. Hungworo [nat], 162
Ngwe Palaung, *alt.* Palaung, Pale
[pce], 466, 342, 516
Ngwele, *alt.* Kwere [cwe], 200
Ng'were, *alt.* Kwere [cwe], 200
Ngweshe, *alt. dial.* Glavda
[glw], 161
Ngweshe-Ndaghan, *alt.* Gvoko
[ngs], 161
Ngwii, *dial.* Mbere [mdt], 89, 121
Ngwo [ngn], 70
dial. Ngwo [ngn], 70
Ngwohi, *alt.* Nggwahyi [ngx], 171
Ngwoi, *alt.* Hungworo [nat], 162
Ngwullaro, *alt.* Laro [lro], 192
Ngyemboon, *alt.* Ngiemboon
[nnh], 69
Ngyeme, *alt.* Njyem [njy], 70, 89
Ngyepu, *alt. dial.* Bari [bfa], 188,
210
Nha Heun, *alt.* Nyaheun [nev], 452
Nhaang, *alt.* Giáy [pcc], 523
N‖hai, *alt. dial.* Naro [nhr], 48
N‖hai-Ntse'e, *alt. dial.* Naro
[nhr], 48
Nhandeva, *alt.* Chiripá [nhd], 284,
220, 226
Nhaneca, *alt.* Nyaneka [nyk], 41
Nhaneka, *alt.* Nyaneka [nyk], 41
Nhang, *dial.* Giáy [pcc], 523
Nharo, *alt.* Naro [nhr], 48, 150
Nharon, *alt.* Naro [nhr], 48
Nhauru, *alt.* Naro [nhr], 48
Nhaurun, *alt.* Naro [nhr], 48
Nhawu, *alt.* Wirangu [wiw], 578
Nhayi, *dial.* Tswa [tsc], 149
Nheengatu, *alt.* Nhengatu [yrl], 230,
246
Nhemba, *alt.* Nyemba [nba], 41
Nhengatu [yrl], 230, 246, 312
Nhengo, *alt.* Nyengo [nye], 41
Nheu, *dial.* Kuy [kdt], 515
Nhlanganu, *alt. dial.* Tsonga
[tso], 186
Nho, *alt. dial.* Bafaw-Balong
[bwt], 56
Nhuon, *alt.* Lü [khb], 524
Nhuwala [nhf], 575
Ni Nyo'o, *dial.* Tunen [baz], 72
Nia Hoen, *alt.* Nyaheun [nev], 452
Niabo, *alt. dial.* Wè Southern [gxx],
95
Niaboua, *alt.* Nyabwa [nwb], 94
Niabre, *alt. dial.* Bété, Gagnoa
[btg], 92
Niahon, *alt.* Nyaheun [nev], 452

Niakaramadougou, *dial.* Senoufo,
Tagwana [tgw], 95
Niakuol, *alt.* Nyahkur [cbn], 516
Niakuoll, *alt.* Nyahkur [cbn], 516
Niamniam, *alt.* Nimbari [nmr], 70
Niang, *alt.* Giáy [pcc], 523
Niangbo, *dial.* Senoufo, Tagwana
[tgw], 95
Niangolo, *alt.* Sénoufo, Senara
[seq], 54
Niangoloko-Diarabakoko, *dial.*
Cerma [cme], 50
Niap, *alt.* Temuan [tmw], 455
Nias [nia], 437
dial. Nias [nia], 437
Nibhatta, *dial.* Bundeli [bns], 357
Nibon, *alt.* Penan, Western [pne], 460
alt. dial. Penan, Western [pne], 325
Nibong, *alt.* Penan, Western
[pne], 460
dial. Penan, Western [pne], 460, 325
Nibulu, *alt.* Nuni, Northern [nuv], 53
alt. Nuni, Southern [nnw], 53
Nibung Terjung, *alt. dial.* Malayic
Dayak [xdy], 394
Nic, *alt. dial.* Udi [udi], 320
Nicaragua Creole English
[bzk], 283
Nicaraguan Sign Language
[ncs], 280
Nicaraguan Tawahka, *dial.*
Sumo-Mayangna [sum], 283
Niçard, *dial.* Provençal [prv], 537,
548
Nicobar, *alt.* Nicobarese, Central
[ncb], 381
Nicobara, *alt.* Nicobarese, Southern
[nik], 381
Nicobarese, Car [caq], 381
Nicobarese, Central [ncb], 381
Nicobarese, Southern [nik], 381
Niçois, *alt. dial.* Provençal [prv], 537,
548
Nicosia, *alt. dial.* Lombard
[lmo], 544
Nicoya, *alt. dial.* Chorotega [cjr], 249
Nide, *alt.* Labo [mwi], 642
Nidem, *alt. dial.* Kaningdon-Nindem
[kdp], 166
Nidi, *alt.* Kwegu [xwg], 116
Nidrou, *dial.* Wè Western [wec], 95
Nidru, *alt. dial.* Wè Western
[wec], 95
Nidzh, *dial.* Udi [udi], 320
Niédéboua, *alt. dial.* Nyabwa
[nwb], 94
Niedersaechsisch, *alt.* Saxon, Low
[nds], 539
Niedersorbisch, *alt.* Sorbian,
Lower [dsb], 539

Niediekaha, *dial.* Senoufo, Tagwana
[tgw], 95
Niel, *alt. dial.* Dinka, Northeastern
[dip], 189
Nielim, *alt.* Niellim [nie], 85
Niellim [nie], 85
dial. Niellim [nie], 85
Niemeng, *alt.* Bamunka [bvm], 57
Niende, *pej. alt.* Mbelime [mql], 45
Niendi, *pej. alt.* Mbelime [mql], 45
Nieng O, *alt.* Mang [zng], 525
Nieni, *dial.* Kuranko [knk], 183
Niergui, *alt. dial.* Bidiyo [bid], 79
Nife, *alt. dial.* Nupe-Nupe-Tako
[nup], 171
Nifilole, *alt.* Ayiwo [nfl], 635
Nigac, *dial.* Mape [mlh], 612
Nigagba, *dial.* Bakwé [bjw], 91
Nigbi, *alt.* Ligbi [lig], 126, 94
dial. Koyaga [kga], 93
Nigeria Mambila, *see* Mambila,
Nigeria [mzk], 169
Nigerian Creole English, *alt.*
Pidgin, Nigerian [pcm], 173
Nigerian Fulfulde, *see* Fulfulde,
Nigerian [fuv], 160
Nigerian Pidgin, *see* Pidgin,
Nigerian [pcm], 173
Nigerian Pidgin English, *alt.*
Pidgin, Nigerian [pcm], 173
Nigerian Sign Language
[nsi], 171
Nigi, *alt. dial.* Yambeta [yat], 73
Nigii, *alt. dial.* Yambeta [yat], 73
Niguecactemigi, *alt. dial.* Guana
[gva], 284
Nigwi, *alt.* Ligbi [lig], 126, 94
Nihal, *alt.* Nihali [nll], 381
Nihali [nll], 381
Nihan, *alt.* Nehan [nsn], 617
Nihang, *alt.* Karbi [mjw], 366
Nii [nii], 618
Niinati, *alt.* Muyu, North [kti], 421
Niitaka, *alt.* Tsou [tsu], 512
Nij, *alt. dial.* Udi [udi], 320
Nijadali [nad], 575
Nijrau, *dial.* Parachi [prc], 317
Nijyamïï Nikyejaada, *alt.* Yagua
[yad], 293
Nika, *alt.* Giryama [nyf], 133
Nikiyama, *dial.* Bo [bpw], 594
Niksek [gbe], 618
Nikuda, *dial.* Onin [oni], 421
Nikulkan-Murnaten-Wakolo, *alt.*
dial. Alune [alp], 396
Nil, *alt.* Paniya [pcg], 382
Nila [nil], 402
Nilamba [nim], 203
Nile Nubian, *alt.* Kenuzi-Dongola
[kzh], 192, 110

alt. Nobiin [fia], 110
Nilotic Kavirondo, *alt.* Luo [luo], 134
Nilyamba, *alt.* Nilamba [nim], 203
Nimadi [noe], 381
Nimalda, *alt.* Adynyamathanha [adt], 567
Nimalto, *alt. dial.* Tera [ttr], 175
Nimana, *alt. dial.* Numana-Nunku-Gbantu-Numbu [nbr], 171
Nimanbur [nmp], 575
Nimanburru, *alt.* Nimanbur [nmp], 575
Nimari, *alt.* Nimadi [noe], 381
Nimbari [nmr], 70
Nimbari-Kebi, *alt.* Nimbari [nmr], 70
Nimbe, *alt. dial.* Ijo, Southeast [ijs], 163
Nimbia, *dial.* Gwandara [gwn], 161
Nimboran [nir], 421
Nimi [nis], 618
Nimi Koro, *alt. dial.* Kono [kno], 183
Nimi Yama, *alt. dial.* Kono [kno], 183
Nimiadi, *alt.* Nimadi [noe], 381
Nimo [niw], 618
Nimo-Wasawai, *alt.* Nimo [niw], 618
Nimoa [nmw], 618
Nimois, *alt. dial.* Provençal [prv], 537
Nimowa, *alt.* Nimoa [nmw], 618
Nimpo, *alt. dial.* Sapo [krn], 139
Nimtep Weng, *dial.* Bimin [bhl], 593
Ninam [shb], 230, 312
Ninatie, *alt.* Muyu, North [kti], 421
Nindem, *dial.* Kaningdon-Nindem [kdp], 166
Nindi [nxi], 203
Nine Hills, *alt. dial.* Sudest [tgo], 625
Ninebulo, *dial.* Sa [sax], 645
Nineia, *alt.* Mato [met], 612
Ning-Long, *dial.* Chinese, Hakka [hak], 329
Ningalami, *alt. dial.* Grangali [nli], 316
Ningebal, *alt.* Bayali [bjy], 569
Ningera [nby], 618
Ningerum, *alt.* Ninggerum [nxr], 618
Ninggera, *alt.* Ningera [nby], 618
Ninggeroem, *alt.* Ninggerum [nxr], 421
Ninggerum [nxr], 618, 421
Ninggirum, *alt.* Ninggerum [nxr], 618, 421

Ninggrum, *alt.* Ninggerum [nxr], 618, 421
Ningi, *dial.* Gamo-Ningi [bte], 160
Ningil [niz], 618
Ningo, *dial.* Dangme [ada], 124
Ningon, *alt.* Nyeng [nfg], 171
Ningraharian Pashto, *dial.* Pashto, Northern [pbu], 488
Ningthaunai, *alt. dial.* Bishnupriya [bpy], 357
Ninguessen, *alt. dial.* Tunen [baz], 72
Ningye [nns], 171
Ninia, *alt.* Yali, Ninia [nlk], 426
Ninia Yali, *see* Yali, Ninia [nlk], 426
Niniari-Piru-Riring-Lumoli, *alt. dial.* Alune [alp], 396
Ninigo, *alt.* Seimat [ssg], 623
Ninkada, *dial.* Bu [jid], 156
Ninkare [gur], 53
Ninong, *dial.* Akoose [bss], 56
Ninzam, *alt.* Ninzo [nin], 171
Ninzne-Udinsk, *dial.* Buriat, Russia [bxr], 504
Ninzo [nin], 171
Nio, *dial.* Lugbara [lgg], 103
Niominka, *dial.* Serer-Sine [srr], 182
Niomoun, *alt. dial.* Jola-Kasa [csk], 180
Niopheng, *alt.* Mru [mro], 376
Niopreng, *alt.* Mru [mro], 321
Niou, *dial.* Niellim [nie], 85
Nipa, *dial.* Angal Heneng [akh], 589
Nüpode Huitoto, *see* Huitoto, Nüpode [hux], 288
Nipode Witoto, *alt.* Huitoto, Nüpode [hux], 288
Niporen, *alt.* Nyang'i [nyp], 212
Nipori, *alt.* Nyang'i [nyp], 212
Nipsan [nps], 421
Niragu, *dial.* Gbiri-Niragu [grh], 160
Niramba, *alt.* Nilamba [nim], 203
Nirere, *alt.* Koalib [kib], 192
Nirmal, *dial.* Gondi, Southern [ggo], 363
Nisa [njs], 421
Nisel, *alt.* Parbate, Eastern [kif], 477
Nisenan [nsz], 306
Nisga'a [ncg], 240
Nishang, *dial.* Nisi [dap], 381
Nishel Kham, *alt.* Parbate, Eastern [kif], 477
Nishga, *alt.* Nisga'a [ncg], 240
Nishi, *alt.* Nisi [dap], 381
Nishinam, *alt.* Nisenan [nsz], 306
Nishka, *alt.* Nisga'a [ncg], 240
Nisi [dap], 381
alt. Parbate, Eastern [kif], 477
Nisi Kham, *alt.* Parbate, Eastern [kif], 477

Nisk'a, *alt.* Nisga'a [ncg], 240
Niska, *alt.* Nisga'a [ncg], 240
Nisqually, *dial.* Salish, Southern Puget Sound [slh], 307
Nissan, *alt.* Nehan [nsn], 617
Nissi, *alt.* Nisi [dap], 381
Nisu, *alt.* Yi, Southern [nos], 348
Niten, *alt.* Eten [etx], 159
Nitinaht, *alt. dial.* Nootka [noo], 240
Nitinat, *dial.* Nootka [noo], 240
Nitu, *dial.* Chin, Mün [mwq], 463
Niuafo'ou [num], 639
Niuatoputapu [nkp], 639
Niue [niu], 586
Niuean, *alt.* Niue [niu], 586
Niuefekai, *pej. alt.* Niue [niu], 586
Niutaji, *dial.* Iowa-Oto [iow], 302
Niutao, *alt. dial.* Tuvaluan [tvl], 640
Nivaclé [cag], 285, 220
Nivaklé, *alt.* Nivaclé [cag], 285
Nive, *dial.* Daba [dbq], 59
Nivkh, *alt.* Gilyak [niv], 504
Nivkhi, *alt.* Gilyak [niv], 504
Nivo, *alt.* Ayiwo [nfl], 635
Niyium, *alt.* Ninggerum [nxr], 618
Nizaa, *alt.* Suga [sgi], 72
Nizh, *alt. dial.* Udi [udi], 320
Nizovsk, *dial.* Negidal [neg], 506
Njabi, *alt.* Njebi [nzb], 121, 89
Njadu, *alt.* Nyadu [nxj], 395
Njai, *alt.* Nzanyi [nja], 171, 71
Njakali, *dial.* Dyaabugay [dyy], 570
Njakambai, *alt.* Nzakambay [nzy], 86
Njalgulgule [njl], 194
Njamal, *alt.* Nyamal [nly], 576
Njamarl, *alt.* Nyamal [nly], 576
Njambeta, *alt.* Yambeta [yat], 73
Njang, *alt. dial.* Kwanja [knp], 65
Njanga, *alt. dial.* Kwanja [knp], 65
Njangga, *alt.* Nyangga [nny], 576
alt. Wirangu [wiw], 578
Njanggala, *alt.* Nyangga [nny], 576
Njangulgule, *alt.* Njalgulgule [njl], 194
Njanti, *alt.* Tibea [ngy], 72
Njanyi, *alt.* Nzanyi [nja], 171, 71
Njao, *alt.* Awyi [auw], 412
alt. Ndau [ndc], 148, 216
Njari, *alt. dial.* Mbembe, Tigon [nza], 66
Njauna, *dial.* Naga, Zeme [nzm], 381
Njawdha, *alt. dial.* Lendu [led], 102
Njawe, *alt.* Jawe [jaz], 584
Njawlo, *dial.* Lendu [led], 102
Njebi [nzb], 121, 89
Njee-Poantu, *dial.* Fe'fe' [fmp], 61
Njegn, *alt.* Nzanyi [nja], 71

Njei, *alt.* Nzanyi [nja], 171, 71
Njeing, *alt.* Nzanyi [nja], 171
Njeleng, *dial.* Mofu-Gudur [mif], 68
Njeli, *alt. dial.* Pande [bkj], 77
Njem, *alt.* Njyem [njy], 70, 89
Njemnjem, *pej. alt.* Suga [sgi], 72
Njemps, *alt. dial.* Samburu
  [saq], 136
Njen [njj], 70
Njeng, *alt.* Nzanyi [nja], 71
Njeny, *alt.* Nzanyi [nja], 171, 71
Njerep [njr], 171
Njerup, *alt.* Njerep [njr], 171
Njesko, *dial.* Kanuri, Central [knc],
  166, 63, 81, 191
Njevi, *alt.* Njebi [nzb], 89
Njigina, *alt.* Nyigina [nyh], 576
Njijapali, *alt.* Nijadali [nad], 575
Njikini, *alt. dial.* Teke, Northern
  [teg], 121
Njikum, *alt.* Jukun Takum [jbu], 63,
  165
Njindo, *alt.* Ngindo [nnq], 202
Njinga, *dial.* Mbundu [kmb], 41
Njiningi, *dial.* Teke, Northern
  [teg], 121
Njiunjiu, *alt.* Teke-Nzikou [nzu], 90
Njo, *alt.* Komering [kge], 436
  alt. Krui [krq], 436
Njong, *dial.* Ngemba [nge], 69
Njoyame, *alt.* Ndoola [ndr], 171, 69
Njuguna, *alt.* Nugunu [nnv], 575
Njuká, *alt.* Aukan [djk], 295
Njumit, *dial.* Lawangan [lbx], 394
Njungene, *alt.* Limbum [lmp], 65
Njwande, *alt.* Bitare [brt], 155, 59
Njyem [njy], 70, 89
Njyunjyu, *alt.* Teke-Nzikou [nzu], 90
Nka', *dial.* Fe'fe' [fmp], 61
Nkafa, *dial.* Kamwe [hig], 166
Nkangala [nkn], 41
Nkap, *alt.* Naki [mff], 69
Nkari [nkz], 171
Nkarigwe, *alt.* Irigwe [iri], 164
Nkem, *dial.* Nkem-Nkum [isi], 171
Nkem-Nkum [isi], 171
Nkembe, *alt. dial.* Mbole [mdq], 104
Nkhonde, *alt.* Nyakyusa-Ngonde
  [nyy], 140
Nkhumbi [khu], 41
Nki, *alt.* Bokyi [bky], 156, 59
Nkim, *alt. dial.* Nkem-Nkum
  [isi], 171
Nkimbe, *dial.* Mbole [mdq], 104
Nklapmx, *alt.* Thompson [thp], 242
Nko, *alt. dial.* Mundani [mnf], 68
Nkojo, *dial.* Mwani [wmw], 148
Nkokolle, *alt.* Nkukoli [nbo], 171
Nkole, *alt.* Nyankore [nyn], 212
  dial. Ntomba [nto], 106

Nkom, *alt.* Kom [bkm], 64
N'komi, *alt. dial.* Myene [mye], 121
Nkomi, *dial.* Myene [mye], 121
Nkonde, *alt.* Nyakyusa-Ngonde
  [nyy], 203, 140
  dial. Nyakyusa-Ngonde [nyy], 140
Nkong, *alt. dial.* Mundani [mnf], 68
Nkongho [nkc], 70
Nkonya [nko], 127
Nkoosi, *alt.* Akoose [bss], 56
Nkoro, *alt.* Nkoroo [nkx], 171
Nkoroo [nkx], 171
Nkosi, *alt.* Akoose [bss], 56
Nkot, *dial.* Yamba [yam], 73
Nkoxo, *alt.* Kako [kkj], 63, 76, 88
Nkoya [nka], 214
  dial. Nkoya [nka], 214
Nkpam, *dial.* Lokaa [yaz], 169
Nkqeshe, *alt.* ‖Xegwi [xeg], 187
Nkriang, *alt.* Ngeq [ngt], 451
Nkuchu, *alt.* Nkutu [nkw], 106
Nkukoli [nbo], 171
Nkum, *dial.* Nkem-Nkum [isi], 171
  dial. Yala [yba], 177
Nkum Akpambe, *dial.* Yala [yba],
  177
Nkuma, *dial.* Tsonga [tso], 186
Nkumabem, *alt. dial.* Mpongmpong
  [mgg], 68
Nkumbi, *alt.* Nkhumbi [khu], 41
Nkundo, *dial.* Mongo-Nkundu
  [lol], 104
Nkundu, *alt. dial.* Mongo-Nkundu
  [lol], 104
  alt. dial. Oroko [bdu], 71
Nkune, *alt. dial.* Ngemba [nge], 69
Nkuraeng, *alt.* Kulango, Bondoukou
  [kzc], 126
  alt. Kulango, Bouna [nku], 94, 126
Nkurange, *alt.* Kulango, Bondoukou
  [kzc], 126
  alt. Kulango, Bouna [nku], 94
Nkutshu, *alt.* Nkutu [nkw], 106
Nkutu [nkw], 106
Nkutuk, *alt.* Samburu [saq], 136
Nkwa, *alt.* Gbari [gby], 160
Nkwaamba, *dial.* Fipa [fip], 198
Nkwen, *dial.* Mendankwe-Nkwen
  [mfd], 67
Nkwifiya, *alt. dial.* Sagala [sbm], 204
Nkwoi, *alt.* Hungworo [nat], 162
Nla Mboo, *alt. dial.* Mbo [mbo], 66
Nlembuu, *alt. dial.* Mbo [mbo], 66
Nlong, *alt. dial.* Akoose [bss], 56
  alt. dial. Bafaw-Balong [bwt], 56
Nnam [nbp], 171
Nnerigwe, *alt.* Irigwe [iri], 164
No, *dial.* Sar [mwm], 86
No-Penge, *dial.* Umbu-Ungu
  [ubu], 629

Noale, *alt.* Mbembe, Tigon [nza], 170
Noanama, *alt.* Woun Meu [noa], 284
Noang, *alt.* Roglai, Northern
  [rog], 526
  alt. dial. Chru [cje], 522
Noatia, *dial.* Kok Borok [trp], 368,
  321
Nobanob, *alt.* Nobonob [gaw], 618
Nobiin [fia], 194, 110
Nobnob, *alt.* Nobonob [gaw], 618
Nobonob [gaw], 618
Nobuk, *alt.* Kwerba Mamberamo
  [xwr], 418
Nocamán [nom], 289
Nochi, *alt.* Notsi [ncf], 618
Nocomán, *alt.* Nocamán [nom], 289
Nocte, *alt.* Naga, Nocte [njb], 379
Nocte Naga, *see* Naga, Nocte
  [njb], 379
Nocten, *alt.* Wichí Lhamtés Nocten
  [mtp], 224, 220
Noctenes, *alt.* Wichí Lhamtés
  Nocten [mtp], 224, 220
Nodup, *dial.* Kuanua [ksd], 608
Noefoor, *alt.* Biak [bhw], 412
Noefoorsch, *alt.* Biak [bhw], 412
Noenama, *alt.* Woun Meu [noa], 284
Nogai [nog], 556
Nogaitsy, *alt.* Nogai [nog], 556
Nogalar, *alt.* Nogai [nog], 556
Nogau, *dial.* Ju|'hoan [ktz], 47, 150
  dial. ǂKx'au‖'ein [aue], 150, 47
Nogay, *alt.* Nogai [nog], 556
Noghai, *alt.* Nogai [nog], 556
Noghay, *alt.* Nogai [nog], 556
Noghaylar, *alt.* Nogai [nog], 556
Nogliki-Val, *alt. dial.* Orok
  [oaa], 506
Nogo, *dial.* Kemak [kem], 351, 407
Nogo-Nogo, *alt. dial.* Kemak
  [kem], 351, 407
Nogugu, *alt.* Nokuku [nkk], 644
Nogukwabai, *alt.* Kwerba
  Mamberamo [xwr], 418
  dial. Kwerba [kwe], 418
Nohina, *pej. alt.* Tolaki [lbw], 433
Noho, *alt.* Batanga [bnm], 110, 58
Nohon, *alt.* Awyu, Central
  [awu], 412
Nohu, *alt.* Batanga [bnm], 110
Nohur, *alt. dial.* Turkmen [tuk], 442
Nohya Sign Language, *alt.*
  Yucatec Maya Sign Language
  [msd], 277
Noie, *pej. alt.* Tolaki [lbw], 433
Noihe, *pej. alt.* Tolaki [lbw], 433
Noikoro, *alt. dial.* Fijian, Western
  [wyy], 580
Noiri [noi], 381
Nokanoka, *alt.* Kwama [kmq], 116

Nokaw, *alt.* Naga, Khiamniungan [nky], 378, 466

Nokchiin Muott, *alt.* Chechen [che], 553

Nokhchiin, *alt.* Chechen [che], 553

Nokhurli, *dial.* Turkmen [tuk], 520, 442

Nokopo, *dial.* Yopno [yut], 634

Nokte, *alt.* Naga, Nocte [njb], 379

Noku, *alt.* Batanga [bnm], 110, 58

Nokuku [nkk], 644

Nokunna, *alt.* Nugunu [nnv], 575

Nomaande [lem], 70

Nomad, *alt.* Gobasi [goi], 600

    alt. Odoodee [kkc], 619

    alt. Samo [smq], 623

Nomadic Fulfulde, *alt. dial.* Fulfulde, Adamawa [fub], 61, 80

    alt. dial. Fulfulde, Kano-Katsina-Bororro [fuv], 61, 80

    alt. dial. Fulfulde, Nigerian [fuv], 160

Nomadic Kubu, *dial.* Kubu [kvb], 436

Nomai, *alt.* Doyayo [dow], 60

Nomane [nof], 618

    dial. Nomane [nof], 618

Nomatsiguenga [not], 289

Nomatsiguenga Campa, *pej. alt.* Nomatsiguenga [not], 289

Nomlaki, *dial.* Wintu [wit], 310

Nomndaa, *alt.* Amuzgo, Guerrero [amu], 259

Nomoi, *alt.* Mortlockese [mrl], 582

Nomopo, *dial.* Sapo [krn], 139

Nomu [noh], 618

Non, *alt.* Noon [snf], 181

Non-Amish Pennsylvania German, *alt. dial.* German, Pennsylvania [pdc], 237

    dial. German, Pennsylvania [pdc], 301

Non-Plain Pennsylvania German, *alt. dial.* German, Pennsylvania [pdc], 301

Nonama, *alt.* Woun Meu [noa], 284

Nonda, *dial.* Bangubangu [bnx], 97

None, *alt.* Noon [snf], 181

Nones, *dial.* Ladin [lld], 544

Nones Blot, *alt. dial.* Ladin [lld], 544

Nonese, *alt. dial.* Ladin [lld], 544

Nonesh, *alt. dial.* Ladin [lld], 544

Nong, *alt.* Batek [btq], 454

    alt. Nung [nut], 525, 452

    alt. dial. Batek [btq], 454

    alt. dial. Mnong, Southern [mnn], 525

Nongtung, *dial.* Pnar [pbv], 384

Noni, *alt.* Noone [nhu], 70

Noniali, *alt.* Lisabata-Nuniali [lcs], 400

Nononke, *alt.* Bozo, Jenaama [bze], 142

    alt. Sorko [bze], 175

Nonukan, *alt.* Tidong [tid], 458

    dial. Tidong [tid], 395

N|oo, *alt. dial.* Shua [shg], 48

N|oo-Khwe, *dial.* Shua [shg], 48

Noocoona, *alt.* Nugunu [nnv], 575

Noogar, *alt. dial.* English [eng], 570

Noohalit, *dial.* Yupik, Central Siberian [ess], 507

Nooka Dora, *alt.* Mukha-Dora [mmk], 376

N||ookhwe, *alt. dial.* Shua [shg], 48

Nookoona, *alt.* Nugunu [nnv], 575

Nooksack [nok], 306

Nooli, *dial.* Santa Cruz [stc], 638

Noomaante, *alt.* Nomaande [lem], 70

Noon [snf], 181

Noone [nhu], 70

Noonga, *alt. dial.* English [eng], 570

Noongaburrah, *alt. dial.* Wangaaybuwan-Ngiyambaa [wyb], 577

Noongar, *alt. dial.* English [eng], 570

Nooni, *alt.* Noone [nhu], 70

Noord-Drents, *alt. dial.* Drents [drt], 548

Noosan, *alt. dial.* !Xóõ [nmn], 48, 151

Nootka [noo], 240

Nootre, *alt.* Notre [bly], 46

Nootsack, *alt.* Nooksack [nok], 306

Nop, *dial.* Koho [kpm], 524

Nopala Chatino, *see* Chatino, Nopala [cya], 259

Nopuk, *alt.* Kwerba Mamberamo [xwr], 418

Nopukw, *alt.* Kwerba Mamberamo [xwr], 418

Nor, *alt.* Mambila, Cameroon [mcu], 66

    alt. Mambila, Nigeria [mzk], 169

    alt. Murik [mtf], 615

Nor Tagbo, *alt.* Mambila, Nigeria [mzk], 169

Nor-Murik Lakes, *alt.* Murik [mtf], 615

Nora, *alt.* Norra [nrr], 466

    dial. Norra [nrr], 466

Nordfriesisch, *alt.* Frisian, Northern [frr], 538

Norfolk, *dial.* English [eng], 565

Norfolk English, *dial.* Pitcairn-Norfolk [pih], 586

Norgorod, *alt. dial.* Karelian [krl], 534

Norio, *dial.* Tolaki [lbw], 433

Norkhana, *dial.* Khana [ogo], 166

Normal Egyptian Arabic, *alt.* Arabic, Egyptian Spoken [arz], 110

Norman, *dial.* French [fra], 536

Normand, *alt. dial.* French [fra], 536

Norn [nrn], 565

Norra [nrr], 466

Norrland, *alt. dial.* Swedish [swe], 562

Nortenyo, *alt.* Buglere [sab], 283

    alt. Teribe [tfr], 284

North Agaw, *alt.* Bilen [byn], 112

North Akoko, *alt.* Arigidi [aqg], 154

North Alaskan Inupiat, *alt.* Inupiatun, North Alaskan [esi], 302, 238

North Alaskan Inupiatun, *see* Inupiatun, North Alaskan [esi], 302, 238

North Albanian, *dial.* Romani, Vlax [rmy], 551

North Ambrym, *see* Ambrym, North [mmg], 640

North Asmat, *see* Asmat, North [nks], 411

North Auckland, *dial.* Maori [mri], 586

North Aunalei, *dial.* One, Molmo [aun], 620

North Awin, *dial.* Aekyom [awi], 587

North Awyu, *see* Awyu, North [yir], 412

North Azerbaijani, *see* Azerbaijani, North [azj], 319, 319

North Babar, *see* Babar, North [bcd], 396

North Balasore Oriya, *dial.* Oriya [ori], 382

North Bangato, *dial.* Bangandu [bgf], 88

North Bavarian, *dial.* Bavarian [bar], 530, 533, 538, 543

North Beami, *dial.* Beami [beo], 593

North Belgium Sign Language, *dial.* Belgian Sign Language [bvs], 530

North Belu, *alt. dial.* Tetun [tet], 410, 351

North Binja, *dial.* Songoora [sod], 108

North Bobe, *dial.* Bube [bvb], 110

North Bolivian Quechua, *see* Quechua, North Bolivian [qul], 223

North Bolivian Quechua, *dial.* Quechua, Puno [qxp], 292

North Borneo Murut, *alt. dial.* Tagal Murut [mvv], 458, 395

North Bunun, *dial.* Bunun [bnn], 511

North Burma Khamti, *dial.* Khamti [kht], 465, 367

North Buru, *alt.* Lisela [lcl], 400

North Central Fore, *dial.* Fore [for], 599

North Central Mixe, *see* Mixe, North Central [neq], 265

North Central Nochixtlán Mixtec, *alt.* Mixtec, Tidaá [mtx], 269

North Central Tarangan, *dial.* Tarangan, West [txn], 404

North Central Yuri, *dial.* Karkar-Yuri [yuj], 603

North Central Zimatlan Zapotec, *alt.* Zapotec, Asunción Mixtepec [zoo], 277

North Chollado, *alt. dial.* Korean [kor], 448

North Ch'ungch'ong, *alt. dial.* Korean [kor], 448

North Coast Mengen, *dial.* Mengen [mee], 613

North Coastal Alune, *dial.* Alune [alp], 396

North Damar, *alt.* Damar, West [drn], 397

North Delta Arabic, *dial.* Arabic, Egyptian Spoken [arz], 110

North Dogri, *dial.* Dogri [dgo], 360

North Drente, *dial.* Drents [drt], 548

North Efate, *see* Efate, North [llp], 641

North Fali, *see* Fali, North [fll], 61

North Finnish, *alt.* Finnish, Kven [fkv], 549
alt. Finnish, Tornedalen [fit], 561

North Giziga, *see* Giziga, North [gis], 62

North Greenlandic, *alt. dial.* Inuktitut, Greenlandic [kal], 252

North Gurage, *alt.* Kistane [gru], 116

North Hamgyongdo, *alt. dial.* Korean [kor], 448

North Hewa, *dial.* Hewa [ham], 602

North Hiberno English, *dial.* English [eng], 542

North Hijazi, *dial.* Arabic, Hijazi Spoken [acw], 508

North Hpon, *dial.* Hpon [hpo], 464

North Ibanag, *dial.* Ibanag [ibg], 494

North Idoma, *alt.* Agatu [agc], 153

North Ile Ape, *dial.* Ile Ape [ila], 407

North Junín Quechua, *see* Quechua, North Junín [qvn], 291

North Kakabai, *dial.* Kakabai [kqf], 603

North Kamayo, *dial.* Kamayo [kyk], 498

North Kamberataro, *dial.* Dera [kbv], 597

North Kati, *alt.* Muyu, North [kti], 421

North Kerala, *dial.* Malayalam [mal], 374

North Khowar, *dial.* Khowar [khw], 486

North Kitui, *dial.* Kamba [kam], 133

North Koma, *alt.* Kwama [kmq], 116

North Kombio, *dial.* Kombio [xbi], 607

North Komedia, *dial.* Armenian [hye], 318

North Konkan, *alt.* Konkani [knn], 369

North Kordofan Arabic, *dial.* Arabic, Sudanese Spoken [apd], 188

North Korowai, *see* Korowai, North [krg], 418

North Kwandu, *dial.* Mashi [mho], 214, 41, 150

North Kyongsangdo, *alt. dial.* Korean [kor], 448

North la Paz Quechua, *alt.* Quechua, North Bolivian [qul], 223

North Laamang, *dial.* Lamang [hia], 168

North Lancashire, *dial.* English [eng], 565

North Lebanese Arabic, *dial.* Arabic, North Levantine Spoken [apc], 453

North Lele, *alt. dial.* Lele [llc], 129

North Levantine Arabic, *alt.* Arabic, North Levantine Spoken [apc], 510

North Levantine Bedawi Arabic, *dial.* Arabic, Eastern Egyptian Bedawi Spoken [avl], 110
dial. Arabic, Levantine Bedawi Spoken [avl], 448, 489

North Levantine Spoken Arabic, *see* Arabic, North Levantine Spoken [apc], 510, 453

North Lole, *dial.* Lole [llg], 408

North Loloda, *alt.* Loloda [loa], 401

North Maewo, *alt.* Marino [mrb], 643

North Makaa, *alt.* Byep [mkk], 59

North Malo, *alt. dial.* Malo [mla], 643

North Marquesan, *see* Marquesan, North [mrq], 581

North Mbundu, *alt.* Mbundu [kmb], 41

North Mekeo, *alt. dial.* Mekeo [mek], 613

North Mesopotamian Spoken Arabic, *see* Arabic, North Mesopotamian Spoken [ayp], 442, 510, 518

North Mianmin, *alt.* Suganga [sug], 625

North Migabac, *dial.* Migabac [mpp], 614

North Modole, *dial.* Modole [mqo], 402

North Moejoe, *alt.* Muyu, North [kti], 421

North Mofu, *see* Mofu, North [mfk], 67

North Moluccan Malay, *see* Malay, North Moluccan [max], 401

North Muyu, *see* Muyu, North [kti], 421

North Najdi, *dial.* Arabic, Najdi Spoken [ars], 508, 442

North Nakama, *dial.* Nakama [nib], 616

North Ngalik, *alt.* Yali, Ninia [nlk], 426
alt. Yali, Pass Valley [yac], 426

North Northern Paiute, *dial.* Paiute, Northern [pao], 306

North Nuaulu, *see* Nuaulu, North [nni], 402

North Nuk, *dial.* Nuk [noc], 618

North Nyali, *alt.* Nyali [nlj], 106

North Olo, *alt. dial.* Olo [ong], 619

North Paama, *dial.* Paama [pma], 644

North Permyak, *dial.* Komi-Permyak [koi], 555

North Puebla Aztec, *alt.* Nahuatl, Northern Puebla [ncj], 271

North P'yong'ando, *alt. dial.* Korean [kor], 448

North Qatari Arabic, *dial.* Arabic, Gulf Spoken [afb], 503

North Quchani, *dial.* Khorasani Turkish [kmz], 439

North Raga, *alt.* Hano [lml], 642

North Russian, *dial.* Russian [rus], 556

North Russian Romani, *dial.* Romani, Baltic [rml], 550, 546

North Saami, *see* Saami, North [sme], 550, 535, 561

North Saiset, *alt. dial.* Saisiyat [xsy], 512

North Sakhalin Gilyak, *dial.* Gilyak [niv], 504

North Sasak, *alt. dial.* Sasak [sas], 409

North Selepet, *dial.* Selepet [spl], 623

North Sena, *alt. dial.* Sena [seh], 149

North Siberut, *dial.* Mentawai [mwv], 436

North Slavey, *see* Slavey, North [scs], 241

North Slope Inupiatun, *dial.* Inupiatun, North Alaskan [esi], 302, 238

North Small Nambas, *dial.* Mae [mme], 643

North Syrian Arabic, *alt.* Arabic, Mesopotamian Spoken [acm], 510

North Tabasaran, *alt. dial.* Tabassaran [tab], 555

North Tabukang, *dial.* Sangir [sxn], 432

North Tairora, *see* Tairora, North [tbg], 626

North Tanna, *see* Tanna, North [tnn], 645

North Tharaka, *alt. dial.* Tharaka [thk], 136

North Timbe, *dial.* Timbe [tim], 627

North Tugen, *see* Tugen, North [tuy], 136

North Tuken, *alt.* Tugen, North [tuy], 136

North Tuvaluan, *dial.* Tuvaluan [tvl], 640

North Udmurt, *dial.* Udmurt [udm], 557

North Urat, *alt. dial.* Urat [urt], 629

North Veluws, *dial.* Veluws [vel], 549

North Veps, *alt. dial.* Veps [vep], 557

North Wahgi, *see* Wahgi, North [whg], 630

North Waibuk, *dial.* Haruai [tmd], 601

North Watut, *see* Watut, North [una], 631

North Wemale, *see* Wemale, North [weo], 405

North Wiltshire, *dial.* English [eng], 565

North Yamdena, *dial.* Yamdena [jmd], 405

North Yawa, *dial.* Yawa [yva], 426

North Yorkshire, *dial.* English [eng], 565

North-Central Lebanese Arabic, *dial.* Arabic, North Levantine Spoken [apc], 453

North-South Udab, *dial.* Fuyug [fuy], 599

North-Western Tunisian, *dial.* Arabic, Tunisian Spoken [aeb], 209

Northeast Ambae, *alt.* Ambae, East [omb], 640

Northeast Ambon, *alt.* Tulehu [tlu], 405

Northeast Aoba, *alt.* Ambae, East [omb], 640

Northeast Awa, *dial.* Awa [awb], 591

Northeast Barito, *alt.* Lawangan [lbx], 394

Northeast Belarusan, *dial.* Belarusan [bel], 530

Northeast Bohemian, *dial.* Czech [ces], 533

Northeast Central Ijo, *alt.* Biseni [ije], 155

Northeast Duguri, *dial.* Duguri [dbm], 158

Northeast Egyptian Bedawi Arabic, *dial.* Arabic, Eastern Egyptian Bedawi Spoken [avl], 110

Northeast Florida Coast, *dial.* Sea Island Creole English [gul], 307

Northeast Fuyug, *dial.* Fuyug [fuy], 599

Northeast Hungarian, *dial.* Hungarian [hun], 542

Northeast Izere, *dial.* Izere [fiz], 164

Northeast Karakalpak, *dial.* Karakalpak [kaa], 316

Northeast Kiwai, *see* Kiwai, Northeast [kiw], 606

Northeast Lampung, *alt. dial.* Abung [abl], 435

Northeast Luba, *alt.* Songe [sop], 108

Northeast Luwu, *dial.* Tae' [rob], 428

Northeast Maidu, *see* Maidu, Northeast [nmu], 304

Northeast Pashayi, *see* Pashayi, Northeast [aee], 317

Northeast Quchani, *alt. dial.* Khorasani Turkish [kmz], 439

Northeast Sahaptin, *alt.* Walla Walla [waa], 309

Northeast Sasak, *alt. dial.* Sasak [sas], 409

Northeast Vanua Levu, *dial.* Fijian [fij], 580

Northeast Viti Levu, *dial.* Fijian [fij], 580

Northeastern Burkina Faso Fulfulde, *see* Fulfulde, Western Niger [fuh], 51

Northeastern Dian Hmong, *see* Hmong, Northeastern Dian [hmd], 334

Northeastern Dinka, *see* Dinka, Northeastern [dip], 189

Northeastern Goe, *alt. dial.* Samo, Maya [sym], 53

Northeastern Grebo, *dial.* Grebo, Northern [gbo], 138

Northeastern Jamiltepec Mixtec, *alt.* Mixtec, Ixtayutla [vmj], 267

Northeastern Jiarong, *alt. dial.* Jiarong [jya], 336

Northeastern Karakalpak, *dial.* Karakalpak [kaa], 521

Northeastern Kazakh, *dial.* Kazakh [kaz], 448, 316, 337

Northeastern Krumen, *alt.* Krumen, Pye [pye], 93

Northeastern Kumauni, *dial.* Kumauni [kfy], 370

Northeastern Mairasi, *dial.* Mairasi [zrs], 419

Northeastern Mixe, *alt.* Mixe, North Central [neq], 265

Northeastern Mongolian, *alt.* Buriat, China [bxu], 329

Northeastern Otomí, *alt.* Otomi, Texcatepec [otx], 273

Northeastern Pashto, *dial.* Pashto, Northern [pbu], 488

Northeastern Pomo, *see* Pomo, Northeastern [pef], 307

Northeastern Pwo Karen, *alt.* Karen, Phrae Pwo [kjt], 514

Northeastern Samo, *alt.* Samo, Maya [sym], 53

Northeastern Sardinian, *alt.* Sardinian, Gallurese [sdn], 545

Northeastern Teke, *alt.* Ngungwel [ngz], 89

Northeastern Thai, *see* Thai, Northeastern [tts], 517

Northeastern Tuvin, *dial.* Tuvin [tyv], 507

Northeastern Yautepec Zapotec, *alt.* Zapotec, Quiavicuzas [zpj], 279

Northeastern Yiddish, *dial.* Yiddish, Eastern [ydd], 446

Northeastern Yunnan Miao, *alt.* Hmong, Northeastern Dian [hmd], 334

Northern Afar, *dial.* Afar [aar], 112, 111

Northern Akhvakh, *alt. dial.* Akhvakh [akv], 552

Northern Alberta Cree, *dial.* Cree, Plains [crk], 236

Northern Alta, *see* Alta, Northern [aqn], 491

Northern Altai, *see* Altai, Northern [atv], 503

Northern Amami-Oshima, *see* Amami-Oshima, Northern [ryn], 446

Northern Amami-Osima, *alt.* Amami-Oshima, Northern [ryn], 446

Northern Ambakich, *dial.* Ambakich [aew], 589

Northern Amis, *alt. dial.* Amis [ami], 511

Northern Arequipa, *alt. dial.* Quechua, Arequipa-La Unión [qxu], 289

Northern Avar, *alt. dial.* Avar [ava], 553

Northern Awu Yi, *dial.* Yi, Awu [yiu], 347

Northern Bai, *see* Bai, Northern [bfc], 327

Northern Baima, *dial.* Baima [bqh], 327

Northern Bakossi, *dial.* Akoose [bss], 56

Northern Balong, *alt. dial.* Kenyang [ken], 64

Northern Bangantu, *alt. dial.* Mpongmpong [mgg], 68

Northern Bantawa, *dial.* Bantawa [bap], 468

Northern Barasano, *alt.* Waimaha [bao], 248, 233

Northern Bashaka, *dial.* Bashkardi [bsg], 438

Northern Bété, *alt.* Bété, Daloa [bev], 92

Northern Betsimisaraka Malagasy, *see* Malagasy, Northern Betsimisaraka [bmm], 140

Northern Birifor, *alt.* Birifor, Malba [bfo], 49

Northern Bobo Madaré, *see* Bobo Madaré, Northern [bbo], 49, 141

Northern Bolon, *alt. dial.* Bolon [bof], 49

Northern Bomitaba, *dial.* Bomitaba [zmx], 88

Northern Buduma, *dial.* Buduma [bdm], 79

Northern Bullom, *alt.* Bullom So [buy], 183, 129

Northern Cagayan Negrito, *alt.* Atta, Pamplona [att], 491

Northern Cakchiquel, *alt.* Kaqkchikel, Northern [ckc], 254

Northern Calabrese-Lucano, *dial.* Napoletano-Calabrese [nap], 545

Northern Catanduanes Bicolano, *see* Bicolano, Northern Catanduanes [cts], 493

Northern Central America Creole English, *alt.* Belize Kriol English [bzj], 221

Northern Chatino, *alt.* Chatino, Zenzontepec [czn], 260

Northern Chinese, *alt.* Chinese, Mandarin [cmn], 329, 461

Northern Chumburung, *dial.* Chumburung [ncu], 124

Northern Cluster Lishán Didán, *dial.* Lishán Didán [trg], 445

Northern Conchucos Ancash Quechua, *see* Quechua, Northern Conchucos Ancash [qxn], 291

Northern Conchucos Quechua, *alt.* Quechua, Northern Conchucos Ancash [qxn], 291

Northern Corsican, *dial.* Corsican [cos], 536

Northern Crimean, *dial.* Crimean Turkish [crh], 521, 518, 532, 551

Northern Cuona, *dial.* Moinba [mob], 340

Northern Dagaare, *alt.* Dagara, Northern [dgi], 50

Northern Dagara, *see* Dagara, Northern [dgi], 50

Northern Dibole, *dial.* Dibole [bvx], 88

Northern Dobel, *dial.* Dobel [kvo], 397

Northern Dong, *see* Dong, Northern [doc], 331

Northern Dos de Mayo, *dial.* Quechua, Huamalíes-Dos de Mayo Huánuco [qvh], 291

Northern East Cree, *see* East Cree, Northern [crl], 237

Northern East-Guizhou Miao, *alt.* Hmong, Northern Qiandong [hea], 335

Northern Eastern James Bay Cree, *alt.* East Cree, Northern [crl], 237

Northern Emberá, *see* Emberá, Northern [emp], 283, 245

Northern Estonian, *alt. dial.* Estonian [est], 534

Northern Extremaduran, *dial.* Extremaduran [ext], 560

Northern Fania, *dial.* Fania [fni], 80

Northern Foothill Yokuts, *dial.* Yokuts [yok], 310

Northern Frisian, *see* Frisian, Northern [frr], 538

Northern Fungom, *alt. dial.* Mmen [bfm], 67

Northern Gabri, *alt.* Tobanga [tng], 87

Northern Ghale, *see* Ghale, Northern [ghh], 471

Northern Gikuyu, *dial.* Gikuyu [kik], 133

Northern Gondi, *see* Gondi, Northern [gno], 362

Northern Gourmanchema, *dial.* Gourmanchéma [gux], 51

Northern Grebo, *see* Grebo, Northern [gbo], 138

Northern Guangdong, *alt. dial.* Chinese, Hakka [hak], 329

Northern Guiyang Hmong, *see* Hmong, Northern Guiyang [huj], 334

Northern Guiyang Miao, *alt.* Hmong, Northern Guiyang [huj], 334

Northern Gunu, *dial.* Nugunu [yas], 70

Northern Gurung, *alt.* Manangba [nmm], 475

Northern Haida, *see* Haida, Northern [hdn], 238, 301

Northern Hanga, *dial.* Hanga [hag], 125

Northern Heiltsuk, *alt. dial.* Heiltsuk [hei], 238

Northern Highland Mazatec, *alt.* Mazatec, San Jerónimo Tecóatl [maa], 265

Northern Hindko, *see* Hindko, Northern [hno], 485

Northern Huishui Hmong, *see* Hmong, Northern Huishui [hmi], 334

Northern Huishui Miao, *alt.* Hmong, Northern Huishui [hmi], 334

Northern Irish, *alt. dial.* Gaelic, Irish [gle], 542

Northern Irula, *dial.* Irula [iru], 365

Northern Isan, *dial.* Thai, Northeastern [tts], 517

Northern Isthmus Zapotec, *alt.* Zapotec, Guevea de Humboldt [zpg], 278

Northern James Bay Cree, *alt.* East Cree, Northern [crl], 237

Northern Kalasha, *dial.* Kalasha [kls], 486

Northern Kalinga, *alt.* Kalinga, Limos [kmk], 497

Northern Kankanay, *see* Kankanay, Northern [xnn], 498

Northern Kaqkchikel, *see* Kaqkchikel, Northern [ckc], 254

Northern Karelian, *dial.* Karelian [krl], 555, 534

Northern Katkari, *dial.* Katkari [kfu], 367

Northern Khams, *dial.* Tibetan, Khams [khg], 345

Northern Khanti, *dial.* Khanty [kca], 505

Northern Khmer, *see* Khmer, Northern [kxm], 515

Northern Kirghiz, *dial.* Kirghiz [kir], 449, 337

Northern Kirinyaga, *alt. dial.* Gikuyu [kik], 133

Northern Kissi, *see* Kissi, Northern [kqs], 129, 183

Northern Kono, *dial.* Kono [kno], 183

Northern Kpele, *alt.* Kpelle, Guinea [gkp], 129

Northern Krahn, *alt.* Krahn, Western [krw], 138, 93

Northern Kurdish, *see* Kurdish, Northern [kmr], 519, 319, 319, 352, 440, 443, 453, 510

Northern Kutai, *dial.* Malay, Tenggarong Kutai [vkt], 394

Northern Lahu, *alt. dial.* Lahu [lhu], 338, 451, 465, 515

Northern Lapp, *alt.* Saami, North [sme], 535

Northern Lappish, *alt.* Saami, North [sme], 561
pej. alt. Saami, North [sme], 550
pej. alt. Saami, South [sma], 550

Northern Lawa, *alt.* Lawa, Eastern [lwl], 515

Northern Lela, *alt. dial.* C'lela [dri], 157

Northern Lengua, *dial.* Lengua [leg], 284

Northern Limba, *dial.* Limba, East [lma], 129, 183

Northern Logo, *alt. dial.* Logo [log], 103

Northern Logudorese, *dial.* Sardinian, Logudorese [src], 545

Northern Lorung, *see* Lorung, Northern [lbr], 474

Northern Low Saxon, *dial.* Saxon, Low [nds], 539

Northern Luba, *alt.* Luna [luj], 103

Northern Lunda, *alt.* Ruund [rnd], 107, 41

Northern Luri, *see* Luri, Northern [lrc], 440

Northern Lushootseed, *dial.* Lushootseed [lut], 304

Northern Lyélé, *dial.* Lyélé [lee], 52

Northern Macedonian, *dial.* Macedonian [mkd], 547

Northern Magahi, *dial.* Magahi [mag], 373

Northern Malimiut Inupiatun, *dial.* Inupiatun, Northwest Alaska [esk], 302

Northern Mam, *see* Mam, Northern [mam], 255, 262

Northern Mamasa, *dial.* Mamasa [mqj], 431

Northern Mandarin, *alt. dial.* Chinese, Mandarin [cmn], 329

Northern Mao, *alt.* Bambassi [myf], 113

Northern Marik, *dial.* Marik [dad], 612

Northern Marwari, *dial.* Marwari [mve], 487

Northern Masalit, *dial.* Masalit [mls], 83

Northern Mashan Hmong, *see* Hmong, Northern Mashan [hmp], 335

Northern Mashan Miao, *alt.* Hmong, Northern Mashan [hmp], 335

Northern Mbene, *alt.* Basaa [bas], 58

Northern Mbula, *dial.* Mbula [mna], 612

Northern Micmac, *dial.* Micmac [mic], 239

Northern Min, *alt.* Chinese, Min Bei [mnp], 330

Northern Mon, *alt. dial.* Mon [mnw], 466

Northern Mongolian, *alt.* Buriat, China [bxu], 329
alt. Buriat, Mongolia [bxm], 461
alt. Buriat, Russia [bxr], 504

Northern Monpa, *alt. dial.* Moinba [mob], 376

Northern Motilón, *alt.* Yukpa [yup], 248, 313

Northern Muna, *alt. dial.* Muna [mnb], 431

Northern Munji, *dial.* Munji [mnj], 316

Northern Murang'a, *alt. dial.* Gikuyu [kik], 133

Northern Nambikuára, *see* Nambikuára, Northern [mbg], 230

Northern Nande, *alt.* Nande [nnb], 105

Northern Ndam, *alt. dial.* Ndam [ndm], 85

Northern Ndebele, *alt.* Ndebele [nde], 216, 48

Northern Ngbandi, *see* Ngbandi, Northern [ngb], 105

Northern Ninam, *dial.* Ninam [shb], 230, 312

Northern Nochixtlán Mixtec, *alt.* Mixtec, Apasco-Apoala [mip], 266

Northern North Hollandish, *dial.* Dutch [nld], 548

Northern Nuni, *see* Nuni, Northern [nuv], 53

Northern Nusu, *dial.* Nusu [nuf], 341

Northern Oaxaca Mixtec, *alt.* Mixtec, Chazumba [xtb], 266

Northern Oaxaca Nahuatl, *see* Nahuatl, Northern Oaxaca [nhy], 271

Northern Ogambi, *dial.* Avokaya [avu], 96

Northern Ohlone, *see* Ohlone, Northern [cst], 306

Northern Ojibwa, *alt.* Ojibwa, Northwestern [ojb], 240
alt. Ojibwa, Severn [ojs], 240

Northern One, *see* One, Northern [onr], 620

Northern Orok, *alt. dial.* Orok [oaa], 506

Northern Paiute, *see* Paiute, Northern [pao], 306

Northern Pame, *see* Pame, Northern [pmq], 273

Northern Pa'o, *dial.* Karen, Pa'o [blk], 464

Northern Pashto, *see* Pashto, Northern [pbu], 488, 317, 520

Northern Pastaza Quichua, *see* Quichua, Northern Pastaza [qvz], 251, 293

Northern Phalura, *dial.* Phalura [phl], 488

Northern Pomo, *see* Pomo, Northern [pej], 307

Northern Popoloca, *alt.* Popoloca, San Marcos Tlalcoyalco [pls], 274

Northern Puebla Nahuatl, *see* Nahuatl, Northern Puebla [ncj], 271

Northern Puget Sound Salish, *alt. dial.* Lushootseed [lut], 304

Northern Pumi, *see* Pumi, Northern [pmi], 342

Northern Qiandong Hmong, *see* Hmong, Northern Qiandong [hea], 335

Northern Qiandong Miao, *alt.* Hmong, Northern Qiandong [hea], 335

Northern Qiang, *see* Qiang, Northern [cng], 342

Northern Quiché, *alt.* K'iche', Cunén [cun], 255

Northern Rengma, *alt.* Naga, Northern Rengma [nnl], 379

Northern Rengma Naga, *see* Naga, Northern Rengma [nnl], 379

Northern Roglai, *see* Roglai, Northern [rog], 526

Northern Romagnolo, *dial.* Emiliano-Romagnolo [eml], 543

Northern Saami, *alt.* Saami, North [sme], 550, 561

Northern Sagara, *alt.* Kagulu [kki], 199

Northern Sakai, *alt.* Temiar [tea], 455

Northern Sakalava, *dial.* Malagasy, Sakalava [skg], 140

Northern Sama, *alt.* Balangingi [sse], 492

Northern Samar, *dial.* Waray-Waray [war], 502

Northern Sangtam, *alt. dial.* Naga, Sangtam [nsa], 379

Northern Sani, *dial.* Yi, Sani [ysn], 347

Northern Saurashtra, *dial.* Saurashtra [saz], 386

Northern Scots, *dial.* Scots [sco], 566

Northern Seeku, *dial.* Seeku [sos], 54

Northern Sel'kup, *alt. dial.* Selkup [sel], 506

Northern Shan, *alt. dial.* Shan [shn], 467

Northern Shilha, *alt.* Tarifit [rif], 146, 40

Northern Shona, *alt. dial.* Shona [sna], 216, 215

Northern Shoshoni, *dial.* Shoshoni [shh], 308

Northern Sierra Miwok, *see* Miwok, Northern Sierra [nsq], 305

Northern Sinama, *alt.* Balangingi [sse], 492, 456

Northern Somali, *dial.* Somali [som], 185

Northern Soqotri, *dial.* Soqotri [sqt], 528

Northern Sorsogon, *alt.* Sorsogon, Masbate [bks], 501

Northern Sotho, *see* Sotho, Northern [nso], 186

Northern Standard Bhojpuri, *dial.* Bhojpuri [bho], 356

Northern Stieng, *alt.* Stieng, Bulo [sti], 526

Northern Stoney, *dial.* Stoney [sto], 241

Northern Subanen, *see* Subanen, Northern [stb], 501

Northern Swedish, *dial.* Swedish [swe], 562

Northern Tagdal, *alt. dial.* Tagdal [tda], 152

Northern Talyshi, *dial.* Talysh [tly], 442

Northern Tarahumara, *see* Tarahumara, Northern [thh], 274

Northern Tats, *dial.* Tat, Muslim [ttt], 556

Northern Taungthu, *alt.* Karen, Pa'o [blk], 464

Northern Tày, *dial.* Tày [tyz], 527

Northern Tehuelche, *alt.* Puelche [pue], 220

Northern Teke, *see* Teke-Tege [teg], 121

Northern Teke, *alt.* Teke-Tege [teg], 90

Northern Tepehuan, *see* Tepehuan, Northern [ntp], 275

Northern Tetun, *dial.* Tetun [tet], 410, 351

Northern Thai, *see* Thai, Northern [nod], 517, 453

Northern Thai, *alt.* Thai, Northern [nod], 517

Northern Thimphu, *dial.* Dzongkha [dzo], 323

Northern Thulung, *dial.* Thulung [tdh], 481

Northern Tiwa, *see* Tiwa, Northern [twf], 308

Northern Tlaxiaco Mixtec, *see* Mixtec, Northern Tlaxiaco [xtn], 267

Northern Toba, *dial.* Toba [tob], 220

Northern Totonac, *alt.* Totonac, Xicotepec de Juárez [too], 276

Northern Toussian, *see* Toussian, Northern [tsp], 55

Northern Tsakonian, *dial.* Tsakonian [tsd], 541

Northern Tujia, *see* Tujia, Northern [tji], 345

Northern Turkana, *dial.* Turkana [tuv], 137

Northern Tutchone, *see* Tutchone, Northern [ttm], 242

Northern Uma, *alt. dial.* Uma [ppk], 434

Northern Uzbek, *see* Uzbek, Northern [uzn], 512, 346

Northern Vietnamese, *dial.* Vietnamese [vie], 527

Northern Villa Alta Zapotec, *alt.* Zapotec, Rincón [zar], 279

Northern Vogul, *dial.* Mansi [mns], 505

Northern Welsh, *dial.* Welsh [cym], 566

Northern Yakha, *dial.* Yakha [ybh], 482

Northern Yali, *alt.* Yali, Angguruk [yli], 426

Northern Yana, *dial.* Yana [ynn], 310

Northern Yau, *dial.* Yau [yuw], 633

Northern Yawuru, *dial.* Yawuru [ywr], 579

Northern Yemeni Arabic, *alt.* Arabic, Sanaani Spoken [ayn], 528

Northern Yi, *alt.* Yi, Sichuan [iii], 348

Northern Yukaghir, *see* Yukaghir, Northern [ykg], 507

Northern Yukagir, *alt.* Yukaghir, Northern [ykg], 507

Northern Zaza, *alt.* Kirmanjki [kiu], 518

Northern Zeme, *alt.* Naga, Mzieme [nme], 379

Northern Zhuang, *see* Zhuang, Northern [ccx], 349

Northumberland, *dial.* English [eng], 565

Northwest Alaska Inupiat, *alt.* Inupiatun, Northwest Alaska [esk], 302

Northwest Alaska Inupiatun, *see* Inupiatun, Northwest Alaska [esk], 302

Northwest Gbaya, *see* Gbaya, Northwest [gya], 75, 61, 160

Northwest Gbaya, *alt.* Gbaya [gya], 88

Northwest Hungarian, *dial.* Hungarian [hun], 542

Northwest Izere, *dial.* Izere [fiz], 164

Northwest Jujuy, *dial.* Quechua, South Bolivian [quh], 223, 220

Northwest Lampung, *alt. dial.* Abung [abl], 435

Northwest Maidu, *see* Maidu, Northwest [mjd], 304

Northwest Marind, *alt.* Marind, Bian [bpv], 419

Northwest Mekeo, *alt. dial.* Mekeo [mek], 613

Northwest Oaxaca Mixtec, *see* Mixtec, Northwest Oaxaca [mxa], 268

Northwest Pashayi, *see* Pashayi, Northwest [glh], 317

Northwest Quchani, *alt. dial.* Khorasani Turkish [kmz], 439

Northwest Ukrainian, *dial.* Ukrainian [ukr], 564

Northwestern, *dial.* Tamang, Western [tdg], 480

Northwestern Arvanitika, *dial.* Albanian, Arvanitika [aat], 540

Northwestern Catalan, *alt. dial.* Catalan-Valencian-Balear [cat], 559

Northwestern Dinka, *see* Dinka, Northwestern [diw], 190

Northwestern Fars, *see* Fars, Northwestern [faz], 439

Northwestern Gurung, *dial.* Gurung, Western [gvr], 471

Northwestern Jiarong, *alt. dial.* Jiarong [jya], 336

Northwestern Karaim, *dial.* Karaim [kdr], 546

Northwestern Kolami, *see* Kolami, Northwestern [kfb], 369

Northwestern Mandarin, *alt. dial.* Chinese, Mandarin [cmn], 329

Northwestern Maninka, *alt.* Maninkakan, Western [mlq], 122, 143

Northwestern Mixe, *alt.* Mixe, Totontepec [mto], 265

Northwestern Nuni. **Northeastern Nuni**, *dial.* Nuni, Northern [nuv], 53

Northwestern Ojibwa, *see* Ojibwa, Northwestern [ojb], 240

Northwestern Oriya, *dial.* Oriya [ori], 382

Northwestern Otomi, *alt.* Otomi, Querétaro [otq], 272

Northwestern Pakhto, *dial.* Pashto, Northern [pbu], 317

Northwestern Pochutla Zapotec, *alt.* Zapotec, San Baltazar Loxicha [zpx], 279

Northwestern Samo, *alt.* Samo, Matya [stj], 53

Northwestern Sardinian, *alt.* Sardinian, Sassarese [sdc], 545

Northwestern Tamang, *see* Tamang, Northwestern [tmk], 479

Northwestern Tehuantepec Zapotec, *alt.* Zapotec, Lachiguiri [zpa], 278

Northwestern Yautepec Zapotec, *alt.* Zapotec, Yautepec [zpb], 281

Northwestern Yiddish, *dial.* Yiddish, Western [yih], 540

Norwegian, *alt.* Norwegian, Bokmål [nob], 549
alt. Norwegian, Nynorsk [nno], 549

Norwegian Lapp, *pej. alt.* Saami, North [sme], 550
pej. alt. Saami, South [sma], 550

Norwegian Saami, *alt.* Saami, North [sme], 561

Norwegian Sign Language [nsl], 549

Norwegian Traveller, *alt.* Norwegian, Traveller [rmg], 550

Norwegian, Bokmål [nob], 549

Norwegian, Nynorsk [nno], 549

Norwegian, Traveller [rmg], 550

Notozer, *dial.* Saami, Skolt [sms], 556

Notre [bly], 46

Notsi [ncf], 618

Nottoway [ntw], 306

Notu, *alt.* Ewage-Notu [nou], 598

Noumoudara-Koumoudara, *dial.* Tiéfo [tiq], 55

Nouna, *dial.* Marka [rkm], 52

Nouni, *alt.* Nuni, Northern [nuv], 53
alt. Nuni, Southern [nnw], 53

Nounouma, *alt.* Nuni, Northern [nuv], 53
alt. Nuni, Southern [nnw], 53

Nova Scotian Sign Language, *alt.* Maritime Sign Language [nsr], 239

Novara, *alt. dial.* Lombard [lmo], 544

Novarese Lombard, *alt. dial.* Lombard [lmo], 544

Novgorod, *alt. dial.* Karelian [krl], 555

Novouygur, *alt.* Uyghur [uig], 448

Nowai, *dial.* Tanna, Southwest [nwi], 645

Nowgong, *alt.* Naga, Ao [njo], 377

Noy [noy], 86

Noza, *alt.* Norra [nrr], 466

Npongué, *alt. dial.* Myene [mye], 121

Npongwe, *alt. dial.* Myene [mye], 121

Nrebele, *alt.* Ndebele [nbl], 186

Nruanghmei, *alt.* Naga, Rongmei [nbu], 379

Nsa, *dial.* Igbo [ibo], 163

Nsadop, *dial.* Bokyi [bky], 156

N'sakara, *alt.* Nzakara [nzk], 77, 106

Nsare, *alt. dial.* Mbembe, Tigon [nza], 66

Nsari [asj], 70

Nsaw, *alt.* Lamnso' [lns], 65, 168

Nsei, *alt.* Kenswei Nsei [ndb], 64

Nsele, *dial.* Nde-Nsele-Nta [ndd], 170

Nsenga [nse], 215, 148, 216
dial. Nsenga [nse], 215

Nshi [nsc], 171

Nsho', *alt.* Lamnso' [lns], 65, 168

Nsihaa, *dial.* Sisaala, Tumulung [sil], 127

Nsimbwa, *dial.* Mwani [wmw], 148

Nsindak, *alt.* Simba [sbw], 121

Nsit, *dial.* Ibibio [ibb], 162

Nso, *alt.* Lamnso' [lns], 65, 168

Nso', *alt.* Lamnso' [lns], 65, 168

Nsongo [nsx], 41

Nsongwa, *alt. dial.* Ngemba [nge], 69

Nsose, *alt.* Bassossi [bsi], 58

Nsuka, *dial.* Igbo [ibo], 163

Nsungali, *alt.* Limbum [lmp], 65

Nsungli, *alt.* Limbum [lmp], 65

Nsungni, *alt.* Limbum [lmp], 65

Nsur, *alt.* Sur [tdl], 175

Nswase, *alt.* Bassossi [bsi], 58

Nswose, *alt.* Bassossi [bsi], 58

Nta, *alt. dial.* Nde-Nsele-Nta [ndd], 170

Ntaapum, *dial.* Ntcham [bud], 209

Ntau, *alt.* Bobot [bty], 397

Ntcham [bud], 209, 127

Ntem, *dial.* Yamba [yam], 73

Ntenyi, *alt.* Naga, Northern Rengma [nnl], 379

Ntenyi Naga, *alt.* Naga, Northern Rengma [nnl], 379

Nthali, *alt. dial.* Tumbuka [tum], 141
dial. Tumbuka [tum], 215

Nthenyi, *alt.* Naga, Northern Rengma [nnl], 379

Ntii, *dial.* Fe'fe' [fmp], 61

Ntili, *dial.* Fipa [fip], 198

Ntlakapmuk, *alt.* Thompson [thp], 242

Ntogapid, *alt.* Karo [arr], 228

Ntogapig, *alt.* Karo [arr], 228

Ntoleh, *dial.* Ligbi [lig], 126

Ntomba [nto], 106
dial. Ntomba [nto], 106

Ntomba-Bikoro, *dial.* Mongo-Nkundu [lol], 104
Ntomba-Bolia, *alt.* Ntomba [nto], 106
Ntomba-Inongo, *dial.* Mongo-Nkundu [lol], 104
Ntong, *dial.* Yamba [yam], 73
Ntoumou, *dial.* Fang [fan], 61
Ntribou, *alt.* Delo [ntr], 124, 207
Ntribu, *alt.* Delo [ntr], 124, 207
Ntrubo, *alt.* Delo [ntr], 124, 207
Ntshanti, *alt.* Ncane [ncr], 69
Ntsiam, *dial.* Mfinu [zmf], 104
Ntswar, *dial.* Mfinu [zmf], 104
Ntugi, *dial.* Tharaka [thk], 136
Ntum, *alt. dial.* Fang [fan], 111
 dial. Fang [fan], 88, 120
Ntumba, *alt.* Ntomba [nto], 106
Ntumu, *alt. dial.* Fang [fan], 111, 61
N|u [ngh], 186
 dial. N|u [ngh], 186
Nu, *alt.* Nung [nun], 466, 341
Nu Baca, *alt.* Nubaca [baf], 70
Nu Gunu, *alt.* Nugunu [yas], 70
Nu Mhou, *alt. dial.* Bunu, Bu-Nao [bwx], 328
Nu River, *dial.* Drung [duu], 332
Nu-San, *alt. dial.* !Xóõ [nmn], 48, 151
Nua, *alt.* Yuaga [nua], 585
Nuadhu, *alt.* Como Karim [cfg], 157
Nuakata, *alt.* 'Auhelawa [kud], 591
Nuangeya, *alt.* Nyang'i [nyp], 212
Nuasue, *alt.* Elip [ekm], 60
 alt. Mmaala [mmu], 67
 alt. Yangben [yav], 72
Nuaulu, *alt.* Nuaulu, North [nni], 402
 alt. Nuaulu, South [nxl], 402
Nuaulu, North [nni], 402
Nuaulu, South [nxl], 402
Nub, *alt.* Mandobo Atas [aax], 419
 alt. Mandobo Bawah [bwp], 419
Nubaca [baf], 70
Nubama, *alt.* Kamo [kcq], 166
Nubi [kcn], 212, 135
Nubia, *dial.* Awar [aya], 591
Nubra Ladakhi, *dial.* Ladakhi [lbj], 372, 338
Nubri [kte], 477
Nubwa, *dial.* Moro [mor], 193
Nuchen, *alt.* Jurchen [juc], 335
Nuclear Western Fijian, *dial.* Fijian, Western [wyy], 580
Nucum, *alt.* Boikin [bzf], 594
Nudoo, *dial.* Vute [vut], 73
|Nu||en, *alt. dial.* !Xóõ [nmn], 48, 151
N|u||en, *alt.* N|u [ngh], 186
Nu||en, *alt. dial.* !Xóõ [nmn], 48, 151
Nuer [nus], 194, 117

Nufawa, *alt.* Nupe-Nupe-Tako [nup], 171
Nufi, *alt.* Fe'fe' [fmp], 61
Nufoor, *alt.* Biak [bhw], 412
Nugane, *dial.* Vute [vut], 73
Nugbo, *dial.* Godié [god], 93
Nuguna, *alt.* Nugunu [nnv], 575
Nugunu (Australia) [nnv], 575
 Nugunu (Cameroon) [yas], 70
Nuguor, *alt.* Nukuoro [nkr], 583
Nuguria, *alt.* Nukuria [nur], 619
Nuhiro, *dial.* Bamu [bcf], 592
Nui, *dial.* Kiribati [gil], 640
Nuian, *alt. dial.* Kiribati [gil], 640
Nujiang, *dial.* Bai, Northern [bfc], 327
Nujum, *dial.* Vute [vut], 73
Nuk [noc], 618
Nuka-Dora, *alt.* Mukha-Dora [mmk], 376
Nukak Makú [mbr], 246
Nukana, *alt.* Nugunu [nnv], 575
Nukapu, *dial.* Pileni [piv], 637
Nukha, *dial.* Azerbaijani, North [azj], 319, 319
Nukna [klt], 619
Nukoro, *alt.* Nukuoro [nkr], 583
Nuku, *alt.* Mehek [nux], 613
Nuku Hiva, *dial.* Marquesan, North [mrq], 581
Nukufetau, *alt. dial.* Tuvaluan [tvl], 640
Nukuini [nuc], 231
Nukulaelae, *alt. dial.* Tuvaluan [tvl], 640
Nukuma, *dial.* Kwoma [kmo], 609
Nukumanu [nuq], 619
Nukuna, *alt.* Nugunu [nnv], 575
Nukunnu, *alt.* Nugunu [nnv], 575
Nukunu, *alt.* Nugunu [nnv], 575
Nukunukubara, *alt.* Wakawaka [wkw], 577
Nukuoro [nkr], 583
Nukuria [nur], 619
Nulibie, *alt.* Elip [ekm], 60
Nulu, *dial.* Rungus [drg], 458
Numadaw, *alt.* Dogon, Bangeri Me [dba], 142
Numana, *dial.* Numana-Nunku-Gbantu-Numbu [nbr], 171
Numana-Nunku-Gbantu-Numbu [nbr], 171
Numand, *alt.* Nomaande [lem], 70
Numangan, *alt.* Numanggang [nop], 619
Numangang, *alt.* Numanggang [nop], 619
Numanggang [nop], 619
Numao, *dial.* Bunu, Bu-Nao [bwx], 328

Numba, *dial.* Ese [mcq], 598
Numbami [sij], 619
Numbu, *dial.* Numana-Nunku-Gbantu-Numbu [nbr], 171
Nume [tgs], 644
Numee [kdk], 585
 dial. Numee [kdk], 585
Numg, *alt.* Rawang [raw], 385
Ñumí Mixtec, *alt.* Mixtec, Northern Tlaxiaco [xtn], 267
Numurana, *alt.* Omurano [omu], 289
Ñuñ, *alt.* Bainouk-Gunyaamolo [bcz], 179
Nuna, *alt.* Koorete [kqy], 116
 alt. Nuni, Northern [nuv], 53
 alt. Nuni, Southern [nnw], 53
Nundoro, *alt.* Ndoola [ndr], 171, 69
Nune, *alt.* Nuni, Northern [nuv], 53
 alt. Nuni, Southern [nnw], 53
Nung (Myanmar) [nun], 466, 341
 Nung (Viet Nam) [nut], 525, 452
 alt. Chinese, Yue [yue], 522
 alt. Rawang [raw], 466
Nùng An, *dial.* Nung [nut], 525
Nùng Cháo, *dial.* Nung [nut], 525
Nùng Fan Slihng, *alt. dial.* Nung [nut], 525
Nùng Inh, *dial.* Nung [nut], 525
Nùng Lòi, *dial.* Nung [nut], 525
Nùng Phan Slình, *dial.* Nung [nut], 525
Nùng Qúy Rin, *dial.* Nung [nut], 525
Nung Rawang, *alt.* Rawang [raw], 466, 385
Nung Ven, *alt.* En [enc], 522
Nungali [nug], 575
Nunggubuju, *alt.* Nunggubuyu [nuy], 575
Nunggubuyu [nuy], 575
Nungu [rin], 171
Nunguda, *alt.* Longuda [lnu], 169
Nungura, *alt.* Longuda [lnu], 169
Nunguraba, *alt.* Longuda [lnu], 169
Nuni, Northern [nuv], 53
Nuni, Southern [nnw], 53
Nuniali, *alt.* Lisabata-Nuniali [lcs], 400
 dial. Lisabata-Nuniali [lcs], 400
Nunku, *dial.* Numana-Nunku-Gbantu-Numbu [nbr], 171
Nunligranskij, *dial.* Chukot [ckt], 504
Nünpa, *alt.* Lepcha [lep], 372, 323, 474
Nunu, *dial.* Bunu, Bu-Nao [bwx], 328
Nunu', *dial.* Sarudu [sdu], 433
Nunukan, *alt. dial.* Tidong [tid], 395
Nunuma, *alt.* Nuni, Northern [nuv], 53

alt. Nuni, Southern [nnw], 53
dial. Kasem [xsm], 125
Nunzo, *alt.* Ninzo [nin], 171
Nuorese, *dial.* Sardinian,
Logudorese [src], 545
Nupani, *dial.* Pileni [piv], 637
Nupbikha [npb], 324
Nupe, *alt.* Nupe-Nupe-Tako
[nup], 171
Nupe Central, *dial.* Nupe-Nupe-
Tako [nup], 171
Nupe Tako, *dial.* Nupe-Nupe-Tako
[nup], 171
Nupe-Nupe-Tako [nup], 171
Nupeci, *alt.* Nupe-Nupe-Tako
[nup], 171
Nupecidji, *alt.* Nupe-Nupe-Tako
[nup], 171
Nupecizi, *alt. dial.* Nupe-Nupe-Tako
[nup], 171
Nupenchi, *alt.* Nupe-Nupe-Tako
[nup], 171
Nupencizi, *alt.* Nupe-Nupe-Tako
[nup], 171
alt. dial. Nupe-Nupe-Tako [nup], 171
Nuquini, *alt.* Nukuini [nuc], 231
Nura, *alt. dial.* Dagara, Northern
[dgi], 50
Nuralda, *alt.* Adynyamathanha
[adt], 567
Nuristani, *alt.* Kati [bsh], 316, 486
Nuro, *alt.* Anuak [anu], 187, 113
Nurpur Sadri, *dial.* Sadri, Oraon
[sdr], 322
Nurra, *alt.* Norra [nrr], 466
Nuru, *alt.* Ogea [eri], 619
Nuruma, *alt.* Nuni, Northern
[nuv], 53
alt. Nuni, Southern [nnw], 53
Nusa Laut [nul], 402
Nusa Penida, *dial.* Bali [ban], 391
Nusa Tadon, *alt.* Adonara
[adr], 406
alt. Ile Ape [ila], 407
Nusalaut, *alt.* Nusa Laut [nul], 402
Nusan, *alt.* N|u [ngh], 186
dial. !Xóõ [nmn], 48, 151
Nusari, *alt.* Wabo [wbb], 424
Nusu [nuf], 341
Nutka, *alt.* Nootka [noo], 240
Nuuchahnulth, *alt.* Nootka
[noo], 240
Nuwakot, *alt. dial.* Tamang,
Western [tdg], 480
Nuxalk, *alt.* Bella Coola [blc], 235
Nuyoo, *dial.* Mixtec, Southwestern
Tlaxiaco [meh], 269
Nuyoo Mixtec, *alt.* Mixtec,
Southwestern Tlaxiaco [meh], 269
Nuzhen, *alt.* Jurchen [juc], 335

Nvhal, *dial.* Tanna, Southwest
[nwi], 645
Nwa, *alt.* Wan [wan], 95
N'walungu, *dial.* Tsonga [tso], 186
Nwe, *alt.* Ngwe [nwe], 70
Nwesi, *dial.* Bemba [bem], 213, 97
Nya Ceriya, *dial.* Longuda [lnu], 169
Nya Dele, *dial.* Longuda [lnu], 169
Nya Guyuwa, *dial.* Longuda
[lnu], 169
Nya Gwanda, *dial.* Longuda
[lnu], 169
Nya Tariya, *dial.* Longuda [lnu], 169
Nyaaja, *dial.* Mumuye [mzm], 170
Nyaana, *alt. dial.* Samo, Southern
[sbd], 54
Nyaanga, *dial.* Kunyi [njx], 88
Nyaani, *alt.* Wanman [wbt], 577
Nyabadan, *dial.* Maba [mde], 83
Nyabasi, *dial.* Kuria [kuj], 134
Nyabea, *alt.* Tibea [ngy], 72
Nyabo, *dial.* Grebo, Southern
[grj], 138
Nyaboa, *alt.* Nyabwa [nwb], 94
Nyabungu, *alt.* Tembo [tbt], 108
Nyabwa [nwb], 94
dial. Nyabwa [nwb], 94
Nyabwa-Nyédébwa, *alt.* Nyabwa
[nwb], 94
Nyada, *alt.* Nyindrou [lid], 619
Nyadu [nxj], 395
Nyag Dii, *alt.* Dii [dur], 60
Nyagali, *alt. dial.* Dyaabugay [dyy],
570
Nyago, *dial.* Godié [god], 93
Nyah Heuny, *alt.* Nyaheun
[nev], 452
Nyah Kur, *alt.* Nyahkur [cbn], 516
Nyaheun [nev], 452
Nyahkur [cbn], 516
Nyahön, *alt.* Nyaheun [nev], 452
Nyai, *dial.* Kalanga [kck], 216, 47
Nyak, *dial.* Ghale, Northern
[ghh], 471
Nyakali, *alt. dial.* Dyaabugay
[dyy], 570
Nyakisisa, *dial.* Haya [hay], 199
Nyaku, *dial.* Bila [bip], 98
Nyakur, *alt.* Nyahkur [cbn], 516
Nyakusa, *alt.* Nyakyusa-Ngonde
[nyy], 203, 140
Nyakwai, *alt. dial.* Acholi [ach], 210
Nyakyak, *alt.* Kyak [bka], 168
Nyakyusa, *dial.* Nyakyusa-Ngonde
[nyy], 203, 140
Nyakyusa-Ngonde [nyy], 203,
140
Nyala, *dial.* Daju, Dar Fur [daj], 189
Nyala, East [nle], 135
Nyala-B, *alt. dial.* Luyia [luy], 134

Nyala-Lagowa, *alt.* Daju, Dar Fur
[daj], 189
Nyâlayu [yly], 585
Nyali [nlj], 106
Nyali-Kilo, *alt.* Nyali [nlj], 106
Nyam [nmi], 171
Nyam-Nyam du Mayo-Kebi, *alt.*
Nimbari [nmr], 70
Nyamal [nly], 576
Nyambara, *alt. dial.* Bari [bfa], 188,
210
Nyambe, *dial.* Tonga [toh], 149
Nyambo [now], 203
Nyambolo, *alt.* Nyam [nmi], 171
Nyambwa, *dial.* Gogo [gog], 198
Nyamel, *alt.* Nyamal [nly], 576
Nyamkat, *alt.* Kinnauri, Bhoti
[nes], 368
Nyamnyam, *alt.* Nimbari [nmr], 70
pej. alt. Suga [sgi], 72
Nyamskad, *alt.* Kinnauri, Bhoti
[nes], 368
Nyamtam, *dial.* Basaa [bas], 58
Nyamuka, *dial.* Manyika [mxc], 216,
148
Nyamusa, *dial.* Nyamusa-Molo
[nwm], 194
Nyamusa-Molo [nwm], 194
Nyamwanga [mwn], 215, 203
Nyamwesi, *alt.* Nyamwezi
[nym], 203
Nyamwezi [nym], 203
Nyamzax, *alt. dial.* Polci [plj], 173
Nyan Wiyau, *alt.* Waja [wja], 177
Nyandang, *alt.* Yendang [yen], 178
Nyandung, *alt. dial.* Kwanja
[knp], 65
Nyaneka [nyk], 41
Nyang, *alt.* Denya [anv], 60
alt. Giáy [pcc], 523
alt. Kenyang [ken], 64
alt. dial. Dinka, Southwestern
[dik], 190
Nyanga [nyj], 106
Nyanga-li [nyc], 106
Nyangala, *alt. dial.* Nande [nnb], 105
Nyanganyatjara, *alt.* Ngaanyatjarra
[ntj], 575
Nyangatom [nnj], 117
Nyangbara, *dial.* Bari [bfa], 188, 210
Nyangbo [nyb], 127
Nyangeya, *alt.* Nyang'i [nyp], 212
Nyangga [nny], 576
alt. Wirangu [wiw], 578
Nyang'i [nyp], 212
Nyangia, *alt.* Nyang'i [nyp], 212
Nyangiya, *alt.* Nyang'i [nyp], 212
Nyango, *alt.* Irigwe [iri], 164
Nyang'ori, *alt. dial.* Kalenjin
[kln], 133

Nyangumarda, *alt.* Nyangumarta [nna], 576
Nyangumarta [nna], 576
Nyangumata, *alt.* Nyangumarta [nna], 576
Nyangwara, *alt. dial.* Bari [bfa], 188, 210
Nyani, *dial.* Ndumu [nmd], 121
Nyanja [nya], 140, 148, 215, 216
dial. Nyanja [nya], 148
Nyanjang, *alt. dial.* Kwanja [knp], 65
Nyankole, *alt.* Nyankore [nyn], 212
Nyankore [nyn], 212
Nyanoun, *dial.* Grebo, Gboloo [gec], 138
Nyanyembe, *dial.* Nyamwezi [nym], 203
Nyanza, *alt.* Mwera [mjh], 202
Nyao, *alt.* Awyi [auw], 412
Nyarafolo Senoufo, *see* Senoufo, Nyarafolo [sev], 95
Nyarafolo-Niafolo, *alt.* Senoufo, Nyarafolo [sev], 95
Nyari, *alt.* Nyali [nlj], 106
Nyaringa, *dial.* Chuwabu [chw], 147
Nyaro, *dial.* Ko [fuj], 192
Nyarong, *alt.* Atuence [atf], 326
Nyarueng, *alt. dial.* Dinka, Southeastern [dks], 190
Nyarweng, *dial.* Dinka, Southeastern [dks], 190
Nyasa, *alt.* Manda [mgs], 201
alt. Mpoto [mpa], 202
alt. Mwera [mjh], 202
dial. Nyanja [nya], 140, 215
Nyasunda, *dial.* Kwanja [knp], 65
Nyatso, *alt.* Kpan [kpk], 167
Nyaturu [rim], 203
Nyatwe, *dial.* Manyika [mxc], 216, 148
Nyaugogo, *dial.* Gogo [gog], 198
Nyaura, *dial.* Iatmul [ian], 602
Nyaw [nyw], 516
Nyawaygi [nyt], 576
Nyayi, *alt. dial.* Kalanga [kck], 47
Nye, *dial.* Shoo-Minda-Nye [bcv], 174
Nyedebwa, *alt. dial.* Nyabwa [nwb], 94
Nyefu, *alt. dial.* Bari [bfa], 188, 210
Nyeku, *dial.* Tabaru [tby], 404
Nyekyosa, *alt.* Nyakyusa-Ngonde [nyy], 203, 140
Nyel, *alt. dial.* Dinka, Northeastern [dip], 189
Nyele, *alt.* Banda-Ndélé [bfl], 75, 188
Nyem, *alt.* Njyem [njy], 70, 89
Nyemathi, *alt. dial.* Tera [ttr], 175
Nyemba [nba], 41

Nyembombo, *alt. dial.* Zimba [zmb], 109
Nyen, *alt.* Njen [njj], 70
Nyenebo, *dial.* Grebo, Central [grv], 138
Nyeng [nfg], 171
Nyengato, *alt.* Nhengatu [yrl], 230, 246
Nyengatú, *alt.* Nhengatu [yrl], 230
Nyengo [nye], 41
dial. Simaa [sie], 215
Nyenkha [neh], 324
Nyenkpa, *dial.* Yeskwa [yes], 178
Nyeo, *dial.* Wè Southern [gxx], 95
Nyepo, *alt. dial.* Bari [bfa], 188, 210
Nyepu, *dial.* Bari [bfa], 188, 210
Nyeri, *alt. dial.* Gikuyu [kik], 133
Nyeshang, *alt.* Manangba [nmm], 475
Nyeshangba, *alt.* Manangba [nmm], 475
Nyeu [nyl], 516
Nyi, *dial.* Lahu [lhu], 338, 451, 465, 515, 524
Nyidu, *alt.* Etkywan [ich], 159
Nyigina [nyh], 576
Nyiha [nih], 203, 215
Nyika, *alt.* Giryama [nyf], 133
alt. Nyiha [nih], 203, 215
Nyikina, *alt.* Nyigina [nyh], 576
Nyikobe, *alt.* Yukuben [ybl], 178, 74
Nyikuben, *alt.* Yukuben [ybl], 178, 74
Nyikyusa, *alt.* Nyakyusa-Ngonde [nyy], 203
Nyilamba, *alt.* Nilamba [nim], 203
Nyilem, *alt.* Niellim [nie], 85
Nyima, *alt.* Ama [nyi], 187
alt. Kamo [kcq], 166
Nyiman, *alt.* Ama [nyi], 187
Nyimang, *alt.* Ama [nyi], 187
Nyimatali, *alt. dial.* Tera [ttr], 175
Nyimatli, *dial.* Tera [ttr], 175
Nyinagbi, *dial.* Bakwé [bjw], 91
Nyindrou [lid], 619
Nyindu [nyg], 106
Nyingwom, *alt.* Kam [kdx], 166
Nyininy, *dial.* Jaru [ddj], 571
Nyisam, *alt.* Kpasam [pbn], 167
Nyishang, *alt.* Manangba [nmm], 475
Nyishi, *alt.* Nisi [dap], 381
Nyising, *alt.* Nisi [dap], 381
Nyisunggu, *alt.* Tanimbili [tbe], 638
Nyiwom, *alt.* Kam [kdx], 166
Nyixa, *alt.* Nyiha [nih], 203, 215
Nyiyabali, *alt.* Nijadali [nad], 575
Nyiypali, *alt.* Nijadali [nad], 575
Nyky, *alt.* Maru [mhx], 340

Nyland Swedish, *dial.* Swedish [swe], 535
Nymylan, *alt.* Koryak [kpy], 505
Nynorsk, *alt.* Norwegian, Nynorsk [nno], 549
Nynorsk Norwegian, *see* Norwegian, Nynorsk [nno], 549
Nyo, *alt.* Nyaw [nyw], 516
Nyo-Kana, *dial.* Khana [ogo], 166
Nyoh, *alt.* Nyaw [nyw], 516
Nyok, *dial.* Dii [dur], 60
Nyoking, *alt.* Nyong [muo], 171
Nyokon, *alt. dial.* Tunen [baz], 72
Nyole [nuj], 212
alt. Nyore [nyd], 135
Nyolge, *alt.* Njalgulgule [njl], 194
Nyong [muo], 71, 171
alt. Yong [yno], 518
Nyongnepa, *alt.* Nyong [muo], 71, 171
Nyongwe, *alt.* Nyungwe [nyu], 148
Nyonyo, *alt.* Kpan [kpk], 167
Nyoole, *alt.* Nyore [nyd], 135
Nyoolne, *alt.* Njalgulgule [njl], 194
Nyo'on, *alt. dial.* Tunen [baz], 72
Nyore [nyd], 135
Nyoro [nyo], 212
alt. Hema [nix], 100
alt. dial. Nyoro [nyo], 212
Nyos, *dial.* Mmen [bfm], 67
Nyoxolonkan, *dial.* Maninkakan, Western [mlq], 143
Nyoyaka, *alt.* Yaka [axk], 78
Nypho, *alt. dial.* Bari [bfa], 188, 210
Nyua, *alt.* Yuaga [nua], 585
Nyuangia, *alt.* Nyang'i [nyp], 212
Nyule, *alt.* Nyole [nuj], 212
Nyuli, *alt.* Nyole [nuj], 212
Nyulnyul [nyv], 576
Nyunga [nys], 576
Nyungar, *alt.* Nyunga [nys], 576
Nyungwe [nyu], 148
Nyuong, *dial.* Nuer [nus], 194
Nyut'chi, *alt. dial.* Iowa-Oto [iow], 302
Nyuwar, *alt. dial.* Longuda [lnu], 169
Nzák Kàráng, *alt.* Karang [kzr], 81
Nzak Mbai, *alt.* Nzakambay [nzy], 86, 71
Nzak Mbay, *alt.* Nzakambay [nzy], 71
Nzaka Mbay, *alt.* Nzakambay [nzy], 86
Nzakambay [nzy], 86, 71
dial. Nzakambay [nzy], 86
Nzakara [nzk], 77, 106
Nzakmbay, *alt.* Nzakambay [nzy], 86, 71
Nzamba, *alt. dial.* Koongo [kng], 101

Nzangi, *alt.* Nzanyi [nja], 171, 71
Nzanyi [nja], 171, 71
Nzare, *alt. dial.* Mbembe, Tigon
    [nza], 170
    dial. Mbembe, Tigon [nza], 66
Nzari, *dial.* Yaka [axk], 78
Nzebi, *alt.* Njebi [nzb], 121, 89
Nzema [nzi], 127, 94
Nzikini, *alt. dial.* Teke, Northern
    [teg], 121
    alt. dial. Teke-Tege [teg], 90
Nzima, *alt.* Nzema [nzi], 127, 94
Nzime, *alt.* Koonzime [ozm], 64
    dial. Koonzime [ozm], 64
Nzin, *alt.* Njen [njj], 70
Nzong, *alt.* Naga, Southern Rengma
    [nre], 379
Nzonyu, *alt.* Naga, Southern Rengma
    [nre], 379
    alt. dial. Naga, Southern Rengma
    [nre], 379
Nzuhwi, *alt.* Duhwa [kbz], 158
O Du, *alt.* O'du [tyh], 525, 452
!'O-!Khung, *alt.* Vasekela Bushman
    [vaj], 151
Oa, *alt.* Tatuyo [tav], 247
Oad, *alt.* Od [odk], 487
Oarte, *alt.* Chin, Paite [pck], 463
Oas, *dial.* Bicolano, Albay [bhk], 493
Oasis Berber, *alt.* Siwi [siz], 110
Oaxaca Amuzgo, *alt.* Amuzgo,
    San Pedro Amuzgos [azg], 259
Oayana, *alt.* Wayana [way], 296,
    234, 252
Oba, *alt.* Ambae, East [omb], 640
Oba-Miwamon, *dial.* Yaqay
    [jaq], 426
Obamba, *alt.* Mbama [mbm], 120
Obang, *alt.* Ejagham [etu], 60
    dial. Befang [bby], 58
Obanliku [bzy], 172
Obe, *dial.* Putukwam [afe], 173
Obelebha, *alt. dial.* Logo [log], 103
Obersorbisch, *alt.* Sorbian, Upper
    [hsb], 539
Oberwart, *dial.* Hungarian
    [hun], 530
Obgwo, *alt.* Ninggerum [nxr], 618
Obi, *alt.* Akoye [miw], 588
    alt. dial. Lese [les], 102
Obian, *alt. dial.* Sama, Southern
    [ssb], 458
    dial. Sama, Southern [ssb], 500
Obileba, *alt. dial.* Logo [log], 103
Obilebha, *dial.* Logo [log], 103
Obini, *alt. dial.* Agwagwune
    [yay], 153
Obio, *dial.* Ikwere [ikw], 164
Obispeño [obi], 306
Obiye, *alt.* Mvuba [mxh], 105

Oblo [obl], 71
Obo Bagobo, *alt.* Manobo, Obo
    [obo], 499
Obo Manobo, *see* Manobo, Obo
    [obo], 499
Obogolo, *alt.* Ogbogolo [ogg], 172
Obogwitai, *alt.* Obokuitai [afz], 421
Obokuitai [afz], 421
Obolo [ann], 172
Obonya, *alt.* Denya [anv], 60
Oboso, *dial.* Putukwam [afe], 173
'Oboyguno, *dial.* Bidiyo [bid], 79
Obulom [obu], 172
Obura-To'okena, *alt. dial.* Tairora,
    South [omw], 626
Obwald, *dial.* Schwyzerdütsch
    [gsw], 563
Ocaina [oca], 289, 246
Occitan, *alt.* Auvergnat [auv], 535
    alt. Gascon [gsc], 537
    alt. Languedocien [lnc], 537
    alt. Limousin [lms], 537
Occitani, *alt.* Languedocien
    [lnc], 537
Ocebe, *alt.* Iceve-Maci [bec], 63
Oceve, *alt.* Iceve-Maci [bec], 163
Ochebe, *alt.* Iceve-Maci [bec], 63,
    163
Ochekwu, *alt.* Agatu [agc], 153
Ocheve, *alt.* Iceve-Maci [bec], 63,
    163
Ochiherero, *alt.* Herero [her], 150,
    47
Ochikwanyama, *alt.* Kwanyama
    [kua], 40, 150
Ochindonga, *alt.* Ndonga
    [ndo], 150, 41
Ocotepec, *dial.* Zoque, Copainalá
    [zoc], 281
Ocotepec Mixe, *dial.* Mixe, Juquila
    [mxq], 265
Ocotepec Mixtec, *see* Mixtec,
    Ocotepec [mie], 268
Ocotepec Mixtec, *alt.* Mixtec,
    Ocotepec [mie], 268
Ocotlán Oeste Zapotec, *alt.*
    Zapotec, Ocotlán [zac], 279
Ocotlán Zapotec, *see* Zapotec,
    Ocotlán [zac], 279
Ocuapa, *alt. dial.* Mixtec,
    Alacatlazala [mim], 265
Ocuiltec, *alt.* Matlatzinca, Atzingo
    [ocu], 263
Ocuilteco, *alt.* Matlatzinca, Atzingo
    [ocu], 263
Od [odk], 487
    alt. Waddar [wbq], 390
Odaje, *dial.* Mbe [mfo], 169
Odasa, *alt. dial.* Kunama [kun], 112
Odawa, *alt.* Ottawa [otw], 240, 306

Oderago, *alt.* Kokoda [xod], 417
Oderiga, *alt.* Mbembe, Cross River
    [mfn], 163
Odiai [bhf], 619
Odienné Jula, *alt.* Wojenaka
    [jod], 95
Odienneka, *dial.* Wojenaka [jod], 95
Odiennekakan, *alt.* Wojenaka
    [jod], 95
Odim, *alt. dial.* Agwagwune
    [yay], 153
Odio, *alt. dial.* Zande [zne], 196
Odionganon, *dial.* Bantoanon
    [bno], 492
Odki, *alt.* Od [odk], 487
Ododei, *alt.* Odoodee [kkc], 619
Ododop, *alt.* Korop [krp], 167, 64
Odoodee [kkc], 619
Odri, *alt.* Oriya [ori], 382
Odrum, *alt.* Oriya [ori], 382
O'du [tyh], 525, 452
Odual [odu], 172
    alt. Sakata [skt], 104
Odul, *alt.* Yukaghir, Northern
    [ykg], 507
    alt. Yukaghir, Southern [yux], 499
Odut [oda], 172
Odyalombito, *alt.* Lombi [lmi], 103
Odzila, *alt. dial.* Avokaya [avu], 188
Odziliwa, *alt. dial.* Avokaya
    [avu], 188
Oe Cusi, *alt.* Baikeno [bkx], 350
Oe Nale, *alt.* Dela-Oenale [row], 406
    alt. dial. Dela-Oenale [row], 406
Oe Pao, *alt. dial.* Ringgou [rgu], 409
Oecussi, *alt.* Baikeno [bkx], 350
Oehoendoeni, *alt.* Damal [uhn], 413
Oekusi, *alt.* Baikeno [bkx], 350
Oeloemanda, *alt.* Ulumanda'
    [ulm], 434
Oema, *alt.* Uma [ppk], 434
Oenale, *dial.* Dela-Oenale [row], 406
Oepao, *alt. dial.* Ringgou [rgu], 409
Oeringoep, *alt.* Dani, Western
    [dnw], 414
Oewaku, *alt.* Arutani [atx], 225, 311
Ofagbe, *dial.* Isoko [iso], 164
Ofaié-Xavante, *alt.* Ofayé
    [opy], 231
Ofayé [opy], 231
Oferikpe, *dial.* Mbembe, Cross River
    [mfn], 163
Offra, *alt.* Gbe, Eastern Xwla
    [gbx], 44
Ofo [ofo], 306
Ofombonga, *dial.* Mbembe, Cross
    River [mfn], 163
Ofonokpan, *dial.* Mbembe, Cross
    River [mfn], 163
Ofor, *alt.* Lubila [kcc], 169

Ofunobwam, *alt.* Mbembe, Cross River [mfn], 163
Ofutop, *alt.* Efutop [ofu], 158
Oga, *alt. dial.* Melanau [mel], 460, 325
Oga Bakung, *dial.* Kenyah, Bakung [boc], 393, 459
Ogaden, *dial.* Somali [som], 136
Ogamaru, *alt. dial.* Logo [log], 103
Ogambi, *dial.* Logo [log], 103
Ogami, *alt. dial.* Miyako [mvi], 447
Ogan [ogn], 437
Ogar, *dial.* Onin [oni], 421
Ogaxpa, *alt.* Quapaw [qua], 307
Ogba, *alt.* Ogbah [ogc], 172
Ogbah [ogc], 172
Ogbakiri, *dial.* Ikwere [ikw], 164
Ogbe Ijo, *dial.* Izon [ijc], 164
Ogbia [ogb], 172
Ogbinya, *alt.* Ogbia [ogb], 172
Ogbogolo [ogg], 172
Ogboin, *dial.* Izon [ijc], 164
Ogboja, *alt. dial.* Nkem-Nkum [isi], 171
Ogbronuagum [ogu], 172
Ogbru, *dial.* Abidji [abi], 88
Òge, *dial.* Arigidi [aqg], 154
Ogea [eri], 619
Oghuz, *dial.* Udi [udi], 320
   dial. Uzbek, Northern [uzn], 512
Ogiek, *alt.* Okiek [oki], 135
Ogit, *alt.* Konda [knd], 417
Ogliastrino, *dial.* Sardinian, Campidanese [sro], 545
Ogoda, *alt.* Boni [bob], 132
Ogoi, *alt.* Baan [bvj], 154
Ogoja, *alt. dial.* Nkem-Nkum [isi], 171
Ogoko, *dial.* Ma'di, Southern [snm], 211
Ogondyan, *alt. dial.* Kunjen [kjn], 573
Ogoni, *alt.* Khana [ogo], 166
Ogori, *alt. dial.* Oko-Eni-Osayen [oks], 172
Ogori-Magongo, *alt.* Oko-Eni-Osayen [oks], 172
Ogowe, *dial.* Fang [fan], 88, 120
Ogua, *dial.* Engenni [enn], 159
Ogugu, *dial.* Igala [igl], 163
Ogulagha, *dial.* Izon [ijc], 164
Oguta, *dial.* Igbo [ibo], 163
Ogwia, *alt.* Mbato [gwa], 94
Ohana-Onyen, *alt. dial.* Mbembe, Cross River [mfn], 163
Ohlone, Northern [cst], 306
Ohlone, Southern [css], 306
Ohuhu, *dial.* Igbo [ibo], 163
Ohumono, *alt.* Kohumono [bcs], 166
Oi, *alt.* Oy [oyb], 452

Oiampí, *alt.* Wayampi [oym], 252, 233
Oiampipucu, *pej. alt.* Wayampi [oym], 233
Oiana, *alt.* Wayana [way], 296, 234
Oiba, *alt. dial.* Gobasi [goi], 600
Oibae, *alt. dial.* Gobasi [goi], 600
Oibu, *dial.* Maria [mds], 612
Oirat, *alt.* Kalmyk-Oirat [xal], 554, 337, 461
   dial. Kalmyk-Oirat [xal], 554
Oirata [oia], 402
Oirot, *alt.* Altai, Southern [alt], 503
Oirya, *alt.* Lokoya [lky], 192
Oium, *alt.* Papel [pbo], 131
Oiumpian, *alt.* Wayampi [oym], 252
Oiyana, *alt. dial.* Gadsup [gaj], 599
Oiyapoque, *dial.* Wayampi [oym], 252
Oiyapoque Wayampi, *dial.* Wayampi [oym], 233
Ojaboli, *alt. dial.* Bagheli [bfy], 354
Ojanjur, *alt.* Majang [mpe], 116
Ojha, *alt. dial.* Bagheli [bfy], 354
Ojhe, *alt. dial.* Bagheli [bfy], 354
Ojhi, *dial.* Bagheli [bfy], 354, 468
Oji-Cree, *alt.* Ojibwa, Severn [ojs], 240
Ojibwa, Central [ojc], 240
Ojibwa, Eastern [ojg], 240
Ojibwa, Northwestern [ojb], 240
Ojibwa, Severn [ojs], 240
Ojibwa, Western [ojw], 240
Ojibway, *alt.* Chippewa [ciw], 299
   alt. Ojibwa, Central [ojc], 240
   alt. Ojibwa, Eastern [ojg], 240
   alt. Ojibwa, Northwestern [ojb], 240
   alt. Ojibwa, Severn [ojs], 240
   alt. Ojibwa, Western [ojw], 240
   alt. Ottawa [otw], 240
Ojibwe, *alt.* Chippewa [ciw], 299
   alt. Ojibwa, Central [ojc], 240
   alt. Ojibwa, Eastern [ojg], 240
   alt. Ojibwa, Northwestern [ojb], 240
   alt. Ojibwa, Severn [ojs], 240
   alt. Ojibwa, Western [ojw], 240
   alt. Ottawa [otw], 240, 306
Ojicree, *alt.* Ojibwa, Severn [ojs], 240
Ojiga, *alt. dial.* Avokaya [avu], 188
Ojila, *dial.* Avokaya [avu], 188, 96
Ojitlán Chinantec, *see* Chinantec, Ojitlán [chj], 260
Ojo, *dial.* Arigidi [aqg], 154
Ojor, *alt.* Lubila [kcc], 169
Oju, *dial.* Igede [ige], 163
Ok Bari, *alt.* Muyu, South [kts], 421
Oka, *dial.* Buriat, Russia [bxr], 504
   dial. Igbo [ibo], 163
Okaina, *alt.* Ocaina [oca], 289, 246

Okak, *alt. dial.* Fang [fan], 61
Okam, *alt.* Mbembe, Cross River [mfn], 163
Okanagan [oka], 240, 306
Okanagan-Colville, *alt.* Okanagan [oka], 240, 306
Okanagon, *alt.* Okanagan [oka], 240, 306
Okande, *alt.* Kande [kbs], 120
Okanisi, *alt.* Aukan [djk], 295
Okanogan, *alt.* Okanagan [oka], 240, 306
Okbap, *dial.* Ketengban [xte], 417
Oke-Agbe, *alt. dial.* Arigidi [aqg], 154
Oke'bu, *alt.* Ndo [ndp], 212, 105
   dial. Ndo [ndp], 212, 105
Okeina, *alt. dial.* Ewage-Notu [nou], 598
Okela, *alt.* Kela [kel], 101
Okena, *alt. dial.* Ewage-Notu [nou], 598
Okene, *dial.* Ebira [igb], 158
Okere, *alt.* Cherepon [cpn], 123
Okhotsk, *dial.* Even [eve], 504
Oki, *alt.* Tuki [bag], 72
Oki-No-Erabu [okn], 447
Okiek [oki], 135, 203
   dial. Okiek [oki], 135
Okii, *alt.* Bokyi [bky], 156, 59
Okinawan, *alt.* Okinawan, Central [ryu], 447
Okinawan, Central [ryu], 447
Oko, *alt.* Oko-Eni-Osayen [oks], 172
   dial. Ese [mcq], 598
   dial. Oko-Eni-Osayen [oks], 172
Oko-Eni-Osayen [oks], 172
Oko-Juwoi [okj], 381
Okobo [okb], 172
Okodia [okd], 172
Okollo, *dial.* Ma'di, Southern [snm], 211
Okolod [kqv], 395, 460
Okolod Murut, *alt.* Okolod [kqv], 395, 460
Okom, *dial.* Mbembe, Cross River [mfn], 163
Okoma, *alt. dial.* Nateni [ntm], 46
Okomanjang, *alt. dial.* Befang [bby], 58
Okoni, *dial.* Nateni [ntm], 46
Okonyong, *alt.* Kiong [kkm], 166
Okordia, *alt.* Okodia [okd], 172
Okorobi, *dial.* Ngwo [ngn], 70
Okoroete, *dial.* Obolo [ann], 172
Okorogung, *dial.* Putukwam [afe], 173
Okoromandjang, *alt. dial.* Befang [bby], 58

Okorotung, *dial.* Putukwam [afe], 173

Okoyong, *alt.* Kiong [kkm], 166

Okpamheri [opa], 172

Okpe (Northwestern Edo) [okx], 172
Okpe (Southwestern Edo) [oke], 172

Okpeden, *dial.* Abua [abn], 153

Okpela, *dial.* Ivbie North-Okpela-Arhe [atg], 164

Okpele, *alt.* Bekwil [bkw], 58

Okpella, *alt. dial.* Ivbie North-Okpela-Arhe [atg], 164

Okpogu, *dial.* Idoma [idu], 163

Okpoto, *dial.* Oring [org], 172

Okrika, *alt.* Kirike [okr], 166

Okro, *dial.* Nali [nss], 616

Oksapmin [opm], 619

Oktenai, *alt.* Wichí Lhamtés Nocten [mtp], 224, 220

Oktengban, *alt.* Ketengban [xte], 417

Oktomberi, *dial.* Udi [udi], 320

Oku [oku], 71
dial. Bokyi [bky], 156

Oku-Juwoi, *alt.* Oko-Juwoi [okj], 381

Okulosho, *dial.* Okpamheri [opa], 172

Okum, *alt.* Akum [aku], 56

Okundi, *alt. dial.* Bokyi [bky], 156

!O!kung, *alt.* !O!ung [oun], 41

Okuni, *dial.* Olulumo-Ikom [iko], 172

Okurikan, *alt.* Agwagwune [yay], 153

Okurosho, *alt. dial.* Okpamheri [opa], 172

Okwasar, *alt.* Isirawa [srl], 415

Ola, *alt. dial.* Ngarinyin [ung], 575
dial. Even [eve], 504

Olal, *dial.* Ambrym, North [mmg], 640

Olam, *dial.* Murle [mur], 117

Olangchung Gola, *alt.* Walungge [ola], 481

Olch, *alt.* Ulch [ulc], 507

Olcha, *alt.* Ulch [ulc], 507

Olchis, *alt.* Ulch [ulc], 507

Old Bargu, *alt. dial.* Buriat, China [bxu], 329

Old Church Slavonic, *see* Slavonic, Old Church [chu], 556

Old Frankish, *alt.* Frankish [frk], 538

Old Hebrew, *alt.* Hebrew, Ancient [hbo], 445

Old Kentish Sign Language [okl], 566

Old Khmer, *alt.* Kuy [kdt], 451

Old Klemtu, *alt. dial.* Tsimshian [tsi], 242

Old Moshi, *alt.* Mochi [old], 202

Old Prussian, *alt.* Prussian [prg], 550

Old Shirazi, *dial.* Farsi, Western [pes], 439

Old Sirenik, *alt.* Yupik, Sirenik [ysr], 508

Old Tupí, *alt.* Tupinambá [tpn], 233

Ole, *dial.* Isoko [iso], 164

Ole Mönpa, *alt.* Olekha [ole], 324

Oleh, *alt. dial.* Isoko [iso], 164

Olekha [ole], 324

'Olelo Hawai'i, *alt.* Hawaiian [haw], 302

'Olelo Hawai'i Makuahine, *alt.* Hawaiian [haw], 302

Olem, *alt.* Angoram [aog], 590

Olga, *alt.* Jumjum [jum], 191

Olgel, *alt. dial.* Kunjen [kjn], 573

Olgol, *alt. dial.* Kunjen [kjn], 573

Olgolo, *alt. dial.* Kunjen [kjn], 573

Olguya, *alt. dial.* Evenki [evn], 332

Oli, *dial.* Duala [dua], 60

Olit, *alt. dial.* Iceve-Maci [bec], 63, 163

Olithi, *alt. dial.* Iceve-Maci [bec], 63, 163

Oliti, *alt. dial.* Iceve-Maci [bec], 163
dial. Iceve-Maci [bec], 63

Oliti-Akwaya, *alt. dial.* Iceve-Maci [bec], 63, 163

Oliya, *alt.* Oriya [ori], 382

Olkoi, *alt.* Elkei [elk], 598

Ollar Gadaba, *alt.* Gadaba, Pottangi Ollar [gdb], 361

Ollari, *alt.* Gadaba, Pottangi Ollar [gdb], 361

Ollaro, *alt.* Gadaba, Pottangi Ollar [gdb], 361

Olo [ong], 619

Ologo, *dial.* Kaluli [bco], 604

Ologuti, *dial.* Yagaria [ygr], 632

Oloh Mangtangai, *alt. dial.* Ngaju [nij], 394

Oloh Mengkatip, *alt. dial.* Bakumpai [bkr], 392

Oloibiri, *dial.* Ogbia [ogb], 172

Oloma [olm], 172

Olombo, *alt.* Lombo [loo], 103

Olomoro, *dial.* Isoko [iso], 164

Olonets, *alt.* Livvi [olo], 555, 535

Olonetsian, *alt.* Livvi [olo], 555, 535

Olossu, *alt.* Russian [rus], 343

Olot, *dial.* Kalmyk-Oirat [xal], 337, 461

Olotepec, *dial.* Mixe, North Central [neq], 265

Olotorit, *alt.* Otuho [lot], 194

Oltean, *alt. dial.* Romanian [ron], 548

Oltenia-Lesser Wallachia, *alt. dial.* Romanian [ron], 548

Olu'bo [lul], 194

Olubogo, *alt.* Olu'bo [lul], 194

Oluboti, *alt.* Olu'bo [lul], 194

Olubwisi, *alt.* Talinga-Bwisi [tlj], 212, 108

Oluchiga, *alt.* Chiga [cgg], 210

Olugwere, *alt.* Gwere [gwr], 210

Oluhanga, *alt. dial.* Luyia [luy], 134

Olukonjo, *alt.* Konjo [koo], 211

Olukonzo, *alt.* Konjo [koo], 211

Olukooki, *alt. dial.* Ganda [lug], 210

Olulu, *dial.* Ipulo [ass], 63

Olulumo, *dial.* Olulumo-Ikom [iko], 172

Olulumo-Ikom [iko], 172

Olumba, *dial.* Siane [snp], 624

Olumuila, *alt. dial.* Nyaneka [nyk], 41

Olunchun, *alt.* Oroqen [orh], 341

Olunyole, *alt.* Nyore [nyd], 135

Olunyore, *alt.* Nyore [nyd], 135

Olusamia, *alt. dial.* Luyia [luy], 134

Olusese, *alt. dial.* Ganda [lug], 210

Olusoga, *alt.* Soga [xog], 212

Oluta Popoluca, *see* Popoluca, Oluta [plo], 274

Oluthimba, *alt.* Zemba [dhm], 42, 151

Oluwanga, *alt. dial.* Luyia [luy], 134

Olyutor, *alt.* Alutor [alr], 503

Omage, *alt.* Yanesha' [ame], 293

Omagua [omg], 289, 231
alt. Carijona [cbd], 244

Omagua-Yete, *alt.* Omagua [omg], 289, 231

Omagwna, *dial.* Ikwere [ikw], 164

Omaha, *dial.* Omaha-Ponca [oma], 306

Omaha-Ponca [oma], 306

Omani, *dial.* Koiari, Grass [kbk], 606

Omani Bedawi Arabic, *alt.* Arabic, Gulf Spoken [afb], 482

Omani Hadari Arabic, *alt.* Arabic, Omani Spoken [acx], 482

Omani Spoken Arabic, *see* Arabic, Omani Spoken [acx], 482, 131, 197

Omati [mgx], 619

Omba, *alt.* Ambae, East [omb], 640

Ombalei, *alt. dial.* Hote [hot], 602

Ombamba [mbm], 89

Omban, *dial.* Ketengban [xte], 417

Ombessa, *alt.* Nugunu [yas], 70

Ombo [oml], 106

Ombule, *alt.* Wambule [wme], 482

Omejes [ome], 246

Omene, *dial.* Sinaugoro [snc], 624

Omerelu, *dial.* Ikwere [ikw], 164

Ometay, *alt. dial.* Gamo-Gofa-Dawro [gmo], 114

Ometepec Aztec, *alt.* Nahuatl, Ometepec [nht], 271

Ometepec Nahuatl, *see* Nahuatl, Ometepec [nht], 271

Ometo, *alt.* Wolaytta [wal], 119

Omi [omi], 106

Ömie [aom], 619

Omkoi, *dial.* Karen, Pwo Northern [pww], 514

Omo, *alt.* Tigak [tgc], 627

Omotic, *alt.* Omotik [omt], 135

Omotik [omt], 135

Ompa, *alt. dial.* Uma [ppk], 434

Omudioga, *dial.* Ikwere [ikw], 164

Omugo, *alt. dial.* Lugbara [lgg], 211

Omurano [omu], 289

Omvang, *dial.* Ewondo [ewo], 61

Omwunra-Toqura, *alt.* Tairora, South [omw], 626

dial. Tairora, South [omw], 626

Omyene, *alt.* Myene [mye], 121

alt. dial. Myene [mye], 121

Ona [ona], 220

dial. Siane [snp], 624

Onabasulu, *alt.* Onobasulu [onn], 620

Onage, *alt.* Fur [fvr], 190

Onandaga, *alt.* Onondaga [ono], 240, 306

Onank, *alt.* Watut, North [una], 631

Ondo, *dial.* Yoruba [yor], 178

Ondoe, *alt.* Olu'bo [lul], 194

Ondoumbo, *alt.* Ndumu [nmd], 121

Ondumbo, *alt.* Ndumu [nmd], 121

One, *dial.* Yasa [yko], 111, 122

One, Inebu [oin], 619

One, Kabore [onk], 619

One, Kwamtim [okk], 620

One, Molmo [aun], 620

One, Northern [onr], 620

One, Southern [osu], 620

Oneida [one], 240, 306

Onele, *alt.* One, Inebu [oin], 619

alt. One, Kabore [onk], 619

alt. One, Molmo [aun], 620

alt. One, Northern [onr], 620

alt. One, Southern [osu], 620

Onesso, *dial.* Aulua [aul], 640

Onëyan, *alt.* Bassari [bsc], 180, 131

Ong [oog], 452

alt. Önge [oon], 381

Ong-Be, *alt.* Lingao [onb], 338

Ongamo, *alt.* Ngasa [nsg], 202

Ongbe, *alt.* Lingao [onb], 338

Önge [oon], 381

Ongom, *alt.* Ngom [nra], 121, 89

'Ongota, *alt.* Birale [bxe], 114

Oni, *alt.* One, Inebu [oin], 619

alt. One, Kabore [onk], 619

alt. One, Kwamtim [okk], 620

alt. One, Molmo [aun], 620

alt. One, Northern [onr], 620

alt. One, Southern [osu], 620

Onian, *alt.* Bassari [bsc], 180, 129, 131

Onim, *alt.* Onin [oni], 421

Onin [oni], 421

Onin Based Pidgin [onx], 421

Onitsha, *dial.* Igbo [ibo], 163

Onjab, *alt.* Onjob [onj], 620

Onjob [onj], 620

Ono [ons], 620

alt. dial. Fijian [fij], 580

dial. Weri [wer], 632

Onobasulu [onn], 620

Onondaga [ono], 240, 306

Onotsu, *dial.* Kikai [kzg], 446

Ontario Delaware, *alt.* Munsee [umu], 239

Ontena, *alt.* Ontenu [ont], 617

Ontenu [ont], 617

Onti, *dial.* Koraga, Korra [kfd], 369

Ontong Java [ojv], 637

Onua, *alt.* Unua [onu], 646

Onya, *dial.* Ketengban [xte], 417

O'odham, *alt.* Tohono O'odham [ood], 309

Oohum, *alt.* Yukuben [ybl], 178

Ööld, *alt. dial.* Kalmyk-Oirat [xal], 337, 461

Oorazhi, *alt.* Urali [url], 389

Oorlams [oor], 186

Oormbur, *alt.* Ngurmbur [nrx], 575

Oormuri, *alt.* Ormuri [oru], 317

Oosima, *alt.* Amami-Oshima, Northern [ryn], 446

Oost-Sumbaas, *alt.* Kambera [xbr], 407

Oost-Vlaams, *dial.* Dutch [nld], 531

Oostvlaams, *dial.* Vlaams [vls], 531

O'othham, *alt.* Tohono O'odham [ood], 309

Ooweekeeno, *dial.* Heiltsuk [hei], 238

Opa, *alt.* Ambae, West [nnd], 640

Opaié-Shavante, *alt.* Ofayé [opy], 231

Opaina, *dial.* Yahuna [ynu], 248

Opalo, *dial.* Bacama [bcy], 154

Opameri, *alt.* Okpamheri [opa], 172

Opao [opo], 620

Opata [opt], 272

Opayé, *alt.* Ofayé [opy], 231

Opëno, *dial.* Anuak [anu], 113

Operemo, *dial.* Izon [ijc], 164

Ophra, *alt.* Gbe, Eastern Xwla [gbx], 44

Opif, *dial.* Biak [bhw], 412

Opo, *alt.* Opuuo [lgn], 117, 194

Opo-Shita, *alt.* Opuuo [lgn], 117, 194

Oporoma, *alt. dial.* Izon [ijc], 164

Oporomo, *dial.* Izon [ijc], 164

Oporoza, *dial.* Izon [ijc], 164

Oporto, *dial.* Portuguese Sign Language [psr], 551

Opotai, *alt.* Aputai [apx], 396

Oprou, *alt.* Aizi, Aproumu [ahp], 91

Opselan, *alt.* Moksela [vms], 402

Opuo, *alt.* Opuuo [lgn], 117, 194

Opuuo [lgn], 117, 194

!Ora, *alt.* Korana [kqz], 186

Ora, *dial.* Emai-Iuleha-Ora [ema], 159

Oraha, *alt.* Oroha [ora], 637

Orak Lawoi', *alt.* Urak Lawoi' [urk], 518

Orakaiva, *alt.* Orokaiva [ork], 620

Orambul, *alt.* Bayali [bjy], 569

Orami, *dial.* Naasioi [nas], 616

Oran, *dial.* Arabic, Algerian Spoken [arq], 39

Orang Bukit, *alt.* Brunei [kxd], 324, 456

alt. Kensiu [kns], 454, 515

Orang Cagayan, *alt.* Mapun [sjm], 499, 457

Orang Gunung, *alt.* Uab Meto [aoz], 410

Orang Hulu, *alt.* Jakun [jak], 454

Orang Kanaq [orn], 455

Orang Kuala, *alt.* Duano' [dup], 454

Orang Laut, *alt.* Bajau, Indonesian [bdl], 427

alt. Loncong [lce], 436

Orang Liar, *alt.* Kensiu [kns], 454, 515

Orang Mamak, *dial.* Minangkabau [min], 436

Orang Negeri, *alt.* Negeri Sembilan Malay [zmi], 455

Orang Seletar [ors], 455, 509

Orang Tanjong of Ulu Langat, *alt. dial.* Semai [sea], 455

Orange River Afrikaans, *dial.* Afrikaans [afr], 185

Orango, *alt. dial.* Bidyogo [bjg], 131

Oranje-Gebergte, *alt.* Una [mtg], 424

Oraoan, *alt.* Kurux [kru], 321

Oraon, *alt.* Kurux [kru], 371

alt. Kurux, Nepali [kxl], 473

dial. Kurux [kru], 371

Oraon Sadri, *see* Sadri, Oraon [sdr], 322

Orase, *alt.* Bussa [dox], 114

Orau, *alt.* Kurux, Nepali [kxl], 473

Ordos, *dial.* Mongolian, Peripheral [mvf], 339, 462

Otapha, *dial.* Abua [abn], 153
Otavalo Quichua, *alt.* Quichua, Imbabura Highland [qvi], 251
Otetela, *alt.* Tetela [tll], 109
Othan, *alt.* Uduk [udu], 119, 196
Oti [oti], 231
Otjidhimba, *alt.* Zemba [dhm], 42, 151
Otjiherero, *alt.* Herero [her], 150, 47
Otjingumbi, *alt.* Nkhumbi [khu], 41
Otjiwambo, *alt.* Kwanyama [kua], 150
  alt. Ndonga [ndo], 150
Oto, *dial.* Iowa-Oto [iow], 302
Otoe, *alt. dial.* Iowa-Oto [iow], 302
Otomí de Huehuetla, *alt.* Otomi, Eastern Highland [otm], 272
Otomí de la Sierra, *alt.* Otomi, Eastern Highland [otm], 272
Otomí de Querétaro, *alt.* Otomi, Querétaro [otq], 272
Otomí de San Felipe Santiago, *alt.* Otomi, Estado de México [ots], 272
Otomí de Tenango, *alt.* Otomi, Tenango [otn], 273
Otomí de Texcatepec, *alt.* Otomi, Texcatepec [otx], 273
Otomí del Estado de México, *alt.* Otomi, Estado de México [ots], 272
Otomí del Oriente, *alt.* Otomi, Eastern Highland [otm], 272
Otomí del Valle del Mezquital, *alt.* Otomi, Mezquital [ote], 272
Otomi, Eastern Highland [otm], 272
Otomi, Estado de México [ots], 272
Otomi, Ixtenco [otz], 272
Otomi, Mezquital [ote], 272
Otomi, Querétaro [otq], 272
Otomi, Temoaya [ott], 273
Otomi, Tenango [otn], 273
Otomi, Texcatepec [otx], 273
Otomi, Tilapa [otl], 273
Otoro [otr], 194
Otsho, *dial.* Lugbara [lgg], 103
Ottawa [otw], 240, 306
Otuho [lot], 194
Otuke [otu], 231
Otukwang, *alt. dial.* Putukwam [afe], 173
Otuo, *alt.* Ghotuo [aaa], 161
Otuque, *alt.* Otuke [otu], 231
Otuqui, *alt.* Otuke [otu], 231
Oturkpo, *alt. dial.* Idoma [idu], 163
Otuxo, *alt.* Otuho [lot], 194
Otvai, *dial.* Kabola [klz], 407
Otwa, *alt.* Ghotuo [aaa], 161

Ouadda, *alt. dial.* Banda-Mbrès [bqk], 75, 188
Ouaddai, *alt.* Maba [mde], 83
Ouaddaien, *alt.* Maba [mde], 83
Ouala, *alt.* Wali [wlx], 128
  alt. Wara [wbf], 55
Ouapadoupou, *dial.* Mòoré [mos], 52
Ouara, *alt.* Wara [wbf], 55
Ouargla, *alt.* Tagargrent [oua], 40
Ouargli, *alt.* Tagargrent [oua], 40
Ouarkoye, *dial.* Buamu [box], 50
Ouassa, *alt. dial.* Banda, Mid-Southern [bjo], 74
Ouatchi, *alt.* Gbe, Waci [wci], 207, 45
Ouatourou-Niasogoni, *dial.* Wara [wbf], 55
Ouayeone, *alt.* Waiwai [waw], 233, 257
Oubatch, *alt.* Jawe [jaz], 584
Oubi, *alt.* Glio-Oubi [oub], 138, 93
  alt. Ubi [ubi], 87
Oubykh, *alt.* Ubykh [uby], 563
Ouedghir, *dial.* Tagargrent [oua], 40
Ouen, *alt.* Numee [kdk], 585
  dial. Numee [kdk], 585
Ouhiguyua, *dial.* Fulfulde, Northeastern Burkina Faso [fuh], 51
Ouinji-Ouinji, *alt.* Anii [blo], 42
Oujda, *dial.* Arabic, Moroccan Spoken [ary], 146
Oujiang, *dial.* Chinese, Wu [wuu], 330
Oula, *alt. dial.* Psikye [kvj], 173
Ouldeme, *alt.* Wuzlam [udl], 73
Ouled Djemma, *dial.* Maba [mde], 83
Ouma [oum], 620
Oune [oue], 620
!O!ung [oun], 41
Ounge, *alt.* Oune [oue], 620
Ouni, *alt.* Honi [how], 335
Ounji-Ounji, *alt.* Anii [blo], 207
Ouobe, *alt.* Wè Northern [wob], 95
Ouolof, *alt.* Wolof [wol], 182, 145
Ouorodougou, *alt.* Worodougou [jud], 96
Ourekabakan, *alt.* Kakabe [kke], 129
Ouri, *alt. dial.* Duala [dua], 60
Ourza, *alt. dial.* Vame [mlr], 73
Ourzo, *alt. dial.* Vame [mlr], 73
Oussouye, *alt. dial.* Jola-Kasa [csk], 180
Outer Seraji, *dial.* Pahari, Kullu [kfx], 382
Outer-Eastern Tamang, *dial.* Tamang, Eastern [taj], 479

Ouzbek, *alt.* Uzbek, Northern [uzn], 346
Ouzza, *alt. dial.* Vame [mlr], 73
Ovambo, *alt.* Kwanyama [kua], 40, 150
Ovand, *alt.* Evant [bzz], 159, 61
Ovande, *alt.* Evant [bzz], 159, 61
Ovando, *alt.* Evant [bzz], 159, 61
Overhill Cherokee, *alt. dial.* Cherokee [chr], 299
Overhill-Middle Cherokee, *dial.* Cherokee [chr], 299
Oviedo, *alt.* Edo [bin], 158
Ovimbundu, *alt.* Umbundu [umb], 42
Ovioba, *alt.* Edo [bin], 158
Owa [stn], 637
Owa Raha, *alt. dial.* Owa [stn], 637
Owa Riki, *alt. dial.* Owa [stn], 637
Owambo, *alt.* Kwanyama [kua], 150
  alt. Ndonga [ndo], 150
Owe, *dial.* Isoko [iso], 164
  dial. Yoruba [yor], 178
Owena, *alt.* Owenia [wsr], 620
Owenda, *alt.* Owenia [wsr], 620
Owenia [wsr], 620
Owenke, *alt.* Evenki [evn], 332
Owerri, *dial.* Igbo [ibo], 163
Owhe, *alt. dial.* Isoko [iso], 164
Owiniga [owi], 620
Owoi, *alt.* Lokoya [lky], 192
Òwòn Àfá, *alt. dial.* Arigidi [aqg], 154
Òwòn Èsé, *alt. dial.* Arigidi [aqg], 154
Òwòn Igásí, *alt. dial.* Arigidi [aqg], 154
Òwòn Ògè, *alt. dial.* Arigidi [aqg], 154
Òwòn Udò, *alt. dial.* Arigidi [aqg], 154
Oxchuc Tzeltal, *see* Tzeltal, Oxchuc [tzh], 276
Oxikuanyama, *alt.* Kwanyama [kua], 40
Oxoriok, *alt.* Lokoya [lky], 192
Oy [oyb], 452
Oya, *alt. dial.* Melanau [mel], 460, 325
Oya', *alt. dial.* Melanau [mel], 460, 325
Oyampí, *alt.* Wayampi [oym], 252, 233
Oyampík, *alt.* Wayampi [oym], 233
Oyampipuku, *pej. alt.* Wayampi [oym], 233
Oyana, *alt.* Wayana [way], 296, 234
  dial. Gadsup [gaj], 599
Oyanpík, *alt.* Wayampi [oym], 233
Oya'oya [oyy], 621

Oyapí, *alt.* Wayampi [oym], 252
Oyaricoulet, *alt.* Akurio [ako], 295
Oyda [oyd], 118
Oyede, *dial.* Isoko [iso], 164
Oyiakiri, *dial.* Izon [ijc], 164
Oyin, *dial.* Arigidi [aqg], 154
Oykangand, *alt. dial.* Kunjen [kjn], 573
Oyo, *dial.* Yoruba [yor], 178
Oyokom, *dial.* Bokyi [bky], 156
Oyrot, *alt.* Altai, Southern [alt], 503
Oyuwi, *alt. dial.* Ma'di [mhi], 211
Oza, *alt. dial.* Bagheli [bfy], 354
Ozbek, *alt.* Uzbek, Northern [uzn], 346
Özbek, *alt.* Uzbek, Northern [uzn], 512
Ozha, *alt. dial.* Bagheli [bfy], 354
Ozolotepec Zapotec, *see* Zapotec, Ozolotepec [zao], 279
Ozoro, *dial.* Isoko [iso], 164
Ozumacín Chinantec, *see* Chinantec, Ozumacín [chz], 261
Ozumatlán Totonac, *see* Totonac, Ozumatlán [tqt], 276
Pa, *alt.* Pare [ppt], 621
   alt. dial. Ghomálá' [bbj], 62
Pa Di [pdi], 341, 525
Pa Hng, *alt.* Pa-Hng [pha], 342, 525
Pà Hung, *alt.* Pa-Hng [pha], 525
Pa Kembaloh, *dial.* Putoh [put], 395
Pa Leng, *alt. dial.* Maleng [pkt], 524
Pa Ngng, *alt.* Pa-Hng [pha], 342
Pa Oh, *alt.* Karen, Pa'o [blk], 464, 514
Pa Then, *alt.* Pa-Hng [pha], 342
Pà Then, *alt.* Pa-Hng [pha], 525
Pa-Hng [pha], 342, 525
Pa-O, *alt.* Karen, Pa'o [blk], 464
   dial. Yamphe [yma], 482
Pa-U, *alt.* Karen, Pa'o [blk], 464, 514
Pa'0, *alt.* Karen, Pa'o [blk], 514
Pa'a [pqa], 173
Paachsai, *dial.* Jumli [jml], 472
Paaci, *alt.* Paicî [pri], 585
Pááfang [pfa], 583
Paama [pma], 644
Paama-Lopevi, *alt.* Paama [pma], 644
Paamese, *alt.* Paama [pma], 644
Pa'an, *dial.* Karen, Pwo Eastern [kjp], 464
Paang, *alt.* Pankhu [pkh], 383
Paasaal [sig], 127
Pa'awa, *alt.* Pa'a [pqa], 173
Pabir, *alt.* Bura-Pabir [bwr], 156
Pabra, *alt.* Pao [ppa], 383
Pacaas-Novos, *alt.* Pakaásnovos [pav], 231

Pacahanovo, *alt.* Pakaásnovos [pav], 231
Pacahuara [pcp], 223
Pacaraos Quechua, *see* Quechua, Pacaraos [qvp], 291
Pacawara, *alt.* Pacahuara [pcp], 223
Pacchmi, *alt.* Bilaspuri [kfs], 356
Pachagan, *dial.* Pashayi, Northwest [glh], 317
Pachien, *alt.* Saaroa [sxr], 512
Pachitea Quechua, *alt.* Quechua, Panao Huánuco [qxh], 292
Pacific Gulf Yupik, *see* Yupik, Pacific Gulf [ems], 310
Pacific Yupik, *alt.* Yupik, Pacific Gulf [ems], 310
Paco, *alt.* Pacoh [pac], 525
Pacoh [pac], 525, 452
Pacu, *alt.* Ipeka-Tapuia [paj], 227
Pa'da, *alt.* Termanu [twu], 410
   dial. Termanu [twu], 410
Pa'da Kona, *dial.* Termanu [twu], 410
Padam, *dial.* Adi [adi], 353
Padamo-Orinoco, *alt. dial.* Yanomamö [guu], 313, 234
Padang, *alt.* Dinka, Northeastern [dip], 189
   alt. Minangkabau [min], 436
   dial. Mamuju [mqx], 431
   dial. Taliabu [tlv], 404
Padar, *dial.* Bhadrawahi [bhd], 355
Padari, *dial.* Bhadrawahi [bhd], 355
Padas, *dial.* Lundayeh [lnd], 460
Padaung, *alt.* Karen, Geko [ghk], 464
   alt. Kayan [pdu], 465
Padaung Karen, *alt.* Kayan [pdu], 465
Padee, *dial.* Noon [snf], 181
Padi, *alt.* Pa Di [pdi], 341, 525
Pa'disua, *dial.* Sahu [saj], 403
Padoa, *dial.* Biak [bhw], 412
Padoe [pdo], 432
Padoé, *alt.* Padoe [pdo], 432
Padogho, *alt. dial.* Kaansa [gna], 51
Padogo, *alt.* Parkwa [pbi], 71
Padokwa, *alt.* Parkwa [pbi], 71
Padorho, *alt. dial.* Kaansa [gna], 51
Padoro, *alt. dial.* Kaansa [gna], 51
Paduko, *alt.* Parkwa [pbi], 71
Padvi, *dial.* Mawchi [mke], 375
Páez [pbb], 246
Pagabete, *alt.* Pagibete [pae], 107
Pagai, *dial.* Mentawai [mwv], 436
Paganyaw, *alt.* Karen, S'gaw [ksw], 464, 514
Pagbahan, *dial.* Iraya [iry], 495
Pagcah, *alt.* Amis [ami], 511
Pagei, *alt.* Pagi [pgi], 621

Pagi [pgi], 621
Pagibete [pae], 107
Pago, *alt.* Pagu [pgu], 403
Pagoe, *alt.* Pagu [pgu], 403
Pagu [pgu], 403
   alt. Karen, Paku [kpp], 464
   alt. dial. Pagu [pgu], 403
Paguana, *dial.* Omagua [omg], 231
Paguara, *alt. dial.* Omagua [omg], 231
Pahadi, *alt. dial.* Bhili [bhb], 356
Pahari, *alt.* Jaunsari [jns], 365
   alt. Kangri [xnr], 366
   alt. Pahari, Kullu [kfx], 382
   alt. Pangwali [pgg], 382
   alt. dial. Newar [new], 476
   dial. Pahari-Potwari [phr], 487
Pahari Bharmauri, *alt.* Gaddi [gbk], 361
Pahari Garhwali, *alt.* Garhwali [gbm], 360
Pahari Kangri, *alt.* Kangri [xnr], 366
Pahari Kullu, *alt.* Pahari, Kullu [kfx], 382
Pahari Mandiyali, *alt.* Mandeali [mjl], 374
Pahari, Kullu [kfx], 382
Pahari, Mahasu [bfz], 382
Pahari-Palpa, *alt.* Palpa [plp], 477
Pahari-Potwari [phr], 487
Paharia, *alt.* Kumarbhag Paharia [kmj], 370
   alt. Mal Paharia [mkb], 373
   alt. dial. Santali [sat], 386
   dial. Santali [sat], 322
Pahariya, *alt.* Kumarbhag Paharia [kmj], 370
Pahavai, *alt.* Tulu-Bohuai [rak], 628
Pahenbaquebo, *dial.* Capanahua [kaq], 287
Paheng, *alt.* Pa-Hng [pha], 342, 525
Pahi [lgt], 621
   dial. Pacoh [pac], 525, 452
Pahlavani [phv], 317
Pahouin, *alt.* Fang [fan], 61, 88, 120
Pahoun, *alt.* Fang [fan], 111
Pahri, *alt. dial.* Newar [new], 476
Pahu, *dial.* Tunjung [tjg], 395
Pahu', *dial.* Dusun, Central [dtp], 456
Pai, *alt.* Bai, Central [bca], 326
   alt. Mala [ped], 611
   alt. Pai Tavytera [pta], 285
   alt. Pe [pai], 173
   alt. Pei [ppq], 621
   dial. Sotho, Northern [nso], 186
Paï, *dial.* Laka [lap], 83
Pai Lisu, *dial.* Lisu [lis], 339
Pai Tavytera [pta], 285

Pai-I, *alt.* Lü [khb], 339, 451, 465, 515, 524

Pai-Yi, *alt.* Lü [khb], 515

Paiawa, *alt.* Guhu-Samane [ghs], 599

Paichien, *alt.* Saaroa [sxr], 512

Paicî [pri], 585

Paidia, *alt.* Pardhi [pcl], 383

Paiela, *dial.* Ipili [ipi], 603

Paiem, *alt.* Fyam [pym], 160

Pai'i', *alt.* Lü [khb], 339

Paiko, *dial.* Gbari [gby], 160

Pailelang, *alt.* Kafoa [kpu], 407

Pailibo, *dial.* Adi [adi], 353

Paimi, *alt.* Naga, Ao [njo], 377

Painara, *alt.* Levuka [lvu], 408

Paipai [ppi], 273

Paiquize, *alt.* Mundurukú [myu], 230

Paitan, *alt.* Tombonuwo [txa], 458

Paitana, *dial.* Waima [rro], 631

Paite, *alt.* Chin, Paite [pck], 359, 463

Paite Chin, *see* Chin, Paite [pck], 359, 463

Paiter, *alt.* Suruí [sru], 232

Paithe, *alt.* Chin, Paite [pck], 359, 463

Paiuan, *alt.* Paiwan [pwn], 511

Paiute, Northern [pao], 306

Paiwa, *alt.* Gapapaiwa [pwg], 599

Paiwan [pwn], 511

Paiyage, *alt.* Silimo [wul], 423

Pajade, *alt.* Badyara [pbp], 128, 130, 179

Pajadinca, *alt.* Badyara [pbp], 130, 179

Pajadinka, *alt.* Badyara [pbp], 128, 130, 179

Pajo, *alt.* Balaesang [bls], 427

Pajokumbuh, *dial.* Minangkabau [min], 436

Pajonal, *alt.* Ashéninka Pajonal [cjo], 286

Pajulu, *alt. dial.* Bari [bfa], 188, 210

Pajungu, *alt.* Bayungu [bxj], 569

Pak, *dial.* Pak-Tong [pkg], 621
dial. Vatrata [vlr], 646

Pak Tai, *alt.* Thai, Southern [sou], 517

Pak Thai, *alt.* Thai, Southern [sou], 517

Pak-Tong [pkg], 621

Paka, *dial.* Nzanyi [nja], 171
pej. alt. dial. Niksek [gbe], 618

Pakaanova, *alt.* Pakaásnovos [pav], 231

Pakaanovas, *alt.* Pakaásnovos [pav], 231

Pakaásnovos [pav], 231

Pakadji, *alt.* Kuuku-Ya'u [kuy], 573

Pakang, *alt.* Pokangá [pok], 231

Pakanha [pkn], 576

Pakara, *alt.* Cara [cfd], 156

Pakarla, *alt.* Banggarla [bjb], 568

Pakatan, *alt.* Bukitan [bkn], 392, 459
dial. Maleng [pkt], 451

Pakawa, *alt. dial.* Kaili, Da'a [kzf], 429

Pakewa, *alt.* Tontemboan [tnt], 434

Pakhto, *alt.* Pashto, Northern [pbu], 488

Pakhtoo, *alt.* Pashto, Northern [pbu], 317, 520
alt. Pashto, Southern [pbt], 520

Pakhtu, *alt.* Pashto, Northern [pbu], 317
alt. Pashto, Southern [pbt], 520

Paki, *alt.* Baki [bki], 641

Pakia-Sideronsi, *dial.* Naasioi [nas], 616

Pakistan Sign Language [pks], 487

Pakkau, *dial.* Bambam [ptu], 427

Pakot, *alt.* Pökoot [pko], 135, 212

Pakpak, *alt.* Batak Dairi [btd], 435

Pakpak Dairi, *alt.* Batak Dairi [btd], 435

Pakse, *dial.* Lao [lao], 445

Paktay, *alt.* Thai, Southern [sou], 517

Paktu, *alt.* Pashto, Northern [pbu], 317
alt. Pashto, Southern [pbt], 441, 520

Paku [pku], 395
alt. Karen, Paku [kpp], 464

Paku Karen, *see* Karen, Paku [kpp], 464

Paku-Tapuya, *alt.* Ipeka-Tapuia [paj], 227

Pakum, *alt.* Kwakum [kwu], 65

Pal [abw], 621

Pal Kurumba, *alt.* Kurumba, Alu [xua], 371

Pala, *alt.* Pa'a [pqa], 173
alt. Pela [bxd], 342
dial. Patpatar [gfk], 621

Pala'au, *alt. dial.* Sama, Southern [ssb], 458

Palachi, *alt. dial.* Karen, S'gaw [ksw], 464, 514

Palai, *alt. dial.* Mócheno [mhn], 545

Palaka, *alt.* Senoufo, Palaka [plr], 95

Palaka Senoufo, *see* Senoufo, Palaka [plr], 95

Palakhi, *alt. dial.* Karen, S'gaw [ksw], 464, 514

Palakka, *alt. dial.* Bugis [bug], 428

Palamata, *alt.* Palumata [pmc], 403

Palampuri, *dial.* Kangri [xnr], 366

Palamul, *alt.* Maden [xmx], 419

Palan, *dial.* Koryak [kpy], 505

Palana, *alt. dial.* Alutor [alr], 503

Palanan Dumagat, *dial.* Paranan [agp], 500

Palanan Valley Agta, *alt. dial.* Paranan [agp], 500

Palanan Valley Dumagat, *alt. dial.* Paranan [agp], 500

Palanenyo, *alt.* Paranan [agp], 500

Palani, *alt.* Paliyan [pcf], 382

Palanskij, *dial.* Alutor [alr], 503

Palantla Chinantec, *see* Chinantec, Palantla [cpa], 261

Palar, *alt.* Palor [fap], 181

Palara, *alt.* Senoufo, Palaka [plr], 95

Palari, *alt.* Polari [pld], 566

Palarie, *alt.* Polari [pld], 566

Palasi, *dial.* Shina, Kohistani [plk], 488

Palasi-Kohistani, *alt.* Shina, Kohistani [plk], 488

Palata, *alt.* Fulfulde, Adamawa [fub], 61, 80

Palattae, *alt. dial.* Bugis [bug], 428

Palau, *alt.* Palauan [pau], 587
dial. Brao [brb], 522
dial. Lave [brb], 451

Palauan [pau], 587

Palauan-Calavite, *dial.* Iraya [iry], 495

Palaui Island, *dial.* Agta, Dupaninan [duo], 490

Palaui Island Agta, *dial.* Agta, Umiray Dumaget [due], 491

Palaung, Pale [pce], 466, 342, 516

Palaung, Rumai [rbb], 466, 342

Palaung, Shwe [pll], 466, 342

Palaw, *dial.* Burmese [mya], 462

Palawan, *alt.* Palawano, Brooke's Point [plw], 500

Palawan Batak, *alt.* Batak [bya], 492

Palawanen, *alt.* Palawano, Central [plc], 500

Palawano, Brooke's Point [plw], 500

Palawano, Central [plc], 500

Palawano, Southwest [plv], 500

Palawanun, *alt.* Palawano, Brooke's Point [plw], 500

Palaweño, *alt.* Palawano, Brooke's Point [plw], 500
alt. Palawano, Central [plc], 500

Palay, *alt.* Palaung, Pale [pce], 466, 342, 516

Palaya, *alt.* Paliyan [pcf], 382

Palayan, *alt.* Paliyan [pcf], 382

Palchi, *alt.* Polci [plj], 173

Palci, *alt.* Polci [plj], 173
alt. dial. Polci [plj], 173

Paldena, *alt.* Fulfulde, Adamawa [fub], 61, 80

Paldida, *alt.* Fulfulde, Adamawa [fub], 61, 80
Pale, *alt.* Palaung, Pale [pce], 466, 342, 516
Pale Palaung, *see* Palaung, Pale [pce], 466, 342, 516
Palee'n, *alt. dial.* Ta'oih, Upper [tth], 453, 527
Palembang [plm], 437
Palembang Malay, *alt.* Palembang [plm], 437
Palenque, *alt.* Palenquero [pln], 246
Palenquero [pln], 246
Palermo, *alt. dial.* Sicilian [scn], 545
Palestanian-Jordanian Arabic, *alt.* Arabic, South Levantine Spoken [ajp], 444
Palestinian-Jordanian Arabic, *alt.* Arabic, South Levantine Spoken [ajp], 448
Paletwa Daai, *dial.* Chin, Daai [dao], 463
Pali [pli], 382, 466, 509
   alt. Bareli, Palya [bpx], 355
Palicur, *alt.* Palikúr [plu], 231, 252
Paliet, *dial.* Dinka, Southwestern [dik], 190
Paliha, *alt.* Bharia [bha], 355
Palijur, *alt.* Palikúr [plu], 231
Palik, *alt.* Apalik [apo], 590
Palikour, *alt.* Palikúr [plu], 231, 252
Palikúr [plu], 231, 252
Palili', *dial.* Toala' [tlz], 433
Palimbei, *dial.* Iatmul [ian], 602
Palin, *alt.* Embaloh [emb], 393
Palín Pocomam, *alt.* Poqomam, Southern [pou], 256
Palioariene, *alt.* Ipeka-Tapuia [paj], 227
Palioping, *alt. dial.* Dinka, Southwestern [dik], 190
Palioupiny, *dial.* Dinka, Southwestern [dik], 190
Palipo, *dial.* Grebo, Northern [gbo], 138
Palisua, *alt. dial.* Sahu [saj], 403
Palitiani, *alt. dial.* Bulgarian [bul], 532, 551
Palityan, *dial.* Bulgarian [bul], 532, 551
Paliyan [pcf], 382
Paliyar, *alt.* Paliyan [pcf], 382
Paljgu, *alt.* Nijadali [nad], 575
Palju, *alt.* Bolyu [ply], 328
Pallakha, *alt.* Senoufo, Palaka [plr], 95
Pallarese, *alt. dial.* Catalan-Valencian-Balear [cat], 559
Palleyan, *alt.* Paliyan [pcf], 382
Palliyar, *alt.* Paliyan [pcf], 382

Palma, *alt.* Makwe [ymk], 148
   alt. Maraba [ymk], 201
   alt. dial. Makwe [ymk], 148
Paloc, *alt. dial.* Dinka, Northeastern [dip], 189
Palodi, *alt.* Bareli, Palya [bpx], 355
Paloesch, *alt.* Kaili, Ledo [lew], 429
Paloic, *alt. dial.* Dinka, Northeastern [dip], 189
Palola, *alt.* Phalura [phl], 488
Palong, *alt.* Dimbong [dii], 60
Palor [fap], 181
Palpa [plp], 477
   dial. Nepali [nep], 381
Palu [pbz], 466
   alt. Kaili, Ledo [lew], 429
   alt. dial. Kaili, Ledo [lew], 429
Palú, *dial.* Mócheno [mhn], 545
Palu Kurumba, *alt.* Kurumba [kfi], 371
Paluan [plz], 458
   dial. Paluan [plz], 458
Palu'e [ple], 409
Palue, *alt.* Palu'e [ple], 409
Palula, *alt.* Phalura [phl], 488
Palumata [pmc], 403
Paluqe, *alt.* Palu'e [ple], 409
Palya Bareli, *see* Bareli, Palya [bpx], 355
Palya Bareli, *alt.* Bareli, Palya [bpx], 355
Palyku, *alt.* Nijadali [nad], 575
Palyu, *alt.* Bolyu [ply], 328
Pam [pmn], 71
   dial. Baluan-Pam [blq], 592
Pama, *alt. dial.* Karipuná [kuq], 228
Pamale, *alt.* Vamale [mkt], 585
Pamana, *alt. dial.* Karipuná [kuq], 228
Pambia [pmb], 107
Pamboang, *alt. dial.* Mandar [mdr], 431
Pambuhan, *dial.* Iraya [iry], 495
Pame de Chichimeca-Jonaz, *alt.* Chichimeca-Jonaz [pei], 260
Pame de Santa María Acapulco, *alt.* Pame, Central [pbs], 273
Pame del Centro, *alt.* Pame, Central [pbs], 273
Pame del Norte, *alt.* Pame, Northern [pmq], 273
Pame, Central [pbs], 273
Pame, Northern [pmq], 273
Pame, Southern [pmz], 273
Pamekasan, *alt. dial.* Madura [mad], 392
Pamekesan, *dial.* Madura [mad], 392
Pamela, *dial.* Sudest [tgo], 625

Pamenyan, *alt.* Bamenyam [bce], 57
Pamié, *alt.* Cubeo [cub], 226
Pamiwa, *alt.* Cubeo [cub], 244, 226
Pammari, *alt. dial.* Paumarí [pad], 231
Pamoa, *alt.* Tatuyo [tav], 247
Pamoa Bara, *dial.* Waimaha [bao], 248
Pamona [bcx], 432
   dial. Pamona [bcx], 432
Pamosu [hih], 621
Pampa, *alt.* Puelche [pue], 220
Pampadeque, *alt.* Cocama-Cocamilla [cod], 287
Pampangan [pam], 500
Pampango, *alt.* Pampangan [pam], 500
Pampangueño, *alt.* Pampangan [pam], 500
Pamplona Atta, *see* Atta, Pamplona [att], 491
Pamue, *alt.* Fang [fan], 111, 61, 88, 120
Pamusa, *dial.* Fore [for], 599
Pan, *alt.* Panchpargania [tdb], 382
Pan Aru, *dial.* Dinka, Northwestern [diw], 190
Pan Sawasi, *alt.* Panchpargania [tdb], 382
Pan Yao, *alt.* Iu Mien [ium], 336, 514
Pana (Burkina Faso) [pnq], 53, 143
   Pana (Central African Republic) [pnz], 77, 71, 86
   alt. Panobo [pno], 289
   dial. Pana [pnz], 77, 86
Pana', *alt.* Phana' [phq], 452
Pana North, *dial.* Pana [pnq], 53, 143
Pana South, *dial.* Pana [pnq], 53, 143
Panaeati, *alt.* Misima-Paneati [mpx], 614
Panags, *alt.* Panang [pcr], 342
Panaieti, *alt.* Misima-Paneati [mpx], 614
Panakha, *alt.* Panang [pcr], 342
Panakha-Panags, *dial.* Tibetan [bod], 388
Panama Embera, *alt.* Emberá, Northern [emp], 283, 245
Panamahka, *dial.* Sumo-Mayangna [sum], 283
Panamanian Creole English [jam], 283
Panamint [par], 306
Panamint Shoshone, *alt.* Panamint [par], 306
Pananag, *alt.* Panang [pcr], 342
Panang [pcr], 342

Panao Huánuco Quechua, *see* Quechua, Panao Huánuco [qxh], 292

Panapanayan, *alt.* Puyuma [pyu], 512

Panapu, *dial.* Karen, S'gaw [ksw], 464, 514

Panará, *alt.* Kreen-Akarore [kre], 229

Panaras, *alt.* Kuot [kto], 608

Panare, *alt.* Eñepa [pbh], 311

Panari, *alt.* Eñepa [pbh], 311

Panasuan [psn], 432

Panatinani, *dial.* Nimoa [nmw], 618

Panawina, *dial.* Nimoa [nmw], 618

Panay, *alt.* Aklanon [akl], 491

Panayano, *alt.* Kinaray-A [krj], 498

Panayeti, *alt.* Misima-Paneati [mpx], 614

Panbe, *alt.* Gimme [kmp], 62
alt. dial. Koma [kmy], 167

Pancana [pnp], 432

Pancaré, *alt.* Pankararú [paz], 231

Pancaru, *alt.* Pankararú [paz], 231

Panchal Lohar, *alt.* Lohar, Gade [gda], 372

Panchali, *dial.* Bhili [bhb], 356

Panchgaunle, *alt.* Thakali [ths], 480

Panchi Brahmauri Rajput, *alt.* Gaddi [gbk], 361

Panchpargania [tdb], 382

Panchthar, *alt. dial.* Limbu [lif], 474

Panchthare, *alt. dial.* Limbu [lif], 474

Panda, *alt. dial.* Ebira [igb], 158
dial. Yeskwa [yes], 178

Pandama, *alt. dial.* Karang [kzr], 63

Pandan, *alt.* Bicolano, Northern Catanduanes [cts], 493
dial. Kinaray-A [krj], 498

Pandaram Basha, *alt.* Malapandaram [mjp], 373

Pandau, *dial.* Pashayi, Northwest [glh], 317

Pande [bkj], 77
dial. Pande [bkj], 77

Pandequebo, *alt.* Cocama-Cocamilla [cod], 287

Pandewan, *dial.* Paluan [plz], 458

Pandewan Murut, *alt. dial.* Paluan [plz], 458

Pandi Muthuvan, *alt. dial.* Muthuvan [muv], 377

Pandicuto, *alt. dial.* Aragonese [arg], 558

Pandikeri, *dial.* Ma'di [mhi], 193

Pandjima, *alt.* Panytyima [pnw], 576

Pandong, *dial.* Sui [swi], 344

Paneate, *alt.* Misima-Paneati [mpx], 614

Paneroa, *alt.* Barasana [bsn], 243

Macuna [myy], 246, 229

Paneyate, *alt.* Misima-Paneati [mpx], 614

Pang, *alt.* Pankhu [pkh], 383

Pang Khua, *alt.* Pankhu [pkh], 383

Pang Pang, *dial.* Eton [etn], 641

Panga, *alt. dial.* Bushoong [buf], 98
dial. Mongo-Nkundu [lol], 104

Pangal, *dial.* Meitei [mni], 375

Pangan, *alt.* Jehai [jhi], 454

Pangasinan [pag], 500

Pangcah, *alt.* Amis [ami], 511

Panggar, *dial.* Kelon [kyo], 407

Panghse, *alt. dial.* Chinese, Mandarin [cmn], 514

Pangi, *alt.* Pangwali [pgg], 382
alt. dial. Lega-Shabunda [lea], 102
dial. Adi [adi], 353

Panginey, *alt. dial.* Gavião do Jiparaná [gvo], 226

Pangjungkho Boli, *dial.* Byangsi [bee], 358

Pangkajene, *alt. dial.* Bugis [bug], 428

Pangkala, *alt.* Banggarla [bjb], 568

Pangkep, *dial.* Bugis [bug], 428

Pangkhu, *alt.* Pankhu [pkh], 321, 383, 466

Pangkumu, *alt.* Rerep [pgk], 645

Pangkumu Bay, *alt.* Rerep [pgk], 645

Pango, *alt.* Pengo [peg], 383

Pango Paraja, *alt.* Pengo [peg], 383

Pangseng [pgs], 173
dial. Pangseng [pgs], 173

Pangsoia-Dolatok, *dial.* Siraya [fos], 512

Pangtsah, *alt.* Amis [ami], 511

Pangu, *alt.* Pongu [png], 173

Pangutaran Sama, *see* Sama, Pangutaran [slm], 500

Pangwa [pbr], 203

Pangwali [pgg], 382

Pangwali Pahari, *alt.* Pangwali [pgg], 382

Pangwe, *alt.* Myene [mye], 121

Pani, *alt.* Dugun [ndu], 60
alt. Pana [pnz], 77, 71, 86

Pani Yerava, *dial.* Ravula [yea], 384

Pania, *alt.* Paniya [pcg], 382

Paniduria, *alt.* Naga, Nocte [njb], 379

Panika, *alt.* Mirgan [zrg], 376

Panikita, *alt. dial.* Páez [pbb], 246

Panim [pnr], 621

Paningesen, *alt. dial.* Tunen [baz], 72

Paniquita, *alt. dial.* Páez [pbb], 246

Panixtlahuaca Chatino, *dial.* Chatino, Western Highland [ctp], 260

Paniya [pcg], 382

Paniyan, *alt.* Paniya [pcg], 382

Panjabi Proper, *dial.* Panjabi, Eastern [pan], 383, 135

Panjabi, Eastern [pan], 383, 135, 509

Panjabi, Mirpur [pmu], 380

Panjabi, Western [pnb], 487, 383

Panjima, *alt.* Panytyima [pnw], 576

Panjiri Yerava, *alt.* Ravula [yea], 384
dial. Ravula [yea], 384

Panjtjima, *alt.* Panytyima [pnw], 576

Panka, *alt.* Mirgan [zrg], 376

Pankalla, *alt.* Banggarla [bjb], 568

Pankarará, *alt.* Pankararú [paz], 231

Pankararé [pax], 231

Pankararú [paz], 231

Pankaravu, *alt.* Pankararú [paz], 231

Pankaré, *alt.* Pankararé [pax], 231

Pankaroru, *alt.* Pankararú [paz], 231

Pankarú, *alt.* Pankararú [paz], 231

Pankho, *alt.* Pankhu [pkh], 321, 383, 466

Pankhu [pkh], 321, 383, 466

Pankhua, *alt.* Pankhu [pkh], 383

Panko, *alt.* Pankhu [pkh], 321, 383, 466

Pankua, *alt.* Pankhu [pkh], 383

Pannei [pnc], 432

Pano, *alt.* Panobo [pno], 289

Panoan Katukína, *see* Katukína, Panoan [knt], 229

Panobo [pno], 289

Pa'non, *alt.* Dugun [ndu], 60

Panon, *alt.* Dugun [ndu], 60

Panso, *alt.* Lamnso' [lns], 65, 168

Pantasmas, *alt.* Matagalpa [mtn], 282

Pantera, *dial.* Nafaanra [nfr], 126

Pantera-Fantera, *alt.* Nafaanra [nfr], 126

Pantesco, *dial.* Sicilian [scn], 545

Pantha, *alt. dial.* Chinese, Mandarin [cmn], 514

Panthare, *dial.* Limbu [lif], 474

Panthare-Yanggrokke-Chaubise-Charkhole, *alt. dial.* Limbu [lif], 474

Pantharey, *alt. dial.* Limbu [lif], 474

Panthe, *alt. dial.* Chinese, Mandarin [cmn], 514

Pantjana, *alt.* Pancana [pnp], 432

Panya, *alt.* Mak [pbl], 169
dial. Mak [pbl], 169

Panyah, *alt.* Paniya [pcg], 382

Panyam, *alt.* Mak [pbl], 169
dial. Mwaghavul [sur], 170
Panyjima, *alt.* Panytyima [pnw], 576
Panytyima [pnw], 576
Pa'o, *alt.* Karen, Pa'o [blk], 464
Pao [ppa], 383
Pa'o Karen, *see* Karen, Pa'o [blk], 464, 514
Paoan, *alt.* Bonan [peh], 328
Paomata, *dial.* Naga, Mao [nbi], 378
Paongan, *alt.* Bonan [peh], 328
Papabuco, *alt.* Zapotec, Elotepec [zte], 278
alt. Zapotec, Texmelucan [zpz], 280
alt. Zapotec, Zaniza [zpw], 281
Papadi, *alt. dial.* Lundayeh [lnd], 394
Papago, *pej. alt. dial.* Tohono O'odham [ood], 309
Papago-Pima, *alt.* Tohono O'odham [ood], 309
Papakene, *dial.* Buang, Mapos [bzh], 595
Papantla Totonac, *see* Totonac, Papantla [top], 276
Papapana [ppn], 621
Papar [dpp], 458
dial. Bajau, West Coast [bdr], 456
Papar Kadazan, *alt.* Kadazan, Coastal [kzj], 457
Papara, *dial.* Senoufo, Cebaara [sef], 94
Papasena [pas], 422
Papavô [ppv], 231
Pape, *alt.* Dugun [ndu], 60
Papei, *alt.* Papel [pbo], 131
Papel [pbo], 131
Paperyn, *alt.* Gugubera [kkp], 571
Papi [ppe], 621
Papia, *alt.* Baba [bbw], 56
Papia Kristang, *alt.* Malaccan Creole Portuguese [mcm], 454, 509
Papiam, *alt.* Papiamentu [pap], 282, 221
Papiamen, *alt.* Papiamentu [pap], 282
Papiamento, *alt.* Papiamentu [pap], 282, 221
Papiamentoe, *alt.* Papiamentu [pap], 282, 221
Papiamentu [pap], 282, 221
Papitalai [pat], 621
Papola, *alt.* Papora-Hoanya [ppu], 512
Papora, *dial.* Papora-Hoanya [ppu], 512
Papora-Hoanya [ppu], 512
Papuan Hiri Motu, *dial.* Motu, Hiri [hmo], 615

Papuan Malay, *dial.* Malay [mly], 436
Papuma [ppm], 422
Para, *alt.* Naga, Khiamniungan [nky], 378, 466
alt. Parawen [prw], 621
Pará Arára, *see* Arára, Pará [aap], 225
Pará Gavião, *see* Gavião, Pará [gvp], 226
Parabhi, *dial.* Konkani [knn], 369
Parachi [prc], 317
Paradi, *alt.* Pardhi [pcl], 383
Paraene, *alt.* Yavitero [yvt], 313
Paraguayan Guaraní, *see* Guaraní, Paraguayan [gug], 284
Paraguayan Toba, *alt.* Emok [emo], 284
Parahujano, *alt.* Paraujano [pbg], 312
Parahuri, *alt.* Yanomámi [wca], 234
Paraja, *alt.* Duruwa [pci], 361
alt. Pengo [peg], 383
Parajhi, *alt.* Bodo Parja [bdv], 357
alt. Duruwa [pci], 361
Parakanã [pak], 231
Parakanân, *alt.* Parakanã [pak], 231
Parakatêjê, *alt.* Gavião, Pará [gvp], 226
Parakuyo, *dial.* Maasai [mas], 134, 201
Parali, *dial.* Nachering [ncd], 476
Paramaccan, *dial.* Aukan [djk], 295
Paran, *alt.* Taroko [trv], 512
alt. dial. Taroko [trv], 512
Paraná Kaingang, *dial.* Kaingáng [kgp], 228
Paranan [agp], 500
Paranapura, *alt.* Chayahuita [cbt], 287
Paranauat, *alt.* Paranawát [paf], 231
Paranawát [paf], 231
Parata, *dial.* Tuamotuan [pmt], 581
Paraujano [pbg], 312
Parauk [prk], 466, 342
Parawen [prw], 621
Parazhghan, *dial.* Pashayi, Northwest [glh], 317
Parbate, Eastern [kif], 477
Parbate, Western [kjl], 477
Parbatiya, *alt.* Nepali [nep], 476, 323, 381
Pardesi, *dial.* Awadhi [awa], 354, 468
Pardhan [pch], 383
Pardhi [pcl], 383
Pare [ppt], 621
alt. Asu [asa], 197
alt. Peere [pfe], 173
Pare-Pare, *alt. dial.* Bugis [bug], 428

Parec, *dial.* Kâte [kmg], 605
Parecís [pab], 231
Parekwa, *alt.* Parkwa [pbi], 71
Paren, *dial.* Koryak [kpy], 505
dial. Naga, Zeme [nzm], 381
Pareng, *alt.* Parenga [pcj], 383
Parenga [pcj], 383
Parenga Parja, *alt.* Parenga [pcj], 383
Parengi, *alt.* Parenga [pcj], 383
Parenji, *alt.* Parenga [pcj], 383
Paresí, *alt.* Parecís [pab], 231
Paressí, *alt.* Parecís [pab], 231
Paret, *dial.* Lamogai [lmg], 609
Pari, *alt.* Embaloh [emb], 393
alt. Mundurukú [myu], 230
Päri [lkr], 194
Paria, *alt.* Pardhi [pcl], 383
Pariana, *alt.* Omagua [omg], 289, 231
Parigi, *alt. dial.* Kaili, Ledo [lew], 429
Parikala, *dial.* Yerukula [yeu], 390
Parima, *alt. dial.* Yanomamö [guu], 313, 234
Parintintín, *dial.* Tenharim [pah], 232
Paripao, *dial.* Lengo [lgr], 637
Parja, *alt.* Bodo Parja [bdv], 357
Parjhi, *alt.* Bodo Parja [bdv], 357
alt. Duruwa [pci], 361
Parji, *alt.* Bodo Parja [bdv], 357
alt. Duruwa [pci], 361
Parkari, *alt.* Koli, Parkari [kvx], 487
Parkari Koli, *see* Koli, Parkari [kvx], 487
Parkwa [pbi], 71
Parlare, *alt.* Polari [pld], 566
Parlary, *alt.* Polari [pld], 566
Parlata Trentina, *alt. dial.* Ladin [lld], 544
Parlyaree, *alt.* Polari [pld], 566
Parnkala, *alt.* Banggarla [bjb], 568
Parnkalla, *alt.* Banggarla [bjb], 568
Parnkarra, *alt.* Warluwara [wrb], 578
Parocana, *alt.* Parakanã [pak], 231
Paroja, *alt.* Bodo Parja [bdv], 357
Parole des Bana, *alt.* Bana [bcw], 57
Parquenahua, *alt.* Yora [mts], 294
Parsee, *alt.* Parsi [prp], 383
Parsee-Dari, *alt.* Parsi-Dari [prd], 441
Parsi [prp], 383
alt. Farsi, Eastern [prs], 315
alt. Farsi, Western [pes], 439
alt. Mal Paharia [mkb], 373
dial. Gujarati [guj], 363
Parsi-Dari [prd], 441

Parsiwan, *dial.* Farsi, Eastern [prs], 315

Parte, *alt.* Chin, Paite [pck], 359

Parti-Maya, *alt.* Badimaya [bia], 568

Parua, *alt.* Kayabí [kyz], 229

Parucutu, *alt.* Hixkaryána [hix], 227
alt. dial. Waiwai [waw], 233

Parukota, *alt.* Waiwai [waw], 257

Parukoto-Charuma, *alt.* Hixkaryána [hix], 227

Parukutu, *alt. dial.* Waiwai [waw], 233

Parun, *alt.* Prasuni [prn], 317

Parvari, *alt. dial.* Konkani [knn], 369

Parvati, *dial.* Garhwali [gbm], 360

Parya [paq], 513, 317

Parya Bhilali, *dial.* Bhilali [bhi], 356

Pasaale, *alt.* Paasaal [sig], 127

Pasaale Sisaala, *alt.* Paasaal [sig], 127

Pasaali, *dial.* Paasaal [sig], 127

Pasan, *alt.* Ratahan [rth], 432

Pasangkayu, *dial.* Bugis [bug], 428

Pasar Malay, *alt.* Malay, Sabah [msi], 457
alt. dial. Malay [mly], 455

Pascuense, *alt.* Rapa Nui [rap], 243

Pase, *dial.* Aceh [ace], 435

Pasemah [pse], 437

Pashagar, *dial.* Pashayi, Northwest [glh], 317

Pashai, *alt.* Pashayi, Southeast [psi], 317

Pashayi, Northeast [aee], 317

Pashayi, Northwest [glh], 317

Pashayi, Southeast [psi], 317

Pashayi, Southwest [psh], 317

Pashto, Central [pst], 488

Pashto, Northern [pbu], 488, 317, 520

Pashto, Southern [pbt], 488, 317, 441, 520

Pashtu, *alt.* Pashto, Northern [pbu], 488, 520
alt. Pashto, Southern [pbt], 488, 441

Pasi [psq], 621
dial. Adi [adi], 353
dial. Mongondow [mog], 431

Pasir, *alt. dial.* Malay [mly], 436
dial. Lawangan [lbx], 394

Pasir Malay, *alt. dial.* Malay [mly], 455

Pasisir, *dial.* Javanese [jav], 391
dial. Rejang [rej], 437

Pasismanua, *alt.* Kaulong [pss], 605

Pasoom, *dial.* Ta'oih, Upper [tth], 453, 527

Paspatian, *dial.* Romani, Balkan [rmn], 532

Pass Valley, *alt.* Yali, Pass Valley [yac], 426
dial. Yali, Pass Valley [yac], 426

Pass Valley Yali, *see* Yali, Pass Valley [yac], 426

Passam, *alt.* Kpasam [pbn], 167

Passamaquoddy, *dial.* Malecite-Passamaquoddy [pqm], 238, 304

Passtoo, *alt.* Pashto, Northern [pbu], 520

Pastaza Quichua, *alt.* Quichua, Northern Pastaza [qvz], 251

Pasuma, *alt.* Kewa, West [kew], 606

Paswam, *alt.* Bitur [mcc], 594

Patagonian Welsh, *dial.* Welsh [cym], 566, 220

Patakai, *alt.* Nuaulu, North [nni], 402
alt. Nuaulu, South [nxl], 402

Patamona [pbc], 257

Patani [ptn], 403
alt. dial. Gujarati [guj], 363

Patapori, *alt.* Peere [pfe], 71, 173

Patara, *dial.* Senoufo, Cebaara [sef], 94

Patashó, *alt.* Pataxó-Hãhaãi [pth], 231

Patasiwa Alfoeren, *alt.* Alune [alp], 396

Pataxi, *alt.* Pataxó-Hãhaãi [pth], 231

Pataxó-Hãhãhãe, *alt.* Pataxó-Hãhaãi [pth], 231

Pataxó-Hãhaãi [pth], 231

Pate, *dial.* Swahili [swh], 136

Patelia, *dial.* Bhili [bhb], 356

Patep [ptp], 621

Pathee, *alt. dial.* Chinese, Mandarin [cmn], 514

Pati, *alt.* Paicî [pri], 585

Patidari, *alt. dial.* Gujarati [guj], 363

Patimitheri, *alt. dial.* Yanomámi [wca], 234

Patimuni, *alt.* Baham [bdw], 412

Patipi, *dial.* Onin [oni], 421

Patjtjamalh, *alt. dial.* Wadjiginy [wdj], 577

Patla-Chicontla Totonac, *see* Totonac, Patla-Chicontla [tot], 276

Patni, *alt.* Pattani [lae], 383

Patnuli, *alt.* Saurashtra [saz], 386
alt. dial. Gujarati [guj], 363

Pato Tapuia, *alt.* Ipeka-Tapuia [paj], 227

Pato-Tapuya, *alt.* Ipeka-Tapuia [paj], 227

Patoé Valdoten, *alt. dial.* Franco-Provençal [frp], 543

Patois, *alt.* Dominican Creole French [acf], 250
alt. Franco-Provençal [frp], 536, 562

alt. Guadeloupean Creole French [gcf], 253

alt. Guianese Creole French [gcr], 252

alt. Jamaican Creole English [jam], 259

alt. Krio [kri], 183

alt. Martiniquan Creole French [gcf], 259

alt. Saint Lucian Creole French [acf], 294

alt. Tayo [cks], 585

alt. Trinidadian Creole French [acf], 296

dial. Grenadian Creole French [acf], 253

Patois de St-Louis, *alt.* Tayo [cks], 585

Patool, *dial.* Gula Iro [glj], 81

Patoxó, *alt.* Pataxó-Hãhaãi [pth], 231

Patpari, *alt.* Patpatar [gfk], 621

Patpatar [gfk], 621
dial. Patpatar [gfk], 621

Patra-Saara, *alt.* Juang [jun], 365

Patrak, *alt. dial.* Kalami [gwc], 485

Patsoka, *alt.* Yurutí [yui], 249

Patta' Binuang, *alt. dial.* Mamasa [mqj], 431

Pattae', *alt. dial.* Mamasa [mqj], 431
dial. Bambam [ptu], 427

Pattan, *alt. dial.* Kohistani, Indus [mvy], 486

Pattani [lae], 383

Pattani Malay, *see* Malay, Pattani [mfa], 516

Pattapu Bhasha, *dial.* Tamil [tam], 388

Pattinjo, *alt. dial.* Enrekang [ptt], 429

Patu, *alt.* Khowar [khw], 486

Patua, *alt.* Juang [jun], 365

Patués, *alt.* Aragonese [arg], 558

Patvi, *alt. dial.* Malvi [mup], 374

Patwa, *alt.* Dominican Creole French [acf], 250
alt. Guadeloupean Creole French [gcf], 253

alt. Guianese Creole French [gcr], 252

alt. Jamaican Creole English [jam], 259

alt. Martiniquan Creole French [gcf], 259

alt. Saint Lucian Creole French [acf], 294

alt. Trinidadian Creole French [acf], 296

dial. Grenadian Creole French [acf], 253

Patwin, *dial.* Wintu [wit], 310

Pau Thin, *alt.* Giáy [pcc], 523
Paucerne, *alt.* Pauserna [psm], 223
Pauhut, *alt. dial.* Teressa [tef], 388
Pauini, *dial.* Jamamadí [jaa], 227
Paulohi [plh], 403
Pauma, *alt.* Paama [pma], 644
Paumarí [pad], 231
Paumarm, *dial.* Paumarí [pad], 231
Paumei, *alt.* Naga, Poumei [pmx], 379
Pa'umotu, *alt.* Tuamotuan [pmt], 581
Paunangis, *dial.* Efate, North [llp], 641
Paupe, *alt.* Papi [ppe], 621
Pauri, *alt.* Bareli, Rathwi [bgd], 355
  alt. dial. Garhwali [gbm], 360
Pauri Bareli, *see* Bareli, Pauri [bfb], 355
Paurong, *alt. dial.* Tibetan [bod], 388
Pauserna [psm], 223
Pauserna-Guarasugwé, *alt.* Pauserna [psm], 223
Pauwi, *alt.* Yoke [yki], 427
Pavaia, *alt.* Pawaia [pwa], 621
Paviotso, *alt.* Paiute, Northern [pao], 306
Pawaia [pwa], 621
Pawana, *alt.* Maquiritari [mch], 312, 229
Pawang, *alt.* Horpa [ero], 335
Pawany, *dial.* Dinka, Northwestern [diw], 190
Pawari, *alt.* Bareli, Rathwi [bgd], 355
  dial. Bundeli [bns], 357
Pawaté, *alt.* Paranawát [paf], 231
Pawdawkwa, *alt.* Parkwa [pbi], 71
Pawixi, *alt. dial.* Kaxuiâna [kbb], 229
Pawiyana, *dial.* Kaxuiâna [kbb], 229
Pawnee [paw], 306
Pawri, *alt.* Bareli, Rathwi [bgd], 355
Paxala, *alt.* Vagla [vag], 128
Pay, *alt.* Mala [ped], 611
  alt. dial. Olo [ong], 619
Paya, *alt.* Pech [pay], 258
Paya-Pucuro, *alt.* Kuna, Border [kvn], 246
Paya-Pucuro Kuna, *alt.* Kuna, Border [kvn], 283
Payagua, *alt.* Orejón [ore], 289
Payap, *alt.* Thai, Northern [nod], 517
Payi, *dial.* Olo [ong], 619
Paynamar [pmr], 621
Payowan, *alt.* Paiwan [pwn], 511
Payualiene, *alt.* Ipeka-Tapuia [paj], 227
Payuliene, *alt.* Ipeka-Tapuia [paj], 227

Payungu, *alt.* Bayungu [bxj], 569
Pazande, *alt.* Zande [zne], 109, 78, 196
Pazend, *alt.* Avestan [ave], 438
Pbharya, *alt.* Parya [paq], 513
Pchcknya, *alt.* Karen, S'gaw [ksw], 464
Pe [pai], 173
  alt. Baima [bqh], 327
  dial. Musey [mse], 68
Pe Miao, *alt.* Hmong Daw [mww], 334, 514
Pe-Bae, *alt.* Enets, Forest [enf], 504
Pe-Holom-Gamé, *dial.* Musey [mse], 85
Pear [pcb], 326
Peawa, *dial.* Wipi [gdr], 632
Pech [pay], 258
Pecixe, *alt. dial.* Mandjak [mfv], 131, 122, 181
Pecok, *alt.* Petjo [pey], 392
Peda, *alt.* Gbe, Xwela [xwe], 45
Pedi, *alt.* Sotho, Northern [nso], 186
  dial. Kgalagadi [xkv], 47
Pedir, *alt. dial.* Aceh [ace], 435
Pedra Branca, *alt. dial.* Kariri-Xocó [kzw], 228
Peekit, *alt. dial.* Yupik, Central Siberian [ess], 507
Peemba, *dial.* Fipa [fip], 198
Peer, *alt.* Peere [pfe], 71, 173
Peer Muure, *dial.* Peere [pfe], 71
Peere [pfe], 71, 173
Peewa, *alt. dial.* Krahn, Western [krw], 93
Pegu, *dial.* Mon [mnw], 466
Peguan, *alt.* Mon [mnw], 466, 516
Pegullo-Bura, *alt.* Yidiny [yii], 579
Peh Miao, *alt.* Hmong Daw [mww], 334, 514
Pehuenche, *dial.* Mapudungun [arn], 242, 220
Pei [ppq], 621
Peigan, *alt. dial.* Blackfoot [bla], 235, 298
Peinan, *alt. dial.* Amis [ami], 511
Pekal [pel], 437
Pekava, *alt. dial.* Kaili, Da'a [kzf], 429
Pekawa, *alt. dial.* Kaili, Da'a [kzf], 429
Pekhi, *alt.* Ubykh [uby], 563
Pekurehua, *alt.* Napu [npy], 432
Pela [bxd], 342
  dial. Bura-Pabir [bwr], 156
Pelado, *alt.* Panobo [pno], 289
Pelam, *alt.* Puyuma [pyu], 512
Pelasla, *alt.* Vame [mlr], 73
  alt. dial. Vame [mlr], 73
Pelau, *dial.* Ontong Java [ojv], 637

Pelauw, *dial.* Haruku [hrk], 398
Pele, *dial.* Pele-Ata [ata], 621
Pele-Ata [ata], 621
Peleata, *alt.* Pele-Ata [ata], 621
Pelende [ppp], 107
Pelimpo, *alt.* Pinyin [pny], 71
Pelipowai, *alt.* Tulu-Bohuai [rak], 628
Pelmung, *dial.* Kulung [kle], 473
Pelta Hay, *alt.* Fulfulde, Adamawa [fub], 61, 80
Pelu, *alt. dial.* Geji [gji], 160
Peluan, *alt. dial.* Paluan [plz], 458
Pelym, *alt. dial.* Mansi [mns], 505
Pem, *alt.* Fyam [pym], 160
Pemba, *dial.* Swahili [swh], 205, 136
Pemon [aoc], 312, 231, 257
  alt. dial. Pemon [aoc], 312
Pemong, *alt.* Pemon [aoc], 312, 231, 257
Pémono [pev], 312
Pen, *alt. dial.* Gulay [gvl], 81
Pen Ti Lolo, *alt.* Qabiao [laq], 526
Peñablanca, *dial.* Agta, Dupaninan [duo], 490
Penampang Kadazan, *alt.* Kadazan, Coastal [kzj], 457
Penan Apo, *dial.* Penan, Western [pne], 460
Penan Apoh, *dial.* Penan, Eastern [pez], 460, 325
Penan Gang, *dial.* Penan, Western [pne], 460, 325
Penan Lanying, *dial.* Penan, Western [pne], 460, 325
Penan Lusong, *dial.* Penan, Western [pne], 460, 325
Penan Nibong, *alt. dial.* Penan, Western [pne], 325
Penan Silat, *dial.* Penan, Western [pne], 460, 325
Penan, Eastern [pez], 460, 325
Penan, Western [pne], 460, 325
Penang Sign Language [psg], 455
Penapo, *dial.* Ambrym, Southeast [tvk], 640
Penasak, *alt.* Penesak [pen], 437
Penasifu, *dial.* Biak [bhw], 412
Penchal [pek], 621
Penchangan, *dial.* Tidong [tid], 395
Pend d'Oreille, *dial.* Kalispel-Pend d'Oreille [fla], 302
Pendau [ums], 432
Pende, *alt.* Phende [pem], 107
Pendia, *alt. dial.* Bakaka [bqz], 57
Penesak [pen], 437
Penghulu, *dial.* Minangkabau [min], 436

Pengo [peg], 383
alt. Vengo [bav], 73
Pengu, *alt.* Pengo [peg], 383
Pengua, *alt.* Pengo [peg], 383
Penguia, *alt. dial.* Kono [kno], 183
Peni, *alt. dial.* Gulay [gvl], 81
Penihing, *alt.* Aoheng [pni], 392
Penin, *alt.* Tunen [baz], 72
Peninsula Sherbro, *dial.* Sherbro [bun], 177
Peninsular Maya, *alt.* Maya, Yucatán [yua], 264
Pennsylvania Deitsh, *alt.* German, Pennsylvania [pdc], 301
Pennsylvania Dutch, *alt.* German, Pennsylvania [pdc], 301, 237
Pennsylvania German, *see* German, Pennsylvania [pdc], 301, 237
Pennsylvanisch, *alt.* German, Pennsylvania [pdc], 237
Pennsylvanisch Deitsch, *alt. dial.* German, Pennsylvania [pdc], 237
Pennsylvanish, *alt.* German, Pennsylvania [pdc], 301
Penobscot, *dial.* Abnaki, Eastern [aaq], 297
Peñoles, *alt. dial.* Mixtec, Peñoles [mil], 268
Peñoles Mixtec, *see* Mixtec, Peñoles [mil], 268
Penrhyn [pnh], 579
Penrhynese, *alt.* Penrhyn [pnh], 579
Pensiangan Murut, *dial.* Tagal Murut [mvv], 458, 395
Pensylvanisch Deitsch, *alt. dial.* German, Pennsylvania [pdc], 301
Pentjangan, *alt. dial.* Tagal Murut [mvv], 458, 395
Pentlatch [ptw], 241
Penyabung Punan, *alt. dial.* Dayak, Land [dyk], 393
Penyin, *alt.* Tunen [baz], 72
Péomé, *alt. dial.* Wè Northern [wob], 95
Peoria, *dial.* Miami [mia], 304
Pepeha, *alt.* Minanibai [mcv], 614
Pepel, *alt.* Papel [pbo], 131
Pepesa, *dial.* Jwira-Pepesa [jwi], 125
Pepesa-Jwira, *alt.* Jwira-Pepesa [jwi], 125
Pepo-Hwan, *alt.* Siraya [fos], 512
Pepohoan, *alt.* Siraya [fos], 512
Pequot-Mohegan, *dial.* Mohegan-Montauk-Narragansett [mof], 305
Perai [wet], 399
Perak, *dial.* Malay [mly], 455
Perak I, *alt. dial.* Semai [sea], 455
Perak II, *alt. dial.* Semai [sea], 455

Peranakan, *alt.* Indonesian, Peranakan [pea], 391
dial. Malay [mly], 436
Peranakan Indonesian, *see* Indonesian, Peranakan [pea], 391
Peräpohja, *dial.* Finnish [fin], 534
Pere, *alt.* Bhele [bhy], 98
alt. Peere [pfe], 71, 173
alt. Wom [wom], 177
alt. dial. Mbum [mdd], 66
Pereba, *alt.* Wom [wom], 177
Perema, *alt.* Wom [wom], 177
Peremka, *alt.* Kunja [pep], 608
Perené Campa, *pej. alt.* Ashéninka Perené [prq], 286
Peri, *alt.* Bhele [bhy], 98
dial. Kalanga [kck], 216, 47
Perim, *dial.* Tunia [tug], 87
Peripheral Mongolian, *see* Mongolian, Peripheral [mvf], 339, 462
Permyak, *alt.* Komi-Permyak [koi], 555
Pero [pip], 173
Persian, *alt.* Farsi, Eastern [prs], 315
alt. Farsi, Western [pes], 439, 443, 482, 503, 513, 520
Persian Azerbaijan Jewish Aramaic, *alt.* Lishán Didán [trg], 445
Persian Sign Language [psc], 441
Peruvian Sign Language [prl], 289
Pesaa, *alt.* Nsari [asj], 70
Pesecham, *alt.* Nduga [ndx], 421
Pesechem, *alt.* Nduga [ndx], 421
Pesegem, *alt.* Nduga [ndx], 421
Peshawar Hindko, *dial.* Hindko, Southern [hnd], 485
Peshawari, *alt. dial.* Hindko, Southern [hnd], 485
Pesii, *alt.* Wushi [bse], 73
Pesisir, Southern [pec], 437
Peske, *alt. dial.* Fali, North [fll], 61
Pessa, *alt.* Kpelle, Guinea [gkp], 129
alt. Kpelle, Liberia [xpe], 138
Pessy, *alt.* Kpelle, Guinea [gkp], 129
alt. Kpelle, Liberia [xpe], 138
Peta, *alt. dial.* Nyanja [nya], 140
dial. Nyanja [nya], 215
Petapa, *alt.* Taje [pee], 433
Petapa Zapotec, *see* Zapotec, Petapa [zpe], 279
Petasia, *dial.* Mori Bawah [xmz], 431
Petats [pex], 621
Petchabun Miao, *dial.* Hmong Daw [mww], 334, 514
Petem, *alt. dial.* Kwakum [kwu], 65

Petén Itzá Maya, *alt.* Itza' [itz], 254
Peterara, *dial.* Maewo, Central [mwo], 643
Peth, *alt. dial.* Dinka, Southwestern [dik], 190
Peti, *alt.* Nyong [muo], 171
Petit Mauresque, *alt.* Lingua Franca [pml], 209
Petjo [pey], 392
Petjoh, *alt.* Petjo [pey], 392
Petlacalancingo Mixtec, *dial.* Mixtec, Alcozauca [xta], 266
Petspets, *dial.* Teop [tio], 627
Peu, *alt.* Karen, Lahta [kvt], 464
Peuhl, *alt.* Pulaar [fuc], 143
Peul, *alt.* Fulfulde, Adamawa [fub], 61, 80
alt. Fulfulde, Borgu [fue], 44, 207
alt. Fulfulde, Central-Eastern Niger [fuq], 151
alt. Fulfulde, Gorgal [fuh], 44
alt. Fulfulde, Kano-Katsina-Bororro [fuv], 61, 80
alt. Fulfulde, Maasina [ffm], 143, 125
alt. Fulfulde, Western Niger [fuh], 151
alt. Pulaar [fuc], 181, 122, 130, 131, 143, 145
Peulh, *alt.* Fulfulde, Adamawa [fub], 61, 80
alt. Fulfulde, Borgu [fue], 44, 207
alt. Fulfulde, Central-Eastern Niger [fuq], 151
alt. Fulfulde, Gorgal [fuh], 44
alt. Fulfulde, Western Niger [fuh], 151
alt. Pulaar [fuc], 181, 122, 130, 131
Pévé [lme], 86, 71
Pevekskij, *dial.* Chukot [ckt], 504
Pewa, *dial.* Krahn, Western [krw], 93
Pewanean, *alt.* Seko Tengah [sko], 433
Pewaneang, *alt.* Seko Tengah [sko], 433
Pfaelzisch [pfl], 538
Pfälzisch, *alt.* Pfaelzisch [pfl], 538
Pfälzische, *alt.* Pfaelzisch [pfl], 538
Pfokomo, *alt.* Pokomo, Lower [poj], 135
Phadang, *dial.* Naga, Tangkhul [nmf], 380
Phai [prt], 516, 452
Phake [phk], 384
Phakey, *alt.* Phake [phk], 384
Phakial, *alt.* Phake [phk], 384
Phalaborwa, *dial.* Sotho, Northern [nso], 186
Phalaburwa, *alt. dial.* Sotho, Northern [nso], 186

Piedmont Sintí, *dial.* Romani, Sinte [rmo], 545
Piedmontese, *alt.* Piemontese [pms], 545
Piegan, *dial.* Blackfoot [bla], 235, 298
Piemontèis, *alt.* Piemontese [pms], 545
Piemontese [pms], 545
Piiga, *alt. dial.* Ukhwejo [ukh], 78
Pijao [pij], 247
Pijdari, *dial.* Kurdish, Central [ckb], 440
Pije [piz], 585
Pijin [pis], 637
Pikanii, *alt.* Blackfoot [bla], 235, 298
Pikaru, *alt.* Bikaru [bic], 593
      dial. Bisorio [bir], 594
Piki, *alt.* Fanagalo [fng], 185, 213, 216
Pikiwa, *alt.* Dibiyaso [dby], 597
Pil, *alt. dial.* Themne [tem], 184
Pila, *alt.* Maia [sks], 610
      alt. Yom [pil], 46
Pilaca, *alt.* Pilagá [plg], 220
Pilagá [plg], 220
Pilam, *alt.* Puyuma [pyu], 512
Pilapila, *alt.* Yom [pil], 46
Pilara, *alt.* Senoufo, Palaka [plr], 95
Pileni [piv], 637
      dial. Pileni [piv], 637
Pilheni, *alt.* Pileni [piv], 637
Pili, *alt.* Bhele [bhy], 98
Pililo, *alt.* Solong [aaw], 625
Pililuna, *alt.* Walmajarri [wmt], 577
Pilinara, *alt. dial.* Ngarinman [nbj], 575
Pilipino, *alt.* Filipino [fil], 494
Pima, *alt. dial.* Tohono O'odham [ood], 309
Pima Bajo [pia], 273
Pimbi, *alt.* Phimbi [phm], 148
Pimbwe [piw], 204
Pimenc, *alt.* Nomaande [lem], 70
Pimi, *alt.* Pumi, Northern [pmi], 342
      alt. Pumi, Southern [pmj], 342
Pimuru, *dial.* Ikobi-Mena [meb], 602
Pin, *alt.* Trieng [stg], 527
Pinai, *alt.* Pinai-Hagahai [pnn], 622
      dial. Pinai-Hagahai [pnn], 622
Pinai-Hagahai [pnn], 622
Pinan, *dial.* Puyuma [pyu], 512
Pinangol, *dial.* Kalinga, Lower Tanudan [kml], 497
Pinata-Konkombira, *alt. dial.* Tairora, South [omw], 626
Pinaye, *alt.* Pinai-Hagahai [pnn], 622
Pinche, *alt.* Taushiro [trr], 293
Pinchi, *alt.* Taushiro [trr], 293
Pinchie, *dial.* Carrier [crx], 236
Pindare, *dial.* Guajajára [gub], 227

Pindi, *alt.* Kwese [kws], 102
      alt. Phende [pem], 107
Pindiga, *dial.* Hõne [juh], 162
Pindiini, *alt.* Pintiini [pti], 576
Pindje, *alt.* Pije [piz], 585
Pine, *alt.* Bine [bon], 593
Pingas, *alt. dial.* Bookan [bnb], 456
Pingelap, *alt.* Pingelapese [pif], 583
Pingelapese [pif], 583
Pingilapese, *alt.* Pingelapese [pif], 583
Pingou, *dial.* Biali [beh], 42
Pingwu Baima, *alt. dial.* Baima [bqh], 327
Pini [pii], 576
Piniari, *alt.* Dogon, Kolum So [dkl], 142
Pinigura [pnv], 576
Pinikura, *alt.* Pinigura [pnv], 576
Pinipel, *alt. dial.* Nehan [nsn], 617
Pinipin, *alt. dial.* Nehan [nsn], 617
Piniritjara, *alt.* Pini [pii], 576
Pinjari, *dial.* Urdu [urd], 389
Pinje, *alt.* Pije [piz], 585
Pinji [pic], 121
      alt. Phende [pem], 107
Pinkangama, *alt.* Mudbura [mwd], 574
Pinneegooroo, *alt.* Burduna [bxn], 569
Pinotepa Nacional Mixtec, *see* Mixtec, Pinotepa Nacional [mio], 268
Pinrang, *alt. dial.* Bugis [bug], 428
Pinrang Utara, *alt. dial.* Bugis [bug], 428
Pintiini [pti], 576
Pintubi, *alt.* Pintupi-Luritja [piu], 576
Pintumbang, *dial.* Kabola [klz], 407
Pintupi-Luritja [piu], 576
Pintuyacu, *dial.* Iquito [iqu], 288
Pinyin [pny], 71
Pioche-Sioni, *alt.* Siona [snn], 247
Pioje, *alt.* Siona [snn], 247
Piojé, *dial.* Secoya [sey], 293
Pipero, *alt.* Pero [pip], 173
Pipikoro, *alt.* Uma [ppk], 434
Pipil [ppl], 252
Pipipaia, *dial.* Rotokas [roo], 623
Piploda, *alt.* Harauti [hoj], 364
Pira, *alt.* Yine [pib], 294
Pira-Tapuya, *alt.* Piratapuyo [pir], 231
Pirabanak, *dial.* Citak [txt], 413
Pirahã [myp], 231
Piratapuyo [pir], 231, 247
Pire, *alt.* Tso [ldp], 176
Piri, *alt.* Bhele [bhy], 98
      alt. Tso [ldp], 176
Pirlatapa [bxi], 576

Pirniritjara, *alt.* Pini [pii], 576
Piro [pie], 307
      pej. alt. Yine [pib], 294
Pirr, *dial.* Naga, Sangtam [nsa], 379
Pirro, *alt.* Yine [pib], 294
Piru [ppr], 403
Pisa, *alt.* Awyu, Asue [psa], 412
Pisabo [pig], 289
Pisaflores Tepehua, *see* Tepehua, Pisaflores [tpp], 275
Pisagua, *alt.* Pisabo [pig], 289
Pisahua, *alt.* Pisabo [pig], 289
Piscataway [psy], 307
Piscimas, *alt.* Bhojpuri [bho], 356
Pishagchi, *dial.* Azerbaijani, South [azb], 438
Pishauco, *alt. dial.* Pemon [aoc], 312
Pisin, *alt.* Tok Pisin [tpi], 628
Piso, *dial.* Kalagan [kqe], 497
Pisquibo, *dial.* Shipibo-Conibo [shp], 293
Pita Pita, *alt.* Pitta Pitta [pit], 576
Pitas Bajau, *dial.* Bajau, West Coast [bdr], 456
Pitas Kimaragang, *dial.* Kimaragang [kqr], 457
Pitayo, *dial.* Páez [pbb], 246
Pitcairn English, *alt.* Pitcairn-Norfolk [pih], 586, 576, 586
      dial. Pitcairn-Norfolk [pih], 634
Pitcairn-Norfolk [pih], 586, 576, 586, 634
Pite, *alt.* Saami, Pite [sje], 561, 550
Pite Saami, *see* Saami, Pite [sje], 561, 550
Pitha-Pitha, *alt.* Pitta Pitta [pit], 576
Pithantjatjarra, *alt. dial.* Pitjantjatjara [pjt], 576
Piti [pcn], 173
Piti Bhoti, *alt.* Spiti Bhoti [spt], 387
Pitiko, *alt.* Kholok [ktc], 166
      alt. Piya-Kwonci [piy], 173
Pitilu, *alt.* Leipon [lek], 609
Pitjantjara, *alt.* Pitjantjatjara [pjt], 576
Pitjantjatjara [pjt], 576
      alt. dial. Pitjantjatjara [pjt], 576
Pitonara, *alt.* Potiguára [pog], 231
Pitt River, *alt.* Achumawi [acv], 297
Pitta Pitta [pit], 576
Pittala Bhasha, *dial.* Pardhi [pcl], 383
Pitti, *alt.* Piti [pcn], 173
Pitu-Ulunna-Salu, *alt.* Bambam [ptu], 427
Pityilu, *alt.* Leipon [lek], 609
Piu [pix], 622
Piva, *alt.* Lawunuia [tgi], 609

Piya, *alt.* Piya-Kwonci [piy], 173
　dial. Piya-Kwonci [piy], 173
Piya-Kwonci [piy], 173
Piyuma, *alt.* Puyuma [pyu], 512
Pizhdar, *dial.* Kurdish, Central
　[ckb], 443
Pla, *alt.* Gbe, Eastern Xwla [gbx], 44
Pladina, *alt.* Fulfulde, Adamawa
　[fub], 61, 80
Plain, *alt. dial.* Longuda [lnu], 169
Plain Angas, *dial.* Ngas [anc], 171
Plain Bura, *alt. dial.* Bura-Pabir
　[bwr], 156
Plain Pennsylvania German, *alt.*
　dial. German, Pennsylvania [pdc],
　301
Plain Tarok, *alt. dial.* Tarok
　[yer], 175
Plain Tetun, *alt. dial.* Tetun
　[tet], 410, 351
Plains Bira, *alt.* Bera [brf], 97
Plains Cree, *see* Cree, Plains
　[crk], 236, 300
Plains Cree, *dial.* Cree, Plains
　[crk], 236
Plains Geta', *dial.* Gata' [gaq], 362
Plains Indian Sign Language
　[psd], 307
Plains Jarawa, *alt.* Bada [bau], 154
Plains Miwok, *see* Miwok, Plains
　[pmw], 305
Plains Ojibway, *alt.* Ojibwa,
　Western [ojw], 240
Plains Sign Language, *alt.* Plains
　Indian Sign Language [psd], 307
Plan de Guadalupe, *dial.* Mixtec,
　Alacatlatzala [mim], 265
Planan, *alt.* Paranan [agp], 500
Plang, *alt.* Blang [blr], 327, 462, 514
Plapo, *alt.* Krumen, Plapo [ktj], 93
　dial. Krumen, Tepo [ted], 138
Plapo Krumen, *see* Krumen, Plapo
　[ktj], 93
Plasla, *alt. dial.* Vame [mlr], 73
Plata, *alt. dial.* Vame [mlr], 73
Platanillo, *dial.* Tlapanec, Acatepec
　[tpx], 275
Plateau Haitian Creole, *dial.*
　Haitian Creole French [hat], 258
Plateau Malagasy, *see* Malagasy,
　Plateau [plt], 140
Plateau Tonga, *alt.* Tonga
　[toi], 215
Platla, *alt. dial.* Vame [mlr], 73
Platt, *alt.* Luxembourgeois [ltz], 537
Plattdütsch, *alt.* Saxon, Low
　[nds], 539
Plautdietsch [pdt], 241, 222, 223,
　231, 249, 273, 285, 307, 448, 539
Playero [gob], 247

Pleikly, *dial.* Jarai [jra], 523, 325
Plo, *dial.* Krahn, Western [krw], 138
Ploskost, *dial.* Chechen [che], 553
Plus, *dial.* Kensiu [kns], 454
Pmasa'a, *dial.* Hamtai [hmt], 601
Pnar [pbv], 384, 322
Pnong, *alt.* Mnong, Central
　[cmo], 525
　alt. dial. Mnong, Southern
　[mnn], 525
Po, *alt.* Bo [bpw], 594
Po Rang, *alt. dial.* Mnong, Southern
　[mnn], 525
Po-Klo, *dial.* Temiar [tea], 455
Po-Nau, *alt.* Bunu, Bu-Nao
　[bwx], 328
Poai, *alt.* Fwâi [fwa], 584
Poamei, *alt.* Pwaamei [pme], 585
Poapoa, *alt.* Pwapwa [pop], 585
Poavosa, *alt.* Babuza [bzg], 511
　dial. Babuza [bzg], 511
Pobyeng, *alt. dial.* Mpongmpong
　[mgg], 68
Pochuri, *alt.* Naga, Pochuri
　[npo], 379
Pochuri Naga, *see* Naga, Pochuri
　[npo], 379
Pochury, *alt.* Naga, Pochuri
　[npo], 379
Pocomam Oriental, *alt.* Poqomam,
　Eastern [poa], 255
Pocomán, *alt.* Poqomam, Central
　[poc], 255
Pocomchí, *alt.* Poqomchi', Eastern
　[poh], 256
　alt. Poqomchi', Western [pob], 256
Poconchí, *alt.* Poqomchi', Eastern
　[poh], 256
Podari, *dial.* Wipi [gdr], 632
Podena [pdn], 422
Podi, *alt. dial.* Me'en [mym], 117
Podia Koya, *dial.* Koya [kff], 370
Podkamennaya Tunguska, *dial.*
　Evenki [evn], 504
Podoba, *alt.* Folopa [ppo], 599
Podogo, *alt.* Parkwa [pbi], 71
Podokge, *dial.* Tupuri [tui], 87
Podoko, *alt.* Parkwa [pbi], 71
Podokwo, *alt.* Parkwa [pbi], 71
Podopa, *alt.* Folopa [ppo], 599
Podra, *alt.* Todrah [tdr], 527
Podzo, *dial.* Sena [seh], 149
Poeng, *alt.* Mengen [mee], 613
　alt. dial. Mengen [mee], 613
Poerah, *alt. dial.* Naga, Tase
　[nst], 380
Pogadi Chib, *alt.* Angloromani
　[rme], 564, 568
Pogara, *dial.* Senoufo, Cebaara
　[sef], 94

Pogaya, *alt.* Bogaya [boq], 594
Pogolo [poy], 204
Pogolu, *alt.* Pogolo [poy], 204
Pogora, *alt.* Pogolo [poy], 204
Pogoro, *alt.* Pogolo [poy], 204
Poguli, *dial.* Kashmiri [kas], 367
Pohbetian, *alt.* Tibetan [bod], 388
Pohing, *alt.* Chukwa [cuw], 470
Pohing Kha, *alt.* Chukwa [cuw], 470
Pohnpeian [pon], 583
Pohoneang, *alt.* Seko Tengah
　[sko], 433
Pohuai, *alt.* Tulu-Bohuai [rak], 628
Poianáua, *alt.* Poyanáwa [pyn], 231
Point Arena, *dial.* Pomo, Central
　[poo], 307
Point Barrow Inupiatun, *alt. dial.*
　Inupiatun, North Alaskan [esi], 302
Point Hope Inupiatun, *dial.*
　Inupiatun, North Alaskan [esi], 302
Poitevin, *dial.* French [fra], 536
Pojoaque, *dial.* Tewa [tew], 308
Pöjulu, *dial.* Bari [bfa], 188, 210
Pok, *alt. dial.* Sabaot [spy], 135
Poka, *dial.* Tumbuka [tum], 141
Pokangá [pok], 231
Pokangá-Tapuya, *alt.* Pokangá
　[pok], 231
Pokau, *alt.* Lala [nrz], 609
Poke [pof], 107
　alt. Tibetan [bod], 388, 481
Poko, *alt.* Pu Ko [puk], 452
　alt. dial. Batanga [bnm], 58
　dial. Lobala [loq], 103
Pokoh, *alt.* Pacoh [pac], 525, 452
Pokomam, *alt.* Poqomam, Central
　[poc], 255
Pokomo, Lower [poj], 135
Pokomo, Upper [pkb], 135
Pokonchí, *alt.* Poqomchi', Eastern
　[poh], 256
Pökoot [pko], 135, 212
Pokot, *alt.* Pökoot [pko], 212
Pökot, *alt.* Pökoot [pko], 135
Pokpok, *dial.* Amis, Nataoran
　[ais], 511
Pol [pmm], 71
　alt. Pomo [pmm], 89
Pola, *alt.* Yi, Poluo [yip], 347
Polabian [pox], 539
Polar Eskimo, *pej. alt. dial.*
　Inuktitut, Greenlandic [kal], 252
Polari [pld], 566
Polchi, *alt.* Polci [plj], 173
Polci [plj], 173
　dial. Polci [plj], 173
Pole, *alt.* Erave [kjy], 598
Poleang, *alt. dial.* Moronene
　[mqn], 431
Poleo, *dial.* Talise [tlr], 638

Poli, *alt. dial.* Doyayo [dow], 60
dial. Yendang [yen], 178
Police Motu, *alt.* Motu, Hiri [hmo], 615
Poligus, *dial.* Evenki [evn], 504
Polish [pol], 550, 446, 533, 539, 551, 558
Polish Romani, *dial.* Romani, Baltic [rml], 550, 546
Polish Sign Language [pso], 550
Poliyar, *alt.* Paliyan [pcf], 382
Polnisch, *alt.* Polish [pol], 550, 539
Polo, *alt.* Pela [bxd], 342
dial. Zaiwa [atb], 349
Pologozom, *dial.* Daba [dbq], 59
Polome, *alt.* Kibiri [prm], 606
Polonombauk [plb], 644
Polopa, *alt.* Folopa [ppo], 599
Polots, *alt. dial.* Belarusan [bel], 530
Polshi, *alt. dial.* Polci [plj], 173
Polski, *alt.* Polish [pol], 550, 446, 533, 539, 551, 558
Poluo Yi, *see* Yi, Poluo [yip], 347
Polyu, *alt.* Bolyu [ply], 328
Pom [pmo], 422
Pomai, *alt.* Naga, Poumei [pmx], 379
Pomak, *alt.* Bulgarian [bul], 563
dial. Bulgarian [bul], 540, 563
Pomakci, *alt. dial.* Bulgarian [bul], 540
Pomakika, *alt. dial.* Bulgarian [bul], 540
Pome, *alt.* Naga, Poumei [pmx], 379
P'ömi, *alt.* Pumi, Northern [pmi], 342
alt. Pumi, Southern [pmj], 342
Pomo [pmm], 89
alt. Pol [pmm], 71
Pomo, Central [poo], 307
Pomo, Eastern [peb], 307
Pomo, Northeastern [pef], 307
Pomo, Northern [pej], 307
Pomo, Southeastern [pom], 307
Pomo, Southern [peq], 307
Ponaal, *alt. dial.* Gula Iro [glj], 81
Ponam [ncc], 622
Ponapean, *alt.* Pohnpeian [pon], 583
dial. Pohnpeian [pon], 583
Ponares [pod], 247
Ponasakan, *alt.* Ponosakan [pns], 432
Ponca, *dial.* Omaha-Ponca [oma], 306
Ponda, *alt.* Luchazi [lch], 41, 214
Pondo, *alt.* Angoram [aog], 590
dial. Pana [pnz], 77
Pondoma, *alt.* Anam [pda], 589
Pondori, *dial.* Bozo, Jenaama [bze], 142
Ponek, *alt.* Tuotomb [ttf], 72
Ponerihouen, *alt.* Paicî [pri], 585

Pong, *alt. dial.* Hung [hnu], 450
dial. Hung [hnu], 523
Pong 1, *alt. dial.* Hung [hnu], 450, 523
Pong 2, *alt. dial.* Hung [hnu], 450, 523
Pong 3, *alt.* Phong-Kniang [pnx], 452
Pongaal, *dial.* Gula Iro [glj], 81
Pongo, *alt.* Pongu [png], 173
dial. Duala [dua], 60
Pong'om, *alt. dial.* Sabaot [spy], 135
Pongoué, *alt. dial.* Myene [mye], 121
Pongpong, *alt.* Mpongmpong [mgg], 68
Pongu [png], 173
Pongyong [pgy], 477
Ponka, *alt.* Omaha-Ponca [oma], 306
Ponna, *alt.* Meitei [mni], 375, 321, 465
Pono, *alt. dial.* Mbum [mdd], 66
Ponorwal, *dial.* Sa [sax], 645
Ponosakan [pns], 432
Ponthai, *alt. dial.* Naga, Nocte [njb], 379
dial. Naga, Tase [nst], 380
Ponthieu, *dial.* Picard [pcd], 537
Pontianak, *alt. dial.* Malay [mly], 436
Pontic [pnt], 541, 563
Pontic Greek, *alt.* Pontic [pnt], 541
Ponyo, *alt.* Naga, Khiamniungan [nky], 378, 466
Ponyon Kulung, *alt.* Pongyong [pgy], 477
Poodena, *alt.* Burduna [bxn], 569
Poonan, *alt.* Gahri [bfu], 361
Poonchi, *alt. dial.* Pahari-Potwari [phr], 487
Poong, *alt. dial.* Hung [hnu], 450, 523
Poono, *alt. dial.* Arop-Lukep [apr], 590
Poordoona, *alt.* Burduna [bxn], 569
Popengare, *alt.* Apurinã [apu], 225
Popo, *alt.* Éwé [ewe], 124, 207
alt. Gbe, Eastern Xwla [gbx], 44
alt. Gen [gej], 207, 45
Popoi, *dial.* Mangbetu [mdj], 104
Popoloca de San Felipe Otlaltepec, *alt.* Popoloca, San Felipe Otlaltepec [pow], 273
Popoloca de San Juan Atzingo, *alt.* Popoloca, San Juan Atzingo [poe], 273
Popoloca de San Luis Temalacayuca, *alt.* Popoloca, San Luís Temalacayuca [pps], 274

Popoloca de San Marcos Tlalcoyalco, *alt.* Popoloca, San Marcos Tlalcoyalco [pls], 274
Popoloca de Santa Inés Ahuatempan, *alt.* Popoloca, Santa Inés Ahuatempan [pca], 274
Popoloca del Oriente, *alt.* Popoloca, San Juan Atzingo [poe], 273
Popoloca del Poniente, *alt.* Popoloca, San Felipe Otlaltepec [pow], 273
Popoloca, Coyotepec [pbf], 273
Popoloca, Mezontla [pbe], 273
Popoloca, San Felipe Otlaltepec [pow], 273
Popoloca, San Juan Atzingo [poe], 273
Popoloca, San Luís Temalacayuca [pps], 274
Popoloca, San Marcos Tlalcoyalco [pls], 274
Popoloca, Santa Inés Ahuatempan [pca], 274
Popoluca de la Sierra, *alt.* Popoluca, Highland [poi], 274
Popoluca, Highland [poi], 274
Popoluca, Oluta [plo], 274
Popoluca, Sayula [pos], 274
Popoluca, Texistepec [poq], 274
Popti', *alt.* Jakalteko, Western [jai], 254
Poqomam, Central [poc], 255
Poqomam, Eastern [poa], 255
Poqomam, Southern [pou], 256
Poqomchi', *alt.* Poqomchi', Western [pob], 256
Poqomchi', Eastern [poh], 256
Poqomchi', Western [pob], 256
Por, *alt.* Pear [pcb], 326
Poraja Katha, *alt.* Bondo [bfw], 357
Porapora, *alt.* Ambakich [aew], 589
Poren, *alt.* Nyang'i [nyp], 212
Porga, *dial.* Biali [beh], 42
Porgera, *dial.* Ipili [ipi], 603
Porhé, *alt.* Purepecha [tsz], 274
Pori, *alt.* Pol [pmm], 71
alt. Pomo [pmm], 89
Pori Asom, *alt. dial.* Pol [pmm], 71
Pori Kinda, *alt. dial.* Pol [pmm], 71
Porja, *alt.* Konda-Dora [kfc], 369
Pormi, *alt.* Ndai [gke], 69
Porohanon [prh], 500
Poroja, *alt.* Bodo Parja [bdv], 357
alt. Parenga [pcj], 383
Porome, *alt.* Kibiri [prm], 606
dial. Kibiri [prm], 606
Poronaisk, *dial.* Orok [oaa], 506
Poros, *dial.* Timugon Murut [tih], 458

Poroto, *dial.* Safwa [sbk], 204
Port Maltese, *dial.* Maltese
  [mlt], 547
Port Sandwich [psw], 645
Port Vato [ptv], 645
Portage, *dial.* Carrier [crx], 236
Português, *alt.* Portuguese
  [por], 551, 351
Português de Bidau, *dial.* Pidgin,
  Timor [tvy], 351
Português de Malaca, *alt.*
  Malaccan Creole Portuguese
  [mcm], 454
Portuguese [por], 551, 41, 74, 131,
  149, 179, 231, 351, 537
Portuguese Calão, *dial.* Caló
  [rmr], 559, 551
Portuguese Creole, *alt.* Crioulo,
  Upper Guinea [pov], 131, 180
Portuguese Patois, *alt.* Malaccan
  Creole Portuguese [mcm], 454
Portuguese Sign Language
  [psr], 551
Posa, *alt. dial.* Polci [plj], 173
Posh 'N' Posh, *alt.* Angloromani
  [rme], 564
Poso, *alt.* Pamona [bcx], 432
  dial. Bajau, Indonesian [bdl], 427
Potafa, *alt.* Massep [mvs], 419
Potawatomi [pot], 307, 241
Pothohari, *alt.* Pahari-Potwari
  [phr], 487
Pothwari, *dial.* Pahari-Potwari
  [phr], 487
Potiguára [pog], 231
Potnariven, *dial.* Sie [erg], 645
Potohari, *alt.* Pahari-Potwari
  [phr], 487
Potoichan, *dial.* Mixtec,
  Alacatlatzala [mim], 265
Potopo, *alt.* Peere [pfe], 71, 173
  alt. dial. Peere [pfe], 71
Potopore, *alt.* Peere [pfe], 71, 173
Potosí, *dial.* Quechua, South
  Bolivian [quh], 223
Potosino Huastec, *alt.* Huastec,
  San Luís Potosí [hva], 262
Pototan, *alt. dial.* Kinaray-A
  [krj], 498
Potsawugok, *alt. dial.* Pemon
  [aoc], 312
Pottangi Ollar Gadaba, *see*
  Gadaba, Pottangi Ollar [gdb], 361
Pottawotomi, *alt.* Potawatomi
  [pot], 307
Pottawottomi, *alt.* Potawatomi
  [pot], 241
Potu, *alt.* Mbato [gwa], 94
Potule, *dial.* Sisaala, Tumulung
  [sil], 127

Poturu, *alt.* Zo'é [pto], 234
Poturujara, *alt.* Zo'é [pto], 234
Potwari, *alt.* Pahari-Potwari
  [phr], 487
  alt. dial. Pahari-Potwari [phr], 487
Pou Hok, *alt.* Puoc [puo], 452
Pouébo, *dial.* Caac [msq], 584
Pougouli, *alt.* Phuie [pug], 53
Poumei, *alt.* Naga, Poumei
  [pmx], 379
Poumei Naga, *see* Naga, Poumei
  [pmx], 379
Poun, *alt.* Bon Gula [glc], 79
Pouno, *alt.* Punu [puu], 121, 89
Pouss, *alt. dial.* Musgu [mug], 68, 85
Pouteng, *alt.* Kháng [kjm], 524
  alt. Khmu [kjg], 451, 337, 465, 515
Pouye [bye], 622
Pove, *alt.* Bubi [buw], 120
Powadhi, *dial.* Panjabi, Eastern
  [pan], 383
Powari [pwr], 384
  alt. dial. Bundeli [bns], 357
  dial. Bagheli [bfy], 354, 468
Powhatan [pim], 307
Poyanáwa [pyn], 231
Poyenisati, *alt.* Caquinte [cot], 287
Ppankka, *alt.* Omaha-Ponca
  [oma], 306
Pradhan, *alt.* Pardhan [pch], 383
Pradhani, *alt.* Pardhan [pch], 383
Prae, *alt.* Karen, Phrae Pwo [kjt], 514
Prai, *alt.* Phai [prt], 516, 452
Prairie French, *dial.* French, Cajun
  [frc], 300
Praistiki, *dial.* Romani, Sinte
  [rmo], 539
Prakaa, *dial.* Manangba [nmm], 475
Pramano, *alt.* Karen, Brek [kvl], 464
Prang, *alt.* Kplang [kph], 126
  dial. Chrau [crw], 522
  dial. Mnong, Southern [mnn], 525
Praok, *alt.* Parauk [prk], 466, 342
Prasun, *alt.* Prasuni [prn], 317
Prasuni [prn], 317
Pray 1, *alt.* Phai [prt], 516, 452
Pray 2, *alt.* Lua' [prb], 516
Pray 3 [pry], 517
Pre, *alt.* Karen, Brek [kvl], 464
  alt. Mbre [mka], 94
  alt. dial. Mnong, Central [cmo], 525
Pre Pisia, *alt.* Mbre [mka], 94
Preh, *dial.* Mnong, Central [cmo], 326
Préh, *dial.* Mnong, Central [cmo], 525
Prehan, *dial.* Melanau [mel], 460
Prekmurski, *dial.* Slovenian
  [slv], 558, 542
Presidio de los Reyes Cora, *dial.*
  Cora, El Nayar [crn], 262
Priangan, *alt.* Sunda [sun], 392

Pribilof Aleut, *alt. dial.* Aleut [ale],
  297
Primmi, *alt.* Pumi, Northern [pmi],
  342
  alt. Pumi, Southern [pmj], 342
Primorski, *dial.* Slovenian [slv], 558,
  545
Prince George, *dial.* Carrier,
  Southern [caf], 236
Principense [pre], 179
Pringan, *dial.* Sunda [sun], 392
Prionezh, *alt. dial.* Veps [vep], 557
Priulian, *alt.* Friulian [fur], 544
Probur, *dial.* Kelon [kyo], 407
Proca Lo, *dial.* Bahing [bhj], 468
Prok, *dial.* Nubri [kte], 477
P'rome, *alt.* Pumi, Northern
  [pmi], 342
  alt. Pumi, Southern [pmj], 342
Proon, *alt.* Tampuan [tpu], 326
Proons, *alt.* Tampuan [tpu], 326
Propontis Tsakonian, *dial.*
  Tsakonian [tsd], 541
Proue, *alt.* Brao [brb], 325, 522
  alt. Lave [brb], 451
Prouvençau, *alt.* Provençal
  [prv], 537
Provençal [prv], 537, 545, 548
Provenzale, *alt.* Provençal [prv], 545
Providencia Sign Language
  [prz], 247
PRSL, *alt.* Puerto Rican Sign
  Language [psl], 294
Pru, *dial.* Koho [kpm], 524
Prussian [prg], 550
Pruumi, *alt.* Pumi, Northern
  [pmi], 342
  alt. Pumi, Southern [pmj], 342
Pshav, *dial.* Georgian [kat], 352
Psikye [kvj], 71, 173
  dial. Psikye [kvj], 71, 173
Psohoh, *alt.* Aigon [aix], 588
  alt. dial. Aigon [aix], 588
Psokhok, *alt. dial.* Aigon [aix], 588
Psokok, *alt. dial.* Aigon [aix], 588
Ptamo, *alt. dial.* Cuiba [cui], 311
Ptep, *alt.* Patep [ptp], 621
Ptsake, *alt.* Psikye [kvj], 71, 173
Pu, *alt.* Nicobarese, Car [caq], 381
Pu Ko [puk], 452
Pú Nà, *alt.* Giáy [pcc], 523
  dial. Giáy [pcc], 523
Pu No, *alt.* Bunu, Younuo [buh], 329
  alt. dial. Bunu, Bu-Nao [bwx], 328
Pu Péo, *alt.* Laqua [laq], 338
  alt. Qabiao [laq], 526
Pu Thenh, *alt.* Khmu [kjg], 451, 465
Pu-I, *alt.* Bouyei [pcc], 328
  alt. Giáy [pcc], 523
Pu-Jui, *alt.* Bouyei [pcc], 328

Pu-Nam, *alt.* Giáy [pcc], 523
Pu-Xian Chinese, *see* Chinese, Pu-Xian [cpx], 330, 454, 508
Pua, *alt.* Puoc [puo], 525
Puan, *dial.* Jarai [jra], 523, 325
Puari [pux], 622
Pubian [pun], 437
Pubiao, *alt.* Laqua [laq], 338
   alt. Qabiao [laq], 526
Puca-Uma, *alt.* Iquito [iqu], 288
Puchikwar, *alt.* A-Pucikwar [apq], 353
Pucikwar, *alt.* A-Pucikwar [apq], 353
Puditara, *dial.* Martu Wangka [mpj], 574
Pudtol Atta, *see* Atta, Pudtol [atp], 491
Pueh, *alt.* Biatah [bth], 392
Puelche [pue], 220
Puerto Rican Sign Language [psl], 294
Pugliese, *dial.* Italian [ita], 544
Pugot, *alt.* Alta, Southern [agy], 491
Puguli, *alt.* Phuie [pug], 53
Puhoc, *alt.* Puoc [puo], 525, 452
Pui, *alt.* Bouyei [pcc], 328
   alt. Giáy [pcc], 523
Puimei, *alt.* Naga, Puimei [npu], 379
Puimei Naga, *see* Naga, Puimei [npu], 379
Puinabe, *alt.* Puinave [pui], 247
Puinahua, *alt.* Poyanáwa [pyn], 231
Puinare, *alt.* Puinave [pui], 312
Puinave [pui], 247, 312
Pujai, *alt.* Bouyei [pcc], 328
Pujuni, *alt.* Nisenan [nsz], 306
Pukamigl-Andegabu, *dial.* Wahgi [wgi], 630
Pukan, *alt.* Bugan [bbh], 328
Pukapuka [pkp], 579
Pukapukan, *alt.* Pukapuka [pkp], 579
Pukaunu, *alt. dial.* Lamaholot [slp], 408
Puki, *alt.* Poke [pof], 107
Pukobjê, *alt.* Gavião, Pará [gvp], 226
Puku, *alt. dial.* Batanga [bnm], 110, 58
   alt. dial. Kag-Fer-Jiir-Koor-Ror-Us-Zuksun [gel], 165
Puku-Geeri-Keri-Wipsi, *alt.* Kag-Fer-Jiir-Koor-Ror-Us-Zuksun [gel], 165
Pukunna, *alt.* Nugunu [nnv], 575
Pul, *alt.* Pol [pmm], 71
   alt. Pomo [pmm], 89
Pula, *alt.* Blang [blr], 327, 462, 514
   alt. Tadyawan [tdy], 502
   alt. Yi, Pula [ypl], 347

Pula Yi, *see* Yi, Pula [ypl], 347
Pulaar [fuc], 181, 122, 130, 131, 143, 145
   alt. dial. Pulaar [fuc], 181, 130, 143, 145
Pulaar Fulfulde, *alt.* Pulaar [fuc], 181, 122, 131, 143
Pulabu [pup], 622
Pulana, *dial.* Sotho, Northern [nso], 186
Pulang, *alt.* Blang [blr], 327, 462, 514
Pulangiyen, *dial.* Manobo, Western Bukidnon [mbb], 499
Pulapese, *dial.* Puluwatese [puw], 583
Pular [fuf], 130, 143, 182, 184
Pulau Guai, *dial.* Jah Hut [jah], 454
Pulaya, *dial.* Malayalam [mal], 374
Pule, *alt.* Fulfulde, Adamawa [fub], 61, 80
Pulei, *alt.* Palaung, Pale [pce], 342
Puleniyan, *dial.* Manobo, Ilianen [mbi], 499
Pulgaon, *dial.* Kolami, Northwestern [kfb], 369
Pulhilh, *alt. dial.* Mandjak [mfv], 131
Pulie-Rauto, *dial.* Lamogai [lmg], 609
Pullo, *alt.* Fulfulde, Adamawa [fub], 61, 80
Pulo Anna, *dial.* Sonsorol [sov], 587
Pulopetak, *dial.* Ngaju [nij], 394
Pulusukese, *dial.* Puluwatese [puw], 583
Puluwat, *alt.* Puluwatese [puw], 583
Puluwatese [puw], 583
   dial. Puluwatese [puw], 583
Puma [pum], 477
   alt. Teanu [tkw], 638
Puma Kala, *alt.* Puma [pum], 477
Puma La, *alt.* Puma [pum], 477
Puma Pima, *alt.* Puma [pum], 477
P'uman, *alt.* U [uuu], 345
Puman, *alt.* U [uuu], 345
Pumbora, *alt.* Puruborá [pur], 232
Pumé [yae], 312
P'umi, *alt.* Pumi, Northern [pmi], 342
   alt. Pumi, Southern [pmj], 342
Pumi, Northern [pmi], 342
Pumi, Southern [pmj], 342
Punan, *alt.* Gahri [bfu], 361
   dial. Dayak, Land [dyk], 393
   pej. alt. Penan, Eastern [pez], 460, 325
   pej. alt. Penan, Western [pne], 460
Punan Aput [pud], 395
Punan Ba, *alt. dial.* Punan Bah-Biau [pna], 460
Punan Bah, *dial.* Punan Bah-Biau [pna], 460

Punan Bah-Biau [pna], 460
Punan Basap, *dial.* Sajau Basap [sjb], 395
Punan Batu 1 [pnm], 460
Punan Batu 2, *dial.* Sajau Basap [sjb], 395
Punan Biau, *dial.* Punan Bah-Biau [pna], 460
Punan Bungan, *alt.* Hovongan [hov], 393
Punan Busang, *dial.* Bukitan [bkn], 392
Punan Merah [puf], 395
Punan Merap [puc], 395
Punan Ratah, *alt. dial.* Dohoi [otd], 393
Punan Sajau, *dial.* Sajau Basap [sjb], 395
Punan Tubu [puj], 395
Punan Ukit, *dial.* Bukitan [bkn], 392
Punapa, *alt.* Bunaba [bck], 569
Punchhi, *dial.* Pahari-Potwari [phr], 487
Punda-Umeda, *dial.* Sowanda [sow], 625
Pungupungu, *dial.* Wadjiginy [wdj], 577
Punial, *alt. dial.* Shina [scl], 488
Punjabi, *alt.* Panjabi, Eastern [pan], 383, 135
Punkalla, *alt.* Banggarla [bjb], 568
Puno, *alt.* Punu [puu], 121, 89
Puno Quechua, *see* Quechua, Puno [qxp], 292
Puno Quechua, *dial.* Quechua, Cusco [quz], 290
Punoi, *alt.* Phunoi [pho], 452, 517
Punthamara, *dial.* Ngura [nbx], 575
Puntlatch, *alt.* Pentlatch [ptw], 241
Punu [puu], 121, 89
   alt. Bunu, Bu-Nao [bwx], 328
   alt. Bunu, Jiongnai [pnu], 328
   alt. Bunu, Wunai [bwn], 328
   alt. Bunu, Younuo [buh], 329
Puoc [puo], 525, 452
Puok, *alt.* Puoc [puo], 525, 452
Pupeo, *alt.* Laqua [laq], 338
   alt. Qabiao [laq], 526
Pupitau, *dial.* Folopa [ppo], 599
Puquina [puq], 289
   alt. Chipaya [cap], 222
Pura, *dial.* Blagar [beu], 406
Puragi [pru], 422
Purai, *dial.* Lawangan [lbx], 394
Puram, *alt.* Purum [pub], 466
Purari [iar], 622
Purbi, *alt. dial.* Bhojpuri [bho], 356
Purduma, *alt.* Burduna [bxn], 569
Purduna, *alt.* Burduna [bxn], 569
Pure Motu, *alt.* Motu [meu], 615

Pureman, *alt. dial.* Wersing [kvw], 410
Purepecha [tsz], 274
Purépecha del Oeste de las Sierras, *alt.* Purepecha, Western Highland [pua], 274
Purepecha, Western Highland [pua], 274
Puri [prr], 231
Purig, *alt.* Purik [prx], 384
Purigskad, *alt.* Purik [prx], 384
Purik [prx], 384
Purik Bhotia, *alt.* Purik [prx], 384
Purisimeño [puy], 307
Purki, *alt.* Purik [prx], 384
Purko, *dial.* Maasai [mas], 134
Puroborá, *alt.* Puruborá [pur], 232
Puroik, *alt.* Sulung [suv], 388
Purr, *alt. dial.* Naga, Sangtam [nsa], 379
Purra, *alt.* Bena [yun], 155
Puruba, *alt.* Puruborá [pur], 232
Puruborá [pur], 232
Purucoto, *alt. dial.* Pemon [aoc], 312
Purum [pub], 466
Purum Naga, *see* Naga, Purum [puz], 379
Purung, *dial.* Lawangan [lbx], 394
Purupurú, *alt.* Paumarí [pad], 231
Pus, *alt. dial.* Musgu [mug], 68, 85
Pusciti, *alt.* Xávante [xav], 234
Pushto, *alt.* Pashto, Northern [pbu], 488, 520
   alt. Pashto, Southern [pbt], 488
Pushtu, *alt.* Pashto, Southern [pbt], 488
Pusto, *alt.* Pashto, Northern [pbu], 520
Puta, *alt.* Karbi [mjw], 366
Putahi, *alt. dial.* Tuamotuan [pmt], 581
Putai [mfl], 173
   alt. Phu Thai [pht], 516, 452, 525
Putatan, *dial.* Bajau, West Coast [bdr], 456
Pute, *alt.* Vute [vut], 73
Puteik, *alt.* Kado [kdv], 464, 337
Putenh, *alt.* Kháng [kjm], 524
Puter-Upper Engadine, *alt. dial.* Romansch [roh], 562
Puthai, *alt.* Phu Thai [pht], 516, 525
Puthay, *alt.* Phu Thai [pht], 452, 525
Puthsu, *alt. dial.* Sena [seh], 149
Putian, *dial.* Chinese, Pu-Xian [cpx], 330
Putoh [put], 395
Putonghua, *alt.* Chinese, Mandarin [cmn], 329, 511
Putru, *dial.* Ronga [rng], 149

Putten, *alt. dial.* Chinese, Pu-Xian [cpx], 330
Puttooas, *alt.* Juang [jun], 365
Putu, *dial.* Sapo [krn], 139
Putujara, *alt. dial.* Martu Wangka [mpj], 574
Putukwam [afe], 173
Puuri, *alt.* Ngong [nnx], 70
Puwa Yi, *see* Yi, Puwa [ypw], 347
Puxi, *dial.* Shangzhai [jih], 343
Puxmetecán, *dial.* Mixe, North Central [neq], 265
Puyallup, *dial.* Salish, Southern Puget Sound [slh], 307
Puyi, *alt.* Bouyei [pcc], 328
   alt. Giáy [pcc], 523
Puyoi, *alt.* Bouyei [pcc], 328
Puyuma [pyu], 512
Pwa, *alt.* Phuie [pug], 53
Pwaamei [pme], 585
Pwakanyaw, *alt.* Karen, S'gaw [ksw], 464, 514
Pwapwa [pop], 585
Pwe, *alt.* Phuie [pug], 53
Pwebo, *alt. dial.* Caac [msq], 584
Pwie, *alt.* Phuie [pug], 53
Pwien, *alt.* Phuie [pug], 53
Pwo, *alt.* Phuie [pug], 53
Pwo Eastern Karen, *see* Karen, Pwo Eastern [kjp], 464
Pwo Northern Karen, *see* Karen, Pwo Northern [pww], 514
Pwo Phrae, *alt.* Karen, Phrae Pwo [kjt], 514
Pwo Western Karen, *see* Karen, Pwo Western [pwo], 464
Pwo Western Thailand Karen, *see* Karen, Pwo Eastern [kjp], 514
Pyapun [pcw], 173
Pye, *alt. dial.* Krumen, Pye [pye], 93
Pye Krumen, *see* Krumen, Pye [pye], 93
Pyem, *alt.* Fyam [pym], 160
Pyen [pyy], 466
Pyeta, *alt.* Ayoreo [ayo], 222
Pyeta Yovai, *alt.* Ayoreo [ayo], 284
Pygmee, *alt.* Baka [bkc], 56
Pygmée de la Lobaye, *alt.* Yaka [axk], 78
Pygmée de Mongoumba, *alt.* Yaka [axk], 78
Pygmées de la Sanghas, *alt.* Yaka [axk], 78
Pygmees de L'est, *alt.* Baka [bkc], 56
Pygmy-E, *alt.* Baka [bkc], 56
P'yong'ando, *dial.* Korean [kor], 448
Pyu [pby], 622
Pyuma, *alt.* Puyuma [pyu], 512

Qabala, *dial.* Azerbaijani, North [azj], 319
Qabekho, *alt. dial.* Naro [nhr], 48
Qabekhoe, *dial.* Naro [nhr], 48
Qabena, *alt. dial.* Kambaata [ktb], 116
Qabiao [laq], 526
   alt. Laqua [laq], 338
Qae, *alt. dial.* Ghari [gri], 636
Qahar, *alt. dial.* Mongolian, Peripheral [mvf], 339
Qajar, *dial.* Azerbaijani, South [azb], 438
Qaladze, *dial.* Lishanid Noshan [aij], 445
Qalmaq, *alt.* Kalmyk-Oirat [xal], 554
Qandahar Pashto, *alt. dial.* Pashto, Southern [pbt], 317
Qanjobal, *alt.* Q'anjob'al, Eastern [kjb], 256
Q'anjob'al, Eastern [kjb], 256
Qaqet [byx], 622
Qaragozlu, *dial.* Azerbaijani, South [azb], 438
Qaraqulpaqs, *alt.* Karakalpak [kaa], 316
Qarawi, *alt.* Shehri [shv], 483
Qarlug, *alt. dial.* Uzbek, Northern [uzn], 512
Qashqa'i [qxq], 441
Qashqai, *alt.* Qashqa'i [qxq], 441
Qashqari, *alt.* Khowar [khw], 486
Qashqay, *alt.* Qashqa'i [qxq], 441
Qatari, *alt.* Arabic, Gulf Spoken [afb], 503
Qatvenua, *alt.* Hano [lml], 642
Qau, *alt.* Gelao, Green [giq], 522
   dial. Gelao [gio], 333
Qawasqar [alc], 243
Qazakh, *dial.* Azerbaijani, North [azj], 319
Qazaq, *alt.* Kazakh [kaz], 448, 316, 461
Qazaqi, *alt.* Kazakh [kaz], 316, 461, 518
Qazvini, *dial.* Farsi, Western [pes], 439
Qebena, *dial.* Kambaata [ktb], 116
Qemant, *alt. dial.* Qimant [ahg], 118
Q'eqchi' [kek], 256
Qhalaxarzi, *alt.* Kgalagadi [xkv], 47
Qheswa, *alt.* Quechua, Cusco [quz], 290
Qi, *dial.* Hlai [lic], 333
Qian Xi, *dial.* Yi, Guizhou [yig], 347
Qiang, Northern [cng], 342
Qiang, Southern [qxs], 342
Qiannan, *dial.* Bouyei [pcc], 328
Qianxi, *dial.* Bouyei [pcc], 328
Qianzhong, *dial.* Bouyei [pcc], 328

Qiao-Wu Yi, *alt.* Yi, Naluo [ylo], 347
Qiaojia-Wuding Yi, *alt.* Yi, Naluo [ylo], 347
Qide, *dial.* Chinese, Huizhou [czh], 329
Qile'en, *alt. dial.* Nanai [gld], 341
Qileng, *dial.* Nanai [gld], 341
Qimant [ahg], 118
    dial. Qimant [ahg], 118
Qin, *alt.* Chin, Asho [csh], 462, 321
Qinati, *dial.* Domari [rmt], 438
Qinghua, *dial.* Pumi, Southern [pmj], 342
Qinlian, *dial.* Chinese, Yue [yue], 331
Qiongshan, *dial.* Lingao [onb], 338
Qiongwen Hua, *alt. dial.* Chinese, Min Nan [nan], 330
Qiqiha'er, *dial.* Daur [dta], 331, 461
Qiqihar, *alt. dial.* Daur [dta], 331, 461
Qiu, *alt.* Drung [duu], 332
Qiubei, *dial.* Zhuang, Northern [ccx], 349
Qiungnai, *alt.* Bunu, Jiongnai [pnu], 328
Qom, *alt.* Toba [tob], 220, 224, 285
Qonaqkend, *dial.* Tat, Muslim [ttt], 320
Qotong, *alt.* Chinese, Mandarin [cmn], 461
Qottu, *pej. alt.* Oromo, Eastern [hae], 118
Qotu Oromo, *alt.* Oromo, Eastern [hae], 118
Qua, *alt. dial.* Ejagham [etu], 159, 60
Quaiquer, *alt.* Awa-Cuaiquer [kwi], 243
Quan Chet, *dial.* Iu Mien [ium], 523
Quan Trang, *dial.* Iu Mien [ium], 523
Quang Dong, *alt.* Chinese, Yue [yue], 522
Quang Lam, *alt.* Kháng [kjm], 524
Quang Tin Katu, *alt.* Takua [tkz], 527
Quang Tri Bru, *alt.* Bru, Eastern [bru], 522
Quapaw [qua], 307
Quaqua, *alt.* Piaroa [pid], 312, 247
Quashie Talk, *alt.* Jamaican Creole English [jam], 259
Quba, *dial.* Azerbaijani, North [azj], 319
    dial. Lezgi [lez], 320
    dial. Tat, Muslim [ttt], 320
Quchani, *alt.* Khorasani Turkish [kmz], 439

Quebec Eskimo, *dial.* Inuktitut, Eastern Canadian [ike], 238
Quebec Sign Language [fcs], 241
Québécois, *dial.* French [fra], 237
Quecchi', *alt.* Q'eqchi' [kek], 256
Quecchí, *alt.* Kekchí [kek], 221, 252
Quechan [yum], 307
Quechua Boliviano, *alt.* Quechua, South Bolivian [quh], 223
Quechua Collao, *alt.* Quechua, Puno [qxp], 292
Quechua Cusco, *alt.* Quechua, Cusco [quz], 290
Quechua de Cusco-Collao, *alt.* Quechua, Cusco [quz], 290
Quechua de Cuzco, *alt.* Quechua, Cusco [quz], 290
Quechua del Este de Apurímac, *alt.* Quechua, Eastern Apurímac [qve], 291
Quechua Qollaw, *alt.* Quechua, Puno [qxp], 292
Quechua Qosqo-Qollaw, *alt.* Quechua, Cusco [quz], 290
Quechua, Ambo-Pasco [qva], 289
Quechua, Arequipa-La Unión [qxu], 289
Quechua, Ayacucho [quy], 289
Quechua, Cajamarca [qvc], 290
Quechua, Cajatambo North Lima [qvl], 290
Quechua, Chachapoyas [quk], 290
Quechua, Chilean [cqu], 243
Quechua, Chincha [qxc], 290
Quechua, Chiquián Ancash [qxa], 290
Quechua, Classical [qwc], 290
Quechua, Corongo Ancash [qwa], 290
Quechua, Cusco [quz], 290
Quechua, Eastern Apurímac [qve], 291
Quechua, Huallaga Huánuco [qub], 291
Quechua, Huamalíes-Dos de Mayo Huánuco [qvh], 291
Quechua, Huaylas Ancash [qwh], 291
Quechua, Huaylla Wanca [qvw], 291
Quechua, Jauja Wanca [qxw], 291
Quechua, Lambayeque [quf], 291
Quechua, Margos-Yarowilca-Lauricocha [qvm], 291

Quechua, Napo Lowland [qvo], 291
Quechua, North Bolivian [qul], 223
Quechua, North Junín [qvn], 291
Quechua, Northern Conchucos Ancash [qxn], 291
Quechua, Pacaraos [qvp], 291
Quechua, Panao Huánuco [qxh], 292
Quechua, Puno [qxp], 292
Quechua, San Martín [qvs], 292
Quechua, Santa Ana de Tusi Pasco [qxt], 292
Quechua, Sihuas Ancash [qws], 292
Quechua, South Bolivian [quh], 223, 220
Quechua, Southern Conchucos Ancash [qxo], 292
Quechua, Southern Pastaza [qup], 292
Quechua, Yanahuanca Pasco [qur], 292
Quechua, Yauyos [qux], 292
Quecl, *alt.* Quechan [yum], 307
Quedah, *alt. dial.* Kensiu [kns], 454
Quemayá, *alt.* Kumiai [dih], 263
Quequexque, *alt.* Teribe [tfr], 284
Querétaro Otomi, *see* Otomi, Querétaro [otq], 272
Quetta Pashto, *dial.* Pashto, Southern [pbt], 488
Quetta-Kandahar Pashto, *alt.* Pashto, Southern [pbt], 488
Quetzaltenango Mam, *alt.* Mam, Southern [mms], 255
Quetzaltepec Mixe, *see* Mixe, Quetzaltepec [pxm], 265
Queuthoe, *alt. dial.* Balanta-Kentohe [ble], 130
Queyu [qvy], 343
Quezon Palawano, *alt.* Palawano, Central [plc], 500
Quiangan, *alt.* Ifugao, Tuwali [ifk], 495
Quiativis, *alt.* Sanapaná [sap], 285
Quiatoni Zapotec, *alt.* Zapotec, San Pedro Quiatoni [zpf], 279
Quiavicuzas Zapotec, *see* Zapotec, Quiavicuzas [zpj], 279
Quicapause, *alt.* Kickapoo [kic], 263
Quiché, *alt.* K'iche', Central [quc], 255
Quichua, Calderón Highland [qud], 251
Quichua, Cañar Highland [qxr], 251

Rakhshani, *dial.* Balochi, Western [bgn], 476, 315, 438
Raklu Un, *alt.* Adabe [adb], 350
Raklu-Un, *alt.* Adabe [adb], 350
Rakunei, *dial.* Kuanua [ksd], 608
Ralam, *alt. dial.* Mnong, Eastern [mng], 525
Ralámuli de la Tarahumara Baja, *alt.* Tarahumara, Lowland [tac], 274
Rälik, *dial.* Marshallese [mah], 582
Ralte [ral], 466, 384
dial. Mizo [lus], 321
Raluana, *dial.* Kuanua [ksd], 608
Ram, *alt. dial.* Fali, South [fal], 61
Rama [rma], 283
Rama Cay Creole English, *dial.* Nicaragua Creole English [bzk], 283
Ramand, *alt. dial.* Takestani [tks], 441
Ramarama, *alt.* Karo [arr], 228
Rambani, *dial.* Kashmiri [kas], 367
Rambatu-Manussa-Rumberu, *alt. dial.* Alune [alp], 396
Rambi, *alt.* Barombi [bbi], 58
Rambia, *alt.* Lambya [lai], 140, 200
Rambuso, *dial.* Sudest [tgo], 625
Ramechap, *alt. dial.* Sherpa [xsr], 478
Ramekhera, *alt.* Korku [kfq], 369
Ramkokamekra, *dial.* Canela [ram], 226
Ramo, *dial.* Adi [adi], 353
Ramoaaina [rai], 622
Ramopa [kjx], 622
Rampi [lje], 432
dial. Rampi [lje], 432
Rampi-Leboni, *alt.* Rampi [lje], 432
Rampuri, *alt. dial.* Pahari, Mahasu [bfz], 382
Ramuaina, *alt.* Ramoaaina [rai], 622
Rana, *alt. dial.* Buru [mhs], 397
dial. Ghale, Kutang [ght], 471
Rana Thakur, *alt.* Tharu, Rana [thr], 481, 388
Rana Tharu, *see* Tharu, Rana [thr], 481, 388
Ranao, *alt.* Maranao [mrw], 499
Ranau [rae], 437
dial. Dusun, Central [dtp], 456
Ranawat, *dial.* Bhili [bhb], 356
Randai, *dial.* Bunun [bnn], 511
Randawaya, *dial.* Ambai [amk], 410
Randile, *alt.* Rendille [rel], 135
Ranei, *alt.* Yinchia [yin], 467
Rang [rax], 173
alt. Byangsi [bee], 358
Rang Glai, *alt.* Roglai, Northern [rog], 526

Rang Po Bhasa, *alt.* Rongpo [rnp], 385
Ranga, *alt. dial.* Enrekang [ptt], 429
Rangah, *alt.* Stieng, Bulo [sti], 526
Rangari, *alt. dial.* Malvi [mup], 374
alt. dial. Varhadi-Nagpuri [vah], 389
dial. Khandesi [khn], 367
Rangdania, *dial.* Rabha [rah], 384
Rangi, *alt.* Langi [lag], 200
Rangkas [rgk], 384
alt. Rongpo [rnp], 385
Rangkhol, *alt.* Hrangkhol [hra], 464, 364
Rangloi, *alt.* Tinani [lbf], 388, 345
Ranglong, *dial.* Chin, Falam [flm], 358
Rangpa, *alt.* Rongpo [rnp], 385
Rangpan, *alt.* Naga, Tase [nst], 466, 380
Rangri, *alt. dial.* Malvi [mup], 374
Rani Bhil, *dial.* Bhili [bhb], 356
Ránmo, *dial.* Blafe [bfh], 594
Rantepao, *dial.* Toraja-Sa'dan [sda], 434
Ranya, *dial.* Gowli [gok], 363
Ranye, *dial.* Lishanid Noshan [aij], 445
Rao [rao], 622
Rao Breri, *alt.* Rao [rao], 622
Raojin, *dial.* Palaung, Pale [pce], 342
Raoping, *alt. dial.* Chinese, Hakka [hak], 329
Raorou, *alt.* Zauzou [zal], 349
Raosiara, *alt. dial.* Teop [tio], 627
Rapa [ray], 581
Rapa Nui [rap], 243
Rapan, *alt.* Rapa [ray], 581
Rapangkaka, *dial.* Pamona [bcx], 432
Rapitok, *dial.* Kuanua [ksd], 608
Rapoisi [kyx], 622
Rappang Buginese, *alt.* Bugis [bug], 428
Rapting [rpt], 622
Rardro Bhil, *dial.* Koli, Wadiyara [kxp], 487
Rarotonga, *dial.* Rarotongan [rar], 579
Rarotongan [rar], 579
Rarotongan-Mangaian, *alt.* Rarotongan [rar], 579
Rarua, *alt.* Saaroa [sxr], 512
Rasawa [rac], 422
Rashaayda, *alt. dial.* Arabic, Najdi Spoken [ars], 508
Rashad, *dial.* Tegali [ras], 195
Rashti, *dial.* Gilaki [glk], 439
Rasuwa, *dial.* Tamang, Western [tdg], 480
Ratagnon [btn], 500

dial. Ratagnon [btn], 500
Ratahan [rth], 432
Ratak, *dial.* Marshallese [mah], 582
Ratchaburi Pwo Karen, *alt. dial.* Karen, Pwo Western Thailand [kjp], 514
Rathawi [rtw], 384
Rathi, *alt.* Bareli, Rathwi [bgd], 355
dial. Garhwali [gbm], 360
Rathia, *alt.* Bareli, Rathwi [bgd], 355
Rathod, *alt.* Dubli [dub], 360
Rathora, *alt. dial.* Bundeli [bns], 357
Rathwi Bareli, *see* Bareli, Rathwi [bgd], 355
Rathwi Pauri, *alt.* Bareli, Rathwi [bgd], 355
Rati, *dial.* Makhuwa-Saka [xsq], 147
Ratnawati, *alt. dial.* Jerung [jee], 472
Rato, *dial.* Rampi [lje], 432
Ratsua, *dial.* Hahon [hah], 601
Rattiyan, *alt.* Vaagri Booli [vaa], 389
Rau, *alt.* T'en [tct], 344
Raua, *alt.* Rawa [rwo], 622
Raut, *alt.* Rawat [jnl], 385
Raute [rau], 478
Rauto, *alt. dial.* Lamogai [lmg], 609
Rautye, *alt.* Raute [rau], 478
Rava, *alt.* Rabha [rah], 384
Ravai, *dial.* Garhwali [gbm], 360
Ravo, *alt. dial.* Bauro [bxa], 635
Ravula [yea], 384
Rawa [rwo], 622
dial. Rawa [rwo], 622
Rawan, *pej. alt.* Uab Meto [aoz], 410
Rawang [raw], 466, 385
alt. Drung [duu], 332
dial. Rawang [raw], 466
Rawas [rws], 437
dial. Rejang [rej], 437
Rawas Ilir, *dial.* Rawas [rws], 437
Rawas Ulu, *dial.* Rawas [rws], 437
Rawat [jnl], 478, 385
Rawe, *alt.* Brao [brb], 522
alt. Lave [brb], 451
Rawo [rwa], 622
alt. dial. Bauro [bxa], 635
Raxshani, *alt. dial.* Balochi, Western [bgn], 476, 315, 438
Rayalseema, *alt. dial.* Telugu [tel], 388
Rayglay, *alt.* Roglai, Northern [rog], 526
Rayón Zoque, *see* Zoque, Rayón [zor], 282
Razajerdi [rat], 441
Razgrad, *dial.* Turkish [tur], 519, 521, 532
Razong, *alt.* Rajong [rjg], 409

Rde, *alt.* Rade [rad], 526
Rde Kpa, *alt. dial.* Rade [rad], 526
Rdzongkha, *alt.* Dzongkha [dzo], 323
Reang, *alt.* Riang [ria], 385, 322
Reao, *dial.* Tuamotuan [pmt], 581
Reasati, *alt.* Seraiki [skr], 386
　alt. dial. Seraiki [skr], 488, 386
Rebar, *dial.* Kuanua [ksd], 608
Rebina, *alt. dial.* Jere [jer], 165
Rebu, *alt.* Baloi [biz], 96
　alt. Bangi [bni], 97
　alt. Bobangi [bni], 88
Red Bobo, *alt.* Buamu [box], 50
Red Dao, *alt.* Iu Mien [ium], 523
Red Gelao, *see* Gelao, Red [gir], 522
Red Indians, *alt.* Beothuk [bue], 235
Red Karen, *alt.* Kayah, Eastern [eky], 465, 515
　alt. Kayah, Western [kyu], 465
Red Lachi, *alt. dial.* Lachi [lbt], 338
Red Lahu, *alt. dial.* Lahu [lhu], 338, 451, 465, 515, 524
Red Lake Chippewa, *dial.* Chippewa [ciw], 299
Red Mantsi, *alt.* Mantsi [nty], 525
Red Meo, *alt.* Hmong, Eastern Xiangxi [muq], 334
　alt. Hmong, Western Xiangxi [mmr], 335
Red Miao, *alt.* Hmong, Eastern Xiangxi [muq], 334
　alt. Hmong, Western Xiangxi [mmr], 335
Red Tai, *alt.* Tai Daeng [tyr], 526
Red Thai, *alt.* Tai Daeng [tyr], 453
Red Trouser Yao, *alt.* Kim Mun [mji], 524
Reddi, *alt.* Mukha-Dora [mmk], 376
Reddi-Dora, *alt.* Mukha-Dora [mmk], 376
Redjang, *alt.* Rejang [rej], 437
Ree, *alt.* Arikara [ari], 298
Reef Islands, *alt.* Ayiwo [nfl], 635
Reefs, *alt.* Ayiwo [nfl], 635
Reel [atu], 195
Rega, *alt.* Lega-Mwenga [lgm], 102
　alt. Lega-Shabunda [lea], 102
Regi, *alt.* Kara [reg], 199
　dial. Cinda-Regi-Tiyal [cdr], 157
Rei, *dial.* Lou [loj], 610
Reikha, *alt.* Dagik [dec], 189
Reiwo, *alt.* Yapunda [yev], 633
Rejang [rej], 437
Rejang Kajan, *alt.* Kayan, Rejang [ree], 459
Rejang Kayan, *see* Kayan, Rejang [ree], 459

Rejang-Lebong, *alt.* Rejang [rej], 437
Rek, *alt.* Dinka, Southwestern [dik], 190
　dial. Dinka, Southwestern [dik], 190
Rekhta, *alt. dial.* Urdu [urd], 389
Rekhti, *alt. dial.* Urdu [urd], 389
Reli [rei], 385
Relli, *alt.* Reli [rei], 385
Rema [bow], 622
Rembarranga, *alt.* Rembarunga [rmb], 576
Rembarrnga, *alt.* Rembarunga [rmb], 576
Rembarunga [rmb], 576
Remboken, *dial.* Tondano [tdn], 434
Rembong [reb], 409
　dial. Rembong [reb], 409
Remi, *alt.* Nyaturu [rim], 203
Remo [rem], 293
　alt. Bondo [bfw], 357
Remontado Agta, *see* Agta, Remontado [agv], 491
Remosum, *alt.* Bondo [bfw], 357
Rempi [rmp], 622
Rempin, *alt.* Rempi [rmp], 622
Remun [lkj], 460
Rendile, *alt.* Rendille [rel], 135
Rendille [rel], 135
Rendre, *alt.* Nungu [rin], 171
Rengao [ren], 526
Rengjongmu, *dial.* Lepcha [lep], 372, 323, 474
Rengma, *alt.* Naga, Southern Rengma [nre], 379
Rengma Naga, *alt.* Naga, Southern Rengma [nre], 379
Rennell, *alt.* Rennell-Belona [mnv], 638
　alt. dial. Rennell-Belona [mnv], 638
Rennell-Belona [mnv], 638
Rennellese, *alt.* Rennell-Belona [mnv], 638
Rennellese Sign Language [rsi], 638
Rennellese-Bellonese, *alt.* Rennell-Belona [mnv], 638
Reo, *alt. dial.* Lyélé [lee], 52
Repanbitip [rpn], 641
Rer Bare [rer], 118
Rerau [rea], 622
Rere, *alt.* Koalib [kib], 192
Rerebere, *alt.* Rer Bare [rer], 118
Rerep [pgk], 645
Reshe [res], 173
Reshiat, *alt.* Daasanach [dsh], 114, 132
Resia, *dial.* Slovenian [slv], 545
Resígaro [rgr], 293
Resígero, *alt.* Resígaro [rgr], 293

Restigouche, *alt.* Micmac [mic], 239, 305
Retta [ret], 409
Retuama, *alt.* Tanimuca-Retuarã [tnc], 247
Retuarã, *alt.* Tanimuca-Retuarã [tnc], 247
　dial. Tanimuca-Retuarã [tnc], 247
Réunion Creole French [rcf], 178
Reval, *alt. dial.* Estonian [est], 534, 534
Rewa, *alt. dial.* Sudest [tgo], 625
Rewandiz, *dial.* Kurdish, Central [ckb], 443
Reyesano [rey], 223
Rgyarong, *alt.* Jiarong [jya], 336
Rhade, *alt.* Rade [rad], 526
Rhaeto-Romance, *alt.* Ladin [lld], 544
　alt. Romansch [roh], 562
Rhathabe, *dial.* Xhosa [xho], 187
Rheno, *alt.* Remo [rem], 293
Rheto-Romance, *alt.* Romansch [roh], 562
Rhinyihinyi, *dial.* Tembo [tbt], 108
Rhiti, *dial.* Kgalagadi [xkv], 47
Rhodanien, *dial.* Provençal [prv], 537
Riahoma, *alt.* Pahi [lgt], 621
Riam, *dial.* Malayic Dayak [xdy], 394
Riang (India) [ria], 385, 322
　Riang (Myanmar) [ril], 467, 343
　dial. Kok Borok [trp], 321
Riang-Lang, *alt.* Riang [ril], 467, 343
Riantana [ran], 422
Riasati, *alt.* Seraiki [skr], 386
　alt. dial. Seraiki [skr], 488, 386
Riasi, *dial.* Kashmiri [kas], 367
Riasiti, *alt.* Seraiki [skr], 488
Riau, *dial.* Malay [mly], 436
Ribagorçan, *alt. dial.* Catalan-Valencian-Balear [cat], 559
Ribagorzano, *alt. dial.* Aragonese [arg], 558
Ribah, *dial.* C'lela [dri], 157
Ribam, *alt. dial.* Piti [pcn], 173
Riban, *dial.* Piti [pcn], 173
Ribaw, *dial.* Bata [bta], 155
Ribbi, *dial.* Loko [lok], 183
Ribe, *dial.* Giryama [nyf], 133
Ribia, *dial.* Themne [tem], 184
Ribina, *dial.* Jere [jer], 165
Ribow, *alt. dial.* Bata [bta], 155
Ribun [rir], 395
Richa, *dial.* Kulere [kul], 167
Ridan, *dial.* Kubu [kvb], 436
Ridarngo, *alt.* Ritarungo [rit], 576

Ridaw, *dial.* Amis, Nataoran [ais], 511
Riddi, *alt.* Mukha-Dora [mmk], 376
Ridharrngu, *alt.* Ritarungo [rit], 576
Rien [rie], 452
Rif, *alt.* Tarifit [rif], 40
Riff, *alt.* Tarifit [rif], 40
Rifi, *alt.* Tarifit [rif], 146, 40
Rifia, *alt.* Tarifit [rif], 146
Rigbo, *dial.* Ma'di, Southern [snm], 211
Rigwe, *alt.* Irigwe [iri], 164
Rihe, *alt. dial.* Giryama [nyf], 133
Rihu'a, *dial.* Fagani [faf], 636
Rik'a, *alt.* Leco [lec], 223
Rikbaktsa [rkb], 232
Rikou, *alt.* Ringgou [rgu], 409
Rikpa, *alt.* Bafia [ksf], 56
Rikpa', *alt.* Bafia [ksf], 56
Rikvani, *dial.* Andi [ani], 553
Rimang-Gudinhma, *alt.* Mbariman-Gudhinma [zmv], 574
Rimatara, *dial.* Austral [aut], 581
Rimi, *alt.* Nyaturu [rim], 203
alt. dial. Nyaturu [rim], 203
Rincón Zapotec, *see* Zapotec, Rincón [zar], 279
Rinconada Bicolano, *alt.* Bicolano, Iriga [bto], 493
Rindi, *alt. dial.* Kambera [xbr], 407
Rindiri, *alt.* Nungu [rin], 171
Rindre, *alt.* Nungu [rin], 171
dial. Nungu [rin], 171
Ringgou [rgu], 409
dial. Ringgou [rgu], 409
Rio, *alt.* Gedaged [gdd], 599
Rio Arauca Guahibo, *alt.* Playero [gob], 247
Río Casacará, *dial.* Yukpa [yup], 248
Río Maracas, *dial.* Yukpa [yup], 248
Río Negro, *dial.* Yukpa [yup], 313
Rio Pongo Baga, *alt.* Baga Sitemu [bsp], 128
Rio Tomo Guahibo, *alt. dial.* Guahibo [guh], 245
Rion, *dial.* Koho [kpm], 524
Riouw-Lingga, *alt. dial.* Malay [mly], 436
Ripere, *alt. dial.* Mbum [mdd], 66
Ripey, *alt.* Bafia [ksf], 56
Ririo [rri], 638
Rirratjingu, *dial.* Dhangu [dhg], 569
Ris, *alt.* Arikara [ari], 298
Rishaidep, *alt.* Musasa [smm], 476
Rishuwa, *alt.* Shuwa-Zamani [ksa], 174
alt. dial. Lere [gnh], 168
Ritaebang, *alt. dial.* Lamaholot [slp], 408

Ritarnugu, *alt.* Ritarungo [rit], 576
Ritarungo [rit], 576
Ritharngu, *alt.* Ritarungo [rit], 576
Ritharrngu, *alt.* Ritarungo [rit], 576
Ritime, *dial.* Gimnime [gmn], 62
Rito, *alt. dial.* Lutos [ndy], 76, 83
Ritok, *dial.* Malay [mly], 436
Riung [riu], 409
alt. dial. Talaud [tld], 433
River Bushman, *pej. alt. dial.* Khwe [xuu], 47
River Cess Gio, *dial.* Dan [daf], 137
River Jarawa, *alt.* Bada [bau], 154
River Jukun, *alt.* Wannu [jub], 177
River Nivaclé, *dial.* Nivaclé [cag], 285, 220
River Ruki, *alt.* Boloki [bkt], 98
Riverain Sango, *see* Sango, Riverain [snj], 77
Rivercess Bassa, *dial.* Bassa [bsq], 137
Riwai, *alt.* Bagheli [bfy], 354, 468
Riyadh, *alt. dial.* Arabic, Najdi Spoken [ars], 508
Riyao, *dial.* Oy [oyb], 452
Rlam, *alt. dial.* Mnong, Eastern [mng], 525
Rmeet, *alt.* Lamet [lbn], 451
Ro, *alt.* Chrau [crw], 522
dial. Folopa [ppo], 599
Ro Bambami, *alt.* Agoi [ibm], 153
Ro-Ngao, *alt.* Rengao [ren], 526
Roamaina, *alt.* Omurano [omu], 289
Roba, *dial.* Lala-Roba [lla], 163
Robba, *alt. dial.* Lala-Roba [lla], 163
Robiana, *alt.* Roviana [rug], 638
Roboda, *alt. dial.* Dobu [dob], 597
Rocky Peak, *alt.* Iteri [itr], 603
Rocoroibo, *alt.* Tarahumara, Lowland [tac], 274
Rodi, *alt.* Norwegian, Traveller [rmg], 550
alt. Traveller Danish [rmd], 534
Rodiya, *dial.* Sinhala [sin], 509
Ro'do Bo', *alt.* Dumi [dus], 471
Rodong, *alt.* Camling [rab], 469
Rodosto, *dial.* Armenian [hye], 318
Rodrigues Creole, *dial.* Morisyen [mfe], 145
Roea, *alt.* Macuna [myy], 246
Rofia, *dial.* Cishingini [asg], 151
Rofik, *alt. dial.* Keiga [kec], 192
Rogede, *dial.* Nzanyi [nja], 171
Roglai, Cacgia [roc], 526
Roglai, Northern [rog], 526
Roglai, Southern [rgs], 526
Rogo [rod], 174
Rohinga, *dial.* Chittagonian [cit], 321, 463

Rohomoni, *dial.* Haruku [hrk], 398
Rohrruri, *alt. dial.* Pahari, Mahasu [bfz], 382
Roinji, *alt.* Ronji [roe], 623
Ro'is, *alt. dial.* Amarasi [aaz], 406
Ro'is Hero, *alt. dial.* Amarasi [aaz], 406
Ro'is Tais Nonof, *alt. dial.* Amarasi [aaz], 406
Rok, *dial.* Khmu [kjg], 451
Rokhung, *dial.* Bahing [bhj], 468
Rokka, *alt.* Ngad'a [nxg], 409
Rolam, *alt. dial.* Mnong, Eastern [mng], 525
Rolom, *alt. dial.* Mnong, Eastern [mng], 525
Rolong, *dial.* Tswana [tsn], 48, 186
Rom, *alt.* Romani, Vlax [rmy], 537, 541, 566
alt. dial. Teso [teo], 213
Roma [rmm], 403
alt. dial. C'lela [dri], 157
Roma-Na, *alt. dial.* C'lela [dri], 157
Romaic, *alt.* Greek [ell], 540
Romam [rmx], 526
Romanau, *alt. dial.* Lobu, Lanas [ruu], 457
Romanche, *alt.* Romansch [roh], 562
Romanés, *alt.* Romani, Vlax [rmy], 541
Romanese, *alt.* Romani, Vlax [rmy], 551
Romang, *alt.* Roma [rmm], 403
Romani English, *alt.* Angloromani [rme], 564, 298
Romani, Balkan [rmn], 557, 441, 532, 537, 539, 541, 542, 545, 547, 548, 551, 563
Romani, Baltic [rml], 550, 546, 546
Romani, Carpathian [rmc], 533, 542, 550, 551, 558, 564
Romani, Kalo Finnish [rmf], 535, 561
Romani, Sinte [rmo], 557, 448, 530, 533, 537, 539, 542, 545, 549, 550, 562
Romani, Tavringer [rmu], 561, 550
Romani, Vlax [rmy], 551, 247, 529, 531, 532, 537, 539, 541, 542, 545, 549, 550, 550, 551, 556, 558, 561, 564, 566
Romani, Welsh [rmw], 566
Romanian [ron], 552, 446, 542, 548, 557, 564
Romanian Sign Language [rms], 552
Romanian, Istro [ruo], 532

Romanian, Macedo [rup], 541, 529, 532, 547, 552, 557
Romanian, Megleno [ruq], 541, 547
Romanichal, *alt.* Angloromani [rme], 564, 298, 568
Romanis, *alt.* Angloromani [rme], 298
Romano-Greek [rge], 541
Romano-Serbian [rsb], 557
Romansch [roh], 562
Romansh, *alt.* Romansch [roh], 562
Rombi, *alt.* Barombi [bbi], 58
alt. Lombi [lmi], 103
Romblomanon [rol], 500
Romblon, *alt.* Romblomanon [rol], 500
dial. Romblomanon [rol], 500
Rombo [rof], 204
Romenes, *alt.* Romani, Vlax [rmy], 537, 566
Romika, *alt.* Romano-Greek [rge], 541
Romkuin, *alt.* Romkun [rmk], 622
Romkun [rmk], 622
Rommanes, *alt.* Romani, Sinte [rmo], 557, 530, 533, 537, 539
Rommani, *alt.* Romani, Tavringer [rmu], 561, 550
Romungre, *alt.* Romani, Vlax [rmy], 542
Romungro, *alt.* Romani, Carpathian [rmc], 533, 558
Ron [cla], 174
alt. Roon [rnn], 422
Roncalese, *dial.* Basque [eus], 559
Rondu, *alt. dial.* Shina [scl], 488
Rone, *alt.* Temein [teq], 195
Rong, *alt.* Changthang [cna], 358
alt. Lepcha [lep], 372, 323, 474
Rong Kethang, *dial.* Karbi [mjw], 366
Rong Kong, *alt.* Lao [lao], 445
Ronga [rng], 149, 186
Rongba, *dial.* Tibetan, Amdo [adx], 344
Rongdani, *alt. dial.* Rabha [rah], 384
Ronge, *alt.* Temein [teq], 195
Rongga [ror], 409
Rongke, *alt.* Lepcha [lep], 372, 323, 474
Rongkong, *alt.* Tae' [rob], 428
dial. Tae' [rob], 428
Rongkong Kanandede, *alt.* Tae' [rob], 428
Rongmahbrogpa, *dial.* Tibetan, Amdo [adx], 344
Rongmai, *alt.* Naga, Rongmei [nbu], 379

Rongmei, *alt.* Naga, Rongmei [nbu], 379
Rongmei Naga, *see* Naga, Rongmei [nbu], 379
Rongo, *alt. dial.* Myene [mye], 121
Rongpa, *alt.* Lepcha [lep], 372, 323, 474
Rongpo [rnp], 385
Rongrang, *dial.* Naga, Tase [nst], 380
Ronji [roe], 623
Ronrang, *dial.* Naga, Tase [nst], 380
Rooi Nasie, *alt.* Nama [naq], 150, 48, 186
Roomarrows, *alt. dial.* Lobu, Lanas [ruu], 457
Roon [rnn], 422
Roongas, *alt.* Rungus [drg], 458
Rootigaanga, *dial.* Datooga [tcc], 198
Roper River Kriol, *dial.* Kriol [rop], 572
Roper River Pidgin, *alt. dial.* Kriol [rop], 572
Roper-Bamyili Creole, *alt.* Kriol [rop], 572
Ropo, *alt. dial.* Krumen, Tepo [ted], 93, 138
Ror, *dial.* Kag-Fer-Jiir-Koor-Ror-Us-Zuksun [gel], 165
Rori, *alt.* Sangu [sbp], 204
Roria [rga], 645
Roro, *alt.* Waima [rro], 631
dial. Waima [rro], 631
Rorovana, *alt.* Torau [ttu], 628
Rosarito Cora, *dial.* Cora, Santa Teresa [cok], 262
Roshani, *alt. dial.* Shughni [sgh], 513
dial. Shughni [sgh], 318
Roshorvi, *alt. dial.* Shughni [sgh], 513
Roso, *dial.* Agta, Dupaninan [duo], 490
Rossel, *alt.* Yele [yle], 633
Rotanese Chamorro, *dial.* Chamorro [cha], 581
Rote, *alt.* Bilba [bpz], 406
alt. Dela-Oenale [row], 406
alt. Dengka [dnk], 406
alt. Lole [llg], 408
alt. Ringgou [rgu], 409
alt. Termanu [twu], 410
alt. Tii [txq], 410
Rote Barat, *alt.* Dela-Oenale [row], 406
alt. Dengka [dnk], 406
alt. Tii [txq], 410
Rote Tengah, *alt.* Lole [llg], 408
alt. Termanu [twu], 410

Rote Timur, *alt.* Bilba [bpz], 406
alt. Ringgou [rgu], 409
Rotea, *alt.* Sedang [sed], 526
Roteang, *alt.* Sedang [sed], 526
Roti, *alt.* Bilba [bpz], 406
alt. Dela-Oenale [row], 406
alt. Dengka [dnk], 406
alt. Lole [llg], 408
alt. Ringgou [rgu], 409
alt. Termanu [twu], 410
alt. Tii [txq], 410
dial. Bajau, Indonesian [bdl], 427
Rotigeenga, *alt. dial.* Datooga [tcc], 198
Rotigenga, *alt. dial.* Datooga [tcc], 198
Rotinese, *alt.* Bilba [bpz], 406
alt. Dela-Oenale [row], 406
alt. Dengka [dnk], 406
alt. Lole [llg], 408
alt. Ringgou [rgu], 409
alt. Termanu [twu], 410
alt. Tii [txq], 410
Roto, *alt. dial.* Lamogai [lmg], 609
Rotokas [roo], 623
Rotorua-Taupo, *dial.* Maori [mri], 586
Rotse, *alt.* Lozi [loz], 214, 150, 216
Rotuman [rtm], 580
Rotuna, *alt.* Rotuman [rtm], 580
Rotvi, *alt.* Lozi [loz], 216
Rotwelsch, *alt.* Traveller Danish [rmd], 534
Rouchi, *alt.* Picard [pcd], 537, 531
Roucouyenne, *alt.* Wayana [way], 296
alt. dial. Wayana [way], 234
Rouku, *alt.* Wára [tci], 631
Roumanian, *alt.* Romanian [ron], 548
Rounga, *alt.* Runga [rou], 86, 77
Roungo, *alt.* Runga [rou], 86
Rourou, *alt.* Zauzou [zal], 349
Routa, *dial.* Bungku [bkz], 428
Routo, *alt. dial.* Lutos [ndy], 76, 83
Rouyi, *alt.* Luyana [lyn], 214, 41
Roviana [rug], 638
Rozi, *alt.* Lozi [loz], 214, 150, 216
Rtahu, *dial.* Tibetan, Amdo [adx], 344
Rtchi, *alt.* Gavar [gou], 61
Rtsamangpa'ikha, *alt.* Chocangacakha [cgk], 323
Rua, *dial.* Wanukaka [wnk], 410
Ruafa, *alt.* Tarifit [rif], 40
Rual, *dial.* Wipi [gdr], 632
Ruanda, *alt.* Rwanda [kin], 178, 107, 212
Ruavatu, *alt.* Lengo [lgr], 637
Rubasa, *alt.* Basa [bzw], 154

Rubassa, *alt.* Basa [bzw], 154
Rubiana, *alt.* Roviana [rug], 638
Ruc, *alt.* Chut [scb], 522, 450
   alt. dial. Chut [scb], 522
   dial. Chut [scb], 450
Rucuyen, *dial.* Wayana [way], 234
Rudbari [rdb], 441
Rue, *dial.* Sena [seh], 149
Rufawa, *alt. dial.* Lame [bma], 168
Rufiji [rui], 204
Rufu, *alt. dial.* Lame [bma], 168
Rufumbira, *dial.* Rwanda [kin], 212
Ruga [ruh], 385
Rugara, *alt.* Terei [buo], 627
Rugciriku, *alt.* Diriku [diu], 149, 40
   alt. Gciriku [diu], 47
Rugnot of Lake Buhi East, *alt.*
   Agta, Mt. Iraya [atl], 490
Rugungu, *alt.* Gungu [rub], 210
Ruguru, *alt.* Luguru [ruf], 200
Ruhaya, *alt.* Haya [hay], 199
Ruhu, *dial.* Lame [bma], 168
Ruihi, *alt.* Rufiji [rui], 204
Ruija, *dial.* Saami, North [sme], 550,
   535, 561
Ruilak, *alt.* Kafoa [kpu], 407
Ruk, *alt.* Chuukese [chk], 582
Rukai [dru], 512
Rukaragwe, *alt.* Nyambo [now], 203
Rukiga, *alt.* Chiga [cgg], 210
Rukobi, *alt.* Hunde [hke], 100
Rukonjo, *alt.* Konjo [koo], 211
   dial. Konjo [koo], 211
Rukuba, *alt.* Che [ruk], 156
Rukul, *dial.* Bo-Rukul [mae], 155
Rukwangali, *alt.* Kwangali
   [kwn], 150, 40
Ruli [ruc], 212
Ruliy, *alt.* Luri, Southern [luz], 440
Rum, *dial.* Giziga, South [giz], 62
Ruma [ruz], 174
   alt. dial. Korku [kfq], 369
Rumai, *alt.* Palaung, Rumai
   [rbb], 466, 342
Rumai Palaung, *see* Palaung,
   Rumai [rbb], 466, 342
Rumaiya, *alt.* Mala [ruy], 169
Rumanau, *alt. dial.* Lobu, Lanas
   [ruu], 457
Rumanau Alab, *alt. dial.* Lobu,
   Lanas [ruu], 457
Rumanian, *alt.* Romanian [ron], 552,
   542, 548, 557, 564
Rumaya, *alt.* Mala [ruy], 169
Rumbala, *alt.* Mbala [mdp], 104
Rumberpon, *dial.* Biak [bhw], 412
Rumbia, *alt. dial.* Moronene [mqn],
   431
Rumbur, *alt. dial.* Kalasha [kls], 486
Rumdali, *alt.* Bahing [bhj], 468

Rumelian, *dial.* Turkish [tur], 519,
   521
Rumli, *alt.* Lombi [lmi], 103
Rumsen, *dial.* Ohlone, Southern
   [css], 306
Rumu [klq], 623
Rumuji, *dial.* Ikwere [ikw], 164
Rumuwa, *alt.* Rumu [klq], 623
Runa [rna], 247
Runa Shimi, *alt.* Quechua, Napo
   Lowland [qvo], 291
   alt. Quichua, Napo Lowland
   [qvo], 251
Runasimi, *alt.* Quechua, Ayacucho
   [quy], 289
Runasimi Qusqu Qullaw, *alt.*
   Quechua, Cusco [quz], 290
Rundi [run], 55, 212
Rundum, *dial.* Tagal Murut
   [mvv], 458, 395
Runga [rou], 86, 77
   alt. Rungwa [rnw], 204
Runga de Ndele, *alt.* Runga
   [rou], 77
Rungu, *alt.* Taabwa [tap], 108, 215
   alt. dial. Myene [mye], 121
   dial. Mambwe-Lungu [mgr], 214,
   201
Rungus [drg], 458
   dial. Rungus [drg], 458
Rungus Dusun, *alt.* Rungus
   [drg], 458
Rungwa [rnw], 204
Runsien, *alt. dial.* Ohlone, Southern
   [css], 306
Runyambo, *alt.* Nyambo [now], 203
Runyankole, *alt.* Nyankore
   [nyn], 212
Runyarwanda, *alt.* Rwanda
   [kin], 212
Runyoro, *alt.* Hema [nix], 100
   alt. Nyoro [nyo], 212
Ruomai, *alt.* Palaung, Rumai
   [rbb], 342
Ruotsi, *alt.* Swedish [swe], 562
Rupini, *dial.* Chin, Falam [flm], 358
Rupit, *dial.* Rawas [rws], 437
Rupshu, *alt.* Changthang [cna], 358
Rupununi, *dial.* Guyanese Creole
   English [gyn], 257
Rural, *alt. dial.* Luri, Northern
   [lrc], 440
Rural Central Maltese, *dial.*
   Maltese [mlt], 547
Rural East Maltese, *dial.* Maltese
   [mlt], 547
Rural Peshawar Hindko, *dial.*
   Hindko, Southern [hnd], 485
Rural West Maltese, *dial.* Maltese
   [mlt], 547

Rurama, *alt.* Ruma [ruz], 174
Ruri, *dial.* Kwaya [kya], 200
Ruruhi'ip, *alt.* Yahang [rhp], 632
Ruruhip, *alt.* Heyo [auk], 602
   alt. Yahang [rhp], 632
Ruruli, *alt.* Ruli [ruc], 212
Ruruma, *alt.* Ruma [ruz], 174
Rurutu, *dial.* Austral [aut], 581
Rushan, *alt. dial.* Shughni [sgh], 513,
   318
Rushani, *alt. dial.* Shughni [sgh], 318
   dial. Shughni [sgh], 513
Russ, *alt.* Russian [rus], 343
Russell Island, *alt.* Lavukaleve
   [lvk], 637
Russia, *alt.* Daasanach [dsh], 114
Russia Buriat, *see* Buriat, Russia
   [bxr], 504
Russian [rus], 556, 307, 343, 446,
   449, 462
Russian Lapp, *alt.* Saami, Skolt
   [sms], 535
   pej. alt. Saami, Skolt [sms], 556
Russian Sign Language
   [rsl], 556, 532
Russit, *alt.* Russian [rus], 446
Russki, *alt.* Russian [rus], 556, 307,
   343, 446, 462
Rustaqa, *dial.* Lishanid Noshan
   [aij], 445
Rusyn [rue], 564, 558
Rut, *dial.* Dinka, Northeastern
   [dip], 189
Rutagwenda, *dial.* Nyoro
   [nyo], 212
Rutah, *dial.* Amahai [amq], 396
Rutal, *alt.* Rutul [rut], 556
Ruteng, *alt. dial.* Manggarai
   [mqy], 409
Ruthenian, *alt.* Rusyn [rue], 564,
   558
Rutkai, *alt.* Rukai [dru], 512
Ruto, *alt.* Lutos [ndy], 76
   alt. dial. Lutos [ndy], 76
   dial. Lutos [ndy], 83
Rutooro, *alt.* Tooro [ttj], 213
Rutoro, *alt.* Tooro [ttj], 213
Rutse, *alt.* Lozi [loz], 214, 150, 216
Rutul [rut], 556
Rutultsy, *alt.* Rutul [rut], 556
Rutuly, *alt.* Rutul [rut], 556
Rutuman, *alt.* Rotuman [rtm], 580
Rutwa, *dial.* Rwanda [kin], 178
Ruund [rnd], 107, 41
Ruviana, *alt.* Roviana [rug], 638
Ruweng, *alt.* Dinka, Northwestern
   [diw], 190
Ruwenzori Kibira, *alt.* Amba
   [rwm], 210, 96
Rwa [rwk], 204

Rwala, *alt. dial.* Arabic, Najdi
    Spoken [ars], 508
Rwamba, *alt.* Amba [rwm], 210, 96
Rwanda [kin], 178, 107, 212
Rwanduz, *dial.* Lishanid Noshan
    [aij], 445
Rwo, *alt.* Rwa [rwk], 204
Sa [sax], 645
    alt. Giáy [pcc], 523
    alt. Samo, Maya [sym], 53
    alt. dial. Ghomálá' [bbj], 62
Sa'a [apb], 638
Saa, *alt.* Dugun [ndu], 60
    alt. Duupa [dae], 60
    alt. Sa'a [apb], 638
Saadje, *alt. dial.* Dii [dur], 60
Saafi, *alt.* Saafi-Saafi [sav], 182
Saafi-Saafi [sav], 182
Saaka, *alt.* Makhuwa-Saka [xsq], 147
Saakye, *alt. dial.* Dii [dur], 60
Saam [raq], 478
    alt. Saami, Inari [smn], 535
    alt. Saami, Kildin [sjd], 556
    alt. Saami, Skolt [sms], 556
    alt. Saami, Ter [sjt], 556
Saam Rai, *alt.* Saam [raq], 478
Saama Kha, *alt.* Saam [raq], 478
Saame, *alt.* Saami, Inari [smn], 535
    alt. Saami, Lule [smj], 550
    alt. Saami, North [sme], 535, 561
    alt. Saami, Skolt [sms], 535
Saami, *alt.* Saami, Kildin [sjd], 556
    alt. Saami, Lule [smj], 561
    alt. Saami, North [sme], 550
    alt. Saami, Pite [sje], 561
    alt. Saami, South [sma], 550
    alt. Saami, Ume [sju], 562
Saami, Akkala [sia], 556
Saami, Inari [smn], 535
Saami, Kemi [sjk], 535
Saami, Kildin [sjd], 556
Saami, Lule [smj], 561, 550
Saami, North [sme], 550, 535, 561
Saami, Pite [sje], 561, 550
Saami, Skolt [sms], 535, 556
Saami, South [sma], 561, 550
Saami, Ter [sjt], 556
Saami, Ume [sju], 562
Saamia, *dial.* Luyia [luy], 134, 211
Saamtaav, *alt.* Kiorr [xko], 451,
    465
Saan, *dial.* Dugun [ndu], 60
    pej. alt. Hai‖om [hgm], 149
Sa'ang, *alt. dial.* Ta'oih, Upper
    [tth], 453, 527
Saanga, *alt.* Makhuwa-Saka
    [xsq], 147
Saanich, *dial.* Salish, Straits
    [str], 241, 307
Saapa, *alt.* Sanapaná [sap], 285

Saaroa [sxr], 512
Saaronge, *alt.* Daju, Dar Daju
    [djc], 79
Saarua, *alt.* Saaroa [sxr], 512
Saawa, *dial.* Mumuye [mzm], 170
Saawii, *dial.* Noon [snf], 181
Saba [saa], 86
Saba Creole English, *dial.*
    Netherlands Antilles Creole English
    [vic], 282
Sabah Bisaya, *see* Bisaya, Sabah
    [bsy], 456
Sabah Malay, *see* Malay, Sabah
    [msi], 457
Sabah Murut, *alt. dial.* Tagal Murut
    [mvv], 458, 395
Sabakor, *alt.* Buruwai [asi], 413
Sa'ban [snv], 460, 395
Sabanê, *alt.* Sabanês [sae], 232
Sabanero, *dial.* Buglere [sab], 283
Sabanês [sae], 232
Sabanga, *dial.* Banda-Mbrès
    [bqk], 75, 188
Sabaot [spy], 135
Sabar, *alt.* Sora [srb], 387
Sabara, *alt.* Sora [srb], 387
Sabari, *alt.* Amis [ami], 511
    dial. Nimoa [nmw], 618
Sabean, *alt.* Mandaic [mid], 441
Sabe'in, *alt.* Mandaic [mid], 441
Sabela, *alt.* Waorani [auc], 251
Sabena, *alt.* Moskona [mtj], 420
Saberi, *alt.* Isirawa [srl], 415
Sabeu, *dial.* Chin, Mara [mrh], 463
Sabi, *dial.* Nyole [nuj], 212
Sabiny, *dial.* Kupsabiny [kpz], 211
Sabir, *alt.* Lingua Franca [pml], 209
Sabon, *dial.* Lele [lle], 609
Sabones, *alt.* Sabanês [sae], 232
Sabu [hvn], 409
    dial. Abu [ado], 586
Sabujá, *dial.* Karirí-Xocó [kzw], 228
Sabüm [sbo], 455
Sabungo, *dial.* Dayak, Land [dyk],
    393
Sabup, *alt.* Kenyah, Sebob [sib], 459
Saburi, *dial.* Logorik [liu], 192
Sabutan, *alt.* Bukar Sadong
    [sdo], 459, 392
Sabuyan, *alt.* Sebuyau [snb], 460
Sabuyau, *alt.* Sebuyau [snb], 460
Sac, *dial.* Mesquakie [sac], 304
Sac And Fox, *alt.* Mesquakie
    [sac], 304
Sacapulas K'iche', *alt.* Sakapulteko
    [quv], 256
Sacapulteco, *alt.* Sakapulteko
    [quv], 256
Sach, *alt.* Chut [scb], 522, 450
    dial. Chut [scb], 522

Saclan, *alt.* Miwok, Bay [mkq], 305
Sada, *alt.* Tae' [rob], 428
    alt. Toala' [tlz], 433
Sadalir, *alt. dial.* Tagal Murut
    [mvv], 458
    alt. dial. Tidong [tid], 395
Sa'dan, *alt.* Toraja-Sa'dan [sda], 434
Sadan, *alt.* Sadri [sck], 385
    alt. Toraja-Sa'dan [sda], 434
Sadana, *alt.* Sadri [sck], 385
Sadang, *alt.* Toraja-Sa'dan [sda], 434
Sadanga, *dial.* Bontoc, Central [bnc],
    493
Sadani, *alt.* Sadri [sck], 385
Sa'dansche, *alt.* Toraja-Sa'dan
    [sda], 434
Sadar, *alt. dial.* Mankanya [knf], 131,
    181
Sadar Bhumij, *alt. dial.* Mundari
    [muw], 376
Sadari, *alt.* Sadri [sck], 385
Sadati, *alt.* Sadri [sck], 385
Sadhan, *alt.* Sadri [sck], 385
Sadhari, *alt.* Sadri [sck], 385
Sadna, *alt.* Sadri [sck], 385
Sado, *alt. dial.* Aja [ajg], 42, 206
Sadong, *alt.* Bukar Sadong
    [sdo], 459, 392
Sadri [sck], 385
    dial. Maithili [mai], 475
Sadri Korwa, *dial.* Chhattisgarhi
    [hne], 358
Sadri, Oraon [sdr], 322
Sadrik, *alt.* Sadri [sck], 385
Saediq, *alt.* Taroko [trv], 512
Saek [skb], 452, 517
Saep [spd], 623
Safalaba, *alt.* Safaliba [saf], 127
Safalba, *alt.* Safaliba [saf], 127
Safali, *alt.* Safaliba [saf], 127
Safaliba [saf], 127
Safan, *alt. dial.* Asmat, Casuarina
    Coast [asc], 411
Safané, *dial.* Marka [rkm], 52
Safen, *alt.* Saafi-Saafi [sav], 182
Safeyoka [apz], 623
Safi, *alt.* Saafi-Saafi [sav], 182
Safi-Safi, *alt.* Saafi-Saafi [sav], 182
Safwa [sbk], 204
Saga-I, *alt. dial.* Kinabatangan, Upper
    [dmg], 457
Sagada Igorot, *alt.* Kankanay,
    Northern [xnn], 498
Sagadin, *dial.* Dido [ddo], 554
Sagai, *dial.* Khakas [kjh], 505, 337
Sagaj, *alt. dial.* Khakas [kjh], 505
Sagaka, *dial.* Koyaga [kga], 93
Sagala [sbm], 204
    alt. Sagalla [tga], 136
Sagalla [tga], 136

Sagamuk, *alt.* Acipa, Eastern [acp], 153
  alt. Acipa, Western [awc], 153
Sagara, *alt.* Sagala [sbm], 204
  dial. Dogon, Tene Kan [dtk], 142
Sagbee, *dial.* Mumuye [mzm], 170
Sageju, *alt.* Segeju [seg], 204
Saghala, *alt.* Sagalla [tga], 136
Saghilin, *alt. dial.* Ainu [ain], 446, 503
Sago, *alt.* Ciwogai [tgd], 157
Sagtengpa, *alt.* Brokpake [sgt], 322
Sagu, *alt.* Adonara [adr], 406
Saguye, *alt. dial.* Borana [gax], 132
Sagwara, *dial.* Wagdi [wbr], 390
Sagzee, *dial.* Dii [dur], 60
Saharan Arabic, *alt.* Arabic, Algerian Saharan Spoken [aao], 39
Sahibganj, *dial.* Sauria Paharia [mjt], 386
Sahidic, *dial.* Coptic [cop], 110
Sahil, *dial.* Arabic, Tunisian Spoken [aeb], 209
Saho [ssy], 112, 118
Sahrawi, *alt.* Arabic, Hassaniyya [mey], 146
Sahu [saj], 403
  alt. dial. Maslam [msv], 66, 84
Sahu'u, *alt.* Sahu [saj], 403
Sai, *alt. dial.* Tai Nüa [tdd], 344
  dial. Gumuz [guk], 191
Saida Sunni Arabic, *dial.* Arabic, North Levantine Spoken [apc], 453
Sa'idi, *alt.* Arabic, Sa'idi Spoken [aec], 110
Sa'idi Spoken Arabic, *see* Arabic, Sa'idi Spoken [aec], 110
Saifi, *dial.* Tehit [kps], 424
Saighani, *alt. dial.* Shughni [sgh], 318
Saija, *alt.* Epena [sja], 245, 251, 283
Sailau, *alt.* Mizo [lus], 376, 321
Sailen, *alt.* Duriankere [dbn], 414
Sailolof, *alt.* Ma'ya [slz], 420
Saingbaun, *dial.* Chin, Asho [csh], 321
Saint Kitts Creole English [aig], 294
Saint Lucian Creole French [acf], 294
Saint Lucian English, *dial.* English [eng], 294
Sainti, *alt.* Santali [sat], 478
Sai'ora, *alt. dial.* Tairora, North [tbg], 626
Saipa, *dial.* Sinsauru [snz], 625
Saipan Carolinian, *alt.* Carolinian [cal], 586
Saiqora, *dial.* Tairora, North [tbg], 626

Sairang, *alt. dial.* Chin, Thado [tcz], 359
  dial. Chin, Thado [tcz], 463
Saiset, *alt.* Saisiyat [xsy], 512
Saisett, *alt.* Saisiyat [xsy], 512
Saisiat, *alt.* Saisiyat [xsy], 512
Saisiett, *alt.* Saisiyat [xsy], 512
Saisirat, *alt.* Saisiyat [xsy], 512
Saisiyat [xsy], 512
Saisyet, *alt.* Saisiyat [xsy], 512
Saisyett, *alt.* Saisiyat [xsy], 512
Saizang, *dial.* Chin, Paite [pck], 359
Sajalong [sjl], 385
Sajau, *alt.* Sajau Basap [sjb], 395
Sajau Basap [sjb], 395
Sak, *alt.* Chak [ckh], 321
  alt. Kado [kdv], 464, 337, 450
Saka, *alt.* Makhuwa-Saka [xsq], 147
  alt. Odual [odu], 172
  alt. Sakata [skt], 104
  alt. dial. Nkutu [nkw], 106
  dial. Makhuwa-Saka [xsq], 147
Sakai, *alt.* Kensiu [kns], 515
Sakai Bukit of Temongoh, *alt. dial.* Temiar [tea], 455
Sakai of Plus Korbu, *dial.* Temiar [tea], 455
Sakai Tanjong of Temongoh, *alt. dial.* Kensiu [kns], 454
Sakaji, *alt.* Nathembo [nte], 148
Sakalagan, *dial.* Mentawai [mwv], 436
Sakalava, *alt.* Bushi [buc], 145
Sakalava Malagasy, *see* Malagasy, Sakalava [skg], 140
Sakam [skm], 623
Sakanyi, *dial.* Ntomba [nto], 106
Sakao [sku], 645
Sakapulteko [quv], 256
Sakar, *dial.* Mbula [mna], 612
Sakara, *alt.* Nzakara [nzk], 77, 106
Sakata [skt], 104
  dial. Sakata [skt], 104
Sakau, *alt.* Sakao [sku], 645
  alt. dial. Kháng [kjm], 524
Sakaya, *dial.* Barein [bva], 78
Sake [sak], 121
Sakechep [sch], 385
  dial. Sakechep [sch], 385
Sakei, *dial.* Kerinci [kvr], 436
Saker, *alt.* Bargam [mlp], 592
Sakha, *alt.* Yakut [sah], 507
Sakhalin, *dial.* Ainu [ain], 446, 503
  dial. Evenki [evn], 504
Sakhur, *alt.* Tsakhur [tkr], 320
Saki, *alt.* Maia [sks], 610
Sakirabiá [skf], 232
Sakirabiák, *alt.* Sakirabiá [skf], 232
Sakirabiáp, *alt.* Sakirabiá [skf], 232
Sakirabiát, *alt.* Sakirabiá [skf], 232

Sakirap, *alt.* Sakirabiá [skf], 232
Sakiray, *alt. dial.* Amis, Nataoran [ais], 511
Sakiraya, *alt. dial.* Amis, Nataoran [ais], 511
Sakiriabar, *alt.* Sakirabiá [skf], 232
Sakizaya, *dial.* Amis, Nataoran [ais], 511
Sakkyryr, *dial.* Even [eve], 504
Saklan, *alt.* Miwok, Bay [mkq], 305
Sakpu, *dial.* Karang [kzr], 63, 81
Sakul, *alt.* Sukur [syk], 175
Sakuye, *dial.* Borana [gax], 132
Sala [shq], 215
  alt. Salar [slr], 343
Salajar, *alt.* Selayar [sly], 433
Salakahadi, *alt.* Molima [mox], 614
Salakau, *alt.* Selako [skl], 395, 461
Salale, *dial.* Oromo, Borana-Arsi-Guji [gax], 117
Salalir, *alt. dial.* Tidong [tid], 395
  dial. Tagal Murut [mvv], 458
Salamãi, *alt.* Mondé [mnd], 230
Salamaikã, *alt.* Mondé [mnd], 230
Salamat, *alt. dial.* Arabic, Chadian Spoken [shu], 78
Salampasu [slx], 107
Salang [hal], 452
  alt. Chut [scb], 522, 450
  alt. Halang [hal], 523
Salani, *dial.* Garhwali [gbm], 360
Salar [slr], 343
Salaru, *alt.* Selaru [slu], 403
Salas [sgu], 403
Salas Gunung, *alt.* Salas [sgu], 403
Salasaca Highland Quichua, *see* Quichua, Salasaca Highland [qxl], 251
Salasaca Quichua, *alt.* Quichua, Salasaca Highland [qxl], 251
Salatav, *dial.* Avar [ava], 553
Salavta, *alt.* Vaghri [vgr], 489
Salawati, *alt.* Ma'ya [slz], 420
Salayar, *alt.* Selayar [sly], 433
Salayer, *alt.* Selayar [sly], 433
Salcha-Goodpaster, *dial.* Tanana, Lower [taa], 308
Salchuq [slq], 441
Sale, *alt.* Che [ruk], 156
Salebabu, *alt. dial.* Talaud [tld], 433
Saleier, *alt.* Selayar [sly], 433
Saleman [sau], 403
Salento, *dial.* Greek [ell], 544
Salewari, *alt. dial.* Telugu [tel], 388
Sali, *alt.* Nsari [asj], 70
Saliany, *dial.* Azerbaijani, North [azj], 319
Saliba [sbe], 623

Sambiu, *alt. dial.* Kwangali
[kwn], 150, 40
Sambla, *alt.* Seeku [sos], 54
Sambo, *alt.* Mbo [mbo], 66
Sambuga, *dial.* Shama-Sambuga
[sqa], 174
Sambup, *alt.* Kenyah, Sebob
[sib], 459
Sambur, *alt.* Samburu [saq], 136
Samburu [saq], 136
Sambya, *dial.* Saam [raq], 478
Sambyu, *dial.* Kwangali [kwn], 150,
40
Same, *alt.* Saami, North [sme], 550,
535, 561
  alt. Saami, Skolt [sms], 535
  alt. Saami, South [sma], 550
Same', *dial.* Bajau, Indonesian
[bdl], 427
Samei [smh], 343
Samg Phang, *alt.* Chinese, Yue
[yue], 522
Sami, *alt.* Saami, Kemi [sjk], 535
Sámi, *alt.* Saami, Inari [smn], 535
  alt. Saami, Kemi [sjk], 535
Samia, *alt. dial.* Luyia [luy], 134
Samic, *alt.* Saami, Inari [smn], 535
  alt. Saami, North [sme], 550, 561
  alt. Saami, South [sma], 550
Samihim, *dial.* Ma'anyan [mhy], 394
Samish, *dial.* Salish, Straits
[str], 241, 307
Sammarinese, *alt.* Emiliano-
Romagnolo [eml], 543
  dial. Emiliano-Romagnolo [eml], 557
Samo [smq], 623
  alt. Owiniga [owi], 620
Sàmó, *alt.* Kalamsé [knz], 51
  alt. Sàmòmá [knz], 143
Samo, Matya [stj], 53
Samo, Maya [sym], 53
Samo, Southern [sbd], 54
Samoan [smo], 634, 567
Samobi, *alt.* Paiwan [pwn], 511
Samoe, *alt.* Wara [wbf], 55
Samogho, *alt.* Duungooma
[dux], 142
  alt. Dzùùngoo [dnn], 51
  alt. Jowulu [jow], 143
  alt. Seeku [sos], 54
Samogitian, *alt. dial.* Lithuanian
[lit], 546
Samogo, *alt.* Duungooma [dux], 142
  alt. Dzùùngoo [dnn], 51
Samogohiri, *alt. dial.* Dzùùngoo
[dnn], 51
Samohai, *alt.* Paiwan [pwn], 511
Sàmòmá [knz], 143
  alt. Kalamsé [knz], 51
Samong, *alt.* Hpon [hpo], 464

Samoro, *alt.* Duungooma [dux], 142
  alt. Dzùùngoo [dnn], 51
Samorogouan, *alt. dial.* Dzùùngoo
[dnn], 51
Samosa [swm], 623
Sampang [rav], 478
  dial. Madura [mad], 392
Sampange Rai, *alt.* Sampang
[rav], 478
Sampara, *dial.* Samba Leko [ndi], 72
Sampit, *alt. dial.* Ngaju [nij], 394
  dial. Malay [mly], 436
Sampolawa, *dial.* Cia-Cia [cia], 429
Sampori, *dial.* Biak [bhw], 412
Sampur, *alt.* Samburu [saq], 136
Samre [sxm], 326
Samtali, *alt.* Santali [sat], 386
Samtao [stu], 467, 343
  alt. Kiorr [xko], 451
Samtao 2, *alt.* Kiorr [xko], 451
Samtau, *alt.* Samtao [stu], 467, 343
Samtuan, *alt.* Samtao [stu], 467, 343
Samurzakan, *dial.* Abkhaz
[abk], 352, 518
Samurzakan-Zugdidi, *dial.* Laz
[lzz], 352
Samvedi [smv], 386
Samya, *alt. dial.* Luyia [luy], 134
San, *alt.* Samo, Matya [stj], 53
  alt. Samo, Maya [sym], 53
  alt. Samo, Southern [sbd], 54
  dial. Bamanankan [bam], 141
  pej. alt. Hai‖om [hgm], 149
San Agustín Loxicha Zapotec,
  dial. Zapotec, Loxicha [ztp], 278
**San Agustín Mixtepec
  Zapotec**, *see* Zapotec, San
  Agustín Mixtepec [ztm], 279
San Agustín Tlacotepec, *dial.*
  Mixtec, Magdalena Peñasco
  [xtm], 267
San Andrés Cohamiata, *dial.*
  Huichol [hch], 263
San Andrés Creole, *alt.* Islander
  Creole English [icr], 246
San Andrés Inga, *dial.* Inga
  [inb], 246
San Andrés K'iche', *see* K'iche',
  San Andrés [qxi], 255
San Andrés Larrainzar Tzotzil,
  see Tzotzil, San Andrés Larrainzar
  [tzs], 277
San Andrés Sajcabajá Quiché,
  alt. K'iche', San Andrés [qxi], 255
**San Antonio Eloxochitlán
  Mazatec**, *dial.* Mazatec, San
  Jerónimo Tecóatl [maa], 265
San Baltazar Loxicha Zapotec,
  see Zapotec, San Baltazar Loxicha
  [zpx], 279

San Baltázar Loxicha Zapotec,
  alt. Zapotec, San Baltazar Loxicha
  [zpx], 279
**San Bartolomé Venustiano
  Carranza Tzotzil**, *alt.* Tzotzil,
  Venustiano Carranza [tzo], 277
San Blas Cuna, *alt.* Kuna, San Blas
  [cuk], 283
San Blas Kuna, *see* Kuna, San Blas
  [cuk], 283
San Blasito Cora, *dial.* Cora, Santa
  Teresa [cok], 262
San Borjano, *alt.* Reyesano
  [rey], 223
San Carlos, *alt. dial.* Ohlone,
  Southern [css], 306
  dial. Apache, Western [apw], 298
San Chay, *alt.* Cao Lan [mlc], 522,
  329
San Chi, *alt.* Cao Lan [mlc], 522,
  329
**San Cristóbal Amoltepec
  Mixtec**, *dial.* Mixtec, Magdalena
  Peñasco [xtm], 267
**San Cristóbal Lachiruaj
  Zapotec**, *alt.* Zapotec, Lachirioag
  [ztc], 278
San Dionisio del Mar Huave, *see*
  Huave, San Dionisio del Mar
  [hve], 262
San Felipe, *dial.* Keres, Eastern
  [kee], 303
**San Felipe Otlaltepec
  Popoloca**, *see* Popoloca, San
  Felipe Otlaltepec [pow], 273
San Felipe Santiago Otomí,
  dial. Otomi, Estado de México
  [ots], 272
**San Francesco Saverio
  Mission**, *alt.* Cochimi [coj], 262
San Francisco, *dial.* Ohlone,
  Northern [cst], 306
San Francisco Cora, *dial.* Cora, El
  Nayar [crn], 262
San Francisco del Mar Huave,
  see Huave, San Francisco del Mar
  [hue], 263
**San Francisco Huehuetlán
  Mazatec**, *dial.* Mazatec, San
  Jerónimo Tecóatl [maa], 265
San Francisco Matlatzinca, *see*
  Matlatzinca, San Francisco [mat],
  264
**San Francisco Xavier de Viggé-
  Biaundo Mission**, *alt.* Cochimi
  [coj], 262
San Fratello, *alt. dial.* Lombard
  [lmo], 544
San Gadaba, *alt.* Gadaba, Pottangi
  Ollar [gdb], 361

San Gregorio Ozolotepec
 Zapotec, *dial.* Zapotec,
 Ozolotepec [zao], 279
San Ignacio de Velazco, *dial.*
 Chiquitano [cax], 222
San Ildefonso, *dial.* Tewa
 [tew], 308
San Javier, *alt.* Cochimi [coj],
 262
 dial. Chiquitano [cax], 222
San Jerónimo Tecóatl
 Mazatec, *see* Mazatec, San
 Jerónimo Tecóatl [maa], 265
San Jerónimo Tecóatl
 Mazatec, *dial.* Mazatec, San
 Jerónimo Tecóatl [maa], 265
San Joaquín, *alt.* Cochimi
 [coj], 262
San Jorge, *alt.* Chimila
 [cbg], 244
San Juan, *dial.* Tewa [tew], 308
San Juan Atzingo Popoloca,
 see Popoloca, San Juan Atzingo
 [poe], 273
San Juan Bautista, *alt. dial.*
 Ohlone, Southern [css], 306
San Juan Colorado Mixtec, *see*
 Mixtec, San Juan Colorado
 [mjc], 268
San Juan Corapan Cora, *dial.*
 Cora, Santa Teresa [cok], 262
San Juan Cotzal Ixil, *see* Ixil, San
 Juan Cotzal [ixl], 254
San Juan Guelavía Zapotec, *see*
 Zapotec, San Juan Guelavía
 [zab], 279
San Juan Ostuncalco Mam, *alt.*
 Mam, Southern [mms], 255
San Juan Piñas, *dial.* Mixtec,
 Western Juxtlahuaca [jmx], 270
San Juan Quiahije Chatino,
 dial. Chatino, Western Highland
 [ctp], 260
San Juan Teita Mixtec, *see*
 Mixtec, San Juan Teita [xtj], 268
San Lorenzo Cuanecuiltitla
 Mazatec, *dial.* Mazatec, San
 Jerónimo Tecóatl [maa], 265
San Lucas Zoquiapan
 Mazatec, *dial.* Mazatec, San
 Jerónimo Tecóatl [maa], 265
San Luís Potosí Huastec, *see*
 Huastec, San Luís Potosí
 [hva], 262
San Luís Temalacayuca
 Popoloca, *see* Popoloca, San
 Luís Temalacayuca [pps], 274
San Marcial Ozolotepec
 Zapotec, *dial.* Zapotec,
 Ozolotepec [zao], 279

San Marcos Comitancillas
 Mam, *alt.* Mam, Central [mvc], 255
San Marcos Tlalcoyalco
 Popoloca, *see* Popoloca, San
 Marcos Tlalcoyalco [pls], 274
San Martín Chile Verde Mam,
 alt. dial. Mam, Southern
 [mms], 255
San Martín Itunyoso Trique, *alt.*
 Triqui, San Martín Itunyoso
 [trq], 276
San Martín Itunyoso Triqui, *see*
 Triqui, San Martín Itunyoso [trq],
 276
San Martín Peras, *dial.* Mixtec,
 Western Juxtlahuaca [jmx], 270
San Martín Quechua, *see*
 Quechua, San Martín [qvs], 292
San Martín Sacatepéquez
 Mam, *dial.* Mam, Southern
 [mms], 255
San Martín Tilcajete Zapotec,
 dial. Zapotec, San Juan Guelavía
 [zab], 279
San Mateo, *dial.* Mazatec, Huautla
 [mau], 264
San Mateo del Mar Huave, *see*
 Huave, San Mateo del Mar
 [huv], 263
San Mateo Peñasco Mixtec,
 dial. Mixtec, Magdalena Peñasco
 [xtm], 267
San Mateo Tepantepec, *dial.*
 Mixtec, Peñoles [mil], 268
San Mateo Zoyamazalco
 Popoloca, *dial.* Popoloca,
 Coyotepec [pbf], 273
San Miguel, *dial.* Chiquitano
 [cax], 222
 dial. Mazatec, Huautla [mau], 264
San Miguel Acatán Kanjobal,
 alt. Akateko [knj], 253
San Miguel Achiutla Mixtec,
 dial. Mixtec, Magdalena Peñasco
 [xtm], 267
San Miguel Chalcatongo, *dial.*
 Mixtec, San Miguel el Grande
 [mig], 268
San Miguel Creole French
 [scf], 284
San Miguel el Grande Mixtec,
 see Mixtec, San Miguel el Grande
 [mig], 268
San Miguel Mitontic, *dial.*
 Tzotzil, Chenalhó [tze], 277
San Miguel Piedras Mixtec, *see*
 Mixtec, San Miguel Piedras
 [xtp], 268
San Miguel Tenango Náhuatl,
 alt. Nahuatl, Tenango [nhi], 272

San Miguel Tenoxtitlán, *dial.*
 Mazahua Central [maz], 264
San Miguel Zapotec, *alt.* Zapotec,
 Coatlán [zps], 278
San Pablo Chalchihuitan, *dial.*
 Tzotzil, Chenalhó [tze], 277
San Pedro Amuzgos Amuzgo,
 see Amuzgo, San Pedro Amuzgos
 [azg], 259
San Pedro Chenalhó, *dial.*
 Tzotzil, Chenalhó [tze], 277
San Pedro de Huacarpana, *dial.*
 Quechua, Yauyos [qux], 292
San Pedro Molinos, *dial.* Mixtec,
 San Miguel el Grande [mig], 268
San Pedro Quiatoni Zapotec,
 see Zapotec, San Pedro Quiatoni
 [zpf], 279
San Pedro Yaspac, *dial.* Zoque,
 Francisco León [zos], 282
San Rafael-Huariaca Quechua,
 alt. Quechua, Ambo-Pasco
 [qva], 289
San Ramon Inagta, *alt.* Agta, Mt.
 Iriga [agz], 491
San Raphael, *alt.* Miwok, Southern
 Sierra [skd], 305
San Raymundo Jalpan
 Zapotec, *alt.* Zapotec, Zaachila
 [ztx], 281
San Salvador Kongo, *see* Kongo,
 San Salvador [kwy], 101, 40
San Sebastián Coatán Chuj, *see*
 Chuj, San Sebastián Coatán
 [cac], 253
San Sebastián-Santa Catarina,
 dial. Huichol [hch], 263
San Simón Zahuatlán, *dial.*
 Mixtec, Silacayoapan [mks], 268
San Tung, *alt. dial.* Sui [swi], 344
San Vicente Coatlán Zapotec,
 see Zapotec, San Vicente Coatlán
 [zpt], 279
San Vicente Coyotepec
 Popoloca, *dial.* Popoloca,
 Coyotepec [pbf], 273
San Xavier, *alt.* Cochimi [coj], 262
Sán-Chi, *alt.* Cao Lan [mlc], 522,
 329
San'a, *dial.* Arabic, Judeo-Yemeni
 [jye], 444, 528
Sanaani Spoken Arabic, *see*
 Arabic, Sanaani Spoken [ayn], 528
Sanaberigi, *alt.* Samberigi
 [ssx], 623
Sanaga, *alt.* Tuki [bag], 72
Sanagage, *alt.* Nathembo [nte], 148
Sanainawa, *alt. dial.* Katukína,
 Panoan [knt], 229
Sanam, *alt.* Sanapaná [sap], 285

Sanamaica, *alt.* Mondé [mnd], 230
Sanamaiká, *alt.* Mondé [mnd], 230
Sanamaykã, *alt.* Mondé [mnd], 230
Sanana, *alt.* Sula [szn], 404
Sanandaj, *dial.* Hulaulá [huy], 445
Sanandaji, *dial.* Kurdish, Central
[ckb], 440
Sanapana, *dial.* Sanapaná [sap], 285
Sanapaná [sap], 285
Sanaroa, *alt. dial.* Dobu [dob], 597
Sanbalbe, *alt.* Malgbe [mxf], 65, 83
Sanbiau, *alt.* Piu [pix], 622
Sancá, *alt.* Malayo [mbp], 246
Sanda, *dial.* Loko [lok], 183
dial. Themne [tem], 184
Sandakan Bajau, *dial.* Bajau, West
Coast [bdr], 456
Sandal, *alt.* Santali [sat], 386, 322,
478
Sandaui, *alt.* Sandawe [sad], 204
Sandawe [sad], 204
Sandaweeki, *alt.* Sandawe
[sad], 204
Sandawi, *alt.* Sandawe [sad], 204
Sandayo, *dial.* Kimaragang
[kqr], 457
Sande, *alt.* Zande [zne], 109, 78, 196
Sandewar, *alt. dial.* Timugon Murut
[tih], 458
Sandia, *dial.* Tiwa, Southern [tix],
309
Sandiwar, *dial.* Timugon Murut
[tih], 458
Sando, *alt. dial.* Kono [kno], 183
Sandong, *dial.* Sui [swi], 344
Sandoway, *dial.* Chin, Asho [csh],
321
Sandu, *alt.* Shendu [shl], 322, 383
Sandwe, *alt.* Sandawe [sad], 204
Sane, *alt.* Samo, Matya [stj], 53
alt. Samo, Southern [sbd], 54
Sanema, *alt.* Sanumá [xsu], 312, 232
Sang, *dial.* Naga, Konyak [nbe], 378
Sanga (Democratic Republic of
Congo) [sng], 107
Sanga (Nigeria) [xsn], 174
alt. Makhuwa-Saka [xsq], 147
alt. Numana-Nunku-Gbantu-Numbu
[nbr], 171
Sangab, *alt.* Mandaya, Sangab
[myt], 498
Sangab Mandaya, *see* Mandaya,
Sangab [myt], 498
Sangaje, *alt. dial.* Koti [eko], 147
Sangaji, *alt.* Nathembo [nte], 148
Sangamesvari, *dial.* Konkani
[knn], 369
Sangangalla', *alt.* Tae' [rob], 428
alt. Toala' [tlz], 433
Sangar, *dial.* Bima [bhp], 406

Sangasanga, *alt.* Bomwali
[bmw], 88
pej. alt. Bomwali [bmw], 59
Sangau, *alt.* Embaloh [emb], 393
Sangbanga, *alt. dial.* Banda-Mbrès
[bqk], 75, 188
Sangche, *dial.* Naga, Tase [nst], 466,
380
Sangesari, *alt.* Sangisari [sgr], 441
Sanggar, *alt. dial.* Bima [bhp], 406
Sanggau [scg], 395
alt. Embaloh [emb], 393
Sanggil, *alt.* Sangil [snl], 501
Sangho, *alt.* Sango [sag], 77, 86, 107
Sangi, *alt.* Sangir [sxn], 432
Sangih, *alt.* Sangir [sxn], 432
Sangihé, *alt.* Sangir [sxn], 432, 501
Sangil [snl], 501
Sangir [sxn], 432, 501
Sangiré, *alt.* Sangil [snl], 501
Sangirese, *alt.* Sangir [sxn], 432,
501
Sangisari [sgr], 441
Sangla, *alt.* Tshangla [tsj], 324, 345,
389
dial. Moinba [mob], 376
Sanglechi, *dial.* Sanglechi-
Ishkashimi [sgl], 317
Sanglechi-Ishkashimi [sgl], 317,
513
Sanglich, *dial.* Sanglechi-Ishkashimi
[sgl], 513
Sangnaur, *alt.* Sunam [ssk], 388
Sango [sag], 77, 86, 107
alt. Sangu [sbp], 204
Sango, Riverain [snj], 77
Sangpang, *alt.* Sampang [rav], 478
alt. dial. Nachering [ncd], 476
Sangpang Gîn, *alt.* Sampang
[rav], 478
Sangpang Gun, *alt.* Sampang [rav],
478
Sangpang Kha, *alt.* Sampang
[rav], 478
Sangrima, *alt.* Naga, Zeme
[nzm], 381
Sangs-Rgyas, *alt.* Kinnauri, Bhoti
[nes], 368
Sangtai, *dial.* Naga, Tase [nst], 466
Sangtal, *alt.* Santali [sat], 386, 322,
478
Sangtam, *alt.* Naga, Sangtam
[nsa], 379
Sangtam Naga, *see* Naga, Sangtam
[nsa], 379
Sangu (Gabon) [snq], 121
Sangu (Tanzania) [sbp], 204
Sangwal, *dial.* Naga, Tase
[nst], 380
Sangwe, *dial.* Sena [seh], 149

Sangyas, *alt.* Kinnauri, Bhoti
[nes], 368
Sanhaja of Srair, *alt.* Senhaja de
Srair [sjs], 146
Sanhsien, *dial.* Chinese, Hakka
[hak], 511
Sani, *dial.* Amami-Oshima, Northern
[ryn], 446
Sani Yi, *see* Yi, Sani [ysn], 347
Sanima, *alt.* Sanumá [xsu], 312
Saninawacana, *alt. dial.* Katukína,
Panoan [knt], 229
Sanio, *alt. dial.* Saniyo-Hiyewe
[sny], 623
Saniyo, *dial.* Saniyo-Hiyewe
[sny], 623
Saniyo-Hiyewe [sny], 623
Sanja, *alt.* Malayo [mbp], 246
Sanjabi, *dial.* Kurdish, Southern
[sdh], 440, 443
Sanjan, *dial.* Pashayi, Northwest
[glh], 317
Sanjo, *alt. dial.* Tonga [toi], 215
Sanka, *alt.* Malayo [mbp], 246
Sankaji, *alt.* Nathembo [nte], 148
Sankara-Yerukala, *dial.* Yerukula
[yeu], 390
Sankaran Maninka, *see* Maninka,
Sankaran [msc], 129
Sankarankan, *alt.* Maninka,
Sankaran [msc], 129
Sanke, *dial.* Naga, Tase [nst], 380
Sankechep, *alt.* Sakechep [sch], 385
Sanketi, *dial.* Tamil [tam], 388
Sankuma, *dial.* Bobo Madaré,
Northern [bbo], 49
Sankura, *dial.* Nuni, Southern [nnw],
53
Sanlong, *dial.* Qiang, Southern
[qxs], 342
Sanna, *alt.* Arabic, Cypriot Spoken
[acy], 350
Sano, *alt.* Gadaba, Pottangi Ollar
[gdb], 361
Sanpoil, *dial.* Okanagan [oka], 240,
306
Sansi [ssi], 386, 488
Sansiboli, *alt.* Sansi [ssi], 386
Sanskrit [san], 386
Sansu [sca], 467
Santa, *alt.* Dongxiang [sce], 332
Santa Ana, *dial.* Keres, Eastern
[kee], 303
dial. Owa [stn], 637
**Santa Ana Ateixtlahuaca
Mazatec**, *dial.* Mazatec, San
Jerónimo Tecóatl [maa], 265
**Santa Ana de Tusi Pasco
Quechua**, *see* Quechua, Santa
Ana de Tusi Pasco [qxt], 292

Santa Ana-Gonzaga, *dial.* Agta, Dupaninan [duo], 490

Santa Catalina, *dial.* Owa [stn], 637

Santa Catarina Albarradas Zapotec, *see* Zapotec, Santa Catarina Albarradas [ztn], 280

Santa Catarina Pantelho, *dial.* Tzotzil, Chenalhó [tze], 277

Santa Catarina Quierí Zapotec, *alt. dial.* Zapotec, Quioquitani-Quierí [ztq], 279

Santa Catarina Quioquitani Zapotec, *alt. dial.* Zapotec, Quioquitani-Quierí [ztq], 279

Santa Catarina Ticuá, *dial.* Mixtec, San Miguel el Grande [mig], 268

Santa Catarina Yosonotu, *dial.* Mixtec, Ocotepec [mie], 268

Santa Clara, *dial.* Ohlone, Northern [cst], 306

dial. Tewa [tew], 308

Santa Crucino, *alt.* Aguano [aga], 285

Santa Cruz [stc], 638

dial. Iraya [iry], 495

dial. Ohlone, Northern [cst], 306

dial. Sambal, Tinà [xsb], 501

Santa Cruz Ocopetatillo Mazatec, *dial.* Mazatec, San Jerónimo Tecóatl [maa], 265

Santa Cruz Verapaz Poqomchi', *dial.* Poqomchi', Western [pob], 256

Santa Eulalia Kanjobal, *alt.* Q'anjob'al, Eastern [kjb], 256

Santa Inés Ahuatempan Popoloca, *see* Popoloca, Santa Inés Ahuatempan [pca], 274

Santa Inés Yatzechi Zapotec, *see* Zapotec, Santa Inés Yatzechi [zpn], 280

Santa Lucía Monteverde Mixtec, *see* Mixtec, Santa Lucía Monteverde [mdv], 268

Santa Magdalena Zoque, *alt.* Zoque, Francisco León [zos], 282

Santa Margarita, *dial.* Agta, Dupaninan [duo], 490

Santa María Acatepec, *dial.* Mixtec, Tututepec [mtu], 269

Santa María Citendejé-Banos, *dial.* Mazahua Central [maz], 264

Santa María de Jesús Cakchiquel, *alt.* Kaqchikel, Santa María de Jesús [cki], 254

Santa María de Jesús Kaqchikel, *see* Kaqchikel, Santa María de Jesús [cki], 254

Santa María del Mar Huave, *see* Huave, Santa María del Mar [hvv], 263

Santa María la Alta Nahuatl, *see* Nahuatl, Santa María la Alta [nhz], 272

Santa María Nativitas, *dial.* Popoloca, San Felipe Otlaltepec [pow], 273

Santa María Pápalo, *dial.* Cuicatec, Tepeuxila [cux], 262

Santa María Peñoles, *dial.* Mixtec, Peñoles [mil], 268

Santa María Quiegolani Zapotec, *see* Zapotec, Santa María Quiegolani [zpi], 280

Santa Maria Tataltepec, *dial.* Mixtec, San Juan Teita [xtj], 268

Santa María Yosoyúa, *dial.* Mixtec, San Miguel el Grande [mig], 268

Santa María Zacatepec Mixtec, *see* Mixtec, Santa María Zacatepec [mza], 268

Santa Rosa, *dial.* Cofán [con], 244

Santa Rosa Quechua, *alt.* Quechua, Napo Lowland [qvo], 291

dial. Quichua, Napo Lowland [qvo], 251

Santa Teresa, *dial.* Ratagnon [btn], 500

Santa Teresa Cora, *see* Cora, Santa Teresa [cok], 262

Santa Teresa Cora, *dial.* Cora, Santa Teresa [cok], 262

Santal, *alt.* Santali [sat], 386, 322, 478

Santali [sat], 386, 322, 478

Santan, *dial.* Dayak, Land [dyk], 393

Santarrosino, *alt.* Quechua, Napo Lowland [qvo], 291

Santchou, *dial.* Mbo [mbo], 66

Santee, *alt. dial.* Dakota [dak], 297, 237

Santee-Sisseton, *alt. dial.* Dakota [dak], 297

Santerre, *alt. dial.* Picard [pcd], 537

Santhal, *alt.* Santali [sat], 478

Santhali, *alt.* Santali [sat], 386, 322, 478

Santhiali, *alt.* Santali [sat], 386

Santiago, *dial.* Chiquitano [cax], 222

Santiago Atitlán Tzutujil, *alt.* Tz'utujil, Eastern [tzj], 256

Santiago del Estero Quichua, *see* Quichua, Santiago del Estero [qus], 220

Santiago Inga, *dial.* Inga [inb], 246

Santiago Lapaguía Zapotec, *see* Zapotec, Santiago Lapaguía [ztl], 280

Santiago Matatlán Zapotec, *dial.* Zapotec, Mitla [zaw], 279

Santiago Tlazoyaltepec, *dial.* Mixtec, Peñoles [mil], 268

Santiago Xanica Zapotec, *see* Zapotec, Santiago Xanica [zpr], 280

Santiagueño Quichua, *alt.* Quichua, Santiago del Estero [qus], 220

Santiam, *alt.* Kalapuya [kyl], 302

Santo, *alt.* Sakao [sku], 645

alt. Tangoa [tgp], 645

Santo Domingo, *dial.* Keres, Eastern [kee], 303

Santo Domingo Albarradas Zapotec, *see* Zapotec, Santo Domingo Albarradas [zas], 280

Santo Domingo Heundío Mixtec, *dial.* Mixtec, Magdalena Peñasco [xtm], 267

Santo Domingo Totonac, *alt.* Totonac, Filomena Mata-Coahuitlán [tlp], 276

Santo Domingo Xenacoj Cakchiquel, *alt.* Kaqchikel, Santo Domingo Xenacoj [ckj], 254

Santo Domingo Xenacoj Kaqchikel, *see* Kaqchikel, Santo Domingo Xenacoj [ckj], 254

Santongeais, *dial.* French [fra], 536

Santora, *alt.* Nara [nrb], 112

Santri, *alt.* Sadri [sck], 385

Santrokofi, *alt.* Selee [snw], 127

Sanumá [xsu], 312, 232

Sanvi, *dial.* Anyin [any], 91

Sanya, *alt.* Sanye [ssn], 136

Sanye [ssn], 136

alt. Boni [bob], 132

alt. Dahalo [dal], 132

alt. dial. Orma [orc], 135

Sanyo, *alt.* Fulfulde, Adamawa [fub], 61, 80

Sanza, *dial.* Konjo [koo], 211, 101

dial. Nande [nnb], 105

Sanzi, *dial.* Bangubangu [bnx], 97

Sao, *alt.* Saho [ssy], 112, 118

alt. Thao [ssf], 512

dial. Maslam [msv], 66, 84

São Paulo Kaingáng, *see* Kaingáng, São Paulo [zkp], 228

São Paulo Sign Language, *alt.* Brazilian Sign Language [bzs], 226

São Tomense, *alt.* Sãotomense [cri], 179

Sa'och [scq], 326
Saonras, *alt.* Sora [srb], 387
Saora, *alt.* Sora [srb], 387
Saotch, *alt.* Sa'och [scq], 326
Sãotomense [cri], 179
Sapa-Sapa, *dial.* Sama, Southern [ssb], 500
Sapalewa, *alt.* Alune [alp], 396
Sapan, *alt. dial.* Asmat, Casuarina Coast [asc], 411
Saparan, *alt.* Maden [xmx], 419
Saparua [spr], 403
Sapé [spc], 312
Sapei, *alt.* Kupsabiny [kpz], 211
Sapiny, *alt. dial.* Kupsabiny [kpz], 211
Sapiteri, *dial.* Huachipaeri [hug], 288
Sapo [krn], 139
Saponi [spi], 422
　alt. Tutelo [tta], 309
Saposa [sps], 623
　alt. dial. Saposa [sps], 623
Sapouan, *alt.* Sapuan [spu], 452
Sapran, *alt.* Maden [xmx], 419
Saprek, *alt.* Paiwan [pwn], 511
Sapsug, *alt. dial.* Adyghe [ady], 552
Saptari, *alt.* Tharu, Kochila [thq], 388
　dial. Tharu, Kochila [thq], 481
Sapuan [spu], 452
Sapudi, *dial.* Madura [mad], 392
Sapulot Murut, *dial.* Tagal Murut [mvv], 458, 395
Sapulut Murut, *alt. dial.* Tagal Murut [mvv], 458, 395
Saputan, *alt.* Bukar Sadong [sdo], 459
Sapwuahfik, *dial.* Pohnpeian [pon], 583
Saqatri, *alt.* Soqotri [sqt], 528
Saqiz, *dial.* Hulaulá [huy], 445
Sar [mwm], 86
　alt. Warji [wji], 177
　dial. Gula [kcm], 76
Sara [sre], 395
　alt. Kaba [ksp], 76
　alt. Ngambay [sba], 85, 69
　alt. Sar [mwm], 86
　alt. dial. Gula [kcm], 76
　alt. dial. Mandjak [mfv], 181
Sara Dinjo, *alt.* Sara Dunjo [koj], 77
Sara Dunjo [koj], 77
Sara Goula, *alt.* Gula [glu], 81
Sara Gula, *alt.* Gula [glu], 81
Sara Kaba [sbz], 77
　alt. Kaba [ksp], 76
　alt. Kaba Na [kwv], 81
Sara Kaba Dem, *alt.* Kaba Deme [kwg], 81
Sara Krowe, *dial.* Sika [ski], 409

Sara Madjingay, *alt.* Sar [mwm], 86
Sara Mbai, *alt.* Mbay [myb], 84
Sara Ngambai, *alt.* Ngambay [sba], 85, 69
Sara Sikka, *alt.* Sika [ski], 409
Sara Toumak, *alt.* Tumak [tmc], 87
Saracatsan, *dial.* Greek [ell], 540
Saraguro Quichua, *alt.* Quichua, Loja Highland [qvj], 251
Sarahole, *alt.* Soninke [snk], 122, 182
Sarahuli, *alt.* Soninke [snk], 122
Saraiki, *alt.* Seraiki [skr], 488, 386
Saraji, *alt. dial.* Pahari, Kullu [kfx], 382
Saraka, *alt.* Tharaka [thk], 136
Saraki, *alt.* Bengali [ben], 355
　dial. Bengali [ben], 469
Sarakole, *alt.* Soninke [snk], 144, 95, 131, 145
Sarakule, *alt.* Soninke [snk], 144
Saralir, *alt. dial.* Tagal Murut [mvv], 458
　alt. dial. Tidong [tid], 395
Saramaccan [srm], 296
Saramo, *alt.* Itonama [ito], 223
　alt. Zaramo [zaj], 206
Sarangani, *dial.* Sangil [snl], 501
Sarangani Blaan, *see* Blaan, Sarangani [bps], 493
Sarangani Manobo, *see* Manobo, Sarangani [mbs], 499
Sarar, *alt. dial.* Mandjak [mfv], 131
　dial. Mandjak [mfv], 122
Sarare, *dial.* Nambikuára, Southern [nab], 230
Sarasira, *dial.* Adzera [azr], 587
Sarassara, *dial.* Jina [jia], 63
Sarasvat Brahmin, *dial.* Konkani, Goanese [gom], 369
Saraveca [sar], 223
Sarawa, *alt.* Warji [wji], 177
Sarawai, *dial.* Dohoi [otd], 393
Sarawak Bisaya, *see* Bisaya, Sarawak [bsd], 459
Sarawak Dayak, *alt.* Jagoi [sne], 459
Sarawak Malay, *dial.* Malay [mly], 455
Sarawak Murut, *alt. dial.* Lundayeh [lnd], 394, 460
Sarawan, *dial.* Brahui [brh], 484, 438
Sarawani, *dial.* Balochi, Western [bgn], 476, 438
Sarawaria, *alt. dial.* Bhojpuri [bho], 356
Sarawule, *alt.* Soninke [snk], 144, 95, 122, 145, 182

Sarayacu Quichua, *alt.* Quichua, Northern Pastaza [qvz], 251
Sarcee, *alt.* Sarsi [srs], 241
Sarchapkkha, *alt.* Tshangla [tsj], 324
Sard, *alt.* Sardinian, Logudorese [src], 545
Sardarese, *alt.* Sardinian, Logudorese [src], 545
Sardinian, Campidanese [sro], 545
Sardinian, Gallurese [sdn], 545
Sardinian, Logudorese [src], 545
Sardinian, Sassarese [sdc], 545
Sardu, *alt.* Sardinian, Campidanese [sro], 545
Sare, *alt. dial.* Sena [seh], 149
Saremdé, *dial.* Mòoré [mos], 52
Sari, *dial.* Enga [enq], 598
Sari Yogur, *alt.* Yugur, West [ybe], 348
Sarig, *alt.* Yugur, West [ybe], 348
Sarikei, *dial.* Melanau [mel], 460
Sarikoli [srh], 343
Sariq, *dial.* Turkmen [tuk], 318
Sarirá, *alt.* Siriano [sri], 232
Sarisen, *alt.* Rukai [dru], 512
Sarkanci, *alt.* Bozo, Jenaama [bze], 142
　alt. Sorko [bze], 175
Sarkawa, *alt.* Bozo, Jenaama [bze], 142
　alt. Sorko [bze], 175
Sarlahi, *dial.* Tharu, Kochila [thq], 481
Sarli [sdf], 443
Sarliya, *alt.* Sarli [sdf], 443
Sarnami Hindi, *alt. dial.* Hindustani, Caribbean [hns], 295
Sarnami Hindustani, *alt. dial.* Hindustani, Caribbean [hns], 295
Sarngam, *alt.* Ngam [nmc], 85
Saroa, *alt.* Saaroa [sxr], 512
　dial. Sinauguro [snc], 624
Sarokama, *alt. dial.* Bobo Madaré, Northern [bbo], 49
Saroua, *alt.* Sarua [swy], 86
Sarpo, *alt.* Sapo [krn], 139
Sarrabense, *dial.* Sardinian, Campidanese [sro], 545
Sarsi [srs], 241
Sart Qalmaq, *alt. dial.* Kalmyk-Oirat [xal]
　dial. Kalmyk-Oirat [xal], 554
Sartenais, *dial.* Corsican [cos], 536
Sartul, *dial.* Mongolian, Halh [khk], 461
Sarua [swy], 86
Sarudu [sdu], 433
Saruga [sra], 623

Sarwa, *alt.* Hietshware [hio], 216
alt. Sarua [swy], 86
alt. Tsoa [hio], 48
Sarwari, *dial.* Mewari [mtr], 375
Sarwaye, *alt.* Sharwa [swq], 72
Sary-Uighur, *alt.* Yugur, West [ybe], 348
Sarygh Uygur, *alt.* Yugur, West [ybe], 348
Sarykoly, *alt.* Sarikoli [srh], 343
Saryq, *dial.* Turkmen [tuk], 520, 442
Sasak [sas], 409
Sasar, *dial.* Vatrata [vlr], 646
Sasaru [sxs], 174
Sasawa, *dial.* Kwerba [kwe], 418
Sasi, *alt.* Sizaki [szk], 204
dial. ‡Hua [huc], 47
Sasime, *alt.* Biyom [bpm], 594
Sassarese, *alt.* Sardinian, Sassarese [sdc], 545
Sassarese Sardinian, *see* Sardinian, Sassarese [sdc], 545
Sastean, *alt.* Shasta [sht], 308
Satar, *alt.* Santali [sat], 386, 322, 478
Sataré, *alt.* Sateré-Mawé [mav], 231
Satawalese [stw], 583
Sate, *alt.* Kumba [ksm], 167
Sateré-Mawé [mav], 231
Saterfriesiesch, *alt.* Saterfriesisch [stq], 539
Saterfriesisch [stq], 539
Saterlandic Frisian, *alt.* Frisian, Eastern [frs], 538
alt. Saterfriesisch [stq], 539
Saterländisch, *alt.* Saterfriesisch [stq], 539
Satpara, *alt. dial.* Shina [scl], 488
Satpariya, *dial.* Koch [kdq], 368, 321
Satre, *alt.* Gawar-Bati [gwt], 316, 484
Satro, *alt.* Dida, Lakota [dic], 92
Satun, *dial.* Tonga [tnz], 518, 456
Satun Malay, *see* Malay, Kedah [meo], 516
Satun Malay, *alt.* Malay, Kedah [meo], 455
Sa'u, *alt.* Sahu [saj], 403
Sau, *alt.* Sahu [saj], 403
alt. Samberigi [ssx], 623
alt. Savi [sdg], 317, 488
alt. Thao [ssf], 512
dial. Dayak, Land [dyk], 393
dial. Enga [enq], 598
Sau Enga, *alt. dial.* Enga [enq], 598
Sauch, *alt.* Sa'och [scq], 326
Saudi Arabian Sign Language [sdl], 508
Sauh, *alt. dial.* Dayak, Land [dyk], 393

Sauji, *alt.* Savi [sdg], 317, 488
Sauk [skc], 623
Sauk-Fox, *alt.* Mesquakie [sac], 304
Sauka, *alt.* Byangsi [bee], 469
alt. Chaudangsi [cdn], 469
alt. Darmiya [drd], 470
Saukas, *alt.* Byangsi [bee], 358
alt. Chaudangsi [cdn], 358
alt. Darmiya [drd], 359
alt. Rangkas [rgk], 384
Saukiya Khun, *alt.* Rangkas [rgk], 384
Saukrang, *dial.* Naga, Tase [nst], 466
Saulteaux, *alt.* Ojibwa, Western [ojw], 240
alt. dial. Ojibwa, Northwestern [ojb], 240
Saumanganja, *dial.* Mentawai [mwv], 436
Saura, *alt.* Sora [srb], 387
Saurashtra [saz], 386
Saurashtra Standard, *alt. dial.* Gujarati [guj], 363
Saurashtri, *alt.* Saurashtra [saz], 386
Sauri [srt], 422
Sauria Paharia [mjt], 386
Sause [sao], 422
Sausi [ssj], 623
Savannakhet, *dial.* Lao [lao], 445
Savara [svr], 386
alt. Sora [srb], 387
Savi [sdg], 317, 488
dial. Gun [guw], 161
Savo, *alt.* Savosavo [svs], 638
dial. Finnish [fin], 534
Savo Island, *alt.* Savosavo [svs], 638
Savolax, *alt. dial.* Finnish [fin], 534
Savosavo [svs], 638
Savoyard, *dial.* Franco-Provençal [frp], 536, 562
Savu, *alt.* Sabu [hvn], 409
Savunese, *alt.* Sabu [hvn], 409
Savusavu, *alt. dial.* Fijian [fij], 580
Saw, *dial.* Ntomba [nto], 106
Sawa, *alt.* Elseng [mrf], 414
Sawabwala, *dial.* Bunama [bdd], 595
Sawai [szw], 403
alt. Saleman [sau], 403
dial. Sawai [szw], 403
Sawaria, *alt.* Sora [srb], 387
Sawatupwa, *dial.* Bunama [bdd], 595
Saweri, *alt.* Isirawa [srl], 415
Saweru [swr], 422
Sawi [saw], 422
alt. Savi [sdg], 317, 488

Sawiat Salmeit, *dial.* Tehit [kps], 424
Sawila [swt], 409
dial. Sawila [swt], 409
Sawitto, *dial.* Bugis [bug], 428
Sawiyanu, *alt.* Ama [amm], 588
Sawk, *alt.* Sok [skk], 452
alt. Sou [sqq], 452
Sawknah [swn], 139
Sawriya Malto, *alt.* Sauria Paharia [mjt], 386
Sawu, *alt.* Sabu [hvn], 409
Sawunese, *alt.* Sabu [hvn], 409
Sawuve, *dial.* Ankave [aak], 590
Sawuy, *alt.* Sawi [saw], 422
Saxon, Low [nds], 539
Saxon, Upper [sxu], 539
Saxwe, *alt.* Gbe, Saxwe [sxw], 44
dial. Gbe, Saxwe [sxw], 44
Saxwe Gbe, *see* Gbe, Saxwe [sxw], 44
Saxwe-Gbe, *alt.* Gbe, Saxwe [sxw], 44
Saxwentesu, *dial.* Nambikuára, Southern [nab], 230
Saya [say], 174
Sayabury, *dial.* Khmu [kjg], 451
Sayaco, *alt.* Amahuaca [amc], 286
Sayacu, *alt.* Amahuaca [amc], 224
Sayan Samoyed, *alt.* Karagas [kim], 505
Sayanci, *alt.* Saya [say], 174
Sayara, *alt.* Saya [say], 174
Sayawa, *alt.* Saya [say], 174
Sayma, *alt.* Chaima [ciy], 311
Saysay, *alt. dial.* Gumuz [guk], 191
Sayula Popoluca, *see* Popoluca, Sayula [pos], 274
Sazek, *alt.* Taroko [trv], 512
Sazin, *alt. dial.* Shina [scl], 488
Sbalt, *alt.* Balti [bft], 355
Sbalti, *alt.* Balti [bft], 483
Sbanag, *alt.* Panang [pcr], 342
Sbranag, *alt.* Panang [pcr], 342
Scanian [scy], 562, 533
Sce, *alt. dial.* Bench [bcq], 113
Schabin-Karahissar, *alt. dial.* Armenian [hye], 318
Schamachi, *alt. dial.* Armenian [hye], 318
Schambala, *alt.* Shambala [ksb], 204
Schekere, *alt.* Khwe [xuu], 214
alt. Kxoe [xuu], 40
Schleiyip, *alt. dial.* Chinese, Yue [yue], 331
Schoe, *alt. dial.* Mpade [mpi], 68
Schouws, *dial.* Zeeuws [zea], 549
Schwäbisch, *alt.* Swabian [swg], 540

Schwaebisch, *alt.* Swabian [swg], 540
Schwytzertuetsch, *alt.* Alemannisch [gsw], 546
Schwyzerdütsch [gsw], 563
  alt. Alemannisch [gsw], 546
Scinacia, *alt.* Boro [bwo], 114
Scots [sco], 566, 543
Scots Gaelic, *alt.* Gaelic, Scottish [gla], 565
Scottish Cant, *alt.* Traveller Scottish [trl], 566
Scottish Gaelic, *see* Gaelic, Scottish [gla], 565
Scottish Traveller Cant, *alt.* Traveller Scottish [trl], 566
Scouse, *dial.* English [eng], 565
Scutari, *dial.* Albanian, Gheg [aln], 529
Se, *dial.* Gbe, Saxwe [sxw], 44
Sea Bajau, *alt. dial.* Sama, Southern [ssb], 458
Sea Dayak, *alt.* Iban [iba], 459, 324, 393
Sea Gypsies, *alt. dial.* Sama, Southern [ssb], 458
Sea Island Creole English [gul], 307
Sea Lappish, *dial.* Saami, North [sme], 550, 535, 561
Seaqaaqaa, *alt. dial.* Fijian [fij], 580
Seaside Grebo, *alt. dial.* Grebo, Southern [grj], 138
  dial. Grebo, Southern [grj], 93
Seba [kdg], 107
  dial. Sabu [hvn], 409
Sebaru', *alt. dial.* Iban [iba], 393
Sebaste, *dial.* Armenian [hye], 318
Sebat Bet Gurage [sgw], 118
Sebaung, *dial.* Dohoi [otd], 393
Sebe, *dial.* Bine [bon], 593
Sebei, *alt.* Kupsabiny [kpz], 211
Seberuang [sbx], 395
  alt. dial. Iban [iba], 393
Sebikotane, *dial.* Saafi-Saafi [sav], 182
Sebob, *alt.* Kenyah, Sebob [sib], 459
Sebob Kenyah, *see* Kenyah, Sebob [sib], 459
Sebop, *alt.* Kenyah, Sebob [sib], 459
Sebuano, *alt.* Cebuano [ceb], 493
Sebunkik, *dial.* Sungor [sjg], 195
Sebutuia, *alt. dial.* Galeya [gar], 599
Sebuyau [snb], 460
Sebyar, *alt.* Arandai [jbj], 411
Sechelt [sec], 241
Sechu, *alt. dial.* Naga, Tase [nst], 380
Sechuana, *alt.* Tswana [tsn], 48, 186, 217
Seco, *alt.* Pech [pay], 258

Secoya [sey], 251, 293
Secumne, *alt.* Maidu, Northwest [mjd], 304
Secunderabad Brahmin, *dial.* Tamil [tam], 388
Secwepemc, *alt.* Shuswap [shs], 241
Sedalir, *dial.* Tidong [tid], 395
Sedálir, *alt. dial.* Tagal Murut [mvv], 458
Sedang [sed], 526
Sedang-Rengao, *dial.* Rengao [ren], 526
Sedanka, *dial.* Itelmen [itl], 505
Sede, *alt. dial.* Jina [jia], 63
Sedehi, *dial.* Farsi, Western [pes], 439
Sedek, *alt.* Taroko [trv], 512
Sedentary Bulgaria, *alt. dial.* Romani, Vlax [rmy], 551
Sedentary Romania, *dial.* Romani, Vlax [rmy], 551
Sedeq, *alt.* Taroko [trv], 512
Sediakk, *alt.* Taroko [trv], 512
Sedik, *alt.* Taroko [trv], 512
Sediq, *alt.* Taroko [trv], 512
Sedoa [tvw], 433
Seduan, *dial.* Sibu [sdx], 461
Seduan-Banyok, *alt.* Sibu [sdx], 461
Seeba-Yaga, *dial.* Fulfulde, Northeastern Burkina Faso [fuh], 51
Seedek, *alt.* Taroko [trv], 512
Seedeq, *alt.* Taroko [trv], 512
Seedik, *alt.* Taroko [trv], 512
Seeku [sos], 54
Seeltersk Frisian, *alt.* Frisian, Eastern [frs], 538
Seeptsa, *alt.* Cholón [cht], 287
Seereer, *alt.* Serer-Sine [srr], 182, 122
Seex, *alt.* Serer-Sine [srr], 182
Sefardi, *alt.* Ladino [lad], 445, 563
Sefwi, *alt.* Sehwi [sfw], 127
Segah, *dial.* Segai [sge], 395
Segahan, *dial.* Melanau [mel], 460
Segai [sge], 395
  alt. dial. Kinabatangan, Upper [dmg], 457
Segalang, *dial.* Melanau [mel], 460
Segar Tor, *alt.* Kwerba [kwe], 418
Segeju [seg], 204
Seget [sbg], 422
Segi, *dial.* Kamasau [kms], 604
Segiddi, *alt. dial.* Saya [say], 174
Seginki, *dial.* Mukulu [moz], 85
Segou, *dial.* Bamanankan [bam], 141
Seguha, *alt.* Zigula [ziw], 206

Segum, *dial.* Serer-Sine [srr], 182, 122
Sehri, *alt.* Shehri [shv], 483
Sehudate, *alt.* Fayu [fau], 415
Sehwi [sfw], 127
Seim, *alt.* Mende [sim], 613
Seimat [ssg], 623
Seira, *alt. dial.* Fordata [frd], 398
Seisirat, *alt.* Saisiyat [xsy], 512
Seit, *dial.* Seit-Kaitetu [hik], 403
Seit-Kaitetu [hik], 403
Seith, *alt. dial.* Seit-Kaitetu [hik], 403
Seiyap, *alt. dial.* Chinese, Yue [yue], 331
Seiyara, *alt.* Saya [say], 174
Sejiq, *alt.* Taroko [trv], 512
Sek, *alt.* Gedaged [gdd], 599
  alt. Saek [skb], 452, 517
Seka, *alt.* Loncong [lce], 436
  alt. Sekar [skz], 422
Sekah, *alt.* Loncong [lce], 436
Sekalaka, *alt.* Kalanga [kck], 47
Sekalaña, *alt.* Kalanga [kck], 216, 47
Sekalau, *alt. dial.* Iban [iba], 393
Sekani [sek], 241
Sekapan [skp], 461
Sekapat, *alt. dial.* Iban [iba], 393
Sekar [skz], 422
Sekare, *dial.* Guhu-Samane [ghs], 599
Sekayu Malay, *dial.* Musi [mui], 437
Seke (Nepal) [skj], 478
  Seke (Vanuatu) [ske], 645
  alt. Seki [syi], 111, 121
Sekepan, *alt.* Sekapan [skp], 461
Sekgoa, *alt.* English [eng], 46
Seki [syi], 111, 121
Sekiana, *alt.* Seki [syi], 111, 121
Sekiani, *alt.* Seki [syi], 111, 121
Sekiyani, *alt.* Seki [syi], 111, 121
Seko, *alt.* Seko Padang [skx], 433
  alt. Seko Tengah [sko], 433
Seko Padang [skx], 433
Seko Tengah [sko], 433
Sekol, *alt.* Skou [skv], 423
Sekou, *alt.* Skou [skv], 423
Sekpele [lip], 127
  dial. Sekpele [lip], 127
Sekumne, *alt.* Maidu, Northwest [mjd], 304
Sekunda, *dial.* Makaa [mcp], 65
Sekwa, *dial.* Kulango, Bouna [nku], 126
  dial. Sekpele [lip], 127
Sekyani, *alt.* Seki [syi], 111, 121
Sela, *alt. dial.* Limba, West-Central [lia], 183
  dial. Korupun-Sela [kpq], 418
Selakau, *alt.* Selako [skl], 461

Selako [skl], 395, 461
Selako Dayak, *alt.* Selako [skl], 395
Selale, *alt. dial.* Oromo, Borana-Arsi-Guji [gax], 117
Selalir, *alt. dial.* Tidong [tid], 395
Selangor Sakai, *dial.* Besisi [mhe], 454
Selangor Sign Language [kgi], 455
Selaru [slu], 403
Selau, *dial.* Halia [hla], 601
Selayar [sly], 433
Sele, *alt.* Selee [snw], 127
Selee [snw], 127
Selek, *alt. dial.* Jola-Kasa [csk], 180
Seleman, *alt.* Saleman [sau], 403
Selemo, *alt.* Isekiri [its], 164
Selepe, *alt.* Selepet [spl], 623
Selepet [spl], 623
Selkirk, *alt.* Tutchone, Northern [ttm], 242
Selknam, *alt.* Ona [ona], 220
Selkup [sel], 506
Selong, *alt.* Moken [mwt], 466, 516
Selti, *alt.* Silt'e [xst], 119
Selung, *alt.* Moken [mwt], 466, 516
Selungai Murut [slg], 395, 458
Seluwasan [sws], 404
  dial. Seluwasan [sws], 404
Selvasa, *alt.* Seluwasan [sws], 404
Selwasa, *alt.* Seluwasan [sws], 404
Selya, *alt. dial.* Nyakyusa-Ngonde [nyy], 203
Selyer, *dial.* Tarok [yer], 175
Sema, *alt.* Naga, Sumi [nsm], 380
Semai [sea], 455
Semakha, *dial.* Azerbaijani, North [azj], 319
Semalinga, *dial.* Zimba [zmb], 109
Semambu, *alt.* Tagal Murut [mvv], 395
  alt. dial. Tagal Murut [mvv], 458
Semandang [sdm], 395
  dial. Semandang [sdm], 395
Semang, *alt.* Awad Bing [bcu], 591
Semaq Beri [szc], 455
Semaq Bri, *alt.* Semaq Beri [szc], 455
Semariji, *dial.* Kunja [pep], 608
Semau, *alt.* Helong [heg], 407
  alt. dial. Helong [heg], 407
Semawa, *alt.* Sumbawa [smw], 409
Sembaan, *alt. dial.* Tringgus [trx], 461
Sembakoeng, *alt.* Sembakung Murut [sbr], 458, 395
Sembakong, *alt.* Sembakung Murut [sbr], 458, 395
Sembakung Murut [sbr], 458, 395

Sembla, *alt.* Seeku [sos], 54
Seme, *alt.* Siamou [sif], 54
Semelai [sza], 455
Semembu, *alt.* Tagal Murut [mvv], 395
  alt. dial. Tagal Murut [mvv], 458, 395
Semendo [sdd], 437
Semiahmoo, *dial.* Salish, Straits [str], 241
Semiang, *alt. dial.* Kayan, Murik [mxr], 459
Sémien, *alt. dial.* Wè Northern [wob], 95
Semigae, *alt.* Andoa [anb], 286
Semimi [etz], 422
Seminole, *alt.* Afro-Seminole Creole [afs], 297
  dial. Muskogee [mus], 305
Semirara, *dial.* Caluyanun [clu], 493
Semitau, *dial.* Malayic Dayak [xdy], 394
Semnam [ssm], 455
Semnani [smy], 441
Semolika, *alt. dial.* Okpamheri [opa], 172
Semolo, *alt. dial.* Zimba [zmb], 109
Semontanés, *alt. dial.* Aragonese [arg], 558
Semoq Beri, *alt.* Semaq Beri [szc], 455
Sempan [xse], 423
Sému, *alt.* Siamou [sif], 54
Semukung Uheng, *dial.* Hovongan [hov], 393
Semulu, *dial.* Zimba [zmb], 109
Semyen, *alt. dial.* Qimant [ahg], 118
Sen Chun, *alt.* Blang [blr], 514
Sena [seh], 149
Sena, Malawi [swk], 140
Sena:ya, *alt.* Senaya [syn], 441
Senadi, *alt.* Senoufo, Cebaara [sef], 94
Senagi, *alt.* Angor [agg], 589
Senaki, *dial.* Laz [lzz], 352
Senara Sénoufo, *see* Sénoufo, Senara [seq], 54
Senare, *alt.* Senoufo, Syenara [shz], 144
Senari, *alt.* Senoufo, Cebaara [sef], 94
  alt. Senoufo, Syenara [shz], 144
Senaya [syn], 441
Senchi, *alt. dial.* C'lela [dri], 157
Sendana, *alt. dial.* Mandar [mdr], 431
Sene [sej], 624
  alt. dial. Gola [gol], 183
Seneca [see], 307, 241
Sened [sds], 209

  dial. Sened [sds], 209
Senga, *alt.* Nsenga [nse], 215, 148, 216
  alt. dial. Babatana [baa], 635
  alt. dial. Tumbuka [tum], 141
  dial. Tumbuka [tum], 215
Sengam, *alt.* Awad Bing [bcu], 591
Sengan, *dial.* Babatana [baa], 635
Sengbe, *dial.* Kuranko [knk], 183
Sengeju, *alt.* Segeju [seg], 204
Sengele [szg], 107
Sengere, *alt.* Sengele [szg], 107
Sengeze, *dial.* Kuni-Boazi [kvg], 608
Sengga, *alt. dial.* Babatana [baa], 635
Senggi [snu], 423
Senggo, *dial.* Citak [txt], 413
Sengima, *alt.* Naga, Zeme [nzm], 381
Sengmai, *dial.* Kado [kdv], 464, 337, 450
Sengo [spk], 624
Sengoi, *alt.* Semai [sea], 455
Sengseng [ssz], 624
Senhaja de Srair [sjs], 146
Seniang, *alt.* South West Bay [sns], 645
Senje, *dial.* Gola [gol], 138, 183
Senji, *alt. dial.* Ndau [ndc], 148
Senkon, *alt. dial.* Sapo [krn], 139
Senoi, *alt.* Semai [sea], 455
Sénoufo, *alt.* Sénoufo, Senara [seq], 54
Senoufo, Cebaara [sef], 94
Senoufo, Djimini [dyi], 95
Senoufo, Mamara [myk], 144
Sénoufo, Nanerigé [sen], 54
Senoufo, Nyarafolo [sev], 95
Senoufo, Palaka [plr], 95
Sénoufo, Senara [seq], 54
Senoufo, Shempire [seb], 95
Sénoufo, Sìcìté [sep], 54, 144
Senoufo, Supyire [spp], 144
Senoufo, Syenara [shz], 144
Senoufo, Tagwana [tgw], 95
Sensi [sni], 293
Sentah, *alt.* Biatah [bth], 459
Sentali, *alt.* Santali [sat], 386, 478
Sentani [set], 423
Senthang, *alt.* Chin, Senthang [sez], 463
Senthang Chin, *see* Chin, Senthang [sez], 463
Senti, *alt.* Sensi [sni], 293
Sentinel [std], 386
Sentinelese, *alt.* Sentinel [std], 386
Sentrokofi, *alt.* Selee [snw], 127
Senya, *dial.* Awutu [afu], 123
Seo, *alt. dial.* Kohistani, Indus [mvy], 486

S'gaw, *alt.* Karen, S'gaw [ksw], 464, 514
S'gaw Karen, *see* Karen, S'gaw [ksw], 464, 514
S'gaw Kayin, *alt.* Karen, S'gaw [ksw], 464, 514
Sguxs, *alt. dial.* Tsimshian [tsi], 242
Sha [scw], 174
  alt. Shan [shn], 467, 517
Shaale, *alt.* Sungor [sjg], 195
Shaanxi, *dial.* Dungan [dng], 449, 448
Shaari, *dial.* Mumuye [mzm], 170
Shaathari, *alt.* Yanomamö [guu], 234
Shabak [sdb], 443
Shabari, *alt.* Sora [srb], 387
Shabin-Karahissar, *dial.* Armenian [hye], 318
Shabo [sbf], 118
Shabogala, *alt.* Atayal [tay], 511
Shabun, *dial.* Shwai [shw], 195
Shachobiikha, *alt.* Tshangla [tsj], 324
Shachopkha, *alt.* Tshangla [tsj], 324
Shacriaba, *alt.* Xakriabá [xkr], 234
Shadal, *dial.* Mankanya [knf], 131, 181
Shaga, *dial.* Kgalagadi [xkv], 47
Shagau, *alt. dial.* Ron [cla], 174
Shagawu, *alt. dial.* Ron [cla], 174
Shah-Mansuri, *dial.* Kashmiri [kas], 367
Shahari, *alt.* Shehri [shv], 483
Shahe, *dial.* Barzani Jewish Neo-Aramaic [bjf], 444
Shahmirzadi [srz], 441
Shaho, *alt.* Saho [ssy], 112, 118
Shahrudi [shm], 441
Shahrudi Kazeruni, *dial.* Farsi, Western [pes], 439
Shahsavani, *dial.* Azerbaijani, South [azb], 438
Shahseven, *alt. dial.* Azerbaijani, South [azb], 438
Shai, *dial.* Dangme [ada], 124
Shaini, *alt.* Sheni [scv], 174
Shaire, *alt.* Sere [swf], 107
Shak, *alt.* Sheko [she], 118
Shaka, *alt.* Ngasa [nsg], 202
Shakacho, *alt.* Shekkacho [moy], 118
Shakara [nfk], 174
Shake, *alt.* Sake [sak], 121
Shako, *alt.* Shabo [sbf], 118
  alt. Sheko [she], 118
Shal, *alt. dial.* Shall-Zwall [sha], 174
Shalkota, *alt. dial.* Midob [mei], 193
Shall, *dial.* Shall-Zwall [sha], 174

Shall-Zwall [sha], 174
Sham, *alt. dial.* Ladakhi [lbj], 372, 338
Shama, *dial.* Shama-Sambuga [sqa], 174
Shama-Sambuga [sqa], 174
Shamaitish, *dial.* Lithuanian [lit], 546
Shamakhi, *dial.* Armenian [hye], 318
  dial. Azerbaijani, North [azj], 319
Shamakot, *dial.* Pashayi, Northwest [glh], 317
Shamang [xsh], 174
Shamatari, *alt.* Yanomamö [guu], 313
Shamatri, *alt.* Yanomamö [guu], 234
Shamba, *dial.* Swahili [swh], 136, 212
Shambaa, *alt.* Shambala [ksb], 204
Shambala [ksb], 204
Shamma, *dial.* Ladakhi [lbj], 372, 338
Shammar, *alt. dial.* Arabic, Najdi Spoken [ars], 442
Shammari, *alt. dial.* Arabic, Najdi Spoken [ars], 508
Shamnyuyanga, *dial.* Naga, Konyak [nbe], 378
Shamskat, *alt. dial.* Ladakhi [lbj], 372, 338
Shamya, *alt.* Sinyar [sys], 86
Shamyan, *alt.* Sinyar [sys], 86
Shan [shn], 467, 517
Shan Gyanan, *alt.* Senaya [syn], 441
Shan Sray, *alt.* Senaya [syn], 441
Shandu, *alt.* Shendu [shl], 322, 383
Shanga [sho], 174
  alt. dial. Ndau [ndc], 216
  dial. Ndau [ndc], 148
Shangaan, *alt.* Tsonga [tso], 186
  alt. dial. Tsonga [tso], 149, 217
Shangama, *dial.* Aari [aiz], 112
Shangana, *alt.* Tsonga [tso], 186
  alt. dial. Tsonga [tso], 149, 217
Shangawa, *alt.* Shanga [sho], 174
Shangge, *alt. dial.* Naga, Tase [nst], 380
Shanghai Sign Language, *dial.* Chinese Sign Language [csl], 329
Shangilla, *pej. alt.* Daasanach [dsh], 114, 132
Shango, *alt.* Sangu [snq], 121
Shangwe, *alt. dial.* Shona [sna], 216
Shangzhai [jih], 343
Shani, *alt.* Sheni [scv], 174
  dial. Dera [kna], 157
Shanjo, *dial.* Tonga [toi], 215
Shankadi, *alt.* Samba [smx], 107

Shankilla, *pej. alt.* Aari [aiz], 112
Shankilligna, *pej. alt.* Aari [aiz], 112
  pej. alt. Gumuz [guk], 115
Shankillinya, *alt.* Gumuz [guk], 191
  pej. alt. Aari [aiz], 112
  pej. alt. Gumuz [guk], 115
Shanlang, *dial.* Naga, Konyak [nbe], 378
Shanqilla, *alt.* Gumuz [guk], 191
  pej. alt. Birale [bxe], 114
  pej. alt. Gumuz [guk], 115
Shantou, *dial.* Chinese, Min Nan [nan], 514
Shanzi Yao, *alt.* Kim Mun [mji], 337
Shao, *alt.* Thao [ssf], 512
Shapra, *alt. dial.* Candoshi-Shapra [cbu], 287
Shapsug, *dial.* Adyghe [ady], 552
Shaqlawa, *dial.* Lishanid Noshan [aij], 445
Sharanahua [mcd], 293, 232
Sharchagpakha, *alt.* Tshangla [tsj], 324
Sharchhopkha, *alt.* Tshangla [tsj], 324
Shark Bay [ssv], 645
Sharoka, *alt.* Tharaka [thk], 136
Sharpa, *alt.* Sherpa [xsr], 478, 343, 387
Sharpa Bhotia, *alt.* Sherpa [xsr], 478, 343, 387
Sharwa [swq], 72
Shasha, *dial.* Nkoya [nka], 214
Shashi, *alt.* Sizaki [szk], 204
Shasta [sht], 308
Shastan, *alt.* Shasta [sht], 308
Shatoi, *alt. dial.* Chechen [che], 553
Shatou, *alt. dial.* Chinese, Yue [yue], 331
Shatt [shj], 195
  alt. Thuri [thu], 195
  dial. Mündü [muh], 193
Shau [sqh], 174
Shauka, *alt.* Byangsi [bee], 469
  alt. Chaudangsi [cdn], 469
  alt. Darmiya [drd], 470
Shaukas, *alt.* Byangsi [bee], 358
  alt. Chaudangsi [cdn], 358
  alt. Darmiya [drd], 359
  alt. Rangkas [rgk], 384
Shausha Wanka Quechua, *alt.* Quechua, Jauja Wanca [qxw], 291
Shavante, *alt.* Xavánte [xav], 234
Shawanawa-Arara, *alt. dial.* Katukína, Panoan [knt], 229
Shawe, *alt. dial.* Mpade [mpi], 68, 84
Shawia, *alt.* Tachawit [shy], 39
Shawiya, *alt.* Tachawit [shy], 39
Shawnee [sjw], 308

Shayabit, *alt.* Chayahuita [cbt], 287
She [shx], 343
  dial. Bench [bcq], 113
Shede, *alt.* Gude [gde], 161, 62
Shedekka, *alt.* Taroko [trv], 512
Sheetshwa, *alt.* Tswa [tsc], 149,
  186, 217
Sheffield Yorkshire, *dial.* English
  [eng], 565
Shehleh, *dial.* Lahu [lhu], 338, 451,
  465, 515, 524
Shehri [shv], 483
Sheikhan, *dial.* Kurdish, Northern
  [kmr], 443
Sheke, *alt.* Seki [syi], 111, 121
Shekgalagadi, *alt.* Kgalagadi
  [xkv], 47
Shekhani, *alt.* Kamviri [xvi], 316,
  486
  alt. dial. Kati [bsh], 316, 486
  dial. Kamviri [xvi], 316, 486
Shekhawati [swv], 386
Shekhawati-Marwari, *alt.*
  Shekhawati [swv], 386
Shekiri, *alt.* Isekiri [its], 164
Shekiyana, *alt.* Seki [syi], 111, 121
Shekka, *alt.* Shekkacho [moy], 118
  alt. Sheko [she], 118
Shekkacho [moy], 118
Shekko, *alt.* Sheko [she], 118
Sheko [she], 118
Shekwan, *alt.* Kavalan [ckv], 511
Sheldru, *alt.* Shelta [sth], 543
Shelknam, *alt.* Ona [ona], 220
Shelkota, *dial.* Midob [mei], 193
Shellen, *dial.* Dera [kna], 157
Shelta [sth], 543
Shemdinani, *dial.* Kurdish,
  Northern [kmr], 519
Shempire Senoufo, *see* Senoufo,
  Shempire [seb], 95
Shemya, *alt.* Sinyar [sys], 86, 195
Shenara, *alt.* Senoufo, Syenara
  [shz], 144
Shendu [shl], 322, 383
Shenge Sherbro, *dial.* Sherbro
  [bun], 177
Shengha, *dial.* Naga, Konyak
  [nbe], 378
Shengwe, *alt.* Tonga [toh], 149
Sheni [scv], 174
Shenpire, *alt.* Senoufo, Shempire
  [seb], 95
Shensi, *alt. dial.* Dungan [dng], 449
Shera Yogur, *alt.* Yugur, East
  [yuy], 348
Sherbro [bun], 177
Sherdukpen [sdp], 387
Shere, *alt.* Sere [swf], 107
Sherenté, *alt.* Xerénte [xer], 234

Sheret, *alt.* Shehri [shv], 483
Sherewyana, *alt.* Hixkaryána
  [hix], 227
Sheri, *alt.* Sere [swf], 107
Sherpa [xsr], 478, 343, 387
Sherwin, *alt.* Sharwa [swq], 72
Sherwood Valley, *dial.* Pomo,
  Northern [pej], 307
Sheshi, *alt.* Kham, Sheshi [kip], 473
Sheshi Kham, *see* Kham, Sheshi
  [kip], 473
Sheta, *alt.* Xetá [xet], 234
Shete Tsere, *alt. dial.* Shua [shg],
  48
Shetebo, *dial.* Shipibo-Conibo [shp],
  293
Sheva, *alt. dial.* Nyanja [nya], 140
Shgip, *alt.* Albanian, Gheg [aln], 557
Shi [shr], 107
  alt. Lahu Shi [kds], 451, 338, 465,
  515, 524
Shi Mun, *dial.* Biao Mon [bmt], 327
Shi Xien, *alt. dial.* Chinese, Hakka
  [hak], 511
Shiba, *alt.* Sherbro [bun], 177
Shibne, *alt.* Somrai [sor], 86
Shibukun, *dial.* Bunun [bnn], 511
Shibushi, *alt.* Bushi [buc], 145
Shibushi Shimaore, *alt.* Bushi
  [buc], 145
Shichopi, *alt.* Chopi [cce], 147
Shicopi, *alt.* Chopi [cce], 147
Shidan, *dial.* Jingpho [kac], 336
Shigen, *alt. dial.* Chinese, Hakka
  [hak], 511
Shighni, *alt. dial.* Shughni [sgh], 513,
  318
Shihhi, *alt.* Arabic, Shihhi Spoken
  [ssh], 520
Shihhi Spoken Arabic, *see*
  Arabic, Shihhi Spoken [ssh], 520
Shihlanganu, *alt. dial.* Tsonga
  [tso], 186
Shiho, *alt.* Saho [ssy], 112, 118
Shihu, *alt.* Arabic, Shihhi Spoken
  [ssh], 520
Shihuh, *alt.* Arabic, Shihhi Spoken
  [ssh], 520
Shii, *alt. dial.* Arabic, North Levantine
  Spoken [apc], 453
Shiita, *alt.* Opuuo [lgn], 117
Shikarijanam, *alt.* Vaagri Booli
  [vaa], 389
Shiki [gua], 174
Shikiana, *alt.* Sikiana [sik], 232, 312
Shikotan, *alt. dial.* Ainu [ain], 446,
  503
Shikou, *alt. dial.* Biao-Jiao Mien
  [bje], 327
Shila, *dial.* Bemba [bem], 97

  dial. Taabwa [tap], 108, 215
Shilanganu, *alt. dial.* Tsonga [tso],
  149, 217
Shile, *alt.* Lega-Mwenga [lgm], 102
Shilengwe, *alt. dial.* Tswa [tsc], 149
Shilha [jbn], 209
  alt. Tachelhit [shi], 146, 39
  alt. Tamazight, Central Atlas
  [tzm], 146
  alt. Tarifit [rif], 146, 40
Shilingol, *dial.* Mongolian,
  Peripheral [mvf], 339
Shilluk [shk], 195
Shimacu, *alt.* Urarina [ura], 293
Shimakonde, *alt.* Makonde
  [kde], 148
Shimalilia, *alt.* Malila [mgq], 201
Shimaore, *alt.* Maore [swb], 146
  dial. Comorian [swb], 140
Shimbogedu, *alt.* Diriku [diu], 149,
  40
  alt. Gciriku [diu], 47
Shimbwera, *alt.* Mbwela [mfu], 41
  alt. dial. Nkoya [nka], 214
Shimigae, *alt.* Andoa [anb], 286
Shimizya, *alt.* Chimila [cbg], 244
Shimla Siraji, *alt. dial.* Pahari,
  Mahasu [bfz], 382
Shimong, *dial.* Adi [adi], 353
Shimwali, *alt.* Comorian, Mwali
  [wlc], 87
Shina [scl], 488, 387
  dial. Rutul [rut], 556
Shina, Kohistani [plk], 488
Shinabo [snh], 223
Shinaki, *alt.* Shina [scl], 488, 387
Shinasha, *alt.* Boro [bwo], 114
Shindzuani, *alt. dial.* Comorian
  [swb], 87
Shindzwani, *alt.* Comorian,
  Ndzwani [wni], 87
  dial. Comorian [swb], 87
Shing Saapa, *alt.* Lhomi [lhm], 474,
  338, 372
Shingazidja, *alt.* Comorian,
  Ngazidja [zdj], 87
Shingsol, *alt. dial.* Chin, Thado
  [tcz], 359
Shingwalungu, *alt. dial.* Tsonga
  [tso], 186, 149, 217
Shinkoya, *alt.* Nkoya [nka], 214
Shinnecock-Poosepatuck, *alt.*
  dial. Mohegan-Montauk-
  Narragansett [mof], 305
Shinyiha, *alt.* Nyiha [nih], 203
Shinzwani, *dial.* Comorian
  [swb], 140
  dial. Maore [swb], 146
Shioko, *alt.* Chokwe [cjk], 99, 40,
  213

Ship, *alt.* Miship [mjs], 170
dial. Albanian, Gheg [aln], 529
Shipaja, *alt.* Xipaya [xiy], 234
Shipi, *alt.* Chinali [cih], 359
Shipibo, *dial.* Shipibo-Conibo
[shp], 293
Shipibo del Madre de Dios,
dial. Shipibo-Conibo [shp], 293
Shipibo-Conibo [shp], 293
Shipinahua, *alt.* Xipináwa
[xip], 234
Shiping-Jianshui Nisu, *alt.* Yi,
Southern [nos], 348
Shiping-Jianshui Yi, *alt.* Yi,
Southern [nos], 348
Shiputhsu, *alt. dial.* Sena [seh], 149
Shiqi, *alt. dial.* Chinese, Yue
[yue], 331
Shir, *alt.* Mandari [mqu], 193
Shira, *alt.* Sira [swj], 121
alt. dial. Machame [jmc], 193
Shira Yugur, *alt.* Yugur, East
[yuy], 348
Shiraho, *dial.* Yaeyama [rys], 447
Shirawa, *dial.* Bade [bde], 154
Shirazi, *dial.* Farsi, Western
[pes], 439
Shirazjahromi, *dial.* Farsi, Western
[pes], 439
Shire, *alt.* Sira [swj], 121
Shiriana, *alt. dial.* Ninam [shb], 230
Shiriana Casapare, *alt.* Ninam
[shb], 230
Shirima, *alt.* Makhuwa-Shirima
[vmk], 147
Shirishana, *alt. dial.* Ninam
[shb], 230
Shirnak-Chizre, *dial.* Chaldean
Neo-Aramaic [cld], 443
Shironga, *alt.* Ronga [rng], 149, 186
Shirumba, *alt.* Shwai [shw], 195
alt. dial. Shwai [shw], 195
Shirwanga, *dial.* Yeyi [yey], 48,
151
Shisa, *alt. dial.* Luyia [luy], 134
Shisambyu, *alt. dial.* Kwangali
[kwn], 150, 40
Shishaban, *alt.* Saaroa [sxr], 512
Shishi, *alt.* Seba [kdg], 107
Shishong, *alt.* Beba [bfp], 58
Shita, *alt.* Opuuo [lgn], 117, 194
Shitako, *alt.* Dibo [dio], 157
Shithlou, *alt. dial.* Chin, Thado
[tcz], 359
Shitshwa, *alt.* Tswa [tsc], 149, 186,
217
Shitsonga, *alt.* Tsonga [tso], 186,
149, 197, 217
Shitta, *alt.* Opuuo [lgn], 194
Shiwi'ma, *alt.* Zuni [zun], 310

Shixien, *alt. dial.* Chinese, Hakka
[hak], 511
Shixing [sxg], 343
Shiyeyi, *alt.* Yeyi [yey], 48, 151
Shkip, *alt.* Albanian, Tosk [als], 529
Sho, *alt.* Chin, Asho [csh], 462, 321
alt. Chin, Chinbon [cnb], 463
alt. Shau [sqh], 174
Shoa, *alt.* Chin, Asho [csh], 462, 321
Shoba, *alt. dial.* Bushoong [buf], 98
Shobang, *alt.* Shom Peng [sii], 387
Shobwa, *alt. dial.* Bushoong
[buf], 98
Shobyo, *alt. dial.* Rwanda [kin], 178
Shoe, *dial.* Mpade [mpi], 68, 84
Shoho, *alt.* Saho [ssy], 112, 118
Sholaga [sle], 387
Sholanayika, *alt.* Sholaga [sle], 387
Sholiga, *alt.* Sholaga [sle], 387
Sholigar, *alt.* Sholaga [sle], 387
Sholio, *dial.* Tyap [kcg], 176
Shom Pen, *alt.* Shom Peng [sii], 387
Shom Peng [sii], 387
Shomba, *dial.* Ngemba [nge], 69
Shomo Karim, *alt.* Como Karim
[cfg], 157
Shomoh, *alt.* Como Karim [cfg], 157
Shomong, *alt.* Como Karim [cfg],
157
Shompen, *alt.* Shom Peng [sii], 387
Shompeng, *alt.* Shom Peng
[sii], 387
Shona [sna], 216, 215
alt. Zezuru [sna], 49
Shong, *alt.* Chong [cog], 325, 514
Shonga, *alt.* Shanga [sho], 174
Shongawa, *alt.* Shanga [sho], 174
Shongo, *alt.* Bushoong [buf], 98
Shongom, *dial.* Tangale [tan], 175
Shonke, *dial.* Argobba [agj], 113
Shonshe, *dial.* Chin, Haka
[cnh], 463, 321, 357
Shoo, *dial.* Shoo-Minda-Nye
[bcv], 174
Shoo-Minda-Nye [bcv], 174
Shopni, *alt.* Albanian, Gheg
[aln], 529
Shor [cjs], 506
dial. Khakas [kjh], 505, 337
Shortsy, *alt.* Shor [cjs], 506
Shosho, *pej. alt.* Berom [bom], 155
Shoshone, *alt.* Shoshoni [shh], 308
Shoshoni [shh], 308
Shpogolu, *alt.* Pogolo [poy], 204
Shqip, *alt.* Albanian, Tosk [als], 529
Shqiperë, *alt.* Albanian, Tosk
[als], 529
Shtafari, *dial.* Thao [ssf], 512
Shtokavski, *alt. dial.* Croatian
[hrv], 532

dial. Serbian [srp], 557
Shu, *dial.* Nande [nnb], 105
Shu-Ai-I, *alt.* Lü [khb], 465
Shua [shg], 48
alt. Arabic, Chadian Spoken [shu], 78
alt. Arabic, Shuwa [shu], 56, 151
Shua Arabic, *alt.* Arabic, Chadian
Spoken [shu], 78
alt. Arabic, Shuwa [shu], 56, 154
Shua-Khwe, *alt.* Shua [shg], 48
dial. Shua [shg], 48
Shuadi, *alt.* Shuadit [sdt], 538
Shuadit [sdt], 538
Shuangbo Lolopho, *dial.* Yi,
Central [ycl], 347
Shuar [jiv], 251
Shuara, *alt.* Shuar [jiv], 251
Shuba, *alt.* Kagate [syw], 472
Shubi [suj], 204
Shugan, *alt. dial.* Shughni [sgh], 513,
318
Shughnani, *alt. dial.* Shughni
[sgh], 318
Shughni [sgh], 513, 318
dial. Shughni [sgh], 513, 318
Shugnan, *alt. dial.* Shughni
[sgh], 513
Shugnan-Rushan, *alt.* Shughni
[sgh], 513
Shugni, *alt. dial.* Shughni [sgh], 318
Shugule, *dial.* Mefele [mfj], 67
Shui, *alt.* Sui [swi], 344
Shui-Pai-I, *alt.* Lü [khb], 339, 451,
515, 524
Shuihu, *alt.* Bouyei [pcc], 328
Shukho, *dial.* Lishana Deni
[lsd], 445
Shukri, *dial.* Arabic, Sudanese
Spoken [apd], 188
Shukulumbwe, *alt.* Ila [ilb], 213
Shulanin, *dial.* Avar [ava], 553
Shuli, *alt.* Acholi [ach], 210, 187
dial. Luri, Southern [luz], 440
Shulla, *alt.* Shilluk [shk], 195
Shumasht, *alt.* Shumashti
[sts], 318
Shumashti [sts], 318
Shumcho [scu], 387
Shumcu, *alt.* Shumcho [scu], 387
Shungo, *alt.* Loo [ldo], 169
Shunhu, *alt.* Loo [ldo], 169
Shunkla, *alt. dial.* Chin, Falam
[flm], 463
Shunyuo, *dial.* Naga, Konyak
[nbe], 378
Shupamem, *alt.* Bamun [bax], 57
Shuri, *alt.* Suri [suq], 119
dial. Okinawan, Central [ryu], 447
Shuro, *alt.* Suri [suq], 119
Shuru, *dial.* Berta [wti], 113, 189

Sierra Oriental Chatino, *alt.*
  Chatino, Eastern Highland
  [cly], 259
Sierra Oriental Otomi, *alt.*
  Otomi, Eastern Highland
  [otm], 272
Sierra Puebla Náhuatl, *alt.*
  Nahuatl, Highland Puebla
  [azz], 271
Sierra Totonac, *alt.* Totonac,
  Highland [tos], 276
Sievemakers, *alt. dial.* Romani,
  Vlax [rmy], 551
Sigarau, *alt. dial.* Iban [iba], 393
Sigawa, *alt.* Sio [xsi], 625
Sigdi, *alt. dial.* Saya [say], 174
Siggoyo, *alt.* Bambassi [myf], 113
Sighu [sxe], 121
Sigi, *alt. dial.* Kaili, Ledo [lew], 429
Sigidi, *dial.* Saya [say], 174
Sigisigero, *alt. dial.* Siwai
  [siw], 625
Siglit, *dial.* Inuktitut, Western
  Canadian [ikt], 238
**Sign Language of the
  Netherlands**, *alt.* Dutch Sign
  Language [dse], 548
Sigumza, *alt.* Gumuz [guk], 115
Siha, *dial.* Machame [jmc], 193
Sihan [snr], 624
  alt. Sian [spg], 461
Sihanaka, *dial.* Malagasy, Plateau
  [plt], 140
Sihong, *dial.* Ma'anyan [mhy], 394
Sihuas Ancash Quechua, *see*
  Quechua, Sihuas Ancash
  [qws], 292
Sihzang, *dial.* Chin, Paite [pck], 359
Sii, *alt.* Wushi [bse], 73
Siime, *dial.* Kaba Deme [kwg], 81
Siis, *alt. dial.* Mandjak [mfv], 131
Siiwa, *dial.* Fipa [fip], 198
Sijali, *alt.* Jumli [jml], 472
Sijiaji, *dial.* Dongxiang [sce], 332
Sika [ski], 409
Sikaiana [sky], 638
Sikami, *alt.* Sikkimese [sip], 387
Sikar, *dial.* Shekhawati [swv], 386
Sikari, *alt.* Sikaritai [tty], 423
Sikaritai [tty], 423
Sikarwari, *dial.* Braj Bhasha
  [bra], 357
Sikasso, *dial.* Bamanankan
  [bam], 141
Sikayana, *alt.* Sikaiana [sky], 638
Sikhota Alin, *dial.* Udihe [ude], 507
Sikhule, *alt.* Sikule [skh], 437
Sikiana [sik], 232, 296, 312
Sikiána, *alt.* Sikiana [sik], 312
Sikiâna, *alt.* Sikiana [sik], 232

Sikïïyana, *alt.* Sikiana [sik], 232
Sikiyana, *alt.* Sikiana [sik], 296
Sikka, *alt.* Sika [ski], 409
Sikka Natar, *dial.* Sika [ski], 409
Sikkanese, *alt.* Sika [ski], 409
Sikkim Bhotia, *alt.* Sikkimese
  [sip], 387
Sikkim Bhutia, *alt.* Sikkimese
  [sip], 387
Sikkimese [sip], 387
Sikpi, *dial.* Aja [ajg], 42, 206
Sikuani, *alt. dial.* Guahibo [guh], 245
  pej. alt. Guahibo [guh], 245
Sikubung, *dial.* Sama, Southern
  [ssb], 458
Sikule [skh], 437
Sikwangali, *alt.* Kwangali
  [kwn], 150, 40
Sila [slt], 452, 526
  alt. Daju, Dar Sila [dau], 80, 189
  dial. Daju, Dar Sila [dau], 189
Silabe, *alt.* Soninke [snk], 144, 95,
  122, 145, 182
Silabu, *dial.* Mentawai [mwv], 436
Silacayoapan Mixtec, *see* Mixtec,
  Silacayoapan [mks], 268
Siladja, *alt.* Selayar [sly], 433
Silajara, *alt.* Selayar [sly], 433
Silakau, *alt.* Selako [skl], 395, 461
Silanke, *alt.* Sininkere [skq], 54
Sileba, *dial.* Sawila [swt], 409
Sileibi [sbq], 624
Silemani, *alt. dial.* Kurdish, Central
  [ckb], 443
Silen, *alt.* Teluti [tlt], 404
Silesian, Lower [sli], 550, 533, 539
Sileti, *alt.* Sylheti [syl], 322, 388
Sili, *alt.* Palor [fap], 181
  alt. Sere [swf], 107
  alt. dial. Shua [shg], 48
Sili-Sili, *alt.* Palor [fap], 181
Siligi, *dial.* Folopa [ppo], 599
Silimo [wul], 423
Silinkere, *alt.* Sininkere [skq], 54
Siliput [mkc], 624
Silisili, *alt.* Watut, Middle [mpl], 631
Sille, *dial.* Cappadocian Greek
  [cpg], 540
Sillok, *alt.* Aka [soh], 187
Silmamo, *alt. dial.* Kacipo-Balesi
  [koe], 115
Silopi [xsp], 624
Siloti, *alt.* Sylheti [syl], 322, 388
Silozi, *alt.* Lozi [loz], 214, 150, 216
Silt'e [xst], 119
Silti, *alt.* Silt'e [xst], 119
Silunguboi, *alt.* Fanagalo [fng], 185
Silver Palaung, *alt.* Palaung, Pale
  [pce], 466, 342, 516
Sim, *dial.* Weri [wer], 632

Sima, *dial.* Naga, Konyak [nbe], 378
Simaa [sie], 215
  dial. Simaa [sie], 215
Simacu, *alt.* Urarina [ura], 293
Simagahi, *alt.* Oya'oya [oyy], 621
Simai, *dial.* Asmat, Central [cns], 411
Simalegi, *dial.* Mentawai [mwv], 436
Simalur, *alt.* Simeulue [smr], 437
Simaranhon, *dial.* Bantoanon
  [bno], 492
Simay, *alt. dial.* Asmat, Central
  [cns], 411
Simba [sbw], 121
  alt. Guaraní, Western Bolivian [gnw],
  223
  alt. Zemba [dhm], 42, 151
Simba Guaraní, *alt.* Guaraní,
  Western Bolivian [gnw], 223
Simbakong, *alt.* Sembakung Murut
  [sbr], 458, 395
Simbali [smg], 624
Simbari [smb], 624
Simberi, *dial.* Mandara [tbf], 612
Simbiti, *dial.* Kuria [kuj], 200, 134
Simbo [sbb], 638
Simbu, *alt.* Kuman [kue], 608
Simeku [smz], 624
Simelungan, *alt.* Batak Simalungun
  [bts], 435
Simeuloë, *alt.* Simeulue [smr], 437
Simeulue [smr], 437
Simi, *alt.* Naga, Sumi [nsm], 380
Simiranch, *alt.* Yine [pib], 294
Simirinche, *pej. alt.* Yine [pib], 294
Simog, *alt.* Auwe [smf], 591
Simori, *dial.* Ekari [ekg], 414
Simpi, *alt.* Esimbi [ags], 61
Simt'anga, *alt.* Xamtanga
  [xan], 119
Simte [smt], 387
Simulul, *alt.* Simeulue [smr], 437
Simunul, *dial.* Sama, Southern
  [ssb], 500, 458
Sina, *alt.* Shina [scl], 488, 387
  dial. Kamwe [hig], 166
Sinabu, *alt. dial.* Kinabatangan,
  Upper [dmg], 457
Sinabu', *dial.* Kinabatangan, Upper
  [dmg], 457
Sinagen [siu], 624
Sinagoro, *alt.* Sinaugoro [snc], 624
Sina'i, *alt. dial.* Kurdish, Central
  [ckb], 440
Sinak Nduga, *dial.* Nduga
  [ndx], 421
Sinaketa, *dial.* Kilivila [kij], 606
Sinaki, *dial.* Suau [swp], 625
Sinale, *alt.* Fembe [agl], 598
Sinama, *alt.* Sama, Central [sml],
  500, 458

alt. Sama, Southern [ssb], 500
alt. Sissano [sso], 625
Sinama Tawi-Tawi, *alt.* Sama, Southern [ssb], 500
Sinan, *dial.* Dayak, Land [dyk], 393
Sinano, *alt.* Sissano [sso], 625
Sinasina [sst], 624
Sinaugoro [snc], 624
Sinauna, *alt.* Agta, Remontado [agv], 491
Sindang Kelingi [sdi], 437
Sindangan Subanun, *alt.* Subanen, Central [syb], 501
Sindebele, *alt.* Ndebele [nde], 216, 48
Sindhi [snd], 488, 387
Sindhi Bhil [sbn], 489
dial. Sindhi Bhil [sbn], 489
Sindhi Ghera, *alt.* Ghera [ghr], 484
Sindhi Meghwar, *dial.* Sindhi Bhil [sbn], 489
Sindhi Musalmani, *dial.* Sindhi [snd], 488
Sindhuli, *alt. dial.* Jerung [jee], 472
Sindhupalchok Pahri, *dial.* Newar [new], 476
Sindhupalcok, *dial.* Thangmi [thf], 480
Sindia, *dial.* Saafi-Saafi [sav], 182
Sindihui Mixtec, *see* Mixtec, Sindihui [xts], 269
Sinding, *alt. dial.* Dayak, Land [dyk], 393
Sindue-Tawaili, *alt. dial.* Kaili, Ledo [lew], 429
Sine, *alt. dial.* Serer-Sine [srr], 122
dial. Serer-Sine [srr], 182
Sine-Saloum, *alt.* Serer-Sine [srr], 182, 122
Sine-Sine, *alt.* Serer-Sine [srr], 182
Sine'i, *alt.* Kurdish, Central [ckb], 440
alt. dial. Kurdish, Central [ckb], 440
Sinesip, *alt.* South West Bay [sns], 645
Sineyi, *alt. dial.* Kurdish, Central [ckb], 440
Sing Mun, *alt.* Puoc [puo], 525
Sing-Fo, *alt.* Singpho [sgp], 387
Singa [sgm], 212
Singala, *dial.* Senoufo, Djimini [dyi], 95
Singali, *alt.* Lambadi [lmn], 372
Singapore Sign Language [sls], 509
Singgai, *alt. dial.* Jagoi [sne], 459
Singge, *dial.* Jagoi [sne], 459
Singgi, *alt. dial.* Jagoi [sne], 459
Singgie, *alt. dial.* Jagoi [sne], 459
Singhala, *alt.* Sinhala [sin], 509

Singhalese, *alt.* Sinhala [sin], 509, 509
Singhi, *alt. dial.* Jagoi [sne], 459
Singja, *alt.* Jumli [jml], 472
Singkarak, *dial.* Minangkabau [min], 436
Singkil, *dial.* Batak Karo [btx], 435
Singli, *alt.* Korwa [kfp], 370
Singorokai, *dial.* Malasanga [mqz], 611
Singpho [sgp], 387
Singson, *alt. dial.* Chin, Thado [tcz], 359
Sinhaja Srir, *alt.* Senhaja de Srair [sjs], 146
Sinhala [sin], 509, 509
Sinhalese, *alt.* Sinhala [sin], 509, 509
Sinicahua Mixtec, *see* Mixtec, Sinicahua [xti], 269
Sininkere [skq], 54
Sinja, *alt.* Shubi [suj], 204
dial. Jumli [jml], 472
Sinjai, *dial.* Bugis [bug], 428
Sinkaling Hkamti, *dial.* Khamti [kht], 465, 367
Sinkiuse, *alt. dial.* Columbia-Wenatchi [col], 300
Sinkon, *dial.* Sapo [krn], 139
Sinohoan, *dial.* Pamona [bcx], 432
Sinsauru [snz], 625
Sintang, *alt. dial.* Malay [mly], 436
Sinte, *alt.* Romani, Sinte [rmo], 557, 530, 533, 539
Sinte Romani, *see* Romani, Sinte [rmo], 557, 448, 530, 533, 537, 539, 542, 545, 549, 550, 562
Sinti, *alt.* Romani, Sinte [rmo], 557, 448, 530, 533, 537, 550
Sintí, *alt.* Romani, Sinte [rmo], 539
Sinug Tausug, *alt.* Tausug [tsg], 502
Sinulihan, *alt. dial.* Dusun, Central [dtp], 456
Sinya, *alt.* Sinyar [sys], 86, 195
Sinyar [sys], 86, 195
Sinyonyoi, *dial.* Mamuju [mqx], 431
Sio [xsi], 625
Siocon, *alt.* Subanon, Western [suc], 501
Siompu, *dial.* Muna [mnb], 431
Siona [snn], 247, 251
Siong, *alt. dial.* Ma'anyan [mhy], 394
Sioni, *alt.* Siona [snn], 247
Siora, *dial.* Zanaki [zak], 206
Sioua, *alt.* Siwi [siz], 110
Sioux, *alt.* Dakota [dak], 297, 237
Sipacapa Quiché, *alt.* Sipakapense [qum], 256
Sipacapeño, *alt.* Sipakapense [qum], 256

Sipacapense, *alt.* Sipakapense [qum], 256
Sipakapense [qum], 256
Sipari, *dial.* Harauti [hoj], 364
Sipeng, *dial.* Penan, Western [pne], 460, 325
Sìpììté, *alt.* Sénoufo, Sìcìté [sep], 54, 144
Sipisi, *dial.* Barapasi [brp], 412
Sipoma, *alt.* Numbami [sij], 619
Sipsongpanna Dai, *alt.* Lü [khb], 339
Sipupu, *dial.* Bunama [bdd], 595
Sipura, *dial.* Mentawai [mwv], 436
Sira [swj], 121
alt. Pawaia [pwa], 621
Siragi, *alt. dial.* Pahari, Kullu [kfx], 382
Siraha, *dial.* Tharu, Kochila [thq], 481
Siraia, *alt.* Siraya [fos], 512
Siraiki, *alt.* Seraiki [skr], 488, 386
Siraiki Hindki, *alt. dial.* Seraiki [skr], 386
Siraiya, *alt.* Siraya [fos], 512
Siraji, *alt. dial.* Pahari, Kullu [kfx], 382
Siraji of Doda, *dial.* Kashmiri [kas], 367
Siraji-Kashmiri, *dial.* Kashmiri [kas], 367
Sirak, *alt.* Nafi [srf], 616
alt. dial. Mefele [mfj], 67
Sirasira, *alt. dial.* Adzera [azr], 587
Sirata, *alt.* Kanuri, Central [knc], 63, 81, 152, 191
Sirawa, *alt.* Siri [sir], 175
Siraya [fos], 512
dial. Siraya [fos], 512
Sirba, *dial.* Gumuz [guk], 115
Sirenik, *alt.* Yupik, Sirenik [ysr], 508
Sirenik Yupik, *see* Yupik, Sirenik [ysr], 508
Sirenikski, *alt.* Yupik, Sirenik [ysr], 508
Sirhe, *alt.* Zire [sih], 585
Siri [sir], 175
alt. Sere [swf], 107
Siri-Sori, *dial.* Saparua [spr], 403
Siria, *dial.* Maasai [mas], 134
Siriana, *alt.* Siriano [sri], 232
Siriane, *alt.* Siriano [sri], 232
Siriano [sri], 247, 232
Sirio, *alt.* Nawaru [nwr], 617
Sirionó [srq], 223
Siripu, *alt. dial.* Cuiba [cui], 244, 311
Siripuria, *alt. dial.* Bengali [ben], 355
dial. Bengali [ben], 469
Sirir, *dial.* Mpur [akc], 420
Sirmauri [srx], 387

Sirmouri, *alt.* Sirmauri [srx], 387
Sirmuri, *alt.* Sirmauri [srx], 387
Sirohi, *dial.* Godwari [gdx], 362
Siroi [ssd], 625
Sironcha, *dial.* Gondi, Southern [ggo], 363
Sirxin, *dial.* Dargwa [dar], 553
Siryon, *alt.* Western Neo-Aramaic [amw], 510
Sisaala, Tumulung [sil], 127
Sisaala, Western [ssl], 128
Sisaali, *alt.* Sissala [sld], 54
Sisai, *alt.* Sisaala, Tumulung [sil], 127
  alt. Sisaala, Western [ssl], 128
Sisaket, *dial.* Khmer, Northern [kxm], 515
Sisala Tumu, *alt.* Sisaala, Tumulung [sil], 127
Sisano, *alt.* Sissano [sso], 625
Sîshëë, *alt.* Zire [sih], 585
Sisi, *dial.* Besisi [mhe], 454
Sisi-Bipi, *alt.* Bipi [biq], 594
Sisiame, *dial.* Bamu [bcf], 592
Sisibna, *dial.* Korupun-Sela [kpq], 418
Sisimin, *alt.* Hewa [ham], 602
Sisingga, *alt. dial.* Babatana [baa], 635
Siska, *alt.* Tonga [tog], 141
Sissala [sld], 54
Sissano [sso], 625
Sisutho, *alt.* Sotho, Southern [sot], 137, 186
Siswati, *alt.* Swati [ssw], 197, 149, 186
Siswazi, *alt.* Swati [ssw], 149, 186
Sisya, *alt.* Tonga [tog], 141
Sisyaban, *alt.* Saaroa [sxr], 512
Sitaang, *alt. dial.* Biatah [bth], 459
Sitangkai, *dial.* Sama, Southern [ssb], 500
Sitemuú, *alt.* Baga Sitemu [bsp], 128
Siteng, *dial.* Melanau [mel], 460
Sitia Sherbro, *dial.* Sherbro [bun], 177
Sitigo, *alt.* Vagla [vag], 128
Sitongwe, *alt.* Tongwe [tny], 205
Situ, *dial.* Jiarong [jya], 336
Siu, *dial.* Swahili [swh], 136
Siuci, *alt. dial.* Baniwa [bwi], 225
Siusi, *alt. dial.* Baniwa [bwi], 225
Siuslaw [sis], 308
Siusy-Tapuya, *dial.* Baniwa [bwi], 225
Sivandi [siy], 441
Sivereki, *dial.* Dimli [diq], 518
Sivukun, *alt. dial.* Bunun [bnn], 511
Siwa, *alt.* Siwi [siz], 110

Siwai [siw], 625
  alt. Amto [amt], 589
Siwane, *dial.* Kgalagadi [xkv], 47
Siwang, *alt.* Chewong [cwg], 454
Siwi [siz], 110
Siwu [akp], 128
Siwuri, *alt.* Tuwuli [bov], 128
Siwusi, *alt.* Siwu [akp], 128
Siyalgir, *dial.* Bhili [bhb], 356
Siyama, *alt.* Sama, Pangutaran [slm], 500
Siyang, *alt.* Chin, Siyin [csy], 463
Siyaowu, *dial.* Guanyinqiao [jiq], 333
Siyi, *dial.* Chinese, Yue [yue], 331
Siyin, *alt.* Chin, Siyin [csy], 463
Siyin Chin, *see* Chin, Siyin [csy], 463
Siyu, *alt. dial.* Swahili [swh], 136
Sizaki [szk], 204
Sizang, *alt.* Chin, Siyin [csy], 463
Sizi, *alt.* Dizi [mdx], 114
Sjaelland, *alt.* Danish [dan], 533
Sjiagha, *alt.* Awyu, Edera [awy], 412
  alt. Awyu, South [aws], 412
Skagit [ska], 308
Skane, *alt.* Scanian [scy], 533
Skånsk, *alt.* Scanian [scy], 562
Skånska, *alt.* Scanian [scy], 562, 533
  dial. Scanian [scy], 562, 533
Skarohreh, *alt.* Tuscarora [tus], 309
Skchip, *alt.* Albanian, Tosk [als], 529
Skepi Creole Dutch [skw], 257
Skidegate, *alt.* Haida, Southern [hax], 238
Skidi, *alt. dial.* Pawnee [paw], 306
Skiri, *alt. dial.* Pawnee [paw], 306
S'klallam, *alt.* Clallam [clm], 300
Sko, *alt.* Skou [skv], 423
Skofro, *alt.* Manem [jet], 612, 419
Skokomish, *alt.* Twana [twa], 309
  dial. Twana [twa], 309
Skolt, *alt.* Saami, Skolt [sms], 556
Skolt Lappish, *alt.* Saami, Skolt [sms], 535
  pej. alt. Saami, Skolt [sms], 556
Skolt Saami, *see* Saami, Skolt [sms], 535, 556
Skou [skv], 423
Skouw, *alt.* Skou [skv], 423
Skow, *alt.* Skou [skv], 423
Skrang, *dial.* Iban [iba], 459
Skrubu, *alt.* Surubu [sde], 175
Slai, *alt.* Hlai [lic], 333
Slave, *pej. alt.* Slavey, North [scs], 241
  pej. alt. Slavey, South [xsl], 241
Slavey, North [scs], 241
Slavey, South [xsl], 241
Slavi, *alt.* Slavey, North [scs], 241

  alt. Slavey, South [xsl], 241
Slavic [mkd], 541
  alt. Macedonian [mkd], 547, 529
Slavonic, Old Church [chu], 556
Sliammon, *dial.* Comox [coo], 236
SLN, *alt.* Dutch Sign Language [dse], 548
Slovak [slk], 558, 542, 558
Slovakian, *alt.* Slovak [slk], 558
Slovakian Sign Language [svk], 558
Slovene, *alt.* Slovenian [slv], 558, 530, 542, 545
Slovenian [slv], 558, 530, 542, 545
Slovenian Sign Language, *dial.* Yugoslavian Sign Language [ysl], 558
Slovenian-Croatian, *dial.* Romani, Sinte [rmo], 545
Slovenian-Croatian Romani, *dial.* Romani, Sinte [rmo], 557
Slovenscina, *alt.* Slovenian [slv], 558
Slovincian, *dial.* Kashubian [csb], 550
Slutska-Mazyrski, *alt. dial.* Belarusan [bel], 530
Slutsko-Mozyr, *alt. dial.* Belarusan [bel], 530
Sm'algyax, *alt.* Tsimshian [tsi], 309
  alt. dial. Tsimshian [tsi], 242
Small Bolgo, *alt. dial.* Bolgo [bvo], 79
Small Flowery Miao, *alt. dial.* Hmong Njua [blu], 334
Small Nambas, *alt.* Letemboi [nms], 642
Smärky Kanum, *see* Kanum, Smärky [kxq], 416
Smith River, *alt.* Tolowa [tol], 309
Smyrna, *dial.* Armenian [hye], 318
Snabi Watubela, *alt.* Watubela [wah], 405
Snohomish [sno], 308
Snoqualmie, *dial.* Salish, Southern Puget Sound [slh], 307
So (Cameroon) [sox], 72
So (Democratic Republic of Congo) [soc], 108
  alt. Aheu [thm], 513, 449
  alt. Soo [teu], 212
  alt. dial. Kulfa [kxj], 82
Sô [sss], 452, 517
So Makon, *alt.* Sô [sss], 452
  dial. Sô [sss], 517
So Phong, *dial.* Sô [sss], 452, 517
So Slouy, *dial.* Sô [sss], 452, 517
So Tri, *alt. dial.* Bru, Eastern [bru], 450

So Trii, *alt. dial.* Bru, Eastern [bru], 450

So Trong, *dial.* Sô [sss], 452, 517

So-Bê, *alt.* Kirmanjki [kiu], 518

So'a [ssq], 409

Soa, *alt.* So [soc], 108
  alt. So'a [ssq], 409
  alt. dial. Kono [kno], 183

Soahuku, *dial.* Amahai [amq], 396

Soai, *alt.* Kuy [kdt], 515, 451

Soba, *alt.* Hupla [hap], 415

Sobané, *alt.* Baga Sobané [bsv], 128

Sobei [sob], 423

Sobo, *pej. alt.* Isoko [iso], 164
  pej. alt. Urhobo [urh], 176

Sobojo, *alt. dial.* Taliabu [tlv], 404

Soboyo, *alt. dial.* Taliabu [tlv], 404

Sobstvenno-Karel'skij-Jazyk, *alt.* Karelian [krl], 555

Socé, *alt.* Mandinka [mnk], 181, 122

Sochi, *dial.* Sansi [ssi], 488

Sochiapan Chinantec, *see* Chinantec, Sochiapan [cso], 261

Sochile, *alt.* Nyakyusa-Ngonde [nyy], 203, 140

Socotri, *alt.* Soqotri [sqt], 528

Soda, *dial.* Gaam [tbi], 190

Soddo, *alt.* Kistane [gru], 116
  dial. Kistane [gru], 116

Soddo Gurage, *alt.* Kistane [gru], 116

Sodia Parja, *alt.* Bodo Parja [bdv], 357

Sodochi, *alt. dial.* Pahari, Mahasu [bfz], 382

Soe, *alt. dial.* Zimba [zmb], 109

Sofala, *alt.* Ndau [ndc], 148, 216

Soga [xog], 212

Sogadas, *alt. dial.* Kunama [kun], 112

Sogal, *dial.* Bine [bon], 593

Sogap, *alt.* Ngala [nud], 618

Sogh, *alt.* Manikion [mnx], 419

Soghai, *alt. dial.* Kinabatangan, Upper [dmg], 457

Soghaua, *alt.* Zaghawa [zag], 196, 87

Sôghoo, *dial.* Senoufo, Mamara [myk], 144

Sogilitan, *alt.* Kadazan, Labuk-Kinabatangan [dtb], 457

Sogoba, *alt.* Sumariup [siv], 626

Sogodas, *alt. dial.* Kunama [kun], 112

Sogokiré, *dial.* Bobo Madaré, Southern [bwq], 49

Sogokiri, *dial.* Bobo Madaré, Northern [bbo], 141

Sogoo, *alt. dial.* Okiek [oki], 135

Sohe, *alt. dial.* Orokaiva [ork], 620

Sohra, *alt. dial.* Khasi [kha], 367

Sohur, *alt.* Yaqay [jaq], 426

Soi [soj], 441

Soibada, *alt. dial.* Tetun [tet], 410, 351

Sok [skk], 452

Sokaka, *alt.* Hixkaryána [hix], 227

Sokhok, *alt. dial.* Aigon [aix], 588

Sokid, *dial.* Dusun, Central [dtp], 456

Sokile, *alt.* Nyakyusa-Ngonde [nyy], 203, 140

Sokili, *alt.* Nyakyusa-Ngonde [nyy], 203

Sokirik, *dial.* Patpatar [gfk], 621

Sokna, *alt.* Sawknah [swn], 139

Soko, *alt.* So [soc], 108
  alt. dial. Kulfa [kxj], 82
  dial. Ntomba [nto], 106

Sokodasa, *dial.* Kunama [kun], 112

Sokoo, *alt. dial.* Okiek [oki], 135

Sokoro [sok], 86
  dial. Sokoro [sok], 86

Sokorok, *alt.* Siliput [mkc], 624

Sokoto, *dial.* Fulfulde, Nigerian [fuv], 160
  dial. Hausa [hau], 162

Sokotri, *alt.* Soqotri [sqt], 528

Sokte, *dial.* Chin, Tedim [ctd], 463, 359

Sokya, *alt.* Kouya [kyf], 93

Sola, *alt.* Miyobe [soy], 45, 208

Solaga, *alt.* Sholaga [sle], 387

Solamba, *alt.* Miyobe [soy], 45, 208

Solanayakkans, *alt.* Sholaga [sle], 387

Sole, *alt. dial.* Zimba [zmb], 109

Soledad, *dial.* Ohlone, Northern [cst], 306

Soli [sby], 215

Soliga, *alt.* Sholaga [sle], 387

Soligar, *alt.* Sholaga [sle], 387

Solla, *alt.* Miyobe [soy], 45, 208

Solo, *dial.* Javanese [jav], 391

Solomons Pidgin, *alt.* Pijin [pis], 637

Solon, *alt.* Evenki [evn], 332, 461, 504

Solong [aaw], 625

Solor, *alt.* Lamaholot [slp], 408

Solorese, *alt.* Lamaholot [slp], 408

Solos [sol], 625

Soloto, *dial.* Yuracare [yuz], 224

Sölreng, *dial.* Frisian, Northern [frr], 538

Solu, *dial.* Sherpa [xsr], 478

Solwa, *alt.* Kagulu [kki], 199

Solwe, *alt. dial.* Sagala [sbm], 204

Som [smc], 625
  alt. Wab [wab], 630

Soma, *alt.* Ditammari [tbz], 207

Somage, *alt.* Momuna [mqf], 420

Somahai, *alt.* Momuna [mqf], 420

Somali [som], 185, 109, 119, 136

Somatu, *alt.* Enets, Tundra [enh], 504

Somba, *dial.* Burum-Mindik [bmu], 595
  pej. alt. Ditammari [tbz], 43, 207

Somba-Siawari, *alt.* Burum-Mindik [bmu], 595

Sombrero Negro, *alt. dial.* Pilagá [plg], 220

Some, *alt.* Ditammari [tbz], 207
  dial. Fasu [faa], 598

Somekhuri, *alt.* Armenian [hye], 437

Somerset, *dial.* English [eng], 565

Somkhuri, *alt.* Armenian [hye], 318, 319, 350, 444, 453, 510, 563

Somono, *dial.* Bamanankan [bam], 141

Somorika, *alt. dial.* Okpamheri [opa], 172

Somra, *alt.* Naga, Tangkhul [nmf], 380

Somrai [sor], 86

Somray [smu], 326

Somre, *alt.* Somrai [sor], 86

Somrei, *alt.* Somrai [sor], 86

Somwadina, *dial.* Duau [dva], 597

Somyev [kgt], 175

Somyewe, *alt.* Somyev [kgt], 175

Son, *dial.* Wa [wbm], 467

Sona, *alt.* Kanasi [soq], 604

Sonahaa, *alt.* Sonha [soi], 479

Sonai, *dial.* Yaeyama [rys], 447

Sonapal, *dial.* Muria, Western [mut], 377

Sonar Boli, *alt.* Kinnauri, Harijan [kjo], 368

Sonde [shc], 108

Sonder, *dial.* Tontemboan [tnt], 434

Sondoang, *dial.* Ulumanda' [ulm], 434

Sondwari, *alt. dial.* Malvi [mup], 374

Song, *alt.* Thai Song [soa], 517

Songa [sgo], 108
  alt. dial. Tsonga [tso], 186
  dial. Luyia [luy], 134, 211

Songai, *alt.* Songhay [hmb], 54
  alt. Songhay, Humburi Senni [hmb], 144
  alt. Songhay, Koyra Chiini [khq], 144
  alt. Songhay, Koyraboro Senni [ses], 144

Songay, *alt.* Songhay [hmb], 54
  alt. Songhay, Humburi Senni [hmb], 144

alt. Songhay, Koyra Chiini
[khq], 144
alt. Songhay, Koyraboro Senni
[ses], 144
Songay Senni, *alt.* Songhay
[hmb], 54
alt. Songhay, Humburi Senni
[hmb], 144
alt. Songhay, Koyraboro Senni
[ses], 144
Songbu, *dial.* Naga, Rongmei
[nbu], 379
Songe [sop], 108
alt. dial. Songe [sop], 108
Songhai, *alt.* Songhay [hmb], 54
alt. Songhay, Humburi Senni
[hmb], 144
alt. Songhay, Koyra Chiini
[khq], 144
alt. Songhay, Koyraboro Senni
[ses], 144
Songhay [hmb], 54
alt. Songhay, Humburi Senni
[hmb], 144
alt. Songhay, Koyra Chiini [khq],
144
alt. Songhay, Koyraboro Senni
[ses], 144
Songhay, Humburi Senni
[hmb], 144
Songhay, Koyra Chiini
[khq], 144
Songhay, Koyraboro Senni
[ses], 144
Songhoy, *alt.* Songhay, Humburi
Senni [hmb], 144
alt. Songhay, Koyra Chiini
[khq], 144
Songish, *dial.* Salish, Straits
[str], 241, 307
Songo [soo], 108
alt. Mbati [mdn], 77
alt. Nsongo [nsx], 41
Songoi, *alt.* Songhay [hmb], 54
alt. Songhay, Humburi Senni
[hmb], 144
alt. Songhay, Koyra Chiini
[khq], 144
alt. Songhay, Koyraboro Senni
[ses], 144
Songola, *alt.* Ombo [oml], 106
alt. Songoora [sod], 108
alt. dial. Nande [nnb], 105
Songomeno [soe], 108
Songoora [sod], 108
Songoy, *alt.* Songhay [hmb], 54
alt. Songhay, Humburi Senni
[hmb], 144
alt. Songhay, Koyra Chiini
[khq], 144

alt. Songhay, Koyraboro Senni
[ses], 144
Songu, *alt. dial.* Folopa [ppo], 599
Songum, *alt.* Sam [snx], 623
Songwa, *dial.* Ngemba [nge], 69
Songwe, *dial.* Safwa [sbk], 204
Songye, *alt.* Songe [sop], 108
Sonha [soi], 479
Sonia [siq], 625
Soninke [snk], 144, 95, 122, 131,
145, 182
Sonjo, *alt.* Temi [soz], 205
Sonora Pima Bajo, *dial.* Pima Bajo
[pia], 273
Sonowal, *alt.* Sunwar [suz], 479
Sonowar, *alt.* Sunwar [suz], 479
Sonpari, *dial.* Bagheli [bfy], 354, 468
Sonrai, *alt.* Songhay [hmb], 54
alt. Songhay, Humburi Senni
[hmb], 144
alt. Songhay, Koyra Chiini [khq], 144
alt. Songhay, Koyraboro Senni
[ses], 144
Sonrhai, *alt.* Songhay [hmb], 54
alt. Songhay, Humburi Senni
[hmb], 144
alt. Songhay, Koyra Chiini [khq], 144
alt. Songhay, Koyraboro Senni
[ses], 144
Sonsogon, *dial.* Kimaragang
[kqr], 457
Sonsorol [sov], 587
Sonsorolese, *alt.* Sonsorol
[sov], 587
dial. Sonsorol [sov], 587
Sonthal, *alt.* Santali [sat], 386, 322,
478
Sonyo, *alt.* Temi [soz], 205
Soo [teu], 212
Sook Murut, *dial.* Paluan [plz], 458
Sooke, *dial.* Salish, Straits [str], 307
Soolevu, *alt. dial.* Fijian [fij], 580
Sooloo, *alt.* Tausug [tsg], 395, 458
Soonde, *alt.* Sonde [shc], 108
Soorath, *alt.* Chaldean Neo-Aramaic
[cld], 443
Sooreth, *alt.* Assyrian Neo-Aramaic
[aii], 442, 319
Soorith, *alt.* Chaldean Neo-Aramaic
[cld], 443
Soow Huhelia, *alt.* Manipa
[mqp], 402
Sop [urw], 625
dial. Koho [kpm], 524
Sopese, *dial.* Folopa [ppo], 599
Sopfomo, *alt.* Naga, Mao [nbi], 378
Sopi, *alt. dial.* Beli [blm], 189
dial. Galela [gbi], 398
Sopocnovskij, *dial.* Itelmen
[itl], 505

Soppeng, *dial.* Bugis [bug], 428
Soppeng Riaja, *alt. dial.* Bugis
[bug], 428
Sopron, *dial.* Hungarian Sign
Language [hsh], 542
Sopvoma, *alt.* Naga, Mao [nbi], 378
Soqotri [sqt], 528
Sor, *alt.* Ngaing [nnf], 618
dial. Biak [bhw], 412
dial. Kupsabiny [kpz], 211
Sora [srb], 387
Soradi, *dial.* Nepali [nep], 476
Sorani, *alt.* Kurdish, Central
[ckb], 443, 440
Sorathi, *alt. dial.* Gujarati [guj], 363
Soray, *alt.* Senaya [syn], 441
Sorbian, Lower [dsb], 539
Sorbian, Upper [hsb], 539
Sorendidori, *dial.* Biak [bhw], 412
Sori, *dial.* Sori-Harengan [sbh], 625
Sori-Harengan [sbh], 625
Sorido, *dial.* Biak [bhw], 412
Sorimi, *alt.* Bo [bpw], 594
Sork, *alt.* Sok [skk], 452
Sorkhei [sqo], 441
Sorko [bze], 175
Soro, *dial.* Hadiyya [hdy], 115
Soroako, *dial.* Mori Bawah
[xmz], 431
Sorogaama, *alt.* Bozo, Jenaama
[bze], 142
Sorogama, *alt.* Sorko [bze], 175
Sorouba, *alt.* Miyobe [soy], 45,
208
Sorsogon Ayta, *see* Ayta, Sorsogon
[ays], 492
Sorsogon Bicolano, *alt.* Sorsogon,
Masbate [bks], 501
Sorsogon, Masbate [bks], 501
Sorsogon, Waray [srv], 501
Sorsogonon, *alt. dial.* Hanunoo
[hnn], 494
Soruba, *alt.* Miyobe [soy], 45, 208
Sorung, *alt. dial.* Sie [erg], 645
Sose, *alt.* Susu [sus], 130, 184
alt. dial. Orokaiva [ork], 620
Sosi, *alt.* Bassossi [bsi], 58
Soso, *alt.* Susu [sus], 130, 184
Sos'va, *alt. dial.* Mansi [mns], 505
Sosyvin, *alt. dial.* Mansi [mns], 505
Sota Kanum, *see* Kanum, Sota
[krz], 416
Sotang, *dial.* Kulung [kle], 473
Sotaring, *alt. dial.* Kulung
[kle], 473
Sotavento, *dial.* Kabuverdianu
[kea], 74
Sotawueng, *alt.* Aheu [thm], 513
Sotho, Northern [nso], 186
Sotho, Southern [sot], 137, 186

Sotipura, *alt. dial.* Maithili [mai], 373

Sotmali, *alt.* Dumi [dus], 471

Soto, *alt.* Maquiritari [mch], 312, 229

Sottaring, *alt. dial.* Kulung [kle], 473

Sou [sqq], 452

Soubakanedougou, *dial.* Cerma [cme], 50

Soubré, *dial.* Béte, Guiberoua [bet], 92

Soudhwari, *alt. dial.* Malvi [mup], 374

Sougb, *alt.* Manikion [mnx], 419

Souk, *alt.* Sou [sqq], 452

Souka, *alt. dial.* Kulfa [kxj], 82

Soulani, *dial.* Wara [wbf], 55

Souletin, *alt.* Basque, Souletin [bsz], 536

Souletin Basque, *see* Basque, Souletin [bsz], 536

Souletino, *alt.* Basque, Souletin [bsz], 536

Souma, *alt.* Suma [sqm], 77

Soumo, *alt.* Sumo Tawahka [sum], 258

alt. Sumo-Mayangna [sum], 283

Soumrai, *alt.* Somrai [sor], 86

Soumray, *alt.* Somrai [sor], 86

Soungor, *alt.* Assangori [sjg], 78

alt. Sungor [sjg], 195

Sounrai, *alt.* Somrai [sor], 86

Sourashtra, *alt.* Saurashtra [saz], 386

Sourbakhal, *alt.* Surbakhal [sbj], 86

Sousse, *alt. dial.* Tachelhit [shi], 39

Soussou, *alt.* Susu [sus], 130, 184

South Africa Tamil, *dial.* Tamil [tam], 388

South African Sign Language [sfs], 186

South Alaska Eskimo, *pej. alt.* Yupik, Pacific Gulf [ems], 310

South Albanian, *alt. dial.* Romani, Vlax [rmy], 551

South Alune, *dial.* Alune [alp], 396

South Ambrym, *alt.* Dakaka [bpa], 641

South Angal Heneng, *alt.* Angal Enen [aoe], 589

South Anjdi, *dial.* Arabic, Najdi Spoken [ars], 508

South Aunalei, *dial.* One, Molmo [aun], 620

South Awa, *dial.* Awa [awb], 591

South Awin, *dial.* Aekyom [awi], 587

South Awyu, *see* Awyu, South [aws], 412

South Azerbaijani, *see* Azerbaijani, South [azb], 438, 315, 443, 510, 518

South Baikeno, *alt. dial.* Baikeno [bkx], 350

South Band, *dial.* Pawnee [paw], 306

South Bavarian, *dial.* Bavarian [bar], 530, 533, 538, 543

South Belgium Sign Language, *dial.* Belgian Sign Language [bvs], 530

South Belu, *alt. dial.* Tetun [tet], 410, 351

South Binja, *dial.* Songoora [sod], 108

South Bolivian Quechua, *see* Quechua, South Bolivian [quh], 223, 220

South Bunun, *dial.* Bunun [bnn], 511

South Buru, *alt. dial.* Buru [mhs], 397

South Buton, *alt.* Cia-Cia [cia], 429

South Carolina, *dial.* Sea Island Creole English [gul], 307

South Central Arvanitika, *dial.* Albanian, Arvanitika [aat], 540

South Central Banda, *see* Banda, South Central [lnl], 74, 97

South Central Cakchiquel, *alt.* Kaqchikel, South Central [ckd], 254

South Central Delta Arabic, *dial.* Arabic, Egyptian Spoken [arz], 110

South Central Dinka, *see* Dinka, South Central [dib], 190

South Central Kaqchikel, *see* Kaqchikel, South Central [ckd], 254

South Central Mixe, *alt.* Mixe, Juquila [mxq], 265

South Central Teke, *alt.* Teke-Fuumu [ifm], 90

South Central Tlaxiaco Mixtec, *alt.* Mixtec, Atatláhuca [mib], 266

South Central Zimatlan Zapotec, *alt.* Zapotec, El Alto [zpp], 278

South Chachapoyas, *alt. dial.* Quechua, Chachapoyas [quk], 290

South Chollado, *alt. dial.* Korean [kor], 448

South Ch'ungch'ong, *alt. dial.* Korean [kor], 448

South Coast Mengen, *dial.* Mengen [mee], 613

South Coast Sikka, *alt. dial.* Sika [ski], 409

South Congo, *dial.* Koongo [kng], 101

South Damar, *alt.* Damar, East [dmr], 397

South Drente, *dial.* Drents [drt], 548

South East Kongo, *dial.* Koongo [kng], 40

South Efate, *see* Efate, South [erk], 641

South Fali, *see* Fali, South [fal], 61

South Fore, *alt. dial.* Fore [for], 599

South Giziga, *see* Giziga, South [giz], 62

South Hamgyongdo, *alt. dial.* Korean [kor], 448

South Hiberno English, *dial.* English [eng], 542

South Hijazi, *dial.* Arabic, Hijazi Spoken [acw], 508

South Hpon, *dial.* Hpon [hpo], 464

South Ibanag, *dial.* Ibanag [ibg], 494

South Ibie, *dial.* Yekhee [ets], 177

South Ile Ape, *dial.* Ile Ape [ila], 407

South Island, *dial.* Maori [mri], 586

South Islands, *alt. dial.* Ramoaaina [rai], 622

South Ivbie, *alt. dial.* Yekhee [ets], 177

South Izere, *dial.* Izere [fiz], 164

South Kakabai, *dial.* Kakabai [kqf], 603

South Kamayo, *dial.* Kamayo [kyk], 498

South Kamberataro, *dial.* Dera [kbv], 597

South Karakelong, *dial.* Talaud [tld], 433

South Kati, *alt.* Muyu, South [kts], 421

South Kerala, *dial.* Malayalam [mal], 374

South Kewa, *alt.* Erave [kjy], 598

South Khowar, *dial.* Khowar [khw], 486

South Kitui, *dial.* Kamba [kam], 133

South Koma, *alt.* Komo [xom], 116

South Kombio, *dial.* Kombio [xbi], 607

South Kongo, *dial.* Koongo [kng], 40

South Kwandu, *dial.* Mashi [mho], 214, 41, 150

South Kyongsangdo, *alt. dial.* Korean [kor], 448

South Laamang, *dial.* Lamang [hia], 168

South Lebanese Arabic, *dial.* Arabic, North Levantine Spoken [apc], 453

South Lele, *alt. dial.* Lele [llc], 129

South Lembata, *see* Lembata, South [lmf], 408

South Levantine Arabic, *alt.* Arabic, South Levantine Spoken [ajp], 448

South Levantine Bedawi Arabic, *dial.* Arabic, Eastern Egyptian Bedawi Spoken [avl], 110 *dial.* Arabic, Levantine Bedawi Spoken [avl], 448, 489

South Levantine Spoken Arabic, *see* Arabic, South Levantine Spoken [ajp], 448, 444, 490

South Lobala, *dial.* Lobala [loq], 103

South Lole, *dial.* Lole [llg], 408

South Loloda, *alt.* Laba [lau], 400

South Luwu, *dial.* Tae' [rob], 428

South Maca, *alt.* Makhuwa-Marrevone [xmc], 147

South Makaa, *alt.* Makaa [mcp], 65

South Malaita, *alt.* Sa'a [apb], 638

South Malo, *alt. dial.* Malo [mla], 643

South Manusela, *dial.* Manusela [wha], 402

South Marquesan, *see* Marquesan, South [mqm], 581

South Mbundu, *alt.* Umbundu [umb], 42

South Mekaa, *alt.* Makaa [mcp], 65

South Mendi, *alt.* Angal Enen [aoe], 589

South Migabac, *dial.* Migabac [mpp], 614

South Modole, *dial.* Modole [mqo], 402

South Moejoe, *alt.* Muyu, South [kts], 421

South Mori, *alt.* Padoe [pdo], 432

South Muyu, *see* Muyu, South [kts], 421

South Nakama, *dial.* Nakama [nib], 616

South Ngada, *dial.* Ngad'a [nxg], 409

South Ngalik, *alt.* Silimo [wul], 423

South Nkundo, *alt. dial.* Mongo-Nkundu [lol], 104

South Northern Paiute, *dial.* Paiute, Northern [pao], 306

South Nuaulu, *see* Nuaulu, South [nxl], 402

South Nuk, *dial.* Nuk [noc], 618

South Olo, *alt. dial.* Olo [ong], 619

South Oran, *dial.* Tamazight, Central Atlas [tzm], 146, 40

South Paama, *dial.* Paama [pma], 644

South Palawano, *dial.* Palawano, Brooke's Point [plw], 500

South Permyak, *dial.* Komi-Permyak [koi], 555

South Pohjanmaa, *dial.* Finnish [fin], 534

South P'yong'ando, *alt. dial.* Korean [kor], 448

South Qatari Arabic, *dial.* Arabic, Gulf Spoken [afb], 503

South Quchani, *dial.* Khorasani Turkish [kmz], 439

South Raga, *alt. dial.* Sa [sax], 645

South Russian, *dial.* Russian [rus], 556

South Saami, *see* Saami, South [sma], 561, 550

South Saiset, *alt. dial.* Saisiyat [xsy], 512

South Sardinian, *alt.* Sardinian, Campidanese [sro], 545

South Selepet, *dial.* Selepet [spl], 623

South Sena, *alt. dial.* Sena [seh], 149

South Siberut, *dial.* Mentawai [mwv], 436

South Slavey, *see* Slavey, South [xsl], 241

South Tabasaran, *dial.* Tabassaran [tab], 555

South Tabukang, *dial.* Sangir [sxn], 432

South Tairora, *see* Tairora, South [omw], 626

South Tetun, *alt. dial.* Tetun [tet], 410, 351

South Tharaka, *alt. dial.* Tharaka [thk], 136

South Tigak, *dial.* Tigak [tgc], 627

South Timbe, *dial.* Timbe [tim], 627

South Toraja, *alt.* Toraja-Sa'dan [sda], 434

South Tugen, *dial.* Kalenjin [kln], 133

South Tuvaluan, *dial.* Tuvaluan [tvl], 640

South Ucayali Ashéninka, *see* Ashéninka, South Ucayali [cpy], 286

South Udmurt, *dial.* Udmurt [udm], 557

South Urat, *alt. dial.* Urat [urt], 629

South Waibuk, *dial.* Haruai [tmd], 601

South Wales, *dial.* English [eng], 565

South Watut, *see* Watut, South [mcy], 631

South Wemale, *see* Wemale, South [tlw], 405

South West Bay [sns], 645

South Yamdena, *dial.* Yamdena [jmd], 405

South Yawa, *dial.* Yawa [yva], 426

South-Central Lebanese Arabic, *dial.* Arabic, North Levantine Spoken [apc], 453

South-Eastern Tunisian, *dial.* Arabic, Tunisian Spoken [aeb], 209

South-Western Tunisian, *dial.* Arabic, Tunisian Spoken [aeb], 209

Southeast Ambrym, *see* Ambrym, Southeast [tvk], 640

Southeast Babar, *see* Babar, Southeast [vbb], 396

Southeast Bobe, *dial.* Bube [bvb], 110

Southeast Cagayan, *alt. dial.* Agta, Dupaninan [duo], 490

Southeast Dobel, *dial.* Dobel [kvo], 397

Southeast Ijo, *see* Ijo, Southeast [ijs], 163

Southeast Kaingang, *dial.* Kaingáng [kgp], 228

Southeast Koba, *dial.* Koba [kpd], 400

Southeast Kongo, *alt. dial.* Koongo [kng], 101

Southeast Lampung, *alt. dial.* Pesisir, Southern [pec], 437

Southeast Marind, *alt.* Marind [mrz], 419 *dial.* Marind [mrz], 419

Southeast Metafonetica, *dial.* Sicilian [scn], 545

Southeast Ngada, *alt.* Ngad'a, Eastern [nea], 409

Southeast Pashayi, *see* Pashayi, Southeast [psi], 317

Southeast Shona, *alt.* Ndau [ndc], 148, 216

Southeast Toba, *dial.* Toba [tob], 220

Southeast Vanua Levu, *dial.* Fijian [fij], 580

Southeast Viti Levu, *dial.* Fijian [fij], 580

Southeastern Dinka, *see* Dinka, Southeastern [dks], 190

Southeastern Finnish, *dial.* Finnish [fin], 534

Southeastern Huastec, *see* Huastec, Southeastern [hsf], 262

Southeastern Huasteca Nahuatl, *dial.* Nahuatl, Eastern Huasteca [nhe], 271

Southeastern Ixtlán Zapotec, *see* Zapotec, Southeastern Ixtlán [zpd], 280

Southeastern Karakalpak, *dial.* Karakalpak [kaa], 521

Southeastern Kolami, *see* Kolami, Southeastern [nit], 369

Southeastern Krumen, *alt.* Krumen, Pye [pye], 93

Southeastern Kumauni, *dial.* Kumauni [kfy], 370

Southeastern Lolo Yi, *see* Yi, Southeastern Lolo [yso], 348

Southeastern Macedonian, *dial.* Macedonian [mkd], 547

Southeastern Mixe, *alt.* Mixe, Coatlán [mco], 265

Southeastern Nochixtlán Mixtec, *see* Mixtec, Southeastern Nochixtlán [mxy], 269

Southeastern Ocotepec Mixtec, *alt.* Mixtec, Southwestern Tlaxiaco [meh], 269

Southeastern Otomí, *alt.* Otomi, Ixtenco [otz], 272

Southeastern Pashto, *dial.* Pashto, Southern [pbt], 488

Southeastern Pomo, *see* Pomo, Southeastern [pom], 307

Southeastern Puebla Nahuatl, *see* Nahuatl, Southeastern Puebla [nhs], 272

Southeastern Tarahumara, *see* Tarahumara, Southeastern [tcu], 275

Southeastern Tepehuan, *see* Tepehuan, Southeastern [stp], 275

Southeastern Tuvin, *dial.* Tuvin [tyv], 507

Southeastern Yautepec Zapotec, *alt.* Zapotec, Tlacolulita [zpk], 280

Southeastern Yi, *alt.* Yi, Guizhou [yig], 347

Southeastern Yiddish, *dial.* Yiddish, Eastern [ydd], 446

Southeastern Zimatlán Zapotec, *alt.* Zapotec, Santa Inés Yatzechi [zpn], 280

Southern Akhvakh, *alt. dial.* Akhvakh [akv], 552

Southern Alta, *see* Alta, Southern [agy], 491

Southern Altai, *see* Altai, Southern [alt], 503

Southern Altai, *alt. dial.* Altai, Southern [alt], 503

Southern Amami-Oshima, *see* Amami-Oshima, Southern [ams], 446

Southern Amami-Osima, *alt.* Amami-Oshima, Southern [ams], 446

Southern Ambakich, *dial.* Ambakich [aew], 589

Southern Amis, *dial.* Amis [ami], 511

Southern Angor, *alt. dial.* Angor [agg], 589

Southern Aragonese, *dial.* Aragonese [arg], 558

Southern Aranda, *dial.* Arrarnta, Western [are], 568

Southern Arapesh, *alt.* Mufian [aoj], 615

Southern Atta, *alt.* Atta, Faire [azt], 491

Southern Awu Yi, *dial.* Yi, Awu [yiu], 347

Southern Aymara, *see* Aymara, Southern [ayc], 287

Southern Baagandji, *alt.* Darling [drl], 569

Southern Bade, *dial.* Bade [bde], 154

Southern Bai, *see* Bai, Southern [bfs], 327

Southern Baima, *dial.* Baima [bqh], 327

Southern Bajau, *alt.* Sama, Southern [ssb], 458

Southern Bakossi, *dial.* Akoose [bss], 56

Southern Balochi, *see* Balochi, Southern [bcc], 483, 438, 482, 520

Southern Bangantu, *alt.* Bangandu [bgf], 57

Southern Bantawa, *dial.* Bantawa [bap], 468

Southern Barasano, *alt.* Barasana [bsn], 243

Southern Bashaka, *dial.* Bashkardi [bsg], 438

Southern Betsimisaraka Malagasy, *see* Malagasy, Southern Betsimisaraka [bjq], 140

Southern Birifor, *see* Birifor, Southern [biv], 123, 92

Southern Bisaya, *alt.* Bisaya, Brunei [bsb], 324

Southern Bobo Madaré, *see* Bobo Madaré, Southern [bwq], 49

Southern Bolon, *alt. dial.* Bolon [bof], 49

Southern Bomitaba, *alt.* Dibole [bvx], 88

Southern Bontoc, *alt.* Finallig [bkb], 494

Southern Buduma, *dial.* Buduma [bdm], 79

Southern Bullom, *alt.* Sherbro [bun], 177

Southern Burun, *alt.* Mabaan [mfz], 193

Southern Butung, *alt.* Cia-Cia [cia], 429

Southern Cakchiquel, *alt.* Kaqkchikel, Southern [ckf], 254

Southern Calabro, *dial.* Sicilian [scn], 545

Southern Carolinian, *alt.* Carolinian [cal], 586

Southern Carrier, *see* Carrier, Southern [caf], 236

Southern Catanduanes Bicolano, *see* Bicolano, Southern Catanduanes [bln], 493

Southern Chumburung, *dial.* Chumburung [ncu], 124

Southern Cluster Lishán Didán, *dial.* Lishán Didán [trg], 445

Southern Coast Kiwai, *dial.* Kiwai, Southern [kjd], 606

Southern Coastal Yawuru, *dial.* Yawuru [ywr], 579

Southern Conchucos Ancash Quechua, *see* Quechua, Southern Conchucos Ancash [qxo], 292

Southern Conchucos Quechua, *alt.* Quechua, Southern Conchucos Ancash [qxo], 292

Southern Crimean, *dial.* Crimean Turkish [crh], 521, 518, 532, 551

Southern Cuona, *dial.* Moinba [mob], 340

Southern Dagaare, *see* Dagaare, Southern [dga], 124

Southern Dagari, *alt.* Dagaare, Southern [dga], 124

Southern Dhatki, *dial.* Dhatki [mki], 484

Southern Dibole, *dial.* Dibole [bvx], 88

Southern Dong, *see* Dong, Southern [kmc], 331

Southern East Cree, *see* East Cree, Southern [crj], 237

Southern East-Guizhou Miao, *alt.* Hmong, Southern Qiandong [hms], 335

Southern Efate, *alt.* Efate, South [erk], 641

Southern Ejagham, *alt. dial.* Ejagham [etu], 60
dial. Ejagham [etu], 159

Southern Ejutla Zapotec, *alt.* Zapotec, San Vicente Coatlán [zpt], 279

Southern Embera, *alt.* Epena [sja], 245, 251, 283

Southern Empera, *alt.* Epena [sja], 245, 251, 283

Southern Estonian, *alt. dial.* Estonian [est], 534

Southern Extremaduran, *dial.* Extremaduran [ext], 560

Southern Fania, *dial.* Fania [fni], 80

Southern Foothill Yokuts, *dial.* Yokuts [yok], 310

Southern French Sign Language, *alt. dial.* French Sign Language [fsl], 536

Southern Gabri, *alt.* Gabri [gab], 80

Southern Ghale, *see* Ghale, Southern [ghe], 471

Southern Gikuyu, *dial.* Gikuyu [kik], 133

Southern Gondi, *see* Gondi, Southern [ggo], 363

Southern Gourmanchema, *dial.* Gourmanchéma [gux], 51

Southern Grebo, *see* Grebo, Southern [grj], 138, 93

Southern Guiyang Hmong, *see* Hmong, Southern Guiyang [hmy], 335

Southern Guiyang Miao, *alt.* Hmong, Southern Guiyang [hmy], 335

Southern Guizhou, *alt. dial.* Bouyei [pcc], 328

Southern Gunu, *dial.* Nugunu [yas], 70

Southern Gurung, *dial.* Gurung, Western [gvr], 471

Southern Haida, *see* Haida, Southern [hax], 238

Southern Hanga, *dial.* Hanga [hag], 125

Southern Heiltsuk, *alt. dial.* Heiltsuk [hei], 238

Southern Hema, *alt.* Hema [nix], 100

Southern Hindko, *see* Hindko, Southern [hnd], 485

Southern Huancayo Quechua, *alt.* Quechua, Huaylla Wanca [qvw], 291

Southern Irish, *alt. dial.* Gaelic, Irish [gle], 542

Southern Irula, *alt. dial.* Irula [iru], 365

Southern Isan. Korat, *dial.* Thai, Northeastern [tts], 517

Southern Itneg, *alt.* Itneg, Maeng [itt], 496

Southern Ivatan, *dial.* Ivatan [ivv], 496

Southern Jafi, *dial.* Kurdish, Central [ckb], 440

Southern Jale, *alt.* Nipsan [nps], 421

Southern Kalasha, *dial.* Kalasha [kls], 486

Southern Kalinga, *see* Kalinga, Southern [ksc], 497

Southern Kannada, *alt.* Kurumba [kfi], 371

Southern Kaqkchikel, *see* Kaqkchikel, Southern [ckf], 254

Southern Karelian, *alt.* Livvi [olo], 555
alt. dial. Karelian [krl], 555, 534

Southern Katkari, *dial.* Katkari [kfu], 367

Southern Kazakh, *dial.* Kazakh [kaz], 448, 316

Southern Khams, *dial.* Tibetan, Khams [khg], 345

Southern Khanti, *alt. dial.* Khanty [kca], 505

Southern Khmer, *dial.* Khmer, Central [khm], 524

Southern Kirghiz, *dial.* Kirghiz [kir], 449, 337

Southern Kirinyaga, *alt. dial.* Gikuyu [kik], 133

Southern Kisagala, *alt.* Sagala [sbm], 204

Southern Kisi, *see* Kisi, Southern [kss], 138, 183

Southern Kiwai, *see* Kiwai, Southern [kjd], 606

Southern Krahn, *alt.* Sapo [krn], 139

Southern Krumen, *alt.* Krumen, Tepo [ted], 93, 138

Southern Kurdish, *see* Kurdish, Southern [sdh], 440, 443

Southern Lahu, *alt. dial.* Lahu [lhu], 338, 451, 465, 515

Southern Lapp, *alt.* Saami, South [sma], 561

Southern Lela, *alt. dial.* C'lela [dri], 157

Southern Lengua, *dial.* Lengua [leg], 284

Southern Libyan Arabic, *dial.* Arabic, Libyan Spoken [ayl], 139
dial. Arabic, Western Egyptian Bedawi Spoken [ayl], 110

Southern Limba, *dial.* Limba, East [lma], 183

Southern Lisu, *alt.* Lisu [lis], 339, 465, 515

Southern Lolopho Yi, *see* Yi, Southern Lolopho [ysp], 348

Southern Lorung, *see* Lorung, Southern [lrr], 474

Southern Luba, *alt.* Sanga [sng], 107

Southern Luri, *see* Luri, Southern [luz], 440

Southern Lushootseed, *dial.* Lushootseed [lut], 304

Southern Lyélé, *dial.* Lyélé [lee], 52

Southern Ma'di, *see* Ma'di, Southern [snm], 211

Southern Ma'di, *alt.* Ma'di, Southern [snm], 211

Southern Magahi, *dial.* Magahi [mag], 373

Southern Maidu, *alt.* Nisenan [nsz], 306

Southern Malay, *alt. dial.* Malay [mly], 455

Southern Malimiut Inupiatun, *alt. dial.* Inupiatun, Northwest Alaska [esk], 302

Southern Mam, *see* Mam, Southern [mms], 255

Southern Mamasa, *alt. dial.* Mamasa [mqj], 431

Southern Maninka, *alt.* Maninkakan, Eastern [emk], 129, 183

Southern Mao, *alt.* Anfillo [myo], 113

Southern Marik, *dial.* Marik [dad], 612

Southern Marwari, *dial.* Marwari [mve], 487

Southern Masalit, *dial.* Masalit [mls], 83

Southern Mashan Hmong, *see* Hmong, Southern Mashan [hma], 335

Southern Mashan Miao, *alt.* Hmong, Southern Mashan [hma], 335

Southern Micmac, *dial.* Micmac [mic], 239

Southern Min, *alt.* Chinese, Min Nan [nan], 330, 508

Southern Mnong, *see* Mnong, Southern [mnn], 525

Southern Mon, *alt. dial.* Mon [mnw], 466

Southern Monpa, *alt. dial.* Moinba [mob], 376

Southern Morocco Arabic, *dial.* Arabic, Moroccan Spoken [ary], 146

Southern Muna, *alt. dial.* Muna [mnb], 431

Southern Munji, *dial.* Munji [mnj], 316

Southern Murang'a, *alt. dial.* Gikuyu [kik], 133

Southern Murut, *alt.* Lundayeh [lnd], 394, 324, 460

Southern Mussau, *dial.* Mussau-Emira [emi], 616

Southern Nambikuára, *see* Nambikuára, Southern [nab], 230

Southern Ndam, *alt. dial.* Ndam [ndm], 85

Southern Ndebele, *alt.* Ndebele [nbl], 186

Southern Ngbandi, *see* Ngbandi, Southern [nbw], 105

Southern Nicobarese, *see* Nicobarese, Southern [nik], 381

Southern Ninam, *dial.* Ninam [shb], 230, 312

Southern Nochixtlan Mixtec, *alt.* Mixtec, Yutanduchi [mab], 270

Southern Nuni, *see* Nuni, Southern [nnw], 53

Southern Nusu, *dial.* Nusu [nuf], 341

Southern Ohlone, *see* Ohlone, Southern [css], 306

Southern Okanogan, *dial.* Okanagan [oka], 240, 306

Southern One, *see* One, Southern [osu], 620

Southern Oriya, *dial.* Oriya [ori], 382

Southern Orok, *alt. dial.* Orok [oaa], 506

Southern Oromo, *alt.* Borana [gax], 132

alt. Oromo, Borana-Arsi-Guji [gax], 117, 185

Southern Paiute, *dial.* Ute-Southern Paiute [ute], 309

Southern Pame, *see* Pame, Southern [pmz], 273

Southern Panjabi, *alt.* Seraiki [skr], 488, 386

Southern Pa'o, *dial.* Karen, Pa'o [blk], 464

Southern Pashto, *see* Pashto, Southern [pbt], 488, 317, 441, 520

Southern Pastaza Quechua, *see* Quechua, Southern Pastaza [qup], 292

Southern Pesisir, *see* Pesisir, Southern [pec], 437

Southern Pokomam, *alt.* Poqomam, Southern [pou], 256

Southern Pomo, *see* Pomo, Southern [peq], 307

Southern Popoloca, *alt.* Popoloca, Mezontla [pbe], 273

alt. Popoloca, San Juan Atzingo [poe], 273

Southern Poqomam, *see* Poqomam, Southern [pou], 256

Southern Puebla Mixtec, *see* Mixtec, Southern Puebla [mit], 269

Southern Puget Sound Salish, *see* Salish, Southern Puget Sound [slh], 307

Southern Puget Sound Salish, *alt. dial.* Lushootseed [lut], 304

Southern Pumi, *see* Pumi, Southern [pmj], 342

Southern Putla Mixtec, *alt.* Mixtec, Santa María Zacatepec [mza], 268

Southern Pwo Karen, *alt.* Karen, Pwo Western Thailand [kjp], 514

alt. dial. Karen, Pwo Eastern [kjp], 464

Southern Qiandong Hmong, *see* Hmong, Southern Qiandong [hms], 335

Southern Qiandong Miao, *alt.* Hmong, Southern Qiandong [hms], 335

Southern Qiang, *see* Qiang, Southern [qxs], 342

Southern Rengma, *alt.* Naga, Southern Rengma [nre], 379

alt. dial. Naga, Southern Rengma [nre], 379

Southern Rengma Naga, *see* Naga, Southern Rengma [nre], 379

Southern Rincon Zapotec, *see* Zapotec, Southern Rincon [zsr], 280

Southern Roglai, *see* Roglai, Southern [rgs], 526

Southern Romagnolo, *dial.* Emiliano-Romagnolo [eml], 543

Southern Sama, *see* Sama, Southern [ssb], 500, 458

Southern Samo, *see* Samo, Southern [sbd], 54

Southern Samo, *alt.* Seeku [sos], 54

Southern Sangtam, *alt. dial.* Naga, Sangtam [nsa], 379

Southern Sani, *dial.* Yi, Sani [ysn], 347

Southern Saurashtra, *dial.* Saurashtra [saz], 386

Southern Scots, *dial.* Scots [sco], 566

Southern Seeku, *dial.* Seeku [sos], 54

Southern Sel'kup, *alt. dial.* Selkup [sel], 506

Southern Shilha, *alt.* Tachelhit [shi], 146, 39

Southern Sierra Miwok, *see* Miwok, Southern Sierra [skd], 305

Southern Sisaala, *alt.* Paasaal [sig], 127

Southern Soqotri, *dial.* Soqotri [sqt], 528

Southern Sorsogon, *alt.* Sorsogon, Waray [srv], 501

Southern Sotho, *see* Sotho, Southern [sot], 137, 186

Southern Standard Bhojpuri, *dial.* Bhojpuri [bho], 356

Southern Standard Maithili, *dial.* Maithili [mai], 373

Southern Stieng, *alt.* Stieng, Budeh [stt], 526

Southern Stoney, *dial.* Stoney [sto], 241

Southern Sudan Arabic, *alt.* Arabic, Sudanese Creole [pga], 187

Southern Sumba, *dial.* Kambera [xbr], 407

Southern Swedish, *alt.* Scanian [scy], 562, 533

Southern Ta-Ang, *alt.* Palaung, Pale [pce], 516

Southern Ta'ang, *alt.* Palaung, Pale [pce], 342

Southern Tagdal, *alt. dial.* Tagdal [tda], 152

Southern Talyshi, *dial.* Talysh [tly], 442

Southern Tày, *dial.* Tày [tyz], 527

Southern Tboli, *dial.* Tboli [tbl], 502

Southern Teke, *alt.* Teke-Kukuya [kkw], 90

Southern Termanu, *alt. dial.* Termanu [twu], 410

Southern Tetun, *dial.* Tetun [tet], 410, 351

Southern Thai, *see* Thai, Southern [sou], 517

Southern Thulung, *dial.* Thulung [tdh], 481

Southern Tiwa, *see* Tiwa, Southern [tix], 309

Southern Tlaxiaco Mixtec, *alt.* Mixtec, Yosondúa [mpm], 270

Southern Tonga, *alt. dial.* Tonga [toi], 215

Southern Toussian, *see* Toussian, Southern [wib], 55

Southern Tsakonian, *dial.* Tsakonian [tsd], 541

Southern Tsimshian, *dial.* Tsimshian [tsi], 242

Southern Tujia, *see* Tujia, Southern [tjs], 345

Southern Turkana, *dial.* Turkana [tuv], 137

Southern Tutchone, *see* Tutchone, Southern [tce], 242

Southern Uma, *dial.* Uma [ppk], 434

Southern Uzbek, *see* Uzbek, Southern [uzs], 318, 520

Southern Veps, *dial.* Veps [vep], 557

Southern Vietnamese, *dial.* Vietnamese [vie], 527

Southern Villa Alta Zapotec, *alt.* Zapotec, Cajonos [zad], 277

Southern Vlax, *dial.* Romani, Vlax [rmy], 531

Southern Vlax Romani, *dial.* Romani, Vlax [rmy], 529

Southern Vogul, *dial.* Mansi [mns], 505

Southern Walloon, *dial.* Walloon [wln], 531

Southern Welsh, *dial.* Welsh [cym], 566

Southern Yakha, *dial.* Yakha [ybh], 482

Southern Yali, *alt.* Yali, Ninia [nlk], 426

Southern Yamalele, *dial.* Iamalele [yml], 602

Southern Yana, *dial.* Yana [ynn], 310

Southern Yemeni Spoken Arabic, *alt.* Arabic, Ta'izzi-Adeni Spoken [acq], 528

Southern Yi, *see* Yi, Southern [nos], 348

Southern Yukaghir, *see* Yukaghir, Southern [yux], 499

Southern Yukagir, *alt.* Yukaghir, Southern [yux], 499

Southern Zaza, *alt.* Dimli [diq], 518

Southern Zhuang, *see* Zhuang, Southern [ccy], 349

Southern-Eastern Mongolian, *alt.* Mongolian, Peripheral [mvf], 339, 462

Southwest Barito, *alt.* Ngaju [nij], 394

Southwest Belarusan, *dial.* Belarusan [bel], 530

Southwest Bobe, *dial.* Bube [bvb], 110

Southwest Bohemian, *dial.* Czech [ces], 533

Southwest Duguri, *dial.* Duguri [dbm], 158

Southwest Ede, *alt.* Ede Nago, Manigri-Kambolé [xkb], 207

Southwest Finland Swedish, *dial.* Swedish [swe], 535

Southwest Gbaya, *see* Gbaya, Southwest [mdo], 76, 62

Southwest Kaingang, *dial.* Kaingáng [kgp], 228

Southwest Karakalpak, *dial.* Karakalpak [kaa], 316

Southwest Lamaholot, *alt.* Lewotobi [lwt], 408

Southwest Lampung, *alt. dial.* Pesisir, Southern [pec], 437

Southwest Palawano, *see* Palawano, Southwest [plv], 500

Southwest Pashayi, *see* Pashayi, Southwest [psh], 317

Southwest Senari, *dial.* Senoufo, Cebaara [sef], 94

Southwest Tanna, *see* Tanna, Southwest [nwi], 645

Southwest Ukrainian, *dial.* Ukrainian [ukr], 564

Southwestern, *dial.* Tamang, Western [tdg], 480

Southwestern Caribbean Creole English, *alt.* Jamaican Creole English [jam], 259
alt. Limón Creole English [jam], 249
alt. Panamanian Creole English [jam], 283

Southwestern Dinka, *see* Dinka, Southwestern [dik], 190

Southwestern Fars, *see* Fars, Southwestern [fay], 439

Southwestern Finnish, *dial.* Finnish [fin], 534

Southwestern Gelao, *alt.* Gelao, White [giw], 522

Southwestern Guiyang Hmong, *see* Hmong, Southwestern Guiyang [hmg], 335

Southwestern Guiyang Miao, *alt.* Hmong, Southwestern Guiyang [hmg], 335

Southwestern Huishui Hmong, *see* Hmong, Southwestern Huishui [hmh], 335

Southwestern Huishui Miao, *alt.* Hmong, Southwestern Huishui [hmh], 335

Southwestern Kazakh, *dial.* Kazakh [kaz], 337

Southwestern Kroumen, *alt.* Krumen, Tepo [ted], 93

Southwestern Logudorese, *dial.* Sardinian, Logudorese [src], 545

Southwestern Mandarin, *alt. dial.* Chinese, Mandarin [cmn], 329

Southwestern Ojibwa, *alt.* Chippewa [ciw], 299

Southwestern Pashto, *dial.* Pashto, Southern [pbt], 317

Southwestern Pomo, *alt.* Kashaya [kju], 303

Southwestern Puebla Nahuatl, *alt.* Nahuatl, Central Puebla [ncx], 270

Southwestern Quiché, *alt.* K'iche', West Central [qut], 255

Southwestern Tamang, *see* Tamang, Southwestern [tsf], 479

Southwestern Tamang, *dial.* Tamang, Eastern [taj], 479

Southwestern Tarahumara, *see* Tarahumara, Southwestern [twr], 275

Southwestern Tarangan, *dial.* Tarangan, West [txn], 404

Southwestern Tepehuan, *see* Tepehuan, Southwestern [tla], 275

Southwestern Tlaxiaco Mixtec, *see* Mixtec, Southwestern Tlaxiaco [meh], 269

Southwestern Udmurt, *alt. dial.* Udmurt [udm], 557

Southwestern Yiddish, *dial.* Yiddish, Western [yih], 540

Souto, *alt.* Sotho, Southern [sot], 137, 186

Sowa [sww], 645
dial. Naga, Konyak [nbe], 378

Sowanda [sow], 625, 423

Sowrashtra, *alt.* Saurashtra [saz], 386

Soyaltepec Mazatec, *see* Mazatec, Soyaltepec [vmp], 265

Soyaltepec Mixtec, *see* Mixtec, Soyaltepec [vmq], 269

Soykin, *dial.* Ingrian [izh], 554

Soyod, *alt.* Tuvin [tyv], 507, 462

Soyon, *alt.* Tuvin [tyv], 507, 462

Soyot, *alt.* Tuvin [tyv], 507, 462

Spanish [spa], 560, 111, 146, 220, 222, 224, 243, 247, 249, 250, 251,

252, 256, 258, 274, 283, 284, 285, 293, 294, 296, 308, 311, 312, 501, 529, 538, 540

Spanish Calo, *dial.* Caló [rmr], 536, 551

Spanish Caló, *dial.* Caló [rmr], 559

Spanish Sign Language [ssp], 561

Spanish, Loreto-Ucayali [spq], 293

Spanyol, *alt.* Ladino [lad], 445, 563

Speng, *alt. dial.* Penan, Western [pne], 460, 325

Spiti Bhoti [spt], 387

Spokan, *alt.* Spokane [spo], 308

Spokane [spo], 308

Spowama, *alt.* Naga, Mao [nbi], 378

Sqoleq, *dial.* Atayal [tay], 511

Squamish [squ], 241

Squliq, *alt. dial.* Atayal [tay], 511

Sradri, *alt.* Sadri [sck], 385

Sranan [srn], 296

Sranan Tongo, *alt.* Sranan [srn], 296

Sray, *alt.* Senaya [syn], 441

Sre, *dial.* Koho [kpm], 524

Srednyaya Ob-Ket, *dial.* Selkup [sel], 506

Srem, *dial.* Albanian, Tosk [als], 529

Sri Lanka Tamil, *dial.* Tamil [tam], 388

Sri Lankan Creole Malay [sci], 509

Sri Lankan Malay, *alt.* Sri Lankan Creole Malay [sci], 509

Sri Lankan Sign Language [sqs], 510

Srihattia, *alt.* Sylheti [syl], 388

Srikakula, *alt. dial.* Telugu [tel], 388

Srinagaria, *dial.* Garhwali [gbm], 360

Srubu, *alt.* Surubu [sde], 175

Ssia, *alt.* Sera [sry], 624

Sso, *alt.* So [sox], 72

Ssu Ghassi, *alt. dial.* Ju|'hoan [ktz], 47, 150

Ssuga, *alt.* Suga [sgi], 72

St. Barth Creole French, *dial.* Guadeloupean Creole French [gcf], 253

St. Barth English, *alt. dial.* English [eng], 253

St. Francis, *alt.* Abnaki, Western [abe], 235

St. Gallen, *dial.* Schwyzerdütsch [gsw], 563

St. Lawrence Iroquoian, *alt.* Laurentian [lre], 238

St. Lawrence Island Eskimo, *pej. alt.* Yupik, Central Siberian [ess], 310

St. Louis, *alt. dial.* Caac [msq], 584

St. Maarten Creole English, *dial.* Netherlands Antilles Creole English [vic], 282

Stado, *alt. dial.* Aja [ajg], 42, 206

Stajerski, *dial.* Slovenian [slv], 558

Stal, *dial.* Lezgi [lez], 555

Standard Adi, *alt. dial.* Adi [adi], 353

Standard Arabic, *see* Arabic, Standard [arb], 508, 39, 78, 87, 109, 110, 112, 139, 146, 184, 187, 197, 209, 320, 442, 444, 448, 449, 453, 482, 490, 503, 510, 520, 528

Standard Assamese, *dial.* Assamese [asm], 354

Standard Bambara, *dial.* Bamanankan [bam], 141

Standard Bundeli, *dial.* Bundeli [bns], 357

Standard Chinese, *alt.* Chinese, Mandarin [cmn], 329

Standard Fijian, *alt.* Fijian [fij], 580

Standard French, *dial.* French [fra], 536

Standard German, *see* German, Standard [deu], 538, 284, 448, 530, 531, 533, 533, 542, 544, 546, 546, 550, 551, 558, 562

Standard Gujarati, *dial.* Gujarati [guj], 363

Standard Hebrew, *dial.* Hebrew [heb], 444

Standard Kashmiri, *dial.* Kashmiri [kas], 367

Standard Konkani, *dial.* Konkani, Goanese [gom], 369

Standard Lebanese Arabic, *dial.* Arabic, North Levantine Spoken [apc], 453

Standard Lugbara, *alt. dial.* Lugbara [lgg], 211

Standard Maithili, *dial.* Maithili [mai], 373

Standard Malay, *alt.* Malay [mly], 455, 324, 436

Standard Maltese, *dial.* Maltese [mlt], 547

Standard Marwari, *alt. dial.* Marwari [rwr], 375

Standard Muna, *dial.* Muna [mnb], 431

Standard Oriya, *alt. dial.* Oriya [ori], 382

Standard Somali, *alt.* Somali [som], 185, 119, 136

Standard Swedish, *dial.* Swedish [swe], 535

Standard Thai, *alt.* Thai [tha], 517

Stang, *dial.* Biatah [bth], 459

Star, *alt.* Gedaged [gdd], 599

Star Harbour, *alt. dial.* Owa [stn], 637

Star-Ragetta, *alt.* Gedaged [gdd], 599

State of Mexico Otomi, *alt.* Otomi, Estado de México [ots], 272

Statia Creole English, *dial.* Netherlands Antilles Creole English [vic], 282

St'at'imcets, *alt.* Lillooet [lil], 238

Stellaquo, *dial.* Carrier, Southern [caf], 236

Stellingwerfs [stl], 549

Stellingwerfstellingwarfs, *alt.* Stellingwerfs [stl], 549

Stem Baga, *alt.* Baga Sitemu [bsp], 128

Stenggang Jagoi, *dial.* Jagoi [sne], 459

Steppe Bashkir, *alt. dial.* Bashkir [bak], 553

Steppe Crimean, *alt. dial.* Crimean Turkish [crh], 521, 518, 532, 551

Stieng, Budeh [stt], 526

Stieng, Bulo [sti], 526, 326

Stimul, *alt.* Paiwan [pwn], 511

Stockbridge, *dial.* Mohegan-Montauk-Narragansett [mof], 305

Stod, *alt.* Stod Bhoti [sbu], 387
     dial. Stod Bhoti [sbu], 387

Stod Bhoti [sbu], 387

Stod-Kad, *alt.* Stod Bhoti [sbu], 387

Stokavian, *alt. dial.* Serbian [srp], 557

Stoney [sto], 241

Stoney Creek, *dial.* Carrier, Southern [caf], 236

Stoney River, *dial.* Tanaina [tfn], 308

Stony, *alt.* Stoney [sto], 241

Stotpa, *alt.* Changthang [cna], 358

Straits, *alt.* Salish, Straits [str], 241, 307

Straits Dobel, *dial.* Dobel [kvo], 397

Straits Malay, *alt.* Malay, Baba [mbf], 509, 455

Straits Salish, *see* Salish, Straits [str], 241, 307

Strieng, *alt.* Trieng [stg], 527

Striped Hmong, *alt. dial.* Hmong Daw [mww], 334, 450, 514

Striped Karen, *alt.* Yinchia [yin], 467

Su, *alt.* Isu [szv], 63

Suruí de Rondônia, *alt.* Suruí [sru], 232

Suruí do Jiparaná, *alt.* Suruí [sru], 232

Suruí do Pará [mdz], 232

Suruviri, *alt. dial.* Ashkun [ask], 315

Suruwahá, *alt.* Suruahá [swx], 232

Suryana, *alt.* Siriano [sri], 232

Süryani, *alt.* Turoyo [tru], 520

Suryaya, *alt.* Syriac [syc], 519

Suryaya Swadaya, *alt.* Assyrian Neo-Aramaic [aii], 442, 510

Suryoyo, *alt.* Mlahsö [lhs], 510
alt. Syriac [syc], 519
alt. Turoyo [tru], 520, 510

Sus, *alt. dial.* Tachelhit [shi], 39

Susa, *dial.* Azerbaijani, North [azj], 319

Sushen, *alt.* Nanai [gld], 341

Susiua, *alt.* Tachelhit [shi], 146
dial. Tachelhit [shi], 39

Susoo, *alt.* Susu [sus], 130, 184

Susquehanna, *alt.* Susquehannock [sqn], 308

Susquehannock [sqn], 308

Sussex, *dial.* English [eng], 565

Susu [sus], 130, 184

Susuami [ssu], 626

Suthu, *alt.* Sotho, Southern [sot], 137, 186

Suti, *dial.* Jagoi [sne], 459

Suto, *alt.* Sotho, Southern [sot], 137, 186

Sutsilvan-Hinterrhein, *alt. dial.* Romansch [roh], 562

Sutu, *alt.* Ngoni [ngo], 202, 148

Suundi [sdj], 90

Suundi de Kimongo, *alt.* Suundi [sdj], 90

Suvalkietiskai, *dial.* Lithuanian [lit], 546

Suwa, *alt.* Arabic, Chadian Spoken [shu], 78
dial. Amba [rwm], 210

Suwannakhet, *alt. dial.* Lao [lao], 445

Suwawa [swu], 433

Suwawa-Bunda, *alt.* Suwawa [swu], 433

Suwurti, *alt. dial.* Kanuri, Tumari [krt], 152

Suyá [suy], 232

Svan [sva], 352

Svanuri, *alt.* Svan [sva], 352

Svea, *dial.* Swedish [swe], 562

Svensk Rommani, *alt.* Romani, Tavringer [rmu], 561, 550

Svenska, *alt.* Swedish [swe], 562

Swabian [swg], 540

Swabou, *dial.* Tso [ldp], 176

Swaga, *dial.* Nande [nnb], 105

Swagup, *alt.* Ngala [nud], 618

Swahili [swh], 205, 55, 136, 146, 149, 185, 186, 212

Swahili, Congo [swc], 108

Swaka, *dial.* Lala-Bisa [leb], 214, 102

Swampy Cree, *see* Cree, Swampy [csw], 236

Swangla, *alt.* Pattani [lae], 383

Swara, *alt.* Sora [srb], 387

Swat Khowar, *dial.* Khowar [khw], 486

Swati [ssw], 197, 149, 186

Swatow, *alt. dial.* Chinese, Min Nan [nan], 514

Swazi, *alt.* Swati [ssw], 197, 149, 186

Swedish [swe], 562, 535

Swedish Sign Language [swl], 562

Swe'nga, *alt.* Yamba [yam], 73

Sweta, *dial.* Kuria [kuj], 200, 134

Swina, *pej. alt.* Shona [sna], 216

Swinomish, *alt.* Skagit [ska], 308

Swiss-French Sign Language [ssr], 563

Swiss-German Sign Language [sgg], 563

Swiss-Italian Sign Language [slf], 563

Swose, *alt.* Bassossi [bsi], 58

Sya, *alt. dial.* Bobo Madaré, Southern [bwq], 49
dial. Bobo Madaré, Northern [bbo], 141

Syabéré, *dial.* Bobo Madaré, Southern [bwq], 49

Syan, *dial.* Masaba [myx], 211

Syang, *alt. dial.* Thakali [ths], 480

Syangja Gurung, *alt. dial.* Gurung, Western [gvr], 471

Syémou, *alt.* Siamou [sif], 54

Syempire, *alt.* Senoufo, Shempire [seb], 95

Syenara, *alt.* Senoufo, Syenara [shz], 144

Syenara Senoufo, *see* Senoufo, Syenara [shz], 144

Syenere, *alt.* Senoufo, Cebaara [sef], 94

Syer, *dial.* Karaboro, Western [kza], 52

Syer-Tenyer, *alt.* Karaboro, Western [kza], 52

Syiagha, *alt.* Awyu, Edera [awy], 412
alt. Awyu, South [aws], 412

Sylheti [syl], 322, 388

Sylheti Bangla, *alt.* Sylheti [syl], 388

Sylheti Bengali, *alt.* Sylheti [syl], 388

Sylhetti, *alt.* Sylheti [syl], 322, 388

Sylhetti Bangla, *alt.* Sylheti [syl], 322

Syloti, *alt.* Sylheti [syl], 322, 388

Syloty, *alt.* Sylheti [syl], 322, 388

Sylt, *alt. dial.* Frisian, Northern [frr], 538

Sym, *dial.* Evenki [evn], 504

Symiarta, *alt.* Sinyar [sys], 86

Synteng, *alt. dial.* Pnar [pbv], 384

Syria, *dial.* Armenian [hye], 318

Syriac [syc], 519

Syrien, *alt. dial.* Armenian [hye], 318

Syrmia, *alt. dial.* Albanian, Tosk [als], 529

Syro-Lebanese Arabic, *alt.* Arabic, North Levantine Spoken [apc], 510, 453

Syro-Mesopotamian Arabic, *alt.* Arabic, North Mesopotamian Spoken [ayp], 510

Syro-Mesopotamian Vernacular Arabic, *alt.* Arabic, North Mesopotamian Spoken [ayp], 442, 518

Syryoyo, *alt.* Turoyo [tru], 520, 510

Syuba, *alt.* Kagate [syw], 472

Szeak-Bagili, *alt.* Gedaged [gdd], 599

Szeged, *dial.* Hungarian Sign Language [hsh], 542

Székely, *dial.* Hungarian [hun], 542

Szi, *alt.* Zaiwa [atb], 349

Szinca, *alt.* Xinca [xin], 256

T-Oy, *alt.* Ta'oih, Upper [tth], 527

T-Valley, *alt.* Eipomek [eip], 414

T. Khullen, *dial.* Naga, Maram [nma], 378

Ta, *alt.* Mubami [tsx], 615

Ta Hoi, *alt.* Ta'oih, Upper [tth], 453, 527

Ta Hua Miao, *alt.* Hmong, Northeastern Dian [hmd], 334

Ta Hwa Miao, *alt.* Hmong, Northeastern Dian [hmd], 334

Ta Sara, *alt.* Sara Kaba [sbz], 77

Tà Sàra, *alt.* Kaba Deme [kwg], 81

Ta-Ang Palaung, *alt.* Palaung, Shwe [pll], 466, 342

Ta-Oi, *alt.* Ta'oih, Upper [tth], 453

Tà-Oi, *alt.* Ta'oih, Upper [tth], 527

Ta-Oy, *alt.* Ta'oih, Upper [tth], 453

Ta-Rieng, *alt.* Trieng [stg], 527

Taa, *alt.* Pamona [bcx], 432
alt. dial. Pamona [bcx], 432
dial. Kaili, Ledo [lew], 429

Taabwa [tap], 108, 215

Ta'adjio, *alt.* Tajio [tdj], 433

Taai, *dial.* Saisiyat [xsy], 512

Ta'am, *dial.* Kei [kei], 399

Taan, *dial.* Yaouré [yre], 96

Taaon, *alt.* Digaro-Mishmi [mhu], 360

Taar Shamyan, *alt.* Sinyar [sys], 86

Taareyo, *alt.* Fulfulde, Adamawa [fub], 61, 80

Taataal, *alt.* Bon Gula [glc], 79

Taba-Damey-Bikha, *alt.* Lhokpu [lhp], 323

Tabaa Zapotec, *see* Zapotec, Tabaa [zat], 280

Tabajari, *dial.* Carib [car], 311

Tabanan, *alt. dial.* Bali [ban], 391

Tabanya, *alt.* Krongo [kgo], 192

Tabar, *alt.* Mandara [tbf], 612
dial. Mandara [tbf], 612

Tabare, *dial.* Sinasina [sst], 624

Tabaru [tby], 404

Tabasaran, *alt.* Tabassaran [tab], 555

Tabasarantsy, *alt.* Tabassaran [tab], 555

Tabasco Aztec, *alt.* Nahuatl, Tabasco [nhc], 272

Tabasco Chontal, *see* Chontal, Tabasco [chf], 262

Tabasco Nahuatl, *see* Nahuatl, Tabasco [nhc], 272

Tabasco Zoque, *see* Zoque, Tabasco [zoq], 282

Tabassaran [tab], 555

Tabeba, *alt.* Tapeba [tbb], 232

Tabehua, *dial.* Zapotec, Zoogocho [zpq], 281

Tabele, *alt.* Ndebele [nde], 216, 48

Tabi, *alt.* Gaam [tbi], 190
alt. Tabla [tnm], 423

Tabilong, *alt.* Tebilung [tgb], 458

Tabla [tnm], 423

Tableng, *dial.* Naga, Konyak [nbe], 378

Tabo [knv], 626

Tabojan, *alt.* Tawoyan [twy], 395

Tabojan Tongka, *alt.* Tawoyan [twy], 395

Taboro, *dial.* Sinaugoro [snc], 624

Taboroma, *alt. dial.* Acipa, Eastern [acp], 153

Tabotiro Jejea, *alt.* Macuna [myy], 246

Taboyan, *alt.* Tawoyan [twy], 395

Tabri, *alt.* Mazanderani [mzn], 441

Tabriak [tzx], 626

Tabriz, *dial.* Azerbaijani, South [azb], 438

Tabu, *alt.* Elseng [mrf], 414
dial. Naga, Konyak [nbe], 378

Tabuid, *alt.* Tawbuid, Eastern [bnj], 502

Tabukan, *alt. dial.* Sangir [sxn], 432

Tabukang, *alt. dial.* Sangir [sxn], 432

Tabulahan, *dial.* Aralle-Tabulahan [atq], 427

Tabun, *alt. dial.* Lundayeh [lnd], 460

Tabuyan, *alt.* Tawoyan [twy], 395

Tabwa, *alt.* Taabwa [tap], 108, 215

Tac Cui, *alt. dial.* Chut [scb], 522

Tacahua Mixtec, *see* Mixtec, Tacahua [xtt], 269

Tacana [tna], 224

Tacana Mam, *alt.* Tacanec [mtz], 274

Tacaná Mam, *alt.* Tacanec [mtz], 256

Tacanec [mtz], 256, 274

Tacaneco, *alt.* Tacanec [mtz], 274

Tacawit, *alt.* Tachawit [shy], 39

Tacep, *alt. dial.* Acipa, Western [awc], 153

Tachawit [shy], 39

Tachelhit [shi], 146, 39

Tachie, *dial.* Carrier [crx], 236

Tachilhit, *alt.* Tachelhit [shi], 146, 39

Tacho, *alt.* Tocho [taz], 196

Tachom, *alt.* Hre [hre], 523

Tachon, *alt. dial.* Bukusu [bxk], 132

Tachoni, *alt. dial.* Bukusu [bxk], 132

Tactic Pokomchí, *alt.* Poqomchi', Eastern [poh], 256

Tactile Sign Language, *dial.* American Sign Language [ase], 298

Tacuate, *pej. alt.* Mixtec, Santa María Zacatepec [mza], 268

Ta'da, *alt. dial.* Kalumpang [kli], 429

Tadaksahak [dsq], 144

Tadavi, *alt.* Dhanki [dhn], 360

Tadghaq, *dial.* Tamasheq, Kidal [taq], 55

Tadha, *dial.* Lendu [led], 102

Tadhaq, *dial.* Tamasheq [taq], 144

Tadianan, *alt.* Tadyawan [tdy], 502

Tadjio, *alt.* Tajio [tdj], 433

Tado, *alt.* Lindu [klw], 430
dial. Aja [ajg], 42, 206
dial. Kaili, Ledo [lew], 429

Tadou, *alt. dial.* Aja [ajg], 42, 206

Tadvi Bhil, *alt.* Dhanki [dhn], 360

Tadyawan [tdy], 502

Tadzhik, *alt.* Tajiki [tgk], 513

Tadzik, *alt.* Sarikoli [srh], 343

Ta'e, *alt.* Toraja-Sa'dan [sda], 434

Tae' [rob], 428
alt. Toraja-Sa'dan [sda], 434
alt. dial. Mamasa [mqj], 431

Tae' Tae', *alt.* Tae' [rob], 428

Taechew, *alt. dial.* Chinese, Min Nan [nan], 508

Taemi, *dial.* Tami [tmy], 626

Taena, *alt.* Makasar [mak], 430

Taeq, *alt.* Tae' [rob], 428

Tafi [tcd], 128

Tafire, *dial.* Senoufo, Tagwana [tgw], 95

Tafota Baruga, *dial.* Baruga [bjz], 592

Tafresh, *dial.* Ashtiani [atn], 438

Tafwap, *dial.* Nicobarese, Southern [nik], 381

Tagabawa [bgs], 502

Tagabawa Bagobo, *alt.* Tagabawa [bgs], 502

Tagabawa Manobo, *alt.* Tagabawa [bgs], 502

Tagabili, *pej. alt.* Tboli [tbl], 502

Tagakaolo, *alt.* Kalagan, Tagakaulu [klg], 497

Tagakaulu Kalagan, *see* Kalagan, Tagakaulu [klg], 497

Tagakawanan, *dial.* Maguindanao [mdh], 498

Tagal, *dial.* Tagal Murut [mvv], 458, 395

Tagal Murut [mvv], 458, 395

Tagalagad, *alt.* Blaan, Koronadal [bpr], 493

Tagale, *alt.* Tegali [ras], 195

Tagalisa, *dial.* Lisela [lcl], 400

Tagalog [tgl], 502

Tagara, *alt.* Duruwa [pci], 361
dial. Senoufo, Cebaara [sef], 94

Tagargrent [oua], 40

Tagaro, *alt. dial.* Dusun, Central [dtp], 456

Tagau, *dial.* Pashayi, Southwest [psh], 317

Tagaur, *dial.* Osetin [oss], 352, 519

Tagba, *alt.* Sénoufo, Sìcìté [sep], 54, 144
alt. Tagbu [tbm], 108

Tagbana, *alt.* Senoufo, Tagwana [tgw], 95

Tagbanua, *alt.* Tagbanwa [tbw], 502

Tagbanwa [tbw], 502

Tagbanwa, Calamian [tbk], 502

Tagbanwa, Central [tgt], 502

Tagbari, *dial.* Senoufo, Cebaara [sef], 94

Tagbo, *alt.* Mambila, Cameroon [mcu], 66
alt. Tagbu [tbm], 108
alt. dial. Banda, Togbo-Vara [tor], 97, 74, 188

Tagboussikan, *alt. dial.* Jula [dyu], 93

Tagbu [tbm], 108

Tagbwali, *alt. dial.* Banda, Togbo-Vara [tor], 74

Tagdal [tda], 152

Tage, *alt.* Kreye [xre], 229

Taggal, *alt. dial.* Tagal Murut [mvv], 458, 395

Taghdansh, *alt. dial.* Soninke [snk], 131

Tagin, *dial.* Nisi [dap], 381

Taginambur, *alt. dial.* Dusun, Central [dtp], 456

Tagish [tgx], 242

Tagkhul, *alt.* Naga, Tangkhul [nmf], 380

Tagle, *alt. dial.* Kadaru [kdu], 191

Tagoi [tag], 195
  dial. Tagoi [tag], 195

Tagol, *alt. dial.* Tagal Murut [mvv], 458, 395

Tagota, *dial.* Meriam [ulk], 574

Tagouna, *alt.* Senoufo, Tagwana [tgw], 95

Tagoy, *alt.* Tagoi [tag], 195

Taguaca, *alt.* Sumo-Mayangna [sum], 283

Tagul, *alt. dial.* Tagal Murut [mvv], 458, 395

Tagula, *alt.* Sudest [tgo], 625

Tagulandang, *alt. dial.* Sangir [sxn], 432

Tagwana, *alt.* Senoufo, Tagwana [tgw], 95

Tagwana Senoufo, *see* Senoufo, Tagwana [tgw], 95

Tahaggart, *alt. dial.* Tamahaq, Tahaggart [thv], 37, 139, 152

Tahaggart Tamahaq, *see* Tamahaq, Tahaggart [thv], 37, 139, 152

Tahamba, *dial.* Bandi [bza], 137

Tahari, *alt.* Guhu-Samane [ghs], 599

Tahit, *alt.* Tehit [kps], 424

Tahitian [tah], 581

Tahltan [tht], 242

Tahoua, *alt.* Tamajaq [ttq], 144
  alt. Tamajaq, Tawallammat [ttq], 152

Tahoua Tamajeq, *alt.* Tamajaq, Tawallammat [ttq], 152, 175

Tahuerh, *alt.* Daur [dta], 331, 461

Tahulandang, *alt. dial.* Sangir [sxn], 432

Tahup, *alt. dial.* Jagoi [sne], 459

Tahur, *alt.* Daur [dta], 331, 461

Tahuta, *dial.* Marquesan, South [mqm], 581

Tai [taw], 626
  alt. Jiamao [jio], 336
  alt. Tee [tkq], 175

Tai Ahom, *alt.* Ahom [aho], 353

Tai Blanc, *alt.* Tai Dón [twh], 526, 453

Tai Boko, *dial.* Baikeno [bkx], 350

Tai Chuang, *alt.* Zhuang, Northern [ccx], 349

Tai Cung, *alt.* Tai Ya [cuu], 344

Tai Daeng [tyr], 526, 453

Tai Dam [blt], 526, 453, 517

Tai Dehong, *alt.* Tai Nüa [tdd], 344

Tai Deng, *alt.* Tai Daeng [tyr], 526, 453

Tai Do [tyj], 526
  alt. Tai Dam [blt], 526

Tai Dón [twh], 526, 453

Tai Hang Tong [thc], 527

Tai Hongjin [tiz], 344

Tai Islam, *alt. dial.* Thai, Southern [sou], 517

Tai Ka, *alt. dial.* Tai Nüa [tdd], 344

Tai Kam Ti, *alt.* Khamti [kht], 465

Tai Kao, *alt.* Tai Dón [twh], 526, 453

Tai Kham Ti, *alt.* Khamti [kht], 367

Tai Khamyang, *alt.* Khamyang [ksu], 367

Tai Khang, *alt.* Kang [kyp], 450

Tai Khun, *alt.* Khün [kkh], 465, 515

Tai Kong, *alt.* Tai Nüa [tdd], 467

Tai Lai, *alt.* Tai Dón [twh], 526, 453

Tai Laka, *alt.* Lakkia [lbc], 338

Tai Lao, *alt.* Lao [lao], 445

Tai Lati, *alt.* Lachi [lbt], 524, 338

Tai Le, *alt.* Tai Nüa [tdd], 344

Tai Loi [tlq], 467, 453
  dial. Tai Loi [tlq], 467, 453

Tai Long [thi], 453
  alt. dial. Shan [shn], 467

Tai Lu, *alt.* Lü [khb], 339, 465, 515, 524

Tai Luang, *alt.* Shan [shn], 467, 517

Tai Lue, *alt.* Lü [khb], 515

Tai Maen, *alt.* Tai Mène [tmp], 453

Tai Man, *alt.* Tai Mène [tmp], 453
  alt. Tai Nüa [tdd], 517

Tai Man Thanh, *alt.* Tai Thanh [tmm], 527

Tai Mao, *alt.* Tai Nüa [tdd], 344
  alt. dial. Shan [shn], 467

Tai Men, *alt.* Tai Mène [tmp], 453

Tai Mene, *alt.* Tai Mène [tmp], 453

Tai Mène [tmp], 453

Tai Mueai, *alt. dial.* Tai Dam [blt], 526

Tai Muei, *alt. dial.* Tai Dam [blt], 453

Tai Muoi, *dial.* Tai Dam [blt], 453

Tai Neua, *alt.* Tai Nüa [tdd], 344, 453, 467, 517

Tai Noir, *alt.* Tai Dam [blt], 526, 453, 517

Tai Nü, *alt.* Tai Nüa [tdd], 344

Tai Nüa [tdd], 344, 453, 467, 517

Tai Nue, *alt.* Tai Nüa [tdd], 344

Tai Nuea, *alt.* Tai Nüa [tdd], 453

Tai Nung, *alt.* Nung [nut], 525

Tai Nya, *alt.* Thai, Northern [nod], 517

Tai Pao [tpo], 453

Tai Pong, *dial.* Tai Nüa [tdd], 344

Tai Rouge, *alt.* Tai Daeng [tyr], 526

Tai Sa', *alt.* Achang [acn], 456

Tai Sa Pa, *alt.* Tày Sa Pa [tys], 527

Tai Sek, *alt.* Saek [skb], 452, 517

Tai Shan, *alt.* Shan [shn], 467, 517

Tai Tac, *alt.* Tày Tac [tyt], 527

Tai Tak Bai, *alt. dial.* Thai, Southern [sou], 517

Tai Thanh [tmm], 527

Tai Tho, *alt.* Tày [tyz], 527

Tai Turung, *alt.* Turung [try], 389

Tai Wang, *dial.* Thai, Northern [nod], 517

Tai Ya [cuu], 344

Tai Yai, *alt.* Shan [shn], 467

Tai Yay, *alt.* Shan [shn], 517

Tai-Chung, *alt.* Tai Ya [cuu], 344

Tai-Cung, *alt.* Tai Ya [cuu], 344

Tai-Khamti, *alt.* Khamti [kht], 465

Tai-Khuen, *alt.* Khün [kkh], 465

Tai-Kong, *alt.* Tai Nüa [tdd], 344

Tai-Le, *alt.* Tai Nüa [tdd], 344

Tai-Maen, *alt.* Tai Mène [tmp], 453

Taiak, *alt.* Kapin [tbx], 605

Taiap [gpn], 626

Taibano, *alt. dial.* Barasana [bsn], 243

Taibei Mandarin, *dial.* Chinese, Mandarin [cmn], 511

Taigi, *dial.* Mator [mtm], 505

Taih-Long, *alt.* Teressa [tef], 388

Taihu, *dial.* Chinese, Wu [wuu], 330

Taijyal, *alt.* Atayal [tay], 511

Taikaku, *dial.* Mentawai [mwv], 436

Taikat [aos], 423

Tailangi, *alt.* Telugu [tel], 388

Tailoi, *alt.* Tai Loi [tlq], 467, 453

Tailung, *alt.* Turung [try], 389

Taimani, *dial.* Aimaq [aiq], 315

Taimouri, *alt. dial.* Aimaq [aiq], 315

Taimuri, *dial.* Aimaq [aiq], 315

Tain-Daware, *alt. dial.* Binandere [bhg], 593

Taina, *alt.* Owiniga [owi], 620

Tainae [ago], 626

Tainan, *dial.* Taiwan Sign Language [tss], 512

Tainbour, *alt. dial.* Dinka, Southwestern [dik], 190

Taino [tnq], 221

Taiof, *dial.* Saposa [sps], 623

Taior, *alt.* Thayore [thd], 576
Taipei, *dial.* Taiwan Sign Language [tss], 512
Taipi, *dial.* Naga, Tase [nst], 380
Tair, *alt.* Panchpargania [tdb], 382
Tairong, *alt.* Turung [try], 389
Tairora, *alt.* Tairora, North [tbg], 626
   dial. Tairora, North [tbg], 626
Tairora, North [tbg], 626
Tairora, South [omw], 626
Tairuma [uar], 626
|**Taise**, *alt. dial.* Shua [shg], 48
Taishan, *alt. dial.* Chinese, Yue [yue], 331
Taita [dav], 136
Taitung, *alt. dial.* Amis [ami], 511
Taivoan, *dial.* Siraya [fos], 512
Taiwaeno, *alt. dial.* Barasana [bsn], 243
Taiwan Kejia, *alt. dial.* Chinese, Hakka [hak], 329
Taiwan Sign Language [tss], 512
Taiwan Ziran Shouyu, *alt.* Taiwan Sign Language [tss], 512
Taiwanese, *alt. dial.* Chinese, Min Nan [nan], 511
Taiwano, *dial.* Barasana [bsn], 243
Taiyal, *alt.* Atayal [tay], 511
Taiyanghe, *dial.* Guanyinqiao [jiq], 333
Taizhou, *dial.* Chinese, Wu [wuu], 330
Ta'izzi, *dial.* Arabic, Ta'izzi-Adeni Spoken [acq], 528
Ta'izzi-Adeni Spoken Arabic, *see* Arabic, Ta'izzi-Adeni Spoken [acq], 528, 109
Tajag, *alt.* Tamajaq [ttq], 144
Taje [pee], 433
Tajiji Arabic, *alt.* Arabic, Tajiki Spoken [abh], 513
Tajik, *alt.* Farsi, Eastern [prs], 484
   alt. Sarikoli [srh], 343
   pej. alt. Fars, Southwestern [fay], 439
Tajiki [tgk], 513
   alt. Sarikoli [srh], 343
   alt. dial. Farsi, Eastern [prs], 315
Tajiki Persian, *alt.* Tajiki [tgk], 513
Tajiki Spoken Arabic, *see* Arabic, Tajiki Spoken [abh], 315, 513
Tajio [tdj], 433
Tajkat, *alt.* Taikat [aos], 423
Tajpuri, *alt.* Rajbanshi [rjb], 384, 322
Tajpuria, *alt.* Rajbanshi [rjb], 477
Tajuasohn [tja], 139
Tajuason, *alt.* Tajuasohn [tja], 139
Tajumulco Mam, *see* Mam, Tajumulco [mpf], 255
Tajuoso, *alt.* Tajuasohn [tja], 139
Tajuosohn, *alt.* Tajuasohn [tja], 139

Tak Bai, *dial.* Thai, Southern [sou], 517
Tak Meo, *alt.* Hmong Njua [blu], 450, 463, 523
Tak Miao, *alt.* Hmong Njua [blu], 334, 514
   dial. Hmong Njua [blu], 334
Taka, *alt. dial.* Lamaholot [slp], 408
Takale, *alt.* Parbate, Western [kjl], 477
   dial. Parbate, Western [kjl], 477
Takale Kham, *alt.* Parbate, Western [kjl], 477
Takam, *alt.* Chakma [ccp], 321, 358
   alt. Miri [mrg], 376
Takama, *dial.* Nyamwezi [nym], 203
Takamanda, *alt.* Denya [anv], 60
   dial. Denya [anv], 60
Takana, *alt.* Tacana [tna], 224
Takankar, *alt.* Pardhi [pcl], 383
Takanoon, *alt.* Mon [mnw], 516
Takapan, *dial.* Paluan [plz], 458
Takaraya, *alt. dial.* Siraya [fos], 512
Takari, *dial.* Pardhi [pcl], 383
Takat, *alt. dial.* Tyap [kcg], 176
Takawa-Béngoro, *dial.* Day [dai], 80
Takaya, *alt. dial.* Lere [gnh], 168
Takazze-Setiit, *dial.* Kunama [kun], 112
Takbanuao, *alt. dial.* Bunun [bnn], 511
Takebakha, *alt. dial.* Bunun [bnn], 511
Takelma [tkm], 308
Takestan, *alt. dial.* Takestani [tks], 441
Takestani [tks], 441
Taketodo, *alt. dial.* Bunun [bnn], 511
Taketomi, *dial.* Yaeyama [rys], 447
Takevatan, *alt. dial.* Bunun [bnn], 511
Taki-Taki, *alt.* Sranan [srn], 296
Takia [tbc], 626
   alt. Pardhi [pcl], 383
Takibakha, *alt. dial.* Bunun [bnn], 511
Takilma, *alt.* Takelma [tkm], 308
Takistani, *alt.* Takestani [tks], 441
Takitudu, *alt. dial.* Bunun [bnn], 511
Takivatan, *alt. dial.* Bunun [bnn], 511
Takonan, *alt.* Atayal [tay], 511
Takopulan, *dial.* Bunun [bnn], 511
Takpa [tkk], 344
   alt. dial. Nupe-Nupe-Tako [nup], 171
   alt. dial. Tibetan [bod], 388

Takpasyeeri, *dial.* Senoufo, Cebaara [sef], 94
Taku, *alt.* Lipo [lpo], 339
   alt. Takuu [nho], 626
Taku Lisu, *alt.* Lipo [lpo], 339
Takua [tkz], 527
Takudh, *alt. dial.* Gwich'in [gwi], 237, 301
Takum, *dial.* Jukun Takum [jbu], 63, 165
   dial. Kpan [kpk], 167
Takuna, *alt.* Tucano [tuo], 233
Takuu [nho], 626
Takwama, *alt.* Kwama [kmq], 116
Takwane [tke], 149
Tal [tal], 175
   alt. Tulu [tcy], 389
Tala [tak], 175
   alt. Mághdì [gmd], 169
   alt. Wemale, South [tlw], 405
   dial. Aja [ajg], 42, 206
   dial. Koho [kpm], 524
Tala Ingod, *dial.* Manobo, Matigsalug [mbt], 499
Tala'ai, *dial.* Molima [mox], 614
Talahundra, *dial.* Kalanga [kck], 216, 47
Tala'i, *dial.* Sahu [saj], 403
Talai [tle], 136
Talaindji, *alt.* Dhalandji [dhl], 569
Talaing, *alt.* Mon [mnw], 466, 516
Talamanca, *alt.* Bribri [bzd], 249
Talandi, *alt.* Dhalandji [dhl], 569
Talandji, *alt.* Dhalandji [dhl], 569
Talang, *dial.* Kerinci [kvr], 436
Talang Padang, *dial.* Pesisir, Southern [pec], 437
Talangee, *alt.* Dhalandji [dhl], 569
Talangit, *dial.* Altai, Southern [alt], 503
Talangit-Tolos, *alt. dial.* Altai, Southern [alt], 503
Talantang, *dial.* Dusun, Sugut [kzs], 456
Talasa, *alt. dial.* Tumtum [tbr], 196
Talassa, *dial.* Tumtum [tbr], 196
Talatui, *alt.* Miwok, Southern Sierra [skd], 305
Talau, *alt. dial.* Logorik [liu], 192
Talaud [tld], 433
Talaut, *alt.* Talaud [tld], 433
Talavia, *alt.* Dubli [dub], 360
Tale, *dial.* Kare [kbn], 76, 63
Talene, *alt. dial.* Farefare [gur], 124
Taleng, *alt.* Mon [mnw], 516
Talensi, *alt. dial.* Farefare [gur], 124
Talesh, *alt.* Talysh [tly], 320, 442
Taleshi, *alt.* Talysh [tly], 442
Tali, *alt. dial.* Kare [kbn], 76
Taliabo, *alt.* Taliabu [tlv], 404

dial. Tamil [tam], 388
Tamil Muthuvan, *alt. dial.* Muthuvan [muv], 377
Tamili, *alt.* Tamil [tam], 388
Tamilouw, *alt.* Sepa [spb], 404
Tamiso, *alt. dial.* Limba, West-Central [lia], 183
Tamkhungnyuo, *dial.* Naga, Konyak [nbe], 378
Tamki [tax], 86
Tamlu, *alt.* Naga, Phom [nph], 379
Tamlu Naga, *alt.* Naga, Phom [nph], 379
Tamma, *alt.* Nama [naq], 150, 48, 186
Tamnim, *alt.* Citak, Tamnim [tml], 413
Tamnim Citak, *see* Citak, Tamnim [tml], 413
Tamok, *alt.* Tama [tma], 86
Tamongobo, *alt.* Tama [tma], 86
Tamorkhole, *alt. dial.* Limbu [lif], 474
Tamot, *alt.* Tama [tma], 86
Tampasok, *alt.* Dusun, Tempasuk [tdu], 456
Tampassuk, *alt.* Dusun, Tempasuk [tdu], 456
Tampasuk, *alt.* Dusun, Tempasuk [tdu], 456
Tampele, *alt.* Tampulma [tpm], 128
Tamphuan, *alt.* Tampuan [tpu], 326
Tampias Lobu, *see* Lobu, Tampias [low], 457
Tampiwi, *dial.* Cuiba [cui], 244
Tamplima, *alt.* Tampulma [tpm], 128
Tampole, *alt.* Tampulma [tpm], 128
Tampolem, *alt.* Tampulma [tpm], 128
Tampolense, *alt.* Tampulma [tpm], 128
Tamprusi, *alt.* Tampulma [tpm], 128
Tampuan [tpu], 326
Tampuen, *alt.* Tampuan [tpu], 326
Tampulma [tpm], 128
Tampuon, *alt.* Tampuan [tpu], 326
Tampur, *dial.* Gayo [gay], 430
Tamsangmu, *dial.* Lepcha [lep], 372, 323, 474
Tamu Kyi, *alt.* Gurung, Western [gvr], 471
dial. Gurung, Eastern [ggn], 471
Tamudes, *alt.* Tomedes [toe], 248
Tamulté de las Sábanas Chontal, *dial.* Chontal, Tabasco [chf], 262
Tamun, *alt.* Chrau [crw], 522
dial. Chrau [crw], 522
Tana, *alt. dial.* Vale [vae], 78

dial. Sampang [rav], 478
Tana Ai, *dial.* Sika [ski], 409
Tana Righu, *dial.* Wejewa [wew], 410
Tana Toa, *dial.* Konjo, Coastal [kjc], 430
Tana Towa, *alt. dial.* Konjo, Coastal [kjc], 430
Tana-Lincha, *dial.* Quechua, Yauyos [qux], 292
Tanacross [tcb], 308
Tanaghai, *alt. dial.* Ghari [gri], 636
Tanah, *alt.* Amis [ami], 511
dial. Minangkabau [min], 436
Tanah Kunu, *alt.* Li'o [ljl], 408
Tanah Merah, *alt.* Tabla [tnm], 423
Tanahmerah [tcm], 423
Tanahmerah 2, *alt.* Tabla [tnm], 423
Tanaina [tfn], 308
Tanala, *dial.* Malagasy, Plateau [plt], 140
Tanan, *dial.* Rukai [dru], 512
Tanana, *alt.* Tanana, Lower [taa], 308
Tanana, Lower [taa], 308
Tanana, Upper [tau], 308, 242
Tanapag [tpv], 587
Tanaslamt, *alt. dial.* Tamasheq [taq], 144
alt. dial. Tamasheq, Kidal [taq], 55
Tanassfarwat, *dial.* Tamajeq, Tayart [thz], 152
Tanay-Paete, *dial.* Tagalog [tgl], 502
Tanchangya, *alt.* Tangchangya [tnv], 322
Tanda, *alt.* Lambadi [lmn], 372
dial. Lobala [loq], 103
Tandai-Nggaria, *dial.* Ghari [gri], 636
Tandam, *alt.* Dogon, Toro Tegu [dtt], 142
Tandanke, *alt.* Budik [tnr], 180
Tandek, *dial.* Kimaragang [kqr], 457
Tandia [tni], 423
Tando, *alt.* Ndolo [ndl], 105
Tandroy, *alt.* Malagasy, Tandroy-Mahafaly [tdx], 140
Tandroy-Mahafaly Malagasy, *see* Malagasy, Tandroy-Mahafaly [tdx], 140
Tandubas, *dial.* Sama, Southern [ssb], 500
Tane, *alt. dial.* Vale [vae], 78
Tanema [tnx], 638
Tanete, *alt. dial.* Bugis [bug], 428
Tang, *alt.* Sedang [sed], 526
dial. Bumthangkha [kjz], 323
dial. Limbum [lmp], 65

dial. Naga, Konyak [nbe], 378
Tanga, *alt.* Tangga [tgg], 627
dial. Tangga [tgg], 627
Tangago, *alt. dial.* Banda-Ndélé [bfl], 75, 188
Tang'ala, *dial.* Kabola [klz], 407
Tangalan, *alt.* Ketangalan [kae], 511
Tangale [tan], 175
Tangalto Lele, *dial.* Lele [llc], 129
Tangam, *dial.* Adi [adi], 353
Tangamma, *dial.* Waama [wwa], 46
Tangao, *alt.* Atayal [tay], 511
Tangara', *alt. dial.* Bookan [bnb], 456
Tangarare, *alt.* Ghari [gri], 636
Tangbago, *dial.* Banda-Ndélé [bfl], 75, 188
Tangbe, *dial.* Seke [skj], 478
Tangchangya [tnv], 322
Tangeta, *dial.* Biali [beh], 42
Tangetti, *alt.* Dyangadi [dyn], 570
Tangga [tgg], 627
Tanggal, *alt.* Dusun, Sugut [kzs], 456
Tanggaraq, *alt. dial.* Bookan [bnb], 456
Tanggu [tgu], 627
Tanggum, *alt.* Tanggu [tgu], 627
Tangi, *dial.* Nande [nnb], 105
Tangier, *dial.* Arabic, Moroccan Spoken [ary], 146
Tangir, *alt. dial.* Shina [scl], 488
Tangkhul, *alt.* Naga, Tangkhul [nmf], 380
Tangkhul Naga, *see* Naga, Tangkhul [nmf], 380
Tangko [tkx], 423
Tangkou, *alt.* Budong-Budong [bdx], 428
Tanglagan, *dial.* Agta, Dupaninan [duo], 490
Tanglapui, *alt.* Kula [tpg], 408
alt. Sawila [swt], 409
Tangle, *alt.* Tangale [tan], 175
Tangoa [tgp], 645
Tangsa, *alt.* Naga, Tase [nst], 466, 380
Tangsarr, *dial.* Rawang [raw], 466
Tangshewi [tnf], 318
Tangshuri, *alt.* Tangshewi [tnf], 318
Tangu, *alt.* Tanggu [tgu], 627
Tanguat [tbs], 627
Tani, *alt.* Maiani [tnh], 610
alt. Miani [pla], 613
Tanima, *alt.* Tanema [tnx], 638
Tanimbar Kei, *dial.* Kei [kei], 399
Tanimbili [tbe], 638
Tanimuca, *dial.* Tanimuca-Retuarã [tnc], 247
Tanimuca-Retuarã [tnc], 247

Tarok [yer], 175
Taroko [trv], 512
Tarom, *alt. dial.* Takestani [tks], 441
Taromi, Upper [tov], 442
Taron, *alt.* Rawang [raw], 466, 385
   dial. Rawang [raw], 466
Tarpia [suf], 423
   alt. dial. Tarpia [suf], 423
Tartar, *alt.* Tatar [tat], 556, 344
Tartu, *dial.* Estonian [est], 534, 534
Taru, *alt.* Karen, Lahta [kvt], 464
   alt. Taungyo [tco], 467
Taruku, *alt.* Taroko [trv], 512
Tarulakhi, *alt.* Karen, Lahta
   [kvt], 464
Tarumbal, *alt.* Bayali [bjy], 569
Taruna, *alt. dial.* Sangir [sxn], 432
Tarunggare, *alt.* Tunggare [trt], 424
Taruw, *alt. dial.* Burmese [mya], 462
Tarya, *alt.* Pongu [png], 173
   dial. Kamoro [kgq], 416
Tasaday, *dial.* Manobo, Cotabato
   [mta], 499
Tasawaq [twq], 152
Tase, *alt.* Naga, Tase [nst], 466
Tase Naga, *see* Naga, Tase
   [nst], 466, 380
Tasemboko, *alt.* Lengo [lgr], 637
Tasey, *alt.* Naga, Tase [nst], 466, 380
Tashelhait, *alt.* Tachelhit [shi], 39
Tashelhayt, *alt.* Tachelhit [shi], 39
Tashelheyt, *alt.* Tachelhit [shi], 146
Tashelhit, *alt.* Tachelhit [shi], 146,
   39
Tashilheet, *alt.* Tachelhit [shi], 146
Tashkent, *dial.* Uzbek, Northern
   [uzn], 346
Tashom, *alt. dial.* Chin, Falam
   [flm], 463
Tashon, *dial.* Chin, Falam [flm], 463
Tasi, *alt.* Halia [hla], 601
Tasi Feto, *alt. dial.* Tetun [tet], 410,
   351
Tasi Mane, *alt. dial.* Tetun [tet], 410,
   351
Tasiko, *dial.* Lewo [lww], 643
Tasing, *alt.* Campalagian [cml], 428
Tasiriki, *alt.* Akei [tsr], 640
Tasman, *alt.* Nukumanu [nuq], 619
Tasmate [tmt], 645
Tasoussit, *alt.* Tachelhit [shi], 146,
   39
Tat, Muslim [ttt], 320, 442, 556
Tata'er, *alt.* Tatar [tat], 344
Tataltepec Chatino, *see* Chatino,
   Tataltepec [cta], 260
Tatana [txx], 458
Tatana', *alt.* Tatana [txx], 458
Tatanaq, *alt.* Tatana [txx], 458
Tatar [tat], 556, 344, 563

Tatau, *dial.* Mandara [tbf], 612
Tate, *alt.* Kaki Ae [tbd], 604
   dial. Bine [bon], 593
Tati, *alt.* Kaki Ae [tbd], 604
   alt. Tat, Muslim [ttt], 320
   alt. Tsoa [hio], 48
   dial. Maithili [mai], 475
Tati Bushman, *alt.* Tsoa [hio], 48
Tatog, *alt.* Datooga [tcc], 198
Tatoga, *alt.* Datooga [tcc], 198
Tatsewalem, *alt.* Kwerba
   Mamberamo [xwr], 418
Tatsienlu, *alt. dial.* Tibetan
   [bod], 388
Tattara, *dial.* Yeskwa [yes], 178
Tattare, *pej. alt.* Romani, Tavringer
   [rmu], 561, 550
Tatu, *alt.* Estonian [est], 534
Taturu, *alt.* Datooga [tcc], 198
Tatutapuyo, *alt.* Tatuyo [tav], 247
Tatuyo [tav], 247
Tau, *alt.* Takuu [nho], 626
   alt. dial. Sotho, Northern [nso], 186
   dial. Kwanga [kwj], 608
Tau Oi, *alt.* Ta'oih, Upper [tth], 453,
   527
Tau Ubian, *alt. dial.* Sama, Southern
   [ssb], 458
Tauade [ttd], 627
Tauata, *alt.* Tauade [ttd], 627
Taubuid, *alt.* Tawbuid, Eastern
   [bnj], 502
Tauch, *alt. dial.* Cimbrian [cim], 543
Tauira, *alt. dial.* Mískito [miq], 282
Taulil [tuh], 627
   dial. Taulil [tuh], 627
Taulipang, *alt. dial.* Pemon
   [aoc], 312, 257
   dial. Pemon [aoc], 231
Taumako, *dial.* Pileni [piv], 637
Tauna, *dial.* Awa [awb], 591
Taung, *dial.* Sotho, Southern
   [sot], 186
Taungtu, *alt.* Karen, Pa'o [blk], 514
Taungyo [tco], 467
Taunita, *dial.* Teop [tio], 627
Taup, *alt. dial.* Jagoi [sne], 459
Taupota [tpa], 627
Taura, *alt. dial.* Lere [gnh], 168
Tauran, *alt.* Amis, Nataoran
   [ais], 511
Taurap, *alt.* Burmeso [bzu], 413
Taurepan, *alt. dial.* Pemon
   [aoc], 231
   dial. Pemon [aoc], 312, 257
Tause [tad], 424
   dial. Tause [tad], 424
Taushiro [trr], 293
Tausog, *alt.* Tausug [tsg], 502, 395,
   458

Tausug [tsg], 502, 395, 458
Tauu, *alt.* Takuu [nho], 626
Tauya [tya], 627
Tava, *alt. dial.* Hre [hre], 523
Tavalong-Vataan, *dial.* Amis
   [ami], 511
Tavara, *alt.* Tawala [tbo], 627
Tavast, *alt. dial.* Finnish [fin], 534
Tavdin, *alt. dial.* Mansi [mns], 505
Taveak, *dial.* Ambrym, Southeast
   [tvk], 640
Taveta [tvs], 136
Tavgi Samoyed, *alt.* Nganasan
   [nio], 506
Tavha-Tsindi, *dial.* Venda
   [ven], 187
Tavhatsindi, *dial.* Venda [ven], 217
Taviak, *alt. dial.* Ambrym, Southeast
   [tvk], 640
Tavola, *alt.* Vaghua [tva], 639
Tavoy, *dial.* Karen, Pwo Eastern
   [kjp], 464
Tavoya, *alt.* Taungyo [tco], 467
Tavoyan [tvn], 467
   alt. Taungyo [tco], 467
Tavringer Romani, *see* Romani,
   Tavringer [rmu], 561, 550
Tavro-Rumeic, *alt. dial.* Greek
   [ell], 564
Tavuki, *alt. dial.* Fijian [fij], 580
Tavula, *alt.* Vaghua [tva], 639
Tavytera, *alt.* Pai Tavytera [pta], 285
Taw Sug, *alt.* Tausug [tsg], 502, 395,
   458
Tawaelia, *alt.* Sedoa [tvw], 433
Tawaili-Sindue, *alt. dial.* Kaili,
   Ledo [lew], 429
Tawakoni, *dial.* Wichita [wic], 310
Tawala [tbo], 627
   alt. Tawara [twl], 149
Tawallammat Tamajaq, *see*
   Tamajaq, Tawallammat [ttq], 152,
   175
Tawallammat Tan Ataram, *dial.*
   Tamajaq [ttq], 144
   dial. Tamajaq, Tawallammat
   [ttq], 152
Tawallammat Tan Dannag, *dial.*
   Tamajaq, Tawallammat [ttq], 152
Tawallammet Tan Dannag, *dial.*
   Tamajaq [ttq], 144
Tawan, *dial.* Tagal Murut
   [mvv], 458, 395
Tawana, *dial.* Tswana [tsn], 48, 151,
   186
Tawang, *alt. dial.* Moinba
   [mob], 376
Tawanxte, *alt. dial.* Nambikuára,
   Northern [mbg], 230
Tawara [twl], 149

alt. Tawala [tbo], 627
Tawara-Chioco, *dial.* Tawara [twl], 149
Tawara-Daque, *dial.* Tawara [twl], 149
Tawarafa, *dial.* Owa [stn], 637
Tawari, *dial.* Gbagyi [gbr], 160
Tawau Murut, *alt.* Kalabakan [kve], 457
    alt. Serudung Murut [srk], 458
Tawbuid, Eastern [bnj], 502
Tawbuid, Western [twb], 502
Tawe-Tavoy, *alt.* Taungyo [tco], 467
Tawini, *alt. dial.* Isnag [isd], 496
Tawira, *dial.* Mískito [miq], 282
Tawit, *alt.* Itawit [itv], 496
Taworta [tbp], 424
Taworta-Aero, *alt.* Taworta [tbp], 424
Tawoyan [twy], 395
Tawoyan Dayak, *alt.* Tawoyan [twy], 395
Tawr, *alt.* Chin, Tawr [tcp], 463
Tawr Chin, *see* Chin, Tawr [tcp], 463
Tawu, *alt.* Yami [tao], 512
Taxmainite, *alt. dial.* Nambikuára, Northern [mbg], 230
Taxwensite, *alt. dial.* Nambikuára, Northern [mbg], 230
Tay, *alt.* Nung [nut], 525
    alt. Tai [taw], 626
Tày [tyz], 527
Tày Bao Lac, *dial.* Tày [tyz], 527
Tay Boi [tas], 527
Tay Boy, *alt.* Tay Boi [tas], 527
Tay Hat, *pej. alt.* O'du [tyh], 525, 452
Tay Hay, *alt.* Kháng [kjm], 524
Tay Khang [tnu], 453
Táy Khao, *alt.* Tai Dón [twh], 526
Tay Mènè, *alt.* Tai Mène [tmp], 453
Tay Mueai, *alt. dial.* Tai Dam [blt], 453
Tay Muoi, *alt.* Tai Do [tyj], 526
Táy Mu'ò'i, *dial.* Tai Dam [blt], 526
Tày Muòng, *alt.* Tai Hang Tong [thc], 527
Tày Nùng, *alt.* Nung [nut], 525
Tay Pong, *alt. dial.* Hung [hnu], 523
Tay Quy Chau, *alt.* Tai Do [tyj], 526
Tày Sa Pa [tys], 527
Tày Tac [tyt], 527
Táy Thanh, *alt.* Tai Thanh [tmm], 527
Tày Trung Khanh, *dial.* Tày [tyz], 527
Tay Yo, *alt.* Tai Do [tyj], 526

Táy-Dam, *alt.* Tai Dam [blt], 526
Tay-Jo, *alt.* Tai Do [tyj], 526
Táy-Môc-Châu, *alt.* Tai Daeng [tyr], 526
Tayaba, *alt. dial.* Nateni [ntm], 46
Tayabas, *dial.* Tagalog [tgl], 502
Tayabas Ayta, *see* Ayta, Tayabas [ayy], 492
Tayal, *alt.* Atayal [tay], 511
Tayan, *dial.* Kombai [tyn], 417
Tayando, *dial.* Kei [kei], 399
Tayari, *dial.* Nateni [ntm], 46
Tayart, *alt. dial.* Tamajeq, Tayart [thz], 152
Tayart Tamajeq, *see* Tamajeq, Tayart [thz], 152
Tayato, *dial.* Enga [enq], 598
Tayek, *alt.* Kapin [tbx], 605
Tayert, *alt. dial.* Tamajeq, Tayart [thz], 152
Tayhay, *alt.* Kháng [kjm], 524
Taying, *alt.* Digaro-Mishmi [mhu], 360
Tayo [cks], 585
Taz, *dial.* Selkup [sel], 506
Taze, *alt.* Kreye [xre], 229
Taznatit [grr], 40
Tazov-Baishyan, *alt. dial.* Selkup [sel], 506
Tbilisi, *dial.* Armenian [hye], 318
T'boli, *alt.* Tboli [tbl], 502
Tboli [tbl], 502
Tcaiti, *alt. dial.* Shua [shg], 48
Tcengui, *alt.* Tsaangi [tsa], 90, 121
Tchaakalaaga, *alt.* Ngadjunmaya [nju], 575
Tchabankeere, *dial.* Fulfulde, Borgu [fue], 44
Tchade, *alt.* Gude [gde], 161, 62
Tchaga, *alt.* Enga [enq], 598
Tchagin, *dial.* Kwang [kvi], 82
Tchakidjebe, *alt.* Dugwor [dme], 60
Tchakin, *alt. dial.* Kwang [kvi], 82
Tchaman, *alt.* Ebrié [ebr], 92
Tchamba, *alt.* Akaselem [aks], 206
    alt. Samba Daka [ccg], 174
Tchambuli, *alt.* Chambri [can], 596
Tchang, *alt.* Yemba [ybb], 74
    alt. dial. Yemba [ybb], 74
Tchangui, *alt.* Tsaangi [tsa], 90, 121
Tchede, *alt.* Tsuvan [tsh], 72
Tcheke, *alt.* Gude [gde], 62
Tchere, *alt.* Giziga, North [gis], 62
Tchere-Aïba, *alt. dial.* Kimré [kqp], 82
Tchevi, *alt.* Sharwa [swq], 72
Tchi, *alt.* Gbe, Ci [cib], 44
Tchide, *dial.* Jina [jia], 63
Tchien, *alt. dial.* Krahn, Eastern [kqo], 138

Tchikai, *alt.* Burarra [bvr], 569
Tchingalee, *alt.* Djingili [jig], 570
Tchini, *dial.* Niellim [nie], 85
Tchire, *dial.* Kimré [kqp], 82
Tchitchege [tck], 121
Tchitem, *alt.* Baga Sitemu [bsp], 128
Tchokossi, *alt.* Anufo [cko], 123, 42, 207
Tchombolo, *alt.* Tchumbuli [bqa], 46
Tchorny, *alt.* Karakalpak [kaa], 521
Tchouvok, *alt.* Cuvok [cuv], 59
Tchumbuli [bqa], 46
    dial. Tchumbuli [bqa], 46
Te, *alt. dial.* Ghomálá' [bbj], 62
Te Mawo, *alt.* Skou [skv], 423
Te Motu, *dial.* Santa Cruz [stc], 638
Tea Mountain Yao, *alt.* Lakkia [lbc], 338
Teanu [tkw], 638
Tebakang, *alt.* Bukar Sadong [sdo], 459, 392
Tebele, *alt.* Ndebele [nde], 216, 48
Tebera, *dial.* Folopa [ppo], 599
Tebilian, *alt.* Tibetan [bod], 388
Tebilung [tgb], 458
Tebou, *alt.* Tedaga [tuq], 86
Tebu, *alt.* Dazaga [dzg], 151
    alt. Tedaga [tuq], 86, 152
Teching, *alt. dial.* Zhuang, Southern [ccy], 349
Techu, *alt. dial.* Chinese, Min Nan [nan], 514
Teco, *alt.* Emerillon [eme], 252
    alt. Tectitec [ttc], 275
    alt. Tektiteko [ttc], 256
Tectitán Mam, *alt.* Tektiteko [ttc], 256
Tectitán Mame, *alt.* Tectitec [ttc], 275
Tectitec [ttc], 275
Tectiteco, *alt.* Tektiteko [ttc], 256
Teda, *alt.* Tedaga [tuq], 86, 152
Tedaga [tuq], 86, 152, 175
Tedesco, *alt.* German, Standard [deu], 538, 544
Tedi, *alt.* Ninggerum [nxr], 618
Tedim, *alt.* Chin, Tedim [ctd], 463, 359
Tedim Chin, *see* Chin, Tedim [ctd], 463, 359
Tedong, *alt.* Tidong [tid], 395, 458
Teduray, *alt.* Tiruray [tiy], 502
Tee [tkq], 175
    dial. Gola [gol], 183
Teel, *alt.* Montol [mtl], 170
Téén [lor], 95, 55
Teenan, *alt.* Tinani [lbf], 388
Teere, *dial.* Doyayo [dow], 60
Tefaro [tfo], 424

Tegal, *dial.* Javanese [jav], 391
Tegali [ras], 195
 dial. Tegali [ras], 195
Tegbo, *alt.* Tafi [tcd], 128
Tege, *alt.* Teke, Northern [teg], 121
 alt. dial. Gola [gol], 183
 alt. dial. Teke, Northern [teg], 121
Tegekali, *dial.* Teke, Northern [teg], 121
Tegele, *alt.* Tegali [ras], 195
Tegem, *alt. dial.* Lafofa [laf], 192
Tegesie, *alt.* Téén [lor], 95, 55
Teghe, *alt.* Teke, Northern [teg], 121
 alt. Teke-Tege [teg], 90
Tegina, *alt. dial.* Cinda-Regi-Tiyal [cdr], 157
Tégué, *alt.* Bozo, Tiéyaxo [boz], 142
 alt. dial. Teke, Northern [teg], 121
Tehid, *alt.* Tehit [kps], 424
Tehit [kps], 424
Tehit Jit, *dial.* Tehit [kps], 424
Tehnu, *alt. dial.* Nicobarese, Central [ncb], 381
Tehoru, *alt.* Teluti [tlt], 404
 alt. dial. Teluti [tlt], 404
Tehrani, *dial.* Farsi, Western [pes], 439
Tehri, *dial.* Garhwali [gbm], 360
Tehua, *alt. dial.* Teluti [tlt], 404
Tehuacán Náhuatl, *alt.* Nahuatl, Southeastern Puebla [nhs], 272
Tehuelche [teh], 220
Teimuri, *alt. dial.* Aimaq [aiq], 315
 dial. Aimaq [aiq], 437
Teimurtash, *alt. dial.* Aimaq [aiq], 437
Teis-Umm-Danab, *alt.* Tese [keg], 195
Teita, *alt.* Taita [dav], 136
Teita Mixtec, *alt.* Mixtec, San Juan Teita [xtj], 268
Teixeira Pinto, *alt. dial.* Mandjak [mfv], 131, 181
 dial. Mandjak [mfv], 122
Teizang, *alt. dial.* Chin, Paite [pck], 359
Tejalapan Zapotec, *see* Zapotec, Tejalapan [ztt], 280
Tejuca, *alt.* Tuyuca [tue], 248
Teke, *alt.* Teke, Northern [teg], 121
 dial. Turkmen [tuk], 520, 318, 442
Teke Alima, *alt.* Teke-Tege [teg], 90
Teke du Pool, *alt.* Teke-Fuumu [ifm], 90
Teke Kali, *alt.* Teke-Tege [teg], 90
Teke, Eboo [ebo], 108
Teke, Ibali [tek], 108
Teke, Northern [teg], 121
Teke-Boma, *alt.* Teke-Eboo [ebo], 90

Teke-Eboo [ebo], 90
Teke-Fuumu [ifm], 90
Teke-Ibali [tek], 90
Teke-Kukuya [kkw], 90
Teke-Laali [lli], 90
Teke-Nzikou [nzu], 90
Teke-Tege [teg], 90
Teke-Tsaayi [tyi], 90
Teke-Tyee [tyx], 90
Tekedaya, *dial.* Taroko [trv], 512
Tekeim, *alt. dial.* Lafofa [laf], 192
Tekel, *alt.* Lehali [tql], 642
Tekela, *alt.* Swati [ssw], 197, 149, 186
Tekele, *alt.* Tegali [ras], 195
Tekeza, *alt.* Swati [ssw], 197, 149, 186
Tekke, *alt. dial.* Turkmen [tuk], 520, 318, 442
Teko, *pej. alt.* Tektiteko [ttc], 256
Tektiteko [ttc], 256
Tekutameso, *alt.* Kauwera [xau], 416
 alt. Kwerba [kwe], 418
Tel Kepe, *dial.* Chaldean Neo-Aramaic [cld], 443
Tela-Masbuar [tvm], 404
Tela'a, *alt.* Tela-Masbuar [tvm], 404
Telaki, *alt.* Tsuvan [tsh], 72
Telangana, *alt. dial.* Telugu [tel], 388
Telangire, *alt.* Telugu [tel], 388
Tele, *alt. dial.* Vale [vae], 78
Teleefool, *alt.* Telefol [tlf], 627
Telefol [tlf], 627
 dial. Telefol [tlf], 627
Telefolmin, *alt.* Telefol [tlf], 627
Telefomin, *alt.* Telefol [tlf], 627
Telegu, *alt.* Telugu [tel], 388
Telei, *alt.* Terei [buo], 627
Teleki, *alt.* Tsuvan [tsh], 72
Telekoson, *alt. dial.* Tagal Murut [mvv], 458, 395
Telemar, *dial.* Ili'uun [ilu], 399
Telengit, *alt.* Altai, Northern [atv], 503
Telengut, *alt.* Altai, Northern [atv], 503
Teleut, *alt.* Altai, Northern [atv], 503
Telgi, *alt.* Telugu [tel], 388
Telha, *dial.* Sandawe [sad], 204
Teli, *alt.* Chhintange [ctn], 470
 dial. Bhojpuri [bho], 469
Telipok, *alt. dial.* Dusun, Central [dtp], 456
Telire, *dial.* Cabécar [cjp], 249
Telom, *alt. dial.* Semai [sea], 455
Telue, *alt.* Gelao, White [giw], 522
Telugu [tel], 388
 alt. dial. Telugu [tel], 388

Telugu Gondi, *alt.* Gondi, Southern [ggo], 363
Telugu Lamani, *alt. dial.* Lambadi [lmn], 372
Teluk Lili, *dial.* Tugutil [tuj], 405
Telukbetung, *dial.* Pesisir, Southern [pec], 437
Teluti [tlt], 404
Telzang, *dial.* Chin, Paite [pck], 359
Tem [kdh], 209, 46, 128
Tema, *alt.* Teme [tdo], 175
Temacin, *dial.* Tagargrent [oua], 40
Temacine Tamazight, *see* Tamazight, Temacine [tjo], 40
Temageri, *dial.* Kanuri, Central [knc], 166, 63, 81, 191
Temainian, *alt.* Temein [teq], 195
Temane, *alt.* Japanese Sign Language [jsl], 446
Temascaltepec Aztec, *alt.* Nahuatl, Temascaltepec [nhv], 272
Temascaltepec Nahuatl, *see* Nahuatl, Temascaltepec [nhv], 272
Temba, *alt.* Tem [kdh], 209, 128
Tembagla, *dial.* Melpa [med], 613
Tembaglo, *alt. dial.* Mbo-Ung [mux], 612
Tembalo, *alt.* Mbo-Ung [mux], 612
 alt. dial. Mbo-Ung [mux], 612
Tembe, *alt.* Tem [kdh], 46
Tembe', *dial.* Temiar [tea], 455
Tembé [tqb], 232
Tembe of Gurupi, *dial.* Guajajára [gub], 227
Tembekuá, *dial.* Kaiwá [kgk], 228
Tembenua, *alt.* Tombonuwo [txa], 458
Tembi, *alt. dial.* Temiar [tea], 455
Tembimbe-Katbol, *alt.* Katbol [tmb], 642
Tembis, *alt.* Tambas [tdk], 175
Tembo (Kitembo) [tbt], 108
 Tembo (Motembo) [tmv], 108
 alt. dial. Nyamwanga [mwn], 215
 dial. Tembo [tbt], 108
Tembung, *dial.* Javanese [jav], 391
Teme [tdo], 175
Temein [teq], 195
Temen, *alt.* Themne [tem], 184
Temer, *alt.* Temiar [tea], 455
Temi [soz], 205
Temiar [tea], 455
Temila, *dial.* Dayak, Land [dyk], 393
Teminabuan, *alt.* Tehit [kps], 424
Temirgoj, *alt. dial.* Adyghe [ady], 552
Temki, *alt.* Tamki [tax], 86
Temne, *alt.* Themne [tem], 184

Temoaya Otomi, *see* Otomi,
Temoaya [ott], 273
Temogun, *alt.* Timugon Murut
[tih], 458
Temoq [tmo], 455
Temoral, *alt.* Panchpargania
[tdb], 382
Tempanye, *alt. dial.* Lefa [lfa], 65
Tempasok, *alt.* Dusun, Tempasuk
[tdu], 456
Tempasuk Dusun, *see* Dusun,
Tempasuk [tdu], 456
Temuan [tmw], 455
dial. Temuan [tmw], 455
T'en [tct], 344
Ten, *alt.* Eten [etx], 159
Ten Kurumba, *alt.* Kurumba, Jennu
[xuj], 371
Ten'a, *alt.* Koyukon [koy], 303
Tena, *alt.* Makasar [mak], 430
Tena Lowland Quichua, *see*
Quichua, Tena Lowland [quw], 251
Tenae, *alt.* Hruso [hru], 364
Tenango, *alt.* Tzeltal, Oxchuc [tzh],
276
dial. Tzeltal, Oxchuc [tzh], 276
Tenango Aztec, *alt.* Nahuatl,
Tenango [nhi], 272
Tenango Nahuatl, *see* Nahuatl,
Tenango [nhi], 272
Tenango Otomi, *see* Otomi,
Tenango [otn], 273
Tench, *alt.* Tenis [tns], 627
Tenda, *alt.* Budik [tnr], 180
alt. Wamey [cou], 130
Tenda Basari, *alt.* Bassari
[bsc], 180, 129
Tendanke, *alt.* Budik [tnr], 180
Tende, *alt.* Kuria [kuj], 200, 134
alt. Tiene [tii], 109
Tendydie, *alt.* Naga, Angami
[njm], 377
Tene Kan, *alt.* Dogon, Tene Kan
[dtk], 142
Tene Kan Dogon, *see* Dogon, Tene
Kan [dtk], 142
Tene Tingi, *alt.* Dogon, Tene Kan
[dtk], 142
Tenejapa, *alt.* Tzeltal, Oxchuc
[tzh], 276
Tenenga, *alt. dial.* Mahou [mxx], 94
Tenere, *dial.* Senoufo, Cebaara
[sef], 94
Tenet, *alt.* Tennet [tex], 195
Tenetehar, *alt.* Guajajára [gub], 227
Tenetehara, *alt.* Tembé [tqb], 232
Tenetehára, *alt.* Guajajára
[gub], 227
Teng, *alt.* Kháng [kjm], 524
dial. Kissi, Northern [kqs], 129, 183

Tenga, *dial.* Soga [xog], 212
Tengah-Tengah, *dial.* Tulehu
[tlu], 405
Tengara, *alt. dial.* Bookan [bnb], 456
Tengganu, *alt. dial.* Jah Hut
[jah], 454
Tenggaraq, *alt. dial.* Bookan
[bnb], 456
Tenggarong, *alt.* Malay,
Tenggarong Kutai [vkt], 394
Tenggarong Kutai, *dial.* Malay,
Tenggarong Kutai [vkt], 394
Tenggarong Kutai Malay, *see*
Malay, Tenggarong Kutai [vkt], 394
Tengger [tes], 392
Tenggerese, *alt.* Tengger [tes], 392
Tengia, *dial.* Kisi, Southern
[kss], 138
Tengima, *alt. dial.* Naga, Angami
[njm], 377
Tengo, *alt.* Mamvu [mdi], 103
Tengoh, *alt. dial.* Jagoi [sne], 459
Tengrela, *alt. dial.* Senoufo, Cebaara
[sef], 94
Tengu, *alt.* Telugu [tel], 388
Tengu Tingi, *dial.* Dogon, Tene Kan
[dtk], 142
Tenh, *alt.* Khmu [kjg], 451, 465
Tenharem, *alt.* Tenharim
[pah], 232
alt. dial. Tenharim [pah], 232
Tenharim [pah], 232
dial. Tenharim [pah], 232
Tenharin, *alt.* Tenharim [pah], 232
alt. dial. Tenharim [pah], 232
Ténhé, *alt.* Téén [lor], 95, 55
Tenino [tqn], 308
Tenis [tns], 627
Tennet [tex], 195
Tenom Murut, *alt.* Timugon Murut
[tih], 458
Tensino, *alt. dial.* Aragonese
[arg], 558
Tent Gypsy, *alt.* Romano-Serbian
[rsb], 557
Tenti, *alt.* Sensi [sni], 293
Tenyer, *dial.* Karaboro, Western
[kza], 52
Tenyidie, *alt. dial.* Naga, Angami
[njm], 377
Tenyidye, *alt. dial.* Naga, Angami
[njm], 377
Teo, *alt. dial.* Teke, Ibali [tek], 108
Teochew, *alt. dial.* Chinese, Min
Nan [nan], 454
dial. Chinese, Min Nan [nan], 508
Teochow, *alt. dial.* Chinese, Min
Nan [nan], 324, 454, 514
Teop [tio], 627
Teor [tev], 404

Teotitlán del Valle Zapotec,
dial. Zapotec, San Juan Guelavía
[zab], 279
Teotitlan Mixtec, *alt.* Mixtec,
Coatzospan [miz], 266
Tepantepec, *alt. dial.* Mixtec,
Peñoles [mil], 268
Tepecano [tep], 275
Tepehua de Hidalgo, *alt.* Tepehua,
Huehuetla [tee], 275
Tepehua de Huehuetla, *alt.*
Tepehua, Huehuetla [tee], 275
Tepehua, Huehuetla [tee], 275
Tepehua, Pisaflores [tpp], 275
Tepehua, Tlachichilco [tpt], 275
Tepehuán del Norte, *alt.*
Tepehuan, Northern [ntp], 275
Tepehuán del Sureste, *alt.*
Tepehuan, Southeastern [stp], 275
Tepehuán del Suroeste, *alt.*
Tepehuan, Southwestern [tla], 275
Tepehuan, Northern [ntp], 275
Tepehuan, Southeastern
[stp], 275
Tepehuan, Southwestern
[tla], 275
Tepehuano, *alt.* Tepehuan,
Southeastern [stp], 275
Tepera, *alt.* Tabla [tnm], 423
dial. Tabla [tnm], 423
Tepes, *alt.* Soo [teu], 212
Tepeth, *alt.* Soo [teu], 212
Tepetotutla Chinantec, *see*
Chinantec, Tepetotutla [cnt], 261
Tepeuxila Cuicatec, *see* Cuicatec,
Tepeuxila [cux], 262
Tepinapa Chinantec, *see*
Chinantec, Tepinapa [cte], 261
Tepo, *dial.* Krumen, Tepo [ted], 93,
138
Tepo Krumen, *see* Krumen, Tepo
[ted], 93, 138
Teq, *alt. dial.* Batek [btq], 454
Teqel, *alt.* Lehali [tql], 642
Tequenica, *alt.* Yámana [yag], 243
Tequistlatec, *alt.* Chontal, Highland
Oaxaca [chd], 261
Tequraca, *alt.* Abishira [ash], 285
Ter Lappish, *pej. alt.* Saami, Ter
[sjt], 556
Ter Saami, *see* Saami, Ter
[sjt], 556
Ter. Tru, *dial.* Toussian, Northern
[tsp], 55
Tera [ttr], 175
alt. Cara [cfd], 156
Terakan, *alt. dial.* Tidong [tid], 395,
458
Terangi, *alt.* Telugu [tel], 388
Terawia, *alt. dial.* Zaghawa [zag], 87

Terebu [trb], 627
Terego, *alt. dial.* Lugbara [lgg], 211
Terei [buo], 627
Terekeme, *dial.* Azerbaijani, North [azj], 319, 319
Terema, *alt. dial.* Suri [suq], 119, 195
Terêna [ter], 232
Tereno, *alt.* Terêna [ter], 232
Terepu, *alt.* Terebu [trb], 627
Teressa [tef], 388
Tereweng [twg], 409
Teri, *alt.* Sagalla [tga], 136
   dial. Sagalla [tga], 136
Teri-Kalwasch, *alt.* Kimaama [kig], 417
Teribe [tfr], 284, 249
Terik, *dial.* Kalenjin [kln], 133
Teriya, *alt.* Cara [cfd], 156
Terki, *alt.* Tsuvan [tsh], 72
Termanu [twu], 410
   alt. dial. Termanu [twu], 410
Terna, *alt. dial.* Suri [suq], 119, 195
Ternate [tft], 404
Ternate Malay, *alt.* Malay, North Moluccan [max], 401
Ternateño [tmg], 404
   dial. Chavacano [cbk], 493
Ternateño Chavacano, *alt. dial.* Chavacano [cbk], 493
Ternatenyo, *alt.* Ternateño [tmg], 404
Terraba, *alt.* Teribe [tfr], 284, 249
Terri, *alt.* Cara [cfd], 156
Terrutong, *alt.* Margu [mhg], 573
Teruku, *dial.* Taroko [trv], 512
Terutong, *alt.* Margu [mhg], 573
Tese [keg], 195
Teshenawa [twc], 175
Teshenna, *alt. dial.* Me'en [mym], 117
Teshina, *alt. dial.* Me'en [mym], 117
Teso [teo], 213, 136
Tessinian, *alt. dial.* Lombard [lmo], 562
Tesu, *dial.* Alumu-Tesu [aab], 153
Tesuque, *dial.* Tewa [tew], 308
Teta, *alt.* Nyungwe [nyu], 148
Tetang, *dial.* Seke [skj], 478
Tete, *alt.* Nyungwe [nyu], 148
Tête de Boule, *alt.* Atikamekw [atj], 235
Teteka, *alt.* Nyong [muo], 171
Tetela [tll], 109
Tetelcingo Aztec, *alt.* Nahuatl, Tetelcingo [nhg], 272
Tetelcingo Nahuatl, *see* Nahuatl, Tetelcingo [nhg], 272
Tetete [teb], 251
Teto, *alt.* Tetun [tet], 410, 351

Teton, *alt.* Lakota [lkt], 303, 238
Tettum, *alt.* Tetun [tet], 410, 351
Tetu, *alt.* Tetun [tet], 410, 351
Tetum, *alt.* Tetun [tet], 410, 351
   alt. Tetun Dili [tdt], 351
Tetum Dili, *alt.* Tetun Dili [tdt], 351
Tetum Praça, *alt.* Tetun Dili [tdt], 351
Tetum Prasa, *alt.* Tetun Dili [tdt], 351
Tetun [tet], 410, 351
   alt. Tetun Dili [tdt], 351
Tetun Belu, *alt.* Tetun [tet], 410, 351
Tetun Dili [tdt], 351
Tetun Loos, *alt. dial.* Tetun [tet], 410, 351
Tetun Los, *alt. dial.* Tetun [tet], 410, 351
Tetun Terik, *alt. dial.* Tetun [tet], 410, 351
Tetun Therik, *alt. dial.* Tetun [tet], 410, 351
Tetung, *alt.* Tetun [tet], 410, 351
Te'uda, *dial.* Taroko [trv], 512
Teueia, *alt.* Macushi [mbc], 229, 257
Teüi, *dial.* Kaiwá [kgk], 228
Teula, *alt.* Liana-Seti [ste], 400
Te'un [tve], 404
Teuso, *alt.* Ik [ikx], 211
Teuth, *alt.* Ik [ikx], 211
Teutila Cuicatec, *see* Cuicatec, Teutila [cut], 262
Teve, *alt.* Tewe [twx], 149
Tevorang, *alt. dial.* Siraya [fos], 512
Tew, *alt.* Tumbuka [tum], 215
Tewa (Indonesia) [twe], 410
   Tewa (USA) [tew], 308
Tewatewa, *dial.* Misima-Paneati [mpx], 614
Tewe [twx], 149
Tewellemet, *alt.* Tamajaq, Tawallammat [ttq], 152
Teweya, *alt.* Macushi [mbc], 229, 257, 312
Tewoyan, *alt.* Tawoyan [twy], 395
Texas, *dial.* Afro-Seminole Creole [afs], 297
Texcatepec Otomi, *see* Otomi, Texcatepec [otx], 273
Texistepec Popoluca, *see* Popoluca, Texistepec [poq], 274
Texmelucan Zapotec, *see* Zapotec, Texmelucan [zpz], 280
Tez, *dial.* Oroch [oac], 506
Tezoatlán, *dial.* Mixtec, Tezoatlán [mxb], 269
Tezoatlán Mixtec, *see* Mixtec, Tezoatlán [mxb], 269
Tfuea, *dial.* Tsou [tsu], 512
Tghuade, *alt.* Dghwede [dgh], 157

Tha [thy], 175
Thaadou Kuki, *alt.* Chin, Thado [tcz], 359
Thaayore, *alt.* Thayore [thd], 576
Thabanggi, *dial.* Parbate, Western [kjl], 477
Thabine-Roka-Nareng, *alt. dial.* Sotho, Northern [nso], 186
Thado Chin, *see* Chin, Thado [tcz], 359, 463
Thado-Pao, *alt.* Chin, Thado [tcz], 359, 463
Thado-Ubiphei, *alt.* Chin, Thado [tcz], 359, 463
Thadou, *alt.* Chin, Thado [tcz], 359, 463
Thae, *alt.* The [thx], 453
Thagichu, *dial.* Tharaka [thk], 136
Thai [tha], 517
Thai Dang, *alt.* Tai Daeng [tyr], 526, 453
Thai Den, *alt.* Tai Dam [blt], 453, 517
Thái Den, *alt.* Tai Dam [blt], 526
Thai Do, *alt.* Tai Daeng [tyr], 526, 453
Thai Isaan, *alt.* Thai, Northeastern [tts], 517
Thai Islam, *alt.* Malay, Pattani [mfa], 516
Thai Lu, *alt.* Lü [khb], 515
Thai Malay, *dial.* Thai, Southern [sou], 517
Thai Sign Language [tsq], 517
Thai Song [soa], 517
Thái Tráng, *alt.* Tai Dón [twh], 526, 453
Thai Yai, *alt.* Shan [shn], 467
Thai Yay, *alt.* Shan [shn], 517
Thai, Northeastern [tts], 517
Thai, Northern [nod], 517, 453
Thai, Southern [sou], 517
Thaiklang, *alt.* Thai [tha], 517
Thaikorat, *alt. dial.* Thai [tha], 517
Thailand Khmer, *alt.* Khmer, Northern [kxm], 515
Thakali [ths], 480
Thakara, *alt.* Duruwa [pci], 361
Thakari, *alt. dial.* Konkani [knn], 369
Thakri, *alt. dial.* Konkani [knn], 369
Thaksaatsaye, *alt. dial.* Thakali [ths], 480
Thaksatsae, *alt. dial.* Thakali [ths], 480
Thaksya, *alt.* Thakali [ths], 480
Thakua, *alt. dial.* Konkani [knn], 369
Thakura, *alt. dial.* Konkani [knn], 369

Thakuri, *dial.* Konkani [knn], 369
Thakwani, *alt.* Takwane [tke], 149
Thal, *dial.* Kalami [gwc], 485
Thalantji, *alt.* Dhalandji [dhl], 569
Thalanyji, *alt.* Dhalandji [dhl], 569
Thali, *alt. dial.* Seraiki [skr], 386
Thalu, *alt.* Tulu [tcy], 389
Thalwepwe, *alt.* Karen, Paku [kpp], 464
Thami, *alt.* Thangmi [thf], 480, 344
Thaminyi, *alt.* Dair [drb], 189
Thang, *dial.* Muong [mtq], 525
Thangal, *alt.* Naga, Thangal [nki], 380
Thangal Naga, *see* Naga, Thangal [nki], 380
Thangatti, *alt.* Dyangadi [dyn], 570
Thangatty, *alt.* Dyangadi [dyn], 570
Thanggal, *alt.* Naga, Thangal [nki], 380
Thangkachep, *dial.* Sakechep [sch], 385
Thangkhulm, *alt.* Naga, Tangkhul [nmf], 380
Thangmi [thf], 480, 344
Thangngen, *alt. dial.* Chin, Thado [tcz], 359
   dial. Chin, Thado [tcz], 463
Thanh, *alt.* Tai Thanh [tmm], 527
Thany, *alt. dial.* Dinka, South Central [dib], 190
Thany Bur, *alt. dial.* Dinka, Southwestern [dik], 190
Thao [ssf], 512
Thar, *alt.* Dhatki [mki], 360
Tharadari Bhil, *dial.* Koli, Wadiyara [kxp], 487
Tharadari Koli, *dial.* Koli, Wadiyara [kxp], 487
Tharaka [thk], 136
   dial. Tharaka [thk], 136
Thareli, *dial.* Sindhi [snd], 488, 387
Thargari, *alt.* Dhargari [dhr], 569
Thari, *dial.* Sindhi [snd], 387
Tharrgari, *alt.* Dhargari [dhr], 569
Tharrkari, *alt.* Dhargari [dhr], 569
Tharu, *dial.* Awadhi [awa], 468
   dial. Bhojpuri [bho], 356
Tharu, Chitwania [the], 480
Tharu, Dangaura [thl], 480, 388
Tharu, Kathoriya [tkt], 480
Tharu, Kochila [thq], 481, 388
Tharu, Rana [thr], 481, 388
Tharumba, *alt.* Dhurga [dhu], 569
Tharumbal, *alt.* Bayali [bjy], 569
That, *alt.* Kado [kdv], 464, 337
Thavung, *alt.* Aheu [thm], 449
Thayetmo, *alt. dial.* Chin, Asho [csh], 462

Thayetmyo, *dial.* Chin, Asho [csh], 462, 321
Thayore [thd], 576
Thayorre, *alt.* Thayore [thd], 576
Thaypan [typ], 576
The [thx], 453
The Cant, *alt.* Shelta [sth], 543
Thebarshad, *alt.* Sunam [ssk], 388
Thebarskad, *alt.* Jangshung [jna], 365
   alt. Kinnauri, Chitkuli [cik], 368
   alt. Shumcho [scu], 387
Thebor, *alt.* Jangshung [jna], 365
   alt. Shumcho [scu], 387
   alt. Sunam [ssk], 388
Thebör Skadd, *alt.* Jangshung [jna], 365
   alt. Shumcho [scu], 387
   alt. Sunam [ssk], 388
Theithei, *alt.* Nathembo [nte], 148
Thembu, *dial.* Xhosa [xho], 187
Themne [tem], 184
Then, *alt.* T'en [tct], 344
Theng, *alt.* Kháng [kjm], 524
   alt. Khmu [kjg], 451, 337, 465
Thephalaborwa, *alt. dial.* Sotho, Northern [nso], 186
Thet, *alt.* Kado [kdv], 464, 337, 450
Thiang, *alt. dial.* Nuer [nus], 194
Thie, *alt.* Tii [txq], 410
Thiin, *alt.* Djiwarli [djl], 570
Thimbukushu, *alt.* Mbukushu [mhw], 150, 41, 47
Thimphu-Punakha, *alt. dial.* Dzongkha [dzo], 323
Thimukushu, *alt.* Mbukushu [mhw], 214
Thin, *alt.* Mal [mlf], 451, 516
Thinglong, *alt.* Naga, Kharam [kfw], 378
Thio, *alt.* Xaragure [axx], 585
Thiro, *alt.* Tira [tic], 196
Thithiza, *alt.* Swati [ssw], 186
Thlan Tan, *alt.* Nga La [hlt], 466
Thlantlang, *alt. dial.* Chin, Haka [cnh], 463, 321, 357
Thlaping, *dial.* Tswana [tsn], 186
Thlaro, *dial.* Tswana [tsn], 186
Thlinget, *alt.* Tlingit [tli], 309, 242
Tho [tou], 527
Thô, *pej. alt.* Tày [tyz], 527
Thognaath, *dial.* Nuer [nus], 194
Thoi, *dial.* Dinka, Northeastern [dip], 189
Thok Cieng Reel, *alt.* Reel [atu], 195
Thok Nath, *alt. dial.* Nuer [nus], 194
Tholong Lo, *alt.* Thulung [tdh], 481
Thompson [thp], 242

Thon, *alt. dial.* Dinka, Southwestern [dik], 190
Thonga, *alt.* Tsonga [tso], 186, 149, 217
Thoorga, *alt.* Dhurga [dhu], 569
Thracean Arvanitika, *dial.* Albanian, Arvanitika [aat], 540
Thro, *alt.* Sô [sss], 452, 517
Thu Lao [tyl], 527
   alt. Tày [tyz], 527
   dial. Tày [tyz], 527
Thuanga, *alt.* Yuaga [nua], 585
   dial. Yuaga [nua], 585
Thudam [thw], 481
Thudam Bhote, *pej. alt.* Thudam [thw], 481
Thui Phum, *dial.* Chin, Matu [hlt], 359
Thukumi, *dial.* Naga, Sangtam [nsa], 379
Thule Inuit, *alt. dial.* Inuktitut, Greenlandic [kal], 252
Thulishi, *alt.* Tulishi [tey], 196
Thulu, *alt.* Tulu [tcy], 389
Thulu Luwa, *alt.* Thulung [tdh], 481
Thululoa, *alt.* Thulung [tdh], 481
Thulung [tdh], 481, 388
Thulung Jemu, *alt.* Thulung [tdh], 481
Thulung La, *alt.* Thulung [tdh], 481
Thulunge Rai, *alt.* Thulung [tdh], 481, 388
Thundai-Kanza, *alt.* Kunja [pep], 608
Thung Chan Pray, *alt.* Phai [prt], 516, 452
Thurawal [tbh], 576
Thuri [thu], 195
Ti, *alt.* Tii [txq], 410
   dial. Mungaka [mhk], 68
Tiaala, *dial.* Gula Iro [glj], 81
Tiadje, *alt.* Tomini [txm], 434
Tiagba, *alt.* Aizi, Tiagbamrin [ahi], 91
Tiagbamrin Aizi, *see* Aizi, Tiagbamrin [ahi], 91
Tial, *dial.* Tulehu [tlu], 405
Tiale [mnl], 646
Tialo, *alt.* Tomini [txm], 434
Tiang [tbj], 627
Tiapi, *alt.* Landoma [ldm], 129
   dial. Landoma [ldm], 129
Tiara, *alt.* Gedaged [gdd], 599
Tiatinagua, *alt.* Ese Ejja [ese], 222, 288
Tiau, *dial.* Citak [txt], 413
Tiayai, *dial.* Kamang [woi], 407
Tiba, *alt.* Gaa [ttb], 160
Tibas Skad, *alt.* Kinnauri [kfk], 368

dial. Tamasheq, Kidal [taq], 55
Timbuktu Songhoy, *alt.* Songhay, Koyra Chiini [khq], 144
Timbunki, *dial.* Maring [mbw], 612
Timene, *alt.* Themne [tem], 184
Timggian, *alt.* Itneg, Banao [bjx], 496
Timigan, *alt.* Timugon Murut [tih], 458
Timigun, *alt.* Timugon Murut [tih], 458
Timiku, *alt. dial.* Seeku [sos], 54
Timingir, *dial.* Arapesh, Bumbita [aon], 590
Timmannee, *alt.* Themne [tem], 184
Timne, *alt.* Themne [tem], 184
Timogon, *alt.* Timugon Murut [tih], 458
Timogun, *alt.* Timugon Murut [tih], 458
Timol, *alt.* Uab Meto [aoz], 410
Timoniko, *alt. dial.* Budu [buu], 98
Timor, *alt.* Uab Meto [aoz], 410
Timor Amarasi, *alt.* Amarasi [aaz], 406
Timor Creole Portuguese, *alt.* Pidgin, Timor [tvy], 351
Timor Dawan, *pej. alt.* Uab Meto [aoz], 410
Timor Pidgin, *see* Pidgin, Timor [tvy], 351
Timoreesch, *alt.* Uab Meto [aoz], 410
Timoreezen, *alt.* Uab Meto [aoz], 410
Timorese, *alt.* Uab Meto [aoz], 410
Timorini, *alt.* Dani, Western [dnw], 414
Timputs, *alt.* Tinputz [tpz], 628
Timu, *alt.* Tem [kdh], 209, 46, 128
　alt. dial. Aceh [ace], 435
　dial. Sabu [hvn], 409
Timugon, *alt.* Timugon Murut [tih], 458
　dial. Timugon Murut [tih], 458
Timugon Murut [tih], 458
Timur, *alt.* Batak Simalungun [bts], 435
　dial. Orya [ury], 422
Timuri, *alt. dial.* Aimaq [aiq], 315
T'in, *alt.* Mal [mlf], 451, 516
Tin, *alt.* Mal [mlf], 451, 516
Tina, *alt.* Sambal, Tinà [xsb], 501
Tinà Sambal, *see* Sambal, Tinà [xsb], 501
Tinagas, *dial.* Dusun, Sugut [kzs], 456
Tinaloctoc, *dial.* Kalinga, Lower Tanudan [kml], 497
Tinam, *alt.* Hatam [had], 415

dial. Hatam [had], 415
Tinan Lahuli, *alt.* Tinani [lbf], 388
Tinani [lbf], 388, 345
Tinata Tuna, *alt.* Kuanua [ksd], 608
Tindakon, *alt.* Kadazan, Labuk-Kinabatangan [dtb], 457
Tindal, *alt.* Dusun, Tempasuk [tdu], 456
　alt. Kuijau [dkr], 457
　alt. Tindi [tin], 557
　dial. Dusun, Central [dtp], 456
Tindi [tin], 557
Tindiga, *pej. alt.* Hadza [hts], 199
Tindin, *alt.* Tindi [tin], 557
Tingal [tie], 196
Tingalun, *alt.* Sembakung Murut [sbr], 458, 395
Tinganeses, *alt.* Cholón [cht], 287
Tingara, *alt. dial.* Bookan [bnb], 456
Tinggalan, *alt.* Sembakung Murut [sbr], 458, 395
Tinggalum, *alt.* Sembakung Murut [sbr], 458, 395
Tinggian, *alt.* Itneg, Inlaod [iti], 496
　alt. Itneg, Moyadan [ity], 496
Tingguian, *alt.* Itneg, Binongan [itb], 496
Tingkala, *alt.* Tikar [tik], 72
Tinglayan, *dial.* Kalinga, Southern [ksc], 497
Tinglayan Kalinga, *alt.* Kalinga, Southern [ksc], 497
Tingong, *dial.* Lefa [lfa], 65
Tingui, *alt.* Tingui-Boto [tgv], 233
Tingui-Boto [tgv], 233
Tinguian, *alt.* Itneg, Banao [bjx], 496
　alt. Itneg, Binongan [itb], 496
　alt. Itneg, Inlaod [iti], 496
　alt. Itneg, Moyadan [ity], 496
Tingzhou, *dial.* Chinese, Hakka [hak], 329
Tinigua [tit], 248
Tiniguas, *alt.* Tinigua [tit], 248
Tinitianes, *alt.* Batak [bya], 492
Tinjar Sibop, *dial.* Kenyah, Sebob [sib], 459
Tinners Romani, *dial.* Romani, Balkan [rmn], 557, 532, 547
Tinoc Kalangoya, *alt.* Kallahan, Tinoc [tne], 498
Tinoc Kallahan, *see* Kallahan, Tinoc [tne], 498
Tinombo, *alt.* Lauje [law], 430
Tinputz [tpz], 628
Tinrin, *alt.* Tiri [cir], 585
Tinta, *alt.* Manta [myg], 66
　dial. Ipulo [ass], 63
Tintekiya, *dial.* Koch [kdq], 368, 321
Tio, *alt. dial.* Teke, Ibali [tek], 108
Tioffo, *dial.* Abé [aba], 90

Tiokossi, *alt.* Anufo [cko], 123, 207
Tiong, *alt.* Kensiu [kns], 515
Tio'or, *alt.* Teor [tev], 404
Tipai, *dial.* Kumiai [dih], 303
Tipai', *alt.* Kumiai [dih], 263
Tipái, *alt.* Kumiai [dih], 263
Tipéi, *alt.* Kumiai [dih], 263
Tipinini, *dial.* Ipili [ipi], 603
Tiple, *dial.* Yale, Kosarek [kkl], 426
Tippera [tpe], 322
Tippera-Bengali, *alt.* Tippera [tpe], 322
Tipperah, *alt.* Tippera [tpe], 322
Tippurah, *alt.* Tippera [tpe], 322
Tipra, *alt.* Riang [ria], 385
　alt. Tippera [tpe], 322
　alt. dial. Kok Borok [trp], 321
Tipun, *alt.* Puyuma [pyu], 512
Tipura, *alt.* Chin, Falam [flm], 358
　alt. Kok Borok [trp], 368, 321
　alt. Tippera [tpe], 322
Tira [tic], 196
Tira Dagig, *alt. dial.* Tira [tic], 196
Tira El Akhdar, *dial.* Tira [tic], 196
Tira Lumum, *dial.* Tira [tic], 196
Tira Mandi, *dial.* Tira [tic], 196
Tirahi [tra], 318
Tirahutia, *alt.* Maithili [mai], 373, 475
Tiran, *alt.* Tidong [tid], 395, 458
Tirhari, *dial.* Bagheli [bfy], 354, 468
　dial. Bundeli [bns], 357
　dial. Kanauji [bjj], 366
Tirhuti, *alt.* Maithili [mai], 373, 475
Tirhutia, *alt.* Maithili [mai], 373, 475
Tiri [cir], 585
Tiribi, *alt.* Teribe [tfr], 284
Tirifie, *alt.* Tarifit [rif], 40
Tiriki, *dial.* Idakho-Isukha-Tiriki [ida], 133
Tirima, *alt. dial.* Suri [suq], 119, 195
Tirio, *alt.* Makayam [aup], 611
Tirió, *alt.* Trió [tri], 296, 233
Tiriya, *dial.* Duruwa [pci], 361
Tiriyó, *alt.* Trió [tri], 233
Tirma, *dial.* Suri [suq], 119, 195
Tirmaga, *alt. dial.* Suri [suq], 119, 195
Tirmagi, *alt. dial.* Suri [suq], 119, 195
Tiro, *alt.* Konjo, Coastal [kjc], 430
　alt. Tira [tic], 196
Tirolean, *alt.* German, Hutterite [geh], 237, 300
Tiron, *alt.* Tawbuid, Eastern [bnj], 502
Tirones, *alt.* Tidong [tid], 395, 458
Tiroon, *alt.* Tidong [tid], 395, 458

Tirrenic, *alt. dial.* Napoletano-Calabrese [nap], 545

Tirribi, *alt.* Teribe [tfr], 284

Tirumbae, *alt.* Tapieté [tpj], 282, 220, 224

Tirurai, *alt.* Tiruray [tiy], 502

Tiruray [tiy], 502

Tishena, *dial.* Me'en [mym], 117

Tisman, *dial.* Rerep [pgk], 645

Tisqopa, *dial.* Chaldean Neo-Aramaic [cld], 443

Tisvel, *alt.* Katbol [tmb], 642

Tit, *dial.* Tamazight, Tidikelt [tia], 40

Tita [tdq], 175

Titan [ttv], 628

Titin Bajaygul, *alt. dial.* Ashkun [ask], 315

Tito, *alt.* Titan [ttv], 628

Titu, *alt. dial.* Mongo-Nkundu [lol], 104

Tiu Chiu, *alt. dial.* Chinese, Min Nan [nan], 391

Tiuchiu, *alt. dial.* Chinese, Min Nan [nan], 324, 514

Tiv [tiv], 175, 72

Tivaghat, *alt. dial.* Vaghat-Ya-Bijim-Legeri [bij], 177

Tiwa [lax], 389

Tiwa, Northern [twf], 308

Tiwa, Southern [tix], 309

Tiwal, *alt. dial.* Ngile [jle], 194

Tiwi [tiw], 576

Tiwirkum, *alt. dial.* Meta' [mgo], 67

Tiwoto, *alt. dial.* Muna [mnb], 431

Tiya, *alt. dial.* Vaghat-Ya-Bijim-Legeri [bij], 177

Tiyal, *alt. dial.* Cinda-Regi-Tiyal [cdr], 157

Tiyar, *alt. dial.* Cinda-Regi-Tiyal [cdr], 157

Tiye, *alt. dial.* Kaba Na [kwv], 81

Tjabakai-Thandji, *alt.* Dyaabugay [dyy], 570

Tjabogaijanji, *alt.* Dyaabugay [dyy], 570

Tjam, *alt.* Cham, Eastern [cjm], 522 *alt.* Cham, Western [cja], 325, 514, 522

Tjamoro, *alt.* Chamorro [cha], 581, 587

Tjampalagian, *alt.* Campalagian [cml], 428

Tjankir, *alt.* Dyaabugay [dyy], 570

Tjankun, *alt.* Dyaabugay [dyy], 570

Tjapukai, *alt.* Dyaabugay [dyy], 570

Tjapunkandji, *alt.* Dyaabugay [dyy], 570

Tjaru, *alt.* Jaru [ddj], 571

Tjendana, *alt. dial.* Mandar [mdr], 431

Tjerait, *alt.* Tyaraity [woa], 577

Tjikalanga, *alt.* Kalanga [kck], 216, 47

Tjimba, *alt.* Zemba [dhm], 42

Tjimundo, *alt.* Angoram [aog], 590

Tjingilu, *alt.* Djingili [jig], 570

Tjirebon, *alt. dial.* Javanese [jav], 391

Tjitak, *alt.* Citak [txt], 413

Tjitjak, *alt.* Citak [txt], 413

Tjiwarli, *alt.* Djiwarli [djl], 570

Tjokwai, *alt.* Wára [tci], 631

Tjuave, *alt.* Chuave [cjv], 596

Tjudun, *alt. dial.* Tulu-Bohuai [rak], 628

Tjunbundji, *alt.* Dyaabugay [dyy], 570

Tjura, *alt.* Nugunu [nnv], 575

Tjurruru [tju], 577

Tjururu, *alt.* Tjurruru [tju], 577

Tjuwalinj, *alt. dial.* Walmajarri [wmt], 577

Tkdaya, *alt. dial.* Taroko [trv], 512

Tla Wilano, *alt.* Unami [unm], 309

Tlachichilco Tepehua, *see* Tepehua, Tlachichilco [tpt], 275

Tlacoapa Tlapanec, *see* Tlapanec, Tlacoapa [tpl], 275

Tlacoatzintepec Chinantec, *see* Chinantec, Tlacoatzintepec [ctl], 261

Tlacolulita Zapotec, *see* Zapotec, Tlacolulita [zpk], 280

Tlahaping, *dial.* Tswana [tsn], 48

Tlahuica, *alt.* Matlatzinca, Atzingo [ocu], 263

Tlahuitoltepec Mixe, *see* Mixe, Tlahuitoltepec [mxp], 265

Tlahura, *alt.* Matlatzinca, Atzingo [ocu], 263

Tlalitzlipa Nahuatl, *see* Nahuatl, Tlalitzlipa [nhj], 272

Tlam Tlaih, *dial.* Nga La [hlt], 466

Tlamacazapa Nahuatl, *see* Nahuatl, Tlamacazapa [nuz], 272

Tlapanec, Acatepec [tpx], 275

Tlapanec, Azoyú [tpc], 275

Tlapanec, Malinaltepec [tcf], 275

Tlapanec, Tlacoapa [tpl], 275

Tlapaneco de Azoyú, *alt.* Tlapanec, Azoyú [tpc], 275

Tlapaneco de Malinaltepec, *alt.* Tlapanec, Malinaltepec [tcf], 275

Tlapaneco de Tlacoapa, *alt.* Tlapanec, Tlacoapa [tpl], 275

Tlapi, *alt. dial.* Tswana [tsn], 48, 186

Tlatsop, *alt. dial.* Chinook [chh], 299

Tlau, *dial.* Mizo [lus], 376

Tlaxcala-Puebla Nahuatl, *alt.* Nahuatl, Central [nhn], 270

Tlazoyaltepec, *alt. dial.* Mixtec, Peñoles [mil], 268

Tlazoyaltepec Mixtec, *see* Mixtec, Tlazoyaltepec [mqh], 269

Tlhaping, *dial.* Tswana [tsn], 151, 217

Tlharo, *dial.* Tswana [tsn], 151

Tlingit [tli], 309, 242

Tlinkit, *alt.* Tlingit [tli], 309, 242

Tlisi, *dial.* Bagvalal [kva], 553

Tlokeang, *alt.* Kato [ktw], 303

Tlokoa, *alt. dial.* Sotho, Northern [nso], 186

Tlokwa, *dial.* Sotho, Northern [nso], 186 *dial.* Tswana [tsn], 48, 186

Tlongsai, *dial.* Chin, Mara [mrh], 359, 463

Tlosai-Siaha, *alt. dial.* Chin, Mara [mrh], 359

Tloue, *alt.* ‖Xegwi [xeg], 187

Tloutle, *alt.* ‖Xegwi [xeg], 187

Tlyadaly, *dial.* Bezhta [kap], 553

Tlyanub, *alt. dial.* Akhvakh [akv], 552

Tmagourt, *dial.* Sened [sds], 209

Tmagurt, *alt. dial.* Sened [sds], 209

Tmooy, *alt.* Khmu [kjg], 515

T'o, *alt.* Tày [tyz], 527

To [toz], 72, 77

To La, *alt. dial.* Koho [kpm], 524

To Pamosean, *alt.* Panasuan [psn], 432

To Panasean, *alt.* Panasuan [psn], 432

To Rete, *alt. dial.* Bungku [bkz], 428

To Rongkong, *alt.* Tae' [rob], 428

To-Bedawie, *alt.* Bedawi [bej], 188

To-Buan, *dial.* Jarai [jra], 523, 325

Toa, *alt.* Toma [tod], 130 *dial.* Paraujano [pbg], 312

To'abaita [mlu], 638

Toak, *dial.* Ambrym, Southeast [tvk], 640

Toaku Lwa, *alt.* Thulung [tdh], 481

Toala, *alt.* Toala' [tlz], 433

Toala' [tlz], 433 *dial.* Toala' [tlz], 433

Toala-Palili, *alt.* Toala' [tlz], 433

Toale, *alt.* Toma [tod], 130

Toali, *alt.* Toma [tod], 130

To'ambaita, *alt.* To'abaita [mlu], 638

Toaripi [tqo], 628 *dial.* Toaripi [tqo], 628

Toba [tob], 220, 224, 285 *alt.* Emok [emo], 284 *dial.* Yemsa [jnj], 119

Toba Batak, *alt.* Batak Toba [bbc], 435

Toba del Oeste, *alt. dial.* Pilagá [plg], 220

Toba of Paraguay, *alt.* Toba-Maskoy [tmf], 285

Toba Qom, *alt.* Toba [tob], 220

Toba Sur, *alt.* Toba [tob], 220
alt. dial. Pilagá [plg], 220

Toba-Emok, *alt.* Emok [emo], 284

Toba-Maskoy [tmf], 285

Toba-Pilagá, *dial.* Pilagá [plg], 220

Toba-Qom, *alt.* Toba [tob], 285

Tobada', *alt.* Bada [bhz], 427

Tobagonian Creole English [tgh], 296

Tobagonian Dialect, *alt.* Tobagonian Creole English [tgh], 296

Tobaku, *dial.* Uma [ppk], 434

Tobalo, *alt. dial.* Pamona [bcx], 432

Tobanga [tng], 87
dial. Tobanga [tng], 87

Tobao, *alt. dial.* Pamona [bcx], 432

Tobaru, *alt.* Tabaru [tby], 404

Tobati [tti], 424

Tobau, *dial.* Pamona [bcx], 432

Tobelo [tlb], 405
alt. dial. Tobelo [tlb], 405

Toberelda, *alt. dial.* Moro [mor], 193

Tobi, *alt.* Tobian [tox], 587

Tobian [tox], 587

Tobilang, *alt.* Tebilung [tgb], 458

Tobilung, *alt.* Tebilung [tgb], 458

Tobo [tbv], 628

Tobote, *alt.* Ntcham [bud], 209, 127

Tobunyuo, *dial.* Naga, Konyak [nbe], 378

Tobwadic, *alt.* Tobati [tti], 424

Tocenga, *dial.* Tuki [bag], 72

Tochipo, *alt. dial.* Acipa, Western [awc], 153

Tocho [taz], 196

Tocod, *alt.* Tukudede [tkd], 351

Tod, *alt.* Stod Bhoti [sbu], 387

Tod-Kad, *alt.* Stod Bhoti [sbu], 387

Toda [tcx], 389
alt. Taroko [trv], 512
alt. Tedaga [tuq], 86

Todaga, *alt.* Tedaga [tuq], 86

Todela, *alt.* Tuxá [tud], 233

Todga, *alt.* Tedaga [tuq], 86

Todi, *alt.* Kaiy [tcq], 416
alt. Toda [tcx], 389

Todii, *alt. dial.* Gola [gol], 138

Todos Santos Almolonga Popoloca, *dial.* Popoloca, Santa Inés Ahuatempan [pca], 274

Todos Santos Cuchumatán Mam, *see* Mam, Todos Santos Cuchumatán [mvj], 255

Todos Santos Mam, *see* Mam, Todos Santos Cuchumatán [mvj], 263

Todrá, *alt.* Todrah [tdr], 527

Todrah [tdr], 527

Todzhin, *alt. dial.* Tuvin [tyv], 507

Toemoetoe, *alt. dial.* Muyu, North [kti], 421

Toende, *dial.* Kusaal [kus], 126, 52

Tof, *alt.* Kulere [kul], 167
dial. Kulere [kul], 167

Tofa, *alt.* Karagas [kim], 505
alt. Tuvin [tyv], 507

Tofalar, *alt.* Karagas [kim], 505

Tofamna, *alt.* Tofanma [tlg], 424

Tofanma [tlg], 424

Tofi, *alt.* Gbe, Tofin [tfi], 44

Tofin, *alt.* Gbe, Tofin [tfi], 44

Tofin Gbe, *see* Gbe, Tofin [tfi], 44

Tofingbe, *alt.* Gbe, Tofin [tfi], 44

Tofoke, *alt.* Poke [pof], 107

Toga [lht], 646

Togbo, *dial.* Banda, Togbo-Vara [tor], 97, 74, 188

Togbo-Vara Banda, *see* Banda, Togbo-Vara [tor], 97, 74, 188

Toghwede, *alt.* Dghwede [dgh], 157

Togo, *dial.* Éwé [ewe], 207

Togo Kan, *dial.* Dogon, Tene Kan [dtk], 142

Togole, *alt.* Tegali [ras], 195

Togoy, *alt.* Togoyo [tgy], 196

Togoyo [tgy], 196

Tohgboh, *alt. dial.* Banda, Togbo-Vara [tor], 97, 74, 188

Tohono O'odam, *dial.* Tohono O'odham [ood], 309

Tohono O'odham [ood], 309

Toi, *alt.* Didinga [did], 189

Toi-Oi, *alt.* Ta'oih, Upper [tth], 527

Toicho, *alt.* Tocho [taz], 196

Toisan, *alt. dial.* Chinese, Yue [yue], 331

Toishanese, *dial.* Chinese, Yue [yue], 454

Tojolabal [toj], 275

Tok Pisin [tpi], 628

Toka, *dial.* Tonga [toi], 215, 217

Tokaimalo, *alt. dial.* Fijian [fij], 580

Tokama, *alt.* Tokano [zuh], 628

Tokano [zuh], 628

Tokat, *alt. dial.* Armenian [hye], 318

Tokelau, *alt.* Tokelauan [tkl], 639

Tokelauan [tkl], 639

Tokha, *alt.* Tuvin [tyv], 507

Tokilor, *alt. dial.* Pulaar [fuc], 181

Tokita, *dial.* Karata [kpt], 555

Tokitin, *alt. dial.* Karata [kpt], 555

Tokkaru, *alt.* Dogri [dgo], 360

Tokko, *dial.* Evenki [evn], 504

Tokmo-Upper Lena, *dial.* Evenki [evn], 504

Tokodé, *alt.* Tukudede [tkd], 351

Tokodede, *alt.* Tukudede [tkd], 351

Tokondindi, *dial.* Pamona [bcx], 432

Tokotu'a, *dial.* Moronene [mqn], 431

Toku-No-Shima [tkn], 447

Tokuni, *dial.* Kopkaka [opk], 418

Tokunu, *alt. dial.* Misima-Paneati [mpx], 614

Tokwa, *alt. dial.* Sotho, Northern [nso], 186

Tokwasa, *alt.* Wára [tci], 631

Tol [jic], 258

Tola, *dial.* Lamja-Dengsa-Tola [ldh], 168

Tolai, *alt.* Kuanua [ksd], 608

Tolaki [lbw], 433

Tolamleinyua, *dial.* Naga, Konyak [nbe], 378

Tolangan, *alt.* Telugu [tel], 388

Tolchha, *dial.* Rongpo [rnp], 385
pej. alt. Rongpo [rnp], 385

Toldil, *dial.* Gola [gol], 183

Tolé, *alt. dial.* Ngäbere [gym], 283

Tolee', *dial.* Uma [ppk], 434

Toli, *alt. dial.* Kono [kno], 183
dial. Gun [guw], 45

Toli-Gbe, *alt.* Gun [guw], 45

Toliliko, *alt. dial.* Pagu [pgu], 403

Tolitai, *alt.* Doutai [tds], 414

Tolitoli, *alt.* Totoli [txe], 434

Toliwiku, *alt. dial.* Pagu [pgu], 403

Tolo, *alt.* Talise [tlr], 638
dial. Bahnar [bdq], 521
dial. Talise [tlr], 638

Tolokiwa, *alt.* Arop-Lukep [apr], 590

Tolokoson, *dial.* Tagal Murut [mvv], 458, 395

Tolomako [tlm], 646

Tolomako-Jereviu, *alt.* Tolomako [tlm], 646

Tolou, *alt.* Tondano [tdn], 434

Tolour, *alt.* Tondano [tdn], 434

Tolowa [tol], 309

Toloweri, *dial.* Bima [bhp], 406

Tolpan, *alt.* Tol [jic], 258

Tolubi, *alt. dial.* Katcha-Kadugli-Miri [xtc], 191

Toluo, *alt. dial.* Gelao [gio], 333

Tom-Kuznets Tatar, *alt.* Shor [cjs], 506

Toma [tod], 130
dial. Samo, Southern [sbd], 54

Toma Ma Dalla, *alt. dial.* Katcha-Kadugli-Miri [xtc], 191

Tomacheck, *alt.* Tamajaq [ttq], 144
alt. Tamajaq, Tawallammat [ttq], 152, 175

alt. Tamajeq, Tayart [thz], 152
alt. Tamasheq [taq], 144
alt. Tamasheq, Kidal [taq], 55
Tomachek, *alt.* Tamahaq, Tahaggart [thv], 37, 139, 152
Tomadino [tdi], 434
Tomahu, *alt. dial.* Buru [mhs], 397
Tomani, *dial.* Tagal Murut [mvv], 458, 395
Tomaraho, *alt. dial.* Chamacoco [ceg], 284
Tomaraxa, *alt. dial.* Chamacoco [ceg], 284
Tomás-Alis, *dial.* Quechua, Yauyos [qux], 292
Tombaggo, *alt. dial.* Banda-Ndélé [bfl], 75, 188
Tombalu, *alt.* Tombulu [tom], 434
Tombatu, *alt.* Tonsawang [tnw], 434
Tombelala [ttp], 434
Tombonuo, *alt.* Tombonuwo [txa], 458
Tombonuva, *alt.* Tombonuwo [txa], 458
Tombonuwo [txa], 458
Tombouctou, *alt. dial.* Tamasheq [taq], 144
alt. dial. Tamasheq, Kidal [taq], 55
Tombucas, *alt.* Tumbuka [tum], 141, 215
Tombula, *alt.* Tombulu [tom], 434
Tombulu [tom], 434
Tombulu', *alt.* Tombulu [tom], 434
Tomea, *alt. dial.* Tukang Besi South [bhq], 434
Tomedes [toe], 248
Tomia, *alt. dial.* Tukang Besi South [bhq], 434
Tomini [txm], 434
Tomliapat, *dial.* Tugun [tzn], 405
Tomman, *alt.* Malfaxal [mlx], 643
Tommot, *dial.* Evenki [evn], 504
Tomo, *alt.* Batek [btq], 454
Tomo Kan Dogon, *see* Dogon, Tomo Kan [dtm], 142, 50
Tomo-Kan, *alt.* Dogon, Tomo Kan [dtm], 142, 50
Tomohon, *dial.* Tombulu [tom], 434
Tomoip [tqp], 628
Tomoive, *alt.* Tomoip [tqp], 628
Tomoni, *dial.* Pamona [bcx], 432
Tomoyp, *alt.* Tomoip [tqp], 628
Tompakewa, *alt.* Tontemboan [tnt], 434
Tompaso, *dial.* Tontemboan [tnt], 434
Tompiro, *alt.* Piro [pie], 307
Tompo, *alt. dial.* Bugis [bug], 428
Tompon, *dial.* Even [eve], 504

Tompulung, *alt.* Kadazan, Labuk-Kinabatangan [dtb], 457
Tomu, *alt.* Odoodee [kkc], 619
alt. dial. Arandai [jbj], 411
Tomu River, *alt.* Odoodee [kkc], 619
Tomyang [tmx], 481
Tomyang Rai, *alt.* Tomyang [tmx], 481
Tona, *dial.* Rukai [dru], 512
Tonda, *alt.* Blafe [bfh], 594
Tondai, *dial.* Bunun [bnn], 511
Tondano [tdn], 434
dial. Tondano [tdn], 434
Tondanou, *alt.* Tondano [tdn], 434
Tong, *alt.* Dong, Northern [doc], 331
alt. Dong, Southern [kmc], 331
alt. Ong [oog], 452
alt. Ta'oih, Lower [tto], 453
dial. Pak-Tong [pkg], 621
dial. Ta'oih, Lower [tto], 453
Tóng, *alt.* Pa-Hng [pha], 342
Tong-Pak, *alt.* Pak-Tong [pkg], 621
Tonga ([toh], 149
   Tonga (Nyasa) [tog], 141
   Tonga (Thailand) [tnz], 518, 456
   Tonga (Zambia) [toi], 215, 217
alt. Tongan [ton], 639
alt. Tsonga [tso], 186, 149, 217
alt. dial. Ndau [ndc], 216
dial. Chopi [cce], 147
Tonga-Inhambane, *alt.* Tonga [toh], 149
Tongan [ton], 639
Tongareva, *alt.* Penrhyn [pnh], 579
Tongariki Island, *dial.* Namakura [nmk], 644
Tongbo, *alt.* Mambila, Cameroon [mcu], 66
alt. Mambila, Nigeria [mzk], 169
Tongeccha, *dial.* Sampang [rav], 478
Tonggu, *dial.* Chinese, Hakka [hak], 329
Tongian 1, *dial.* Bajau, Indonesian [bdl], 427
Tongian 2, *dial.* Bajau, Indonesian [bdl], 427
Tongkou, *alt.* Budong-Budong [bdx], 428
Tonglim, *dial.* Naga, Tase [nst], 380
Tongoa, *alt. dial.* Efate, North [llp], 641
Tongoa Island, *dial.* Namakura [nmk], 644
Tongoyna, *alt.* Tupuri [tui], 72
Tongren, *dial.* Bonan [peh], 328
Tongshi-Qiandui-Baocheng, *alt. dial.* Hlai [lic], 333
Tongwe [tny], 205

Toni, *alt. dial.* Gwandara [gwn], 161
Tonj Bongo, *dial.* Bongo [bot], 189
Tonjo, *dial.* Tuki [bag], 72
Tonjon [tjn], 95
Tonkawa [tqw], 309
Tonkinese, *alt. dial.* Vietnamese [vie], 527
Tonko, *alt.* Mabaan [mfz], 193
alt. dial. Limba, West-Central [lia], 183
Tonore, *alt.* Ikpeng [txi], 227
Tonsawang [tnw], 434
Tonsea [txs], 434
Tonsea', *alt.* Tonsea [txs], 434
Tontemboan [tnt], 434
Tonto, *dial.* Apache, Western [apw], 298
Tontoli, *alt.* Totoli [txe], 434
Toodii, *alt. dial.* Gola [gol], 183
To'olaki, *alt.* Tolaki [lbw], 433
Tooma, *alt.* Toma [tod], 130
To'on Savi, *alt.* Mixtec, Alacatlatzala [mim], 265
Toongo, *dial.* Gbaya, Southwest [mdo], 76
Tooro [ttj], 213
alt. dial. Hema [nix], 100
Toototobi, *alt. dial.* Yanomámi [wca], 234
Topada, *alt. dial.* Pamona [bcx], 432
Topoiyo [toy], 434
Topoke, *alt.* Poke [pof], 107
Toposa [toq], 196
Topotaa, *alt. dial.* Pamona [bcx], 432
Topotha, *alt.* Toposa [toq], 196
Topura, *dial.* Wedau [wed], 631
Tora, *dial.* Bangba [bbe], 97
Torá [trz], 233
Toradja, *alt.* Toraja-Sa'dan [sda], 434
Toraja, *alt.* Toraja-Sa'dan [sda], 434
Toraja Barat, *dial.* Toraja-Sa'dan [sda], 434
Toraja Timur, *alt.* Tae' [rob], 428
alt. Toala' [tlz], 433
Toraja-Sa'dan [sda], 434
Toram [trj], 87
Torau [ttu], 628
Toraz, *alt.* Torá [trz], 233
Torbi, *alt.* Mambila, Cameroon [mcu], 66
alt. dial. Mambila, Cameroon [mcu], 66
Torete, *dial.* Bungku [bkz], 428
Torghoud, *alt. dial.* Kalmyk-Oirat [xal], 554
Torghud, *alt. dial.* Kalmyk-Oirat [xal], 554

Torgon, *dial.* Nanai [gld], 506
Torgut, *dial.* Kalmyk-Oirat [xal], 554
Torguud, *alt. dial.* Kalmyk-Oirat [xal], 554
Torguut, *alt. dial.* Kalmyk-Oirat [xal], 554
Tori, *alt.* Sikaritai [tty], 423
Tori Aikwakai, *alt.* Sikaritai [tty], 423
Toriko, *alt.* Lika [lik], 102
Torishima, *dial.* Okinawan, Central [ryu], 447
Torki, *alt.* Azerbaijani, South [azb], 438
Torkomani, *alt.* Turkmen [tuk], 442
Tornasi, *alt.* Kelo [xel], 192
Torne, *dial.* Saami, North [sme], 550, 535, 561
Torne Valley Finnish, *alt.* Finnish, Tornedalen [fit], 561
  dial. Finnish, Tornedalen [fit], 561
Tornedalen, *alt.* Finnish, Tornedalen [fit], 561
Tornedalen Finnish, *see* Finnish, Tornedalen [fit], 561, 534
Tornedalsfinska, *alt.* Finnish, Tornedalen [fit], 561
Toro [tdv], 175
  alt. Tooro [ttj], 213
  alt. dial. Fali, South [fal], 61
  dial. Hema [nix], 100
Toro So, *alt.* Dogon, Toro So [dts], 142
Toro So Dogon, *see* Dogon, Toro So [dts], 142
Toro Tegu Dogon, *see* Dogon, Toro Tegu [dtt], 142
Toroko, *alt.* Taroko [trv], 512
Torom, *alt.* Toram [trj], 87
Toromona, *alt.* Toromono [tno], 224
Toromono [tno], 224
Torona [tqr], 196
Torr, *alt.* Chin, Tawr [tcp], 463
Torres, *alt.* Hiw [hiw], 642
  alt. Toga [lht], 646
Torres Island, *alt.* Hiw [hiw], 642
Torres Strait Broken, *alt.* Torres Strait Creole [tcs], 577
Torres Strait Creole [tcs], 577
Torres Strait Pidgin, *alt.* Torres Strait Creole [tcs], 577
Torricelli [tei], 628
Toru, *alt.* Taungyo [tco], 467
Torum, *alt.* Toram [trj], 87
Torwali [trw], 489
Tosila'ai, *dial.* Molima [mox], 614
Tosk, *alt.* Albanian, Tosk [als], 529
Tosk Albanian, *see* Albanian, Tosk [als], 529, 540, 563

Totali, *dial.* Newar [new], 476
Totcha, *alt.* Naga, Tutsa [tvt], 380
Totela [ttl], 215, 151
Toto [txo], 389
Totok, *dial.* Naga, Konyak [nbe], 378
Totoli [txe], 434
Totomachapan Zapotec, *see* Zapotec, Totomachapan [zph], 280
Totonac, Coyutla [toc], 276
Totonac, Filomena Mata-Coahuitlán [tlp], 276
Totonac, Highland [tos], 276
Totonac, Ozumatlán [tqt], 276
Totonac, Papantla [top], 276
Totonac, Patla-Chicontla [tot], 276
Totonac, Xicotepec de Juárez [too], 276
Totonac, Yecuatla [tlc], 276
Totonaco de Coyutla, *alt.* Totonac, Coyutla [toc], 276
Totonaco de Filomena Mata-Coahuitlán, *alt.* Totonac, Filomena Mata-Coahuitlán [tlp], 276
Totonaco de la Sierra, *alt.* Totonac, Highland [tos], 276
Totonaco de Ozumatlán, *alt.* Totonac, Ozumatlán [tqt], 276
Totonaco de Papantla, *alt.* Totonac, Papantla [top], 276
Totonaco de Patla y Chicontla, *alt.* Totonac, Patla-Chicontla [tot], 276
Totonaco de Villa Juárez, *alt.* Totonac, Xicotepec de Juárez [too], 276
Totontepec Mixe, *see* Mixe, Totontepec [mto], 265
Totoro [ttk], 248
Tototepec, *dial.* Mixtec, Alacatlatzala [mim], 265
Touaouru, *alt.* Numee [kdk], 585
  alt. dial. Numee [kdk], 585
Touareg, *alt.* Tamahaq, Tahaggart [thv], 37, 152
  alt. Tamajaq, Tawallammat [ttq], 152
  alt. Tamajeq, Tayart [thz], 152
Touat, *dial.* Taznatit [grr], 40
Toubakai, *alt.* Soninke [snk], 144, 95, 122, 145, 182
Toubou, *alt.* Dazaga [dzg], 151
  alt. Tedaga [tuq], 86, 152
Toubouri, *alt.* Tupuri [tui], 72, 87
Toucouleur, *dial.* Pulaar [fuc], 181, 122, 130, 143, 145
Toudougouka, *alt. dial.* Wojenaka [jod], 95
Tougan, *alt.* Samo, Matya [stj], 53

Touggourt, *alt.* Tamazight, Temacine [tjo], 40
Tougourt, *alt.* Tamazight, Temacine [tjo], 40
Toulonnais, *alt. dial.* Provençal [prv], 537
Touloun, *dial.* Halia [hla], 601
Toulour, *alt.* Tondano [tdn], 434
Toum, *dial.* Hung [hnu], 450
Toum Phong, *alt. dial.* Hung [hnu], 523
Toumak, *alt.* Tumak [tmc], 87
Toumbulu, *alt.* Tombulu [tom], 434
Tounia, *alt.* Tunia [tug], 87
Tounkoul, *alt. dial.* Bidiyo [bid], 79
Tountemboan, *alt.* Tontemboan [tnt], 434
Touo [tqu], 639
Toupouri, *alt.* Tupuri [tui], 72, 87
Toura (Côte d'Ivoire) [neb], 95
  Toura (Papua New Guinea) [don], 628
Tourage, *alt.* Tamahaq, Tahaggart [thv], 37, 139, 152
  alt. Tamajaq, Tawallammat [ttq], 152
  pej. alt. Tamajaq [ttq], 144
Tourai, *dial.* Mouk-Aria [mwh], 615
Toureg, *alt.* Tamahaq, Tahaggart [thv], 139
Tourka, *alt.* Turka [tuz], 55
Tourou, *alt.* Hide [xed], 162
  alt. dial. Hdi [xed], 62
Toussian, Northern [tsp], 55
Toussian, Southern [wib], 55
Tovoke, *alt.* Poke [pof], 107
Towa, *alt.* Jemez [tow], 302
Towal, *alt. dial.* Ngile [jle], 194
Toware, *alt.* Tae' [rob], 428
  alt. Toala' [tlz], 433
Towargarhi, *alt. dial.* Bundeli [bns], 357
Towe, *alt.* Towei [ttn], 424
Towei [ttn], 424
Towetan, *alt.* Malavedan [mjr], 374
Towi, *alt.* Neyo [ney], 94
Town Bemba, *dial.* Bemba [bem], 213
Towolhi, *alt.* Maca [mca], 285
Toyeri, *dial.* Huachipaeri [hug], 288
Toyoeri, *alt. dial.* Huachipaeri [hug], 288
Tozhuma, *alt.* Naga, Yimchungru [yim], 380
Tozluk Turks, *alt. dial.* Balkan Gagauz Turkish [bgx], 563
Tozvi, *alt.* Lozi [loz], 214, 150, 216
Trabzon, *dial.* Armenian [hye], 318
Trade Jula, *alt. dial.* Jula [dyu], 93

Trade Malay, *alt. dial.* Malay [mly], 455

Trai, *pej. alt.* Iu Mien [ium], 523

Trakay, *dial.* Karaim [kdr], 546

Transalpin, *dial.* Provençal [prv], 537, 545

Transitional Kanauji, *dial.* Kanauji [bjj], 366

Transvaal Ndebele, *alt.* Ndebele [nbl], 186

Transvaal Sotho, *alt.* Sotho, Northern [nso], 186

Transylvania, *dial.* German, Standard [deu], 551

Transylvanian, *dial.* Romani, Carpathian [rmc], 542, 550, 551

dial. Romanian [ron], 552

Trapani, *alt. dial.* Sicilian [scn], 545

Trapezunt, *alt. dial.* Armenian [hye], 318

Trappist Sign Language, *dial.* Monastic Sign Language [mzg], 566

Tràu, *alt. dial.* Cua [cua], 522

Traude, *alt.* Dghwede [dgh], 157

Traveller Danish [rmd], 534

Traveller Norwegian, *see* Norwegian, Traveller [rmg], 550

Traveller Scottish [trl], 566

Traveller Swedish, *alt.* Romani, Tavringer [rmu], 561, 550

Traw, *dial.* Cua [cua], 522

Tredici Communi Cimbrian, *dial.* Cimbrian [cim], 543

Tregami [trm], 318

Tregorrois, *dial.* Breton [bre], 536

Trembo, *dial.* Grebo, Central [grv], 138

Tremembé [tme], 233

Treng, *alt.* Trieng [stg], 527

alt. dial. Lundayeh [lnd], 460

Trengganu, *dial.* Malay [mly], 455

Trentino Western, *alt. dial.* Lombard [lmo], 544

Trepo, *dial.* Krumen, Pye [pye], 93

Tretine, *dial.* Venetian [vec], 532

Tri, *dial.* Bru, Eastern [bru], 450, 514, 522

Tribal Oriya, *alt.* Oriya, Adivasi [ort], 382

Trieng [stg], 527

Triestino, *dial.* Venetian [vec], 545

Trièu Chau, *alt.* Chinese, Yue [yue], 522

Trigami, *alt.* Tregami [trm], 318

Trimuris [tip], 424

Tring [tgq], 461

dial. Koho [kpm], 524

Tringgus [trx], 461

dial. Tringgus [trx], 461

Tringus, *alt.* Tringgus [trx], 461

Trinh, *alt. dial.* Koho [kpm], 524

Trinidad Bhojpuri, *alt.* Hindustani, Caribbean [hns], 296

dial. Hindustani, Caribbean [hns], 295

Trinidadian Creole English [trf], 296

Trinidadian Creole French [acf], 296

Trinitario [trn], 224

Trinkat, *alt. dial.* Nicobarese, Central [ncb], 381

Trinkut, *dial.* Nicobarese, Central [ncb], 381

Trió [tri], 296, 233

Triometesem, *alt.* Akurio [ako], 295

Triometesen, *alt.* Akurio [ako], 295

Triperah, *alt.* Tippera [tpe], 322

Tripolita'it, *alt.* Arabic, Judeo-Tripolitanian [yud], 444

Tripolitanian Arabic, *dial.* Arabic, Libyan Spoken [ayl], 139

dial. Arabic, Western Egyptian Bedawi Spoken [ayl], 110

Tripolitanian Judeo-Arabic, *alt.* Arabic, Judeo-Tripolitanian [yud], 444

Tripura, *alt.* Kok Borok [trp], 368, 321

alt. Tippera [tpe], 322

Tripuri, *alt.* Kok Borok [trp], 368, 321

Triqui de San Andrés Chicahuaxtla, *alt.* Triqui, Chicahuaxtla [trs], 276

Triqui de San Juan Copala, *alt.* Triqui, Copala [trc], 276

Triqui de San Martín Itunyoso, *alt.* Triqui, San Martín Itunyoso [trq], 276

Triqui, Chicahuaxtla [trs], 276

Triqui, Copala [trc], 276

Triqui, San Martín Itunyoso [trq], 276

Trisuli, *dial.* Tamang, Western [tdg], 480

Trobiawan, *dial.* Basay [byq], 511

Tromowa, *alt.* Groma [gro], 333, 363

Trondheim, *dial.* Norwegian Sign Language [nsl], 549

Trong Ggia, *alt.* Giáy [pcc], 523

True Motu, *alt.* Motu [meu], 615

Truj, *alt. dial.* Tulishi [tey], 196

Truk, *alt.* Chuukese [chk], 582

Truká [tka], 233

Trukese, *alt.* Chuukese [chk], 582

Trukhmen, *alt.* Turkmen [tuk], 520, 519

Trukhmeny, *alt.* Turkmen [tuk], 520

Trukmen, *alt.* Turkmen [tuk], 318

dial. Turkmen [tuk], 442

Truku, *alt.* Taroko [trv], 512

alt. dial. Taroko [trv], 512

Trumaí [tpy], 233

Trung, *alt.* Drung [duu], 332

Trusan, *dial.* Lundayeh [lnd], 324, 460

Tsaam, *alt.* Samba [smx], 107

alt. dial. Mandjak [mfv], 131, 181

Tsaamo, *dial.* Mandjak [mfv], 122

Tsaangi [tsa], 90, 121

Tsachila, *alt.* Colorado [cof], 250

Tsafiki, *alt.* Colorado [cof], 250

Tsaga, *alt.* Enga [enq], 598

Tsagkaglingpa'ikha, *alt.* Chocangacakha [cgk], 323

Tsagu, *alt.* Ciwogai [tgd], 157

Tsaiwa, *alt.* Zaiwa [atb], 349, 467

Tsakhur [tkr], 320, 557

Tsakhury, *alt.* Tsakhur [tkr], 320, 557

Tsakma, *alt.* Chakma [ccp], 358

Tsakonia, *alt.* Tsakonian [tsd], 541

Tsakonian [tsd], 541

Tsakwambo [kvz], 424

Tsalagi, *alt.* Cherokee [chr], 299

Tsalisen, *alt.* Rukai [dru], 512

Tsama, *alt.* Ebrié [ebr], 92

Tsamai [tsb], 119

Tsamak, *alt.* Maidu, Northwest [mjd], 304

Tsamakko, *alt.* Tsamai [tsb], 119

Tsamako, *alt.* Tsamai [tsb], 119

Ts'amay, *alt.* Tsamai [tsb], 119

Tsamba, *alt.* Samba [smx], 107

alt. Samba Daka [ccg], 174

Tsang, *alt. dial.* Tibetan, Central [bod], 344

Tsangi, *alt.* Tsaangi [tsa], 121

Tsangla, *alt.* Tshangla [tsj], 324, 345, 389

Tsanglo, *alt.* Naga, Angami [njm], 377

alt. Tshangla [tsj], 345

Tsanuma, *alt.* Sanumá [xsu], 312, 232

Ts'ao, *alt. dial.* Naro [nhr], 48

Ts'aokhoe, *dial.* Naro [nhr], 48

Tsaokhwe, *alt. dial.* Naro [nhr], 48

Tsarisen, *alt.* Rukai [dru], 512

Tsasi, *alt.* !Xóõ [nmn], 48

Tsat [huq], 345

Tsaudangsi, *alt.* Chaudangsi [cdn], 358, 469

Tsaukwe, *alt. dial.* Naro [nhr], 48

Tsaurasya, *alt.* Wambule [wme], 482
Tsaxur, *alt.* Tsakhur [tkr], 320, 557
Tsaya, *alt.* Teke-Tsaayi [tyi], 90
Tsaye, *alt.* Teke-Tsaayi [tyi], 90
Tsayi, *alt.* Teke-Tsaayi [tyi], 90
Tschako, *alt.* Sheko [she], 118
Tschetti, *dial.* Ifè [ife], 208
Tschiokloe, *alt.* Chokwe [cjk], 40
Tschiokwe, *alt.* Chokwe [cjk], 99, 213
Tschopi, *alt.* Chopi [cce], 147
Tsegob, *alt. dial.* Akhvakh [akv], 552
Tseku [tsk], 345, 324, 481
Tsenap, *alt.* Chenapian [cjn], 596
Tsepang, *alt.* Chepang [cdm], 469
Tserekwe, *dial.* Naro [nhr], 48
Tsesungún, *dial.* Huilliche [huh], 242
Tsetsaut [txc], 242
Ts'exa, *alt.* ǁAni [hnh], 46
Ts'éxa, *alt.* ǁAni [hnh], 46
Tsez, *alt.* Dido [ddo], 554
Tsezy, *alt.* Dido [ddo], 554
Tshaahui, *alt.* Chayahuita [cbt], 287
Tshala, *alt.* Chala [cll], 123
Tshali, *alt.* Chalikha [tgf], 323
Tshalingpa, *alt.* Chalikha [tgf], 323
Tshamberi, *alt.* Chambri [can], 596
Tshangkha, *alt.* Lakha [lkh], 323
Tshangla [tsj], 324, 345, 389
Tsheenya, *alt.* Enya [gey], 99
Tshidi-Khwe, *dial.* Shua [shg], 48
Tshiga, *alt. dial.* Rwanda [kin], 178
Tshikiana, *alt.* Sikiana [sik], 296
Tshiluba, *alt.* Luba-Kasai [lua], 103
Tshirambo, *alt.* Bambalang [bmo], 56
Tsh'iti, *alt. dial.* Shua [shg], 48
Tshivenda, *alt.* Venda [ven], 217
Tshogo, *alt. dial.* Rwanda [kin], 178
Tshokwe, *alt.* Chokwe [cjk], 99, 40, 213
Tshom-Djapa, *dial.* Kanamarí [knm], 228
Tshumakwe, *alt.* Shua [shg], 48
Tshumkwe, *alt.* Juǀʼhoan [ktz], 150
Tshummbuli, *alt.* Tchumbuli [bqa], 46
Tshuosh, *alt.* Malinguat [sic], 611
Tshuwau, *alt.* Hietshware [hio], 216
alt. Tsoa [hio], 48
Tshwa, *alt.* Tsoa [hio], 48
alt. Tswa [tsc], 149, 186, 217
dial. Tswa [tsc], 149, 186, 217
Tshwana, *alt.* Tswana [tsn], 217
Tshwosh, *alt.* Malinguat [sic], 611
Tsia, *alt.* Zia [zia], 634
Tsie, *alt.* Ligbi [lig], 126

Tsigane, *alt.* Romani, Sinte [rmo], 448, 533, 537, 550
alt. Romani, Vlax [rmy], 537, 566
Tsigene, *alt.* Domari [rmt], 438, 448, 510, 563
alt. Romani, Vlax [rmy], 551, 531, 542
Tsíhuli, *alt.* Kinnauri, Chitkuli [cik], 368
Tsikimba [kdl], 175
Tsilmano, *alt. dial.* Kacipo-Balesi [koe], 115
Tsimajeega, *dial.* Datooga [tcc], 198
Tsimané [cas], 224
Tsimihety, *alt.* Malagasy, Tsimihety [xmw], 140
Tsimihety Malagasy, *see* Malagasy, Tsimihety [xmw], 140
Tsimpshean, *alt.* Tsimshian [tsi], 242
Tsimshean, *alt.* Tsimshian [tsi], 309
Tsimshian [tsi], 242, 309
Tsíndíí, *alt.* Tlapanec, Azoyú [tpc], 275
Tsindir, *alt.* Naga, Lotha [njh], 378
Tsinga, *dial.* Tuki [bag], 72
Tsingani, *alt.* Romani, Vlax [rmy], 541
Tsinghwele, *alt.* Kwere [cwe], 200
Tsinuk Wawa, *alt.* Chinook Wawa [chn], 299
Tsiracua, *dial.* Ayoreo [ayo], 284
Tsírà'khàmájíín, *alt. dial.* Tlapanec, Malinaltepec [tcf], 275
Tsiricua, *dial.* Ayoreo [ayo], 222
Tsiripá, *alt.* Chiripá [nhd], 284, 220, 226
Tsishima, *alt. dial.* Ainu [ain], 446
Tsishingini [tsw], 176
Tsitkhuli, *alt.* Kinnauri, Chitkuli [cik], 368
Tsitsikhar, *alt. dial.* Daur [dta], 331, 461
Tsivili, *alt.* Vili [vif], 90, 121
Tsiwaha, *alt.* Tswana [tsn], 186
Tslagi, *alt.* Cherokee [chr], 299
Tso [ldp], 176
alt. Tsou [tsu], 512
Tsoa [hio], 48
Tsóbó, *alt.* Tso [ldp], 176
Tsobwa, *alt. dial.* Bushoong [buf], 98
Tsochiang, *alt. dial.* Zhuang, Southern [ccy], 349
Tsoghami, *alt.* Naga, Angami [njm], 377
Tsogo [tsv], 121
Tsokwambo, *alt.* Tsakwambo [kvz], 424
Tsola, *dial.* Tuyuca [tue], 233

Ts'ole', *dial.* Atayal [tay], 511
Tsonga [tso], 186, 149, 197, 217
Tsongol, *dial.* Mongolian, Halh [khk], 461
Tsontsii, *alt.* Naga, Lotha [njh], 378
Tsontsu, *dial.* Naga, Lotha [njh], 378
Tsoo, *alt.* Tsou [tsu], 512
Ts'ooke, *dial.* Salish, Straits [str], 241
Tsorokwe, *alt. dial.* Naro [nhr], 48
Tsotsitaal [fly], 186
Tsotso, *dial.* Luyia [luy], 134
Tsou [tsu], 512
Tsova-Tush, *alt.* Bats [bbl], 352
Tsu-U, *alt.* Tsou [tsu], 512
Tsu-Wo, *alt.* Tsou [tsu], 512
Tsudakhar, *alt. dial.* Dargwa [dar], 553
Tsugumi, *alt.* Naga, Angami [njm], 377
Tsuku, *alt.* Tseku [tsk], 345, 324, 481
Tsum [ttz], 481
Tsumanggorun, *dial.* Adzera [azr], 587
Tsumge, *alt.* Tsum [ttz], 481
Tsumkwe, *alt.* Juǀʼhoan [ktz], 47
Ts'ün-Lao [tsl], 527
Tsunari, *alt.* Bannoni [bcm], 592
Tsuntin, *alt.* Dido [ddo], 554
Tsuou, *alt.* Tsou [tsu], 512
Tsureja, *alt.* Reshe [res], 173
Tsureshe, *alt.* Reshe [res], 173
Tsuu T'ina, *alt.* Sarsi [srs], 241
Tsuvadi [tvd], 176
Tsuvan [tsh], 72
Tsuwenki, *dial.* Maring [mbw], 612
Tswa [tsc], 149, 186, 217
Tswana [tsn], 48, 151, 186, 217
Tswapong [two], 48
Tswene, *dial.* Sotho, Northern [nso], 186
Tsweni, *alt. dial.* Sotho, Northern [nso], 186
Tta'o, *alt. dial.* Siraya [fos], 512
Tu [mjg], 345
Tú Du, *alt.* Gelao, White [giw], 522
Tu Guangdonghua, *alt.* Chinese, Hakka [hak], 329
Tu Ngoro, *alt. dial.* Tuki [bag], 72
Tu-Dí, *dial.* Giáy [pcc], 523
Tu-Dìn, *alt.* Giáy [pcc], 523
Tu-Lop, *alt. dial.* Koho [kpm], 524
Tual, *dial.* Osetin [oss], 352, 519
Tuam, *alt.* Mutu [tuc], 616
dial. Mutu [tuc], 616
Tuam-Mutu, *alt.* Mutu [tuc], 616
Tuamotuan [pmt], 581
Tuan Tet, *dial.* Karen, Pwo Western [pwo], 464

Tuaran Dusun, *alt.* Lotud [dtr], 457
Tuareg, *alt.* Tamahaq, Tahaggart
   [thv], 37, 139, 152
   alt. Tamajaq, Tawallammat
   [ttq], 152, 175
   alt. Tamajeq, Tayart [thz], 152
   alt. Tamasheq, Kidal [taq], 55
   pej. alt. Tamajaq [ttq], 144
   pej. alt. Tamasheq [taq], 144
Tuat, *alt. dial.* Taznatit [grr], 40
Tuauru, *alt.* Numee [kdk], 585
Tuba, *alt.* Ligbi [lig], 126, 94
   alt. Tuvin [tyv], 507, 462
   alt. dial. Zaghawa [zag], 196
Tuba-Kizhi, *dial.* Tuvin [tyv], 507
Tubai, *dial.* Namosi-Naitasiri-Serua
   [bwb], 580
Tubal, *dial.* Lamma [lev], 408
Tubaniwai, *alt. dial.* Fijian, Western
   [wyy], 580
Tubar [tbu], 276
Tubarão [tba], 233
Tubare, *alt.* Tarahumara,
   Southwestern [twr], 275
   alt. Tubar [tbu], 276
Tübatulabal [tub], 309
Tubbi, *alt.* Ulumanda' [ulm], 434
Tube, *alt. dial.* Lamma [lev], 408
Tubeta, *alt.* Taveta [tvs], 136
Tubetube, *alt.* Bwanabwana
   [tte], 596
Tubiruasa, *alt.* Uruangnirin
   [urn], 424
Tu'boro, *alt. dial.* Karang [kzr], 63
Tuboy Subanon, *alt.* Subanen,
   Northern [stb], 501
Tubu, *alt.* Dazaga [dzg], 151
   alt. Tedaga [tuq], 86, 152
Tubuai, *dial.* Austral [aut], 581
Tubuai-Rurutu, *alt.* Austral
   [aut], 581
Tubulamo, *dial.* Sinaugoro
   [snc], 624
Tuburi, *alt.* Tupuri [tui], 72, 87
Tucano [tuo], 233, 248
Tuchia, *alt.* Tujia, Northern [tji], 345
   alt. Tujia, Southern [tjs], 345
Tuchinaua, *alt.* Tuxináwa [tux], 233
Tucuna, *alt.* Ticuna [tca], 248
Tuda, *alt.* Tedaga [tuq], 86
   alt. Toda [tcx], 389
Tudaga, *alt.* Tedaga [tuq], 86
Tudahwe, *alt.* Pawaia [pwa], 621
Tudanchi, *alt. dial.* Kag-Fer-Jiir-
   Koor-Ror-Us-Zuksun [gel], 165
Tudja, *alt.* Tujia, Northern [tji], 345
Tuer-Gala, *dial.* Zaghawa [zag], 87
Tuerke, *alt.* Ili Turki [ili], 336, 448
Tuftera, *alt.* Hwana [hwo], 162
Tufungwa, *alt.* Fungwa [ula], 160

Tugara, *alt.* Duruwa [pci], 361
Tugen, North [tuy], 136
Tugeri, *alt.* Marind [mrz], 419
   dial. Marind [mrz], 419
Tugun [tzn], 405
Tugura, *alt. dial.* Lame [bma], 168
Tuguro-Chumikan, *dial.* Evenki
   [evn], 504
Tugurt, *alt.* Tamazight, Temacine
   [tjo], 40
Tugutil [tuj], 405
Tuhup, *dial.* Hupdë [jup], 227
Tuic, *dial.* Dinka, Southeastern
   [dks], 190
   dial. Dinka, Southwestern [dik], 190
Tuichiap, *dial.* Chin, Paite [pck], 359
Tuiuca, *alt.* Tuyuca [tue], 233
Tujia, *alt.* Bouyei [pcc], 328
Tujia, Northern [tji], 345
Tujia, Southern [tjs], 345
Tuka, *dial.* Gagu [ggu], 93
Tukaimi, *alt.* Naga, Thangal
   [nki], 380
Tukana, *alt.* Tucano [tuo], 248
Tukána, *alt.* Tucano [tuo], 233
Tukang Besi North [khc], 434
Tukang Besi South [bhq], 434
Tukang-Besi, *alt.* Tukang Besi
   South [bhq], 434
Tukche, *dial.* Thakali [ths], 480
Tuken, *alt.* Tugen, North [tuy], 136
   alt. dial. Kalenjin [kln], 133
Tuki [bag], 72
Tukkongo, *alt.* Wongo [won], 109
Tukolor, *alt. dial.* Pulaar [fuc], 181,
   122, 130, 143
Tukombe, *alt. dial.* Tuki [bag], 72
Tukongo, *alt.* Wongo [won], 109
Tukpa [tpq], 389
Tuku, *dial.* Tooro [ttj], 213
Tukude, *alt.* Tukudede [tkd], 351
Tukudede [tkd], 351
   dial. Tukudede [tkd], 351
Tukudh, *alt.* Gwich'in [gwi], 237
   alt. dial. Gwich'in [gwi], 237, 301
Tukulor, *alt. dial.* Pulaar [fuc], 181,
   122, 130, 143, 145
Tukulu, *alt. dial.* Swahili [swh], 136
Tukumanféd [tkf], 233
Tukun, *alt.* Mbembe, Tigon
   [nza], 170
Tukuna, *alt.* Ticuna [tca], 233, 293
Tukúna, *alt.* Ticuna [tca], 248
Tukurina, *dial.* Jamamadí [jaa], 227
Tula [tul], 176
Tulai, *alt. dial.* Zeem [zua], 178
Tulambatu, *dial.* Bungku
   [bkz], 428
Tulehu [tlu], 405
   dial. Tulehu [tlu], 405

Tulem, *alt.* Dani, Mid Grand Valley
   [dnt], 413
Tulesh, *alt.* Tulishi [tey], 196
Tulim, *dial.* Naga, Tase [nst], 466
Tuling, *alt. dial.* Tunen [baz], 72
Tulishi [tey], 196
   dial. Tulishi [tey], 196
Tullu, *alt.* Tulu [tcy], 389
Tulon, *alt. dial.* Halia [hla], 601
Tulu [tcy], 389
   alt. dial. Tulu-Bohuai [rak], 628
Tulu-Bohuai [rak], 628
Tulun, *alt. dial.* Halia [hla], 601
   alt. dial. Tulu-Bohuai [rak], 628
Tulung, *alt.* Drung [duu], 332
Tuluva Bhasa, *alt.* Tulu [tcy], 389
Tum, *alt. dial.* Hung [hnu], 450
Tuma, *alt.* Tuma-Irumu [iou], 628
Tuma-Irumu [iou], 628
Tumac, *alt.* Tumak [tmc], 87
Tumag, *alt.* Tumak [tmc], 87
Tumak [tmc], 87
   dial. Tumak [tmc], 87
Tumala, *alt.* Mala [ruy], 169
Tumale, *dial.* Tagoi [tag], 195
Tumanao, *alt.* Blaan, Sarangani
   [bps], 493
Tumaniq, *alt. dial.* Tagal Murut
   [mvv], 458, 395
Tumara, *alt.* Juwal [mwb], 603
Tumari, *dial.* Kanuri, Tumari
   [krt], 152
Tumari Kanuri, *see* Kanuri, Tumari
   [krt], 152
Tumariya, *alt.* Panchpargania
   [tdb], 382
Tumaru, *alt.* Juwal [mwb], 603
Tumawo, *alt.* Skou [skv], 423
Tumba, *dial.* Gogo [gog], 198
   dial. Kagulu [kki], 199
Tumbalá Chol, *see* Chol, Tumbalá
   [ctu], 261
Tumbele, *alt. dial.* Tuki [bag], 72
Tumboka, *alt.* Tumbuka [tum], 141,
   215
Tumbuka [tum], 141, 215
Tumbunwha, *alt.* Tombonuwo
   [txa], 458
Tumet, *alt. dial.* Mongolian,
   Peripheral [mvf], 339, 462
Tumi [kku], 176
Tumie, *alt.* Tomoip [tqp], 628
Tumleo [tmq], 628
Tumma, *dial.* Katcha-Kadugli-Miri
   [xtc], 191
Tummok, *alt.* Tumak [tmc], 87
Tümpisa Shoshoni, *alt.* Panamint
   [par], 306
Tumtum [tbr], 196
   dial. Tumtum [tbr], 196

dial. Iau [tmu], 415
Turu-Hide, *alt.* Hdi [xed], 62
alt. Hide [xed], 162
Turuba, *alt. dial.* Longuda [lnu], 169
Turubu, *alt.* Terebu [trb], 627
Turuj, *alt. dial.* Tulishi [tey], 196
Turuka, *alt.* Turka [tuz], 55
Turumawa, *alt.* Etulo [utr], 159
Turumbu, *alt.* Lombo [loo], 103
Turumsa [tqm], 629
Turung [try], 389
Turunggare, *alt.* Tunggare [trt], 424
Turupu, *alt.* Terebu [trb], 627
Turutap, *alt.* Maia [sks], 610
Turvali, *alt.* Torwali [trw], 489
Tuscan, *dial.* Italian [ita], 544
Tuscarora [tus], 242, 309
Tush, *alt.* Bats [bbl], 352
dial. Georgian [kat], 352
Tusha, *alt.* Tuxá [tud], 233
Tushama, *alt.* Shama-Sambuga
[sqa], 174
Tusia, *alt.* Toussian, Northern
[tsp], 55
alt. Toussian, Southern [wib], 55
Tusian, *alt.* Toussian, Northern [tsp],
55
alt. Toussian, Southern [wib], 55
Tutapi, *alt.* Orejón [ore], 289
Tutchone, Northern [ttm], 242
Tutchone, Southern [tce], 242
Tutelo [tta], 309
Tutet, *alt.* Chaura [crv], 358
Tutla Mixe, *alt.* Mixe, Mazatlán
[mzl], 265
Tutoh Kenya, *alt.* Kenyah, Tutoh
[ttw], 460
Tutoh Kenyah, *see* Kenyah, Tutoh
[ttw], 460
Tutoncana, *dial.* Evenki [evn], 504
Tutong 1 [ttx], 325, 461
Tutong 2 [ttg], 325
Tutrugbu, *alt.* Nyangbo [nyb], 127
Tutsa, *alt.* Naga, Tutsa [tvt], 380
Tutsa Naga, *see* Naga, Tutsa [tvt],
380
Tutsingo, *alt. dial.* Tuki [bag], 72
Tutuba [tmi], 646
Tutumi, *alt.* Tumi [kku], 176
Tutung, *alt.* Tutong 2 [ttg], 325
Tutunohan, *alt.* Aputai [apx], 396
alt. Perai [wet], 399
alt. Tugun [tzn], 405
Tututepec Mixtec, *see* Mixtec,
Tututepec [mtu], 269
Tututni [tuu], 309
Tuuda, *alt. dial.* Taroko [trv], 512
Tu'un Va'a, *alt.* Mixtec, Santa María
Zacatepec [mza], 268
Tuuno, *alt.* Doyayo [dow], 60

Tuva, *alt.* Tuvin [tyv], 507, 462
Tuva-Uriankhai, *alt.* Tuvin [tyv],
462
Tuvalu, *alt.* Tuvaluan [tvl], 640
Tuvaluan [tvl], 640
Tuvan, *alt.* Tuvin [tyv], 507, 462
Tuvia, *alt.* Tuvin [tyv], 507, 462
Tuvin [tyv], 507, 345, 462
Tuvinian, *alt.* Tuvin [tyv], 507, 462
Tuwa, *alt.* Tuvin [tyv], 345
Tuwa-Uriankhai, *alt.* Tuvin
[tyv], 462
Tuwali, *alt.* Ifugao, Tuwali [ifk], 495
Tuwali Ifugao, *see* Ifugao, Tuwali
[ifk], 495
Tuwang, *dial.* Lawangan [lbx], 394
Tuwari [tww], 629
Tuwat, *alt. dial.* Taznatit [grr], 40
Tuwili, *alt.* Tuwuli [bov], 128
Tuwuli [bov], 128
Tuxá [tud], 233
Tuxináwa [tux], 233
Tuyuca [tue], 248, 233
Tuyuka, *alt.* Tuyuca [tue], 248, 233
Tuyuneri, *alt. dial.* Huachipaeri
[hug], 288
Tuzanteco, *dial.* Mocho [mhc], 270
Tver, *alt. dial.* Karelian [krl], 555,
534
Twa, *alt. dial.* Rwanda [kin], 178
dial. Lenje [leh], 214
dial. Rwanda [kin], 107, 212
T'wa Kwama, *alt.* Kwama
[kmq], 116
Twa of Bangweulu, *dial.* Bemba
[bem], 213
Twa of Kafwe, *dial.* Tonga
[toi], 215
Twabo, *dial.* Glaro-Twabo [glr], 137
Twampa, *alt.* Uduk [udu], 119, 196
Twana [twa], 309
Twar, *alt.* Zangwal [zah], 178
Twendi [twn], 72
Twente, *alt.* Twents [twd], 549
Twents [twd], 549
Twer, *alt. dial.* Zaghawa [zag], 196
Twi, *alt.* Bwamu, Cwi [bwy], 50
alt. dial. Akan [aka], 123
alt. dial. Dinka, Southeastern
[dks], 190
Twic, *alt. dial.* Dinka, Southwestern
[dik], 190
Twich, *alt. dial.* Dinka, Southwestern
[dik], 190
Twii, *alt. dial.* Kenyang [ken], 64
Twij, *alt. dial.* Dinka, Southwestern
[dik], 190
Twoyu, *alt.* Dizi [mdx], 114
Twumwu, *dial.* Tikar [tik], 72
Txikân, *alt.* Ikpeng [txi], 227

Txikão, *alt.* Ikpeng [txi], 227
Txiripá, *alt.* Chiripá [nhd], 284, 220,
226
Txitxopi, *alt.* Chopi [cce], 147
Txopi, *alt.* Chopi [cce], 147
Txunhuã Dyapá, *alt. dial.*
Kanamarí [knm], 228
Txunhuã-Djapá, *alt. dial.* Kanamarí
[knm], 228
Txuwabo, *alt.* Chuwabu [chw], 147
Tyal, *alt.* Atayal [tay], 511
Tyama, *alt.* Ebrié [ebr], 92
Tyamuhi, *alt.* Cemuhî [cam], 584
Tyanga, *alt.* Kyenga [tye], 168
Tyap [kcg], 176
alt. dial. Tyap [kcg], 176
Tyapi, *alt.* Landoma [ldm], 129
Tyaraity [woa], 577
Tyebala, *alt.* Senoufo, Cebaara
[sef], 94
Tyebara, *dial.* Senoufo, Cebaara
[sef], 94
Tyefo, *alt.* Tiéfo [tiq], 55
Tyeforo, *alt.* Tiéfo [tiq], 55
Tyemeri, *dial.* Nangikurrunggurr
[nam], 574
Tyenga, *alt.* Kyenga [tye], 168, 45
Tyeyaxo, *alt.* Bozo, Tiéyaxo
[boz], 142
Tyhua, *alt.* Kua [tyu], 47
Tym, *dial.* Selkup [sel], 506
Tyneside Northumberland, *dial.*
English [eng], 565
Tyo, *alt. dial.* Teke, Ibali [tek], 108
Tyopi, *alt.* Landoma [ldm], 129
Tyrewuju, *dial.* Carib [car], 226,
252, 295
Tyrolese, *alt.* German, Hutterite
[geh], 237, 300
Tyua, *alt.* Kua [tyu], 47
Tyura, *alt.* Nugunu [nnv], 575
Tyurama, *alt.* Turka [tuz], 55
Tyva, *alt.* Tuvin [tyv], 507
Tzeltal de Ocosingo, *alt.* Tzeltal,
Bachajón [tzb], 276
Tzeltal, Bachajón [tzb], 276
Tzeltal, Oxchuc [tzh], 276
Tzilkotin, *alt.* Chilcotin [clc], 236
Tzimbro, *alt.* Cimbrian [cim], 543
Tzo, *alt.* Tsou [tsu], 512
Tzotzil de Huixtán, *alt.* Tzotzil,
Huixtán [tzu], 277
**Tzotzil de San Andrés
Larrainzar**, *alt.* Tzotzil, San
Andrés Larrainzar [tzs], 277
Tzotzil, Chamula [tzc], 277
Tzotzil, Chenalhó [tze], 277
Tzotzil, Huixtán [tzu], 277
Tzotzil, San Andrés Larrainzar
[tzs], 277

Tzotzil, Venustiano Carranza [tzo], 277

Tzotzil, Zinacantán [tzz], 277

Tzuku, *alt.* Tseku [tsk], 345, 324, 481

Tzutuhil, *alt.* Tz'utujil, Eastern [tzj], 256

Tzutujil Oriental, *alt.* Tz'utujil, Eastern [tzj], 256

Tz'utujil, Eastern [tzj], 256

Tz'utujil, Western [tzt], 256

U [uuu], 345

  alt. Tibetan, Central [bod], 344

  dial. Khmu [kjg], 451

U Ní, *alt.* Hani [hni], 523

Ua Huka, *dial.* Marquesan, North [mrq], 581

Ua Pou, *dial.* Marquesan, North [mrq], 581

Uab Atoni Pah Meto, *alt.* Uab Meto [aoz], 410

Uab Meto [aoz], 410

  alt. Baikeno [bkx], 350

Uab Pah Meto, *alt.* Baikeno [bkx], 350

  alt. Uab Meto [aoz], 410

Uadzoli, *dial.* Carútana [cru], 226

Uageo, *alt.* Wogeo [woc], 632

Uai Ma'a, *alt.* Waima'a [wmh], 351

Uaiai, *dial.* Paumarí [pad], 231

Uaiana, *alt.* Piratapuyo [pir], 231

  alt. Wayana [way], 296, 234, 252

Uaicana, *alt.* Piratapuyo [pir], 231

Uaieue, *alt.* Waiwai [waw], 233, 257

Uaikena, *alt.* Piratapuyo [pir], 231, 247

Uaimirí, *alt. dial.* Atruahí [atr], 225

Uaimo'a, *alt.* Waima'a [wmh], 351

Uainana, *alt.* Piratapuyo [pir], 231

Uaiora, *alt.* Wayoró [wyr], 234

Uaiquiare, *alt. dial.* Yabarana [yar], 313

Uairã, *alt.* Tanimuca-Retuarã [tnc], 247

Uaiuai, *alt.* Waiwai [waw], 233, 257

Ualamo, *alt.* Wolaytta [wal], 119

Uamué [uam], 233

Uanana, *alt.* Guanano [gvc], 227

Uanano, *alt.* Guanano [gvc], 245

Uapixana, *alt.* Wapishana [wap], 257, 233

Uardai, *alt.* Orma [orc], 135

Uare [ksj], 629

  dial. Uare [ksj], 629

Uari, *alt.* Tubarão [tba], 233

Uaripi, *alt.* Tairuma [uar], 626

Uase, *alt.* Pele-Ata [ata], 621

Uasi, *alt.* Pele-Ata [ata], 621

Uasilau, *alt.* Pele-Ata [ata], 621

Uasona, *alt. dial.* Tucano [tuo], 233

Uaura, *alt.* Waurá [wau], 233

Uba, *alt.* Wolaytta [wal], 119

Ubach, *alt.* Jawe [jaz], 584

Ubae, *dial.* Nakanai [nak], 616

Ubaghara [byc], 176

Ubamer, *alt. dial.* Aari [aiz], 112

Ubang [uba], 176

Ubani, *alt.* Ibani [iby], 162

Ubdé, *alt.* Hupdë [jup], 227, 246

Ubeteng, *alt. dial.* Ukpet-Ehom [akd], 176

Ubi [ubi], 87

  alt. Glio-Oubi [oub], 138, 93

Ubian, *dial.* Sama, Southern [ssb], 458

Ubili, *alt.* Meramera [mxm], 613

Ubima, *dial.* Ikwere [ikw], 164

Ubir [ubr], 629

Ubiri, *alt.* Ubir [ubr], 629

Uboi, *alt.* Kobiana [kcj], 131, 181

Ubu, *dial.* Wambule [wme], 482

Ubu Ugu, *alt.* Umbu-Ungu [ubu], 629

Ubuia, *alt. dial.* Dobu [dob], 597

Ubwebwe, *dial.* Pongu [png], 173

Ubye, *dial.* Ekpeye [ekp], 159

Ubykh [uby], 563

Ubyx, *alt.* Ubykh [uby], 563

Ucanja Kamuku, *alt.* Rogo [rod], 174

Ucayali, *alt.* Cocama-Cocamilla [cod], 287

  alt. Quechua, San Martín [qvs], 292

Ucayali Ashéninca, *alt.* Ashéninka, Ucayali-Yurúa [cpb], 286, 225

Ucayali-Yurúa Ashéninka, *see* Ashéninka, Ucayali-Yurúa [cpb], 286, 225

Uchai Sadri, *dial.* Sadri, Oraon [sdr], 322

Uchama, *dial.* Evenki [evn], 504

Uchean, *alt.* Yuchi [yuc], 310

Uchur, *dial.* Evenki [evn], 504

Ucinda, *alt. dial.* Cinda-Regi-Tiyal [cdr], 157

Uda [uda], 176

Udai, *alt.* Mamuju [mqx], 431

  dial. Temuan [tmw], 455

Udayapur, *dial.* Tharu, Kochila [thq], 481

Udegeis, *alt.* Udihe [ude], 507

Udehe, *alt.* Udihe [ude], 507

Udekama, *pej. alt.* Degema [deg], 157

Udekhe, *alt.* Udihe [ude], 507

Uderi, *dial.* Maria [mds], 612

Udi [udi], 320

Udihe [ude], 507

Udin, *alt.* Udi [udi], 320

Udjir, *alt.* Ujir [udj], 405

Udlam, *alt.* Wuzlam [udl], 73

Udmurt [udm], 557

  alt. dial. Udmurt [udm], 557

Udo, *dial.* Arigidi [aqg], 154

Udom, *alt. dial.* Nde-Nsele-Nta [ndd], 170

Udu, *dial.* Urhobo [urh], 176

Uduk [udu], 119, 196

Udung, *alt.* Wutung [wut], 632

Uélé, *dial.* Kango [kty], 100

Uellanskij, *dial.* Chukot [ckt], 504

‖U‖en, *alt. dial.* !Xóõ [nmn], 48, 151

|U‖en, *alt. dial.* !Xóõ [nmn], 48, 151

Uen, *alt.* Numee [kdk], 585

Uerequema, *alt.* Guarequena [gae], 311, 227

Ufaina, *alt.* Tanimuca-Retuarã [tnc], 247

Ufaufa, *dial.* Iduna [viv], 602

Ufia, *dial.* Oring [org], 172

Ufim [ufi], 629

Ufiom, *dial.* Oring [org], 172

Ufufu, *dial.* Iduna [viv], 602

Ugana, *dial.* Lavatbura-Lamusong [lbv], 609

Ugandan Sign Language [ugn], 213

Ugare, *alt.* Mesaka [iyo], 67

Ugawng, *alt.* Ugong [ugo], 518

Ugbala, *dial.* Kukele [kez], 167

Ugbe, *alt.* Alege [alf], 153

Ugbem, *alt. dial.* Ubaghara [byc], 176

Uge, *alt.* Alege [alf], 153

Ugele, *alt.* Ughele [uge], 639

Ugep, *dial.* Lokaa [yaz], 169

Ughbug, *alt. dial.* Dargwa [dar], 553

Ughele [uge], 639

Ugi, *alt.* Bugis [bug], 428

  alt. dial. Sa'a [apb], 638

Ugi Riawa, *alt. dial.* Bugis [bug], 428

Ugie, *alt.* Ngie [ngj], 69

'Ugong, *alt.* Ugong [ugo], 518

Ugong [ugo], 518

Uguano, *alt.* Aguano [aga], 285

Uhak, *dial.* Perai [wet], 399

Uhami [uha], 176

Uhei Kachlakan, *alt.* Benggoi [bgy], 397

  alt. Liana-Seti [ste], 400

Uhei Kaclakin, *alt.* Liana-Seti [ste], 400

Uhei Kahlakim, *alt.* Liana-Seti [ste], 400

Uhei-Kaclakin, *alt.* Benggoi [bgy], 397

Uhei-Kahlakim, *alt.* Benggoi [bgy], 397

Uhumkhegi, *alt.* Yukuben [ybl], 178

Umaua, *alt.* Omagua [omg], 289, 231

Umawa, *alt.* Carijona [cbd], 244

Umayam, *dial.* Manobo, Agusan [msm], 499

Umbaia, *alt.* Wambaya [wmb], 577

Umbertana, *alt.* Adynyamathanha [adt], 567

Umbewaha, *alt.* Kumbewaha [xks], 430

Umbindhamu [umd], 577

Umboi, *alt.* Kovai [kqb], 607

Umbrian, *dial.* Italian [ita], 544

Umbu Ratu Nggai, *alt. dial.* Kambera [xbr], 407

Umbu-Ungu [ubu], 629

Umbugarla [umr], 577

Umbule, *alt.* Wambule [wme], 482

Umbundo, *alt.* Umbundu [umb], 42

Umbundu [umb], 42

Umbuygamu [umg], 577

Ume, *alt.* Saami, Ume [sju], 562
    dial. Isoko [iso], 164
    dial. Wipi [gdr], 632

Ume Saami, *see* Saami, Ume [sju], 562

Umeda [upi], 629

Umera, *dial.* Gebe [gei], 398

Umiray Agta, *alt.* Agta, Umiray Dumaget [due], 491

Umiray Dumaget Agta, *see* Agta, Umiray Dumaget [due], 491

Umirey Dumagat, *alt.* Agta, Umiray Dumaget [due], 491

Umm Dorein, *dial.* Moro [mor], 193

Umm Gabralla, *dial.* Moro [mor], 193

Umo, *alt.* Arem [aem], 521, 450

Umon [umm], 176

Umotína [umo], 233

Umpila [ump], 577

Umraya, *dial.* Hértevin [hrt], 518

Umua, *alt.* Macuna [myy], 246
    dial. Mangseng [mbh], 612

Umuahia, *dial.* Igbo [ibo], 163

Umurano, *alt.* Omurano [omu], 289

Umuruta, *dial.* Bo [bpw], 594

Umutina, *alt.* Umotína [umo], 233

Una [mtg], 424

Unalaskan, *alt. dial.* Aleut [ale], 297

Unambal, *alt.* Wunambal [wub], 578

Unami [unm], 309

Unangan, *alt.* Aleut [ale], 495
    alt. dial. Aleut [ale], 297

Unangany, *alt.* Aleut [ale], 495
    alt. dial. Aleut [ale], 297

Unangg, *alt.* Watut, North [una], 631

Unanghan, *alt.* Aleut [ale], 495

Unank, *alt.* Watut, North [una], 631

'Unar, *alt.* Besme [bes], 79

Unde Kaili, *see* Kaili, Unde [unz], 429

Undimeha, *dial.* Nda'nda' [nnz], 69

Undri, *alt.* Urdu [urd], 389

Undu, *dial.* Berta [wti], 113, 189

Undup, *dial.* Iban [iba], 459

Uneapa [bbn], 629

Uneme [une], 176

Unga, *dial.* Bemba [bem], 213
    dial. Buriat, Russia [bxr], 504

Ungameha, *dial.* Nda'nda' [nnz], 69

Ungarinjin, *alt.* Ngarinyin [ung], 575

Ungarinyin, *alt.* Ngarinyin [ung], 575

Unggumi, *dial.* Worora [unp], 578

Ungie, *alt.* Ngie [ngj], 69

Ungoe, *dial.* Suba [suh], 136

Ungom, *alt.* Ngom [nra], 121, 89

Ungorri, *alt.* Kunggari [kgl], 572

Ungu, *alt.* Idun [ldb], 163

Unguja, *dial.* Swahili [swh], 205

Ungwe, *alt.* Hungworo [nat], 162

Unhan, *pej. alt.* Inonhan [loc], 495

Unhun, *dial.* Curripaco [kpc], 226

Uni, *alt.* Hani [hni], 523
    alt. Honi [how], 335

Unietti, *alt.* Afitti [aft], 187

Uningangk, *alt.* Urningangg [urc], 577

Unogboko, *dial.* Isoko [iso], 164

Unserdeutsch [uln], 629

Unshoi, *alt.* Usui [usi], 322

Unsuiy, *alt.* Usui [usi], 322

Untib, *dial.* Avar [ava], 553

Unua [onu], 646

Unwana, *dial.* Igbo [ibo], 163

Unyama, *dial.* Manyika [mxc], 216, 148

Unyamootha, *alt.* Adynyamathanha [adt], 567

Unyeada, *dial.* Obolo [ann], 172

Unza, *alt.* Naga, Southern Rengma [nre], 379

Uokha [uok], 176

Uollamo, *alt.* Wolaytta [wal], 119

Uomo, *alt.* Pakaásnovos [pav], 231

Upale, *alt.* Nyang'i [nyp], 212

Upata, *dial.* Ekpeye [ekp], 159

Upella, *alt. dial.* Ivbie North-Okpela-Arhe [atg], 164

Upland Yuman, *alt.* Havasupai-Walapai-Yavapai [yuf], 301

Upoto, *alt. dial.* Lusengo [lse], 103

Upper Adele, *dial.* Adele [ade], 206, 122

Upper Asaro, *alt.* Dano [aso], 596
    dial. Dano [aso], 596

Upper August River, *dial.* Mian [mpt], 613

Upper Bal, *dial.* Svan [sva], 352

Upper Balong, *alt. dial.* Kenyang [ken], 64

Upper Bamu, *dial.* Bamu [bcf], 592

Upper Baram Kenja, *alt.* Kenyah, Upper Baram [ubm], 460, 394

Upper Baram Kenyah, *see* Kenyah, Upper Baram [ubm], 460, 394

Upper Bele, *dial.* Dani, Lower Grand Valley [dni], 413

Upper Bisaya, *dial.* Bisaya, Sarawak [bsd], 459

Upper Bondo, *dial.* Bondo [bfw], 357

Upper Carniola, *dial.* Slovenian [slv], 558

Upper Chehalis, *see* Chehalis, Upper [cjh], 299

Upper Cherokee, *alt. dial.* Cherokee [chr], 299

Upper Chinook, *alt.* Wasco-Wishram [wac], 310

Upper Circassian, *alt.* Kabardian [kbd], 554

Upper Colorado River Yuman, *alt.* Havasupai-Walapai-Yavapai [yuf], 301

Upper Coquille, *alt.* Coquille [coq], 300

Upper Egypt Arabic, *alt.* Arabic, Sa'idi Spoken [aec], 110
    dial. Arabic, Sa'idi Spoken [aec], 110

Upper Engadine, *dial.* Romansch [roh], 562

Upper Gio, *dial.* Dan [daf], 137

Upper Grand Valley Dani, *see* Dani, Upper Grand Valley [dna], 414

Upper Groma, *dial.* Groma [gro], 333, 363

Upper Guinea Crioulo, *see* Crioulo, Upper Guinea [pov], 131, 180

Upper Inlet, *dial.* Tanaina [tfn], 308

Upper Irumu, *alt.* Tuma-Irumu [iou], 628

Upper Kenyang, *dial.* Kenyang [ken], 64

Upper Kheng, *dial.* Khengkha [xkf], 323

Upper Kinabatangan, *see* Kinabatangan, Upper [dmg], 457

Upper Kolyma, *dial.* Even [eve], 504

Upper Kuskokwim, *see* Kuskokwim, Upper [kuu], 303

Upper Ladakhi, *alt.* Changthang [cna], 358

Upper Lagaip, *dial.* Hewa [ham], 602

Upper Lamet, *dial.* Lamet [lbn], 451, 515

Upper Lozyvin, *alt. dial.* Mansi [mns], 505

Upper Lusatian, *alt.* Sorbian, Upper [hsb], 539

Upper Luzh, *alt. dial.* Ingrian [izh], 554

Upper Mahasu Pahari, *dial.* Pahari, Mahasu [bfz], 382

Upper Managalasi, *alt.* Ömie [aom], 619

Upper Mbo, *alt.* Nkongho [nkc], 70

Upper Michian-Wisconsin Chippewa, *dial.* Chippewa [ciw], 299

Upper Morehead, *alt.* Arammba [stk], 590
alt. Wára [tci], 631

Upper Mori, *alt.* Mori Atas [mzq], 431

Upper Mortlock, *dial.* Mortlockese [mrl], 582

Upper Mustang, *dial.* Lowa [loy], 474

Upper Nar, *alt. dial.* Nar Phu [npa], 476

Upper Navarran, *alt. dial.* Basque [eus], 559

Upper Piman, *alt.* Tohono O'odham [ood], 309

Upper Pokomo, *see* Pokomo, Upper [pkb], 135

Upper Pyramid, *dial.* Dani, Lower Grand Valley [dni], 413

Upper Saxon, *see* Saxon, Upper [sxu], 539

Upper Silesian, *dial.* Polish [pol], 550

Upper Sorbian, *see* Sorbian, Upper [hsb], 539

Upper Stieng, *alt.* Stieng, Bulo [sti], 526

Upper Tanana, *see* Tanana, Upper [tau], 308, 242

Upper Tanudan, *alt.* Kalinga, Upper Tanudan [kgh], 497

Upper Tanudan Kalinga, *see* Kalinga, Upper Tanudan [kgh], 497

Upper Ta'oih, *see* Ta'oih, Upper [tth], 453, 527

Upper Taromi, *see* Taromi, Upper [tov], 442

Upper Tor, *alt.* Berik [bkl], 412

Upper Ugu River, *dial.* Umanakaina [gdn], 629

Upper Wasi-Weri, *dial.* Prasuni [prn], 317

Upper Yazgulyam, *dial.* Yazgulyam [yah], 513

Upper Yei, *dial.* Yei [jei], 426

Upper Zyphe, *dial.* Zyphe [zyp], 467, 391

Upstream Lese, *alt. dial.* Lese [les], 102

Upurui, *alt.* Wayana [way], 296, 234, 252

Ura (Papua New Guinea) [uro], 629
Ura (Vanuatu) [uur], 646
alt. Fungwa [ula], 160
dial. Bumthangkha [kjz], 323

Ura Madzarin, *alt. dial.* Fali [fli], 159

'Urada, *alt.* 'Auhelawa [kud], 591

Uradhi [urf], 577

Urahuli, *alt. dial.* Fali [fli], 159

Urak Lawoi' [urk], 518

Urakha-Akhush, *alt. dial.* Dargwa [dar], 553

Urali [url], 389

Urali Irula, *alt. dial.* Irula [iru], 365

Urali Kurumba, *alt.* Kurumba, Betta [xub], 371

Uraly, *alt.* Urali [url], 389

Urama, *dial.* Kiwai, Northeast [kiw], 606

Uramät, *alt.* Ura [uro], 629

Urambal, *alt.* Bayali [bjy], 569

Urambween, *alt. dial.* Fali [fli], 159

Uramet, *alt.* Ura [uro], 629

Uramit, *alt.* Ura [uro], 629

Uramot, *alt.* Ura [uro], 629

Uran, *alt.* Hatam [had], 415
dial. Hatam [had], 415

Urang, *alt.* Kurux [kru], 371

Uraon, *alt.* Kurux [kru], 371, 321
alt. Kurux, Nepali [kxl], 473

Urapmin [urm], 629

Uraricaa-Paragua, *alt. dial.* Ninam [shb], 230

Urarina [ura], 293

Urat [urt], 629
alt. dial. Mongolian, Peripheral [mvf], 339
dial. Mongolian, Halh [khk], 505
dial. Mongolian, Peripheral [mvf], 462

Uraxa-Axusha, *dial.* Dargwa [dar], 553

Urban Indian Sign Language, *alt.* Indian Sign Language [ins], 365

Urbareg, *alt. dial.* Silt'e [xst], 119

Urdu [urd], 489, 145, 187, 389

Ureng, *alt. dial.* Asilulu [asl], 396

Ureparapara, *alt.* Lehalurup [urr], 642

Urequema, *alt.* Guarequena [gae], 311, 227

Urfa, *dial.* Turkish [tur], 519, 521

Urhobo [urh], 176

Uri [uvh], 629
alt. Naga, Ao [njo], 377
alt. dial. Pawaia [pwa], 621

Uri Vehees, *alt.* Uri [uvh], 629

Uria, *alt.* Orya [ury], 422

Uriai, *alt.* Odiai [bhf], 619

Uriankhai, *alt.* Tuvin [tyv], 507, 462
dial. Kalmyk-Oirat [xal], 461

Uriankhai-Monchak, *alt.* Tuvin [tyv], 507

Urigina [urg], 629

Uriginau, *alt.* Urigina [urg], 629

Urii, *alt.* Uri [uvh], 629

Urim [uri], 630

Urimo [urx], 630

Uripiv, *dial.* Uripiv-Wala-Rano-Atchin [upv], 646

Uripiv-Wala-Rano-Atchin [upv], 646

Urita, *dial.* Arapesh, Bumbita [aon], 590

Uriya, *alt.* Oriya [ori], 382

Urkarax, *alt. dial.* Dargwa [dar], 553

Urli, *alt.* Urali [url], 389

Urmia-Maragha, *alt. dial.* Armenian [hye], 318

Urmia-Maragheh, *dial.* Armenian [hye], 318, 437

Urmuri, *alt.* Ormuri [oru], 487

Urningangg [urc], 577

Uro, *dial.* Arigidi [aqg], 154

Urogo, *alt.* Rogo [rod], 174

Uroovin, *alt. dial.* Fali [fli], 159

Urrighel, *dial.* Tarifit [rif], 146

Urrti, *alt. dial.* Midob [mei], 193

Ursári, *dial.* Romani, Balkan [rmn], 551

Urtsun, *alt. dial.* Kalasha [kls], 486

Uru [ure], 224
dial. Mochi [old], 202

Uru-Eu-Uau-Uau, *alt.* Uru-Eu-Wau-Wau [urz], 233

Uru-Eu-Wau-Wau [urz], 233

Uru-Pa-In [urp], 233

Urua, *alt. dial.* Galeya [gar], 599

Uruak, *alt.* Arutani [atx], 225, 311

Uruangnirin [urn], 424

Uruava [urv], 630

Urubu, *dial.* Carútana [cru], 226

Urubú, *alt.* Urubú-Kaapor [urb], 233

Urubú Sign Language, *alt.* Urubú-Kaapor Sign Language [uks], 233

Urubú-Kaapor [urb], 233

Urubú-Kaapor Sign Language [uks], 233

Urubu-Tapuya, *alt.* Piratapuyo [pir], 247

Urucena, *alt. dial.* Wayana [way], 234

Urucuiana, *dial.* Wayana [way], 234

Urudu, *alt.* Urdu [urd], 389

Uruewawau, *alt.* Uru-Eu-Wau-Wau [urz], 233

Uruguayan Sign Language [ugy], 311

Uruku, *alt.* Karo [arr], 228

Urukun, *dial.* Isebe [igo], 603

Urum [uum], 352, 564

Urumi [uru], 233

Urundi, *alt.* Edopi [dbf], 414
alt. Iau [tmu], 415
alt. Rundi [run], 55

Urunyaruanda, *alt.* Rwanda [kin], 178

Urupaya, *alt. dial.* Maritsauá [msp], 230

Ururagwe, *alt.* Nyambo [now], 203

Ururi, *alt.* Edopi [dbf], 414
alt. Iau [tmu], 415

Urushubi, *alt.* Shubi [suj], 204

Urutani, *alt.* Arutani [atx], 225, 311

Uruund, *alt.* Ruund [rnd], 107, 41

Uruwa, *alt.* Yau [yuw], 633

Uryankhai, *alt.* Tuvin [tyv], 507

Uryankhai-Monchak, *alt.* Tuvin [tyv], 462

Us, *dial.* Kag-Fer-Jiir-Koor-Ror-Us-Zuksun [gel], 165

Usage, *dial.* Mian [mpt], 613

Usaghade [usk], 72, 176

Usak, *alt.* Silimo [wul], 423

Usakade, *alt.* Usaghade [usk], 72, 176

Usakedet, *alt.* Usaghade [usk], 72, 176

Usamba, *alt.* Samba [smx], 107

Usan [wnu], 630

Usari, *alt. dial.* Romani, Balkan [rmn], 551
dial. Karkar-Yuri [yuj], 603

Usarufa [usa], 630

Usbaki, *alt.* Uzbek, Northern [uzn], 346

Usbeki, *alt.* Uzbek, Northern [uzn], 346
alt. Uzbek, Southern [uzs], 318

Usen, *dial.* Barok [bjk], 592

Ushaku, *dial.* Befang [bby], 58

Usheida, *alt. dial.* Befang [bby], 58

Ushi, *alt.* Aushi [auh], 213, 96

Ushoi, *alt.* Usui [usi], 322

Ushojo [ush], 489

Ushu, *dial.* Kalami [gwc], 485

Ushuji, *alt.* Ushojo [ush], 489

Ushut, *alt. dial.* Prasuni [prn], 317

Usi, *alt.* Aushi [auh], 213, 96

Usiai, *alt.* Lele [lle], 609

Usila Chinantec, *see* Chinantec, Usila [cuc], 261

Usilele, *alt.* Lele [lel], 102

Usino, *alt.* Sop [urw], 625

Usipi, *alt.* Kok Borok [trp], 321

Usipi Mrung, *alt.* Kok Borok [trp], 368

Usirampia, *alt. dial.* Baruya [byr], 592

Usku [ulf], 424

USL, *alt.* Ugandan Sign Language [ugn], 213

Usokun, *alt. dial.* Degema [deg], 157

Uspanteco, *alt.* Uspanteko [usp], 256

Uspanteko [usp], 256

Usseri, *dial.* Rombo [rof], 204

Ussuri, *dial.* Nanai [gld], 506

Ustutun, *dial.* Ili'uun [ilu], 399

Usu, *alt.* Uya [usu], 630

Usui [usi], 322

Usurufa, *alt.* Usarufa [usa], 630

Ut, *dial.* Teor [tev], 404

Uta', *alt. dial.* Meta' [mgo], 67

Utabi, *dial.* Ikobi-Mena [meb], 602

Utaha, *alt.* Ifo [iff], 642

'Utaiba, *alt. dial.* Arabic, Najdi Spoken [ars], 508

Utalo, *dial.* Diodio [ddi], 597

Utama, *alt. dial.* Ubaghara [byc], 176

Utamu, *alt. dial.* Ubaghara [byc], 176

Utanga, *alt.* Otank [uta], 173

Utange, *alt.* Otank [uta], 173

Utank, *alt.* Otank [uta], 173

Utarmbung [omo], 627

Utatu, *alt. dial.* Datooga [tcc], 198

Ütbü, *alt.* Chin, Chinbon [cnb], 463

Ute, *dial.* Ute-Southern Paiute [ute], 309

Ute-Southern Paiute [ute], 309

Uti, *alt.* Udi [udi], 320
dial. Isoko [iso], 164

Utkali, *alt.* Oriya [ori], 382

Utnoor, *dial.* Gondi, Southern [ggo], 363

Utnur, *dial.* Kolami, Southeastern [nit], 369

Utonkon, *alt. dial.* Oring [org], 172

Utoro, *alt.* Otoro [otr], 194

Utsang, *dial.* Tibetan [bod], 481

Utsat, *alt.* Tsat [huq], 345

Utse, *alt.* Iceve-Maci [bec], 63, 163

Utser, *alt.* Iceve-Maci [bec], 63, 163

Utset, *alt.* Tsat [huq], 345

Utseu, *alt.* Iceve-Maci [bec], 63, 163

Uttari, *dial.* Awadhi [awa], 354, 468

Uttarkashi, *alt. dial.* Garhwali [gbm], 360

Utu [utu], 630

Utugwang, *alt.* Putukwam [afe], 173

dial. Putukwam [afe], 173

Utuma, *alt. dial.* Ubaghara [byc], 176

Utupua, *alt.* Amba [utp], 634

Utur, *alt.* Etulo [utr], 159

Uturupa, *alt.* Usarufa [usa], 630

Uud Danum, *alt.* Dohoi [otd], 393

Uuhum, *alt.* Yukuben [ybl], 178, 74

Uuhum-Gigi, *alt.* Yukuben [ybl], 178, 74

Uurti, *alt. dial.* Midob [mei], 193

Uusimaa Swedish, *dial.* Swedish [swe], 535

Uut Danum, *alt.* Dohoi [otd], 393

Uvbie [evh], 176

Uvean, *alt.* Wallisian [wls], 647, 585

Uvean, West [uve], 585

Uvhria, *alt.* Uvbie [evh], 176

Uvin, *alt.* Fali [fli], 159

Uvol, *alt.* Lote [uvl], 610

Uvwie, *alt.* Uvbie [evh], 176

U'wa, *alt.* Tunebo, Central [tuf], 248
alt. Tunebo, Western [tnb], 248

Uwenpantai, *dial.* Wemale, North [weo], 405

Uwepa-Uwano, *dial.* Yekhee [ets], 177

Uwet, *alt.* Bakpinka [bbs], 154

Uwi, *alt. dial.* Akposo [kpo], 123
alt. dial. Ikposo [kpo], 208

Uy Lo, *alt. dial.* Tho [tou], 527

Uya [usu], 630
alt. Sausi [ssj], 623

Uyalipa Pii, *alt.* Lembena [leq], 609

Uyanga, *alt.* Doko-Uyanga [uya], 158

Uyghur [uig], 346, 318, 448, 462, 520

Uyghuri, *alt.* Uyghur [uig], 318

Uygur, *alt.* Uyghur [uig], 346, 448, 462, 520

Uyobe, *alt.* Miyobe [soy], 45, 208

Uzairue, *dial.* Yekhee [ets], 177

Uzam, *alt.* Wuzlam [udl], 73

Uzbak, *alt.* Uzbek, Southern [uzs], 318

Uzbek, Northern [uzn], 512, 346

Uzbek, Southern [uzs], 318, 520

Uzbeki, *alt.* Uzbek, Southern [uzs], 318

Uzbeki Arabic, *alt.* Arabic, Uzbeki Spoken [auz], 521

Uzbeki Spoken Arabic, *see* Arabic, Uzbeki Spoken [auz], 521

Uzbin, *dial.* Pashayi, Northwest [glh], 317

Uzekwe [eze], 176

Uzemchin, *alt. dial.* Mongolian, Peripheral [mvf], 462

Uzere, *dial.* Isoko [iso], 164

Uzhil, *alt.* Aushi [auh], 213

Uzhili, *alt.* Aushi [auh], 96
Uzlam, *alt.* Wuzlam [udl], 73
Uzo, *alt.* Izon [ijc], 164
Va, *alt.* Wa [wbm], 467, 346
 dial. Wa [wbm], 346
Va Lang, *dial.* Nga La [hlt], 466
Vaagri Booli [vaa], 389
Vaalpens, *alt. dial.* !Xóõ [nmn], 48, 151
Vaaneroki, *alt.* Bokyi [bky], 156, 59
Vaazin, *dial.* Dii [dur], 60
Vacacocha, *alt.* Abishira [ash], 285
Vacamwe, *alt.* Kamwe [hig], 166
Vach, *alt. dial.* Khanty [kca], 505
Vadaga, *alt. dial.* Telugu [tel], 388
Vadagu, *alt.* Badaga [bfq], 354
Vadanda, *alt. dial.* Ndau [ndc], 148
Vadara, *alt. dial.* Banda-Banda [bpd], 75, 188
Vadari, *alt.* Waddar [wbq], 390
 alt. dial. Telugu [tel], 388
Vadda Beldar, *alt.* Waddar [wbq], 390
Vadiya, *alt.* Oriya [ori], 382
Vado, *dial.* Tinputz [tpz], 628
Vado-Vaene', *dial.* Tinputz [tpz], 628
Vadodari, *alt. dial.* Gujarati [guj], 363
Vadonde, *dial.* Makonde [kde], 148
Vadval, *alt.* Phudagi [phd], 384
Vaedda, *alt.* Veddah [ved], 510
Vaene', *dial.* Tinputz [tpz], 628
Vafsi [vaf], 442
Vagadi, *alt.* Wagdi [wbr], 390
Vagala, *alt.* Vagla [vag], 128
Vagari, *alt.* Koli, Kachi [gjk], 486, 369
 alt. Wagdi [wbr], 390
Vagaria, *alt.* Koli, Kachi [gjk], 486, 369
Vagdi, *alt.* Wagdi [wbr], 390
Vaged, *alt.* Wagdi [wbr], 390
Vageri, *alt.* Wagdi [wbr], 390
Vaghat, *dial.* Vaghat-Ya-Bijim-Legeri [bij], 177
Vaghat-Ya-Bijim-Legeri [bij], 177
Vaghri [vgr], 489
 alt. Bauria [bge], 355
 alt. Koli, Kachi [gjk], 369
Vaghri Koli, *alt.* Vaghri [vgr], 489
Vaghua [tva], 639
Vagi, *alt.* Wagdi [wbr], 390
Vagily, *alt. dial.* Mansi [mns], 505
Vagla [vag], 128
Vagri, *dial.* Koli, Kachi [gjk], 486, 369
Vagua, *alt.* Vaghua [tva], 639
Vah Cuengh, *alt.* Zhuang, Northern [ccx], 349

Vahitu, *dial.* Tuamotuan [pmt], 581
Vai [vai], 139, 184
Vai Fordata, *alt.* Fordata [frd], 398
Vai Tnebar, *alt.* Fordata [frd], 398
Vaidida, *alt.* Fordata [frd], 398
Vaikenu, *alt.* Baikeno [bkx], 350
Vaikino, *alt.* Baikeno [bkx], 350
Vailala, *alt.* Orokolo [oro], 620
Vaipei, *alt.* Vaiphei [vap], 389
Vaiphei [vap], 389
Vaira-Ntosara, *dial.* Tairora, South [omw], 626
Vaitupu, *alt. dial.* Tuvaluan [tvl], 640
Vaiverang, *alt.* Adonara [adr], 406
Vajieng, *dial.* Chrau [crw], 522
Vakam, *dial.* Citak [txt], 413
Vakhan, *alt.* Wakhi [wbl], 489, 318, 346, 513
Vakuta, *dial.* Kilivila [kij], 606
Vakweli, *alt.* Mokpwe [bri], 68
Val-Nogliki, *dial.* Orok [oaa], 506
Valaisan, *dial.* Franco-Provençal [frp], 562
Valdostano, *alt. dial.* Franco-Provençal [frp], 543
Valdotain, *alt. dial.* Franco-Provençal [frp], 543
Vale [vae], 78
 alt. Glavda [glw], 62
 dial. Vale [vae], 78
Valeien, *alt. dial.* Provençal [prv], 537
Valencià, *alt. dial.* Catalan-Valencian-Balear [cat], 559
Valencian, *dial.* Catalan-Valencian-Balear [cat], 559
Valenciano, *alt. dial.* Catalan-Valencian-Balear [cat], 559
Valiente, *alt.* Ngäbere [gym], 283
 dial. Ngäbere [gym], 283
Vallader-Lower Engadine, *alt. dial.* Romansch [roh], 562
Valle D'aosta, *dial.* Franco-Provençal [frp], 543
Valle Nacional Chinantec, *see* Chinantec, Valle Nacional [cvn], 261
Valley Cove, *dial.* Agta, Dupaninan [duo], 490
Valley Maidu, *see* Maidu, Valley [vmv], 304
Valley Miwok, *alt.* Miwok, Plains [pmw], 305
Valley Tihaamah, *dial.* Arabic, Hijazi Spoken [acw], 508
Valley Tonga, *alt. dial.* Tonga [toi], 215
Valley Yokuts, *dial.* Yokuts [yok], 310

Valman [van], 630
Valmiki, *alt.* Kupia [key], 371
Valongi, *alt. dial.* Bafaw-Balong [bwt], 56
Valpay, *alt.* Valpei [vlp], 646
Valpei [vlp], 646
Valpei-Hukua, *alt.* Valpei [vlp], 646
Valserisch, *alt. dial.* Schwyzerdütsch [gsw], 563
Valuga, *alt. dial.* Motlav [mlv], 644
Valuva, *alt. dial.* Motlav [mlv], 644
Valuwa, *alt. dial.* Motlav [mlv], 644
Valvideiru, *dial.* Fala [fax], 560
Vamakonde, *dial.* Makonde [kde], 148
Vamale [mkt], 585
 dial. Vamale [mkt], 585
Vambeng, *alt.* Mokpwe [bri], 68
Vame [mlr], 73
Vamwalu, *dial.* Makonde [kde], 148
Vamwambe, *dial.* Makonde [kde], 148
Van, *dial.* Armenian [hye], 318
Van Kieu, *alt.* Bru, Eastern [bru], 522
Vana, *alt. dial.* Mbum [mdd], 66
Vanambere, *alt.* Wanambre [wnb], 631
Vanatina, *alt.* Sudest [tgo], 625
Vanavara, *dial.* Evenki [evn], 504
Vancouver Cantonese, *dial.* Chinese, Yue [yue]
Vanda, *alt.* Wanda [wbh], 205
Vandougouka, *alt. dial.* Wojenaka [jod], 95
Vandu Gelao, *alt.* Gelao, Red [gir], 522
Vanechi, *alt.* Waneci [wne], 489
Vanga, *alt.* Sudest [tgo], 625
Vangunu [mpr], 639
 dial. Vangunu [mpr], 639
Vanikolo, *alt.* Vano [vnk], 639
Vanikoro, *alt.* Vano [vnk], 639
Vanimo [vam], 630
Vanjari, *alt.* Lambadi [lmn], 372
Vannetais, *dial.* Breton [bre], 536
Vano [vnk], 639
Vanua Balavu, *dial.* Lauan [llx], 580
Vanua Lava, *alt.* Vatrata [vlr], 646
Vanuma [vau], 109
Vanumami, *dial.* Kuanua [ksd], 608
Vao [vao], 646
Vapidiana, *alt.* Wapishana [wap], 257, 233
Vapopeo', *dial.* Tinputz [tpz], 628
Vapopeo'-Rausaura, *dial.* Tinputz [tpz], 628
Vara, *alt.* Wára [tci], 631
 dial. Banda, Togbo-Vara [tor], 74

Varese, *alt.* Varisi [vrs], 639
Varhadi-Nagpuri [vah], 389
Variegated Miao, *alt.* Hmong,
    Northeastern Dian [hmd], 334
Varihío, *alt.* Huarijio [var], 262
Varisi [vrs], 639
    dial. Varisi [vrs], 639
Varjan, *dial.* Waigali [wbk], 318
Varli [vav], 390
Varmali, *alt.* Lamenu [lmu], 642
Varois, *alt. dial.* Provençal [prv], 537
Varsu, *alt.* Lewo [lww], 643
Vartashen, *alt. dial.* Udi [udi], 320
Vartavo, *alt.* Burmbar [vrt], 641
Varto, *dial.* Kirmanjki [kiu], 518
Vasava, *alt.* Vasavi [vas], 390
Vasava Bhil, *alt.* Vasavi [vas], 390
Vasave, *alt.* Vasavi [vas], 390
Vasavi [vas], 390
Vascuense, *alt.* Basque [eus], 559
Vasekela Bushman [vaj], 151
Vaskia, *alt.* Waskia [wsk], 631
Vasorontu, *alt. dial.* Kwadi
    [kwz], 40
Vasui, *alt.* Tinputz [tpz], 628
    dial. Tinputz [tpz], 628
Vasuii, *alt.* Tinputz [tpz], 628
Vasyugan, *alt. dial.* Khanty
    [kca], 505
Vata, *dial.* Dida, Lakota [dic], 92
Vateve, *alt.* Tewe [twx], 149
Vatka-Havoutsi, *alt. dial.*
    Tsakonian [tsd], 541
Vatrata [vlr], 646
Vaturanga, *alt. dial.* Ghari
    [gri], 636
Vaudois, *dial.* Franco-Provençal
    [frp], 562
Vaupés Cacua, *dial.* Cacua [cbv],
    244
Vavoehpoa', *dial.* Tinputz
    [tpz], 628
Vawngtu, *alt.* Zyphe [zyp], 391
Vayu, *alt.* Wayu [vay], 482
Vazama, *alt.* Khwe [xuu], 214
    alt. Kxoe [xuu], 40
Vazezuru, *alt. dial.* Shona
    [sna], 216
Vazhiyammar, *alt.* Malaryan
    [mjq], 374
Veda, *alt.* Veddah [ved], 510
Vedans, *alt.* Malavedan [mjr], 374
Veddah [ved], 510
Veddha, *alt.* Veddah [ved], 510
Veen Colony, *alt. dial.* Gronings
    [gos], 548
Veenkoloniaals, *dial.* Gronings
    [gos], 548
Vegliote, *alt.* Dalmatian [dlm], 532
Vehees, *alt.* Vehes [val], 630

Vehes [val], 630
Vei, *alt.* Vai [vai], 139, 184
Veiao, *alt.* Yao [yao], 141, 149, 206,
    215
Veiphei, *alt.* Vaiphei [vap], 389
Vejos, *alt.* Wichí Lhamtés Vejoz
    [wlv], 220
Vele, *alt. dial.* Nakanai [nak], 616
Veliche, *alt.* Huilliche [huh], 242
Veliperi, *alt. dial.* Ipeka-Tapuia
    [paj], 227
Vella Lavella, *alt.* Bilua [blb], 635
Veluwe, *alt.* Veluws [vel], 549
Veluws [vel], 549
Vemgo, *dial.* Vemgo-Mabas
    [vem], 177, 73
Vemgo-Mabas [vem], 177, 73
Venaambakaia, *alt.* Pomo, Central
    [poo], 307
Venaco, *dial.* Corsican [cos], 536
Venambakaiia, *alt.* Pomo, Central
    [poo], 307
Venda [ven], 187, 217
Vendo, *dial.* Yasa [yko], 111, 122
Venet, *alt.* Venetian [vec], 545
Venetian [vec], 545, 532
Venetian Proper, *dial.* Venetian
    [vec], 545, 532
Veneto, *alt.* Venetian [vec], 545
Venezuelan Sign Language
    [vsl], 312
Vengi, *alt.* Vengo [bav], 73
Vengo [bav], 73
Vengoo, *alt.* Vengo [bav], 73
Ventimigliese, *alt. dial.* Ligurian
    [lij], 548
Ventureño [veo], 309
Venustiano Carranza Tzotzil,
    see Tzotzil, Venustiano Carranza
    [tzo], 277
Veps [vep], 557
Vepsian, *alt.* Veps [vep], 557
Veqaura, *dial.* Tairora, South
    [omw], 626
Vera, *alt. dial.* Banda, Togbo-Vara
    [tor], 74
Veracruz Huastec, *see* Huastec,
    Veracruz [hus], 262
Veraguas Sabanero, *alt.* Buglere
    [sab], 283
Vere, *alt.* Mom Jango [ver], 170, 68
    dial. Nakanai [nak], 616
Verkhovsk, *dial.* Negidal
    [neg], 506
Vermandois, *alt. dial.* Picard
    [pcd], 537
Veron, *alt.* Prasuni [prn], 317
Verou, *alt.* Prasuni [prn], 317
Verre, *alt.* Mom Jango [ver], 170,
    68

Veruni, *alt.* Prasuni [prn], 317
Vesi, *alt.* Wushi [bse], 73
Vetan, *dial.* Malavedan [mjr], 374
Veteng, *alt.* Kenswei Nsei
    [ndb], 64
Vette Kada Irula, *dial.* Irula [iru],
    365
Vettuvan, *dial.* Malavedan
    [mjr], 374
Vetumboso, *dial.* Mosina
    [msn], 644
Vetweng, *alt.* Kenswei Nsei
    [ndb], 64
Veveu Evav, *alt.* Kei [kei], 399
Veveva, *alt.* Wejewa [wew], 410
Vezo, *dial.* Malagasy, Sakalava
    [skg], 140
Vhe, *alt.* Éwé [ewe], 124, 207
Viccholi, *alt. dial.* Sindhi
    [snd], 488
    dial. Sindhi [snd], 387
Vice-Arxava, *dial.* Laz [lzz], 352
Vicholi, *alt. dial.* Sindhi [snd], 488
Vicholo, *dial.* Sindhi [snd], 488
Vico-Ajaccio, *dial.* Corsican [cos],
    536
Vicxin, *dial.* Lak [lbe], 555
Vidar, *dial.* Alviri-Vidari [avd], 437
Vidari, *alt. dial.* Alviri-Vidari [avd],
    437
Vidiri, *alt. dial.* Banda-Banda
    [bpd], 75
    dial. Banda-Banda [bpd], 188
Vidri, *alt. dial.* Banda-Banda
    [bpd], 75, 188
Vidunda [vid], 205
Vidzeme, *alt. dial.* Liv [liv], 546
Viemo [vig], 55
Vientiane, *dial.* Lao [lao], 445
Viet, *alt.* Vietnamese [vie], 527
Viet Go Mien, *alt.* Khmer, Central
    [khm], 524
Vietnamese [vie], 527, 346
Vietnamese Pidgin French, *alt.*
    Tay Boi [tas], 527
Vige, *alt.* Viemo [vig], 55
Vigué, *alt.* Viemo [vig], 55
Vigye, *alt.* Viemo [vig], 55
Vigzar, *alt. dial.* Saya [say], 174
Viipekeel, *alt.* Estonian Sign
    Language [eso], 534
Viittomakieli, *alt.* Finnish Sign
    Language [fse], 534
Vikhlin, *alt. dial.* Lak [lbe], 555
Vikzar, *alt. dial.* Saya [say], 174
Vil, *alt.* Bhili [bhb], 356
Vila, *alt. dial.* Tsonga [tso], 149,
    217
Vilela [vil], 220
Vili [vif], 90, 121

Villa Alta Zapotec, *alt.* Zapotec, Yatzachi [zav], 281

Villa Corzo, *dial.* Tzotzil, Huixtán [tzu], 277

Villa Viciosa Agta, *see* Agta, Villa Viciosa [dyg], 491

Village Bokobaru, *dial.* Bokobaru [bus], 156

Vimeu, *alt. dial.* Picard [pcd], 537

Vimtim, *alt.* Fali [fli], 159
alt. dial. Fali [fli], 159

Vin, *dial.* Fali [fli], 159

Vinaata-Konkompira, *dial.* Tairora, South [omw], 626

Vinahe, *alt.* Kariya [kil], 166

Vincentian, *dial.* Carib, Island [crb], 295

Vincentian Creole English [svc], 295

Vinmavis [vnm], 646

Vinza [vin], 205

Vira, *alt.* Joba [job], 100

Virac, *alt.* Bicolano, Southern Catanduanes [bln], 493

Virgin Islands Creole English [vic], 297, 234
alt. Netherlands Antilles Creole English [vic], 282

Virginia Algonkian, *alt.* Powhatan [pim], 307

Virginia Algonquian, *alt.* Powhatan [pim], 307

Viri, *alt.* Belanda Viri [bvi], 189
alt. Birri [bvq], 75
alt. dial. Masana [mcn], 83, 66

Viro, *alt.* Estonian [est], 534, 534

Viryal, *dial.* Chuvash [chv], 553

Visayak, *alt.* Bisaya, Brunei [bsb], 324
alt. Bisaya, Sarawak [bsd], 459

Visayan, *alt.* Cebuano [ceb], 493

Vishakhapatnam, *alt. dial.* Telugu [tel], 388

Vishavan [vis], 390

Visholi, *dial.* Sindhi [snd], 387

Visigoth, *dial.* Gothic [got], 564

Visik, *alt. dial.* Vemgo-Mabas [vem], 177

Vita, *alt. dial.* Banda, West Central [bbp], 74

Vital-Arkhava, *alt. dial.* Laz [lzz], 352

Viteb-Mogilev, *alt. dial.* Belarusan [bel], 530

Viti [vit], 177

Vitskhin, *alt. dial.* Lak [lbe], 555

Vittangi Finnish, *dial.* Finnish, Tornedalen [fit], 561

Vitu, *alt.* Muduapa [wiv], 615

Vivigana, *alt.* Iduna [viv], 602

Vivigani, *alt.* Iduna [viv], 602

Viwivakeu, *dial.* Amahuaca [amc], 224

Viwulu-Aua, *alt.* Wuvulu-Aua [wuv], 632

Vixaritari Vaniuqui, *alt.* Huichol [hch], 263

Vixlin, *dial.* Lak [lbe], 555

Vizaritari Vaniuki, *alt.* Huichol [hch], 263

Vizcaino, *alt. dial.* Basque [eus], 559

Vizik, *alt. dial.* Vemgo-Mabas [vem], 177

Vlaams [vls], 531, 538, 549

Vlach, *alt.* Romanian, Macedo [rup], 541, 529

Vlaemsch, *alt.* Vlaams [vls], 531, 538
alt. dial. Vlaams [vls], 531, 538, 549

Vlax, *alt.* Romani, Vlax [rmy], 531, 537

Vlax Romani, *see* Romani, Vlax [rmy], 551, 247, 529, 531, 532, 537, 539, 541, 542, 545, 549, 550, 550, 551, 556, 558, 561, 564, 566

Vlax Romany, *alt.* Romani, Vlax [rmy], 551

Vlin, *dial.* Éwé [ewe], 207

Vlum, *alt. dial.* Musgu [mug], 68, 85

Vo, *alt.* Wa [wbm], 467, 346
dial. Éwé [ewe], 207

Vo Limkou, *alt.* Lingao [onb], 338

Voa Dê, *alt.* Gelao, Red [gir], 522

Vod [vot], 557

Vodere, *alt. dial.* Banda-Banda [bpd], 75, 188

Vodian, *alt.* Vod [vot], 557

Vogelkop, *dial.* Biak [bhw], 412

Vogherese-Pavese, *dial.* Emiliano-Romagnolo [eml], 543

Vogul, *alt.* Mansi [mns], 505

Vogulich, *alt.* Mansi [mns], 505

Voguly, *alt.* Mansi [mns], 505

Voko, *alt.* Longto [wok], 65

Volga, *alt. dial.* Mari, Eastern [mhr], 555

Volga Oirat, *alt.* Kalmyk-Oirat [xal], 554

Volof, *alt.* Wolof [wol], 182, 145

Volow, *dial.* Motlav [mlv], 644

Vomni, *alt. dial.* Koma [kmy], 167

Vonkutu, *alt. dial.* Lese [les], 102

Vono [kch], 177

Vonun, *alt.* Bunun [bnn], 511

Voqtwaq, *dial.* Chrau [crw], 522

Vora, *alt. dial.* Banda, Togbo-Vara [tor], 74
dial. Sinaugoro [snc], 624

Vore, *dial.* Bobo Madaré, Northern [bbo], 141

Voré, *dial.* Bobo Madaré, Southern [bwq], 49

Voro [vor], 177

Voru, *alt. dial.* Estonian [est], 534

Vôru, *dial.* Estonian [est], 534

Vote, *alt.* Vod [vot], 557

Votiak, *alt.* Udmurt [udm], 557

Votian, *alt.* Vod [vot], 557

Votic, *alt.* Vod [vot], 557

Votish, *alt.* Vod [vot], 557

Vötö, *alt.* Viti [vit], 177

Votyak, *alt.* Udmurt [udm], 557

Vouaousi, *alt.* Aushi [auh], 213, 96

Voute, *alt.* Vute [vut], 73

Voutere, *alt.* Vute [vut], 73

Vovo, *alt.* Bieria [brj], 641
alt. dial. Bieria [brj], 641

Vowak, *alt. dial.* Lengua [leg], 284

Vuite, *alt.* Chin, Paite [pck], 463

Vukutu, *dial.* Lese [les], 102

Vulaa, *alt.* Hula [hul], 602

Vulava, *dial.* Bughotu [bgt], 635

Vulum, *dial.* Musgu [mug], 68, 85

Vulung, *alt.* Thao [ssf], 512

Vumbu [vum], 121

Vunadidir, *dial.* Kuanua [ksd], 608

Vunapu [vnp], 646

Vungunya, *dial.* Yombe [yom], 109, 42, 90

Vunjo [vun], 205

Vunmarama, *alt.* Hano [lml], 642

Vunum, *alt.* Bunun [bnn], 511

Vunun, *alt.* Bunun [bnn], 511

Vunung, *alt.* Bunun [bnn], 511

Vupuran, *alt.* Papora-Hoanya [ppu], 512

Vuras, *alt. dial.* Mosina [msn], 644

Vureas, *alt. dial.* Mosina [msn], 644

Vures, *alt. dial.* Mosina [msn], 644

Vute [vut], 73, 177

Vute de Banyo, *alt. dial.* Vute [vut], 73

Vute de Doume, *alt. dial.* Vute [vut], 73

Vute de Linte, *alt. dial.* Vute [vut], 73

Vute de Mbandjok, *alt. dial.* Vute [vut], 73

Vute de Ngorro, *alt. dial.* Vute [vut], 73

Vute de Sangbe, *alt. dial.* Vute [vut], 73

Vute de Tibati, *alt. dial.* Vute [vut], 73

Vute de Yangba, *alt. dial.* Vute [vut], 73

Vute Mbanjo, *dial.* Vute [vut], 73

Vuteen, *alt.* Yupik, Sirenik [ysr], 508

Vutere, *alt.* Vute [vut], 177

Vwela, *alt. dial.* Ligbi [lig], 126
Vwezhi, *alt. dial.* Gbagyi [gbr], 160
Vy, *alt.* Vai [vai], 139, 184
Vyneganga Powari, *dial.* Powari [pwr], 384
Vyrus, *dial.* Estonian [est], 534
Wa [wbm], 467, 346
  alt. Blang [blr], 514
  alt. Lawa, Western [lcp], 338
  alt. Parauk [prk], 466, 342
Wa Bambani, *alt.* Agoi [ibm], 153
Wa Khawk, *dial.* Maru [mhx], 465
Wa Lon, *dial.* Wa [wbm], 467
Wa Maathi, *alt.* Mbugu [mhd], 202
Wa Proper, *alt.* Lawa, Western [lcp], 338
Wa Pwi, *alt.* Wa [wbm], 467, 346
Wa-Duku, *dial.* Bacama [bcy], 154
Wa'a, *alt.* Dghwede [dgh], 157
Wáádú, *dial.* Toura [neb], 95
Waagai, *alt.* Wagaya [wga], 577
Waagi, *alt.* Wagaya [wga], 577
Waali, *alt.* Wali [wlx], 128
Waama [wwa], 46
  dial. Waama [wwa], 46
Waamwang [wmn], 585
Waanjama, *dial.* Mende [men], 183
Waano, *alt.* Wano [wno], 425
Waanyi, *alt. dial.* Garawa [gbc], 570
Waar, *alt.* War [aml], 322
Waat, *alt.* Sanye [ssn], 136
Waata, *alt.* Boni [bob], 132
  alt. Sanye [ssn], 136
  dial. Orma [orc], 135
Wab [wab], 630
Wabag, *alt. dial.* Enga [enq], 598
Wabo [wbb], 424
Waboda [kmx], 630
Waboni, *alt.* Boni [bob], 132
Wabuda, *alt.* Waboda [kmx], 630
Wabui, *alt.* Hixkaryána [hix], 227
Wabula, *dial.* Cia-Cia [cia], 429
Wachi, *alt.* Gbe, Waci [wci], 207
Waci, *alt.* Gbe, Waci [wci], 207, 45
Waci Gbe, *see* Gbe, Waci [wci], 207, 45
Waci-Gbe, *alt.* Gbe, Waci [wci], 207, 45
Wacipaire, *alt.* Huachipaeri [hug], 288
Waciri, *dial.* Pashto, Central [pst], 488
Waco, *dial.* Wichita [wic], 310
Waçu, *alt.* Wasu [wsu], 233
Wad, *alt. dial.* Lutos [ndy], 76
Wada, *dial.* Banda-Mbrès [bqk], 75, 188
  dial. Lutos [ndy], 76
Wada Thuri, *alt.* Thuri [thu], 195
Wadaginam [wdg], 630

Wadaginamb, *alt.* Wadaginam [wdg], 630
Wadai, *alt.* Maba [mde], 83
  alt. Orma [orc], 135
Wadalei, *dial.* Galeya [gar], 599
Wadaman, *alt.* Wardaman [wrr], 578
Wadamkong, *dial.* Rawang [raw], 466
Wadapi-Laut, *alt. dial.* Ambai [amk], 410
Wadaria, *alt.* Koli, Wadiyara [kxp], 369, 487
Wadau, *dial.* Pashayi, Northwest [glh], 317
Waddar [wbq], 390
Waddayen, *alt.* Maba [mde], 83
Wadega, *alt.* Jumjum [jum], 191
Wadema, *alt. dial.* Yanomámi [wca], 234
Waderman, *alt.* Wardaman [wrr], 578
Wadhiara, *alt.* Koli, Wadiyara [kxp], 369, 487
Wadi, *alt. dial.* Tagargrent [oua], 40
  dial. Bata [bta], 155
  dial. Jimi [jim], 63
Wadibu, *dial.* Biak [bhw], 412
Wadimbisa, *dial.* Budu [buu], 98
Wadiri, *alt.* Yanyuwa [jao], 579
Wadiwadi, *dial.* Thurawal [tbh], 576
Wadiyara Koli, *see* Koli, Wadiyara [kxp], 369, 487
Wadiyara Koli, *dial.* Koli, Wadiyara [kxp], 487
Wadjari, *alt.* Wajarri [wbv], 577
Wadjeri, *alt.* Wajarri [wbv], 577
Wadjiginy [wdj], 577
Wadjigu [wdu], 577
Wadondo, *alt. dial.* Ndau [ndc], 148
Waduman, *alt.* Wardaman [wrr], 578
Wadzoli, *alt. dial.* Carútana [cru], 226
Wae Geren, *alt. dial.* Buru [mhs], 397
Wae Kabo, *alt. dial.* Buru [mhs], 397
Wae Rana [wrx], 410
Wae Sama, *dial.* Buru [mhs], 397
Wa'ema [wag], 630
Waengatu, *alt.* Nhengatu [yrl], 230, 246, 312
Waerana, *alt.* Wae Rana [wrx], 410
Waesama, *alt. dial.* Buru [mhs], 397
Waffa [waj], 630
Waga, *alt.* Wakawaka [wkw], 577
Waga-Waga, *alt.* Wakawaka [wkw], 577
Wagadi, *alt.* Wagdi [wbr], 390
Wagai, *alt.* Wagaya [wga], 577
Wagaja, *alt.* Wagaya [wga], 577

Waganga, *alt. dial.* Nyanja [nya], 140, 215
Wagap, *alt.* Cemuhî [cam], 584
Wagarabai, *alt.* Suganga [sug], 625
Wagari, *alt.* Wagdi [wbr], 390
Wagarindem, *alt.* Yafi [wfg], 426
Wagau, *dial.* Buang, Mapos [bzh], 595
Wagawaga [wgw], 630
  alt. Wakawaka [wkw], 577
  alt. dial. Tawala [tbo], 627
  dial. Wagawaga [wgw], 630
  dial. Wakawaka [wkw], 577
Wagaya [wga], 577
Wagaydy, *alt.* Wadjiginy [wdj], 577
Wagdi [wbr], 390
Wage, *alt.* Angal Heneng [akh], 589
Wagelak, *alt.* Ritarungo [rit], 576
Wageman [waq], 577
Waggaia, *alt.* Wagaya [wga], 577
Waghari, *alt.* Wagdi [wbr], 390
Wagholi, *alt.* Wagdi [wbr], 390
Wagi [fad], 630
  dial. Zaghawa [zag], 196
Wagifa, *dial.* Bwaidoka [bwd], 596
Wagiman, *alt.* Wageman [waq], 577
Wagimuda, *alt.* Maiani [tnh], 610
Wagoi, *alt.* Agoi [ibm], 153
Wagow, *alt.* Tamagario [tcg], 423
Wagri, *alt.* Wagdi [wbr], 390
Waha, *alt.* Lamang [hia], 168
Wahai, *alt.* Manusela [wha], 402
  alt. Saleman [sau], 403
Wahakaim, *dial.* Liana-Seti [ste], 400
Wahau Kajan, *alt.* Kayan, Wahau [whu], 393
Wahau Kayan, *see* Kayan, Wahau [whu], 393
Wahau Kenya, *alt.* Kenyah, Wahau [whk], 394
Wahau Kenyah, *see* Kenyah, Wahau [whk], 394
Wahe, *dial.* Gbari [gby], 160
Wahgi [wgi], 630
Wahgi, North [whg], 630
Wahibo, *alt.* Guahibo [guh], 245, 311
Wahinama, *alt.* Manusela [wha], 402
Wahke, *dial.* Rawang [raw], 466
Wahmirí, *alt. dial.* Atruahí [atr], 225
Wa'i, *alt. dial.* Bata [bta], 155
  alt. dial. Jimi [jim], 63
Wai, *alt.* Ajië [aji], 584
  alt. Waigali [wbk], 318
  dial. Naga, Yimchungru [yim], 380
Wai Jilu, *alt. dial.* Kambera [xbr], 407
Wai-Ala, *alt.* Waigali [wbk], 318

Waia, *dial.* Bungku [bkz], 428
Waiampi, *alt.* Wayampi [oym], 233
Waiãpi, *alt.* Wayampi [oym], 233
Waibuk, *alt.* Haruai [tmd], 601
Waibula, *dial.* Iduna [viv], 602
Waicá, *alt.* Akawaio [ake], 311
   alt. Yanomámi [wca], 234
Waidina, *alt. dial.* Fijian [fij], 580
Waidjelu, *alt. dial.* Kambera
   [xbr], 407
Waidjewa, *alt.* Wejewa [wew], 410
Waidoro, *dial.* Gizrra [tof], 600
Waiema, *alt.* Wa'ema [wag], 630
Waigala, *alt.* Waigali [wbk], 318
Waigali [wbk], 318
Waigalii, *alt.* Waigali [wbk], 318
Waigan, *dial.* Hanunoo [hnn], 494
Waigeli, *alt.* Waigali [wbk], 318
Waigeo [wgo], 424
Waigiu, *alt.* Waigeo [wgo], 424
Waijara, *alt.* Owenia [wsr], 620
Waijelo, *alt. dial.* Kambera
   [xbr], 407
Waika, *alt. dial.* Yanomámi
   [wca], 234
Waiká, *alt.* Yanomámi [wca], 234
Waikala, *dial.* Kowiai [kwh], 418
Waikhara, *alt.* Piratapuyo [pir], 231
Waikino, *alt.* Piratapuyo [pir], 231,
   247
Waikisu, *dial.* Nambikuára, Southern
   [nab], 230
Waiku, *alt. dial.* Suyá [suy], 232
Wailaki [wlk], 309
Wailapa [wlr], 646
Wailbi, *alt.* Adynyamathanha
   [adt], 567
Wailbri, *alt.* Warlpiri [wbp], 578
Wailemi, *alt.* Ikobi-Mena
   [meb], 602
Wailpi, *alt.* Adynyamathanha
   [adt], 567
Wailu, *alt.* Ajië [aji], 584
Waima [rro], 631
   dial. Waima [rro], 631
Waima'a [wmh], 351
Waimaha [bao], 248, 233
   alt. Waima'a [wmh], 351
Waimaja, *alt.* Waimaha [bao], 248,
   233
Waimirí, *dial.* Atruahí [atr], 225
Waimoa, *alt.* Waima'a [wmh], 351
Wain, *alt.* Nabak [naf], 616
Waina, *alt.* Piratapuyo [pir], 231
   alt. Sowanda [sow], 625, 423
   dial. Sowanda [sow], 625
Waina-Sowanda, *alt.* Sowanda
   [sow], 423
Wainanana, *dial.* Teop [tio], 627
Waing, *alt.* Duwet [gve], 598

Wainungomo, *alt. dial.* Maquiritari
   [mch], 229
Wainyi, *alt. dial.* Garawa [gbc], 570
Waioli [wli], 405
Waipu, *alt.* Mekwei [msf], 420
Waisara, *alt.* Owenia [wsr], 620
Waisika, *alt.* Kamang [woi], 407
Waiwai [waw], 233, 257
Waiwerang, *alt.* Adonara [adr], 406
Waja [wja], 177
   dial. Waja [wja], 177
Wajakes, *alt. dial.* Safeyoka
   [apz], 623
Wajamli, *alt. dial.* Buli [bzq], 397
Wajan Dutse, *alt. dial.* Waja
   [wja], 177
Wajan Kasa, *alt. dial.* Waja [wja],
   177
Wajana, *alt.* Wayana [way], 296
Wajao, *alt.* Yao [yao], 141, 149, 206,
   215
Wajapae, *alt.* Wayampi [oym], 233
Wajapi, *alt.* Wayampi [oym], 252
Wajapuku, *alt.* Wayampi [oym], 233
   dial. Wayampi [oym], 252
Wajarri [wbv], 577
Wajaru, *alt.* Wayoró [wyr], 234
Wajewa, *alt.* Wejewa [wew], 410
Wajiaraye, *alt.* Yurutí [yui], 249
Wajo, *dial.* Bugis [bug], 428
Wajoli, *alt.* Waioli [wli], 405
Waka [wav], 177
Wakaja, *alt.* Wagaya [wga], 577
Wakal, *dial.* Hitu [htu], 398
Wakalanga, *alt.* Kalanga [kck], 216
Wakalitesu, *dial.* Nambikuára,
   Southern [nab], 230
Wakande, *alt.* Mbembe, Cross River
   [mfn], 163
Wakari, *alt.* Wapan [juk], 177
Wakasihu, *dial.* Larike-Wakasihu
   [alo], 396
Wakatobi, *alt.* Tukang Besi North
   [khc], 434
   alt. Tukang Besi South [bhq], 434
Wakawaka [wkw], 577
Wakaya, *alt.* Wagaya [wga], 577
Wakchali, *alt. dial.* Sampang
   [rav], 478
Wakde [wkd], 425
Wake, *alt. dial.* Gbari [gby], 160
Wakhani, *alt.* Wakhi [wbl], 489, 318,
   346, 513
Wakhi [wbl], 489, 318, 346, 513
Wakhigi, *alt.* Wakhi [wbl], 489, 318,
   346, 513
Wakindiga, *alt.* Hadza [hts], 199
Wakka, *alt.* Wakawaka [wkw], 577
Wakkaja, *alt.* Wagaya [wga], 577
Wakombe, *alt. dial.* Tuki [bag], 72

Wakoná [waf], 233
Wakore, *alt.* Soninke [snk], 144, 95,
   122, 145
Wakorikori, *alt. dial.* Shona
   [sna], 215
Wakue, *dial.* Ese [mcq], 598
Wakut, *alt.* Tai Loi [tlq], 467, 453
   alt. Wa [wbm], 467, 346
Wala [lgl], 639
   alt. Dagaari Dioula [dgd], 50
   alt. Wali [wlx], 128
   alt. dial. Angal Heneng [akh], 589
Wala-Rano, *alt. dial.* Uripiv-Wala-
   Rano-Atchin [upv], 646
Walachian, *alt. dial.* Romanian
   [ron], 552, 548
Walad Dulla, *dial.* Assangori
   [sjg], 78
   dial. Sungor [sjg], 195
Walaf, *alt.* Wolof [wol], 182, 145
Walaha, *dial.* Ambae, West
   [nnd], 640
Walak [wlw], 425
Walamo, *alt.* Wolaytta [wal], 119
Walane, *alt. dial.* Silt'e [xst], 119
Walang, *alt.* Kunbarlang [wlg], 572
Walangu, *dial.* Gupapuyngu
   [guf], 571
Walapai, *dial.* Havasupai-Walapai-
   Yavapai [yuf], 301
Walar, *alt. dial.* Ngarinyin
   [ung], 575
Walari, *alt.* Wali [wll], 196
Walarishe, *alt.* Wali [wll], 196
Walbiri, *alt.* Warlpiri [wbp], 578
Walchers, *dial.* Zeeuws [zea], 549
Wâldfrysk, *dial.* Frisian, Western
   [fri], 548
Wale, *dial.* Bwanabwana [tte], 596
   dial. Parbate, Western [kjl], 477
Walese, *alt.* Lese [les], 102
Wali (Ghana) [wlx], 128
   Wali (Sudan) [wll], 196
Wali Banuah, *alt.* Sikule
   [skh], 437
Walia, *alt.* Masana [mcn], 66
   dial. Malgbe [mxf], 83
   dial. Masana [mcn], 83
Waling [wly], 481
Walio [wla], 631
Waliperi, *dial.* Ipeka-Tapuia
   [paj], 227
Walisi, *alt.* Lese [les], 102
Waljbi, *alt.* Adynyamathanha
   [adt], 567
Waljwan, *alt. dial.* Wangaaybuwan-
   Ngiyambaa [wyb], 577
Walla Walla [waa], 309
Wallace, *dial.* Bajau, Indonesian
   [bdl], 427

Wallamo, *alt.* Wolaytta [wal], 119
Wallaroo, *alt.* Nugunu [nnv], 575
Wallis, *dial.* Schwyzerdütsch [gsw], 563
Wallisian [wls], 647, 585
Wallisien, *alt.* Wallisian [wls], 647, 585
Wallon, *alt.* Walloon [wln], 531
Walloon [wln], 531
Walmajarri [wmt], 577
Walmajiri, *alt.* Walmajarri [wmt], 577
Walmala, *alt.* Warlmanpa [wrl], 578
Walmama, *alt.* Warlpiri [wbp], 578
Walmatjari, *alt.* Walmajarri [wmt], 577
Walmatjiri, *alt.* Walmajarri [wmt], 577
Walomwe, *alt.* Lomwe [ngl], 147
Walookera, *alt.* Warluwara [wrb], 578
Walpiri, *alt.* Warlpiri [wbp], 578
Walpre, *alt.* Soninke [snk], 182
Walsa, *alt.* Waris [wrs], 631, 425
Walscher, *alt.* Walser [wae], 563, 530, 545, 546
Walser [wae], 563, 530, 545, 546
Walugera, *alt.* Warluwara [wrb], 578
Walulu, *dial.* Kaluli [bco], 604
Walung, *alt.* Waling [wly], 481
alt. Walungge [ola], 481
Walüng, *alt.* Waling [wly], 481
Walungchung Gola, *alt.* Walungge [ola], 481
Walungge [ola], 481
Walunggi Keccya, *alt.* Walungge [ola], 481
Waluridji, *alt.* Muluridyi [vmu], 574
Walurigi, *alt.* Ambae, East [omb], 640
Waluwara, *alt.* Warluwara [wrb], 578
Walya, *alt. dial.* Masana [mcn], 83
dial. Masana [mcn], 66
Wam, *alt.* Wom [wmo], 632
Wama, *alt.* Akurio [ako], 295
Wama'a, *alt.* Mbugu [mhd], 202
Wamai, *alt. dial.* Ashkun [ask], 315
Wamais, *alt.* Ashkun [ask], 315
Wamak, *dial.* Kuni-Boazi [kvg], 608
Wamanyika, *alt.* Manyika [mxc], 216
Wamar, *alt.* Manombai [woo], 402
Wamas [wmc], 631
Wamay, *alt.* Wamey [cou], 182, 130
Wamayi, *alt.* Ashkun [ask], 315
Wambaia, *alt.* Wambaya [wmb], 577

Wambaja, *alt.* Wambaya [wmb], 577
Wambaya [wmb], 577
dial. Wambaya [wmb], 577
Wambisa, *alt.* Huambisa [hub], 288
Wambon [wms], 425
alt. Mandobo Atas [aax], 419
Wambule [wme], 482
Wambutu, *alt.* Mangbutu [mdk], 104
Wamdiu, *dial.* Marghi South [mfm], 169
Wamei, *alt.* Wamey [cou], 182, 130
Wamesa, *alt.* Wandamen [wad], 425
dial. Wandamen [wad], 425
Wamey [cou], 182, 130
Wamia, *alt.* Teso [teo], 213
Wamin [wmi], 577
Wamoang, *alt.* Waamwang [wmn], 585
Wamola, *alt. dial.* Kâte [kmg], 605
Wamora, *dial.* Kâte [kmg], 605
Wampanoag [wam], 309
Wampar [lbq], 631
Wampukuamp, *alt. dial.* Kombio [xbi], 607
Wampur [waz], 631
Wamwan, *dial.* Muyuw [myw], 616
Wan [wan], 95
alt. dial. Armenian [hye], 318
Wan Wan, *alt.* Heyo [auk], 602
Wana, *alt.* Pamona [bcx], 432
alt. dial. Pamona [bcx], 432
dial. Kâte [kmg], 605
Wanai, *alt.* Mapoyo [mcg], 312
Wanam, *alt.* Yale, Kosarek [kkl], 426
dial. Tami [tmy], 626
Wanambre [wnb], 631
Wanami, *dial.* Manam [mva], 611
Wanana, *alt.* Guanano [gvc], 245
Wanâna, *alt.* Guanano [gvc], 227
Wanang, *dial.* Koch [kdq], 368, 321
Wanano, *alt.* Guanano [gvc], 227
Wanap [wnp], 631
Wancheng, *alt. dial.* Chinese, Yue [yue], 331
Wancho, *alt.* Naga, Wancho [nnp], 380
Wancho Naga, *see* Naga, Wancho [nnp], 380
Wanci, *dial.* Tukang Besi North [khc], 434
Wand Tuan, *alt.* Kamasau [kms], 604
Wanda [wbh], 205
Wandabong, *dial.* Yopno [yut], 634
Wandala [mfi], 73, 177
dial. Wandala [mfi], 73
Wandamen [wad], 425
Wandamen-Windesi, *alt.* Wandamen [wad], 425

Wandaran, *alt.* Wandarang [wnd], 577
Wandarang [wnd], 577
Wandi, *dial.* Dass [dot], 157
Wandia, *alt.* Wanda [wbh], 205
Wandji [wdd], 122
Wandjirra, *alt. dial.* Gurinji [gue], 571
Wando, *dial.* Siane [snp], 624
Wando Bando, *alt.* Menka [mea], 67
Wandya, *dial.* Nyiha [nih], 215
Wané [hwa], 95
Wanechi, *alt.* Waneci [wne], 489
Waneci [wne], 489
Wanetsi, *alt.* Waneci [wne], 489
Wang, *dial.* Muong [mtq], 525
Wang-The, *dial.* Dzongkha [dzo], 323
Wanga, *dial.* Luyia [luy], 134
Wangaaybuwan, *dial.* Wangaaybuwan-Ngiyambaa [wyb], 577
Wangaaybuwan-Ngiyambaa [wyb], 577
Wangada, *alt.* Pintiini [pti], 576
Wanganui, *dial.* Maori [mri], 586
Wangata, *dial.* Mongo-Nkundu [lol], 104
Wangday, *alt. dial.* Dass [dot], 157
Wanggaji, *alt.* Pintiini [pti], 576
Wanggamadu, *alt.* Kokata [ktd], 572
Wanggamala [wnm], 577
Wangganguru [wgg], 577
Wanggo, *alt.* Wanggom [wng], 425
Wanggom [wng], 425
Wangi- Wangi, *alt. dial.* Tukang Besi North [khc], 434
Wangjiaji, *dial.* Dongxiang [sce], 332
Wangka, *dial.* Rembong [reb], 409
Wangkajunga, *dial.* Martu Wangka [mpj], 574
Wangkajungka, *alt. dial.* Martu Wangka [mpj], 574
Wangkatja, *alt.* Pintiini [pti], 576
Wangki, *alt. dial.* Mískito [miq], 282
Wangkumara, *alt. dial.* Ngura [nbx], 575
Wango, *dial.* Arosi [aia], 635
Wangom, *alt.* Wanggom [wng], 425
Wangumarra, *alt. dial.* Ngura [nbx], 575
Wangurri, *dial.* Dhangu [dhg], 569
Wani, *dial.* Kolami, Northwestern [kfb], 369
Wanib, *alt.* Heyo [auk], 602

Wanigela, *dial.* Keapara [khz], 605
Wanimo, *alt.* Vanimo [vam], 630
Wanindilyaugwa, *alt.*
    Anindilyakwa [aoi], 568
Waninnawa, *alt.* Katukína, Panoan
    [knt], 229
Wanja, *alt.* Sowanda [sow], 625, 423
Wanje, *alt. dial.* Tukang Besi North
    [khc], 434
Wanji [wbi], 205
    alt. Lambadi [lmn], 372
    alt. dial. Tukang Besi North
    [khc], 434
    dial. Garawa [gbc], 570
Wanki, *dial.* Mískito [miq], 282
Wanman [wbt], 577
Wannu [jub], 177
Wano [wno], 425
Wanokaka, *alt.* Wanukaka
    [wnk], 410
Wanoni, *alt.* Kahua [agw], 636
    alt. Owa [stn], 637
Wanse, *alt.* Puinave [pui], 312
Wansum, *alt.* Pahi [lgt], 621
Wantakia, *dial.* Baruya [byr], 592
Wantji, *alt. dial.* Tukang Besi North
    [khc], 434
Wantoat [wnc], 631
Wanukaka [wnk], 410
    dial. Wanukaka [wnk], 410
Wanuma, *alt.* Usan [wnu], 630
Wanya, *alt.* Sowanda [sow], 625,
    423
Wanyai, *alt. dial.* Kalanga [kck], 216
Wanyika, *alt.* Manyika [mxc], 216
Wanyjirra, *alt. dial.* Gurinji
    [gue], 571
Wanyoro, *dial.* Alur [alz], 210
Waodani, *alt.* Waorani [auc], 251
Waola, *dial.* Angal Heneng
    [akh], 589
Waorani [auc], 251
Wapã, *alt.* Wapan [juk], 177
Wapan [juk], 177
Wapatu, *alt.* Kalapuya [kyl], 302
Wape, *alt. dial.* Olo [ong], 619
Wãpha [juw], 177
Wapi, *alt.* Pinai-Hagahai [pnn], 622
    alt. dial. Enga [enq], 598
    dial. Olo [ong], 619
Wapi Pii, *alt.* Lembena [leq], 609
Wapichan, *alt.* Wapishana
    [wap], 257
Wapichana, *alt.* Wapishana
    [wap], 257
Wapisana, *alt.* Wapishana
    [wap], 257
Wapishana [wap], 257, 233
Wapishiana, *alt.* Wapishana
    [wap], 233

Wapishshiana, *alt.* Wapishana
    [wap], 257
Wapisiana, *alt.* Wapishana
    [wap], 257, 233
Wapitxana, *alt.* Wapishana
    [wap], 257
Wapixana, *alt.* Wapishana
    [wap], 257
Wapixiana, *alt.* Wapishana
    [wap], 233
Wapixiána, *alt.* Wapishana
    [wap], 233
Wappo [wao], 309
Wapu, *dial.* Wantoat [wnc], 631
Wapumni, *alt.* Nisenan [nsz], 306
War [aml], 322, 390
    alt. Meoswar [mvx], 420
    dial. Khasi [kha], 367
War-Jaintia, *dial.* War [aml], 322,
    390
War-Khasi, *dial.* War [aml], 322,
    390
Wara [wbf], 55
    alt. dial. Bugis [bug], 428
Wára [tci], 631
    dial. Wára [tci], 631
Wärä, *alt.* Wára [tci], 631
Warabal, *alt.* Bayali [bjy], 569
    dial. Lola [lcd], 401
Warabori, *dial.* Marau [mvr], 415
Waraga, *dial.* Folopa [ppo], 599
Warandgeri, *alt.* Wiradhuri [wrh],
    578
Warang, *alt. dial.* Nga La [hlt], 466
Warao [wba], 312, 257, 296
Warapiche, *alt.* Chaima [ciy], 311
Warapu [wra], 631
Warasai, *alt. dial.* Yessan-Mayo
    [yss], 633
Warat, *alt.* Madngele [zml], 573
Warau, *alt.* Warao [wba], 257
Warawara, *alt. dial.* Limba, East
    [lma], 129, 183
Waray [wrz], 577
    alt. Waray-Waray [war], 502
    dial. Waray-Waray [war], 502
Waray Sorsogon, *see* Sorsogon,
    Waray [srv], 501
Waray-Waray [war], 502
Warda'man, *alt.* Wardaman
    [wrr], 578
Wardaman [wrr], 578
Warday, *alt.* Orma [orc], 135
Wardei, *alt.* Orma [orc], 135
Wardman, *alt.* Wardaman
    [wrr], 578
Wardo, *dial.* Biak [bhw], 412
Warduji [wrd], 318
Warduman, *alt.* Wardaman
    [wrr], 578

Ware [wre], 206
    alt. dial. Bwanabwana [tte], 596
Warekena, *alt.* Guarequena
    [gae], 311
Warekéna, *alt.* Guarequena
    [gae], 227
Warema, *alt. dial.* Yanomámi
    [wca], 234
Waremboivoro, *alt.* Warembori
    [wsa], 425
Warembori [wsa], 425
    alt. dial. Marau [mvr], 415
Warenbori, *alt.* Warembori
    [wsa], 425
Wares [wai], 425
Wargarindem, *alt.* Yafi [wfg], 426
Wargla, *alt.* Tagargrent [oua], 40
Wari, *alt.* Pakaásnovos [pav], 231
    alt. Tubarão [tba], 233
    alt. Waritai [wbe], 425
    alt. dial. Bwanabwana [tte], 596
    dial. Biak [bhw], 412
Wariadai, *alt.* Morigi [mdb], 615
Wariagar, *alt.* Kemberano [bzp], 412
Wariapano, *alt.* Panobo [pno], 289
Warihío, *alt.* Huarijio [var], 262
Warikiana, *alt.* Kaxuiâna [kbb], 229
Warikyana, *alt.* Kaxuiâna [kbb], 229
Warilau, *alt.* Kola [kvv], 400
Warimi, *alt.* Worimi [kda], 578
Waris [wrs], 631, 425
Waritai [wbe], 425
Wariyangga [wri], 578
Warja, *alt.* Warji [wji], 177
Warjawa, *alt.* Warji [wji], 177
Warji [wji], 177
Warkay-Bipim [bgv], 425
Warki, *alt.* Dilling [dil], 189
Warkimbe, *alt.* Dilling [dil], 189
Warkya, *alt.* Wagaya [wga], 577
Warlang, *alt.* Kunbarlang
    [wlg], 572
Warli, *alt.* Varli [vav], 390
Warlmanpa [wrl], 578
Warlpiri [wbp], 578
Warluwara [wrb], 578
Warm Springs, *alt.* Tenino
    [tqn], 308
Warmawa, *dial.* Kurdish, Central
    [ckb], 443
Warn, *dial.* Kisi, Southern [kss], 138
Warnang [wrn], 196
Warndarang, *alt.* Wandarang
    [wnd], 577
Warnman, *alt.* Wanman [wbt], 577
Waro, *alt.* Palor [fap], 181
Waro-Waro, *alt.* Wolof [wol], 182
Waropen [wrp], 425
Waropen Kai, *dial.* Waropen [wrp],
    425

Wazegua, *alt.* Zigula [ziw], 206
Wazezuru, *alt. dial.* Shona [sna], 216
Wazhazhe, *alt.* Osage [osa], 306
Waziri, *alt. dial.* Pashto, Central [pst], 488
We, *alt. dial.* Ghomálá' [bbj], 62
alt. dial. Mmen [bfm], 67
dial. Tonga [toi], 215, 217
Wè Northern [wob], 95
Wè Southern [gxx], 95
Wè Western [wec], 95
Weasisi, *dial.* Whitesands [tnp], 646
Weda, *alt.* Sawai [szw], 403
alt. Veddah [ved], 510
dial. Sawai [szw], 403
Weda-Sawai, *alt.* Sawai [szw], 403
Wedau [wed], 631
Wedaun, *alt.* Wedau [wed], 631
Wedawan, *alt.* Wedau [wed], 631
Weddo, *alt.* Veddah [ved], 510
Wedebo, *dial.* Grebo, Barclayville [gry], 138
Wedebo Grebo, *alt.* Grebo, Barclayville [gry], 138
Wedjah, *alt. dial.* Sapo [krn], 139
Wèè, *alt.* Wè Northern [wob], 95
alt. Wè Southern [gxx], 95
alt. Wè Western [wec], 95
Weela, *alt.* Ligbi [lig], 126
alt. dial. Ligbi [lig], 126
Ween, *alt.* Toura [neb], 95
Weenhayek, *alt.* Wichí Lhamtés Nocten [mtp], 224
Wegal, *dial.* Pashayi, Southeast [psi], 317
Wegam, *alt.* Kugama [kow], 167
Wegele, *alt.* Gengle [geg], 161
Weh [weh], 73
Wei, *alt.* Tibetan, Central [bod], 344
Weidyenye, *alt.* Mundurukú [myu], 230
Weigu, *dial.* Qiang, Northern [cng], 342
Weila, *alt.* Ligbi [lig], 126
alt. dial. Ligbi [lig], 126
Weilate, *alt.* Kalmyk-Oirat [xal], 337
Weim, *alt.* Gal [gap], 599
Weining Yi, *dial.* Yi, Wusa [ywu], 348
Weirate, *dial.* Tause [tad], 424
Weiwuer, *alt.* Uyghur [uig], 346
Weizang, *alt.* Tibetan, Central [bod], 344
Wejewa [wew], 410
Welam, *alt.* Naga, Khiamniungan [nky], 378, 466
Welamo, *alt.* Wolaytta [wal], 119
Welaung [weu], 467
Wele, *alt.* Weri [wer], 632

Weleki, *alt.* Weliki [klh], 632
Welemur, *dial.* Aputai [apx], 396
Weli, *alt.* Weri [wer], 632
Weliki [klh], 632
Wellamo, *alt.* Wolaytta [wal], 119
Welsh [cym], 566, 220
Welsh Romani, *see* Romani, Welsh [rmw], 566
Wemale, North [weo], 405
Wemale, South [tlw], 405
Wemba, *alt.* Bemba [bem], 213, 97
Wembera, *dial.* Boro [bwo], 114
Wembi, *alt.* Manem [jet], 612, 419
Weme, *alt.* Gbe, Weme [wem], 45
dial. Gun [guw], 161
Weme Gbe, *see* Gbe, Weme [wem], 45
Weme-Gbe, *alt.* Gbe, Weme [wem], 45
Wemo, *dial.* Kâte [kmg], 605
Wen, *alt.* Numee [kdk], 585
Wen Baima, *alt. dial.* Baima [bqh], 327
Wen-Ma, *dial.* Zhuang, Southern [ccy], 349
Wenatchee, *alt. dial.* Columbia-Wenatchi [col], 300
Wenatchi, *dial.* Columbia-Wenatchi [col], 300
Wenatchi-Columbia, *alt.* Columbia-Wenatchi [col], 300
Wenbera, *dial.* Gumuz [guk], 115
Wenchang, *alt. dial.* Chinese, Min Nan [nan], 330
Wendat, *alt.* Wyandot [wya], 310
Wendish, *alt.* Sorbian, Lower [dsb], 539
alt. Sorbian, Upper [hsb], 539
Wenma, *alt. dial.* Zhuang, Southern [ccy], 349
Wenta, *dial.* Hamtai [hmt], 601
Wenteene, *dial.* Toussian, Northern [tsp], 55
Wenya, *alt. dial.* Tumbuka [tum], 141
dial. Tumbuka [tum], 215
Weppa Wano, *alt. dial.* Yekhee [ets], 177
Werchikwar, *alt. dial.* Burushaski [bsk], 484
Werders, *alt.* Waddar [wbq], 390
Were [wei], 632
alt. Mom Jango [ver], 170, 68
alt. Sawai [szw], 403
Wèré, *dial.* Wára [tci], 631
Werekena, *alt.* Guarequena [gae], 227
Weretai, *alt.* Waritai [wbe], 425
Weri [wer], 632
alt. Arapesh, Bumbita [aon], 590

Weriagar, *dial.* Kemberano [bzp], 412
Werikena, *alt.* Guarequena [gae], 227
Weril, *dial.* Arapesh, Bumbita [aon], 590
Werinama, *alt.* Bobot [bty], 397
Werir, *dial.* Arapesh, Bumbita [aon], 590
Werni, *alt.* Warnang [wrn], 196
Werogery, *alt.* Wiradhuri [wrh], 578
Werria, *dial.* Moro [mor], 193
Werro, *alt. dial.* Estonian [est], 534
Wersin, *alt.* Wersing [kvw], 410
Wersing [kvw], 410
Werugha, *dial.* Taita [dav], 136
Wes Cos, *alt.* Pidgin, Cameroon [wes], 71
Wesa, *dial.* Nyole [nuj], 212
Wesi, *alt.* Watubela [wah], 405
Wesrau, *alt.* Semimi [etz], 422
West Adonara, *dial.* Adonara [adr], 406
West Ambae, *see* Ambae, West [nnd], 640
West Angal Heneng, *alt.* Angal Heneng [akh], 589
West Arabian Colloquial Arabic, *alt.* Arabic, Hijazi Spoken [acw], 508
West Arctic Inupiatun, *dial.* Inupiatun, North Alaskan [esi], 302, 238
West Asturian, *dial.* Asturian [ast], 551
West Awin, *alt.* Aekyom [awi], 587
West Bafwangada, *dial.* Budu [buu], 98
West Baikeno, *alt. dial.* Baikeno [bkx], 350
West Banggai, *dial.* Banggai [bgz], 427
West Berawan, *dial.* Berawan [lod], 459
West Boikin, *dial.* Boikin [bzf], 594
West Borneo Coast Malay, *dial.* Malay [mly], 436
West Cape Afrikaans, *alt. dial.* Afrikaans [afr], 185
West Central Banda, *see* Banda, West Central [bbp], 74, 188
West Central Goe, *alt.* Samo, Matya [stj], 53
West Central K'iche', *see* K'iche', West Central [qut], 255
West Central Klaoh, *dial.* Klao [klu], 138
West Central Komba, *dial.* Komba [kpf], 607

West Central Kwomtari, *dial.* Kwomtari [kwo], 609

West Central Mixe, *alt.* Mixe, Tlahuitoltepec [mxp], 265

West Central Oromo, *see* Oromo, West Central [gaz], 118

West Chachapoyas, *alt. dial.* Quechua, Chachapoyas [quk], 290

West Circassian, *alt.* Adyghe [ady], 552, 442, 444, 447, 510, 547

West Coast Bajao, *alt.* Bajau, West Coast [bdr], 456

West Coast Bajau, *see* Bajau, West Coast [bdr], 456

West Country, *dial.* English [eng], 565

West Damar, *see* Damar, West [drn], 397

West Dangaléat, *dial.* Dangaléat [daa], 80

West Danube, *dial.* Hungarian [hun], 542

West Elema, *alt.* Orokolo [oro], 620

West Ende, *alt. dial.* Ende [end], 406

West Futuna, *dial.* Futuna-Aniwa [fut], 641

West Futuna-Aniwa, *alt.* Futuna-Aniwa [fut], 641

West Fuyug, *dial.* Fuyug [fuy], 599

West Gimi, *alt. dial.* Gimi [gim], 600

West Gogo, *alt. dial.* Gogo [gog], 198

West Gorontalo, *dial.* Gorontalo [gor], 429

West Greenlandic, *dial.* Inuktitut, Greenlandic [kal], 252

West Groningen, *dial.* Gronings [gos], 548

West Gronings, *alt. dial.* Gronings [gos], 548

West Guadalcanal, *alt.* Ghari [gri], 636

West Gurage, *alt.* Sebat Bet Gurage [sgw], 118

West Gwari, *alt.* Gbari [gby], 160

West Hunan Miao, *alt.* Hmong, Western Xiangxi [mmr], 335

West Hungarian, *dial.* Hungarian [hun], 542

West Kalamsé, *alt. dial.* Kalamsé [knz], 51

alt. dial. Sàmòmá [knz], 143

West Kara, *dial.* Kara [leu], 605

West Karekare, *alt. dial.* Karekare [kai], 166

West Kasem, *dial.* Kasem [xsm], 52

West Kewa, *see* Kewa, West [kew], 606

West Koita, *dial.* Koitabu [kqi], 607

West Komba, *dial.* Komba [kpf], 607

West Kongo, *dial.* Koongo [kng], 101, 40

West Lamaholot, *dial.* Lamaholot [slp], 408

West Latvian, *dial.* Latvian [lav], 546

West Lembata, *see* Lembata, West [lmj], 408

West Mafa, *dial.* Mafa [maf], 65

West Main Cree, *alt.* Cree, Moose [crm], 236

alt. Cree, Swampy [csw], 236

West Makian, *see* Makian, West [mqs], 401

West Makua, *alt.* Makhuwa-Shirima [vmk], 147

West Marsela, *alt.* Masela, West [mss], 402

West Masela, *see* Masela, West [mss], 402

West Mbum, *alt. dial.* Mbum [mdd], 66

West Mekeo, *alt. dial.* Mekeo [mek], 613

West Mendi, *alt.* Angal Heneng [akh], 589

West Mori, *alt.* Mori Atas [mzq], 431

West Mwerelawa, *dial.* Merlav [mrm], 644

West Nda'nda'-South Nda'nda', *alt. dial.* Nda'nda' [nnz], 69

West Nek, *dial.* Nek [nif], 617

West Numanggang, *dial.* Numanggang [nop], 619

West Nyala, *dial.* Luyia [luy], 134

West Oki-No-Erabu, *dial.* Oki-No-Erabu [okn], 447

West Olodiama, *dial.* Izon [ijc], 164

West Orya, *alt. dial.* Orya [ury], 422

West Pokot, *dial.* Pökoot [pko], 135

West Quchani, *dial.* Khorasani Turkish [kmz], 439

West Sentani, *dial.* Sentani [set], 423

West Shore Cree, *alt.* Cree, Moose [crm], 236

alt. Cree, Swampy [csw], 236

West Slovakian Romani, *dial.* Romani, Carpathian [rmc], 533, 558

West Solor, *dial.* Lamaholot [slp], 408

West Songhoy, *alt.* Songhay, Koyra Chiini [khq], 144

West Sumbanese, *alt.* Wejewa [wew], 410

West Tanna, *dial.* Tanna, North [tnn], 645

West Tarakiri, *dial.* Izon [ijc], 164

West Tarangan, *see* Tarangan, West [txn], 404

West Teke, *alt.* Teke-Tyee [tyx], 90 *alt.* Yaka [iyx], 90

West Teluti, *dial.* Teluti [tlt], 404

West Tigak, *dial.* Tigak [tgc], 627

West Toraja, *alt. dial.* Toraja-Sa'dan [sda], 434

West Torres, *alt.* Torres Strait Creole [tcs], 577

West Torricelli, *dial.* Torricelli [tei], 628

West Trangan, *alt.* Tarangan, West [txn], 404

West Urii, *dial.* Uri [uvh], 629

West Uvean, *see* Uvean, West [uve], 585

West Vanua Levu, *dial.* Fijian [fij], 580

West Vlaams, *dial.* Vlaams [vls], 549

West Vod, *dial.* Vod [vot], 557

West Waylla, *dial.* Quechua, Huaylla Wanca [qvw], 291

West Wosera, *alt.* Hanga Hundi [wos], 601

West Yambes, *dial.* Yambes [ymb], 633

West Yawa, *dial.* Yawa [yva], 426

West Yorkshire, *dial.* English [eng], 565

West Yugur, *see* Yugur, West [ybe], 348

West-Central Kombio, *dial.* Kombio [xbi], 607

West-Central Limba, *see* Limba, West-Central [lia], 183

West-Central Manggarai, *dial.* Manggarai [mqy], 409

West-Central Mese, *dial.* Mese [mci], 613

Westerlauwers Fries, *dial.* Frisian, Western [fri], 548

Western, *alt. dial.* Sherpa [xsr], 478 *dial.* Muthuvan [muv], 377

Western Abnaki, *see* Abnaki, Western [abe], 235

Western Acheron, *dial.* Acheron [acz], 187

Western Acipa, *see* Acipa, Western [awc], 153

Western Acipanci, *alt. dial.* Acipa, Western [awc], 153

Western Addasen, *dial.* Itneg, Adasen [tiu], 496

Western Agaw, *alt.* Qimant [ahg], 118

Western Aka, *alt. dial.* Aka [axk], 87

Western Aleut, *dial.* Aleut [ale], 297

Western Angami, *alt. dial.* Naga, Angami [njm], 377

Western Anmatyerre, *alt. dial.* Anmatyerre [amx], 568

Western Apache, *see* Apache, Western [apw], 298

Western Aragonese, *dial.* Aragonese [arg], 558

Western Aranda, *dial.* Arrarnta, Western [are], 568

Western Argentine Guaraní, *see* Guaraní, Eastern Bolivian [gui], 220

Western Armenian, *dial.* Armenian [hye], 319, 350, 442, 444, 448, 453, 510

Western Arrarnta, *see* Arrarnta, Western [are], 568

Western Assamese, *dial.* Assamese [asm], 354

Western Asturian, *dial.* Asturian [ast], 559

Western Bade, *dial.* Bade [bde], 154

Western Baima, *dial.* Baima [bqh], 327

Western Bakossi, *dial.* Akoose [bss], 56

Western Balochi, *see* Balochi, Western [bgn], 476, 315, 438, 520

Western Bantawa, *dial.* Bantawa [bap], 468

Western Bashkir, *alt. dial.* Bashkir [bak], 553

Western Bété, *alt.* Béte, Guiberoua [bet], 92

Western Bila, *alt.* Bila [bip], 98

Western Bisa, *alt. dial.* Bissa [bib], 123

Western Bobo Oule, *alt.* Bomu [bmq], 137

Western Bobo Wule, *alt.* Bomu [bmq], 49

Western Bolivian Guaraní, *see* Guaraní, Western Bolivian [gnw], 223

Western Bontoc, *alt.* Kankanay, Northern [xnn], 498

Western Bru, *see* Bru, Western [brv], 514

Western Bukidnon Manobo, *see* Manobo, Western Bukidnon [mbb], 499

Western Bwamu, *alt.* Bomu [bmq], 137

Western Cajamarca, *dial.* Quechua, Cajamarca [qvc], 290

Western Cakchiquel, *alt.* Kaqchikel, Western [ckw], 254

Western Campidenese, *dial.* Sardinian, Campidanese [sro], 545

Western Canada Gwich'in, *dial.* Gwich'in [gwi], 237, 301

Western Canadian Inuktitut, *see* Inuktitut, Western Canadian [ikt], 238

Western Cappadocian, *dial.* Cappadocian Greek [cpg], 540

Western Carib, *alt. dial.* Carib [car], 257, 295

Western Central Sierra Miwok, *dial.* Miwok, Central Sierra [csm], 305

Western Cham, *see* Cham, Western [cja], 325, 514, 522

Western Chepang, *alt.* Bujhyal [byh], 469
dial. Chepang [cdm], 469

Western Cherokee, *alt. dial.* Cherokee [chr], 299

Western Cree, *alt.* Cree, Plains [crk], 236, 300

Western Dan, *alt. dial.* Dan [daf], 92

Western Dani, *see* Dani, Western [dnw], 414

Western Dani of Bokondini, *dial.* Dani, Western [dnw], 414

Western Dani of Pyramid, *dial.* Dani, Western [dnw], 414

Western Danish, *alt.* Jutish [jut], 533

Western Dengka, *dial.* Dengka [dnk], 406

Western Dhimal, *dial.* Dhimal [dhi], 470

Western Dinka, *alt.* Dinka, Southwestern [dik], 190

Western Ditammari, *alt. dial.* Ditammari [tbz], 43, 207

Western Duka, *dial.* Hun-Saare [dud], 162

Western Duun, *alt.* Duungooma [dux], 142

Western Duvle, *dial.* Duvle [duv], 414

Western Edolo, *dial.* Edolo [etr], 598

Western Egyptian Bedawi Arabic, *dial.* Arabic, Western Egyptian Bedawi Spoken [ayl], 110

Western Egyptian Bedawi Spoken Arabic, *see* Arabic, Libyan Spoken [ayl], 110

Western Ejagham, *dial.* Ejagham [etu], 159, 60

Western Ejutla Zapotec, *alt.* Zapotec, Ayoquesco [zaf], 277

Western Emiliano, *dial.* Emiliano-Romagnolo [eml], 543

Western Ergong, *alt. dial.* Horpa [ero], 335

Western Ersu, *alt. dial.* Ersu [ers], 332

Western Farsi, *see* Farsi, Western [pes], 439, 443, 482, 503, 513, 520

Western Fas, *dial.* Fas [fqs], 598

Western Fijian, *see* Fijian, Western [wyy], 580

Western Frisian, *see* Frisian, Western [fri], 548

Western Friulian, *dial.* Friulian [fur], 544

Western Garifuna, *dial.* Garifuna [cab], 258

Western Gitsken, *alt. dial.* Gitxsan [git], 237

Western Gizra, *dial.* Gizrra [tof], 600

Western Guizhou, *alt. dial.* Bouyei [pcc], 328

Western Gujari, *dial.* Gujari [gju], 485

Western Gurung, *see* Gurung, Western [gvr], 471, 363

Western Helambu Sherpa, *dial.* Helambu Sherpa [scp], 472

Western Highland Chatino, *see* Chatino, Western Highland [ctp], 260

Western Highland Purepecha, *see* Purepecha, Western Highland [pua], 274

Western Highland Purépecha, *alt.* Purepecha, Western Highland [pua], 274

Western Hmong, *alt.* Hmong Njua [blu], 334

Western Horpa, *alt. dial.* Horpa [ero], 335

Western Huasteca Aztec, *alt.* Nahuatl, Western Huasteca [nhw], 272

Western Huasteca Nahuatl, *see* Nahuatl, Western Huasteca [nhw], 272

Western Huasteca Náhuatl, *dial.* Nahuatl, Western Huasteca [nhw], 272

Western Huichol, *alt. dial.* Huichol [hch], 263

Western Irish, *alt. dial.* Gaelic, Irish [gle], 542

Western Isirawa, *dial.* Isirawa [srl], 415

Western Itelmen, *alt.* Itelmen [itl], 505

Western Ixtlán Zapotec, *alt.* Zapotec, Yareni [zae], 281

Western Jacaltec, *see* Jakalteko, Western [jai], 263

Western Jacalteco, *alt.* Jakalteko, Western [jai], 254

Western Jakalteko, *see* Jakalteko, Western [jai], 254

Western Jamiltepec Mixtec, *alt.* Mixtec, Pinotepa Nacional [mio], 268

Western Japanese, *dial.* Japanese [jpn], 446

Western Jiarong, *alt.* Guanyinqiao [jiq], 333
alt. Horpa [ero], 335
alt. Shangzhai [jih], 343

Western Jibbali, *dial.* Shehri [shv], 483

Western Jikany, *dial.* Nuer [nus], 194

Western Juxtlahuaca Mixtec, *see* Mixtec, Western Juxtlahuaca [jmx], 270

Western Kaba, *alt.* Kaba [ksp], 81

Western Kalebwe, *dial.* Songe [sop], 108

Western Kalibugan, *alt. dial.* Subanon, Western [suc], 501

Western Kanjobal, *see* Akateko [knj], 263

Western Kanjobal, *alt.* Akateko [knj], 253

Western Kaqkchikel, *see* Kaqkchikel, Western [ckw], 254

Western Karaboro, *see* Karaboro, Western [kza], 52

Western Kativiri, *dial.* Kati [bsh], 316, 486

Western Katu, *see* Katu, Western [kuf], 450

Western Kayah, *see* Kayah, Western [kyu], 465

Western Kazakh, *dial.* Kazakh [kaz], 448, 316

Western Kele, *alt.* Kélé [keb], 120
dial. Kélé [keb], 120

Western Keliko, *dial.* Keliko [kbo], 192

Western Kenya, *alt.* Kenyah, Western [xky], 460

Western Kenyah, *see* Kenyah, Western [xky], 460

Western Keres, *see* Keres, Western [kjq], 303

Western Keres Pueblo, *alt.* Keres, Western [kjq], 303

Western Khams, *dial.* Tibetan, Khams [khg], 345

Western K'iche', *dial.* K'iche', West Central [qut], 255

Western Kilmeri, *dial.* Kilmeri [kih], 606

Western Kituba, *dial.* Kituba [ktu], 101

Western Klaoh, *dial.* Klao [klu], 138

Western Kolibugan, *dial.* Subanon, Western [suc], 501

Western Koromfe, *dial.* Koromfé [kfz], 143

Western Krahn, *see* Krahn, Western [krw], 138, 93

Western Kran, *alt.* Krahn, Western [krw], 138

Western Kumauni, *dial.* Kumauni [kfy], 370

Western Kundu, *alt. dial.* Oroko [bdu], 71

Western Kusaal, *alt. dial.* Kusaal [kus], 126, 52

Western Lalu Yi, *see* Yi, Western Lalu [ywl], 348

Western Lampung, *alt.* Krui [krq], 436

Western Laotian, *alt.* Thai, Northern [nod], 517

Western Lawa, *see* Lawa, Western [lcp], 338, 515

Western Limba, *dial.* Limba, West-Central [lia], 183

Western Livonian, *dial.* Liv [liv], 546

Western Lombard, *dial.* Lombard [lmo], 544

Western Low Navarrese, *dial.* Basque, Navarro-Labourdin [bqe], 535

Western Luba, *alt.* Luba-Kasai [lua], 103

Western Macedonian, *dial.* Macedonian [mkd], 547

Western Macina, *dial.* Fulfulde, Maasina [ffm], 143

Western Magar, *see* Magar, Western [mrd], 475

Western Maithili, *dial.* Maithili [mai], 373

Western Makua, *alt.* Lomwe [ngl], 147

Western Malinke, *alt.* Maninkakan, Western [mlq], 181, 143

Western Mam, *alt.* Mam, Central [mvc], 255
alt. Tacanec [mtz], 256

Western Mampruli, *dial.* Mampruli [maw], 126

Western Mandarin, *alt. dial.* Chinese, Mandarin [cmn], 514

Western Manggarai, *dial.* Manggarai [mqy], 409

Western Maninkakan, *see* Maninkakan, Western [mlq], 181, 122, 143

Western Mari, *see* Mari, Western [mrj], 555

Western Marik, *dial.* Marik [dad], 612

Western Masalit, *dial.* Masalit [mls], 83

Western Mashan Hmong, *see* Hmong, Western Mashan [hmw], 335

Western Mashan Miao, *alt.* Hmong, Western Mashan [hmw], 335

Western Mbube, *alt.* Mbe [mfo], 169

Western Mehri, *dial.* Mehri [gdq], 528

Western Meohang, *see* Meohang, Western [raf], 476

Western Miahuatlán Zapotec, *alt.* Zapotec, Coatlán [zps], 278

Western Miao, *alt.* Hmong Njua [blu], 334, 514

Western Mongol, *alt.* Kalmyk-Oirat [xal], 337, 461

Western Mongolian, *alt.* Kalmyk-Oirat [xal], 554

Western Montagnais, *dial.* Montagnais [moe], 239

Western Motu, *dial.* Motu [meu], 615

Western Muria, *see* Muria, Western [mut], 377

Western Mussau, *dial.* Mussau-Emira [emi], 616

Western Muya, *dial.* Muya [mvm], 340

Western Namuyi, *dial.* Namuyi [nmy], 341

Western Naskapi, *dial.* Naskapi [nsk], 239

Western Neo-Aramaic [amw], 510

Western Niger Fulfulde, *see* Fulfulde, Western Niger [fuh], 151

Western Nihiri, *dial.* Varli [vav], 390

Western Nyasa, *alt.* Tonga [tog], 141

Western Ojibwa, *see* Ojibwa, Western [ojw], 240

Western Okpamheri, *dial.* Okpamheri [opa], 172

Western Oriya, *dial.* Oriya [ori], 382

Western Oromo, *dial.* Oromo, West Central [gaz], 118

Western Otomi, *alt.* Otomi, Querétaro [otq], 272

Western Pagi, *dial.* Pagi [pgi], 621

Western Panjabi, *see* Panjabi, Western [pnb], 487, 383

Western Parbate, *see* Parbate, Western [kjl], 477

Western Pattani, *alt. dial.* Pattani [lae], 383

Western Penan, *see* Penan, Western [pne], 460, 325

Western Pochutla Zapotec, *alt.* Zapotec, Loxicha [ztp], 278

Western Pocomchí, *alt.* Poqomchi', Western [pob], 256

Western Point, *dial.* Nimoa [nmw], 618

Western Pokomchí, *alt.* Poqomchi', Western [pob], 256

Western Popoloca, *alt.* Popoloca, San Felipe Otlaltepec [pow], 273

Western Poqomchi', *see* Poqomchi', Western [pob], 256

Western Punjabi, *alt.* Panjabi, Western [pnb], 487, 383

Western Q'anjob'al, *alt.* Akateko [knj], 253

Western Rajbanshi, *dial.* Rajbanshi [rjb], 384, 477

Western Red Bobo, *alt.* Bomu [bmq], 137

Western Rengao, *dial.* Rengao [ren], 526

Western Rote, *alt.* Dela-Oenale [row], 406
alt. Dengka [dnk], 406
alt. Tii [txq], 410

Western Ruli, *dial.* Ruli [ruc], 212

Western She, *alt. dial.* She [shx], 343

Western Shona, *alt.* Kalanga [kck], 216

Western Shoshoni, *dial.* Shoshoni [shh], 308

Western Shuswap, *dial.* Shuswap [shs], 241

Western Sicilian, *dial.* Sicilian [scn], 545

Western Sisaala, *see* Sisaala, Western [ssl], 128

Western Sola de Vega Mixtec, *alt.* Mixtec, Amoltepec [mbz], 266

Western Sola de Vega Zapotec, *alt.* Zapotec, Zaniza [zpw], 281

Western Soqotri, *dial.* Soqotri [sqt], 528

Western Standard Bhojpuri, *dial.* Bhojpuri [bho], 356

Western Subanon, *see* Subanon, Western [suc], 501

Western Sudanese, *dial.* Arabic, Sudanese Spoken [apd], 188

Western Sumi, *alt. dial.* Naga, Sumi [nsm], 380

Western Suri, *alt. dial.* Kacipo-Balesi [koe], 115
dial. Kacipo-Balesi [koe], 191

Western Swampy Cree, *dial.* Cree, Swampy [csw], 236

Western Syriac, *dial.* Syriac [syc], 519

Western Tamang, *see* Tamang, Western [tdg], 480

Western Tarahumara, *alt.* Tarahumara, Lowland [tac], 274

Western Tatar, *dial.* Tatar [tat], 556

Western Taubuid, *alt.* Tawbuid, Western [twb], 502

Western Tawbuid, *see* Tawbuid, Western [twb], 502

Western Tboli, *dial.* Tboli [tbl], 502

Western Temne, *dial.* Themne [tem], 184

Western Thami, *dial.* Thangmi [thf], 480

Western Tlacolula Zapotec, *alt.* Zapotec, San Juan Guelavía [zab], 279

Western Tlapanec, *alt.* Tlapanec, Acatepec [tpx], 275

Western Toposa, *dial.* Toposa [toq], 196

Western Tunebo, *see* Tunebo, Western [tnb], 248

Western Tuvin, *dial.* Tuvin [tyv], 507

Western Tz'utujil, *see* Tz'utujil, Western [tzt], 256

Western Uma, *alt. dial.* Uma [ppk], 434

Western Vogul, *dial.* Mansi [mns], 505

Western Wakhi, *dial.* Wakhi [wbl], 513

Western Walloon, *dial.* Walloon [wln], 531

Western West-Hunan Miao, *alt.* Hmong, Western Xiangxi [mmr], 335

Western Xiangsi Miao, *alt.* Hmong, Western Xiangxi [mmr], 335

Western Xiangxi Hmong, *see* Hmong, Western Xiangxi [mmr], 335

Western Xwla Gbe, *see* Gbe, Western Xwla [xwl], 45, 207

Western Yagnobi, *dial.* Yagnobi [yai], 513

Western Yali, *alt.* Yali, Pass Valley [yac], 426

Western Yanomami, *dial.* Yanomamö [guu], 313, 234

Western Yautepec Zapotec, *alt.* Zapotec, Santa María Quiegolani [zpi], 280

Western Yi, *see* Yi, Western [ywt], 348

Western Yiddish, *see* Yiddish, Western [yih], 540

Western York Cree, *dial.* Cree, Plains [crk], 236

Western Zimatlán Zapotec, *alt.* Zapotec, Totomachapan [zph], 280

Westerwold, *alt. dial.* Gronings [gos], 548

Westerwolds, *dial.* Gronings [gos], 548

Westfaelisch, *alt.* Westphalien [wep], 540

Westfälisch, *alt.* Westphalien [wep], 540

Westfries, *alt. dial.* Dutch [nld], 548

Westmorland, *dial.* English [eng], 565

Westphalien [wep], 540

Westvlaams, *dial.* Vlaams [vls], 531

Wetamut [wwo], 646

Wetan, *dial.* Luang [lex], 401

Wetang, *alt. dial.* Luang [lex], 401

Wetawit, *alt.* Berta [wti], 113, 189

Wete, *dial.* Dehu [dhv], 584

Wetere, *alt.* Vute [vut], 177

Wetu, *dial.* Jur Modo [bex], 191

Wewau, *alt.* Wewaw [wea], 467

Wewaw [wea], 467

Wewewa, *alt.* Wejewa [wew], 410

Wewjewa, *alt.* Wejewa [wew], 410

Weyewa, *alt.* Wejewa [wew], 410
dial. Wejewa [wew], 410

Weyoko, *dial.* Bunama [bdd], 595

Weyt'o, *alt.* Weyto [woy], 119

Weyto [woy], 119

Whelngo, *alt.* Mizo [lus], 376, 321, 466

Whilkut, *dial.* Hupa [hup], 302

White Bolon, *dial.* Bolon [bof], 49

White Clay People, *alt.* Gros Ventre [ats], 301

White Gelao, *see* Gelao, White [giw], 522

White Karen, *alt.* Karen, Geba [kvq], 458
 alt. Karen, S'gaw [ksw], 464, 514
White Khoany, *dial.* Phunoi [pho], 452, 517
White Lachi, *see* Lachi, White [lwh], 524
White Lachi, *alt.* Lachi, White [lwh], 524
White Lahu, *alt. dial.* Lahu [lhu], 524
White Lisu, *alt. dial.* Lisu [lis], 339
 dial. Lisu [lis], 465
White Lum, *alt.* Hmong Daw [mww], 334, 450, 514, 523
White Meo, *alt.* Hmong Daw [mww], 334, 450, 514, 523
White Miao, *alt.* Hmong Daw [mww], 334, 450, 514
White Mountain, *dial.* Apache, Western [apw], 298
White Nile Dinka, *alt.* Dinka, Northeastern [dip], 189
White Nogai, *dial.* Nogai [nog], 556
White Russia Romani, *dial.* Romani, Baltic [rml], 546
White Russian, *alt.* Belarusan [bel], 530, 550
White Russian Romani, *dial.* Romani, Baltic [rml], 550
White Ruthenian, *alt.* Belarusan [bel], 530
White Tai, *alt.* Tai Dón [twh], 526, 453
Whitesands [tnp], 646
Whitsands, *alt.* Whitesands [tnp], 646
Wi, *alt. dial.* Gbari [gby], 160
Wiakei, *alt.* Wiaki [wii], 632
Wiaki [wii], 632
Wiang Jan, *alt. dial.* Lao [lao], 445
Wiang Papao Lua, *alt.* Lawa, Eastern [lwl], 515
Wiaoe, *alt.* Rahambuu [raz], 432
Wiarumus [tua], 632
Wiase, *dial.* Dwang [nnu], 120
Wiau, *alt.* Rahambuu [raz], 432
Wibo, *dial.* Mwani [wmw], 148
Wichí Lhamtés Güisnay [mzh], 220
Wichí Lhamtés Nocten [mtp], 224, 220
Wichí Lhamtés Vejoz [wlv], 220
Wichita [wic], 310
Widala, *alt.* Kholok [ktc], 166
 alt. Mághdì [gmd], 169
Widekum, *alt. dial.* Meta' [mgo], 67
Widikum-Tadkon, *alt.* Meta' [mgo], 67

Widimaya, *alt.* Badimaya [bia], 568
Wiga, *alt.* Uyghur [uig], 346
 dial. Sinaugoro [snc], 624
Wighor, *alt.* Uyghur [uig], 318
Wihe, *alt.* Kariya [kil], 166
Wiila, *alt.* Ligbi [lig], 126
 alt. dial. Ligbi [lig], 126
Wiindza-Baali, *dial.* Ngombe [ngc], 106
Wiiratheri, *alt.* Wiradhuri [wrh], 578
Wik Muminh, *alt.* Kuku-Muminh [xmh], 572
Wik Njinturawik-Nganhcara, *alt.* Wikngenchera [wua], 578
Wik-Em'an, *alt.* Wik-Me'anha [wih], 578
Wik-Ep, *alt.* Wik-Epa [wie], 578
Wik-Epa [wie], 578
Wik-liyanh [wij], 578
Wik-Keyangan [wif], 578
Wik-Me'anha [wih], 578
Wik-Mumin, *alt.* Kuku-Muminh [xmh], 572
Wik-Mungkan [wim], 578
Wik-Mungkhn, *alt.* Wik-Mungkan [wim], 578
Wik-Munkan, *alt.* Wik-Mungkan [wim], 578
Wik-Nantjara, *alt.* Wikngenchera [wua], 578
Wik-Ngandjara, *dial.* Wikalkan [wik], 578
Wik-Ngathana [wig], 578
Wik-Ngathara, *alt.* Wikalkan [wik], 578
Wik-Ngatharra, *alt.* Wikalkan [wik], 578
Wik-Ngathrr, *alt.* Wikalkan [wik], 578
Wikalkan [wik], 578
Wikngatara, *alt.* Wikalkan [wik], 578
Wikngenchera [wua], 578
Wila-Wila, *alt.* Wilawila [wil], 578
Wilawila [wil], 578
 dial. Ngarinyin [ung], 575
Wild 'Ali, *alt. dial.* Arabic, Najdi Spoken [ars], 508
Wile, *dial.* Birifor, Malba [bfo], 49
Wiljakali, *dial.* Darling [drl], 569
Willong Circle, *dial.* Naga, Maram [nma], 378
Wilyagali, *alt. dial.* Darling [drl], 569
Wimbum, *alt.* Limbum [lmp], 65, 169
Win, *alt.* Toussian, Southern [wib], 55
Wina, *alt.* Desano [des], 226, 245
 alt. Sowanda [sow], 625, 423
 alt. Tupuri [tui], 72
 dial. Masana [mcn], 83, 66

Winatu, *dial.* Uma [ppk], 434
Windesi, *alt.* Wandamen [wad], 425
 dial. Wandamen [wad], 425
Windessi, *alt.* Wandamen [wad], 425
Windisch, *dial.* Slovenian [slv], 530
Wingei, *dial.* Ambulas [abt], 589
Winisk River Ojibwa, *dial.* Ojibwa, Severn [ojs], 240
Winiv, *dial.* Merei [lmb], 643
 dial. Vinmavis [vnm], 646
Winjawindjagu, *alt.* Yawuru [ywr], 579
Winji-Winji, *alt.* Anii [blo], 42, 207
Winnebago, *alt.* Ho-Chunk [win], 302
Wins, *dial.* Buang, Mapos [bzh], 595
Wintu [wit], 310
 dial. Wintu [wit], 310
Wintun, *alt.* Wintu [wit], 310
Winyé [kst], 55
Wipi [gdr], 632
Wipie, *alt.* Adynyamathanha [adt], 567
Wipim, *dial.* Wipi [gdr], 632
Wipsi-Ni, *alt. dial.* Kag-Fer-Jiir-Koor-Ror-Us-Zuksun [gel], 165
Wira, *dial.* Jur Modo [bex], 191
Wirã, *alt.* Desano [des], 226
Wira-Athoree, *alt.* Wiradhuri [wrh], 578
Wiradhuri [wrh], 578
Wiradhurri, *alt.* Wiradhuri [wrh], 578
Wiradjuri, *alt.* Wiradhuri [wrh], 578
Wiraduri, *alt.* Wiradhuri [wrh], 578
Wiraféd [wir], 234
Wiraidyuri, *alt.* Wiradhuri [wrh], 578
Wirajeree, *alt.* Wiradhuri [wrh], 578
Wiram, *alt.* Suki [sui], 626
Wirangu [wiw], 578
Wirashuri, *alt.* Wiradhuri [wrh], 578
Wiratheri, *alt.* Wiradhuri [wrh], 578
Wiregi, *dial.* Suba [suh], 136
Wiri, *alt.* Duvle [duv], 414
Wiroféd, *alt.* Wiraféd [wir], 234
Wirongu, *alt.* Wirangu [wiw], 578
Wironguwongga, *alt.* Wirangu [wiw], 578
Wirracharee, *alt.* Wiradhuri [wrh], 578
Wirrai'yarrai, *alt.* Wiradhuri [wrh], 578
Wirri, *alt.* Biri [bzr], 569
Wirrung, *alt.* Wirangu [wiw], 578
Wirrunga, *alt.* Wirangu [wiw], 578
Wiru [wiu], 632
Wisa, *alt. dial.* Lala-Bisa [leb], 214
Wisconsin, *dial.* Ho-Chunk [win], 302

Wita Ea, *dial.* Moronene [mqn], 431
Witoto, *alt.* Huitoto, Murui [huu], 288, 245
Witsuwit'en, *alt.* Babine [bcr], 235
Witu, *alt.* Muduapa [wiv], 615
  alt. Wiru [wiu], 632
Wiwa, *alt.* Malayo [mbp], 246
Wiwirano, *dial.* Tolaki [lbw], 433
Wiyaa, *alt.* Waja [wja], 177
Wiyagar, *alt.* Kayagar [kyt], 417
Wiyagwa, *dial.* Ankave [aak], 590
Wiyap, *alt.* Jiru [jrr], 165
Wiyau, *alt.* Haruai [tmd], 601
Wiyaw, *alt.* Haruai [tmd], 601
Wiyeh, *dial.* Limbum [lmp], 65
Wiyot [wiy], 310
Wiza, *alt. dial.* Lala-Bisa [leb], 214, 102
Wlepo, *dial.* Krumen, Pye [pye], 93
Wlopo, *dial.* Krumen, Tepo [ted], 93, 138
Wluwe-Hawlo, *dial.* Krumen, Pye [pye], 93
Wo, *alt.* Bassari [bsc], 180, 129, 131
  alt. Kulung [bbu], 167
  dial. Yoruba [yor], 178
Wobé, *alt.* Wè Northern [wob], 95
Wocokeso, *alt. dial.* Safeyoka [apz], 623
Woda, *alt.* Wolani [wod], 425
Woda-Mo, *alt.* Wolani [wod], 425
Wodaabe, *dial.* Fulfulde, Central-Eastern Niger [fuq], 151
Wodani, *alt.* Wolani [wod], 425
Wodde, *alt.* Waddar [wbq], 390
Wodiwodi, *alt. dial.* Thurawal [tbh], 576
Wodo, *alt.* Walak [wlw], 425
Wogaity, *alt.* Wadjiginy [wdj], 577
Wogamusin [wog], 632
Wogang, *alt.* Waxianghua [wxa], 346
Wogeman, *alt.* Wageman [waq], 577
Wogeo [woc], 632
Woggil, *alt.* Yidiny [yii], 579
Wogri Boli, *alt.* Vaagri Booli [vaa], 389
Wogri-Boli, *dial.* Domari [rmt], 360
Wogu, *alt.* Bahinemo [bjh], 591
Woi [wbw], 425
Woigo, *dial.* Wipi [gdr], 632
Woisika, *alt.* Kamang [woi], 407
Wojenaka [jod], 95
Wojo, *alt. dial.* Banda, West Central [bbp], 74
Wokam, *alt.* Manombai [woo], 402
Wokeimin, *alt.* Faiwol [fai], 598
Wokiare, *alt. dial.* Yabarana [yar], 313
Woko, *alt.* Longto [wok], 65

Wolaita, *alt.* Wolaytta [wal], 119
Wolaitta, *alt.* Wolaytta [wal], 119
Wolane, *dial.* Silt'e [xst], 119
Wolani [wod], 425
Wolataita, *alt.* Wolaytta [wal], 119
Wolayta, *alt.* Wolaytta [wal], 119
Wolaytta [wal], 119
Woleaian [woe], 583
  dial. Woleaian [woe], 583
Wolio [wlo], 435, 458
Wollamo, *alt.* Wolaytta [wal], 119
Wollegara, *alt.* Warluwara [wrb], 578
Wolmeri, *alt.* Walmajarri [wmt], 577
Wolof [wol], 182, 145
Wolof, Gambian [wof], 122
Wolu, *alt.* Teluti [tlt], 404
  alt. dial. Teluti [tlt], 404
Wolyamidi, *alt. dial.* Ngarinyin [ung], 575
Wom (Nigeria) [wom], 177
  Wom (Papua New Guinea) [wmo], 632
Wom-By-A, *alt.* Wambaya [wmb], 577
Womboko, *alt.* Wumboko [bqm], 73
Wombungee, *alt. dial.* Wangaaybuwan-Ngiyambaa [wyb], 577
Wombya, *alt.* Wambaya [wmb], 577
Wonarua, *dial.* Awabakal [awk], 568
Wonga, *alt.* Pintiini [pti], 576
Wongagibun, *alt. dial.* Wangaaybuwan-Ngiyambaa [wyb], 577
Wongai-I, *alt.* Pintiini [pti], 576
Wongaibon, *alt. dial.* Wangaaybuwan-Ngiyambaa [wyb], 577
Wongaidya, *alt.* Nugunu [nnv], 575
Wongamardu, *alt.* Kokata [ktd], 572
Wongamusin, *alt.* Wogamusin [wog], 632
Wonggaii, *alt.* Pintiini [pti], 576
Wonghi, *alt. dial.* Wangaaybuwan-Ngiyambaa [wyb], 577
Wonghibon, *alt. dial.* Wangaaybuwan-Ngiyambaa [wyb], 577
Wongkumara, *dial.* Ngura [nbx], 575
Wongo [won], 109
Woni, *alt.* Honi [how], 335
  alt. Kado [kdv], 464
Wonie, *dial.* Wipi [gdr], 632
Wonjhibon, *alt. dial.* Wangaaybuwan-Ngiyambaa [wyb], 577

Wono, *alt.* Seko Padang [skx], 433
  alt. dial. Seko Padang [skx], 433
Wonti, *alt.* Waropen [wrp], 425
Woods Cree, *see* Cree, Woods [cwd], 236
Wo'oi, *alt.* Woi [wbw], 425
Woolwa, *alt.* Sumo-Mayangna [sum], 283
Wooragurie, *alt.* Wiradhuri [wrh], 578
Wooteelit, *dial.* Yupik, Central Siberian [ess], 507
Wopkeimin, *dial.* Faiwol [fai], 598
Worase, *alt. dial.* Gawwada [gwd], 115
Wordaman, *alt.* Wardaman [wrr], 578
Wordjerg, *alt.* Wiradhuri [wrh], 578
Worgai, *alt.* Wagaya [wga], 577
Worgaia, *alt.* Wagaya [wga], 577
Woria [wor], 426
Woriasi, *alt.* Wabo [wbb], 424
Worimi [kda], 578
Workai, *alt.* Barakai [baj], 396
Workia, *alt.* Wagaya [wga], 577
Worku, *dial.* Igede [ige], 163
Worla, *alt. dial.* Ngarinyin [ung], 575
Worlaja, *alt. dial.* Ngarinyin [ung], 575
Woro, *alt.* Voro [vor], 177
  alt. dial. Gbaya [krs], 190
Worodougou [jud], 96
Worodougou Jula, *alt.* Worodougou [jud], 96
Worodougouka, *dial.* Worodougou [jud], 96
Worodougoukakan, *alt.* Worodougou [jud], 96
Worodugu, *alt.* Worodougou [jud], 96
Worora [unp], 578
  dial. Worora [unp], 578
Worpen, *alt.* Waropen [wrp], 425
Worrorra, *alt.* Worora [unp], 578
Worugl, *alt. dial.* Folopa [ppo], 599
Wosera-Kamu, *dial.* Ambulas [abt], 589
Wosera-Mamu, *dial.* Ambulas [abt], 589
Woskia, *alt.* Waskia [wsk], 631
Wotaf, *alt.* Massep [mvs], 419
Wotapuri-Katarqalai [wsv], 318
Wotu [wtw], 435
Wotuja, *alt.* Maco [wpc], 312
Woulki, *dial.* Mpade [mpi], 68, 84
Woun Meu [noa], 284, 248
Wounaan, *alt.* Woun Meu [noa], 284
Wounmeu, *alt.* Woun Meu [noa], 284

Wouri, *alt. dial.* Duala [dua], 60
Woute, *alt.* Vute [vut], 73
Wovan, *alt.* Haruai [tmd], 601
Wovea, *alt.* Bubia [bbx], 59
Wowo, *alt.* Bieria [brj], 641
   alt. dial. Bieria [brj], 641
Wowonii, *alt.* Wawonii [wow], 435
Wrelpo, *dial.* Grebo, Southern [grj], 138
Wu, *alt.* Chinese, Wu [wuu], 330
   dial. Wa [wbm], 467
Wu Chinese, *see* Chinese, Wu [wuu], 330
Wu-Lu Yi, *alt.* Yi, Wuding-Luquan [ywq], 348
Wuasinkishu, *alt. dial.* Maasai [mas], 134
Wubahamer, *dial.* Aari [aiz], 112
Wubomei, *dial.* Loma [lom], 138
Wubulkarra, *dial.* Gupapuyngu [guf], 571
Wubuy, *alt.* Nunggubuyu [nuy], 575
Wuding Naisu, *dial.* Yi, Wuding-Luquan [ywq], 348
Wuding-Luquan Yi, *see* Yi, Wuding-Luquan [ywq], 348
Wudu [wud], 209
Wudufu, *alt.* Mburku [bbt], 170
Wuhána, *alt.* Macuna [myy], 246, 229
Wukan, *dial.* Wapan [juk], 177
Wukari, *alt.* Wapan [juk], 177
Wula, *alt. dial.* Ngarinyin [ung], 575
   alt. dial. Psikye [kvj], 173
   dial. Bokyi [bky], 156
Wuladja, *alt. dial.* Ngarinyin [ung], 575
Wuladjangari, *alt. dial.* Ngarinyin [ung], 575
Wulaki, *dial.* Djinang [dji], 570
Wulamba, *alt.* Dhuwal [duj], 569
Wulanga, *dial.* Yele [yle], 633
Wule, *dial.* Dagara, Northern [dgi], 50
Wulik, *alt.* Silimo [wul], 423
Wulima, *dial.* Lala-Bisa [leb], 102
Wuliwuli [wlu], 578
Wulna [wux], 578
Wulu, *dial.* Beli [blm], 189
Wulukoha, *dial.* Bandi [bza], 137
Wum, *alt.* Aghem [agq], 56
Wumboko [bqm], 73
Wumbu, *alt. dial.* Teke-Fuumu [ifm], 90
Wumbvu [wum], 122, 90
Wumeng Yi, *see* Yi, Wumeng [ywm], 348
Wumnabal, *alt.* Wunambal [wub], 578

Wumvu, *alt.* Wumbvu [wum], 122, 90
Wuna, *alt.* Mbum [mdd], 66
   alt. Muna [mnb], 431
Wunai, *alt.* Bunu, Wunai [bwn], 328
Wunai Bunu, *see* Bunu, Wunai [bwn], 328
Wunamara, *alt.* Maykulan [mnt], 574
Wunambal [wub], 578
   alt. Kwini [gww], 573
   dial. Wunambal [wub], 578
Wunambullu, *alt.* Wunambal [wub], 578
Wunavai, *dial.* Ankave [aak], 590
Wunci, *alt.* Ghulfan [ghl], 191
Wuncimbe, *alt.* Ghulfan [ghl], 191
Wundu, *dial.* Banda-Banda [bpd], 188
Wungu, *alt.* Bungu [wun], 197
Wuningak, *alt.* Urningangg [urc], 577
Wunjo, *alt.* Vunjo [vun], 205
Wupijiang, *dial.* Zauzou [zal], 349
Wupiwi, *alt. dial.* Cuiba [cui], 244
Wuranci, *alt. dial.* Gwamhi-Wuri [bga], 161
Wurawa, *alt. dial.* Gwamhi-Wuri [bga], 161
Wureidbug, *alt.* Amarag [amg], 567
Wurga, *dial.* Marghi Central [mrt], 169
Wuri, *alt. dial.* Duala [dua], 60
   dial. Gwamhi-Wuri [bga], 161
Wurkum, *alt.* Kholok [ktc], 166
   alt. Kulung [bbu], 167
   alt. Piya-Kwonci [piy], 173
Wurla, *alt. dial.* Ngarinyin [ung], 575
Wurlayi, *alt.* Gurinji [gue], 571
Wurrugu [wur], 578
Wusa Yi, *see* Yi, Wusa [ywu], 348
Wuse Hua, *pej. alt.* E [eee], 332
Wusehua, *pej. alt.* E [eee], 332
Wushi [bse], 73
Wusi [wsi], 646
Wusi-Kerepua, *alt.* Wusi [wsi], 646
Wusyep Tep, *dial.* Urat [urt], 629
Wusyep Yehre, *dial.* Urat [urt], 629
Wute, *alt.* Vute [vut], 73, 177
Wutun, *alt.* Wutunhua [wuh], 346
Wutung [wut], 632
Wutunhua [wuh], 346
Wuu, *alt. dial.* Wuvulu-Aua [wuv], 632
Wuumu, *dial.* Teke-Fuumu [ifm], 90
Wuvulu, *alt. dial.* Wuvulu-Aua [wuv], 632
Wuvulu-Aua [wuv], 632
Wuya, *alt.* Waja [wja], 177

Wuyarrawala, *alt.* Wandarang [wnd], 577
Wuzhou, *dial.* Chinese, Wu [wuu], 330
Wuzlam [udl], 73
Wuzuraabya, *alt. dial.* Baruya [byr], 592
Wyandot [wya], 310
   dial. Wyandot [wya], 310
Wyandotte, *alt.* Wyandot [wya], 310
Wyendat, *alt.* Wyandot [wya], 310
X-Ray, *pej. alt.* Dao [daz], 414
Xa, *alt.* Kháng [kjm], 524
Xá, *pej. alt.* Iu Mien [ium], 523
Xa Ai, *alt.* Kháng [kjm], 524
Xa Bung, *alt.* Kháng [kjm], 524
Xa Cau, *alt.* Khmu [kjg], 524
   alt. dial. Kháng [kjm], 524
Xá Chien, *alt.* Laha [lha], 524
Xa Chung Chá, *alt.* Giáy [pcc], 523
Xa Coong, *pej. alt.* Côông [cnc], 522
Xa Dang, *alt.* Kháng [kjm], 524
   alt. Sedang [sed], 526
Xa Don, *alt.* Kháng [kjm], 524
Xa Hoc, *alt.* Kháng [kjm], 524
Xa Khao, *alt. dial.* Kháng [kjm], 524
Xá Khao, *alt.* Kháng [kjm], 524
   alt. Laha [lha], 524
Xa La Vang, *alt. dial.* Hung [hnu], 523
Xá Lá Vàng, *alt.* Mang [zng], 525
Xá Lay, *alt.* Laha [lha], 524
Xá Mang, *alt.* Mang [zng], 525
Xá Ó, *alt.* Mang [zng], 525
Xá Phó, *alt.* Laghuu [lgh], 524
Xá U Ní, *alt.* Hani [hni], 523
Xa Xam, *pej. alt.* Côông [cnc], 522
Xa Xeng, *pej. alt.* Côông [cnc], 522
Xa Xua, *alt.* Kháng [kjm], 524
Xa-Dieng, *alt.* Stieng, Bulo [sti], 526
Xaasonga, *alt.* Xaasongaxango [kao], 145
   alt. Xasonga [kao], 182
Xaasongaxango [kao], 145
   alt. Xasonga [kao], 182
Xadani Zapotec, *see* Zapotec, Xadani [zax], 281
Xadi, *alt.* Hdi [xed], 62
Xagua, *alt.* Achagua [aca], 243
|Xaise, *dial.* Shua [shg], 48
Xaixai, *alt.* Juǀ'hoan [ktz], 47, 150
Xajdak, *alt. dial.* Dargwa [dar], 553
Xajrjuzovskij, *dial.* Itelmen [itl], 505
Xakriabá [xkr], 234
Xakuchi, *dial.* Adyghe [ady], 552
|Xam [xam], 187
|Xam-Ka-!k'e, *alt.* |Xam [xam], 187

Xamang, *alt.* Mang [zng], 339
Xamatari, *alt.* Sanumá [xsu], 312, 232
Xambioá, *alt.* Karajá [kpj], 228
Xamir, *alt.* Xamtanga [xan], 119
Xamta, *alt.* Xamtanga [xan], 119
Xamtanga [xan], 119
Xan, *alt.* Bozo, Hainyaxo [bzx], 142
Xanaguía Zapotec, *see* Zapotec, Xanaguía [ztg], 281
Xananwa, *alt. dial.* Sotho, Northern [nso], 186
Xanga, *alt. dial.* Ndau [ndc], 148
Xanica Zapotec, *alt.* Zapotec, Santiago Xanica [zpr], 280
Xanty, *alt.* Khanty [kca], 505
Xanyaxo, *alt.* Bozo, Hainyaxo [bzx], 142
Xaput, *dial.* Kryts [kry], 319
Xaracii, *alt.* Xârâcùù [ane], 585
Xârâcùù [ane], 585
Xaragure [axx], 585
Xarbuk, *dial.* Dargwa [dar], 553
Xaroxa, *alt.* Didinga [did], 189
Xarua, *alt. dial.* Bola [bnp], 594
Xasa, *alt.* Tigré [tig], 112, 195
Xasonga [kao], 182
   alt. Xaasongaxango [kao], 145
Xasonke, *alt.* Xaasongaxango [kao], 145
   alt. Xasonga [kao], 182
Xatia, *dial.* !Xóõ [nmn], 48, 151
Xatyrskij, *alt. dial.* Kerek [krk], 505
   dial. Chukot [ckt], 504
   dial. Koryak [kpy], 505
∥X'au∥'e, *alt.* ǂKx'au∥'ein [aue], 150, 47
Xauni, *alt.* Hani [hni], 523
Xavánte [xav], 234
Xavierano, *alt. dial.* Chiquitano [cax], 222
Xebero, *alt.* Jebero [jeb], 288
Xedi, *alt.* Hdi [xed], 62
   alt. Hide [xed], 162
∥Xegwe, *alt.* ∥Xegwi [xeg], 187
∥Xegwi [xeg], 187
∥Xekwi, *alt.* ∥Xegwi [xeg], 187
Xenacoj, *alt.* Kaqkchikel, Santo Domingo Xenacoj [ckj], 254
Xenqenna, *dial.* Soninke [snk], 144
Xerénte [xer], 234
Xereu, *alt.* Hixkaryána [hix], 227
Xerewyana, *alt.* Hixkaryána [hix], 227
Xesibe, *dial.* Xhosa [xho], 187
Xetá [xet], 234
Xevsur, *dial.* Georgian [kat], 352
Xhosa [xho], 187, 137
Xiaerba, *alt.* Sherpa [xsr], 478, 343, 387

Xiamen, *alt. dial.* Chinese, Min Nan [nan], 508
   dial. Chinese, Min Nan [nan], 330
Xiandao [xia], 346
Xiandaohua, *alt.* Xiandao [xia], 346
Xiang, *alt.* Chinese, Xiang [hsn], 331
Xiang Chinese, *see* Chinese, Xiang [hsn], 331
Xianghua, *alt.* Waxianghua [wxa], 346
Xiangyun, *dial.* Bai, Southern [bfs], 327
Xianyou, *dial.* Chinese, Pu-Xian [cpx], 330
Xiao Hua Miao, *dial.* Hmong Njua [blu], 334
Xiaonan, *alt. dial.* Dongxiang [sce], 332
Xiaoshanhua, *alt.* Zaiwa [atb], 349
Xiaoyili, *dial.* Guanyinqiao [jiq], 333
Xibe [sjo], 347
Xibei Guanhua, *dial.* Chinese, Mandarin [cmn], 329
Xiberoera, *alt.* Basque, Souletin [bsz], 536
Xibita, *alt.* Hibito [hib], 288
Xibitaoan, *alt.* Cocama-Cocamilla [cod], 287
Xibo, *alt.* Xibe [sjo], 347
Xicaque, *alt.* Tol [jic], 258
Xichangana, *alt.* Tsonga [tso], 197
   alt. dial. Tsonga [tso], 149, 217
Xicotepec de Juárez Totonac, *see* Totonac, Xicotepec de Juárez [too], 276
Xidzivi, *alt. dial.* Tswa [tsc], 149
Xihuila, *alt.* Jebero [jeb], 288
Xijia Miao, *alt.* Hmong, Luopohe [hml], 334
Xikiyana, *alt.* Sikiana [sik], 232
Xikrin, *dial.* Kayapó [txu], 229
Xikujana, *alt.* Sikiana [sik], 232
Xiluleke, *alt. dial.* Tsonga [tso], 186
Ximahe Miao, *alt.* Hmong, Luopohe [hml], 334
Xin Mul, *alt.* Puoc [puo], 525, 452
Xinalug, *alt.* Khinalugh [kjj], 319
Xinan Guanhua, *dial.* Chinese, Mandarin [cmn], 329
Xinca [xin], 256
Xing Mun, *alt.* Puoc [puo], 452
Xinghua, *alt. dial.* Chinese, Pu-Xian [cpx], 330, 508
   dial. Chinese, Min Dong [cdo], 391
   dial. Chinese, Pu-Xian [cpx], 454
Xingú Asuriní, *see* Asuriní, Xingú [asn], 225
Xinh Mul, *alt.* Puoc [puo], 525, 452
Xinh-Mun, *alt.* Puoc [puo], 525

Xinjiang Mongolian, *alt.* Kalmyk-Oirat [xal], 337
Xinminhua, *alt.* Chinese, Hakka [hak], 329
Xinping Nisu, *dial.* Yi, Eshan-Xinping [yiv], 347
Xipaia, *alt.* Xipaya [xiy], 234
Xipaya [xiy], 234
Xipináwa [xip], 234
Xiri [xii], 187
Xiriana, *alt.* Ninam [shb], 312
Xirianá, *alt.* Ninam [shb], 230
Xiriâna [xir], 234
Xirikwa, *alt.* Xiri [xii], 187
Xirima, *alt.* Makhuwa-Shirima [vmk], 147
Xiriwai, *alt.* Nadëb [mbj], 230
Xironga, *alt.* Ronga [rng], 149
Xishan Lalu Yi, *see* Yi, Xishan Lalu [yik], 348
Xishuangbanna Dai, *alt.* Lü [khb], 339
Xitibo, *alt. dial.* Shipibo-Conibo [shp], 293
Xitshwa, *alt.* Tswa [tsc], 149, 186, 217
Xitsonga, *alt.* Tsonga [tso], 149, 197, 217
Xiuyi, *dial.* Chinese, Huizhou [czh], 329
Xivaro, *alt.* Shuar [jiv], 251
!Xo, *alt.* Ju∣'hoan [ktz], 47, 150
∥Xo-Kxoe, *dial.* Khwe [xuu], 214
   dial. Kxoe [xuu], 150
Xochapa Mixtec, *dial.* Mixtec, Alcozauca [xta], 266
Xocó, *alt.* Karirí-Xocó [kzw], 228
Xodang, *alt.* Sedang [sed], 526
Xokleng [xok], 234
Xokó, *alt.* Karirí-Xocó [kzw], 228
Xokó-Karirí, *alt.* Karirí-Xocó [kzw], 228
∥Xom-Kxoe, *dial.* Kxoe [xuu], 150
Xong, *alt.* Chong [cog], 325, 514
Xonga, *dial.* Tsonga [tso], 186
!Xóõ [nmn], 48, 151
Xopa, *dial.* Laz [lzz], 352
Xosa, *alt.* Xhosa [xho], 187
Xoshnaw, *dial.* Kurdish, Central [ckb], 443
Xre Nop, *alt. dial.* Koho [kpm], 524
Xrikwa, *alt.* Xiri [xii], 187
Xtieng, *alt.* Stieng, Bulo [sti], 526
!Xu, *alt.* Kung-Ekoka [knw], 150, 40
Xu, *alt.* Khwe [xuu], 214
   alt. Kxoe [xuu], 40
Xû, *alt.* Ju∣'hoan [ktz], 47, 150
Xuanzhou, *dial.* Chinese, Wu [wuu], 330

Xuhwe, *alt.* Khwe [xuu], 214
    alt. Kxoe [xuu], 40
Xui, *alt.* Chinese, Mandarin
    [cmn], 461
Xukru, *alt. dial.* Kayapó [txu], 229
Xukurú [xoo], 234
    alt. Kariří-Xocó [kzw], 228
Xukuru Kariri, *alt.* Kariří-Xocó
    [kzw], 228
!Xun, *alt.* Kung-Ekoka [knw], 150
Xun, *alt.* Ju|'hoan [ktz], 47, 150
    alt. Khwe [xuu], 47, 214
    alt. Kxoe [xuu], 150, 40, 186
!Xung, *alt.* Kung-Ekoka [knw], 150
Xunzal, *alt.* Hunzib [huz], 554
Xunzax, *alt. dial.* Avar [ava], 553
Xuòng, *dial.* Nung [nut], 525
Xurima, *alt.* Yanomámi [wca], 234
Xuriwai, *alt.* Nadëb [mbj], 230
Xvarshi, *alt.* Khvarshi [khv], 555
    dial. Khvarshi [khv], 555
Xwela, *alt.* Gbe, Xwela [xwe], 45
Xwela Gbe, *see* Gbe, Xwela
    [xwe], 45
Xwela-Gba, *alt.* Gbe, Xwela
    [xwe], 45
Xwla, *alt.* Gbe, Eastern Xwla
    [gbx], 44
    alt. Gbe, Western Xwla [xwl], 45
Xwla-Gbe, *alt.* Gbe, Western Xwla
    [xwl], 45
Y Mia, *alt.* Lachi [lbt], 524, 338
Y Pí, *alt.* Lachi [lbt], 524
Y Póng, *alt.* Lachi [lbt], 524
Y Poong, *alt.* Lachi [lbt], 338
Y To, *alt.* Lachi [lbt], 524, 338
Y-Lang, *alt. dial.* Bahnar [bdq], 521
Ya, *alt.* Tai Ya [cuu], 344
    alt. dial. Tai Nüa [tdd], 344
    dial. Vaghat-Ya-Bijim-Legeri [bij],
    177
Ya Lu, *alt.* Yugur, West [ybe], 348
Ya-Tuka, *dial.* Kallahan, Keley-I
    [ify], 497
Yaa, *alt.* Yaka [iyx], 90
    dial. Mumuye [mzm], 170
Yáá Mòò, *alt.* Moo [gwg], 170
Yaadré, *dial.* Mòoré [mos], 52
Yaaga, *alt. dial.* Fulfulde,
    Northeastern Burkina Faso
    [fuh], 51
Yaako, *alt.* Margu [mhg], 573
Yaaku [muu], 137
Yaakua, *alt.* Yaaku [muu], 137
Yaali, *alt.* Kendeje [klf], 82
    dial. Kendeje [klf], 82
Yaamba, *dial.* Mbole [mdq], 104
Yaan, *alt. dial.* Mòoré [mos], 209
    dial. Yaouré [yre], 96
Yaande, *dial.* Mòoré [mos], 52

Yaáyuwee, *alt. dial.* Gbaya,
    Northwest [gya], 61
    dial. Gbaya, Northwest [gya], 75
Yaba, *dial.* Bobo Madaré, Northern
    [bbo], 49
Yabaâna [ybn], 234
Yaban, *alt.* Arandai [jbj], 411
Yabarana [yar], 313
    alt. Yabaâna [ybn], 234
Yabeka, *dial.* Ewondo [ewo], 61
Yabekanga, *dial.* Ewondo [ewo], 61
Yabekolo, *dial.* Ewondo [ewo], 61
Yabem [jae], 632
Yaben [ybm], 632
Yabi, *dial.* Ekari [ekg], 414
Yabim, *alt.* Yabem [jae], 632
Yabin, *alt.* Konda [knd], 417
Yabin Yahadian, *alt.* Yahadian
    [ner], 426
Yabin-Konda, *alt.* Konda [knd], 417
Yabio, *alt.* Yawiyo [ybx], 633
Yabiyufa, *alt.* Yaweyuha [yby], 633
Yabong [ybo], 632
Yabutí, *alt.* Jabutí [jbt], 227
Yabyang, *dial.* Bakoko [bkh], 57
Yabyang-Yapeke, *alt. dial.* Bakoko
    [bkh], 57
Yacan, *alt.* Yakan [yka], 502, 458
Yace [ekr], 177
Yacham, *alt. dial.* Naga, Ao
    [njo], 377
Yache, *alt.* Yace [ekr], 177
Yachumi, *alt.* Naga, Yimchungru
    [yim], 380
Yacoua, *alt. dial.* Banda, Mid-
    Southern [bjo], 74, 97
Yacouba, *alt.* Dan [daf], 92, 129,
    137
Yade, *alt.* Yale [nce], 633
Yadena, *alt.* Buduma [bdm], 59
Yadu, *dial.* Qiang, Northern [cng],
    342
Yaeyama [rys], 447
Yaffi, *alt.* Yafi [wfg], 426
Yafi [wfg], 426
Yag Dii, *alt.* Dii [dur], 60
Yaga, *dial.* Agta, Dupaninan
    [duo], 490
Yagán, *alt.* Yámana [yag], 243
Yaganiza-Xagacía Zapotec, *dial.*
    Zapotec, Cajonos [zad], 277
Yagar Yagar, *alt.* Kala Lagaw Ya
    [mwp], 571
Yagaria [ygr], 632
Yagawak, *alt. dial.* Wantoat
    [wnc], 631
Yagba, *dial.* Yoruba [yor], 178
Yage, *dial.* Dungan [dng], 449
Yagele, *alt.* Gengle [geg], 161
Yaghan, *alt.* Yámana [yag], 243

Yaghwatadaxa, *alt. dial.* Guduf-
    Gava [gdf], 161
Yagnob, *alt.* Yagnobi [yai], 513
Yagnobi [yai], 513
Yagomi [ygm], 632
Yagoua, *alt. dial.* Masana [mcn], 83,
    66
Yagua [yad], 293
Yagwa, *dial.* Masana [mcn], 83, 66
Yagwoia [ygw], 632
Yahadian [ner], 426
Yahang [rhp], 632
Yaheun, *alt.* Nyaheun [nev], 452
Yahi, *dial.* Yana [ynn], 310
Yahow, *alt. dial.* Chin, Falam
    [flm], 463
Yahua, *alt.* Yagua [yad], 293
Yahuanahua, *alt.* Yawanawa
    [ywn], 234
Yahudic, *alt.* Arabic, Judeo-Iraqi
    [yhd], 444, 442
Yahuna [ynu], 248
Yahup, *alt.* Yuhup [yab], 234
Yahup Makú, *alt.* Yuhup [yab], 234
Yai, *alt.* Giáy [pcc], 523
    alt. Iaai [iai], 584
Yaikole, *dial.* Mbole [mdq], 104
Yair, *alt.* Awyu, North [yir], 412
Yaisu, *dial.* Mbole [mdq], 104
Yaitepec Chatino, *dial.* Chatino,
    Western Highland [ctp], 260
Yaiwe, *alt. dial.* Gbaya, Northwest
    [gya], 75, 61
Yajima, *alt. dial.* Mongo-Nkundu
    [lol], 104
Yaka (Central African Republic)
    [axk], 78
    Yaka (Congo) [iyx], 90
    Yaka (Democratic Republic of
    Congo) [yaf], 109, 42
    alt. Aka [axk], 87
    alt. Kako [kkj], 63, 76, 88
    dial. Ganzi [gnz], 75
    dial. Yaka [yaf], 42
Yakahanga, *dial.* Nyambo
    [now], 203
Yakaikeke [ykk], 632
Yakalag, *alt. dial.* Bakoko [bkh], 57
Yakalak, *dial.* Bakoko [bkh], 57
Yakamul [ykm], 632
    dial. Yakamul [ykm], 632
Yakan [yka], 502, 458
    alt. Arakanese [mhv], 462, 354
Yakha [ybh], 482, 390
Yakhain, *alt. dial.* Arakanese
    [mhv], 320
Yakhaing, *alt.* Arakanese [mhv], 462,
    354
Yakiba, *alt.* Maia [sks], 610
Yakima [yak], 310

dial. Yakima [yak], 310
Yakkha, *alt.* Yakha [ybh], 482, 390
Yakkhaba, *alt.* Yakha [ybh], 482, 390
Yakkhaba Cea, *alt.* Lumba-Yakkha [luu], 475
alt. Yakha [ybh], 482
Yakkhaba Lorung, *alt.* Lorung, Southern [lrr], 474
Yakkhaba Sala, *alt.* Yakha [ybh], 482
Yako, *alt.* Margu [mhg], 573
Yakö, *alt.* Lokaa [yaz], 169
Yakoko, *dial.* Mumuye [mzm], 170
Yakoma [yky], 78, 109
Yakon, *alt. dial.* Alsea [aes], 298
Yakona, *alt. dial.* Alsea [aes], 298
Yakoro, *alt.* Bekwarra [bkv], 155
Yakpa, *dial.* Banda, Mid-Southern [bjo], 74, 97
Yakpwa, *alt. dial.* Banda, Mid-Southern [bjo], 74, 97
Yakthung Pan, *alt.* Limbu [lif], 474
alt. dial. Limbu [lif], 474
Yakuba, *alt.* Dan [daf], 92, 129, 137
Yakule, *alt. dial.* Yendang [yen], 178
Yakurr, *alt.* Lokaa [yaz], 169
Yakusu, *alt.* Kele [khy], 101
Yakut [sah], 507
Yakut-Sakha, *alt.* Yakut [sah], 507
Yakwa, *alt. dial.* Banda, Mid-Southern [bjo], 74, 97
Yakwina, *alt. dial.* Alsea [aes], 298
Yala [yba], 177
Yala Ikom, *alt. dial.* Yala [yba], 177
Yala Obubra, *alt. dial.* Yala [yba], 177
Yala Ogoja, *dial.* Yala [yba], 177
Yalach, *alt. dial.* Czech [ces], 533
Yalahatan [jal], 405
Yalálag Zapotec, *see* Zapotec, Yalálag [zpu], 281
Yalang, *dial.* Buyang [byu], 329
Yalapmunxte, *alt. dial.* Nambikuára, Northern [mbg], 230
Yalarnnga [ylr], 578
Yalayu, *dial.* Nyâlayu [yly], 585
Yaldiye-Ho, *alt.* Kanju [kbe], 572
Yale [nce], 633
Yale, Kosarek [kkl], 426
Yale-Kosarek, *alt.* Yale, Kosarek [kkl], 426
Yale-Nipsan, *alt.* Nipsan [nps], 421
Yaleba, *alt.* Buhutu [bxh], 595
dial. Tawala [tbo], 627
Yalgawarra, *alt.* Flinders Island [fln], 570
Yali Selatan, *alt.* Yali, Ninia [nlk], 426
Yali, Angguruk [yli], 426

Yali, Ninia [nlk], 426
Yali, Pass Valley [yac], 426
Yaliambi, *dial.* Budza [bja], 98
Yalima, *dial.* Mongo-Nkundu [lol], 104
Yalimo, *alt.* Yali, Angguruk [yli], 426
Yalina, *dial.* Zapotec, Zoogocho [zpq], 281
Yallof, *alt.* Wolof [wol], 182, 145
Yalmbau, *alt.* Mangala [mem], 573
Yalu, *alt.* Aribwaung [ylu], 590
Yalunka [yal], 130, 184
alt. Jalunga [yal], 143, 180
Yalunke, *alt.* Jalunga [yal], 143, 180
alt. Yalunka [yal], 130, 184
Yaly, *alt.* Yali, Pass Valley [yac], 426
Yam, *alt. dial.* Mòoré [mos], 209
Yamai, *dial.* Awad Bing [bcu], 591
Yamale, *alt.* Kugama [kow], 167
Yamalele, *alt.* Iamalele [yml], 602
Yamalo, *alt.* Kugama [kow], 167
Yamaltu, *alt. dial.* Tera [ttr], 175
Yamamadí, *alt.* Jamamadí [jaa], 227
Yámana [yag], 243
Yamanawa, *alt.* Yaminahua [yaa], 293, 224, 234
Yamap [ymp], 633
Yamba [yam], 73, 177
Yambasa, *alt.* Nugunu [yas], 70
Yambassa, *alt.* Nugunu [yas], 70
Yambes [ymb], 633
Yambeta [yat], 73
Yambetta, *alt.* Yambeta [yat], 73
Yambiyambi, *alt.* Bisis [bnw], 594
Yambo, *alt.* Anuak [anu], 187, 113
Yamdena [jmd], 405
Yamegi, *alt.* Gula [kcm], 76, 191
Yameo [yme], 293
Yami [tao], 512
Yamiaca, *alt.* Atsahuaca [atc], 286
Yaminahua [yaa], 293, 224, 234
dial. Yaminahua [yaa], 293
Yaminawa, *alt.* Yaminahua [yaa], 293, 224
Yamináwa, *alt.* Yaminahua [yaa], 234
Yamna [ymn], 426
Yamod, *dial.* Gor [gqr], 80
Yamofowe, *dial.* Siane [snp], 624
Yamongeri [ymg], 109
Yamongiri, *alt.* Yamongeri [ymg], 109
Yamphe [yma], 482
alt. Yamphu [ybi], 482
Yamphe Kha, *alt.* Yamphe [yma], 482
Yamphu [ybi], 482
alt. Yamphe [yma], 482
Yamphu Kha, *alt.* Yamphu [ybi], 482

Yamphu Rai, *alt.* Yamphu [ybi], 482
Yamur, *dial.* Kamoro [kgq], 416
Yan, *alt. dial.* Mòoré [mos], 209
Yan-Guang, *dial.* Zhuang, Southern [ccy], 349
Yan-Nhangu, *alt.* Jarnango [jay], 571
Yana [ynn], 310
alt. dial. Mòoré [mos], 209
dial. Mòoré [mos], 52
Yanaba, *dial.* Muyuw [myw], 616
Yanadi, *alt. dial.* Telugu [tel], 388
Yanahuanca Pasco Quechua, *see* Quechua, Yanahuanca Pasco [qur], 292
Yanaigua, *alt.* Tapieté [tpj], 282, 220, 224
Yanam, *alt.* Ninam [shb], 230, 312
Yanamam, *dial.* Yanomámi [wca], 234
Yanangu, *alt.* Jarnango [jay], 571
Yanbe, *alt.* Yangbye [ybd], 467
Yanbye, *alt.* Yangbye [ybd], 467
Yanchunger, *alt.* Naga, Yimchungru [yim], 380
Yandang, *alt.* Yendang [yen], 178
Yandapo, *dial.* Enga [enq], 598
Yanderika, *alt.* Indri [idr], 191
Yandime, *dial.* Siane [snp], 624
Yandirika, *alt.* Indri [idr], 191
Yandruwandha [ynd], 578
Yanesha' [ame], 293
Yang, *alt.* Riang [ril], 467
Yang Daeng, *alt.* Kayah, Western [kyu], 465
Yang Khao, *alt.* Karen, S'gaw [ksw], 464, 514
Yang Sek, *alt.* Riang [ril], 343
Yang Wan Kun, *alt.* Riang [ril], 467, 343
Yanga, *alt. dial.* Mòoré [mos], 52
dial. Mòoré [mos], 209
Yang'an, *alt. dial.* Sui [swi], 344
Yangarella, *alt.* Nyangga [nny], 576
Yangaro, *pej. alt.* Yemsa [jnj], 119
Yangatalet, *alt.* Karen, Yintale [kvy], 465
Yangben [yav], 72
Yangbye [ybd], 467
Yangeborong, *dial.* Borong [ksr], 594
Yangele, *dial.* Gbaya, Southwest [mdo], 76
Yangere, *alt.* Banda-Yangere [yaj], 75
Yangeru, *alt.* Bena [yun], 155
Yanggal, *alt.* Nyangga [nny], 576
Yangho [ynh], 122
Yanghuang, *alt.* T'en [tct], 344

Yangkaal, *alt.* Nyangga [nny], 576
Yangkam [bsx], 177
Yangkolen, *dial.* Urim [uri], 630
Yanglam, *alt.* Riang [ril], 467, 343
Yangman [jng], 579
Yango [yng], 109
Yangonda, *dial.* Mbole [mdq], 104
Yangoru, *alt.* Boikin [bzf], 594
Yangtadai, *alt.* Karen, Yintale
　[kvy], 465
Yangtsebikha, *alt.* Dzalakha
　[dzl], 323
Yanguere, *alt.* Banda-Yangere [yaj],
　75
Yangulam [ynl], 633
Yangye, *alt.* Yangbye [ybd], 467
Yani, *alt.* Akha [ahk], 462, 326, 449,
　513, 521
Yanimoi, *alt. dial.* Kombio [xbi], 607
Yanito, *dial.* English [eng], 540
Yankam, *alt.* Yangkam [bsx], 177
Yankowan, *alt.* Wasembo [gsp], 631
Yankton, *alt. dial.* Dakota
　[dak], 297, 237
Yankton-Yanktonais, *alt. dial.*
　Dakota [dak], 297
Yankunjtjatjarra, *alt.*
　Yankunytjatjara [kdd], 579
Yankuntatjara, *alt.* Yankunytjatjara
　[kdd], 579
Yankunytjatjara [kdd], 579
　dial. Pitjantjatjara [pjt], 576
Yanoam, *alt.* Yanomámi [wca], 234
Yanoma, *dial.* Sanumá [xsu], 312
Yanomam, *alt.* Yanomámi
　[wca], 234
　dial. Yanomámi [wca], 234
Yanomame, *alt.* Yanomamö
　[guu], 313
Yanomamé, *alt.* Yanomámi
　[wca], 234
Yanomami, *alt.* Yanomamö [guu],
　313, 234
Yanomámi [wca], 234
Yanomamö [guu], 313, 234
Yanomay, *dial.* Yanomámi
　[wca], 234
Yanphu, *alt.* Yamphu [ybi], 482
Yanrakinot, *dial.* Chukot [ckt], 504
Yans, *alt.* Yansi [yns], 109
Yansi [yns], 109
Yanta, *dial.* Gorakor [goc], 600
Yanula, *alt.* Yanyuwa [jao], 579
Yanyula, *alt.* Yanyuwa [jao], 579
Yanyuwa [jao], 579
Yanzhou, *dial.* Chinese, Huizhou
　[czh], 329
Yanzi, *alt.* Kimbu [kiv], 200
　alt. Yansi [yns], 109
Ya'o, *alt.* Kuuku-Ya'u [kuy], 573

Yao [yao], 141, 149, 206, 215
　alt. Iu Mien [ium], 336, 450, 514,
　523
Yao Kimmien, *alt.* Iu Mien
　[ium], 523
Yao Min, *alt.* Dzao Min [bpn], 332
Yao Ogang, *alt.* Iu Mien [ium], 523
Yao Yen, *alt.* Lisu [lis], 339, 465, 515
Yao'an Lolopho, *dial.* Yi, Central
　[ycl], 347
Yaosakor, *alt.* Asmat, Yaosakor
　[asy], 411
Yaosakor Asmat, *see* Asmat,
　Yaosakor [asy], 411
Yaounde, *alt.* Ewondo [ewo], 61
Yaouré [yre], 96
Yapanani, *alt.* Yawa [yva], 426
Yapeli, *alt.* Nyong [muo], 171
Yapese [yap], 583
Yapo, *dial.* Krumen, Pye [pye], 93
Yapoa, *dial.* Wedau [wed], 631
Yapoma, *dial.* Bakoko [bkh], 57
Yaprería, *alt.* Japrería [jru], 311
Yapsi-Taja, *dial.* Orya [ury], 422
Yapunda [yev], 633
Yaqai, *alt.* Yaqay [jaq], 426
Yaqay [jaq], 426
Yaqui [yaq], 277, 310
Yaquina, *dial.* Alsea [aes], 298
Yarahuuraxi-Capanapara, *alt.*
　dial. Cuiba [cui], 311
　dial. Cuiba [cui], 244
Yaralde, *alt.* Narrinyeri [nay], 575
Yaran, *dial.* Mari, Western [mrj], 555
Yarawara, *alt.* Jaruára [jap], 227
Yarawata [yrw], 633
Yarawe, *alt.* Suena [sue], 625
Yarawi, *alt.* Suena [sue], 625
Yare, *alt.* Kantosi [xkt], 125, 51
Yarë, *alt.* Yale [nce], 633
Yareba [yrb], 633
Yareni Zapotec, *see* Zapotec,
　Yareni [zae], 281
Yari, *alt.* Dagaari Dioula [dgd], 50
　dial. Beembe [beq], 88
Yarí [yri], 248
Yariba, *alt.* Yoruba [yor], 178, 46
Yarkandi, *alt. dial.* Uyghur
　[uig], 318
Yarkhun, *dial.* Wakhi [wbl], 489
Yarluyandji, *alt.* Ngamini
　[nmv], 575
Yarsi, *alt.* Kantosi [xkt], 125, 51
Yarsun [yrs], 426
Yarukula, *alt.* Yerukula [yeu], 390
Yaruma, *dial.* Suyá [suy], 232
Yarumarra, *dial.* Ngura [nbx], 575
Yaruro, *alt.* Pumé [yae], 312
Yaruru, *alt.* Pumé [yae], 312
Yarus, *dial.* Adzera [azr], 587

Yas, *alt.* Asmat, Central [cns], 411
Yasa [yko], 73, 111, 122
　alt. Pawaia [pwa], 621
Yasgua, *alt.* Yeskwa [yes], 178
Yashi, *alt.* Hasha [ybj], 162
Yasichi, *alt. dial.* Luri, Southern
　[luz], 440
Yasin, *alt. dial.* Burushaski [bsk], 484
　dial. Wakhi [wbl], 489
Yasing, *alt. dial.* Mundang [mua], 85,
　68
Yaso, *dial.* Gumuz [guk], 115
Yasoukou, *alt. dial.* Bakoko
　[bkh], 57
Yassa, *alt.* Yasa [yko], 73, 111, 122
Yassing, *alt. dial.* Mundang [mua],
　68
Yassuku, *alt. dial.* Bakoko [bkh], 57
Yasua, *alt. dial.* Gbaya, Southwest
　[mdo], 76
Yasug, *alt. dial.* Bakoko [bkh], 57
Yasuji, *dial.* Luri, Southern [luz], 440
Yasuku, *alt. dial.* Bakoko [bkh], 57
Yasyin, *alt.* Yessan-Mayo [yss], 633
Yate, *alt.* Inoke-Yate [ino], 603
Yatê, *alt.* Fulniô [fun], 226
　dial. Fulniô [fun], 226
Yatee Zapotec, *see* Zapotec, Yatee
　[zty], 281
Yatini, *dial.* Nuni, Southern [nnw], 53
Yatye, *alt.* Yace [ekr], 177
Yatzachi Zapotec, *see* Zapotec,
　Yatzachi [zav], 281
Yau (Morobe Province) [yuw], 633
　Yau (Sandaun Province) [yyu], 633
　alt. Edopi [dbf], 414
　alt. Iau [tmu], 415
　alt. dial. Yessan-Mayo [yss], 633
Yau Min, *alt.* Dzao Min [bpn], 332
Yauan, *alt.* Bragat [aof], 594
Yauaperi, *alt. dial.* Atruahí [atr], 225
Yauarana, *alt.* Yabarana [yar], 313
Yaudijbaia, *alt.* Yawuru [ywr], 579
Yaudjibara, *alt.* Yawuru [ywr], 579
Yaugiba, *alt.* Urimo [urx], 630
Yauke, *alt.* Yoke [yki], 427
Yaul [yla], 633
Yaulapiti, *alt.* Yawalapití [yaw],
　234
Yauma [yax], 42, 215
Yaúna, *alt.* Yahuna [ynu], 248
Yaunde, *alt.* Ewondo [ewo], 61
Ya'unk, *alt.* Yahang [rhp], 632
Yaur [jau], 426
Yaurawa, *alt.* Reshe [res], 173
Yaure, *alt.* Yaouré [yre], 96
Yauri, *alt.* Cishingini [asg], 151
Yautefa, *alt.* Tobati [tti], 424
Yautepec Zapotec, *see* Zapotec,
　Yautepec [zpb], 281

Yauyos Quechua, *see* Quechua, Yauyos [qux], 292
Yava, *alt.* Yagua [yad], 293
  alt. Yawa [yva], 426
Yavapai, *dial.* Havasupai-Walapai-Yavapai [yuf], 301
Yavatmal, *dial.* Gondi, Northern [gno], 362
Yavesía Zapotec, *alt.* Zapotec, Southeastern Ixtlán [zpd], 280
Yavita, *alt.* Baré [bae], 311
  alt. Mandahuaca [mht], 312
Yavitero [yvt], 313
Yaw, *alt. dial.* Yessan-Mayo [yss], 633
  dial. Burmese [mya], 462
Yaw Yin, *alt.* Lisu [lis], 339, 465, 515
Yaw-Yen, *alt.* Lisu [lis], 339, 465, 515
Yawa [yva], 426
  alt. Kalou [ywa], 604
Yawalapití [yaw], 234
Yawanawa [ywn], 234
Yawarana, *alt.* Yabarana [yar], 313
Yawarawarga [yww], 579
Yawarete Tapuya, *alt. dial.* Carútana [cru], 226
Yawdwin, *alt.* Chin, Mün [mwq], 463
Yawenian, *alt.* Iwam, Sepik [iws], 603
Yaweyuha [yby], 633
Yawiyo [ybx], 633
Yawiyuha, *alt.* Yaweyuha [yby], 633
Yawjibara, *alt.* Yawuru [ywr], 579
Yawotataxa, *alt. dial.* Guduf-Gava [gdf], 161
Yawu, *dial.* Yessan-Mayo [yss], 633
Yawuru [ywr], 579
Yawyin, *alt.* Lisu [lis], 372
Yay, *alt.* Giáy [pcc], 523
Yayeyama, *alt.* Yaeyama [rys], 447
Yayuna, *alt.* Yahuna [ynu], 248
Yazdi, *dial.* Farsi, Western [pes], 439
  pej. alt. Dari, Zoroastrian [gbz], 438
Yazgulam, *alt.* Yazgulyam [yah], 513
Yazgulyam [yah], 513
Yazgulyami, *alt.* Yazgulyam [yah], 513
Yazva, *dial.* Komi-Zyrian [kpv], 555
Ybanag, *alt.* Ibanag [ibg], 494
Ye, *dial.* Mon [mnw], 466
Yeba, *alt.* Macuna [myy], 246
Yebamasã, *alt.* Macuna [myy], 229
Yebekolo, *alt. dial.* Ewondo [ewo], 61
Yebu, *alt.* Awak [awo], 154
Yeci, *dial.* Holu [hol], 40

Ye'cuana, *alt.* Maquiritari [mch], 312
  alt. dial. Maquiritari [mch], 229
Yecuatla Totonac, *see* Totonac, Yecuatla [tlc], 276
Yedana, *alt.* Yedina [bdm], 177
Yedima, *alt.* Buduma [bdm], 79, 59
  alt. Yedina [bdm], 177
Yedina [bdm], 177
  alt. Buduma [bdm], 79, 59
Yedji, *alt. dial.* Chumburung [ncu], 124
Yeei, *alt.* Yeyi [yey], 48, 151
  dial. Yansi [yns], 109
Yega, *alt.* Keiga [kec], 192
  alt. dial. Ewage-Notu [nou], 598
  alt. dial. Korafe [kpr], 607
Yegha, *alt. dial.* Korafe [kpr], 607
Yeghe, *dial.* Khana [ogo], 166
Yeghuye, *alt.* Yagwoia [ygw], 632
Yegua, *alt.* Yagua [yad], 293
Yeh, *alt.* Jeh [jeh], 523, 450
Yeh-Jeh, *alt.* Lisu [lis], 465
Yeh-Jen, *alt.* Lisu [lis], 339, 515
Yehen, *alt.* Fwâi [fwa], 584
Yehpá Majsá, *alt.* Macuna [myy], 229
Yëhup, *alt.* Yuhup [yab], 234
Yei [jei], 426
  alt. Yeyi [yey], 48, 151
Yei-Nan, *alt.* Yei [jei], 426
Yeidji, *alt.* Wunambal [wub], 578
Yeinbaw, *alt.* Karen, Yinbaw [kvu], 464
Yeithi, *alt.* Wunambal [wub], 578
Yeji, *dial.* Chumburung [ncu], 124
Yekhee [ets], 177
Yekora [ykr], 633
Yekuana, *alt.* Maquiritari [mch], 312
  alt. dial. Maquiritari [mch], 229
Yela [yel], 109
  alt. Yele [yle], 633
Yele [yle], 633
Yelejong, *alt.* Yele [yle], 633
Yeletnye, *alt.* Yele [yle], 633
Yelidnye, *alt.* Yele [yle], 633
Yelinda, *dial.* Bulu [bum], 59
Yellow Lahu, *alt.* Lahu Shi [kds], 451, 338, 465, 515, 524
Yellow Leaf, *alt.* Mlabri [mra], 516, 451
Yellow River, *alt.* Namia [nnm], 617
Yellow Uighur, *alt.* Yugur, West [ybe], 348
Yellowknife, *dial.* Chipewyan [chp], 236
Yelmek [jel], 426
Yelmo, *alt. dial.* C'lela [dri], 157
Yelogu [ylg], 633
Yelong, *dial.* Guanyinqiao [jiq], 333
Yem, *alt.* Yemsa [jnj], 119

Yema, *alt.* Suena [sue], 625
Yemba [ybb], 74
  dial. Yemba [ybb], 74
Yembana, *dial.* Bulu [bum], 59
Yembe, *alt.* Songe [sop], 108
Yembo, *alt.* Anuak [anu], 113
Yemchidi, *alt. dial.* Aimaq [aiq], 315
Yemenite Hebrew, *alt. dial.* Hebrew [heb], 444
Yemenite Judeo-Arabic, *alt.* Arabic, Judeo-Yemeni [jye], 444, 528
Yemma, *alt.* Yemsa [jnj], 119
Yemsa [jnj], 119
Yenadi, *alt. dial.* Telugu [tel], 388
Yendam, *alt.* Yendang [yen], 178
Yendang [yen], 178
Yengen, *alt.* Fwâi [fwa], 584
Yengono, *dial.* Bulu [bum], 59
Yengoru, *alt.* Boikin [bzf], 594
Yeni [yei], 74
Yeniche [yec], 540
Yenimu, *alt.* Awyu, Edera [awy], 412
  alt. Awyu, South [aws], 412
Yenisei Ostyak, *alt.* Ket [ket], 505
Yenisei Samoyedic, *alt.* Enets, Forest [enf], 504
  alt. Enets, Tundra [enh], 504
Yenisei Tatar, *alt.* Khakas [kjh], 505, 337
Yenisey Ostiak, *alt.* Ket [ket], 505
Yenishe, *alt.* Yeniche [yec], 540
Yenkuang, *alt. dial.* Zhuang, Southern [ccy], 349
Yepá Maxsã, *alt.* Macuna [myy], 229
Yepá-Mahsá, *alt.* Macuna [myy], 246, 229
Yepocapa Southwestern Cakchiquel, *alt.* Kaqchikel, Yepocapa Southwestern [cbm], 255
Yepocapa Southwestern Kaqchikel, *see* Kaqchikel, Yepocapa Southwestern [cbm], 255
Yerakai [yra], 633
Yeral, *alt.* Nhengatu [yrl], 230, 246, 312
Yerani, *alt.* Gorovu [grq], 600
Yerava, *alt.* Ravula [yea], 384
Yerawa, *alt.* Aka-Jeru [akj], 353
Yerbogocen, *dial.* Evenki [evn], 504
Yere, *alt.* Bwamu, Láá Láá [bwj], 50
Yerekai, *alt.* Yerakai [yra], 633
Yeretuar [gop], 426
Yerevan, *dial.* Azerbaijani, North [azj], 319
Yergam, *alt.* Tarok [yer], 175
Yerge, *alt.* Fur [fvr], 190

Yergum, *alt.* Tarok [yer], 175
Yergyuch, *dial.* Budukh [bdk], 319
Yergyudzh, *dial.* Kryts [kry], 319
Yeri Waali, *dial.* Wali [wlx], 128
Yerington-Schurz, *alt. dial.* Paiute, Northern [pao], 306
Yerisiam, *alt.* Iresim [ire], 415
Yerjungkhu Boli, *dial.* Byangsi [bee], 358
Yerkula, *alt.* Yerukula [yeu], 390
Yerong [yrn], 347
Yeru, *dial.* Koma [kmy], 64
Yerukala, *alt.* Yerukula [yeu], 390
Yerukala-Korava, *alt.* Yerukula [yeu], 390
Yerukla, *alt.* Yerukula [yeu], 390
Yerukula [yeu], 390
Yerukula-Bhasha, *alt.* Yerukula [yeu], 390
Yerwa, *dial.* Kanuri, Central [knc], 166
Yerwa Kanuri, *alt.* Kanuri, Central [knc], 166, 63, 81, 152, 191
Yes Firan, *alt.* Firan [fir], 160
Yesan, *alt.* Yessan-Mayo [yss], 633
Yeskwa [yes], 178
Yesoum, *alt. dial.* Ewondo [ewo], 61
Yessan-Mayo [yss], 633
Yetfa [yet], 426, 633
Yeti, *alt.* Manem [jet], 612, 419
Yetimarala, *alt.* Bayali [bjy], 569
Yetinji, *alt.* Yidiny [yii], 579
Yeu, *alt.* Nyeu [nyl], 516
Yevanic [yej], 446
Yevanitika, *alt.* Yevanic [yej], 446
Yewena-Yongsu, *dial.* Tabla [tnm], 423
Yewu, *alt. dial.* Bwa [bww], 99
Yey, *alt.* Yei [jei], 426
  alt. dial. Yansi [yns], 109
Yeyeza, *alt.* Swati [ssw], 186
Yeyi [yey], 48, 151
Yezo, *alt. dial.* Ainu [ain], 446, 503
Yezum, *alt. dial.* Ewondo [ewo], 61
Yholmo, *alt.* Helambu Sherpa [scp], 472
Yhuata, *alt.* Omagua [omg], 289, 231
Yhulkasom, *alt. dial.* Thakali [ths], 480
Yi Be Wu, *alt.* Bebe [bzv], 58
Yi, Ache [yif], 347
Yi, Awu [yiu], 347
Yi, Axi [yix], 347
Yi, Azhe [yiz], 347
Yi, Central [ycl], 347
Yi, Dayao [yio], 347
Yi, Eastern Lalu [yit], 347
Yi, Eshan-Xinping [yiv], 347
Yi, Guizhou [yig], 347

Yi, Limi [ylm], 347
Yi, Mili [ymh], 347
Yi, Miqie [yiq], 347
Yi, Muji [ymj], 347
Yi, Naluo [ylo], 347
Yi, Poluo [yip], 347
Yi, Pula [ypl], 347
Yi, Puwa [ypw], 347
Yi, Sani [ysn], 347
Yi, Sichuan [iii], 348
Yi, Southeastern Lolo [yso], 348
Yi, Southern [nos], 348
Yi, Southern Lolopho [ysp], 348
Yi, Western [ywt], 348
Yi, Western Lalu [ywl], 348
Yi, Wuding-Luquan [ywq], 348
Yi, Wumeng [ywm], 348
Yi, Wusa [ywu], 348
Yi, Xishan Lalu [yik], 348
Yi, Yuanjiang-Mojiang [yym], 348
Yi-Liu, *dial.* Chinese, Gan [gan], 329
Yibarambu, *alt.* Barama [bbg], 120
Yibwa, *alt.* Tima [tms], 195
Yichira, *alt.* Sira [swj], 121
Yidana, *alt.* Buduma [bdm], 79
  alt. Yedina [bdm], 177
Yidda, *alt.* Mada [mda], 169
Yiddinji, *alt.* Yidiny [yii], 579
Yiddish, *alt.* Yiddish, Eastern [ydd], 446
  alt. Yiddish, Western [yih], 540
Yiddish Sign Language [yds], 446
Yiddish, Eastern [ydd], 446, 546
Yiddish, Western [yih], 540
Yidena, *alt.* Buduma [bdm], 79
Yidga, *alt.* Yidgha [ydg], 489
Yidgha [ydg], 489
Yidi, *alt. dial.* Kwegu [xwg], 116
Yidin, *alt.* Yidiny [yii], 579
Yidindji, *alt.* Yidiny [yii], 579
Yidini, *alt.* Yidiny [yii], 579
Yidinich, *dial.* Kwegu [xwg], 116
Yidinit, *alt. dial.* Kwegu [xwg], 116
Yidiny [yii], 579
  dial. Yidiny [yii], 579
Yidish, *alt.* Yiddish, Western [yih], 540
Yidu, *alt.* Luoba, Yidu [clk], 339
Yidu Luoba, *see* Idu-Mishmi [clk], 339
Yidu Luoba, *alt.* Idu-Mishmi [clk], 364
Yigai, *alt.* Bahinemo [bjh], 591
Yigha, *alt.* Leyigha [ayi], 168
Yiive, *alt.* Iyive [uiv], 63, 164
Yil [yll], 630
Yili, *dial.* Tula [tul], 176
Yiligele, *dial.* Toura [neb], 95

Yillaro, *alt.* Laro [lro], 192
Yilparitja, *alt. dial.* Martu Wangka [mpj], 574
Yimas [yee], 633
Yimba, *alt.* Limba, East [lma], 129, 183
  alt. Limba, West-Central [lia], 183
Yimbun, *alt.* Abun [kgr], 410
Yimchunger, *alt.* Naga, Yimchungru [yim], 380
Yimchungre, *alt.* Naga, Yimchungru [yim], 380
Yimchungru, *alt.* Naga, Yimchungru [yim], 380
  dial. Naga, Yimchungru [yim], 380
Yimchungru Naga, *see* Naga, Yimchungru [yim], 380
Yimtim, *alt.* Fali [fli], 159
Yimwom, *alt.* Kam [kdx], 166
Yin, *alt.* Riang [ril], 467, 343
Yinbaw, *alt.* Karen, Yinbaw [kvu], 464
Yinbaw Karen, *see* Karen, Yinbaw [kvu], 464
Yinchia [yin], 467
Yindi, *dial.* Chin, Khumi [cnk], 463, 321
Yindjibarndi [yij], 579
Yindjilandji [yil], 579
Yindu, *alt. dial.* Chin, Khumi [cnk], 463, 321
Yine [pib], 294
Ying-Yi, *dial.* Chinese, Gan [gan], 329
Yinggarda [yia], 579
Yingkarta, *alt.* Yinggarda [yia], 579
Yingkwira, *alt.* Nunggubuyu [nuy], 575
Yinglish [yib], 310, 566
Yinibu, *alt.* Iteri [itr], 603
Yinjebi, *alt.* Njebi [nzb], 121, 89
Yinjtjipartnti, *alt.* Yindjibarndi [yij], 579
Yinnet, *alt.* Yinchia [yin], 467
Yintale, *alt.* Karen, Yintale [kvy], 465
Yintale Karen, *see* Karen, Yintale [kvy], 465
Yintalet, *alt.* Karen, Yintale [kvy], 465
Yinuo Yi, *dial.* Yi, Sichuan [iii], 348
Yinzebi, *alt.* Njebi [nzb], 121, 89
Yipma, *alt.* Baruya [byr], 592
Yipounou, *alt.* Punu [puu], 121
Yipunu, *alt.* Punu [puu], 121, 89
Yir, *alt.* Ir [irr], 450
Yir Thangedl, *alt. dial.* Yir Yoront [yiy], 579
Yir Yiront, *alt.* Yir Yoront [yiy], 579

Yir Yoront [yiy], 579
Yira, *dial.* Nande [nnb], 105
Yirmel, *alt. dial.* Yir Yoront [yiy], 579
Yirtangettle, *alt. dial.* Yir Yoront [yiy], 579
Yirtutiym, *alt. dial.* Yir Yoront [yiy], 579
Yiru, *alt.* Nali [nss], 616
Yiryo, *dial.* Berakou [bxv], 79
Yis [yis], 633
Yisangou, *alt.* Sangu [snq], 121
Yisangu, *alt.* Sangu [snq], 121
Yishengzha Yi, *dial.* Yi, Sichuan [iii], 348
Yitintyi, *alt.* Yidiny [yii], 579
Yiu Mien, *alt.* Iu Mien [ium], 336, 514
Yivoumbou, *alt.* Vumbu [vum], 121
Yiwom [gek], 178
Ylanos, *alt.* Iranun [ill], 457
Ynã, *alt.* Karajá [kpj], 228
Yo, *alt.* Nyaw [nyw], 516
   alt. Yos [yos], 467
Yoabou, *alt.* Waama [wwa], 46
Yoabu, *alt.* Waama [wwa], 46
Yoadabe-Watoare, *alt.* Maring [mbw], 612
Yoana, *alt.* Yuwana [yau], 313
Yoangen, *alt. dial.* Kube [kgf], 608
Yoanggeng, *alt. dial.* Kube [kgf], 608
Yoari, *alt. dial.* Yanomámi [wca], 234
Yoba [yob], 634
Yobin, *alt.* Lisu [lis], 372
Yocoboue, *alt. dial.* Dida, Yocoboué [gud], 92
Yocoboué Dida, *see* Dida, Yocoboué [gud], 92
Yocot'an, *alt.* Chontal, Tabasco [chf], 262
Yoe, *alt.* Nyeu [nyl], 516
Yofo, *alt.* Kumba [ksm], 167
   dial. Yendang [yen], 178
Yofuaha, *alt.* Chorote, Iyojwa'ja [crt], 220
Yogad [yog], 503
Yogam, *alt. dial.* Ghomálá' [bbj], 62
Yogli, *dial.* Naga, Tase [nst], 380
Yogor, *alt.* Yugur, East [yuy], 348
Yögur, *alt.* Yugur, East [yuy], 348
Yohlmu Tam, *alt.* Helambu Sherpa [scp], 472
Yohoraa, *dial.* Tucano [tuo], 233
Yohowré, *alt.* Yaouré [yre], 96
Yoi, *alt.* Yoy [yoy], 518, 453
Yoidik [ydk], 634
Yoit, *alt.* Yupik, Central Siberian [ess], 507
Yokaia, *alt.* Pomo, Central [poo], 307

Yokan, *dial.* Saami, Skolt [sms], 556
Yokari, *dial.* Tabla [tnm], 423
Yoke [yki], 427
Yoki, *alt.* Yoke [yki], 427
Yokouboué, *alt. dial.* Dida, Yocoboué [gud], 92
Yoku, *dial.* Sie [erg], 645
Yokula, *alt.* Ganggalida [gcd], 570
Yokuts [yok], 310
Yola, *alt.* Jola-Fonyi [dyo], 180, 118
Yolox Chinanteco, *dial.* Chinantec, Quiotepec [chq], 261
Yoloxochitl Mixtec, *see* Mixtec, Yoloxochitl [xty], 270
Yom [pil], 46
   dial. Bedjond [bjv], 79
Yom Gawac, *alt.* Bugawac [buk], 595
Yombe [yom], 109, 42, 90
   alt. dial. Vili [vif], 90
   dial. Tumbuka [tum], 141, 215
Yombe Classique, *alt. dial.* Yombe [yom], 109, 42, 90
Yombiro Lele, *dial.* Lele [llc], 129
Yomud, *dial.* Turkmen [tuk], 520, 442
Yomut, *alt. dial.* Turkmen [tuk], 442
   dial. Turkmen [tuk], 318
Yonaguni [yoi], 447
Yong [yno], 518
Yongbei, *dial.* Zhuang, Northern [ccx], 349
Yonggom [yon], 634
   alt. Muyu, North [kti], 421
   alt. Muyu, South [kts], 421
Yongho, *alt.* Yangho [ynh], 122
Yongkom, *alt.* Muyu, North [kti], 421
   alt. Muyu, South [kts], 421
   alt. Yonggom [yon], 634
Yongkuk, *dial.* Naga, Tase [nst], 380
Yongnan, *dial.* Zhuang, Southern [ccy], 349
Yongo, *dial.* Mbangala [mxg], 41
Yongolei, *dial.* Biangai [big], 593
Yongom, *alt.* Muyu, North [kti], 421
   alt. Muyu, South [kts], 421
   alt. Yonggom [yon], 634
Yongomugi, *dial.* Kuman [kue], 608
Yongor, *alt.* Bena [yun], 155
Yongren, *dial.* Tai Nüa [tdd], 344
Yongyasha, *dial.* Naga, Phom [nph], 379
Yoni, *dial.* Themne [tem], 184
Yoo, *dial.* Yaouré [yre], 96
Yooba, *alt.* Yoruba [yor], 178, 46
Yooi, *alt.* Yoy [yoy], 518, 453
Yoombe, *dial.* Vili [vif], 90, 121

Yooy, *alt.* Yoy [yoy], 518, 453
Yopará, *alt. dial.* Guaraní, Paraguayan [gug], 284
Yopno [yut], 634
Yora [mts], 294
Yoranahua, *alt.* Yora [mts], 294
Yorda, *alt.* Kpan [kpk], 167
Yori, *dial.* Awad Bing [bcu], 591
York Cree, *alt.* Cree, Moose [crm], 236
   alt. Cree, Swampy [csw], 236
Yoro, *alt.* Mumuye [mzm], 170
   dial. Mumuye [mzm], 170
Yoron [yox], 447
Yoruba [yor], 178, 46
   alt. Ravula [yea], 384
Yoruk, *alt. dial.* Balkan Gagauz Turkish [bgx], 563, 547
Yos [yos], 467
Yosemite, *alt.* Miwok, Southern Sierra [skd], 305
Yoshkar-Olin, *alt. dial.* Mari, Eastern [mhr], 555
Yosoñama, *dial.* Mixtec, Northern Tlaxiaco [xtn], 267
Yosondúa Mixtec, *see* Mixtec, Yosondúa [mpm], 270
Yot, *alt. dial.* Cua [cua], 522
Yotafa, *alt.* Tobati [tti], 424
Yote, *alt.* Yos [yos], 467
Yoti, *dial.* Yendang [yen], 178
Yotowawa, *alt.* Kisar [kje], 400
Yotubo, *alt.* Gimnime [gmn], 62
You, *alt. dial.* Tai Nüa [tdd], 344
Youanne, *pej. alt.* Thai, Northern [nod], 453
Youjiang, *dial.* Zhuang, Northern [ccx], 349
Youle, *alt.* Jinuo, Youle [jiu], 336
Youle Jinuo, *see* Jinuo, Youle [jiu], 336
Youlou, *alt.* Yulu [yul], 78, 109, 196
Youmian, *alt.* Iu Mien [ium], 336, 514
Younuo, *alt.* Bunu, Younuo [buh], 329
Younuo Bunu, *see* Bunu, Younuo [buh], 329
Youon, *pej. alt.* Thai, Northern [nod], 453
Youré, *alt.* Yaouré [yre], 96
Youtubo, *alt. dial.* Koma [kmy], 167
Yovai, *alt.* Ayoreo [ayo], 222
Yowera, *alt.* Alyawarr [aly], 567
Yoy [yoy], 518, 453
Yoza, *dial.* Haya [hay], 199
Yrapa, *dial.* Yukpa [yup], 313
Yrepo, *dial.* Krumen, Tepo [ted], 93, 138

Ethnologue

Yurmaty, *dial.* Bashkir [bak], 553
Yurok [yur], 310
Yuruk, *alt. dial.* Balkan Gagauz Turkish [bgx], 563, 547
Yürük, *dial.* Domari [rmt], 438
Yurúna, *alt.* Jurúna [jur], 228
Yurupari Tapuya, *alt. dial.* Carútana [cru], 226
Yurutí [yui], 249, 234
Yuruti-Tapuya, *alt.* Yurutí [yui], 249
Yusufzai Pashto, *alt.* Pashto, Northern [pbu], 488
Yuta, *dial.* Wipi [gdr], 632
Yutanduchi Mixtec, *see* Mixtec, Yutanduchi [mab], 270
Yuwana [yau], 313
Za, *alt.* Hya [hya], 62, 162
Zaa, *alt.* Dii [dur], 60
  dial. Wè Southern [gxx], 95
Zaachila, *dial.* Zapotec, Santa Inés Yatzechi [zpn], 280
Zaachila Zapotec, *see* Zapotec, Zaachila [ztx], 281
Zaakosa, *alt.* Fulfulde, Adamawa [fub], 61, 80
Zaar, *dial.* Saya [say], 174
Zaba, *alt.* Zhaba [zhb], 349
Zabana [kji], 639
Zabarma, *alt.* Zarma [dje], 152, 55, 178
  alt. Zarmaci [dje], 145
Zacapoaxtla Náhuat, *alt.* Nahuatl, Highland Puebla [azz], 271
Zacatepec, *dial.* Mixe, North Central [neq], 265
Zacatepec Chatino, *see* Chatino, Zacatepec [ctz], 260
Zacatepec Mixtec, *alt.* Mixtec, Santa María Zacatepec [mza], 268
Zadar, *alt. dial.* Albanian, Tosk [als], 529
Zadgaali, *alt. dial.* Balochi, Southern [bcc], 482
Zadie, *alt. dial.* Bété, Gagnoa [btg], 92
Zagaoua, *alt.* Zaghawa [zag], 196, 87
Zagaran Mran, *dial.* Maru [mhx], 465
Zagawa, *alt.* Zaghawa [zag], 196, 87
Zaghawa [zag], 196, 87
Zaghvana, *alt.* Dghwede [dgh], 157
Zagna, *dial.* Wè Southern [gxx], 95
Zagne, *dial.* Wè Southern [gxx], 95
Zagundzi, *alt. dial.* Romani, Vlax [rmy], 551
Zaha, *alt. dial.* Wè Southern [gxx], 95

Zahao, *dial.* Chin, Falam [flm], 463
Zahau, *alt. dial.* Chin, Falam [flm], 463
Zahau-Shimhrin, *alt. dial.* Chin, Falam [flm], 463
Zainal, *dial.* Aimaq [aiq], 315
Zaïre Swahili, *alt.* Swahili, Congo [swc], 108
Zaiwa [atb], 349, 467
  alt. Zakhring [zkr], 390
  dial. Zaiwa [atb], 349
Zaka, *alt.* Tokano [zuh], 628
Zakara, *alt.* Nzakara [nzk], 77, 106
Zakataly, *alt. dial.* Avar [ava], 319
  dial. Avar [ava], 553
  dial. Azerbaijani, North [azj], 319
Zakho, *dial.* Kurdish, Northern [kmr], 443
  dial. Lishana Deni [lsd], 445
Zakhring [zkr], 390
Zaki, *dial.* Lugbara [lgg], 103
Zaksa, *alt. dial.* Zari [zaz], 178
Zakshi, *dial.* Zari [zaz], 178
Zala, *dial.* Wolaytta [wal], 119
Zalamo, *alt.* Zaramo [zaj], 206
Zalavaria Koli, *dial.* Koli, Kachi [gjk], 486, 369
Zama, *alt.* Khwe [xuu], 214
  alt. Kxoe [xuu], 40
Zaman, *dial.* Bulu [bum], 59
Zambezi, *alt.* Tonga [toi], 215, 217
Zambian Sign Language [zsl], 215
Zamboangueño, *alt.* Chavacano [cbk], 493
  dial. Chavacano [cbk], 493
Zame, *alt. dial.* Jimi [jim], 63
Zamfarawa, *dial.* Hausa [hau], 162
Zamre, *dial.* Mesme [zim], 84
Zamyaki, *alt. dial.* Grangali [nli], 316
Zan, *alt.* Laz [lzz], 519, 352
  dial. Zan Gula [zna], 87
Zan Gula [zna], 87
Zana, *alt.* Baatonum [bba], 154
Zanaki [zak], 206
Zande [zne], 109, 78, 196
Zandi, *alt.* Zande [zne], 109, 78, 196
Zang, *alt.* Tibetan, Central [bod], 344
  dial. Ngwo [ngn], 70
Zang Wen, *alt.* Tibetan [bod], 481
Zanga, *dial.* Dyan [dya], 51
Zangnte, *alt.* Tibea [ngy], 72
Zangram, *alt.* Jangshung [jna], 365
Zangskari [zau], 390
Zangwal [zah], 178
Zani, *alt.* Nzanyi [nja], 171, 71
Zaniza Zapotec, *see* Zapotec, Zaniza [zpw], 281

Zanjan, *alt. dial.* Takestani [tks], 441
Zanniat, *dial.* Chin, Falam [flm], 463, 321
Zanskari, *alt.* Zangskari [zau], 390
Zanu, *dial.* Koma [kmy], 64
Zany, *alt.* Nzanyi [nja], 171, 71
Zanzibar, *alt. dial.* Swahili [swh], 205
Zao, *alt.* Chin, Mara [mrh], 359, 463
Zaomin, *alt.* Dzao Min [bpn], 332
Zaore, *dial.* Mòoré [mos], 52
Zápara, *alt.* Záparo [zro], 252
Záparo [zro], 252
Zapotec, Aloápam [zaq], 277
Zapotec, Amatlán [zpo], 277
Zapotec, Asunción Mixtepec [zoo], 277
Zapotec, Ayoquesco [zaf], 277
Zapotec, Cajonos [zad], 277
Zapotec, Chichicapan [zpv], 278
Zapotec, Choapan [zpc], 278
Zapotec, Coatecas Altas [zca], 278
Zapotec, Coatlán [zps], 278
Zapotec, El Alto [zpp], 278
Zapotec, Elotepec [zte], 278
Zapotec, Guevea de Humboldt [zpg], 278
Zapotec, Güilá [ztu], 278
Zapotec, Isthmus [zai], 278
Zapotec, Lachiguiri [zpa], 278
Zapotec, Lachirioag [ztc], 278
Zapotec, Lachixío [zpl], 278
Zapotec, Loxicha [ztp], 278
Zapotec, Mazaltepec [zpy], 278
Zapotec, Miahuatlán [zam], 279
Zapotec, Mitla [zaw], 279
Zapotec, Mixtepec [zpm], 279
Zapotec, Ocotlán [zac], 279
Zapotec, Ozolotepec [zao], 279
Zapotec, Petapa [zpe], 279
Zapotec, Quiavicuzas [zpj], 279
Zapotec, Quioquitani-Quierí [ztq], 279
Zapotec, Rincón [zar], 279
Zapotec, San Agustín Mixtepec [ztm], 279
Zapotec, San Baltazar Loxicha [zpx], 279
Zapotec, San Juan Guelavía [zab], 279
Zapotec, San Pedro Quiatoni [zpf], 279
Zapotec, San Vicente Coatlán [zpt], 279
Zapotec, Santa Catarina Albarradas [ztn], 280

Zapotec, Santa Inés Yatzechi
[zpn], 280

**Zapotec, Santa María
Quiegolani** [zpi], 280

Zapotec, Santiago Lapaguía
[ztl], 280

Zapotec, Santiago Xanica [zpr],
280

**Zapotec, Santo Domingo
Albarradas** [zas], 280

Zapotec, Sierra de Juárez [zaa],
280

Zapotec, Southeastern Ixtlán
[zpd], 280

Zapotec, Southern Rincon
[zsr], 280

Zapotec, Tabaa [zat], 280

Zapotec, Tejalapan [ztt], 280

Zapotec, Texmelucan [zpz],
280

Zapotec, Tilquiapan [zts], 280

Zapotec, Tlacolulita
[zpk], 280

Zapotec, Totomachapan [zph],
280

Zapotec, Xadani [zax], 281

Zapotec, Xanaguía [ztg], 281

Zapotec, Yalálag [zpu], 281

Zapotec, Yareni [zae], 281

Zapotec, Yatee [zty], 281

Zapotec, Yatzachi [zav], 281

Zapotec, Yautepec [zpb], 281

Zapotec, Zaachila [ztx], 281

Zapotec, Zaniza [zpw], 281

Zapotec, Zoogocho [zpq], 281

Zapoteco de Aloápam, *alt.*
Zapotec, Aloápam [zaq], 277

**Zapoteco de Asunción
Mixtepec**, *alt.* Zapotec, Asunción
Mixtepec [zoo], 277

**Zapoteco de Asunción
Tlacolulita**, *alt.* Zapotec,
Tlacolulita [zpk], 280

Zapoteco de Atepec, *alt.*
Zapotec, Sierra de Juárez
[zaa], 280

Zapoteco de Choapan, *alt.*
Zapotec, Choapan [zpc], 278

**Zapoteco de Guevea de
Humboldt**, *alt.* Zapotec, Guevea
de Humboldt [zpg], 278

Zapoteco de Lachixío, *alt.*
Zapotec, Lachixío [zpl], 278

Zapoteco de Loxicha, *alt.*
Zapotec, Loxicha [ztp], 278

Zapoteco de Miahuatlán, *alt.*
Zapotec, Miahuatlán [zam],
279

Zapoteco de Ozolotepec, *alt.*
Zapotec, Ozolotepec [zao], 279

Zapoteco de Quiavicuzas, *alt.*
Zapotec, Quiavicuzas [zpj], 279

**Zapoteco de Quioquitani Y
Quierí**, *alt.* Zapotec, Quioquitani-
Quierí [ztq], 279

Zapoteco de Rincón Sur, *alt.*
Zapotec, Southern Rincon
[zsr], 280

**Zapoteco de San Baltazar
Chichicapan**, *alt.* Zapotec,
Chichicapan [zpv], 278

**Zapoteco de San Baltázar
Loxicha**, *alt.* Zapotec, San
Baltazar Loxicha [zpx], 279

**Zapoteco de San Bartolo
Yautepec**, *alt.* Zapotec, Yautepec
[zpb], 281

**Zapoteco de San Bartolomé
Zoogocho**, *alt.* Zapotec,
Zoogocho [zpq], 281

**Zapoteco de San Cristóbal
Amatlán**, *alt.* Zapotec, Amatlán
[zpo], 277

**Zapoteco de San Dionisio
Ocotepec**, *alt.* Zapotec, Güilá
[ztu], 278

**Zapoteco de San Felipe
Tejalapan**, *alt.* Zapotec,
Tejalapan [ztt], 280

**Zapoteco de San Juan
Coatecas Altas**, *alt.* Zapotec,
Coatecas Altas [zca], 278

**Zapoteco de San Juan
Elotepec**, *alt.* Zapotec, Elotepec
[zte], 278

**Zapoteco de San Juan
Guelavía**, *alt.* Zapotec, San Juan
Guelavía [zab], 279

**Zapoteco de San Juan
Lachixila O**, *alt.* Zapotec,
Quiavicuzas [zpj], 279

**Zapoteco de San Juan
Mixtepec**, *alt.* Zapotec, Mixtepec
[zpm], 279

**Zapoteco de San Lorenzo
Texmelucan**, *alt.* Zapotec,
Texmelucan [zpz], 280

**Zapoteco de San Miguel
Tilquiapan**, *alt.* Zapotec,
Tilquiapan [zts], 280

Zapoteco de San Pablo Güilá,
alt. Zapotec, Güilá [ztu], 278

**Zapoteco de San Pedro
Cajonos**, *alt.* Zapotec, Cajonos
[zad], 277

Zapoteco de San Pedro el Alto,
alt. Zapotec, El Alto [zpp], 278

**Zapoteco de San Pedro
Quiatoni**, *alt.* Zapotec, San Pedro
Quiatoni [zpf], 279

**Zapoteco de San Pedro
Totomachapan**, *alt.* Zapotec,
Totomachapan [zph], 280

**Zapoteco de San Vicente
Coatlán**, *alt.* Zapotec, San
Vicente Coatlán [zpt], 279

Zapoteco de Santa Ana Yareni,
alt. Zapotec, Yareni [zae], 281

**Zapoteco de Santa Catarina
Albarradas**, *alt.* Zapotec, Santa
Catarina Albarradas [ztn], 280

**Zapoteco de Santa Catarina
Xanaguía**, *alt.* Zapotec, Xanaguía
[ztg], 281

**Zapoteco de Santa Inés
Yatzechi**, *alt.* Zapotec, Santa Inés
Yatzechi [zpn], 280

**Zapoteco de Santa María
Ayoquesco**, *alt.* Zapotec,
Ayoquesco [zaf], 277

**Zapoteco de Santa María
Coatlán**, *alt.* Zapotec, Coatlán
[zps], 278

**Zapoteco de Santa María
Petapa**, *alt.* Zapotec, Petapa
[zpe], 279

**Zapoteco de Santa María
Quiegolani**, *alt.* Zapotec, Santa
María Quiegolani [zpi], 280

**Zapoteco de Santa María
Xadani**, *alt.* Zapotec, Xadani
[zax], 281

**Zapoteco de Santa María
Zaniza**, *alt.* Zapotec, Zaniza
[zpw], 281

**Zapoteco de Santiago
Lachiguiri**, *alt.* Zapotec,
Lachiguiri [zpa], 278

**Zapoteco de Santiago
Lapaguía**, *alt.* Zapotec, Santiago
Lapaguía [ztl], 280

**Zapoteco de Santo Domingo
Albarradas**, *alt.* Zapotec, Santo
Domingo Albarradas [zas], 280

**Zapoteco de Santo Tomás
Mazaltepec**, *alt.* Zapotec,
Mazaltepec [zpy], 278

Zapoteco de Tabaa, *alt.* Zapotec,
Tabaa [zat], 280

Zapoteco de Tejalápam, *alt.*
Zapotec, Tejalapan [ztt], 280

**Zapoteco de Teococuilco de
Marcos Pérez**, *alt.* Zapotec,
Yareni [zae], 281

Zapoteco de Yagallo, *alt.*
Zapotec, Rincón [zar], 279

Zapoteco de Yalálag, *alt.* Zapotec,
Yalálag [zpu], 281

Zapoteco de Yatee, *alt.* Zapotec,
Yatee [zty], 281

Language Code Index

This index gives an alphabetical listing of all 7,299 three-letter codes that are used in this volume to uniquely identify languages. The referenced page contains the main entry that describes the language.

313 of the codes are defined by the ISO 639-2 standard; these codes are indicated by italics. All other codes are part of ISO/DIS 639-3; see "History of the *Ethnologue*" on page 7.

ahr	Ahirani, 353	***ale***	Aleut, 297	**ant**	Antakarinya, 568
ahs	Ashe, 154	**alf**	Alege, 153	**anu**	Anuak, 187
aht	Ahtena, 297	**alh**	Alawa, 567	**anv**	Denya, 60
aia	Arosi, 635	**ali**	Amaimon, 588	**anw**	Anaang, 153
aib	Ainu (China), 326	**alj**	Alangan, 491	**anx**	Andra-Hus, 589
aic	Ainbai, 588	**alk**	Alak, 449	**any**	Anyin, 91
aid	Alngith, 567	**all**	Allar, 353	**anz**	Anem, 589
aie	Amara, 589	**alm**	Amblong, 640	**aoa**	Angolar, 179
aif	Agi, 588	**aln**	Albanian, Gheg, 557	**aob**	Abom, 587
aig	Antigua and Barbuda Creole English, 219	**alo**	Larike-Wakasihu, 396	**aoc**	Pemon, 312
		alp	Alune, 396	**aod**	Andarum, 589
aih	Ai-Cham, 326	**alq**	Algonquin, 235	**aoe**	Angal Enen, 589
aii	Assyrian Neo-Aramaic, 442	**alr**	Alutor, 503	**aof**	Bragat, 594
aij	Lishanid Noshan, 445	**als**	Albanian, Tosk, 529	**aog**	Angoram, 590
aik	Ake, 153	**alt**	Altai, Southern, 503	**aoh**	Arma, 243
ail	Aimele, 588	**alu**	'Are'are, 634	**aoi**	Anindilyakwa, 568
aim	Aimol, 353	**alw**	Alaba, 112	**aoj**	Mufian, 615
ain	Ainu (Japan), 446	**alx**	Alatil, 588	**aok**	Arhö, 584
aio	Aiton, 353	**aly**	Alyawarr, 567	**aol**	Alor, 406
aip	Burumakok, 413	**alz**	Alur, 96	**aom**	Ömie, 619
aiq	Aimaq, 315	**ama**	Amanayé, 224	**aon**	Arapesh, Bumbita, 590
air	Airoran, 410	**amb**	Ambo, 153	**aor**	Aore, 640
ais	Amis, Nataoran, 511	**amc**	Amahuaca, 286	**aos**	Taikat, 423
ait	Arikem, 225	**amd**	Amapá Creole, 224	**aot**	A'tong, 354
aix	Aigon, 588	**ame**	Yanesha', 293	**aox**	Atorada, 257
aiy	Ali, 74	**amf**	Hamer-Banna, 115	**aoz**	Uab Meto, 410
aiz	Aari, 112	**amg**	Amarag, 567	**apb**	Sa'a, 638
aja	Aja (Sudan), 187	***amh***	Amharic, 113	**apc**	Arabic, North Levantine Spoken, 510
ajg	Aja (Benin), 42	**ami**	Amis, 511		
aji	Ajië, 584	**amj**	Amdang, 78	**apd**	Arabic, Sudanese Spoken, 188
ajp	Arabic, South Levantine Spoken, 448	**amk**	Ambai, 410	**ape**	Bukiyip, 595
		aml	War, 322	**apg**	Ampanang, 392
ajt	Arabic, Judeo-Tunisian, 444	**amm**	Ama (Papua New Guinea), 588	**aph**	Athpariya, 468
aju	Arabic, Judeo-Moroccan, 444	**amn**	Amanab, 589	**api**	Apiacá, 225
ajw	Ajawa, 153	**amo**	Amo, 153	**apj**	Apache, Jicarilla, 298
ajz	Amri, 353	**amp**	Alamblak, 588	**apk**	Apache, Kiowa, 298
aka	Akan, 123	**amq**	Amahai, 396	**apl**	Apache, Lipan, 298
akb	Batak Angkola, 435	**amr**	Amarakaeri, 286	**apm**	Apache, Mescalero-Chiricahua, 298
akc	Mpur, 420	**ams**	Amami-Oshima, Southern, 446		
akd	Ukpet-Ehom, 176	**amt**	Amto, 589	**apn**	Apinayé, 225
ake	Akawaio, 256	**amu**	Amuzgo, Guerrero, 259	**apo**	Apalik, 590
akf	Akpa, 153	**amv**	Ambelau, 396	**app**	Apma, 640
akg	Anakalangu, 406	**amw**	Western Neo-Aramaic, 510	**apq**	A-Pucikwar, 353
akh	Angal Heneng, 589	**amx**	Anmatyerre, 568	**apr**	Arop-Lukep, 590
aki	Aiome, 588	**amy**	Ami, 568	**aps**	Arop-Sissano, 590
akj	Aka-Jeru, 353	**amz**	Atampaya, 568	**apt**	Apatani, 354
akl	Aklanon, 491	**ana**	Andaqui, 243	**apu**	Apurinã, 225
akm	Aka-Bo, 353	**anb**	Andoa, 286	**apw**	Apache, Western, 298
akn	Amikoana, 224	**anc**	Ngas, 171	**apx**	Aputai, 396
ako	Akurio, 295	**and**	Ansus, 411	**apy**	Apalaí, 224
akp	Siwu, 128	**ane**	Xârâcùù, 585	**apz**	Safeyoka, 623
akq	Ak, 588	**anf**	Animere, 123	**aqc**	Archi, 553
akr	Araki, 640	**anh**	Nend, 617	**aqg**	Arigidi, 154
aks	Akaselem, 206	**ani**	Andi, 553	**aqm**	Atohwaim, 411
akt	Akolet, 588	**anj**	Anor, 590	**aqn**	Alta, Northern, 491
aku	Akum, 56	**ank**	Goemai, 161	**aqp**	Atakapa, 298
akv	Akhvakh, 552	**anl**	Anu, 462	**aqr**	Arhâ, 584
akw	Akwa, 88	**anm**	Anal, 354	**arb**	Arabic, Standard, 508
akx	Aka-Kede, 353	**ann**	Obolo, 172	**ard**	Arabana, 568
aky	Aka-Kol, 353	**ano**	Andoque, 243	**are**	Arrarnta, Western, 568
akz	Alabama, 297	**anp**	Angika, 354	**arf**	Arafundi, 590
ala	Alago, 153	**anq**	Jarawa (India), 365	***arg***	Aragonese, 558
alc	Qawasqar, 243	**anr**	Andh, 354	**arh**	Arhuaco, 243
ald	Alladian, 91	**ans**	Anserma, 243	**ari**	Arikara, 298

jct	Judeo-Crimean Tatar, 521	jra	Jarai, 523	kbp	Kabiyé, 208
jda	Jad, 365	jrr	Jiru, 165	kbq	Kamano, 604
jdg	Jadgali, 485	jrt	Jorto, 165	kbr	Kafa, 116
jdt	Judeo-Tat, 445	jru	Japrería, 311	kbs	Kande, 120
jeb	Jebero, 288	jsl	Japanese Sign Language, 446	kbt	Abadi, 587
jee	Jerung, 472	jua	Júma, 227	kbu	Kabutra, 485
jeg	Jeng, 450	jub	Wannu, 177	kbv	Dera (Indonesia), 414
jeh	Jeh, 523	juc	Jurchen, 335	kbw	Kaiep, 603
jei	Yei, 426	jud	Worodougou, 96	kbx	Ap Ma, 590
jek	Jeri Kuo, 93	juh	Hõne, 162	kby	Kanuri, Manga, 152
jel	Yelmek, 426	juk	Wapan, 177	kbz	Duhwa, 158
jen	Dza, 158	jul	Jirel, 472	kca	Khanty, 505
jer	Jere, 165	jum	Jumjum, 191	kcb	Kawacha, 605
jet	Manem, 612	jun	Juang, 365	kcc	Lubila, 169
jeu	Jonkor Bourmataguil, 81	juo	Jiba, 165	kcd	Kanum, Ngkâlmpw, 416
jgb	Ngbee, 106	jup	Hupdë, 227	kce	Kaivi, 165
jge	Judeo-Georgian, 445	jur	Jurúna, 228	kcf	Ukaan, 176
jgo	Ngomba, 69	jut	Jutish, 533	kcg	Tyap, 176
jhi	Jehai, 454	juu	Ju, 165	kch	Vono, 177
jia	Jina, 63	juw	Wãpha, 177	kci	Kamantan, 166
jib	Jibu, 165	juy	Juray, 365	kcj	Kobiana, 131
jic	Tol, 258	jvn	Javanese, Caribbean, 295	kck	Kalanga, 216
jid	Bu, 156	jwi	Jwira-Pepesa, 125	kcl	Kela (Papua New Guinea), 605
jie	Jilbe, 165	jya	Jiarong, 336	kcm	Gula (Central African
jig	Djingili, 570	jye	Arabic, Judeo-Yemeni, 444		Republic), 76
jih	Shangzhai, 343	jyy	Jaya, 81	kcn	Nubi, 212
jii	Jiiddu, 184	*kaa*	Kara-Kalpak, 521	kco	Kinalakna, 606
jil	Jilim, 603	*kab*	Kabyle, 39	kcp	Kanga, 191
jim	Jimi (Cameroon), 63	*kac*	Kachin, 464	kcq	Kamo, 166
jio	Jiamao, 336	kad	Kadara, 165	kcr	Katla, 192
jiq	Guanyinqiao, 333	kae	Ketangalan, 511	kcs	Koenoem, 166
jit	Jita, 199	kag	Kajaman, 459	kct	Kaian, 603
jiu	Jinuo, Youle, 336	kah	Kara (Central African	kcu	Kami (Tanzania), 199
jiv	Shuar, 251		Republic), 76	kcv	Kete, 101
jiy	Jinuo, Buyuan, 336	kai	Karekare, 166	kcw	Kabwari, 100
jko	Kubo, 608	kaj	Jju, 165	kcx	Kachama-Ganjule, 115
jku	Labir, 168	kak	Kallahan, Kayapa, 497	kcy	Korandje, 39
jle	Ngile, 194	*kal*	Kalaallisut, 252	kcz	Konongo, 200
jma	Dima, 597	*kam*	Kamba (Kenya), 133	kda	Worimi, 578
jmb	Zumbun, 178	*kan*	Kannada, 366	kdc	Kutu, 200
jmc	Machame, 193	kao	Xaasongaxango, 145	kdd	Yankunytjatjara, 579
jmd	Yamdena, 405	kap	Bezhta, 553	kde	Makonde, 201
jmi	Jimi (Nigeria), 165	kaq	Capanahua, 287	kdf	Mamusi, 611
jmk	Jamtska, 561	*kas*	Kashmiri, 367	kdg	Seba, 107
jml	Jumli, 472	*kat*	Georgian, 352	kdh	Tem, 209
jmr	Kamara, 125	kav	Katukína, 228	kdi	Kumam, 211
jms	Mashi (Nigeria), 169	kax	Kao, 399	kdj	Karamojong, 211
jmx	Mixtec, Western	kay	Kamayurá, 228	kdk	Numee, 585
	Juxtlahuaca, 270	*kaz*	Kazakh, 448	kdl	Tsikimba, 175
jna	Jangshung, 365	kba	Kalarko, 572	kdm	Kagoma, 165
jnd	Jandavra, 485	kbb	Kaxuiâna, 229	kdn	Kunda, 216
jng	Yangman, 579	kbc	Kadiwéu, 228	kdp	Kaningdon-Nindem, 166
jni	Janji, 164	*kbd*	Kabardian, 554	kdq	Koch, 368
jnj	Yemsa, 119	kbe	Kanju, 572	kdr	Karaim, 546
jnl	Rawat, 478	kbf	Kakauhua, 242	kds	Lahu Shi, 451
jns	Jaunsari, 365	kbg	Khamba, 367	kdt	Kuy, 515
job	Joba, 100	kbh	Camsá, 244	kdu	Kadaru, 191
jod	Wojenaka, 95	kbj	Kari, 101	kdv	Kado, 464
jor	Jorá, 223	kbk	Koiari, Grass, 606	kdw	Koneraw, 417
jos	Jordanian Sign Language, 448	kbl	Kanembu, 81	kdx	Kam, 166
jow	Jowulu, 143	kbm	Iwal, 603	kdy	Keder, 417
jpn	Japanese, 446	kbn	Kare (Central African	kdz	Kwaja, 65
jpr	Judeo-Persian, 444		Republic), 76	kea	Kabuverdianu, 74
jqr	Jaqaru, 288	kbo	Keliko, 192	keb	Kélé, 120

ktg	Kalkutung, 572	**kvt**	Karen, Lahta, 464	**kyf**	Kouya, 93
kth	Karanga, 82	**kvu**	Karen, Yinbaw, 464	**kyg**	Keyagana, 606
kti	Muyu, North, 421	**kvv**	Kola, 400	**kyh**	Karok, 303
ktj	Krumen, Plapo, 93	**kvw**	Wersing, 410	**kyi**	Kiput, 460
ktk	Kaniet, 604	**kvx**	Koli, Parkari, 487	**kyj**	Karao, 498
ktl	Koroshi, 440	**kvy**	Karen, Yintale, 465	**kyk**	Kamayo, 498
ktm	Kurti, 608	**kvz**	Tsakwambo, 424	**kyl**	Kalapuya, 302
ktn	Karitiâna, 228	**kwa**	Dâw, 226	**kym**	Kpatili, 76
kto	Kuot, 608	**kwb**	Kwa, 167	**kyn**	Karolanos, 498
ktp	Kaduo, 450	**kwc**	Likwala, 89	**kyo**	Kelon, 407
ktq	Katabaga, 498	**kwd**	Kwaio, 637	**kyp**	Kang, 450
ktr	Kota Marudu Tinagas, 457	**kwe**	Kwerba, 418	**kyq**	Kenga, 82
kts	Muyu, South, 421	**kwf**	Kwara'ae, 637	**kyr**	Kuruáya, 229
ktt	Ketum, 417	**kwg**	Kaba Deme, 81	**kys**	Kayan, Baram, 459
ktu	Kituba (Democratic Republic of Congo), 101	**kwh**	Kowiai, 418	**kyt**	Kayagar, 417
		kwi	Awa-Cuaiquer, 243	**kyu**	Kayah, Western, 465
ktv	Katu, Eastern, 523	**kwj**	Kwanga, 608	**kyv**	Kayort, 473
ktw	Kato, 303	**kwk**	Kwakiutl, 238	**kyw**	Kudmali, 370
ktx	Kaxararí, 229	**kwl**	Kofyar, 166	**kyx**	Rapoisi, 622
kty	Kango (Bas-Uélé District), 100	**kwm**	Kwambi, 150	**kyy**	Kambaira, 604
ktz	Ju|'hoan, 47	**kwn**	Kwangali, 150	**kyz**	Kayabí, 229
kua	Kuanyama, 40	**kwo**	Kwomtari, 609	**kza**	Karaboro, Western, 52
kub	Kutep, 167	**kwp**	Kodia, 93	**kzb**	Kaibobo, 399
kud	'Auhelawa, 591	**kwq**	Kwak, 168	**kzc**	Kulango, Bondoukou, 94
kue	Kuman, 608	**kwr**	Kwer, 418	**kzd**	Kadai, 399
kuf	Katu, Western, 450	**kws**	Kwese, 102	**kze**	Kosena, 607
kug	Kupa, 167	**kwt**	Kwesten, 418	**kzf**	Kaili, Da'a, 429
kuh	Kushi, 167	**kwu**	Kwakum, 65	**kzg**	Kikai, 446
kui	Kuikúro-Kalapálo, 229	**kwv**	Kaba Na, 81	**kzh**	Kenuzi-Dongola, 192
kuj	Kuria, 200	**kww**	Kwinti, 296	**kzi**	Kelabit, 459
kuk	Kepo', 407	**kwx**	Khirwar, 368	**kzj**	Kadazan, Coastal, 457
kul	Kulere, 167	**kwy**	Kongo, San Salvador, 101	**kzk**	Kazukuru, 636
kum	Kumyk, 555	**kwz**	Kwadi, 40	**kzl**	Kayeli, 399
kun	Kunama, 112	**kxa**	Kairiru, 603	**kzm**	Kais, 415
kuo	Kumukio, 608	**kxb**	Krobu, 93	**kzn**	Kokola, 140
kup	Kunimaipa, 608	**kxc**	Komso, 116	**kzo**	Kaningi, 120
kuq	Karipuná, 228	**kxd**	Brunei, 324	**kzp**	Kaidipang, 429
kus	Kusaal, 126	**kxe**	Kakihum, 166	**kzq**	Kaike, 473
kut	Kutenai, 238	**kxf**	Karen, Manumanaw, 464	**kzr**	Karang, 63
kuu	Kuskokwim, Upper, 303	**kxg**	Katingan, 393	**kzs**	Dusun, Sugut, 456
kuv	Kur, 400	**kxh**	Karo (Ethiopia), 116	**kzt**	Dusun, Tambunan, 456
kuw	Kpagua, 76	**kxi**	Keningau Murut, 457	**kzu**	Kayupulau, 417
kux	Kukatja, 572	**kxj**	Kulfa, 82	**kzv**	Komyandaret, 417
kuy	Kuuku-Ya'u, 573	**kxk**	Karen, Zayein, 465	**kzw**	Kariri-Xocó, 228
kuz	Kunza, 242	**kxl**	Kurux, Nepali, 473	**kzx**	Kamarian, 399
kva	Bagvalal, 553	**kxm**	Khmer, Northern, 515	**kzy**	Kango (Tshopo District), 100
kvb	Kubu, 436	**kxn**	Kanowit, 459	**kzz**	Kalabra, 416
kvc	Kove, 607	**kxo**	Kanoé, 228	**laa**	Subanun, Lapuyan, 501
kvd	Kui (Indonesia), 408	**kxp**	Koli, Wadiyara, 369	**lac**	Lacandon, 263
kve	Kalabakan, 457	**kxq**	Kanum, Smärky, 416	*lad*	Ladino, 445
kvf	Kabalai, 81	**kxr**	Koro (Papua New Guinea), 607	**lae**	Pattani, 383
kvg	Kuni-Boazi, 608	**kxs**	Kangjia, 337	**laf**	Lafofa, 192
kvh	Komodo, 408	**kxt**	Koiwat, 607	**lag**	Langi, 200
kvi	Kwang, 82	**kxu**	Kui (India), 370	**lai**	Lambya, 140
kvj	Psikye, 71	**kxv**	Kuvi, 371	**laj**	Lango (Uganda), 211
kvk	Korean Sign Language, 449	**kxw**	Konai, 607	**lak**	Laka (Nigeria), 168
kvl	Karen, Brek, 464	**kxx**	Likuba, 89	**lal**	Lalia, 102
kvm	Kendem, 63	**kxy**	Kayong, 515	*lam*	Lamba, 214
kvn	Kuna, Border, 246	**kxz**	Kerewo, 606	**lan**	Laru, 168
kvo	Dobel, 397	**kya**	Kwaya, 200	*lao*	Lao, 445
kvp	Kompane, 400	**kyb**	Kalinga, Butbut, 497	**lap**	Laka (Chad), 83
kvq	Karen, Geba, 458	**kyc**	Kyaka, 609	**laq**	Qabiao, 526
kvr	Kerinci, 436	**kyd**	Karey, 399	**lar**	Larteh, 126
kvs	Kunggara, 572	**kye**	Krache, 126	**las**	Lama (Togo), 208

lat	Latin, 566	**len**	Lenca, 258	**lje**	Rampi, 432
lau	Laba, 400	**leo**	Leti (Cameroon), 65	**lji**	Laiyolo, 430
lav	Latvian, 546	**lep**	Lepcha, 372	**ljl**	Li'o, 408
law	Lauje, 430	**leq**	Lembena, 609	**ljp**	Lampung, 436
lax	Tiwa, 389	**ler**	Lenkau, 609	**lka**	Lakalei, 351
lay	Lama (Myanmar), 465	**les**	Lese, 102	**lke**	Kenyi, 211
laz	Aribwatsa, 590	**let**	Lesing-Gelimi, 610	**lkh**	Lakha, 323
lba	Lui, 465	**leu**	Kara (Papua New Guinea), 605	**lki**	Laki, 440
lbb	Label, 609	**lev**	Lamma, 408	**lkj**	Remun, 460
lbc	Lakkia, 338	**lew**	Kaili, Ledo, 429	**lkl**	Laeko-Libuat, 609
lbe	Lak, 555	**lex**	Luang, 401	**lkn**	Lakona, 642
lbf	Tinani, 388	**ley**	Lemolang, 430	**lkr**	Päri, 194
lbg	Laopang, 465	*lez*	Lezghian, 555	**lkt**	Lakota, 303
lbi	La'bi, 65	**lfa**	Lefa, 65	**lky**	Lokoya, 192
lbj	Ladakhi, 372	**lga**	Lungga, 637	**lla**	Lala-Roba, 163
lbm	Lodhi, 372	**lgb**	Laghu, 637	**llb**	Lolo, 147
lbn	Lamet, 451	**lgg**	Lugbara, 211	**llc**	Lele (Guinea), 129
lbo	Laven, 451	**lgh**	Laghuu, 524	**lld**	Ladin, 544
lbq	Wampar, 631	**lgi**	Lengilu, 394	**lle**	Lele (Papua New Guinea), 609
lbr	Lorung, Northern, 474	**lgk**	Lingarak, 643	**llf**	Hermit, 602
lbs	Libyan Sign Language, 139	**lgl**	Wala, 639	**llg**	Lole, 408
lbt	Lachi, 524	**lgm**	Lega-Mwenga, 102	**lli**	Teke-Laali, 90
lbu	Labu, 609	**lgn**	Opuuo, 117	**llk**	Lelak, 460
lbv	Lavatbura-Lamusong, 609	**lgq**	Logba, 126	**lll**	Lilau, 610
lbw	Tolaki, 433	**lgr**	Lengo, 637	**llm**	Lasalimu, 430
lbx	Lawangan, 394	**lgt**	Pahi, 621	**lln**	Lele (Chad), 83
lby	Lamu-Lamu, 573	**lgu**	Longgu, 637	**llo**	Khlor, 450
lbz	Lardil, 573	**lgz**	Ligenza, 102	**llp**	Efate, North, 641
lcc	Legenyem, 418	**lha**	Laha (Viet Nam), 524	**llq**	Lolak, 430
lcd	Lola, 401	**lhh**	Laha (Indonesia), 400	**lls**	Lithuanian Sign Language, 546
lce	Loncong, 436	**lhl**	Lohar, Lahul, 372	**llu**	Lau, 637
lcf	Lubu, 436	**lhm**	Lhomi, 474	**llx**	Lauan, 580
lch	Luchazi, 41	**lhn**	Lahanan, 460	**lma**	Limba, East, 129
lcl	Lisela, 400	**lhp**	Lhokpu, 323	**lmb**	Merei, 643
lcm	Tungag, 628	**lhs**	Mlahsö, 510	**lmc**	Limilngan, 573
lcp	Lawa, Western, 338	**lht**	Toga, 646	**lmd**	Lumun, 193
lcq	Luhu, 401	**lhu**	Lahu, 338	**lme**	Pévé, 86
lcs	Lisabata-Nuniali, 400	**lia**	Limba, West-Central, 183	**lmf**	Lembata, South, 408
ldb	Idun, 163	**lib**	Likum, 610	**lmg**	Lamogai, 609
ldd	Luri, 169	**lic**	Hlai, 333	**lmh**	Lambichhong, 474
ldg	Lenyima, 168	**lid**	Nyindrou, 619	**lmi**	Lombi, 103
ldh	Lamja-Dengsa-Tola, 168	**lie**	Likila, 103	**lmj**	Lembata, West, 408
ldi	Laari, 88	**lif**	Limbu, 474	**lmk**	Lamkang, 372
ldj	Lemoro, 168	**lig**	Ligbi, 126	**lml**	Hano, 642
ldk	Leelau, 168	**lih**	Lihir, 610	**lmm**	Lamam, 325
ldl	Kaan, 165	**lii**	Lingkhim, 474	**lmn**	Lambadi, 372
ldm	Landoma, 129	**lij**	Ligurian, 544	**lmo**	Lombard, 544
ldo	Loo, 169	**lik**	Lika, 102	**lmp**	Limbum, 65
ldp	Tso, 176	**lil**	Lillooet, 238	**lmq**	Lamatuka, 408
ldq	Lufu, 169	*lim*	Limburgish, Limburger, Limburgan, 548	**lmr**	Lamalera, 408
lea	Lega-Shabunda, 102			**lms**	Limousin, 537
leb	Lala-Bisa, 214	*lin*	Lingala, 103	**lmt**	Lematang, 436
lec	Leco, 223	**lio**	Liki, 418	**lmu**	Lamenu, 642
led	Lendu, 102	**lip**	Sekpele, 127	**lmv**	Lomaiviti, 580
lee	Lyélé, 52	**liq**	Libido, 116	**lmw**	Miwok, Lake, 305
lef	Lelemi, 126	**lir**	Liberian English, 138	**lmx**	Laimbue, 65
leg	Lengua, 284	**lis**	Lisu, 339	**lmy**	Lamboya, 408
leh	Lenje, 214	*lit*	Lithuanian, 546	**lmz**	Lumbee, 304
lei	Lemio, 609	**liu**	Logorik, 192	**lna**	Langbashe, 76
lej	Lengola, 102	**liv**	Liv, 546	**lnb**	Mbalanhu, 150
lek	Leipon, 609	**liw**	Lembak, 436	**lnc**	Languedocien, 537
lel	Lele (Democratic Republic of Congo), 102	**lix**	Liabuku, 430	**lnd**	Lundayeh, 394
		liy	Banda-Bambari, 75	**lnh**	Lanoh, 454
lem	Nomaande, 70	**liz**	Libinza, 102	**lni**	Lantanai, 609

lnj	Leningitij, 573	**lud**	Ludian, 555	**mbg**	Nambikuára, Northern, 230
lnl	Banda, South Central, 74	**lue**	Luvale, 214	**mbh**	Mangseng, 612
lnm	Langam, 609	**luf**	Laua, 609	**mbi**	Manobo, Ilianen, 499
lnn	Lorediakarkar, 643	*lug*	Ganda, 210	**mbj**	Nadëb, 230
lno	Lango (Sudan), 192	*lui*	Luiseno, 304	**mbk**	Malol, 611
lns	Lamnso', 65	**luj**	Luna, 103	**mbl**	Maxakalí, 230
lnt	Lintang, 436	**luk**	Lunanakha, 323	**mbm**	Ombamba, 89
lnu	Longuda, 169	**lul**	Olu'bo, 194	**mbn**	Macaguán, 246
lnz	Lonzo, 103	**lum**	Luimbi, 41	**mbo**	Mbo (Cameroon), 66
loa	Loloda, 401	*lun*	Lunda, 214	**mbp**	Malayo, 246
lob	Lobi, 52	*luo*	Luo (Kenya and Tanzania), 134	**mbq**	Maisin, 610
loc	Inonhan, 495	**lup**	Lumbu, 120	**mbr**	Nukak Makú, 246
lod	Berawan, 459	**luq**	Lucumi, 249	**mbs**	Manobo, Sarangani, 499
loe	Saluan, Coastal, 432	**lur**	Laura, 408	**mbt**	Manobo, Matigsalug, 499
lof	Logol, 192	*lus*	Lushai, 376	**mbu**	Mbula-Bwazza, 170
log	Logo, 103	**lut**	Lushootseed, 304	**mbv**	Mbulungish, 130
loh	Narim, 194	**luu**	Lumba-Yakkha, 475	**mbw**	Maring, 612
loi	Loma (Côte d'Ivoire), 94	**luv**	Luwati, 483	**mbx**	Mari (East Sepik Province), 612
loj	Lou, 610	**luw**	Luo, 65	**mby**	Memoni, 487
lok	Loko, 183	**luy**	Luyia, 134	**mbz**	Mixtec, Amoltepec, 266
lol	Mongo, 104	**luz**	Luri, Southern, 440	**mca**	Maca, 285
lom	Loma (Liberia), 138	**lva**	Maku'a, 351	**mcb**	Machiguenga, 288
lon	Lomwe, Malawi, 140	**lvk**	Lavukaleve, 637	**mcc**	Bitur, 594
loo	Lombo, 103	**lvu**	Levuka, 408	**mcd**	Sharanahua, 293
lop	Lopa, 169	**lwa**	Lwalu, 103	**mce**	Mixtec, Itundujia, 265
loq	Lobala, 103	**lwe**	Lewo Eleng, 408	**mcf**	Matsés, 288
lor	Téén, 95	**lwh**	Lachi, White, 524	**mcg**	Mapoyo, 312
los	Loniu, 610	**lwl**	Lawa, Eastern, 515	**mch**	Maquiritari, 312
lot	Otuho, 194	**lwo**	Luwo, 193	**mci**	Mese, 613
lou	Louisiana Creole French, 304	**lwt**	Lewotobi, 408	**mcj**	Mvanip, 170
lov	Lopi, 465	**lww**	Lewo, 643	**mck**	Mbunda, 214
low	Lobu, Tampias, 457	**lya**	Layakha, 323	**mcl**	Macaguaje, 246
lox	Loun, 401	**lyn**	Luyana, 214	**mcm**	Malaccan Creole
loy	Lowa, 474	**lzl**	Litzlitz, 643		Portuguese, 454
loz	Lozi, 214	**lzz**	Laz, 519	**mcn**	Masana, 83
lpa	Lelepa, 642	**maa**	Mazatec, San Jerónimo	**mco**	Mixe, Coatlán, 265
lpe	Lepki, 418		Tecóatl, 265	**mcp**	Makaa, 65
lpo	Lipo, 339	**mab**	Mixtec, Yutanduchi, 270	**mcq**	Ese, 598
lpx	Lopit, 193	*mad*	Madurese, 392	**mcr**	Menya, 613
lra	Lara', 460	**mae**	Bo-Rukul, 155	**mcs**	Mambai, 66
lrc	Luri, Northern, 440	**maf**	Mafa, 65	**mct**	Mengisa, 67
lre	Laurentian, 238	*mag*	Magahi, 373	**mcu**	Mambila, Cameroon, 66
lrg	Laragia, 573	*mah*	Marshall, 582	**mcv**	Minanibai, 614
lrk	Loarki, 480	*mai*	Maithili, 373	**mcw**	Mawa (Chad), 84
lrl	Lari, 440	**maj**	Mazatec, Jalapa De Díaz, 264	**mcx**	Mpiemo, 77
lrn	Lorang, 401	*mak*	Makasar, 430	**mcy**	Watut, South, 631
lro	Laro, 192	*mal*	Malayalam, 374	**mcz**	Mawan, 612
lrr	Lorung, Southern, 474	**mam**	Mam, Northern, 255	**mda**	Mada (Nigeria), 169
lrv	Larevat, 642	**maq**	Mazatec, Chiquihuitlán, 264	**mdb**	Morigi, 615
lsa	Lasgerdi, 440	*mar*	Marathi, 374	**mdc**	Male (Papua New Guinea), 611
lsd	Lishana Deni, 445	*mas*	Masai, 134	**mdd**	Mbum, 66
lse	Lusengo, 103	**mat**	Matlatzinca, San Francisco, 264	**mde**	Maba (Chad), 83
lsg	Lyons Sign Language, 537	**mau**	Mazatec, Huautla, 264	*mdf*	Moksha, 556
lsi	Lashi, 465	**mav**	Sateré-Mawé, 231	**mdg**	Massalat, 84
lsl	Latvian Sign Language, 546	**maw**	Mampruli, 126	**mdh**	Maguindanao, 498
lso	Laos Sign Language, 451	**max**	Malay, North Moluccan, 401	**mdi**	Mamvu, 103
lsr	Aruop, 591	**maz**	Mazahua Central, 264	**mdj**	Mangbetu, 104
lss	Lasi, 487	**mba**	Higaonon, 494	**mdk**	Mangbutu, 104
lti	Leti (Indonesia), 400	**mbb**	Manobo, Western	**mdl**	Maltese Sign Language, 547
ltu	Latu, 400		Bukidnon, 499	**mdm**	Mayogo, 104
ltz	Letzeburgesch, 546	**mbc**	Macushi, 229	**mdn**	Mbati, 77
lua	Luba-Lulua, 103	**mbd**	Manobo, Dibabawon, 499	**mdo**	Gbaya, Southwest, 76
lub	Luba-Katanga, 103	**mbe**	Molale, 305	**mdp**	Mbala, 104
luc	Aringa, 210	**mbf**	Malay, Baba, 509	**mdq**	Mbole, 104

msm Manobo, Agusan, 499
msn Mosina, 644
mso Mombum, 420
msp Maritsauá, 230
msq Caac, 584
msr Mongolian Sign Language, 461
mss Masela, West, 402
mst Mandaya, Cataelano, 498
msu Musom, 616
msv Maslam, 66
msw Mansoanka, 131
msx Moresada, 615
msy Aruamu, 591
msz Momare, 614
mta Manobo, Cotabato, 499
mtb Anyin Morofo, 91
mtc Munit, 615
mtd Mualang, 394
mte Mono (Solomon Islands), 637
mtf Murik, 615
mtg Una, 424
mth Munggui, 421
mti Maiwa (Papua New
       Guinea), 611
mtj Moskona, 420
mtk Mbe', 66
mtl Montol, 170
mtm Mator, 505
mtn Matagalpa, 282
mto Mixe, Totontepec, 265
mtp Wichí Lhamtés Nocten, 224
mtq Muong, 525
mtr Mewari, 375
mts Yora, 294
mtt Mota, 644
mtu Mixtec, Tututepec, 269
mtv Asaro'o, 591
mtw Magahat, 498
mtx Mixtec, Tidaá, 269
mty Nabi, 616
mtz Tacanec, 256
mua Mundang, 85
mub Mubi, 84
muc Mbu', 66
mud Aleut, Mednyj, 503
mue Media Lengua, 251
mug Musgu, 68
muh Mündü, 193
mui Musi, 437
muj Mabire, 83
muk Mugom, 476
mum Maiwala, 611
muo Nyong, 71
mup Malvi, 374
muq Hmong, Eastern Xiangxi, 334
mur Murle, 193
mus Creek, 305
mut Muria, Western, 377
muu Yaaku, 137
muv Muthuvan, 377
muw Mundari, 376
mux Mbo-Ung, 612
muy Muyang, 69
muz Mursi, 117

mva Manam, 611
mvb Mattole, 304
mvc Mam, Central, 255
mvd Mamboru, 408
mve Marwari (Pakistan), 487
mvf Mongolian, Peripheral, 339
mvg Mixtec, Yucuañe, 270
mvh Mire, 84
mvi Miyako, 447
mvj Mam, Todos Santos
       Cuchumatán, 255
mvk Mekmek, 613
mvl Mbara (Australia), 574
mvm Muya, 340
mvn Minaveha, 614
mvo Marovo, 637
mvp Duri, 429
mvq Moere, 614
mvr Marau, 415
mvs Massep, 419
mvt Mpotovoro, 644
mvu Marfa, 83
mvv Tagal Murut, 458
mvw Machinga, 201
mvx Meoswar, 420
mvy Kohistani, Indus, 486
mvz Mesqan, 117
mwa Mwatebu, 616
mwb Juwal, 603
mwc Are, 590
mwd Mudbura, 574
mwe Mwera (Chimwera), 202
mwf Murrinh-Patha, 574
mwg Aiklep, 588
mwh Mouk-Aria, 615
mwi Labo, 642
mwj Maligo, 41
mwk Maninkakan, Kita, 143
mwl Mirandese, 551
mwm Sar, 86
mwn Nyamwanga, 215
mwo Maewo, Central, 643
mwp Kala Lagaw Ya, 571
mwq Chin, Mün, 463
mws Mwimbi-Muthambi, 135
mwt Moken, 466
mwu Mittu, 193
mwv Mentawai, 436
mww Hmong Daw, 334
mwx Mediak, 202
mwy Mosiro, 202
mwz Moingi, 104
mxa Mixtec, Northwest Oaxaca, 268
mxb Mixtec, Tezoatlán, 269
mxc Manyika, 216
mxd Modang, 394
mxe Mele-Fila, 643
mxf Malgbe, 65
mxg Mbangala, 41
mxh Mvuba, 105
mxi Mozarabic, 560
mxj Miju-Mishmi, 375
mxk Monumbo, 614
mxl Gbe, Maxi, 44

mxm Meramera, 613
mxn Moi (Indonesia), 420
mxo Mbowe, 214
mxp Mixe, Tlahuitoltepec, 265
mxq Mixe, Juquila, 265
mxr Kayan, Murik, 459
mxs Mixtec, Huitepec, 267
mxt Mixtec, Jamiltepec, 267
mxu Mada (Cameroon), 65
mxv Mixtec, Metlatónoc, 267
mxw Namo, 617
mxx Mahou, 94
mxy Mixtec, Southeastern
       Nochixtlán, 269
mxz Masela, Central, 402
mya Burmese, 462
myb Mbay, 84
myc Mayeka, 104
myd Maramba, 612
mye Myene, 121
myf Bambassi, 113
myg Manta, 66
myh Makah, 304
myi Mina (India), 376
myj Mangayat, 193
myk Senoufo, Mamara, 144
myl Moma, 431
mym Me'en, 117
myo Anfillo, 113
myp Pirahã, 231
myq Maninka, Forest, 94
myr Muniche, 289
mys Mesmes, 117
myt Mandaya, Sangab, 498
myu Mundurukú, 230
myv Erzya, 554
myw Muyuw, 616
myx Masaba, 211
myy Macuna, 246
myz Mandaic, Classical, 441
mza Mixtec, Santa María
       Zacatepec, 268
mzb Tumzabt, 40
mzc Madagascar Sign
       Language, 140
mzd Malimba, 66
mze Morawa, 614
mzf Aiku, 588
mzg Monastic Sign Language, 566
mzh Wichí Lhamtés Güisnay, 220
mzi Mazatec, Ixcatlán, 264
mzj Manya, 139
mzk Mambila, Nigeria, 169
mzl Mixe, Mazatlán, 265
mzm Mumuye, 170
mzn Mazanderani, 441
mzo Matipuhy, 230
mzp Movima, 223
mzq Mori Atas, 431
mzr Marúbo, 230
mzs Macanese, 339
mzt Mintil, 455
mzu Inapang, 603
mzv Manza, 76

mzw	Deg, 124	nck	Nakara, 574	nfl	Ayiwo, 635
mzx	Mawayana, 257	ncl	Nahuatl, Michoacán, 271	nfr	Nafaanra, 126
mzy	Mozambican Sign Language, 148	ncm	Nambo, 617	nfu	Mfumte, 67
		ncn	Nauna, 617	nga	Ngbaka, 105
mzz	Maiadomu, 610	nco	Sibe, 624	ngb	Ngbandi, Northern, 105
nab	Nambikuára, Southern, 230	ncp	Ndaktup, 69	ngc	Ngombe (Democratic Republic of Congo), 106
nac	Narak, 617	ncr	Ncane, 69		
nad	Nijadali, 575	ncs	Nicaraguan Sign Language, 280	ngd	Ngando (Central African Republic), 77
nae	Naka'ela, 402	nct	Naga, Chothe, 377		
naf	Nabak, 616	ncu	Chumburung, 124	nge	Ngemba, 69
nag	Naga Pidgin, 377	ncx	Nahuatl, Central Puebla, 270	ngg	Ngbaka Manza, 77
naj	Nalu, 130	ncz	Natchez, 305	ngh	N|u, 186
nak	Nakanai, 616	nda	Ndasa, 89	ngi	Ngizim, 171
nal	Nalik, 617	ndb	Kenswei Nsei, 64	ngj	Ngie, 69
nam	Nangikurrunggurr, 574	ndc	Ndau, 148	ngk	Ngalkbun, 575
nan	Chinese, Min Nan, 330	ndd	Nde-Nsele-Nta, 170	ngl	Lomwe, 147
nao	Naaba, 476	*nde*	Ndebele, North, 216	ngm	Ngatik Men's Creole, 582
nap	Neapolitan, 545	ndg	Ndengereko, 202	ngn	Ngwo, 70
naq	Nama (Namibia), 150	ndh	Ndali, 202	ngo	Ngoni, 202
nar	Iguta, 163	ndi	Samba Leko, 174	ngp	Ngulu, 203
nas	Naasioi, 616	ndj	Ndamba, 202	ngq	Ngurimi, 203
nat	Hungworo, 162	ndk	Ndaka, 102	ngr	Nanggu, 637
nau	Nauru, 583	ndl	Ndolo, 105	ngs	Gvoko, 161
nav	Navajo, 305	ndm	Ndam, 85	ngt	Ngeq, 451
naw	Nawuri, 127	ndn	Ngundi, 89	ngu	Nahuatl, Guerrero, 271
nax	Nakwi, 616	*ndo*	Ndonga, 150	ngv	Nagumi, 69
nay	Narrinyeri, 575	ndp	Ndo, 212	ngw	Ngwaba, 171
naz	Nahuatl, Coatepec, 270	ndq	Ndombe, 41	ngx	Nggwahyi, 171
nba	Nyemba, 41	ndr	Ndoola, 171	ngy	Tibea, 72
nbb	Ndoe, 170	*nds*	Low German; Low Saxon, 539	ngz	Ngungwel, 89
nbc	Naga, Chang, 377	ndt	Ndunga, 105	nhb	Beng, 92
nbd	Ngbinda, 106	ndu	Dugun, 60	nhc	Nahuatl, Tabasco, 272
nbe	Naga, Konyak, 378	ndv	Ndut, 181	nhd	Chiripá, 284
nbf	Naxi, 341	ndw	Ndobo, 105	nhe	Nahuatl, Eastern Huasteca, 271
nbg	Nagarchal, 381	ndx	Nduga, 421	nhf	Nhuwala, 575
nbh	Ngamo, 171	ndy	Lutos, 76	nhg	Nahuatl, Tetelcingo, 272
nbi	Naga, Mao, 378	ndz	Ndogo, 194	nhh	Nahari, 381
nbj	Ngarinman, 575	nea	Ngad'a, Eastern, 409	nhi	Nahuatl, Tenango, 272
nbk	Nake, 616	neb	Toura (Côte d'Ivoire), 95	nhj	Nahuatl, Tlalitzlipa, 272
nbl	Ndebele, South, 186	nec	Nedebang, 409	nhk	Nahuatl, Isthmus-Cosoleacaque, 271
nbm	Ngbaka Ma'bo, 77	ned	Nde-Gbite, 170		
nbn	Kuri, 418	nee	Kumak, 584	nhm	Nahuatl, Morelos, 271
nbo	Nkukoli, 171	nef	Nefamese, 381	nhn	Nahuatl, Central, 270
nbp	Nnam, 171	neg	Negidal, 506	nho	Takuu, 626
nbq	Nggem, 421	neh	Nyenkha, 324	nhp	Nahuatl, Isthmus-Pajapan, 271
nbr	Numana-Nunku-Gbantu-Numbu, 171	nej	Neko, 617	nhq	Nahuatl, Huaxcaleca, 271
		nek	Neku, 585	nhr	Naro, 48
nbs	Namibian Sign Language, 150	nem	Nemi, 585	nhs	Nahuatl, Southeastern Puebla, 272
nbt	Na, 377	nen	Nengone, 585		
nbu	Naga, Rongmei, 379	neo	Ná-Meo, 525	nht	Nahuatl, Ometepec, 271
nbv	Ngamambo, 69	*nep*	Nepali, 476	nhu	Noone, 70
nbw	Ngbandi, Southern, 105	neq	Mixe, North Central, 265	nhv	Nahuatl, Temascaltepec, 272
nbx	Ngura, 575	ner	Yahadian, 426	nhw	Nahuatl, Western Huasteca, 272
nby	Ningera, 618	nes	Kinnauri, Bhoti, 368	nhx	Nahuatl, Isthmus-Mecayapan, 271
nca	Iyo, 603	net	Nete, 618		
ncb	Nicobarese, Central, 381	nev	Nyaheun, 452	nhy	Nahuatl, Northern Oaxaca, 271
ncc	Ponam, 622	*new*	Newari, 476	nhz	Nahuatl, Santa María La Alta, 272
ncd	Nachering, 476	nex	Neme, 617		
nce	Yale, 633	ney	Neyo, 94	*nia*	Nias, 437
ncf	Notsi, 618	nez	Nez Perce, 306	nib	Nakama, 616
ncg	Nisga'a, 240	nfa	Dhao, 406	nid	Ngandi, 575
nch	Nahuatl, Central Huasteca, 270	nfd	Ndun, 171	nie	Niellim, 85
nci	Nahuatl, Classical, 270	nfg	Nyeng, 171	nif	Nek, 617
ncj	Nahuatl, Northern Puebla, 271	nfk	Shakara, 174	nig	Ngalakan, 575

otn	Otomi, Tenango, 273	**pcb**	Pear, 326	**pht**	Phu Thai, 516
otq	Otomi, Querétaro, 272	**pcc**	Bouyei, 328	**phu**	Phuan, 516
otr	Otoro, 194	**pcd**	Picard, 537	**phv**	Pahlavani, 317
ots	Otomi, Estado de México, 272	**pce**	Palaung, Pale, 466	**phw**	Phangduwali, 477
ott	Otomi, Temoaya, 273	**pcf**	Paliyan, 382	**pia**	Pima Bajo, 273
otu	Otuke, 231	**pcg**	Paniya, 382	**pib**	Yine, 294
otw	Ottawa, 240	**pch**	Pardhan, 383	**pic**	Pinji, 121
otx	Otomi, Texcatepec, 273	**pci**	Duruwa, 361	**pid**	Piaroa, 312
otz	Otomi, Ixtenco, 272	**pcj**	Parenga, 383	**pie**	Piro, 307
oua	Tagargrent, 40	**pck**	Chin, Paite, 359	**pif**	Pingelapese, 583
oub	Glio-Oubi, 138	**pcl**	Pardhi, 383	**pig**	Pisabo, 289
oue	Oune, 620	**pcm**	Pidgin, Nigerian, 173	**pih**	Pitcairn-Norfolk, 586
oum	Ouma, 620	**pcn**	Piti, 173	**pii**	Pini, 576
oun	!O!ung, 41	**pcp**	Pacahuara, 223	**pij**	Pijao, 247
owi	Owiniga, 620	**pcr**	Panang, 342	**pil**	Yom, 46
oyb	Oy, 452	**pcw**	Pyapun, 173	**pim**	Powhatan, 307
oyd	Oyda, 118	**pda**	Anam, 589	**pin**	Piame, 621
oym	Wayampi, 252	**pdc**	German, Pennsylvania, 301	**pio**	Piapoco, 247
oyy	Oya'oya, 621	**pdi**	Pa Di, 341	**pip**	Pero, 173
ozm	Koonzime, 64	**pdn**	Podena, 422	**pir**	Piratapuyo, 231
pab	Parecís, 231	**pdo**	Padoe, 432	**pis**	Pijin, 637
pac	Pacoh, 525	**pdt**	Plautdietsch, 241	**pit**	Pitta Pitta, 576
pad	Paumarí, 231	**pdu**	Kayan, 465	**piu**	Pintupi-Luritja, 576
pae	Pagibete, 107	**pea**	Indonesian, Peranakan, 391	**piv**	Pileni, 637
paf	Paranawát, 231	**peb**	Pomo, Eastern, 307	**piw**	Pimbwe, 204
pag	Pangasinan, 500	**pec**	Pesisir, Southern, 437	**pix**	Piu, 622
pah	Tenharim, 232	**ped**	Mala (Papua New Guinea), 611	**piy**	Piya-Kwonci, 173
pai	Pe, 173	**pee**	Taje, 433	**piz**	Pije, 585
paj	Ipeka-Tapuia, 227	**pef**	Pomo, Northeastern, 307	**pjt**	Pitjantjatjara, 576
pak	Parakanã, 231	**peg**	Pengo, 383	**pkb**	Pokomo, Upper, 135
pam	Pampanga, 500	**peh**	Bonan, 328	**pkg**	Pak-Tong, 621
pan	Panjabi, 383	**pei**	Chichimeca-Jonaz, 260	**pkh**	Pankhu, 321
pao	Paiute, Northern, 306	**pej**	Pomo, Northern, 307	**pkn**	Pakanha, 576
pap	Papiamento, 282	**pek**	Penchal, 621	**pko**	Pökoot, 135
paq	Parya, 513	**pel**	Pekal, 437	**pkp**	Pukapuka, 579
par	Panamint, 306	**pem**	Phende, 107	**pks**	Pakistan Sign Language, 487
pas	Papasena, 422	**pen**	Penesak, 437	**pkt**	Maleng, 451
pat	Papitalai, 621	**pep**	Kunja, 608	**pku**	Paku, 395
pau	Palauan, 587	**peq**	Pomo, Southern, 307	**pla**	Miani, 613
pav	Pakaásnovos, 231	**pes**	Farsi, Western, 439	**plb**	Polonombauk, 644
paw	Pawnee, 306	**pev**	Pémono, 312	**plc**	Palawano, Central, 500
pax	Pankararé, 231	**pex**	Petats, 621	**pld**	Polari, 566
pay	Pech, 258	**pey**	Petjo, 392	**ple**	Palu'e, 409
paz	Pankararú, 231	**pez**	Penan, Eastern, 460	**plg**	Pilagá, 220
pbb	Páez, 246	**pfa**	Pááfang, 583	**plh**	Paulohi, 403
pbc	Patamona, 257	**pfe**	Peere, 71	*pli*	Pali, 382
pbe	Popoloca, Mezontla, 273	**pfl**	Pfaelzisch, 538	**plj**	Polci, 173
pbf	Popoloca, Coyotepec, 273	**pga**	Arabic, Sudanese Creole, 187	**plk**	Shina, Kohistani, 488
pbg	Paraujano, 312	**pgg**	Pangwali, 382	**pll**	Palaung, Shwe, 466
pbh	Eñepa, 311	**pgi**	Pagi, 621	**plm**	Palembang, 437
pbi	Parkwa, 71	**pgk**	Rerep, 645	**pln**	Palenquero, 246
pbl	Mak (Nigeria), 169	**pgs**	Pangseng, 173	**plo**	Popoluca, Oluta, 274
pbn	Kpasam, 167	**pgu**	Pagu, 403	**plp**	Palpa, 477
pbo	Papel, 131	**pgy**	Pongyong, 477	**plr**	Senoufo, Palaka, 95
pbp	Badyara, 128	**pha**	Pa-Hng, 342	**pls**	Popoloca, San Marcos Tlalcoyalco, 274
pbr	Pangwa, 203	**phd**	Phudagi, 384	
pbs	Pame, Central, 273	**phg**	Phuong, 525	**plt**	Malagasy, Plateau, 140
pbt	Pashto, Southern, 488	**phh**	Phula, 525	**plu**	Palikúr, 231
pbu	Pashto, Northern, 488	**phk**	Phake, 384	**plv**	Palawano, Southwest, 500
pbv	Pnar, 384	**phl**	Phalura, 488	**plw**	Palawano, Brooke's Point, 500
pby	Pyu, 622	**phm**	Phimbi, 148	**ply**	Bolyu, 328
pbz	Palu, 466	**pho**	Phunoi, 452	**plz**	Paluan, 458
pca	Popoloca, Santa Inés Ahuatempan, 274	**phq**	Phana', 452	**pma**	Paama, 644
		phr	Pahari-Potwari, 487	**pmb**	Pambia, 107

tve	Te'un, 404	**tzn**	Tugun, 405	**umo**	Umotína, 233
tvk	Ambrym, Southeast, 640	**tzo**	Tzotzil, Venustiano	**ump**	Umpila, 577
tvl	Tuvalu, 640		Carranza, 277	**umr**	Umbugarla, 577
tvm	Tela-Masbuar, 404	**tzs**	Tzotzil, San Andrés	**ums**	Pendau, 432
tvn	Tavoyan, 467		Larrainzar, 277	**umu**	Munsee, 239
tvo	Tidore, 405	**tzt**	Tzutujil, Western, 256	**una**	Watut, North, 631
tvs	Taveta, 136	**tzu**	Tzotzil, Huixtán, 277	**une**	Uneme, 176
tvt	Naga, Tutsa, 380	**tzx**	Tabriak, 626	**ung**	Ngarinyin, 575
tvw	Sedoa, 433	**tzz**	Tzotzil, Zinacantán, 277	**unk**	Enawené-Nawé, 226
tvy	Pidgin, Timor, 351	**uam**	Uamué, 233	**unm**	Unami, 309
twa	Twana, 309	**uan**	Kuan, 451	**unp**	Worora, 578
twb	Tawbuid, Western, 502	**uar**	Tairuma, 626	**unz**	Kaili, Unde, 429
twc	Teshenawa, 175	**uba**	Ubang, 176	**uok**	Uokha, 176
twd	Twents, 549	**ubi**	Ubi, 87	**upi**	Umeda, 629
twe	Tewa (Indonesia), 410	**ubm**	Kenyah, Upper Baram, 460	**upv**	Uripiv-Wala-Rano-Atchin, 646
twf	Tiwa, Northern, 308	**ubr**	Ubir, 629	**ura**	Urarina, 293
twg	Tereweng, 409	**ubu**	Umbu-Ungu, 629	**urb**	Urubú-Kaapor, 233
twh	Tai Dón, 526	**uby**	Ubykh, 563	**urc**	Urningangg, 577
twl	Tawara, 149	**uda**	Uda, 176	*urd*	Urdu, 489
twn	Twendi, 72	**ude**	Udihe, 507	**ure**	Uru, 224
two	Tswapong, 48	**udi**	Udi, 320	**urf**	Uradhi, 577
twp	Ere, 598	**udj**	Ujir, 405	**urg**	Urigina, 629
twq	Tasawaq, 152	**udl**	Wuzlam, 73	**urh**	Urhobo, 176
twr	Tarahumara, Southwestern, 275	*udm*	Udmurt, 557	**uri**	Urim, 630
twt	Turiwára, 233	**udu**	Uduk, 119	**urk**	Urak Lawoi', 518
twu	Termanu, 410	**ues**	Kioko, 429	**url**	Urali, 389
tww	Tuwari, 629	**ufi**	Ufim, 629	**urm**	Urapmin, 629
twx	Tewe, 149	**ugb**	Kuku-Ugbanh, 572	**urn**	Uruangnirin, 424
twy	Tawoyan, 395	**uge**	Ughele, 639	**uro**	Ura (Papua New Guinea), 629
txa	Tombonuwo, 458	**ugn**	Ugandan Sign Language, 213	**urp**	Uru-Pa-In, 233
txc	Tsetsaut, 242	**ugo**	Ugong, 518	**urr**	Lehalurup, 642
txe	Totoli, 434	**ugy**	Uruguayan Sign Language, 311	**urt**	Urat, 629
txi	Ikpeng, 227	**uha**	Uhami, 176	**uru**	Urumi, 233
txm	Tomini, 434	**uhn**	Damal, 413	**urv**	Uruava, 630
txn	Tarangan, West, 404	*uig*	Uighur, 346	**urw**	Sop, 625
txo	Toto, 389	**uis**	Uisai, 629	**urx**	Urimo, 630
txq	Tii, 410	**uiv**	Iyive, 63	**ury**	Orya, 422
txs	Tonsea, 434	**uji**	Tanjijili, 175	**urz**	Uru-Eu-Wau-Wau, 233
txt	Citak, 413	**uka**	Kaburi, 415	**usa**	Usarufa, 630
txu	Kayapó, 229	**ukg**	Ukuriguma, 629	**ush**	Ushojo, 489
txx	Tatana, 458	**ukh**	Ukhwejo, 78	**usi**	Usui, 322
txy	Malagasy, Tanosy, 140	**ukl**	Ukrainian Sign Language, 564	**usk**	Usaghade, 72
tya	Tauya, 627	**ukp**	Ukpe-Bayobiri, 176	**usp**	Uspanteco, 256
tye	Kyenga, 168	**ukq**	Ukwa, 176	**usu**	Uya, 630
tyh	O'du, 525	*ukr*	Ukrainian, 564	**uta**	Otank, 173
tyi	Teke-Tsaayi, 90	**uks**	Urubú-Kaapor Sign	**ute**	Ute-Southern Paiute, 309
tyj	Tai Do, 526		Language, 233	**utp**	Amba (Solomon Islands), 634
tyl	Thu Lao, 527	**uku**	Ukue, 176	**utr**	Etulo, 159
tyn	Kombai, 417	**ukw**	Ukwuani-Aboh-Ndoni, 176	**utu**	Utu, 630
typ	Thaypan, 576	**ula**	Fungwa, 160	**uum**	Urum, 352
tyr	Tai Daeng, 526	**ulb**	Ulukwumi, 176	**uun**	Kulon-Pazeh, 511
tys	Tày Sa Pa, 527	**ulc**	Ulch, 507	**uur**	Ura (Vanuatu), 646
tyt	Tày Tac, 527	**ulf**	Usku, 424	**uuu**	U, 345
tyu	Kua, 47	**uli**	Ulithian, 583	**uve**	Uvean, West, 585
tyv	Tuvinian, 507	**ulk**	Meriam, 574	**uvh**	Uri, 629
tyx	Teke-Tyee, 90	**ull**	Ullatan, 389	**uvl**	Lote, 610
tyz	Tày, 527	**ulm**	Ulumanda', 434	**uwa**	Kuku-Uwanh, 572
tza	Tanzanian Sign Language, 205	**uln**	Unserdeutsch, 629	**uya**	Doko-Uyanga, 158
tzb	Tzeltal, Bachajón, 276	**uma**	Umatilla, 309	**uzn**	Uzbek, Northern, 512
tzc	Tzotzil, Chamula, 277	*umb*	Umbundu, 42	**uzs**	Uzbek, Southern, 318
tze	Tzotzil, Chenalhó, 277	**umd**	Umbindhamu, 577	**vaa**	Vaagri Booli, 389
tzh	Tzeltal, Oxchuc, 276	**umg**	Umbuygamu, 577	**vae**	Vale, 78
tzj	Tzutujil, Eastern, 256	**umi**	Ukit, 461	**vaf**	Vafsi, 442
tzm	Tamazight, Central Atlas, 146	**umm**	Umon, 176	**vag**	Vagla, 128

vah	Varhadi-Nagpuri, 389	**vmr**	Marenje, 148	**wdd**	Wandji, 122
vai	Vai, 139	**vms**	Moksela, 402	**wdg**	Wadaginam, 630
vaj	Vasekela Bushman, 151	**vmu**	Muluridyi, 574	**wdj**	Wadjiginy, 577
val	Vehes, 630	**vmv**	Maidu, Valley, 304	**wdu**	Wadjigu, 577
vam	Vanimo, 630	**vmw**	Makhuwa, 147	**wea**	Wewaw, 467
van	Valman, 630	**vmx**	Mixtec, Tamazola, 269	**wec**	Wè Western, 95
vao	Vao, 646	**vmy**	Mazatec, Ayautla, 264	**wed**	Wedau, 631
vap	Vaiphei, 389	**vmz**	Mazatec, Mazatlán, 264	**weh**	Weh, 73
var	Huarijio, 262	**vnk**	Vano, 639	**wei**	Were, 632
vas	Vasavi, 390	**vnm**	Vinmavis, 646	**wem**	Gbe, Weme, 45
vau	Vanuma, 109	**vnp**	Vunapu, 646	**weo**	Wemale, North, 405
vav	Varli, 390	**vor**	Voro, 177	**wep**	Westphalien, 540
vay	Wayu, 482	*vot*	Votic, 557	**wer**	Weri, 632
vbb	Babar, Southeast, 396	**vrs**	Varisi, 639	**wes**	Pidgin, Cameroon, 71
vec	Venetian, 545	**vrt**	Burmbar, 641	**wet**	Perai, 399
ved	Veddah, 510	**vsi**	Moldova Sign Language, 548	**weu**	Welaung, 467
vel	Veluws, 549	**vsl**	Venezuelan Sign	**wew**	Wejewa, 410
vem	Vemgo-Mabas, 177		Language, 312	**wfg**	Yafi, 426
ven	Venda, 187	**vum**	Vumbu, 121	**wga**	Wagaya, 577
veo	Ventureño, 309	**vun**	Vunjo, 205	**wgg**	Wangganguru, 577
vep	Veps, 557	**vut**	Vute, 73	**wgi**	Wahgi, 630
ver	Mom Jango, 170	**waa**	Walla Walla, 309	**wgo**	Waigeo, 424
vgr	Vaghri, 489	**wab**	Wab, 630	**wgw**	Wagawaga, 630
vic	Virgin Islands Creole	**wac**	Wasco-Wishram, 310	**wgy**	Warrgamay, 578
	English, 297	**wad**	Wandamen, 425	**wha**	Manusela, 402
vid	Vidunda, 205	**wae**	Walser, 563	**whg**	Wahgi, North, 630
vie	Vietnamese, 527	**waf**	Wakoná, 233	**whk**	Kenyah, Wahau, 394
vif	Vili, 90	**wag**	Wa'ema, 630	**whu**	Kayan, Wahau, 393
vig	Viemo, 55	**wah**	Watubela, 405	**wib**	Toussian, Southern, 55
vil	Vilela, 220	**wai**	Wares, 425	**wic**	Wichita, 310
vin	Vinza, 205	**waj**	Waffa, 630	**wie**	Wik-Epa, 578
vis	Vishavan, 390	*wal*	Walamo, 119	**wif**	Wik-Keyangan, 578
vit	Viti, 177	**wam**	Wampanoag, 309	**wig**	Wik-Ngathana, 578
viv	Iduna, 602	**wan**	Wan, 95	**wih**	Wik-Me'anha, 578
vka	Kariyarra, 572	**wao**	Wappo, 309	**wii**	Wiaki, 632
vki	Ija-Zuba, 163	**wap**	Wapishana, 257	**wij**	Wik-Iiyanh, 578
vkj	Kujarge, 82	**waq**	Wageman, 577	**wik**	Wikalkan, 578
vkk	Kaur, 436	*war*	Waray (Philippines), 502	**wil**	Wilawila, 578
vkl	Kulisusu, 430	*was*	Washo, 310	**wim**	Wik-Mungkan, 578
vkm	Kamakan, 228	**wat**	Kaninuwa, 604	**win**	Ho-Chunk, 302
vko	Kodeoha, 430	**wau**	Waurá, 233	**wir**	Wiraféd, 234
vkp	Korlai Creole Portuguese, 370	**wav**	Waka, 177	**wit**	Wintu, 310
vkt	Malay, Tenggarong Kutai, 394	**waw**	Waiwai, 233	**wiu**	Wiru, 632
vku	Kurrama, 572	**wax**	Watam, 631	**wiv**	Muduapa, 615
vky	Kayu Agung, 436	**way**	Wayana, 296	**wiw**	Wirangu, 578
vlp	Valpei, 646	**waz**	Wampur, 631	**wiy**	Wiyot, 310
vlr	Vatrata, 646	**wba**	Warao, 312	**wja**	Waja, 177
vls	Vlaams, 531	**wbb**	Wabo, 424	**wji**	Warji, 177
vma	Martuyhunira, 574	**wbe**	Waritai, 425	**wka**	Kw'adza, 200
vmb	Mbabaram, 574	**wbf**	Wara, 55	**wkd**	Wakde, 425
vmc	Mixtec, Juxtlahuaca, 267	**wbh**	Wanda, 205	**wkw**	Wakawaka, 577
vmd	Koraga, Mudu, 369	**wbi**	Wanji, 205	**wla**	Walio, 631
vme	Masela, East, 402	**wbj**	Alagwa, 197	**wlc**	Comorian, Mwali, 87
vmf	Mainfränkisch, 539	**wbk**	Waigali, 318	**wlg**	Kunbarlang, 572
vmg	Minigir, 614	**wbl**	Wakhi, 489	**wli**	Waioli, 405
vmh	Maraghei, 441	**wbm**	Wa, 467	**wlk**	Wailaki, 309
vmi	Miwa, 574	**wbp**	Warlpiri, 578	**wll**	Wali (Sudan), 196
vmj	Mixtec, Ixtayutla, 267	**wbq**	Waddar, 390	*wln*	Walloon, 531
vmk	Makhuwa-Shirima, 147	**wbr**	Wagdi, 390	**wlo**	Wolio, 435
vml	Malgana, 573	**wbt**	Wanman, 577	**wlr**	Wailapa, 646
vmm	Mixtec, Mitlatongo, 267	**wbv**	Wajarri, 577	**wls**	Wallisian, 647
vmo	Muko-Muko, 436	**wbw**	Woi, 425	**wlu**	Wuliwuli, 578
vmp	Mazatec, Soyaltepec, 265	**wca**	Yanomámi, 234	**wlv**	Wichí Lhamtés Vejoz, 220
vmq	Mixtec, Soyaltepec, 269	**wci**	Gbe, Waci, 207	**wlw**	Walak, 425

Country Index